PARKERSBURG & WOOD COUNTY PUBLIC LIBRARY
5091 000428052 4

W9-CKM-423
DO NOT
CHECK OUT

68TH EDITION

AMERICAN LIBRARY DIRECTORY™

2015-2016

American Library Directory™
68th Edition

Publisher
Thomas H. Hogan

Vice President, Content
Dick Kaser

Director, ITI Reference Group
Owen O'Donnell

Managing Editors
Beverley McDonough
Stephen L. Torpie

Associate Editor
Jennifer Williams

Operations Manager, Tampa Editorial
Debra James

Associate Project Coordinator, Tampa Editorial
Paula Watts

CONTENTS

VOLUME 1

VOLUME 2

PREFACE

Welcome to the 68th edition of the *American Library Directory*. Now in its 107th year, the directory was published biennially from 1908 to 1978 and annually since. The *American Library Directory* is edited and compiled by Information Today, Inc. of New Providence, New Jersey.

ARRANGEMENT AND COVERAGE

The major section of the directory contains listings of public, academic, government, and specialized libraries in the United States and in Canada. Listings are arranged geographically by the U.S. and Canada, then alphabetized by states, provinces, cities, and finally by the institution or library name.

Each state and province opens with statistical information regarding public libraries. Where feasible, these statistics were supplied by the state or provincial library authorities. Some are derived from public sources.

Entries include the name and address of the library, names of key personnel, and information on the library's holdings. In addition, the entries for the majority of libraries provide information on some or all of these additional areas: Income; Expenditures including salaries; E-Mail; Subject Interests; Special Collections; Automation; and Publications. Also included in each entry is a Standard Address Number (SAN), a unique address identification code used to expedite billing, shipping, and electronic ordering. For SAN assignments or questions, contact SAN@bowker.com. See the sample entry on page xi for a comprehensive guide to information that can be included in each entry.

Information within each library entry came either from the library staff itself, the library's web site, or from public sources. Each library received a copy of the previous edition's entry for updating. If the material was not returned, the data were verified, as much as possible, through telephone, e-mail, and web research. Entries verified from public sources are indicated by an asterisk (*) following the library name.

Non-listed libraries that have come to our attention since the previous edition are sent questionnaires. If the library returns the form with sufficient information, it is included. Entries new to the directory are indicated by a section indicator (§) to the left of the classification letter that precedes the entry.

Each library listed is identified by a code that indicates the type of library it is. The following codes are used:

A — Armed Forces
C — College or University
E — Electronic
G — Government, from local to federal
J — Community College
L — Law
M — Medical
P — Public and State Libraries
R — Religious
S — Special, including industry and company libraries as well as libraries serving associations, clubs, foundations, institutes, and societies.

ADDITIONAL SECTIONS

Library Award Recipients 2014. This section includes awards for outstanding librarianship or services, major development grants, and research projects.

Volume 2 of the directory serves as a support or auxiliary to the Library Section, and includes a variety of specialized information:

1. *Networks, Consortia, and Other Cooperative Library Organizations* includes automation networks, statewide networking systems, book processing and purchasing centers, and other specialized cooperating organizations. Entries indicate the number of members and the primary functions of each.

2. *Library Schools and Training Courses* includes a variety of community college, college, and university library science programs. Entries indicate entrance requirements, tuition, type of training offered, degrees and hours offered, and special courses offered. A dagger (†) indicates a program accredited by the American Library Association Committee on Accreditation.

3. *Library Systems* provides a listing of all state and provincial library systems. A brief statement indicating system functions within the state or province precedes the alphabetically arranged list of the state or province's systems. Cities are also included so that the user can locate a system's entry in the Library Section of the directory, or in cases where the state is followed by (N), in the Network Section of the directory.

4. *Libraries for the Blind and Physically Handicapped* provides a listing of all libraries designated by the National Library Service for the Blind and Physically Handicapped as regional and sub-regional libraries serving print handicapped patrons. It also includes Canadian libraries that have facilities for assisting these patrons.

5. *Libraries Serving the Deaf and Hearing Impaired* provides a similar listing of all libraries that have indicated that they have a TDD reference service for deaf patrons or other specialized equipment and services. The list is arranged by state and then by library name. The city is included so the user can find the entry in the Library Section and determine the TDD number as well as other services by reading the paragraph "Special Services for the Deaf" included in the library's entry.

6. *State and Provincial Public Library Agencies* indicates name, address, person-in-charge, and telephone number of the state agency that is responsible for public libraries.

7. *State School Library Agencies* indicates the same information for the state agency that is responsible for elementary and high school programs.

8. *The Interlibrary Loan Code for the United States* is reprinted with the permission of the American Library Association.

9. *United States Armed Forces Libraries Overseas* is a listing, by military branch, of all overseas libraries and is arranged in geographic order. Entries generally include the state-side military PO Box and SAN number correlated to each overseas library.

10. The *Organization Index* provides an alphabetical listing of all libraries and networks. Cross-references are included as needed.

11. The *Personnel Index* is an alphabetical listing of individuals who are included within entries for libraries, consortia, and library schools.

RELATED SERVICES

American Library Directory is also available online at **www.americanlibrarydirectory.com**. You can identify all libraries that meet certain criteria such as holdings, staff size, expenditures, income, and more with a single search. Feel free to visit the site and take advantage of our free trial offer.

The editors and researchers have made every effort to include all material submitted as accurately and completely as possible within the confines of format and scope. However, the publishers do not assume and hereby disclaim any liability to any party for any loss or damage caused by errors or omissions in the *American Library Directory* whether such errors and omissions resulted from negligence, accident, or any other cause. In the event of a publication error, the sole responsibility of the publisher will be the entry of corrected information in succeeding editions.

ACKNOWLEDGEMENTS

The editors wish to thank all of those who responded to our requests for information; without their efforts, the *American Library Directory* could not be published.

The editors also wish to express their appreciation for the cooperation of the officers of the state, regional, and provincial libraries who have provided statistics and other information concerning libraries in their areas.

Finally, Information Today would like to acknowledge the recent retirement of Beverley McDonough, Managing Editor for *American Library Directory*. In 1984, Beverley traveled to Tempe, Arizona, with her R. R. Bowker colleagues to begin the transition of this directory from the Jacques Cattell Press to the Bowker offices in New York City.

There has been considerable change over those thirty years, from three office moves to a change in ownership to the advent of the Internet. But one thing did not change. Beverley remained the steady, dedicated, and conscientious steward of the *American Library Directory*. We appreciate Beverley's tireless efforts to make this product the best it can be and we wish her well in her retirement.

Stephen L. Torpie
Managing Editor

Return this form by e-mail or fax to:

aldsupport@infotoday.com
Fax: 908-219-0192

Information Today, Inc.

American Library Directory
121 Chanlon Road, Suite G-20
New Providence, NJ 07974

AMERICAN LIBRARY DIRECTORY EDITORIAL REVISION FORM

☐ Please check here if you are nominating this library for a new listing in the directory

☐ Please check if this library is already listed

Library Name: ______________________________

Address: ______________________________

City: ______________ State or Province: ______________ Postal Code: ________

E-Mail: ______________ Web Site: ______________

Phone: ______________ Fax: ______________

Brief Description of Library: ______________________________

Personnel

☐ Addition ☐ Deletion ☐ Correction

First Name: ______________ Last Name: ______________ Title: ______________

☐ Addition ☐ Deletion ☐ Correction

First Name: ______________ Last Name: ______________ Title: ______________

☐ Addition ☐ Deletion ☐ Correction

First Name: ______________ Last Name: ______________ Title: ______________

(Continued on back)

Other Information

Indicate other information to be added to or corrected in this listing. Please be as specific as possible, noting erroneous data to be corrected or deleted.

____

____

____

____

____

____

____

Verification

Data for this listing will not be updated without the following information.

Your Name: ______________ Your Title: ______________

Organization Name: ______________

Address: ______________

City: ______________ State or Province: ______________ Postal Code: ______________

E-Mail: ______________ Web Site: ______________

Indicate if you are a: ☐ Representative of this organization ☐ User of this directory ☐ Other

If other, please specify: ______________

Thank you for helping Information Today, Inc. maintain the most up-to-date information available.

SAMPLE ENTRY

(fictional)

[1]**P** [2]McNeil & Foster, [3]Prescott Memorial Library, [4]500 Terra Cotta Dr, 85005-3126. [5]SAN 360-9070. [6]Tel: 602-839-9108. Toll Free Tel: 800-625-3848. FAX: 602-839-2020. TDD: 602-839-9202. E-mail: mcneilfoster@prescott.org. Web Site: www.prescottlib.com. [7]*Dir* Troy Alan; Tel: 602-839-5522; *Asst Dir* Tasha Brunnell; *Tech Serv* Beverly Greene; *Pub Servs* Tanya Peeley. Subject Specialists: *Bus* Cecil Brown; *Folklore* Peggy Shoree.

[8]Staff 20 (MLS 15, Non-MLS 5)

[9]Founded 1903. Pop served 92,540; Circ 210,000

[10]July 2013-Jun 2014 Income (Main Library and Branch(es)) $750,500, State $600,000, City $150,500. Mats Exp $118,400, Books $53,400, Per/Ser (Incl. Access Fees) $60,000, Micro $2,000, AV Equip $3,000. Sal $97,100 (Prof $32,000)

[11]**Library Holdings:** Bk Vols 110,000; Bk Titles 72,000; Per subs 245

[12]**Special Collections:** Local History (Lehi College)

[13]**Subject Interests:** Child psychology, genetics

[14]**Automation Activity & Vendor Info:** (Acquisitions) Innovative Interfaces Inc.; (Cataloging) Innovative Interfaces Inc.; (Circulation) Gaylord

[15]**Database Vendor:** EBSCO Online, OCLC WorldCat

[16]Wireless access

[17]Mem of Southwestern Library System

[18]Partic in Amigos Library Services, Inc.; Library Interchange Network (LINK)

[19]Special Services for the Deaf-TDD. Staff member who knows sign language; projector & captioned films

[20]Friends of Library Group

[21]**Bookmobiles:** 1

[22]**Branches:** 1

EASTSIDE, 9807 Post St, 85007-3184. SAN 360-9083. Tel 602-839-9178; *Librn* Linda Rhodes

Library Holdings: Bk Vols 23,000

1. Classification key (see "Arrangement & Coverage" in the Preface for explanation).
2. Official library name.
3. Other name by which library may be known.
4. Address.
5. SAN (Standard Address Number).
6. Communication information.
7. Personnel.
8. Number and professional status of staff.
9. Library background—Data on enrollment and the highest degree offered are included for academic libraries.
10. Income figures—Library income is broken down by source when reported.
    Expenditure figures—Material expenditure figures are requested for AV equipment, books, electronic reference materials (including access fees), manuscripts and archives, microforms, other print materials, periodicals/serials (including access fees), and preservation. In addition, salary figures are broken down by professional status when given.

LIBRARY COUNT

Provided here are totals for major types of libraries in the United States and Canada. Included are counts for public, academic, armed forces, government, and special libraries. Excluded from the counts are branch, departmental, and divisional libraries not listed with a full address in the directory. Some categories, such as academic, provide counts for specialized libraries such as law or medical libraries. As counts for only certain types of special libraries are given, these subcategories may not add up to the total count for each type of library.

PUBLIC—Each public library is counted once and then each branch is counted separately. Because the organization of systems varies from state to state, the method of counting these libraries varies also. In some cases, the libraries forming the systems were designated as member libraries, while in others they were given as branch libraries. In yet other instances, systems maintain branches as well as member libraries. If listed in this directory as a branch, the library was recorded in the branch count; however, member libraries were counted independently and recorded in the number of public libraries. Special public libraries are also included in the Total Special Libraries count.

ACADEMIC—The figure for academic libraries includes all libraries listed in the directory as part of academic institutions, whether they are main, departmental, or special. Specialized libraries and library departments at these colleges, such as law, medical, religious, or science libraries, are also counted in the Total Special Libraries figure.

GOVERNMENT and ARMED FORCES—Counts include all government and armed forces-related libraries listed in the directory, including specialized ones. Those libraries that are also defined as special libraries are included in the Total Special Libraries figure.

NOTE: Branch records for academic and government libraries are no longer counted within these breakdowns, causing some discrepancy when comparing figures with previous editions. This does not affect the total number of libraries listed in the *American Library Directory*.

SPECIAL—The special libraries count includes only specialized libraries that are not public, academic, armed forces, or government institutions. The Total Special Libraries count includes all law, medical, religious, business, and other special libraries found in the *American Library Directory* regardless of who operates them.

LIBRARIES IN THE UNITED STATES

A. **PUBLIC LIBRARIES**....................................*16,833
Public Libraries, excluding Branches......................9,622
Main Public Libraries that have branches........1,416
Public Library Branches..7,211

B. **ACADEMIC LIBRARIES**.................................*3,675
Community College Libraries..............................1,132
Departmental..201
Medical...6
Religious..8
University & College...2,543
Departmental..1,204
Law...189
Medical...235
Religious...249

C. **ARMED FORCES LIBRARIES**..........................*252
Air Force..72
Medical...5
Army..118
Medical..24
Marine...12
Navy..50
Law..1
Medical...10

D. **GOVERNMENT LIBRARIES**...........................*934
Law...369
Medical...140

E. **SPECIAL LIBRARIES** (Excluding Public, Academic, Armed Forces, and Government)..........................*5,730
Law...757
Medical..1,167
Religious...447

F. **TOTAL SPECIAL LIBRARIES** (Including Public, Academic, Armed Forces, and Government)...........6,966
Total Law..1,316

Total Medical....1,587
Total Religious....912

G. **TOTAL LIBRARIES COUNTED (*)**....27,424

LIBRARIES IN REGIONS ADMINISTERED BY THE UNITED STATES

A. **PUBLIC LIBRARIES**....*27
Public Libraries, excluding Branches....9
Main Public Libraries that have branches....3
Public Library Branches....18

B. **ACADEMIC LIBRARIES**....*37
Community College Libraries....3
Departmental....1
University & College....34
Departmental....20
Law....3
Medical....2
Religious....1

C. **ARMED FORCES LIBRARIES**....*2
Air Force....1
Army....1
Navy....0

D. **GOVERNMENT LIBRARIES**....*3
Law....1
Medical....1

E. **SPECIAL LIBRARIES** (Excluding Public, Academic, Armed Forces, and Government)....*6
Law....3
Medical....1
Religious....1

F. **TOTAL SPECIAL LIBRARIES** (Including Public, Academic, Armed Forces, and Government)....14
Total Law....7
Total Medical....4
Total Religious....2

G. **TOTAL LIBRARIES COUNTED (*)**....75

LIBRARIES IN CANADA

A. **PUBLIC LIBRARIES**....*2,032
Public Libraries, excluding Branches....798
Main Public Libraries that have branches....139
Public Library Branches....1,234

B. **ACADEMIC LIBRARIES**....*328
Community College Libraries....76
Departmental....12
Religious....1
University & College....252
Departmental....174
Law....16
Medical....18
Religious....34

C. **GOVERNMENT LIBRARIES**....*203
Law....29
Medical....5

D. **SPECIAL LIBRARIES** (Excluding Public, Academic, Armed Forces, and Government)....*670
Law....90
Medical....154
Religious....21

E. **TOTAL SPECIAL LIBRARIES** (Including Public, Academic, Armed Forces, and Government)....773
Total Law....135
Total Medical....177
Total Religious....75

F. **TOTAL LIBRARIES COUNTED (*)**....3,233

SUMMARY

TOTAL UNITED STATES LIBRARIES....27,424

TOTAL LIBRARIES ADMINISTERED BY THE UNITED STATES....75

TOTAL CANADIAN LIBRARIES....3,233

GRAND TOTAL OF LIBRARIES LISTED....30,732

Library Award Recipients 2014

Listed below are major awards given to libraries and librarians in the calendar year 2014. These entries were selected from the more inclusive list of scholarships and grant awards found in the *Library and Book Trade Almanac*, 60th edition (Information Today, Inc., 2015). Included here are awards for outstanding librarianship or service, development grants, and research projects larger than an essay or monograph. Awards are listed alphabetically by organization.

American Association of School Librarians (AASL)

AASL/BAKER & TAYLOR DISTINGUISHED SERVICE AWARD ($3,000). For outstanding contributions to librarianship and school library development. Donor: Baker & Taylor. Winner: Debra Kachel, Mansfield University.

American Library Association (ALA)

ALA/INFORMATION TODAY, INC. LIBRARY OF THE FUTURE AWARD ($1,500). For a library, consortium, group of librarians, or support organization for innovative planning for, applications of, or development of patron training programs about information technology in a library setting. Donors: Information Today, Inc. and IIDA. Winners: Queens Library, Jamaica, New York, for its "Enriching the Lives of a Challenged Community by Lending Tablets" in the wake of 2012's Hurricane Sandy.

BETA PHI MU AWARD ($1,000). For distinguished service in library education. Donor: Beta Phi Mu International Library & Information Science Honorary Society. Winner: Beth M. Paskoff, director, Louisiana State University School of Library and Information Science.

EQUALITY AWARD ($1,000). To an individual or group for an outstanding contribution that promotes equality in the library profession. Donor: Rowman & Littlefield. Winner: Ann K. Symons.

ELIZABETH FUTAS CATALYST FOR CHANGE AWARD ($1,000). A biennial award to recognize a librarian who invests time and talent to make positive change in the profession of librarianship. Donor: Elizabeth Futas Memorial Fund. Winner: Karen G. Schneider.

GALE CENGAGE LEARNING FINANCIAL DEVELOPMENT AWARD ($2,500). To a library organization for a financial development project to secure new funding resources for a public or academic library. Donor: Gale Cengage Learning. Winner: Cedar Park (Texas) Public Library for Fable Fest, an annual fundraising festival.

JOHN AMES HUMPHRY/OCLC/FOREST PRESS AWARD ($1,000). To one or more individuals for significant contributions to international librarianship. Donor: OCLC/Forest Press. Winner: Shali Zhang.

JOSEPH W. LIPPINCOTT AWARD ($1,000). For distinguished service to the library profession. Donor: Joseph W. Lippincott III. Winner: Maurice "Mitch" Freedman.

H. W. WILSON LIBRARY STAFF DEVELOPMENT GRANT ($3,500). To a library organization for a program to further its staff development goals and objectives. Donor: H. W. Wilson Company. Winner: Martin County (Florida) Library System.

Association for Library Collections and Technical Services (ALCTS)

ESTHER J. PIERCY AWARD ($1,500). To a librarian with no more than ten years' experience for contributions and leadership in the field of library collections and technical services. Donor: YBP Library Services. Winner: Patrick Carr.

ULRICH'S SERIALS LIBRARIANSHIP AWARD ($1,500). For distinguished contributions to serials librarianship. Sponsor: ProQuest. Winner: Les Hawkins.

Association for Library Service to Children (ALSC)

ALSC/BAKER & TAYLOR SUMMER READING PROGRAM GRANT ($3,000). For implementation of an outstanding public library summer reading program for children. Donor: Baker & Taylor. Winner: Ames (Iowa) Public Library.

ALSC/CANDLEWICK PRESS "LIGHT THE WAY: LIBRARY OUTREACH TO THE UNDERSERVED" GRANT ($3,000). To a library conducting exemplary outreach to underserved populations. Donor: Candlewick Press. Winner: LGBT Center of Raleigh (North Carolina) Library.

Association of College and Research Libraries (ACRL)

ACRL ACADEMIC OR RESEARCH LIBRARIAN OF THE YEAR AWARD ($5,000). For outstanding contribution to academic and research librarianship and library development. Donor: YBP Library Services. Winner: Tim Bucknall, University of North Carolina, Greensboro.

ACRL/CLS PROQUEST INNOVATION IN COLLEGE LIBRARIANSHIP AWARD ($3,000). To academic librarians who show a capacity for innovation in the areas of programs, services, and operations; or creating innovations for library colleagues that facilitate their ability to better serve the library's community. Winners: Tish Hayes, Terra B. Jacobson, and Troy A. Swanson, Moraine Valley Community College Library.

ACRL/EBSS DISTINGUISHED EDUCATION AND BEHAVIORAL SCIENCES LIBRARIAN AWARD ($2,500). To an academic librarian who has made an outstanding contribution as an education and/or behavioral sciences librarian through accomplishments and service to the profession. Donor: John Wiley & Sons. Winner: Stephanie Davis-Kahl, Illinois Wesleyan University.

EXCELLENCE IN ACADEMIC LIBRARIES AWARDS ($3,000). To recognize outstanding college and university libraries. Donor: YBP Library Services. Winners: (university) Cal Poly State University; (college) Lafayette College; (community college) Illinois Central College.

INSTRUCTION SECTION INNOVATION AWARD ($3,000). To librarians or project teams in recognition of a project that demonstrates creative, innovative, or unique approaches to information literacy instruction or programming. Donor: ProQuest. Winners: Meredith Farkas, Amy Hofer, Lisa Molinelli, and Kimberly Willson-St. Clair, Portland State University Libraries.

Black Caucus of the American Library Association (BCALA)

DEMCO/BCALA EXCELLENCE IN LIBRARIANSHIP AWARD. To a librarian who has made significant contributions to promoting the status of African Americans in the library profession. Winner: Emily R. Guss, City Colleges of Chicago.

Library Leadership and Management Association (LLAMA)

JOHN COTTON DANA LIBRARY PUBLIC RELATIONS AWARDS. To libraries or library organizations of all types for public relations programs or special projects ended during the preceding year. Donors: H. W. Wilson Foundation and EBSCO. Winners: Birmingham (Alabama) Public Library for "Letter from Birmingham Jail: A Worldwide Celebration"; Champaign (Illinois) Public Library for "Show Some Library Love"; Kitsap Regional Library, Kitsap County, Washington, for its "Traveling Book Campaign"; James B. Hunt, Jr. Library, North Carolina State University, for "The Library of the Future"; Sacramento (California) Public Library for "The Poe Project"; Texas A&M University for "Deeper Than Swords: A Two-Day Celebration of George R.R. Martin"; University of Texas, San Antonio, for "Ask Us Anything"; Wells County (Indiana) Public Library for "Your Go-To Spot."

Public Library Association (PLA)

EBSCO EXCELLENCE IN SMALL AND/OR RURAL PUBLIC SERVICE AWARD ($1,000). Honors a library serving a population of 10,000 or less that demonstrates excellence of service to its community as exemplified by an overall service program or a special program of significant accomplishment. Donor: EBSCO. Winner: Bertha Voyer Memorial Library, Honey Grove, Texas.

ALLIE BETH MARTIN AWARD ($3,000). To honor a public librarian who has demonstrated extraordinary range and depth of knowledge about books or other library materials and has distinguished ability to share that knowledge. Donor: Baker & Taylor. Winner: Rollie James Welch, Cleveland (Ohio) Public Library.

ROMANCE WRITERS OF AMERICA LIBRARY GRANT ($4,500). To a library to build or expand a fiction collection and/or host romance fiction programming. Donor: Romance Writers of America. Winner: Red Wing (Minnesota) Public Library.

Reference and User Services Association (RUSA)

VIRGINIA BOUCHER-OCLC DISTINGUISHED ILL LIBRARIAN AWARD ($2,000). To a librarian for outstanding professional achievement, leadership, and contributions to interlibrary loan and document delivery. Winner: David Larsen, University of Chicago.

ISADORE GILBERT MUDGE AWARD ($5,000). For distinguished contributions to reference librarianship. Donor: Gale Cengage Learning: Winner: William Miller, Florida Atlantic University.

CANADA

Canadian Library Association (CLA)

CLA/ACB DAFOE SCHOLARSHIP ($C5,000). Winner: Alexander Herd.

CLA OUTSTANDING SERVICE TO LIBRARIANSHIP AWARD. Donor: ProQuest. Winner: Linda Cook, Edmonton Public Library.

CLA/H. W. WILSON SCHOLARSHIP ($2,000). Winner: Zoe Dickinson.

KEY TO SYMBOLS AND ABBREVIATIONS

KEY TO SYMBOLS

A - Armed Forces libraries
C - College and University libraries
E - Electronic libraries
G - Government libraries
J - Community College libraries
L - Law libraries
M - Medical libraries
P - Public and State libraries
R - Religious libraries
S - Special libraries
* - No response received directly from the library; data gathered from other sources
§ - New library and/or listed for the first time
† - Library school program accredited by the American Library Association Committee on Accreditation

KEY TO ABBREVIATIONS

A-tapes - Audio Tapes
Acad - Academic, Academy
Acctg - Accounting
Acq - Acquisition Librarian, Acquisitions
Actg - Acting
Ad - Adult Services Librarian
Add - Address
Admin - Administration, Administrative
Adminr - Administrator
Adv - Adviser, Advisor, Advisory
Advan - Advanced, Advancement
Aeronaut - Aeronautics
AFB - Air Force Base
Agr - Agricultural, Agriculture
Ala - Alabama
Alta - Alberta
Am - America, American
Ann - Annual, Annually
Anthrop - Anthropology
APO - Air Force Post Office, Army Post Office
Approp - Appropriation
Approx - Approximate, Approximately
Appt - Appointment
Archaeol - Archaeology
Archit - Architecture
Ariz - Arizona
Ark - Arkansas
Asn - Association
Assoc - Associate
Asst - Assistant
AV - Audiovisual, Audiovisual Materials
Ave - Avenue
BC - British Columbia
Bd - Binding, Bound
Behav - Behaviorial
Bibliog - Bibliographic, Bibliographical, Bibliography
Bibliogr - Bibliographer
Biog - Biographer, Biographical, Biography
Biol - Biology
Bk(s) - Book(s)
Bkmobile - Bookmobile
Bldg - Building
Blvd - Boulevard
Bot - Botany
Br - Branch, Branches
Bro - Brother
Bur - Bureau
Bus - Business
Calif - California
Can - Canada, Canadian
Cap - Capital
Cat(s) - Cataloging Librarian, Cataloging, Catalog(s)
Cent - Central
Ch - Children, Children's Librarian, Children's Services
Chem - Chemical, Chemistry
Chmn - Chairman
Cht(s) - Chart(s)
Circ - Circulation
Cler - Clerical Staff
Co - Company
Col - College
Coll - Collection, Collections
Colo - Colorado
COM - Computer Output Microform
Commun - Community
Comn - Commission
Comt - Committee
Conn - Connecticut
Conserv - Conservation
Consult - Consultant
Coop - Cooperates, Cooperating, Cooperation, Cooperative, Corporate
Coord - Coordinating
Coordr - Coordinator
Corp - Corporation
Coun - Council
CP - Case Postale
Ct - Court
Ctr - Center, Centre
Curric - Curriculum
DC - District of Columbia
Del - Delaware
Den - Denominational
Dent - Dentistry
Dep - Deputy, Depository
Dept - Department
Develop - Development
Dir - Director
Div - Division
Doc - Document, Documents
Dr - Doctor, Drive
E - East
Econ - Economic
Ed - Edited, Edition, Editor
Educ - Education, Educational
Elem - Elementary
Eng - Engineering
Enrl - Enrollment
Ent - Entrance
Environ - Environmental
Equip - Equipment
ERDA - Energy Research & Development Administration
Est - Estimate, Estimation
Estab - Established
Excl - Excluding
Exec - Executive
Exp - Expenditure
Ext - Extension of Telephone
Fac - Faculty, Facilities
Fed - Federal
Fedn - Federation
Fel - Fellowship
Fla - Florida
Flm - Films
Flr - Floor
Found - Foundation
FPO - Fleet Post Office

Fr - French
Fs - Filmstrips
Ft - Fort
FT - Full Time
FTE - Full Time Equivalent
Ga - Georgia
Gen - General, Generated
Geog - Geographical, Geography
Geol - Geological, Geology
Govt - Government
Grad - Graduate
Hist - Historical, History
Hort - Horticulture
Hq - Headquarters
Hrs - Hours
Hwy - Highway, Highways
Hydrol - Hydrology
Ill - Illinois
ILL - Interlibrary Loan
Illustr - Illustrator, Illustration
Inc - Income, Incorporated
Incl - Including
Ind - Indiana
Indust - Industrial, Industry
Info - Information
Ins - Insurance
Inst - Institute, Institutions
Instrul - Instructional
Instr - Instructor
Intl - International
Jr - Junior
Juv - Juvenile
Kans - Kansas
Ky - Kentucky
La - Louisiana
Lab - Laboratories, Laboratory
Lang(s) - Language(s)
Lectr - Lecturer
Legis - Legislative, Legislature
Libr - Libraries, Library
Librn - Librarian
Lit - Literary, Literature
Ltd - Limited
Mag(s) - Magazine(s)
Man - Manitoba
Mass - Massachusetts
Mat(s) - Material(s)
Math - Mathematical, Mathematics
Md - Maryland
Med - Medical, Medicine
Media - Media Specialist
Mem - Member
Metaphys - Metaphysical, Metaphysics
Metrop - Metropolitan
Mgr - Manager, Managerial
Mgt - Management
Mich - Michigan
Micro - Microform
Mil - Military
Misc - Miscellaneous
Miss - Mississippi
Minn - Minnesota
Mkt - Marketing
Mo - Missouri
Ms - Manuscript, Manuscripts
Mus - Museum
N - North
NASA - National Aeronautics & Space Administration
Nat - National
NB - New Brunswick
NC - North Carolina
NDak - North Dakota
NE - Northeast, Northeastern
Nebr - Nebraska
Nev - Nevada
New Eng - New England
Newsp - Newspaper, Newspapers
Nfld - Newfoundland
NH - New Hampshire
NJ - New Jersey
NMex - New Mexico
Nonfict - nonfiction
NS - Nova Scotia
NW - Northwest, Northwestern
NY - New York
Oceanog - Oceanography
Off - Office
Okla - Oklahoma
Ont - Ontario
Ore - Oregon
Ornith - Ornithology
Pa - Pennsylvania
Pac - Pacific
Partic - Participant, Participates
Per(s) - Periodical(s)
Pharm - Pharmacy
Philos - Philosophical, Philosophy
Photog - Photograph, Photography
Phys - Physical
Pkwy - Parkway
Pl - Place
PO - Post Office
Polit Sci - Political Science
Pop - Population
PR - Puerto Rico
Prep - Perparation, Preparatory
Pres - President, Presidents
Presv - Preservation
Proc - Process, Processing
Prof - Professional, Professor
Prog - Program, Programming
Prov - Province, Provincial
Psychiat - Psychiatrist, Psychiatry, Psychiatric
Psychol - Psychological, Psychology
PT - Part Time
Pub - Public
Pub Rel - Public Relations Head
Publ(s) - Publisher, Publishing, Publication(s)
Pvt - Private
Qtr - Quarter
Que - Quebec
R&D - Research & Development
Rd - Road
Read - Readable
Rec - Record, Recording, Records
Ref - Reference
Relig - Religion, Religious
Rep - Representative
Reprod - Reproduction
Req - Requirement
Res - Research, Resource, Resources
RI - Rhode Island
RLIN - Research Libraries Information Network
Rm - Room
Rpt(s) - Report(s)
RR - Rural Route
Rte - Route
S - South
Sal - Salary
SAN - Standard Address Number
Sask - Saskatchewan
SC - South Carolina
Sch - School
Sci - Science, Scientific
Sci Fict - Science Fiction
SDak - South Dakota
SE - Southeast, Southeastern
Secy - Secretary
Sem - Semester, Seminary
Ser - Serials, Serials Librarian
Serv(s) - Service(s)
Soc - Social, Society, Societies
Sociol - Sociology
Spec - Special, Specialist
Sq - Square
Sr - Senor, Senior, Sister
St - Saint, Street
Sta - Station
Sub(s) - Subscription(s)
Subj - Subject, Subjects
Sup - Supplies
Supv - Supervising, Supervision
Supvr - Supervisor
Supvry - Supervisory
SW - Southwest, Southwestern
Syst - System, Systems
TDD - Telecomm. Device for the Deaf
Tech - Technical, Technician, Technology
Tel - Telephone
Tenn - Tennessee
Tex - Texas
Theol - Theological, Theology
Tpk - Turnpike
Treas - Treasurer
TTY - Teletypewriter
TV - Television
TVA - Tennessee Valley Authority
UN - United Nations
Undergrad - Undergraduate
Univ - University
US - United States
VPres -Vice President
V-tapes - Video Tapes
Va - Virginia
Vet - Veteran
VF - Vertical Files
VI - Virgin Islands
Vis - Visiting
Vols - Volumes, Volunteers
Vt - Vermont
W - West
Wash - Washington
Wis - Wisconsin
WLN - Washington Library Network
WVa - West Virginia
Wyo - Wyoming
YA - Young Adult Librarian, Young Adult Services
Zool - Zoology

68TH EDITION

AMERICAN LIBRARY DIRECTORY™

2015-2016

LIBRARIES IN THE UNITED STATES

ALABAMA

Date of Statistics: FY 2013
Population, 2010 U.S. Census: 4,779,736
Population, 2011 U.S. Census (est.): 4,802,740
Population Served by Public Libraries: 4,802,740
Total Volumes in Public Libraries: 12,784,635
Volumes Per Capita: 2.66
Total Public Library Circulation: 20,873,534
Circulation Per Capita: 4.35
Total Public Library Income: $100,881,915
Source of Income: Mainly public funds
Expenditures Per Capita: $20.43
Number of County & Multi-county Public Library Systems: 16
Counties Served: 67
Grants-in-Aid to Public Libraries:
State: $3,777,745
Federal: $1,243,116

ABBEVILLE

P ABBEVILLE MEMORIAL LIBRARY*, 301 Kirkland St, 36310. SAN 330-2822. Tel: 334-585-2818. FAX: 334-585-2819. *Librn,* Debbie McLain Creel; E-mail: dmclain@cityofabbeville.org
Library Holdings: Bk Vols 25,534
Automation Activity & Vendor Info: (Cataloging) Book Systems; (Circulation) Book Systems; (OPAC) Book Systems
Open Mon-Fri 9-5, Sat 9-12
Friends of the Library Group

ADAMSVILLE

P ADAMSVILLE PUBLIC LIBRARY, 4825 Main St, 35005-1947. (Mail add: PO Box 309, 35005-0309), SAN 376-7620. Tel: 205-674-3399. FAX: 205-674-5405. Web Site: www.adamsville.lib.al.us. *Interim Dir,* Gina Antolini; E-mail: gantolini@cityofadamsville.org
Library Holdings: Bk Vols 14,000
Wireless access
Open Mon-Fri 9-5

AKRON

P AKRON PUBLIC LIBRARY*, 207 First Ave S, 35441. (Mail add: PO Box 8, 35441-0008), SAN 300-0001. Tel: 205-372-3148. FAX: 205-372-3198. *Dir,* Carthenia Blackmon; E-mail: carthenia@yahoo.com; Staff 14 (MLS 5, Non-MLS 9)
Library Holdings: Bk Vols 1,000; Per Subs 10
Mem of Public Library of Anniston-Calhoun County
Open Mon, Wed & Thurs 9-5

ALABASTER

P ALBERT L SCOTT LIBRARY*, 100 Ninth St NW, 35007-9172. SAN 371-9332. Tel: 205-664-6822. FAX: 205-664-6839. *Dir,* Nan Abbott; E-mail: nabbott@shelbycounty-al.org; Staff 14 (MLS 3, Non-MLS 11)
Pop 28,240; Circ 164,783
Oct 2006-Sept 2007 Income $810,603, State $30,164, City $780,439. Mats Exp $89,360, Books $65,000, Per/Ser (Incl. Access Fees) $7,260, AV Mat $17,100
Library Holdings: DVDs 3,278; Bk Vols 50,935; Per Subs 128; Talking Bks 1,658; Videos 534
Subject Interests: Cooking, Decorating, Gardening, Local hist
Automation Activity & Vendor Info: (Circulation) Innovative Interfaces, Inc; (OPAC) Innovative Interfaces, Inc
Wireless access
Mem of Harrison Regional Library System
Open Mon, Tues & Thurs 9-8, Wed & Fri 9-6, Sat 10-5, Sun 1-5
Friends of the Library Group

ALBERTVILLE

P ALBERTVILLE PUBLIC LIBRARY*, 200 Jackson St, 35950. (Mail add: PO Box 430, 35950-0008), SAN 300-001X. Tel: 256-891-8290. FAX: 256-891-8295. Web Site: www.albertvillelibrary.org. *Dir,* Lisa Rowell; E-mail: lrowell@albertvillelibrary.org; *Circ,* Pam Burgess; Staff 5 (MLS 1, Non-MLS 4)
Pop 80,000; Circ 150,095
Library Holdings: Bk Titles 85,000; Per Subs 100
Special Collections: Civil War Coll; Rare Books Room; War Between the States
Automation Activity & Vendor Info: (Cataloging) Book Systems; (Circulation) Book Systems; (OPAC) Book Systems
Mem of Marshall County Cooperative Library
Open Mon 10-7, Tues-Fri 8-5, Sat 9-1
Friends of the Library Group

P MARSHALL COUNTY COOPERATIVE LIBRARY*, 600 College St, Ste 100, 35950-2722. (Mail add: PO Box 185, 35950-0003), SAN 324-1424. Tel: 256-878-8523. FAX: 256 878 9562. *Dir,* Debra Slaton
Founded 1974
Library Holdings: Bk Vols 7,000
Member Libraries: Albertville Public Library; Boaz Public Library; Grant Public Library; Guntersville Public Library
Open Mon-Thurs 8-1
Bookmobiles: 1

ALEXANDER CITY

J CENTRAL ALABAMA COMMUNITY COLLEGE*, Thomas D Russell Library, 1675 Cherokee Rd, 35010. (Mail add: PO Box 699, 35011-0699), SAN 330-0005. Tel: 256-234-6346. Circulation Tel: 256-215-4290. FAX: 256-234-0384. Web Site: www.cacc.cc.al.us/alexcitylibrar/default.htm. *Librn,* Denita Oliver; Tel: 256-215-4293, E-mail: doliver@cacc.edu; *Cat, Ref,* Carolyn Ingram; Tel: 256-215-4291, E-mail: cingram@cacc.edu; Staff 5 (MLS 1, Non-MLS 4)
Founded 1965. Enrl 2,000; Fac 60; Highest Degree: Associate
Library Holdings: Bk Titles 25,273; Bk Vols 30,469; Per Subs 280
Special Collections: Alabama & Local History (Alabama Room)
Automation Activity & Vendor Info: (Cataloging) Follett Software; (Circulation) Follett Software; (OPAC) Follett Software
Database Vendor: Dialog, OCLC FirstSearch, OVID Technologies
Partic in Ala Union List & Serials
Open Mon-Thurs 7:45am-8pm, Fri 7:45-4
Friends of the Library Group
Departmental Libraries:
CHILDERSBURG CAMPUS LIBRARY, 34091 US Hwy 280, Childersburg, 35044, SAN 370-4548. Tel: 256-378-2041. FAX: 256-378-2040. *Librn,* Deborah Waller; Tel: 256-378-5576, Ext 2041; Staff 1.5 (MLS 1, Non-MLS 0.5)
Founded 1989. Enrl 2,365; Fac 75; Highest Degree: Associate

Library Holdings: CDs 65; DVDs 35; e-books 6,183; Bk Vols 8,417; Per Subs 118; Talking Bks 19; Videos 233
Database Vendor: EBSCOhost
Open Mon-Thurs 7:30-7, Fri 8-12
Restriction: Open to students, fac & staff

P ADELIA M RUSSELL LIBRARY*, 318 Church St, 35010-2516. SAN 376-5601. Tel: 256-329-6796. FAX: 256-329-6797. E-mail: alexcity@amrlibrary.net. *Dir,* Amy Huff
Library Holdings: Bk Vols 38,000; Per Subs 87
Automation Activity & Vendor Info: (Cataloging) Book Systems; (Circulation) Book Systems; (OPAC) Book Systems
Mem of Horseshoe Bend Regional Library
Open Mon-Thurs 8-7, Fri 8-5, Sat 8-12
Branches: 1
MAMIE'S PLACE CHILDREN'S LIBRARY & LEARNING CENTER, 284 Church St, 35010. Tel: 256-234-4644. *Ch,* Kathryn Reed
Library Holdings: Bk Vols 400,000
Open Mon-Thurs 8-7, Fri 8-5, Sat 8-12

ALICEVILLE

P ALICEVILLE PUBLIC LIBRARY*, 416 Third Ave N, 35442. SAN 300-0028. Tel: 205-373-6691. FAX: 205-373-6691. E-mail: apl@nctv.com. Web Site: home.nctv.com/apl. *Dir,* Nelda B Hudgins; *Asst Librn,* Teresa Gibson; *Asst Librn,* Katie McFarlin
Founded 1955. Pop 3,227; Circ 12,000
Library Holdings: Bk Titles 20,000
Automation Activity & Vendor Info: (Acquisitions) Follett Software; (Cataloging) Follett Software; (Circulation) Follett Software; (ILL) OCLC WorldShare Interlibrary Loan
Wireless access
Function: Copy machines, Fax serv, ILL available, Music CDs, Prog for children & young adult, Summer reading prog, Tax forms, VHS videos
Mem of Pickens County Cooperative Library
Open Mon-Wed & Fri 10-11:30 & 12:30-5, Thurs 10-11:30 & 12:30-8, Sat 9-12
Friends of the Library Group

ANDALUSIA

P ANDALUSIA PUBLIC LIBRARY*, 212 S Three Notch St, 36420. SAN 300-0036. Tel: 334-222-6612. FAX: 334-222-6612. E-mail: andylibrary@andycable.com. Web Site: www.andylibrary.com. *Dir,* Karin Taylor; *Ch Serv,* Betty Harrelson; *Ref,* La Ferne D Griggs; *Tech Serv,* Joan Herring
Founded 1920. Pop 8,000; Circ 50,000
Library Holdings: Bk Titles 53,000; Per Subs 48
Special Collections: American Ancestors, bks, micro; One Hundred Years of County Newspapers, micro. Oral History
Automation Activity & Vendor Info: (Acquisitions) TLC (The Library Corporation); (Cataloging) TLC (The Library Corporation); (Circulation) TLC (The Library Corporation); (OPAC) TLC (The Library Corporation)
Open Mon-Fri 8-5, Sat 8-12

J LURLEEN B WALLACE COMMUNITY COLLEGE LIBRARY, 1000 Dannelly Blvd, 36420. (Mail add: PO Box 1418, 36420-1418), SAN 300-0044. Tel: 334-881-2265. Interlibrary Loan Service Tel: 334-881-2269. Administration Tel: 334-881-2266. FAX: 334-881-2300. Web Site: www.lbwcc.edu/library.aspx. *Dir, Learning Res,* Hugh Carter; E-mail: hcarter@lbwcc.edu; Staff 2 (MLS 1, Non-MLS 1)
Founded 1969. Enrl 1,585; Fac 51; Highest Degree: Associate
Oct 2013-Sept 2014 Income $298,855. Mats Exp $37,490, Books $12,965, Per/Ser (Incl. Access Fees) $17,000, AV Mat $7,525
Library Holdings: AV Mats 1,331; e-books 25,299; Bk Titles 33,774; Bk Vols 39,616
Special Collections: Alabama Coll; LBW Community College Archives
Automation Activity & Vendor Info: (Acquisitions) Auto-Graphics, Inc; (Cataloging) Auto-Graphics, Inc; (Circulation) Auto-Graphics, Inc; (Course Reserve) Auto-Graphics, Inc; (ILL) Auto-Graphics, Inc; (Media Booking) Auto-Graphics, Inc; (OPAC) Auto-Graphics, Inc; (Serials) Auto-Graphics, Inc
Database Vendor: EBSCOhost, Gale Cengage Learning, OCLC WorldShare Interlibrary Loan, ProQuest, PubMed, SerialsSolutions, WebMD
Wireless access
Publications: Annual Report
Partic in Lyrasis
Open Mon-Thurs 7:45am-8pm, Fri 8-Noon

ANNISTON

M NORTHEAST ALABAMA REGIONAL MEDICAL CENTER*, William Bruce Mitchell Medical Library, 400 E Tenth St, 36207. SAN 324-5950. Tel: 256-235-5224, 256-235-5800. Web Site: www.rmccares.org. *Coordr,* Kathy Phillips
Founded 1940
Library Holdings: e-books 50; e-journals 52; Per Subs 3
Database Vendor: MD Consult
Wireless access
Special Services for the Deaf - ADA equip

R PARKER MEMORIAL BAPTIST CHURCH LIBRARY*, 1205 Quintard Ave, 36207. (Mail add: PO Box 2140, 36202-2104), SAN 300-0052. Tel: 256-236-5628. FAX: 256-236-5441.
Founded 1951
Library Holdings: Bk Vols 7,500

P PUBLIC LIBRARY OF ANNISTON-CALHOUN COUNTY*, 108 E Tenth St, 36201. (Mail add: PO Box 308, 36202-0308), SAN 330-003X. Tel: 256-237-8501, 256-237-8503. FAX: 256-238-0474. E-mail: library@publiclibrary.cc. Web Site: www.anniston.lib.al.us. *Dir,* Teresa Kiser; E-mail: tkiser@publiclibrary.cc; *Spec Coll Librn,* Tom Mullins; *Acq,* Sandra Underwood; *Adult Serv,* Mary Connor; *Ref,* Sunny Addison; Staff 19 (MLS 4, Non-MLS 15)
Founded 1965. Circ 169,295
Library Holdings: Bk Vols 114,748; Per Subs 225
Special Collections: Alabama History; Andrea Coll (Alabama Room); Anniston Room Coll; Genealogy (Alabama Room)
Subject Interests: Genealogy, Local hist
Automation Activity & Vendor Info: (Circulation) SirsiDynix; (OPAC) SirsiDynix
Publications: Serendipity Library (Newsletter)
Member Libraries: Akron Public Library; Piedmont Public Library
Open Mon-Thurs 9-6:30, Fri 9-5, Sat 10-5, Sun 1-5
Friends of the Library Group
Branches: 1
CARVER BRANCH, 722 W 14th St, 36201, SAN 330-0099. Tel: 256-237-7271. FAX: 256-237-7271. E-mail: carver@publiclibrary.cc. *Librn,* Brenda Manning
Open Mon-Thurs 9-5
Friends of the Library Group
Bookmobiles: 1

ARAB

P ARAB PUBLIC LIBRARY*, 325 Second St NW, 35016-1999. SAN 300-0060. Tel: 256-586-3366. FAX: 256-586-5638. E-mail: library@arabcity.org. *Dir,* Kathy Handle
Founded 1963. Circ 71,269
Library Holdings: Bk Vols 52,000; Per Subs 40
Subject Interests: Ala, Civil War
Automation Activity & Vendor Info: (Cataloging) Book Systems; (Circulation) Book Systems; (OPAC) Book Systems
Database Vendor: ComPanion Corp
Wireless access
Open Mon & Tues 10-8, Wed & Fri 10-6, Sat 9-3
Friends of the Library Group

ARLEY

P ARLEY PUBLIC LIBRARY*, 6788 Hwy 41, 35541. (Mail add: PO Box 146, 35541), SAN 300-0079. Tel: 205-387-0129. FAX: 205-387-0129. E-mail: arleylibrary@bellsouth.net. *Librn,* Susie Barber
Founded 1974
Library Holdings: Bk Vols 3,800
Mem of Carl Elliott Regional Library System
Open Mon, Tues, Thurs & Fri 10-5, Wed 10-4:30

ASHLAND

P ASHLAND CITY PUBLIC LIBRARY*, 113 Second Ave N, 36251. (Mail add: PO Box 296, 36251-0296), SAN 376-561X. Tel: 256-354-3427. FAX: 256-354-3427. E-mail: ashlibrary@centurytel.net. Web Site: www.cheaharegionallibrary.org/libraries/ashland. *Librn,* Tina Nolen
Library Holdings: Bk Vols 14,000
Automation Activity & Vendor Info: (Cataloging) Follett Software; (Circulation) Follett Software
Mem of Cheaha Regional Library
Open Mon-Fri 8:30-4:30
Friends of the Library Group

ASHVILLE

P SAINT CLAIR COUNTY PUBLIC LIBRARY*, 139 Fifth Ave, 35953. (Mail add: PO Box 308, 35953-0308), SAN 330-3217. Tel: 205-594-3694. FAX: 205-594-3695. E-mail: countylibrary.stclair@gmail.com. *Dir,* Judy Douglas
Founded 1957. Pop 60,000; Circ 57,046

Oct 2008-Sept 2009 Income $143,619, State $31,227, Federal $5,700, County $94,878, Locally Generated Income $1,500, Other $10,314. Mats Exp $173,742. Sal $94,718 (Prof $37,000)
Library Holdings: Audiobooks 241; DVDs 857; Bk Vols 14,447; Per Subs 19
Automation Activity & Vendor Info: (Acquisitions) Book Systems; (Cataloging) Book Systems; (Circulation) Book Systems; (OPAC) Book Systems
Publications: History of St Clair County, 1539-1846
Open Mon-Fri 9-5
Branches: 4
ASHVILLE BRANCH, Sixth Ave, 35953. (Mail add: PO Box 187, 35953), SAN 330-3241. Tel: 205-594-7954. *Librn,* Barbara Stewart
Library Holdings: Bk Vols 10,475
Open Mon-Fri 9-12 & 1-4
RAGLAND BRANCH, 26 Providence Rd, Ragland, 35131, SAN 330-3330. Tel: 205-472-2007. FAX: 205-472-2007. E-mail: libby81@ragland.net. *Librn,* Patricia Poe
Library Holdings: Bk Vols 9,321
Open Mon 8-2, Tues-Fri 1-6
SPRINGVILLE BRANCH, 6496 US Hwy 11, Springville, 35146, SAN 374-6526. Tel: 205-467-2339. FAX: 205-467-2339. *Librn,* Betty Wisner; E-mail: spvli@windstream.net
Library Holdings: Bk Vols 19,565; Per Subs 11
Automation Activity & Vendor Info: (Acquisitions) Book Systems; (Cataloging) Book Systems; (Circulation) Book Systems; (OPAC) Book Systems
Open Mon, Wed & Fri 10-5, Tues & Thurs 10-8, Sat 10-1, Sun 2-5
Friends of the Library Group
STEELE BRANCH, 78 Hill Top, Steele, 35987. (Mail add: PO Box 548, Steele, 35987). Tel: 256-538-0811. FAX: 256 538-0811. *Librn,* Linda Fann
Pop 1,248; Circ 3,301
Oct 2008-Sept 2009 Income $18,244, State $1,561, City $10,612, Federal $3,880, County $221, Locally Generated Income $970, Other $1,000. Mats Exp $6,632, Books $1,586, Per/Ser (Incl. Access Fees) $196, AV Mat $4,850. Sal $6,316
Library Holdings: DVDs 447; Bk Titles 8,840
Open Mon-Wed 11-5, Thurs 1-5

ATHENS

P ATHENS-LIMESTONE PUBLIC LIBRARY*, 405 E South St, 35611. SAN 300-0087. Tel: 256-232-1233. FAX: 256-232-1250. Web Site: www.athenslimestone.lib.al.us. *Dir,* Paula Laurita; E-mail: allibrarydirector@gmail.com; Staff 4 (MLS 1, Non-MLS 3)
Founded 1970. Pop 65,676
Automation Activity & Vendor Info: (Acquisitions) Innovative Interfaces, Inc; (Cataloging) Innovative Interfaces, Inc; (Circulation) Innovative Interfaces, Inc; (OPAC) Innovative Interfaces, Inc
Wireless access
Open Mon 1-6, Tues & Thurs 10-8, Wed 10-6, Fri & Sat 10-5
Friends of the Library Group

C ATHENS STATE UNIVERSITY LIBRARY*, 407 E Pryor St, 35611. (Mail add: 300 N Beaty St, 35611), SAN 300-0095. Tel: 256-216-6661. FAX: 256-216-6674. E-mail: refdesk@athens.edu. Web Site: www.athens.edu/library. *Dir,* Dr Robert Burkhardt; E-mail: robert.burkhardt@athens.edu; *Acq, Asst Dir,* Barbara Burks; *Writing Ctr Dir,* Tony Ricks; *Ref, Instruction & Emerging Technologies Librn,* Del O'Neal; *Archivist,* Sara Love; *Cat/Ref/Syst,* Mary Aquila; *Circ, E-Learning & Instruction,* Jennifer Wolfe; *ILL,* Judy Stinnett; *Ref Serv,* Tim Williams; Staff 6 (MLS 6)
Founded 1842. Enrl 3,203; Fac 84; Highest Degree: Bachelor
Library Holdings: e-books 92,000; Bk Vols 123,000; Per Subs 317
Subject Interests: Local hist, Rare bks
Automation Activity & Vendor Info: (Cataloging) Innovative Interfaces, Inc; (Circulation) Innovative Interfaces, Inc; (ILL) OCLC; (OPAC) Innovative Interfaces, Inc
Publications: Libary Handbook
Partic in Lyrasis; Network of Alabama Academic Libraries; OCLC Online Computer Library Center, Inc
Open Mon-Thurs 8am-10pm, Fri 8-5, Sat 9-5, Sun 2-5
Friends of the Library Group

ATMORE

P ATMORE PUBLIC LIBRARY*, 700 E Church St, 36502. SAN 330-0153. Tel: 251-368-5234. FAX: 251-368-7064. Web Site: www.atmorelibrary.com. *Dir,* Cathy McKinley; E-mail: cmckinley@atmorelibrary.com; Staff 1 (MLS 1)
Founded 1923. Pop 15,000; Circ 54,927
Library Holdings: Bk Titles 50,000; Per Subs 54
Special Collections: Cancer & Heart Coll; Forestry (Atmores Industries Coll); Scout Books Coll
Automation Activity & Vendor Info: (Cataloging) Follett Software; (Circulation) Follett Software; (OPAC) Follett Software
Mem of Escambia County Cooperative Library System
Open Mon-Fri 10-6, Sat 8-1
Friends of the Library Group

P ESCAMBIA COUNTY COOPERATIVE LIBRARY SYSTEM*, 700 E Church St, 36502. SAN 324-0754. Tel: 251-368-4130. FAX: 251-368-4130. E-mail: escolib@frontiernet.net. *Adminr,* Pat Hetzel; Staff 2 (Non-MLS 2)
Founded 1980
Library Holdings: Bk Vols 10,000; Per Subs 14
Function: Homebound delivery serv
Member Libraries: Atmore Public Library; Brewton Public Library; Flomaton Public Library
Special Services for the Blind - Talking bks
Open Mon-Fri 7:30-3:30

ATTALLA

P ATTALLA-ETOWAH COUNTY PUBLIC LIBRARY*, 604 N Fourth St, 35954. SAN 300-0109. Tel: 256-538-9266. FAX: 256-538-9223. *Dir,* Lisa Spears; *Asst Librn,* Connie Beddingfield
Founded 1967. Pop 8,000; Circ 14,284
Library Holdings: Bk Vols 26,000; Per Subs 72
Wireless access
Open Mon-Fri 9-5:30, Sat 10-2

AUBURN

P AUBURN PUBLIC LIBRARY, 749 E Thach Ave, 36830. SAN 300-0117. Tel: 334-501-3190. Web Site: www.auburnalabama.org/library. *Dir,* Chris Warren; *Asst Dir,* Tyler Whitten; *Ch Serv,* Eve Engle; *Electronic Serv,* Dianne Ballentine; Staff 9 (MLS 5, Non-MLS 4)
Pop 42,987; Circ 167,338
Library Holdings: AV Mats 2,608; High Interest/Low Vocabulary Bk Vols 62; Large Print Bks 5,000; Bk Vols 70,000; Per Subs 135; Talking Bks 850
Special Collections: English as a Second Language
Automation Activity & Vendor Info: (Cataloging) Innovative Interfaces, Inc; (Circulation) Innovative Interfaces, Inc; (OPAC) Innovative Interfaces, Inc
Database Vendor: EBSCOhost, Gale Cengage Learning, OCLC FirstSearch
Wireless access
Function: AV serv, Handicapped accessible, ILL available, Magnifiers for reading, Photocopying/Printing, Prog for children & young adult, Ref serv available, Summer reading prog, Telephone ref, Wheelchair accessible
Publications: What's New? (Newsletter)
Special Services for the Blind - Aids for in-house use; Assistive/Adapted tech devices, equip & products; Bks available with recordings; Bks on cassette; Bks on CD; Computer with voice synthesizer for visually impaired persons; Copier with enlargement capabilities; HP Scan Jet with photo-finish software; Info on spec aids & appliances; Large print bks; Large screen computer & software; Networked computers with assistive software; PC for handicapped; Reader equip; Screen enlargement software for people with visual disabilities; Screen reader software; Talking bks
Open Mon-Thurs 9-9, Fri & Sat 9-5, Sun 2-6
Friends of the Library Group

AUBURN UNIVERSITY
C RALPH BROWN DRAUGHON LIBRARY*, 231 Mell St, 36849. Tel: 334-844-4500. Circulation Tel: 334-844-1701. Interlibrary Loan Service Tel: 334-844-1728. Reference Tel: 334-844-1737. Administration Tel: 334-844-1741. Toll Free Tel: 800-446-0387. FAX: 334-844-4424. Web Site: www.lib.auburn.edu/. *Dean, Libr Serv,* Bonnie MacEwan; Tel: 334-844-1715, E-mail: macewbj@auburn.edu; *Asst Dean, Coll Develop,* Glenn Anderson; *Head, Acq,* Paula Sullenger; Tel: 334-844-1725; *Head Archivist, Head, Spec Coll,* Dwayne Cox; Tel: 334-844-1707; *Head, Syst,* Aaron Trehub; Tel: 334-844-1716, E-mail: trehuaj@auburn.edu; *Outreach Serv Librn,* Linda Thornton; *Mgr,* Bob Yerkey; Tel: 334-844-2704; *Cat,* Helen Goldman; Tel: 334-844-0241; *Circ, Reserves,* Susan Hinds; Tel: 334-844-1579; *Digital Serv,* Gary Hawkins; *Doc Delivery,* Pambanisha King. Subject Specialists: *Bus,* Bob Yerkey; Staff 47 (MLS 47)
Founded 1856. Enrl 23,547; Fac 1,142; Highest Degree: Doctorate
Oct 2006-Sept 2007. Mats Exp $5,543,546. Sal $4,535,114 (Prof $2,858,377)
Library Holdings: e-books 285,137; e-journals 13,850; Bk Vols 3,016,986; Per Subs 36,395
Special Collections: Alabama Coll; Architecture Coll, slides; Auburn University Coll; US Government Publications; USGS Map Reference Coll. US Document Depository
Subject Interests: Genealogy, Relig hist, Sports
Automation Activity & Vendor Info: (Acquisitions) Ex Libris Group; (Cataloging) Ex Libris Group; (Circulation) Ex Libris Group; (Course Reserve) Docutek; (ILL) Ex Libris Group; (OPAC) Ex Libris Group; (Serials) Ex Libris Group

Partic in Association of Research Libraries (ARL); Association of Southeastern Research Libraries; BRS; CAS Online; Dialog Corp; Lyrasis; NAAL; Nat Ground Water; National Network of Libraries of Medicine; Network of Alabama Academic Libraries; RLIN (Research Libraries Information Network); SDC Info Servs; USDC
Open Mon-Thurs 7:45-2, Fri 7:45am-9pm, Sat 9-9, Sun 1pm-2am

C THE LIBRARY OF ARCHITECTURE, DESIGN & CONSTRUCTION*, Dudley Hall Commons, 36849. Tel: 334-844-1752. FAX: 334-844-1756. Web Site: www.lib.auburn.edu/architecture/. *Librn,* Boyd Childress
Library Holdings: Bk Vols 36,500
Open Mon-Thurs 7:45am-Midnight, Fri 7:45-5, Sat 9-6, Sun 1-Midnight

CM VETERINARY MEDICAL*, 101 Greene Hall, 36849-5606. Tel: 334-844-1749. Administration Tel: 334-844-1750. FAX: 334-844-1758. *Librn,* Bob Buchanan; E-mail: buchara@auburn.edu; Staff 3 (MLS 1, Non-MLS 2)
Library Holdings: Bk Vols 30,000
Partic in NASA Libraries Information System-NASA Galaxie
Open Mon-Thurs 7:30am-10:30pm, Fri 7:30-6, Sat 10-2, Sun 1-10:30

G UNITED STATES FOREST SERVICE*, Forest Engineering Research Library, George W Andrews Forestry Sciences Lab, 521 Devall Dr, 36849-5418. SAN 373-3777. Tel: 334-826-8700. FAX: 334-821-0037. Web Site: srs.fs.usda.gov/forestops.
Library Holdings: Bk Vols 12,000
Special Collections: Foreign publications; Forest Engineering; Forest operations literature
Subject Interests: Forestry
Partic in WiLS
Open Mon-Fri 8-4:30

BAY MINETTE

P BAY MINETTE PUBLIC LIBRARY*, 205 W Second St, 36507. SAN 300-0133. Tel: 251-580-1648. FAX: 251-937-0339. Web Site: www.bayminettepubliclibrary.org. *Dir, Libr Serv,* Joanna M Bailey; E-mail: jbailey@ci.bay-minette.al.us; *Cat, Tech Serv,* Kimberly Watson; Staff 7 (Non-MLS 7)
Founded 1922. Pop 8,000; Circ 25,000
Library Holdings: Bk Vols 36,000; Per Subs 60
Subject Interests: Ala, Genealogy
Automation Activity & Vendor Info: (Acquisitions) TLC (The Library Corporation); (Cataloging) TLC (The Library Corporation); (Circulation) TLC (The Library Corporation)
Mem of Baldwin County Library Cooperative, Inc
Open Mon, Wed & Fri 9-6, Tues & Thurs 9-8, Sat 10-2
Friends of the Library Group

J FAULKNER STATE COMMUNITY COLLEGE*, Austin R Meadows Library, 1900 Hwy 31 S, 36507. SAN 300-0141. Tel: 251-580-2145. FAX: 251-937-5140. *Dir,* Rheena Elmore; E-mail: rheena.elmore@faulknerstate.edu; Staff 5 (MLS 1, Non-MLS 4)
Founded 1965. Enrl 4,500; Fac 120; Highest Degree: Associate
Library Holdings: AV Mats 2,500; Bks on Deafness & Sign Lang 30; High Interest/Low Vocabulary Bk Vols 30; Bk Titles 65,815; Bk Vols 68,343; Per Subs 200
Special Collections: Baldwin Coll
Automation Activity & Vendor Info: (Cataloging) Book Systems; (Circulation) Book Systems; (OPAC) Book Systems
Wireless access
Open Mon-Thurs 7:30am-9pm, Fri 7:30-3:30, Sat 9-12

BAYOU LA BATRE

P MOSE HUDSON TAPIA PUBLIC LIBRARY*, 13885 S Wintzell Ave, 36509. SAN 300-015X. Tel: 251-824-4213. FAX: 251-824-3196. E-mail: tapialibrary@yahoo.com. *Asst Librn,* Jessica Perot; Staff 1 (Non-MLS 1)
Pop 3,500; Circ 5,700
Library Holdings: Bk Vols 17,680; Per Subs 15
Automation Activity & Vendor Info: (Cataloging) Book Systems; (Circulation) Book Systems; (OPAC) Book Systems
Friends of the Library Group

BESSEMER

P BESSEMER PUBLIC LIBRARY*, 701 Ninth Ave N, 35020-5305. SAN 300-0168. Tel: 205-428-7882. FAX: 205-428-7885. E-mail: bessemerlibrary@gmail.com. Web Site: www.bessemer.lib.al.us. *Dir,* Carole McDowell Castine; Tel: 205-428-7868; *Adult Serv,* Leslie Cost West; E-mail: lwest@bham.lib.al.us; *Youth Serv,* Priscilla Renee Ward; E-mail: pward@bham.lib.al.us; Staff 12 (MLS 2, Non-MLS 10)
Founded 1908. Pop 29,672; Circ 112,903
Library Holdings: AV Mats 4,065; Bk Titles 71,622; Per Subs 124; Talking Bks 2,448
Database Vendor: EBSCOhost, Gale Cengage Learning, Innovative Interfaces, Inc
Partic in Jefferson County Libr Coop
Open Mon-Fri 9-6, Sat 10-4

J LAWSON STATE COMMUNITY COLLEGE LIBRARY*, Bessemer Campus, 1100 Ninth Ave SW, 35022. Tel: 205-929-3434, 205-929-6333. Administration Tel: 205-929-3490. FAX: 205-925-3716. *Libr Dir,* Sandra Henderson; E-mail: shenderson@lawsonstate.edu; *Librn,* Jacqueline Cooper; E-mail: jnazzeri@lawsonstate.edu; *Librn,* Tonja Hunter; E-mail: thunter@lawsonstate.edu; *Extended Day Librn,* Sheryl Howard; E-mail: swhoward@lawsonstate.edu; *AV Tech,* Harold Dennard; E-mail: hdennard@lawsonstate.edu; *Automation Spec,* LeighAnn Carroll; E-mail: lcarroll@lawsonstate.edu
Founded 1949. Enrl 3,500; Fac 167; Highest Degree: Associate
Library Holdings: Audiobooks 80; AV Mats 1,196; CDs 758; DVDs 322; e-books 26,000; Bk Titles 53,516; Bk Vols 55,000; Per Subs 160; Videos 847
Automation Activity & Vendor Info: (Acquisitions) SirsiDynix; (Cataloging) SirsiDynix; (Circulation) SirsiDynix; (Course Reserve) SirsiDynix; (OPAC) SirsiDynix
Database Vendor: Baker & Taylor, EBSCOhost, OVID Technologies, ProQuest, SirsiDynix
Wireless access
Function: Art exhibits
Partic in Lyrasis
Open Mon-Thurs 8am-8:30pm, Fri 8-4, Sat 8-Noon

BIRMINGHAM

S ALABAMA POWER CO, Research Services, 600 N 18th St, 35203-2206. (Mail add: PO Box 2641, 35291-0277), SAN 300-0184. Tel: 205-257-4466. FAX: 205-257-2075. E-mail: w2xaplib@southernco.com. *Coordr,* Sherie Mattox; E-mail: samattox@southernco.com; *Res Librn,* Lisa Mitchell; E-mail: lrmitche@southernco.com; Staff 3 (MLS 2, Non-MLS 1)
Founded 1925
Library Holdings: Audiobooks 300; Bk Titles 7,500; Bk Vols 8,000; Per Subs 30; Videos 500
Subject Interests: Bus & mgt, Computer sci, Electric utilities, Eng
Automation Activity & Vendor Info: (Cataloging) EOS International; (Circulation) EOS International; (OPAC) EOS International; (Serials) EOS International
Database Vendor: Dun & Bradstreet, EOS International, IEEE (Institute of Electrical & Electronics Engineers), IHS, Ingram Library Services, LexisNexis, OCLC WorldShare Interlibrary Loan
Function: 24/7 Online cat, Bks on CD, ILL available, Microfiche/film & reading machines, Online searches, Res libr
Partic in Lyrasis
Restriction: Access for corporate affiliates, Circulates for staff only, Co libr, Employees only, External users must contact libr

M AMERICAN SPORTS MEDICINE INSTITUTE*, Sports Medicine Library, 2660 Tenth Ave S, Ste 505, 35205. SAN 327-0327. Tel: 205-918-2130. Administration Tel: 205-918-2135. FAX: 205-918-2178. Administration FAX: 205-918-2177. Web Site: www.asmi.org. *Med Librn,* Susan McWhorter; E-mail: susan@asmi.org; *Asst Librn,* DeBora Hall
Library Holdings: Bk Titles 500; Bk Vols 700; Per Subs 95
Subject Interests: Orthopedics
Partic in Alabama Health Libraries Association, Inc; Medical Library Association (MLA); SEND

L BALCH & BINGHAM ATTORNEYS LIBRARY*, 1901 Sixth Ave N, Ste 1500, 35203. SAN 300-0192. Tel: 205-251-8100. FAX: 205-226-8798. *Dir,* Christina Tabereaux; Tel: 205-226-8710; Staff 3 (MLS 1, Non-MLS 2)
Library Holdings: Bk Titles 2,000; Bk Vols 35,000; Per Subs 200
Subject Interests: State law
Partic in Westlaw
Restriction: Private libr

S BIRMINGHAM MUSEUM OF ART, Clarence B Hanson Jr Library, 2000 Rev Abraham Wood Jr Blvd, 35203-2278. SAN 300-0214. Tel: 205-297-8065. E-mail: library@artsbma.org. Web Site: www.artsbma.org. *Librn,* Lindsey Reynolds; E-mail: lreynolds@artsbma.org; Staff 1 (MLS 1)
Founded 1966
Library Holdings: Bk Titles 26,000; Bk Vols 26,000; Per Subs 50
Special Collections: Buten Wedgwood Coll; Chellis Wedgwood Coll; The Dwight & Lucille Beeson Wedgwood Coll
Subject Interests: Art
Automation Activity & Vendor Info: (Cataloging) ByWater Solutions; (OPAC) ByWater Solutions
Database Vendor: ARTstor, OCLC FirstSearch, OCLC WorldShare Interlibrary Loan
Wireless access
Function: For res purposes, ILL available, Telephone ref
Restriction: In-house use for visitors, Non-circulating, Open by appt only

P BIRMINGHAM PUBLIC LIBRARY, Central, 2100 Park Pl, 35203-2744. SAN 330-0307. Tel: 205-226-3600. Circulation Tel: 205-226-3602. Interlibrary Loan Service Tel: 205-226-3730. Administration Tel: 205-226-3610. FAX: 205-226-3743. Web Site: www.bplonline.org. *Interim Dir,* Angela Fisher Hall; E-mail: ahall@bham.lib.al.us; *Br Coordr, Head, Info Literacy,* Janine Langston; Tel: 205-322-6371, E-mail: jlangston@bham.lib.al.us; *Br Coordr,* Sandra Crawley; E-mail: scraw@bham.lib.al.us; *Pub Relations Coordr,* Chanda Temple; Tel: 205-226-3604, E-mail: ctemple@bham.lib.al.us; *Pub Serv,* Karyn David; E-mail: kdavid@bham.lib.al.us; Staff 75 (MLS 65, Non-MLS 10)
Founded 1902. Pop 656,700; Circ 1,217,148
Jul 2008-Jun 2009 Income (Main Library and Branch(s)) $16,937,357, State $207,684, City $16,459,673, County $270,000. Mats Exp $16,297,908, Books $805,479, Per/Ser (Incl. Access Fees) $2,063, Micro $1,463, AV Mat $83,480, Electronic Ref Mat (Incl. Access Fees) $425. Sal $10,292,903
Library Holdings: AV Mats 82,159; CDs 17,810; Large Print Bks 19,471; Music Scores 2,362; Bk Vols 899,404; Per Subs 2,500; Talking Bks 15,848; Videos 48,501
Special Collections: Affiliate Agency-Alabama Data Center; Ballet, Dance (Collins Coll of the Dance), bks, photog, programs; Cartography (Agee-Woodward Coll), bks, maps; Drama Coll; Early Children's Books (Hardie Coll); Foundation Center New York (Cooperating Coll); Genealogy, Southern History (Tutwiler Coll), bks, micro, pamphlets, per, VF; Philately (Scruggs Coll), bks, stamps, pamphlets; Rare Books (Bowron Coll). UN Document Depository; US Document Depository
Subject Interests: Genealogy
Automation Activity & Vendor Info: (Acquisitions) Innovative Interfaces, Inc; (Cataloging) Innovative Interfaces, Inc; (Circulation) Innovative Interfaces, Inc; (OPAC) Innovative Interfaces, Inc; (Serials) Innovative Interfaces, Inc
Wireless access
Partic in Jefferson County Libr Coop
Special Services for the Deaf - TDD equip
Open Mon & Tues 9-8, Wed-Sat 9-6, Sun 2-6
Friends of the Library Group

Branches: 18

AVONDALE, 509 40th St S, 35222-3309, SAN 330-0390. Tel: 205-226-4000. FAX: 205-595-5824. *Librn,* Felita Yarbrough; Staff 18 (MLS 5, Non-MLS 13)
Library Holdings: CDs 723; DVDs 1,028; Large Print Bks 841; Bk Vols 37,160; Talking Bks 1,297; Videos 2,170
Open Mon & Tues 9-8, Wed-Sat 9-6, Sun 2-6

EAST ENSLEY BRANCH, 900 14th St, Ensley, 35218-1206, SAN 330-0455. Tel: 205-787-1928. FAX: 205-786-7219. *Librn,* Christopher Hare
Library Holdings: CDs 76; DVDs 596; Large Print Bks 19; Bk Vols 16,569; Talking Bks 90; Videos 955
Open Mon, Tues, Thurs & Fri 9-12 & 1-6, Wed 1-6
Friends of the Library Group

EAST LAKE, Five Oporto-Madrid Blvd, 35206-4800, SAN 330-048X. Tel: 205-836-3341. FAX: 205-833-8055. *Librn,* William Darby; E-mail: wdarby@bham.lib.al.us
Library Holdings: Bk Vols 17,585
Open Mon-Fri 9-6, Sat 9-1 & 2-6

EASTWOOD, 4500 Montevallo Rd, Ste 107, 35210, SAN 330-0498. Tel: 205-591-4944. FAX: 205-956-2503. *Librn,* William Darby; E-mail: wdarby@bham.lib.al.us; Staff 7 (MLS 1, Non-MLS 6)
Library Holdings: CDs 6; Large Print Bks 412; Bk Vols 7,571; Per Subs 50; Talking Bks 623
Open Mon-Sat 9-6, Sun 1-5

ENSLEY BRANCH, 1201 25th St, Ensley, 35218-1944, SAN 330-051X. Tel: 205-785-2625. FAX: 205-785-6625. *Librn,* Alisha Johnson
Library Holdings: DVDs 630; Large Print Bks 17; Bk Vols 11,728; Videos 591
Open Mon, Tues, Thurs & Fri 9-12 & 1-6, Wed 1-6

FIVE POINTS WEST, 4812 Avenue W, 35208-4726, SAN 330-0528. Tel: 205-226-4013. FAX: 205-780-8152. *Librn,* Janine Langston; E-mail: jlangston@bham.lib.al.us; Staff 4 (MLS 4)
Library Holdings: CDs 618; DVDs 1,346; Large Print Bks 778; Bk Vols 48,232; Talking Bks 1,310; Videos 1,618
Open Mon & Tues 9-8, Wed-Sat 9-6, Sun 2-6

INGLENOOK, 4100 N 40th Terrace, 35217-4162, SAN 330-0595. Tel: 205-849-8739. FAX: 205-841-2551. *Librn,* Karnecia Williams
Library Holdings: DVDs 560; Large Print Bks 2; Bk Vols 7,715; Videos 648
Open Mon, Tues, Thurs & Fri 9-12 & 1-6, Wed 1-6

NORTH AVONDALE, 501 43rd St N, 35222-1417, SAN 330-0544. Tel: 205-592-2082. FAX: 205-595-9871. *Librn,* Saundra Ross; E-mail: sross@bham.lib.al.us; Staff 3 (MLS 1, Non-MLS 2)
Library Holdings: CDs 269; DVDs 610; Bk Vols 10,906; Talking Bks 80; Videos 1,175
Open Mon, Tues, Thurs & Fri 9-12 & 1-6, Wed 1-6

NORTH BIRMINGHAM, 2501 31st Ave N, 35207-4423, SAN 330-0633. Tel: 205-226-4025. FAX: 205-250-0725. *Librn,* Sandra Crawley; E-mail: scraw@bham.lib.al.us
Library Holdings: CDs 670; DVDs 970; Large Print Bks 7; Bk Vols 33,530; Talking Bks 968; Videos 1,680
Open Mon & Tues 9-8, Wed-Sat 9-6, Sun 2-6

POWDERLY, 3301 Jefferson Ave SW, 35221-1241, SAN 330-0684. Tel: 205-925-6178. FAX: 205-925-1276. *Br Mgr,* Loretta Bitten; E-mail: lbitten@bham.lib.al.us
Library Holdings: Bks-By-Mail 7,401; CDs 259; DVDs 592; Large Print Bks 932; Bk Vols 13,424; Talking Bks 497; Videos 1,077
Open Mon, Tues, Thurs & Fri 9-12 & 1-6, Wed 1-6

PRATT CITY BRANCH, 509 Dugan Ave, 35214-5224, SAN 330-0692. Tel: 205-791-4997. *Br Mgr,* Deborah Drake-Blackman; E-mail: ddrake@bham.lib.al.us
Library Holdings: CDs 230; DVDs 622; Large Print Bks 126; Bk Vols 22,013; Talking Bks 570; Videos 2,000
Open Mon-Fri 9-6, Sat 9-1 & 2-6

SMITHFIELD, One Eighth Ave W, 35204-3724, SAN 330-0757. Tel: 205-324-8428. FAX: 205-254-8851. *Librn,* Yolanda T Hardy; E-mail: yhardy@bham.lib.al.us
Library Holdings: CDs 257; DVDs 628; Large Print Bks 21; Bk Vols 25,017; Talking Bks 278; Videos 898
Open Mon-Fri 9-6, Sat 9-1 & 2-6

SOUTHSIDE, 1814 11th Ave S, 35205-4808, SAN 330-0668. Tel: 205-933-7776. FAX: 205-918-0723. *Librn,* Teresa Ceravolo; E-mail: tceravolo@bham.lib.al.us; Staff 1 (MLS 1)
Library Holdings: Audiobooks 600; CDs 300; DVDs 1,700; Large Print Bks 500; Bk Vols 23,394; Videos 60
Special Services for the Deaf - Closed caption videos; High interest/low vocabulary bks
Special Services for the Blind - Large print bks
Open Mon-Fri 9-6, Sat 9-1 & 2-6
Friends of the Library Group

SPRINGVILLE ROAD, 1224 Springville Rd, 35215-7512, SAN 330-0579. Tel: 205-226-4081. FAX: 205-856-0825. *Librn,* Sandra Lee; E-mail: slee@bham.lib.al.us
Library Holdings: CDs 738; DVDs 1,114; Large Print Bks 2,474; Bk Vols 58,938; Talking Bks 2,880; Videos 3,283
Open Mon & Tues 9-8, Wed-Sat 9-6, Sun 2-6

TITUSVILLE, Two Sixth Ave SW, 35211-2909, SAN 330-0781. Tel: 205-322-1140. FAX: 205-328-2149. *Librn,* Darlene Worford; E-mail: dworford@bham.lib.al.us
Library Holdings: Bk Vols 21,000; Talking Bks 400
Open Mon-Fri 9-6, Sat 9-1 & 2-6

WEST END, 1348 Tuscaloosa Ave SW, 35211-1948, SAN 330-0811. Tel: 205-226-4089. FAX: 205-785-6260. *Br Head,* Maya N Jones; E-mail: mjones@bham.lib.al.us; Staff 3 (MLS 1, Non-MLS 2)
Library Holdings: CDs 175; DVDs 527; Bk Vols 16,000; Per Subs 25; Talking Bks 150
Special Services for the Deaf - Bks on deafness & sign lang; Staff with knowledge of sign lang
Open Mon-Fri 9-6, Sat 9-1 & 2-6
Friends of the Library Group

WOODLAWN, 5709 First Ave N, 35212-1603, SAN 330-0846. Tel: 205 595 2001. FAX: 205-595-9654. *Librn,* Pamela Jessie; E-mail: pjessie@bham.lib.al.us
Library Holdings: CDs 373; DVDs 650; Large Print Bks 424; Bk Vols 16,550; Videos 1,549
Open Mon, Tues, Thurs & Fri 9-12 & 1-6, Wed 1-6

WYLAM BRANCH, 4300 Seventh Ave, 35224-2624, SAN 330-0870. Tel: 205-785-0349. FAX: 205-781-6571. *Librn,* Jean Shanks
Library Holdings: CDs 45; DVDs 2,000; Bk Vols 11,000; Videos 75
Open Mon, Tues, Thurs & Fri 9-12 & 1-6, Wed 1-6

C BIRMINGHAM-SOUTHERN COLLEGE*, Charles Andrew Rush Learning Center & N E Miles Library, 900 Arkadelphia Rd, 35254. (Mail add: PO Box 549020, 35254-0001), SAN 300-0230. Tel: 205-226-4740. Interlibrary Loan Service Tel: 205-226-4748. Reference Tel: 205-226-4766. Administration Tel: 205-226-4744. FAX: 205-226-4743. Web Site: www.bsc.edu. *Dir,* Charlotte Ford; E-mail: cford@bsc.edu; *Cat Librn,* Janice J Poplau; E-mail: jpoplau@bsc.edu; *Archivist, Ref Librn,* Guy Hubbs; Tel: 205-226-4752, E-mail: ghubbs@bsc.edu; *Ref Librn,* Steve Laughlin; E-mail: slaughli@bsc.edu; *Ref Librn,* Stacey Thornberry; E-mail: sthornbe@bsc.edu; *Circ Supvr,* Eric Kennedy; E-mail: ekennedy@bsc.edu; *Ref Serv Coordr,* Pam Sawallis; Tel: 205-226-4749, E-mail: psawalli@bsc.edu. Subject Specialists: *Southern hist,* Guy Hubbs; *Bus,* Steve Laughlin; Staff 6.5 (MLS 5.5, Non-MLS 1)
Founded 1856. Enrl 1,389; Fac 107; Highest Degree: Master
Jun 2007-May 2008 Income $1,262,533. Mats Exp $555,614, Books $193,950, Per/Ser (Incl. Access Fees) $152,654, Micro $23,930, AV Equip $5,000, AV Mat $11,312, Electronic Ref Mat (Incl. Access Fees) $150,600, Presv $18,168. Sal $565,411 (Prof $305,397)

Library Holdings: AV Mats 31,826; CDs 5,522; DVDs 1,576; e-books 42,404; e-journals 38,517; Music Scores 2,200; Bk Titles 189,573; Bk Vols 259,572; Per Subs 540; Videos 5,325
Special Collections: Alabama Authors; Alabama History; Alabama Methodism. US Document Depository
Subject Interests: Americana
Automation Activity & Vendor Info: (Acquisitions) SirsiDynix; (Cataloging) SirsiDynix; (Circulation) SirsiDynix; (OPAC) SirsiDynix; (Serials) SirsiDynix
Database Vendor: ABC-CLIO, American Chemical Society, American Mathematical Society, Annual Reviews, BioOne, Cambridge Scientific Abstracts, CQ Press, CredoReference, EBSCOhost, Elsevier, Gale Cengage Learning, JSTOR, LexisNexis, Mergent Online, OCLC FirstSearch, Oxford Online, Project MUSE, ProQuest, ScienceDirect, SerialsSolutions, SirsiDynix, Wiley InterScience, Wilson - Wilson Web
Wireless access
Partic in Associated Colleges of the South; Lyrasis; Network of Alabama Academic Libraries
Open Mon-Thurs 8am-Midnight, Fri 8-5, Sat 9-5, Sun 2-Midnight

L BRADLEY, ARANT, ROSE & WHITE*, Law Library, One Federal Pl, 1819 Fifth Ave N, 35203. SAN 300-0249. Tel: 205-521-8000. FAX: 205-521-8800. Web Site: www.bradleyarant.com. *Head of Libr,* Lori D Martin
Library Holdings: Bk Vols 27,000
Partic in Dialog Corp; Westlaw
Restriction: Private libr

L BURR & FORMAN LIBRARY*, Southtrust Tower, Ste 3100, 420 20th St N, 35203. SAN 300-0419. Tel: 205-251-3000. FAX: 205-458-5100. *Librn,* Helen Walker
Library Holdings: Bk Vols 18,000; Per Subs 25
Special Collections: Labor, Corporate law

M CALLAHAN EYE FOUNDATION HOSPITAL*, John E Meyer Eye Library, 1720 University Blvd, 35233-1895. SAN 324-6523. Tel: 205-325-8505. FAX: 205-325-8506. *Librn,* Kenneth Tow; E-mail: ktow@uabmc.edu
Library Holdings: Bk Titles 1,650; Per Subs 42
Subject Interests: Ophthalmology
Wireless access
Partic in National Network of Libraries of Medicine
Open Mon-Fri 7:30-4

SR INDEPENDENT PRESBYTERIAN CHURCH*, John N Lukens Library, 3100 Highland Ave S, 35205-1400. SAN 328-5138. Tel: 205-933-1830. FAX: 205-933-1836. *Librn,* Ginni Robertson
Library Holdings: Bk Vols 4,500; Per Subs 10
Subject Interests: Relig, Theol
Open Mon, Tues, Thurs & Fri 8:30-4:30, Wed 8:30-7:30, Sun 8:30-1

GL JEFFERSON COUNTY LAW LIBRARY, Jefferson County Court House, Ste 530, 716 Richard Arrington Jr Blvd N, 35203. SAN 300-029X. Tel: 205-325-5628. FAX: 205-322-5915. Web Site: jeffconline.jccal.org/law_library. *Law Librn,* Position Currently Open; *Law Libr Asst,* Karen W Bussey; E-mail: busseyk@jccal.org; Staff 2 (MLS 1, Non-MLS 1)
Founded 1885
Oct 2007-Sept 2008 Income $457,000. Mats Exp $179,546, Books $34,500, Per/Ser (Incl. Access Fees) $575, Electronic Ref Mat (Incl. Access Fees) $144,000, Presv $471. Sal $240,800
Subject Interests: Law
Database Vendor: HeinOnline, LexisNexis, Westlaw
Wireless access
Open Mon-Fri 8:30-5
Restriction: Non-circulating to the pub

J JEFFERSON STATE COMMUNITY COLLEGE*, James B Allen Library, 2601 Carson Rd, 35215-3098. SAN 300-0303. Tel: 205-856-8524. FAX: 205-856-8512. *Coordr,* Lynda Dickinson; Tel: 205-520-5530, Fax: 205-530-5931; *Circ,* Miriam Ford; Tel: 205-856-7788; *Info Serv, Ref,* Judy Dawson; Tel: 205-856-7786; Staff 6 (MLS 3, Non-MLS 3)
Founded 1965. Enrl 7,400; Highest Degree: Associate
Library Holdings: AV Mats 2,931; Bk Vols 70,207; Per Subs 294
Special Collections: US Document Depository
Automation Activity & Vendor Info: (Cataloging) SirsiDynix; (Circulation) SirsiDynix
Database Vendor: EBSCOhost, Gale Cengage Learning, OCLC FirstSearch, ProQuest
Publications: LRC Quarterly
Open Mon-Thurs 7:30am-9pm, Fri 7:30-4, Sat 9-Noon

J LAWSON STATE COMMUNITY COLLEGE LIBRARY*, Birmingham Campus, 3060 Wilson Rd SW, 35221. SAN 320-5487. Tel: 205-925-2515, Ext 6333, 205-929-6333. Circulation Tel: 205-929-2068. Reference Tel: 205-929-2021. FAX: 205-925-3716. Web Site: www.lawsonstate.edu. *Dir,* Sandra L Henderson; E-mail: shenderson@lawsonstate.edu; *Ref,* Jackie Nazeri Cooper; *Ref,* Tonja Hunter
Founded 1965. Enrl 2,000
Library Holdings: Bk Vols 31,000; Per Subs 165
Special Collections: Martin Luther King Jr Afro-American Coll
Automation Activity & Vendor Info: (Acquisitions) SirsiDynix; (Cataloging) SirsiDynix; (Circulation) SirsiDynix; (Course Reserve) SirsiDynix; (OPAC) SirsiDynix
Database Vendor: ProQuest, SirsiDynix
Wireless access
Publications: Annual Report; Booktalk (Newsletter); Policy Manual; Student Handbook
Open Mon-Thurs 8am-8:30pm, Fri 8-4, Sat 8-Noon
Friends of the Library Group

S THE LIBRARY AT BIRMINGHAM BOTANICAL GARDEN*, 2612 Lane Park Rd, 35223. SAN 324-0061. Tel: 205-414-3920. FAX: 205-414-3922. E-mail: thelibrary@bbgardens.org. Web Site: www.bbgardens.org/library. *Dir of Libr,* Hope Long; Tel: 205-414-3931, E-mail: hopel@bham.lib.al.us; *Librn,* Elizabeth Drewry; Tel: 205-414-3932, E-mail: edrewry@bham.lib.al.us; Staff 3 (MLS 2, Non-MLS 1)
Founded 1973
Library Holdings: Audiobooks 10; AV Mats 200; CDs 30; DVDs 50; Electronic Media & Resources 20; Bk Titles 7,500; Per Subs 60; Videos 125
Subject Interests: Botany, Hort, Nature
Automation Activity & Vendor Info: (Circulation) Innovative Interfaces, Inc; (OPAC) Innovative Interfaces, Inc
Database Vendor: EBSCOhost, Factset, Gale Cengage Learning, LexisNexis, Newsbank, OCLC FirstSearch, OCLC WorldShare Interlibrary Loan, ProQuest, ScienceDirect
Function: Adult bk club, Art exhibits, Audiobks via web, Bks on CD, CD-ROM, Children's prog, Computers for patron use, Copy machines, e-mail serv, E-Reserves, Electronic databases & coll, Exhibits, Holiday prog, Homebound delivery serv, ILL available, Online cat, Online searches, OverDrive digital audio bks, Photocopying/Printing, Prog for adults, Prog for children & young adult, Pub access computers, Ref serv available, Ref serv in person, Res libr, Telephone ref, VHS videos, Web-catalog, Wheelchair accessible, Workshops
Publications: Garden Dirt (Newsletter)
Partic in Jefferson County Libr Coop
Open Mon-Fri 9-4, Sat 10-4, Sun 2-5

L MAYNARD, COOPER & GALE*, Law Library, Amsouth Harbert Plaza, Ste 2400, 1901 Sixth Ave N, 35203-2602. SAN 372-2627. Tel: 205-254-1000, 205-488-3570. FAX: 205-254-1999. Web Site: www.mcglaw.com. *Librn,* Sean Reese; Staff 2 (MLS 1, Non-MLS 1)
Library Holdings: Bk Titles 10,000

P NORTH SHELBY COUNTY LIBRARY*, 5521 Cahaba Valley Rd, 35242. SAN 371-9367. Tel: 205-439-5500. Circulation Tel: 205-439-5508. Reference Tel: 205-439-5510. Administration Tel: 205-439-5555. FAX: 205-439-5503. Web Site: www.northshelbylibrary.org. *Dir of Libr Serv,* Katie Guerin; Tel: 205-439-5540, E-mail: katie.guerin@gmail.com; Staff 10 (MLS 7, Non-MLS 3)
Pop 60,000; Circ 250,000
Library Holdings: Bk Vols 63,000; Per Subs 95
Automation Activity & Vendor Info: (Acquisitions) Innovative Interfaces, Inc; (Cataloging) Innovative Interfaces, Inc; (Circulation) Innovative Interfaces, Inc; (OPAC) Innovative Interfaces, Inc
Wireless access
Mem of Harrison Regional Library System
Open Mon & Thurs 10-8, Tues, Wed & Fri 10-6, Sat 10-4, Sun 1-5
Friends of the Library Group

M SAINT VINCENT'S HOSPITAL*, Cunningham Wilson Library & Resource Center, 810 St Vincent's Dr, 35205-1695. SAN 324-5306. Tel: 205-939-7830. FAX: 205-930-2182. *Info Spec,* Sister Anne Marie Schreiner; Tel: 205-939-7832, E-mail: srannema@stv.org; Staff 2 (MLS 1, Non-MLS 1)
Library Holdings: e-books 20; e-journals 250; Bk Titles 2,000; Per Subs 120; Videos 100
Subject Interests: Career develop, Consumer health, Nursing, Spiritual life
Database Vendor: Dialog, OVID Technologies
Partic in Alabama Health Libraries Association, Inc; SEND
Open Mon-Fri 8-4:30

C SAMFORD UNIVERSITY LIBRARY, 800 Lakeshore Dr, 35229. SAN 330-0900. Tel: 205-726-2846. Circulation Tel: 205-726-2748. Interlibrary Loan Service Tel: 205-726-2983. Reference Tel: 205-726-2196. FAX:

205-726-4009. E-mail: library@samford.edu. Web Site: www.samford.edu/library. *Dean,* Kimmetha Herndon; E-mail: kherndon@samford.edu; *Assoc Dean, Chair, Coll Develop & Acq,* Lori Northrup; Tel: 205-726-2518; *Chair, Cat, Tech Serv,* Jaro Szurek; Tel: 205-726-4136; *Chair, Circ,* Cheryl Cecil; Tel: 205-726-2699, E-mail: cscecil@samford.edu; *Chair, Ref & Res Serv,* Carla Waddell; Tel: 205-726-2755, E-mail: ctwaddel@samford.edu; *Chair, Spec Coll, Librn,* Jennifer Taylor; Tel: 205-726-4103, E-mail: jrtaylor@samford.edu; *Automation Syst Coordr, Online Serv,* Ed Cherry; Tel: 205-726-2506, E-mail: cecherry@samford.edu; *Acq,* Regina Coleman; Tel: 205-726-2520, E-mail: srcolema@samford.edu; Staff 29 (MLS 14, Non-MLS 15)
Founded 1841. Highest Degree: Doctorate
Library Holdings: e-books 81,980; Microforms 664,474; Bk Vols 504,709; Per Subs 13,204
Special Collections: Alabama History & Literature, bks, ms, maps, microfilm, newsp; Baptist History, bks, ms, microfilm; Douglas McMurtrie Coll, bks, pamphlets; Genealogy Coll, bks, ms, per; Hearn Coll; History & Genealogy (Casey Coll), bks, ms, maps; Irish Coll; John Ruskin First Edition Books; Masefield First Edition Books & Critical Works; Tennyson First Edition Books & Critical Works. Oral History; US Document Depository
Automation Activity & Vendor Info: (Cataloging) Innovative Interfaces, Inc - Millenium; (Circulation) Innovative Interfaces, Inc - Millenium; (ILL) OCLC ILLiad; (OPAC) Innovative Interfaces, Inc - Millenium; (Serials) Innovative Interfaces, Inc - Millenium
Database Vendor: 3M Library Systems, Baker & Taylor, Cambridge Scientific Abstracts, EBSCO Information Services, EBSCOhost, H W Wilson, HeinOnline, Innovative Interfaces, Inc, JSTOR, LexisNexis, Marcive, Inc, OCLC FirstSearch, OCLC WorldShare Interlibrary Loan, Oxford Online, ProQuest, SerialsSolutions, ValueLine, Wiley InterScience, Wilson - Wilson Web, YBP Library Services
Function: Computers for patron use, Copy machines, Doc delivery serv, e-mail & chat, e-mail serv, Electronic databases & coll, Exhibits, Fax serv, Govt ref serv, Handicapped accessible, ILL available, Instruction & testing, Libr develop, Mail & tel request accepted, Mail loans to mem, Music CDs, Newsp ref libr, Notary serv, Online cat, Online info literacy tutorials on the web & in blackboard, Online ref, Online searches, Orientations, Outreach serv, Photocopying/Printing, Pub access computers, Ref & res, Ref serv available, Ref serv in person, Res libr, Scanner, Spoken cassettes & CDs, Tax forms, Telephone ref, VCDs, VHS videos, Web-catalog, Wheelchair accessible
Publications: Folklore in the Samford University Library; History of Marion, Alabama, by Samuel A Townes, reprint of 1844 Edition; Ireland, The Albert E Casey Coll & Other Irish Materials in the Samford University Library; Maps in the Samford University Library; Maud McLure Kelly, Alabama's First Woman Lawyer, by C Newman (Samford University Library Research Series, paper No 6); Samford University Library Research Series, paper No 7
Partic in Lyrasis; Network of Alabama Academic Libraries
Friends of the Library Group

Departmental Libraries:

CL LUCILLE STEWART BEESON LAW LIBRARY, 800 Lakeshore Dr, 35229, SAN 330-0994. Tel: 205-726-2714. FAX: 205-726-2644. Web Site: www.lawlib.samford.edu. *Dir,* Gregory K Laughlin; *Computer Librn,* Grace Simms; *Acq,* Cherie Feenker; *Cat,* Rebecca Hutto; *Ref,* Edward L Craig, Jr; *Ref,* Brenda K Jones; *Ser,* Michael Manasco; Staff 14 (MLS 7, Non-MLS 7)
Founded 1847. Enrl 494; Fac 21
Library Holdings: Bk Titles 37,991; Bk Vols 202,951; Per Subs 2,029
Database Vendor: Gale Cengage Learning, H W Wilson, HeinOnline, LexisNexis, Westlaw
Restriction: Open to researchers by request, Open to students, fac & staff

CURRICULUM MATERIALS CENTER, Beeson Education Bldg, 800 Lakeshore Dr, 35229, SAN 330-096X. Tel: 205-726-2558. FAX: 205-726-2068. *Dir,* Michele Haralson; E-mail: mkharals@samford.edu
Library Holdings: Bk Titles 5,000; Per Subs 12
Open Mon-Thurs 8am-9pm, Fri 8-3, Sat 10-2

GLOBAL DRUG INFORMATION CENTER MCWHORTER SCHOOL OF PHARMACY, Ingalls Bldg, 800 Lakeshore Dr, 35229, SAN 330-0935. Tel: 205-726-2161, 205-726-2891. FAX: 205-726-4012. Web Site: www.samford.edu/schools/pharmacy/dic/index.html. *Dir,* Michael G Kendrach; *Librn,* Robert Schrimsher
Library Holdings: Bk Vols 900; Per Subs 80
Open Mon-Wed 8am-9pm, Thurs & Fri 8-4:30

L SIROTE & PERMUTT PC, Law Library, 2311 Highland Ave S, 35205-2792. (Mail add: PO Box 55727, 35255-5727), SAN 326-3088. Tel: 205-930-5233. FAX: 205-930-5101. *Librn,* William Preston Peyton; E-mail: ppeyton@sirote.com
Founded 1946
Library Holdings: Bk Vols 8,000; Per Subs 45
Database Vendor: LexisNexis, Westlaw
Restriction: Staff use only

CR SOUTHEASTERN BIBLE COLLEGE LIBRARY, Gannett-Estes Library, 2545 Valleydale Rd, 35244. SAN 300-0346. Tel: 205-970-9233. FAX: 205-970-9207. E-mail: library@sebc.edu. Web Site: www.sebc.edu. *Librn,* Paul A Roberts; E-mail: proberts@sebc.edu; *Libr Asst,* Becky Owens; Staff 1.75 (MLS 1, Non-MLS 0.75)
Founded 1935. Enrl 170; Fac 26; Highest Degree: Bachelor
Library Holdings: AV Mats 1,600; CDs 1,500; DVDs 178; e-books 42,850; e-journals 155,186; Bk Titles 58,552; Bk Vols 60,525; Per Subs 98; Videos 735
Subject Interests: Educ, Pre-seminary
Automation Activity & Vendor Info: (Cataloging) EOS International; (Circulation) EOS International; (Course Reserve) EOS International; (ILL) OCLC ILLiad; (OPAC) EOS International; (Serials) EOS International
Database Vendor: EBSCO Information Services, EBSCOhost, EOS International, Ingram Library Services, OCLC, OCLC FirstSearch, OCLC WorldShare Interlibrary Loan
Wireless access

S SOUTHERN RESEARCH INSTITUTE*, Thomas Martin Memorial Library, 2000 Ninth Ave S, 35205. (Mail add: PO Box 55305, 35255-5305), SAN 300-0362. Tel: 205-581-2000, Ext 2272. FAX: 205-581-2008. *Mgr, Online Serv,* Richard J Remy; E-mail: r.remy@sri.org
Founded 1945
Library Holdings: Bk Vols 14,200; Per Subs 300
Subject Interests: Biol, Cancer, Chem, Eng, Genetics, Mechanical eng, Metallurgy, Microbiology, Physics, Pollution, Virology
Partic in CAS Online; Dialog Corp

R TEMPLE EMANU EL*, Engel Library, 2100 Highland Ave, 35205. SAN 300-0397. Tel: 205-933-8037, Ext 240. FAX: 205-933-8099. E-mail: library@ourtemple.org.
Founded 1914
Library Holdings: Bk Vols 4,500
Open Mon-Fri 8:30-4

UNIVERSITY OF ALABAMA AT BIRMINGHAM

CM DEPARTMENT OF ANESTHESIOLOGY LIBRARY*, 619 19th St S, J965, 35249-6810, SAN 324-5284. Tel: 205-975-0158. FAX: 205-975-5963. Web Site: medicine.uab.edu/anesthesiology. *Librn,* A J Wright; E-mail: ajwright@uab.edu; Staff 1 (MLS 1)
Founded 1979
Library Holdings: CDs 125; DVDs 60; Bk Vols 3,348
Special Collections: Alice McNeal, MD Coll, bks & other mats related to first dept Chair, 1946-1964; Anesthesia History Coll, bks & other mats; Departmental History Coll, correspondence, photog & other mats, 1946 to present
Subject Interests: Anesthesia, Critical care, Pain mgt
Partic in National Network of Libraries of Medicine
Open Mon-Fri 7-5

CM LISTER HILL LIBRARY OF THE HEALTH SCIENCES*, 1700 University Blvd, 35294-0013. (Mail add: 1720 Second Ave S, 35294-0013), SAN 330-1176. Tel: 205-934-5460. Circulation Tel: 205-934-3306. Interlibrary Loan Service Tel: 205-934-2356. Information Services Tel: 205-934-2230. FAX: 205-934-3545. Information Services FAX: 204-975-8313. Web Site: www.uab.edu/lister. *Dir,* T Scott Plutchak; E-mail: tscott@uab.edu; *Assoc Dir, Hist Coll,* Mike Flannery; E-mail: flannery@uab.edu; *Assoc Dir, Pub Serv,* Patricia Higginbottom; E-mail: phiggin@uab.edu; *Asst Dir, Access & Doc Delivery,* Michael Fitts; E-mail: fitts@uab.edu; *Head, Cat,* Valerie Gordon; E-mail: vgordon@uab.edu; *Syst Librn,* Lisa Ennis; E-mail: scorbett@uab.edu; *Archivist,* Tim Pennycuff; E-mail: tpenny@uab.edu; *Ser,* Sylvia McAphee; E-mail: smcaphee@uab.edu; Staff 40 (MLS 19, Non-MLS 21)
Founded 1945. Highest Degree: Doctorate
Library Holdings: Bk Vols 337,728
Special Collections: Alabama Museum of the Health Sciences; Reynolds Historical Library; UAB Archives
Subject Interests: Allied health, Dentistry, Med, Nursing, Optometry, Pub health
Automation Activity & Vendor Info: (Acquisitions) SirsiDynix; (Cataloging) SirsiDynix; (Circulation) SirsiDynix; (ILL) OCLC ILLiad; (OPAC) SirsiDynix; (Serials) SirsiDynix
Database Vendor: EBSCOhost, OCLC FirstSearch, OVID Technologies, SirsiDynix
Partic in Association of Southeastern Research Libraries; Consortium of Southern Biomedical Libraries; Network of Alabama Academic Libraries
Publications: Lister Hill Letter; Newsletter of the Reynolds Library Assocs
Friends of the Library Group

C MERVYN H STERNE LIBRARY, 917 13th St S, 35205. (Mail add: 1720 Second Ave S, SL 172, 35294-0014). Tel: 205-934-6364. Circulation Tel: 205-934-4338. Interlibrary Loan Service Tel: 205-934-6365. Administration Tel: 205-934-6360. Interlibrary Loan Service FAX: 205-975-6230. Administration FAX: 205-934-0238. Web Site: www.mhsl.uab.edu. *Inaugural Dean of Libr & Prof of UAB Libr,* John M

Meador, Jr; Tel: 205-934-5460, E-mail: jmmj@uab.edu; *Head, Cat & Coll Mgt,* Carolyn Walden; Tel: 205-934-0633, E-mail: cwalden@uab.edu; *Head, Ref,* Linda Harris; E-mail: lharris@uab.edu; *Head, User Serv/Circ,* Dr Fred J Olive, III; E-mail: folive@uab.edu; *Digital Res/Presv Librn,* Yan Wang; Tel: 205-934-6357, E-mail: yanwang3@uab.edu; *Electronic Res Librn,* Peggy Kain; Tel: 205-934-9939, E-mail: pkain@uab.edu; *Ref Librn,* Craig Beard; E-mail: cbeard@uab.edu; *Ref Librn,* Brooke Becker; E-mail: babecker@uab.edu; *Ref Librn,* Jeffery Graveline; E-mail: jgraveli@uab.edu; *Ref Librn,* Dana Hettich; E-mail: dhettich@uab.edu; *Ref Librn,* Jennifer Long; E-mail: jmlong@uab.edu; *Ref Librn,* Heather Martin; E-mail: hmartin@uab.edu; *Ref Librn,* Imelda Vetter; E-mail: ivetter@uab.edu; *Ref Librn, Instruction & Outreach,* Delores Carlito; E-mail: delo@uab.edu; *Cataloger,* Tony Schimizzi; Tel: 205-934-3512, E-mail: senecas@uab.edu; *Cataloger,* Laura Simpson; E-mail: simle@uab.edu; *Cataloger,* Irina Stanishevskaya; E-mail: istan@uab.edu; *ILL,* Eddie Luster; E-mail: eluster@uab.edu. Subject Specialists: *Eng,* Craig Beard; *Behav sci, Soc sci,* Brooke Becker; *Bus, Govt doc, Legal,* Jeffery Graveline; *Gen,* Dana Hettich; *Math, Sci,* Jennifer Long; *Arts, Humanities,* Heather Martin; *Educ,* Imelda Vetter; Staff 25 (MLS 17, Non-MLS 8)
Founded 1966. Enrl 17,999; Fac 2,322; Highest Degree: Doctorate
Oct 2012-Sept 2013 Income $5,555,795, State $3,819,487, Locally Generated Income $27,075, Parent Institution $1,609,682, Other $99,551. Mats Exp $1,797,041, Books $232,989, Per/Ser (Incl. Access Fees) $708,440, Other Print Mats $4,699, AV Mat $8,296, Electronic Ref Mat (Incl. Access Fees) $822,910, Presv $19,707. Sal $2,513,046 (Prof $1,111,569)
Library Holdings: AV Mats 10,565; CDs 9,594; e-books 80,620; e-journals 4,221; Microforms 1,267,569; Bk Titles 1,120,007; Bk Vols 1,159,102; Per Subs 20,846; Videos 6,844
Special Collections: Proust Coll. Oral History
Automation Activity & Vendor Info: (Acquisitions) Ex Libris Group; (Cataloging) Ex Libris Group; (Circulation) Ex Libris Group; (Course Reserve) Ex Libris Group; (ILL) OCLC ILLiad; (OPAC) Ex Libris Group; (Serials) Ex Libris Group
Database Vendor: ACM (Association for Computing Machinery), Alexander Street Press, American Chemical Society, American Mathematical Society, American Psychological Association (APA), Annual Reviews, ARTstor, Baker & Taylor, BioOne, Blackwell, Bowker, Cambridge Scientific Abstracts, CQ Press, ebrary, EBSCOhost, Elsevier, Gale Cengage Learning, Hoovers, IEEE (Institute of Electrical & Electronics Engineers), IOP, JSTOR, LexisNexis, Modern Language Association, OCLC, OCLC ArticleFirst, OCLC CAMIO, OCLC FirstSearch, OCLC WorldShare Interlibrary Loan, Paratext, Project MUSE, ProQuest, Springer-Verlag, ValueLine, Wiley, YBP Library Services
Partic in Association of Southeastern Research Libraries; Lyrasis; Network of Alabama Academic Libraries; OCLC Online Computer Library Center, Inc
Publications: Mervyn H Sterne Library Directions (Newsletter)
Open Mon-Thurs 7:30am-2am, Fri 7:30-7, Sat 9-5, Sun 1pm-2am
Friends of the Library Group

BLOUNTSVILLE

P BLOUNTSVILLE PUBLIC LIBRARY*, 65 Chestnut St, 35031. (Mail add: PO Box 219, 35031-0219), SAN 300-0443. Tel: 205-429-3156. FAX: 205-429-4806. E-mail: blountsvillelib@hotmail.com. Web Site: www.blountsvillepubliclibrary.com. *Dir,* Yvonne Murphree; *Asst Librn,* Dorothy Yarbrough
Pop 1,400; Circ 23,000
Library Holdings: Bk Titles 22,000; Bk Vols 23,000; Per Subs 40
Subject Interests: Local hist
Automation Activity & Vendor Info: (Cataloging) Follett Software; (Circulation) Follett Software
Open Mon & Thurs 9-7, Tues, Wed & Fri 9-5, Sat 9-2
Friends of the Library Group

BOAZ

P BOAZ PUBLIC LIBRARY*, 404 Thomas Ave, 35957. SAN 300-0451. Tel: 256-593-8056. FAX: 256-593-8153. E-mail: library@cityofboaz.org. Web Site: www.cityofboaz.org. *Dir,* Lynn Burgess; Staff 1 (Non-MLS 1)
Founded 1971. Pop 8,000; Circ 10,000
Library Holdings: Bk Titles 55,000; Bk Vols 60,000; Per Subs 100
Special Collections: Paperback Coll
Subject Interests: Ala, Genealogy
Automation Activity & Vendor Info: (Cataloging) Follett Software; (Circulation) Follett Software; (OPAC) Follett Software
Mem of Marshall County Cooperative Library
Open Mon-Thurs 9-8, Fri 9-5, Sat 9-3
Friends of the Library Group

J SNEAD STATE COMMUNITY COLLEGE*, Virgil B McCain Jr Learning Resource Center, 220 N Walnut, 35957-1650. (Mail add: PO Box 734, 35957-0734), SAN 300-046X. Tel: 256-840-4173. Administration Tel: 256-840-4195. FAX: 256-593-3098. Web Site: www.snead.edu/library/. *Librn,* John M Miller, II; E-mail: jmiller@snead.edu; Staff 4 (MLS 1, Non-MLS 3)
Founded 1935. Enrl 1,472; Fac 40
Library Holdings: AV Mats 1,038; e-books 30,825; Bk Titles 38,044; Bk Vols 40,196; Per Subs 172
Special Collections: Alabama Authors (Borden Deal, Babs Deal, William B Huie, William Heath, Elise Sanguinetti, Thomas Wilkerson); Alabama Coll; College Archives
Automation Activity & Vendor Info: (Cataloging) Innovative Interfaces, Inc; (Circulation) Innovative Interfaces, Inc; (OPAC) Innovative Interfaces, Inc
Database Vendor: EBSCOhost, Facts on File
Wireless access
Partic in Library Management Network, Inc
Open Mon-Thurs 7:30am-9pm, Fri 7:30-12
Restriction: Open to pub for ref & circ; with some limitations, Open to students, fac & staff

BRANTLEY

P BRANTLEY PUBLIC LIBRARY, Ten MLK Dr, 36009. (Mail add: PO Box 45, 36009-0045), SAN 300-0478. Tel: 334-527-8624. FAX: 334-527-3216. E-mail: brantleypublib@hotmail.com. *Dir,* Davina Mount
Pop 1,151; Circ 4,207
Library Holdings: Large Print Bks 300; Bk Vols 3,600; Per Subs 24
Open Mon-Fri 1-5, Sat 10-Noon

BREWTON

P BREWTON PUBLIC LIBRARY*, 206 W Jackson St, 36426. SAN 300-0494. Tel: 251-867-4626. FAX: 251-809-1749. Web Site: www.cityofbrewton.org. *Dir,* Glenda Lammers; Tel: 251-867-4626, Ext 1743, E-mail: glammers@cityofbrewton.org; *Cat,* Stacey Owens; E-mail: stowens_7@hotmail.com; *Tech Serv,* Wanda Wilson; E-mail: sissybar14@hotmail.com. Subject Specialists: *Cataloging,* Stacey Owens; Staff 10 (MLS 1, Non-MLS 9)
Founded 1960. Pop 5,498; Circ 13,500
Library Holdings: AV Mats 5,848; Bks on Deafness & Sign Lang 4; Large Print Bks 3,200; Bk Titles 45,806; Bk Vols 39,849; Per Subs 96
Special Collections: Rare Books Coll; Wildflowers of Escambia County
Automation Activity & Vendor Info: (Cataloging) Follett Software; (Circulation) Follett Software; (OPAC) Follett Software
Function: Home delivery & serv to Sr ctr & nursing homes, Homebound delivery serv, ILL available, Photocopying/Printing, Prog for children & young adult, Summer reading prog, Wheelchair accessible
Mem of Escambia County Cooperative Library System
Restriction: Circ limited

J JEFFERSON DAVIS COMMUNITY COLLEGE*, Leigh Library, 220 Alco Dr, 36426. (Mail add: PO Box 958, 36427-0958), SAN 300-0508. Tel: 251-809-1584. FAX: 251-809-1548. E-mail: library@jdcc.edu. Web Site: www.jdcc.edu/library/. *Dir, Libr Serv,* Jeffrey Faust; Tel: 251-809-1581, E-mail: jeffrey.faust@jdcc.edu; *Tech Serv,* Kim Coale; Tel: 251-809-1582; Staff 3 (MLS 2, Non-MLS 1)
Founded 1965. Enrl 1,200
Library Holdings: Bk Titles 33,500; Per Subs 218
Special Collections: Alabama Coll
Automation Activity & Vendor Info: (OPAC) LibraryWorld, Inc
Wireless access
Function: ILL available
Partic in National Network of Libraries of Medicine South Central Region

BRIDGEPORT

P LENA CAGLE PUBLIC LIBRARY*, 401 Alabama Ave, 35740. (Mail add: PO Box 875, 35740-0875). Tel: 256-495-2259. FAX: 256-495-2119. E-mail: cbridgep@bellsouth.net. *Librn,* Charlean Rutherford; Staff 1 (Non-MLS 1)
Founded 1993. Pop 3,000
Library Holdings: Bk Vols 7,600; Per Subs 23
Automation Activity & Vendor Info: (Acquisitions) Follett Software; (Cataloging) Follett Software; (Circulation) Follett Software
Open Mon 9-5, Tues, Thurs & Fri 8-5, Wed 1-5
Friends of the Library Group

G RUSSELL CAVE NATIONAL MONUMENT LIBRARY*, 3729 County Rd 98, 35740. SAN 323-6927. Tel: 256-495-2672. FAX: 256-495-9220. Web Site: www.nps.gov/ruca. *Superintendent,* John Bundy
Founded 1962
Library Holdings: Bk Titles 600
Subject Interests: Archaeology
Open Mon-Sun 8-4:30

BRUNDIDGE

P TUPPER LIGHTFOOT MEMORIAL LIBRARY*, 164 S Main St, 36010. SAN 330-2911. Tel: 334-735-2145. FAX: 334-735-2145. E-mail: bdgelib@email.com. *Dir,* Jean Carroll
Library Holdings: Bk Vols 14,500; Per Subs 40
Open Mon-Fri 9-5, Sat 9-12

BUTLER

P CHOCTAW COUNTY PUBLIC LIBRARY*, 124 N Academy Ave, 36904. SAN 330-1206. Tel: 205 459 2542. E-mail: ccpl1@hotmail.com. Web Site: choctawbookworm.wetpaint.com. *Dir,* Ashley Kay Taylor; *Br Head,* Patsy Ray; Tel: 251-542-9379
Founded 1954. Pop 15,000; Circ 62,646
Oct 2008-Sept 2009 Income (Main Library and Branch(s)) $83,500, State $16,000, City $25,000, County $25,000, Locally Generated Income $7,500, Other $10,000
Library Holdings: Bk Vols 75,000; Per Subs 30
Subject Interests: Ala
Automation Activity & Vendor Info: (Cataloging) Follett Software; (Circulation) Follett Software; (OPAC) Follett Software
Function: Computers for patron use, Electronic databases & coll, Summer reading prog, Tax forms, Video lending libr
Open Wed-Fri 9-7
Friends of the Library Group
Branches: 1
SILAS BRANCH, 130 Indian Way, Silas, 36919. (Mail add: PO Box 92, Silas, 36919), SAN 330-1265. Tel: 251 542 9379. *Br Mgr,* Patsy Ray
Open Mon & Wed 9:30-4:30
Friends of the Library Group

CALERA

P CALERA PUBLIC LIBRARY*, 9700 Hwy 25, 35040. (Mail add: PO Box 690, 35040-0690), SAN 371-9340. Tel: 205-668-3514. FAX: 205-668-3515. Web Site: www.shelbycounty-al.org. *Librn,* Janet Greathouse; E-mail: jgreathouse@calera.org
Pop 4,000
Library Holdings: Bk Vols 16,000; Per Subs 13
Automation Activity & Vendor Info: (Cataloging) Innovative Interfaces, Inc; (Circulation) Innovative Interfaces, Inc; (ILL) Innovative Interfaces, Inc; (OPAC) Innovative Interfaces, Inc
Mem of Harrison Regional Library System
Open Mon, Tues & Thurs 8-7, Wed & Fri 8-6, Sat 9-2
Friends of the Library Group

CAMDEN

P WILCOX COUNTY LIBRARY*, 100 Broad St, 36726-1702. SAN 324-0738. Tel: 334-682-4355. FAX: 334-682-5437. E-mail: wilcoxlibrary@frontiernet.net. *Dir,* Bettie Morgan; E-mail: betmorgan@frontiernet.net; Staff 3 (MLS 1, Non-MLS 2)
Founded 1979. Pop 14,000
Library Holdings: Bk Titles 36,444; Per Subs 60
Special Collections: Census Records Coll, micro. State Document Depository
Subject Interests: Ala, Genealogy
Automation Activity & Vendor Info: (Acquisitions) Follett Software; (Cataloging) Follett Software; (Circulation) Follett Software; (Course Reserve) Follett Software; (ILL) Follett Software; (OPAC) Follett Software; (Serials) Follett Software
Open Mon 9-6, Tues-Fri 8-5
Branches: 2
PINE APPLE BRANCH, 124 County Rd 59, Pine Apple, 36768, SAN 300-1881. Tel: 251-746-2698. *Librn,* Dale Winters
Pop 298; Circ 763
Library Holdings: Bk Titles 5,000
Open Tues & Fri 2:30-5
PINE HILL BRANCH, 530 Oak Grove St, Pine Hill, 36769, SAN 324-2692. Tel: 334-963-4351. FAX: 334-963-4352. *Librn,* Darlene Williamson
Library Holdings: Bk Titles 15,000
Open Mon 9-1, Tues-Fri 1-5

CARBON HILL

P CARBON HILL CITY LIBRARY*, 414 NW Fifth Ave, 35549. SAN 300-0524. Tel: 205-924-4254. *Dir,* Nancy Rhea Stewart; E-mail: nrstewart@hotmail.com; Staff 1 (MLS 1)
Founded 1931. Pop 5,000
Library Holdings: AV Mats 24; Bk Titles 7,000; Per Subs 20
Mem of Carl Elliott Regional Library System
Open Mon-Thurs 1-5

CARROLLTON

P CARROLLTON PUBLIC LIBRARY*, 225 Commerce Ave, 35447. (Mail add: PO Box 92, 35447-0092), SAN 325-1551. Tel: 205-367-2142. FAX: 205-367-2142. *Librn,* Sue Yarbrough
Founded 1981. Pop 963; Circ 6,010
Library Holdings: Bk Vols 10,500
Automation Activity & Vendor Info: (Cataloging) Follett Software; (Circulation) Follett Software
Mem of Pickens County Cooperative Library
Open Mon, Wed & Thurs 12-5, Tues 9-3, Sat 9-12

P PICKENS COUNTY COOPERATIVE LIBRARY*, Service Ctr Bldg, 155 Reform St, 35447. (Mail add: PO Box 489, 35447-0489). Tel: 205-367-8407. E-mail: pccl@nctv.com. Web Site: www.pickenslibrary.com. *Dir,* Melanie Wood; Staff 1 (Non-MLS 1)
Library Holdings: Bk Vols 50,000
Special Collections: Pickens County Historical Coll
Automation Activity & Vendor Info: (Acquisitions) Book Systems; (Cataloging) Book Systems; (Circulation) Book Systems
Wireless access
Member Libraries: Aliceville Public Library; Carrollton Public Library; Reform Public Library; Ruth Holliman Public Library
Open Mon-Fri 8-4
Restriction: Not a lending libr, Ref only to non-staff

CENTRE

P CHEROKEE COUNTY PUBLIC LIBRARY, 310 Mary St, 35960. SAN 300-0532. Tel: 256-927-5838. FAX: 256-927-2800. E-mail: cpi@tds.net. Web Site: www.cheaharegionallibrary.org. *Librn,* Elaine J Henry; Staff 1 (MLS 1)
Founded 1946. Pop 18,200; Circ 28,295
Library Holdings: Bk Titles 24,000; Bk Vols 27,000; Per Subs 20
Automation Activity & Vendor Info: (Cataloging) Book Systems; (Circulation) Book Systems; (OPAC) Book Systems
Open Mon, Tues, Thurs & Fri 8-5, Sat 8-12

CENTREVILLE

P BRENT-CENTREVILLE PUBLIC LIBRARY*, 20 Library St, 35042. SAN 300-0486. Tel: 205-926-4736. FAX: 205-926-4736. *Dir,* Cindy Snuggs
Pop 16,000
Library Holdings: Bk Vols 20,000; Per Subs 55
Automation Activity & Vendor Info: (Cataloging) Follett Software; (Circulation) Follett Software
Special Services for the Deaf - Captioned film dep
Open Mon 9-8, Tues-Fri 9-5, Sat 9-12
Friends of the Library Group

CHATOM

P WASHINGTON COUNTY PUBLIC LIBRARY*, 14102 Saint Stephens Ave, 36518. (Mail add: PO Box 1057, 36518), SAN 300-0540. Tel: 251-847-2097. FAX: 251-847-2098. Web Site: www.wcpls.net. *Dir,* Jessica Ross; E-mail: jross@wcpls.org; Staff 1 (MLS 1)
Founded 1956. Pop 18,000; Circ 43,275
Oct 2008-Sept 2009 Income $261,060, State $18,780, City $16,000, Federal $42,680, County $3,000, Locally Generated Income $34,600, Other $146,000. Mats Exp $25,200. Sal $181,985 (Prof $42,000)
Library Holdings: Bk Vols 55,000; Per Subs 116
Special Collections: African Artifacts (Dr Paul Petcher Coll); Washington County History Coll
Subject Interests: Consumer health, Gardening
Automation Activity & Vendor Info: (Acquisitions) Book Systems; (Cataloging) Book Systems; (Circulation) Book Systems; (Course Reserve) Book Systems; (ILL) Book Systems; (Media Booking) Book Systems; (OPAC) Book Systems; (Serials) Book Systems
Function: Accelerated reader prog, Adult literacy prog, Archival coll, Art exhibits, Audio & video playback equip for onsite use, Audiobks via web, AV serv, Bk club(s), Bk reviews (Group), Bks on cassette, Bks on CD, CD-ROM, Children's prog, Citizenship assistance, Computer training, Computers for patron use, Copy machines, Distance learning, Doc delivery serv, e-mail & chat, e-mail serv, E-Reserves, Electronic databases & coll, Exhibits, Family literacy, Fax serv, Games & aids for the handicapped, Genealogy discussion group, Handicapped accessible, Health sci info serv, Holiday prog, Home delivery & serv to Sr ctr & nursing homes, Homebound delivery serv, Homework prog, ILL available, Instruction & testing, Jail serv, Learning ctr, Libr develop, Literacy & newcomer serv, Magnifiers for reading, Mail & tel request accepted, Mail loans to mem, Music CDs, Newsp ref libr, Online cat, Online info literacy tutorials on the web & in blackboard, Online ref, Online searches, Orientations, Outreach serv, Outside serv via phone, mail, e-mail & web, Photocopying/Printing, Preschool outreach, Prof lending libr, Prog for adults, Prog for children & young adult, Provide serv for the mentally ill, Pub access computers, Ref & res, Ref serv available, Ref serv in person, Referrals accepted, Res libr,

Res performed for a fee, Satellite serv, Scanner, Senior computer classes, Senior outreach, Serves mentally handicapped consumers, Specialized serv in classical studies, Spoken cassettes & CDs, Spoken cassettes & DVDs, Story hour, Summer reading prog, Tax forms, Teen prog, Telephone ref, VCDs, VHS videos, Video lending libr, Visual arts prog, Web-Braille, Web-catalog, Wheelchair accessible, Workshops, Writing prog
Open Mon, Wed, Thurs & Fri 9-5, Tues 9-7
Friends of the Library Group
Branches: 1
MCINTOSH BRANCH, Melva Jean Daughtery Bldg, 83 Olin Rd, McIntosh, 36553. (Mail add: PO Box 55, McIntosh, 36553). Tel: 251-944-2047. FAX: 251-944-2041. *Libr Asst,* Jeanine Payne
Open Mon & Wed 1-5, Thurs 11-5
Bookmobiles: 1

CHEROKEE

P CHEROKEE PUBLIC LIBRARY*, 118 Church St, 35616. (Mail add: PO Box 333, 35616-0333). Tel: 256-359-4384. FAX: 256-359-4016. E-mail: cherokeelibrary@yahoo.com. *Admin Dir,* Sheila D Graham; *Asst Librn,* Dorothy Todd; Staff 2 (Non-MLS 2)
Circ 2,850
Library Holdings: Bk Vols 20,000
Automation Activity & Vendor Info: (Cataloging) Book Systems; (Circulation) Book Systems
Mem of Northwest Iowa Library Services
Special Services for the Blind - Bks on cassette
Open Mon-Fri 10-5, Sat 10-2
Friends of the Library Group

CHICKASAW

P CHICKASAW PUBLIC LIBRARY*, Ina Pullen Smallwood Memorial Library, 224 Grant St, 36611. (Mail add: PO Box 11449, 36671-0449), SAN 300-0559. Tel: 251-452-6465. FAX: 251-452-6465. Web Site: www.chickasawlibrary.org. *Libr Dir,* Teresa Goolsby
Founded 1948. Pop 6,649; Circ 35,126
Library Holdings: Bk Vols 20,000; Per Subs 75
Automation Activity & Vendor Info: (Cataloging) Book Systems; (Circulation) Book Systems; (OPAC) Book Systems
Open Mon-Fri Noon-6, Sat 1-6
Friends of the Library Group

CHILDERSBURG

P EARLE A RAINWATER MEMORIAL LIBRARY*, 124 Ninth Ave SW, 35044. SAN 300-0567. Tel: 256-378-7239. FAX: 256-378-7287. *Dir,* Barbara A Rich; E-mail: brich@childersburg.org; Staff 5 (Non-MLS 5)
Founded 1946. Pop 4,997; Circ 36,243
Oct 2006-Sept 2007 Income $150,944, State $5,134, City $89,890, County $30,061, Locally Generated Income $25,859. Mats Exp $46,275, Books $26,275, AV Mat $969. Sal $71,745
Library Holdings: Bk Vols 42,562; Per Subs 30; Talking Bks 1,436; Videos 1,484
Special Collections: Army Ordinance Works Records. US Document Depository
Subject Interests: World War II power plant
Automation Activity & Vendor Info: (Acquisitions) Book Systems; (Cataloging) Book Systems; (Circulation) Book Systems; (OPAC) Book Systems; (Serials) Book Systems
Mem of Cheaha Regional Library
Open Mon-Fri 9-6, Sat 8-1
Restriction: Circ to mem only

CITRONELLE

P CITRONELLE MEMORIAL LIBRARY*, 7855 State St, 36522. SAN 300-0575. Tel: 251-866-7319. FAX: 251-866-5210. E-mail: clib4@yahoo.com. *Dir,* Deborah Craft; *Librn,* Robin Blackwell
Founded 1893. Pop 5,000; Circ 23,177
Library Holdings: Bk Titles 24,000; Per Subs 20
Automation Activity & Vendor Info: (Cataloging) Book Systems; (Circulation) Book Systems; (OPAC) Book Systems
Open Mon 10-12 & 2-6, Tues & Thurs 2-8, Fri 2-6, Sat 9-5

CLANTON

P CHILTON CLANTON LIBRARY*, 100 First Ave, 35045. SAN 300-0583. Tel: 205-755-1768. FAX: 205-755-1374. Web Site: ccpl.lib.al.us. *Dir,* Mary Jo Abernathy; E-mail: ccpljo@bellsouth.net; Staff 5 (Non-MLS 5)
Founded 1963. Pop 40,516
Oct 2005-Sept 2006 Income $194,063, State $37,401, City $89,838, County $45,000, Locally Generated Income $21,824. Mats Exp $14,779, Books $10,447, Per/Ser (Incl. Access Fees) $1,836, AV Equip $297, AV Mat $2,199. Sal $112,837
Library Holdings: AV Mats 625; Bk Titles 70,100; Bk Vols 69,339; Per Subs 25
Subject Interests: Genealogy
Automation Activity & Vendor Info: (Cataloging) Follett Software; (Circulation) Follett Software; (OPAC) Follett Software
Database Vendor: EBSCOhost, OCLC FirstSearch
Open Mon-Fri 8-6, Sat 9-12
Branches: 3
JEMISON PUBLIC LIBRARY, 14 Padgett Lane, Jemison, 35085. (Mail add: PO Box 609, Jemison, 35085-0609), SAN 300-127X. Tel: 205-688-4492. FAX: 205-688-1109. *Librn,* Jeannette Brasher
Founded 1945. Pop 1,828; Circ 3,669
Open Mon-Fri 8-4
MAPLESVILLE PUBLIC LIBRARY, 9400 AL Hwy 22, Maplesville, 36750. (Mail add: PO Box 9, Maplesville, 36750-0009), SAN 300-1377. Tel: 334-366-4211. FAX: 334-366-4210. *Librn,* Sheila Haigler
Pop 680; Circ 3,099
Open Mon-Fri 7:30-4
THORSBY PUBLIC LIBRARY, City Hall, Hwy 31, Main St, Thorsby, 35171. (Mail add: PO Box 608, Thorsby, 35171-0608), SAN 370-0909. Tel: 205-646-3575. *Admin Serv,* Julie Lockhart
Open Mon-Fri 8-12 & 1-4

CLAYTON

P CLAYTON TOWN & COUNTY LIBRARY*, 45 N Midway St, 36016. (Mail add: PO Box 518, 36016-0518), SAN 330-2946. Tel: 334-775-3506. FAX: 334-775-3538. E-mail: town.library@yahoo.com. Web Site: www.towncounty.lib.al.us. *Libr Dir,* Denise Allain; *Asst Libr Dir,* Robbie Mitchell
Library Holdings: Bk Vols 18,000; Per Subs 25
Special Collections: Genealogical Resources
Automation Activity & Vendor Info: (Cataloging) Book Systems; (Circulation) Book Systems; (OPAC) Book Systems
Wireless access
Open Mon-Fri 1-6
Friends of the Library Group

COLLINSVILLE

P COLLINSVILLE PUBLIC LIBRARY*, 4299 Alabama Hwy 68, 35961. (Mail add: PO Box 743, 35961-0743), SAN 376-740X. Tel: 256-524-2323. FAX: 256-524-2323. *Librn,* Jennifer Wilkins; E-mail: jencollib@hotmail.com
Library Holdings: Bk Vols 7,000; Talking Bks 810; Videos 450
Automation Activity & Vendor Info: (Cataloging) Book Systems; (Circulation) Book Systems; (OPAC) Book Systems
Open Mon 12:30-6:30, Tues & Wed 10:30-6:30, Thurs 1:30-5, Fri 2:30-5
Friends of the Library Group

COLUMBIANA

P COLUMBIANA PUBLIC LIBRARY*, 50 Lester St, 35051. (Mail add: PO Box 1459, 35051-1459), SAN 321-6063. Tel: 205-669-5812. FAX: 205-669-5803. Web Site: www.shelbycounty-al.org. *Dir,* Jane Marie Bailey; E-mail: cpldirector@shelbycounty-al.org; *Asst Librn,* Shelia Gallups; Staff 2 (Non-MLS 2)
Founded 1963. Pop 5,000; Circ 70,000
Library Holdings: AV Mats 1,500; Bk Titles 26,000; Per Subs 24; Talking Bks 1,200
Automation Activity & Vendor Info: (Acquisitions) Innovative Interfaces, Inc; (Cataloging) Innovative Interfaces, Inc; (Circulation) Innovative Interfaces, Inc; (ILL) Innovative Interfaces, Inc; (Media Booking) Innovative Interfaces, Inc; (OPAC) Innovative Interfaces, Inc; (Serials) Innovative Interfaces, Inc
Function: Adult bk club, Adult literacy prog, After school storytime, AV serv, Bk club(s), Computer training, Copy machines, e-mail serv, E-Reserves, Electronic databases & coll, Family literacy, Fax serv, Handicapped accessible, Homework prog, ILL available, Mail & tel request accepted, Music CDs, Newsp ref libr, Online ref, Online searches, Photocopying/Printing, Prog for adults, Prog for children & young adult, Ref serv available, Spoken cassettes & CDs, Spoken cassettes & DVDs, Summer reading prog, Tax forms, Telephone ref, VHS videos
Mem of Harrison Regional Library System
Special Services for the Deaf - Bks on deafness & sign lang; Staff with knowledge of sign lang
Open Mon, Wed & Fri 9-5, Tues & Thurs 9-8, Sat 9-1
Friends of the Library Group

P HARRISON REGIONAL LIBRARY SYSTEM*, 50 Lester St, 35051. SAN 330-129X. Tel: 205-669-3910. Circulation Tel: 205-669-3892. Interlibrary Loan Service Tel: 205-669-8772. Reference Tel: 205-669-3894. Administration Tel: 205-669-3891. Automation Services Tel: 205-669-3895. FAX: 205-669-3940. Web Site: www.shelbycounty-al.org. *Dir,* Barbara Roberts; Tel: 205-669-3893, E-mail: broberts@pelhamonline.com; *Adminr,* Mary Hedrick; E-mail: mhedrick@shelbycounty-al.org; *Mgr,* Kathy Arnett;

E-mail: karnett@shelbycounty-al.org; *Coll Develop, Head, Ref, ILL,* Cindy Reed; E-mail: creed@shelbycounty-al.org; Staff 12 (MLS 1, Non-MLS 11)
Founded 1940. Pop 143,293; Circ 600,000
Library Holdings: Bk Titles 11,998; Bk Vols 13,931; Per Subs 56
Special Collections: Alabama & Shelby County History Coll; George Washington Museum & Coll
Automation Activity & Vendor Info: (Acquisitions) Innovative Interfaces, Inc; (Cataloging) Innovative Interfaces, Inc; (Circulation) Innovative Interfaces, Inc; (ILL) Innovative Interfaces, Inc; (OPAC) Innovative Interfaces, Inc; (Serials) Innovative Interfaces, Inc
Database Vendor: Baker & Taylor, EBSCOhost, Gale Cengage Learning, OCLC FirstSearch, Wilson - Wilson Web
Function: Games & aids for the handicapped, Handicapped accessible, Home delivery & serv to Sr ctr & nursing homes, Homebound delivery serv, ILL available, Newsp ref libr, Online searches, Prog for adults, Ref serv available, Telephone ref, Wheelchair accessible, Workshops
Member Libraries: Albert L Scott Library; Calera Public Library; Chelsea Public Library; Columbiana Public Library; James Boyd Holmes Public Library; Lallouise Florey McGraw Public Library; North Shelby County Library; Pelham Public Library
Special Services for the Deaf - Assistive tech; Bks on deafness & sign lang; Closed caption videos; High interest/low vocabulary bks; Spec interest per; Staff with knowledge of sign lang
Special Services for the Blind - Assistive/Adapted tech devices, equip & products; BiFolkal kits; Bks available with recordings; Bks on cassette; Bks on CD; Braille bks; Braille equip; Computer with voice synthesizer for visually impaired persons; Home delivery serv; Large print bks; Large screen computer & software; Magnifiers; Reader equip; Talking bks; ZoomText magnification & reading software
Open Mon-Thurs 8-6, Fri 8-5

COURTLAND

P COURTLAND PUBLIC LIBRARY*, 215 College St, 35618. (Mail add: PO Box 467, 35618-0171), SAN 376-7639. Tel: 256-637-9988. E-mail: courtland@lmn.lib.al.us. *Librn,* Kathrine Cosby
Library Holdings: Bk Vols 3,800
Wireless access
Partic in Library Management Network, Inc
Open Mon-Thurs 1-5

CROSSVILLE

P CROSSVILLE PUBLIC LIBRARY*, 8075 AL Hwy 227, 35962. (Mail add: PO Box 308, 35962-0308). Tel: 256-528-2628. FAX: 256-528-2628. Web Site: webmini.apls.state.al.us/apls_web/crossville. *Librn,* Elizabeth Hearn
Founded 1971
Library Holdings: Bk Vols 9,000
Automation Activity & Vendor Info: (Acquisitions) Brodart; (Cataloging) Brodart
Open Mon-Thurs 9-5, Fri 9-3, Sat 9-1
Friends of the Library Group

CULLMAN

P CULLMAN COUNTY PUBLIC LIBRARY SYSTEM*, 200 Clark St NE, 35055. SAN 330-1567. Tel: 256-734-1068. Circulation Tel: 256-734-2720. Reference Tel: 256-736-2011. Information Services Tel: 256-734-4824. FAX: 256-734-6902. Web Site: www.ccpls.com. *Dir,* Max Hand; E-mail: handm@ccpls.com; *Asst Dir,* Sharon Townson; E-mail: townsonsd@ccpls.com; *Coordr, Circ,* Brenda Waldrep; E-mail: waldrepb@ccpls.com; *Coordr, Info Serv, Adult Prog, Fiction & Media,* Lesia J Coleman; E-mail: colemanl@ccpls.com; *Coordr, Ref (Info Serv),* Barbara Lee; E-mail: leeb@ccpls.com; Staff 4 (MLS 3, Non-MLS 1)
Founded 1928. Pop 77,000; Circ 121,000
Oct 2005-Sept 2006 Income (Main Library and Branch(s)) $510,000, State $85,000, City $90,000, Federal $30,000, County $285,000, Locally Generated Income $20,000. Mats Exp $65,000. Sal $285,000 (Prof $110,000)
Library Holdings: AV Mats 4,800; Bks on Deafness & Sign Lang 15; CDs 1,500; DVDs 300; e-books 45,000; Large Print Bks 3,500; Bk Titles 70,000; Bk Vols 87,615; Per Subs 167; Videos 2,000
Special Collections: Archival (W C Bates Coll, City of Cullman Records, Geo Parker Diaries, Pittman Gin Records, Memorabilia Coll, Coterie Club Records); Genealogy (Daughters of the American Revolution Coll, United Daughters of the Confederacy Coll); Maps (Fuller Coll, Dan J Scott Coll); Photographs (Cullman-Johnson Coll, Hazel Karter-Daniel Coll). Oral History
Subject Interests: Ala, Civil War
Automation Activity & Vendor Info: (Cataloging) Book Systems; (Circulation) Book Systems; (ILL) OCLC Connexion; (OPAC) Book Systems
Database Vendor: EBSCOhost, Electric Library, Gale Cengage Learning, Grolier Online, OCLC FirstSearch, OCLC WorldShare Interlibrary Loan, ProQuest, WebMD, Wilson - Wilson Web
Wireless access
Function: Adult literacy prog, Archival coll, Art exhibits, Audio & video playback equip for onsite use, AV serv, Computer training, Copy machines, Doc delivery serv, e-mail serv, E-Reserves, Electronic databases & coll, Equip loans & repairs, Family literacy, Fax serv, Govt ref serv, Handicapped accessible, Health sci info serv, Home delivery & serv to Sr ctr & nursing homes, Homework prog, ILL available, Learning ctr, Mail & tel request accepted, Music CDs, Online searches, Orientations, Photocopying/Printing, Preschool outreach, Prog for adults, Prog for children & young adult, Provide serv for the mentally ill, Ref & res, Ref serv available, Senior computer classes, Spoken cassettes & CDs, Spoken cassettes & DVDs, Summer reading prog, Tax forms, Telephone ref, VHS videos, Video lending libr, Wheelchair accessible
Partic in OCLC Online Computer Library Center, Inc
Open Mon, Wed & Fri (Winter) 9-6, Tues & Thurs 9-8, Sat 9-4; Mon-Fri (Summer) 9-6, Sat 9-4
Restriction: Non-resident fee
Branches: 4
TOM BEVILL PUBLIC, 151 Byars Rd, Hanceville, 35077, SAN 330-1621. Tel: 256-287-1573. FAX: 256-287-1573. *Br Head,* Helen Johnson
Founded 1996. Pop 298
Library Holdings: Bk Vols 1,500; Per Subs 12
Subject Interests: Adult educ, African-Am
FAIRVIEW PUBLIC, 7525 Alabama Hwy, 69 North, 35058. Tel: 256-796-5424. FAX: 256-796-5424. *Br Head,* Debbie Shedd
Open Mon-Thurs 8-5
GARDEN CITY PUBLIC, Municipal Bldg, Hwy 31, Garden City, 35070, SAN 330-1591. Tel: 256-352-4552. FAX: 256-734-6902. *Br Head,* Mary Griffin
Founded 1946. Pop 604; Circ 5,504
Subject Interests: Local hist
HANCEVILLE PUBLIC, 108 S Main St, Hanceville, 35077, SAN 377-7812. Tel: 256-352-0685. FAX: 256-352-1111. *Br Head,* Shirley Burden
Open Tues & Thurs 3-7, Wed & Fri 1-5, Sat 9-12
Bookmobiles: 2. Coordr, Extn Servs, Jeremy Weissend. Bk titles 3000

DADEVILLE

P DADEVILLE PUBLIC LIBRARY*, 205 N West St, 36853. SAN 300-0613. Tel: 256-825-7820. FAX: 256-825-7820. E-mail: dpl@lakemartin.net. *Dir,* Amy Huff; Staff 3 (MLS 1, Non-MLS 2)
Founded 1907. Pop 3,212; Circ 18,684
Library Holdings: Bk Vols 10,300; Per Subs 12
Function: ILL available
Mem of Horseshoe Bend Regional Library
Open Mon, Tues, Thurs & Fri 9-5, Sat 9-12
Friends of the Library Group

P HORSESHOE BEND REGIONAL LIBRARY*, 207 N West St, 36853. SAN 300-0621. Tel: 256-825-9232. FAX: 256-825-4314. E-mail: horseshoebend@bellsouth.net. Web Site: www.horseshoebendlibrary.org. *Dir,* Susie Anderson; *Asst Dir,* Regina Strickland; Staff 2 (MLS 2)
Founded 1940. Pop 178,200
Library Holdings: AV Mats 2,992; Bk Vols 119,644; Per Subs 32
Automation Activity & Vendor Info: (Cataloging) Brodart; (Circulation) Brodart
Function: Home delivery & serv to Sr ctr & nursing homes, Homebound delivery serv, ILL available, Ref serv available
Member Libraries: Adelia M Russell Library; Dadeville Public Library; Goodwater Public Library; Millbrook Public Library; Tallassee Community Library; Wetumpka Public Library
Open Mon-Fri 8-5
Bookmobiles: 1

DALEVILLE

P DALEVILLE PUBLIC LIBRARY*, 308 Donnell Blvd, 36322. SAN 330-3004. Tel: 334-503-9119. FAX: 334-503-9119. E-mail: dalevillepubliclibrary@troycable.net. *Librn,* Kathryn Brown
Library Holdings: Bk Vols 18,000; Per Subs 20
Automation Activity & Vendor Info: (Cataloging) Evergreen; (Circulation) Evergreen; (OPAC) Evergreen
Wireless access
Open Mon-Thurs 10-6, Fri & Sat 10-3
Friends of the Library Group

DAPHNE

P DAPHNE PUBLIC LIBRARY*, 2607 US Hwy 98, 36526. (Mail add: PO Box 1225, 36526-1225), SAN 300-063X. Tel: 251-621-2818. Circulation Tel: 251-621-2818, Ext 200. Reference Tel: 251-621-2818, Ext 207. Administration Tel: 251-621-2818, Ext 201. FAX: 251-621-3086. E-mail: daphlib3@bellsouth.net. Web Site: www.daphneal.com/library. *Libr Dir,*

Tonja Young; E-mail: tonjadpl@bellsouth.net; Staff 10 (MLS 3, Non-MLS 7)
Founded 1969. Pop 18,600; Circ 270,871
Oct 2008-Oct 2009 Income $551,774, State $18,974, City $489,850, Federal $17,950, Locally Generated Income $25,000. Mats Exp $109,597, Books $72,822, Per/Ser (Incl. Access Fees) $3,200, Manu Arch $2,000, AV Mat $31,375, Presv $200. Sal $262,169
Library Holdings: Audiobooks 4,330; AV Mats 12,507; Bks on Deafness & Sign Lang 50; Braille Volumes 100; CDs 648; DVDs 3,275; Electronic Media & Resources 89; Large Print Bks 2,548; Bk Vols 51,374; Per Subs 91; Talking Bks 7,045; Videos 4,254
Special Collections: Ecology & Environmental Sciences (Earth Matters Environmental Resource Coll); Local History, Oral History & Alabama Authors (Daphne Special Coll); Small Business Resource Center
Automation Activity & Vendor Info: (Circulation) TLC (The Library Corporation)
Wireless access
Function: Adult bk club, After school storytime, Archival coll, Art exhibits, Audio & video playback equip for onsite use, Bk club(s), Bks on cassette, Bks on CD, Children's prog, Computer training, Computers for patron use, Copy machines, Electronic databases & coll, Exhibits, Family literacy, Free DVD rentals, Govt ref serv, Handicapped accessible, Holiday prog, ILL available, Instruction & testing, Large print keyboards, Magnifiers for reading, Music CDs, Online cat, Online searches, Outreach serv, Preschool outreach, Prog for adults, Prog for children & young adult, Pub access computers, Ref serv available, Senior computer classes, Senior outreach, Story hour, Summer reading prog, Tax forms, Teen prog, VHS videos, Wheelchair accessible, Workshops
Mem of Baldwin County Library Cooperative, Inc
Special Services for the Deaf - Bks on deafness & sign lang
Special Services for the Blind - Aids for in-house use; Audio mat; Bks & mags in Braille, on rec, tape & cassette; Bks on cassette; Bks on CD; Braille bks; Cassettes; Children's Braille; Closed circuit TV; Computer access aids; Extensive large print coll; IBM screen reader; Large print bks; Large screen computer & software; Low vision equip; Magnifiers; Newsletter (in large print, Braille or on cassette); Recorded bks; Screen enlargement software for people with visual disabilities; Sound rec; Variable speed audiotape players; Videos on blindness & phys handicaps; ZoomText magnification & reading software
Open Mon-Thurs 9-8, Fri 9-5, Sat 9-2
Restriction: Non-resident fee
Friends of the Library Group

S UNITED STATES SPORTS ACADEMY LIBRARY*, One Academy Dr, 36526. SAN 324-5098. Tel: 251-626-3303, Ext 268. Interlibrary Loan Service Tel: 251-626-3303, Ext 269. Reference Tel: 251-626-3303, Ext 265. FAX: 251-626-1149. E-mail: library@ussa.edu. Web Site: www.ussa.edu/library. *Libr Dir,* Position Currently Open
Library Holdings: Bk Titles 10,000; Per Subs 247
Special Collections: Foreign Countries (International Coll), bks, flms, vf
Subject Interests: Fitness, Sport coaching, Sport mgt, Sport res, Sports med
Database Vendor: EBSCOhost, Gale Cengage Learning, OCLC WorldShare Interlibrary Loan, ProQuest, PubMed, SBRnet (Sports Business Research Network), SerialsSolutions, WebMD
Wireless access
Publications: Shelflist (Acquisition list)
Partic in Lyrasis; National Network of Libraries of Medicine; Network of Alabama Academic Libraries; OCLC Online Computer Library Center, Inc
Open Mon-Fri (Winter) 8-5; Mon-Thurs (Summer) 8am-9pm, Fri 8-5, Sat 9-12

DAUPHIN ISLAND

G DEPARTMENT OF CONSERVATION & NATURAL RESOURCES*, Two North Iberville St, 36528-0189. (Mail add: PO Box 189, 36528), SAN 327-8883. Tel: 251-861-2882. FAX: 251-861-8741.
Library Holdings: Bk Vols 500
Open Mon-Fri 8-5

DEATSVILLE

J J F INGRAM STATE TECHNICAL COLLEGE LIBRARY*, Murry C Gregg Learning Resources & Professional Development Center, 5375 Ingram Rd, 36022. (Mail add: PO Box 220350, 36022-0350). Tel: 334-285-5177. FAX: 334-285-5328.
Library Holdings: Bk Vols 5,349; Per Subs 124
Automation Activity & Vendor Info: (Acquisitions) LibraryWorld, Inc; (Cataloging) LibraryWorld, Inc; (Circulation) LibraryWorld, Inc; (OPAC) LibraryWorld, Inc; (Serials) LibraryWorld, Inc
Open Mon-Fri 7-3

DECATUR

J CALHOUN COMMUNITY COLLEGE, Albert P Brewer Library, Hwy 31 N, 35609. (Mail add: PO Box 2216, 35609-2216), SAN 330-1656. Tel: 256-306-2774. Reference Tel: 256-306-2777. Administration Tel: 256-306-2775, 256-306-2784. FAX: 256-306-2780. Web Site: www.calhoun.edu/library. *Dir of Libr Serv,* Position Currently Open; *Cat/Ref Serv/Tech Serv,* Brenda P Parris; Tel: 256-306-2778, E-mail: bsp@calhoun.edu
Founded 1965. Highest Degree: Associate
Special Collections: Alabama Coll; Center for the Study of Southern Political Culture
Automation Activity & Vendor Info: (Cataloging) SirsiDynix; (Circulation) SirsiDynix; (ILL) OCLC WorldShare Interlibrary Loan; (OPAC) SirsiDynix
Database Vendor: ARTstor, Cinahl, CredoReference, EBSCO Information Services, EBSCOhost, Gale Cengage Learning, OCLC WorldShare Interlibrary Loan, ProQuest, SirsiDynix, YBP Library Services
Wireless access
Special Services for the Blind - Screen enlargement software for people with visual disabilities
Open Mon-Thurs 7:45am-8pm, Fri 7:45am-11:45am

Departmental Libraries:

HUNTSVILLE CAMPUS LIBRARY, 102-B Wynn Dr, Huntsville, 35805. (Mail add: PO Box 2216, 35609-2216). Tel: 256-890-4774. Reference Tel: 256-890-4777. FAX: 256-890-4713. *Librn,* Gerald D Jackson; Tel: 256-890-4771, E-mail: gdj@calhoun.edu
Open Mon-Thurs 7:45am-8pm, Fri 7:45am-11:45am, Sat 7:45-1

SR CENTRAL UNITED METHODIST CHURCH LIBRARY*, 616 Jackson St SE, 35601-3124. SAN 373-3785. Tel: 256-353-6941. *Librn,* Betty Tull
Library Holdings: Bk Vols 5,000

P DECATUR PUBLIC LIBRARY*, 504 Cherry St NE, 35601. SAN 300-0656. Tel: 256-353-2993. FAX: 256-350-6736. Web Site: www.decatur.lib.al.us. *Dir,* Sandra McCandless; Tel: 256-353-2993, Ext 102, E-mail: director@decatur.lib.al.us; Staff 25 (MLS 2, Non-MLS 23)
Founded 1905. Pop 113,740; Circ 246,853
Jul 2005-Jun 2006 Income $914,553, State $89,068, City $360,000, Federal $35,920, County $101,163, Other $328,402. Mats Exp $95,931, Books $56,297, Per/Ser (Incl. Access Fees) $19,634, AV Mat $20,000. Sal $354,715
Library Holdings: Bk Vols 98,063; Per Subs 200; Talking Bks 2,726
Subject Interests: Genealogy, Local hist
Automation Activity & Vendor Info: (Cataloging) TLC (The Library Corporation); (Circulation) TLC (The Library Corporation); (Course Reserve) TLC (The Library Corporation)
Database Vendor: Baker & Taylor, BWI, EBSCO Information Services, EBSCOhost, Facts on File, Gale Cengage Learning, Ingram Library Services, LearningExpress, OCLC ArticleFirst, OCLC FirstSearch, OCLC WebJunction, OCLC WorldShare Interlibrary Loan, ProQuest, TLC (The Library Corporation), World Book Online
Wireless access
Publications: INDEX-Friends of the Library (Newsletter)
Mem of Wheeler Basin Regional Library
Open Mon-Wed 9-8, Thurs 9-6, Fri & Sat 9-5, Sun 2-5
Friends of the Library Group

DEMOPOLIS

P MARENGO LIBRARY SYSTEM*, Demopolis Public Library, 211 E Washington, 36732. SAN 300-0664. Tel: 334-289-1595. FAX: 334-289-8260. Web Site: www.demopolislibrary.info. *Dir,* Morgan Grimes; E-mail: morgan.grimes@demopolisal.gov
Founded 1922. Pop 8,000; Circ 41,170
Library Holdings: Bk Vols 25,000; Per Subs 66
Special Collections: Demopolis History Coll
Subject Interests: Genealogy
Automation Activity & Vendor Info: (Cataloging) Book Systems; (Circulation) Book Systems; (OPAC) Book Systems
Wireless access
Open Mon, Tues, Thurs & Fri 9-5:30, Wed & Sat 9-1
Friends of the Library Group

DOTHAN

P HOUSTON LOVE MEMORIAL LIBRARY*, 212 W Burdeshaw St, 36303. (Mail add: PO Box 1369, 36302-1369), SAN 330-1710. Tel: 334-793-9767. FAX: 334-793-6645. Web Site: www.houstonlovelibrary.org. *Dir,* Bettye Forbus; E-mail: blforbus@yahoo.com; *AV,* Brenda Muhammad; *Ch Serv,* Kristin North; *Circ,* Glenda Cain; *ILL, Ref,* Susan Veasey; *Reader Serv,* Christi Armstrong; Staff 11 (MLS 4, Non-MLS 7)
Founded 1900. Pop 90,000; Circ 317,074
Library Holdings: Large Print Bks 9,357; Bk Vols 192,000; Per Subs 116; Talking Bks 1,066; Videos 2,634

Automation Activity & Vendor Info: (Cataloging) SirsiDynix; (Circulation) SirsiDynix; (OPAC) SirsiDynix
Open Mon, Tues & Thurs 9-9, Wed & Fri 9-6, Sat 9-5, Sun 1-5
Branches: 3
ASHFORD BRANCH, 305 Sixth Ave, Ashford, 36312, SAN 330-1745. Tel: 334-899-3121. *Librn,* Anna Todd
Library Holdings: Bk Vols 17,384
Open Tues 2-6, Wed 1-5, Thurs 9-12 & 2-5, Fri 9-12 & 1-5, Sat 9-12

P DIVISION FOR THE BLIND & PHYSICALLY HANDICAPPED, PO Box 1369, 36302, SAN 330-1729. Tel: 334-793-9767. *Librn,* Glenda Cain; *Librn,* Christi Armstrong
Founded 1971. Circ 5,500
Library Holdings: Bk Vols 6,500
Special Collections: Braille; Reference materials on blindness & other handicaps; Religious books on cassette & disc
Open Mon, Tues & Thurs 9-9, Wed & Fri 9-6, Sat 9-5, Sun 1-5
Friends of the Library Group

ROSSIE PURCELL BRANCH, 200 S Main St, Columbia, 36319. (Mail add: PO Box 309, Columbia, 36319), SAN 330-177X. Tel: 334-696-4417. *Librn,* Donna Cooper
Library Holdings: Bk Vols 10,387
Open Tues 3-6, Wed & Sat 9-12, Thurs 9-12 & 2-5
Bookmobiles: 2

M SOUTHEAST ALABAMA MEDICAL CENTER*, Medical Library, 1108 Ross Clark Circle, Hwy 84 E, 36301-3024. (Mail add: PO Box 6987, 36302-6987), SAN 320-362X. Tel: 334-793-8102. *Dir,* Pat McGee
Founded 1964
Library Holdings: Bk Titles 705; Per Subs 100
Subject Interests: Clinical med
Partic in SE-Atlantic Regional Med Libr Servs
Restriction: Staff use only

C TROY UNIVERSITY*, Dothan Library, 502 University Dr, 36304. SAN 300-0885. Tel: 334-983-6556, Ext 1320. Circulation Tel: 334-983-6556, Ext 1331. Interlibrary Loan Service Tel: 334-983-6556, Ext 1323. Reference Tel: 334-983-6556, Ext 1321. FAX: 334-983-6327. Web Site: dothan.troy.edu/library. *Libr Dir,* Christopher Shaffer; E-mail: shafferc@troy.edu; *Ref/Info Serv Librn,* Donna S Miller; E-mail: dmiller@troy.edu; *Tech Serv Librn,* Olga Knyaz; Tel: 334-983-6556, Ext 1325, E-mail: oknyaz@troy.edu; *Archivist,* Dr Martin Olliff; Tel: 334-983-6556, Ext 1327, E-mail: molliff@troy.edu; *Circ, ILL,* Mary B McCruter; E-mail: mmccruter@troy.edu; *Media Spec,* Jim Jones; Tel: 334-983-6556, Ext 1393, E-mail: ojones73957@troy.edu; *Per,* Kasie Patrick; Tel: 334-983-6556, Ext 1322, E-mail: klpatrick@troy.edu; *Spec Coll & Archives Librn,* Tina Bernath, Tel: 334-983-6556, Ext 1321, E mail: tbernath@troy.edu; *Tech Serv,* Jana Tew; E-mail: jatew@troy.edu; Staff 9 (MLS 3, Non-MLS 6)
Founded 1973. Enrl 1,800; Fac 95; Highest Degree: Doctorate
Library Holdings: e-books 40,000; Bk Vols 102,000; Per Subs 410
Special Collections: Wiregrass History Coll
Subject Interests: Bus & mgt, Computer sci, Criminal law & justice, Educ, Hist
Automation Activity & Vendor Info: (Cataloging) SirsiDynix; (Circulation) SirsiDynix; (Course Reserve) SirsiDynix; (OPAC) SirsiDynix; (Serials) SirsiDynix
Database Vendor: EBSCOhost, Emerald, Gale Cengage Learning, LexisNexis, OCLC FirstSearch, OVID Technologies, ProQuest, Wilson - Wilson Web
Wireless access
Partic in Lyrasis; Network of Alabama Academic Libraries
Open Mon-Thurs 8am-9pm, Fri 8-12, Sat 10-2, Sun 1-5

J WALLACE COMMUNITY COLLEGE*, Phillip G Hamm Library-LRC, 1141 Wallace Dr, 36303. SAN 300-0680. Tel: 334-556-2225, 334-983-3521, Ext 2225. Toll Free Tel: 800-543-2426. FAX: 334-556-2283. TDD: 800-548-2546. Web Site: www.wallace.edu. *Dir,* A P Hoffman; E-mail: ahoffman@wallace.edu; Staff 1 (MLS 1)
Founded 1965. Enrl 3,500; Fac 90; Highest Degree: Associate
Library Holdings: AV Mats 350; e-books 40,000; Bk Titles 35,000; Bk Vols 40,000; Per Subs 275; Talking Bks 50
Subject Interests: Ala, Allied health, Children's educ, Nursing
Automation Activity & Vendor Info: (Acquisitions) Ex Libris Group; (Cataloging) Ex Libris Group; (Circulation) Ex Libris Group; (Course Reserve) Ex Libris Group; (OPAC) Ex Libris Group; (Serials) Ex Libris Group
Wireless access
Open Mon-Thurs 7:30am-8:30pm, Fri 7:30am-11:30pm

DOUBLE SPRINGS

P DOUBLE SPRINGS PUBLIC LIBRARY*, 637 Blake Dr, 35553. (Mail add: PO Box 555, 35553-0555), SAN 300-0699. Tel: 205-489-2412. FAX: 205-489-2412. *Librn,* Beth Kendrick; E-mail: bekendrick@hotmail.com
Library Holdings: AV Mats 2,000; Bk Vols 9,000
Mem of Carl Elliott Regional Library System
Open Mon-Fri 9-5

ELBA

P ELBA PUBLIC LIBRARY*, 406 Simmons St, 36323. SAN 300-0710. Tel: 334-897-6921. FAX: 334-897-6921. E-mail: elbalibrary@gmail.com. Web Site: www.elbaalabama.net/quality-of-life/library. *Dir,* Kay Wilson; Staff 1 (MLS 1)
Pop 4,355; Circ 18,525
Library Holdings: CDs 222; Bk Titles 12,682; Per Subs 24; Talking Bks 643; Videos 429
Automation Activity & Vendor Info: (Cataloging) Book Systems; (Circulation) Book Systems; (OPAC) Book Systems
Open Mon & Fri 8-5, Tues, Thurs & Sat 9-5
Friends of the Library Group

ELMORE

S ALABAMA DEPARTMENT OF CORRECTIONS*, Draper Correctional Facility Library, PO Box 1107, 36025-9900. Tel: 334-567-2221, Ext 260. FAX: 334-567-1519. *In Charge,* Rhonda Williams
Library Holdings: Bk Vols 3,000
Database Vendor: LexisNexis

ENTERPRISE

P ENTERPRISE PUBLIC LIBRARY*, 101 E Grubbs St, 36330. SAN 300-0729. Tel: 334-347-2636. FAX: 334-393-6477. Web Site: www.enterpriselibrary.org. *Libr Dir,* Denise Unruh-Kitch; *Acq,* Jo Thompson; *Ch Serv,* Louise Peters; *Circ,* Kay Knop
Founded 1923. Pop 21,176; Circ 116,000
Library Holdings: AV Mats 175; Large Print Bks 500; Bk Vols 59,000; Per Subs 9; Talking Bks 500
Special Collections: Audio Books, Large Print, Videos
Subject Interests: Ala
Automation Activity & Vendor Info: (Acquisitions) TLC (The Library Corporation); (Cataloging) TLC (The Library Corporation); (Circulation) TLC (The Library Corporation); (ILL) OCLC; (OPAC) TLC (The Library Corporation)
Wireless access
Mem of North Central Kansas Libraries System
Special Services for the Blind - Audio mat; Large print bks
Open Mon, Wed & Fri 9-5:30, Tues & Thurs 9-7, Sat 9-4
Friends of the Library Group

J ENTERPRISE STATE COMMUNITY COLLEGE*, Learning Resource Center, 600 Plaza Dr, 36330. (Mail add: PO Box 1300, 36331-1300), SAN 300-0737. Tel: 334-347-2623, Ext 2271. FAX: 334-347-0146. Web Site: www.escc.edu. *Dir,* Susan Sumblin; *Bibliog Instr,* Phyllis Tanner; *Tech Serv,* Linda Stephens; Staff 3 (MLS 3)
Founded 1966. Enrl 1,800; Fac 52
Library Holdings: Bk Vols 50,000
Special Collections: US Document Depository
Subject Interests: Genealogy
Automation Activity & Vendor Info: (Cataloging) SirsiDynix; (Circulation) SirsiDynix; (OPAC) SirsiDynix
Partic in Lyrasis; OCLC Online Computer Library Center, Inc

EUFAULA

P EUFAULA CARNEGIE LIBRARY*, 217 N Eufaula Ave, 36027. SAN 330-3039. Tel: 334-687-2337. Administration Tel: 334-687-8190. FAX: 334-687-8143. E-mail: eufaulacl@yahoo.com. Web Site: www.ecl.lib.al.us. *Dir,* Ronnie Smith; E-mail: dir_ecl@yahoo.com; Staff 11 (MLS 1, Non-MLS 10)
Founded 1904. Pop 31,633
Oct 2005-Sept 2006 Income $127,396, State $15,186, City $75,000, Federal $10,662, Locally Generated Income $11,190, Other $15,358. Mats Exp $8,601, Books $6,119, AV Mat $2,482. Sal $134,724 (Prof $41,500)
Library Holdings: Bk Vols 33,640; Per Subs 90
Special Collections: Local History & Genealogy Coll
Automation Activity & Vendor Info: (Cataloging) Follett Software; (Circulation) Follett Software; (OPAC) Follett Software
Database Vendor: Baker & Taylor, TLC (The Library Corporation)
Wireless access
Open Mon & Wed 9-6, Tues & Thurs 9-8, Fri 9-5, Sat 9-2
Friends of the Library Group

J WALLACE COMMUNITY COLLEGE*, Eufaula Campus Learning Resources Center, 3235 S Eufaula Ave, 36027-3542. (Mail add: PO Drawer 580, 36072-0580). Tel: 334-687-3543. Toll Free Tel: 800-543-2426. FAX: 334-687-0255. Web Site: www.wallace.edu/student_resources/lrc/lrc_sparks.htm. *Librn,* Clara West Martin; Tel: 334-687-3543, Ext 4202, E-mail: cmartin@wallace.edu; Staff 1 (Non-MLS 1)

Founded 2000. Enrl 640; Fac 32; Highest Degree: Associate
Library Holdings: CDs 50; DVDs 36; e-books 49,070; e-journals 56; Bk Vols 6,000; Per Subs 32; Videos 437
Database Vendor: EBSCO Information Services
Open Mon-Thurs 7:30am-10pm, Fri 7:30am-12:15pm

EUTAW

P JAMES C POOLE JR MEMORIAL LIBRARY*, 420 Prairie Ave, 35462-1165. Tel: 205-372-9026. FAX: 205-372-9026. E-mail: jcpoolelibrary@yahoo.com. *Librn,* Marilyn Gibson
Pop 9,880
Library Holdings: Bk Vols 15,000; Per Subs 22
Automation Activity & Vendor Info: (Cataloging) Book Systems; (Circulation) Book Systems; (Course Reserve) Book Systems; (ILL) Book Systems; (Media Booking) Book Systems
Wireless access
Open Mon-Wed & Fri 9-12 & 3-5, Thurs & Sat 9-12

EVA

P EVA PUBLIC LIBRARY, 4549 Hwy 55 E, 35621. (Mail add: PO Box 99, 35621-0099), SAN 376-7647. Tel: 256-796-8638. FAX: 256-796-8638. E-mail: evalibrary@att.net. Web Site: www2.youseemore.com/eva. *Dir,* Betty Golden
Founded 1980
Library Holdings: Bk Vols 12,000; Per Subs 6
Wireless access
Open Mon 3-7, Tues & Sat 10-1, Wed & Fri 2-5, Thurs 2-6
Friends of the Library Group

EVERGREEN

P EVERGREEN-CONECUH COUNTY PUBLIC LIBRARY*, 119 Cemetery Ave, 36401. SAN 300-0753. Tel: 251-578-2670. FAX: 251-578-2316. *Dir,* Diann Lee; *Ch Serv,* Diane Sosebee
Pop 14,500; Circ 30,000
Library Holdings: Bk Vols 35,000; Per Subs 10
Special Collections: Lucy C Warren Heritage Section
Subject Interests: Genealogy
Automation Activity & Vendor Info: (Cataloging) Book Systems; (Circulation) Book Systems; (ILL) OCLC WorldShare Interlibrary Loan; (OPAC) Book Systems
Open Mon-Fri 9-5, Sat 9-12

FAIRFIELD

P WALTER J HANNA MEMORIAL LIBRARY*, 4615 Gary Ave, 35064. SAN 300-0761. Tel: 205-783-6007. FAX: 205-783-6041. Web Site: www.fairfield.lib.al.us. *Dir,* Lora R Perry; E-mail: lperry@bham.lib.al.us
Circ 12,179
Library Holdings: Bk Vols 37,000; Per Subs 33
Automation Activity & Vendor Info: (Cataloging) Innovative Interfaces, Inc; (Circulation) Innovative Interfaces, Inc; (OPAC) Innovative Interfaces, Inc
Function: Music CDs, Prog for children & young adult, Summer reading prog, VHS videos
Open Mon-Fri 9-6, Sat 9-12

C MILES COLLEGE*, C A Kirkendoll Learning Resources Center, 5500 Myron Massey Blvd, 35064. (Mail add: PO Box 39800, Birmingham, 35208-0937), SAN 300-0311. Tel: 205-929-1709, 205-929-1714. Reference Tel: 205-929-1748. Automation Services Tel: 205-929-1715. FAX: 205-929-1635. Web Site: www.miles.edu. *Dir,* Dr Geraldine Bell; E-mail: gbell@miles.edu; *Ref Librn,* Laurie Hackney; Tel: 205-929-1713, E-mail: lhackney@miles.edu; *Media Spec,* Kim Gordon Moore; E-mail: kmoore@miles.edu; *Cataloger,* Candice Murdock; E-mail: cmurdock@miles.edu; *Circ,* Lynne Bobbs; Tel: 205-929-1710, E-mail: lbobbs@miles.edu; *Per,* Patrice Tutt; Tel: 205-929-1711, E-mail: htutt@miles.edu; *Pub Serv,* Christopher Anderson; Tel: 205-929-1712, E-mail: canderson@miles.edu; Staff 9 (MLS 3, Non-MLS 6)
Founded 1978. Enrl 1,875; Fac 110; Highest Degree: Bachelor
Jul 2008-Jun 2009 Income $428,623. Mats Exp $135,000, Books $75,000, Per/Ser (Incl. Access Fees) $50,000, AV Equip $5,000, Electronic Ref Mat (Incl. Access Fees) $5,000. Sal $245,123 (Prof $208,563)
Library Holdings: AV Mats 2,473; Bk Vols 100,000; Per Subs 400
Special Collections: Afro-American Coll; Children's Coll
Automation Activity & Vendor Info: (Acquisitions) Innovative Interfaces, Inc; (Cataloging) Innovative Interfaces, Inc; (Circulation) Innovative Interfaces, Inc; (Course Reserve) Innovative Interfaces, Inc; (ILL) Innovative Interfaces, Inc; (OPAC) Innovative Interfaces, Inc; (Serials) Innovative Interfaces, Inc
Database Vendor: EBSCOhost, Facts on File, OCLC WorldShare Interlibrary Loan
Wireless access
Function: ILL available, Ref serv available
Partic in HBCU Library Alliance; Lyrasis
Open Mon-Thurs 8am-Midnight, Fri 8am-10pm, Sat & Sun 1pm-Midnight
Friends of the Library Group

FAIRHOPE

P FAIRHOPE PUBLIC LIBRARY*, 501 Fairhope Ave, 36532. SAN 300-0788. Tel: 251-928-7483. Administration Tel: 251-929-0366. FAX: 251-928-9717. Web Site: www.fairhopelibrary.org. *Dir,* Tamara Dean; E-mail: director@fairhopelibrary.org; *Cat,* Susan Diemert; E-mail: cataloguer@fairhopelibrary.org; *Circ,* Carole Kaiser; E-mail: circulation@fairhopelibrary.org; *Ref Serv,* Cheryl Bradley; *Youth Serv,* Genie Jones; E-mail: youthservices@fairhopelibrary.org; Staff 7 (MLS 1, Non-MLS 6)
Founded 1894. Pop 15,702; Circ 224,312
Library Holdings: AV Mats 10,674; Bks on Deafness & Sign Lang 21; e-books 20,000; High Interest/Low Vocabulary Bk Vols 99; Large Print Bks 2,747; Bk Vols 70,695; Per Subs 140; Talking Bks 3,030
Special Collections: Alabama Poetry (Frances Ruffin Durham); Area History Coll; Local Authors Coll. Oral History
Subject Interests: Local hist, Theosophy
Automation Activity & Vendor Info: (Cataloging) TLC (The Library Corporation); (Circulation) TLC (The Library Corporation); (OPAC) TLC (The Library Corporation)
Wireless access
Publications: Alabama A to Z
Mem of Baldwin County Library Cooperative, Inc
Open Mon, Tues & Thurs 9-8, Wed 1-6, Fri 9-5, Sat 9-3
Friends of the Library Group

FALKVILLE

P FALKVILLE PUBLIC LIBRARY*, Seven N First Ave, 35622. (Mail add: PO Box 407, 35622-0407), SAN 376-737X. Tel: 256-784-5822. FAX: 256-784-5525. E-mail: falkvillepubliclibrary@yahoo.com. Web Site: www.falkville.org/departments/library. *Dir,* Jennifer Asherbranner
Founded 1989. Pop 1,109
Library Holdings: Bk Vols 11,000
Automation Activity & Vendor Info: (Acquisitions) TLC (The Library Corporation)
Database Vendor: TLC (The Library Corporation)
Wireless access
Mem of Wheeler Basin Regional Library
Open Mon, Tues, Thurs & Fri 8-12 & 1-5, Wed 8-12

FAYETTE

J BEVILL STATE COMMUNITY COLLEGE*, Learning Resources Center, 2631 Temple Ave N, 35555. SAN 300-0796. Tel: 205-932-3221, Ext 5141. FAX: 205-932-8821. Web Site: www.bscc.edu. *Head Librn,* Sally Middleton; E-mail: samiddleton@bscc.edu; Staff 1 (MLS 1)
Founded 1969. Enrl 1,600; Fac 30
Library Holdings: Bk Vols 40,000
Special Collections: Albert P Brewer Coll. State Document Depository; US Document Depository
Automation Activity & Vendor Info: (Cataloging) Follett Software; (Circulation) Follett Software; (OPAC) Follett Software
Publications: BSCC LRC Handbook
Open Mon-Thurs 7:30am-8:30pm, Fri 7:30-3:30

P FAYETTE COUNTY MEMORIAL LIBRARY*, 326 Temple Ave N, 35555. SAN 300-080X. Tel: 205-932-6625. FAX: 205-932-4152. E-mail: faycomemlib@cyberjoes.com. Web Site: www.fcml.org. *Dir,* Amia Baker; Staff 1 (MLS 1)
Founded 1923. Pop 17,182; Circ 34,890
Special Collections: Alabama Room, including Census Records through 1920; Genealogy Coll
Automation Activity & Vendor Info: (Cataloging) Book Systems; (Circulation) Book Systems; (OPAC) Book Systems
Wireless access
Function: Bks on cassette, Bks on CD, Computer training, Computers for patron use, Copy machines, Electronic databases & coll, Fax serv, Free DVD rentals, Homework prog, Microfiche/film & reading machines, Newsp ref libr, Online cat, OverDrive digital audio bks, Photocopying/Printing, Preschool reading prog, Printer for laptops & handheld devices, Prog for children & young adult, Pub access computers, Ref serv available, Spoken cassettes & CDs, Story hour, Summer reading prog, Tax forms, VHS videos
Open Mon-Thurs 9-6, Fri 9-5, Sat 9-12

FLOMATON

P FLOMATON PUBLIC LIBRARY*, 436 Houston St, 36441. SAN 300-0818. Tel: 251-296-3552. FAX: 251-296-3355. E-mail: fpl_1@bellsouth.net. Web Site: www.apls.state.al.us/libraries/flomaton. *Libr Dir,* Faye Knowles; *Asst Dir,* Kaci Boutwell

Pop 15,033; Circ 25,238
Library Holdings: Bk Titles 22,000; Per Subs 30
Automation Activity & Vendor Info: (Cataloging) Follett Software; (Circulation) Follett Software; (OPAC) Follett Software
Mem of Escambia County Cooperative Library System
Open Mon-Fri 8:15-5, Sat 8-12

FLORALA

P FLORALA PUBLIC LIBRARY*, 1214 Fourth St, 36442-3810. SAN 300-0826. Tel: 334-858-3525. FAX: 334-858-3525. Web Site: webmini.apls.state.al.us/apls_web/florala/?q=home. *Dir,* Judy Petry; E-mail: fpldirector@fairpoint.net
Founded 1934. Pop 2,011; Circ 22,681
Library Holdings: Audiobooks 80; AV Mats 964; DVDs 938; Large Print Bks 50; Bk Vols 15,983; Per Subs 43; Talking Bks 345; Videos 285
Special Collections: Historic Photographs of Florala, Ala
Wireless access
Open Mon-Fri 8:30-5

FLORENCE

P FLORENCE-LAUDERDALE PUBLIC LIBRARY*, 350 N Wood Ave, 35630. SAN 300-0834. Tel: 256-764-6564. FAX: 256-764-6629. Web Site: flpl.org. *Dir,* Nancy Sanford; E-mail: nsanford@flpl.org; *Coll Develop & Automation Serv Librn,* Elisabeth G South; E-mail: esouth@flpl.org; *Daily Operations & Tech Serv Supvr,* Melissa Dial; E-mail: mdial@flpl.org; *Info Serv Supvr,* Abby Carpenter; E-mail: acouch@flpl.org; Staff 18.5 (MLS 3.5, Non-MLS 15)
Founded 1945. Pop 80,000; Circ 275,000
Oct 2010-Sept 2011 Income $999,000. Mats Exp $60,000
Library Holdings: AV Mats 7,500; Electronic Media & Resources 60; Microforms 1,200; Bk Vols 85,000; Per Subs 100
Special Collections: Digital Archive of Local History
Subject Interests: Genealogy, Local hist
Automation Activity & Vendor Info: (Acquisitions) Innovative Interfaces, Inc; (Cataloging) Innovative Interfaces, Inc; (Circulation) Innovative Interfaces, Inc; (ILL) OCLC; (OPAC) Innovative Interfaces, Inc
Database Vendor: EBSCOhost, Gale Cengage Learning, LearningExpress, OCLC WorldShare Interlibrary Loan, ProQuest, Wilson - Wilson Web
Wireless access
Open Mon-Thurs 10-7, Fri & Sat 10-5, Sun 1-5
Friends of the Library Group

C UNIVERSITY OF NORTH ALABAMA, Collier Library, One Harrison Plaza, Box 5028, 35632-0001. SAN 300-0850. Tel: 256-765-4241. Circulation Tel: 256-765-4469. Interlibrary Loan Service Tel: 256-765-4308. FAX: 256-765-4438. Web Site: www.una.edu/library. *Dir, Libr Serv,* Dr Melvin Davis, E-mail: mdavis2@una.edu; *Head, Acq & Electronic Res,* Amy Butler; Tel: 256-765-4266; *Head, Cat,* Darlene Townsend; Tel: 256-765-4473; *Head, Circ, Head, Per,* Doris McDaniel; *Instrul Serv Librn,* D Leigh Thompson; Tel: 256-765-4466; *Ref & ILL Serv Coordr,* Celia Reynolds; Tel: 256-765-4625; *Tech Coordr,* Jonathan Simms; Tel: 256-765-4470, *Web Coordr,* Phillip Oliver; Tel: 256-765-4559; Staff 11.53 (MLS 10.53, Non-MLS 1)
Founded 1830. Enrl 7,260; Fac 348; Highest Degree: Master
Oct 2007-Sept 2008 Income $2,705,675. Mats Exp $816,800, Books $206,944, Per/Ser (Incl. Access Fees) $217,520, Micro $12,811, AV Mat $47,232, Electronic Ref Mat (Incl. Access Fees) $308,688, Presv $12,512. Sal $1,325,768 (Prof $730,382)
Library Holdings: AV Mats 13,303; CDs 1,756; DVDs 3,635; e-books 241,784; e-journals 3,408; Electronic Media & Resources 137; Bk Titles 277,016; Bk Vols 398,512; Per Subs 3,815; Videos 5,968
Special Collections: Alabama Historical Coll; Congressman Flippo Coll; Film Script Archives; Local History Archives. US Document Depository
Subject Interests: Bus & mgt, Educ, Hist, Humanities, Nursing, Soc sci & issues
Automation Activity & Vendor Info: (Acquisitions) Ex Libris Group; (Cataloging) Ex Libris Group; (Circulation) Ex Libris Group; (Course Reserve) Ex Libris Group; (ILL) Ex Libris Group; (Media Booking) Ex Libris Group; (OPAC) Ex Libris Group; (Serials) Ex Libris Group
Database Vendor: ACM (Association for Computing Machinery), Alexander Street Press, American Chemical Society, BioOne, Cambridge Scientific Abstracts, Career Guidance Foundation, Children's Literature Comprehensive Database Company (CLCD), College Source, EBSCOhost, Elsevier, Facts on File, Gale Cengage Learning, H W Wilson, Hoovers, IOP, JSTOR, LexisNexis, OCLC FirstSearch, OCLC WorldShare Interlibrary Loan, OVID Technologies, Oxford Online, Project MUSE, ProQuest, Sage, ScienceDirect, SerialsSolutions, ValueLine, Wiley InterScience, Wilson - Wilson Web
Wireless access
Function: ILL available
Publications: Pathfinder Series Finding Aids (Reference guide)
Partic in Lyrasis; Network of Alabama Academic Libraries
Open Mon-Thurs 7:30am-1am, Fri 7:30-4:30, Sat 9-5, Sun 2pm-1am

FOLEY

P FOLEY PUBLIC LIBRARY*, 319 E Laurel Ave, 36535. SAN 300-0869. Tel: 251-943-7665. FAX: 251-943-8637. E-mail: fpllib@hotmail.com, library@gulftel.com. Web Site: www.foleylibrary.org. *Dir,* Donna Soto; E-mail: dsoto@hotmail.com; Staff 7 (MLS 1, Non-MLS 6)
Founded 1923. Pop 12,000; Circ 170,739
Library Holdings: Bk Vols 43,395; Per Subs 81
Subject Interests: Ala, Genealogy
Automation Activity & Vendor Info: (Cataloging) TLC (The Library Corporation); (Circulation) TLC (The Library Corporation); (OPAC) TLC (The Library Corporation)
Mem of Baldwin County Library Cooperative, Inc
Open Mon-Wed 9-8, Thurs 1-8, Fri & Sat 9-5
Friends of the Library Group

FORT PAYNE

P DEKALB COUNTY PUBLIC LIBRARY*, 504 Grand Ave NW, 35967. SAN 300-0877. Tel: 256-845-2671. FAX: 256-845-2671. *Dir,* Elizabeth Tucker; *Asst Librn,* Yvonne Toombs
Circ 102,000
Oct 2005-Sept 2006 Income $260,000. Mats Exp $40,000, Books $38,000, Per/Ser (Incl. Access Fees) $2,000. Sal $147,500
Library Holdings: Bk Vols 81,000; Per Subs 34
Special Collections: Indian Coll
Subject Interests: Indians, Local hist
Automation Activity & Vendor Info: (Cataloging) Innovative Interfaces, Inc; (Circulation) Innovative Interfaces, Inc; (OPAC) Innovative Interfaces, Inc
Partic in Library Management Network, Inc
Open Mon 10-8, Tues-Fri 10-6, Sat 10-3
Branches: 1
HENAGAR BRANCH, 17163 Alabama Hwy 75, Henagar, 35978. Tel: 256-657-1380. *Br Mgr,* Juanita Hadden
Open Tues & Thurs 1-5, Sat 9-1
Bookmobiles: 1

FORT RUCKER

UNITED STATES ARMY
A AVIATION TECHNICAL LIBRARY*, Bldg 9204, Fifth Ave, 36362, SAN 330-1923. Tel: 334-255-2944. Interlibrary Loan Service Tel: 334-255-3177. Administration Tel: 334-255-3912.
Founded 1955
Special Collections: Army Regulations; DTIC Technical Reports
Subject Interests: Aviation, Mil hist
Automation Activity & Vendor Info: (Cataloging) SirsiDynix; (Circulation) SirsiDynix; (OPAC) SirsiDynix
A CENTER LIBRARY*, Bldg 212, Corner of Ruf Ave & Novosel, 36362-5000, SAN 330-1869. Tel: 334-255-3885. FAX: 334-255-1567. *Head Librn,* Alfred Edwards; E-mail: al.edwards@us.army.mil; *Tech Serv Librn,* Laurie Richardson; Staff 6 (MLS 2, Non-MLS 4)
Founded 1954
Library Holdings: AV Mats 4,500; Bks on Deafness & Sign Lang 22; High Interest/Low Vocabulary Bk Vols 212; Large Print Bks 450; Bk Titles 63,500; Bk Vols 65,000, Per Subs 112
Special Collections: Christian Fiction Coll; German Language Coll; World War II Coll
Automation Activity & Vendor Info: (Acquisitions) Baker & Taylor; (Cataloging) SirsiDynix; (Circulation) SirsiDynix; (Media Booking) Baker & Taylor; (Serials) EBSCO Online
Function: Story hour
Special Services for the Blind - Talking bks
Open Mon & Fri 9-5, Tues-Thurs 9-7, Sat Noon-5
Restriction: Open to authorized patrons

FULTONDALE

P FULTONDALE PUBLIC LIBRARY*, PO Box 549, 35068-0549. SAN 300-0893. Tel: 205-849-6335. FAX: 205-841-3620. Web Site: www.fultondale.lib.al.us. *Dir,* Cristi Starkey; E-mail: cstarkey@bham.lib.al.us
Pop 7,000; Circ 42,000
Library Holdings: Bk Vols 25,000; Per Subs 52
Automation Activity & Vendor Info: (Cataloging) Innovative Interfaces, Inc; (Circulation) Innovative Interfaces, Inc; (OPAC) Innovative Interfaces, Inc
Open Mon, Wed & Fri 9-5, Tues & Thurs 9-8, Sat 9-1

GADSDEN

R FIRST PRESBYTERIAN CHURCH OF GADSDEN LIBRARY*, 530 Chestnut St, 35901. (Mail add: PO Box 676, 35902-0676), SAN 300-0923. Tel: 256-547-5747. FAX: 256-547-5789. *Mgr,* Diane Alford
Founded 1960

Library Holdings: Bk Vols 3,000
Open Mon-Fri 9-12 & 1-4:30

P GADSDEN PUBLIC LIBRARY*, 254 College St, 35901. SAN 330-1958. Tel: 256-549-4699. Reference Tel: 256-549-4699, Ext 29. FAX: 256-549-4766. E-mail: gpl@gadsdenlibrary.org. Web Site: www.gadsdenlibrary.org. *Dir, Libr Serv,* Amanda Jackson; *Cat,* Debbie Walker; *Circ,* Paula Spears; *ILL,* Paulette Makary; Staff 26 (MLS 2, Non-MLS 24)
Founded 1906. Pop 103,975; Circ 237,188
Library Holdings: Bk Titles 166,285; Bk Vols 202,166
Special Collections: Alabama History Coll. US Document Depository
Subject Interests: Genealogy
Automation Activity & Vendor Info: (Cataloging) Book Systems; (Circulation) Book Systems; (ILL) Book Systems; (OPAC) Book Systems
Database Vendor: EBSCOhost, Gale Cengage Learning, OCLC FirstSearch
Wireless access
Open Mon, Tues & Thurs 9-7, Wed, Fri & Sat 9-5
Branches: 2
EAST GADSDEN, 919 Wilson St, 35903, SAN 330-2016. Tel: 256-549-4691. *Br Mgr,* Lashunda Williams
Library Holdings: Bk Vols 5,000
Function: Ref serv available, Res libr
Open Mon-Fri 1-5
HOYT WARSHAM, 2700 W Meighan Blvd, 35904, SAN 330-1982. Tel: 256-549-4688. *Br Mgr,* Kay Henderson
Library Holdings: Bk Vols 2,725
Open Mon-Fri 9-5

J GADSDEN STATE COMMUNITY COLLEGE*, Meadows Library, 1001 George Wallace Dr, 35902. (Mail add: PO Box 227, 35902-0227), SAN 324-3435. Tel: 256-549-8333. Reference Tel: 256-549-8411. FAX: 256-549-8401. Web Site: www.gadsdenstate.edu/library. *Dir, Libr Serv,* Dusty Folds; Tel: 256-549-8421, Fax: 256-549-8410; *Cat,* Dorothy Burgess; Tel: 256-549-8496, E-mail: dmburgess@gadsdenstate.edu; *Ref,* Melinda Harvey; Tel: 256-549-8412, E-mail: mharvey@gadsdenstate.edu; Staff 9 (MLS 4, Non-MLS 5)
Founded 1965. Enrl 3,500; Fac 125; Highest Degree: Associate
Library Holdings: Bk Vols 110,000; Per Subs 282
Special Collections: Gadsden State Archives; Mary Cooper Coll
Subject Interests: Ala, Law, Southern lit
Automation Activity & Vendor Info: (Cataloging) Innovative Interfaces, Inc; (Circulation) Innovative Interfaces, Inc; (ILL) Innovative Interfaces, Inc; (OPAC) Innovative Interfaces, Inc
Database Vendor: EBSCOhost, Gale Cengage Learning, OCLC FirstSearch, ProQuest, Westlaw
Function: For res purposes
Publications: Faculty Handbook; Library Skills Handbook; New-Acquisitions (annual); Student Handbook
Partic in Library Management Network, Inc
Special Services for the Blind - Low vision equip
Open Mon-Thurs 7:30am-8:30pm, Fri 7:30-3
Departmental Libraries:
PIERCE C CAIN LEARNING RESOURCE CENTER, 1801 Coleman Rd, Anniston, 36207-6858. (Mail add: PO Box 1647, Anniston, 36202-1647). Tel: 256-835-5435. FAX: 256-835-5476. *Pub Serv Librn,* Michael Gibson; E-mail: mgibson@gadsdenstate.edu
Library Holdings: Bk Titles 14,000; Per Subs 40
Function: AV serv, Satellite serv
Open Mon-Thurs 7:30am-8:30pm, Fri 7:30am-11:30am
MCCLELLAN CENTER, 100 Gamecock Dr, Anniston, 36205. Tel: 256-238-9352. *Ref Librn,* Melinda Harvey; E-mail: mharvey@gadsdenstate.edu
Open Mon-Wed 8-7, Thurs 8-5, Fri 8am-11pm

GARDENDALE

P GARDENDALE PUBLIC LIBRARY*, 995 Mt Olive Rd, 35071. SAN 300-0958. Tel: 205-631-6639. FAX: 205-631-0146. Web Site: www.gardendale.lib.org. *Dir,* Connie Smith; *Adult Serv,* Lisa Keith; *Adult Serv,* Jina Robertson; *Ch Serv,* Lucy Siddiqui; *Circ,* Angie Coburn
Founded 1959. Pop 15,000; Circ 193,303
Library Holdings: Bk Vols 51,261; Per Subs 120
Automation Activity & Vendor Info: (Cataloging) Innovative Interfaces, Inc; (Circulation) Innovative Interfaces, Inc; (OPAC) Innovative Interfaces, Inc
Partic in Jefferson County Library System
Open Mon, Tues & Thurs 9-8, Wed & Fri 9-5, Sat 9-1

GENEVA

P GENEVA PUBLIC LIBRARY, 312 S Commerce St, 36340. (Mail add: PO Box 550, 36340-0550), SAN 300-0966. Tel: 334-684-2459. FAX: 334-219-4223. E-mail: genevapubliclibrary@gmail.com. Web Site: www.genevapubliclibrary.org. *Dir,* Marian Wynn; Staff 1 (Non-MLS 1)
Founded 1904. Pop 8,401; Circ 15,000
Library Holdings: Bk Vols 15,000; Per Subs 25
Automation Activity & Vendor Info: (Acquisitions) Book Systems; (Cataloging) Book Systems; (Circulation) Book Systems; (ILL) OCLC WorldShare Interlibrary Loan
Database Vendor: EBSCOhost, OCLC WebJunction, OCLC WorldShare Interlibrary Loan
Wireless access
Function: Pub access computers, Summer reading prog, Tax forms
Open Mon-Fri 10-5

GERALDINE

P GERALDINE PUBLIC LIBRARY*, 13543 Alabama Hwy 227, 35974-0268. (Mail add: PO Box 268, 35974-0268), SAN 376-6454. Tel: 256-659-6663. FAX: 256-659-6663. E-mail: geraldn2@farmerstel.com. *Dir,* Diane Maddox
Circ 3,661
Library Holdings: Bk Titles 34,534
Special Collections: Civil war
Special Services for the Blind - Audio mat; Bks available with recordings
Open Mon, Tues, Thurs & Fri 11-5, Wed 10-4, Sat 9-1

GOODWATER

P GOODWATER PUBLIC LIBRARY*, 36 Weogufka St, 35072. (Mail add: PO Box 140, 35072-0140), SAN 300-0974. Tel: 256-839-5741. FAX: 256-839-5741. E-mail: gplibrary2003@yahoo.com. *Dir,* Shirley Thompson; *Asst Librn,* Bonnie Rogers
Founded 1945. Pop 1,550; Circ 2,932
Library Holdings: Bk Titles 10,000
Function: Bks on cassette, Bks on CD, Computers for patron use, Copy machines, Fax serv, Free DVD rentals, ILL available, Online info literacy tutorials on the web & in blackboard, Pub access computers, Summer reading prog, VHS videos, Wheelchair accessible
Mem of Horseshoe Bend Regional Library
Open Mon-Fri 9-5

GORDO

P RUTH HOLLIMAN PUBLIC LIBRARY*, 287 Main St, 35466. (Mail add: PO Box 336, 35466-0336), SAN 300-0982. Tel: 205-364-7148. FAX: 205-364-7148. *Dir,* Melba Hollingsworth
Pop 4,250; Circ 10,500
Library Holdings: Bk Vols 12,500
Automation Activity & Vendor Info: (Cataloging) Follett Software; (Circulation) Follett Software
Mem of Pickens County Cooperative Library
Open Mon, Thurs & Fri 12-5, Tues 10-5, Wed 12-3, Sat 8-12
Friends of the Library Group

GRANT

P GRANT PUBLIC LIBRARY*, 5379 Main St, 35747. (Mail add: PO Box 401, 35747-0401), SAN 376-5628. Tel: 256-728-5128. FAX: 256-728-5128. E-mail: readme@nehp.net. Web Site: users.nehp.net/readme. *Librn,* Karen Kirkland
Library Holdings: Bk Vols 15,000
Mem of Marshall County Cooperative Library
Open Mon 11-7, Tues & Thurs 10-4, Fri 12-6, Sat 9-3
Friends of the Library Group

GRAYSVILLE

P GRAYSVILLE PUBLIC LIBRARY*, 315 S Main St, 35073. SAN 300-0990. Tel: 205-674-3040. FAX: 205-674-3296. *Dir,* Judy Smith; E-mail: jsmith@bham.lib.al.us
Founded 1978. Pop 2,400; Circ 60,000
Library Holdings: Bk Vols 24,000; Per Subs 45
Automation Activity & Vendor Info: (Cataloging) Innovative Interfaces, Inc; (Circulation) Innovative Interfaces, Inc; (OPAC) Inmagic, Inc.
Partic in Jefferson County Libr Coop
Open Mon, Tues, Thurs & Fri 9-5:30, Wed & Sat 10-1

GREENSBORO

P HALE COUNTY PUBLIC LIBRARY, 1103 Main St, 36744. (Mail add: PO Box 399, 36744-0399), SAN 300-1008. Tel: 334-624-3409. FAX: 334-624-3409. E-mail: halecountylibrar@bellsouth.net. Web Site: www.hcplgreensboro.org. *Dir,* Carolyn Hemstreet; *Asst Librn,* Robin Cooper; Staff 1.4 (Non-MLS 1.4)

Founded 1925. Pop 6,800; Circ 13,000
Oct 2013-Sept 2014 Income $43,773, State $7,022, City $4,000, County $6,751, Locally Generated Income $15,000, Other $11,000. Mats Exp $5,757, Books $4,000, Per/Ser (Incl. Access Fees) $412, Other Print Mats $300, Micro $50, Electronic Ref Mat (Incl. Access Fees) $995. Sal $25,000
Library Holdings: Audiobooks 504; Bks on Deafness & Sign Lang 2; CDs 13; DVDs 424; e-books 13; High Interest/Low Vocabulary Bk Vols 100; Large Print Bks 325; Bk Titles 15,529; Per Subs 25; Videos 527
Special Collections: Alabama History & Literature Coll; Genealogy Coll (area families)
Automation Activity & Vendor Info: (Cataloging) Book Systems; (Circulation) Book Systems; (OPAC) Book Systems
Wireless access
Function: Bilingual assistance for Spanish patrons, Bks on cassette, Computer training, Computers for patron use, Copy machines, Fax serv, Handicapped accessible, ILL available, Magazines, Magnifiers for reading, Microfiche/film & reading machines, Newsp ref libr, Online cat, Online searches, Photocopying/Printing, Preschool reading prog, Printer for laptops & handheld devices, Prog for children & young adult, Ref & res, Senior computer classes, Story hour, Summer reading prog, Tax forms, VHS videos, Web-catalog
Open Mon-Wed & Fri 10-5:15, Sat 9-12
Friends of the Library Group

GREENVILLE

G BUTLER COUNTY HISTORICAL-GENEALOGICAL SOCIETY LIBRARY*, 309 Fort Dale St, 36037. (Mail add: PO Box 561, 36037-0561), SAN 375-8346. Tel: 334-383-9564. E-mail: historyroom@camelliacom.com. *Dir,* Judy Taylor; Tel: 334-382-6852
Library Holdings: Bk Titles 600; Per Subs 50
Function: Ref serv available

P GREENVILLE-BUTLER COUNTY PUBLIC LIBRARY*, 309 Ft Dale St, 36037. Tel: 334-382-3216. FAX: 334-382-9769. E-mail: gbcpl@alaweb.com. *Dir,* Burke McFerrin
Library Holdings: Bk Vols 40,000; Per Subs 20
Automation Activity & Vendor Info: (Cataloging) Book Systems; (Circulation) Book Systems
Open Mon-Fri 9-5:30, Sat 9-2

GROVE HILL

P GROVE HILL PUBLIC LIBRARY*, 108 Dubose Ave, 36451-9502. SAN 300-1016. Tel: 251-275-8157. FAX: 251-275-8157. *Librn,* Betsy West; E-mail: betsywest43@yahoo.com
Pop 2,266; Circ 10,800
Library Holdings: Bk Vols 19,000; Per Subs 25
Special Collections: Census Rec; Family Research
Automation Activity & Vendor Info: (Circulation) Follett Software
Open Mon-Fri 10:30-5

GULF SHORES

P THOMAS B NORTON PUBLIC LIBRARY*, 221 W 19th Ave, 36542. SAN 300-1024. Tel: 251-968-1176. FAX: 251-968-1184. Web Site: www.thomasbnortonlibrary.com. *Dir,* Wendy Congiardo; *Ref Librn,* Jane C Daugherty; E-mail: thomasbnortonlibrary@gmail.com; Staff 5 (MLS 2, Non-MLS 3)
Founded 1963
Library Holdings: AV Mats 1,926; High Interest/Low Vocabulary Bk Vols 34; Large Print Bks 1,300; Bk Vols 35,419; Per Subs 110
Special Collections: Alabama Room
Subject Interests: Hist
Automation Activity & Vendor Info: (Acquisitions) TLC (The Library Corporation); (Cataloging) TLC (The Library Corporation); (Circulation) TLC (The Library Corporation); (OPAC) TLC (The Library Corporation)
Database Vendor: infoUSA, Overdrive, Inc
Wireless access
Function: Adult bk club, Art exhibits, Audiobks via web, Bks on cassette, Bks on CD, CD-ROM, Children's prog, Computer training, Computers for patron use, Copy machines, e-mail & chat, Electronic databases & coll, Fax serv, Free DVD rentals, Handicapped accessible, Holiday prog, ILL available, Instruction & testing, Magnifiers for reading, Microfiche/film & reading machines, Music CDs, Notary serv, Online cat, Online ref, Online searches, Orientations, Photocopying/Printing, Prog for adults, Prog for children & young adult, Pub access computers, Ref serv available, Ref serv in person, Scanner, Senior computer classes, Spanish lang bks, Summer reading prog, Tax forms, Teen prog, VHS videos, Web-catalog, Wheelchair accessible, Workshops, Writing prog
Mem of Baldwin County Library Cooperative, Inc
Open Mon & Tues 10-8, Wed-Fri 10-6, Sat 10-3
Friends of the Library Group

GUNTERSVILLE

P GUNTERSVILLE PUBLIC LIBRARY*, 1240 O'Brig Ave, 35976. SAN 300-1032. Tel: 256-571-7595. FAX: 256-571-7596. Web Site: www.guntersvillelibrary.org. *Dir,* Beth Dean; *Asst Dir,* Marie Harmon; E-mail: marie2@guntersvillelibrary.org; *Ch,* Amanda Shumate; Staff 4 (MLS 2, Non-MLS 2)
Founded 1947. Pop 10,343; Circ 75,400
Library Holdings: AV Mats 300; DVDs 300; Large Print Bks 500; Bk Vols 50,000; Per Subs 65; Talking Bks 600; Videos 2,000
Special Collections: Genealogical materials of Marshall County; Historical Coll of Guntersville's newspapers
Publications: Friends Newsletter; Library Notes (Newsletter)
Mem of Marshall County Cooperative Library
Open Tues 9-8, Wed-Fri 9-6, Sat 9-2
Friends of the Library Group

HALEYVILLE

P HALEYVILLE PUBLIC LIBRARY*, 913 20th St, 35565. SAN 300-1040. Tel: 205-486-7450. FAX: 205-486-7450. *Librn,* Waldrup Carla
Library Holdings: Bk Vols 12,000; Per Subs 45
Mem of Carl Elliott Regional Library System
Open Mon-Fri 8-5, Sat 9-12

HAMILTON

J BEVILL STATE COMMUNITY COLLEGE*, Hamilton Campus Library, PO Box 9, 35570-0009. Tel: 205-921-3177, Ext 5313. Toll Free Tel: 800-648-3271. FAX: 205-952-9617. Web Site: www.bscc.edu. *Head Librn,* Tammy Sanders; Tel: 205-921-3177, Ext 5356, E-mail: tsanders@bscc.edu
Library Holdings: Bk Vols 13,500
Wireless access
Function: ILL available, Photocopying/Printing, Ref serv available
Open Mon-Thurs 7:30am-8:30pm, Fri 7:30am-11:30am

HANCEVILLE

J WALLACE STATE COLLEGE*, Hanceville Library, 801 Main St NW, 35077-2000. (Mail add: PO Box 2000, 35077-2000). Tel: 256-352-8260. FAX: 256-352-8254. Web Site: www.wallacestate.edu. *Head Librn,* William Simpson
Library Holdings: Bk Vols 55,000
Automation Activity & Vendor Info: (Cataloging) Follett Software; (Circulation) Follett Software; (OPAC) Follett Software
Function: AV serv
Open Mon-Thurs 7:30am-8:30pm, Fri 7:30-4, Sat 9-3

HARTFORD

P MCGREGOR-MCKINNEY PUBLIC LIBRARY*, Hartford Public Library, 101 E Fulton St, 36344. SAN 300-1059. Tel: 334-588-2384. FAX: 334-588-2384. E-mail: mmplhartford@centurytel.net. *Dir,* Stephanie Riley; *Asst Dir,* Kelly King
Pop 2,649; Circ 14,280
Library Holdings: Large Print Bks 1,500; Bk Vols 17,000; Per Subs 35; Talking Bks 600
Automation Activity & Vendor Info: (Cataloging) Book Systems; (Circulation) Book Systems; (OPAC) Book Systems
Function: ILL available, Prog for children & young adult, Summer reading prog
Partic in Lyrasis
Open Mon, Wed & Fri 8-5, Tues 8-5:30

HARTSELLE

P HARTSELLE PUBLIC LIBRARY*, 152 NW Sparkman St, 35640. SAN 300-1067. Tel: 256-773-9880. FAX: 256-773-9884. *Librn,* Emily Love; E-mail: elove@hartselle.org
Pop 10,860; Circ 47,280
Library Holdings: Bk Vols 29,000; Per Subs 20
Special Collections: William Bradford Huie Coll
Publications: Friends of the Library (Newsletter)
Mem of Wheeler Basin Regional Library
Open Mon-Thurs 10-6, Fri 9-5
Friends of the Library Group

HAYNEVILLE

P HAYNEVILLE-LOWNDES COUNTY PUBLIC LIBRARY*, 215B Tuskeena St, 36040. (Mail add: PO Box 425, 36040-0425). Tel: 334-548-2686. FAX: 334-548-5427. E-mail: htcard@htcnet.net. *Dir,* Jimmie Felder
Founded 1988. Pop 9,000; Circ 3,000
Library Holdings: Audiobooks 25; Bks on Deafness & Sign Lang 2; High Interest/Low Vocabulary Bk Vols 300; Large Print Bks 25; Bk Vols 24,000; Per Subs 14

Wireless access
Function: Art exhibits, Bks on cassette, Citizenship assistance, Copy machines, e-mail serv, Fax serv, Handicapped accessible, Online ref, Online searches, Photocopying/Printing, Ref serv available, Ref serv in person, Summer reading prog, Tax forms, Wheelchair accessible, Workshops
Open Mon, Wed & Fri 10-3, Tues & Thurs 10-4:30

HEADLAND

P BLANCHE R SOLOMON MEMORIAL LIBRARY*, 17 Park St, 36345. SAN 330-3063. Tel: 334-693-2706. FAX: 334-693-5023. *Libr Dir,* Joan Moulton; Chase Bryant
Pop 3,523
Library Holdings: Bk Vols 48,461; Per Subs 43
Automation Activity & Vendor Info: (Cataloging) Book Systems; (Circulation) Book Systems; (OPAC) Book Systems
Open Mon 9-8, Tues-Fri 9-5

HEFLIN

P CHEAHA REGIONAL LIBRARY*, 935 Coleman St, 36264. SAN 320-1430. Tel: 256-463-7125. FAX: 256-463-7125. E-mail: cheahareglibrary@centurytel.net. Web Site: www.cheaharegionallibrary.org. *Dir,* Evi Jones
Founded 1976. Pop 65,000
Library Holdings: Audiobooks 5,681; Bks on Deafness & Sign Lang 243; CDs 862; DVDs 358; e-books 2,985; e-journals 12; Electronic Media & Resources 98; High Interest/Low Vocabulary Bk Vols 8,594; Large Print Bks 7,948; Bk Vols 35,489; Talking Bks 24
Automation Activity & Vendor Info: (Acquisitions) Book Systems; (Cataloging) Book Systems; (Circulation) Book Systems; (OPAC) Book Systems
Database Vendor: EBSCOhost, OCLC FirstSearch
Wireless access
Member Libraries: Annie L Awbrey Public Library; Ashland City Public Library; Earle A Rainwater Memorial Library; Lineville Public Library; Lucile L Morgan Public Library
Special Services for the Deaf - Bks on deafness & sign lang; High interest/low vocabulary bks; TDD equip
Special Services for the Blind - Braille bks; Home delivery serv; Talking bks
Open Mon-Fri 8:30-4:30
Bookmobiles: 2. Librn, Kayron Triplett

P LUCILE L MORGAN PUBLIC LIBRARY*, 541 Ross St, 36264. SAN 300-1075. Tel: 256-463-2259. FAX: 256-463-2259. Web Site: www.cheaharegionllibrary.org. *Librn,* Joyce Dryden
Founded 1964. Pop 3,014; Circ 5,691
Library Holdings: AV Mats 82; Large Print Bks 146; Bk Vols 14,500; Per Subs 25; Talking Bks 130
Special Collections: Old Book Coll
Mem of Cheaha Regional Library
Open Mon-Fri 1-5, Sat 10-1

HELENA

P JAMES BOYD HOLMES PUBLIC LIBRARY*, 230 Tucker Rd, 35080-7036. SAN 371-9359. Tel: 205-664-8308. FAX: 205-664-4593. Web Site: www.shelbycounty-al.org. *Dir,* Daniel Dearing; E-mail: ddearing@shelbycounty-al.org; Staff 5 (Non-MLS 5)
Founded 1960. Pop 13,000
Library Holdings: Bk Vols 26,000; Per Subs 20
Automation Activity & Vendor Info: (Cataloging) Innovative Interfaces, Inc; (Circulation) Innovative Interfaces, Inc; (OPAC) Innovative Interfaces, Inc
Mem of Harrison Regional Library System
Open Mon & Thurs 10-8, Tues & Wed 10-6, Fri 10-5, Sat 10-2
Friends of the Library Group

HOMEWOOD

P HOMEWOOD PUBLIC LIBRARY*, 1721 Oxmoor Rd, 35209-4085. SAN 300-1083. Tel: 205-332-6600. FAX: 205-802-6424. Web Site: www.homewoodpubliclibrary.org. *Dir,* Deborah Fout; E-mail: dfout@bham.lib.al.us; *Head, Adult Serv,* Leslie West; Tel: 205-332-6620, E-mail: lwest@bham.lib.al.us; *Head, Ch,* Dona Smith; Tel: 205-332-6616, E-mail: dhsmith@bham.lib.al.us; *Head, Circ Serv,* Lonnie Jones; Tel: 205-332-6611, E-mail: ljones@bham.lib.al.us; *Ref Librn,* Beth Hutcheson; Tel: 205-332-6622, E-mail: bhutcheson@bham.lib.al.us; *Spec Projects Librn,* Heather Cover; Tel: 205-332-6621, E-mail: hcover@bham.lib.al.us; *IT Mgr,* Brooks Fancher; Tel: 205-332-6630, E-mail: bfancher@bham.lib.al.us; *Webmaster,* Cheryl Burnette; Tel: 205-332-6631, E-mail: cburnette@bham.lib.al.us; Staff 33.13 (MLS 9.4, Non-MLS 23.73)
Founded 1942. Pop 25,262; Circ 519,683
Library Holdings: Audiobooks 5,590; AV Mats 327; CDs 2,901; DVDs 15,770; e-books 4,991; Electronic Media & Resources 77; Large Print Bks 2,397; Bk Vols 73,301; Per Subs 220
Automation Activity & Vendor Info: (Cataloging) Innovative Interfaces, Inc - Millenium; (Circulation) Innovative Interfaces, Inc - Millenium; (OPAC) Innovative Interfaces, Inc
Wireless access
Partic in Jefferson County Libr Coop
Open Mon, Tues & Thurs 9-9, Wed, Fri & Sat 9-6, Sun 2-6
Friends of the Library Group

HOOVER

P HOOVER PUBLIC LIBRARY*, 200 Municipal Dr, 35216. SAN 329-1839. Tel: 205-444-7810. Circulation Tel: 205-444-7800. FAX: 205-444-7878. Web Site: www.hoover.lib.al.us. *Dir,* Linda R Andrews; E-mail: lindaa@bham.lib.al.us; *Coordr,* Matina Johnson; *Adult Serv,* Patricia Guarino; *Ch Serv,* Amanda Bonner; *Circ,* Billie Page; *Ref,* Susan L Spafford; *Tech Coordr,* Carrie Speinmehl. Subject Specialists: *Fine arts,* Matina Johnson; Staff 62 (MLS 14, Non-MLS 48)
Founded 1983. Pop 65,000; Circ 1,081,202
Library Holdings: Bk Vols 171,567; Per Subs 347
Automation Activity & Vendor Info: (Cataloging) Innovative Interfaces, Inc; (Circulation) Innovative Interfaces, Inc; (OPAC) Innovative Interfaces, Inc
Publications: Quarterly Calendar
Open Mon-Thurs 9-9, Fri 9-6, Sat 10-6, Sun 2-6
Friends of the Library Group

HUEYTOWN

P HUEYTOWN PUBLIC LIBRARY, 1372 Hueytown Rd, 35023-2443. SAN 300-1091. Tel: 205-491-1443. FAX: 205-491-6319. Web Site: www.hueytownlibrary.org. *Dir,* Virginia Allen; E-mail: vallen@bham.lib.al.us; Staff 5 (Non-MLS 5)
Founded 1969. Pop 15,734; Circ 61,053
Library Holdings: Bk Vols 45,000; Per Subs 42
Subject Interests: Ala
Automation Activity & Vendor Info: (Cataloging) Innovative Interfaces, Inc - Sierra; (Circulation) Innovative Interfaces, Inc - Sierra; (OPAC) Innovative Interfaces, Inc - Sierra
Wireless access
Partic in Jefferson County Libr Coop
Open Mon-Fri 10-6, Sat 9-1

HUNTSVILLE

C ALABAMA A&M UNIVERSITY*, Joseph F Drake Memorial Learning Resources Center, 4900 Meridian St, 35762. SAN 300-1792. Tel: 256-372-4747. Circulation Tel: 256-372-4723. Interlibrary Loan Service Tel: 256-372-4728. Reference Tel: 256-372-4712. FAX: 256-372-5768. E-mail: info@aamu.edu. Web Site: www.aamu.edu. *Actg Dir,* Gary Bush; *Head, Ref,* Prudence Bryant; Tel: 256-372-4729; *Syst Librn,* Diane McArthur; Tel: 256-372-4715; *Cat,* Delorise Pruitt; Tel: 256-372-4730; Staff 21 (MLS 11, Non-MLS 10)
Founded 1875. Enrl 6,500; Fac 280; Highest Degree: Doctorate
Library Holdings: Bk Titles 254,000; Per Subs 1,600
Special Collections: Archival & Historical Colls; Audio Visual Coll; Black Coll; Carnegie-Mydral Coll; Curriculum Coll; ERIC Coll; Government Documents Coll; International Studies Coll; J F Kennedy Memorial Coll; Schomburg Coll; Textbook Coll; YA Coll. Oral History; US Document Depository
Subject Interests: Agr, Art & archit, Bus & mgt, Econ, Educ, Eng, Food sci, Forestry, Hist, Humanities, Music, Natural sci, Physics, Soc sci & issues, Urban planning
Automation Activity & Vendor Info: (Acquisitions) SirsiDynix; (Cataloging) SirsiDynix; (Circulation) SirsiDynix; (Serials) SirsiDynix
Database Vendor: EBSCOhost
Wireless access
Publications: Bulldogbytes (Newsletter)
Partic in Lyrasis; Network of Alabama Academic Libraries
Open Mon-Thurs (Sept-June) 8am-11pm, Fri 8-5, Sat 11-3, Sun 1-10
Friends of the Library Group

P HUNTSVILLE-MADISON COUNTY PUBLIC LIBRARY*, 915 Monroe St, 35801. (Mail add: PO Box 443, 35804-0443), SAN 330-2105. Tel: 256-532-5940. Circulation Tel: 256-532-5984. Interlibrary Loan Service Tel: 256-532-5967. Administration Tel: 256-532-5950. Automation Services Tel: 256-532-5963. Information Services Tel: 256-532-5975. FAX: 256-532-5997. Information Services FAX: 256-532-5994. E-mail: askus@hmcpl.org. Web Site: www.hmcpl.org. *Exec Dir,* Laurel Best; E-mail: lbest@hmcpl.org; *Dep Dir,* Susan B Royer; Tel: 256-532-5952; *Assoc Dir, Extn & Outreach Serv,* Susan Markham; Tel: 256-532-5961, E-mail: smarkham@hmcpl.org; *Assoc Dir, Main Libr Pub Serv,* Position Currently Open; *Ref & Adult Serv Mgr,* Mary Moore; E-mail: mmoore@hmcpl.org; *Cat, Tech Serv,* Barbara Liaw; Tel: 256-532-5976;

Coll Develop, Ann Phillips; Tel: 256-532-5993; *Genealogist,* Position Currently Open; *ILL,* Pamela Payne
Founded 1818. Pop 304,307; Circ 2,094,469
Oct 2010-Sept 2011 Income (Main Library and Branch(s)) $5,792,413. Mats Exp $812,194. Sal $3,646,087
Library Holdings: AV Mats 84,900; e-books 1,525; Electronic Media & Resources 86; Bk Vols 446,042; Per Subs 714
Special Collections: Civil War & Southern History (Zeitler Room Coll), bks, maps & newsp; Foreign Language Materials; Genealogy & Local History (Heritage Room Coll), bks, micro & ms
Subject Interests: Foreign lang
Automation Activity & Vendor Info: (Acquisitions) SirsiDynix; (Cataloging) SirsiDynix; (Circulation) SirsiDynix; (OPAC) SirsiDynix; (Serials) SirsiDynix
Database Vendor: SirsiDynix
Wireless access
Publications: Cover to Cover (Newsletter)
Special Services for the Blind - Talking bks & player equip
Open Mon-Thurs 9-9, Fri & Sat 9-5, Sun 1-5
Friends of the Library Group
Branches: 12
BAILEY COVE LIBRARY, 1409 Weatherly Plaza, 35803, SAN 377-6581. Tel: 256-881-0257. *Br Mgr,* Patsy Ducote
Open Mon-Thurs 9-8, Fri & Sat 9-5, Sun 1-5
Friends of the Library Group
ELIZABETH CARPENTER PUBLIC LIBRARY OF NEW HOPE, 5498 Main St, New Hope, 35760, SAN 329-6148. Tel: 256-723-2995. *Br Mgr,* Katy Kalil
Founded 1989
Library Holdings: Bk Vols 20,930
Open Mon 2-8, Tues & Thurs 10-6, Fri 10-1, Sat 10-7
Friends of the Library Group
GURLEY PUBLIC LIBRARY, 225 Walker St, Gurley, 35748, SAN 329-6121. Tel: 256-776-2102. *Br Mgr,* Alisa Watson
Library Holdings: Bk Vols 9,849
Open Mon 12-7, Tues 12-5, Wed 10-5, Thurs & Fri 2-5, Sat 10-2
Friends of the Library Group
TILLMAN D HILL PUBLIC LIBRARY, 131 Knowledge Dr, Hazel Green, 35750, SAN 372-5103. Tel: 256-828-9529. *Br Mgr,* Lesia Flynn; E-mail: aflynn@hmcpl.org
Library Holdings: Bk Vols 29,000
Open Mon & Thurs 12-6, Tues 12-8, Wed, Fri & Sat 9-1
Friends of the Library Group
MADISON PUBLIC LIBRARY, 130 Plaza Blvd, Madison, 35758, SAN 330-2229. Tel: 256-461-0046. FAX: 256 461 0530. *Br Mgr,* Sarah Sledge
Library Holdings: Bk Vols 80,000
Open Mon-Thurs 9-8, Fri & Sat 9-5, Sun 1-5
Friends of the Library Group
OSCAR MASON LIBRARY, 149 Mason Ct, 35805, SAN 376-8929. Tel: 256-535-2249. *Br Mgr,* Yuki Lewis
Function: Ref serv available
Open Mon-Thurs 9-5, Fri 12-5
Friends of the Library Group
MONROVIA PUBLIC LIBRARY, 254 Allen Drake Dr, 35806, SAN 377-6603. Tel: 256-489-3392. *Br Mgr,* Cindy Hewitt; E-mail: chewitt@hmcpl.org
Library Holdings: Bk Vols 11,127
Open Mon & Thurs 10-6, Tues 2-8, Fri & Sat 10-2
Friends of the Library Group
ELEANOR E MURPHY LIBRARY, 7910 Charlotte Dr SW, 35802, SAN 330-2164. Tel: 256-881-5620. FAX: 256-881-9181. *Br Mgr,* Connie Chow
Open Mon-Thurs 9-8, Fri & Sat 9-5
Friends of the Library Group
BESSIE K RUSSELL BRANCH LIBRARY, 3011 C Sparkman Dr, 35810, SAN 330-2253. Tel: 256-859-9050. *Br Mgr,* Patti Ehmen
Founded 1962
Open Mon-Thurs 9-6, Fri & Sat 9-5
Friends of the Library Group
R SHOWERS CENTER, 4600 Blue Spring Rd, 35810, SAN 377-6964. Tel: 256-851-7492. *Br Mgr,* Lillie Cawthron
Library Holdings: Bk Vols 6,835
Open Mon-Thurs 9-6, Fri 9-5
Friends of the Library Group

P SUBREGIONAL LIBRARY FOR THE BLIND & PHYSICALLY HANDICAPPED, 915 Monroe St, 35801-5007. (Mail add: PO Box 443, 35804-0443). Tel: 256-532-5980. FAX: 256-532-5997. *Librn,* Bobby Lipscomb; E-mail: blipscomb@hmcpl.org
Founded 1967
Open Mon-Fri 9-4:30
TRIANA YOUTH CENTER LIBRARY, 640 Sixth St, Madison, 35756, SAN 376-8937. Tel: 256-772-3677. *Br Mgr,* Blanche Orr
Open Mon-Fri 12-5
Friends of the Library Group
Bookmobiles: 2

J J F DRAKE STATE TECHNICAL COLLEGE*, S C O'Neal Library & Technology Center, 3421 Meridan St N, 35811-1544. Tel: 256-539-8161, Ext 120, 256-551-3120. Reference Tel: 256-551-5208. Toll Free Tel: 888-413-7253. FAX: 256-551-3134. Web Site: www.drakestate.edu. *Librn, Media Spec,* Kathryn B Neal; E-mail: nealk@drakestate.edu; *Asst Librn,* Lesley N Shotts; Tel: 256-551-5206, E-mail: shotts@drakestate.edu; Staff 2 (MLS 2)
Founded 1961. Enrl 695; Highest Degree: Associate
Sept 2006-Aug 2007. Mats Exp $150,000, Books $118,000, Per/Ser (Incl. Access Fees) $15,000, Other Print Mats $2,000, AV Mat $11,000, Electronic Ref Mat (Incl. Access Fees) $4,000. Sal $132,383
Library Holdings: AV Mats 3,817; CDs 14; DVDs 139; Bk Titles 12,936; Bk Vols 14,872; Per Subs 129
Special Collections: Black Coll
Automation Activity & Vendor Info: (Cataloging) Follett Software; (Circulation) Follett Software; (Course Reserve) Follett Software; (OPAC) Follett Software
Database Vendor: Baker & Taylor, EBSCO Information Services, ProQuest
Wireless access
Function: AV serv, Photocopying/Printing
Open Mon-Thurs 8-7, Fri 8-4:30

C OAKWOOD COLLEGE*, Eva B Dykes Library, 7000 Adventist Blvd, 35896. SAN 300-1164. Tel: 256-726-7246. Interlibrary Loan Service Tel: 256-726-7248. FAX: 256-726-7538. Web Site: www.oakwood.edu/library. *Acq, Dir,* Paulette L Johnson; Tel: 256-726-7250, E-mail: pjohnson@oakwood.edu; *Archivist,* Minneola Dixon; *Cat, Tech Serv,* Morris Iheanacho; *ILL, Ref,* Elizabeth Mosby; Staff 9 (MLS 4, Non-MLS 5)
Founded 1896. Enrl 1,800; Fac 100; Highest Degree: Bachelor
Library Holdings: Bk Vols 135,000; Per Subs 565
Special Collections: Black Studies; Oakwood College History; Seventh-Day Adventist Black History. Oral History
Automation Activity & Vendor Info: (Cataloging) SirsiDynix; (Circulation) SirsiDynix; (OPAC) SirsiDynix
Database Vendor: EBSCOhost, Gale Cengage Learning, JSTOR, OCLC FirstSearch, SirsiDynix
Wireless access
Partic in Network of Alabama Academic Libraries
Open Mon-Thurs 7:45am-11pm, Fri 7:45-1, Sun 10am-11pm

S US SPACE & ROCKET CENTER*, Von Braun Library & Archives, One Tranquility Base, 35805-3399. SAN 327-9340. Tel: 256-721-7148. FAX: 256-722-5600. *Exec Dir,* Larry Capps; *Archivist, Curator,* Irene Willhite; E-mail: irenew@spacecamp.com
Library Holdings: Bk Vols 4,500
Restriction: Open by appt only

C UNIVERSITY OF ALABAMA IN HUNTSVILLE*, M Louis Salmon Library, 301 Sparkman Dr NW, 35899. SAN 300-1199. Tel: 256-824-6530. Interlibrary Loan Service Tel: 256-890-6124. Reference Tel: 256-824-6529. Administration Tel: 256-824-6540. FAX: 256-824-6083. Circulation FAX: 256-824-6552. Web Site: www.uah.edu/library. *Interim Dir,* David Phillip Moore; Tel: 256-824-6285; *Head, Circ,* Lelon Oliver; E-mail: oliverl@email.uah.edu; *Head, ILL,* Charoltte Olson; Tel: 256-824-6522, Fax: 256-824-6862; *Head, Tech Serv,* Susan McCreless; Tel: 256-824-6537, E-mail: mccrels@email.uah.edu; *Archivist, Art Librn, Govt Doc,* Anne Coleman; Tel: 256-824-6418, E-mail: colemana@email.uah.edu; *Ref Librn,* Dr Belinda Ong; Tel: 256-824-6432, E-mail: ongb@email.uah.edu; *Syst Librn,* Jack Drost; Tel: 256-824-7407, E-mail: drostj@email.uah.edu. Subject Specialists: *Bus, Libr sci,* David Phillip Moore; Staff 33 (MLS 8, Non-MLS 25)
Founded 1967. Enrl 6,200; Fac 301; Highest Degree: Doctorate
Library Holdings: e-books 46,172; e-journals 17,500; Bk Titles 283,948; Bk Vols 329,686; Per Subs 1,044
Special Collections: Harvie Jone Architectural Coll; Robert E Jones Congressional Papers; Robert Forward Space Coll; Saturn V History Documentation Coll; Skylab Space Station Coll; Willy Ley Space Coll. US Document Depository
Subject Interests: Bus, Eng
Automation Activity & Vendor Info: (Acquisitions) SirsiDynix; (Cataloging) SirsiDynix; (Circulation) SirsiDynix; (Course Reserve) SirsiDynix; (ILL) SirsiDynix; (OPAC) SirsiDynix; (Serials) SirsiDynix
Database Vendor: Baker & Taylor, Cambridge Scientific Abstracts, Dialog, EBSCOhost, Gale Cengage Learning, JSTOR, LexisNexis, OCLC FirstSearch, OCLC WorldShare Interlibrary Loan, OVID Technologies, ProQuest, ScienceDirect, SirsiDynix
Function: For res purposes, Ref serv available, Res libr, Wheelchair accessible
Publications: Guide to the Salmon Library (Library handbook)

Partic in Lyrasis; Network of Alabama Academic Libraries; OCLC Online Computer Library Center, Inc
Special Services for the Blind - Assistive/Adapted tech devices, equip & products; Computer with voice synthesizer for visually impaired persons
Open Mon-Thurs 8am-12am, Fri 8-8, Sat 9-6, Sun 1-10

IDER

P IDER PUBLIC LIBRARY*, 10808 Alabama Hwy 75, 35981. (Mail add: PO Box 202, 35981-0202), SAN 376-5636. Tel: 256-657-2170. FAX: 256-657-3178. E-mail: iderpl1@farmerstel.com. *Librn,* Virginia Adams
Library Holdings: Bk Vols 12,000
Open Tues-Fri 12:45-5, Sat 9-12
Friends of the Library Group

IRONDALE

P IRONDALE PUBLIC LIBRARY*, 105 20th St S, 35210. SAN 300-1210. Tel: 205-951-1415. FAX: 205-951-7715. Web Site: www.irondalelibrary.com. *Dir,* Madelyn M Wilson; E-mail: dwilson@bham.lib.al.us; Staff 5.53 (MLS 2, Non-MLS 3.53)
Founded 1951. Pop 9,704; Circ 67,367
Library Holdings: Audiobooks 1,025; DVDs 1,896; Bk Vols 41,313; Per Subs 85
Automation Activity & Vendor Info: (Cataloging) Innovative Interfaces, Inc; (Circulation) Innovative Interfaces, Inc; (OPAC) Innovative Interfaces, Inc
Wireless access
Partic in Jefferson County Libr Coop
Open Mon, Tues & Thurs 9:30-7, Wed 9:30-6, Fri 9-1, Sat 11-3, Sun 2-5

JACKSON

P WHITE SMITH MEMORIAL LIBRARY*, 213 College Ave, 36545. (Mail add: PO Box 265, 36545), SAN 300-1229. Tel: 251-246-4962. FAX: 251-246-9791. E-mail: wsmlibrary@yahoo.com. *Coordr,* Debra Grayson; *Pub Relations,* Shelia Finch
Founded 1937. Pop 7,000; Circ 29,521
Library Holdings: Large Print Bks 200; Bk Titles 18,500; Bk Vols 21,000; Per Subs 15
Special Collections: Video Coll
Automation Activity & Vendor Info: (Cataloging) Book Systems; (Circulation) Book Systems; (OPAC) Book Systems
Open Mon & Thurs 9-6, Tues, Wed & Fri 9-5
Friends of the Library Group

JACKSONVILLE

P JACKSONVILLE PUBLIC LIBRARY*, 200 Pelham Rd S, 36265. SAN 300-1245. Tel: 256-435-6332. FAX: 256-435-4459. E-mail: jplkids@hotmail.com, lotsabooks@hotmail.com. Web Site: www.jacksonvillepubliclibrary.org. *Dir,* Barbara Rowell; *Acq,* Amy Miller; *Computer Tech,* Christy Wallace; Staff 9 (MLS 1, Non-MLS 8)
Founded 1957. Pop 9,000; Circ 94,000
Oct 2010-Sept 2011 Income $491,979, State $9,005, City $467,974, Federal $15,000. Mats Exp $83,626, Books $64,798, AV Mat $15,687, Electronic Ref Mat (Incl. Access Fees) $2,941, Presv $200. Sal $266,650
Library Holdings: Audiobooks 677; DVDs 2,447; e-books 3,249; Bk Vols 58,216; Per Subs 61
Special Collections: Col John Pelham Papers; Jacksonville History Museum Coll; John Francis Papers (Civil War Roster & Letters)
Automation Activity & Vendor Info: (Cataloging) SirsiDynix; (Circulation) SirsiDynix; (OPAC) SirsiDynix
Wireless access
Open Tues-Fri 8-6, Sat 8-4

C JACKSONVILLE STATE UNIVERSITY LIBRARY*, Houston Cole Library, 700 Pelham Rd N, 36265. SAN 300-1237. Tel: 256-782-5255. Interlibrary Loan Service Tel: 256-782-5243. FAX: 256-782-5872. Web Site: www.jsu.edu/library. *Dean of Libr Serv,* John-Bauer Graham; E-mail: jgraham@jsu.edu; *Head, Tech Serv,* Jodi Poe; *Cat Librn,* Arland Henning; *Cat Librn,* Kim Stevens; *Electronic Res Librn,* Bethany Latham; *Electronic Res Librn,* Yingqi Tang; *Acq, Per Librn,* Mary Bevis; *Ref & Instruction Librn,* Charlcie Pettway Vann; *Ref Librn,* Paula Barnett-Ellis; *Ref Librn,* Linda Cain; *Ref Librn,* Laurie Charnigo; *Ref Librn,* Carley Knight; *Ref Librn,* Harry Nuttall; *Ref Librn,* Doug Taylor; *Ref Librn,* Hanrong Wang; *Syst Coordr,* Donald Walter; *Access Serv, ILL,* Debra Deering-Barrett; *AV,* Tony Gravette. Subject Specialists: *Math, Sci,* Paula Barnett-Ellis; *Geog, Hist,* Linda Cain; *Educ,* Laurie Charnigo; *Art, Lang arts, Music,* Carley Knight; *Lit,* Harry Nuttall; *Bus & mgt,* Doug Taylor; *Law, Tech,* Hanrong Wang; Staff 18 (MLS 15, Non-MLS 3)
Founded 1883. Enrl 9,000; Fac 453; Highest Degree: Master
Oct 2008-Sept 2009 Income $3,119,799. Mats Exp $785,397, Books $314,797, Per/Ser (Incl. Access Fees) $450,600, AV Mat $10,000, Presv $10,000. Sal $1,459,369
Library Holdings: AV Mats 38,940; e-books 19,067; Bk Vols 714,960; Per Subs 1,802
Special Collections: Alabama; Old & Rare Books. Oral History; US Document Depository
Automation Activity & Vendor Info: (Acquisitions) Ex Libris Group; (Cataloging) Ex Libris Group; (Circulation) Ex Libris Group; (OPAC) Ex Libris Group; (Serials) Ex Libris Group
Database Vendor: 3M Library Systems, American Chemical Society, Baker & Taylor, Cambridge Scientific Abstracts, EBSCOhost, Emerald, Ex Libris Group, Gale Cengage Learning, H W Wilson, JSTOR, OCLC WorldShare Interlibrary Loan, ProQuest, SerialsSolutions, Westlaw
Wireless access
Partic in Lyrasis; Network of Alabama Academic Libraries
Open Mon-Thurs 7:30am-11pm, Fri 7:30-4:30, Sat 9-5, Sun 3-11
Friends of the Library Group

JASPER

J BEVILL STATE COMMUNITY COLLEGE, Irma D Nicholson Library, 1411 Indiana Ave, 35501-4967. SAN 300-1261. Tel: 205-387-0511, Ext 5748. FAX: 205-387-5190. Web Site: www.bscc.edu. *Chief Librn,* Rebecca E Whitten; *Libr Asst,* Pat Bowden; Staff 2 (MLS 2)
Enrl 1,000; Highest Degree: Associate
Library Holdings: Bk Vols 25,930; Per Subs 85
Automation Activity & Vendor Info: (Cataloging) Follett Software; (Circulation) Follett Software; (OPAC) Follett Software
Open Mon-Thurs 7:30am-8:30pm, Fri 7:30am-11:30am

P CARL ELLIOTT REGIONAL LIBRARY SYSTEM*, 98 E 18th St, 35501. SAN 300-1253. Tel: 205-221-2568. E-mail: contact@carlelliottregionallibrary.com. *Dir,* Sandra Underwood; *Cat, Tech Serv,* Martha R Baldwin; *Extn Serv,* Christy Cagle; E-mail: cerls.ill.cd@gmail.com; *Syst Adminr,* Stephen Underwood; E-mail: sunderwood@carlelliottregionallibrary.org
Founded 1957. Pop 95,000; Circ 165,000
Library Holdings: Bk Titles 87,000; Bk Vols 98,000; Per Subs 132
Special Collections: Literature (Musgrove Coll)
Automation Activity & Vendor Info: (Cataloging) TLC (The Library Corporation); (Circulation) TLC (The Library Corporation); (OPAC) TLC (The Library Corporation)
Wireless access
Publications: Regional Messenger
Member Libraries: Arley Public Library; Carbon Hill City Library; Double Springs Public Library; Haleyville Public Library; Jasper Public Library; Sumiton Public Library
Open Mon-Fri 8-5

P JASPER PUBLIC LIBRARY*, 98 18th St E, 35501. SAN 320-8915. Tel: 205-221-8512. E-mail: jasperpubliclibrary@hotmail.com. *Librn,* Colleen Miller
Library Holdings: Bk Titles 60,000; Per Subs 124
Open Mon-Fri 9-6

KILLEN

P KILLEN PUBLIC LIBRARY*, 325 J C Malden Hwy, 35645. SAN 376-5644. Tel: 256-757-5471. FAX: 256-757-5471. E-mail: killenlibrary@bellsouth.net. *Librn,* Pamela White; *Asst Librn,* Linda Baskins
Library Holdings: CDs 67; DVDs 78; Large Print Bks 3,467; Bk Titles 19,000; Bk Vols 20,000; Talking Bks 145
Automation Activity & Vendor Info: (Acquisitions) Book Systems; (Cataloging) Book Systems; (Circulation) Book Systems; (OPAC) Book Systems
Wireless access
Open Mon-Wed & Fri 9-5, Thurs 11-7, Sat 9-1
Friends of the Library Group

LEEDS

P LEEDS JANE CULBRETH PUBLIC LIBRARY*, 8104 Parkway Dr, 35094-2225. SAN 300-130X. Tel: 205-699-5962. FAX: 205-699-6843. Web Site: www.leedslibrary.com. *Dir,* Mondretta Williams; E-mail: mwilliams@bham.lib.al.us; Staff 4 (MLS 1, Non-MLS 3)
Founded 1923. Pop 10,455; Circ 95,786
Oct 2005-Sept 2006 Income $285,195, State $7,000, City $232,477, Locally Generated Income $45,718. Mats Exp $20,352, Books $9,633, Other Print Mats $4,648, AV Mat $6,071. Sal $205,435
Library Holdings: AV Mats 4,068; e-books 472; Bk Vols 31,424; Per Subs 92; Talking Bks 1,570
Subject Interests: Ala
Automation Activity & Vendor Info: (Circulation) Innovative Interfaces, Inc
Database Vendor: EBSCOhost, OVID Technologies, ProQuest
Function: Ref serv available
Partic in Jefferson County Libr Coop

Special Services for the Deaf - Staff with knowledge of sign lang
Special Services for the Blind - Bks on cassette
Open Mon & Thurs 9:30-7, Tues & Wed 9:30-5:30, Fri & Sat 9:30-1
Friends of the Library Group

LEIGHTON

P LEIGHTON PUBLIC LIBRARY*, 8740 Main St, 35646. (Mail add: PO Box 484, 35646-0484), SAN 300-1318. Tel: 256-446-5380. FAX: 256-446-5380. E-mail: lepubli2@hiwaay.net. *Librn,* Polly King
Pop 988; Circ 7,100
Library Holdings: Bk Vols 10,000; Per Subs 22
Open Tues-Fri 1-5, Sat 10-2
Friends of the Library Group

LEXINGTON

P BURCHELL CAMPBELL MEMORIAL LIBRARY*, 11075 Hwy 101, 35648-0459. SAN 376-7590. Tel: 256-229-5579. FAX: 256-229-5579. E-mail: lexlibrary@bellsouth.net. *Librn,* Sherri Burgess; Staff 1 (Non-MLS 1)
Pop 2,000
Library Holdings: Bk Vols 7,500
Open Tues-Fri 11-4, Sat 9-12
Friends of the Library Group

LILLIAN

P LILLIAN PERDIDO BAY LIBRARY*, 12634 Ickler Ave, 36549. (Mail add: PO Box 237, 36549-0237). Tel: 251-962-4700. FAX: 251-962-4700. *Pres,* Barbara Kuntz; E-mail: lperdblib@gulftel.com; *Librn,* Doris Palmer
Founded 1993
Library Holdings: CDs 188; DVDs 41; Large Print Bks 277; Bk Vols 16,269; Talking Bks 360; Videos 634
Mem of Baldwin County Library Cooperative, Inc
Open Tues & Thurs 10-2 & 4-6, Wed, Fri & Sat 10-2

LINCOLN

P LINCOLN PUBLIC LIBRARY*, 49 Complex Dr, 35096-5096. SAN 376-5520. Tel: 205-763-7244. FAX: 205-763-7244. E-mail: lincolnpubliclibrary@lincolnalabama.com. *Head Librn,* Melanie Harris
Founded 1975. Pop 4,800
Library Holdings: AV Mats 300; Large Print Bks 100; Bk Vols 14,000; Per Subs 27; Talking Bks 210
Automation Activity & Vendor Info: (Cataloging) Book Systems; (Circulation) Book Systems; (OPAC) Book Systems
Mem of Mountain-Valley Library System; Washington County Library System
Partic in Minuteman Library Network; Ocean State Libraries
Open Mon 10-7, Tues-Fri 8-5, Sat 8-12

LINDEN

P MARENGO COUNTY PUBLIC LIBRARY, 210 N Shiloh St, 36748. SAN 300-1326. Tel: 334-295-2246. FAX: 334-295-2265. E-mail: marengocounty933@bellsouth.net. *Dir,* Joyce Morgan; *Asst Librn,* Sandra Creel
Founded 1941. Pop 23,819; Circ 60,069
Library Holdings: Audiobooks 359; DVDs 117; Bk Vols 8,725
Automation Activity & Vendor Info: (Acquisitions) Book Systems; (Cataloging) Book Systems; (Circulation) Book Systems; (OPAC) Book Systems
Wireless access
Open Mon-Fri 10-5
Bookmobiles: Librarian, James Creel, 4,000 books

LINEVILLE

P LINEVILLE PUBLIC LIBRARY*, 60119 Hwy 49, 36266. (Mail add: PO Box 482, 36266-0482), SAN 376-7388. Tel: 256-396-5162. FAX: 256-396-5162. E-mail: linevillelibrary@centurytel.net. Web Site: www.cheaharegionallibrary.org. *Dir,* Faye Cole
Library Holdings: Bk Vols 10,000
Mem of Cheaha Regional Library
Open Mon-Fri 9:30-4:30

LIVINGSTON

P SUMTER COUNTY LIBRARY SYSTEM*, 201 Monroe St, 35470. (Mail add: PO Drawer U, 35470-0377), SAN 324-0746. Tel: 205-652-2349. E-mail: rptlibrary@bellsouth.net. *Dir,* Margie Hutcheson; Staff 1 (MLS 1)
Founded 1979. Pop 14,500
Automation Activity & Vendor Info: (Cataloging) Book Systems; (Circulation) Book Systems
Member Libraries: Ruby Pickens Tartt Public Library
Open Mon, Tues & Thurs 9-6, Wed & Fri 9-5, Sat 9-12

P RUBY PICKENS TARTT PUBLIC LIBRARY*, 201 Monroe St, 35470. (Mail add: PO Drawer U, 35470), SAN 300-1342. Tel: 205-652-2349. FAX: 205-652-6688. E-mail: rptlibrary@bellsouth.net. *Dir,* Margie Hutcheson; Staff 3 (MLS 1, Non-MLS 2)
Founded 1905. Pop 14,500; Circ 31,715
Oct 2009-Sept 2010 Income $141,097, State $6,635, City $110,000, Federal $4,000, County $10,000, Locally Generated Income $8,676, Other $1,786. Mats Exp $22,219, Books $20,033, AV Mat $2,186. Sal $88,000 (Prof $49,000)
Library Holdings: Audiobooks 1,032; DVDs 521; Bk Vols 31,214; Per Subs 40
Automation Activity & Vendor Info: (Acquisitions) Book Systems; (Cataloging) Book Systems; (Circulation) Book Systems
Wireless access
Mem of Sumter County Library System
Open Mon, Tues & Thurs 9-6, Wed & Fri 9-5, Sat 9-12
Friends of the Library Group

C UNIVERSITY OF WEST ALABAMA*, Julia Tutwiler Library, UWA Station 12, 35470. SAN 300-1334. Tel: 205-652-3613. Interlibrary Loan Service Tel: 205-652-3842. Administration Tel: 205-652-3614. Automation Services Tel: 205-652-3677. FAX: 205-652-2332. E-mail: uwalibrary@uwa.edu. Web Site: www.library.uwa.edu. *Acq, Dir,* Dr Monroe C Snider; E-mail: nsnider@uwa.edu
Founded 1835. Enrl 3,500; Fac 110; Highest Degree: Master
Library Holdings: Bk Titles 130,000; Bk Vols 250,000; Per Subs 200
Special Collections: Alabama Room; Folklore (Ruby Pickens Tartt Coll), mss; Microfiche Coll
Automation Activity & Vendor Info: (Acquisitions) Ex Libris Group; (Cataloging) Ex Libris Group; (Circulation) Ex Libris Group; (Course Reserve) Ex Libris Group; (ILL) Ex Libris Group; (Media Booking) Ex Libris Group; (OPAC) Ex Libris Group; (Serials) Ex Libris Group
Database Vendor: EBSCOhost, Gale Cengage Learning, OCLC FirstSearch, ProQuest
Wireless access
Partic in Lyrasis
Open Mon-Thurs 8am-11pm, Fri 8-5, Sat 9:30-4, Sun 4-11

LOUISVILLE

P LOUISVILLE PUBLIC LIBRARY*, 1951 Main St, 36048. (Mail add: PO Box 125, 36048), SAN 330-3098. Tel: 334-266-5210. FAX: 334-266-5630. *Librn,* Debra Vinson
Pop 618
Library Holdings: Bk Vols 5,500; Videos 17
Open Mon-Wed & Fri 8-11:30 & 12:30-3

LOXLEY

P LOXLEY PUBLIC LIBRARY*, 1001 Loxley Ave, 36551. (Mail add: PO Box 527, 36551-0527), SAN 300-1350. Tel: 251-964-5695. E-mail: loxlib@gulftel.com. *Librn,* Debbie Zonker
Circ 3,760
Library Holdings: Bk Vols 8,000
Mem of Baldwin County Library Cooperative, Inc
Open Mon, Wed & Fri 9-5, Tues & Sat 10-2

LUVERNE

P LUVERNE PUBLIC LIBRARY*, 148 E Third St, 36049. SAN 300-1369. Tel: 334-335-5326. FAX: 334-335-6402. E-mail: library@luverne.org. Web Site: library.luverne.org. *Dir,* Kathryn Tomlin; *Asst Dir,* Regina Grayson; Staff 2 (Non-MLS 2)
Founded 1954. Pop 10,242; Circ 13,424
Oct 2009-Sept 2010 Income $111,533, State $9,119, City $85,000, County $6,000, Locally Generated Income $7,000, Other $4,414. Mats Exp $9,452, Books $6,500, Other Print Mats $952, AV Mat $2,000. Sal $73,554
Library Holdings: Audiobooks 747; AV Mats 1,181; CDs 323; DVDs 581; Large Print Bks 114; Bk Vols 13,823; Per Subs 33
Automation Activity & Vendor Info: (Cataloging) Book Systems; (Circulation) Book Systems; (ILL) OCLC WorldShare Interlibrary Loan; (OPAC) Book Systems
Wireless access
Function: Bks on cassette, Bks on CD, CD-ROM, Children's prog, Computers for patron use, Copy machines, Electronic databases & coll, Free DVD rentals, Holiday prog, ILL available, Music CDs, Online cat, Online info literacy tutorials on the web & in blackboard, Online searches, Photocopying/Printing, Prog for adults, Prog for children & young adult, Ref serv available, Summer reading prog, Tax forms, Wheelchair accessible
Open Mon 11-7, Tues & Thurs 11-5:30, Wed 11-6, Fri 11-5, Sat 9-12
Friends of the Library Group

MARION

C JUDSON COLLEGE*, Bowling Library, 306 E Dekalb St, 36756. SAN 300-1393. Tel: 334-683-5182. FAX: 334-683-5188. Web Site: www.judson.edu. *Dir of Libr Serv,* George Washburn; Tel: 334-683-5281, E-mail: gwashburn@judson.edu; *Librn,* Andrea Abernathy; E-mail: aabernathy@judson.edu
Founded 1838. Enrl 425; Fac 37; Highest Degree: Bachelor
Library Holdings: Bk Titles 58,000; Bk Vols 72,000; Per Subs 429
Special Collections: Alabama Women's Hall of Fame Coll
Subject Interests: British hist, Relig
Automation Activity & Vendor Info: (Cataloging) Ex Libris Group; (Circulation) Ex Libris Group; (OPAC) Ex Libris Group
Database Vendor: EBSCOhost, Gale Cengage Learning, ProQuest
Wireless access
Partic in Lyrasis; NAAL
Open Mon-Thurs 8-6 & 7-10, Fri 8-12 & 1-4, Sun 6pm-10pm

J MARION MILITARY INSTITUTE*, Baer Memorial Library, 1101 Washington St, 36756. SAN 300-1407. Tel: 334-683-2371. Web Site: www.marionmilitary.edu. *Dir,* Glenda Lammers; E-mail: glammers@marionmilitary.edu; Staff 2 (MLS 1, Non-MLS 1)
Founded 1887. Enrl 325
Library Holdings: Bk Titles 22,853; Bk Vols 32,131; Per Subs 60
Automation Activity & Vendor Info: (Cataloging) Book Systems; (Circulation) Book Systems; (OPAC) Book Systems
Wireless access
Restriction: Authorized patrons

P MARION-PERRY COUNTY LIBRARY*, 202 Washington St, 36756. SAN 300-1415. Tel: 334-683-6411. FAX: 334-683-0599. E-mail: librar_p@bellsouth.net.
Founded 1934. Pop 14,872
Library Holdings: Bk Vols 20,000; Per Subs 20
Special Collections: Genealogy, filmstrips, audiobooks, videos
Subject Interests: Art
Open Mon, Wed, Thurs & Fri 9-1 & 2-5:30, Tues 9-1, 2-5:30 & 7-9
Friends of the Library Group

MAXWELL AFB

UNITED STATES AIR FORCE
A AIR UNIVERSITY - MUIR S FAIRCHILD RESEARCH INFORMATION CENTER, 600 Chennault Circle, 36112-6010, SAN 300-1431. Tel: 334-953-2606. Circulation Tel: 334-953-2230. Interlibrary Loan Service Tel: 334-953-7223. Reference Tel: 334-953-2888. Web Site: www.au.af.mil/au/aul/aul.htm. *Dir,* Dr Jeff Luzius; E-mail: jeff.luzius@us.af.mil; *Assoc Dir,* Martha McCrary; E-mail: martha.mccrary@us.af.mil; *Head, Reader Serv,* Terry Hawkins; Tel: 334-953-2237, Fax: 334-953-2329, E-mail: terry.hawkins@us.af.mil; *Head, Ref,* Ron Dial; Tel: 334-953-2347, E-mail: ron.dial@us.af.mil; *Head, Syst,* Martha M Stewart; Tel: 334-953-2474, E-mail: martha.stewart@us.af.mil; *Head, Tech Serv,* Tyler S Evans; Tel: 334-953-7691, E-mail: tyler.evans.1@us.af.mil; *Acq,* Deborah Barone; Tel: 334-953-2410, E-mail: deborah.barone@us.af.mil; *Automation Syst Coordr,* Wendy Ng; Tel: 334-953-6498, E-mail: wendy.ng@us.af.mil; *Bibliographer,* Kimberly Hunter; Tel: 334-953-9811, E-mail: kimberly.hunter@us.af.mil; *Cat,* Patricia Fogler; Tel: 334-953-2135, E-mail: patricia.fogler@us.af.mil; *Electronic Serv,* Vicki Watkins; Tel: 334-953-8301, E-mail: vicki.watkins@us.af.mil; Staff 30 (MLS 30)
Founded 1946. Enrl 8,593; Highest Degree: Master
Library Holdings: AV Mats 769; CDs 1,090; e-books 46,816; Microforms 959,522; Bk Titles 564,911; Per Subs 1,255; Videos 2,326
Special Collections: Air University Coll, rare bks & per related to flight
Subject Interests: Bus & mgt, Econ, Educ, Foreign relations, Hist, Mil sci
Automation Activity & Vendor Info: (Acquisitions) Ex Libris Group; (Cataloging) Ex Libris Group; (Circulation) Ex Libris Group; (Course Reserve) Ex Libris Group; (ILL) Ex Libris Group; (OPAC) Ex Libris Group; (Serials) Ex Libris Group
Database Vendor: CountryWatch, EBSCOhost, Gale Cengage Learning, Jane's, JSTOR, LexisNexis, OCLC FirstSearch, ProQuest
Partic in Association of Southeastern Research Libraries; Lyrasis; Military Education Coordination Conference (MECC); Network of Alabama Academic Libraries
Publications: Air University Library Index to Military Periodicals; Air University Library Master List of Periodicals; Special Bibliography Series
Open Mon-Thurs 7:30am-9pm, Fri 7:30-5, Sat 11-5
Restriction: Pub use on premises
A HISTORICAL RESEARCH AGENCY*, AFHRA, 600 Chennault Circle, Bldg 1405, 36112-6424, SAN 330-2288. Tel: 334-953-2395. FAX: 334-953-4096. E-mail: afhranews@maxwell.af.mil. Web Site: afhra.maxwell.af.mil. *Archivist,* Lynn Gamma; E-mail: lynn.gamma@maxwell.af.mil
Founded 1942
Special Collections: End of Tour Reports; German Air Force (Karlsruhe Document Coll) & GAF Monograph Series, doc, micro; Gulf War Coll; Historical Monographs; Histories of Air Force Organizations; Personal Papers of Air Force Leaders USAF (Individual Aircraft Record Card Coll), doc, micro. Oral History
A MAXWELL AIR FORCE BASE LIBRARY FL3300*, FL 3300, Bldg 28, 355 Kirkpatrick Ave E, 36112, SAN 330-2075. Tel: 334-953-6484. FAX: 334-953-7643.
Founded 1958. Pop 6,800
Library Holdings: Bk Vols 68,000; Per Subs 275
A MAXWELL GUNTER COMMUNITY LIBRARY SYSTEM*, MSD/MSEL, 481 Williamson St, Bldg 1110 Gunter Annex, 36114, SAN 330-2342. Tel: 334-416-3179. FAX: 334-416-2949. *Dir,* Bernadette Roche; Staff 8 (MLS 1, Non-MLS 7)
Library Holdings: Bk Vols 41,000

MIDFIELD

P MIDFIELD PUBLIC LIBRARY, 400 Breland Dr, 35228-2732. SAN 376-5091. Tel: 205-923-1027. FAX: 205-923-3015. Web Site: midfield.lib.al.us. *Dir,* Priscilla Ward; E-mail: pward@bham.lib.al.us
Founded 1976. Pop 6,000; Circ 8,000
Oct 2005-Sept 2006 Income $65,500, State $3,000, City $61,000, Locally Generated Income $1,500. Mats Exp $12,000. Sal $28,000
Library Holdings: DVDs 30; Large Print Bks 515; Bk Vols 14,000; Per Subs 25; Talking Bks 425; Videos 1,549
Subject Interests: Ala, Career, College, Educ, Occupational, State hist
Automation Activity & Vendor Info: (Cataloging) Innovative Interfaces, Inc; (Circulation) Innovative Interfaces, Inc; (OPAC) Innovative Interfaces, Inc
Wireless access
Partic in Jefferson County Libr Coop
Open Mon-Fri 10-6, Sat 11-3
Friends of the Library Group

MIDLAND CITY

P MARY BERRY BROWN MEMORIAL LIBRARY*, 1318 Hinton Waters, 36350. (Mail add: PO Box 713, 36350-0713), SAN 330-2881. Tel: 334-983-3511. *Librn,* Kay Armstrong
Library Holdings: Bk Vols 10,000; Per Subs 10
Open Mon-Fri 12:30-4:30

MILLBROOK

P MILLBROOK PUBLIC LIBRARY*, 3650 Grandview Rd, 36054. (Mail add: PO Box 525, 36054-0525), SAN 300-144X. Tel: 334-285-6688. FAX: 334-285-0152. E-mail: millbrooklib@elmore.rr.com. Web Site: www.library.cityofmillbrook.org. *Dir,* Linda Moore; Tel: 334-285-6688, Ext 22; *Ch Serv,* Angela Dewberry; Tel: 334-285-6688, Ext 21; *Circ,* Kathy Ziegler; Tel: 334-285-6688, Ext 23; Staff 3 (Non-MLS 3)
Founded 1964. Pop 20,000; Circ 76,737
Library Holdings: Bk Vols 33,000; Per Subs 60
Special Collections: Oral History
Automation Activity & Vendor Info: (Cataloging) Follett Software; (Circulation) Follett Software
Database Vendor: EBSCOhost, Gale Cengage Learning, ProQuest
Wireless access
Function: Accelerated reader prog, Adult literacy prog, Bk club(s), Bks on cassette, Bks on CD, Children's prog, Computers for patron use, Copy machines, Handicapped accessible, ILL available, Music CDs, Online cat, OverDrive digital audio bks, Photocopying/Printing, Preschool reading prog, Prog for adults, Prog for children & young adult, Spoken cassettes & CDs, Spoken cassettes & DVDs, Story hour, Summer reading prog, VHS videos, Web-catalog, Wheelchair accessible
Mem of Horseshoe Bend Regional Library
Open Mon, Wed & Fri 8-5, Tues 8-8, Thurs 8-6, Sat 8-3
Friends of the Library Group

MOBILE

J BISHOP STATE COMMUNITY COLLEGE*, Minnie Slade Bishop Library, 351 N Broad St, 36603-5898. SAN 300-1512. Tel: 251 405-7111. Circulation Tel: 251 405-7112. Administration Tel: 251 405-7113. FAX: 251-438-2463. Web Site: www.bishop.edu.
Founded 1943
Library Holdings: Bk Vols 53,883; Per Subs 207
Special Collections: Black Coll
Automation Activity & Vendor Info: (Cataloging) Follett Software; (Circulation) Follett Software; (OPAC) Follett Software
Special Services for the Deaf - Captioned film dep; Staff with knowledge of sign lang
Open Mon-Fri 7:30-5:30

Departmental Libraries:
BAKER-GAINES CENTRAL CAMPUS, 1365 Dr Martin Luther King Jr Ave, 36603-5362. Tel: 251-405-4424. FAX: 251-405-4423. Web Site: www.bscc.cc.al.us. *Librn,* Marsha Mickles; E-mail: mmickles@bishop.edu
Founded 1995
Library Holdings: Bk Vols 4,442; Per Subs 25
Open Mon-Fri 8-5
CARVER CAMPUS, 414 Stanton St, 36617-2399. Tel: 251-662-5391. FAX: 251-471-5961. *Libr Tech,* Aleathia L Phifer; Fax: 251-479-9071, E-mail: aphifer@bishop.edu
Founded 1991
Library Holdings: Bk Vols 6,979; Per Subs 33
Open Mon-Fri 8-4:30
SOUTHWEST CAMPUS, 925 Dauphin Island Pkwy, 36605-3299. Tel: 251-665-4091. FAX: 251-479-7091. *Dir,* Fr Robert L Parker; *Libr Assoc,* Lydia W Hollins; E-mail: lhollins@bishop.edu
Founded 1954
Library Holdings: Bk Vols 1,479; Per Subs 24
Open Mon-Fri 8am-9:30pm

S HISTORIC MOBILE PRESERVATION SOCIETY*, Minnie Mitchell Archives, 300 Oakleigh Pl, 36604. SAN 327-8654. Tel: 251-432-6161. E-mail: hmps@bellsouth.net. Web Site: www.historicmobile.org. *Exec Dir,* Rhonda Davis; *Archives Dir,* Position Currently Open
Founded 1936
Library Holdings: Bk Vols 800
Special Collections: 19th Century Original Documents (deeds, letters, newsp); Civil War Diaries; George Rogers Library Coll; Local History Coll; Wilson Photograph Coll
Subject Interests: 19th Century
Function: Archival coll, Ref & res
Open Tues-Fri 9-3
Restriction: Access at librarian's discretion, Not a lending libr

GL MOBILE COUNTY PUBLIC LAW LIBRARY*, Mobile Government Plaza, 205 Government St, 36644-2308. SAN 300-1482. Tel: 251-574-8436. FAX: 251-574-4757. *Librn,* Jacquelyn Carson; E-mail: jcarson@justice.com
Library Holdings: Bk Titles 500; Bk Vols 60,000; Per Subs 59
Database Vendor: LexisNexis, Westlaw
Partic in LexisNexis; Westlaw
Open Mon-Fri 8-5

P MOBILE PUBLIC LIBRARY*, Ben May Main Library, 701 Government St, 36602. SAN 330-2407. Tel: 251-208-7073. Interlibrary Loan Service Tel: 251-208-7402. FAX: 251-208-5865. E-mail: circulation@mplonline.org. Web Site: www.mplonline.org. *Dir,* Scott Kinney; E-mail: director@mplonline.org; *Asst Dir,* Mary Laughlin; E-mail: asstdirector@mplonline.org; *Mgr,* Margie Calhoun; Staff 33 (MLS 33)
Founded 1928. Pop 400,236; Circ 1,335,076
Library Holdings: Bk Vols 471,737; Per Subs 800
Special Collections: Mobile History, 1702-present; Mobile Mardi Gras Coll, misc
Subject Interests: Genealogy
Automation Activity & Vendor Info: (Acquisitions) SirsiDynix; (Cataloging) SirsiDynix; (Circulation) SirsiDynix; (OPAC) SirsiDynix
Database Vendor: Newsbank, ReferenceUSA
Publications: MPL Today (Newsletter)
Special Services for the Deaf - Bks on deafness & sign lang; Staff with knowledge of sign lang; TTY equip
Open Mon-Thurs 9-8, Fri & Sat 9-6, Sun (Sept-May) 1-5
Friends of the Library Group
Branches: 7
MOORER/SPRING HILL BRANCH, Four McGregor Ave, 36608, SAN 330-2466. Tel: 251-470-7770. FAX: 251-470-7774. *Br Mgr,* Stephen Prager
Library Holdings: Bk Vols 36,894
Open Mon, Wed, Fri & Sat 9-6, Tues & Thurs 9-8
Friends of the Library Group
PARKWAY BRANCH, 1924-B Dauphin Island Pkwy, 36605-3004, SAN 330-2490. Tel: 251-470-7712. FAX: 251-470-7766. E-mail: parkwaybranch@mplonline.org. *Br Mgr,* Betty Kidd
Library Holdings: Bk Vols 36,894
Open Mon, Wed, Fri & Sat 9-6, Tues & Thurs 12-8
Friends of the Library Group
SARALAND PUBLIC LIBRARY, 111 Saraland Loop, Saraland, 36571-2418, SAN 330-2520. Tel: 251-675-2879. FAX: 251-675-2879. E-mail: saralandbranch@mplonline.org. *Br Mgr,* Sheryl Somathilake
Library Holdings: Bk Vols 24,181
Open Mon, Wed, Fri & Sat 10-6, Tues & Thurs 12-9
Friends of the Library Group
SEMMES BRANCH, 9150 Moffett Rd, Semmes, 36575. Tel: 251-645-6840. FAX: 251-645-6856. E-mail: sembranch@mplonline.org. *Mgr,* Heather Williams
Open Mon & Wed 10-6, Tues & Thurs Noon-7:30, Sat 10-5
THEODORE OAKS BRANCH, 5808 Hwy 90 W, Ste E, Theodore, 36582. Tel: 251-653-5012. FAX: 251-653-8176. E-mail: theodoreoaksbranch@mplonline.org. *Mgr,* Lynn Hudson
Open Mon & Tues 10-7, Wed-Sat 10-5
TOULMINVILLE, 601 Stanton Rd, 36617-2209, SAN 330-2555. Tel: 251-438-7075. FAX: 251-438-7058. E-mail: tvlebranch@mplonline.org. *Br Mgr,* Gloria Williams
Library Holdings: Bk Vols 45,000
Open Mon & Thurs 12-8, Tues, Wed, Fri & Sat 9-6
Friends of the Library Group
WEST REGIONAL BRANCH, 5555 Grelot Rd, 36609, SAN 330-2431. Tel: 251-340-8555. FAX: 251-304-2160. E-mail: westregionalbranch@mplonline.org. *Br Mgr,* Janet Curry
Library Holdings: Bk Vols 190,000
Open Mon-Thurs 9-8, Fri & Sat 9-6
Friends of the Library Group
Bookmobiles: 1. Elaine Crook, Mgr

S MUSEUM OF MOBILE*, Reference Library, 111 S Royal St, 36602-3101. SAN 300-1504. Tel: 251-208-7569. FAX: 251-208-7686. E-mail: museum@cityofmobile.org. Web Site: www.museumofmobile.com. *Dir,* George Ewert
Founded 1962
Library Holdings: Bk Titles 3,000
Subject Interests: City hist, Civil War
Restriction: Open by appt only

CR SPRING HILL COLLEGE*, Marnie & John Burke Memorial Library, 4000 Dauphin St, 36608. SAN 300-1520. Tel: 251-380-3870. Interlibrary Loan Service Tel: 251-380-4178. Reference Tel: 251-380-3880. FAX: 251-460-2107. Interlibrary Loan Service FAX: 251-380-2179. Web Site: shclibrary.shc.edu. *Dir,* Gentry L Holbert; E-mail: gholbert@shc.edu; *Tech Serv Librn,* Janie Mathews; Fax: jmathews@shc.edu; Staff 16 (MLS 4, Non-MLS 12)
Founded 1830. Enrl 1,216; Fac 94; Highest Degree: Master
Library Holdings: Bk Titles 99,500; Bk Vols 173,000; Per Subs 543
Special Collections: Jesuitica Coll; Mobiliana Coll. US Document Depository
Subject Interests: Rare bks
Automation Activity & Vendor Info: (Acquisitions) SirsiDynix; (Cataloging) SirsiDynix; (Circulation) SirsiDynix; (Course Reserve) SirsiDynix; (OPAC) SirsiDynix; (Serials) SirsiDynix
Database Vendor: Dialog, EBSCOhost, Gale Cengage Learning, LexisNexis, OCLC FirstSearch, OVID Technologies, ProQuest
Wireless access
Function: Archival coll
Publications: Friends of the Library Newsletter
Partic in Association of Jesuit Colleges & Universities (AJCU); Lyrasis; Network of Alabama Academic Libraries; OCLC Online Computer Library Center, Inc
Open Mon-Thurs 7:30am-Midnight, Fri 7:30-5, Sat 9-7, Sun 1-Midnight
Friends of the Library Group

A UNITED STATES ARMY CORPS OF ENGINEERS*, Mobile District Library, 109 Saint Joseph St, 36628-0001. (Mail add: PO Box 2288, 36628-0001). Tel: 251-690-3182. FAX: 251-694-4350. E-mail: CESAM-Library@sam.usace.army.mil. Web Site: www.sam.usace.army.mil/im/im-p/liblinks.html. *Librn,* Cheryl Martin
Library Holdings: Bk Vols 7,800; Per Subs 15
Subject Interests: Sci, Tech
Wireless access
Restriction: Staff use only

C UNIVERSITY OF MOBILE*, J L Bedsole Library, 5735 College Pkwy, 36613-2842. SAN 330-2377. Tel: 251-442-2242. Circulation Tel: 251-442-2246. Interlibrary Loan Service Tel: 251-442-2423. FAX: 251-442-2515. Web Site: library.umobile.edu. *Dir of Libr Serv,* Jeffrey D Calametti; Tel: 251-442-2243, E-mail: jeffc@umobile.edu; *Ref Librn,* Matthew Fraser; Tel: 251-442-2244, E-mail: mfraser@umobile.edu; *Ref Librn,* Chuck Hodgin; E-mail: chodgin@umobile.edu; *Cat, Tech Serv,* Donna Ramer; Tel: 251-442-2478, E-mail: donnae@umobile.edu; *Pub Serv,* Lindy White; E-mail: lindyw@mail.umobile.edu; Staff 5 (MLS 2, Non-MLS 3)
Founded 1961. Enrl 1,600; Fac 90; Highest Degree: Master
Library Holdings: AV Mats 1,833; e-books 39,944; e-journals 33,294; Bk Titles 62,350; Bk Vols 71,341; Per Subs 323
Special Collections: Southern Baptist History
Subject Interests: Ala, Civil War, Educ, Local hist, Relig
Automation Activity & Vendor Info: (Cataloging) TLC (The Library Corporation); (Circulation) TLC (The Library Corporation); (Course

Reserve) TLC (The Library Corporation); (OPAC) TLC (The Library Corporation)
Database Vendor: 3M Library Systems, American Chemical Society, American Mathematical Society, American Psychological Association (APA), Bowker, Cinahl, CQ Press, EBSCOhost, Facts on File, Gale Cengage Learning, H W Wilson, Hoovers, McGraw-Hill, Medline, Modern Language Association, Newsbank, OCLC ArticleFirst, OCLC FirstSearch, OCLC WorldShare Interlibrary Loan, Oxford Online, ProQuest, PubMed, TLC (The Library Corporation), ValueLine, Wiley InterScience, Wilson - Wilson Web
Wireless access
Partic in Lyrasis; Network of Alabama Academic Libraries; OCLC Online Computer Library Center, Inc; Southern Baptist Libr Asn
Open Mon, Tues & Thurs 7:45am-10pm, Wed 7:45am-9pm, Fri 7:45-4:30, Sat 10-5 (Summer 10-2)

C UNIVERSITY OF SOUTH ALABAMA, Marx Library, 5901 USA Dr N, Rm 145, 36688. Tel: 251-460-7021. Circulation Tel: 251-460-7028. Interlibrary Loan Service Tel: 251-460-7034. Reference Tel: 251-460-7025. Information Services Tel: 251-460-7924. FAX: 251-460-7181. Interlibrary Loan Service FAX: 251-460-7636. Information Services FAX: 251-460-7181. Web Site: library.southalabama.edu. *Dean,* Dr Richard Wood; E-mail: rwood@southalabama.edu; *Asst Dean, Head, Coll Mgt,* Mary Duffy; E-mail: mduffy@southalabama.edu; *Head, Cat & Proc,* Nero Muriel; Tel: 251-460-2837, E-mail: mero@southalabama.edu; *Head, Coll Develop,* Kathyrn Jones; Tel: 251-460-7033, E-mail: kjones@southalabama.edu; *Head, Govt Doc & Ser,* Vicki Tate; Tel: 251-460-2822, E-mail: vtate@southalabama.edu; *Head, Ref & Instruction,* Kathy Wheeler; Tel: 251-460-7938, E-mail: kwheeler@southalabama.edu; *ILL,* Deborah Cobb; E-mail: dcobb@southalabama.edu. Subject Specialists: *Cataloging, Philos,* Nero Muriel; *Communications, Soc sci,* Kathyrn Jones; *Math, Statistics,* Kathy Wheeler; Staff 38 (MLS 14, Non-MLS 24)
Founded 1964. Enrl 16,000; Fac 500; Highest Degree: Doctorate
Oct 2012-Sept 2013 Income (Main Library Only) $4,348,315. Mats Exp $1,471,177. Sal $1,936,587
Special Collections: Albert Schweitzer Coll; Doy Leale McCall Rare Book & Manuscript Library (Strong photog archives; Alabama hist); Holocaust Coll; Photog Archives of Mobile; US Government Documents. State Document Depository; US Document Depository
Subject Interests: City hist, Local hist
Automation Activity & Vendor Info: (Acquisitions) Ex Libris Group; (Cataloging) Ex Libris Group; (Circulation) Ex Libris Group; (Course Reserve) Ex Libris Group; (ILL) OCLC Online; (OPAC) Ex Libris Group; (Serials) Ex Libris Group
Database Vendor: ACM (Association for Computing Machinery), Agricola, American Chemical Society, American Mathematical Society, American Psychological Association (APA), ARTstor, Baker & Taylor, BioOne, Cinahl, College Source, Dialog, Ebooks Corporation, ebrary, EBSCO Discovery Service, EBSCO Information Services, EBSCOhost, Elsevier, Emerald, Ex Libris Group, Facts on File, Gale Cengage Learning, Haworth Pres Inc, HeinOnline, Hoovers, IEEE (Institute of Electrical & Electronics Engineers), JSTOR, LexisNexis, Marcive, Inc, MD Consult, Medline, Mergent Online, Newsbank, Newsbank-Readex, OCLC, OCLC FirstSearch, OCLC WorldShare Interlibrary Loan, OVID Technologies, Oxford Online, Project MUSE, ProQuest, PubMed, Sage, ScienceDirect, Scopus, Springer-Verlag, Wiley InterScience, YBP Library Services
Wireless access
Function: Art exhibits, AV serv, CD-ROM, Computers for patron use, Copy machines, e-mail & chat, E-Reserves, Electronic databases & coll, Exhibits, Govt ref serv, ILL available, Music CDs, Online cat, Online ref, Online searches, Photocopying/Printing, Printer for laptops & handheld devices, Pub access computers, Ref & res, Ref serv available, Ref serv in person, Scanner, Study rm, Tax forms, Telephone ref, Web-catalog, Wheelchair accessible
Partic in Lyrasis; Network of Alabama Academic Libraries
Restriction: In-house use for visitors, Open to students, fac & staff
Departmental Libraries:
CM BIOMEDICAL LIBRARY, Biomedical Library Bldg, 5791 USA Dr N, 36688-0002, SAN 330-258X. Tel: 251-460-7043. Interlibrary Loan Service Tel: 251-460-7850. Reference Tel: 251-460-7044. FAX: 251-460-6958. Interlibrary Loan Service FAX: 251-460-7638. Web Site: biomedicallibrary.southalabama.edu/library. *Interim Dir,* Geneva Staggs; Tel: 251-460-6885; *Asst Dir, Coll Mgt,* Jie Li; Tel: 251-460-6890; *Asst Dir, Hospital Serv,* Geneva Staggs; *Asst Dir, Pub Serv,* Clista Clanton; Staff 26 (MLS 9, Non-MLS 17)
Founded 1972. Enrl 2,862; Fac 236; Highest Degree: Doctorate
Oct 2013-Sept 2014 Income $2,785,460. Mats Exp $968,000, Books $39,000, Per/Ser (Incl. Access Fees) $929,000. Sal $1,052,931
Library Holdings: Bk Titles 21,606
Partic in Consortium of Southern Biomedical Libraries
Publications: Biofeedback (Newsletter)
Open Mon-Thurs 7:15am-10:45pm, Fri 7:15-6, Sat 9-6, Sun 1-9:45

MONROEVILLE

J ALABAMA SOUTHERN COMMUNITY COLLEGE*, John Dennis Forte Library, 2800 S Alabama Ave, 36460. (Mail add: PO Box 2000, 36461-2000), SAN 300-1547. Tel: 251-575-3156. FAX: 251-575-5116. Web Site: www.ascc.edu. *Dir,* LaShannon Hollinger; Tel: 251-575-3156, Ext 8271, E-mail: lhollinger@ascc.edu; *Asst Dir,* Deborah Rankins; Tel: 334-637-3146, E-mail: drankins@ascc.edu
Founded 1965. Enrl 1,218
Library Holdings: Bk Vols 34,741; Per Subs 36
Special Collections: Alabamiana Coll; Professional Coll
Subject Interests: Careers
Automation Activity & Vendor Info: (Cataloging) Book Systems; (Circulation) Book Systems
Wireless access
Open Mon-Thurs 7:30am-8:30pm, Fri 7:30-3
Departmental Libraries:
GILBERTOWN CAMPUS, 251 College St, Gilbertown, 36908. (Mail add: PO Box 2000, Gilbertown, 36908-2000). Tel: 334-843-5265. FAX: 334-843-2420. *Dir,* LaShannon Hollinger; Tel: 251-575-3156, Ext 8271, E-mail: lhollinger@ascc.edu
Library Holdings: Bk Vols 33,500; Per Subs 60
Open Mon-Thurs 7:30-2 & 5:30-9:30
KATHRYN TUCKER WINDHAM MUSEUM LIBRARY, 30755 Hwy 43, Thomasville, 36784-2519. (Mail add: PO Box 2000, Thomasville, 36784), SAN 322-8827. Tel: 334-636-9642, Ext 3146. FAX: 334-636-1478. *Dir,* LaShannon Hollinger; Tel: 251-575-3156, Ext 8271, E-mail: lhollinger@ascc.edu; *Asst Dir,* Deborah Rankins; Tel: 334-637-3146, E-mail: drankins@ascc.edu; Staff 4 (MLS 2, Non-MLS 2)
Enrl 1,100; Fac 40
Library Holdings: Bk Vols 47,000; Per Subs 60
Open Mon-Thurs 7:30-7:30, Fri 7:30-2, Sat 10-2, Sun 2-6

P MONROE COUNTY PUBLIC LIBRARY*, 121 Pineville Rd, 36460. SAN 300-1539. Tel: 251-743-3818. FAX: 251-575-7357. E-mail: monroli2@frontiernet.net. *Head of Libr,* Bunny Hines Nobles; *Ch Serv, Circ,* Mary Ann Harris
Founded 1927. Pop 25,043; Circ 62,000
Library Holdings: CDs 40; DVDs 10; Large Print Bks 265; Bk Vols 26,091; Per Subs 27; Talking Bks 1,077; Videos 552
Special Collections: Alabama Coll; Forestry Coll; Genealogy Coll; Paperback Coll
Automation Activity & Vendor Info: (Acquisitions) Baker & Taylor; (Cataloging) Follett Software; (Circulation) Follett Software
Database Vendor: Baker & Taylor
Partic in Midwest Collaborative for Library Services (MCLS)
Open Mon-Fri 9-5
Friends of the Library Group

MONTEVALLO

P PARNELL MEMORIAL LIBRARY*, 277 Park Dr, 35115-3882. SAN 321-5660. Tel: 205-665-9207. FAX: 205-665-9214. *Dir,* Pauline Beach; Staff 1 (Non-MLS 1)
Founded 1958. Pop 4,500; Circ 25,866
Oct 2005-Sept 2006 Income $98,475, State $5,128, City $93,347. Mats Exp $6,070. Sal $68,057
Library Holdings: CDs 180; Bk Titles 17,356; Talking Bks 291; Videos 640
Special Collections: Alabama Authors Coll; Large Print Coll
Automation Activity & Vendor Info: (Cataloging) Innovative Interfaces, Inc; (Circulation) Innovative Interfaces, Inc; (OPAC) Innovative Interfaces, Inc
Function: ILL available, Music CDs, Photocopying/Printing, Prog for children & young adult, Summer reading prog, VHS videos, Wheelchair accessible
Open Mon-Fri 10-5, Sat 10-2

C UNIVERSITY OF MONTEVALLO*, Oliver Cromwell Carmichael Library, Station 6100, 35115-6100. SAN 300-1555. Tel: 205-665-6100. FAX: 205-665-6112. E-mail: library@montevallo.edu. Web Site: www.montevallo.edu/library. *Dir,* Kathleen Lowe; E-mail: lowek@montevallo.edu; *Coll Mgt Librn, Metadata Librn,* Amanda Melcher; Tel: 205-665-6104, E-mail: melcheras@montevallo.edu; *Archivist, Ref Librn,* Carey Heatherly; Tel: 205-665-6107, E-mail: heatherlycw@montevallo.edu; *Syst & Emerging Tech Librn,* Jason Cooper; Tel: 205-665-6114, E-mail: cooperjd@montevallo.edu; *Circ Supvr,* Gloria Beasley; Tel: 205-665-6101, E-mail: beasleygj@montevallo.edu; *Evening Circ Supvr,* Barbara Belisle; Staff 14 (MLS 6, Non-MLS 8)
Founded 1896. Enrl 2,494; Fac 168; Highest Degree: Master
Library Holdings: Bk Titles 156,531; Bk Vols 252,120; Per Subs 738
Special Collections: Alabama Authors; Alabama History & Descriptions
Database Vendor: SirsiDynix

Partic in Lyrasis; Network of Alabama Academic Libraries; OCLC Online Computer Library Center, Inc
Open Mon-Wed 8am-1am, Thurs 8am-11pm, Fri 8-5, Sat 10-2, Sun 2-11

MONTGOMERY

S ALABAMA DEPARTMENT OF ARCHIVES & HISTORY RESEARCH ROOM, 624 Washington Ave, 36130-0100. SAN 300-1571. Tel: 334-242-4435. Interlibrary Loan Service Tel: 334-353-4706. FAX: 334-240-3433. Web Site: www.archives.alabama.gov. *Asst Dir, Pub Serv,* Debbie Pendleton; E-mail: debbie.pendleton@archives.alabama.gov; *Ref Archivist,* Norwood A Kerr; E-mail: norwood.kerr@archives.alabama.gov; Staff 4 (MLS 4)
Founded 1901
Library Holdings: Bk Vols 40,000
Special Collections: Alabama Newspapers; Historical Records of State of Alabama, bks, ms, maps, pamphlets & photog; Private Manuscript Coll. State Document Depository
Subject Interests: State govt, State hist
Automation Activity & Vendor Info: (Cataloging) Ex Libris Group; (OPAC) Ex Libris Group
Wireless access
Function: Archival coll, Outside serv via phone, mail, e-mail & web, Pub access computers, Workshops
Open Tues-Fri 8:30-4:30
Restriction: Non-circulating coll
Friends of the Library Group

G ALABAMA LEAGUE OF MUNICIPALITIES LIBRARY*, PO Box 1270, 36102-1270. SAN 327-0114. Tel: 334-262-2566. FAX: 334-263-0200. Web Site: www.alalm.org. *Librn,* Rachel Wagner
Library Holdings: Bk Titles 1,500; Per Subs 42

P ALABAMA PUBLIC LIBRARY SERVICE*, 6030 Monticello Dr, 36130. SAN 330-2644. Tel: 334-213-3900. Reference Tel: 334-213-3950. Automation Services Tel: 334-213-3938. Toll Free Tel: 800-723-8459 (Alabama only). FAX: 334-213-3993. Reference FAX: 334-213-3960. TDD: 334-213-3905. Web Site: www.apls.state.al.us. *Dir,* Nancy Pack; *Financial Serv,* Scott Burbank; Tel: 334-213-3629; Staff 30 (MLS 12, Non-MLS 18)
Founded 1959. Pop 4,802,740
Oct 2013-Sept 2014 Income (Main Library Only) $9,348,824, State $6,792,737, Federal $2,556,087
Library Holdings: Bk Titles 137,893; Bk Vols 147,026; Per Subs 1,249, Talking Bks 306,212
Subject Interests: Ala
Automation Activity & Vendor Info: (Acquisitions) Evergreen; (Cataloging) Evergreen; (Circulation) Evergreen; (Course Reserve) Evergreen; (ILL) Evergreen; (OPAC) Evergreen; (Serials) Evergreen
Database Vendor: EBSCOhost, Gale Cengage Learning, LearningExpress, OCLC FirstSearch, OCLC WorldShare Interlibrary Loan, World Book Online
Wireless access
Function: Audio & video playback equip for onsite use, Games & aids for the handicapped, Govt ref serv, Handicapped accessible, ILL available, Libr develop, Online searches, Ref serv available, Summer reading prog, Telephone ref, Wheelchair accessible, Workshops
Publications: APLSeed (Online only); What's Line (Quarterly)
Special Services for the Deaf - Assistive tech; Bks on deafness & sign lang; TDD equip
Special Services for the Blind - Accessible computers; Assistive/Adapted tech devices, equip & products; Bks & mags in Braille, on rec, tape & cassette; Bks on cassette; Bks on flash-memory cartridges; Daisy reader; Digital talking bk; Digital talking bk machines; Free checkout of audio mat; Home delivery serv; Newsline for the Blind; Spec cats; Talking bks; Talking bks & player equip; Volunteer serv
Open Mon-Fri 8-5
Branches: 1
ALABAMA REGIONAL LIBRARY FOR THE BLIND & PHYSICALLY HANDICAPPED
See Separate Entry

P ALABAMA PUBLIC LIBRARY SERVICE, Alabama Regional Library for the Blind & Physically Handicapped, 6030 Monticello Dr, 36117-1907. SAN 300-1598. Tel: 334-213-3906. Administration Tel: 334-213-3921. Toll Free Tel: 800-392-5671. FAX: 334-213-3993. E-mail: bphhelpdesk@apls.state.al.us. *Regional Dir,* Ruth Evans; *Reader Serv,* Dorothy Baker; *Reader Serv,* Mike Coleman; *Reader Serv,* Tim Emmons. Subject Specialists: *Adaptive tech, Braille,* Tim Emmons; Staff 5 (MLS 4, Non-MLS 1)
Founded 1978. Pop 5,496; Circ 138,508
Oct 2006-Sept 2007 Income $420,225, State $398,529, Federal $21,696
Library Holdings: Bks on Deafness & Sign Lang 50; Braille Volumes 2,265; Talking Bks 390,000
Special Collections: Alabamiana Coll; Blindness & Physically Handicapped (Core Coll)
Subject Interests: Adaptive tech, Braille
Automation Activity & Vendor Info: (Cataloging) Keystone Systems, Inc (KLAS); (Circulation) Keystone Systems, Inc (KLAS); (ILL) Keystone Systems, Inc (KLAS); (Serials) Keystone Systems, Inc (KLAS)
Database Vendor: Keystone Systems, Inc (KLAS)
Wireless access
Function: Accelerated reader prog, Audiobks via web, Bks on cassette, Children's prog, Computers for patron use, Copy machines, Digital talking bks, Equip loans & repairs, Games & aids for the handicapped, Handicapped accessible, ILL available, Mail & tel request accepted, Mail loans to mem, Prog for adults, Prog for children & young adult, Web-Braille, Wheelchair accessible
Publications: What's Line (Newsletter)
Partic in Network of Alabama Academic Libraries
Special Services for the Deaf - Closed caption videos; Coll on deaf educ; Deaf publ; Spec interest per; Staff with knowledge of sign lang; TDD equip
Special Services for the Blind - Accessible computers; Assistive/Adapted tech devices, equip & products; Bks & mags in Braille, on rec, tape & cassette; Bks on cassette; Braille & cassettes; Braille alphabet card; Braille bks; Cassette playback machines; Cassettes; Children's Braille; Digital talking bk; Info on spec aids & appliances; Machine repair; Musical scores in Braille & large print; Newsline for the Blind; PC for handicapped; Tel Pioneers equip repair group; Web-Braille; ZoomText magnification & reading software
Open Mon-Fri 8-5
Restriction: Closed stack

C ALABAMA STATE UNIVERSITY*, Levi Watkins Learning Resource Center, 915 S Jackson St, 36104. (Mail add: PO Box 271, 36101-0271), SAN 300 161X. Tel: 334-229-4106, 334-229-6890. Circulation Tel: 334-229-4109. Interlibrary Loan Service Tel: 334-229-1078. Reference Tel: 334-229-4110. Automation Services Tel: 334-229-6998. FAX: 334-229-4911, 334-229-4940. Web Site: www.lib.alasu.edu. *Dean,* Dr Janice R Franklin; E-mail: jfranklin@alasu.edu; *Access Serv, Cat,* Jian Zhang; *Acq,* Kevin Walker; *Archives, Spec Coll,* Dr Howard Robinson; *Circ,* Rebecca Mohr; *Coll Develop,* Neil Foulger; E-mail: nfoulger@alasu.edu; *Info Literacy, ILL,* Natasha Jenkins; *Tech Serv,* Freddie Siler; Staff 33 (MLS 16, Non-MLS 17)
Founded 1921. Enrl 5,565; Fac 427; Highest Degree: Doctorate
Library Holdings: Bk Titles 209,149; Bk Vols 417,404; Per Subs 2,082
Special Collections: E D Nixon Coll; Ollie L Brown Afro-American Heritage Coll, bks, micro
Subject Interests: Acctg, Biological sci, Educ, Health sci
Automation Activity & Vendor Info: (Acquisitions) Ex Libris Group; (Cataloging) Ex Libris Group; (Circulation) Ex Libris Group; (Course Reserve) Ex Libris Group; (ILL) Ex Libris Group; (Media Booking) Ex Libris Group; (OPAC) Ex Libris Group; (Serials) Ex Libris Group
Publications: Libretto
Partic in Lyrasis; Montgomery Higher Education Librs; Network of Alabama Academic Libraries
Open Mon-Thurs 8-10, Fri 8-5, Sat 10-4, Sun 2-9
Friends of the Library Group

GL ALABAMA SUPREME COURT & STATE LAW LIBRARY, Heflin-Torbert Judicial Bldg, 300 Dexter Ave, 36104. SAN 300-1628. Tel: 334-229-0578. Circulation Tel: 334-229-0581. Interlibrary Loan Service Tel: 334-229-0571. Reference Tel: 334-229-0563. Toll Free Tel: 800-236-4069. FAX: 334-229-0543. Reference FAX: 334-229-0544, 334-229-0545. E-mail: ALSCReference@gmail.com. Web Site: judicial.alabama.gov/library.cfm. *Dir, State Law Librn,* Timothy A Lewis; E-mail: tlewis@appellate.state.al.us; *Electronic Serv Librn,* Myra Sabel; Tel: 334-229-0580, E-mail: msabel@appellate.state.al.us; *Pub Serv Librn,* Alma Surles; Tel: 334-229-0569, E-mail: asurles@appellate.state.al.us; *Acq,* Susan Wilkinson; E-mail: swilkinson@appellate.state.al.us; *Pub Serv,* Courtney Britt; E-mail: cbritt@appellate.state.al.us; *Ser,* Zack Camerio; Staff 10.5 (MLS 4, Non-MLS 6.5)
Founded 1828
Oct 2008-Sept 2009 Income $1,490,671. Mats Exp $446,749, Books $209,277, Electronic Ref Mat (Incl. Access Fees) $237,472. Sal $636,908
Library Holdings: AV Mats 342; Bk Titles 58,847; Bk Vols 235,834; Per Subs 776
Special Collections: Alabama Supreme Court Briefs (1965-present); Judicial College Papers. State Document Depository; US Document Depository
Subject Interests: Ala, Law
Automation Activity & Vendor Info: (Acquisitions) Innovative Interfaces, Inc; (Cataloging) Innovative Interfaces, Inc; (Circulation) Innovative Interfaces, Inc; (Course Reserve) Innovative Interfaces, Inc; (ILL) OCLC; (OPAC) Innovative Interfaces, Inc; (Serials) Innovative Interfaces, Inc
Database Vendor: HeinOnline, Innovative Interfaces, Inc, LexisNexis, Westlaw
Wireless access

Function: Archival coll
Publications: Court Brief (Newsletter); The Rotunda (Newsletter); The Update (Current awareness service)
Partic in Lyrasis; Network of Alabama Academic Libraries; OCLC Online Computer Library Center, Inc
Open Mon-Fri 8-6

CR AMRIDGE UNIVERSITY LIBRARY*, 1200 Taylor Rd, 36117. SAN 371-9936. Tel: 334-387-7546. Toll Free Tel: 800-351-4040. FAX: 334-387-3878. E-mail: library@amridgeuniversity.edu. Web Site: www.amridgeuniversity.edu/au_library.html. *Libr Dir,* Terence Sheridan; Staff 5 (MLS 2, Non-MLS 3)
Founded 1967. Enrl 700; Highest Degree: Doctorate
Library Holdings: AV Mats 800; Bk Titles 80,000; Per Subs 1,200
Subject Interests: Counseling, Theol
Automation Activity & Vendor Info: (Cataloging) Book Systems; (Circulation) Book Systems; (OPAC) Book Systems
Database Vendor: OCLC FirstSearch, ProQuest
Function: Online cat
Open Mon 8-5, Tues-Thurs 8-6:30, Fri 8-12

C AUBURN UNIVERSITY, Montgomery Library, 7440 East Dr, 36117. (Mail add: PO Box 244023, 36124-4023), SAN 300-1636. Tel: 334-244-3200. Circulation Tel: 334-244-3416, 334-244-3647. Interlibrary Loan Service Tel: 334-244-3447. Reference Tel: 334-244-3649. Automation Services Tel: 334-244-3420. FAX: 334-244-3720. E-mail: Reference@aum.edu. Web Site: aumnicat.aum.edu. *Coordr, Libr Instruction, Dean of Libr,* Barbara Hightower; E-mail: bhighto1@aum.edu; *Head, Tech Serv,* John Gantt; E-mail: jgantt2@aum.edu; *Access Serv/ILL Librn,* Karen Williams; E-mail: kwilli16@aum.edu; *Automation Librn,* Tim Bailey; E-mail: tbailey1@aum.edu; *Coll Develop Librn,* Rickey D Best; Tel: 334-244-3276, E-mail: rbest@aum.edu. Subject Specialists: *Nursing,* Barbara Hightower; Staff 23 (MLS 7, Non-MLS 16)
Founded 1969. Enrl 4,500; Fac 213; Highest Degree: Doctorate
Oct 2013-Sept 2014 Income $2,011,630. Mats Exp $548,105, Books $62,746, Per/Ser (Incl. Access Fees) $478,726, AV Mat $5,633, Presv $1,000. Sal $1,247,653 (Prof $457,120)
Library Holdings: CDs 1,602; DVDs 975; e-books 65,000; e-journals 256; Bk Vols 515,000; Per Subs 432; Videos 2,000
Special Collections: Local & Regional Studies; University Archives. US Document Depository
Subject Interests: Genealogy
Automation Activity & Vendor Info: (Acquisitions) Ex Libris Group; (Cataloging) Ex Libris Group; (Circulation) Ex Libris Group; (Course Reserve) Ex Libris Group; (ILL) Ex Libris Group; (Media Booking) Ex Libris Group; (OPAC) Ex Libris Group; (Serials) Ex Libris Group
Database Vendor: ABC-CLIO, American Chemical Society, American Mathematical Society, American Psychological Association (APA), ARTstor, Baker & Taylor, BioOne, Blackwell, Bowker, Cinahl, CQ Press, Dun & Bradstreet, EBSCOhost, Elsevier, JSTOR, LexisNexis, Majors, Marcive, Inc, Mergent Online, Newsbank, OCLC ArticleFirst, OCLC FirstSearch, OCLC WorldShare Interlibrary Loan, OVID Technologies, Oxford Online, Project MUSE, ProQuest, Sage, ScienceDirect, Standard & Poor's, Thomson - Web of Science, Westlaw, Wiley InterScience, YBP Library Services
Wireless access
Publications: Friends of the AUM Library (Newsletter)
Partic in Lyrasis; Montgomery Higher Education Librs; OCLC Online Computer Library Center, Inc
Open Mon-Thurs 7:30am-10pm, Fri 7:30-5, Sat 1-5, Sun 1-9
Friends of the Library Group

M BAPTIST MEDICAL CENTER LIBRARY*, 2105 E South Blvd, 36116-2001. (Mail add: PO Box 11010, 36111-0010), SAN 324-5640. Tel: 334-286-2952. FAX: 334-286-5691. *Coordr,* Pamela Phillips; Tel: 334-286-2718, E-mail: pphillips@baptistfirst.org
Founded 1963
Library Holdings: Bk Titles 1,247; Per Subs 58
Subject Interests: Cardiology, Dermatology, Gynecology, Internal med, Neurology, Neurosurgery, Obstetrics, Orthopedics, Pediatrics, Surgery
Partic in National Network of Libraries of Medicine

CR FAULKNER UNIVERSITY*, Gus Nichols Library, 5345 Atlanta Hwy, 36109-3398. SAN 300-1563. Tel: 334-386-7207. Interlibrary Loan Service Tel: 334-386-7541. Reference Tel: 334-386-7209. Administration Tel: 334-386-7299. FAX: 334-386-7481. Web Site: www.faulkner.edu/gnl.asp. *Dir,* Barbara Kelly; E-mail: bkelly@faulkner.edu; *Coll Develop,* Jim Womack; E-mail: jwomack@faulkner.edu; *Extended Serv,* Dena Luce; Tel: 334-386-7482, E-mail: dluce@faulkner.edu; *ILL,* Gloria Boles; E-mail: gboles@faulkner.edu; *Ref,* Angela Barry; E-mail: abarry@faulkner.edu; *Tech Serv,* Joy Smith; E-mail: jsmith@faulkner.edu; Staff 10 (MLS 5, Non-MLS 5)
Founded 1944. Enrl 2,300; Fac 75; Highest Degree: Doctorate
Library Holdings: Bk Vols 107,000; Per Subs 504
Special Collections: Churches of Christ Materials
Subject Interests: Art & archit, Bus & mgt, Econ, Educ, Health sci, Hist, Lit, Math, Natural sci, Psychol, Relig, Soc sci & issues
Automation Activity & Vendor Info: (Acquisitions) Innovative Interfaces, Inc; (Cataloging) Innovative Interfaces, Inc; (Circulation) Innovative Interfaces, Inc; (OPAC) Innovative Interfaces, Inc; (Serials) Innovative Interfaces, Inc
Wireless access
Function: Archival coll, ILL available, Photocopying/Printing, Ref serv available, Res libr
Partic in Christian Col Libr; Lyrasis; Montgomery Higher Education Librs; Network of Alabama Academic Libraries; OCLC Online Computer Library Center, Inc
Restriction: In-house use for visitors, Open to students, fac & staff

J H COUNCILL TRENHOLM STATE TECHNICAL COLLEGE LIBRARY*, 3086 Mobile Hwy, 36108. (Mail add: 1225 Air Base Blvd, 36108). Tel: 334-420-4457. Circulation Tel: 334-420-4357, 334-420-4455. FAX: 334-420-4458. Web Site: www.trenholmtech.cc.al.us. *Head Librn,* Paul Blackmon; E-mail: pblackmon@trenholmstate.edu; Staff 3 (MLS 2, Non-MLS 1)
Enrl 1,134; Highest Degree: Associate
Library Holdings: AV Mats 395; e-books 25,000; Bk Titles 5,425; Bk Vols 7,123; Per Subs 101
Special Collections: Archives
Subject Interests: Voting rights
Automation Activity & Vendor Info: (Cataloging) OCLC Online; (Circulation) Follett Software; (Course Reserve) Follett Software; (Media Booking) Follett Software; (OPAC) Follett Software; (Serials) Follett Software
Database Vendor: EBSCOhost, Gale Cengage Learning, OCLC FirstSearch, ProQuest
Function: Archival coll, Photocopying/Printing, Ref serv available, Telephone ref, Wheelchair accessible
Open Mon-Thurs 7:30am-8pm, Fri 7:30am-11:30pm
Restriction: In-house use for visitors, Open to pub for ref only

C HUNTINGDON COLLEGE*, Houghton Memorial Library, 1500 E Fairview Ave, 36106. SAN 300-1660. Tel: 334-833-4421. Interlibrary Loan Service Tel: 334-833-4537. Reference Tel: 334-833-4560. Administration Tel: 334-833-4512. FAX: 334-263-4465. Web Site: www.library.huntingdon.edu. *Dir, Libr Serv,* Eric A Kidwell; E-mail: ekidwell@huntingdon.edu; *Head, Circ,* Margaret Kinney; Tel: 334-833-4422, E-mail: margaretk@huntingdon.edu; *Syst/Electronic Res Librn,* Brenda Kerwin; Tel: 334-833-4529, E-mail: bkerwin@huntingdon.edu; *Tech Serv Librn,* Position Currently Open; *Evening/Weekend Supvr,* Donna Clements; E-mail: dclements@huntingdon.edu; *Acq, Admin Serv,* Mrs Joel Godfrey; E-mail: jgodfrey@huntingdon.edu; *Archivist,* Sharon Tucker; Tel: 334-833-4413, E-mail: stucker@huntingdon.edu; *Asst Archivist,* Mary Ann Pickard; Tel: 334-833-4418, E-mail: mpickard@huntingdon.edu; *Cat Asst,* Yvonne Williams; E-mail: ywilliams@huntingdon.edu; *ILL, Ref Serv,* Nordis Smith; E-mail: nosmith@huntingdon.edu; Staff 4 (MLS 3, Non-MLS 1)
Founded 1854. Enrl 960; Fac 57; Highest Degree: Bachelor
Jun 2012-May 2013 Income $520,530
Library Holdings: AV Mats 4,421; DVDs 2,177; e-books 72,405; e-journals 13,306; Electronic Media & Resources 102; Microforms 61,551; Bk Vols 113,364; Per Subs 191; Videos 1,536
Special Collections: Alabama-West Florida Conference of the United Methodist Church; Alabamiana; Archives & History of United Methodist Church; Autographed Book Coll; College Archives; Rare Book Coll
Automation Activity & Vendor Info: (Acquisitions) OCLC; (Cataloging) OCLC; (Circulation) OCLC; (OPAC) OCLC; (Serials) OCLC
Database Vendor: BioOne, Bowker, College Source, CQ Press, CredoReference, EBSCOhost, Facts on File, Gale Cengage Learning, JSTOR, McGraw-Hill, OCLC FirstSearch, OCLC WorldShare Interlibrary Loan, ProQuest, PubMed, Sage, Springshare, LLC
Wireless access
Partic in Lyrasis; Montgomery Higher Education Librs; Network of Alabama Academic Libraries
Open Mon-Thurs 7:30am-11pm, Fri 7:30-4:45, Sat 12-4:45, Sun 5pm-11pm

M JACKSON HOSPITAL & CLINIC, INC*, Medical Library, 1725 Pine St, 36106. SAN 325-9501. Tel: 334-293-8696. FAX: 334-293-8791.
Library Holdings: Bk Titles 340; Bk Vols 663
Open Mon-Fri 9-4

P MONTGOMERY CITY-COUNTY PUBLIC LIBRARY SYSTEM, Library Administration, 245 High St, 36104. (Mail add: PO Box 1950, 36102-1950), SAN 330-2709. Tel: 334-240-4300. FAX: 334-240-4977. Web Site: www.mccpl.lib.al.us. *Libr Dir,* Jaunita M Owes; Tel: 334-240-4989, E-mail: jowes@mccpl.lib.al.us; *Asst Libr Dir,* Vivian B White; Tel: 334-240-4922, E-mail: vwhite@mccpl.lib.al.us; *Coll Develop Librn, Head, Tech Serv,* Thomas Anderson; Tel: 334-240-4975, E-mail:

tanderson@mccpl.lib.al.us; *Coordr, Extn Serv, Librn IV,* Position Currently Open; *Libr Develop Coordr,* Rebie Morris; Tel: 334-240-4924, E-mail: rmorris@mccpl.lib.al.us; *Tech Coordr,* Samuel Jackson, Jr; Tel: 334-240-4986, E-mail: sjackson@mccpl.lib.al.us
Founded 1899. Pop 230,149; Circ 435,477
Automation Activity & Vendor Info: (Acquisitions) SirsiDynix; (Cataloging) OCLC; (Circulation) SirsiDynix; (ILL) OCLC; (OPAC) SirsiDynix
Database Vendor: Baker & Taylor, Booklist Online, Bowker, EBSCO Information Services, EBSCOhost, Facts on File, Foundation Center, Gale Cengage Learning, LearningExpress, Medline, Newsbank, OCLC, OCLC FirstSearch, OCLC WorldShare Interlibrary Loan, Overdrive, Inc, Oxford Online, ProQuest, PubMed, SirsiDynix, TumbleBookLibrary, ValueLine, World Book Online
Wireless access
Function: Libr develop, Outreach serv
Publications: Black History Month Program Guide (Annual); Guide to Services & Programs (Library handbook); MCCPL Staff Read Into the Holidays (Annual); Montgomery City-County Public Library Annual Report; National Library Week Program Guide (Annual); Summer Reading Program Guide (Annual); Things to Do @ Your Library (Monthly bulletin)
Open Mon-Fri 8-5 (Admin Office)
Friends of the Library Group
Branches: 11
COLISEUM BOULEVARD BRANCH LIBRARY, 840 Coliseum Blvd, 36109, SAN 330-2768. Tel: 334-271-7005. FAX: 334-244-5754. E-mail: coliseumcirc@mccpl.lib.al.us. *Br Mgr, Librn III,* Gertie Scott; E-mail: gscott@mccpl.lib.al.us; *Asst Br Mgr, Ch, Librn I,* Floyd W Little, Jr; E-mail: wlittle@mccpl.lib.al.us; Staff 4 (MLS 1, Non-MLS 3)
Special Collections: US Dep of Transportation Plume Investigation Reports, Dec 1999 to present
Special Services for the Deaf - Staff with knowledge of sign lang
Open Mon-Fri 9-6
GOVERNORS SQUARE BRANCH LIBRARY, 2885-B E South Blvd, 36111, SAN 330-2725. Tel: 334-284-7929. FAX: 334-240-4839. E-mail: govercirc@mccpl.lib.al.us. *Br Mgr, Librn III,* Joan Means; E-mail: jmeans@mccpl.lib.al.us; *Asst Br Mgr, Ch, Librn I,* Anita Berry; E-mail: aberry@mccpl.lib.al.us; Staff 4.5 (MLS 2, Non-MLS 2.5)
Open Mon-Fri 9-6
HAMPSTEAD BRANCH LIBRARY, 5251 Hampstead High St, Ste 107, 36116. Tel: 334-244-5770. FAX: 334-244-5773. E-mail: hampsteadcirc@mccpl.lib.al.us. *Asst Br Mgr, Ch, Librn I,* Kathryn Powell; E-mail: kpowell@mccpl.lib.al.us; Staff 3 (MLS 2, Non-MLS 1)
Open Mon-Fri 9-6
RUFUS A LEWIS REGIONAL LIBRARY, 3095 Mobile Hwy, 36108, SAN 374-6860. Tel: 334-240-4848. FAX: 334-240-4847. E-mail: lewiscirc@mccpl.lib.al.us. *Br Mgr, Librn III,* Glenda Walker; E-mail: gwalker@mccpl.lib.al.us; *Asst Br Mgr, Ch, Librn I,* Minnie Stringer; E-mail: mstringer@mccpl.lib.al.us; Staff 5 (MLS 2, Non-MLS 3)
Open Mon & Tues 9-9, Wed-Fri 9-6, Sat 9-1
E L LOWDER REGIONAL LIBRARY, 2590 Bell Rd, 36117, SAN 374-6879. Tel: 334-244-5717. FAX: 334-240-4893. E-mail: lowdercirc@mccpl.lib.al.us. *Br Mgr, Librn III,* Julia-Ann Jenkins; E-mail: jjenkins@mccpl.lib.al.us; *Asst Br Mgr, Ch, Librn I,* Shirley Toston; E-mail: stoston@mccpl.lib.al.us; *Asst Br Mgr, Ch, Librn I,* Stacie Williams; E-mail: sworthy@mccpl.lib.al.us; Staff 5.5 (MLS 1, Non-MLS 4.5)
Open Mon & Wed 9-9, Tues, Thurs & Fri 9-6, Sat 9-1
JULIETTE HAMPTON MORGAN MEMORIAL LIBRARY (MAIN LIBRARY), 245 High St, 36104. Tel: 334-240-4999. Circulation Tel: 334-240-4997, 334-240-4998. Reference Tel: 334-240-4982, 334-240-4992. FAX: 334-240-4980. E-mail: maincirc@mccpl.lib.al.us. *Head Librn, Librn IV, Mgr,* Timothy E Berry; Tel: 334-240-4996, E-mail: tberry@mccpl.lib.al.us; *Head, Circ Serv, Librn II,* Zella'Ques S Brown; E-mail: zbrown@mccpl.lib.al.us; *Head, Ref & Info Serv, Librn III,* Suzanne Horton; E-mail: shorton@mccpl.lib.al.us; *Ch, Librn II,* Fredriatta Brown; Tel: 334-240-4991, E-mail: fbrown@mccpl.lib.al.us; *Librn II, Ref Librn,* Brenda Davis; E-mail: bdavis@mccpl.lib.al.us; *Librn II, Ref Librn,* Khalilah Hayes; E-mail: khayes@mccpl.lib.al.us; *Librn II, Ref Librn,* Sharon Phillips; E-mail: sphillips@mccpl.lib.al.us; *Librn II, Ref Librn,* Mary B Wilhoite; E-mail: mwilhoite@mccpl.lib.al.us; *Computer Lab Mgr, Librn II, Webmaster,* LaRuth Martin; Tel: 334-240-4994, E-mail: lmartin@mccpl.lib.al.us; Staff 20.5 (MLS 5, Non-MLS 15.5)
Pop 230,149; Circ 115,818
Special Collections: Alabama Journal Newspaper Coll, June 1952 to April 1993, microfilm; Alabamiana & Rare Book Coll; Arms & Military Coll; Descriptive Video Coll; Montgomery Advertiser, March 1952 to present, microfilm; New York Times Newspaper Coll, Jan 1972 to present, microfilm; Wall Street Journal, Jan 1972 to present, microfilm
Automation Activity & Vendor Info: (ILL) OCLC WorldShare Interlibrary Loan; (Serials) SirsiDynix
Function: Adult bk club, Archival coll, AV serv, Bk club(s), Bks on cassette, Children's prog, Computer training, Computers for patron use, Copy machines, E-Reserves, Electronic databases & coll, Fax serv, Handicapped accessible, Homework prog, ILL available, Music CDs, Newsp ref libr, Online cat, OverDrive digital audio bks, Photocopying/Printing, Prog for adults, Prog for children & young adult, Ref & res, Ref serv available, Story hour, Summer reading prog, Tax forms, Teen prog, Telephone ref, VHS videos
Publications: Reference Notes (Reference guide)
Special Services for the Deaf - TTY equip
Special Services for the Blind - Bks on cassette; Descriptive video serv (DVS); Large print bks; Ref serv
Open Mon-Wed 9-9, Thurs & Fri 9-6, Sat 9-1, Sun 2-6
Restriction: In-house use for visitors, Non-circulating of rare bks, Non-resident fee, Restricted borrowing privileges
Friends of the Library Group
PIKE ROAD BRANCH LIBRARY, 9585 Vaughn Rd, Pike Road, 36064. (Mail add: PO Box 640036, Pike Road, 36064-0036), SAN 378-1720. Tel: 334-244-8679. FAX: 334-240-4887. E-mail: pikeroadcirc@mccpl.lib.al.us. *Asst Br Mgr, Ch, Librn I,* Charles Matthew Williams; E-mail: cmwilliams@mccpl.lib.al.us; Staff 3 (MLS 2, Non-MLS 1)
Open Mon-Fri 9-6
Friends of the Library Group
PINE LEVEL BRANCH LIBRARY, 20 Kohn Dr, Pine Level, 36065. (Mail add: 20 Kohn Dr, Ramer, 36069), SAN 378-1747. Tel: 334-584-7144. E-mail: pinelevelcirc@mccpl.lib.al.us. *Br Mgr, Extn Serv Librn, Librn IV,* David Blackledge; Tel: 334-240-4843, Fax: 334-240-4839, E-mail: dblackledge@mccpl.lib.al.us; *Libr Asst II,* Sabrina Wells; Staff 2 (MLS 1, Non-MLS 1)
Closed October 2014-September 2015, or until further notice
Open Mon, Wed & Fri 9-1, Tues & Thurs 2-6
Friends of the Library Group
PINTLALA BRANCH LIBRARY, 255 Federal Rd, Pintlala, 36043-9781, SAN 378-1704. Tel: 334-281-8069. FAX: 334-240-4860. E-mail: pintlalacirc@mccpl.lib.al.us. *Asst Br Mgr, Ch, Librn I,* Sandra S Berry; E-mail: ssavage@mccpl.lib.al.us; Staff 3 (MLS 1, Non-MLS 2)
Open Mon-Fri 9-6
Friends of the Library Group
RAMER BRANCH LIBRARY, 5444 State Hwy 94, Ramer, 36069-5008, SAN 330-2741. Tel: 334-562-3364. FAX: 334-562-3889. E-mail: ramercirc@mccpl.lib.al.us. *Br Mgr, Librn III,* James A Greer; E-mail: jgreer@mccpl.lib.al.us; *Asst Br Mgr, Ch, Librn I,* Diane Griffin; E-mail: dgriffin@mccpl.lib.al.us; Staff 2 (MLS 1, Non-MLS 1)
Open Mon-Fri 9-6
Friends of the Library Group
BERTHA PLEASANT WILLIAMS LIBRARY - ROSA L PARKS AVENUE BRANCH, 1276 Rosa L Parks Ave, 36108, SAN 330-2733. Tel: 334-240-4979. FAX: 334-240-4925. E-mail: rosacirc@mccpl.lib.al.us. *Br Mgr, Librn III,* Glenda Walker; E-mail: gwalker@mccpl.lib.al.us; *Asst Br Mgr, Ch, Librn I,* Lauren Kiefer; E-mail: lkiefer@mccpl.lib.al.us; Staff 3.5 (MLS 2, Non-MLS 1.5)
Open Mon-Fri 9-6
Friends of the Library Group

GL MONTGOMERY COUNTY LAW LIBRARY*, 251 S Lawrence St, 36104. SAN 300-1679. Tel: 334-832-1394. FAX: 334-265-9536. *Librn,* Suzanne Duffey
Library Holdings: Bk Titles 215
Database Vendor: LexisNexis, Westlaw
Open Mon-Fri 8-5
Restriction: Ref only to non-staff

C SOUTH UNIVERSITY LIBRARY*, Montgomery Campus, 5355 Vaughn Rd, 36116-1120. SAN 375-4383. Tel: 334-395-8800. Circulation Tel: 334-395-8861. Reference Tel: 334-395-8891. Administration Tel: 334-395-8860. FAX: 334-395-8859. E-mail: sumonadm@southuniversity.edu. Web Site: www.southuniversity.edu/montgomery.aspx. *Dir,* Jessica Hayes; E-mail: jehayes@southuniversity.edu; *Ref Librn, Ref/ILL/Instruction,* Rachel Chenault; Staff 3 (MLS 2, Non-MLS 1)
Enrl 580; Highest Degree: Master
Library Holdings: Audiobooks 50; AV Mats 976; CDs 296; DVDs 500; e-books 50,000; Bk Vols 20,000; Per Subs 22
Special Collections: Fiction & Non-Fiction by Alabama Authors (Alabama Coll); Law Coll
Subject Interests: Bus, Counseling, Info tech, Law, Med, Phys therapy
Automation Activity & Vendor Info: (Acquisitions) Ex Libris Group; (Cataloging) Ex Libris Group; (Circulation) Ex Libris Group; (Course Reserve) Ex Libris Group; (ILL) Ex Libris Group; (OPAC) Ex Libris Group; (Serials) Ex Libris Group
Database Vendor: EBSCOhost, Gale Cengage Learning, OVID Technologies, ProQuest, Westlaw
Wireless access
Function: Audio & video playback equip for onsite use, Bks on cassette, Bks on CD, CD-ROM, Computers for patron use, Copy machines, Distance learning, e-mail serv, Electronic databases & coll, Free DVD rentals, ILL available, Instruction & testing, Mail & tel request accepted, Notary serv,

Online searches, Orientations, Photocopying/Printing, Ref & res, Ref serv available, Spoken cassettes & CDs, Spoken cassettes & DVDs, Telephone ref, Video lending libr, Web-catalog, Workshops
Open Mon-Thurs 8am-9:30pm, Fri & Sat 8:30-4:30

C TROY UNIVERSITY, MONTGOMERY CAMPUS, Rosa Parks Library, 252 Montgomery St, 36104-3425. SAN 300-1709. Tel: 334-241-9576. Interlibrary Loan Service Tel: 334-241-9784. Reference Tel: 334-241-8605. FAX: 334-241-9590. E-mail: m01library@troy.edu. Web Site: montgomery.troy.edu/library/default.htm. *Libr Dir,* Kent E Snowden; Tel: 334-241-9783, E-mail: kesnowden@troy.edu; *Coll Develop/Ref Librn,* Debbie West; Tel: 334-241-5820, E-mail: debwest@troy.edu; *Ref & Instruction Librn,* Alyssa Martin; Tel: 334-241-8601, E-mail: almartin@troy.edu; Staff 3 (MLS 3)
Founded 1964. Enrl 3,500; Fac 190; Highest Degree: Doctorate
Library Holdings: AV Mats 1,045; e-books 59,930; Bk Vols 32,230; Per Subs 355
Subject Interests: Nursing
Automation Activity & Vendor Info: (Acquisitions) SIRSI WorkFlows; (Cataloging) SIRSI WorkFlows; (Circulation) SIRSI WorkFlows; (OPAC) SIRSI WorkFlows; (Serials) SIRSI WorkFlows
Database Vendor: Cinahl, EBSCOhost, Elsevier, JSTOR, ProQuest
Wireless access
Partic in Montgomery Higher Education Librs; Network of Alabama Academic Libraries
Open Mon-Thurs 8am-9pm, Fri 8-4:30, Sun 2-6
Restriction: Borrowing privileges limited to fac & registered students

S VALIDATA COMPUTER & RESEARCH CORP LIBRARY*, 428 S Perry St, 36104-4236. (Mail add: PO Box 4720, 36103-4720), SAN 373-3831. Tel: 334-834-2324. FAX: 334-262-5648. E-mail: marketing@validata.org. Web Site: www.validata.com. *In Charge,* Warren Philips
Library Holdings: Bk Vols 7,000; Per Subs 10

MOODY

P DORIS STANLEY MEMORIAL LIBRARY*, 1515 Bookmark Lane, 35004. SAN 325-402X. Tel: 205-640-2517. FAX: 205-640-2534. E-mail: dsml@moodyalabama.gov. *Libr Dir,* Patsy Spradley
Open Mon-Thurs 8-6

MOULTON

P LAWRENCE COUNTY PUBLIC LIBRARY*, 401 College St, 35650. SAN 300-1733. Tel: 256-974-0883. FAX: 256-974-0890. E-mail: info@lawrencecpl.org. Web Site: www.lawrencecpl.org. *Dir,* Ball Anderton; Staff 4 (MLS 1, Non-MLS 3)
Founded 1961. Pop 34,800
Library Holdings: DVDs 362; Large Print Bks 707; Bk Titles 37,241; Talking Bks 845; Videos 1,371
Automation Activity & Vendor Info: (Acquisitions) Follett Software; (Cataloging) Follett Software; (ILL) OCLC Online
Wireless access
Function: ILL available, Photocopying/Printing, Prog for children & young adult, Summer reading prog, Telephone ref
Open Mon-Thurs 9:30-6, Fri 9:30-5
Friends of the Library Group

MOUNDVILLE

P MOUNDVILLE PUBLIC LIBRARY*, 411 Market St, 35474. (Mail add: PO Box 336, 35474-0336), SAN 300-1741. Tel: 205-371-2283. FAX: 205-371-2283. E-mail: moundville.library@yahoo.com. *Dir, Librn,* Linda Davis
Pop 6,000; Circ 4,700
Library Holdings: Bk Vols 8,500; Per Subs 10
Special Collections: Alabamaian Coll
Automation Activity & Vendor Info: (Acquisitions) Book Systems; (Cataloging) Book Systems; (Circulation) Book Systems; (ILL) Book Systems; (OPAC) Book Systems; (Serials) Book Systems
Wireless access
Open Tues-Fri 9-5:30, Sat 9-12

MOUNT VERNON

P MOUNT VERNON PUBLIC LIBRARY*, 1220 Military Rd, 36560. Tel: 251-829-9497. FAX: 251-829-5546. E-mail: mtvernonlibrary@yahoo.com. *Dir,* Willard Sims; *Librn,* David Alexander Ori; E-mail: adrrrienne031000@yahoo.com
Library Holdings: Bk Vols 8,000; Per Subs 30
Wireless access
Mem of Westchester Library System
Open Mon-Thurs 1-5, Sat 9-1

M SEARCY HOSPITAL PATIENT LIBRARY*, 325 E Coy S Hwy, 36560. SAN 300-175X. Tel: 251-662-6700, 251-662-6842. FAX: 251-829-9075. *Dir,* Renee Reynolds
Library Holdings: Bk Titles 7,000; Bk Vols 7,500; Per Subs 85
Friends of the Library Group

MOUNTAIN BROOK

P EMMET O'NEAL LIBRARY*, 50 Oak St, 35213. SAN 300-1768. Tel: 205-879-0459. Circulation Tel: 205-445-1101. Reference Tel: 205-445-1121. Administration Tel: 205-879-0492. FAX: 205-879-5388. Web Site: www.eolib.org. *Dir,* Susan DeBrecht Murrell; E-mail: smurrell@bham.lib.al.us; *Acq, Cat,* Nancy D Sexton; E-mail: nsexton@bham.lib.al.us; *Adult Serv,* Katie Moellering; E-mail: kmoellering@bham.lib.al.us; *Ch Serv,* Carol Melton; E-mail: carolm@bham.lib.al.us; *Circ,* Doris Young; E-mail: dyoung@bham.lib.al.us; *Ref,* Holley Wesley; E-mail: hwesley@bham.lib.al.us; Staff 5 (MLS 3, Non-MLS 2)
Founded 1964. Pop 20,183; Circ 327,189
Library Holdings: Bk Titles 106,044; Bk Vols 123,638; Per Subs 132
Special Collections: Gardening Coll; Travel Coll
Subject Interests: Gardening
Automation Activity & Vendor Info: (Cataloging) Innovative Interfaces, Inc; (Circulation) Innovative Interfaces, Inc; (OPAC) Innovative Interfaces, Inc
Publications: Friends of the Library Bookends
Partic in Jefferson County Libr Coop
Open Mon, Tues & Thurs (Winter) 9-9, Wed 9-6, Fri & Sat 9-5, Sun 1-5; Mon, Wed & Thurs (Summer) 9-6, Tues 9-9, Fri & Sat 9-5
Friends of the Library Group

MUSCLE SHOALS

S IFDC LIBRARY, Travis P Hignett Memorial Library, Reservation Rd, COMPLEX F, 35661. (Mail add: PO Box 2040, 35662-2040), SAN 325-9072. Tel: 256-381-6600. FAX: 256-381-7408. E-mail: librarian@ifdc.org. Web Site: www.ifdc.org. *Interim Librn,* Drucilla S Gambrell; Staff 1 (MLS 1)
Founded 1977
Library Holdings: CDs 100; e-journals 20; Bk Titles 23,500; Per Subs 183
Special Collections: Audio Visuals; Country File; International Agricultural Organization File; Organization File; Patent Files; Training Programs
Subject Interests: Agr, Agr bus, Develop countries, Fertilizers, Mkt
Automation Activity & Vendor Info: (Cataloging) EOS International; (Circulation) EOS International; (ILL) OCLC; (OPAC) EOS International; (Serials) EOS International
Database Vendor: Agricola, American Chemical Society, Baker & Taylor, Dialog, Elsevier, EOS International, OCLC FirstSearch, OCLC WorldShare Interlibrary Loan, ProQuest, ReferenceUSA, ScienceDirect, SirsiDynix, SoutronGLOBAL, STN International, Wiley InterScience
Wireless access
Function: 24/7 Online cat
Publications: Library Information (Reference guide)
Open Mon-Fri 7;30-4:15
Restriction: Access for corporate affiliates, Authorized patrons, Badge access after hrs

P MUSCLE SHOALS PUBLIC LIBRARY, 1918 E Avalon, 35661. SAN 300-1776. Tel: 256-386-9212. FAX: 256-386-9211. E-mail: mspl@muscleshoals.lib.al.us. Web Site: cityofmuscleshoals.com/Default.asp?ID=65. *Libr Mgr,* Denita Lester; E-mail: dlester@muscleshoals.lib.al.us; *Acq,* Anna Cathernine Thompson; *Ch Serv,* Kay Lesley; *Circ,* Christina Johnson; *Tech Asst,* Melanie Emerson; *Youth Serv,* Anna Kaitlan Isom; Staff 1 (MLS 1)
Pop 17,589; Circ 241,547
Library Holdings: Bk Vols 46,000; Per Subs 50
Automation Activity & Vendor Info: (Acquisitions) TLC (The Library Corporation); (Cataloging) TLC (The Library Corporation); (Circulation) TLC (The Library Corporation); (OPAC) TLC (The Library Corporation); (Serials) TLC (The Library Corporation)
Database Vendor: EBSCOhost, OCLC, OCLC FirstSearch, OCLC WebJunction, OCLC WorldShare Interlibrary Loan
Wireless access
Function: VHS videos
Open Mon 12-5, Tues & Thurs 10-7, Wed, Fri & Sat 10-5
Restriction: Open to pub upon request
Friends of the Library Group

J NORTHWEST-SHOALS COMMUNITY COLLEGE*, Larry W McCoy Learning Resource Center, 800 George Wallace Blvd, 35661-3206. (Mail add: PO Box 2545, 35662-2545). Tel: 256-331-5283. FAX: 256-331-5269. Web Site: www.nwscc.edu. *Librn,* Rachel Trapp; E-mail: rachel.trapp@nwscc.edu

Library Holdings: Bk Vols 30,000; Per Subs 150
Function: ILL available
Open Mon-Thurs 7:30am-9pm, Fri 7:30-4, Sat 8am-12:30pm

NEWTON

P NEWTON PUBLIC LIBRARY*, 209 Oates Dr, 36352. SAN 330-3128. Tel: 334-299-3316. E-mail: library@newtonplks.org. *Libr Dir,* Tammy Forbes
Library Holdings: Bk Vols 12,000
Automation Activity & Vendor Info: (Cataloging) Book Systems; (Circulation) Book Systems
Mem of South Central Kansas Library System
Open Mon-Fri 10:30-4:30

ODENVILLE

P ODENVILLE PUBLIC LIBRARY*, 200 Alabama St, 35120. (Mail add: PO Box 249, 35120), SAN 330-3276. Tel: 205-629-5901. FAX: 205-629-5324. E-mail: odenlib@windstream.net. Web Site: www.odenlib.org. *Libr Dir,* Betty Corley
Founded 1960
Library Holdings: Audiobooks 524; CDs 65; DVDs 444; e-books 97; High Interest/Low Vocabulary Bk Vols 146; Large Print Bks 275; Bk Vols 16,500; Per Subs 9; Spec Interest Per Sub 5
Automation Activity & Vendor Info: (Acquisitions) Biblionix; (Cataloging) Biblionix; (Circulation) Biblionix; (OPAC) OCLC
Wireless access
Open Tues-Fri 9-6
Friends of the Library Group

ONEONTA

P ONEONTA PUBLIC LIBRARY, 221 Second St S, 35121. SAN 300-1806. Tel: 205-274-7641. FAX: 205-274-7643. E-mail: oplib@otelco.net. Web Site: www.oneontapubliclibrary.org. *Dir,* Rebekah F Wood; *Asst Dir,* Kay Butts; *Programming Librn,* Amy Woods; *Cat,* Pam Guin; *Circ,* Ricky Statham; Staff 7 (MLS 2, Non-MLS 5)
Founded 1948. Circ 50,867
Library Holdings: Bk Vols 37,091; Per Subs 127
Subject Interests: Genealogy, Rare bks, Video
Automation Activity & Vendor Info: (Cataloging) Book Systems; (Circulation) Book Systems; (OPAC) Book Systems
Database Vendor: Overdrive, Inc, ProQuest, TumbleBookLibrary
Special Services for the Deaf - Bks on deafness & sign lang
Special Services for the Blind - Aids for in-house use; Audio mat; Bks on CD; Closed circuit TV; Copier with enlargement capabilities; Large print bks; Large screen computer & software; Micro-computer access & training
Open Mon & Thurs 9-7, Tues, Wed & Fri 9-5, Sat 9-2
Friends of the Library Group

OPELIKA

P LEWIS COOPER JUNIOR MEMORIAL LIBRARY*, 200 S Sixth St, 36801. SAN 300-1814. Tel: 334-705-5380. FAX: 334-705-5381. Web Site: www.opelika.org/depts/library/index.html. *Dir,* Susan Delmas; Staff 10 (MLS 3, Non-MLS 7)
Founded 1941. Pop 23,000
Oct 2008-Sept 2009 Income $777,181, State $28,000, City $749,181. Mats Exp $82,500, Books $70,000, Per/Ser (Incl. Access Fees) $2,000, Micro $500, AV Mat $10,000. Sal $55,305
Library Holdings: Audiobooks 5,000; CDs 1,000; DVDs 5,000; Large Print Bks 1,000; Microforms 100; Bk Titles 61,000; Bk Vols 65,000; Per Subs 60; Videos 1,000
Special Collections: Alabama Coll
Subject Interests: Genealogy
Automation Activity & Vendor Info: (Cataloging) Innovative Interfaces, Inc; (Circulation) Innovative Interfaces, Inc; (OPAC) Innovative Interfaces, Inc
Wireless access
Open Mon & Tues 8:30-7:30, Wed 8:30-5, Sat 9-5, Sun 1-5
Friends of the Library Group

OPP

P OPP PUBLIC LIBRARY*, 1604 N Main St, 36467. SAN 300-1830. Tel: 334-493-6423. FAX: 334-493-6423. E-mail: staff@opplibrary.com. *Dir,* Gayle P Clare; *Librn,* Janet L Davis; *Librn,* Sally A Shaner; Staff 2 (Non-MLS 2)
Founded 1937. Pop 12,946; Circ 31,753
Oct 2005-Sept 2006 Income $96,919, State $13,526, City $64,793, County $7,100, Locally Generated Income $4,500, Other $7,000. Mats Exp $20,600, Books $18,000, Per/Ser (Incl. Access Fees) $600, AV Mat $2,000. Sal $50,073 (Prof $18,211)
Library Holdings: CDs 150; DVDs 50; Large Print Bks 575; Bk Vols 18,444; Per Subs 23; Talking Bks 210; Videos 265
Automation Activity & Vendor Info: (Cataloging) Book Systems; (Circulation) Book Systems; (ILL) OCLC FirstSearch; (OPAC) Book Systems; (Serials) EBSCO Online
Database Vendor: EBSCOhost, Gale Cengage Learning, OCLC FirstSearch, OCLC WebJunction, OCLC WorldShare Interlibrary Loan, PubMed
Wireless access
Function: Art exhibits, Audio & video playback equip for onsite use, Bk club(s), CD-ROM, Computer training, Copy machines, e-mail serv, E-Reserves, Electronic databases & coll, Fax serv, Handicapped accessible, Homework prog, ILL available, Magnifiers for reading, Music CDs, Photocopying/Printing, Preschool outreach, Prog for children & young adult, Senior computer classes, Spoken cassettes & CDs, Summer reading prog, Tax forms, VHS videos, Video lending libr, Wheelchair accessible
Special Services for the Deaf - TTY equip
Open Mon-Thurs 8-6, Fri 8-5
Restriction: Open to pub for ref & circ; with some limitations
Friends of the Library Group

ORANGE BEACH

P ORANGE BEACH PUBLIC LIBRARY*, 26267 Canal Rd, 36561-3917. (Mail add: PO Box 1649, 36561-1649), SAN 373-7004. Tel: 251-981-2923. FAX: 251-981-2920. E-mail: askobpl@cityoforangebeach.com. Web Site: www.orangebeachlibrary.org. *Dir,* Bonnie Lee; E-mail: blee@cityoforangebeach.com; *Asst Dir,* Patricia P Underwood; *Circ Supvr,* Sherry Brandler; *Admin Serv,* Andrea Y Mewbourn; *Adult Serv, Ref Serv,* Maria Baroco; *Ch Serv,* Patsy Rose; *Circ, YA Serv,* Meagan Bing; *Circ,* Seth Bowling; Staff 8 (MLS 3, Non-MLS 5)
Founded 1992. Pop 5,441; Circ 110,674
Jan 2011-Dec 2011 Income $501,660, State $2,748, City $431,435, Federal $5,250, Locally Generated Income $50,000. Mats Exp $24,500, Books $17,000, Per/Ser (Incl. Access Fees) $2,200, AV Mat $5,000, Electronic Ref Mat (Incl. Access Fees) $300. Sal $409,000 (Prof $118,265)
Library Holdings: Audiobooks 4,221; Bks on Deafness & Sign Lang 20; CDs 2,556; DVDs 700; e-books 2,786; Electronic Media & Resources 68; Large Print Bks 754; Bk Vols 49,343; Per Subs 52; Videos 636
Automation Activity & Vendor Info: (Cataloging) TLC (The Library Corporation); (Circulation) TLC (The Library Corporation); (Course Reserve) TLC (The Library Corporation); (OPAC) TLC (The Library Corporation)
Database Vendor: Tech Logic, TLC (The Library Corporation)
Wireless access
Function: Accelerated reader prog, Adult bk club, Audiobks via web, Bk club(s), Bks on cassette, Bks on CD, Children's prog, Computer training, Computers for patron use, Copy machines, Digital talking bks, Distance learning, e-mail & chat, Electronic databases & coll, Fax serv, Free DVD rentals, Handicapped accessible, Homebound delivery serv, Homework prog, ILL available, Large print keyboards, Mail & tel request accepted, Music CDs, Newsp ref libr, Notary serv, Online cat, Online ref, Online searches, Outside serv via phone, mail, e-mail & web, OverDrive digital audio bks, Photocopying/Printing, Printer for laptops & handheld devices, Prog for adults, Prog for children & young adult, Pub access computers, Ref serv in person, Res libr, Scanner, Senior computer classes, Spoken cassettes & CDs, Spoken cassettes & DVDs, Story hour, Summer & winter reading prog, Summer reading prog, Tax forms, Teen prog, Telephone ref, VHS videos, Web-catalog, Wheelchair accessible, Winter reading prog
Mem of Baldwin County Library Cooperative, Inc
Special Services for the Deaf - Bks on deafness & sign lang
Special Services for the Blind - Bks on CD; Home delivery serv; Large print bks; Recorded bks
Open Mon, Tues & Fri 9-6, Wed & Thurs 9-8, Sat 9-3
Friends of the Library Group

OXFORD

P OXFORD PUBLIC LIBRARY*, 213 Choccolocco St, 36203. SAN 300-1849. Tel: 256-831-1750. FAX: 256-835-6798. E-mail: library@oxfordalabama.org. Web Site: www.oxfordalabama.org. *Dir,* Irene Sparks; *Librn,* Alayne Livingston; *Ch,* June Fulmer
Founded 1927. Pop 14,592; Circ 37,311
Library Holdings: Bk Vols 24,000; Per Subs 35
Automation Activity & Vendor Info: (Cataloging) Book Systems; (Circulation) Book Systems; (OPAC) Book Systems
Open Tues-Fri 9-5:30, Sat 8-4:30

OZARK

J ENTERPRISE STATE COMMUNITY COLLEGE*, Ozark Aviation Campus Learning Resource Center, 3405 US Hwy 231 S, 36360. SAN 322-6824. Tel: 334-774-5113.
Highest Degree: Associate
Special Collections: Civil, Commercial & General Aviation
Subject Interests: Automotive, Aviation, Electronics
Automation Activity & Vendor Info: (Acquisitions) SirsiDynix; (Cataloging) SirsiDynix; (Circulation) SirsiDynix; (Course Reserve)

SirsiDynix; (ILL) SirsiDynix; (Media Booking) SirsiDynix; (OPAC) SirsiDynix; (Serials) SirsiDynix
Database Vendor: SirsiDynix
Wireless access
Open Mon & Wed 8-4:45, Tues & Thurs 9-7:30, Fri 8-Noon
Restriction: Open to fac, students & qualified researchers
Departmental Libraries:
MOBILE AVIATION CENTER, 1975 Ave C, Mobile, 36615, SAN 370-0119. Tel: 251-438-2816. FAX: 251-438-2816.
Library Holdings: Bk Vols 2,500; Per Subs 20
Open Mon-Thurs 7:30-4:30, Fri 7:30-2

P OZARK-DALE COUNTY PUBLIC LIBRARY, INC*, 416 James St, 36360. SAN 330-2970. Tel: 334-774-2399, 334-774-5480. E-mail: library@odcpl.com. Web Site: www.odcpl.com. *Dir,* Sandra J Holmes; *Ch Serv,* Marla Drake; *Circ,* Charlene Paschall; *ILL,* Elaine Land; *Ref Serv,* Jocelyn Rayford; *Tech Serv,* Angie Walsh; *Tech Support,* Karen Speck. Subject Specialists: *Genealogy,* Jocelyn Rayford; Staff 6 (Non-MLS 6)
Founded 1945. Pop 37,106
Library Holdings: AV Mats 4,619; CDs 666; DVDs 55; Large Print Bks 2,053; Bk Titles 57,848; Per Subs 113; Talking Bks 1,888; Videos 2,010
Special Collections: Autry Religious Coll; Creel R Richardson Genealogy Coll
Automation Activity & Vendor Info: (Cataloging) Follett Software; (Circulation) Follett Software; (OPAC) Follett Software
Function: Prog for children & young adult
Open Tues-Thurs 9-8, Fri & Sat 9-5
Friends of the Library Group

PELHAM

P PELHAM PUBLIC LIBRARY*, 3160 Pelham Pkwy, 35124. (Mail add: PO Box 1627, 35124-5627), SAN 325-0407. Tel: 205-620-6418. FAX: 205-620-6469. E-mail: library@pelhamonline.com. Web Site: www.pelhamlibrary.com. *Dir,* Barbara Roberts; E-mail: broberts@pelhamonline.com; Staff 17 (MLS 5, Non-MLS 12)
Founded 1975. Pop 17,000; Circ 200,000
Library Holdings: Bk Vols 50,000; Per Subs 50
Automation Activity & Vendor Info: (Cataloging) Innovative Interfaces, Inc; (Circulation) Innovative Interfaces, Inc; (OPAC) Innovative Interfaces, Inc
Mem of Harrison Regional Library System
Open Mon-Thurs 9-8, Fri 9-5, Sat 10-5, Sun 1-5

PELL CITY

P PELL CITY LIBRARY*, 1923 First Ave N, 35125. SAN 330-3306. Tel: 205-884-1015. FAX: 205-814-4798. Web Site: www.pc.lib.al.us. *Dir,* Danny Stewart; E-mail: danny@asc.edu; *Asst Dir,* Susan Mann; E-mail: smannpcl@yahoo.com
Pop 25,000
Library Holdings: Bk Vols 36,000
Special Collections: Oral History
Automation Activity & Vendor Info: (Cataloging) Book Systems; (Circulation) Book Systems; (OPAC) Book Systems
Open Mon, Wed & Fri 9-6, Tues & Thurs 9-7, Sat 9-2
Friends of the Library Group

PHENIX CITY

J CHATTAHOOCHEE VALLEY COMMUNITY COLLEGE*, Learning Resource Center, 2602 College Dr, 36869-7960. Tel: 334-291-4978. FAX: 334-291-4980. Web Site: www.cv.edu/library. *Dir,* Chen Xueying; Tel: 334-291-4979, E-mail: xueying.chen@cv.edu
Founded 1981. Enrl 2,000
Library Holdings: AV Mats 300; e-books 8,000; Bk Vols 53,000; Per Subs 210
Special Collections: Southern States Genealogy Coll
Automation Activity & Vendor Info: (Acquisitions) SirsiDynix; (Circulation) SirsiDynix; (Course Reserve) SirsiDynix; (OPAC) SirsiDynix
Function: ILL available
Partic in Lyrasis
Open Mon-Thurs 8am-9pm, Fri 8-2, Sun 2-6

P PHENIX CITY-RUSSELL COUNTY LIBRARY*, 1501 17th Ave, 36867. SAN 300-1857. Tel: 334-297-1139. FAX: 334-298-8452. E-mail: phenixcitylibrary@gmail.com. *Dir,* Michele Squier Kilday; Tel: 334-664-1700, E-mail: mkilday@phenixcityal.us; Staff 4 (Non-MLS 4)
Founded 1957. Pop 50,000; Circ 71,134
Library Holdings: Audiobooks 501; Bks on Deafness & Sign Lang 10; DVDs 1,516; Large Print Bks 1,862; Bk Titles 38,279; Per Subs 91; Talking Bks 513; Videos 572
Automation Activity & Vendor Info: (Cataloging) Book Systems; (Circulation) Book Systems; (OPAC) Book Systems
Wireless access
Special Services for the Deaf - Bks on deafness & sign lang
Special Services for the Blind - Extensive large print coll
Open Mon-Thurs 9:30-6:30, Fri 9:30-6, Sat 10-2, Sun 1-5
Restriction: Authorized scholars by appt
Friends of the Library Group

PHIL CAMPBELL

J NORTHWEST-SHOALS COMMUNITY COLLEGE*, James A Glasgow Library, 2080 College Rd, 35581. (Mail add: PO Box 2345, Muscle Shoals, 35662), SAN 300-1865. Tel: 256-331-6271. FAX: 256-331-6202. E-mail: library@nwscc.edu. Web Site: www.nwscc.edu. *Coll Develop, Librn,* Rachel Trapp; Staff 2 (MLS 1, Non-MLS 1)
Founded 1963. Enrl 1,000; Fac 33
Library Holdings: Bk Vols 31,100; Per Subs 210
Special Collections: Alabama Professional; Alabama Room Coll, bks, microflm; Children's Coll; Nursing Coll, multi media mat
Subject Interests: Lang arts, Nursing, Soc sci & issues
Automation Activity & Vendor Info: (Cataloging) SirsiDynix; (Circulation) SirsiDynix; (OPAC) SirsiDynix
Function: ILL available
Publications: AV Catalog; Policy & Procedures Manual
Open Mon-Thurs 7:30am-9pm, Fri 8-3:30

PIEDMONT

P PIEDMONT PUBLIC LIBRARY*, 106 N Main St, 36272. SAN 300-1873. Tel: 256-447-3369. FAX: 256-447-3383. Web Site: publiclibrary.cc/piedmont. *Librn,* Kim Mills; E-mail: kim.mills@piedmontcity.org
Founded 1969. Circ 40,000
Library Holdings: Bk Vols 35,000; Per Subs 40
Automation Activity & Vendor Info: (Cataloging) SirsiDynix; (Circulation) SirsiDynix; (OPAC) SirsiDynix
Mem of Public Library of Anniston-Calhoun County
Open Mon & Fri 9-5, Tues & Thurs 9-6, Sat 9-4

PLEASANT GROVE

P PLEASANT GROVE PUBLIC LIBRARY*, 501 Park Rd, 35127. (Mail add: PO Box 339, 35127-0339), SAN 324-122X. Tel: 205-744-1731. FAX: 205-744-5479. Web Site: www.pleasantgrove.lib.al.us. *Dir,* Donna Sartain; E-mail: dsartain@bham.lib.al.us
Founded 1948. Pop 7,102; Circ 30,228
Library Holdings: Bk Vols 30,000; Per Subs 43
Automation Activity & Vendor Info: (Cataloging) Innovative Interfaces, Inc; (Circulation) Innovative Interfaces, Inc; (OPAC) Innovative Interfaces, Inc
Open Mon-Fri 9-5, Sat 9-12

PRATTVILLE

P AUTAUGA PRATTVILLE PUBLIC LIBRARY*, 254 Doster St, 36067-3933. SAN 300-1903. Tel: 334-365-3396. FAX: 334-365-3397. Web Site: www.appl.info. *Dir,* Janice Yates Earnest; E-mail: jearnest@appl.info; *Admin Serv, Asst Dir,* Karen Millton; E-mail: kmillton@appl.info; *Children & Youth Serv Librn,* Barbara Curry; E-mail: bcurry@appl.info; Staff 5 (MLS 2, Non-MLS 3)
Founded 1956. Pop 54,000; Circ 120,000
Library Holdings: Bk Vols 85,000; Per Subs 145
Special Collections: Local History & Genealogical Materials for Autauga County & Surrounding Alabama Counties (Alabama History Coll)
Automation Activity & Vendor Info: (Cataloging) SirsiDynix; (Circulation) SirsiDynix
Wireless access
Function: Accelerated reader prog, Audiobks via web, Bk club(s), Bks on CD, Children's prog, Computers for patron use, Copy machines, Genealogy discussion group, ILL available, Notary serv, Preschool outreach, Preschool reading prog, Ref serv available, Story hour
Publications: APPLe Newsletter (Online only)
Open Mon, Tues & Thurs 9-7, Wed, Fri & Sat 9-5
Friends of the Library Group
Branches: 3
AUTAUGAVILLE PUBLIC, 207 N Taylor St, Autaugaville, 36003. (Mail add: PO Box 178, Autaugaville, 36003-0178), SAN 300-0125. Tel: 334-365-9322. *Br Librn,* Amelia Bishop
Open Mon-Wed 8-5
Friends of the Library Group
BILLINGSLEY PUBLIC, 2021 Office St, Billingsley, 36006. (Mail add: PO Box 42, Billingsley, 3606-0034), SAN 300-0176. Tel: 205-755-9809. E-mail: contact@appl.info. *Br Mgr,* Mary Ellen Williams
Open Mon & Thurs 8-5

MARBURY COMMUNITY, 205 County Rd 20 E, Marbury, 36051. (Mail add: PO Box 200, Marbury, 36051-0200), SAN 300-1385. Tel: 205-755-8575. *Librn,* Amelia Bishop
Open Tues-Thurs 9-5
Friends of the Library Group

PRICEVILLE

P PRICEVILLE PUBLIC LIBRARY*, 103 Faye Dr, 35603. Tel: 256-584-0230. FAX: 256-584-0230. E-mail: prv_library@charter.net. *Librn,* April Dean
Library Holdings: Bk Vols 15,200; Per Subs 15
Open Mon, Tues & Thurs 9-7, Fri 9-5, Sat 9-1

PRICHARD

P PRICHARD PUBLIC LIBRARY*, 300 W Love Joy Loop, 36610. SAN 300-1911. Tel: 251-452-7847. FAX: 251-452-7935. *Dir,* Autherine Caponis
Pop 39,000
Library Holdings: Bk Vols 77,000; Per Subs 215
Open Mon-Thurs 9-8, Fri & Sat 9-5
Branches: 1
MITCHELL, 4440 Highpoint Blvd, Eight Mile, 36613, SAN 377-807X. Tel: 251-452-7846. FAX: 251-452-6517. *Librn,* Lucille Chapman
Library Holdings: Bk Vols 25,000
Open Mon & Wed 12-6, Fri 10-4

RAINBOW CITY

P RAINBOW CITY PUBLIC LIBRARY*, 3702 Rainbow Dr, 35906. SAN 374-4604. Tel: 256-442-8477. FAX: 256-442-4128. E-mail: library@rbcalabama.com. Web Site: www.rbclibrary.org. *Dir,* Tina M Brooks; *Cat,* Joan Roark; Staff 9 (MLS 1, Non-MLS 8)
Founded 1981. Pop 9,324; Circ 126,865
Library Holdings: Audiobooks 3,041; CDs 216; DVDs 1,129; Large Print Bks 912; Bk Vols 50,743; Per Subs 80; Videos 923
Automation Activity & Vendor Info: (Cataloging) Book Systems; (Circulation) Book Systems; (ILL) OCLC; (OPAC) Book Systems
Database Vendor: ProQuest
Wireless access
Open Mon-Thurs 9-7, Fri & Sat 9-5

RAINSVILLE

J NORTHEAST ALABAMA COMMUNITY COLLEGE*, Cecil B Word Learning Resources Center, 138 Alabama Hwy 35, 35986, (Mail add: PO Box 159, 35986-0159), SAN 300-192X. Tel: 256-228-6001, 256-638-4418. FAX: 256-228-4350. E-mail: nac_circ@lmn.lib.al.us. Web Site: www.nacc.edu. *Dir, Libr Serv,* Julia B Everett; Tel: 256-228-6001, Ext 226, E-mail: everettj@nacc.edu; *Librn,* Renee Goss; Tel: 256-228-6001, Ext 329, E-mail: gossr@nacc.edu; Staff 5 (MLS 3, Non-MLS 2)
Founded 1965. Enrl 2,500; Fac 135; Highest Degree: Associate
Library Holdings: Bk Vols 60,000; Per Subs 120
Automation Activity & Vendor Info: (Cataloging) Innovative Interfaces, Inc; (Circulation) Innovative Interfaces, Inc; (OPAC) Innovative Interfaces, Inc
Database Vendor: EBSCOhost, Gale Cengage Learning, Wilson - Wilson Web
Wireless access
Function: ILL available
Partic in Library Management Network, Inc
Open Mon-Thurs 7:30am-9:30pm, Fri 7:30-3

P RAINSVILLE PUBLIC LIBRARY*, 941 E Main St, 35986. (Mail add: PO Box 509, 35986), SAN 300-1938. Tel: 256-638-3311. FAX: 256-638-3314. E-mail: rpl1@farmerstel.com. Web Site: www.rainsvillepublibrary.homestead.com. *Dir,* Ruth Hammon; *Asst Dir, Ch,* Carolyn Wooten; *Acq Librn,* Nadine Shipp; *Automation Spec,* Sarah Cruce
Founded 1968. Pop 9,900; Circ 38,000
Library Holdings: Bk Vols 42,000; Per Subs 35
Automation Activity & Vendor Info: (Cataloging) Follett Software; (Circulation) Follett Software; (OPAC) Follett Software
Open Mon, Wed, Thurs & Fri 8-5, Tues 8-7, Sat 8-12

REDSTONE ARSENAL

UNITED STATES ARMY

A REDSTONE ARSENAL FAMILY & MWR LIBRARY*, 3323 Redeye Rd, 35898, SAN 330-3454. Tel: 256-876-4741. FAX: 256-876-3949. Web Site: www.redstonemwr.com. *Dir,* Gail M Alden; E-mail: gail.alden@us.army.mil; *Head, Tech Serv,* Martha A Burns; E-mail: martha.a.burns@us.army.mil; *Ref Librn,* Barbara McGroary; E-mail: barbara.s.mcgroary@us.army.mil; *Ref Librn,* Sara Kate Roberts; E-mail: sara.kate.roberts@us.army.mil; Staff 6 (MLS 3, Non-MLS 3)
Founded 1952
Library Holdings: DVDs 9,990; Bk Vols 34,000; Per Subs 30; Talking Bks 2,500
Automation Activity & Vendor Info: (Cataloging) OCLC Connexion; (Circulation) Innovative Interfaces, Inc - Millenium; (ILL) OCLC Connexion; (OPAC) Innovative Interfaces, Inc - Millenium
Database Vendor: Baker & Taylor, EBSCOhost, Gale Cengage Learning, Innovative Interfaces, Inc, OCLC FirstSearch
Open Tues-Sat 10-6:30
Restriction: Authorized patrons

A REDSTONE SCIENTIFIC INFORMATION CENTER, Bldg 4484, Martin Rd, 35898-5000, SAN 330-342X. Tel: 256-876-9309. Interlibrary Loan Service Tel: 256-842-1268. Reference Tel: 256-876-5181. Information Services Tel: 256 876-5195. FAX: 256-842-7415. Reference FAX: 256-876-6000. E-mail: usarmy.redstone.amrdec.mbx.rsic-gov@mail.mil. Web Site: https://rsic.amrdec.army.mil. *Libr Dir,* Elizabeth Lloyd; Staff 8 (MLS 6, Non-MLS 2)
Founded 1949
Library Holdings: Bk Vols 263,000
Special Collections: Guidance & Control; Helicopter; Peenemuende Papers; Rocket Technology; Space Defense
Subject Interests: Aeronaut, Aviation, Chem, Computer sci, Electrical eng, Electronics, Mechanical eng, Nuclear sci, Physics
Automation Activity & Vendor Info: (Cataloging) SirsiDynix; (Circulation) SirsiDynix; (OPAC) SirsiDynix
Function: Electronic databases & coll, ILL available, Microfiche/film & reading machines, Online cat, Ref serv available
Partic in Fedlink
Open Mon-Thurs 8-4
Restriction: Authorized personnel only

REFORM

P REFORM PUBLIC LIBRARY*, 302 First St S, 35481. (Mail add: PO Box 819, 35481-0819), SAN 324-0630. Tel: 205-375-6240. FAX: 205-375-6240. E-mail: rpl@nctv.com. Web Site: pickenslibrary.com/reform. *Dir,* Curtis Wheat; Staff 1 (Non-MLS 1)
Founded 1975. Pop 2,100; Circ 5,030
Library Holdings: Bk Vols 12,000; Per Subs 27
Automation Activity & Vendor Info: (Cataloging) Follett Software; (Circulation) Follett Software
Wireless access
Mem of Pickens County Cooperative Library
Open Mon, Thurs & Fri 9-12 & 1-5, Tues 9-12 & 1-7, Sat 9-Noon
Friends of the Library Group

ROANOKE

P ANNIE L AWBREY PUBLIC LIBRARY*, 736 College St, 36274-1617. SAN 300-1946. Tel: 334-863-2632. FAX: 334-863-8997. E-mail: annielawbrey@yahoo.com. *Dir,* Autum Hill; Staff 1 (MLS 1)
Founded 1934. Pop 20,400
Library Holdings: Bk Titles 21,000; Bk Vols 22,500; Per Subs 50
Special Collections: Adult Readers
Automation Activity & Vendor Info: (Cataloging) Follett Software; (Circulation) Follett Software
Mem of Cheaha Regional Library
Open Mon-Fri 9-12 & 1-5, Sat 9-12
Friends of the Library Group

ROBERTSDALE

P BALDWIN COUNTY LIBRARY COOPERATIVE, INC*, 22251 Palmer St, 36567. (Mail add: PO Box 399, 36567-0399), SAN 300-1954. Tel: 251-970-4010. FAX: 251-970-4011. Web Site: www.gulftel.com/bclc. *Dir,* Liz Reed; E-mail: bclcdirector@gulftel.com; *ILL,* Susan Koier; *Tech Serv,* Kim Mumbower; Staff 3 (Non-MLS 3)
Founded 1966. Pop 82,990
Oct 2005-Sept 2006 Income $188,736, State $76,618, County $76,618, Locally Generated Income $3,500, Parent Institution $30,000, Other $2,000. Mats Exp $3,900, Books $2,500, Per/Ser (Incl. Access Fees) $900, AV Mat $500. Sal $118,000 (Prof $33,500)
Library Holdings: AV Mats 889; Bks on Deafness & Sign Lang 39; DVDs 10; Large Print Bks 3,000; Bk Titles 17,129; Per Subs 86; Videos 187
Subject Interests: Adult educ
Automation Activity & Vendor Info: (Cataloging) TLC (The Library Corporation); (Circulation) TLC (The Library Corporation); (OPAC) TLC (The Library Corporation)
Function: ILL available, Ref serv available, Telephone ref
Member Libraries: Bay Minette Public Library; Daphne Public Library; Fairhope Public Library; Foley Public Library; Lillian Perdido Bay Library; Loxley Public Library; Orange Beach Public Library; Oscar Johnson Memorial Library; Robertsdale Public Library; Thomas B Norton Public Library
Open Mon-Fri 8-5:30
Bookmobiles: 1. Bk titles 3000

P ROBERTSDALE PUBLIC LIBRARY*, 18301 Pennsylvania St, 36567. SAN 300-1962. Tel: 251-947-8960. FAX: 251-947-5521. E-mail: library@robertsdale.org. Web Site: www.robertsdale.org. *Dir,* Cynthia Nall; *Asst Librn,* Joyce Allen
Founded 1914. Pop 3,600; Circ 51,000
Library Holdings: Bk Titles 30,000; Per Subs 60
Automation Activity & Vendor Info: (Cataloging) TLC (The Library Corporation); (Circulation) TLC (The Library Corporation); (OPAC) TLC (The Library Corporation)
Mem of Baldwin County Library Cooperative, Inc
Open Mon & Wed 9-6, Tues & Thurs 9-8, Fri 9-5, Sat 9-1

ROCKFORD

P ROCKFORD PUBLIC LIBRARY*, 9688 US Hwy 231, 35136. (Mail add: PO Box 128, 35136-0128), SAN 300-1970. Tel: 256-377-4911. FAX: 256-377-4489. *Librn,* Glenda Cardwell; E-mail: glenda@gcardwell.net
Founded 1962. Pop 480; Circ 5,140
Library Holdings: AV Mats 70; Bk Vols 4,600; Per Subs 19
Wireless access
Open Mon-Fri 7-5

ROGERSVILLE

P ROGERSVILLE PUBLIC LIBRARY*, 74 Bank St, 35652. (Mail add: PO Box 190, 35652-0190), SAN 300-1989. Tel: 256-247-0151. FAX: 256-247-0144. E-mail: information@rogersvillelibrary.org. Web Site: www.rogersvillelibrary.org. *Librn,* Teresa Garner; Staff 4 (MLS 1, Non-MLS 3)
Pop 11,000; Circ 35,359
Library Holdings: Bk Vols 26,000; Per Subs 32
Subject Interests: Genealogy
Automation Activity & Vendor Info: (Cataloging) Book Systems; (Circulation) Book Systems; (OPAC) Book Systems
Open Tues 9-7, Wed & Fri 9-5, Thurs 12-7, Sat 9-3
Friends of the Library Group

RUSSELLVILLE

P RUSSELLVILLE PUBLIC LIBRARY, 110 E Lawrence St, 35653. SAN 330-4175. Tel: 256-332-1535. E-mail: ruslib110@yahoo.com. *Libr Dir,* Ashley Copeland Cummins
Pop 25,000
Library Holdings: Bk Vols 16,500
Open Tues-Fri 10-5, Sat 10-2
Friends of the Library Group

SAMSON

P SAMSON PUBLIC LIBRARY*, 200 N Johnson St, 36477-2006. SAN 300-2012. Tel: 334-898-7806. FAX: 334-898-7806. *Librn,* Heather Beverley
Founded 1928. Pop 5,722; Circ 3,022
Library Holdings: CDs 154; Electronic Media & Resources 72; Large Print Bks 555; Bk Vols 8,641; Per Subs 15; Videos 75
Special Collections: 1500 Centenniel Photos Coll
Open Mon-Fri 10-12 & 1-5

SARDIS CITY

P SARDIS CITY PUBLIC LIBRARY*, 1310 Church St, 35956-2200. (Mail add: 1335 Sardis Dr, 35956-2862). Tel: 256-593-5634. FAX: 256-593-6258. *Librn,* Georgia Lipscomb
Library Holdings: Large Print Bks 200; Bk Vols 9,500; Per Subs 10
Partic in Lyrasis
Open Tues, Wed & Fri 1-5, Thurs & Sat 9-1

SATSUMA

P SATSUMA PUBLIC LIBRARY*, 5466 Old Hwy 43, 36572. (Mail add: PO Box 579, 36572-0579). Tel: 251-679-0700. FAX: 251-679-0973. Web Site: www.satsumalibrary.org. *Dir,* Cindy Ingram
Founded 1994
Library Holdings: Bk Titles 11,900; Bk Vols 13,000; Per Subs 21
Automation Activity & Vendor Info: (Acquisitions) Book Systems; (Cataloging) Book Systems; (Circulation) Book Systems; (Course Reserve) Book Systems; (OPAC) Book Systems
Wireless access
Open Mon, Wed & Fri 10-5, Tues & Thurs 10-6, Sat 9-2
Friends of the Library Group

SCOTTSBORO

P SCOTTSBORO PUBLIC LIBRARY*, 1002 S Broad St, 35768. SAN 300-2039. Tel: 256-574-4335. FAX: 256-259-4457. E-mail: scottsboropubliclibrary@gmail.com. Web Site: www.scottsborolibrary.org. *Librn,* Laura Pitts
Founded 1929. Pop 49,900; Circ 101,183
Library Holdings: Bk Vols 42,000; Per Subs 105
Special Collections: Alabama Genealogy Coll
Automation Activity & Vendor Info: (Cataloging) Innovative Interfaces, Inc; (Circulation) Innovative Interfaces, Inc; (OPAC) Innovative Interfaces, Inc
Open Mon-Thurs 9-6, Fri 9-5, Sat 9-1
Friends of the Library Group

SELMA

C CONCORDIA COLLEGE*, Ellwanger Hunt Learning Resource Center, 1712 Broad St, 36701. Tel: 334-874-5700, Ext 19745. FAX: 334-874-5755. Web Site: www.ccal.edu/?q=library. *Libr Dir,* Scott Whiting; Tel: 334-874-5700, Ext 19739, E-mail: jswhiting@ccal.edu; *Asst Librn,* Rosalind Harris; Tel: 334-874-5700, Ext 19734, E-mail: roharris@ccal.edu; *Asst Librn,* Joyce Kendrick; E-mail: jkendrick@ccal.edu; *Asst Librn,* Minnie McMillan; Staff 2 (MLS 2)
Founded 1980. Enrl 500; Fac 45; Highest Degree: Bachelor
Library Holdings: Bk Vols 55,000
Automation Activity & Vendor Info: (Acquisitions) Follett Software; (Cataloging) Follett Software; (Circulation) Follett Software; (Course Reserve) Follett Software; (ILL) OCLC FirstSearch; (Media Booking) Follett Software; (OPAC) Follett Software; (Serials) EBSCO Online
Database Vendor: Alexander Street Press, Gale Cengage Learning, H W Wilson, LexisNexis, OCLC FirstSearch, OCLC WorldShare Interlibrary Loan, ProQuest, Wilson - Wilson Web
Wireless access
Function: Computers for patron use, Copy machines, Electronic databases & coll, Exhibits, Handicapped accessible, ILL available, Instruction & testing, Literacy & newcomer serv, Online info literacy tutorials on the web & in blackboard, Online ref, Online searches, Orientations, Photocopying/Printing, Wheelchair accessible
Partic in Lyrasis; OCLC Online Computer Library Center, Inc
Open Mon-Thurs 8am-9pm, Fri 8-5, Sat 8-2; Mon-Fri (Summer) 8-5
Restriction: Access at librarian's discretion

P PUBLIC LIBRARY OF SELMA & DALLAS COUNTY*, 1103 Selma Ave, 36703-4445. SAN 300-2055. Tel: 334-874-1725. FAX: 334-874-1729. Web Site: www.selmalibrary.org. *Dir,* Becky Nichols; E-mail: becky@selmalibrary.org
Founded 1903. Pop 45,000; Circ 142,586
Library Holdings: Bk Titles 72,568; Bk Vols 72,701; Per Subs 61
Subject Interests: Local hist
Automation Activity & Vendor Info: (Cataloging) SirsiDynix; (Circulation) SirsiDynix; (OPAC) SirsiDynix
Open Mon-Sat 9-5
Friends of the Library Group

C SELMA UNIVERSITY*, Stone-Robinson Library, 1501 Lapsley St, 36701. SAN 300-2063. Tel: 334-874-7673. FAX: 334-872-7746. E-mail: selmau4@bellsouth.net. Web Site: selmauniversity.org/library.htm. *Dir,* Edna Green; E-mail: green_edna@yahoo.com
Founded 1959. Highest Degree: Master
Library Holdings: Bk Titles 23,000; Per Subs 154
Special Collections: Black Studies Coll
Wireless access
Open Mon, Wed & Thurs 8-5, Tues 8-7, Fri 8-2:30

J WALLACE COMMUNITY COLLEGE, Selma Library, 3000 Earl Goodwin Pkwy, 36701. (Mail add: PO Box 2530, 36702-2530), SAN 300-2047. Tel: 334-876-9344, 334-876-9345. FAX: 334-876-9314. Web Site: www.wccs.edu/library.html. *Dir,* Minnie Carstarphen; E-mail: minnie.carstarphen@wccs.edu; *Asst Librn,* Glenda Davis; *Asst Librn,* Brenda Powell; Staff 4 (MLS 3, Non-MLS 1)
Founded 1974. Enrl 1,976; Fac 60; Highest Degree: Associate
Oct 2013-Sept 2014 Income $182,741. Mats Exp $24,751, Books $8,260, Per/Ser (Incl. Access Fees) $7,244, Other Print Mats $1,332, AV Mat $1,915, Electronic Ref Mat (Incl. Access Fees) $6,000. Sal $121,698 (Prof $57,689)
Library Holdings: AV Mats 975; CDs 220; e-books 104; Bk Vols 21,892; Per Subs 70; Videos 680
Subject Interests: Lit, Nursing, Soc sci & issues
Automation Activity & Vendor Info: (Cataloging) MITINET, Inc; (Circulation) Follett Software; (OPAC) Follett Software
Database Vendor: EBSCO Information Services, EBSCOhost, MITINET, Inc, OCLC FirstSearch, OCLC WorldShare Interlibrary Loan, ProQuest
Wireless access
Function: Res libr
Publications: Audio-Visual Catalog; Library Handbook; Nursing Video Catalog; Periodical Catalog
Open Mon-Thurs 7am-8:30pm, Fri 7-Noon
Restriction: Open to students, fac & staff

SHEFFIELD

P SHEFFIELD PUBLIC LIBRARY*, 316 N Montgomery Ave, 35660. SAN 300-2101. Tel: 256-386-5633. FAX: 256-386-5608. Web Site: www1.youseemore.com/sheffieldpl. *Dir,* Beth Ridgeway; *Cat,* Sandy Kirsch; *Ch Serv,* Lynne Martin; *Tech Serv,* Evallou Richardson
Pop 15,000; Circ 52,125
Library Holdings: e-books 27,000; Bk Vols 57,000; Per Subs 50
Special Collections: Local History & Genealogy Coll
Automation Activity & Vendor Info: (Cataloging) Innovative Interfaces, Inc; (Circulation) Innovative Interfaces, Inc; (OPAC) Innovative Interfaces, Inc
Open Mon-Fri 9-5
Friends of the Library Group

SILVERHILL

P OSCAR JOHNSON MEMORIAL LIBRARY*, 21967 Sixth St, 36576. (Mail add: PO Box 309, 36576-0309). Tel: 251-945-5201. Web Site: www.gulftel.com/bclc/bclibraries/silverhi.htm. *Librn,* Tonja Young; E-mail: tonjadpl@bellsouth.net; Staff 1 (Non-MLS 1)
Founded 1907. Pop 630; Circ 3,050
Library Holdings: Bk Vols 10,000
Mem of Baldwin County Library Cooperative, Inc
Open Mon 2-7, Tues, Wed & Fri 2-4, Thurs 10-5, Sat 1-4

SLOCOMB

P SLOCOMB PUBLIC LIBRARY*, 134 S Dalton St, 36375. (Mail add: PO Box 1026, 36375-1026), SAN 376-7418. Tel: 334-886-9009. E-mail: slocomb.library@yahoo.com. *Librn,* Kacey Dillon
Library Holdings: Bk Vols 8,000
Wireless access
Open Mon-Fri 1-5

SPRINGVILLE

S ALABAMA DEPARTMENT OF CORRECTIONS*, St Clair Correctional Facility Library, 1000 Saint Clair Rd, 35146-9790. Tel: 205-467-6111, Ext 610. *Librn,* Keith Cunningham
Founded 1983
Library Holdings: Bk Vols 7,000
Database Vendor: Westlaw
Open Mon-Sun 9-7:30

STEVENSON

P STEVENSON PUBLIC LIBRARY*, 102 W Main St, 35772. SAN 374-4507. Tel: 256-437-3008. FAX: 256-437-0031. *Librn,* Monica Davis
Library Holdings: Bk Vols 12,000; Per Subs 40
Automation Activity & Vendor Info: (Cataloging) Follett Software; (Circulation) Follett Software
Open Mon-Wed & Fri 10-5, Thurs 1-5, Sat 10-2
Friends of the Library Group

SUMITON

J BEVILL STATE COMMUNITY COLLEGE*, Sumiton Campus Library, 101 S State St, 35148. (Mail add: PO Box 800, 35148-0800). Tel: 205-648-3271. Information Services Tel: 205-648-3271, Ext 5238. Toll Free Tel: 800-648-3271. FAX: 205-648-7152. Web Site: www.bscc.edu. *Dir,* Tyrone Webb; E-mail: twebb@bscc.edu
Founded 1965. Enrl 1,800; Fac 75; Highest Degree: Associate
Library Holdings: AV Mats 1,250; Bk Titles 25,000; Per Subs 75; Talking Bks 54
Automation Activity & Vendor Info: (Cataloging) Follett Software; (Circulation) Follett Software; (OPAC) Follett Software
Function: ILL available, Photocopying/Printing, Ref serv available
Open Mon-Thurs 7:30am-8:30pm, Fri 7:30-3:30

P SUMITON PUBLIC LIBRARY*, Town Hall, 416 State St, 35148. (Mail add: PO Box 10, 35148-0010), SAN 300-2136. Tel: 205-648-7451. FAX: 205-648-7451. *Dir,* Sharon Black
Pop 4,000
Library Holdings: e-books 4,000; Bk Titles 9,000
Wireless access
Mem of Carl Elliott Regional Library System
Open Mon-Thurs 8-12 & 1-5, Fri 8-12 & 1-4

SYLACAUGA

P B B COMER MEMORIAL LIBRARY*, 314 N Broadway, 35150-2528. SAN 300-2144. Tel: 256-249-0961. Web Site: www.sylacauga.net/library. *Dir,* Dr Shirley K Spears; E-mail: sspears@sylacauga.net; *Asst Dir,* Tracey Thomas; Staff 2 (MLS 2)
Founded 1939
Library Holdings: Bk Vols 100,000; Per Subs 170
Special Collections: Alabama History Coll
Subject Interests: Genealogy
Automation Activity & Vendor Info: (Cataloging) Innovative Interfaces, Inc; (Circulation) Innovative Interfaces, Inc; (OPAC) Innovative Interfaces, Inc
Open Mon, Wed & Fri 9-5, Tues & Thurs 9-7:30, Sat 9-3, Sun 1-4

TALLADEGA

P ALABAMA INSTITUTE FOR THE DEAF & BLIND*, Library & Resource Center for the Blind & Physically Handicapped, 705 South St, 35160. (Mail add: PO Box 698, 35161), SAN 300-2152. Tel: 256-761-3237. FAX: 256-761-3561. Toll Free FAX: 800-848-4722. Web Site: www.aidb.org. *Dir,* Teresa Lacy; E-mail: lacy.teresa@aidb.state.al.us; *Reader Serv,* Carol Fowler; E-mail: fowler.carol@aidb.state.al.us; Staff 2 (MLS 1, Non-MLS 1)
Founded 1965. Circ 20,000
Library Holdings: Bk Vols 60,000; Per Subs 62
Special Collections: Alabama History, cassettes
Automation Activity & Vendor Info: (Acquisitions) Book Systems; (Cataloging) Book Systems; (Circulation) Book Systems; (Course Reserve) Book Systems; (ILL) Book Systems; (Media Booking) Book Systems; (OPAC) Book Systems; (Serials) Book Systems
Wireless access
Publications: Newsletter (irregular)
Special Services for the Blind - Bks on cassette; Braille bks; Large print bks
Friends of the Library Group

C TALLADEGA COLLEGE*, Savery Library, 627 W Battle St, 35160. SAN 300-2160. Tel: 256-761-6279. FAX: 256-362-0497. Web Site: www.talladega.edu. *Librn,* Juliette S Smith; E-mail: jssmith@talladega.edu; Staff 2 (MLS 2)
Founded 1939. Enrl 706; Fac 30; Highest Degree: Bachelor
Library Holdings: Bk Titles 120,687; Per Subs 211
Special Collections: Amistad Mutiny - Murals; Black Studies; Talladega Historical Coll. Oral History
Automation Activity & Vendor Info: (Acquisitions) Innovative Interfaces, Inc; (Cataloging) Innovative Interfaces, Inc; (Circulation) Innovative Interfaces, Inc; (OPAC) Innovative Interfaces, Inc
Wireless access
Publications: New Acquisitions; Student Handbook
Partic in Lyrasis; Network of Alabama Academic Libraries
Open Mon-Thurs 8am-10pm, Fri 8-5, Sat 10-6, Sun 1:30-9:30
Friends of the Library Group

GL TALLADEGA COUNTY LAW LIBRARY*, Talladega County Judicial Bldg, Northeast St, 35161. (Mail add: PO Box 459, 35161-0459), SAN 300-2179. Tel: 256-761-2116. FAX: 256-480-5293. *Librn,* Megan Campbell; *Librn,* Cindy Currie
Founded 1955
Library Holdings: Bk Vols 35,000; Per Subs 100
Wireless access
Open Mon-Fri 8-4

P TALLADEGA PUBLIC LIBRARY*, 202 South St E, 35160. SAN 300-2187. Tel: 256-362-4211. FAX: 256-362-0653. E-mail: talladeg@yahoo.com. *Librn,* Vickie Harkins; E-mail: yardbrough@yahoo.com; Staff 7 (MLS 1, Non-MLS 6)
Founded 1906. Pop 72,601; Circ 118,641
Library Holdings: Bk Vols 100,000; Per Subs 100
Special Collections: Talladega History & Alabana History
Automation Activity & Vendor Info: (Cataloging) Book Systems; (Circulation) Book Systems
Open Mon-Thurs 9-6, Fri 9-4, Sat 9-3

TALLASSEE

P TALLASSEE COMMUNITY LIBRARY*, 99 S Freeman Ave, 36078. SAN 300-2195. Tel: 334-283-2732. FAX: 334-283-2732. E-mail: tallasseecitylib@gmail.com. *Librn,* Sharon Johnson
Pop 5,500; Circ 18,750
Library Holdings: Bk Titles 20,000; Per Subs 15
Automation Activity & Vendor Info: (Cataloging) Follett Software; (Circulation) Follett Software
Mem of Horseshoe Bend Regional Library
Open Tues-Sat 11-6

TARRANT

P TARRANT PUBLIC LIBRARY*, 1143 Ford Ave, 35217-2437. SAN 300-2209. Tel: 205-849-2825. Web Site: www.tarrant.lib.al.us. *Librn,* Patrick Coleman; E-mail: pjc6165@hotmail.com
Founded 1930. Pop 8,046
Library Holdings: Bk Vols 31,000; Per Subs 66

Special Collections: Arrowhead Coll; Petrified Wood; Shell Coll
Subject Interests: Ala
Automation Activity & Vendor Info: (Cataloging) Innovative Interfaces, Inc; (Circulation) Innovative Interfaces, Inc; (OPAC) Innovative Interfaces, Inc
Publications: Newsletter
Open Mon-Fri 8-5, Sat 8-12

THOMASVILLE

P THOMASVILLE PUBLIC LIBRARY*, 1401 Mosley Dr, 36784. SAN 300-2225. Tel: 334-636-5343. FAX: 334-636-4305. E-mail: tvillelibrary@gmail.com. Web Site: www.thomasvillepubliclibrary.org. *Dir,* Gina Wilson; *Asst Dir, Youth Serv Librn,* Melanie Cornelson; E-mail: tplkids@bellsouth.net; *Tech Serv & Automation,* Ruby Hightower; E-mail: tpltech@bellsouth.net; Staff 6 (MLS 1, Non-MLS 5)
Pop 5,000; Circ 33,200
Oct 2005-Sept 2006 Income $130,733, State $10,543, City $98,190, Federal $4,000, Locally Generated Income $18,000. Mats Exp $27,700, Books $16,400, Per/Ser (Incl. Access Fees) $800, Other Print Mats $3,500, AV Mat $7,000. Sal $101,379 (Prof $37,000)
Library Holdings: CDs 71; DVDs 22; Large Print Bks 1,054; Bk Titles 19,133; Bk Vols 23,503; Per Subs 21; Videos 659
Automation Activity & Vendor Info: (Acquisitions) Book Systems; (Cataloging) Book Systems; (Circulation) Book Systems; (ILL) OCLC FirstSearch; (OPAC) Book Systems
Wireless access
Function: Bk club(s), e-mail serv, Home delivery & serv to Sr ctr & nursing homes, ILL available, Prog for children & young adult, Ref serv available, Senior computer classes, Spoken cassettes & CDs, Spoken cassettes & DVDs, Summer reading prog, Tax forms
Open Mon, Wed & Fri 9-5, Tues & Thurs 9-7, Sat 9-1
Friends of the Library Group

TROY

P TROY PUBLIC LIBRARY*, 300 N Three Notch St, 36081. SAN 330-3152. Tel: 334-566-1314. FAX: 334-566-4392. Web Site: publiclibrary.troy.al.us. *Dir,* William White; E-mail: wwhite@troycitylibrary.org; *Asst Dir,* Karen Bullard; Staff 8 (MLS 1, Non-MLS 7)
Pop 29,605
Library Holdings: AV Mats 528; Large Print Bks 3,342; Bk Titles 75,000; Per Subs 136; Talking Bks 2,771
Subject Interests: Antiques, Genealogy, State hist
Automation Activity & Vendor Info: (Cataloging) Book Systems; (Circulation) Book Systems; (OPAC) Book Systems
Open Mon & Wed (Winter) 9-5:30, Tues & Thurs 9-8, Fri 9-5, Sat 9-3; Mon-Thurs (Summer) 9-5:30, Fri 9-5, Sat 9-3
Friends of the Library Group

C TROY UNIVERSITY LIBRARY*, 309 Wallace Hall, 501 University Ave, 36082. SAN 330-3489. Tel: 334-670-3266. Interlibrary Loan Service Tel: 334-670-3256. Reference Tel: 334-670-3255. Automation Services Tel: 334-670-3470. FAX: 334-670-3694. Reference FAX: 334-670-3955. E-mail: libhelp@troy.edu. Web Site: trojan.troy.edu/library/. *Dean, Univ Libr,* Dr Henry R Stewart; Tel: 334-670-3263, E-mail: hstewart@troy.edu; *Head, Ref & Pub Serv,* Dr William Garrett; Tel: 334-670-3257, E-mail: wagarrett@troy.edu; *Global Campus Librn,* Jay Brandes; Tel: 334-670-6344, E-mail: jayb777@troy.edu; *Ref Librn,* Rachel Hooper; Tel: 334-670-3269, E-mail: hooperr@troy.edu; *Acq,* Jana Slay; Tel: 334-670-3258, E-mail: jslay@troy.edu; *Cataloger,* Ruth E Elder; Tel: 334-670-3874, E-mail: relder@troy.edu; *ILL,* Belinda C Edwards; E-mail: bedwards@troy.edu; *Ref,* Brian Webb; Tel: 334-670-3198, E-mail: bwebb@troy.edu; *Ref Serv,* Dr Kristine Stillwell; Tel: 334-670-3261; *Ref Serv,* Lisa Vardaman; Tel: 334-670-3262, E-mail: lisavardaman@troy.edu. Subject Specialists: *Humanities,* Dr William Garrett; *Bus,* Rachel Hooper; *Sci,* Brian Webb; *Govt doc, Soc sci,* Dr Kristine Stillwell; *Educ,* Lisa Vardaman; Staff 10 (MLS 9, Non-MLS 1)
Founded 1887. Enrl 7,500; Fac 524; Highest Degree: Doctorate
Oct 2013-Sept 2014 Income $10,000. Mats Exp $1,004,000, Books $175,000, Per/Ser (Incl. Access Fees) $260,000, Micro $61,000, AV Mat $18,000, Electronic Ref Mat (Incl. Access Fees) $480,000, Presv $10,000. Sal $1,312,584 (Prof $518,936)
Library Holdings: Audiobooks 369; AV Mats 42,809; Bks on Deafness & Sign Lang 160; CDs 960; DVDs 4,745; e-books 79,184; e-journals 4; Microforms 1,217,631; Music Scores 1,830; Bk Vols 571,152; Per Subs 1,902; Talking Bks 15
Special Collections: Alabamiana. US Document Depository
Subject Interests: Educ, Indians
Automation Activity & Vendor Info: (Acquisitions) SirsiDynix; (Cataloging) OCLC Connexion; (Circulation) SirsiDynix; (Course Reserve) SirsiDynix; (ILL) OCLC ILLiad; (OPAC) SirsiDynix; (Serials) SirsiDynix
Database Vendor: Alexander Street Press, American Chemical Society, American Mathematical Society, Baker & Taylor, BioOne, Bowker, CQ Press, CredoReference, Ebooks Corporation, EBSCOhost, Elsevier, Emerald, Gale Cengage Learning, H W Wilson, JSTOR, LearningExpress, LexisNexis, Majors, Medline, Newsbank, OCLC FirstSearch, OCLC WorldShare Interlibrary Loan, OVID Technologies, Oxford Online, ProQuest, PubMed, Safari Books Online, SBRnet (Sports Business Research Network), ScienceDirect, SerialsSolutions, Westlaw, Wiley InterScience, Wilson - Wilson Web
Wireless access
Function: Wheelchair accessible
Partic in Lyrasis; NAAL; OCLC Online Computer Library Center, Inc
Open Mon-Wed 8am-Midnight, Thurs 8am-11pm, Fri 8-6, Sat 10-5, Sun 2-Midnight

TRUSSVILLE

P TRUSSVILLE PUBLIC LIBRARY*, 201 Parkway Dr, 35173. SAN 300-2241. Tel: 205-655-2022. FAX: 205-661-1645. Web Site: www.trussvillelibrary.com. *Dir,* Emily Tish; E-mail: etish@bham.lib.al.us
Circ 50,000
Library Holdings: Bk Vols 60,000; Per Subs 95
Special Collections: Trussville & Alabama History Coll
Automation Activity & Vendor Info: (Cataloging) Innovative Interfaces, Inc; (Circulation) Innovative Interfaces, Inc; (OPAC) Innovative Interfaces, Inc
Open Mon & Tues 9-8, Wed & Fri 9-6, Sat 10-4, Sun 1-5
Friends of the Library Group

TUSCALOOSA

GM DEPARTMENT OF VETERANS AFFAIRS*, Hospital Medical Center Library, 3701 Loop Rd E, 35404. SAN 300-2284. Tel: 205-554-2000, Ext 2355. FAX: 205-554-2033. *Libr Tech,* Ruby Brown; E-mail: ruby.brown@va.gov
Founded 1932
Library Holdings: Bk Vols 1,000; Per Subs 75
Special Collections: Alcoholism Coll, bk & tapes; Community Mental Health Coll, bks & tapes; Psychiatry Coll, bks & tapes
Subject Interests: Geriatrics & gerontology
Partic in Veterans Affairs Libr Network (VALNET)
Open Mon-Fri 8-4:30

G GEOLOGICAL SURVEY OF ALABAMA LIBRARY, Walter Bryan Jones Hall, 420 Hackberry Lane, 35401. (Mail add: PO Box 869999, 35486-6999), SAN 300-2322. Tel: 205-247-3634. FAX: 205-349-2861. E-mail: library@gsa.state.al.us. Web Site: www.gsa.state.al.us. Staff 1 (MLS 1)
Founded 1873
Library Holdings: Bk Titles 150,911
Special Collections: Aerial Photography; Satellite Imagery for Alabama
Subject Interests: Geol, Paleontology
Publications: Bibliographies; publications of the Geological Survey of Alabama & State Oil & Gas Board
Open Mon-Fri 8-5

J SHELTON STATE COMMUNITY COLLEGE, Brooks-Cork Library, Martin Campus, 9500 Old Greensboro Rd, 35405. SAN 300-225X. Tel: 205-391-3925. Administration Tel: 205-391-2233. FAX: 205-391-3926. E-mail: library@sheltonstate.edu. Web Site: www.sheltonstate.edu/libraries.aspx. *Dir,* Position Currently Open; *Asst Dir, Libr Serv, Electronic Res Librn,* Kelly Ann Griffiths; Tel: 205-391-2268, E-mail: kgriffiths@sheltonstate.edu; *Evening Librn,* Don C Bell; Tel: 205-391-2245, E-mail: dbell@sheltonstate.edu; *Coll Mgt, Pub Serv Librn,* Glen Johnson; Tel: 205-391-2327, E-mail: gjohnson@sheltonstate.edu; *AV,* Jean Epps; Tel: 205-391-2970, E-mail: jepps@sheltonstate.edu; *Cat,* Liz Jones; Tel: 205-391-2405, E-mail: ejones@sheltonsate.edu; *Circ,* Tracy Williams; Tel: 205-391-2203, E-mail: twilliams@sheltonstate.edu; *Outreach Serv,* Tamara Gainous; Tel: 205-391-2248, E-mail: tgainous@sheltonstate.edu; Staff 9 (MLS 4, Non-MLS 5)
Founded 1979. Enrl 5,072; Fac 95; Highest Degree: Associate
Library Holdings: AV Mats 3,000; DVDs 175; e-books 17,000; Bk Vols 50,000; Per Subs 375; Videos 1,600
Special Collections: Lon Alexander Sr Coll; Phifer Family Coll
Automation Activity & Vendor Info: (Acquisitions) Innovative Interfaces, Inc; (Cataloging) Innovative Interfaces, Inc; (Circulation) Innovative Interfaces, Inc; (Course Reserve) Innovative Interfaces, Inc; (ILL) OCLC; (Media Booking) Innovative Interfaces, Inc; (OPAC) Innovative Interfaces, Inc
Database Vendor: 3M Library Systems, Baker & Taylor, Blackwell, Bowker, Brodart, EBSCO Information Services, Gale Cengage Learning, H W Wilson, ProQuest, Wilson - Wilson Web
Wireless access
Partic in HBCU Library Alliance; Lyrasis; OCLC Online Computer Library Center, Inc
Special Services for the Deaf - ADA equip

Special Services for the Blind - Accessible computers
Open Mon-Thurs 7:30am-10pm, Fri 8-Noon

C STILLMAN COLLEGE*, William H Sheppard Library, 3601 Stillman Blvd, 35403. (Mail add: PO Box 1430, 35403-1430), SAN 300-2268. Tel: 205-366-8851. FAX: 205-247-8042. Web Site: www.stillman.edu. *Dean,* Robert Heath; E-mail: rheath@stillman.edu; Staff 5 (MLS 4, Non-MLS 1)
Founded 1876. Enrl 1,065; Fac 71; Highest Degree: Bachelor
Library Holdings: Bk Vols 118,000
Special Collections: Afro-American Coll; Black History & Literature, 19th Century & Early 20th Century (microfilm). Oral History
Subject Interests: Relig
Automation Activity & Vendor Info: (Cataloging) Ex Libris Group; (Circulation) Ex Libris Group; (OPAC) Ex Libris Group
Database Vendor: Gale Cengage Learning, JSTOR, Wilson - Wilson Web
Wireless access
Partic in OCLC Online Computer Library Center, Inc
Open Mon-Thurs 8am-Midnight, Fri 8-5, Sat 10-2, Sun 5pm-Midnight

P TUSCALOOSA PUBLIC LIBRARY, 1801 Jack Warner Pkwy, 35401-1027. SAN 330-3519. Tel: 205-345-5820. FAX: 205-758-1735. Web Site: www.tuscaloosa-library.org. *Interim Dir,* Rick Freeman; Tel: 205-345-5820, Ext 1102; *Dir, Pub Affairs & Communication,* Vince Bellofatto; Tel: 205-345-5820, Ext 1110, E-mail: vbellofatto@tuscaloosa-library.org; Staff 48 (MLS 11, Non-MLS 37)
Founded 1921. Pop 192,000
Library Holdings: Bk Vols 186,595; Per Subs 700
Subject Interests: Genealogy, Local hist
Automation Activity & Vendor Info: (Acquisitions) Innovative Interfaces, Inc - Sierra; (Cataloging) Innovative Interfaces, Inc - Sierra; (Circulation) Innovative Interfaces, Inc - Sierra; (ILL) Innovative Interfaces, Inc - Sierra; (OPAC) Innovative Interfaces, Inc - Sierra; (Serials) Innovative Interfaces, Inc - Sierra
Wireless access
Open Mon-Thurs 9-9, Fri 12-5, Sat 9-5, Sun 2-6
Friends of the Library Group
Branches: 2
BROWN LIBRARY, 300 Bobby Miller Pkwy, 35405. Tel: 205-391-9989. FAX: 205-391-9355. *Head Librn,* Kelly Butler; Staff 3 (MLS 1, Non-MLS 2)
Open Mon, Wed & Thurs 10-6, Tues 1-8, Fri 1-5
WEAVER-BOLDEN LIBRARY, 2522 Lanier Ave, 35401, SAN 330-3578. Tel: 205-758-8291. FAX: 205-464-0906. *Head Librn,* Marti Ball
Open Mon-Thurs 9-7, Fri 1-5
Friends of the Library Group
Bookmobiles: 2

CM UNIVERSITY OF ALABAMA*, Health Sciences Library, 850 Fifth Ave E, 35401. (Mail add: Box 870378, 35487-0378), SAN 330-3608. Tel: 205-348-1360. FAX: 205-348-9563. *Libr Dir,* Nelle Williams; Tel: 205-348-1364, E-mail: nwilliam@cchs.ua.edu; *Tech Serv & Syst Librn,* Suhua Fan
Founded 1973. Enrl 22,000; Fac 1,122; Highest Degree: Doctorate
Library Holdings: Bk Vols 17,863; Per Subs 295
Subject Interests: Med, Nursing
Automation Activity & Vendor Info: (Cataloging) Ex Libris Group; (Circulation) Ex Libris Group; (OPAC) Ex Libris Group
Wireless access
Partic in Association of Southeastern Research Libraries; Lyrasis; National Network of Libraries of Medicine; Network of Alabama Academic Libraries; OCLC Online Computer Library Center, Inc
Open Mon-Thurs 8am-9:30pm, Fri 8-4:45

UNIVERSITY OF ALABAMA
CL SCHOOL OF LAW LIBRARY*, 101 Paul Bryant Dr, 35487. (Mail add: Box 870383, 35487-0383), SAN 330-3969. Tel: 205-348-5925. Reference Tel: 205-348-1114. FAX: 205-348-1112. Web Site: www.law.ua.edu. *Dir,* James Leonard; E-mail: jleonard@law.ua.edu; *Assoc Dir,* Robert Marshall; *Asst Dir,* Ruth Weeks; *Head, Ref (Info Serv),* Iain Barksdale; *Cat,* Julie Griffith-Kees; *Coll Develop,* Paul Pruitt; *Computer Serv,* David Lowe; *Curator of Archival Coll,* David Durham; *Ref,* Penny Gibson; Staff 9 (MLS 8, Non-MLS 1)
Founded 1872. Enrl 592; Fac 35; Highest Degree: Doctorate
Library Holdings: Bk Titles 134,603; Bk Vols 438,444; Per Subs 3,368
Special Collections: Former US Senator Howell Heflin; Former US Supreme Court Justice Hugo L Black
Automation Activity & Vendor Info: (Acquisitions) Innovative Interfaces, Inc; (Cataloging) Innovative Interfaces, Inc; (Circulation) Innovative Interfaces, Inc; (Course Reserve) Innovative Interfaces, Inc; (OPAC) Innovative Interfaces, Inc; (Serials) Innovative Interfaces, Inc
Database Vendor: LexisNexis, Westlaw
Partic in Association of Research Libraries (ARL); Dialog Corp; NAAL; Westlaw
Publications: CASE; User Guides Series
Open Mon-Fri 7:30am-Midnight, Sat 9am-10pm, Sun 10am-Midnight

C UNIVERSITY LIBRARIES*, University of Alabama Campus, Capstone Dr, 35487. (Mail add: Box 870266, 35487-0266), SAN 330-3845. Tel: 205-348-7561. Circulation Tel: 205-348-9748. Interlibrary Loan Service Tel: 205-348-6345. Reference Tel: 205-348-6047. Automation Services Tel: 205-348-4608. FAX: 205-348-8833. Interlibrary Loan Service FAX: 205-348-9564. Reference FAX: 205-348-0760. Web Site: www.lib.ua.edu. *Dean of Libr,* Dr Louis A Pitschmann; E-mail: lpitschm@bama.ua.edu; *Assoc Dean,* Karen Croneis; Tel: 205-348-5569, E-mail: kcroneis@bama.ua.edu; *Head, Acq,* Beth Holley; Tel: 205-348-1493, Fax: 205-348-6358, E-mail: bholley@bama.ua.edu; *Curator,* Clark Center; Tel: 205-348-0513, Fax: 205-348-1699, E-mail: ccenter@bama.ua.edu; Staff 46 (MLS 40, Non-MLS 6)
Founded 1831. Enrl 23,878; Fac 811; Highest Degree: Doctorate
Library Holdings: e-books 40,389; e-journals 73,449; Bk Vols 2,175,700; Per Subs 29,374
Special Collections: 17th & 18th Century Cartography (Warner Map Coll); Alabama & Southern Manuscripts & University Archives; Confederate Imprints Coll; David Walker Lupton African American Cookbook Coll; First Editions (19th Century Literature Coll); Rucker Agee Coll of Alabamiana; Sheet Music Coll; Southern Americana Coll; Southern History & Culture (Wade Hall Coll), photogs, sound rec; William Campbell March & Numerous Southern Authors Coll; World War II Armed Services Editions. State Document Depository; US Document Depository
Automation Activity & Vendor Info: (Acquisitions) Ex Libris Group; (Cataloging) Ex Libris Group; (Circulation) Ex Libris Group; (Course Reserve) Ex Libris Group; (OPAC) Ex Libris Group; (Serials) Ex Libris Group
Database Vendor: EBSCOhost, Gale Cengage Learning, LexisNexis, OCLC FirstSearch, OVID Technologies, ProQuest, Wilson - Wilson Web
Partic in Association of Southeastern Research Libraries; Lyrasis
Publications: Library Horizons (Newsletter)
Special Services for the Deaf - TTY equip
Special Services for the Blind - Assistive/Adapted tech devices, equip & products
Open Mon-Thurs 7:45am-Midnight, Sat 10-8, Sun 1pm-Midnight
Friends of the Library Group

R UNIVERSITY PRESBYTERIAN CHURCH*, Ann Inglett Library, 1127 Eighth St, 35401. SAN 300-2276. Tel: 205-758-5422. FAX: 205-758-5422. E-mail: upsa@bellsouth.net. Web Site: bama.ua.edu/~upsa. *Librn,* Nancy Dupree
Founded 1964
Library Holdings: Bk Vols 4,000; Per Subs 10
Subject Interests: Biblical studies, Relig, Sociol, Theol

TUSCUMBIA

P HELEN KELLER PUBLIC LIBRARY, 511 N Main St, 35674. SAN 300-2292. Tel: 256-383-7065. FAX: 256-389-9057. Web Site: www2.youseemore.com/helenkeller. *Librn,* Heather McWilliams; E-mail: heather.mcwilliams@comcast.net; Staff 3 (Non-MLS 3)
Founded 1893. Pop 9,137; Circ 48,220
Oct 2006-Sept 2007 Income $106,809. Mats Exp $19,486. Sal $45,312
Library Holdings: AV Mats 1,120; e-books 27,000; Bk Vols 22,664; Per Subs 25; Talking Bks 836
Automation Activity & Vendor Info: (Cataloging) TLC (The Library Corporation); (Circulation) TLC (The Library Corporation); (OPAC) TLC (The Library Corporation)
Wireless access
Partic in Library Management Network, Inc
Open Mon & Thurs 10-6, Tues, Wed & Fri 10-5
Friends of the Library Group

TUSKEGEE

P MACON COUNTY-TUSKEGEE PUBLIC LIBRARY*, 302 S Main St, 36083-1894. SAN 330-3667. Tel: 334-727-5192. FAX: 334-727-5989. *Libr Dir,* Pepre Bridges; Staff 2 (Non-MLS 2)
Founded 1968. Pop 25,000
Library Holdings: Bk Vols 26,000; Per Subs 63
Special Collections: Children's Literature (Sammy Young Coll), A-tapes, fs, flm
Publications: American Libraries; Library Journal; Library Scene
Open Mon & Wed 9-6, Tues & Thurs 1-6, Fri 9-4:30
Friends of the Library Group

C TUSKEGEE UNIVERSITY*, Ford Motor Company Library-Learning Resource Center, Hollis Burke Frissell Bldg, 1200 W Old Montgomery Rd, 36088. SAN 330-3721. Tel: 334-727-8892, 334-727-8894. Circulation Tel: 334-724-4744, 334-727-8900. Interlibrary Loan Service Tel: 334-724-4688, 334-727-8895. Reference Tel: 334-724-4231, 334-727-8896. Automation Services Tel: 334-724-4740. FAX: 334-727-9282. Web Site:

www.tuskegee.edu/libraries. *Dir, Libr Serv - Univ Archives & Mus,* Juanita M Roberts; E-mail: jroberts@mytu.tuskegee.edu; *Head, Cat & Tech Serv,* Deborah Haile; Tel: 334-727-8898, E-mail: deborahhaile@hotmail.com; *Head, Circ & Reserves,* Brother Deloris Player; Tel: 334-727-8900, E-mail: dplayer@mytu.tuskegee.edu; *Head, Ref Serv,* Eunice G Samuel; E-mail: gbanks@mytu.tuskegee.edu; *Archit Librn,* Shakuntala Singh; Tel: 334-727-4572; *Eng Librn,* Leigh Jones; Tel: 334-727-8901; *Govt Doc/Ref Librn,* Asteria Ndulute; Tel: 334-727-8891, E-mail: ndulutea@mytu.tuskegee.edu; *Media/Ser/ILL Librn,* Rose Frazier; *Veterinary Med Librn,* Margaret Alexander; Tel: 334-727-8780, Fax: 334-727-8442; *Curator,* Dr Jontyule Robinson; Tel: 334-727-8888, Fax: 334-725-2400; *Info Literacy,* Charlene Major; Tel: 334-727-8676; *Spec Coll,* Lakishia Richardson; Tel: 334-727-8890; *Univ Archivist,* Dana Chandler; E-mail: dchalder@mytu.tuskegee.edu; Staff 9 (MLS 9)
Founded 1881. Enrl 3,000; Highest Degree: Doctorate
Library Holdings: Bk Vols 310,000; Per Subs 1,500
Special Collections: Blacks (Washington Coll). US Document Depository
Automation Activity & Vendor Info: (Acquisitions) SirsiDynix; (Cataloging) SirsiDynix; (Circulation) SirsiDynix; (ILL) SirsiDynix; (OPAC) SirsiDynix; (Serials) SirsiDynix
Database Vendor: ABC-CLIO, Agricola, Alexander Street Press, American Chemical Society, American Mathematical Society, American Physical Society, BioOne, Children's Literature Comprehensive Database Company (CLCD), Cinahl, College Source, EBSCO Auto Repair Reference, EBSCOhost, Elsevier, Emerald, Gale Cengage Learning, IEEE (Institute of Electrical & Electronics Engineers), Ingenta, JSTOR, LexisNexis, MD Consult, Medline, OCLC FirstSearch, OVID Technologies, Project MUSE, ProQuest, PubMed, ScienceDirect, Scopus, SerialsSolutions, SirsiDynix, Wiley InterScience
Wireless access
Partic in Coop Col Libr Ctr, Inc; NAAL
Open Mon-Thurs 8am-10pm, Fri 8-4:30, Sat 1-5, Sun 2-10

UNION SPRINGS

P UNION SPRINGS PUBLIC LIBRARY*, 103 Prairie St N, 36089. SAN 330-3187. Tel: 334-738-2760. FAX: 334-738-2780. Web Site: www.unionspringslibrary.com. *Librn,* Frances Brown
Library Holdings: Bk Vols 10,000; Per Subs 31
Wireless access
Open Mon-Wed 9-5, Thurs 11-5

UNIONTOWN

P UNIONTOWN PUBLIC LIBRARY*, PO Box 637, 36786-0637. Tel: 334-628-6681. FAX: 334-628-6681. E-mail: uniontownbookworm@yahoo.com. *Librn,* JoAnn Robinson
Library Holdings: Bk Vols 1,500
Open Mon-Fri 11-4

VALLEY

P H GRADY BRADSHAW CHAMBERS COUNTY LIBRARY*, 3419 20th Ave, 36854. SAN 320-1155. Tel: 334-768-2161. FAX: 334-768-7272. E-mail: chamberscountylibrary@yahoo.com. Web Site: www.chamberscountylibrary.org. *Dir,* Mary H Hamilton; *Asst Dir,* Bonnie L Strength; *Cat,* Anne Alsobrook; *Ch Serv,* Tabitha Truitt; Staff 9 (MLS 4, Non-MLS 5)
Founded 1976. Pop 39,965; Circ 60,217
Library Holdings: Bk Titles 52,808; Bk Vols 62,912; Per Subs 153
Special Collections: Cobb Memorial Archives. Oral History
Subject Interests: Genealogy
Open Mon & Tues 10-8, Wed-Fri 10-6, Sat 10-2
Friends of the Library Group
Branches: 1
LAFAYETTE PILOT PUBLIC LIBRARY, 198 First St SE, Lafayette, 36862, SAN 300-1288. Tel: 334-864-0012. E-mail: lafayette@chamberscountylibrary.org. *Dir,* Mary Hamilton; *Br Mgr,* Betty Barrett
Circ 8,299
Library Holdings: Bk Vols 8,418; Per Subs 25
Open Mon-Fri 12:30-5, Sat 9-12
Friends of the Library Group

VESTAVIA HILLS

P VESTAVIA HILLS LIBRARY IN THE FOREST*, 1112 Montgomery Hwy, 35216. SAN 300-2349. Tel: 205-978-0155. FAX: 205-978-0156. Web Site: www.vestavia.lib.al.us. *Dir,* Taneishe Tucker; *Ref,* Thomas M Lesley; *Tech Serv,* Lonny W Terry
Founded 1969. Pop 20,384; Circ 131,238
Library Holdings: Bk Vols 82,000; Per Subs 135
Special Collections: American Heritage, National Geographic, 1955-82, Readers Digest
Automation Activity & Vendor Info: (Cataloging) Innovative Interfaces, Inc; (Circulation) Innovative Interfaces, Inc; (OPAC) Innovative Interfaces, Inc
Publications: American Libraries; Booklist
Partic in Jefferson County Libr Coop
Open Mon-Thurs 9-8, Fri & Sat 9-6, Sun 1-5
Friends of the Library Group

VINCENT

P LALLOUISE FLOREY MCGRAW PUBLIC LIBRARY*, 42860 Hwy 25, 35178-6156. (Mail add: PO Box 3, 35178-0003), SAN 371-9375. Tel: 205-672-2749. FAX: 205-672-2749. E-mail: vincentlibrary@shelbycounty-al.org. Web Site: www.shelbycounty-al.org. *Librn,* Heather Baker
Library Holdings: Bk Vols 10,500
Automation Activity & Vendor Info: (Cataloging) Innovative Interfaces, Inc; (Circulation) Innovative Interfaces, Inc; (OPAC) Innovative Interfaces, Inc
Mem of Harrison Regional Library System
Open Mon & Thurs 12-6, Tues & Wed 10-4, Sat 8-12

WADLEY

J SOUTHERN UNION STATE COMMUNITY COLLEGE*, McClintock-Ensminger Library, 750 Robert St, 36276. (Mail add: PO Box 1000, 36276), SAN 300-2357. Tel: 256-395-2211, Ext 5130. FAX: 256-395-2215. Web Site: www.suscc.edu. *Dir,* Kathy E Reynolds; E-mail: kreynolds@suscc.edu; *Tech Serv,* Donna Franklin; *Tech Serv,* Kathy Thrash; Staff 7 (MLS 2, Non-MLS 5)
Founded 1922
Library Holdings: Bk Vols 90,000; Per Subs 370
Special Collections: Alabama History Coll
Automation Activity & Vendor Info: (Acquisitions) SirsiDynix; (Cataloging) SirsiDynix; (Circulation) SirsiDynix; (OPAC) SirsiDynix; (Serials) SirsiDynix
Publications: A/V Catalog; Student Handbook
Partic in Alabama Libr Asn
Open Mon & Fri 7:30-4, Tues-Thurs 7:30am-9pm
Departmental Libraries:
OPELIKA CAMPUS, 1701 Lafayette Pkwy, Opelika, 36801. Tel: 334-745-6437. FAX: 334-749-5505. *Dir,* Kathy E Reynolds; E-mail: kreynolds@suscc.edu
Open Mon-Thurs 7:30am-9pm, Fri 7:30-3
VALLEY CAMPUS, 321 Fob James Dr, Valley, 36854, SAN 300-1296. Tel: 334-756-4151. FAX: 334-756-5183. *Dir,* Kathy Reynolds; E-mail: kreynolds@suscc.edu
Open Mon-Thurs 8:30-1:30 & 4:30-8:30

WALNUT GROVE

P WESTSIDE PUBLIC LIBRARY*, 5151 Walnut Grove Rd, 35990. (Mail add: PO Box 100, 35990-0100), SAN 374-5678. Tel: 205-589-6699. FAX: 205-589-6699. *Dir,* Tina Goss; *Head Librn,* Stacy Richards; Staff 2 (MLS 1, Non-MLS 1)
Founded 1991. Pop 3,500
Library Holdings: Bk Vols 7,500; Per Subs 20
Automation Activity & Vendor Info: (Cataloging) Book Systems; (Circulation) Book Systems; (OPAC) Book Systems
Open Mon & Thurs 1-7, Tues & Fri 9-1

WARRIOR

P WARRIOR PUBLIC LIBRARY*, Ten First St, 35180-1501. SAN 376-5539. Tel: 205-647-3006. FAX: 205-647-9280. Web Site: warrior.lib.al.us. *Librn,* Erica Calvert; E-mail: ecalvert@bham.lib.al.us
Library Holdings: Bk Titles 22,800; Bk Vols 23,000; Per Subs 32
Automation Activity & Vendor Info: (Cataloging) Innovative Interfaces, Inc; (Circulation) Innovative Interfaces, Inc; (OPAC) Innovative Interfaces, Inc
Partic in Jefferson County Libr Coop
Open Mon, Wed & Fri 9-5, Tues & Thurs 9-8, Sat 9-12
Friends of the Library Group

WEST BLOCTON

P WEST BLOCTON PUBLIC LIBRARY*, 62 Walter Owens Dr, 35184. (Mail add: PO Box 292, 35184-0292). Tel: 205-938-3570. FAX: 205-938-7803. *Librn,* Emma Hicks
Library Holdings: Bk Vols 15,000
Automation Activity & Vendor Info: (Cataloging) Follett Software; (Circulation) Follett Software
Open Tues 1-6 & 6:30-9, Wed & Fri 1-6, Thurs 1-6 & 6:30-9:30, Sat 9-12

WETUMPKA

P WETUMPKA PUBLIC LIBRARY*, 212 S Main St, 36092. (Mail add: PO Box 249, 36092-0005), SAN 300-2365. Tel: 334-567-1308. FAX: 334-567-1309. E-mail: library@cityofwetumpka.com. Web Site: www.wetumpkalibrary.com. *Dir,* Susan Hayes; *Librn,* Joyce Hancock; *Librn,* Myrna Hays; Staff 5 (MLS 1.5, Non-MLS 3.5)
Founded 1957. Pop 6,528; Circ 76,000
Library Holdings: Bk Vols 23,000; Per Subs 55
Special Collections: Local Artists Art Coll
Wireless access
Function: Bk club(s), Bks on CD, Children's prog, Computers for patron use, Copy machines, Free DVD rentals, ILL available, Music CDs, Photocopying/Printing, Story hour, Summer reading prog, Tax forms
Mem of Horseshoe Bend Regional Library
Open Mon-Fri 8-6, Sat 9-5
Friends of the Library Group

WHITEHALL

P WHITE HALL PUBLIC LIBRARY*, 643 Freedom, 36040. Tel: 334-874-7323. FAX: 334-874-7323. *Dir,* Ethel J Williams; E-mail: e.williams@mindspring.com
Library Holdings: High Interest/Low Vocabulary Bk Vols 3,000; Bk Vols 20,000
Automation Activity & Vendor Info: (Acquisitions) Book Systems; (Cataloging) Book Systems; (Circulation) Book Systems; (ILL) Book Systems; (Serials) Book Systems
Open Mon-Thurs 10-2

WILSONVILLE

P WILSONVILLE PUBLIC LIBRARY*, PO Box 70, 35186 0070. SAN 371-9383. Tel: 205-669-6180. FAX: 205-669-6205. *Librn,* Vernice Stoudenmire
Library Holdings: Bk Titles 5,500
Open Mon & Fri 3-4:30, Tues-Thurs 9-4:30

WINFIELD

P NORTHWEST REGIONAL LIBRARY*, 185 Ashwood Dr, 35594-5436. (Mail add: PO Box 1527, 35594-1527), SAN 330-4027. Tel: 205 487-2330. FAX: 205-487-4815. *Dir,* Ann Lynn
Founded 1961
Library Holdings: Bk Vols 80,176; Per Subs 10
Automation Activity & Vendor Info: (Cataloging) Follett Software; (Circulation) Follett Software; (OPAC) Follett Software
Open Mon-Thurs 8-5
Branches: 8
MARY WALLACE COBB MEMORIAL LIBRARY, 44425 Hwy 17, Vernon, 35592. (Mail add: PO Box 357, Vernon, 35592-0357), SAN 330-423X. Tel: 205 695 6123. FAX: 205-695-1006. Web Site: webmini.apls.state.al.us/apls_web/northwest/?q=wallace. *Libr Dir,* Amanda Glasgow
Circ 16,000
Library Holdings: Bk Vols 5,454
Open Mon-Fri 9-5:30
KENNEDY PUBLIC LIBRARY, 17885 Hwy 96, Kennedy, 35574. (Mail add: PO Box 70, Kennedy, 35574-0070), SAN 330-4086. Tel: 205-596-3670. FAX: 205-596-3956. *Librn,* James Vice
Circ 800
Library Holdings: Bk Vols 4,595
Open Mon, Tues, Thurs & Fri 8-12 & 1-5
MCHS COMMUNITY LIBRARY, 8115 US Hwy 43, Guin, 35563. (Mail add: PO Box 549, Guin, 35563-0549), SAN 330-4116. Tel: 205-468-2544. FAX: 205-468-2544. *Librn,* Margaret Masengale
Pop 3,000; Circ 20,400
Library Holdings: Bk Vols 15,938; Per Subs 83
MILLPORT PUBLIC LIBRARY, 920 Black St, Millport, 35576. (Mail add: PO Box 159, Millport, 35576-0159), SAN 330-4124. Tel: 205-662-4286. Web Site: webmini.apls.state.al.us/apls_web/northwest/?q=millport. *Librn,* Position Currently Open
Circ 2,500
Library Holdings: Bk Vols 7,460
Open Mon & Wed 9-Noon, Tues, Thurs & Fri 9-12 & 1-5
Friends of the Library Group
CLYDE NIX PUBLIC LIBRARY, 350 Bexar Ave W, Hamilton, 35570. (Mail add: PO Box 1944, Hamilton, 35570-1944), SAN 330-4051. Tel: 205-921-4290. FAX: 205-921-4290. E-mail: clydenix@yahoo.com. *Librn,* Starr Homer
Circ 33,400
Library Holdings: Bk Vols 15,646; Per Subs 29
Open Mon, Tues, Thurs & Fri 10-5, Wed 12-4, Sat 10-12
Friends of the Library Group
SULLIGENT PUBLIC LIBRARY, 514 Elm St, Sulligent, 35586-9053. (Mail add: PO Box 215, Sulligent, 35586-0215), SAN 330-4205. Tel: 205-698-8631. FAX: 205-698-0232. E-mail: sullpl@yahoo.com. *Librn,* Cathy Collins
Circ 13,000
Library Holdings: Bk Vols 11,948
Open Mon 9-6, Tues-Fri 9-5, Sat 9-12
WEATHERFORD PUBLIC LIBRARY, 307 Fourth Ave, Red Bay, 35582. (Mail add: PO Box 870, Red Bay, 35582-0870), SAN 330-4140. Tel: 256-356-9255. E-mail: rblibrary@bellsouth.net. *Librn,* Linda Ezzeal
Founded 1974. Circ 13,300
Library Holdings: Bks on Deafness & Sign Lang 10; Bk Vols 9,703; Per Subs 10
Subject Interests: Biographies, Fiction
Open Mon & Wed 1-5, Tues 10-5, Thurs & Fri 12-5
WINFIELD PUBLIC LIBRARY, 185 Ashwood Dr, 35594. (Mail add: PO Box 688, 35594-0688), SAN 330-4264. Tel: 205-487-2484. FAX: 205-487-5146. E-mail: library@winfieldcity.org. *Dir & Librn,* Regina Sperry
Circ 43,000
Library Holdings: Bk Vols 27,000; Per Subs 44
Open Mon & Thurs 9-6, Tues & Fri 9-5, Wed 12-5, Sat 9-Noon
Friends of the Library Group

WOODVILLE

P WOODVILLE PUBLIC LIBRARY, 26 Venson St, 35776. (Mail add: PO Box 116, 35776-0116), SAN 325-4402. Tel: 256-776-2796. FAX: 256-776-3294. E-mail: publicw@bellsouth.net. Web Site: www.woodvilleonline.com. *Dir,* Karen Chambers
Founded 1985. Pop 775; Circ 14,500
Library Holdings: CDs 10; DVDs 10; High Interest/Low Vocabulary Bk Vols 135; Large Print Bks 250; Bk Vols 19,051; Per Subs 24; Videos 100
Subject Interests: Genealogy
Open Tues-Fri 9-5
Friends of the Library Group

YORK

P HIGHTOWER MEMORIAL LIBRARY*, 630 Ave A, 36925. SAN 300-2373. Tel: 205-392-2004. *Dir,* Thelma McCann
Pop 5,859; Circ 11,514
Library Holdings: AV Mats 217; Bk Vols 12,000; Per Subs 20
Open Mon-Wed & Fri 9-4:30, Thurs & Sat 9-12

Date of Statistics: FY 2013
Population, 2010 U.S. Census: 710,231
Population, FY 2013 (State Demographer): 736,399
Population Served by Public Libraries: 652,860
Total Volumes in Public Libraries: 2,798,510 (print 2,439,730, ebooks 358,780)
Total Public Library Circulation: 4,625,365
Public Library Income:
Operating Revenue: $36,236,466
Operating Expenditures: $35,890,855
Capital Revenue: $24,171,996
Capital Expenditures: $36,222,524
Number of County Libraries: Alaska is divided into 19 organized boroughs and one unorganized borough. Twelve boroughs fund borough-wide service
Public Library Assistance & Interlibrary Cooperation Grants: Continuing to offer these grants, as well as Continuing Education Grants
State Appropriations: $891,400

ANCHOR POINT

P ANCHOR POINT PUBLIC LIBRARY*, 72551 Milo Fritz Ave, 99556. (Mail add: PO Box 129, 99556-0129). Tel: 907-235-5692. FAX: 907-235-5692. E-mail: anchorpointlibrary@gmail.com. Web Site: www.anchorpointlibrary.com. *Dir,* Lora L Craig
Founded 1947. Pop 2,500
Jul 2007-Jun 2008 Income $14,000, State $6,350, Locally Generated Income $7,650. Mats Exp $5,000, Books $3,500, Per/Ser (Incl. Access Fees) $100, AV Mat $1,100, Electronic Ref Mat (Incl. Access Fees) $300. Sal $4,800
Library Holdings: Audiobooks 70; CDs 5; DVDs 300; Large Print Bks 25; Bk Titles 11,750; Bk Vols 12,000; Per Subs 3; Videos 2,500
Automation Activity & Vendor Info: (Acquisitions) Follett Software; (Cataloging) Follett Software; (Circulation) Follett Software
Wireless access
Function: Alaskana res, Art exhibits, Bks on cassette, Bks on CD, CD-ROM, Computers for patron use, Copy machines, Fax serv, Free DVD rentals, Handicapped accessible, ILL available, Music CDs, Online cat, Preschool outreach, Pub access computers, Story hour, Summer reading prog, VHS videos, Wheelchair accessible
Open Mon, Wed & Fri 10-5, Sat 11-5
Friends of the Library Group

ANCHORAGE

ALASKA DEPARTMENT OF NATURAL RESOURCES
G DIVISION OF MINING, LAND & WATER LIBRARY*, 550 W Seventh Ave, Ste 1070, 99501-3579, SAN 320-8095. Tel: 907-269-8600. FAX: 907-269-8904. TDD: 907-269-8411.
Library Holdings: Bk Vols 500; Per Subs 10
Special Collections: Coal Application Permits for Alaska; Division Reports; Geology & Mining Magazines; Large Mine Applications & Permitting in Alaska; US Bureaus of Mines Reports on Southeast Alaska
Subject Interests: Alaska
Open Mon-Fri 8-4:30

G PUBLIC INFORMATION CENTER*, 550 W Seventh Ave, Ste 1260, 99501, SAN 374-602X. Tel: 907-269-8400. FAX: 907-269-8901. TDD: 907-269-8411. E-mail: dnr.pic@alaska.gov. Web Site: dnr.alaska.gov. *Mgr,* Kathy Johnson
Publications: Fact Sheets; Pamphlets on ADNR programs
Special Services for the Deaf - TTY equip
Open Mon-Fri 10-5

S ALASKA HERITAGE MUSEUM & LIBRARY AT WELLS FARGO*, 301 W Northern Lights Blvd, K3212-051, 99503. SAN 329-7209. Tel: 907-265-2834. FAX: 907-265-2860. *Curator,* Tom D Bennett; E-mail: tom.d.bennett@wellsfargo.com; *Mus Asst,* Walter Van Horn; Staff 2 (Non-MLS 2)
Founded 1968
Library Holdings: AV Mats 24; Bk Titles 2,500
Special Collections: Alaskan History
Subject Interests: Alaska
Function: Ref serv available
Publications: Heritage of Alaska
Partic in Alaska Libr Asn
Open Mon-Fri 12-4

S ALASKA HOUSING FINANCE CORP*, Research Information Center Library, 4300 Boniface Pkwy, 99504. (Mail add: PO Box 101020, 99510), SAN 321-446X. Tel: 907-330-8166. FAX: 907-338-1747. Web Site: www.ahfc.us. *Librn,* Betty Hall
Founded 1984
Library Holdings: Bk Titles 6,000; Per Subs 20
Open Mon-Fri 8-5

S ALASKA MASONIC LIBRARY & MUSEUM*, 518 E 14th St, 99501-5330. Tel: 907-561-1477. *Exec Dir,* Joe Dahl
Library Holdings: Bk Vols 2,000
Restriction: Open by appt only

M ALASKA NATIVE MEDICAL CENTER*, Bonnie Williams Memorial Library, 4315 Diplomacy Dr, 99508-5999. Tel: 907-729-2943. E-mail: library@anthc.org.
Founded 1959
Database Vendor: EBSCOhost, Elsevier, OVID Technologies, UpToDate
Wireless access
Function: ILL available
Restriction: Med staff only

G ALASKA OIL & GAS CONSERVATION COMMISSION LIBRARY*, 333 W Seventh Ave, Ste 100, 99501. SAN 373-3335. Tel: 907-279-1433. FAX: 907-276-7542. Web Site: www.aogcc.alaska.gov. *Librn,* Christine Mahnken
Library Holdings: Bk Vols 3,000; Per Subs 10
Partic in Alaska Library Network
Open Mon-Fri 8-4:30

G ALASKA RESOURCES LIBRARY & INFORMATION SERVICES*, Library Bldg, 3211 Providence Dr, Ste 111, 99508-4614. SAN 377-841X. Tel: 907-272-7547. Interlibrary Loan Service Tel: 907-786-7677. FAX: 907-786-7652. Interlibrary Loan Service FAX: 907-786-7680. E-mail: reference@arlis.org. Web Site: www.arlis.org. *Librn,* Juli Braund-Allen; Tel: 907-786-7666, E-mail: anjb1@uaa.alaska.edu; *Govt Doc Librn,* Kevin Keating; Tel: 907-786-7688, E-mail: kevin@arlis.org; *Coll Develop Coordr,* Celia Rozen; Tel: 907-786-7676, E-mail: celia@arlis.org; *Ref Serv Coordr,* Carrie Holba; Tel: 907-786-7660, E-mail: carrie@arlis.org; *Syst Coordr,* Steve Johnson; Tel: 907-786-7661, E-mail: steve@arlis.org; *Cataloger,* Ed Kazzimir; Tel: 907-786-7672, E-mail: edwardk@arlis.org; *ILL,* Sharon Prien; Tel: 907-786-7677, E-mail: sharon@arlis.org; Staff 15 (MLS 6, Non-MLS 9)
Founded 1997
Library Holdings: Bk Titles 90,000; Bk Vols 200,000; Per Subs 700

Special Collections: US Document Depository
Subject Interests: Cultural res, Natural res
Automation Activity & Vendor Info: (Cataloging) OCLC; (Circulation) SirsiDynix; (ILL) OCLC; (OPAC) SirsiDynix
Database Vendor: Dialog, LexisNexis, OCLC FirstSearch, OVID Technologies, SirsiDynix
Function: Doc delivery serv, Govt ref serv, ILL available, Outside serv via phone, mail, e-mail & web, Ref serv available, Res libr, Wheelchair accessible
Partic in OCLC Online Computer Library Center, Inc; OCLC-LVIS
Open Mon-Fri 8-5
Friends of the Library Group

GL ALASKA STATE COURT LAW LIBRARY*, 303 K St, 99501. SAN 300-2381. Tel: 907-264-0585. Toll Free Tel: 888-282-2082. FAX: 907-264-0733. E-mail: library@courts.state.ak.us. Web Site: www.courts.alaska.gov/library.htm. *State Law Librn,* Susan Falk; E-mail: sfalk@courts.state.ak.us; *Pub Serv Librn,* Buck Sterling; E-mail: wsterling@courts.state.ak.us; *Syst Librn,* Ken Wheaton; E-mail: kwheaton@courts.state.ak.us; *Tech Serv Librn,* Beth Odsen; E-mail: bodsen@courts.state.ak.us
Founded 1959
Library Holdings: Bk Vols 363,735; Per Subs 328
Special Collections: US Document Depository
Automation Activity & Vendor Info: (Acquisitions) Horizon; (Cataloging) Horizon; (Circulation) Horizon; (OPAC) Horizon; (Serials) Horizon
Database Vendor: OCLC FirstSearch
Wireless access
Open Mon-Thurs 8-6, Fri 8-4:30, Sun 12-5

Branches:

JUNEAU BRANCH, Dimond Court Bldg, 123 Fourth St, Juneau, 99811. (Mail add: PO Box 114100, Juneau, 99811-4100). Tel: 907-463-4761. FAX: 907-463-4784. *Librn,* Marinke Van Gelder; E-mail: mvangelder@courts.state.ak.us
Open Mon-Fri 8-4:30

KETCHIKAN BRANCH, 415 Main St, Rm 206, Ketchikan, 99901. Tel: 907-225-0500. FAX: 907-225-7420. *Librn,* Debra Hilron; E-mail: dhilton@courts.state.ak.us
Open Mon-Fri 1:30-4:30

ALASKA STATE LIBRARY

G LIBRARY DEVELOPMENT, 344 W Third Ave, Ste 125, 99501, SAN 375-2852. Tel: 907-269-6570. Toll Free Tel: 800-776-6566. FAX: 907-269-6580. E-mail: aslanc@alaska.gov. Web Site: library.alaska.gov/dev/libdev.html. *Head, Libr Develop,* Patience Frederiksen; E-mail: patience.frederiksen@alaska.gov; *Network Coordr,* Shane Southwick; E-mail: shane.southwick@alaska.gov; Staff 8 (MLS 4, Non-MLS 4)
Founded 1971
Library Holdings: Bk Vols 850; Per Subs 5
Subject Interests: Libr sci
Automation Activity & Vendor Info: (Acquisitions) SirsiDynix; (Cataloging) SirsiDynix; (Circulation) SirsiDynix; (OPAC) SirsiDynix; (Serials) SirsiDynix
Special Services for the Blind - Bks & mags in Braille, on rec, tape & cassette; Bks on cassette; Large print bks; Talking bks & player equip
Open Mon-Fri 8-4:30

P TALKING BOOK CENTER, 344 W Third Ave, Ste 125, 99501, SAN 300-2403. Tel: 907-269-6575. Toll Free Tel: 800-776-6566 (Alaska only). FAX: 907-269-6580. E-mail: tbc@alaska.gov. Web Site: talkingbooks.alaska.gov. *Regional Librn,* Patience Frederiksen; Tel: 907-269-6566, E-mail: patience.frederiksen@alaska.gov; Staff 3 (MLS 1, Non-MLS 2)
Founded 1968
Library Holdings: Large Print Bks 2,700; Talking Bks 79,000
Function: ILL available
Special Services for the Blind - Braille alphabet card; Cassette playback machines; Cassettes; Digital talking bk; Digital talking bk machines; Extensive large print coll; Volunteer serv
Open Mon-Fri 8-4:30
Restriction: Registered patrons only

S ANCHORAGE DAILY NEWS LIBRARY*, 1001 Northway Dr, 99508. (Mail add: PO Box 14-9001, 99514-9001), SAN 329-7721. Tel: 907-257-4593. FAX: 907-258-2157. Web Site: www.adnsearch.com. *Librn,* Sharon Palmisano; E-mail: spalmisano@adn.com; *Asst Librn,* Lynn Hallquist; Staff 2 (MLS 2)
Library Holdings: Bk Titles 1,000; Per Subs 25

S ANCHORAGE MUSEUM*, Atwood Alaska Resource Center, 625 C St, 99501. SAN 300-242X. Tel: 907-929-9235. FAX: 907-929-9233. E-mail: resourcecenter@anchoragemuseum.org. Web Site: www.anchoragemuseum.org. *Librn, Res Ctr Mgr,* Teressa Williams; *Photo Archivist,* Sara Piasecki; Staff 3 (MLS 2, Non-MLS 1)
Founded 1968
Library Holdings: Bk Titles 10,000; Bk Vols 12,000; Per Subs 45
Special Collections: ADAK Coll (Adak Historical Society); Alaska Railroad Coll, photog; Alexander Creek (Fred Winters Coll), diaries; Barrow & Diomede Islands (Eide Coll), photog; Otto Goetze Coll; Reindeer Herding (Ickes Coll), photog; Steve McCutcheon Coll, photog; Valdez History (Crary-Henderson Coll), photog; Vern Brickley Coll; Ward Wells Coll, photog
Subject Interests: Alaskana, Art, Ethnology, Hist, Sci
Automation Activity & Vendor Info: (Acquisitions) SirsiDynix; (Cataloging) SirsiDynix; (Circulation) SirsiDynix; (ILL) OCLC FirstSearch; (OPAC) SirsiDynix; (Serials) SirsiDynix
Wireless access
Function: Alaskana res, Archival coll, e-mail serv, ILL available, Mail & tel request accepted, Telephone ref, Web-catalog
Partic in Alaska Library Network
Open Tues-Fri 10-2
Restriction: In-house use for visitors, Lending to staff only, Non-circulating to the pub, Open to pub for ref only

P ANCHORAGE PUBLIC LIBRARY, Z J Loussac Public Library, 3600 Denali St, 99503. SAN 330-4329. Tel: 907-343-2975. Interlibrary Loan Service Tel: 907-343-2822. Reference Tel: 907-343-2863. Administration Tel: 907-343-2965. FAX: 907-343-2930. TDD: 907-563-0872. Web Site: www.anchoragelibrary.org. *Dir,* Mary Jo Torgeson; Tel: 907-343-2892, E-mail: torgesonmj@muni.org; *Coll Develop Coordr,* Laura Baldwin; Tel: 907-343-2980, E-mail: baldwinls@muni.org; *Adult Serv,* Rayette Sterling; Tel: 907-343-2856, E-mail: sterlingrs@muni.org; *ILL,* Eleanor Spees; *Youth Serv,* Elizabeth Nicolai; Tel: 907-343-2840, E-mail: nicolaiel@muni.org; Staff 78.9 (MLS 20.6, Non-MLS 58.3)
Founded 1945. Pop 301,134; Circ 1,876,368
Jan 2013-Dec 2013 Income (Main Library and Branch(s)) $11,226,490, State $320,250, City $10,448,481, Locally Generated Income $111,000, Other $337,750. Mats Exp $1,152,300, Books $649,934, Per/Ser (Incl. Access Fees) $50,813, Other Print Mats $16,732, AV Mat $236,379, Electronic Ref Mat (Incl. Access Fees) $198,442. Sal $6,068,101 (Prof $6,068,101)
Library Holdings: Audiobooks 46,845; AV Mats 63,779; e-books 9,150; Bk Vols 481,861; Per Subs 751
Special Collections: Alaska Coll, bks, mss, maps, micro, newsp clippings, personal papers, photos; Loussac Children's Literature Coll; Patent & Trademark. Oral History; State Document Depository; US Document Depository
Automation Activity & Vendor Info: (Acquisitions) SirsiDynix; (Cataloging) SirsiDynix; (Circulation) SirsiDynix
Database Vendor: EBSCOhost, Gale Cengage Learning, OCLC FirstSearch
Wireless access
Function: Adult bk club, After school storytime, Alaskana res, Audiobks via web, Bks on CD, Children's prog, Computers for patron use, Copy machines, Digital talking bks, Electronic databases & coll, Exhibits, Family literacy, Free DVD rentals, Genealogy discussion group, Handicapped accessible, Holiday prog, Homework prog, ILL available, Magnifiers for reading, Mail & tel request accepted, Music CDs, Outside serv via phone, mail, e-mail & web, OverDrive digital audio bks, Photocopying/Printing, Preschool outreach, Prog for adults, Prog for children & young adult, Pub access computers, Ref serv in person, Senior outreach, Story hour, Summer reading prog, Teen prog, Telephone ref, Wheelchair accessible, Workshops
Publications: Activities Calendar (Monthly); Annual Report
Partic in OCLC Online Computer Library Center, Inc
Special Services for the Deaf - Adult & family literacy prog; Sign lang interpreter upon request for prog; Staff with knowledge of sign lang; TDD equip
Special Services for the Blind - BiFolkal kits; Bks available with recordings; Bks on CD; Large print bks; Magnifiers; Playaways (bks on MP3); Sound rec
Open Mon-Thurs 10-9, Fri & Sat 10-6, Sun 1-5
Friends of the Library Group

Branches: 4

CHUGIAK-EAGLE RIVER BRANCH, Eagle River Town Ctr, 12001 Business Blvd, No 176, Eagle River, 99577-7743, SAN 330-4353. Tel: 907-343-1530. FAX: 907-694-2955. *Br Mgr,* Nancy Clark; Tel: 907-343-1533, E-mail: clarkne@muni.org
Open Tues 12-7, Wed & Thurs 11-7, Fri & Sat 10-6
Friends of the Library Group

SCOTT & WESLEY GERRISH LIBRARY, 250 Egloff Dr, Girdwood, 99587. (Mail add: PO Box 169, Girdwood, 99587-0169), SAN 330-4388. Tel: 907-343-4024. FAX: 907-783-3118. *Br Mgr,* Position Currently Open
Open Tues & Thurs 1-6, Wed 1-8, Fri & Sat 10-6
Friends of the Library Group

MOUNTAIN VIEW BRANCH, 120 Bragaw St, 99508-1307. *Br Mgr,* Position Currently Open
Automation Activity & Vendor Info: (Acquisitions) SirsiDynix; (Cataloging) SirsiDynix; (Circulation) SirsiDynix
Database Vendor: EBSCOhost, Gale Cengage Learning, OCLC FirstSearch
Special Services for the Deaf - Sign lang interpreter upon request for prog; Staff with knowledge of sign lang
Special Services for the Blind - BiFolkal kits; Bks on CD; Cassettes; Large print bks; Playaways (bks on MP3); Recorded bks; Sound rec; Talking bks from Braille Inst
Open Tues 2-7, Wed-Fri 11-6, Sat 10-6
Friends of the Library Group

MULDOON BRANCH, 1251 Muldoon Rd, Ste 158, 99504, SAN 325-4380. Tel: 907-343-4223. Circulation Tel: 907-343-4032. FAX: 907-337-2122. *Br Mgr,* Linda Klein
Publications: Business & Company ASAP; Computer Database; General Reference Center (Index to periodicals); Health Reference Center; National Newspapers Index (Index to newspapers)
Open Tues 3-7, Wed-Fri 10-6, Sat 12-6
Friends of the Library Group

C CHARTER COLLEGE LIBRARY*, 2221 E Northern Lights Blvd, 99508. Tel: 907-277-1000, 907-777-1309. FAX: 907-274-3342. *Coordr,* Christopher Horner; E-mail: chris.horner@chartercollege.edu
Founded 1985. Highest Degree: Master
Library Holdings: Bk Vols 20,000; Per Subs 70
Automation Activity & Vendor Info: (Cataloging) LibraryWorld, Inc; (Circulation) LibraryWorld, Inc; (OPAC) LibraryWorld, Inc; (Serials) LibraryWorld, Inc
Wireless access
Open Mon-Thurs 8am-10pm, Fri 8-5

L COOK INLET PRE-TRIAL FACILITY LIBRARY*, 1300 E Fourth Ave, 99501. Tel: 907-269-0943. FAX: 907-269-0905. *Educ Coordr,* Miriam Yeager
Library Holdings: Bk Vols 1,000
Database Vendor: LexisNexis
Open Mon-Thurs 8:30am-11am

S SPECIAL EDUCATION SERVICE AGENCY LIBRARY, 3501 Denali St, Ste 101, 99503. SAN 371-7720. Tel: 907-334-1301. FAX: 907-562-0545. TDD: 907-563-8284. Web Site: www.sesa.org. *Librn,* Anne Freitag; E-mail: afreitag@sesa.org; Staff 1 (MLS 1)
Founded 1987
Library Holdings: Audiobooks 1, AV Mats 550; Bks on Deafness & Sign Lang 244; Braille Volumes 503; CDs 135; DVDs 374; e-books 35; e-journals 12; High Interest/Low Vocabulary Bk Vols 45; Large Print Bks 6; Music Scores 8; Bk Titles 3,092; Bk Vols 4,184; Per Subs 18; Spec Interest Per Sub 18; Videos 532
Special Collections: Alaska Autism Resource Center; Assistive Technology Equipment
Subject Interests: Autism Spectrum disorders & related topics, Blindness, Deafness, Emotional disabilities, Hearing impaired, Low vision, Spec educ
Automation Activity & Vendor Info: (Acquisitions) LibraryWorld, Inc; (Cataloging) LibraryWorld, Inc; (Circulation) LibraryWorld, Inc; (OPAC) LibraryWorld, Inc; (Serials) LibraryWorld, Inc
Wireless access
Function: CD-ROM, Computers for patron use, Copy machines, Electronic databases & coll, Free DVD rentals, Games & aids for the handicapped, Handicapped accessible, Health sci info serv, Magazines, Magnifiers for reading, Mail & tel request accepted, Online cat, Online ref, Online searches, Orientations, Outside serv via phone, mail, e-mail & web, Photocopying/Printing, Ref serv available, Scanner, Telephone ref, VHS videos
Partic in OCLC Online Computer Library Center, Inc
Special Services for the Deaf - Am sign lang & deaf culture; Assistive tech; Bks on deafness & sign lang; Closed caption videos; Coll on deaf educ; High interest/low vocabulary bks; Spec interest per; TTY equip; Videos & decoder
Special Services for the Blind - Braille bks; Braille equip; Cassette playback machines; Children's Braille; Closed circuit TV magnifier; Computer access aids; Dragon Naturally Speaking software; Info on spec aids & appliances; Inspiration software; Large print bks; Large type calculator; Lending of low vision aids; Low vision equip; Magnifiers; Talking calculator; Videos on blindness & phys handicaps
Restriction: Open to pub by appt only

GL UNITED STATES COURTS LIBRARY, 222 W Seventh Ave, Rm 181, 99513-7586. SAN 300-2470. Tel: 907-271-5655. FAX: 907-271-5640. *Librn,* Catherine A Davidson; Staff 1 (MLS 1)
Library Holdings: Bk Titles 9,000; Bk Vols 26,000; Per Subs 12
Special Collections: Alaska National Interest Lands Conservation Act; Alaska Native Claims Settlement Act & other Alaska Titles
Subject Interests: Law
Automation Activity & Vendor Info: (Cataloging) OCLC; (OPAC) SirsiDynix
Database Vendor: LexisNexis, Westlaw
Function: Res libr
Publications: Audio Visual Holdings List; Microfiche Holdings List; Pathfinders; Periodicals List
Partic in OCLC Online Computer Library Center, Inc
Open Mon-Fri 10-4
Restriction: Restricted access

UNIVERSITY OF ALASKA ANCHORAGE

C CONSORTIUM LIBRARY*, 3211 Providence Dr, 99508-8176, SAN 300-2497. Tel: 907-786-1871. Reference Tel: 907-786-1848. FAX: 907-786-1834. Web Site: www.consortiumlibrary.org. *Dean of Libr,* Stephen Rollins; Tel: 907-786-1825, E-mail: sjrollins@uaa.alaska.edu; *Head, Admin Budget,* Kate Gordon; Tel: 907-786-1903; *Head, Alaska Med Libr,* Kathy Murray; Tel: 907-786-1870; *Head, Archives & Spec Coll,* Arlene Schmuland; Tel: 907-786-1849; *Head, Circ, Head, ILL,* Robin Hanson; Tel: 907-786-1871; *Acq, Head, Coll Develop,* Jodee Kuden; Tel: 907-786-1875; *Head, Libr Syst,* Mike Robinson; Tel: 907-786-1001; *Govt Doc Librn, Head, Tech Serv,* Rebecca Moorman; Tel: 907-786-1974; *Head, Ref & Instruction,* Page Brannon; Tel: 907-786-1873, E-mail: ayref@uaa.alaska.edu; *Med Ref Librn,* Sally Bremner; *Web Librn,* Coral Sheldon-Hess; *Archives,* Megan Friedel; *Archivist,* Mariecris Gatlabayan; *E-Res Mgt,* Christie Ericson; Tel: 907-786-1990; *Ref & Instruction,* Anna Bjartmarsdottir; *Ref & Instruction,* Juli Braund-Allen; *Ref & Instruction,* Daria Carle; *Ref & Instruction,* Christina Carter; *Ref & Instruction,* Ralph Courtney; *Ref & Instruction,* Judy Green; *Ref & Instruction,* Kevin Keating; *Ref & Instruction,* Deborah Mole; *Ref Serv,* Nancy Lesh. Subject Specialists: *Eng,* Kate Gordon; *Health sci,* Kathy Murray; *Culinary, Phys educ, Recreation,* Robin Hanson; *Computer sci,* Mike Robinson; *Govt doc,* Rebecca Moorman; *Justice,* Page Brannon; *Health sci,* Sally Bremner; *Eng,* Coral Sheldon-Hess; *Women's studies,* Mariecris Gatlabayan; *Foreign lang,* Christie Ericson; *English,* Anna Bjartmarsdottir; *Art, Philos, Relig,* Juli Braund-Allen; *Sciences,* Daria Carle; *Bus,* Christina Carter; *Anthrop, Music, Soc sci,* Ralph Courtney; *Educ,* Judy Green; *Hist, Polit sci,* Kevin Keating; *Communications,* Deborah Mole; *Alaskana,* Nancy Lesh; Staff 21 (MLS 21)
Founded 1973. Enrl 11,650; Fac 576; Highest Degree: Master
Jul 2011-Jun 2012. Mats Exp $1,890,000, Books $200,000, Per/Ser (Incl. Access Fees) $1,600,000, Other Print Mats $20,000, Micro $2,500, AV Mat $17,500, Electronic Ref Mat (Incl. Access Fees) $50,000
Library Holdings: e-books 13,266; e-journals 48,952; Music Scores 1,500; Bk Titles 499,697; Bk Vols 789,648; Per Subs 3,700
Special Collections: Alaskana & Polar Regions Coll; Archives & Manuscripts Coll; Music Coll. State Document Depository; US Document Depository
Subject Interests: Health sci
Automation Activity & Vendor Info: (Acquisitions) SirsiDynix; (Cataloging) SirsiDynix; (Circulation) SirsiDynix; (Course Reserve) SirsiDynix; (ILL) OCLC; (OPAC) SirsiDynix; (Serials) SirsiDynix
Function: Alaskana res, Archival coll, Art exhibits, Audiobks via web, Computers for patron use, Copy machines, Distance learning, Doc delivery serv, e-mail & chat, Electronic databases & coll, Govt ref serv, Handicapped accessible, Health sci info serv, ILL available, Microfiche/film & reading machines, Music CDs, Online cat, Online ref, Scanner, Video lending libr, Web-catalog

C ENVIRONMENT & NATURAL RESOURCES INSTITUTE ARCTIC ENVIRONMENT & DATA INFORMATION CENTER LIBRARY*, 707 A St, 99501, SAN 300-2500. Tel: 907-257-2732. FAX: 907-257-2707. *Info Spec,* Judy Alward; E-mail: anjaa@uaa.alaska.edu
Founded 1972
Library Holdings: Bk Titles 8,800
Special Collections: Alaska Department of Transportation & Public Facilities Statewide Research, rpts; Alaska Native Regional Corporations Annual Reports; Alaska Oil & Gas Association Reports; Alaska Oil Spill Commission Coll; Alyeska's Port Valdez Environmental Monitoring Studies; ARCO Arctic Environmental Reports; Arctic Petroleum Operators Association Publications; Climatological Data for Alaska; Depository for Arctic Petroleum Operators Association & for Alaska Oil & Gas Association; National Association of Corrosion Engineers, Alaska Section, Corrosion Book & Technical Reports Coll; Report Series of Various State Agencies; University of Alaska Institute Reports. State Document Depository; US Document Depository
Subject Interests: Alaska climate res, Alaska environ studies, Arctic res, Natural sci
Partic in Alaska Library Network
Publications: Bibliographies; Climate & Environmental Atlases; Maps; Pamphlets; Posters; Technical Reports

BARROW

P TUZZY CONSORTIUM LIBRARY*, 5421 North Star St, 99723. (Mail add: PO Box 2130, 99723-2130), SAN 376-3609. Tel: 907-852-4050. Toll Free Tel: 800-478-6916. FAX: 907-852-4059. E-mail: tuzzy@tuzzy.org. Web Site: www.tuzzy.org. *Dir,* David Ongley; E-mail: david.ongley@tuzzy.org; *Youth Serv,* Erin Hollingsworth; E-mail: erin.hollingsworth@tuzzy.org; Staff 2 (MLS 2)
Founded 1989. Pop 7,481; Circ 36,094
Jul 2011-Jun 2012 Income $835,944, State $52,000, Federal $56,000, Parent Institution $643,585, Other $84,359. Mats Exp $73,216, Books $29,782, Per/Ser (Incl. Access Fees) $16,312, Other Print Mats $1,100, AV Mat $9,475, Electronic Ref Mat (Incl. Access Fees) $16,547. Sal $346,814 (Prof $153,335)
Library Holdings: CDs 1,300; DVDs 4,000; e-books 4,803; Bk Titles 50,903; Bk Vols 55,000; Per Subs 153; Talking Bks 335; Videos 6,498
Special Collections: Arctic Related Rare Books
Automation Activity & Vendor Info: (Cataloging) SirsiDynix; (Circulation) SirsiDynix; (Course Reserve) SirsiDynix; (ILL) OCLC FirstSearch; (OPAC) SIRSI-iBistro; (Serials) SirsiDynix
Database Vendor: CredoReference, EBSCO Auto Repair Reference, EBSCOhost, Evanced Solutions, Inc, Newsbank, OCLC FirstSearch, World Book Online
Wireless access
Open Mon-Thurs 9-9, Fri & Sat 12-6
Friends of the Library Group

BETHEL

P KUSKOKWIM CONSORTIUM LIBRARY*, 420 State Hwy, 99559. (Mail add: PO Box 368, 99559-0368), SAN 300-2535. Tel: 907-543-4516. Interlibrary Loan Service Tel: 907-543-4517. Administration Tel: 907-543-4571. FAX: 907-543-4503. *Head of Libr,* Catherine Powers; *Asst Librn,* Maxine Beaver; *Asst Librn,* Hector Teran; Staff 3 (MLS 1, Non-MLS 2)
Founded 1970. Pop 15,000
Library Holdings: Bk Vols 35,700; Per Subs 63; Talking Bks 2,454; Videos 1,405
Special Collections: Alaska History
Automation Activity & Vendor Info: (Cataloging) SirsiDynix; (Circulation) SirsiDynix; (ILL) OCLC; (OPAC) SirsiDynix
Friends of the Library Group

S YUKON-KUSKOKWIM CORRECTIONAL CENTER LIBRARY*, PO Box 400, 99559. Tel: 907-543-5245. FAX: 907-543-3097. *Educ Coordr,* Susan Taylor
Database Vendor: LexisNexis

BIG LAKE

P BIG LAKE PUBLIC LIBRARY*, 3140 S Big Lake Rd, 99652. (Mail add: PO Box 520829, 99652-0829), SAN 376-3625. Tel: 907-892-6475. FAX: 907-892-6546. E-mail: biglake.library@matsugov.us. Web Site: www.matsulibraries.org/biglake. *Librn,* Jo Cassidy; E-mail: jcassidy@matsugov.us
Founded 1986. Pop 25,615; Circ 74,041
Jul 2005-Jun 2006 Income $205,015, State $6,200, County $198,815. Mats Exp $18,750. Sal $101,038
Library Holdings: AV Mats 1,342; Large Print Bks 257; Bk Titles 18,769; Per Subs 58; Talking Bks 1,238
Automation Activity & Vendor Info: (Cataloging) SirsiDynix; (Circulation) SirsiDynix; (ILL) SirsiDynix; (OPAC) SirsiDynix
Database Vendor: OCLC FirstSearch, OCLC WorldShare Interlibrary Loan
Wireless access
Open Mon, Wed & Fri 10-6, Tues & Thurs 10-8, Sat 11-6
Friends of the Library Group

CANTWELL

P CANTWELL COMMUNITY-SCHOOL LIBRARY*, Mile 133-5 Denali Hwy, 99729. (Mail add: PO Box 68, 99729-0068). Tel: 907-768-2372. FAX: 907-768-2500. *Dir,* JoElla Blanchard; E-mail: jblanchard@dbsd.org
Library Holdings: Bk Vols 11,312; Per Subs 30
Automation Activity & Vendor Info: (Cataloging) Chancery SMS; (Circulation) Chancery SMS; (OPAC) Chancery SMS
Database Vendor: OCLC FirstSearch
Open Mon & Tues (Winter) 3-8, Sat 11-3; Mon & Tues (Summer) 12-6, Sat 12-3

CHINIAK

P CHINIAK PUBLIC LIBRARY*, 42650 Chiniak Hwy, 99615. (Mail add: PO Box 5610, 99615-5610), SAN 376-3641. Tel: 907-486-3022. FAX: 907-486-3022. *Dir,* Susan Baker
Pop 75
Jul 2011-Jun 2012 Income $9,300, State $6,300, County $3,000. Mats Exp $6,300, Books $3,500, Per/Ser (Incl. Access Fees) $1,000, AV Mat $1,000
Library Holdings: Audiobooks 10; CDs 100; DVDs 100; Bk Titles 17,000; Per Subs 23; Videos 300
Wireless access
Open Mon 11-12, Tues 4-6, Wed 11-1, Thurs 12-7, Sat 10-12

COOPER LANDING

P COOPER LANDING COMMUNITY LIBRARY*, Mile .8 Bean Creek Rd, 99572. (Mail add: PO Box 517, 99572-0517), SAN 322-8460. Tel: 907-595-1241. E-mail: ourlibrary@arctic.net. Web Site: www.arctic.net/~alibrary/. *Dir,* Kay Thomas; Tel: 907-599-1643, E-mail: qenqay@arctic.net; Staff 15 (Non-MLS 15)
Founded 1984. Pop 500
Library Holdings: Audiobooks 450; DVDs 238; Large Print Bks 20; Bk Titles 5,000
Subject Interests: Alaskana, Civil War
Database Vendor: Brodart
Wireless access
Open Mon 10-12 & 2-4, Tues 1-3 & 7-9, Wed 1-3, Fri 10-12, 2-4 & 7-9, Thurs & Sat 1-4
Friends of the Library Group

COPPER CENTER

P THE FRANCES KIBBLE KENNY LAKE PUBLIC LIBRARY*, Mile 5 Edgerton Hwy, 99573-9703. (Mail add: Box 223, HC 60, 99573-0223). Tel: 907-822-3015. FAX: 907-822-3015. E-mail: kennylakelibrary@yahoo.com. *Librn,* Lil Gilmore; *Librn,* Tana Finnesand; *Librn,* Sandy Libby; *Librn,* Marian Lightwood; *Librn,* Ruth McHenry; *Librn,* Levi Wenger
Pop 410; Circ 3,802
Library Holdings: AV Mats 1,300; Bk Vols 6,000
Open Mon & Thurs-Sat 1-4, Tues 4-7, Wed 11-3
Friends of the Library Group
Bookmobiles: 1

CORDOVA

P CORDOVA PUBLIC LIBRARY*, 622 First St, 99574. (Mail add: PO Box 1170, 99574-1170), SAN 300-2543. Tel: 907-424-6667. FAX: 907-424-6666. E-mail: infoservices@cityofcordova.net. Web Site: www.cityofcordova.net. *Dir,* Cathy Sherman
Founded 1908. Pop 3,000; Circ 27,397
Library Holdings: Bk Titles 25,000; Per Subs 70
Special Collections: State Document Depository
Subject Interests: Alaskana, Arts & crafts, Educ, Local hist, Natural sci
Open Tues-Fri 10-8, Sat 1-5
Friends of the Library Group

CRAIG

P CRAIG PUBLIC LIBRARY*, 504 Third St, 99921. (Mail add: PO Box 769, 99921-0769), SAN 300-2551. Tel: 907-826-3281. FAX: 907-826-3280. E-mail: library@craigak.com. Web Site: www.craigpubliclibrary.org. *Libr Dir,* Amy K Marshall
Founded 1935. Pop 5,000; Circ 14,000
Library Holdings: Bk Titles 10,900; Per Subs 73
Subject Interests: Alaska
Automation Activity & Vendor Info: (Cataloging) OCLC WorldShare Interlibrary Loan; (Circulation) Follett Software; (OPAC) Follett Software
Wireless access
Open Mon 12-5 & 7-9, Tues-Thurs 10-5 & 7-9, Fri 10-5, Sat Noon-4

DEERING

P IPNATCHIAQ PUBLIC LIBRARY*, 59 Main St, 99736. (Mail add: PO Box 70, 99736-0070). Tel: 907-363-2136. FAX: 907-363-2156. *Librn,* Nellie M Brown
Founded 1983. Pop 158; Circ 467
Library Holdings: Bk Titles 6,434; Bk Vols 8,184; Per Subs 21
Special Collections: Oral History
Open Mon-Sat 6pm-8pm

DELTA JUNCTION

P DELTA COMMUNITY LIBRARY, 2291 Deborah St, 99737. (Mail add: PO Box 229, 99737-0229). Tel: 907-895-4102. FAX: 907-895-4457. E-mail: deltalibrary@wildak.net. Web Site: mydeltalibrary.org. *Dir,* Joyce McCombs; Staff 1 (Non-MLS 1)
Founded 1960. Pop 5,000; Circ 45,386
Jul 2014-Jun 2015 Income $202,197, State $7,600, City $171,462, Locally Generated Income $9,035, Other $14,100. Mats Exp $12,214, Books $8,771, Per/Ser (Incl. Access Fees) $385, AV Mat $1,500, Electronic Ref Mat (Incl. Access Fees) $1,558. Sal $80,024 (Prof $49,920)

Library Holdings: Audiobooks 744; Bks on Deafness & Sign Lang 21; CDs 381; DVDs 3,378; Bk Titles 15,411; Bk Vols 16,022; Per Subs 12
Special Collections: Local Alaskana; Newspapers (Walker's Weekly, Midnight Sun & Delta Paper). Municipal Document Depository
Automation Activity & Vendor Info: (Cataloging) Follett Software; (Circulation) Follett Software; (OPAC) Follett Software
Database Vendor: Baker & Taylor, Brodart, EBSCO Auto Repair Reference, EBSCOhost, H W Wilson, OCLC WebJunction, OCLC WorldShare Interlibrary Loan, Overdrive, Inc
Wireless access
Function: 24/7 Electronic res, 24/7 Online cat, Adult bk club, Alaskana res, Audiobks via web, Bk club(s), Bks on CD, Children's prog, Computers for patron use, Copy machines, Electronic databases & coll, Fax serv, Free DVD rentals, Handicapped accessible, Holiday prog, ILL available, Large print keyboards, Magazines, Magnifiers for reading, Mail & tel request accepted, Mango lang, Movies, Music CDs, Notary serv, Online cat, OverDrive digital audio bks, Photocopying/Printing, Preschool reading prog, Printer for laptops & handheld devices, Prog for adults, Prog for children & young adult, Pub access computers, Ref serv available, Ref serv in person, Scanner, Story hour, Summer reading prog, Tax forms, Telephone ref, Wheelchair accessible
Special Services for the Deaf - Assisted listening device; Closed caption videos
Special Services for the Blind - Accessible computers; Bks on CD; Copier with enlargement capabilities; Home delivery serv; Internet workstation with adaptive software; Magnifiers; Playaways (bks on MP3)
Open Mon, Wed & Fri 10-6, Tues & Thurs 10-7, Sat 11-5
Friends of the Library Group

DILLINGHAM

P DILLINGHAM PUBLIC LIBRARY*, 306 D St W, 99576. (Mail add: PO Box 870, 99576-0870), SAN 322-6557. Tel: 907-842-5610. FAX: 907-842-4237. E-mail: librarian@dillinghamak.us. Web Site: www.dillinghamak.us. *Librn,* Sonja Marx; Staff 1 (Non-MLS 1)
Founded 1949. Pop 2,413
Automation Activity & Vendor Info: (Acquisitions) ComPanion Corp; (Circulation) ComPanion Corp; (OPAC) ComPanion Corp
Wireless access
Special Services for the Deaf - Bks on deafness & sign lang
Open Mon, Tues & Thurs 10-5, Wed 10-6, Fri 12-7, Sat 10-2
Friends of the Library Group

EAGLE

P EAGLE PUBLIC LIBRARY*, Second & Amundsen, 99738. (Mail add: PO Box 45, 99738), SAN 376-7957. Tel: 907-547-2334. *Pres,* Betty Borg; *Dir,* Theresa Dean
Library Holdings: AV Mats 1,840; Bk Vols 10,000; Per Subs 40
Open Mon (Winter) 2-5, Thurs 1-8, Sat 2-4; Mon (Summer) 2-8, Tues-Thurs 2-5, Fri 5-9

EAGLE RIVER

S ALASKA STATE DEPARTMENT OF CORRECTIONS*, Hiland Mountain Correctional Center Library, 9101 Hesterberg Rd, 99577. SAN 321-026X. Tel: 907-694-9511. FAX: 907-694-4507. *Educ Coordr,* Karen Jenkins; Staff 1 (Non-MLS 1)
Founded 1974
Library Holdings: Bk Titles 4,000; Bk Vols 4,719; Per Subs 27
Open Mon-Thurs 11-6
Restriction: Not open to pub

EGEGIK

P EGEGIK VILLAGE LIBRARY*, 289 Airport Way, 99579. (Mail add: PO Box 29, 99579-0029), SAN 376-6535. Tel: 907-563-0556, 907-563-0557.
Library Holdings: AV Mats 690; Bk Vols 4,500; Per Subs 126

EIELSON AFB

A UNITED STATES AIR FORCE, Eielson Air Force Base Library, 2518 Central Ave, Bldg 3310, 99702. SAN 330-4620. Tel: 907-377-3174. FAX: 907-377-1683. *Librn,* Arnessa Jeffery; E-mail: arnessa.jeffery.2@us.af.mil; Staff 6 (MLS 1, Non-MLS 5)
Founded 1946
Library Holdings: AV Mats 3,700; e-books 11; Bk Vols 29,800; Per Subs 63
Special Collections: Arctic Coll; Professional Military Education
Automation Activity & Vendor Info: (Cataloging) SirsiDynix; (Circulation) SirsiDynix; (OPAC) SirsiDynix
Database Vendor: EBSCO Auto Repair Reference, EBSCOhost, Gale Cengage Learning, Newsbank, OCLC FirstSearch, OCLC WorldShare Interlibrary Loan, Overdrive, Inc, ProQuest, SirsiDynix
Wireless access
Restriction: Not open to pub

ELIM

P ELIM COMMUNITY LIBRARY*, Ernest Nylin Memorial Library, 101 Hillside St, 99739. (Mail add: PO Box 39070, 99739). Tel: 907-890-3501. FAX: 907-890-2363. *Librn,* Jerri Nagaruk; E-mail: jerrinagaruk@hotmail.com
Pop 300
Library Holdings: Bk Titles 7,201; Bk Vols 7,445; Per Subs 38
Function: Audio & video playback equip for onsite use, CD-ROM, Digital talking bks, Distance learning, Handicapped accessible, ILL available, Music CDs, Online searches, Photocopying/Printing, Spoken cassettes & CDs, Summer reading prog, VHS videos, Wheelchair accessible
Open Mon-Fri 1-3, Tues & Thurs 7:30pm-10pm

ELMENDORF AFB

AM UNITED STATES AIR FORCE*, Joint Venture Hospital Library, 5955 Zeamer Ave, 3MDG/SGSOL, 99506-3700. SAN 330-471X. Tel: 907-580-6490. FAX: 907-580-5527. *Med Librn,* Jarmila Henderson; Tel: 907-580-3024, Fax: 907-257-6768; Staff 1.5 (MLS 1.5)
Library Holdings: Bk Vols 4,000; Per Subs 80
Special Collections: Popular Medicine
Partic in National Network of Libraries of Medicine
Open Mon-Fri 8-5

A UNITED STATES ARMY*, Corps of Engineers Alaska District, 2218 Third St, 99506-6898. (Mail add: PO Box 6898, 99506-0898), SAN 330-4590. Tel: 907-753-2527. FAX: 907-753-2526. Web Site: www.poa.usace.army.mil. *Librn,* Natalia Soto; E-mail: natalia.d.soto@usace.army.mil; Staff 1 (MLS 1)
Automation Activity & Vendor Info: (Cataloging) EOS International; (Circulation) EOS International; (OPAC) EOS International

FAIRBANKS

G BUREAU OF LAND MANAGEMENT LIBRARY*, Fairbanks District Office, 1150 University Ave, 99709-3844. SAN 300-256X. Tel: 907-474-2200. FAX: 907-474-2280, 907-474-2282. Web Site: aurora.ak.blm.gov. *Natural Res Mgr,* Elliott Lowe; Tel: 907-474-2307
Library Holdings: Bk Vols 3,000
Special Collections: Alaska Statutes Coll; Department of the Interior Decisions Coll; Interior Board of Land Appeals (IBLA) decisions; United States Codes of Federal Regulations Coll; United States Statutes at Large Coll
Subject Interests: Natural res mgt
Restriction: Non-circulating to the pub

SR CATHOLIC DIOCESE OF FAIRBANKS*, Library Resource Center, Chancery Bldg, 1316 Peger Rd, 99709-5199. Tel: 907-374-9500. FAX: 907-374-9580. E-mail: library@cbna.org. Web Site: www.cbna.info. *Coordr, Res Serv,* David Schienle
Library Holdings: Bk Vols 4,541
Special Collections: Alaskana Coll
Subject Interests: Theol
Open Mon-Fri 8:30-4:30

S FAIRBANKS CORRECTIONAL CENTER LIBRARY*, 1931 Eagan St, 99701. Tel: 907-458-6700. FAX: 907-458-6751. *In Charge,* Jerry Watson
Database Vendor: LexisNexis

M FAIRBANKS MEMORIAL HOSPITAL LIBRARY*, 1650 Cowles St, 99701-5998. Tel: 907-458-5584. *Librn,* Doreen Smith; E-mail: doreen.smith@bannerhealth.com; Staff 0.9 (MLS 0.9)
Library Holdings: Bk Vols 1,000; Per Subs 150
Database Vendor: DynaMed, EBSCOhost, Majors, Medlib, Medline, PubMed, ScienceDirect
Function: Doc delivery serv, Electronic databases & coll, For res purposes, Health sci info serv, ILL available, Mail & tel request accepted, Online searches, Orientations, Photocopying/Printing, Ref serv available
Restriction: Hospital employees & physicians only, Not open to pub, Prof mat only

P FAIRBANKS NORTH STAR BOROUGH LIBRARIES, Noel Wien Library, 1215 Cowles St, 99701. SAN 300-2578. Tel: 907-459-1020. FAX: 907-459-1024. E-mail: library@fnsblibrary.us. Web Site: library.fnsb.lib.ak.us. *Dir,* Mary Ellen Baker; Tel: 907-459-1022, E-mail: mbaker@fnsblibrary.us; *Circ Librn,* Stephanie Stucky; Tel: 907-459-1043, E-mail: stephanies@fnsblibrary.us; *Ref Librn,* Ann Pittman; E-mail: apittman@fnsblibrary.us
Founded 1909. Pop 87,650; Circ 561,979
Jul 2005-Jun 2006 Income $4,431,108. Mats Exp $474,091. Sal $3,334,328
Library Holdings: AV Mats 32,096; e-journals 25; Bk Vols 293,609; Per Subs 999
Special Collections: State Document Depository

Subject Interests: Alaska
Automation Activity & Vendor Info: (Acquisitions) SirsiDynix; (Serials) SirsiDynix
Wireless access
Open Mon-Thurs 10-9, Fri 10-6, Sat 10-5, Sun (Sept-May) 1-5
Friends of the Library Group
Branches: 1
NORTH POLE BRANCH, 656 NPHS Blvd, North Pole, 99705-7808, SAN 324-2463. Tel: 907-488-6101. FAX: 907-488-8465. E-mail: northpole@fnsblibrary.us. *Librn,* Ingrid Clauson
Open Tues & Wed 11-9, Thurs & Fri 11-6, Sat 11-5
Friends of the Library Group

S GEOPHYSICAL INSTITUTE, Keith B Mather Library, Int Arctic Research Ctr, 930 Koyukuk Dr, 99775. (Mail add: PO Box 757355, 99775-7355), SAN 330-4833. Tel: 907-474-7503. Interlibrary Loan Service Tel: 907-474-1561. Administration Tel: 907-474-7512. E-mail: gilibrary@gi.alaska.edu. Web Site: www.gi.alaska.edu/facilities/mather. *Librn,* Flora Grabowska; Staff 1.5 (MLS 1.5)
Founded 1945
Library Holdings: Bk Vols 68,000; Per Subs 325
Special Collections: Alaska Department of Transportation Library; International Association of Volcanology & Chemistry of the Earth's Interior Coll; International Geophysical Year (IGY) Coll
Subject Interests: Atmospheric sci, Geophysics, Glaciology, Remote sensing, Seismology, Space sci, Volcanology
Wireless access
Open Mon-Fri 8-5

C UNIVERSITY OF ALASKA FAIRBANKS*, Elmer E Rasmuson Library, 310 Tanana Dr, 99775. (Mail add: PO Box 756800, 99775-6800), SAN 330-4779. Tel: 907-474-7224. Circulation Tel: 907-474-7481. Interlibrary Loan Service Tel: 907-474-5348. Reference Tel: 907-474-7482. FAX: 907-474-6841. Interlibrary Loan Service FAX: 907-474-5744. E-mail: fydir@uaf.edu. Web Site: www.library.uaf.edu. *Dean of Libr,* James Huesmann; E-mail: JLHuesmann@alaska.edu; *Bibliog Serv, Head, Acq,* Natalie Forshaw; Tel: 907-474-7401, E-mail: fnncf@uaf.edu; *Head, Info Serv,* Rheba Dupras; Tel: 907-474-6692, E-mail: rheba.dupras@uaf.edu; *Libr Syst Mgr,* Walker Wheeler; Tel: 907-474-7173, E-mail: walker.wheeler@uaf.edu; *Bioscience Librn,* Anne Christie; Tel: 907-474-7442, E-mail: anne.christie@uaf.edu; *Digital Projects Librn,* Yi Yu; Tel: 907-474-5364, E-mail: fxyy@uaf.edu; *Instruction Librn,* Lisa Lehman; Tel: 907-474-5350, E-mail: fflml@uaf.edu; *Outreach Serv Librn,* Diane Ruess; Tel: 907-474-6349, E-mail: ffder@uaf.edu; *Web Librn,* Ilana Kingsley; Tel: 907-474-7518, E-mail: ffimk@uaf.edu; *Metadata Coordr,* Paul Adasiak; Tel: 907-474-5354, E-mail: fnpfa@uaf.edu; *Coll Develop Officer,* Karen Jensen; Tel: 907-474-6695, E-mail: karen.jensen@uaf.edu; *Fiscal Officer,* Anne Aleshire; Tel: 907-474-6696, E-mail: fnama@uaf.edu; *Univ Archivist,* Anne Foster; Tel: 907-474-5590, E-mail: ffalf@uaf.edu; *Artic Bibliogr, Curator, Rare Bks & Maps,* Tamara Lincoln; Tel: 907-474-6671, E-mail: fftpl@uaf.edu; *Assoc Archivist,* Peggy Asbury; Tel: 907-474-6595, E-mail: fnmaa1@uaf.edu; *Curator, Oral Hist,* William Schneider; Tel: 907-474-5355, E-mail: ffwss@uaf.edu; *Circ/ILL/Media,* Jennifer Stutesman; Tel: 907-474-2676, E-mail: fnjcs1@uaf.edu; *Film Archivist,* Dirk Tordoff; Tel: 907-474-5357, E-mail: fndit@uaf.edu; *Govt Doc,* John Kawula; Tel: 907-474-6730, E-mail: ffjdk@uaf.edu; *ILL,* Deb Knutsen; Tel: 907-474-6691, E-mail: fyrill@uaf.edu; *Media Spec,* Marie Johnson; Tel: 907-474-7024, E-mail: fnmhj@uaf.edu; *Off-Campus Libr Serv,* Suzan Hahn; Tel: 907-474-5241, E-mail: ffslh1@uaf.edu; Staff 66 (MLS 12, Non-MLS 54)
Founded 1917. Enrl 5,423; Fac 622; Highest Degree: Doctorate
Jul 2007-Jun 2008 Income $8,600,524, State $29,391, Provincial $359,728, Federal $208,661, County $18,170, Locally Generated Income $551,297, Parent Institution $7,433,277. Mats Exp $4,845,513, Books $350,433, Per/Ser (Incl. Access Fees) $836,608, Micro $14,307, AV Mat $57,337, Electronic Ref Mat (Incl. Access Fees) $883,392, Presv $15,827. Sal $3,292,910 (Prof $1,423,673)
Library Holdings: Audiobooks 417; AV Mats 27,880; CDs 2,301; DVDs 5,150; Electronic Media & Resources 55,086; Microforms 163,910; Music Scores 6,079; Bk Vols 809,372; Per Subs 7,716; Videos 17,312
Special Collections: Alaska and Polar Regions (Film; Archives; Manuscrips). Oral History; State Document Depository; US Document Depository
Subject Interests: Alaska & Polar regions
Automation Activity & Vendor Info: (Circulation) SirsiDynix; (Course Reserve) Docutek; (ILL) OCLC; (OPAC) SirsiDynix
Database Vendor: EBSCOhost, Gale Cengage Learning, JSTOR, OCLC FirstSearch, ProQuest
Wireless access
Function: Alaskana res, Archival coll, Audio & video playback equip for onsite use, Bus archives, CD-ROM, Copy machines, Distance learning, Doc delivery serv, E-Reserves, Electronic databases & coll, Equip loans & repairs, Govt ref serv, ILL available, Music CDs, Newsp ref libr, Photocopying/Printing, Ref & res, VHS videos, Video lending libr, Wheelchair accessible
Partic in EPSCoR Science Information Group
Special Services for the Deaf - TTY equip

FORT RICHARDSON

A FORT RICHARDSON POST LIBRARY*, IMPA-FRA-HRE PL, Bldg 7, Chilkoot Ave, 99505-0055. SAN 376-6314. Tel: 907-384-1648. FAX: 907-384-7534. *Dir,* Brian Moher; *Head, Tech Serv,* Jyll Yahne; *Tech Serv,* Jody Evans; *Tech Serv,* Leon Williams; Staff 4 (MLS 1, Non-MLS 3)
Founded 1950
Library Holdings: Bk Titles 50,000; Per Subs 125
Special Collections: Artic Coll
Subject Interests: Arctic
Automation Activity & Vendor Info: (Circulation) Horizon; (OPAC) Horizon
Database Vendor: EBSCOhost, Gale Cengage Learning, OCLC FirstSearch
Open Tues, Wed & Thurs 10-8, Fri & Sat 10-5

FORT WAINWRIGHT

UNITED STATES ARMY
AM BASSET ARMY HOSPITAL MEDICAL LIBRARY*, 1060 Gaffney Rd, No 7440, 99703-7440. Tel: 907-361-5194. FAX: 907-361-4845. *Libr Tech,* Thomas Bracher
Library Holdings: Bk Titles 1,800; Bk Vols 2,000; Per Subs 119
Subject Interests: Obstetrics & gynecology, Orthopedics, Surgery
A FORT WAINWRIGHT POST LIBRARY, Santiago Ave, Bldg 3700, 99703. (Mail add: 1060 Gaffney Rd, No 6600, 99703-6600), SAN 330-4957. Tel: 907-353-2642. Administration Tel: 907-353-2645. FAX: 907-353-2609. *Supvr,* Joann Ogreenc; Staff 5 (MLS 1, Non-MLS 4)
Founded 1951
Library Holdings: CDs 1,121; DVDs 1,529; Bk Vols 41,097; Per Subs 75; Talking Bks 556; Videos 2,816
Special Collections: Alaskana; Children's Coll
Database Vendor: CountryWatch, EBSCO Auto Repair Reference, EBSCOhost, Facts on File, Gale Cengage Learning, Newsbank, OCLC FirstSearch, OCLC WorldShare Interlibrary Loan, Oxford Online, ProQuest
Function: Audio & video playback equip for onsite use, Bks on cassette, Bks on CD, Children's prog, Computers for patron use, Copy machines, Electronic databases & coll, Handicapped accessible, ILL available, Mail & tel request accepted, Music CDs, Online cat, Photocopying/Printing, Pub access computers, Ref serv available, Scanner, Story hour, Summer reading prog, VCDs, VHS videos, Wheelchair accessible
Partic in Fedlink; OCLC Online Computer Library Center, Inc
Open Mon-Thurs 10-7, Fri 10-6, Sat 10-4
Restriction: Authorized patrons
A MILITARY OCCUPATIONAL SPECIALTY LIBRARY*, Bldg 2110, Montgomery Rd, 99703. (Mail add: 1060 Gaffnee Rd, Box 6600, 99703). Tel: 907-353-7297. FAX: 907-353-7472. *Librn,* Nikki Tuck
Library Holdings: Bk Vols 5,000; Per Subs 100
Restriction: Mil only

GALENA

P CHARLES EVANS COMMUNITY LIBRARY*, 299 Antoski Dr, 99741. (Mail add: PO Box 149, 99741-0149), SAN 376-6934. Tel: 907-656-1883, Ext 127. FAX: 907-656-1769. Web Site: library.galenaalaska.org. *Librn,* Genny Brown; *Librn,* Alyson Esmailka; Staff 2 (Non-MLS 2)
Founded 1976. Pop 675; Circ 6,852
Library Holdings: AV Mats 175; DVDs 300; Bk Vols 25,000; Per Subs 25; Videos 400
Automation Activity & Vendor Info: (Cataloging) Follett Software; (Circulation) Follett Software; (OPAC) Follett Software
Open Mon-Thurs 4:30pm-6:45pm, Sun 10-3

GLENNALLEN

P COPPER VALLEY COMMUNITY LIBRARY*, Mile 186 Glenn Hwy, 99588. (Mail add: PO Box 173, 99588-0173), SAN 372-5316. Tel: 907-822-5427. Automation Services Tel: 907-259-8526. FAX: 907-822-5427. E-mail: cvcla@cvinternet.net. Web Site: www.cvinternet.net/~cvcla. *Coordr,* Sharron Ables
Founded 1954. Pop 3,500; Circ 18,000
Library Holdings: Bk Vols 18,523; Per Subs 29
Automation Activity & Vendor Info: (Acquisitions) Follett Software; (Cataloging) Follett Software; (Circulation) Follett Software
Wireless access
Open Tues & Wed 1-6, Thurs & Sat 11-6, Fri 1-8
Bookmobiles: 1

GUSTAVUS

P GUSTAVUS PUBLIC LIBRARY*, PO Box 279, 99826-0279. Tel: 907-697-2350. FAX: 907-697-2249. E-mail: librarian@gustavus.lib.ak.us. Web Site: www.gustavus.lib.ak.us. *Librn,* Sylvia Martinez
Library Holdings: Bk Vols 8,200; Per Subs 30
Open Mon & Wed 1:30-4:30 & 7-9, Tues & Fri 1:30-4:30, Thurs 10-12, Sat 11-3

S NATIONAL PARK SERVICE*, Glacier Bay National Park & Preserve Library, PO Box 140, 99826-0140. Tel: 907-697-2675. FAX: 907-697-2654. Web Site: www.nps.gov/glba/naturescience/bibliography.htm. *Coll/Libr Mgr,* Rusty Yerxa
Library Holdings: Bk Vols 2,000
Subject Interests: Ethnography, Geol, Glaciology, Hist, Marine biol
Function: Res libr
Open Mon-Fri 8-5

HAINES

P HAINES BOROUGH PUBLIC LIBRARY*, 111 Third Ave, 99827-1089. (Mail add: PO Box 1089, 99827), SAN 300-2632. Tel: 907-766-2545. FAX: 907-766-2551. Web Site: haineslibrary.org. *Dir,* Patricia Brown; E-mail: director@haineslibrary.org; *Asst Dir,* Reba Heaton; E-mail: operations@haineslibrary.org; Staff 6.2 (Non-MLS 6.2)
Founded 1928. Pop 2,503; Circ 103,523
Library Holdings: Bk Titles 25,450; Per Subs 142
Special Collections: Alaska Coll
Automation Activity & Vendor Info: (Cataloging) Evergreen; (Circulation) Evergreen; (ILL) OCLC CatExpress; (OPAC) Evergreen
Database Vendor: OCLC FirstSearch
Wireless access
Function: Adult bk club, After school storytime, Alaskana res, Art exhibits, Audiobks via web, Bks on cassette, Bks on CD, Chess club, Children's prog, Computer training, Computers for patron use, Copy machines, Digital talking bks, Distance learning, e-mail serv, E-Reserves, Electronic databases & coll, Equip loans & repairs, Exhibits, Free DVD rentals, Govt ref serv, Holiday prog, Homework prog, ILL available, Instruction & testing, Large print keyboards, Music CDs, Online cat, Online ref, Online searches, Outside serv via phone, mail, e-mail & web, OverDrive digital audio bks, Photocopying/Printing, Preschool outreach, Prog for adults, Story hour, Summer reading prog, Tax forms, VHS videos, Web-catalog, Workshops
Open Mon Thurs 10-9, Fri 10-6, Sat & Sun 12:30-4:30
Friends of the Library Group

S SHELDON MUSEUM & CULTURAL CENTER LIBRARY*, 11 Main St, 99827. (Mail add: PO Box 269, 99827), SAN 329-1995. Tel: 907-766-2366. FAX: 907-766-2368. E-mail: director@sheldonmuseum.net. Web Site: www.sheldonmuseum.org. *Dir,* Helen Alten; Staff 2 (MLS 2)
Founded 1925
Library Holdings: Bk Titles 1,100; Bk Vols 1,150
Subject Interests: Local hist, State hist, Tlingit art, Tlingit culture
Wireless access
Function: Archival coll, AV serv, Res libr
Restriction: Not a lending libr, Open by appt only

HEALY

P TRI-VALLEY SCHOOL - COMMUNITY LIBRARY*, Suntrana Rd, 99743. (Mail add: PO Box 518, 99743-0518), SAN 376-3404. Tel: 907-683-2507. FAX: 907-683-2517. *Librn,* Amanda Austin; E-mail: aaustin@dbsd.org; *Librn,* Peggy Menke; E-mail: pmenke@dbsd.org; Staff 2 (Non-MLS 2)
Founded 1980. Pop 1,000
Library Holdings: Bk Vols 22,000; Per Subs 45
Automation Activity & Vendor Info: (Cataloging) Chancery SMS; (Circulation) Chancery SMS; (OPAC) Chancery SMS
Open Mon-Wed 3:30-8:30, Sun 12-4:30
Friends of the Library Group

HOLLIS

P HOLLIS PUBLIC LIBRARY*, PO Box 5, 99950. SAN 376-3595. Tel: 907-530-7112. *Dir,* Annette Sharpe
Founded 1985
Library Holdings: Bk Titles 9,500; Bk Vols 16,000
Mem of Southern Prairie Library System
Open Mon & Thurs 9-1, Tues 2-5, Wed 1-4, Sat 10-2
Friends of the Library Group

HOMER

P HOMER PUBLIC LIBRARY, 500 Hazel Ave, 99603. SAN 320-1414. Tel: 907-235-3180. FAX: 907-235-3136. E-mail: library@ci.homer.ak.us. Web Site: library.ci.homer.ak.us. *Dir,* Ann Dixon; Tel: 907-235-3180, Ext 21, E-mail: adixon@ci.homer.ak.us; Staff 8 (MLS 2, Non-MLS 6)
Founded 1944. Pop 13,016; Circ 118,157
Library Holdings: Audiobooks 2,597; DVDs 2,451; Bk Vols 39,954; Per Subs 145
Automation Activity & Vendor Info: (Acquisitions) Evergreen; (Cataloging) Evergreen; (Circulation) Evergreen; (ILL) Clio; (OPAC) Evergreen; (Serials) Evergreen
Database Vendor: Bowker, EBSCO Auto Repair Reference, EBSCOhost, H W Wilson, OCLC FirstSearch, OCLC WorldShare Interlibrary Loan, Overdrive, Inc, ProQuest, TumbleBookLibrary
Wireless access
Function: 24/7 Electronic res, 24/7 Online cat, Adult bk club, Archival coll, Art exhibits, Audiobks via web, AV serv, Bks on cassette, Bks on CD, Children's prog, Computer training, Computers for patron use, Copy machines, Digital talking bks, E-Reserves, Electronic databases & coll, Equip loans & repairs, eReaders, Exhibits, Family literacy, Free DVD rentals, Genealogy discussion group, Handicapped accessible, Holiday prog, Homebound delivery serv, ILL available, Life-long learning prog for all ages, Magazines, Magnifiers for reading, Mail & tel request accepted, Mango lang, Microfiche/film & reading machines, Music CDs, Online cat, Online info literacy tutorials on the web & in blackboard, Online searches, Outreach serv, OverDrive digital audio bks, Photocopying/Printing, Preschool outreach, Preschool reading prog, Prof lending libr, Prog for adults, Prog for children & young adult, Pub access computers, Ref serv available, Scanner, Senior computer classes, Serves mentally handicapped consumers, Spoken cassettes & CDs, Spoken cassettes & DVDs, Story hour, Study rm, Summer reading prog, Tax forms, Teen prog, Telephone ref, VHS videos, Video lending libr, Web-catalog, Wheelchair accessible
Special Services for the Deaf - Sorenson video relay syst
Open Mon, Wed, Fri & Sat 10-6, Tues & Thurs 10-8
Friends of the Library Group

HYDER

P HYDER PUBLIC LIBRARY*, 50 Main St, 99923. (Mail add: PO Box 50, 99923-0050), SAN 328-0381. Tel: 250-636-2637. FAX: 250-636-2714. *Librn,* Caroline Beadsby; E-mail: beadsbycaroline@hotmail.com
Circ 1,517
Library Holdings: AV Mats 550; Bk Titles 5,961; Bk Vols 15,000; Per Subs 70

JUNEAU

GL ALASKA DEPARTMENT OF LAW*, Attorney General's Library, PO Box 110300, 99811-0300. SAN 371-0270. Tel: 907-465-3600. FAX: 907-465-2417. Web Site: www.law.state.ak.us.
Library Holdings: Bk Vols 2,500; Per Subs 35

G ALASKA STATE LEGISLATURE*, Legislative Reference Library, State Capitol, 99801 1182. SAN 321-074X. Tel: 907-465-3808. FAX: 907-465-4844. E-mail: legislative_library@legis.state.ak.us. Web Site: www.legis.state.ak.us. *Librn,* Brooke Daly; *Librn,* Brien Daugherty; *Head Librn,* Mary Pagenkopf; Staff 2 (Non-MLS 2)
Special Collections: Alaska State Legislature Committee Records; Alaska State Legislature Publications Coll
Open Mon-Fri 8-5

P ALASKA STATE LIBRARY, State Office Bldg, 8th Flr, 333 Willoughby Ave, 99801. (Mail add: PO Box 110571, 99811-0571), SAN 330-4981. Tel: 907-465-2920. Interlibrary Loan Service Tel: 907-465-2988. Reference Tel: 907-465-2921. Administration Tel: 907-465-2910. FAX: 907-465-2665. Administration FAX: 907-465-2151. E-mail: asl@alaska.gov. Web Site: library.alaska.gov. *Dir, Libr, Archives & Mus,* Linda Thibodeau; Tel: 907-465-2911, E-mail: linda.thibodeau@alaska.gov; *Head, Historical Coll,* Jim Simard; E-mail: james.simard@alaska.gov; *Head, Info Serv,* Freya Anderson; *Head, Libr Develop,* Patience Frederiksen; E-mail: patience.frederiksen@alaska.gov; *Digital Librn,* Daniel Cornwall; *Govt Pub Librn,* Maeghan Kearney; E-mail: maeghan.kearney@alaska.gov; *Librn,* Sara Bornstein; *Librn,* Katie Fearer; *Librn,* Sorrel Goodwin; *Librn,* Anastasia Tarmann; Staff 16 (MLS 16)
Founded 1957. Pop 626,932
Library Holdings: AV Mats 775; Bk Vols 110,000; Per Subs 350
Special Collections: Alaska History (Wickersham Coll of Alaskana), photos; Alaska Marine History (L H Bayers Coll), doc; Can, Calif & Wash; Salmon Canneries (Alaska Packers Association Records), flm; Trans-Alaska Pipeline Impact, slides. Oral History; State Document Depository; US Document Depository
Subject Interests: Educ, Hist, Libr & info sci, State govt
Automation Activity & Vendor Info: (Cataloging) SirsiDynix; (Circulation) SirsiDynix; (OPAC) SirsiDynix; (Serials) SirsiDynix

Database Vendor: EBSCOhost, Gale Cengage Learning
Wireless access
Function: Alaskana res, Govt ref serv, ILL available, Libr develop
Publications: Indexes to Collection; Information Empowered; Statistics of Alaska Public Libraries
Partic in Dialog Corp; OCLC Online Computer Library Center, Inc
Special Services for the Blind - Talking bks
Open Mon-Wed & Fri 10-4:30, Thurs 10-6
Branches: 2
ALASKA HISTORICAL COLLECTIONS, State Office Bldg, 8th Flr, 333 Willoughby Ave, 99801. (Mail add: PO Box 110571, 99811-0571), SAN 300-2667. Tel: 907-465-2925. FAX: 907-465-2990. E-mail: asl.historical@alaska.gov. Web Site: library.alaska.gov/hist/hist.html, www.eed.state.ak.us/lam. *Hist Coll Librn,* James Simard; Tel: 907-465-2926, E-mail: james.simard@alaska.gov; Staff 3 (MLS 3)
Founded 1900
Library Holdings: Bk Vols 37,000
Special Collections: Alaska Juneau Mining Company Records; Alaska Packers Association Records; Alaska-Artic Research; Alaskana (Wickersham Coll); Juneau Area Mining Records; Marine History (L H Bayers), doc; Russian American Coll; Russian History-General & Military (Dolgopolov Coll); Salmon Canneries; Trans-Alaska Pipeline Impact; Vinokouroff Coll; Winter & Pond Photograph Coll. State Document Depository; US Document Depository
Subject Interests: Alaska, Arctic
Function: Res libr
Partic in OCLC Online Computer Library Center, Inc
Publications: Alaska Historical Monograph Series; Alaska Newspapers on Microfilm, 1866-1998; Some Books About Alaska Received (annual)
Open Mon-Fri 10-4:30
Restriction: Non-circulating to the pub
TALKING BOOK CENTER
See Alaska State Library, Anchorage

P JUNEAU PUBLIC LIBRARIES*, 292 Marine Way, 99801. SAN 330-5104. Tel: 907-586-5324. FAX: 907-586-3419. Web Site: www.juneau.org/library. *Dir,* Barbara Berg; *Network Adminr,* Aaron Johnson; *Circ,* Mark Whitman; *Coll Develop,* Catherine Melville; *Electronic Serv,* Jonas Lamb; *Info Serv,* Jenna Guenther; *ILL,* Kate Enge; *Youth Serv,* M.J. Grande; *Webmaster,* Patrick McGonegal; Staff 5 (MLS 5)
Founded 1913. Pop 32,000; Circ 300,000
Library Holdings: Bk Vols 122,383; Per Subs 364
Subject Interests: Alaska
Automation Activity & Vendor Info: (Cataloging) SirsiDynix; (Circulation) SirsiDynix; (OPAC) SirsiDynix
Wireless access
Publications: The Resource: A Directory of Juneau's Community Organizations
Open Mon-Thurs 11-9, Fri-Sun 12-5
Friends of the Library Group
Branches: 2
DOUGLAS PUBLIC, 1016 Third St, Douglas, 99824, SAN 330-5139. Tel: 907-364-2378. FAX: 907-364-2627. *Br Mgr,* Carol Race
Open Mon-Wed 2-8, Thurs 11-5, Fri-Sun 1-5
Friends of the Library Group
MENDENHALL VALLEY, 9105 Mendenhall Mall Rd, Ste 350, 99801, SAN 330-5163. Tel: 907-789-0125. FAX: 907-790-2213. *Br Mgr,* Mark Whitman
Open Mon-Thurs 10-8, Fri 10-7, Sat 10-6, Sun 12-5
Friends of the Library Group

G NATIONAL MARINE FISHERIES SERVICE*, Auke Bay Lab/TSMRI Library, NOAA, 17109 Point Lena Loop Rd, 99801. SAN 300-2519. Tel: 907-789-6010. FAX: 907-789-6094.
Founded 1960
Library Holdings: Bk Titles 20,000; Per Subs 84
Subject Interests: Ecology, Fisheries
Automation Activity & Vendor Info: (Cataloging) OCLC
Partic in Dialog Corp
Open Mon-Fri 8-4:30

C UNIVERSITY OF ALASKA SOUTHEAST*, William A Egan Library, 11120 Glacier Hwy, 99801-8676. SAN 300-2691. Tel: 907-796-6483. Circulation Tel: 907-796-6300. Interlibrary Loan Service Tel: 907-796-6470. Reference Tel: 907-796-6502. FAX: 907-796-6249. Administration FAX: 907-796-6302. E-mail: egan.library@uas.alaska.edu. Web Site: www.uas.alaska.edu/library. *Regional Libr Dir,* Elise Tomlinson; Tel: 907-796-6467, E-mail: elise.tomlinson@uas.alaska.edu; *Info Literacy Librn,* Bethany Wilkes; Tel: 907-796-6515, E-mail: bethany.wilkes@uas.alaska.edu; *Outreach Serv Librn,* Jennifer Ward; Tel: 907-796-6285, E-mail: jennifer.brown@uas.alaska.edu; *Tech Serv Librn,* Caroline Hassler; Tel: 907-796-6345, E-mail: hchassler@uas.alaska.edu; *ILL,* Beatrice Franklin; E-mail: beatrice.franklin@uas.alaska.edu; *Pub Serv,* Jonas Lamb; Tel: 907-796-6440, E-mail: jonas.lamb@uas.alaska.edu. Subject Specialists: *Humanities, Soc sci,* Bethany Wilkes; *Bus, Educ,* Jennifer Ward; *Sciences,* Jonas Lamb; Staff 12 (MLS 5, Non-MLS 7)
Founded 1956. Enrl 1,760; Fac 88; Highest Degree: Master
Library Holdings: e-books 36,938; Electronic Media & Resources 6,350; Bk Titles 142,000; Bk Vols 154,500; Per Subs 465
Special Collections: US Document Depository
Automation Activity & Vendor Info: (Cataloging) SirsiDynix; (Circulation) SirsiDynix; (ILL) OCLC ILLiad; (OPAC) SirsiDynix
Database Vendor: CQ Press, ebrary, EBSCOhost, Gale Cengage Learning, JSTOR, Newsbank, OCLC FirstSearch, OCLC WorldShare Interlibrary Loan, ProQuest, ScienceDirect, SirsiDynix
Wireless access
Partic in Leian; New Mexico Consortium of Academic Libraries
Open Mon-Thurs 8am-10pm, Fri 8-5, Sat 11-5, Sun 11-8

KASILOF

P KASILOF PUBLIC LIBRARY*, 5800 Sterling Hwy, 99610. (Mail add: PO Box 176, 99610-0176), SAN 320-4650. Tel: 907-260-3959. FAX: 907-262-8477. *Librn,* Katja Wolfe; Staff 1 (MLS 1)
Founded 1962. Pop 1,132; Circ 7,000
Library Holdings: Bk Vols 14,000
Special Collections: Alaska Coll
Automation Activity & Vendor Info: (Acquisitions) ComPanion Corp; (Cataloging) ComPanion Corp; (Circulation) ComPanion Corp; (OPAC) ComPanion Corp
Wireless access
Partic in Alaska Library Network
Open Mon-Thurs (Winter) 2-5; Mon & Thurs (Summer) 2-7

KENAI

P KENAI COMMUNITY LIBRARY*, 163 Main St Loop, 99611-7723. SAN 300-2705. Tel: 907-283-4378. FAX: 907-283-2266. E-mail: kenailibrary@ci.kenai.ak.us. Web Site: www.kenailibrary.org, www.kenalibrary.org. *Dir,* Mary Jo Joiner; E-mail: mjoiner@ci.kenai.ak.us; *Asst Dir, Cat,* Mary Lucia White; E-mail: mwhite@ci.kenai.ak.us; *Children's & YA Librn,* Kyrstin Floodeen; E-mail: kfloodeen@ci.kenai.ak.us; *Cat, Ref Serv,* Joy Morgan; *Computer Serv, Ref Serv,* Ryanna Thurman; E-mail: rthurman@ci.kenai.ak.us; *ILL, Ref Serv,* Janina Efta; E-mail: jefta@ci.kenai.ak.us; *Ref Serv, Ser,* Susan Wesley; Staff 8 (MLS 2, Non-MLS 6)
Founded 1949. Pop 13,560; Circ 123,000
Library Holdings: AV Mats 1,664; Bks on Deafness & Sign Lang 45; High Interest/Low Vocabulary Bk Vols 350; Bk Titles 65,185; Bk Vols 77,772; Per Subs 275
Subject Interests: Alaska, Fishing, Genealogy
Automation Activity & Vendor Info: (Cataloging) SirsiDynix; (Circulation) SirsiDynix; (ILL) OCLC Connexion; (OPAC) SIRSI-iBistro
Database Vendor: EBSCOhost, OCLC FirstSearch, SirsiDynix
Wireless access
Function: AV serv, ILL available, Ref serv available
Open Mon-Thurs 9-7, Fri 9-6, Sat 9-5, Sun (Winter) 1-4
Friends of the Library Group

S WILDWOOD CORRECTIONAL COMPLEX LIBRARY*, Ten Chugach Ave, 99611. Tel: 907-260-7200. FAX: 907-260-7208. *Educ Coordr,* Lloyd Steward
Database Vendor: LexisNexis

S WILDWOOD PRE-TRIAL FACILITY LIBRARY*, Five Chugach Ave, 99611. Tel: 907-260-7265. FAX: 907-260-7265. *Educ Coordr,* Laurel Luddy
Database Vendor: LexisNexis

KETCHIKAN

P KETCHIKAN PUBLIC LIBRARY*, 1110 Copper Ridge Lane, 99901. SAN 300-2721. Tel: 907-225-3331. FAX: 907-225-0153. E-mail: library@firstcitylibraries.org. Web Site: www.firstcitylibraries.org. *Dir,* Linda S Lyshol; *Sr Librn, Adult/Tech Serv,* Lisa Pearson; *Sr Librn, Ch Serv,* Position Currently Open; Staff 3 (MLS 3)
Founded 1901. Pop 13,779; Circ 141,728
Jan 2014-Dec 2014 Income $1,733,060, City $121,664, County $397,799, Other $228,020. Mats Exp $91,477, Books $77,638, Per/Ser (Incl. Access Fees) $8,290, Electronic Ref Mat (Incl. Access Fees) $5,549. Sal Prof $64,087
Library Holdings: Bk Vols 60,000; Per Subs 130
Special Collections: Alaskana (SE Alaska history)
Automation Activity & Vendor Info: (Acquisitions) SIRSI WorkFlows; (Cataloging) SIRSI WorkFlows; (Circulation) SIRSI WorkFlows; (ILL) OCLC WorldShare Interlibrary Loan; (OPAC) SirsiDynix; (Serials) EBSCO Online
Database Vendor: EBSCOhost
Wireless access

Function: Accelerated reader prog, Accessibility serv available based on individual needs, Alaskana res, Audio & video playback equip for onsite use, Bks on cassette, Bks on CD, Children's prog, Computers for patron use, Copy machines, Digital talking bks, Free DVD rentals, Home delivery & serv to Sr ctr & nursing homes, ILL available, Large print keyboards, Magnifiers for reading, Online cat, Outreach serv, Photocopying/Printing, Prog for adults, Prog for children & young adult, Provide serv for the mentally ill, Ref serv available, Ref serv in person, Scanner, Senior outreach, Story hour, Summer reading prog, Tax forms, Teen prog, Telephone ref, VHS videos, Wheelchair accessible
Special Services for the Deaf - ADA equip; Assistive tech; Bks on deafness & sign lang; Closed caption videos
Special Services for the Blind - Bks on CD; Bks on flash-memory cartridges; Large print & cassettes; Large print bks; Large print bks & talking machines; Large screen computer & software; Lending of low vision aids; Talking bks; Talking bks & player equip
Open Mon-Wed 10-8, Thurs-Sat 10-6
Restriction: ID required to use computers (Ltd hrs), Photo ID required for access
Friends of the Library Group

S TONGASS HISTORICAL MUSEUM, Reference Room, 629 Dock St, 99901. SAN 327-6805. Tel: 907-225-5600. FAX: 907-225-5602. *Dir,* Lacey Simpson; E-mail: lacys@ketchikan.ak.us; *Curator,* Hayley Chambers; E-mail: hayleyc@city.ketchikan.ak.us; Staff 3 (Non-MLS 3)
Founded 1961
Library Holdings: Bk Vols 2,500
Subject Interests: Ethnology
Publications: Bibliography of Ketchikan History
Open Tues (Winter) 1-5, Sat 10-4; Mon-Fri (Summer) 8-5

C UNIVERSITY OF ALASKA SOUTHEAST, Ketchikan Campus Library, 2600 Seventh Ave, 99901. SAN 300-2713. Tel: 907-228-4567. Toll Free Tel: 888-550-6177. FAX: 907-228-4520. Web Site: www.ketch.alaska.edu/library. *Supv Librn-Tech, Outreach, Delivery Serv,* Kathleen Wiechelman; Tel: 907-228-4517, E-mail: kwiechelman@uas.alaska.edu; Staff 2 (MLS 1, Non-MLS 1)
Founded 1954
Library Holdings: Bk Vols 30,000; Per Subs 100
Special Collections: US Document Depository
Subject Interests: Native people, Western Americana
Database Vendor: ARTstor, Cambridge Scientific Abstracts, ebrary, EBSCOhost, JSTOR, OCLC FirstSearch, OCLC WorldShare Interlibrary Loan, ProQuest, RefWorks, ScienceDirect, SirsiDynix
Wireless access
Open Mon-Thurs 10-7, Fri 10-6, Sat 9-1

KODIAK

C KODIAK COLLEGE*, Carolyn Floyd Library, 117 Benny Benson Dr, 99615-6643. SAN 320-5517. Tel: 907-486-1238. FAX: 907-486-1257. Web Site: www.koc.alaska.edu/current-students/library-catalog, www.koc.alaska.edu/library.asp. *Dir,* Margaret Holm; E-mail: meholm@uaa.alaska.edu; Staff 2 (MLS 1, Non-MLS 1)
Library Holdings: DVDs 1,200; Bk Titles 27,000; Per Subs 12
Special Collections: Alaskana Coll
Database Vendor: EBSCOhost, OCLC FirstSearch, OVID Technologies, SirsiDynix
Wireless access
Open Mon-Thurs 11-8, Fri 9-5, Sat 10-5

P KODIAK PUBLIC LIBRARY*, A Holmes Johnson Memorial Library, 319 Lower Mill Bay Rd, 99615. SAN 300-273X. Tel: 907-486-8686. FAX: 907-486-8681. Web Site: www.city.kodiak.ak.us. *Dir,* Joseph D'Elia; Tel: 907-486-8688, E-mail: jdelia@city.kodiak.ak.us; *Acq,* Shelly Egle; Tel: 907-486-8685, E-mail: segle@city.kodiak.ak.us; *Ch Serv,* Kristina Hinkle; Tel: 907-486-8683, E-mail: khinkle@city.kodiak.ak.us; *Circ,* Theresa Dietrich; Tel: 907-486-8682, E-mail: tdietrich@city.kodiak.ak.us; *Tech Serv,* Lisa Booch; Tel: 907-486-8684, E-mail: lbooch@city.kodiak.ak.us; Staff 9 (MLS 1, Non-MLS 8)
Founded 1946. Pop 15,839; Circ 95,000
Jul 2006-Jun 2007 Income $730,710. Mats Exp $49,770. Sal $613,560
Library Holdings: CDs 5,517; DVDs 300; Bk Vols 67,681; Per Subs 275; Videos 2,670
Special Collections: Alaska. Oral History
Subject Interests: Fisheries
Automation Activity & Vendor Info: (Cataloging) SirsiDynix; (Circulation) SirsiDynix; (OPAC) SirsiDynix
Publications: Library Lines (Monthly)
Partic in Alaska Library Network
Open Mon-Fri 10-9, Sat 10-5, Sun 1-5
Friends of the Library Group

G NATIONAL MARINE FISHERIES SERVICE*, W F Thompson Memorial Library, 301 Research Ct, 99615-7400. SAN 300-2748. Tel: 907-481-1712. FAX: 907-481-1702. Web Site: www.afsc.noaa.gov/kodiak/library/libraryhomepage.htm. *Librn,* Maria Bello; E-mail: maria.bello@noaa.gov; Staff 1 (Non-MLS 1)
Founded 1971
Library Holdings: Bk Vols 4,500; Per Subs 50
Special Collections: INPFC Annual Reports & Bulletins; US Fish Commission Reports; W F Thompson Coll
Subject Interests: Fisheries, Marine biol
Function: Res libr
Restriction: Circulates for staff only

R SAINT HERMAN THEOLOGICAL SEMINARY LIBRARY*, 414 Mission Rd, 99615. SAN 320-5525. Tel: 907-486-3524. FAX: 907-486-5935. Web Site: www.dioceseofalaska.org. *Librn,* Mark Harrison; Staff 2 (Non-MLS 2)
Founded 1973
Library Holdings: Bk Vols 10,000; Per Subs 10
Subject Interests: Alaskan native studies, Orthodox theol, Rare bks, Relig hist
Automation Activity & Vendor Info: (Cataloging) Follett Software
Restriction: Open to students, fac & staff

KOTZEBUE

C UNIVERSITY OF ALASKA FAIRBANKS*, Chukchi Consortium Library, 604 Third St, 99752. (Mail add: PO Box 297, 99752-0297), SAN 376-3560. Tel: 907-442-2410. FAX: 907-442-2322. *Dir,* Pauline Harvey; E-mail: pharvey1@alaska.edu; *Libr Mgr,* Stacy Glaser; E-mail: slglaser@alaska.edu
Library Holdings: AV Mats 1,400; Bk Titles 14,000; Per Subs 120; Talking Bks 275
Automation Activity & Vendor Info: (Acquisitions) SirsiDynix; (Cataloging) SirsiDynix; (Circulation) SirsiDynix; (Course Reserve) SirsiDynix; (ILL) SirsiDynix; (Media Booking) SirsiDynix; (OPAC) SirsiDynix; (Serials) SirsiDynix
Open Mon-Fri 12-8, Sat 12-6

KOYUKUK

P KOYUKUK COMMUNITY LIBRARY*, 300 Vista Rd, 99754. (Mail add: PO Box 49, 99754-0049), SAN 373-8612. Tel: 907-927-2224. *Chief Librn,* April Dayton; Tel: 907-927-2245, Ext 2301; *Librn,* Douglas Dayton
Founded 1983. Pop 101; Circ 2,422
Library Holdings: AV Mats 55; Bk Titles 1,739; Bk Vols 3,000; Per Subs 12
Special Services for the Deaf - Staff with knowledge of sign lang

MCGRATH

P MCGRATH COMMUNITY LIBRARY*, 12 Chinana Ave, 99627. (Mail add: PO Box 249, 99627-0249), SAN 374-437X. Tel: 907-524-3843. FAX: 907-524-3335. *Dir,* Loretta Maillelle; Staff 3 (MLS 1, Non-MLS 2)
Founded 1942. Pop 466; Circ 3,291
Library Holdings: Bk Titles 12,000; Per Subs 12
Special Collections: Alaskana, bks, per, res papers & v-tapes
Automation Activity & Vendor Info: (Acquisitions) Follett Software; (Cataloging) Follett Software; (Circulation) Follett Software; (OPAC) Follett Software
Partic in Alaska Library Network
Open Mon-Thurs 12-2 & 7-9, Sun 7-9

MOOSE PASS

P MOOSE PASS PUBLIC LIBRARY*, 33675 Depot Rd, 99631. (Mail add: PO Box 154, 99631). Tel: 907-288-3111. FAX: 907-288-3111. E-mail: bookmoose@gmail.com. Web Site: www.moosepasslibrary.webs.com. *Head Librn,* Kindra Leaders; Staff 1 (Non-MLS 1)
Pop 375
Library Holdings: AV Mats 700; Bk Vols 6,000; Per Subs 10
Special Collections: Alaskana
Wireless access
Open Wed 11-7, Thurs 6pm-8pm, Fri 10-3
Friends of the Library Group

NAKNEK

P BRISTOL BAY BOROUGH LIBRARIES*, Martin Monsen Regional Library, 101 Main St, 99633. (Mail add: PO Box 147, 99633-0147). Tel: 907-246-4465. Web Site: bristolbayboroughak.us/administration/libraries/index.html. *Dir,* Sheila Ring
Pop 1,257
Jul 2005-Jun 2006 Income (Main Library and Branch(s)) $125,000. Sal $65,668

Library Holdings: Bks on Deafness & Sign Lang 20; Bk Vols 10,000; Per Subs 24
Automation Activity & Vendor Info: (Cataloging) Follett Software; (Circulation) Follett Software
Wireless access
Open Tues & Thurs 10-6, Wed, Fri & Sat 9-5
Branches: 1
SOUTH NAKNEK BRANCH, PO Box 70045, South Naknek, 99670. Tel: 907-246-6513. FAX: 907-246-6513.
Library Holdings: Bk Vols 5,000; Per Subs 12
Open Tues-Fri 1-5:30, Sat 1-5

NENANA

P NENANA PUBLIC LIBRARY*, 202 E Second & Market, 99760. (Mail add: PO Box 40, 99760-0040). Tel: 907-832-5812. FAX: 907-832-5899. E-mail: nenanalibrary@hotmail.com. *Dir,* Darcia M Grace; Staff 1 (Non-MLS 1)
Founded 1981. Pop 549
Jul 2005-Jun 2006 Income $69,646. Mats Exp $5,500. Sal $39,849
Library Holdings: CDs 310; DVDs 113; Bk Titles 13,307; Per Subs 12; Talking Bks 290; Videos 1,580
Special Collections: Nenana Historical Coll. Oral History
Automation Activity & Vendor Info: (Cataloging) Follett Software; (Circulation) Follett Software; (ILL) OCLC; (OPAC) Follett Software
Function: CD-ROM, Homebound delivery serv, ILL available, Photocopying/Printing, Prog for children & young adult, Serves mentally handicapped consumers, Summer reading prog, Telephone ref, VHS videos, Video lending libr
Special Services for the Blind - Computer with voice synthesizer for visually impaired persons
Open Wed & Thurs 11-7, Fri 9-5, Sat 12-8
Friends of the Library Group

NIKOLAI

P NIKOLAI PUBLIC LIBRARY*, PO Box 90, 99691-0090. SAN 376-0090. Tel: 907-293-2427. FAX: 907-293-2115. *Adminr,* Roger Jenkins
Library Holdings: Bk Titles 12,000; Bk Vols 25,000; Per Subs 15

NINILCHIK

P NINILCHIK COMMUNITY LIBRARY*, 15850 Sterling Hwy, 99639. (Mail add: PO Box 39165, 99639-0165), SAN 325-3031. Tel: 907-567-3333. *Librn,* Danielle Nolan; Staff 1 (Non-MLS 1)
Founded 1948. Pop 780; Circ 21,000
Open Mon & Fri 1-6, Tues-Thurs 11-4, Sat 11-2

NOME

S ANVIL MOUNTAIN CORRECTIONAL CENTER LIBRARY*, PO Box 730, 99762-0730. Tel: 907-443-2241. FAX: 907-443-5195. *Educ Coordr,* Howard Appel
Library Holdings: Bk Vols 2,000
Database Vendor: LexisNexis
Open Mon-Fri 7am-11am, Sat & Sun 1-4

P KEGOAYAH KOZGA PUBLIC LIBRARY*, 223 Front St, 99762. (Mail add: PO Box 1168, 99762-1168), SAN 300-2756. Tel: 907-443-6628. FAX: 907-443-3762. E-mail: library@nomealaska.org. *Dir,* Marguerite La Riviere; E-mail: mlariviere@nomealaska.org
Founded 1902. Pop 3,508
Library Holdings: AV Mats 993; Bk Titles 17,000; Bk Vols 18,372; Per Subs 50
Special Collections: Alaskana Rare Book Coll (Kozga); Alice Green Coll; Bilingual Inupiat; Bilingual Inupiat/English; Elders Conference Recordings for the Inupiat Eskimo; Seward Peninsula; Siberian Yupik/English
Subject Interests: Local hist
Automation Activity & Vendor Info: (Circulation) Follett Software; (OPAC) Follett Software
Database Vendor: OCLC FirstSearch
Partic in Alaska Library Network
Open Mon-Thurs 12-8, Fri & Sat 12-6

OUZINKIE

S OUZINKIE TRIBAL COUNCIL, Media Center, 130 Third St, 99644. (Mail add: PO Box 130, 99644). Tel: 907-680-2323. FAX: 907-680-2214. E-mail: library@ouzinkie.org. Web Site: www.ouzinkie.org. *Librn,* Lorena Wallace; E-mail: lorenawallace@live.com
Library Holdings: Bk Vols 2,000; Per Subs 10
Wireless access
Open Mon-Thurs 10-4, Sat 1-4

PALMER

CR ALASKA BIBLE COLLEGE LIBRARY, 248 E Elmwood Ave, 99645. SAN 300-2616. Tel: 907-745-3201. FAX: 907-822-5027. E-mail: library@akbible.edu. *Dir,* Harley Bowerman; Staff 3 (Non-MLS 3)
Founded 1966. Enrl 32; Fac 11; Highest Degree: Bachelor
Jun 2006-May 2007. Mats Exp $7,500, Books $4,000, Per/Ser (Incl. Access Fees) $1,800, AV Mat $250
Library Holdings: Bk Titles 22,000; Bk Vols 30,000; Per Subs 102
Special Collections: Alaska-Arctic
Subject Interests: Relig
Database Vendor: EBSCOhost
Open Mon-Fri 9am-10pm, Sat 1-9

PALMER CORRECTIONAL CENTER
S MEDIUM SECURITY FACILITY LIBRARY*, PO Box 919, 99645-0919. Tel: 907-746-8270. FAX: 907-746-8222.
Library Holdings: Bk Vols 2,000
Open Mon-Sun 8am-9pm
S MINIMUM SECURITY FACILITY LIBRARY*, PO Box 919, 99645-0919. Tel: 907-746-8250. FAX: 907-746-8248.
Library Holdings: Bk Vols 2,700
Open Mon-Sun 8am-9pm

P PALMER PUBLIC LIBRARY, 655 S Valley Way, 99645. SAN 300-2772. Tel: 907-745-4690. FAX: 907-746-3570. Web Site: pplak.org, www.cityofpalmer.org/library. *Dir,* Beth Skow; E-mail: bskow@palmerak.org; *Prog Coordr, Youth Serv Coordr,* Katie Schweisthal; E-mail: kschweisthal@palmerak.org; *Cat,* Jessie Giyer; E-mail: jgiyer@palmerak.org; Staff 5 (MLS 1, Non-MLS 4)
Founded 1945. Pop 17,000; Circ 100,000
Jan 2005-Dec 2005 Income $502,515, City $298,215, Federal $6,300, County $195,000, Other $3,000. Mats Exp $50,000. Sal $238,000 (Prof $55,000)
Library Holdings: AV Mats 625; Large Print Bks 625; Bk Titles 41,700; Bk Vols 45,000; Talking Bks 600
Special Collections: Jewish Holocaust Memorial Coll; Matanuska Valley Pioneer, Valley Settler & Matanuska Valley Record; Matanuska Valley Settlement Newspapers (1937-1959)
Automation Activity & Vendor Info: (Cataloging) SirsiDynix; (Circulation) SirsiDynix
Database Vendor: EBSCOhost
Wireless access
Function: ILL available, Prog for adults, Prog for children & young adult, Summer reading prog, VHS videos
Publications: Friends of the Library Newsletter (Quarterly)
Partic in Alaska Library Network
Open Mon & Wed 10-8, Tues & Thurs 10-6, Fri & Sat 10-2
Restriction: Residents only
Friends of the Library Group

C UNIVERSITY OF ALASKA ANCHORAGE, MAT-SU COLLEGE, Alvin S Okeson Library, 8295 E College Dr, 99645. (Mail add: PO Box 2889, 99645-2889), SAN 300-2780. Tel: 907-745-9740. Interlibrary Loan Service Tel: 907-745-9735. FAX: 907-745-9777. Web Site: matsu.alaska.edu/office/library. *Dir,* Craig Ballain; E-mail: cballain@matsu.alaska.edu; Staff 6 (MLS 2, Non-MLS 4)
Founded 1961
Library Holdings: AV Mats 4,800; e-books 20,000; Bk Vols 49,000; Per Subs 93
Special Collections: Local History. Oral History
Subject Interests: Art, Educ, Renewable energy, Soc sci
Wireless access
Partic in OCLC Online Computer Library Center, Inc
Open Mon-Thurs 8:30-8, Fri 8:30-6, Sat 9-3

PELICAN

P PELICAN PUBLIC LIBRARY*, 166 Salmon Way, 99832. (Mail add: PO Box 712, 99832-0712), SAN 376-7302. Tel: 907-735-2500. FAX: 907-735-2258. *Dir,* Linda Ady
Library Holdings: Bk Vols 8,000; Per Subs 35
Wireless access
Open Mon & Fri 5:30-7:30, Tues & Thurs 7:30pm-9:30pm, Wed & Sat 2:30-5:30
Friends of the Library Group

PETERSBURG

P PETERSBURG PUBLIC LIBRARY, 14 S Second St, 99833. (Mail add: PO Box 549, 99833-0549), SAN 300-2799. Tel: 907-772-3349. FAX: 907-772-3759. Web Site: www.psglib.org. *Librn,* Tara Alcock; E-mail: talcock@petersburgak.gov; *Tech Serv,* Chris Weiss
Founded 1913. Pop 3,200; Circ 28,000
Library Holdings: Bk Vols 33,036; Per Subs 72

Automation Activity & Vendor Info: (Cataloging) SirsiDynix; (Circulation) SirsiDynix; (OPAC) SirsiDynix
Wireless access
Publications: Petersburg, Heritage of the Sea
Partic in Alaska Library Network; OCLC Online Computer Library Center, Inc
Open Mon-Thurs 11-8, Fri & Sat 11-6
Friends of the Library Group

PORT LIONS

P JESSE WAKEFIELD MEMORIAL LIBRARY*, 207 Spruce Dr, 99550. (Mail add: PO Box 49, 99550-0049). Tel: 907-454-2288. FAX: 907-454-2420. *Head Librn,* Lisa Pennington
Circ 3,495
Library Holdings: AV Mats 260; Bk Vols 11,356; Per Subs 20
Open Mon & Wed 6pm-9pm, Tues & Thurs 2-5, Fri 9-12

RUBY

P RUBY COMMUNITY LIBRARY*, Ten Kennedy Way, 99768. FAX: 907-468-4443. *Librn,* Karen Gurtler
Pop 204; Circ 4,847
Library Holdings: AV Mats 142; Bk Vols 3,700; Per Subs 14
Open Wed-Fri 3-6, Sat 2-5

SELDOVIA

P SELDOVIA PUBLIC LIBRARY*, 260 Seldovia St, 99663. (Mail add: PO Box H, 99663-0190), SAN 376-3390. Tel: 907-234-7662. E-mail: seldovia.library@gmail.com. *Libr Dir,* Position Currently Open
Founded 1935. Pop 500
Library Holdings: Audiobooks 331; AV Mats 2,262; CDs 132; Bk Titles 8,336; Per Subs 16; Videos 1,799
Automation Activity & Vendor Info: (Cataloging) JayWil Software Development, Inc; (Circulation) JayWil Software Development, Inc
Wireless access
Function: After school storytime, Alaskana res, Archival coll, Bks on cassette, Bks on CD, CD-ROM, Children's prog, Computer training, Computers for patron use, Copy machines, Distance learning, e-mail & chat, Electronic databases & coll, Free DVD rentals, Handicapped accessible, ILL available, Magnifiers for reading, Music CDs, Outside serv via phone, mail, e-mail & web, Photocopying/Printing, Preschool outreach, Prog for adults, Prog for children & young adult, Pub access computers, Ref & res, Senior outreach, Spoken cassettes & CDs, Story hour, Telephone ref, VHS videos, Video lending libr, Wheelchair accessible
Open Mon 3-5:30, Tues 2-4:30 & 6:30-8:30, Wed 12-2, Thurs 2-5:30 & 6:30-8:30, Sat 3-7, Sun 1-3

SEWARD

J ALASKA VOCATIONAL TECHNICAL CENTER, Jack Werner Memorial Library, 519 Fourth Ave, 99664. (Mail add: PO Box 889, 99664-0889). Tel: 907-224-6114. FAX: 907-224-4406. *Librn,* Lisa Rininger; E-mail: lisa.rininger@avtec.edu
Founded 1970. Enrl 250; Fac 50
Library Holdings: Bk Vols 8,000
Subject Interests: Alaska, Prof
Automation Activity & Vendor Info: (Cataloging) Follett Software; (Circulation) Follett Software; (ILL) OCLC; (OPAC) Follett Software
Wireless access
Open Mon-Thurs 11:30-1 & 3:30-10, Fri-Sun 4-9

P SEWARD COMMUNITY LIBRARY & MUSEUM*, 239 Six Ave, 99664. (Mail add: PO Box 2389, 99664-2389), SAN 300-2802. Tel: 907-224-4082. Interlibrary Loan Service Tel: 907-224-4009. Administration Tel: 907-224-4008. FAX: 907-224-3521. E-mail: library@cityofseward.net. *Dir,* Patricia Linville; *Coll Coordr,* Amy Carney; Tel: 907-224-4010, E-mail: acarney@cityofseward.net; *Prog Coordr/Ch,* Rachel James; E-mail: rjames@cityofseward.net; *Tech Serv Coordr,* Tember Eliason; E-mail: teliason@cityofseward.net. Subject Specialists: *Archives, Mus, Tech,* Amy Carney; *Prog,* Rachel James; *Cataloging, Ill,* Tember Eliason; Staff 5 (MLS 1, Non-MLS 4)
Founded 1933. Pop 5,250; Circ 50,378
Library Holdings: High Interest/Low Vocabulary Bk Vols 50; Bk Titles 27,000; Bk Vols 30,000; Per Subs 75
Special Collections: Local Historical Photo Coll
Subject Interests: Japanese
Database Vendor: EBSCOhost
Function: Adult bk club, Alaskana res, Archival coll, Art exhibits, Audio & video playback equip for onsite use, Audiobks via web, Bi-weekly Writer's Group, Bk club(s), Bks on CD, Children's prog, Citizenship assistance, Computer training, Computers for patron use, Copy machines, Digital talking bks, Distance learning, Electronic databases & coll, Equip loans & repairs, Exhibits, Free DVD rentals, Govt ref serv, Handicapped accessible, Holiday prog, Homebound delivery serv, ILL available, Instruction & testing, Jail serv, Mail & tel request accepted, Microfiche/film & reading machines, Mus passes, Music CDs, Notary serv, Online cat, Online searches, Outreach serv, Outside serv via phone, mail, e-mail & web, OverDrive digital audio bks, Passport agency, Photocopying/Printing, Preschool reading prog, Printer for laptops & handheld devices, Prog for adults, Prog for children & young adult, Provide serv for the mentally ill, Pub access computers, Ref serv available, Scanner, Story hour, Summer & winter reading prog, Summer reading prog, Tax forms, Telephone ref, Web-catalog, Wheelchair accessible, Winter reading prog, Writing prog
Publications: Index to the Seward Gateway (1904-1910); Seward Gateway Prosperity, 1925 ed reprint
Friends of the Library Group

S SPRING CREEK CORRECTIONAL CENTER LIBRARY*, PO Box 2109, 99664. Tel: 907-224-8200. FAX: 907-224-8062. *In Charge,* Larry Deboard
Database Vendor: LexisNexis

SITKA

P KETTLESON MEMORIAL LIBRARY*, 320 Harbor Dr, 99835-7553. SAN 300-2810. Tel: 907-747-8708. FAX: 907-747-8755. E-mail: library@cityofsitka.com. Web Site: www.cityofsitka.com/dept/library/library.html. *Dir,* Cheryl Pearson; *Ch Serv,* Tina Johnson; Staff 1 (MLS 1)
Founded 1923. Pop 8,835; Circ 131,021
Library Holdings: AV Mats 9,940; Bk Titles 56,293; Bk Vols 59,767; Per Subs 283
Special Collections: Local History (Louise Brightman Room), bk, micro
Automation Activity & Vendor Info: (Cataloging) SirsiDynix; (Circulation) SirsiDynix
Database Vendor: OCLC FirstSearch
Open Mon-Thurs 10-9, Fri 10-6, Sat & Sun 1-5
Friends of the Library Group

S NATIONAL PARK SERVICE*, Sitka National Historical Park Library, 103 Monastery, 99835-7603. SAN 323-8784. Tel: 907-747-6281. FAX: 907-747-5938. Web Site: www.nps.gov/sitk. *In Charge,* Michele Simmons
Founded 1950
Library Holdings: Bk Titles 2,400
Special Collections: Russian American History, bks, tapes, film; SE Alaska Native Coll; Tlingit Indian Culture. Oral History
Restriction: Open by appt only

SKAGWAY

P SKAGWAY PUBLIC LIBRARY*, 769 State St, 99840. (Mail add: PO Box 394, 99840-0394), SAN 300-2837. Tel: 907-983-2665. FAX: 907-983-2666. E-mail: library@skagway.org. *Librn,* Julene Fairbanks
Pop 811; Circ 17,290
Jul 2005-Jun 2006 Income $120,000. Mats Exp $10,000. Sal $72,000
Library Holdings: Music Scores 16; Bk Titles 106,000; Per Subs 67; Talking Bks 200
Automation Activity & Vendor Info: (Circulation) Follett Software; (ILL) OCLC; (OPAC) Follett Software
Open Mon-Fri (Winter) 1-8, Sat & Sun 1-5; Mon Fri (Summer) 12-9, Sat & Sun 1-5

G UNITED STATES NATIONAL PARK SERVICE*, Klondike Gold Rush International Historical Park Library, Park Headquarters, Second Ave & Broadway, 99840. (Mail add: PO Box 517, 99840-0517), SAN 372-7157. Tel: 907-983-2921. FAX: 907-983-9249. TDD: 907-983-9200. Web Site: www.nps.gov/klgo. *Div Chief,* Theresa Thibault; Tel: 907-983-9236, E-mail: theresa_thibault@nps.gov; *Historian,* Karl Gurcke
Founded 1976
Library Holdings: Bk Titles 1,000
Special Collections: Dyea & the Chilkoot Trail; Klondike Gold Rush, especially Skagway & the White Pass
Special Services for the Deaf - TDD equip
Restriction: Open by appt only

SOLDOTNA

C ALASKA CHRISTIAN COLLEGE*, Learning Resource Center, 35109 Royal Pl, 99669. Tel: 907-260-7422. FAX: 907-260-6722. *Dir, Learning Res,* Dale W Solberg; Staff 1.5 (MLS 1, Non-MLS 0.5)
Founded 2000. Enrl 40; Fac 7; Highest Degree: Associate
Jun 2011-May 2012. Mats Exp $10,000
Library Holdings: AV Mats 100; Electronic Media & Resources 35; Bk Vols 14,000; Per Subs 40
Automation Activity & Vendor Info: (Circulation) Follett Software; (OPAC) Follett Software
Partic in Christian Library Consortium; OCLC Online Computer Library Center, Inc
Open Mon-Thurs 1-9, Fri 10-4, Sat 1:30-5:30, Sun 6pm-9pm

C KENAI PENINSULA COLLEGE LIBRARY*, 156 College Rd, 99669. SAN 300-2845. Tel: 907-262-0385. FAX: 907-262-0386. E-mail: iylib@uaa.alaska.edu. Web Site: www.kpc.alaska.edu. *Dir,* Jane E Fuerstenau; E-mail: ifjef@uaa.alaska.edu; *Asst Librn,* Meagan Zimpelmann; Tel: 907-262-0384, E-mail: inmaz@uaa.alaska.edu; Staff 2 (MLS 1, Non-MLS 1)
Founded 1964. Enrl 700; Fac 18; Highest Degree: Bachelor
Jul 2008-Jun 2009 Income $104,000. Mats Exp $24,600, Books $6,000, Per/Ser (Incl. Access Fees) $8,000, AV Equip $300, AV Mat $2,300, Electronic Ref Mat (Incl. Access Fees) $5,000, Presv $3,000. Sal $79,000 (Prof $49,000)
Library Holdings: Bk Vols 23,000; Per Subs 60
Subject Interests: Alaska
Automation Activity & Vendor Info: (Cataloging) SirsiDynix; (Circulation) SirsiDynix
Database Vendor: EBSCO Auto Repair Reference, EBSCOhost, JSTOR, LexisNexis, OCLC FirstSearch, OCLC WorldShare Interlibrary Loan, Project MUSE, ProQuest, SirsiDynix, ValueLine
Wireless access
Function: Art exhibits, Audio & video playback equip for onsite use, AV serv, Computers for patron use, Electronic databases & coll, Fax serv, Handicapped accessible, Magnifiers for reading, Music CDs, Online cat, Online ref, Pub access computers, Ref & res, Scanner, VHS videos, Video lending libr, Web-catalog, Wheelchair accessible
Partic in University of Alaska GNOSIS Libr Syst
Open Mon-Thurs 8:30-7:30, Fri 8-5
Restriction: Open to pub for ref & circ; with some limitations

P SOLDOTNA PUBLIC LIBRARY*, Joyce Carver Memorial Library, 235 N Binkley St, 99669. SAN 300-2853. Tel: 907-262-4227. FAX: 907-262-6856. *Librn,* Terri Burdick; *Asst Librn,* Kathlyne McLeod
Founded 1965. Pop 4,000; Circ 100,345
Library Holdings: Bk Titles 43,930; Bk Vols 36,986; Per Subs 95
Automation Activity & Vendor Info: (Circulation) Follett Software
Database Vendor: EBSCOhost
Wireless access
Open Mon-Thurs 9-8, Fri 12-6, Sat 9-6
Friends of the Library Group

SUTTON

P SUTTON PUBLIC LIBRARY*, 11317 N Jonesville Mine Rd, 99674. (Mail add: PO Box 266, 99674-0266), SAN 376-7329. Tel: 907-745-4467. FAX: 907-745-1057. Web Site: www.matsulibraries.org. *Librn,* Nancy Bertels; E-mail: nbertels@matsugov.us; Staff 2 (Non-MLS 2)
Pop 52,322
Jul 2006-Jun 2007 Income $169,270, State $6,300, Locally Generated Income $162,970. Mats Exp $18,000. Sal $81,960
Library Holdings: Bk Titles 9,976; Bk Vols 10,206; Per Subs 35
Automation Activity & Vendor Info: (Cataloging) SirsiDynix; (Circulation) SirsiDynix; (ILL) OCLC FirstSearch; (OPAC) SirsiDynix
Function: After school storytime, ILL available, Photocopying/Printing, Prog for adults, Prog for children & young adult, Ref serv available, Spoken cassettes & CDs, Summer reading prog, Telephone ref, VHS videos, Wheelchair accessible
Open Tues & Thurs 11-8, Wed & Fri 10-7, Sat 11-4
Friends of the Library Group

TAKOTNA

P TAKOTNA COMMUNITY LIBRARY*, PO Box 86, 99675. Tel: 907-298-2229. FAX: 907-298-2325. *Librn,* Misty Wachter
Library Holdings: Bk Vols 3,000
Open Mon-Sat 3-5

TALKEETNA

P TALKEETNA PUBLIC LIBRARY*, 23151 S Talkeetna Spur Rd, 99676-0768. (Mail add: PO Box 768, 99676), SAN 376-3706. Tel: 907-733-2359. FAX: 907-733-3017. E-mail: talkeetna.library@matsugov.us. Web Site: www.matsulibraries.org. *Librn,* Ann Yadon
Library Holdings: Audiobooks 965; Bk Titles 14,588; Per Subs 39; Videos 2,025
Automation Activity & Vendor Info: (Acquisitions) SirsiDynix; (Cataloging) SirsiDynix; (Circulation) SirsiDynix; (Media Booking) SirsiDynix; (OPAC) SirsiDynix
Partic in Matanuska-Susitna Library Network
Open Mon-Sat 11-6
Friends of the Library Group

TANANA

P TANANA COMMUNITY-SCHOOL LIBRARY*, 89 Front St, 99777. (Mail add: PO Box 109, 99777). Tel: 907-366-7211. FAX: 907-366-7201. E-mail: talcomlib@hotmail.com. *Librn,* Barbara Martin
Library Holdings: Bk Vols 8,000; Per Subs 20
Open Mon 4-8, Wed & Fri 5-8

TENAKEE SPRINGS

P DERMOTT O'TOOLE MEMORIAL LIBRARY*, PO Box 35, 99841-0035. SAN 376-7965. Tel: 907-736-2248. FAX: 907-736-2249. *Dir,* Mary Almy
Pop 104
Library Holdings: Bk Titles 8,000
Wireless access
Open Tues & Wed 1-5, Thurs 6-8, Sat 10-2, Sun 2-4
Friends of the Library Group

THORNE BAY

P THORNE BAY PUBLIC LIBRARY, 120 Freeman Dr, 99919. Tel: 907-828-3303. E-mail: library@thornebay-ak.gov. Web Site: thornebayalaska.net. *Dir,* Lana Clark
Founded 2001. Pop 500
Library Holdings: AV Mats 300; Bk Titles 4,000; Per Subs 10
Special Collections: Alaskana Section
Subject Interests: Local hist
Friends of the Library Group

TOK

P TOK COMMUNITY LIBRARY, Mile 1314 Alaska Hwy, 99780. (Mail add: PO Box 227, 99780-0227), SAN 322-7669. Tel: 907-883-5623. FAX: 907-883-5623. E-mail: library@tokak.us. Web Site: www.tokak.us/library. *Librn,* Kathy Morgan; Tel: 907-940-0046, E-mail: kathy@tokak.us
Founded 1955. Pop 1,258; Circ 3,808
Jul 2010-Jun 2011 Income $18,827, State $8,300, Federal $6,365, Locally Generated Income $3,162. Mats Exp $4,159, Books $2,089, Per/Ser (Incl. Access Fees) $271, AV Mat $1,347, Electronic Ref Mat (Incl. Access Fees) $452
Library Holdings: Bk Titles 10,000; Bk Vols 16,000; Per Subs 30
Automation Activity & Vendor Info: (Acquisitions) Follett Software; (Cataloging) Follett Software; (Circulation) Follett Software
Function: Alaskana res, Bks on cassette, Bks on CD, Children's prog, Computers for patron use, Copy machines, Fax serv, Free DVD rentals, Handicapped accessible, ILL available, Instruction & testing, Music CDs, Photocopying/Printing, Pub access computers, Spoken cassettes & CDs, Story hour, VHS videos, Video lending libr, Wheelchair accessible
Open Mon 1-4, Tues 10-12 & 5-8, Wed 9:30-12, Thurs 9-12, Sat 10-1, Sun 10-4
Restriction: In-house use for visitors, Non-resident fee, Registered patrons only

TRAPPER CREEK

P TRAPPER CREEK PUBLIC LIBRARY*, Mile 115 Parks Hwy, 99683. (Mail add: PO Box 13388, 99683-0388), SAN 376-6497. Tel: 907-733-1546. FAX: 907-733-1546. Web Site: www.matsulibraries.org/trappercreek/. *Librn,* Jennie Earles; E-mail: jennie.earles@matsugov.us
Jul 2005-Jun 2006 Income $93,483
Library Holdings: Bk Vols 10,500; Per Subs 30
Subject Interests: Alaska
Automation Activity & Vendor Info: (Acquisitions) SirsiDynix; (Cataloging) SirsiDynix; (Circulation) SirsiDynix; (OPAC) SirsiDynix; (Serials) SirsiDynix
Open Mon & Wed 12-7, Thurs 9-2, Sat 12-6
Friends of the Library Group

TULUKSAK

P TULUKSAK SCHOOL-COMMUNITY LIBRARY*, Tulkisarmute Yupiit School, 115 Main Rd, 99679. SAN 376-6926. Tel: 907-695-5608. Web Site: www.yupiit.org/Domain/10. *Librn,* Dora Napoka; E-mail: DNapoka@yupiit.org
Library Holdings: CDs 100; Large Print Bks 50; Bk Vols 1,000
Automation Activity & Vendor Info: (Cataloging) Follett Software; (Circulation) Follett Software; (OPAC) Follett Software
Open Mon, Tues & Thurs 10-3:30 & 4-7, Wed & Fri 10-3:30, Sat 12-2

UNALAKLEET

P TICASUK LIBRARY*, PO Box 28, 99684-0028. Tel: 907-624-3053. FAX: 907-624-3130. *Librn,* Doris Ivanoff
Founded 1982. Pop 780; Circ 2,474
Library Holdings: Bk Vols 4,537; Per Subs 18

Special Collections: Oral History
Subject Interests: Ethnography
Wireless access
Partic in Alaska Library Network
Open Wed-Sat 1-5

UNALASKA

P UNALASKA PUBLIC LIBRARY*, 64 Eleanor Dr, 99685. (Mail add: PO Box 1370, 99685-1370). Tel: 907-581-5060. FAX: 907-581-5266. E-mail: akunak@ci.unalaska.ak.us, unalaskacitylibrary@gmail.com. *Dir,* Position Currently Open
Founded 1995. Pop 4,376; Circ 228,841
Jul 2010-Jun 2011 Income $587,396, State $6,300, City $550,578, Federal $10,518, Other $20,000. Mats Exp $87,172, Books $64,152, Per/Ser (Incl. Access Fees) $6,787, Micro $500, AV Mat $4,582, Electronic Ref Mat (Incl. Access Fees) $4,280, Presv $6,871. Sal $394,047 (Prof $87,118)
Library Holdings: Audiobooks 71; Bks on Deafness & Sign Lang 142; DVDs 17,940; Electronic Media & Resources 51; High Interest/Low Vocabulary Bk Vols 4,492; Bk Titles 34,241; Bk Vols 35,847; Per Subs 135; Videos 8,491
Special Collections: Alaskana Coll; Aleutian Region Newspaper Coll
Automation Activity & Vendor Info: (Acquisitions) Baker & Taylor; (Cataloging) OCLC FirstSearch; (Circulation) SirsiDynix; (Course Reserve) SirsiDynix; (ILL) OCLC WorldShare Interlibrary Loan; (OPAC) SirsiDynix; (Serials) SirsiDynix
Database Vendor: EBSCOhost, Electric Library, OCLC FirstSearch, OCLC WorldShare Interlibrary Loan, SirsiDynix
Function: After school storytime
Partic in Alaska Library Network
Special Services for the Deaf - TDD equip
Open Mon-Fri 10-9, Sat & Sun 12-6
Restriction: Non-circulating of rare bks
Friends of the Library Group

VALDEZ

P VALDEZ CONSORTIUM LIBRARY, 212 Fairbanks St, 99686. (Mail add: PO Box 609, 99686-0609), SAN 300-2861. Tel: 907-835-4632. FAX: 907-835-4876. E-mail: vdzlib@ci.valdez.ak.us. Web Site: www.ci.valdez.ak.us/library. *Head Librn,* Mollie Good; *Circ Supvr,* Sara Baker; Staff 1 (MLS 1)
Founded 1930. Pop 4,036; Circ 48,442
Jan 2005-Dec 2005 Income $329,369
Library Holdings: Bks on Deafness & Sign Lang 111; DVDs 64; High Interest/Low Vocabulary Bk Vols 54; Large Print Bks 140; Bk Titles 44,750; Bk Vols 45,786; Per Subs 136; Talking Bks 1,700; Videos 1,455
Special Collections: Alaska Coll
Automation Activity & Vendor Info: (Acquisitions) SirsiDynix; (Cataloging) SirsiDynix; (Circulation) SirsiDynix; (OPAC) SirsiDynix
Database Vendor: OCLC FirstSearch
Wireless access
Open Mon & Fri 10-6, Tues-Thurs 10-8, Sat 12-5, Sun 1-5

WASILLA

P WASILLA META-ROSE PUBLIC LIBRARY*, 391 N Main St, 99654-7085. SAN 300-287X. Tel: 907-376-5913. Administration Tel: 907-864-9170. FAX: 907-376-2347. E-mail: library@ci.wasilla.ak.us. Web Site: www.cityofwasilla.com/library. *Dir,* K J Martin-Albright; E-mail: kmartin-albright@ci.wasilla.ak.us; *Electronic & Ad,* Jean Powell; Tel: 907-864-9177, E-mail: jpowell@ci.wasilla.ak.us; *Youth Serv Librn,* Sara Saxton; Tel: 907-864-9173, E-mail: ssaxton@ci.wasilla.ak.us; *ILL Coordr,* Trudy Toomey; Tel: 907-864-9175, E-mail: ttoomey@ci.wasilla.ak.us; Staff 10 (MLS 3, Non-MLS 7)
Founded 1938. Pop 39,736; Circ 169,567
Jul 2011-Jun 2012 Income $1,011,800, State $6,500, City $891,961, Federal $4,187, County $72,089, Locally Generated Income $37,063. Mats Exp $97,357, Books $76,316, Per/Ser (Incl. Access Fees) $3,424, AV Mat $16,036, Electronic Ref Mat (Incl. Access Fees) $1,581. Sal $463,684
Library Holdings: Audiobooks 2,112; e-books 6,280; Electronic Media & Resources 7,871; Bk Titles 55,277; Bk Vols 53,914; Per Subs 79; Videos 2,985
Special Collections: Municipal Document Depository
Subject Interests: Alaskana
Automation Activity & Vendor Info: (Cataloging) SirsiDynix; (Circulation) SirsiDynix; (ILL) OCLC WorldShare Interlibrary Loan; (OPAC) SirsiDynix
Database Vendor: WT Cox
Wireless access
Function: Alaskana res, Audiobks via web, Bks on cassette, Bks on CD, Children's prog, Computers for patron use, Copy machines, Digital talking bks, Doc delivery serv, Electronic databases & coll, Exhibits, Free DVD rentals, Handicapped accessible, Homework prog, ILL available, Microfiche/film & reading machines, Music CDs, Online cat, Online searches, Outside serv via phone, mail, e-mail & web, OverDrive digital audio bks, Photocopying/Printing, Preschool reading prog, Printer for laptops & handheld devices, Prog for adults, Prog for children & young adult, Pub access computers, Ref serv available, Ref serv in person, Serves mentally handicapped consumers, Story hour, Summer & winter reading prog, Summer reading prog, Tax forms, Teen prog, Telephone ref, VHS videos, Wheelchair accessible, Winter reading prog
Partic in Alaska Library Network; Matanuska-Susitna Library Network
Open Mon 2-6, Tues & Thurs 10:30-7, Wed & Fri 10:30-6, Sat 1-5
Friends of the Library Group

WILLOW

P WILLOW PUBLIC LIBRARY*, 23557 W Willow Community Center Circle, 99688. (Mail add: PO Box 129, 99688-0129), SAN 320-4677. Tel: 907-495-7323. FAX: 907-495-5014. E-mail: willow.library@matsugov.us. Web Site: www.matsulibraries.org.willow. *Librn,* Julie Mitchell; *Asst Librn,* Nina Zwahlen; Staff 2 (Non-MLS 2)
Founded 1967. Circ 33,377
Library Holdings: Audiobooks 1,345; DVDs 2,091; Bk Vols 23,306; Per Subs 55
Special Collections: Alaskana
Automation Activity & Vendor Info: (Acquisitions) SirsiDynix; (Cataloging) SirsiDynix; (ILL) SirsiDynix; (OPAC) Innovative Interfaces, Inc
Wireless access
Open Mon, Tues & Thurs 12-8, Wed & Fri 10:30-6, Sat 10.30-3:30
Friends of the Library Group

WRANGELL

P IRENE INGLE PUBLIC LIBRARY*, Wrangell Public Library, 124 Second Ave, 99929. (Mail add: PO Box 679, 99929-0679), SAN 300-2888. Tel: 907-874-3535. FAX: 907-874-2520. E-mail: wrangelllibrary@gci.net. Web Site: www.wrangell.com/library. *Librn,* Kay Jabusch; *Assoc Librn,* Margaret Villarma; Staff 3 (Non-MLS 3)
Founded 1921. Pop 2,348; Circ 40,209
Jul 2012-Jun 2013 Income $292,590, State $6,250, City $280,340, Federal $6,000. Mats Exp $286,340
Library Holdings: Bk Titles 28,000; Per Subs 62
Subject Interests: Alaska
Automation Activity & Vendor Info: (Acquisitions) The Library Co-Op, Inc; (Cataloging) The Library Co-Op, Inc; (Circulation) The Library Co-Op, Inc; (ILL) OCLC FirstSearch; (OPAC) The Library Co-Op, Inc
Database Vendor: EBSCO Auto Repair Reference, EBSCO Information Services, EBSCOhost, OCLC, Overdrive, Inc
Wireless access
Open Mon & Fri 10-12 & 1-5, Tues-Thurs 1-5 & 7-9, Sat 9-5
Friends of the Library Group

ARIZONA

Date of Statistics: FY 2012-2013
Population, 2010 U.S. Census: 6,392,017
Population Served by Public Libraries: 6,581,054
Total Volumes in Public Libraries: 10,092,562
Volumes Per Capita: 1.5
Total Public Library Circulation: 47,443,670
Circulation Per Capita: 7.2
Total Public Library Income: $178,915,988
Number of County Libraries: 15
Counties Served: 15
Number of Bookmobiles in State: 10
Grants-in-Aid to Public Libraries: (FY 2012-2013)
Federal: $2,060,104
State Aid: $1,571,269

APACHE JUNCTION

P APACHE JUNCTION PUBLIC LIBRARY, 1177 N Idaho Rd, 85119. SAN 300-290X. Tel: 480-474-8555. FAX: 480-671-8037. TDD: 480-983-6012. E-mail: lstaff@ajcity.net. Web Site: www.ajpl.org. *Dir,* Spencer Paden; E-mail: spaden@ajcity.net; *Librn,* Linda Konopitski; *Youth Serv Supvry Librn,* Pam Standhart; *Libr Mgr,* Tracie Curtis; *Supvr,* Trish Pelletier; Staff 5 (MLS 4, Non-MLS 1)
Founded 1965. Pop 37,263; Circ 578,126
Jul 2013-Jun 2014 Income $1,118,952, City $1,093,952, County $25,000
Library Holdings: AV Mats 34,402; e-books 27,626; Bk Titles 92,310; Bk Vols 122,022; Per Subs 127
Special Collections: Arizona Coll; Superstition Mountain Reserve Coll. US Document Depository
Automation Activity & Vendor Info: (Acquisitions) Innovative Interfaces, Inc; (Cataloging) Innovative Interfaces, Inc; (Circulation) Innovative Interfaces, Inc; (OPAC) Innovative Interfaces, Inc
Database Vendor: 3M Library Systems, Alexander Street Press, Baker & Taylor, Booksite, EBSCOhost, Facts on File, HeinOnline, infoUSA, Ingram Library Services, Innovative Interfaces, Inc, LearningExpress, LexisNexis, Medline, Newsbank, OCLC WebJunction, OCLC WorldShare Interlibrary Loan, Overdrive, Inc, ReferenceUSA, TumbleBookLibrary, ValueLine
Wireless access
Mem of Pinal County Library District
Special Services for the Deaf - TDD equip; Videos & decoder
Special Services for the Blind - Bks on cassette; Bks on CD; Large print bks; Magnifiers; Screen enlargement software for people with visual disabilities; ZoomText magnification & reading software
Friends of the Library Group

C CENTRAL ARIZONA COLLEGE*, Superstition Mountain Campus Learning Resource Center, 273 E Old West Hwy (US 60), 85219-5231. Tel: 480-677-7747. FAX: 480-677-7738. Web Site: www.centralaz.edu. *Librn,* Rhonda Jackson; *Learning Res Ctr Spec,* Julie Oneil; E-mail: julie.oneil@centralaz.edu
Library Holdings: Bk Vols 10,000; Per Subs 10
Wireless access
Open Mon-Thurs (Winter) 8-7, Fri 8-4:30; Mon-Thurs (Summer) 8-6

ARIZONA CITY

P ARIZONA CITY COMMUNITY LIBRARY*, 13254 Sunland Gin Rd, 85223. (Mail add: PO Box 118, 85223-0118), SAN 300-2918. Tel: 520-466-5565. FAX: 520-466-6050. *Librn,* Delise Christensen
Founded 1963. Pop 5,000; Circ 9,942
Library Holdings: AV Mats 600; Bk Vols 22,000; Talking Bks 450
Special Collections: Arizona Coll
Automation Activity & Vendor Info: (Cataloging) Horizon; (Circulation) Horizon; (OPAC) Horizon
Publications: Newsletter
Mem of Pinal County Library District
Special Services for the Blind - Audio mat; Talking bks
Open Tues & Fri 11-5, Wed & Thurs 11-7, Sat 11-3
Friends of the Library Group

ASH FORK

P ASH FORK PUBLIC LIBRARY*, 450 W Lewis Ave, 86320. (Mail add: PO Box 295, 86320-0295), SAN 323-7796. Tel: 928-637-2442. FAX: 928-637-2442. Web Site: www.yavapailibrary.org/yavapai/ashfork.asp. *Commun Librn,* Mary Rigby
Library Holdings: Bk Vols 8,000
Automation Activity & Vendor Info: (Cataloging) SirsiDynix; (OPAC) SirsiDynix
Mem of Yavapai County Free Library District
Open Mon-Fri 10-4

AVONDALE

P AVONDALE PUBLIC LIBRARY*, Sam Garcia Western Avenue Library, 495 E Western Ave, 85323. SAN 300-2926. Tel: 623-333-2601, 623-333-2665. E-mail: emailLibrary@avondale.org. Web Site: www.avondalelibrary.org. *Libr Mgr,* Ava Gutwein
Founded 1930. Pop 60,000; Circ 150,000
Library Holdings: Bk Vols 45,000; Per Subs 52
Subject Interests: Spanish (Lang)
Automation Activity & Vendor Info: (Cataloging) Innovative Interfaces, Inc; (Circulation) Innovative Interfaces, Inc; (OPAC) Innovative Interfaces, Inc
Wireless access
Open Mon-Thurs 10-7, Fri & Sat 10-5
Branches: 1
AVONDALE CIVIC CENTER LIBRARY, 11350 W Civic Ctr Dr, 85323. Tel: 623-333-2602. *Libr Mgr,* Ava Gutwein
Founded 2007

J ESTRELLA MOUNTAIN COMMUNITY COLLEGE LIBRARY*, 3000 N Dysart Rd, 85392. SAN 374-7417. Tel: 623-935-8191. FAX: 623-935-8060. Web Site: www.estrellamountain.edu. *Div Chair,* Nikol Price; E-mail: nikol.price@estrellamountain.edu; *Librn,* Terry Meyer; *Librn,* Jennifer Wong; *Librn,* Christopher Zagar; Staff 7.5 (MLS 4, Non-MLS 3.5)
Founded 1992. Enrl 5,000; Fac 92; Highest Degree: Associate
Library Holdings: Bk Titles 15,000; Per Subs 100
Automation Activity & Vendor Info: (Acquisitions) Horizon; (Cataloging) Horizon; (Circulation) Horizon; (Course Reserve) Horizon; (ILL) Horizon; (Media Booking) Horizon; (OPAC) Horizon; (Serials) Horizon
Wireless access
Open Mon-Thurs 7am-10pm, Fri 7-5, Sat 8-5

BAGDAD

P BAGDAD PUBLIC LIBRARY*, 700 Palo Verde, Bldg C, 86321. (Mail add: PO Box 95, 86321-0095), SAN 323-7818. Tel: 928-633-2325. FAX: 928-633-2054. Web Site: www.yavapailibrary.org/yavapai/bagdad.asp. *Commun Librn,* Kimberly Silveira
Library Holdings: Bk Titles 10,000
Automation Activity & Vendor Info: (Cataloging) SirsiDynix; (Circulation) SirsiDynix; (OPAC) SirsiDynix
Mem of Yavapai County Free Library District
Open Mon, Tues & Thurs 10-4, Wed 10-5

BENSON

P BENSON PUBLIC LIBRARY*, 300 S Huachuca, 85602-6650. SAN 300-2934. Tel: 520-586-9535. FAX: 520-586-3224. E-mail: bensonpubliclibrary@cityofbenson.com. *Dir,* Peggy Scott; E-mail: pscott@bensonpl.lib.az.us; *Asst Dir,* Kelli Jeter; Staff 7 (Non-MLS 7)
Founded 1916. Pop 8,000; Circ 74,000
Library Holdings: Bk Vols 36,625; Per Subs 51
Special Collections: Arizoniana
Subject Interests: Arizona, Gen fiction
Automation Activity & Vendor Info: (Cataloging) SirsiDynix; (Circulation) SirsiDynix
Database Vendor: SirsiDynix
Wireless access
Function: ILL available, Photocopying/Printing, Prof lending libr, Ref serv available, Telephone ref
Mem of Cochise County Library District
Partic in Southwest Area Multicounty Multitype Interlibrary Exchange
Special Services for the Deaf - Bks on deafness & sign lang; Spec interest per
Special Services for the Blind - Bks on cassette
Open Mon & Thurs 10-7, Tues & Wed 10-6, Fri 10-5, Sat 10-1
Friends of the Library Group

BISBEE

S BISBEE MINING & HISTORICAL MUSEUM*, Lemuel C Shattuck Memorial Archival Library, Five Copper Queen Plaza, 85603. (Mail add: PO Box 14, 85603-0014), SAN 300-2942. Tel: 520-432-7071. FAX: 520-432-7800. Web Site: bisbeemuseum.org. *Dir,* Carrie Gustavson; E-mail: carrie@bisbeemuseum.org; *Coll Mgr,* Annie Larkin; E-mail: annie@bisbeemuseum.org; Staff 4 (MLS 1, Non-MLS 3)
Founded 1974
Library Holdings: AV Mats 450; Bk Titles 1,200
Special Collections: Bisbee Newspapers 1898-1970, microfilm; City of Bisbee Voter Registration Records; Cochise County Original Geological Survey Maps; County Great Registers & County Census for 1880 (1882 Special Census), 1900 & 1910; Historic Image Photographic Coll; Historic Preservation & Restoration File; Hospital Records, pre-1900; Manuscript Coll; Tombstone Newspapers 1877-1901. Municipal Document Depository; Oral History
Subject Interests: Geol, Local hist, Mining
Open Sat-Sun 10-4
Restriction: Non-circulating
Friends of the Library Group

GL COCHISE COUNTY LAW LIBRARY*, 100 Quality Hill, 85603. (Mail add: PO Drawer P, 85603-0050), SAN 300-2950. Tel: 520-432-8513. Administration Tel: 520-432-8500. FAX: 520-432-2630. Web Site: www.co.cochise.az.us. *Librn,* Frances Simmons; E-mail: fsimmons@cochise.az.gov
Founded 1930
Library Holdings: Bk Titles 27,000
Open Mon-Fri 8-5

P COCHISE COUNTY LIBRARY DISTRICT*, Old High School, 2nd Flr, 100 Clawson, 85603. (Mail add: PO Drawer AK, 85603-0099), SAN 330-5228. Tel: 520-432-8930. FAX: 520-432-7339. Web Site: cochise.lib.az.us. *Dir,* Lise Gilliland; E-mail: lgilliland@co.cochise.az.us; *Pub Serv,* Kimberly Holman; E-mail: kholman@cochisecold.lib.az.us; *Syst Adminr,* Larry Scritchfield; E-mail: lscritch@cochisecold.lib.az.us; *Tech Serv,* Susan Mathews; E-mail: smathews@cochisecold.lib.az.us; Staff 9 (MLS 4, Non-MLS 5)
Founded 1970. Pop 135,000
Library Holdings: Bk Titles 70,000; Bk Vols 120,000
Automation Activity & Vendor Info: (Cataloging) SirsiDynix; (Circulation) SirsiDynix; (ILL) SirsiDynix; (OPAC) SirsiDynix
Database Vendor: OCLC FirstSearch
Function: Homebound delivery serv
Member Libraries: Benson Public Library; Copper Queen Library; Douglas Public Library; Elsie S Hogan Community Library; Huachuca City Public Library; Sierra Vista Public Library; Tombstone Reading Station-Tombstone City Library
Open Mon-Fri 8-5
Friends of the Library Group
Branches: 5
ELFRIDA LIBRARY, 10552 N Hwy 191, Elfrida, 85610-9021. (Mail add: PO Box 98, Elfrida, 85610-0098). Tel: 520-642-1744. FAX: 520-642-1744. *Br Coordr,* Charlene Kennedy; Staff 1 (Non-MLS 1)
Pop 1,200; Circ 9,434
Library Holdings: Bk Vols 6,440
Function: Prog for children & young adult, Summer reading prog
Open Tues 1-8, Thurs 9-12 & 2-5, Fri 1-5, Sat 9-12
Friends of the Library Group
MYRTLE KRAFT LIBRARY, 2393 S Rock House Rd, Portal, 85632. (Mail add: PO Box 16552, Portal, 85632-6552), SAN 330-5430. Tel: 520-558-2468. FAX: 520-558-2468. *Br Mgr,* Kathleen Talbot; E-mail: ktalbot@cochise.az.gov; *Asst Librn,* Penny Johnston; Staff 1 (Non-MLS 1)
Founded 1979. Pop 300; Circ 4,913
Library Holdings: Bk Vols 4,800
Function: Summer reading prog
Open Tues-Sat 10-2
Friends of the Library Group
JIMMIE LIBHART LIBRARY, 201 N Central, Bowie, 85605. (Mail add: PO Box 417, Bowie, 85605-0417), SAN 325-3910. Tel: 520-847-2522. FAX: 520-847-2522. *Br Mgr,* Richard Bergquist; E-mail: rbergquist@cochise.az.gov; Staff 1 (Non-MLS 1)
Founded 1985. Pop 300; Circ 5,070
Library Holdings: Bk Vols 4,897
Function: Prog for children & young adult, Summer reading prog
Open Mon-Fri 10-3
SUNSITES COMMUNITY LIBRARY, 210 N Ford Rd, Pearce, 85625. (Mail add: PO Box 544, Pearce, 85625-0544), SAN 330-5252. Tel: 520-826-3866. FAX: 520-826-3866. *Br Mgr,* Jennifer Davis; E-mail: JRDavis@cochise.az.gov; Staff 1 (Non-MLS 1)
Founded 1979. Pop 1,200; Circ 13,290
Library Holdings: Bk Vols 10,166
Function: Prog for children & young adult, Summer reading prog
Open Mon, Wed, Thurs & Fri 9:30-4:30, Sat 9:30-11:30
Friends of the Library Group
ALICE WOODS SUNIZONA LIBRARY AT ASH CREEK SCHOOL, 6460 E Hwy 181, Pearce, 85625, SAN 330-549X. Tel: 520-824-3145. FAX: 520-824-3145. *Br Coordr,* Marian Baker Gierlach; Staff 1 (Non-MLS 1)
Founded 1979. Pop 300; Circ 9,639
Library Holdings: Bk Vols 9,536
Function: Summer reading prog
Open Tues 2-4, Wed 9:30-11:30, Thurs 9-11:30, Fri 11:30-5, Sat 9-12
Bookmobiles: 2. Librn, Ted Weller

P COPPER QUEEN LIBRARY, Bisbee City Library, Six Main St, 85603. (Mail add: PO Box 1857, 85603-2857), SAN 300-2969. Tel: 520-432-4232. FAX: 520-432-7061. *Dir,* Peg White; E-mail: pwhite@bisbeepl.lib.az.us; *Access/Tech Serv Coordr,* Jason Macoviak; *Prog Coordr,* Chandra Curtin; Staff 4 (MLS 1, Non-MLS 3)
Founded 1882. Pop 6,090; Circ 42,196
Library Holdings: Bk Vols 30,000; Per Subs 40
Special Collections: Southwest & Arizona Coll
Automation Activity & Vendor Info: (Cataloging) SirsiDynix; (Circulation) SirsiDynix
Database Vendor: SirsiDynix
Wireless access
Mem of Cochise County Library District
Open Mon & Tues Noon-7, Wed-Fri 10-5
Friends of the Library Group

BLACK CANYON CITY

P BLACK CANYON CITY COMMUNITY LIBRARY*, 34701 S Old Black Canyon Hwy, 85324. (Mail add: PO Box 87, 85324-0087), SAN 323-7834. Tel: 623-374-5866. FAX: 623-374-0465. Web Site: yavapailibrary.org/bcc.htm. *Commun Librn,* Melina Reylek; E-mail: melina.reylek@co.yavapai.az.us
Library Holdings: Audiobooks 300; Bks on Deafness & Sign Lang 5; DVDs 1,000; Large Print Bks 200; Bk Titles 19,000; Per Subs 6; Videos 500
Automation Activity & Vendor Info: (Cataloging) SirsiDynix; (Circulation) SirsiDynix; (OPAC) SirsiDynix
Mem of Yavapai County Free Library District
Open Tues-Thurs 9-7, Fri & Sat 9-5

BUCKEYE

S ARIZONA DEPARTMENT OF CORRECTIONS - ADULT INSTITUTIONS*, Arizona State Prison Complex - Lewis Library, 26700 S Hwy 85, 85326. (Mail add: PO Box 70, 85326-0070). Tel: 623-386-6160,

Ext 4908. FAX: 623-386-6160, Ext 4910. *Librn,* Steve Latto; *Librn,* Roxanne Moore; *Librn,* Janet Tabor; *Libr Supvr-Popular Libr,* Ruby Padilla
Library Holdings: Bk Vols 30,000
Open Mon-Fri 7-3:30

P BUCKEYE PUBLIC LIBRARY, 310 N Sixth St, 85326-2439. SAN 300-2977. Tel: 623-349-6300. FAX: 623-349-6310. Web Site: www.buckeyeaz.gov/library. *Libr Mgr,* Jana White; E-mail: jwhite@buckeyeaz.gov; *Librn,* Denise Baker; E-mail: dbaker@buckeyeaz.gov; *Libr Supvr,* Christine Larson; E-mail: clarson@buckeyeaz.gov; Staff 9.75 (MLS 2, Non-MLS 7.75)
Founded 1956. Pop 54,000
Library Holdings: Bk Vols 25,000; Per Subs 60
Special Collections: Arizona History & Culture (Southwest Coll)
Automation Activity & Vendor Info: (Cataloging) Innovative Interfaces, Inc; (Circulation) Innovative Interfaces, Inc; (OPAC) Innovative Interfaces, Inc
Wireless access
Open Mon, Wed & Fri 9-5, Tues & Thurs 9-7, Sat 9-4
Friends of the Library Group
Bookmobiles: 1

CAMP VERDE

P CAMP VERDE COMMUNITY LIBRARY, 130 Black Bridge Rd, 86322. SAN 323-7850. Tel: 928-554-8380. FAX: 928-567-9583. E-mail: library@campverde.az.gov. Web Site: www.campverde.az.gov/government/library. *Dir,* Kathy D Hellman; Tel: 928-554-8381, E-mail: kathy.hellman@campverde.az.gov; *Youth Serv Librn,* Dianna Manasse; Tel: 928-554-8387, E-mail: dianna.manasse@campverde.az.gov; *Cat, Tech Serv,* Valerie Foster; Tel: 928-554-8388, E-mail: valerie.foster@campverde.az.gov; *Ch Serv,* Wendy Cook-Roberts, E-mail: wendy.roberts@campverde.az.gov; *Circ/Adult Serv,* Gerry Laurito; Tel: 928-554-8384, E-mail: gerry.laurito@campverde.az.gov; *Circ/Vols Serv,* Alice R Gottschalk; Tel: 928-554-8383, E-mail: alice.gottschalk@campverde.az.gov; *Libr Spec - Teens,* Sebra Choe; Tel: 928-554-8391, E-mail: sebra.choe@campverde.az.gov; *Tech Serv,* Dee Thompson; Tel: 938-554-8392, E-mail: dee.thompson@campverde.az.gov; *Youth Serv,* Denise Alm; Tel: 928-554-8393, E-mail: denise.alm@campverde.az.gov; Staff 7 (MLS 3, Non-MLS 4)
Founded 1958. Pop 12,000; Circ 93,855
Jul 2014-Jun 2015 Income $419,145, City $290,945, Federal $45,700, County $80,000, Locally Generated Income $2,500. Mats Exp $26,700, Books $17,700, Other Print Mats $1,700, AV Mat $7,300. Sal $310,935 (Prof $144,227)
Library Holdings: Audiobooks 555; AV Mats 6; Bks-By-Mail 200; CDs 302; DVDs 1,110; e-books 77; Large Print Bks 2,052; Bk Titles 28,771; Bk Vols 28,771; Per Subs 46
Special Collections: Southwest US Information & Culture
Automation Activity & Vendor Info: (Cataloging) SirsiDynix, (Circulation) SirsiDynix; (ILL) OCLC WorldShare Interlibrary Loan; (OPAC) SirsiDynix
Database Vendor: Gale Cengage Learning, OCLC WorldShare Interlibrary Loan, Overdrive, Inc, SirsiDynix, TumbleBookLibrary
Wireless access
Function: 24/7 Electronic res, 24/7 Online cat, Accelerated reader prog, Adult bk club, Adult literacy prog, Art exhibits, Audiobks via web, Bi-weekly Writer's Group, Bk club(s), Bk reviews (Group), Bks on CD, Children's prog, Computer training, Computers for patron use, Copy machines, Digital talking bks, Electronic databases & coll, eReaders, Fax serv, Free DVD rentals, Handicapped accessible, Holiday prog, Home delivery & serv to Sr ctr & nursing homes, Homework prog, ILL available, Instruction & testing, Jail serv, Jazz prog, Life-long learning prog for all ages, Magazines, Magnifiers for reading, Mail & tel request accepted, Mango lang, Movies, Music CDs, Newsp ref libr, Online cat, Online searches, Outreach serv, Outside serv via phone, mail, e-mail & web, OverDrive digital audio bks, Photocopying/Printing, Preschool outreach, Preschool reading prog, Printer for laptops & handheld devices, Prog for adults, Prog for children & young adult, Pub access computers, Ref serv available, Ref serv in person, Scanner, Senior computer classes, Senior outreach, Story hour, Summer reading prog, Tax forms, Teen prog, Telephone ref, Web-catalog, Wheelchair accessible, Workshops, Writing prog
Publications: Subject Handouts
Partic in Yavapai Libr Network
Open Tues-Thurs 8:30-7, Fri & Sat 8:30-3:30

CASA GRANDE

P CASA GRANDE PUBLIC LIBRARY*, 449 N Dry Lake, 85222. SAN 300-2993. Tel: 520-421-8710. FAX: 520-421-8701. TDD: 520-421-2035. Web Site: casagrandeaz.us/rec/library. *City Librn,* Amber Kent; E-mail: akent@casagrandeaz.gov; *Ad,* Kevin Sahey; Tel: 520-421-8710, Ext 5160, E-mail: ksahey@casagrandeaz.gov; *Ad,* Julie Yen; Tel: 520-421-8710, Ext 5240, E-mail: jyen@casagrandeaz.gov; *Youth Serv Librn,* Julie Lash; Tel: 520-421-8710, Ext 5150, E-mail: jlash@casagrandeaz.gov; Staff 12 (MLS 4, Non-MLS 8)
Founded 1958. Pop 42,455; Circ 230,000
Library Holdings: AV Mats 8,365; CDs 494; DVDs 696; Electronic Media & Resources 12; High Interest/Low Vocabulary Bk Vols 100; Large Print Bks 3,241; Bk Titles 75,433; Per Subs 312; Talking Bks 100; Videos 6,933
Special Collections: Municipal Document Depository
Subject Interests: Local hist
Automation Activity & Vendor Info: (Acquisitions) Innovative Interfaces, Inc; (Cataloging) Innovative Interfaces, Inc; (Circulation) Innovative Interfaces, Inc; (Course Reserve) Innovative Interfaces, Inc; (ILL) Innovative Interfaces, Inc; (Media Booking) Innovative Interfaces, Inc; (OPAC) Innovative Interfaces, Inc; (Serials) Innovative Interfaces, Inc
Database Vendor: ALLDATA Online, Amigos Library Services, Backstage Library Works, Booksite, EBSCO - WebFeat, EBSCO Auto Repair Reference, EBSCO Information Services, EBSCOhost, Gale Cengage Learning, Grolier Online, Ingram Library Services, OCLC ArticleFirst, OCLC FirstSearch, OCLC WebJunction, OCLC WorldShare Interlibrary Loan, Overdrive, Inc, ProQuest, ReferenceUSA, Wilson - Wilson Web
Wireless access
Function: Archival coll, Art exhibits, Audiobks via web, BA reader (adult literacy), Bk club(s), Bks on cassette, Bks on CD, Children's prog, Computer training, Computers for patron use, Copy machines, Digital talking bks, e-mail serv, E-Reserves, Electronic databases & coll, Family literacy, Free DVD rentals, Handicapped accessible, Holiday prog, Homebound delivery serv, Homework prog, ILL available, Instruction & testing, Learning ctr, Music CDs, Newsp ref libr, Online cat, Online searches, Outside serv via phone, mail, e-mail & web, OverDrive digital audio bks, Pub access computers, Ref & res, Ref serv available, Res libr, Senior computer classes, Senior outreach, Spoken cassettes & CDs, Spoken cassettes & DVDs, Story hour, Summer reading prog, Tax forms, Teen prog, Telephone ref, VHS videos, Video lending libr, Web-catalog, Wheelchair accessible
Mem of Pinal County Library District
Special Services for the Deaf - TTY equip
Open Mon-Thurs 9-7, Fri 9-5, Sun 1-5
Friends of the Library Group
Branches: 1
VISTA GRANDE LIBRARY, 1556 N Arizola Rd, 85122. Tel: 520-421-8652. FAX: 520-836-0819. *Mgr,* Amber Kent; *YA Librn,* Julie Andersen
Library Holdings: AV Mats 10,000; Bk Vols 30,000; Per Subs 50
Open Mon-Fri 8-5, Sat 9-5
Friends of the Library Group
Bookmobiles: 1. Librn, Chuck Okafor

S CASA GRANDE VALLEY HISTORICAL SOCIETY*, Museum Library, 110 W Florence Blvd, 85122. SAN 327-7089. Tel: 520-836-2223. E-mail: info@cgvhs.org. Web Site: www.cgvhs.org. *Archivist,* Kay Benedict
Founded 1964
Library Holdings: Bk Titles 300
Subject Interests: Local hist
Open Mon-Fri 9-1
Restriction: Non-circulating to the pub

CAVE CREEK

P DESERT FOOTHILLS LIBRARY, 38443 N Schoolhouse Rd, 85331. (Mail add: PO Box 4070, 85327-4070), SAN 376-8414. Tel: 480-488-2286. FAX: 480-595-8353. Web Site: www.dfla.org. *Exec Dir,* David G Court; E-mail: dcourt@dfla.org; *Mkt & Prog Mgr,* Dereth DeHaan; E-mail: ddehaan@dfla.org; Staff 10 (MLS 2, Non-MLS 8)
Founded 1953. Pop 8,498; Circ 123,000
Jul 2014-Jun 2015 Income $670,000, County $60,000, Locally Generated Income $610,000. Mats Exp $78,000, Books $42,000, Per/Ser (Incl. Access Fees) $4,000, AV Equip $14,000, AV Mat $18,000. Sal $361,000 (Prof $94,000)
Library Holdings: AV Mats 5,300; e-books 1,000; Large Print Bks 1,200; Bk Titles 50,000; Per Subs 100; Talking Bks 3,340; Videos 7,000
Special Collections: Southwest Coll
Wireless access
Function: Adult bk club, Art exhibits, Bk club(s), Bks on CD, Children's prog, Computer training, Computers for patron use, Copy machines, Digital talking bks, Electronic databases & coll, Exhibits, Fax serv, Free DVD rentals, Handicapped accessible, Holiday prog, Home delivery & serv to Sr ctr & nursing homes, Homebound delivery serv, ILL available, Mus passes, Music CDs, Notary serv, Online cat, Online ref, Online searches, Orientations, Outreach serv, OverDrive digital audio bks, Passport agency, Photocopying/Printing, Preschool outreach, Preschool reading prog, Prog for adults, Prog for children & young adult, Pub access computers, Senior computer classes, Spanish lang bks, Spoken cassettes & CDs, Spoken cassettes & DVDs, Story hour, Summer & winter reading prog, Summer reading prog, Tax forms, Teen prog, Video lending libr, Wheelchair accessible, Writing prog

Open Mon-Thurs 9-7, Fri 9-5, Sat 10-4, Sun 12-4
Friends of the Library Group

CHANDLER

J CHANDLER-GILBERT COMMUNITY COLLEGE LIBRARY*, 2626 E Pecos Rd, 85225-2499. Tel: 480-857-5100. Circulation Tel: 480-857-5102. Web Site: www.cgc.maricopa.edu/library. *Dir,* Carol Dichtenberg; Tel: 480-857-5133, E-mail: carol.dichtenberg@cgcmail.maricopa.edu; *Access Serv,* Barbara Stott; Tel: 480-857-5137, Fax: 480-857-5136, E-mail: barbara.stott@cgcmail.maricopa.edu; Staff 9 (MLS 4, Non-MLS 5)
Founded 1987. Enrl 12,000; Highest Degree: Associate
Library Holdings: Bk Vols 27,000; Per Subs 180
Automation Activity & Vendor Info: (Acquisitions) SirsiDynix; (Cataloging) SirsiDynix; (Circulation) SirsiDynix; (ILL) OCLC ILLiad; (OPAC) SirsiDynix
Database Vendor: EBSCOhost, Gale Cengage Learning, Newsbank, OCLC FirstSearch, SirsiDynix, Wilson - Wilson Web
Wireless access
Open Mon-Thurs (Winter) 7:30am-9pm, Fri 7:30-2, Sat 9-2; Mon-Thurs (Summer) 8am-9pm

P CHANDLER PUBLIC LIBRARY, 22 S Delaware, 85225. (Mail add: MS601, PO Box 4008, 85244-4008), SAN 300-3000. Tel: 480-782-2800. FAX: 480-782-2823. TDD: 800-367-8939. Web Site: www.chandlerlibrary.org. *Libr Mgr,* Brenda Brown; Tel: 480-782-2817, E-mail: brenda.brown@chandleraz.gov; *Asst Libr Mgr, Pub Serv,* Kris Sherman; Tel: 480-782-2818, E-mail: kris.sherman@chandleraz.gov; *Asst Libr Mgr, Tech,* Daniel Lee; Tel: 480-782-2813, E-mail: dan.lee@chandleraz.gov; *Admin Librn,* Marybeth Gardner; Tel: 480-782-2816, E-mail: marybeth.gardner@chandleraz.gov. Subject Specialists: *Adult educ,* Marybeth Gardner; Staff 36 (MLS 10, Non-MLS 26)
Founded 1954. Pop 250,000
Special Collections: Arizona & Southwest Coll; Arizona Indian Coll; Large Print Book Coll; New Reader Coll; Spanish Language Coll
Database Vendor: Gale Cengage Learning, OCLC FirstSearch
Wireless access
Function: Adult bk club, Homebound delivery serv, Homework prog, ILL available, Summer reading prog, Telephone ref
Special Services for the Deaf - TDD equip
Open Mon-Wed 9-9, Thurs-Sat 9-5, Sun 1-5
Friends of the Library Group
Branches: 3
BASHA, 5990 S Val Vista Dr, 85249. (Mail add: MS 920, PO Box 4008, 85244-4008). Tel: 480-782-2800. FAX: 480-782-2855. *Admin Librn,* George Delalis; Tel: 480-782-2856, E-mail: george.delalis@chandleraz.gov; Staff 8 (MLS 3, Non-MLS 5)
Founded 2003
Function: Adult bk club, Prog for adults, Prog for children & young adult, Summer reading prog
Open Mon-Wed 7:30am-8pm, Thurs & Fri 7:30-5, Sat 10-2
Friends of the Library Group
HAMILTON, 3700 S Arizona Ave, 85248-4500. (Mail add: MS917, PO Box 4008, 85244-4008). Tel: 480-782-2800. FAX: 480-782-2833. *Admin Librn,* Phyllis Saunders; Tel: 480-782-2831, E-mail: phyllis.saunders@chandleraz.gov; Staff 8 (MLS 2, Non-MLS 6)
Function: Adult bk club, Photocopying/Printing
Open Mon-Wed 7:30am-8pm, Thurs & Fri 7:30-5, Sat 1-5
Friends of the Library Group
SUNSET, 4930 W Ray Rd, 85226-6219. (Mail add: MS918, PO Box 4008, 85244-4008). Tel: 480-782-2800. FAX: 480-782-2848. *Admin Librn,* Susan Hoffman; E-mail: susan.hoffman@chandleraz.gov; Staff 12.5 (MLS 4.5, Non-MLS 8)
Function: Adult bk club, After school storytime, Audiobks via web, Bks on CD, Chess club, Children's prog, Computer training, Computers for patron use, Copy machines, Digital talking bks, e-mail & chat, E-Reserves, Fax serv, ILL available, Mus passes, Music CDs, Newsp ref libr, Online cat, Online searches, OverDrive digital audio bks, Photocopying/Printing, Prog for adults, Prog for children & young adult, Ref serv in person, Scanner, Story hour, Tax forms, Teen prog, Telephone ref, Wheelchair accessible, Writing prog
Open Mon-Wed 7:30am-8pm, Thurs & Fri 7:30-5, Sat 1-5
Friends of the Library Group

CHINO VALLEY

P CHINO VALLEY PUBLIC LIBRARY*, 1020 W Palomino Rd, 86323-5500. (Mail add: PO Box 1188, 86323-1188), SAN 323-7877. Tel: 928-636-2687. FAX: 928-636-9129. Web Site: www.ci.chino-valley.az.us. *Dir,* Scott A Bruner; *Asst Librn,* Julia A Diener; *Cat,* Patricia Lobdell; *Ch Serv,* Darlene J Westcott; *Circ,* Dennis Dingley; *Circ,* Christa Kerbstat; *Circ,* Gillian McArthur; Staff 7 (MLS 1, Non-MLS 6)
Library Holdings: Bk Vols 40,000
Database Vendor: SirsiDynix
Mem of Yavapai County Free Library District
Partic in Amninet; Libr Network of Arizona; Yavapai Libr Network
Open Mon-Thurs 9-7, Fri & Sat 9-5
Friends of the Library Group

CIBECUE

P CIBECUE COMMUNITY LIBRARY*, Six W Third St, 85911. (Mail add: PO Box 80008, 85911), SAN 376-6047. Tel: 928-332-2621. FAX: 928-332-2442. E-mail: cbqlibrary@wmat.us. *Dir,* Verna Cromwell
Library Holdings: Bk Vols 3,200
Open Mon-Thurs 9-4:45

CLARKDALE

P CLARK MEMORIAL LIBRARY*, 39 N Ninth St, 86324. (Mail add: PO Box 308, 86324-0308), SAN 323-7893. Tel: 928-639-2480. FAX: 928-639-2489. E-mail: library@clarkdale.az.gov. Web Site: www.clarkdale.az.gov/library2.html. *Commun Serv Supvr,* Dawn Norman; E-mail: dawn.norman@clarkdale.az.gov; *Circ,* Margie Hardie; E-mail: margie.hardie@clarkdale.az.gov
Pop 3,824
Library Holdings: Bk Vols 10,000; Per Subs 32
Automation Activity & Vendor Info: (Cataloging) SirsiDynix; (Circulation) SirsiDynix; (OPAC) SirsiDynix
Database Vendor: Overdrive, Inc
Wireless access
Function: Accelerated reader prog, Adult bk club, Archival coll, Art exhibits, Audio & video playback equip for onsite use, Audiobks via web, AV serv, Bk club(s), Bks on CD, CD-ROM, Children's prog, Computer training, Computers for patron use, Copy machines, Distance learning, e-mail & chat, e-mail serv, E-Reserves, Electronic databases & coll, Exhibits, Fax serv, Free DVD rentals, Handicapped accessible, Homework prog, ILL available, Newsp ref libr, Notary serv, Online ref, Online searches, OverDrive digital audio bks, Photocopying/Printing, Printer for laptops & handheld devices, Prog for adults, Prog for children & young adult, Pub access computers, Spoken cassettes & CDs, Story hour, Summer reading prog, Web-catalog, Wheelchair accessible
Mem of Yavapai County Free Library District
Partic in Yavapai Libr Network
Open Mon-Thurs 8:30-5:30, Fri 8-Noon

CLAY SPRINGS

P CLAY SPRINGS PUBLIC LIBRARY*, 2106 Granite Rd, 85923. (Mail add: PO Box 428, 85923-0428), SAN 377-0737. Tel: 928-739-4848. E-mail: cpl@navajo.lib.az.us. *In Charge,* Beverly Jackson
Library Holdings: AV Mats 215; Large Print Bks 50; Bk Titles 2,000; Bk Vols 3,500; Talking Bks 60
Open Mon-Fri 1-4

CLIFTON

P CLIFTON PUBLIC LIBRARY*, 588 Turner Ave, 85533. (Mail add: PO Box 1226, 85533-1226), SAN 300-3027. Tel: 928-865-2461. FAX: 928-865-3014. *Dir,* Norine Lawrence; E-mail: lawrence@townofclifton.com; Staff 1 (Non-MLS 1)
Founded 1941. Pop 9,000
Library Holdings: Bk Vols 25,000; Per Subs 20
Special Collections: Arizona Coll
Mem of Greenlee County Library System
Open Mon & Tues 10-6, Wed & Thurs 10-5, Fri 10-4

CONGRESS

P CONGRESS PUBLIC LIBRARY*, 26750 Santa Fe Rd, 85332. (Mail add: PO Box 280, 85332-0280), SAN 323-7915. Tel: 928-427-3945. FAX: 928-427-3945. Web Site: www.yavapailibrary.org/yavapai/congress.asp. *Commun Librn,* Mary Ann Paulic; Staff 1 (Non-MLS 1)
Founded 1984. Pop 1,700; Circ 8,036
Jul 2006-Jun 2007 Income $4,620. Mats Exp $4,064, Books $3,984, Per/Ser (Incl. Access Fees) $80. Sal $16,000
Library Holdings: DVDs 100; Bk Titles 3,500; Per Subs 3; Videos 300
Automation Activity & Vendor Info: (Circulation) SirsiDynix
Database Vendor: EBSCOhost, OCLC FirstSearch, SirsiDynix
Mem of Yavapai County Free Library District
Special Services for the Blind - Bks on cassette; Bks on CD; Large print bks; Magnifiers
Open Wed, Thurs & Fri 10-4, Sat 9-1

COOLIDGE

C CENTRAL ARIZONA COLLEGE*, Signal Peak Library, 8470 N Overfield Rd, 85128. SAN 300-3043. Tel: 520-494-5286. FAX: 520-494-5284. Web Site: www.centralaz.edu/library. *Dir,* Adriana Saavedra; E-mail: adriana.saavedra@centralaz.edu; *Librn,* Rhonda Jackson;

Librn, Scott Snellman; *Librn,* McKay Wellikson; Staff 9 (MLS 5, Non-MLS 4)
Founded 1969. Highest Degree: Associate
Library Holdings: Bk Vols 90,000; Per Subs 105
Special Collections: US Document Depository
Automation Activity & Vendor Info: (Acquisitions) SirsiDynix; (Cataloging) SirsiDynix; (Circulation) SirsiDynix; (Course Reserve) SirsiDynix; (ILL) SirsiDynix; (Media Booking) SirsiDynix; (OPAC) SirsiDynix; (Serials) SirsiDynix
Database Vendor: ABC-CLIO, Alexander Street Press, CQ Press, EBSCOhost, Facts on File, Gale Cengage Learning, Greenwood Publishing Group, H W Wilson, OCLC, SirsiDynix
Wireless access
Partic in Amigos Library Services, Inc; OCLC Online Computer Library Center, Inc
Special Services for the Blind - Accessible computers; Audio mat; Bks on CD; Copier with enlargement capabilities; Large screen computer & software; Low vision equip
Open Mon-Thurs 7:30am-8pm, Fri 7:30-6, Sun Noon-6
Departmental Libraries:
ARAVAIPA CAMPUS LEARNING RESOURCE CENTER
See Separate Entry in Winkelman
SUPERSTITION MOUNTAIN CAMPUS LEARNING RESOURCE CENTER
See Separate Entry in Apache Junction

P COOLIDGE PUBLIC LIBRARY*, 160 W Central Ave, 85128. SAN 300-3051. Tel: 520-723-6030. FAX: 520-723-7026. Web Site: www.coolidgeaz.com. *Libr Mgr,* Joyce Baker; Staff 1 (MLS 1)
Pop 11,300; Circ 99,590
Library Holdings: Bk Titles 27,775; Per Subs 40
Special Collections: Large Print Coll
Automation Activity & Vendor Info: (Cataloging) Innovative Interfaces, Inc; (Circulation) Innovative Interfaces, Inc; (OPAC) Innovative Interfaces, Inc
Wireless access
Mem of Pinal County Library District
Open Mon-Fri 8-6, Sat 8-1
Friends of the Library Group

CORDES LAKES

P CORDES LAKES PUBLIC LIBRARY*, 20445 E Quailrun Dr, 86333. (Mail add: PO Box 69, Mayer, 86333), SAN 323-7931. Tel: 928-632-5492. *Librn,* Becky Madaras
Library Holdings: Bk Vols 5,079
Automation Activity & Vendor Info: (Cataloging) SirsiDynix; (Circulation) SirsiDynix; (OPAC) SirsiDynix
Open Tues 2-7, Thurs 1-6, Fri 10-3

COTTONWOOD

P COTTONWOOD PUBLIC LIBRARY*, 100 S Sixth St, 86326. SAN 300-306X. Tel. 928-634-7559. FAX: 928 634 0253. *Libr Mgr,* Vanessa Ward; E-mail: vward@cottonwoodaz.gov; Staff 5 (MLS 2, Non-MLS 3)
Founded 1960. Pop 40,000; Circ 349,783
Jul 2008-Jun 2009 Income $869,760, City $683,360, County $186,400. Mats Exp $82,500, Books $47,500, Per/Ser (Incl. Access Fees) $3,000, Other Print Mats $2,000, AV Mat $30,000. Sal $420,700 (Prof $77,671)
Library Holdings: Audiobooks 750; CDs 830; DVDs 1,806; Large Print Bks 6,283; Bk Titles 83,559; Per Subs 60; Videos 3,244
Automation Activity & Vendor Info: (Circulation) SirsiDynix
Function: ILL available
Partic in Yavapai Libr Network
Open Mon & Sat 10-2, Tues-Fri 9-6
Friends of the Library Group

M VERDE VALLEY MEDICAL CENTER*, David G Wells MD Memorial Library, 269 S Candy Lane, 86326. Tel: 928-639-6444. Administration Tel: 928-634-2251. FAX: 928-639-6457. Web Site: verdevalleymedicalcenter.com. *Coordr, Libr Assoc,* Karen Fanning; E-mail: fannink@nahealth.com
Founded 1996
Library Holdings: Bk Titles 300
Restriction: Not a lending libr

DOUGLAS

S ARIZONA DEPARTMENT OF CORRECTIONS - ADULT INSTITUTIONS*, Arizona State Prison Complex - Douglas Library, 6911 N BDI Blvd, 85608. (Mail add: PO Drawer 3867, 85608-3867). Tel: 520-364-7521, Ext 34522. FAX: 520-805-5971. *Librn III,* Kathleen Fry; E-mail: kfry@azcorrections.gov
Library Holdings: Bk Vols 26,880

J COCHISE COLLEGE LIBRARY*, Charles Di Peso Library, 4190 W Hwy 80, 85607. SAN 330-5643. Tel: 520-417-4082. FAX: 520-417-4120. E-mail: library@cochise.edu. Web Site: www.cochise.edu/information/library/index.asp. *Dir,* Patricia Hotchkiss; Staff 12 (MLS 3, Non-MLS 9)
Founded 1964. Enrl 5,000; Fac 105; Highest Degree: Associate
Library Holdings: AV Mats 3,000; Bk Vols 66,950; Per Subs 325; Talking Bks 230; Videos 2,400
Subject Interests: Aviation, Hist, Nursing
Automation Activity & Vendor Info: (Cataloging) OCLC; (Circulation) SirsiDynix; (Course Reserve) SirsiDynix; (ILL) OCLC; (Media Booking) SirsiDynix; (OPAC) SirsiDynix
Database Vendor: ProQuest
Function: For res purposes, Homebound delivery serv, ILL available, Magnifiers for reading, Outside serv via phone, mail, e-mail & web, Photocopying/Printing, Ref serv available, Telephone ref
Publications: Annual Report; Monthly Acquisitions Report; Periodical Holdings List
Partic in Amigos Library Services, Inc
Open Mon-Thurs (Winter) 8-8, Fri 8-4, Sat 10-2; Mon & Thurs (Summer) 9-3, Tues & Wed 2-8
Restriction: In-house use for visitors, Residents only, Students only
Departmental Libraries:
ANDREA CRACCHIOLO LIBRARY, 901 N Colombo Ave, Sierra Vista, 85635, SAN 300-4295. Tel: 520-515-5320. FAX: 520-515-5464. *Dir,* Patricia Hotchkiss; *Libr & Instrul Tech Adminr,* Philip Patton; Tel: 520-515-5390, E-mail: pattonp@cochise.edu; *Emerging Tech Librn,* Alexandra Felton; Tel: 520-515-5421, E-mail: feltona@cochise.edu; *Pub Serv/Instruction Librn,* Tetima Parnprome; Tel: 520-515-5383, E-mail: parnpromet@cochise.edu; *Tech Serv & Info Technology Librn,* John Walsh; Tel: 520-417-4081, E-mail: walshj@cochise.edu; Staff 5 (MLS 4, Non-MLS 1)
Founded 1974. Enrl 4,600; Fac 100; Highest Degree: Associate
Automation Activity & Vendor Info: (Cataloging) SirsiDynix; (Serials) EBSCO Online
Database Vendor: Gale Cengage Learning, Grolier Online, JSTOR, Marcive, Inc, Newsbank, OCLC FirstSearch, OCLC WorldShare Interlibrary Loan
Function: Art exhibits, Audio & video playback equip for onsite use, AV serv, Bks on CD, Computers for patron use, Copy machines, Distance learning, Doc delivery serv, e-mail serv, Electronic databases & coll, Equip loans & repairs, Exhibits, Free DVD rentals, Handicapped accessible, Instruction & testing, Mail & tel request accepted, Online cat, Online searches, Photocopying/Printing, Pub access computers, Ref & res, Tax forms, VHS videos, Video lending libr
Open Mon-Thurs 8am-9pm, Fri 8-4, Sat 10-4, Sun 12-5; Mon-Thurs (Summer) 8-8
Restriction: Authorized patrons, ID required to use computers (Ltd hrs), In-house use for visitors, Open to students, fac & staff
Friends of the Library Group

P DOUGLAS PUBLIC LIBRARY*, 560 Tenth St, 85607. SAN 300-3078. Tel: 520-417-7357. FAX: 520-805-5503. Web Site: cochise.lib.az.us/douglas. *Interim Dir,* Ana Urquijo; E-mail: ana.urquijo@douglasaz.gov; Staff 7 (MLS 1, Non-MLS 6)
Founded 1902. Pop 21,000; Circ 72,302
Jul 2005-Jun 2006. Mats Exp $35,200
Library Holdings: AV Mats 3,949; Bk Vols 42,500; Per Subs 102
Special Collections: Arizona Coll; Spanish Language Coll
Database Vendor: Wilson - Wilson Web
Mem of Cochise County Library District
Open Mon-Thurs 10-7, Fri 10-5, Sat 10-2, Sun (Sept-May) 1-5
Friends of the Library Group

DRAGOON

S AMERIND FOUNDATION, INC*, Fulton-Hayden Memorial Library, 2100 N Amerind Rd, 85609. (Mail add: PO Box 400, 85609-0400), SAN 300-3086. Tel: 520-586-3666. FAX: 520-586-4679. E-mail: libros@amerind.org. Web Site: www.amerind.org. *Librn,* Sally Newland
Founded 1962
Library Holdings: Bk Titles 25,000; Per Subs 150
Special Collections: El Archivo de Hidalgo del Parral, 1631-1821, micro; Facsimile Editions of Major Mesoamerican Codices; Records of the Colonial Period of New Spain (northern Mexico); Southwest Americana
Subject Interests: Anthrop, Archaeology
Wireless access
Restriction: Open by appt only

DUNCAN

P DUNCAN PUBLIC LIBRARY, 379401 State Hwy 75, 85534. (Mail add: PO Box 115, 85534-0115), SAN 300-3094. Tel: 928-359-2094. FAX: 928-359-2094. E-mail: duncanlibrary@vtc.net. *Libr Serv Dir,* Barbara Blackburn; Staff 1 (Non-MLS 1)

Founded 1947. Pop 850
Library Holdings: Bk Titles 10,000
Special Collections: Southwest Coll
Subject Interests: Am Indians
Automation Activity & Vendor Info: (Acquisitions) Follett Software; (Cataloging) Follett Software; (Circulation) Follett Software
Wireless access
Function: ILL available, Photocopying/Printing, Prog for children & young adult, Summer reading prog
Mem of Greenlee County Library System
Open Mon & Wed 1-6, Tues & Thurs 9-5, Fri 1-5

ELOY

P ELOY SANTA CRUZ LIBRARY*, 1000 N Main St, 85131. SAN 300-3116. Tel: 520-466-3814. FAX: 520-466-4433. Web Site: www.eloyaz.org/library.html. *Dir,* Russell Ketcham; E-mail: rus.ketcham@pinalcountyaz.gov; *Assoc Librn,* Position Currently Open; *Circ, Libr Asst,* Anthony Rodriquez; *Libr Asst, Tech Serv,* Vivianna Flores. Subject Specialists: *Hist,* Russell Ketcham; Staff 4.45 (MLS 1, Non-MLS 3.45)
Founded 1952. Pop 11,000; Circ 35,687
Library Holdings: Audiobooks 114; CDs 700; DVDs 3,494; e-books 2,000; Electronic Media & Resources 100; Large Print Bks 500; Bk Vols 17,605; Per Subs 72
Special Collections: Adult Literacy Coll; African-American & Hispanic Coll; Arizona Coll; Audio Visual Coll; Southwest Coll
Automation Activity & Vendor Info: (Acquisitions) Innovative Interfaces, Inc; (Cataloging) Innovative Interfaces, Inc; (Circulation) Innovative Interfaces, Inc; (ILL) OCLC WorldShare Interlibrary Loan; (OPAC) Innovative Interfaces, Inc
Database Vendor: EBSCO - WebFeat, EBSCO Auto Repair Reference, EBSCO Discovery Service, EBSCO Information Services, Evanced Solutions, Inc, infoUSA, Innovative Interfaces, Inc
Wireless access
Function: Audiobks via web, CD-ROM, Children's prog, Computer training, Computers for patron use, Copy machines, Digital talking bks, E-Reserves, Electronic databases & coll, Exhibits, Family literacy, Fax serv, Free DVD rentals, Handicapped accessible, ILL available, Music CDs, Online cat, Online searches, Photocopying/Printing, Prog for adults, Prog for children & young adult, Pub access computers, Ref serv in person, Scanner, Spanish lang bks, Spoken cassettes & DVDs, Summer reading prog, Tax forms, Teen prog
Open Mon-Fri 7:30-6
Friends of the Library Group

FLAGSTAFF

S THE ARBORETUM AT FLAGSTAFF LIBRARY*, 4001 S Woody Mountain Rd, 86001. SAN 373-3866. Tel: 928-774-1442, Ext 109. FAX: 928-774-1441. Web Site: www.thearb.org. *Exec Dir,* Lynne Nemeth; Staff 0.1 (Non-MLS 0.1)
Founded 1981
Library Holdings: Bk Titles 1,650
Subject Interests: Botany, Colorado Plateau, Ecology, Environ educ, Forestry, Hort, Natural hist, Nonprofit mgt
Function: For res purposes, Res libr
Restriction: By permission only, Circulates for staff only, Open by appt only, Staff & prof res

S ARIZONA HISTORICAL SOCIETY LIBRARY*, Northern Arizona Division, 2340 N Fort Valley Rd, 86001. Tel: 928-774-6272. FAX: 928-774-1596. E-mail: AHSFlagstaff@azhs.gov. Web Site: www.arizonahistoricalsociety.org. *Dir,* Joseph M Meehan; *Curator,* Susan Wilcox
Library Holdings: Bk Vols 50,000
Open Mon-Sat 9-5

GL COCONINO COUNTY LAW LIBRARY & SELF-HELP CENTER*, 200 N San Francisco St, 86001. SAN 300-3124. Tel: 928-679-7540. Toll Free Tel: 877-806-3187. Web Site: www.coconino.az.gov/lawlibrary. *Librn,* Gretchen Hornberger
Function: Res libr
Open Mon-Fri 8-5
Restriction: Not a lending libr

P FLAGSTAFF CITY-COCONINO COUNTY PUBLIC LIBRARY SYSTEM*, 300 W Aspen, 86001. SAN 330-5678. Tel: 928-213-2331. Circulation Tel: 928-213-2334. Interlibrary Loan Service Tel: 928-213-2379. Administration Tel: 928-213-2351. FAX: 928-774-9573. Web Site: www.flagstaffpubliclibrary.org. *Dir,* Heidi Holland; *Head, Pub Serv,* H Christie; *Acq,* Ilean Casey; *Ch Serv,* Molly Sadler; *Circ,* Barbara Griffiths; *ILL,* Jessica Cadiente; *Tech Serv,* Janine Veinus; Staff 11 (MLS 7, Non-MLS 4)
Founded 1890. Pop 106,000; Circ 752,724
Library Holdings: Bk Vols 207,000; Per Subs 400
Subject Interests: Arizona, Local hist, SW
Automation Activity & Vendor Info: (Acquisitions) SirsiDynix; (Cataloging) SirsiDynix; (Circulation) SirsiDynix; (Course Reserve) SirsiDynix; (ILL) SirsiDynix; (Media Booking) SirsiDynix; (OPAC) SirsiDynix; (Serials) SirsiDynix
Database Vendor: OCLC FirstSearch
Publications: The Friends of the Library (Newsletter)
Member Libraries: Fredonia Public Library; Grand Canyon-Tusayan Community Library; Page Public Library; Williams Public Library
Partic in OCLC Online Computer Library Center, Inc
Special Services for the Deaf - High interest/low vocabulary bks; Spec interest per
Special Services for the Blind - Closed circuit TV; Magnifiers; Reader equip; Talking bks
Open Mon-Thurs 10-9, Fri 10-7, Sat 10-6
Friends of the Library Group
Branches: 3
EAST FLAGSTAFF COMMUNITY LIBRARY, 3000 N Fourth St, 86004, SAN 330-5767. Tel: 928-774-8434. *Br Mgr,* Erin McCusker; Staff 10 (MLS 1, Non-MLS 9)
Library Holdings: Bk Vols 18,000
Open Mon-Thurs 9-9, Fri 9-6, Sat 9-1, Sun 1-5
Friends of the Library Group
FOREST LAKES COMMUNITY LIBRARY, 417 Old Rim Rd, Forest Lakes, 85931. (Mail add: PO Box 1799, Forest Lakes, 85931-1799), SAN 376-320X. Tel: 928-535-9125. FAX: 928-535-4729. *Mgr, Libr Serv,* Cheryl Rife
Library Holdings: Bk Titles 5,500; Bk Vols 7,700
Open Tues & Thurs (Winter) 10:30-5, Fri 11-5, Sat 9-2; Tues-Sat (Summer) 8:30-3
TUBA CITY PUBLIC LIBRARY, 78 Main St, Tuba City, 86045. (Mail add: PO Box 190, Tuba City, 86045-0190), SAN 300-4465. Tel: 928-283-5856. FAX: 928-283-6188. *Mgr,* Pearl Goldtooth
Founded 1957. Pop 10,000; Circ 14,031
Library Holdings: Bk Vols 12,000; Per Subs 30
Special Collections: Navaho History & Culture
Subject Interests: Native Am
Open Mon-Thurs 10-7, Sun 1-5
Bookmobiles: 2

S FLAGSTAFF MEDICAL CENTER*, John B Jamison MD Memorial Library, 1200 N Beaver St, 86001. SAN 374-8235. Tel: 928-773-2418. FAX: 928-773-2253. *Coordr,* Suzanne Tackitt; E-mail: suzanne.tackitt@nahealth.com; Staff 1 (MLS 1)
Library Holdings: Bk Vols 1,000
Database Vendor: EBSCOhost, Gale Cengage Learning, OVID Technologies, PubMed, STAT!Ref (Teton Data Systems)
Function: Computer training, Copy machines, Electronic databases & coll, ILL available, Mail & tel request accepted, Online ref, Photocopying/Printing, Ref serv available, Spoken cassettes & CDs, Telephone ref, VHS videos
Partic in Arizona Health Information Network (AZHIN)
Open Mon-Fri 8-4:30
Restriction: Hospital staff & commun, In-house use for visitors

S LOWELL OBSERVATORY LIBRARY*, 1400 W Mars Hill Rd, 86001. SAN 300-3132. Tel: 928-233-3216. FAX: 928-774-6296. Web Site: www.lowell.edu/. *Librn & Archivist,* Lauren Amundson; Tel: 928-233-3265, E-mail: amundson@lowell.edu
Founded 1894
Library Holdings: Bk Titles 4,873; Per Subs 25
Subject Interests: Astronomy, Math, Physics
Restriction: Staff use only

S MUSEUM OF NORTHERN ARIZONA, Harold S Colton Memorial Library, 3101 N Fort Valley Rd, 86001. SAN 300-3140. Tel: 928-774-5211, Ext 256. FAX: 928-779-1527. E-mail: library@mna.mus.az.us. Web Site: www.musnaz.org. *Coll Mgr,* Elaine Hughes; Tel: 928-774-5211, Ext 228, E-mail: ehughes@mna.mus.az.us; *Archivist,* Patricia Walker; E-mail: pwalker@mna.mus.az.us; Staff 1 (MLS 1)
Founded 1928
Library Holdings: Bk Vols 100,000; Per Subs 60
Special Collections: Hopi & Navajo Culture
Subject Interests: Archaeology, Botany, Cultural hist, Ethnology, Fine arts, Geol, Natural hist, Zoology
Function: Res libr
Restriction: Non-circulating

C NORTHERN ARIZONA UNIVERSITY*, Cline Library, Bldg 028, Knoles Dr, 86011. (Mail add: PO Box 6022, 86011-6022), SAN 300-3159. Tel: 928-523-2173. Administration Tel: 928-523-6802. Information Services Tel: 928-523-6805. Toll Free Tel: 800-247-3380 (Arizona only). FAX:

928-523-3770. E-mail: cline.library@nau.edu, library.administration@nau.edu. Web Site: library.nau.edu. *Dean & Univ Librn,* Cynthia Childrey; E-mail: cynthia.childrey@nau.edu; *Assoc Univ Librn,* Beth Schuck; Tel: 928-523-6779, E-mail: beth.schuck@nau.edu; *Coordr, Commun Affairs, Grants & Develop,* Kathleen L Schmand; Tel: 928-523-0341, E-mail: kathleen.schmand@nau.edu; *Coordr, Content, Access & Delivery Serv,* Julie Swann; Tel: 928-523-4939, E-mail: julie.swann@nau.edu; *Spec Coll & Archives Librn,* Karen J Underhill; Tel: 928-523-6502, E-mail: karen.underhill@nau.edu; Staff 69 (MLS 32, Non-MLS 37)
Founded 1912. Enrl 25,204; Fac 813; Highest Degree: Doctorate
Jul 2010-Jun 2011 Income $6,381,589. Mats Exp $1,765,090, Books $17,944, Per/Ser (Incl. Access Fees) $40,224, Manu Arch $4,997, Micro $9,600, AV Mat $69,023, Electronic Ref Mat (Incl. Access Fees) $1,379,280. Sal $3,101,530 (Prof $1,901,782)
Library Holdings: AV Mats 28,163; e-books 107,058; e-journals 59,863; Electronic Media & Resources 67,707; Bk Titles 498,508; Bk Vols 576,598; Per Subs 60,085; Videos 13,602
Special Collections: A F Whiting Coll; Arizona History (Historical Society Coll), archives, photos; Bill Belknap Coll; Bruce Babbitt Coll; Colorado Plateau Coll; Emery Kolb Coll; Fred Harvey Coll; Harvey Butchart Coll; James J Hanks Coll; Josef Muench Coll, photos; NAU Archives; Philip Johnston Coll; Tad Nichols Coll. Oral History; US Document Depository
Subject Interests: Colorado Plateau, Environ sci, Land use & develop, Native Am hist
Automation Activity & Vendor Info: (Acquisitions) Innovative Interfaces, Inc; (Cataloging) Innovative Interfaces, Inc; (Circulation) Innovative Interfaces, Inc; (Course Reserve) Blackboard Inc; (ILL) OCLC ILLiad; (Media Booking) Innovative Interfaces, Inc; (OPAC) Innovative Interfaces, Inc; (Serials) Innovative Interfaces, Inc
Database Vendor: ACM (Association for Computing Machinery), Alexander Street Press, American Chemical Society, American Mathematical Society, American Psychological Association (APA), Amigos Library Services, ARTstor, BioOne, Cambridge Scientific Abstracts, ebrary, EBSCO Information Services, EBSCOhost, Elsevier, Emerald, Gale Cengage Learning, H W Wilson, IEEE (Institute of Electrical & Electronics Engineers), Innovative Interfaces, Inc, ISI Web of Knowledge, JSTOR, McGraw-Hill, Medline, Modern Language Association, Nature Publishing Group, Newsbank, OCLC FirstSearch, OCLC WorldShare Interlibrary Loan, OVID Technologies, Oxford Online, Project MUSE, ProQuest, PubMed, RefWorks, Sage, ScienceDirect, SerialsSolutions, Springer-Verlag, Standard & Poor's, Swets Information Services, Thomson - Web of Science, ValueLine, Westlaw, Wiley, Wiley InterScience
Wireless access
Function: Archival coll, Doc delivery serv, e-mail & chat, e-mail serv, E-Reserves, Electronic databases & coll, Govt ref serv, Handicapped accessible, Health sci info serv, ILL available, Music CDs, Online cat, Online ref, Online searches, Pub access computers, Ref & res, Ref serv available, Ref serv in person, Scanner, Telephone ref, Wheelchair accessible
Publications: Library E-news (Online only); Library Insights (Newsletter)
Partic in Ariz Univ Librs Coun; Arizona Health Information Network (AZHIN); Greater Western Library Alliance; OCLC Online Computer Library Center, Inc
Special Services for the Deaf - Assistive tech; TTY equip
Special Services for the Blind - Assistive/Adapted tech devices, equip & products

G US GEOLOGICAL SURVEY LIBRARY*, 2255 N Gemini Dr, 86001. SAN 300-3167. Tel: 928-556-7272. FAX: 928-556-7237. E-mail: flag_lib@usgs.gov. *Admin Librn,* Donita Polly; Tel: 928-556-7008, E-mail: dpolly@usgs.gov
Founded 1964
Library Holdings: Bk Vols 40,000; Per Subs 210
Special Collections: Astro-Geology Coll
Subject Interests: Earth sci, Geol, Space sci
Open Mon-Fri 8-4:30

FLORENCE

S ARIZONA DEPARTMENT OF CORRECTIONS - ADULT INSTITUTIONS*, Arizona State Prison Complex - Eyman Library, 4374 Butte Ave, 85232. (Mail add: PO Box 3500, 85232-3500). Tel: 520-868-0201. FAX: 520-868-8556. *Librn,* Patricia Dixon; Tel: 520-868-0201, Ext 6850; *Librn,* Terry Hernandez; Tel: 520-868-0201, Ext 4026; *Librn,* Frances Owens; Tel: 520-868-0201, Ext 6207; *Librn,* Victor Ruboyianes; Tel: 520-868-0201, Ext 5022; *Supvr,* G Arhin
Library Holdings: Bk Vols 28,952

S ARIZONA STATE PRISON COMPLEX FLORENCE LIBRARIES*, 1305 E Butte Ave, 85232. (Mail add: PO Box 629, 85232-0629), SAN 324-1130. Tel: 520-868-4011, Ext 6010. FAX: 520-868-8288. *Librn,* Kerry Hernandez
Founded 1914
Library Holdings: Bk Titles 60,000; Per Subs 28
Special Services for the Deaf - Bks on deafness & sign lang; Staff with knowledge of sign lang

P FLORENCE COMMUNITY LIBRARY*, 1000 S Willow St, 85232. (Mail add: PO Box 985, 85232), SAN 300-3175. Tel: 520-868-8311. FAX: 520-868-8316. Web Site: www.florenceaz.gov/library. *Dir,* Rosemary Bebris; Staff 6 (Non-MLS 6)
Pop 11,540; Circ 19,718
Library Holdings: Bk Titles 26,000; Per Subs 38
Automation Activity & Vendor Info: (Cataloging) SirsiDynix; (Circulation) SirsiDynix; (OPAC) SirsiDynix
Database Vendor: EBSCOhost, OCLC FirstSearch
Function: ILL available
Mem of Pinal County Library District
Open Mon-Thurs 7am-8pm, Fri 7-4, Sat & Sun 12-4
Friends of the Library Group

S PINAL COUNTY HISTORICAL SOCIETY, INC LIBRARY*, 715 S Main St, 85132. (Mail add: PO Box 851, 85132-0851), SAN 328-672X. Tel: 520-868-4382. *Res,* Chris Reid
Founded 1958
Library Holdings: Bk Titles 1,000; Bk Vols 1,500; Per Subs 3; Spec Interest Per Sub 3; Videos 35
Special Collections: 1870-1950's Arizona State Prisoner Ledgers, microfilm; Arizona History, doc; Arizona State Prison & Pinal County (Della Meadows Coll); Florence Historic Pioneer Letters, doc; Southwest Native American Coll. Oral History
Subject Interests: Local hist
Function: Ref serv available, Res libr
Publications: Newsletter
Open Tues-Sat 11-4, Sun 12-4
Restriction: Authorized patrons

P PINAL COUNTY LIBRARY DISTRICT*, 92 W Butte Ave, 85132. (Mail add: PO Box 2974, 85132-3056), SAN 300-3183. Tel: 520-866-6457. Reference Tel: 520-866-6473. FAX: 520-866-6533. *Dir,* Denise Keller; *Dep Libr Dir,* Alexander Conrad; E-mail: alexander.conrad@pinalcountyaz.gov; *Emerging Tech Librn,* Ann Leonard; Tel: 520-855-6024, E-mail: ann.leonard@pinalcountyaz.gov; *Ref Librn,* Shirley Condit; E-mail: shirley.condit@pinalcountyaz.gov; *Bibliog Database Mgr,* Eileen Jaffe; E-mail: eileen.jaffe@pinalcountyaz.gov; *Libr Tech II,* Pamela Beerens; E-mail: pamela.beerens@pinalcountyaz.gov; *Libr Tech II,* Kathryn Clemans; E-mail: kathryn.clemans@pinalcountyaz.gov; *Libr Tech II,* Nyla Davis-Valencia; E-mail: nyla.davis-valencia@pinalcountyaz.gov; *Outreach Serv,* Position Currently Open; Staff 9 (MLS 5, Non-MLS 4)
Founded 1960. Pop 320,000
Jul 2012-Jun 2013 Income $2,339,583, State $23,000, Federal $36,880, County $2,279,703. Mats Exp $3,445,385, Books $534,362, Electronic Ref Mat (Incl. Access Fees) $94,828. Sal $470,895 (Prof $46,945)
Library Holdings: e-journals 180; Electronic Media & Resources 16; Bk Titles 1,269; Bk Vols 1,341; Per Subs 16
Subject Interests: Prof
Automation Activity & Vendor Info: (Acquisitions) Innovative Interfaces, Inc; (Cataloging) Innovative Interfaces, Inc; (Circulation) Innovative Interfaces, Inc; (ILL) Innovative Interfaces, Inc; (OPAC) Innovative Interfaces, Inc; (Serials) Innovative Interfaces, Inc
Wireless access
Publications: PCLD (Newsletter)
Member Libraries: Apache Junction Public Library; Arizona City Community Library; Casa Grande Public Library; Coolidge Public Library; Florence Community Library; Mammoth Public Library; Maricopa Public Library; Oracle Public Library; San Manuel Public Library; Superior Public Library
Special Services for the Deaf - Bks on deafness & sign lang; High interest/low vocabulary bks
Special Services for the Blind - Accessible computers; Audio mat; Bks on CD; Copier with enlargement capabilities; Digital talking bk; Extensive large print coll; Large print & cassettes; Large print bks; Playaways (bks on MP3)
Open Mon-Fri 8-5

FORT GRANT

S ARIZONA DEPARTMENT OF CORRECTIONS, ARIZONA STATE PRISON COMPLEX-SAFFORD*, Fort Grant Library, NW Sulphur Springs Valley, Graham County, 85643. (Mail add: 896 S Cook Rd, Safford, 85546). Tel: 928-828-3393, Ext 4217. *Librn II,* Shannon McGlaughlin; E-mail: smcglaug@azcorrections.gov. Subject Specialists: *Western US hist,* Shannon McGlaughlin; Staff 1 (Non-MLS 1)
Founded 1881
Jul 2012-Jun 2013 Income $4,824, Locally Generated Income $4,824. Mats Exp $4,824, Books $3,500, Per/Ser (Incl. Access Fees) $324, Presv $1,000. Sal $39,000

Library Holdings: Audiobooks 6; Bks on Deafness & Sign Lang 4; High Interest/Low Vocabulary Bk Vols 1,000; Large Print Bks 60; Bk Titles 7,600; Bk Vols 8,000; Per Subs 30
Special Collections: Addiction & Recovery Coll; Adult Basic Education Coll; African American Coll; Distance Learning Reference Coll; General Equivalency Diploma Coll; Hispanic Coll; Lewis vs Casey Legal Reference Coll; Man-Woman Relationships Coll; Marriage Coll; Methamphetamine Addiction & Recovery Coll; Native American Coll; Parenting Coll; Southwestern States History Coll; Spanish Language Coll; Transition/Life Skills Coll
Subject Interests: Fantasy, Mystery, SW hist, Western
Automation Activity & Vendor Info: (Cataloging) MC2 Systems; (Circulation) MC2 Systems
Database Vendor: Autolib Library & Information Management Systems
Function: Bilingual assistance for Spanish patrons, Distance learning, Govt ref serv, Learning ctr, Literacy & newcomer serv, Notary serv, Orientations, Outreach serv, Photocopying/Printing, Prog for adults, Ref serv available
Open Mon-Wed 8:30-3, Thurs 12-7:30
Restriction: Not open to pub, Secured area only open to authorized personnel, Staff & inmates only

FREDONIA

P FREDONIA PUBLIC LIBRARY*, 130 N Main, 86022. (Mail add: PO Box 218, 86022-0218), SAN 300-3205. Tel: 928-643-7137. FAX: 928-643-7137. E-mail: flibrary@gmail.com. *Head Librn,* Lisa Findlay; Staff 1.5 (Non-MLS 1.5)
Founded 1958. Pop 1,335
Library Holdings: Bk Titles 21,929; Per Subs 13
Special Collections: Jonreed Lauritzen Books & Jensen Memorial Coll
Automation Activity & Vendor Info: (Cataloging) Follett Software; (Circulation) Follett Software
Mem of Flagstaff City-Coconino County Public Library System; Southeast Kansas Library System
Open Mon-Thurs 8-6, Fri 10-2

P KAIBAB PAIUTE PUBLIC LIBRARY*, 250 N Pipe Springs Rd, 86022. (Mail add: HC 65, Box 2, 86022), SAN 376-317X. Tel: 928-643-6004. FAX: 928-643-7260. *Librn,* Ona Segundo; E-mail: osegundo@kaibabpaiute-nsn.gov
Library Holdings: Bk Titles 10,000; Bk Vols 11,000; Per Subs 12
Open Mon-Thurs 9-6, Fri 8-5

GANADO

G US NATIONAL PARK SERVICE*, Hubbell Trading Post National Historic Site Library, PO Box 150, 86505-0150. SAN 375-6459. Tel: 928-755-3475. FAX: 928-755-3405. Web Site: www.nps.gov/hutr. *Adminr,* Yolanda Lincoln
Library Holdings: Bk Titles 15,000
Open Mon-Fri 8-5

GLENDALE

J GLENDALE COMMUNITY COLLEGE*, John F Prince Library Media Center, 6000 W Olive Ave, 85302. SAN 300-3256. Tel: 623-845-3101. Circulation Tel: 623-845-3109. Interlibrary Loan Service Tel: 623-845-3107. Reference Tel: 623-845-3112. FAX: 623-845-3102. E-mail: gcclibrarymedia@gccaz.edu. Web Site: lib.gccaz.edu/lmc. *Dept Chair,* Frank Torres; Tel: 623-845-3904, E-mail: frank.torres@gccaz.edu; *Librn,* Dede Elrobeh; Tel: 623-845-3108, E-mail: dorothy.elrobeh@gccaz.edu; *Librn,* Mark Floor; Tel: 623-845-3165, E-mail: mark.floor@gccaz.edu; *Librn,* Ed McKennon; Tel: 623-845-3195, E-mail: edward.mckennon@gccaz.edu; *Librn,* Christine Moore; Tel: 623-845-3425, E-mail: christine.moore@gccaz.edu; *Librn,* David M Rodriguez; Tel: 623-845-3125, E-mail: david.m.rodriguez@gccaz.edu; *Librn,* Renee Smith; Tel: 623-845-3110, E-mail: renee.smith@gccaz.edu; *N Campus Librn,* Jose Aguinaga; Tel: 623-845-4105, E-mail: jose.aguinaga@gccaz.edu; *Supvr, Access Serv,* Judy Fleming; Tel: 623-845-3117, E-mail: j.fleming@gccaz.edu; *Coordr, Media Serv,* Scott Kozakiewicz; Tel: 623 845-3115, E-mail: scott.kozakiewicz@gccaz.edu; Staff 21 (MLS 9, Non-MLS 12)
Founded 1965. Enrl 21,300; Fac 30; Highest Degree: Associate
Library Holdings: Bk Titles 173,244; Bk Vols 173,244; Per Subs 34,276
Automation Activity & Vendor Info: (Acquisitions) SirsiDynix; (Cataloging) SirsiDynix; (Circulation) SirsiDynix; (Course Reserve) SirsiDynix; (ILL) OCLC ILLiad; (Media Booking) SirsiDynix; (OPAC) SirsiDynix; (Serials) SirsiDynix
Database Vendor: EBSCOhost, Gale Cengage Learning, JSTOR, LexisNexis, Newsbank, OCLC FirstSearch, ProQuest, SerialsSolutions, Wilson - Wilson Web
Wireless access
Open Mon-Thurs 6:30am-10pm, Fri 6:30-5, Sat 7-5, Sun Noon-5
Friends of the Library Group

P GLENDALE PUBLIC LIBRARY, 5959 W Brown St, 85302-1248. SAN 300-3264. Tel: 623-930-3530. Interlibrary Loan Service Tel: 623-930-3558. Reference Tel: 623-930-3531. Administration Tel: 623-930-3561. Automation Services Tel: 623-930-3586. FAX: 623-842-4209. Reference FAX: 623-842-4227. TDD: 623-842-2161. Web Site: www.glendaleaz.com/library. *Dir,* Michael Beck; *Libr Mgr,* Karen Reed; E-mail: KMReed@GLENDALEAZ.com; *Admin Serv Mgr,* Kathy Curley; Tel: 623-930-3556, E-mail: khamel@glendaleaz.com; Staff 114 (MLS 39, Non-MLS 75)
Founded 1895. Pop 240,000; Circ 2,631,465
Jul 2007-Jun 2008 Income (Main Library and Branch(s)) $8,477,238
Automation Activity & Vendor Info: (Acquisitions) Horizon; (Cataloging) Horizon; (Circulation) Horizon; (ILL) OCLC Connexion; (OPAC) Horizon; (Serials) Horizon
Wireless access
Open Mon-Thurs & Sat 9-5, Fri 9-6, Sun 1-5
Branches: 2
FOOTHILLS, 19055 N 57th Ave, 85308. Tel: 623-930-3830. Reference Tel: 623-930-3831. FAX: 623-930-3855. Reference FAX: 623-930-3866. *Libr Mgr,* Karen Reed; E-mail: kmreed@glendaleaz.com
VELMA TEAGUE BRANCH, 7010 N 58th Ave, 85301, SAN 376-8821. Tel: 623-930-3430. Reference Tel: 623-930-3431. FAX: 602-937-8798. *Libr Mgr,* Karen Reed

C THUNDERBIRD SCHOOL OF GLOBAL MANAGEMENT*, Merle A Hinrichs International Business Information Centre, One Global Pl, 85306-6000. SAN 300-3248. Tel: 602-978-7300. Circulation Tel: 602-978-7232. Interlibrary Loan Service Tel: 602-978-7236. Reference Tel: 602-978-7306. FAX: 602-978-7762. Web Site: students.thunderbird.edu/campus-resources/ibic-library. *Dir,* Wes Edens; E-mail: wes.edens@thunderbird.edu; *Archivist,* Shannon Walker; Staff 14 (MLS 5, Non-MLS 9)
Founded 1946. Enrl 1,200; Fac 110; Highest Degree: Master
Library Holdings: AV Mats 4,000; Bk Titles 70,000; Per Subs 1,400
Special Collections: Foreign Language Feature Films, video; Foreign Language Newspapers & Periodicals
Subject Interests: Acctg, Finance, Intl, Mkt, Polit sci
Automation Activity & Vendor Info: (Acquisitions) SirsiDynix; (Cataloging) SirsiDynix; (Circulation) SirsiDynix; (Course Reserve) SirsiDynix; (ILL) SirsiDynix; (Media Booking) SirsiDynix; (OPAC) SirsiDynix; (Serials) SirsiDynix
Wireless access
Publications: Library Guides
Partic in OCLC Online Computer Library Center, Inc
Open Mon-Wed 7am-Midnight, Thurs & Fri 7am-10pm, Sat 10-10, Sun 10am-Midnight
Restriction: Open to students, fac & staff

GLOBE

S ARIZONA DEPARTMENT OF CORRECTIONS - ADULT INSTITUTIONS*, Arizona State Prison Complex - Globe Library, PO Box 2799, 85502-2799. Tel: 928-425-8141. FAX: 928-425-0621. *Librn,* John Ellison
Library Holdings: Bk Vols 2,930

S GILA COUNTY HISTORICAL MUSEUM LIBRARY*, 1330 N Broad St, 85501. (Mail add: PO Box 2891, 85502-2891), SAN 374-8251. Tel: 928-425-7385. Web Site: gilahistorical.com. *Dir,* Donna Anderson
Founded 1972
Library Holdings: Bk Vols 250; Spec Interest Per Sub 1
Subject Interests: Local hist
Open Mon-Fri 10-4, Sat 11-3
Restriction: Not a lending libr

GL GILA COUNTY LAW LIBRARY*, 1400 E Ash St, 85501. SAN 300-3272. Tel: 928-425-3231. FAX: 928-425-0319. *Librn,* Mary Stemm; Tel: 908-402-8768; Staff 1 (Non-MLS 1)
Founded 1908
Library Holdings: Bk Vols 1,000; Per Subs 10
Database Vendor: Westlaw
Restriction: Prof mat only, Pub use on premises

P GILA COUNTY LIBRARY DISTRICT*, 1400 E Ash St, 85501-1414. SAN 375-3182. Tel: 928-402-8768, 928-402-8770. Toll Free Tel: 800-304-4452, Ext 8768. FAX: 928-425-3462. Web Site: gcldaz.org/gila/. *Dir,* Jacque Griffin; E-mail: jgriffin@co.gila.az.us; *ILL, Ref, Res,* Mary A Stemm; E-mail: mstemm@gcldaz.org; *Syst Programmer, Syst Coordr,* Yodona Pennell; Tel: 928-402-8769, E-mail: ypenne@gila.lib.az.us; Staff 3 (Non-MLS 3)
Founded 1971. Pop 54,060
Library Holdings: AV Mats 19,306; CDs 4,476; DVDs 1,680; Large Print Bks 6,316; Bk Titles 270,790; Per Subs 150; Videos 8,215

Automation Activity & Vendor Info: (Cataloging) Innovative Interfaces, Inc; (Circulation) Innovative Interfaces, Inc; (ILL) OCLC FirstSearch; (OPAC) Innovative Interfaces, Inc
Database Vendor: OCLC FirstSearch, Wilson - Wilson Web
Member Libraries: Globe Public Library; Hayden Public Library; Isabelle Hunt Memorial Public Library; Payson Public Library; San Carlos Public Library; Tonto Basin Public Library; Young Public Library
Special Services for the Deaf - TDD equip
Open Mon-Fri 8-5

P GLOBE PUBLIC LIBRARY*, 339 S Broad St, 85501-1744. SAN 300-3299. Tel: 928-425-6111. FAX: 928-425-3357. *Dir,* Marion Steele; E-mail: msteele@gcldaz.org; *Dep Librn,* Mary Helen Avalos; E-mail: mavalos@gcldaz.org; *ILL, Libr Asst,* Emily Leverance; E-mail: eleverance@gcldaz.org; Staff 1 (Non-MLS 1)
Pop 7,495; Circ 44,649
Jul 2010-Jun 2011 Income $242,978, City $116,739, County $116,739, Locally Generated Income $9,500. Mats Exp $22,100, Books $18,000, Per/Ser (Incl. Access Fees) $1,600, AV Mat $2,500. Sal $98,609 (Prof $39,499)
Library Holdings: AV Mats 2,294; Bks on Deafness & Sign Lang 21; CDs 144; DVDs 848; High Interest/Low Vocabulary Bk Vols 11; Large Print Bks 364; Bk Titles 19,951; Bk Vols 20,239; Per Subs 67; Talking Bks 655; Videos 185
Special Collections: Arizona Southwest
Automation Activity & Vendor Info: (Cataloging) Innovative Interfaces, Inc; (Circulation) Innovative Interfaces, Inc; (ILL) OCLC FirstSearch; (OPAC) Innovative Interfaces, Inc
Database Vendor: OCLC FirstSearch, OCLC WorldShare Interlibrary Loan, ProQuest, Wilson - Wilson Web
Wireless access
Mem of Gila County Library District
Open Mon, Tues, Fri & Sat 10-5:30, Wed & Thurs 10-7
Friends of the Library Group

GOODYEAR

S ARIZONA DEPARTMENT OF CORRECTIONS - ADULT INSTITUTIONS*, Arizona State Prison Complex - Perryville Library, 2014 N Citrus Rd, 85338. (Mail add: PO Box 3000, 85338-3000). Tel: 623-853-0304. FAX: 623-853-0304. *Librn,* Joyce Kelly; Tel: 623-853-0304, Ext 25574; *Librn,* Michael Maynard; Tel: 623-853-0304, Ext 24967
Library Holdings: Bk Vols 16,000
Open Mon-Fri 8-4

GRAND CANYON

G GRAND CANYON NATIONAL PARK RESEARCH LIBRARY*, Park Headquarters Bldg, 20 S Entrance Rd, 86023. (Mail add: PO Box 129, 86023-0129), SAN 300-3329. Tel: 928-638-7768. FAX: 928-638-7776.
Founded 1920
Library Holdings: AV Mats 500; Bk Titles 7,000; Bk Vols 12,000; Per Subs 25
Special Collections: Rare Books
Subject Interests: Anthrop, Astronomy, Biol, Environment, Geol, Native Am, SW states hist
Automation Activity & Vendor Info: (Acquisitions) EOS International; (Cataloging) OCLC Connexion; (Circulation) EOS International; (ILL) OCLC; (OPAC) EOS International; (Serials) EOS International
Database Vendor: Amigos Library Services, EBSCOhost, Gale Cengage Learning, HeinOnline, JSTOR, Newsbank-Readex, OCLC FirstSearch, ProQuest, ScienceDirect
Wireless access
Function: Archival coll, Doc delivery serv, For res purposes, Govt ref serv, ILL available, Pub access computers, Ref serv available, Res libr, Video lending libr, Web-catalog
Partic in Amigos Library Services, Inc; OCLC-LVIS
Open Mon-Fri 8:30-4:30
Restriction: Non-circulating of rare bks, Open to pub for ref only

P GRAND CANYON-TUSAYAN COMMUNITY LIBRARY*, 11 Navajo St, 86023. (Mail add: PO Box 99, 86023-0099), SAN 300-3310. Tel: 928-638-2718. FAX: 928-638-2718. E-mail: gccl518@yahoo.com. *Br Mgr,* Mindy Karlsberger
Founded 1932. Pop 1,500; Circ 9,000
Library Holdings: DVDs 250; Large Print Bks 65; Bk Vols 15,000; Per Subs 30; Talking Bks 250; Videos 300
Subject Interests: SW
Automation Activity & Vendor Info: (Cataloging) Follett Software; (Circulation) Follett Software; (OPAC) Follett Software
Mem of Flagstaff City-Coconino County Public Library System
Open Mon-Fri 11-5, Sat 9-2

HAYDEN

P HAYDEN PUBLIC LIBRARY*, 219 E Fifth Ave, 85135. (Mail add: PO Box 99, 85135-0099), SAN 300-3337. Tel: 520-356-7031. FAX: 520-356-7031. *Librn,* Mary Helen Lopez
Founded 1966. Pop 3,000; Circ 21,116
Library Holdings: Bk Titles 12,000; Bk Vols 14,000
Special Collections: Spanish, bks & records
Mem of Gila County Library District
Open Mon, Wed-Fri 9-5, Tues 9-5 & 7-8:30
Friends of the Library Group

HEBER

P RIM COMMUNITY LIBRARY*, 3404 Mustang Ave, 85928. (Mail add: PO Box 305, 85928-0305). Tel: 928-535-5749. FAX: 928-535-6409. E-mail: rcl@navajo.lib.az.us. Web Site: www.navajoco.lib.az.us. *Mgr,* Kathleen Shea
Founded 1985. Pop 4,800; Circ 13,500
Library Holdings: AV Mats 200; Bks on Deafness & Sign Lang 10; Large Print Bks 300; Bk Titles 13,300
Special Services for the Blind - Talking bks
Open Tues 12-6, Wed-Fri 11-5, Sat 9-12
Friends of the Library Group

HOLBROOK

P HOLBROOK PUBLIC LIBRARY, 403 Park St, 86025. SAN 300-3345. Tel: 928-524-3732. FAX: 928-524-2159. E-mail: holbrookpl@gmail.com. *Dir,* Wendy Skevington; Staff 2 (MLS 1, Non-MLS 1)
Founded 1958. Pop 5,300; Circ 65,000
Library Holdings: Bk Titles 45,000; Per Subs 52
Automation Activity & Vendor Info: (Cataloging) SirsiDynix; (Circulation) SirsiDynix; (OPAC) SirsiDynix
Wireless access
Partic in Ariz Resources Consortium; Navajo County Libr District
Open Tues 8-3, Wed & Thurs 12-7, Fri 12-5, Sat 10-3
Friends of the Library Group

J NORTHLAND PIONEER COLLEGE LIBRARIES*, PO Box 610, 86025. SAN 376-8791. Interlibrary Loan Service Tel: 928-532-6120. Administration Tel: 928-524-7320. Interlibrary Loan Service FAX: 928-532-6121. Administration FAX: 928-524-7321. E-mail: npcref@npc.edu. Web Site: www.npc.edu/library. *Head Librn,* Stan Pirog; Tel: 928-524-7324, E-mail: stan.pirog@npc.edu; *Access Serv, Electronic Res, Ser,* Susan Acton; Tel: 928-532-6123, E-mail: susan.acton@npc.edu; *Govt Doc,* Deb Holbrook; Tel: 928-289-6523, E-mail: deborah.holbrook@npc.edu; *ILL,* Denise Rominger; Tel: 928-532-6122, E-mail: denise.rominger@npc.edu; Staff 3 (MLS 2, Non-MLS 1)
Founded 1975. Enrl 2,100; Fac 210; Highest Degree: Associate
Library Holdings: Audiobooks 469; Bks on Deafness & Sign Lang 164; Braille Volumes 39; CDs 299; DVDs 774; e-books 399; e-journals 2; Electronic Media & Resources 10,426; Large Print Bks 28; Microforms 18,345; Bk Titles 72,509; Bk Vols 83,830; Per Subs 25; Videos 1,235
Special Collections: US Document Depository
Automation Activity & Vendor Info: (Acquisitions) EOS International; (Cataloging) EOS International; (Circulation) EOS International; (ILL) OCLC; (Media Booking) EOS International; (OPAC) EOS International; (Serials) EOS International
Database Vendor: Alexander Street Press, Baker & Taylor, EBSCOhost, EOS International, Gale Cengage Learning, JSTOR, OCLC, OCLC WebJunction, OCLC WorldShare Interlibrary Loan, Oxford Online, ProQuest
Wireless access
Open Mon-Thurs 8am-9pm, Fri 8-4

HUACHUCA CITY

P HUACHUCA CITY PUBLIC LIBRARY, 506 N Gonzales Blvd, 85616-9610. SAN 300-3361. Tel: 520-456-1063. FAX: 520-456-8852. Web Site: cochise.lib.az.us/hcity.html. *Dir, Libr Serv,* Kelly Ferguson; E-mail: kferguson@huachucacity.gov; *Circ,* Jann Frampton; Staff 3 (Non-MLS 3)
Founded 1958. Pop 12,000
Library Holdings: AV Mats 695; CDs 100; DVDs 95; High Interest/Low Vocabulary Bk Vols 5,335; Large Print Bks 400; Music Scores 160; Bk Titles 15,000; Bk Vols 20,144; Per Subs 26; Talking Bks 875; Videos 958
Special Collections: Cochise County History & Tourism Coll
Subject Interests: Arizona, Literacy, Local hist, Music, SW, Tourism, Video
Automation Activity & Vendor Info: (Cataloging) SirsiDynix; (Circulation) SirsiDynix; (ILL) SirsiDynix; (OPAC) SirsiDynix
Database Vendor: OCLC FirstSearch, SirsiDynix
Function: After school storytime, AV serv, Handicapped accessible, Homework prog, ILL available, Music CDs, Photocopying/Printing, Prog for children & young adult, Ref serv available, Spoken cassettes & CDs,

Spoken cassettes & DVDs, Summer reading prog, VHS videos, Video lending libr, Wheelchair accessible
Publications: LC's Bookmark (Newsletter)
Mem of Cochise County Library District
Special Services for the Deaf - Bks on deafness & sign lang; Closed caption videos; High interest/low vocabulary bks
Special Services for the Blind - Home delivery serv; Large print bks; Ref serv; Videos on blindness & phys handicaps
Open Mon-Fri 10-6, Sat 10-3
Restriction: Authorized patrons, Circ to mem only, In-house use for visitors, Open to pub for ref & circ; with some limitations
Friends of the Library Group

JEROME

P JEROME PUBLIC LIBRARY*, 600 Clark St, 86331. (Mail add: PO Drawer I, 86331-0247), SAN 300-337X. Tel: 928-639-0574. FAX: 928-639-0574. *Librn,* Kathleen Jarvis; Staff 1 (Non-MLS 1)
Founded 1919. Pop 500; Circ 12,000
Library Holdings: Bk Titles 9,500; Bk Vols 10,000
Special Collections: Arizona & the Southwest (National Geographic 1949-1976, Arizona Highways 1953-1977)
Automation Activity & Vendor Info: (Cataloging) SirsiDynix; (Circulation) SirsiDynix; (OPAC) SirsiDynix
Mem of Yavapai County Free Library District
Open Mon & Wed 10-5, Tues & Thurs 12-8, Fri 12-6, Sun 10-2

KEARNY

P ARTHUR E POMEROY PUBLIC LIBRARY*, Kearny Library, 912A Tilbury Rd, 85237. (Mail add: PO Box 220, 85237-0220), SAN 300-3388. Tel: 520-363-5861. FAX: 520-363-5214. *Head Librn,* Joyce Danilow; E-mail: Janet.Danilow@pinalcountyaz.gov
Founded 1958. Pop 2,500; Circ 39,399
Library Holdings: Bk Vols 18,400; Per Subs 10
Special Collections: History (Southwestern Coll)
Subject Interests: Local hist
Automation Activity & Vendor Info: (Cataloging) SirsiDynix; (Circulation) SirsiDynix; (OPAC) SirsiDynix
Publications: Booklist; Library Journal; School Library Journal
Open Mon-Thurs 10-5
Friends of the Library Group

KINGMAN

J MOHAVE COMMUNITY COLLEGE LIBRARY*, 1971 Jagerson Ave, 86409-1238. SAN 330-6186. Tel: 928-757-4331. Reference Tel: 928-757-0856. Administration Tel: 928-757-0883. FAX: 928-757-0896. Administration FAX: 928-757-0871. Web Site: www.mohave.edu. *Librn,* Adele Maxson; Tel: 928-757-0802, E-mail: amaxson@mohave.edu; Staff 12 (MLS 3, Non-MLS 9)
Founded 1971. Enrl 7,887; Fac 52; Highest Degree: Associate
Library Holdings: CDs 53; DVDs 33; Bk Titles 76,789; Bk Vols 65,651; Per Subs 415; Talking Bks 1,375; Videos 1,393
Automation Activity & Vendor Info: (Acquisitions) Innovative Interfaces, Inc; (Cataloging) SirsiDynix; (Circulation) Innovative Interfaces, Inc; (Course Reserve) Innovative Interfaces, Inc; (ILL) Innovative Interfaces, Inc; (Media Booking) Innovative Interfaces, Inc; (OPAC) Innovative Interfaces, Inc; (Serials) EBSCO Online
Database Vendor: Amigos Library Services, Baker & Taylor, Bowker, College Source, CQ Press, EBSCO Information Services, EBSCOhost, Facts on File, Gale Cengage Learning, Ingram Library Services, OCLC FirstSearch, Oxford Online, SerialsSolutions, Standard & Poor's
Wireless access
Open Mon-Thurs 8am-9:30pm, Fri 8-5, Sat 9-1
Departmental Libraries:
BULLHEAD CITY CAMPUS, 3400 Hwy 95, Bullhead City, 86442-8204. Tel: 928-758-2420. FAX: 928-758-4436. *Campus Librn,* Sara Brandel; E-mail: sbrandel@mohave.edu; Staff 3 (MLS 1, Non-MLS 2)
Library Holdings: Per Subs 219
KINGMAN CAMPUS, 1971 Jagerson Ave, 86401. Tel: 928-757-0856. FAX: 928-757-0871. *Campus Librn,* Adele Maxson; Tel: 928-757-0802; Staff 3 (MLS 1, Non-MLS 2)
Library Holdings: Bk Vols 30,000; Per Subs 420
LAKE HAVASU CITY CAMPUS, 1977 W Acoma Blvd, Lake Havasu City, 86403-2999. Tel: 928-453-5809. Interlibrary Loan Service Tel: 928-505-3311. Administration Tel: 928-505-3337. FAX: 928-453-8335. *Campus Librn,* Wendi Birkhead; E-mail: wbirkhead@mohave.edu; *ILL/Doc Delivery Serv,* Mary Jo Powell; E-mail: mpowell@mohave.edu; Staff 3 (MLS 1, Non-MLS 2)
Founded 1971. Highest Degree: Associate
Library Holdings: Bk Vols 40,000; Per Subs 88
NORTH MOHAVE CAMPUS, 480 S Central, Colorado City, 86021. (Mail add: PO Box 980, Colorado City, 86021-0980). Tel: 928-875-2799, Ext 2224. FAX: 928-875-2831. *Librn,* Kim Naylor; E-mail: knaylor@mohave.edu
Library Holdings: Bk Vols 2,000; Per Subs 10

S MOHAVE COUNTY HISTORICAL SOCIETY*, Mohave Museum of History & Arts Library, 400 W Beale St, 86401. SAN 300-3396. Tel: 928-753-3195. FAX: 928-718-1562. E-mail: library@mohavemuseum.org. *Dir,* Shannon Rossiter; E-mail: mmdirector@citlink.net; *Librn,* Kay Ellermann; E-mail: mmlibrary@citlink.net
Founded 1966
Library Holdings: Bk Titles 4,000
Special Collections: Camp Beale's Springs Coll, bks, ms, micro; Genealogical Coll; Maps; Photographs from 1880 Related to Mohave County. Oral History
Subject Interests: Arizona, Indians, Mining, Ranching
Restriction: Non-circulating to the pub

P MOHAVE COUNTY LIBRARY DISTRICT*, 3269 N Burbank St, 86402-7000. (Mail add: PO Box 7000, 86402-7000), SAN 330-6038. Administration Tel: 928-692-5717. Toll Free Tel: 800-525-8987. Administration FAX: 928-692-5762. Web Site: www.mohavecountylibrary.info. *Libr District Dir,* Kathryn Pennell; *Asst Dir,* Julie Huelsbeck; Tel: 928-692-5711, E-mail: julie.huelsbeck@co.mohave.az.us; *Commun Libr Mgr,* Stella Carlzen; Tel: 928-692-5714, Fax: 928-757-0458, E-mail: stella.carlzen@co.mohave.az.us; *Tech Serv Mgr,* Bruce Carter; Tel: 928-692-5744, E-mail: bruce.carter@co.mohave.az.us; Staff 9 (MLS 6, Non-MLS 3)
Founded 1926. Pop 205,000; Circ 660,182
Jul 2008-Jun 2009 Income (Main Library and Branch(s)) $10,363,002, State $25,000, Federal $9,820, County $10,328,182. Mats Exp $718,749, Books $371,245, Per/Ser (Incl. Access Fees) $62,097, AV Mat $119,727, Electronic Ref Mat (Incl. Access Fees) $165,680. Sal $2,667,323 (Prof $38,605)
Library Holdings: AV Mats 36,502; Bk Vols 209,633; Per Subs 564
Subject Interests: Arizona
Automation Activity & Vendor Info: (Acquisitions) SIRSI Unicorn; (Cataloging) SIRSI Unicorn; (Circulation) SIRSI Unicorn; (ILL) OCLC; (OPAC) SIRSI-iBistro
Database Vendor: EBSCO - WebFeat, EBSCO Auto Repair Reference, ProQuest
Wireless access
Function: Bks on cassette, Bks on CD, Children's prog, Computer training, Computers for patron use, Copy machines, Digital talking bks, e-mail serv, Fax serv, Free DVD rentals, Handicapped accessible, Holiday prog, Home delivery & serv to Sr ctr & nursing homes, Homebound delivery serv, Homework prog, ILL available, Music CDs, Online cat, Online searches, Prog for adults, Prog for children & young adult, Pub access computers, Story hour, Summer reading prog, Tax forms, Teen prog, Telephone ref, VHS videos
Partic in Amigos Library Services, Inc; OCLC Online Computer Library Center, Inc
Special Services for the Deaf - Bks on deafness & sign lang; Closed caption videos; High interest/low vocabulary bks
Special Services for the Blind - Bks on cassette; Bks on CD; Copier with enlargement capabilities; Large print & cassettes; Large print bks; Large print bks & talking machines; Playaways (bks on MP3); Recorded bks; Ref serv; Sound rec; Talking bks; VisualTek equip
Friends of the Library Group
Branches: 10
BULLHEAD CITY BRANCH, 1170 E Hancock Rd, Bullhead City, 86442, SAN 330-6062. Tel: 928-758-0714. FAX: 928-758-0720. E-mail: library@mohavecounty.us. *Libr Serv Mgr,* Stella Carlzen; Tel: 928-758-0740, E-mail: stella.carlzen@mohavecounty.us; Staff 2 (MLS 2)
Founded 1942. Circ 187,143
Library Holdings: Audiobooks 2,604; AV Mats 7,087; Bks-By-Mail 502; Bks on Deafness & Sign Lang 31; Braille Volumes 3; CDs 3,864; DVDs 2,843; e-books 3,988; e-journals 4,031; Electronic Media & Resources 134; High Interest/Low Vocabulary Bk Vols 36; Large Print Bks 2,575; Music Scores 37; Bk Titles 44,377; Bk Vols 46,798; Per Subs 102; Videos 130
Special Collections: Arizona Region
Automation Activity & Vendor Info: (Acquisitions) SirsiDynix; (Cataloging) SirsiDynix; (Circulation) SirsiDynix; (ILL) OCLC; (OPAC) SirsiDynix
Database Vendor: Baker & Taylor, EBSCO Auto Repair Reference, EBSCOhost, Ingram Library Services, OCLC, Overdrive, Inc, ProQuest, SirsiDynix, TumbleBookLibrary, World Book Online
Function: Audiobks via web, Bks on CD, Copy machines, Electronic databases & coll, Fax serv, Free DVD rentals, Handicapped accessible, Home delivery & serv to Sr ctr & nursing homes, ILL available, Online cat, OverDrive digital audio bks, Prog for adults, Prog for children & young adult, Pub access computers, Spanish lang bks

Special Services for the Blind - Bks on CD; Large print bks; Playaways (bks on MP3); Talking bk serv referral
Open Mon & Wed 9-6, Tues & Thurs 9-8, Fri & Sat 9-5
Friends of the Library Group

CHLORIDE COMMUNITY LIBRARY, 4901 Pay Roll Ave, Chloride, 86431. (Mail add: PO Box 111, Chloride, 86431-0111). Tel: 928-565-2200. Administration Tel: 928-692-5718. FAX: 928-565-2200. E-mail: library@mohavecounty.us. *Commun Libr Rep,* Janice Garoutte; E-mail: janice.garoutte@mohavecounty.us
Founded 1994. Circ 9,577
Library Holdings: Audiobooks 139; AV Mats 1,218; Bks on Deafness & Sign Lang 2; CDs 130; DVDs 1,051; e-books 3,988; e-journals 4,031; Electronic Media & Resources 16; High Interest/Low Vocabulary Bk Vols 4; Large Print Bks 29; Bk Titles 2,680; Bk Vols 2,782; Per Subs 17; Videos 5
Special Collections: Arizona Region
Automation Activity & Vendor Info: (Acquisitions) SirsiDynix; (Cataloging) SirsiDynix; (Circulation) SirsiDynix; (OPAC) SirsiDynix
Database Vendor: Baker & Taylor, EBSCOhost, Ingram Library Services, OCLC, Overdrive, Inc, SirsiDynix, TumbleBookLibrary, World Book Online
Function: Audiobks via web, Bks on CD, Copy machines, Electronic databases & coll, Fax serv, Free DVD rentals, Handicapped accessible, Home delivery & serv to Sr ctr & nursing homes, ILL available, Online cat, OverDrive digital audio bks, Prog for adults, Prog for children & young adult, Pub access computers
Special Services for the Blind - Bks on CD; Large print bks; Playaways (bks on MP3); Talking bk serv referral
Open Tues & Thurs 9am-12:30pm, Wed 2-6, Sat 10-2
Friends of the Library Group

DOLAN SPRINGS COMMUNITY LIBRARY, 16140 N Pierce Ferry Rd, Dolan Springs, 86441. (Mail add: PO Box 427, Dolan Springs, 86441-0427). Tel: 928-767-4292. Administration Tel: 928-692-5718. FAX: 928-767-4292. E-mail: library@mohavecounty.us. *Commun Libr Rep,* Position Currently Open
Founded 1975. Circ 17,528
Library Holdings: Audiobooks 396; AV Mats 1,746; CDs 448; DVDs 1,189; e-books 3,988; e-journals 4,031; Electronic Media & Resources 30; High Interest/Low Vocabulary Bk Vols 4; Large Print Bks 341; Music Scores 1; Bk Titles 5,297; Bk Vols 5,340; Per Subs 18; Videos 68
Special Collections: Arizona Region
Automation Activity & Vendor Info: (Acquisitions) SirsiDynix; (Cataloging) SirsiDynix; (Circulation) SirsiDynix; (OPAC) SirsiDynix
Database Vendor: Baker & Taylor, EBSCOhost, Ingram Library Services, OCLC, Overdrive, Inc, SirsiDynix, TumbleBookLibrary, World Book Online
Function: Audiobks via web, Bks on CD, Copy machines, Electronic databases & coll, Fax serv, Free DVD rentals, Handicapped accessible, Home delivery & serv to Sr ctr & nursing homes, ILL available, Online cat, OverDrive digital audio bks, Prog for adults, Prog for children & young adult, Pub access computers
Special Services for the Blind - Bks on CD; Large print bks; Playaways (bks on MP3); Talking bk serv referral
Open Tues & Fri 8-1, Thurs 12-6, Sat 8-12
Friends of the Library Group

GOLDEN SHORES COMMUNITY LIBRARY, 13136 S Golden Shores Pkwy, Topock, 86436-1086. (Mail add: PO Box 1086, Topock, 86436-1086), SAN 371-361X. Tel: 928-768-2235. Administration Tel: 928-692-5718. FAX: 928-768-2235. E-mail: library@mohavecounty.us. *Commun Libr Rep,* Kim Stoddard; E-mail: kim.stoddard@mohavecounty.us
Founded 1991. Circ 11,801
Library Holdings: Audiobooks 247; AV Mats 1,223; Bks on Deafness & Sign Lang 2; CDs 235; DVDs 923; e-books 3,988; e-journals 4,031; Electronic Media & Resources 24; High Interest/Low Vocabulary Bk Vols 3; Large Print Bks 233; Bk Titles 4,875; Bk Vols 4,958; Per Subs 9; Videos 7
Special Collections: Arizona Region
Automation Activity & Vendor Info: (Acquisitions) SirsiDynix; (Cataloging) SirsiDynix; (Circulation) SirsiDynix; (ILL) OCLC; (OPAC) SirsiDynix
Database Vendor: Baker & Taylor, EBSCO Auto Repair Reference, EBSCOhost, Ingram Library Services, OCLC, Overdrive, Inc, ProQuest, SirsiDynix, TumbleBookLibrary, World Book Online
Function: Audiobks via web, Bks on CD, Copy machines, Electronic databases & coll, Fax serv, Free DVD rentals, Handicapped accessible, Home delivery & serv to Sr ctr & nursing homes, ILL available, Online cat, OverDrive digital audio bks, Prog for adults, Prog for children & young adult, Pub access computers
Special Services for the Blind - Bks on CD; Large print bks; Playaways (bks on MP3); Talking bk serv referral
Open Tues, Thurs & Sat 9-1, Wed 2-5
Friends of the Library Group

GOLDEN VALLEY COMMUNITY LIBRARY, 3417 N Verde Rd, Golden Valley, 86413-0671. (Mail add: 4195 Hwy 68, Unit C PMB 671, Golden Valley, 86413-8115). Tel: 928-565-2989. Administration Tel: 928-692-5718. FAX: 928-565-2989. E-mail: library@mohavecounty.us. *Commun Libr Rep,* Otis Brooks; E-mail: otis.brooks@mohavecounty.us
Founded 2005. Circ 13,037
Library Holdings: Audiobooks 452; AV Mats 1,439; Bks on Deafness & Sign Lang 1; CDs 416; DVDs 816; e-books 3,988; e-journals 4,031; Electronic Media & Resources 15; High Interest/Low Vocabulary Bk Vols 6; Large Print Bks 252; Bk Titles 4,625; Bk Vols 4,749; Per Subs 8; Videos 7
Special Collections: Arizona Region
Automation Activity & Vendor Info: (Acquisitions) SirsiDynix, (Cataloging) SirsiDynix; (Circulation) SirsiDynix; (OPAC) SirsiDynix
Database Vendor: Baker & Taylor, EBSCOhost, Ingram Library Services, OCLC, Overdrive, Inc, SirsiDynix, TumbleBookLibrary, World Book Online
Function: Audiobks via web, Bks on CD, Copy machines, Electronic databases & coll, Fax serv, Free DVD rentals, Handicapped accessible, Home delivery & serv to Sr ctr & nursing homes, ILL available, Online cat, OverDrive digital audio bks, Prog for adults, Prog for children & young adult, Pub access computers
Special Services for the Blind - Bks on CD; Large print bks; Playaways (bks on MP3); Talking bk serv referral
Open Tues 9-3, Thurs 12-6, Sat 10-1
Friends of the Library Group

KINGMAN LIBRARY, 3269 N Burbank St, 86401. (Mail add: PO Box 7000, 86402-7000). Tel: 928-692-2665. Circulation Tel: 928-692-5702. FAX: 928-692-5788. E-mail: library@mohavecounty.us. *Libr Serv Mgr,* Bev Clouse; Tel: 928-692-5795, E-mail: bev.clouse@mohavecounty.us; Staff 2 (MLS 2)
Founded 1926. Circ 251,535
Library Holdings: Audiobooks 2,680; AV Mats 8,240; Bks-By-Mail 502; Bks on Deafness & Sign Lang 34; Braille Volumes 109; CDs 3,583; DVDs 1,436; e-books 3,988; e-journals 4,031; Electronic Media & Resources 132; High Interest/Low Vocabulary Bk Vols 99; Large Print Bks 3,385; Music Scores 12; Bk Titles 50,548; Bk Vols 52,067; Per Subs 135; Videos 148
Special Collections: Arizona Region
Automation Activity & Vendor Info: (Acquisitions) SirsiDynix; (Cataloging) SirsiDynix; (Circulation) SirsiDynix; (OPAC) SirsiDynix
Database Vendor: Baker & Taylor, EBSCOhost, Ingram Library Services, OCLC, Overdrive, Inc, SirsiDynix, TumbleBookLibrary, World Book Online
Function: Audiobks via web, Bks on CD, Copy machines, Electronic databases & coll, Fax serv, Free DVD rentals, Handicapped accessible, Home delivery & serv to Sr ctr & nursing homes, ILL available, Magnifiers for reading, Online cat, OverDrive digital audio bks, Prog for adults, Prog for children & young adult, Pub access computers, Spanish lang bks
Special Services for the Blind - Assistive/Adapted tech devices, equip & products; Bks on CD; Braille equip; Children's Braille; Copier with enlargement capabilities; Large print bks; Photo duplicator for making large print; Playaways (bks on MP3); Talking bk serv referral
Open Mon & Wed 9-6, Tues & Thurs 9-8, Fri & Sat 9-5
Friends of the Library Group

LAKE HAVASU CITY BRANCH LIBRARY, 1770 N McCulloch Blvd, Lake Havasu City, 86403-8847, SAN 330-6097. Tel: 928-453-0718. FAX: 928-453-0720. E-mail: library@mohavecounty.us. *Libr Serv Mgr,* Cynthia Amador; E-mail: cynthia.amador@mohavecounty.us; Staff 2 (MLS 2)
Founded 1968. Circ 2,254,427
Library Holdings: Audiobooks 2,900; AV Mats 8,332; Bks-By-Mail 502; Bks on Deafness & Sign Lang 40; Braille Volumes 2; CDs 3,556; DVDs 3,839; e-books 3,988; e-journals 4,031; Electronic Media & Resources 292; High Interest/Low Vocabulary Bk Vols 740; Large Print Bks 3,226; Music Scores 11; Bk Titles 45,471; Bk Vols 48,288; Per Subs 183; Videos 99
Special Collections: Arizona Region; Health
Subject Interests: Adult literacy, Graphic novels, Spanish
Automation Activity & Vendor Info: (Acquisitions) SirsiDynix; (Cataloging) SirsiDynix; (Circulation) SirsiDynix; (ILL) OCLC; (OPAC) SirsiDynix
Database Vendor: Baker & Taylor, EBSCO Auto Repair Reference, EBSCOhost, Ingram Library Services, OCLC, Overdrive, Inc, ProQuest, SirsiDynix, TumbleBookLibrary, World Book Online
Function: Audiobks via web, Bk club(s), Bks on CD, Copy machines, Electronic databases & coll, Fax serv, Free DVD rentals, Handicapped accessible, Home delivery & serv to Sr ctr & nursing homes, ILL available, Online cat, OverDrive digital audio bks, Prog for adults, Prog for children & young adult, Pub access computers, Spanish lang bks
Special Services for the Blind - Bks on CD; Large print bks; Magnifiers; Playaways (bks on MP3); Talking bk serv referral
Open Mon & Wed 9-6, Tues & Thurs 9-8, Fri & Sat 9-5
Friends of the Library Group

MEADVIEW COMMUNITY LIBRARY, 149 E Meadview Blvd, Meadview, 86444. (Mail add: PO Box 187, Meadview, 86444-0187), SAN 370-906X. Tel: 928-564-2535. Administration Tel: 928-692-5718. FAX: 928-564-2535. E-mail: library@mohavecounty.us. *Commun Libr Rep,* Pinkey Elliott; E-mail: pinkey.elliott@mohavecounty.us
Founded 1990. Circ 4,100
Library Holdings: Audiobooks 435; AV Mats 1,427; CDs 377; DVDs 918; e-books 3,988; e-journals 4,031; Electronic Media & Resources 9; High Interest/Low Vocabulary Bk Vols 2; Large Print Bks 151; Bk Titles 4,575; Bk Vols 4,706; Per Subs 7; Videos 1
Special Collections: Arizona Region
Automation Activity & Vendor Info: (Acquisitions) SirsiDynix; (Cataloging) SirsiDynix; (Circulation) SirsiDynix; (ILL) OCLC; (OPAC) SirsiDynix
Database Vendor: Baker & Taylor, EBSCO Auto Repair Reference, EBSCOhost, Ingram Library Services, OCLC, Overdrive, Inc, ProQuest, SirsiDynix, TumbleBookLibrary, World Book Online
Function: Audiobks via web, Bks on CD, Copy machines, Electronic databases & coll, Fax serv, Free DVD rentals, Handicapped accessible, Home delivery & serv to Sr ctr & nursing homes, ILL available, Online cat, OverDrive digital audio bks, Prog for adults, Prog for children & young adult, Pub access computers
Special Services for the Blind - Bks on CD; Large print bks; Playaways (bks on MP3); Talking bk serv referral
Open Tues 10-5, Thurs 11-6, Sat 10-4
Friends of the Library Group

SOUTH MOHAVE VALLEY COMMUNITY LIBRARY, 8045 Hwy 95, Ste D, Mohave Valley, 86446. (Mail add: PO Box 5661, Mohave Valley, 86440-5661), SAN 373-191X. Tel: 928-768-1151. Administration Tel: 928-692-5718. FAX: 928-768-1151. E-mail: library@mohavecounty.us. *Commun Libr Rep,* Amber Benkle; E-mail: amber.benkle@mohavecounty.us
Founded 1992. Circ 21,791
Library Holdings: Audiobooks 322; AV Mats 1,326; Bks on Deafness & Sign Lang 2; CDs 318; DVDs 933; e-books 3,988; e-journals 4,031; Electronic Media & Resources 37; High Interest/Low Vocabulary Bk Vols 3; Large Print Bks 222; Bk Titles 5,239; Bk Vols 5,314; Per Subs 10; Videos 1
Special Collections: Arizona Region
Automation Activity & Vendor Info: (Acquisitions) SirsiDynix; (Cataloging) SirsiDynix; (Circulation) SirsiDynix; (OPAC) SirsiDynix
Database Vendor: Baker & Taylor, EBSCOhost, Ingram Library Services, OCLC, Overdrive, Inc, SirsiDynix, TumbleBookLibrary, World Book Online
Function: Audiobks via web, Bks on CD, Copy machines, Electronic databases & coll, Fax serv, Free DVD rentals, Handicapped accessible, Home delivery & serv to Sr ctr & nursing homes, ILL available, Online cat, OverDrive digital audio bks, Prog for adults, Prog for children & young adult, Pub access computers
Special Services for the Blind - Bks on CD; Large print bks; Playaways (bks on MP3); Talking bk serv referral
Open Tues & Fri 1-5, Thurs 10-5, Sat 10-3
Friends of the Library Group

VALLE VISTA COMMUNITY LIBRARY, 7264 E Concho Dr, Ste B, 86401-9466, SAN 378-1666. Tel: 928-692-7662. Administration Tel: 928-692-5718. FAX: 928-692-7662. E-mail: library@mohavecounty.us. *Commun Libr Rep,* Kelly Dreyer; E-mail: kelly.dreyer@mohavecounty.us
Founded 1998. Circ 10,786
Library Holdings: Audiobooks 225; AV Mats 1,497; Bks on Deafness & Sign Lang 1; Braille Volumes 1; CDs 258; DVDs 1,123; e-books 3,988; e-journals 4,031; Electronic Media & Resources 30; High Interest/Low Vocabulary Bk Vols 2; Large Print Bks 295; Bk Titles 4,924; Bk Vols 4,994; Per Subs 10; Videos 71
Special Collections: Arizona Region
Automation Activity & Vendor Info: (Acquisitions) SirsiDynix; (Cataloging) SirsiDynix; (Circulation) SirsiDynix; (OPAC) SirsiDynix
Database Vendor: Baker & Taylor, EBSCOhost, Ingram Library Services, OCLC, Overdrive, Inc, SirsiDynix, TumbleBookLibrary, World Book Online
Function: Audiobks via web, Bks on CD, Copy machines, Electronic databases & coll, Fax serv, Free DVD rentals, Handicapped accessible, Home delivery & serv to Sr ctr & nursing homes, ILL available, Online cat, OverDrive digital audio bks, Prog for adults, Prog for children & young adult, Pub access computers
Special Services for the Blind - Bks on CD; Large print bks; Playaways (bks on MP3); Talking bk serv referral
Open Tues & Thurs 2:30-6, Wed & Sat 10-2
Friends of the Library Group

Bookmobiles: 2. Librn, Stella Carlzen. Bk titles 9,106

LAKESIDE

P LARSON MEMORIAL PUBLIC LIBRARY*, 1595 Johnson Dr, 85929. SAN 300-340X. Tel: 928-368-6688. Administration Tel: 928-368-0624. Toll Free Tel: 877-368-0624. FAX: 928-368-8963. E-mail: larsonlibrary@navajocountylibraries.org. Web Site: www.navajocountylibraries.org. *Dir,* Jeff Collins; Staff 5 (MLS 1, Non-MLS 4)
Founded 1954. Pop 20,000; Circ 80,000
Jul 2006-Jun 2007 Income $181,300, State $1,300, City $180,000. Mats Exp $16,000, Books $13,000, Per/Ser (Incl. Access Fees) $3,000. Sal $147,000 (Prof $43,000)
Library Holdings: CDs 40; DVDs 200; Large Print Bks 13,000; Bk Titles 31,000; Bk Vols 32,000; Per Subs 70
Special Collections: National Geographic Coll
Subject Interests: Arizona, Indians
Automation Activity & Vendor Info: (Acquisitions) SirsiDynix; (Cataloging) SirsiDynix; (Circulation) SirsiDynix; (OPAC) SirsiDynix
Database Vendor: OVID Technologies
Wireless access
Function: ILL available, Photocopying/Printing, Prog for children & young adult, Summer reading prog, Telephone ref
Partic in Navajo County Libr District
Special Services for the Blind - Talking bks
Open Tues-Sat 9:30-6
Friends of the Library Group

LUKE AFB

A UNITED STATES AIR FORCE, Luke Air Force Base Library, Bldg 219, 7424 N Homer Dr, 56 SVS/SVMG FL 4887, 85309. SAN 330-6216. Tel: 623-856-7191. FAX: 623-935-2023. *Dir,* Dr George Marangoly; Staff 2 (MLS 2)
Founded 1951
Library Holdings: AV Mats 4,000; e-books 450; Large Print Bks 1,000; Bk Vols 49,500; Per Subs 225; Talking Bks 4,500
Special Collections: Arizona, Mission Support. Oral History
Subject Interests: Aeronaut, Mil hist
Automation Activity & Vendor Info: (Cataloging) SirsiDynix; (Circulation) SirsiDynix; (ILL) OCLC
Database Vendor: OCLC FirstSearch
Publications: Bibliographies; Library Links (Newsletter)
Partic in Dialog Corp; OCLC Online Computer Library Center, Inc
Open Mon & Tues 9:30-7:30, Wed-Fri 9:30-5:30, Sat 10-4

MAMMOTH

P MAMMOTH PUBLIC LIBRARY, 125 N Clark St, 85618. (Mail add: PO Box 549, 85618-0549), SAN 300-3434. Tel: 520-487-2026. FAX: 520-487-2364. *Librn,* Position Currently Open
Founded 1962. Pop 1,850; Circ 7,833
Library Holdings: Bk Titles 8,000; Bk Vols 8,500; Per Subs 40
Automation Activity & Vendor Info: (Cataloging) SirsiDynix; (Circulation) SirsiDynix; (OPAC) SirsiDynix
Wireless access
Mem of Pinal County Library District
Open Tues & Wed 12-6, Thurs 2-6, Fri & Sat 10-2

MARANA

S ARIZONA DEPARTMENT OF CORRECTIONS - ADULT INSTITUTIONS*, Marana Community Correctional Facility Library, 12610 W Silverbell Rd, 85653. Tel: 520-682-2077. FAX: 520-682-4080.
Library Holdings: Bk Vols 25,000; Per Subs 24
Automation Activity & Vendor Info: (Cataloging) Autolib Library & Information Management Systems; (Circulation) Autolib Library & Information Management Systems
Open Mon & Wed 3-4, Tues & Thurs 1-4 & 8-9, Sat & Sun 9am-11pm

MARICOPA

P MARICOPA PUBLIC LIBRARY*, 41600 W Smith-Enke Rd, Bldg 10, 85138. Tel: 520-568-2926. FAX: 520-568-2680. Web Site: www.maricopa-az.gov/web/marcopiapubliclibrary. *Libr Mgr,* Erik Surber; E-mail: erik.surber@pinalcountyaz.gov; *Asst Librn,* Position Currently Open; *Libr Asst,* Timothy Provenzano; Staff 9 (MLS 4, Non-MLS 5)
Founded 1958. Pop 33,000
Library Holdings: Bk Vols 18,515; Per Subs 42
Special Collections: Arizona Coll
Automation Activity & Vendor Info: (Cataloging) Horizon; (Circulation) Horizon
Function: Bilingual assistance for Spanish patrons, Bks on CD, Children's prog, Citizenship assistance, Computer training, Computers for patron use, Copy machines, Digital talking bks, E-Reserves, Electronic databases & coll, Exhibits, Free DVD rentals, Govt ref serv, Health sci info serv, Holiday prog, ILL available, Music CDs, Online cat, Photocopying/Printing, Preschool reading prog, Prog for adults, Prog for children & young adult, Provide serv for the mentally ill, Pub access computers, Senior computer classes, Spanish lang bks, Story hour, Summer & winter reading prog, Summer reading prog, Tax forms, Teen prog, Telephone ref, Video lending libr, Winter reading prog

Mem of Pinal County Library District
Open Mon & Wed 10-7, Tues & Thurs 9-6, Fri & Sat 9-5
Friends of the Library Group

MAYER

P MAYER PUBLIC LIBRARY*, 10004 Wicks Ave, 86333. (Mail add: PO Box 1016, 86333-1016), SAN 323-7974. Tel: 928-632-7370. FAX: 928-632-7370. Web Site: www.prescottlib.az.us/maylib.htm. *Dir,* Daniel Collins
Founded 1965
Library Holdings: Bk Vols 10,000
Subject Interests: SW
Automation Activity & Vendor Info: (Cataloging) SirsiDynix; (Circulation) SirsiDynix; (OPAC) SirsiDynix
Mem of Yavapai County Free Library District
Open Mon-Fri 10-4, Sat 10-12
Friends of the Library Group

MCNARY

P MCNARY COMMUNITY LIBRARY*, 208 W Pine St, 85930. (Mail add: PO Box 586, 85930-0586). Tel: 928-334-2101. FAX: 928-334-2102. E-mail: mcl@navajo.lib.az.us. Web Site: www.navajoco.lib.az.us. *Dir,* Carmen Perry
Library Holdings: Bk Vols 11,025
Automation Activity & Vendor Info: (Cataloging) SirsiDynix; (Circulation) SirsiDynix; (OPAC) SirsiDynix
Open Mon & Thurs 10-2, Tues & Wed 2-6

MESA

CM A T STILL UNIVERSITY*, A T Still Memorial Library, 5850 E Still Circle, 85206-6091. Tel: 480-219-6090. FAX: 480-219-6100. E-mail: libaz@atsu.edu. Web Site: www.atsu.edu/atsmlib. *Dir,* Michael R Kronenfeld; E-mail: mkronenfeld@atsu.edu; *Dir, Educ Tech Develop Ctr,* William Coombs; Tel: 480-219-6259, E-mail: wcoombs@atsu.edu; *Distance Support Librn,* Cynthia Porter; Tel: 480-219-6192, E-mail: cporter@atsu.edu; *Electronic Res Librn,* Harold Bright; Tel: 480-219-6036, E-mail: hbright@atsu.edu; Staff 5 (MLS 4, Non-MLS 1)
Founded 2002. Enrl 4,074; Highest Degree: Doctorate
Library Holdings: e-books 150,000; e-journals 25,000; Bk Vols 800; Per Subs 90
Automation Activity & Vendor Info: (Acquisitions) CyberTools for Libraries; (Cataloging) OCLC; (OPAC) CyberTools for Libraries; (Serials) EBSCO Online
Database Vendor: Cinahl, CyberTools for Libraries, EBSCO - WebFeat, EBSCO Discovery Service, EBSCOhost, Elsevier, Lexi-Comp, McGraw-Hill, Medline, Micromedex, Natural Standard, OCLC, OVID Technologies, PubMed, ScienceDirect, Springshare, LLC, STAT!Ref (Teton Data Systems), UpToDate, Wiley
Wireless access
Partic in Arizona Health Information Network (AZHIN); MOBIUS (Missouri Bibliographic Information User System)
Open Mon-Sun 8am-11pm

S ARIZONA MUSEUM FOR YOUTH LIBRARY*, 35 N Robson St, 85201. SAN 375-7161. Tel: 480-644-2467. FAX: 480-644-2466. Web Site: www.arizonamuseumforyouth.com, www.cityofmesa.org. *Curator,* Jeffory Morris; Tel: 480-644-5769, E-mail: Jeffory.Morris@MesaAZ.gov
Library Holdings: Bk Titles 1,000
Open Tues-Sun 9-5

M BANNER DESERT MEDICAL CENTER*, Health Science Library, 1400 S Dobson Rd, 85202. Tel: 480-512-3024. FAX: 480-512-8720. *Librn,* Kathy Bilko; E-mail: kathy.bilko@bannerhealth.com
Library Holdings: Bk Titles 750; Bk Vols 1,200; Per Subs 200
Open Mon-Fri 7-4

S CHURCH OF JESUS CHRIST OF LATTER-DAY SAINTS*, Mesa FamilySearch Library, 41 S Hobson, 85204. SAN 300-3450. Tel: 480-964-1200. FAX: 480-964-7137. E-mail: admin@mesarfhc.org. Web Site: mesafsl.org. *Dir,* Sherril Harmon; *Asst Dir,* Bruce Evans; *Asst Dir,* Adrian Kuzdas
Founded 1930
Library Holdings: Bk Titles 35,000
Special Collections: Family Histories & Biographies; International Genealogical Index; US Census Records. Oral History
Subject Interests: Genealogy
Open Mon & Fri 9-5, Tues-Thurs 9-9, Sat 10-5

J MESA COMMUNITY COLLEGE LIBRARY*, Paul A Elsner Library, 1833 W Southern Ave, 85202. SAN 300-3469. Tel: 480-461-7671. Circulation Tel: 480-461-7680. Reference Tel: 480-461-7682. FAX: 480-461-7681. TDD: 480-969-5387. Web Site: www.mesacc.edu/library/. *Chair,* Ann Tolzman; E-mail: ann.tolzman@mesacc.edu; *Libr Mgr,* Julie Yen; E-mail: julie.yen@mesacc.edu; Staff 29 (MLS 10, Non-MLS 19)
Founded 1963. Enrl 24,470; Fac 350; Highest Degree: Associate
Jul 2006-Jun 2007 Income (Main and Other College/University Libraries) $2,235,686. Mats Exp $342,801, Books $227,841, Per/Ser (Incl. Access Fees) $78,261, Micro $10,891, Electronic Ref Mat (Incl. Access Fees) $25,808. Sal $1,372,796 (Prof $713,110)
Library Holdings: AV Mats 679; e-books 28,752; Bk Vols 85,184; Per Subs 528
Automation Activity & Vendor Info: (Acquisitions) SirsiDynix; (Cataloging) SirsiDynix; (Circulation) SirsiDynix; (Course Reserve) SirsiDynix; (ILL) SirsiDynix; (Media Booking) SirsiDynix; (OPAC) SirsiDynix; (Serials) EBSCO Online
Database Vendor: Amigos Library Services, ARTstor, Baker & Taylor, Cinahl, CQ Press, ebrary, EBSCO - WebFeat, EBSCOhost, Elsevier, Gale Cengage Learning, Newsbank, OCLC FirstSearch, Oxford Online, ProQuest, SerialsSolutions, SirsiDynix, ValueLine
Wireless access
Function: Electronic databases & coll, Handicapped accessible, ILL available, Online ref, Ref serv available, Tax forms
Special Services for the Blind - Computer with voice synthesizer for visually impaired persons
Open Mon-Thurs 6am-Midnight, Fri 6-5, Sat 8-5, Sun Noon-10

Departmental Libraries:

RED MOUNTAIN, 7110 E McKellips Rd, 85207. Tel: 480-654-7741. Reference Tel: 480-654-7740. FAX: 480-654-7401. *Dir,* Marie C Brown; E-mail: marie.brown@mesacc.edu
Library Holdings: Per Subs 85
Open Mon-Thurs (Fall & Spring) 7am-8:30pm, Fri 7-4, Sat 10-2

P MESA PUBLIC LIBRARY, 64 E First St, 85201-6768. SAN 300-3477. Tel: 480-644-3100. Interlibrary Loan Service Tel: 480-644-2732. Administration Tel: 480-644-2739. Automation Services Tel: 480-644-3986. FAX: 480-644-2991. Interlibrary Loan Service FAX: 480-644-5710. Administration FAX: 480-644-3490. E-mail: library.info@mesaaz.gov. Web Site: www.mesalibrary.org. *Dir,* Heather Wolf; Tel: 480-644-2712, E-mail: heather.wolf@mesaaz.gov; *Br Operations Supvr, Circ, Fac Serv,* Tom Naylor; Tel: 480-644-4144, E-mail: tom.naylor@mesaaz.gov; *Coll Support Serv Supvr,* Jill S London; Tel: 480-644-3725, E-mail: jill.london@mesaaz.gov; *Br Coordr,* Kathy Little; Tel: 480-644-2726, E-mail: kathy.little@mesaaz.gov; *Coll Develop, Res Develop Coordr,* Liz Costanzo-Lee; Tel: 480-644-4709, E-mail: liz.costanzo-lee@mesaaz.gov; *Tech Adminr,* Brandon Williams; Tel: 480-644-2472, E-mail: brandon.williams@mesaaz.gov; Staff 33.1 (MLS 12.6, Non-MLS 20.5)
Founded 1926. Pop 450,000; Circ 2,346,586
Jul 2013-Jun 2014 Income (Main Library and Branch(s)) $7,754,952, State $22,099, City $7,637,000, Federal $33,471, Locally Generated Income $62,382. Mats Exp $1,016,400, Books $507,900, AV Mat $256,000, Electronic Ref Mat (Incl. Access Fees) $252,500
Library Holdings: Audiobooks 27,261; AV Mats 37,091; Braille Volumes 50; DVDs 5,913; e-books 76; Large Print Bks 15,864; Bk Titles 285,527; Bk Vols 585,127; Per Subs 280
Special Collections: Oral History
Subject Interests: Local hist, Spanish (Lang)
Automation Activity & Vendor Info: (Acquisitions) Innovative Interfaces, Inc; (Cataloging) Innovative Interfaces, Inc; (Circulation) Innovative Interfaces, Inc; (ILL) OCLC ILLiad; (OPAC) Innovative Interfaces, Inc; (Serials) Innovative Interfaces, Inc
Database Vendor: 3M Library Systems, Atlas Systems, Baker & Taylor, Brodart, infoUSA, Ingram Library Services, Innovative Interfaces, Inc, OCLC FirstSearch, OCLC WorldShare Interlibrary Loan, Overdrive, Inc, ProQuest, ReferenceUSA, TumbleBookLibrary, WT Cox
Wireless access
Partic in OCLC Online Computer Library Center, Inc
Special Services for the Deaf - ADA equip; Bks on deafness & sign lang; Closed caption videos; TTY equip
Special Services for the Blind - Braille bks; Copier with enlargement capabilities; Large print bks
Open Mon-Thurs 10-8, Fri & Sat 10-5

Branches: 3

DOBSON RANCH BRANCH, 2425 S Dobson Rd, 85202, SAN 328-6800. Tel: 480-644-3444. FAX: 602-644-3445. *Br Coordr,* Polly Bonnett; Tel: 480-644-3448, E-mail: polly.bonnett@mesaaz.gov; Staff 9 (MLS 3, Non-MLS 6)
Founded 1987
Function: Bks on CD, Children's prog, Computers for patron use, Copy machines, Electronic databases & coll, Free DVD rentals, ILL available, OverDrive digital audio bks, Prog for adults, Prog for children & young adult, Pub access computers, Story hour, Summer reading prog
Open Mon-Thurs 10-8, Fri & Sat 10-5

MESA EXPRESS LIBRARY, 2055 S Power Rd, Ste 1031, 85209. Tel: 480-644-3300.
Founded 2011

Function: Bks on CD, Computers for patron use, Copy machines, Electronic databases & coll, Free DVD rentals, ILL available, Online cat, OverDrive digital audio bks, Photocopying/Printing, Pub access computers, Summer reading prog, Wheelchair accessible

RED MOUNTAIN BRANCH, 635 N Power Rd, 85205, SAN 325-3791. Tel: 480-644-3183. Circulation Tel: 480-644-3182. FAX: 480-644-3559. *Br Operations Supvr,* Terese Crary; Tel: 480-644-3862, E-mail: terese.crary@mesaaz.gov; Staff 21 (MLS 6, Non-MLS 15)
Founded 1985
Function: Bks on CD, Children's prog, Computers for patron use, Copy machines, Electronic databases & coll, Exhibits, Free DVD rentals, ILL available, Large print keyboards, Magnifiers for reading, Mus passes, Music CDs, Online cat, Photocopying/Printing, Prog for adults, Prog for children & young adult, Ref & res, Ref serv in person, Story hour, Summer reading prog, Teen prog, Telephone ref, Video lending libr, Web-catalog
Open Mon-Thurs 10-8, Fri & Sat 10-5

MIAMI

P MIAMI MEMORIAL-GILA COUNTY LIBRARY*, 282 S Adonis Ave, 85539. SAN 300-3493. Tel: 928-473-2621. FAX: 928-473-2567. *Libr Mgr,* Delvan Hayward; E-mail: dhayward@gcldaz.org
Pop 37,098
Library Holdings: Bk Vols 70,000; Per Subs 10
Open Tues-Fri 10-6, Sat 9-1

MORENCI

P MORENCI COMMUNITY LIBRARY*, 346 Morenci Plaza, 85540. (Mail add: PO Box 1060, 85540-1060), SAN 376-3269. Tel: 928-865-2775. FAX: 928-865-3130. *Dir,* Lourdes Campus
Library Holdings: Bk Titles 18,327; Bk Vols 19,127; Per Subs 58
Subject Interests: Arizona, Mining
Mem of Greenlee County Library System
Open Mon-Thurs 9-5, Fri 9-8, Sat 10-5, Sun 1-5
Friends of the Library Group

NOGALES

P NOGALES-SANTA CRUZ COUNTY PUBLIC LIBRARY*, Nogales Public Library, 518 N Grand Ave, 85621. SAN 300-3507. Tel: 520-287-3343. Reference Tel: 520-285-5712. FAX: 520-287-4823. TDD: 520-287-6571. *Dir,* Suzanne Haddock; *Sr Libr Asst,* Mirna Navarro; *Cat,* Alicia Fleischer; *Ch Serv,* Danitza Lopez; *ILL,* Sandra Mascarenas; Staff 6 (MLS 1, Non-MLS 5)
Founded 1923. Pop 44,575; Circ 143,748
Jul 2008-Jun 2009 Income (Main Library and Branch(s)) $590,216, City $339,305, County $226,203, Locally Generated Income $1,708. Mats Exp $41,482, Books $32,942, AV Mat $8,540. Sal $269,990
Library Holdings: CDs 1,590; DVDs 2,163; Bk Titles 62,720; Per Subs 92; Videos 2,163
Special Collections: Arizona & Southwest History Coll; Spanish Language Coll
Automation Activity & Vendor Info: (Cataloging) Innovative Interfaces, Inc; (Circulation) Innovative Interfaces, Inc
Function: Adult bk club, Bilingual assistance for Spanish patrons, Bks on cassette, Bks on CD, Chess club, Children's prog, Computer training, Computers for patron use, Copy machines, Handicapped accessible, Homework prog, ILL available, Music CDs, Online cat, Online searches, Photocopying/Printing, Pub access computers, Senior computer classes, Spoken cassettes & CDs, Spoken cassettes & DVDs, Story hour, Summer reading prog, Tax forms
Partic in OCLC Online Computer Library Center, Inc
Special Services for the Deaf - TDD equip
Open Mon & Wed 10-6 (9:30-6 Summer), Tues & Thurs 9:30-7, Fri 9-5, Sat 9-4
Restriction: Borrowing requests are handled by ILL
Friends of the Library Group
Branches: 3
RIO RICO LIBRARY, 1060 Yavapai Dr, Rio Rico, 85648, SAN 320-9520. Tel: 520-281-8067. *Asst Librn,* Danitza Lopez; Staff 1 (Non-MLS 1)
Founded 1982
Friends of the Library Group
SONOITA COMMUNITY LIBRARY, County Complex Bldg, 3147 State Rte 83, Sonoita, 85637. (Mail add: 518 N Grand Ave, 85621), SAN 373-1820. Tel: 520-455-5517. *Br Mgr,* Mirna Navarro
Friends of the Library Group
TUBAC COMMUNITY LIBRARY, 50 Bridge Rd, Tubac, 85646, SAN 326-7911. Tel: 520-398-9814. *Br Mgr,* Mirna Navarro
Open Mon-Wed 10-2, Thurs & Fri 10-4
Friends of the Library Group

S PIMERIA ALTA HISTORICAL SOCIETY LIBRARY & MUSEUM*, 136 N Grand Ave, 85621. (Mail add: PO Box 2281, 85628-2281), SAN 326-5609. Tel: 520-287-4621. *Pres,* Kathleen Escalada
Founded 1942
Library Holdings: Bk Titles 1,500; Bk Vols 1,600; Per Subs 10
Special Collections: Municipal Document Depository; Oral History; US Document Depository
Wireless access
Open Fri-Sun 10-4

ORACLE

P ORACLE PUBLIC LIBRARY*, 565 American Ave, 85623. (Mail add: PO Box 960, 85623), SAN 300-3515. Tel: 520-896-2121. FAX: 520-896-2149. *Dir,* Pauly Skiba
Founded 1920. Pop 5,500; Circ 12,000
Library Holdings: Bk Titles 12,000; Per Subs 20
Special Collections: Southwest Coll
Automation Activity & Vendor Info: (Cataloging) Horizon; (Circulation) Horizon; (OPAC) Horizon
Mem of Pinal County Library District
Open Mon 9-4, Tues 8-6, Thurs 9-6, Wed 9-3, Fri 8-Noon, Sat 9-3

PAGE

P PAGE PUBLIC LIBRARY*, 479 S Lake Powell Blvd, 86040. (Mail add: PO Box 1776, 86040-1776), SAN 300-354X. Tel: 928-645-4270. Administration Tel: 928-645-5803. FAX: 928-645-5804. TDD: 928-645-4133. *Libr Dir,* Debbie Winlock; Tel: 928-645-4272, E-mail: debbie@cityofpage.org; *Acq, Cat,* Deanna Bigman; E-mail: deanna@cityofpage.org; *Adult Serv, Ref,* Chana Burney; E-mail: chana@cityofpage.org; *Circ, ILL,* Semra Gorst; Tel: 928-645-4131, E-mail: sgorst@cityofpage.org; Staff 8 (MLS 1, Non-MLS 7)
Founded 1959. Pop 25,000
Jul 2007-Jun 2008. Mats Exp $45,000
Library Holdings: CDs 3,788; DVDs 3,132; Bk Titles 55,697; Bk Vols 58,585; Per Subs 50
Subject Interests: Arizona, Native Am
Automation Activity & Vendor Info: (Acquisitions) TLC (The Library Corporation); (Cataloging) TLC (The Library Corporation); (Circulation) TLC (The Library Corporation); (OPAC) TLC (The Library Corporation)
Database Vendor: Gale Cengage Learning, Innovative Interfaces, Inc, OVID Technologies
Wireless access
Publications: Annual Report; Library Board Policy Manual
Mem of Flagstaff City-Coconino County Public Library System
Open Tues-Thurs 9-8, Fri 9-6, Sat 10-6
Friends of the Library Group

S JOHN WESLEY POWELL MEMORIAL MUSEUM LIBRARY*, Six N Lake Powell Blvd, 86040. (Mail add: PO Box 547, 86040-0547), SAN 371-1560. Tel: 928-645-9496. FAX: 928-645-3412. Web Site: www.powellmuseum.org. *Actg Dir,* Mark Law; E-mail: director@powellmuseum.org; Staff 1 (Non-MLS 1)
Founded 1969
Library Holdings: Bk Vols 500
Special Collections: John Wesley Powell Coll; State History - Glen Canyon Dam, Colorado River, Lake Powell. Oral History
Function: Archival coll
Restriction: Non-circulating

PARKER

P COLORADO RIVER INDIAN TRIBES PUBLIC LIBRARY*, Second Ave & Mohave Rd, Rte 1, Box 23-B, 85344. SAN 300-3558. Tel: 928-669-1332. FAX: 928-669-8262. E-mail: crit.library@crit-nsn.gov. Web Site: www.critlibrary.com. *Dir,* Gilford Harper
Founded 1958. Circ 4,376
Library Holdings: Bks on Deafness & Sign Lang 16; Bk Titles 12,000; Bk Vols 22,000
Special Collections: Archival documents, History & Culture (Indian Coll), micro, photo
Automation Activity & Vendor Info: (Acquisitions) Follett Software; (Cataloging) Follett Software; (Circulation) Follett Software

P PARKER PUBLIC LIBRARY*, 1001 S Navajo Ave, 85344. SAN 300-3566. Tel: 928-669-2622. Toll Free Tel: 877-852-6657. FAX: 928-669-8668. Web Site: www.parkerpubliclibraryaz.org. *Libr Mgr,* Ruthie Davis; *Adult, Children & Teen Serv,* Jeannie Smith. Subject Specialists: *Bilingual,* Jeannie Smith; Staff 4 (Non-MLS 4)
Founded 1957. Pop 12,000; Circ 43,000
Library Holdings: Bk Vols 22,000
Subject Interests: Arizona
Automation Activity & Vendor Info: (Cataloging) Follett Software; (Circulation) Follett Software

Database Vendor: OCLC FirstSearch
Function: ILL available
Special Services for the Deaf - Bks on deafness & sign lang; High interest/low vocabulary bks
Special Services for the Blind - Bks on cassette
Open Mon-Fri 9-7, Sat 9-2
Friends of the Library Group
Branches: 2
BOUSE PUBLIC LIBRARY, 44031 Plomosa Rd, Bouse, 85325. (Mail add: PO Box 840, Bouse, 85325-0840). Tel: 928-851-1023. FAX: 928-851-2758. *Mgr,* Heather Huhtala
Open Tues 9-4, Wed & Thurs 9-3, Sat 10-3
CENTENNIAL PUBLIC LIBRARY, 69725 Centennial Rd, Salome, 85348, SAN 377-0303. Tel: 928-859-4271. FAX: 928-859-4364. Web Site: www.parkerpubliclibraryaz.org/centennial.php. *Mgr,* Sharon Hillhouse
Library Holdings: Bk Titles 4,500
Open Mon-Wed 9-3:30, Thurs 12-6

PATAGONIA

P PATAGONIA PUBLIC LIBRARY*, 346 Duquesne, 85624. (Mail add: PO Box 415, 85624), SAN 320-2054. Tel: 520-394-2010. FAX: 520-394-2113. E-mail: info@patagoniapubliclibrary.org. Web Site: www.patagoniapubliclibrary.org. *Librn,* Abbie Zeltzer; Staff 1.75 (MLS 1, Non-MLS 0.75)
Founded 1957. Pop 3,200; Circ 22,500
Jul 2011-Jun 2012 Income $111,800, City $58,000, County $21,300, Locally Generated Income $29,500, Other $3,000. Mats Exp $23,455, Books $12,500, Per/Ser (Incl. Access Fees) $2,230, Manu Arch $575, AV Mat $4,750, Electronic Ref Mat (Incl. Access Fees) $3,400. Sal $35,000 (Prof $28,750)
Library Holdings: Audiobooks 785; Braille Volumes 1; CDs 317; DVDs 1,234; Electronic Media & Resources 40; Large Print Bks 558; Bk Titles 12,433; Bk Vols 12,487; Per Subs 52; Videos 211
Special Collections: Foreign Language Video & DVD Coll; Library of Congress Classic DVD & Video Coll; Southwest & Local History Coll
Automation Activity & Vendor Info: (OPAC) Biblionix
Wireless access
Function: Adult bk club, Computer training, Copy machines, Electronic databases & coll, Fax serv, Handicapped accessible, Homebound delivery serv, ILL available, Mail & tel request accepted, Music CDs, Online ref, Online searches, Photocopying/Printing, Preschool outreach, Prog for adults, Prog for children & young adult, Spoken cassettes & CDs, Spoken cassettes & DVDs, Summer reading prog, Tax forms, VHS videos, Video lending libr, Wheelchair accessible
Open Mon-Fri 10-5, Sat 10-2
Friends of the Library Group

PAYSON

P PAYSON PUBLIC LIBRARY*, 328 N McLane Rd, 85541. SAN 300-3574. Tel: 928-474-9260. FAX: 928-474-2679. *Dir,* Emily Linkey; *Asst Mgr,* Elaine Votruba; *Ch,* Katie Sanchez; *Circ,* Bobbie Scott
Founded 1923. Pop 13,000; Circ 101,000
Library Holdings: Bk Vols 85,000; Per Subs 90
Special Collections: History (Southwest Coll); Native Americans
Automation Activity & Vendor Info: (Cataloging) Innovative Interfaces, Inc; (Circulation) Innovative Interfaces, Inc; (OPAC) Innovative Interfaces, Inc
Mem of Gila County Library District
Open Mon, Tues, Thurs & Fri 10-6, Wed 10-8, Sat 10-5
Friends of the Library Group

PEACH SPRINGS

P EDWARD MCELWAIN MEMORIAL LIBRARY*, 460 Hualapai Way, 86434. (Mail add: PO Box 179, 86434-0179). Tel: 928-769-2200. FAX: 928-769-2250. *Dir,* Cheryle Beecher; E-mail: nyachyu@yahoo.com
Library Holdings: Bk Vols 10,000
Open Mon-Fri 8-5

PEORIA

P PEORIA PUBLIC LIBRARY, 8463 W Monroe St, 85345. (Mail add: 8401 W Monroe, 85345), SAN 300-3590. Tel: 623-773-7555. Interlibrary Loan Service Tel: 623-773-7530. Reference Tel: 623-773-7556. Administration Tel: 623-773-7557. FAX: 623-773-7567. Web Site: library.peoriaaz.gov. *Libr Mgr,* Mary Roberts; E-mail: mary.roberts@peoriaaz.gov; *Librn II,* Ali Scherzay; Tel: 623-773-7540; *Librn II,* Dawn Marie Schmidt; Tel: 623-773-7562, E-mail: dawnmarie.schmidt@peoriaaz.gov; *Circ, Libr Serv Coordr,* Jill Thomsen; Tel: 623-773-7566, E-mail: jill.thomsen@peoriaaz.gov; Staff 8 (MLS 4, Non-MLS 4)
Founded 1920. Circ 111,819
Library Holdings: Bk Titles 198,050; Per Subs 105
Subject Interests: Spanish (Lang)
Automation Activity & Vendor Info: (Acquisitions) Innovative Interfaces, Inc; (Cataloging) Innovative Interfaces, Inc; (Circulation) Innovative Interfaces, Inc; (OPAC) Innovative Interfaces, Inc; (Serials) Innovative Interfaces, Inc
Database Vendor: SirsiDynix
Wireless access
Function: Art exhibits, Bks on CD, Children's prog, Computers for patron use, Copy machines, Electronic databases & coll, eReaders, Fax serv, Free DVD rentals, Handicapped accessible, ILL available, Jazz prog, Magazines, Movies, Music CDs, Online ref, Online searches, Story hour, Study rm, Teen prog, Telephone ref
Open Mon-Thurs 9-8, Fri & Sat 9-6, Sun 1-5
Restriction: Borrowing requests are handled by ILL
Friends of the Library Group
Branches: 1
SUNRISE MOUNTAIN, 21109 N 98th Ave, 85382, SAN 377-7553. Tel: 623-773-8650. FAX: 623-773-8670. *Librn III,* Pattie Fransen; Tel: 623-773-8655, E-mail: pattie.fransen@peoriaaz.gov; *Librn II,* Kathie Jackson; Tel: 623-773-8667, E-mail: kathie.jackson@peoriaaz.gov; *Circ, Libr Serv Coordr,* Heather Sorden; Tel: 623-773-8656; Staff 5 (MLS 5)
Founded 1996
Library Holdings: Bk Titles 75,000
Open Mon-Thurs 9-8, Fri & Sat 9-6, Sun 1-5
Friends of the Library Group

PETRIFIED FOREST NATIONAL PARK

S NATIONAL PARK SERVICE*, Petrified Forest National Park Library, One Park Rd, 86028. (Mail add: PO Box 2217, 86028-0217), SAN 300-3604. Tel: 928-524-6228. FAX: 928-524-3567. *In Charge,* Pat Thompson
Founded 1906
Library Holdings: Bk Vols 5,000
Special Collections: Triassic Period
Subject Interests: Natural hist
Open Mon-Fri 8-4
Restriction: In-house use for visitors, Staff & prof res

PHOENIX

S AMEC EARTH & ENVIRONMENTAL TECHNICAL LIBRARY*, 4600 E Wshington St, Ste 600, 85034. SAN 371-5191. Tel: 602-733-6000.
Library Holdings: Bk Titles 12,000; Per Subs 120
Subject Interests: Eng, Environment, Geol
Open Mon-Fri 8-5

CR AMERICAN INDIAN COLLEGE, Dorothy Cummings Library, 10020 N 15th Ave, 85021-2199. SAN 300-3639. Tel: 602-944-3335, Ext 251. Circulation Tel: 602-944-3335, Ext 252. Toll Free Tel: 800-933-3828. E-mail: library@aicag.edu. Web Site: www.aicag.edu/academics/library/. *Librn,* Deborah Ramm; E-mail: dramm@aicag.edu; *Tech Serv Librn,* Marsha Cleaveland; Tel: 602-944-3335, E-mail: mcleaveland@aicag.edu; Staff 1 (MLS 0.5, Non-MLS 0.5)
Founded 1965. Enrl 68; Fac 15; Highest Degree: Bachelor
Jul 2011-Jun 2012. Mats Exp $14,250, Books $5,000, Per/Ser (Incl. Access Fees) $2,250, Electronic Ref Mat (Incl. Access Fees) $7,000
Library Holdings: Bk Vols 25,000; Per Subs 50; Videos 670
Special Collections: Native American Coll; Religion, Bible
Subject Interests: Relig, Theol
Automation Activity & Vendor Info: (Cataloging) OPALS (Open-source Automated Library System); (Circulation) OPALS (Open-source Automated Library System); (Course Reserve) OPALS (Open-source Automated Library System); (OPAC) OPALS (Open-source Automated Library System)
Database Vendor: EBSCOhost
Wireless access
Function: Computers for patron use, Copy machines, Online ref, Online searches, Orientations, Photocopying/Printing, Scanner, VHS videos, Web-catalog
Partic in Theological Library Cooperative of Arizona
Open Mon & Tues 1-9, Wed-Fri 9-11 & 1-5
Restriction: Open to students, fac, staff & alumni

C ARGOSY UNIVERSITY, Phoenix Library, 2233 W Dunlap Ave, Ste 150, 85021. Tel: 602-216-2600. FAX: 602-216-3150. *Libr Serv Spec,* Dr Robert Campbell; Tel: 602-216-3124, E-mail: rcampbell@argosy.edu
Library Holdings: Bk Titles 10,000; Per Subs 150
Wireless access
Open Mon-Fri 8:30am-9pm, Sat & Sun 10-5

CR ARIZONA CHRISTIAN UNIVERSITY LIBRARY*, 2625 E Cactus Rd, 85032-7097. SAN 300-3949. Tel: 602-992-6101, Ext 117. FAX: 602-404-2159. Web Site: arizonachristian.edu/library. *Dir,* Sean McNulty; E-mail: Sean.Mcnulty@arizonachristian.edu; Staff 1 (MLS 1)
Founded 1960. Enrl 267; Fac 32; Highest Degree: Bachelor

Jul 2005-Jun 2006 Income $149,283. Mats Exp $34,300, Books $17,500, Per/Ser (Incl. Access Fees) $6,500, Micro $2,900, AV Mat $3,000, Presv $4,400. Sal $84,864 (Prof $48,190)
Library Holdings: AV Mats 2,334; CDs 78; DVDs 21; e-books 19,300; e-journals 2,047; Music Scores 41; Bk Titles 22,343; Bk Vols 27,332; Per Subs 130; Videos 745
Subject Interests: Biblical studies, Theol
Automation Activity & Vendor Info: (Cataloging) Follett Software; (Circulation) Follett Software; (ILL) OCLC
Database Vendor: EBSCOhost
Partic in OCLC Online Computer Library Center, Inc

ARIZONA DEPARTMENT OF CORRECTIONS - ADULT INSTITUTIONS

S ARIZONA STATE PRISON COMPLEX - PHOENIX LIBRARY*, 2500 E Van Buren St, 85008. (Mail add: PO Box 52109, 85072-2109). Tel: 602-685-3100. FAX: 602-685-3129. *Educ Supvr,* Ron Brugman; Tel: 602-685-3100, Ext 3758
Library Holdings: Bk Vols 15,000

S ARIZONA STATE PRISON PHOENIX-WEST*, 3402 W Cocopah St, 85009. Tel: 602-352-0350, Ext 109. FAX: 602-352-0357. Web Site: www.librarything.com/profile/PrisonLib. *Librn,* Alexandra Rowland; E-mail: arowland@geogroup.com; Staff 1 (MLS 1)
Jul 2011-Jun 2012. Mats Exp $500. Sal $32,000
Library Holdings: Audiobooks 204; Bk Vols 6,116; Per Subs 8
Automation Activity & Vendor Info: (Cataloging) DEMCO; (Circulation) DEMCO
Function: Accelerated reader prog, Accessibility serv available based on individual needs, Adult bk club, Adult literacy prog, BA reader (adult literacy), Bilingual assistance for Spanish patrons, Copy machines, Distance learning, ILL available, Legal assistance to inmates, Literacy & newcomer serv, Notary serv, Orientations
Restriction: Internal circ only

G ARIZONA DEPARTMENT OF EDUCATION LIBRARY, 1535 W Jefferson St, Bin 6, 85007. SAN 300-3647. Tel: 602-542-5416. *Dir,* Linda Edgington; Staff 1 (MLS 1)
Library Holdings: Bk Titles 500; Per Subs 2
Subject Interests: Educ

G ARIZONA DEPARTMENT OF ENVIRONMENTAL QUALITY LIBRARY*, 1110 W Washington St, 85007. SAN 374-9029. Administration Tel: 602-771-2300. Toll Free Tel: 800-234-5677 (AZ only). FAX: 602-771-2399. *Librn, Ref Serv,* Norleen Lara; Tel: 602-771-4712
Founded 1988
Library Holdings: Bk Titles 2,000; Bk Vols 2,500
Subject Interests: Air, Environ, Pollution prevention, Sustainable develop, Topographic maps, Waste, Water
Automation Activity & Vendor Info: (Cataloging) Inmagic, Inc.; (Circulation) Inmagic, Inc.
Database Vendor: OCLC FirstSearch
Function: Archival coll, Electronic databases & coll, Govt ref serv, ILL available, Online ref, Photocopying/Printing, Ref serv available, Telephone ref
Open Mon-Fri 8-5
Restriction: Circ limited, Open to pub for ref & circ; with some limitations

G ARIZONA DEPARTMENT OF TRANSPORTATION LIBRARY*, 206 S 17th Ave, Rm 198, MD O75R, 85007. SAN 374-5198. Tel: 602-712-3138. FAX: 602-712-3400. E-mail: library@azdot.gov. Web Site: www.azdot.gov/planning/research-center/library. *Librn,* Dale Steele; Staff 1 (MLS 1)
Founded 1989
Library Holdings: CDs 240; Bk Vols 36,686; Per Subs 69
Subject Interests: Civil eng, Transportation
Automation Activity & Vendor Info: (Cataloging) Inmagic, Inc.; (Circulation) Inmagic, Inc.; (OPAC) Inmagic, Inc.; (Serials) Inmagic, Inc.
Partic in OCLC Online Computer Library Center, Inc
Open Mon-Fri 8-4

P ARIZONA STATE BRAILLE & TALKING BOOK LIBRARY, 1030 N 32nd St, 85008. SAN 300-368X. Tel: 602-255-5578. Toll Free Tel: 800-255-5578. FAX: 602-286-0444. Web Site: www.azlibrary.gov/braille. *Dir,* Linda A Montgomery; E-mail: lmontgomery@azlibrary.gov; *Asst Dir,* Ron Bryant; *Coll Develop,* Erin Pawlus; *Tech Serv,* Lorin Lindsay; Staff 9 (MLS 6, Non-MLS 3)
Founded 1970
Library Holdings: Braille Volumes 435; DVDs 502; Bk Vols 485; Per Subs 15; Talking Bks 240,000; Videos 487
Special Collections: Arizona & Spanish Language Cassettes, locally produced; Reference Materials on Blindness & Disablities, print
Automation Activity & Vendor Info: (Circulation) Keystone Systems, Inc (KLAS)
Publications: Adaptive Technology In Arizona Libraries (Annual); Talking Book News (Newsletter)
Special Services for the Blind - Bks & mags in Braille, on rec, tape & cassette; Braille equip; Cassette playback machines; Descriptive video serv (DVS); Home delivery serv; Info on spec aids & appliances; Machine repair; Newsletter (in large print, Braille or on cassette); Newsline for the Blind; Production of talking bks; Volunteer serv
Open Mon-Fri 8-5
Restriction: Authorized patrons, Restricted pub use
Friends of the Library Group

M ARIZONA STATE HOSPITAL LIBRARY*, 2500 E Van Buren St, 85008. SAN 330-6240. Tel: 602-220-6045. FAX: 602-629-7285. Web Site: www.azdhs.gov/azsh/library.htm. *Med Librn,* Gail Bacani; E-mail: bacanig@azdhs.gov. Subject Specialists: *Mental health,* Gail Bacani; Staff 1 (MLS 1)
Founded 1965
Library Holdings: AV Mats 500; DVDs 200; Large Print Bks 50; Bk Titles 10,000; Bk Vols 850; Per Subs 20; Talking Bks 80; Videos 300
Special Collections: State Document Depository
Subject Interests: Drug abuse, Mental health, Nursing, Psychiat, Psychol, Psychotherapy, Soc serv (soc work)
Automation Activity & Vendor Info: (Cataloging) CyberTools for Libraries; (Circulation) CyberTools for Libraries; (ILL) OCLC FirstSearch; (OPAC) CyberTools for Libraries; (Serials) CyberTools for Libraries
Database Vendor: EBSCOhost, Gale Cengage Learning, LexisNexis, OCLC FirstSearch, OCLC WorldShare Interlibrary Loan, OVID Technologies, PubMed, STAT!Ref (Teton Data Systems), WebMD
Function: ILL available, Ref serv available, Res libr
Partic in Asn of Mental Health Librn (AMHL); Cent Ariz Biomed Librns; Pacific Southwest Regional Medical Library (PSRML)
Open Mon-Fri 7:30-12 & 1-4
Restriction: Non-circulating to the pub

P ARIZONA STATE LIBRARY, ARCHIVES & PUBLIC RECORDS, 1700 W Washington, Rm 200, 85007. SAN 300-3701. Tel: 602-926-4035. Toll Free Tel: 800-228-4710 (AZ only). FAX: 602-256-7983. E-mail: research@azlibrary.gov. Web Site: www.azlibrary.gov. *State Librn,* Joan Clark; Tel: 602-926-3805, E-mail: jclark@azlibrary.gov; *Dep Dir,* Ted Hale; Tel: 602-926-3736, E-mail: thale@azlibrary.gov; *Dir, Archives & Rec Mgt,* Melanie Sturgeon, PhD; Tel: 602-926-3720, E-mail: msturgeo@azlibrary.gov; *Dir, Coll & External Relations,* Janet Fisher; Tel: 602-926-3870, Fax: 602-256-7984, E-mail: jfisher@azlibrary.gov; *Dir, E-rate & Pub Serv,* Malavika Muralidharan; Tel: 602-926-3601, E-mail: mala@azlibrary.gov; *Dir, Libr Develop,* Holly Henley; E-mail: hhenley@azlibrary.gov; Staff 27 (MLS 24, Non-MLS 3)
Founded 1864
Jul 2013-Jun 2014 Income $12,630,377, State $7,156,200, Federal $3,934,176, Locally Generated Income $1,540,001. Mats Exp $183,332, Books $25,987, Per/Ser (Incl. Access Fees) $29,701, Micro $30,481, Electronic Ref Mat (Incl. Access Fees) $97,163. Sal $6,107,447
Library Holdings: Audiobooks 49,600; AV Mats 812; e-books 278,531; Microforms 2,307,482; Bk Vols 1,363,983; Per Subs 2,015; Talking Bks 10,423
Subject Interests: Arizona, Genealogy, Law
Automation Activity & Vendor Info: (Acquisitions) SirsiDynix; (Cataloging) SirsiDynix; (Circulation) SirsiDynix; (ILL) SirsiDynix; (OPAC) SirsiDynix; (Serials) SirsiDynix
Database Vendor: Gale Cengage Learning, HeinOnline, LexisNexis, Newsbank, OCLC WorldShare Interlibrary Loan, Overdrive, Inc, ProQuest, ReferenceUSA, SirsiDynix, Westlaw
Wireless access
Function: ILL available
Publications: Arizona Public Library Statistics; Arizona Reading Program Manual; Library Development Newsletter; Talking Book News
Partic in OCLC Online Computer Library Center, Inc
Open Mon-Fri 8-5
Restriction: Circ limited

CL ARIZONA SUMMIT LAW SCHOOL*, One N Central Ave, 85004. Tel: 602-682-6898. Circulation Tel: 602-682-6897. FAX: 602-682-6996. E-mail: circdept@AZSummitlaw.edu. Web Site: www.azsummitlaw.edu. *Interim Dir,* Christy Ryan; Staff 12 (MLS 5, Non-MLS 7)
Founded 2005. Enrl 200; Fac 22; Highest Degree: Doctorate
Automation Activity & Vendor Info: (Acquisitions) Innovative Interfaces, Inc; (Cataloging) Innovative Interfaces, Inc; (Circulation) Innovative Interfaces, Inc; (Course Reserve) Innovative Interfaces, Inc; (ILL) OCLC; (OPAC) Innovative Interfaces, Inc; (Serials) Innovative Interfaces, Inc
Database Vendor: Cassidy Cataloguing Services, Inc, HeinOnline, LexisNexis, ProQuest, Westlaw
Wireless access
Partic in Amigos Library Services, Inc
Open Mon-Fri 8am-10pm, Sat & Sun 10-9
Restriction: Open to students, fac & staff

C THE ART INSTITUTE OF PHOENIX*, Learning Resource Center, 2233 W Dunlap Ave, 85021-2859. Tel: 602-331-7500. Reference Tel: 602-331-7571. Administration Tel: 602-331-7580. Toll Free Tel: 800-474-2479, Ext 7580. FAX: 602-216-3150. Web Site: www.artinstitutes.edu/phoenix. *Libr Dir,* Traci E Cushmeer; *Ref Librn,* Laura Artusio; Staff 2 (MLS 2)
Founded 1995. Enrl 1,100; Highest Degree: Bachelor
Library Holdings: AV Mats 4,000; e-journals 12; Electronic Media & Resources 12; Large Print Bks 15; Bk Titles 30,252; Per Subs 206
Subject Interests: Art, Culinary, Design, Digital video, Graphic design, Interior design, Photog, Web design
Automation Activity & Vendor Info: (Acquisitions) Baker & Taylor; (Cataloging) Follett Software; (Circulation) Follett Software; (OPAC) Follett Software
Wireless access
Function: CD-ROM, Computers for patron use, Copy machines, e-mail serv, Electronic databases & coll, Instruction & testing, Literacy & newcomer serv, Online cat, Online ref, Online searches, Orientations, Outreach serv, Ref & res, Ref serv available, Scanner, Telephone ref
Restriction: Authorized patrons, Borrowing privileges limited to fac & registered students, Circ privileges for students & alumni only, Not a lending libr, Not open to pub, Open to students, fac & staff

M BANNER GOOD SAMARITAN MEDICAL CENTER*, Merril W Brown Health Sciences Library, 1111 E McDowell Rd, 85006. SAN 300-3736. Tel: 602-839-4353. FAX: 602-839-3493. Web Site: www.bannerhealth.com. *Dir,* Sally Harvey; Staff 6 (MLS 3, Non-MLS 3)
Founded 1965
Library Holdings: Bk Vols 10,000; Per Subs 750
Special Collections: GSRMC Heritage Coll
Subject Interests: Clinical med, Consumer health, Hospital admin, Nursing
Database Vendor: Gale Cengage Learning, OVID Technologies
Function: ILL available
Partic in Arizona Health Information Network (AZHIN); Cent Ariz Biomed Librns; Medical Library Group of Southern California & Arizona (MLGSCA)
Special Services for the Blind - Reader equip
Open Mon-Fri 7:30-5

Branches:

GRACE MIDDLEBROOK FAMILY LEARNING CENTER, 1111 E McDowell Rd, 85006. Tel: 602-839-4970. FAX: 602-839-4971. *Librn,* Terry Ratner; E-mail: terry.ratner@bannerhealth.com; Staff 2 (MLS 1, Non-MLS 1)
Database Vendor: Gale Cengage Learning, OVID Technologies
Open Mon-Fri 11-5

L BURCH & CRACCHIOLO PA*, Law Library, 702 E Osborn Rd, Ste 200, 85014. SAN 323-6854. Tel: 602-234-8704. FAX: 602-344-3704. Web Site: www.bcattorneys.com. *Libr Mgr,* Diane Abazarnia; E-mail: dbabazarnia@bcattorneys.com; Staff 1 (MLS 1)
Library Holdings: Bk Vols 12,000
Restriction: Staff use only

S DESERT BOTANICAL GARDEN LIBRARY*, Schilling Library, 1201 N Galvin Pkwy, 85008. SAN 321-0324. Tel: 480-481-8133. FAX: 480-481-8124. E-mail: library@dbg.org. Web Site: dbg.org. *Librn,* Beth Brand; Staff 1 (Non-MLS 1)
Founded 1939
Library Holdings: Bk Vols 8,000; Per Subs 50
Special Collections: Cactaceae; Desert Landscape Design
Subject Interests: Agavaceae, Agro-ecology, Arid land plants, Cactaceae, Endangered, Ethnobotany, Rare plants
Automation Activity & Vendor Info: (Cataloging) OCLC Connexion; (OPAC) EOS International
Database Vendor: EOS International
Wireless access
Function: Adult bk club, Archival coll, Copy machines, Online cat
Publications: Index Seminum; Sonoran Quarterly (Newsletter)
Partic in Council on Botanical & Horticultural Libraries, Inc (CBHL)
Open Mon-Fri 12-4
Restriction: In-house use for visitors, Not a lending libr, Ref only to non-staff

C DEVRY UNIVERSITY LIBRARY*, Phoenix Campus Community Library, 2149 W Dunlap Ave, 85021-2982. SAN 375-7587. Tel: 602-749-4638. Interlibrary Loan Service Tel: 603-870-9222, Ext 710. Information Services Tel: 602-870-9222, Ext 712. FAX: 602-734-1999. Web Site: www.phx.devry.edu/library.html. *Dir of Libr Serv,* Margot Cassidy; E-mail: mcassidy@devry.edu; Staff 1 (MLS 1)
Founded 1931. Enrl 1,200; Fac 45; Highest Degree: Master
Jul 2005-Jun 2006. Mats Exp $66,000, Books $15,000, Per/Ser (Incl. Access Fees) $5,000, Other Print Mats $2,500, Micro $500, Electronic Ref Mat (Incl. Access Fees) $40,000, Presv $3,000. Sal $80,000 (Prof $48,000)
Library Holdings: AV Mats 1,300; CDs 25; e-books 12,000; High Interest/Low Vocabulary Bk Vols 30; Bk Titles 25,000; Per Subs 75
Special Collections: Directories: Arizona High Tech, Rocky Mt High Tech; Nikola Tesla Coll
Subject Interests: Computer sci, Electronics
Automation Activity & Vendor Info: (Acquisitions) Ex Libris Group; (Cataloging) Marcive, Inc; (Circulation) Ex Libris Group; (Course Reserve) Ex Libris Group; (ILL) Ex Libris Group; (Media Booking) Ex Libris Group; (OPAC) Ex Libris Group; (Serials) Ex Libris Group
Database Vendor: Gale Cengage Learning, Newsbank, ProQuest, ReferenceUSA
Wireless access
Function: Bus archives, For res purposes, ILL available, Photocopying/Printing, Ref serv available
Open Mon-Thurs 8am-9pm, Fri 8-6, Sat 9-1
Restriction: In-house use for visitors, Not open to pub, Open to students, fac & staff

L FENNEMORE CRAIG, Law Library, 2394 E Camelback Rd, 85016. SAN 372-3712. Tel: 602-916-5280. FAX: 602-916-5964. *Librn,* Alexis Soard
Library Holdings: Per Subs 250
Automation Activity & Vendor Info: (Acquisitions) EOS International; (Cataloging) EOS International; (Circulation) EOS International; (Course Reserve) EOS International; (ILL) EOS International; (Media Booking) EOS International; (OPAC) EOS International; (Serials) EOS International
Open Mon-Fri 8-5
Restriction: Not open to pub

S FOUNDATION FOR BLIND CHILDREN LIBRARY & MEDIA CENTER*, Arizona Instructional Resource Center, 1235 E Harmont Dr, 85020-3864. SAN 300-4163. Tel: 602-678-5810, 602-678-5816. Toll Free Tel: 800-322-4870. FAX: 602-678-5811. Web Site: www.seeitourway.org. *Dir,* Vivian Seki; E-mail: vseki@seeitourway.org; Staff 8 (Non-MLS 8)
Founded 1952
Library Holdings: Braille Volumes 5,000; e-books 100; High Interest/Low Vocabulary Bk Vols 100; Large Print Bks 8,000; Bk Titles 20,000; Bk Vols 60,000; Per Subs 25; Videos 40
Special Collections: Braille, Large Print, Print/Braille & Electronic Files for Blind & Visually Impaired Students
Special Services for the Blind - Braille bks; Descriptive video serv (DVS); Large print bks
Open Mon-Fri 8-4:30

L GALLAGHER & KENNEDY*, Law Library, 2575 E Camelback Rd, 85016-4240. SAN 372-2619. Tel: 602-530-8000, 602-530-8149. FAX: 602-530-8500. Web Site: www.gknet.com. *Librn,* Jeffrey D Mcguire; E-mail: jdm@gknet.com
Library Holdings: Bk Titles 750; Per Subs 200

C GRAND CANYON UNIVERSITY LIBRARY, 3300 W Camelback Rd, 85017-3030. SAN 300-3744. Tel; 602-639-6641. Toll Free Tel: 800-800-9776. FAX: 602-639-7835. E-mail: library@gcu.edu. Web Site: library.gcu.edu. *Dir, Libr Serv,* Nita Mailander; E-mail: nita.mailander@gcu.edu; Staff 20 (MLS 14, Non-MLS 6)
Founded 1949. Highest Degree: Doctorate
Automation Activity & Vendor Info: (Circulation) Innovative Interfaces, Inc; (OPAC) Innovative Interfaces, Inc
Wireless access
Open Mon-Fri 7am-10pm, Sat & Sun 10-10
Restriction: Open to others by appt, Open to students, fac & staff

S HALL OF FLAME*, Richard S Fowler Memorial Library, 6101 E Van Buren, 85008. SAN 300-3752. Tel: 602-275-3473. FAX: 602-275-0896. Web Site: www.hallofflame.org. *Dir,* Peter Molloy; E-mail: petermolloy@hallofflame.org; *Librn,* Leslie Marshall
Founded 1968
Library Holdings: Bk Vols 6,000; Per Subs 12
Special Collections: History of Firefighting in the US & Europe
Wireless access
Restriction: Staff use only

S HEARD MUSEUM*, Billie Jane Baguley Library & Archives, 2301 N Central Ave, 85004-1323. SAN 300-3760. Tel: 602-252-8840. FAX: 602-252-9757. Web Site: www.heard.org. *Dir,* Mario Nick Klimiades; Tel: 602-251-0228, E-mail: mario@heard.org; Staff 3 (MLS 1, Non-MLS 2)
Founded 1929
Library Holdings: AV Mats 1,500; Bk Titles 31,000; Per Subs 240
Special Collections: Atlatl Coll; Barry Goldwater Color Photography Coll; Fred Harvey Company Papers & Photographs; Native American Artists Resource Coll; Native American Boarding School Coll; North American Indian (Curtis Coll); R Brownell McCrew Papers & Photographs
Subject Interests: Anthrop, Archaeology, Native Am art
Automation Activity & Vendor Info: (Cataloging) OCLC; (OPAC) CARL.Solution (TLC)

Database Vendor: OCLC FirstSearch
Function: Photocopying/Printing, Ref serv available
Publications: Archival Collections Guide; Native American Artist Directory
Partic in Consortium of Arizona Museum Archives & Libraries (CAZMAL)
Open Mon-Fri 10-4:45
Restriction: Non-circulating, Open to pub by appt only
Friends of the Library Group

M INDIAN HEALTH SERVICES*, Phoenix Indian Medical Center Library, 4212 N 16th St, 85016. SAN 320-9075. Tel: 602-263-1676. FAX: 602-263-1577. Web Site: pimc.azhin.org. *Dir, Med Libr,* Rebecca Swift; E-mail: rebecca.swift@ihs.gov; Staff 1 (MLS 1)
Founded 1950
Special Collections: Diseases of Native Americans Coll
Subject Interests: Endocrinology
Partic in Arizona Health Information Network (AZHIN); Cent Ariz Biomed Librns
Open Mon-Fri 8-4:30

L JABURG & WILK PC*, Law Library, Great American Tower, Ste 2000, 3200 N Central Ave, 85012. SAN 372-3720. Tel: 602-248-1000. FAX: 602-248-0522. E-mail: info@jaburgwilk.com.
Library Holdings: Bk Vols 2,500
Restriction: Staff use only

L JENNINGS, STROUSS & SALMON*, Law Library, One E Washington St, Ste 1900, 85004-2554. SAN 372-3739. Tel: 602-262-5911. FAX: 602-253-3255. Web Site: www.jsslaw.com. *Librn,* Renee Stanbery; E-mail: rstanbery@jsslaw.com
Library Holdings: Bk Vols 20,000

CR KINO INSTITUTE DIOCESAN LIBRARY*, 400 E Monroe St, 85004-2336. SAN 325-268X. Tel: 602-354-2311. Web Site: www.kinoinstitute.org. *Librn,* Darcy Peletich; E-mail: dpeletich@diocesephoenix.org
Founded 1978. Enrl 130; Fac 7
Library Holdings: AV Mats 3,850; CDs 60; DVDs 60; Bk Titles 26,000; Per Subs 120; Videos 1,800
Subject Interests: Sacred scripture, Spirituality, Theol
Automation Activity & Vendor Info: (Circulation) Book Systems
Database Vendor: Amigos Library Services, OCLC FirstSearch
Function: ILL available
Open Tues, Wed & Thurs 12:30-6:30

L LEWIS & ROCA LIBRARY*, Renaisance Tower, No 2, 40 N Central Ave, Ste 1900, 85004-4429. SAN 326-5641. Tel: 602-262-5303. FAX: 602-734-3739. Web Site: lrlaw.com. *Dir, Libr Serv,* Michael Reddy; Staff 4 (MLS 2, Non-MLS 2)
Library Holdings: Bk Titles 5,500; Bk Vols 40,000; Per Subs 100
Subject Interests: Corporate law, Real estate
Partic in Dialog Corp; Westlaw
Restriction: Staff use only

M JOHN C LINCOLN HEALTH NETWORK*, Grigg Medical Library, 250 E Dunlap Ave, 85020. Tel: 602-870-6328. FAX: 602-997-9325. Web Site: www.jcl.com. *Med Librn,* Sue Shelly; Staff 2 (MLS 2)
Founded 1983
Library Holdings: Bk Titles 5,000; Per Subs 300
Special Collections: Medical Libraries
Open Mon-Fri 8-4:30

S MARICOPA COUNTY JAIL LIBRARY*, 3150 W Lower Buckeye Rd, 85009. Tel: 602-876-5633, 602-876-5638. FAX: 602-353-1546. *Libr Mgr,* Lisa Poulin; E-mail: l_poulin@mcso.maricopa.gov
Library Holdings: Bk Vols 20,000
Restriction: Staff & inmates only

P MARICOPA COUNTY LIBRARY DISTRICT, 2700 N Central Ave, Ste 700, 85004. SAN 300-3809. Tel: 602-652-3000. FAX: 602-652-3071. Web Site: www.mcldaz.org. *Dir,* Cindy Kolaczynski; Tel: 602-652-3030, Fax: 602-652-3079, E-mail: cindykolaczynski@mcldaz.org; *Dep Dir,* Jeremy Reeder; Tel: 602-652-3036, E-mail: jeremyreeder@mcldaz.org; *Br Operations Adminr,* Alicia Snarr; Tel: 602-652-3015, E-mail: aliciasnarr@mcldaz.org; *Br Operations Adminr-Innovations & Strategies,* Michael Porter; Tel: 602-652-3005, E-mail: michaelporter@mcldaz.org; *Customer Experience Adminr,* Caris O'Malley; Tel: 602-652-3056, E-mail: carisomalley@mcldaz.org; *Adult Serv Mgr,* Tony Apodaca; Tel: 602-652-3006, E-mail: tonyapodaca@mcldaz.org; *Coll Develop Mgr,* Helen Gutierrez; Tel: 602-652-3039, E-mail: helengutierrez@mcldaz.org; *Finance Mgr,* John Werbach; Tel: 602-652-3051, E-mail: johnwerbach@mcldaz.org; *Human Res Mgr,* Lena Beecher; Tel: 602-652-3033, Fax: 602-652-3078, E-mail: lenabeecher@mcldaz.org; *Teen Serv Mgr,* Brianna King; Tel: 602-652-3032, E-mail: briannaking@mcldaz.org; *Youth Serv Mgr,* Danette Barton; Tel: 602-652-3052, E-mail: danettebarton@mcldaz.org; *Mkt/Pub Relations Coordr,* Nelson Mitchell; Tel: 602-652-3045, E-mail: nelsonmitchell@mcldaz.org; *Chief Tech Officer,* Matt Miller; Tel: 602-652-3060, E-mail: mattmiller@mcldaz.org; Staff 258 (MLS 57, Non-MLS 201)
Founded 1986. Pop 797,840; Circ 7,454,130
Jul 2012-Jun 2013 Income (Main Library and Branch(s)) $21,477,596. Mats Exp $4,782,000
Automation Activity & Vendor Info: (Acquisitions) Innovative Interfaces, Inc; (Cataloging) Innovative Interfaces, Inc; (Circulation) Innovative Interfaces, Inc; (ILL) OCLC WorldShare Interlibrary Loan; (OPAC) Innovative Interfaces, Inc
Wireless access
Friends of the Library Group
Branches: 17
AGUILA BRANCH, 51300 W US Hwy 60, Aguila, 85320, SAN 378-2328. Tel: 602-652-3000. FAX: 602-652-3484.
Library Holdings: Bk Titles 6,312
Open Mon 10-7, Tues-Thurs 10-6, Fri & Sat 10-5
EL MIRAGE BRANCH, 14011 N First Ave, El Mirage, 85335, SAN 378-2344. Tel: 602-652-3000. FAX: 602-652-3390.
Library Holdings: Bk Titles 12,526
Open Mon-Wed 9-5, Thurs 10-7, Fri & Sat 9-5
FAIRWAY BRANCH, 10600 W Peoria Ave, Rm 144, Sun City, 85351, SAN 330-7026. Tel: 602-652-3000.
Library Holdings: Bk Titles 10,444
Open Mon-Fri 9-4
Friends of the Library Group
FOUNTAIN HILLS BRANCH, 12901 N La Montana Dr, Fountain Hills, 85268, SAN 376-8422. Tel: 602-652-3000. FAX: 602-652-3270.
Library Holdings: Bk Titles 43,520
Open Mon-Thurs 9-9, Fri & Sat 9-5
Friends of the Library Group
GILA BEND BRANCH, 202 N Euclid, Gila Bend, 85337. (Mail add: PO Box B, Gila Bend, 85337), SAN 378-2387. Tel: 602-652-3000. FAX: 602-652-3398.
Library Holdings: Bk Titles 9,064
Open Mon 10-7, Tues-Thurs 10-6, Fri 10-5
Friends of the Library Group
GOODYEAR BRANCH LIBRARY, 14415 W Van Buren St, Ste C101, Goodyear, 85338. Tel: 602-652-3000. FAX: 602-652-3475.
Library Holdings: Bk Titles 18,031
Open Mon-Wed 10-7, Thurs-Sat 10-5
Friends of the Library Group
GUADALUPE BRANCH, 9241 S Avenida del Yaqui, Guadalupe, 85283, SAN 376-8449. FAX: 602-652-3296.
Library Holdings: Bk Titles 9,676
Open Mon 10-7, Tues-Thurs 10-6, Fri 10-5
HOLLYHOCK BRANCH, 15844 N Hollyhock St, Surprise, 85374, SAN 376-849X. Tel: 602-652-3000. FAX: 602-652-3489.
Library Holdings: Bk Titles 3,526
Open Tues & Thurs 1-6
LITCHFIELD PARK BRANCH, 101 W Wigwam Blvd, Litchfield, 85340, SAN 378-2360. Tel: 302-652-3000. FAX: 602-652-3470.
Library Holdings: Bk Titles 36,289
Open Mon-Wed 10-8, Thurs-Sat 10-5
Friends of the Library Group
NORTH VALLEY REGIONAL, 40410 N Gavilan Peak Pkwy, Anthem, 85086. Tel: 602-652-3000. FAX: 602-652-3320.
Library Holdings: Bk Titles 69,286
Open Mon-Thurs 9-9, Fri & Sat 9-5, Sun 1-5
Friends of the Library Group
NORTHWEST REGIONAL, 16089 N Bullard Ave, Surprise, 85374. Tel: 602-652-3000. FAX: 602-652-3420.
Library Holdings: Bk Titles 96,639
Open Mon-Thurs 9-9, Fri & Sat 9-5, Sun 1-5
Friends of the Library Group
PERRY BRANCH, 1965 E Queen Creek Rd, Gilbert, 85297. Tel: 302-652-3000. FAX: 602-651-3575.
Library Holdings: Bk Titles 45,132
Open Mon-Thurs 10-7, Fri & Sat 10-4
Friends of the Library Group
QUEEN CREEK BRANCH, 21802 S Ellsworth Rd, Queen Creek, 85242, SAN 376-8465. Tel: 602-652-3000. FAX: 602-652-3360.
Library Holdings: Bk Titles 75,182
Open Mon-Thurs 9-8, Fri & Sat 9-5
Friends of the Library Group
ED ROBSON BRANCH, 9330 E Riggs Rd, Sun Lakes, 85248, SAN 376-8481. Tel: 602-652-3000. FAX: 602-652-3280.
Library Holdings: Bk Titles 14,346
Open Mon-Wed 9-5, Thurs 10-7, Fri & Sat 9-5
Friends of the Library Group

SOUTHEAST REGIONAL, 775 N Greenfield Rd, Gilbert, 85234. Tel: 302-652-3000. FAX: 602-652-3240.
Library Holdings: Bk Titles 143,399
Open Mon-Thurs 10-9, Fri & Sat 10-5, Sun 1-5
Friends of the Library Group

SUN CITY BRANCH, 16828 N 99th Ave, Sun City, 85351. Tel: 602-652-3000. FAX: 602-651-2015.
Library Holdings: Bk Titles 32,998
Friends of the Library Group

WHITE TANK BRANCH, 20304 W White Tank Mountain Rd, Waddell, 85355. Tel: 602-652-3000. FAX: 602-651-2225.
Open Mon-Wed 10-7, Thurs-Sat 10-5
Friends of the Library Group

L MAYNARD CRONIN ERICKSON CURRAN & REITER, PLC*, Law Library, 3200 N Central, Ste 1800, 85012. SAN 375-8273. Tel: 602-279-8500. FAX: 602-263-8185. *Dir, Human Res,* Heidi Burnett
Library Holdings: Bk Titles 13,000

L OSBORN MALEDON*, Law Library, 2929 N Central, 21st Flr, 85012-2794. SAN 372-2635. Tel: 602-640-9000. FAX: 602-640-9050. *Librn,* Theresa Greco; Tel: 602-640-9210
Library Holdings: Bk Titles 10,000
Partic in OCLC Online Computer Library Center, Inc
Open Mon-Fri 8-5

J PARADISE VALLEY COMMUNITY COLLEGE, Buxton Library, 18401 N 32nd St, 85032-1200. Tel: 602-787-7200. Interlibrary Loan Service Tel: 602-787-7258. Reference Tel: 602-787-7215. Administration Tel: 606-787-7222. FAX: 602-787-7205. Web Site: www.paradisevalley.edu/library. *Chair,* John U Chavez; E-mail: j.chavez@paradisevalley.edu; *Instrul Librn,* Karen Anderson; E-mail: karen.anderson@paradisevalley.edu; *Instrul Librn,* Paula Crossman; Tel: 602-787-7203, E-mail: paula.crossmand@paradisevalley.edu; *Instrul Librn,* Sylvia Frost; E-mail: sylvia.frost@paradisevalley.edu; *Instrul Librn,* Dixie Klatt; E-mail: dixie.klatt@paradisevalley.edu; *Instrul Librn,* Alexandra Rowland; E-mail: alexandra.rowland@gcc.edu; *Instrul Librn,* Joe Schallan; E-mail: joe.schallan@paradisevalley.edu; *Supvr, Libr Access Serv,* Cindy Nieves; Tel: 602-787-7207, E-mail: cindy.nieves@paradisevalley.edu; *Div Coordr,* Christina McDonough; Tel: 602-787-7259, E-mail: christina.mcdonough@paradisevalley.edu; *Circ/Reserves, Libr Asst,* Jerice Eckels; E-mail: jerice.eckels@pvmail.maricopa.edu; *Libr Asst, Acq/Receiving,* Denise Cole; Tel: 602-787-7238, E-mail: denise.cole@paradisevalley.edu; *Acq, Libr Asst, ILL,* Nicole Almanza; Tel: 602-787-7213, E-mail: nicole.almanza@paradisevalley.edu; *E-Res & Coll Develop,* Kande Mickelsen; Tel: 602-787-6692, E-mail: kandice.mickelsen@paradisevalley.edu; *Instrul Serv, Assessment, Developmental Educ,* Lili Kang; Tel: 602-787-7209, E-mail: li.kang@paradisevalley.edu. Subject Specialists: *Bus, Math,* John U Chavez; *Behav & soc sci, Fine arts, Performing arts,* Paula Crossman; *Archives,* Dixie Klatt; *Health & wellness, Nursing sci,* Kande Mickelsen; *Communications, English, Humanities,* Lili Kang; Staff 9 (MLS 4, Non-MLS 5)
Founded 1987. Enrl 8,908; Highest Degree: Associate
Jul 2013-Jun 2014 Income $1,115,859, Locally Generated Income $10,027, Parent Institution $1,105,832. Mats Exp $175,626, Books $75,923, Per/Ser (Incl. Access Fees) $30,162, Micro $4,336, AV Mat $32,391, Electronic Ref Mat (Incl. Access Fees) $32,814. Sal $691,484 (Prof $492,888)
Library Holdings: Audiobooks 164; AV Mats 7,572; Bks on Deafness & Sign Lang 63; CDs 1,636; DVDs 3,948; e-books 860; High Interest/Low Vocabulary Bk Vols 203; Music Scores 67; Bk Vols 38,414; Per Subs 151; Videos 1,037
Special Collections: Caldecott & Newbury Coll; Career & College Resources Coll; Children's Fiction/Nonfiction/Picture Books Coll; General Coll; Leisure Reading Coll; Literacy Coll; Maps Coll; McNaughton Coll; Music CDs Coll; Periodicals - Current Coll; Popular Movies Coll; Young Adults Coll
Automation Activity & Vendor Info: (Acquisitions) Horizon; (Cataloging) Horizon; (Circulation) Horizon; (Course Reserve) Horizon; (ILL) OCLC ILLiad; (OPAC) Horizon; (Serials) Horizon
Database Vendor: CQ Press, ebrary, EBSCO - WebFeat, EBSCOhost, Facts on File, Gale Cengage Learning, Greenwood Publishing Group, H W Wilson, Knovel, LearningExpress, McGraw-Hill, Natural Standard, Newsbank, OCLC FirstSearch, OCLC WorldShare Interlibrary Loan, Oxford Online, ProQuest, ReferenceUSA, SerialsSolutions, Wilson - Wilson Web
Wireless access
Function: Archival coll, Art exhibits, Audio & video playback equip for onsite use, Bilingual assistance for Spanish patrons, Bks on CD, Computers for patron use, Copy machines, e-mail serv, Electronic databases & coll, Exhibits, Free DVD rentals, Handicapped accessible, ILL available, Music CDs, Online cat, Online info literacy tutorials on the web & in blackboard, Online ref, Online searches, Orientations, Photocopying/Printing, Pub access computers, Ref serv available, Ref serv in person, Scanner, Spanish lang bks, Tax forms, Telephone ref, Web-catalog, Wheelchair accessible
Special Services for the Deaf - Assistive tech; Closed caption videos; High interest/low vocabulary bks
Special Services for the Blind - Accessible computers; Audio mat; Bks on CD; Closed circuit TV magnifier; Computer with voice synthesizer for visually impaired persons; Copier with enlargement capabilities; Dragon Naturally Speaking software; Internet workstation with adaptive software; Radio reading serv; Reader equip; Ref serv; Screen reader software
Open Mon-Thurs 7am-8pm, Fri 7-2, Sat 12-4
Restriction: Open to pub for ref & circ; with some limitations, Open to students, fac & staff

L PERKINS COIE LIBRARY*, 2901 N Central Ave, Ste 2000, 85012. SAN 329-8191. Tel: 602-351-8213. Web Site: www.perkinscoie.com. *Librn,* Karen Anderson; Staff 1 (MLS 1)
Library Holdings: Bk Vols 20,000; Per Subs 150
Subject Interests: Law
Wireless access
Restriction: Not open to pub, Private libr

S PHOENIX ART MUSEUM LIBRARY, 1625 N Central Ave, 85004-1685. SAN 300-3868. Tel: 602-257-2136. FAX: 602-253-8662. E-mail: library@phxart.org. Web Site: www.phxart.org. *Librn,* Abigail Nersesian; Staff 2 (MLS 2)
Founded 1959
Library Holdings: Electronic Media & Resources 6; Bk Vols 52,000; Per Subs 65
Special Collections: American Art Coll; Auction Records Coll; Latin American Art Coll; One-Person Exhibition Coll; Rembrandt Print Catalogs from 1751 (Orme Lewis Coll); Vertical Files (Subject Artist Museum)
Subject Interests: Art & archit, Decorative art, European art, Fashion, Graphic arts, Sculpture, Western Am art
Wireless access
Function: Archival coll, Online cat, Ref serv available
Open Wed-Fri 10-4
Restriction: Non-circulating coll

M PHOENIX CHILDREN'S HOSPITAL, Emily Center Library, 1919 E Thomas Rd, 85016. SAN 373-3386. Tel: 602-933-1400. Toll Free Tel: 866-933-6459. FAX: 602-933-1409. E-mail: emilycenter@phoenixchildrens.com. Web Site: www.theemilycenter.com. *Dir,* Teresa Boeger; Staff 4 (Non-MLS 4)
Founded 1990
Library Holdings: AV Mats 200; Bk Titles 6,000
Special Collections: Spanish Information about Child Health & Illness Issues
Subject Interests: Pediatrics
Automation Activity & Vendor Info: (Cataloging) Innovative Interfaces, Inc; (Circulation) Innovative Interfaces, Inc
Database Vendor: OCLC, OCLC WorldShare Interlibrary Loan
Wireless access
Function: Computers for patron use, Handicapped accessible, Mail & tel request accepted, Online searches, Spanish lang bks, Wheelchair accessible
Open Mon-Fri 9-7, Sat & Sun 10-4

J PHOENIX COLLEGE*, Fannin Library, 1202 W Thomas Rd, 85013. SAN 300-3876. Tel: 602-285-7457. Circulation Tel: 602-285-7473. Interlibrary Loan Service Tel: 602-285-7480. Reference Tel: 602-285-7470. FAX: 602-285-7368. E-mail: circulation@pcmail.maricopa.edu. Web Site: www.phoenixcollege.edu/library. *Chair,* Linda Soland; E-mail: linda.soland@phoenixcollege.edu; *Librn,* Michelle Dyer-Hurdon; E-mail: michelle.dyer-hurdon@phoenixcollege.edu; *Librn,* Ann Roselle; *Librn,* Elizabeth Saliba; *ILL,* Linda Frakes; Staff 6 (MLS 6)
Founded 1925. Fac 181; Highest Degree: Associate
Library Holdings: Bk Vols 80,000; Per Subs 330
Subject Interests: Arizona

P PHOENIX PUBLIC LIBRARY*, 1221 N Central Ave, 85004. SAN 330-6429. Tel: 602-262-4636. Administration Tel: 602-262-6157. FAX: 602-261-8836. TDD: 602-254-8205. Web Site: www.phoenixpubliclibrary.org. *City Librn,* Rita Hamilton; E-mail: rita.hamilton@phoenix.gov; *Dep Dir, Coll & Prog,* Karl Kendall; E-mail: karl.kendall@phoenix.gov; *Dep Dir, Info Tech & Digital Initiatives,* Aimee Fifarek; E-mail: aimee.fifarek@phoenix.gov; *Dep Dir, Mgt Serv,* Tammy Ryan; E-mail: tammy.ryan@phoenix.gov; *Dep Dir, Pub Serv,* Paula Fortier; E-mail: paula.fortier@phoenix.gov; Staff 85.7 (MLS 83.7, Non-MLS 2)
Founded 1898. Pop 1,488,750; Circ 10,427,548
Jul 2013-Jun 2014 Income (Main Library and Branch(s)) $1,079,884. Mats Exp $4,606,967
Special Collections: Arizona History Coll; Art of Book Coll; Center for Children's Literature; Map Room; Rare Book Room. US Document Depository
Automation Activity & Vendor Info: (Acquisitions) Innovative Interfaces, Inc; (Cataloging) Innovative Interfaces, Inc; (Circulation) Innovative

Interfaces, Inc; (OPAC) Innovative Interfaces, Inc; (Serials) Innovative Interfaces, Inc
Wireless access
Special Services for the Deaf - TDD equip; TTY equip
Special Services for the Blind - Assistive/Adapted tech devices, equip & products; Braille bks; Descriptive video serv (DVS); Talking bks
Open Mon, Fri & Sat 9-5, Tues-Thurs 9-9, Sun 1-5
Friends of the Library Group
Branches: 16
ACACIA LIBRARY, 750 E Townley Ave, 85020, SAN 330-6453. FAX: 602-943-4399. *Br Mgr,* Tom Gemberling; E-mail: tom.gemberling@phoenix.gov
Founded 1969
Special Services for the Deaf - TDD equip
Open Tues-Thurs 11-7, Fri & Sat 9-5
Friends of the Library Group
AGAVE LIBRARY, 23550 N 36th Ave, 85310. FAX: 623-582-9003. *Br Mgr,* Marijo Kist; E-mail: marijo.kist@phoenix.gov
Open Tues-Thurs 10-8, Fri & Sat 9-5
CENTURY LIBRARY, 1750 E Highland Ave, 85016-4648, SAN 330-6488. FAX: 602-277-0317. TDD: 602-254-8205. *Br Mgr,* Karen Idehara; E-mail: karen.idehara@phoenix.gov
Founded 1973
Open Tues-Thurs 11-7, Fri & Sat 9-5
Friends of the Library Group
CESAR CHAVEZ LIBRARY, 3635 W Baseline Rd, Laveen, 85339. FAX: 602-237-7514. *Br Mgr,* Annette Vigil; E-mail: annette.vigil@phoenix.gov
Founded 2007
Special Services for the Deaf - TDD equip
Open Mon & Sat 9-5, Tues-Thurs 10-8, Sun 1-5
CHOLLA LIBRARY, 10050 Metro Pkwy E, 85051, SAN 330-6518. FAX: 602-261-8641. *Br Mgr,* Nicole Ney; E-mail: nicole.ney@phoenix.gov
Founded 1975
Special Services for the Deaf - TDD equip
Open Mon & Sat 9-5, Tues-Thurs 10-8, Sun 1-5
Friends of the Library Group
DESERT BROOM LIBRARY, 29710 N Cave Creek Rd, 85331. FAX: 602-534-7189. *Br Mgr,* Mimi McCain; E-mail: mimi.mccain@phoenix.gov
Founded 2005
Special Services for the Deaf - TDD equip
Open Tues-Thurs 11-7, Fri & Sat 9-5
Friends of the Library Group
DESERT SAGE LIBRARY, 7602 W Encanto Blvd, 85035, SAN 377-7960. FAX: 623-849-8913. *Br Mgr,* Dawn Porfirio-Milton; E-mail: dawn.porfiriomilton@phoenix.gov
Founded 1997
Special Services for the Deaf - TDD equip
Open Tues-Thurs 11-7, Fri & Sat 9-5
Friends of the Library Group
HARMON LIBRARY, 1325 S Fifth Ave, 85003, SAN 330-6542. FAX: 602-261-8591. *Br Mgr,* Stephanie Martinez; E-mail: stephanie.martinez@phoenix.gov
Founded 1950
Special Services for the Deaf - TDD equip
Open Tues-Thurs 11-7, Fri & Sat 9-5
Friends of the Library Group
IRONWOOD LIBRARY, 4333 E Chandler Blvd, 85048, SAN 372-0195. FAX: 602-261-8949. *Br Mgr,* Lisa Tharp; E-mail: lisa.tharp@phoenix.gov
Founded 1991
Special Services for the Deaf - TDD equip
Open Mon & Sat 9-5, Tues-Thurs 10-8, Sun 1-5
Friends of the Library Group
JUNIPER LIBRARY, 1825 W Union Hills Dr, 85027, SAN 370-8098. FAX: 602-942-1870. *Br Mgr,* Judy DeBolt; E-mail: judy.debolt@phoenix.gov
Founded 1996
Database Vendor: 3M Library Systems, Baker & Taylor, EBSCOhost, LearningExpress, ProQuest, ReferenceUSA
Open Mon & Sat 9-5, Tues-Thurs 10-8, Sun 1-5
Friends of the Library Group
MESQUITE LIBRARY, 4525 E Paradise Village Pkwy N, 85032, SAN 330-6577. FAX: 602-569-9001. *Br Mgr,* Yvonne Murphy; E-mail: yvonne.murphy@phoenix.gov
Founded 1982
Special Services for the Deaf - TDD equip
Open Mon & Sat 9-5, Tues-Thurs 10-8, Sun 1-5
Friends of the Library Group
OCOTILLO LIBRARY & WORKFORCE LITERACY CENTER, 102 W Southern Ave, 85041, SAN 330-6607. FAX: 602-268-4831. *Br Mgr,* Mary Mitchell; E-mail: mary.mitchell@phoenix.gov
Founded 1967
Special Services for the Deaf - TDD equip
Open Tues-Thurs 11-7, Fri & Sat 9-5
Friends of the Library Group
PALO VERDE LIBRARY, 4402 N 51st Ave, 85031, SAN 330-6631. FAX: 602-261-8455. *Br Mgr,* Carole Towles; E-mail: carole.towles@phoenix.gov
Founded 1966
Special Services for the Deaf - TDD equip
Open Mon & Sat 9-5, Tues-Thurs 10-8, Sun 1-5
Friends of the Library Group
SAGUARO LIBRARY, 2808 N 46th St, 85008, SAN 330-6666. FAX: 602-956-2031. *Br Mgr,* Theresa Shaw; E-mail: theresa.shaw@phxlib.org
Founded 1964
Special Services for the Deaf - TDD equip
Open Mon & Sat 9-5, Tues-Thurs 10-8, Sun 1-5
Friends of the Library Group
SOUTH MOUNTAIN COMMUNITY LIBRARY, 7050 S 24th St, 85042. *Br Mgr,* Robb Barr; E-mail: robb.barr@phoenix.gov
Open Mon-Thurs 7:30am-9pm, Fri & Sat 7:30-5, Sun 1-5
Friends of the Library Group
YUCCA LIBRARY, 5648 N 15th Ave, 85015, SAN 330-6690. FAX: 602-261-8986. *Br Mgr,* Sabrena Adams; E-mail: sabrena.adams@phoenix.gov
Founded 1969
Special Services for the Deaf - TDD equip
Open Tues-Thurs 10-8, Fri & Sat 9-5
Friends of the Library Group

§R PHOENIX SEMINARY LIBRARY, 4222 E Thomas Rd, Ste 100, 85018. Tel: 602-429-4973. FAX: 602-850-8085. Web Site: www.ps.edu/library. *Dir, Libr Serv,* Doug Olbert; E-mail: drolbert@ps.edu; *Acq/Ref Librn,* Mitch Miller; E-mail: mmiller@ps.edu; *Tech Serv Librn,* Jim Santeford; E-mail: jsanteford@ps.edu
Wireless access
Open Mon-Wed 9:30-9:30, Thurs 11:30-8, Fri 8:30-5

GM PHOENIX VA HEALTH CARE SYSTEM*, Medical Library, 650 E Indian School Rd, 85012. SAN 300-4023. Tel: 602-222-6411. FAX: 602-222-6472. *Librn,* Mark Simmons; E-mail: mark.simmons@med.va.gov; Staff 4 (MLS 1, Non-MLS 3)
Founded 1951
Library Holdings: e-journals 190; Bk Titles 3,000; Bk Vols 7,000; Per Subs 350
Subject Interests: Consumer health, Med, Nursing
Automation Activity & Vendor Info: (Cataloging) EOS International; (Circulation) EOS International; (OPAC) EOS International
Database Vendor: Dialog, Gale Cengage Learning, OCLC FirstSearch, OVID Technologies
Partic in Arizona Health Information Network (AZHIN); Cent Ariz Biomed Librns; Dept of Vet Affairs Libr Network; Medical Library Group of Southern California & Arizona (MLGSCA)
Open Mon-Fri 8-4:30

S PUEBLO GRANDE MUSEUM & ARCHAEOLOGICAL PARK*, Research Library, 4619 E Washington St, 85034-1909. SAN 372-7629. Tel: 602-495-0901. FAX: 602-495-5645. E-mail: pueblo.grande.museum.pks@phoenix.gov. Web Site: www.pueblogrande.com. *Coordr,* Holly Young; E-mail: holly.young@phoenix.org
Library Holdings: Bk Titles 5,000; Spec Interest Per Sub 75
Special Collections: Halseth Coll; Hayden Coll; Hohokam Coll, bks, ms; Pueblo Grande Museum Archives; Schroeder Coll
Subject Interests: Archaeology
Function: Archival coll, ILL available, Photocopying/Printing, Res libr, Telephone ref
Open Mon-Fri 9-4
Restriction: Non-circulating to the pub

M SAINT JOSEPH'S HOSPITAL & MEDICAL CENTER*, Health Sciences Library, 350 W Thomas Rd, 85013. (Mail add: PO Box 2071, 85013-2071), SAN 300-3906. Tel: 602-406-3299. FAX: 602-406-4171. *Mgr,* Molly Harrington; E-mail: molly.harrington@chw.edu; Staff 2 (MLS 2)
Founded 1942
Library Holdings: Bk Vols 5,000; Per Subs 320
Special Collections: Neurological Sciences (Barrow Neurological Institute of Neurological Sciences Coll)
Subject Interests: Med, Nursing
Partic in Arizona Health Information Network (AZHIN); Cent Ariz Biomed Librns
Open Mon-Fri 8-5

J SOUTH MOUNTAIN COMMUNITY COLLEGE LIBRARY*, 7050 S 24th St, 85042. SAN 320-9989. Tel: 602-243-8187. Reference Tel: 602-243-8194. FAX: 602-243-8180. Web Site: library.southmountaincc.edu. *Div Chair, Libr & Teaching & Learning Ctr,* Amy MacPherson; Tel:

602-305-5714, E-mail: amy.macpherson@southmountaincc.edu; *Librn,* Lydia Johnson; E-mail: jydia.johnson@southmountaincc.edu; *Instruction Librn,* Lora Largo; Tel: 602-243-8345, E-mail: lora.largo@southmountaincc.edu; *Tech Librn,* Cate McNamara; Tel: 602-243-8192, E-mail: cate.mcnamara@southmountaincc.edu; Staff 8 (MLS 3, Non-MLS 5)
Founded 1980. Enrl 3,937; Highest Degree: Associate
Library Holdings: Bk Titles 38,000; Bk Vols 40,000
Automation Activity & Vendor Info: (Cataloging) SirsiDynix; (Circulation) SirsiDynix
Partic in Amigos Library Services, Inc
Open Mon-Thurs 7;30am-9pm, Fri & Sat 7:30-5, Sun 1-5

GL SUPERIOR COURT LAW LIBRARY*, 101 W Jefferson, 85003. SAN 300-3795. Tel: 602-506-3461. FAX: 602-506-3677. E-mail: services@scll.maricopa.gov. Web Site: www.superiorcourt.maricopa.gov/lawlibrary. *Dir,* Ray Billotte; E-mail: billotter@superiorcourt.maricopa.gov; *Asst Dir,* Jennifer Murray; Fax: 602-506-2940, E-mail: murrayj006@scll.maricopa.gov; *Automation Syst Coordr, Tech Serv,* Liz Fairman; Tel: 602-506-3462, E-mail: lfairman@scll.maricopa.gov; *Acq, Coll Develop,* Valerie Lerma; Tel: 602-506-1647, E-mail: vlerma@scll.maricopa.gov; *Ref,* Susan Armstrong; E-mail: armstrongs001@scll.maricopa.gov; Staff 15 (MLS 7, Non-MLS 8)
Founded 1913
Library Holdings: Bk Titles 20,000; Bk Vols 140,000
Subject Interests: Law
Wireless access
Publications: Court Informer; En Banc (Newsletter)
Partic in Dialog Corp; Westlaw
Open Mon-Fri 8-5

S U-HAUL INTERNATIONAL*, Library & Research Services, 2727 N Central Ave, 85036. (Mail add: PO Box 21502, 85036-1502), SAN 300-3981. Tel: 602-263-6011. *Librn,* Meg Maher; E-mail: meg-maher@fc.uhaul.com
Library Holdings: Bk Vols 6,850; Per Subs 250
Special Collections: Truck & Trailer Design & Safety
Subject Interests: Bus & mgt, Eng, Indust safety, Law, Manufacturing, Mkt, Transportation
Publications: Publication Catalogs; Publication Index
Restriction: Access for corporate affiliates

GL UNITED STATES COURTS LIBRARY*, Sandra Day O'Connor United States Courthouse, Ste 410, 401 W Washington St, SPC16, 85003-2135. SAN 321-8023. Tel: 602-322-7295. FAX: 602-322-7299. *Satellite Librn,* Tim Blake, E-mail: tim_blake@lb9.uscourts.gov; *Asst Satellite Librn,* Margaret A Ackroyd; Staff 3 (MLS 2, Non-MLS 1)
Founded 1980
Library Holdings: Bk Titles 3,951; Bk Vols 33,764
Database Vendor: HeinOnline, LexisNexis, OCLC FirstSearch, OCLC WorldShare Interlibrary Loan, SirsiDynix, Westlaw
Function: Archival coll, Ref & res, Ref serv available, Res libr, Tax forms
Publications: Library Guide; Library Newsletter (Monthly)
Partic in OCLC Online Computer Library Center, Inc
Restriction: Open to staff only, Prof mat only, Restricted pub use

PIMA

P PIMA PUBLIC LIBRARY, 50 S 200 West, 85543. (Mail add: PO Box 489, 85543-0489), SAN 300-404X. Tel: 928-485-2822. FAX: 928-485-0701. E-mail: librarian@pimalibrary.org. Web Site: www.pimalibrary.org. *Dir,* Rane Jones; *Asst Librn,* Skyler Beals; *Asst Librn,* Jean O'Dell; Staff 3 (Non-MLS 3)
Founded 1960. Pop 2,458; Circ 20,000
Jul 2013-Jun 2014 Income $56,128, State $2,000, City $52,000, Locally Generated Income $2,128. Mats Exp $22,000, Books $8,831, Per/Ser (Incl. Access Fees) $103, AV Mat $230. Sal $27,158
Library Holdings: Audiobooks 212; Bks on Deafness & Sign Lang 6; DVDs 1,034; Bk Titles 11,440; Per Subs 2
Automation Activity & Vendor Info: (Acquisitions) Baker & Taylor; (Cataloging) Follett Software; (Circulation) Follett Software; (ILL) OCLC WorldShare Interlibrary Loan; (OPAC) Follett Software
Database Vendor: OCLC FirstSearch, OCLC WorldShare Interlibrary Loan
Function: Activity rm, Bks on CD, Computers for patron use, Copy machines, Fax serv, Free DVD rentals, ILL available, Magazines, Movies, Music CDs, Online searches, Photocopying/Printing, Preschool outreach, Preschool reading prog, Prog for children & young adult, Pub access computers, Spanish lang bks, Story hour, Summer reading prog, Wheelchair accessible
Open Mon-Thurs 10-7, Fri 10-2

PINE

P ISABELLE HUNT MEMORIAL PUBLIC LIBRARY*, 6124 N Randall Pl, 85544. (Mail add: PO Box 229, 85544-0229), SAN 300-4058. Tel: 928-476-3678. FAX: 928-476-2914. Web Site: www.pinepubliclibrary.com. *Mgr,* Becky L Waer; E-mail: beckywaer@gmail.com; Staff 2 (Non-MLS 2)
Founded 1974. Pop 3,000; Circ 27,513
Jul 2012-Jun 2013 Income $104,000
Library Holdings: Bk Vols 16,000
Special Collections: Arizona Coll, bks, pamphlets
Automation Activity & Vendor Info: (ILL) OCLC FirstSearch
Database Vendor: Baker & Taylor, OCLC FirstSearch, SirsiDynix
Wireless access
Function: Homebound delivery serv, ILL available, Photocopying/Printing, Prog for children & young adult, Summer reading prog, Wheelchair accessible
Mem of Gila County Library District
Open Tues & Fri 10-5, Wed 10-4, Thurs 10-6, Sat 9-2
Restriction: Open to pub for ref & circ; with some limitations
Friends of the Library Group

PRESCOTT

DEPARTMENT OF VETERANS AFFAIRS
GM NORTHERN ARIZONA VA HEALTH CARE SYSTEM LIBRARY*, 500 Hwy 89 N, 86313, SAN 321-2424. Tel: 928-445-4860, Ext 6492. Interlibrary Loan Service Tel: 928-776-6031. FAX: 928-776-6094. *Librn,* Terri Smiley
Library Holdings: AV Mats 460; CDs 100; DVDs 50; Large Print Bks 620; Bk Titles 3,000; Per Subs 120; Talking Bks 440; Videos 500
Partic in Medical Library Group of Southern California & Arizona (MLGSCA)
Restriction: Not open to pub

C EMBRY-RIDDLE AERONAUTICAL UNIVERSITY, Christine & Steven F Udvar-Hazy Library & Learning Center, 3700 Willow Creek Rd, 86301-3720. SAN 323-7621. Tel: 928-777-3811. Reference Tel: 928-777-3761. Interlibrary Loan Service FAX: 928-777-6988. Administration FAX: 928-777-6987. E-mail: prlib@erau.edu. Web Site: library.pr.erau.edu. *Dir,* Sarah K Thomas; Tel: 928-777-3812, E-mail: sarah@erau.edu; *Assoc Dir,* Dr Akos Delneky; Tel: 928-777-6658, E-mail: akos.delneky@erau.edu; *Digital Learning Design/Res Librn,* Brittany Blanchard; Tel: 928-777-6656, E-mail: brittany.blanchard@erau.edu; *Res Librn & Info Resources Coordr,* Patricia Watkins; Tel: 928-777-3920, E-mail: patricia.watkins@erau.edu; *Res Librn & Instruction Serv Coordr,* Suzie Roth; Tel: 928 777-3858, E-mail: suzie.roth@erau.edu; *Libr Syst & Tech Mgr,* Joanne Evanoff; Tel: 928-777-3802, E-mail: joanne.evanoff@erau.edu; Staff 11 (MLS 6, Non-MLS 5)
Founded 1978. Enrl 2,035; Fac 128; Highest Degree: Master
Jul 2013-Jun 2014 Income $1,071,340. Mats Exp $161,210, Books $6,954, Per/Ser (Incl. Access Fees) $33,952, AV Equip $5,203, AV Mat $3,667, Electronic Ref Mat (Incl. Access Fees) $111,086, Presv $348. Sal $584,926 (Prof $373,238)
Library Holdings: DVDs 2,042; e-books 152,222; e-journals 56,116; Microforms 100,077; Bk Titles 29,966; Per Subs 150
Special Collections: Aviation History Coll; Kalusa Miniature Aircraft Coll
Subject Interests: Aeronaut sci, Aerospace eng, Aviation safety, Global security & intelligence studies, Space physics
Automation Activity & Vendor Info: (Acquisitions) SirsiDynix; (Cataloging) SirsiDynix; (Circulation) SirsiDynix; (ILL) Clio; (OPAC) SirsiDynix
Database Vendor: ACM (Association for Computing Machinery), Alexander Street Press, Amigos Library Services, Annual Reviews, ASCE Research Library, CQ Press, CredoReference, EBSCOhost, Emerald, Facts on File, H W Wilson, IEEE (Institute of Electrical & Electronics Engineers), Jane's, JSTOR, LexisNexis, Mergent Online, Newsbank, OCLC FirstSearch, OCLC WorldShare Interlibrary Loan, Plunkett Research, Ltd, ProQuest, RefWorks, Sage, ScienceDirect, SerialsSolutions, SirsiDynix, ValueLine, Wilson - Wilson Web, WT Cox
Wireless access
Function: Online info literacy tutorials on the web & in blackboard
Publications: Annual Report; Annual Student Survey Results; Assessment Plan
Partic in Florida Library Information Network; Yavapai Libr Network
Open Mon-Thurs 7am-1am, Fri 7am-9pm, Sat 10-7, Sun 10am-1am

C PRESCOTT COLLEGE LIBRARY*, 217 Garden St, 86301. (Mail add: 220 Grove Ave, 86301), SAN 321-4656. Tel: 928-350-1300. Toll Free Tel: 877-350-2100, Ext 1300. FAX: 928-776-5224. E-mail: library@prescott.edu. Web Site: www.prescott.edu/library. *Dir,* Rich Lewis; *Ref & Instruction Librn,* Michaela Willi Hooper; Staff 7 (MLS 3, Non-MLS 4)
Founded 1966. Enrl 1,000; Fac 75; Highest Degree: Doctorate
Library Holdings: e-books 107,000; e-journals 32,000; Bk Titles 29,844; Bk Vols 33,027; Per Subs 220; Videos 1,665

Subject Interests: Adventure educ, Arts & letters, Counseling psychol, Environ studies, Experiential educ, Peace studies, Sustainability studies
Database Vendor: SirsiDynix
Wireless access
Mem of Yavapai County Free Library District
Partic in OCLC Online Computer Library Center, Inc

S PRESCOTT HISTORICAL SOCIETY*, Sharlot Hall Archives & Library, 115 S McCormick St, 86301. Tel: 928-445-3122. Reference Tel: 928-445-3122, Ext 14. FAX: 928-776-9053. Web Site: www.sharlot.org. *Archivist,* Brenda Taylor; *Asst Archivist,* Scott Anderson; E-mail: scottanderson@sharlot.org
Founded 1928
Library Holdings: Bk Titles 10,000
Special Collections: Archives Coll; Arizona History Coll, newspaper, mss; Early Arizona & Indian Coll, photog. Oral History
Open Mon-Sat 10-5, Sat 12-4

P PRESCOTT PUBLIC LIBRARY*, 215 E Goodwin St, 86303. SAN 330-6720. Tel: 928-777-1500. Circulation Tel: 928-777-1524. Interlibrary Loan Service Tel: 928-777-1510. Reference Tel: 928-777-1526. FAX: 928-771-5829. Web Site: www.prescottlibrary.info. *Dir,* Roger Saft; Tel: 928-777-1523, E-mail: roger.saft@prescott-az.gov; *Circ Librn,* Cindy Campbell; Tel: 928-777-1508, E-mail: cindy.campbell@prescott-az.gov; *Pub Serv Mgr,* Martha Baden; Tel: 928-777-1519, E-mail: martha.baden@prescott-az.gov; *Mgr, Support Serv,* Teresa Vonk; Tel: 928-777-1504, E-mail: teresa.vonk@prescott-az.gov; *Adult Serv,* Norm Zeeman; Tel: 928-777-1509, E-mail: norm.zeeman@prescott-az.gov; *Tech Serv,* Lisa Zierke; Tel: 928-777-1507, E-mail: lisa.zierke@prescott-az.gov; *Youth Serv,* Leona Vittum-Jones; Tel: 928-777-1506, E-mail: leona.vittum.jones@prescott-az.gov; Staff 13.4 (MLS 7.4, Non-MLS 6)
Founded 1903. Pop 39,865; Circ 808,048
Jul 2012-Jun 2013 Income $2,260,241. Mats Exp $203,889, Books $130,551, Per/Ser (Incl. Access Fees) $17,000, AV Mat $29,160, Electronic Ref Mat (Incl. Access Fees) $27,178. Sal $1,434,196 (Prof $711,526)
Library Holdings: Audiobooks 4,842; AV Mats 16,643; CDs 5,425; DVDs 11,218; e-books 8,237; Large Print Bks 5,239; Bk Vols 151,223; Per Subs 285
Automation Activity & Vendor Info: (Circulation) SirsiDynix
Database Vendor: Baker & Taylor, Ebooks Corporation, EBSCO Auto Repair Reference, EBSCOhost, Evanced Solutions, Inc, Facts on File, Foundation Center, Gale Cengage Learning, Grolier Online, OCLC FirstSearch, Overdrive, Inc, ProQuest, ReferenceUSA, ValueLine
Wireless access
Publications: Roundup
Partic in Yavapai Libr Network
Open Mon, Fri & Sat 9-5, Tues & Thurs 9-9, Wed 1-9, Sun 1-5
Friends of the Library Group

S SMOKI MUSEUM, AMERICAN INDIAN ART & CULTURE*, Smoki Museum Library, 147 N Arizona St, 86301. (Mail add: PO Box 10224, 86304-0224), SAN 375-3913. Tel: 928-445-1230. FAX: 928-777-0573. E-mail: info@smokimuseum.org. Web Site: www.smokimuseum.org. *Dir,* Cindy Gresser; E-mail: director@smokimuseum.org
Founded 1995
Library Holdings: Bk Vols 1,000
Special Collections: E S Curtis Coll, photogravures; Kate T Cory Coll, diary, dictionary of Hopi words, paintings, photogs
Subject Interests: Anthrop, Archeology, SW
Mem of Yavapai County Free Library District
Open Mon-Fri 1-4

C YAVAPAI COLLEGE LIBRARY, Bldg 19, 1100 E Sheldon St, 86301. SAN 300-4104. Tel: 928-776-2260. Interlibrary Loan Service Tel: 928-776-2059. Reference Tel: 928-776-2261. Toll Free Tel: 800-922-6787. FAX: 928-776-2275. E-mail: library@yc.edu. Web Site: www.yc.edu/library. *Dir,* Mike Byrnes; Tel: 928-771-6124, E-mail: mike.byrnes@yc.edu; *Tech Serv Mgr,* Ustadza Ely; Tel: 928-776-2264, E-mail: ustadza.ely@yc.edu; Staff 6 (MLS 4, Non-MLS 2)
Founded 1969. Enrl 9,063; Fac 427; Highest Degree: Associate
Library Holdings: AV Mats 15,464; CDs 804; Electronic Media & Resources 34; Bk Vols 114,125; Per Subs 557
Special Collections: College Archives
Subject Interests: SW
Automation Activity & Vendor Info: (Acquisitions) SirsiDynix; (Cataloging) SirsiDynix; (Circulation) SirsiDynix; (Course Reserve) SirsiDynix; (OPAC) SirsiDynix
Database Vendor: EBSCOhost, JSTOR, LexisNexis, OCLC FirstSearch, ProQuest, SerialsSolutions, Westlaw, Wilson - Wilson Web
Wireless access
Function: Archival coll, Audio & video playback equip for onsite use, AV serv, Govt ref serv, ILL available, Online searches, Photocopying/Printing, Ref serv available, Wheelchair accessible, Workshops
Partic in Yavapai Libr Network

Departmental Libraries:
VERDE VALLEY CAMPUS, 601 Black Hills Dr, Clarkdale, 86324, SAN 370-0224. Tel: 928-634-6541. FAX: 928-634-6543. *Libr Mgr,* Sheri Kinney; Staff 5 (MLS 1, Non-MLS 4)
Library Holdings: CDs 534; DVDs 584; Electronic Media & Resources 51; Bk Titles 33,990; Per Subs 149; Videos 6,272
Open Mon-Thurs 8-8, Fri 8-4, Sat 10-2

P YAVAPAI COUNTY FREE LIBRARY DISTRICT*, 1971 Commerce Ctr Circle, Ste D, 86301. SAN 323-8091. Tel: 928-771-3191. FAX: 928-771-3113. Web Site: yavapailibrary.org. *Dir,* Barbara Kile; E-mail: barbara.kile@co.yavapai.az.us; *Asst Dir,* Susan Lapis; *Libr Spec,* Megan Hammond; Staff 4 (MLS 1, Non-MLS 3)
Library Holdings: Bk Titles 3,500
Automation Activity & Vendor Info: (Acquisitions) SirsiDynix; (Cataloging) SirsiDynix; (Circulation) SirsiDynix; (Course Reserve) SirsiDynix; (OPAC) SirsiDynix; (Serials) SirsiDynix
Database Vendor: OCLC FirstSearch, SirsiDynix
Member Libraries: Ash Fork Public Library; Bagdad Public Library; Black Canyon City Community Library; Chino Valley Public Library; Clark Memorial Library; Congress Public Library; Jerome Public Library; Mayer Public Library; Prescott College Library; Prescott Valley Public Library; Sedona Public Library; Seligman Public Library; Smoki Museum, American Indian Art & Culture; Wilhoit Public Library; Yarnell Public Library
Open Mon-Fri 8-5

GL YAVAPAI COUNTY LAW LIBRARY*, Yavapai County Courthouse, 120 S Cortez St, Rm 112, 86303. SAN 300-4090. Tel: 928-771-3309. FAX: 928-771-3503. E-mail: YavLawLib@courts.az.gov. *Librn,* Charlotte Anthony; Staff 1 (Non-MLS 1)
Database Vendor: LexisNexis, Westlaw
Function: Res libr
Open Mon-Fri 8-5

S YAVAPAI-PRESCOTT TRIBAL LIBRARY*, 530 E Merritt, 86301-2038. SAN 375-1813. Tel: 928-515-7321. FAX: 928-442-1450. *Dir,* Barbara Royer; E-mail: broyer@ypit.com; Staff 1.75 (Non-MLS 1.75)
Library Holdings: AV Mats 40; Bk Titles 5,000; Per Subs 21; Talking Bks 20
Wireless access
Function: After school storytime, Audio & video playback equip for onsite use, Bks on cassette, Children's prog, Computer training, Computers for patron use, Copy machines, e-mail serv, Family literacy, Homework prog, Online searches, Photocopying/Printing, Preschool outreach, Ref serv in person, Senior outreach, Story hour, Summer & winter reading prog, VHS videos
Restriction: Open to tribal commun mem only

PRESCOTT VALLEY

P PRESCOTT VALLEY PUBLIC LIBRARY*, 7401 E Civic Circle, 86314. SAN 323-7990. Tel: 928-759-3040. FAX: 928-759-3121. Web Site: www.pvlib.net. *Dir,* Stuart Mattson; Tel: 928-759-3041; *Asst Dir,* Ted Johnson; *Circ Supvr,* Casey VanHaren; *Cat,* Barbara Tieman; *Ch Serv,* Anne Pieszak
Library Holdings: Bk Vols 80,000; Per Subs 81
Automation Activity & Vendor Info: (Cataloging) SirsiDynix; (Circulation) SirsiDynix; (OPAC) SirsiDynix
Mem of Yavapai County Free Library District
Open Mon-Thurs 10-9, Fri 10-6, Sat 10-4
Friends of the Library Group

QUARTZSITE

P QUARTZSITE PUBLIC LIBRARY*, 465 N Plymouth Ave, 85346. (Mail add: PO Box 2812, 85346-2812), SAN 377-032X. Tel: 928-927-6593. FAX: 928-927-3593. E-mail: qsitelib@hotmail.com. Web Site: www.qlib.org. *Dir,* Elizabeth Braswell; Staff 4 (MLS 1, Non-MLS 3)
Founded 1968. Pop 3,600; Circ 55,000
Library Holdings: Audiobooks 1,200; CDs 150; DVDs 1,200; High Interest/Low Vocabulary Bk Vols 100; Large Print Bks 1,421; Bk Titles 34,000; Per Subs 58; Talking Bks 30; Videos 3,500
Special Collections: Arizona Coll; Arizona Western College Coll; Caregiver Resource Zone Coll
Automation Activity & Vendor Info: (Acquisitions) Book Systems; (Cataloging) Book Systems; (Circulation) Book Systems; (ILL) OCLC CatExpress; (OPAC) Book Systems; (Serials) Book Systems
Wireless access
Function: Accelerated reader prog, Children's prog, Computers for patron use, Copy machines, Distance learning, Electronic databases & coll, Free DVD rentals, Games & aids for the handicapped, ILL available, Music CDs, Online cat, Online searches, Photocopying/Printing, Prog for adults, Prog for children & young adult, Pub access computers, Senior outreach,

Spoken cassettes & CDs, Spoken cassettes & DVDs, Story hour, Summer reading prog, Tax forms, VHS videos, Wheelchair accessible
Special Services for the Blind - Talking bks
Open Mon-Fri 8-5
Friends of the Library Group

SACATON

P IRA H HAYES MEMORIAL LIBRARY, 94 N Church St, 85147. (Mail add: PO Box 97, 85147-0097), SAN 376-3188. Tel: 520-562-3225. FAX: 520-562-3903. *Head Librn,* Ramona Tecumseh; E-mail: ramona.tecumseh1@gric.nsn.us
Library Holdings: Bk Titles 15,000
Open Mon-Fri 9-6

SAFFORD

S ARIZONA DEPARTMENT OF CORRECTIONS - ADULT INSTITUTIONS*, Arizona State Prison Complex - Safford Resource Library, 896 S Cook Rd, 85546. Tel: 928-428-4698. *Librn II,* Matt Angleton; E-mail: mangleton@azcorrections.gov
Library Holdings: Bk Vols 9,000
Open Mon-Fri 8-4

P SAFFORD CITY-GRAHAM COUNTY LIBRARY*, 808 S Seventh Ave, 85546. SAN 300-4112. Tel: 928-432-4165. FAX: 928-348-3209. E-mail: librarystaff@ci.safford.az.us. Web Site: www.saffordlibrary.org. *Libr Dir,* Leanne McElroy; Tel: 928-432-4151, E-mail: lmcelroy@ci.safford.az.us; Staff 1 (MLS 0, Non-MLS 1)
Founded 1916. Pop 36,000; Circ 107,225
Jul 2011-Jun 2012 Income $697,752, State $133,000, City $418,952, Federal $66,000, County $32,800, Locally Generated Income $47,000. Mats Exp $29,625, Books $22,200, Per/Ser (Incl. Access Fees) $300, AV Mat $4,625, Electronic Ref Mat (Incl. Access Fees) $2,500. Sal $228,300 (Prof $67,000)
Library Holdings: Audiobooks 4,115; Bks on Deafness & Sign Lang 51; CDs 1,353; DVDs 1,547; e-books 327; Electronic Media & Resources 2; Large Print Bks 2,277; Microforms 201; Bk Vols 38,343; Per Subs 12; Videos 12
Special Collections: Arizona Coll
Automation Activity & Vendor Info: (Acquisitions) Baker & Taylor; (Cataloging) OCLC CatExpress; (Circulation) Follett Software; (Course Reserve) Follett Software; (ILL) OCLC; (OPAC) Follett Software
Database Vendor: EBSCO Auto Repair Reference, EBSCOhost, HeinOnline, OCLC FirstSearch, OCLC WorldShare Interlibrary Loan
Wireless access
Function: Adult bk club, Art exhibits, Audiobks via web, Bks on CD, Children's prog, Computer training, Computers for patron use, Copy machines, Electronic databases & coll, Exhibits, Family literacy, Free DVD rentals, Handicapped accessible, Homework prog, ILL available, Literacy & newcomer serv, Magnifiers for reading, Music CDs, Online cat, Online ref, Online searches, OverDrive digital audio bks, Preschool outreach, Prog for adults, Prog for children & young adult, Pub access computers, Ref & res, Ref serv in person, Senior computer classes, Spanish lang bks, Story hour, Summer reading prog, Tax forms, Telephone ref, Web-catalog, Wheelchair accessible
Special Services for the Blind - Talking bk & rec for the blind cat; Talking bks
Open Mon-Thurs 10-7
Restriction: ID required to use computers (Ltd hrs), Lending limited to county residents
Friends of the Library Group

SAINT DAVID

SR HOLY TRINITY MONASTERY LIBRARY, Hwy 80, Milepost 302, 85630. (Mail add: PO Box 298, 85630-0298), SAN 375-3832. Tel: 520-720-4642, Ext 22. FAX: 520-720-4202. E-mail: hermitable@yahoo.com. Web Site: www.holytrinitymonastery.org. *Librn,* Sister Jeanne Hill; Staff 1 (Non-MLS 1)
Founded 1974
Library Holdings: Bk Titles 47,300; Bk Vols 49,300; Per Subs 40
Special Collections: Great Books; Monastic Coll; Southwest/Native American Coll, bks, mags. Oral History
Wireless access

SAINT JOHNS

P APACHE COUNTY LIBRARY DISTRICT, 30 S Second W, 85936. (Mail add: PO Box 2760, 85936-2760), SAN 300-4120. Web Site: www.apachecountylibraries.com. *Dir,* Judith Pepple; E-mail: jpepple@co.apache.az.us; Staff 9.2 (MLS 1, Non-MLS 8.2)
Founded 1986. Pop 18,591; Circ 166,939
Jul 2012-Jun 2013 Income (Main Library and Branch(s)) $1,718,831, State $25,000, Federal $60,333, County $1,602,892, Other $30,606. Sal $685,735
Library Holdings: Audiobooks 4,393; DVDs 8,451; e-books 2,191; Bk Vols 61,695; Per Subs 143
Special Collections: Southwest Coll
Automation Activity & Vendor Info: (Cataloging) Innovative Interfaces, Inc; (Circulation) Innovative Interfaces, Inc; (ILL) OCLC; (OPAC) Innovative Interfaces, Inc
Database Vendor: EBSCOhost, OCLC FirstSearch
Wireless access
Function: Adult bk club, Art exhibits, Bks on CD, Children's prog, Computers for patron use, Copy machines, Exhibits, Fax serv, Free DVD rentals, ILL available, Online cat, Prog for adults, Scanner, Story hour, Summer reading prog, Teen prog, Workshops
Open Mon-Thurs 8-5
Restriction: Lending limited to county residents
Branches: 7
ALPINE PUBLIC, 17 County Rd 2061, Alpine, 85920. (Mail add: PO Box 528, Alpine, 85920-0528), SAN 328-0314. *Mgr,* Evelyn Williams; E-mail: evelynw@co.apache.az.us; Staff 1 (Non-MLS 1)
Open Mon-Fri 10-11:30 & 12:30-5
Friends of the Library Group
CONCHO PUBLIC, 18 County Rd 5101, Concho, 85924. (Mail add: PO Box 339, Concho, 85924-0339), SAN 371-3490. *Libr Mgr,* Daniela Rovida; E-mail: drovida@co.apache.az.us; Staff 0.8 (Non-MLS 0.8)
Open Mon-Thurs 12-6
GREER MEMORIAL, 74A Main St, Greer, 85927. (Mail add: PO Box 144, Greer, 85927-0144), SAN 371-3520. *Libr Mgr,* Ramona K Harp; E-mail: rharp@co.apache.az.us; Staff 0.55 (Non-MLS 0.55)
Open Tues & Wed 10-1 & 2-6, Thurs 3-7, Fri & Sat 9-2
Friends of the Library Group
ROUND VALLEY PUBLIC, 179 S Main St, Eagar, 85925. (Mail add: PO Box 1180, Eagar, 85925-1180), SAN 371-3482. Web Site: www.roundvalleylibrary.com. *Libr Mgr,* Felipa Earl; E-mail: fearl@co.apache.az.us; Staff 1 (Non-MLS 1)
Open Mon, Wed & Fri 10-5, Tues & Thurs 10-7, Sat 10-2
SAINT JOHNS PUBLIC, 35 S Third W, 85936. (Mail add: PO Box 766, 85936-0766), SAN 371-3547. *Libr Mgr,* Carolyn Des Champs; Staff 1 (Non-MLS 1)
Open Mon, Wed & Fri 10-5, Tues & Thurs 10-7, Sat 10-2
SANDERS PUBLIC, I-40, Exit 339, 191 N Frontage Rd E, Sanders, 86512. (Mail add: PO Box 1000, Sanders, 86512-1000), SAN 371-3539. *Libr Mgr,* Tresa Cox; E-mail: tcox@co.apache.az.us; Staff 0.8 (Non-MLS 0.8)
Open Mon-Thurs 12-6
VERNON PUBLIC, Ten County Rd 3142, Vernon, 85940. (Mail add: PO Box 600, Vernon, 85940-0600). *Libr Mgr,* Tamara Applegate; E-mail: tapplegate@co.apache.az.us; Staff 0.8 (Non-MLS 0.8)
Open Mon & Wed 10-12 & 1-5, Tues & Thurs 1-7

SAN CARLOS

P SAN CARLOS PUBLIC LIBRARY*, 89 San Carlos Ave, 85550. (Mail add: PO Box 545, 85550), SAN 300-4139. Tel: 928-475-2611. FAX: 928-475-2611. *Dir,* Emma Victor; E-mail: emma_victor08@yahoo.com
Founded 1971. Pop 7,000
Library Holdings: Bk Vols 10,000; Per Subs 18
Special Collections: Arizona Indian Coll
Mem of Gila County Library District
Open Mon-Fri 8-4:30

SAN LUIS

S ARIZONA DEPARTMENT OF CORRECTIONS - ADULT INSTITUTIONS*, Arizona State Prison Complex - Yuma Library, 7125 E Juan Sanchez Blvd, 85349. (Mail add: PO Box 13004, Yuma, 85366-3004). Tel: 928-627-8871. FAX: 928-627-6503.
Library Holdings: Bk Vols 12,000
Open Mon-Fri 7-3:30

SAN MANUEL

P SAN MANUEL PUBLIC LIBRARY*, 108 Fifth Ave, 85631. SAN 300-4147. Tel: 520-385-4470. FAX: 520-385-2910. Web Site: www.co.pinal.az.us/library. *Dir,* Denise Keller
Founded 1959. Pop 4,300; Circ 18,112
Library Holdings: Bk Vols 12,000
Automation Activity & Vendor Info: (Cataloging) Innovative Interfaces, Inc; (Circulation) Innovative Interfaces, Inc; (OPAC) Innovative Interfaces, Inc
Mem of Pinal County Library District
Open Mon-Fri 9-12 & 1-6, Sat 9-12

SCOTTSDALE

R MARIAN & RALPH FEFFER LIBRARY*, 10460 N 56th St, 85253. SAN 300-3973. Tel: 480-951-0323. FAX: 480-951-7150. E-mail: library@cbiaz.org. Web Site: www.cbiaz.org. *Libr Dir,* Carol Reynolds
Founded 1958
Library Holdings: Bk Titles 12,000
Special Collections: Holocaust Books; Judaica Coll
Open Tues & Wed 10-4, Thurs 10-6, Sun 9-12

C FRANK LLOYD WRIGHT SCHOOL OF ARCHITECTURE, William Wesley Peters Library, PO Box 4430, 85261-4430. SAN 374-8243. Tel: 480-391-4011. FAX: 480-860-8472. E-mail: wwplib@taliesin.edu. Web Site: www.franklloydwright.org. *Dir,* Elizabeth Dawsari; E-mail: edawsari@taliesin.edu
Library Holdings: Bk Titles 31,500; Per Subs 100
Special Collections: Frank Lloyd Wright Coll
Subject Interests: Archit
Automation Activity & Vendor Info: (ILL) Surpass
Database Vendor: Coutts Information Service, Surpass
Wireless access
Publications: Subject Bibliographies (Architecture)
Open Mon-Fri 8-5

R GOLDEN GATE BAPTIST THEOLOGICAL SEMINARY LIBRARY, Arizona Campus, 2240 N Hayden Rd, Ste 101, 85257-2801. Tel: 480-941-1993. FAX: 480-945-4199. E-mail: azlibrary@ggbts.edu. Web Site: library.ggbts.edu. *Campus Librn,* Julie Hines; Tel: 480-941-1993, Ext 213
Wireless access
Partic in Theological Library Cooperative of Arizona
Open Mon-Fri 9-4:30

M MAYO CLINIC SCOTTSDALE LIBRARIES, 13400 E Shea Blvd, 85259. SAN 370-5366. Tel: 480-301-8443. FAX: 480-301-7005. *Dir,* Lisa Marks; *Asst Librn,* Diana Rogers; Staff 7 (MLS 2, Non-MLS 5)
Founded 1987
Library Holdings: Bk Titles 2,000; Per Subs 320
Subject Interests: Clinical med, Molecular biol
Database Vendor: Innovative Interfaces, Inc, OVID Technologies
Function: ILL available
Restriction: Staff use only

P SALT RIVER TRIBAL LIBRARY, 1880 N Longmore Rd, 85256. (Mail add: 10005 E Osborn Rd, 85256). SAN 300-4198. Tel: 480-362-2557. FAX: 480-362-2556. *Librn,* Leigh Thomas; E-mail: leigh.thomas@srpmic-ed.org
Founded 1969. Pop 4,000; Circ 4,500
Library Holdings: Bk Vols 8,600; Per Subs 45
Automation Activity & Vendor Info: (Cataloging) Follett Software; (Circulation) Follett Software
Open Mon, Wed & Fri 8-5, Tues & Thurs 8-8

J SCOTTSDALE COMMUNITY COLLEGE LIBRARY*, 9000 E Chaparral Rd, 85256. SAN 300-4201. Tel: 480-423-6651. Reference Tel: 480-423-6650. FAX: 480-423-6666. E-mail: scc.library@scottsdalecc.edu. Web Site: www.scottsdalecc.edu/library/. *Dir,* Dr Patricia Lokey; Tel: 480-423-6653, E-mail: pat.lokey@sccmail.maricopa.edu; *Tech Serv Librn,* Marsha Ballard; Tel: 480-423-6638, E-mail: marsha.ballard@sccmail.maricopa.edu; Staff 9.5 (MLS 6, Non-MLS 3.5)
Founded 1971. Enrl 10,000; Fac 160; Highest Degree: Associate
Library Holdings: AV Mats 1,724; Bks on Deafness & Sign Lang 32; CDs 170; DVDs 686; e-books 31,110; e-journals 72; Electronic Media & Resources 12; High Interest/Low Vocabulary Bk Vols 20; Large Print Bks 20; Music Scores 26; Bk Titles 40,000; Bk Vols 36,796; Per Subs 319; Talking Bks 37; Videos 693
Special Collections: Colleges and Careers; Indians of the Southwest Coll; Language
Automation Activity & Vendor Info: (Acquisitions) SirsiDynix; (Cataloging) SirsiDynix; (Circulation) SirsiDynix; (Course Reserve) SirsiDynix; (ILL) OCLC ILLiad; (Media Booking) SirsiDynix; (OPAC) SirsiDynix; (Serials) SirsiDynix
Database Vendor: 3M Library Systems, Amigos Library Services, Baker & Taylor, CQ Press, ebrary, EBSCOhost, Gale Cengage Learning, Greenwood Publishing Group, LearningExpress, LexisNexis, Newsbank, OCLC FirstSearch, OCLC WebJunction, OCLC WorldShare Interlibrary Loan, Oxford Online, ProQuest, SerialsSolutions, SirsiDynix, Wilson - Wilson Web, World Book Online
Wireless access
Open Mon-Thurs 7:30am-9:30pm, Fri 7:30-4, Sat 10-2

SCOTTSDALE HEALTHCARE
M DR ROBERT C FOREMAN HEALTH SCIENCES LIBRARY*, Scottsdale Healthcare Osborn, 7400 E Osborn Rd, 85251, SAN 300-421X. Tel: 480-882-4870. FAX: 480-882-4200. E-mail: olibrary@shc.org. *Supvr,* Evonda Copeland; E-mail: ecopeland@shc.org; Staff 3 (MLS 2, Non-MLS 1)
Founded 1968
Library Holdings: Bk Titles 2,000; Per Subs 250
Special Collections: Family Practice; Obstetrics, Gynecology & Urology
Subject Interests: Internal med, Nursing, Obstetrics & gynecology, Orthopedics, Pediatrics, Radiology, Surgery
Automation Activity & Vendor Info: (Cataloging) CyberTools for Libraries; (OPAC) CyberTools for Libraries; (Serials) CyberTools for Libraries
Database Vendor: EBSCOhost, OVID Technologies, PubMed, RefWorks, ScienceDirect, UpToDate
Partic in Arizona Health Information Network (AZHIN); Cent Ariz Biomed Librns; Medical Library Group of Southern California & Arizona (MLGSCA)
Open Mon-Fri 7:30-5:30

M HEALTH SCIENCES LIBRARY*, 9003 E Shea Blvd, 85260, SAN 375-2836. Tel: 480-323-3870. FAX: 480-323-3864. E-mail: slibrary@shc.org. Web Site: www.shc.org. *Supvr,* Evonda Copeland; Staff 4 (MLS 2, Non-MLS 2)
Library Holdings: Bk Vols 1,200; Per Subs 150
Automation Activity & Vendor Info: (Cataloging) CyberTools for Libraries; (OPAC) CyberTools for Libraries; (Serials) CyberTools for Libraries
Database Vendor: CyberTools for Libraries, EBSCOhost, OVID Technologies, PubMed, RefWorks, ScienceDirect
Partic in Arizona Health Information Network (AZHIN); Cent Ariz Biomed Librns; Medical Library Group of Southern California & Arizona (MLGSCA)
Open Mon-Fri 7:30-5:30

P SCOTTSDALE PUBLIC LIBRARY*, 3839 N Drinkwater Blvd, 85251-4467. (Mail add: PO Box 1000 LI 101, 85252-1000), SAN 300-4228. Tel: 480-312-7323. FAX: 480-312-7993. TDD: 480-312-7670. Web Site: library.ci.scottsdale.az.us. *Dir,* Carol Damaso; E-mail: cdamaso@scottsdaleaz.gov; *Adult Serv Sr Libr Mgr,* Dana Braccia; E-mail: dbraccia@scottsdaleaz.gov; *Support Serv Sr Mgr, Youth Serv Sr Libr Mgr,* Kathy Coster; E-mail: kcoster@scottsdaleaz.gov; *Tech & Content Sr Mgr,* Position Currently Open; *Adult Serv Coordr,* Michael Beck; E-mail: mbeck@scottsdaleaz.gov; *Coll Develop Coordr,* Rebekka Jones; E-mail: rjones@scottsdaleaz.gov; *Communications Coordr,* Ann Porter; E-mail: aporter@scottsdaleaz.gov; *Early Literacy Coordr,* Marie Raymond; E-mail: mraymond@scottsdaleaz.gov; *Youth/Teen Serv Coordr,* Medina Zick; E-mail: mzick@scottsdaleaz.gov; *Sr Mgt Analyst,* Cheryl Thomsen; E-mail: cthomsen@scottsdaleaz.gov; Staff 24 (MLS 24)
Founded 1959. Pop 217,379; Circ 1,518,000
Jul 2011-Jun 2012 Income (Main Library and Branch(s)) $9,233,994, State $11,566, City $8,558,890, Federal $95,036, Locally Generated Income $210,502, Other $358,000. Mats Exp $1,211,493, Books $843,306, Per/Ser (Incl. Access Fees) $69,000, AV Mat $155,320, Electronic Ref Mat (Incl. Access Fees) $69,724. Sal $6,750,231
Library Holdings: Audiobooks 11,952; CDs 25,409; DVDs 64,303; e-books 113,766; Bk Vols 419,647
Special Collections: Scottsdale Coll. Oral History
Subject Interests: Hist of Scottsdale
Automation Activity & Vendor Info: (Acquisitions) Innovative Interfaces, Inc - Millenium; (Cataloging) Innovative Interfaces, Inc - Millenium; (Circulation) Innovative Interfaces, Inc - Millenium; (Course Reserve) Innovative Interfaces, Inc - Millenium; (ILL) Innovative Interfaces, Inc - Millenium; (OPAC) Innovative Interfaces, Inc - Millenium; (Serials) Innovative Interfaces, Inc - Millenium
Database Vendor: EBSCOhost, OCLC FirstSearch, OCLC WorldShare Interlibrary Loan, ProQuest, ReferenceUSA, ValueLine
Wireless access
Function: Homebound delivery serv, ILL available, Magnifiers for reading, Prog for children & young adult, Summer reading prog, Wheelchair accessible
Partic in Amigos Library Services, Inc; OCLC Online Computer Library Center, Inc
Special Services for the Deaf - TDD equip
Special Services for the Blind - Home delivery serv
Open Mon-Thurs 9-9, Fri & Sat 10-6, Sun 1-5
Friends of the Library Group
Branches: 3
ARABIAN LIBRARY, 10215 E McDowell Mountain Ranch Rd, 85255-8601, SAN 376-8945. *Br Mgr,* Ann Mathews; Tel: 480-312-6225, E-mail: AMathews@scottsdaleaz.gov
Open Mon-Thurs 9-8, Fri & Sat 10-6, Sun 1-5
Friends of the Library Group
MUSTANG LIBRARY, 10101 N 90th St, 85258-4404. (Mail add: PO Box 1000, 85252-1000), SAN 374-4493. *Br Mgr,* Melissa Orr; Tel: 480-312-6031, E-mail: morr@scottsdaleaz.gov
Special Services for the Deaf - TTY equip

Open Mon-Thurs 9-8, Fri & Sat 10-6, Sun 1-5
Friends of the Library Group
PALOMINO LIBRARY, 12575 E Via Linda, Ste 102, 85259-4310. (Mail add: PO Box 1000, 85252-1000), SAN 376-8953. *Coordr,* Melissa Orr; Tel: 480-312-6011, E-mail: morr@scottsdaleaz.gov
Open Mon-Thurs 9-8, Fri 10-6, Sat 10-2
Friends of the Library Group

SEDONA

P SEDONA PUBLIC LIBRARY*, 3250 White Bear Rd, 86336. SAN 300-4252. Tel: 928-282-7714. FAX: 928-282-5789. E-mail: director@sedonalibrary.org. Web Site: www.sedonalibrary.org. *Dir,* Virginia Volkman; *Head, Circ,* Mia Fliers; *Coordr,* Cheryl Yeates; *Ref Serv,* Patricia Lowell; *Youth Serv,* Karen Mack; Staff 12 (MLS 4, Non-MLS 8)
Founded 1958. Pop 15,000; Circ 123,702
Library Holdings: Bk Vols 80,000; Per Subs 230
Special Collections: Arizona Coll
Automation Activity & Vendor Info: (Acquisitions) SirsiDynix; (Cataloging) SirsiDynix; (Circulation) SirsiDynix; (OPAC) SirsiDynix
Database Vendor: EBSCOhost, OCLC FirstSearch
Mem of Yavapai County Free Library District
Partic in Yavapai Libr Network
Open Mon & Wed 10-8, Tues & Thurs 10-6, Fri & Sat 10-5, Sun 12-5
Friends of the Library Group

S WORLD RESEARCH FOUNDATION LIBRARY*, 41 Bell Rock Plaza, 86351. (Mail add: PO Box 20828, 86341), SAN 373-1030. Tel: 928-284-3300. FAX: 928-284-3530. E-mail: info@wrf.org. Web Site: www.wrf.org. *Pres,* Steve Ross
Library Holdings: Bk Vols 30,000
Open Mon-Fri 10-12 & 1-5

SELIGMAN

P SELIGMAN PUBLIC LIBRARY*, 54170 N Floyd St, 86337. (Mail add: PO Box 623, 86337), SAN 323-8016. Tel: 928-422-3633. FAX: 928-422-3633. *Mgr,* Charlotte Lindemuth
Library Holdings: Bk Vols 4,500
Automation Activity & Vendor Info: (Cataloging) SirsiDynix; (Circulation) SirsiDynix; (OPAC) SirsiDynix
Mem of Yavapai County Free Library District
Open Mon-Fri 9:30-5

SELLS

P VENITO GARCIA PUBLIC LIBRARY & ARCHIVES*, PO Box 837, 85634-0837. Tel: 520-383-5756. FAX: 520-383-2429. *Librn,* Wendy Begay
Pop 1,300; Circ 9,000
Library Holdings: Bk Vols 6,000; Per Subs 20
Open Mon-Fri 8-5
Friends of the Library Group
Branches: 1
SAN LUCY DISTRICT, 1125 C St, Gila Bend, 85337. (Mail add: PO Box GG, Gila Bend, 85337-0479). Tel: 928-683-2012, 928-683-2796. FAX: 928-683-2802. Reference FAX: 928-683-6956. *Librn,* E Frances Venegas; E-mail: fecv5@yahoo.com
Open Mon-Fri 8-5
Friends of the Library Group

J TOHONO O'ODHAM COMMUNITY COLLEGE LIBRARY*, Hwy 86 Milepost 115.5 N, 85634. (Mail add: PO 3129, 85634-3129). Tel: 520-383-0032. FAX: 520-383-8403. Web Site: www.youseemore.com/tocc. *Col Librn,* Elaine Cubbins; E-mail: ecubbins@tocc.edu; *Libr Asst,* Elizabeth Ortega; *Libr Asst,* Carmella Pablo; E-mail: cpablo@tocc.edu. Subject Specialists: *Am Indian, Humanities,* Elaine Cubbins
Founded 2001. Enrl 200; Fac 18; Highest Degree: Associate
Library Holdings: CDs 122; DVDs 1,498; e-books 10; Large Print Bks 20; Bk Titles 9,600; Bk Vols 10,000; Per Subs 28; Talking Bks 15; Videos 725
Special Collections: O'odham Materials Coll; Rare Materials; Tohono O'odham Community College Special Colls
Subject Interests: Agr, Am Indian, Bus, Early childhood educ, Educ, Environ studies
Automation Activity & Vendor Info: (Acquisitions) TLC (The Library Corporation); (Cataloging) TLC (The Library Corporation); (Circulation) TLC (The Library Corporation); (Course Reserve) TLC (The Library Corporation); (ILL) TLC (The Library Corporation); (OPAC) TLC (The Library Corporation)
Database Vendor: TLC (The Library Corporation)
Wireless access
Function: Archival coll, Audio & video playback equip for onsite use, Bks on cassette, Bks on CD, CD-ROM, Computer training, Computers for patron use, Copy machines, e-mail & chat, e-mail serv, Electronic databases & coll, Equip loans & repairs, Fax serv, Govt ref serv, Health sci info serv, Jail serv, Learning ctr, Magnifiers for reading, Music CDs, Online cat, Online ref, Online searches, Orientations, Outreach serv, Photocopying/Printing, Pub access computers, Ref & res, Scanner, Spoken cassettes & CDs, Spoken cassettes & DVDs, Telephone ref, VHS videos, Web-catalog, Wheelchair accessible
Open Mon-Thurs 8-7, Fri 8-5
Restriction: Non-circulating of rare bks, Open to fac, students & qualified researchers, Open to pub for ref & circ; with some limitations, Open to students, fac, staff & alumni
Friends of the Library Group

SHOW LOW

P SHOW LOW PUBLIC LIBRARY*, 180 N Ninth St, 85901. SAN 300-4287. Tel: 928-532-4070. FAX: 928-532-4079. Web Site: www.ci.show-low.az.us/departments/library. *Dir,* Wendy Kochheiser; Tel: 928-532-4073; *Head, Tech Serv,* Kathy Tippets; Tel: 928-532-4076, E-mail: ktippets@ci.show-low.az.us; *Ch Serv,* Gabrielle Zornes; Tel: 928-532-4074, E-mail: gzornes@ci.show-low.az.us; *Electronic Res,* Don Fogle; Tel: 928-532-4065, E-mail: dfogle@ci.show-low.az.us; Staff 9 (MLS 1, Non-MLS 8)
Pop 15,000; Circ 129,000
Jul 2006-Jun 2007 Income $560,000. Mats Exp $55,300, Books $47,300, Per/Ser (Incl. Access Fees) $2,000, AV Mat $5,000, Electronic Ref Mat (Incl. Access Fees) $1,000. Sal $260,000
Library Holdings: CDs 1,460; DVDs 2,245; Electronic Media & Resources 40; High Interest/Low Vocabulary Bk Vols 200; Bk Titles 40,324; Bk Vols 39,372; Per Subs 90
Special Collections: Adult Basic Education Coll
Subject Interests: Arizona
Automation Activity & Vendor Info: (Cataloging) SirsiDynix; (Circulation) SirsiDynix; (ILL) OCLC Connexion; (OPAC) SirsiDynix; (Serials) DEMCO
Database Vendor: EBSCO - WebFeat, OCLC FirstSearch
Wireless access
Open Mon, Tues, Thurs & Fri 8-6, Wed 8-8, Sat 10-5
Friends of the Library Group

SIERRA VISTA

P SIERRA VISTA PUBLIC LIBRARY*, 2600 E Tacoma, 85635-1399. SAN 300-4309. Tel: 520-458-4225. Administration Tel: 520-458-4239. FAX: 520-458-5377. E-mail: library@sierravistaaz.gov. Web Site: www.sierravistaaz.gov/svlibrary. *Dir, Libr Serv,* Victoria Yarbrough; E-mail: victoria.yarbrough@sierravistaaz.gov; *Libr Adminr,* Emily Scherrer; *Circ Coordr,* Louise Mella; *Circ Coordr,* Teri Miller; *Adult Serv,* Susan Abend; *ILL,* Debra Chatham; *Tech Serv,* Joyce Fernandez; *Youth Serv,* Megan Sneary; Staff 4 (MLS 4)
Founded 1959. Pop 45,000; Circ 310,000
Library Holdings: Bk Vols 105,000; Per Subs 180
Special Collections: Arizona Coll. Oral History
Automation Activity & Vendor Info: (Cataloging) OCLC; (Circulation) SIRSI WorkFlows; (ILL) OCLC; (OPAC) SIRSI-iBistro
Wireless access
Mem of Cochise County Library District
Special Services for the Blind - Talking bks
Open Mon & Sun 12-5, Tues-Thurs 10-7, Fri & Sat 10-6
Friends of the Library Group

SNOWFLAKE

P SNOWFLAKE-TAYLOR PUBLIC LIBRARY*, 418 S Fourth W, 85937. SAN 321-7779. Tel: 928-536-7103. FAX: 928-536-3057. E-mail: library@ci.snowflake.az.us. Web Site: www.ci.snowflake.az.us/res-library.htm. *Dir,* Cathryn McDowell; Staff 3 (Non-MLS 3)
Founded 1965. Pop 8,000; Circ 60,000
Library Holdings: Audiobooks 1,450; Bk Vols 39,000; Per Subs 36
Special Collections: Snowflake Herald, 1903-1914
Automation Activity & Vendor Info: (Cataloging) SirsiDynix; (Circulation) SirsiDynix; (ILL) OCLC Online; (OPAC) SirsiDynix
Database Vendor: OCLC FirstSearch, ProQuest, SirsiDynix
Wireless access
Partic in Navajo County Libr District
Special Services for the Deaf - Closed caption videos
Special Services for the Blind - Assistive/Adapted tech devices, equip & products
Open Tues-Thurs 10-6, Fri 11-5, Sat 10-2
Friends of the Library Group

SOMERTON

P COCOPAH TRIBAL LIBRARY*, 14250 S Avenue 1, 85350. (Mail add: 14515 S Veterans Dr, 85350), SAN 376-3196. Tel: 928-627-8026. FAX: 928-627-2510. E-mail: cococvt@cocopah.com. *Dir,* Sandy L Johnson
Library Holdings: Bk Titles 2,400; Per Subs 14
Open Mon-Fri 8-5

SUN CITY

M BANNER BOSWELL MEDICAL CENTER*, Medical Library/Patient & Family Learning Center, 10401 W Thunderbird Blvd, 85351. SAN 373-3874. Tel: 623-832-6668. FAX: 623-832-5574. Web Site: shc.azhin.org. *Librn,* Dawn Humay; E-mail: dawn.humay@bannerhealth.com; Staff 1 (MLS 1)
Library Holdings: Bk Vols 600; Per Subs 120
Subject Interests: Gerontology, Internal med, Surgery
Automation Activity & Vendor Info: (Cataloging) EOS International; (Circulation) EOS International; (Serials) EBSCO Online
Database Vendor: EBSCOhost, OVID Technologies, PubMed
Wireless access
Function: Doc delivery serv, Health sci info serv, ILL available, Online searches, Photocopying/Printing, Ref serv available
Partic in Arizona Health Information Network (AZHIN); Cent Ariz Biomed Librns
Open Mon-Fri 8-4:30
Restriction: Access at librarian's discretion, Authorized patrons, Circulates for staff only, In-house use for visitors, Lending to staff only, Non-circulating to the pub, Open to pub for ref only, Pub use on premises

SUN CITY WEST

S R H JOHNSON LIBRARY*, Sun City West Library, 13801 W Meeker Blvd, 85375-4406. SAN 321-110X. Tel: 623-544-6130. Administration Tel: 623-544-6160. FAX: 623-544-6131. Web Site: rcscw.com. *Dir,* Carol Foutts; *Asst Dir,* Margaret Anderson; *AV,* Frances Buchanan; Staff 6 (Non-MLS 6)
Founded 1979
Library Holdings: AV Mats 2,875; DVDs 1,959; Large Print Bks 8,832; Bk Titles 38,000; Bk Vols 39,000; Per Subs 197; Talking Bks 705
Special Collections: Southwest Coll
Subject Interests: Arizona
Automation Activity & Vendor Info: (Circulation) Follett Software
Wireless access
Open Tues-Sat 9-4
Restriction: Residents only
Friends of the Library Group

SUPERIOR

P SUPERIOR PUBLIC LIBRARY*, 99 Kellner Ave, 85273. SAN 300-435X. Tel: 520-689-2327. FAX: 520-689-5809. Web Site: pinalcountyaz.gov/library. *Dir,* Josie O Campos; E-mail: josie.campos@pinalcountyaz.gov
Founded 1952. Pop 3,400; Circ 24,000
Library Holdings: Bk Titles 12,000; Bk Vols 12,300; Per Subs 35
Automation Activity & Vendor Info: (Acquisitions) Horizon
Wireless access
Publications: Library News (Monthly newsletter)
Mem of Pinal County Library District
Open Mon-Thurs 9-7
Friends of the Library Group

TEMPE

S AMERICAN FEDERATION OF ASTROLOGERS, INC LIBRARY*, 6535 S Rural Rd, 85283-3746. SAN 300-4368. Tel: 480-838-1751. Toll Free Tel: 888-301-7630. FAX: 480-838-8293. *Exec Dir,* Kris Brandt-Riske
Founded 1938
Library Holdings: Bk Vols 3,000
Special Collections: Various Out-of-Print Publications (1600-1800)
Publications: Today's Astrologer (Monthly)
Restriction: Private libr

S ARIZONA HISTORICAL SOCIETY MUSEUM LIBRARY & ARCHIVES*, 1300 N College Ave, 85281. SAN 321-8813. Tel: 480-929-0292. Reference Tel: 480-929-0292, Ext 174. FAX: 480-929-9973. Web Site: www.arizonahistoricalsociety.org. *Archivist/Librn, Dir,* Whitaker D Linda; Tel: 480-929-0292, Ext 127, E-mail: lwhitaker@azhs.gov; Staff 4 (MLS 1, Non-MLS 3)
Founded 1973
Library Holdings: Bk Titles 2,000; Per Subs 20
Special Collections: A J Bayless Coll; Arizona Homebuilders Association Coll; Arizona Quilt Project; Betty Puckle Photo Coll; Charles A Stauffer Coll; Elton Kunselman Photo Coll; George M Aurelius Theater Coll; Laura Danieli Coll; LeForgee Photo Coll; Lescher-Mahoney Architectural Drawing Coll; Orpheus Men's Choir Coll; Papago Park German POW Camp Photo Coll; Phoenix History Project Coll; Phoenix Streetcar Company; Photograph Coll; Robert Isbell Coll; Smarthwaite Family Coll; Snell Family Papers. Oral History
Subject Interests: Cent Ariz in 20th Century, Phoenix
Open Tues & Wed 1-4, Thurs & Fri 10-1
Restriction: Non-circulating to the pub

CL ARIZONA STATE UNIVERSITY, COLLEGE OF LAW*, Ross-Blakley Law Library, 110 S McAllister Ave, 85287-7806. (Mail add: PO Box 877806, 85287-7806), SAN 330-714X. Tel: 480-965-6141. FAX: 480-965-4283. Web Site: www.lawlib.asu.edu. *Assoc Dean,* Victoria Trotta; Tel: 480-965-2521, E-mail: victoria.trotta@asu.edu; *Assoc Dir, Head, Pub Serv,* Beth DiFelice; Tel: 480-965-4871, E-mail: beth.difelice@asu.edu; *Acq/Ser Librn,* Kerry Skinner; Tel: 480-965-4872, E-mail: kerry.skinner@asu.edu; *Access Serv,* Leslie Pardo; *Bibliog Serv,* Position Currently Open; *Ref,* William David Gay; Tel: 480-965-4860, E-mail: david.gay@asu.edu; *Ref Serv,* Position Currently Open. Subject Specialists: *Legal res,* Victoria Trotta; *Legal res,* Beth DiFelice; Staff 16 (MLS 5, Non-MLS 11)
Founded 1966. Enrl 600; Fac 50; Highest Degree: Doctorate
Library Holdings: AV Mats 651; Bk Vols 406,853; Per Subs 3,901
Special Collections: State Document Depository; US Document Depository
Automation Activity & Vendor Info: (Course Reserve) Innovative Interfaces, Inc; (ILL) OCLC Online; (OPAC) Innovative Interfaces, Inc
Wireless access
Partic in OCLC Online Computer Library Center, Inc
Restriction: 24-hr pass syst for students only, Access at librarian's discretion, Access for corporate affiliates, Authorized patrons, Authorized personnel only, Authorized scholars by appt, Badge access after hrs, Borrowing privileges limited to anthropology fac & libr staff, Borrowing privileges limited to fac & registered students, Borrowing requests are handled by ILL, By permission only, Circ limited, Circ privileges for students & alumni only, Circ to mem only, Circ to mil employees only, Circulates for staff only, Clients only, Closed stack, Co libr, Employee & client use only, Teacher & adminr only

C ARIZONA STATE UNIVERSITY LIBRARIES, 300 E Orange Mall Dr, 85287-1006. (Mail add: PO Box 871006, 85287-1006), SAN 330-7050. Tel: 480-965-3417. Circulation Tel: 480-965-3605. Interlibrary Loan Service Tel: 480-965-3282. Information Services Tel: 480-965-4236. FAX: 480-965-9169. Web Site: lib.asu.edu. *Univ Librn,* James J O'Donnell; *Assoc Univ Librn & Chief Tech Officer,* Philip Konomos; Tel: 480-965-9654, E-mail: konomos@asu.edu; *Head, Bibliog & Metadata Serv,* Marcia Anderson; Tel: 480-965-9392, Fax: 480-965-1043, E-mail: marcia.anderson@asu.edu; *Access Serv, ILL,* Ginny Sylvester; Tel: 480-965-4919, E-mail: ginny.sylvester@asu.edu; *Archivist,* Robert Spindler; Tel: 480-965-9277, E-mail: robert.spindler@asu.edu; *Coll & Scholarly Communications,* Jeanne Richardson; Tel: 480-965-5345, E-mail: jeanne.richardson@asu.edu; *Govt Doc,* Dan Stanton; Tel: 480-965-1798, E-mail: dan.stanton@asu.edu; Staff 197.5 (MLS 68, Non-MLS 129.5)
Founded 1891. Enrl 72,254; Fac 2,513; Highest Degree: Doctorate
Library Holdings: e-books 403,504; Microforms 7,700,000; Bk Vols 45,000,000; Per Subs 65,586
Special Collections: Alberto Pradeau Archives; American Indian, Arizona & Southwest History; Barry Goldwater Archives; Carl Hayden Archives; Jimmy Starr Archives; John R Rhodes Archives; Mexican Numismatics; Solar Energy Archives; Spain; Theatre for Youth Coll; Victorian Literature including Pre-Raphaelites & New; William Burroughs Archives. US Document Depository
Automation Activity & Vendor Info: (Acquisitions) Innovative Interfaces, Inc; (Circulation) Innovative Interfaces, Inc; (Serials) Innovative Interfaces, Inc
Wireless access
Function: Res libr
Publications: Bibliographies (Newsletter)
Partic in Amigos Library Services, Inc; Association of Research Libraries (ARL); Center for Research Libraries; Greater Western Library Alliance
Friends of the Library Group

Departmental Libraries:

ARCHITECTURE & ENVIRONMENTAL DESIGN LIBRARY, 810 Forest Mall, Design N Bldg, 85287-1705. (Mail add: PO Box 871006, 85287-1006). Tel: 480-965-6400. FAX: 480-727-6965. Web Site: lib.asu.edu/architecture. *Head of Libr,* Deborah Koshinsky; E-mail: deborah.koshinsky@asu.edu. Subject Specialists: *Archit, Interior design, Visual communications,* Deborah Koshinsky; Staff 3 (MLS 1, Non-MLS 2)
Library Holdings: Bk Vols 50,000

BIBLIOGRAPHIC & METADATA SERVICES, PO Box 871006, 85287-1006. Tel: 480-965-5889. FAX: 480-965-1043. *Head, Bibliog & Metadata Serv,* Marcia Anderson
Automation Activity & Vendor Info: (Acquisitions) Innovative Interfaces, Inc; (Cataloging) Innovative Interfaces, Inc; (OPAC) Innovative Interfaces, Inc; (Serials) Innovative Interfaces, Inc

COLLECTIONS & SCHOLARLY COMMUNICATION, PO Box 871006, 85287-1006. Tel: 480-965-5250. FAX: 480-965-9127. *Chief Officer, Coll Serv, Scholarly Communications Officer,* Jeanne Richardson; E-mail: jeanne.richardson@asu.edu; Staff 10.5 (MLS 7, Non-MLS 3.5)
Jun 2008-Jun 2009. Mats Exp $11,179,512, Books $1,176,474, Per/Ser (Incl. Access Fees) $8,962,161, Electronic Ref Mat (Incl. Access Fees) $1,040,877
Library Holdings: Audiobooks 67,179; e-books 325,320; Microforms 7,614,192; Bk Vols 4,393,156; Per Subs 95,515
Open Mon-Fri 8-5

DOWNTOWN PHOENIX CAMPUS LIBRARY, UCENT Bldg, Ste L1-62, 411 N Central Ave, Phoenix, 85004-1213. Tel: 602-496-0300. Automation Services Tel: 602-496-0315. FAX: 602-496-0312. E-mail: dpclib@asu.edu. Web Site: lib.asu.edu/Downtown. *Dir & Librn,* Scott Muir; Tel: 602-496-0311, E-mail: scott.muir@asu.edu; *Health Sci Librn,* Virginia Pannabecker; Tel: 602-496-0683, E-mail: virginia.pannabecker@asu.edu; *Instruction Librn,* Alexandra Humphreys; Tel: 602-496-1188, E-mail: humphreys.alexandra@asu.edu; *Soc Sci Librn,* Deborah Abston; Tel: 602-496-0307, E-mail: deborah.abston@asu.edu; *Access Serv Mgr,* Federico Martinez-Garcia Jr; Tel: 602-496-0318, E-mail: federico.martinezjr@asu.edu; *Admin Assoc,* Rayleen Myers; E-mail: rayleen.myers@asu.edu; Staff 10 (MLS 4, Non-MLS 6)
Jul 2012-Jun 2013. Mats Exp $135,000, Books $35,000, Electronic Ref Mat (Incl. Access Fees) $100,000
Library Holdings: Bk Vols 9,500; Per Subs 195
Automation Activity & Vendor Info: (Acquisitions) Innovative Interfaces, Inc; (Cataloging) Innovative Interfaces, Inc; (Circulation) Innovative Interfaces, Inc
Open Mon-Thurs 7am-11pm, Fri 7-6, Sat 10-6, Sun 1-9
Friends of the Library Group

FLETCHER LIBRARY, 4701 W Thunderbird Rd, Glendale, 85306. (Mail add: PO Box 37100, Phoenix, 85069-7100), SAN 323-7788. Tel: 602-543-5718. Reference Tel: 602-543-8567. FAX: 602-543-8540. E-mail: westlib@asu.edu. Web Site: library.west.asu.edu/. *Libr Dir,* Dennis Isbell; Tel: 602-543-8508, E-mail: dennis.isbell@asu.edu; *Librn,* Bee Gallegos; *Librn,* Lisa Kammerlocher; *Mgr, Access Serv,* Christina Peck. Subject Specialists: *Arts, Humanities,* Dennis Isbell; *Educ, Hist,* Bee Gallegos; *Soc sci,* Lisa Kammerlocher; *Educ, Hist,* Christina Peck; Staff 11 (MLS 3, Non-MLS 8)
Founded 1984. Enrl 13,504; Fac 221; Highest Degree: Doctorate
Library Holdings: Bk Vols 338,711
Automation Activity & Vendor Info: (Acquisitions) Innovative Interfaces, Inc; (Circulation) Innovative Interfaces, Inc; (Course Reserve) Innovative Interfaces, Inc; (ILL) Innovative Interfaces, Inc; (Media Booking) Innovative Interfaces, Inc; (OPAC) Innovative Interfaces, Inc; (Serials) Innovative Interfaces, Inc
Database Vendor: Cambridge Scientific Abstracts, CQ Press, EBSCOhost, ISI Web of Knowledge, LexisNexis, Newsbank, OCLC FirstSearch, ProQuest, ReferenceUSA, RefWorks, Thomson - Web of Science, Wilson - Wilson Web
Partic in Ariz Univ Librs Coun; Greater Western Library Alliance

LIBRARY AT THE POLYTECHNIC CAMPUS, Academic Ctr, Bldg 20, 5988 S Backus Mall, Mesa, 85212. Tel: 480-727-1037. FAX: 480-727-1077. Web Site: lib.asu.edu/poly. *Interim Dir,* Dennis P Muir; Tel: 480-727-1974, E-mail: scott.muir@asu.edu; *Assoc Librn,* Ellen Welty; Tel: 480-727-1157, E-mail: ellen.welty@asu.edu; *Librn,* Jeanette Mueller Alexander; Tel: 480-965-3084, E-mail: jenny.muller-alexander@asu.edu; *Mgr, Access Serv,* Laura Cox; Tel: 480-727-1911, E-mail: Laura.M.Cox.1@asu.edu; *Sr Bus Mgr,* Sally Forney; Tel: 480-727-1059, E-mail: sally.forney@asu.edu; Staff 8.5 (MLS 3, Non-MLS 5.5)
Founded 1996. Enrl 4,877; Highest Degree: Doctorate
Automation Activity & Vendor Info: (Cataloging) Innovative Interfaces, Inc; (Circulation) Innovative Interfaces, Inc; (OPAC) Innovative Interfaces, Inc
Open Mon-Thurs 8am-Midnight, Fri 8-7, Sat 10-6, Sun 2-10

MUSIC, Music Bldg, 85287. (Mail add: PO Box 870505, 85287-0505), SAN 330-7174. Tel: 480-965-3513. FAX: 480-965-9598. *Head of Libr,* Dr Christopher Mehrens; Tel: 480-965-4267, E-mail: christopher.mehrens@asu.edu; Staff 3 (MLS 1, Non-MLS 2)
Highest Degree: Doctorate
Library Holdings: CDs 11,871; DVDs 863; Microforms 1,620; Music Scores 75,039; Bk Vols 30,648; Per Subs 244; Videos 937
Open Mon-Thurs 8am-10pm, Fri 8-6, Sat 11-5, Sun 12-10

DANIEL E NOBLE SCIENCE & ENGINEERING LIBRARY, 601 E Tyler, 85287-1006. (Mail add: PO Box 871006, 85287-1006), SAN 330-7123. Tel: 480-965-2600. Administration Tel: 480-965-7609. FAX: 480-965-0883. Web Site: lib.asu.edu/noble. *Head of Libr,* Brad Vogus; Staff 20 (MLS 8, Non-MLS 12)
Library Holdings: Bk Vols 425,000
Special Collections: Map Coll, aerial photos, sheet maps

C COLLINS COLLEGE LIBRARIES*, Tempe Campus Library, 1140 S Priest Dr, 85281. Tel: 480-446-1185. Circulation Tel: 480-966-3000, Ext 436. Toll Free Tel: 800-876-7070. FAX: 480-902-0663. E-mail: library@collinscollege.edu. *Libr Dir,* Lisa Shaughnessy; Staff 3 (MLS 1, Non-MLS 2)
Founded 1978. Highest Degree: Bachelor
Jan 2006-Dec 2006. Mats Exp $67,000. Sal $105,000
Wireless access

J RIO SALADO COLLEGE, Knowledge Commons, 2323 W 14th St, 85281. SAN 321-4745. Tel: 480-517-8424. Toll Free Tel: 866-670-8420. FAX: 480-517-8449. Web Site: www.riosalado.edu/library. *Fac Chair, Libr Serv,* Hazel Davis; Tel: 480-517-8273, Fax: 480-377-4873, E-mail: hazel.davis@riosalado.edu; *Ref & Instruction Librn,* Janelle Underhill; Tel: 480-517-8281, E-mail: janelle.underhill@riosalado.edu; *Supvr, Libr Access Serv,* Melanie Fritz; Tel: 480-517-8428, E-mail: melanie.fritz@riosalado.edu; *Instrul Coordr, Libr Serv,* Kirstin Thomas; Tel: 480-517-8423, E-mail: kirstin.thomas@riosalado.edu; Staff 8 (MLS 4, Non-MLS 4)
Founded 1982. Enrl 65,047; Fac 1,584; Highest Degree: Associate
Automation Activity & Vendor Info: (Acquisitions) SirsiDynix; (Cataloging) SirsiDynix; (Circulation) SirsiDynix; (Course Reserve) SirsiDynix; (OPAC) SirsiDynix; (Serials) SirsiDynix
Wireless access
Open Mon-Thurs 8-7, Fri 9-5, Sat 9-2

S SALT RIVER PROJECT LIBRARY*, ISB/PAB Library, 1600 N Priest Dr, 85281-1213. Tel: 602-236-5676. FAX: 602-629-8585. E-mail: isblib@srpnet.com. *Librn,* Cathy Large; Tel: 602-236-2259, Fax: 602-236-2664, E-mail: calarge@srpnet.com; Staff 2 (MLS 1, Non-MLS 1)
Founded 1958
Library Holdings: Bk Titles 22,000; Per Subs 115
Special Collections: Career Resources
Subject Interests: Bus & mgt, Computers, Electric utilities, Eng, Info tech, Utilities industry, Water
Automation Activity & Vendor Info: (Acquisitions) SydneyPlus; (Cataloging) SydneyPlus; (Circulation) SydneyPlus; (ILL) OCLC; (OPAC) SydneyPlus; (Serials) SydneyPlus
Database Vendor: Dialog, IEEE (Institute of Electrical & Electronics Engineers), LexisNexis
Function: For res purposes, ILL available, Photocopying/Printing, Telephone ref
Restriction: Co libr

CM SOUTHWEST COLLEGE OF NATUROPATHIC MEDICINE & HEALTH SCIENCES LIBRARY*, 2140 E Broadway Rd, 85282-1751. Tel: 480-222-9247. Administration Tel: 480-222-9245. FAX: 480-222-9447. E-mail: library@scnm.edu. Web Site: my.scnm.edu/ICS/Library/. *Dir,* Dr Bryan Stansfield; E-mail: b.stansfield@scnm.edu; *Libr Tech,* Mayu Muralidharan; E-mail: m.muralidharan@scnm.edu; Staff 3 (MLS 1, Non-MLS 2)
Founded 1996. Enrl 340; Fac 50; Highest Degree: Doctorate
Library Holdings: Bk Titles 14,000; Per Subs 100
Special Collections: Randolph Environmental Medicine Coll
Subject Interests: Alternative med, Health, Wellness
Automation Activity & Vendor Info: (Cataloging) EOS International; (Circulation) EOS International; (OPAC) EOS International; (Serials) EOS International
Database Vendor: EBSCOhost, Medline, PubMed
Wireless access
Partic in Asn Col & Res Librs; Cent Ariz Biomed Librns; Medical Library Group of Southern California & Arizona (MLGSCA)
Open Mon-Thurs 7-7, Fri 7-5
Friends of the Library Group

P TEMPE PUBLIC LIBRARY*, 3500 S Rural Rd, 85282. SAN 300-4406. Tel: 480-350-5500. FAX: 480-350-5544. Web Site: www.tempe.gov/library. *Libr Operations Mgr,* Clay Workman; Tel: 480-350-5540, E-mail: clay_workman@tempe.gov; *Mgr, Pub Serv,* Sherry Warren; Tel: 480-350-5554, E-mail: sherry_warren@tempe.gov; *Mgr, Support Serv,* Kimberlee Garza; Tel: 480-350-5557, E-mail: kim_garza@tempe.gov; Staff 13 (MLS 13)
Founded 1935. Pop 169,712; Circ 1,015,578
Jul 2011-Jun 2012 Income $3,645,784. Mats Exp $412,912
Library Holdings: Bk Titles 210,449; Bk Vols 314,947
Automation Activity & Vendor Info: (Acquisitions) Innovative Interfaces, Inc; (Cataloging) Innovative Interfaces, Inc; (Circulation) Innovative Interfaces, Inc; (OPAC) Innovative Interfaces, Inc; (Serials) Innovative Interfaces, Inc
Database Vendor: 3M Library Systems, Baker & Taylor, Booksite, BWI, EBSCOhost, Facts on File, Gale Cengage Learning, Innovative Interfaces, Inc, LearningExpress, OCLC WorldShare Interlibrary Loan, Overdrive, Inc, Oxford Communications, ProQuest
Wireless access

Function: Art exhibits, Audiobks via web, Bilingual assistance for Spanish patrons, Bk club(s), Bks on CD, Children's prog, Computer training, Computers for patron use, Copy machines, Electronic databases & coll, Fax serv, Free DVD rentals, Handicapped accessible, Homebound delivery serv, ILL available, Music CDs, Online cat, Online searches, OverDrive digital audio bks, Prog for adults, Prog for children & young adult, Pub access computers, Ref serv in person, Story hour, Summer reading prog, Teen prog, Telephone ref, Video lending libr, Web-catalog, Wheelchair accessible
Open Mon 10-6, Tues-Thurs 10-8, Fri & Sat 10:30-5, Sun 12-5
Friends of the Library Group

THATCHER

J EASTERN ARIZONA COLLEGE*, Alumni Library, 615 N Stadium Ave, 85552. SAN 300-4414. Tel: 928-428-8304. FAX: 928-428-8390. E-mail: library@eac.edu. Web Site: www.eac.edu/academics/library. *Dir, Libr Serv,* Karen Jaggers; Tel: 928-428-8308, E-mail: karen.jaggers@eac.edu; Staff 10 (MLS 1, Non-MLS 9)
Founded 1888. Enrl 5,710; Fac 237; Highest Degree: Associate
Library Holdings: AV Mats 391; e-books 253; Bk Titles 47,244; Bk Vols 51,063; Per Subs 64
Automation Activity & Vendor Info: (Acquisitions) Innovative Interfaces, Inc; (Cataloging) Innovative Interfaces, Inc; (Circulation) Innovative Interfaces, Inc; (OPAC) Innovative Interfaces, Inc
Database Vendor: CQ Press, ebrary, EBSCO Discovery Service, EBSCOhost, Facts on File, Gale Cengage Learning, Newsbank, ProQuest, Westlaw
Wireless access
Open Mon-Thurs 7am-10pm, Fri 7-5, Sat 10-4, Sun 6pm-10pm

TOLLESON

P TOLLESON PUBLIC LIBRARY*, 9555 W Van Buren St, 85353. SAN 300-4422. Tel: 623-936-7111, Ext 2746. FAX: 623-936-9793. Web Site: www.tollesonaz.org. *Dir,* John Paul Lopez; *Libr Asst,* Lisa Gallegos; Tel: 623-936-2748, E-mail: lgallegos@tollesonaz.org; Staff 4 (Non-MLS 4)
Founded 1949. Pop 5,445; Circ 29,556
Library Holdings: Bks on Deafness & Sign Lang 10; CDs 100; DVDs 1,200; Bk Vols 23,000; Per Subs 40; Talking Bks 269
Special Collections: Prehistoric Arizona Indian Pottery, Kachinas & Artifacts; Spanish Language Materials; Young Adult Coll
Automation Activity & Vendor Info: (Acquisitions) Innovative Interfaces, Inc; (Cataloging) OCLC CatExpress; (Circulation) Innovative Interfaces, Inc; (OPAC) Innovative Interfaces, Inc
Database Vendor: EBSCOhost
Wireless access
Function: Bilingual assistance for Spanish patrons, Bks on CD, Children's prog, Computers for patron use, Copy machines, Electronic databases & coll, Fax serv, Free DVD rentals, Music CDs, Online cat, Online searches, Preschool outreach, Prog for adults, Prog for children & young adult, Ref serv available, Spoken cassettes & CDs, Story hour, Summer reading prog, Tax forms, Telephone ref
Partic in OCLC Online Computer Library Center, Inc
Open Mon-Wed 9-7, Thurs & Fri 9-5, Sat 9-1

TOMBSTONE

P TOMBSTONE READING STATION-TOMBSTONE CITY LIBRARY*, Fourth & Toughnut Sts, 85638. (Mail add: PO Box 218, 85638-0218), SAN 300-4430. Tel: 520-457-3612. FAX: 520-457-3612. Web Site: www.cochise.lib.az.us. *Librn,* Mary Buchanan; E-mail: mbuchanan@tombstonepl.lib.az.us; Staff 2 (Non-MLS 2)
Founded 1961
Library Holdings: Bk Vols 15,000
Subject Interests: Arizona
Mem of Cochise County Library District
Open Mon-Fri 8-12 & 1-5
Friends of the Library Group

TONTO BASIN

P TONTO BASIN PUBLIC LIBRARY*, 415 Old Hwy 188, 85553. (Mail add: PO Box 368, 85553-0368), SAN 376-7280. Tel: 928-479-2355. FAX: 928-479-2355. *Libr Mgr,* Kathy Womack
Founded 1983. Pop 1,424; Circ 38,000
Library Holdings: Bk Titles 15,000; Per Subs 2
Automation Activity & Vendor Info: (Cataloging) Innovative Interfaces, Inc; (Circulation) Innovative Interfaces, Inc; (OPAC) Innovative Interfaces, Inc
Wireless access
Mem of Gila County Library District
Open Mon-Fri 8-4

TSAILE

C DINE COLLEGE*, Kinyaa'aanii Charlie Benally Library, One Circle Dr, Rte 12, 86556. (Mail add: PO Box 1000, 86556), SAN 300-4457. Tel: 928-724-6758. Reference Tel: 928-724-6757. Administration FAX: 928-724-6759. E-mail: library@dinecollege.edu. Web Site: library.dinecollege.edu. *Col Librn,* Herman Peterson; E-mail: hpeterson@dinecollege.edu; *AV,* Cindy Slivers; *Cat,* Rosita Klee; *Circ,* Ruby Johnson; *Ser,* Mary Norcross
Founded 1969. Enrl 2,000; Fac 51
Library Holdings: Bk Vols 55,000; Per Subs 260
Special Collections: North American Indians (Moses Donner Coll), bks & film; RC German Coll
Wireless access
Open Mon-Thurs 8am-9pm, Fri 8-4, Sun 5-9

TUCSON

S ARABIAN HORSE OWNERS FOUNDATION*, W R Brown Memorial Library, 4101 N Bear Canyon Rd, 85749. SAN 327-912X. Tel: 520-760-0682. Toll Free Tel: 800-892-0682. FAX: 520-749-2572. E-mail: ahof001@aol.com. Web Site: www.ahof.org. *Exec Dir,* Howard Shenk
Founded 1956
Library Holdings: Bk Titles 1,000
Special Collections: Horse books dating from 1587
Restriction: Open by appt only

S ARIZONA DEPARTMENT OF CORRECTIONS - ADULT INSTITUTIONS*, Arizona State Prison Complex - Tucson Library, 10000 S Wilmot Rd, 85734. (Mail add: PO Box 24400, 85734-4400). Tel: 520-574-0024, Ext 37919. FAX: 520-574-7308. *Head Librn,* Sally Berg; *Librn,* Renee Hermsen; *Librn,* Jon Meade; *Librn,* Jeffery St Clair
Library Holdings: Bk Vols 46,225
Open Mon-Fri 7-3:30

S ARIZONA GEOLOGICAL SURVEY*, Reference Library, 416 W Congress St, Ste 100, 85701. SAN 370-338X. Tel: 520-770-3500. FAX: 520-770-3505. Web Site: www.azgs.az.gov. *In Charge,* Michael Conway; Tel: 520-209-4146, E-mail: michael.conway@azgs.az.gov
Library Holdings: Bk Titles 300; Per Subs 10
Special Collections: Arizona Theses & Dissertations; Mine Coll. US Document Depository
Subject Interests: Geol
Open Mon-Fri 8-5
Restriction: Open to pub for ref only

S ARIZONA HISTORICAL SOCIETY*, Library Archives-Southern Arizona Division, 949 E Second St, 85719. SAN 300-449X. Tel: 520-628-5774. FAX: 520-629-8966. E-mail: ahsref@azhs.gov. Web Site: www.arizonahistoricalsociety.org/library-and-archives/. *Archivist/Librn,* Laura Hoft; *Archivist/Librn,* Erin Wahl; *Curator,* Julia Arriola; E-mail: jarriola@azhs.gov; Staff 4.5 (MLS 2.5, Non-MLS 2)
Founded 1884
Library Holdings: Microforms 9,000; Bk Titles 50,000; Per Subs 40
Subject Interests: Arizona, Mexico
Automation Activity & Vendor Info: (Acquisitions) Ex Libris Group; (Cataloging) Ex Libris Group; (Media Booking) Ex Libris Group; (OPAC) Ex Libris Group
Database Vendor: Ex Libris Group, OCLC FirstSearch, OCLC WebJunction
Function: For res purposes, Mail & tel request accepted, Newsp ref libr, Online cat, Online ref, Outreach serv, Ref & res, Ref serv available, Ref serv in person, Res libr, Res performed for a fee
Open Mon-Fri 10-3, Sat 10-1
Restriction: Non-circulating

S ARIZONA-SONORA DESERT MUSEUM LIBRARY*, 2021 N Kinney Rd, 85743. SAN 330-7204. Tel: 520-883-1380, Ext 264. FAX: 520-883-2500. E-mail: info@desertmuseum.org. Web Site: www.desertmuseum.org. *Head, Info Serv,* Peggy Larson; Staff 1 (MLS 1)
Founded 1952
Library Holdings: AV Mats 200; Bk Titles 7,000; Per Subs 58
Special Collections: Natural History Coll, slides
Subject Interests: Botany, Ecology, Geol, Natural hist, SW region, Zoology
Automation Activity & Vendor Info: (Cataloging) LibraryWorld, Inc; (Circulation) LibraryWorld, Inc; (Course Reserve) LibraryWorld, Inc; (ILL) LibraryWorld, Inc; (Media Booking) LibraryWorld, Inc; (OPAC) LibraryWorld, Inc
Function: Res libr
Publications: ASDM News; Sonorensis
Restriction: Open by appt only

S ARIZONA STATE MUSEUM LIBRARY*, University of Arizona, 1013 E University Blvd, 85721-0026. (Mail add: PO Box 210026, 85721-0026), SAN 300-4678. Tel: 520-621-4695. FAX: 520-621-2976. Web Site: www.statemuseum.arizona.edu. *Librn,* Mary Graham; E-mail: megraham@email.arizona.edu; *Asst Librn, Cataloger,* Marly Helm; E-mail: mhelm@email.arizona.edu; Staff 2 (MLS 2)
Founded 1957
Library Holdings: Bk Vols 50,000; Per Subs 30
Subject Interests: Anthrop, Archaeology, Museology, SW
Automation Activity & Vendor Info: (Acquisitions) Ex Libris Group; (Cataloging) Ex Libris Group; (Circulation) Ex Libris Group; (OPAC) Ex Libris Group
Wireless access
Open Mon-Thurs 10-3
Restriction: Non-circulating

S ARIZONA STATE SCHOOLS FOR THE DEAF & THE BLIND LIBRARY, 1200 W Speedway, 85745. (Mail add: PO Box 85000, 85754-5000), SAN 300-4503. Tel: 520-770-3671. FAX: 520-770-3752. *Librn,* Peg Hartman; Tel: 520-770-3462, E-mail: peg.hartman@asdb.az.gov; Staff 2 (MLS 1, Non-MLS 1)
Library Holdings: Bk Vols 30,000; Per Subs 25
Special Collections: Braille; Deaf & Visually Impaired (Professional Coll); Deaf Studies; Described & Captioned Media Accessible Learning Center; Descriptive Videos; Parent Lending Library, Shared Reading Project
Subject Interests: Regional
Automation Activity & Vendor Info: (Cataloging) Follett Software; (Circulation) Follett Software; (OPAC) Follett Software
Database Vendor: TumbleBookLibrary
Wireless access
Special Services for the Deaf - Am sign lang & deaf culture; Bks on deafness & sign lang; Closed caption videos; Coll on deaf educ; Deaf publ; Interpreter on staff; Staff with knowledge of sign lang; Video relay serv
Special Services for the Blind - Descriptive video serv (DVS); Digital talking bk machines; Large print bks; ZoomText magnification & reading software

S EDWARD F BARRINS MEMORIAL LIBRARY*, 2023 E Adams St, 85719-4320. SAN 371-6422. Tel: 520-327-7956. *In Charge,* P C Barrins
Founded 1979
Library Holdings: Bk Titles 11,000; Per Subs 54
Special Collections: Alexandria O'Sullivan Mystery Coll; Phyllis C Barrins Coll (complete works); Religion (Catherine M Willy Commemorative Coll)
Subject Interests: Braille, Hypnotherapy in med, Nursing, Psychol, Reincarnation, Relig
Restriction: By permission only, Private libr

M CARONDELET SAINT MARY'S HOSPITAL*, Ralph Henry Fuller Medical Library, 1601 W St Mary's Rd, 85745. SAN 300-4600. Tel: 520-872-4974. FAX: 520-872-4936. *Librn,* Catherine Dimenstein
Founded 1937
Library Holdings: e-books 240; e-journals 900; Bk Titles 340; Per Subs 25
Subject Interests: Allied health, Med, Nursing
Publications: Serials list (annual)
Partic in Arizona Health Information Network (AZHIN); Medical Library Group of Southern California & Arizona (MLGSCA); Pacific Southwest Regional Medical Library (PSRML)
Restriction: Not open to pub

DEPARTMENT OF VETERANS AFFAIRS

GM PATIENT EDUCATION RESOURCE CENTER*, 3601 S Sixth Ave, 7-14A, 85723. Tel: 520-792-1450, Ext 6516. FAX: 520-629-4638. *Librn,* Sharon Hammond
Library Holdings: Bk Vols 250
Open Mon-Fri 8-4:30

GM SOUTHERN ARIZONA VA HEALTHCARE SYSTEM*, 3601 S Sixth Ave, 85723, SAN 300-4686. Tel: 520-629-1836. FAX: 520-629-4638. E-mail: tucson.library@va.gov. *Librn,* Lynn Flance; Staff 1 (MLS 1)
Library Holdings: Bk Vols 1,400; Per Subs 200
Subject Interests: Med, Nursing, Psychiat, Psychol
Partic in Pacific Southwest Regional Medical Library (PSRML); Veterans Affairs Libr Network (VALNET)
Open Mon-Fri 8-4:30

S INTERNATIONAL SOCIETY FOR VEHICLE PRESERVATION LIBRARY*, 8987 E Tonque Verde, No 309-300, 85749-9399. SAN 373-3912. Tel: 520-749-2260. E-mail: isvp@earthlink.net. Web Site: iamc-isvp.org. *Dir,* Elaine C Haessner
Library Holdings: Bk Vols 600
Subject Interests: Aircraft, Automobiles, Motorcycle, Trains, Transportation
Restriction: Open by appt only

S NATIONAL PARK SERVICE*, Western Archeological & Conservation Center Library, 255 N Commerce Park Loop, 85745. SAN 300-4570. Tel: 520-791-6400. FAX: 520-791-6465. *Prog Dir,* Stephanie Rodeffer; Tel: 520-791-6401
Founded 1952
Oct 2006-Sept 2007. Mats Exp $5,000
Library Holdings: Bk Titles 14,000; Per Subs 40
Special Collections: Archives of Archeological Records of Southwestern US; Stabilization & Environmental Impact Statements; Unpublished Reports & Manuscripts on Archaeological Excavations
Subject Interests: Anthrop, Natural res
Automation Activity & Vendor Info: (Cataloging) Ex Libris Group; (Serials) EBSCO Online
Partic in OCLC Online Computer Library Center, Inc
Restriction: Open by appt only, Staff use only

J PIMA COMMUNITY COLLEGE*, West Campus Library, 2202 W Anklam Rd, 85709-0001. SAN 330-7328. Tel: 520-206-6821. FAX: 520-206-3059. Web Site: www.pima.edu/library. *Dir,* Joseph Labuda; E-mail: jlabuda@pima.edu; *Librn,* Jim Berger; E-mail: jbberger@pima.edu; *Librn,* Eric Comport; E-mail: ecomport@pima.edu; Staff 4 (MLS 3, Non-MLS 1)
Founded 1970. Enrl 12,500; Fac 203; Highest Degree: Associate
Library Holdings: Bk Vols 165,000; Per Subs 550
Automation Activity & Vendor Info: (Acquisitions) Innovative Interfaces, Inc; (Circulation) Innovative Interfaces, Inc; (Serials) Innovative Interfaces, Inc
Wireless access
Special Services for the Deaf - Closed caption videos; Deaf publ; Videos & decoder
Special Services for the Blind - Assistive/Adapted tech devices, equip & products; Computer with voice synthesizer for visually impaired persons
Open Mon-Thurs 8am-9pm, Fri 8-5, Sat 9-3

Departmental Libraries:

DESERT VISTA, 5901 S Calle Santa Cruz, 85709-6055, SAN 373-0069. Tel: 520-206-5095. FAX: 520-206-5090. *Dir,* Antonio Arroyo; Tel: 520-206-5068, E-mail: antonio.arroyo@pima.edu
Library Holdings: Bk Titles 18,017; Per Subs 145
Open Mon-Thurs 8am-9pm, Fri 8-5, Sat 9-3

DISTRICT LIBRARY SERVICES, 4905B E Broadway Blvd, 85709-1010, SAN 374-8189. Tel: 520 206-4607. FAX: 520-206-4890. *Dir,* Michael Hanson; Tel: 520-206-4608, E-mail: mhanson6@pima.edu; Staff 9 (MLS 2, Non-MLS 7)
Founded 1969. Enrl 20,000; Fac 363; Highest Degree: Associate
Function: Doc delivery serv, ILL available
Partic in OCLC Online Computer Library Center, Inc
Restriction: Open to pub for ref & circ; with some limitations, Open to students, fac & staff, Residents only

DOWNTOWN, 1255 N Stone Ave, 85709-3035, SAN 330-7352. Tel: 520-206-7267. FAX: 520-206-7217. *Dir,* Theresa Stanley; Tel: 520-206-7245; Staff 8 (MLS 4, Non-MLS 4)
Founded 1978. Enrl 4,000; Fac 88; Highest Degree: Associate
Library Holdings: Bk Titles 22,829; Bk Vols 24,764; Per Subs 162
Subject Interests: Automotive eng, Graphic arts
Open Mon-Thurs 8am-9pm, Fri 8-5, Sat 9-3

EAST, 8181 E Irvington Rd, 85709-4000, SAN 330-7387. Tel: 520-206-7693. FAX: 520-206-7690. *Dir,* Charles Becker; E-mail: cbecker@pima.edu; *Librn,* Becky Moore; Staff 4 (MLS 2, Non-MLS 2)
Founded 1976. Enrl 2,070; Fac 40
Library Holdings: Bk Vols 29,000; Per Subs 63
Open Mon-Thurs 8am-9pm, Fri 8-5, Sat 9-3

G PIMA COUNTY JUVENILE COURT CENTER LIBRARY*, 2225 E Ajo Way, 85713-6295. SAN 326-3266. Tel: 520-740-2082. FAX: 520-740-4570. *Librn,* Gwen Reid; E-mail: gwen.reid@pcjcc.pima.gov; Staff 1 (MLS 1)
Founded 1976
Library Holdings: Bk Titles 2,000; Per Subs 25; Spec Interest Per Sub 10
Subject Interests: Juv delinquency, Mental disorders of children, Sexual abuse
Function: Prof lending libr
Restriction: Staff use only

GL PIMA COUNTY LAW LIBRARY*, Superior Court Bldg, 110 W Congress, Rm 256, 85701-1317. SAN 300-4597. Tel: 520-724-8456. FAX: 520-724-9122. E-mail: pcll@sc.pima.gov. Web Site: www.sc.co.pima.gov/lawlib/. *Dir,* Sol Gomez; Staff 4 (MLS 1, Non-MLS 3)
Founded 1915
Library Holdings: Bk Titles 2,252; Bk Vols 35,000
Subject Interests: Law
Automation Activity & Vendor Info: (Cataloging) LibraryWorld, Inc; (Circulation) LibraryWorld, Inc; (OPAC) LibraryWorld, Inc; (Serials) LibraryWorld, Inc
Open Mon-Fri 8-5

P PIMA COUNTY PUBLIC LIBRARY*, 101 N Stone Ave, 85701. SAN 330-7417. Tel: 520-564-5600. FAX: 520-594-5621. Web Site: www.library.pima.gov. *Exec Dir,* Melinda Cervantes; *Dep Dir,* Pat Corella; *Dep Dir,* Amber Mathewson; *Dep Dir,* Karyn Prechtel; *Coll Develop Mgr,* Richard DiRusso; *Commun Relations Mgr,* Kenya Johnson; Staff 79 (MLS 77, Non-MLS 2)
Founded 1883. Pop 992,394; Circ 7,220,685
Library Holdings: CDs 43,222; DVDs 18,311; Bk Vols 1,427,983; Per Subs 3,403; Talking Bks 35,641; Videos 38,212
Special Collections: Arizona Coll; Business Coll; Southwestern Literature for Children; Spanish Language Coll. US Document Depository
Subject Interests: Arizona, Bus & mgt, Govt
Automation Activity & Vendor Info: (Acquisitions) Innovative Interfaces, Inc; (Cataloging) Innovative Interfaces, Inc; (Circulation) Innovative Interfaces, Inc; (OPAC) Innovative Interfaces, Inc
Member Libraries: Pima County Public Library
Partic in OCLC Online Computer Library Center, Inc
Special Services for the Deaf - Closed caption videos; TTY equip
Special Services for the Blind - Assistive/Adapted tech devices, equip & products; Computer with voice synthesizer for visually impaired persons
Friends of the Library Group
Branches: 27
WHEELER TAFT ABBETT SR LIBRARY, 7800 N Schisler Dr, 85743. Tel: 520-594-5200. Web Site: www.library.pima.gov/locations/abbett. *Br Mgr,* Cat Strong; Tel: 520-594-5210
Library Holdings: Bk Vols 60,000
Open Mon-Thurs 10-8, Fri 10-5, Sat 9-5, Sun 1-5
CAVIGLIA-ARIVACA, 17050 W Arivaca Rd, Arivaca, 85601. (Mail add: PO Box 668, Arivaca, 85601), SAN 371-9685. Tel: 520-594-5235. FAX: 520-594-5236. Web Site: www.library.pima.gov/locations/arivaca. *Br Mgr,* Leesa Jacobson
Library Holdings: Bk Vols 15,939
Open Tues & Wed 11-8, Thurs 10-6, Fri 11-5, Sat 9-5
Friends of the Library Group
MARTHA COOPER LIBRARY, 1377 N Catalina Ave, 857-12. Tel: 520-594-5315. Web Site: www.library.pima.gov/locations/marthacooper. *Br Mgr,* Dianna Thor; Tel: 520-594-5320
Library Holdings: Bk Vols 20,000
Open Mon-Thurs 10-8, Fri 10-5, Sat 9-5, Sun 1-5
DEWHIRST CATALINA, 15631 N Oracle Rd, No 199, Catalina, 85739, SAN 371-9693. Tel: 520-594-5240. FAX: 520-594-5241. Web Site: www.library.pima.gov/locations/catalina. *Br Mgr,* Bethany Wilson
Library Holdings: Bk Vols 15,746
Open Mon, Wed & Thurs 10-6, Tues 10-7, Fri 10-5, Sat 9-5
QUINCIE DOUGLAS, 1585 E 36th St, 85713. Tel: 520-594-5335. FAX: 520-594-5336. Administration FAX: 520-594-5621. Web Site: www.library.pima.gov/locations/quinciedouglas. *Br Mgr,* Sharla Darby
Open Mon-Thurs 10-8, Fri 10-5, Sat 9-5, Sun 1-5
DUSENBERRY-RIVER BRANCH, 5605 E River Rd, 85750, SAN 371-9707. Tel: 520-594-5345. FAX: 520-594-5346. Web Site: www.library.pima.gov/locations/river. *Br Mgr,* Dianna Thor
Library Holdings: Bk Vols 85,201
Open Mon-Thurs 10-8, Fri 10-5, Sat 9-5, Sun 1-5
ECKSTROM-COLUMBUS, 4350 E 22nd St, 85711, SAN 330-7476. Tel: 520-594-5285. FAX: 520-770-4102. Web Site: www.library.pima.gov/locations/columbus. *Br Mgr,* Mary Sanchez
Library Holdings: Bk Vols 76,166
Open Mon-Thurs 10-8, Fri 10-5, Sat 9-5, Sun 1-5
EL PUEBLO, 101 W Irvington Rd, 85714, SAN 330-7743. Tel: 520-594-5250. FAX: 520-594-5251. Web Site: www.library.pima.gov/locations/elpueblo. *Br Mgr,* Aaron Valdivia
Library Holdings: Bk Vols 18,524
Open Mon & Tues 9-6, Wed & Thurs 10-6, Fri 10-5, Sat 9-5
EL RIO, 1390 W Speedway Blvd, 85745, SAN 330-7778. Tel: 520-594-5245. FAX: 520-594-5246. Web Site: www.library.pima.gov/locations/elrio. *Br Mgr,* Emily Lane
Library Holdings: Bk Vols 7,738
Open Mon & Tues 9-6, Wed & Thurs 10-6, Fri 10-5
FLOWING WELLS BRANCH, 1730 W Wetmore Rd, 85705. Tel: 520-594-5225. Web Site: www.library.pima.gov/locations/flowingwells. *Br Mgr,* Manager Bradford; Tel: 508-594-5230
Library Holdings: Bk Vols 13,000
Open Mon-Thurs 10-8, Fri 10-5, Sat 9-5, Sun 1-5
GEASA-MARANA, 13370 N Lon Adams Rd, Marana, 85653, SAN 330-7808. Tel: 520-594-5255. FAX: 520-594-5256. Web Site: www.library.pima.gov/locations/marana. *Br Mgr,* Vicki Ann Duraine
Library Holdings: Bk Vols 11,963
Open Tues & Thurs 10-6, Wed 10-7, Fri 10-5, Sat 9-5
HIMMEL PARK, 1035 N Treat Ave, 85716, SAN 330-7565. Tel: 520-594-5305. FAX: 520-594-5306. Web Site: www.library.pima.gov/locations/himmel. *Br Mgr,* Sharla Darby
Library Holdings: Bk Vols 49,199
Open Mon-Thurs 10-8, Fri 10-5, Sat 9-5, Sun 1-5
JOYNER-GREEN VALLEY, 601 N La Canada Dr, Green Valley, 85614, SAN 330-7530. Tel: 520-594-5295. FAX: 520-770-4113. Web Site: www.library.pima.gov/locations/greenvalley. *Br Mgr,* Donie Gignac
Library Holdings: Bk Vols 70,968
Open Mon-Thurs 9-7, Fri 10-5, Sat 9-5, Sun 1-5
Friends of the Library Group
KIRK-BEAR CANYON, 8959 E Tanque Verde Rd, 85749, SAN 371-9715. Tel: 520-594-5275. FAX: 520-594-5276. Web Site: www.library.pima.gov/locations/bearcanyon. *Br Mgr,* Daphne Daly
Library Holdings: Bk Vols 77,066
Open Mon-Thurs 10-8, Fri 10-5, Sat 9-5, Sun 1-5
Friends of the Library Group
SAM LENA-SOUTH TUCSON, 1607 S Sixth Ave, 85713, SAN 330-7867. Tel: 520-594-5265. FAX: 520-594-5266. Web Site: www.library.pima.gov/locations/southtucson. *Br Mgr,* Marissa Alcorta
Library Holdings: Bk Vols 20,548
Open Mon-Thurs 10-6, Fri 10-5, Sat 9-5, Sun 1-5
MILLER-GOLF LINKS, 9640 E Golf Links Rd, 85730. Tel: 520-594-5355. FAX: 520-770-4104. Web Site: www.library.pima.gov/locations/golflinks. *Br Mgr,* Mary McKinney
Library Holdings: Bk Vols 82,444
Open Mon-Thurs 10-8, Fri 10-5, Sat 9-5, Sun 1-5
MISSION, 3770 S Mission Rd, 85713, SAN 330-762X. Tel: 520-594-5325. FAX: 520-770-4106. Web Site: www.library.pima.gov/locations/mission. *Br Mgr,* Margaret Wilkie
Library Holdings: Bk Vols 65,786
Open Mon-Thurs 10-8, Fri 10-5, Sat 9-5, Sun 1-5
MURPHY-WILMOT, 530 N Wilmot Rd, 85711, SAN 330-7719. Tel: 520-594-5620. FAX: 520-770-4110. Web Site: www.library.pima.gov/locations/wilmot. *Br Mgr,* Daphne Daly
Library Holdings: Bk Vols 123,253
Open Mon-Thurs 10-8, Fri 10-5, Sat 9-5, Sun 1-5
NANINI, 7300 N Shannon Rd, 85741, SAN 330-7654. Tel: 520-594-5365. FAX: 520-594-5366. Web Site: www.library.pima.gov/locations/nanini. *Br Mgr,* Kristi Bradford
Library Holdings: Bk Vols 118,187
Open Mon-Thurs 10-8, Fri 10-5, Sat 9-5, Sun 1-5
ORO VALLEY PUBLIC LIBRARY, 1305 W Naranja Dr, Oro Valley, 85737. Tel: 520-594-5580. Web Site: www.library.pima.gov/locations/orovalley. *Br Mgr,* Ruth Grant; Tel: 520-594-5581; Staff 28.5 (MLS 5.5, Non-MLS 23)
Founded 2002. Pop 41,000; Circ 305,766
Library Holdings: AV Mats 9,944; CDs 2,794; DVDs 1,792; Large Print Bks 1,849; Bk Vols 76,765; Per Subs 227; Talking Bks 2,751; Videos 2,607
Automation Activity & Vendor Info: (Cataloging) Innovative Interfaces, Inc; (Circulation) Innovative Interfaces, Inc; (OPAC) Innovative Interfaces, Inc
Function: Adult bk club, Adult literacy prog, Chess club, Computer training, Copy machines, Digital talking bks, e-mail serv, Electronic databases & coll, Handicapped accessible, Homework prog, ILL available, Music CDs, Online ref, Prog for adults, Prog for children & young adult, Ref serv available, Senior computer classes, Spoken cassettes & CDs, Summer reading prog, Telephone ref, VHS videos, Wheelchair accessible
Mem of Pima County Public Library
Open Mon-Thurs 9-7, Fri 10-5, Sat 9-5, Sun 1-5
Friends of the Library Group
SAHUARITA, 725 W Via Rancho Sahuarita, Sahuarita, 85629. Tel: 520-594-5490. Web Site: www.library.pima.gov/locations/sahuarita. *Br Mgr,* Michelle White; Tel: 520-594-5495
Open Tues-Thurs 10-6, Fri 10-5, Sat 9-5
SALAZAR-AJO BRANCH, 15 W Plaza St, Ste 179, Ajo, 85321, SAN 330-7441. Tel: 520-387-6075. FAX: 520-387-5345. Web Site: www.library.pima.gov/locations/ajo. *Br Mgr,* Linda Lam
Library Holdings: Bk Vols 21,935
Open Mon-Thurs 9-7, Fri & Sat 9-5
SANTA ROSA BRANCH, 1075 S Tenth Ave, 85701. Tel: 520-594-5260. Web Site: www.library.pima.gov/locations/santarosa. *Br Mgr,* Susan Husband
Open Tues & Thurs 9-7, Wed 9-6, Fri 10-5, Sat 9-5
SOUTHWEST, 6855 S Mark Rd, 85757. Tel: 520-594-5270. Web Site: www.library.pima.gov/locations/southwest. *Br Mgr,* Paulina Aguirre-Clinch
Library Holdings: Bk Vols 21,071
Open Mon & Tues 10-6, Wed & Thurs 10-7, Fri 10-5, Sat 9-5
JOEL D VALDEZ, 101 N Stone Ave, 85701, SAN 330-759X. Tel: 520-594-5500. FAX: 520-594-5501. Web Site: www.library.pima.gov/locations/main. *Br Mgr,* Sandy White
Library Holdings: Bk Vols 186,219
Open Mon-Wed 9-8, Thurs 9-6, Fri 9-5, Sat 10-5, Sun 1-5
Friends of the Library Group

VALENCIA, 202 W Valencia Rd, 85706, SAN 330-7689. Tel: 520-594-5390. FAX: 520-594-5391. Web Site: www.library.pima.gov/locations/valencia. *Br Mgr,* Kathy Konecny
Library Holdings: Bk Vols 83,633
Open Mon-Thurs 10-8, Fri 10-5, Sat 9-5, Sun 1-5
WOODS MEMORIAL BRANCH, 3455 N First Ave, 85719, SAN 330-7506. Tel: 520-594-5445. FAX: 520-770-4111. Web Site: www.library.pima.gov/locations/woods. *Br Mgr,* Coni Weatherford
Library Holdings: Bk Vols 99,013
Open Mon-Thurs 10-8, Fri 10-5, Sat 9-5, Sun 1-5
Bookmobiles: 1

M PIMA MEDICAL INSTITUTE LIBRARY*, 3350 E Grant Rd, 85716. SAN 375-6785. Tel: 520-326-1600. FAX: 520-795-3463. *Fac Coordr,* Judy Bodzioney
Library Holdings: Bk Titles 2,000; Bk Vols 5,000; Per Subs 78
Open Mon-Thurs 7:30am-9:30pm, Fri 7:30-4:30

S RAYTHEON TECHNICAL LIBRARY*, Bldg 811/T, 1151 E Hermans Rd, 85756. (Mail add: PO Box 11337, 85734-1337), SAN 375-7722. Tel: 520-794-8807. *Librn,* Amy C Smith
Library Holdings: Bk Titles 18,604; Per Subs 300
Subject Interests: Aeronaut, Electronics, Math, Physics, Radar
Automation Activity & Vendor Info: (Cataloging) SirsiDynix; (Circulation) SirsiDynix; (OPAC) SirsiDynix; (Serials) SirsiDynix
Database Vendor: EBSCOhost, OCLC FirstSearch, OVID Technologies, SirsiDynix
Function: Res libr
Restriction: Authorized patrons, Circ limited, Employees only, No access to competitors, Not open to pub

M SAINT JOSEPH'S HOSPITAL*, Bruce Cole Memorial Library, 350 N Wilmot Rd, 85711. SAN 328-588X. Tel: 520-873-3925. FAX: 520-873-6554. *Librn, Supvr,* Michelle Bureau; E-mail: mbureau@carondelet.org
Library Holdings: Bk Vols 800
Subject Interests: Ophthalmology
Wireless access
Open Mon-Fri 8-4:30

SR SAINT MARK'S PRESBYTERIAN CHURCH LIBRARY*, 3809 E Third St, 85716. SAN 373-3890. Tel: 520-325-1001. FAX: 520-327-4599. *Librn,* Don Dickinson
Jan 2007-Dec 2007. Mats Exp $500
Library Holdings: AV Mats 100; Bk Titles 2,500; Bk Vols 4,000
Subject Interests: Border studies, Counseling, Marriage, Philos, Relig, Theol
Open Sun 8-Noon

SR ST THOMAS MORE CATHOLIC NEWMAN CENTER*, 1615 E Second St, 85719, SAN 300-4589. Tel: 520-327-6662. FAX: 520-327-6559. E-mail: newman@uacatholic.org. Web Site: www.uacatholic.org. *Dir,* Fr Bartholomew Hutcherson; E-mail: frbart@uacatholic.org
Founded 1952
Library Holdings: Bk Vols 4,100; Per Subs 15
Subject Interests: Catholicism, Philos, Psychol, Theol
Open Mon-Fri 11-8, Sat 11-6, Sun 8am-8:30pm

S SAN XAVIER LEARNING CENTER LIBRARY*, 2018 W San Xavier Rd, 85746. SAN 377-0761. Tel: 520-807-8621. FAX: 520-807-8689. *Dir,* Yvonne Corella; *Coordr,* Gertie Lopez; E-mail: glopez@waknet.org
Library Holdings: Bk Vols 2,000
Open Mon-Fri 8-5

R TEMPLE EMANUEL LIBRARY*, 225 N Country Club Rd, 85716. SAN 300-4619. Tel: 520-327-4501. FAX: 520-327-4504. Web Site: www.templeemanueltucson.org. *Exec Dir,* Donna Beyer; E-mail: dbeyer@templeemanueltucson.org
Founded 1910
Library Holdings: Bk Titles 9,500; Per Subs 10
Subject Interests: Fiction, Judaica (lit or hist of Jews), Relig orders

S TOHONO CHUL PARK LIBRARY*, 7366 N Paseo del Norte, 85704. SAN 375-6572. Tel: 520-742-6455, Ext 228. FAX: 520-797-1213. *Pub Prog Dir,* Jo Falls; E-mail: jfalls@tohonochul.org
Founded 1985
Library Holdings: Bk Titles 600
Special Collections: Desert Plants (Boyce Thompson Arboretum); Journal of Arizona Archaelogical & Historical Society; Journal of Arizona History
Function: Ref serv available, Res libr

S TUCSON ELECTRIC POWER CO LIBRARY*, 3950 E Irvington, 85714-2114. (Mail add: PO Box 711, 85702-0711), SAN 300-4635. Tel: 520-745-3318. FAX: 520-571-4019. *Mgr, Libr Serv,* Jan Prideaux; E-mail: jprideaux@tucsonelectric.com
Founded 1974
Library Holdings: Bk Vols 1,100; Per Subs 325

S TUCSON MUSEUM OF ART*, Research Library, 140 N Main Ave, 85701-8290. SAN 300-466X. Tel: 520-624-2333, Ext 122. FAX: 520-624-7202. E-mail: library@tucsonmuseumofart.org. Web Site: www.tucsonmuseumofart.org. *Chief Exec Officer,* Robert Knight; *Res Librn,* Lisa Bunker; Staff 13 (MLS 1, Non-MLS 12)
Founded 1974
Jul 2006-Jun 2007. Mats Exp $10,000
Library Holdings: AV Mats 25; DVDs 20; Bk Titles 13,000; Bk Vols 13,500; Per Subs 18; Videos 150
Special Collections: American Art (Lee & Pam Parry Coll); Archival Papers of Arizona Artists, including John Maul, Charles Clement & Ray Strang; Artists Biography Files; Dorcas Worsley Contemporary & Latin American Coll; Extensive Print & Slide Colls of Precolumbian, Art of the Americas, Art of the West, 20th Century European & American Art, Folk Art, Contemporary Art, Arts & Crafts Movement, African & Oceanic Art; Folk Art (Berta Wright Coll); Precolumbian Art (Frederick Pleasant Coll)
Subject Interests: Art hist, Art of the Americas, Contemporary art, Folk art, Modern art, Pre-Columbian art, Spanish colonial art
Automation Activity & Vendor Info: (OPAC) Innovative Interfaces, Inc; (Serials) EBSCO Online
Function: Archival coll, Outside serv via phone, mail, e-mail & web, Photocopying/Printing, Ref serv available, Referrals accepted, Res libr, Telephone ref
Open Tues-Thurs 10-3
Restriction: Circ limited
Friends of the Library Group

SR UNITARIAN UNIVERSALIST CHURCH LIBRARY*, 4831 E 22nd St, 85711-4903. SAN 374-7719. Tel: 520-748-1551. FAX: 520-748-0178. E-mail: uu1@qwestoffice.net. Web Site: www.uuctucson.org. *Adminr,* Mary Wiese
Library Holdings: Bk Vols 300
Open Mon-Fri 8-5

C UNIVERSITY OF ARIZONA*, Main Library, 1510 E University Blvd, 85721. (Mail add: PO Box 210055, 85721-0055), SAN 330-7891. Tel: 520-621-6442, 520-621-6443. Circulation Tel: 520-621-6406. Interlibrary Loan Service Tel: 520-621-6438. Administration Tel: 520-621-5079. Interlibrary Loan Service FAX: 520-621-4619. Administration FAX: 520-621-9733. Web Site: www.library.arizona.edu. *Dean of Libr,* Karen Williams; E-mail: karenwilliams@email.arizona.edu; *Asst Dean, Tech Strategy,* Jeremy Frumkin; Staff 186 (MLS 71, Non-MLS 115)
Founded 1891. Enrl 36,805; Fac 2,101; Highest Degree: Doctorate
Library Holdings: Bk Vols 5,050,074; Per Subs 23,280
Special Collections: Arizoniana; Drama (W Stevens Coll); Fine Arts (Hanley Coll); Food & Agr Orgn & European Econ Community; Mexican Colonial History Coll; Photography as an Art Form (Center for Creative Photography); Private Press (Frank Holme Coll); Southwestern Americana. Oral History; US Document Depository
Subject Interests: Fiction, Hist of sci
Automation Activity & Vendor Info: (Acquisitions) Innovative Interfaces, Inc; (Cataloging) Innovative Interfaces, Inc; (Circulation) Innovative Interfaces, Inc
Database Vendor: EBSCOhost, Gale Cengage Learning, Innovative Interfaces, Inc, LexisNexis, OCLC FirstSearch, OVID Technologies, ProQuest, Wilson - Wilson Web
Wireless access
Function: Res libr
Publications: Arizona Index; Center for Creative Photography (Journal); Guide to Chicano Resources; Index to Arizona News in the Arizona Daily Star; Library Information Guides
Partic in Association of Research Libraries (ARL)
Special Services for the Deaf - Bks on deafness & sign lang; High interest/low vocabulary bks; Spec interest per
Friends of the Library Group
Departmental Libraries:
CM ARIZONA HEALTH SCIENCES LIBRARY, 1501 N Campbell Ave, 85724. (Mail add: PO Box 245079, 85724-5079), SAN 330-7921. Tel: 520-626-6121. Interlibrary Loan Service Tel: 520-626-6438. Information Services Tel: 520-626-6125. FAX: 520-626-2922. E-mail: refdesk@ahsl.arizona.edu. Web Site: ahsl.arizona.edu. *Dir,* Gary A Freiburger; E-mail: garyf@ahsl.arizona.edu; *Dep Dir,* Jeanette L Ryan; Tel: 520-626-6143, E-mail: jeanette@ahsl.arizona.edu; *Asst Dir, Info & Access,* Joan B Schlimgen; Tel: 520-626-6140, E-mail: joan@ahsl.arizona.edu; *Asst Dir, User Support & Serv,* Sandra Kramer; E-mail: skramer@ahsl.arizona.edu; *Head, Coll Serv,* Mary Holcomb; Tel: 520-626-2924, E-mail: mholcomb@ahsl.arizona.edu; *AZHIN Librn,*

Brooke Billman; Tel: 520-626-1544, E-mail: Brooke.billman@ahsl.arizona.edu; *Digital Res Librn,* Dave Piper; Tel: 520-626-2529, E-mail: dpiper@ahsl.arizona.edu; *Emerging Tech Librn,* Position Currently Open; *Info Serv Librn,* Dr Carol Howe; Tel: 520-626-2739, E-mail: chowe@ahsl.arizona.edu; *Info Serv Librn,* Jennifer Martin; Tel: 520-626-6344, E-mail: jennifer@ahsl.arizona.edu; *Info Serv Librn,* Annabelle Nunez; Tel: 520-626-7172, E-mail: anunez@ahsl.arizona.edu; *Info Serv Librn,* Mary Riordan; Tel: 520-626-3510, E-mail: mriordan@ahsl.arizona.edu; *Info Serv Librn,* Dr Ahlam Saleh; Tel: 520-626-5450, E-mail: Asaleh@ahsl.arizona.edu; *Info Serv Librn,* Mari Stoddard; Tel: 520-626-2925, E-mail: stoddard@ahsl.arizona.edu; *Outreach Serv Librn,* Yamila El-Khayat; E-mail: yme@ahsl.arizona.edu. Subject Specialists: *Med,* Dr Carol Howe; *Pharm,* Jennifer Martin; *Pub health,* Annabelle Nunez; *Med res,* Dr Ahlam Saleh; *Pub health,* Mari Stoddard; Staff 23.96 (MLS 16.33, Non-MLS 7.63)
Founded 1965. Highest Degree: Doctorate
Library Holdings: Bk Titles 88,029; Bk Vols 219,193; Per Subs 2,194
Special Collections: Arizona Health Sciences Center & History of Health Care; The Healing Arts in the Southwest, archives
Subject Interests: Med, Nursing, Pharm, Pub health
Automation Activity & Vendor Info: (Acquisitions) Innovative Interfaces, Inc - Millenium; (Cataloging) Innovative Interfaces, Inc - Millenium; (Circulation) Innovative Interfaces, Inc - Millenium; (OPAC) Innovative Interfaces, Inc - Millenium; (Serials) Innovative Interfaces, Inc - Millenium
Partic in Ariz Univ Librs Coun; Arizona Health Information Network (AZHIN); Greater Western Library Alliance; National Network of Libraries of Medicine; Pacific Southwest Regional Medical Library (PSRML)
Restriction: Borrowing privileges limited to fac & registered students, In-house use for visitors, Med & nursing staff, patients & families

EAST ASIAN COLLECTION, 1510 E University Blvd, 85720. (Mail add: PO Box 210055, 85721-0055). Tel: 520-307-2773. Reference Tel: 520-621-6384. FAX: 520-621-3655. TDD: 520-621-6443. *Librn,* Ping Situ; E-mail: psitu@email.arizona.edu. Subject Specialists: *Chinese studies,* Ping Situ
Library Holdings: Bk Titles 86,500; Bk Vols 200,000; Per Subs 239
Subject Interests: Chinese, Japanese studies
Friends of the Library Group

MUSIC COLLECTION, 1510 E University Blvd, 85721-0055. Tel: 520-621-7009. *Libr Operations Supvr,* Michelle Monroe-Menjugas

CL JAMES E ROGERS COLLEGE OF LAW LIBRARY, 1201 E Speedway, 85721. (Mail add: PO Box 210176, 85721-0176). Circulation Tel: 520-626-8023. Reference Tel: 520-621-5455. FAX: 520-621-3138. Web Site: www.law.arizona.edu/library. *Assoc Dean, Info,* Michael G Chiorazzi; E-mail: chiorazm@email.arizona.edu; *Head, Pub Serv,* Shaun Esposito; E-mail: sesposit@email.arizona.edu; *Coll Mgt Librn,* Jezerik Gaddoura; *Ref Librn,* Sarah Gotschall; E-mail: sgotscha@email.arizona.edu; *Access Serv,* Maureen Garmon; E-mail: mgarmon@email.arizona.edu; *Cat,* Kerin McPherson; *Ref,* Leah Sandwell-Weiss; E-mail: rsweiss@email.arizona.edu
Founded 1915
Library Holdings: Bk Titles 66,000; Bk Vols 400,000; Per Subs 4,500
Subject Interests: Natural res
Function: Photocopying/Printing
Partic in OCLC Online Computer Library Center, Inc
Restriction: Not a lending libr, Open to fac, students & qualified researchers

SCIENCE-ENGINEERING, 744 N Highland, Bldg 54, 85721. (Mail add: PO Box 210054, 85721-0054). Tel: 520-621-6384. FAX: 520-621-3655. *Br Head,* Jeanne Pfander; E-mail: jpfander@email.arizona.edu
Open Mon-Thurs 7:30-1, Fri 7:30-6, Sat 9-6, Sun 11-1

SPACE IMAGERY CENTER, 1629 E University Blvd, 85721-0092, SAN 321-6721. Tel: 520-621-2870. FAX: 520-621-4933. Web Site: www.lpl.arizona.edu/sic. *Dir,* Timothy Swindle; *Librn,* Lisa Martin
Founded 1977
Special Collections: Apollo; Clementine; Lunar Orbiter; Magellan, etc; Mariner 6, 7, 9, 10; Mars Global Surveyor; Pioneer 10 & 11; Space Probes - Gemini; Viking 1 & 2; Voyager 1 & 2
Subject Interests: Planetary sci
Open Mon, Wed & Fri 8-12 & 1-5, Tues & Thurs 10:30-5

SPECIAL COLLECTIONS, 1510 E University, 85721. (Mail add: PO Box 210055, 85721-0055). Tel: 520-621-6423. FAX: 520-621-2709. *Archivist,* Roger Myers; Tel: 520-621-4345, E-mail: jrmyers@email.arizona.edu
Partic in Arizona Universities Library Consortium (AULC)
Friends of the Library Group

WHITERIVER

P WHITERIVER PUBLIC LIBRARY*, 100 E Walnut St, 85941. (Mail add: PO Box 370, 85941-0370), SAN 300-4716. Tel: 928-338-4884. FAX: 928-338-4470. *Librn,* Carmen Perry
Founded 1934. Pop 10,000
Library Holdings: Bk Titles 12,000; Per Subs 25
Special Collections: Arizona Coll
Automation Activity & Vendor Info: (Cataloging) SirsiDynix; (Circulation) SirsiDynix; (OPAC) SirsiDynix
Open Mon-Thurs 10-5

WICKENBURG

S DESERT CABALLEROS WESTERN MUSEUM*, Blossom Memorial Library, 21 N Frontier St, 85390. SAN 375-7579. Tel: 928-684-2272. FAX: 928-684-5794. Web Site: www.westernmuseum.org. *Exec Dir,* W James Burns, PhD
Founded 1960
Library Holdings: Bk Titles 1,500
Open Mon-Fri 10-5

P WICKENBURG PUBLIC LIBRARY, 164 E Apache St, 85390. SAN 300-4724. Tel: 928-684-2665. Web Site: wickenburg.polarislibrary.com. *Librn,* Jane Horsefield; Staff 4 (MLS 1, Non-MLS 3)
Founded 1942. Pop 11,000; Circ 134,687
Library Holdings: Audiobooks 506; CDs 874; DVDs 1,206; Large Print Bks 1,484; Bk Titles 40,000; Bk Vols 41,110; Per Subs 32; Talking Bks 822; Videos 1,671
Special Collections: History (Southwest Coll)
Automation Activity & Vendor Info: (Cataloging) Innovative Interfaces, Inc; (Circulation) Innovative Interfaces, Inc
Wireless access
Function: Adult bk club, Bks on cassette, Bks on CD, Children's prog, Computers for patron use, Free DVD rentals, Handicapped accessible, Music CDs, Online cat, Summer reading prog, Tax forms, VHS videos, Web-catalog
Open Mon-Fri 8:30-5
Friends of the Library Group

WILHOIT

P WILHOIT PUBLIC LIBRARY*, 9325 Donegal Dr, Ste B, 86332. Tel: 928-442-3611. FAX: 928-442-2407. Web Site: www.yavapailibrary.org/yavapai/wilhoit.asp. *Librn,* Marcia Schmitt; E-mail: marcia.schmitt@yavapai.us; *Asst Librn,* Lanny LeForte
Library Holdings: Bk Vols 3,600
Automation Activity & Vendor Info: (Cataloging) SirsiDynix; (Circulation) SirsiDynix; (OPAC) SirsiDynix
Wireless access
Mem of Yavapai County Free Library District
Open Tues-Sat 11-4

WILLCOX

P ELSIE S HOGAN COMMUNITY LIBRARY*, 100 N Curtis Ave, 85643. SAN 330-5376. Tel: 520-766-4250. FAX: 520-384-0126. *Dir,* Tom Miner; E-mail: tminer@willcoxcity.org; Staff 4 (Non-MLS 4)
Founded 1923. Pop 6,415; Circ 35,497
Library Holdings: Bk Titles 30,016; Per Subs 30
Automation Activity & Vendor Info: (Acquisitions) Baker & Taylor; (Cataloging) SirsiDynix; (Circulation) SirsiDynix; (ILL) SirsiDynix; (OPAC) SirsiDynix
Database Vendor: EBSCOhost, HeinOnline, OCLC FirstSearch
Wireless access
Function: e-mail serv, E-Reserves, Electronic databases & coll, Equip loans & repairs, Exhibits, Games & aids for the handicapped, Genealogy discussion group, Handicapped accessible, Holiday prog, ILL available, Instruction & testing, Literacy & newcomer serv, Magnifiers for reading, Mail & tel request accepted, Microfiche/film & reading machines, Music CDs, Newsp ref libr, Notary serv, Online cat, Online searches, Outreach serv, Outside serv via phone, mail, e-mail & web, OverDrive digital audio bks, Photocopying/Printing, Preschool outreach, Preschool reading prog, Printer for laptops & handheld devices, Prog for adults, Prog for children & young adult, Pub access computers, Ref & res, Senior computer classes, Senior outreach, Serves mentally handicapped consumers, Spanish lang bks, Spoken cassettes & DVDs, Story hour, Summer reading prog, Tax forms, Teen prog, VHS videos, Video lending libr, Wheelchair accessible, Workshops
Mem of Cochise County Library District
Special Services for the Blind - Aids for in-house use; Assistive/Adapted tech devices, equip & products; Audio mat; Bks & mags in Braille, on rec, tape & cassette; Bks available with recordings
Open Mon-Wed 10-6, Thurs 10-7, Fri 9-5, Sat 9-2
Friends of the Library Group

G UNITED STATES NATIONAL PARK SERVICE*, Chiricahua National Monument Library, 13063 E Bonita Canyon Rd, 85643-9737. SAN 375-2259. Tel: 520-824-3560. FAX: 520-824-3421. Web Site: www.nps.gov/chir. *In Charge,* Julena Campbell
Founded 1924
Library Holdings: Bk Titles 4,000

Function: For res purposes
Restriction: Access at librarian's discretion

WILLIAMS

P WILLIAMS PUBLIC LIBRARY*, 113 S First St, 86046. SAN 300-4740. Tel: 928-635-2263. FAX: 928-635-4495. *Librn,* Andrea Mary Dunn; Staff 1 (Non-MLS 1)
Founded 1895. Pop 2,800; Circ 14,450
Library Holdings: Bk Titles 10,000; Bk Vols 11,000; Per Subs 20
Subject Interests: Arizona
Mem of Flagstaff City-Coconino County Public Library System
Open Tues-Thurs 9-5 & 6-8, Fri 9-5:30, Sat 9-1

WINDOW ROCK

S OFFICE OF NAVAJO NATION LIBRARY*, Hwy 264, Post Office Loop Rd, 86515. (Mail add: PO Box 9040, 86515-9040), SAN 321-0693. Tel: 928-871-6376, 928-871-6526. FAX: 928-871-7304. Web Site: nnlib.org. *Supvr,* Irving Nelson; Tel: 928-871-7303, E-mail: inelson979@yahoo.com; Staff 14 (MLS 6, Non-MLS 8)
Founded 1941
Library Holdings: Bk Titles 66,290; Per Subs 135
Special Collections: Navajo History & Culture
Subject Interests: Archaeology
Wireless access
Open Mon 8-5, Tues-Fri 8-8, Sat 9-5

WINKELMAN

C CENTRAL ARIZONA COLLEGE*, Aravaipa Campus Learning Resource Center, 80440 E Aravaipa Rd, 85292. Tel: 520-357-2821. FAX: 520-357-2832. Web Site: www.centralaz.edu. *Dir,* Adriana Saavedra; E-mail: adriana.saavedra@centralaz.edu
Enrl 260; Fac 6; Highest Degree: Associate
Library Holdings: Bk Vols 35,000
Database Vendor: Gale Cengage Learning, Newsbank
Function: AV serv
Special Services for the Deaf - Assistive tech
Open Mon-Thurs 8am-7:30pm, Fri 8-4:30

WINSLOW

S ARIZONA DEPARTMENT OF CORRECTIONS - ADULT INSTITUTIONS*, Arizona State Prison Complex Winslow Library, 2100 S Hwy 87, 86047. Tel: 928-289-9551, Ext 6538. FAX: 928-289-9551, Ext 6553.
Library Holdings: Bk Vols 15,000
Open Mon-Fri 7-3:30

S ARIZONA STATE PARKS*, Homolovi Ruins State Park Library, Homolovi Ruins Visitor Center, SR 87 one mile N of I-40, 86047. (Mail add: HC63 Box 5, 86047), SAN 371-2788. Tel: 928-289-4106. FAX: 928-289-2021. E-mail: library@homolovi.com. *Librn,* Chad Muiner
Library Holdings: Bk Vols 3,000
Special Collections: Indian Culture Archeolology

P WINSLOW PUBLIC LIBRARY*, 420 W Gilmore St, 86047. SAN 300-4767. Tel: 928-289-4982. FAX: 928-289-4182. E-mail: win@winslow.lib.az.us. Web Site: www.navajoco.lib.az.us, www.winslowarizona.com. *Dir,* Docia Blalock; *Adult Serv,* Michele Hernandez; *Circ,* Sandy Fulton; Staff 5 (MLS 2, Non-MLS 3)
Founded 1969. Pop 15,000; Circ 31,000
Library Holdings: High Interest/Low Vocabulary Bk Vols 100; Bk Titles 27,000; Bk Vols 29,250; Per Subs 90
Special Collections: Arizona History
Subject Interests: Indians
Automation Activity & Vendor Info: (Cataloging) SirsiDynix; (Circulation) SirsiDynix; (OPAC) SirsiDynix
Database Vendor: OCLC FirstSearch
Mem of Washington County Library System
Partic in Channeled Ariz Info Network; Navajo County Libr District
Special Services for the Deaf - TDD equip
Special Services for the Blind - Talking bks
Open Tues, Thurs & Fri 10-5, Wed 10-7, Sat 10-2
Friends of the Library Group

WOODRUFF

P WOODRUFF COMMUNITY LIBRARY, 6414 W First St, 85942. (Mail add: PO Box 77, 85942-0077). Tel: 928-524-3885. FAX: 928-524-3885. E-mail: wcl@navajo.lib.az.us. Web Site: www.navajoco.lib.az.us. *Dir,* Darlynn Mobley; E-mail: darlynnmobley@hotmail.com
Library Holdings: Bk Vols 4,500
Automation Activity & Vendor Info: (Cataloging) SirsiDynix; (Circulation) SirsiDynix
Database Vendor: OCLC FirstSearch
Open Tues & Thurs 10-12 & 4-6, Sat 10-2

YARNELL

P YARNELL PUBLIC LIBRARY*, 22278 N Hwy 89, 85362. (Mail add: PO Box 808, 85362), SAN 323-8032. Tel: 928-427-3191. FAX: 928-427-3191. Web Site: www.yavapailibrary.org/yavapai/yarnell.asp. *Commun Librn,* Christina Cooper
Library Holdings: AV Mats 800; Bk Vols 7,000; Per Subs 20; Talking Bks 1,000
Special Collections: Local Archives
Automation Activity & Vendor Info: (Cataloging) SirsiDynix; (Circulation) SirsiDynix; (OPAC) SirsiDynix
Mem of Yavapai County Free Library District
Open Mon-Fri 9:30-4:30, Sat 9:30-2:30

YOUNG

P YOUNG PUBLIC LIBRARY, 123 S Midway Ave, 85554. (Mail add: PO Box 150, 85554), SAN 300-4783. Tel: 928-462-3588. FAX: 928-462-3588. *Dir,* Elizabeth J Hutton; E-mail: ejhutton@gcldaz.org; *Asst Librn,* Lynnette Carter
Founded 1984. Pop 850; Circ 3,790
Library Holdings: AV Mats 250; Bks on Deafness & Sign Lang 25; CDs 150; Large Print Bks 350; Bk Vols 18,000; Per Subs 4; Talking Bks 120; Videos 800
Special Collections: Southwest Nonfiction; Western Fiction
Wireless access
Function: Adult literacy prog, Handicapped accessible, ILL available, Photocopying/Printing, Prog for children & young adult, Summer reading prog, Wheelchair accessible
Mem of Gila County Library District
Open Tues-Fri 12-5, Sat 10-2

YOUNGTOWN

P YOUNGTOWN PUBLIC LIBRARY*, 12035 Clubhouse Sq, 85363. SAN 300-4791. Tel: 623-974-3401. *Libr Mgr,* Heidi Speed; E-mail: hspeed@youngtownaz.org
Founded 1956. Pop 2,500; Circ 14,000
Library Holdings: Bk Titles 8,500
Special Collections: Arizona & Southwestern
Automation Activity & Vendor Info: (Cataloging) Follett Software; (Circulation) Follett Software
Open Mon-Wed & Fri 10-4, Thurs 10-7, Sat 10-1

YUMA

S ARIZONA HISTORICAL SOCIETY LIBRARY*, Rio Colorado Division, 240 Madison Ave, 85364. SAN 300-4821. Tel: 928-782-1841. FAX: 928-783-0680. E-mail: ahsyuma@azhs.gov. Web Site: arizonahistoricalsociety.org. *Curator,* Joseph Meehan; E-mail: jmeehan@azhs.gov
Founded 1963
Library Holdings: Bk Titles 500
Special Collections: Lower Colorado River Area Historical Photographs; Military Oral History Tapes-WWII Period. Oral History
Open Tues-Fri 10-4
Restriction: Non-circulating, Open by appt only

J ARIZONA WESTERN COLLEGE*, Academic Library, 2020 S Ave 8E, 85366. (Mail add: PO Box 929, 85366-0929), SAN 300-4805. Tel: 928-344-7777. FAX: 928-344-7751. E-mail: library@azwestern.edu. Web Site: www.azwestern.edu/library. *Dir, Libr Serv,* Angie Creel; E-mail: angie.creel@azwestern.edu; *Acq Librn,* Tymmi Woods; *IT Librn,* Wendy Hoag; *Circ,* Julie Williamson; *Distance Educ,* Tina Sibley; *ILL,* Rickley Prewitt; *Ref,* Camille O'Neill; *Ref,* Renee Westphal; Staff 11 (MLS 6, Non-MLS 5)
Founded 1963. Enrl 5,000; Fac 150; Highest Degree: Associate
Library Holdings: Bk Titles 84,000; Bk Vols 90,000; Per Subs 463
Special Collections: SouthWest Border Coll
Automation Activity & Vendor Info: (Acquisitions) SirsiDynix; (Cataloging) SirsiDynix; (Circulation) SirsiDynix; (Course Reserve) SirsiDynix; (OPAC) SirsiDynix; (Serials) SirsiDynix
Database Vendor: OCLC FirstSearch
Function: Audio & video playback equip for onsite use, Bks on cassette, Bks on CD, Computers for patron use, Copy machines, Distance learning, Doc delivery serv, e-mail & chat, Electronic databases & coll, Free DVD rentals, Govt ref serv, Music CDs, Online info literacy tutorials on the web & in blackboard, Online ref, Orientations, Outside serv via phone, mail, e-mail & web, Photocopying/Printing, Pub access computers, Ref & res, Ref serv in person, Tax forms, VHS videos
Partic in OCLC Online Computer Library Center, Inc

A UNITED STATES ARMY*, Yuma Proving Ground Post Library, Bldg 530, 301 C St, 85365-9848. SAN 330-8286. Tel: 928-328-2558. Interlibrary Loan Service Tel: 928-328-3068. FAX: 928-328-3055. *Librn,* Carol A Cowperthwaite; Staff 2 (Non-MLS 2)
Founded 1953
Library Holdings: AV Mats 1,774; Bk Vols 43,256; Per Subs 24; Talking Bks 704
Subject Interests: Arizona
Automation Activity & Vendor Info: (Acquisitions) Bibliomation Inc; (Cataloging) OCLC; (Circulation) Horizon; (ILL) OCLC; (OPAC) Horizon
Partic in OCLC Online Computer Library Center, Inc
Open Tues-Thurs 10-7, Fri & Sat 10-6

A UNITED STATES MARINE CORPS*, Station Library, Bldg 633, 85369. (Mail add: PO Box 99119, 85369-9119), SAN 330-8340. Tel: 928-269-2785. FAX: 928-344-5592. *Mgr,* Bonnie Miller
Founded 1948
Library Holdings: Bk Vols 20,500; Per Subs 93
Subject Interests: Aviation

GL YUMA COUNTY LAW LIBRARY*, 168 S Second Ave, Ste L, 85364-2364. SAN 300-483X. Tel: 928-817-4165. *Librn,* Margi Castaneda
Library Holdings: Bk Vols 16,000
Subject Interests: Law
Open Mon-Fri 8-5

P YUMA COUNTY LIBRARY DISTRICT, Main Library, 2951 S 21st Dr, 85364. SAN 330-8375. Tel: 928-782-1871. Circulation Tel: 928-373-6492. Interlibrary Loan Service Tel: 928-373-6504. Administration Tel: 928-373-6460. Automation Services Tel: 928-373-6467. Information Services Tel: 928-373-6482, 928-373-6513. FAX: 928-782-9420. E-mail: librarian@yumalibrary.org. Web Site: yumalibrary.org. *Dir of Libr,* Susan M Evans; Tel: 928-373-6462, E-mail: sevans@yumalibrary.org; *Asst Dir,* Position Currently Open; *Electronic Serv Librn,* Jocelyn Bates; Tel: 928-314-2440, E-mail: jocelyn.bates@yumalibrary.org; *Librn,* Rebecca Brendel; Tel: 928-373-2453, E-mail: becky.brendel@yumalibrary.org; *Librn,* James Patrick; Tel: 928-373-6484, E-mail: jpatrick@yumalibrary.org; *Bus Off Adminr,* Arthur S Duran; Tel: 928-373-6463, E-mail: sduran@yumalibrary.org; *Fund Develop Officer,* Cecilia Young; Tel: 928-373-6495, E-mail: cyoung@yumalibrary.org; *Admin Mgr,* Lana L Heston; E-mail: lheston@yumalibrary.org; *Coll Mgr,* Bryan Summers; Tel: 928-373-6502, E-mail: bsummers@yumalibrary.org; *Commun Relations Mgr,* Sarah Wisdom; Tel: 928-373-6483, E-mail: swisdom@yumalibrary.org; *Info Serv Mgr,* Brian Franssen; Tel: 928-373-6480, E-mail: bfranssen@yumalibrary.org; *IT Mgr,* Joanne Jin; E-mail: jlee@yumalibrary.org; *Teen Serv Mgr,* Lauren Regenhardt; Tel: 928-373-6487, E-mail: lauren.regenhardt@yumalibrary.org; *Youth Serv Mgr,* Hannah Stewart; Tel: 928-373-6494, E-mail: hannah.stewart@yumalibrary.org; *Circ Supvr,* Sandra Nicasio; Tel: 928-373-6491, E-mail: snicasio@yumalibrary.org; *Computer Lab/Per Supvr,* Jerry Mendez; Tel: 928-314-2456, E-mail: jmendez@yumalibrary.org; *Adul Prog Coordr/LAII,* Nicole Perez; E-mail: nicole.perez@yumalibrary.org; *LAII Teen/Spanish Outreach Coordr,* Alex Garcia; Tel: 928-373-6481, E-mail: agarcia@yumalibrary.org; *Homebound Serv, ILL,* Sylvia Moore; Tel: 928-373-6488, E-mail: smoore@yumalibrary.org; *Homebound Serv/Computer Access,* David Monypeny; E-mail: dmonypeny@yumalibrary.org. Subject Specialists: *Pub relations,* Sarah Wisdom; Staff 95.58 (MLS 20, Non-MLS 75.58)
Founded 2009. Pop 209,323; Circ 765,249
Jul 2013-Jun 2014 Income (Main Library and Branch(s)) $6,528,634, State $23,000, Federal $30,000, County $6,021,556, Other $454,078. Mats Exp $1,344,674, Books $511,471, Other Print Mats $206,777, AV Mat $626,426. Sal $4,341,948 (Prof $39,542)
Library Holdings: Audiobooks 36,631; e-books 39,836; Bk Vols 427,616; Per Subs 669; Videos 26,259
Special Collections: AHS Rio Colorado Coll (Yuma History Coll); Arizona Room (Arizona & Local History)
Subject Interests: Arizona, Local hist
Automation Activity & Vendor Info: (Acquisitions) SirsiDynix; (Circulation) SirsiDynix; (ILL) OCLC ILLiad; (OPAC) SirsiDynix; (Serials) SirsiDynix
Database Vendor: 3M Library Systems, Amigos Library Services, Baker & Taylor, Booksite, Bowker, Brodart, BWI, EBSCO Auto Repair Reference, EBSCO Information Services, EBSCOhost, Foundation Center, Gale Cengage Learning, Grolier Online, Newsbank, Norman Lathrop Enterprises, OCLC FirstSearch, OCLC WebJunction, OCLC WorldShare Interlibrary Loan, Overdrive, Inc, ProQuest, SirsiDynix, WebMD
Wireless access
Function: Adult bk club, Adult literacy prog, After school storytime, Audiobks via web, Bilingual assistance for Spanish patrons, Bk club(s), Bk reviews (Group), Children's prog, Computer training, Computers for patron use, Copy machines, Free DVD rentals, Genealogy discussion group, Handicapped accessible, Holiday prog, Home delivery & serv to Sr ctr & nursing homes, Homebound delivery serv, Homework prog, ILL available, Microfiche/film & reading machines, Music CDs, Newsp ref libr, Notary serv, Online cat, Online ref, Online searches, Outreach serv, OverDrive digital audio bks, Photocopying/Printing, Preschool outreach, Preschool reading prog, Prog for adults, Prog for children & young adult, Pub access computers, Ref serv available, Ref serv in person, Senior computer classes, Senior outreach, Spanish lang bks, Spoken cassettes & DVDs, Story hour, Summer & winter reading prog, Summer reading prog, Tax forms, Teen prog, Telephone ref, Wheelchair accessible, Winter reading prog, Words travel prog, Workshops, Writing prog
Special Services for the Deaf - Assisted listening device; Assistive tech; Bks on deafness & sign lang; TDD equip; TTY equip
Special Services for the Blind - Assistive/Adapted tech devices, equip & products; Audio mat; BiFolkal kits; Bks on cassette; Bks on CD; Computer with voice synthesizer for visually impaired persons; Copier with enlargement capabilities; Home delivery serv; Large print bks; Lending of low vision aids; Magnifiers
Open Mon-Thurs 9-9, Fri & Sat 9-5
Friends of the Library Group
Branches: 7
DATELAND BRANCH, Ave 64E & Interstate 8, Dateland, 85333. (Mail add: PO Box 3000, Dateland, 85333). Tel: 928-454-2242. FAX: 928-454-2217. *Libr Asst II,* Lucy Shaw; E-mail: lshaw@yumalibrary.org; Staff 0.5 (Non-MLS 0.5)
Pop 584; Circ 3,218
Library Holdings: Audiobooks 1,214; Bk Vols 14,316; Videos 474
Open Mon, Wed & Fri 8:30-3, Tues & Thurs 8:30-5
FOOTHILLS BRANCH, 13226 E South Frontage Rd, 85367. SAN 328-6827. Tel: 928-342-1640. Circulation Tel: 928-373-6522. Information Services Tel: 928-314-2444. FAX: 928-305-0497. *Br Mgr,* Dorey Conway; Tel: 928-373-6509, E-mail: dorey.conway@yumalibrary.org; *Librn,* Vanna Nguyen; Tel: 928-373-6524, E-mail: vanna.nguyen@yumalibrary.org; Staff 9.03 (MLS 2, Non-MLS 7.03)
Pop 28,135; Circ 140,690
Library Holdings: Audiobooks 4,754; Bk Vols 57,404; Videos 3,184
Open Tues-Thurs 10-7, Fri & Sat 10-5
Friends of the Library Group
HERITAGE BRANCH, 350 Third Ave, 85364. Tel: 928-783-5415. Circulation Tel: 928-373-6515. Information Services Tel: 928-373-6516. FAX: 928-783-5840. *Br Mgr,* Bryce Rumbles; Tel: 928-373-6531, E-mail: bryce.rumbles@yumalibrary.org; *Librn,* Rand Alkire; Tel: 928-373-6486, E-mail: rand.beltran@yumalibrary.org; *Librn,* James Patrick; E-mail: jpatrick@yumalibrary.org; *Spec Coll Librn,* Laurie Boone; Tel: 928-373-6468, E-mail: lboone@yumalibrary.org; Staff 7.45 (MLS 2.5, Non-MLS 4.95)
Circ 44,208
Library Holdings: Audiobooks 4,832; Bk Vols 58,079; Videos 3,296
Special Collections: Arizona Historical Society Rio Colorado Coll
Open Tues-Thurs 10-7, Fri & Sat 10-5
Friends of the Library Group
ROLL BRANCH, 5151 S Ave 39E, Roll, 85347. Tel: 928-785-3701. FAX: 928-785-3701. *Libr Asst II,* Lucy Shaw; Tel: 928-785-9575, E-mail: lshaw@yumalibrary.org; Staff 0.5 (Non-MLS 0.5)
Pop 573; Circ 2,597
Library Holdings: Audiobooks 1,348; Bk Vols 15,208; Videos 551
Open Mon, Tues & Thurs 8:30-3:30, Wed & Fri 8:30-5
SAN LUIS BRANCH, 1075 N Sixth Ave, San Luis, 85349. (Mail add: PO Box 1630, San Luis, 85349-1630), SAN 328-8900. Tel: 928-627-8344. FAX: 928-627-8296. *Br Mgr,* Lorenia Diaz; Tel: 928-314-2447, E-mail: lorenia.diaz@yumalibrary.org; *Librn,* Jack Hallin; Tel: 928-317-2448, E-mail: jack.hallin@yumalibrary.org; Staff 11.59 (MLS 2, Non-MLS 9.59)
Pop 31,180; Circ 66,613
Library Holdings: Audiobooks 3,788; Bk Vols 47,954; Videos 3,143
Open Tues & Wed 9-7, Thurs 9-8, Fri & Sat 9-5
Friends of the Library Group
SOMERTON BRANCH, 240 Canal St, Somerton, 85350. (Mail add: PO Box 460, Somerton, 85350-0460), SAN 330-8464. Tel: 928-627-2149. FAX: 928-627-8345. *Br Supvr,* Frances Murrietta; Tel: 928-373-6543, E-mail: fmurrietta@yumalibrary.org; Staff 5.5 (Non-MLS 5.5)
Pop 14,994; Circ 32,320
Library Holdings: Audiobooks 5,275; Bk Vols 44,861; Per Subs 50; Videos 2,223
Open Tues-Thurs 10-7, Fri & Sat 10-5
Friends of the Library Group
WELLTON BRANCH, 28790 San Jose Ave, Wellton, 85356. (Mail add: PO Box 577, Wellton, 85356-0577), SAN 330-8499. Tel: 928-785-9575. FAX: 928-785-4410. *Br Supvr,* Carol Finfrock; Tel: 928-373-6552, E-mail: cfinfrock@yumalibrary.org; Staff 4.5 (Non-MLS 4.5)
Pop 2,908; Circ 30,328
Library Holdings: Audiobooks 1,818; Bk Vols 31,416; Videos 2,202
Function: Adult bk club, Adult literacy prog, After school storytime, Audiobks via web, Bilingual assistance for Spanish patrons, Bk club(s), Bks on cassette, Bks on CD, Children's prog, Computer training, Computers for patron use, Copy machines, Electronic databases & coll, Free DVD rentals, Handicapped accessible, Holiday prog, Music CDs,

Online cat, Online ref, Online searches, OverDrive digital audio bks, Photocopying/Printing, Preschool outreach, Preschool reading prog, Prog for adults, Prog for children & young adult, Pub access computers, Ref serv available, Ref serv in person, Senior computer classes, Spanish lang bks, Story hour, Summer & winter reading prog, Telephone ref, Wheelchair accessible
Open Tues-Thurs 10-7, Fri & Sat 10-5
Restriction: Registered patrons only
Friends of the Library Group

ARKANSAS

Date of Statistics: FY 2012
Population, 2010 U.S. Census: 2,915,918
Population Served by Public Libraries: 2,718,655
Unserved: 197,263
Total Volumes in Public Libraries: 7,183,563
Volumes Per Capita: 2.46
Total Public Library Circulation: 13,934,552
Circulation Per Capita: 5.39
Total Public Library Income (including federal and state funds): $69,810,329
Sources of Income: Property tax, sales tax, state funds, gifts, and donations
Local Tax Rate: Varies from three-tenths mill to three mill

Expenditures Per Capita: $25.70
Number of County or Multi-County (Regional) Libraries:
City Public Libraries: 12
Single County Systems: 25
Multi-county Systems: 16
Counties Served: 75
Number of Bookmobiles in State: 3
Federal (Title I LSTA): nil
Total State Aid: $5,578,500 (for public libraries)
Total Federal Funds (spent for state library purposes): $1,800,586
Formula for Apportionment: Stratified
Special Uses of Two Funds: Regional library systems, automation, books, other library materials, bookmobile services

ALMA

P ALMA PUBLIC LIBRARY*, 624 Fayetteville Ave, 72921. SAN 330-9878. Tel: 479-632-4140. FAX: 479-632-6099. E-mail: alma@crawfordcountylib.org. *Br Mgr,* Melanie Allen
Library Holdings: Bk Vols 45,626
Database Vendor: EBSCOhost, OCLC FirstSearch
Mem of Crawford County Library System
Open Mon-Fri 8-6, Sat 10-2
Friends of the Library Group

ARKADELPHIA

P CLARK COUNTY LIBRARY*, 609 Caddo St, 71923. SAN 330-8553. Tel: 870-246-2271. FAX: 870-246-4189. E-mail: library22@yahoo.com. *Dir,* Judy Golden
Founded 1897. Pop 24,932; Circ 118,000
Jan 2005-Dec 2005 Income (Main Library and Branch(s)) $300,000. Mats Exp $35,000. Sal $180,000
Library Holdings: Bk Titles 90,000; Per Subs 80
Special Collections: Genealogy (Daughters of the American Revolution); History of Arkansas
Automation Activity & Vendor Info: (Cataloging) Follett Software; (Circulation) Follett Software; (OPAC) Follett Software
Open Tues-Fri 8:30-5, Sat 9-1
Branches: 1
GURDON PUBLIC, 204 E Walnut, Gurdon, 71743, SAN 330-8618. Tel: 870-353-2911. *Dir,* Judy Golden
Library Holdings: Bk Vols 20,000
Open Tues-Fri 9:30-5

C HENDERSON STATE UNIVERSITY*, Huie Library, 1100 Henderson, 71999-0001. SAN 300-4848. Tel: 870-230-5258. Reference Tel: 870-230-5292. Administration Tel: 870-230-5014. FAX: 870-230-5365. Web Site: library.hsu.edu. *Dir,* Robert Yehl; E-mail: yehlb@hsu.edu; *Cat Librn, Ref Librn,* Kathie Buckman; Tel: 870-230-5307; *Spec Coll Librn,* Lea Ann Alexander; Staff 18 (MLS 6, Non-MLS 12)
Founded 1890. Enrl 3,500; Highest Degree: Master
Library Holdings: Bk Titles 212,825; Bk Vols 255,567; Per Subs 1,478
Special Collections: Graphic novels; History of comics
Automation Activity & Vendor Info: (Acquisitions) Innovative Interfaces, Inc; (Cataloging) Innovative Interfaces, Inc; (Circulation) Innovative Interfaces, Inc; (OPAC) Innovative Interfaces, Inc; (Serials) Innovative Interfaces, Inc
Database Vendor: EBSCOhost, Gale Cengage Learning, LexisNexis, OCLC FirstSearch, OVID Technologies, ProQuest
Wireless access
Partic in BRS
Friends of the Library Group

C OUACHITA BAPTIST UNIVERSITY*, Riley-Hickingbotham Library, 410 Ouachita, OBU Box 3742, 71998-0001. SAN 330-8677. Tel: 870-245-5119. FAX: 870-245-5245. Web Site: www.obu.edu. *Dir,* Dr Ray Granade; Tel: 870-245-5121, E-mail: granade@obu.edu; *Circ, Head, Ref,* Kristi Smith; E-mail: smithk@obu.edu; *Per Librn,* Margaret Reed; Tel: 870-245-5117, E-mail: reedm@obu.edu; *Circ, Ref Librn,* Lacy S Wolfe; E-mail: wolfel@obu.edu; *Archivist,* Phyllis Kinnison; Tel: 870-245-5332; *Govt Doc,* Janice Ford; Tel: 870-245-5122, E-mail: fordj@obu.edu; *Tech Serv,* Anping Wu; Tel: 870-245-5115, E-mail: wua@obu.edu; Staff 7 (MLS 7)
Founded 1886. Enrl 1,697; Highest Degree: Bachelor
Jun 2011-May 2012 Income $760,685. Mats Exp $760,685, Books $90,000, Manu Arch $34,264, Micro $93,700, AV Mat $1,098, Electronic Ref Mat (Incl. Access Fees) $34,200
Library Holdings: Per Subs 1,032
Special Collections: Associational Minutes of the Arkansas Baptist State Convention; Papers of Governor Mike Huckabee; Papers of Representative Mike Ross; Papers of Senator John L McClellan 1940-1977. Oral History; State Document Depository; US Document Depository
Subject Interests: Educ, Humanities, Music
Automation Activity & Vendor Info: (Acquisitions) Innovative Interfaces, Inc - Millenium; (Cataloging) Innovative Interfaces, Inc - Millenium; (Circulation) Innovative Interfaces, Inc - Millenium; (Course Reserve) Innovative Interfaces, Inc - Millenium; (Media Booking) Innovative Interfaces, Inc - Millenium; (OPAC) Innovative Interfaces, Inc - Millenium; (Serials) Innovative Interfaces, Inc - Millenium
Wireless access
Open Mon-Thurs 8am-11pm, Fri 8-5, Sat 11:30-5:30, Sun 6pm-11pm

BATESVILLE

CR LYON COLLEGE, Mabee-Simpson Library, 2300 Highland Rd, 72501-3699. SAN 300-4856. Tel: 870-307-7205. Interlibrary Loan Service Tel: 870-307-7505. FAX: 870-307-7279. Web Site: library.lyon.edu. *Dir,* Dean Covington; Tel: 870-307-7206, E-mail: dean.covington@lyon.edu; *Asst Dir,* Camille Beary; Tel: 870-307-7444, E-mail: camille.beary@lyon.edu; *ILL,* Kathy Whittenton; E-mail: katherine.whittenton@lyon.edu; Staff 5 (MLS 3, Non-MLS 2)
Founded 1872. Enrl 600; Fac 42; Highest Degree: Bachelor
Jul 2014-Jun 2015. Mats Exp $184,000, Books $10,000, Per/Ser (Incl. Access Fees) $24,000, Electronic Ref Mat (Incl. Access Fees) $150,000
Library Holdings: Audiobooks 60; CDs 1,186; DVDs 1,734; e-books 23,199; e-journals 36,676; Microforms 2,928; Bk Vols 145,884; Per Subs 334; Videos 1,290
Special Collections: Arkansas & Ozark History & Culture; John Quincy Wolf Folk Music/Folklore Coll. State Document Depository
Automation Activity & Vendor Info: (Acquisitions) SirsiDynix; (Cataloging) SirsiDynix; (Circulation) SirsiDynix; (Course Reserve) SirsiDynix; (ILL) OCLC FirstSearch; (OPAC) SirsiDynix; (Serials) SirsiDynix
Database Vendor: American Chemical Society, American Psychological Association (APA), Amigos Library Services, ARTstor, BioOne,

CredoReference, EBSCO Information Services, EBSCOhost, Elsevier, JSTOR, LexisNexis, Modern Language Association, Nature Publishing Group, OCLC, OCLC FirstSearch, OCLC WorldShare Interlibrary Loan, Oxford Online, Project MUSE, ProQuest, ScienceDirect, SirsiDynix, Springshare, LLC, WT Cox
Wireless access
Partic in ARKLink
Open Mon-Thurs 8am-Midnight, Fri 8-7, Sat 1-7, Sun 2pm-Midnight
Friends of the Library Group

J ROY ROW, SR & IMOGENE ROW JOHNS LIBRARY*, 2005 White Dr, 72501. (Mail add: PO Box 3350, 72503-3350). Tel: 870-612-2020. Reference Tel: 870-612-2019. Toll Free Tel: 800-508-7878. *Dir,* Linda L Bennett; E-mail: lbennett@uaccb.edu; Staff 4 (MLS 1, Non-MLS 3)
Founded 1998. Enrl 1,300; Fac 50; Highest Degree: Associate
Jul 2006-Jun 2007. Mats Exp $24,719, Books $14,000, Per/Ser (Incl. Access Fees) $7,000, Electronic Ref Mat (Incl. Access Fees) $3,719. Sal $71,263 (Prof $44,000)
Library Holdings: e-books 9,000; Bk Titles 15,000; Bk Vols 18,000; Per Subs 150
Special Collections: Independence County Law Library
Automation Activity & Vendor Info: (Cataloging) Innovative Interfaces, Inc; (Circulation) Innovative Interfaces, Inc; (Course Reserve) Innovative Interfaces, Inc; (ILL) OCLC; (OPAC) Innovative Interfaces, Inc; (Serials) EBSCO Online
Database Vendor: EBSCOhost, Facts on File, Gale Cengage Learning, LexisNexis, OCLC WorldShare Interlibrary Loan
Function: ILL available, Online cat, Online searches, Orientations, Ref serv available, VHS videos
Open Mon-Thurs 7:30am-9pm, Fri 7:30-5, Sat 11-4
Restriction: Authorized patrons, Open to students, Open to students, fac & staff, Pub use on premises

P WHITE RIVER REGIONAL LIBRARY*, 368 E Main St, 72501. SAN 300-4864. Tel: 870-793-8814. FAX: 870-793-8896. E-mail: indcolib@hotmail.com. Web Site: www.indcolib.com. *Dir,* Debra Sutterfield; *ILL,* Janet Swaim; Staff 2 (MLS 2)
Founded 1978. Pop 91,428; Circ 394,482
Library Holdings: Bk Vols 151,905; Per Subs 462
Special Collections: Arkansas History (Vela Jernigan Memorial)
Automation Activity & Vendor Info: (Acquisitions) Follett Software
Wireless access
Member Libraries: Cleburne County Library; Izard County Library; Stone County Library
Open Mon 9-6, Tues-Sat 9-5, Sun 1:30-5
Branches: 5
FULTON COUNTY MAMMOTH SPRING BRANCH, 315 Main St, Mammoth Spring, 72554. (Mail add: PO Box 256, Mammoth Spring, 72554-3205). Tel: 870-625-3205. *Librn,* Carole Howell
Library Holdings: Audiobooks 100; Bks on Deafness & Sign Lang 5; CDs 100; DVDs 20; Large Print Bks 200; Bk Vols 10,000; Per Subs 5; Videos 500
Open Mon & Wed-Fri 9:30-4:30, Sat 9-3
Friends of the Library Group
FULTON COUNTY - VIOLA BRANCH, 199 Hwy 223, Viola, 72583. (Mail add: PO Box 258, Viola, 72583-0258). Tel: 870-458-3070. *Librn,* Terry Wineland
Library Holdings: Bk Vols 4,000
Open Tues & Wed 11:30-4:30, Fri 10-4:30, Sat 9:30-1
SHARP COUNTY - CAVE CITY BRANCH, 120 Spring St, Cave City, 72521. (Mail add: PO Box 240, Cave City, 72521-0240). Tel: 870-283-6947. *Librn,* Vera Anderson
Library Holdings: Bk Vols 4,000; Per Subs 21
Open Mon & Wed 10-5, Fri 10:30-5:30
Friends of the Library Group
SHARP COUNTY - EVENING SHADE BRANCH, 222 Main St, Evening Shade, 72532. (Mail add: PO Box 118, Evening Shade, 72532-0118). Tel: 870-266-3873. *Librn,* Angela Haley
Library Holdings: Bk Vols 4,500
Open Tues, Thurs & Fri 10-5
Friends of the Library Group
SHARP COUNTY - WILLIFORD BRANCH, 232 Main St, Williford, 72482. (Mail add: PO Box 94, Williford, 72482-0094). Tel: 870-966-4227. *Librn,* Crystal Coble
Library Holdings: Bk Vols 4,000
Open Mon & Fri 10:30-4:30

BEEBE

J ARKANSAS STATE UNIVERSITY*, Abington Memorial Library, Palm & Iowa Sts, 72012. (Mail add: PO Box 1000, 72012), SAN 300-4872. Tel: 501-882-8976. Interlibrary Loan Service Tel: 501-882-8991. Administration Tel: 501-882-8807. FAX: 501-882-8833. TDD: 501-882-8969. E-mail: circ@asub.edu. *Libr Dir,* Tracy D Smith; Tel: 501-882-8806, E-mail: tdsmith@asub.edu; *Instrul & Electronic Res Librn,* Ronald S Russ; Tel: 501-882-8959, E-mail: rsruss@asub.edu; Staff 8 (MLS 2, Non-MLS 6)
Founded 1929. Enrl 2,640; Fac 150; Highest Degree: Associate
Library Holdings: AV Mats 3,600; e-books 38,000; e-journals 32,000; Bk Vols 76,000; Per Subs 251; Talking Bks 70
Subject Interests: Ark
Automation Activity & Vendor Info: (Cataloging) TLC (The Library Corporation); (Circulation) TLC (The Library Corporation); (Serials) TLC (The Library Corporation)
Database Vendor: EBSCOhost, Gale Cengage Learning, LexisNexis, OCLC FirstSearch, ProQuest
Wireless access
Function: Audio & video playback equip for onsite use, CD-ROM, Digital talking bks, Distance learning, Handicapped accessible, Health sci info serv, ILL available, Mail loans to mem, Music CDs, Online searches, Orientations, Outside serv via phone, mail, e-mail & web, Photocopying/Printing, Ref serv available, Spoken cassettes & CDs, Telephone ref, VHS videos, Wheelchair accessible, Workshops
Partic in ARKLink
Special Services for the Deaf - Closed caption videos; TDD equip; TTY equip
Special Services for the Blind - Assistive/Adapted tech devices, equip & products; Audio mat; Bks on cassette; Bks on CD; Cassette playback machines; Computer with voice synthesizer for visually impaired persons; HP Scan Jet with photo-finish software; Large print bks; PC for handicapped; Rec; Ref serv; Talking bks; Videos on blindness & phys handicaps
Restriction: Open to pub for ref & circ; with some limitations, Restricted borrowing privileges

BELLA VISTA

S BELLA VISTA HISTORICAL SOCIETY MUSEUM LIBRARY*, 1885 Bella Vista Way, 72714. SAN 371-7100. Tel: 479-855-2335. *Pres,* Carole Westby
Founded 1976
Library Holdings: Bk Titles 400; Per Subs 12
Special Collections: Anthropology-Archaeology, bks, per, slides; History Coll, bks, chts, docs, maps. Oral History
Subject Interests: Local hist
Function: Res libr
Open Thurs-Sun 1-4
Restriction: Non-circulating

P BELLA VISTA PUBLIC LIBRARY, 11 Dickens Pl, 72714-4603. Tel: 479-855-1753. FAX: 479-855-4475. Web Site: www.bvpl.org. *Dir,* Roxie Wright; E-mail: rwright@bellavistacityar.com; *Asst Librn,* Myrna McGee; Staff 6 (MLS 2, Non-MLS 4)
Founded 1981. Pop 26,000; Circ 73,678
Jan 2008-Dec 2008 Income $295,332, Locally Generated Income $284,832, Other $10,500. Mats Exp $42,583, Books $31,063, Per/Ser (Incl. Access Fees) $5,463, Other Print Mats $250, AV Mat $5,807. Sal $73,011 (Prof $50,143)
Library Holdings: Audiobooks 930; Bks on Deafness & Sign Lang 10; CDs 330; DVDs 3,336; High Interest/Low Vocabulary Bk Vols 3,024; Large Print Bks 3,673; Bk Vols 55,000; Per Subs 40; Talking Bks 930
Special Collections: Arkansas Coll; Classic Films Coll; Easy Readers Coll; Quilting Coll
Subject Interests: Civil War, World War II
Automation Activity & Vendor Info: (Cataloging) Innovative Interfaces, Inc; (Circulation) Innovative Interfaces, Inc; (OPAC) Innovative Interfaces, Inc
Database Vendor: EBSCOhost
Wireless access
Special Services for the Blind - Free checkout of audio mat
Open Mon & Wed 9-8, Tues & Thurs-Sat 9-5
Friends of the Library Group

BENTON

P SALINE COUNTY PUBLIC LIBRARY*, Bob Herzfeld Memorial Library, 1800 Smithers Dr, 72015. SAN 330-8855. Tel: 501-778-4766. Toll Free Tel: 800-476-4466. FAX: 501-778-0536. E-mail: administrator@salinecountylibrary.org. Web Site: www.salinecountylibrary.org. *Dir,* Erin Waller; *Head, Ch,* Jill Martin; *Head, Coll & Tech,* Alissa Turner; *Acq Mgr,* Pat Struble; *Bus Mgr,* Erin Cozart; *Cataloger,* Julie Syler; *ILS Adminr,* Tina Hardister; Staff 26 (MLS 4, Non-MLS 22)
Founded 1928. Pop 83,529; Circ 418,231
Jan 2005-Dec 2005 Income (Main Library and Branch(s)) $250,000, State $75,000, County $175,000. Mats Exp $435,000, Books $410,000, Electronic Ref Mat (Incl. Access Fees) $25,000. Sal $923,522 (Prof $193,102)
Library Holdings: DVDs 11,550; e-books 5,201; Bk Titles 138,435; Per Subs 175; Talking Bks 9,888

Subject Interests: Ark
Automation Activity & Vendor Info: (Acquisitions) Innovative Interfaces, Inc; (Cataloging) Innovative Interfaces, Inc; (Circulation) Innovative Interfaces, Inc; (OPAC) Innovative Interfaces, Inc
Database Vendor: 3M Library Systems, Baker & Taylor, BWI, EBSCOhost, Grolier Online, OCLC FirstSearch, SirsiDynix
Wireless access
Open Mon, Wed & Thurs 9-8, Tues & Fri 9-5:30, Sat 9-4
Branches: 1
MABEL BOSWELL MEMORIAL LIBRARY - BRYANT, 201 Pricket Rd, Bryant, 72022, SAN 330-888X. Tel: 501-847-2166. FAX: 501-847-4524. *Br Mgr,* Brad Crumby; Staff 4 (Non MLS 4)
Open Mon & Wed-Fri 9-5:30, Tues 9-8, Sat 9-4

BENTONVILLE

P BENTONVILLE PUBLIC LIBRARY, 405 S Main St, 72712. SAN 300-4880. Tel: 479-271-3192. FAX: 479-271-6775. E-mail: library@bentonvillear.com. Web Site: www.bentonvillelibrary.org. *Dir,* Hadi Dudley; Staff 12 (MLS 1, Non-MLS 11)
Founded 1947. Pop 19,730; Circ 92,500
Library Holdings: AV Mats 2,335; Large Print Bks 4,000; Bk Vols 62,000; Per Subs 205; Talking Bks 3,500
Special Collections: Arkansas History, bk & microfilm; Benton County Daily Record, large print, micro
Automation Activity & Vendor Info: (Cataloging) TLC (The Library Corporation); (Circulation) TLC (The Library Corporation); (OPAC) TLC (The Library Corporation)
Database Vendor: EBSCOhost
Wireless access
Open Mon-Thurs 9-8, Fri & Sat 9-5
Friends of the Library Group

P CAVE SPRINGS PUBLIC LIBRARY*, Midway Ave, 72712. (Mail add: 9588 Phillips Lane, 72712-6657). Tel: 479-248-7117. *Librn,* Jackie Morris; *Librn,* Marlene Sands
Library Holdings: Bk Vols 1,600
Open Sat 10-2
Friends of the Library Group

J NORTHWEST ARKANSAS COMMUNITY COLLEGE*, Pauline Whitaker Library, One College Dr, 72712-5091. Tel: 479-619-4244. FAX: 479-619-4115. E-mail: library@nwacc.edu. Web Site: www.nwacc.edu/library. *Dir,* Gwen Dobbs; *Librn,* Rachel Ackerman; *Librn,* Joel Tonyan; *Librn,* Janelle Wilkinson; *Librn,* Stacy Winchester
Highest Degree: Associate
Library Holdings: Bk Vols 30,000; Per Subs 100
Automation Activity & Vendor Info: (Cataloging) LibLime; (Circulation) LibLime; (OPAC) LibLime
Database Vendor: ARTstor, Baker & Taylor, ebrary, EBSCOhost, LexisNexis, LibLime, ProQuest
Wireless access
Function: ILL available, Photocopying/Printing
Open Mon-Thurs (Winter) 8-8, Fri & Sat 9-3; Mon & Tues (Summer) 8-8, Wed & Thurs 8-6, Fri 9-3

S NORTHWEST ARKANSAS GENEALOGY SOCIETY, Library & Archives, 405 S Main St, Bentonville Public Library, 72712. SAN 371-1889. Tel: 479-271-6820. E-mail: genealogy@bentonvillear.com. *Web Coordr,* Wilma Fields
Library Holdings: Bk Vols 5,000; Spec Interest Per Sub 13
Special Collections: Mount Meadows Massacre - Utah 1857, doc, rec
Wireless access
Open Mon-Thurs 9-8, Fri & Sat 9-5

BERRYVILLE

P BERRYVILLE PUBLIC LIBRARY, 104 Spring St, 72616. SAN 331-0922. Tel: 870-423-2323. FAX: 870-423-2432. E-mail: info@berryvillelibrary.org. *Dir,* Mark Schuster; *Asst Librn,* Carla Youngblood
Founded 1978
Library Holdings: Bks on Deafness & Sign Lang 10; High Interest/Low Vocabulary Bk Vols 150; Bk Vols 26,000; Per Subs 80
Wireless access
Mem of Carroll & Madison Library System
Open Mon-Fri 9-6, Sat 9-1, Sun 1-5
Friends of the Library Group

P CARROLL & MADISON LIBRARY SYSTEM, 106 Spring St, 72616. Tel: 870-423-5300. FAX: 870-423-7117. E-mail: admin@camals.org. Web Site: www.carrollmadisonlibraries.org. *Adminr,* Johnice Dominick; Staff 2 (MLS 1, Non-MLS 1)
Founded 2000
Member Libraries: Berryville Public Library; Carnegie Public Library; Green Forest Public Library; Huntsville Public Library; Kingston Community Library; St Paul Public Library
Open Mon-Fri 9-5

BLYTHEVILLE

J ARKANSAS NORTHEASTERN COLLEGE*, Adams-Vines Library, 2501 S Division St, 72315-5111. Tel: 870-762-3189. FAX: 870-762-5534. *Dir, Libr Serv,* Bronwyn Morgan; E-mail: bmorgan@smail.anc.edu; Staff 3 (MLS 1, Non-MLS 2)
Founded 1993. Enrl 1,200; Fac 75; Highest Degree: Associate
Library Holdings: DVDs 125; High Interest/Low Vocabulary Bk Vols 100; Bk Vols 21,000; Per Subs 225; Videos 1,500
Special Collections: Arkansas Coll
Automation Activity & Vendor Info: (Cataloging) Innovative Interfaces, Inc; (Circulation) Innovative Interfaces, Inc; (ILL) OCLC; (OPAC) Innovative Interfaces, Inc
Wireless access
Partic in Amigos Library Services, Inc
Open Mon-Thurs 8-8, Fri 9-4, Sat 9-Noon

P MISSISSIPPI COUNTY LIBRARY SYSTEM*, 200 N Fifth St, 72315-2709. SAN 330-891X. Tel: 870-762-2431. FAX: 870-762-2242. E-mail: info@mclibrary.net. Web Site: www.mclibrary.net. *Dir,* Kevin Barron; Staff 2 (MLS 2)
Founded 1921. Pop 46,480; Circ 299,571
Library Holdings: Bk Vols 200,000; Per Subs 250; Talking Bks 500; Videos 200
Database Vendor: EBSCOhost
Wireless access
Function: Adult literacy prog, Copy machines, Electronic databases & coll, Handicapped accessible, ILL available, Photocopying/Printing, Prog for children & young adult, Ref serv available, Spoken cassettes & CDs, Summer reading prog, Tax forms, Telephone ref, VHS videos, Video lending libr, Wheelchair accessible
Partic in OCLC Online Computer Library Center, Inc
Open Mon, Tues & Thurs 9-8, Wed & Fri 9-5, Sat 10-5, Sun 1-4
Branches: 7
BLYTHEVILLE PUBLIC, 200 N Fifth St, 72315. Tel: 870-762-2431. FAX: 870-762-2242. *Br Mgr,* Mary Razor; Staff 1 (MLS 1)
Founded 1921. Pop 15,620; Circ 100,000
Library Holdings: Bk Vols 150,000; Per Subs 100; Talking Bks 250
Database Vendor: EBSCOhost
Function: After school storytime, Copy machines, Handicapped accessible, ILL available, Photocopying/Printing, Prog for children & young adult, Spoken cassettes & CDs, Summer reading prog, Tax forms, VHS videos, Video lending libr, Wheelchair accessible
Open Mon, Tues & Thurs 9-8, Wed 9-5, Sat 10-5, Sun 1-4
KEISER PUBLIC, 112 E Main St, Keiser, 72351, SAN 330-8944. Tel: 870-526-2073. *Br Mgr,* Karen Harrison
Pop 759; Circ 20,000
Library Holdings: Bk Titles 4,000; Per Subs 15; Talking Bks 20
Function: Prog for children & young adult, Summer reading prog, Tax forms
Open Mon, Wed & Fri 1-5
LEACHVILLE PUBLIC, 105 S Main St, Leachville, 72438. (Mail add: PO Box 686, Leachville, 72438-0686), SAN 330-8979. Tel: 870-539-6485. *Br Mgr,* Mandy Hill
Pop 1,993; Circ 20,000
Library Holdings: Bk Vols 4,000; Per Subs 15; Talking Bks 20
Function: Prog for children & young adult, Spoken cassettes & CDs, Summer reading prog, Tax forms, Wheelchair accessible
Open Mon, Wed & Fri 10:30-5:30
LUXORA PUBLIC, 215 Washington St, Luxora, 72358. (Mail add: PO Box 189, Luxora, 72358-1089), SAN 376-2408. Tel: 870-658-2421. FAX: 870-658-2421. *Br Mgr,* Wana Jones
Pop 1,400; Circ 10,000
Library Holdings: Bk Vols 4,000; Per Subs 15; Talking Bks 20
Function: After school storytime, Copy machines, Electronic databases & coll, Photocopying/Printing, Prog for children & young adult, Summer reading prog, Tax forms
Open Mon, Wed & Fri 1-5
MANILA PUBLIC, 103 N Dewey Ave, Manila, 72442. (Mail add: PO Box 569, Manila, 72442-0559), SAN 330-9002. Tel: 870-561-3525. FAX: 870-561-3525. *Br Mgr,* Mary Alice Ketchum
Pop 3,324; Circ 30,000
Library Holdings: Bk Vols 4,000; Per Subs 15; Talking Bks 20
Function: After school storytime, Handicapped accessible, Prog for children & young adult, Summer reading prog, Tax forms, Wheelchair accessible
Open Mon, Wed & Fri 12-5:30, Sat 10-4

OSCEOLA PUBLIC, 320 West Hale Ave, Osceola, 72370-2530, SAN 330-9037. Tel: 870-563-2721. FAX: 870-563-6550. *Br Mgr,* Denise Hester; Staff 2 (MLS 1, Non-MLS 1)
Founded 1948. Pop 7,757; Circ 50,000
Library Holdings: Large Print Bks 300; Bk Titles 30,000; Per Subs 75; Talking Bks 200
Special Collections: Arkansas genealogy
Subject Interests: Local genealogy
Function: Computer training, Copy machines, e-mail serv, Fax serv, Handicapped accessible, ILL available, Online searches, Photocopying/Printing, Prog for adults, Prog for children & young adult, Ref serv available, Senior computer classes, Spoken cassettes & CDs, Summer reading prog, Tax forms, Telephone ref, VHS videos, Video lending libr, Wheelchair accessible
Special Services for the Deaf - Bks on deafness & sign lang
Open Mon, Tues & Thurs 9-8, Wed & Fri 9-5, Sat 10-5, Sun 1-4

WILSON PUBLIC, One Park St, Wilson, 72395, SAN 330-9061. Tel: 870-655-8414. FAX: 870-655-8414. *Br Mgr,* Linda Dawson
Pop 903; Circ 20,000
Library Holdings: Bk Vols 4,000; Per Subs 15; Talking Bks 20
Function: After school storytime, Handicapped accessible, Prog for children & young adult, Spoken cassettes & CDs, Summer reading prog, Tax forms, Wheelchair accessible
Open Mon, Wed & Fri 11:30-4:30

BULL SHOALS

P BULL SHOALS LIBRARY, 1218 Central Blvd, 72619. (Mail add: PO Box 406, 72619-0406), SAN 329-5419. Tel: 870-445-4265. E-mail: bullslibrary@hotmail.com. Web Site: www.bullshoalslibrary.org. *Pres,* Michelle Skinner; E-mail: mckendreep@outlook.com; *IT Mgr,* Larry Kanturek; Tel: 713-857-4325, E-mail: biglarryk56@suddenlink.net; *Libr Tech,* Barbara Repta; E-mail: barrod711@hotmail.com
Pop 3,000
Library Holdings: DVDs 30; Bk Vols 20,000; Per Subs 50; Talking Bks 403; Videos 705
Automation Activity & Vendor Info: (Cataloging) LiBRARYSOFT; (Circulation) LiBRARYSOFT; (OPAC) LiBRARYSOFT
Database Vendor: LiBRARYSOFT
Wireless access
Function: Computers for patron use, Free DVD rentals, Handicapped accessible, Magazines, Movies, Printer for laptops & handheld devices, Pub access computers
Open Tues-Fri 10-3, Sat 10-12:30
Friends of the Library Group

CALICO ROCK

P IZARD COUNTY LIBRARY*, Calico Rock Public Library, 301 Second St, 72519. Tel: 870-297-3785. E-mail: calicorocklibrary@yahoo.com. Web Site: www.calicorocklibrary.com. *Regional Dir,* Debra Sutterfield; Tel: 870-793-8814; *Librn,* Aimee Watts
Library Holdings: Audiobooks 125; CDs 50; DVDs 200; Large Print Bks 225; Bk Titles 11,535; Bk Vols 11,973; Per Subs 15; Videos 350
Special Collections: Genealogy Coll
Mem of White River Regional Library
Open Mon-Thurs 9:30-4:30, Sat 9:30-1:30
Friends of the Library Group

CAMDEN

J SOUTHERN ARKANSAS UNIVERSITY TECH-LIBRARY*, Dr George J Brown Learning Resource Center, 6415 Spellman Rd, 71701. (Mail add: PO Box 3499, 71711-1599), SAN 300-4961. Tel: 870-574-4518, 870-574-4544. FAX: 870-574-4568. Web Site: library.sautech.edu. *Dir,* Allison Malone; E-mail: amalone@sautech.edu; Staff 3 (MLS 1, Non-MLS 2)
Founded 1967
Automation Activity & Vendor Info: (Cataloging) SirsiDynix; (Circulation) SirsiDynix; (Course Reserve) SirsiDynix; (ILL) OCLC WorldShare Interlibrary Loan; (OPAC) SirsiDynix; (Serials) EBSCO Online
Database Vendor: 3M Library Systems, Amigos Library Services, Bowker, CredoReference, EBSCOhost, Facts on File, Gale Cengage Learning, Grolier Online, LearningExpress, Newsbank, OCLC FirstSearch, OCLC WorldShare Interlibrary Loan, SirsiDynix, YBP Library Services
Wireless access
Partic in ARKLink
Open Mon-Thurs 8-7, Fri 8-Noon

CEDARVILLE

P CEDARVILLE PUBLIC LIBRARY*, 639 Pirates Way, 72932. (Mail add: PO Box 95, 72932-0095), SAN 330-9908. Tel: 479-410-1853. FAX: 479-410-1853. E-mail: cedarvillelibrary@hotmail.com. Web Site: www.crawfordcountylib.org. *Librn,* Michele Mullen
Library Holdings: Bk Vols 11,334
Database Vendor: EBSCOhost, OCLC FirstSearch
Mem of Crawford County Library System
Open Mon-Fri 9:30-5:30
Friends of the Library Group

CLARKSVILLE

C UNIVERSITY OF THE OZARKS*, Robson Library, 415 N College Ave, 72830. SAN 300-4899. Tel: 479-979-1382. FAX: 479-979-1477. Web Site: www.ozarks.edu. *Dir,* Stuart P Stelzer; E-mail: sstelzer@ozarks.edu; *Tech Serv,* Janice Blackard; Staff 4 (MLS 1, Non-MLS 3)
Founded 1891. Enrl 612; Fac 54; Highest Degree: Bachelor
Library Holdings: e-books 38,000; e-journals 25,000; Bk Vols 88,000; Per Subs 450; Videos 1,275
Special Collections: State Document Depository
Automation Activity & Vendor Info: (Acquisitions) Ex Libris Group; (Cataloging) Ex Libris Group; (Circulation) Ex Libris Group; (OPAC) Ex Libris Group; (Serials) SerialsSolutions
Database Vendor: ABC-CLIO, Alexander Street Press, American Psychological Association (APA), Amigos Library Services, ARTstor, BioOne, Children's Literature Comprehensive Database Company (CLCD), CQ Press, EBSCOhost, Ex Libris Group, Ingram Library Services, LexisNexis, Mergent Online, Modern Language Association, Newsbank, OCLC ArticleFirst, OCLC FirstSearch, OCLC WorldShare Interlibrary Loan, Oxford Online, ProQuest, SerialsSolutions, Westlaw, Wilson - Wilson Web
Function: Wheelchair accessible
Partic in ARKnet (Arkansas Academic & Research Network); OCLC Online Computer Library Center, Inc
Restriction: Open to pub for ref & circ; with some limitations, Open to students, fac & staff

CONWAY

CR CENTRAL BAPTIST COLLEGE, J E Cobb Library, 1501 College Ave, 72034. SAN 300-4902. Tel: 501-329-6872. FAX: 501-329-2941. Web Site: www.cbc.edu. *Dir,* Rachel Whittingham; E-mail: rwhittingham@cbc.edu; Staff 3 (MLS 2, Non-MLS 1)
Founded 1952. Enrl 385; Highest Degree: Bachelor
Library Holdings: AV Mats 1,658; Bks on Deafness & Sign Lang 15; Bk Titles 48,135; Bk Vols 54,236; Per Subs 310
Special Collections: Baptist Missionary Association of Arkansas History
Automation Activity & Vendor Info: (Acquisitions) TLC (The Library Corporation); (Cataloging) TLC (The Library Corporation); (Circulation) TLC (The Library Corporation); (ILL) TLC (The Library Corporation); (OPAC) TLC (The Library Corporation)
Database Vendor: EBSCO Discovery Service
Wireless access
Partic in ARKLink
Special Services for the Blind - Assistive/Adapted tech devices, equip & products
Open Mon-Thurs 7:30am-11:30pm, Fri 7:30-4, Sat 11-4, Sun 7pm-11:30pm

P FAULKNER-VAN BUREN REGIONAL LIBRARY SYSTEM*, 1900 Tyler St, 72032. SAN 330-9126. Tel: 501-327-7482. Administration Tel: 501-450-4981. FAX: 501-327-9098. Web Site: www.fcl.org. *Dir,* Tina Murdock; Staff 20.5 (MLS 2.5, Non-MLS 18)
Founded 1938. Pop 112,206; Circ 436,411
Jan 2005-Dec 2005 Income (Main Library and Branch(s)) $1,328,092, State $98,489, City $44,276, County $1,125,217, Other $104,386. Mats Exp $167,059, Books $138,436, Per/Ser (Incl. Access Fees) $9,000, AV Mat $19,623. Sal $478,612 (Prof $80,000)
Library Holdings: AV Mats 15,162; Large Print Bks 100; Bk Titles 120,000; Bk Vols 183,005; Per Subs 309
Special Collections: Arkansas Coll; Genealogy Coll
Automation Activity & Vendor Info: (Acquisitions) LibraryWorld, Inc; (Cataloging) LibraryWorld, Inc; (Circulation) LibraryWorld, Inc; (ILL) OCLC; (OPAC) LibraryWorld, Inc; (Serials) EBSCO Online
Wireless access
Publications: Newsletter
Special Services for the Deaf - Assistive tech
Open Mon-Thurs 9-7, Fri & Sat 9-5, Sun 1-5
Restriction: Open to pub for ref & circ; with some limitations
Friends of the Library Group
Branches: 5
GREENBRIER BRANCH, 13 Wilson Farm Rd, Greenbrier, 72058, SAN 377-7723. Tel: 501-679-6344. FAX: 501-679-6934. *Librn,* Judy Lovell
Open Mon-Fri Noon-6
MAYFLOWER BRANCH, Six Ashmore Dr, Mayflower, 72106. (Mail add: PO Box 240, Mayflower, 72106-0240), SAN 377-774X. Tel: 501-470-9678. FAX: 501-470-9039. *Librn,* Jean Smith
Open Mon-Fri Noon-6

TWIN GROVES BRANCH, Ten Twin Groves Lane, Twin Groves, 72039. Tel: 501-335-8088. FAX: 501-335-8088. *Librn,* Sheena Cain
Library Holdings: Bk Vols 3,000
Open Mon-Fri Noon-6

VAN BUREN COUNTY, 119 Shake Rag Rd, Clinton, 72031, SAN 330-9215. Tel: 501-745-2100. FAX: 501-745-5860. *Br Mgr,* Karla Fultz
Library Holdings: Bk Vols 22,000
Friends of the Library Group

VILONIA BRANCH, Three Bise Dr, Vilonia, 72173. (Mail add: PO Box 388, Vilonia, 72173-0388), SAN 374-4388. Tel: 501-796-8520. FAX: 501-796-8753. *Br Mgr,* Shelia Biggins
Open Mon Fri 12-6
Friends of the Library Group

C HENDRIX COLLEGE, Olin C Bailey Library, 1600 Washington Ave, 72032. SAN 300-4910. Tel: 501-450-1289. Circulation Tel: 501-450-1303. FAX: 501-450-3800. E-mail: libraryreference@hendrix.edu. Web Site: www.hendrix.edu/baileylibrary. *Dir & Librn,* Britt Anne Murphy; Tel: 501-450-1288, E-mail: murphyb@hendrix.edu; *Access Serv Librn,* Peggy Morrison; E-mail: morrison@hendrix.edu; *Asst Librn, Pub Serv, Col Archivist,* Christina Thompson Shutt; Tel: 501-450-4558, E-mail: thompsonc@hendrix.edu; *Asst Librn, Tech Serv,* Matthew Windsor; Tel: 501-450-1287, E-mail: windsor@hendrix.edu; Staff 10 (MLS 4, Non-MLS 6)
Founded 1876. Enrl 1,375; Fac 108; Highest Degree: Master
Library Holdings: CDs 1,096; DVDs 2,992; e-books 30,942; e-journals 65,518; Microforms 67,497; Bk Titles 229,775; Bk Vols 264,400; Per Subs 393
Special Collections: Arkansas Methodist Archives; Arkansasiana; Hendrix College Archives; Stebbins Coll of Arkansiana; Wilbur D Mills Archives. State Document Depository
Automation Activity & Vendor Info: (Acquisitions) Innovative Interfaces, Inc; (Cataloging) Innovative Interfaces, Inc; (Circulation) Innovative Interfaces, Inc; (Course Reserve) Innovative Interfaces, Inc; (OPAC) Innovative Interfaces, Inc; (Serials) Innovative Interfaces, Inc
Database Vendor: Alexander Street Press, American Chemical Society, American Physical Society, Amigos Library Services, Annual Reviews, ARTstor, Baker & Taylor, Cambridge Scientific Abstracts, EBSCO Information Services, EBSCOhost, Elsevier, Gale Cengage Learning, H W Wilson, Innovative Interfaces, Inc, ISI Web of Knowledge, JSTOR, LexisNexis, Medline, Modern Language Association, Nature Publishing Group, OCLC FirstSearch, OCLC WorldShare Interlibrary Loan, Project MUSE, ProQuest, ScienceDirect, SerialsSolutions, Springer-Verlag, Thomson - Web of Science
Wireless access
Partic in Amigos Library Services, Inc; ARKLink; Associated Colleges of the South

C UNIVERSITY OF CENTRAL ARKANSAS*, Torreyson Library, 201 Donaghey Ave, 72035. SAN 300-4929. Tel: 501-450-3174. Interlibrary Loan Service Tel: 501-450-5205. Reference Tel: 501-450-5224. Administration Tel: 501-450-5201. FAX: 501-450-5208. Web Site: www.uca.edu/library. *Dir,* Art A Lichtenstein; E-mail: artl@uca.edu; *Coordr, Tech Serv,* Kaye Talley; *Archivist,* Jimmy Bryant; Staff 40 (MLS 12, Non-MLS 28)
Founded 1907. Enrl 11,600; Highest Degree: Doctorate
Subject Interests: Ark
Wireless access
Partic in ARKLink; OCLC Online Computer Library Center, Inc; OCLC-LVIS

CORNING

P CORNING PUBLIC LIBRARY, 613 Pine St, 72422. SAN 331-3239. Tel: 870-857-3453. FAX: 870-857-3453. E-mail: corning@mylibrarynow.org. Web Site: www.mylibrarynow.org/corning. *Dir & Librn,* Kathy Butler; *Asst Dir, Cataloger,* Karen Debord; *Circ,* Peggy Renee Bliss; Staff 3 (Non-MLS 3)
Founded 1926. Pop 6,000; Circ 36,000
Library Holdings: Bk Titles 32,000; Per Subs 10
Subject Interests: Genealogy
Automation Activity & Vendor Info: (Cataloging) Book Systems; (Circulation) Book Systems; (OPAC) Book Systems; (OPAC) Book Systems
Database Vendor: EBSCOhost, OCLC FirstSearch
Wireless access
Mem of Northeast Arkansas Regional Library System
Open Mon, Tues & Thurs 8:30-5:30, Wed 8:30-5, Fri 8:30-4, Sat 9-1

CROSSETT

P CROSSETT PUBLIC LIBRARY*, 1700 Main St, 71635. SAN 300-4937. Tel: 870-364-2230. FAX: 870-364-2231. Web Site: www.crossett.lib.ar.us. *Dir,* David Anderson; Staff 2 (MLS 2)
Founded 1938. Pop 14,000; Circ 103,789
Library Holdings: Bk Vols 44,000; Per Subs 65
Special Collections: Arkansas Coll
Open Mon, Tues, Thurs & Fri 9-6:30, Wed 9-5:30, Sat 9-3
Friends of the Library Group

C UNIVERSITY OF ARKANSAS AT MONTICELLO*, College of Technology-Crossett Library, 1326 Hwy 52 W, 71635. Tel: 870-364-6414. FAX: 870-364-5707. Web Site: www.uamont.edu. *Adminr,* Janie Carter; E-mail: carter@uamont.edu
Enrl 3,000
Library Holdings: AV Mats 500; Bk Vols 6,500; Per Subs 12
Automation Activity & Vendor Info: (Cataloging) Follett Software; (Circulation) Follett Software; (Course Reserve) Follett Software; (ILL) Follett Software
Special Services for the Deaf - Adult & family literacy prog; Assistive tech; Bks on deafness & sign lang; High interest/low vocabulary bks
Special Services for the Blind - Assistive/Adapted tech devices, equip & products
Open Mon-Thurs 8-4, Fri 8-Noon

DARDANELLE

P ARKANSAS RIVER VALLEY REGIONAL LIBRARY SYSTEM*, Headquarters, 501 N Front St, 72834-3507. SAN 330-924X. Tel: 479-229-4418. FAX: 479-229-2595. E-mail: arvrls@centurytel.net, darlib@centurytel.net. Web Site: www.arvrls.com. *Dir,* Donna McDonald
Founded 1959. Pop 71,434; Circ 358,759
Jan 2005-Dec 2005 Income (Main Library and Branch(s)) $1,220,239. Mats Exp $229,599. Sal $520,582
Library Holdings: Bk Vols 266,526; Per Subs 250
Special Collections: Arkansas; Local History Coll
Automation Activity & Vendor Info: (Cataloging) SirsiDynix; (Circulation) SirsiDynix; (OPAC) SirsiDynix
Wireless access
Open Mon 9-7, Tues-Fri 9-5
Branches: 6

CHARLESTON BRANCH, 12 S School St, Charleston, 72933-0338, SAN 330-9304. Tel: 479-965-2605. FAX: 479-965-2755. E-mail: chpublibrary@yahoo.com. *Librn,* Kimberly Wilder
Open Mon-Fri 9-5, Sat 10-12

FRANKLIN COUNTY, 407 W Market St, Ozark, 72949-2727, SAN 330-9363. Tel: 479-667-2724. FAX: 479-667-9021. E-mail: ozlib@centurytel.net. *Librn,* Nancy Smith
Open Mon 12-7, Tues-Fri 9-5

BOYD T & MOLLIE GATTIS-LOGAN COUNTY LIBRARY, 100 E Academy, Paris, 72855-4432, SAN 330-9452. Tel: 479-963-2371. FAX: 479-963-9243. *Librn,* Rita Eckart
Open Mon & Thurs 10-6, Tues, Wed & Fri 9-5, Sat 9-1
Friends of the Library Group

JOHNSON COUNTY, Two Taylor Circle, Clarksville, 72830-3653, SAN 330-9398. Tel: 479-754-3135. FAX: 479-754-6343. E-mail: jclib@centurytel.net. *Librn,* Kathy Jones
Library Holdings: Bk Titles 30,000
Open Mon 12-7, Tues-Fri 9:30-5, Sat 9:30 12

LOGAN COUNTY, 419 N Kennedy, Booneville, 72927-3630, SAN 330-9428. Tel: 479-675-2735. FAX: 479-675-2735. E mail: bblog@centurytel.net. *Librn,* Danita Harger
Open Mon & Thurs 10-6, Tues, Wed & Fri 9-5, Sat 9-1
Friends of the Library Group

YELL COUNTY, 904 Atlanta St, Danville, 72833. (Mail add: PO Box 850, Danville, 72833-0850), SAN 330-9517. Tel: 479-495-2911. FAX: 479-495-2822. E-mail: ycl@arkwest.com. Web Site: www.arvrls.com/yell.htm. *Librn,* Stacey Beatty
Open Mon 9-6, Tues-Fri 9-5

DE QUEEN

J COSSATOT COMMUNITY COLLEGE OF THE UNIVERSITY OF ARKANSAS, Kimball Library, 195 College Dr, 71832. Tel: 870-584-4471. FAX: 870-642-3320. Web Site: www2.youseemore.com/cccua. *Res Coordr,* Relinda Ruth; E-mail: rruth@cccua.edu
Library Holdings: Bk Vols 10,000; Per Subs 50
Database Vendor: Community of Science (COS), EBSCOhost, Facts on File, Gale Cengage Learning, Grolier Online, OCLC FirstSearch, OCLC WorldShare Interlibrary Loan, ProQuest, PubMed
Wireless access
Open Mon-Thurs 7:30-7, Fri 7:30-4

P SEVIER COUNTY LIBRARY*, De Queen Branch, 200 W Stillwell, 71832. SAN 331-1287. Tel: 870-584-4364. FAX: 870-642-8319. E-mail: seviercountylibrary@yahoo.com. Web Site: www.seviercountylibrary.com. *Head Librn,* Johnye Fisher; *Asst Head Librn,* Annette Eastwood; *Librn,* Lou Colbert

Function: Children's prog, Computers for patron use, Copy machines, Free DVD rentals, Internet access
Open Mon, Wed & Fri 8-6, Tues & Thurs Noon-6, Sat 9-Noon
Branches: 2
GILLHAM BRANCH, 202 N Second St, Gillham, 71841-9511. (Mail add: PO Box 173, Gillham, 71842-0173), SAN 331-1376. Tel: 870-386-5665. FAX: 870-386-5665. E-mail: libgillham@yahoo.com. *Librn,* Susie Tollett
Open Tues & Thurs 9:30-5, Sat 9-12
HORATIO BRANCH, 108 Main St, Horatio, 71842, SAN 331-1430. Tel: 870-832-6882. FAX: 870-832-6882. *Librn,* Joan Moore
Open Tues & Thurs 8:30-5:30, Sat 9-12

DECATUR

P IVA JANE PEEK PUBLIC LIBRARY, 121 N Main St, 72722. (Mail add: PO Box 247, 72722-0247). Tel: 479-752-7323. FAX: 479-752-7323. E-mail: ijppublib121@yahoo.com. *Librn,* Karen Jones; Staff 1 (Non-MLS 1)
Founded 2001. Pop 3,408; Circ 1,864
Library Holdings: Audiobooks 31; Bks on Deafness & Sign Lang 3; CDs 77; DVDs 70; High Interest/Low Vocabulary Bk Vols 70; Large Print Bks 211; Bk Vols 9,236; Per Subs 2; Videos 399
Automation Activity & Vendor Info: (Cataloging) Book Systems; (Circulation) Book Systems; (OPAC) Book Systems
Wireless access
Open Mon-Fri 3:30-7, Wed 10:30-1

DEWITT

P DEWITT PUBLIC LIBRARY*, 205 W Maxwell, 72042. SAN 300-4945. Tel: 870-946-1151. FAX: 870-946-1151. *Dir,* Virginia D Platt
Founded 1926. Pop 4,000; Circ 14,000
Library Holdings: Bk Vols 43,000
Open Mon-Fri 9-5, Sat 9-1
Branches: 1
CLEON COLLIER MEMORIAL LIBRARY, 211 Main St, Gillett, 72055, SAN 320-0817. Tel: 870-548-2821. FAX: 870-548-2821. *Librn,* Stacey Clawson
Founded 1976. Circ 4,388
Library Holdings: Bk Titles 3,928
Open Mon-Wed & Fri 12:30-5:30

J PHILLIPS COMMUNITY COLLEGE OF THE UNIVERSITY OF ARKANSAS*, DeWitt Campus Library, 1210 Ricebelt Ave, 72042. (Mail add: PO Box 427, 72042-0427). Tel: 870-946-3506, Ext 1621. FAX: 870-946-2644. Web Site: www.pccua.edu/library/dewitt_library_information.htm. *Dir,* Jerrie Townsend; Tel: 870-946-3506, Ext 1818, E-mail: jtownsend@pccua.edu; *Librn,* Raylyn Boyd
Library Holdings: Bk Vols 6,500; Per Subs 50
Automation Activity & Vendor Info: (Cataloging) Innovative Interfaces, Inc; (Circulation) Innovative Interfaces, Inc; (OPAC) Innovative Interfaces, Inc
Database Vendor: Gale Cengage Learning, OCLC FirstSearch, ProQuest
Open Mon-Fri 8-4:30; Mon-Thurs (Summer) 7-4:30

DYESS

P DYESS PUBLIC LIBRARY*, 101 E Fourth St, 72330. Tel: 870-764-2101 (city hall). *Librn,* Brenda Barnes
Library Holdings: Bk Vols 2,000
Open Mon (Winter) 3:30-5; Mon (Summer) 1-3

EDMONDSON

P EDMONDSON PUBLIC LIBRARY*, 61 Waterford St, 72332. (Mail add: PO Box 300, 72332-0300). Tel: 870-735-6946. FAX: 870-735-6988. *Librn,* Bonnie Ellis
Library Holdings: Bk Vols 2,400
Open Mon-Fri 1-5

EL DORADO

P BARTON LIBRARY*, 200 E Fifth St, 71730-3897. SAN 330-9541. Tel: 870-863-5447. FAX: 870-862-3944. E-mail: inquiries@bartonlibrary.org. Web Site: www.bartonlibrary.org. *Dir,* Nancy Arn; E-mail: narn@bartonlibrary.org; Staff 1 (MLS 1)
Founded 1958. Pop 43,165; Circ 61,506
Jan 2008-Dec 2008 Income (Main Library and Branch(s)) $568,739, State $81,707, City $308,869, County $141,815, Locally Generated Income $13,747, Other $22,601. Mats Exp $49,077, Books $37,864, Per/Ser (Incl. Access Fees) $3,500, AV Equip $1,105, AV Mat $4,500, Electronic Ref Mat (Incl. Access Fees) $2,108. Sal $332,408 (Prof $44,162)
Library Holdings: Audiobooks 2,016; Bks on Deafness & Sign Lang 7; DVDs 1,613; Electronic Media & Resources 87; Microforms 618; Bk Titles 75,872; Per Subs 107
Special Collections: Arkansas Coll, monographs & periodicals; Genealogy Coll, micro, monographs; Large Print Coll
Automation Activity & Vendor Info: (Cataloging) TLC (The Library Corporation); (Circulation) TLC (The Library Corporation); (Course Reserve) TLC (The Library Corporation); (ILL) TLC (The Library Corporation); (Media Booking) TLC (The Library Corporation); (OPAC) TLC (The Library Corporation)
Database Vendor: EBSCOhost, TLC (The Library Corporation)
Wireless access
Function: Bk club(s), Bks on CD, Children's prog, Computers for patron use, Copy machines, Fax serv, Genealogy discussion group, Handicapped accessible, Holiday prog, Homebound delivery serv, Homework prog, ILL available, Mail & tel request accepted, Notary serv, Online cat, Outreach serv, Photocopying/Printing, Preschool outreach, Prog for adults, Prog for children & young adult, Pub access computers, Ref serv in person, Story hour, Summer reading prog, Tax forms, Teen prog
Publications: Come Together (Monthly newsletter)
Partic in Amigos Library Services, Inc; OCLC Online Computer Library Center, Inc
Special Services for the Deaf - Bks on deafness & sign lang
Special Services for the Blind - Bks on CD; Large print bks; Ref serv
Open Mon, Wed & Fri 9:30-5:30, Tues & Thurs 1-9, Sat 1-5
Friends of the Library Group
Branches: 5
HARPER MEMORIAL, 301 N Myrtle, Junction City, 71749. (Mail add: PO Box 730, Junction City, 71749-0730), SAN 330-9606. Tel: 870-924-5556. FAX: 870-924-5556. *Librn,* Pam Smith
Library Holdings: Bk Vols 5,255
Open Mon, Tues, Thurs & Fri 12-5 (1-6 Summer)
Friends of the Library Group
HUTTIG BRANCH, Frost St, Huttig, 71747. (Mail add: PO Box 396, Huttig, 71747-0458), SAN 330-9576. Tel: 870-943-3411. FAX: 870-943-3411. *Librn,* Gelynn Little
Library Holdings: Bk Vols 7,000
Open Mon, Tues, Thurs & Fri 11-4
NORPHLET PUBLIC, City Hall Bldg, 101 E Padgett St, Norphlet, 71759. (Mail add: PO Box 44, Norphlet, 71759-0044), SAN 330-9630. Tel: 870-546-2274. FAX: 870-546-2274. *Librn,* Amy Kitchens
Library Holdings: Bk Vols 3,605
Open Mon, Tues, Thurs & Fri 11-4
SMACKOVER PUBLIC, 700 N Broadway, Smackover, 71762, SAN 330-969X. Tel: 870-725-3741. FAX: 870-725-3798. *Librn,* Melba Bussell
Library Holdings: Bk Vols 8,230
Subject Interests: Genealogy, Local hist
Open Mon, Thurs & Fri 8:30-5
Friends of the Library Group
STRONG PUBLIC, 246 Second Ave, Strong, 71765. (Mail add: PO Box 157, Strong, 71765-0157), SAN 330-972X. Tel: 870-797-2165. FAX: 870-797-2165. *Librn,* Rhonda Bagwell
Pop 626; Circ 6,000
Library Holdings: Audiobooks 10; Bks on Deafness & Sign Lang 3; CDs 20; Large Print Bks 1,000; Bk Vols 5,400; Per Subs 10; Spec Interest Per Sub 3
Function: Summer reading prog
Open Mon, Tues, Thurs & Fri 11-4

J SOUTH ARKANSAS COMMUNITY COLLEGE*, Library Media Center, 300 Summit, 71730. (Mail add: PO Box 7010, 71731), SAN 321-1754. Tel: 870-864-7115. FAX: 870-864-7134. Web Site: www.southark.edu. *Dir,* Francis Kuykendall; Tel: 870-864-7116, E-mail: fkuykendall@southark.edu; *Tech Serv,* Lauri Wilson; Staff 2 (MLS 1, Non-MLS 1)
Founded 1976. Enrl 1,250; Fac 75; Highest Degree: Associate
Library Holdings: Bk Titles 22,000; Bk Vols 24,000; Per Subs 98
Automation Activity & Vendor Info: (Acquisitions) LS 2000; (Cataloging) LS 2000; (Circulation) LS 2000; (Course Reserve) LS 2000; (OPAC) LS 2000; (Serials) LS 2000
Database Vendor: EBSCOhost, Gale Cengage Learning, ProQuest
Function: AV serv
Partic in Ark Libr Asn
Open Mon-Thurs (Winter) 7:30-7, Fri 7:30-5, Sun 1-5; Mon-Fri (Summer) 8-5

CM UNIVERSITY OF ARKANSAS FOR MEDICAL SCIENCES SOUTH ARKANSAS LIBRARY*, Carroll Medical Library, 460 W Oak, 71730. SAN 300-4996. Tel: 870-881-4403, 870-881-4404. FAX: 870-862-0570. Web Site: www.ahecsa.uams.edu/library.asp. *Dir,* Vicki J De Yampert; E-mail: vdeyampert@ahecsa.uams.edu; *Libr Tech,* Deborah G Johnson; E-mail: djohnson@ahecsa.uams.edu
Founded 1974
Library Holdings: Bk Vols 1,000; Per Subs 100
Special Collections: Consumer Health Information Coll
Wireless access
Partic in OCLC Online Computer Library Center, Inc; S Cent Regional Med Libr Program

ELKINS

P ELKINS PUBLIC LIBRARY*, 352 N Center St, 72727. SAN 328-6843. Tel: 479-643-2904. E-mail: elkins@wcls.lib.ar.us. Web Site: Elkinspubliclibrary.com, www.wcls.lib.ar.us. *Libr Dir,* Margaret Harrelson
Library Holdings: Bk Vols 10,000
Automation Activity & Vendor Info: (Acquisitions) Innovative Interfaces, Inc; (Cataloging) Innovative Interfaces, Inc; (Circulation) Innovative Interfaces, Inc; (OPAC) Innovative Interfaces, Inc
Wireless access
Mem of Washington County Library System
Open Mon-Fri 10-6, Sat 10-2
Friends of the Library Group

EUREKA SPRINGS

P CARNEGIE PUBLIC LIBRARY*, 194 Spring St, 72632. SAN 331-0957. Tel: 479-253-8754. FAX: 479-253-7807. E-mail: info@eurekalibrary.org. Web Site: www.eurekalibrary.org. *Dir,* Jean Elderwind; *Asst Dir,* Kate Zakar; Staff 3 (MLS 1, Non-MLS 2)
Founded 1910. Pop 8,500; Circ 65,000
Library Holdings: Bks on Deafness & Sign Lang 20; High Interest/Low Vocabulary Bk Vols 75; Bk Vols 38,000; Per Subs 55
Special Collections: Local History Coll
Wireless access
Open Mon & Wed 9-6, Tues & Thurs 9-8, Fri & Sat 9-5
Friends of the Library Group

FAIRFIELD BAY

P FAIRFIELD BAY LIBRARY, INC*, 369 Dave Creek Pkwy, 72088. SAN 330-9150. Tel: 501-884-4930. E-mail: ffblib@artelco.com. *Mgr,* Sara Michael
Wireless access
Special Services for the Deaf - Adult & family literacy prog; Bks on deafness & sign lang; Closed caption videos
Open Mon, Tues & Thurs 1-4, Wed & Fri 10-5, Sat 10-12:30
Friends of the Library Group

FAYETTEVILLE

P FAYETTEVILLE PUBLIC LIBRARY*, Blair Library, 401 W Mountain St, 72701. SAN 330-9932. Tel: 479-856-7000. FAX: 479-571-0222. E-mail: questions@faylib.org. Web Site: www.faylib.org. *Exec Dir,* David Johnson; Tel: 479-856-7100, E-mail: djohnson@faylib.org; *Dir of Libr Serv,* Laura Speer; E-mail: lspeer@faylib.org; *Head, Circ,* Denise Wax; *Head, Tech Serv,* Sarah Houk; *Actg Head of Ref,* Willow Fitzgibbon; E-mail: wfitzgibbon@faylib.org; *Actg Head, Youth Serv,* Caitlyn Walsh; E-mail: cwalsh@faylib.org; *Mgr, Info Tech,* Lynn Yandell; Staff 23 (MLS 10, Non-MLS 13)
Founded 1916. Pop 68,980; Circ 951,872
Jan 2008-Dec 2008 Income $3,603,361, State $118,996, City $1,891,365, Locally Generated Income $1,070,000, Other $523,000. Mats Exp $406,294, Books $227,526, Per/Ser (Incl. Access Fees) $20,314, Other Print Mats $20,314, AV Mat $89,385, Electronic Ref Mat (Incl. Access Fees) $48,755. Sal $17,217,961
Library Holdings: Bk Vols 238,079; Per Subs 357
Subject Interests: Genealogy
Automation Activity & Vendor Info: (Acquisitions) Innovative Interfaces, Inc; (Cataloging) Innovative Interfaces, Inc; (Circulation) Innovative Interfaces, Inc; (OPAC) Innovative Interfaces, Inc; (Serials) Innovative Interfaces, Inc
Database Vendor: Baker & Taylor, Comprise Technologies Inc, EBSCOhost, Gale Cengage Learning, OCLC FirstSearch, ReferenceUSA
Wireless access
Function: After school storytime, Audio & video playback equip for onsite use, Bi-weekly Writer's Group, Games & aids for the handicapped, Handicapped accessible, Homebound delivery serv, ILL available, Music CDs, Prog for adults, Prog for children & young adult, Ref serv available, Spoken cassettes & CDs, Summer reading prog, Wheelchair accessible, Workshops
Special Services for the Blind - Assistive/Adapted tech devices, equip & products
Open Mon-Thurs 9-8, Fri & Sat 9-5, Sun 1-5
Restriction: Non-resident fee
Friends of the Library Group

C UNIVERSITY OF ARKANSAS LIBRARIES, 365 N McIlroy Ave, 72701-4002. SAN 331-0264. Tel: 479-575-4101. Circulation Tel: 479-575-4104. Interlibrary Loan Service Tel: 479-575-6424. Reference Tel: 479-575-6645. Administration Tel: 479-575-6702. FAX: 479-575-6656. Interlibrary Loan Service FAX: 479-575-5558. Reference FAX: 479-575-4592. Web Site: libinfo.uark.edu. *Dean,* Carolyn Henderson Allen; E-mail: challen@uark.edu; *Dir of Admin Serv,* Marco DeProsperis; Tel: 479-575-3079, E-mail: mdeprosp@uark.edu; *Dir, Acad Res & Serv,* Lora Lennertz; Tel: 479-575-5545, E-mail: lennertz@uark.edu; *Dir, Coll Mgt & IT Serv,* Judy Ganson; Tel: 479-575-2130, E-mail: jganson@uark.edu; *Develop Dir,* Ben Carter; Tel: 479-575-4663, E-mail: bcarter@uark.edu; *Asst Dir, Human Res,* Jeff Banks; Tel: 479-575-4769, E-mail: jbbanks@uark.edu; *Head, ILL,* Tess Gibson; Tel: 479-575-2925, E-mail: tmgibso@uark.edu; *Head, Monographs,* Mary Gilbertson; Tel: 479-575-5417, E-mail: mag@uark.edu; *Head, Music Cat/Database Maintenance,* Deb Kulczak; Tel: 479-575-4811, E-mail: dkulczak@uark.edu; *Head, Performing Arts & Media,* Tim Zou; Tel: 479-575-5514, E-mail: tzou@uark.edu; *Head, Ser,* Marilyn Rogers; E-mail: mrogers@uark.edu; *Head, Spec Coll,* Timothy G Nutt; Tel: 479-575-8443, E-mail: timn@uark.edu; *Head, Spec Coll Cat,* Mikey King; Tel: 479-575-4657, E-mail: mikey@uark.edu; *Head, Tech Serv,* Position Currently Open; *Bus Librn,* Position Currently Open; *Educ Librn,* Elizabeth McKee; Tel: 479-575-5313, E-mail: emckee@uark.edu; *Eng & Math Librn,* Patricia Kirkwood; Tel: 479-575-2480, E-mail: pkirkwo@uark.edu; *Geosciences & Maps Librn,* Position Currently Open; *Life Sci Librn,* Tony Stankus; Tel: 479-575-4031, E-mail: tstankus@uark.edu; *Ref Librn,* Norma Johnson; Tel: 479-575-3498, E-mail: njohns@uark.edu; *Ref Librn,* Sarah Spiegel; Tel: 479-575-8415, E-mail: sspiegel@uark.edu; *Sci Librn,* Necia Parker-Gibson; Tel: 479-575-8421, E-mail: neciap@uark.edu; *Spec Coll Res & Outreach Serv Librn,* Joshua Youngblood; Tel: 479-575-7251, E-mail: jcyoungb@uark.edu; *Syst Librn,* Position Currently Open; *Web Serv Librn,* Beth Juhl; Tel: 479-575-4665, E-mail: bjuhl@uark.edu; *Librn in Residence,* Martha Parker; Tel: 479-575-2032, E-mail: map012@uark.edu; *Fac Coordr,* Sheri Gallaher; Tel: 479-575-3808, E-mail: sgallahe@uark.edu; *Govt Doc & Soc Sci Serv,* Donna Daniels; Tel: 479-575-8417, E-mail: donnad@uark.edu; *Univ Archivist,* Amy Allen; Tel: 479-575-6370, E-mail: ala005@uark.edu. Subject Specialists: *Asian studies, Chinese lang & lit, Japanese lang & lit,* Lora Lennertz; *Asian studies, Chinese lang & lit, Japanese lang & lit,* Tim Zou; *Eng, Math, Transportation,* Patricia Kirkwood; Staff 50 (MLS 32, Non-MLS 18)
Founded 1872. Enrl 28,724; Fac 1,035; Highest Degree: Doctorate
Jul 2012-Jun 2013. Mats Exp $6,864,015, Books $947,444, Per/Ser (Incl. Access Fees) $5,012,236, Other Print Mats $495,153. Sal $5,768,379 (Prof $3,329,667)
Library Holdings: CDs 32,005; DVDs 6,374; Electronic Media & Resources 9,013; Microforms 5,583,650; Bk Vols 2,100,885; Per Subs 51,403
Special Collections: Arkansas Coll; William J Fulbright Coll. Oral History; US Document Depository
Subject Interests: Agr, Archit, Creative writing, Intl relations
Automation Activity & Vendor Info: (Acquisitions) Innovative Interfaces, Inc; (Cataloging) Innovative Interfaces, Inc; (Circulation) Innovative Interfaces, Inc; (Course Reserve) Innovative Interfaces, Inc; (ILL) Innovative Interfaces, Inc, (Media Booking) Innovative Interfaces, Inc; (OPAC) Innovative Interfaces, Inc; (Serials) Innovative Interfaces, Inc
Database Vendor: ACM (Association for Computing Machinery), Agricola, Alexander Street Press, American Chemical Society, American Mathematical Society, Amigos Library Services, ARTstor, ASCE Research Library, BioOne, Bowker, Cambridge Scientific Abstracts, Cinahl, CQ Press, CRC Press/Taylor & Francis Group, ebrary, EBSCOhost, Elsevier MDL, Emerald, Foundation Center, Gale Cengage Learning, Gallup, IEEE (Institute of Electrical & Electronics Engineers), Ingenta, Innovative Interfaces, Inc, IOP, ISI Web of Knowledge, JSTOR, Knovel, LexisNexis, Luna Imaging/Insight, Marcive, Inc, Marquis Who's Who, McGraw-Hill, Medline, Mergent Online, Modern Language Association, OCLC ArticleFirst, OCLC FirstSearch, OCLC WorldShare Interlibrary Loan, OVID Technologies, Oxford Online, Project MUSE, ProQuest, PubMed, RefWorks, Sage, ScienceDirect, Standard & Poor's, ValueLine, Wiley, Wiley InterScience, Wilson - Wilson Web, YBP Library Services
Wireless access
Publications: Arkansauce (Newsletter); Arkansian (Special Collections) (Newsletter); Retrospective (Annual report)
Partic in Amigos Library Services, Inc; ARKnet (Arkansas Academic & Research Network); Center for Research Libraries; Council of University of Arkansas Research Libraries (CUARL); EPSCoR Science Information Group; Greater Western Library Alliance
Special Services for the Blind - Assistive/Adapted tech devices, equip & products
Open Mon-Thurs 7am-2am, Fri 7-6, Sat 10-6, Sun Noon-2am

Departmental Libraries:

CHEMISTRY & BIOCHEMISTRY, University of Arkansas, 225 CHEM, 72701-4002. Tel: 479-575-2557. Administration Tel: 479-575-8418. Web Site: libinfo.uark.edu/chemistry. *Head of Libr,* Lutishoor Salisbury; Fax: 479-575-6656, E-mail: lsalisbu@uark.edu. Subject Specialists: *Biochem, Chem,* Lutishoor Salisbury; Staff 2 (MLS 1, Non-MLS 1)
Enrl 330; Fac 23; Highest Degree: Doctorate

FINE ARTS, 104 Fine Arts Bldg, 72701. (Mail add: 365 N McIlroy Ave, 72701-4002). Tel: 479-575-4708. Web Site: libinfo.uark.edu/fal. *Head of Libr,* Phillip J Jones; Tel: 479-575-3081, E-mail: pjj01@uark.edu; *Supvr,* Gale Golden; Tel: 479-575-3499, E-mail: gcgolden@uark.edu; *Evening Supvr,* Aiden Guzman; Tel: 479-575-4236, E-mail: aeguzman@uark.edu. Subject Specialists: *Archit, Art, Interior design,* Phillip J Jones; Staff 3 (MLS 1, Non-MLS 2)
Enrl 876; Fac 48; Highest Degree: Bachelor

Library Holdings: Bk Vols 36,231
Automation Activity & Vendor Info: (Circulation) Innovative Interfaces, Inc; (OPAC) Innovative Interfaces, Inc
Open Mon-Thurs 8am-11pm, Fri 8-6, Sat 1-6, Sun 2-11
Friends of the Library Group

PHYSICS, 221 Physics, 72701. (Mail add: 365 N McIlroy Ave, 72701-4002). Tel: 479-575-2505. E-mail: physlib@uark.edu. Web Site: libinfo.uark.edu/physics. *Head of Libr,* Kathleen Lehman; Tel: 479-575-7048, E-mail: kalehman@uark.edu. Subject Specialists: *Physics, Planetary sci, Space sci,* Kathleen Lehman; Staff 2 (MLS 1, Non-MLS 1)
Library Holdings: Bk Vols 19,407

CL ROBERT A & VIVIAN YOUNG LAW LIBRARY, School of Law, Waterman Hall 107, 72701-1201, SAN 331-0353. Tel: 479-575-5601. FAX: 479-575-2053. Web Site: law.uark.edu/library/research. *Dir,* Randall Thompson; Tel: 479-575-5831, E-mail: rjthomps@uark.edu; *Assoc Dir,* Monika Szakasits; Tel: 479-575-2839, E-mail: mszakas@uark.edu; *Bus Mgr,* Jackie Dunn; Tel: 479-575-5310, E-mail: jmd03@uark.edu; *Ref Serv Coordr,* Lorraine Lorne; Tel: 479-575-5834, E-mail: llorne@uark.edu; *Cat Supvr,* Nancy Phillips; Tel: 479-575-5984, E-mail: nphillips@uark.edu; *Circ,* Jo Anna Collins; Tel: 479-575-5051, E-mail: jcollins@uark.edu; *Ref,* Cathy Chick; Tel: 479-575-5835, E-mail: cchick@uark.edu; Staff 13 (MLS 6, Non-MLS 7)
Founded 1924. Enrl 400; Fac 35; Highest Degree: Doctorate
Library Holdings: Bk Titles 89,462; Bk Vols 158,353; Per Subs 545
Special Collections: State Document Depository; UN Document Depository; US Document Depository
Subject Interests: Law
Automation Activity & Vendor Info: (Acquisitions) Innovative Interfaces, Inc; (Cataloging) Innovative Interfaces, Inc; (Circulation) Innovative Interfaces, Inc; (Course Reserve) Innovative Interfaces, Inc; (ILL) Innovative Interfaces, Inc; (Media Booking) Innovative Interfaces, Inc; (OPAC) Innovative Interfaces, Inc; (Serials) Innovative Interfaces, Inc
Database Vendor: LexisNexis
Partic in OCLC Online Computer Library Center, Inc
Publications: Young in a Nutshell (Newsletter)

P WASHINGTON COUNTY LIBRARY SYSTEM*, 1080 W Clydesdale Dr, 72701. Tel: 479-442-6253. FAX: 479-442-6812. E-mail: info@wcls.lib.ar.us. Web Site: wcls.lib.ar.us. *Dir,* Glenda Audrain; *Asst Dir,* Steven Thomas; E-mail: stevent@wcls.lib.ar.us; Staff 2 (MLS 2)
Founded 2000. Pop 199,060; Circ 1,051,830
Library Holdings: Bk Vols 350,000
Database Vendor: EBSCOhost, Gale Cengage Learning, LearningExpress, OCLC FirstSearch
Function: ILL available
Member Libraries: Burgettstown Community Library; California Area Public Library; Donora Public Library; Elkins Public Library; Frank Sarris Public Library; Heritage Public Library; Lincoln Public Library; Monongahela Area Library; Peters Township Public Library; Prairie Grove Public Library; Springdale Public Library; Washington County Library System; Winslow Public Library
Friends of the Library Group
Branches: 2
GREENLAND BRANCH LIBRARY, PO Box 67, 8 E Ross, Greenland, 72737, SAN 330-9967. Tel: 479-582-5992. E-mail: greenlandbranch@wcls.lib.ar.us. *Librn,* Terri Underhill
Library Holdings: Bk Vols 7,500
Mem of Washington County Library System
Open Mon, Tues, Thurs & Fri 12-5
WINSLOW BRANCH LIBRARY, 351 South Hwy 71, Winslow, 72959, SAN 331-023X. Tel: 479-634-5405. E-mail: winslowbranch@wcls.lib.ar.us. *Br Mgr,* Pam Kugel
Library Holdings: Bk Titles 6,000
Open Tues-Thurs & Sat 9-5

FORDYCE

P DALLAS COUNTY LIBRARY*, 501 E Fourth St, 71742. (Mail add: PO Box 584, 71742-0584), SAN 331-0418. Tel: 870-352-3592. FAX: 870-352-3508. E-mail: dalcolib@yahoo.com. *Libr Mgr,* Amy Ketzer
Founded 1934. Pop 9,168; Circ 32,000
Library Holdings: Large Print Bks 75; Bk Vols 34,295
Automation Activity & Vendor Info: (Cataloging) Follett Software; (Circulation) Follett Software; (OPAC) Follett Software
Open Mon-Wed & Fri 9-4:30
Branches: 1
SPARKMAN BRANCH, 186 Dallas 208, Sparkman, 71763, SAN 331-0477. *Librn,* Katie Freeman
Open Tues & Wed 2-4

FORREST CITY

J EAST ARKANSAS COMMUNITY COLLEGE*, Learning Resources Center, 1700 Newcastle Rd, 72335. SAN 320-1201. Tel: 870-633-4480, Ext 322. FAX: 870-633-7222. Web Site: www.eacc.edu. *Librn,* Daniel Page; Staff 4 (MLS 1, Non-MLS 3)
Founded 1974. Enrl 972
Library Holdings: Bk Vols 30,000; Per Subs 100
Automation Activity & Vendor Info: (Cataloging) TLC (The Library Corporation); (Circulation) TLC (The Library Corporation); (OPAC) TLC (The Library Corporation)
Database Vendor: EBSCOhost, Gale Cengage Learning, ProQuest
Open Mon-Thurs 7:45am-8pm, Fri 7:45-4:30, Sat 8-12

P FORREST CITY PUBLIC LIBRARY*, 421 S Washington, 72335-3839. SAN 300-502X. Tel: 870-633-5646. FAX: 870-633-5647. Web Site: www.forrestcitylibrary.org. *Dir,* Arlisa Price; Staff 3 (Non-MLS 3)
Founded 1921. Pop 15,000; Circ 34,019
Library Holdings: Bk Titles 29,156; Per Subs 31
Subject Interests: Ark

FORT SMITH

S WILLIAM O DARBY RANGER MEMORIAL FOUNDATION INC*, Museum & Heritage Centre, 311 General Darby St, 72902. (Mail add: PO Box 1625, 72902-1625), SAN 375-3514. Tel: 479-782-3388. FAX: 479-782-3388. E-mail: gendarby@att.net, gendarby@yahoo.com. Web Site: www.darbyrangerfoundation.com. *Pres,* Emory S Dockery, Jr
Founded 1977
Library Holdings: Bk Vols 5,000
Special Collections: Victor L Cary Civil War Book Coll; World War II Coll
Wireless access
Open Mon-Fri 8-1

P FORT SMITH PUBLIC LIBRARY*, 3201 Rogers Ave, 72903. SAN 331-0507. Tel: 479-783-0229. FAX: 479-782-8571. TDD: 479-785-1413. Web Site: www.fortsmithlibrary.org. *Dir,* Jennifer Goodson; E-mail: jgoodson@fortsmithlibrary.org; *Asst Dir,* Diane Holwick; E-mail: dholwick@fortsmithlibrary.org; *Syst Coordr,* P J Williams; E-mail: pwilliams@fortsmithlibrary.org; *Circ,* Jeane Pillar; E-mail: jpillar@fortsmithlibrary.org; *Info Spec,* Diana Curry; E-mail: dcurry@fortsmithlibrary.org; *Ref Serv,* Ashley Hagan; E-mail: ahagan@fortsmithlibrary.org; *Tech Serv,* Jennie Ballinger; E-mail: jballinger@fortsmithlibrary.org; *Youth Serv,* Robin Kelly; E-mail: rkelly@fortsmithlibrary.org. Subject Specialists: *Genealogy,* Diana Curry; Staff 14 (MLS 6, Non-MLS 8)
Founded 1906. Pop 80,268; Circ 686,013
Library Holdings: AV Mats 12,477; Bk Titles 169,249; Bk Vols 252,952; Per Subs 475
Special Collections: Local, State History & Genealogy (Arkansas Coll), bks & micro; Mathew C Clark American Sign Language Coll; Vietnamese Coll
Subject Interests: Spanish
Automation Activity & Vendor Info: (Cataloging) Innovative Interfaces, Inc; (Circulation) Innovative Interfaces, Inc; (OPAC) Innovative Interfaces, Inc
Database Vendor: EBSCOhost, Facts on File, OCLC FirstSearch
Wireless access
Partic in OCLC Online Computer Library Center, Inc
Special Services for the Deaf - TDD equip
Open Mon-Thurs 9-9, Fri 9-6, Sat 10-5, Sun 1-5
Friends of the Library Group
Branches: 3
DALLAS STREET, 8100 Dallas St, Forth Smith, 72903. Tel: 479-484-5650. *Br Mgr,* Mike Ezell; Fax: 479-484-5658, E-mail: mezell@fortsmithlibrary.org; Staff 1 (Non-MLS 1)
Library Holdings: Bk Vols 24,730
MILLER, 8701 S 28th St, 72908. Tel: 479-646-3945. FAX: 479-646-3965. *Br Mgr,* Tiffany Nelson; E-mail: tnelson@fortsmithlibrary.org; Staff 1 (Non-MLS 1)
Library Holdings: Bk Vols 26,786
WINDSOR DRIVE, 4701 Windsor Dr, 72904. Tel: 479-785-0405. FAX: 479-785-0431. *Br Mgr,* Janine Jamison; E-mail: jjamison@fortsmithlibrary.org; Staff 1 (Non-MLS 1)
Library Holdings: Bk Vols 24,829

M REGIONAL MEDICAL CENTER*, Health Sciences Library, 1001 Towson Ave, 72901-4915. (Mail add: PO Box 17006, 72917-7006), SAN 300-5054. Tel: 479-441-5337. FAX: 479-441-5339. Web Site: www.sparks.org. *Dir, Online Serv,* Grace Anderson; E-mail: grace@sparks.org; *Asst Librn,* Jean Stewart
Founded 1972
Library Holdings: Bk Titles 3,000; Per Subs 227

Automation Activity & Vendor Info: (Cataloging) Innovative Interfaces, Inc
Database Vendor: OCLC FirstSearch, OVID Technologies
Function: ILL available
Partic in ARIEL; OCLC Online Computer Library Center, Inc
Open Mon-Fri 8-4:30

M SAINT EDWARD MERCY MEDICAL CENTER LIBRARY*, 7301 Rogers Ave, 72917. (Mail add: PO Box 17000, 72917-7000), SAN 300-5038. Tel: 479-314-6520. FAX: 479-314-5646. *Dir,* Pat Morris; E-mail: pmorris@ftsm.mercy.net
Library Holdings: Bk Vols 1,600, Per Subs 52
Subject Interests: Med, Nursing
Wireless access
Open Mon-Fri 7:30-4

GL SEBASTIAN COUNTY LAW LIBRARY*, 623 Garrison Ave, Ste 418, 72901. SAN 300-5046. Tel: 479-783-4730. FAX: 479-783-4730. E-mail: sebcoll@sbcglobal.net. *Librn,* Brenda Elliott
Library Holdings: Bk Vols 18,000
Database Vendor: Westlaw
Wireless access
Open Mon, Wed & Fri 9-5

C UNIVERSITY OF ARKANSAS FORT SMITH, Boreham Library, 5210 Grand Ave, 72903. (Mail add: PO Box 3649, 72913-3649), SAN 300-5062. Tel: 479-788-7200. Interlibrary Loan Service Tel: 479-788-7201. Reference Tel: 479-788-7204, 479-788-7208. FAX: 479-424-6236. E-mail: library@uafs.edu. Web Site: www.uafs.edu. *Dir of Libr Serv,* Robert Frizzell; Tel: 479-788-7205, E-mail: Robert.Frizzell@uafs.edu; *Digital Coll Librn, Ref,* Carolyn Filippelli; E-mail: Carolyn.Filippelli@uafs.edu; *Pub Serv & Instruction Librn,* Jordan Ruud; E-mail: jordan.ruud@uafs.edu; *Pub Serv Librn,* Jason Phillips; Tel: 479-788-7217, E-mail: Jason.Phillips@uafs.edu; *Cat, Tech Serv,* Dennis G Van Arsdale; E-mail: Dennis.Vanarsdale@uafs.edu. Subject Specialists: *Non-N Am hist, Philos,* Robert Frizzell; *Educ, Soc sci,* Carolyn Filippelli; *Lang, Lit,* Jordan Ruud; *Biol, Geol, Polit sci,* Jason Phillips; *Computing, Sci, Tech,* Dennis G Van Arsdale; Staff 6 (MLS 6)
Founded 1928. Enrl 5,400; Fac 240; Highest Degree: Bachelor
Library Holdings: CDs 354; DVDs 2,316; e-books 163,000; e-journals 56,000; Music Scores 500; Bk Titles 62,408; Bk Vols 66,646; Per Subs 240
Special Collections: Grantsmanship Coll; Olive, Kathleen & Rosa Belle A Pebley Historical & Cultural Center; Wilder Historical Coll
Automation Activity & Vendor Info: (Cataloging) Innovative Interfaces, Inc; (Circulation) Innovative Interfaces, Inc; (Course Reserve) Innovative Interfaces, Inc; (ILL) OCLC ILLiad; (OPAC) Innovative Interfaces, Inc; (Serials) Innovative Interfaces, Inc
Database Vendor: ABC-CLIO, ACM (Association for Computing Machinery), Agricola, American Chemical Society, American Psychological Association (APA), Amigos Library Services, ARTstor, BioOne, Cambridge Scientific Abstracts, Career Guidance Foundation, Cinahl, College Source, Commonwealth Business Media, CredoReference, EBSCOhost, Foundation Center, Gale Cengage Learning, H W Wilson, JSTOR, LexisNexis, Medline, Modern Language Association, OCLC FirstSearch, OVID Technologies, Project MUSE, ProQuest, PubMed, RefWorks, Sage, ScienceDirect, SerialsSolutions, Swets Information Services, Wiley
Wireless access
Function: 24/7 Online cat
Partic in Amigos Library Services, Inc; ARKLink; OCLC Online Computer Library Center, Inc
Open Mon-Thurs (Fall & Spring) 7am-9:30pm, Fri 7-5, Sat 11-3, Sun 2-8

GARFIELD

S US NATIONAL PARK SERVICE, Pea Ridge Military Park Library, 15930 Hyw 62, 72732. SAN 370-2855. Tel: 479-451-8122. FAX: 479-451-8639. Web Site: www.nps.gov/peri. *In Charge,* Troy Banzhaf; E-mail: troy_banzhaf@nps.gov
Library Holdings: Bk Vols 500
Special Collections: Battle of Pea Ridge, microfilm, rpts
Restriction: Open to pub by appt only, Open to pub for ref only

GENTRY

P GENTRY PUBLIC LIBRARY, 105 E Main St, 72734. Tel: 479-736-2054. FAX: 479-736-8567. E-mail: library@cityofgentry.com. Web Site: www.gentrylibrary.us. *Librn,* Darla Threet; E-mail: darla.threet@cityofgentry.com; Staff 2 (Non-MLS 2)
Founded 1975. Pop 15,359; Circ 25,397
Jan 2011-Dec 2011 Income $148,994, City $144,394, Locally Generated Income $4,600. Mats Exp $6,400, Books $6,000, Per/Ser (Incl. Access Fees) $400. Sal $41,794
Library Holdings: Audiobooks 983; Bks on Deafness & Sign Lang 14; DVDs 1,702; Large Print Bks 72; Bk Titles 19,961; Per Subs 25

Special Collections: American Civil War (Quantrill Special Coll Research)
Automation Activity & Vendor Info: (Acquisitions) Book Systems; (Cataloging) Book Systems; (Circulation) Book Systems
Wireless access
Open Mon & Thurs 9-7, Tues, Wed & Fri 9-5, Sat 9-12
Friends of the Library Group

GLENWOOD

P BAINUM LIBRARY & LEARNING CENTER, Glenwood City Library, 210 N Second St, Ste L, 71943. SAN 331-1406. Tel: 870-356-4643. FAX: 870-356-4643. E-mail: library@bainum.org. Web Site: bainum.org. *Librn,* Marjorie Melichar
Wireless access
Open Tues-Fri 9-5, Sat 9-2

GRAVETTE

P GRAVETTE PUBLIC LIBRARY*, 407 Charlotte St SE, 72736-9363. Tel: 479-787-6955. FAX: 479-787-9780. E-mail: librarygravette@yahoo.com. Web Site: www.cityofgravette-ar.gov/gravettelibrary.html. *Libr Mgr,* Kim Schneider
Pop 2,500
Library Holdings: Bk Vols 20,000; Per Subs 10
Automation Activity & Vendor Info: (Acquisitions) SirsiDynix; (Cataloging) SirsiDynix; (Circulation) SirsiDynix
Database Vendor: Overdrive, Inc
Wireless access
Special Services for the Blind - Accessible computers; Audio mat
Open Mon-Fri 10-6, Sat 9-5
Friends of the Library Group
Bookmobiles: 1

GREEN FOREST

P GREEN FOREST PUBLIC LIBRARY, 206 E Main St, 72638-2627. (Mail add: PO Box 746, 72638-0746), SAN 331-0981. Tel: 870-438-6700. FAX: 870-438-4586. E-mail: info@greenforestlibrary.org. Web Site: www.greenforestlibrary.org. *Libr Dir,* Tiffany Newton; E-mail: tnewton@greenforestlibrary.org; *Asst Librn,* LeAnn Stark; *Libr Assoc,* Tammy Martin; *Libr Assoc,* Amber Staley; Staff 4 (MLS 1, Non-MLS 3)
Founded 1935
Library Holdings: Audiobooks 1,174; Bks on Deafness & Sign Lang 29; Braille Volumes 2; CDs 10; DVDs 2,099; High Interest/Low Vocabulary Bk Vols 150; Large Print Bks 300; Bk Vols 23,973; Per Subs 50; Videos 175
Automation Activity & Vendor Info: (Acquisitions) Innovative Interfaces, Inc; (Cataloging) Innovative Interfaces, Inc; (Circulation) Innovative Interfaces, Inc; (OPAC) Innovative Interfaces, Inc; (Serials) Innovative Interfaces, Inc
Database Vendor: EBSCOhost, ProQuest
Wireless access
Mem of Carroll & Madison Library System
Open Mon-Thurs 9-6, Fri & Sat 9-5
Friends of the Library Group

GREENWOOD

P SCOTT-SEBASTIAN REGIONAL LIBRARY*, 18 N Adair, 72936. (Mail add: PO Box 400, 72936-0400), SAN 331-0566. Tel: 479-996-2856. FAX: 479-996-2236. *Dir,* Judy Beth Clevenger; E-mail: judybc111@yahoo.com; Staff 9 (MLS 1, Non-MLS 8)
Founded 1954. Pop 42,000
Library Holdings: Bk Vols 92,000; Per Subs 150
Special Collections: Arkansas History Coll
Automation Activity & Vendor Info: (Cataloging) Follett Software; (Circulation) Follett Software
Database Vendor: OCLC FirstSearch
Open Mon 9-7:30, Tues-Fri 9-5, Sat 9-12
Friends of the Library Group
Branches: 5
HARTFORD LIBRARY, 22 Broadway, Hartford, 72938. (Mail add: PO Box 236, Hartford, 72938-0236), SAN 331-0655. *Br Mgr,* Linda Morgan
Library Holdings: Bk Vols 4,000
Open Tues & Thurs 10:30-12:30 & 1:30-4:30
Friends of the Library Group
LAVACA LIBRARY, 100 S Davis, Lavaca, 72941, SAN 331-071X. *Br Mgr,* Peggy Helton
Library Holdings: Bk Vols 4,000
Open Tues 1-5
Friends of the Library Group
MANSFIELD LIBRARY, 200 N Sebascott Ave, Mansfield, 72944. (Mail add: PO Box 476, Mansfield, 72944-0476), SAN 331-0744. *Br Mgr,* Anna Carter
Library Holdings: Bk Vols 3,700

Open Tues 9-4, Thurs 10-2:30
Friends of the Library Group
SCOTT COUNTY LIBRARY, 141 Second St, Waldron, 72958. (Mail add: PO Box 957, Waldron, 72958-0957), SAN 331-0809. Tel: 479-637-3516. FAX: 479-637-3516. *Librn,* Elva Garzini
Library Holdings: Bk Vols 34,000
Special Collections: Arkansas History
Open Tues-Fri 9-5
Friends of the Library Group
SEBASTIAN COUNTY LIBRARY, 18 N Adair, 72936. (Mail add: PO Box 400, 72936). Tel: 479-996-2856. *Librn,* Gayle Taylor
Library Holdings: AV Mats 925; Bk Vols 78,000; Per Subs 145; Videos 1,881
Special Collections: Arkansas History; Gifted & Talented Children; Large Print; Reference
Open Mon 9-7:30, Tues-Fri 9-5, Sat 9-12
Friends of the Library Group

HAMBURG

P ASHLEY COUNTY LIBRARY*, 211 E Lincoln, 71646. SAN 300-5070. Tel: 870-853-2078. FAX: 870-853-2079. E-mail: ashlib@sbcglobal.net. *Librn,* Henrietta Thompson
Founded 1935. Pop 24,319; Circ 69,500
Library Holdings: Large Print Bks 350; Bk Titles 53,830; Per Subs 64; Talking Bks 1,088
Subject Interests: Genealogy
Publications: Weekly newspaper column
Open Mon-Fri 9-5:30

HAMPTON

P CALHOUN COUNTY LIBRARY*, 109 Second St, 71744. (Mail add: PO Box 1162, 71744-1162), SAN 373-1863. Tel: 870-798-4492. FAX: 870-798-4492. E-mail: calcolib@yahoo.com. *Librn,* Brenda Barfell
Library Holdings: Bk Vols 30,000
Open Mon-Wed & Fri 12-5
Branches: 1
THORNTON PUBLIC LIBRARY, 220 Second St, Rte 1, Thornton, 71766. (Mail add: PO Box 40, Thornton, 71766), SAN 331-2844. Tel: 870-352-5990. *Librn,* Venita Ann Ables; Tel: 870-352-7619, E-mail: venita43@windstream.net
Open Mon, Tues, Thurs & Fri 2-5

HARDY

P SHARP COUNTY LIBRARY*, 201 Church St, 72542. Tel: 870-856-3934. *Librn,* Cecilia Mullins
Founded 1934
Library Holdings: Bk Vols 28,500; Per Subs 49
Open Mon-Fri 8:30-5, Sat 9-1
Friends of the Library Group

HARRISON

P BOONE COUNTY LIBRARY*, 221 W Stephenson, 72601-4225. SAN 331-0892. Tel: 870-741-5913. FAX: 870-741-5946. E-mail: boonecolibrary@hotmail.com. Web Site: www.boonecountylibrary.org. *Librn,* LaVoyce Ewing; E-mail: lewing@boonecountylibrary.org; Staff 9 (MLS 1, Non-MLS 8)
Founded 1903. Pop 33,000; Circ 170,363
Jan 2007-Dec 2007 Income $507,322, State $60,266, County $419,142, Locally Generated Income $27,914. Mats Exp $73,424, Books $40,000, Per/Ser (Incl. Access Fees) $3,824, AV Mat $15,000, Electronic Ref Mat (Incl. Access Fees) $9,600, Presv $5,000. Sal $260,565 (Prof $181,960)
Library Holdings: Bk Vols 81,000
Automation Activity & Vendor Info: (Cataloging) TLC (The Library Corporation); (Circulation) TLC (The Library Corporation); (Course Reserve) TLC (The Library Corporation); (ILL) OCLC WorldShare Interlibrary Loan; (OPAC) TLC (The Library Corporation); (Serials) TLC (The Library Corporation)
Database Vendor: Amigos Library Services, EBSCOhost, Facts on File, Gale Cengage Learning, OCLC FirstSearch, OCLC WorldShare Interlibrary Loan, ProQuest, TLC (The Library Corporation), World Book Online
Wireless access
Function: Accelerated reader prog, Art exhibits, Bk reviews (Group), CD-ROM, Children's prog, Computers for patron use, Copy machines, E-Reserves, Electronic databases & coll, Genealogy discussion group, Handicapped accessible, Homebound delivery serv, ILL available, Music CDs, Online cat, Online ref, Online searches, Preschool outreach, Prog for children & young adult, Scanner, Summer reading prog, Tax forms, Teen prog, Telephone ref, VHS videos, Wheelchair accessible
Special Services for the Deaf - Bks on deafness & sign lang; Closed caption videos; High interest/low vocabulary bks
Special Services for the Blind - Aids for in-house use; Bks & mags in Braille, on rec, tape & cassette; Bks available with recordings; Bks on cassette; Bks on CD; Braille & cassettes; Braille bks; Children's Braille; Copier with enlargement capabilities; Home delivery serv; Large print & cassettes; Large print bks; Magnifiers; Talking bks
Open Mon, Wed, Fri & Sat 9-5, Tues & Thurs 9-7
Restriction: Sub libr
Friends of the Library Group

C NORTH ARKANSAS COLLEGE LIBRARY*, South Campus, 1515 Pioneer Dr, 72601. SAN 378-391X. Tel: 870-391-3359. Interlibrary Loan Service Tel: 870-391-3122. Reference Tel: 870-391-3358. FAX: 870-391-3245. Web Site: www.northark.net/academics/library/index.htm. *Dir,* Jim Robb; E-mail: jrobb@northark.edu; *Asst Librn, Ser,* Michelle Palmer; Tel: 870-391-3356; *Cat,* Karen Tablish; E-mail: ktablish@northark.edu; Staff 5 (MLS 2, Non-MLS 3)
Founded 1974. Enrl 1,500; Fac 121; Highest Degree: Bachelor
Library Holdings: AV Mats 2,800; Bk Titles 22,500; Bk Vols 25,200; Per Subs 212
Subject Interests: Ark
Automation Activity & Vendor Info: (Cataloging) TLC (The Library Corporation); (Circulation) TLC (The Library Corporation); (ILL) OCLC; (OPAC) TLC (The Library Corporation); (Serials) TLC (The Library Corporation)
Database Vendor: EBSCOhost, Gale Cengage Learning, Newsbank, OCLC FirstSearch, ProQuest, ScienceDirect, Wilson - Wilson Web
Wireless access
Function: For res purposes
Partic in OCLC Online Computer Library Center, Inc
Open Mon-Thurs (Winter) 7:30am-9pm, Fri 7:30-5, Sat 8-5; Mon-Fri (Summer) 7:30-5
Friends of the Library Group
Departmental Libraries:
NORTH CAMPUS, 1320 Spring Rd, 72601. (Mail add: 1515 Pioneer Dr, 72601-5508). Tel: 870-391-3368. FAX: 870-391-3341. *Dir,* Jim Robb; Tel: 870-391-3359, E-mail: jrobb@northark.edu; *Libr Mgr,* Donette Smith; E-mail: dsmith@northark.edu
Library Holdings: AV Mats 377; Bk Titles 3,104; Per Subs 42
Function: ILL available, Photocopying/Printing, Telephone ref
Open Mon-Fri 7:30-4:30

HEBER SPRINGS

P CLEBURNE COUNTY LIBRARY*, 1010 W Searcy St, 72543. SAN 377-8592. Tel: 501-362-2477. FAX: 501-362-2606. *County Librn,* Zack Cothren; Staff 5 (Non-MLS 5)
Founded 1935
Library Holdings: Bk Vols 42,000; Per Subs 95
Automation Activity & Vendor Info: (Cataloging) Follett Software; (Circulation) Follett Software; (Course Reserve) Follett Software; (OPAC) Follett Software; (Serials) Follett Software
Mem of White River Regional Library
Open Mon 12-8, Tues, Wed & Fri 9-5, Thurs 9-8, Sat 9-4
Friends of the Library Group
Branches: 1
GREERS FERRY BRANCH, Greers Ferry Lake Plaza, 8249 Edgemont Rd, Ste 9, Greers Ferry, 72067, SAN 372-5138. Tel: 501-825-8677. *Librn,* Constance Jean Cothren; Staff 1 (Non-MLS 1)
Founded 1974
Library Holdings: Bk Vols 9,000
Function: Art exhibits
Open Mon, Wed & Fri 12-4:30, Sat 9-12
Restriction: 24-hr pass syst for students only, Access at librarian's discretion, Access for corporate affiliates, Authorized personnel only, Authorized scholars by appt, Badge access after hrs
Friends of the Library Group

HELENA

J PHILLIPS COMMUNITY COLLEGE OF THE UNIVERSITY OF ARKANSAS*, Helena Campus-Lewis Library, 1000 Campus Dr, 72342. (Mail add: PO Box 785, 72342-0785), SAN 300-5097. Tel: 870-338-6474. FAX: 870-338-2783. Web Site: www.pccua.edu/library/library.htm. *Dir,* Jerrie Townsend; E-mail: jtownsend@pccua.edu; *Asst Librn,* Ruthie L Pride; *Circ,* Betty Boydstun; *ILL, Ser,* Linda Washington; *Purchasing,* Rhita Walker; E-mail: Rhita@pccua.edu; Staff 4 (MLS 1, Non-MLS 3)
Founded 1966. Enrl 1,486
Library Holdings: Bk Titles 43,550; Per Subs 351
Partic in Libr & Info Resources Network (LIRN)

P PHILLIPS-LEE-MONROE REGIONAL LIBRARY*, Phillips County Library, 623 Pecan St, 72342. SAN 331-1139. Tel: 870-338-3537. FAX: 870-338-8855. *Dir,* Linda Bennett; Staff 1 (Non-MLS 1)
Founded 1961. Pop 50,000; Circ 53,302
Library Holdings: Bk Vols 219,786; Per Subs 121
Subject Interests: Ark, Genealogy, Local hist

Wireless access
Open Mon-Fri 7-5
Branches: 5
ELAINE LIBRARY, 126 Main St, Elaine, 72333. (Mail add: PO Box 328, Elaine, 72333), SAN 331-1147. Tel: 870-827-6628. *Librn,* Clara Williamson
Founded 1974
Open Mon-Wed & Fri 9-12 & 1-4
LEE COUNTY LIBRARY, 77 W Main St, Marianna, 72360-2297, SAN 321-8511. Tel: 870-295-2688. E-mail: leecountylibrary@sbcglobal.net. *Librn,* Betsy Bowman
Open Mon, Tues & Fri 9-12 & 1-4:30, Sat 9-12
MARVELL LIBRARY, 806 Carruth, Marvell, 72366. (Mail add: PO Box 625, Marvell, 72366-0625), SAN 331-1163. Tel: 870-829-3183. *Librn,* Edwynne Story
Founded 1924
Open Tues-Fri 9:30-12 & 1-4:30
MONROE COUNTY LIBRARY, 270 Madison St, Clarendon, 72029-2792, SAN 331-1155. Tel: 870-747-5593. FAX: 870-747-5593. E-mail: clarendonlibrary@centurytel.net. *Br Librn,* Jim Rogers
Open Mon-Fri 8-12 & 1-5
WEST HELENA LIBRARY, 721 Plaza St, West Helena, 72390-2698, SAN 331-118X. Tel: 870-572-2861. *Br Coordr,* Jean Smith; E-mail: jsmith72390@yahoo.com
Founded 1916
Open Mon-Fri 10-5

HOPE

P HEMPSTEAD COUNTY LIBRARY, 500 S Elm St, 71801. Tel: 870-777-4564. FAX: 870-777-2915. E-mail: hempcolib@gmail.com. Web Site: www.hempcolib.org. *Dir,* Courtney McNiel; Staff 3 (MLS 1, Non-MLS 2)
Founded 1948. Pop 22,500; Circ 28,200
Library Holdings: Audiobooks 586; DVDs 341; e-books 701; Large Print Bks 1,427; Bk Vols 43,897; Per Subs 15
Wireless access
Open Mon 12-8, Tues-Thurs 9-5:30
Friends of the Library Group

J UNIVERSITY OF ARKANSAS COMMUNITY COLLEGE AT HOPE*, 2500 S Main St, 71801. (Mail add: PO Box 140, 71801), SAN 375-4197. Tel: 870-722-8250. FAX: 870-777-8254. Web Site: www.uacch.edu. *Dir, Libr & Info Serv,* Marielle McFarland; Tel: 870 722-8251, E-mail: marielle.mcfarland@uacch.edu; Staff 3 (MLS 1, Non-MLS 2)
Founded 1992. Enrl 1,485; Fac 45; Highest Degree: Associate
Library Holdings: AV Mats 1,100; e-books 30,000; Bk Vols 11,500
Automation Activity & Vendor Info: (Course Reserve) Follett Software
Database Vendor: CQ Press, CredoReference, EBSCOhost, Gale Cengage Learning, Grolier Online, SerialsSolutions
Function: CD-ROM, Computers for patron use, Copy machines, Electronic databases & coll, Handicapped accessible, ILL available, Online cat, Online ref, Photocopying/Printing, Ref serv in person, VHS videos, Wheelchair accessible
Open Mon-Thurs 7-7, Fri 7-3

HORSESHOE BEND

P IZARD COUNTY LIBRARY*, Horseshoe Bend Public Library, Nine Club Rd, 72512-2717. Tel: 870-670-4318. E-mail: horseshoebendlib@centurytel.net. *Head Librn,* Fran M McGrew
Founded 1974. Pop 3,500
Library Holdings: Bk Titles 12,000
Wireless access
Function: Adult bk club, Art exhibits, Copy machines, e-mail serv, Handicapped accessible, Magnifiers for reading, Music CDs, Newsp ref libr, Photocopying/Printing, Prog for children & young adult, Spoken cassettes & CDs, Summer reading prog, Tax forms, VHS videos, Video lending libr, Wheelchair accessible
Special Services for the Deaf - Bks on deafness & sign lang
Special Services for the Blind - Bks on cassette; Bks on CD; Closed circuit TV magnifier; Large print bks; Low vision equip
Open Mon-Fri 11-5, Sat 10-2:30
Restriction: Mem only, Open to pub for ref & circ; with some limitations
Friends of the Library Group

HOT SPRINGS

P GARLAND COUNTY LIBRARY*, 1427 Malvern Ave, 71901. SAN 372-767X. Tel: 501-623-4161. FAX: 501-623-5647. E-mail: gclhsar@hotmail.com. Web Site: www.garland.lib.ar.us. *Dir,* John W Wells; Staff 3 (MLS 3)
Founded 1948. Pop 88,034; Circ 523,787
Library Holdings: Bk Vols 110,000; Per Subs 450
Special Collections: Arkansas History & Genealogy Coll
Automation Activity & Vendor Info: (Acquisitions) SirsiDynix; (Cataloging) SirsiDynix; (Circulation) SirsiDynix; (OPAC) SirsiDynix
Database Vendor: SirsiDynix
Function: Mail loans to mem
Open Mon, Fri & Sat 9-5, Tues, Wed & Thurs 9-8, Sun 12:30-5:30
Friends of the Library Group
Bookmobiles: 1

J NATIONAL PARK COMMUNITY COLLEGE LIBRARY*, 101 College Dr, 71913. SAN 300-5100. Tel: 501-760-4101, 501-760-4110. Interlibrary Loan Service Tel: 501-760-4105. FAX: 501-760-4106. Web Site: www.youseemore.com/npcc. *Dir,* Sara Seaman; E-mail: sseaman@npcc.edu; *Librn,* Kristen Quintanilla; E-mail: kquintanilla@npcc.edu; Staff 6 (MLS 2, Non-MLS 4)
Founded 1973. Enrl 3,500; Fac 150; Highest Degree: Associate
Jul 2011-Jun 2012 Income $516,017. Mats Exp $87,662, Books $35,000, Per/Ser (Incl. Access Fees) $16,962, Micro $5,200, AV Equip $1,000, AV Mat $5,500, Electronic Ref Mat (Incl. Access Fees) $24,000. Sal $196,783 (Prof $94,037)
Library Holdings: CDs 164; DVDs 732; e-books 25,398; Bk Titles 26,703; Per Subs 180; Videos 200
Special Collections: Arkansas Coll; Arkansas Democrat Gazette, 1977-present, microfilm
Subject Interests: Art, Hist, Lit, Nursing
Automation Activity & Vendor Info: (Acquisitions) TLC (The Library Corporation); (Cataloging) TLC (The Library Corporation); (Circulation) TLC (The Library Corporation); (Course Reserve) TLC (The Library Corporation); (ILL) OCLC FirstSearch; (OPAC) TLC (The Library Corporation); (Serials) EBSCO Online
Database Vendor: Alexander Street Press, Amigos Library Services, CredoReference, ebrary, EBSCOhost, Facts on File, Foundation Center, Gale Cengage Learning, Greenwood Publishing Group, H W Wilson, LexisNexis, OCLC FirstSearch, OCLC WorldShare Interlibrary Loan, ProQuest, TLC (The Library Corporation)
Wireless access
Publications: NPCC Library Newsletter (Quarterly)
Partic in Amigos Library Services, Inc; ARIEL; ARKLink; ARKnet (Arkansas Academic & Research Network); OCLC Online Computer Library Center, Inc
Special Services for the Deaf - Bks on deafness & sign lang; Closed caption videos
Special Services for the Blind - Bks on CD; Copier with enlargement capabilities; Low vision equip
Open Mon-Thurs 7am-8pm, Fri 7-4:30

HUNTSVILLE

P MADISON PUBLIC LIBRARY*, 827 N College Ave, 72740. (Mail add: PO Box 745, 72740-0745), SAN 331-1015. Tel: 479-738-2754. FAX: 479-738-5542. E-mail: info@madisoncountylibraries.org. Web Site: www.carrollmadisonlibraries.org/library.aspx?lib=huntsville. *Libr Dir,* Billie Whorton; *Asst Librn,* Rose Fowler; *Libr Asst,* Charlotte Holiday
Library Holdings: Bk Vols 15,000; Per Subs 20
Wireless access
Open Mon & Tues 8-6, Wed-Fri 8-4:30, Sat 9-1
Friends of the Library Group

JASPER

P NEWTON COUNTY PUBLIC LIBRARY*, Hwy 7 S, 72641. (Mail add: HC31, Box 8, 72641), SAN 331-1074. Tel: 870-446-2983. FAX: 870-446-2983. E-mail: newtonark@yahoo.com. Web Site: www.newtoncountylibrary.com. *Librn,* Teresa Hayes
Library Holdings: Bk Vols 15,000
Open Mon-Fri 9:30-5:30, Sat 10-2
Friends of the Library Group

JONESBORO

P CROWLEY RIDGE REGIONAL LIBRARY, 315 W Oak Ave, 72401. SAN 331-1821. Tel: 870-935-5133. FAX: 870-935-7987. Web Site: www.libraryinjonesboro.org. *Dir,* David Eckert; Tel: 870-935-5133, Ext 9964, E-mail: david@libraryinjonesboro.org; *Dir, Info Tech,* Ben Bizzle; Tel: 870-935-5133, Ext 9951, E-mail: ben@libraryinjonesboro.org; *Dir, Youth Serv,* Kay Taylor; Tel: 870-935-5133, Ext 9973, E-mail: kay@libraryinjonesboro.org; *Caraway Br Librn,* Stacey Hart; Tel: 870-482-3394, E-mail: shart@libraryinjonesboro.org; *Goldsby Br Librn,* Tamala Ingram; Tel: 870-475-6144, E-mail: tingram@libraryinjonesboro.org; *Kohn Memorial Br Librn,* Connie McDonald; Tel: 870-486-2515, E-mail: cmcdonald@libraryinjonesboro.org; *Marked Tree Br Librn,* Fran Bell; Tel: 870-358-3190, E-mail: fbell@libraryinjonesboro.org; *McAdams Br Librn,* Donna Vickers; Tel: 870-237-4407, E-mail: dvickers@libraryinjonesboro.org; *Poinsett County Br Librn,* Angie Lacy; Tel: 870-578-4465, E-mail: alacy@libraryinjonesboro.org; *Teen Librn,* Nina Darley; Tel: 870-935-5133,

Ext 9984, E-mail: ndarley@libraryinjonesboro.org; *W Poinsett County Br Librn,* Valerie Riley; Tel: 870-684-2235, E-mail: vriley@libraryinjonesboro.org; *Bus Mgr,* Nancy Dobbins; Tel: 870-935-5133, Ext 9981, E-mail: nancy@libraryinjonesboro.org; *Asst Bus Mgr,* Sarah Keath; Tel: 870-935-5133, Ext 9989, E-mail: skeath@libraryinjonesboro.org; *Asst Youth Serv Mgr,* Morgan Sallee; Tel: 870-935-5133, Ext 9980, E-mail: morgan@libraryinjonesboro.org; *Circ Mgr,* LaTonya Jones; Tel: 870-935-5133, Ext 9976, E-mail: tonya@libraryinjonesboro.org; *Info Serv Mgr,* Nechia Whittingham; Tel: 870-935-5133, Ext 9983, E-mail: nwhittin@libraryinjonesboro.org; *Pub Relations Mgr,* Brandi Hodges; Tel: 870-935-5133, Ext 9953, E-mail: bhodges@libraryinjonesboro.org; *Tech Serv Mgr,* Nathan Whitmire; Tel: 870-935-5133, Ext 9982, E-mail: nwhitmire@libraryinjonesboro.org; *Outreach Coordr,* Valerie Carroll; Tel: 870-935-5133, Ext 9991, E-mail: vcarroll@libraryinjonesboro.org; *Educ Spec,* Margo Reiser; Tel: 870-935-5133, Ext 9978, E-mail: margo@libraryinjonesboro.og; Staff 18 (MLS 5, Non-MLS 13)
Founded 1966. Pop 97,018; Circ 398,655
Automation Activity & Vendor Info: (Acquisitions) Innovative Interfaces, Inc - Millenium; (Cataloging) Innovative Interfaces, Inc - Millenium; (Circulation) Innovative Interfaces, Inc - Millenium; (OPAC) Innovative Interfaces, Inc - Millenium
Database Vendor: EBSCOhost, Newsbank, ProQuest, SirsiDynix
Wireless access
Function: Adult bk club, Adult literacy prog, Art exhibits, Audio & video playback equip for onsite use, Bk club(s), CD-ROM, Digital talking bks, Games & aids for the handicapped, Handicapped accessible, ILL available, Magnifiers for reading, Music CDs, Online searches, Photocopying/Printing, Prog for adults, Prog for children & young adult, Satellite serv, Summer reading prog, VHS videos, Wheelchair accessible, Workshops
Open Mon & Tues 9-8:30, Wed-Fri 9-6, Sat 9-5, Sun 1-5
Friends of the Library Group

CM UNIVERSITY OF ARKANSAS*, Regional Medical Library, 223 E Jackson, 72401. SAN 300-5135. Tel: 870-972-1290. FAX: 870-931-0839. Web Site: www.uark.edu. *Dir, Libr Serv,* Position Currently Open
Founded 1974
Library Holdings: Bk Vols 2,015; Per Subs 145
Subject Interests: Family practice
Publications: Updates (NE Arkansas Hosp Libr Consortium)
Partic in Docline; Northeast Arkansas Hospital Library Consortium; OCLC Online Computer Library Center, Inc; Univ of Ark for Med Sci
Open Mon-Fri 8-5

KINGSTON

P KINGSTON COMMUNITY LIBRARY*, PO Box 6, 72742-0006. Tel: 479-665-2745. FAX: 479-665-2745. E-mail: klibrary@madisoncounty.net. Web Site: www.klibrary.org. *Librn,* Linda Davidson
Library Holdings: Bk Vols 5,000
Wireless access
Open Mon 10-1, Tues-Fri 2-6, Sat 9-12
Friends of the Library Group

LEWISVILLE

P LAFAYETTE COUNTY LIBRARY*, 219 E Third St, 71845. SAN 331-2720. Tel: 870-921-4757. FAX: 870-921-4756. E-mail: lewisvillelibrary2004@yahoo.com. Web Site: www.youseemore.com/columbia. *Librn,* Laura Cleveland
Library Holdings: Bk Titles 9,651
Open Mon-Fri 12-6

LINCOLN

P LINCOLN PUBLIC LIBRARY, 107 W Bean, 72744. (Mail add: PO Box 555, 72744-0555), SAN 330-9991. Tel: 479-824-3294. E-mail: library@lincolnarkansas.com. *Dir,* Dianna Payne
Library Holdings: Bk Vols 28,000; Per Subs 3
Automation Activity & Vendor Info: (Cataloging) Innovative Interfaces, Inc; (Circulation) Innovative Interfaces, Inc; (OPAC) Innovative Interfaces, Inc
Wireless access
Open Tues 12-8, Wed 9-5, Thurs 9:30-5:30, Fri & Sat 1-5

LITTLE ROCK

S THE ARKANSAS ARTS CENTER, Elizabeth Prewitt Taylor Memorial Library, MacArthur Park, 501 E Ninth St, 72202. (Mail add: PO Box 2137, 72203-2137), SAN 300-5151. Tel: 501-396-0341. FAX: 501-375-8053. E-mail: library@arkansasartscenter.org. Web Site: www.arkansasartscenter.org. *Librn,* AJ Bufford; E-mail: abufford@arkansasartscenter.org; Staff 1 (MLS 1)
Founded 1963
Library Holdings: Bk Vols 7,000; Per Subs 25
Special Collections: George Fisher Political Cartoons; John Reid Coll of Early American Jazz
Subject Interests: Art, Decorative art
Automation Activity & Vendor Info: (Acquisitions) Innovative Interfaces, Inc; (Cataloging) Innovative Interfaces, Inc; (Circulation) Innovative Interfaces, Inc; (Course Reserve) Innovative Interfaces, Inc; (ILL) Innovative Interfaces, Inc; (Media Booking) Innovative Interfaces, Inc; (OPAC) Innovative Interfaces, Inc; (Serials) Innovative Interfaces, Inc
Database Vendor: EBSCOhost, OCLC FirstSearch, ProQuest
Wireless access
Restriction: Non-circulating

C ARKANSAS BAPTIST COLLEGE LIBRARY*, 1621 Martin Luther King Dr, 72202. SAN 300-516X. Tel: 501-244-5109. FAX: 501-244-5102. Web Site: www.arkansasbaptist.edu. *Dir of Libr Serv,* Sonya Locket
Library Holdings: Bk Titles 20,000; Bk Vols 30,000; Per Subs 98
Automation Activity & Vendor Info: (Cataloging) Follett Software; (ILL) Follett Software
Database Vendor: EBSCOhost
Wireless access
Open Mon-Fri 8-8

G ARKANSAS GEOLOGICAL SURVEY LIBRARY*, 3815 W Roosevelt Rd, 72204-6369. SAN 300-5208. Tel: 501-296-1877. FAX: 501-663-7360. E-mail: agc@arkansas.gov. Web Site: www.arkansas.gov/agc/agc.htm. *In Charge,* Susan Young
Founded 1923
Library Holdings: Bk Titles 10,000; Per Subs 11
Publications: Bulletins; Guidebooks; Information Circulars, Miscellaneous Publications; Water Resources Circulars & Summaries
Open Mon-Fri 8-4:30

S ARKANSAS HISTORY COMMISSION LIBRARY*, One Capitol Mall, 2nd Flr, 72201. SAN 326-7008. Tel: 501-682-6900. FAX: 501-682-6916. Web Site: www.ark-ives.com. *Dir,* Lisa Spear; *Librn,* Sheila Bevill; E-mail: sheila.bevill@arkansas.gov; *Managing Archivist,* Mary Dunn; *Curator,* Julienne Crawford; Staff 6 (MLS 2, Non-MLS 4)
Library Holdings: Microforms 53,000; Bk Vols 20,000; Per Subs 1,000
Subject Interests: Ark, State hist
Open Mon-Sat 8-4:30

P ARKANSAS REGIONAL LIBRARY FOR THE BLIND & PHYSICALLY HANDICAPPED, 900 W Capitol Ave, Ste 100, 72201-3108. SAN 300-5224. Tel: 501-682-1155. Toll Free Tel: 866-660-0885. TDD: 501-682-1002. E-mail: nlsbooks@library.arkansas.gov. Web Site: www.library.arkansas.gov/libraryForTheBlind/Pages/default.aspx. *Libr Mgr,* John JD Hall; E-mail: jd@library.arkansas.gov; *Reader Serv,* Jeff Kersey; Tel: 501-682-2856, E-mail: jeff@library.arkansas.gov; *Reader Serv, Ch,* Eva Jane Harrison; Tel: 501-682-2871, E-mail: eva@library.arkansas.gov; Staff 9 (MLS 3, Non-MLS 6)
Founded 1969. Pop 4,000; Circ 214,010
Library Holdings: Braille Volumes 29,080; Bk Titles 77,863; Talking Bks 145,934
Subject Interests: Braille
Function: Handicapped accessible, Mail loans to mem
Special Services for the Blind - Bks & mags in Braille, on rec, tape & cassette; Bks on flash-memory cartridges; Braille bks; Digital talking bk; Digital talking bk machines; Free checkout of audio mat; Web-Braille
Open Mon-Fri 8-4:30
Restriction: Authorized patrons, Free to mem, Lending libr only via mail

S ARKANSAS SCHOOL FOR THE DEAF LIBRARY*, 2400 W Markham St, 72205. (Mail add: PO Box 3811, 72203-3811), SAN 300-5240. Tel: 501-324-9515. FAX: 501-324-9553. TDD: 501-324-9506. *Librn,* Fran Miller; E-mail: franm@asd.k12.ar.us
Library Holdings: Bks on Deafness & Sign Lang 600; Bk Vols 10,000; Per Subs 75
Automation Activity & Vendor Info: (Cataloging) Follett Software; (Circulation) Follett Software
Open Mon-Fri 9-5

P ARKANSAS STATE LIBRARY*, 900 W Capitol, Ste 100, 72201. SAN 331-2097. Tel: 501-682-2053. Interlibrary Loan Service Tel: 501-682-2866. Administration Tel: 501-682-1527. Automation Services Tel: 501-682-6052. FAX: 501-682-1899. Interlibrary Loan Service FAX: 501-682-1529. Administration FAX: 501-682-1533. Automation Services FAX: 501-682-1531. TDD: 501-682-1002. E-mail: reference@library.arkansas.gov. Web Site: www.library.arkansas.gov. *State Librn,* Carolyn Ashcraft; Tel: 501-682-1526, E-mail: carolyn@library.arkansas.gov; *Dep Dir, Libr Develop & Serv,* Dwain Gordon; Tel: 501-682-2863, E-mail: dwain@library.arkansas.gov; *Div Mgr, Coll Develop,* Mary Brewer; Tel: 501-682-2840, E-mail: mary@library.arkansas.gov; *Admin Serv Mgr,* Mindy Hodges; E-mail: mindy@library.arkansas.gov; *Mgr, Grants & Spec Project,* Deborah Hall;

E-mail: debbie@library.arkansas.gov; *Mgr, Network Serv,* Sally Hawkes; E-mail: sally@library.arkansas.gov; *Pub Info Spec,* Danny Koonce; Tel: 501-682-2837, E-mail: danny@library.arkansas.gov. Subject Specialists: *Tech,* Sally Hawkes; Staff 52 (MLS 18, Non-MLS 34)
Founded 1935. Pop 2,538,303
Library Holdings: Bk Vols 492,204; Per Subs 2,500
Special Collections: Arkansiana; Blind & Physically Handicapped Coll; CIS Coll, microfiche; Library & Information Science (Professional Coll); Patent Depository. State Document Depository; US Document Depository
Subject Interests: Bus & mgt, Computer sci, US industries
Automation Activity & Vendor Info: (Acquisitions) SirsiDynix; (Circulation) SirsiDynix; (OPAC) SirsiDynix; (Serials) SirsiDynix
Database Vendor: Dialog, EBSCOhost, Gale Cengage Learning, OCLC FirstSearch, ProQuest, Wilson - Wilson Web
Publications: Arkansas Documents; directories; indexes; The News
Partic in BRS; OCLC Online Computer Library Center, Inc
Open Mon-Fri 8-4:30

GL ARKANSAS SUPREME COURT LIBRARY*, 625 Marshall St, Ste 1500, 72201. SAN 300-5267. Tel: 501-682-2147. FAX: 501-682-6877. Web Site: courts.state.ar.us/courts/sc_library.html. *Dir,* Ava M Hicks; E-mail: ava.hicks@arkansas.gov; *Pub Serv Coordr,* Rod Miller; *Tech Serv,* Shawn Pierce; Tel: 501-682-6878; Staff 3 (MLS 2, Non-MLS 1)
Founded 1851
Library Holdings: Bk Vols 90,000
Special Collections: State Document Depository; US Document Depository
Subject Interests: Law
Automation Activity & Vendor Info: (Acquisitions) Innovative Interfaces, Inc; (Cataloging) Innovative Interfaces, Inc; (Circulation) Innovative Interfaces, Inc; (OPAC) Innovative Interfaces, Inc; (Serials) Innovative Interfaces, Inc
Database Vendor: LexisNexis, OCLC FirstSearch, Westlaw
Partic in OCLC Online Computer Library Center, Inc
Open Mon-Fri 8-5

P CENTRAL ARKANSAS LIBRARY SYSTEM*, 100 Rock St, 72201-4698. SAN 331-2216. Tel: 501-918-3000. Circulation Tel: 501-918-3041. Interlibrary Loan Service Tel: 501-918-3014. Reference Tel: 501-918-3003. Administration Tel: 501-918-3030. Interlibrary Loan Service FAX: 501-376-1830. Administration FAX: 501-375-7451. TDD: 501-918-3048. E-mail: calsinfo@cals.lib.ar.us, refdesk@cals.lib.ar.us Web Site: www.cals.org. *Dir,* Dr Bobby Roberts; Tel: 501-918-3037, E-mail: bobbyr@cals.org; *Assoc Dir,* Jennifer Chilcoat; Tel: 501-918-3031, E-mail: chilcoat@cals.org; *Assoc Dir,* Carol Coffey; Tel: 501-918-3008, E-mail: ccoffey@cals.org; *Coll Develop,* Philip Jones; Tel: 501-918-3070, E-mail: pjones@cals.org; *Curator,* Dr David Stricklin; Tel: 501-320-5710, E-mail: dstricklin@cals.org; *ILL,* Lee Razer; E-mail: lrazer@cals.org; *Pub Relations,* Susan Gele; Tel: 501-918-3086, E-mail: sgele@cals.org; *Ref,* John McGraw; Tel: 501-918-3010, E-mail: jmcgraw@cals.org; *Tech Serv,* Tracy Hamby; Tel: 501-918-3071, E-mail: tracyh@cals.org; Staff 232 (MLS 33, Non-MLS 199)
Founded 1910. Pop 332,076; Circ 2,494,114
Jan 2011-Dec 2011 Income (Main Library and Branch(s)) $15,606,563, State $582,548, City $12,351,673, County $2,100,446, Locally Generated Income $571,896. Mats Exp $1,989,251, Books $1,066,387, AV Mat $506,223, Electronic Ref Mat (Incl. Access Fees) $416,461. Sal $7,852,925
Library Holdings: AV Mats 64,128; Bk Titles 356,805; Bk Vols 869,104; Per Subs 1,599
Special Collections: Charlie May Simon Awards Coll; Clinton Gubernatorial Papers; Foundation Center Regional Coll. Oral History; State Document Depository; US Document Depository
Subject Interests: Genealogy, Local hist, State hist
Automation Activity & Vendor Info: (Acquisitions) Innovative Interfaces, Inc; (Cataloging) Innovative Interfaces, Inc; (Circulation) Innovative Interfaces, Inc; (ILL) OCLC; (OPAC) Innovative Interfaces, Inc; (Serials) Innovative Interfaces, Inc
Database Vendor: ABC-CLIO, Baker & Taylor, Booklist Online, Booksite, BWI, College Source, EBSCOhost, Facts on File, Gale Cengage Learning, Grolier Online, infoUSA, LearningExpress, Marcive, Inc, Mergent Online, OCLC FirstSearch, OCLC WorldShare Interlibrary Loan, ProQuest, ReferenceUSA
Wireless access
Function: Adult bk club, After school storytime, Archival coll, Art exhibits, Audiobks via web, Bk club(s), Bks on CD, Children's prog, Computer training, Computers for patron use, Copy machines, Electronic databases & coll, Exhibits, Fax serv, Free DVD rentals, Handicapped accessible, Homebound delivery serv, ILL available, Magnifiers for reading, Mail & tel request accepted, Microfiche/film & reading machines, Music CDs, Notary serv, Online cat, Online ref, OverDrive digital audio bks, Photocopying/Printing, Preschool outreach, Printer for laptops & handheld devices, Prog for adults, Prog for children & young adult, Pub access computers, Ref serv available, Ref serv in person, Spanish lang bks, Spoken cassettes & CDs, Story hour, Summer & winter reading prog, Summer reading prog, Tax forms, Teen prog, Telephone ref, Web-catalog, Wheelchair accessible, Winter reading prog
Partic in OCLC Online Computer Library Center, Inc
Special Services for the Deaf - Closed caption videos; TDD equip
Special Services for the Blind - Audio mat; Bks on CD
Open Mon-Thurs 9-8, Fri & Sat 9-6, Sun 1-5
Friends of the Library Group
Branches: 10
DEE BROWN BRANCH, 6325 Baseline, 72209-4810, SAN 331-2364. Tel: 501-568-7494. *Br Mgr,* Joseph Hudak
Library Holdings: Bk Vols 63,566
Open Mon, Tues & Thurs 10-8, Wed, Fri & Sat 10-6
JOHN GOULD FLETCHER BRANCH, 823 N Buchanan St, 72205-3211, SAN 331-2240. Tel: 501-663-5457. *Br Mgr,* Freddy Hudson
Library Holdings: Bk Vols 95,437
Open Mon-Wed 9-8, Thurs-Sat 9-6
MAUMELLE BRANCH, Ten Lake Point Dr, Maumelle, 72113-6230, SAN 378-2492. Tel: 501-851-2551. *Br Mgr,* Pam Rudkin
Library Holdings: Bk Vols 51,189
Open Mon, Tues & Thurs 10-8, Wed, Fri & Sat 10-6
SIDNEY S MCMATH BRANCH, 2100 John Barrow Rd, 72204. Tel: 501-225-0066. *Br Mgr,* John McGraw
Library Holdings: Bk Vols 44,199
Open Mon & Wed 9-8, Tues & Thurs-Sat 9-6
MAX MILAM BRANCH, 609 Aplin Ave, Perryville, 72126, SAN 331-2305. Tel: 501-889-2554. *Br Mgr,* Janice Guffey
Library Holdings: Bk Vols 37,535
Open Mon, Wed-Sat 10-6, Tues 10-8
ESTHER NIXON BRANCH, 308 W Main St, Jacksonville, 72076-4507, SAN 331 2275. Tel: 501-982-5533. *Br Mgr,* Kathy Seymour
Library Holdings: Bk Vols 62,091
Open Mon, Wed, Fri & Sat 10-6, Tues & Thurs 10-8
AMY SANDERS BRANCH, 31 Shelby Dr, Sherwood, 72120-3197, SAN 331-233X. Tel: 501-835-7756. *Br Mgr,* Ginann Swindle
Library Holdings: Bk Vols 48,960
Open Mon, Wed, Fri & Sat 9:30-6, Tues & Thurs 9:30-8
ADOLPHINE FLETCHER TERRY BRANCH, 2015 Napa Valley Dr, 72212, SAN 370-5773. Tel: 501-228-0129. *Br Mgr,* Leslie Blanchard
Library Holdings: Bk Vols 104,368
Open Mon, Wed & Thurs 9-8, Tues, Fri & Sat 9-6
ROOSEVELT THOMPSON BRANCH, 38 Rahling Circle, 72223. Tel: 501-821-3060. *Br Mgr,* Mary Louise Cantwell
Library Holdings: Bk Vols 49,723
Open Mon, Tues & Thurs 10-8, Wed, Fri & Sat 10-6
SUE COWAN WILLIAMS BRANCH, 1800 S Chester St, 72206-1010, SAN 378-2514. Tel: 501-376-4282. *Br Mgr,* Latina Sheard
Library Holdings: Bk Vols 20,579
Open Mon, Wed, Fri & Sat 10-6, Tues & Thurs 10-8

G CENTRAL ARKANSAS VETERANS HEALTHCARE SYSTEM*, Health Sciences Library, 4300 W Seventh St, 72205-5484. SAN 300-5321. Tel: 501-257-5620. Administration Tel: 501-257-5622. FAX: 501-257-5626. *Chief Librn,* Edward Poletti; *Librn,* Glenna Collett; Staff 4 (MLS 3, Non-MLS 1)
Founded 1950
Library Holdings: AV Mats 1,404; Bk Titles 3,651; Per Subs 373
Automation Activity & Vendor Info: (Cataloging) Follett Software; (Circulation) Follett Software; (OPAC) Follett Software
Database Vendor: EBSCOhost
Function: Health sci info serv
Partic in OCLC-LVIS

M MARGARET CLARK GILBREATH LIBRARY*, Baptist Health Medical Center Library, 9601 Interstate 630, Exit 7, 72205. SAN 331-2151. Tel: 501-202-2671. FAX: 501-202-1318. *Head of Libr,* Carolyn Baker; Staff 2 (MLS 1, Non-MLS 1)
Founded 1974
Library Holdings: e-books 20; e-journals 90; Bk Vols 5,000; Per Subs 194
Subject Interests: Med, Nursing
Automation Activity & Vendor Info: (Cataloging) CyberTools for Libraries; (Circulation) CyberTools for Libraries; (OPAC) CyberTools for Libraries; (Serials) CyberTools for Libraries
Database Vendor: EBSCOhost, Elsevier, OVID Technologies
Wireless access
Partic in Docline; National Network of Libraries of Medicine
Open Mon-Fri 8-5

S HISTORIC ARKANSAS MUSEUM LIBRARY, LeFevre Research Library, 200 E Third St, 72201-1608. SAN 370-3355. Tel: 501-324-9351. FAX: 501-324-9345. Web Site: www.historicarkansas.org. *Exec Dir,* William B Worthen; Tel: 501-324-9308, E-mail: billw@arkansasheritage.org; *Curator, Dep Dir,* Swannee Bennett; Tel: 501-324-9395, E-mail: swannee@arkansasheritage.org. Subject Specialists: *State hist,* William B

Worthen; *Fine arts, Mechanical, State hist,* Swannee Bennett; Staff 1 (Non-MLS 1)
Library Holdings: Bk Titles 2,600; Bk Vols 3,300
Subject Interests: State hist
Database Vendor: JayWil Software Development, Inc
Wireless access
Open Mon-Sat 9-5, Sun 1-5
Restriction: Not a lending libr

S NATIONAL ARCHIVES & RECORDS ADMINISTRATION*, William J Clinton Presidential Library & Museum, 1200 President Clinton Ave, 72201. Tel: 501-374-4242. FAX: 501-244-2883. E-mail: clinton.library@nara.gov. Web Site: www.clintonlibrary.gov.
Special Collections: Music Exhibit; Presidential Archives, official recs, papers, photogs, v-tapes
Open Mon-Sat 9-5, Sun 1-5

C PHILANDER SMITH COLLEGE, Donald W Reynolds Library, 900 Daisy Bates Dr, 72202. SAN 300-5291. Tel: 501-370-5262. FAX: 501-370-5307. Web Site: www.philander.edu. *Dir,* Teresa I Ojezua; E-mail: tojezua@philander.edu; *Archivist, Digital Serv Librn,* Elonda Clay; E-mail: eclay@philander.edu. Subject Specialists: *Sci,* Teresa I Ojezua; *Digital humanities, STEM,* Elonda Clay; Staff 4 (MLS 2, Non-MLS 2)
Founded 1920. Enrl 540; Highest Degree: Bachelor
Library Holdings: CDs 200; DVDs 383; e-books 150; e-journals 14,878; Microforms 2,375; Bk Titles 72,910; Bk Vols 74,500; Per Subs 312; Videos 935
Special Collections: African American/Black History; PSC Archives
Subject Interests: African-Am (ethnic), Ark, Bus & mgt, Ethnic studies
Automation Activity & Vendor Info: (Acquisitions) EOS International; (Cataloging) EOS International; (Circulation) Follett Software; (ILL) OCLC WorldShare Interlibrary Loan; (OPAC) EOS International; (Serials) EBSCO Online
Database Vendor: Amigos Library Services, EBSCOhost, Gale Cengage Learning, JSTOR, LearningExpress, Nature Publishing Group, OCLC ArticleFirst, OCLC FirstSearch, OCLC WorldShare Interlibrary Loan, ProQuest, PubMed, ReferenceUSA, YBP Library Services
Wireless access
Function: Microfiche/film & reading machines, Movies, Music CDs, Online cat, Online info literacy tutorials on the web & in blackboard, Online searches, Orientations, Outreach serv, Outside serv via phone, mail, e-mail & web, Photocopying/Printing, Pub access computers, Scanner, Serves mentally handicapped consumers, Web-catalog, Workshops
Publications: Knowledge is Freedom (Newsletter)
Partic in Amigos Library Services, Inc; ARKLink; HBCU Library Alliance; OCLC Online Computer Library Center, Inc
Special Services for the Blind - Accessible computers; Assistive/Adapted tech devices, equip & products; Computer with voice synthesizer for visually impaired persons; Low vision equip; PC for handicapped
Open Mon-Thurs 7:30am-10pm, Fri 7:30am-8:30pm, Sat 9-9, Sun 1-10
Restriction: Borrowing privileges limited to fac & registered students

M SAINT VINCENT HEALTH SYSTEMS LIBRARY*, Frank T Padberg Medical Library, Two Saint Vincent Circle, 72205. SAN 300-5305. Tel: 501-552-3231. FAX: 501-552-4311. E-mail: medlib@stvincenthealth.com. *Coll Develop, Librn,* Mandy Weeks
Founded 1900
Library Holdings: Bk Vols 4,048; Per Subs 142
Subject Interests: Health sci, Med
Open Mon-Fri 8-4:30

G UNITED STATES COURT OF APPEALS, Branch Library, 600 W Capitol Ave, Rm A302, 72201. SAN 324-6701. Tel: 501-604-5215. FAX: 501-604-5217. Web Site: www.ca8.uscourts.gov. *Librn,* Crata Castleberry; E-mail: crata_castleberry@ca8.uscourts.gov; Staff 2 (MLS 1, Non-MLS 1)
Founded 1981
Library Holdings: Bk Titles 5,000; Bk Vols 16,000; Per Subs 65
Subject Interests: Fed law
Automation Activity & Vendor Info: (Acquisitions) SirsiDynix; (Cataloging) SirsiDynix; (Circulation) SirsiDynix; (Course Reserve) SirsiDynix; (ILL) SirsiDynix; (Media Booking) SirsiDynix; (OPAC) SirsiDynix
Database Vendor: LexisNexis, Westlaw
Partic in Dialog Corp; Lexis, Solinet, Westlaw; OCLC Online Computer Library Center, Inc
Open Mon-Fri 8:15-5

C UNIVERSITY OF ARKANSAS AT LITTLE ROCK*, Ottenheimer Library, 2801 S University Ave, 72204. SAN 331-2429. Tel: 501-569-3123. Interlibrary Loan Service Tel: 501-569-8812. Reference Tel: 501-569-8806. Administration Tel: 501-569-8803. Automation Services Tel: 501-569-8813. FAX: 501-569-3017. Administration FAX: 501-569-8814. E-mail: library@ualr.edu. Web Site: www.library.ualr.edu. *Interim Dean,* J B Hill; *Dean,* Position Currently Open; *Dir of Admin Serv,* C Suzanne Martin; Tel: 501-569-8805, E-mail: csmartin@ualr.edu; *Dir, Pub Serv,* Position Currently Open; *Dir, Tech & Tech Serv,* Claire Anne Liebst; Tel: 501-569-3248, Fax: 501-569-8128, E-mail: caliebst@ualr.edu; *Head, Cat,* Donna Rose; Tel: 501-569-8817, E-mail: dkrose@ualr.edu; *Head, Info Tech,* Linda Wen; E-mail: wxwen@ualr.edu; *Head, Ref,* Carol Macheak; Tel: 501-569-8809, E-mail: cimacheak@ualr.edu; *Coll Develop Librn,* Maureen James; Tel: 501-569-8816, Fax: 501-569-8128, E-mail: mejames@ualr.edu; *Doc Librn, Ref,* Karen Russ; Tel: 501-569-8444, E-mail: kmruss@ualr.edu; *Ref Librn,* Lisa Li; Tel: 501-569-8811, E-mail: hxli@ualr.edu; *Ref Librn,* Brent Nelson; Tel: 501-569-8807, E-mail: banelson@ualr.edu; *Instruction Coordr, Ref Librn,* John Siegel; Tel: 501-569-3536, E-mail: jxsiegel@ualr.edu; *Cataloger,* Lixia Zhao; Tel: 501-569-3454, E-mail: lxzhao@ualr.edu; Staff 17 (MLS 13, Non-MLS 4)
Founded 1927. Enrl 13,167; Fac 442; Highest Degree: Doctorate
Jul 2009-Jun 2010 Income (Main Library Only) $4,643,405, State $3,606,973, Other $1,036,432. Mats Exp $1,659,464, Books $311,888, Per/Ser (Incl. Access Fees) $826,206, Electronic Ref Mat (Incl. Access Fees) $518,370, Presv $3,000. Sal $1,184,625 (Prof $750,118)
Library Holdings: AV Mats 5,963; e-books 31,057; e-journals 62,682; Microforms 233,938; Music Scores 2,182; Bk Vols 512,661; Per Subs 49,134; Talking Bks 273; Videos 4,778
Special Collections: US Document Depository
Subject Interests: Bus & mgt, Educ, Govt, Humanities, Psychol
Automation Activity & Vendor Info: (Acquisitions) Innovative Interfaces, Inc; (Cataloging) Innovative Interfaces, Inc; (Circulation) Innovative Interfaces, Inc; (Course Reserve) Innovative Interfaces, Inc; (OPAC) Innovative Interfaces, Inc; (Serials) Innovative Interfaces, Inc
Database Vendor: Cambridge Scientific Abstracts, EBSCOhost, JSTOR, LexisNexis, OCLC FirstSearch, OCLC WorldShare Interlibrary Loan, OVID Technologies, ProQuest, SerialsSolutions, Wilson - Wilson Web
Wireless access
Function: Computers for patron use, Copy machines, Doc delivery serv, e-mail & chat, E-Reserves, Electronic databases & coll, Music CDs, Online cat, Online ref, Orientations, Pub access computers, Telephone ref
Publications: Ottenheimer News (Newsletter)
Partic in ARKLink
Special Services for the Deaf - TDD equip
Open Mon-Fri 7:45am-10:45pm
Restriction: Access at librarian's discretion

Departmental Libraries:

CL PULASKI COUNTY LAW LIBRARY, 1203 McMath Ave, 72202-5142, SAN 331-2453. Tel: 501-324-9444. FAX: 501-324-9447. Web Site: www.law.ualr.edu/library. *Dir, Reader Serv,* June Stewart; Tel: 501-324-9975, E-mail: jlstewart@ualr.edu; *Ref Serv, Spec Coll Librn,* Kathryn Fitzhugh; *Acq, Ser,* Jada Aitchison; *Cat, Ref Serv,* Susan D Goldner; *Circ,* Jessie Burchfield; *Electronic Res, Ref Serv,* Melissa Serfass; Staff 16 (MLS 6, Non-MLS 10)
Founded 1965. Enrl 400; Fac 22; Highest Degree: Doctorate
Library Holdings: Bk Titles 36,877; Bk Vols 277,950; Per Subs 3,252
Special Collections: Ark Supreme Court Records and Briefs, 1836-1926. State Document Depository; US Document Depository
Automation Activity & Vendor Info: (Acquisitions) Innovative Interfaces, Inc; (Cataloging) Innovative Interfaces, Inc; (Circulation) Innovative Interfaces, Inc; (ILL) Innovative Interfaces, Inc; (OPAC) Innovative Interfaces, Inc; (Serials) Innovative Interfaces, Inc
Publications: Law Library Guide; Legal Reader (Newsletter)
Open Mon-Thurs 7am-11pm, Fri 7-10, Sat 9-6, Sun 1-11
Friends of the Library Group

CM UNIVERSITY OF ARKANSAS FOR MEDICAL SCIENCES LIBRARY*, 4301 W Markham St, SLOT 586, 72205-7186. SAN 331-2488. Tel: 501-686-5980. Interlibrary Loan Service Tel: 501-686-6744. Reference Tel: 501-686-6734. FAX: 501-686-6745. Web Site: www.library.uams.edu. *Dir,* Mary Ryan; Tel: 501-686-6730, Fax: 501-296-1423, E-mail: ryanmaryl@uams.edu; Staff 13 (MLS 12, Non-MLS 1)
Founded 1879. Enrl 2,820; Fac 1,354; Highest Degree: Doctorate
Library Holdings: AV Mats 468; e-books 883; e-journals 4,509; Electronic Media & Resources 250; Bk Titles 34,056; Bk Vols 40,956; Per Subs 3,618
Special Collections: History of Medicine in Arkansas; Pathology (Schlumberger Coll)
Automation Activity & Vendor Info: (Acquisitions) Innovative Interfaces, Inc; (Cataloging) Innovative Interfaces, Inc; (Circulation) Innovative Interfaces, Inc; (Course Reserve) Innovative Interfaces, Inc; (ILL) Innovative Interfaces, Inc; (OPAC) Innovative Interfaces, Inc; (Serials) Innovative Interfaces, Inc
Wireless access
Publications: UAMS Library (Newsletter)
Partic in ARKLink; OCLC Online Computer Library Center, Inc; South Central Academic Medical Libraries Consortium
Open Mon-Thurs 7:30am-10pm, Fri 7:30-6, Sat 9-6, Sun 2-10
Friends of the Library Group

L WILLIAMS & ANDERSON*, Law Library, 111 Center, 22nd Flr, 72201. SAN 372-2597. Tel: 501-372-0800. FAX: 501-372-6453. E-mail: info@williamsanderson.com. Web Site: www.williamsanderson.com. *Librn,* Anthony Okaro
Founded 1989
Library Holdings: Bk Vols 4,000
Subject Interests: Environ law, Real estate, Securities

LITTLE ROCK AFB

A UNITED STATES AIR FORCE*, Little Rock Air Force Base Library, 976 Cannon Dr, FL 4460, 72099-5289. SAN 331-2518. Tel: 501-987-6979. *Librn,* Bethry J Becker; E-mail: bethry.becker@littlerock.af.mil
Founded 1956
Library Holdings: Bk Vols 21,000
Subject Interests: Aeronaut, Bus & mgt

LONOKE

P LONOKE PRAIRIE COUNTY REGIONAL LIBRARY HEADQUARTERS*, 204 E Second St, 72086-2858. SAN 324-041X. Tel: 501-676-6635. FAX: 501-676-7687. Web Site: www.lpregional.lib.ar.us. *Dir,* Leroy Gattin; E-mail: lgattin@lpregional.lib.ar.us; *Librn,* Shirley McGraw; E-mail: smcgraw@lpregional.lib.ar.us; Staff 8 (MLS 1, Non-MLS 7)
Founded 1937. Pop 70,000; Circ 165,000
Library Holdings: Bk Titles 80,000; Bk Vols 131,000; Per Subs 240
Special Collections: Genealogy Coll; Local History Coll
Open Mon-Wed & Fri 9-5, Thurs 9-7, Sat 9-1
Branches: 8
CARLISLE PUBLIC, 105 E Fifth, Carlisle, 72024, SAN 324-0665. Tel: 870-552-3976. FAX: 870-552-9306. *Librn,* Lynnette Ward; E-mail: lward@lpregional.lib.ar.us
Founded 1972. Pop 2,304
Function: Bks on CD, Children's prog, Computers for patron use, Copy machines, Electronic databases & coll, Free DVD rentals, Holiday prog, ILL available, Music CDs, Photocopying/Printing, Preschool outreach, Prog for children & young adult, Senior outreach, Story hour, Summer reading prog, Tax forms, Teen prog
Open Mon, Wed & Thurs 9-5, Tues 10-6, Fri 8-4
ARLENE CHERRY MEMORIAL, 506 N Grant St, Cabot, 72023, SAN 324-0649. Tel: 501-843-7661. FAX: 501 843 6316. *Librn,* Christine Williams; E-mail: cwilliams@lpregional.lib.ar.us
Open Mon-Thurs 8:30-7, Fri 8:30-5, Sat 9-1
Friends of the Library Group
DES ARC PUBLIC, 408 Curran St, Des Arc, 72040. (Mail add: PO Box 546, Des Arc, 72040-0546), SAN 373-5036. Tel: 870-256-3003. FAX: 870-256-3003. *Librn,* Ashley Newton; E-mail: anewton@lpregional.lib.ar.us
Open Tues, Wed & Thurs 10-5
DEVALLS BLUFF PUBLIC, 173 Market St, Devalls Bluff, 72041. (Mail add: PO Box 504, Devalls Bluff, 72041), SAN 373-5044. Tel: 870-998-7010. FAX: 870-998-7010. *Librn,* Julie Ingram; E-mail: jingram@lpregional.lib.ar.us
Open Tues, Wed & Thurs 9:30-12 & 1-5
WILLIAM F FOSTER PUBLIC, 100 E Taylor St, England, 72046-2181, SAN 324-0673. Tel: 501-842-2051. FAX: 501-842-2051. *Librn,* Nanette Palmer; E-mail: npalmer@lpregional.lib.ar.us
Open Mon & Sat 9-12, Tues-Fri 9-5:30
HAZEN PUBLIC, 121 US Hwy 70 E, Hazen, 72064. (Mail add: PO Box 428, Hazen, 72064-0428), SAN 324-8070. Tel: 870-255-3576. FAX: 870-255-3576. *Librn,* Patsy McMullen; E-mail: pmcmullen@lpregional.lib.ar.us
Open Mon-Fri 10-12 & 1-5:30
MARJORIE WALKER MCCRARY MEMORIAL, 204 E Second St, 72086. Tel: 501-676-6635. FAX: 501-676-7687. *Librn,* Shirley McGraw
Open Mon-Wed & Fri 9-5, Thurs 9-7, Sat 9-1
Friends of the Library Group
WARD PUBLIC LIBRARY, 405 Hickory St, Ste 100, Ward, 72176. Tel: 501-941-3220. FAX: 501-941-3359. *Librn/Br Mgr,* Venessa Ford; E-mail: vford@lpregional.lib.ar.us
Founded 1999. Pop 4,076
Function: AV serv, Bks on CD, CD-ROM, Children's prog, Computers for patron use, Copy machines, Fax serv, Free DVD rentals, Handicapped accessible, ILL available, Magazines, Movies, Music CDs, Online cat, Online searches, Prog for adults, Prog for children & young adult, Pub access computers, Summer reading prog, Tax forms, Teen prog, VHS videos, Video lending libr, Web-catalog, Wheelchair accessible
Open Mon & Tues 9-6, Wed & Thurs 9-5:30, Fri 9-2
Restriction: ID required to use computers (Ltd hrs), In-house use for visitors, Lending limited to county residents

MAGNOLIA

P COLUMBIA COUNTY LIBRARY*, 2057 N Jackson St, 71754. (Mail add: PO Box 668, 71754), SAN 331-2542. Tel: 870-234-1991. FAX: 870-234-5077. E-mail: library@cocolib.org. *Dir,* Rhonda Rolen; *Asst Dir,* Dana Thornton; E-mail: dana.thornton@colcnty.lib.ar.us; Staff 1 (MLS 1)
Founded 1929. Pop 71,734
Library Holdings: Bk Vols 125,000; Per Subs 58
Special Collections: Arkansas Coll; Genealogy Coll
Automation Activity & Vendor Info: (Cataloging) TLC (The Library Corporation); (Circulation) TLC (The Library Corporation); (OPAC) TLC (The Library Corporation)
Database Vendor: EBSCOhost, Grolier Online, OCLC FirstSearch, OCLC WorldShare Interlibrary Loan, TLC (The Library Corporation)
Wireless access
Function: Bks on cassette, Bks on CD, CD-ROM, Children's prog, Computers for patron use, Copy machines, Homebound delivery serv, ILL available, Online cat, Online ref, Prog for adults, Prog for children & young adult, Pub access computers, Summer reading prog, Tax forms, Teen prog, VHS videos
Open Mon & Thurs 12-8, Tues, Wed & Fri 9-6, Sat 9-12
Restriction: Circ to mem only, Non-circulating coll, Registered patrons only
Branches: 4
BEARDEN PUBLIC LIBRARY, 210 N Cedar, Bearden, 71720. (Mail add: PO Box 136, Bearden, 71720-0536), SAN 331-2577. Tel: 870-687-2634. *Librn,* Lucy Shurtleff
Open Mon-Thurs 2-5
PUBLIC LIBRARY OF CAMDEN & OUACHITA COUNTY, 120 Harrison Ave SW, Camden, 71701. SAN 331-2631. Tel: 870-836-5083. FAX: 870-836-0163. *Dir,* Lisa Pickett
Library Holdings: Bk Titles 43,000
Open Mon-Fri 9:30-5:30, Sat 9-12
STEPHENS PUBLIC LIBRARY, 108 W Ruby St, Stephens, 71764. (Mail add: PO Box 104, Stephens, 71764-0104), SAN 331-278X. Tel: 870-786-5231. *Librn,* Nettie Tribble
Open Mon-Thurs 1-4
TAYLOR PUBLIC LIBRARY, 101 W Pope, Taylor, 71861, SAN 331-281X. Tel: 870-694-2051. *Librn,* Betty Ann Jackson; Staff 1 (MLS 1)
Open Mon-Fri 2-5

C SOUTHERN ARKANSAS UNIVERSITY*, Magale Library, 100 E University, 71753-5000. (Mail add: SAU Box 9401, 71754-9401), SAN 300-533X. Tel: 870-235-4170. Reference Tel: 870-235-5083. FAX: 870-235-5018. Web Site: www.saumag.edu/library. *Dir,* Peggy Walters; Tel: 870-235-4171, E-mail: ppwalters@saumag.edu; *Access Serv, Asst Libr Dir, Syst Tech,* Margo Pierson; Tel: 870-235-4177, E-mail: mmpierson@saumag.edu; *Bibliog Instr, Pub Serv,* Julie Metro; Tel: 870-235-4174, E-mail: jmetro@saumag.edu; *Circ & User Serv, Electronic Res Librn/Libr Webmaster,* Del Duke; Tel: 870-235-4175, E-mail: dgduke@saumag.edu; *Govt Doc, Per,* Peggy Rogers; Tel: 870-235-5066, E-mail: pvrogers@saumag.edu; *ILL, Ref,* Donna McCloy; Tel: 870-235-4178, E-mail: dmmccloy@saumag.edu; Staff 9 (MLS 5, Non-MLS 4)
Founded 1909. Enrl 3,100; Fac 135; Highest Degree: Master
Library Holdings: AV Mats 12,214; Bks on Deafness & Sign Lang 24; Bk Titles 132,755; Bk Vols 149,000; Per Subs 612
Special Collections: Arkansiana. State Document Depository; US Document Depository
Automation Activity & Vendor Info: (Acquisitions) SirsiDynix; (Cataloging) SirsiDynix; (Circulation) SirsiDynix; (Course Reserve) SirsiDynix; (OPAC) SirsiDynix; (Serials) SirsiDynix
Database Vendor: American Chemical Society, Amigos Library Services, Annual Reviews, Baker & Taylor, Cambridge Scientific Abstracts, Checkpoint Systems, Inc, Cinahl, CQ Press, Dialog, Dun & Bradstreet, EBSCO - WebFeat, EBSCO Information Services, EBSCOhost, Facts on File, Gale Cengage Learning, H W Wilson, JSTOR, LexisNexis, Marcive, Inc, Mergent Online, Modern Language Association, Newsbank, OCLC FirstSearch, OCLC WorldShare Interlibrary Loan, OVID Technologies, ProQuest, SerialsSolutions, SirsiDynix, STN International, Wilson - Wilson Web, YBP Library Services
Wireless access
Partic in ARKLink; OCLC Online Computer Library Center, Inc
Friends of the Library Group

MALVERN

J COLLEGE OF THE OUACHITAS, Library & Learning Resource Center, (Formerly Ouachita Technical College), One College Circle, 72104. Tel: 501-337-5000. Interlibrary Loan Service Tel: 501-332-0208. Information Services Tel: 501-332-0210. FAX: 501-337-9382. Web Site: www1.youseemore.com/otc. *Dir,* Mary Ann Harper; E-mail: mharper@coto.edu; Staff 1 (MLS 1)
Founded 1991. Enrl 823; Fac 56; Highest Degree: Associate

Library Holdings: Bk Vols 12,000; Per Subs 32
Automation Activity & Vendor Info: (Acquisitions) TLC (The Library Corporation); (Cataloging) TLC (The Library Corporation); (Circulation) TLC (The Library Corporation); (OPAC) TLC (The Library Corporation)
Database Vendor: Gale Cengage Learning, ProQuest
Wireless access
Function: Adult bk club, Art exhibits, Audio & video playback equip for onsite use, Bk club(s), Bks on cassette, Bks on CD, CD-ROM, Computer training, Computers for patron use, Copy machines, e-mail & chat, e-mail serv, E-Reserves, Electronic databases & coll, Free DVD rentals, Handicapped accessible, ILL available, Instruction & testing, Magnifiers for reading, Mail & tel request accepted, Mail loans to mem, Music CDs, Newsp ref libr, Online cat, Online ref, Online searches, Orientations, Outside serv via phone, mail, e-mail & web, Photocopying/Printing, Pub access computers, Ref & res, Ref serv available, Ref serv in person, Res libr, Scanner, Spoken cassettes & CDs, Spoken cassettes & DVDs, Telephone ref, VHS videos, Video lending libr, Wheelchair accessible
Partic in Amigos Library Services, Inc; ARKLink; Educ Resources Info Ctr
Open Mon-Thurs (Winter) 7:30-7:30, Fri 7:30-4:30; Mon-Fri (Summer) 7:30-4:30
Restriction: Authorized patrons, Circ limited, In-house use for visitors, Lending libr only via mail, Non-circulating coll, Open to pub for ref & circ; with some limitations, Open to students, fac & staff, Photo ID required for access

P MALVERN-HOT SPRING COUNTY LIBRARY, Mid-Arkansas Regional Library, 202 E Third St, 72104. SAN 300-5348. Tel: 501-332-5441. FAX: 501-332-6679. E-mail: hotspringcountylibrary@yahoo.com. Web Site: www.hsc.lib.ar.us. *Libr Dir,* Ashley Parker-Graves; E-mail: Ashley.parker@arkansas.gov; *Libr Mgr,* Charlotte Smith; E-mail: Charlotte.m.smith@arkansas.gov; *Libr Serv Mgr,* Jan Lambert; *Circ Mgr,* Arnescia Lee; Staff 1 (Non-MLS 1)
Founded 1928. Pop 29,000; Circ 120,000
Library Holdings: Bk Vols 74,000; Per Subs 70
Subject Interests: Ark, Genealogy
Automation Activity & Vendor Info: (Cataloging) Innovative Interfaces, Inc; (Circulation) Innovative Interfaces, Inc; (OPAC) Innovative Interfaces, Inc
Database Vendor: EBSCOhost, Gale Cengage Learning
Wireless access
Open Mon, Wed & Fri 9-5, Tues 9-7, Thurs 12-7, Sat 9-1
Friends of the Library Group
Bookmobiles: 1

MARION

P CRITTENDEN COUNTY LIBRARY*, Margaret Woolfolk Library, 100 N Currie St, 72364. SAN 300-5364. Tel: 870-739-3238. FAX: 870-739-4624. E-mail: woolfolklibrary@yahoo.com. *County Librn,* Tracy Pahls; Staff 4 (Non-MLS 4)
Pop 22,140; Circ 24,000
Library Holdings: Bk Vols 41,000; Per Subs 75
Special Collections: Arkansas Coll
Wireless access
Open Mon-Fri 9-6, Sat 9-12
Friends of the Library Group
Branches: 4
CRAWFORDSVILLE BRANCH, 5444 Main St, Crawfordsville, 72327. (Mail add: PO Box 28, Crawfordsville, 72327-0028), SAN 321-9143. Tel: 870-823-5204. *Librn,* Jennifer Sexton
Founded 1963. Pop 514
Function: Summer reading prog
Open Mon & Tues 9-4:30, Wed 11:30-4:30
Friends of the Library Group
EARLE BRANCH, 703 Commerce St, Earle, 72331, SAN 321-9135. Tel: 870-792-8500. *Librn,* Linda McCain
Open Tues-Thurs 9-4:30
Friends of the Library Group
GILMORE BRANCH, 87 Front St, Gilmore, 72339, SAN 321-916X. Tel: 870-343-2697. FAX: 870-343-2601. *Librn,* Cathy Moore
Open Mon-Fri 3-5
Friends of the Library Group
HORSESHOE BRANCH, 3181 Horseshoe Circle, Hughes, 72348, SAN 321-9178. Tel: 870-339-3862. E-mail: horseshoelakelibrary@gmail.com. *Librn,* Jennifer Sexton
Pop 2,000; Circ 5,000
Function: Homebound delivery serv
Open Tues & Thurs 9:30-6
Friends of the Library Group

MARSHALL

P SEARCY COUNTY LIBRARY*, Jim G Ferguson Memorial, 202 E Main St, 72650. SAN 331-1104. Tel: 870-448-2420. FAX: 870-448-5453. *Librn,* Pat Halsted
Library Holdings: Bk Vols 35,000
Open Mon, Wed & Fri 10-5, Tues & Thurs 10-7, Sat 10-12:30
Friends of the Library Group

MELBOURNE

P IZARD COUNTY LIBRARY*, Melbourne Public Library, 1007 E Main St, 72556. (Mail add: PO Box 343, 72556-0343), SAN 326-7121. Tel: 870-368-7467. FAX: 870-368-3242. Web Site: www.melbournelibrary.webs.com. *Libr Mgr,* Tammi Trotter
Founded 1957. Pop 1,673
Library Holdings: Bk Titles 10,000; Per Subs 10
Mem of White River Regional Library
Open Mon-Thurs 9-4:30, Fri 9:30-4:30, Sat 10:30-1:30

J OZARKA COLLEGE, Paul Weaver Library, 218 College Dr, 72556-8708. (Mail add: PO Box 10, 72556). Tel: 870-368-7371. Circulation Tel: 870-368-2054. Interlibrary Loan Service Tel: 870-368-2055. Toll Free Tel: 800-821-4335. FAX: 870-368-2091. Web Site: www.ozarka.edu/library.cfm. *Libr Dir,* Mary Ellen Hawkins; E-mail: mhawkins@ozarka.edu; Staff 3 (MLS 2, Non-MLS 1)
Founded 1991. Enrl 1,500; Fac 50; Highest Degree: Associate
Library Holdings: Bks on Deafness & Sign Lang 12; DVDs 508; e-books 1,200; e-journals 6,500; Large Print Bks 10; Bk Vols 16,500; Per Subs 125; Videos 1,530
Automation Activity & Vendor Info: (Acquisitions) OpenBiblio; (Cataloging) OpenBiblio; (Circulation) OpenBiblio; (Course Reserve) OCLC; (ILL) OpenBiblio; (Media Booking) OpenBiblio; (OPAC) OpenBiblio; (Serials) OpenBiblio
Database Vendor: ALLDATA Online, Amigos Library Services, Bowker, Cinahl, CredoReference, EBSCOhost, Gale Cengage Learning, LearningExpress, Medline, Newsbank, OCLC FirstSearch, OCLC WorldShare Interlibrary Loan, OpenBiblio, ProQuest, World Book Online
Wireless access
Function: Free DVD rentals
Partic in ARKLink
Open Mon-Thurs 8-7:30, Fri 8-4:30
Restriction: Authorized patrons, Badge access after hrs
Friends of the Library Group

MENA

P POLK COUNTY LIBRARY*, 410 Eighth St, 71953. SAN 331-1589. Tel: 479-394-2314. FAX: 479-394-2314. Web Site: menapolkcountylibrary.org. *County Librn,* Shirley Philpot
Wireless access
Function: Copy machines, Fax serv, ILL available, Pub access computers, Story hour
Mem of Ouachita Mountains Regional Library
Open Mon-Wed & Fri 9-5, Thurs 9-6, Sat 9-2
Friends of the Library Group

J RICH MOUNTAIN COMMUNITY COLLEGE*, Saint John Library, 1100 College Dr, 71953-2503. Tel: 479-394-7622. FAX: 479-394-2828. Web Site: www.rmcc.edu/library.htm. *Dir,* Clara O'Daniel; Tel: 501-394-7622, Ext 1370, E-mail: codaniel@rmcc.edu
Founded 1983
Library Holdings: Bk Vols 15,000; Per Subs 90
Automation Activity & Vendor Info: (Cataloging) Mandarin Library Automation; (Circulation) Mandarin Library Automation; (OPAC) Mandarin Library Automation
Database Vendor: LexisNexis, ProQuest
Function: ILL available, Ref serv available
Open Mon-Thurs (Winter) 8-8, Fri 8-3:30; Mon-Thurs (Summer) 8-4:30, Fri 8:30-3:30

MONTICELLO

P SOUTHEAST ARKANSAS REGIONAL LIBRARY*, 114 E Jackson St, 71655. SAN 331-2879. Tel: 870-367-8584. FAX: 870-367-5166. Web Site: www1.youseemore.com/seark. *Dir,* Judy Calhoun; E-mail: director@searl@gmail.com; Staff 44 (MLS 1, Non-MLS 43)
Founded 1947. Pop 75,000; Circ 203,204
Library Holdings: Bk Titles 80,000; Bk Vols 183,000; Per Subs 495
Subject Interests: Ark
Automation Activity & Vendor Info: (Cataloging) TLC (The Library Corporation); (Circulation) TLC (The Library Corporation)
Open Mon-Fri 9-5:30, Sat 9-2

Branches: 12
ARKANSAS CITY BRANCH, PO Box 447, Arkansas City, 71630, SAN 331-2909. *Mgr,* Joyce Douthit
Open Thurs 10-5
DERMOTT BRANCH, 117 S Freeman St, Dermott, 71638, SAN 321-9518. Tel: 870-538-3514. FAX: 870-538-3514. *Br Mgr,* Kelly Washington
Open Mon-Fri 12:30-5:30, Sat 9-12
Friends of the Library Group
DUMAS BRANCH, 120 E Choctow, Dumas, 71639, SAN 331-2968. Tel: 870-382-5763. FAX: 870-382-5763. *Mgr,* Debra Dardenne
Open Mon-Fri 9-6, Sat 10-2
Friends of the Library Group
EUDORA BRANCH, 161 N Cherry St, Eudora, 71640, SAN 321-9526. Tel: 870-355-2450. FAX: 870-355-2450. *Mgr,* Mary Bates
Open Mon-Fri 12:30-5:30, Sat 9-12
HERMITAGE BRANCH, PO Box 98, Hermitage, 71647-0098, SAN 331-3034. Tel: 870-463-8962. FAX: 870-463-8962. *Mgr,* Elvie Belin
Open Mon-Fri 12-5, Sat 9-11
LAKE VILLAGE BRANCH, 108 Church St, Lake Village, 71653, SAN 300-5143. Tel: 870-265-6116. FAX: 870-265-6116. E-mail: lakevillage.searl@gmail.com. *Mgr,* Judy Fava
Open Mon-Fri 9-6
Friends of the Library Group
MCGEHEE BRANCH, 211 N Fourth St, McGehee, 71654, SAN 331-3050. Tel: 870-222-4097. FAX: 870-222-4097. *Mgr,* Debbie Fowler
Open Mon-Fri 9-6, Sat 10-2
Friends of the Library Group
MONTICELLO BRANCH, 114 E Jackson, 71655, SAN 331-3069. Tel: 870-367-8583. FAX: 870-367-5166. *Mgr,* Brandy Horne
Open Mon-Fri 9-5:30, Sat 9-2
Friends of the Library Group
STAR CITY BRANCH, 200 E Wiley, Star City, 71667, SAN 331 3085. Tel: 870-628-4711. FAX: 870-628-4711. *Br Mgr,* Simone Kirk
Open Mon-Fri 9-6, Sat 9-2
Friends of the Library Group
TILLAR BRANCH, PO Box 136, Tillar, 71670-0136, SAN 331-3115. Tel: 870-367-8584. *Mgr,* Joyce Douthit
Open Tues 10-5
WARREN BRANCH, 115 W Cypress, Warren, 71671, SAN 331-3131. Tel: 870-226-2536. FAX: 870 226 2536. *Mgr,* Roxie Wright
Open Mon-Fri 10-6, Sat 10-2
Friends of the Library Group
WATSON BRANCH, PO Box 205, Watson, 71674, SAN 331-314X. Tel: 870-644-3655. FAX: 870-644-3655. *Mgr,* Joyce Douthit
Open Wed 10-5

C UNIVERSITY OF ARKANSAS-MONTICELLO LIBRARY*, Taylor Library & Technology Center, 514 University Dr, 71656. (Mail add: PO Box 3599, 71656-3599), SAN 300-5372. Tel: 870-460-1080. FAX: 870-460-1980. Web Site: www.uamont.edu/library. *Dir,* Sandra Campbell; Tel: 870-460-1180, E-mail: campbell@uamont.edu; *Assoc Librn, Head, Ref & Ser,* Helen Guenter; *Asst Librn,* Kathy Davis; *Asst Librn, Head, Doc Delivery/ILL, Ref Serv,* Lanee Dunlap; *Asst Librn, Chair, Spec Coll & Archives, Ref Serv,* Mary Heady; *Asst Librn, Head, Tech Serv, Ref Serv,* Paula Reaves; *Br Head, Info Literacy,* Janie Carter; *Circ Mgr, Coordr,* Annette Vincent; *ILL, Libr Tech,* Linda Forrest; *Ser,* Kay Crook; Staff 10 (MLS 4, Non-MLS 6)
Founded 1909. Enrl 2,942; Fac 150; Highest Degree: Master
Library Holdings: Bk Vols 151,176; Per Subs 1,000
Special Collections: State Document Depository; US Document Depository
Subject Interests: Ark, Forestry
Automation Activity & Vendor Info: (Acquisitions) Innovative Interfaces, Inc; (Cataloging) Innovative Interfaces, Inc; (Circulation) Innovative Interfaces, Inc; (Course Reserve) Innovative Interfaces, Inc; (OPAC) Innovative Interfaces, Inc; (Serials) Innovative Interfaces, Inc
Database Vendor: Innovative Interfaces, Inc
Publications: Annual Report
Partic in ARKLink
Open Mon-Thurs (Aug-May) 8am-10pm, Fri 8-4:30, Sat 2-5, Sun 2-10; Mon-Thurs (June & July) 8-8, Fri 8-4:30, Sun 5-9

MORRILTON

P CONWAY COUNTY LIBRARY HEADQUARTERS*, 101 W Church St, 72110-3399. SAN 300-5380. Tel: 501-354-5204. FAX: 501-354-5206. Web Site: www.youseemore.com/conwaycl. *Dir,* Jay Carter; E-mail: jay.carter@conwaycountylibrary.org; Staff 4 (MLS 1, Non-MLS 3)
Founded 1916. Pop 21,273; Circ 64,840
Library Holdings: Bk Titles 35,000; Per Subs 34
Automation Activity & Vendor Info: (Cataloging) TLC (The Library Corporation); (Circulation) TLC (The Library Corporation); (ILL) OCLC FirstSearch; (OPAC) TLC (The Library Corporation)
Wireless access
Function: Bk club(s), Computers for patron use, Fax serv, ILL available, Preschool outreach, Prog for adults, Prog for children & young adult, Pub access computers, Spoken cassettes & CDs, Spoken cassettes & DVDs, Story hour, Summer reading prog, Teen prog, Web-catalog
Open Tues-Fri 9-6:30, Sat 9-1
Friends of the Library Group

JR UNIVERSITY OF ARKANSAS COMMUNITY COLLEGE AT MORRILTON*, Gordon Library, Kirk Bldg, 1537 University Blvd, 72110-9601. Tel: 501-977-2033. FAX: 501-354-9948. *Librn,* Linda Julian; Fax: 501-977-2134, E-mail: julian@uaccm.edu
Founded 1961. Highest Degree: Associate
Library Holdings: Bk Titles 13,440; Bk Vols 16,469; Per Subs 44
Automation Activity & Vendor Info: (Cataloging) SirsiDynix; (Circulation) SirsiDynix
Open Mon-Thurs 8-7, Fri 8-4

MOUNT IDA

P MONTGOMERY COUNTY LIBRARY*, 145A Whittington St, 71957-9404. (Mail add: PO Box 189, 71957-0189), SAN 300-5399. Tel: 870-867-3812. FAX: 870-867-3812. E-mail: montlibrary@hotmail.com. Web Site: www.montgomerycountyarlibrary. *County Librn,* Joann Whisenhunt
Founded 1958. Pop 9,245; Circ 25,168
Jan 2005-Dec 2005 Income $40,000
Library Holdings: Bk Titles 14,000
Special Collections: Montgomery County Genealogy Coll
Function: Copy machines, Fax serv, ILL available, Pub access computers
Mem of Ouachita Mountains Regional Library
Open Mon-Fri 9:30-4:30
Friends of the Library Group

MOUNTAIN HOME

C ARKANSAS STATE UNIVERSITY*, Norma Wood Library, 1600 S College St, 72653-5326. Tel: 870-508-6112. FAX: 870-508-6291. Web Site: www.asumh.edu. *Dir,* Tina Bradley; E-mail: tbradley@asumh.edu; Staff 5 (MLS 2, Non-MLS 3)
Library Holdings: Bk Vols 17,000; Per Subs 167
Automation Activity & Vendor Info: (Acquisitions) Ex Libris Group; (Cataloging) Ex Libris Group; (Circulation) Ex Libris Group; (Course Reserve) Ex Libris Group; (ILL) Ex Libris Group; (OPAC) Ex Libris Group
Database Vendor: EBSCOhost, LexisNexis, OCLC FirstSearch, ProQuest
Wireless access
Function: ILL available, Photocopying/Printing, Ref serv available, Telephone ref
Open Mon-Thurs 7:30am-8pm, Fri 7:30-5
Restriction: Open to students, fac & staff, Pub use on premises

P BAXTER COUNTY LIBRARY*, Donald W Reynolds Library, 300 Library Hill, 72653. Tel: 870-580-0987. FAX: 870-580-0935. E-mail: baxlib@baxtercountylibrary.org. Web Site: www.baxtercountylibrary.org. *Librn,* Gwen Khayat; Staff 19 (MLS 2, Non-MLS 17)
Founded 1952. Pop 42,000; Circ 340,605
Library Holdings: Bk Vols 73,000
Automation Activity & Vendor Info: (Cataloging) TLC (The Library Corporation); (Circulation) TLC (The Library Corporation); (OPAC) TLC (The Library Corporation)
Wireless access
Open Mon & Wed-Fri 10-6:30, Tues 10-8, Sat 10-4, Sun 1-5
Friends of the Library Group
Branches: 1
GASSVILLE BRANCH, 6469 Hwy 62 W, Gassville, 72635. (Mail add: 300 Library Hill, 72653). Tel: 870-435-2180. Administration Tel: 870-425-3598. Administration FAX: 870-425-7226. *Dir,* Gwen Khayat
Pop 3,000; Circ 4,300
Library Holdings: Bk Vols 3,000
Automation Activity & Vendor Info: (Cataloging) The Library Co-Op, Inc; (ILL) OCLC; (Media Booking) TLC (The Library Corporation)
Function: Bks on cassette, Bks on CD, Copy machines, Electronic databases & coll, ILL available, Magnifiers for reading, Online cat, Online searches, Photocopying/Printing, Spoken cassettes & CDs, Spoken cassettes & DVDs, VHS videos, Web-catalog, Wheelchair accessible
Open Mon-Fri 1-5, Sat 10-2

MOUNTAIN VIEW

P STONE COUNTY LIBRARY*, Bessie Boehm Moore Library, 326 W Washington St, 72560. Tel: 870-269-3100. E-mail: stonecolibrary@mvtel.net. *Br Mgr,* Lenora Duncan
Library Holdings: Bk Vols 25,000; Per Subs 45
Automation Activity & Vendor Info: (Cataloging) Follett Software; (Circulation) Follett Software
Wireless access

Open Mon, Wed & Fri 9:30-5, Tues 9:30-6, Thurs 9:30-7, Sat 9:30-1
Friends of the Library Group

MOUNTAINBURG

P MOUNTAINBURG PUBLIC LIBRARY*, 1300 Hwy 71 N, 72946. SAN 331-0027. Tel: 479-369-1600. FAX: 479-369-1600. Web Site: www.crawfordcountylib.org. *Librn,* Sue Yount
Library Holdings: Bk Vols 18,889
Automation Activity & Vendor Info: (Cataloging) TLC (The Library Corporation); (Circulation) TLC (The Library Corporation); (ILL) OCLC; (OPAC) TLC (The Library Corporation)
Database Vendor: EBSCOhost, OCLC FirstSearch
Mem of Crawford County Library System
Open Mon-Fri 8-6, Sat 9-12
Friends of the Library Group

MULBERRY

P MULBERRY PUBLIC LIBRARY*, 220 N Main St, 72947. (Mail add: PO Box 589, 72947-0589), SAN 331-0051. Tel: 479-997-1226. Interlibrary Loan Service Tel: 479-471-3226. FAX: 479-997-1226. Interlibrary Loan Service FAX: 479-471-3227. E-mail: mulberrylibrary@hotmail.com. Web Site: www.crawfordcounty.lib.org. *Br Mgr,* Cindy Whitson
Pop 1,600
Library Holdings: Bk Vols 16,553
Automation Activity & Vendor Info: (Cataloging) TLC (The Library Corporation); (Circulation) TLC (The Library Corporation); (OPAC) TLC (The Library Corporation)
Database Vendor: EBSCOhost, OCLC FirstSearch
Wireless access
Open Mon-Fri 8:15-5:15, Sat 11-2
Friends of the Library Group

MURFREESBORO

P PIKE COUNTY LIBRARY*, 210 Second Ave, 71958. (Mail add: PO Box 153, 71958-0153), SAN 331-149X. Tel: 870-295-4520. E-mail: murfreesborolibrary@gmail.com. *Librn,* Gladys Leeper
Friends of the Library Group
Branches: 1
DELIGHT BRANCH LIBRARY, 401 E Antioch St, Delight, 71940. (Mail add: PO Box 88, Delight, 71940-0142), SAN 331-1252. Tel: 870-379-2456. E-mail: delightlib1@hotmail.com. *Librn,* Virginia Evans
Open Tues-Fri 10-5

NASHVILLE

P TRI-COUNTY REGIONAL LIBRARY*, Howard County Library, 426 N Main St, Ste 5, 71852. SAN 331-1643. Tel: 870-845-2566. FAX: 870-845-7533. E-mail: Tri-countyreglibsystem@hotmail.com. *Mgr,* Janice Curry
Pop 6,000; Circ 34,000
Subject Interests: Ark
Open Mon 11-7, Tues-Sat 10-5
Branches: 8
ASHDOWN COMMUNITY LIBRARY, 160 E Commerce St, Ashdown, 71822, SAN 331-1228. Tel: 870-898-3233. FAX: 870-898-3233. E-mail: ashcomlib@yahoo.com. *Mgr,* Nora Johnson
Pop 2,944
Open Mon 12-7, Tues-Fri 9-6
DIERKS PUBLIC LIBRARY, 202 W Third St, Dierks, 71833. (Mail add: PO Box 10, Dierks, 71833-0010), SAN 331-1317. Tel: 870-286-3228. FAX: 870-286-2570. E-mail: dierkslib@yahoo.com. *Mgr,* Ruth White
Open Tues-Thurs 8:30-4:30
FOREMAN PUBLIC LIBRARY, 216 Schumann St, Foreman, 71836. (Mail add: PO Box 7, Foreman, 71836-0007), SAN 331-1341. Tel: 870-542-7409. FAX: 870-542-7409. E-mail: foremanpublib@yahoo.com. *Mgr,* Tammy Whitlow
Open Mon-Fri 8:30-5
LOCKESBURG PUBLIC LIBRARY, 112 E Main St, Lockesburg, 71846. (Mail add: PO Box 46, Lockesburg, 71846). Tel: 870-289-2233. FAX: 870-289-2233. E-mail: loxlib@hotmail.com. *Mgr,* Wendy Clay
Open Wed & Thurs 9:30-5, Sat 9-12
BEN LOMOND PUBLIC LIBRARY, 148 Wilson Creek, Ben Lomond, 71823. (Mail add: PO Box 142, Ben Lomond, 71823-0142). Tel: 870-287-4374. FAX: 870-287-4374. E-mail: benlomondlib@yahoo.com. *Mgr,* Pamela Farquhar
Open Tues & Thurs 9:30-5, Sat 9-Noon
MINERAL SPRINGS PUBLIC LIBRARY, 310 E Runnels, Mineral Springs, 71851. (Mail add: PO Box 309, Mineral Springs, 71851-0309), SAN 331-152X. Tel: 870-287-7162. *Mgr,* Cheryl Burcham
Open Tues & Wed 11-5
TOLLETTE PUBLIC LIBRARY, 205 Town Hall Dr, Tollette, 71851. (Mail add: PO Box 418, Tollette, 71851-0418), SAN 331-1651. Tel: 870-287-7166. E-mail: tollettebranchlibrary@yahoo.com. *Librn,* Wilma Lafferty
Library Holdings: Bk Vols 5,000
Open Mon-Wed 9-3
WINTHROP PUBLIC LIBRARY, 720 High St, Winthrop, 71866. (Mail add: PO Box 193, Winthrop, 71866-0193), SAN 331-1554. Tel: 870-381-7580. FAX: 870-381-7580. E-mail: chunbug@yahoo.com. *Mgr,* Vonnie Chewning
Open Mon-Fri 10-5
Friends of the Library Group

NEWPORT

C ARKANSAS STATE UNIVERSITY*, Newport Library, 7648 Victory Blvd, 72112-8912. Tel: 870-512-7861. Interlibrary Loan Service Tel: 870-512-7862. FAX: 870-512-7870. Web Site: www.asun.edu/library. *Librn,* Jennifer Ballard
Library Holdings: Bk Titles 6,400; Bk Vols 8,000; Per Subs 76
Automation Activity & Vendor Info: (Acquisitions) Ex Libris Group; (Cataloging) Ex Libris Group; (Circulation) Ex Libris Group; (ILL) OCLC FirstSearch; (OPAC) Ex Libris Group
Database Vendor: EBSCOhost, OCLC FirstSearch, ProQuest
Wireless access
Open Mon-Thurs (Fall & Spring) 8-6, Fri 8-4:30, Sat 9-1

P JACKSON COUNTY LIBRARY*, W A Billingsley Memorial Library, 213 Walnut St, 72112-3325. (Mail add: PO Box 748, 72112-0748), SAN 300-5402. Tel: 870-523-2952. FAX: 870-523-5218. Web Site: www.jacksoncolibrary.net/library. *Dir,* Connie Cook; E-mail: connie@jacksoncolibrary.net; *Ref Librn,* Ellen Crain; *Children's Prog, Circ,* Sally Dunkin
Founded 1930. Pop 18,944
Library Holdings: Large Print Bks 2,750; Bk Titles 53,000; Per Subs 70
Subject Interests: Ark, Genealogy
Automation Activity & Vendor Info: (Cataloging) Follett Software; (Circulation) Follett Software; (ILL) OCLC
Database Vendor: EBSCOhost, OCLC FirstSearch
Open Mon-Fri 9:30-5, Sat 9:30-Noon
Branches: 1
TUCKERMAN BRANCH, 200 W Main St, Tuckerman, 72473. (Mail add: PO Box 1117, Tuckerman, 72473-1117). Tel: 870-349-5336. FAX: 870-349-5336. *Librn,* Margaret Campbell
Pop 1,741
Library Holdings: Bk Vols 59,750
Open Mon-Fri 8-12 & 12:30-4:30

NORTH LITTLE ROCK

P WILLIAM F LAMAN PUBLIC LIBRARY*, 2801 Orange St, 72114-2296. SAN 300-5429. Tel: 501-758-1720. FAX: 501-758-3539. Web Site: www.laman.net. *Dir,* Jeffrey L Baskin; Fax: 501-753-0524, E-mail: jeff.baskin@laman.net; *Asst Dir,* Butler Zoe; E-mail: zoe.butler@laman.net; Staff 22 (MLS 4, Non-MLS 18)
Founded 1945. Pop 61,741; Circ 206,078
Jan 2005-Dec 2005 Income $1,977,612. Mats Exp $306,000
Library Holdings: e-books 25; Bk Titles 165,057; Per Subs 252
Special Collections: Ark History; Genealogy Coll
Automation Activity & Vendor Info: (OPAC) Innovative Interfaces, Inc
Wireless access
Partic in OCLC Online Computer Library Center, Inc

J PULASKI TECHNICAL COLLEGE LIBRARY*, 3000 W Scenic Dr, 72118-3347. Tel: 501-812-2272. FAX: 501-812-2315. Web Site: www.pulaskitech.edu/library. *Dir,* Deborah Kirby; E-mail: dkirby@pulaskitech.edu; *Asst Dir,* Wendy Davis; Staff 7 (MLS 4, Non-MLS 3)
Enrl 8,500; Highest Degree: Associate
Library Holdings: AV Mats 2,228; Bk Titles 28,633; Bk Vols 32,530; Per Subs 275
Automation Activity & Vendor Info: (Acquisitions) Ex Libris Group; (Cataloging) Ex Libris Group; (Circulation) Ex Libris Group; (Course Reserve) Ex Libris Group; (OPAC) Ex Libris Group; (Serials) Ex Libris Group
Database Vendor: American Psychological Association (APA), Bowker, EBSCOhost, Gale Cengage Learning, LexisNexis, OCLC FirstSearch, Oxford Online, ProQuest
Wireless access
Function: Distance learning, ILL available, Photocopying/Printing, Ref serv available
Partic in ARKLink
Open Mon-Thurs 7:30-7:30, Fri 7:30-3, Sat 7:30-12:30

PARAGOULD

M ARKANSAS METHODIST HOSPITAL*, Doctors' Memorial Library, 900 W Kings Hwy, 72450. (Mail add: PO Box 339, 72451-0339), SAN 320-1236. Tel: 870-239-7101. FAX: 870-239-7400. *Librn,* Kim Nelson
Founded 1970
Library Holdings: Bk Titles 800; Per Subs 20
Subject Interests: Med, Nursing
Restriction: Staff use only

J CROWLEY'S RIDGE COLLEGE LIBRARY*, 100 College Dr, 72450. SAN 300-5445. Tel: 870-236-6901. Toll Free Tel: 800-264-1096. FAX: 870-236-7748. Web Site: www.crowleysridgecollege.edu. *Dir,* Mark Warnick; E-mail: mwarnick@crc.edu
Founded 1964. Enrl 100; Fac 8
Library Holdings: Bk Vols 15,400; Per Subs 60
Subject Interests: Relig
Database Vendor: EBSCOhost, OCLC FirstSearch, ProQuest
Open Mon, Tues & Thurs 8am-10pm, Wed & Fri 8-5

P GREENE COUNTY PUBLIC LIBRARY*, 120 N 12th St, 72450. Tel: 870-236-8711. FAX: 870-236-1442. E-mail: greene@mylibrarynow.org. Web Site: www.mylibrarynow.org/greene. *County Librn,* Sandra Rogers; E-mail: sandy@mylibrarynow.org; *Librn,* Adam Broom; E-mail: adam@mylibrarynow.org; *ILL/Ref Librn,* Cathy Howard; E-mail: cathy@mylibrarynow.org; *Cat,* Kellie Cole; E-mail: kelly@mylibrarynow.org; *Circ,* Connie Sorrentino; E-mail: connie@mylibrarynow.org; Staff 7 (Non-MLS 7)
Founded 1965. Pop 68,194; Circ 274,503
Subject Interests: Ark, Genealogy
Automation Activity & Vendor Info: (Acquisitions) Follett Software; (Cataloging) Follett Software; (Circulation) Follett Software; (Course Reserve) Follett Software; (ILL) Follett Software; (Serials) EBSCO Online
Wireless access
Mem of Northeast Arkansas Regional Library System
Partic in SouthWest Ohio & Neighboring Libraries
Open Mon-Thurs 8-6, Fri & Sat 8-1
Friends of the Library Group

P NORTHEAST ARKANSAS REGIONAL LIBRARY SYSTEM*, 120 N 12th St, 72450. SAN 331-3204. Tel: 870-236-8711. FAX: 870-236-1442. *Dir,* Mike E Rogers; Staff 1 (MLS 1)
Founded 1965. Pop 71,000
Automation Activity & Vendor Info: (Circulation) Book Systems; (ILL) Book Systems; (OPAC) Book Systems
Wireless access
Function: Adult bk club, Bk club(s), Computer training, Copy machines, e-mail serv, Electronic databases & coll, Handicapped accessible, ILL available, Libr develop, Magnifiers for reading, Music CDs, Online ref, Online searches, Photocopying/Printing, Prog for adults, Prog for children & young adult, Ref & res, Senior computer classes, Serves mentally handicapped consumers, Spoken cassettes & CDs, Spoken cassettes & DVDs, Summer reading prog, Tax forms, VHS videos, Video lending libr, Wheelchair accessible
Member Libraries: Corning Public Library; Greene County Public Library; Piggott Public Library; Randolph County Library; Rector Public Library
Open Mon-Thurs 8-6, Fri 8-4, Sat 8-1

PEA RIDGE

P PEA RIDGE COMMUNITY LIBRARY*, 161 E Pickens Rd, 72751-2306. (Mail add: PO Box 9, 72751-0009). Tel: 479-451-8442. E-mail: library@pearidgecommunitylibrary.org. Web Site: pearidgecommunitylibrary.org. *Librn,* Peggy Maddox
Pop 5,500; Circ 3,000
Library Holdings: High Interest/Low Vocabulary Bk Vols 900; Large Print Bks 55; Bk Vols 13,100; Talking Bks 58
Special Collections: Arkansas History Coll
Function: Accelerated reader prog
Open Tues 4-8, Wed & Thurs 10-12 & 1-5
Restriction: ID required to use computers (Ltd hrs)

PIGGOTT

P PIGGOTT PUBLIC LIBRARY, 361 W Main, 72454. SAN 331-3263. Tel: 870-598-3666. FAX: 870-598-3669. E-mail: piggottlibrary@yahoo.com. Web Site: mylibrarynow.org/piggott. *Dir,* Gay Johnson; E-mail: gjohnson1953@yahoo.com; Staff 3 (Non-MLS 3)
Founded 1935
Library Holdings: AV Mats 122; CDs 803; DVDs 730; Large Print Bks 1,255; Microforms 122; Bk Titles 26,721; Per Subs 12; Videos 295
Automation Activity & Vendor Info: (Cataloging) Book Systems; (Circulation) Book Systems; (OPAC) Book Systems
Database Vendor: EBSCOhost, Gale Cengage Learning, OCLC FirstSearch
Wireless access
Mem of Northeast Arkansas Regional Library System
Open Mon, Tues & Thurs 8:30-5:30, Wed 8:30-5, Fri 8:30-4, Sat 9-1

PINE BLUFF

S ARKANSAS DEPARTMENT OF CORRECTION
DIAGNOSTIC UNIT LIBRARY*, 7500 Correction Circle, 71603-1498. Tel: 870-267-6410. FAX: 870-267-6721. *Supvr,* Cathy Herring; E-mail: cathy.herring@arkansas.gov
Library Holdings: Bk Vols 1,297; Per Subs 16
Database Vendor: LexisNexis
Open Mon-Fri 8-11, 1-4 & 6-8

S PINE BLUFF WORK COMPLEX CHAPEL LIBRARY*, 890 Freeline Dr, 71603-1498. Tel: 870-267-6510. FAX: 870-267-6529. *In Charge,* John Mark Wheeler; E-mail: john.wheeler@arkansas.gov
Library Holdings: Bk Vols 6,000; Per Subs 40
Open Tues-Fri 8-10 & 2-4

P PINE BLUFF & JEFFERSON COUNTY LIBRARY SYSTEM, Main Library, 200 E Eighth Ave, 71601. SAN 300-5453. Tel: 870-534-4802. Circulation Tel: 870-534-4818. Reference Tel: 870-534-2159. FAX: 870-534-8707. E-mail: info@pinebluffllibrary.org. Web Site: www.pinebluffllibrary.org. *Dir,* Michael Sawyer; Tel: 870-534-4615, E-mail: msawyer@pinebluffllibrary.org; *Computer & Info Res Librn,* Terrance Griffin; *Children's Mgr,* Danielle McNealy; *Circ Mgr,* Vernitta Love; *Circ Mgr,* Jeannine Matthews; *Ref Mgr,* Jana Mitchell; *Tech Serv,* Tammie Harris. Subject Specialists: *Info syst,* Terrance Griffin; Staff 17 (MLS 1, Non-MLS 16)
Founded 1913. Pop 47,000; Circ 78,481
Jan 2014-Dec 2014 Income (Main Library and Branch(s)) $1,304,500, State $134,000, City $585,000, County $560,000, Locally Generated Income $25,500. Mats Exp $205,186, Books $127,000, Per/Ser (Incl. Access Fees) $10,000, AV Mat $30,000, Electronic Ref Mat (Incl. Access Fees) $38,186
Library Holdings: Audiobooks 1,005; DVDs 3,079; Microforms 5,686; Bk Titles 57,172; Bk Vols 64,771; Per Subs 62
Special Collections: Arkansas Coll; Genealogy with Emphasis on Arkansas, North Carolina, South Carolina, Tennessee & Virginia; Index to Deaths for Pine Bluff & Jefferson County Newspapers; Regional History of Arkansas & Mississippi Valley, bks, maps, micro
Automation Activity & Vendor Info: (Acquisitions) TLC (The Library Corporation); (Cataloging) TLC (The Library Corporation); (Circulation) TLC (The Library Corporation); (OPAC) TLC (The Library Corporation); (Serials) TLC (The Library Corporation)
Database Vendor: EBSCOhost, Gale Cengage Learning, Grolier Online, Newsbank, OCLC FirstSearch, OCLC WorldShare Interlibrary Loan, ProQuest
Wireless access
Function: AV serv, ILL available, Photocopying/Printing, Prog for children & young adult, Ref serv available, Summer reading prog, Telephone ref, Wheelchair accessible
Partic in OCLC Online Computer Library Center, Inc
Open Mon, Tues & Thurs 9-8, Wed 9-6, Fri & Sat 9-4
Restriction: Open to pub for ref & circ; with some limitations
Friends of the Library Group
Branches: 4
ALTHEIMER PUBLIC LIBRARY, 222 S Edline, Altheimer, 72004-8589. Tel: 870-766-8499. FAX: 870-766-8499. *Br Mgr,* Melony Darrough; Staff 0.75 (Non-MLS 0.75)
Founded 2001. Pop 5,000; Circ 2,007
Library Holdings: Audiobooks 38; DVDs 384; Bk Titles 13,831; Bk Vols 13,611; Per Subs 11
Open Tues-Fri (May-Aug) 10-4, Sat 9-1; Mon-Thurs (Sept-Apr) Noon-6, Sat 9-1
REDFIELD PUBLIC LIBRARY, 310 Brodie St, Redfield, 72132. (Mail add: PO Box 70, Redfield, 72132-0070). Tel: 501-397-5070. FAX: 501-397-5070. *Br Mgr,* Cathy Ackerman; Staff 1.25 (Non-MLS 1.25)
Founded 1999. Pop 2,500; Circ 15,418
Library Holdings: Audiobooks 238; DVDs 701; Bk Titles 20,468; Bk Vols 19,664; Per Subs 10
Open Mon-Thurs (May-Aug) 10-4, Sat 9-1; Mon-Thurs (Sept-April) 12-6, Sat 9-1
Friends of the Library Group
WATSON CHAPEL PUBLIC LIBRARY, 4120 Camden Rd, 71603, SAN 322-6204. Tel: 870-879-3406. FAX: 870-879-6437. *Br Mgr,* Shay Green; Staff 1.5 (Non-MLS 1.5)
Founded 1985. Pop 2,500; Circ 44,461
Library Holdings: Audiobooks 521; DVDs 1,306; Bk Titles 31,457; Bk Vols 29,985; Per Subs 24
Open Mon-Thurs 9-6, Fri 9-4, Sat 9-1

WHITE HALL PUBLIC LIBRARY, 300 Anderson St, White Hall, 71602, SAN 320-0825. Tel: 870-247-5064. FAX: 870-247-2613. *Asst Br Mgr,* Ellen Bauer; *Br Supvr,* Mary Ellis; Tel: 870-267-1564; Staff 2.5 (Non-MLS 2.5)
Founded 1978. Pop 5,000; Circ 68,297
Library Holdings: Audiobooks 812; DVDs 1,588; Bk Titles 41,532; Bk Vols 40,365; Per Subs 26
Open Mon, Tues & Thurs 9-8, Wed 9-6, Fri 9-4, Sat 9-1
Friends of the Library Group

C SOUTHEAST ARKANSAS COLLEGE*, SEARK Library & Center for E-Learning, 1900 Hazel St, 71603. Tel: 870-543-5936, 870-850-4815. Interlibrary Loan Service Tel: 870-850-4814. Toll Free Tel: 888-732-7582. FAX: 870-850-4815. Interlibrary Loan Service FAX: 870-850-4814. E-mail: library@seark.edu. Web Site: www.youseemore.com/searkcollege. *Librn,* Kimberly Williams; E-mail: kwilliams@seark.edu; *Libr Support Spec,* TiKeecha Spikes; Tel: 870-850-4840, Fax: 870-850-4840, E-mail: tspikes@seark.edu; *Libr Tech,* Joyce Chamel; E-mail: jchamel@seark.edu. Subject Specialists: *Cataloging, Ill,* Joyce Chamel; Staff 4.5 (MLS 2, Non-MLS 2.5)
Founded 1993. Highest Degree: Associate
Library Holdings: Bk Titles 11,000; Bk Vols 14,000; Per Subs 120
Special Collections: Early Childhood Paraprofessional Coll
Automation Activity & Vendor Info: (Cataloging) TLC (The Library Corporation); (Circulation) TLC (The Library Corporation); (ILL) OCLC FirstSearch; (OPAC) TLC (The Library Corporation)
Database Vendor: EBSCOhost, Gale Cengage Learning, LexisNexis, OCLC FirstSearch, OCLC WorldShare Interlibrary Loan, ProQuest, TLC (The Library Corporation), YBP Library Services
Wireless access
Function: AV serv, Distance learning, ILL available, Photocopying/Printing, Ref serv available
Partic in ARKLink
Open Mon-Thurs 7:30am-8pm, Fri 7:30-5

C UNIVERSITY OF ARKANSAS-PINE BLUFF*, Watson Memorial Library-Learning & Instructional Resources Centers, 1200 N University Dr, 71601. SAN 331-3352. Tel: 870-575-8411. Circulation Tel: 870-575-8848. Reference Tel: 870-575-8896. FAX: 870-575-4651. Web Site: www.uapb.edu. *Dir,* Edward J Fontenette; Tel: 870-575-8000, Ext 8410, E-mail: fontenettee@uapb.edu; *Assoc Dir, Coordr, Spec Coll & Libr Develop,* Georgia Watley; *Coordr, Spec Serv,* Evelyn Yeats; Staff 7 (MLS 7)
Founded 1938. Enrl 2,917; Fac 140; Highest Degree: Bachelor
Library Holdings: Bk Vols 351,229
Special Collections: Afro American Coll; Arkansas (Raley Coll); Literature (Rare Books Coll); State Government (Knox Nelson Coll). State Document Depository; UN Document Depository; US Document Depository
Subject Interests: Agr, Educ, Indust arts, Nursing
Automation Activity & Vendor Info: (Acquisitions) Innovative Interfaces, Inc; (Cataloging) Innovative Interfaces, Inc; (Circulation) Innovative Interfaces, Inc; (Course Reserve) Innovative Interfaces, Inc; (ILL) Innovative Interfaces, Inc; (Media Booking) Innovative Interfaces, Inc; (OPAC) Innovative Interfaces, Inc; (Serials) Innovative Interfaces, Inc
Database Vendor: EBSCOhost, ProQuest
Publications: Acquisitions List (Monthly)
Open Mon-Thurs 7:30am-11pm, Fri 7:30-5, Sat 8:30-4:30, Sun 3:30-11

Departmental Libraries:

FINE ARTS, Art Department, Mail Slot 4925, 71601. Tel: 870-575-8236. FAX: 870-575-4636. *In Charge,* Henri Linton; E-mail: lintonhao@uapb.edu
Open Mon-Fri 8:30-4:30

HUMAN SCIENCES, Mail Slot 4971, 71601. Tel: 870-575-8817. *Chairperson,* Valerie Colyard; E-mail: colyardv@uapb.edu

CM MELVILLE LIBRARY, 4010 S Mulberry St, 71603, SAN 331-3387. Tel: 870-541-7629. FAX: 870-541-7628. *Dir, Libr Serv,* Julie Dobbins; E-mail: jdobbins@ahecpb.uams.edu
Library Holdings: Bk Vols 185,000
Subject Interests: Med, Nursing
Automation Activity & Vendor Info: (Cataloging) Innovative Interfaces, Inc; (Circulation) Innovative Interfaces, Inc; (OPAC) Innovative Interfaces, Inc
Partic in OCLC Online Computer Library Center, Inc
Publications: The Collection (bimonthly newsletter)
Open Mon-Thurs 8-6, Fri 8-5

MUSIC LAB, 1200 N University Dr, 71601. Tel: 870-575-8905. *Librn,* James Mincy; Tel: 870-575-7036, E-mail: mincyj@uapb.edu

NURSING LAB, 1200 University Dr, Mail Slot 4973, 71611. Tel: 870-575-8220. FAX: 870-575-8229. *Librn,* Patrice Fisher; E-mail: fisherp@uapb.edu
Library Holdings: Bk Vols 100
Open Mon-Fri 8-5

POCAHONTAS

J BLACK RIVER TECHNICAL COLLEGE LIBRARY*, 1410 Hwy 304 E, 72455. (Mail add: PO Box 468, 72455-0468). Tel: 870-248-4060. FAX: 870-248-4100. Web Site: library.blackrivertech.edu. *Dir,* Anne Simpson; E-mail: anne.simpson@blackrivertech.edu
Library Holdings: Bk Vols 25,000; Per Subs 200
Automation Activity & Vendor Info: (Cataloging) SirsiDynix; (Circulation) SirsiDynix
Database Vendor: Gale Cengage Learning, OCLC FirstSearch, ProQuest
Function: Ref serv available
Open Mon-Thurs (Spring & Fall) 7:30am-8pm, Fri 7:30-4:30; Mon-Thurs (Summer) 7-5

P RANDOLPH COUNTY LIBRARY, 111 W Everett St, 72455. SAN 331-3298. Tel: 870-892-5617. FAX: 870-892-1142. E-mail: randolph@mylibrarynow.org. Web Site: www.mylibrarynow.org/randolph. *Dir,* Jackie Salyards; E-mail: jackie@mylibrarynow.org; Staff 5 (Non-MLS 5)
Founded 1939. Pop 18,195; Circ 8,500
Jan 2014-Dec 2014 Income $296,000. Mats Exp $296,000. Sal $105,000
Library Holdings: AV Mats 1,500; Bks on Deafness & Sign Lang 25; Braille Volumes 1; CDs 1,500; DVDs 350; Large Print Bks 5,200; Bk Titles 55,000; Per Subs 40; Talking Bks 1,246; Videos 800
Special Collections: Arkansas Reference, microfilm, newsp, family histories; Genealogy Coll; History Coll
Automation Activity & Vendor Info: (Cataloging) Book Systems; (Circulation) Book Systems; (OPAC) Book Systems
Database Vendor: EBSCOhost
Wireless access
Mem of Northeast Arkansas Regional Library System
Special Services for the Deaf - Bks on deafness & sign lang
Open Mon-Fri 9-5, Sat 9-12
Friends of the Library Group
Bookmobiles: 1. In Charge, Diane Evans

PRAIRIE GROVE

P PRAIRIE GROVE PUBLIC LIBRARY, 123 S Neal St, 72753. (Mail add: PO Box 10, 72753-0010), SAN 331-0086. Tel: 479-846-3782. FAX: 479-846-3428. E-mail: prairiegrove@wcls.lib.ar.us. Web Site: www.library.arkansasusa.com/prairie_grove. *Librn,* Iva Sorrell
Library Holdings: Bk Vols 25,000
Wireless access
Mem of Washington County Library System
Open Mon-Sat 9:30-5:30
Friends of the Library Group

PRESCOTT

P PRESCOTT/NEVADA COUNTY LIBRARY*, 121 W Main St, 71857. SAN 331-1619. Tel: 870-887-5846. FAX: 870-887-8226. *Librn,* Terri Vandiver
Wireless access
Open Tues-Fri 9:30-5:30
Friends of the Library Group

RECTOR

P RECTOR PUBLIC LIBRARY, 121 W Fourth St, 72461. SAN 331-3328. Tel: 870-595-2410. FAX: 870-595-2410. E-mail: rectorlibrary@yahoo.com. Web Site: www.rectorlibrary.com. *Dir,* Deana Mills; *Asst Dir,* Brenda Shelton; *Ch,* Virginia Shipley; Staff 4 (Non-MLS 4)
Founded 1934. Pop 3,000
Automation Activity & Vendor Info: (Acquisitions) Book Systems
Database Vendor: Baker & Taylor, BWI, EBSCOhost, Gale Cengage Learning, Ingram Library Services
Wireless access
Mem of Northeast Arkansas Regional Library System
Open Mon, Tues & Thurs 8:30-5:30, Wed 8:30-5, Fri 8:30-4, Sat 9-1
Friends of the Library Group

RISON

P ROY & CHRISTINE STURGIS LIBRARY*, Cleveland County Mid-Arkansas Regional Library, 203 W Magnolia St, 71665. (Mail add: PO Box 388, 71665-0388), SAN 300-5461. Tel: 870-325-7270. FAX: 870-325-7008. E-mail: clecolib@yahoo.com. *Librn,* Hilda Terry
Pop 7,781; Circ 14,160
Library Holdings: Bk Vols 29,153; Per Subs 36
Open Mon & Thurs 8:30-6, Tues, Wed & Fri 8:30-4:30, Sat 9-12
Friends of the Library Group

ROGERS

P ROGERS PUBLIC LIBRARY*, 711 S Dixieland Rd, 72758. SAN 331-0116. Tel: 479-621-1152. Circulation Tel: 479-621-1152, Ext 10. Interlibrary Loan Service Tel: 479-621-1152, Ext 18. Reference Tel: 479-621-1152, Ext 15. FAX: 479-621-1165. Web Site: library.rpl.lib.ar.us. *Dir,* Judy Faye Casey; Tel: 479-621-1152, Ext 11, E-mail: jcasey@rogersark.org; *Head, Ref,* Robert Finch; Tel: 479-621-1152, Ext 19, E-mail: rfinch@rogersark.org; *Tech Serv Supvr,* Chad Pollock; Tel: 479-621-1152, Ext 12, E-mail: cpollock@rogersark.org; *Automation Syst Coordr,* John Henry; Tel: 479-621-1152, Ext 13, E-mail: jhenry@rogersark.org; *Ch Serv,* Rebecca Willhite; Tel: 479-621-1152, Ext 31, E-mail: rwillhite@rogersark.org; *Reader Serv,* Lesley Knieriem; Tel: 479-621-1152, Ext 22, E-mail: lknieriem@rogersark.org; *YA Serv,* Evan Day; Tel: 479-621-1152, Ext 32, E-mail: eday@rogersark.org; Staff 34 (MLS 7, Non-MLS 27)
Founded 1904. Pop 48,666; Circ 456,115
Jan 2009-Dec 2009 Income $1,011,840, State $75,000, City $66,840, County $830,000, Other $40,000. Mats Exp $222,085, Books $127,000, Per/Ser (Incl. Access Fees) $7,025, AV Equip $22,000, AV Mat $48,600, Electronic Ref Mat (Incl. Access Fees) $17,460. Sal $950,447 (Prof $437,053)
Library Holdings: Audiobooks 4,633; AV Mats 5,269; CDs 2,486; DVDs 3,900; e-books 4,134; Electronic Media & Resources 28; High Interest/Low Vocabulary Bk Vols 177; Large Print Bks 5,176; Bk Titles 96,755; Bk Vols 118,518; Per Subs 314; Videos 3,909
Automation Activity & Vendor Info: (Acquisitions) Innovative Interfaces, Inc; (Cataloging) Innovative Interfaces, Inc; (Circulation) Innovative Interfaces, Inc; (ILL) OCLC; (OPAC) Innovative Interfaces, Inc
Database Vendor: EBSCOhost, OCLC FirstSearch
Wireless access
Function: Homebound delivery serv, ILL available, Magnifiers for reading, Online searches, Photocopying/Printing, Prog for children & young adult, Ref serv available, Summer reading prog, Telephone ref, Wheelchair accessible
Open Mon-Thurs 9-9, Fri & Sat 9-5, Sun 1-5
Friends of the Library Group

RUSSELLVILLE

C ARKANSAS TECH UNIVERSITY*, Ross Pendergraft Library & Technology Center, 305 West Q St, 72801-2222. SAN 300-547X. Tel: 479-968-0289. Circulation Tel: 479-964-0569. Interlibrary Loan Service Tel: 479-968-0416. Reference Tel: 479-964-0570. Toll Free Tel: 855-761-0006. FAX: 479-964-0559. Interlibrary Loan Service FAX: 479-968-2185. Web Site: library.atu.edu. *Dir,* Bill Parton; Tel: 479-968-0417, E-mail: wparton@atu.edu; *Acq Librn,* Frances Hager; Tel: 479-964-0561, E-mail: fhager@atu.edu; *Electronic Res Librn,* Carol Hanan; Tel: 479-968-0288, E-mail: chanan@atu.edu; *Music & Media Librn,* Dr Lowell Lybarger; Tel: 479-964-0584, E-mail: llybarger@atu.edu; *Pub Serv Librn,* Sherry Tinerella; Tel: 479-964-0571, E-mail: stinerella@atu.edu; *Syst Librn,* Philippe Van Houtte; Tel: 479-498-6042, E-mail: pvanhoutte@atu.edu; *Tech Serv Librn,* Angela Black; Tel: 479-964-0558, E-mail: ablack9@atu.edu. Subject Specialists: *Ethnomusicology,* Dr Lowell Lybarger; Staff 7 (MLS 7)
Founded 1909. Enrl 11,350; Fac 330; Highest Degree: Master
Jul 2012-Jun 2013 Income $1,638,956, Federal $18,460, Parent Institution $1,620,496. Mats Exp $559,811, Books $64,173, Per/Ser (Incl. Access Fees) $145,263, Micro $23,357, AV Mat $22,374, Electronic Ref Mat (Incl. Access Fees) $298,457, Presv $6,187. Sal $765,201 (Prof $367,089)
Library Holdings: Audiobooks 200; AV Mats 15,500; e-books 20,000; e-journals 40,000; Microforms 902,200; Music Scores 4,000; Bk Vols 174,600; Per Subs 756
Special Collections: Parks & Recreation Administration, bk & micro. State Document Depository; US Document Depository
Subject Interests: Eng, Humanities, Music, Nursing
Automation Activity & Vendor Info: (Acquisitions) Ex Libris Group; (Cataloging) Ex Libris Group; (Circulation) Ex Libris Group; (Course Reserve) Ex Libris Group; (ILL) OCLC WorldShare Interlibrary Loan; (Media Booking) Ex Libris Group; (OPAC) Ex Libris Group; (Serials) Ex Libris Group
Database Vendor: ABC-CLIO, ACM (Association for Computing Machinery), Amigos Library Services, BioOne, Cambridge Scientific Abstracts, CredoReference, EBSCOhost, Ex Libris Group, Gale Cengage Learning, ISI Web of Knowledge, JSTOR, LexisNexis, OCLC, OCLC WorldShare Interlibrary Loan, OVID Technologies, Oxford Online, Project MUSE, ProQuest
Wireless access
Function: ILL available
Publications: Arkansas Gazette Index (Index to newspapers)
Partic in ARKLink
Open Mon-Thurs 7am-Midnight, Fri 7-6, Sat 10-6, Sun 2-Midnight

P POPE COUNTY LIBRARY SYSTEM*, Russellville Headquarters Branch, 116 E Third St, 72801. SAN 371-7992. Tel: 479-968-4368. FAX: 479-968-3222. Web Site: www.popelibrary.org. *Syst Dir,* Shawn Pierce; *Dir, Br,* Position Currently Open; *Cat,* Lorie Darter; *Ch Prog,* Emily Moore; *Circ,* Peggy Belcher; *ILL,* Jackie Blaney; *Teen & Adult Serv Prog,* Sherry Simpson; Staff 8 (MLS 2, Non-MLS 6)
Founded 1920. Pop 52,063; Circ 391,425
Library Holdings: AV Mats 4,200; Bks on Deafness & Sign Lang 45; High Interest/Low Vocabulary Bk Vols 3,000; Large Print Bks 2,362; Bk Titles 76,493; Bk Vols 115,125; Per Subs 142
Special Collections: Arkansas Hist, films; Genealogy (Katie Murdoch Coll), bks, docs; Local Hist Coll
Automation Activity & Vendor Info: (Cataloging) Innovative Interfaces, Inc; (Circulation) Innovative Interfaces, Inc; (OPAC) Innovative Interfaces, Inc
Wireless access
Special Services for the Deaf - Bks on deafness & sign lang; High interest/low vocabulary bks; Staff with knowledge of sign lang
Open Mon-Wed & Fri 8:30-5:30, Thurs 11-8, Sat 9-1
Friends of the Library Group
Branches: 3
ATKINS CENTENNIAL BRANCH, 216 NE First St, Atkins, 72823, SAN 371-800X. Tel: 479-641-7904. FAX: 479-641-1169. *Br Mgr,* Robbie Duvall
Library Holdings: Bk Vols 10,000
Open Mon-Fri 9-5
DOVER BRANCH, 80 Library Rd, Dover, 72837, SAN 371-8018. Tel: 479-331-2173. FAX: 479-331-4151. *Br Librn,* Glenda McMillan
Library Holdings: Bk Vols 9,000
Open Mon-Fri 9-12 & 1-5
Friends of the Library Group
HECTOR BRANCH, PO Box 293, Hector, 72843, SAN 377-5925. Tel: 479-284-0907. FAX: 479-284-0907. *Head of Libr,* Ednita Condley
Library Holdings: Bk Vols 4,000
Open Mon & Wed 1-5, Tues 9-1, Thurs 2-6
Bookmobiles: 1

SAINT PAUL

P ST PAUL PUBLIC LIBRARY*, 145 Fifth St, 72760. (Mail add: PO Box 123, 72760-0123). Tel: 479-677-2907. E-mail: library72760@gmail.com. Web Site: www.carrollmadisonlibraries.org/library.aspx?lib=stpaul. *Libr Dir,* Bonnie Rodgers
Library Holdings: e-books 700; High Interest/Low Vocabulary Bk Vols 100, Large Print Bks 250; Bk Vols 4,600; Per Subs 10; Talking Bks 10
Wireless access
Mem of Carroll & Madison Library System
Open Mon & Wed 1-4, Tues 9-2, Thurs 1-6, Fri 9-6, Sat 9-1
Friends of the Library Group

SALEM

P FULTON COUNTY LIBRARY*, 131 Pickren St, 72576. (Mail add: PO Box 277, 72576-0277). Tel: 870-895-2014. FAX: 870-895-2014. *Librn,* Betty J Roork
Pop 12,000; Circ 14,000
Library Holdings: Bk Vols 20,260; Per Subs 19; Talking Bks 100
Open Mon-Fri 8:30-4:30

SEARCY

J ARKANSAS STATE UNIVERSITY*, Media Center, 1800 E Moore, 72143-4710. (Mail add: PO Box 909, 72145-0909). Tel: 501-207-4031. FAX: 501-268-0263. *Librn,* Zettie Holland; E-mail: zholland@searcy.asub.edu
Founded 1988. Enrl 700; Fac 92; Highest Degree: Associate
Library Holdings: Bk Vols 4,500
Open Mon-Fri 8-4:30

CR HARDING UNIVERSITY, Brackett Library, 915 E Market St, 72149-2267. (Mail add: PO Box 12267, 72149-0001), SAN 300-5488. Tel: 501-279-4354. Circulation Tel: 501-279-4279. Interlibrary Loan Service Tel: 501-279-4238. Reference Tel: 501-279-4775. Interlibrary Loan Service FAX: 501-279-4268. Web Site: www.harding.edu/library. *Libr Dir,* Jean Waldrop; Tel: 501-279-4011, E-mail: jwaldrop@harding.edu; *Archives & Spec Coll Librn,* Hannah Wood; Tel: 501-279-4205, E-mail: hwood@harding.edu; *E-Res & Ser Librn,* Gerald Cox; Tel: 501-279-4349, E-mail: gcox@harding.edu; *Pub Serv Librn,* Whitney Hammes; Tel: 501-279-4228, E-mail: khammes1@harding.edu; *Ref & Theol Librn,* Justin Lillard; Tel: 501-279-4251, E-mail: jlillard@harding.edu; *Syst Librn,* Brenda Breezeel; Tel: 501-279-5387, E-mail: bbreezell@harding.edu; *E-Learning & Instruction,* Lisa Burley; Tel: 501-279-4185, E-mail: lburley@harding.edu; *Tech Serv,* Shirley Williams; Tel: 501-279-4376, E-mail: swilliams@harding.edu. Subject Specialists: *Health sci,* Jean Waldrop; *Communication, Hist, Theatre,* Hannah Wood; *Biol, Chem,*

Physics, Gerald Cox; *Educ, Music,* Whitney Hammes; *Bible, Bus, Kinesiology,* Justin Lillard; *English, Psychol, Soc work,* Lisa Burley; *Art, Foreign lang, Math,* Shirley Williams; Staff 14.75 (MLS 7.75, Non-MLS 7)
Founded 1924. Enrl 6,075; Fac 357; Highest Degree: Doctorate
Library Holdings: Audiobooks 3,271; CDs 829; DVDs 1,084; Electronic Media & Resources 72,002; Microforms 20,477; Bk Vols 365,162; Per Subs 717; Videos 305
Special Collections: Harding History; LAC; Williams-Miles Science History Coll. Oral History
Automation Activity & Vendor Info: (Acquisitions) Ex Libris Group; (Cataloging) Ex Libris Group; (Circulation) Ex Libris Group; (ILL) Ex Libris Group; (OPAC) Ex Libris Group; (Serials) Ex Libris Group
Database Vendor: 3M Library Systems, ABC-CLIO, American Chemical Society, Amigos Library Services, Annual Reviews, BCR: Christian Periodical Index, BioOne, Bowker, Children's Literature Comprehensive Database Company (CLCD), Cinahl, CountryWatch, CredoReference, DynaMed, EBSCO Information Services, EBSCOhost, Elsevier, Emerald, Ex Libris Group, Facts on File, Faulkner Information Services, Gale Cengage Learning, H W Wilson, Hoovers, Ingenta, ISI Web of Knowledge, JSTOR, Lexi-Comp, LexisNexis, Marcive, Inc, Marquis Who's Who, McGraw-Hill, MD Consult, Medline, Micromedex, Modern Language Association, Natural Standard, OCLC, OCLC ArticleFirst, OCLC FirstSearch, OCLC WorldShare Interlibrary Loan, ProQuest, PubMed, Sage, ScienceDirect, STN International, ValueLine, Wiley, Wilson - Wilson Web, World Book Online
Wireless access
Function: Archival coll, Distance learning, Doc delivery serv, e-mail & chat, E-Reserves, Electronic databases & coll, ILL available, Music CDs, Online cat, Online ref, Outside serv via phone, mail, e-mail & web, Photocopying/Printing, Ref serv available, Telephone ref, VHS videos, Web-catalog
Partic in Amigos Library Services, Inc; ARKLink; OCLC Online Computer Library Center, Inc
Special Services for the Blind - Bks on cassette; Bks on CD; Cassettes
Open Mon-Thurs 7:45am-11pm, Fri 7:45-5, Sun 1:30-11
Restriction: Authorized patrons, ID required to use computers (Ltd hrs), In-house use for visitors, Non-circulating of rare bks

P WHITE COUNTY REGIONAL LIBRARY SYSTEM*, 113 E Pleasure Ave, 72143-7798. SAN 331-3417. Tel: 501-268-2449, 501-279-2870. Circulation Tel: 501-269-2449, Ext 22. Interlibrary Loan Service Tel: 501-279-2870, Ext 21. Administration Tel: 501-279-2870, Ext 2. FAX: 501-268-5682. Web Site: www.wcrls.org. *Dir,* Darla Ino; Staff 1 (MLS 1)
Founded 1896. Pop 72,560; Circ 289,686
Jan 2006-Dec 2006 Income (Main Library Only) $965,027, State $85,813, City $116,000, County $603,932, Locally Generated Income $14,265, Other $145,017. Mats Exp $129,494, Books $109,741, Per/Ser (Incl. Access Fees) $11,756, Micro $302, AV Mat $7,695. Sal $243,106 (Prof $36,547)
Library Holdings: AV Mats 6,722; Bks on Deafness & Sign Lang 30; CDs 1,610; DVDs 12; High Interest/Low Vocabulary Bk Vols 89; Large Print Bks 1,200; Bk Titles 11,380; Bk Vols 113,795; Per Subs 720; Talking Bks 1,200; Videos 1,774
Special Collections: Mental Illness
Subject Interests: Ark
Automation Activity & Vendor Info: (Acquisitions) SIRSI-iBistro; (Cataloging) OCLC; (Circulation) SirsiDynix; (ILL) OCLC; (OPAC) SirsiDynix
Database Vendor: EBSCOhost, Facts on File, Grolier Online, H W Wilson, OCLC ArticleFirst, OCLC FirstSearch, OCLC WebJunction, OCLC WorldShare Interlibrary Loan, ProQuest, SirsiDynix, ValueLine
Function: Accelerated reader prog, After school storytime, AV serv, Bks on cassette, Bks on CD, Children's prog, Computers for patron use, Copy machines, Doc delivery serv, e-mail serv, E-Reserves, Electronic databases & coll, Fax serv, Free DVD rentals, Handicapped accessible, ILL available, Mail & tel request accepted, Online cat, Online ref, Online searches, Outside serv via phone, mail, e-mail & web, Photocopying/Printing, Preschool outreach, Prog for children & young adult, Provide serv for the mentally ill, Ref serv available, Summer reading prog, Tax forms, Telephone ref, VHS videos, Video lending libr, Web-catalog, Wheelchair accessible
Open Mon & Thurs 9-8, Tues & Wed 9-6, Fri 9-5, Sat 10-5
Branches: 7
BALDWIN MEMORIAL, 612 Van Buren, Judsonia, 72081, SAN 331-3476. Tel: 501-729-3995. FAX: 501-729-5994. *Librn,* Travis Allen
Library Holdings: AV Mats 574; Bk Vols 15,569
Open Mon-Thurs & Sat 9-12 & 1-5
BEEBE PUBLIC, 115 W Illinois, Beebe, 72012-3245, SAN 331-3506. Tel: 501-882-3235. FAX: 501-882-3235. *Librn,* Ramona Howell
Circ 17,141
Library Holdings: AV Mats 488; Bk Vols 10,247
Open Mon, Wed & Thurs 12-6, Tues 10-6, Sat 10-2
BRADFORD BRANCH, 302 W Walnut, Bradford, 72020. (Mail add: PO Box 282, Bradford, 72020-0282), SAN 377-7707. Tel: 501-344-2558. FAX: 501-344-2558. *Librn,* Brenda Lewis
Library Holdings: AV Mats 410; Bk Vols 3,704
Open Mon-Fri 1-5, Sat 10-2
LYDA MILLER LIBRARY, 2609 Hwy 367 N, Bald Knob, 72010. (Mail add: PO Box 287, Bald Knob, 72010-0287), SAN 331-3441. Tel: 501-724-5452. *Librn,* Teresa Scritchfield
Library Holdings: AV Mats 514; Bk Vols 8,268
Open Mon-Thurs 2-6, Sat 10-2
PANGBURN PUBLIC, 914 Main St, Pangburn, 72121. (Mail add: PO Box 333, Pangburn, 72121-0333), SAN 331-3530. Tel: 501-728-4612. FAX: 501-728-4612. *Librn,* Peggy Taylor
Library Holdings: AV Mats 310; Bk Vols 6,686
Open Mon, Tues, Thurs & Fri 12-5
ROSE BUD PUBLIC, 548 Hwy 5 S, Rose Bud, 71237. (Mail add: PO Box 327, Rose Bud, 72137-0327). Tel: 501-556-4447. FAX: 501-556-4447. *Librn,* Gina Rooks
Library Holdings: AV Mats 225; Bk Vols 5,848
Open Mon-Fri 11-5
Friends of the Library Group
SEARCY PUBLIC, 113 E Pleasure Ave, 72143, SAN 331-3565. FAX: 501-268-5682. *Librn,* Rita Starling
Library Holdings: AV Mats 4,201; Bk Vols 59,236
Open Mon & Thurs 9-8, Tues & Wed 9-6, Fri 9-5, Sat 10-5 (10-1 Summer)

SHERIDAN

P GRANT COUNTY LIBRARY*, 210 N Oak St, 72150-2495. SAN 300-5496. Tel: 870-942-4436. FAX: 870-942-7500. *Dir,* Pam Withers; Staff 4 (MLS 1, Non-MLS 3)
Library Holdings: Bk Vols 34,000
Automation Activity & Vendor Info: (Cataloging) Innovative Interfaces, Inc; (Circulation) Innovative Interfaces, Inc; (OPAC) Innovative Interfaces, Inc
Open Mon 9-8, Tues, Wed & Fri 9-5, Sat 10-2

SILOAM SPRINGS

C JOHN BROWN UNIVERSITY LIBRARY*, Arutunoff Learning Resource Center, 2000 W University, 72761. SAN 300-550X. Tel: 479-524-7202. Interlibrary Loan Service Tel: 479-524-7276. Reference Tel: 479-524-7153. Administration Tel: 479-524-7203. FAX: 479-524-7335. E-mail: library@jbu.edu. Web Site: www.jbu.edu/library. *Dir,* Mary E Habermas; E-mail: mhaberma@jbu.edu; *Instrul Serv Librn,* Brent Swearingen; Tel: 479-524-7207, E-mail: bswearingen@jbu.edu; *ILL Librn,* Simone Schroder; E-mail: simones@jbu.edu; *Ref Librn,* Steve Paschold; E-mail: spaschold@jbu.edu; Staff 9 (MLS 4, Non-MLS 5)
Founded 1956. Enrl 1,900; Fac 80; Highest Degree: Master
Library Holdings: AV Mats 3,751; e-books 10,000; e-journals 12,000; Bk Titles 87,958; Bk Vols 107,055; Per Subs 450
Special Collections: J Vernon McGee Coll; Oliver Coll; Romig Coll
Automation Activity & Vendor Info: (Cataloging) TLC (The Library Corporation); (Circulation) TLC (The Library Corporation); (Course Reserve) TLC (The Library Corporation); (ILL) OCLC; (OPAC) TLC (The Library Corporation)
Database Vendor: American Chemical Society, American Psychological Association (APA), Amigos Library Services, Annual Reviews, BCR: Christian Periodical Index, BioOne, CQ Press, CredoReference, EBSCOhost, Facts on File, Gale Cengage Learning, Gallup, Hoovers, JSTOR, LexisNexis, Modern Language Association, OCLC FirstSearch, OCLC WorldShare Interlibrary Loan, ProQuest, ScienceDirect, TLC (The Library Corporation)
Wireless access
Partic in ARKLink; Westchester Academic Library Directors Organization (WALDO)
Open Mon-Thurs 7:30am-Midnight, Fri 7:30-5, Sat 11-4, Sun 3-Midnight

P SILOAM SPRINGS PUBLIC LIBRARY, 401 W University St, 72761. SAN 300-5518. Tel: 479-524-4236. FAX: 479-524-3908. E-mail: Library@siloamsprings.com. Web Site: www.siloamsprings.com/departments/library. *Libr Mgr,* Dolores Deuel; Staff 1 (MLS 1)
Founded 1966. Pop 25,000; Circ 112,562
Library Holdings: Audiobooks 1,380; CDs 986; DVDs 3,256; e-books 9,701; Large Print Bks 1,612; Bk Titles 41,596; Per Subs 23
Automation Activity & Vendor Info: (Cataloging) Innovative Interfaces, Inc; (Circulation) Innovative Interfaces, Inc; (ILL) OCLC
Database Vendor: OCLC FirstSearch
Wireless access
Function: 24/7 Online cat, Adult bk club, After school storytime, Audiobks via web, Bk club(s), Bks on CD, Children's prog, Computers for patron use, Copy machines, e-mail & chat, E-Reserves, Fax serv, Free DVD rentals, Holiday prog, Laminating, Magazines, Magnifiers for

reading, Movies, Music CDs, Prog for adults, Prog for children & young adult, Pub access computers, Story hour, Summer reading prog, Tax forms, Teen prog, Web-catalog
Open Mon-Fri 9-7, Sat 9-4
Friends of the Library Group

SPRINGDALE

J NORTHWEST TECHNICAL INSTITUTE*, Walter Turnbow Library, 709 S Old Missouri Rd, 72764. Tel: 479-751-8824, Ext 140. FAX: 479-756-8744. E-mail: NTILibrary@nwti.edu. Web Site: www.nti.tec.ar.us. *Librn,* Becky Echols; Staff 2 (Non-MLS 2)
Highest Degree: Certificate
Library Holdings: Bk Vols 7,000; Per Subs 120
Automation Activity & Vendor Info: (Cataloging) Follett Software; (Circulation) Follett Software; (Course Reserve) Follett Software
Database Vendor: EBSCOhost, Gale Cengage Learning, OCLC FirstSearch, ProQuest
Function: Photocopying/Printing
Open Mon-Thurs 7:30-4, Fri 7:30-2

S SHILOH MUSEUM OF OZARK HISTORY LIBRARY, 118 W Johnson Ave, 72764. SAN 373-3947. Tel: 479-750-8165. FAX: 479-750-8693. E-mail: shiloh@springdalear.gov. Web Site: www.shilohmuseum.org. *Archivist, Librn,* Marie Demeroukas; E-mail: mdemeroukas@springdalear.gov. Subject Specialists: *Ark Ozarks,* Marie Demeroukas; Staff 1.75 (Non-MLS 1.75)
Founded 1968
Library Holdings: Bk Vols 900
Special Collections: Photos of Arkansas Ozarks
Open Mon-Sat 10-5
Restriction: In-house use for visitors, Internal use only, Not a lending libr, Open to researchers by request
Friends of the Library Group

P SPRINGDALE PUBLIC LIBRARY*, 405 S Pleasant St, 72764. SAN 331-0140. Tel: 479-750-8180. FAX: 479-750-8182. Web Site: www.springdalelibrary.org. *Dir,* Marcia Ransom; E-mail: mransom@springdalelibrary.org; *Asst Dir,* Ellen Andes; E-mail: eandes@springdalelibrary.org; *Automated Serv Coordr,* Lisa Caldwell; E-mail: lcaldwell@springdalelibrary.org; *Tech Coordr,* Cindy McCauley; E-mail: cmccauley@springdalelibrary.org; *Ch Serv,* Trudy Hill; *Ref Serv, Ad,* Claudia Driver; E-mail: cdriver@springdalelibrary.org; *Tech Serv,* Angel Hutchison; E-mail: ahutchison@springdalelibrary.org; *YA Serv,* Sharon Christian; E-mail: sharonchristian@springdalelibrary.org; Staff 7 (MLS 5, Non-MLS 2)
Founded 1923. Pop 45,578; Circ 623,000
Library Holdings: AV Mats 18,732; Bk Vols 140,753; Per Subs 277
Automation Activity & Vendor Info: (Cataloging) Innovative Interfaces, Inc; (Circulation) Innovative Interfaces, Inc; (OPAC) Innovative Interfaces, Inc
Wireless access
Publications: Newsletter (Quarterly)
Mem of Washington County Library System
Open Mon-Thurs 9-8, Fri 9-6, Sat 9-5, Sun 1-5
Friends of the Library Group

STATE UNIVERSITY

C ARKANSAS STATE UNIVERSITY, Dean B Ellis Library, 322 University Loop West Circle, 72401. (Mail add: PO Box 2040, 72467-2040), SAN 331-1678. Tel: 870-972-3077. Circulation Tel: 870-972-2460. Reference Tel: 870-972-3208. Administration Tel: 870-972-3099. FAX: 870-972-3199. Interlibrary Loan Service FAX: 870-972-5706. E-mail: refdesk@astate.edu. Web Site: www.library.astate.edu. *Libr Dir,* Jeff Bailey; Tel: 870-972-2724, E-mail: jbailey@astate.edu; *Asst Libr Dir,* Myron Flugstad; E-mail: mflugstad@astate.edu; *Asst Libr Dir,* April Sheppard; *Head, Archives,* Dr Brady Banta, PhD; E-mail: bbanta@astate.edu; *Acq & Ser Librn,* Linda Creibaum; *Outreach Librn,* Sherry L Eskridge; *Ref & Instruction Librn,* Laura Downing; *Ref & Instruction Librn,* Dominique Hallett; *Ref & Instruction Librn,* Robin Payne; *Ref & Instruction Librn,* Robert Robinette; *Ser Access Librn,* Star Holloway; *Syst Librn,* F Tracy Farmer; *Web Serv Librn,* Wendy Crist; Staff 37 (MLS 15, Non-MLS 22)
Founded 1909. Enrl 12,185; Highest Degree: Doctorate
Jul 2013-Jun 2014 Income $4,650,612, Parent Institution $2,830,612, Other $1,820,000. Sal $1,204,787 (Prof $753,706)
Library Holdings: Bk Vols 1,093,849
Special Collections: Cass Hough Aeronautica Coll; Children (Lois Lenski Coll); Iraf Twist Coll; Judd Hill Plantation Records; Legal Research Coll; Library Science (Reference & Periodical Coll); Midsouth Center for Oral History; Saint Francis Levee District Tax Coll Records; US Representative Bill Alexander Coll; US Representative E C Took Gathings Coll. State Document Depository; US Document Depository
Automation Activity & Vendor Info: (Acquisitions) Ex Libris Group; (Cataloging) Ex Libris Group; (Circulation) Ex Libris Group; (Course Reserve) Ex Libris Group; (ILL) Ex Libris Group; (OPAC) Ex Libris Group; (Serials) Ex Libris Group
Database Vendor: EBSCO Discovery Service, EBSCOhost, Emerald, Facts on File, Gale Cengage Learning, ISI Web of Knowledge, JSTOR, LexisNexis, Marquis Who's Who, Mergent Online, OCLC FirstSearch, OVID Technologies, Project MUSE, ProQuest, ScienceDirect, Westlaw
Wireless access
Partic in ARKLink; OCLC Online Computer Library Center, Inc
Open Mon-Thurs (Fall & Spring) 7am-1am, Fri 7-6, Sat 10-6, Sun 2pm-1am; Mon-Thurs (Summer) 7:15am-10pm, Fri 7:15-5, Sat 12-6, Sun 2-9

STUTTGART

J PHILLIPS COMMUNITY COLLEGE OF THE UNIVERSITY OF ARKANSAS*, Stuttgart Campus Library, 2807 Hwy 165 S, Box A, 72160. Tel: 870-673-4201, Ext 1819. Automation Services Tel: 870-673-4201, Ext 1818. FAX: 870-673-8166. Web Site: www.pccua.edu/library/library.htm. *Dir,* Jerrie Townsend; E-mail: jtownsend@pccua.edu; *Librn,* Susan Leder; E-mail: sleder@pccua.edu
Library Holdings: Bk Vols 3,000
Open Mon-Thurs (Winter) 8-8, Fri 8-1:30; Mon-Fri (Summer)7:30-7:30

P STUTTGART PUBLIC LIBRARY*, Arkansas County Library Headquarters, 2002 S Buerkle St, 72160-6508. SAN 300-5526. Tel: 870-673-1966. FAX: 870-673-4295. E-mail: legalbookie@lycos.com, stuttgart006@centurytel.net. Web Site: www.stuttgartpubliclibrary.org. *Dir,* Ted T Campbell; Staff 5 (MLS 2, Non-MLS 3)
Founded 1922. Pop 21,653; Circ 92,465
Library Holdings: AV Mats 891; Bks on Deafness & Sign Lang 12; Braille Volumes 10; CDs 288; DVDs 70; High Interest/Low Vocabulary Bk Vols 300; Large Print Bks 1,284; Music Scores 192; Bk Titles 62,675; Bk Vols 83,650; Per Subs 135; Spec Interest Per Sub 14; Talking Bks 27; Videos 495
Special Collections: Arkansas Coll; Rare Books (Queeny Coll)
Subject Interests: Agr, Antiques, Genealogy
Open Mon, Wed & Fri 9-6, Tues 1-7:30, Thurs & Sat 1-6

G US DEPARTMENT OF AGRICULTURE*, Agricultural Research, 2955 Hwy 130 E, 72160. (Mail add: PO Box 1050, 72160-1050), SAN 325-5271. Tel: 870-673-4483. FAX: 870-673-7710. Web Site: www.snarc.ars.usda.gov.
Library Holdings: Bk Titles 985; Per Subs 125
Special Collections: Reprint Coll Cross indexed & filed numerically (subject & author)
Subject Interests: Aquaculture, Fish culture, Water quality
Partic in OCLC Online Computer Library Center, Inc
Restriction: Open by appt only

SULPHUR SPRINGS

P SULPHUR SPRINGS PUBLIC LIBRARY*, 512 S Black Ave, 72768. (Mail add: PO Box 275, 72768-0275). Tel: 479-298-3753. FAX: 479-298-3963. E-mail: sspringslib@yahoo.com. *Librn,* Lily Mae Buckley
Library Holdings: Audiobooks 20; CDs 100; DVDs 20; Large Print Bks 96; Bk Vols 20,000; Videos 143
Open Mon 8-5, Tues & Wed 8-2:30
Friends of the Library Group

TEXARKANA

CM UNIVERSITY OF ARKANSAS FOR MEDICAL SCIENCES*, Area Health Education Center-Southwest Library, 300 E Sixth St, 71854. SAN 300-5534. Tel: 870-779-6023. FAX: 870-779-6050. Web Site: www.ahectxk.uams.edu. *Libr Dir,* Destiny Carter; E-mail: dncarter@uams.edu; *ILL, Libr Tech,* Kayla Lance; Staff 2 (Non-MLS 2)
Founded 1976
Library Holdings: AV Mats 600; Bk Titles 2,000; Per Subs 200
Special Collections: Consumer Health (Books, A/V materials, brochures, and pamphlets)
Automation Activity & Vendor Info: (Circulation) Innovative Interfaces, Inc
Database Vendor: Innovative Interfaces, Inc, OCLC FirstSearch, OVID Technologies
Publications: Union Catalog of Monographs; Union Catalog of Serials

TRUMANN

P TRUMANN PUBLIC LIBRARY*, 1200 W Main St, 72472. (Mail add: PO Box 73, 72472-0073), SAN 371-8379. Tel: 870-483-7744. FAX: 870-483-7744. *Dir,* Janie Teague; Staff 1 (Non-MLS 1)
Founded 1975. Pop 6,000
Jan 2010-Dec 2010 Income $43,600, City $24,800, County $18,000. Mats Exp $7,000. Sal $20,000 (Prof $15,000)

Library Holdings: Bks on Deafness & Sign Lang 2; CDs 25; DVDs 70; Large Print Bks 425; Bk Titles 11,565; Bk Vols 12,000; Per Subs 6; Talking Bks 410; Videos 79
Automation Activity & Vendor Info: (Cataloging) Follett Software; (Circulation) Follett Software
Wireless access
Special Services for the Blind - Bks on cassette
Open Mon-Fri 11:30-5:30

VAN BUREN

P VAN BUREN PUBLIC LIBRARY, 1409 Main St, 72956. SAN 331-0175. Tel: 479-474-6045. FAX: 479-471-3227. Web Site: www.crawfordcountylib.org. *Br Mgr,* Danalene Porter; Staff 5 (Non-MLS 5)
Founded 1899. Pop 19,000
Library Holdings: Bk Vols 60,000; Per Subs 20
Subject Interests: Genealogy, State hist
Automation Activity & Vendor Info: (Acquisitions) TLC (The Library Corporation); (Cataloging) TLC (The Library Corporation); (Circulation) TLC (The Library Corporation); (ILL) OCLC; (OPAC) TLC (The Library Corporation)
Database Vendor: EBSCOhost, OCLC FirstSearch
Wireless access
Mem of Crawford County Library System
Open Mon-Thurs 9-7, Fri & Sat 9-5:30, Sun 1-4
Friends of the Library Group

WALNUT RIDGE

P LAWRENCE COUNTY LIBRARY*, 1315 W Main St, 72476. SAN 331-359X. Tel: 870-886-3222. FAX: 870-886-9520. E-mail: lawcolib@yahoo.com. Web Site: www.lawcolibrary.com. *Dir,* Ashley Burris
Founded 1942. Pop 17,457; Circ 111,708
Library Holdings: Bk Vols 62,285; Per Subs 92
Automation Activity & Vendor Info: (Cataloging) Follett Software; (Circulation) Follett Software; (ILL) OCLC
Open Mon 8-8, Tues 8-6, Wed-Fri 8-5, Sat 9-1
Friends of the Library Group
Branches: 2
BOBBI JEAN MEMORIAL, 102 Hendrix St, Imboden, 72434, SAN 331-362X. Tel: 870-869-2093. FAX: 870-869-2093. *Librn,* Laura McLeod
Library Holdings: Bk Vols 10,000
Open Mon 10-5, Tues, Thurs & Fri 12-5, Sat 9-12
Friends of the Library Group
DRIFTWOOD, 28 Hwy 25, Lynn, 72440. (Mail add: PO Box 7, Lynn, 72440-0007), SAN 372-7866. Tel: 870-528-3506. FAX: 870-528-3506. *Br Mgr,* Katheryn Bates
Library Holdings: Audiobooks 389; CDs 223; DVDs 151; Large Print Bks 250; Bk Titles 13,097; Per Subs 10; Videos 87
Open Mon 10-5, Tues-Thurs 12-5, Sat 9-12

CR WILLIAMS BAPTIST COLLEGE*, Felix Goodson Library, 91 W Fulbright, 72476. (Mail add: PO Box 3738 WBC, 72476-4669), SAN 300-5542. Tel: 870-759-4139. Toll Free Tel: 800-722-4434. Web Site: www.wbcoll.edu/library. *Dir, Libr Serv,* Pamela Meridith; *Cat,* Peggy Chadwick; E-mail: pchadwick@wbcoll.edu; *Pub Serv,* Joel D Olive; E-mail: jolive@wbcoll.edu; Staff 3 (MLS 1, Non-MLS 2)
Founded 1941. Enrl 521; Fac 35; Highest Degree: Bachelor
Library Holdings: Audiobooks 7; AV Mats 11; CDs 29; e-books 121; Bk Vols 59,964; Per Subs 84; Videos 14
Special Collections: Harrison Coll
Automation Activity & Vendor Info: (Cataloging) OCLC CatExpress
Database Vendor: ABC-CLIO, Amigos Library Services, BioOne, Cinahl, Dun & Bradstreet, EBSCOhost, Gale Cengage Learning, Hoovers, JSTOR, Medline, Modern Language Association, OCLC ArticleFirst, OCLC CAMIO, OCLC FirstSearch, OCLC WorldShare Interlibrary Loan, World Book Online, WT Cox
Wireless access
Function: Alaskana res, Archival coll, Art exhibits, Audio & video playback equip for onsite use, AV serv, Bks on cassette, Bks on CD, CD-ROM, Computers for patron use, Copy machines, Digital talking bks, e-mail & chat, Electronic databases & coll, Equip loans & repairs, Exhibits, Handicapped accessible, ILL available, Literacy & newcomer serv, Newsp ref libr, Online cat, Online ref, Online searches, Orientations, Outreach serv, Photocopying/Printing, Printer for laptops & handheld devices, Prof lending libr, Pub access computers, Ref & res, Ref serv available, Res libr, Spanish lang bks, Video lending libr, Web-catalog, Wheelchair accessible, Workshops
Partic in Amigos Library Services, Inc; ARKLink; OCLC Online Computer Library Center, Inc
Special Services for the Deaf - Bks on deafness & sign lang
Special Services for the Blind - Bks on cassette; Bks on CD
Open Mon-Thurs 8am-Midnight, Fri 8-4:30, Sat 12-4, Sun 1-5
Restriction: Limited access for the pub, Open to students, fac & staff

WASHINGTON

S SOUTHWEST ARKANSAS REGIONAL ARCHIVES, Historic Washington State Park, 201 Hwy 195S, 71862. (Mail add: PO Box 134, 71862), SAN 328-3399. Tel: 870-983-2633. FAX: 870-983-2636. E-mail: southwest.archives@arkansas.gov. Web Site: www.ark-ives.com/sara. *Archives Mgr,* Peggy Lloyd; E-mail: peggy.lloyd@arkansas.gov. Subject Specialists: *English, State hist,* Peggy Lloyd; Staff 2 (Non-MLS 2)
Founded 1978
Library Holdings: Bk Vols 1,100
Special Collections: Cemetery Records; Census Coll, microfilm & print; Genealogical Research Materials & Family Histories; Land Records; Marriage Records; Newspaper Coll, microfilm; Obituaries; Tax Lists
Subject Interests: Civil War, Hist SW Ark
Function: Archival coll, Ref serv available
Open Tues-Sat 8-4:30
Friends of the Library Group

WEST FORK

P WEST FORK MUNICIPAL LIBRARY*, 198 Main St, 72774. (Mail add: PO Box 304, 72774-0304), SAN 331-0205. Tel: 479-839-2626. FAX: 479-839-2626. E-mail: westfork@wcls.lib.ar.us. Web Site: www.wcls.lib.ar.us. *Librn,* Joan Bachman
Library Holdings: Audiobooks 690; DVDs 3,200; Large Print Bks 1,800; Bk Vols 30,000
Open Mon-Fri 9:30-5, Sat 9:30-2:30
Friends of the Library Group

WEST MEMPHIS

J MID-SOUTH COMMUNITY COLLEGE, Sandra C Goldsby Library, Donald W Reynolds Ctr, 2000 W Broadway, 72301-3829. Tel: 870-733-6768. FAX: 870-733-6719. E-mail: library@midsouthcc.edu. Web Site: www.midsouthcc.edu/students/library/. *Dir,* Claire Jones; *Libr Tech,* Patricia McGarrity; Staff 2.5 (MLS 1, Non-MLS 1.5)
Library Holdings: Audiobooks 654; AV Mats 3,318; CDs 334; DVDs 439; Large Print Bks 600; Bk Titles 19,456; Bk Vols 22,105; Per Subs 51; Videos 1,948
Automation Activity & Vendor Info: (Cataloging) TLC (The Library Corporation); (Circulation) TLC (The Library Corporation); (ILL) OCLC WorldShare Interlibrary Loan; (OPAC) TLC (The Library Corporation)
Database Vendor: CredoReference, EBSCOhost, Gale Cengage Learning, OCLC FirstSearch, OCLC WorldShare Interlibrary Loan, Oxford Online, ProQuest, TLC (The Library Corporation)
Wireless access
Function: 24/7 Electronic res, 24/7 Online cat, Audio & video playback equip for onsite use, Bks on cassette, Bks on CD, Computers for patron use, Copy machines, Electronic databases & coll, Handicapped accessible, ILL available, Magazines, Online cat, Orientations, Ref & res, Wheelchair accessible
Open Mon-Thurs 7:30-7, Fri 7:30-4:30

P WEST MEMPHIS PUBLIC LIBRARY, 213 N Avalon, 72301. SAN 331-3654. Tel: 870-732-7590. FAX: 870-732-7636. *Dir,* Caroline Redfearn
Pop 29,800; Circ 50,000
Library Holdings: Bk Vols 50,000; Per Subs 47
Open Mon 10-8, Tues-Thurs 10-7, Fri 10-5, Sat 10-3
Friends of the Library Group

WYNNE

P EAST CENTRAL ARKANSAS REGIONAL LIBRARY*, 410 E Merriman Ave, 72396. SAN 324-0797. Tel: 870-238-3850. FAX: 870-238-5434. *Dir,* Holly Mercer; Staff 7 (MLS 1, Non-MLS 6)
Founded 1951. Pop 28,267; Circ 101,535
Library Holdings: Bk Vols 39,405; Per Subs 136
Automation Activity & Vendor Info: (Cataloging) Follett Software; (Circulation) Follett Software; (OPAC) Follett Software
Database Vendor: EBSCOhost, OCLC FirstSearch
Wireless access
Open Mon & Thurs 9-8, Tues, Wed & Fri 9-5
Friends of the Library Group
Branches: 4
CHERRY VALLEY BRANCH, 166 Hwy 1B, Cherry Valley, 72324-8704. (Mail add: PO Box 130, Cherry Valley, 72324-0130). Tel: 870-588-3323. FAX: 870-588-4311. *Librn,* Stacey Bennett
Library Holdings: Bk Vols 500
Open Mon-Fri 8:30-4:30
CROSS COUNTY, 410 E Merriman Ave, 72396, SAN 300-5569. Tel: 870-238-3850. FAX: 870-238-5434. Web Site: ccl.lib.ar.us. *Librn,* Caprisha Page
Founded 1951

Library Holdings: Bk Titles 25,000; Bk Vols 30,000
Open Mon & Thurs 9-8, Tues, Wed & Fri 9-5
HICKORY RIDGE BRANCH, 135 S Front, Hickory Ridge, 72347. (Mail add: PO Box 34, Hickory Ridge, 72347). Tel: 870-697-2201. FAX: 870-697-2201. *Librn,* Lynnette Imboden
Library Holdings: Bk Vols 1,000
Open Mon-Fri 8-4
Friends of the Library Group
WOODRUFF COUNTY, 201 Mulberry St, Augusta, 72006, SAN 330-8766. Tel: 870-347-5331. FAX: 870-347-5331. Web Site: wcl.lib.ar.us. *Librn,* Angie Meachum
Library Holdings: Bk Titles 15,000; Bk Vols 20,000
Open Mon 12-7, Tues-Fri 10-5

YELLVILLE

P MARION COUNTY LIBRARY*, 308 Old Main, 72687. (Mail add: PO Box 554, 72687-0554). Tel: 870-449-6015. FAX: 870-449-6015. *Dir of Libr Serv,* Anita Paulson; *Asst Dir, Libr Serv,* Ed Davis; Staff 3 (Non-MLS 3)
Library Holdings: Bk Vols 21,000
Function: ILL available, Photocopying/Printing, Summer reading prog, Wheelchair accessible
Open Mon-Fri 9-5, Sat 10-2
Restriction: Open to pub for ref & circ; with some limitations

CALIFORNIA

Date of Statistics: FY 2012-2013
Population 2010 U.S. Census: 37,253,956
Population Served by Public Libraries: 37,966,034
Total Volumes in Public Libraries: 77,586,737
Volumes Per Capita: 2.04
Total Public Library Circulation: 222,549,002
Circulation Per Capita: 5.86
Total Public Library Expenditure: $1,337,257,015
Expenditures Per Capita: $35.22
Number of County Libraries: 50
Counties Served: 58
Number of Bookmobiles: 53
Grants-in-Aid to Public Libraries:
Federal (Library Services & Technology Act): $15,029,503
Matching Local Funds: $1,844,429
State Aid: $4,700,000
Public Libraries Share from Both Sources: $14,284,182
State Library's Share: $5,445,320

ALAMEDA

P ALAMEDA FREE LIBRARY*, 1550 Oak St, 94501-2932. SAN 331-3719. Circulation Tel: 510-747-7777. Interlibrary Loan Service Tel: 510-747-7743. Reference Tel: 510-747-7713. Administration Tel: 510-747-7720. Administration FAX: 510-865-1230. E-mail: alamedafree@ci.alameda.ca.us, ill@ci.alameda.ca.us. Web Site: www.alamedafree.org. *Dir,* Jane Chisaki; E-mail: jchisaki@ci.alameda.ca.us; *Adult Serv/Young Adult Librarian,* Position Currently Open; *Circ Supvr, ILL,* Position Currently Open; *Supvr, Ad Serv,* Cosette Ratliff; Tel: 510-747-7716, E-mail: cratliff@ci.alameda.ca.us; *Supvr, Ch Serv,* Eva Volin; Tel: 510-747-7707, E-mail: evolin@ci.alameda.ca.us; *Tech Serv Supvr,* David Hall; Tel: 510-747-7730, E-mail: dhall@ci.alameda.ca.us; *Acq Tech,* Sherry Carrai; Tel: 510-747-7725, E-mail: scarrai@ci.alameda.ca.us. Subject Specialists: *Graphic novels,* Eva Volin; Staff 33 (MLS 12, Non-MLS 21)
Founded 1877. Pop 74,000; Circ 516,814
Library Holdings: Bks on Deafness & Sign Lang 60; High Interest/Low Vocabulary Bk Vols 90; Large Print Bks 1,719; Bk Titles 120,000; Bk Vols 178,573; Per Subs 322
Special Collections: Asian Languages Coll (Chinese, Japanese & Tagalog); Audio Book Coll; City, County & State History Coll; Large Print Coll, Leap Frog Coll (bk/cassette kits & reading machines); Media Coll, DVDs & videocassettes; Spanish Language Coll
Automation Activity & Vendor Info: (Acquisitions) Horizon; (Cataloging) Horizon; (Circulation) Horizon; (ILL) OCLC FirstSearch; (OPAC) Horizon
Database Vendor: Alexander Street Press, Baker & Taylor, Evanced Solutions, Inc, Facts on File, Gale Cengage Learning, Grolier Online, infoUSA, LearningExpress, Newsbank, Overdrive, Inc, ProQuest, ReferenceUSA, SirsiDynix
Wireless access
Mem of Pacific Library Partnership (PLP)
Partic in Califa
Special Services for the Deaf - Bks on deafness & sign lang; High interest/low vocabulary bks; Staff with knowledge of sign lang
Special Services for the Blind - Closed circuit TV; Reader equip
Open Mon-Wed 12-8, Thurs 10-6, Fri & Sat 10-5, Sun 1-5
Friends of the Library Group
Branches: 2
BAY FARM ISLAND, 3221 Mecartney Rd, 94502, SAN 331-3727. Tel: 510-747-7787. FAX: 510-337-1426. *Sr Librn,* Lynda Williams; E-mail: lwilliam@ci.alameda.ca.us; Staff 2 (MLS 1, Non-MLS 1)
Founded 1980. Pop 12,039; Circ 99,636
Library Holdings: Bk Vols 23,862
Open Mon & Thurs 10-6, Tues 12-8, Sat 10-5
WEST END, 788 Santa Clara Ave, 94501-3334, SAN 331-3743. Tel: 510-747-7767. FAX: 510-337-0877. *Sr Librn,* Karin Lundstrom; Tel: 510-747-7780, E-mail: klunstr@ci.alameda.ca.us; *Libr Tech,* Valerie Levitt; Staff 3 (MLS 1, Non-MLS 2)
Founded 1933. Pop 25,078; Circ 64,407
Library Holdings: Bk Vols 32,131
Open Mon 12-8, Wed & Thurs 10-6, Sat 10-5

C ARGOSY UNIVERSITY, Information Commons Library, 1005 Atlantic Ave, 94501-1148. SAN 321-6217. Tel: 510-215-0277, 510-217-4794. Circulation Tel: 510-217-4795. FAX: 510-215-0381. E-mail: ausflibrary@argosy.edu. Web Site: www.argosy.edu. *In Charge,* Heath Momon; Tel: 510-217-4793
Founded 1998. Enrl 750; Fac 50; Highest Degree: Doctorate
Library Holdings: Bk Titles 4,500; Per Subs 70
Automation Activity & Vendor Info: (Cataloging) Ex Libris Group; (Circulation) Ex Libris Group; (OPAC) Ex Libris Group
Database Vendor: EBSCOhost, ProQuest
Wireless access
Publications: Annual report
Partic in Northern & Central California Psychology Libraries
Open Mon-Thurs 8:30am-9:15pm, Fri & Sat 8:30-6

J COLLEGE OF ALAMEDA*, Library & Learning Resources Center, 555 Ralph Appezzato Memorial Pkwy, 94501. SAN 300-5577. Tel: 510-522-7221, 510-748-2365. FAX: 510-748-2380. Web Site: alameda.peralta.edu/library. *Head Librn/Tech Serv & Syst,* David Hatfield Sparks; Tel: 510-748-2253, E-mail: dsparks@peralta.edu; *Pub Serv Librn,* Jane McKenna; Tel: 510-748-2366, E-mail: jmckenna@peralata.edu; *Ref & Instruction Librn,* Steven Gerstle; Tel: 510-748-5217, E-mail: sgerstle@peralta.edu; Staff 10 (MLS 3, Non-MLS 7)
Founded 1970
Library Holdings: Electronic Media & Resources 13; Bk Vols 34,000; Per Subs 30
Automation Activity & Vendor Info: (Acquisitions) Horizon; (Cataloging) Horizon; (Circulation) Horizon; (Course Reserve) Horizon; (Media Booking) Horizon; (OPAC) Horizon; (Serials) Horizon
Database Vendor: EBSCOhost, Gale Cengage Learning, LexisNexis, ProQuest, SirsiDynix
Open Mon-Thurs 7:45-7, Fri 7:45-5, Sat 11-3

S LATHAM FOUNDATION LIBRARY*, Latham Plaza Bldg, 1826 Clement Ave, 94501-1397. SAN 326-3290. Tel: 510-521-0920. FAX: 510-521-9861. E-mail: info@latham.org. Web Site: www.latham.org. *Pres,* Hugh H Tebault, III
Founded 1917
Library Holdings: Bk Titles 100; Bk Vols 300
Special Collections: H/CAB (Human Companion Animal Bond), films & tapes
Publications: Great Dog Adoptions: A Guide for Shelters; Teaching Compassion 1999; Teaching Empathy 2004
Restriction: Not a lending libr

ALHAMBRA

P ALHAMBRA PUBLIC LIBRARY*, 101 S First St, 91801-3432. SAN 331-3832. Tel: 626-570-5008. Circulation Tel: 626-570-5028. Reference Tel: 626-570-3212. FAX: 626-457-1104. E-mail: refdesk@alhambralibrary.org. Web Site: alhambralibrary.org. *Dir,* Carmen M Hernandez; Tel: 626-570-5079; *ILL,* Estella Reyes; *Ref,* Connie Chan; *Ref,* Robert Herberg; *Ref,* Patricia Todd; *Ref Serv,* Lori Kremer; *Tech Serv,* David Brown; *Libr Spec,* Shannen Dang; Staff 8 (MLS 8)
Founded 1906. Pop 89,700; Circ 550,000
Library Holdings: AV Mats 7,933; Bk Vols 158,047; Per Subs 213
Automation Activity & Vendor Info: (Acquisitions) SirsiDynix; (Cataloging) SirsiDynix; (Circulation) SirsiDynix; (OPAC) SirsiDynix; (Serials) SirsiDynix
Database Vendor: EBSCOhost, Gale Cengage Learning, SirsiDynix
Partic in Califa; Southern California Library Cooperative
Open Mon 1-9, Tues & Wed 11-9, Thurs 10-9, Fri & Sat 10-5, Sun 1-5
Friends of the Library Group

C ALLIANT INTERNATIONAL UNIVERSITY*, Los Angeles Campus Library, 1000 S Fremont Ave, Unit 5, 91803. SAN 300-9009. Tel: 626-270-3270. Administration Tel: 626-270-3275. FAX: 626-284-1682. Web Site: library.alliant.edu. *Libr Dir,* Shawna Hellenius; E-mail: shellenius@alliant.edu; *Res & Instruction Librn,* Sherry Youssef; Tel: 626-270-3272, E-mail: syoussef@alliant.edu; Staff 3 (MLS 2, Non-MLS 1)
Founded 1969. Enrl 607; Fac 60; Highest Degree: Doctorate
Jul 2010-Jun 2011. Mats Exp $67,591, Books $5,169, Per/Ser (Incl. Access Fees) $24,579, Other Print Mats $34,782, AV Mat $930, Presv $2,131. Sal $134,896
Library Holdings: AV Mats 627; DVDs 222; Bk Vols 22,580; Per Subs 41; Videos 534
Special Collections: Psychology Assessement Coll (Restricted access)
Subject Interests: Multiculturalism, Psychol
Automation Activity & Vendor Info: (Acquisitions) Innovative Interfaces, Inc - Millenium; (Cataloging) Innovative Interfaces, Inc - Millenium; (Circulation) Innovative Interfaces, Inc - Millenium; (Course Reserve) Innovative Interfaces, Inc - Millenium; (ILL) Innovative Interfaces, Inc - Millenium; (Media Booking) Innovative Interfaces, Inc - Millenium; (OPAC) Innovative Interfaces, Inc - Millenium; (Serials) Innovative Interfaces, Inc - Millenium
Database Vendor: Alexander Street Press, American Psychological Association (APA), Annual Reviews, Blackwell, ebrary, EBSCOhost, Elsevier, Emerald, Haworth Pres Inc, JSTOR, LexisNexis, Medline, OCLC WorldShare Interlibrary Loan, ProQuest, Sage, ScienceDirect, Wiley, YBP Library Services
Wireless access
Partic in Link+; Pacific Southwest Regional Medical Library (PSRML); Statewide California Electronic Library Consortium (SCELC)
Open Mon-Thurs 8:30-8, Fri 8:30-6, Sat & Sun 12-5
Restriction: Borrowing privileges limited to fac & registered students, In-house use for visitors

R FIRST UNITED METHODIST CHURCH*, Dorothy Hooper Memorial Library, Nine N Almansor St, 91801-2699. SAN 300-5615. Tel: 626-289-4258. FAX: 626-289-4316. *Librn,* Marge Brann
Founded 1940
Library Holdings: Bk Titles 5,500

ALTADENA

P ALTADENA LIBRARY DISTRICT*, 600 E Mariposa St, 91001. SAN 300-5631. Tel: 626-798-0833. FAX: 626-798-5351. Web Site: altadenalibrary.org. *Dir,* Barbara Pearson; *Acq,* Victoria Escobar; *Adult Serv, Ref Serv, Ad,* Laureen McCoy; *Ch Serv,* Laurel Sharp; *Circ, Tech Serv,* Pauline Dutton; *Circ,* Michelle Hoskin; *ILL,* Michelle Hoskins; *YA Serv,* Cassandra Sterns; Staff 7 (MLS 7)
Founded 1908. Pop 44,000; Circ 165,879
Library Holdings: AV Mats 8,412; Large Print Bks 1,224; Bk Titles 115,790; Bk Vols 141,558; Per Subs 230; Talking Bks 2,465; Videos 2,237
Special Collections: Altadena History Coll
Automation Activity & Vendor Info: (OPAC) Innovative Interfaces, Inc
Publications: Friends of Altadena Newsletter; Poetry & Cookies (Annual)
Partic in Southern California Library Cooperative
Open Mon & Tues 10-9, Wed-Sat 10-6
Friends of the Library Group
Branches: 1
BOB LUCAS MEMORIAL LIBRARY & LITERACY CENTER, 2659 N Lincoln Ave, 91001-4963, SAN 375-524X. Tel: 626-798-8338. FAX: 626-798-3968. Web Site: library.altadena.ca.us. *Librn,* Erica Buss; Staff 2 (MLS 1, Non-MLS 1)
Open Mon-Fri 10-6
Friends of the Library Group

S THEOSOPHICAL UNIVERSITY LIBRARY*, 2416 N Lake Ave, 91001. (Mail add: PO Box C, Pasadena, 91109-7107), SAN 300-5666. Tel: 626-798-8020. FAX: 626-798-4749. E-mail: tslibrary@theosociety.org. *Head of Libr,* James T Belderis; *Ref,* I Belderis
Founded 1919
Library Holdings: Bk Titles 40,000; Bk Vols 45,000; Per Subs 30
Special Collections: Theosophy Coll, bks, per
Subject Interests: Art, Philos, World relig
Publications: Sunrise Magazine

ALTURAS

P MODOC COUNTY LIBRARY*, 212 W Third St, 96101. SAN 331-3891. Tel: 530-233-6340. FAX: 530-233-3375. E-mail: library@co.modoc.ca.us. Web Site: www.modoccountylibrary.org/. *County Librn,* Cheryl Baker; *Tech Serv Coordr,* Joanne Cain
Founded 1906. Pop 9,825
Library Holdings: Bk Vols 62,733; Per Subs 65
Special Collections: California Indian Library Coll; Modoc County History Coll
Mem of NorthNet Library System
Open Mon & Fri 10-5, Tues 12-6, Thurs 12-7
Friends of the Library Group
Branches: 3
ADIN BRANCH, Adin Community Hall, Hwy 299, Adin, 96006, SAN 331-3921. Tel: 530-299-3502. *Br Assoc,* Kathie Nelson
Library Holdings: Bk Vols 5,000
Open Tues 1-6
CEDARVILLE BRANCH, 460 Main St, Cedarville, 96104. (Mail add: PO Box 573, Cedarville, 96104-0573), SAN 331-4073. Tel: 530-279-2614. *Br Assoc,* Peggy Duncan
Library Holdings: Bk Vols 5,000
Open Tues & Fri 12-6
LOOKOUT BRANCH, Lookout Park, Lookout, 96054, SAN 331-4049. Tel: 530-294-5776. *Br Assoc,* Betty Hallberg
Library Holdings: Bk Vols 1,000
Open Wed 1-6

ANAHEIM

P ANAHEIM PUBLIC LIBRARY*, 500 W Broadway, 92805-3699. SAN 331-4103. Tel: 714-765-1880. Administration Tel: 714-765-1810. Administration FAX: 714-765-1730. Web Site: www.anaheim.net/library.html. *Actg City Librn,* Audrey Lujan; *Acq of New Ser/Per,* James Drews; Tel: 714-765-1840; Staff 44 (MLS 44)
Founded 1901
Library Holdings: Bk Vols 263,000
Special Collections: Anaheim History Coll (Anaheim History Room), bks, pamphlets, pictures
Subject Interests: Bus & mgt, Law, Local hist
Automation Activity & Vendor Info: (Acquisitions) SirsiDynix; (Circulation) SirsiDynix
Database Vendor: Gale Cengage Learning
Partic in Southern California Library Cooperative
Open Mon-Fri 11-8, Sat 10-6
Friends of the Library Group
Branches: 4
CANYON HILLS, 400 Scout Trail, 92807-4763, SAN 331-412X. Tel: 714-974-7630. *Mgr, Libr Serv,* Marianne Hugo
Library Holdings: Bk Vols 97,000
Open Mon-Thurs 11-8, Fri 10-6
Friends of the Library Group
EUCLID, 1340 S Euclid St, 92802-2008, SAN 331-4138. Tel: 714-765-3625. FAX: 714-765-3624. *Br Mgr,* Tas Watts
Library Holdings: Bk Vols 48,000
Open Mon-Thurs 12-8, Fri 12-6
Friends of the Library Group
ELVA L HASKETT BRANCH, 2650 W Broadway, 92804, SAN 331-4162. Tel: 714-765-5075. FAX: 714-765-5076. *Br Mgr,* Luz Cayabyab
Library Holdings: Bk Vols 74,000
Open Mon-Thurs 11-8, Fri & Sat 12-6
Friends of the Library Group
SUNKIST, 901 S Sunkist St, 92806-4739, SAN 331-4197. Tel: 714-765-3576. FAX: 714-765-3574. *Libr Serv Mgr,* Joe Purtell; *Librn,* Catherine St Clair
Library Holdings: Bk Vols 57,000
Open Mon-Thurs 12-8, Fri 12-6
Friends of the Library Group
Bookmobiles: 2. Principal Librn. Keely Hall

M ANAHEIM REGIONAL MEDICAL CENTER*, Medical Library, 1111 W La Palma Ave, 92801. SAN 300-5674. Tel: 714-999-6020. FAX: 714-999-3907. *Librn,* Carol Schechter
Founded 1975
Library Holdings: Bk Titles 411; Bk Vols 451; Per Subs 50

Wireless access
Function: ILL available
Restriction: Staff use only

CM SOUTH BAYLO UNIVERSITY LIBRARY*, Main Campus, 1126 N Brookhurst St, 92801-1704. SAN 300-6581. Tel: 714-533-1495. Administration Tel: 714-533-6077. FAX: 714-533-6040. *Dir, Libr & Info Serv,* Dr Edwin Duane Follick; E-mail: edfollick@southbaylo.edu; *Assoc Dir,* Dr Kwang-hee Park; E-mail: pkwanghee@southbaylo.edu. Subject Specialists: *Alternative med, Law, Theol,* Dr Edwin Duane Follick; *Theol,* Dr Kwang-hee Park; Staff 2 (MLS 1, Non-MLS 1)
Founded 1978. Enrl 681; Fac 45; Highest Degree: Doctorate
Library Holdings: Bk Vols 10,000
Special Collections: Traditional Chinese Medicine
Wireless access
Function: Archival coll, Health sci info serv, Online searches, Photocopying/Printing, Ref serv available, Res libr, Satellite serv

ANGWIN

C PACIFIC UNION COLLEGE*, W E Nelson Memorial Library, One Angwin Ave, 94508-9705. Tel: 707-965-6241, 707-965-6311. Interlibrary Loan Service Tel: 707-965-6244. Reference Tel: 707-965-6639. FAX: 707-965-6504. Web Site: www.library.puc.edu. *Dir,* Adu Worku; E-mail: aworku@puc.edu; *Archivist, Spec Coll Librn,* Gary Shearer; Tel: 707-965-6675, E-mail: gshearer@puc.edu; *Pub Serv, Syst Coordr,* Joel Lutes; Tel: 707-965-6674, E-mail: jlutes@puc.edu; *Cat,* Linda Maberly; Tel: 707-965-6640, E-mail: lmaberly@puc.edu; *Media Spec,* Trevor Murtagh; Tel: 707-965-7221, E-mail: tmurtagh@puc.edu; *Ref,* Abella Gilbert; Tel: 707-965-6244, E-mail: gabella@puc.edu; Staff 9 (MLS 5, Non-MLS 4)
Founded 1882. Enrl 1,662; Fac 104; Highest Degree: Master
Library Holdings: CDs 768; e-books 2,297; Music Scores 3,861; Bk Titles 119,118; Bk Vols 142,407; Per Subs 812; Videos 3,001
Special Collections: Ellen G White Study Center; Pitcairn Islands Study Center; Seventh-Day Adventist Study Center
Automation Activity & Vendor Info: (Cataloging) TLC (The Library Corporation); (Circulation) TLC (The Library Corporation); (ILL) OCLC Connexion; (OPAC) TLC (The Library Corporation)
Database Vendor: EBSCOhost, Gale Cengage Learning, LexisNexis, OCLC FirstSearch, OCLC WorldShare Interlibrary Loan, OVID Technologies, ProQuest
Publications: Special Collection Bibliographies (Reference guide)
Partic in Adventist Librs Info Coop; OCLC Online Computer Library Center, Inc; Statewide California Electronic Library Consortium (SCELC)

APTOS

J CABRILLO COLLEGE*, Robert E Swenson Library, 6500 Soquel Dr, 95003-3198. SAN 300-578X. Tel: 831-479-6537. FAX: 831-479-6500. Web Site: www.cabrillo.edu. *Dir,* Georg Romero; E-mail: geromero@cabrillo.edu; *Ref Serv,* Sylvia Winder; E-mail: sywinder@cabrillo.edu; *Tech Serv,* Stephanie Staley; E-mail: ststaley@cabrillo.edu; Staff 8 (MLS 8)
Founded 1959. Enrl 14,000; Fac 250; Highest Degree: Associate
Library Holdings: Bk Vols 80,000
Automation Activity & Vendor Info: (Acquisitions) Innovative Interfaces, Inc; (Cataloging) Innovative Interfaces, Inc; (Circulation) Innovative Interfaces, Inc; (Course Reserve) Innovative Interfaces, Inc; (ILL) OCLC; (OPAC) Innovative Interfaces, Inc; (Serials) Innovative Interfaces, Inc
Database Vendor: ARTstor, CountryWatch, CQ Press, EBSCOhost, Gale Cengage Learning, JSTOR, Medline, Oxford Online, ProQuest
Wireless access
Publications: Library Research Guides
Partic in Monterey Bay Area Cooperative Library System
Open Mon-Thurs 8-8, Fri 8-4, Sat 12-4

S SAVING & PRESERVING ARTS & CULTURAL ENVIRONMENTS*, Library & Archives, 9053 Soquel Dr, Ste 205, 95003. SAN 328-2139. Tel: 831-662-2907. FAX: 831-662-2918. Web Site: www.spacesarchives.org. *Dir,* Jo Farb Hernández; E-mail: jfh@spacesarchives.org; Staff 0.5 (MLS 0.5)
Founded 1978
Special Collections: Art Environments Coll; Popular Culture Coll; Self-taught Artists
Subject Interests: Archit, Art

ARCADIA

P ARCADIA PUBLIC LIBRARY, 20 W Duarte Rd, 91006. SAN 300-5798. Tel: 626-821-5567. Circulation Tel: 626-821-5571. Interlibrary Loan Service Tel: 626-294-4806. Reference Tel: 626-821-5569. Administration Tel: 626-821-5573. Information Services Tel: 626-821-4326. FAX: 626-447-8050. Interlibrary Loan Service FAX: 626-447-9753. E-mail: ref247@ci.arcadia.ca.us. Web Site: library.ci.arcadia.ca.us. *Dir, Libr & Mus Serv,* Mary Beth Hayes; Tel: 626-821-4364, E-mail: mhayes@ci.arcadia.ca.us; *Head, Adult/Teen Serv,* David Dolim; Tel: 626-821-4327, E-mail: ddolim@ci.arcadia.ca.us; *Head, Ch,* Petra Morris; Tel: 626-821-5568, E-mail: pmorris@ci.arcadia.ca.us; *Head, Circ,* Samantha Alba; Tel: 626-294-4804, E-mail: salba@ci.arcadia.ca.us; *Head, Info Syst,* Cathi Wiggins; E-mail: cwiggins@ci.arcadia.ca.us; *Head, Tech Serv,* Kathy Meacham; Tel: 626-821-5574, E-mail: kmeacham@ci.arcadia.ca.us; *Mgr, Libr Serv,* Darlene Bradley; Tel: 626-821-5570, E-mail: dbradley@ci.arcadia.ca.us; *Mgr, Libr Serv,* Roger Hiles; Tel: 626-821-5565, E-mail: rhiles@ci.arcadia.ca.us; *Acq, ILL,* Christina Vallejo; E-mail: cvallejo@ci.arcadia.ca.us; *Adult & Teen Serv,* Debbie Marks; Tel: 626-294-4801, E-mail: dmarks@ci.arcadia.ca.us; *Adult & Teen Serv,* Yvonne Ng; Tel: 626-294-4808, E-mail: yng@ci.arcadia.ca.us; Staff 11.5 (MLS 11.5)
Founded 1920. Pop 56,546; Circ 775,481
Jul 2012-Jun 2013 Income $3,164,546, State $15,211, City $3,082,435, Locally Generated Income $66,900. Mats Exp $308,956, Books $193,843, Per/Ser (Incl. Access Fees) $18,855, Micro $6,000, AV Mat $29,000, Electronic Ref Mat (Incl. Access Fees) $59,258, Presv $2,000. Sal $1,565,260 (Prof $60,216)
Library Holdings: Audiobooks 2,943; AV Mats 10,563; Braille Volumes 43; CDs 5,677; DVDs 4,373; e-books 3,234; Large Print Bks 1,852; Bk Vols 185,072; Per Subs 221
Special Collections: US Document Depository
Subject Interests: Local hist
Automation Activity & Vendor Info: (Acquisitions) Baker & Taylor; (Cataloging) ByWater Solutions; (Circulation) ByWater Solutions; (ILL) OCLC; (OPAC) ByWater Solutions; (Serials) ByWater Solutions
Database Vendor: Baker & Taylor, EBSCO Information Services, Gale Cengage Learning, Grolier Online, H W Wilson, Ingram Library Services, LearningExpress, OCLC WebJunction, OCLC WorldShare Interlibrary Loan, ProQuest, Wilson - Wilson Web
Wireless access
Function: Adult bk club, After school storytime, Archival coll, Audiobks via web, Bk club(s), Bks on CD, CD-ROM, Children's prog, Computer training, Computers for patron use, Copy machines, Digital talking bks, e-mail & chat, Electronic databases & coll, Exhibits, Free DVD rentals, Handicapped accessible, Homebound delivery serv, ILL available, Magnifiers for reading, Microfiche/film & reading machines, Music CDs, Online cat, Online ref, OverDrive digital audio bks, Photocopying/Printing, Prog for adults, Prog for children & young adult, Pub access computers, Ref serv available, Ref serv in person, Spanish lang bks, Spoken cassettes & CDs, Story hour, Summer reading prog, Tax forms, Teen prog, Telephone ref, VHS videos, Web-catalog, Wheelchair accessible
Partic in Southern California Library Cooperative
Special Services for the Deaf - ADA equip; Bks on deafness & sign lang
Special Services for the Blind - Assistive/Adapted tech devices, equip & products; Audio mat; Bks & mags in Braille, on rec, tape & cassette; Braille bks; Magnifiers
Open Mon-Thurs 10-9, Fri & Sat 10-6
Friends of the Library Group

S CALIFORNIA THOROUGHBRED BREEDERS ASSOCIATION, Carleton F Burke Memorial Library, 201 Colorado Pl, 91007. (Mail add: PO Box 60018, 91066-6018), SAN 300-5801. Tel: 626-445-7800. Toll Free Tel: 800-573-2822. FAX: 626-574-0852. Web Site: www.ctba.com. *Librn,* Vivian Montoya; E-mail: vivian@ctba.com
Founded 1964
Library Holdings: Bk Titles 3,000; Bk Vols 10,000; Per Subs 20
Special Collections: American Breeding (C C Moseley Coll), bks & flm; Foreign Racing & Breeding (Edward Lasker Coll); Kent Cochran Coll
Open Mon-Fri 9-4
Restriction: Open to pub for ref only

S LOS ANGELES COUNTY ARBORETUM & BOTANIC GARDEN*, Arboretum Library, 301 N Baldwin Ave, 91007-2697. SAN 300-581X. Tel: 626-821-3213. FAX: 626-445-1217. Web Site: www.arboretum.org/explore/library. *Plant Sci Librn,* Susan C Eubank; E-mail: susan.eubank@arboretum.org. Subject Specialists: *Botany, Gardening, Plants,* Susan C Eubank; Staff 1 (MLS 1)
Founded 1948
Jul 2011-Jun 2012 Income $72,000, County $66,000, Locally Generated Income $6,000. Mats Exp $15,500, Books $2,500, Per/Ser (Incl. Access Fees) $13,000. Sal $55,000 (Prof $55,000)
Library Holdings: DVDs 2; Bk Titles 27,000; Bk Vols 28,000; Per Subs 150; Spec Interest Per Sub 150
Special Collections: Plants, Gardens & Travel in California (William Aplin Slide Coll), 1940-1980
Subject Interests: Botany, Gardening, Hort, Local hist
Automation Activity & Vendor Info: (Cataloging) OCLC Connexion; (Circulation) EOS International; (ILL) EOS International; (OPAC) EOS International
Database Vendor: Agricola, EOS International, OCLC FirstSearch, OCLC WorldShare Interlibrary Loan

Function: Art exhibits, Bk club(s), Children's prog, ILL available, Mail loans to mem, Online ref, Online searches, Orientations, Photocopying/Printing, Prog for adults, Ref & res, Ref serv available, Referrals accepted, Story hour
Partic in Council on Botanical & Horticultural Libraries, Inc (CBHL)
Open Tues-Fri 8:30-5:30, Sat 8:30-5, Sun 12-4
Restriction: Circ to mem only, Non-circulating of rare bks

M METHODIST HOSPITAL OF SOUTHERN CALIFORNIA*, Medical Library, 300 W Huntington Dr, 91007. SAN 300-5828. Tel: 626-898-8000. FAX: 626-574-3712. *Coordr,* Joyce Ogle
Founded 1957
Library Holdings: Bk Vols 100; Per Subs 5
Restriction: Staff use only

ARCATA

C HUMBOLDT STATE UNIVERSITY LIBRARY*, One Harpst St, 95521-8299. SAN 300-5836. Tel: 707-826-3441. Circulation Tel: 707-826-3431. Interlibrary Loan Service Tel: 707-826-4824, 707-826-4889. Reference Tel: 707-826-3418. FAX: 707-826-3440. Interlibrary Loan Service FAX: 707-826-5590. Web Site: library.humboldt.edu. *Dean of Libr,* Teresa Grenot; *Chair, Access Serv,* Wayne Perryman; Tel: 707-826-5598, E-mail: wayne.perryman@humboldt.edu; *Chair, Coll Develop,* Mary Kay; Tel: 707-826-3414, E-mail: mhk1@humboldlt.edu; *Chair, Ref Serv,* Robert Sathrum; Tel: 707-826-5617, E-mail: robert.sathrum@humboldt.edu; *Circ Supvr,* John Taloff; Tel: 707-826-5599, E-mail: john.taloff@humboldt.edu; *Syst Coordr,* Jeremy Shellhase; Tel: 707-826-3144, E-mail: jeremy.shellhase@humboldt.edu; *Cat,* George Wrenn; Tel: 707-826-3412, E-mail: george.wren@humboldt.edu; *Spec Coll & Archives Librn,* Joan Berman; Tel: 707-826-4939, E-mail: joan.berman@humboldt.edu; Staff 39 (MLS 14, Non-MLS 25)
Founded 1913. Enrl 8,046; Fac 517; Highest Degree: Master
Library Holdings: e-books 22,561; Bk Vols 595,208; Per Subs 1,714
Special Collections: Regional History (Humboldt County Coll, Humboldt State University Archives). State Document Depository; US Document Depository
Automation Activity & Vendor Info: (Acquisitions) Ex Libris Group; (Cataloging) Ex Libris Group; (Circulation) Ex Libris Group; (Course Reserve) Ex Libris Group; (ILL) OCLC ILLiad; (OPAC) Ex Libris Group; (Serials) Ex Libris Group
Database Vendor: Dialog, EBSCOhost, LexisNexis, OCLC FirstSearch, OVID Technologies, ProQuest, SirsiDynix, TLC (The Library Corporation)
Mem of NorthNet Library System
Partic in OCLC Online Computer Library Center, Inc

ARMONA

P ARMONA COMMUNITY LIBRARY*, 11115 C St, 93202. (Mail add: PO Box 368, 93202-0368). Tel: 559-583-5005. FAX: 559-583-5004. Web Site: www.sjvls.lib.ca.us/kings. *Librn,* Mary Diaz
Library Holdings: Bk Vols 14,000
Automation Activity & Vendor Info: (Acquisitions) Horizon; (Cataloging) Horizon; (Circulation) Horizon; (OPAC) Horizon
Database Vendor: Gale Cengage Learning
Open Mon-Fri 8-4:30

ATASCADERO

S ATASCADERO HISTORICAL SOCIETY MUSEUM LIBRARY, 6600 Lewis Ave, 93423. (Mail add: PO Box 1047, 93423-1047), SAN 370-341X. Tel: 805-466-8341. E-mail: atascaderocolonymuseum@gmail.com. Web Site: www.atascaderohistoricalsociety.org. *Curator,* Ann Wright
Founded 1965
Library Holdings: Bk Vols 300
Special Collections: Atascadero High School Yearbooks; Atascadero Newspapers; E G Lewis Photograph Coll
Open Wed & Sat 1-4

ATASCADERO STATE HOSPITAL

M LOGAN PATIENT'S LIBRARY*, 10333 El Camino Real, 93422. (Mail add: PO Box 7003, 93423-7003), SAN 331-4227. Tel: 805-468-2520. FAX: 805-468-3027. *Librn,* Nancy Gulliver; *Law Librn,* Veronica Gutierrez; Tel: 805-468-3343. Subject Specialists: *Med,* Nancy Gulliver; Staff 3 (MLS 1, Non-MLS 2)
Founded 1957
Library Holdings: AV Mats 400; High Interest/Low Vocabulary Bk Vols 500; Bk Titles 9,000; Bk Vols 15,000; Per Subs 29
Special Collections: Law (California & Federal Laws & Codes)
Partic in Gold Coast Library Network
Special Services for the Deaf - Bks on deafness & sign lang; High interest/low vocabulary bks
Special Services for the Blind - Audio mat; Bks on cassette; Cassette playback machines; Cassettes; Large print bks; Magnifiers
Restriction: Not open to pub, Staff & patient use

M LOGAN PROFESSIONAL LIBRARY, 10333 El Camino Real, 93422. (Mail add: PO Box 7003, 93423-7003), SAN 331-4251. Tel: 805-468-2491. FAX: 805-468-3027. *Librn,* Nancy Gulliver; E-mail: ngullive@ashdsh.ca.gov; Staff 2 (MLS 1, Non-MLS 1)
Founded 1957
Library Holdings: Bk Titles 8,500; Bk Vols 9,000; Videos 200
Special Collections: Treatment Enhancement Coll
Subject Interests: Med, Nursing, Psychiat, Psychotherapy, Rehabilitation
Database Vendor: PubMed, Westlaw
Function: ILL available
Partic in Gold Coast Library Network; Medical Library Group of Southern California & Arizona (MLGSCA); National Network of Libraries of Medicine
Restriction: Not open to pub

ATHERTON

C MENLO COLLEGE, Bowman Library, 1000 El Camino Real, 94027-4300. SAN 301-0511. Tel: 650-543-3826. Circulation Tel: 650-543-3825. FAX: 650-543-3833. Web Site: www.menlo.edu/library. *Interim Dean, Libr Serv,* Linda K Smith; E-mail: lsmith@menlo.edu; *Info & Access Serv Librn,* Anne Linvill; E-mail: alinvill@menlo.edu; *Info Serv Librn,* Melissa Pincus; E-mail: melissa.pincus@menlo.edu; *Info Serv Librn,* Tricia Soto; E-mail: tricia.soto@menlo.edu; *Info Serv Librn,* Marie Varelas; E-mail: marie.varelas@menlo.edu; *Col Archivist, Tech Serv Librn,* Cheryl S Collins; E-mail: ccollins@menlo.edu; Staff 6 (MLS 6)
Founded 1927. Enrl 750; Fac 85; Highest Degree: Bachelor
Library Holdings: Bk Vols 60,000; Per Subs 40,000
Subject Interests: Bus, Soc sci
Automation Activity & Vendor Info: (Acquisitions) Innovative Interfaces, Inc; (Cataloging) Innovative Interfaces, Inc; (Circulation) Innovative Interfaces, Inc; (Course Reserve) Innovative Interfaces, Inc; (ILL) Innovative Interfaces, Inc; (Media Booking) Innovative Interfaces, Inc; (OPAC) Innovative Interfaces, Inc; (Serials) Innovative Interfaces, Inc
Wireless access
Function: Archival coll, Audio & video playback equip for onsite use, Computers for patron use, Copy machines, E-Reserves, Electronic databases & coll, ILL available, Magnifiers for reading, Online cat, Online searches, Photocopying/Printing, Pub access computers, Ref serv available, Telephone ref, Workshops
Partic in Bay Area Library & Information Network; MLC; Statewide California Electronic Library Consortium (SCELC)
Special Services for the Blind - Assistive/Adapted tech devices, equip & products
Open Mon-Thurs 8am-11pm, Fri 8-6, Sat 11-5, Sun 1-11
Restriction: Open to pub for ref & circ; with some limitations, Open to students, fac, staff & alumni

AUBURN

L PLACER COUNTY LAW LIBRARY*, 1523 Lincoln Way, 95603. SAN 377-7766. Tel: 530-823-2573. FAX: 530-823-9470. *Librn,* Christopher Christman
Library Holdings: Bk Vols 7,800
Open Mon & Tues 8-8, Wed-Fri 8-5, Sat 10-2

P PLACER COUNTY LIBRARY*, 350 Nevada St, 95603-3789. SAN 331-4286. Tel: 530-886-4500, 530-886-4550. Reference Tel: 530-886-4510. FAX: 530-886-4555. E-mail: library@placerlibrary.org. Web Site: www.placer.ca.gov/library. *Dir, Libr Serv,* Mary George; E-mail: mgeorge@placer.ca.gov; *Asst Dir, Libr Serv,* JoAnn Collins; E-mail: jcollins@placer.ca.gov
Founded 1937. Pop 145,500; Circ 732,106
Library Holdings: Bk Vols 115,300
Special Collections: State Document Depository
Database Vendor: Gale Cengage Learning
Open Mon 10-7, Tues-Thurs 10-6, Fri & Sat 10-5
Friends of the Library Group
Branches: 10
APPLEGATE BRANCH, 18018 Applegate Rd, Applegate, 95703. (Mail add: PO Box 267, Applegate, 97503), SAN 331-4316. Tel: 530-878-2721. FAX: 530-878-2721. *Br Mgr,* Annette Long
Library Holdings: Bk Vols 15,300
Open Tues 10-4, Wed 3-7, Thurs-Sat 1-5
Friends of the Library Group
COLFAX BRANCH, Two Church St, Colfax, 95713. (Mail add: PO Box 719, Colfax, 95713-0719), SAN 331-4340. Tel: 530-346-8211. FAX: 530-346-8211. *Br Mgr,* Andrea Spark
Open Tues 1-7, Wed & Thurs 12-5, Fri & Sat 10-2
Friends of the Library Group

FORESTHILL BRANCH, 24580 Main St, Foresthill, 95631. (Mail add: PO Box 419, Foresthill, 95631-0419), SAN 331-4405. Tel: 530-367-2785. FAX: 530-367-4721. *Br Mgr,* Robin Guthrie
Library Holdings: Bk Vols 14,400
Open Tues 11-5, Wed 1-7, Thurs 10-2, Fri 1-5, Sat 11-3
Friends of the Library Group
GRANITE BAY BRANCH, 6475 Douglas Blvd, Granite Bay, 95746, SAN 373-5737. Tel: 916-791-5590. FAX: 916-791-1837. *Br Mgr,* Bron Cancilla
Library Holdings: Bk Titles 44,900
Open Tues 10-8, Wed 12-8, Thurs 10-6, Fri & Sat 10-5
Friends of the Library Group
KINGS BEACH BRANCH, 301 Secline Dr, Kings Beach, 96143. (Mail add: PO Box 246, Kings Beach, 96143-0246), SAN 331-443X. Tel: 530-546-2021. FAX: 530-546-2126. *Br Mgr,* Louise Jensen
Library Holdings: Bk Vols 14,500
Open Tues & Fri 1-5, Wed 2-6, Thurs 10-2, Sat 11-3
Friends of the Library Group
LOOMIS BRANCH, 6050 Library Dr, Loomis, 95650. (Mail add: PO Box 610, Loomis, 95650-0610), SAN 331-4464. Tel: 916-652-7061. FAX: 916-652-5156. *Br Mgr,* Beth Enright
Library Holdings: Bk Vols 22,200
Open Tues, Thurs & Fri 10-5, Wed 12-7, Sat 12-4
Friends of the Library Group
MEADOW VISTA BRANCH, 16981 Placer Hills Rd, Ste B6, Meadow Vista, 95722. Tel: 530-878-2647. FAX: 530-878-4983. *Br Mgr,* Debbie Centi
Founded 2001
Library Holdings: Bk Vols 14,200
Open Tues 10-3, Wed 3-8, Thurs & Fri 12-5, Sat 10-2
PENRYN BRANCH, 2215 Rippey Rd, Penryn, 95663. (Mail add: PO Box 405, Penryn, 95663-0405), SAN 331-4499. Tel: 916-663-3621. FAX: 916-663-3621. *Br Mgr,* Kathy Padilla
Library Holdings: Bk Vols 8,500
Open Tues 2-6, Wed & Sat 10-2, Thurs & Fri 1-5
Friends of the Library Group
ROCKLIN BRANCH, 4890 Granite Dr, Rocklin, 95677-2547, SAN 331-4529. Tel: 916-624-3133. FAX: 916-632-9152. *Asst Dir,* Mary George
Library Holdings: Bk Vols 57,300
Open Mon & Tues 10-8, Wed & Thurs 10-6, Fri & Sat 10-5
Friends of the Library Group
TAHOE CITY BRANCH, 740 N Lake Blvd, Tahoe City, 96145. (Mail add: PO Box 6570, Tahoe City, 96145-6570), SAN 331-4553. Tel: 530-583-3382. FAX: 530-583-5805.
Library Holdings: Bk Vols 20,900
Open Tues, Thurs & Fri 10-5, Wed 12-7, Sat 10-2
Friends of the Library Group
Bookmobiles: 1. Bk vols 5300

AZUSA

P AZUSA CITY LIBRARY*, 729 N Dalton Ave, 91702-2586. SAN 300-5844. Tel: 626-812-5232. Circulation Tel: 626-812-5477. Reference Tel: 626-812-5268. FAX: 626-334-4368. E-mail: library_staff@ci.azusa.ca.us. Web Site: www.ci.azusa.ca.us. *Dir,* Nancy Johnson; Staff 22 (MLS 3, Non-MLS 19)
Founded 1898. Pop 44,712; Circ 126,600
Library Holdings: Bk Vols 100,000; Per Subs 163
Special Collections: Indians of North America Coll; Spanish Language Coll
Subject Interests: Local hist
Automation Activity & Vendor Info: (Cataloging) SirsiDynix; (Circulation) SirsiDynix; (OPAC) SirsiDynix
Partic in Southern California Library Cooperative
Open Mon-Wed 10-9, Thurs 10-6, Fri & Sat 10-5
Friends of the Library Group

BAKER

C CALIFORNIA STATE UNIVERSITY*, Desert Studies Center Library, PO Box 490, 92309. SAN 373-4935. Tel: 714-936-0461. Web Site: biology.fullerton.edu. *Mgr,* Robert Fulton; E-mail: rfulton@fullerton.edu
Library Holdings: Bk Vols 1,800
Open Mon-Fri 8-5
Restriction: Open by appt only, Open to pub for ref only

BAKERSFIELD

J BAKERSFIELD COLLEGE*, Grace Van Dyke Bird Library, 1801 Panorama Dr, 93305-1298. SAN 300-5879. Tel: 661-395-4461. FAX: 661-395-4397. Web Site: www.bakersfieldcollege.edu. *Chair,* Anna Agenjo; E-mail: aagenjo@bakersfieldcollege.edu; *Ref Librn,* Dawn Dobie; *Ref Librn,* Nancy Guidry; *Ref Librn,* Marci Lingo; E-mail: mlingo@bakersfieldcollege.edu; *Tech Serv Librn,* Kirk Russell; *Libr Asst,* Dora Hare; *Libr Asst I,* Stephanie Vidales; *Libr Asst II,* Deborah Carmona; *Libr Tech II,* Carol Paschal; *Libr Tech II,* Karen Valenzuela; Staff 10 (MLS 5, Non-MLS 5)
Founded 1913. Enrl 16,000; Fac 236
Library Holdings: Bk Vols 80,000; Per Subs 145
Special Collections: Bell British Plays, 1776-1795; Grove Plays of the Bohemian Club of San Francisco, 1911-1958
Subject Interests: Calif
Automation Activity & Vendor Info: (Acquisitions) Horizon; (Cataloging) Horizon; (Circulation) Horizon; (Course Reserve) Horizon; (ILL) Horizon; (OPAC) Horizon; (Serials) Horizon
Database Vendor: EBSCOhost, Gale Cengage Learning
Publications: Bulletin
Open Mon-Thurs 8-8, Fri 8-2, Sat 11-3

C CALIFORNIA STATE UNIVERSITY*, Walter W Stiern Library, 60 LIB, 9001 Stockdale Hwy, 93311-1022. SAN 300-5895. Tel: 661-654-3172. Interlibrary Loan Service Tel: 661-654-2159. Reference Tel: 661-654-3231. Administration Tel: 661-654-3042. FAX: 661-654-3238. Interlibrary Loan Service FAX: 661-654-2259. E-mail: csub_library@csub.edu. Web Site: www.lib.csub.edu. *Interim Dean,* Curt Asher; E-mail: casher@csub.edu; *Bibliog Control Librn, Govt Doc,* Norm Hutcherson; Tel: 661-654-2061, E-mail: nhutcherson@csub.edu; *Distance Serv Librn,* Kristine Holloway; Tel: 661-654-5072, E-mail: kholloway2@csub.edu; *Distance Serv Librn,* Jamie Jacks; Tel: 661-654-3372, E-mail: jjacks@csub.edu; *First Year Experience Librn, Instrul Tech Librn,* Sandra Bozarth; E-mail: sbozarth2@csub.edu; *Instruction Librn,* Christy Gavin; Tel: 661-654-3237, E-mail: cgavin@csub.edu; *Database Mgt,* Roxanne Starbuck; Tel: 661-654-3258, E-mail: rstarbuck@csub.edu; *Circ Mgr,* Vickie Melton; Tel: 661-654-3236, E mail: vmelton@csub.edu; *Tech Serv Mgr,* Sherry Bennett; Tel: 661-654-3254, E-mail: sbennett@csub.edu; *Admin Support Coordr,* Eileen Montoya; E-mail: emontoya@csub.edu; *Ref Serv Coordr,* Johanna Alexander; Tel: 661-664-3256, E-mail: jalexander@csub.edu; *Web Serv Coordr,* Ying Zhong; Tel: 661-654-3119, E-mail: yzhong@csub.edu; *Syst Analyst,* Frank Aguirre; Tel: 661-664-2274, E-mail: faguirre@csub.edu; *Acq,* Darline Norris; Tel: 661-654-3262, E-mail: dnorris@csub.edu; *Circ,* Kristi Chavez; E-mail: kchavez4@csub.edu; *Circ,* F Javier Llamas; Tel: 661-654-3233, E-mail: fllamas@csub.edu; *Circ,* Aide Zaragoza; Tel: 661-654-3234, E-mail: azaragoza@csub.edu; *ILL,* Janet Gonzales; Tel: 661-654-2129, E-mail: jgonzales@csub.edu; *ILL,* Ariel Lauricio; Tel: 661-664-3189, E-mail: alauricio@csub.edu; *Ser,* Monica Ibarra; Tel: 661-664-3249, E-mail: mgarcia@csub.edu. Subject Specialists: *Geol, Physics, Polit sci,* Norm Hutcherson; *Educ, Multicultural studies,* Sandra Bozarth; *English,* Christy Gavin; *Bus, Econ,* Johanna Alexander; *Computer sci, Math, Nursing,* Ying Zhong
Founded 1970. Enrl 8,002; Fac 366; Highest Degree: Master
Library Holdings: AV Mats 10,097; Bk Titles 358,808; Bk Vols 461,829; Per Subs 1,208
Special Collections: Oral History; State Document Depository; US Document Depository
Automation Activity & Vendor Info: (Acquisitions) Ex Libris Group; (Cataloging) Ex Libris Group; (Circulation) Ex Libris Group; (ILL) Ex Libris Group; (Serials) Ex Libris Group
Database Vendor: EBSCOhost, Gale Cengage Learning, LexisNexis, OVID Technologies, TLC (The Library Corporation), Wilson - Wilson Web
Partic in Dialog Corp; OCLC Online Computer Library Center, Inc; SDC Search Serv; Southern Calif Answering Network
Open Mon-Thurs 9am-10pm, Fri 9-5, Sun 11-7
Friends of the Library Group

GL KERN COUNTY LAW LIBRARY*, 1415 Truxtun Ave, Rm 301, 93301. SAN 300-5917. Tel: 661-868-5320. FAX: 661-868-5368. Web Site: www.kclawlib.org. *Librn,* Annette Heath; Staff 5 (Non-MLS 5)
Founded 1891
Library Holdings: CDs 28; Bk Vols 18,261; Videos 5
Special Collections: State Document Depository
Subject Interests: Legal
Open Mon-Fri 8-4

P KERN COUNTY LIBRARY, 701 Truxtun Ave, 93301-4816. SAN 331-4588. Tel: 661-868-0700. Circulation Tel: 661-868-0760. Interlibrary Loan Service Tel: 661-868-0787. Reference Tel: 661-868-0770. Information Services Tel: 661-868-0745. FAX: 661-868-0799. Reference FAX: 661-868-0831. Web Site: www.kerncountylibrary.org. *Dir,* Nancy Kerr; E-mail: nancy.kerr@kerncountylibrary.org; *Asst Dir, Operations,* Sarah Bleyl; E-mail: sarah.bleyl@kerncountylibrary.org; *Asst Dir, Pub Serv,* Andrea Apple; E-mail: andrea.apple@kerncountylibrary.org; *Asst Dir, Support Serv,* Georgia Wages; E-mail: georgia.wages@kerncountylibrary.org; Staff 28.5 (MLS 27.5, Non-MLS 1)
Founded 1900. Pop 857,882; Circ 1,502,126
Library Holdings: AV Mats 65,000; e-books 1,000; Bk Vols 1,810,000; Per Subs 191
Special Collections: California Geology-Mining-Petroleum Coll, bks & micro; Kern County Historical Coll, bks & micro. State Document Depository; US Document Depository

Subject Interests: Hist, Natural sci
Wireless access
Mem of San Joaquin Valley Library System
Open Mon-Fri 8-5
Friends of the Library Group
Branches: 25
ARVIN BRANCH, 201 Campus Dr, Arvin, 93203, SAN 331-4596. Tel: 661-854-5934. FAX: 661-584-3744. *Br Supvr,* Rafael Moreno
Founded 1914. Pop 17,147; Circ 21,123
Library Holdings: Bk Vols 29,542
Open Mon-Thurs 11-7
Friends of the Library Group
BAKER BRANCH, 1400 Baker St, 93305-3731, SAN 331-4618. Tel: 661-861-2390. *Br Supvr,* Josie Salas
Founded 1910. Pop 29,878; Circ 5,822
Library Holdings: Bk Vols 17,430
Open Mon & Wed 11-7
Friends of the Library Group
BEALE MEMORIAL, 701 Truxtun Ave, 93301-4816, SAN 331-4816. Tel: 661-868-0701. FAX: 661-868-0831. *Head of Libr,* Maria Rutledge
Founded 1900. Pop 36,728; Circ 362,692
Library Holdings: Bk Vols 292,354
Special Collections: Genealogy Coll; Geology Mining & Petroleum Coll; Kern County History Coll
Open Mon-Thurs 11-7, Fri & Sat 10-6
Friends of the Library Group
BORON BRANCH, 26967 20 Mule Team Rd, Boron, 93516-1550, SAN 331-460X. Tel: 760-762-5606. *Br Supvr,* Shannon Grace
Founded 1955. Pop 2,314; Circ 6,744
Library Holdings: Bk Vols 12,232
Open Mon, Wed & Fri 10-6
Friends of the Library Group
BUTTONWILLOW BRANCH, 101 Main St, Buttonwillow, 93206. (Mail add: PO Box 476, Buttonwillow, 93206), SAN 331-4626. Tel: 661-764-5337. FAX: 661-764-5337. *Br Supvr,* David Squires; Staff 0.4 (Non-MLS 0.4)
Founded 1913. Pop 3,238; Circ 2,793
Library Holdings: Bk Vols 9,268
Open Mon, Wed & Fri 11-6
Friends of the Library Group
CALIFORNIA CITY BRANCH, 9507 California City Blvd, California City, 93505-2280, SAN 331-2280. Tel: 760-373-4757. FAX: 760-373-4757. *Br Supvr,* Jake Cairns
Founded 1963. Pop 13,595; Circ 33,298
Library Holdings: Bk Vols 21,129
Open Tues & Thurs 11-7, Fri & Sat 9-5
Friends of the Library Group
DELANO BRANCH, 925 Tenth Ave, Delano, 93215-2229, SAN 331-4677. Tel: 661-725-1078. *Br Supvr,* Rosaalia Aguirre
Founded 1919. Pop 52,509; Circ 61,758
Library Holdings: Bk Vols 34,000
Open Tues-Thurs 11-7, Sat 9-5
Friends of the Library Group
FRAZIER PARK BRANCH, 3732 Park Dr, Frazier Park, 93225, SAN 321-8686. Tel: 661-245-1267. *Br Supvr,* Marie Smith
Founded 1982. Pop 8,480; Circ 20,434
Library Holdings: Bk Vols 15,963
Open Tues-Thurs 11-7, Fri & Sat 9-5
HOLLOWAY-GONZALES BRANCH, 506 E Brundage Lane, 93307-3337, SAN 331-4707. Tel: 661-861-2083. *Br Supvr,* Joe DeRamus
Founded 1975. Pop 21,930; Circ 3,879
Library Holdings: Bk Vols 21,670
Open Wed & Fri 9-5
Friends of the Library Group
CLARA M JACKSON BRANCH, 500 W Kern Ave, McFarland, 93250-1355, SAN 377-6662. Tel: 661-792-2318. FAX: 661-792-6588. *Br Supvr,* Rosaalia Aguirre
Founded 1913. Pop 12,146; Circ 11,174
Library Holdings: Bk Vols 20,000
Open Wed-Fri 10-6
Friends of the Library Group
KERN RIVER VALLEY BRANCH, 7054 Lake Isabella Blvd, Lake Isabella, 93240-9205, SAN 331-4685. Tel: 760-549-2083. *Br Supvr,* Peggy Hickey; E-mail: peggy.hickey@kerncountylibrary.org
Founded 1914. Pop 13,519; Circ 63,590
Library Holdings: Bk Vols 37,377
Open Tues & Thurs 11-7, Fri & Sat 9-5
Friends of the Library Group
KERNVILLE BRANCH, 48 Tobias St, Kernville, 93238. (Mail add: PO Box 1907, Kernville, 93238-1907), SAN 331-4693. Tel: 760-376-6180. *Br Supvr,* Peggy Hickey
Founded 1914. Pop 2,011; Circ 7,469
Library Holdings: Bk Vols 5,307
Open Tues & Thurs 10-5
Friends of the Library Group
WANDA KIRK BRANCH, 3611 Rosamond Blvd, Rosamond, 93560-7653, SAN 378-2093. Tel: 661-256-3236. FAX: 661-256-2906. *Br Supvr,* Michele Carey
Founded 1914. Pop 25,455; Circ 61,211
Library Holdings: Bk Vols 45,000
Open Tues & Thurs 11-7, Fri & Sat 9-5
Friends of the Library Group
LAMONT BRANCH, 8304 Segrue Rd, Lamont, 93241-2123, SAN 331-4715. Tel: 661-845-3471. FAX: 661-845-7701. *Br Supvr,* Rafael Moreno
Founded 1911. Pop 21,031; Circ 24,781
Library Holdings: Bk Vols 35,444
Open Wed & Thurs 11-7, Fri & Sat 9-5
Friends of the Library Group
MOJAVE BRANCH, 16916 1/2 Hwy 14 Space D-2, Mojave, 93501-1226, SAN 331-474X. Tel: 661-824-2243. *Br Supvr,* Michele Carey; Staff 2 (MLS 1, Non-MLS 1)
Founded 1914. Pop 7,104; Circ 7,213
Library Holdings: Bk Vols 12,000
Function: Bks on cassette, Bks on CD, CD-ROM, Computers for patron use, Copy machines, Electronic databases & coll, Holiday prog, Music CDs, Online searches, OverDrive digital audio bks, Photocopying/Printing, Pub access computers, Ref serv available, Summer reading prog, Tax forms, VHS videos
Open Mon, Wed & Fri 10-6
Friends of the Library Group
NORTHEAST BRANCH, 3725 Columbus St, 93306-2719, SAN 331-4847. Tel: 661-871-9017. *Br Supvr,* Taarna Long
Founded 1982. Pop 81,649; Circ 92,182
Library Holdings: Bk Vols 52,000
Open Tues & Thurs 11-7, Sat 9-5
Friends of the Library Group
BRYCE C RATHBUN BRANCH, 200 W China Grade Loop, 93308-1709, SAN 331-4731. Tel: 661-393-6431. FAX: 661-393-6432. *Br Supvr,* Joe DeRamus
Founded 1917. Pop 33,753; Circ 42,414
Library Holdings: Bk Vols 38,702
Open Tues & Thurs 11-7, Sat 9-5
Friends of the Library Group
RIDGECREST BRANCH, 131 E Las Flores Ave, Ridgecrest, 93555-3648, SAN 331-4766. Tel: 760-384-5870. FAX: 760-384-3211. *Br Supvr,* Marsha R Lloyd; E-mail: marsha.lloyd@kerncountylibrary.org; Staff 3 (MLS 1, Non-MLS 2)
Founded 1941. Pop 37,012; Circ 119,787
Library Holdings: Audiobooks 200; Bks on Deafness & Sign Lang 20; CDs 500; DVDs 250; e-books 100; High Interest/Low Vocabulary Bk Vols 30; Large Print Bks 500; Bk Vols 54,098; Per Subs 100; Talking Bks 20
Special Collections: Flora & Fauna of Indian Wells Valley; Local History Coll; Petroglyphs
Automation Activity & Vendor Info: (Circulation) SirsiDynix
Database Vendor: EBSCOhost, Gale Cengage Learning
Open Tues-Thurs 11-7, Fri & Sat 9-5
Friends of the Library Group
SHAFTER BRANCH, 236 James St, Ste 2, Shafter, 93263-2031, SAN 331-4774. Tel: 661-746-2156. *Br Supvr,* Mandy Walters
Founded 1915. Pop 26,468; Circ 20,086
Library Holdings: Bk Vols 25,412
Open Tues & Thurs 11-7, Sat 9-5
Friends of the Library Group
SOUTHWEST BRANCH, 8301 Ming Ave, 93311-2020, SAN 331-4839. Tel: 661-664-7716. Reference Tel: 661-665-1258. FAX: 661-664-7717. *Br Supvr,* Sherry Wade
Founded 1981. Pop 169,671; Circ 317,917
Library Holdings: Bk Vols 79,939
Open Tues-Thurs 11-7, Fri & Sat 9-5
Friends of the Library Group
TAFT BRANCH, 27 Cougar Ct, Taft, 93268-2327, SAN 331-4820. Tel: 661-763-3294. FAX: 661-763-1237. *Br Supvr,* Catherine Edgecomb; E-mail: catherine.edgecomb@kerncountylibrary.org
Founded 1912. Pop 23,542; Circ 31,510
Library Holdings: Bk Vols 34,352
Open Tues-Thurs 11-7, Sat 9-5
Friends of the Library Group
TEHACHAPI BRANCH, 1001 W Tehachapi Blvd, Ste A-400, Tehachapi, 93561-2551, SAN 331-4782. Tel: 661-822-4938. FAX: 661-823-8406. *Br Supvr,* Jacob Cairns
Founded 1912. Pop 34,142; Circ 121,421
Library Holdings: Bk Vols 37,000
Open Mon & Wed 11-7, Fri & Sat 9-5
Friends of the Library Group
WASCO BRANCH, 1102 Seventh St, Wasco, 93280-1801, SAN 331-4804. Tel: 661-758-2114. *Br Supvr,* Ernestina Garcia
Founded 1912. Pop 29,931; Circ 23,109
Library Holdings: Bk Vols 26,289

Open Mon, Wed & Fri 10-6
Friends of the Library Group
ELEANOR N WILSON BRANCH, 1901 Wilson Rd, 93304-5612, SAN 331-4790. Tel: 661-834-4044. *Br Supvr,* Taarna Long
Founded 1970. Pop 94,010; Circ 55,288
Library Holdings: Bk Vols 35,424
Open Mon & Wed 11-7, Fri 9-5
Friends of the Library Group
WOFFORD HEIGHTS BRANCH, 6400-B Wofford Blvd, Wofford Heights, 93285. (Mail add: PO Box 1285, Wofford Heights, 93285-1285), SAN 331-4812. Tel: 760-376-6160. *Br Supvr,* Nancy Moore
Founded 1953. Pop 2,721; Circ 17,927
Library Holdings: Bk Vols 8,101
Open Mon & Wed 10-6, Fri 9-5
Friends of the Library Group
Bookmobiles: 2. In Charge, Mary White & Peggy Hickey. Bk vols 7,844

S KERN COUNTY MUSEUM, Historical Reference Library, 3801 Chester Ave, 93301-1395. SAN 300-5925. Tel: 661-868-8400. FAX: 661-322-6415. E-mail: info@kerncountymuseum.org. Web Site: www.kcmuseum.org. *Chief Curator,* Lori Wear; E-mail: wearl@kerncountymuseum.org; Staff 1 (Non-MLS 1)
Founded 1941
Library Holdings: Bk Vols 2,500
Special Collections: Archives; City Directories; Photographs; Product Catalogs; Reference Books
Subject Interests: Archaeology, Calif hist, Local hist, Museology
Restriction: Not a lending libr, Open by appt only, Open to researchers by request

M KERN MEDICAL CENTER*, Health Sciences Library, 1700 Mt Vernon Ave, 93306. SAN 300-5933. Tel: 661-326-2227. FAX: 661-862-7654. *In Charge,* Lalaine Garin
Founded 1945
Jul 2005-Jun 2006. Mats Exp $115,000, Books $10,000, Per/Ser (Incl. Access Fees) $85,000, Electronic Ref Mat (Incl. Access Fees) $13,000, Presv $6,000
Library Holdings: Bk Vols 3,000; Per Subs 205
Database Vendor: EBSCOhost
Partic in Medical Library Association (MLA); Medical Library Group of Southern California & Arizona (MLGSCA); National Network of Libraries of Medicine
Open Mon-Fri 8-5

M MERCY HEALTHCARE*, Medical Library, 2215 Truxtun Ave, 93301-3602. (Mail add: PO Box 119, 93302-0119), SAN 323-598X. Tel: 661-632-5231. Web Site: www.mercybakersfield.org.
Library Holdings: Bk Titles 156; Bk Vols 200
Subject Interests: Oncology
Friends of the Library Group

BANNING

P BANNING LIBRARY DISTRICT*, 21 W Nicolet St, 92220. Tel: 951-849-3192. E-mail: bld@banninglibrarydistrict.org. Web Site: www.banninglibrarydistrict.org. *Dir,* Robert Lippman; *Ch,* Andres Calderon; *Tech Serv,* Fernando Morales; E-mail: fernandom@banninglibrarydistrict.org
Pop 26,400; Circ 116,088
Library Holdings: AV Mats 5,420; Bk Vols 72,292; Per Subs 138
Mem of Inland Library System
Open Mon-Wed 9-6, Thurs 10-7, Fri 10-5, Sat 10-3

M SAN GORGONIO MEMORIAL HOSPITAL*, Medical Library, 600 N Highland Springs Ave, 92220. SAN 327-5930. Tel: 951-845-1121, Ext 6226. FAX: 951-845-2836.
Library Holdings: Bk Vols 151
Restriction: Staff use only

BARSTOW

J BARSTOW COLLEGE*, Thomas Kimball Library, 2700 Barstow Rd, 92311. SAN 300-595X. Tel: 760-252-2411, Ext 7270. FAX: 760-252-6725. Web Site: www.barstow.edu/lrc/library/default.asp. *Librn,* Kyri A Freeman; E-mail: kfreeman@barstow.edu; Staff 1 (MLS 1)
Founded 1960
Library Holdings: Bk Vols 41,000
Subject Interests: Am Civil War, Desert ecology, Native Am studies
Automation Activity & Vendor Info: (Acquisitions) Ex Libris Group; (Cataloging) Ex Libris Group; (Course Reserve) Ex Libris Group; (OPAC) Ex Libris Group; (Serials) Ex Libris Group
Database Vendor: EBSCOhost
Wireless access
Function: Archival coll, Art exhibits, Audio & video playback equip for onsite use, AV serv, Copy machines, Digital talking bks, Distance learning, Electronic databases & coll, Games & aids for the handicapped, Handicapped accessible, Mail & tel request accepted, Music CDs, Online ref, Online searches, Orientations, Outside serv via phone, mail, e-mail & web, Photocopying/Printing, Ref serv available, Spoken cassettes & CDs, Spoken cassettes & DVDs, Tax forms, Telephone ref, VHS videos, Wheelchair accessible
Open Mon-Thurs (Summer) 8-5; Mon-Thurs (Winter) 8-8, Fri 8-4

BEALE AFB

A UNITED STATES AIR FORCE*, Beale Air Force Base Library FL4686, Nine SVS/SVMG, 17849 16th St, Bldg 25219, 95903-1611. SAN 331-4944. Tel: 530-634-2314. FAX: 530-634-2032. *Dir,* Bonnie Williams
Library Holdings: Bk Vols 44,000; Per Subs 150
Special Collections: Aeronautics & California Coll
Open Mon-Thurs 10-8, Fri 10-3, Sat & Sun 12-5

BEAUMONT

P BEAUMONT LIBRARY DISTRICT*, 125 E Eighth St, 92223-2194. SAN 300-5968. Tel: 951-845-1357. FAX: 951-845-6217. E-mail: beaumontlib@telis.org. Web Site: www.bld.lib.ca.us. *Dir,* Clara DiFelice; *Young Reader's Serv,* Janelle Ramsay; Staff 8 (MLS 7, Non-MLS 1)
Founded 1911. Pop 52,500; Circ 180,000
Jul 2009-Jun 2010 Income $1,200,000. Mats Exp $132,000, Books $100,000, Per/Ser (Incl. Access Fees) $2,500, AV Mat $25,000, Electronic Ref Mat (Incl. Access Fees) $4,500
Library Holdings: Audiobooks 702; DVDs 5,300; Large Print Bks 3,840; Bk Vols 60,000; Per Subs 65; Videos 570
Automation Activity & Vendor Info: (Cataloging) TLC (The Library Corporation); (Circulation) TLC (The Library Corporation); (OPAC) TLC (The Library Corporation)
Database Vendor: EBSCOhost
Wireless access
Mem of Inland Library System
Partic in OCLC Online Computer Library Center, Inc
Open Mon, Wed, Fri & Sat 10-6, Tues & Thurs 10-8, Sun 1-6
Friends of the Library Group

BELLFLOWER

M KAISER-PERMANENTE MEDICAL CENTER*, Health Sciences Library & Media Center, 9400 E Rosecrans Ave, 90706. SAN 300-5984. Tel: 562-461-4247. FAX: 562-461-4948. *Dir,* Cindy Runnels
Founded 1965
Library Holdings: Bk Vols 8,720; Per Subs 500
Subject Interests: Hospital admin, Med, Nursing
Partic in San Bernardino, Inyo, Riverside Counties United Library Services

BELMONT

C NOTRE DAME DE NAMUR UNIVERSITY LIBRARY, The Carl Gellert & Celia Berta Gellert Library, 1500 Ralston Ave, 94002-1908. SAN 300-5992. Tel: 650-508-3748. Interlibrary Loan Service Tel: 650-508-3747. Administration Tel: 650-508-3745. FAX: 650-508-3697. E-mail: library@ndnu.edu. Web Site: www.ndnu.edu/Gellertlibrary. *Dir,* Mary Wegmann; E-mail: mwegmann@ndnu.edu; *Acq of Monographs, Cat,* Hai Huynh; Tel: 650-508-3486, E-mail: hhuynh@cnd.edu; *Circ,* Patricia Medina; Staff 8 (MLS 4.5, Non-MLS 3.5)
Founded 1922. Enrl 1,600; Fac 104; Highest Degree: Master
Jul 2005-Jun 2006 Income $571,494. Mats Exp $156,278. Sal $406,403 (Prof $291,319)
Library Holdings: e-journals 10,000; Bk Vols 90,702; Per Subs 500; Videos 1,461
Special Collections: California Coll
Automation Activity & Vendor Info: (Cataloging) Auto-Graphics, Inc; (Circulation) Auto-Graphics, Inc; (OPAC) Auto-Graphics, Inc
Database Vendor: CQ Press, EBSCOhost, Elsevier MDL, Gale Cengage Learning, Hoovers, OCLC FirstSearch, ProQuest, ScienceDirect, Wilson - Wilson Web
Wireless access
Partic in CAL/PALS; Statewide California Electronic Library Consortium (SCELC)
Open Mon-Thurs 8am-11pm, Fri 8-4, Sat 10-6, Sun 12-9

BENICIA

P BENICIA PUBLIC LIBRARY*, 150 East L St, 94510-3281. SAN 300-6018. Tel: 707-746-4343. FAX: 707-747-8122. Web Site: www.BeniciaLibrary.org. *Dir,* Diane Smikahl; E-mail: dsmikahl@ci.benicia.ca.us; *Head, Ch,* Allison Angell; E-mail: aangell@ci.benicia.ca.us; *Head, Pub Serv,* Fran Martinez-Coyne; E-mail: fmartinezcoyne@ci.benicia.ca.us; *Head, Tech Serv,* Daveta Cooper; Tel: 707-746-4347, E-mail: dcooper@ci.benicia.ca.us; Staff 52 (MLS 6, Non-MLS 46)
Founded 1911. Pop 28,086; Circ 384,056

Jul 2010-Jun 2011 Income $2,154,130, State $125,520, City $1,210,570, Locally Generated Income $688,010, Other $130,030. Mats Exp $146,860, Books $88,904, Per/Ser (Incl. Access Fees) $7,511, AV Equip $8,430, AV Mat $31,814, Electronic Ref Mat (Incl. Access Fees) $10,201. Sal $1,230,455
Library Holdings: AV Mats 7,783; DVDs 5,068; e-books 11,988; Electronic Media & Resources 25; Bk Titles 89,803; Bk Vols 95,888; Per Subs 159
Special Collections: California Coll; Local Newspaper (1899-present). Oral History
Subject Interests: Local hist
Automation Activity & Vendor Info: (Cataloging) CARL.Solution (TLC); (Circulation) CARL.Solution (TLC); (ILL) OCLC Online; (OPAC) CARL.Solution (TLC)
Database Vendor: TLC (The Library Corporation)
Wireless access
Function: Homebound delivery serv, ILL available
Mem of NorthNet Library System
Partic in Solano Napa & Partners Library Consortium (SNAP)
Open Mon-Thurs 10-9, Fri-Sun 12-6
Restriction: Access for corporate affiliates
Friends of the Library Group

BERKELEY

M BAYER HEALTHCARE*, Berkeley Library & Information Services, 800 Dwight Way, 94701. SAN 300-6107. Tel: 510-705-5000.
Founded 1948
Library Holdings: e-journals 3,000; Bk Vols 28,795
Subject Interests: Pharmaceutical sci
Automation Activity & Vendor Info: (Cataloging) OCLC; (ILL) OCLC; (OPAC) Ex Libris Group; (Serials) EBSCO Online
Database Vendor: Dialog, STN International
Publications: Acquisitions List (Quarterly); Current Awareness Biological (weekly); Periodical Holdings List
Restriction: Co libr, Not open to pub

J BERKELEY CITY COLLEGE LIBRARY*, 2050 Center St, Rm 131, 94704. SAN 323-5726. Circulation Tel: 510-981-2824. *Librn,* Joshua Boatright; Tel: 510-981-2991, E-mail: jboatright@peralta.edu; *Librn,* Fred Cisin; Tel: 510-981-2964, E-mail: fcisin@peralta.edu; Staff 2 (MLS 2)
Enrl 5,000
Library Holdings: Bk Vols 7,000; Per Subs 33
Open Mon-Thurs (Sept-May) 8:30-7:30, Fri 8:30-4; Mon-Fri (June-Aug) 8:45-5

P BERKELEY PUBLIC LIBRARY*, 2090 Kittredge St, 94704-1427. SAN 331-5428. Tel: 510-981-6100. Circulation Tel: 510-981-6203. Reference Tel: 510-981-6148. Administration Tel: 510-981-6195. FAX: 510-981-6111. Reference FAX: 510-981-6219. TDD: 510-548-1240. Web Site: www.berkeleypubliclibrary.org. *Dir of Libr Serv,* Position Currently Open; *Dep Dir,* Suzanne Olawski; Staff 71 (MLS 71)
Founded 1893. Pop 102,743; Circ 1,541,221
Library Holdings: Bk Vols 446,703; Per Subs 1,524
Special Collections: Swingle Coll of Berkeley History, bks, maps, oral hist, pamphlets, photog, misc; World War I & World War II Poster Coll
Subject Interests: Art & archit, Civil rights, Ethnic studies, Feminism, Music
Automation Activity & Vendor Info: (Circulation) Innovative Interfaces, Inc; (OPAC) Innovative Interfaces, Inc
Database Vendor: Innovative Interfaces, Inc
Wireless access
Mem of Bay Area Library & Information System
Special Services for the Deaf - TDD equip
Special Services for the Blind - Reader equip
Open Mon 12-8, Tues 10-8, Wed-Sat 10-6, Sun 1-5
Friends of the Library Group
Branches: 2
CLAREMONT BRANCH, 2940 Benvenue Ave, 94705, SAN 331-5452. Tel: 510-981-6280. FAX: 510-843-1603. *Br Supvr,* Shani Leonards
Founded 1924. Circ 139,672
Library Holdings: Bk Vols 49,236
Open Mon, Tues, Fri & Sat 10-6, Wed & Thurs 12-8
Friends of the Library Group
NORTH BRANCH, 1170 The Alameda, 94707, SAN 331-5487. Tel: 510-981-6250. FAX: 510-528-8975. *Br Mgr,* Marge Sussman; Staff 17 (MLS 4, Non-MLS 13)
Founded 1936. Circ 235,556
Library Holdings: Bk Vols 45,807
Open Mon, Tues, Fri & Sat 10-6, Wed & Thurs 12-8
Friends of the Library Group

CR GRADUATE THEOLOGICAL UNION LIBRARY*, Flora Lamson Hewlett Library, 2400 Ridge Rd, 94709-1212. SAN 331-5630. Tel: 510-649-2500. Interlibrary Loan Service Tel: 510-649-2502. Reference Tel: 510-649-2501. FAX: 510-649-2508. E-mail: library@gtu.edu. Web Site: www.gtu.edu/library. *Libr Dir,* Robert Benedetto; Tel: 510-649-2540, E-mail: rbenedetto@gtu.edu; *Head, Cat,* Melodie Frances; Tel: 510-649-2521, E-mail: mfrances@gtu.edu; *Head, Coll Develop,* Clay-Edward Dixon; Tel: 510-649-2509, E-mail: cedixon@gtu.edu; *Ref Librn,* Phillippa Caldeira; E-mail: pcaldeira@gtu.edu; *Conservator,* Bonnie Jo Cullison; Tel: 510-649-2527, E-mail: bcullison@gtu.edu; *Spec Coll,* David Stiver; Tel: 510-649-2523, E-mail: dstiver@gtu.edu; Staff 16 (MLS 7, Non-MLS 9)
Founded 1969. Enrl 1,100; Fac 110; Highest Degree: Doctorate
Jul 2008-Jun 2009. Mats Exp $554,517, Books $348,651, Per/Ser (Incl. Access Fees) $136,193, AV Mat $1,287, Electronic Ref Mat (Incl. Access Fees) $43,534, Presv $24,852. Sal $745,080 (Prof $542,391)
Library Holdings: AV Mats 294,910; CDs 1,000; DVDs 637; Electronic Media & Resources 54; Bk Vols 494,364; Per Subs 1,512; Videos 1,237
Special Collections: Archival Collections with emphasis in the area of Ecumenical & Inter-Religious Activity in the Western United States & Pacific Rim; Institutional Record of the Graduate Theological Union; Manuscript Coll; New Religious Movements Research Coll; Rare Book Coll, bks, pamphlets
Subject Interests: Biblical studies, Christianity, Relig, Theol, World relig
Automation Activity & Vendor Info: (Acquisitions) Innovative Interfaces, Inc; (Cataloging) Innovative Interfaces, Inc; (Circulation) Innovative Interfaces, Inc; (Course Reserve) Innovative Interfaces, Inc; (ILL) OCLC Connexion; (OPAC) Innovative Interfaces, Inc; (Serials) Innovative Interfaces, Inc
Database Vendor: OCLC FirstSearch, OVID Technologies, ProQuest, Wilson - Wilson Web
Wireless access
Function: e-mail serv, Electronic databases & coll, Exhibits, Free DVD rentals, Handicapped accessible, ILL available, Instruction & testing, Music CDs, Online cat, Online ref, Orientations, Outside serv via phone, mail, e-mail & web, Photocopying/Printing, Pub access computers, Ref serv available, Ref serv in person, Telephone ref, VCDs, VHS videos, Workshops
Partic in Statewide California Electronic Library Consortium (SCELC)
Special Services for the Blind - Reader equip
Open Mon-Thurs 8:30am-10pm, Fri 8:30-6, Sat 10-6, Sun 12-7; Mon, Tues & Fri (Summer) 8:30-5, Wed & Thurs 8:30-7, Sat 11-6
Friends of the Library Group

C INSTITUTE OF TRANSPORTATION STUDIES LIBRARY*, Harmer E Davis Transportation Library, 412 McLaughlin Hall, MC 1720, 94720-1720. SAN 331-7013. Tel: 510-642-3604. FAX: 510-642-9180. E-mail: itslib@.berkeley.edu. Web Site: library.its.berkeley.edu. *Dir,* Rita Evans; Tel: 510-643-3564, E-mail: revans@library.berkeley.edu; *Ref Librn,* Kendra Levine; E-mail: klevine@library.berkeley.edu
Founded 1948
Library Holdings: Bk Vols 149,426
Automation Activity & Vendor Info: (Acquisitions) Innovative Interfaces, Inc - Millenium; (Cataloging) OCLC Connexion; (Circulation) Innovative Interfaces, Inc - Millenium; (Course Reserve) Innovative Interfaces, Inc - Millenium; (OPAC) Innovative Interfaces, Inc
Wireless access
Partic in OCLC Online Computer Library Center, Inc
Open Mon-Fri 1-5

SR SWEDENBORGIAN LIBRARY & ARCHIVES, 1798 Scenic Ave, 94709. SAN 307-5672. Tel: 510-849-8228, 510-849-8248. FAX: 510-849-8296. Web Site: www.shs.psr.edu.
Founded 1866
Library Holdings: Bk Vols 24,000; Per Subs 15
Special Collections: Emanuel Swedenborg Coll; New Church Coll; New Jerusalem Church Coll; Swedenborgian Church Coll
Subject Interests: New church hist, Theol
Function: Archival coll, Ref serv available
Restriction: Non-circulating to the pub, Open by appt only

S UNIVERSITY OF CALIFORNIA-BERKELEY*, Institute of Govermental Studies, 109 Moses Hall, IGS-UC Berkeley, 94720. Tel: 510-642-1472. FAX: 510-643-0866. Web Site: www.igs.berkeley.edu. *Dir, Libr Serv,* Nick Robinson
Library Holdings: Bk Vols 400,000; Per Subs 1,100
Automation Activity & Vendor Info: (Cataloging) OCLC; (Serials) OCLC
Open Mon-Fri 9-5
Restriction: Restricted pub use

C UNIVERSITY OF CALIFORNIA, BERKELEY*, 255 Doe Library, 94720-6000. SAN 331-6025. Tel: 510-642-6657. Circulation Tel: 510-643-4331. Interlibrary Loan Service Tel: 510-642-7365. FAX: 510-643-8179. Interlibrary Loan Service FAX: 510-643-8476. Web Site: www.lib.berkeley.edu. *Univ Librn,* Thomas C Leonard; *Assoc Univ Librn,* Elizabeth Dupuis

Founded 1871. Enrl 32,000; Fac 1,482; Highest Degree: Doctorate
Library Holdings: Bk Vols 10,000,000; Per Subs 89,750
Special Collections: Letters, Literary Manuscripts & Scrapbooks of Samuel Clemens (Mark Twain Coll); Music History, bks, mss, scores; Radio Carbon Date Cards, Photographic Plates, Rubbings, University Archive Photographs, Aerial Photographs, VF mat; Recollections of Persons Who Have Contributed to the Development of the West (Regional Oral History Office). State Document Depository; UN Document Depository; US Document Depository
Publications: A Program for the Conservation & Preservation of Library Materials in the General Library; Bene Legere Newsletter for Library Associates; Bibliographic Guides to Research Resources in Selected Subjects; Collection Development Policy Statement; Faculty Newsletter (Quarterly); Orientation Leaflets; Titles Classified by the Library of Congress Classification: National Shelflist Count
Partic in Association of Research Libraries (ARL); BRS; Dialog Corp; OCLC Online Computer Library Center, Inc; OCLC Research Library Partnership; RLIN (Research Libraries Information Network); Westlaw; Wilsonline
Special Services for the Deaf - TDD equip
Special Services for the Blind - Blind students ctr; Reader equip; Rental typewriters & computers
Friends of the Library Group

Departmental Libraries:

ART HISTORY/CLASSICS, 308 Doe Library, 94720-6000, SAN 331-684X. Tel: 510-642-7361. Reference Tel: 510-642-5358. FAX: 510-643-2185. Web Site: www.lib.berkeley.edu/arth. *Fine Arts Librn,* Kathryn Wayne

BANCROFT LIBRARY, 94720-6000. Tel: 510-642-3781. FAX: 510-642-7589. E-mail: bancref@library.berkeley.edu. Web Site: bancroft.berkeley.edu. *Dir,* Elaine C Tennant
Library Holdings: Bk Vols 600,000
Special Collections: Fine Printing Coll; History of Science & Technology (Rare Books Coll); History of Western North America, especially California & Mexico (Bancroft Coll), bks, ms; Humanities Coll; Mark Twain Coll, bks, ms; Modern Poetry Coll; North & Central America Coll; Rare Imprints of Western Europe; University Archives. Oral History
Open Mon-Fri 10-5
Friends of the Library Group

CATALOGING & METADATA SERVICES, 250 Moffit Library, 94720-6000, SAN 320-944X. Tel: 510-643-2038. FAX: 510-642-4956. *Head, Cat & Metadata Serv,* Lisa Rowlison de Ortiz; E-mail: lrowliso@library.berkeley.edu

CHEMISTRY, 100 Hildebrand Hall, 94720-6000, SAN 331-6718. Tel: 510-642-3753. E-mail: chem@library.berkeley.edu. Web Site: www.lib.berkeley.edu/chem. *Operations Mgr,* Agnes Concepcion; Tel: 510-643-4477, E-mail: aconcepc@library.berkeley.edu
Library Holdings: e journals 700; Bk Vols 70,000
Open Mon-Fri 9-5

EARTH SCIENCES & MAPS, 50 McCone Hall, 94720-6000, SAN 331-6742. Tel: 510-642-2997. E-mail: eart@library.berkeley.edu. Web Site: www.lib.berkeley.edu/eart. *Actg Dir,* Brian Quigley; Staff 6 (MLS 1, Non MLS 5)
Library Holdings: Bk Vols 118,228; Per Subs 2,000
Automation Activity & Vendor Info: (Acquisitions) Innovative Interfaces, Inc; (Serials) Innovative Interfaces, Inc
Database Vendor: OCLC FirstSearch

EDUCATION PSYCHOLOGY, 2600 Tolman Hall, 94720-6000, SAN 331-6203. Tel: 510-642-4209. Reference Tel: 510-642-2475. FAX: 510-642-8224. Web Site: lib.berkeley.edu/edp. *Head, Educ & Psychol Libr,* Susan Edwards; E-mail: sedwards@library.berkeley.edu; *Head, Circ,* Brian Light; E-mail: blight@library.berkeley.edu; *Librn,* Margaret L Phillips; E-mail: mphillip@library.berkeley.edu; Staff 5 (MLS 2, Non-MLS 3)
Highest Degree: Doctorate
Library Holdings: Bk Vols 185,000; Per Subs 802
Open Mon-Thurs 9-9, Fri 9-5, Sat & Sun 1-5

ENVIRONMENTAL DESIGN, 210 Wurster Hall, 94720-6000, SAN 331-6238. Tel: 510-642-4818. Reference Tel: 510-643-7421. Web Site: www.lib.berkeley.edu/ENVI. *Interim Head Librn,* David Eifler; Tel: 510-643-7422, E-mail: deifler@library.berkeley.edu; *Operations Mgr,* Dori Hsiao; Tel: 510-643-7220, E-mail: dori.hsiao@berkeley.edu; Staff 5.3 (MLS 2.3, Non-MLS 3)
Founded 1903. Enrl 1,010; Fac 84; Highest Degree: Doctorate
Library Holdings: Bk Vols 210,000; Per Subs 500; Spec Interest Per Sub 750
Special Collections: Beatrix Farrand Rare Books
Subject Interests: Archit, City planning, Landscape archit
Function: Doc delivery serv, Electronic databases & coll, Handicapped accessible, ILL available, Online cat, Online info literacy tutorials on the web & in blackboard, Photocopying/Printing, Ref serv available, Wheelchair accessible
Restriction: Borrowing privileges limited to fac & registered students, In-house use for visitors, Non-circulating of rare bks, Off-site coll in storage - retrieval as requested

ETHNIC STUDIES, 30 Stephens Hall, MC 2360, 94720-2360, SAN 376-9518. Tel: 510-643-1234. FAX: 510-643-8433. E-mail: esl@library.berkeley.edu. Web Site: eslibrary.berkeley.edu. *Head Librn,* Lillian Castillo-Speed; Tel: 510-642-3947, E-mail: csl@library.berkeley.edu; Staff 5 (MLS 3, Non-MLS 2)
Special Collections: AAS Archives; AAS Special Coll; Asian American Studies; CS A/V; CS Archives; CS Locked Case; NAS California Coll & NAS A/V Coll
Subject Interests: Chicano studies, Ethnic studies, Native Am studies

GEORGE & MARY FOSTER ANTHROPOLOGY LIBRARY, 230 Kroeber Hall, 94720-3710, SAN 331-6173. Tel: 510-642-2400. FAX: 510-643-9293. *Interim Head Librn,* Hilary Schiraldi; E-mail: hschiral@library.berkeley.edu; *Operations Mgr,* Lillian Lee; Tel: 510-642-2419, E-mail: llee@library.berkeley.edu
Library Holdings: Bk Vols 93,000
Open Mon-Fri 10-5

GIANNINI FOUNDATION LIBRARY, 248 Giannini Hall, 94720-3310, SAN 331-6890. Tel: 510-642-7121. FAX: 510-643-8911. E-mail: gflibrary@berkeley.edu. Web Site: are.berkeley.edu/library. *Libr Asst,* Jeffrey Cole; Staff 3 (MLS 1, Non-MLS 2)
Founded 1930. Fac 30; Highest Degree: Doctorate
Library Holdings: Bk Vols 200,000
Special Collections: Federal-State market reports on microfilm form 1900 to 1982
Subject Interests: Natural res
Automation Activity & Vendor Info: (Cataloging) Inmagic, Inc.
Restriction: Staff use, pub by appt

JEAN GRAY HARGROVE MUSIC LIBRARY, Hargrove Music Library, 94720-6000, SAN 331-6297. Tel: 510-642-2623. Reference Tel: 510-642-2624. FAX: 510-642-8237. Web Site: www.lib.berkeley.edu/musi. *Head Music Libr,* John Shepard; *Asst Head, Music Libr,* Manuel Erviti; Tel: 510-642-6197, E-mail: merviti@library.berkeley.edu; *Circ Supvr,* Angela Arnold; Tel: 510-643-6196, E-mail: musicirc@library.berkeley.edu; *Acq & Ser,* Allison Rea; Tel: 510-643-6198, E-mail: area@library.berkeley.edu
Library Holdings: Bk Vols 165,326

INSTITUTE FOR RESEARCH ON LABOR & EMPLOYMENT LIBRARY, 2521 Channing Way, MC 5555, 94720-5555, SAN 331-6955. Tel: 510-642-1705. FAX: 510-642-6432. E-mail: iirl@library.berkeley.edu. Web Site: www.irle.berkeley.edu/library. *Dir, Libr & Info Res,* Terence K Huwe; E-mail: thuwe@library.berkeley.edu
Founded 1945. Enrl 30,000; Fac 65; Highest Degree: Doctorate
Library Holdings: Bk Vols 45,000

INSTITUTE OF GOVERNMENTAL STUDIES, 109 Moses Hall, Ground flr, 94720-2370, SAN 331-6920. Tel: 510-642-1472. FAX. 510-642-3020. E-mail: igsl@berkeley.edu. Web Site: www.igs.berkeley.edu/library. *Dir,* Nick Robinson; *Digital Serv Librn,* Julie Lefevre
Library Holdings: Bk Vols 400,000

INSTRUCTION & USER SERVICES, 302 Moffitt Library, 94720-6000, SAN 331-6114. Tel: 510-643-9959. FAX. 510-642-9454. *Head, Instruction & User Serv,* Jennifer Dorner; Tel: 510-768-7059, E-mail: jdorner@library.berkeley.edu

MARIAN KOSHLAND BIOSCIENCE & NATURAL RESOURCES LIBRARY, 2101 Valley Life Science Bldg, No 6500, 94720-6500, SAN 331-6475. Tel: 510-642-2531. Web Site: www.lib.berkeley.edu/bios/. *Interim Head Librn,* Susan Koskinen; Staff 4 (MLS 4)
Library Holdings: Bk Vols 500,000; Per Subs 6,500

KRESGE ENGINEERING LIBRARY, 110 Bechtel Engineering Ctr, 94720-1796, SAN 331-6777. Tel: 510-642-3366. FAX: 510-643-6771. Web Site: www.lib.berkeley.edu/engi. *Actg Dir,* Brian Quigley; Staff 3 (MLS 3)
Library Holdings: Bk Vols 236,257; Per Subs 1,804
Subject Interests: Eng

CL LAW, School of Law, Boalt Hall, 94720-7210, SAN 331-7072. Tel: 510-642-0621. FAX: 510-643-5039. Web Site: www.law.berkeley.edu/library. *Dir,* Kathleen Vanden Heuvel; E-mail: kvandenh@law.berkeley.edu; *Sr Ref & Coll Develop Librn,* Lucia Diamond; E-mail: diamondl@law.berkeley.edu; *Ref Librn,* Jennifer K Nelson; E-mail: jnelson@law.berkeley.edu; *Ref,* Marlene Harmon; E-mail: mharmon@law.berkeley.edu
Founded 1912. Highest Degree: Doctorate
Special Collections: Anglo-American, Foreign & International Law Research Coll; Canon, Medieval & Roman Law Coll
Partic in RLIN (Research Libraries Information Network); Westlaw
Publications: Acquisitions list

THOMAS J LONG BUSINESS LIBRARY, Haas School of Business, Rm S350, 2220 Piedmont Ave, 94720-1990, SAN 331-6327. Tel: 510-642-0370. Interlibrary Loan Service Tel: 510-642-7367. Reference Tel: 510-642-0400. FAX: 510-643-5277. Reference FAX: 510-643-8476. Web Site: www.lib.berkeley.edu/BUSI. *Head Librn,* Hilary Schiraldi;

E-mail: hschiral@library.berkeley.edu; *Ref & Instruction Librn,* Lydia Petersen; E-mail: lpeterse@library.berkeley.edu
Library Holdings: Bk Vols 159,000
Subject Interests: Bus admin, Econ

SHELDON MARGEN PUBLIC HEALTH LIBRARY, One University Hall, No 7360, 94720-7360, SAN 331-6629. Tel: 510-642-2511. FAX: 510-642-7623. E-mail: publ@library.berkeley.edu. Web Site: www.lib.berkeley.edu/publ. *Head of Libr,* Deborah Jan; Staff 11 (MLS 5, Non-MLS 6)
Founded 1955
Library Holdings: Bk Vols 104,000
Open Mon-Thurs 9-8, Fri 9-5, Sat & Sun 1-5

MATHEMATICS-STATISTICS, 100 Evans Hall, No 6000, 94720-6000, SAN 331-6688. Tel: 510-642-3381. FAX: 510-642-8257. E-mail: math@library.berkeley.edu. Web Site: www.lib.berkeley.edu/math. *Head Librn,* Brian Quigley; E-mail: bquigley@library.berkeley.edu
Library Holdings: Bk Vols 85,205

OPTOMETRY & HEALTH SCIENCES LIBRARY, 490 Minor Hall, 94720-2020, SAN 331-6599. Tel: 510-642-1020. FAX: 510-643-8600. Web Site: www.lib.berkeley.edu/opto. *Actg Head, Ref & Selector Librn,* Susan Koskinen; Staff 4 (MLS 1, Non-MLS 3)
Founded 1949. Highest Degree: Doctorate
Library Holdings: Bk Vols 15,000
Subject Interests: Med, Ophthalmology, Optometry, Vision sci
Partic in Association of Vision Science Librarians (AVSL)
Open Mon-Fri 9-5

PACIFIC EARTHQUAKE ENGINEERING RESEARCH (PEER) CENTER LIBRARY - NISEE, UCB-RFS Bldg 453, 1301 S 46th St, Richmond, 94804, SAN 331-6912. Tel: 510-665-3419. E-mail: nisee@berkeley.edu. Web Site: nisee2.berkeley.edu. *Info Syst Mgr,* Charles James
Founded 1972
Library Holdings: Bk Vols 56,000
Special Collections: Godden International Structural Slide Library; Kovak Historical Image Coll; Steinbrugge Image Coll
Subject Interests: Earthquakes, Eng, Geotech eng, Seismology, Structural eng
Database Vendor: OCLC FirstSearch
Open Mon-Fri 9-5

PHILOSOPHY, 305 Moses Hall, 94720, SAN 331-7021. Tel: 510-642-2722. *In Charge,* Jan Carter
Library Holdings: Bk Vols 10,000; Per Subs 60
Restriction: Non-circulating coll

PHYSICS-ASTRONOMY LIBRARY, 351 LeConte Hall, 94720-6000, SAN 331-6807. Tel: 510-642-3122. FAX: 510-642-8350. Web Site: www.lib.berkeley.edu/phys. *Head Librn,* Samantha Teplitzky
Library Holdings: Bk Vols 48,321

SOCIAL WELFARE, 227 Haviland Hall, 94720-6000, SAN 331-6351. Tel: 510-642-4432. FAX: 510-643-1476. Web Site: www.lib.berkeley.edu/socw. *Head of Libr,* Susan Edwards; E-mail: sedwards@library.berkeley.edu; *Operations Mgr,* Craig Alderson; E-mail: calderso@library.berkeley.edu
Library Holdings: Bk Vols 33,000; Per Subs 200

SOUTH-SOUTHEAST ASIA LIBRARY, 120 Doe Library, 94720-6000, SAN 331-6831. Tel: 510-642-3095. FAX: 510-643-8817. Web Site: www.lib.berkeley.edu/SSEAL. *Librn,* Virginia Jing-yi Shih; Tel: 510-643-0850, E-mail: vshih@library.berkeley.edu
Library Holdings: Bk Vols 400,000

C V STARR EAST ASIAN LIBRARY, 94720-6000, SAN 331-6084. Tel: 510-642-2556. FAX: 510-642-3817. E-mail: eal@library.berkeley.edu. Web Site: www.lib.berkeley.edu/eal. *Dir,* Peter Zhou; Tel: 510-643-6579, E-mail: pzhou@library.berkeley.edu
Library Holdings: Bk Vols 900,000
Open Mon-Thurs 9-9, Fri 9-5, Sat 10-5, Sun 12-5

S WRIGHT INSTITUTE LIBRARY*, 2728 Durant Ave, 94704. SAN 323-4649. Tel: 510-841-9230, Ext 121. FAX: 510-841-0167. Web Site: www.wrightinst.edu. *Dir of Libr Serv,* Jason Strauss; Tel: 510-841-9230, Ext 140, E-mail: jstrauss@wi.edu; *Librn,* Lona French
Library Holdings: Bk Titles 10,000; Per Subs 115
Subject Interests: Psychol
Open Mon-Fri 8:30-5, Sat 9-4:30

BEVERLY HILLS

S ACADEMY OF MOTION PICTURE ARTS & SCIENCES*, Margaret Herrick Library, 333 S La Cienega Blvd, 90211. SAN 300-6212. Tel: 310-247-3000. Reference Tel: 310-247-3020. FAX: 310-657-5193. Web Site: www.oscars.org. *Libr Dir,* Linda Harris Mehr; Tel: 310-247-3000, Ext 2201, E-mail: lmehr@oscars.org; *Head, Ref Serv,* Sandra Archer; Tel: 310-247-3000, Ext 2205; *Acq Librn,* Susan Oka; Tel: 310-247-3000, Ext 2216; *Graphic Arts Librn,* Anne Coco; Tel: 310-247-3000, Ext 2274; *Librn/Acad Files,* Libby Wertin; Tel: 310-247-3000, Ext 2208; *Librn/Scripts/Festivals & Awards,* Greg Walsh; Tel: 310-247-3000, Ext 2209; *Syst Librn,* Zoe Friedlander; Tel: 310-247-3000, Ext 2239; *Info Syst Coordr,* Vionnette Dover Sellers; Tel: 310-247-3000, Ext 2299; *Photographic Serv Adminr,* Matthew Severson; Tel: 310-247-3000, Ext 2227; *Acq Archivist,* Howard Prouty; Tel: 310-247-3000, Ext 2225; *Coll Archivist,* Val Almendarez; Tel: 310-247-3000, Ext 2224; *Res Archivist,* Barbara Hall; Tel: 310-247-3000, Ext 2218; *Monographs Cataloger,* Don Lee; Tel: 310-247-3000, Ext 2207; *Ser,* Lea Whittington; Tel: 310-247-3000, Ext 2223. Subject Specialists: *Graphic arts,* Anne Coco; Staff 62 (MLS 10, Non-MLS 52)
Founded 1927
Library Holdings: Bk Vols 50,013; Per Subs 200
Special Collections: Adolph Zukor Coll; Alfred Hitchcock Coll; Andrew Marton Coll; Arthur Hiller Coll; Barry Lyndon Coll; Cary Grant Coll; Cecil B DeMille Coll, stills; Charlton Heston Coll; Colleen Moore Coll, scrapbks, stills; David Niven Coll; Edith Head Coll, sketches & stills; Elmer-Dyer Coll; Endre Bohem Coll; Fred Renaldo Coll; Fred Zinnemann Coll; George Cukor Coll, correspondence & scripts; George Steven Coll, correspondence, financial rec, production files, scripts & stills; Gregory Peck Coll; Hal B Wallis Coll; Hedda Hopper Coll; J Roy Hunt Coll, correspondence, scripts & stills; Jackie Coogan Coll; James Wong Howe Coll; Jean Hersholt Coll; John Engstead Coll; John Paxton Coll; John Sturges Coll; Joseph Biroc Coll; Jules White Coll; Kay Van Pipper Coll; Leo Kuter Coll; Leonard Goldstein Coll; Lewis Milestone, Mary Pickford, Martin Ritt, Paul Mazursky, William Friedkin, Hal Ashby, George Roy Hill & Bryan Forbes (Hollywood Museum Coll), papers & stills; Louella Parsons Coll; Mack Sennett Coll, contracts, financial rec, scripts & stills; Merle Oberon Coll; Metro-Goldwyn-Mayer Inc Coll, stills; MGM Scripts Coll; Milton Krims Coll; MPAA Production Code, case files; Paramount Pictures Coll, scripts, still bks & stills; Paul Ivano Coll; Pete Smith Coll; Ring Lardner Jr Coll; RKO Radio Pictures Coll, stills; Robert Lees Coll; Sam Peckinpah Coll; Saul Bass Coll; Selig Coll, copyrights, scripts & stills; Sid Avery Coll, stills; Sidney Skolsky Coll; Steve McQueen Coll; Thomas Ince Coll; Valentine Davies Coll; Vaudeville (Buster Keaton Coll); William Beaudine Coll. Oral History
Automation Activity & Vendor Info: (Acquisitions) Ex Libris Group; (Cataloging) Ex Libris Group; (OPAC) Ex Libris Group
Wireless access
Open Mon, Thurs & Fri 10-6, Tues 10-8

P BEVERLY HILLS PUBLIC LIBRARY*, 444 N Rexford Dr, 90210-4877. SAN 300-6239. Tel: 310-288-2220. Circulation Tel: 310-288-2222. Interlibrary Loan Service Tel: 310-288-2240. Reference Tel: 310-288-2244. FAX: 310-278-3387. E-mail: library@beverlyhills.org. Web Site: www.bhpl.org. *Asst Dir, Commun Serv, City Librn,* Nancy Hunt-Coffey; *Librn III/Outreach Serv,* Suzanne Mulhare; *Librn III/Ref,* Madeline Gabriel; *Librn III/Youth Serv,* Sandra Abini; *Libr Serv Mgr/Access Serv,* Karen Buth; *Libr Serv Mgr/Pub Serv,* Marilyn Taniguchi; *ILL,* Loc Huynh; Staff 26 (MLS 26)
Founded 1929. Pop 34,000; Circ 682,000
Library Holdings: Bk Titles 233,382; Per Subs 236
Special Collections: 19th & 20th Century Art & Artists; Beverly Hills Coll
Subject Interests: Art, Dance
Automation Activity & Vendor Info: (Acquisitions) Innovative Interfaces, Inc; (Cataloging) Innovative Interfaces, Inc; (Circulation) Innovative Interfaces, Inc; (ILL) OCLC; (OPAC) Innovative Interfaces, Inc; (Serials) Innovative Interfaces, Inc
Database Vendor: Innovative Interfaces, Inc
Wireless access
Open Mon-Thurs 10-8, Fri & Sat 10-6, Sun Noon-5
Friends of the Library Group

P BEVERLY HILLS PUBLIC LIBRARY*, Roxbury Community Center Library, 471 S Roxbury Dr, 90212-4113. (Mail add: 444 N Rexford Dr, 90210). Tel: 310-285-6849. Web Site: www.bhpl.org. *Libr Serv Mgr,* Karen Buth; Tel: 310-288-2251, E-mail: KButh@BeverlyHills.org; *Libr Serv Mgr,* Marilyn Taniguchi; Tel: 310-288-2270, E-mail: MTaniguchi@BeverlyHills.org
Founded 1982. Pop 4,800; Circ 9,900
Library Holdings: Bk Vols 1,800; Per Subs 50
Partic in Southern California Library Cooperative
Open Mon-Fri 9:30am-1:30pm

BISHOP

S LAWS RAILROAD MUSEUM & HISTORICAL SITE LIBRARY*, Library & Arts Bldg, Silver Canyon Rd, 93515. (Mail add: PO Box 363, 93515-0363), SAN 375-4685. Tel: 760-873-5950. E-mail: lawsmuseum@aol.com. Web Site: www.lawsmuseum.org. *In Charge,* Barbara Moss
Founded 1966
Library Holdings: Bk Vols 500

M NORTHERN INYO HOSPITAL*, Medical Library, 150 Pioneer Lane, 93514. SAN 325-0962. Tel: 760-873-5811, Ext 2279. FAX: 760-872-5879. Web Site: www.nih.org. *Librn,* Annette Gaskin; Staff 1 (MLS 1)
Library Holdings: Bk Titles 551; Per Subs 51
Special Collections: High Altitude Sickness, Pulmonary Edema; Mountain, Wilderness Emergencies

BLYTHE

J PALO VERDE COLLEGE*, Harry A Faull Library, One College Dr, 92225-9561. SAN 300-628X. Tel: 760-921-5518. Administration Tel: 760-921-5558. FAX: 760-921-5581. E-mail: pvc-library@paloverde.edu. Web Site: www.paloverde.edu/library. *Librn,* June Turner; E-mail: june.turner@paloverde.edu; Staff 1 (MLS 1)
Founded 1947. Enrl 4,500; Fac 36; Highest Degree: Associate
Library Holdings: AV Mats 1,477; High Interest/Low Vocabulary Bk Vols 116; Bk Titles 16,978; Bk Vols 17,665; Per Subs 47; Talking Bks 51
Automation Activity & Vendor Info: (Cataloging) ComPanion Corp; (Circulation) ComPanion Corp; (OPAC) ComPanion Corp
Database Vendor: EBSCOhost
Wireless access
Partic in SIRCULS
Open Mon-Thurs 8-8, Fri 8-4:30

P PALO VERDE VALLEY LIBRARY DISTRICT*, 125 W Chanslorway, 92225-1293. SAN 300-6298. Tel: 760-922-5371. FAX: 760-922-5334. E-mail: pvvdl@global101.com. *Libr Dir,* Brenda Reed; *Asst Dir, Controller,* Brenda S Lugo; Staff 4 (Non-MLS 4)
Founded 1959. Pop 40,700; Circ 39,378
Library Holdings: AV Mats 324; Bks on Deafness & Sign Lang 16; Bk Titles 44,105; Bk Vols 51,588; Per Subs 79
Special Collections: Palo Verde Times (local) 1911 to present (microfilm); Palo Verde Valley Local History (complete set)
Automation Activity & Vendor Info: (Cataloging) Brodart; (Circulation) SirsiDynix
Wireless access
Mem of Inland Library System
Open Mon-Wed 10-6, Thurs 10-8, Fri 10-5, Sat 10-4
Friends of the Library Group

BRAWLEY

P BRAWLEY PUBLIC LIBRARY*, 400 Main St, 92227-2491. SAN 300-631X. Tel: 760-344-1891. FAX: 760 344 0212. *Dir,* Marjo Mello; Tel: 760-344-1891, Ext 10; Staff 2 (MLS 1, Non-MLS 1)
Founded 1921. Pop 23,000; Circ 72,000
Library Holdings: AV Mats 800; Bk Titles 55,000; Per Subs 60; Talking Bks 950
Partic in Serra Cooperative Library System
Open Tues-Thurs 12-8, Fri & Sat 9-5
Friends of the Library Group
Bookmobiles: 1

BREA

R GOLDEN GATE BAPTIST THEOLOGICAL SEMINARY*, Southern California Campus Library, 251 S Randolph Ave, Ste A, 92821-5759. Tel: 714-256-1311. FAX: 714-256-9284. Web Site: www.ggbts.edu. *Mgr, Libr Serv,* Harvey Martindill; E-mail: HarveyMartindill@ggbts.edu
Library Holdings: Bk Vols 24,678
Wireless access
Open Mon & Wed 7am-9:30pm, Tues & Thurs 7am-9pm, Fri 7am-8:30pm, Sat 8:30-2

BRIDGEPORT

GL MONO COUNTY LAW LIBRARY*, Courthouse, Main St, 93517. (Mail add: PO Box 617, 93517-0617), SAN 320-555X. Tel: 760-932-5550.
Library Holdings: Bk Vols 2,258
Restriction: Not a lending libr

BUENA PARK

P BUENA PARK LIBRARY DISTRICT*, 7150 La Palma Ave, 90620-2547. SAN 300-6352. Tel: 714-826-4100. FAX: 714-826-5052. E-mail: library@buenapark.lib.ca.us. Web Site: www.buenaparklibrary.org. *Dir,* Mary McCasland; E-mail: marymac@buenapark.lib.ca.us; Staff 1 (MLS 1)
Founded 1919. Pop 82,000; Circ 459,392
Library Holdings: CDs 3,531; DVDs 5,872; Large Print Bks 1,387; Bk Titles 95,286; Bk Vols 118,125; Per Subs 185; Talking Bks 2,123; Videos 2,023
Automation Activity & Vendor Info: (Acquisitions) SirsiDynix; (Cataloging) SirsiDynix; (Circulation) SirsiDynix; (ILL) OCLC Online; (OPAC) SirsiDynix; (Serials) SirsiDynix
Database Vendor: Baker & Taylor, EBSCOhost, Facts on File, Gale Cengage Learning, Newsbank, ProQuest, ReferenceUSA, SirsiDynix
Wireless access
Function: Adult bk club, Bilingual assistance for Spanish patrons, Bk club(s), Bks on CD, Children's prog, Computers for patron use, Copy machines, E-Reserves, Electronic databases & coll, Fax serv, ILL available, Music CDs, Notary serv, Online cat, Online ref, Outside serv via phone, mail, e-mail & web, Passport agency, Preschool outreach, Prog for adults, Prog for children & young adult, Pub access computers, Ref serv available, Ref serv in person, Story hour, Summer reading prog, Tax forms, Teen prog, Telephone ref
Partic in Southern California Library Cooperative
Special Services for the Deaf - Bks on deafness & sign lang; High interest/low vocabulary bks
Special Services for the Blind - Bks available with recordings; Copier with enlargement capabilities; Large print bks; Ref serv; Talking bks; Videos on blindness & phys handicaps
Open Tues-Thurs 10-8, Fri & Sat 10-5
Friends of the Library Group

BURBANK

P BURBANK PUBLIC LIBRARY*, 110 N Glenoaks Blvd, 91502-1203. SAN 331-7161. Tel: 818-238-5600. Reference Tel: 818-238-5580. Administration Tel: 818-238-5551. FAX: 818-238-5553. TDD: 818-238-5575. E-mail: library@ci.burbank.ca.us. Web Site: www.burbankLibrary.com. *Libr Serv Dir,* Sharon Cohen; E-mail: scohen@ci.burbank.ca.us; *Asst Libr Serv Dir,* Helen Wang; E-mail: hwang@ci.burbank.ca.us; *Coordr, Ch Serv,* Cathleen Bowley; Tel: 818-238-5610, E-mail: cbowley@ci.burbank.ca.us; *Coordr, Ref (Info Serv),* Patrice Samko; E-mail: psamko@ci.burbank.ca.us; Staff 61.85 (MLS 24.1, Non-MLS 37.75)
Founded 1938. Pop 104,427; Circ 1,385,672
Library Holdings: AV Mats 76,998; Large Print Bks 6,630; Bk Titles 457,520; Per Subs 466
Automation Activity & Vendor Info: (Acquisitions) SirsiDynix; (Cataloging) SirsiDynix; (Circulation) SirsiDynix; (OPAC) SirsiDynix; (Serials) SirsiDynix
Database Vendor: Gale Cengage Learning, Grolier Online, infoUSA, LexisNexis, Newsbank, OCLC WorldShare Interlibrary Loan, ProQuest, ReferenceUSA, TumbleBookLibrary
Wireless access
Function: Accelerated reader prog, Adult bk club, Adult literacy prog, After school storytime, AV serv, Bilingual assistance for Spanish patrons, Bk club(s), Bk reviews (Group), Bks on cassette, Bks on CD, Children's prog, Computer training, Computers for patron use, Copy machines, e-mail serv, E-Reserves, Electronic databases & coll, Exhibits, Family literacy, Free DVD rentals, Health sci info serv, Homebound delivery serv, Homework prog, ILL available, Magnifiers for reading, Music CDs, Online cat, Online ref, Orientations, Outreach serv, Photocopying/Printing, Prog for adults, Prog for children & young adult, Pub access computers, Ref serv available, Ref serv in person, Senior computer classes, Senior outreach, Spoken cassettes & CDs, Spoken cassettes & DVDs, Story hour, Summer reading prog, Tax forms, Teen prog, Web-Braille, Web-catalog
Partic in Califa; OCLC Online Computer Library Center, Inc; Southern California Library Cooperative
Special Services for the Blind - Braille bks; Talking bks
Open Mon-Thurs 9:30-9, Fri 9:30-6, Sat 10-6, Sun 1-5
Friends of the Library Group
Branches: 2
BUENA VISTA, 300 N Buena Vista St, 91505-3208, SAN 331-7196. Tel: 818-238-5620. Reference Tel: 818-238-5625. FAX: 818-238-5623. *Supv Librn,* Christine Rodriguez
Pop 30,600; Circ 655,959
Library Holdings: Bk Vols 179,281
Automation Activity & Vendor Info: (Course Reserve) SirsiDynix
Open Mon-Thurs 10-9, Fri 10-6, Sat 10-5, Sun 1-5
Friends of the Library Group
NORTHWEST, 3323 W Victory Blvd, 91505-1543, SAN 331-7226. Tel: 818-238-5640. FAX: 818-238-5642. *Supv Librn,* Melissa Gwynne
Pop 16,000; Circ 72,562
Library Holdings: Bk Vols 61,107
Open Mon-Fri 12-6
Friends of the Library Group

M PROVIDENCE SAINT JOSEPH MEDICAL CENTER*, Health Science Library, 501 S Buena Vista St, 91505-4866. SAN 300-6425. Tel: 818-847-3822. FAX: 818-847-3823. *Mgr, Libr Serv,* Jacqueline Steltz-Lenarsky; E-mail: jacqueline.steltz-lenarsky@providence.org; Staff 2 (MLS 1, Non-MLS 1)
Founded 1943
Library Holdings: Bk Vols 7,314; Per Subs 150
Subject Interests: Cardiology, Mgt, Nursing, Oncology
Automation Activity & Vendor Info: (Cataloging) EOS International; (Circulation) EOS International; (OPAC) EOS International; (Serials) EOS International

Partic in Medical Library Group of Southern California & Arizona (MLGSCA); Medlars; Pacific Southwest Regional Medical Library (PSRML)
Open Mon-Thurs 7:30-3:30, Fri 8-Noon
Restriction: Circulates for staff only, In-house use for visitors

S SOUTHERN CALIFORNIA GENEALOGICAL SOCIETY*, Family Research Library, 417 Irving Dr, 91504-2408. SAN 324-5675. Tel: 818-843-7247. FAX: 818-843-7262. Web Site: www.scgsgenealogy.com. *Pres,* Pam Wiedenbeck; *Libr Operations,* Linda Golovko; *Acq,* Sally Emerson; *Per,* Beverly Truesdale
Founded 1964
Library Holdings: Microforms 1,000; Bk Vols 3,600; Per Subs 1,200
Special Collections: Cornwall, England (Ross Coll); French Canadian Heritage Society of California; German Genealogical Society of America Coll; Hispanic-America
Subject Interests: Calif, Fr Canadian, Genealogy, Hispanic, Tex
Publications: The Searcher (Quarterly)
Partic in Genealogical Alliance
Open Tues 10-9, Wed, Thurs & Fri 10-4
Restriction: Open to pub for ref only

C WOODBURY UNIVERSITY LIBRARY, 7500 Glenoaks Blvd, 91510-1099. (Mail add: PO Box 7846, 91510-7846), SAN 301-0236. Tel: 818-252-5200. Interlibrary Loan Service Tel: 818-252-5211. Reference Tel: 818-252-5201. FAX: 818-767-4534. Web Site: library.woodbury.edu. *Univ Librn,* Nedra Peterson; E-mail: nedra.peterson@woodbury.edu; *Access Serv Librn,* Raida Gatten; E-mail: raida.gatten@woodbury.edu; *Outreach Librn,* Barret Havens; E-mail: barret.havens@woodbury.edu; *Syst Librn,* Jenny Rosenfeld; E-mail: jennifer.rosenfeld@woodbury.edu; *Coordr, Libr Instruction,* Diane Zwemer; E-mail: diane.zwemer@woodbury.edu; Staff 13 (MLS 6, Non-MLS 7)
Founded 1884. Enrl 1,550; Fac 277; Highest Degree: Master
Library Holdings: e-books 2,575; Bk Vols 66,654; Per Subs 307; Videos 1,896
Subject Interests: Archit, Bus, Design, Fashion, Interior archit
Automation Activity & Vendor Info: (Cataloging) OCLC; (Circulation) OCLC; (ILL) OCLC WorldShare Interlibrary Loan; (OPAC) OCLC; (Serials) EBSCO Online
Database Vendor: Alexander Street Press, ARTstor, Baker & Taylor, College Source, CountryWatch, CQ Press, CredoReference, EBSCOhost, Emerald, Gale Cengage Learning, H W Wilson, Hoovers, JSTOR, LexisNexis, McGraw-Hill, Newsbank-Readex, OCLC FirstSearch, OCLC WorldShare Interlibrary Loan, Oxford Online, Project MUSE, ProQuest, RefWorks, SerialsSolutions, Wilson - Wilson Web
Wireless access
Partic in Statewide California Electronic Library Consortium (SCELC)
Friends of the Library Group
Departmental Libraries:
SAN DIEGO CAMPUS, 2212 Main St, San Diego, 92113. Tel: 619-235-2900. E-mail: san.diego@woodbury.edu. Web Site: library.woodbury.edu/services/sd. *Librn,* Cathryn Copper; Tel: 619-235-2900, Ext 22, E-mail: cathryn.copper@woodbury.edu. Subject Specialists: *Archit,* Cathryn Copper
Library Holdings: Bk Titles 5,000; Per Subs 30
Subject Interests: Archit, Real estate
Function: ILL available

BURLINGAME

P BURLINGAME PUBLIC LIBRARY*, 480 Primrose Rd, 94010-4083. SAN 331-7315. Tel: 650-558-7400. Interlibrary Loan Service Tel: 650-558-7417. Reference Tel: 650-558-7444. Administration Tel: 650-558-7474. Automation Services Tel: 650-558-7412. FAX: 650-342-1948. Administration FAX: 650-342-6295. E-mail: bplref@plsinfo.org. Web Site: www.burlingame.org/library. *Dir,* Patricia Harding; Tel: 650-558-7401, E-mail: harding@plsinfo.org; *Dir, Tech Serv,* Barry Mills; E-mail: mills@plsinfo.org; *Br Coordr,* Patti Flynn; Tel: 650-340-6180, E-mail: flynn@plsinfo.org; *AV,* Kelly Keefer; Tel: 650-558-7415, E-mail: keefer@plsinfo.org; *Circ,* Amy Gettle; Tel: 650-558-7450, E-mail: gettle@plsinfo.org; *Ch Serv,* Susan Reiterman; Tel: 650-558-7440, E-mail: reiterman@plsinfo.org; *Per,* Dorothy Ezquerro; Tel: 650-558-7431, E-mail: ezquerro@plsinfo.org; Staff 22 (MLS 10, Non-MLS 12)
Founded 1909. Pop 35,602; Circ 624,000
Jul 2005-Jun 2006 Income (Main Library Only) $3,592,086, State $175,000, City $3,417,086. Mats Exp $361,451, Books $250,451, Per/Ser (Incl. Access Fees) $34,000, Micro $7,000, AV Mat $50,000, Electronic Ref Mat (Incl. Access Fees) $20,000. Sal $2,551,370
Library Holdings: Audiobooks 4,046; AV Mats 14,782; CDs 3,191; DVDs 7,545; Bk Vols 182,926; Per Subs 200
Automation Activity & Vendor Info: (Acquisitions) Innovative Interfaces, Inc; (Cataloging) Innovative Interfaces, Inc; (Circulation) Innovative Interfaces, Inc; (ILL) OCLC; (OPAC) Innovative Interfaces, Inc; (Serials) EBSCO Online
Database Vendor: Baker & Taylor, EBSCOhost, Gale Cengage Learning, OCLC FirstSearch, OCLC WorldShare Interlibrary Loan, ProQuest, ReferenceUSA
Wireless access
Partic in Peninsula Libraries Automated Network
Open Mon-Thurs 10-9, Fri & Sat 10-5, Sun 1-5
Friends of the Library Group
Branches: 1
EASTON DRIVE BRANCH, 1800 Easton Dr, 94010. Tel: 650-340-6180. FAX: 650-340-6184. *Br Mgr,* Sue Reiterman; E-mail: reiterman@plsinfo.org; Staff 2 (MLS 1, Non-MLS 1)
Pop 5,000; Circ 60,000
Jul 2005-Jun 2006 Income $100,000. Mats Exp $40,000, Books $30,000, AV Mat $10,000. Sal $50,000
Library Holdings: Audiobooks 591; AV Mats 1,649; DVDs 1,058; Bk Vols 14,557
Partic in Peninsula Libraries Automated Network
Open Mon-Thurs 2-8, Fri & Sat 2-5
Friends of the Library Group

M MILLS-PENINSULA HEALTH SERVICES LIBRARY*, 1501 Trousdale Dr, 94010. SAN 300-6433. Tel: 650-696-5621. FAX: 650-696-5484. Web Site: www.mills-peninsula.org. *Librn,* Debbie Martin
Library Holdings: Bk Vols 5,000; Per Subs 200
Subject Interests: Med, Nursing
Partic in National Network of Libraries of Medicine
Open Mon-Fri 7:30-4

CALABASAS

P CITY OF CALABASAS LIBRARY*, 200 Civic Center Way, 91302. Tel: 818-225-7616. Web Site: www.cityofcalabasas.com/library.html. *City Librn,* Barbara Lockwood; E-mail: blockwood@cityofcalabasas.com; *Librn,* Karilyn Steward; E-mail: ksteward@cityofcalabasas.com; *Supvr, Circ,* Anita Torres; E-mail: atorres@cityofcalabasas.com; *Tech Serv Coordr,* Suchandra Ghosh; E-mail: sghosh@cityofcalabasas.com; Staff 8 (MLS 3, Non-MLS 5)
Founded 1998. Pop 23,000; Circ 120,000
Library Holdings: AV Mats 2,650; Bks on Deafness & Sign Lang 76; CDs 757; DVDs 3,014; Large Print Bks 493; Music Scores 41; Bk Vols 36,000; Per Subs 93; Talking Bks 1,964; Videos 1,400
Subject Interests: Local hist
Automation Activity & Vendor Info: (Acquisitions) Innovative Interfaces, Inc; (Cataloging) Innovative Interfaces, Inc; (Circulation) Innovative Interfaces, Inc; (ILL) OCLC; (OPAC) Innovative Interfaces, Inc; (Serials) Innovative Interfaces, Inc
Database Vendor: Gale Cengage Learning, Newsbank, ReferenceUSA
Wireless access
Partic in Southern California Library Cooperative
Open Tues-Thurs 10-9, Fri & Sat 10-5, Sun 12-5
Friends of the Library Group

CALEXICO

P CAMARENA MEMORIAL LIBRARY*, 850 Encinas Ave, 92231. SAN 300-6441. Tel: 760-768-2170. FAX: 760-357-0404. E-mail: library@calexico.ca.gov. Web Site: www.calexicolibrary.org. *Dir, Commun Serv,* Sandra Tauler; *Ref Librn,* Norma Gerardo; *Ref Librn,* Lizeth Legaspi; *Libr Asst II,* Julio Manriquez; *Libr Tech,* Sonia Garcia; Staff 3 (MLS 1, Non-MLS 2)
Founded 1919. Pop 37,000; Circ 106,455
Jul 2007-Jun 2008 Income $877,477, State $77,963, City $776,353, Federal $20,000, Other $3,161. Sal $434,860
Library Holdings: Audiobooks 602; AV Mats 1,502; High Interest/Low Vocabulary Bk Vols 150; Large Print Bks 600; Bk Titles 68,750; Bk Vols 75,000; Per Subs 104; Talking Bks 100
Special Collections: History of Imperial Valley
Automation Activity & Vendor Info: (Cataloging) Innovative Interfaces, Inc; (Circulation) Innovative Interfaces, Inc; (OPAC) Innovative Interfaces, Inc
Database Vendor: EBSCOhost
Partic in Serra Cooperative Library System
Open Mon-Thurs 10-8
Friends of the Library Group

C SAN DIEGO STATE UNIVERSITY*, Imperial Valley Campus Library, 720 Heber Ave, 92231-0550. SAN 331-7374. Tel: 760-768-5585. Reference Tel: 760-768-5633. FAX: 760-768-5525. Web Site: www.ivcampus.sdsu.edu/library/. *Ref Librn,* William Payne; Tel: 760-768-5626, E-mail: bpayne@mail.sdsu.edu; Staff 3 (MLS 1, Non-MLS 2)
Founded 1959. Highest Degree: Master
Library Holdings: Bk Titles 60,000; Bk Vols 115,000; Per Subs 150
Special Collections: US-Mexico Borderlands (Border Coll)
Subject Interests: Criminal justice, Liberal studies, Psychol, Pub admin, Spanish, Teacher educ

Automation Activity & Vendor Info: (Cataloging) Innovative Interfaces, Inc; (Circulation) Innovative Interfaces, Inc
Database Vendor: Innovative Interfaces, Inc
Partic in OCLC Online Computer Library Center, Inc; San Diego Greater Metro Area Libr & Info Agency Coun
Open Mon-Thurs 10-9, Fri 10-4, Sat 10-3

CAMARILLO

P CAMARILLO PUBLIC LIBRARY*, 4101 Las Posas Rd, 93010. SAN 335-2269. Tel: 805-388-5222. Reference Tel: 805-388-5811. E-mail: askus@camarillolibrary.org. Web Site: librarycatalog.info. *Librn,* Barbara Wolfe
Open Mon-Thurs 10-9, Fri-Sun 10-5

G DIVISION OF JUVENILE JUSTICE OF DEPARTMENT OF CORRECTIONS*, Ventura Youth Correctional Facility Library, 3100 Wright Rd, 93010-8307. SAN 322-8681. Tel: 805-485-7951. FAX: 805-485-2801. *Sr Librn,* Claudia Deardorff; E-mail: cdeardorff@cdcr.ca.gov
Founded 1962
Library Holdings: Bk Titles 6,000; Per Subs 20
Special Collections: Law Coll
Subject Interests: Law, Sociol
Database Vendor: ProQuest
Open Mon-Fri 7-3

CAMERON PARK

M MARSHALL COMMUNITY HEALTH LIBRARY, 3581 Palmer Dr, Ste 101, 95682. Tel: 530-626-2778. FAX: 530-626-2779. Web Site: www.marshallmedical.org/library.cfm. *Librn,* Alison Clement; Tel: 530-626-5459, E-mail: aclement@marshallmedical.org; Staff 1 (MLS 1)
Library Holdings: Bks on Deafness & Sign Lang 10; CDs 30; DVDs 30; Large Print Bks 10; Bk Vols 4,000; Per Subs 10
Special Collections: Children's Picture Books on Health & Wellness
Automation Activity & Vendor Info: (Cataloging) SirsiDynix; (Circulation) SirsiDynix; (OPAC) SirsiDynix
Function: Computers for patron use, Online searches, Pub access computers, Ref & res, Ref serv available, Telephone ref, Wheelchair accessible
Open Mon-Thurs 9-4

CAMP PENDLETON

UNITED STATES MARINE CORPS

A LIBRARY SERVICES*, Bldg 1146, 92055. (Mail add: PO Box 555005, 92055-5005), SAN 331-7528. Tel: 760-725-5104, 760-725-5669. FAX: 760-725-6569. Web Site: library.usmc-mccs.org. *Dir,* Sandra Jensen; *Asst Librn,* Ariel Gasper; Staff 19 (MLS 4, Non-MLS 15)
Founded 1950
Library Holdings: Bk Vols 16,000
Subject Interests: Mil hist
Partic in San Diego Greater Metro Area Libr & Info Agency Coun
Open Mon-Thurs 9-8, Fri-Sun 9-5

A SEASIDE SQUARE LIBRARY*, San Onofre, Bldg 51093, 92055. Tel: 760-725-7325. FAX: 760-763-1360. *Tech Serv,* Geraldine Hagen
Library Holdings: Bk Vols 10,124; Per Subs 70
Open Mon-Thurs 12-8, Fri-Sun 12-5

UNITED STATES NAVY

A CREW'S LIBRARY, Naval Hospital, 200 Mercy Circle, 92055-5191. (Mail add: Box 555191, 92055-5191), SAN 331-7587. Tel: 760-719-3463, 760-719-4636. FAX: 760-725-4156. *Libr Dir,* Kathleen Dunning-Torbett; E-mail: kathleen.dunning-torbett@med.navy.mil
Founded 1943
Library Holdings: Audiobooks 500; DVDs 2,500; Bk Vols 500; Per Subs 200
Automation Activity & Vendor Info: (Cataloging) EOS International
Function: Bks on CD, Computers for patron use, Free DVD rentals, Handicapped accessible, ILL available, Magazines, Online cat, Online searches, Ref serv available
Open Mon-Fri 6:30-3:45
Restriction: Not open to pub

AM MEDICAL LIBRARY*, Naval Hospital, Box 555191, 92055-5191, SAN 331-7617. Tel: 760-725-1322. FAX: 760-725-4156. *Libr Dir,* Kathleen Dunning-Torbett; Tel: 760-725-1229, E-mail: kathleen.dunning-torbett@med.navy.mil; *Dept Head,* Position Currently Open; Staff 2 (MLS 1, Non-MLS 1)
Founded 1947
Library Holdings: AV Mats 300; CDs 600; DVDs 130; e-books 350; e-journals 150; Bk Titles 2,000; Per Subs 235
Subject Interests: Dentistry, Med, Nursing
Automation Activity & Vendor Info: (Acquisitions) Baker & Taylor; (Cataloging) EOS International; (OPAC) EOS International; (Serials) EOS International
Database Vendor: Dialog, DynaMed, EBSCOhost, EOS International, Lexi-Comp, MD Consult, Medline, OVID Technologies, PubMed, ScienceDirect, STAT!Ref (Teton Data Systems), UpToDate, WT Cox
Partic in Consortium of Naval Libraries (CNL); Docline; Medical Library Association (MLA); OCLC Online Computer Library Center, Inc; Pacific Southwest Regional Medical Library (PSRML)
Publications: Newsletter
Open Mon-Fri 6:30-3:45

CANOGA PARK

S PRATT & WHITNEY ROCKETDYNE, INC*, Library Services, 6633 Canoga Ave, 91309. Tel: 818-586-2575. FAX: 818-586-9150. *Librn,* Fern Willis; *Res,* Dennis Bowyer; Staff 4 (MLS 3, Non-MLS 1)
Founded 1955
Library Holdings: Microforms 10,000; Bk Titles 25,000; Per Subs 27
Special Collections: Historic Rocketdyne Photos; Technical Reports
Subject Interests: Fluid mechanics, Knowledge mgt, Nuclear eng, Physics, Thermodynamics
Function: Res libr
Restriction: Co libr

CANYON LAKE

R CANYON LAKE COMMUNITY CHURCH LIBRARY*, 30515 Railroad Canyon Rd, 92587. Tel: 951-244-1877. E-mail: library@canyonlakechurch.org. *Mgr,* Bob Haskins
Jul 2012-Jun 2013 Income $1,000, Parent Institution $600, Other $400. Mats Exp $1,000, Books $800, AV Mat $200
Library Holdings: Audiobooks 81; CDs 291; DVDs 252; Large Print Bks 40; Bk Titles 6,450; Bk Vols 6,505; Videos 160
Automation Activity & Vendor Info: (Cataloging) LibraryWorld, Inc; (Circulation) LibraryWorld, Inc; (OPAC) LibraryWorld, Inc
Database Vendor: LibraryWorld, Inc
Wireless access
Function: Bks on cassette, Bks on CD, Free DVD rentals, Music CDs, Story hour, Summer reading prog, Video lending libr
Open Tues 6pm-9pm, Wed 8:30-Noon, Thurs 6pm-8pm, Sun 7:30am-12:30pm
Restriction: Congregants only. Lending limited to county residents

CARLSBAD

P CARLSBAD CITY LIBRARY, Dove Library, 1775 Dove Lane, 92011-4048. SAN 300-6492. Tel: 760-602-2011. FAX: 760-602-7942. E-mail: librarian@carlsbadca.gov. Web Site: www.carlsbadca.gov/services/depts/library/. *Dep Libr Dir,* Diane Bednarski; Tel: 760-602-2010, E-mail: Diane.Bednarski@carlsbadca.gov; *Tech Serv Supvr,* Chris Pickavet; Tel: 760-602-2029; *Libr Prog & Venues Coordr,* Keith Gemmell; Tel: 760-602-2024, E-mail: keith.gemmell@carlsbadca.gov; *Ch Serv,* Barbara Chung; Tel: 760-602-2064; *ILL,* Darin Williamson; Tel: 760-602-2058; *Sr Mgt Analyst,* Steven Didier; Tel: 760-602-2014, E-mail: Steven.Didier@carlsbadca.gov; Staff 112 (MLS 23, Non MLS 89)
Founded 1956. Pop 110,972; Circ 1,369,396
Library Holdings: Audiobooks 16,633; Bks on Deafness & Sign Lang 60; Braille Volumes 3; CDs 31,963; DVDs 21,757; e-books 2,786; Electronic Media & Resources 29; High Interest/Low Vocabulary Bk Vols 1,135; Large Print Bks 6,938; Microforms 231,066; Bk Titles 212,150; Bk Titles 212,150; Bk Titles 212,150; Bk Vols 267,666; Per Subs 541
Subject Interests: Genealogy, Local hist
Automation Activity & Vendor Info: (Cataloging) SirsiDynix; (Circulation) SirsiDynix; (OPAC) SirsiDynix
Database Vendor: OCLC FirstSearch, ReferenceUSA, SirsiDynix, Wilson - Wilson Web
Wireless access
Publications: Carlsbad: A Village by the Sea; Carlsbad: An Unabashed History of the Village by the Sea; Seekers of the Spring: A History of Carlsbad
Partic in OCLC Online Computer Library Center, Inc; Serra Cooperative Library System
Special Services for the Deaf - Closed caption videos
Special Services for the Blind - Vantage closed circuit TV magnifier
Open Mon-Thurs 9-9, Fri & Sat 9-5, Sun 1-5
Friends of the Library Group
Branches: 2
GEORGINA COLE LIBRARY, 1250 Carlsbad Village Dr, 92008, SAN 322-5550. Tel: 760-434-2870. FAX: 760-434-9975. *Dep Libr Dir,* Suzanne Smithson; Tel: 760-434-2876
Open Mon-Thurs 9-9, Fri 9-5, Sun 1-5
Friends of the Library Group

LIBRARY LEARNING CENTER, 3368 Eureka Pl, 92008, SAN 375-5428. Tel: 760-931-4500. FAX: 760-729-8335. *Principal Librn,* Callie Ahrens; Tel: 760-931-4520; *Commun Outreach Supvr-Bilingual,* Lizeth Simonson; Tel: 760-931-4509; *Commun Outreach Supvr-Literacy,* Carrie Scott; Tel: 760-931-4515
Open Mon-Thurs 11-6, Fri 11-5
Friends of the Library Group

S RICHARD T LIDDICOAT GEMOLOGICAL LIBRARY & INFORMATION CENTER, GIA Library, 5345 Armada Dr, 92008. SAN 301-5866. Tel: 760-603-4046, 760-603-4068. Toll Free Tel: 800-421-7250, Ext 4046, 800-421-7250, Ext 4068. FAX: 760-603-4256. E-mail: library@gia.edu. Web Site: www.gia.edu/library. *Dir,* Dona Mary Dirlam; Tel: 760-603-4154, E-mail: ddirlam@gia.edu; *Sr Librn,* Rosemary Tozer; Tel: 760-603-4016, E-mail: rtozer@gia.edu; *Mgr,* Judy Colbert; Tel: 760-603-4075, E-mail: jcolbert@gia.edu; *Mgr,* Paula Jean Rucinski; Tel: 760-603-4174, E-mail: paula.rucinski@gia.edu. Subject Specialists: *Gemology, Geol, Jewelry,* Dona Mary Dirlam; *Rare bks,* Rosemary Tozer; *Digital asset mgt, Gemology, Visual res,* Judy Colbert; *Bus, Gemology,* Paula Jean Rucinski; Staff 18 (MLS 4, Non-MLS 14)
Founded 1931
Library Holdings: CDs 250; DVDs 333; Bk Vols 57,000; Per Subs 230; Videos 1,103
Special Collections: Auction Catalogs; Gemology & Mineralogy (Joseph A Freilich Library, John & Marjorie Jane Sinkankas Coll & Henry Polissack Library); Jewelry & Jewelry History (Theodore Horovitz Library); Science & Mineralogy (Clifford J Awald Library). Oral History
Subject Interests: Gemology, Geol, Jewelry hist, Jewelry manufacturing, Mineralogy
Automation Activity & Vendor Info: (Acquisitions) EOS International; (Cataloging) EOS International; (Circulation) EOS International; (ILL) OCLC Online; (OPAC) EOS International; (Serials) EOS International
Database Vendor: EBSCOhost, OCLC WorldShare Interlibrary Loan
Wireless access
Function: For res purposes
Partic in Libr & Info Resources Network (LIRN)
Open Mon-Fri 7:30-5
Restriction: Circ limited, Closed stack, Co libr, Non-circulating coll, Non-circulating to the pub, Open to pub for ref only, Photo ID required for access, Pub use on premises

CARMEL

P HARRISON MEMORIAL LIBRARY, Carmel Public Library, Ocean Ave & Lincoln St, 93921. (Mail add: PO Box 800, 93921-0800), SAN 300-6514. Tel: 831-624-4629. Reference Tel: 831-624-7323. Administration Tel: 831-624-1366. FAX: 831-624-0407. E-mail: hml.reference@gmail.com. Web Site: www.hm-lib.org. *Libr Dir,* Janet Bombard; E-mail: jbombard@ci.carmel.ca.us; *Head Archivist,* Ashlee Wright; Tel: 831-624-1615, E-mail: awright@ci.carmel.ca.us; *Head, Ref,* Jean Chapin; E-mail: jchapin@ci.carmel.ca.us; *Head, Youth Serv,* Grace Melady; Tel: 831-624-4664, E-mail: gmelady@ci.carmel.ca.us; *Circ Supvr,* Amy Rector; E-mail: arector@ci.carmel.ca.us; *ILL/Doc Delivery Serv,* Jeanette Campbell; E-mail: jcampbell@ci.carmel.ca.us; Staff 11.33 (MLS 4.75, Non-MLS 6.58)
Founded 1906. Pop 3,738; Circ 153,227
Jul 2013-Jun 2014 Income $1,285,477, City $966,177, Locally Generated Income $319,300. Mats Exp $206,776, Books $112,434, Per/Ser (Incl. Access Fees) $12,000, Manu Arch $2,500, AV Equip $34,987, AV Mat $26,000, Electronic Ref Mat (Incl. Access Fees) $15,500, Presv $2,500. Sal $595,000
Library Holdings: Audiobooks 2,941; AV Mats 6,940; DVDs 3,591; e-books 2,934; Large Print Bks 2,165; Bk Titles 69,229; Bk Vols 75,615; Per Subs 112; Talking Bks 2,390; Videos 247
Special Collections: Carmel History Coll, photog; Carmel Pine Cone Local Newspaper Coll, 1915-present; Edward Weston Photographs; Robinson Jeffers Coll
Automation Activity & Vendor Info: (Acquisitions) Baker & Taylor; (Cataloging) OCLC Connexion; (Circulation) ByWater Solutions; (ILL) OCLC FirstSearch; (OPAC) ByWater Solutions
Database Vendor: Baker & Taylor, ByWater Solutions, EBSCOhost, Gale Cengage Learning, Marquis Who's Who, OCLC WorldShare Interlibrary Loan, Overdrive, Inc, ProQuest, ReferenceUSA
Wireless access
Function: 24/7 Electronic res, 24/7 Online cat, Adult literacy prog, Audiobks via web, Bks on CD, Children's prog, Computers for patron use, Copy machines, Digital talking bks, e-mail & chat, Electronic databases & coll, eReaders, Free DVD rentals, Homebound delivery serv, ILL available, Magazines, Magnifiers for reading, Mail & tel request accepted, Mango lang, Microfiche/film & reading machines, Online cat, Outreach serv, Outside serv via phone, mail, e-mail & web, OverDrive digital audio bks, Photocopying/Printing, Preschool outreach, Preschool reading prog, Prog for adults, Prog for children & young adult, Pub access computers, Ref serv available, Scanner, Spanish lang bks, Story hour, Summer reading prog, Tax forms, Teen prog, Telephone ref, Web-catalog
Partic in Monterey Bay Area Cooperative Library System
Open Mon & Sat 1-5, Tues & Wed 11-8, Thurs & Fri 10-6
Friends of the Library Group

CARSON

C CALIFORNIA STATE UNIVERSITY DOMINGUEZ HILLS*, University Library, 1000 E Victoria St, 90747. SAN 300-6549. Tel: 310-243-3700. Circulation Tel: 310-243-3712. Interlibrary Loan Service Tel: 310-243-3716. Reference Tel: 310-243-3582, 310-243-3586. Information Services Tel: 310-243-3715. FAX: 310-516-4219. Web Site: www.csudh.edu. *Dean,* Sandra Parham; Tel: 310-243-2200, E-mail: sparham@csudh.edu; *Dir, Archives & Spec Coll,* Gregory Williams; Tel: 310-243-3013, E-mail: gwilliams@csudh.edu; *Head, Acq & Coll Develop,* John Calhoun; Tel: 310-243-2830, E-mail: jccalhoun@csudh.edu; *Head, Ref Serv,* Naomi Moy; Tel: 310-243-2086, E-mail: nmoy@csudh.edu; *Cat Librn,* Joanna Dunklee; Tel: 310-243-3062, E-mail: jdunklee@csudh.edu; *Electronic Serv Librn,* Wei Ma; Tel: 310-243-2085, E-mail: wma@csudh.edu; *Ref Librn, Web Serv,* Stewart Baker; Tel: 310-243-2062, E-mail: sbaker@csudh.edu; *Ref Librn,* Jeff Broude; Tel: 310-243-3709, E-mail: jbroude@csudh.edu; *Ref Librn,* Vivian Linderman; Tel: 310-243-2308, E-mail: vlinderman@csudh.edu; *Admin Serv Mgr,* Jo Ellen Davis; Tel: 310-243-2207, E-mail: jedavis@csudh.edu; *Night Supvr,* Olivia Hook; Tel: 310-243-3407, E-mail: ohook@csudh.edu; *Coordr, Distance Learning,* Carol Dales; Tel: 310-243-2088, E-mail: cdales@csudh.edu; *Coordr, Info/Student Serv,* Elizabeth Davis; Tel: 310-243-3679, E-mail: edavis@csudh.edu; *Admin Support Coordr,* Johna Taylor; Tel: 310-243-2305, E-mail: jtaylor@csudh.edu; *Bibliog Instruction Coordr,* Caroline Bordinaro; Tel: 310-243-2084, E-mail: cbordinaro@csudh.edu; *Circ Serv Coordr,* Robert Downs; Tel: 310-243-2404, E-mail: rdowns@csudh.edu; *Archivist, Cataloger,* Thomas Philo; Tel: 310-243-3361, E-mail: tphilo@csudh.edu; *ILL,* Faye Phinsee-Clack; Tel: 310-243-3758, E-mail: fclack@csudh.edu; *Acq Asst,* Shilo Moreno; Tel: 310-243-2850, E-mail: smoreno@csudh.edu. Subject Specialists: *Develop, Grants,* Gregory Williams; Staff 12 (MLS 10, Non-MLS 2)
Founded 1965. Enrl 9,038; Fac 680; Highest Degree: Master
Jul 2006-Jun 2007 Income $2,539,795. Mats Exp $2,539,795, Books $170,723, Per/Ser (Incl. Access Fees) $193,340, Electronic Ref Mat (Incl. Access Fees) $293,372, Presv $23,726. Sal $1,741,498 (Prof $1,026,439)
Library Holdings: AV Mats 10,438; Bk Vols 434,328; Per Subs 669
Special Collections: American Best Sellers (Claudia Buckner Coll); Archives of California State Univ Syst. State Document Depository; US Document Depository
Automation Activity & Vendor Info: (Acquisitions) Innovative Interfaces, Inc; (Cataloging) Innovative Interfaces, Inc; (Circulation) Innovative Interfaces, Inc; (Course Reserve) Innovative Interfaces, Inc; (ILL) Innovative Interfaces, Inc; (Serials) Innovative Interfaces, Inc
Database Vendor: American Chemical Society, American Mathematical Society, Blackwell, CountryWatch, EBSCOhost, Elsevier, Innovative Interfaces, Inc, JSTOR, LexisNexis, Mergent Online, OCLC FirstSearch, OCLC WorldShare Interlibrary Loan, OVID Technologies, ProQuest, Springer-Verlag, ValueLine, Wilson - Wilson Web
Wireless access
Function: Distance learning, Electronic databases & coll, Govt ref serv, ILL available, Online cat, Ref serv available, Telephone ref
Partic in OCLC Online Computer Library Center, Inc
Open Mon-Thurs 8-7, Fri 8-5, Sat 10-5
Friends of the Library Group

CERRITOS

P CERRITOS LIBRARY*, 18025 Bloomfield Ave, 90703. SAN 300-6611. Tel: 562-916-1350. Circulation Tel: 562-916-1340. Reference Tel: 562-916-1342. Administration Tel: 562-916-1378. FAX: 562-916-1375. E-mail: library@ci.cerritos.ca.us. Web Site: www.ci.cerritos.ca.us/library. *City Librn,* Don Buckley; *Head, Adult Serv,* Marie Furrows; E-mail: marie_furrows@ci.cerritos.ca.us; *Syst Librn,* Steve Henderson; E-mail: steve_henderson@ci.cerritos.ca.us; *Ch Serv,* Jocelle Liong; E-mail: jocelle_liong@ci.cerritos.ca.us; *Circ,* Claudra Herrgra; *Tech Serv,* Jeanny Chan; Tel: 562-916-1345; *YA Serv,* Padmini Prabhakar; E-mail: padmini_prabhakar@ci.cerritos.ca.us; Staff 11 (MLS 9.5, Non-MLS 1.5)
Founded 1973. Pop 54,834; Circ 971,057
Jul 2010-Jun 2011 Income $5,215,954, State $18,794, City $5,197,160. Mats Exp $457,966, Books $303,293, Per/Ser (Incl. Access Fees) $19,844, AV Mat $41,030, Electronic Ref Mat (Incl. Access Fees) $92,865, Presv $934. Sal $2,732,970 (Prof $683,410)
Library Holdings: AV Mats 23,992; CDs 4,296; DVDs 6,442; e-books 2,700; Bk Titles 266,133; Bk Vols 237,797; Per Subs 243; Talking Bks 2,053; Videos 12,715
Special Collections: Art of the Book: the Book as Art (Artists' Books); First Ladies' Coll; Performing Arts Coll
Automation Activity & Vendor Info: (Acquisitions) BiblioMondo; (Cataloging) BiblioMondo; (Circulation) BiblioMondo; (ILL) OCLC; (OPAC) BiblioMondo

Database Vendor: Baker & Taylor, EBSCOhost, Gale Cengage Learning, Newsbank, OCLC FirstSearch, OCLC WorldShare Interlibrary Loan
Wireless access
Function: Archival coll, Art exhibits, Bk club(s), CD-ROM, Computer training, Copy machines, Electronic databases & coll, Fax serv, Games & aids for the handicapped, Handicapped accessible, ILL available, Large print keyboards, Magnifiers for reading, Mail & tel request accepted, Music CDs, Online ref, Online searches, Orientations, Photocopying/Printing, Prog for adults, Prog for children & young adult, Ref & res, Ref serv available, Senior computer classes, Spoken cassettes & CDs, Spoken cassettes & DVDs, Summer reading prog, Tax forms, Telephone ref, VHS videos, Video lending libr, Wheelchair accessible, Workshops
Partic in OCLC Online Computer Library Center, Inc
Special Services for the Deaf - Assisted listening device; Assistive tech; Bks on deafness & sign lang; Closed caption videos
Special Services for the Blind - Assistive/Adapted tech devices, equip & products; Audio mat; Bks on cassette; Bks on CD; Closed circuit TV magnifier; Computer with voice synthesizer for visually impaired persons; Copier with enlargement capabilities; Large print & cassettes; Large print bks; Low vision equip; Magnifiers; Networked computers with assistive software; PC for handicapped; Scanner for conversion & translation of mats; Screen enlargement software for people with visual disabilities; Screen reader software; Text reader; ZoomText magnification & reading software
Open Mon-Fri 10-9, Sat 9-5, Sun 1-5
Friends of the Library Group

CHATSWORTH

S CHATSWORTH HISTORICAL SOCIETY*, Frank H Schepler Jr & William F Schepler Memorial Library, 10385 Shadow Oak Dr, 91311. SAN 371-2435. Tel: 818-882-5614. FAX: 818-882-5614. E-mail: chatsmimi@aol.com. Web Site: historicalsocieties.net. *Pres,* Linda van der Valk; *Curator,* Virginia Faye Watson; Tel: 818-341-3053, Fax: 818-341-3053. Subject Specialists: *Chatsworth hist,* Virginia Faye Watson
Library Holdings: Bk Titles 500
Special Collections: Photographs of San Fernando Valley History; San Fernando Valley & California History (Lila & Bill Schepler Book Coll); Slide Coll
Subject Interests: Geog, Local authors
Function: Res libr
Restriction: Open by appt only

S NATIONAL INVESTIGATIONS COMMITTEE ON UNIDENTIFIED FLYING OBJECTS*, Research Library, 21601 Devonshire St, Ste 217, 91311. SAN 375-1570. Tel: 818-882-0052. FAX: 818-882-0047. Web Site: www.nicufo.org.
Founded 1967
Library Holdings: Bk Titles 3,000; Per Subs 500
Subject Interests: Space, Spirituality, UFO phenomenon
Publications: Inter Space Link (Monthly) (Newsletter); UFO Journal (Quarterly)
Restriction: Open by appt only

C PHILLIPS GRADUATE INSTITUTE LIBRARY*, 19900 Plummer St, 91311. SAN 300-8908. Tel: 818-386-5640. FAX: 818-386-5696. E-mail: library@pgi.edu. Web Site: www.pgi.edu. *Dir, Libr Serv,* Caroline Sisneros; Tel: 818-386-5642, E-mail: csisneros@pgi.edu; *Circ,* Linda Folse; Staff 3 (MLS 1, Non-MLS 2)
Founded 1981. Highest Degree: Doctorate
Library Holdings: AV Mats 1,800; e-books 1,000; Bk Titles 9,000; Per Subs 75
Subject Interests: Family therapy, Marriage, Organizational behavior, Psychol, Sch counseling
Automation Activity & Vendor Info: (Acquisitions) EOS International; (Cataloging) EOS International; (Circulation) EOS International; (OPAC) EOS International; (Serials) EOS International
Database Vendor: EBSCOhost, LexisNexis, Sage
Wireless access
Function: Res libr
Partic in Medical Library Group of Southern California & Arizona (MLGSCA); OCLC Online Computer Library Center, Inc; Statewide California Electronic Library Consortium (SCELC)
Special Services for the Deaf - Coll on deaf educ

CHICO

C CALIFORNIA STATE UNIVERSITY, CHICO*, Meriam Library, 400 W First St, 95929-0295. SAN 300-6646. Tel: 530-898-5862. Circulation Tel: 530-898-6501. Interlibrary Loan Service Tel: 530-898-6479. Reference Tel: 530-898-5833. FAX: 530-898-4443. Web Site: www.csuchico.edu/library. *Interim Univ Librn,* Sarah Blakeslee; Tel: 530-898-4244, E-mail: sblakeslee@csuchico.edu; *Vice Provost & CIO, Info Res,* Michael Schilling; Tel: 530-898-6212, E-mail: mlschilling@csuchico.edu; *Head, Circ & Reserves,* Joe Crotts; Tel: 530-898-6675, E-mail: jcrotts@csuchico.edu; *Head, Coll Mgt & Tech Serv,* Marc Langston; Tel: 530-898-4587, E-mail: mlangston@csuchico.edu; *Head, ILL,* JoAnn Bradley; E-mail: jbradley@csuchico.edu; *Head, Ref & Instruction,* Jodi Shepherd; Tel: 530-898-5499, E-mail: jrshepherd@csuchico.edu; *Head, Spec Coll & Archives,* George Thompson; Tel: 530-898-6603, E-mail: ghthompson@csuchico.edu; Staff 35.25 (MLS 11, Non-MLS 24.25)
Founded 1887. Enrl 16,470; Fac 862; Highest Degree: Master
Jul 2011-Jun 2012 Income $3,882,965. Mats Exp $1,072,576, Books $223,382, Per/Ser (Incl. Access Fees) $104,120, Manu Arch $1,910, Micro $15,257, AV Mat $6,295, Electronic Ref Mat (Incl. Access Fees) $713,748, Presv $7,864. Sal $2,185,244 (Prof $842,663)
Library Holdings: Bk Vols 930,321; Per Subs 534
Special Collections: Northeast California Coll, photog & print. Oral History; US Document Depository
Automation Activity & Vendor Info: (Acquisitions) Innovative Interfaces, Inc; (Cataloging) Innovative Interfaces, Inc; (Circulation) Innovative Interfaces, Inc; (Course Reserve) Innovative Interfaces, Inc; (ILL) OCLC ILLiad; (OPAC) Innovative Interfaces, Inc; (Serials) Innovative Interfaces, Inc
Database Vendor: Alexander Street Press, ARTstor, EBSCOhost, Elsevier, Gale Cengage Learning, JSTOR, Newsbank, ProQuest, Springer-Verlag
Wireless access
Mem of NorthNet Library System
Open Mon-Thurs 7:30am-11:45pm, Fri 7:30-4:45, Sat Noon-4:45, Sun Noon-11:45

CHINA LAKE

A UNITED STATES NAVY*, Naval Air Warfare Center Weapons Division Technical Library, One Administration Circle, Stop 6203, 93555-6100. Tel: 760-939-3389. Interlibrary Loan Service Tel: 760-939-4132. FAX: 760-939-2431. E-mail: nwtechlib@navy.mil. *Dir,* Barbara Lupei; Staff 11 (MLS 5, Non-MLS 6)
Founded 1946
Library Holdings: Bk Vols 40,000; Per Subs 400
Subject Interests: Aerospace, Chem, Computer sci, Electronics, Eng, Math, Naval sci, Physics, Weapons
Automation Activity & Vendor Info: (Acquisitions) SirsiDynix; (Cataloging) SirsiDynix; (Circulation) SirsiDynix; (ILL) OCLC; (OPAC) SirsiDynix; (Serials) SirsiDynix
Database Vendor: Cambridge Scientific Abstracts, Dialog, ISI Web of Knowledge, Jane's, OCLC FirstSearch, ProQuest, SirsiDynix
Partic in Consortium of Naval Libraries (CNL)
Restriction: Authorized personnel only, Not open to pub, Restricted access

CHULA VISTA

S AMERICAN SCIENTIFIC CORP LIBRARY*, 3250 Holly Way, 91910-3217. SAN 328-1388. Tel: 619-422-1754. FAX: 619-426-1280. *Mgr,* Louis Gerken; E-mail: gerkenlc@att.net; *Tech Serv,* Valerie Brault
Founded 1974
Library Holdings: Bk Titles 300; Per Subs 12
Subject Interests: World War II

P CHULA VISTA PUBLIC LIBRARY*, Civic Center, 365 F St, 91910-2697. SAN 300-6662. Tel: 619-691-5069. Administration Tel: 619-585-5689. FAX: 619-427-4246. Web Site: www.chulavistalibrary.com. *Libr Dir,* Betty Waznis; Tel: 619-691-5170, E-mail: bwaznis@chulavista.lib.ca.us; *Pub Serv Mgr,* Stephanie Loney; Tel: 619-691-5288, E-mail: sloney@chulavista.lib.ca.us; *Digital Serv, Tech Serv Mgr,* Jodie Sawina; Tel: 619-691-5138, E-mail: jsawina@chulavista.lib.ca.us; Staff 12 (MLS 10, Non-MLS 2)
Founded 1891. Pop 246,496; Circ 952,847
Jul 2010-Jun 2011 Income (Main Library and Branch(s)) $3,851,008. Mats Exp $495,278, Books $280,350, Per/Ser (Incl. Access Fees) $17,933, Manu Arch $4,000, AV Mat $65,387, Electronic Ref Mat (Incl. Access Fees) $124,878, Presv $2,730. Sal $2,812,603
Library Holdings: CDs 15,041; DVDs 16,701; Electronic Media & Resources 750; Bk Vols 412,649
Subject Interests: Genealogy, Local hist
Automation Activity & Vendor Info: (Acquisitions) Baker & Taylor; (Cataloging) Innovative Interfaces, Inc - Millenium; (Circulation) Innovative Interfaces, Inc - Millenium; (OPAC) Innovative Interfaces, Inc - Millenium; (Serials) Innovative Interfaces, Inc - Millenium
Database Vendor: Gale Cengage Learning, Innovative Interfaces, Inc, LearningExpress, ReferenceUSA, TumbleBookLibrary, World Book Online
Wireless access
Function: Audiobks via web, Bilingual assistance for Spanish patrons, Bk club(s), Bks on CD, Children's prog, Computers for patron use, Copy machines, Digital talking bks, E-Reserves, Electronic databases & coll, Exhibits, Genealogy discussion group, Handicapped accessible, Holiday prog, ILL available, Music CDs, Online cat, OverDrive digital audio bks, Passport agency, Photocopying/Printing, Prog for adults, Prog for children & young adult, Story hour, Summer & winter reading prog, Tax forms, Telephone ref, VCDs, Wheelchair accessible

Publications: Calendar of Events (Monthly); Library Brochure; Library Buzz (Newsletter)
Partic in OCLC Online Computer Library Center, Inc; Serra Cooperative Library System
Open Mon-Thurs 10-8, Fri & Sat 10-5, Sun 1-5
Friends of the Library Group
Branches: 1
SOUTH CHULA VISTA, 389 Orange Ave, 91911-4116, SAN 370-2952. Tel: 619-585-5750. FAX: 619-420-1591. *Br Mgr,* Joy Whatley; Tel: 619-585-5786, E-mail: jwhatley@chulavista.lib.ca.us; Staff 4 (MLS 4)
Founded 1995. Pop 21,727; Circ 350,084
Library Holdings: Bk Vols 160,395
Function: Adult literacy prog, After school storytime, Art exhibits, Bilingual assistance for Spanish patrons, Bks on CD, Children's prog, Citizenship assistance, Computer training, Computers for patron use, E-Reserves, Electronic databases & coll, Exhibits, Holiday prog, Homework prog, ILL available, Literacy & newcomer serv, Mail & tel request accepted, Music CDs, Online cat, Outreach serv, Photocopying/Printing, Preschool outreach, Prog for adults, Prog for children & young adult, Pub access computers, Ref & res, Story hour, Summer reading prog, Tax forms, Teen prog, Telephone ref
Open Mon-Wed 11-8, Thurs & Fri 10-6, Sat 10-2
Friends of the Library Group

J SOUTHWESTERN COLLEGE LIBRARY*, 900 Otay Lakes Rd, 91910-7299. SAN 300-6689. Tel: 619-216-6619, 619-482-6373. Circulation Tel: 619-482-6397. Interlibrary Loan Service Tel: 619-482-6431. Information Services Tel: 619-421-6700, Ext 5381. FAX: 619-482-6417. TDD: 619-482-6490. E-mail: library@swccd.edu. Web Site: www.swc.cc.ca.us/~library/. *Dean,* Mink Stavenga; Tel: 619-482-6542, E-mail: mstavenga@swccd.edu; *Librn,* Diane Gustafson; Tel: 619-482-6433, E-mail: dgustafson@swc.cc.ca.us; *Librn,* Mark Hammond; Tel: 619-421-6700, Ext 5781, E-mail: mhammond@swc.cc.ca.us; *Librn,* Tony McGee; *Librn,* Naomi Trapp; Tel: 619-421-6700, Ext 5893, E-mail: ntrapp@swc.cc.ca.us; *Librn,* Ron Vess; E-mail: rvess@swc.cc.ca.us; Staff 11 (MLS 6, Non-MLS 5)
Founded 1961. Enrl 18,597; Fac 752; Highest Degree: Associate
Library Holdings: High Interest/Low Vocabulary Bk Vols 487; Bk Titles 79,946; Bk Vols 86,539; Per Subs 240
Automation Activity & Vendor Info: (Cataloging) SirsiDynix; (Circulation) SirsiDynix; (OPAC) SirsiDynix
Database Vendor: EBSCOhost, Gale Cengage Learning, OCLC FirstSearch, ProQuest, SirsiDynix
Partic in OCLC Online Computer Library Center, Inc
Special Services for the Deaf - TDD equip
Friends of the Library Group

CITY OF INDUSTRY

S WORKMAN & TEMPLE FAMILY HOMESTEAD MUSEUM LIBRARY*, 15415 E Don Julian Rd, 91745-1029. SAN 374-793X. Tel: 626-968-8492. FAX: 626-968-2048. E-mail: info@homesteadmuseum.org. Web Site: www.homesteadmuseum.org. *Dir,* Karen Wade; E-mail: k.wade@homesteadmuseum.org; *Coll Mgr,* Paul R Spitzzeri; E-mail: p.spitzzeri@homesteadmuseum.org
Founded 1981
Jul 2005-Jun 2006 Income $3,500. Mats Exp $3,500, Books $3,000, Per/Ser (Incl. Access Fees) $500
Library Holdings: Bk Vols 3,250; Per Subs 45
Special Collections: Pre-1930 Imprints; Southern California & California History, 1830-1930
Subject Interests: Archit, Decorative art, Interior design, Mus admin
Database Vendor: OCLC FirstSearch
Function: Photocopying/Printing
Restriction: Non-circulating

CLAREMONT

C CLAREMONT COLLEGES LIBRARY*, Honnold-Mudd Library, 800 Dartmouth Ave, 91711. SAN 331-7765. Tel: 909-621-8014. Web Site: libraries.claremont.edu. Staff 74 (MLS 28, Non-MLS 46)
Founded 1887. Enrl 7,000; Fac 800; Highest Degree: Doctorate
Library Holdings: e-books 25,000; Bk Vols 2,678,000; Per Subs 5,958
Special Collections: Cartography of the Pacific Coast; Claremont Colleges Archives; Honnold Library: Calif & Western Americana; Irving Wallace; Northern Europe & Scandinavia; Oxford & its Colleges; Philbrick Library of Dramatic Arts; Renaissance; Water Resources of Southern Calif, bk, mss. Oral History; State Document Depository; US Document Depository
Subject Interests: Art, Bus & mgt, Econ, Educ, Environ studies, Hist, Law, Lit, Music, Natural sci, Relig, Soc sci & issues, Women's studies
Automation Activity & Vendor Info: (Acquisitions) Innovative Interfaces, Inc; (Cataloging) Innovative Interfaces, Inc; (Circulation) Innovative Interfaces, Inc; (Course Reserve) Docutek; (OPAC) Innovative Interfaces, Inc; (Serials) Innovative Interfaces, Inc
Wireless access
Partic in OCLC Online Computer Library Center, Inc; RLIN (Research Libraries Information Network)
Restriction: Restricted access
Departmental Libraries:
ELLA STRONG DENISON LIBRARY, Scripps College, 1030 N Columbia Ave, 91711, SAN 331-779X. Tel: 909-607-3941. FAX: 909-607-1548. *Dir,* Judy Harvey Sahak; Tel: 909-621-8973, E-mail: judy.sahak@scrippscollege.edu; Staff 4 (MLS 2, Non-MLS 2)
Library Holdings: Bk Vols 55,000; Per Subs 40
Special Collections: Bookplates; Ellen Browning Scripps; Gertrude Stein Coll; History of Book & Book Arts; Juvenilia; Latin America Coll; Macpherson Coll on Women; Melville Coll; Robert & Elizabeth Browning Coll; Southwest Coll
Subject Interests: Art & archit, Humanities, Women's studies
Open Mon-Thurs 10am-Midnight, Fri 10-5, Sat 12-5, Sun Noon-Midnight

CR CLAREMONT SCHOOL OF THEOLOGY LIBRARY*, 1325 N College Ave, 91711. SAN 300-676X. Tel: 909-447-2589. Reference Tel: 909-447-2511. E-mail: library@cst.edu. Reference E-mail: reference@cst.edu. Web Site: www.cst.edu/library. *Dir,* John Dickason; Tel: 909-447-2512, E-mail: jdickason@cst.edu; *Cat,* Eugene Fieg; Tel: 909-447-2513, E-mail: efieg@cst.edu; *Circ,* Elaine Walker; Tel: 909-447-2510, E-mail: ewalker@cst.edu; *Ref,* Betty Clements; E-mail: bclements@cst.edu; *Libr Asst,* Koala Jones; E-mail: kjones@cst.edu; Staff 7 (MLS 4, Non-MLS 3)
Founded 1957. Enrl 395; Fac 33; Highest Degree: Doctorate
Library Holdings: Bk Vols 192,000; Per Subs 641
Special Collections: James C Baker Manuscripts; Kirby Page Manuscripts; Robert H Mitchell Hymnology Coll
Subject Interests: Biblical studies
Partic in OCLC Online Computer Library Center, Inc
Open Mon-Thurs 8:30am-10pm, Fri 8:30-7, Sat 9-5
Departmental Libraries:
CENTER FOR PROCESS STUDIES, 1325 N College Ave, 91711-3154. Tel: 909-447-2533, 909-621-5330. FAX: 909-621-2760. E-mail: process@ctr4process.org. Web Site: www.ctr4process.org. *Librn,* Steven W Hulbert; E-mail: steve@ctr4process.org
Library Holdings: Bk Vols 2,400
Special Collections: Charles Birch Coll; Charles Hartshorne Archive; Daniel Day Williams Archive; David Ray Griffin Coll; John B Cobb Coll; John Spencer Archive; Mary Elizabeth Moore Coll; Philip Clayton Coll; William A Beardslee Archive
Subject Interests: Philos, Relig, Theol
Publications: Process Perspectives (Newsletter); Process Studies (Bi-annually)
Open Mon-Fri 9-5

S RANCHO SANTA ANA BOTANIC GARDEN LIBRARY, 1500 N College Ave, 91711. SAN 300-6751. Tel: 909-625-8767, Ext 210. FAX: 909-626-7670. Web Site: www.rsabg.org. *Libr Spec,* Irene Holiman; E-mail: iholiman@rsabg.org; Staff 2 (MLS 1, Non-MLS 1)
Founded 1927
Library Holdings: Bk Vols 47,000; Per Subs 600
Special Collections: Californiana; Marcus E Jones Archival Materials
Subject Interests: Biol, Botany, Conserv, Evolution, Hort
Automation Activity & Vendor Info: (Cataloging) OCLC
Database Vendor: OCLC FirstSearch
Partic in OCLC Online Computer Library Center, Inc; OCLC Western Service Center
Open Mon-Fri 9-4
Restriction: Non-circulating

CLOVIS

CL SAN JOAQUIN COLLEGE OF LAW LIBRARY*, 901 Fifth St, 93612. SAN 300-7669. Tel: 559-323-2100, Ext 121. FAX: 559-323-5566. Web Site: www.sjcl.edu/library. *Librn,* Pete Rooney; E-mail: prooney@sjcl.edu
Founded 1969
Library Holdings: Bk Vols 56,500; Per Subs 300
Automation Activity & Vendor Info: (Acquisitions) EOS International; (Cataloging) EOS International; (Circulation) EOS International; (Serials) EOS International
Open Mon-Thurs 9am-10pm, Fri 9-5, Sat & Sun 8:30-6

COALINGA

P COALINGA-HURON LIBRARY DISTRICT*, Coalinga District Library, 305 N Fourth St, 93210. SAN 331-8060. Tel: 559-935-1676. FAX: 559-935-1058. *Dir of Libr Serv,* Sylvia Archibald; *Circ,* Hilda Crawford; *Tech Serv,* Diana Baker; Staff 1 (Non-MLS 1)
Founded 1912. Pop 30,274; Circ 58,058
Jul 2009-Jun 2010 Income (Main Library and Branch(s)) $10,127,000, State $10,643, County $943,063, Other $1,406,685. Mats Exp $112,500,

Books $91,000, Other Print Mats $6,500, Electronic Ref Mat (Incl. Access Fees) $8,000. Sal $69,568
Library Holdings: Audiobooks 979; AV Mats 3,614; CDs 109; Large Print Bks 1,060; Bk Titles 78,130; Bk Vols 78,276; Per Subs 125; Talking Bks 1,833; Videos 4,260
Subject Interests: Calif, Genealogy, Local hist, Native Am
Automation Activity & Vendor Info: (Acquisitions) Horizon; (Cataloging) Horizon
Mem of San Joaquin Valley Library System
Open Mon-Thurs 10-8, Fri & Sat 10-5
Branches: 1
HURON BRANCH, 36050 O St, Huron, 93234. (Mail add: PO Box 190, Huron, 93234-0190), SAN 331-8095. Tel: 559-945-2284. FAX: 559-945-2855. *Br Spec,* Melba McHaney
Library Holdings: Bk Vols 18,000; Per Subs 45
Open Mon-Thurs 10-7

J WEST HILLS COMMUNITY COLLEGE*, Fitch Library, 300 Cherry Lane, 93210. SAN 331-8125. Tel: 559-934-2420. FAX: 559-935-2633. Web Site: www.westhillscollege.com. *Librn,* Matthew Magnuson; E-mail: matthewmagnuson@whccd.edu; Staff 3 (MLS 1, Non-MLS 2)
Founded 1956. Enrl 2,100; Fac 41
Library Holdings: High Interest/Low Vocabulary Bk Vols 2,000; Bk Vols 44,000; Per Subs 112
Subject Interests: Chicano studies, Corrections, English as a second lang, Graphic novels, Studio art
Automation Activity & Vendor Info: (Cataloging) SirsiDynix; (Circulation) SirsiDynix; (Course Reserve) SirsiDynix
Database Vendor: CountryWatch, CQ Press, EBSCOhost, Gale Cengage Learning, ProQuest
Wireless access
Partic in Heartland Regional Library Network of the Library of California
Open Mon-Thurs (Fall & Spring) 7:30am-8pm, Fri 7:30-4

COLTON

M ARROWHEAD REGIONAL MEDICAL CENTER, Health Sciences Library, 400 N Pepper Ave, 92324-1819. SAN 301-3014. Tel: 909-580-1300. FAX: 909-580-1310. *Dir, Libr Serv,* Gloria Arredondo; Tel: 909-580-1385, E-mail: arredondog@armc.sbcounty.gov; *ILL,* Marisa Luna; Tel: 909-580-1308, E-mail: lunam@armc.sbcounty.gov; Staff 2 (MLS 1, Non-MLS 1)
Library Holdings: e-books 1,296; e-journals 5,200; Bk Titles 2,800; Per Subs 307
Subject Interests: Med
Automation Activity & Vendor Info: (Acquisitions) EOS International; (Cataloging) EOS International; (Circulation) EOS International; (OPAC) EOS International; (Serials) EOS International
Database Vendor: 3M Library Systems, Elsevier, EOS International, Lexi-Comp, Majors, Marcive, Inc, McGraw-Hill, OVID Technologies, ProQuest, UpToDate, Wiley InterScience
Wireless access
Function: ILL available, Res libr
Publications: San Bernardino County Medical Center Library Brochure
Partic in Docline; Inland Empire Med Libr Coop; Medical Library Group of Southern California & Arizona (MLGSCA); Pacific Southwest Regional Medical Library (PSRML); San Bernardino, Inyo, Riverside Counties United Library Services
Restriction: Med staff only

P COLTON PUBLIC LIBRARY*, 656 N Ninth St, 92324. SAN 300-6778. Tel: 909-370-5083. Web Site: www.ci.colton.ca.us/cs_l.html. *Libr Dir,* Edward Pedroza; Tel: 909-370-5189, E-mail: epedroza@ci.colton.ca.us; Staff 14 (MLS 1, Non-MLS 13)
Founded 1906. Pop 49,100; Circ 353,365
Library Holdings: Bk Titles 88,060; Bk Vols 99,826; Per Subs 300
Automation Activity & Vendor Info: (Cataloging) SirsiDynix; (Circulation) SirsiDynix; (OPAC) SirsiDynix
Database Vendor: SirsiDynix
Mem of Inland Library System
Open Mon, Fri & Sat 10-6, Wed 12-8
Friends of the Library Group
Branches: 1
LUQUE BRANCH, 294 East O St, 92324, SAN 329-2673. Tel: 909-370-5182. FAX: 909-370-5182. *Br Supvr,* Edward Pedroza; Tel: 909-370-5189, E-mail: epedroza@ci.colton.ca.us; Staff 1 (Non-MLS 1)

S WORLD LIFE RESEARCH INSTITUTE LIBRARY*, 23000 Grand Terrace Rd, 92324. SAN 300-6786. Tel: 909-825-4773. FAX: 909-783-3477. *Dir,* Bruce Halstead
Founded 1959
Library Holdings: Bk Vols 30,000
Subject Interests: Marine biol, Nutrition, Pollution, Toxicology

COLUSA

P COLUSA COUNTY FREE LIBRARY*, 738 Market St, 95932. SAN 376-3722. Tel: 530-458-7671. FAX: 530-458-7358. E-mail: ccl@countyofcolusa.org. *Dir,* Wendy Burke; E-mail: wburke@countyofcolusa.org; *Fiscal Officer,* Candy Grimm; E-mail: cagrimm@countyofcolusa.org; Staff 6 (MLS 1, Non-MLS 5)
Founded 1915. Pop 21,951; Circ 39,651
Library Holdings: AV Mats 4,700; Bk Vols 96,835; Per Subs 77; Videos 5,814
Special Collections: California Indian Library Coll (Colusa County); Colusa County History Coll
Automation Activity & Vendor Info: (Cataloging) Innovative Interfaces, Inc; (Circulation) Innovative Interfaces, Inc; (ILL) Innovative Interfaces, Inc; (OPAC) Innovative Interfaces, Inc
Function: Adult literacy prog, Bilingual assistance for Spanish patrons, Bks on cassette, Bks on CD, Children's prog, Computers for patron use, Copy machines, Family literacy, ILL available, Online cat, Ref serv available, Story hour, Summer reading prog, Telephone ref, VHS videos, Video lending libr, Wheelchair accessible
Mem of Mountain-Valley Library System
Open Mon-Wed 10-5, Thurs 10-8, Fri 12-5
Friends of the Library Group
Branches: 6
ARBUCKLE BRANCH, 610 King St, Arbuckle, 95912. (Mail add: PO Box 893, Arbuckle, 95912-0893). Tel: 530-476-2526. FAX: 530-476-2526. E-mail: arbucklelibrary@yahoo.com. *Br Mgr,* Michelle Dennis
Library Holdings: Bk Vols 2,500
Open Mon 1-6, Tues 10-3, Wed 1-7
GRIMES BRANCH, 240 Main St, Grimes, 95950. (Mail add: PO Box 275, Grimes, 95950-0275). Tel: 530-437-2428. FAX: 530-437-2428. E-mail: grimeslibrary@yahoo.com. *Br Mgr,* Roseann Ellis
Library Holdings: Bk Vols 7,600
Open Tues & Thurs 2-5:30, Wed 9:30-11:30
MAXWELL BRANCH, 34 Oak St, Maxwell, 95955. Tel: 530-438-2250. FAX: 530-438-2250. E-mail: maxwelllibrary@countyofcolusa.org. *Br Mgr,* Sharron Johnson
Library Holdings: Bk Vols 7,000
Open Tues-Thurs 12:30-6
PRINCETON BRANCH, 232 Prince St, Princeton, 95970. (Mail add: PO Box 97, Princeton, 95970-0097). Tel: 530-439-2235. FAX: 530-439-2235. *Br Mgr,* Mary Beth Massa; E-mail: mbmassa2002@yahoo.com
Library Holdings: Bk Vols 10,000
Open Tues 8-1, Wed 8-5
STONYFORD BRANCH, 5080 Stonyford-Lodoga Rd, Stonyford, 95979. (Mail add: PO Box 238, Stonyford, 95979-0238). Tel: 530-963-3722. *Br Mgr,* Jeff Applegate
Library Holdings: Bk Vols 3,000
Open Wed 1-6, Thurs 3-7, Sat 10-1:30
WILLIAMS BRANCH, 901 E St, Williams, 95987. (Mail add: PO Box 517, Williams, 95987-0517). Tel: 530-473-5955. FAX: 530-473-5955. E-mail: williamslibrary@countyofcolusa.org. *Br Mgr,* Rebecca Christy
Library Holdings: Bk Vols 8,500
Open Tues-Thurs 12-6, Sat 10-2

COMMERCE

P CITY OF COMMERCE PUBLIC LIBRARY*, 5655 Jillson St, 90040-1485. SAN 331-8338. Tel: 323-722-6660. Reference Tel: 323-722-6660, Ext 2275. FAX: 323-724-1978. E-mail: referencel@ci.commerce.ca.us. Web Site: www.cocpl.org. *Dir of Libr Serv,* Beatriz Sarmiento; E-mail: beatrizs@ci.commerce.ca.us; *Ch Serv,* Sigrid Hudson; Tel: 323-722-6660, Ext 2829, E-mail: sigridh@ci.commerce.ca.us; *Circ,* Yolanda Cardenas-Parra; E-mail: yolandac@ci.commerce.ca.us; Staff 70 (MLS 8, Non-MLS 62)
Founded 1961. Pop 13,504; Circ 259,861
Library Holdings: AV Mats 11,994; CDs 4,053; DVDs 3,446; High Interest/Low Vocabulary Bk Vols 600; Large Print Bks 884; Bk Titles 80,098; Bk Vols 131,796; Per Subs 399; Talking Bks 978; Videos 5,540
Automation Activity & Vendor Info: (Cataloging) SirsiDynix; (Circulation) SirsiDynix; (ILL) OCLC Online; (OPAC) SirsiDynix; (Serials) SirsiDynix
Database Vendor: Gale Cengage Learning, Newsbank, OCLC FirstSearch, Westlaw
Function: Art exhibits, BA reader (adult literacy), Home delivery & serv to Sr ctr & nursing homes, ILL available, Magnifiers for reading, Music CDs, Photocopying/Printing, Prog for adults, Prog for children & young adult, Ref serv available, Spoken cassettes & CDs, Summer reading prog, VHS videos, Workshops
Partic in Southern California Library Cooperative
Open Mon-Thurs 10-8, Fri 10-6, Sat 10-2

Branches: 3

ATLANTIC BRANCH, 2269 S Atlantic Blvd, 90040, SAN 377-5712. Tel: 323-780-1176. FAX: 323-780-0308. *Mgr,* Cris Muniz; Staff 7 (Non-MLS 7)
Founded 1996. Circ 34,031
Library Holdings: CDs 857; DVDs 558; Bk Titles 12,532; Bk Vols 13,909; Per Subs 46; Videos 544
Function: Photocopying/Printing, Prog for children & young adult, Ref serv available, Summer reading prog
Open Mon-Thurs 1-8, Fri 1-6

BRISTOW PARK BRANCH, 1466 S McDonnell Ave, 90040, SAN 378-1852. Tel: 323-265-1787. FAX: 323-269-6608. *Mgr,* Luis Martinez; Staff 7 (Non-MLS 7)
Founded 1988. Circ 54,667
Library Holdings: CDs 475; DVDs 662; Bk Titles 14,214; Bk Vols 16,386; Per Subs 71; Videos 882
Function: Photocopying/Printing, Prog for children & young adult, Ref serv available, Summer reading prog
Open Mon & Tues 2-8, Wed & Thurs 1-8, Fri 2-6

GREENWOOD BRANCH, 6134 Greenwood Ave, 90040, SAN 378-1879. Tel: 562-927-1516. FAX: 562-927-2076. *Br Mgr,* Olivia Audoma; Staff 7 (Non-MLS 7)
Founded 1966. Circ 45,712
Jul 2007-Jun 2008 Income $148,587. Mats Exp $25,000. Sal $100,925
Library Holdings: CDs 512; DVDs 633; Bk Titles 14,017; Bk Vols 15,514; Per Subs 59; Videos 791
Function: Adult bk club, After school storytime, Bilingual assistance for Spanish patrons, Bks on CD, Children's prog, Computer training, Computers for patron use, Copy machines, Free DVD rentals, Handicapped accessible, Holiday prog, Homebound delivery serv, Homework prog, ILL available, Learning ctr, Mail & tel request accepted, Music CDs, Online cat, Online info literacy tutorials on the web & in blackboard, Online searches, Orientations, Photocopying/Printing, Preschool outreach, Prog for children & young adult, Pub access computers, Summer reading prog, Tax forms, Teen prog, VHS videos, Wheelchair accessible, Workshops
Open Mon-Thurs 1-8, Fri & Sat 10-3

COMPTON

J COMPTON COMMUNITY COLLEGE LIBRARY*, Emily B Hart-Holifield Library, 1111 E Artesia Blvd, 90221. SAN 300-6816. Tel: 310-900-1600, Ext 2175. FAX: 310-900-1693. Web Site: www.compton.edu/library. *Acq,* Andree Valdry; *Bibliog Instr, Cat,* Eleanor Sonido; *Ref Serv,* Roberta Hawkins; *Ref Serv,* Elizabeth Martin; *Ref Serv,* Estina Pratt
Founded 1927. Highest Degree: Associate
Library Holdings: AV Mats 384; CDs 100; High Interest/Low Vocabulary Bk Vols 804; Bk Titles 32,391; Bk Vols 39,277; Per Subs 139
Automation Activity & Vendor Info: (Acquisitions) Ex Libris Group; (Cataloging) Ex Libris Group; (Circulation) Ex Libris Group; (OPAC) Ex Libris Group
Database Vendor: EBSCOhost, Gale Cengage Learning, OCLC WorldShare Interlibrary Loan, ProQuest
Function: For res purposes
Open Mon-Thurs (Winter) 8-8, Fri & Sat 8-4; Mon-Thurs (Summer) 8-6

CONCORD

S CALRECOVERY INC LIBRARY*, 2454 Stanwell Dr, 94520. SAN 373-4951. Tel: 925-356-3700. FAX: 925-356-7956. E-mail: mail@calrecovery.com. Web Site: www.calrecovery.com. *Librn,* Cheryl Henry
Library Holdings: Bk Vols 7,000; Per Subs 20
Open Mon-Fri 8-4

J HEALD COLLEGE*, Learning Resource Center-Concord Campus, 5130 Commercial Circle, 94520. Tel: 925-288-5800. Toll Free Tel: 800-755-3550. FAX: 925-288-5896. Web Site: www.heald.edu.
Library Holdings: AV Mats 150; Bk Vols 800; Per Subs 20
Database Vendor: EBSCOhost
Wireless access
Open Mon-Thurs 7am-10:30pm, Fri 7-6

CORONA

P CORONA PUBLIC LIBRARY*, 650 S Main St, 92882. SAN 300-6824. Tel: 951-736-2381. Circulation Tel: 951-736-2382. Interlibrary Loan Service Tel: 951-279-3586. Administration Tel: 951-736-2384. FAX: 951-736-2499. Web Site: www.coronapubliclibrary.org. *Dir,* Julie Fredericksen; *Div Mgr, Pub Serv,* Abigail Schellberg; *Adult Serv,* Christina Smith; *Ch Serv,* Suzanne MacConnell; *Circ,* Gabrielle MacKay; *Tech Serv,* Betty Luscher; Staff 9 (MLS 9)
Founded 1899. Pop 123,000; Circ 370,002
Library Holdings: Bk Vols 160,000; Per Subs 400
Special Collections: Calif; Corona Newspaper Archives, photographs. Oral History
Subject Interests: Local hist
Automation Activity & Vendor Info: (Acquisitions) SirsiDynix; (Cataloging) SirsiDynix; (Circulation) SirsiDynix; (Course Reserve) SirsiDynix; (ILL) SirsiDynix; (Media Booking) SirsiDynix; (OPAC) SirsiDynix; (Serials) SirsiDynix
Mem of Inland Library System
Open Mon & Tues 12-9, Wed & Thurs 10-6, Sat 10-5
Friends of the Library Group

CORONA DEL MAR

S SHERMAN RESEARCH LIBRARY & GARDENS*, 2647 E Pacific Coast Hwy, 92625. SAN 300-6832. Tel: 949-673-1880. FAX: 949-675-5458. Web Site: www.slgardens.org/the_library. *Librn,* Jill Thrasher; E-mail: jill@slgardens.org; Staff 3 (MLS 1, Non-MLS 2)
Founded 1966
Library Holdings: Bk Vols 25,000
Subject Interests: Hist of the Pacific Southwest
Open Tues-Thurs 9-1 & 2-4:30
Restriction: Not a lending libr

CORONADO

P CORONADO PUBLIC LIBRARY*, 640 Orange Ave, 92118-1526. SAN 300-6840. Tel: 619-522-7390. Reference Tel: 619-522-2484. Administration Tel: 619-522-2475. FAX: 619-435-4205. Web Site: www.coronado.ca.us/library. *Dir of Libr Serv,* Christian R Esquevin; Tel: 619-522-7395, E-mail: c.esquevin@coronado.lib.ca.us; *Head, Tech & Vols,* Phyllis Belter; Tel: 619-522-2474, E-mail: p.belter@coronado.lib.ca.us; *Head, Circ,* Cheryl Grove; Tel: 619-522-2472, E-mail: c.grove@coronado.lib.ca.us; *Head, Tech Serv,* Vy Tu; Tel: 619-522-2473, E-mail: v.tu@coronado.lib.ca.us; Staff 9 (MLS 9)
Founded 1890. Pop 23,916; Circ 357,841
Jul 2009-Jun 2010 Income $2,411,854, State $19,698, City $2,325,028. Mats Exp $286,175, Books $121,267, Per/Ser (Incl. Access Fees) $18,912, Manu Arch $2,500, Micro $14,500, AV Mat $95,326, Electronic Ref Mat (Incl. Access Fees) $28,670, Presv $5,000. Sal $1,333,859
Library Holdings: Audiobooks 3,357; AV Mats 21,168; CDs 6,908; DVDs 12,260; Large Print Bks 2,910; Microforms 86; Bk Titles 137,040; Bk Vols 161,048; Per Subs 339; Videos 727
Special Collections: Coronado Government Documents; Coronado Local History Photograph & Map Coll
Subject Interests: Gardening, Local hist, Spec operations, World War II
Automation Activity & Vendor Info: (Acquisitions) Innovative Interfaces, Inc - Millenium; (Cataloging) Innovative Interfaces, Inc; (Circulation) Innovative Interfaces, Inc; (OPAC) Innovative Interfaces, Inc - Millenium
Database Vendor: Baker & Taylor, Bowker, Grolier Online, ProQuest, ReferenceUSA
Wireless access
Function: Web-catalog
Publications: Calendar of Events; Summer Reading Brochure; The Story of the Ramos Martinez Murals & the La Avenida Cafe
Partic in OCLC Online Computer Library Center, Inc; Serra Cooperative Library System
Open Mon-Thurs 10-9, Fri & Sat 10-6, Sun 1-5
Friends of the Library Group

COSTA MESA

J ORANGE COAST COLLEGE LIBRARY, 2701 Fairview Rd, 92626. (Mail add: PO Box 5005, 92626-5005), SAN 300-6905. Tel: 714-432-5885. FAX: 714-432-6850. Web Site: www.orangecoastcollege.edu/academics/library/Pages/default.aspx. *Dean,* Joseph Poshek; *Instrul Serv Librn,* Vinta Oviatt; *Acq,* Carl Morgan; *Archives, Cat, Per,* Jodi Della Marna; *Online Serv,* Lori Cassidy; *Pub Serv,* John Dale
Founded 1948. Fac 400
Library Holdings: AV Mats 3,462; e-books 18,747; Bk Titles 93,529; Bk Vols 95,000; Per Subs 212
Automation Activity & Vendor Info: (Cataloging) Ex Libris Group; (Circulation) Ex Libris Group; (Course Reserve) Ex Libris Group; (OPAC) Ex Libris Group; (Serials) Ex Libris Group
Database Vendor: Baker & Taylor, CountryWatch, CQ Press, EBSCOhost, Gale Cengage Learning, JSTOR, LexisNexis, Marcive, Inc, ProQuest, SerialsSolutions, Springer-Verlag
Wireless access
Partic in OCLC Online Computer Library Center, Inc
Friends of the Library Group

L RUTAN & TUCKER LIBRARY*, 611 Anton, Ste 1400, 92626. SAN 301-5424. Tel: 714-641-5100. FAX: 714-546-9035. Web Site: www.rutan.com/libinfo. *Sr Librn,* Arlen Bristol; E-mail: abristol@rutan.com
Library Holdings: Bk Vols 30,000; Per Subs 150

C VANGUARD UNIVERSITY OF SOUTHERN CALIFORNIA*, O Cope Budge Library, 55 Fair Dr, 92626. SAN 300-6913. Tel: 714-556-3610, Ext 2400. FAX: 714-966-5478. *Head of Libr,* Alison English; *Archives Librn,* Pam Crenshaw; *Ref Librn,* Melvyn Covetta; *Cat, Ref,* Mary Wilson; *Circ,* Jack Morgan; *Purchasing,* Elena Nipper; Staff 6 (MLS 4, Non-MLS 2)
Founded 1920. Enrl 1,900; Fac 100; Highest Degree: Master
Jul 2008-Jun 2009. Mats Exp $222,000, Books $80,000, Manu Arch $2,000, Electronic Ref Mat (Incl. Access Fees) $140,000. Sal $318,600 (Prof $164,600)
Library Holdings: e-books 37,000; Bk Titles 75,000; Bk Vols 180,000; Per Subs 800
Special Collections: Christian Religion & Judaic Coll; Drama Coll; Nursing Coll; Pentecostal Coll; Spanish Coll
Automation Activity & Vendor Info: (Cataloging) Follett Software; (Circulation) Follett Software; (ILL) OCLC; (OPAC) Follett Software
Partic in OCLC Online Computer Library Center, Inc; Statewide California Electronic Library Consortium (SCELC)
Open Mon-Thurs 7:30am-11pm, Fri 7:30-5, Sat 10-5, Sun 2-8
Friends of the Library Group

CL WHITTIER COLLEGE*, School of Law Library, 3333 Harbor Blvd, 92626. SAN 301-0201. Tel: 714-444-4141. Circulation Tel: 714-444-4141, Ext 482. Interlibrary Loan Service Tel: 714-444-4141, Ext 487. FAX: 714-444-3609. Web Site: wollfpac.law.whittier.edu. *Dir,* J Denny Haythorn; Staff 15 (MLS 7, Non-MLS 8)
Founded 1966. Enrl 900; Fac 45; Highest Degree: Doctorate
Library Holdings: Bk Vols 360,000; Per Subs 4,700
Special Collections: State Document Depository; US Document Depository
Automation Activity & Vendor Info: (Cataloging) Innovative Interfaces, Inc; (Circulation) Innovative Interfaces, Inc; (Course Reserve) Innovative Interfaces, Inc; (OPAC) Innovative Interfaces, Inc; (Serials) Innovative Interfaces, Inc
Database Vendor: Innovative Interfaces, Inc
Open Mon-Thurs 8am-Midnight, Fri 8am-10pm, Sat 10-8, Sun 10am-Midnight

L WOODRUFF, SPRADLIN & SMART LIBRARY*, 555 Anton Blvd, Ste 1200, 92626-7670. SAN 301-5416. Tel: 714-558-7000. *Librn,* Cristi Anne Kirk
Library Holdings: Bk Vols 5,000
Subject Interests: Law

COVINA

C AMERICAN GRADUATE UNIVERSITY LIBRARY*, 733 N Dodsworth Ave, 91724-2499. SAN 373-0239. Tel: 626-966-4576, Ext 1003. FAX: 626-915-1709. E-mail: info@agu.edu. Web Site: www.agu.edu. *Librn,* Marie Sirney
Library Holdings: Bk Titles 3,500; Per Subs 30
Restriction: Staff use only

P COVINA PUBLIC LIBRARY*, 234 N Second Ave, 91723-2198. SAN 300-6921. Tel: 626-384-5300. Reference Tel: 626-384-5290. Administration Tel: 626-384-5297. FAX: 626-384-5315. Web Site: www.covinaca.gov. *Libr Serv Supvr,* Jennifer Blair; Tel: 626-384-5293, E-mail: jblair@covinaca.gov; *Ref Serv,* Krizia Virbia; Staff 9.5 (MLS 1, Non-MLS 8.5)
Founded 1897. Pop 49,541; Circ 162,855
Jul 2008-Jun 2009 Income $1,432,874, State $41,936, City $1,288,207, Federal $23,055, Other $79,676. Mats Exp $111,494, Books $74,311, Per/Ser (Incl. Access Fees) $17,716. Sal $931,785
Library Holdings: CDs 4,443; DVDs 4,014; Bk Vols 94,295; Per Subs 161
Automation Activity & Vendor Info: (Cataloging) SirsiDynix; (Circulation) SirsiDynix; (OPAC) SirsiDynix
Database Vendor: Gale Cengage Learning
Wireless access
Function: Accelerated reader prog, Adult bk club, Adult literacy prog, After school storytime, Bks on CD, Children's prog, Computers for patron use, Copy machines, Electronic databases & coll, Family literacy, Holiday prog, Homework prog, ILL available, Large print keyboards, Literacy & newcomer serv, Music CDs, Photocopying/Printing, Preschool reading prog, Prog for adults, Prog for children & young adult, Ref serv available, Ref serv in person, Scanner, Senior computer classes, Story hour, Telephone ref
Open Tues & Wed 12-8, Thurs & Fri 11-6, Sat 10-5
Restriction: Non-circulating of rare bks
Friends of the Library Group

CRESCENT CITY

S DEL NORTE COUNTY HISTORICAL SOCIETY MUSEUM LIBRARY*, 577 H St, 95531. SAN 327-3202. Tel: 707-464-3922. FAX: 707-464-7186. E-mail: manager@delnortehistory.org. Web Site: www.delnortehistory.org. *Coordr,* Karen Betlejewski
Founded 1951
Library Holdings: Bk Vols 1,000
Special Collections: Historical Files of Settlement of Del Norte County Area (circa 1800-1900)
Subject Interests: Local hist
Open Mon-Sat 10-4
Friends of the Library Group

P DEL NORTE COUNTY LIBRARY DISTRICT*, 190 Price Mall, 95531-4395. SAN 300-693X. Tel: 707-464-9793. FAX: 707-464-6726. Web Site: www.delnortecountylibrary.org. *Dir,* Linda Kaufmann; *Librn,* Rebecca Tipton; Staff 7 (MLS 1, Non-MLS 6)
Founded 1978. Pop 27,850
Library Holdings: Bk Vols 60,000; Per Subs 48
Special Collections: California Indian Library Coll - Del Norte; Del Norte County History
Automation Activity & Vendor Info: (Cataloging) ByWater Solutions; (Circulation) ByWater Solutions; (OPAC) ByWater Solutions
Wireless access
Function: Family literacy, ILL available, Summer reading prog, Telephone ref
Mem of NorthNet Library System
Open Tues-Fri 11-6, Sat 12-4; Tues-Fri (Summer) 10-6
Friends of the Library Group
Bookmobiles: 1

M SUTTER COAST HOSPITAL LIBRARY*, 800 E Washington Blvd, 95531-3699. SAN 325-2566. Tel: 707-464-8880. FAX: 707-464-8886. *Dir,* Janet Wardlaw
Founded 1960
Library Holdings: Bk Titles 300; Per Subs 80

CULVER CITY

S MAYME A CLAYTON LIBRARY & MUSEUM*, 4130 Overland Ave, 90230-3734. Tel: 310-202-1647. FAX: 310-202-1617. E-mail: info@claytonmuseum.org. Web Site: www.claytonmuseum.org. *Exec Dir,* Larry Earl; E-mail: learl@claytonmuseum.org
Library Holdings: AV Mats 1,700; Bk Vols 30,000
Subject Interests: African-Am hist & culture
Wireless access
Restriction: Non-circulating, Researchers by appt only

S PROSPEROS SERVERS' CENTER LIBRARY*, PO Box 4969, 90231-4969. SAN 371-3407. Tel: 310-287-1663. FAX: 310-287-0157. E-mail: info@theprosperos.org. Web Site: www.theprosperos.org. *In Charge,* Clair Gold
Library Holdings: Bk Vols 1,200
Subject Interests: Hist, Psychol

J WEST LOS ANGELES COLLEGE LIBRARY*, Heldman Learning Resource Center, 9000 Overland Ave, 90230. SAN 309-4618. Tel: 310-287-4408. Interlibrary Loan Service Tel: 310-287-4580. Reference Tel: 310-287-4269. Administration Tel: 310-287-4401. FAX: 310-287-4366. Web Site: www.wlac.edu/library/index.html. *Chair,* Judy Chow; *Circ/Per, Prof, Libr Sci, Ref Librn,* Ken Lee; Tel: 310-287-4402, E-mail: leeken@wlac.edu; *Asst Prof, Libr Sci, Ref, Syst Librn,* Ken Lin; Tel: 310-287-4437, E-mail: link@wlac.edu. Subject Specialists: *Art,* Judy Chow; *Bus, Law, Lit,* Ken Lee; *Sci,* Ken Lin; Staff 7 (MLS 3, Non-MLS 4)
Founded 1969. Enrl 12,000; Fac 199; Highest Degree: Associate
Jul 2011-Jun 2012. Mats Exp $71,500, Books $20,000, Per/Ser (Incl. Access Fees) $7,500, AV Equip $4,000, AV Mat $4,000, Electronic Ref Mat (Incl. Access Fees) $36,000
Library Holdings: AV Mats 150; DVDs 25; e-books 15,000; e-journals 10,500; Bk Titles 69,000; Bk Vols 70,500; Per Subs 95; Videos 350
Special Collections: Law Coll
Automation Activity & Vendor Info: (Acquisitions) Baker & Taylor; (Cataloging) SIRSI WorkFlows; (Circulation) SIRSI Unicorn; (Course Reserve) SIRSI Unicorn; (OPAC) SIRSI Unicorn; (Serials) EBSCO Online
Database Vendor: CountryWatch, EBSCOhost, Facts on File, Gale Cengage Learning, H W Wilson, JSTOR, LexisNexis, ProQuest
Wireless access
Special Services for the Blind - Low vision equip
Open Mon-Thurs 7:30am-8pm, Fri 9-1, Sat 11-3

CUPERTINO

J DE ANZA COLLEGE, A Robert DeHart Learning Center, 21250 Stevens Creek Blvd, 95014-5793. SAN 300-6999. Circulation Tel: 408-864-8761. Reference Tel: 408-864-8479. FAX: 408-864-8603. Web Site:

www.deanza.edu/library. *Dir,* Tom Dolen; Tel: 408-864-8764, E-mail: dolentom@deanza.edu; *Head, Ref,* Lena Chang; Tel: 408-864-8728, E-mail: changlena@deanza.edu; *Librn,* Pauline Yeckley; Tel: 408-864-8303, E-mail: yeckleypauline@deanza.edu; *Access Serv Librn,* Alex Swanner; Tel: 408-864-8486, E-mail: swanneralex@deanza.edu; *Syst Librn,* Cecilia Hui; Tel: 408-864-8383, E-mail: huicecilia@deanza.edu; *Syst Coordr,* Trung Thai; Tel: 408-846-8438, E-mail: trungthai@deanza.edu; *Syst Coordr,* Quang Thanh; Tel: 408-864-8494, E-mail: thanhquang@deanza.edu; *Acq,* Tracy Lam; Tel: 408-864-8439; *Cat,* Lisa Hatt; Tel: 408-864-8459, E-mail: hattlisa@deanza.edu; *Circ,* Irene Niazov; Tel: 408-864-8763, E-mail: niazovirene@deanza.edu; *Circ/Reserves,* David Byars; Tel: 408-864-8759, E-mail: byarsdavid@deanza.edu; *ILL,* Kathy Munson; Tel: 408-864-8335, E-mail: munsonkathy@deanza.edu; *Media Spec,* Sandy Cardoza; Tel: 408-864-8771, E-mail: cardozasandy@deanza.edu; *Media Spec,* Keri Kirkpatrick; Tel: 408-864-8581, E-mail: kirkpatrickkeri@deanza.edu; Staff 15 (MLS 5, Non-MLS 10)
Founded 1967. Enrl 22,000; Fac 935; Highest Degree: Associate
Library Holdings: Bk Titles 87,000; Bk Vols 110,000; Per Subs 300
Special Collections: Vietnam Conflict (De Cillis Coll). Oral History
Subject Interests: Art & archit, Hist, Spec educ
Automation Activity & Vendor Info: (Acquisitions) SirsiDynix; (Cataloging) SirsiDynix; (OPAC) SirsiDynix
Database Vendor: EBSCOhost, Gale Cengage Learning, ProQuest
Wireless access
Function: Ref serv available
Special Services for the Deaf - TDD equip
Open Mon-Thurs 8am-9pm, Fri 8-4

M PLANETREE HEALTH LIBRARY*, PlaneTree Health Information Center at Cupertino Library, 10800 Torre Ave, 2nd Flr, 95014, (Mail add: 15891 Los Gatos-Almaden Rd, Mission Oaks, Los Gatos, 95032). Tel: 408-358-5668, 408-446-1677, Ext 3350. FAX: 408-356-7312. E-mail: webmail@planetree-sccl.org. Web Site: www.planetree-sccl.org. *Dir,* Candace Ford; Staff 1.5 (MLS 1, Non-MLS 0.5)
Founded 1989
Special Collections: Spanish Coll
Automation Activity & Vendor Info: (Cataloging) Inmagic, Inc.; (Circulation) Inmagic, Inc.; (OPAC) Inmagic, Inc.
Database Vendor: EBSCOhost, Gale Cengage Learning
Wireless access
Open Tues 4-8, Wed 10-2, Thurs, Fri & Sat 2-6

CYPRESS

J CYPRESS COLLEGE LIBRARY, 9200 Valley View St, 90630-5897. SAN 300-7049. Tel: 714-484-7125. Reference Tel: 714-484-7069. FAX: 714-826-6723. E-mail: librarian@cypresscollege.edu. Web Site: www.cypresscollege.edu/academics/academicPrograms/LibraryLearningResourceCenter/Library. *Dean, Libr & Learning Res,* Dr Treisa Cassens; Tel: 714-484-7302, E-mail: tcassens@cypresscollege.edu; *Ref Librn,* Joyce Peacock; Tel: 714-484-7068, E-mail: jpeacock@cypresscollege.edu; *Coordr, Acq & Per,* Peggy Austin; Tel: 714-484-7066, E-mail: paustin@cypresscollege.edu; *Cat, Syst,* Monica Doman; Tel: 714-484-7067, E-mail: mdoman@cypresscollege.edu; *Instruction & Outreach,* Billy Pashaie; Tel: 714-484-7418, E-mail: wpashaie@cypresscollege.edu; Staff 4 (MLS 4)
Founded 1966. Enrl 20,034; Fac 4; Highest Degree: Associate
Jul 2006-Jun 2007. Mats Exp $190,596, Books $127,000, Per/Ser (Incl. Access Fees) $14,250, Electronic Ref Mat (Incl. Access Fees) $49,346. Sal $684,093 (Prof $308,413)
Library Holdings: CDs 572; DVDs 2,085; e-books 5,100; Bk Titles 53,948; Bk Vols 62,089; Per Subs 40
Automation Activity & Vendor Info: (Acquisitions) Ex Libris Group; (Cataloging) Ex Libris Group; (Circulation) Ex Libris Group; (Course Reserve) Ex Libris Group; (ILL) OCLC; (OPAC) Ex Libris Group; (Serials) Ex Libris Group
Database Vendor: Cinahl, EBSCOhost, Gale Cengage Learning, Newsbank, OCLC WorldShare Interlibrary Loan
Wireless access
Open Mon-Thurs (Winter) 8am-9pm, Fri 8-1; Mon-Thurs (Summer) 11-7

DALY CITY

P DALY CITY PUBLIC LIBRARY, 40 Wembley Dr, 94015-4399. SAN 331-8664. Tel: 650-991-8023. FAX: 650-991-5726. E-mail: dcplref@plsinfo.org. Web Site: www.dalycitylibrary.org. Staff 28.6 (MLS 6.6, Non-MLS 22)
Founded 1925. Pop 106,160; Circ 259,703
Special Collections: Philippine History, Culture & Arts (Filipiana)
Automation Activity & Vendor Info: (Acquisitions) Innovative Interfaces, Inc; (Cataloging) Innovative Interfaces, Inc; (Circulation) Innovative Interfaces, Inc; (ILL) OCLC Online; (OPAC) BiblioCommons
Database Vendor: BiblioCommons, Comprise Technologies Inc, Gale Cengage Learning, Grolier Online, Innovative Interfaces, Inc, LearningExpress, Overdrive, Inc, Safari Books Online, TumbleBookLibrary
Wireless access
Function: ILL available
Mem of Peninsula Library System
Special Services for the Blind - Screen reader software
Branches: 3
BAYSHORE, 460 Martin St, 94014, SAN 331-8699. Tel: 650-991-8074. FAX: 415-508-0860. *Br Head,* Karen Engle; Staff 2 (MLS 1, Non-MLS 1)
Circ 22,648
Library Holdings: DVDs 1,809; Bk Vols 20,173; Per Subs 41; Talking Bks 335; Videos 460
Open Mon & Wed 2-8, Tues, Thurs & Fri 12-6
Friends of the Library Group
JOHN D DALY BRANCH, 134 Hillside Blvd, 94014, SAN 331-8729. Tel: 650-991-8073. FAX: 650-746-8373. *Br Head,* Position Currently Open
Circ 86,857
Library Holdings: DVDs 2,583; Bk Vols 27,769; Per Subs 60; Talking Bks 469; Videos 281
Open Mon, Wed & Fri 12-6, Tues & Thurs 2-8
Friends of the Library Group
WESTLAKE, 275 Southgate Ave, 94015-3471, SAN 331-8753. Tel: 650-991-8071. FAX: 650-991-8180. *Br Head,* Sheila Uriarte; Staff 6 (MLS 1, Non-MLS 5)
Circ 184,932
Library Holdings: DVDs 3,087; Bk Vols 52,982; Per Subs 40; Talking Bks 972; Videos 1,011
Open Mon, Wed & Thurs 10-6, Tues 1-9, Fri 1-6, Sat 10-5
Friends of the Library Group

M SETON MEDICAL CENTER*, Health Sciences Library, 1900 Sullivan Ave, Ground Flr Hospital, 94015. SAN 300-7057. Tel: 650-991-6315, 650-991-6700. FAX: 650-991-6638. E-mail: smclibrary@dochs.org. Web Site: www.setonlibrary.org. *Med Librn,* Jeanie Fraser; Staff 0.5 (MLS 0.5)
Library Holdings: Bk Vols 1,300; Per Subs 128
Subject Interests: Cardiology, Infectious diseases, Med, Orthopedics
Database Vendor: EBSCOhost, OVID Technologies
Wireless access
Partic in National Network of Libraries of Medicine; Northern California & Nevada Medical Library Group (NCNMLG); San Francisco Biomedical Library Network

DANVILLE

S THE BLACKHAWK MUSEUM*, Automotive Research Library, 3700 Blackhawk Plaza Circle, 94506. SAN 300-7812. Tel: 925-736-2277, Ext 254. FAX: 925-736-4818. E-mail: museum@blackhawkmuseum.org. Web Site: www.blackhawkmuseum.org. *Archivist, Librn,* Herb Jorgensen
Founded 1984
Library Holdings: Bk Titles 750; Per Subs 14
Special Collections: Automobile Quarterly Coll; Manufacturer Press Kits & Owner's Materials
Wireless access
Open Tues 9-12, Wed-Sun 10-5
Restriction: Non-circulating

DAVIS

R DAVIS COMMUNITY CHURCH LIBRARY*, 412 C St, 95616. SAN 300-7073. Tel: 530-753-2894. FAX: 530-753-0182. E-mail: office@dccpres.org. Web Site: www.dccpres.org. *Librn,* Carol May; *Librn,* Mary L Stephens
Library Holdings: Bk Vols 3,015
Automation Activity & Vendor Info: (Cataloging) Follett Software
Open Mon-Thurs 9-2

SR DAVIS FRIENDS MEETING LIBRARY, 345 L St, 95616. SAN 371-6562. Tel: 530-758-8492.
Library Holdings: Bk Titles 1,700; Per Subs 20
Special Collections: Quaker History Coll
Subject Interests: Quaker info
Publications: Annual Report (cumulative 1986-1993); Subject Headings with Supplements

S MONSANTO-CALGENE CAMPUS LIBRARY*, 1920 Fifth St, 95616. SAN 325-0539. Tel: 530-753-6313. FAX: 530-792-2453. *Br Mgr, Librn,* Deanna Johnson; Staff 1 (MLS 1)
Founded 1982
Library Holdings: Bk Titles 1,865; Bk Vols 1,900; Per Subs 75
Subject Interests: Molecular biol, Plant sci
Automation Activity & Vendor Info: (Acquisitions) LibraryWorld, Inc; (Cataloging) LibraryWorld, Inc; (Circulation) LibraryWorld, Inc; (OPAC) LibraryWorld, Inc; (Serials) LibraryWorld, Inc
Database Vendor: Dialog, OCLC FirstSearch, SirsiDynix
Function: Res libr
Restriction: Staff use only

C UNIVERSITY OF CALIFORNIA, DAVIS, University Library, 100 NW Quad, 95616-5292. SAN 331-8788. Tel: 530-752-1203. Interlibrary Loan Service Tel: 530-752-2251. Reference Tel: 530-752-1126. Administration Tel: 530-752-2110. Automation Services Tel: 530-752-1202. FAX: 530-752-3148. Interlibrary Loan Service FAX: 530-752-7815. Administration FAX: 530-752-6899. Web Site: www.lib.ucdavis.edu. *Univ Librn,* MacKenzie Smith; *Dep Univ Librn,* William Garrity; *Assoc Univ Librn,* Helen Henry; *Assoc Univ Librn,* Amy Kautzman; *Assoc Univ Librn,* Gail Yokote; *Co-Head, Content Support Serv,* Karleen Darr; *Co-Head, Content Support Serv,* Xiaoli Li; *Head, Access & Delivery Serv,* Robin Gustafson; *Head, Coll Strategies,* Myra Appel; *Head, HR & Financial Serv,* Kobe Childs-Floyd; *Head, Info Tech Support Serv,* Dale Snapp; *Head, Res Support Serv,* Beth Callahan; *Head, Spec Coll,* Daryl Morrison. Subject Specialists: *Humanities,* Myra Appel; Staff 109 (MLS 36, Non-MLS 73)
Founded 1908. Enrl 34,175; Fac 1,596; Highest Degree: Doctorate
Special Collections: 16th-20th Century British Coll, bks, pamphlets; 18th-Early 20th Century American History & Literature; Agricultural Technology, advertising mat, archives, bks, manufacturer's cat, mss pamphlets, per, photog, repair manuals; Apiculture, bks, cat, ms, pamphlets, per, photog; Asian History, bks, ms, pamphlets; Botany, bks, ms, per, photog; California Agricultural & Northern California History, bks, ms, oral hist, pamphlets, per, photog, promotional mats; California Artists & Architecture, bibliographies, cat, drawings & paintings, ms, photog; Chicano History, bks, ms, oral history, pamphlets; Civil Rights, bks, broadsides, ms, pamphlets; Ecology, archives, bks, ms, pamphlets; Enology & Viticulture, bks, ms, oral hist, pamphlets, per, photog, posters, promotional mats; Fine Printing, bks, broadsides, pamphlets; Food Industry & Technology, archives, bks, ms, menus, pamphlets, photog; French Revolution, doc, engravings, ms; German Literature, bks, clippings, ms; Horticulture & Pomology, advertising mat, archives, bks, cats, drawings, ms, paintings, pamphlets, photog, posters; Michael & Margaret B Harrison Western Research Center; Native American History, bks, broadsides, ms, pamphlets; Performing Arts, archives, bks, clippings, engravings, ms, photog, playbills, posters, programs, scripts, stage & lighting designs; Poetry (US Avant Garde & British 1789-1972), bks, broadsides, ms, pamphlets, per; Russian History, engravings, ms, photog; Water & Irrigation, archives, bks, ms, pamphlets, photog; Western American History & Thought, bks, clippings, ethnographic reports, pamphlets, photog, pictures; World War I & II, bks, ms, pamphlets, posters. Oral History
Subject Interests: Agr, Agr econ, Art & archit, Biochem, Biol, Botany, Bus & mgt, Chem, Econ, Educ, Entomology, Ethnic studies, Genetics, Geol, Hist, Hort, Law, Lit, Math, Med, Music, Natural sci, Nutrition, Philos, Physics, Physiology, Toxicology, Veterinary med, Women's studies
Automation Activity & Vendor Info: (Acquisitions) Ex Libris Group; (Cataloging) Ex Libris Group; (Circulation) Ex Libris Group; (Course Reserve) Ex Libris Group; (Serials) Ex Libris Group
Wireless access
Partic in Association of Research Libraries (ARL); OCLC Online Computer Library Center, Inc; Pacific Southwest Regional Medical Library (PSRML); Univ of Calif Librs
Friends of the Library Group

Departmental Libraries:

AGRICULTURAL & RESOURCE ECONOMICS LIBRARY, One Shields Ave, 95616-8512, SAN 331-8966. Tel: 530-752-1540. E-mail: arel@primal.ucdavis.edu. Web Site: arc.ucdavis.edu/en/department/library.
Founded 1950. Highest Degree: Doctorate
Library Holdings: Bk Vols 9,284; Per Subs 763
Subject Interests: Agr econ, Develop economics, Environ econ, Natural res econ
Restriction: Non-circulating coll

CM LOREN D CARLSON HEALTH SCIENCES LIBRARY, Med Sci 1B, One Shields Ave, 95616-5291, SAN 331-8990. Tel: 530-752-1162. Circulation Tel: 530-752-8041. Interlibrary Loan Service Tel: 530-752-6379. Reference Tel: 530-752-7042. Administration Tel: 530-752-6207. FAX: 530-752-4718. E-mail: hslref@ucdavis.edu. Web Site: www.lib.ucdavis.edu/dept/hsl.
Founded 1966. Highest Degree: Doctorate
Special Collections: Veterinary Historical Coll

CL MABIE LAW LIBRARY, 400 Mrak Hall Dr, 95616. Tel: 530-752-3327. FAX: 530-752-8766. E-mail: lawlibref@ucdavis.edu. Web Site: law.ucdavis.edu/library. *Dir,* Judy Janes; E-mail: jcjanes@ucdavis.edu; Staff 23 (MLS 7, Non-MLS 16)
Founded 1964. Enrl 610; Fac 60; Highest Degree: Doctorate
Library Holdings: Bk Titles 112,139; Bk Vols 307,988; Per Subs 5,436
Special Collections: State Document Depository; US Document Depository
Automation Activity & Vendor Info: (Acquisitions) Innovative Interfaces, Inc; (Cataloging) Innovative Interfaces, Inc; (Circulation) Innovative Interfaces, Inc; (Course Reserve) Innovative Interfaces, Inc; (ILL) Innovative Interfaces, Inc; (OPAC) Innovative Interfaces, Inc; (Serials) Innovative Interfaces, Inc
Database Vendor: EBSCO Information Services, Gale Cengage Learning, HeinOnline, LexisNexis, Wilson - Wilson Web

MEDICAL CENTER LIBRARY
See Separate Entry under F William Blaisdell Medical Library, Sacramento

PHYSICAL SCIENCES & ENGINEERING LIBRARY, One Shields Ave, 95616-8676, SAN 331-9059. Tel: 530-752-0540. FAX: 530-752-4719. E-mail: pse@ucdavis.edu. Web Site: www.lib.ucdavis.edu/dept/pse.
Subject Interests: Astrophysics, Atmospheric sci, Chem, Eng, Geol, Meteorology, Physics

CM TOXICOLOGY DOCUMENTATION CENTER, Environ Toxicology Dept, One Shields Ave, 95616-8588, SAN 331-8842. Tel: 530-752-2587. FAX: 530-752-3394. *Mgr,* Loreen Kleinschmidt
Library Holdings: Bk Vols 6,000; Per Subs 32
Open Mon-Fri 8-12 & 1-5

DEATH VALLEY

S NATIONAL PARK SERVICE*, Death Valley National Park Research Libraries, Hwy 190, Park Headquarters, 92328. (Mail add: PO Box 579, 92328-0579), SAN 300-7081. Tel: 760-786-3200, Ext 287. FAX: 760-786-2169. *Curator,* Blair Davenport; E-mail: blair_davenport@nps.gov
Founded 1933
Library Holdings: Bk Titles 10,000
Special Collections: Death Valley National Park; Natural Sciences Coll, Chiefly Geology. Oral History
Friends of the Library Group

DIXON

P DIXON PUBLIC LIBRARY, 230 N First St, 95620-3028. SAN 300-712X. Tel: 707-678-5447. FAX: 707-678-3515. Web Site: www.dixonlibrary.com. *Dir,* Steve Arozena; *Ref & Ad Serv Librn,* Catherine Dunn; E-mail: dunnc@dixonlibrary.com; Staff 16 (MLS 3, Non-MLS 13)
Founded 1911. Pop 19,100; Circ 45,115
Jul 2011-Jun 2012 Income $912,853, State $26,000, City $24,398, Locally Generated Income $310,915, Other $551,428. Mats Exp $115,000, Books $86,000, Per/Ser (Incl. Access Fees) $8,500, Other Print Mats $1,000, AV Mat $7,500, Electronic Ref Mat (Incl. Access Fees) $12,000. Sal $614,202 (Prof $416,109)
Library Holdings: Bk Titles 45,000; Per Subs 150
Special Collections: Local History Photograph & Scrapbook Coll. Oral History
Automation Activity & Vendor Info: (Acquisitions) CARL.Solution (TLC); (Cataloging) CARL.Solution (TLC); (Circulation) CARL.Solution (TLC); (ILL) CARL.Solution (TLC); (OPAC) CARL.Solution (TLC); (Serials) CARL.Solution (TLC)
Database Vendor: Baker & Taylor, BWI, EBSCOhost, Gale Cengage Learning, Newsbank, OCLC WorldShare Interlibrary Loan, ProQuest
Wireless access
Function: Adult bk club, After school storytime, Archival coll, Bk club(s), Bks on CD, Digital talking bks, Doc delivery serv, Electronic databases & coll, Handicapped accessible, Homebound delivery serv, ILL available, Music CDs, Online searches, Photocopying/Printing, Preschool outreach, Prog for adults, Prog for children & young adult, Ref serv available, Summer reading prog, Telephone ref, VCDs, Workshops
Publications: Dixon Public Library News (Newsletter)
Mem of NorthNet Library System
Partic in Solano Napa & Partners Library Consortium (SNAP)
Friends of the Library Group

DOWNEY

P COUNTY OF LOS ANGELES PUBLIC LIBRARY, 7400 E Imperial Hwy, 90242-3375. (Mail add: PO Box 7011, 90241-7011), SAN 332-3765. Tel: 562-940-8462. Interlibrary Loan Service Tel: 562-940-8561. FAX: 562-803-3032. TDD: 562-940-8477. E-mail: colapl@library.lacounty.gov. Web Site: www.colapublib.org. *County Librn,* Margaret Donnellan Todd; Tel: 562-940-8400, E-mail: mdtodd@library.lacounty.gov; *Dir, Pub Serv,* Barbara Custen; Tel: 562-940-8409, E-mail: bcusten@library.lacounty.gov; *Asst Dir, Adm Serv, Chief Dep,* Yolanda De Ramus; Tel: 562-940-8406, E-mail: yderamus@library.lacounty.gov; *Asst Dir, Cap Projects & Fac Serv,* Jim Allen; Tel: 562-940-4145, E-mail: jallen@library.lacounty.gov; *Chief Info Officer, Interim Asst Dir, Info Syst,* Migell Acosta; Tel: 562-940-8418, E-mail: macosta@library.lacounty.gov; *Interim Head of Tech Serv,* Melody Holzman; Tel: 562-940-8543, E-mail: mholzman@library.lacounty.gov; *Youth Serv Adminr,* Deborah Anderson; Tel: 562-940-8522, E-mail: danderson@library.lacounty.gov; *Coll Develop Coordr,* Wendy Crutcher; Tel: 562-940-8503, E-mail: wcrutcher@library.lacounty.gov; Staff 322 (MLS 245, Non-MLS 77)
Founded 1912. Pop 3,358,197; Circ 14,115,156
Jul 2013-Jun 2014 Income (Main Library and Branch(s)) $131,674,899, State $1,065,422, Federal $5,871, County $127,454,546, Locally Generated Income $3,149,060. Mats Exp $8,292,464, Books $5,749,398, Per/Ser (Incl. Access Fees) $10,563, AV Mat $1,163,238, Electronic Ref Mat (Incl. Access Fees) $1,354,656, Presv $14,609. Sal $48,992,269
Library Holdings: Bk Titles 924,318; Per Subs 5,443

Special Collections: American Indian Resource Center; Arkel Erb Memorial Mountaineering Coll; Asian Pacific Resource Center; Black Resource Center; Californiana; Chicano Resource Center; HIV Information Center; Nautical Coll. Oral History; State Document Depository; US Document Depository
Automation Activity & Vendor Info: (Acquisitions) SirsiDynix; (Cataloging) SirsiDynix; (Circulation) SirsiDynix; (OPAC) SirsiDynix
Database Vendor: SirsiDynix
Wireless access
Publications: Annual Report
Partic in OCLC Online Computer Library Center, Inc; Southern California Library Cooperative
Special Services for the Deaf - Assistive tech; High interest/low vocabulary bks; Staff with knowledge of sign lang; TDD equip
Special Services for the Blind - Magnifiers; Screen enlargement software for people with visual disabilities
Restriction: Access at librarian's discretion
Friends of the Library Group
Branches: 88
ACTON AGUA DULE LIBRARY, 33792 Crown Valley Rd, Acton, 93510. Tel: 661-259-7101. FAX: 661-269-7101. *Commun Libr Mgr,* Valerie Bailey
Pop 10,461; Circ 125,820
Library Holdings: Bk Vols 57,564; Per Subs 106
Friends of the Library Group
AGOURA HILLS LIBRARY, 29901 Ladyface Ct, Agoura Hills, 91301, SAN 332-5598. Tel: 818-889-2278. FAX: 818-991-5019. Web Site: www.colapublib.org/libs/lasvirgenes. *Commun Libr Mgr,* Nina Hull
Founded 2001. Pop 20,625; Circ 194,838
Library Holdings: Bk Vols 98,222; Per Subs 15
Friends of the Library Group
ALONDRA LIBRARY, 11949 Alondra Blvd, Norwalk, 90650-7108, SAN 332-4303. Tel: 562-868-7771. FAX: 562-863-8620. Web Site: www.colapublib.org/libs/alondra. *Commun Libr Mgr,* Sue Kane
Founded 1970. Pop 44,145; Circ 69,844
Library Holdings: Bk Vols 35,431; Per Subs 26
Friends of the Library Group
ANTELOPE VALLEY BOOKMOBILE, 601 W Lancaster Blvd, Lancaster, 93534. Tel: 661-948-8270. FAX: 661-949-7386. Web Site: www.colapublib.org/libs/antelopevalley/bookmobile.html. *Commun Libr Mgr,* Diane Gavin
Founded 1981. Circ 29,577
Library Holdings: Bk Vols 18,851; Per Subs 25
ARTESIA LIBRARY, 18722 S Clarkdale Ave, Artesia, 90701-5817, SAN 332-4338. Tel: 562-865-6614. FAX: 562-924-4644. Web Site: www.colapublib.org/libs/artesia. *Commun Libr Mgr,* Barbara Nightingale
Founded 1968. Pop 16,776; Circ 100,450
Library Holdings: Bk Vols 42,397; Per Subs 36
Friends of the Library Group
AVALON LIBRARY, 215 Sumner Ave, Avalon, 90704. (Mail add: PO Box 585, Avalon, 90704), SAN 332-4362. Tel: 310-510-1050. FAX: 310-510-1645. Web Site: www.colapublib.org/libs/avalon. *Commun Libr Mgr,* Kelly Conn
Founded 1961. Pop 3,820; Circ 31,044
Library Holdings: Bk Vols 14,637; Per Subs 27
Friends of the Library Group
BALDWIN PARK LIBRARY, 4181 Baldwin Park Blvd, Baldwin Park, 91706-3203, SAN 332-4397. Tel: 626-962-6947. FAX: 626-337-6631. Web Site: www.colapublib.org/libs/baldwinpark. *Commun Libr Mgr,* Rafael Gonzalez
Founded 1969. Circ 29,688
Library Holdings: Bk Vols 70,746; Per Subs 74
Friends of the Library Group
BELL GARDENS LIBRARY, 7110 S Garfield Ave, Bell Gardens, 90201-3244, SAN 332-4451. Tel: 562-927-1309. FAX: 562-928-4512. Web Site: www.colapublib.org/libs/bellgardens. *Commun Libr Mgr,* Cheryl Gilera
Founded 1968. Pop 42,667; Circ 74,080
Library Holdings: Bk Vols 33,650; Per Subs 14
Friends of the Library Group
BELL LIBRARY, 4411 E Gage Ave, Bell, 90201-1216, SAN 332-4427. Tel: 323-560-2149. FAX: 323-773-7557. Web Site: www.colapublib.org/libs/bell. *Commun Libr Mgr,* Gabriela Torres
Founded 1960. Pop 35,972; Circ 63,973
Library Holdings: Bk Vols 33,739; Per Subs 21
Friends of the Library Group
A C BILBREW LIBRARY, 150 E El Segundo Blvd, Los Angeles, 90061-2356, SAN 332-4516. Tel: 310-538-3350. FAX: 310-327-0824. Web Site: www.colapublib.org/libs/bilbrew. *Commun Libr Mgr,* Yolande Wilburn
Founded 1974. Pop 26,475; Circ 129,294
Library Holdings: Bk Vols 102,854; Per Subs 98
Special Collections: Black Resource Center
Friends of the Library Group
CLIFTON M BRAKENSIEK LIBRARY, 9945 E Flower St, Bellflower, 90706-5486, SAN 332-4575. Tel: 562-925-5543. FAX: 562-920-9249. Web Site: www.colapublib.org/libs/brakensiek. *Commun Libr Mgr,* Lauren Talbott
Founded 1975. Pop 77,741; Circ 178,832
Library Holdings: Bk Vols 103,384; Per Subs 52
Friends of the Library Group
CARSON LIBRARY, 151 E Carson St, Carson, 90745-2797, SAN 332-463X. Tel: 310-830-0901. FAX: 310-830-6181. Web Site: www.colapublib.org/libs/carson. *Commun Libr Mgr,* Leticia Tan
Founded 1972. Pop 79,838; Circ 231,042
Library Holdings: Bk Vols 149,178; Per Subs 180
Friends of the Library Group
CASTAIC LIBRARY, 27955 Sloan Canyon Rd, Castaic, 91384. Tel: 661-257-7410. FAX: 661-257-5959. Web Site: www.colapublib.org/libs/castaic. *Commun Libr Mgr,* Matthew Gill
Founded 2008. Pop 18,538; Circ 83,975
Library Holdings: Bk Vols 43,057; Per Subs 54
Friends of the Library Group
CHARTER OAK LIBRARY, 20540 E Arrow Hwy, Ste K, Covina, 91724-1238, SAN 332-4664. Tel: 626-339-2151. FAX: 626-339-2799. Web Site: www.colapublib.org/libs/charteroak. *Commun Libr Mgr,* Denise Dilley
Founded 1990. Pop 47,633; Circ 98,189
Library Holdings: Bk Vols 42,619; Per Subs 44
Friends of the Library Group
MAYWOOD CESAR CHAVEZ LIBRARY, 4323 E Slauson Ave, Maywood, 90270-2837, SAN 332-5989. Tel: 323-771-8600. FAX: 323-560-0515. Web Site: www.colapublib.org/libs/maywood. *Commun Libr Mgr,* Edmond Osborn
Founded 1949. Pop 27,758; Circ 74,459
Library Holdings: Bk Vols 32,698; Per Subs 26
Friends of the Library Group
CITY TERRACE LIBRARY, 4025 E City Terrace Dr, Los Angeles, 90063-1297, SAN 332-4699. Tel: 323-261-0295. FAX: 323-261-1790. Web Site: www.colapublib.org/libs/cityterrace. *Commun Libr Mgr,* Stacey Walter
Founded 1979. Pop 25,436; Circ 81,811
Library Holdings: Bk Vols 48,103; Per Subs 60
Friends of the Library Group
CLAREMONT LIBRARY, 208 N Harvard Ave, Claremont, 91711, SAN 332-4729. Tel: 909-621-4902. FAX: 909-621-2366. Web Site: www.colapublib.org/libs/claremont. *Commun Libr Mgr,* Amy Crow
Founded 1971. Pop 35,920; Circ 255,479
Library Holdings: Bk Vols 123,344; Per Subs 60
Friends of the Library Group
COMPTON LIBRARY, 240 W Compton Blvd, Compton, 90220-3109, SAN 332-4753. Tel: 310-637-0202. FAX: 310-537-1141. Web Site: www.colapublib.org/libs/compton. *Commun Libr Mgr,* Sharon Johnson
Founded 1975. Pop 98,082; Circ 99,915
Library Holdings: Bk Vols 73,690; Per Subs 58
Friends of the Library Group
CUDAHY LIBRARY, 5218 Santa Ana St, Cudahy, 90201-6098, SAN 332-4788. Tel: 323-771-1345. FAX: 323-771-6973. Web Site: www.colapublib.org/libs/cudahy. *Commun Libr Mgr,* Jose Parra
Founded 1968. Pop 24,142; Circ 53,818
Library Holdings: Bk Vols 21,538; Per Subs 44
Friends of the Library Group
GARDENA MAYME DEAR LIBRARY, 1731 W Gardena Blvd, Gardena, 90247-4726, SAN 332-5148. Tel: 310-323-6363. FAX: 310-327-0992. Web Site: www.colapublib.org/libs/gardena. *Commun Libr Mgr,* Elmita Brown
Founded 1964. Pop 51,517; Circ 142,421
Library Holdings: Bk Vols 106,334; Per Subs 49
Friends of the Library Group
DIAMOND BAR LIBRARY, 21800 Copley Dr, Diamond Bar, 91765-2299, SAN 332-4877. Tel: 909-861-4978. FAX: 909-860-3054. Web Site: www.colapublib.org/libs/diamondbar. *Commun Libr Mgr,* Pui-Ching Ho
Founded 1977. Pop 56,400; Circ 388,627
Library Holdings: Bk Vols 75,134; Per Subs 74
Friends of the Library Group
CULVER CITY JULIAN DIXON LIBRARY, 4975 Overland Ave, Culver City, 90230-4299, SAN 332-4818. Tel: 310-559-1676. FAX: 310-559-2994. Web Site: www.colapublib.org/libs/culvercity. *Commun Libr Mgr,* Laura Frakes
Founded 1970. Pop 39,579; Circ 363,842
Library Holdings: Bk Vols 120,392; Per Subs 147
Special Collections: Judaica Coll
Friends of the Library Group
DUARTE LIBRARY, 1301 Buena Vista St, Duarte, 91010-2410, SAN 332-4931. Tel: 626-358-1865. FAX: 626-303-4917. Web Site: www.colapublib.org/libs/duarte. *Commun Libr Mgr,* Joanna Gee
Founded 1966. Pop 21,668; Circ 100,973

Library Holdings: Bk Vols 57,597; Per Subs 31
Friends of the Library Group

EAST LOS ANGELES LIBRARY, 4837 E Third St, Los Angeles, 90022-1601, SAN 332-4990. Tel: 323-264-0155. FAX: 323-264-5465. Web Site: www.colapublib.org/libs/eastla. *Commun Libr Mgr,* Alice Medina
Founded 1965. Pop 126,019; Circ 332,762
Library Holdings: Bk Vols 131,661; Per Subs 146
Special Collections: Chicano Resource Center
Friends of the Library Group

EAST RANCHO DOMINGUEZ LIBRARY, 4420 E Rose St, East Rancho Dominguez, 90221-3664, SAN 332-4966. Tel: 310-632-6193. FAX: 310-608-0294. Web Site: www.colapublib.org/libs/dominguez. *Commun Libr Mgr,* Betty Marlow
Founded 1966. Pop 14,658; Circ 68,847
Library Holdings: Bk Vols 38,308; Per Subs 32
Friends of the Library Group

EL CAMINO REAL LIBRARY, 4264 E Whittier Blvd, Los Angeles, 90023-2036, SAN 332-5059. Tel: 323-269-8102. FAX: 323-268-5186. Web Site: www.colapublib.org/libs/elcaminoreal. *Commun Libr Mgr,* Rebecca Garcia
Founded 1971. Pop 45,728
Library Holdings: Bk Vols 39,471; Per Subs 43
Friends of the Library Group

EL MONTE LIBRARY, 3224 Tyler Ave, El Monte, 91731-3356, SAN 332-5083. Tel: 626-444-9506. FAX: 626-443-5864. Web Site: www.colapublib.org/libs/elmonte. *Commun Libr Mgr,* Gina Quesenberry
Founded 1961. Pop 58,707; Circ 123,801
Library Holdings: Bk Vols 52,581; Per Subs 29
Friends of the Library Group

FLORENCE LIBRARY, 1610 E Florence Ave, Los Angeles, 90001-2522, SAN 332-5113. Tel: 323-581-8028. FAX: 323-587-3240. Web Site: www.colapublib.org/libs/florence. *Commun Libr Mgr,* Angel Nicolas
Founded 1970. Pop 38,189; Circ 101,463
Library Holdings: Bk Vols 50,148; Per Subs 62
Friends of the Library Group

GRAHAM LIBRARY, 1900 E Firestone Blvd, Los Angeles, 90001-4126, SAN 332-5172. Tel: 323-582-2903. FAX: 323-581-8478. Web Site: www.colapublib.org/libs/graham. *Commun Libr Mgr,* Angel Nicolas
Founded 1969. Pop 24,244; Circ 108,465
Library Holdings: Bk Vols 47,393; Per Subs 65
Friends of the Library Group

HACIENDA HEIGHTS LIBRARY, 16010 La Monde St, Hacienda Heights, 91745-4299, SAN 332-5202. Tel: 626-968-9356. FAX: 626-336-3126. Web Site: www.colapublib.org/libs/haciendahts. *Actg Commun Libr Mgr,* Amy Botcilho
Founded 1972. Pop 53,561; Circ 313,761
Library Holdings: Bk Vols 74,280; Per Subs 95
Friends of the Library Group

HAWAIIAN GARDENS LIBRARY, 11940 Carson St, Hawaiian Gardens, 90716-1137, SAN 332-5229. Tel: 562-496-1212. FAX: 562-425-0410. Web Site: www.colapublib.org/libs/hawaiiangardens. *Commun Libr Mgr,* Karen Cavanaugh
Founded 1972. Pop 14,456; Circ 63,510
Library Holdings: Bk Vols 42,001; Per Subs 34

HAWTHORNE LIBRARY, 12700 S Grevillea Ave, Hawthorne, 90250-4396, SAN 332-5237. Tel: 310-679-8193. FAX: 310-679-4846. Web Site: www.colapublib.org/libs/hawthorne. *Commun Libr Mgr,* Daniel Granados
Founded 1961. Pop 73,339; Circ 149,133
Library Holdings: Bk Vols 85,552; Per Subs 59
Friends of the Library Group

HERMOSA BEACH LIBRARY, 550 Pier Ave, Hermosa Beach, 90254-3892, SAN 332-5261. Tel: 310-379-8475. FAX: 310-374-0746. Web Site: www.colapublib.org/libs/hermosa. *Commun Libr Mgr,* Don Gould
Founded 1962. Pop 19,750; Circ 143,618
Library Holdings: Bk Vols 49,236; Per Subs 22
Friends of the Library Group

CHET HOLIFIELD LIBRARY, 1060 S Greenwood Ave, Montebello, 90640-6030, SAN 332-5296. Tel: 323-728-0421. FAX: 323-888-6053. Web Site: www.colapublib.org/libs/holifield. *Commun Libr Mgr,* Hilda Loh-Guan
Founded 1969. Pop 15,880; Circ 34,315
Library Holdings: Bk Vols 30,993; Per Subs 48
Friends of the Library Group

HOLLYDALE LIBRARY, 12000 S Garfield Ave, South Gate, 90280-7894, SAN 332-5326. Tel: 562-634-0156. FAX: 562-531-9530. Web Site: www.colapublib.org/libs/hollydale. *Commun Libr Mgr,* Grisel Oquendo
Founded 1966. Pop 10,925; Circ 39,626
Library Holdings: Bk Vols 43,528; Per Subs 33
Friends of the Library Group

HUNTINGTON PARK LIBRARY, 6518 Miles Ave, Huntington Park, 90255-4388, SAN 332-5385. Tel: 323-583-1461. FAX: 323-587-2061. Web Site: www.colapublib.org/libs/huntingtonpark. *Commun Libr Mgr,* Martin Delgado
Founded 1970. Pop 59,033; Circ 126,724
Library Holdings: Bk Vols 98,304; Per Subs 65
Special Collections: American Indian Resource Center
Subject Interests: N Am Indians
Friends of the Library Group

ANGELO M IACOBONI LIBRARY, 4990 Clark Ave, Lakewood, 90712-2676, SAN 332-5415. Tel: 562-866-1777. FAX: 562-866-1217. Web Site: www.colapublib.org/libs/iacoboni. *Commun Libr Mgr,* Sarah Comfort
Founded 1972. Pop 51,090; Circ 355,880
Library Holdings: Bk Vols 133,923; Per Subs 121
Friends of the Library Group

DR MARTIN LUTHER KING, JR LIBRARY, 17906 S Avalon Blvd, Carson, 90746-1598, SAN 332-6705. Tel: 310-327-4830. FAX: 310-327-3630. Web Site: www.colapublib.org/libs/victoria. *Commun Libr Mgr,* Sarah Harper
Founded 1973. Pop 11,524; Circ 33,642
Library Holdings: Bk Vols 20,187; Per Subs 16
Friends of the Library Group

LA CANADA FLINTRIDGE LIBRARY, 4545 N Oakwood Ave, La Canada Flintridge, 91011-3358, SAN 332-544X. Tel: 818-790-3330. FAX: 818-952-1754. Web Site: www.colapublib.org/libs/lacanada. *Commun Libr Mgr,* Mark Totten
Founded 1971. Pop 20,535; Circ 229,768
Library Holdings: Bk Vols 68,784; Per Subs 57
Friends of the Library Group

LA CRESCENTA LIBRARY, 2809 Foothill Blvd, La Crescenta, 91214-2999, SAN 332-5474. Tel: 818-248-5313. FAX: 818-248-1289. Web Site: www.colapublib.org/libs/lacrescenta. *Commun Libr Mgr,* Marta Wiggins
Founded 1963. Pop 19,176; Circ 328,460
Library Holdings: Bk Vols 71,703; Per Subs 48
Friends of the Library Group

LA MIRADA LIBRARY, 13800 La Mirada Blvd, La Mirada, 90638-3098, SAN 332-5504. Tel: 562-943-0277. FAX: 562-943-3920. Web Site: www.colapublib.org/libs/lamirada. *Commun Libr Mgr,* Jennifer McCarty
Founded 1969. Pop 49,178; Circ 204,974
Library Holdings: Bk Vols 96,017; Per Subs 44
Friends of the Library Group

LA PUENTE LIBRARY, 15920 E Central Ave, La Puente, 91744-5499, SAN 332-5563. Tel: 626-968-4613. FAX: 626-369-0294. Web Site: www.colapublib.org/libs/lapuente. *Commun Libr Mgr,* Jeanette Freels
Founded 1968. Pop 23,970; Circ 54,120
Library Holdings: Bk Vols 49,947; Per Subs 31
Friends of the Library Group

LA VERNE LIBRARY, 3640 D St, La Verne, 91750-3572, SAN 332-5628. Tel: 909-596-1934. FAX: 909-596-7303. Web Site: www.colapublib.org/libs/laverne. *Commun Libr Mgr,* George May
Founded 1985. Pop 32,228; Circ 155,748
Library Holdings: Bk Vols 56,785; Per Subs 40
Friends of the Library Group

LAKE LOS ANGELES LIBRARY, 16921 E Ave O, Ste A, Palmdale, 93591, SAN 373-563X. Tel: 661-264-0593. FAX: 661-264-0859. Web Site: www.colapublib.org/libs/lakelosangeles. *Commun Libr Mgr,* Mary MacTaggart
Founded 1991. Pop 11,851; Circ 101,202
Library Holdings: Bk Vols 37,032; Per Subs 45
Friends of the Library Group

LANCASTER LIBRARY, 601 W Lancaster Blvd, Lancaster, 93534, SAN 332-5539. Tel: 661-948-5029. FAX: 661-945-0480. Web Site: www.colapublib.org/libs/lancaster. *Commun Libr Mgr,* Judy Hist
Founded 1997. Pop 159,878; Circ 491,517
Library Holdings: Bk Vols 203,463; Per Subs 239
Friends of the Library Group

LAWNDALE LIBRARY, 14615 Burin Ave, Lawndale, 90260-1431, SAN 332-5652. Tel: 310-676-0177. FAX: 310-973-0498. Web Site: www.colapublib.org/libs/lawndale. *Commun Libr Mgr,* Melissa McCollum
Founded 1955. Pop 32,507; Circ 162,482
Library Holdings: Bk Vols 76,903; Per Subs 26
Friends of the Library Group

LENNOX LIBRARY, 10828 Condon Ave, Lennox, 90304-2398, SAN 332-5687. Tel: 310-674-0385. FAX: 310-673-6508. Web Site: www.colapublib.org/libs/lennox. *Commun Libr Mgr,* Peter Hsu
Founded 1949. Pop 22,276; Circ 46,378
Library Holdings: Bk Vols 45,057; Per Subs 49
Friends of the Library Group

LITTLEROCK LIBRARY, 35119 80th St E, Littlerock, 93543, SAN 332-5717. Tel: 661-944-4138. FAX: 661-944-4150. Web Site: www.colapublib.org/libs/littlerock. *Commun Libr Mgr,* Trisha Pritchard
Founded 1998. Pop 12,465; Circ 107,866

Library Holdings: Bk Vols 37,603; Per Subs 65
Friends of the Library Group
LIVE OAK LIBRARY, 4153-55 E Live Oak Ave, Arcadia, 91006-5895, SAN 332-5741. Tel: 626-446-8803. FAX: 626-446-9418. Web Site: www.colapublib.org/libs/liveoak. *Commun Libr Mgr,* Dina Malakoff
Founded 1966. Pop 56,247; Circ 97,346
Library Holdings: Bk Vols 41,922; Per Subs 42
Friends of the Library Group
LOMITA LIBRARY, 24200 Narbonne Ave, Lomita, 90717-1188, SAN 332-5776. Tel: 310-539-4515. FAX: 310-534-8649. Web Site: www.colapublib.org/libs/lomita. *Commun Libr Mgr,* Linda Shimane
Founded 1976. Pop 20,630; Circ 102,424
Library Holdings: Bk Vols 44,193; Per Subs 67
Friends of the Library Group
LOS NIETOS LIBRARY, 11644 E Slauson Ave, Whittier, 90606-3396, SAN 332-5806. Tel: 562-695-0708. FAX: 562-699-3876. Web Site: www.colapublib.org/libs/losnietos. *Commun Libr Mgr,* Theresa Cazares
Founded 1979. Pop 8,654; Circ 48,565
Library Holdings: Bk Vols 35,128; Per Subs 46
Friends of the Library Group
LYNWOOD LIBRARY, 11320 Bullis Rd, Lynwood, 90262-3661, SAN 332-5830. Tel: 310-635-7121. FAX: 310-635-4967. Web Site: www.colapublib.org/libs/lynwood. *Commun Libr Mgr,* Don Slaven
Founded 1977. Pop 70,980; Circ 193,312
Library Holdings: Bk Vols 91,660; Per Subs 64
Friends of the Library Group
MALIBU LIBRARY, 23519 W Civic Center Way, Malibu, 90265-4804, SAN 332-5865. Tel: 310-456-6438. FAX: 310-456-8681. Web Site: www.colapublib.org/libs/malibu. *Commun Libr Mgr,* Melissa Stallings
Founded 1970. Pop 12,865; Circ 88,964
Library Holdings: Bk Vols 63,349; Per Subs 53
Special Collections: Arkel Erb Memorial Mountaineering Coll
Friends of the Library Group
MANHATTAN BEACH LIBRARY, 1320 Highland Ave, Manhattan Beach, 90266-4789, SAN 332-589X. Tel: 310-545-8595. FAX: 310-545-5394. Web Site: www.colapublib.org/libs/manhattan. *Commun Libr Mgr,* Don Gould
Founded 1975. Pop 35,619; Circ 42,837
Library Holdings: Bk Vols 77,500; Per Subs 24
Friends of the Library Group
MONTEBELLO LIBRARY, 1550 W Beverly Blvd, Montebello, 90640-3993, SAN 332-6012. Tel: 323-722-6551. FAX: 323-722-3018. Web Site: www.colapublib.org/libs/montebello. *Commun Libr Mgr,* Rosemary Gurrola
Founded 1966. Pop 46,077; Circ 148,292
Library Holdings: Bk Vols 113,951; Per Subs 153
Special Collections: Asian-Pacific Resource Center
Friends of the Library Group
NORWALK LIBRARY, 12350 Imperial Hwy, Norwalk, 90650-3199, SAN 332-6071. Tel: 562-868-0775. FAX: 562-929-1130. Web Site: www.colapublib.org/libs/norwalk. *Commun Libr Mgr,* Sue Kane
Founded 1969. Pop 63,527; Circ 220,326
Library Holdings: Audiobooks 8,514; Bk Vols 228,439; Per Subs 129; Videos 7,817
Special Collections: Business Subject Specialty Center; Edelman Public Policy Coll
Subject Interests: Bus
Friends of the Library Group
NORWOOD LIBRARY, 4550 N Peck Rd, El Monte, 91732-1998, SAN 332-6101. Tel: 626-443-3147. FAX: 626-350-6099. Web Site: www.colapublib.org/libs/norwood. *Commun Libr Mgr,* Stephen Trumble
Founded 1977. Pop 55,927; Circ 149,621
Library Holdings: Bk Vols 61,928; Per Subs 31
Friends of the Library Group
GEORGE NYE JR LIBRARY, 6600 Del Amo Blvd, Lakewood, 90713-2206, SAN 332-6136. Tel: 562-421-8497. FAX: 562-496-3943. Web Site: www.colapublib.org/libs/nye. *Commun Libr Mgr,* Carol Burke
Founded 1972. Pop 28,530; Circ 76,954
Library Holdings: Bk Vols 48,087; Per Subs 29
Friends of the Library Group
PARAMOUNT LIBRARY, 16254 Colorado Ave, Paramount, 90723-5085, SAN 332-6160. Tel: 562-630-3171. FAX: 562-630-3968. Web Site: www.colapublib.org/libs/paramount. *Commun Libr Mgr,* Katherine Adams
Founded 1967. Pop 55,051; Circ 103,143
Library Holdings: Bk Vols 54,375; Per Subs 53
Friends of the Library Group
PICO RIVERA LIBRARY, 9001 Mines Ave, Pico Rivera, 90660-3098, SAN 332-6195. Tel: 562-942-7394. FAX: 562-942-7779. Web Site: www.colapublib.org/libs/picorivera. *Commun Libr Mgr,* Christiane Warburton
Founded 1961. Pop 38,803; Circ 139,753
Library Holdings: Bk Vols 76,896; Per Subs 28
Friends of the Library Group
QUARTZ HILL LIBRARY, 42018 N 50th St W, Quartz Hill, 93536-3509, SAN 332-6225. Tel: 661-943-2454. FAX: 661-943-6337. Web Site: www.colapublib.org/libs/quartzhill. *Commun Libr Mgr,* Victoria Vallejos
Founded 1959. Pop 10,435; Circ 178,603
Library Holdings: Bk Vols 40,690; Per Subs 44
Friends of the Library Group
ANTHONY QUINN LIBRARY, 3965 Cesar E Chavez Ave, Los Angeles, 90063, SAN 332-4486. Tel: 323-264-7715. FAX: 323-262-7121. Web Site: www.colapublib.org/libs/quinn. *Commun Libr Mgr,* Maribel Alvarez
Founded 1973. Pop 26,493; Circ 73,950
Library Holdings: Bk Vols 47,882; Per Subs 52
Friends of the Library Group
RIVERA LIBRARY, 7828 S Serapis Ave, Pico Rivera, 90660-4600, SAN 332-625X. Tel: 562-949-5485. FAX: 562-948-3455. Web Site: www.colapublib.org/libs/rivera. *Commun Libr Mgr,* Christiane Warburton
Founded 1969. Pop 23,598; Circ 68,836
Library Holdings: Bk Vols 37,061; Per Subs 22
Friends of the Library Group
ROSEMEAD LIBRARY, 8800 Valley Blvd, Rosemead, 91770-1788, SAN 332-6284. Tel: 626-573-5220. FAX: 626-280-8523. Web Site: www.colapublib.org/libs/rosemead. *Commun Libr Mgr,* Sue Yamamoto
Founded 1965. Pop 54,762; Circ 314,418
Library Holdings: Bk Vols 128,339; Per Subs 74
Friends of the Library Group
ROWLAND HEIGHTS LIBRARY, 1850 Nogales St, Rowland Heights, 91748-2945, SAN 332-6314. Tel: 626-912-5348. FAX: 626-810-3538. Web Site: www.colapublib.org/libs/rowlandhts. *Commun Libr Mgr,* Desiree Lee
Founded 1979. Pop 48,516; Circ 440,202
Library Holdings: Bk Vols 117,535; Per Subs 87
Friends of the Library Group
SAN DIMAS LIBRARY, 145 N Walnut Ave, San Dimas, 91773-2603, SAN 332-6349. Tel: 909-599-6738. FAX: 909-592-4490. Web Site: www.colapublib.org/libs/sandimas. *Commun Libr Mgr,* Nora Chen
Founded 1971. Pop 34,072; Circ 226,918
Library Holdings: Bk Vols 86,632; Per Subs 80
Friends of the Library Group
SAN FERNANDO LIBRARY, 217 N Maclay Ave, San Fernando, 91340-2433, SAN 332-6373. Tel: 818-365-6928. FAX: 818-365-3820. Web Site: www.colapublib.org/libs/sanfernando. *Commun Libr Mgr,* Hilda Casas
Founded 2001. Pop 24,222; Circ 115,390
Library Holdings: Bk Vols 56,436; Per Subs 50
Friends of the Library Group
SAN GABRIEL LIBRARY, 500 S Del Mar Ave, San Gabriel, 91776-2408, SAN 332-6403. Tel: 626-287-0761. FAX: 626-285-2610. Web Site: www.colapublib.org/libs/sangabriel. *Commun Libr Mgr,* Julie Sorensen
Founded 1967. Pop 40,313; Circ 226,283
Library Holdings: Bk Vols 62,911; Per Subs 25
Friends of the Library Group
SANTA CLARITA VALLEY BOOKMOBILE, 21182 Center Pointe Pkwy, Ste 130, Santa Clarita, 91350. Tel: 661-260-1792. FAX: 661-254-5999. *Commun Libr Mgr,* Steve Lowe
Library Holdings: Bk Vols 10,108; Per Subs 24
MASAO W SATOW LIBRARY, 14433 S Crenshaw Blvd, Gardena, 90249-3142, SAN 332-6462. Tel: 310-679-0638. FAX: 310-970-0275. Web Site: www.colapublib.org/libs/satow. *Commun Libr Mgr,* Elaine Fukumoto
Founded 1977. Pop 7,221; Circ 96,931
Library Holdings: Bk Vols 55,505; Per Subs 66
Friends of the Library Group
SORENSEN LIBRARY, 6934 Broadway Ave, Whittier, 90606-1994, SAN 377-6549. Tel: 562-695-3979. FAX: 562-695-8925. Web Site: www.colapublib.org/libs/sorensen. *Commun Libr Mgr,* Leticia Polizzi
Founded 1956. Pop 23,002; Circ 139,038
Library Holdings: Bk Vols 56,582; Per Subs 43
Friends of the Library Group
SOUTH EL MONTE LIBRARY, 1430 N Central Ave, South El Monte, 91733-3302, SAN 332-6527. Tel: 626-443-4158. FAX: 626-575-7450. Web Site: www.colapublib.org/libs/selmonte. *Commun Libr Mgr,* Roberta Marquez
Founded 1966. Pop 20,426; Circ 9,294
Library Holdings: Bk Vols 30,024; Per Subs 30
Friends of the Library Group
SOUTH WHITTIER LIBRARY, 14433 Leffingwell Rd, Whittier, 90604-2966, SAN 332-6551. Tel: 562-946-4415. FAX: 562-941-6138. Web Site: www.colapublib.org/libs/swhittier. *Actg Commun Libr Mgr,* Kelly Baggett
Founded 1988. Pop 39,189; Circ 77,308
Library Holdings: Bk Vols 62,365; Per Subs 64
Friends of the Library Group

STEVENSON RANCH EXPRESS LIBRARY, 26233 W Faulkner Dr, Stevenson Ranch, 91381. Tel: 661-287-5954. FAX: 661-257-5959. *Commun Libr Mgr,* Matthew Gill
Pop 17,080; Circ 37,041
Library Holdings: Bk Vols 6,021; Per Subs 30
SUNKIST LIBRARY, 840 N Puente Ave, La Puente, 91746-1316, SAN 332-6586. Tel: 626-960-2707. FAX: 626-338-5141. Web Site: www.colapublib.org/libs/sunkist. *Commun Libr Mgr,* Yaa Sefa-Boakye
Founded 1977. Pop 15,153; Circ 163,885
Library Holdings: Bk Vols 58,855; Per Subs 54
LLOYD TABER-MARINA DEL REY LIBRARY, 4533 Admiralty Way, Marina del Rey, 90292-5416, SAN 332-5954. Tel: 310 821-3415. FAX: 310-306-3372. Web Site: www.colapublib.org/libs/marina. *Commun Libr Mgr,* Winona Phillabaum
Founded 1975. Pop 8,389; Circ 177,248
Library Holdings: Bk Vols 61,899; Per Subs 76
Special Collections: Nautical Coll
Friends of the Library Group
TEMPLE CITY LIBRARY, 5939 Golden West Ave, Temple City, 91780-2292, SAN 332-6640. Tel: 626-285-2136. FAX: 626-285-2314. Web Site: www.colapublib.org/libs/templecity. *Commun Libr Mgr,* Jing Li
Founded 1962. Pop 36,134; Circ 260,989
Library Holdings: Bk Vols 59,329; Per Subs 49
Friends of the Library Group
TOPANGA LIBRARY, 122 N Topanga Canyon Blvd, Topanga, 90290. Tel: 310-455-3480. FAX: 310-455-3491. *Commun Libr Mgr,* Oleg Kagan
Pop 7,812; Circ 110,054
Library Holdings: Bk Vols 54,406; Per Subs 47
URBAN OUTREACH BOOKMOBILE, 1601 W Covina Pkwy, West Covina, 91790. Tel: 626-338-8373. FAX: 626-337-5166. Web Site: www.colapublib.org/libs/urban/bookmobile.html. *Commun Libr Mgr,* Emma Guerrero
Founded 2001. Circ 59,680
Library Holdings: Bk Vols 29,456; Per Subs 28
VIEW PARK LIBRARY, 3854 W 54th St, Los Angeles, 90043-2297, SAN 332-673X. Tel: 323-293-5371. FAX: 323-292-4330. Web Site: www.colapublib.org/libs/viewpark. *Commun Libr Mgr,* Linda Dickerson
Founded 1977. Pop 10,598; Circ 91,654
Library Holdings: Bk Vols 65,727; Per Subs 43
Friends of the Library Group
WALNUT LIBRARY, 21155 La Puente Rd, Walnut, 91789-2017, SAN 332-6829. Tel: 909-595-0757. FAX: 909-595-7553. Web Site: www.colapublib.org/libs/walnut. *Commun Libr Mgr,* Jenny Cheng
Founded 1985. Pop 30,112; Circ 191,826
Library Holdings: Bk Vols 46,793; Per Subs 25
Friends of the Library Group
LELAND R WEAVER LIBRARY, 4035 Tweedy Blvd, South Gate, 90280-6199, SAN 332-6853. Tel: 323-567-8853. FAX: 323-563-1046. Web Site: www.colapublib.org/libs/weaver. *Commun Libr Mgr,* Grisel Oquendo
Founded 1973. Circ 63,153
Library Holdings: Bk Vols 82,356; Per Subs 64
Friends of the Library Group
WEST COVINA LIBRARY, 1601 W Covina Pkwy, West Covina, 91790-2786, SAN 332-6888. Tel: 626-962-3541. FAX: 626-962-1507. Web Site: www.colapublib.org/libs/wcovina. *Commun Libr Mgr,* Wen Wen Zhang
Founded 1960. Pop 107,828; Circ 415,688
Library Holdings: Bk Vols 151,831; Per Subs 169
Friends of the Library Group
WEST HOLLYWOOD LIBRARY, 625 N San Vicente Blvd, West Hollywood, 90069-5020, SAN 332-6438. Tel: 310-652-5340. FAX: 310-652-2580. Web Site: www.colapublib.org/libs/whollywood. *Commun Libr Mgr,* Melissa McCollum
Founded 1962. Pop 35,072; Circ 299,038
Library Holdings: Bk Vols 106,655; Per Subs 125
Special Collections: Ron Shipton HIV Information Center
Friends of the Library Group
WESTLAKE VILLAGE LIBRARY, 31220 Oak Crest Dr, Westlake Village, 91361, SAN 373-5648. Tel: 818-865-9230. FAX: 818-865-0724. Web Site: www.colapublib.org/libs/westlake. *Commun Libr Mgr,* Katharine Schwartz
Founded 2001. Pop 8,386; Circ 156,378
Library Holdings: Bk Vols 50,716; Per Subs 19
Friends of the Library Group
WILLOWBROOK LIBRARY, 11838 Wilmington Ave, Los Angeles, 90059-3016, SAN 332-6918. Tel: 323-564-5698. FAX: 323-564-7709. Web Site: www.colapublib.org/libs/willowbrook. *Commun Libr Mgr,* Alice Tang
Founded 1988. Pop 35,506; Circ 64,335
Library Holdings: Bk Vols 30,240; Per Subs 42
Friends of the Library Group
WISEBURN LIBRARY, 5335 W 135th St, Hawthorne, 90250-4948, SAN 332-6942. Tel: 310-643-8880. FAX: 310-536-0749. Web Site: www.colapublib.org/libs/wiseburn. *Commun Libr Mgr,* Barbara Johnson
Founded 1966. Pop 10,553; Circ 82,711
Library Holdings: Bk Vols 37,694; Per Subs 13
Friends of the Library Group
WOODCREST LIBRARY, 1340 W 106th St, Los Angeles, 90044-1626, SAN 332-6977. Tel: 323-757-9373. FAX: 323-756-4907. Web Site: www.colapublib.org/libs/woodcrest. *Commun Libr Mgr,* Catherine Bueno
Founded 1967. Pop 87,687; Circ 93,198
Library Holdings: Bk Vols 57,386; Per Subs 65
Friends of the Library Group
Bookmobiles: 3

P DOWNEY CITY LIBRARY*, 11121 Brookshire Ave, Caller Box 7015, 90241-7015. SAN 300-7146. Tel: 562-904-7360. Circulation Tel: 562-904-7360, Ext 128. Interlibrary Loan Service Tel: 562-904-7360, Ext 121. Reference Tel: 562-904-7360, Ext 132. FAX: 562-923-3763. Web Site: www.downeylibrary.org. *Sr Librn,* Jan Palen; Tel: 562-904-7357, E-mail: jpalen@downeyca.org; Staff 7 (MLS 7)
Founded 1958. Pop 110,000; Circ 491,355
Library Holdings: Audiobooks 1,800; AV Mats 6,000; CDs 1,300; DVDs 2,900; Large Print Bks 891; Bk Titles 96,345; Bk Vols 137,219; Per Subs 240
Special Collections: US Document Depository
Automation Activity & Vendor Info: (Cataloging) Horizon; (ILL) OCLC FirstSearch; (OPAC) SirsiDynix
Database Vendor: EBSCOhost, Gale Cengage Learning
Function: Accelerated reader prog, Adult bk club, Adult literacy prog, AV serv, Bilingual assistance for Spanish patrons, Bks on CD, Children's prog, Computer training, Computers for patron use, Copy machines, Electronic databases & coll, Exhibits, Family literacy, Govt ref serv, Handicapped accessible, Home delivery & serv to Sr ctr & nursing homes, ILL available, Magnifiers for reading, Music CDs, Online ref, Online searches, Outside serv via phone, mail, e-mail & web, Photocopying/Printing, Preschool outreach, Prog for adults, Prog for children & young adult, Pub access computers, Ref serv in person, Story hour, Summer reading prog, Tax forms, Teen prog, Telephone ref, Video lending libr, Web-catalog, Wheelchair accessible
Partic in Southern California Library Cooperative
Open Mon-Thurs 10-8, Fri & Sat 10-5
Friends of the Library Group

S DOWNEY HISTORICAL SOCIETY*, Downey History Center Library, 12540 Rives Ave, 90242-3444. (Mail add: PO Box 554, 90241-0554), SAN 328-2406. Tel: 562-862-2777. E-mail: downey.historicalsociety@verizon.net. *Pres,* John Vincent
Founded 1965
Library Holdings: Bk Titles 800
Special Collections: Aerospace; Clipping File; Downey Court Dockets (1871-1957); Local Newspapers (1888-present); Los Angeles County District Attorney's Records of Arrests (1883- 1919); Photographs; School, Insurance & Agriculture Records
Subject Interests: Aerospace, Governor Downey, Local hist, Los Nietos Valley pioneers

S LOS ANGELES COUNTY OFFICE OF EDUCATION*, eLibrary Services, 9300 Imperial Hwy, 90242-2813. Tel: 562-922-6359. FAX: 562-940-1699. E-mail: prc_reference_desk@lacoe.edu. Web Site: els.ito.lacoe.edu. *Coordr,* Jennifer Ormsby; E-mail: ormsby_jennifer@lacoe.edu; Staff 2 (MLS 2)
Founded 1974
Library Holdings: Per Subs 300
Subject Interests: Curric, Educ
Wireless access
Open Mon-Fri 8-5

M RANCHO LOS AMIGOS MEDICAL CENTER*, Health Sciences Library, 7601 E Imperial Hwy, Rm 1109, 90242-3456. SAN 300-7154. Tel: 562-401-7696. *In Charge,* Evelyn Marks
Founded 1959
Library Holdings: Bk Titles 9,010; Per Subs 450
Subject Interests: Orthopedics, Phys therapy
Partic in BRS; Dialog Corp; SDC Info Servs
Open Mon-Thurs 8-5:30, Fri 8-5
Friends of the Library Group

DOWNIEVILLE

L SIERRA COUNTY LAW LIBRARY*, Courthouse, PO Box 457, 95936. SAN 373-1871. Tel: 530-289-3269. FAX: 530-289-2822. *Librn,* Sandi Marshall
Library Holdings: Bk Vols 3,000
Subject Interests: State law
Open Mon-Fri 8-5

DUARTE

M CITY OF HOPE, Lee Graff Medical & Scientific Library, 1500 E Duarte Rd, 91010. SAN 300-7170. Tel: 626-301-8497. FAX: 909-357-1929. E-mail: library@coh.org. Web Site: www.cityofhope.org/library. *Dir,* Andrea Lynch; E-mail: alynch@coh.org; *Libr Asst III,* Susan Koscielski; Staff 6.5 (MLS 3, Non-MLS 3.5)
Founded 1954
Library Holdings: e-journals 12,000; Bk Titles 20,000; Per Subs 73
Subject Interests: Biol, Cancer, Endocrinology, Genetics, Hematology, Immunology, Pathology, Respiratory diseases
Automation Activity & Vendor Info: (Cataloging) Innovative Interfaces, Inc - Millenium; (Circulation) Innovative Interfaces, Inc - Millenium; (ILL) OCLC ILLiad; (OPAC) Innovative Interfaces, Inc - Millenium; (Serials) Innovative Interfaces, Inc - Millenium
Database Vendor: American Chemical Society, American Physical Society, American Psychological Association (APA), Annual Reviews, Atlas Systems, Bowker, Brodart, Cinahl, EBSCO Information Services, EBSCOhost, Elsevier, Haworth Pres Inc, Ingenta, Innovative Interfaces, Inc, IOP, ISI Web of Knowledge, LexisNexis, MD Consult, Nature Publishing Group, OCLC WorldShare Interlibrary Loan, OVID Technologies, Oxford Online, ProQuest, PubMed, Sage, ScienceDirect, Scopus, Springer-Verlag, Springshare, LLC, Thomson - Web of Science, UpToDate, Wiley, Wiley InterScience, YBP Library Services
Partic in OCLC Online Computer Library Center, Inc; Statewide California Electronic Library Consortium (SCELC)
Open Mon-Fri 8-6

EAST PALO ALTO

L DLA PIPER US LLP*, Law Library, 2000 University Ave, 94303. Tel: 650-833-2000. Interlibrary Loan Service Tel: 650-833-1588. Administration Tel: 650-833-2070. FAX: 650-833-2001. *Res Serv Mgr,* Julia Fuerst; E-mail: julia.fuerst@dlapiper.com; *Libr Asst,* Galina Budman; E-mail: galina.budman@dlapiper.com; Staff 2 (MLS 1, Non-MLS 1)
Library Holdings: Bk Titles 3,490; Bk Vols 11,178; Per Subs 95
Automation Activity & Vendor Info: (Acquisitions) Innovative Interfaces, Inc; (Cataloging) Innovative Interfaces, Inc; (Circulation) Innovative Interfaces, Inc; (OPAC) Innovative Interfaces, Inc; (Serials) Innovative Interfaces, Inc

EDWARDS AFB

G NASA DRYDEN FLIGHT RESEARCH CENTER*, Research Library, 4825 Lilly Ave M/S 2412, 93523. (Mail add: PO Box 273 M/S 2412, 93523-0273), SAN 300-7197. Tel: 661-276-3702. FAX: 661-276-2244. Web Site: nasagalaxie.larc.nasa.gov, www.dfrc.nasa.gov. *Librn,* Carla Bender; Staff 2 (MLS 1, Non-MLS 1)
Founded 1949
Oct 2005-Sept 2006. Mats Exp $50,000, Books $5,000, Per/Ser (Incl. Access Fees) $25,000, Other Print Mats $10,000, Micro $8,000, Electronic Ref Mat (Incl. Access Fees) $2,000
Library Holdings: AV Mats 100; Bk Titles 5,000; Bk Vols 5,200; Per Subs 100; Spec Interest Per Sub 70
Special Collections: AGARD/NATO Reports; Air Force Reports; NACA Wartime Reports & RM's; NASA Reports; National Aerospace Laboratory of the Netherlands Reports
Subject Interests: Aeronaut
Automation Activity & Vendor Info: (Cataloging) SirsiDynix; (Circulation) SirsiDynix; (OPAC) SirsiDynix
Partic in DOD-Drols; NASA Libraries Information System-NASA Galaxie; OCLC Online Computer Library Center, Inc
Open Mon-Fri 7:30-4
Restriction: Circ limited

UNITED STATES AIR FORCE

A AIR FORCE FLIGHT TEST CENTER TECHNICAL RESEARCH LIBRARY*, 812 TSS/ENTL, 307 E Popson Ave, Bldg 1400, Rm 106, 93524-6630, SAN 331-9113. Tel: 661-277-3606. FAX: 661-277-6451. *Chief Librn,* Marie L Nelson; *Librn,* Jennie Paton; Tel: 661-275-5516, Fax: 661-275-6070; *Asst Librn,* Darrell Shiplett; Staff 5 (MLS 3, Non-MLS 2)
Founded 1955
Library Holdings: Bk Vols 32,000
Subject Interests: Aeronaut, Chem, Eng, Math, Physics
Automation Activity & Vendor Info: (Cataloging) OCLC Connexion; (Circulation) SirsiDynix; (ILL) OCLC; (OPAC) SirsiDynix; (Serials) SirsiDynix
Database Vendor: Cambridge Scientific Abstracts, Dialog, EBSCOhost, IEEE (Institute of Electrical & Electronics Engineers), Newsbank, OCLC FirstSearch, OCLC WorldShare Interlibrary Loan, SerialsSolutions, SirsiDynix
Partic in OCLC Online Computer Library Center, Inc
Restriction: Authorized patrons

A EDWARDS AIR FORCE BASE LIBRARY*, Five W Yeager Blvd, 93524-1295, SAN 331-9083. Tel: 661-275-2665. FAX: 661-277-6100. *Dir,* Alison Vasquez; Staff 1 (MLS 1)
Founded 1942
Library Holdings: Bk Vols 28,000; Per Subs 54
Subject Interests: Educ, Recreation
Function: Web-Braille
Partic in OCLC Online Computer Library Center, Inc
Restriction: Access at librarian's discretion

EL CAJON

J CUYAMACA COLLEGE LIBRARY*, 900 Rancho San Diego Pkwy, 92019-4304. SAN 322-872X. Tel: 619-660-4416. Circulation Tel: 619-660-4446. Interlibrary Loan Service Tel: 619-660-4499. Reference Tel: 619-660-4421. Administration Tel: 619-660-4400. FAX: 619-660-4493. TDD: 619-660-4418. Web Site: www.cuyamaca.edu. *Assoc Dean of Libr,* Lawrence Sherwood; E-mail: larry.sherwood@gcccd.edu; *Librn,* Angela Nesta; Tel: 619-660-4403, E-mail: angela.nesta@gcccd.edu; *Librn,* Jeri Resto; Tel: 619-660-4423, E-mail: jeri.resto@gcccd.edu; *Librn,* Kari Wergeland; Tel: 619-660-4412, E-mail: kari.wergeland@gcccd.edu; Staff 9 (MLS 4, Non-MLS 5)
Founded 1978. Enrl 8,000; Fac 89; Highest Degree: Associate
Jul 2005-Jun 2006 Income $1,474,880. Mats Exp $1,474,880, Books $40,000, Per/Ser (Incl. Access Fees) $22,238, AV Mat $5,000, Electronic Ref Mat (Incl. Access Fees) $38,635. Sal $818,266 (Prof $379,146)
Library Holdings: AV Mats 2,029; Bks on Deafness & Sign Lang 59; CDs 44; DVDs 155; e-books 1,810; Large Print Bks 22; Bk Vols 32,052; Per Subs 109; Videos 1,649
Automation Activity & Vendor Info: (Cataloging) SirsiDynix; (Circulation) SirsiDynix; (Course Reserve) SirsiDynix; (ILL) OCLC Online; (OPAC) SirsiDynix; (Serials) SirsiDynix
Database Vendor: Gale Cengage Learning
Wireless access
Open Mon-Thurs 7:30am-9pm, Fri 7:30-1, Sat 9-3

SR EL CAJON FIRST PRESBYTERIAN CHURCH LIBRARY, 500 Farragut Circle, 92020. SAN 374-8448. Tel: 619-442-2583. FAX: 619-442-2588. E-mail: firstpresec@sbcglobal.net. Web Site: www.firstpres-elcajon.org. *Librn,* Michelle Blackman; Staff 3 (MLS 1, Non-MLS 2)
Founded 1981
Library Holdings: AV Mats 57; CDs 5; DVDs 19; Large Print Bks 14; Bk Vols 2,942; Per Subs 1; Videos 193
Subject Interests: Christian fiction
Partic in Church & Synagogue Libr Asn

CR SAN DIEGO CHRISTIAN COLLEGE*, Southern California Seminary Library, 2100 Greenfield Dr, 92019-1161. SAN 331-9148. Tel: 619-201-8747. Interlibrary Loan Service Tel: 619-201-8683. FAX: 619-201-8799. Web Site: www.sdcc.edu/library. *Dir, Libr Serv,* Ruth Martin; *Operations Librn,* Mona Hsu; Tel: 619-201-8681, E-mail: mhsu@sdcc.edu; *Syst Librn,* Matt Owen; E-mail: mowen@sdcc.edu; *Cat, Ref Serv,* Jennifer Ewing; Tel: 619-201-8682, E-mail: jewing@socalsem.edu; *Cat,* Kathie Russell; E-mail: krussell@socalsem.edu; Staff 4 (MLS 3.5, Non-MLS 0.5)
Founded 1971. Enrl 900; Highest Degree: Doctorate
Jul 2011-Jun 2012. Mats Exp $175,351, Books $26,729, Per/Ser (Incl. Access Fees) $23,896, AV Mat $3,279, Electronic Ref Mat (Incl. Access Fees) $21,230
Library Holdings: Audiobooks 305; AV Mats 61,522; CDs 502; DVDs 347; e-books 150,332; e-journals 30,325; Electronic Media & Resources 85; Music Scores 29,933; Bk Titles 55,139; Bk Vols 65,005; Per Subs 150; Videos 200
Subject Interests: Biblical studies, Psychol
Automation Activity & Vendor Info: (Acquisitions) OCLC; (Cataloging) OCLC Connexion; (Circulation) OCLC; (ILL) OCLC; (OPAC) OCLC; (Serials) OCLC
Database Vendor: 3M Library Systems, ABC-CLIO, Alexander Street Press, CIOS (Communication Institute for Online Scholarship), CredoReference, ebrary, EBSCOhost, Facts on File, Gale Cengage Learning, H W Wilson, McGraw-Hill, Modern Language Association, OCLC, OCLC FirstSearch, OCLC WorldShare Interlibrary Loan, OCLC Worldshare Management Services, Oxford Online, Paratext, ProQuest, Sage, SerialsSolutions, Springer-Verlag, Springshare, LLC
Wireless access
Partic in Association of Christian Librarians; Christian Library Consortium; OCLC Online Computer Library Center, Inc; Statewide California Electronic Library Consortium (SCELC)
Open Mon-Thurs 7:30am-10:30pm, Fri 7:30-5, Sat 11-4

EL CENTRO

P EL CENTRO PUBLIC LIBRARY*, 1140 N Imperial Ave, 92243. SAN 331-9202. Tel: 760-337-4565. FAX: 760-352-1384. Web Site: www.eclib.org. *Dir,* Roland Banks; E-mail: rbanks@ci.el-centro.ca.us;

Supvr, Lois Shelton; E-mail: lshelton@eclib.org; Staff 5 (MLS 1, Non-MLS 4)
Founded 1909. Pop 42,000; Circ 147,000
Library Holdings: Bk Titles 95,000; Per Subs 45
Special Collections: Imperial Valley California Coll, bks & pamphlets. State Document Depository
Automation Activity & Vendor Info: (Acquisitions) Innovative Interfaces, Inc; (Cataloging) Innovative Interfaces, Inc; (Circulation) Innovative Interfaces, Inc; (ILL) Innovative Interfaces, Inc; (Media Booking) Innovative Interfaces, Inc; (OPAC) Innovative Interfaces, Inc; (Serials) Innovative Interfaces, Inc
Database Vendor: EBSCOhost, LearningExpress, Overdrive, Inc
Wireless access
Function: Prog for children & young adult
Partic in Serra Cooperative Library System
Open Mon-Thurs 9-7, Fri 9-5, Sat 9-1
Friends of the Library Group
Branches: 1
EL CENTRO COMMUNITY CENTER, 375 S First St, 92243, SAN 331-9237. Tel: 760-336-8977. *Librn,* Michelle Aris
Library Holdings: Bk Vols 1,500
Open Thurs 9-6, Fri 9-5

P IMPERIAL COUNTY FREE LIBRARY*, Headquarters, 1331 S Clark Rd, Bldg 24, 92243. (Mail add: 1125 Main St, 92243-2748), SAN 332-1606. Tel: 760-339-6460. FAX: 760-339-6465. E-mail: imperialcountylibrary@co.imperial.ca.us. Web Site: www.co.imperial.ca.us/library. *County Librn,* Connie Barrington; Staff 6.5 (MLS 1, Non-MLS 5.5)
Founded 1912. Pop 55,740
Jul 2008-Jun 2009 Income (Main Library and Branch(s)) $523,500, State $28,500, County $495,000. Mats Exp $38,702, Books $29,946, Per/Ser (Incl. Access Fees) $2,471, AV Mat $2,630, Electronic Ref Mat (Incl. Access Fees) $3,655. Sal $353,735 (Prof $113,000)
Library Holdings: Audiobooks 1,490; AV Mats 1,974; Bks on Deafness & Sign Lang 25; Electronic Media & Resources 1; Large Print Bks 1,000; Bk Titles 47,631; Bk Vols 53,378; Per Subs 45; Videos 1,974
Special Collections: Local History (Holtville & Imperial Valley Coll); Spanish Language Coll, audios, bks, pers, videos
Wireless access
Function: Adult literacy prog, CD-ROM, Computer training, Copy machines, Electronic databases & coll, Family literacy, Fax serv, Homework prog, ILL available, Music CDs, Photocopying/Printing, Prog for adults, Prog for children & young adult, Ref serv available, Spoken cassettes & CDs, Spoken cassettes & DVDs, Summer reading prog, Tax forms, VHS videos
Partic in Serra Cooperative Library System
Special Services for the Blind - Assistive/Adapted tech devices, equip & products; Audio mat; Bks available with recordings; Bks on cassette; Bks on CD; Cassette playback machines; Cassettes; Large print bks; Screen enlargement software for people with visual disabilities
Friends of the Library Group
Branches: 4
CALIPATRIA BRANCH, 105 S Lake, Calipatria, 92233. (Mail add: PO Box 707, Calipatria, 92233-0707), SAN 332-1630. Tel: 760-348-2630. FAX: 760-348-5575. *Br Mgr,* Connie Barrington
Function: Audio & video playback equip for onsite use, CD-ROM, Computer training, Copy machines, Electronic databases & coll, Family literacy, ILL available, Photocopying/Printing, Prog for adults, Prog for children & young adult, Ref serv available, Spoken cassettes & CDs, Spoken cassettes & DVDs, Summer reading prog, Tax forms, Telephone ref, VHS videos, Video lending libr
Open Mon-Wed 9-6, Thurs 10-7, Fri 9-5
Friends of the Library Group
HEBER BRANCH, 1078 Dogwood Rd, Heber, 92257. (Mail add: 1125 Main St, 92243-2748). Tel: 760-336-0737. FAX: 760-336-0748. *In Charge,* Rebecca Mendoza
Pop 5,000; Circ 14,084
Open Tues 10-1 & 2-7, Fri 9-5
HOLTVILLE BRANCH, 101 E Sixth St, Holtville, 92250-1228. (Mail add: PO Box 755, Holtville, 92250-0755), SAN 332-1665. Tel: 760-356-2385. FAX: 760-356-2437. *In Charge,* Lorenza Carpenter
Pop 7,000
Special Collections: Local History (Holtville & Imperial County History Coll); Spanish Language Coll
Function: Adult literacy prog, CD-ROM, Computer training, Copy machines, Electronic databases & coll, Family literacy, Fax serv, Handicapped accessible, Homework prog, ILL available, Online info literacy tutorials on the web & in blackboard, Orientations, Photocopying/Printing, Prog for adults, Prog for children & young adult, Ref serv available, Spoken cassettes & CDs, Summer reading prog, Tax forms, VHS videos
Open Mon, Tues & Thurs 9-6, Wed 9-7, Fri 9-5
Friends of the Library Group
SALTON CITY BRANCH, 2098 Frontage Rd, Salton City, 92275. (Mail add: PO Box 5340, Salton City, 92275-5340). Tel: 760-604-6956. *In Charge,* Eric Garcia
Library Holdings: Bk Vols 3,500
Database Vendor: EBSCOhost, ProQuest
Open Mon & Wed 9-12 & 1-4

GL IMPERIAL COUNTY LAW LIBRARY*, Courthouse, 939 W Main St, 2nd Flr, 92243. SAN 300-7227. Tel: 760-482-2271. FAX: 760-482-4530. Web Site: www.imperialcountylawlibrary.org. *In Charge,* Maribel Martinez
Library Holdings: Bk Vols 4,000
Wireless access
Open Mon-Fri 8-12 & 1-5

A UNITED STATES NAVY*, Naval Air General Library, MWR Library, 2003 D St, Bldg 318, 92243. SAN 331-9261. Tel: 760-339-2470. FAX: 760-339-2470. *Librn,* Letti Earle
Library Holdings: Bk Titles 8,000; Per Subs 14

EL MONTE

S EL MONTE MUSEUM OF HISTORY LIBRARY*, Museum Library, 3150 N Tyler Ave, 91731-6307. SAN 327-3148. Tel: 626-444-3813, 626-580-2232. FAX: 626-444-8142. *Curator,* Donna Crippen; E-mail: museum@elmonteca.gov
Library Holdings: Bk Titles 1,700; Bk Vols 3,000; Per Subs 20
Open Tues-Fri 10-4, Sun 1-3

EL SEGUNDO

S AEROSPACE CORP*, Charles C Lauritsen Library, 2360 E El Segundo Blvd, 90245-4691. (Mail add: PO Box 80966, Mail Station M1/199, Los Angeles, 90009-0966), SAN 300-7251. Tel: 310-336-6093. FAX: 310-336-0624. Web Site: www.aero.org/education/tai/library. *Dir, Mgr, Archives & Rec Mgt,* Patricia W Green; E-mail: patricia.w.green@aero.org; *Mgr, Res Serv,* Christine L Lincoln; Tel: 310-336-6738, E-mail: christine.l.lincoln@aero.org; *Mgr, Tech Serv,* Shirley L Tanaka; E-mail: shirley.l.tanaka@aero.org
Founded 1960
Library Holdings: e-journals 450; Electronic Media & Resources 22; Bk Titles 99,800; Bk Vols 100,000; Per Subs 700
Special Collections: Aerospace Corporation Authors
Subject Interests: Aeronaut, Aerospace sci, Astronautics, Eng
Automation Activity & Vendor Info: (Acquisitions) Ex Libris Group; (Cataloging) Ex Libris Group; (Circulation) Ex Libris Group; (OPAC) Ex Libris Group; (Serials) Ex Libris Group
Database Vendor: ACM (Association for Computing Machinery), American Chemical Society, Bowker, Cambridge Scientific Abstracts, Carroll Publishing, CQ Press, CRC Press/Taylor & Francis Group, Dialog, Dun & Bradstreet, Elsevier, Ex Libris Group, IEEE (Institute of Electrical & Electronics Engineers), IHS, Jane's, Knovel, LexisNexis, Marquis Who's Who, McGraw-Hill, Open Text Corporation, Oxford Online, ProQuest, Safari Books Online, ScienceDirect, STN International, Thomson - Web of Science
Wireless access
Function: Res libr
Publications: Library Services Announcements; Professional Papers
Partic in Statewide California Electronic Library Consortium (SCELC)
Restriction: Authorized personnel only

P EL SEGUNDO PUBLIC LIBRARY, 111 W Mariposa Ave, 90245-2299. SAN 300-7286. Tel: 310-524-2722. Reference Tel: 310-524-2728. Administration Tel: 310-524-2770. FAX: 310-648-7560. Web Site: www.eslib.org. *Dir,* Debra F Brighton; E-mail: brighton@elsegundo.org; *Sr Librn, Adult Serv, Literacy Prog/Author Fair Coordr,* Ellen Cunningham; Tel: 310-524-2729, E-mail: ecunningham@elsegundo.org; *Sr Librn, Circ, Cat & Tech Support,* Mark Herbert; Tel: 310-524-2732, E-mail: mherbert@elsegundo.org; *Librn II/Youth Serv, Sch Serv,* Sindee Pickens; Tel: 310-524-2771, E-mail: spicken@elsegundio.org; Staff 16.5 (MLS 4.5, Non-MLS 12)
Founded 1948. Pop 16,654; Circ 220,000
Library Holdings: Audiobooks 5,500; AV Mats 6,000; Bks on Deafness & Sign Lang 20; CDs 5,600; DVDs 7,350; e-books 6,150; Electronic Media & Resources 10; High Interest/Low Vocabulary Bk Vols 500; Large Print Bks 5,000; Microforms 400; Bk Titles 149,880; Bk Vols 159,000; Per Subs 112; Spec Interest Per Sub 20; Videos 1,000
Special Collections: Adult Literacy; Archival Photos Online; El Segundo Local History Coll
Subject Interests: Art, Biographies, Cooking, Job search, Local hist, Popular fiction, Sci fict, Spanish lang, Travel
Automation Activity & Vendor Info: (Acquisitions) Baker & Taylor; (Cataloging) Innovative Interfaces, Inc; (Circulation) Innovative Interfaces, Inc; (ILL) Innovative Interfaces, Inc; (OPAC) Innovative Interfaces, Inc; (Serials) Innovative Interfaces, Inc

Database Vendor: Baker & Taylor, EBSCO Information Services, Gale Cengage Learning, OCLC WorldShare Interlibrary Loan, Overdrive, Inc, ProQuest, World Book Online
Wireless access
Publications: El Segundo Public Library News (Online only)
Partic in Southern California Library Cooperative
Open Mon-Thurs 9-9, Fri 10-5, Sat 9-5
Friends of the Library Group

S WYLE LABORATORIES*, Research Library, 128 Maryland St, 90245-4100. SAN 326-6346. Tel: 310-322-1763, Ext 6730. FAX: 310-322-9799. Web Site: www.wylelabs.com. *Librn,* Myra Alarcon
Library Holdings: Bk Titles 400; Per Subs 40
Subject Interests: Aeronaut, Noise pollution
Restriction: Private libr

ELDRIDGE

M SONOMA DEVELOPMENTAL CENTER*, Staff Library, PO Box 1493, 95431-1493. SAN 331-9385. Tel: 707-938-6244. FAX: 707-938-6244. *Sr Librn,* Ann Amman
Founded 1951. Pop 1,800
Library Holdings: Bk Vols 4,800; Per Subs 104
Special Collections: History of Sonoma State Hospital, bks, journals & newsp
Subject Interests: Mentally retarded, Pediatrics, Psychiat, Psychol, Soc serv (soc work)
Publications: Journal Holdings
Partic in N Bay Health Sci Libr Consortium; Pacific Southwest Regional Medical Library (PSRML)
Restriction: Staff use only

EMERYVILLE

S ALCOHOL RESEARCH GROUP LIBRARY, 6475 Christie Ave, Ste 400, 94608-1010. SAN 329-8272. Tel: 510-597-3440. FAX: 510-985-6459. E-mail: library@arg.org. Web Site: www.arg.org. *Info Spec,* Debbie Cluney; E-mail: dcluney@arg.org; Staff 1 (Non-MLS 1)
Founded 1959
Library Holdings: Bk Vols 6,100; Per Subs 249
Subject Interests: Alcohol abuse, Drug abuse, Smoking, Socio-cultural aspects of alcohol, Tobacco
Automation Activity & Vendor Info: (Acquisitions) Inmagic, Inc.; (Cataloging) Inmagic, Inc.; (Serials) Inmagic, Inc.
Restriction: Authorized scholars by appt, Circulates for staff only, Open by appt only

ENCINITAS

S QUAIL BOTANICAL GARDENS FOUNDATION INC LIBRARY*, 230 Quail Gardens Dr, 92024-0005. SAN 373-3998. Tel: 760-436-3036. FAX: 760-632-0917. Web Site: www.qbgardens.com. *Librn,* Kenneth Hayward
Library Holdings: Bk Vols 2,000
Special Collections: Out-of-Print Botanical Coll, bks, slides & videos
Subject Interests: Botany, Gardening, Hort
Open Wed 12-4, Sun 10-4

ESCONDIDO

S ESCONDIDO HISTORY CENTER, 321 N Broadway, 92025. (Mail add: PO Box 263, 92033-0263), SAN 373-4013. Tel: 760-743-8207. FAX: 760-743-8267. Web Site: www.escondidohistory.org. *Exec Dir,* Wendy Barker; E-mail: barker@escondidohistory.org; *Bus Mgr,* Robin Fox; E-mail: fox@escondidohistory.org
Library Holdings: Bk Vols 919
Subject Interests: Calif, Furniture, Local hist, State hist
Wireless access
Open Tues-Sat 10-4
Restriction: Open to pub for ref only

P ESCONDIDO PUBLIC LIBRARY*, 239 S Kalmia St, 92025. SAN 300-7340. Tel: 760-839-4683. Circulation Tel: 760-839-4684. Interlibrary Loan Service Tel: 760-839-4840. Reference Tel: 760-839-4839. Administration Tel: 760-839-4601. FAX: 760-741-4255. Web Site: library.escondido.org. *City Librn,* Position Currently Open; *Dep City Librn,* Cynthia Smith; Tel: 760-839-4329, E-mail: csmith@escondido.org; *Dir, Tech Serv,* Donna Feddern; Tel: 760-839-4624, E-mail: dfeddern@escondido.org; *Adult Serv,* Paul Crouthamel; Tel: 760-839-4814, E-mail: pcrouthamel@escondido.org; *Coll Develop,* Neva Robinson; Tel: 760-839-4214, E-mail: nrobinson@ci.escondido.ca.us; *Youth Serv,* Cindi Bouvier; Tel: 760-839-4827, E-mail: cbouvier@escondido.org; Staff 27 (MLS 12, Non-MLS 15)
Founded 1898. Pop 138,015; Circ 753,415
Library Holdings: AV Mats 32,472; e-books 2,000; Bk Titles 160,259; Per Subs 200
Special Collections: Local & Family History (Pioneer Room)
Subject Interests: Bus & mgt, Local hist
Automation Activity & Vendor Info: (Circulation) Horizon; (ILL) OCLC
Wireless access
Function: Adult literacy prog, Bilingual assistance for Spanish patrons, Bk club(s), Bks on CD, Chess club, Children's prog, Computer training, Computers for patron use, Copy machines, E-Reserves, Electronic databases & coll, Exhibits, Family literacy, Fax serv, Handicapped accessible, Home delivery & serv to Sr ctr & nursing homes, Homework prog, Music CDs, Online cat, Online ref, Outreach serv, Prog for adults, Prog for children & young adult, Pub access computers, Senior computer classes, Story hour, Summer reading prog, Tax forms, Teen prog, Telephone ref, VHS videos, Wheelchair accessible
Publications: 100 Years of Library History in Escondido
Partic in Califa
Open Mon & Tues 10-8, Wed-Fri 10-6, Sat 10-5
Friends of the Library Group
Bookmobiles: 1

M PPH MEDICAL LIBRARY*, Palomar Medical Ctr, 555 E Valley Pkwy, 92025. SAN 371-6325. Tel: 760-739-3146. FAX: 760-739-3229. Web Site: www.pph.org. *Med Librn,* Bill Dodge
Founded 1988
Library Holdings: e-journals 22; Bk Titles 643; Bk Vols 720; Per Subs 74
Subject Interests: Med, Nursing
Partic in Medical Library Group of Southern California & Arizona (MLGSCA); National Network of Libraries of Medicine
Open Mon-Fri 7:30-5

S SAN DIEGO ZOO GLOBAL LIBRARY*, Beckman Ctr, 15600 Psaqual Valley Rd, 92027. Tel: 760-291-8702. FAX: 760-291-5478. Web Site: library.sandiegozoo.org. *Assoc Dir, Libr Serv,* Amy Jankowski; Tel: 760-291-5479, E-mail: AJankowski@sandiegozoo.org; *Asst Librn,* Kathy Elliott; Tel: 760-747-8702, Ext 5736, E-mail: KElliott@sandiegozoo.org; *Libr Res Spec,* Melody Brooks; Tel: 760-747-8702, Ext 5735; Staff 2 (MLS 1, Non-MLS 1)
Founded 1916
Library Holdings: Bk Vols 11,000; Per Subs 680
Special Collections: Ernst Schwarz Coll, reprints; Herpetology (Charles E Shaw Coll), bks, reprints; Zoo Publications (annual reports, guidebooks, newsletters)
Subject Interests: Hort, Veterinary med
Publications: Accessions list (Monthly)
Partic in Coop Libr Agency for Syst & Servs; Dialog Corp; OCLC Online Computer Library Center, Inc; San Diego Greater Metro Area Libr & Info Agency Coun
Open Mon-Fri 8-4:30
Restriction: Staff use only

R WESTMINSTER SEMINARY CALIFORNIA LIBRARY*, 1725 Bear Valley Pkwy, 92027. SAN 321-236X. Tel: 760-480-8474. FAX: 760-480-0252. Web Site: www.wscal.edu. *Dir, Libr Serv,* John Bales; E-mail: jbales@wscal.edu; *Circ,* Dan Wagner; E-mail: dwagner@wscal.edu; Staff 6 (MLS 1, Non-MLS 5)
Founded 1980. Enrl 147; Fac 13; Highest Degree: Master
Library Holdings: Bk Vols 63,420; Per Subs 260
Special Collections: 16th/17th Century Reformation & Puritanism, micro
Subject Interests: Biblical studies, Theol
Automation Activity & Vendor Info: (Cataloging) Follett Software; (Circulation) Follett Software; (OPAC) Follett Software
Database Vendor: OCLC FirstSearch, ProQuest
Partic in Statewide California Electronic Library Consortium (SCELC)
Open Mon-Fri 7:45am-10pm, Sat 9-5

EUREKA

J COLLEGE OF THE REDWOODS*, 7351 Tompkins Hill Rd, 95501. SAN 300-7375. Tel: 707-476-4260. Reference Tel: 707-476-4263. FAX: 707-476-4432. *Dir,* Mary Grace McGovern; Tel: 707-476-4264, E-mail: marygrace-mcgovern@Redwoods.edu; *Librn,* Ruth Moon; E-mail: ruth-moon@redwoods.edu; Staff 2 (MLS 2)
Founded 1965. Enrl 6,673; Highest Degree: Associate
Library Holdings: Bk Titles 60,000; Bk Vols 66,313
Subject Interests: Nursing
Automation Activity & Vendor Info: (Cataloging) ByWater Solutions; (Circulation) ByWater Solutions; (Course Reserve) ByWater Solutions; (ILL) ByWater Solutions; (OPAC) ByWater Solutions
Database Vendor: EBSCOhost, Gale Cengage Learning, ProQuest
Mem of NorthNet Library System
Partic in OCLC Online Computer Library Center, Inc
Open Mon-Thurs 7:45am-9pm, Fri 7:45-5

GL HUMBOLDT COUNTY LAW LIBRARY*, Courthouse, 825 Fourth St, RM 812, 95501. SAN 300-7383. Tel: 707-476-2356. FAX: 707-445-6297. E-mail: redgar@co.humboldt.ca.us. Web Site:

co.humboldt.ca.us/law-library. *Libr Spec,* Richard Edgar; *Libr Spec,* Stephanie Richter
Founded 1907
Library Holdings: Bk Vols 18,000
Wireless access
Open Mon-Fri 8:30-5

P HUMBOLDT COUNTY LIBRARY*, Library Administration, 1313 Third St, 95501-0553. SAN 331-9415. Tel: 707-269-1918. TDD: 718-442-0462. Web Site: co.humboldt.ca.us/library. *County Librn,* Victor Zazueta; E-mail: vzazueta@co.humboldt.ca.us; *Supv Librn,* Jo Ann Bauer; *Supv Librn,* Christopher Cooper; *Librn II,* Nick Wilczek; *Div Mgr, Acq & Tech Serv,* Janet Smith; *Div Mgr, Circ Serv,* Ronda Wittenberg; *Div Mgr, Pub Serv,* Kitty Yancheff; E-mail: kyancheff@co.humboldt.ca.us; Staff 12 (MLS 12)
Founded 1878. Pop 121,000
Library Holdings: Bk Titles 148,308; Bk Vols 239,625; Per Subs 332
Special Collections: American Indians Coll, especially California Indians; Humboldt County History Coll; NRC Nuclear Power Plants LDR
Automation Activity & Vendor Info: (Circulation) Innovative Interfaces, Inc
Wireless access
Mem of NorthNet Library System
Special Services for the Deaf - TDD equip
Open Tues-Sat 8-5
Friends of the Library Group
Branches: 11
ARCATA BRANCH, 500 Seventh St, Arcata, 95521-6315, SAN 331-944X. Tel: 707-822-5954. *Br Mgr,* Nicolas Wilczek
Library Holdings: Bk Vols 12,000
Open Tues & Fri 12-5, Wed & Sat 10-5, Thurs 12-8
Friends of the Library Group
BLUE LAKE BRANCH, City Hall, 111 Greenwood Ave, Blue Lake, 95525. (Mail add: PO Box 236, Blue Lake, 95525-0236), SAN 331-9474. Tel: 707-668-4207. *Br Mgr,* Charlene Stearns
Library Holdings: Bk Vols 3,000
Open Wed 2-7, Sat 11-4
Friends of the Library Group
EUREKA (MAIN LIBRARY), 1313 Third St, 95501, SAN 331-9490. Tel: 707-269-1900. Reference Tel: 707-269-1905. *Br Mgr,* Victor Zazueta; *Supv Librn, Ch,* JoAnn Bauer; *Ref Librn II,* Rachel Harwood; *Ref Librn II,* Debra Hill
Library Holdings: Bk Vols 161,860
Open Tues & Thurs 12-5, Wed 12-8, Fri 10-5, Sat 11-4
Friends of the Library Group
FERNDALE BRANCH, 807 Main St, Ferndale, 95536. (Mail add: PO Box 397, Ferndale, 95536-0397), SAN 331-9504. Tel: 707-786-9559. *Br Mgr,* Bonnie Von Braun
Library Holdings: Bk Vols 10,000
Open Tues & Thurs 12-5 & 7-9, Wed & Sat 12-5, Fri 12-4
Friends of the Library Group
FORTUNA BRANCH, 753 14th St, Fortuna, 95540-2113, SAN 331-9539. Tel: 707-725-3460. *Br Mgr,* Chris Cooper
Library Holdings: Bk Vols 7,000
Open Tues 12-5, Wed 12-9, Thurs-Sat 10-5
Friends of the Library Group
GARBERVILLE BRANCH, 715 Cedar St, Garberville, 95542-3201, SAN 331-9563. Tel. 707-923-2230. FAX: 707 923 2230. *Br Mgr,* John Christianson; E-mail: jchristianson@co.humboldt.ca.us
Library Holdings: Bk Vols 7,000
Open Wed 12-7, Thurs & Fri 12-6, Sat 12-4
Friends of the Library Group
MCKINLEYVILLE BRANCH, 1606 Pickett Rd, McKinleyville, 95519, SAN 331-9652. Tel: 707-839-4459. *Br Mgr,* Sunny Falling-Rain
Library Holdings: Bk Vols 2,500
Open Tues & Fri 12-5, Wed 12-8, Thurs & Sat 10-5
Friends of the Library Group
RIO DELL BRANCH, 715 Wildwood Ave, Rio Dell, 95562-1321, SAN 331-9687. Tel: 707-764-3333. *Br Mgr,* Jeanine Lancaster
Library Holdings: Bk Vols 3,600
Open Tues & Sat 11-4, Wed 1-6
Friends of the Library Group
TRINIDAD BRANCH, Janis Ct, Trinidad, 95570. (Mail add: PO Box 856, Trinidad, 95570), SAN 331-9717. Tel: 707-677-0227. *Br Mgr,* Kenzie Mullen; Staff 0.4 (Non-MLS 0.4)
Library Holdings: Bk Vols 2,500
Open Tues 2:30-8, Sat 10:30-4
Friends of the Library Group
WILLOW CREEK BRANCH, Hwy 299 & Hwy 96, Willow Creek, 95573-0466. (Mail add: PO Box 466, Willow Creek, 95573), SAN 331-9628. Tel: 530-629-2146. *Br Mgr,* Elizabeth Young; Staff 1 (MLS 0, Non-MLS 1)
Library Holdings: Bk Vols 5,458
Open Wed & Thurs 12-5, Fri & Sat 12-4
Friends of the Library Group
KIM YERTON MEMORIAL BRANCH, Ten Loop Rd, Hoopa, 95546. (Mail add: PO Box 1407, Hoopa, 95546). Tel: 530-625-5082. FAX: 530-625-5022. *Br Mgr,* Jacqueline E Letalien
Open Tues, Thurs & Sat 10-1 & 2-5, Wed 10-1 & 2-8
Friends of the Library Group
Bookmobiles: 1

S KIM YERTON INDIAN ACTION LIBRARY*, 2905 Hubbard Ln, Ste C, 95501. SAN 324-2773. Tel: 707-443-8401. FAX: 707-443-9281. E-mail: indianaction@att.net. *Dir,* Coleen Bruno
Founded 1974
Library Holdings: Bk Titles 3,000
Special Collections: American Indians; California Northwest Coast Tribes (Yurok, Hupa, Karok Coll), bks, flms, photogs, tapes; Photographs (Ericson, Curtis, Boyle, Roberts Coll), bd vols
Open Mon-Fri 9-5

M SAINT JOSEPH HEALTH SYSTEM*, Saint Joseph Hospital Medical Library, 2700 Dolbeer St, 95501. SAN 300-7391. Tel: 707-445-8121, Ext 7514. FAX: 707-269-3836. *Dir,* Elizabeth Brown
Founded 1950
Library Holdings: Bk Vols 300; Per Subs 100
Publications: SJH Library flyer, SJH-Table of Contents
Partic in Docline; Pacific Southwest Regional Medical Library (PSRML)
Restriction: Open by appt only

FAIRFIELD

J SOLANO COMMUNITY COLLEGE LIBRARY*, 4000 Suisun Valley Rd, 94534. SAN 301-6838. Tel: 707-864-7132. FAX: 707-864-7231. Web Site: www.solano.cc.ca.us/library/index.html. *VPres, Tech & Learning Res,* Jay Field; *Access Serv,* Erin Duane; *Pub Serv,* Quentin Carter; E-mail: quentin.carter@solano.edu; *Tech Serv,* Rashmi Johal; Staff 8 (MLS 4, Non-MLS 4)
Founded 1965. Enrl 10,377; Fac 146; Highest Degree: Associate
Library Holdings: High Interest/Low Vocabulary Bk Vols 200; Bk Titles 30,550; Bk Vols 36,500; Per Subs 165
Automation Activity & Vendor Info: (Circulation) TLC (The Library Corporation); (OPAC) TLC (The Library Corporation)
Database Vendor: EBSCOhost, OCLC FirstSearch
Mem of NorthNet Library System
Partic in Coop Libr Agency for Syst & Servs; OCLC Online Computer Library Center, Inc; Solano Napa & Partners Library Consortium (SNAP)
Open Mon-Thurs 7:45am-7:50pm, Fri (Aug-May) 7:45-2:50

P SOLANO COUNTY LIBRARY*, 1150 Kentucky St, 94533-5799. SAN 331-9741. Toll Free Tel: 866-572-7587. FAX: 707-421-7474. Web Site: www.solanolibrary.com. *Dir, Libr Serv,* Bonnie A Katz; *Dep Dir, Pub Serv,* Margaret Yost; *Dep Dir, Support Serv,* Lynne Williams; Staff 111 (MLS 33, Non-MLS 78)
Pop 360,023; Circ 3,700,433
Jul 2011-Jun 2012 Income $12,061,898. Mats Exp $1,057,920, Books $494,916, Per/Ser (Incl. Access Fees) $42,620, Electronic Ref Mat (Incl. Access Fees) $520,384. Sal $7,638,342
Library Holdings: Audiobooks 50,000, AV Mats 160,316; e-books 24,831; Electronic Media & Resources 4,352; Bk Vols 534,219; Per Subs 1,119
Special Collections: Printing (Donovan J McCune Coll), rare bks, specimens; Solano County History Coll; Vallejo History Coll
Automation Activity & Vendor Info: (Acquisitions) TLC (The Library Corporation); (Cataloging) OCLC; (Circulation) TLC (The Library Corporation); (Course Reserve) TLC (The Library Corporation); (ILL) OCLC; (OPAC) TLC (The Library Corporation); (Serials) TLC (The Library Corporation)
Wireless access
Mem of NorthNet Library System
Partic in Solano Napa & Partners Library Consortium (SNAP)
Friends of the Library Group
Branches: 9
FAIRFIELD CIVIC CENTER, 1150 Kentucky St, 94533, SAN 331-9776. Toll Free Tel: 866-572-7587. FAX: 707-421-7207.
Pop 106,379; Circ 576,462
Friends of the Library Group
FAIRFIELD CORDELIA LIBRARY, 5050 Business Ctr Dr, 94534. FAX: 707-863-7311. Toll Free FAX: 866-572-7587.
Pop 26,959; Circ 282,916
Friends of the Library Group
JOHN F KENNEDY BRANCH, 505 Santa Clara St, Vallejo, 94590, SAN 331-9806. Toll Free Tel: 866-572-7587. FAX: 707-553-5667.
Pop 115,928; Circ 485,549
Friends of the Library Group

L LAW LIBRARY, Hall of Justice, 600 Union Ave, 94533, SAN 300-7405. Tel: 707-421-6520. FAX: 707-421-6516. *Librn,* Jonathan Watson; Staff 2 (MLS 1, Non-MLS 1)
Founded 1911

Special Collections: California Statutes; Codes of Solano Co & Cities therein
Open Mon-Fri 8-4:30
RIO VISTA LIBRARY, 44 S Second St, Rio Vista, 94571, SAN 331-9830. Toll Free Tel: 866-572-7587. FAX: 707-374-2919.
Pop 7,418; Circ 86,506
Friends of the Library Group
SPRINGSTOWNE LIBRARY, 1003 Oakwood Ave, Vallejo, 94591, SAN 331-9865. Toll Free Tel: 866-572-7587. FAX: 707-553-5656.
Pop 46,371; Circ 190,246
Friends of the Library Group
SUISUN CITY LIBRARY, 601 Pintail Dr, Suisun City, 94585, SAN 373-8760. Toll Free Tel: 866-572-7587. FAX: 707-784-1426.
Pop 27,978; Circ 200,757
Friends of the Library Group
VACAVILLE PUBLIC LIBRARY-CULTURAL CENTER, 1020 Ulatis Dr, Vacaville, 95687, SAN 331-989X. Toll Free Tel: 866-572-7587. FAX: 707-451-0987.
Pop 92,092; Circ 554,430
Open Mon-Thurs 10-9, Fri & Sat 10-5, Sun 1-5
Friends of the Library Group
VACAVILLE PUBLIC LIBRARY-TOWN SQUARE, One Town Square Pl, Vacaville, 95688. Toll Free Tel: 866-572-7587. FAX: 707-455-7509.
Pop 36,837; Circ 305,696
Friends of the Library Group

FOLSOM

C FOLSOM LAKE COLLEGE LIBRARY*, Ten College Pkwy, 95630. Tel: 916-608-6613. Reference Tel: 916-608-6612. FAX: 916-608-6533. Web Site: www.flc.losrios.edu/libraries.htm. *Librn,* Rebecca Mendell; Tel: 916-608-6708, E-mail: mendelr@flc.losrios.edu; *Librn,* Lorilie Roundtree; Tel: 916-608-6818, E-mail: roundtl@flc.losrios.edu; *Librn,* James Telles; Tel: 916-608-6528, E-mail: tellesj@flc.losrios.edu; *Librn,* Stacia S Thiessen; Tel: 916-608-6557, E-mail: thiess@flc.losrios.edu; *Access Serv,* Demetria Deary; Tel: 916-608-6704; *Access Serv,* Kevin Webb; Tel: 916-608-6703; *Tech Serv,* Tanya George; Tel: 916-608-6587; Staff 4 (MLS 4)
Automation Activity & Vendor Info: (Cataloging) Innovative Interfaces, Inc; (Circulation) Innovative Interfaces, Inc; (OPAC) Innovative Interfaces, Inc
Wireless access
Open Mon-Thurs 8-8, Fri 8-5

P FOLSOM PUBLIC LIBRARY*, 411 Stafford St, 95630. SAN 375-4987. Tel: 916-355-7374. FAX: 916-355-7332. E-mail: libstaff@folsom.ca.us. Web Site: www.folsomlibrary.com. *Libr Mgr,* Lisa Dale; E-mail: ldale@folsom.ca.us
Founded 1993. Pop 72,000; Circ 570,000
Automation Activity & Vendor Info: (Cataloging) Innovative Interfaces, Inc; (Circulation) Innovative Interfaces, Inc
Database Vendor: Baker & Taylor, Brodart, Civica, EBSCOhost, Gale Cengage Learning, Innovative Interfaces, Inc, OCLC, OCLC FirstSearch, Overdrive, Inc
Wireless access
Open Tues 10-8, Wed-Sat 10-5, Sun 12-5
Friends of the Library Group

FONTANA

M KAISER-PERMANENTE MEDICAL CENTER*, Health Sciences Library, 9961 Sierra Ave, 92335. SAN 300-743X. Tel: 909-427-5086. FAX: 909-427-6288. *Asst Librn,* Grace Johnston; Staff 4 (MLS 2, Non-MLS 2)
Founded 1950
Library Holdings: CDs 1,300; DVDs 50; e-books 150; e-journals 4,566; Electronic Media & Resources 52; Bk Vols 1,000; Per Subs 42
Subject Interests: Dermatology, Family med, Internal med, Neurology, Obstetrics & gynecology, Orthopedics, Pediatrics, Radiology, Sports med, Surgery, Urology
Automation Activity & Vendor Info: (Cataloging) Innovative Interfaces, Inc - Millenium; (Circulation) Innovative Interfaces, Inc - Millenium; (Serials) Innovative Interfaces, Inc - Millenium
Database Vendor: EBSCO Information Services, EBSCOhost, Majors, MD Consult, Micromedex, PubMed, ScienceDirect
Partic in Inland Empire Med Libr Coop; Medical Library Association (MLA)
Open Mon-Fri 7:30-5
Restriction: Access at librarian's discretion

FORT IRWIN

UNITED STATES ARMY
A FORT IRWIN POST LIBRARY*, National Training Ctr, Bldg 331, Second St & F Ave, 92310. (Mail add: PO Box 105091, 92310-5091), SAN 321-8716. Tel: 760-380-3462. FAX: 760-380-5071. Web Site: www.fortirwinmwr.com/recreation-2/the-post-library. *Librn,* Cara Bates; Staff 4.5 (MLS 1, Non-MLS 3.5)
Founded 1981
Library Holdings: CDs 812; DVDs 1,146; Bk Vols 30,916; Per Subs 94; Talking Bks 859; Videos 1,464
Subject Interests: Calif, Mil hist, Mil sci
Automation Activity & Vendor Info: (Acquisitions) Horizon; (Cataloging) Horizon; (Circulation) Horizon; (OPAC) Horizon
Database Vendor: EBSCOhost, Gale Cengage Learning
Function: Adult bk club, Bilingual assistance for Spanish patrons, Bks on cassette, Bks on CD, Children's prog, Computers for patron use, Copy machines, Family literacy, Fax serv, Free DVD rentals, Handicapped accessible, Holiday prog, ILL available, Music CDs, Online cat, Online searches, Photocopying/Printing, Prog for adults, Prog for children & young adult, Pub access computers, Ref serv available, Story hour, Telephone ref, VHS videos, Video lending libr, Wheelchair accessible, Workshops
Partic in OCLC Online Computer Library Center, Inc
Special Services for the Deaf - Bks on deafness & sign lang
Special Services for the Blind - Aids for in-house use; Bks on cassette; Bks on CD; Cassette playback machines; Cassettes; Copier with enlargement capabilities; Large print bks; Magnifiers; Recorded bks; Sound rec
Open Mon-Fri 10-7, Sat 10-2
Restriction: Authorized patrons, Circ to mil employees only, Photo ID required for access
AM WEED ARMY COMMUNITY HOSPITAL, MEDICAL LIBRARY*, PO Box 105109, 92310-5109, SAN 324-153X. Tel: 760-380-6889. FAX: 760-380-5734. *Tech Info Spec,* Peggy Makie; Staff 1 (MLS 1)
Library Holdings: Bk Titles 326; Per Subs 35
Subject Interests: Dentistry, Emergency room, Nursing, Pharm, Preventive med

FREMONT

P ALAMEDA COUNTY LIBRARY*, 2450 Stevenson Blvd, 94538-2326. SAN 332-091X. Tel: 510-745-1500. FAX: 510-793-2987. TDD: 888-663-0660. Web Site: www.aclibrary.org. *Interim County Librn,* Carmen Martinez; *Dep County Librn,* Cindy Chadwick; Tel: 510-745-1504, E-mail: cchadwick@aclibrary.org; *Head, Br Libr,* Peggy Watson; Tel: 510-745-1512, E-mail: pwatson@aclibrary.org; *Br Mgr,* Sallie Pine; Staff 56 (MLS 43, Non-MLS 13)
Founded 1910. Pop 540,620; Circ 6,056,555
Library Holdings: Bk Vols 1,051,767; Per Subs 2,201
Special Collections: State Document Depository
Subject Interests: Bus & mgt, Local hist, Spanish (Lang)
Automation Activity & Vendor Info: (Acquisitions) Innovative Interfaces, Inc; (Cataloging) Innovative Interfaces, Inc; (Circulation) Innovative Interfaces, Inc; (OPAC) Innovative Interfaces, Inc; (Serials) Innovative Interfaces, Inc
Database Vendor: Gale Cengage Learning, Grolier Online, infoUSA, Innovative Interfaces, Inc, LearningExpress, OCLC FirstSearch, ProQuest, Safari Books Online, Telus
Wireless access
Mem of Bay Area Library & Information System
Open Mon-Fri 8:30-5
Friends of the Library Group
Branches: 11
ALBANY BRANCH, 1247 Marin Ave, Albany, 94706-2043, SAN 332-0944. Tel: 510-526-3720. *Br Mgr,* Deborah Sica; E-mail: dsica@aclibrary.org
Library Holdings: Bk Vols 80,000; Per Subs 125
Special Services for the Deaf - TDD equip
Open Mon 12-6, Tues & Wed 12-8, Thurs 10-6, Sat 10-5, Sun 1-5
Friends of the Library Group
CASTRO VALLEY BRANCH, 3600 Norbridge Ave, Castro Valley, 94546-5878, SAN 332-1002. Tel: 510-667-7900. *Br Mgr,* Carolyn Moskovitz; E-mail: cmoskovitz@aclibrary.org
Library Holdings: Bk Vols 96,296; Per Subs 190
Special Services for the Deaf - TDD equip
Open Mon & Tues 12-8, Wed & Thurs 10-6, Sat 10-5, Sun 1-5
Friends of the Library Group
CENTERVILLE, 3801 Nicolet Ave, 94536-3409, SAN 332-1037. Tel: 510-795-2629. *Br Mgr,* Sallie Pine
Library Holdings: Bk Vols 44,000; Per Subs 100
Open Tues 1-8, Thurs 11-6
Friends of the Library Group
DUBLIN BRANCH, 200 Civic Plaza, Dublin, 94568, SAN 332-1061. Tel: 925-803-7252. *Br Mgr,* Lee Jouthas; E-mail: ljouthas@aclibrary.org
Library Holdings: Bk Vols 145,700; Per Subs 448
Special Services for the Deaf - TDD equip
Open Mon & Tues 10-8, Wed 12-8, Thurs 10-6, Sat 10-5, Sun 1-5
Friends of the Library Group

EXTENSION SERVICES, 2450 Stevenson Blvd, 94538-2326. Tel: 510-745-1477. *Dep County Librn,* Cindy Chadwick
Library Holdings: Bk Vols 33,001; Per Subs 71
FREMONT LIBRARY, 2400 Stevenson Blvd, 94538-2326, SAN 332-1096. Tel: 510-745-1400. *Br Mgr,* Sallie Pine
Library Holdings: Bk Vols 286,209; Per Subs 531
Special Services for the Deaf - Bks on deafness & sign lang; Staff with knowledge of sign lang; TDD equip
Open Mon & Tues 1-9, Wed 12-6, Thurs & Fri 11-6, Sat 10-5, Sun 1-5
Friends of the Library Group
IRVINGTON, 41825 Greenpark Dr, 94538-4084, SAN 332-1150. Tel: 510-795-2631. *Br Mgr,* Sallie Pine
Library Holdings: Bk Vols 37,500; Per Subs 44
Open Wed 10-5
Friends of the Library Group
NEWARK BRANCH, 6300 Civic Terrace Ave, Newark, 94560-3766, SAN 332-1185. Tel: 510-795-2627. *Actg Mgr,* Brian Edwards
Library Holdings: Bk Vols 73,297; Per Subs 158
Open Tues & Thurs 1-9, Wed & Fri 10-6, Sat 10-5
Friends of the Library Group
NILES, 150 I St, 94536-2907, SAN 332-1215. Tel: 510-795-2626. *Br Mgr,* Sallie Pine
Library Holdings: Bk Vols 11,000; Per Subs 34
Open Tues 10-5
Friends of the Library Group
SAN LORENZO BRANCH, 395 Paseo Grande, San Lorenzo, 94580-2453, SAN 332-1274. Tel: 510-670-6283. *Actg Br Mgr,* Lorraine Marcille
Library Holdings: Bk Vols 83,646; Per Subs 251
Open Mon & Tues 12-8, Wed & Thurs 10-6, Sat 10-5, Sun 1-5
Friends of the Library Group
UNION CITY BRANCH, 34007 Alvarado-Niles Rd, Union City, 94587-4498, SAN 332-1304 Tel: 510-745-1464. FAX: 510-487-7241. *Br Mgr,* Tracey Firestone; E-mail: tfirestone@aclibrary.org
Library Holdings: Bk Vols 100,000
Subject Interests: Spanish (Lang)
Open Mon 10-6, Tues & Thurs 1-8, Fri 2-6, Sat 10-5, Sun 1-5
Friends of the Library Group

P CALIFORNIA SCHOOL FOR THE BLIND, Library Media Center, 500 Walnut Ave, 94536. SAN 300-6069. Tel: 510-794-3800, Ext 259. FAX: 510-794-3813. *In Charge,* Elizabeth Hart; E-mail: ehart@csb-cde.ca.gov; Staff 1 (Non-MLS 1)
Founded 1926
Library Holdings: Braille Volumes 4,884; Large Print Bks 2,164; Per Subs 27; Talking Bks 3,330; Videos 168
Special Collections: Audio Books, Fiction & Non-Fiction; Braille Fiction & Non-Fiction; Large Print Fiction & Non-Fiction; Manipulative & Tactile Items for Students; Print/Braille Books, Fiction & Non-Fiction; Professional Coll; Reading/Language Arts, Science, Mathematic & Social Studies Textbooks, audio, braille, large print, print
Automation Activity & Vendor Info: (Cataloging) Book Systems; (Circulation) Book Systems; (OPAC) Book Systems
Function: Audio & video playback equip for onsite use, Bks on cassette, Bks on CD, Computers for patron use, Copy machines, Games & aids for the handicapped, ILL available, Online cat, Spoken cassettes & CDs, VHS videos
Special Services for the Blind - Accessible computers; Bks & mags in Braille, on rec, tape & cassette; Bks available with recordings; Bks on cassette; Bks on CD; Braille bks; Braille equip; Braille Webster's dictionary; Children's Braille; Closed circuit TV; Computer with voice synthesizer for visually impaired persons; Copier with enlargement capabilities; Daisy reader; Descriptive video serv (DVS); Large print & cassettes; Large print bks; Recorded bks; Screen enlargement software for people with visual disabilities; Screen reader software; Sound rec
Open Mon-Thurs 7:30-4:30, Fri 7:30-2
Restriction: Open to students, fac & staff, Use of others with permission of librn

C DEVRY UNIVERSITY*, Fremont Campus Library, 6600 Dumbarton Circle, 94555. Tel: 510-574-1220. Web Site: library.devry.edu. *Libr Dir,* Louise Pasternack; Tel: 510-574-1221, E-mail: lpasternack@devry.edu
Library Holdings: Audiobooks 175; Bk Titles 20,000; Per Subs 55
Database Vendor: ebrary, EBSCOhost, Faulkner Information Services, LexisNexis, ProQuest, Safari Books Online
Wireless access
Open Mon-Thurs 9-9, Fri 9-6, Sat 10-4

J OHLONE COLLEGE*, Blanchard Learning Resources Center, 43600 Mission Blvd, 94539. SAN 300-7480. Tel: 510-659-6160. Interlibrary Loan Service Tel: 510-659-6171. Administration Tel: 510-659-6166. Automation Services Tel: 510-659-6164. FAX: 510-659-6265. E-mail: librarians@ohlone.edu. Web Site: www.ohlone.cc.ca.us/org/library. *Librn,* K G Greenstein; Tel: 510-659-6000, Ext 5272, E-mail: kgreenstein@ohlone.edu; *Librn,* Jim Landavazo; Tel: 510-659-6163, E-mail: jlandavazo@ohlone.edu; *Librn,* Elizabeth Silva; Tel: 510-659-6000, Ext 7484, E-mail: esilva@ohlone.edu; *Tech Serv,* Kathy Sparling; E-mail: ksparling@ohlone.edu; Staff 9 (MLS 4, Non-MLS 5)
Founded 1967. Enrl 10,442; Fac 650; Highest Degree: Associate
Library Holdings: CDs 13,100; Bk Titles 69,116; Per Subs 194; Videos 3,290
Automation Activity & Vendor Info: (Acquisitions) Ex Libris Group; (Cataloging) Ex Libris Group; (Circulation) Ex Libris Group; (OPAC) Ex Libris Group; (Serials) Ex Libris Group
Database Vendor: EBSCOhost, OCLC FirstSearch
Function: AV serv, ILL available, Photocopying/Printing, Ref serv available
Partic in Bay Area Library & Information Network
Special Services for the Blind - Assistive/Adapted tech devices, equip & products
Restriction: Non-circulating to the pub

J QUEEN OF THE HOLY ROSARY COLLEGE LIBRARY*, 43326 Mission Blvd, 94539. SAN 321-4265. Tel: 510-657-2468. Web Site: www.qhrc.org. *Librn,* Mary Ellen D Parker; *Asst Librn,* Sister Claudine Hammer; Staff 3 (MLS 1, Non-MLS 2)
Founded 1908
Library Holdings: AV Mats 731; Bk Titles 24,188; Bk Vols 30,224; Per Subs 150
Special Collections: Art (Dresden Coll), slides
Subject Interests: Philos, Relig, Theol
Automation Activity & Vendor Info: (Cataloging) Follett Software; (Circulation) Follett Software; (OPAC) Follett Software
Wireless access
Publications: Lumen

M WASHINGTON HOSPITAL HEALTHCARE SYSTEM*, Community Health Resource Library, 2500 Mowry Ave, 94538. Tel. 510-494-7030. FAX: 510-742-9285. TDD: 510-494-7050. Web Site: www.healthlibrary.org. *Operations Coordr/Mgr,* Castillo Lucy; E-mail: lucy_castillo@whhs.com; Staff 1 (MLS 1)
Library Holdings: AV Mats 400; Bk Vols 7,000; Per Subs 30
Automation Activity & Vendor Info: (Cataloging) Follett Software; (Circulation) Follett Software; (OPAC) Follett Software
Database Vendor: ProQuest
Open Mon-Fri 10-6

FRENCH CAMP

M SAN JOAQUIN GENERAL HOSPITAL*, Medical Library, 500 W Hospital Rd, 95231. (Mail add: PO Box 1020, Stockton, 95201). SAN 300-7499. Tel: 209-468-6628. FAX: 209-468-6642.
Library Holdings: Bk Titles 800; Bk Vols 1,000; Per Subs 238
Subject Interests: Ethics, Med, Mgt, Nursing
Wireless access
Partic in Docline; Northern California & Nevada Medical Library Group (NCNMLG)
Open Mon-Fri 8-4:30

FRESNO

C ALLIANT INTERNATIONAL UNIVERSITY*, Kauffman Library - Fresno Campus, 5130 E Clinton Way, 93727. SAN 300-7510. Tel: 559-253-2265. Circulation Tel: 559-253-2288. Interlibrary Loan Service Tel: 559-253-2291. Administration Tel: 559-253-2252. FAX: 559-253-2223. Web Site: library.alliant.edu. *Libr Dir,* Louise A Colbert-Mar; E-mail: lcolbert@alliant.edu; *Electronic Res & ILL Librn,* Glenn Tozier; E-mail: gtozier@alliant.edu; *Libr Tech, Sacramento Location,* Barbara Wallace; Tel: 916-561-3202, E-mail: bwallace@alliant.edu; Staff 5 (MLS 2, Non-MLS 3)
Founded 1973. Enrl 547; Fac 51; Highest Degree: Doctorate
Jul 2010-Jun 2011. Mats Exp $48,659, Books $5,500, Per/Ser (Incl. Access Fees) $15,721, Other Print Mats $25,435, AV Mat $2,003. Sal $79,446
Library Holdings: Audiobooks 176; DVDs 142; Bk Vols 10,609; Per Subs 47; Videos 738
Special Collections: Children's Therapy Coll; Psychological Testing Materials
Subject Interests: Clinical psychol, Forensic psychol, Psychol
Automation Activity & Vendor Info: (Acquisitions) Innovative Interfaces, Inc - Millenium; (Cataloging) Innovative Interfaces, Inc - Millenium; (Circulation) Innovative Interfaces, Inc - Millenium; (Course Reserve) Innovative Interfaces, Inc - Millenium; (ILL) Innovative Interfaces, Inc - Millenium; (Media Booking) Innovative Interfaces, Inc - Millenium; (OPAC) Innovative Interfaces, Inc - Millenium; (Serials) Innovative Interfaces, Inc - Millenium
Database Vendor: Alexander Street Press, American Psychological Association (APA), Annual Reviews, Blackwell, ebrary, EBSCOhost, Elsevier, Emerald, Haworth Pres Inc, ISI Web of Knowledge, JSTOR, LexisNexis, Medline, OCLC FirstSearch, OCLC WorldShare Interlibrary Loan, ProQuest, Sage, ScienceDirect, Springer-Verlag, Wiley InterScience, YBP Library Services

Wireless access
Partic in Asn of Mental Health Librn (AMHL); Link+; Statewide California Electronic Library Consortium (SCELC)
Open Mon-Thurs 8-9, Fri 8-6, Sat & Sun 10-4
Restriction: Borrowing privileges limited to fac & registered students

L BAKER, MANOCK & JENSEN LIBRARY*, 5260 N Palm Ave, Ste 421, 93704. SAN 372-266X. Tel: 559-432-5400. *Librn,* Lori Sanders; Tel: 559-436-2086
Library Holdings: Bk Vols 20,000
Restriction: Non-circulating, Staff use only

C CALIFORNIA CHRISTIAN COLLEGE*, Cortese Library, 4881 E University Ave, 93703. SAN 300-7502. Tel: 559-251-5025. Administration Tel: 559-251-4215. FAX: 559-251-4231. Web Site: calchristiancollege.org. *Librn,* Nan Singh
Founded 1955. Highest Degree: Bachelor
Library Holdings: Bk Vols 22,000; Per Subs 15
Special Collections: California Free Will Baptist History; Free Will Baptist Denominational History
Subject Interests: Relig
Automation Activity & Vendor Info: (OPAC) LibraryWorld, Inc
Open Mon, Tues & Thurs 8-5 & 6-9, Wed & Fri 8-5
Friends of the Library Group

L CALIFORNIA COURT OF APPEAL FIFTH APPELLATE DISTRICT LIBRARY*, 2424 Ventura St, 93721. SAN 372-2678. Tel: 559-445-5686. FAX: 559-445-6684. Web Site: www.courts.ca.gov. *Librn,* Tara Crabtree
Library Holdings: Bk Vols 10,000; Per Subs 50
Database Vendor: LexisNexis, Westlaw
Restriction: Staff use only

CALIFORNIA STATE UNIVERSITY, FRESNO

C HENRY MADDEN LIBRARY*, 5200 N Barton Ave, Mail Stop ML-34, 93740-8014, SAN 300-7529. Tel: 559-278-2403. Circulation Tel: 559-278-2551. Interlibrary Loan Service Tel: 559-278-3032. Reference Tel: 559-278-2174. Information Services Tel: 559-278-2596. FAX: 559-278-6952. Web Site: www.csufresno.edu/library. *Assoc Univ Librn,* Dave Tyckoson; Tel: 559-278-5678, E-mail: davety@csufresno.edu; *Asst Univ Librn, Coll Develop,* Kimberley Smith; Tel: 559-278-4578, E-mail: kimberle@csufresno.edu; *Dean, Libr Serv,* Peter McDonald; E-mail: pmcdonald@csufresno.edu; *Dir, Libr Develop,* Marcia Morrison; Tel: 559-278-7177, E-mail: marciamo@csufresno.edu; *Head, Admin Serv,* Glenda Harada; Tel: 559-278-2142, E-mail: gharada@csufresno.edu; *Head, Circ Serv,* Christine Evans; E-mail: chevans@csufresno.edu; *Head, Info & Outreach Serv,* Monica Fusich; Tel: 559-278-7673, E-mail: monicaf@csufresno.edu; *Head, Libr Info Tech,* Patrick Newell; Tel: 559-278-6528, E-mail: pnewell@csufresno.edu; *Head, Pub Serv,* Paula Popma; Tel: 559-278-5794, E-mail: ppopma@csufresno.edu; *Head, Ref,* Allison Cowgill; Tel: 559-278-1022, E-mail: acowgill@csufresno.edu; *Head, Resource Sharing,* Gretchen Higginbottom; Tel: 559-278-3032, E-mail: ghigginbottom@csufresno.edu; *Maps & Govt Info Librn,* Carol Doyle; Tel: 559-278-2335, E-mail: caroldo@csufresno.edu; *Spec Coll Librn,* Tammy Lau; Tel: 559-278-2595, E-mail: tammyl@csufresno.edu; *Teacher Res Ctr Librn,* Mike Tillman; Tel: 559-278-2054, E-mail: miket@csufresno.edu; *Coordr, Bldg Mgt,* Susan Christensen; Tel: 559-278-5792, E-mail: susanm@csufresno.edu; *Cataloger,* Janet Bochin; Tel: 559-278-2158, E-mail: janetbo@csufresno.edu. Subject Specialists: *Eng,* Dave Tyckoson; *Educ,* Patrick Newell; *Soc sci,* Allison Cowgill; *Agr, Sciences,* Carol Doyle; *Eng,* Mike Tillman; *Music,* Janet Bochin; Staff 61.98 (MLS 23.15, Non-MLS 38.83)
Founded 1911. Enrl 18,229; Fac 1,142; Highest Degree: Doctorate
Jul 2010-Jun 2011 Income $6,610,250. Mats Exp $2,580,078, Books $230,617, Per/Ser (Incl. Access Fees) $1,351,626, AV Mat $26,005, Electronic Ref Mat (Incl. Access Fees) $962,576, Presv $9,254. Sal $4,411,908 (Prof $1,993,537)
Library Holdings: AV Mats 92,426; CDs 83,321; DVDs 9,105; e-books 89,192; e-journals 12,581; Microforms 1,430,346; Bk Titles 1,044,948; Bk Vols 1,151,598; Per Subs 42,585
Special Collections: Arne Nixon Center for the Study of Children's Literature; Central Valley Political Archives; Credit Foncier Colony, Topolobampo, Sinaloa (Mexico Coll); Enology; History (Roy J Woodward Memorial Library of California); International Exhibitions; Literature (William Saroyan Coll). State Document Depository; US Document Depository
Automation Activity & Vendor Info: (Acquisitions) Innovative Interfaces, Inc - Millenium; (Cataloging) Innovative Interfaces, Inc - Millenium; (Circulation) Innovative Interfaces, Inc - Millenium; (ILL) OCLC ILLiad; (Media Booking) Innovative Interfaces, Inc - Millenium; (OPAC) Innovative Interfaces, Inc - Millenium; (Serials) Innovative Interfaces, Inc - Millenium
Database Vendor: ABC-CLIO, ACM (Association for Computing Machinery), Agricola, Alexander Street Press, American Chemical Society, American Mathematical Society, American Physical Society, American Psychological Association (APA), Annual Reviews, ARTstor, ASCE Research Library, Backstage Library Works, Cambridge Scientific Abstracts, Children's Literature Comprehensive Database Company (CLCD), Cinahl, CQ Press, ebrary, EBSCOhost, Elsevier, Emerald, Ex Libris Group, Factiva.com, Foundation Center, Gale Cengage Learning, H W Wilson, Haworth Pres Inc, Hoovers, IBISWorld, IEEE (Institute of Electrical & Electronics Engineers), Innovative Interfaces, Inc, IOP, ISI Web of Knowledge, JSTOR, LexisNexis, Medline, Mergent Online, Modern Language Association, Nature Publishing Group, Newsbank, OCLC, OCLC FirstSearch, OCLC WorldShare Interlibrary Loan, Oxford Online, Project MUSE, ProQuest, PubMed, Safari Books Online, Sage, ScienceDirect, Springer-Verlag, Thomson - Web of Science, ValueLine, Wiley InterScience, Wilson - Wilson Web, YBP Library Services
Function: Art exhibits, CD-ROM, Computers for patron use, Copy machines, e-mail & chat, e-mail serv, Electronic databases & coll, Exhibits, Free DVD rentals, Handicapped accessible, ILL available, Learning ctr, Libr develop, Mail & tel request accepted, Microfiche/film & reading machines, Music CDs, Online cat, Online info literacy tutorials on the web & in blackboard, Online ref, Orientations, Photocopying/Printing, Printer for laptops & handheld devices, Pub access computers, Ref & res, Ref serv available, Scanner, Spanish lang bks, Tax forms, Telephone ref, VHS videos, Web-catalog, Wheelchair accessible, Workshops
Partic in Link+; OCLC Online Computer Library Center, Inc
Publications: Madden Library Update & Friendscript (Newsletter); The Magic Mirror (Newsletter)
Special Services for the Deaf - Am sign lang & deaf culture; Assistive tech; Bks on deafness & sign lang; Closed caption videos; Coll on deaf educ
Special Services for the Blind - Accessible computers; Assistive/Adapted tech devices, equip & products; Cassette playback machines; Copier with enlargement capabilities; Internet workstation with adaptive software; Networked computers with assistive software
Open Mon-Thurs 7:45am-11pm, Fri 7:45-5, Sat 10-6, Sun 2-10
Friends of the Library Group

C SAHATDJIAN LIBRARY*, Armenian Studies Program, 5245 N Backer Ave PB4, 93740-8001. Tel: 559-278-2669. FAX: 559-278-2129. Web Site: armenianstudies.csufresno.edu. *Dir,* Dr Barlow Der Mugrdechian; E-mail: barlowd@csufresno.edu
Founded 1988. Enrl 225; Fac 2; Highest Degree: Master
Library Holdings: Bk Titles 2,000; Per Subs 30
Special Collections: Armenian Film Archive; Elbrecht Historic Churches Archive; Index of Armenian Art; William Saroyan Coll
Subject Interests: Archives
Open Mon-Fri 8-4

S FRESNO BEE*, Editorial Library, 1626 E St, 93786-0001. SAN 300-7545. Tel: 559-441-6111. Circulation Toll Free Tel: 800-877-3400. Toll Free Tel: 800-877-7300. FAX: 559-495-6803. Web Site: www.fresnobee.com. *Chief Librn,* Ashley Wayte; Tel: 559-441-6381; Staff 5 (MLS 5)
Founded 1922
Library Holdings: Bk Vols 963
Special Collections: Newspaper clippings, fiche, microfilm from 1922-present
Database Vendor: Dialog, LexisNexis
Restriction: Open by appt only

S FRESNO CITY & COUNTY HISTORICAL SOCIETY ARCHIVES*, 7160 W Kearney Blvd, 93706. SAN 300-7553. Tel: 559-441-0862. FAX: 559-441-1372. E-mail: info@valleyhistory.org. Web Site: www.valleyhistory.org. *Curator of Coll,* Sharon Hiigel; E-mail: shiigel@valleyhistory.org. Subject Specialists: *Local hist, Photog,* Sharon Hiigel
Founded 1919
Library Holdings: Bk Titles 3,000
Special Collections: Agriculture, Fresno City & County, Ethnic & Cultural Groups, Logging (Photograph Colls); Ben R Walker History Files, 1850-1953, newsp clippings; Ephemera Coll, ad mats, calendars, invitations, paper currency, postcards, posters, programs, trade cats; Municipal & County Records; Personal, Family, Organization & Business Records, ms; Vertical Files, ann reports, brochures, church & organization anniversary publs, newsp clippings, pamphlets. Oral History
Subject Interests: Calif Cent Valley, Fresno City, Fresno County
Restriction: Researchers by appt only

J FRESNO CITY COLLEGE LIBRARY, 1101 E University Ave, 93741. SAN 300-7561. Tel: 559-442-8204. Circulation Tel: 559-442-8205. Administration Tel: 559-265-5709. FAX: 559-265-5758. Web Site: www.fresnocitycollege.edu/library. *Dean, Instruction, Libr & Student Learning Support Serv,* Position Currently Open; *Bibliog Instruction Librn,* Donna Chandler; E-mail: donna.chandler@fresnocitycollege.edu; *Librn,* Laurel Doud; E-mail: laurel.doud@fresnocitycollege.edu; *Librn,* Mai Yang; E-mail: mai.yang@fresnocitycollege.edu; *Tech Serv Librn,* Paula Demanett; E-mail: paula.demanett@fresnocitycollege.edu; Staff 7 (MLS 7)
Founded 1910. Enrl 25,000; Fac 530; Highest Degree: Associate

Library Holdings: AV Mats 1,000; e-books 24,000; Electronic Media & Resources 15; Bk Titles 90,000; Per Subs 150
Automation Activity & Vendor Info: (Cataloging) Innovative Interfaces, Inc - Millenium; (Circulation) Innovative Interfaces, Inc - Millenium; (Course Reserve) Innovative Interfaces, Inc - Millenium; (ILL) OCLC; (OPAC) Innovative Interfaces, Inc - Millenium
Database Vendor: 3M Library Systems, ABC-CLIO, ARTstor, Bowker, Cinahl, CountryWatch, EBSCOhost, Gale Cengage Learning, Greenwood Publishing Group, Innovative Interfaces, Inc, JSTOR, LexisNexis, OCLC, Oxford Online, ProQuest
Wireless access
Publications: Library News (Newsletter)
Partic in Community College League of California (CCLC)
Special Services for the Deaf - ADA equip; Closed caption videos; Sign lang interpreter upon request for prog
Special Services for the Blind - Assistive/Adapted tech devices, equip & products; Copier with enlargement capabilities; Dragon Naturally Speaking software; Magnifiers; Screen enlargement software for people with visual disabilities
Open Mon-Thurs 7:30-7:30, Fri 7:30-2
Friends of the Library Group

S FRESNO COUNTY GENEALOGICAL SOCIETY LIBRARY, San Joaquin Valley Heritage & Genealogy Center, Fresno Public Library, 2420 Mariposa St, 93721-2285. (Mail add: PO Box 1429, 93716-1429), SAN 370-6834. Tel: 559-600-6230. FAX: 559-448-1971. E-mail: infofcgs@gmail.com. Web Site: www.fresnolibrary.org/calif, www.rootsweb.ancestry.com/~cafcgs. *Librn,* Kathleen Coleman
Founded 1965
Library Holdings: CDs 568; Microforms 2,079; Bk Titles 12,508; Per Subs 87; Videos 29
Subject Interests: Genealogy, State hist
Automation Activity & Vendor Info: (Cataloging) SirsiDynix; (Circulation) SirsiDynix; (OPAC) SirsiDynix
Wireless access
Publications: Ash Tree Echo; The Jotted Line (Newsletter)
Open Mon-Wed 10-6, Thurs 10-7, Fri & Sat 10-5, Sun 12-5
Restriction: Non-circulating
Friends of the Library Group

GL FRESNO COUNTY PUBLIC LAW LIBRARY, Fresno County Courthouse, Rm 600, 1100 Van Ness Ave, 93721-2017. SAN 300-7626. Tel: 559-600-2227. E-mail: lawlibrary@co.fresno.ca.us. Web Site: www.fresnolawlibrary.org. *Dir,* Sharon E Borbon; *Acq/ILL Librn, Ref Librn,* Mark Masters; E-mail: mmasters@co.fresno.ca.us; *Circ Serv,* Karina Martinez
Founded 1891
Library Holdings: Bk Titles 3,277; Bk Vols 46,980
Automation Activity & Vendor Info: (Cataloging) EOS International; (Circulation) EOS International; (OPAC) EOS International; (Serials) EOS International
Database Vendor: EBSCO Information Services, HeinOnline, Westlaw
Open Mon-Fri 8-5

P FRESNO COUNTY PUBLIC LIBRARY*, 2420 Mariposa St, 93721-2204. SAN 331-9989. Tel: 559-600-7323. Administration Tel: 559-600-6237. Administration FAX: 559-600-7628. Web Site: www.fresnolibrary.org. *County Librn,* Laurel Prysiazny; E-mail: laurel.prysiazny@fresnolibrary.org; *Assoc County Librn,* Kelley Worman-Landano; E-mail: kelley.worman-landano@fresnolibrary.org; *Br Cluster Mgr,* Terry Sterling; Tel: 559-600-6243, E-mail: terry.sterling@fresnolibrary.org; *Hq Div Mgr,* Deborah Janzen; E-mail: deborah.janzen@fresnolibrary.org; *Mgt Serv Mgr,* Carina Gil; E-mail: carina.gil@fresnolibrary.org; *Br Supvr,* Kerry Eckman; E-mail: kerry.eckman@fresnolibrary.org; *Br Supvr,* Wendy Eisenberg; E-mail: wendy.eisenberg@fresnolibrary.org; *Br Supvr,* Penny Hill; E-mail: penny.hill@fresnolibrary.org; *Br Supvr,* Lisa Lindsay; Tel: 559-600-6267, E-mail: lisa.lindsay@fresnolibrary.org; *Literacy Coordr,* Jeremy Boriack; E-mail: jeremy.boriack@fresnolibrary.org; *Vols Serv Coordr,* Elizabeth Finkle; Tel: 559-600-9230, E-mail: elizabeth.finkle@fresnolibrary.org; *Develop Officer,* Linda Calandra; E-mail: linda.calandra@fresnolibrary.org; *Fac Serv,* Patrick Heintz; Tel: 559-600-6246, E-mail: patrick.heintz@fresnolibrary.org; *Spec Coll,* Nance Espinosa; E-mail: nance.espinosa@fresnolibrary.org; Staff 48 (MLS 48)
Founded 1910. Pop 919,379; Circ 3,989,774
Jul 2012-Jun 2013 Income (Main Library and Branch(s)) $25,542,779. Mats Exp $2,344,278. Sal $16,563,158
Library Holdings: Audiobooks 104,866; CDs 50,011; DVDs 88,377; e-books 6,647; Large Print Bks 17,258; Microforms 11,611; Bk Vols 981,536; Talking Bks 27,751
Special Collections: Gary Soto Coll; Leo Politi Coll; Manly Australia (Sister City) Coll; Miwok & Yokut Native American Coll; Mother Goose Coll; Oral History Coll (Japanese & Fresno County); William Saroyan Coll. Oral History; State Document Depository; US Document Depository
Subject Interests: Calif, City hist, Genealogy, Local hist, Punjabi (Lang), Spanish (Lang)
Automation Activity & Vendor Info: (Acquisitions) SirsiDynix; (Cataloging) SirsiDynix; (Circulation) SirsiDynix; (OPAC) SirsiDynix; (Serials) SirsiDynix
Wireless access
Function: Adult literacy prog, Archival coll, Audiobks via web, Bilingual assistance for Spanish patrons, Bks on CD, Children's prog, Computer training, Computers for patron use, Copy machines, Digital talking bks, Electronic databases & coll, Family literacy, Free DVD rentals, Govt ref serv, Handicapped accessible, Home delivery & serv to Sr ctr & nursing homes, Homebound delivery serv, Homework prog, ILL available, Jail serv, Music CDs, Online cat, Online ref, Outside serv via phone, mail, e-mail & web, Photocopying/Printing, Preschool outreach, Prog for adults, Prog for children & young adult, Pub access computers, Ref serv available, Senior outreach, Story hour, Summer reading prog, Tax forms, Teen prog, Telephone ref, Web-catalog, Wheelchair accessible
Publications: Book Notes & Footnotes (Newsletter); Talking Book Library (Newsletter)
Mem of San Joaquin Valley Library System
Partic in Califa; CLA; OCLC Online Computer Library Center, Inc
Special Services for the Deaf - Closed caption videos; Staff with knowledge of sign lang
Special Services for the Blind - Bks on CD; Digital talking bk; Digital talking bk machines; Home delivery serv; Large print bks; Playaways (bks on MP3); Talking bks & player equip; Tel Pioneers equip repair group
Friends of the Library Group
Branches: 36
AUBERRY BRANCH, 33049 Auberry Rd, Auberry, 93602. (Mail add: PO Box 279, Auberry, 93602-0279), SAN 374-4094. Tel: 559-855-8523. FAX: 559-855-8523. *Br Supvr,* Connie Urquhart; Staff 1 (MLS 1)
Founded 1918. Pop 7,330; Circ 70,372
Special Collections: Miwok & Yokut Native American Coll
Friends of the Library Group
BEAR MOUNTAIN NEIGHBORHOOD, 30733 E Kings Canyon Rd, Squaw Valley, 93675-9305, SAN 378-2239. Tel: 559-332-2528. *Br Supvr,* Wendy Eisenberg
Founded 1981. Pop 3,187; Circ 38,250
Friends of the Library Group
BIG CREEK STATION, 55185 Point Rd, Big Creek, 93605. (Mail add: PO Box 25, Big Creek, 93605-0025), SAN 378-2255. Tel: 559-893-6614. *Br Supvr,* Connie Urquhart
Founded 1917. Pop 1,503; Circ 4,110
BIOLA BRANCH, 4885 N Biola Ave, 93723. Tel: 559-843-2001. *Supvr,* Penny Hill; Tel: 559-600-4071
Open Mon & Thurs 3-7, Sat 10-2
CARUTHERS NEIGHBORHOOD, 13382 S Henderson Rd, Caruthers, 93609. (Mail add: PO Box 95, Caruthers, 93609-0095), SAN 378-2271. Tel: 559-864-8766. *Br Supvr,* Sean Aragon
Founded 1911. Pop 10,204; Circ 27,085
Friends of the Library Group
CEDAR CLINTON NEIGHBORHOOD, 4150 E Clinton Ave, 93703-2520, SAN 378-2298. Tel: 559-442-1770. *Br Supvr,* Connie Urquhart; Staff 1 (MLS 1)
Founded 1922. Pop 71,717; Circ 212,281
Friends of the Library Group
CLOVIS REGIONAL, 1155 Fifth St, Clovis, 93612-1314, SAN 332-0103. Tel: 559-600-9531. *Br Supvr,* Connie Urquhart; Staff 1 (MLS 1)
Founded 1915. Pop 113,000; Circ 482,678
Friends of the Library Group
EASTON NEIGHBORHOOD, 25 E Fantz Ave, Easton, 93706-5911, SAN 378-231X. Tel: 559-237-3929. *Br Supvr,* Sean Aragon
Founded 1910. Pop 4,666; Circ 22,190
FIG GARDEN REGIONAL, 3071 W Bullard Ave, 93711, SAN 332-0162. Tel: 559-600-4071. *Br Supvr,* Penny Hill; Staff 1 (MLS 1)
Founded 1962. Pop 81,442; Circ 402,812
Friends of the Library Group
FIREBAUGH NEIGHBORHOOD, 1315 O St, Firebaugh, 93622-2319, SAN 378-2336. Tel: 559-600-9274. *Br Supvr,* Penny Hill
Founded 1923. Pop 9,244; Circ 17,989
FOWLER BRANCH, 306 S Seventh St, Fowler, 93625, SAN 377-6387. Tel: 559-600-9281. *Br Supvr,* Sean Aragon; Staff 1 (MLS 1)
Founded 1913. Pop 13,149; Circ 52,660
Friends of the Library Group
FRESNO COUNTY JAIL, 2200 Fresno St, 93721-2204. (Mail add: 2420 Mariposa St, 93721), SAN 377-6409. Tel: 559-600-7323. FAX: 559-600-7628.
Restriction: Staff & inmates only
GILLIS NEIGHBORHOOD, 629 W Dakota Ave, 93705-2820, SAN 377-6425. Tel: 559-225-0140. *Br Supvr,* Sean Aragon; Staff 1 (MLS 1)
Founded 1940. Pop 94,346; Circ 207,711
Friends of the Library Group
KERMAN BRANCH, 15081 W Kearney Plaza, Kerman, 93630-1357, SAN 377-6093. Tel: 559-846-8804. *Br Supvr,* Penny Hill
Founded 1907. Pop 29,054; Circ 80,477
Special Collections: Panjabi Language Materials
Friends of the Library Group

KINGSBURG BRANCH, 1399 Draper St, Kingsburg, 93631-1906, SAN 377-6115. Tel: 559-897-3710. *Br Supvr,* Sean Aragon
Founded 1910. Pop 12,921; Circ 77,435
Friends of the Library Group

LATON STATION, 6313 DeWoody St, Laton, 93242. (Mail add: PO Box 38, Laton, 93242-0038), SAN 377-6131. Tel: 559-923-4554. *Br Supvr,* Sean Aragon
Founded 1904. Pop 3,587; Circ 7,551

LITERACY SERVICES CENTER, 2420 Mariposa St, 93721. Tel: 559-600-9240. *Coordr,* Jeremy Boriack
Subject Interests: Adult literacy, Early childhood literacy & learning, Parenting
Function: Adult literacy prog

MENDOTA BRANCH, 1246 Belmont Ave, Mendota, 93640-2667, SAN 378-2352. Tel: 559-600-9291. *Br Supvr,* Penny Hill; Staff 1 (MLS 1)
Founded 1919. Pop 12,689; Circ 29,242

MOSQUEDA CENTER NEIGHBORHOOD, 4670 E Butler Ave, 93702-4608, SAN 377-6174. Tel: 559-600-4072. *Br Supvr,* Connie Urquhart
Founded 1976. Pop 38,528; Circ 51,813
Special Collections: Gary Soto Coll

ORANGE COVE BRANCH, 815 Park Blvd, Orange Cove, 93646, SAN 378-2379. Tel: 559-600-9292. *Br Supvr,* Wendy Eisenberg; Staff 1 (MLS 1)
Founded 1915. Pop 10,940; Circ 50,763
Friends of the Library Group

PARLIER NEIGHBORHOOD, 1130 E Parlier Ave, Parlier, 93648-2433, SAN 377-6190. Tel: 559-646-3835. *Br Supvr,* Wendy Eisenberg
Founded 1910. Pop 16,715; Circ 20,224

PIEDRA STATION, 25385 Trimmer Springs Rd, Piedra, 93657, (Mail add: PO Box 389, Piedra, 93649-0389), SAN 377-6212. Tel: 559-787-3266. *Br Supvr,* Wendy Eisenberg
Founded 1983. Pop 5,668; Circ 6,258
Friends of the Library Group

PINEDALE NEIGHBORHOOD, 7170 N San Pablo Ave, Pinedale, 93650-1143, SAN 377-6239. Tel: 559-439-0486. *Br Supvr,* Terrence Eckman
Founded 1948. Pop 3,595; Circ 25,479

LEO POLITI BRANCH, 5771 N First St, 93710-6203, SAN 378-2395. Tel: 559-431-6450. *Br Supvr,* Terrence Eckman; E-mail: terrence.eckman@fresnolibrary.org; Staff 1 (MLS 1)
Founded 1974. Pop 59,033; Circ 200,794
Special Collections: Leo Politi Coll
Friends of the Library Group

REEDLEY BRANCH, 1027 E St, Reedley, 93654-2918, SAN 332-0227. Tel: 559-638-2818. *Br Supvr,* Wendy Eisenberg; Staff 1 (MLS 1)
Founded 1910. Pop 29,482; Circ 134,623
Friends of the Library Group

RIVERDALE NEIGHBORHOOD, 20975 Malsbary Ave, Riverdale, 93656. (Mail add: PO Box 757, Riverdale, 93656-0757), SAN 377-6255. Tel: 559-867-3381. *Br Supvr,* Sean Aragon
Founded 1913. Pop 5,661; Circ 25,238

SAN JOAQUIN NEIGHBORHOOD, 8781 Main St, San Joaquin, 93660. (Mail add: PO Box 948, San Joaquin, 93660-0948), SAN 377-6271. Tel: 559-693-2171. *Br Supvr,* Penny Hill
Founded 1916. Pop 6,461; Circ 31,207

SANGER BRANCH, 1812 Seventh St, Sanger, 93657-2805, SAN 332-0251. Tel: 559-875-2435. *Br Supvr,* Wendy Eisenberg

SELMA BRANCH, 2200 Selma St, Selma, 93662-3151, SAN 332-0286. Tel: 559-896-3393. *Br Supvr,* Sean Aragon; Staff 1 (MLS 1)
Founded 1913. Pop 30,893; Circ 115,137
Special Collections: Sister City Coll (Sister City with Manly, Australia)
Friends of the Library Group

SENIOR RESOURCE CENTER, 2025 E Dakota Ave, 93726, SAN 378-2433. Tel: 559-600-6767. *Br Supvr,* Lisa Lindsay
Founded 2005. Circ 10,643
Special Collections: Large Print & Nonprint Colls; Programs to Seniors & Caregivers

SHAVER LAKE STATION, 41344 Tollhouse Rd, Shaver Lake, 93664. (Mail add: PO Box 169, Shaver Lake, 93664-0169), SAN 378-2417. Tel: 559-841-3330. *Br Supvr,* Connie Urquhart
Founded 1934. Pop 1,502; Circ 5,279

SUNNYSIDE REGIONAL, 5566 E Kings Canyon Rd, 93727-4526. Tel: 559-600-6594. FAX: 559-255-6599. *Br Supvr,* Wendy Eisenberg; Staff 1 (MLS 1)
Founded 1965. Pop 61,131; Circ 247,999
Friends of the Library Group

P TALKING BOOK LIBRARY FOR THE BLIND, 770 N San Pablo Ave, 93728-3640, SAN 332-0014. Tel: 559-600-3217. *Br Supvr,* Lisa Lindsay; Staff 1 (MLS 1)
Founded 1975. Circ 81,834
Special Services for the Blind - Assistive/Adapted tech devices, equip & products; Digital talking bk; Digital talking bk machines; Talking bks & player equip; Tel Pioneers equip repair group
Friends of the Library Group

TRANQUILLITY STATION, 25561 Williams St, Tranquillity, 93668. (Mail add: PO Box 246, Tranquillity, 93668-0246), SAN 377-6298. Tel: 559-698-5158. *Br Supvr,* Penny Hill
Founded 1913. Pop 3,527; Circ 16,029

WEST FRESNO BRANCH, 188 E California Ave, 93706. Tel: 559-455-6066. *Br Supvr,* Penny Hill; Staff 1 (MLS 1)
Founded 1973. Pop 30,591; Circ 62,751

WOODWARD PARK REGIONAL, 944 E Perrin Ave, 93720. Tel: 559-600-3135. Information Services Tel: 559-600-9236. FAX: 559-600-1348. *Br Supvr,* Terrence Eckman; Staff 2 (MLS 2)
Founded 2004. Pop 60,809; Circ 623,845
Special Collections: Chinese Language Materials
Friends of the Library Group

Bookmobiles: 2

C FRESNO PACIFIC UNIVERSITY, Hiebert Library, 1717 S Chestnut Ave, 93702. SAN 300-7642. Tel: 559-453-2090. FAX: 559-453-2124. Web Site: www.fresno.edu/library. *Dir,* Kevin Enns-Rempel; Tel: 559-453-2225, E-mail: kevin.enns-rempel@fresno.edu; *Assoc Libr Dir, Circ,* Anne Guenther; Tel: 599-453-2121, E-mail: aguenthe@fresno.edu; *Acq,* Hope Nisly; Tel: 559-453-2223, E-mail: nhope@fresno.edu; *Archivist,* Hannah Keeney; Tel: 559-453-3437, E-mail: hannah.keeney@fresno.edu; *Cat, Tech Serv,* Vern Carter; Tel: 559-453-7124, E-mail: vern.carter@fresno.edu; *Ref,* Ernest Carrere; Tel: 559-453-2131, E-mail: ernest.carrere@fresno.edu; Staff 6 (MLS 5, Non-MLS 1)
Founded 1944. Enrl 3,800; Fac 150; Highest Degree: Master
Library Holdings: AV Mats 6,666; e-books 139,159; e-journals 20,010; Electronic Media & Resources 15,520; Bk Vols 139,453; Per Subs 572
Special Collections: Mennonite Library & Archives
Subject Interests: Hist, Relig
Automation Activity & Vendor Info: (Acquisitions) Innovative Interfaces, Inc - Millenium; (Cataloging) Innovative Interfaces, Inc - Millenium; (Circulation) Innovative Interfaces, Inc - Millenium; (Course Reserve) Innovative Interfaces, Inc - Millenium; (OPAC) Innovative Interfaces, Inc - Millenium; (Serials) Innovative Interfaces, Inc - Millenium
Database Vendor: Alexander Street Press, American Psychological Association (APA), Annual Reviews, Cinahl, ebrary, EBSCOhost, Innovative Interfaces, Inc, JSTOR, Sage, Springer-Verlag, Wiley
Wireless access
Function: 24/7 Online cat, Archival coll, Art exhibits, Audio & video playback equip for onsite use, Copy machines, e-mail & chat, Electronic databases & coll, Online cat
Partic in Link+; OCLC Online Computer Library Center, Inc; Statewide California Electronic Library Consortium (SCELC)
Open Mon-Thurs 8am-10pm, Fri 8-5, Sat 9-5

J HEALD COLLEGE*, Learning Resource Center-Fresno Campus, 255 W Bullard Ave, 93704. Tel: 559-438-4222. FAX: 559-438-0948. Web Site: www.heald.edu. *Mgr,* Martha Espinoza; E-mail: martha_espinoza@fresno.heald.edu
Library Holdings: Bk Vols 500
Database Vendor: EBSCOhost
Open Mon-Thurs 7am-10:45pm, Fri 8-6, Sat 10-3

L MCCORMICK, BARSTOW, SHEPPARD, WAYTE & CARRUTH, Law Library, 7647 N Freso St, 93720. SAN 373-7446. Tel: 559-433-1300. FAX: 559-433-2300. Web Site: www.mccormickbarstow.com/. *Librn,* Pat Sullivan; E-mail: pat.sullivan@mccormickbarstow.com
Library Holdings: Bk Titles 1,300; Bk Vols 12,000

M WILLIAM O OWEN MEDICAL LIBRARY*, Saint Agnes Medical Ctr, 1303 E Herndon Ave, MS 70, 93720-1234. SAN 320-5592. Tel: 559-450-3322. Reference Tel: 559-450-3325. FAX: 559-450-3315. E-mail: medlib@samc.com. *Med Librn,* Nancy Crossfield; Staff 1 (MLS 1)
Founded 1974
Jul 2013-Jun 2014. Mats Exp $94,000, Books $8,000, Per/Ser (Incl. Access Fees) $66,000, Electronic Ref Mat (Incl. Access Fees) $20,000. Sal $130,000
Library Holdings: Bk Vols 900; Per Subs 125
Subject Interests: Cardiology, Gen surgery, Med, Nursing
Automation Activity & Vendor Info: (Cataloging) Marcive, Inc; (Circulation) CyberTools for Libraries; (OPAC) CyberTools for Libraries
Database Vendor: Cinahl, EBSCO Information Services, EBSCOhost, Elsevier, MD Consult, OVID Technologies, PubMed, STAT!Ref (Teton Data Systems), Wiley
Wireless access
Function: Health sci info serv, ILL available, Online searches, Orientations, Photocopying/Printing, Ref serv available
Partic in Medical Library Group of Southern California & Arizona (MLGSCA); Northern California & Nevada Medical Library Group (NCNMLG)
Open Mon-Fri 8:30-4
Restriction: Authorized patrons, Circulates for staff only

SR ROMAN CATHOLIC DIOCESE OF FRESNO LIBRARY*, 1550 N Fresno St, 93703-3788. SAN 300-7537. Tel: 559-488-7400. FAX: 559-488-7464. E-mail: archives@dioceseoffresno.org. Web Site: www.dioceseoffresno.org.
Founded 1934
Library Holdings: Bk Vols 20,000
Subject Interests: Relig, Western Americana
Restriction: Open by appt only

P SAN JOAQUIN VALLEY LIBRARY SYSTEM*, 2420 Mariposa St, 93721. SAN 300-7677. Tel: 559-600-6283. Automation Services Tel: 559-600-6285. FAX: 559-600-6295. Web Site: www.sjvls.org. *Admin Librn,* Jeffrey E Crosby; E-mail: jeffrey.crosby@sjvls.org; Staff 7 (MLS 4, Non-MLS 3)
Founded 1960. Pop 2,350,208; Circ 6,290,642
Automation Activity & Vendor Info: (Acquisitions) SirsiDynix; (Cataloging) SirsiDynix; (Circulation) SirsiDynix; (ILL) SirsiDynix; (OPAC) SirsiDynix; (Serials) SirsiDynix
Database Vendor: EBSCOhost
Member Libraries: Coalinga-Huron Library District; Fresno County Public Library; Kern County Library; Kings County Library; Madera County Library; Mariposa County Library; Merced County Library; Porterville Public Library; Tulare County Library; Tulare Public Library
Special Services for the Blind - Talking bks
Restriction: Non-circulating to the pub

SR TEMPLE BETH ISRAEL LIBRARY*, 6622 N Maroa Ave, 93704. SAN 320-5606. Tel: 559-432-3600. FAX: 559-432-3685. Web Site: www.tbifresno.org/study/library. *Pres,* David Sicherman
Jan 2005-Dec 2005. Mats Exp Books $500
Library Holdings: Bk Titles 2,000
Special Collections: Holocaust Coll
Automation Activity & Vendor Info: (Cataloging) JayWil Software Development, Inc

S THE VINEYARD*, Real Estate Library, 100 W Shaw Ave, 93704. SAN 300-7650. Tel: 559-222-0182. *Librn,* Richard Erganian
Founded 1956
Library Holdings: Bk Titles 3,000
Special Collections: Mixed Use Development, Real Estate (Shopping Center Development), Hotels & Motels
Subject Interests: Archit, Urban planning
Restriction: Staff use only

L UNITED STATES COURTS LIBRARY*, 2500 Tulare St, Ste 2401, 93721. SAN 372-2686. Tel: 559-499-5615. *Librn,* Martin Schwartz; Staff 1 (MLS 1)
Library Holdings: Bk Titles 884; Bk Vols 17,000
Automation Activity & Vendor Info: (Acquisitions) SIRSI WorkFlows; (Cataloging) SIRSI WorkFlows; (OPAC) SirsiDynix; (Serials) SIRSI WorkFlows
Database Vendor: HeinOnline, LexisNexis, OCLC WorldShare Interlibrary Loan, ProQuest, SirsiDynix, Westlaw
Wireless access
Open Mon-Fri 9-12 & 1-4

FULLERTON

C CALIFORNIA STATE UNIVERSITY, FULLERTON*, Paulina June & George Pollak Library, 800 N State College Blvd, 92834. (Mail add: PO Box 4150, 92834-4150), SAN 300-774X. Tel: 657-278-2633. FAX: 657-278-2439. E-mail: libraryanswers@fullerton.edu. Web Site: www.library.fullerton.edu. *Interim Univ Librn,* Susan Tschabrun; Tel: 657-278-7556, E-mail: stschabrun@fullerton.edu; *Chair, Tech Serv,* Barbara Miller; Tel: 657-278-7544, E-mail: bmiller@fullerton.edu; *Head of Instruction & Info Serv,* Adolfo Prieto; Tel: 657-278-2538, E-mail: aprieto@fullerton.edu; *Head, Access Serv,* Ron Rodriguez; E-mail: rrodriguez@fullerton.edu; Staff 62 (MLS 25, Non-MLS 37)
Founded 1959. Enrl 37,000; Fac 2,100; Highest Degree: Master
Library Holdings: Bk Titles 743,945; Bk Vols 1,111,419; Per Subs 2,476
Special Collections: State Document Depository; US Document Depository
Automation Activity & Vendor Info: (Cataloging) Innovative Interfaces, Inc; (Circulation) Innovative Interfaces, Inc
Publications: Exhibition Catalogue for Maps Illustrating the History of Cartography; Reference Department Bibliographies & Guides
Partic in BRS; Dow Jones News Retrieval; OCLC Online Computer Library Center, Inc; SDC Info Servs
Friends of the Library Group

J FULLERTON COLLEGE*, William T Boyce Library, 321 E Chapman Ave, 92832-2095. SAN 300-7758. Tel: 714-992-7039. Interlibrary Loan Service Tel: 714-992-5682. Administration Tel: 714-992-7040. FAX: 714-992-9961. Interlibrary Loan Service FAX: 714-992-9960. E-mail: librarian@fullcoll.edu. Web Site: library.fullcoll.edu. *Actg Dean of Libr & Learning Res, Dea, Soc Sci,* Dan Tesar; Tel: 714-992-7040, E-mail: dtesar@fullcoll.edu; *Acq Librn,* Monique Delatte Starkey; Tel: 714-992-7379, E-mail: mdelatte@fullcoll.edu; *Cat Librn,* Dave Brown; Tel: 714-992-7376, E-mail: dbrown@fullcoll.edu; *Circ Librn,* Jane Ishibashi; Tel: 714-992-7378, E-mail: jishibashi@fullcoll.edu; *Instruction Librn,* Jill Okamura; Tel: 714-992-7380, E-mail: jokamura@fullcoll.edu; *Syst Librn,* Erica Bennett; Tel: 714-992-7375, E-mail: ebennett@fullcoll.edu; Staff 15 (MLS 5, Non-MLS 10)
Founded 1913. Enrl 18,890; Fac 315; Highest Degree: Associate
Library Holdings: Audiobooks 6; AV Mats 2,751; Bks on Deafness & Sign Lang 111; CDs 463; DVDs 122; e-books 173,108; e-journals 37; Electronic Media & Resources 10; High Interest/Low Vocabulary Bk Vols 694; Large Print Bks 22; Microforms 7,036; Bk Titles 80,355; Bk Vols 88,083; Per Subs 120
Special Collections: Topographic Maps of California (United States Geological Survey Coll). Oral History
Subject Interests: Calif, Libr & info sci, Literary criticism, Local hist, Music, Women's studies
Automation Activity & Vendor Info: (Acquisitions) Ex Libris Group; (Cataloging) Ex Libris Group; (Circulation) Ex Libris Group; (Course Reserve) Ex Libris Group; (OPAC) Ex Libris Group; (Serials) Ex Libris Group
Database Vendor: CQ Press, EBSCOhost, Gale Cengage Learning, JSTOR, LexisNexis, McGraw-Hill, Springer-Verlag
Wireless access
Partic in OCLC Online Computer Library Center, Inc
Special Services for the Blind - Closed circuit TV magnifier
Open Mon-Thurs 7:30am-9pm, Fri 7:30-4, Sat 10-2
Friends of the Library Group

P FULLERTON PUBLIC LIBRARY*, 353 W Commonwealth Ave, 92832-1796. SAN 332-0340. Tel: 714-738-6380. Circulation Tel: 714-738-6334. Reference Tel: 714-738-6326. FAX: 714-447-3280. Reference E-mail: reference@fullertonlibrary.org. Web Site: www.fullertonlibrary.org. *Dir,* Maureen Gebelein; E-mail: maureeng@ci.fullerton.ca.us; *Div Mgr, Tech Serv,* Andrea Taylor; Tel: 714-738-6392; *Adult Serv, Ref,* Tim Mountain; Tel: 714-738-6325, E-mail: timm@ci.fullerton.ca.us; *Cat,* Carol Wright; Tel: 714-738-6395, E-mail: carolwr@ci.fullerton.ca.us; *Ch Serv,* Janine Jacobs; Tel: 714-738-6343, E-mail: janinej@ci.fullerton.ca.us; *YA Serv,* Shirley Ku; Tel: 714-773-5719, E-mail: shirleyk@ci.fullerton.ca.us; Staff 30 (MLS 15, Non-MLS 15)
Founded 1906. Pop 134,100; Circ 997,013
Library Holdings: Bk Titles 250,000; Per Subs 400
Special Collections: Local History Room; Mary Campbell Children's Coll
Subject Interests: Chinese lang, Korean (Lang), Spanish (Lang)
Automation Activity & Vendor Info: (Acquisitions) SirsiDynix; (Cataloging) SirsiDynix; (Circulation) SirsiDynix; (ILL) SirsiDynix; (Media Booking) SirsiDynix; (OPAC) SirsiDynix; (Serials) SirsiDynix
Database Vendor: EBSCOhost, Gale Cengage Learning, LexisNexis, Newsbank, OCLC FirstSearch, SirsiDynix
Wireless access
Open Mon-Thurs 10-9, Fri & Sat 10-5, Sun 1-5
Friends of the Library Group
Branches: 1
HUNT BRANCH, 201 S Basque Ave, 92833-3372, SAN 332-0375. Tel: 714-738-3122. *Sr Librn,* Judy Booth; Tel: 714-738-5364, E-mail: judyb@ci.fullerton.ca.us
Library Holdings: Bk Vols 30,024
Open Tues 10-6, Thurs 12-8
Friends of the Library Group
Bookmobiles: 1. In Charge, Judy Booth. Bk vols 5,000

C HOPE INTERNATIONAL UNIVERSITY, Hugh & Hazel Darling Library, 2500 E Nutwood Ave, 92831. SAN 300-7782. Tel: 714-879-3901, Ext 1234. E-mail: darlinglibrary@hiu.edu. Web Site: library.hiu.edu. *Dir of Libr Serv,* Robin R Hartman; Tel: 714-879-3901, Ext 1212, E-mail: rhartman@hiu.edu; *Ref & Instruction Librn,* Terri L Bogan; Tel: 714-879-3901, Ext 1261, E-mail: tbogan@hiu.edu; *Syst & Tech Serv Librn,* Jennifer Rich; Tel: 714-879-3901, Ext 1218, E-mail: jarich@hiu.edu; *Libr Serv Mgr,* Katy Lines; Tel: 714-879-3901, Ext 1223, E-mail: kelines@hiu.edu; Staff 4 (MLS 3, Non-MLS 1)
Founded 1928. Enrl 1,200; Fac 3; Highest Degree: Master
Jun 2014-May 2015 Income $489,250, Parent Institution $486,250, Other $3,000. Mats Exp $130,500, Books $25,000, Per/Ser (Incl. Access Fees) $45,000, Electronic Ref Mat (Incl. Access Fees) $60,500. Sal $290,752 (Prof $207,130)
Library Holdings: AV Mats 2,287; e-books 124,635; Bk Vols 68,763; Per Subs 164
Special Collections: George P Taubman Coll; Restoration Movement (Rare Book Coll)
Subject Interests: Restoration movement
Automation Activity & Vendor Info: (Acquisitions) OCLC; (Cataloging) OCLC; (Circulation) OCLC; (Course Reserve) OCLC; (ILL) OCLC; (OPAC) OCLC; (Serials) OCLC

Database Vendor: ebrary, Gale Cengage Learning, LexisNexis, OCLC FirstSearch, OCLC WorldShare Interlibrary Loan, ProQuest, SerialsSolutions
Wireless access
Partic in OCLC Online Computer Library Center, Inc; Statewide California Electronic Library Consortium (SCELC)
Open Mon-Thurs 7:45am-11pm, Fri 7:45-5, Sun 2-11

M SAINT JUDE MEDICAL CENTER*, Medical Library, 101 E Valencia Mesa Dr, 92835. SAN 327-4098. Tel: 714-871-3280. FAX: 714-447-6481. *Librn,* Carol Schechter; Staff 1 (MLS 1)
Jul 2005-Jun 2006. Mats Exp $56,000, Books $7,000, Per/Ser (Incl. Access Fees) $49,000. Sal $59,824
Library Holdings: Bk Vols 1,000; Per Subs 70
Special Collections: Consumer Health Coll
Subject Interests: Med, Nursing
Automation Activity & Vendor Info: (Cataloging) Surpass; (OPAC) Surpass
Database Vendor: EBSCO Information Services, ProQuest
Partic in Medical Library Group of Southern California & Arizona (MLGSCA)

C SOUTHERN CALIFORNIA COLLEGE OF OPTOMETRY, M B Ketchum Memorial Library, Marshall B Ketchum University, 2575 Yorba Linda Blvd, 92831-1699. SAN 300-7790. Tel: 714-449-7440. FAX: 714-879-0481. E-mail: library@ketchum.edu. Web Site: ketchum.edu/library/index.html. *Dir, Libr Serv,* D J Matthews; E-mail: djmatthews@ketchum.edu; Staff 3 (MLS 1, Non-MLS 2)
Founded 1950. Enrl 400; Fac 100; Highest Degree: Doctorate
Library Holdings: Bk Titles 13,000; Per Subs 130
Special Collections: Historical Vision Coll
Subject Interests: Ophthalmology, Optics, Optometry
Publications: Faculty Publications; Library's Latest Additions (Bi-monthly); Student Research Papers (Annual)
Partic in Coop Libr Agency for Syst & Servs; OCLC Online Computer Library Center, Inc
Restriction: Open to students, fac & staff, Pub use on premises

CL WESTERN STATE LAW LIBRARY*, 1111 N State College Blvd, 92831-3014. SAN 300-7804. Tel: 714-459-1113. FAX: 714-871-4806. Web Site: www.wsulaw.edu. *Dir,* Patricia O'Connor; Tel: 714-459-1175, E-mail: poconnor@wsulaw.edu; *Assoc Dir,* Anne Rimmer; *Cat, Mgr, Bibliog Serv, Ref,* Dan Blackaby; *Acq Librn,* Pat Plumb; *Ref Librn,* Judy Andresen; *Ref Librn,* Scott Frey
Library Holdings: Bk Titles 34,713; Bk Vols 98,923
Subject Interests: Anglo-Am law
Partic in OCLC Online Computer Library Center, Inc
Open Mon-Fri 7am-11:30pm, Sat 8-7, Sun 8am-11:30pm

GILROY

J GAVILAN COLLEGE LIBRARY*, 5055 Santa Teresa Blvd, 95020. SAN 300-7839. Tel: 408-848-4812. Circulation Tel: 408-848-4810. Reference Tel: 408-848-4806. FAX: 408-846-4927. Web Site: www.gavilan.edu/library. *Dir,* Douglas Achterman; Tel: 408-848-4809, E-mail: dachterman@gavilan.edu; *Acq,* Diane Hanks; *Ref,* Dana Young; Staff 2 (MLS 2)
Founded 1963. Enrl 4,838; Fac 70
Library Holdings: e-books 9,332; Bk Titles 56,500; Bk Vols 65,227
Automation Activity & Vendor Info: (Acquisitions) Ex Libris Group; (Cataloging) Ex Libris Group; (Circulation) Ex Libris Group; (Course Reserve) Ex Libris Group; (OPAC) Ex Libris Group; (Serials) Ex Libris Group
Database Vendor: EBSCOhost
Wireless access
Publications: Bibliographies; Handouts
Mem of Pacific Library Partnership (PLP)
Partic in Monterey Bay Area Cooperative Library System; OCLC Online Computer Library Center, Inc
Open Mon-Thurs 8-8, Fri 8-4

S LUCAS SIGNATONE CORP LIBRARY*, 393 Tomkins Ct Ste J, 95020. SAN 328-2031. Tel: 408-848-2851. FAX: 408-848-5763. E-mail: sales@signatone.com. Web Site: www.signatone.com. *Librn,* Richard Dixon
Library Holdings: Bk Vols 1,000

GLENDALE

S AMERICAN HERITAGE LIBRARY & MUSEUM*, 600 S Central Ave, 91204-2009. SAN 300-7928. Tel: 818-240-1775. E-mail: library@srcalifornia.com. Web Site: www.srcalifornia.com. *Libr Dir,* Richard H Breithaupt, Jr; E-mail: rick@srcalifornia.com
Founded 1893
Library Holdings: AV Mats 2,000; CDs 500; Electronic Media & Resources 1,000; Bk Titles 23,000; Bk Vols 25,000; Spec Interest Per Sub 5,000
Special Collections: Family Histories; Photographic; Vital Records
Subject Interests: 17th-20th Century Am, Am colonial hist, English genealogy, English hist, Genealogy, Mil hist (US)
Automation Activity & Vendor Info: (Acquisitions) Inmagic, Inc.; (Cataloging) OCLC WorldShare Interlibrary Loan
Database Vendor: Bowker, OCLC WorldShare Interlibrary Loan
Wireless access
Function: Ref serv available
Partic in OCLC Online Computer Library Center, Inc
Open Fri-Sat 10-4
Restriction: Not a lending libr
Friends of the Library Group

S FOREST LAWN MUSEUM LIBRARY*, 1712 S Glendale Ave, 91205. SAN 300-7847. Tel: 323-340-4707. E-mail: info@forestlawn.com. Web Site: www.forestlawn.com. *Curator,* Joan Adan
Founded 1951
Library Holdings: Bk Vols 3,000
Special Collections: American Bronze Statuary; American History; Autographs; Gems; Pre-Christian & Christian Era Coins
Restriction: Staff use only

M GLENDALE ADVENTIST MEDICAL CENTER LIBRARY*, 1509 Wilson Terrace, 91206. SAN 300-7855. Tel: 818-409-8034. Administration Tel: 818-409-8575. FAX: 818-546-5633. Web Site: www.glendaleadventist.com. *Dir,* June Levy; *Sr Librn,* Zahra Fotovat; E-mail: zahra.fotovat@ah.org; Staff 1 (MLS 1)
Founded 1957
Library Holdings: AV Mats 700; Bk Titles 8,500; Per Subs 650
Subject Interests: Allied health, Med, Nursing
Automation Activity & Vendor Info: (Cataloging) SydneyPlus; (Circulation) SydneyPlus; (OPAC) SydneyPlus
Partic in CinaHL; Dialog Corp; Docline; Medical Library Group of Southern California & Arizona (MLGSCA)
Open Mon, Tues & Thurs 8:30-5, Wed 8:30-8, Fri 8:30-3
Restriction: Mem only

J GLENDALE COMMUNITY COLLEGE LIBRARY*, 1500 N Verdugo Rd, 91208-2894. SAN 300-7863. Tel: 818-240-1000, Ext 5574. FAX: 818-246-5107. Web Site: www.glendale.edu/library. *Assoc Dean, Libr & Learning Res,* James S Krusling; E-mail: krusling@glendale.edu; *Instrul Serv Librn,* Suzy Chen; E-mail: schen@glendale.edu; *Instrul Serv Librn,* Nancy Getty; E-mail: ngetty@glendale.edu; *Pub Serv Librn, Ref Serv,* Brenda Jones; E-mail: bjones@glendale.edu; *Tech Serv & Web Librn,* Zohara Kaye; E-mail: zkaye@glendale.edu; *Circ Mgr,* Russell Beckett; E-mail: rbeckett@glendale.edu; *Coll Develop,* Shelley Aronoff; E-mail: saronoff@glendale.edu; Staff 17.61 (MLS 6.16, Non-MLS 11.45)
Founded 1927. Enrl 22,593; Fac 752; Highest Degree: Associate
Jul 2011-Jun 2012 Income $1,628,147. Mats Exp $241,153, Books $108,059, Per/Ser (Incl. Access Fees) $23,622, Electronic Ref Mat (Incl. Access Fees) $107,972, Presv $1,500. Sal $1,335,469 (Prof $693,973)
Library Holdings: e-books 24,000; Bk Titles 92,170; Bk Vols 113,000; Per Subs 166
Automation Activity & Vendor Info: (Acquisitions) Ex Libris Group; (Cataloging) Ex Libris Group; (Circulation) Ex Libris Group; (Course Reserve) Ex Libris Group; (OPAC) Ex Libris Group; (Serials) Ex Libris Group
Wireless access
Partic in Council of Chief Librn (CCL); OCLC Online Computer Library Center, Inc
Open Mon-Thurs 8am-9pm, Fri & Sat 10-2

P GLENDALE LIBRARY, ARTS & CULTURE, Glendale Public Library, 222 E Harvard St, 91205-1075. SAN 332-043X. Tel: 818-548-2030. Circulation Tel: 818-548-2021. Interlibrary Loan Service Tel: 818-548-6430. Reference Tel: 818-548-2027. FAX: 818-548-7225. TDD: 818-543-0368. Web Site: library.ci.glendale.ca.us, www.glendalepubliclibrary.org. *Dir, Libr, Arts & Culture,* Cindy Cleary; Tel: 818-548-2043, E-mail: ccleary@glendaleca.gov; *Adminr, Bldg Mgt & Capital Projects,* Carolyn Flemming; Tel: 818-548-3999, Fax: 818-548-2030, E-mail: cflemming@glendaleca.gov; *Adminr, Prog & Serv,* Nora Goldsmith; Tel: 818-548-4020, E-mail: ngoldsmith@glendaleca.gov; *Adminr, Tech, Coll Serv & Develop,* Alyssa Resnick; Tel: 818-548-2180, E-mail: aresnick@glendaleca.gov; Staff 94 (MLS 31, Non-MLS 63)
Founded 1906. Pop 191,719; Circ 1,097,061
Jul 2013-Jun 2014 Income (Main Library and Branch(s)) $8,246,769, City $8,062,909, Federal $5,000, Locally Generated Income $178,860. Mats Exp $716,308, Books $453,346, Per/Ser (Incl. Access Fees) $4,700, Micro $14,100, AV Mat $61,718, Electronic Ref Mat (Incl. Access Fees) $182,444. Sal $4,002,047 (Prof $2,108,985)
Library Holdings: Bk Vols 571,942

Special Collections: Domestic Cat Genealogy; Original Art Coll; Piano Roll Coll; Sheet Music Coll
Subject Interests: Art, Calif, Local hist, Music
Automation Activity & Vendor Info: (Acquisitions) SirsiDynix; (Cataloging) SirsiDynix; (Circulation) SirsiDynix; (ILL) SirsiDynix; (OPAC) SirsiDynix
Database Vendor: Dialog, Gale Cengage Learning
Wireless access
Partic in Dialog Corp; OCLC Online Computer Library Center, Inc
Special Services for the Deaf - TDD equip
Special Services for the Blind - Cassettes; Computer with voice synthesizer for visually impaired persons; Large print bks; Magnifiers; Rec; Talking bks
Open Mon-Thurs 10-8, Fri & Sat 10-6, Sun 1-5
Friends of the Library Group
Branches: 7
BRAND LIBRARY & ART CENTER, 1601 W Mountain St, 91201-1209, SAN 332-0464. Tel: 818-548-2051. FAX: 818-548-5079. Web Site: www.brandlibrary.org. *Sr Libr Supvr,* Cathy Billings; Tel: 818-548-2010; *Librn Spec,* Caley Cannon; Tel: 818-548-2713, E-mail: ccannon@glendaleca.gov; *Librn Spec,* Blair Whittington; Tel: 818-548-2050, E-mail: bwhittington@glendaleca.gov. Subject Specialists: *Art,* Cathy Billings; *Art,* Caley Cannon; *Music,* Blair Whittington; Staff 3 (MLS 3)
Circ 150,000
Library Holdings: CDs 32,337; DVDs 1,515; Bk Vols 78,069
Subject Interests: Art, Music
Function: Art exhibits, Computers for patron use, Copy machines, Music CDs, Prog for adults
Open Tues & Thurs 12-8, Wed 12-6, Fri & Sat 10-5
Friends of the Library Group
CASA VERDUGO, 1151 N Brand Blvd, 91202-2503, SAN 332-0499. Tel: 818-548-2047. FAX: 818-548-8052. *Br Mgr,* Katherine Loeser; E-mail: kloeser@ci.glendale.ca.us; *Ch Serv,* Vivian Dulay; E-mail: vdulay@ci.glendale.ca.us; Staff 2 (MLS 2)
Founded 1951. Pop 26,526; Circ 50,000
Library Holdings: Bk Vols 55,000
Open Mon & Wed 1-8, Tues 1-6, Thurs 10-6, Sat 10-5
Friends of the Library Group
CHEVY CHASE, 3301 E Chevy Chase Dr, 91206-1416, SAN 332-0529. Tel: 818-548-2046. FAX: 818-548-7713. *Br Mgr,* Tiffany Lacayanga; E-mail: tbarrios@ci.glendale.ca.us
Circ 6,000
Library Holdings: Bk Vols 30,895
Open Wed 2-8, Sat 12-5
GRANDVIEW, 1535 Fifth St, 91201-1985, SAN 332-0553. Tel: 818-548-2049. FAX: 818-549-0678. *Br Mgr,* Katherine Loeser; E-mail: kloeser@ci.glendale.ca.us; *Ch Serv,* Lyda Truick
Circ 44,253
Library Holdings: Bk Vols 44,115
Open Mon 1-8, Tues & Thurs 1-6, Wed 10-6, Fri 10-5
Friends of the Library Group
LIBRARY CONNECTION @ ADAMS SQUARE, 1100 E Chevy Chase Dr, 91205. Tel: 818-548-3833. FAX: 818-500-1039. *Br Mgr,* Hala Shonouda; E-mail: hshonouda@ci.glendale.ca.us
Open Mon-Wed 1-8, Thurs 10-6, Sat 10-5
MONTROSE-CRESCENTA BRANCH, 2465 Honolulu Ave, Montrose, 91020-1803, SAN 332-0588. Tel: 818-548-2048. FAX: 818-248-6987. *Br Mgr,* Tiffany Lacayanga; E-mail: tbarrios@ci.glendale.ca.us
Pop 35,016; Circ 134,428
Library Holdings: Bk Vols 66,033
Special Services for the Deaf - TDD equip
Open Mon & Tues 1-8, Wed & Thurs 11-6, Sat 10-5
Friends of the Library Group
PACIFIC PARK, 501 S Pacific Ave, 91204. Tel: 818-548-3760. FAX: 818-409-7154. *Br Mgr,* Hala Shonouda; E-mail: hshonouda@ci.glendale.ca.us; *Ch Serv,* Arpine Eloyan; E-mail: aeloyan@ci.glendale.ca.us
Open Mon & Wed 2-8, Tues 2-6, Thurs 10-6, Sat 10-5
Bookmobiles: 1. Librn, Mindy Liberman. Bk vols 7777

CL GLENDALE UNIVERSITY*, College of Law Library, 220 N Glendale Ave, 91206. SAN 300-7871. Tel: 818-247-0770. FAX: 818-247-0872. Web Site: www.glendalelaw.edu. *Dean,* Darrin Greitzer; *Librn,* Enid Levy
Founded 1967
Library Holdings: Bk Vols 50,000; Per Subs 125
Special Collections: English Common Law Coll; Rare Law Books
Friends of the Library Group

L KNAPP, PETERSEN & CLARKE*, Law Library, 550 N Brand Blvd, Ste 1500, 91203-1922. SAN 372-3194. Tel: 818-547-5000. FAX: 818-547-5329. Web Site: www.kpclegal.com. *Pres,* Cynthia Trangsrud; *Librn,* Position Currently Open
Library Holdings: Bk Vols 14,250; Per Subs 28

S WALT DISNEY IMAGINEERING*, Information Research Center, 1401 Flower St, 91201. (Mail add: PO Box 25020, 91221-5020), SAN 300-7952. Tel: 818-544-6594. FAX: 818-544-7845. *In Charge,* Aileen Kutaka; Staff 1 (MLS 1)
Founded 1962
Library Holdings: Bk Vols 50,000; Per Subs 500
Subject Interests: Art & archit, Bus & mgt, Costume design, Eng, Hist, Interior design, Travel
Special Services for the Deaf - Staff with knowledge of sign lang
Open Mon-Fri 9-5

GLENDORA

J CITRUS COLLEGE*, Hayden Memorial Library, 1000 W Foothill Blvd, 91741-1899. SAN 300-5860. Tel: 626-914-8640. Interlibrary Loan Service Tel: 626-914-8646. Reference Tel: 626-914-8644. FAX: 626-963-2531. Web Site: www.citruscollege.edu/library. *Dean,* Eric Rabitoy; E-mail: erabitoy@citruscollege.edu; *Head, Ref,* Sarah Bosler; E-mail: sbosler@citruscollege.edu; *Syst & Tech Serv Librn,* Lanette Granger; E-mail: lgranger@citruscollege.edu; Staff 11 (MLS 7, Non-MLS 4)
Founded 1915. Enrl 11,000; Fac 170; Highest Degree: Associate
Library Holdings: e-books 20,000; Bk Titles 38,607; Bk Vols 50,000; Per Subs 140
Special Collections: Astronomy (Schlesinger Coll); Hayden Coll ((Education))
Subject Interests: Art & archit, Music, Soc sci & issues
Automation Activity & Vendor Info: (Circulation) Innovative Interfaces, Inc - Millenium
Database Vendor: EBSCOhost, Gale Cengage Learning
Function: Archival coll, Art exhibits, Audio & video playback equip for onsite use, AV serv, ILL available, Music CDs, Orientations, Photocopying/Printing, Ref & res, VHS videos, Wheelchair accessible
Partic in Community College League of California (CCLC); Inland Empire Acad Libr Coop (IEALC); OCLC Online Computer Library Center, Inc
Open Mon-Thurs 7:30am-8pm, Fri 7:30-4
Restriction: Borrowing privileges limited to fac & registered students, In-house use for visitors, Open to students, fac & staff

P GLENDORA PUBLIC LIBRARY & CULTURAL CENTER, 140 S Glendora Ave, 91741. SAN 300-7979. Tel: 626-852-4891. FAX: 626-852-4899. E-mail: library@glendoralibrary.org. Web Site: www.glendoralibrary.org. *Libr Dir,* Janet Stone; Tel: 626-852-4896, E-mail: jstone@glendoralibrary.org; *Mgr, Sr Librn,* Cindy Romero; Tel: 626-852-4813, E-mail: cromero@glendoralibrary.org; *Support Serv Mgr,* Carlos Baffigo, Tel: 626-852-4827, E-mail: cbaffigo@glendoralibrary.org; *Mgt Analyst,* Elke Cathel; Tel: 626-852-4895, E-mail: ecathel@glendoralibrary.org; Staff 9 (MLS 7, Non-MLS 2)
Founded 1912. Pop 51,000; Circ 370,341
Jul 2014-Jun 2015 Income $1,906,436, City $1,800,342, Federal $12,582, Locally Generated Income $93,512. Mats Exp $131,820, Books $50,634, Per/Ser (Incl. Access Fees) $12,600, AV Mat $13,479, Electronic Ref Mat (Incl. Access Fees) $55,107
Library Holdings: AV Mats 19,518; DVDs 9,297; e-books 11,796; Electronic Media & Resources 31; Bk Vols 102,826; Per Subs 231
Automation Activity & Vendor Info: (Acquisitions) Innovative Interfaces, Inc; (Cataloging) Innovative Interfaces, Inc; (Circulation) Innovative Interfaces, Inc; (ILL) OCLC; (OPAC) Innovative Interfaces, Inc
Wireless access
Function: Adult bk club, Adult literacy prog, After school storytime, Audiobks via web, AV serv, Bk club(s), Bks on cassette, Bks on CD, Children's prog, Computers for patron use, Copy machines, Digital talking bks, Doc delivery serv, e-mail serv, E-Reserves, Electronic databases & coll, Fax serv, Handicapped accessible, Home delivery & serv to Sr ctr & nursing homes, Homebound delivery serv, ILL available, Libr develop, Magnifiers for reading, Music CDs, Online ref, Outreach serv, Outside serv via phone, mail, e-mail & web, OverDrive digital audio bks, Photocopying/Printing, Preschool outreach, Prog for adults, Prog for children & young adult, Pub access computers, Ref & res, Ref serv available, Ref serv in person, Referrals accepted, Scanner, Spoken cassettes & CDs, Spoken cassettes & DVDs, Story hour, Summer reading prog, Tax forms, Teen prog, Telephone ref, VHS videos, Video lending libr, Web-catalog, Wheelchair accessible, Workshops
Partic in Southern California Library Cooperative
Special Services for the Deaf - ADA equip; Adult & family literacy prog; Bks on deafness & sign lang; Closed caption videos; High interest/low vocabulary bks; TDD equip
Special Services for the Blind - ZoomText magnification & reading software
Open Mon-Wed 10-8, Thurs-Sat 10-5
Friends of the Library Group

GRASS VALLEY

J SIERRA COLLEGE LIBRARY*, Nevada County Campus, 250 Sierra College Dr, 95945. SAN 375-4243. Tel: 530-274-5304. FAX: 530-274-5333. Web Site: www.sierracollege.edu. *Learning Res Coordr,* Patricia Saulsbury; E-mail: psaulsbury@sierracollege.edu
Library Holdings: Bk Titles 16,000; Bk Vols 17,000; Per Subs 100
Automation Activity & Vendor Info: (Cataloging) Ex Libris Group; (Circulation) Ex Libris Group; (ILL) OCLC; (OPAC) Ex Libris Group
Open Mon-Thurs (Winter) 9-8, Fri 9-1; Mon-Thurs (Summer) 10-7

M SIERRA NEVADA MEMORIAL HOSPITAL*, Health Sciences Library, 155 Glasson Way, 95945-5723. (Mail add: PO Box 1029, 95945-1029), SAN 370-6753. Tel: 530-274-6064. FAX: 530-274-6214. *Mgr, Libr Serv,* Susi Petrillo; E-mail: spetrillo@chw.edu
Founded 1981
Library Holdings: Bk Vols 1,200; Per Subs 120
Partic in Sacramento Area Health Sciences Librs
Open Mon-Fri 8-4:30

GREENBRAE

M MARIN GENERAL HOSPITAL*, Medical Library, 250 Bon Air Rd, 94904. (Mail add: PO Box 8010, San Rafael, 94912-8010), SAN 322-8886. Tel: 415-925-7393. FAX: 415-925-7396. Web Site: www.maringeneral.sutterhealth.org. *Librn,* Katherine Renick
Library Holdings: Bk Vols 2,500; Per Subs 100
Special Collections: History of Psychiatry
Subject Interests: Consumer health, Med
Open Mon-Fri 9-4
Restriction: Ref only to non-staff

HANFORD

GL KINGS COUNTY LAW LIBRARY*, Kings County Govt Ctr, 1400 W Lacey Blvd, 93230. SAN 320-5649. Tel: 559-582-3211, Ext 4430. Web Site: www.countyofkings.com/lawlibrary. *Librn,* Dale Lefkowitz
Founded 1898
Library Holdings: Bk Vols 8,500
Wireless access
Open Mon-Fri 8-5

P KINGS COUNTY LIBRARY*, 401 N Douty St, 93230. SAN 332-0618. Tel: 559-582-0261. Circulation Tel: 559-582-0261, Ext 101. Administration Tel: 559-582-0262. Information Services Tel: 559-582-0261, Ext 103. FAX: 559-583-6163. Web Site: www.kingscountylibrary.org. *Dir,* Natalie Rencher; E-mail: natalie.rencher@kingscountylibrary.org; *Ch Serv,* Jennifer Riordan; *Ref Librn,* Lee Sherman; Staff 3 (MLS 3)
Founded 1911. Pop 144,000; Circ 110,829
Library Holdings: AV Mats 1,373; Bk Titles 120,000; Bk Vols 191,747; Per Subs 249; Spec Interest Per Sub 10
Special Collections: Kings County and California History; The Jewish Holocaust
Automation Activity & Vendor Info: (Acquisitions) SirsiDynix; (Cataloging) SirsiDynix; (Circulation) SirsiDynix; (ILL) OCLC
Database Vendor: Gale Cengage Learning, OCLC FirstSearch, SirsiDynix
Wireless access
Mem of San Joaquin Valley Library System
Open Mon-Wed 10-8, Thurs 10-6, Sat 12-5
Friends of the Library Group
Branches: 6
AVENAL BRANCH, 501 E King St, Avenal, 93204, SAN 332-0677. Tel: 559-386-5741. FAX: 559-386-1418. *Br Mgr,* Sheryl Tune
Circ 7,051
Library Holdings: Large Print Bks 150; Bk Titles 12,000; Bk Vols 14,850; Per Subs 30
Open Mon 11-8, Tues & Wed 11-7, Thurs 12-5, Fri 1-5
Friends of the Library Group
CORCORAN BRANCH, 1001-A Chittenden, Corcoran, 93212, SAN 332-0731. Tel: 559-992-3314. FAX: 559-992-3364. *Br Mgr,* Allison Peyton
Pop 21,554; Circ 9,335
Library Holdings: Large Print Bks 500; Bk Titles 16,240; Bk Vols 24,541; Per Subs 40
Open Mon 11-8, Tues & Wed 11-7, Thurs 12-5, Fri 1-5
HANFORD BRANCH, 401 N Douty St, 93230, SAN 332-0790. Tel: 559-582-0261. FAX: 559-583-6163. *Br Mgr,* Gail Lucas; E-mail: gail.lucas@kingscountylibrary.org
Pop 43,575; Circ 110,829
Library Holdings: Large Print Bks 2,500; Bk Vols 159,504
Open Mon-Wed 10-8, Thurs 10-6, Fri & Sat 12-5
Friends of the Library Group
KETTLEMAN CITY BRANCH, PO Box 158, Kettleman City, 93239-0158, SAN 332-0820. Tel: 559-386-9804. *Libr Asst III,* Eugenie Todd
Library Holdings: Bk Titles 11,807; Bk Vols 9,356; Per Subs 45
Open Tues-Thurs 1-6
Friends of the Library Group
LEMOORE BRANCH, 457 C St, Lemoore, 93245, SAN 332-0855. Tel: 559-924-2188. FAX: 559-924-1521. *Libr Asst III,* Christine Baize
Pop 20,850; Circ 31,543
Library Holdings: Bk Titles 17,500; Bk Vols 20,850; Per Subs 100
Open Mon-Wed 10-8, Thurs 10-6, Fri & Sat 12-5
STRATFORD BRANCH, 20300 Main St, Stratford, 93266. (Mail add: 401 N Douty St, 93230), SAN 332-088X. Tel: 559-947-3003. *Br Mgr,* Allison Peyton
Pop 1,264; Circ 1,744
Library Holdings: Large Print Bks 200; Bk Titles 10,640; Bk Vols 12,504; Per Subs 25
Open Tues-Thurs 1-6

HAYWARD

C CALIFORNIA STATE UNIVERSITY, EAST BAY LIBRARY, CSU East Bay Library, 25800 Carlos Bee Blvd, 94542-3052. SAN 300-8142. Tel: 510-885-3664. Circulation Tel: 510-885-3612. Interlibrary Loan Service Tel: 510-885-2986. Reference Tel: 510-885-3765. FAX: 510-885-2049. E-mail: circservices@csueastbay.edu, libhelp@csueastbay.edu. Web Site: library.csueastbay.edu. *Dean of Libr,* John E Wenzler; E-mail: john.wenzler@csueastbay.edu; *Librn,* Doug Highsmith; Tel: 510-885-3610, E-mail: doug.highsmith@csueastbay.edu; *Librn,* Aline Soules; Tel: 510-885-4596, E-mail: aline.soules@csueastbay.edu; *Librn/Concord Campus Libr,* Liz Ginno; Tel: 510-885-2969, Fax: 510-885-2969, E-mail: liz.ginno@csueastbay.edu; *Assoc Librn,* Stephanie Alexander; Tel: 510-885-7674, E-mail: stephanie.alexander@csueastbay.edu; *Assoc Librn,* Tom Bickley; Tel: 510-885-7554, E-mail: tom.bickley@csueastbay.edu; *Assoc Librn,* Dana Edwards; Tel: 510-885-3632, E-mail: dana.edwards@csueastbay.edu; *Assoc Librn,* Kyzyl Fenno-Smith; Tel: 510-885-2974, E-mail: kyzyl.fenno-smith@csueastbay.edu; *Assoc Librn,* Sharon Radcliff; Tel: 510-885-7452, E-mail: sharon.radcliff@csueastbay.edu; *Assoc Librn,* Diana Wakimoto; Tel: 510-885-4287, E-mail: diana.wakimoto@csueastbay.edu; *Assoc Librn, Syst,* Jiannan Wang; Tel: 510-885-2973, E-mail: jiannan.wang@csueastbay.edu; *Sr Asst Librn,* Jeffra Bussmann; Tel: 510-885-3780, E-mail: jeffra.bussmann@csueastbay.edu; *Sr Asst Librn,* Andrew Carlos; Tel: 510-885-2303, E-mail: andrew.carlos@csueastbay.edu; *Sr Asst Librn,* Gretchen Keer; Tel: 510-885-2968, E-mail: gretchen.keer@csueastbay.edu; *Access Serv Mgr,* Paula Kapteyn; Tel: 510-885-4905, E-mail: paula.kapteyn@csueastbay.edu; *Adminr/Acq Mgr,* Susan Rath; Tel: 510-885-3627, E-mail: susan.rath@csueastbay.edu; *Bibliog Control Mgr,* Tom Holt; Tel: 510-885-2429, E-mail: tom.holt@csueastbay.edu; *Learning Commons Mgr,* Paulette Washington; Tel: 510-885-2651, E-mail: paulette.washington@csueastbay.edu; *Media Res & Reserves Mgr,* Jason Chavez; Tel: 510-885-2299, E-mail: jason.chavez@csueastbay.edu; Staff 33 (MLS 16, Non-MLS 17)
Founded 1957. Enrl 14,000; Fac 752; Highest Degree: Master
Jul 2013-Jun 2014 Income $3,486,995, State $3,178,057, Federal $8,938. Mats Exp $1,070,309, Books $298,204, Per/Ser (Incl. Access Fees) $261,965, Micro $850, AV Mat $12,415, Electronic Ref Mat (Incl. Access Fees) $494,516, Presv $2,359. Sal $2,111,502 (Prof $1,086,718)
Library Holdings: AV Mats 36,610; CDs 4,562; DVDs 1,294; e-books 189,228; e-journals 103,000; Electronic Media & Resources 310,000; Microforms 12,803; Music Scores 21,219; Bk Titles 684,571; Bk Vols 922,749; Per Subs 390; Videos 22,434
Special Collections: Artists Book Coll; Bay Area Poetry Coll; Early Voyages & Travels Coll; Marco Polo Coll. State Document Depository; US Document Depository
Automation Activity & Vendor Info: (Acquisitions) Innovative Interfaces, Inc; (Cataloging) Innovative Interfaces, Inc; (Circulation) Innovative Interfaces, Inc; (Course Reserve) Innovative Interfaces, Inc; (ILL) OCLC ILLiad; (Media Booking) Innovative Interfaces, Inc; (OPAC) Innovative Interfaces, Inc; (Serials) Innovative Interfaces, Inc
Database Vendor: Agricola, Cambridge Scientific Abstracts, EBSCOhost, Factiva.com, Gale Cengage Learning, Innovative Interfaces, Inc, JSTOR, LexisNexis, OCLC FirstSearch, OCLC WorldShare Interlibrary Loan, OVID Technologies, ProQuest, ScienceDirect, Wilson - Wilson Web
Wireless access
Function: Doc delivery serv, E-Reserves, Electronic databases & coll, ILL available, Orientations, Photocopying/Printing, Ref & res, Ref serv available, Spoken cassettes & CDs, Spoken cassettes & DVDs, Telephone ref, VHS videos, Wheelchair accessible
Partic in Bay Area Library & Information Network; OCLC Online Computer Library Center, Inc
Special Services for the Deaf - TTY equip
Open Mon-Thurs 8am-10pm, Fri 8-5, Sat 11-5, Sun 12-7
Restriction: In-house use for visitors, Open to fac, students & qualified researchers

J CHABOT COLLEGE LIBRARY*, 25555 Hesperian Blvd, 94545. SAN 332-1339. Circulation Tel: 510-723-7513. Reference Tel: 510-723-6764, 510-723-7006. Administration Tel: 510-723-6778. Information Services Tel:

510-723-6765. Administration FAX: 510-723-7005. E-mail: chabotref@clpccd.cc.ca.us. Web Site: www.chabotcollege.edu/library. *Coordr, Libr Serv, Info Literacy,* Kim Morrison; Tel: 510-723-6762, E-mail: kmorrison@chabotcollege.edu; *Acq,* Heather Hernandez; Tel: 510-723-6763, E-mail: hherandez@chabotcollege.edu; *Bibliog Instr, Info Tech,* Norman I Buchwald; Tel: 510-723-6993, E-mail: nbuchwald@chabotcollege.edu; *Cataloger, Syst,* Debbie Buti; Tel: 510-723-6768, E-mail: dbuti@chabotcollege.edu; *Coll Develop, Ref,* James E Matthews; E-mail: jmatthews@chabotcollege.edu; *Instruction & Outreach,* Pedro Reynoso; Tel: 510-723-6767, E-mail: preynoso@chabotcollege.edu; Staff 10 (MLS 5, Non-MLS 5)
Founded 1961. Enrl 15,000; Fac 264; Highest Degree: Associate
Jul 2008-Jun 2009 Income $894,372. Mats Exp $204,600, Books $115,600, Per/Ser (Incl. Access Fees) $22,000, AV Mat $25,000, Electronic Ref Mat (Incl. Access Fees) $42,000. Sal $790,000 (Prof $460,000)
Library Holdings: AV Mats 11,855; Bk Titles 65,460; Per Subs 201
Special Collections: California History Coll
Subject Interests: Fire sci, Nursing
Automation Activity & Vendor Info: (Cataloging) OCLC Online; (Circulation) SirsiDynix; (OPAC) SirsiDynix
Database Vendor: EBSCOhost, LexisNexis
Wireless access
Partic in California Community College Library Consortium (CCLC)

P HAYWARD PUBLIC LIBRARY, 835 C St, 94541-5120. SAN 332-1363. Tel: 510-293-8685. Administration Tel: 510-881-7954. Administration FAX: 510-733-6669. TDD: 510-537-7593. E-mail: library@hayward-ca.gov. Web Site: www.library.hayward-ca.gov. *Dir, Libr & Commun Serv,* Sean Reinhart; Tel: 510-881-7956, E-mail: sean.reinhart@hayward-ca.gov; *Adult Serv, Electronic Serv Mgr,* Clio Hathaway; Tel: 510-881-7948, E-mail: clio.hathaway@hayward-ca.gov; *Operations Mgr,* Vince Ang; Tel: 510-881-7987, E-mail: vince.ang@hayward-ca.gov; *Educ Serv Coordr,* Cynthia Breeden-Johnson; *Literacy Prog Coordr,* Cynthia Breeden-Johnson; Tel: 510-881-7911, Fax: 510-293-5093; Staff 12.5 (MLS 9, Non-MLS 3.5)
Founded 1897. Pop 148,756; Circ 1,087,737
Jul 2010-Jun 2011 Income (Main Library and Branch(s)) $4,099,101, State $103,989, City $3,811,591, Federal $138,521, Locally Generated Income $45,000. Mats Exp $295,569, Books $127,468, Per/Ser (Incl. Access Fees) $24,163, AV Mat $121,143, Electronic Ref Mat (Incl. Access Fees) $22,795. Sal $2,402,318
Library Holdings: Audiobooks 3,664; AV Mats 36,762; Bks on Deafness & Sign Lang 75; CDs 8,870; DVDs 24,855; e-books 8,074; Large Print Bks 844; Bk Vols 124,928; Per Subs 159
Automation Activity & Vendor Info: (Acquisitions) Innovative Interfaces, Inc; (Cataloging) Innovative Interfaces, Inc; (Circulation) Innovative Interfaces, Inc; (ILL) Innovative Interfaces, Inc; (OPAC) Innovative Interfaces, Inc
Database Vendor: ALLDATA Online, EBSCOhost, Newsbank, Overdrive, Inc, World Book Online
Wireless access
Function: Adult bk club, Adult literacy prog, After school storytime, Audiobks via web, Bilingual assistance for Spanish patrons, Bk club(s), Bks on CD, Children's prog, Computers for patron use, Copy machines, Electronic databases & coll, Family literacy, Free DVD rentals, Handicapped accessible, Home delivery & serv to Sr ctr & nursing homes, Homebound delivery serv, Homework prog, Literacy & newcomer serv, Mus passes, Music CDs, Online cat, Online searches, OverDrive digital audio bks, Photocopying/Printing, Preschool outreach, Printer for laptops & handheld devices, Prog for adults, Prog for children & young adult, Pub access computers, Ref serv available, Satellite serv, Senior outreach, Spanish lang bks, Spoken cassettes & CDs, Story hour, Summer reading prog, Tax forms, Teen prog, Web-catalog, Workshops, Writing prog
Mem of Bay Area Library & Information System
Partic in Califa; Link+
Special Services for the Deaf - TDD equip
Special Services for the Blind - Large print bks
Open Mon-Wed 11-8, Thurs-Sat 10-5
Friends of the Library Group
Branches: 1
WEEKES BRANCH, 27300 Patrick Ave, 94544, SAN 332-1398. Tel: 510-782-2155. FAX: 510-259-0429. *Br Mgr,* Melesha Owen; Tel: 510-293-5239, E-mail: melesha.owen@hayward-ca.gov; Staff 7 (MLS 3, Non-MLS 4)
Circ 353,910
Function: After school storytime, Audiobks via web, Bilingual assistance for Spanish patrons, Bks on CD, Children's prog, Computers for patron use, Copy machines, Electronic databases & coll, Family literacy, Free DVD rentals, Handicapped accessible, Homebound delivery serv, ILL available, Music CDs, Online cat, OverDrive digital audio bks, Photocopying/Printing, Printer for laptops & handheld devices, Prog for adults, Prog for children & young adult, Pub access computers, Ref serv available, Senior outreach, Spoken cassettes & CDs, Story hour, Summer reading prog, Teen prog, Telephone ref
Open Mon-Wed 11-8, Thurs-Sat 10-5
Friends of the Library Group

J HEALD COLLEGE, Learning Resource Center-Hayward Campus, 25500 Industrial Blvd, 94545. Tel: 510-783-2100. FAX: 510-783-3287. Web Site: www.heald.edu. *Learning Res Ctr Coordr,* David Arita
Highest Degree: Associate
Library Holdings: Bk Vols 889; Per Subs 20
Database Vendor: EBSCOhost
Function: ILL available, Instruction & testing, Learning ctr, Online searches, Video lending libr, Wheelchair accessible
Open Mon-Thurs 7:30am-10pm, Fri 7:30-7
Restriction: Borrowing privileges limited to fac & registered students, Circ privileges for students & alumni only

M LIFE CHIROPRACTIC COLLEGE-WEST LIBRARY*, 25001 Industrial Blvd, 94545. SAN 327-9162. Tel: 510-780-4507. Reference Tel: 510-780-4500, Ext 2730. FAX: 510-780-4590. E-mail: library@lifewest.edu. Web Site: www.lifewest.edu/library. *Dir,* Annette Osenga; E-mail: aosenga@lifewest.edu; *Syst Coordr,* Barbara Delli-Gatti; E-mail: bdelligatti@lifewest.edu; Staff 4 (MLS 2, Non-MLS 2)
Founded 1981. Enrl 350; Highest Degree: Doctorate
Jul 2008-Jun 2009 Income $7,220. Mats Exp $104,566, Books $13,504, Per/Ser (Incl. Access Fees) $73,200, AV Equip $6,575, AV Mat $3,450, Electronic Ref Mat (Incl. Access Fees) $7,300, Presv $537. Sal $404,675
Library Holdings: AV Mats 5,300; e-journals 116; Bk Titles 8,500; Bk Vols 10,300; Per Subs 200
Special Collections: Chiropractic Rare Book Coll; College Archives
Automation Activity & Vendor Info: (Cataloging) SirsiDynix; (Circulation) SirsiDynix; (OPAC) SirsiDynix
Database Vendor: EBSCOhost, Wiley
Wireless access
Function: Audio & video playback equip for onsite use, AV serv, CD-ROM, Computers for patron use, Copy machines, Distance learning, Doc delivery serv, e-mail serv, E-Reserves, Electronic databases & coll, Health sci info serv, ILL available, Online cat, Online searches, Photocopying/Printing, Ref serv available, Ref serv in person, Res performed for a fee, Telephone ref, Web-catalog
Publications: New Materials (Acquisition list)
Partic in Chiropractic Libr Consortium; National Network of Libraries of Medicine; Northern California & Nevada Medical Library Group (NCNMLG); OCLC Online Computer Library Center, Inc
Open Mon-Thurs 7am-8pm, Fri 7-5, Sat 12-5
Restriction: Borrowing privileges limited to fac & registered students, Borrowing requests are handled by ILL, Circ to mem only, In-house use for visitors

HEMET

P HEMET PUBLIC LIBRARY*, 300 E Latham, 92543. SAN 300-8177. Tel: 951-765-2440. FAX: 951-765-2446. Web Site: www.cityofhemet.org. *Dir,* Kathye Caines; Tel: 951-765-2447, E-mail: kcaines@cityofhemet.org; Staff 7 (MLS 3, Non-MLS 4)
Founded 1907. Pop 72,000; Circ 470,000
Library Holdings: CDs 1,457; DVDs 7,000; Bk Vols 105,000; Per Subs 192; Talking Bks 2,520; Videos 1,000
Subject Interests: Local hist
Automation Activity & Vendor Info: (Circulation) Horizon
Wireless access
Function: Adult literacy prog, Handicapped accessible, Homebound delivery serv, ILL available, Music CDs, Photocopying/Printing, Prog for adults, Prog for children & young adult, Ref serv available, Spoken cassettes & CDs, Summer reading prog, Telephone ref, VHS videos, Wheelchair accessible
Mem of Inland Library System
Partic in San Bernardino, Inyo, Riverside Counties United Library Services
Special Services for the Deaf - Closed caption videos
Special Services for the Blind - Talking bks; Talking bks & player equip
Open Wed & Thurs 9-7, Fri & Sat 9-6
Friends of the Library Group

HOLLISTER

P SAN BENITO COUNTY FREE LIBRARY*, 470 Fifth St, 95023-3885. SAN 300-8185. Tel: 831-636-4107. FAX: 831-636-4099. E-mail: sanbenlib@sbcglobal.net. Web Site: www.sanbenitofl.org. *County Librn,* Nora Conte; Tel: 831-636-4097; Staff 7.5 (MLS 1.5, Non-MLS 6)
Founded 1918. Pop 55,871; Circ 93,667
Jul 2007-Jun 2008 Income $510,732, State $23,219, City $15,000, Federal $3,000, County $441,347, Other $28,166. Mats Exp $31,478, Books $14,407, Per/Ser (Incl. Access Fees) $9,523, Other Print Mats $785, AV Mat $785, Electronic Ref Mat (Incl. Access Fees) $5,978. Sal $302,171 (Prof $80,000)
Library Holdings: Bk Titles 63,860; Bk Vols 81,595; Per Subs 220

Special Collections: American Indian Coll; Automotive Coll; Japanese Language Coll; Large Print Coll; Local & State (California Coll); Mysteries Coll; Science Fiction Coll; Spanish Language Coll
Automation Activity & Vendor Info: (ILL) OCLC WorldShare Interlibrary Loan
Database Vendor: Gale Cengage Learning, LibLime, OCLC WorldShare Interlibrary Loan, World Book Online
Wireless access
Function: Children's prog, Citizenship assistance, Computer training, Computers for patron use, Copy machines
Partic in Monterey Bay Area Cooperative Library System
Special Services for the Blind - Audio mat; Bks on cassette; Cassettes; Copier with enlargement capabilities; Large print bks; Magnifiers; Ref serv; Talking bks
Open Mon & Wed 10-6, Tues & Thurs 12-8
Friends of the Library Group
Bookmobiles: 2. Bk titles 3000

GL SAN BENITO COUNTY LAW LIBRARY*, Courthouse, 440 Fifth St, 95023. SAN 320-5665. Tel: 831-636-4016, 831-636-4040. FAX: 831-636-4044. *Dir,* Karen Forcum
Library Holdings: Bk Titles 5,200; Bk Vols 12,537
Special Collections: Federal & California Case Law & Statutes

HOLLYWOOD

S HOLLYWOOD FILM ARCHIVE LIBRARY*, PMB 321, 8391 Beverly Blvd, 90048. SAN 320-1570. Tel: 323-655-4968. *Dir,* D Richard Baer
Founded 1973
Library Holdings: Bk Titles 2,300
Special Collections: Computerized Review Indexes, Motion Picture Exhibitor, Monthly Film Bulletin, Harrison's Reports; Film Reference (The Hollywood Film Archive Catalog)
Subject Interests: Movies, Television
Restriction: Staff use only, Use of others with permission of librn

HOPLAND

S HOPLAND RESEARCH & EXTENSION CENTER LIBRARY*, 4070 University Rd, 95449. SAN 373-4943. Tel: 707-744-1424. FAX: 707-744-1040. Web Site: ucanr.org/sites/hopland. *Dir,* Dr Robert M Timm; E-mail: rmtimm@ucanr.edu
Library Holdings: Bk Vols 200
Wireless access
Open Mon-Fri 12-6

HUNTINGTON BEACH

S AMERICAN AVIATION HISTORICAL SOCIETY*, Reference Library, 15211 Springdale St, 92649-1156. (Mail add: PO Box 3023, 92649-1156), SAN 371-2834. Tel: 714-549-4818. FAX: 714-549-3657. Web Site: aahs-online.org. *Pres,* Jerri Bergen
Founded 1956
Library Holdings: Bk Vols 15,000; Per Subs 5,000
Open Wed 10-5
Restriction: Mem only

J GOLDEN WEST COLLEGE*, R Dudley Boyce Library & Learning Center, 15744 Golden West St, 92647. (Mail add: PO Box 2748, 92647-2748), SAN 300-8215. Tel: 714-895-8741. FAX: 714-895-8926. TDD: 714-895-8957. Web Site: www.goldenwestcollege.edu/library. *Dir, Pub Serv,* Treisa Cassens; Tel: 714-895-8741, Ext 51214, E-mail: tcassens@gwc.cccd.edu; *Acq, Cat,* Julie A Davis; Tel: 714-895-8741, Ext 55207, E-mail: jadavis@gwc.cccd.edu; *Pub Serv,* Vanessa Aguirre; Tel: 714-895-8741, Ext 51243, E-mail: vgarcia@gwc.cccd.edu; *Online Serv, Ref, Syst,* Gonzalo Garcia; Tel: 714-895-8741, Ext 55250, E-mail: ggarcia@gwc.cccd.edu; Staff 11 (MLS 5, Non-MLS 6)
Founded 1966. Highest Degree: Associate
Subject Interests: Art, Nursing, Soc sci & issues
Automation Activity & Vendor Info: (Acquisitions) Baker & Taylor; (Cataloging) Baker & Taylor; (Circulation) Baker & Taylor; (Course Reserve) Baker & Taylor; (OPAC) Baker & Taylor
Database Vendor: Baker & Taylor, CountryWatch, CQ Press, EBSCOhost, Gale Cengage Learning, Project MUSE, ProQuest
Wireless access
Function: ILL available, Instruction & testing, Ref & res, Wheelchair accessible
Special Services for the Deaf - Bks on deafness & sign lang; Closed caption videos; High interest/low vocabulary bks; TDD equip; TTY equip
Special Services for the Blind - Computer with voice synthesizer for visually impaired persons
Open Mon-Thurs 8am-8:45pm, Fri 8-3

P HUNTINGTON BEACH PUBLIC LIBRARY SYSTEM, Information & Cultural Resource Center, 7111 Talbert Ave, 92648. SAN 332-1428. Tel: 714-842-4481. FAX: 714-375-5180. E-mail: library@hbpl.org. Web Site: www.hbpl.org. *Dir, Libr Serv,* Stephanie Beverage; E-mail: stephanie.beverage@surfcity-hb.org; *Principal Librn,* Mary Wilson; E-mail: mwilson@surfcity-hb.org; *ILL,* Bonnie Nowak; Staff 28.25 (MLS 10, Non-MLS 18.25)
Founded 1909. Pop 190,377; Circ 960,747
Oct 2012-Sept 2013 Income (Main Library and Branch(s)) $4,044,917, State $37,577, City $3,677,170, Federal $17,200, Other $312,970. Mats Exp $395,267, Books $257,457, Per/Ser (Incl. Access Fees) $21,490, AV Mat $32,000, Electronic Ref Mat (Incl. Access Fees) $84,320. Sal $3,273,323
Library Holdings: Audiobooks 796; AV Mats 20,334; Bks on Deafness & Sign Lang 124; CDs 7,854; DVDs 8,075; e-books 1,891; Electronic Media & Resources 18; Large Print Bks 5,297; Bk Titles 302,266; Bk Vols 388,588; Per Subs 277
Special Collections: Genealogy (Orange County, CA, Genealogical Society Coll)
Automation Activity & Vendor Info: (Cataloging) Horizon; (Circulation) Horizon; (OPAC) Horizon
Database Vendor: EBSCOhost, Newsbank, ProQuest, ReferenceUSA
Wireless access
Function: Adult literacy prog, After school storytime, Art exhibits, Audiobks via web, Bks on cassette, Bks on CD, Children's prog, Computers for patron use, Copy machines, Digital talking bks, E-Reserves, Electronic databases & coll, Family literacy, Genealogy discussion group, Holiday prog, Homework prog, ILL available, Music CDs, Online cat, Online searches, OverDrive digital audio bks, Photocopying/Printing, Prog for adults, Prog for children & young adult, Pub access computers, Story hour, Summer reading prog, Teen prog, Wheelchair accessible
Open Mon 1-9, Tues-Thurs 9-9, Fri & Sat 9-5
Restriction: Non-resident fee
Friends of the Library Group
Branches: 4
BANNING, 9281 Banning Ave, 92646-8302, SAN 332-1517. Tel: 714-375-5005. FAX: 714-375-5091.
Open Wed & Thurs 10-7, Fri & Sat 9-5
Friends of the Library Group
MAIN STREET BRANCH, 525 Main St, 92648-5133, SAN 332-1452. Tel: 714-375-5071. FAX: 714-375-5072. *Br Mgr, Libr Spec,* Robin Ott
Open Tues-Thurs 10-7, Fri & Sat 9-5
Friends of the Library Group
HELEN MURPHY BRANCH, 15882 Graham St, 92649-1724, SAN 332-1487. Tel: 714-375-5006. FAX: 714-373-3088. *Librn,* Susan Foster; E-mail: susan.foster@surfcity-hb.org
Open Tues-Thurs 10-7
Friends of the Library Group
OAK VIEW, 17251 Oak Lane, 92648, SAN 377-0265. Tel: 714-375-5068. FAX: 714-375-5073. *Br Mgr, Libr Spec,* Claudia Locke
Open Mon-Thurs 10-7, Fri 9-5
Friends of the Library Group

IMPERIAL

P IMPERIAL PUBLIC LIBRARY*, 200 W Ninth St, 92251. SAN 300-8231. Tel: 760-355-1332. FAX: 760-355-4857. Web Site: imperial.polarislibrary.com, www.cityofimperial.org/dept.php?id=32. *Libr Adminr,* Christina Carter; E-mail: ccarter@cityofimperial.org
Founded 1904. Pop 14,758; Circ 39,523
Library Holdings: Bk Vols 34,600
Wireless access
Partic in Serra Cooperative Library System
Open Mon-Thurs 10-8, Fri 10-5, Sat 11-3

J IMPERIAL VALLEY COLLEGE*, Spencer Library Media Center, 380 E Ira Aten Rd, 92251. (Mail add: PO Box 158, 92251-0158), SAN 300-824X. Tel: 760-355-6378. Circulation Tel: 760-355-6490. Reference Tel: 760-355-6445. FAX: 760-355-1090. Web Site: www.imperial.edu. *Dean,* Taylor Ruhl; E-mail: taylor.ruhl@imperial.edu; *Lead Librn,* Cathy Zazueta; E-mail: cathy.zazueta@imperial.edu; *Ref Librn,* Frank Hoppe; Tel: 760-355-6193, E-mail: frank.hoppe@imperial.edu; *Tech Serv,* Mary Ann Smith; Tel: 760-355-6380, E-mail: maryann.smith@imperial.edu; Staff 9 (MLS 3, Non-MLS 6)
Founded 1922. Enrl 7,633; Fac 119; Highest Degree: Associate
Library Holdings: AV Mats 778; Bk Titles 55,789; Bk Vols 59,571; Per Subs 463
Subject Interests: Local hist
Automation Activity & Vendor Info: (Cataloging) OCLC Online; (Circulation) SirsiDynix; (ILL) OCLC; (OPAC) SirsiDynix
Database Vendor: EBSCOhost, LexisNexis, ProQuest
Wireless access
Open Mon-Thurs 8-8, Fri 8-3

INDEPENDENCE

P INYO COUNTY FREE LIBRARY*, 168 N Edwards St, 93526. (Mail add: PO Drawer K, 93526-0610), SAN 332-169X. Tel: 760-878-0260. Administration Tel: 760-878-0359. FAX: 760-878-0360. E-mail: inyocolib@qnet.com. Web Site: www.inyocounty.us/library. *Libr Dir,* Nancy Masters; E-mail: nmasters@inyocounty.us; *Tech Serv Librn,* Joe Frankel; E-mail: jfrankel@inyocounty.us; *Cat Spec,* Leah Tubbs
Founded 1913. Pop 18,400; Circ 130,000
Library Holdings: Bk Vols 101,500; Per Subs 129
Special Collections: Mary Hunter Austin Coll
Subject Interests: Inyo County
Mem of Inland Library System
Partic in San Bernardino, Inyo, Riverside Counties United Library Services
Open Mon-Fri 12-5, Wed 6pm-9pm, Sat 10-1
Branches: 5
BIG PINE BRANCH, 500 S Main St, Big Pine, 93513. (Mail add: PO Box 760, Big Pine, 93513-0760), SAN 377-6018. Tel: 760-938-2420. E-mail: bplibrary@qnet.com. *Librn,* Lydia Baldwin; *Libr Spec,* Arline Rogers
Library Holdings: Bk Vols 16,000; Per Subs 11
Open Mon, Tues, Thurs & Fri 12-5, Wed 2-7, Sat 10-1
Friends of the Library Group
BISHOP BRANCH, 210 Academy Ave, Bishop, 93514-2693, SAN 375-5509. Tel: 760-873-5115. Reference Tel: 760-873-5119. FAX: 760-873-5356. E-mail: bishoplib@qnet.com. *Librn,* Ann Kothman; E-mail: akothman@inyocounty.us; *Libr Spec,* Reece Parker; E-mail: rparker@inyocounty.us
Library Holdings: Bk Vols 30,200; Per Subs 33
Open Mon, Wed & Fri 10-6, Tues & Thurs 12-8, Sat 10-1
Friends of the Library Group
FURNACE CREEK, 201 Nevares Rd, Cow Creek, Death Valley, 92328. (Mail add: PO Box 568, Death Valley, 92328-0568). Tel: 760-786-2408. *Libr Spec,* Crystal Taylor
Library Holdings: Bk Vols 2,450; Per Subs 6
Open Wed 4:30-8:30, Sat 9-12
LONE PINE BRANCH, 127 Bush St, Lone Pine, 93545. (Mail add: PO Box 745, Lone Pine, 93545-0745), SAN 377-6034. Tel: 760-876-5031. E-mail: lplibrary@qnet.com. *Libr Spec,* Kathy Chambers
Library Holdings: Bk Vols 12,500; Per Subs 33
Open Mon & Wed 12:30-7, Tues, Thurs & Fri 10-12 & 1-5, Sat 10-1
Friends of the Library Group
TECOPA BRANCH, 408 Tecopa Hot Springs Rd, Tecopa, 92389. (Mail add: PO Box 177, Tecopa, 92389-0177). Tel: 760-852-4171. FAX: 760-852-4171. *Libr Spec,* Nancy Good; E-mail: ngood@inyocounty.us
Library Holdings: Bk Vols 4,500; Per Subs 6
Open Mon, Tues & Thurs (Winter) 7 11:30 & 12-3; Tues & Thurs (Summer) 7-11:30 & 12-3

GL INYO COUNTY LAW LIBRARY*, 168 N Edwards St, 93526. (Mail add: PO Drawer K, 93526-0610), SAN 320-1562. Tel: 760-878-0260. FAX. 760-878-0360. *Law Libr Operations Mgr,* Nancy Masters; E-mail: nmasters@inyocounty.us
Library Holdings: Bk Vols 3,700
Subject Interests: Calif
Open Mon-Fri Noon-5

INDIO

GL RIVERSIDE COUNTY LAW LIBRARY*, Indio Branch, 46-900A Monroe St, Ste 101, 92201. SAN 300-8258. Tel: 760-848-7151. FAX: 760-347-4500. E-mail: lawlibrary.indio@rclawlibrary.org. Web Site: rclawlibrary.org. *Libr Asst,* Gina Dreyer; *Libr Asst,* Carrol Magder
Library Holdings: Bk Vols 23,402; Per Subs 14
Subject Interests: Law
Database Vendor: SirsiDynix
Wireless access
Open Mon-Fri 8-4

INGLEWOOD

M CENTINELA HOSPITAL MEDICAL CENTER*, Edwin W Dean Sr Memorial Library, 555 E Hardy St, 90301-4011. SAN 321-1258. Tel: 310-673-4660, Ext 7266. FAX: 310-419-8275. *In Charge,* Helen Wiley; E-mail: hwiley@primehealthcare.com; Staff 2 (MLS 1, Non-MLS 1)
Founded 1975
Library Holdings: e-journals 100; Bk Titles 250
Subject Interests: Arthritis, Cardiology, Diabetes, Med, Obstetrics & gynecology, Orthopedics, Sports med
Automation Activity & Vendor Info: (Cataloging) EOS International; (Serials) Ex Libris Group
Partic in Docline
Open Tues & Thurs 9-4:30, Fri 9-2

P INGLEWOOD PUBLIC LIBRARY, 101 W Manchester Blvd, 90301-1771. SAN 332-172X. Tel: 310-412-5380. Circulation Tel: 310-412-5620. Reference Tel: 310-412-4280. Administration Tel: 310-412-5397. Information Services Tel: 310-412-5123. FAX: 310-412-8848. TDD: 310-412-4343. E-mail: publiclibrary@cityofinglewood.org. Web Site: library.cityofinglewood.org. *Libr Mgr,* Frances Tracht; E-mail: FTracht@cityofinglewood.org; *Act Principal Librn, Adult Serv,* Joel J Rane; E-mail: JRane@cityofinglewood.org; *Principal Librn, Children's/Youth Services, Br Serv,* Angela Citizen; E-mail: ACitizen@cityofinglewood.org; *Assoc Librn, Circ Serv,* Adrienne Dodson; E-mail: ADodson@cityofinglewood.org; *Ch Serv Librn,* Dawn Fechter; E-mail: DFite@cityofinglewood.org; *Br Serv Supvr,* Lori Williams; E-mail: LWilliams@cityofinglewood.org; *Circ Serv Supvr,* Susan Cunningham; E-mail: SCunningham@cityofinglewood.org; *Supvr, Ser,* Frank Francis; E-mail: FFrancis@cityofinglewood.org; *Supvr, Tech Serv,* Luz Torres-Eckhard; E-mail: LTorres@cityofinglewood.org; Staff 15 (MLS 7, Non-MLS 8)
Founded 1913. Pop 110,623; Circ 160,107
Oct 2011-Sept 2012 Income (Main Library and Branch(s)) $2,542,521, City $2,517,277, Other $25,244. Mats Exp $270,107, Books $70,912, Per/Ser (Incl. Access Fees) $116,343, Other Print Mats $8,652, Electronic Ref Mat (Incl. Access Fees) $73,313, Presv $887. Sal $2,034,026
Library Holdings: Audiobooks 2,996; e-books 9; Electronic Media & Resources 32; Bk Vols 411,955; Per Subs 590
Special Collections: Inglewood (Local History Coll); Large Print; Military History (Special Coll of Local); Rare Books (Includes some rare books published in Southern California); Spanish. Municipal Document Depository; State Document Depository; US Document Depository
Automation Activity & Vendor Info: (Acquisitions) Innovative Interfaces, Inc; (Cataloging) Innovative Interfaces, Inc; (Circulation) Innovative Interfaces, Inc; (ILL) Innovative Interfaces, Inc; (OPAC) Innovative Interfaces, Inc; (Serials) Innovative Interfaces, Inc
Database Vendor: 3M Library Systems, EBSCO Information Services, Gale Cengage Learning, Innovative Interfaces, Inc, Natural Standard, ProQuest, WT Cox
Wireless access
Function: 24/7 Electronic res, 24/7 Online cat, Activity rm, After school storytime, Archival coll, Art exhibits, Audio & video playback equip for onsite use, Audiobks via web, AV serv, Bilingual assistance for Spanish patrons, Bks on cassette, Bks on CD, CD-ROM, Children's prog, Citizenship assistance, Computer training, Computers for patron use, Copy machines, Electronic databases & coll, Exhibits, Fax serv, Free DVD rentals, Govt ref serv, Holiday prog, ILL available, Life-long learning prog for all ages, Magazines, Mail & tel request accepted, Microfiche/film & reading machines, Movies, Music CDs, Newsp ref libr, Online cat, Online ref, Online searches, Orientations, Passport agency, Photocopying/Printing, Prog for adults, Prog for children & young adult, Pub access computers, Ref serv available, Ref serv in person, Senior computer classes, Spanish lang bks, Spoken cassettes & CDs, Spoken cassettes & DVDs, Story hour, Study rm, Summer reading prog, Tax forms, Teen prog, Telephone ref, VHS videos, Video lending libr, Web-catalog, Wheelchair accessible
Partic in Califa; Southern California Library Cooperative
Open Mon-Wed 11 8, Thurs 11-6, Sat 10-2
Restriction: Circ to mem only, Closed stack, Free to mem, ID required to use computers (Ltd hrs), In-house use for visitors, Non-circulating coll, Non-circulating of rare bks
Friends of the Library Group
Branches: 1
CRENSHAW-IMPERIAL BRANCH LIBRARY, 11141 Crenshaw Blvd, 90303-2338, SAN 332-1754. Tel: 310-412-5403. FAX: 310-412-5684.
Library Holdings: Bk Vols 43,841
Open Mon, Tues & Thurs 11-6

CL UNIVERSITY OF WEST LOS ANGELES*, Law School Library, 9920 S LaCienega Blvd, 90301-4423. SAN 331-863X. Tel: 310-342-5206. FAX: 310-342-5298. Web Site: www.uwla.edu/Academics/library.aspx. *Dir, Libr Serv,* Jimmy Rimonte; E-mail: jrimonte@uwla.edu
Founded 1968. Enrl 400
Library Holdings: Bk Vols 31,000; Per Subs 100
Database Vendor: Westlaw
Partic in Westlaw
Open Mon, Tues & Wed 12:30-8:30, Thurs & Fri 1:30-8:30, Sat 9:30-1:30

IRVINE

CR CONCORDIA UNIVERSITY LIBRARY*, 1530 Concordia W, 92612. SAN 322-7065. Tel: 949-854-8002, Ext 1500. E-mail: librarian@cui.edu. Web Site: www.cui.edu/library. *Dir, Libr Serv,* Carolina Barton; Tel: 949-214-3093, E-mail: carolina.barton@cui.edu; Staff 3 (MLS 2, Non-MLS 1)
Founded 1976. Enrl 2,100; Fac 72; Highest Degree: Master
Library Holdings: CDs 250; Bk Titles 85,000; Bk Vols 90,000; Per Subs 850
Special Collections: Dale Hartmann Curriculum Coll; Gehrke Reformation Coll; Robert C Baden Memorial Children's Coll
Subject Interests: Lutheran theol, Reformation hist
Automation Activity & Vendor Info: (Acquisitions) TLC (The Library Corporation); (Cataloging) TLC (The Library Corporation); (Circulation)

TLC (The Library Corporation); (Course Reserve) TLC (The Library Corporation); (OPAC) TLC (The Library Corporation); (Serials) TLC (The Library Corporation)
Database Vendor: EBSCOhost, JSTOR, LexisNexis, SerialsSolutions
Wireless access
Function: Music CDs, Orientations, Photocopying/Printing, Spoken cassettes & CDs, VHS videos, Wheelchair accessible
Partic in Concordia Univ Syst; Orbis Cascade Alliance; Southern Calif Area Theol Librns Asn; Statewide California Electronic Library Consortium (SCELC)
Open Mon-Thurs 8am-10pm, Fri 8-4:30, Sun 3-10
Restriction: Fee for pub use, Open to students, fac & staff

S FASHION INSTITUTE OF DESIGN & MERCHANDISING LIBRARY*, 17590 Gillette Ave, 92614. SAN 328-6622. Tel: 949-851-6200. Circulation Tel: 949-851-6200, Ext 1737. Reference Tel: 949-851-6200, Ext 1738. FAX: 949-851-6808. Web Site: www.fidm.edu. *Librn,* Rebecca Markman; E-mail: rmarkman@fidm.edu; Staff 3 (MLS 1, Non-MLS 2)
Library Holdings: AV Mats 1,200; Bk Vols 2,100; Per Subs 65
Wireless access
Restriction: Open by appt only

J IRVINE VALLEY COLLEGE LIBRARY, 5500 Irvine Center Dr, 92618-4399. SAN 324-7333. Tel: 949-451-5261. FAX: 949-451-5796. Web Site: www.ivc.edu/library. *Librn,* Cheryl Delson; E-mail: cdelson@ivc.edu; *Librn,* Tony Lin; E-mail: alin@ivc.edu; Staff 4 (MLS 4)
Founded 1979. Enrl 14,768; Fac 70
Library Holdings: Bk Vols 45,000; Per Subs 120
Partic in Dialog Corp; OCLC Online Computer Library Center, Inc
Open Mon-Thurs 8am-9pm, Fri 8-4, Sat 10-2

S MOTORCYCLE INDUSTRY COUNCIL*, Two Jenner St, Ste 150, 92618-3806. SAN 373-0255. Tel: 949-727-4211. FAX: 949-727-4217. Web Site: www.mic.org. *Dir,* Pat Murphy
Library Holdings: Bk Vols 150; Per Subs 25
Restriction: Mem only

S PARKER HANNIFIN CORP, Engineering Library, 16666 Von Karman Ave, M/S A-17, 92606-4997. SAN 377-4244. Tel: 949-851-3352. FAX: 949-851-3571. *Librn,* Kristi Susan Anderson; E-mail: ksanderson@parker.com; Staff 1 (MLS 1)
Founded 1981
Jul 2005-Jun 2006. Mats Exp $46,500, Books $500, Other Print Mats $1,000, Electronic Ref Mat (Incl. Access Fees) $45,000. Sal $50,000
Library Holdings: Bk Titles 10,000
Function: Res libr

C UNIVERSITY OF CALIFORNIA IRVINE LIBRARIES*, Langson Library, PO Box 19557, 92623-9557. SAN 300-8355. Tel: 949-824-6836. Administration Tel: 949-824-5212. Web Site: www.lib.uci.edu. *Univ Librn,* Lorelei Tanji; *Assoc Univ Librn, Pub Serv,* Carol Ann Hughes; Tel: 949-824-9753; *Admin Serv, Asst Univ Librn,* Kevin Ruminson; Tel: 949-824-4440; *Asst Univ Librn, Res Resources,* John Renaud; Tel: 949-824-5216
Founded 1965. Highest Degree: Doctorate
Special Collections: Bibliotheca Neurologica Courville Coll, artifacts, bks; Book Art Coll; British Naval History Coll; Contemporary Small Press Poetry Coll; Dance Coll; History of Literary Criticism (Wellek Coll); Neurology, Neuropathology (Courville Coll); Orchids & Horticulture (Menninger Coll); Regional California History Coll; Southeast Asian Archive; Thomas Mann (Waldmuller Coll). State Document Depository; US Document Depository
Wireless access
Publications: Library Update (Newsletter); UCI Libraries for Library Partners & Friends (Newsletter)
Partic in Association of Research Libraries (ARL); Center for Research Libraries; OCLC Online Computer Library Center, Inc; Univ of Calif Librs
Special Services for the Deaf - Assistive tech
Friends of the Library Group
Departmental Libraries:
AYALA SCIENCE LIBRARY, PO Box 19557, 92623-9557, SAN 326-7091. Tel: 949-824-3681. FAX: 949-824-3114. *Univ Librn,* Lorelei Tanji; Tel: 949-824-5212
Open Mon-Thurs 7:30am-3am, Fri 7:30am-9pm, Sat 10-9, Sun 10am-3am
CM GRUNIGEN MEDICAL LIBRARY, Bldg 22A Rt 81, 101 The City Dr S, Orange, 92868, SAN 326-713X. Tel: 714-456-5585. Web Site: grunigen.lib.uci.edu. *Actg Dir,* Cynthia Johnson

IRWINDALE

P IRWINDALE PUBLIC LIBRARY*, 5050 N Irwindale Ave, 91706. SAN 300-8363. Tel: 626-430-2229. Administration Tel: 626-430-2228. Web Site: www.ci.irwindale.ca.us/departments/library. *City Librn,* Ryan Baker; Staff 4 (MLS 1, Non-MLS 3)
Founded 1961. Pop 1,445; Circ 23,440
Library Holdings: Bk Vols 16,055; Per Subs 45
Special Collections: Irwindale City History Coll
Wireless access
Function: After school storytime, Archival coll, Homebound delivery serv, Online cat, Photocopying/Printing, Tax forms
Partic in Southern California Library Cooperative
Open Mon-Thurs 9-7

JACKSON

GL AMADOR COUNTY LAW LIBRARY*, 530 Sutter St, 95642. Interlibrary Loan Service Tel: 209-223-6405. E-mail: library@amadorgov.org. Web Site: www.amadorgov.org/library. *County Librn,* Laura Einstadler
Founded 1891
Library Holdings: Audiobooks 4,049; AV Mats 5,630; Electronic Media & Resources 7; Bk Vols 90,000; Per Subs 60
Database Vendor: SirsiDynix
Wireless access
Partic in 49-99 Cooperative Library System
Open Mon-Wed 10-6, Thurs & Fri 10-5, Sat 12-4
Friends of the Library Group

P AMADOR COUNTY LIBRARY, Main Library, 530 Sutter St, 95642. SAN 300-8371. Tel: 209-223-6400. FAX: 209-223-6303. E-mail: library@amadorgov.org. Web Site: www.amadorgov.org/library. *County Librn,* Laura Einstadter; E-mail: leinstadter@amadorgov.org
Pop 38,000; Circ 97,219
Library Holdings: Audiobooks 4,287; Microforms 1,037; Bk Vols 86,631; Per Subs 71; Videos 4,760
Special Collections: Amador County History Coll (local mining, history, genealogy); Index of Amador County Newspapers (microfilm); Mines & Mineral Research Coll
Automation Activity & Vendor Info: (Acquisitions) SirsiDynix; (Cataloging) SirsiDynix; (Circulation) SirsiDynix; (OPAC) SIRSI-iBistro
Database Vendor: SirsiDynix
Wireless access
Publications: Friends of Library Newsletter (Quarterly)
Partic in 49-99 Cooperative Library System
Open Mon & Tue 10-6, Wed 10-7, Thurs & Fri 10-5
Friends of the Library Group
Branches: 4
IONE BRANCH, 25 E Main St, Ione, 95640. Tel: 209-274-2560.
Open Mon & Wed 10-1, Tues 2-7, Thurs 1-5, Fri 1-4
PINE GROVE BRANCH, 19889 Hwy 88, Pine Grove, 95665. Tel: 209-296-3111. *In Charge,* Brad Barrow
Library Holdings: Bk Vols 6,360
Open Tues & Wed 12-5
Friends of the Library Group
PIONEER BRANCH, 25070 Buckhorn Ridge Rd, Pioneer, 95666. (Mail add: PO Box 821, Pioneer, 95666-0821). Tel: 209-295-7330. *Libr Asst,* Brad Barrow
Library Holdings: Bk Vols 5,000
Open Thurs & Fri 12-5
Friends of the Library Group
PLYMOUTH BRANCH, 9375 Main St, Plymouth, 95669. (Mail add: PO Box 61, Plymouth, 95669-0061). Tel: 209-245-6476. *In Charge,* Rae LeGrande
Library Holdings: Bk Vols 7,000
Open Tues 1:30-5, Wed 10-12 & 1-5, Thurs & Fri 1:30-5
Friends of the Library Group

JOLON

A UNITED STATES ARMY*, Fort Hunter Liggett Library, PO Box 896, 93928-0896. Tel: 831-386-2719. FAX: 831-386-2002. *Libr Mgr,* Cassandra Belcher
Library Holdings: Bk Vols 10,000
Restriction: Mil only

JOSHUA TREE

J COPPER MOUNTAIN COLLEGE*, Greenleaf Library, 6162 Rotary Way, 92252. (Mail add: PO Box 1398, 92251-0879), SAN 301-6722. Tel: 760-366-3791. FAX: 760-366-5256. Web Site: library.cmccd.edu. *Librn,* Carolyn Hopkins; Tel: 760-366-3791, Ext 5293, E-mail: chopkins@cmccd.edu; *Libr Spec,* Dena Gast; Tel: 760-366-3791, Ext 5902; *Libr Spec,* Cathy Inscore; Tel: 760-366-3791, Ext 5901; *Libr Tech,* Shannon Frechette; *Libr Tech,* Cassandra Nafziger; Tel: 760-366-3794, Ext 5901; Staff 3 (MLS 1, Non-MLS 2)
Enrl 2,400; Fac 26; Highest Degree: Associate
Library Holdings: CDs 34; DVDs 15; e-books 2,708; Bk Titles 11,161; Bk Vols 12,925; Per Subs 70; Videos 1,159
Special Collections: Desert Studies

Automation Activity & Vendor Info: (Cataloging) TLC (The Library Corporation); (Circulation) TLC (The Library Corporation); (OPAC) TLC (The Library Corporation)
Database Vendor: EBSCOhost, Gale Cengage Learning, LexisNexis, Newsbank, ProQuest
Wireless access
Partic in SIRCULS
Open Mon-Thurs 8am-8:30pm, Fri 8-6

KENTFIELD

J COLLEGE OF MARIN LIBRARY*, 835 College Ave, 94904. SAN 300-8398. Tel: 415-457-8811, 415-485-9656. Reference Tel: 415-485-9475. FAX: 415-457-5395. Web Site: www.marin.edu. *Coordr, Librn,* Carl Cox; E-mail: carl.cox@marin.edu; *Librn,* Matthew Priewe; *Librn,* Joan Risch; Staff 5 (MLS 5)
Founded 1926
Library Holdings: Bk Titles 92,100; Bk Vols 137,000; Per Subs 331
Open Mon-Thurs (Winter) 8am-9pm, Fri 8-4; Mon-Thurs (Summer) 8-4
Friends of the Library Group

LA JOLLA

S LIBRARY ASSOCIATION OF LA JOLLA*, Athenaeum Music & Arts Library, 1008 Wall St, 92037. SAN 300-8479. Tel: 858-454-5872. FAX: 858-454-5835. E-mail: athlib@pacbell.net. Web Site: www.ljathenaeum.org. *Librn,* Kathi Bower Peterson; Staff 15 (MLS 2, Non-MLS 13)
Founded 1899
Jul 2008-Jun 2009 Income $1,230,000. Mats Exp $60,000
Library Holdings: AV Mats 17,300; Bk Titles 19,000; Per Subs 71
Special Collections: Artists Books; Music (Bach Gesellschaft Coll)
Subject Interests: Art, Music
Automation Activity & Vendor Info: (Cataloging) EOS International; (Circulation) EOS International; (OPAC) EOS International; (Serials) EOS International
Wireless access
Publications: Annual Report; Art Exhibition Catalogues; Newsletter (Bi-monthly); School Brochures (Quarterly)
Open Tues & Thurs-Sat 10-5:30, Wed 10-8:30
Restriction: Non-circulating to the pub

S MUSEUM OF CONTEMPORARY ART SAN DIEGO*, Helen Palmer Geisel Library, 700 Prospect St, 92037. SAN 300-8460. Tel: 858-454-3541, Ext 132. FAX: 858-454-6985. Web Site: www.mcasd.org. *Librn,* Andrea Hales; Staff 1 (Non-MLS 1)
Founded 1941
Library Holdings: Bk Titles 6,373; Per Subs 47
Special Collections: Artists Vertical Files; Interviews with Artists, audio & video. Oral History
Subject Interests: Contemporary art, Modern art
Restriction: Not a lending libr

S SALK INSTITUTE FOR BIOLOGICAL STUDIES*, Salk Institute Library, 10010 N Torrey Pines Rd, 92037-1099. SAN 300-8495. Tel: 858-453-4100, Ext 1235. FAX: 858-452-7472. E-mail: library@salk.edu. Web Site: jonas.salk.edu. *Mgr,* Carol Bodas; E-mail: bodas@salk.edu; *Libr Assoc,* Rosa Lopez; E-mail: lopez@salk.edu; Staff 2 (Non-MLS 2)
Founded 1962. Enrl 119; Fac 60
Library Holdings: DVDs 1,600; e-books 1,000; e-journals 500; Bk Vols 2,000; Per Subs 10
Subject Interests: Biochem, Genetics, Immunology, Molecular biol, Neuroscience, Plant biol, Proteomics, Virology
Database Vendor: Elsevier, FileMaker, LibLime, Medline, Nature Publishing Group, PubMed, ScienceDirect
Wireless access
Function: Res libr
Partic in Statewide California Electronic Library Consortium (SCELC)
Restriction: Limited access for the pub

M THE SCRIPPS RESEARCH INSTITUTE*, Kresge Library, 10550 N Torrey Pines Rd, 92037. SAN 300-8509. Tel: 858-784-8705. FAX: 858-784-2035. E-mail: helplib@scripps.edu. Web Site: www.scripps.edu. *Dir,* Paula King; Staff 8 (MLS 5, Non-MLS 3)
Founded 1962
Library Holdings: Bk Vols 4,400; Per Subs 720
Subject Interests: Biochem, Chem, Immunology, Med, Molecular biol, Neurobiol
Automation Activity & Vendor Info: (OPAC) OCLC WorldShare Interlibrary Loan
Database Vendor: American Chemical Society, Annual Reviews, Elsevier, ISI Web of Knowledge, JSTOR, Nature Publishing Group, OCLC, OVID Technologies, PubMed, ScienceDirect, Springer-Verlag, Wiley
Wireless access
Function: For res purposes, ILL available
Partic in National Network of Libraries of Medicine; OCLC Online Computer Library Center, Inc; Statewide California Electronic Library Consortium (SCELC)
Restriction: Authorized personnel only, Not open to pub

G UNITED STATES DEPARTMENT OF COMMERCE, NATIONAL OCEANIC & ATMOSPHERIC ADMINISTRATION*, Southwest Fisheries Science Center Library, 8901 La Jolla Shores Dr, 92037-1509. SAN 300-8487. Tel: 858-546-7038, 858-546-7196. FAX: 858-546-7003. *Librn,* Debra A Losey; E-mail: debra.losey@noaa.gov; Staff 2 (MLS 1, Non-MLS 1)
Founded 1965
Library Holdings: Per Subs 88
Special Collections: Inter-American Tropical Tuna Commission
Subject Interests: Antarctic, Fisheries, Fisheries econ, Marine biol, Marine mammals, Oceanography
Database Vendor: Cambridge Scientific Abstracts, JSTOR, OCLC, ScienceDirect, SirsiDynix, Springer-Verlag, Swets Information Services, Thomson - Web of Science, WT Cox
Wireless access
Publications: FYI (inhouse, irregular); New Acquisitions (inhouse, irregular)
Partic in Fedlink; OCLC Online Computer Library Center, Inc
Restriction: Open to others by appt, Restricted access

C UNIVERSITY OF CALIFORNIA, SAN DIEGO*, University Libraries, 9500 Gilman Dr, Mail Code 0175G, 92093-0175. SAN 332-1878. Tel: 858-534-3336. Interlibrary Loan Service Tel: 858-534-2528. Administration Tel. 858-534-3061. FAX: 858-534-4970. Web Site: www.ucsd.edu/library/index.html. *Univ Librn,* Brian E C Schottlaender; Tel: 858-534-3060, E-mail: becs@ucsd.edu; *Assoc Univ Librn, Admin Serv,* Tammy Dearie; *Assoc Univ Librn, Coll & Serv,* Martha Hruska; Tel: 858-534-1235; *Assoc Univ Librn, Tech Serv,* Luc Declerck; *Assoc Univ Librn, User Serv,* Catherine R Friedman; Tel: 858-534-1278; *Admin Dir,* Maureen Harden; Tel: 858-534-1277; *Dir of Develop,* Barbara Brink; *Head, Acq,* Tony Harvell; Tel: 858-534-3305, Fax: 858-534-1256; *Head, Metadata & Content Mgt,* Linda Barnhart; Tel: 858-534-3307, Fax: 858-822-0349; *Head, Tech Serv,* Declan Fleming; Tel: 858-534-7476, Fax: 858-534-6206; *ILL,* Laura Chipps; Staff 286 (MLS 61, Non-MLS 225)
Founded 1959. Enrl 27,682; Fac 7,126; Highest Degree: Doctorate
Library Holdings: AV Mats 144,225; CDs 53,399; e-books 231,216; Microforms 3,309,102; Music Scores 44,157; Bk Vols 3,372,785; Per Subs 7,861
Special Collections: Baja, CA; Contemporary American Poetry (Archive for New Poetry); Contemporary Music; European Communities Common Market Publications; Melanesian Ethnography; Pacific Voyages; Renaissance; Science & Public Policy; Spanish Civil War. State Document Depository; US Document Depository
Automation Activity & Vendor Info: (Acquisitions) Innovative Interfaces, Inc; (Circulation) Innovative Interfaces, Inc; (OPAC) Innovative Interfaces, Inc; (Serials) Innovative Interfaces, Inc
Database Vendor: OCLC FirstSearch
Wireless access
Publications: Faculty/Friends (Newsletter); Melanesian Acquisition; Pacific Voyages Collection Bibliography, Renaissance Collection Bibliography
Partic in Am Asn of Health Sci Librs; Coalition for Networked Information (CNI); Coun of Libr Info Resources; Dialog Corp; Medical Library Association (MLA); National Initiative for a Networked Cultural Heritage; OCLC Online Computer Library Center, Inc; Pacific Southwest Regional Medical Library (PSRML); Scholarly Publ & Acad Resources Coalition; SDC Search Serv
Friends of the Library Group

Departmental Libraries:

THE ARTS LIBRARY, 9500 Gilman Dr, 0175Q, 92093-0175. Administration Tel: 858-534-0245. Information Services Tel: 858-534-8074. Administration FAX: 858-534-0189. *Head of Libr,* Leslie Abrams; E-mail: labrams@ucsd.edu
Library Holdings: CDs 92,344; Music Scores 43,867; Bk Vols 172,689; Videos 15,001
Friends of the Library Group

CM BIOMEDICAL LIBRARY, 9500 Gilman Dr, 0699, 92093-0699. Tel: 858-534-3418. Circulation Tel: 858-534-3253. Interlibrary Loan Service Tel: 858-534-4779. Reference Tel: 858-534-1201. FAX: 858-822-2219. Interlibrary Loan Service FAX: 858-534-0746. *Interim Dir,* Sue McGuinness; *Asst Dir,* Jenny Reiswig; *Instruction & Outreach Librn,* Mary Wickline; *Undergrad Serv Librn,* Dominique Turnbow
Founded 1963
Library Holdings: AV Mats 99; CDs 615; Bk Vols 216,327; Per Subs 779
Automation Activity & Vendor Info: (Circulation) Insignia Software
Friends of the Library Group

MANDEVILLE SPECIAL COLLECTIONS, UCSD Libraries 0175S, 9500 Gilman Dr, 92093-0175. Tel: 858-534-2533. Reference Tel: 858-534-1276. FAX: 858-534-5950. E-mail: spcoll@ucsd.edu. Web Site:

libraries.ucsd.edu/collections/sca/index.html. *Dir,* Lynda C Claassen; E-mail: lclaassen@ucsd.edu
Open Mon, Tues, Thurs & Fri 9-5, Wed 9-7
Friends of the Library Group

SCIENCE & ENGINEERING, 9500 Gilman Dr, Dept 0175E, 92093-0175. Tel: 858-534-4579. Circulation Tel: 858-534-3257. Interlibrary Loan Service Tel: 858-534-1219. Reference Tel: 858-534-3258. FAX: 858-534-5583. E-mail: scilib@ucsd.edu. *Head of Libr,* Mary Linn Bergstrom; E-mail: mlbergstrom@library.ucsd.edu; *Head, Outreach Serv, Head, Ref & Instruction,* Susan Shepherd; *Digital Serv Librn,* SuHui Ho
Library Holdings: AV Mats 624; CDs 2,299; Microforms 440,570; Bk Vols 291,466; Per Subs 717
Friends of the Library Group

LA MIRADA

C BIOLA UNIVERSITY LIBRARY, 13800 Biola Ave, 90639-0002. SAN 300-8525. Tel: 562-903-4834. Circulation Tel: 562-903-4835. Interlibrary Loan Service Tel: 562-903-4833. Reference Tel: 562-903-4838. FAX: 562-903-4840. Web Site: library.biola.edu. *Dean, Libr & Media Serv,* Dr Gregg Geary; Tel: 562-944-0351, Ext 5605, E-mail: gregg.geary@biola.edu; *Assoc Dean, Libr & Media Serv,* Sue Whitehead; Tel: 562-944-0351, Ext 5611, E-mail: sue.whitehead@biola.edu; *Asst Dean, Libr & Media Serv,* Juliana Morley; Tel: 562-944-0351, Ext 5620, E-mail: juliana.morley@biola.edu; *Head, Access Serv,* Julie Ellis; Tel: 562-944-0351, Ext 5604, E-mail: julie.ellis@biola.edu; *Electronic Res/Ser Librn,* Bob Krauss; Tel: 562-903-4837, E-mail: bob.krauss@biola.edu; *Metadata Librn,* John Tiffin; Tel: 562-944-0351, Ext 5153, E-mail: john.tiffin@biola.edu; *Music & Media Librn,* John Redford; Tel: 562-944-0351, Ext 5613, E-mail: john.redford@biola.edu; *Ref & Instruction Librn,* Stacie Schmidt; Tel: 562-944-0351, Ext 5154, E-mail: stacie.schmidt@biola.edu; *Tech Serv Librn,* Eileen Walraven; Tel: 562-944-0351, Ext 3653, E-mail: eileen.walraven@biola.edu; *Mgr, Libr Info Tech,* Simon Heres; Tel: 562-944-0351, Ext 5612, E-mail: simon.heres@biola.edu; Staff 22 (MLS 9, Non-MLS 13)
Founded 1908. Enrl 6,339; Fac 461; Highest Degree: Doctorate
Jul 2013-Jun 2014 Income $3,206,870, Locally Generated Income $53,896, Parent Institution $3,152,974. Mats Exp $1,596,439, Books $298,666, Per/Ser (Incl. Access Fees) $104,517, AV Equip $30,309, Electronic Ref Mat (Incl. Access Fees) $957,363. Sal $1,428,647 (Prof $671,850)
Library Holdings: AV Mats 3,049; Bks on Deafness & Sign Lang 112; Braille Volumes 55; CDs 5,079; DVDs 4,481; e-books 398,721; e-journals 56,484; Large Print Bks 12; Microforms 5,993; Music Scores 6,706; Bk Vols 265,056; Per Subs 433; Videos 2,672
Special Collections: Bible Versions & Translations Coll; Biola University Archives
Subject Interests: Nursing, Psychol, Relig
Automation Activity & Vendor Info: (Acquisitions) Innovative Interfaces, Inc; (Cataloging) Innovative Interfaces, Inc; (Circulation) Innovative Interfaces, Inc; (Course Reserve) Innovative Interfaces, Inc; (ILL) Innovative Interfaces, Inc; (Media Booking) Innovative Interfaces, Inc; (OPAC) Innovative Interfaces, Inc; (Serials) Innovative Interfaces, Inc
Database Vendor: Alexander Street Press, American Chemical Society, American Psychological Association (APA), ARTstor, College Source, CRC Press/Taylor & Francis Group, CredoReference, ebrary, EBSCOhost, Elsevier, Gale Cengage Learning, Ingenta, JSTOR, LexisNexis, OCLC, OVID Technologies, Oxford Online, Paratext, Project MUSE, ProQuest, Sage, SerialsSolutions, Springer-Verlag, Springshare, LLC, Wiley
Wireless access
Function: Archival coll, Art exhibits, Audio & video playback equip for onsite use, AV serv, Bks on CD, CD-ROM, Computers for patron use, Copy machines, Distance learning, Doc delivery serv, e-mail & chat, E-Reserves, Electronic databases & coll, Equip loans & repairs, ILL available, Learning ctr, Microfiche/film & reading machines, Music CDs, Online cat, Online info literacy tutorials on the web & in blackboard, Online ref, Online searches, Orientations, Outside serv via phone, mail, e-mail & web, Photocopying/Printing, Printer for laptops & handheld devices, Ref serv available, Ref serv in person, Scanner, VHS videos, Web-catalog, Wheelchair accessible
Publications: Year in Review (Annual report)
Partic in Christian Library Consortium; Inland Empire Acad Libr Coop (IEALC); OCLC Online Computer Library Center, Inc; Southern Calif Area Theol Librns Asn; Southern California Theological Library Association (SCATLA); Statewide California Electronic Library Consortium (SCELC); Westchester Academic Library Directors Organization (WALDO)
Special Services for the Deaf - Assistive tech; Bks on deafness & sign lang
Special Services for the Blind - Assistive/Adapted tech devices, equip & products; Braille bks
Open Mon-Thurs 7:30am-Midnight, Fri 7:30-6, Sat Noon-6, Sun 2-Midnight

LA VERNE

C UNIVERSITY OF LA VERNE*, Elvin & Betty Wilson Library, 2040 Third St, 91750. SAN 332-205X. Tel: 909-593-3511, Ext 4305. Circulation Tel: 909-593-3511, Ext 4301. Interlibrary Loan Service Tel: 909-593-3511, Ext 4309. Administration Tel: 909-593-3511, Ext 4304. Automation Services Tel: 909-593-3511, Ext 4307. FAX: 909-392-2733. E-mail: reference@ulv.edu. Web Site: www.ulv.edu/library. *Prof, Univ Librn,* Vinaya Tripuraneni; E-mail: vtripuraneni@laverne.edu; *Prof, User Serv Librn,* Dona Bentley; *Prof, Res & Instruction Librn,* Linda Gordon; *Asst Prof, Res & Instruction Librn,* Andre Ambrus; *Asst Prof, Instrul Tech Librn, Web Librn,* Erin Gratz; *Asst Prof, Info Literacy Librn,* Shelley Urbizagastegui; *Assessment Librn, Asst Prof,* Darryl Swarm; *Evening/Weekend Librn,* Alex Valdivia; Staff 18 (MLS 9, Non-MLS 9)
Founded 1891. Enrl 5,947; Fac 263; Highest Degree: Doctorate
Library Holdings: e-books 2,476; e-journals 11,400; Bk Vols 148,790; Per Subs 11,585; Videos 2,462
Automation Activity & Vendor Info: (Acquisitions) Innovative Interfaces, Inc; (Cataloging) Innovative Interfaces, Inc; (Circulation) Innovative Interfaces, Inc; (ILL) OCLC; (OPAC) Innovative Interfaces, Inc; (Serials) Innovative Interfaces, Inc
Database Vendor: Cambridge Scientific Abstracts, EBSCOhost, LexisNexis, OCLC WorldShare Interlibrary Loan, ProQuest, SerialsSolutions, Wilson - Wilson Web
Function: Archival coll, ILL available
Partic in Inland Empire Acad Libr Coop (IEALC); New England Law Library Consortium, Inc; OCLC Western Service Center; Statewide California Electronic Library Consortium (SCELC)
Friends of the Library Group

LAFAYETTE

R LAFAYETTE-ORINDA PRESBYTERIAN CHURCH LIBRARY*, 49 Knox Dr, 94549. SAN 300-855X. Tel: 925-283-8722. FAX: 925-283-0138. Web Site: www.lopc.org. *Librn,* Betty Graves
Library Holdings: Bk Vols 1,957
Open Mon-Fri 8:30-5, Sun 8-1

S SOYINFO CENTER LIBRARY*, 1021 Dolores Dr, 94549-2907. (Mail add: PO Box 234, 94549-0234), SAN 325-4925. Tel: 925-283-2991. Web Site: www.soyinfocenter.com. *Head Librn,* William Shurtleff; Staff 1 (MLS 1)
Founded 1976
Library Holdings: e-books 38; Bk Titles 2,613; Per Subs 12
Special Collections: Soybeans & Soyfoods Coll, archives, bks, databases (1100 BC-present), reprints. Oral History
Subject Interests: Soybeans, Soyfoods, Vegitarianism
Publications: Bibliographies of Soya Series; Digital History of Soy Series; History of Soybeans & Soyfoods Series; Soyfoods Industry & Market Directory & Databook; Thesaurus for Soya
Restriction: Open to pub by appt only
Friends of the Library Group

R TEMPLE ISAIAH*, Cantor Ted Cotler Memorial Library, 3800 Mount Diablo Blvd, 94549. Tel: 925-283-8575, Ext 322. FAX: 925-283-8355. Web Site: www.temple-isaiah.org, www.temple-isaiah.org/temple/isaiah/community/C50. *Librn,* Val Morehouse; E-mail: valm.library@temple-isaiah.org; Staff 2 (MLS 1, Non-MLS 1)
Jun 2008-May 2009 Income $50,000, Locally Generated Income $1,000, Parent Institution $2,500, Other $4,120. Mats Exp $4,300, Books $3,000, Per/Ser (Incl. Access Fees) $600, AV Mat $600, Electronic Ref Mat (Incl. Access Fees) $100. Sal $28,700
Library Holdings: AV Mats 665; Bk Vols 6,886; Per Subs 26; Spec Interest Per Sub 26; Talking Bks 30; Videos 455
Special Collections: Children's Coll; Jewish Music Coll; Jewish Parenting Coll; Jewish Videos & Audios; Multicultural Judaism Coll
Subject Interests: Judaica
Automation Activity & Vendor Info: (Cataloging) Follett Software; (Circulation) Follett Software; (OPAC) Follett Software
Wireless access
Function: CD-ROM, Handicapped accessible, ILL available, Music CDs, Online searches, Photocopying/Printing, Prog for adults, Prog for children & young adult, Ref serv available, Spoken cassettes & CDs, Telephone ref, VHS videos
Publications: Ruach/Library Column (Monthly bulletin)
Special Services for the Deaf - Closed caption videos
Open Tues 1-6, Wed 1-8:30, Thurs 8:30-1, Sun 9-1
Restriction: In-house use for visitors, Non-circulating to the pub, Open to fac, students & qualified researchers, Pub use on premises

LAKEPORT

S HISTORIC COURTHOUSE MUSEUM LIBRARY, 255 N Main St, 95453. (Mail add: 255 N Forbes, 95453), SAN 329-966X. Tel: 707-263-4555. FAX: 707-263-7918. E-mail: museum@lakecountyca.gov. *Curator,* Linda Lake
Library Holdings: Bk Vols 500
Special Collections: Historic County Court Records; Lake County, California History Coll
Wireless access
Open Wed-Sat 10-4
Friends of the Library Group

GL LAKE COUNTY LAW LIBRARY*, 175 Third St, 95453. (Mail add: 255 N Forbes St, 95453), SAN 320-5673. Tel: 707-263-2205. FAX: 707-263-2207. Web Site: www.lakecountyca.gov/law. *Law Librn,* Casse Waldman Forczek
Library Holdings: Bk Vols 7,500
Special Collections: Federal Cases, micro; Local Ordinances
Database Vendor: LexisNexis
Function: Computers for patron use, Copy machines, ILL available, Pub access computers
Open Mon-Fri 10-4:30
Restriction: Circ limited, Lending limited to county residents

P LAKE COUNTY LIBRARY*, Lakeport Library, 1425 N High St, 95453-3800. SAN 332-2114. Tel: 707-263-8816. FAX: 707-263-6796. E-mail: Library@co.lake.ca.us. Web Site: www.co.lake.ca.us/library/library.html. *County Librn,* Susan Jean Clayton; *Circ,* Barbara Green; *Circ, Tech Serv,* Amy Patton; *Circ, Tech Serv,* Christopher Veach; *ILL, Tech Serv,* Jan Cook; Staff 2 (MLS 2)
Founded 1974. Pop 63,000; Circ 207,000
Library Holdings: Bk Vols 145,000; Per Subs 174
Special Collections: Geothermal Resources; Lake County History; Pomo Indians
Automation Activity & Vendor Info: (Cataloging) SirsiDynix; (Circulation) SirsiDynix; (OPAC) SirsiDynix
Database Vendor: OCLC FirstSearch
Wireless access
Mem of NorthNet Library System
Open Tues & Thurs-Sat 10-5, Wed 12-8
Friends of the Library Group
Branches: 3
MIDDLETOWN BRANCH, 21256 Washington St, Middletown, 95461. (Mail add: PO Box 578, Middletown, 95461-0578), SAN 332-2149. Tel: 707-987-3674. FAX: 707-987-3674. *Br Mgr,* Gehlen Palmer
Library Holdings: Bk Vols 10,238
Open Tues, Thurs & Fri 1-6, Wed 1-6, Sat 10-3
Friends of the Library Group
REDBUD, 14785 Burns Valley Rd, Clearlake, 95422-0600, SAN 332-2173. Tel: 707-994-5115. FAX: 707-995-6012. *Librn,* Irwin Feldman; Staff 1 (MLS 1)
Library Holdings: Bk Vols 35,129
Open Tues & Thurs-Sat 10-5, Wed 12-8
Friends of the Library Group
UPPER LAKE BRANCH, 310 Second St, Upper Lake, 95485. (Mail add: PO Box 486, Upper Lake, 95485-0486), SAN 332-2203. Tel: 707-275-2049. *Br Mgr,* Linda Bushta
Library Holdings: Bk Vols 10,478
Open Tues-Fri 1-6, Sat 10-3
Friends of the Library Group

LANCASTER

J ANTELOPE VALLEY COLLEGE LIBRARY*, 3041 W Ave K, 93536-5426. SAN 300-8584. Tel: 661-722-6533. FAX: 661-722-6456. E-mail: libraryinfo@avc.edu. Web Site: www.avc.edu/studentservices/library. *Dean, Institutional Effectiveness, Res & Planning,* Meeta Goel; E-mail: mgoel@avc.edu; *Info Competency Librn,* Scott Lee; *Ref & Instrul Serv Librn,* Van Rider; *Ref/Electronic Res Librn,* Carolyn Burrell; E-mail: cburrell@avc.edu; Staff 3 (MLS 3)
Founded 1962. Enrl 8,800; Fac 320
Library Holdings: Bk Vols 50,000
Automation Activity & Vendor Info: (Acquisitions) SirsiDynix; (Cataloging) SirsiDynix; (Circulation) SirsiDynix; (Course Reserve) SirsiDynix; (ILL) OCLC; (OPAC) SirsiDynix; (Serials) SirsiDynix
Database Vendor: EBSCOhost

LARKSPUR

P LARKSPUR PUBLIC LIBRARY*, 400 Magnolia Ave, 94939. SAN 300-8592. Tel: 415-927-5005. FAX: 415-927-5136. Web Site: www.larkspurlibrary.org. *Dir,* Frances Gordon
Pop 12,000; Circ 98,000
Library Holdings: Bk Titles 55,000; Per Subs 100
Wireless access
Friends of the Library Group

LEMON GROVE

S PRICE-POTTENGER NUTRITION FOUNDATION LIBRARY, 7890 Broadway, 91945. SAN 371-4268. Tel: 619-462-7600. Toll Free Tel: 800-366-3748. FAX: 619-433-3136. E-mail: info@ppnf.org. Web Site: www.ppnf.org.
Founded 1965
Library Holdings: CDs 1,273; DVDs 385; Bk Titles 7,014; Per Subs 20; Videos 385
Special Collections: Bernard Jensen Coll; Dr Emmanuel Cheraskin Coll; Dr Francis M Pottenger Jr Coll; Dr George E Meinig, DDS Coll; Dr Granville Knight, MD Coll; Dr Henry Bieler Coll; Dr John Myers Coll; Dr Martha Jones, PhD Coll; Dr Melvin Page Coll; Dr Royal Lee Coll, Lee Foundation; Dr Weston A Price, DDS Coll; Dr William Albrecht Coll; Edgar Cayce Coll; Edward Rosenow Coll; George Chapman Coll; Lee Foundation Coll
Subject Interests: Dental, Ecology, Gardening, Health, Nutrition
Function: Res libr
Publications: Journal of Health and Healing (Quarterly)
Restriction: Mem only, Not a lending libr, Open by appt only

LEMOORE

J WEST HILLS COLLEGE LEMOORE LIBRARY*, 555 College Ave, 93245. SAN 300-7421. Tel: 559-925-3403. Circulation Tel: 559-925-3420. FAX: 559-924-1662. TDD: 559-924-8158. Web Site: www.westhillscollege.com/lemoore/academics/library/index.asp. *Librn,* Ron Lynn Oxford; E-mail: ronoxford@westhillscollege.com; Staff 3 (MLS 1, Non-MLS 2)
Founded 2002. Enrl 2,000; Highest Degree: Associate
Jul 2007-Jun 2008 Income $200,000. Mats Exp $75,000, Books $27,500, AV Equip $10,000, AV Mat $1,500, Electronic Ref Mat (Incl. Access Fees) $36,000. Sal $94,000 (Prof $56,000)
Library Holdings: CDs 1,500; DVDs 1,004; e-books 11,400; Bk Vols 35,000; Per Subs 97
Automation Activity & Vendor Info: (Acquisitions) SirsiDynix; (Cataloging) SirsiDynix; (Circulation) SirsiDynix; (Course Reserve) SirsiDynix; (ILL) SirsiDynix; (Media Booking) SirsiDynix; (OPAC) SirsiDynix; (Serials) SirsiDynix
Database Vendor: Alexander Street Press, Baker & Taylor, EBSCOhost, Gale Cengage Learning, OCLC WorldShare Interlibrary Loan, ProQuest, SirsiDynix
Wireless access
Function: Archival coll, AV serv, Copy machines, Distance learning, Handicapped accessible, Homework prog, Learning ctr, Online searches, Orientations, Ref & res, Ref serv available, VHS videos
Partic in Community College League of California (CCLC)
Special Services for the Blind - Computer with voice synthesizer for visually impaired persons; Reader equip
Open Mon-Thurs 7:30am-8pm, Fri 7:30-4
Restriction: Borrowing privileges limited to fac & registered students, Circ to mem only, In-house use for visitors, Open to students, fac & staff

LINCOLN

P LINCOLN PUBLIC LIBRARY*, 485 Twelve Bridges Dr, 95648. SAN 300-8622. Tel: 916-434-2410. Administration Tel: 916-434-2409. FAX: 919-409-9235. E-mail: library@ci.lincoln.ca.us. Web Site: www.libraryatlincoln.org. *Coordr,* Renae Mahaffey; E-mail: rmahaffey@ci.lincoln.ca.us; Staff 2.9 (MLS 0.5, Non-MLS 2.4)
Founded 1906. Pop 40,000; Circ 328,768
Library Holdings: Bk Vols 101,387
Automation Activity & Vendor Info: (Acquisitions) Ex Libris Group; (Cataloging) Ex Libris Group; (Circulation) Ex Libris Group; (ILL) OCLC; (OPAC) Ex Libris Group; (Serials) Ex Libris Group
Database Vendor: Gale Cengage Learning, ProQuest
Wireless access
Function: Adult bk club, Art exhibits, Audio & video playback equip for onsite use, Bks on CD, Children's prog, Computer training, Computers for patron use, Copy machines, Free DVD rentals, Genealogy discussion group, Holiday prog, Homework prog, ILL available, Music CDs, Online cat, Prog for adults, Prog for children & young adult, Pub access computers, Ref serv available, Ref serv in person, Story hour, Summer reading prog, Teen prog, Telephone ref, Wheelchair accessible
Special Services for the Deaf - Bks on deafness & sign lang; Closed caption videos; Staff with knowledge of sign lang
Special Services for the Blind - Bks on cassette; Bks on CD; Large print bks; Low vision equip
Friends of the Library Group

LIVERMORE

J LAS POSITAS COLLEGE LIBRARY*, 3000 Campus Hill Dr, 94551-7623. SAN 300-8630. Tel: 925-424-1150. Circulation Tel: 925-424-1151. FAX: 925-606-7249. Web Site: www.laspositascollege.edu/library. *Coordr,* Cheryl Warren; *Ref Serv,* Frances Hui; *Ref,* Angela Amaya; *Ref,* Tina Inzerilla; Staff 4 (MLS 4)
Founded 1975. Enrl 4,665
Library Holdings: Bk Titles 34,000; Per Subs 100
Automation Activity & Vendor Info: (Acquisitions) SirsiDynix; (Cataloging) SirsiDynix; (Circulation) SirsiDynix; (Course Reserve) SirsiDynix; (OPAC) SirsiDynix; (Serials) SirsiDynix
Wireless access
Partic in Bay Area Library & Information Network; California Community College Library Consortium (CCLC); OCLC Online Computer Library Center, Inc
Open Mon-Thurs 8-7, Fri 8-2

S LAWRENCE LIVERMORE NATIONAL LABORATORY LIBRARY*, 7000 East Ave, 94550. (Mail add: PO Box 5500, 94550-5500), SAN 300-8665. Tel: 925-424-6105. FAX: 925-424-2921. E-mail: library-reference@llnl.gov. Web Site: www.llnl.gov/library. *Libr Mgr,* Mary Allen; Tel: 925-423-8386; Staff 8 (MLS 5, Non-MLS 3)
Founded 1952
Library Holdings: Bk Vols 335,000; Per Subs 7,179
Automation Activity & Vendor Info: (Acquisitions) SirsiDynix; (Cataloging) SirsiDynix; (Circulation) SirsiDynix; (Course Reserve) SirsiDynix; (ILL) Relais International; (Media Booking) SirsiDynix; (OPAC) SirsiDynix; (Serials) SirsiDynix
Database Vendor: STN International
Wireless access
Publications: New Titles
Partic in BRS; Dialog Corp; NASA Libraries Information System-NASA Galaxie; RLIN (Research Libraries Information Network)
Restriction: Authorized patrons, Authorized personnel only, Restricted loan policy

P LIVERMORE PUBLIC LIBRARY, 1188 S Livermore Ave, 94550. SAN 300-8649. Tel: 925-373-5500. Circulation Tel: 925-373-5502. Reference Tel: 925-373-5505. Administration Tel: 925-373-5509. Automation Services Tel: 925-373-5512. FAX: 925-373-5503. E-mail: lib@livermore.lib.ca.us. Web Site: www.livermorelibrary.net. *Dir,* Tamera LeBeau; E-mail: tklebeau@livermore.lib.ca.us; Staff 28 (MLS 11.5, Non-MLS 16.5)
Founded 1896. Pop 84,852; Circ 849,145
Jul 2013-Jun 2014 Income (Main Library and Branch(s)) $3,792,698, State $42,694, City $3,690,004, Locally Generated Income $60,000. Mats Exp $324,640, Books $157,000, Per/Ser (Incl. Access Fees) $22,000, Other Print Mats $4,740, Micro $2,500, AV Mat $28,400, Electronic Ref Mat (Incl. Access Fees) $110,000. Sal $2,812,109 (Prof $1,406,055)
Library Holdings: Audiobooks 3,765; CDs 858; DVDs 9,178; e-books 19,008; Electronic Media & Resources 39; Microforms 3,076; Bk Titles 145,045; Bk Vols 214,094; Per Subs 290
Subject Interests: Local hist
Automation Activity & Vendor Info: (Acquisitions) Innovative Interfaces, Inc; (Cataloging) Innovative Interfaces, Inc; (Circulation) Innovative Interfaces, Inc; (OPAC) Innovative Interfaces, Inc; (Serials) Innovative Interfaces, Inc
Database Vendor: American Physical Society, Baker & Taylor, Bowker, Brodart, Civica, CQ Press, EBSCO Auto Repair Reference, Evanced Solutions, Inc, Gale Cengage Learning, Ingram Library Services, Innovative Interfaces, Inc, LearningExpress, OCLC WorldShare Interlibrary Loan, Overdrive, Inc, ProQuest, Tech Logic
Wireless access
Function: 24/7 Electronic res, 24/7 Online cat, Accelerated reader prog, Adult bk club, Adult literacy prog, Art exhibits, Audiobks via web, Bilingual assistance for Spanish patrons, Bk club(s), Bks on CD, Children's prog, Computer training, Computers for patron use, Copy machines, Digital talking bks, e-mail & chat, E-Reserves, Electronic databases & coll, Exhibits, Fax serv, Free DVD rentals, Handicapped accessible, Holiday prog, ILL available, Jazz prog, Magazines, Mail & tel request accepted, Microfiche/film & reading machines, Online cat, Online ref, Online searches, Outside serv via phone, mail, e-mail & web, OverDrive digital audio bks, Photocopying/Printing, Preschool outreach, Preschool reading prog, Prog for adults, Prog for children & young adult, Pub access computers, Ref serv available, Scanner, Senior computer classes, Spoken cassettes & CDs, Story hour, Study rm, Summer reading prog, Tax forms, Teen prog, Telephone ref, Web-catalog
Publications: Annual Report; Strategic Services Plan; Technology Plan
Mem of Pacific Library Partnership (PLP)
Open Mon-Thurs 10-9, Fri 10-6, Sat 10-5, Sun 12-6
Friends of the Library Group
Branches: 2
RINCON, 725 Rincon Ave, 94550, SAN 377-5933. Tel: 925-373-5540.
Founded 1996. Pop 15,000; Circ 50,226
Library Holdings: Audiobooks 311; DVDs 1,699; Large Print Bks 145; Bk Vols 20,010; Per Subs 25
Function: Bilingual assistance for Spanish patrons, Bks on CD, Children's prog, Computers for patron use, Copy machines, Digital talking bks, Electronic databases & coll, Free DVD rentals, Handicapped accessible, Holiday prog, Homework prog, ILL available, Online cat, OverDrive digital audio bks, Preschool reading prog, Prog for children & young adult, Pub access computers, Story hour, Summer reading prog
Open Mon 12-8, Wed 10-6, Fri 10-5
SPRINGTOWN, 998 Bluebell Dr, 94550, SAN 377-595X. Tel: 925-373-5517.
Founded 1986. Pop 12,000
Library Holdings: Audiobooks 268; DVDs 1,337; Large Print Bks 78; Bk Vols 18,196; Per Subs 10
Open Tues 12-8, Thurs 9-1
Friends of the Library Group

S SANDIA NATIONAL LABORATORIES*, Technical Library, 7011 East Ave, 94550. (Mail add: PO Box 969, MS 9960, 94551-0969), SAN 300-8657. Tel: 925-294-1029. FAX: 925-294-2355. *Mgr,* Karen Cardwell; E-mail: kjcardw@sandia.gov
Founded 1956
Library Holdings: Bk Titles 12,000; Per Subs 575
Subject Interests: Chem, Computer sci, Energy, Eng, Math, Nuclear sci, Physics
Automation Activity & Vendor Info: (Acquisitions) SirsiDynix; (Cataloging) SirsiDynix; (Circulation) SirsiDynix; (Serials) SirsiDynix
Function: Res libr
Restriction: Not open to pub

LODI

P LODI PUBLIC LIBRARY*, 201 W Locust St, 95240. SAN 300-8681. Tel: 209-333-5566. Reference Tel: 209-333-5503. Administration Tel: 209-333-5534. FAX: 209-367-5944. E-mail: library@lodi.gov. Web Site: www.lodi.gov/library. *Dir, Libr Serv,* Nancy Martinez; Tel: 209-333-5540, E-mail: nmartinez@lodi.gov; *Libr Serv Mgr,* Andrea D Woodruff; Tel: 209-333-5505, E-mail: awoodruff@lodi.gov; *Ch Serv,* James Tinder; Tel: 209-333-6800, Ext 2008, E-mail: jtinder@lodi.gov; *Ref Serv,* Behjat Kerdegari; E-mail: bkerdegari@lodi.gov; *Ref Serv,* Sandy Sue Smith; E-mail: ssmith@lodi.gov; Staff 5 (MLS 5)
Founded 1907. Pop 63,000; Circ 260,000
Library Holdings: Bk Titles 130,000; Per Subs 150; Videos 2,000
Special Collections: Lodi History & Californiana, micro, photog
Automation Activity & Vendor Info: (Acquisitions) SirsiDynix; (Cataloging) SirsiDynix; (Circulation) SirsiDynix; (ILL) SirsiDynix; (OPAC) SirsiDynix; (Serials) SirsiDynix
Database Vendor: ALLDATA Online, Gale Cengage Learning, infoUSA, LearningExpress
Wireless access
Function: Adult bk club, Adult literacy prog, Art exhibits, Computer training, Handicapped accessible, Homework prog, ILL available, Magnifiers for reading, Prog for children & young adult, Pub access computers, Summer reading prog, Teen prog, VHS videos
Partic in 49-99 Cooperative Library System
Open Mon Noon-9, Tues & Wed 9-9, Thurs 9-6, Sat 9-2, Sun 1-5
Friends of the Library Group

S SAN JOAQUIN COUNTY HISTORICAL MUSEUM, Gerald D Kennedy Reference Library, 11793 N Micke Grove Rd, 95241. (Mail add: PO Box 30, 95241-0030), SAN 327-8905. Tel: 209-331-2055. FAX: 209-331-2057. E-mail: info@sanjoaquinhistory.org. Web Site: www.sanjoaquinhistory.org. *Librn & Archivist,* Dr Leigh Johnsen; E-mail: leighjohnsen@sanjoaquinhistory.org; Staff 1 (MLS 0.5, Non-MLS 0.5)
Founded 1986
Library Holdings: Bk Vols 3,000; Per Subs 12
Special Collections: Agricultural Technology Manuals; City of Lodi Records; City of Stockton Records; San Joaquin County Records; UC Cooperative Agricultural Extension Records, San Joaquin County; Weber Family Papers. Oral History
Subject Interests: Local county hist
Function: Archival coll, Photocopying/Printing, Ref serv available, Res libr
Partic in Califa
Restriction: In-house use for visitors, Not a lending libr, Open by appt only

S SRI AUROBINDO SADHANA PEETHAM LIBRARY*, 2621 W Hwy 12, 95242. SAN 327-1668. Tel: 209-339-1342, 209-339-3710. FAX: 209-339-3715. E-mail: sasp@lodinet.com. Web Site: sasp.collaboration.org. *Librn,* Dakshina Vanzetti
Library Holdings: Bk Titles 2,000

Special Collections: Ayurveda & Health; Classical Indian Spiritual Tradition; Collected Works of Sri Aurobindo; Collected Works of the Mother; Yoga
Restriction: Open by appt only

LOMA LINDA

GM DEPARTMENT OF VETERANS AFFAIRS*, Medical Center Library Service, 11201 Benton St, 92357. SAN 300-869X. Tel: 909-422-3000, Ext 2970. FAX: 909-422-3164. *Librn,* Erica Bass; *Tech Serv,* Lynn LaVigueur; Staff 2 (MLS 1, Non-MLS 1)
Founded 1977
Library Holdings: Bk Titles 2,000; Per Subs 201
Subject Interests: Med
Automation Activity & Vendor Info: (Cataloging) Innovative Interfaces, Inc; (Circulation) Innovative Interfaces, Inc
Database Vendor: OVID Technologies, PubMed
Wireless access
Open Mon-Fri 7:30-4:30

C LOMA LINDA UNIVERSITY*, Del E Webb Memorial Library, 11072 Anderson St, 92350-0001. SAN 332-2297. Tel: 909-558-4581. Circulation Tel: 909-558-4550. Interlibrary Loan Service Tel: 909-558-4925. Reference Tel: 909-558-4588. FAX: 909-558-4121. Interlibrary Loan Service FAX: 909-558-4188. Web Site: library.llu.edu. *Dir,* Carlene Drake; *Cat Librn,* Warren Johns; *Access Serv,* Elisa Cortez; *Per,* Shirley Rais; *Ref,* Gurmeet Sehgal; *Ref,* Shan Tamares; *Spec Coll & Archives Librn,* Lori Curtis; *Tech Serv,* Nelia Wurangian; Staff 30 (MLS 8, Non-MLS 22)
Founded 1907. Enrl 4,026; Highest Degree: Doctorate
Jul 2010-Jun 2011. Mats Exp $1,735,938, Books $82,707, Per/Ser (Incl. Access Fees) $1,033,334, Electronic Ref Mat (Incl. Access Fees) $619,897. Sal $1,551,352
Library Holdings: e-journals 11,299; Bk Titles 212,712; Bk Vols 385,015
Special Collections: Archival Coll; Medicine (Peter C Remondino Coll), bks, Archives of American Dental Society of Anesthesiology; Seventh-Day Adventist Church (Heritage Coll). Oral History
Subject Interests: Health sci, Med, Relig
Automation Activity & Vendor Info: (Acquisitions) Innovative Interfaces, Inc; (Cataloging) Innovative Interfaces, Inc; (Circulation) Innovative Interfaces, Inc; (Course Reserve) Innovative Interfaces, Inc; (ILL) Innovative Interfaces, Inc; (Media Booking) Innovative Interfaces, Inc; (OPAC) Innovative Interfaces, Inc; (Serials) Innovative Interfaces, Inc
Database Vendor: Innovative Interfaces, Inc
Wireless access
Partic in Adventist Librs Info Coop; Inland Empire Acad Libr Coop (IEALC); National Network of Libraries of Medicine; Statewide California Electronic Library Consortium (SCELC)
Open Mon-Thurs 7:30am-11pm, Fri 7:30-2, Sun 10am-11pm

LOMPOC

P LOMPOC PUBLIC LIBRARY, 501 E North Ave, 93436-3498. SAN 332-2351. Tel: 805-875-8775. Reference Tel: 805-875-8778. Administration Tel: 805-875-8787. FAX: 805-736-6440. E-mail: lomref@blackgold.org. Web Site: www.cityoflompoc.com/library. *Libr Dir,* Jessica Cadiente; Tel: 805-875-8785, E-mail: j_cadiente@ci.lompoc.ca.us; *Libr Mgr,* Position Currently Open, *Youth Serv,* Lezlee Hurtado; Tel: 805-875-8781; *Ref Asst,* Michelle Davenport; *Ref Asst,* Elizabeth Hamilton; *Ref Asst,* Maria Parker; Staff 27 (MLS 2, Non-MLS 25)
Founded 1907. Pop 66,000
Special Collections: Local History Coll
Subject Interests: Gardening, Hort
Automation Activity & Vendor Info: (Acquisitions) Innovative Interfaces, Inc; (Cataloging) Innovative Interfaces, Inc; (Circulation) Innovative Interfaces, Inc; (OPAC) Innovative Interfaces, Inc; (Serials) Innovative Interfaces, Inc
Database Vendor: Baker & Taylor, Overdrive, Inc
Wireless access
Mem of Black Gold Cooperative Library System
Open Mon-Thurs 10-7, Fri & Sat 1-5
Friends of the Library Group
Branches: 2
BUELLTON BRANCH, 140 W Hwy 246, Buellton, 93427. (Mail add: PO Box 187, Buellton, 93427), SAN 332-2386. Tel: 805-688-3115. FAX: 805-688-3115. E-mail: buellton@blackgold.org. *Br Supvr,* Elizabeth Chapman; Staff 4.5 (Non-MLS 4.5)
Founded 1923. Pop 5,382
Open Mon & Tues 11-8, Wed-Fri 10-6, Sat 12:30-5:30
Friends of the Library Group
VILLAGE, 3755 Constellation Rd, 93436, SAN 332-2416. Tel: 805-733-3323. FAX: 805-733-3323. *Br Mgr,* Stacy Brigman; Staff 2.5 (Non-MLS 2.5)
Founded 1976
Open Tues & Wed 10-6, Thurs 1-8, Fri & Sat 1-6
Friends of the Library Group

LONG BEACH

C CALIFORNIA STATE UNIVERSITY, LONG BEACH*, University Library, 1250 N Bellflower Blvd, 90840. SAN 300-8711. Tel: 562-985-4047. FAX: 562-985-8131. Web Site: www.csulb.edu/library. *Dean & Dir, Libr Serv,* Roman V Kochan; Staff 21 (MLS 19, Non-MLS 2)
Founded 1949. Enrl 32,686; Fac 2,001; Highest Degree: Doctorate
Jul 2012-Jun 2013. Mats Exp $1,817,152, Books $149,475, Per/Ser (Incl. Access Fees) $601,013, Other Print Mats $43,412, AV Mat $10,640, Electronic Ref Mat (Incl. Access Fees) $1,011,759, Presv $853. Sal $3,571,488 (Prof $1,726,114)
Library Holdings: Audiobooks 1,866; CDs 8,920; DVDs 4,834; e-books 378,254; e-journals 74,790; Microforms 1,502,855; Bk Titles 663,099; Bk Vols 1,102,003; Per Subs 1,956
Special Collections: Abolition Movement (Dumond Coll); Art Prints & Photography Coll; Arts in Southern California Archive; California History (Bekeart Coll); Radical Politics in California (Dorothy Healey Coll); Theater History (Pasadena Playhouse Coll), playscripts; United States Revolutionary War; University Archives. Oral History; State Document Depository; US Document Depository
Automation Activity & Vendor Info: (Acquisitions) Innovative Interfaces, Inc; (Cataloging) Innovative Interfaces, Inc; (Circulation) Innovative Interfaces, Inc; (Course Reserve) Innovative Interfaces, Inc; (ILL) OCLC ILLiad; (OPAC) Innovative Interfaces, Inc; (Serials) Innovative Interfaces, Inc
Database Vendor: ABC-CLIO, ACM (Association for Computing Machinery), Agricola, Alexander Street Press, American Chemical Society, American Geophysical Union, American Mathematical Society, American Physical Society, American Psychological Association (APA), Amigos Library Services, Annual Reviews, ARTstor, ASCE Research Library, Baker & Taylor, Blackwell, Cambridge Scientific Abstracts, Checkpoint Systems, Inc, Cinahl, CIOS (Communication Institute for Online Scholarship), College Source, CountryWatch, CQ Press, CRC Press/Taylor & Francis Group, ebrary, EBSCO Information Services, EBSCOhost, Emerald, Ex Libris Group, Factiva.com, H W Wilson, Haworth Pres Inc, HeinOnline, Hoovers, IBISWorld, IEEE (Institute of Electrical & Electronics Engineers), Ingenta, Innovative Interfaces, Inc, IOP, ISI Web of Knowledge, Jane's, JSTOR, LexisNexis, Marcive, Inc, Medline, Mergent Online, Nature Publishing Group, OCLC FirstSearch, OCLC WorldShare Interlibrary Loan, OVID Technologies, Oxford Online, Paratext, Project MUSE, ProQuest, PubMed, RefWorks, Safari Books Online, Sage, ScienceDirect, SerialsSolutions, Springer-Verlag, Standard & Poor's, STN International, Thomson - Web of Science, ValueLine, Westlaw, Wiley InterScience
Wireless access
Publications: Library Skills
Partic in Statewide California Electronic Library Consortium (SCELC)
Open Mon-Fri 6:45am-11pm, Sat 10-5, Sun 12:30-11
Friends of the Library Group

M COLLEGE MEDICAL CENTER, Harris Memorial Library, (Formerly Pacific Hospital of Long Beach), 2776 Pacific Ave, 90806. SAN 300-8800. Tel: 562 997-2182. FAX: 562-595-0271. *Med Librn,* Phillip Garcia; E-mail: phillip.garcia@molinahealthcare.com; Staff 1 (MLS 1)
Founded 1964
Library Holdings: Bk Titles 722; Per Subs 145
Subject Interests: Acupuncture, Med, Nursing, Osteopathology, Osteopathy, Podiatry
Function: Bks on cassette, ILL available, Online searches, Ref serv available
Partic in Medical Library Group of Southern California & Arizona (MLGSCA)
Open Mon-Fri 8-5

C DEVRY UNIVERSITY*, Long Beach Campus Library, 3880 Kilroy Airport Way, 90806. Tel: 562-997-5507. FAX: 562-997-5389. Web Site: www.lb.devry.edu/campus_library.html, www.library.devry.edu. *Librn,* Heather L Burke; Tel: 562-997-5581, E-mail: hburke@devry.edu; *Libr Assoc,* Colleen Mulhall-Briski; Tel: 562-997-5351, E-mail: cbriski@devry.edu; Staff 2 (MLS 1, Non-MLS 1)
Highest Degree: Master
Library Holdings: AV Mats 2,250; Bk Vols 15,000; Per Subs 80
Automation Activity & Vendor Info: (Acquisitions) Baker & Taylor; (Cataloging) Baker & Taylor; (Circulation) Baker & Taylor; (ILL) OCLC; (OPAC) Baker & Taylor
Database Vendor: Agricola, Baker & Taylor, Checkpoint Systems, Inc, Cinahl, CredoReference, EBSCOhost, Faulkner Information Services, IBISWorld, OCLC WorldShare Interlibrary Loan, Oxford Online, Plunkett Research, Ltd, PubMed, Safari Books Online
Wireless access
Function: CD-ROM, Copy machines, Electronic databases & coll, ILL available, Online ref, Ref serv available, Spoken cassettes & CDs, Telephone ref
Open Mon-Thurs 9-8, Fri 9-5

R FIRST BAPTIST CHURCH OF LAKEWOOD LIBRARY*, 5336 E Arbor Rd, 90808. SAN 300-872X. Tel: 562-420-1471, Ext 247. FAX: 562-420-9140. E-mail: info@1bl.org. Web Site: www.fbcol.org. *In Charge,* Sonja Friese
Founded 1950
Library Holdings: Bk Vols 9,500
Subject Interests: Biblical studies, Children's lit, Marriage, Missions & missionaries
Open Thurs & Sun 9-Noon

S HISTORICAL SOCIETY OF LONG BEACH*, 4260 Atlantic Ave, 90807. SAN 326-4807. Tel: 562-424-2220. FAX: 562-424-2262. E-mail: newspaper@hslb.org. Web Site: hslb.org. *Exec Dir,* Julie Bartolotto; E-mail: julieb@hslb.org; Staff 2 (Non-MLS 2)
Founded 1962
Library Holdings: Bk Titles 400
Special Collections: Documents; Historical Newspaper Coll; Pamphlets; Photograph Coll; Scrapbooks. Oral History
Subject Interests: Artifacts, Local hist, Maps
Function: Ref serv available
Publications: Photograph Journals
Open Tues, Wed & Fri 1-5, Thurs 1-7, Sat 11-5
Restriction: Non-circulating

J LONG BEACH CITY COLLEGE*, Liberal Arts Campus & Pacific Coast Campus Libraries, 4901 E Carson St, 90808. SAN 332-2475. Tel: 562-938-3028 (PCC Campus), 562-938-4232 (LAC Campus). Circulation Tel: 562-928-3029 (PCC Campus), 562-928-4231 (LAC Campus). Interlibrary Loan Service Tel: 562-938-4576, 562-938-4809. FAX: 562-938-3062, 562-938-4777. E-mail: pcclibrary@lbcc.edu. Web Site: www.lib.lbcc.edu. *Dept Head,* Position Currently Open; *Interim Dept Head,* Kim Barclay; E-mail: kbarclay@lbcc.edu; *Access Serv & Electronic Res Librn,* Nenita Buenaventura; E-mail: nbuenaventura@lbcc.edu; *Bibliog Instruction Librn,* Kim Barclay; Tel: 562-938-4708, E-mail: kbarclay@lbcc.edu; *Cat Librn,* Dele Ukwu; Tel: 562-938-4581, E-mail: dukwu@lbcc.edu; *Syst Librn,* Dena Laney; Tel: 562-938-4714, E-mail: dlaney@lbcc.edu; *Br Coordr,* Dr Ramachandran Sethuraman; Tel: 562-938-3115, E-mail: rsethuraman@lbcc.edu. Subject Specialists: *Allied health, Med, Sci,* Nenita Buenaventura; *Fine arts,* Kim Barclay; *Soc sci,* Dena Laney; Staff 28 (MLS 19, Non-MLS 9)
Founded 1927. Enrl 24,828; Highest Degree: Associate
Library Holdings: Bk Vols 145,639; Per Subs 466
Automation Activity & Vendor Info: (Cataloging) OCLC; (Circulation) OCLC; (ILL) OCLC FirstSearch; (OPAC) OCLC; (Serials) EBSCO Online
Database Vendor: 3M Library Systems, Bowker, CountryWatch, CQ Press, CRC Press/Taylor & Francis Group, EBSCOhost, Ex Libris Group, Facts on File, Gale Cengage Learning, H W Wilson, JSTOR, LearningExpress, Newsbank, OCLC FirstSearch, Oxford Online, ProQuest, SerialsSolutions
Wireless access
Open Mon-Thurs (LAC Campus) 7am-10pm, Fri 7-4, Sat 10-4; Mon-Thurs (PCC Campus) 8am-9pm, Fri 9-2:30, Sat 10-2
Friends of the Library Group

S LONG BEACH JEWISH COMMUNITY CENTER - THE ALPERT JCC*, Stanley S Zack Library, 3801 E Willow St, 90815. SAN 300-8762. Tel: 562-426-7601. FAX: 562-424-3915. Web Site: www.jewishlongbeach.org. *Exec Dir,* Jeff Antonoff; E-mail: jantonoff@alpertjcc.org
Founded 1961
Library Holdings: Bk Titles 3,500; Bk Vols 3,500; Per Subs 20
Subject Interests: Judaica (lit or hist of Jews)
Wireless access
Open Mon-Thurs 6am-10pm, Fri 6-6, Sat & Sun 7-6

M LONG BEACH MEMORIAL/MILLER CHILDREN'S HOSPITAL LONG BEACH*, Health Sciences & Parks Medical Libraries, 2801 Atlantic Ave, 90806-1737. SAN 300-8797. Tel: 562-933-3841. Administration Tel: 562-933-3851. FAX: 562-933-3847. E-mail: parksmedicallibrary@memorialcare.org. *Dir,* Judy Kraemer; E-mail: jkraemer@memorialcare.org; *Med Librn,* Carol Schechter; *Libr Tech,* Elizabeth Mason; E-mail: emrenteria@memorialcare.org. Subject Specialists: *Bus, Info tech, Med,* Judy Kraemer; *Med,* Carol Schechter; Staff 2 (MLS 1, Non-MLS 1)
Founded 1927
Library Holdings: Bk Titles 1,000; Bk Vols 2,100; Per Subs 600
Subject Interests: Allied health, Bus, Med, Nursing
Automation Activity & Vendor Info: (Acquisitions) SirsiDynix; (Cataloging) SirsiDynix; (Circulation) SirsiDynix; (OPAC) SirsiDynix; (Serials) SirsiDynix
Database Vendor: Cinahl, EBSCO Information Services, Elsevier, MD Consult, Medline, Micromedex, Natural Standard, OVID Technologies, PubMed, ScienceDirect, SirsiDynix, STAT!Ref (Teton Data Systems), UpToDate, Wiley InterScience
Wireless access
Function: Audio & video playback equip for onsite use, Computers for patron use, Copy machines, Doc delivery serv, E-Reserves, Electronic databases & coll, Handicapped accessible, Health sci info serv, ILL available, Online cat, Online ref, Online searches, Orientations, Outreach serv, Outside serv via phone, mail, e-mail & web, Photocopying/Printing, Prof lending libr, Ref & res, Ref serv available, Telephone ref, Web-catalog, Wheelchair accessible, Workshops
Publications: Fact Sheet (Documents)
Partic in Medical Library Group of Southern California & Arizona (MLGSCA); Statewide California Electronic Library Consortium (SCELC)
Restriction: Authorized personnel only

S LONG BEACH MUSEUM OF ART LIBRARY*, 2300 E Ocean Blvd, 90803. SAN 300-8770. Tel: 562-439-2119, Ext 226. FAX: 562-439-3587. Web Site: www.lbma.org. *Dir,* Ronald C Nelson
Founded 1957
Library Holdings: Bk Titles 2,000; Bk Vols 2,600
Wireless access
Open Thurs 11-8, Fri-Sun 11-5

P LONG BEACH PUBLIC LIBRARY*, 101 Pacific Ave, 90822-1097. SAN 332-2564. Tel: 562-570-7500. Circulation Tel: 562-570-6901. Interlibrary Loan Service Tel: 562-570-6053. FAX: 562-570-7408. TDD: 562-570-6744. Web Site: www.lbpl.org. *Dir,* Glenda Williams; *Mgr, Main Libr,* Darla Wegener; *Mgr, Cent & W Neighborhood Libr,* Position Currently Open; Staff 187 (MLS 47, Non-MLS 140)
Founded 1896. Pop 460,000; Circ 1,644,125
Oct 2011-Sept 2012 Income (Main Library and Branch(s)) $13,229,859. Mats Exp $1,079,000, Books $438,623, Per/Ser (Incl. Access Fees) $84,927, Electronic Ref Mat (Incl. Access Fees) $324,601. Sal $9,778,290
Library Holdings: Audiobooks 8,476; AV Mats 54,689; CDs 21,754; DVDs 24,459; e-books 79; e-journals 5,846; Electronic Media & Resources 17; Large Print Bks 8,974; Bk Titles 382,107; Bk Vols 844,950
Special Collections: Bertrand L Smith Rare Book; Long Beach History; Marilyn Horne Archives, pictures, press clippings, rec. State Document Depository; US Document Depository
Subject Interests: Petroleum
Automation Activity & Vendor Info: (Acquisitions) Innovative Interfaces, Inc - Millenium; (Cataloging) Innovative Interfaces, Inc - Millenium; (Circulation) Innovative Interfaces, Inc - Millenium; (ILL) Innovative Interfaces, Inc - Millenium; (OPAC) Innovative Interfaces, Inc - Millenium; (Serials) Innovative Interfaces, Inc - Millenium
Wireless access
Function: Adult bk club, Adult literacy prog, Audiobks via web, Bks on cassette, Bks on CD, Computer training, Computers for patron use, Copy machines, Electronic databases & coll, Family literacy, Handicapped accessible, Homework prog, ILL available, Magnifiers for reading, Music CDs, Online cat, Online ref, OverDrive digital audio bks, Photocopying/Printing, Prog for children & young adult, Ref & res, Ref serv in person, Story hour, Summer reading prog, Tax forms, Telephone ref, Wheelchair accessible
Mem of Nassau Library System
Partic in Coop Libr Agency for Syst & Servs; Southern Calif Interlibr Loan Network
Special Services for the Deaf - Assistive tech; Closed caption videos; TTY equip
Special Services for the Blind - Bks on cassette; Bks on CD; Reader equip; Screen reader software
Open Tues 10-8, Wed & Thurs 10-6, Fri & Sat 10-5
Friends of the Library Group
Branches: 11
ALAMITOS, 1836 E Third St, 90802, SAN 332-2599. Tel: 562-570-1037. *Br Mgr,* Silke Kinoshita
Library Holdings: Bk Vols 38,922
Open Tues & Thurs 12-7, Wed 12-6, Fri & Sat 10-5
Friends of the Library Group
RUTH BACH BRANCH, 4055 Bellflower Blvd, 90808, SAN 332-2629. Tel: 562-570-1038. *Br Mgr,* Chenda Yong; E-mail: chenda.yong@lbpl.org
Library Holdings: Bk Vols 45,946
Open Tues & Thurs 12-7, Wed 12-6, Fri & Sat 10-5
Friends of the Library Group
BAY SHORE, 195 Bay Shore Ave, 90803, SAN 332-2653. Tel: 562-570-1039. *Br Mgr,* Debbie Vilander; E-mail: debbie.vilander@lbpl.org
Library Holdings: Bk Vols 37,970
Open Tues & Thurs 12-7, Wed 12-6, Fri & Sat 10-5
Friends of the Library Group
BREWITT, 4036 E Anaheim St, 90804, SAN 332-2688. Tel: 562-570-1040. *Br Mgr,* Lynda Poling; E-mail: lynda.poling@lbpl.org
Library Holdings: Bk Vols 37,295
Open Tues & Thurs 12-7, Wed 12-6, Fri & Sat 10-5
Friends of the Library Group

BURNETT, 560 E Hill St, 90806, SAN 332-2718. Tel: 562-570-1041. *Br Mgr,* Erica Lansdown; E-mail: erica.lansdown@lbpl.org
Library Holdings: Bk Vols 53,713
Open Tues & Thurs 12-7, Wed 12-6, Fri & Sat 10-5
Friends of the Library Group

DANA, 3680 Atlantic Ave, 90807, SAN 332-2742. Tel: 562-570-1042. *Br Mgr,* Jennifer Songster; E-mail: jennifer.songster@lbpl.org
Library Holdings: Bk Vols 40,218
Open Tues & Thurs 12-7, Wed 12-6, Fri & Sat 10-5
Friends of the Library Group

EL DORADO, 2900 Studebaker Rd, 90815, SAN 332-2777. Tel: 562-570-3136. *Br Mgr,* Lynda Salem-Poling; E-mail: lynda.poling@lbpl.org
Library Holdings: Bk Vols 56,782
Open Tues & Thurs 12-7, Wed 12-6, Fri & Sat 10-5
Friends of the Library Group

BRET HARTE BRANCH, 1595 W Willow St, 90810, SAN 332-2807. Tel: 562-570-1044. *Br Mgr,* Stephen Quinney; E-mail: stephen.quinney@lbpl.org
Library Holdings: Bk Vols 53,391
Open Tues & Thurs 12-7, Wed 12-6, Fri & Sat 10-5
Friends of the Library Group

LOS ALTOS, 5614 E Britton Dr, 90815, SAN 332-2831. Tel: 562-570-1045. *Br Mgr,* Josephine Caron; E-mail: josephine.caron@lbpl.org; Staff 2 (MLS 2)
Founded 1957. Pop 41,286; Circ 141,286
Library Holdings: Bk Vols 49,287
Open Tues & Thurs 12-7, Wed 12-6, Fri & Sat 10-5
Friends of the Library Group

NORTH, 5571 Orange Ave, 90805, SAN 332-2920. Tel: 562-570-1047. *Br Mgr,* Cynthia Effraim; E-mail: cynthia.effraim@lbpl.org
Library Holdings: Bk Vols 37,342
Open Tues & Thurs 12-7, Wed 12-6, Fri & Sat 10-5
Friends of the Library Group

MARK TWAIN BRANCH, 1401 E Anaheim St, 90813, SAN 332-2890. Tel: 562-570-1046. *Br Mgr,* Jennifer Songster; E-mail: jennifer.songster@lbpl.org
Library Holdings: Bk Vols 63,000
Open Tues & Thurs 12-7, Wed 12-6, Fri & Sat 10-5
Friends of the Library Group

S RMS FOUNDATION, INC*, Hotel Queen Mary Historical Archives, 1126 Queens Hwy, 90802. SAN 326-2936. Tel: 562-435-3511. FAX: 562-437-4531. Web Site: www.queenmary.com. *Archivist,* Ron Smith; Staff 4 (MLS 3, Non-MLS 1)
Founded 1967
Library Holdings: Bk Titles 200
Special Collections: Original logbooks, manuals, plans and misc recs

M SAINT MARY MEDICAL CENTER*, Bellis Medical Library, 1050 Linden Ave, 90813. (Mail add: PO Box 887, 90801-0887), SAN 300-8819. Tel: 562-491-9295. FAX: 562-491-9293. *Mgr,* Linda Rubin; E-mail: linda.rubin@chw.edu
Founded 1955
Library Holdings: Bk Vols 1,500; Per Subs 100
Subject Interests: Hospital admin, Nursing
Partic in Medical Library Group of Southern California & Arizona (MLGSCA)
Open Mon-Thurs 8-4:30
Restriction: Med staff only

S SCS ENGINEERS LIBRARY*, 3900 Kilroy Airport Way, Ste 100, 90806-6816. SAN 373-028X. Tel: 562-426-9544. FAX: 562-427-0805. Web Site: www.scsengineers.com. *Librn,* Loran Bures; E-mail: lbures@scsengineers.com; Staff 1 (Non-MLS 1)
Founded 1970
Library Holdings: Bk Vols 55,000; Per Subs 120
Function: Res libr
Open Mon-Fri 8-5
Restriction: Access at librarian's discretion

GM VA LONG BEACH HEALTH CARE SYSTEM*, Health Care Sciences Library, 5901 E Seventh St, Bldg 2, Rm 345, 90822-5201. SAN 300-8835. Tel: 562-826-8000, ext 5463. FAX: 562-826-5447. Web Site: www.longbeach.va.gov. *Libr Mgr,* Marie Carter; *Libr Tech,* William Stradwer; Staff 2 (MLS 1, Non-MLS 1)
Founded 1946
Library Holdings: Bk Titles 3,000; Per Subs 7,000
Special Collections: Management Coll
Subject Interests: Clinical med
Database Vendor: Innovative Interfaces, Inc, OVID Technologies
Partic in Docline; Veterans Affairs Libr Network (VALNET)
Open Mon-Fri 8-4:30

LOS ALTOS HILLS

R CONGREGATION BETH AM LIBRARY*, 26790 Arastradero Rd, 94022. SAN 300-8878. Tel: 650-493-4661. FAX: 650-494-8248. *Librn,* Diane Rauchwerger
Library Holdings: Bk Vols 10,000
Special Collections: Judaica

J FOOTHILL COLLEGE*, Hubert H Semans Library, 12345 El Monte Rd, 94022-4599. SAN 300-8894. Circulation Tel: 650-949-7611. Interlibrary Loan Service Tel: 650-949-7029. Reference Tel: 650-949-7608. FAX: 650-949-7123. Web Site: www.foothill.edu/library. *Dean,* Paul Starer; E-mail: starerpaul@fhda.edu; *Coll Develop Librn,* Mary Thomas; *Librn,* Micaela Agyare; *Librn,* Kay Jones; Tel: 650-949-7602, E-mail: jonekay@foothill.edu; *Librn,* Pam Wilkes; Staff 10 (MLS 4, Non-MLS 6)
Founded 1958. Enrl 14,976; Fac 334; Highest Degree: Associate
Library Holdings: Bk Titles 80,193; Bk Vols 89,022; Per Subs 250
Subject Interests: Art, Lit, Philos, Relig
Automation Activity & Vendor Info: (Acquisitions) SirsiDynix; (Cataloging) SirsiDynix; (Circulation) SirsiDynix; (ILL) SirsiDynix; (Serials) SirsiDynix
Database Vendor: ARTstor, Career Guidance Foundation, EBSCOhost, Gale Cengage Learning, Newsbank
Wireless access
Publications: Student Handbook
Partic in Colorado Alliance of Research Libraries; OCLC Online Computer Library Center, Inc
Special Services for the Deaf - Closed caption videos
Special Services for the Blind - Assistive/Adapted tech devices, equip & products
Open Mon-Thurs 8-6, Fri 8-4
Restriction: Open to pub for ref only
Friends of the Library Group

LOS ANGELES

S AMERICAN FILM INSTITUTE*, Louis B Mayer Library, 2021 N Western Ave, 90027. SAN 300-6220. Tel: 323-856-7654. FAX: 323-856-7803. E-mail: library@afi.com. Web Site: www.afi.com. *Librn/Exec Ed, AFI Cat,* Robert Baughn; Tel: 323-856-7661. Subject Specialists: *Am film hist,* Robert Baughn; Staff 6 (MLS 1, Non-MLS 5)
Founded 1969
Library Holdings: Bk Titles 7,000; Per Subs 20
Special Collections: Film Daily Coll (1923-1969); Film Index (1930-1969); Fritz Lang Coll; Manuscript Coll; Martin Scorsese Coll; Motion Picture & Television Scripts Coll; Oral History Transcripts Coll; Radio-TV Daily (1939-1964); RKO Radio Flash Coll (1932-1955); Robert Aldrich Coll; Seminar Transcripts & Tape Coll; TV Guide (1948-present). Oral History
Subject Interests: Am film production
Automation Activity & Vendor Info: (Circulation) LibraryWorld, Inc
Function: Res libr
Partic in Statewide California Electronic Library Consortium (SCELC)
Restriction: Non-circulating to the pub

R AMERICAN JEWISH UNIVERSITY, Ostrow Library, 15600 Mulholland Dr, 90077. SAN 301-0155. Tel: 310-476-9777, Ext 238. E-mail: library@aju.edu. Web Site: library.aju.edu. *Dir, Libr Serv,* Paul Miller; E-mail: pmiller@aju.edu
Library Holdings: Bk Vols 115,000; Per Subs 150
Special Collections: Judaica & Hebraica Coll
Subject Interests: Educ, Humanities, Judaica (lit or hist of Jews)
Automation Activity & Vendor Info: (Cataloging) OCLC; (Circulation) OCLC; (OPAC) OCLC; (Serials) OCLC
Open Mon-Thurs 8-8, Fri 8-2:30, Sun 1-5

L ANDERSON, MCPHARLIN & CONNERS LLP LIBRARY, 444 S Flower St, No 3100, 90071. Tel: 213-236-1677. FAX: 213-622-7594. E-mail: sml@amclaw.com. *Librn,* Shihmei Lin; Staff 1 (MLS 1)
Founded 1947
Library Holdings: High Interest/Low Vocabulary Bk Vols 30; Bk Titles 1,000; Bk Vols 5,000; Per Subs 20
Database Vendor: LexisNexis
Function: For res purposes
Publications: (Collection catalog)

AUTRY NATIONAL CENTER

S AUTRY LIBRARY*, 4700 Western Heritage Way, 90027-1462, SAN 372-6606. Tel: 323-667-2000, Ext 349. FAX: 323-660-5721. E-mail: rroom@theautry.org. Web Site: theautry.org/research/autry-library. *Dir,* Marva Felchlin; *Sr Mgr, Tech Serv,* Cheryl Miller; Staff 5 (MLS 4, Non-MLS 1)
Founded 1988
Library Holdings: Bk Vols 25,000; Per Subs 100

Special Collections: Dime Novels; Dude Ranch Brochures; Gene Autry Archive; Nudie's Rodeo Tailor Coll, customer files, photog; Postcards; Saddle & Western Wear Trade Catalogs; Western Americana (Fred Rosenstock Coll), archival coll, bks, maps, photog, postcards; Western Character Comic Books; Western Film Posters & Stills; Western Music Coll, rec, sheet music, WLS radio family yearbks; Western TV Scripts & Photographic Stills; Women of the West Museum Coll
Subject Interests: Bus of western entertainment, Hist & mythology of Am W
Automation Activity & Vendor Info: (Cataloging) Innovative Interfaces, Inc; (OPAC) Innovative Interfaces, Inc; (Serials) EBSCO Online
Database Vendor: Innovative Interfaces, Inc
Partic in Dialog Corp; OCLC Online Computer Library Center, Inc
Restriction: Circulates for staff only, In-house use for visitors, Non-circulating to the pub, Open to others by appt

S BRAUN RESEARCH LIBRARY*, 234 Museum Dr, 90065. Tel: 323-221-2164. FAX: 322-221-8223. E-mail: rroom@theautry.org. Web Site: theautry.org/research/braun-research-library. *Dir,* Kim Walters; Tel: 323-221-2164, Ext 255, E-mail: kwalters@theautry.org; *Ref Librn,* Liza Posas; Tel: 323-221-2164, Ext 256, E-mail: lposas@theautry.org; Staff 3 (MLS 2, Non-MLS 1)
Library Holdings: Bk Vols 50,000
Special Collections: Manuscript Coll (History & Founding of Archaeology & Anthropology in the US); Photo Archives (Primarily Native Americans 1890s-1940s); Sound Recording Archives (California Hispanic Folk Songs, 1900-1908 & Native American Recordings), wax cylinder recs
Automation Activity & Vendor Info: (Cataloging) Innovative Interfaces, Inc; (OPAC) Innovative Interfaces, Inc; (Serials) EBSCO Online
Partic in OCLC Online Computer Library Center, Inc
Open Mon-Fri 9-5
Restriction: Non-circulating to the pub

L BLECHER & COLLINS*, Law Library, 515 S Figueroa St, 17th Flr, Ste 1750, 90071. SAN 372-2775. Tel: 213-622-4222. FAX: 213-622-1656. Web Site: www.blechercollins.com. *Librn,* Antoinette V Shilkevich
Library Holdings: Bk Vols 1,500
Database Vendor: LexisNexis, Westlaw
Restriction: Staff use only

P BRAILLE INSTITUTE LIBRARY SERVICES, 741 N Vermont Ave, 90029-3514. SAN 300-8975. Tel: 323-660-3880. Toll Free Tel: 800-808-2555 (Southern California only). FAX: 323-662-2440. E-mail: bils@braillelibrary.org. Reference E-mail: reference@braillelibrary.org. Web Site: www.braillelibrary.org. *Dir, Libr Serv,* Dr Henry C Chang; Tel: 323-663-1111, Ext 3185, E-mail: dls@braillelibrary.org; *Info Res Librn,* Kathryn Hayes; Tel: 323-663-1111, Ext 1283, E-mail: khayes@braillelibrary.org; *Circ Serv Mgr,* Hung-Ming Cheng; Tel: 323-663-1111, Ext 1317, E-mail: ming@brailleinstitute.org; *Reader Serv Mgr,* Tina Herbison; Tel: 323-663-1111, Ext 1382, E-mail: tina@braillelibrary.org; *Support Serv Mgr,* Edith Gavino; Tel: 323-663-1111, Ext 1284, E-mail: edith@braillelibrary.org; *Mat Develop Coordr,* Ivan G Johnson; Tel: 323-663-1111, Ext 1388, E-mail: igjohnson@braillelibrary.org; Staff 33 (MLS 3, Non-MLS 30)
Founded 1919
Jul 2013-Jun 2014 Income (Main Library and Branch(s)) $2,927,000, State $443,262, Parent Institution $2,483,738. Mats Exp $48,000, Books $45,000, Per/Ser (Incl. Access Fees) $3,000. Sal $1,686,441
Library Holdings: Audiobooks 657,677; Braille Volumes 53,099; Large Print Bks 930; Bk Titles 94,957; Bk Vols 713,579; Per Subs 12; Videos 2,924
Special Collections: Blindness & Other Handicap Reference Material; Southern California Coll
Subject Interests: Blindness, Physically handicapped
Automation Activity & Vendor Info: (Cataloging) Keystone Systems, Inc (KLAS); (Circulation) Keystone Systems, Inc (KLAS); (OPAC) Keystone Systems, Inc (KLAS); (Serials) Keystone Systems, Inc (KLAS)
Database Vendor: ProQuest
Wireless access
Function: Audiobks via web, Bk club(s), Bks on cassette, Computers for patron use, Digital talking bks, Handicapped accessible, ILL available, Online cat, Wheelchair accessible
Publications: Fiction Classics Catalog; Librarian Newsletter; Record Books on Tapes about California; Subject Bibliographies; Transcribe Books into Braille
Special Services for the Blind - Accessible computers; Bks on cassette; Cassette playback machines; Computer with voice synthesizer for visually impaired persons; Digital talking bk; Digital talking bk machines; Large print bks; Newsletter (in large print, Braille or on cassette); Newsp reading serv; Volunteer serv; Web-Braille
Open Mon-Fri 8:30-5
Restriction: Authorized patrons, Limited access based on advanced application, Limited access for the pub, Registered patrons only, Restricted borrowing privileges

Branches: 4
DESERT CENTER, 70-251 Ramon Rd, Rancho Mirage, 92270, SAN 372-7637. Tel: 760-321-1111. FAX: 760-321-9715. *Coordr,* Gayle Wormell; E-mail: gpwormell@brailleinstitute.org; Staff 1 (Non-MLS 1)
Library Holdings: Audiobooks 8,417; Braille Volumes 20; Bk Titles 6,156; Videos 47
Special Services for the Blind - Bks on cassette; Digital talking bk; Digital talking bk machines
Open Mon-Fri 8:30-5
ORANGE COUNTY CENTER, 527 N Dale Ave, Anaheim, 92801, SAN 372-7645. Tel: 714-821-5000. FAX: 714-527-7621. *Coordr,* Benjamin Gabriel; Tel: 714-821-5000, Ext 2126, E-mail: BGabriel@brailleinstitute.org; Staff 2 (Non-MLS 2)
Library Holdings: Audiobooks 8,344; Braille Volumes 163; Bk Titles 6,236; Videos 126
Special Services for the Blind - Bks on cassette; Cassette playback machines; Digital talking bk; Digital talking bk machines
Open Mon-Fri 8:30-5
Friends of the Library Group
SAN DIEGO CENTER, 4555 Executive Dr, San Diego, 92121-3021, SAN 372-7653. Tel: 858-452-1111. FAX: 858-452-1688. *Coordr,* Louise Zuckerman; Tel: 858-452-1111, Ext 5011, E-mail: lmzuckerman@brailleinstitute.org; Staff 1 (MLS 1)
Library Holdings: Audiobooks 9,611; Braille Volumes 193; Bk Titles 7,020; Videos 237
Special Services for the Blind - Bks on cassette; Cassette playback machines; Digital talking bk; Digital talking bk machines
Open Mon-Fri 8:30-5
Friends of the Library Group
SANTA BARBARA CENTER, 2031 De La Vina St, Santa Barbara, 93105, SAN 372-7661. Tel: 805-682-6222. FAX: 805-687-6141. *Coordr,* Nate Streeper; E-mail: nkstreeper@brailleinstitute.org; Staff 1 (Non-MLS 1)
Library Holdings: Audiobooks 7,709; Braille Volumes 68; Bk Titles 7,626; Videos 172
Special Services for the Blind - Digital talking bk; Digital talking bk machines

L BUCHALTER NEMER*, Law Library, 1000 Wilshire Blvd, Ste 1500, 90017. SAN 372-2740. Tel: 213-891-0700. Administration Tel: 213-891-5655. FAX: 213-896-0400. Web Site: www.buchalter.com. *Dir, Libr Serv,* Michelle Kuczma
Library Holdings: Bk Vols 20,000
Database Vendor: Dialog, LexisNexis, Westlaw
Restriction: Staff use only

M CALIFORNIA HOSPITAL MEDICAL CENTER LOS ANGELES*, Information Center Medical Library, 1401 S Grand Ave, 90015. SAN 320-4448. Tel: 213-742-5872. Administration Tel: 213-742-5811. FAX: 213-765-4046. Web Site: www.chmcla.org/library. *Librn,* Brian Marshall; Staff 2 (MLS 1, Non-MLS 1)
Founded 1964
Library Holdings: Bk Vols 1,200; Per Subs 9
Subject Interests: Clinical med, Nursing, Oncology
Automation Activity & Vendor Info: (Cataloging) EOS International; (Circulation) EOS International; (OPAC) EOS International
Database Vendor: Cinahl, EBSCOhost, Elsevier, Medline, Micromedex, OVID Technologies, ProQuest, PubMed, UpToDate, Wiley
Partic in National Network of Libraries of Medicine
Restriction: Not open to pub

L CALIFORNIA SECOND DISTRICT COURT OF APPEALS*, 300 S Spring St, Rm 3547, 90013. SAN 300-9114. Tel: 213-830-7241. FAX: 213-897-2429. *Head Librn,* Carol David Ebbinghouse; E-mail: carol.ebbinghouse@jud.ca.gov; Staff 3 (MLS 2, Non-MLS 1)
Founded 1967
Library Holdings: Bk Vols 65,000
Subject Interests: Calif
Database Vendor: LexisNexis
Restriction: Not open to pub

C CALIFORNIA STATE UNIVERSITY, LOS ANGELES, John F Kennedy Memorial Library, 5151 State University Dr, 90032-8300. SAN 300-9017. Tel: 323-343-3950. Circulation Tel: 323-343-3987. Interlibrary Loan Service Tel: 323-343-3983, 323-343-4983. Reference Tel: 323-343-4927, 323-343-4928. Administration Tel: 323-343-3929, 323-343-3953. Information Services Tel: 323-343-3994. FAX: 323-343-5600. Interlibrary Loan Service FAX: 323-343-6401. Web Site: www.calstatela.edu/library. *Univ Librn,* Alice Kawakami; E-mail: akawaka@calstatela.edu; *Assoc Univ Librn,* Marla Peppers; E-mail: mpepper@calstatela.edu; Staff 33.5 (MLS 13.5, Non-MLS 20)
Founded 1947. Enrl 23,258; Fac 12; Highest Degree: Master
Jul 2013-Jun 2014. Mats Exp $1,425,650. Sal $2,597,875 (Prof $2,390,234)

Library Holdings: CDs 5,918; DVDs 4,001; e-books 168,920; e-journals 67,700; Electronic Media & Resources 15,562; Microforms 808,960; Bk Vols 983,229; Per Subs 63,861
Special Collections: Carlos Montes Papers & Gloria Arellanes Papers; East LA Archives; Film Scripts (Anthony Quinn Coll); Joseph Wambaugh Manuscript Coll; Mexican American Baseball: From the Barrios to the Big Leagues; Musical Scores (Eugene List & Carol Glenn Coll); Musical Scores (Otto Klemperer Coll); Printing Books (Perry R Long Coll); Public Officials Papers: Mervyn Dymally, Julian Nava, Julian Dixon, Richard Alatorre; Roy Harris & Stan Kenton Music Archives; Theatre Arts (Arthur M Applebaum Coll). State Document Depository; US Document Depository
Automation Activity & Vendor Info: (Acquisitions) Innovative Interfaces, Inc; (Cataloging) Innovative Interfaces, Inc; (Circulation) Innovative Interfaces, Inc; (Course Reserve) Docutek; (Media Booking) Innovative Interfaces, Inc; (OPAC) Innovative Interfaces, Inc; (Serials) Innovative Interfaces, Inc
Database Vendor: EBSCOhost, Gale Cengage Learning, Innovative Interfaces, Inc, LexisNexis, OCLC FirstSearch, OVID Technologies, ProQuest
Wireless access
Partic in Metronet; OCLC Online Computer Library Center, Inc
Friends of the Library Group

S CAPITAL GROUP COMPANIES, INC*, Research Library, 333 S Hope St, 90071. SAN 300-9025. Tel: 213-486-9261. FAX: 213-486-9571. *Sr VPres,* Vickie H Taylor; E-mail: vht@capgroup.com; Staff 26 (MLS 17, Non-MLS 9)
Founded 1965
Library Holdings: Bk Vols 3,000; Per Subs 2,500
Special Collections: Economic & Financial Information on Global Companies
Subject Interests: Bus & mgt, Econ, Stock market
Automation Activity & Vendor Info: (Acquisitions) Sydney; (Cataloging) Sydney; (OPAC) Sydney; (Serials) Sydney
Database Vendor: Dialog, Factiva.com, LexisNexis
Restriction: Staff use only

M CDU HEALTH SCIENCES LIBRARY*, 1731 E 120th St, 90059. SAN 300-9424. Tel: 323-563-4869. FAX: 323-563-4861. E-mail: smc@cdrewu.edu. Web Site: www.cdrewu.edu. *Dir, Learning Res,* Darlene Kelly; Staff 10 (MLS 3, Non-MLS 7)
Founded 1972
Library Holdings: Bk Titles 14,000; Bk Vols 48,000; Per Subs 760
Special Collections: Clinical Medicine
Automation Activity & Vendor Info: (Cataloging) EOS International; (Circulation) EOS International
Partic in Docline
Open Mon-Thurs 8am-9pm, Fri 8-7, Sat & Sun 11-4:45

M CEDARS-SINAI MEDICAL CENTER*, Medical Library, South Tower, Rm 2815, 8700 Beverly Blvd, 90048-1865. (Mail add: PO Box 48956, 90048-0956), SAN 300-9033. Tel: 310-423-3751. Interlibrary Loan Service Tel: 310-423-3647. FAX: 310-423-0138. E-mail: library@cshs.org. Web Site: www.csmc.edu/mlic. *Mgr, Libr Serv,* Janet L Hobbs; E-mail: hobbsjl@cshs.org; Staff 8 (MLS 4, Non-MLS 4)
Library Holdings: e-books 2,000; e-journals 12,000; Bk Vols 10,000
Special Collections: Judaica; History of Medicine
Automation Activity & Vendor Info: (Acquisitions) SirsiDynix; (Cataloging) OCLC; (Circulation) SirsiDynix; (Course Reserve) SirsiDynix; (OPAC) Mandarin Library Automation; (Serials) SirsiDynix
Database Vendor: Dialog, OCLC FirstSearch, OVID Technologies, SirsiDynix
Function: Archival coll, Doc delivery serv, For res purposes, Govt ref serv, ILL available, Newsp ref libr, Photocopying/Printing, Prof lending libr, Ref serv available
Publications: Current Book List
Restriction: Med staff only

M CHILDREN'S HOSPITAL LOS ANGELES*, Health Sciences Library, 4650 Sunset Blvd, MS41, 90027-0700. SAN 300-9068. Tel: 323-361-2254. FAX: 323-361-4844. E-mail: librarygroup@chla.usc.edu. *Libr Mgr,* Joan Godell; E-mail: jgodell@chla.usc.edu; Staff 2 (MLS 1, Non-MLS 1)
Founded 1928
Library Holdings: Per Subs 7
Subject Interests: Pediatrics
Database Vendor: Swets Information Services
Open Mon-Thurs 8-6, Fri 8-5

L COX, CASTLE & NICHOLSON LLP LIBRARY*, 2049 Century Park E, 28th Flr, 90067. SAN 300-9122. Tel: 310-277-4222, Ext 2444. FAX: 310-277-7889. Web Site: www.coxcastle.com/info/home.html. *Librn,* Janet Kasabian; E-mail: jkasabian@coxcastle.com
Library Holdings: Bk Vols 17,000; Per Subs 500

M DAUGHTERS OF CHARITY HEALTH CARE SYSTEM*, Saint Vincent Medical Center-Health Science Library, 2131 W Third St, 90057. SAN 325-7177. Tel: 213-484-5530. FAX: 213-484-7092. Web Site: stvincentmedicalcenter.com. *Librn,* Evelyn Walker; E-mail: evelynwalker@dochs.org
Library Holdings: Bk Titles 4,000; Per Subs 240
Subject Interests: Cardiology, Nephrology, Oncology, Transplantation
Automation Activity & Vendor Info: (Cataloging) CyberTools for Libraries; (Circulation) CyberTools for Libraries; (OPAC) CyberTools for Libraries; (Serials) CyberTools for Libraries
Database Vendor: EBSCOhost, OVID Technologies
Partic in National Network of Libraries of Medicine Pacific Northwest Region
Open Mon-Fri 8:30-5

M DOHENY EYE INSTITUTE*, Norris Visual Science Library, 1450 San Pablo St, DEI3400, 90033. SAN 321-6128. Tel: 323-442-7139. *Med Ed/Libr Mgr,* Susan Clarke; E-mail: sclarke@doheny.org; Staff 1 (MLS 1)
Founded 1976
Library Holdings: Bk Vols 1,975
Subject Interests: Ophthalmology
Automation Activity & Vendor Info: (Cataloging) LibraryWorld, Inc; (OPAC) LibraryWorld, Inc
Wireless access
Function: ILL available, Pub access computers, Scanner, Web-catalog
Partic in Association of Vision Science Librarians (AVSL); Medical Library Group of Southern California & Arizona (MLGSCA); Pacific Southwest Regional Medical Library (PSRML)
Open Mon-Fri 8-4
Restriction: Badge access after hrs

S EDUCATIONAL COMMUNICATIONS, INC, Environmental Resources Library, PO Box 351419, 90035-9119. SAN 326-1654. Tel: 310-559-9160. FAX: 310-559-9160. E-mail: ECNP@aol.com. Web Site: www.ecoprojects.org. *Exec Dir,* Nancy Pearlman; Tel: 213-705-4992
Founded 1958
Library Holdings: AV Mats 3,000; DVDs 100; e-journals 36; Bk Titles 2,000; Per Subs 40; Spec Interest Per Sub 50; Videos 600
Special Collections: Autographed Books by Authors on Environmental Topics; Compendium Newsletter Coll; Ecology & Ecotourism (ECONEWS Television Series & Environmental Directions Radio Series Coll); Environment
Subject Interests: Conserv, Ecology, Environment, Land use, Natural res, Sustainability, Wildlife
Publications: The Compendium (Newsletter)
Restriction: Open by appt only

S FARMERS INSURANCE GROUP LIBRARY*, 4680 Wilshire Blvd, 90010-3807. (Mail add: PO Box 2478, 90051-2478), SAN 300-919X. Tel: 323-932-3200. FAX: 323-932-3101. Web Site: www.farmers.com. *Librn,* Maria Palma
Library Holdings: Bk Vols 5,800
Restriction: Staff use only

S FASHION INSTITUTE OF DESIGN & MERCHANDISING, 919 S Grand Ave, 90015-1421. SAN 375-4774. Tel: 213-486-2009. FAX: 213-624-9365. E-mail: library@fidm.com. Web Site: www.fidm.com. *Coll Mgr, Head Librn,* Robin Dodge; Staff 32 (MLS 7, Non-MLS 25)
Founded 1969
Wireless access
Open Mon-Thurs 7am-10pm, Fri 7-7, Sat 8-6

L FOLEY & LARDNER LLP*, Los Angeles Library, 555 S Flower St, Ste 3500, 90071-2411. SAN 371-6007. Tel: 213-972-4500. Reference Tel: 213-972-4657. FAX: 213-486-0065. *Dir of Southern California Libr Serv,* Stefanie Frame; E-mail: sframe@foley.com; Staff 2 (MLS 1, Non-MLS 1)
Library Holdings: Bk Titles 800; Bk Vols 8,000; Per Subs 142
Subject Interests: Health law, Intellectual property, Litigation, Securities law
Automation Activity & Vendor Info: (Acquisitions) Inmagic, Inc.; (Cataloging) Inmagic, Inc.; (Circulation) Inmagic, Inc.; (OPAC) Inmagic, Inc.; (Serials) Inmagic, Inc.
Database Vendor: Checkpoint Systems, Inc, Dun & Bradstreet, HeinOnline, Hoovers, Infotrieve, LexisNexis, Loislaw, ScienceDirect
Wireless access
Restriction: Staff use only

L FULBRIGHT & JAWORSKI LLP*, Law Library, 555 S Flower St, 41st Flr, 90071. SAN 372-2805. Tel: 213-892-9262. FAX: 213-892-9494. Web Site: www.fulbright.com. *Librn,* Nina A Clark; E-mail: naclark@fulbright.com
Library Holdings: Bk Vols 25,000

Automation Activity & Vendor Info: (Cataloging) Inmagic, Inc.; (Serials) Inmagic, Inc.
Open Mon-Fri 9-5

S GETTY RESEARCH INSTITUTE*, Research Library, 1200 Getty Center Dr, Ste 1100, 90049-1688. SAN 301-0325. Tel: 310-440-7390. Interlibrary Loan Service Tel: 310-440-7395. FAX: 310-440-7780. E-mail: reference@getty.edu. Web Site: www.getty.edu/research. *Asst Dir,* David Farneth; E-mail: dfarneth@getty.edu; *Asst Dir,* Kathleen Salomon; E-mail: ksalomon@getty.edu; *Head, Coll Develop,* Marcia Reed; E-mail: mreed@getty.edu; *Head, Conserv & Presv,* Mary Sackett; E-mail: msackett@getty.edu; *Head, Dept of Archit,* Wim De Wit; E-mail: wdwit@getty.edu. Subject Specialists: *Conserv,* Mary Sackett; Staff 120 (MLS 30, Non-MLS 90)
Founded 1983
Library Holdings: AV Mats 17,343; Microforms 10,725; Bk Titles 731,277; Bk Vols 1,006,148; Per Subs 2,981
Special Collections: Collecting, Display & Visual Resources for the Study of Art History; Historiography of Art; Modern Period
Subject Interests: Archaeology, Archit, Archives, Drawings, Manuscripts, Prints, Rare bks
Automation Activity & Vendor Info: (Acquisitions) Ex Libris Group; (Cataloging) Ex Libris Group; (Circulation) Ex Libris Group; (ILL) Ex Libris Group; (OPAC) Ex Libris Group; (Serials) Ex Libris Group
Database Vendor: ABC-CLIO, ARTstor, CredoReference, EBSCOhost, Ex Libris Group, Gale Cengage Learning, JSTOR, LexisNexis, OCLC FirstSearch, Oxford Online, Paratext, Project MUSE, ProQuest, ScienceDirect, Scopus, SerialsSolutions, Springer-Verlag, Wiley
Wireless access
Function: Res libr
Publications: Getty Research Journal (Annual); Getty Thesaurus of Geographic Names (Online only); Getty Vocabularies: Art & Architecture (Online only); Issues & Debates Series; Text & Document Series; Union List of Artists Names (Online only)
Partic in Independent Res Libr Asn; OCLC Online Computer Library Center, Inc; OCLC Research Library Partnership; Statewide California Electronic Library Consortium (SCELC)
Open Mon-Fri 9:30-5

L GIBSON, DUNN & CRUTCHER*, Law Library, 333 S Grand Ave, 90071-3197. SAN 300-9238. Tel: 213-229-7000. FAX: 213-229-7520. *Chief Librn,* Dena Hollingsworth; *Librn,* Reed Nelson; Staff 12 (MLS 6, Non-MLS 6)
Library Holdings: Bk Vols 50,000
Wireless access
Restriction: Private libr

M GOOD SAMARITAN HOSPITAL*, Medical Library, 637 S Lucas Ave, 90017. SAN 300-9300. Tel: 213-977-2047, 213-977-2323. FAX: 213-977-2325. E-mail: library@goodsam.org. Web Site: www.goodsam.org/support/library. *Managing Dir,* Andrea Harrow; Staff 1 (MLS 1)
Founded 1941
Jan 2012-Dec 2012. Mats Exp $54,000, Books $2,000, Per/Ser (Incl. Access Fees) $22,000, Electronic Ref Mat (Incl. Access Fees) $30,000. Sal $68,000
Library Holdings: Bk Vols 2,500; Per Subs 150
Database Vendor: EBSCOhost, Elsevier, MD Consult, Micromedex, OVID Technologies
Partic in Medical Library Group of Southern California & Arizona (MLGSCA); National Network of Libraries of Medicine
Open Mon-Fri 8:30-4:30
Restriction: Non-circulating to the pub

L GREENBERG GLUSKER FIELDS CLAMAN & MACHTINGER LLP LIBRARY*, 1900 Avenue of the Stars, Ste 2100, 90067. SAN 300-9246. Tel: 310-553-3610. FAX: 310-553-0687. *Dir, Libr & Res Serv,* Marjorie Jay; Staff 1 (MLS 1)
Library Holdings: CDs 70; DVDs 5; Bk Titles 2,050; Bk Vols 14,290; Per Subs 275
Subject Interests: Law
Wireless access
Restriction: Not open to pub

S GRIFFITH OBSERVATORY LIBRARY*, 2800 E Observatory Rd, 90027. SAN 300-9254. Tel: 213-473-0800. FAX: 213-473-0818. Web Site: www.griffithobservatory.org. *Dir,* Dr Edwin C Krupp; E-mail: edwin.c.krupp@lacity.org
Founded 1935
Library Holdings: Bk Vols 9,446; Per Subs 20
Subject Interests: Astronomy
Publications: Griffith Observer
Restriction: Non-circulating to the pub

CR HEBREW UNION COLLEGE-JEWISH INSTITUTE OF RELIGION*, Frances-Henry Library, 3077 University Ave, 90007. SAN 300-9262. Tel: 213-749-3424. Reference Tel: 213-765-2127, 213-765-2170. Administration Tel: 213-765-2125. Toll Free Tel: 800-899-0925. FAX: 213-749-1937. Web Site: www.huc.edu/libraries/la. *Dir,* Dr Yaffa Weisman; E-mail: yweisman@huc.edu; *Sr Assoc Librn,* Sheryl Stahl; E-mail: sstahl@huc.edu. Subject Specialists: *Bible, Hebrew, Judaica,* Dr Yaffa Weisman; *Music,* Sheryl Stahl; Staff 6.5 (MLS 2.5, Non-MLS 4)
Founded 1958. Enrl 300; Fac 65; Highest Degree: Doctorate
Library Holdings: Bks on Deafness & Sign Lang 25; Bk Vols 112,000; Per Subs 500
Special Collections: American Jewish Archives, West Coast Microfilm Branch; American Jewish Periodical Center, West Coast Microfilm Branch
Subject Interests: Ethics, Jewish hist & lit, Judaica (lit or hist of Jews), Relig
Automation Activity & Vendor Info: (Circulation) Innovative Interfaces, Inc; (Course Reserve) Innovative Interfaces, Inc; (ILL) Innovative Interfaces, Inc; (OPAC) Innovative Interfaces, Inc; (Serials) Innovative Interfaces, Inc
Partic in OCLC Research Library Partnership; Southern Calif Area Theol Librns Asn; SouthWest Ohio & Neighboring Libraries
Special Services for the Blind - Audio mat; Braille bks
Restriction: Fee for pub use, Open to pub for ref & circ; with some limitations, Open to students, fac & staff

M HOUSE EAR INSTITUTE*, Athalie Irvine Clarke Library, 2100 W Third St, 4th Flr, 90057-1922. SAN 325-7215. Tel: 213-483-4431. Toll Free Tel: 800-388-8612. FAX: 213-413-8789. Web Site: www.hei.org. *In Charge,* Rene Rivers; E-mail: rrivers@houseresearch.org; Staff 1 (MLS 1)
Founded 1975
Library Holdings: Bks on Deafness & Sign Lang 80; Bk Vols 2,800; Per Subs 190; Videos 250
Subject Interests: Audiology, Otolaryngology, Rare bks
Function: Photocopying/Printing, VHS videos
Partic in Medical Library Group of Southern California & Arizona (MLGSCA)
Restriction: Non-circulating to the pub, Open to pub by appt only

L JONES DAY*, Law Library, 555 S Flower St, 50th Flr, 90013-90071. SAN 329-9953. Tel: 213-489-3939. FAX: 213-243-2539. Web Site: www.jonesday.com. *Ref,* Jim Center; E-mail: j.senter@jonesday.com
Library Holdings: Bk Vols 3,000
Automation Activity & Vendor Info: (Acquisitions) Innovative Interfaces, Inc - Millenium; (Cataloging) Innovative Interfaces, Inc - Millenium; (Circulation) Innovative Interfaces, Inc - Millenium; (OPAC) Innovative Interfaces, Inc - Millenium; (Serials) Innovative Interfaces, Inc - Millenium
Database Vendor: LexisNexis, Westlaw
Open Mon-Fri 9-5:30

S C G JUNG INSTITUTE OF LOS ANGELES, Max & Lore Zeller Library, 10349 W Pico Blvd, 90064. SAN 300-9378. Tel: 310-556-1193, Ext 229. FAX: 310-556-2290. E-mail: library@junginla.org. Web Site: www.junginla.org. *Librn,* Nancy Forbes; Staff 0.5 (Non-MLS 0.5)
Founded 1948
Library Holdings: Bk Vols 7,000; Per Subs 15
Special Collections: Analytical Psychology Club of Los Angeles, lectures 1944-76; ARAS (Archive for Research in Archetypal Symbolism), cat sheets, photog, slides
Subject Interests: Analytical psychol
Wireless access
Function: Ref serv available, Res libr, Spoken cassettes & CDs, Spoken cassettes & DVDs, Telephone ref, VHS videos
Open Wed, Fri & Sat 12-5
Restriction: Mem only
Friends of the Library Group

M KAISER-PERMANENTE MEDICAL CENTER, Irving P Ackerman MD Health Sciences Library, 4733 Sunset Blvd, 1st Flr, 90027. SAN 300-9394. Tel: 323-783-8568. Administration Tel: 323-783-4687. FAX: 323-783-4192. E-mail: iamclibrary@kp.org. *Mgr, Libr Serv,* Thomas E Shreves; Staff 5 (MLS 2, Non-MLS 3)
Founded 1953
Library Holdings: e-books 200; Bk Titles 1,200
Subject Interests: Clinical med, Nursing, Psychiat, Psychol
Open Mon-Fri 8-5

L KAYE SCHOLER LLP*, Law Library, 1999 Avenue of the Stars, Ste 1700, 90067. SAN 372-2694. Tel: 310-788-1000. FAX: 310-788-1200. *Librn,* Position Currently Open
Library Holdings: Bk Vols 12,000

S KOREAN CULTURAL CENTER LIBRARY*, 5505 Wilshire Blvd, 90036. SAN 327-5795. Tel: 323-936-7141. FAX: 323-936-5712. E-mail: librarian@kccla.org. Web Site: kccla.org. *Librn,* Daniel Kim; Staff 2 (MLS 1, Non-MLS 1)
Founded 1980
Library Holdings: Bk Vols 25,000; Per Subs 52
Publications: Korean Culture (Quarterly)

S KPMG LLP*, Tax Library, 355 S Grand Ave, Ste 2000, 90017-1568. SAN 300-9823. Tel: 213-972-4000. FAX: 213-622-1217. Web Site: www.kpmg.com. *Sr Libr Assoc,* Alison Leathley; Staff 1 (Non-MLS 1)
Library Holdings: Bk Vols 300; Per Subs 20
Database Vendor: LexisNexis
Wireless access
Function: Res libr
Restriction: Not open to pub

S LA84 FOUNDATION, Sports Library, 2141 W Adams Blvd, 90018. SAN 300-9076. Tel: 323-730-4646. FAX: 323-730-0546. E-mail: library@la84.org. Web Site: www.la84.org. *VPres, Communications & Educ,* Dr Wayne V Wilson; E-mail: wwilson@la84.org; *AV Coordr, Cat, Ref,* Michael W Salmon; E-mail: msalmon@la84.org; *Syst Adminr, Webmaster,* Shirley S Ito; E-mail: sito@la84.org; Staff 3.5 (MLS 3, Non-MLS 0.5)
Founded 1936
Library Holdings: Bk Titles 30,000; Bk Vols 35,000; Per Subs 350; Videos 5,000
Special Collections: Digital Archive; National Track & Field Research Coll; Olympic Games Coll; Ralph Miller Golf Coll; Sport Films; Sport Photographs
Subject Interests: Coaches educ, Olympic games, Sports
Automation Activity & Vendor Info: (Cataloging) EOS International; (Circulation) EOS International; (OPAC) EOS International; (Serials) EOS International
Database Vendor: Dialog, EBSCO Information Services, EBSCOhost, OCLC FirstSearch, OVID Technologies
Function: Ref & res
Publications: SportsLetter (Online only)
Partic in OCLC Online Computer Library Center, Inc

L LEGAL AID FOUNDATION OF LOS ANGELES, Law Library, 1102 Crenshaw Blvd, 90019. SAN 372-2937. Tel: 323-801-7940. FAX: 323-801-7921. *Librn,* Pamela L Hall; E-mail: phall@lafla.org; Staff 1 (MLS 1)
Library Holdings: Bk Vols 1,100
Subject Interests: Consumer, Domestic violence, Employment, Evictions, Family law, Govt benefits, Housing, Human trafficking, Immigration
Database Vendor: LexisNexis, Westlaw
Function: Res libr
Restriction: Not open to pub

L LEWIS, BRISBOIS, BISGAARD & SMITH*, Law Library, 221 N Figueroa St, Ste 1300, 90012. SAN 372-2708. Tel: 213-580-7908. FAX: 213-250-7900. Web Site: www.lbbs.com. *Dir,* Jill Robins; Staff 2 (MLS 1, Non-MLS 1)
Founded 1978
Library Holdings: Bk Titles 1,550
Subject Interests: Environ law

J LOS ANGELES CITY COLLEGE LIBRARY*, 855 N Vermont Ave, 90029. SAN 300-9491. Tel: 323-953-4000. Circulation Tel: 323-953-4000, Ext 2395. Interlibrary Loan Service Tel: 323-953-4000, Ext 2401. Reference Tel: 323-953-4000, Ext 2406. Administration Tel: 323-953-4000, Ext 2407. FAX: 323-953-4013. Web Site: www.lacitycollege.edu/resource/library. *Chair,* Barbara J Vasquez; E-mail: vasquebj@lacitycollege.edu; *Bibliog Instruction/Ref,* Rosalind Goddard; Tel: 323-953-4000, Ext 2399, E-mail: goddarrk@lacitycollege.edu; *Bibliog Instruction/Ref,* Andy Mezynski; Tel: 323-953-4000, Ext 2403, E-mail: mezynsab@lacitycollege.edu; *Acq, Circ, Ref,* Dorothy Fuhrmann; E-mail: fuhrmadm@lacitycollege.edu; *Cat, Ref,* Elizabeth Gnerre; Tel: 323-953-4000, Ext 2409, E-mail: gnerreeo@lacitycollege.edu; Staff 13 (MLS 5, Non-MLS 8)
Founded 1929. Enrl 16,268; Fac 1,212; Highest Degree: Associate
Library Holdings: Bk Titles 115,880; Bk Vols 146,900; Per Subs 159
Automation Activity & Vendor Info: (Acquisitions) SirsiDynix; (Cataloging) SirsiDynix; (Circulation) SirsiDynix; (Course Reserve) SirsiDynix; (OPAC) SirsiDynix; (Serials) SirsiDynix
Database Vendor: Alexander Street Press, Baker & Taylor, CountryWatch, CQ Press, Gale Cengage Learning, LexisNexis, Newsbank, OCLC FirstSearch, ProQuest, SirsiDynix, Wilson - Wilson Web
Wireless access
Function: For res purposes, Handicapped accessible, ILL available, Magnifiers for reading, Online searches, Orientations, Photocopying/Printing, Ref serv available, Res libr, Wheelchair accessible
Restriction: In-house use for visitors, Open to students, fac & staff, Photo ID required for access, Pub use on premises

L LOS ANGELES COUNTY COUNSEL LAW LIBRARY*, 500 W Temple St, Rm 610, 90012. SAN 372-3704. Tel: 213-974-1982. FAX: 213-626-7446. Web Site: www.lacounty.info. *Librn,* Beth Barney
Library Holdings: Bk Vols 15,000
Automation Activity & Vendor Info: (Cataloging) Inmagic, Inc.
Restriction: Staff use only

L LOS ANGELES COUNTY LAW LIBRARY*, Mildred L Lillie Bldg, 301 W First St, 90012-3100. SAN 332-334X. Tel: 213-785-2529. Reference Tel: 213-785-2513. FAX: 213-613-1329. *Exec Dir,* Marcia J Koslov; *Sr Dir, Admin Serv,* Patrick K O'Leary; *Sr Dir, Info Serv,* Jaye Nelson; *Dir of Communications,* Douglas Myers; *Dir, Prog & Partnerships,* Malinda Muller; *Dir, Ref,* Ralph Stahlberg; *Dir of Tech,* Meilling Li; Staff 66 (MLS 12, Non-MLS 54)
Founded 1891
Library Holdings: Bk Titles 189,150; Bk Vols 992,060; Per Subs 11,876
Special Collections: State Document Depository; US Document Depository
Subject Interests: Comparative law, Fed law, Foreign law, Intl law, State law
Automation Activity & Vendor Info: (Cataloging) Ex Libris Group; (Circulation) Ex Libris Group; (OPAC) Ex Libris Group; (Serials) Ex Libris Group
Database Vendor: Dialog
Wireless access
Open Mon-Fri 8:30-6, Sat 9-5
Friends of the Library Group
Branches:
LONG BEACH, County Bldg, Rm 505, 415 W Ocean Blvd, Long Beach, 90802, SAN 332-3439. Tel: 562-983-7088. *Br Asst,* Pedro Orellana
Subject Interests: Fed law, State law
Open Mon-Fri 8:30-1:30
Friends of the Library Group
NORWALK, SE Superior Courts Bldg, Rm 714, 12720 Norwalk Blvd, Norwalk, 90650, SAN 332-3463. Tel: 562-807-7310. FAX: 562-868-8936. *Br Asst,* Kay Mayorga
Subject Interests: Fed law, State law
Open Mon-Fri 8:30-1:30
Friends of the Library Group
SANTA MONICA, County Bldg, 1725 Main St, Rm 219, Santa Monica, 90401, SAN 332-3552. Tel: 310-260-3644. FAX: 310-917-9230. *Br Asst,* Judith Yontef
Subject Interests: Fed law, State law
Open Mon-Fri 8:30-1:30
Friends of the Library Group
TORRANCE, S Bay County Bldg, Rm 110, 825 Maple Ave, Torrance, 90503, SAN 332-3587. Tel. 310-222-8816. FAX: 310-320-9734. *Br Asst,* Paula Hart
Subject Interests: Fed law, State law
Open Mon-Fri 8:30-1:30
Friends of the Library Group

G LOS ANGELES COUNTY METROPOLITAN TRANSPORTATION AUTHORITY*, Dorothy Peyton Gray Transportation Library & Archive, One Gateway Plaza, 15th Flr, Mail Stop 99-15-1, 90012-2952. SAN 325-4933. Tel: 213-922-4859. TDD: 800-735-2922. E-mail: library@metro.net. Web Site: www.metro.net/library. *Adminr, Librn,* Matthew Barrett; *Digital Res Librn,* Kenneth Bicknell; Tel: 213-933-4861, E-mail: bicknellk@metro.net; Staff 2 (MLS 2)
Founded 1971
Library Holdings: CDs 300; Bk Titles 48,000; Bk Vols 200,000; Per Subs 165; Videos 1,000
Special Collections: Deeds; Local Transit; Photographs 1871 to present; Urban Transportation & Urban Planning
Subject Interests: Transportation
Automation Activity & Vendor Info: (Circulation) CyberTools for Libraries; (ILL) OCLC; (OPAC) CyberTools for Libraries; (Serials) EBSCO Online
Wireless access
Function: ILL available
Publications: Acquisitions List
Partic in OCLC Online Computer Library Center, Inc
Special Services for the Deaf - TDD equip
Open Mon & Thurs 9-4
Restriction: Circ limited, Employees & their associates, In-house use for visitors

S LOS ANGELES COUNTY MUSEUM OF ART*, Mr & Mrs Allan C Balch Art Research Library, 5905 Wilshire Blvd, 90036-4597. SAN 332-3641. Tel: 323-857-6118. FAX: 323-857-4790. E-mail: library@lacma.org. Web Site: www.lacma.org. *Head Librn,* Alexis Curry; Tel: 323-857-6122, E-mail: acurry@lacma.org; *Sr Librn,* Pauline Wolstencroft; Tel: 323-857-6121, E-mail: pwolsten@lacma.org; *Ser & Electronic Res Librn,* Douglas Cordell; Tel: 323-857-6531, E-mail: dcordell@lacma.org; *Archivist,* Jessica Gambling; E-mail: jgambling@lacma.org; Staff 8 (MLS 4, Non-MLS 4)
Founded 1965
Library Holdings: Bk Titles 175,000; Bk Vols 176,000; Per Subs 400
Special Collections: Costume & Textiles Rare Books (Doris Stearns Coll); Rifkind Center for German Expressionist Studies (Library & Print Coll)
Subject Interests: Art hist
Automation Activity & Vendor Info: (Acquisitions) OCLC; (Cataloging) OCLC; (Circulation) OCLC; (OPAC) OCLC; (Serials) OCLC
Database Vendor: ARTstor, EBSCOhost, JSTOR, OCLC FirstSearch, Wilson - Wilson Web
Function: e-mail serv, For res purposes, Handicapped accessible, ILL available, Photocopying/Printing, Ref serv available, Res libr, Telephone ref
Partic in OCLC Online Computer Library Center, Inc; Statewide California Electronic Library Consortium (SCELC)
Restriction: Circulates for staff only, In-house use for visitors, Open to pub by appt only
Friends of the Library Group
Branches:
ROBERT GORE RIFKIND CENTER FOR GERMAN EXPRESSIONIST STUDIES, 5905 Wilshire Blvd, 90036, SAN 320-3646. Tel: 323-857-4752, 323-857-6165. FAX: 323-857-4790. E-mail: library@lacma.org. *Librn,* Julia Kim; E-mail: jkim@lacma.org
Founded 1979
Library Holdings: Bk Titles 6,000; Bk Vols 6,500
Special Collections: German Expressionist Graphics Coll
Publications: Bibliography of German Expressionism: Catalog of the Robert Gore Rifkind Center for German Expressionist Studies at the Los Angeles County Museum of Art (G K Hall, 1990)
Restriction: Open by appt only
Friends of the Library Group

M LOS ANGELES COUNTY-UNIVERSITY OF SOUTHERN CALIFORNIA*, IPT-Medical Library, Medical Center, Inpatient Tower -3K111, 2051 Marengo St, 90033. SAN 332-7000. Tel: 323-409-7006. FAX: 323-441-8291. E-mail: iptmedicallibrary@dhs.lacounty.gov. *Med Librn,* Bella Kwong; Staff 3.5 (MLS 1, Non-MLS 2.5)
Library Holdings: e-journals 350; Bk Vols 6,300; Per Subs 80
Subject Interests: Clinical med
Partic in Docline
Open Mon-Fri 8:30-6

P LOS ANGELES PUBLIC LIBRARY SYSTEM*, Central Library, 630 W Fifth St, 90071-2002. SAN 332-7124. Tel: 213-228-7000. Information Services Tel: 213-228-7272. FAX: 213-228-7519. Web Site: www.lapl.org. *City Librn,* John F Szabo; E-mail: jszabo@lapl.org; *Asst City Librn,* Kristina Morita; Tel: 213-228-7461, E-mail: kmorita@lapl.org; *Dir, Pub Relations,* Peter Persic; Tel: 213-228-7556, Fax: 213-228-7569, E-mail: ppersic@lapl.org; *Dir, Br,* Cheryl Collins; *Coll Serv Mgr,* Peggy Murphy; Tel: 213-228-7191, Fax: 213-228-7041; *Children's Serv Coordr,* Eva Mitnick; Tel: 213-228-7483, Fax: 213-228-7485, E-mail: emitnick@lapl.org; Staff 443.5 (MLS 443.5)
Founded 1872. Pop 4,390,379; Circ 15,574,773
Library Holdings: Bk Vols 6,433,567
Special Collections: Automotive Repair Manuals; California History Coll; California in Fiction; Catholicism of Early Spanish Southwest; Children's Literature Coll; Cookery; Corporation Records; Dobinson Coll of Drama & Theatre, bks, programs; Fiction by & about Blacks; Film Study; Genealogy Coll; Government Specifications & Standards; Japanese Prints; Language Study; Large Type Books; Menus Coll; Orchestral Scores & Parts; Rare Books Coll; United States Patents. State Document Depository; UN Document Depository; US Document Depository
Wireless access
Partic in OCLC Online Computer Library Center, Inc; Southern California Library Cooperative
Special Services for the Deaf - Staff with knowledge of sign lang; TDD equip
Open Mon-Thurs 10-8, Fri & Sat 10-5:30, Sun 1-5
Friends of the Library Group
Branches: 77
ANGELES MESA, 2700 W 52nd St, 90043-1953, SAN 332-7272. Tel: 323-292-4328. FAX: 323-296-3508. *Sr Librn,* Langdon Faust
Library Holdings: Bk Vols 27,511
Open Mon & Wed 10-8, Tues & Thurs 12:30-8, Fri & Sat 10-5:30
Friends of the Library Group
ARROYO SECO REGIONAL, 6145 N Figueroa St, 90042-3565, SAN 332-7302. Tel: 323-255-0537. FAX: 323-255-1710. *Sr Librn,* Dora Suarez
Library Holdings: Bk Vols 46,758
Open Mon & Wed 10-8, Tues & Thurs 12:30-8, Fri & Sat 10-5:30, Sun 1-5
Friends of the Library Group
ASCOT, 120 W Florence Ave, 90003, SAN 332-7337. Tel: 323-759-4817. FAX: 323-758-6578. *Sr Librn,* Ellen Tanner
Library Holdings: Bk Vols 34,751
Open Mon & Wed 10-8, Tues & Thurs 12:30-8, Fri & Sat 10-5:30
ATWATER, 3379 Glendale Blvd, 90039-1825, SAN 332-7361. Tel: 323-664-1353. FAX: 323-913-4765. *Sr Librn,* Stella Nahapetian
Library Holdings: Bk Vols 37,343
Open Mon & Wed 10-8, Tues & Thurs 12:30-8, Fri & Sat 10-5:30
Friends of the Library Group
BALDWIN HILLS, 2906 S La Brea Ave, 90016-3902, SAN 332-7396. Tel: 323-733-1196. FAX: 323 733-0774. *Sr Librn,* Zakkiyya Rivers
Library Holdings: Bk Vols 46,297
Open Mon & Wed 10-8, Tues & Thurs 12:30-8, Fri & Sat 10-5:30
Friends of the Library Group
EXPOSITION PARK - DR MARY MCLEOD BETHUNE REGIONAL BRANCH, 3900 S Western Ave, 90062, SAN 332-7752. Tel: 323-290-3113. FAX: 323-290-3153. *Sr Librn,* JoAnn Morgan
Library Holdings: Bk Vols 44,556
Open Mon & Wed 10-8, Tues & Thurs 12:30-8, Fri & Sat 10-5:30, Sun 1-5
CAHUENGA, 4591 Santa Monica Blvd, 90029-1937, SAN 332-7485. Tel: 323-664-6418. FAX: 323-664-6200. *Sr Librn,* Jie Ren
Library Holdings: Bk Vols 34,203
Open Mon & Wed 10-8, Tues & Thurs 12:30-8, Fri & Sat 10-5:30
Friends of the Library Group
CANOGA PARK BRANCH, 20939 Sherman Way, Canoga Park, 91303, SAN 332-7515. Tel: 818-887-0320. FAX: 818-346-1074. *Sr Librn,* Connie Topete
Library Holdings: Bk Vols 61,866
Open Mon & Wed 10-8, Tues & Thurs 12:30-8, Fri & Sat 10-5:30
Friends of the Library Group
CENTRAL SOUTHERN AREA, 931 S Gaffey St, San Pedro, 90731, SAN 332-7140. Tel: 310-548-7785. FAX: 310-548-2096. *Mgr,* Kren Malone
CHATSWORTH BRANCH, 21052 Devonshire St, Chatsworth, 91311, SAN 332-754X. Tel: 818-341-4276. FAX: 818-341-7905. *Sr Librn,* Janet Metzler
Library Holdings: Bk Vols 50,382
Open Mon & Wed 10-8, Tues & Thurs 12:30-8, Fri & Sat 10-5:30
Friends of the Library Group
CHINATOWN, 639 N Hill St, 90012-2317, SAN 332-7574. Tel: 213-620-0925. FAX: 213-620-9956. *Sr Librn,* Shan Liang
Library Holdings: Bk Vols 69,165
Open Mon & Wed 10-8, Tues & Thurs 12:30-8, Fri & Sat 10-5:30
Friends of the Library Group
CYPRESS PARK, 1150 Cypress Ave, 90065-1144, SAN 332-7604. Tel: 323-224-0039. FAX: 323-224-0454. *Sr Librn,* Erika Caswell
Library Holdings: Bk Vols 36,013
Open Mon & Wed 10-8, Tues & Thurs 12:30-8, Fri & Sat 10-5:30
Friends of the Library Group
WILL & ARIEL DURANT BRANCH, 7140 W Sunset Blvd, 90046, SAN 332-8899. Tel: 323-876-2741. FAX: 323-876-0485. *Sr Librn,* John Frank
Library Holdings: Bk Vols 55,475
Open Mon & Wed 10-8, Tues & Thurs 12:30-8, Fri & Sat 10-5:30
Friends of the Library Group
EAGLE ROCK, 5027 Caspar Ave, 90041-1901, SAN 332-7639. Tel: 323-258-8078. FAX: 323-478-9530. *Sr Librn,* Sonja Hannah
Library Holdings: Bk Vols 52,160
Open Mon & Wed 10-8, Tues & Thurs 12:30-8, Fri & Sat 10-5:30
Friends of the Library Group
EAST VALLEY AREA, 5211 Tujunga Ave, 91601, SAN 332-7159. Tel: 818-755-7666. FAX: 818-760-8924. *Mgr,* Emily Fate
ECHO PARK, 1410 W Temple St, 90026-5605, SAN 332-7663. Tel: 213-250-7808. FAX: 213-580-3744. *Sr Librn,* Victoria Sikora
Library Holdings: Bk Vols 45,414
Open Mon & Wed 10-8, Tues & Thurs 12:30-8, Fri & Sat 10-5:30
Friends of the Library Group
EDENDALE, 2011 W Sunset Blvd, 90026. Tel: 213-207-3000. FAX: 213-207-3097. E-mail: eden@lapl.org. *Sr Librn,* Niels Bartels
Open Mon & Wed 10-8, Tues & Thurs 12:30-8, Fri & Sat 10-5:30
EL SERENO, 5226 Huntington Dr S, 90032, SAN 332-7698. Tel: 323-225-9201. FAX: 323-441-0112. *Sr Librn,* Eugene Estrada
Library Holdings: Bk Vols 56,742
Open Mon & Wed 10-8, Tues & Thurs 12:30-8, Fri & Sat 10-5:30
Friends of the Library Group

ENCINO-TARZANA BRANCH, 18231 Ventura Blvd, Tarzana, 91356-3620, SAN 332-7728. Tel: 818-343-1983. FAX: 818-343-7867. E-mail: enctar@lapl.org. *Sr Librn,* David Hagopian
Library Holdings: Bk Vols 62,724
Friends of the Library Group

FAIRFAX, 161 S Gardner St, 90036-2717, SAN 332-7787. Tel: 323-936-6191. FAX: 323-934-2675. *Sr Librn,* Roy Stone
Library Holdings: Bk Vols 50,379
Open Mon & Wed 10-8, Tues & Thurs 12:30-8, Fri & Sat 10-5:30
Friends of the Library Group

FELIPE DE NEVE BRANCH, 2820 W Sixth St, 90057-3114, SAN 332-7817. Tel: 213-384-7676. FAX: 213-368-7667. *Sr Librn,* Cathie Ehle
Library Holdings: Bk Vols 34,122
Open Mon & Wed 10-8, Tues & Thurs 12:30-8, Fri & Sat 10-5:30
Friends of the Library Group

BENJAMIN FRANKLIN BRANCH, 2200 E First St, 90033, SAN 332-7426. Tel: 323-263-6901. FAX: 323-526-3043. *Sr Librn,* Alicia Moguel; Staff 9 (MLS 4, Non-MLS 5)
Founded 1916
Library Holdings: Bk Vols 39,246
Open Mon & Wed 10-8, Tues & Thurs 12:30-8, Fri & Sat 10-5:30
Friends of the Library Group

JOHN C FREMONT BRANCH, 6121 Melrose Ave, 90038-3501, SAN 332-7841. Tel: 323-962-3521. FAX: 323-962-4553. *Sr Librn,* Beth Feinberg; Staff 10 (MLS 4, Non-MLS 6)
Library Holdings: Bk Vols 38,847
Open Mon & Wed 10-8, Tues & Thurs 12:30-8, Fri & Sat 10-5:30
Friends of the Library Group

FRANCES HOWARD GOLDWYN-HOLLYWOOD REGIONAL BRANCH, 1623 N Ivar Ave, 90028-6304, SAN 332-7906. Tel: 323-856-8260. FAX: 323-467-5707. *Sr Librn,* Kian Daizadeh
Library Holdings: Bk Vols 87,279
Subject Interests: Motion pictures
Open Mon & Wed 10-8, Tues & Thurs 12:30-8, Fri & Sat 10-5:30, Sun 1-5
Friends of the Library Group

GRANADA HILLS BRANCH, 10640 Petit Ave, Granada Hills, 91344-6452, SAN 332-7876. Tel: 818-368-5687. FAX: 818-756-9286. *Sr Librn,* Pamela Rhodes
Library Holdings: Bk Vols 63,670
Open Mon & Wed 10-8, Tues & Thurs 12:30-8, Fri & Sat 10-5:30
Friends of the Library Group

HARBOR CITY-HARBOR GATEWAY, 24000 S Western Ave, 90710, SAN 377-6492. Tel: 310-534-9520. FAX: 310-534-9532. *Sr Librn,* John Pham
Library Holdings: Bk Vols 50,882
Open Mon & Wed 10-8, Tues & Thurs 12:30-8, Fri & Sat 10-5:30

HOLLYWOOD AREA, 694 S Oxford St, 90005, SAN 332-7167. Tel: 213-368-7689. FAX: 213-639-1654. *Mgr,* Paul Montgomerie

HYDE PARK MIRIAM MATTHEWS BRANCH, 2205 Florence Ave, 90043, SAN 332-7930. Tel: 323-750-7241. FAX: 323-752-7861. *Actg Sr Librn,* Jennifer Murphy
Library Holdings: Bk Vols 32,880
Open Mon & Wed 10-8, Tues & Thurs 12:30-8, Fri & Sat 10-5:30
Friends of the Library Group

WASHINGTON IRVING BRANCH, 4117 W Washington Blvd, 90018-1053, SAN 332-7965. Tel: 323-734-6303. FAX: 323-731-2416. *Sr Librn,* Marcie Jones
Library Holdings: Bk Vols 41,265
Open Mon & Wed 10-8, Tues & Thurs 12:30-8, Fri & Sat 10-5:30
Friends of the Library Group

JEFFERSON BRANCH, 2211 W Jefferson Blvd, 90018-3741, SAN 332-799X. Tel: 323-734-8573. FAX: 323-737-2885. *Sr Librn,* Karla Valdez
Library Holdings: Bk Vols 29,369
Open Mon & Wed 10-8, Tues & Thurs 12:30-8, Fri & Sat 10-5:30
Friends of the Library Group

JUNIPERO SERRA, 4607 S Main St, 90037-2735, SAN 332-8023. Tel: 323-234-1685. FAX: 323-846-5389. *Sr Librn,* Haewon Paick
Library Holdings: Bk Vols 42,901
Open Mon & Wed 10-8, Tues & Thurs 12:30-8, Fri & Sat 10-5:30
Friends of the Library Group

DONALD BRUCE KAUFMAN-BRENTWOOD BRANCH, 11820 San Vicente Blvd, 90049-5002, SAN 332-7450. Tel: 310-575-8273. FAX: 310-575-8276. *Sr Librn,* Henry Gambill
Library Holdings: Bk Vols 44,357
Open Mon & Wed 10-8, Tues & Thurs 12:30-8, Fri & Sat 10-5:30
Friends of the Library Group

LAKE VIEW TERRACE, 12002 Osborne St, 91342, SAN 332-8112. Tel: 818-890-7404. FAX: 818-897-2738. *Sr Librn,* Constance Dosch
Library Holdings: Bk Vols 53,032
Open Mon & Wed 10-8, Tues & Thurs 12:30-8, Fri & Sat 10-5:30
Friends of the Library Group

LINCOLN HEIGHTS, 2530 Workman St, 90031-2322, SAN 332-8058. Tel: 323-226-1692. FAX: 323-226-1691. *Sr Librn,* Steven Cheng
Library Holdings: Bk Vols 37,273
Open Mon & Wed 10-8, Tues & Thurs 12:30-8, Fri & Sat 10-5:30
Friends of the Library Group

LITTLE TOKYO, 203 S Los Angeles St, 90012, SAN 329-658X. Tel: 213-612-0525. FAX: 213-612-0424. *Sr Librn,* James Sherod
Library Holdings: Bk Vols 67,900
Open Mon & Wed 10-8, Tues & Thurs 12:30-8, Fri & Sat 10-5:30
Friends of the Library Group

LOS FELIZ, 1874 Hillhurst Ave, 90027-4427, SAN 332-8082. Tel: 323-913-4710. FAX: 323-913-4714. *Sr Librn,* Pearl Yonezawa
Library Holdings: Bk Vols 54,325
Open Mon & Wed 10-8, Tues & Thurs 12:30-8, Fri & Sat 10-5:30
Friends of the Library Group

MALABAR, 2801 Wabash Ave, 90033-2604, SAN 332-8147. Tel: 323-263-1497. FAX: 323-612-0416. *Sr Librn,* Yan Wen
Library Holdings: Bk Vols 34,328
Open Mon & Wed 10-8, Tues & Thurs 12:30-8, Fri & Sat 10-5:30
Friends of the Library Group

MAR VISTA, 12006 Venice Blvd, 90066-3810, SAN 332-8171. Tel: 310-390-3454. FAX: 310-391-0531. *Sr Librn,* Carole Kealoha
Library Holdings: Bk Vols 44,910
Open Mon & Wed 10-8, Tues & Thurs 12:30-8, Fri & Sat 10-5:30
Friends of the Library Group

MEMORIAL, 4625 W Olympic Blvd, 90019-1832, SAN 332-8201. Tel: 323-938-2732. FAX: 323-938-3378. *Sr Librn,* Johathan Pitre
Library Holdings: Bk Vols 38,116
Open Mon & Wed 10-8, Tues & Thurs 12:30-8, Fri & Sat 10-5:30
Friends of the Library Group

MID-VALLEY REGIONAL, 16244 Nordhoff St, North Hills, 91343, SAN 377-6476. Tel: 818-895-3650. FAX: 818-895-3657. *Sr Librn,* Victoria Magaw
Library Holdings: Bk Vols 133,455
Open Mon & Wed 10-8, Tues & Thurs 12:30-8, Fri & Sat 10-5:30, Sun 1-5
Friends of the Library Group

JOHN MUIR BRANCH, 1005 W 64th St, 90044-3605, SAN 332-8236. Tel: 323-789-4800. FAX: 323-789-5758. *Actg Sr Librn,* Marc Horton
Library Holdings: Bk Vols 27,329
Open Mon & Wed 10-8, Tues & Thurs 12:30-8, Fri & Sat 10-5:30
Friends of the Library Group

NORTH HOLLYWOOD AMELIA EARHART REGIONAL, 5211 Tujunga Ave, North Hollywood, 91601-3119, SAN 332-8260. Tel: 818-766-7185. FAX: 818-755-7671. *Sr Librn,* Jeanne Rankin
Library Holdings: Bk Vols 51,036
Open Mon & Wed 10-8, Tues & Thurs 12:30-8, Fri & Sat 10-5:30, Sun 1-5
Friends of the Library Group

NORTHEAST AREA, 6145 N Figueroa St, 90042, SAN 332-7175. Tel: 323-255-1863. FAX: 323-256-8459. *Mgr,* Sylva Galan-Garcia

NORTHRIDGE BRANCH, 9051 Darby Ave, Northridge, 91325-2743, SAN 332-8295. Tel: 818-886-3640. FAX: 818-886-6850. *Sr Librn,* Leslie Chudnoff
Library Holdings: Bk Vols 61,323
Open Mon & Wed 10-8, Tues & Thurs 12:30-8, Fri & Sat 10-5:30
Friends of the Library Group

PACOIMA BRANCH, 13605 Van Nuys Blvd, Pacoima, 91331-3613, SAN 332-8325. Tel: 818-899-5203. FAX: 818-899-5336. *Sr Librn,* Laura Contin
Library Holdings: Bk Vols 51,293
Open Mon & Wed 10-8, Tues & Thurs 12:30-8, Fri & Sat 10-5:30
Friends of the Library Group

PALISADES BRANCH, 861 Alma Real Dr, Pacific Palisades, 90272-3730, SAN 332-835X. Tel: 310-459-2754. FAX: 310-454-3198. *Sr Librn,* Mary Hopf
Library Holdings: Bk Vols 44,984
Open Mon & Wed 10-8, Tues & Thurs 12:30-8, Fri & Sat 10-5:30
Friends of the Library Group

PALMS-RANCHO PARK, 2920 Overland Ave, 90064-4220, SAN 332-8384. Tel: 310-840-2142. FAX: 310-202-4597. *Sr Librn,* Maggie L Johnson
Library Holdings: Bk Vols 50,853
Open Mon & Wed 10-8, Tues & Thurs 12:30-8, Fri & Sat 10-5:30
Friends of the Library Group

PANORAMA CITY BRANCH, 14345 Roscoe Blvd, Panorama City, 91402-4222, SAN 332-8414. Tel: 818-894-4071. FAX: 818-895-6482. *Sr Librn,* Teri Markson
Library Holdings: Bk Vols 46,076
Open Mon & Wed 10-8, Tues & Thurs 12:30-8, Fri & Sat 10-5:30
Friends of the Library Group

PICO UNION, 1030 S Alvarado St, 90006. Tel: 213-368-7545. FAX: 213-368-7543. E-mail: punion@lapl.org. *Sr Librn,* Kathleen Ellison
Open Mon & Wed 10-8, Tues & Thurs 12:30-8, Fri & Sat 10-5:30

PIO PICO-KOREATOWN, 694 S Oxford, 90005-2872, SAN 332-8449. Tel: 213-368-7647. FAX: 213-639-1653. *Sr Librn,* Myungcha Miki Lim
Library Holdings: Bk Vols 88,184
Open Mon & Wed 10-8, Tues & Thurs 12:30-8, Fri & Sat 10-5:30
Friends of the Library Group

PLATT, 23600 Victory Blvd, Woodland Hills, 91367, SAN 377-0117. Tel: 818-340-9386. FAX: 818-340-9645. *Sr Librn,* Janet Gast
Library Holdings: Bk Vols 61,612
Open Mon & Wed 10-8, Tues & Thurs 12:30-8, Fri & Sat 10-5:30
Friends of the Library Group

PLAYA VISTA, 6400 Playa Vista Dr, 90094. Tel: 310-437-6680. FAX: 310-437-6690. E-mail: pvista@lapl.org. *Sr Librn,* Joseph Atkinson
Open Mon & Wed 10-8, Tues & Thurs 12:30-8, Fri & Sat 10-5:30

PORTER RANCH, 11371 Tampa Ave, Northridge, 91326, SAN 377-0095. Tel: 818-360-5706. FAX: 818-360-3106. *Sr Librn,* Shayeri Tangri
Library Holdings: Bk Vols 58,427
Open Mon & Wed 10-8, Tues & Thurs 12:30-8, Fri & Sat 10-5:30
Friends of the Library Group

ROBERTSON, 1719 S Robertson Blvd, 90035-4315, SAN 332-8473. Tel: 310-840-2147. FAX: 310-840-2156. *Sr Librn,* Carol Duan
Library Holdings: Bk Vols 39,584
Open Mon & Wed 10-8, Tues & Thurs 12:30-8, Fri & Sat 10-5:30, Sun 1-5
Friends of the Library Group

SAN PEDRO REGIONAL, 931 S Gaffey St, San Pedro, 90731-3606, SAN 332-8503. Tel: 310-548-7779. FAX: 310-548-7453. *Sr Librn,* David Ellis
Library Holdings: Bk Vols 71,553
Open Mon & Wed 10-8, Tues & Thurs 12:30-8, Fri & Sat 10-5:30, Sun 1-5

SHERMAN OAKS MARTIN POLLARD BRANCH, 14245 Moorpark St, Sherman Oaks, 91423-2722, SAN 332-8538. Tel: 818-205-9716. FAX: 818-205-9866. *Sr Librn,* Arthur Pond
Library Holdings: Bk Vols 62,855
Open Mon & Wed 10-8, Tues & Thurs 12:30-8, Fri & Sat 10-5:30
Friends of the Library Group

SILVER LAKE, 2411 Glendale Ave, 90039. Tel: 323-913-7451. FAX: 323-913-7460. E-mail: silver@lapl.org. *Sr Librn,* Lisa Palombi
Open Mon & Wed 10-8, Tues & Thurs 12:30-8, Fri & Sat 10-5:30

ROBERT LOUIS STEVENSON BRANCH, 803 Spence St, 90023-1727, SAN 332-8562. Tel: 323-268-4710. FAX: 213-268-7622. *Sr Librn,* Lupie Leyva
Library Holdings: Bk Vols 31,341
Open Mon & Wed 10-8, Tues & Thurs 12:30-8, Fri & Sat 10-5:30
Friends of the Library Group

STUDIO CITY BRANCH, 12511 Moorpark St, Studio City, 91604-1372, SAN 332-8597. Tel: 818-755-7873. FAX: 818-755-7878. *Sr Librn,* Karen Pickard-Four
Library Holdings: Bk Vols 60,988
Open Mon & Wed 10-8, Tues & Thurs 12:30-8, Fri & Sat 10-5:30
Friends of the Library Group

SUN VALLEY BRANCH, 7935 Vineland Ave, Sun Valley, 91352-4477, SAN 332-8627. Tel: 818-764-1338. FAX: 818-764-2245. *Sr Librn,* Guadalupe Canales
Library Holdings: Bk Vols 47,183
Open Mon & Wed 10-8, Tues & Thurs 12:30-8, Fri & Sat 10-5:30
Friends of the Library Group

SUNLAND-TUJUNGA BRANCH, 7771 Foothill Blvd, Tujunga, 91042-2137, SAN 332-8651. Tel: 818-352-4481. FAX: 818-352-2501. *Actg Sr Librn,* Florence L Jacinto
Library Holdings: Bk Vols 47,281
Open Mon & Wed 10-8, Tues & Thurs 12:30-8, Fri & Sat 10-5:30
Friends of the Library Group

SYLMAR BRANCH, 14561 Polk St, Sylmar, 91342-4055, SAN 332-8686. Tel: 818-367-6102. FAX: 818-367-5872. *Sr Librn,* Faegheh Mofidi
Library Holdings: Bk Vols 47,162
Open Mon & Wed 10-8, Tues & Thurs 12:30-8, Fri & Sat 10-5:30
Friends of the Library Group

MARK TWAIN BRANCH, 9621 S Figueroa St, 90003, SAN 332-8716. Tel: 323-755-4088. FAX: 323-755-3185. *Sr Librn,* Martha Sherod; Staff 8 (MLS 2, Non-MLS 6)
Library Holdings: Bk Vols 41,888
Open Mon & Wed 10-8, Tues & Thurs 12:30-8, Fri & Sat 10-5:30
Friends of the Library Group

VALLEY PLAZA, 12311 Vanowen St, North Hollywood, 91605, SAN 332-9100. Tel: 818-765-9251. FAX: 818-765-9260. *Sr Librn,* Patricia Rostomian
Library Holdings: Bk Vols 45,937
Open Mon & Wed 10-8, Tues & Thurs 12:30-8, Fri & Sat 10-5:30
Friends of the Library Group

VAN NUYS BRANCH, 6250 Sylmar Ave Mall, Van Nuys, 91401-2707, SAN 332-8740. Tel: 818-756-8453. FAX: 818-756-9291. *Sr Librn,* Kelly Tyler
Library Holdings: Bk Vols 63,478
Open Mon & Wed 10-8, Tues & Thurs 12:30-8, Fri & Sat 10-5:30
Friends of the Library Group

VENICE-ABBOT KINNEY MEMORIAL, 501 S Venice Blvd, Venice, 90291-4201, SAN 332-9070. Tel: 310-821-1769. FAX: 310-306-9124. *Sr Librn,* Rachel Bindman
Library Holdings: Bk Vols 47,358
Open Mon & Wed 10-8, Tues & Thurs 12:30-8, Fri & Sat 10-5:30
Friends of the Library Group

VERMONT SQUARE, 1201 W 48th St, 90037-2838, SAN 332-8864. Tel: 323-290-7405. FAX: 323-290-7408. *Actg Sr Librn,* Soo Jin Kim; Staff 8 (MLS 3, Non-MLS 5)
Library Holdings: Bk Vols 29,199
Subject Interests: African-Am hist
Open Mon & Wed 10-8, Tues & Thurs 12:30-8, Fri & Sat 10-5:30
Friends of the Library Group

LEON H WASHINGTON JR MEMORIAL-VERNON BRANCH, 4504 S Central Ave, 90011-3632, SAN 332-8953. Tel: 213-234-9106. FAX: 213-231-4291. *Sr Librn,* Ana Campos
Library Holdings: Bk Vols 41,126
Open Mon & Wed 10-8, Tues & Thurs 12:30-8, Fri & Sat 10-5:30
Friends of the Library Group

WEST LOS ANGELES REGIONAL, 11360 Santa Monica Blvd, 90025-3152, SAN 332-9046. Tel: 310-575-8323. FAX: 310-575-8475. *Sr Librn,* Claudia Martinez
Library Holdings: Bk Vols 43,805
Open Mon & Wed 10-8, Tues & Thurs 12:30-8, Fri & Sat 10-5:30, Sun 1-5
Friends of the Library Group

WEST VALLEY AREA, 19036 Vanowen St, Reseda, 91335, SAN 332-7213. Tel: 818-895-3662. FAX: 818-895-3656. *Mgr,* Ruth E Seid
Open Mon & Wed 10-8, Tues & Thurs 12:30-8, Fri & Sat 10-5:30, Sun 1-5

WEST VALLEY REGIONAL, 19036 Vanowen St, Receda, 91335, SAN 332-8929. Tel: 818-345-9806. FAX: 818-345-4288. *Sr Librn,* Ken Blum
Library Holdings: Bk Vols 74,362
Open Mon & Wed 10-8, Tues & Thurs 12:30-8, Fri & Sat 10-5:30, Sun 1-5
Friends of the Library Group

WESTCHESTER-LOYOLA VILLAGE, 7114 W Manchester Ave, 90045-3509. Tel: 310-348-1096. FAX: 310-348-1082. *Sr Librn,* Jennifer Ishimoto
Library Holdings: Bk Vols 34,374
Open Mon & Wed 10-8, Tues & Thurs 12:30-8, Fri & Sat 10-5:30
Friends of the Library Group

WESTWOOD, 1246 Glendon Ave, 90024, SAN 332-7221. Tel: 310-474-1739, 310-575-8476. FAX: 310-470-3892, 310-575-8433. *Area Mgr,* Adam Mendelsohn; *Sr Librn,* Shahla Chamanara
Open Mon & Wed 10-8, Tues & Thurs 12:30-8, Fri & Sat 10-5:30

WILMINGTON, 1300 N Avalon Blvd, 90744, SAN 332-883X. Tel: 310-834-1082. FAX: 310-548-7418. *Sr Librn,* Denise Nossett
Library Holdings: Bk Vols 56,745
Open Mon & Wed 10-8, Tues & Thurs 12:30-8, Fri & Sat 10-5:30
Friends of the Library Group

WILSHIRE, 149 N Saint Andrew Pl, 90004, SAN 332-8805. Tel: 323-957-4550. FAX: 323-957-4555. *Sr Librn,* Madeleine Kerr Ildefonso
Library Holdings: Bk Vols 38,172
Open Mon & Wed 10-8, Tues & Thurs 12:30-8, Fri & Sat 10-5:30
Friends of the Library Group

WOODLAND HILLS BRANCH, 22200 Ventura Blvd, Woodland Hills, 91364-1517, SAN 332-8988. Tel: 818-226-9056. FAX: 818-226-0017. *Sr Librn,* Jane Dobija
Library Holdings: Bk Vols 53,346
Open Mon & Wed 10-8, Tues & Thurs 12:30-8, Fri & Sat 10-5:30
Friends of the Library Group

ALMA REAVES WOODS-WATTS BRANCH, 10205 Compton Ave, 90002-2804, SAN 332-8775. Tel: 323-789-2850. FAX: 323-789-2859. *Sr Librn,* David Tulanian
Library Holdings: Bk Vols 46,116
Open Mon & Wed 10-8, Tues & Thurs 12:30-8, Fri & Sat 10-5:30
Friends of the Library Group

J LOS ANGELES SOUTHWEST COLLEGE*, Founders Library, Cox Bldg, 1600 W Imperial Hwy, 90047-4899. SAN 300-9580. Tel: 323-241-5235. FAX: 323-241-5221. *Head of Libr,* Werts Shelley; *Cat,* Gabrielle Arvig; Staff 8 (MLS 4, Non-MLS 4)
Founded 1967. Enrl 7,169; Fac 250; Highest Degree: Associate
Library Holdings: AV Mats 700; Bk Vols 48,970; Per Subs 265
Subject Interests: African-Am, Hispanic
Automation Activity & Vendor Info: (Cataloging) SirsiDynix; (Circulation) SirsiDynix; (OPAC) SirsiDynix
Database Vendor: SirsiDynix
Publications: Library Brochure; Los Angeles Southwest College - A Selected List of New Books; Periodicals Holding List
Partic in Lyrasis
Special Services for the Blind - Reader equip
Open Mon-Thurs 7:45am-8pm, Fri 7:45-1

S LOS ANGELES TIMES*, Editorial Library, 202 W First St, 90012-0267. SAN 300-9599. Tel: 213-237-7181. Web Site: www.latimes.com. *Dir,* Cary Schneider; *Librn,* Scott Wilson; Staff 7 (MLS 7)
Founded 1905
Library Holdings: Bk Titles 10,000
Special Collections: Core Reference Coll; Los Angeles Times, clippings, flm, photogs
Subject Interests: Current events
Publications: Library Information Notes; Library Updates
Partic in OCLC Online Computer Library Center, Inc; Southern California Library Cooperative

J LOS ANGELES TRADE TECHNICAL COLLEGE LIBRARY*, 400 W Washington Blvd, 90015. SAN 300-9602. Tel: 213-763-3958. Circulation Tel: 213-763-3950. Administration Tel: 213-763-3978. FAX: 213-763-5393. Web Site: college.lattc.edu/library. *Dept Chair,* Lisa Nitsch; E-mail: nitschlm@lattc.edu; *Librn,* Judith Samuel; E-mail: samuelJC@lattc.edu; Staff 2 (MLS 2)
Founded 1927. Enrl 6,440; Fac 500
Library Holdings: e-books 5,312; Microforms 114; Bk Titles 84,963; Bk Vols 85,487; Per Subs 193
Special Collections: Blanche Gottlieb Culinary Arts Coll
Subject Interests: Fashion
Automation Activity & Vendor Info: (Cataloging) SIRSI WorkFlows; (Circulation) SIRSI WorkFlows; (Course Reserve) SIRSI WorkFlows; (ILL) SIRSI WorkFlows; (OPAC) SirsiDynix
Database Vendor: CountryWatch, EBSCO Auto Repair Reference, EBSCOhost, Gale Cengage Learning, ProQuest, SirsiDynix
Wireless access
Open Mon-Thurs 9-6, Fri 8-1

CL LOYOLA LAW SCHOOL*, William M Rains Law Library, 919 S Albany St, 90015-1211. SAN 332-916X. Tel: 213-736-1117. Interlibrary Loan Service Tel: 213-736-8119. Administration Tel: 213-736-1198. FAX: 213-487-2204. Administration FAX: 213-385-5950. Web Site: www.library.lls.edu. *Dir,* Daniel W Martin; Tel: 213-736-1197, E-mail: daniel.martin@lls.edu; *Assoc Dir,* Karen Verdugo; Tel: 213-736-1181, E-mail: karen.verdugo@lls.edu; *Head, Libr Computing Serv,* David Burch; Tel: 213-736-1115, E-mail: david.burch@lls.edu; *Head, Ref,* Laura Cadra; Tel: 213-736-1141, E-mail: laura.cadra@lls.edu; *Head, Tech Serv,* Edward St John; Tel: 213-736-1146, Fax: 213-385-7614, E-mail: edward.stjohn@lls.edu; *Acq/Ser Librn,* Dawn Smith; Tel: 213-736-1174, E-mail: dawn.smith@lls.edu; *Cat Librn,* Vera Aronoff; Tel: 213-736-1419, E-mail: vera.aronoff@lls.edu; *Computing Serv Librn,* Florante Ibanez; Tel: 213-736-1431, E-mail: florante.ibanez@lls.edu; *Ref/Digital Mgt Librn,* Suzanna Shatarevyan; Tel: 213-736-1147, E-mail: suzanna.shatarevyan@lls.edu; *Ref Librn,* Thomas Boone; Tel: 213-736-1329, E-mail: thomas.boone@lls.edu; *Ref Librn,* Amber Kennedy Madole; Tel: 213-736-8389, E-mail: amber.madole@lls.edu; *Ref Librn,* Joshua Phillips; Tel: 213-736-1413, E-mail: joshua.phillips@lls.edu; *Ref Librn,* Lisa Schultz; Tel: 213-736-8132, E-mail: lisa.schultz@lls.edu.
Subject Specialists: *Foreign/Intl law,* Laura Cadra
Founded 1920. Highest Degree: Doctorate
Special Collections: Loyola Law School Archive Coll; Rare Books on Law. State Document Depository; US Document Depository
Subject Interests: Acid rain
Database Vendor: Dialog, EBSCOhost, HeinOnline, Innovative Interfaces, Inc, JSTOR, LexisNexis, Loislaw, OCLC FirstSearch, Oxford Online, Westlaw, Wilson - Wilson Web
Wireless access
Publications: Acquisitions List; Annual report; Occasional Showers (Newsletter)

C LOYOLA MARYMOUNT UNIVERSITY*, William H Hannon Library, One LMU Dr, MS 8200, 90045-2659. SAN 332-9135. Tel: 310-338-2788. Circulation Tel: 310-338-5709. Interlibrary Loan Service Tel: 310-338-5705. Reference Tel: 310-338-2790. Administration Tel: 310-338-4593. FAX: 310-338-4366. Circulation FAX: 310-338-3006. Administration FAX: 310-338-4484. E-mail: library@lmu.edu. Web Site: library.lmu.edu, lmulibrary.typepad.com. *Dean of Libr,* Kristine R Brancolini; E-mail: brancoli@lmu.edu; *Assoc Dean,* Tobeylynn Birch; Tel: 310-338-3088, E-mail: tobeylynn.birch@lmu.edu; *Head, Acq & Ser,* Charles Hillen; Tel: 310-338-4458, E-mail: charles.hillen@lmu.edu; *Head, Archives & Spec Coll,* Cynthia Becht; Tel: 310-338-2780, E-mail: cbecht@lmu.edu; *Head, Cat,* Walt Walker; Tel: 310-338-7687, E-mail: wwalker@lmu.edu; *Head, Coll Develop,* Glenn Johnson-Grau; Tel: 310-338-6063, E-mail: gjohnson@lmu.edu; *Head, Ref & Instruction,* Susan Gardner; Tel: 310-338-7680, E-mail: Susan.Gardner@lmu.edu; *Circ Serv Librn,* Rhonda Rosen; Tel: 310-338-4584, E-mail: rrosen@lmu.edu; *Digital Prog Librn,* Shilpa Rele; Tel: 310-338-2792, E-mail: shilpa.rele@lmu.edu; *Emerging Tech Librn, Ref & Instruction,* Tara Radniecki; Tel: 310-337-7686; *Syst Librn,* Meghan Weeks; Tel: 310-338-5929, E-mail: meghan.weeks@lmu.edu; *Instruction Coordr, Ref & Instruction,* Elisa Slater Acosta; Tel: 310-338-7679, E-mail: eslater@lmu.edu; Staff 26 (MLS 24, Non-MLS 2)
Founded 1929. Enrl 8,307; Fac 521; Highest Degree: Doctorate
Library Holdings: AV Mats 30,436; e-books 196,376; e-journals 55,939; Bk Vols 510,283; Per Subs 1,151
Special Collections: 20th Century Theater & Film Coll; Arthur P Jacobs Coll; Oliver Goldsmith Coll; Rare Books; Saint Thomas Moore Coll; Werner von Boltenstern Postcard Coll
Automation Activity & Vendor Info: (Acquisitions) Innovative Interfaces, Inc; (Cataloging) Innovative Interfaces, Inc; (Circulation) Innovative Interfaces, Inc; (Course Reserve) Docutek; (ILL) OCLC ILLiad; (Media Booking) Innovative Interfaces, Inc; (OPAC) Innovative Interfaces, Inc; (Serials) Innovative Interfaces, Inc
Database Vendor: ABC-CLIO, ACM (Association for Computing Machinery), Alexander Street Press, American Chemical Society, American Geophysical Union, American Mathematical Society, American Physical Society, American Psychological Association (APA), Annual Reviews, ARTstor, BioOne, Bowker, Cambridge Scientific Abstracts, CIOS (Communication Institute for Online Scholarship), CountryWatch, CQ Press, CRC Press/Taylor & Francis Group, CredoReference, Dun & Bradstreet, ebrary, EBSCOhost, Elsevier, Emerald, Facts on File, Gale Cengage Learning, Gallup, H W Wilson, Hoovers, IEEE (Institute of Electrical & Electronics Engineers), Innovative Interfaces, Inc, Innovative Interfaces, Inc, IOP, JSTOR, LexisNexis, Medline, Mergent Online, Nature Publishing Group, Newsbank, OCLC FirstSearch, OCLC WorldShare Interlibrary Loan, Oxford Online, Project MUSE, ProQuest, Sage, ScienceDirect, SerialsSolutions, SirsiDynix, Springer-Verlag, Standard & Poor's, Thomson - Web of Science, ValueLine, Wiley InterScience, YBP Library Services
Wireless access
Partic in Association of Jesuit Colleges & Universities (AJCU); Link+; OCLC Online Computer Library Center, Inc; Statewide California Electronic Library Consortium (SCELC)
Open Mon-Thurs 8am-2am, Fri 8-8, Sat 11-8, Sun 11-2
Restriction: Open to students, fac & staff, Restricted pub use

L MESERVE, MUMPER & HUGHES*, Law Library, 300 S Grand Ave, 24th Flr, 90071-3185. SAN 328-4093. Tel: 213-620-0300. FAX: 213-625-1930. Web Site: www.mmhllp.com. *Adminr,* Kirk Simons
Library Holdings: Bk Vols 10,000
Subject Interests: Labor
Restriction: Not open to pub

L MILBANK, TWEED, HADLEY & MCCLOY*, Law Library, 601 S Figueroa St, 30th Flr, 90017. SAN 372-3046. Tel: 213-892-4468, 213-892-4475. FAX: 213-892-4798. Web Site: www.milbank.com.
Library Holdings: Bk Titles 1,000; Bk Vols 2,000; Per Subs 218
Partic in OCLC Online Computer Library Center, Inc
Restriction: Not a lending libr, Not open to pub

L MITCHELL SILBERBERG & KNUPP LLP*, Law Library, 11377 W Olympic Blvd, 90064-1683. SAN 300-9696. Tel: 310-312-2000. FAX: 310-312-3100. E-mail: library@msk.com. Web Site: www.msk.com. *Librn,* Carolyn A Pratt; *Asst Librn,* Sunan Xing; Staff 3 (MLS 2, Non-MLS 1)
Library Holdings: Bk Vols 35,000
Automation Activity & Vendor Info: (Cataloging) EOS International; (OPAC) EOS International; (Serials) EOS International
Wireless access
Restriction: Staff use only

S MORRISON & FOERSTER LLP LIBRARY*, 555 W Fifth St, Ste 3500, 90013-1024. SAN 370-1662. Tel: 213-892-5359. FAX: 213-892-5454. Web Site: www.mofo.com. *Librn,* Lee Nemchek
Library Holdings: Bk Titles 20,000; Per Subs 500
Special Collections: California City Charters; California Municipal Planning & Zoning Ordinances
Subject Interests: Labor, Law, Real estate
Partic in CDB Infotek; CourtLink; Dialog Corp; Dun & Bradstreet Info Servs; Westlaw
Restriction: Staff use only

C MOUNT SAINT MARY'S COLLEGE*, Charles Willard Coe Memorial Library, 12001 Chalon Rd, 90049-1599. SAN 332-9194. Tel: 310-954-4370. FAX: 310-954-4379. Web Site: www.msmc.la.edu. *Dir,* Claudia Reed; E-mail: creed@msmc.la.edu; *Access Serv,* Susan Shapiro; *Ref,* Rozha Popovitch-Krekic; *Tech Serv,* Mary Sedgwick; Staff 6 (MLS 6)
Founded 1925. Enrl 1,200; Fac 89; Highest Degree: Master
Library Holdings: Bk Titles 115,000; Bk Vols 132,201; Per Subs 800
Special Collections: Cardinal Newman Coll
Subject Interests: Humanities, Nursing, Phys therapy
Automation Activity & Vendor Info: (Cataloging) Innovative Interfaces, Inc; (Circulation) Innovative Interfaces, Inc
Partic in Dialog Corp; National Network of Libraries of Medicine; OCLC Online Computer Library Center, Inc
Open Mon-Thurs 8-5, Fri 8-4, Sat 10-6, Sun 10-10

Departmental Libraries:
DOHENY CAMPUS LIBRARY, Ten Chester Pl, 90007, SAN 332-9224. Tel: 213-477-2750. FAX: 213-749-8111. *Librn,* Mary Kranz
Open Mon-Thurs 8am-9pm, Fri 8-4:30, Sat & Sun 10-6

L MUNGER, TOLLES & OLSON LLP*, Law Library, 355 S Grand Ave, 35th Flr, 90071-1560. SAN 300-970X. Tel: 213-683-9100. Reference Tel: 213-683-9100, Ext 3550. FAX: 213-683-5173. *Head Librn,* Joan Schipper; *Assoc Librn,* Helen Kim; *Ref Serv,* Ramon Barajas; Staff 3 (MLS 3)
Founded 1963
Library Holdings: Bk Vols 15,000
Subject Interests: Am law

S THE MUSIC CENTER OF LOS ANGELES COUNTY ARCHIVES*, 135 N Grand Ave, 90012-3013. SAN 332-9259. Tel: 213-972-7499. FAX: 213-972-3132. *Archivist,* Julio C Gonzalez; E-mail: jgonzalez@musiccenter.org. Subject Specialists: *Theatre,* Julio C Gonzalez; Staff 1 (MLS 1)
Founded 1969
Library Holdings: Bk Titles 381; Bk Vols 500
Special Collections: Costumes; Los Angeles (Raymond Barnes Coll), bks, clippings, photog, programs; Los Angeles Philharmonic Orchestra-Hollywood Bowl (John Orlando Northcutt Coll), bks, photog; Opera (Richard Crooks Coll), stage; Otto Rothschild Photo Coll; Theatre-Early; Theatre-New York, Los Angeles (Kenneth Randall Coll), bks, clippings, photog, programs. Oral History
Subject Interests: Music, Performing arts
Restriction: Open by appt only

L MUSICK, PEELER & GARRETT LIBRARY*, One Wilshire Bldg, 624 S Grand Ave, Ste 2000, 90017. SAN 300-9718. Tel: 213-629-7600. FAX: 213-624-1376. Web Site: www.mpgweb.com. *Librn,* Lisa L Baker
Library Holdings: Bk Vols 20,000; Per Subs 400
Subject Interests: Corporate, Labor, Law, Litigation, Real estate, Tax
Automation Activity & Vendor Info: (Cataloging) Inmagic, Inc.; (OPAC) Inmagic, Inc.

S NATIONAL ECONOMIC RESEARCH ASSOCIATES, INC LIBRARY*, 777 S Figueroa St, Ste 4200, 90017. SAN 300-9726. Tel: 213-346-3000. FAX: 213-346-3030. Web Site: www.nera.com. *In Charge,* Linda Dorman
Library Holdings: Bk Vols 2,500; Per Subs 95
Subject Interests: Antitrust law

S NEW CENTER FOR PSYCHOANALYSIS LIBRARY*, 2014 Sawtelle Blvd, 90025. SAN 300-6271. Tel: 310-478-6541. FAX: 310-477-5968. E-mail: info@n-c-p.org. Web Site: n-c-p.org. *Coordr,* Pat Wright
Founded 1958
Library Holdings: Bk Titles 3,200; Bk Vols 4,500; Per Subs 20
Subject Interests: Humanities, Psychiat, Psychoanalysis, Psychol, Soc sci
Partic in Pacific Southwest Regional Medical Library (PSRML)

NORTHROP GRUMMAN CORP
S CORPORATE RESEARCH LIBRARY*, 1840 Century Park E, 90067-2199, SAN 371-7232. Tel: 310-201-3132, 310-201-3231. FAX: 310-201-3023. *Librn,* Michelle Tate; Staff 3 (MLS 2, Non-MLS 1)
Library Holdings: Bk Titles 3,245; Per Subs 90
Partic in OCLC Western Service Center

L NOSSAMAN LLP LIBRARY, 777 S Figueroa St, Ste 3400, 90017. SAN 300-9742. Tel: 213-612-7800. FAX: 213-612-7801. E-mail: library@nossaman.com. Web Site: www.nossaman.com.
Library Holdings: Bk Vols 12,000; Per Subs 350
Automation Activity & Vendor Info: (Cataloging) EOS International; (Circulation) EOS International; (OPAC) EOS International; (Serials) EOS International
Wireless access
Open Mon-Fri 9-5
Restriction: Authorized personnel only
Branches:
IRVINE, 18101 Von Karman Ave, Ste 1800, Irvine, 92612.
SACRAMENTO, 621 Capitol Mall, 25th Fl, Sacramento, 95814.
SAN FRANCISCO, 50 California St, 34th Fl, San Francisco, 94111. Tel: 415-398-3600. FAX: 415-398-2438. E-mail: library@nossaman.com.
Automation Activity & Vendor Info: (Cataloging) EOS International

C OCCIDENTAL COLLEGE LIBRARY, Mary Norton Clapp Library, 1600 Campus Rd, 90041. SAN 300-9750. Circulation Tel: 323-259-2640. Interlibrary Loan Service Tel: 323-259-2628. Administration Tel: 323-259-2832. FAX: 323-341-4991. Interlibrary Loan Service FAX: 323-259-2815. Web Site: www.oxy.edu/library. *Col Librn,* Robert Kieft; Tel: 323-259-2504, E-mail: kieft@oxy.edu; *Librn, Data Mgt & Integrity,* John De La Fontaine; Tel: 323-259-2914, E-mail: delafo@oxy.edu; *Col Archivist & Spec Coll Librn,* Dale Stieber; Tel: 323-259-2852, E-mail: dstieber@oxy.edu; *Circ & Reserves Mgr,* Hoda Abdelghani; E-mail: habdelghani@oxy.edu; *Asst Archivist,* Anne Mar; E-mail: amar@oxy.edu; Staff 5 (MLS 4, Non-MLS 1)
Founded 1887. Highest Degree: Master
Automation Activity & Vendor Info: (Acquisitions) Innovative Interfaces, Inc; (Cataloging) Innovative Interfaces, Inc; (Circulation) Innovative Interfaces, Inc; (Course Reserve) Innovative Interfaces, Inc; (ILL) Innovative Interfaces, Inc; (Media Booking) Innovative Interfaces, Inc; (OPAC) Innovative Interfaces, Inc; (Serials) Innovative Interfaces, Inc
Wireless access
Partic in Link+; OCLC Online Computer Library Center, Inc; Statewide California Electronic Library Consortium (SCELC)

L O'MELVENY & MYERS LLP*, Law Library, 400 S Hope St, 90071-2899. SAN 300-9769. Tel: 213-430-6000. FAX: 213-430-6407. *Dir,* Cheryl Smith; *Head Librn,* Gail Okazaki; E-mail: gokazaki@omm.com; *Head, Ref,* Cindy Spadoni; Staff 14 (MLS 8, Non-MLS 6)
Founded 1885
Library Holdings: Bk Vols 45,000; Per Subs 500
Automation Activity & Vendor Info: (Cataloging) Horizon
Partic in Dialog Corp; Dow Jones News Retrieval; OCLC Online Computer Library Center, Inc; Westlaw
Restriction: Staff use only

S ONE INSTITUTE & ARCHIVES*, ONE National Gay & Lesbian Archives at USC, 909 W Adams Blvd, 90007. SAN 300-9297. Tel: 213-741-0094. E-mail: askone@oneinstitute.org. Web Site: www.oneinstitute.org. *Dir,* Joseph Hawkins, PhD; *Archivist,* Kyle Morgan; E-mail: kylem@onearchives.org; *Archivist,* Michael Oliveira; E-mail: mikeo@onearchives.org; *Archivist,* Loni Shibuyama; Fax: lonis@onearchives.org
Founded 1952
Library Holdings: Bk Vols 25,000
Special Collections: Homophile & Gay Liberation Movements, 1948-present
Subject Interests: Gay & lesbian, Lesbian culture & hist
Wireless access
Function: Archival coll, For res purposes, Photocopying/Printing, Res libr
Restriction: Open by appt only

M ORTHOPAEDIC HOSPITAL*, Lt Robert J Rubel Memorial Library, 2400 S Flower St, 90007. SAN 300-9785. Tel: 213-742-1000. FAX: 213-742-1100. *Dir,* Margo Holmes; E-mail: MargoHolmes@mednet.ucla.edu. Subject Specialists: *Orthopaedic,* Margo Holmes
Founded 1945
Library Holdings: Bk Titles 3,660; Per Subs 38
Subject Interests: Orthopedics
Database Vendor: EBSCOhost
Partic in Pacific Southwest Regional Medical Library (PSRML)
Open Thurs 7-2:45
Restriction: Not open to pub

C PACIFIC STATES UNIVERSITY LIBRARY*, 3450 Wilshire Blvd, Ste 500, 90010. SAN 300-9807. Tel: 323-731-2383. FAX: 323-731-7276. Web Site: www.psuca.edu. *Univ Librn,* Deborah Hull; E-mail: dhull@psuca.edu; Staff 1 (MLS 1)
Founded 1928. Enrl 300; Fac 30; Highest Degree: Master
Library Holdings: DVDs 20; Electronic Media & Resources 1; Bk Titles 900; Bk Vols 1,000; Per Subs 1; Spec Interest Per Sub 1
Database Vendor: ProQuest
Wireless access
Restriction: Borrowing privileges limited to fac & registered students

L PAUL HASTINGS LLP*, Law Library, 515 S Flower, 25th Flr, 90071. SAN 329-9333. Tel: 213-683-6000. FAX: 213-627-0705. Web Site: www.paulhastings.com. *Mgr, Info Serv,* Liana Juliano; E-mail: lianajuliano@paulhastings.com
Library Holdings: Bk Vols 30,000; Per Subs 400
Subject Interests: Labor law

S PHILOSOPHICAL RESEARCH SOCIETY LIBRARY*, 3910 Los Feliz Blvd, 90027. SAN 300-9831. Tel: 323-663-2167. Toll Free Tel: 800-548-4062. FAX: 323-663-9443. E-mail: library@prs.org. Web Site: www.prs.org/library.htm, www.uprs.edu/resources/library.php. *Librn,* Maja D'Aoust; Staff 2 (Non-MLS 2)
Founded 1934
Library Holdings: Bk Titles 50,000
Special Collections: Bohn Coll; E T Seton Coll; Edwin Parker Coll; Le Plongeon Coll; Manly P Hall Coll; Max Muller Coll; Oliver L Reiser Coll
Subject Interests: Ancient philos, Art, Astrology, Comparative relig, Egypt, Metaphysics, Modern philos, Mythology, Psychol
Friends of the Library Group

S POLAND'S MILLENNIUM LIBRARY IN LOS ANGELES*, 3424 W Adams Blvd, 90018. SAN 327-6414. Tel: 310-234-0279. *Pres,* Danuta Zawadzki; Staff 4 (MLS 1, Non-MLS 3)
Founded 1966
Library Holdings: Bk Titles 14,200; Bk Vols 16,250
Special Collections: Genocide of Poles, 1939-1945
Subject Interests: Poland
Open Sun 11-11:45 & 1-2

L PROSKAUER ROSE LLP*, Law Library, 2049 Century Park E, Ste 3200, 90067. SAN 372-3054. Tel: 310-284-5683, 310-557-2900. FAX: 310-557-2193. Web Site: www.proskauer.com. *Head of Libr,* Lisa Winslow; E-mail: lwinslow@proskauer.com; *Asst Librn,* Audrey Gauna; Staff 2 (MLS 1, Non-MLS 1)
Founded 1875
Library Holdings: Bk Vols 15,000; Per Subs 100

S REISS-DAVIS CHILD STUDY CENTER*, Research Library, 3200 Motor Ave, 90034-3710. SAN 300-9874. Tel: 310-204-1666, Ext 359. FAX: 310-838-4637. Web Site: www.vistadelmar.org. *Librn,* Dawn Saunders
Founded 1950
Library Holdings: Bk Titles 9,000; Bk Vols 14,500; Per Subs 95
Special Collections: Freud Coll
Partic in Pacific Southwest Regional Medical Library (PSRML)
Open Mon-Fri 9-12 & 1-5

L SEYFARTH SHAW LIBRARY*, 2029 Century Park E, Ste 3300, 90067. SAN 325-7614. Tel: 310-277-7200. FAX: 310-201-5219. *Librn,* Beth Bernstein
Library Holdings: Bk Vols 10,000

L SHEPPARD, MULLIN, RICHTER & HAMPTON LIBRARY*, 333 S Hope, 42nd flr, 90071. SAN 300-9912. Tel: 213-617-4127. FAX: 213-620-1398. *Head Librn,* Martin Korn; Staff 5 (MLS 2, Non-MLS 3)
Library Holdings: e-books 250; e-journals 150; Bk Titles 7,000; Bk Vols 50,000; Per Subs 225
Subject Interests: Antitrust law, Banking, Intellectual property, Labor, Litigation, Real estate, Securities
Restriction: Staff use only

L SIDLEY AUSTIN LLP LIBRARY*, 555 W Fifth St, Ste 4000, 90013. SAN 371-6309. Tel: 213-896-6193. FAX: 213-896-6600. *Dir,* Position Currently Open; *Assoc Librn,* Lisa Kiguchi Shin; *Access Serv/Reserves/Ref Librn,* Glen Gustafson; Staff 5 (MLS 3, Non-MLS 2)
Founded 1980
Library Holdings: Bk Vols 25,000
Subject Interests: Bankruptcy, Corporate law, Intellectual property, Labor, Litigation, Real estate, Tax
Restriction: Not open to pub

C SIMON WIESENTHAL CENTER & MUSEUM OF TOLERANCE*, Library & Archives, 1399 S Roxbury Dr, 90035-4709. SAN 320-5681. Tel: 310-772-7605. FAX: 310-277-6568. E-mail: library@wiesenthal.net. Web Site: www.weisenthal.com/library. *Dir,* Adaire J Klein; *Ref,* Nancy Saul; *Tech Serv,* Margo Gutstein
Founded 1978
Library Holdings: Bk Vols 50,000; Per Subs 200
Special Collections: Books by & about Simon Wiesenthal; Primary Anti-Semitica & Holocaust Denial
Subject Interests: Holocaust, Judaica (lit or hist of Jews), Racism

SR SINAI TEMPLE*, Blumenthal Library, 10400 Wilshire Blvd, 90024. SAN 300-9920. Tel: 310-474-1518, 310-481-3218. FAX: 310-474-6801. E-mail: info@sinaitemple.org. Web Site: www.sinaitemple.org. *Dir,* Lisa Silverman; E-mail: lsilverman@sinaitemple.org
Founded 1969
Library Holdings: Bk Titles 20,899; Bk Vols 30,000; Per Subs 38
Special Collections: Haggadot Coll; Parenting Coll; Sinai Akiba Day School Coll for General Studies; William R Blumenthal Rare Book Coll
Subject Interests: Children's lit, Judaica (lit or hist of Jews), Lit
Publications: Articles for Association of Jewish Libraries (bulletins); Articles on children's literature with Jewish themes; Central Cataloging Service for Libraries of Judaica; Reform Judaism
Partic in Metronet

C SOUTHERN CALIFORNIA INSTITUTE OF ARCHITECTURE*, Kappe Library, 960 E Third St, 90013. SAN 301-5947. Tel: 213-613-2200, Ext 323. FAX: 213-613-2260. Web Site: www.sciarc.edu. *Mgr,* Kevin McMahon
Founded 1972. Enrl 380; Fac 50; Highest Degree: Master
Library Holdings: Bk Titles 50,000; Bk Vols 50,325; Per Subs 120
Subject Interests: Art & archit, Urban planning
Open Mon-Fri 10-6

S SOUTHERN CALIFORNIA LIBRARY FOR SOCIAL STUDIES & RESEARCH*, 6120 S Vermont Ave, 90044. SAN 300-9955. Tel: 323-759-6063. FAX: 323-759-2252. E-mail: archives@socallib.org. Web Site: www.socallib.org. *Dir,* Yusef Omowale; E-mail: omowale@socallib.org; *Dir, Communications,* Michele Welsing; E-mail: mwelsing@socallib.org; *Librn,* Rukshana Singh; E-mail: rukshana@socallib.org; Staff 7 (MLS 2, Non-MLS 5)
Founded 1963
Special Collections: Calif Democratic Council Records; Chicano & Black Liberation, newsp files; Civil Rights Congress Records; Committee for the Protection of Foreign Born Files; Folk Music (Earl Robinson & William Wolff Colls); Harry Bridges Deportation Case Records; Morris Kominsky Coll (American Right); Organization History (Peace, Civil Rights, Political & Social Action Groups as well as Civil Rights & Civil Liberties Ad Hoc Committees), files from turn of century to present; Smith Act Case Records
Subject Interests: African-Am hist, Civil liberties, Civil rights, Labor, Latino hist
Function: Archival coll, Art exhibits, Computers for patron use, Copy machines, e-mail serv, Electronic databases & coll, Exhibits, For res purposes, Handicapped accessible, Photocopying/Printing, Prog for adults, Prog for children & young adult, Pub access computers, Ref & res, Ref serv available, Ref serv in person, Res libr, Telephone ref, VHS videos, Video lending libr, Workshops
Publications: Heritage (Newsletter)
Open Tues-Sat 10-6

CL SOUTHWESTERN LAW SCHOOL*, Leigh H Taylor Law Library, 3050 Wilshire Blvd, 90010. Tel: 213-738-5771. Interlibrary Loan Service Tel: 213-738-6728. Reference Tel: 213-738-6725. FAX: 213-738-5792. E-mail: library@swlaw.edu. Web Site: library.swlaw.edu. *Assoc Dean, Libr Serv,* Linda A Whisman; *Assoc Dir,* Carole Weiner; *Ref Librn,* David McFadden; *Syst Librn,* Tracy Tsui; *Cat,* Connie Deng; *Ref,* Sharrel Gerlach; *Ref,* Dennis Ladd; Staff 10 (MLS 7, Non-MLS 3)
Founded 1911. Enrl 875; Fac 55; Highest Degree: Doctorate
Library Holdings: e-books 22,000; Bk Titles 135,800; Bk Vols 492,400; Per Subs 4,000
Special Collections: State Document Depository; US Document Depository
Automation Activity & Vendor Info: (Acquisitions) Innovative Interfaces, Inc; (Cataloging) Innovative Interfaces, Inc; (Circulation) Innovative Interfaces, Inc; (Course Reserve) Innovative Interfaces, Inc; (ILL) OCLC; (OPAC) Innovative Interfaces, Inc; (Serials) Innovative Interfaces, Inc
Database Vendor: JSTOR, LexisNexis, Loislaw, Marcive, Inc, OCLC WorldShare Interlibrary Loan, SerialsSolutions, Westlaw, Wilson - Wilson Web
Wireless access
Function: ILL available
Restriction: Not open to pub

S RALPH STONE & CO, INC*, Engineers Library, 10954 Santa Monica Blvd, 90025. SAN 300-9971. Tel: 310-478-1501. FAX: 310-478-7359. *In Charge,* Richard Kahle
Founded 1950
Library Holdings: Bk Vols 3,094; Per Subs 13
Subject Interests: Chem, Environ eng, Geol, Geotechnical
Restriction: Staff use only

L STROOCK & LAVAN*, Law Library, 2029 Century Park E, Ste 1800, 90067. SAN 372-3747. Tel: 310-556-5800. FAX: 310-556-5959.
Library Holdings: Bk Vols 12,000
Restriction: Staff use only

L TRANSAMERICA OCCIDENTAL LIFE INSURANCE*, Law Library, 1150 S Olive St, Ste T-2100, 90015-2211. SAN 370-4106. Tel: 213-742-3123. FAX: 213-741-6623. *Librn,* Pauline Leary; Tel: 213-742-5237
Library Holdings: Bk Vols 9,000; Per Subs 11
Restriction: Employees only

L TROY & GOULD*, Law Library, 1801 Century Park E, 16th Flr, 90067. SAN 372-3755. Tel: 310-553-4441. FAX: 310-201-4746. Web Site: www.troygould.com. *Librn,* Larry Zamora; E-mail: lzamora@troygould.com
Library Holdings: Bk Vols 5,000; Per Subs 12
Restriction: Employees only

S TWENTIETH CENTURY FOX FILM CORP*, Frances C Richardson Research Center, 10201 W Pico Blvd, No 89/105, 90035. (Mail add: PO Box 900, Beverly Hills, 90213-0900), SAN 301-0031. Tel: 310-369-2782. FAX: 310-369-3645. *Dir,* Lisa Fredsti; E-mail: lisa.fredsti@fox.com; Staff 4 (MLS 1, Non-MLS 3)
Founded 1924
Library Holdings: Bk Vols 35,000; Per Subs 90

Special Collections: Peggy Hoyt Fashion Design Coll; US & German Armies; WW II Combat Photos
Subject Interests: Art & archit, Costume design, Hist, Militaria, Photog
Restriction: Employees only, Non-circulating to the pub

GL UNITED STATES COURTS LIBRARY*, 255 E Temple St, Rm 132, 90012. SAN 301-0104. Tel: 213-894-8900. FAX: 213-894-8906. *Librn,* Zora Maynard
Library Holdings: Bk Vols 30,000
Subject Interests: Law
Automation Activity & Vendor Info: (Acquisitions) SirsiDynix; (Cataloging) SirsiDynix; (Circulation) SirsiDynix; (Serials) SirsiDynix
Partic in OCLC Online Computer Library Center, Inc; Westlaw
Open Mon-Fri 8:30-4:30

GL UNITED STATES DEPARTMENT OF JUSTICE*, United States Attorney Central District of California Library, 1214 US Courthouse, 312 N Spring St, 90012. SAN 301-0090. Tel: 213-894-2419. FAX: 213-894-1381. *Librn,* Cornell Winston
Founded 1888
Library Holdings: Bk Vols 15,000
Restriction: Not open to pub

UNIVERSITY OF CALIFORNIA, LOS ANGELES
C RALPH J BUNCHE CENTER FOR AFRICAN-AMERICAN STUDIES LIBRARY & MEDIA CENTER*, 135 Haines Hall, Box 951545, 90095-1545, SAN 332-9550. Tel: 310-825-6060. FAX: 310-825-5019. Web Site: www.bunchecenter.ucla.edu. *Librn,* Dalena E Hunter. Subject Specialists: *African-Am studies,* Dalena E Hunter; Staff 1 (MLS 1)
Founded 1969
Jul 2007-Jun 2008 Income $14,000. Mats Exp $6,100, Books $5,000, Per/Ser (Incl. Access Fees) $1,000, AV Mat $100. Sal $46,000
Library Holdings: Audiobooks 10; CDs 50; DVDs 250; Bk Vols 8,479; Per Subs 21; Videos 205
Special Collections: African Student Union (ASU) Archive; Carlos Moore Archive; Kenny Burrell Archive
Subject Interests: African-Am studies
Function: e-mail & chat, Electronic databases & coll, Orientations, Ref serv in person, Scanner, VHS videos
Partic in Association of Research Libraries (ARL)
Open Mon-Thurs 9-6, Fri 9-3
Restriction: In-house use for visitors, Non-circulating
C INSTRUCTIONAL MEDIA LIBRARY*, Powell Library, Rm 46, 90095-1517, SAN 332-9585. Tel: 310-825-0755. FAX: 310-206-5392. E-mail: imlib@ucla.edu. Web Site: www.oid.ucla.edu/lmlib. *Mgr,* Kathleen Ford
Founded 1963
Subject Interests: Bus & mgt, Ethnic studies, Hist, Performing arts, Soc sci & issues
Publications: Video periodicals & directories

C UNIVERSITY OF CALIFORNIA LOS ANGELES LIBRARY*, PO Box 951575, 90095-1575. Tel: 310-825-1201. Circulation Tel: 310-825-4732. Interlibrary Loan Service Tel: 310-825-1263. Reference Tel: 310-825-1323. Automation Services Tel: 310-825-9188. Information Services Tel: 310-825-7143. FAX: 310-206-4109. Web Site: www.library.ucla.edu. *Univ Librn,* Virginia Steel
Founded 1919. Enrl 37,221; Fac 11,163; Highest Degree: Doctorate
Library Holdings: Bk Vols 8,157,182; Per Subs 77,509
Special Collections: 19th & 20th Century British & American Literature; 19th Century British Fiction (Michael Sadlier Coll); British Commonwealth History, especially Australia & New Zealand; British History; California History; Contemporary Western Writers, including special collections on individual authors; Early English Children's Books; Early Italian Printing (Ahmanson-Murphy Coll); Elmer Belt Library of Vinciana; Folklore; History of Medicine; Latin American Studies; Mazarinades; Mountaineering Literature (Farquhar Coll); National Parks & Conservation (Albright Coll); Organizational; Southern California Imprints, pamphlets; Spinoza Coll; Western Americana. Oral History; UN Document Depository; US Document Depository
Automation Activity & Vendor Info: (Acquisitions) Ex Libris Group; (Cataloging) Ex Libris Group; (Circulation) Ex Libris Group; (Course Reserve) Ex Libris Group; (OPAC) Ex Libris Group
Wireless access
Publications: Faculty News From the UCLA Library; UCLA Librarian; UCLA Library Guide
Partic in Association of Research Libraries (ARL)
Friends of the Library Group
Departmental Libraries:
THE ARTS LIBRARY, 1400 Public Policy Bldg, 90095-9203. (Mail add: Box 951392, 90095-1392), SAN 332-9704. Tel: 310-206-5425. FAX: 310-825-1303. Web Site: www.library.ucla.edu/libraries/arts/arts-library. *Interim Head of Libr,* Kevin Mulroy; *Archit, Design & Digital Serv Librn,* Janine Henri; Tel: 310-206-4587; *Film, Television & Theater Librn,* Diana King; Tel: 310-206-4823; *Visual Arts Librn,* Robert Gore; Tel: 310-206-5426; Staff 4 (MLS 4)
Library Holdings: Bk Vols 285,680; Per Subs 1,987
Special Collections: Art of the Low Countries Decimal Index; Bookworks & Artist Publications (Hoffberg Coll); Leonardo da Vinci (Elmer Belt Library of Vinciana)
Subject Interests: Archit, Art, Ceramics, Film, Photog, Television, Textiles
Partic in BRS; OCLC Online Computer Library Center, Inc
Publications: Art Catalogs
Open Mon-Fri 9-5, Sat 1-5
CHICANO STUDIES RESEARCH CENTER LIBRARY & ARCHIVE, 144 Haines Hall, 90095-1544. Tel: 310-206-6052. FAX: 310-206-1784. E-mail: library@chicano.ucla.edu. Web Site: www.chicano.ucla.edu/library. *Librn,* Lizette Guerra; E-mail: lguerra@chicano.ucla.edu; *Archives Mgr,* Michael Stone
Founded 1969
Library Holdings: AV Mats 1,030; Bk Titles 1,500; Bk Vols 16,536
Special Collections: Microfilm reels, digital objects, posters & archival coll
Subject Interests: Chicano hist & culture
Automation Activity & Vendor Info: (Cataloging) Ex Libris Group; (OPAC) Ex Libris Group
Open Mon-Fri 10-5
Restriction: Non-circulating, Researchers only
WILLIAM ANDREWS CLARK MEMORIAL LIBRARY, 2520 Cimarron St, 90018, SAN 332-9798. Tel: 323-731-8529. FAX: 323-731-8617. Web Site: www.clarklibrary.ucla.edu. *Dir,* Barbara Fuchs; Staff 6 (MLS 5, Non-MLS 1)
Founded 1934
Library Holdings: Per Subs 97,259; Spec Interest Per Sub 678
Special Collections: 17th & early 18th Century English & European Civilization; Eric Gill Coll; John Dryden Coll; Modern Fine Printing; Montana History Coll; Oscar Wilde & the Nineties; Robert Boyle Coll; Robert Gibbings Coll
Open Mon-Fri 9-4:45
Friends of the Library Group
COLLEGE LIBRARY, Powell Library Bldg, 90095. (Mail add: Box 951450, 90095-1450), SAN 332-964X. Tel: 310-825-1938. FAX: 310-206-9312. Automation Services FAX: 310-825-9389. *Head of Libr,* Kelly Miller; *Circ,* Richard Jones; *Ref,* Catherine M Brown; *Ref,* Miki Goral; *Ref,* Simon Lee
Library Holdings: Bk Vols 235,421; Per Subs 559
Publications: General Information Guide; Self-Guided Tour
CL HUGH & HAZEL DARLING LAW LIBRARY, 1112 Law Bldg, Box 951458, 385 Charles E Young Dr E, 90095-1458, SAN 332-9941. Tel: 310-825-7826. Circulation Tel: 310-825-4743. Reference Tel: 310-825-6414. FAX: 310-825-1372. Web Site: www.law.ucla.edu/library. *Dir, Law Libr,* Kevin Gerson; E-mail: gerson@law.ucla.edu; *Dir, Ref, Dir, Res Serv,* Amy Atchinsen; *Dir, Access Serv, Dir, Info Serv,* Donna Gulnac; *Dir, Bibliog Serv, Dir, Coll Mgt,* Cindy Spadoni; *Head, Cat,* Melissa Beck; *Head, Coll, Ref Librn,* Jennifer Lentz; *Sr Ref Librn,* June Kim; *Acq Librn,* Michelle Gorospe; *Law Librn,* John Wilson; *Ref Librn,* Cheryl Kelly Fischer; *Ref Librn,* Lynn McClelland; *Ref Librn,* Vicki Steiner
Library Holdings: Bk Vols 592,266; Per Subs 8,258
Special Collections: David Bernard Memorial Aviation Law Library. State Document Depository; US Document Depository
Subject Interests: E Asia, Islam, Latin Am
Partic in Legal Lexis; Metronet; OCLC Online Computer Library Center, Inc; Westlaw
Open Mon-Thurs 8am-11:30pm, Fri 8am-8:30pm, Sat 9-5:30, Sun 1pm-11:30pm
CM LOUISE M DARLING BIOMEDICAL LIBRARY, 12-077 Center for the Health Sciences, 90095. (Mail add: PO Box 951798, 90095-1798), SAN 332-9739. Tel: 310-825-4904. Interlibrary Loan Service Tel: 310-825-4055. FAX: 310-825-0465. Interlibrary Loan Service FAX: 310-206-8675. *Dir,* Judy Consales; Tel: 310-825-5781; *Assoc Dir,* Julie Kwan
Library Holdings: Bk Vols 651,167; Per Subs 3,471
Special Collections: Dr M N Beigelman Coll (opthalmology); Florence Nightingale Coll; History of the Health Sciences; History of the Life Sciences; Japanese Medical Books & Prints, 17th-19th Centuries; S Weir Mitchell Coll; Slide, Portrait, Realia & Print Coll
Subject Interests: Dentistry, Med, Neurology, Nursing, Pub health
Partic in Cap Area Libr Network Inc; Coop Libr Agency for Syst & Servs
GRACE M HUNT MEMORIAL ENGLISH READING ROOM, 235 Humanities Bldg, 415 Portola Plaza, 90095, SAN 332-9887. Tel: 310-825-4511. *Librn,* Lynda Tolly; E-mail: tolly@english.ucla.edu
Library Holdings: Bk Vols 34,396; Per Subs 167
Special Collections: Josephine Miles Poetry Coll; Modern Contemporary Poetry (1500 vols)
Subject Interests: Am lit, English lit, Literary criticism

EUGENE & MAXINE ROSENFELD MANAGEMENT LIBRARY, 110 Westwood Plaza, E-301, 90095, SAN 332-9976. Tel: 310-825-3138. Administration Tel: 310-825-3047. FAX: 310-825-6632. Web Site: www.anderson.ucla.edu/rosenfeld-library. *Head of Libr,* Angela Horne; *Coll & Donations of Libr Mat,* Michael Oppenheim; Tel: 310-825-0769; Staff 8 (MLS 4, Non-MLS 4)
Founded 1961. Enrl 1,700; Highest Degree: Doctorate
Library Holdings: Microforms 548,495; Bk Vols 182,663
Special Collections: Corporate History Coll; Goldsmiths-Kress Library of Economic Literature Microfilm Coll (Pre-1850); New York Stock Exchange Listing Applications (1957-1999); Rare Books in Business & Economics, 16th-18th Centuries (Robert E Gross Coll)
Subject Interests: Bus, Mgt
Open Mon-Thurs 7:30am-11pm, Fri 7:30am-8pm, Sat 9-7, Sun 1-11

RICHARD C RUDOLPH EAST ASIAN LIBRARY, 21617 Research Library YRL, 90095, SAN 333-0060. Tel: 310-825-4836. FAX: 310-206-4960. *Dir,* Su Chen; Tel: 310-825-1401; *Librn,* Sanghun Cho; Tel: 310-825-9535; *Librn,* Position Currently Open; *Cat,* Hui Li; Tel: 310-206-9606. Subject Specialists: *Korea,* Sanghun Cho; *Chinese,* Hui Li; Staff 12 (MLS 5, Non-MLS 7)
Founded 1948
Library Holdings: Bk Vols 673,215; Per Subs 3,124
Special Collections: Chinese Archeology Coll; Fine Arts Coll; Japanese Buddhism Coll; Korean Literature Coll - Classical & Modern; Religion Coll
Subject Interests: E Asia
Partic in OCLC Online Computer Library Center, Inc
Publications: Richard C Rudolph East Asian Library Bibliographic Series
Open Mon-Thurs 7:30am-11pm, Fri 7:30-6, Sat 9-5, Sun 1-5

SCIENCE & ENGINEERING LIBRARIES, 8270 Boelter Hall, 90095, SAN 332-9852. Tel: 310-825-4951. Interlibrary Loan Service Tel: 310-825-3646. FAX: 310-206-9872. Interlibrary Loan Service FAX: 310-206-3908. *Assoc Dir,* Julie Kwan; *Actg Head, Libr,* Judy Consales
Library Holdings: Bk Vols 602,152; Per Subs 4,461
Special Collections: Technical Reports Coll (including depository items from DOE, NASA, NTIS, Rand Corp)
Subject Interests: Astronomy
Partic in Dialog Corp

C UNIVERSITY OF SOUTHERN CALIFORNIA LIBRARIES*, University Park Campus, 3550 Trousdale Pkwy, 90089-0182. SAN 333-0184. Tel: 213-740-7119. Interlibrary Loan Service Tel: 213-740-4020. Reference Tel: 213-740-4039. Administration Tel: 213-821-2344. Information Services Tel: 213-740-5555. FAX: 213-740-9962. Web Site: www.usc.edu/libraries.
Founded 1880. Enrl 38,000; Fac 3,440; Highest Degree: Doctorate
Jul 2010-Jul 2011. Mats Exp $34,969,066. Sal $13,992,582
Library Holdings: e-books 721,441; Bk Vols 3,978,705
Special Collections: American Literature Coll (1850-); Cinematic Arts Coll; East Asian Coll; German Literature in Exile Coll; Latin American (Boeckmann Coll); Natural History Coll (Hancock); Philosophy (Gomperz Coll); Southern California Regional History. Can & Prov; State Document Depository; UN Document Depository; US Document Depository
Automation Activity & Vendor Info: (Acquisitions) SirsiDynix; (Cataloging) SirsiDynix; (Circulation) SirsiDynix; (Course Reserve) SirsiDynix; (ILL) OCLC ILLiad; (OPAC) SirsiDynix; (Serials) SirsiDynix
Wireless access
Function: Res libr
Partic in Association of Research Libraries (ARL); Center for Research Libraries; Greater Western Library Alliance; OCLC Online Computer Library Center, Inc; Pacific Rim Digital Library Alliance (PRDLA); Southern Calif Electronic Libr Consortium
Friends of the Library Group

Departmental Libraries:

CL ASA V CALL LAW LIBRARY, 699 Exposition Blvd, LAW 202, MC 0072, 90089-0072, SAN 333-0753. Tel: 213-740-6482. FAX: 213-740-7179. Web Site: law.usc.edu. *Dir, Law Libr, Assoc Dean & Chief Info Officer,* Pauline Aranas; E-mail: paranas@law.usc.edu; *Assoc Dir, Law Libr for Coll & Admin Serv,* Leonette Williams; E-mail: lwilliams@law.usc.edu; *Asst Dir, Pub Serv,* Brian Raphael; E-mail: braphael@law.usc.edu; *Bus Coordr,* Steven Benson; E-mail: sbenson@law.usc.edu
Special Collections: State Document Depository; US Document Depository
Database Vendor: LexisNexis, Westlaw
Publications: Asa V Call Law Guide to Legal Secondary Source in the Law Library

CM NORRIS MEDICAL LIBRARY, 2003 Zonal Ave, 90089-9130, SAN 333-0788. Tel: 323-442-1116. Reference Tel: 323-442-1111. Administration Tel: 323-442-1130. FAX: 323-221-1235. E-mail: medlib@usc.edu. Web Site: www.usc.edu/nml. *Assoc Dir, Educ & Res Serv,* Eileen Eandi; Tel: 323-442-1133, E-mail: eeandi@usc.edu; Staff 36 (MLS 12, Non-MLS 24)
Founded 1928. Enrl 3,849; Fac 1,365; Highest Degree: Doctorate
Jul 2007-Jun 2008 Income $557,626. Mats Exp $2,769,239, Books $334,870, Per/Ser (Incl. Access Fees) $2,152,438, AV Mat $5,026, Electronic Ref Mat (Incl. Access Fees) $228,100, Presv $48,805. Sal $1,721,535 (Prof $815,585)
Library Holdings: AV Mats 13,741; DVDs 57; e-books 545; e-journals 2,425; Bk Titles 43,672; Bk Vols 48,099; Per Subs 2,219
Special Collections: American Indian Ethnopharmacology Coll; Far West Medicine Coll; Salerni Collegium History of Medicine Coll
Subject Interests: Med, Nursing, Occupational therapy, Pharm, Phys therapy
Automation Activity & Vendor Info: (Acquisitions) Horizon; (Cataloging) Horizon; (Circulation) Horizon; (Course Reserve) Docutek; (ILL) OCLC ILLiad; (OPAC) Horizon; (Serials) SerialsSolutions
Database Vendor: 3M Library Systems, Annual Reviews, BioOne, Cinahl, Community of Science (COS), EBSCO - WebFeat, Elsevier, Elsevier MDL, ISI Web of Knowledge, JSTOR, Lexi-Comp, Majors, MD Consult, Medline, Micromedex, Natural Standard, Nature Publishing Group, OCLC WorldShare Interlibrary Loan, OVID Technologies, Oxford Online, PubMed, RefWorks, Safari Books Online, ScienceDirect, SerialsSolutions, SirsiDynix, Springer-Verlag, STAT!Ref (Teton Data Systems), Swets Information Services, Thomson - Web of Science, UpToDate, WebMD, Wiley, Wiley InterScience
Function: Health sci info serv
Partic in National Network of Libraries of Medicine Pacific Southwest Region; Statewide California Electronic Library Consortium (SCELC)
Open Mon-Thurs 7am-Midnight, Fri 7am-8pm, Sat 9-5, Sun 9am-10pm
Friends of the Library Group

CM JENNIFER ANN WILSON DENTAL LIBRARY & LEARNING CENTER, 925 W 34th St, DEN 21, University Park - MC 0641, 90089-0641, SAN 333-0729. Tel: 213-740-6476. Circulation Tel: 213-740-0008. Interlibrary Loan Service Tel: 213-740-8578. Reference Tel: 213-740-1441. FAX: 213-748-8565. E-mail: wdl@usc.edu. Web Site: wdl.usc.edu. *Dir,* John P Glueckert; E-mail: gluecker@usc.edu; *Info Serv Librn,* Annie Hughes; E-mail: amhughes@usc.edu; Staff 8 (MLS 2, Non-MLS 6)
Founded 1897. Enrl 928; Fac 116; Highest Degree: Doctorate
Library Holdings: Audiobooks 248; AV Mats 5,296; DVDs 40; e-books 283; e-journals 237; Bk Titles 17,408; Bk Vols 20,257; Per Subs 317; Videos 229
Special Collections: Dentistry Rare Books Coll
Automation Activity & Vendor Info: (Acquisitions) Horizon; (Cataloging) Horizon; (Circulation) Horizon; (Course Reserve) Horizon; (OPAC) Horizon; (Serials) Horizon
Database Vendor: 3M Library Systems, Alexander Street Press, Annual Reviews, Community of Science (COS), CRC Press/Taylor & Francis Group, ebrary, EBSCO - WebFeat, EBSCOhost, Elsevier, Elsevier MDL, H W Wilson, ISI Web of Knowledge, JSTOR, Lexi-Comp, Medline, Nature Publishing Group, OCLC FirstSearch, OCLC WorldShare Interlibrary Loan, OVID Technologies, PubMed, RefWorks, ScienceDirect, Scopus, SerialsSolutions, STAT!Ref (Teton Data Systems), Swets Information Services, Thomson - Web of Science, UpToDate, WebMD, Wiley InterScience
Function: Copy machines, Doc delivery serv, ILL available
Partic in Center for Research Libraries; National Network of Libraries of Medicine; Pacific Southwest Regional Medical Library (PSRML)
Restriction: Access at librarian's discretion, Access for corporate affiliates, Authorized patrons, Authorized scholars by appt, Borrowing privileges limited to fac & registered students, Circ limited, In-house use for visitors, Non-circulating of rare bks, Non-circulating to the pub, Open to fac, students & qualified researchers, Open to qualified scholars, Open to researchers by request, Restricted loan policy, Restricted pub use

GM VA GREATER LOS ANGELES HEALTH CARE SYSTEM*, West Los Angeles Health Care Center, 11301 Wilshire Blvd, W142D, 90073. SAN 333-0842. Tel: 310-268-3003. FAX: 310-268-4919. *Chief Librn,* Susan Efteland; Staff 1 (MLS 1)
Founded 1936
Library Holdings: Bk Vols 2,500; Per Subs 784
Subject Interests: Med, Psychiat, Psychol
Partic in Dialog Corp
Open Mon-Fri 8-4:30

M WHITE MEMORIAL MEDICAL CENTER*, Courville-Abbott Memorial Library, 1720 Cesar E Chavez Ave, 90033-2462. SAN 301-0198. Tel: 323-260-5715. FAX: 323-260-5748. *Libr Dir,* June Levy; E-mail: levyjr@ah.org; *Med Librn,* Zahra Fotovat; E-mail: fotovaz@ah.org; *Med Librn,* Myrna Y Uyengco-Harooch; E-mail: uyengcmy@ah.org; Staff 2 (MLS 1, Non-MLS 1)
Founded 1920
Library Holdings: Bk Vols 43,000; Per Subs 350
Special Collections: History & Religion (Percy T Magan Coll); History Coll; History of Medicine (Margaret & H James Hara Memorial Coll)
Subject Interests: Med, Nursing
Automation Activity & Vendor Info: (Cataloging) SydneyPlus; (Circulation) SydneyPlus

Partic in National Network of Libraries of Medicine Pacific Northwest Region
Restriction: Staff & mem only
Friends of the Library Group

SR WILSHIRE BOULEVARD TEMPLE - LIBRARIES*, 3663 Wilshire Blvd, 90010-2798. (Mail add: 11661 W Olympic Blvd, 90064), SAN 301-021X. Tel: 213-388-2401. Administration Tel: 424-208-8934. E-mail: info@wbtla.org. Web Site: www.wbtla.org. *Librn,* Karen Morgenstern; Tel: 424-208-8945, Fax: 310-689-4569, E-mail: kmorgenstern@brawerman.org
Founded 1929
Library Holdings: Bk Vols 17,050
Special Collections: Judaica
Wireless access

R STEPHEN S WISE TEMPLE LIBRARY*, 15500 Stephen S Wise Dr, 90077. SAN 301-0228. Tel: 310-889-2241. FAX: 310-476-2353. *Dir,* Roberta Lloyd; E-mail: rlloyd@sswt.org; *Librn,* Teri Markson; E-mail: tmarkson@sswt.org; Staff 4 (MLS 3, Non-MLS 1)
Founded 1967
Subject Interests: Judaica (lit or hist of Jews)
Friends of the Library Group

LOS GATOS

M EL CAMINO LOS GATOS HEALTH LIBRARY*, 815 Pollard Rd, 95032. SAN 370-5676. Tel: 408-866-4044. FAX: 408-866-3829. E-mail: communityhealthlibrary@gmail.com. *Sr Librn,* Michael Liddicoat; Staff 5 (MLS 1, Non-MLS 4)
Founded 1989
Library Holdings: DVDs 40; e-books 104; e-journals 16; Bk Titles 1,500; Per Subs 50
Subject Interests: Consumer health, Med, Nursing
Automation Activity & Vendor Info: (Cataloging) EOS International; (Circulation) EOS International; (Serials) Basch Subscriptions, Inc
Database Vendor: EBSCO Information Services
Wireless access
Partic in Coop Libr Agency for Syst & Servs
Open Mon-Thurs 9-3:30

P LOS GATOS PUBLIC LIBRARY, 100 Villa Ave, 95030-6981. SAN 301-0260. Tel: 408-354-6891. Interlibrary Loan Service Tel: 408-399-5784. Reference Tel: 408-354-6896. Administration Tel: 408-354-6898. FAX: 408-399-6008. E-mail: library@losgatosca.gov. Web Site: library.losgatosca.gov. *Town Librn,* Henry Bankhead; E-mail: hbankhead@losgatosca.gov; *Town Librn,* Heidi Murphy; E-mail: hmurphy@losgatosca.gov; Staff 5 (MLS 5)
Founded 1898. Pop 29,500; Circ 450,000
Jul 2012-Jun 2013 Income $2,192,690
Library Holdings: Large Print Bks 1,077; Bk Titles 130,000; Per Subs 150
Subject Interests: Local hist
Automation Activity & Vendor Info: (Acquisitions) ByWater Solutions; (Cataloging) ByWater Solutions; (Circulation) ByWater Solutions; (ILL) OCLC CatExpress; (OPAC) ByWater Solutions; (Serials) ByWater Solutions
Database Vendor: 3M Library Systems, EBSCOhost, OCLC FirstSearch
Wireless access
Open Mon & Tues 11-8, Wed-Fri 10-6, Sat 10-5, Sun 12-5
Friends of the Library Group

R SACRED HEART JESUIT CENTER*, House Library, 300 College Ave, 95030. (Mail add: PO Box 128, 95031-0128), SAN 301-0252. Tel: 408-884-1700. Administration Tel: 408-884-1702. FAX: 408-884-1747. E-mail: shjclibrary@calprov.org. *Librn,* Fr Gerald John Lentz; E-mail: glentz@calprov.org; Staff 1 (Non-MLS 1)
Founded 1851
Library Holdings: Bk Vols 4,000
Special Collections: Catholic Theology; Jesuitica
Restriction: Private libr

P SANTA CLARA COUNTY LIBRARY DISTRICT*, 14600 Winchester Blvd, 95032. SAN 334-7281. Tel: 408-293-2326. Toll Free Tel: 800-286-1991. FAX: 408-364-0161. Web Site: www.santaclaracountylib.org. *County Librn,* Nancy Howe; E-mail: nhowe@sccl.org; *Info Syst Mgr,* Sanjeev Singla; Tel: 408-293-2326, Ext 3051, E-mail: ssingla@sccl.org; *Serv Mgr, Coll Develop & Reading Serv,* Gail Mason; E-mail: gmason@sccl.org; *Serv Mgr, Outreach & Pub Awareness,* Patricia Lorenzo; Tel: 408-293-2326, Ext 3010, E-mail: plorenzo@sccl.org; Staff 82 (MLS 75, Non-MLS 7)
Founded 1912. Pop 424,918; Circ 11,319,133
Jun 2009-Jul 2010 Income (Main Library and Branch(s)) $33,402,100, State $1,440,600, City $1,290,500, Locally Generated Income $29,648,000, Other $1,023,000. Mats Exp $4,210,500, Books $3,622,380, Per/Ser (Incl. Access Fees) $161,120, Electronic Ref Mat (Incl. Access Fees) $427,000. Sal $5,932,812 (Prof $15,528,614)
Library Holdings: High Interest/Low Vocabulary Bk Vols 3,871; Large Print Bks 34,518; Bk Titles 386,308; Bk Vols 1,700,000; Per Subs 2,831; Talking Bks 30,498
Special Collections: California Western Americana. State Document Depository; US Document Depository
Automation Activity & Vendor Info: (Acquisitions) SirsiDynix; (Cataloging) SirsiDynix; (Circulation) SirsiDynix; (ILL) OCLC WorldShare Interlibrary Loan; (OPAC) SirsiDynix; (Serials) SirsiDynix
Database Vendor: Alexander Street Press, ALLDATA Online, EBSCOhost, Gale Cengage Learning, Grolier Online, OCLC FirstSearch, OCLC WorldShare Interlibrary Loan, ProQuest, ReferenceUSA
Wireless access
Function: Accelerated reader prog, Adult bk club, Adult literacy prog, After school storytime, Archival coll, Art exhibits, Audio & video playback equip for onsite use, Audiobks via web, AV serv, BA reader (adult literacy), Bi-weekly Writer's Group, Bilingual assistance for Spanish patrons, Bk club(s), Bk reviews (Group), Bks on cassette, Bks on CD, CD-ROM, Chess club, Children's prog, Citizenship assistance, Computer training, Computers for patron use, Copy machines, Digital talking bks, e-mail & chat, e-mail serv, E-Reserves, Electronic databases & coll, Exhibits, Family literacy, For res purposes, Free DVD rentals, Games & aids for the handicapped, Genealogy discussion group, Govt ref serv, Handicapped accessible, Health sci info serv, Holiday prog, Home delivery & serv to Sr ctr & nursing homes, Homebound delivery serv, Homework prog, ILL available, Jail serv, Large print keyboards, Learning ctr, Legal assistance to inmates, Libr develop, Literacy & newcomer serv, Magnifiers for reading, Mail & tel request accepted, Mail loans to mem, Mus passes, Music CDs, Newsp ref libr, Online cat, Online info literacy tutorials on the web & in blackboard, Online ref, Online searches, Orientations, Outreach serv, Outside serv via phone, mail, e-mail & web, OverDrive digital audio bks, Photocopying/Printing, Preschool outreach, Prof lending libr, Prog for adults, Prog for children & young adult, Pub access computers, Ref & res, Ref serv available, Ref serv in person, Referrals accepted, Res libr, Senior computer classes, Senior outreach, Serves mentally handicapped consumers, Spoken cassettes & CDs, Spoken cassettes & DVDs, Story hour, Summer reading prog, Tax forms, Teen prog, Telephone ref, VHS videos, Video lending libr, Web-catalog, Wheelchair accessible
Partic in Califa
Friends of the Library Group
Branches: 8
CAMPBELL PUBLIC, 77 Harrison Ave, Campbell, 95008-1409, SAN 334-7370. Tel: 408-866-1991. FAX: 408-866-1433. *Commun Librn,* Cheryl Houts; Staff 10 (MLS 9, Non-MLS 1)
Pop 49,733; Circ 912,112
Library Holdings: Bk Vols 189,662
Friends of the Library Group
CUPERTINO LIBRARY, 10800 Torre Ave, Cupertino, 95014-3254, SAN 334-7435. Tel: 408-446-1677. FAX: 408-252-8749. E-mail: cupertino_manager@sccl.org. Web Site: www.sccl.org/cupertino. *Commun Librn,* Mark Fink; Tel: 408-446-1677, Ext 3300, E-mail: mfink@sccl.org; Staff 15 (MLS 15)
Pop 58,302; Circ 2,800,000
Library Holdings: Bk Vols 370,000
Special Collections: Local History (California Western Americana Coll)
Friends of the Library Group
GILROY LIBRARY, 7387 Rosanna St, Gilroy, 95020-6193, SAN 334-746X. Tel: 408-842-8207. FAX: 408-842-0489. *Head Librn,* Lani Yoshimura; Tel: 408-842-8208; Staff 6 (MLS 6)
Pop 54,848; Circ 428,347
Library Holdings: Bk Titles 111,282; Bk Vols 142,468
Friends of the Library Group
LOS ALTOS MAIN LIBRARY, 13 S San Antonio Rd, Los Altos, 94022-3049, SAN 334-7494. Tel: 650-948-7683. FAX: 650-941-6308. *Commun Librn,* Cynthia Wilson; Staff 11 (MLS 11)
Pop 41,348; Circ 1,515,157
Library Holdings: Bk Vols 262,826
Function: Adult bk club, Adult literacy prog, Art exhibits, Audio & video playback equip for onsite use, Audiobks via web, Bk club(s), Bks on CD, CD-ROM, Children's prog, Computers for patron use, Copy machines, Digital talking bks, e-mail & chat, Electronic databases & coll, Family literacy, Free DVD rentals, Handicapped accessible, Health sci info serv, Homebound delivery serv, ILL available, Large print keyboards, Magnifiers for reading, Microfiche/film & reading machines, Music CDs, Online cat, Online ref, Online searches, Outreach serv, OverDrive digital audio bks, Photocopying/Printing, Preschool outreach, Prog for adults, Prog for children & young adult, Pub access computers, Ref serv available, Ref serv in person, Scanner, Senior computer classes, Senior outreach, Spanish lang bks, Spoken cassettes & CDs, Spoken cassettes & DVDs, Story hour, Summer reading prog, Tax forms, Teen prog, Telephone ref, Web-catalog, Wheelchair accessible
Open Mon-Thurs 10-9, Fri & Sat 10-6, Sun 12-6
Friends of the Library Group

LOS ALTOS-WOODLAND BRANCH, 1975 Grant Rd, Los Altos, 94022-6984, SAN 334-7672. Tel: 650-969-6030. FAX: 650-969-4922. *Librn,* Paul Miller
Circ 229,542
Library Holdings: Bk Titles 40,177; Bk Vols 46,582
Friends of the Library Group

MILPITAS PUBLIC, 160 N Main St, Milpitas, 95035-4323, SAN 334-7346. Tel: 408-262-1171. Reference Tel: 408-262-1171, Ext 3616. FAX: 408-262-5806. *Commun Librn,* Linda E Arbaugh; Staff 10 (MLS 8, Non-MLS 2)
Pop 70,000; Circ 1,960,000
Library Holdings: Bk Vols 300,000
Open Mon-Wed 1-9, Thurs-Sat 10-6, Sun 12-6
Friends of the Library Group

MORGAN HILL BRANCH, 660 W Main Ave, Morgan Hill, 95037-4128, SAN 334-7524. Tel: 408-779-3196. FAX: 408-779-0883. *Commun Librn,* Peggy Tomasso; E-mail: ptomasso@sccl.org; *Adult & Teen Serv, Supv Librn,* Jeff Grubb; E-mail: jgrubb@sccl.org; *Supv Librn, Ch,* Saralyn Otter; E-mail: sotter@sccl.org; Staff 22 (MLS 8, Non-MLS 14)
Pop 45,763; Circ 841,673
Library Holdings: Bk Titles 125,771; Bk Vols 160,689
Automation Activity & Vendor Info: (Circulation) Horizon; (Serials) EBSCO Online
Database Vendor: 3M Library Systems, ABC-CLIO, Baker & Taylor, BiblioCommons, EBSCO Auto Repair Reference, EBSCO Information Services, Electric Library, Greenwood Publishing Group, H W Wilson, Ingram Library Services, LearningExpress, Marquis Who's Who, McGraw-Hill, Medline, Newsbank, OCLC, Overdrive, Inc, Oxford Online, PubMed, Safari Books Online, Standard & Poor's, TumbleBookLibrary, ValueLine, Wilson - Wilson Web, World Book Online
Function: Adult bk club, Adult literacy prog, Audio & video playback equip for onsite use, Audiobks via web, Bilingual assistance for Spanish patrons, Bks on CD, CD-ROM, Children's prog, Computers for patron use, Copy machines, Digital talking bks, Electronic databases & coll, Free DVD rentals, Handicapped accessible, Holiday prog, Home delivery & serv to Sr ctr & nursing homes, Homebound delivery serv, ILL available, Large print keyboards, Magnifiers for reading, Microfiche/film & reading machines, Mus passes, Music CDs, Online ref, Online searches, Outreach serv, OverDrive digital audio bks, Photocopying/Printing, Preschool outreach, Preschool reading prog, Printer for laptops & handheld devices, Prog for adults, Prog for children & young adult, Pub access computers, Ref serv available, Ref serv in person, Scanner, Senior outreach, Spanish lang bks, Story hour, Summer reading prog, Tax forms, Teen prog, Telephone ref, Web-catalog, Wheelchair accessible, Workshops
Special Services for the Deaf - ADA equip; Adult & family literacy prog; Bks on deafness & sign lang; Closed caption videos; High interest/low vocabulary bks; TTY equip
Special Services for the Blind - Children's Braille; Computer access aids; Computer with voice synthesizer for visually impaired persons; Extensive large print coll; Free checkout of audio mat; Home delivery serv; Large print bks; Magnifiers; PC for handicapped; Talking bks
Open Tues 1-9, Wed & Thurs 10-9, Fri & Sat 10-6
Restriction: Non-resident fee
Friends of the Library Group

SARATOGA COMMUNITY LIBRARY, 13650 Saratoga Ave, Saratoga, 95070-5099, SAN 334-7559. Tel: 408-867-6129. Circulation Tel: 408-867-6127. FAX: 408-867-9806. *Commun Librn,* Barbara Morrow Williams; Staff 8 (MLS 8)
Pop 35,558; Circ 1,359,483
Library Holdings: Bk Titles 149,953; Bk Vols 204,583
Open Mon & Tues 1-9, Wed & Thurs 10-9, Fri & Sat 10-6, Sun 1-5.
Friends of the Library Group

Bookmobiles: 2

LYNWOOD

M SAINT FRANCIS MEDICAL CENTER*, Medical Library, 3630 E Imperial Hwy, 90262. SAN 301-0287. Tel: 310-900-8671. FAX: 310-639-5936. *Coordr,* Beth Araya; E-mail: betharaya@dochs.org; Staff 2 (MLS 1, Non-MLS 1)
Founded 1971
Library Holdings: Bk Titles 1,800; Per Subs 212
Open Mon-Fri 8:30-5
Friends of the Library Group

MADERA

M CHILDREN'S HOSPITAL CENTRAL CALIFORNIA*, Nathalie Wolfe Pediatric Sciences Library, 9300 Valley Children's Pl, 93638-8762. SAN 320-5614. Tel: 559-353-6170. Interlibrary Loan Service Tel: 559-353-6178. FAX: 559-353-6176. Web Site: www.childrenscentralcal.org. Staff 3 (MLS 1, Non-MLS 2)
Founded 1989
Library Holdings: Bk Vols 1,500; Per Subs 200
Subject Interests: Pediatrics
Automation Activity & Vendor Info: (Cataloging) CyberTools for Libraries; (Circulation) CyberTools for Libraries; (OPAC) CyberTools for Libraries; (Serials) CyberTools for Libraries
Database Vendor: EBSCOhost, Elsevier, PubMed, UpToDate
Function: Computers for patron use, Copy machines, Doc delivery serv, Electronic databases & coll, Fax serv, Handicapped accessible, Health sci info serv, Online cat, Online searches
Partic in Northern California & Nevada Medical Library Group (NCNMLG)
Open Mon-Fri 7-5
Restriction: Circulates for staff only, Hospital staff & commun, Med staff & students, Pub use on premises

S MADERA COUNTY HISTORICAL SOCIETY*, Museum-Library, 210 W Yosemite Ave, 93637-3533. (Mail add: PO Box 150, 93639-0150), SAN 371-7267. Tel: 559-673-0291. *Curator,* Dorothy Foust
Library Holdings: Bk Vols 130
Special Collections: County
Open Tues 9-12

L MADERA COUNTY LAW LIBRARY, County Government Ctr, 209 W Yosemite Ave, 93637-3596. SAN 301-0309. Tel: 559-673-0378. FAX: 559-673-0378. E-mail: director@maderalawlibrary.com, frontdesk@maderalawlibrary.com. *Law Libr Dir/Law Librn,* Kristina R Olvera; *Asst Law Librn,* Trudy Burke
Founded 1909
Subject Interests: Legal ref mat
Wireless access
Open Mon-Fri 9-1

P MADERA COUNTY LIBRARY*, 121 North G St, 93637-3592. SAN 333-0966. Tel: 559-675-7871. FAX: 559-675-7998. Web Site: www.maderacountylibrary.org. *County Librn,* Ellen Mester; *Managing Librn,* Position Currently Open
Founded 1910
Library Holdings: DVDs 7,321; e-books 523; Bk Vols 241,458; Per Subs 210
Subject Interests: Calif, Civil War, Genealogy
Automation Activity & Vendor Info: (Acquisitions) Horizon; (Cataloging) Horizon; (Circulation) Horizon; (Course Reserve) Horizon; (ILL) Horizon; (OPAC) Horizon; (Serials) Horizon
Database Vendor: Gale Cengage Learning
Mem of San Joaquin Valley Library System
Open Mon-Thurs 11-6, Fri & Sat 11-3
Friends of the Library Group

Branches: 4

CHOWCHILLA BRANCH, 300 Kings Ave, Chowchilla, 93610-2059, SAN 333-0990. Tel: 559-665-2630. FAX: 559-665-4216. *Br Mgr,* Nellie Serna
Library Holdings: Bk Vols 34,523
Open Tues 11-6, Wed & Thurs 11-5, Fri & Sat 11-3
Friends of the Library Group

NORTH FORK BRANCH, 32908 Rd 222, North Fork, 93643, SAN 333-1024. Tel: 559-877-2387. FAX: 559-877-3527.
Library Holdings: Bk Vols 21,328
Open Tues 11-6, Wed & Thurs 11-5, Fri & Sat 11-3
Friends of the Library Group

OAKHURST BRANCH, 49044 Civic Circle, Oakhurst, 93644-0484, SAN 333-1059. Tel: 559-683-4838. FAX: 559-642-4591. *Br Mgr,* Dale Rushing
Library Holdings: Bk Vols 42,000
Open Mon-Thurs 10-5, Fri & Sat 10-2
Friends of the Library Group

RANCHOS BRANCH, 37167 Avenue 12, Ste 4C, 93638-8725, SAN 371-9537. Tel: 559-645-1214. *Br Mgr,* Amanda Jude; E-mail: amanda.jude@maderacountylibrary.org
Founded 1990
Library Holdings: Bk Vols 18,000
Open Tues 11-6, Wed & Thurs 11-5, Fri & Sat 11-3
Friends of the Library Group

MALIBU

C PEPPERDINE UNIVERSITY LIBRARIES*, Payson Library, 24255 Pacific Coast Hwy, 90263. SAN 333-1083. Tel: 310-506-4252. Circulation Tel: 310-506-7273. Reference Tel: 310-506-4238. FAX: 310-506-7225. Interlibrary Loan Service FAX: 310-506-7515. Web Site: library.pepperdine.edu. *Dean of Libr,* Mark Roosa; E-mail: mark.roosa@pepperdine.edu; *Assoc Univ Librn, Coll & Serv,* Lynne Jacobsen; *Assoc Univ Librn, Pub Serv,* Melinda Raine; *Access Serv Librn,* Sally Bryant; *Ser & Electronic Res Librn,* Elizabeth Parang; *Tech Serv Librn,* Erin Carlson; *Cat,* Patricia Richmond; *ILL,* Melissa Nicholls; *Ref,* Ken Fink; *Ref,* Marc Vinyard; Staff 25 (MLS 14, Non-MLS 11)
Founded 1937. Enrl 6,269; Fac 382; Highest Degree: Doctorate

Library Holdings: Music Scores 3,827; Bk Vols 350,467; Per Subs 1,515
Special Collections: French Coll on 19th Century Paris (Mlynarsky Coll); Religious History (Churches of Christ). US Document Depository
Automation Activity & Vendor Info: (Acquisitions) Ex Libris Group; (Cataloging) Ex Libris Group; (Circulation) Ex Libris Group; (Course Reserve) Docutek; (OPAC) Ex Libris Group; (Serials) SerialsSolutions
Wireless access
Partic in OCLC Online Computer Library Center, Inc; Statewide California Electronic Library Consortium (SCELC)
Open Mon-Thurs 7:30am-3am, Fri 7:30am-9pm, Sat 10-9, Sun Noon-3am
Friends of the Library Group
Departmental Libraries:
ENCINO GRADUATE CAMPUS LIBRARY, 16830 Ventura Blvd, Ste 200, Encino, 91436, SAN 373-5567. Tel: 818-501-1615. FAX: 815-501-1605. *Info Serv Librn,* Lizette Gabriel; E-mail: lizette.gabriel@pepperdine.edu; Staff 1 (Non-MLS 1)
Subject Interests: Bus & mgt, Educ, Psychol
Open Mon-Thurs 2:30-10:30, Fri 11-7, Sat 9-5
CL SCHOOL OF LAW-JERENE APPLEBY HARNISH LAW LIBRARY, 24255 Pacific Coast Hwy, 90263. Tel: 310-506-4643. Administration Tel: 310-506-4647. FAX: 310-506-4836. Web Site: www.law.pepperdine.edu. *Assoc Dean, Libr & Info Serv,* Herb Cihak; *Assoc Dir,* Phillip Bohl; *Assoc Dir,* Katie Kerr; *Pub Serv,* Jessica Drewitz; *Ref,* Jennifer Allison; *Ref,* Don Buffaloe; *Ref,* Jodi Kruger; *Ref,* Gina McCoy; *Tech Serv,* Joy Humphrey
Library Holdings: Bk Titles 125,000; Bk Vols 400,000; Per Subs 3,603
Special Collections: American Arbitration Association Library & Information Center Coll
Automation Activity & Vendor Info: (Course Reserve) Ex Libris Group; (ILL) Ex Libris Group; (Media Booking) Ex Libris Group; (OPAC) Ex Libris Group; (Serials) Ex Libris Group
Open Mon-Thurs 7am-Midnight, Fri 7am-8pm, Sat 9am-10pm, Sun Noon-Midnight
IRVINE CENTER LIBRARY, Lakeshore Towers III, 18111 Von Karman Ave, Irvine, 92715, SAN 321-4044. Tel: 949-223-2520. FAX: 949-223-2559. *Librn,* Toby Berger
Subject Interests: Bus & mgt, Educ, Psychol
Function: ILL available
Open Mon-Thurs 12-9, Fri 12-7, Sat 9-5, Sun 1-7
WEST LOS ANGELES GRADUATE CAMPUS LIBRARY, 6100 Center Dr, Los Angeles, 90045, SAN 332-9402. Tel: 310-568-5717. Circulation Tel: 310-568-5685. Reference Tel: 310-568-5670. FAX: 310-568-5789. *Coordr,* Cindy Lundquist; *Ref,* Maria Brahme
Subject Interests: Bus & mgt, Educ, Psychol
Open Mon-Thurs 12-9, Fri 12-7, Sat 9-5, Sun 1-7
WESTLAKE VILLAGE GRADUATE CAMPUS LIBRARY, Westlake Ctr 2, 2829 Townsgate Rd, Ste 180, Westlake Village, 91361. Tel: 805-449-1181.
Open Mon-Thurs 12-9, Fri 12-7, Sat 9-5, Sun 1-7

MAMMOTH LAKES

P MONO COUNTY FREE LIBRARY*, Mammoth Lakes, 400 Sierra Park Blvd, 93546. (Mail add: PO Box 1120, 93546-1120), SAN 377-8576. Tel: 760-934-4777. FAX: 760-934-6268. *Librn,* Doug Oldham; Tel: 760-934-8670, E-mail: doldham@monocoe.org
Pop 10,800; Circ 100,000
Library Holdings: Bk Titles 45,000; Per Subs 120
Automation Activity & Vendor Info: (Circulation) SirsiDynix; (ILL) OCLC; (OPAC) SirsiDynix
Database Vendor: OCLC FirstSearch, SirsiDynix
Wireless access
Open Mon-Fri 10-7, Sat 9-5:30
Friends of the Library Group
Branches: 4
BRIDGEPORT, 94 N School St, Bridgeport, 93517. (Mail add: PO Box 398, Bridgeport, 93517-0398), SAN 300-6344. Tel: 760-932-7482. FAX: 760-932-7539. *Librn,* Abbie Bridges; E-mail: abridges@monocoe.org
Founded 1965. Pop 11,200; Circ 63,391
Library Holdings: Bk Vols 26,000; Per Subs 19
Special Collections: Native American Coll
Publications: Bibliographies
Open Tues, Thurs & Fri 10-5, Wed 10-8, Sat 10-5
Friends of the Library Group
COLEVILLE, 111591 Hwy 395, Coleville, 96107, SAN 377-8428. Tel: 530-495-2788. FAX: 530-495-2295. *Librn,* Olga Gilbert; E-mail: ogilbert@monocoe.org
Library Holdings: Bk Vols 30,000
Automation Activity & Vendor Info: (Cataloging) SirsiDynix; (Circulation) SirsiDynix
Open Tues & Thurs 1-6, Wed 1-7, Sat 9-1
Friends of the Library Group
CROWLEY LAKE, 3627 Crowley Lake Dr, Crowley Lake, 93546. Tel: 760-935-4505. FAX: 760-935-4560. *Sr Librn,* Diane Thoman; E-mail: dthoman@monocoe.org
Open Tues, Thurs & Fri 1-6, Sat 10-3
JUNE LAKE, 90 W Granite Ave, June Lake, 93529. (Mail add: PO Box 145, June Lake, 93529-0145), SAN 377-8444. Tel: 760-648-7284. FAX: 760-648-7284. *Librn,* Vineca Hess
Library Holdings: Bk Vols 14,000; Per Subs 3
Open Tues-Thurs & Sat 1-6
Friends of the Library Group
Bookmobiles: 1

MARINA

P MONTEREY COUNTY FREE LIBRARIES*, 188 Seaside Ctr, 93933-2500. SAN 334-0953. Tel: 831-883-7573. FAX: 831-883-7574. E-mail: 611-seaside-ref@co.monterey.ca.us. Web Site: www.co.montereycountyfreelibraries.org. *County Librn,* Jayanti Addleman; *Managing Librn,* Chris Ricker; Tel: 831-883-7567, E-mail: rickercm@co.monterey.ca.us; Staff 25 (MLS 11, Non-MLS 14)
Founded 1912. Pop 220,825; Circ 649,117
Jul 2012-Jun 2013 Income (Main Library and Branch(s)) $7,445,942, County $6,881,904, Locally Generated Income $564,038. Mats Exp $7,272,407, Books $337,822. Sal $2,887,221
Library Holdings: Audiobooks 7,763; AV Mats 26,202; CDs 7,763; DVDs 14,551; e-books 6,005; Large Print Bks 4,379; Microforms 2,846; Bk Titles 186,602; Bk Vols 389,074; Per Subs 440; Talking Bks 7,763; Videos 2,497
Special Collections: Californiana Coll
Automation Activity & Vendor Info: (Acquisitions) Innovative Interfaces, Inc; (Cataloging) Innovative Interfaces, Inc; (Circulation) Innovative Interfaces, Inc; (OPAC) Innovative Interfaces, Inc
Database Vendor: 3M Library Systems, Baker & Taylor, BioOne, Brodart, BWI, Comprise Technologies Inc, EBSCO Information Services, Foundation Center, Gale Cengage Learning, McGraw-Hill, OCLC, Overdrive, Inc, ReferenceUSA, TumbleBookLibrary, World Book Online
Wireless access
Function: Adult bk club, Adult literacy prog, Archival coll, Art exhibits, Audiobks via web, Bilingual assistance for Spanish patrons, Bk club(s), Bks on cassette, Bks on CD, Children's prog, Computer training, Computers for patron use, Copy machines, Digital talking bks, e-mail & chat, e-mail serv, Electronic databases & coll, Family literacy, Fax serv, Free DVD rentals, Handicapped accessible, Homebound delivery serv, Homework prog, ILL available, Magnifiers for reading, Microfiche/film & reading machines, Online cat, Online ref, Online searches, OverDrive digital audio bks, Photocopying/Printing, Prog for adults, Prog for children & young adult, Pub access computers, Spanish lang bks, Story hour, Summer reading prog, Tax forms, VHS videos, Web-catalog, Wheelchair accessible, Workshops
Partic in Monterey Bay Area Cooperative Library System
Special Services for the Deaf - Bks on deafness & sign lang; Closed caption videos
Special Services for the Blind - Bks on cassette; Bks on CD; Extensive large print coll; Free checkout of audio mat; Home delivery serv; Large print bks; Magnifiers; Recorded bks; Talking bks
Open Mon-Fri 8-5
Friends of the Library Group
Branches: 17
AROMAS BRANCH, 389-D Blohm Ave, Aromas, 95004. (Mail add: PO Box 298, Aromas, 95004-0298), SAN 334-0988. Tel: 831-726-3240. FAX: 831-726-0102. *Br Mgr,* Hillary Bussio
Pop 2,797; Circ 9,711
Library Holdings: Bk Vols 8,852
Function: Prog for adults, Prog for children & young adult, Summer reading prog
Open Wed & Fri 2-6, Thurs & Sat 10-12 & 1-5
Friends of the Library Group
BIG SUR BRANCH, Hwy 1 at Ripplewood Resort, Big Sur, 93920. (Mail add: PO Box 217, Big Sur, 93920-0217), SAN 334-1135. Tel: 831-667-2537. FAX: 831-667-0708. *Br Mgr,* Julia Begin
Pop 1,336; Circ 9,956
Library Holdings: Bk Vols 10,647
Function: Prog for children & young adult
Open Wed & Thurs 2-6, Fri & Sat 11-4
Friends of the Library Group
BRADLEY BRANCH, Dixie St, Bradley, 93426. (Mail add: PO Box 330, Bradley, 93426-0330), SAN 334-1046. Tel: 805-472-9407. FAX: 805-472-9565. *Br Mgr,* Darlene Lloyd
Pop 450; Circ 4,814
Library Holdings: Bk Vols 3,476
Function: Prog for children & young adult, Summer reading prog
Open Wed 8-3, Fri 8-12
BUENA VISTA, 18250 Tara Dr, Salinas, 93908, SAN 378-0376. Tel: 831-455-9699. FAX: 831-455-0369. *Br Mgr,* Jane Wallace; Staff 1 (Non-MLS 1)
Pop 16,069; Circ 38,298

Library Holdings: Bk Vols 18,139
Function: Prog for children & young adult, Summer reading prog
Open Tues 10-8, Wed & Thurs 10-5, Fri 10-4, Sat 11-5
CARMEL VALLEY BRANCH, 65 W Carmel Valley Rd, Carmel Valley, 93924, SAN 334-1070. Tel: 831-659-2377. FAX: 831-659-0589. *Br Mgr,* Jennifer Smith; Staff 1 (MLS 1)
Pop 6,819; Circ 50,776
Library Holdings: Bk Vols 30,725
Function: Prog for adults, Prog for children & young adult, Summer reading prog
Open Tues & Thurs 11-7, Wed & Fri 10-5, Sat 11-5
Friends of the Library Group
CASTROVILLE BRANCH, 11160 Speegle St, Castroville, 95012, SAN 334-1100. Tel: 831-769-8724. FAX: 831-633-6315. *Br Mgr,* Kurt Ellison; Staff 1 (MLS 1)
Pop 9,525; Circ 36,019
Library Holdings: Bk Vols 31,322
Function: Prog for children & young adult, Summer reading prog
Open Tues-Thurs 11-7, Fri & Sat 11-5
Friends of the Library Group
GONZALES BRANCH, 851 Fifth St, Ste T, Gonzales, 93926, SAN 334-116X. Tel: 831-675-2209. FAX: 831-675-9525. *Br Mgr,* Courtney Amparo; Staff 1 (MLS 1)
Pop 8,364; Circ 19,612
Library Holdings: Bk Vols 20,616
Function: Bilingual assistance for Spanish patrons, Computers for patron use, Copy machines, Fax serv, Homework prog, Photocopying/Printing, Prog for children & young adult, Spanish lang bks, Story hour, Summer reading prog
Open Tues & Wed 11-7, Thurs 11-5, Fri & Sat 10-5
GREENFIELD BRANCH, 315 El Camino Real, Greenfield, 93927, SAN 334-1194. Tel: 831-674-2614. FAX: 831-674-2688. *Br Mgr,* Elizabeth Lopez; Staff 1 (Non-MLS 1)
Pop 16,629; Circ 599,886
Library Holdings: Bk Vols 25,352
Function: Prog for children & young adult, Summer reading prog
Open Tues & Wed 12-8, Thurs 10-6, Fri 12-5, Sat 10-5
KING CITY BRANCH, 402 Broadway, King City, 93930, SAN 370-7946. Tel: 831-385-3677. FAX: 831-385-0918. *Br Mgr,* Robin Cauntay; Staff 1 (MLS 1)
Pop 11,518; Circ 60,249
Library Holdings: Bk Vols 36,075
Function: Prog for children & young adult, Summer reading prog
Open Mon-Thurs 10-8, Fri & Sat 10 5
Friends of the Library Group
MARINA BRANCH, 190 Seaside Circle, 93933, SAN 334-1224. Tel: 831-883-7507. FAX: 831-883-9473. *Br Mgr,* Samuel Daniels; Tel: 831-883-7506; Staff 1 (MLS 1)
Pop 21,750; Circ 85,761
Library Holdings: Bk Vols 26,677
Function: Prog for children & young adult, Summer reading prog
Open Tues & Wed 12-8, Thurs & Fri 10-5, Sat 10-4
Friends of the Library Group
PAJARO BRANCH, 29 Bishop St, Pajaro, 95076, SAN 376-9186. Tel: 831-761-2545. FAX: 831-768-7782. *Br Mgr,* Joseantonio Gonzalez
Pop 3,600; Circ 4,916
Library Holdings: Bk Vols 8,517
Function: Prog for children & young adult, Summer reading prog
Open Tues & Thurs 10-1:30 & 2:30-6, Sat 10-2
PARKFIELD, 70643 Parkfield-Coalinga Rd, San Miguel, 93451, SAN 334-1283. Tel: 805-463-2347. FAX: 805-463-2347. *Br Mgr,* Marlene Thomason
Library Holdings: Bk Vols 6,039
Function: Prog for children & young adult, Summer reading prog
Branch is temporarily closed
PRUNEDALE, 17822 Moro Rd, Salinas, 93907, SAN 334-1313. Tel: 831-663-2292. FAX: 831-663-0203. *Br Mgr,* Tamara Del Conte; Staff 1 (Non-MLS 1)
Pop 16,432; Circ 69,255
Library Holdings: Bk Vols 41,488
Function: Prog for children & young adult, Summer reading prog
Open Mon-Thurs 10-8, Fri & Sat 10-5
Friends of the Library Group
SAN ARDO BRANCH, 62350 College St, San Ardo, 93450. (Mail add: PO Box 127, San Ardo, 93450-0127), SAN 334-1348. Tel: 831-627-2503. FAX: 831-627-4229. *Br Mgr,* Maria Lomeli
Pop 873; Circ 8,806
Library Holdings: Bk Vols 8,111
Function: Prog for children & young adult, Summer reading prog
Open Wed-Fri 11-5
SAN LUCAS BRANCH, 54692 Teresa St, San Lucas, 93954. (Mail add: PO Box 28, San Lucas, 93954-0028), SAN 334-1372. Tel: 831-382-4382. FAX: 831-382-4677.
Library Holdings: Bk Vols 7,290
Function: Prog for children & young adult, Summer reading prog
Open Tues-Thurs 12-6
SEASIDE BRANCH, 550 Harcourt Ave, Seaside, 93955, SAN 334-1402. Tel: 831-899-2055. FAX: 831-899-2735. *Br Mgr,* Sharon Freed; Staff 3 (MLS 1, Non-MLS 2)
Pop 36,568; Circ 113,217
Library Holdings: Bk Vols 69,049
Function: Adult literacy prog, Prog for children & young adult, Summer reading prog
Open Mon-Thurs 10-8, Fri & Sat 10-5
Friends of the Library Group
SOLEDAD BRANCH, 401 Gabilan Dr, Soledad, 93960, SAN 334-1437. Tel: 831-678-2430. FAX: 831-678-3087. *Br Mgr,* Denise Campos; Staff 1 (Non-MLS 1)
Pop 24,502; Circ 42,191
Library Holdings: Bk Vols 33,570
Function: Prog for children & young adult, Summer reading prog
Open Tues & Wed 12-8, Thurs 10-6, Fri & Sat 10-4
Bookmobiles: 3. Bk Titles 10,125

S MONTEREY INSTITUTE FOR RESEARCH & ASTRONOMY*, Priscilla Fairfield Bok Library, 200 Eighth St, 93933. SAN 327-7119. Tel: 831-883-1000. FAX: 831-883-1031. E-mail: mira@mira.org. Web Site: www.mira.org. *Librn,* Clasina Shane; E-mail: cs@mira.org
Library Holdings: Bk Vols 3,000; Per Subs 8,000
Restriction: Open by appt only

MARIPOSA

L MARIPOSA COUNTY LAW LIBRARY*, 4978 10th St, 95338. (Mail add: PO Box 106, 95338), SAN 324-3532. Web Site: mariposalibrary.org. *Head Librn,* Janet Chase-Williams; E-mail: janet.chase-williams@sjvls.org; *Asst Librn II,* Lea-Ann Nichols
Library Holdings: Bk Vols 1,993
Wireless access

P MARIPOSA COUNTY LIBRARY*, 4978 Tenth St, 95338. (Mail add: PO Box 106, 95338-0106), SAN 374-6291. Tel: 209-966-2140. FAX: 209-742-7527. Web Site: www.mariposalibrary.org. *Librn,* Janet Chase-Williams; *Asst Librn,* Catherine Adams; Staff 9 (MLS 1, Non-MLS 8)
Founded 1926. Pop 16,000; Circ 81,133
Library Holdings: Bk Vols 33,000; Per Subs 75
Mem of San Joaquin Valley Library System
Special Services for the Deaf Bks on deafness & sign lang; Captioned film dep; High interest/low vocabulary bks
Open Mon & Sat 9:30-2, Tues & Thurs 9:30-6, Wed & Fri 9:30-5
Friends of the Library Group
Branches: 4
BASSETT MEMORIAL, 7971 Chilnualna Falls Rd, Wawona, 95389. (Mail add: PO Box 2008, Wawona, 95389-2008), SAN 374-6321. Tel: 209-375-6510. *Br Head,* Diane Mello; Staff 3 (Non-MLS 3)
Open Wed & Fri (Winter) 12-5, Sat 10-3; Mon-Fri (Summer) 1-5, Sat 10-2
Friends of the Library Group
EL PORTAL BRANCH, 9670 Rancheria Flat Rd, 1st Flr, El Portal, 95318. (Mail add: PO Box 160, El Portal, 95318-0160), SAN 374-6305. Tel: 209-379-2401. *Br Head,* Andrea Canapary; Staff 3 (Non-MLS 3)
Open Mon & Thurs 10-6:30, Sun & Mon (Summer) 12-7
RED CLOUD, 10332-C Fiske Rd, Coulterville, 95311, SAN 374-6313. Tel: 209-878-3692. *Br Librn,* Pam Lagomarsino; Staff 3 (Non-MLS 3)
Open Tues, Wed & Fri 11-3, Sat (Winter) 12-4
Friends of the Library Group
YOSEMITE NATIONAL PARK BRANCH, Girls Club Bldg, 58 Cedar Ct, Yosemite National Park, 95389. (Mail add: PO Box 395, Yosemite National Park, 95389-0395), SAN 374-633X. Tel: 209-372-4552. *Br Head,* Alice Rosenfeld; Staff 3 (Non-MLS 3)
Open Mon 12-3, Tues & Wed 10-2, Thurs 3-6

MARKLEEVILLE

S ALPINE COUNTY HISTORICAL SOCIETY*, Alpine County Museum Library, One School St, 96120. (Mail add: PO Box 517, 96120-0517), SAN 371-7038. Tel: 530-694-2317. FAX: 530-694-1087. E-mail: alpinemuseum@yahoo.com. Web Site: www.alpinecountymuseum.com. *Dir,* Wanda Coyan
Founded 1964
Library Holdings: Bk Titles 600; Per Subs 16
Special Collections: Alpine County First Familes Coll; Spicer Archealogical Coll. Oral History
Wireless access
Function: Res libr
Publications: Alpine Review (Quarterly)
Restriction: Not a lending libr

P ALPINE COUNTY LIBRARY*, 270 Laramie St, 96120. (Mail add: PO Box 187, 96120-0187), SAN 301-0406. Tel: 530-694-2120. FAX: 530-694-2408. E-mail: library@alpinecountyca.gov. Web Site: www.alpinecountyca.gov/departments/library. *Dir,* Rita Lovell; Staff 3 (MLS 1, Non-MLS 2)
Founded 1969. Pop 1,200; Circ 1,265
Library Holdings: CDs 192; Large Print Bks 47; Bk Titles 14,044; Bk Vols 15,832; Per Subs 70; Talking Bks 474; Videos 1,532
Special Collections: Local History Coll
Subject Interests: Local hist
Automation Activity & Vendor Info: (Cataloging) TLC (The Library Corporation); (Circulation) TLC (The Library Corporation); (OPAC) TLC (The Library Corporation)
Database Vendor: OCLC FirstSearch
Function: Archival coll, ILL available, Photocopying/Printing, Prog for adults, Prog for children & young adult, Ref serv available, Summer reading prog, Wheelchair accessible
Publications: Library Newsletter (Bi-monthly)
Open Wed & Thurs 10-6, Fri & Sat 10-5
Friends of the Library Group
Branches: 1
BEAR VALLEY BRANCH, 367 Creekside Dr, Bear Valley, 95223. (Mail add: PO Box 5237, Bear Valley, 95223-5237), SAN 370-4904. Tel: 209-753-6219. FAX: 209-753-2219. *Libr Tech,* Thea Schoettgen
Circ 5,011
Library Holdings: Bk Titles 4,776; Bk Vols 4,808; Per Subs 44; Talking Bks 262; Videos 662
Function: AV serv, ILL available, Photocopying/Printing, Prog for adults, Prog for children & young adult, Ref serv available, Summer reading prog, Wheelchair accessible
Open Wed & Fri 12:30-5:30, Thurs 1-6, Sat 9-2
Friends of the Library Group
Bookmobiles: 1

MARTINEZ

GL CONTRA COSTA COUNTY PUBLIC LAW LIBRARY, 1020 Ward St, 1st Flr, 94553-1360. SAN 301-0414. Tel: 925-646-2783. FAX: 925-646-2438. Web Site: www.cccpllib.org. *Dir,* Carey Rowan; E-mail: carey.rowan@ll.cccounty.us; *Admin Serv,* Naomi Little; Staff 4 (Non-MLS 4)
Founded 1893
Library Holdings: Bk Vols 36,450; Per Subs 15
Automation Activity & Vendor Info: (Acquisitions) Sydney; (Cataloging) Sydney; (OPAC) Sydney; (Serials) Sydney
Database Vendor: Fastcase, HeinOnline, LexisNexis, Westlaw
Wireless access
Open Mon-Fri 8-5
Restriction: Non-circulating
Branches:
PITTSBURG BRANCH, Richard E Arnason Justice Ctr, Ste 1045, 1000 Center Dr, Pittsburg, 94565. Tel: 925-252-2800.
RICHMOND BRANCH, George D Carroll Courthouse, Rm 237, 100 37th St, Richmond, 94805. Tel: 510-374-3019.

MARYSVILLE

J YUBA COMMUNITY COLLEGE*, Learning Resources Center, 2088 N Beale Rd, 95901. SAN 301-0449. Tel: 530-741-6762. Circulation Tel: 530-741-6755. Reference Tel: 530-741-6756. FAX: 530-741-6824. *Dean,* Kevin Dobbs; Staff 2.1 (MLS 1.6, Non-MLS 0.5)
Founded 1927. Enrl 3,100; Fac 145; Highest Degree: Associate
Library Holdings: Bk Titles 65,000; Per Subs 250
Automation Activity & Vendor Info: (Acquisitions) Baker & Taylor; (Circulation) SirsiDynix; (Course Reserve) SirsiDynix; (OPAC) SirsiDynix; (Serials) EBSCO Online
Wireless access
Open Mon-Thurs 7:30am-9pm, Fri 7:30-5

GL YUBA COUNTY LAW LIBRARY*, 915 Eighth St, 95901. Tel: 530-749-7565. FAX: 530-749-7513. *In Charge,* Esther O Davis
Library Holdings: Bk Vols 2,500

P YUBA COUNTY LIBRARY*, 303 Second St, 95901-6099. SAN 301-0430. Tel: 530-749-7380. Interlibrary Loan Service Tel: 530-749-7323. Reference Tel: 530-749-7386. FAX: 530-741-3098. E-mail: library@co.yuba.ca.us. Web Site: library.yuba.org. *Dir,* Position Currently Open; *Archival & Ref Librn,* Regina Zurakowski; E-mail: gzurakowski@co.yuba.ca.us; Staff 6 (MLS 1, Non-MLS 5)
Founded 1858. Pop 72,615; Circ 156,382
Jul 2011-Jun 2012 Income $699,686. Mats Exp $30,000. Sal $311,057
Library Holdings: Bk Vols 123,229; Per Subs 45
Special Collections: California History
Automation Activity & Vendor Info: (Cataloging) SirsiDynix; (Circulation) SirsiDynix; (Course Reserve) SirsiDynix; (ILL) OCLC; (OPAC) SIRSI-iBistro
Database Vendor: Baker & Taylor, Booklist Online, Booksite, EBSCO - WebFeat, LearningExpress, Newsbank, OCLC FirstSearch, OCLC WebJunction, OCLC WorldShare Interlibrary Loan, SirsiDynix
Wireless access
Function: Archival coll, Art exhibits, Audio & video playback equip for onsite use, Bilingual assistance for Spanish patrons, Bks on cassette, Bks on CD, CD-ROM, Children's prog, Computer training, Computers for patron use, Copy machines, E-Reserves, Electronic databases & coll, Free DVD rentals, Handicapped accessible, Holiday prog, Homebound delivery serv, ILL available, Instruction & testing, Mail & tel request accepted, Music CDs, Online cat, Online ref, Online searches, Outreach serv, Photocopying/Printing, Preschool outreach, Prog for adults, Prog for children & young adult, Pub access computers, Ref & res, Ref serv available, Referrals accepted, Scanner, Senior computer classes, Spoken cassettes & CDs, Story hour, Summer reading prog, Tax forms, Teen prog, Telephone ref, VHS videos, Video lending libr, Web-catalog, Wheelchair accessible, Workshops, Writing prog
Mem of Mountain-Valley Library System
Open Tues, Wed & Sat 10:30-6, Thurs & Fri 12-6
Friends of the Library Group

MENDOCINO

S KELLEY HOUSE MUSEUM, INC*, 45007 Albion St, 95460. (Mail add: PO Box 922, 95460-0922), SAN 373-4102. Tel: 707-937-5791. FAX: 707-937-2156. Web Site: www.kelleyhousemuseum.org. *Exec Dir,* Nancy Freeze
Founded 1973
Jan 2010-Dec 2010 Income $100,000. Mats Exp $25,000. Sal $60,000
Library Holdings: DVDs 50; Bk Vols 300
Special Collections: Oral History
Open Mon & Fri-Sun (Winter) 11-3; Tues-Thurs (Summer) 11-3

S MENDOCINO ART CENTER LIBRARY*, Visual Arts, 45200 Little Lake St, 95460. (Mail add: PO Box 765, 95460-0765), SAN 333-1202. Tel: 707-937-5818. Toll Free Tel: 800-653-3328. FAX: 707-937-4625. E-mail: register@mendocinoartcenter.org. Web Site: www.mendocinoartcenter.org. *Exec Dir,* Lindsay Shields; E-mail: director@mendocinoartcenter.org
Founded 1962
Library Holdings: Bk Titles 500
Subject Interests: Visual arts
Wireless access
Restriction: Mem only

MENLO PARK

S EXPONENT*, Information Resources, 149 Commonwealth Dr, 94025. SAN 371-7453. Tel: 650-688-7171. FAX: 650-329-9526. Web Site: www.exponent.com. *Mgr,* Lee Pharis; Tel: 650-688-7141, E-mail: lpharis@exponent.com; Staff 4 (MLS 2, Non-MLS 2)
Founded 1984
Library Holdings: Bk Titles 5,000; Bk Vols 7,500; Per Subs 3
Subject Interests: Electronics, Eng
Automation Activity & Vendor Info: (Acquisitions) Cuadra Associates, Inc; (Cataloging) Cuadra Associates, Inc
Database Vendor: Dialog, LexisNexis, STN International, Westlaw
Restriction: Private libr

P MENLO PARK PUBLIC LIBRARY*, 800 Alma St, Alma & Ravenswood, 94025-3455. SAN 301-052X. Tel: 650-330-2500. Information Services Tel: 650-330-2520. FAX: 650-327-7030. Web Site: www.menloparklibrary.org. *Dir,* Susan Holmer; Staff 16.5 (MLS 6.75, Non-MLS 9.75)
Founded 1916. Pop 32,513; Circ 624,669
Library Holdings: Bk Vols 149,927
Automation Activity & Vendor Info: (Acquisitions) Innovative Interfaces, Inc; (Cataloging) Innovative Interfaces, Inc; (Circulation) Innovative Interfaces, Inc; (OPAC) Innovative Interfaces, Inc
Database Vendor: Gale Cengage Learning
Wireless access
Mem of Pacific Library Partnership (PLP)
Open Mon & Wed 10-9, Tues 12-9, Thurs & Fri 10-6, Sat 10-5, Sun 12-5
Friends of the Library Group
Branches: 1
BELLE HAVEN, 413 Ivy Dr, 94025. Tel: 650-330-2540. *Br Mgr,* Judy Fagerholm
Library Holdings: Bk Vols 10,000; Per Subs 30
Open Tues & Wed 12-7, Thurs & Fri 12-6, Sat 12-5

R SAINT PATRICK'S SEMINARY, Carl Gellert & Celia Berta Gellert Foundation Memorial Library, 320 Middlefield Rd, 94025. SAN 301-0546. Tel: 650-321-5655. FAX: 650-323-5447. Web Site: www.stpatricksseminary.org. *Dir,* David Kriegh; Tel: 650-289-3350, Ext 20,

E-mail: david.kriegh@stpsu.org; *Librn,* Cheryl Collins; *Pub Serv Librn,* Gabriel Ortiz; *Cataloger,* Wayne Davison; *Tech Asst,* Sharon Hamrick; Staff 4 (MLS 4)
Founded 1898. Enrl 96; Fac 20; Highest Degree: Master
Jul 2008-Jun 2009 Income $292,179. Mats Exp $81,148, Books $36,968, Per/Ser (Incl. Access Fees) $24,738, AV Mat $58, Electronic Ref Mat (Incl. Access Fees) $16,437, Presv $2,947. Sal $192,022 (Prof $179,838)
Library Holdings: AV Mats 2,484; Bk Vols 109,716; Per Subs 300; Videos 770
Special Collections: Californiana & Western Americana (C Albert Shumate MD Coll); Library of Archbishop Alemany (First Archbishop of San Francisco Coll)
Subject Interests: Scripture, Theol
Automation Activity & Vendor Info: (Cataloging) OCLC Connexion; (ILL) OCLC; (OPAC) Cassidy Cataloguing Services, Inc
Database Vendor: Cassidy Cataloguing Services, Inc
Wireless access
Function: Computers for patron use, Copy machines, ILL available, Online cat, Photocopying/Printing, Pub access computers, Ref serv available, Wheelchair accessible
Partic in Califa; OCLC Online Computer Library Center, Inc; Statewide California Electronic Library Consortium (SCELC)
Restriction: Restricted borrowing privileges

S SRI INTERNATIONAL*, Research Information Services, 333 Ravenswood Ave, 94025. SAN 333-1261. Tel: 650-859-5506. FAX: 650-859-2757. E-mail: library@sri.com. Web Site: www.sri.com. *Mgr,* Lisa Beffa; *Info Spec,* Roger Sherman; Staff 3 (MLS 3)
Founded 1948
Library Holdings: Bk Titles 25,000; Per Subs 2,200
Restriction: Staff use only
Branches:
LIFE SCIENCES LIBRARY, 333 Ravenswood Ave, 94025, SAN 333-1296. Tel: 650-859-3549. *Circ Asst,* Jim Johnson

G UNITED STATES GEOLOGICAL SURVEY LIBRARY, 345 Middlefield Rd, Bldg 15 (MS-955), 94025-3591. SAN 301-0554. Tel: 650-329-5027. Circulation Tel: 650-329-5026. Toll Free Tel: 888-275-8747. FAX: 650-329-5132. E-mail: men_lib@usgs.gov. Web Site: library.usgs.gov. *Br Mgr,* Joseph Langdon; Tel: 650-329-5013, E-mail: jlangdon@usgs.gov; *Digital Res Librn,* Lakegan Harris; Tel: 650-329-5034, E-mail: lharris@usgs.gov; *ILL/Tech Serv Librn,* Mike Moore; Tel: 650-329-5009, E-mail: mmmoore@usgs.gov; *Ref Librn, Tech Serv,* Angelica Bravos; Tel: 650-329-5025, E-mail: abravos@usgs.gov; *Ref Librn,* Charles Wenger; Tel: 650-329-5427, E-mail: cwenger@usgs.go; *Circ Tech,* Sharon Sachse; E-mail: ssachse@usgs.gov; *Doc Delivery,* Jon Debord; Tel: 650-329-5144, E-mail: jdebord@usgs.gov; *Tech Support,* Anna Tellez; Tel: 650-329-5128, E-mail: amtellez@usgs.gov; Staff 8 (MLS 4, Non-MLS 4)
Founded 1953
Special Collections: Aerial Photo Coll; California History Coll
Subject Interests: Calif, Earth sci, Hist, Maps, Natural hazards, Water res
Automation Activity & Vendor Info: (Acquisitions) SirsiDynix; (Cataloging) SirsiDynix; (Circulation) SirsiDynix; (ILL) OCLC GovDoc; (OPAC) SirsiDynix; (Serials) SirsiDynix
Database Vendor: Blackwell, EBSCOhost, Elsevier, OCLC FirstSearch, OCLC WorldShare Interlibrary Loan, SirsiDynix
Function: Copy machines, Govt ref serv, Handicapped accessible, ILL available, Online cat, Wheelchair accessible
Open Mon-Fri 8:30-4:30
Restriction: Open to pub for ref only

MERCED

J MERCED COLLEGE, Learning Resources Center, 3600 M St, 95348. SAN 333-1326. Tel: 209-384-6080. Circulation Tel: 209-384-6081. Reference Tel: 209-384-6083. FAX: 209-384-6084. E-mail: walsh.s@mccd.edu. Web Site: www.mccd.edu/lrc/index.html. *Dir,* Dr Susan Walsh; Tel: 209-384-6082, E-mail: walsh.s@mccd.edu; *Assoc Librn,* Joey Merritt; Tel: 209-384-6283, E-mail: joey.merritt@mccd.edu; *Electronic Res Librn,* Nancy Golz; Tel: 209-386-6703, E-mail: nancy.golz@mccd.edu; *Ref Librn,* Dee Near; Tel: 209-384-6086, E-mail: near.d@mccd.edu; *Mgr, Tech Serv,* Omar Amavizca; Tel: 209-384-6145, E-mail: amavizca.o@mccd.edu; Staff 9 (MLS 3, Non-MLS 6)
Founded 1972. Enrl 11,263; Fac 310; Highest Degree: Associate
Library Holdings: Bk Vols 44,272; Per Subs 235
Automation Activity & Vendor Info: (Circulation) SirsiDynix; (Course Reserve) SirsiDynix; (OPAC) SirsiDynix; (Serials) SirsiDynix
Database Vendor: ABC-CLIO, CountryWatch, CQ Press, EBSCO Auto Repair Reference, EBSCOhost, Facts on File, LexisNexis, Newsbank
Wireless access
Partic in 49-99 Cooperative Library System
Open Mon-Thurs 8am-8:30pm, Fri 8-2; Mon & Tues (Summer) 12-8, Wed & Thurs 8-4
Friends of the Library Group

GL MERCED COUNTY LAW LIBRARY*, 670 W 22nd St, 95340-3780. SAN 301-0570. Tel: 209-385-7332. FAX: 209-385-7448. E-mail: ll01@co.merced.ca.us. *Librn,* Susan Nenagh; Staff 1 (Non-MLS 1)
Library Holdings: Bk Titles 10,000
Partic in Westlaw

P MERCED COUNTY LIBRARY, 2100 O St, 95340-3637. SAN 333-1350. Tel: 209-385-7646. Circulation Tel: 209-385-7643. FAX: 209-726-7912. E-mail: info@mercedcountylibrary.org. Web Site: www.co.merced.ca.us. *County Librn,* Amy Taylor; E-mail: ataylor@co.merced.ca.us; Staff 13 (MLS 3, Non-MLS 10)
Founded 1910. Pop 255,793; Circ 264,427
Jul 2013-Jun 2014 Income $148,898. Mats Exp $2,752,075
Library Holdings: Bk Titles 191,537; Bk Vols 372,920; Per Subs 150
Special Collections: California History Coll; California Telephone Books; Cookery Coll; Genealogy Coll. Oral History
Wireless access
Mem of San Joaquin Valley Library System
Partic in OCLC Online Computer Library Center, Inc
Open Mon-Thurs 10-6, Fri & Sat 10-5
Friends of the Library Group
Branches: 11
ATWATER BRANCH, 1600 Third St, Atwater, 95301-3607, SAN 333-1415. Tel: 209-358-6651. *In Charge,* Kathy Lund
Library Holdings: Bk Vols 24,435
Open Tues-Thurs 10-6, Fri & Sat 10-5
Friends of the Library Group
DELHI EDUCATIONAL PARK COMMUNITY, 16881 Schendel Rd, Delhi, 95315, SAN 333-1539. Tel: 209-656-2049. *In Charge,* Allyssa Tidwell
Library Holdings: Bk Vols 5,643
Open Mon-Fri 8-4, Sat 10-3
DOS PALOS BRANCH, 2002 Almond St, Dos Palos, 93620-2304, SAN 333-1563. Tel: 209-392-2155. *In Charge,* Patricia Leisman
Library Holdings: Bk Vols 15,982
Open Wed 10-6, Fri 10-5, Sat 10-3
Friends of the Library Group
GUSTINE BRANCH, 205 Sixth St, Gustine, 95322-1112, SAN 333-1687. Tel: 209-854-3013. *In Charge,* Nola Ramirez; Staff 1 (Non-MLS 1)
Library Holdings: High Interest/Low Vocabulary Bk Vols 100; Large Print Bks 600; Bk Vols 11,470; Per Subs 19
Function: ILL available, Prog for children & young adult, Summer reading prog, Tax forms
Open Tues & Thurs 10-6, Sat 10-5
IRWIN-HILMAR BRANCH, 20041 W Falke St, Hilmar, 95324-9778, SAN 333-1717. Tel: 209-632-0746. *In Charge,* Debbie Hutchins
Library Holdings: Bk Vols 14,911
Open Wed 10-6, Fri 10-5, Sat 10-3
Friends of the Library Group
LE GRAND BRANCH, 12949 Le Grand Rd, Le Grand, 95333, SAN 333-1741. Tel: 209-389-4541. *In Charge,* Dana Moroni
Founded 1910. Circ 4,000
Library Holdings: Bk Vols 17,706
Open Mon-Fri 10-5, Sat 10-3
Friends of the Library Group
LIVINGSTON BRANCH, 1212 Main St, Livingston, 95334-1215, SAN 333-1776. Tel: 209-394-7330. *In Charge,* Yvette Enos
Library Holdings: Bk Vols 22,303
Open Tues & Thurs 10-6, Sat 10-5
Friends of the Library Group
LOS BANOS BRANCH, 1312 Seventh St, Los Banos, 93635-4757, SAN 333-1806. Tel: 209-826-5254. *In Charge,* Lenny Costa
Library Holdings: Bk Vols 21,518
Open Tues-Thurs 10-6, Fri & Sat 10-5
Friends of the Library Group
SANTA NELLA BRANCH, 29188 W Centinella Ave, Santa Nella, 95322-9625, SAN 333-1911. Tel: 209-826-6059. *In Charge,* Antonina Wuthrich
Library Holdings: Bk Vols 8,973
Open Tues & Sat 10-3
Friends of the Library Group
SNELLING BRANCH, 15916 N Hwy 59, Snelling, 95369, SAN 333-192X. Tel: 209-563-6616. *In Charge,* Margaret Wise
Founded 1932
Library Holdings: Bk Vols 6,514
Open Thurs & Sat 10-3
Friends of the Library Group
WINTON BRANCH, 7057 W Walnut, Winton, 95388, SAN 333-2012. Tel: 209-358-3651. *In Charge,* Lisa Simms
Library Holdings: Bk Vols 11,106
Open Wed & Sat 10-3
Friends of the Library Group

C UNIVERSITY OF CALIFORNIA, MERCED LIBRARY, 5200 N Lake Rd, 95343-5001. Tel: 209-228-4444. FAX: 209-228-4271. E-mail: library@ucmerced.edu. Web Site: library.ucmerced.edu. *Interim Univ Librn,* Donald Barclay; Tel: 209-201-9724, E-mail: dbarclay@ucmerced.edu; *Assoc Univ Librn, Libr Operations,* Eric Scott; Tel: 209-675-8040, E-mail: escott@ucmerced.edu; *Head, Coll Serv,* Jim Dooley; Tel: 209-658-7161, E-mail: jdooley@ucmerced.edu; *Head, Digital Assets,* Emily S Lin; Tel: 209-658-7146, E-mail: elin@ucmerced.edu; *Head, User Communication & Instruction,* Sara Davidson Squibb; Tel: 209-205-8237, E-mail: sdavidson2@ucmerced.edu; *Instruction & Scholarly Communications Librn,* Susan Mikkelsen; Tel: 209-228-4615, E-mail: smikkelsen@ucmerced.edu; *Tech Mgr,* Tom Bustos; Tel: 209-337-8710, E-mail: tbustos@ucmerced.edu; *Libr Serv Supvr,* Joe Ameen; Tel: 209-201-5013, E-mail: sameen@ucmerced.edu; *Interlibrary Serv Coordr,* Denice Sawatzky; Tel: 209-228-2963, E-mail: dsawatzky@ucmerced.edu; *Night/Weekend Serv Coordr,* Brent Patrick; Tel: 209-406-9688, E-mail: bpatrick@ucmerced.edu; *Res Access Cordr,* Heather Gillis; Tel: 209-228-2945, E-mail: hgillis@ucmerced.edu; *Tech Serv Coordr,* Sarah Sheets; Tel: 209-228-4422, E-mail: ssheets@ucmerced.edu; Staff 19 (MLS 8, Non-MLS 11)
Founded 2005. Enrl 4,200; Fac 230; Highest Degree: Doctorate
Jul 2008-Jun 2009. Mats Exp $1,317,497. Sal $1,107,288 (Prof $891,459)
Library Holdings: CDs 78; DVDs 1,182; e-books 616,647; e-journals 36,554; Electronic Media & Resources 300; Bk Vols 81,570; Per Subs 13
Special Collections: US Document Depository
Automation Activity & Vendor Info: (Acquisitions) Innovative Interfaces, Inc - Millenium; (Cataloging) Innovative Interfaces, Inc - Millenium; (Circulation) Innovative Interfaces, Inc - Millenium; (ILL) Innovative Interfaces, Inc; (OPAC) Innovative Interfaces, Inc - Millenium; (Serials) Innovative Interfaces, Inc - Millenium
Database Vendor: ACM (Association for Computing Machinery), Alexander Street Press, American Chemical Society, American Mathematical Society, American Physical Society, American Psychological Association (APA), Annual Reviews, ARTstor, BioOne, Cambridge Scientific Abstracts, Checkpoint Systems, Inc, CISTI Source, Community of Science (COS), CountryWatch, Coutts Information Service, CQ Press, CRC Press/Taylor & Francis Group, CredoReference, Ebooks Corporation, ebrary, EBSCOhost, Elsevier, Ex Libris Group, Factiva.com, IEEE (Institute of Electrical & Electronics Engineers), Ingenta, Innovative Interfaces, Inc, IOP, ISI Web of Knowledge, JSTOR, Knovel, LexisNexis, Luna Imaging/Insight, Marcive, Inc, Medline, Modern Language Association, Nature Publishing Group, Newsbank, OCLC ArticleFirst, OCLC FirstSearch, OCLC WorldShare Interlibrary Loan, OVID Technologies, Oxford Online, Project MUSE, ProQuest, PubMed, RefWorks, Safari Books Online, Sage, ScienceDirect, Springer-Verlag, Swets Information Services, Thomson - Web of Science, Wiley InterScience, Wilson - Wilson Web, YBP Library Services
Wireless access
Function: Archival coll, Art exhibits, Computers for patron use, Copy machines, Doc delivery serv, e-mail & chat, e-mail serv, E-Reserves, Electronic databases & coll, Exhibits, Govt ref serv, ILL available, Mail & tel request accepted, Music CDs, Online cat, Online ref, Pub access computers, Ref serv in person, Telephone ref, Web-catalog, Wheelchair accessible
Open Mon-Thurs 7am-Midnight, Fri 7-6, Sat 12-6, Sun Noon-Midnight

MILL VALLEY

R GOLDEN GATE BAPTIST THEOLOGICAL SEMINARY LIBRARY*, 201 Seminary Dr, 94941. SAN 301-0589. Tel: 415-380-1300. Circulation Tel: 415-380-1660. Reference Tel: 415-380-1663. FAX: 415-380-1652. Web Site: www.ggbts.edu. *Dir, Libr Serv,* Kelly Campbell; Tel: 415-380-1678, E-mail: kellycampbell@ggbts.edu; *Ref & Instruction Librn,* T R Parker; E-mail: trparker@ggbts.edu; *Cat,* HaeSook Kim; E-mail: haesookkim@ggbts.edu; Staff 7 (MLS 2, Non-MLS 5)
Founded 1944. Enrl 1,307; Fac 30
Library Holdings: Bks on Deafness & Sign Lang 40; Bk Titles 98,000; Per Subs 276
Special Collections: Baptist History; Music Coll; Rare Book Coll; William O Crews Leadership Coll
Subject Interests: Music, Relig, Theol
Automation Activity & Vendor Info: (Acquisitions) Ex Libris Group; (Cataloging) Ex Libris Group; (Circulation) Ex Libris Group; (OPAC) Ex Libris Group; (Serials) Ex Libris Group
Database Vendor: EBSCOhost, OCLC FirstSearch
Partic in OCLC Online Computer Library Center, Inc
Open Mon-Thurs 7:30am-11pm, Fri 7:30am-7pm, Sat Noon-5

P MILL VALLEY PUBLIC LIBRARY*, 375 Throckmorton Ave, 94941-2698. SAN 301-0597. Tel: 415-389-4292. FAX: 415-388-8929. E-mail: refdesk@cityofmillvalley.org. Web Site: millvalleylibrary.org. *City Librn,* Anji Brenner; Tel: 415-389-4292, Ext 115, E-mail: abrenner@cityofmillvalley.org; *Ch Serv Librn,* Yolanda Fletcher; Tel: 415-389-4292, Ext 119, E-mail: yfletcher@cityofmillvalley.org; *Hist Rm Librn,* David Grossman; Tel: 415-389-4292, Ext 131, E-mail: dgrossman@cityofmillvalley.org; *Sr Librn,* Gail Jones; Tel: 415-389-4292, Ext 133, E-mail: gjones@cityofmillvalley.org; *Web Librn,* Sean Mooney; Tel: 415-389-4292, Ext 107, E-mail: smooney@cityofmillvalley.org; *YA Librn,* Katie MacBride; Tel: 415-389-4292, Ext 129, E-mail: kmacbride@cityofmillvalley.org; *Operations Mgr,* Kristen Clark; Tel: 415-389-4292, Ext 113, E-mail: kclark@cityofmillvalley.org; *Circ Supvr,* Cara Brancoli-Monchicourt; Tel: 415-389-4292, Ext 112, E-mail: cbrancoli@cityofmillvalley.org; Staff 20 (MLS 7, Non-MLS 13)
Founded 1908. Pop 13,686; Circ 317,694
Library Holdings: Bk Titles 102,117; Per Subs 359
Special Collections: Local History Room; Lucretia Little History Room, bks, clippings, pamphlets, photog; Miwok Indians. Oral History
Automation Activity & Vendor Info: (Acquisitions) Innovative Interfaces, Inc; (Cataloging) Innovative Interfaces, Inc; (Circulation) Innovative Interfaces, Inc; (ILL) OCLC; (OPAC) Innovative Interfaces, Inc; (Serials) Innovative Interfaces, Inc
Database Vendor: Baker & Taylor, EBSCOhost, Gale Cengage Learning, Innovative Interfaces, Inc, OCLC FirstSearch, OCLC WorldShare Interlibrary Loan, ProQuest
Wireless access
Function: Archival coll, Art exhibits, Audio & video playback equip for onsite use, Handicapped accessible, Homebound delivery serv, ILL available, Music CDs, Online searches, Photocopying/Printing, Prog for adults, Prog for children & young adult, Summer reading prog, Wheelchair accessible
Mem of NorthNet Library System
Partic in Califa; Marin Automated Resources & Information Network (MARINet)
Special Services for the Blind - Bks on cassette; Bks on CD
Open Mon-Thurs 10-9, Fri 12-6, Sat 10-5, Sun 1-5
Friends of the Library Group

MILPITAS

R CHRIST COMMUNITY CHURCH*, 1000 S Park Victoria Dr, 95035-7099. SAN 374-4981. Tel: 408-262-8000. FAX: 408-262-1635. Web Site: www.cccmilpitas.org. *In Charge,* Emily Smith; Staff 1 (MLS 1)
Founded 1981
Library Holdings: Bk Titles 7,000
Special Collections: Bibles, 50 variations & languages
Open Wed 11:30am-Noon, Sun 10:15-10:45 & 12-12:20

J HEALD COLLEGE*, Learning Resource Center-Milpitas Campus, 341 Great Mall Pkwy, 95035-8027. SAN 326-4165. Tel: 408-934-4900. FAX: 408-876-5202. Web Site: www.heald.edu. *Librn,* Redgie Dancel; Tel: 408-934-4900, Ext 5127, E-mail: redgie_dancel@heald.edu; Staff 2 (MLS 1, Non-MLS 1)
Founded 1980. Enrl 1,600; Fac 70; Highest Degree: Associate
Library Holdings: Bk Titles 1,876; Per Subs 65
Special Collections: Databooks & Technical Manuals
Subject Interests: Acctg, Bus, Career, Computers, Criminal justice, Electronics, Legal, Networks
Database Vendor: EBSCOhost
Function: Ref serv available
Publications: Library Handbook; Research Procedures; Subject Bibliographies
Open Mon-Thurs 7am-10:30pm, Fri 7am-9pm
Restriction: Open to students, fac & staff

MINERAL

S NATIONAL PARK SERVICE*, Lassen Volcanic National Park Library, PO Box 100, 96063-0100. SAN 301-0619. Tel: 530-595-4444. FAX: 530-595-3408. Web Site: www.nps.gov/lavo. *In Charge,* Cari Kreshak; E-mail: cari_kreshak@nps.gov
Library Holdings: Bk Vols 800
Subject Interests: Natural hist
Restriction: Staff use only

MISSION HILLS

M PROVIDENCE HOLY CROSS MEDICAL CENTER*, Strazzeri Medical Library, 15031 Rinaldi St, 91345. (Mail add: PO Box 9600, 91346-9600), SAN 329-3963. Tel: 818-496-4545. FAX: 818-496-4481. E-mail: phcmc.library@providence.org. *Ref Librn,* Pamela Gay; Staff 2 (MLS 1, Non-MLS 1)
Library Holdings: Bk Titles 2,400; Bk Vols 2,500; Per Subs 171
Subject Interests: Allied health, Nursing
Automation Activity & Vendor Info: (Cataloging) EOS International; (Circulation) EOS International; (OPAC) EOS International; (Serials) EOS International
Function: Health sci info serv, ILL available, Photocopying/Printing
Partic in Medical Library Group of Southern California & Arizona (MLGSCA)
Restriction: In-house use for visitors, Lending to staff only, Non-circulating to the pub, Restricted pub use

SR ROMAN CATHOLIC ARCHDIOCESE OF LOS ANGELES*, Archival Center Library & Historical Museum, 15151 San Fernando Mission Blvd, 91345. SAN 371-1099. Tel: 818-365-1501. FAX: 818-361-3276. Web Site: archivalcenter.org. *Archivist,* Francis J Weber; E-mail: msgrweber@archivalcenter.org
Library Holdings: Bk Vols 15,000
Open Mon-Fri 9-4:30
Friends of the Library Group

MISSION VIEJO

P MISSION VIEJO LIBRARY, 100 Civic Ctr, 92691. SAN 375-4227. Tel: 949-830-7100. Circulation Tel: 949-830-7100, Ext 5101. Interlibrary Loan Service Tel: 949-830-7100, Ext 5119. Reference Tel: 949-830-7100, Ext 5105. Administration Tel: 949-830-7100, Ext 5128. FAX: 949-586-8447. E-mail: generalreference@cityofmissionviejo.org. Web Site: www.cmvl.org. *Dir, Libr & Cultural Serv,* Genesis Hansen; Tel: 949-470-3076, E-mail: ghansen@cityofmissionviejo.org; *Circ Serv Mgr,* Kathleen Kelton; Tel: 949-830-7100, Ext 5130, E-mail: kkelton@cityofmissionviejo.org; *Mgr, Pub Serv,* Gayle Meldau; Tel: 949-830-7100, Ext 5132, E-mail: gmeldau@cityofmissionviejo.org; *Mgr, Support Serv,* Tony Dillehunt; Tel: 949-830-7100, Ext 5123, E-mail: tdillehunt@cityofmissionviejo.org; Staff 34 (MLS 10, Non-MLS 24)
Founded 1997. Pop 98,000; Circ 939,734
Jul 2010-Jun 2011 Income $3,268,097. Mats Exp $212,045, Books $144,084, Per/Ser (Incl. Access Fees) $9,245, Electronic Ref Mat (Incl. Access Fees) $58,716. Sal $1,606,824
Library Holdings: e-books 895; Bk Titles 130,000; Bk Vols 155,406; Per Subs 169
Subject Interests: Genealogy, Local hist
Automation Activity & Vendor Info: (Acquisitions) SirsiDynix; (Cataloging) SirsiDynix; (Circulation) SirsiDynix; (ILL) OCLC FirstSearch; (OPAC) SirsiDynix; (Serials) EBSCO Online
Database Vendor: EBSCOhost, Gale Cengage Learning, Grolier Online, Overdrive, Inc, ProQuest, ReferenceUSA
Wireless access
Function: Archival coll, Art exhibits, Audiobks via web, Bk club(s), Bks on CD, Children's prog, Computers for patron use, Copy machines, Electronic databases & coll, Exhibits, Free DVD rentals, ILL available, Magnifiers for reading, Music CDs, Online cat, OverDrive digital audio bks, Passport agency, Prog for adults, Prog for children & young adult, Pub access computers, Summer reading prog, Teen prog, Web-catalog
Partic in Southern California Library Cooperative
Special Services for the Blind - Large print bks; Low vision equip; Magnifiers
Open Mon-Thurs 10-9, Fri 1-5, Sat 10-5, Sun 12-5
Friends of the Library Group

J SADDLEBACK COLLEGE*, James B Utt Library, 28000 Marguerite Pkwy, 92692. SAN 301-0635. Tel: 949-582-4523. Interlibrary Loan Service Tel: 949-582-4533. Reference Tel: 949-582-4525. FAX: 949-364-0284. Web Site: www.saddleback.edu. *Dean,* Dr Kevin O'Connor; Tel: 949-582-4366, E-mail: koconnor@saddleback.edu; *Asst Admin,* Khaver Akhter; Tel: 949-582-4516, E-mail: kakhter@saddleback.edu; *Instrul Serv Librn,* Eric Garant; Tel: 949-582-4627, E-mail: egarant@saddleback.edu; *Acq, Cat, Circ,* Dawn Collings; Tel: 949-582-4526, E-mail: dcollings@saddleback.edu; *Acq, AV, Cat,* James Locke; Tel: 949-582-4874, E-mail: jlocke@saddleback.edu; *Acq,* Tom Weisrock; Tel: 949-528-4921, E-mail: tweisrock@saddleback.edu; *AV, Distance Educ,* Steve Tash; Tel: 949-582-4543, E-mail: stash@saddleback.edu; *AV, Per,* Lori Cassidy; Tel: 949-582-4875, E-mail: lcassidy@saddleback.edu; *AV, Per,* Andralee Hayes; Tel: 949-582-4873, E-mail: ahayes@saddleback.edu; *Bibliog Instr,* Pamela Perry; Tel: 949-582-4966, E-mail: pperry@saddleback.edu; *Bibliog Instr, Distance Educ,* Gita Satyendra; Tel: 949-582-4654, E-mail: gsatyendra@saddleback.edu; *Circ,* Ana Maria Cobos; Tel: 949-528-4542, E-mail: acobos@saddleback.edu; *Circ,* Kian Farshidpour; Tel: 949-582-4876, E-mail: kfarshidapou@saddleback.edu; *Circ, ILL,* Debbie Immel; E-mail: dimmel@saddleback.edu; *Circ,* Vannie Pham; Tel: 949-582-2523, E-mail: vpham@saddleback.edu; *Per,* Lucila Soria; E-mail: lsoria@saddleback.edu; *Ref Serv,* Wendy Gordon; Tel: 949-582-4932, E-mail: wgordon@saddleback.edu; Staff 14 (MLS 6, Non-MLS 8)
Founded 1968. Enrl 25,000; Fac 270; Highest Degree: Associate
Library Holdings: AV Mats 9,000; Bks on Deafness & Sign Lang 65; Bk Titles 87,611; Bk Vols 101,438; Per Subs 283
Automation Activity & Vendor Info: (Circulation) SirsiDynix; (OPAC) SirsiDynix
Database Vendor: OCLC FirstSearch
Function: AV serv, Distance learning, ILL available, Photocopying/Printing, Ref serv available, Telephone ref
Publications: Library Skills Workbook
Partic in Coop Libr Agency for Syst & Servs; OCLC Online Computer Library Center, Inc
Friends of the Library Group

MODESTO

M DOCTORS MEDICAL CENTER*, Professional Library, 1441 Florida Ave, 95352-4418. (Mail add: PO Box 4138, 95352-4138), SAN 321-5628. Tel: 209-576-3782. FAX: 209-576-3595. E-mail: dmc.library@tenethealth.com. *Med Librn,* Sherri Husman; E-mail: sherri.husman@tenethealth.com; Staff 1 (MLS 1)
Founded 1966
Library Holdings: Bk Titles 586; Bk Vols 625; Per Subs 166
Subject Interests: Med, Nursing
Partic in National Network of Libraries of Medicine
Open Mon-Fri 7:30-4:00

S THE MODESTO BEE*, Information Center, 1325 H St, 95354. SAN 301-066X. Tel: 209-578-2333, 209-578-2370. FAX: 209-578-2207. Web Site: www.modbee.com/man/archive. *Chief Librn,* Karen Aiello; E-mail: kaiello@modbee.org; Staff 4 (Non-MLS 4)
Library Holdings: Bk Titles 500; Per Subs 20
Function: Newsp ref libr
Restriction: Not open to pub

J MODESTO JUNIOR COLLEGE LIBRARY, 435 College Ave, 95350. SAN 301-0678. Circulation Tel: 209-575-6228, 209-575-6676. Interlibrary Loan Service Tel: 209-575-6663. Reference Tel: 209-575-6230, 209-575-6949. Administration Tel: 209-575-6235. Automation Services Tel: 209-575-6254. Information Services Tel: 209-575-6868. FAX: 209-575-6669. Web Site: mjc.edu/instruction/library/. *Dean, Libr & Learning Res,* Jillian Daly; Tel: 209-575-6062, E-mail: dalyj@mjc.edu; *Coll Develop Librn,* Sue Adler; Tel: 209-575-6807, E-mail: adlers@mjc.edu; *Instruction Librn,* Kathleen Ennis; Tel: 209-575-6409, E-mail: ennisk@mjc.edu; *Ref Serv Librn,* Iris Carroll; Tel: 209-575-6082, E-mail: carrolli@mjc.edu; *Syst Librn,* Ellen Dambrosio; E-mail: dambrosioe@mjc.edu; *West Campus Librn,* Brian Greene; E-mail: greeneb@mjc.edu; Staff 6 (MLS 5.5, Non-MLS 0.5)
Founded 1935. Enrl 6,371; Fac 565; Highest Degree: Associate
Jul 2013-Jun 2014 Income $1,495,500. Mats Exp $81,975, Books $32,612, Per/Ser (Incl. Access Fees) $789, Electronic Ref Mat (Incl. Access Fees) $48,574. Sal $924,817 (Prof $470,626)
Library Holdings: CDs 190; DVDs 250; e-books 22,563; e-journals 60,000; Electronic Media & Resources 3; High Interest/Low Vocabulary Bk Vols 434; Large Print Bks 4; Music Scores 25; Bk Titles 23,773; Bk Vols 24,327; Per Subs 139
Special Collections: Archives (bks on geographical area, college newspaper, photographs & yearbooks; Area Newspapers (The Modesto Bee, The New York Times, San Francisco Chronicle, Stanislaus Connections, USA Today, Vida en el valle, The Wall Street Journal; Children's bks; Rare bks
Automation Activity & Vendor Info: (Acquisitions) OCLC; (Cataloging) OCLC; (Circulation) OCLC; (Course Reserve) OCLC; (ILL) OCLC; (OPAC) OCLC; (Serials) OCLC
Database Vendor: ABC-CLIO, CountryWatch, CQ Press, EBSCOhost, Facts on File, Gale Cengage Learning, Greenwood Publishing Group, Newsbank, OCLC ArticleFirst, OCLC WorldShare Interlibrary Loan, OCLC Worldshare Management Services, Springshare, LLC
Wireless access
Function: 24/7 Online cat, Archival coll, Computers for patron use, Copy machines, Electronic databases & coll, Equip loans & repairs, Handicapped accessible, ILL available, Learning ctr, Magazines, Music CDs, Online cat, Online info literacy tutorials on the web & in blackboard, Online ref, Online searches, Outreach serv, Outside serv via phone, mail, e-mail & web, Ref & res, Ref serv available, Ref serv in person, Scanner, Spanish lang bks, Study rm, Telephone ref, Web-catalog, Wheelchair accessible, Workshops
Partic in Community College League of California (CCLC); Council of Chief Librn (CCL); OCLC Online Computer Library Center, Inc
Special Services for the Deaf - Bks on deafness & sign lang; Closed caption videos
Special Services for the Blind - Internet workstation with adaptive software
Open Mon-Fri 7:30-8:30, Sat 8-5
Restriction: Fee for pub use, ID required to use computers (Ltd hrs), Limited access for the pub, Non-circulating of rare bks, Open to students, fac, staff & alumni
Friends of the Library Group

GL STANISLAUS COUNTY LAW LIBRARY*, 1101 13th St, 95354. SAN 301-0716. Tel: 209-558-7759. FAX: 209-558-8284. TDD: 209-558-8285. E-mail: lawlibrary@arrival.net. Web Site: www.stanislauslawlibrary.arrival.net. *Librn,* Janice K Milliken; E-mail: milliken@arrival.net; *Asst Librn,* Alex Kern; E-mail: kern@arrival.net
Jul 2008-Jun 2009 Income $469,116. Mats Exp $116,591, Electronic Ref Mat (Incl. Access Fees) $57,595. Sal $126,902
Library Holdings: CDs 139; DVDs 10; Bk Vols 18,689; Per Subs 51
Special Collections: Local Municipal & County Codes
Automation Activity & Vendor Info: (Cataloging) LibraryWorld, Inc; (Serials) LibraryWorld, Inc

Wireless access
Open Mon-Fri 8-5

P STANISLAUS COUNTY LIBRARY*, 1500 I St, 95354-1166. SAN 333-2101. Tel: 209-558-7800. Reference Tel: 209-558-7814. Administration Tel: 209-558-7801. FAX: 209-529-4779. E-mail: refquest@scfl.lib.ca.us. Web Site: www.stanislauslibrary.org. *County Librn,* Diane McDonnell; *Libr Mgr,* Amy Taylor; *Br Operations Mgr,* Charles Teval; *Virtual Serv Mgr,* John Fleming; *Acq,* Stacey Chen; Staff 16 (MLS 16)
Founded 1912. Pop 519,940; Circ 2,101,936
Jul 2011-Jun 2012 Income (Main Library and Branch(s)) $9,168,587, State $9,582, County $491,810, Locally Generated Income $8,667,195. Mats Exp $1,579,861, Books $422,756, Electronic Ref Mat (Incl. Access Fees) $35,033. Sal $5,711,621
Library Holdings: Bk Vols 777,429; Per Subs 184
Special Collections: Californiana; Selections in Spanish & Vietnamese; Song File; Stanislaus County Hist Coll
Subject Interests: Genealogy
Automation Activity & Vendor Info: (Acquisitions) Brodart; (Cataloging) OCLC; (Circulation) SirsiDynix; (ILL) OCLC; (OPAC) SirsiDynix; (Serials) EBSCO Online
Database Vendor: 3M Library Systems, Gale Cengage Learning, infoUSA, SirsiDynix
Wireless access
Partic in 49-99 Cooperative Library System
Special Services for the Deaf - Closed caption videos; TDD equip
Special Services for the Blind - Bks on cassette; Bks on CD; Computer with voice synthesizer for visually impaired persons; Reader equip
Open Mon-Thurs 10-9, Sat 10-5
Friends of the Library Group
Branches: 12
NORA BALLARD LIBRARY (WATERFORD BRANCH), 324 E St, Waterford, 95386-9005, SAN 333-2497. Tel: 209-874-2191. FAX: 209-874-2191. *Br Mgr,* Cindy Scott
Pop 8,763; Circ 60,782
Library Holdings: Bk Vols 21,756
Special Collections: Oral History
Subject Interests: Relig
Open Mon, Tues & Thurs 10-6, Fri 10-5, Sat 12-5
DAVID F BUSH LIBRARY (OAKDALE BRANCH), 151 S First Ave, Oakdale, 95361-3902, SAN 333-2314. Tel: 209-847-4204. FAX: 209-847-4205. *Br Mgr,* Bryan Sontag
Pop 17,440; Circ 134,989
Library Holdings: Bk Vols 45,883
Open Mon & Wed 10-6, Tues & Thurs 10-8, Sat 10-5
Friends of the Library Group
DENAIR BRANCH, 4801 Kersey Rd, Denair, 95316-9350. (Mail add: PO Box 190, Denair, 95316-0190), SAN 333-2160. Tel: 209-634-1283. FAX: 209-634-1283. *Br Mgr,* Karina Mendoza
Pop 3,719; Circ 26,181
Library Holdings: Bk Vols 15,117
Open Tues-Thurs 12-6, Fri & Sat 12-5
Friends of the Library Group
EMPIRE BRANCH, 18 S Abbie, Empire, 95319. (Mail add: PO Box 7, Empire, 95319-0007), SAN 333-2195. Tel: 209-524-5505. FAX: 209-524-5505. *Br Mgr,* Heather Bailey
Pop 4,203; Circ 18,362
Library Holdings: Bk Vols 11,180
Open Tues-Sat 12-6
FLORENCE L GONDRING LIBRARY, 2250 Magnolia, Ceres, 95307-3209, SAN 333-2136. Tel: 209-537-8938. FAX: 209-537-8939. *Br Mgr,* Carol Blomquist
Pop 45,854; Circ 114,464
Library Holdings: Bk Vols 36,817
Open Mon 10-8, Tues-Thurs 10-6, Sat 12-5
Friends of the Library Group
HUGHSON BRANCH, 2412 Third St, Ste A, Hughson, 95326. (Mail add: PO Box 1025, Hughson, 95326-1025), SAN 333-2225. Tel: 209-883-2293. FAX: 209-883-2293. *Br Mgr,* Isabel Fiqueroa
Pop 6,187; Circ 25,183
Library Holdings: Bk Vols 12,888
Open Tues-Sat 12-6
Friends of the Library Group
KEYES BRANCH, 4420 Maud Ave, Keyes, 95328-0367. (Mail add: PO Box 369, Keyes, 95328-0369), SAN 333-225X. Tel: 209-664-8006. FAX: 209-664-8006. *Br Mgr,* Fernando Linares
Pop 4,928; Circ 18,742
Library Holdings: Bk Vols 14,436
Open Mon 9-5, Tues, Wed & Fri 8:30-5, Thurs 8:30-7, Sat 12-4
NEWMAN BRANCH, 1305 Kern St, Newman, 95360-1603, SAN 333-2284. Tel: 209-862-2010. FAX: 209-862-2010. *Br Mgr,* Barbara Alexander
Founded 1909. Pop 10,586; Circ 34,309
Library Holdings: Bk Vols 17,657
Open Tues 12-8, Wed-Sat 10-5
PATTERSON BRANCH, 46 N Salado, Patterson, 95363-2587, SAN 333-2349. Tel: 209-892-6473. FAX: 209-892-5100. *Br Mgr,* Jo Roullard
Founded 1976. Pop 19,337; Circ 124,350
Library Holdings: Bk Vols 25,764
Automation Activity & Vendor Info: (OPAC) SirsiDynix
Open Mon, Tues & Thurs 10-6, Wed 10-8, Fri 10-5, Sat 12-5
Friends of the Library Group
RIVERBANK BRANCH, 3442 Santa Fe Ave, Riverbank, 95367-2319, SAN 333-2373. Tel: 209-869-7008. FAX: 209-869-7008. *Br Mgr,* Becky Parrott
Pop 21,757; Circ 66,142
Library Holdings: Bk Vols 25,763
Open Tues & Thurs 10-6, Wed 10-8, Fri 10-5, Sat 12-5
SALIDA BRANCH, 4835 Sisk Rd, Salida, 95368-9445, SAN 333-2403. Tel: 209-543-7353. FAX: 209-543-7318. *Br Mgr,* Stacey Chen
Pop 16,000; Circ 302,753
Library Holdings: Bk Vols 77,547
Open Mon 10-8, Wed & Thurs 10-6, Fri & Sat 10-5
Friends of the Library Group
TURLOCK BRANCH, 550 Minaret Ave, Turlock, 95380-4198, SAN 333-2438. Tel: 209-664-8100. FAX: 209-664-8101. *Br Mgr,* Diane Bartlett
Pop 70,158; Circ 316,098
Library Holdings: Bk Vols 88,744
Open Mon-Thurs 10-9, Fri & Sat 10-5
Friends of the Library Group

M SUTTER HEALTH CENTRAL VALLEY REGION*, Health Sciences Library, 1800 Coffee Rd, Ste 43, 95355-2700. (Mail add: PO Box 942, 95353-0942), SAN 328-4344. Tel: 209-569-7722. FAX: 209-569-7469. Web Site: www.memorialmedicalcenter.org. *Med Librn,* Jean Lei; E-mail: leij4@sutterhealth.org; Staff 1 (MLS 1)
Library Holdings: e-books 1,500; e-journals 2,000; Bk Titles 1,000; Per Subs 74; Videos 100
Subject Interests: Med, Nursing, Pharmacology
Database Vendor: EBSCOhost, MD Consult, OVID Technologies, PubMed, UpToDate
Wireless access
Partic in Medical Library Association (MLA); Northern California & Nevada Medical Library Group (NCNMLG)
Restriction: Staff use only

MOFFETT FIELD

NASA AMES RESEARCH CENTER
S LIFE SCIENCES LIBRARY*, Mail Stop 239-13, 94035-1000, SAN 333-2527. Tel: 650-604-5387. FAX: 650-604-7741. E-mail: arc-dl-library@mail.nasa.gov. Web Site: www.library.arc.nasa.gov. *Librn,* Lisa Sewell; Staff 2 (MLS 1, Non-MLS 1)
Founded 1965
Library Holdings: e-journals 2,000; Bk Titles 18,500; Bk Vols 20,000; Per Subs 112
Special Collections: Aerospace Biology & Medicine; Biochemistry (Origin of Life Coll); Biogenesis Coll; Evolution Genetics
Subject Interests: Aerospace med, Aviation med, Biochem, Human factors, Physiology, Planetary sci
Automation Activity & Vendor Info: (Cataloging) SirsiDynix; (Circulation) SirsiDynix
Partic in Dialog Corp
S TECHNICAL LIBRARY*, Bldg 202, Mail Stop 202-3, 94035-1000, SAN 333-2551. Tel: 650-604-6325. FAX: 650-604-4988. E-mail: arc-dl-library@mail.nasa.gov. Web Site: www.ameslib.arc.nasa.gov. *Head, Ref,* Dan Pappas; E-mail: daniel.t.pappas@nasa.gov; *Mgr,* Evelyn Warren; Tel: 650-604-5681; *Acq Librn,* Donna Kleiner; Staff 4 (MLS 3, Non-MLS 1)
Founded 1940
Library Holdings: e-books 400; e-journals 1,000; Bk Titles 39,000; Per Subs 250
Special Collections: NASA & NACA Reports
Subject Interests: Aeronaut, Astronomy, Astrophysics, Chem, Computer sci, Eng, Life sci, Math
Automation Activity & Vendor Info: (Acquisitions) SirsiDynix; (Cataloging) SirsiDynix; (Circulation) SirsiDynix; (OPAC) SirsiDynix; (Serials) SirsiDynix

MONROVIA

R FIRST PRESBYTERIAN CHURCH LIBRARY*, 101 E Foothill Blvd, 91016. SAN 374-843X. Tel: 626-358-3297. FAX: 626-358-5997. E-mail: church@fpcmonrovia.org. Web Site: www.fpcmonrovia.org.
Library Holdings: Bk Vols 100; Per Subs 20
Open Mon-Fri 9-4

P MONROVIA PUBLIC LIBRARY, 321 S Myrtle Ave, 91016-2848. SAN 301-0732. Tel: 626-256-8274. Reference Tel: 626-256-8259. Administration Tel: 626-256-8250. FAX: 626-256-8255. *Dir, Commun Serv,* Tina Cherry; Tel: 626-256-8246, E-mail: tcherry@ci.monrovia.ca.us; *Actg Div Mgr,* Linda Granicy; Tel: 626-256-8253, E-mail: lgranicy@ci.monrovia.ca.us; Staff 9.61 (MLS 7.55, Non-MLS 2.06)
Founded 1895. Pop 39,006; Circ 110,203
Library Holdings: Bk Vols 120,000; Per Subs 161
Automation Activity & Vendor Info: (Acquisitions) SirsiDynix; (Cataloging) SirsiDynix; (Circulation) SirsiDynix; (OPAC) SirsiDynix; (Serials) SirsiDynix
Database Vendor: EBSCOhost, Gale Cengage Learning, OCLC WorldShare Interlibrary Loan, SirsiDynix
Wireless access
Function: Adult literacy prog, Handicapped accessible, Home delivery & serv to Sr ctr & nursing homes, ILL available, Photocopying/Printing, Prog for children & young adult, Ref serv available, Summer reading prog, Wheelchair accessible
Special Services for the Deaf - Assistive tech; TDD equip; TTY equip
Open Mon-Wed 10-8, Thurs-Sat Noon-5
Restriction: Open to pub for ref & circ; with some limitations
Friends of the Library Group

MONTEBELLO

M BEVERLY HOSPITAL*, Breitman Memorial Library, 309 W Beverly Blvd, 90640. SAN 373-4129. Tel: 323-725-4305. FAX: 323-889-2424. *Librn,* Irene Bogner; Staff 0.5 (Non-MLS 0.5)
Founded 1978
Library Holdings: AV Mats 177; e-books 2,118; Bk Vols 500; Per Subs 37
Subject Interests: Med, Nutrition, Pharmacology
Database Vendor: PubMed
Partic in Docline
Restriction: Not open to pub

MONTEREY

G AISO LIBRARY*, 543 Lawton Rd, Ste 617A, 93944-3214. SAN 301-2212. Tel: 831-242-5572. Interlibrary Loan Service Tel: 831-242-4792. Reference Tel: 831-242-6948. Automation Services Tel: 831-242-6889. FAX: 831-242-5816. Web Site: www.dliflc.edu/libraries.html. *Librn,* Melanie Barney; E-mail: melanie.barney1@us.army.mil; *Cat Librn,* Kurt Kuss; E-mail: kurt.kuss@us.army.mil; *Chamberlin Librn,* Carl C Chan; Tel: 831-242-7680, E-mail: carl.chanc@us.army.mil; *Electronic Serv Librn,* Tammy Lowery; E-mail: tammy.t.lowery@us.army.mil; *Syst Librn,* William D Mace; E-mail: william.mace1@us.army.mil; *Ref Serv,* Rita L Smith; E-mail: rita.louise.smith@us.army.mil; Staff 14 (MLS 7, Non-MLS 7)
Founded 1943
Library Holdings: Bk Titles 110,000; Bk Vols 115,000; Per Subs 800
Special Collections: Foreign Language Coll
Subject Interests: Foreign lang
Automation Activity & Vendor Info: (Cataloging) TLC (The Library Corporation); (Circulation) TLC (The Library Corporation); (ILL) OCLC; (OPAC) TLC (The Library Corporation); (Serials) TLC (The Library Corporation)
Database Vendor: Gale Cengage Learning, OCLC FirstSearch, TLC (The Library Corporation)
Function: ILL available, Ref serv available
Partic in Fedlink
Open Mon-Thurs 7:45am-9pm, Fri 7:45-4:45, Sat 12-5, Sun 12:30-9
Restriction: Open to pub for ref only

S COLTON HALL MUSEUM LIBRARY*, 570 Pacific St, 93940. SAN 327-8158. Tel: 831-646-5640, 831-646-5648. FAX: 831-646-3917. E-mail: rygg@ci.monterey.ca.us. Web Site: www.monterey.org.
Library Holdings: Bk Vols 2,500; Per Subs 15
Special Collections: Monterey History American Period, 1846-present. Oral History
Open Sun-Sat 10-4

S CTB/MCGRAW-HILL LIBRARY*, 20 Ryan Ranch Rd, 93940-5703. SAN 301-0759. Tel: 831-393-0700, 831-393-7008. FAX: 831-393-7825. Web Site: www.ctb.com. *Coordr, Libr Serv,* Debbie Uvalles; Tel: 831-393-6555
Founded 1965
Library Holdings: Bk Vols 6,087; Per Subs 11,923
Special Collections: Test Archives
Subject Interests: Educ, Psychol, Statistics
Automation Activity & Vendor Info: (Cataloging) LAC Group
Publications: Acquisitions List (Monthly)
Partic in Cooperative Information Network
Open Mon-Fri 9-4:30

S MONTEREY BAY AQUARIUM LIBRARY*, 886 Cannery Row, 93940-1085. SAN 373-031X. Tel: 831-648-4849. FAX: 831-648-4884. Web Site: www.mbayaq.org. *Info Serv, Mgr,* Fran Wolfe; *Cat,* Gail Skidmore
Library Holdings: Bk Vols 5,000; Per Subs 100
Subject Interests: Oceanography
Partic in Monterey Bay Area Cooperative Library System
Restriction: Open by appt only

S MONTEREY HISTORY & ART ASSOCIATION*, Mayo Hayes O'Donnell Library, 155 Van Buren St, 93940. (Mail add: Five Custom House Plaza, 93940), SAN 301-0775. Tel: 831-372-1838. Web Site: www.montereyhistory.org. *Exec Dir,* Lisa Coscino; *Librn,* Faye Messinger; Fax: 831-624-9579
Founded 1970
Library Holdings: Bk Vols 3,000
Special Collections: Californiana; Western United States, especially Monterey. Oral History
Subject Interests: Calif
Function: Res libr
Restriction: Open by appt only

C MONTEREY INSTITUTE OF INTERNATIONAL STUDIES*, William Tell Coleman Library, 425 Van Buren St, 93940. (Mail add: 460 Pierce St, 93940), SAN 301-0783. Tel: 831-647-4133. Interlibrary Loan Service Tel: 831-647-4134. Reference Tel: 831-647-4135. FAX: 831-647-3518. Web Site: monti.miis.edu. *Dir,* Peter Y Liu; Tel: 831-647-4139; *Access Serv,* Anna West; *Cat,* Wang Hsueh-Ying; Tel: 831-647-4136; *Ref,* Ann Flower; Staff 9 (MLS 4, Non-MLS 5)
Founded 1955. Enrl 700; Fac 70; Highest Degree: Master
Library Holdings: e-books 3,050; Bk Vols 92,000; Per Subs 600
Special Collections: Foreign Language; General & Technical Dictionaries (English & Foreign Languages); International Business; MIIS Theses; Monterey Institute of International Studies Archives
Subject Interests: Econ, Humanities, Intl, Lit, Trade
Automation Activity & Vendor Info: (Acquisitions) Innovative Interfaces, Inc; (Cataloging) Innovative Interfaces, Inc; (Circulation) Innovative Interfaces, Inc; (Course Reserve) Innovative Interfaces, Inc; (OPAC) Innovative Interfaces, Inc; (Serials) Innovative Interfaces, Inc
Database Vendor: Innovative Interfaces, Inc
Publications: MIIS/List of Periodicals
Partic in Monterey Bay Area Cooperative Library System; OCLC Research Library Partnership; Statewide California Electronic Library Consortium (SCELC)
Open Mon-Thurs 8:30am-11pm, Fri 8:30-8, Sat 10-8, Sun 10am-11pm

J MONTEREY PENINSULA COLLEGE LIBRARY*, 980 Fremont Blvd, 93940-4704. SAN 301-0791. Tel: 831-646-4095. Circulation Tel: 831-646-3098. Reference Tel: 831-646-4262. FAX: 831-645-1308. Web Site: www.mpc.edu/library. *Pub Serv Librn,* Deborah Ruiz; Tel: 831-646-3097; *Electronic Res & Instruction Librn,* Stephanie Tetter; Tel: 831-646-4082, E-mail: stetter@mpc.edu; *Instruction & Ref Librn,* Bill Easton; Tel: 831-645-1382, E-mail: weaston@mpc.edu; *Tech Serv Librn,* Bernadine Abbott; Tel: 831-646-4204, E-mail: babbott@mpc.edu
Founded 1947. Enrl 12,500; Highest Degree: Associate
Library Holdings: Bk Vols 60,000; Per Subs 225
Automation Activity & Vendor Info: (Acquisitions) Ex Libris Group; (Cataloging) Ex Libris Group; (Circulation) Ex Libris Group; (Course Reserve) Ex Libris Group; (ILL) Ex Libris Group; (OPAC) Ex Libris Group; (Serials) Ex Libris Group
Partic in Monterey Bay Area Cooperative Library System; OCLC Online Computer Library Center, Inc
Open Mon-Thurs 8am-9pm, Fri 8-2, Sun 1-5

P MONTEREY PUBLIC LIBRARY*, 625 Pacific St, 93940-2866. SAN 301-0805. Tel: 831-646-3932. Circulation Tel: 831-646-3930. Interlibrary Loan Service Tel: 831-646-3743. Reference Tel: 831-646-3933. FAX: 831-646-5618. E-mail: refdesk@ci.monterey.ca.us. Web Site: www.monterey.org/library. *Dir,* Kim Bui-Burton; Tel: 831-646-5601, E-mail: buiburto@ci.monterey.ca.us; *Asst Libr Dir,* Douglas Holtzman; Tel: 831-646-3745, E-mail: holtzman@ci.monterey.ca.us; *Circ, Reader Serv,* Inga Labeaune; Tel: 831-646-3477, E-mail: labeaune@ci.monterey.ca.us; *ILL,* Bridget McConnell; E-mail: mcconnel@ci.monterey.ca.us; *Youth Serv,* Karen Brown; Tel: 831-646-3744, E-mail: brownk@ci.monterey.ca.us; Staff 11 (MLS 11)
Founded 1849. Pop 30,000; Circ 418,989
Library Holdings: AV Mats 9,182; Bk Titles 114,612; Per Subs 340
Special Collections: Monterey History
Automation Activity & Vendor Info: (Acquisitions) Innovative Interfaces, Inc; (Cataloging) Innovative Interfaces, Inc; (Circulation) Innovative Interfaces, Inc; (OPAC) Innovative Interfaces, Inc; (Serials) Innovative Interfaces, Inc
Publications: Annual Report; Calendar of Events
Partic in Monterey Bay Area Cooperative Library System
Friends of the Library Group
Bookmobiles: 1

C NAVAL POSTGRADUATE SCHOOL, Dudley Knox Library, 411 Dyer Rd, 93943. SAN 301-0813. Tel: 831-656-2975. Circulation Tel: 831-656-2947. Interlibrary Loan Service Tel: 831-656-7735 (lending), 831-656-7782 (borrowing). Reference Tel: 831-656-2485. Administration Tel: 831-656-2341. FAX: 831-656-2050. Interlibrary Loan Service FAX: 831-656-2842. E-mail: refdesk@nps.edu. Web Site: www.nps.edu/library. *Univ Librn,* Eleanor Uhlinger; *Outreach & Coll Develop Mgr,* Greta Marlatt; Tel: 831-656-3500, E-mail: gmarlatt@nps.edu; Staff 20 (MLS 11, Non-MLS 9)
Founded 1946. Enrl 2,964; Fac 393; Highest Degree: Doctorate
Oct 2013-Sept 2014 Income $5,290,000. Sal $2,139,679 (Prof $1,210,873)
Library Holdings: Audiobooks 224; DVDs 1,469; e-books 273,223; Microforms 20,417; Bk Titles 314,327
Special Collections: Hotel Del Monte, Naval Postgraduate School Special Coll & Archives; Intelligence Coll; Military & Naval History (Buckley Coll). US Document Depository
Subject Interests: Bus, Computer sci, Econ, Eng, Finance, Hist, Math, Mgt, Nat security, Physics, Polit sci
Automation Activity & Vendor Info: (Acquisitions) SirsiDynix; (Cataloging) SirsiDynix; (Circulation) SirsiDynix; (ILL) OCLC ILLiad; (OPAC) SirsiDynix; (Serials) SirsiDynix
Wireless access
Function: ILL available
Publications: Periodical Holdings
Mem of Pacific Library Partnership (PLP)
Partic in Califa; Consortium of Naval Libraries (CNL); Federal Library & Information Center Committee (FLICC); Military Education Coordination Conference (MECC); Nat Res Libr Alliance (NRLA)
Open Mon-Thurs 7am-8pm, Fri 7-5, Sat 9-5, Sun 12-8
Restriction: Open by appt only

MONTEREY PARK

C EAST LOS ANGELES COLLEGE*, Helen Miller Bailey Library, 1301 Avenida Cesar Chaves, 91754. SAN 301-083X. Tel: 323-265-8758. FAX: 323-267-3714. Web Site: library.elac.edu. *Chairperson,* Choonhee Rhim; E-mail: rhimcl@elac.edu; Staff 15 (MLS 7, Non-MLS 8)
Founded 1946. Enrl 20,000; Fac 350; Highest Degree: Associate
Library Holdings: Bk Titles 100,000; Bk Vols 110,000; Per Subs 100
Automation Activity & Vendor Info: (Cataloging) SirsiDynix; (Circulation) SirsiDynix; (OPAC) SirsiDynix
Database Vendor: CQ Press, EBSCOhost, Gale Cengage Learning, SirsiDynix
Wireless access
Publications: Bibliographic Instructional Handouts; Library handbook
Open Mon-Fri 8-4

P MONTEREY PARK BRUGGEMEYER LIBRARY*, Monterey Park Public Library, 318 S Ramona Ave, 91754-3399. SAN 301-0821. Tel: 626-307-1368. Circulation Tel: 626-307-1366. Interlibrary Loan Service Tel: 626-307-1399. Administration Tel: 626-307-1269. Automation Services Tel: 626-307-1379. FAX: 626-288-4251. TDD: 626-307-2540. E-mail: library@montereypark.ca.gov. Web Site: montereyparklibrary.llwip.org. *City Librn, Libr Dir,* Position Currently Open; *Interim City Librn,* Norma Arvizu; Tel: 626-307-1418, E-mail: narvizu@montereypark.ca.gov; *Adult & Teen Serv Mgr, Sr Librn,* Cindy Costales; Tel: 626-307-1398, E-mail: ccostales@montereypark.ca.gov; *Mgr, Ch Serv, Sr Librn,* Christina Yueh; Tel: 626-307-1412, E-mail: cyueh@montereypark.ca.gov; *Mgr, Tech Serv, Sr Librn,* Evena Shu; E-mail: eshu@montereypark.ca.gov; *Teen Serv Librn,* Darren Braden; E-mail: dbraden@montereypark.ca.gov; *Circ Supvr,* Julie Villanueva; E-mail: jvillanueva@montereypark.ca.gov; *Adult Ref, AV,* Maggie Wang; E-mail: mwang@montereypark.ca.gov. Subject Specialists: *Citizen prep, TESL literacy,* Norma Arvizu; *Adult prog, Fiction,* Cindy Costales; *Children's lit, Chinese lang mat,* Christina Yueh; *Teen lit, Young adult lit,* Darren Braden; *Chinese lang & lit,* Maggie Wang; Staff 6 (MLS 5, Non-MLS 1)
Founded 1929. Pop 63,300; Circ 460,000
Jul 2010-Jun 2011 Income $2,130,104, State $31,991, City $1,574,990, Federal $30,388, Locally Generated Income $492,735. Mats Exp $152,390, Books $103,218, Per/Ser (Incl. Access Fees) $4,910, Micro $4,322, AV Mat $27,089, Electronic Ref Mat (Incl. Access Fees) $10,551, Presv $2,300. Sal $728,953 (Prof $463,582)
Library Holdings: Audiobooks 1,362; AV Mats 10,548; CDs 2,744; DVDs 3,572; e-books 1; Large Print Bks 728; Microforms 661; Bk Titles 135,666; Bk Vols 148,586; Per Subs 93; Videos 2,860
Special Collections: Chinese, Japanese, Korean, Spanish & Vietnamese Languages Coll. US Document Depository
Subject Interests: Calif, Local hist
Automation Activity & Vendor Info: (Cataloging) Innovative Interfaces, Inc; (Circulation) Innovative Interfaces, Inc; (ILL) OCLC Online; (OPAC) Innovative Interfaces, Inc
Database Vendor: Gale Cengage Learning, LearningExpress, McGraw-Hill, Newsbank, OCLC WorldShare Interlibrary Loan, ProQuest
Wireless access
Function: Computer training, Computers for patron use, Copy machines, e-mail serv, Electronic databases & coll, Exhibits, Family literacy, Govt ref serv, Holiday prog, Homework prog, ILL available, Literacy & newcomer serv, Mail & tel request accepted, Music CDs, Newsp ref libr, Online cat, Online ref, Online searches, Outreach serv, Photocopying/Printing, Preschool outreach, Prof lending libr, Prog for adults, Prog for children & young adult, Pub access computers, Ref serv available, Ref serv in person, Res libr, Senior computer classes, Senior outreach, Spoken cassettes & CDs, Story hour, Summer & winter reading prog, Summer reading prog, Teen prog, Telephone ref, Video lending libr, Wheelchair accessible, Winter reading prog, Workshops, Writing prog
Publications: Message from the City Librarian (Online only)
Partic in Califa; Southern California Library Cooperative
Special Services for the Deaf - Adult & family literacy prog; Closed caption videos; TDD equip
Special Services for the Blind - Bks available with recordings; Bks on cassette; Bks on CD; Large print bks
Open Mon & Tues 12-9, Wed & Thurs 10-6, Sun 1-5
Restriction: Access at librarian's discretion, Authorized personnel only, Badge access after hrs, Borrowing requests are handled by ILL, Circ to mem only, ID required to use computers (Ltd hrs), Mem only
Friends of the Library Group

MOORPARK

P MOORPARK CITY LIBRARY*, 699 Moorpark Ave, 93021. SAN 335-2471. Tel: 805-517-6370. FAX: 805-523-2736. Web Site: www.moorparklibrary.org.
Wireless access
Open Mon-Thurs 10-8, Fri & Sat 10-5, Sun 1-5
Friends of the Library Group

J MOORPARK COLLEGE LIBRARY*, 7075 Campus Rd, 93021-1695. SAN 301-0848. Tel: 805-378-1450. Reference Tel: 805-378-1472. FAX: 805-378-1470. Web Site: www.moorparkcollege.edu/services_for_students/library/index.shtml. *Dept Chair,* Mrs Faten Habib; E-mail: fhabib@vcccd.edu; *Assoc Librn,* Mary LaBarge; *Libr Tech,* Penny Hahn; Staff 3 (MLS 3)
Founded 1967. Enrl 13,704; Fac 621
Library Holdings: Bk Vols 74,139; Per Subs 338
Automation Activity & Vendor Info: (Acquisitions) Ex Libris Group; (Cataloging) Ex Libris Group; (Circulation) Ex Libris Group; (Course Reserve) Ex Libris Group; (ILL) Ex Libris Group; (OPAC) Ex Libris Group; (Serials) Ex Libris Group
Database Vendor: OCLC WorldShare Interlibrary Loan
Open Mon-Thurs 8am-8:30pm, Fri 8-2:30, Sat 9-4

S SCHUYLER TECHNICAL LIBRARY*, 4519 N Ashtree St, 93021. SAN 317-3607. Tel: 805-529-7922. *In Charge,* Dr Gilbert S Bahn
Founded 1952
Special Collections: Professional Papers of Gilbert S Bahn
Restriction: Staff use only

MORAGA

S MORAGA HISTORICAL SOCIETY ARCHIVES*, 1500 Saint Mary's Rd, 94556-2037. (Mail add: PO Box 103, 94556-0103), SAN 372-7343. Tel: 925-377-8734. Web Site: www.moragahistory.org. *Archivist,* Margaret DePriester; *Archivist,* Elsie Mastick; Staff 1 (MLS 1)
Library Holdings: Bk Titles 600
Special Collections: Rancho Land Case No 590 (1852). Oral History
Subject Interests: Genealogy
Wireless access
Publications: El Rancho (historical journal); Newsletter
Open Mon, Wed & Fri 1-3
Restriction: Open to pub for ref only
Friends of the Library Group

C SAINT MARY'S COLLEGE LIBRARY*, Saint Albert Hall Library, 1928 Saint Mary's Rd, 94575. (Mail add: PO Box 4290, 94575-4290), SAN 301-0856. Tel: 925-631-4229. Administration Tel: 925-631-4525. FAX: 925-376-6097. Web Site: library.stmarys-ca.edu. *Dean of Libr,* Tom Carter; E-mail: tcarter@stmarys-ca.edu; *Head, Coll Mgt,* Linda Wobbe; *Head, Cat & Coll,* Hannah Thomas; *Head, Access Serv,* Sharon Walters; *Electronic Reserves Librn,* Gemma Pavon; *Ref/Cat Librn,* Elise Wong; *Ref & Instruction Librn,* Susan Birkenseer; *Ref & Instruction Librn,* Margaret Brown-Salazar; *Ref & Instruction Librn,* Martin Cohen; *Ref & Instruction Librn,* Susan Garbarino; *Ref & Instruction Librn,* Sharon Radcliff; *Ref & Instruction Librn,* Sarah Vital; *Mgr, Electronic Res,* Hansen Dave; *Mgr, Per,* Diane Nolting; *Mgr, ILL,* Alle Porter; *Circ Serv Supvr,* Norm Patridge; *Circ Serv Supvr,* Steve Stonewell; *Coordr, Instrul Serv,* Richard Lemberg; *Coordr, Ref Serv-Adult,* Patricia Wade; Staff 20 (MLS 11, Non-MLS 9)
Founded 1863. Enrl 3,400; Fac 230; Highest Degree: Doctorate
Jul 2009-Jun 2010 Income $2,500,000. Mats Exp $836,000, Books $279,000, Per/Ser (Incl. Access Fees) $199,000, AV Mat $25,000,

Electronic Ref Mat (Incl. Access Fees) $317,000, Presv $16,000. Sal $1,143,000 (Prof $802,000)
Library Holdings: AV Mats 9,645; e-books 651; e-journals 178; Electronic Media & Resources 117; Bk Titles 177,034; Bk Vols 227,104; Per Subs 773
Special Collections: Byron Bryant Film Coll, v-tapes; Califorina Mathematical Society Archives; College Archives; Oxford Movement (Newman Coll); Spirituality of 17th & 18th Century (Lasallian Research Center). Oral History
Subject Interests: Hist, Philos, Relig
Automation Activity & Vendor Info: (Acquisitions) Innovative Interfaces, Inc; (Cataloging) Innovative Interfaces, Inc; (Circulation) Innovative Interfaces, Inc; (Course Reserve) Innovative Interfaces, Inc; (ILL) OCLC ILLiad; (OPAC) Innovative Interfaces, Inc; (Serials) Innovative Interfaces, Inc
Database Vendor: Baker & Taylor, Blackwell, Cambridge Scientific Abstracts, Dialog, EBSCOhost, Gale Cengage Learning, Innovative Interfaces, Inc, OVID Technologies, ProQuest, SerialsSolutions, Wiley
Wireless access
Partic in OCLC Online Computer Library Center, Inc; RLIN (Research Libraries Information Network); Statewide California Electronic Library Consortium (SCELC)
Open Mon-Thurs 8am-Midnight, Fri 8-5, Sat 10-6, Sun 10am-Midnight

MORENO VALLEY

P MORENO VALLEY PUBLIC LIBRARY*, 25480 Alessandro Blvd, 92553. SAN 378-2565. Tel: 951-413-3880. FAX: 951-413-3895. E-mail: citylibrary@moval.org. Web Site: library.booksite.com/7252/, www.moval.org. *Librn,* Loes Knutson; E-mail: loesk@moval.org; *Librn,* April Nava; E-mail: apriln@moval.org; *Librn,* Sharon Navarro; E-mail: sharonn@moval.org; *Librn,* Jennifer Rapier; E-mail: jenniferr@moval.org; *Div Mgr, Libr Serv,* Paula Smus; Tel: 951-413-3881, E-mail: paulas@moval.org; *Circ,* Karen Morales; E-mail: karenmo@moval.org; Staff 5 (MLS 5)
Founded 1987. Pop 195,000; Circ 429,072
Jul 2010-Jun 2011. Mats Exp $107,583, Books $86,297, Per/Ser (Incl. Access Fees) $3,810, Electronic Ref Mat (Incl. Access Fees) $17,476
Library Holdings: Bk Vols 146,948; Per Subs 77
Automation Activity & Vendor Info: (Acquisitions) SirsiDynix; (Cataloging) SirsiDynix; (Circulation) SirsiDynix; (Serials) SirsiDynix
Wireless access
Function: Bilingual assistance for Spanish patrons, Bk club(s), Bks on cassette, Bks on CD, Computers for patron use, Copy machines, Digital talking bks, e-mail & chat, e-mail serv, Electronic databases & coll, Fax serv, Free DVD rentals, Handicapped accessible, ILL available, Magnifiers for reading, Music CDs, Online cat, Online ref, Online searches, Photocopying/Printing, Pub access computers, Ref serv available, Ref serv in person, Spoken cassettes & CDs, Story hour, Summer reading prog, Web-catalog, Wheelchair accessible
Mem of Inland Library System
Open Mon-Thurs 9-8, Sat 9-6
Friends of the Library Group

J RIVERSIDE COMMUNITY COLLEGE DISTRICT*, Moreno Valley Campus Library, 16130 Lasselle St, 92551-2045. SAN 371-9626. Tel: 951-571-6112. Circulation Tel: 951-571-6111. Reference Tel: 951-571-6109. FAX: 951-571-6191. Web Site: library.rcc.edu/moreno. *Dean, Tech & Instrul Support Serv,* Cid Tenpas; Tel: 951-571-6344, E-mail: cid.tenpas@rcc.edu; Staff 4 (MLS 2, Non-MLS 2)
Founded 1991. Enrl 7,000; Fac 55; Highest Degree: Associate
Library Holdings: Bk Titles 20,000; Bk Vols 22,000; Per Subs 150
Database Vendor: 3M Library Systems, Innovative Interfaces, Inc
Wireless access
Open Mon-Thurs 8-7, Fri 8-1

M RIVERSIDE COUNTY REGIONAL MEDICAL CENTER LIBRARY*, 26520 Cactus Ave, 92555. SAN 301-2557. Tel: 951-486-5101. FAX: 951-486-5045. *Coordr,* Sherry Allen; E-mail: sheallen@co.riverside.ca.us
Founded 1957
Library Holdings: Bk Titles 995; Bk Vols 1,025; Per Subs 209
Subject Interests: Bacteriology, Dermatology, Internal med, Mental health, Neurology, Nursing, Obstetrics & gynecology, Ophthalmology, Otolaryngology, Pediatrics, Radiology, Surgery
Open Mon-Fri 8:30-5
Restriction: Med staff only

MOSS LANDING

CM CALIFORNIA STATE UNIVERSITY*, Moss Landing Marine Laboratories Library, 8272 Moss Landing Rd, 95039. SAN 301-0864. Tel: 831-771-4400. FAX: 831-632-4403. E-mail: library@mlml.calstate.edu. Web Site: www.mlml.calstate.edu. *Dir,* Joan Parker; E-mail: parker@mlml.calstate.edu
Founded 1966. Enrl 150; Fac 9; Highest Degree: Master
Library Holdings: Bk Vols 15,000; Per Subs 100
Special Collections: Elkhorn Slough Coll
Subject Interests: Calif, Mammals, Marine biol, Oceanography
Open Mon-Fri 8:30-5
Friends of the Library Group

S SHAKESPEARE SOCIETY OF AMERICA*, New Shakespeare Sanctuary Library, 7981 Moss Landing Rd, 95039. SAN 371-134X. Tel: 831-633-2989. E-mail: admin@shakespearesocietyofamerica.org. Web Site: www.shakespearesocietyofamerica.org. *Pres & Dir,* Terry Taylor
Founded 1968
Library Holdings: Bk Vols 3,000
Subject Interests: Elizabethan studies, Shakespeare studies
Restriction: Open by appt only

MOUNTAIN VIEW

M EL CAMINO HOSPITAL LIBRARY & INFORMATION CENTER*, 2500 Grant Rd, 94039. SAN 370-2006. Tel: 650-940-7210. FAX: 650-940-7299. E-mail: healthlib@elcaminohospital.org. Web Site: www.elcaminohospital.org. *Mgr,* Jack Black
Library Holdings: Bk Vols 4,460; Per Subs 200
Subject Interests: Ethics, Med, Nursing
Automation Activity & Vendor Info: (Acquisitions) EOS International; (Cataloging) EOS International; (Circulation) EOS International; (OPAC) EOS International; (Serials) EOS International
Publications: Holdings Lists; Special Selected Bibliographies
Partic in Northern California & Nevada Medical Library Group (NCNMLG); Southnet

L FENWICK & WEST LLP, LIBRARY*, Silicon Valley Ctr, 801 California St, 94041. SAN 373-739X. Tel: 650-335-7575. FAX: 650-938-5200. E-mail: library@fenwick.com. Web Site: www.fenwick.com. *Libr Mgr,* Sharon McNally Lahey; Tel: 650-335-7249, E-mail: slahey@fenwick.com; Staff 5 (MLS 3, Non-MLS 2)
Founded 1975
Automation Activity & Vendor Info: (Cataloging) EOS International; (OPAC) EOS International; (Serials) EOS International
Database Vendor: Dialog, Dun & Bradstreet, EOS International, Factset, HeinOnline, LexisNexis, Loislaw, MicroPatent, Westlaw
Wireless access

P MOUNTAIN VIEW PUBLIC LIBRARY*, 585 Franklin St, 94041-1998. SAN 301-0899. Tel: 650-903-6335. Circulation Tel: 650-903-6336. Interlibrary Loan Service Tel: 650-903-6864. Reference Tel: 650-903-6337. FAX: 650-962-0438. Web Site: www.library.ci.mtnview.ca.us. *Dir,* Rosanne Macek; E-mail: rosanne.macek@mountainview.gov; *Libr Serv Mgr,* Laura Shea-Clark; Staff 18 (MLS 18)
Founded 1905. Pop 74,066; Circ 1,799,000
Jul 2006-Jun 2007 Income $4,679,682. Mats Exp $471,837, Books $305,329, Per/Ser (Incl. Access Fees) $36,444, AV Mat $99,838, Electronic Ref Mat (Incl. Access Fees) $30,226. Sal $3,577,100
Library Holdings: AV Mats 39,619; e-books 1,662; Bk Vols 228,856; Per Subs 326
Special Collections: Automobiles, Maintenance & Repair; Local History. Oral History
Automation Activity & Vendor Info: (Acquisitions) Innovative Interfaces, Inc; (Cataloging) Innovative Interfaces, Inc; (Circulation) Innovative Interfaces, Inc; (ILL) Innovative Interfaces, Inc; (OPAC) Innovative Interfaces, Inc; (Serials) Innovative Interfaces, Inc
Database Vendor: Gale Cengage Learning, LearningExpress, TumbleBookLibrary
Wireless access
Special Services for the Blind - Braille bks; Reader equip
Open Mon-Thurs 10-9, Fri & Sat 10-6, Sun 1-5
Friends of the Library Group
Bookmobiles: 1

S PACIFIC STUDIES CENTER*, 278A Hope St, 94041. SAN 320-1597. Tel: 650-969-1545. FAX: 650-961-8918. *Dir,* Lenny Siegel; E-mail: lsiegel@cpeo.org
Founded 1969
Library Holdings: Bk Titles 4,500; Per Subs 30
Special Collections: Alternative Magazines; Newspaper Clippings, vf
Restriction: Open by appt only

MURRIETA

P MURRIETA PUBLIC LIBRARY, Eight Town Sq, 92562. Tel: 951-304-2665. Reference Tel: 951-461-6626. FAX: 951-696-0165. Web Site: www.murrietalibrary.info. *Libr Mgr,* Elise Malkowski; E-mail: emalkowski@murrieta.org; *Supv Librn, Ch,* Allison Eagans; Staff 17.5 (MLS 5.5, Non-MLS 12)
Founded 1999. Pop 104,985; Circ 439,694
Library Holdings: Bk Vols 85,000; Per Subs 100

Automation Activity & Vendor Info: (Cataloging) Innovative Interfaces, Inc; (Circulation) Innovative Interfaces, Inc; (OPAC) Innovative Interfaces, Inc; (Serials) Innovative Interfaces, Inc
Wireless access
Mem of Inland Library System
Open Mon & Tues 10-8, Wed & Thurs 10-6, Fri & Sat 12-5
Friends of the Library Group

NAPA

S NAPA COUNTY HISTORICAL SOCIETY*, Goodman Library Bldg, 1219 First St, 94559. SAN 326-6338. Tel: 707-224-1739. E-mail: director@napahistory.org. Web Site: www.napahistory.org. *Exec Dir,* Nancy Levenberg; Staff 14 (MLS 1, Non-MLS 13)
Founded 1948
Library Holdings: Bk Titles 3,686; Bk Vols 7,000
Special Collections: City & Co of Napa
Function: Archival coll
Restriction: Non-circulating to the pub, Open by appt only

GL NAPA COUNTY LAW LIBRARY*, Old Courthouse, Rm 132, 825 Brown St, 94559. SAN 301-0945. Tel: 707-299-1201. FAX: 707-253-4229. *Librn,* Maxine C Oellien
Library Holdings: Bk Vols 14,696

P NAPA COUNTY LIBRARY, Napa Main Library, 580 Coombs St, 94559-3396. SAN 301-0929. Tel: 707-253-4241. Circulation Tel: 707-253-4243. Reference Tel: 707-253-4235. Administration Tel: 707-253-4242. FAX: 707-253-4615. TDD: 707-253-6088. E-mail: Library@countyofnapa.org. Web Site: www.countyofnapa.org/Library. *Dir,* Danis Kreimeier; E-mail: danis.kreimeier@countyofnapa.org; *Asst Libr Dir,* Anthony Halstead; Tel: 707-253-4061, E-mail: anthony.halstead@countyofnapa.org; *Head, Circ,* Tina Jolley; Tel: 707-253-4072, E-mail: tina.jolley@countyofnapa.org; *Supvr, Ch Serv,* Ann Davis; Tel: 707-253-4079, E-mail: adavis2@co.napa.ca.us; *Coll Serv Supvr,* Nancy Bradford; Tel: 707-253-4281, E-mail: nancy.bradford@countyofnapa.org; *Supvr, Extn Serv,* Nicole Shields; *Literacy Supvr,* Robin Rafael; Tel: 707-253-4283, E-mail: robin.rafael@countyofnapa.org; *Ref Supvr,* Position Currently Open.
Subject Specialists: *Literacy,* Robin Rafael; Staff 24.1 (MLS 9.8, Non-MLS 14.3)
Founded 1916. Pop 105,353; Circ 615,089
Special Collections: Local Newspaper Index
Subject Interests: County hist
Automation Activity & Vendor Info: (Acquisitions) TLC (The Library Corporation); (Cataloging) TLC (The Library Corporation); (Circulation) TLC (The Library Corporation); (OPAC) TLC (The Library Corporation)
Database Vendor: Baker & Taylor, BWI, EBSCOhost, Gale Cengage Learning, OCLC FirstSearch, ProQuest, TLC (The Library Corporation)
Wireless access
Function: Adult bk club, Adult literacy prog, Art exhibits, CD-ROM, Computer training, Copy machines, Electronic databases & coll, Family literacy, Handicapped accessible, ILL available, Magnifiers for reading, Music CDs, Preschool outreach, Prog for adults, Prog for children & young adult, Senior computer classes, Spoken cassettes & CDs, Spoken cassettes & DVDs, Summer reading prog, Tax forms, Telephone ref, VHS videos, Wheelchair accessible
Publications: Local History Indexer's Manual
Mem of NorthNet Library System
Partic in Solano Napa & Partners Library Consortium (SNAP)
Special Services for the Deaf - TDD equip
Open Mon-Thurs 10-9, Fri 10-5:30, Sat 10-5, Sun 2-9
Friends of the Library Group
Branches: 3
AMERICAN CANYON BRANCH, 3421 Broadway-Hwy 29, Ste E-3, American Canyon, 94503. Tel: 707-644-1136. *In Charge,* Susan Ryan; E-mail: sryan@co.napa.ca.us
Pop 16,031; Circ 76,090
Friends of the Library Group
CALISTOGA BRANCH, 1108 Myrtle, Calistoga, 94515-1730, SAN 321-7353. Tel: 707-942-4833. FAX: 707-942-0941. *In Charge,* Anne Scott; E-mail: ascott@co.napa.ca.us
Pop 5,302; Circ 35,001
Subject Interests: Local hist
Friends of the Library Group
YOUNTVILLE BRANCH, 6548 Yount St, Yountville, 94599-1271, SAN 328-7769. Tel: 707-944-1888. *In Charge,* Louise Myatt
Pop 3,290; Circ 14,950
Friends of the Library Group

M NAPA STATE HOSPITAL*, Wrenshall A Oliver Professional Library, 2100 Napa-Vallejo Hwy, 94558. SAN 332-1541. Tel: 707-253-5477. FAX: 707-253-5873. *Sr Librn,* Carl A Seele; Staff 1 (MLS 1)
Founded 1957
Library Holdings: e-journals 16; Bk Titles 4,000; Per Subs 18
Special Collections: Contemporary Psychotherapies (Laskay Coll); History of Psychiatry (Argens Coll)
Subject Interests: Mental illness, Neurology, Psychiat, Psychol, Soc serv (soc work), Therapy
Automation Activity & Vendor Info: (Acquisitions) LibraryWorld, Inc; (Cataloging) LibraryWorld, Inc; (Circulation) LibraryWorld, Inc; (OPAC) LibraryWorld, Inc; (Serials) LibraryWorld, Inc
Database Vendor: PubMed
Function: For res purposes, ILL available
Open Mon-Thurs 7:30-5
Restriction: Open to researchers by request
Branches:
JOHN STEWART RICHIE PATIENTS' LIBRARY, 2100 Napa-Vallejo Hwy, 94558-6293. Tel: 707-253-5351. FAX: 707-253-5682. *Actg Librn,* Jacquie Fitch
Library Holdings: Bk Vols 6,500; Per Subs 40
Open Mon-Fri 1:30-5

J NAPA VALLEY COLLEGE LIBRARY, 1700 Bldg, 2277 Napa-Vallejo Hwy, 94558. SAN 301-0937. Tel: 707-256-7400. Interlibrary Loan Service Tel: 707-256-7416. Reference Tel: 707-256-7430. FAX: 707-253-3015. *Dean, Libr & Learning Res,* Rebecca Scott; Tel: 707-256-7438, E-mail: rscott@napavalley.edu; *Librn,* Nancy McEnery; Tel: 707-256-7430, E-mail: nmcenery@napavalley.edu; *Acq, Circ, Tech Serv,* Jan Schardt; Tel: 707-256-7412, E-mail: jschardt@napavalley.edu; *Circ,* Tereasa Snowder; Tel: 707-256-7457, E-mail: tsnowder@napavalley.edu; *Coll Develop, Ref Serv,* Stephanie Grohs; E-mail: sgrohs@napavalley.edu; *Ser, Tech Serv,* Amy Guan; E-mail: aguan@napavalley.edu
Founded 1942. Enrl 10,000; Fac 200; Highest Degree: Associate
Jul 2013-Jun 2014 Income $492,874. Mats Exp $74,500, Books $5,000, Per/Ser (Incl. Access Fees) $13,000, Other Print Mats $5,000, AV Mat $6,500, Electronic Ref Mat (Incl. Access Fees) $45,000. Sal $357,803
Library Holdings: AV Mats 5,120; CDs 100; Bk Titles 57,000; Bk Vols 59,000; Per Subs 295
Special Collections: Cookbook Coll; Copia Coll; Jessamyn West Coll; Napa History Coll; Winery & Viticulture Technology Coll
Automation Activity & Vendor Info: (Acquisitions) CARL.Solution (TLC); (Cataloging) OCLC; (Circulation) CARL.Solution (TLC); (Course Reserve) CARL.Solution (TLC); (ILL) OCLC; (OPAC) CARL.Solution (TLC); (Serials) CARL.Solution (TLC)
Database Vendor: ARTstor, EBSCOhost, JSTOR, Newsbank, OCLC FirstSearch, ProQuest, Safari Books Online, TLC (The Library Corporation)
Mem of NorthNet Library System
Partic in Solano Napa & Partners Library Consortium (SNAP)
Open Mon-Thurs 7:30am-8pm, Fri 7:30-Noon

NATIONAL CITY

S BEAUCHAMP BOTANICAL LIBRARY*, 1434 E 24th St, 91950-6010. (Mail add: PO Box 985, 91951-0985), SAN 324-7325. Tel: 619-477-0295. FAX: 619-477-5380. *Librn,* R Mitchel Beauchamp; E-mail: mitch@psbs.com
Founded 1970
Jan 2005-Dec 2005. Mats Exp $4,300, Books $1,800, Per/Ser (Incl. Access Fees) $2,500
Library Holdings: Bk Titles 6,700; Per Subs 49
Special Collections: Floristic Monographs
Subject Interests: Petaloid monocots (esp amaryllidaceae), Vascular floras of the world

P NATIONAL CITY PUBLIC LIBRARY, 1401 National City Blvd, 91950-4401. SAN 301-0953. Tel: 619-470-5800. FAX: 619-470-5880. Web Site: www.cl.national-city.ca.us. *Dir,* Minh Duong; E-mail: minh.duong@nationalcitylibrary.org; Staff 8 (MLS 4, Non-MLS 4)
Founded 1896. Pop 55,600; Circ 303,370
Library Holdings: Bk Titles 110,500; Per Subs 350
Special Collections: Local History, bks, tapes; Spanish bks, per. Oral History
Subject Interests: Ethnic studies, Hist
Automation Activity & Vendor Info: (Cataloging) SirsiDynix; (Circulation) SirsiDynix
Wireless access
Publications: Pee Wee Press; Project READ (Newsletter); Teacher's Topics (Newsletter)
Open Mon-Thurs 10-8, Sat & Sun 1-5
Friends of the Library Group

NEVADA CITY

S AMERICAN HERB ASSOCIATION LIBRARY*, PO Box 1673, 95959. SAN 370-9914. Tel: 530-265-9552. FAX: 530-274-3140. Web Site: www.ahaherb.com. *Dir,* Kathi Keville
Library Holdings: Bk Vols 6,000; Per Subs 40

S NEVADA COUNTY HISTORICAL SOCIETY*, Searls Historical Library, 214 Church St, 95959. SAN 301-0961. Tel: 530-265-5910. *Dir,* Patricia J Chesnut; E-mail: pchesnut@hughes.net
Founded 1972
Library Holdings: CDs 250; Bk Titles 2,790
Special Collections: Nevada County Photographs. Oral History
Subject Interests: Local hist, State hist
Open Mon-Sat 1-4
Restriction: Open to pub for ref only

P NEVADA COUNTY LIBRARY*, Madelyn Helling Library, 980 Helling Way, 95959. SAN 373-5931. Tel: 530-265-7050. Interlibrary Loan Service Tel: 530-470-2773. Reference Tel: 530-470-2748. Administration Tel: 530-265-1407. Administration Toll Free Tel: 888-831-1407. Administration FAX: 530-265-9863. E-mail: library.reference@co.nevada.ca.us. Web Site: www.mynevadacounty.com/nc/library. *Br Mgr, County Librn,* Jessica Hudson; Tel: 530-265-7078, E-mail: jessica.hudson@co.nevada.ca.us
Founded 1991. Pop 97,182; Circ 634,488
Jul 2011-Jun 2012 Income (Main Library and Branch(s)) $2,341,275, State $12,392, Federal $15,176, Locally Generated Income $2,093,186, Other $220,521. Mats Exp $831,324, Books $72,192, Per/Ser (Incl. Access Fees) $12,080, Other Print Mats $668,303, AV Mat $30,377, Electronic Ref Mat (Incl. Access Fees) $48,372. Sal $1,424,579
Library Holdings: Audiobooks 15,347; e-books 4,959; Bk Titles 184,205; Per Subs 302; Videos 17,083
Automation Activity & Vendor Info: (Acquisitions) SirsiDynix; (Cataloging) SirsiDynix; (Circulation) SirsiDynix; (ILL) OCLC; (OPAC) SirsiDynix
Database Vendor: Booklist Online, Gale Cengage Learning, Ingram Library Services, LearningExpress, OCLC FirstSearch, OCLC WorldShare Interlibrary Loan, Overdrive, Inc, ProQuest, SirsiDynix, TumbleBookLibrary
Wireless access
Function: Adult literacy prog, After school storytime, Audiobks via web, Bks on cassette, Bks on CD, Children's prog, Computers for patron use, Copy machines, Electronic databases & coll, Free DVD rentals, Handicapped accessible, Home delivery & serv to Sr ctr & nursing homes, Homebound delivery serv, ILL available, Literacy & newcomer serv, Music CDs, Online cat, OverDrive digital audio bks, Photocopying/Printing, Prog for adults, Prog for children & young adult, Pub access computers, Story hour, Summer reading prog, Tax forms, VHS videos, Wheelchair accessible
Special Services for the Blind - Audio mat; Bks on cassette; Bks on CD; Extensive large print coll; Magnifiers; Talking bk serv referral
Open Mon & Thurs 11-7, Tues, Wed & Fri 11-6, Sat 11-5
Friends of the Library Group
Branches: 5
BEAR RIVER STATION, 11130 Magnolia Rd, Grass Valley, 95949, SAN 333-2640. Circulation Tel: 530-271-4147. *Libr Tech,* Eckholt Cheri; E-mail: cheri.eckholt@co.nevada.ca.us
Founded 2002
Function: Adult bk club, Adult literacy prog, Bks on cassette, Bks on CD, Children's prog, Computers for patron use, Copy machines, Electronic databases & coll, Handicapped accessible, Home delivery & serv to Sr ctr & nursing homes, Homebound delivery serv, ILL available, Music CDs, Online cat, Online ref, Photocopying/Printing, Prog for adults, Prog for children & young adult, Pub access computers, Ref serv available, Summer reading prog, Tax forms, Telephone ref, VHS videos, Web-catalog, Wheelchair accessible
Open Mon & Wed 3-7, Sat 9-12 & 1-4
Friends of the Library Group
DORIS FOLEY LIBRARY FOR HISTORICAL RESEARCH, 211 N Pine St, 95959-2592, SAN 333-2705. Tel: 530-265-4606. E-mail: foley@ncfol.org. *Libr Tech,* Leslie Vera; E-mail: leslie.vera@co.nevada.ca.us
Founded 1907
Special Collections: Nevada County Court Records
Subject Interests: Local hist, Mining
Open Wed-Sat 10-4
Friends of the Library Group
GRASS VALLEY LIBRARY - ROYCE BRANCH, 207 Mill St, Grass Valley, 95945-6789, SAN 333-2675. Tel: 530-273-4117. *Br Mgr,* Laura Pappani; E-mail: laura.pappani@co.nevada.ca.us
Founded 1916
Open Tues 10-6, Wed-Fri 10-5, Sat 10-4
Friends of the Library Group
PENN VALLEY STATION, 11336 Pleasant Valley Rd, Penn Valley, 95946. Tel: 530-432-5764. *Libr Tech,* Claire Stafford; E-mail: claire.stafford@co.nevada.ca.us
Founded 2002
Open Tues & Thurs 2-6, Wed & Fri 10-2, Sat 1-5
Friends of the Library Group
TRUCKEE LIBRARY, 10031 Levon Ave, Truckee, 96161-4800, SAN 333-273X. Tel: 530-582-7846. *Br Mgr,* Lucinda deLorimier; E-mail: lucinda.delorimier@co.nevada.ca.us
Founded 1976
Open Mon-Wed & Fri 10:30-6, Thurs 11-7
Friends of the Library Group

NEWPORT BEACH

M HOAG MEMORIAL HOSPITAL PRESBYTERIAN*, Robert & Winifred Bacon Memorial Medical Library, One Hoag Dr, 92658. (Mail add: PO Box 6100, 92658-6100), SAN 301-102X. Tel: 949-764-8308. FAX: 949-764-5729. Web Site: www.hoag.org. *Librn,* Barbara Garside; Staff 1 (MLS 1)
Founded 1959
Library Holdings: Bk Vols 1,000; Per Subs 300
Special Collections: Psychiatry (Krukas Memorial Coll)
Subject Interests: Nursing
Open Mon-Fri 6:30-3

P NEWPORT BEACH PUBLIC LIBRARY*, 1000 Avocado Ave, 92660-6301. SAN 333-2764. Tel: 949-717-3800. FAX: 949-640-5681. E-mail: nbplref@newportbeachca.gov. Web Site: www.newportbeachlibrary.org. *Dir,* Position Currently Open; *Coll Develop Librn,* Melissa Hartson; Tel: 949-717-3827, Fax: 949-640-5648, E-mail: mhartson@newportbeachca.gov; *Libr Serv Mgr,* Tim Hetherton; Tel: 949-717-3819, E-mail: thetherton@newportbeachca.gov; *Br & Youth Serv Coordr,* Debbie Walker; Tel: 949-717-3829, E-mail: dwalker@newportbeachca.gov; *Coordr, Ref Serv-Adult,* Natalie Basmaciyan; Tel: 949-717-3823, E-mail: nbasmaciyan@newportbeachca.gov; *Support Serv Coordr,* Melissa Kelly; Tel: 949-717-3852, E-mail: mkelly@newportbeachca.gov; Staff 65.5 (MLS 19.5, Non-MLS 46)
Founded 1920. Pop 83,120; Circ 1,622,573
Library Holdings: Bk Titles 282,874; Bk Vols 325,890; Per Subs 708
Special Collections: Nautical Coll; Newport Beach History Coll
Automation Activity & Vendor Info: (Acquisitions) Innovative Interfaces, Inc; (Cataloging) Innovative Interfaces, Inc; (Circulation) Innovative Interfaces, Inc; (OPAC) Innovative Interfaces, Inc; (Serials) Innovative Interfaces, Inc
Database Vendor: ProQuest
Wireless access
Publications: Bookends (Newsletter); Lighthouse (Newsletter)
Partic in Califa; Metro Coop Libr Syst; Southern California Library Cooperative
Friends of the Library Group
Branches: 4
BALBOA BRANCH, 100 E Balboa Blvd, Balboa, 92661, SAN 333-2799. Tel: 949-644-3076. FAX: 949-675-8524. *Librn,* Andrea Jason; E-mail: ajason@city.newport-beach.ca.us
Library Holdings: Bk Vols 50,353
CENTRAL LIBRARY, 1000 Avocado Ave, 92660-6301, SAN 333-2888. Tel: 949-717-3800. FAX: 949-640-5681. ; Staff 24 (MLS 22, Non-MLS 2)
Founded 1920. Pop 75,662; Circ 1,002,877
Library Holdings: Bk Vols 226,811
Subject Interests: Am hist, Art, Bus
Open Mon-Thurs 9-9, Fri & Sat 9-6, Sun 12-5
CORONA DEL MAR BRANCH, 420 Marigold Ave, Corona del Mar, 92625, SAN 333-2829. Tel: 949-717-3800. FAX: 949-673-4917. *Librn,* Andrew Kachaturian; Staff 1 (MLS 1)
Library Holdings: Bk Vols 32,653
MARINERS, 1300 Irvine Ave, 92660, SAN 333-2853. Tel: 949-717-3800. FAX: 949-642-4848. *Librn,* Mary Ellen Bowman; Staff 2 (MLS 2)
Founded 1950
Library Holdings: Bk Vols 64,582
Open Mon-Thurs 9-9, Fri & Sat 9-6, Sun 12-5

L O'MELVENY & MYERS LLP*, Law Library, 610 Newport Center Dr, 92660-6429. SAN 372-3801. Tel: 949-760-9600. FAX: 949-823-6994. Web Site: www.omm.com. *Dir,* Cheryl Smith; *Librn,* Kirsten Anderson
Founded 1979
Library Holdings: Bk Vols 5,000
Restriction: Staff use only

S ORANGE COUNTY MUSEUM OF ART LIBRARY*, 850 San Clemente Dr, 92660. SAN 301-1046. Tel: 949-759-1122. FAX: 949-759-5623. Web Site: www.ocma.net. *Librn,* Ruth E Roe
Founded 1965
Library Holdings: Bk Titles 200
Subject Interests: Calif, Contemporary art
Restriction: Staff use only

S STRADLING, YOCCA, CARLSON & RAUTH*, Law Library, 660 Newport Ctr, Ste 1600, 92660. SAN 373-9007. Tel: 949-725-4000. FAX: 949-725-4100. Web Site: www.sycr.com. *Librn,* Lynn Connor Merring; Tel: 949-725-4023, E-mail: lmerring@sycr.com. Subject Specialists: *Law,* Lynn Connor Merring; Staff 2 (MLS 1, Non-MLS 1)

Founded 1975
Library Holdings: Bk Titles 1,100; Bk Vols 9,000; Per Subs 250
Restriction: Not open to pub

NORCO

GL CALIFORNIA DEPARTMENT OF CORRECTIONS*, California Rehabilitation Center Library, Fifth St & Western, 92860. (Mail add: PO Box 1841, 92860), SAN 300-838X. Tel: 951-737-2683, Ext 4202. FAX: 951-273-2380. *Sr Librn,* Mitchell Lindenbaum; E-mail: mitch.lindenbaum@cdcr.ca.gov; *Librn,* Mike Ludwig; Staff 3 (MLS 2, Non-MLS 1)
Founded 1966
Library Holdings: Bk Vols 43,077
Special Collections: Federal & California Law, cases & statutes

NORTH HIGHLANDS

R ZION LUTHERAN CHURCH*, 3644 Bolivar Ave, 95660. SAN 301-1070. Tel: 916-332-4001. FAX: 916-332-4030. Web Site: www.zionlutherannh.org. *Librn,* JoAnne Schramm; E-mail: jo82732@aol.com; Staff 4 (Non-MLS 4)
Founded 1955
Library Holdings: AV Mats 250; High Interest/Low Vocabulary Bk Vols 500; Bk Vols 1,200
Open Fri 9am-11am, Sun 9-10:30 & 11:45-12:15
Restriction: Not open to pub

NORTH HOLLYWOOD

S PACIFICA FOUNDATION*, Pacifica Radio Archives, 3729 Cahuenga Blvd W, 91604. SAN 326-0577. Tel: 818-506-1077. Toll Free Tel: 800-735-0230. FAX: 818-506-1084. E-mail: pacarchive@aol.com. Web Site: www.pacificaradioarchives.org. *Dir,* Brian DeShazor; Tel: 818-506-1077, Ext 263; *Cat,* Andrea Hull; Tel: 818-506-1077, Ext 265; Staff 2 (MLS 1, Non-MLS 1)
Founded 1970
Library Holdings: Bk Titles 40,000
Subject Interests: Polit sci, Pub affairs
Automation Activity & Vendor Info: (Cataloging) Inmagic, Inc.
Function: Archival coll
Publications: Annual Cassette & Reel to Reel Catalogues (print)
Partic in OCLC Online Computer Library Center, Inc
Open to public to listen to tapes in house, by appointment

S WESTERN COSTUME CO*, Research Library, 11041 Vanowen St, 91605. SAN 326-3800. Tel: 818-760-0902, Ext 148. Reference Tel: 818-508-2148. FAX: 818-508-2182. Web Site: www.westerncostume.com. *Dir,* Bobi Garland; E-mail: research@westerncostume.com; Staff 1 (MLS 1)
Founded 1915
Library Holdings: Bk Titles 12,500; Bk Vols 13,500; Per Subs 60
Special Collections: Godey, Peterson & Vogue, mags; Sears & Montgomery Ward Catalogs (1895 to present); Twentieth Century Fox Costume Still Coll
Subject Interests: Costume, Fashion
Open Mon-Fri 8-5

NORTHRIDGE

C CALIFORNIA STATE UNIVERSITY, NORTHRIDGE, Delmar T Oviatt Library, 18111 Nordhoff St, 91330. SAN 333-2918. Tel: 818-677-2285. Circulation Tel: 818-677-2274. Interlibrary Loan Service Tel: 818-677-2294. Administration Tel: 818-677-2271. FAX: 818-677-2676. Interlibrary Loan Service FAX: 818-677-3325. Reference FAX: 818-677-4136. TDD: 818-677-6519. Web Site: library.csun.edu. *Dean,* Mark Stover, PhD; E-mail: mark.stover@csun.edu; *Interim Assoc Dean,* Lynn Lampert; E-mail: Lynn.lampert@csun.edu; *Mgr, Acad Res,* Lara Clary; Tel: 818-677-2205, E-mail: laura.clary@csun.edu; Staff 89 (MLS 32, Non-MLS 57)
Founded 1958. Enrl 35,000; Fac 1,929; Highest Degree: Doctorate
Jul 2013-Jun 2014 Income (Main Library Only) $9,820,818. Sal $5,723,609 (Prof $2,368,788)
Library Holdings: e-books 570,151; e-journals 74,181; Microforms 3,184,894; Bk Titles 1,575,695; Bk Vols 2,170,589; Videos 45,992
Special Collections: 19th Century English & American Playbills (Theater Program Coll, 1809-1930); 19th Century English Theatre Playbills Coll; California & Local History Coll; California Tourism & Promotional Literature Coll; Carl Sandburg Coll, bks, news clippings, pamphlets; Catherine Mulholland Coll; Chinese Antiquities (Tseng Coll); Contemporary 20th Century American Writers (McDermott Coll); Edwin Booth Coll; Francis Gilbert Webb Correspondence, 1898-1934; Gwen Driston Papers; Haldeman-Julius Publications, Big & Little Blue Books, etc; History of Printing (Lynton Kistler-Merle Armitage Coll); Human Sexuality (Vern & Bonnie Bullough Coll); International Guitar Research Archives; Japanese-American World War II Relocation Camps, doc, newsp; Migrant Farm Labor Camp Newsletters, 1930s; Milton Geiger Papers; Old China Hands Coll; Radio & Film Scripts, NBC Radio Plays, 1935-1943; Ray Martin Coll, music scores; Revolutionary & Political Movements in Russia, 1875-1937 (Patrick Coll); San Fernando Valley Digital History Library; Slaves & Slavery (American Plantation Documents, 1756-1869); Urban Archives Coll; Vern & Bonnie Bullough Coll; Voluntary Labor & Civic Associations Papers; Women Music Composers (Aaron Cohen Coll, Ruth Shaw Wylie Scores, Ardis O Higgin Coll). State Document Depository; US Document Depository
Subject Interests: Local hist, Music
Automation Activity & Vendor Info: (Acquisitions) Innovative Interfaces, Inc; (Cataloging) Innovative Interfaces, Inc; (Circulation) Innovative Interfaces, Inc; (Course Reserve) Innovative Interfaces, Inc; (ILL) OCLC; (OPAC) Innovative Interfaces, Inc; (Serials) Innovative Interfaces, Inc
Database Vendor: Alexander Street Press, American Chemical Society, ebrary, EBSCOhost, Elsevier, Factiva.com, Gale Cengage Learning, ISI Web of Knowledge, JSTOR, LexisNexis, Mergent Online, Newsbank-Readex, OCLC, OVID Technologies, Project MUSE, ProQuest, ScienceDirect, Wiley
Wireless access
Function: Archival coll, Audio & video playback equip for onsite use, Bks on cassette, Bks on CD, Computers for patron use, Copy machines, Doc delivery serv, e-mail & chat, E-Reserves, Electronic databases & coll, Equip loans & repairs, Exhibits, Govt ref serv, Handicapped accessible, ILL available, Large print keyboards, Libr develop, Online cat, Online info literacy tutorials on the web & in blackboard, Online ref, Online searches, Orientations, Outreach serv, Outside serv via phone, mail, e-mail & web, Photocopying/Printing, Ref & res, Ref serv available, Ref serv in person, Video lending libr, Web-catalog, Wheelchair accessible
Publications: Faculty Guide to the Oviatt Library; Library eNews (Quarterly newsletter); Oviatt Friends (Newsletter); Student Guide to the Oviatt Library; University Library (Annual report)
Partic in OCLC Online Computer Library Center, Inc
Special Services for the Deaf - Assistive tech; Bks on deafness & sign lang; Closed caption videos; Staff with knowledge of sign lang; TTY equip
Special Services for the Blind - Assistive/Adapted tech devices, equip & products; Audio mat; Bks on cassette; Bks on CD; Braille equip; Talking bks; Talking calculator
Open Mon-Thurs 7:45am-12am, Fri 7:45-5, Sat 11-5, Sun Noon-8
Restriction: Authorized patrons, Borrowing privileges limited to fac & registered students, Borrowing requests are handled by ILL, External users must contact libr, ID required to use computers (Ltd hrs), Open to students, fac, staff & alumni
Friends of the Library Group

Departmental Libraries:

GEOGRAPHY MAP LIBRARY, Sierra Hall 171, 18111 Nordhoff St, 91330-8249, SAN 333-2977. Tel: 818-677-3465. FAX: 818-677-7840. E-mail: map.library@csun.edu. Web Site: www.csun.edu/maplibrary. *Curator,* Kris Tacsik; Staff 2 (Non-MLS 2)
Library Holdings: Bk Vols 1,600
Special Collections: Sanborn Fire Insurance Maps
Open Mon-Fri 8:30-4:30

NATIONAL CENTER ON DEAFNESS-PEPNET RESOURCE CENTER, 18111 Nordhoff St, 91330-8267, SAN 333-2942. Tel: 818-677-2611. FAX: 818-677-7963. TDD: 818-677-2665. E-mail: prc@csun.edu. Web Site; www.csun.edu/ncod. *Librn for Deaf, Spec Coll Librn,* Anthony Karl Ivankovic; Tel: 818-435-8174; Staff 1 (Non-MLS 1)
Library Holdings: Bks on Deafness & Sign Lang 11,865; CDs 15; DVDs 2,280; Large Print Bks 15; Bk Vols 7,232; Per Subs 169; Videos 2,154
Function: Audio & video playback equip for onsite use, Res libr
Special Services for the Deaf - Bks on deafness & sign lang; Closed caption videos; Coll on deaf educ; Deaf publ; Spec interest per; Staff with knowledge of sign lang; Videos & decoder
Open Mon-Fri 9-4:30
Restriction: Open to pub for ref & circ; with some limitations, Restricted borrowing privileges

M NORTHRIDGE HOSPITAL*, Atcherley Medical Library, 18300 Roscoe Blvd, 91328. SAN 321-5601. Tel: 818-885-8500, Ext 4608. FAX: 818-885-0372. Web Site: www.chwconnect.com. *Librn,* Eva Perkins
Founded 1975
Library Holdings: Bk Titles 3,000; Per Subs 190
Open Mon-Fri 7:30-5:30
Restriction: Staff use only

NORWALK

J CERRITOS COLLEGE LIBRARY*, 11110 Alondra Blvd, 90650. SAN 301-1127. Tel: 562-860-2451, Ext 2430. Circulation Tel: 562-860-2451, Ext 2424. Interlibrary Loan Service Tel: 562-860-2451, Ext 2422. Reference Tel: 562-860-2451, Ext 2425. Administration Tel: 562-860-2451, Ext 2412. FAX: 562-467-5002. E-mail: refuser@cerritos.edu. Web Site: www.cerritos.edu/library. *Dean, Libr/Learning Res Ctr,* Carl Bengston; E-mail: cbengston@cerritos.edu; *Librn, Ref Coordr,* Lorraine Gersitz; Tel:

562-860-2451, Ext 2414, E-mail: lgersitz@cerritos.edu; *Coll Develop & Acq Librn,* Monica Lopez; *Syst & Tech Serv Librn,* Debra Moore; Tel: 562-860-2451, Ext 2418, E-mail: dmoore@cerritos.edu; *Adjunct Ref Librn,* Valencia Mitchell; Tel: 562-860-2451, Ext 2416, E-mail: vmitchell@cerritos.edu; *Adjunct Ref Librn,* Lynda Sampson; Staff 14 (MLS 7, Non-MLS 7)
Founded 1956. Enrl 24,000; Highest Degree: Associate
Library Holdings: Bk Titles 110,000; Per Subs 200
Automation Activity & Vendor Info: (Acquisitions) SirsiDynix; (Cataloging) SirsiDynix; (Circulation) SirsiDynix; (Course Reserve) SirsiDynix; (ILL) OCLC; (OPAC) SirsiDynix; (Serials) SirsiDynix
Database Vendor: EBSCOhost, Gale Cengage Learning, Newsbank, ProQuest
Wireless access
Function: Distance learning, ILL available, Orientations, Photocopying/Printing
Partic in California Community College Library Consortium (CCLC); OCLC Online Computer Library Center, Inc
Special Services for the Deaf - Bks on deafness & sign lang
Special Services for the Blind - Text reader; ZoomText magnification & reading software
Open Mon-Thurs 7:30am-9pm, Fri 7:30-3

M METROPOLITAN STATE HOSPITAL*, Staff Library, 11401 Bloomfield Ave, 90650. SAN 333-306X. Tel: 562-651-3274. FAX: 562-651-4439. Web Site: www.dmh.ca.gov. *Sr Librn,* James Church; E-mail: james.church@msh.dsh.ca.gov; Staff 1 (MLS 1)
Founded 1950
Library Holdings: CDs 200; Large Print Bks 100; Bk Vols 3,600; Talking Bks 200; Videos 1,000
Subject Interests: Psychiat, Psychol, Sociol
Open Mon-Fri 8-4

NOVATO

S MUSEUM OF THE AMERICAN INDIAN LIBRARY*, Miwok Park, 2200 Novato Blvd, 94947. (Mail add: PO Box 864, 94948-0864), SAN 329-0662. Tel: 415-897-4064. FAX: 415-892-7804. Web Site: www.marinindian.com. *Exec Dir,* Colleen Hicks
Founded 1967
Library Holdings: Bk Vols 600
Subject Interests: Am Indian art, Calif, Native people
Function: Ref serv available
Restriction: Non-circulating to the pub, Open by appt only

OAKLAND

M ALAMEDA COUNTY MEDICAL CENTER*, Medical Library, 1411 E 31st St, 94602. SAN 301-1135. Tel: 510-437-4701. Interlibrary Loan Service Tel: 510-437-8392. FAX: 510-537-7592. Web Site: www.acmedctr.org. *Mgr, Supv Librn,* Kathy Yue; E-mail: cyue@acmedctr.org; Staff 2 (MLS 1, Non-MLS 1)
Founded 1917
Library Holdings: CDs 300; e-books 50; e-journals 180; Bk Vols 4,000; Per Subs 200
Subject Interests: Clinical med
Automation Activity & Vendor Info: (Acquisitions) CyberTools for Libraries; (Cataloging) CyberTools for Libraries; (Circulation) CyberTools for Libraries; (OPAC) CyberTools for Libraries; (Serials) SerialsSolutions
Database Vendor: MD Consult, Micromedex, UpToDate
Wireless access
Function: ILL available, Res libr
Partic in Docline; National Network of Libraries of Medicine; Northern California & Nevada Medical Library Group (NCNMLG); Pacific Southwest Regional Medical Library (PSRML)
Restriction: Circ limited, Circulates for staff only, Employees & their associates, Internal circ only, Lending to staff only, Mem organizations only, Not a lending libr, Not open to pub, Prof mat only, Restricted access, Restricted loan policy, Secured area only open to authorized personnel, Staff use only

S BERKELEY PLANNING ASSOCIATES LIBRARY*, 440 Grand Ave, Ste 500, 94610. SAN 371-2389. Tel: 510-465-7884. FAX: 510-465-7885. Web Site: www.bpacl.com. *Librn,* Sabrina Williams
Library Holdings: Bk Vols 550; Per Subs 20
Open Mon-Fri 8:30-5

C CALIFORNIA COLLEGE OF THE ARTS LIBRARIES*, Meyer Library, 5212 Broadway, 94618. SAN 301-1186. Circulation Tel: 510-594-3658. Reference Tel: 510-594-3659. Administration Tel: 510-594-3660. E-mail: refdesk@cca.edu. Web Site: libraries.cca.edu. *Dir of Libr,* Janice Woo; E-mail: jwoo@cca.edu; *Librn, Syst & Serv,* Cody Hennesy; E-mail: chennesy@cca.edu; *Digital Archivist,* Annemarie Poniz Haar; E-mail: ahaar@cca.edu; Staff 3 (MLS 3)
Founded 1926. Enrl 1,800; Fac 250; Highest Degree: Master
Library Holdings: Bk Titles 35,000; Bk Vols 38,000; Per Subs 125; Videos 2,200
Special Collections: Capp Street Project Archives; College Archives; Hamaguchi Study Print Coll
Subject Interests: Fine arts
Automation Activity & Vendor Info: (OPAC) Innovative Interfaces, Inc
Database Vendor: ARTstor, EBSCO - WebFeat, Gale Cengage Learning, JSTOR, Material ConneXion, Oxford Online, ProQuest, SerialsSolutions, Wilson - Wilson Web
Wireless access
Partic in BayNet Library Association; Statewide California Electronic Library Consortium (SCELC)
Open Mon-Wed 8am-11pm, Thurs 8-8, Fri 8-5, Sat 2-6, Sun 2-11
Restriction: Open to others by appt, Open to students, fac & staff

Departmental Libraries:

SIMPSON LIBRARY, 1111 Eighth St, San Francisco, 94107. Administration Tel: 415-703-9574. Information Services Tel: 415-703-9558. *Dir of Libr,* Janice Woo; E-mail: jwoo@cca.edu; *Assoc Dir of Libr,* Position Currently Open; *Fine Arts Librn,* Teri Dowling; E-mail: tdowling@cca.edu. Subject Specialists: *Art,* Teri Dowling; Staff 2 (MLS 2)
Founded 1986
Library Holdings: Bk Titles 17,000; Bk Vols 19,000; Per Subs 130; Videos 600
Special Collections: Joseph Sinel Coll; Small Press Traffic Archives
Subject Interests: Archit, Design
Automation Activity & Vendor Info: (OPAC) Innovative Interfaces, Inc
Database Vendor: ARTstor, EBSCOhost, Gale Cengage Learning, JSTOR, Material ConneXion, Oxford Online, ProQuest, SerialsSolutions
Partic in Southern Calif Electronic Libr Consortium
Restriction: Open to others by appt, Open to students, fac & staff

G CALIFORNIA STATE DEPARTMENT OF HEALTH SERVICES*, Office of Environmental Health Hazard Assessment, 1515 Clay St, 16th Flr, 94612. Tel: 510-622-3204. FAX: 510-622-3197. *Head Librn,* Charleen Kubota
Library Holdings: Bk Vols 10,000
Automation Activity & Vendor Info: (Cataloging) Inmagic, Inc.
Database Vendor: Dialog, OVID Technologies
Open Mon-Fri 9-5
Restriction: Staff use only

M CHILDREN'S HOSPITAL & RESEARCH CENTER OAKLAND*, Gordon Health Sciences Library, 747 52nd St, 4th Flr, 94609. SAN 301-1208. Tel: 510-428-3448. FAX: 510-601-3963. E-mail: cholibrary@mail.cho.org. *Librn,* Mina Davenport; Staff 1 (MLS 1)
Founded 1938
Jan 2010-Dec 2011. Mats Exp $154,000, Books $8,000, Per/Ser (Incl. Access Fees) $75,000, Electronic Ref Mat (Incl. Access Fees) $71,000. Sal $51,000
Library Holdings: e-journals 150; Bk Titles 3,100; Bk Vols 3,600; Per Subs 292; Videos 75
Subject Interests: Pediatrics
Automation Activity & Vendor Info: (Acquisitions) EOS International; (Cataloging) EOS International; (Circulation) EOS International; (ILL) OCLC ILLiad; (OPAC) EOS International; (Serials) EOS International
Database Vendor: EBSCOhost, Elsevier MDL, OCLC FirstSearch, OVID Technologies, PubMed, UpToDate
Function: ILL available, Online searches, Photocopying/Printing, Ref serv available
Publications: Online Acquisitions List; Online Newsletter; Serials Holdings
Partic in Docline; Northern California & Nevada Medical Library Group (NCNMLG); OCLC Online Computer Library Center, Inc; San Francisco Biomedical Library Network
Restriction: Circulates for staff only, Not open to pub
Friends of the Library Group

C HOLY NAMES UNIVERSITY*, Paul J Cushing Library, 3500 Mountain Blvd, 94619. SAN 301-1267. Tel: 510-436-1332. FAX: 510-436-1260. Web Site: www.hnu.edu. *Dir,* Karen Schneider; Tel: 510-436-1160, E-mail: schneider@hnu.edu; Staff 3 (MLS 2, Non-MLS 1)
Founded 1880. Enrl 930; Fac 90; Highest Degree: Master
Library Holdings: AV Mats 4,975; e-books 25,000; Bk Titles 75,000; Bk Vols 111,174; Talking Bks 85
Subject Interests: Music, Nursing, Relig
Wireless access
Function: For res purposes, ILL available, Res libr
Open Mon-Thurs 9am-10pm, Fri 9-5, Sat 10-5, Sun 12-10
Restriction: Non-circulating to the pub

S INDEPENDENT INSTITUTE LIBRARY*, 100 Swan Way, 94621-1428. SAN 371-7410. Tel: 510-632-1366. FAX: 510-568-6040. E-mail: info@independent.org. Web Site: www.independent.org. *Librn,* Sanjeev Saini; Tel: 510-632-1366, Ext 143; Staff 1 (MLS 1)

Founded 1986
Library Holdings: Bk Titles 6,500; Per Subs 85
Subject Interests: Econ, Hist, Law, Polit sci, Sociol
Open Mon-Fri 8:30-5:30

M KAISER-PERMANENTE MEDICAL CENTER*, Oakland Medical Center-Health Sciences Library, 280 W MacArthur Blvd, 94611-5693. SAN 301-1283. Tel: 510-752-6158. FAX: 510-752-1500. *Librn,* Ysabel Bertolucci; Staff 2 (MLS 1, Non-MLS 1)
Founded 1949
Library Holdings: Bk Titles 1,000
Subject Interests: Arthritis, Cancer, Nutrition
Automation Activity & Vendor Info: (Cataloging) Innovative Interfaces, Inc; (Circulation) Innovative Interfaces, Inc; (OPAC) Innovative Interfaces, Inc; (Serials) Innovative Interfaces, Inc
Wireless access
Open Mon-Fri 8:30-4:30

J LANEY COLLEGE*, Library-Learning Resources Center, 900 Fallon St, 94607. SAN 301-1291. Tel: 510-464-3493. FAX: 510-464-3264. Web Site: laney.edu/library. *Exec VPres, Student Learning,* Steve Cohen; *Head Librn,* Evelyn Lord; *Media/Instruction Librn,* Ann Buchalter; Staff 5 (MLS 5)
Founded 1956. Enrl 10,508; Fac 177
Library Holdings: DVDs 600; Bk Titles 80,634; Bk Vols 89,000; Per Subs 108
Automation Activity & Vendor Info: (Cataloging) Innovative Interfaces, Inc - Millenium; (Circulation) Innovative Interfaces, Inc - Millenium
Wireless access
Open Mon-Thurs 8-8, Fri 8-6

C LINCOLN UNIVERSITY LIBRARY*, 401 15th St, 94612. SAN 321-9380. Tel: 510-628-8011. FAX: 510-628-8012. E-mail: library@lincolnuca.edu. Web Site: www.lincolnuca.edu/studentlife/library. *Head Librn,* Nicole Y Marsh; E-mail: librarian@lincolnuca.edu; Staff 3 (MLS 1, Non-MLS 2)
Founded 1962. Enrl 400; Fac 25; Highest Degree: Doctorate
Library Holdings: Bk Titles 19,500; Bk Vols 21,500; Per Subs 657; Spec Interest Per Sub 20
Automation Activity & Vendor Info: (Acquisitions) LibraryWorld, Inc
Database Vendor: ebrary, EBSCOhost, Gale Cengage Learning, LexisNexis, LibraryWorld, Inc, Plunkett Research, Ltd
Wireless access
Open Mon-Thurs (Winter) 9-7, Fri 9-4, Sat 9-5; Mon-Thurs (Summer) 9-7, Fri 9-4
Restriction: Authorized personnel only

J MERRITT COLLEGE LIBRARY*, 12500 Campus Dr, 94619. SAN 301-1305. Tel: 510-436-2461. Circulation Tel: 510-436-2457. Reference Tel: 510-436-2557. FAX: 510-531-4960. E-mail: merrittlib@peralta.edu. Web Site: merritt.peralta.edu/library. *Dean of Instruction,* Stacy Thompson; *Head Librn,* Tim Hackett; *Tech Serv Librn,* Eva Ng-Chin; Staff 6 (MLS 3, Non-MLS 3)
Founded 1954. Enrl 2,500; Fac 128; Highest Degree: Associate
Library Holdings: Bk Titles 55,000; Per Subs 100
Special Collections: Black Panthers Archive Coll
Automation Activity & Vendor Info: (Acquisitions) Innovative Interfaces, Inc; (Cataloging) Innovative Interfaces, Inc; (Circulation) Innovative Interfaces, Inc; (Course Reserve) Innovative Interfaces, Inc; (OPAC) Innovative Interfaces, Inc
Database Vendor: CQ Press, EBSCOhost, LexisNexis
Wireless access
Special Services for the Blind - Computer with voice synthesizer for visually impaired persons; Reader equip
Open Mon-Thurs 8-7, Fri 8-3

G METROPOLITAN TRANSPORTATION COMMISSION*, MTC-ABAG Library, 101 Eighth St, 94607. SAN 331-5363. Tel: 510-817-5836. FAX: 510-817-5932. E-mail: library@mtc.ca.gov. Web Site: www.mtc.ca.gov. *Head Librn,* Julie Tunnell; E-mail: jtunnell@mtc.ca.gov; Staff 3 (MLS 2, Non-MLS 1)
Founded 1972
Library Holdings: Bk Vols 25,000; Per Subs 1,000
Special Collections: Environmental Impact Reports; San Francisco Bay Region Planning & Transportation History
Subject Interests: Census, City planning, Regional planning, Transportation
Wireless access
Partic in OCLC Online Computer Library Center, Inc
Open Mon-Fri 8:30-5

C MILLS COLLEGE*, F W Olin Library, 5000 MacArthur Blvd, 94613. SAN 333-3159. Tel: 510-430-2385. Circulation Tel: 510-430-2196. FAX: 510-430-2278. Web Site: www.mills.edu. *Ref,* Michael Beller; Tel: 510-430-2051, E-mail: mbeller@mills.edu; *Ser,* Stella Tang; Tel: 510-430-2382, E-mail: stellat@mills.edu; *Spec Coll & Archives Librn,* Janice Braun; Tel: 510-430-2047, E-mail: jbraun@mills.edu; *Tech Serv,* John Winsor; Tel: 510-430-2466, E-mail: jwinsor@mills.edu; Staff 14 (MLS 7, Non-MLS 7)
Founded 1852. Enrl 1,256; Fac 155; Highest Degree: Doctorate
Library Holdings: Bk Titles 183,674; Bk Vols 224,059; Per Subs 920
Special Collections: 19th & 20th Century English & American Dance (Jane Bourne Parton Coll); Fine Press Books; Music (Darius Milhaud Archive); Rare Americana
Subject Interests: Art, Bk arts, Dance, Lit, Shakespeare
Automation Activity & Vendor Info: (Acquisitions) Innovative Interfaces, Inc; (Cataloging) Innovative Interfaces, Inc; (Circulation) Innovative Interfaces, Inc; (Course Reserve) Innovative Interfaces, Inc; (ILL) Innovative Interfaces, Inc; (Media Booking) Innovative Interfaces, Inc; (OPAC) Innovative Interfaces, Inc; (Serials) Innovative Interfaces, Inc
Database Vendor: EBSCOhost, Gale Cengage Learning, Innovative Interfaces, Inc, JSTOR, LexisNexis, OCLC FirstSearch, ProQuest, Wilson - Wilson Web
Wireless access
Function: Res libr
Publications: Literary & Cultural Journeys: Selected Letters to Arturo Torres-Rioseco; Salon at Larkmead; The Flying Cloud & Her First Passengers
Partic in Statewide California Electronic Library Consortium (SCELC)
Open Mon-Thurs 8:30am-Midnight, Fri 8:30-6, Sat Noon-6, Sun Noon-11

P OAKLAND PUBLIC LIBRARY*, 125 14th St, 94612. SAN 333-3213. Tel: 510-238-3282. Circulation Tel: 510-238-3144. Reference Tel: 510-238-3136, 510-238-3138. Administration Tel: 510-238-3281. Automation Services Tel: 510-238-6719. Information Services Tel: 510-238-3134. FAX: 510-238-2232. Automation Services FAX: 510-238-6722. TDD: 510-834-7446. Web Site: www.oaklandlibrary.org. *Dep Dir, Interim Dir,* Gerard G Garzon; Tel: 510-238-6720, E-mail: gggarzon@oaklandnet.com; *Dir,* Position Currently Open; *Chief Financial Officer,* Gene Tom; Tel: 510-238-6609, Fax: 510-238-6866, E-mail: gtom@oaklandnet.com; *Supv Librn, Commun Relations,* Kathleen Hirooka; Tel: 510-238-6713, Fax: 510-238-4923, E-mail: khirooka@oaklandlibrary.org; *Mgr, Purchasing,* Nora Haron; Tel: 510-238-6572, E-mail: nharon@oaklandlibrary.org; *Mgr, Grants & Develop,* Leslie Rodd; Tel: 510-238-6932, E-mail: lrodd@oaklandlibrary.org; *Human Res Mgr,* Crystal Ramie; Tel: 510-238-6716, E-mail: cramie@oaklandlibrary.com; *Mgr, Policy & Strategic Planning,* Julie Odofin; Tel: 510-238-6610, E-mail: jodofin@oaklandnet.com; *Br Coordr,* Marjorie Li; Tel: 510-238-3670, E-mail: mli@oaklandlibrary.org; *Br Coordr,* Gracie Woodard; Tel: 510-238-3479, E-mail: gwoodard@oaklandlibrary.org; *Acq,* Kathleen DiGiovanni; Tel: 510-238-4704, E-mail: kdigiovanni@oaklandlibrary.org; *Cat,* Jiao Han; Tel: 510-238-2217, Fax: 510-238-6722, E-mail: jhan@oaklandlibrary.org; *Chief Curator,* Rick Moss; Tel: 510-637-0197, Fax: 510-637-0204, E-mail: rmoss@oaklandlibrary.org; *Ch Serv,* Nina Lindsay; E-mail: nlindsay@oaklandlibrary.org; *Ref Serv,* Douglas Smith; Tel: 510-238-6611, E-mail: dsmith@oaklandlibrary.org; *Tech Serv & Automation,* Daniel Hersh; Tel: 510-238-3270, E-mail: dhersh@oaklandlibrary.org; Staff 79.61 (MLS 79.61)
Founded 1878. Pop 431,291; Circ 2,317,505
Jul 2005-Jun 2006 Income (Main Library and Branch(s)) $23,325,985, State $302,698, City $22,575,554, Other $447,733. Mats Exp $1,996,558, Books $1,270,521, Per/Ser (Incl. Access Fees) $236,694, Micro $31,150, AV Mat $252,193, Electronic Ref Mat (Incl. Access Fees) $206,000. Sal $10,792,812
Library Holdings: AV Mats 76,021; e-books 7,457; Electronic Media & Resources 37; Large Print Bks 4,881; Music Scores 27,000; Bk Titles 526,574; Bk Vols 1,148,809; Per Subs 3,359; Videos 38,581
Special Collections: African-American Museum & Library (Archival Coll); Asian Coll; Local History Coll; Oakland History Room; Tool Lending Library; USGS Topographical Maps. State Document Depository; US Document Depository
Subject Interests: Art, Asia, Bus, Local hist, Music
Automation Activity & Vendor Info: (Acquisitions) Innovative Interfaces, Inc; (Cataloging) Innovative Interfaces, Inc; (Circulation) Innovative Interfaces, Inc; (ILL) Innovative Interfaces, Inc; (OPAC) Innovative Interfaces, Inc
Database Vendor: Baker & Taylor, BWI, Gale Cengage Learning, Newsbank, OCLC FirstSearch, OCLC WorldShare Interlibrary Loan, PubMed
Function: Adult literacy prog, Archival coll, AV serv, CD-ROM, E-Reserves, Electronic databases & coll, Family literacy, Govt ref serv, Handicapped accessible, ILL available, Magnifiers for reading, Newsp ref libr, Online searches, Photocopying/Printing, Prog for adults, Prog for children & young adult, Ref serv available, Summer reading prog, Tax forms, Wheelchair accessible
Publications: Annual Reports; Calendar of Events; Staff Newsletter
Mem of Bay Area Library & Information System
Special Services for the Deaf - Assistive tech; Bks on deafness & sign lang; TTY equip

Special Services for the Blind - ABE/GED & braille classes for the visually impaired & print handicapped; Aids for in-house use; Assistive/Adapted tech devices, equip & products; Audio mat; Computer with voice synthesizer for visually impaired persons; Reader equip
Open Mon, Tues & Sat 10-5:30, Wed & Thurs 12-8:30, Fri 12-5:30, Sun 1-5
Friends of the Library Group
Branches: 16
ASIAN, 388 Ninth St, Ste 190, 94612, SAN 333-3248. Tel: 510-238-3400. FAX: 510-238-4732. *Actg Br Mgr,* Steve Lavoie; E-mail: slavoie@oaklandlibrary.org; Staff 3.4 (MLS 3.4)
Founded 1975. Pop 12,200; Circ 335,797
Library Holdings: Bk Vols 75,334
Special Collections: Asian American Coll, English; Asian Materials in Asian Languages (Chinese, Japanese, Korean, Vietnamese, Thai, Cambodian, Tagalog & Laotian) gen subj titles, major ref titles; Asian Studies Coll
Friends of the Library Group
BROOKFIELD, 9255 Edes Ave, 94603, SAN 333-3272. Tel: 510-615-5725. FAX: 510-615-5862. *Br Mgr,* Cynthia Hegedus; E-mail: chegedus@oaklandlibrary.org; Staff 2 (MLS 2)
Founded 1992. Pop 11,347; Circ 27,494
Library Holdings: Bk Vols 34,534
Function: Computers for patron use, Copy machines, Digital talking bks, E-Reserves, Electronic databases & coll, Free DVD rentals, Handicapped accessible, Music CDs, Online cat, Online searches, OverDrive digital audio bks, Photocopying/Printing, Preschool outreach, Prog for adults, Prog for children & young adult, Pub access computers, Ref serv available, Ref serv in person, Spanish lang bks, Story hour, Summer reading prog, Tax forms, Teen prog, Telephone ref, VHS videos, Wheelchair accessible
Restriction: 24-hr pass syst for students only
Friends of the Library Group
CESAR E CHAVEZ BRANCH, 3301 E 12th St, Ste 271, 94601, SAN 333-3515. Tel: 510-535-5620. FAX: 510-535-5622. *Br Mgr,* Jane Lopez; E-mail: jlopez@oaklandlibrary.org; Staff 3 (MLS 3)
Founded 1966. Pop 32,889; Circ 108,874
Library Holdings: Bk Vols 49,668
Special Collections: Spanish Language Coll
Friends of the Library Group
DIMOND, 3565 Fruitvale Ave, 94602, SAN 333-3302. Tel: 510-482-7844. FAX: 510-482-7824. *Br Mgr,* Sarah Hodgson; E-mail: shodgson@oaklandlibrary.org; Staff 5 (MLS 5)
Founded 1915. Pop 45,319; Circ 221,079
Library Holdings: Bk Vols 75,532
Special Collections: American Indian Coll
Function: Adult literacy prog, Prog for adults, Prog for children & young adult, Summer reading prog
Friends of the Library Group
EASTMONT, Eastmont Town Ctr, Ste 211, 7200 Bancroft Ave, 94605, SAN 333-3337. Tel: 510-615-5726. FAX: 510-615-5863. *Actg Br Mgr,* Veronica Lee; E-mail: vlee@oaklandlibrary.org; Staff 2 (MLS 2)
Founded 1945. Pop 31,716; Circ 35,375
Library Holdings: Bk Vols 41,786
Friends of the Library Group
ELMHURST, 1427 88th Ave, 94621, SAN 333-3361. Tel: 510-615-5727. FAX: 510-615-5869. *Br Mgr,* Anna Pavon; E-mail: apavon@oaklandlibrary.org; Staff 2 (MLS 2)
Founded 1911. Pop 31,811; Circ 26,643
Library Holdings: Bk Vols 29,063
Open Tues 11:30-7, Wed, Thurs & Sat 10-5:30, Fri 12-5:30
GOLDEN GATE, 5606 San Pablo Ave, 94608, SAN 333-3426. Tel: 510-597-5023. FAX: 510-597-5030. *Br Mgr,* Sandra Toscano; E-mail: stoscano@oaklandlibrary.org; Staff 2 (MLS 2)
Pop 22,866; Circ 49,071
Library Holdings: Bk Vols 32,978
Special Collections: Materials in Hindi & Punjabi (East Indian Coll)
Function: Adult bk club, Chess club, Homework prog, Jazz prog, Prog for adults, Prog for children & young adult, Summer reading prog
Open Tues 12:30-8, Wed, Thurs & Sat 10-5:30, Fri 12-5:30
Friends of the Library Group
MARTIN LUTHER KING BRANCH, 6833 International Blvd, 94621, SAN 333-3450. Tel: 510-615-5728. FAX: 510-615-5739. *Br Mgr,* Ajoke Kokodoko; E-mail: akokodoko@oaklandlibrary.org; Staff 2 (MLS 2)
Founded 1916. Pop 20,188; Circ 23,308
Library Holdings: Bk Vols 29,123
LAKEVIEW, 550 El Embarcadero, 94610, SAN 333-3485. Tel: 510-238-7344. FAX: 510-238-6760. *Br Mgr,* Mary Farrell; E-mail: mfarrell@oaklandlibrary.org; Staff 2 (MLS 2)
Founded 1949. Pop 39,768; Circ 110,651
Library Holdings: Bk Vols 40,966
Function: Prog for adults, Prog for children & young adult, Summer reading prog
MAIN LIBRARY, 125 14th St, 94612, SAN 333-3221. Tel: 510-238-3134. FAX: 510-238-2232. TDD: 510-834-7446. *Dir, Libr Serv,* Gerry Garzon; E-mail: gggarzon@oaklandlibrary.org; *Assoc Dir,* Jamie Turbak; E-mail: jturbak@oaklandlibrary.org; *Supv Librn,* Daniel Hersh; *Supv Librn,* Nina Lindsay; *Supv Librn,* Jane Lopez; *Supv Librn,* Mary Schrader; E-mail: mschrader@oaklandlibrary.org; *Chief Curator, African Am Mus & Libr,* Rick Moss; *Chief Financial Officer,* Gene Tom; *Human Res Mgr,* Crystal Ramie; *Mgr, Grants & Develop,* Winifred Walters; Staff 20.7 (MLS 20.7)
Founded 1878. Pop 432,291; Circ 588,835
Library Holdings: Bk Vols 355,257
Function: Archival coll, ILL available, Newsp ref libr, Photocopying/Printing, Prog for adults, Prog for children & young adult, Ref serv available, Summer reading prog, VHS videos
Special Services for the Deaf - Assistive tech; Closed caption videos; TTY equip
Special Services for the Blind - Descriptive video serv (DVS); Reader equip; ZoomText magnification & reading software
Open Mon, Tues & Sat 10-5:30, Wed & Thurs 12-8, Fri 12-5:30, Sun 1-5
MELROSE, 4805 Foothill Blvd, 94601, SAN 333-3574. Tel: 510-535-5623. Interlibrary Loan Service FAX: 510-535-5641. *Br Mgr,* Sandra Toscano; E-mail: stoscano@oaklandlibrary.org; Staff 2 (MLS 2)
Founded 1916. Pop 39,822; Circ 34,704
Library Holdings: Bk Vols 31,951
Friends of the Library Group
MONTCLAIR, 1687 Mountain Blvd, 94611, SAN 333-3604. Tel: 510-482-7810. FAX: 510-482-7865. *Br Mgr,* Lynne Cutler; E-mail: lcutler@oaklandlibrary.org; Staff 2 (MLS 2)
Founded 1930. Pop 21,112; Circ 159,148
Library Holdings: Bk Vols 47,840
PIEDMONT AVENUE, 160 41st St, 94611, SAN 333-3663. Tel: 510-597-5011. FAX: 510-597-5078. *Br Mgr,* Jamie Turbak; E-mail: jturbak@oaklandlibrary.org; Staff 2 (MLS 2)
Founded 1912. Pop 19,174; Circ 182,599
Library Holdings: Bk Vols 39,930
Friends of the Library Group
ROCKRIDGE, 5366 College Ave, 94618, SAN 333-3698. Tel: 510-597-5017. FAX: 510-597-5067. *Br Mgr,* Patricia Lichter; E-mail: plichter@oaklandlibrary.org; Staff 4 (MLS 4)
Founded 1919. Pop 9,026; Circ 261,723
Library Holdings: Bk Vols 84,218
Friends of the Library Group
TEMESCAL, 5205 Telegraph Ave, 94609, SAN 333-3728. Tel: 510-597-5049. FAX: 510-597-5062. *Br Mgr,* Steve Lavoie; E-mail: slavoie@oaklandlibrary.org; Staff 2 (MLS 2)
Founded 1918. Pop 17,657; Circ 58,107
Library Holdings: Bk Vols 29,000
Special Collections: Amharic & Tigrinya Language Coll; Tool Lending Library, bks, tools, videos
Open Tues 12:30-8, Wed, Thurs & Sat 10-5:30, Fri 12-5:30
Friends of the Library Group
WEST OAKLAND, 1801 Adeline St, 94607, SAN 333-3752. Tel: 510-238-7352. FAX: 510-238-7551. *Br Mgr,* Christine Saed; E-mail: csaed@oaklandlibrary.org; Staff 2 (MLS 2)
Founded 1878. Circ 27,106
Library Holdings: Bk Vols 51,519
Bookmobiles: 1. Sr Librn, Christine Saed. Bk titles 2,500

S PACIFIC INSTITUTE FOR RESEARCH & EVALUATION*, Prevention Research Center Library, 180 Grand Ave, Ste 1200, 94612. SAN 374-8553. Tel: 510-486-1111, 510-883-5746. FAX: 510-644-0594. Web Site: www.prev.org. *Mgr, Info Serv, Mgr, Libr Serv,* Julie Murphy; E-mail: jmurphy@prev.org; Staff 1 (MLS 1)
Founded 1984
Library Holdings: Bk Titles 3,500; Per Subs 28
Subject Interests: Alcohol, drug & tobacco prevention
Open Mon-Fri 9-5:30
Restriction: Staff use only

C PATTEN UNIVERSITY, Patten Learning Commons, 2433 Coolidge Ave, 94601. SAN 301-133X. Tel: 510-485-7830. E-mail: librarian@patten.edu. Web Site: www.patten.edu. *Dir,* Lisa Hubbell; Tel: 510-261-8500, Ext 7830, E-mail: lhubbell@patten.edu; Staff 1 (MLS 1)
Founded 1960. Enrl 465; Fac 34; Highest Degree: Master
Library Holdings: AV Mats 670; Bks on Deafness & Sign Lang 15; Bk Titles 36,886; Per Subs 120
Special Collections: Business Management in Chinese
Subject Interests: Biblical studies, Educ, Judaica, Music
Partic in Statewide California Electronic Library Consortium (SCELC)
Open Mon-Fri 9-5
Restriction: Not open to pub

L REED SMITH LLP*, Law Library, 1999 Harrison St, 94612. SAN 301-1232. Tel: 510-466-6195. Interlibrary Loan Service Tel: 510-466-6192. Reference Tel: 510-466-6194. FAX: 510-273-8832. Web Site:

www.reedsmith.com. *Head Ref Librn,* D Cunningham; E-mail: dcunningham@reedsmith.com; Staff 6 (MLS 3, Non-MLS 3)
Founded 1967
Library Holdings: Bk Vols 12,000; Per Subs 300
Automation Activity & Vendor Info: (Acquisitions) SirsiDynix; (Serials) SirsiDynix
Database Vendor: Dialog, LexisNexis, Westlaw
Open Mon-Fri 9-5
Branches:
LAW LIBRARY, 355 S Grand Ave, Ste 2900, Los Angeles, 90017, SAN 370-7571. Tel: 213-457-8000. FAX: 213-457-8080. *Librn,* Ralph Prado; Staff 2 (MLS 1, Non-MLS 1)
Library Holdings: Bk Titles 200; Bk Vols 5,000; Per Subs 24
Open Mon-Fri 8-5

CM SAMUEL MERRITT COLLEGE*, John A Graziano Memorial Library, 400 Hawthorne Ave, 94609. SAN 301-1313. Tel: 510-869-8900. FAX: 510-869-6633. Web Site: www.samuelmerritt.edu. *Dir,* Barbara Ryken; Tel: 510-869-8692, E-mail: bryken@samuelmerritt.edu; *Access Serv,* Huyen Ho; Tel: 510-869-8694, E-mail: hho@samuelmerritt.edu; *Ref Serv,* Kristi Wessenberg; Tel: 510-869-6833, E-mail: kwessenberg@samuelmerritt.edu; *Tech Serv,* Ann Barnard; Tel: 510-869-8693, E-mail: abarnard@samuelmerritt.edu; Staff 2 (MLS 2)
Founded 1909. Enrl 600; Fac 102; Highest Degree: Doctorate
Library Holdings: Bk Vols 15,548; Per Subs 437
Subject Interests: Health sci, Nursing, Occupational therapy, Phys therapy, Podiatric med
Automation Activity & Vendor Info: (Acquisitions) SirsiDynix; (Cataloging) SirsiDynix; (Circulation) SirsiDynix; (Course Reserve) SirsiDynix; (OPAC) SirsiDynix; (Serials) SirsiDynix
Database Vendor: OVID Technologies, ProQuest
Partic in Docline; National Network of Libraries of Medicine South Central Region; Northern & Central California Psychology Libraries; Northern California & Nevada Medical Library Group (NCNMLG); Pacific Southwest Regional Medical Library (PSRML)
Open Mon-Thurs 8am-9pm, Fri 8-5, Sat 12-4, Sun 12-9
Restriction: Non-circulating to the pub

CL UNIVERSITY OF CALIFORNIA*, Continuing Education of the Bar Library, 300 Frank H Ogawa Plaza, Ste 410, 94612. SAN 300-6204. Tel: 510-302-2000. FAX: 510-302-2001. *Dir,* Pamela J Jester; Staff 1 (MLS 1)
Founded 1960

GL BERNARD E WITKIN ALAMEDA COUNTY LAW LIBRARY*, 12th & Oak St Bldg, 125 Twelfth St, 94607-4912. SAN 301-1143. Tel: 510-208-4800. Circulation Tel: 510-208-4835. Reference Tel: 510-208-4832. Administration Tel: 510-272-6483. FAX: 510-208-4823. E-mail: lawlib@acgov.org. Web Site: www.acgov.org/law. *Dir,* Mark E Estes; Tel: 510-272-6481; *Pub Serv Librn,* Patricia Monk; Tel: 510-272-6484, E-mail: patricia.monk@acgov.org; *Ref Librn,* Emily Bergfeld; Tel: 510-272-6486, E-mail: emily.bergfeld@acgov.org; *Ref Serv,* Claudia Cook; Tel: 510-208-4830, E-mail: claudia.cook@acgov.org; Staff 13 (MLS 5, Non-MLS 8)
Founded 1891. Pop 1,454,300
Library Holdings: AV Mats 524; CDs 95; DVDs 4; Electronic Media & Resources 351; Microforms 551,872; Bk Titles 13,177; Bk Vols 74,637; Per Subs 1,898; Videos 38
Special Collections: Alameda County Ordinance Code, Administrative Code, Budgets & Other Special Publications; California Supreme Court & Appellate Briefs, microfiche; Federal & State Statutes, Indexes & Digests; Legal Periodical Coll, California & US Law Schools; Legal Practice Material, California & Federal; Local Municipal Codes. Municipal Document Depository; State Document Depository; US Document Depository
Automation Activity & Vendor Info: (Acquisitions) SydneyPlus; (Cataloging) SydneyPlus; (Circulation) SydneyPlus; (OPAC) SydneyPlus
Database Vendor: EBSCOhost, HeinOnline, LexisNexis, OCLC, OCLC WorldShare Interlibrary Loan, Westlaw
Wireless access
Function: Audio & video playback equip for onsite use, CD-ROM, Computers for patron use, Copy machines, Doc delivery serv, Electronic databases & coll, Handicapped accessible, ILL available, Magnifiers for reading, Online searches, Photocopying/Printing, Printer for laptops & handheld devices, Pub access computers, Ref & res, Ref serv available, Scanner, Spoken cassettes & CDs, Telephone ref, Web-catalog, Wheelchair accessible
Publications: ACLL (Newsletter); MCLE Titles (Acquisition list); Recent Acquisitions List
Partic in Califa; Law Library Microform Consortium (LLMC); OCLC Online Computer Library Center, Inc
Open Mon, Wed & Fri 8:30-6, Tues & Thurs 8:30am-9pm

Departmental Libraries:
SOUTH COUNTY BRANCH, 224 W Winton Ave, Rm 162, Hayward, 94544, SAN 300-810X. Tel: 510-670-5230. FAX: 510-670-5292. *Dir,* Mark E Estes; E-mail: mark.estes@acgov.org; Staff 1 (MLS 1)
Founded 1967
Library Holdings: Electronic Media & Resources 4; Bk Titles 1,819; Bk Vols 30,292
Special Collections: Local Municipal Codes & City Ordinances. Municipal Document Depository
Subject Interests: Legal res
Automation Activity & Vendor Info: (Serials) SydneyPlus
Function: Res libr
Open Mon-Fri 8:30-5

OCEANSIDE

J MIRACOSTA COLLEGE LIBRARY*, Oceanside Campus, One Barnard Dr, 92056-3899. SAN 301-1372. Circulation Tel: 760-795-6715. Reference Tel: 760-795-6716. FAX: 760-795-6723. Web Site: www.miracosta.edu/library. *Dean,* Mario Valente; Tel: 760-795-6720, E-mail: mvalente@miracosta.edu; *Chair,* Myla Stokes Kelly; Tel: 760-634-7836, E-mail: mkelly@miracosta.edu; *Coll Develop Librn, Tech Serv,* Glorian Sipman; Tel: 760-795-6722, E-mail: gsipman@miracosta.edu; *Online Serv Librn,* Pamela Perry; Tel: 760-795-6719, E-mail: pperry@miracosta.edu; *Electronic Res,* Jennifer Paris; Tel: 760-634-7814, E-mail: jparis@miracosta.edu; Staff 12 (MLS 6, Non-MLS 6)
Founded 1934. Enrl 10,840; Fac 875; Highest Degree: Associate
Library Holdings: AV Mats 7,186; e-books 16,508; Bk Titles 61,292; Bk Vols 72,743; Per Subs 214
Automation Activity & Vendor Info: (Cataloging) SirsiDynix; (Circulation) SirsiDynix; (Course Reserve) SirsiDynix; (ILL) OCLC; (OPAC) SirsiDynix; (Serials) SirsiDynix
Database Vendor: Alexander Street Press, ARTstor, Gale Cengage Learning, JSTOR, OVID Technologies, ProQuest
Wireless access
Function: AV serv, Distance learning, For res purposes, Handicapped accessible, ILL available, Photocopying/Printing, Ref serv available, Telephone ref, Wheelchair accessible
Publications: Citation Guides (Reference guide)
Partic in N County Higher Educ Alliance; OCLC Online Computer Library Center, Inc
Special Services for the Deaf - Closed caption videos
Special Services for the Blind - Braille bks; Computer with voice synthesizer for visually impaired persons
Open Mon-Thurs 8am-9:30pm, Fri 8-3, Sat 10-5
Friends of the Library Group
Departmental Libraries:
SAN ELIJO CAMPUS, 3333 Manchester Ave, Cardiff, 92007-1516. Circulation Tel: 760-634-7850. Reference Tel: 760-634-7864. FAX: 760-634-7890. *Librn,* Myla Stokes Kelly; Tel: 760-634-7836, E-mail: mkelly@miracosta.edu
Open Mon-Thurs 8am-9:30pm, Fri 8-3, Sat 10-5

P OCEANSIDE PUBLIC LIBRARY, 330 N Coast Hwy, 92054-2824. SAN 301-1380. Tel: 760-435-5600. FAX: 760-435-9614. E-mail: public.library@ci.oceanside.ca.us. Web Site: www.oceansidepubliclibrary.org. *Dir,* Sherri Cosby; Tel: 760-435-5609, E-mail: scosby@ci.oceanside.ca.us; *Libr Div Mgr/Pub Serv,* Bradley Penner; Tel: 760-435-5575, E-mail: bpenner@ci.oceanside.ca.us; *Mgr, Ad Serv,* Monica Chapa-Domercq; Tel: 760-435-5586, E-mail: mcdomercq@ci.oceanside.ca.us; *Commun Outreach Coordr,* Kristine Moralez; Tel: 760-435-5571, E-mail: kmoralez@ci.oceanside.ca.us; *Tech Analyst,* Samuel Liston; Tel: 760-435-5628, E-mail: sliston@ci.oceanside.ca.us; *Youth Serv,* Marie Town; Tel: 760-435-5597, E-mail: mtown@ci.oceanside.ca.us; *Br Mgr,* CJ Di Mento; Tel: 760-435-5614, E-mail: cdimento@ci.oceanside.ca.us. Subject Specialists: *Concert ser,* Kristine Moralez; Staff 21.4 (MLS 15, Non-MLS 6.4)
Founded 1904. Pop 179,681; Circ 553,323
Jul 2009-Jun 2010 Income (Main Library and Branch(s)) $6,312,980, State $19,273, City $6,227,270, Locally Generated Income $66,437. Mats Exp $355,144, Books $221,853, Per/Ser (Incl. Access Fees) $24,619, Other Print Mats $14,000, AV Mat $58,300, Electronic Ref Mat (Incl. Access Fees) $36,372. Sal $3,361,400
Library Holdings: Audiobooks 2,991; CDs 7,348; DVDs 9,265; e-books 3,500; Microforms 3,815; Bk Titles 189,929; Bk Vols 255,115; Per Subs 493; Videos 4,628
Special Collections: Caldecott-Newberry Memorial Coll; Martin Luther King Jr Coll; Parents Resource Coll; Samoan Culture Coll; Teachers Resource Center
Subject Interests: Bus & mgt, Children's lit, Employment, Parent
Automation Activity & Vendor Info: (Acquisitions) SirsiDynix; (Cataloging) SirsiDynix; (Circulation) SirsiDynix; (ILL) SirsiDynix; (OPAC) SirsiDynix; (Serials) SirsiDynix
Database Vendor: Gale Cengage Learning, OCLC FirstSearch, ProQuest, Wilson - Wilson Web

Wireless access
Partic in Serra Cooperative Library System
Friends of the Library Group
Branches: 2
MISSION BRANCH, 3861 B Mission Ave, 92058, SAN 370-3819. Tel: 760-435-5600. FAX: 760-433-6850. *Sr Librn,* CJ Di Mento; Tel: 760-435-5614, E-mail: cdimento@ci.oceanside.ca.us; *Librn I,* Elizabeth Aaron; Tel: 760-435-5595, E-mail: eaaron@ci.oceanside.ca.us; *Circ Supvr,* Israel Vazquez; Tel: 760-435-5593, E-mail: ivazquez@ci.oceanside.ca.us; Staff 2 (MLS 2)
Open Mon-Wed 10-7, Thurs & Fri 10-6, Sat 12-5, Sun 1-5
OCEANSIDE READS LEARNING CENTER, 321 N Nevada St, 92054-2811, SAN 378-1240. Tel: 760-435-5680. FAX: 760-435-5681. *Literacy Coordr,* Corrie Miles; Tel: 760-435-5682, E-mail: cmiles@ci.oceanside.ca.us; Staff 2 (Non-MLS 2)
Bookmobiles: 2

OJAI

S KRISHNAMURTI FOUNDATION OF AMERICA LIBRARY*, Educational Center Library, 1098 McAndrew Rd, 93023. (Mail add: PO Box 1560, 93024), SAN 374-4817. Tel: 805-646-4948. Web Site: www.kfa.org/library.htm. *Librn,* Michael Krohnen
Founded 1984
Library Holdings: Bk Vols 2,000
Special Collections: J Krishnamurti, bks & teachings
Open Thurs & Fri 1-5, Sun 10-5

SR KROTONA INSTITUTE OF THEOSOPHY LIBRARY, Two Krotona Hill, 93023-3901. SAN 301-1399. Tel: 805-646-2653. E-mail: library@krotonainstitute.org. *Head of Libr,* Lakshmi Narayan
Founded 1926
Library Holdings: DVDs 250; Bk Titles 15,000; Videos 200
Subject Interests: Astrology, Eastern philosophy, Philos, Psychol, Relig, Theosophy
Wireless access
Open Tues-Fri 10-5, Sat & Sun 1-5

ONTARIO

P ONTARIO CITY LIBRARY*, Ovitt Family Community Library, 215 East C St, 91764-4111. SAN 301-1429. Tel: 909-395-2004. Circulation Tel: 909-395-2521. Reference Tel: 909-395-2205. FAX: 909-395-2043. Web Site: www.ci.ontario.ca.us/index.aspx?page=386. *Libr Dir,* Helen Fisher; Staff 71 (MLS 13, Non-MLS 58)
Founded 1885. Pop 173,690
Jul 2007-Jun 2008 Income (Main Library and Branch(s)) $3,216,553, State $134,215, City $2,942,359, Other $139,979. Mats Exp $763,279, Books $243,179, Per/Ser (Incl. Access Fees) $380,000, Micro $3,500, AV Mat $70,600, Electronic Ref Mat (Incl. Access Fees) $65,000, Presv $1,000. Sal $2,164,330
Library Holdings: AV Mats 28,658; CDs 16,378; DVDs 8,552; Bk Titles 145,245; Bk Vols 208,912; Per Subs 686; Videos 10,902
Special Collections: Oral History; State Document Depository; US Document Depository
Subject Interests: Local hist
Automation Activity & Vendor Info: (Acquisitions) SirsiDynix; (Cataloging) SirsiDynix; (Circulation) SirsiDynix; (OPAC) SirsiDynix; (Serials) SirsiDynix
Wireless access
Function: Accelerated reader prog, Adult bk club, Adult literacy prog, After school storytime, Archival coll, AV serv, BA reader (adult literacy), Bk club(s), Bks on cassette, Bks on CD, CD-ROM, Children's prog, Computer training, Computers for patron use, Copy machines, E-Reserves, Electronic databases & coll, Family literacy, Fax serv, Free DVD rentals, Govt ref serv, Handicapped accessible, Holiday prog, Home delivery & serv to Sr ctr & nursing homes, Homebound delivery serv, Homework prog, ILL available, Learning ctr, Literacy & newcomer serv, Mail & tel request accepted, Newsp ref libr, Online cat, Online ref, Online searches, Outreach serv, Photocopying/Printing, Preschool outreach, Prog for adults, Prog for children & young adult, Pub access computers, Ref & res, Ref serv available, Senior computer classes, Spoken cassettes & CDs, Spoken cassettes & DVDs, Story hour, Summer reading prog, Tax forms, Telephone ref, VHS videos, Video lending libr, Web-catalog
Mem of Inland Library System
Open Mon-Thurs 10-9, Fri & Sat 10-6, Sun 1-4
Friends of the Library Group
Branches: 1
COLONY HIGH, 3850 E Riverside Dr, 91761-1623. Tel: 909-395-2014. FAX: 909-930-0836. *Br Mgr,* Heather Withrow; E-mail: hwithrow@ci.ontario.ca.us; Staff 13 (MLS 2, Non-MLS 11)
Library Holdings: AV Mats 5,200; CDs 1,500; DVDs 1,000; Bk Titles 54,085; Bk Vols 55,849; Per Subs 57; Videos 875
Open Mon-Wed 12-8, Thurs-Sat 10-6

CL UNIVERSITY OF LA VERNE*, College of Law Library, 320 E D St, 91764. SAN 329-6679. Tel: 909-460-2070. FAX: 909-460-2083. Web Site: lawlibrary.laverne.edu. *Dir,* Kenneth Rudolf; Tel: 909-460-2065, E-mail: krudolf@laverne.edu; *Head, Coll Mgt,* Darlene Gaetano; Tel: 909-460-2064, E-mail: dgaetano@laverne.edu; *Head, Instruction & Res,* Teresa Conaway; Tel: 909-460-2067, E-mail: tconaway@laverne.edu; *Ref Serv,* Bill Ketchum; Tel: 909-460-2063, E-mail: wketchum@laverne.edu; *Ref Serv,* Young Lee; Tel: 909-460-2062, E-mail: ylee@laverne.edu; Staff 5 (MLS 5)
Founded 1970. Enrl 350; Fac 20; Highest Degree: Doctorate
Library Holdings: Microforms 217,000; Bk Titles 28,000; Bk Vols 80,000; Per Subs 475; Videos 75
Special Collections: State Document Depository; US Document Depository
Automation Activity & Vendor Info: (Acquisitions) Innovative Interfaces, Inc - Millenium; (Cataloging) Innovative Interfaces, Inc; (Circulation) Innovative Interfaces, Inc - Millenium; (ILL) OCLC; (OPAC) Innovative Interfaces, Inc - Millenium; (Serials) Innovative Interfaces, Inc - Millenium
Database Vendor: Fastcase, Gale Cengage Learning, HeinOnline, LexisNexis, Oxford Online, ProQuest, Westlaw, Wilson - Wilson Web
Wireless access
Partic in Inland Empire Acad Libr Coop (IEALC); OCLC Online Computer Library Center, Inc
Open Mon-Thurs 8am-11pm, Fri 8am-9pm, Sat 9-9, Sun 12-9
Restriction: Prof mat only

ORANGE

C CHAPMAN UNIVERSITY, Leatherby Libraries, One University Dr, 92866-1099. SAN 301-1437. Tel: 714-532-7756. Circulation Tel: 714-532-7723. Interlibrary Loan Service Tel: 714-532-7717. Reference Tel: 714-532-7714. FAX: 714-532-7743. E-mail: libweb@chapman.edu. Web Site: www.chapman.edu/library. *Dean, Leatherby Libr,* Charlene Baldwin; E-mail: baldwin@chapman.edu; *Assoc Dean,* Kevin Ross; *Chair, Coll Mgt,* Julie Artman; E-mail: artman@chapman.edu; *Chair, Libr Syst & Tech,* Brett Fisher; E-mail: bfisher@chapman.edu; *Chair, Pub Serv,* Carolyn Radcliff; E-mail: cradclif@chapman.edu; *Head, Acq,* Theresa Paulsrud; *Head, Circ,* Eddie Sauceda; E-mail: sauceda@chapman.edu; *Head, Ser,* Andrew Valbuena; E-mail: valbuen@chapman.edu; *Archives Librn, Spec Coll Librn,* Randolph Boyd; *Cat Librn,* Nancy Gonzalez; *Coordr, Brandman Univ Libr Serv,* Lugene Rosen; E-mail: lrosen@chapman.edu; *Coordr, Cat & Gifts,* Shahrzad Khasrowpour; E-mail: shahrza@chapman.edu; *Coordr, Scholarly Communications & Electronic Res,* Kristin Laughtin-Dunker; E-mail: laughtin@chapman.edu; *Coordr, ILL,* Jessica Bower; E-mail: jbower@chapman.edu; *Coordr, Spec Coll & Archives,* Rand Boyd; E-mail: rboyd@chapman.edu; *Libr Develop Coordr,* Essraa Nawar; E-mail: nawar@chapman.edu
Founded 1923. Enrl 13,216; Fac 857; Highest Degree: Doctorate
Library Holdings: Audiobooks 25,594; CDs 3,212; DVDs 6,912; e-books 16,009; e-journals 62,782; Bk Vols 326,423; Per Subs 752
Special Collections: Center for American War Letters; Charles C Chapman Rare Book Coll; Disciple of Christ Church History; Huell Howser Archive
Subject Interests: Orange County hist
Automation Activity & Vendor Info: (Acquisitions) Innovative Interfaces, Inc; (Cataloging) Innovative Interfaces, Inc; (Circulation) Innovative Interfaces, Inc; (Course Reserve) Innovative Interfaces, Inc; (ILL) OCLC ILLiad; (OPAC) Innovative Interfaces, Inc; (Serials) Innovative Interfaces, Inc
Database Vendor: Alexander Street Press, ARTstor, Cinahl, CQ Press, EBSCO Discovery Service, EBSCOhost, Gale Cengage Learning, Innovative Interfaces, Inc, ISI Web of Knowledge, JSTOR, LexisNexis, Mergent Online, Oxford Online, ProQuest, PubMed, Sage, ScienceDirect, Thomson - Web of Science
Wireless access
Function: ILL available, Ref serv available
Partic in OCLC Online Computer Library Center, Inc; Statewide California Electronic Library Consortium (SCELC)
Open Mon-Fri 7-2 , Sat & Sun 10-2

CL CHAPMAN UNIVERSITY SCHOOL OF LAW*, Harry & Diane Rinker Law Library, 370 N Glassell St, Rm 325, 92866. SAN 378-438X. Tel: 714-628-2537. Circulation Tel: 714-628-2553. Reference Tel: 714-628-2548. Information Services Tel: 714-628-2595. Web Site: www.chapman.edu/law/student-resources/library/index.aspx. *Libr Dir,* Linda Kawaguchi; Tel: 714-628-2538, E-mail: kawaguch@chapman.edu; *Head, Info Serv,* Isa Lang; E-mail: ilang@chapman.edu; *Acq Librn,* Tracie Hall; Tel: 714-628-2539, E-mail: trhall@chapman.edu; *Cat Librn,* Tanya Cao; Tel: 714-628-2546, E-mail: cao@chapman.edu; *Librn,* Lorin Geitner; Tel: 714-628-0829, E-mail: loge@chapman.edu; *Librn,* Patricia Hart; Tel: 714-628-2544, E-mail: hart@chapman.edu; Staff 11 (MLS 5, Non-MLS 6)
Library Holdings: Bk Vols 300,000
Database Vendor: HeinOnline, LexisNexis, Westlaw
Open Mon-Thurs 8am-Midnight, Fri 8am-11pm, Sat 8am-10pm, Sun 10am-Midnight

J ITT TECHNICAL INSTITUTE*, Orange Campus Library, 4000 W Metropolitan Dr, Ste 100, 92868. Tel: 714-941-2400. FAX: 714-535-1802. Web Site: www.itt-tech.edu. *Libr Asst,* Mary Ann Coleville
Library Holdings: Bk Vols 2,000; Per Subs 12
Automation Activity & Vendor Info: (Cataloging) Follett Software; (Circulation) Follett Software; (OPAC) Follett Software
Database Vendor: EBSCOhost, ProQuest
Partic in Capital District Library Council
Open Mon-Fri 9-9, Sat 9-2

P ORANGE PUBLIC LIBRARY & HISTORY CENTER, 407 E Chapman Ave, 92866-1509. SAN 333-483X. Tel: 714-288-2400. Reference Tel: 714-288-2410. Administration Tel: 714-288-2471. FAX: 714-771-6126. Web Site: www.cityoforange.org/library. *Libr Dir,* Yolanda Moreno; E-mail: ymoreno@cityoforange.org; *Sr Librn, Children's & Br Serv,* Rosanne Miller; E-mail: rmiller@cityoforange.org; Staff 62 (MLS 14, Non-MLS 48)
Founded 1885. Pop 137,800; Circ 436,106
Jul 2005-Jun 2006. Mats Exp $266,300, Books $153,000, Per/Ser (Incl. Access Fees) $8,400, Micro $15,000, AV Mat $23,000, Electronic Ref Mat (Incl. Access Fees) $66,900. Sal $1,650,000
Library Holdings: AV Mats 24,500; Bk Vols 221,165; Per Subs 60
Special Collections: Local History Coll
Automation Activity & Vendor Info: (Acquisitions) SirsiDynix; (Cataloging) SirsiDynix; (Circulation) SirsiDynix; (OPAC) SirsiDynix
Database Vendor: EBSCOhost, Gale Cengage Learning, ProQuest
Wireless access
Function: Copy machines, E-Reserves, Electronic databases & coll, Handicapped accessible, Homebound delivery serv, ILL available, Online ref, Prog for children & young adult, Spoken cassettes & CDs, Summer reading prog, Tax forms
Partic in Southern California Library Cooperative
Open Mon-Wed 10-9, Thurs-Sat 10-6
Friends of the Library Group
Branches: 2
EL MODENA BRANCH, 380 S Hewes St, 92869, SAN 333-4864. Tel: 714-288-2450. FAX: 714-771-6126.
Founded 1978. Pop 138,792; Circ 646,807
Open Mon-Wed 2-7, Thurs-Sat 1-6
Friends of the Library Group
TAFT BRANCH, 740 E Taft Ave, 92865-4406, SAN 333-4899. Tel: 714-288-2430. Circulation Tel: 714-288-2433. Reference Tel: 714-288-2436. FAX: 714-282-8663. *Librn III,* Kurt Keesling; Tel: 714-288-2440; Staff 4 (MLS 1, Non-MLS 3)
Founded 1969. Pop 40,644; Circ 218,235
Open Mon-Wed 1-8, Thurs-Sat 1-6
Friends of the Library Group

M SAINT JOSEPH HOSPITAL & CHILDRENS HOSPITAL OF ORANGE COUNTY*, Burlew Medical Library, 1100 W Stewart Dr, 92863. (Mail add: PO Box 5600, 92863-5600), SAN 301-147X. Tel: 714-771-8291. FAX: 714-744-8533. Web Site: www.burlewmedicallibrary.org. *Libr Mgr,* Danielle Linden; E-mail: Danielle.Linden@stjoe.org; Staff 3 (MLS 1, Non-MLS 2)
Founded 1955
Library Holdings: e-books 10; e-journals 400; Bk Titles 6,000; Per Subs 400
Subject Interests: Cardiology, Ethics, Internal med, Nursing, Orthopedics, Pediatrics, Surgery
Automation Activity & Vendor Info: (Cataloging) Sydney; (Serials) Sydney
Database Vendor: OVID Technologies
Function: Doc delivery serv, ILL available, Ref serv available, Res libr
Partic in BRS; Coop Libr Agency for Syst & Servs; National Network of Libraries of Medicine Pacific Northwest Region; SDC
Open Mon-Fri 8:30-5
Restriction: In-house use for visitors, Lending to staff only

CR SAINT JOSEPH LIBRARY*, 480 S Batavia St, 92868-3907. SAN 333-3965. Tel: 714-633-8121, Ext 7765. E-mail: sjlibrary@csjorange.org. *Coordr,* Margie Catahan; E-mail: mcatahan@csjorange.org; Staff 2 (Non-MLS 2)
Founded 1953
Library Holdings: AV Mats 600; Bk Titles 12,750; Per Subs 50; Talking Bks 1,320
Subject Interests: Art, Christian, Relig, Roman Catholic relig, Spirituality, Theol
Automation Activity & Vendor Info: (Acquisitions) Follett Software; (Cataloging) Follett Software
Wireless access
Friends of the Library Group

C SANTIAGO CANYON COLLEGE*, 8045 E Chapman Ave, 92869. SAN 329-3017. Tel: 714-628-5000. Reference Tel: 714-628-5005, 714-628-5006. Administration Tel: 714-628-5001. FAX: 714-633-2842. Web Site: www.sccollege.edu/library. *Dean,* Dr Marilyn Flores; E-mail: flores_marilyn@sccollege.edu
Founded 1978. Enrl 26,672; Fac 158
Library Holdings: High Interest/Low Vocabulary Bk Vols 354; Bk Titles 65,000
Database Vendor: EBSCOhost, Gale Cengage Learning
Open Mon-Thurs 7:30-7:30
Restriction: Open to students, fac & staff
Friends of the Library Group

ORLAND

P ORLAND FREE LIBRARY*, 333 Mill St, 95963. SAN 333-4929. Tel: 530-865-1640. Web Site: www.orlandfreelibrary.net. *Youth Serv Librn,* Nancy Leek; Staff 6 (MLS 2, Non-MLS 4)
Founded 1909. Pop 14,616; Circ 51,040
Jul 2007-Jun 2008 Income $380,598, City $320,229, County $60,369. Mats Exp $11,740. Sal $201,943 (Prof $95,000)
Library Holdings: Bk Vols 62,000; Per Subs 80
Automation Activity & Vendor Info: (Cataloging) TLC (The Library Corporation); (Circulation) TLC (The Library Corporation); (ILL) OCLC WorldShare Interlibrary Loan; (OPAC) TLC (The Library Corporation)
Wireless access
Function: Adult literacy prog, Computer training, Family literacy, Handicapped accessible, ILL available, Magnifiers for reading, Photocopying/Printing, Prog for children & young adult, Summer reading prog, Telephone ref
Mem of NorthNet Library System
Open Mon, Wed & Fri 11-6, Tues & Thurs 11-7
Friends of the Library Group

OROVILLE

J BUTTE COLLEGE LIBRARY, Frederick S Montgomery Library, 3536 Butte Campus Dr, 95965-8399. SAN 301-1518. Tel: 530-879-4017. Interlibrary Loan Service Tel: 530-879-4066. Reference Tel: 530-879-4024. Administration Tel: 530-879-4050. Administration FAX: 530-879-6164. E-mail: referenceli@butte.edu. Web Site: www.butte.edu/library. *Dir, Libr Serv,* Dr Luozhu Cen; Fax: 530-895-2849, E-mail: cenlu@butte.edu; *Ref & Instruction Librn,* Morgan Brynnan; Tel: 530-879-4020, E-mail: brynnanmo@butte.edu; *Libr Tech/Cir & Reserves,* Jennifer Lasell; Tel: 530-879-4060; *Tech Serv,* Tiyebeh Jobari; Tel: 530-879-4022; Staff 8 (MLS 4, Non-MLS 4)
Founded 1967. Enrl 13,700; Highest Degree: Associate
Jul 2011-Jun 2012. Mats Exp $190,982, Books $59,000, Per/Ser (Incl. Access Fees) $31,200, Electronic Ref Mat (Incl. Access Fees) $100,782
Library Holdings: e-books 610,000; e-journals 28,000; High Interest/Low Vocabulary Bk Vols 600; Bk Titles 72,000; Bk Vols 73,829; Per Subs 165
Automation Activity & Vendor Info: (Acquisitions) OCLC; (Cataloging) OCLC; (Circulation) OCLC; (Course Reserve) OCLC; (ILL) OCLC WorldShare Interlibrary Loan; (Media Booking) OCLC; (OPAC) OCLC; (Serials) EBSCO Online
Database Vendor: CountryWatch, CQ Press, EBSCOhost, Facts on File, Gale Cengage Learning, JSTOR, McGraw-Hill, Newsbank, OCLC WorldShare Interlibrary Loan, Oxford Online, ProQuest
Wireless access
Function: ILL available, Instruction & testing, Online cat, Online info literacy tutorials on the web & in blackboard, Online ref, Online searches, Orientations, Outreach serv, Outside serv via phone, mail, e-mail & web, Pub access computers, Ref & res, Ref serv available, Workshops
Mem of NorthNet Library System
Partic in Commun Col Libr Automation Consortium; OCLC Online Computer Library Center, Inc
Open Mon-Thurs 7:30-5:45, Fri 7:30am-11:45pm; Mon-Thurs (Summer) 7-5
Restriction: Open to students, fac, staff & alumni, Pub use on premises

P BUTTE COUNTY LIBRARY*, 1820 Mitchell Ave, 95966-5387. SAN 333-4988. Tel: 530-538-7525. Circulation Tel: 530-538-7355. Interlibrary Loan Service Tel: 530-538-7326. Reference Tel: 530-538-7642. FAX: 530-538-7235. E-mail: lib@buttecounty.net. Web Site: www.buttecounty.net/bclibrary. *Br Mgr,* Brenda Crotts; Tel: 530-538-7196; Staff 6 (MLS 5, Non MLS 1)
Founded 1913. Pop 221,000; Circ 826,821
Jul 2006-Jun 2007 Income (Main Library and Branch(s)) $3,094,988, State $142,003, Federal $39,091, Locally Generated Income $2,718,314, Other $195,580. Mats Exp $199,557, Other Print Mats $186,754, Electronic Ref Mat (Incl. Access Fees) $12,803. Sal $2,310,251
Library Holdings: AV Mats 17,043; e-books 4; Bk Vols 276,528; Per Subs 526
Special Collections: Butte County History Coll. State Document Depository
Subject Interests: County hist

Automation Activity & Vendor Info: (Cataloging) TLC (The Library Corporation); (Circulation) TLC (The Library Corporation); (OPAC) TLC (The Library Corporation)
Database Vendor: EBSCOhost, Gale Cengage Learning, TLC (The Library Corporation), World Book Online
Function: Adult literacy prog, Handicapped accessible, ILL available, Magnifiers for reading, Photocopying/Printing, Prog for children & young adult, Summer reading prog, Wheelchair accessible
Mem of NorthNet Library System
Partic in OCLC Online Computer Library Center, Inc
Special Services for the Deaf - Bks on deafness & sign lang
Special Services for the Blind - Assistive/Adapted tech devices, equip & products; Bks on cassette; Bks on CD; Braille bks; Extensive large print coll; Large print bks; Low vision equip; Reader equip
Open Tues & Wed 11-6, Thurs-Sat 10-5
Friends of the Library Group
Branches: 5
BIGGS BRANCH, 464A B St, Biggs, 95917-9796. (Mail add: PO Box 516, Biggs, 95917-0516), SAN 370-7938. Tel: 530-868-5724. *Br Librn,* Cynthia Pustejovsky
Open Tues 12-6
CHICO BRANCH, 1108 Sherman Ave, Chico, 95926-3575, SAN 333-5046. Tel: 530-891-2762. FAX: 530-891-2978. E-mail: chicolibrary@buttecounty.net. *Br Librn,* Sarah Vantrease; *Ch,* Lydia Neeley; Staff 1 (MLS 1)
Function: Photocopying/Printing, Prog for adults, Prog for children & young adult, Ref serv available, Summer reading prog, Telephone ref, VHS videos
Open Mon, Fri & Sat 9-5, Tues-Thurs 9-7
Friends of the Library Group
DURHAM BRANCH, 2545 Durham-Dayton Hwy, Durham, 95938-9615. (Mail add: PO Box 119, Durham, 95938-0119), SAN 333-5100. Tel: 530-879-3835. *Br Librn,* Cynthia Pustejovsky
Open Tues & Wed 12-6, Thurs-Sat 10-4
Friends of the Library Group
GRIDLEY BRANCH, 299 Spruce St, Gridley, 95948-0397, SAN 333-516X. Tel: 530-846-3323. *Br Librn,* Cynthia Pustejovsky; Staff 1 (MLS 1)
Open Tues & Wed 12-6, Thurs-Sat 10-4
Friends of the Library Group
PARADISE BRANCH, 5922 Clark Rd, Paradise, 95969-4896, SAN 333-5194. Tel: 530-872-6320. FAX: 530-872-6322. *Br Librn,* Brenda Crotts; Staff 1 (MLS 1)
Function: Art exhibits, Handicapped accessible, ILL available, Photocopying/Printing, Prog for adults, Prog for children & young adult, Ref serv available, Summer reading prog, Telephone ref, VHS videos, Wheelchair accessible
Open Tues & Wed 11-6, Thurs-Sat 10-5
Friends of the Library Group
Bookmobiles: 1

GL BUTTE COUNTY PUBLIC LAW LIBRARY*, 1675 Montgomery St, 95965. SAN 301-1526. Tel: 530-538-7122. FAX: 530-534 1499. E-mail: publiclawlibrarian@gmail.com. Web Site: home.surewest.net/buttelaw. *Dir,* John A Zorbas; E-mail: jzorbas@sbcglobal.net; *Librn,* Joyce Monday; Staff 1.75 (MLS 1, Non-MLS 0.75)
Founded 1907
Jul 2012-Jun 2013 Income $175,000. Mats Exp $45,000, Books $30,000, Electronic Ref Mat (Incl. Access Fees) $15,000. Sal $130,000
Library Holdings: Bk Titles 600; Bk Vols 5,000; Per Subs 15
Subject Interests: Law
Database Vendor: EBSCOhost, LexisNexis, Westlaw
Wireless access
Function: Citizenship assistance, Computers for patron use, Copy machines, Doc delivery serv, e-mail serv, Electronic databases & coll, Govt ref serv, Online searches, Photocopying/Printing, Pub access computers, Ref & res, Ref serv available, Ref serv in person, Tax forms
Open Mon-Fri 8:30-4:30
Restriction: Restricted borrowing privileges

M OROVILLE HOSPITAL*, Goddard Memorial Library, 2767 Olive Hwy, 95966. SAN 301-1534. Tel: 530-554-1309. Toll Free FAX: 866-789-4223. *Dir,* Roger Brudno; E-mail: rbrudno@orohosp.com; Staff 1.1 (MLS 1, Non-MLS 0.1)
Founded 1968
Library Holdings: e-books 40; e-journals 80
Function: Doc delivery serv, Health sci info serv, Online searches, Outreach serv, Ref serv available
Partic in National Network of Libraries of Medicine; Northern California & Nevada Medical Library Group (NCNMLG); Pacific Southwest Regional Medical Library (PSRML)
Restriction: External users must contact libr, Hospital employees & physicians only, Med & nursing staff, patients & families, Not a lending libr, Not open to pub

OXNARD

J OXNARD COLLEGE LIBRARY*, 4000 S Rose Ave, 93033-6699. SAN 321-4788. Tel: 805-986-5949. Circulation Tel: 805-986-5819. Reference Tel: 805-986-5820. Administration Tel: 805-986-5818. FAX: 805-986-5888. Web Site: www.oxnardcollege.edu. *Supvr, Learning Res Ctr,* Diva Ward; E-mail: dward@vcccd.edu; *Assoc Librn,* Tom Stough; E-mail: tstough@vcccd.edu; *Libr Tech,* Ray Acosta; Tel: 805-986-5800, Ext 1971, E-mail: racosta@vcccd.edu; Staff 1 (MLS 1)
Founded 1975. Enrl 7,233; Fac 88
Library Holdings: e-books 19,000; Bk Titles 36,630; Bk Vols 43,384; Per Subs 70
Subject Interests: Soc sci
Automation Activity & Vendor Info: (Cataloging) Ex Libris Group; (Circulation) Ex Libris Group; (OPAC) Ex Libris Group; (Serials) Ex Libris Group
Database Vendor: ARTstor, CountryWatch, CQ Press, EBSCO Auto Repair Reference, EBSCO Information Services, EBSCOhost, Ex Libris Group, Gale Cengage Learning, JSTOR, LexisNexis, ProQuest, World Book Online
Wireless access
Open Mon-Thurs 8am-9pm, Fri 8-5

P OXNARD PUBLIC LIBRARY, 251 South A St, 93030. SAN 301-1542. Tel: 805-385-7500. Circulation Tel: 805-385-7507. Reference Tel: 805-385-7532. Administration Tel: 805-385-7528. FAX: 805-385-7526. E-mail: Library@ci.oxnard.ca.us. Web Site: www.oxnardlibrary.net. *Libr Dir,* Barbara J Murray; Tel: 805-385-7522, E-mail: barbara.murray@ci.oxnard.ca.us; *Head, Circ,* Yvonne Harper; Tel: 805-385-7512, E-mail: yvonne.harper@ci.oxnard.ca.us; *Head, Pub Serv, Head, Ref, Music,* Sofia Kimsey; Tel: 805-385-7529, E-mail: sofia.kimsey@ci.oxnard.ca.us; *Ch,* Vanesa Chua; Tel: 805 240-7339, E-mail: vanesa.chua@ci.oxnard.ca.us; *Ch,* Laura Duncan; Tel: 805 385-7504, E-mail: laura.duncan@ci.oxnard.ca.us; *Hist Coll Librn,* Judy Weston; Tel: 805-385-7531, E-mail: judy.weston@ci.oxnard.ca.us; *Ref Librn,* Karen Schatz; E-mail: karen.schatz@ci.oxnard.ca.us; *YA Librn,* Kristina Hernandez; Tel: 805-240-7309, E-mail: kristina.hernandez@ci.oxnard.ca.us. Subject Specialists: *Local hist,* Judy Weston; Staff 50 (MLS 13, Non-MLS 37)
Founded 1907. Pop 203,645; Circ 568,664
Jul 2013-Jun 2014 Income (Main Library and Branch(s)) $5,198,323, State $218,971, City $4,707,707, Other $271,645. Mats Exp $319,424, Books $219,456, Per/Ser (Incl. Access Fees) $11,434, Other Print Mats $60,440, Electronic Ref Mat (Incl. Access Fees) $27,466, Presv $628. Sal $2,981,705
Library Holdings: AV Mats 15,129; e-books 703; Bk Vols 331,061; Per Subs 235
Subject Interests: Local govt, Local hist, Spanish (Lang)
Automation Activity & Vendor Info: (Acquisitions) SirsiDynix; (Cataloging) SirsiDynix, (Circulation) SirsiDynix; (Media Booking) SirsiDynix; (OPAC) SirsiDynix; (Serials) SirsiDynix
Database Vendor: Baker & Taylor, Bowker, Gale Cengage Learning, Ingram Library Services, LearningExpress, Newsbank, OCLC WorldShare Interlibrary Loan, WT Cox
Wireless access
Function: Bilingual assistance for Spanish patrons, Bk club(s), Bks on cassette, Bks on CD, CD-ROM, Children's prog, Computer training, Computers for patron use, Copy machines, Electronic databases & coll, Free DVD rentals, Handicapped accessible, ILL available, Mail & tel request accepted, Music CDs, Passport agency, Prog for adults, Prog for children & young adult, Summer reading prog, Teen prog, VHS videos, Wheelchair accessible
Partic in Southern California Library Cooperative
Special Services for the Deaf - ADA equip
Special Services for the Blind - Braille bks; Reader equip
Open Mon-Thurs 9-8, Sat 9-5:30, Sun 1-5
Friends of the Library Group
Branches: 2
COLONIA, 1500 Camino del Sol, No 26, 93030, SAN 377-5917. Tel: 805-385-8108. FAX: 805-385-8323. *Librn,* Pamela Wood; Tel: 805-385-7984, E-mail: pamela.wood@ci.oxnard.ca.us; Staff 3 (MLS 1, Non-MLS 2)
Founded 1978. Pop 28,510; Circ 14,537
Library Holdings: Bk Vols 11,422
Function: Summer reading prog
Open Mon-Thurs 12-6
Friends of the Library Group
SOUTH OXNARD, 4300 Saviers Rd, 93033, SAN 377-8401. Tel: 805-385-8129. FAX: 805-488-1336. *Br Librn,* Alan Neal; Tel: 805-247-8951, E-mail: alan.neal@ci.oxnard.ca.us; Staff 5 (MLS 3, Non-MLS 2)
Founded 2007. Pop 91,641; Circ 413,897
Library Holdings: Bk Vols 329,628
Open Mon-Thurs 9-8, Sat 9-5:30
Friends of the Library Group

M SAINT JOHN'S REGIONAL MEDICAL CENTER*, Health Sciences Library, 1600 N Rose Ave, 93030. SAN 301-1550. Tel: 805-988-2820. FAX: 805-981-4419. Web Site: www.stjohnslibrary.org. *Dir, Libr Serv,* Joanne Kennedy; E-mail: jkennedy@chw.edu
Founded 1973
Library Holdings: Bk Titles 3,500; Per Subs 100
Open Mon-Fri 8:30-5

PACIFIC GROVE

P PACIFIC GROVE PUBLIC LIBRARY*, 550 Central Ave, 93950-2789. SAN 301-1585. Tel: 831-648-5760. Reference Tel: 831-648-5762. FAX: 831-373-3268. Web Site: www.pacificgrove.lib.ca.us. *Ch, Sr Librn,* Lisa Maddalena; Tel: 831-648-5760, Ext 11, E-mail: lmaddale@pacificgrove.lib.ca.us; *Adult Serv, Ref Serv,* Mary Byrne Elturk; Tel: 831-648-5760, Ext 17, E-mail: melturk@ci.pg.ca.us; Staff 12 (MLS 5, Non-MLS 7)
Founded 1908. Pop 15,114; Circ 215,182
Library Holdings: Audiobooks 4,301; AV Mats 5,782; CDs 1,574; DVDs 3,581; e-books 3,355; Large Print Bks 3,613; Bk Titles 97,498; Bk Vols 98,094; Per Subs 206; Talking Bks 1,461; Videos 1,035
Automation Activity & Vendor Info: (Acquisitions) Innovative Interfaces, Inc; (Cataloging) Innovative Interfaces, Inc; (Circulation) Innovative Interfaces, Inc; (OPAC) Innovative Interfaces, Inc; (Serials) Innovative Interfaces, Inc
Database Vendor: Gale Cengage Learning, Innovative Interfaces, Inc, OCLC FirstSearch
Wireless access
Function: Bilingual assistance for Spanish patrons, Bks on CD, Children's prog, Computers for patron use, Copy machines, Electronic databases & coll, Exhibits, Free DVD rentals, Handicapped accessible, Home delivery & serv to Sr ctr & nursing homes, Magnifiers for reading, Music CDs, Outside serv via phone, mail, e-mail & web, OverDrive digital audio bks, Prog for adults, Prog for children & young adult, Pub access computers, Ref serv in person, Story hour, Summer reading prog, Tax forms, Teen prog, Telephone ref, VHS videos, Web-catalog, Wheelchair accessible
Partic in Califa; Monterey Bay Area Cooperative Library System
Special Services for the Deaf - Assistive tech; Bks on deafness & sign lang; Closed caption videos; TTY equip
Special Services for the Blind - Bks on cassette; Bks on CD; Large print bks; Magnifiers; Reader equip; VisualTek equip
Open Tues-Thurs 11-7, Fri & Sat 12-5
Friends of the Library Group

PACIFIC PALISADES

R KEHILLAT ISRAEL RECONSTRUCTIONIST CONGREGATION OF PACIFIC PALISADES*, Berrie Library, 16019 Sunset Blvd, 90272. SAN 301-1607. Tel: 310-459-2328. FAX: 310-573-2098. *Exec Dir,* Jane Krantz
Founded 1968
Library Holdings: Bk Titles 2,500; Per Subs 25
Special Collections: Reconstructionist Judaism
Subject Interests: Judaica (lit or hist of Jews)
Open Mon-Thurs 9-5, Fri 9-3:30
Restriction: Mem only

PALM DESERT

C COLLEGE OF THE DESERT LIBRARY*, 43-500 Monterey, 92260. SAN 301-1615. Tel: 760-773-2563. FAX: 760-568-5955. Web Site: www.collegeofthedesert.edu. *Coordr, Libr Serv,* Jonathan Fernald; Tel: 760-679-3775, E-mail: jfernald@collegeofthedesert.edu; *Ref Serv,* Claudia Derum; E-mail: cderum@collegeofthedesert.edu; Staff 3 (Non-MLS 3)
Founded 1962. Enrl 8,360; Fac 417; Highest Degree: Doctorate
Library Holdings: AV Mats 929; Bks on Deafness & Sign Lang 35; e-books 4,700; High Interest/Low Vocabulary Bk Vols 14; Bk Vols 51,602; Per Subs 200
Special Collections: Desert Coll, rare books; Winston S Churchill Coll, bks, pamphlets, rare bks
Subject Interests: Rare bks
Automation Activity & Vendor Info: (Cataloging) OCLC; (Circulation) SirsiDynix; (ILL) OCLC; (OPAC) SirsiDynix
Database Vendor: EBSCOhost, Gale Cengage Learning, Newsbank, ProQuest, SirsiDynix
Partic in Coop Libr Agency for Syst & Servs; Inland Empire Acad Libr Coop (IEALC); San Bernardino, Inyo, Riverside Counties United Library Services
Open Mon-Thurs 8-8, Fri 8-5
Friends of the Library Group

PALM SPRINGS

S PALM SPRINGS ART MUSEUM LIBRARY, 101 Museum Dr, 92262. (Mail add: PO Box 2310, 92263-2310), SAN 301-1631. Tel: 760-325-7186. FAX: 760-327-5069. Web Site: www.psmuseum.org. *Librn,* Frank Lopez; Tel: 760-322-4833, E-mail: flopez@psmuseum.org; Staff 1 (MLS 1)
Founded 1938
Library Holdings: Bk Vols 8,000; Per Subs 20
Special Collections: Artist Files; Auction Catalogs
Subject Interests: Archit, Art, Design, Glass, Native Am, Photog
Automation Activity & Vendor Info: (Cataloging) LibraryWorld, Inc; (Circulation) LibraryWorld, Inc; (OPAC) LibraryWorld, Inc
Restriction: Non-circulating to the pub, Open by appt only

P PALM SPRINGS PUBLIC LIBRARY, 300 S Sunrise Way, 92262-7699. SAN 333-5224. Tel: 760-323-7323. Administration Tel: 760-322-8375. FAX: 760-320-9834. E-mail: library.info@palmspringsca.gov. Web Site: www.palmspringslibrary.org. *Dir of Libr Serv,* Jeannie Kays; E-mail: jeannie.kays@palmspringsca.gov; *Libr Operation & Coll Mgr,* Jeff Clayton; Tel: 760-323-8387, E-mail: jeff.clayton@palmspringsca.gov; *Libr Serv & Pub Relations Mgr,* Julie Warren; Tel: 760-416-6731, E-mail: julie.warren@palmspringsca.gov; Staff 6 (MLS 5, Non-MLS 1)
Founded 1919. Pop 47,601; Circ 429,910
Jul 2010-Jun 2011 Income $3,994,562, State $18,739, City $1,997,281, Locally Generated Income $1,978,542. Mats Exp $278,105, Books $113,300, Per/Ser (Incl. Access Fees) $7,800, AV Mat $122,400, Electronic Ref Mat (Incl. Access Fees) $34,605. Sal $812,495
Library Holdings: Audiobooks 564; Bks on Deafness & Sign Lang 40; CDs 7,560; DVDs 12,138; e-books 353; Electronic Media & Resources 8; Large Print Bks 5,307; Microforms 3,345; Bk Vols 98,996; Per Subs 140
Special Collections: Spanish Language Coll. Oral History
Subject Interests: Genealogy, Hist, Local hist
Automation Activity & Vendor Info: (Acquisitions) Baker & Taylor; (Cataloging) OCLC; (Circulation) Innovative Interfaces, Inc; (ILL) OCLC WorldShare Interlibrary Loan; (OPAC) Innovative Interfaces, Inc; (Serials) Innovative Interfaces, Inc
Database Vendor: Baker & Taylor, Brodart, Gale Cengage Learning, Medline, Newsbank, OCLC FirstSearch, OCLC WorldShare Interlibrary Loan, Overdrive, Inc, ProQuest, ValueLine, WebMD, World Book Online
Wireless access
Function: 24/7 Online cat, Activity rm, Adult bk club, Art exhibits, Audiobks via web, Bilingual assistance for Spanish patrons, Bk club(s), Bks on CD, Children's prog, Computer training, Computers for patron use, Copy machines, e-mail & chat, E-Reserves, Electronic databases & coll, Exhibits, Free DVD rentals, Genealogy discussion group, Handicapped accessible, Holiday prog, ILL available, Life-long learning prog for all ages, Magazines, Mail & tel request accepted, Mango lang, Microfiche/film & reading machines, Movies, Music CDs, Newsp ref libr, Online cat, Online info literacy tutorials on the web & in blackboard, Online ref, Orientations, OverDrive digital audio bks, Photocopying/Printing, Preschool outreach, Prog for adults, Prog for children & young adult, Pub access computers, Ref serv in person, Res performed for a fee, Spanish lang bks, Story hour, Summer reading prog, Teen prog, Web-catalog, Wheelchair accessible, Workshops
Partic in Califa
Special Services for the Blind - Audio mat; Bks on CD
Open Mon & Thurs 10-6, Tues & Wed 10-8, Fri & Sat 10-5
Restriction: Ref only
Friends of the Library Group

PALMDALE

P PALMDALE CITY LIBRARY*, 700 E Palmdale Blvd, 93550. SAN 324-2781. Tel: 661-267-5600. FAX: 661-267-5606. Web Site: www.palmdalelibrary.org. *Dir,* Thomas Vose; Staff 7 (MLS 6, Non-MLS 1)
Founded 1977. Pop 136,734; Circ 431,290
Library Holdings: AV Mats 8,200; Bk Vols 127,760; Per Subs 453
Special Collections: Local History Coll
Automation Activity & Vendor Info: (Acquisitions) SirsiDynix; (Cataloging) SirsiDynix; (Circulation) SirsiDynix; (OPAC) SirsiDynix
Partic in Southern California Library Cooperative
Open Mon-Thurs 10-8, Fri & Sat 10-5, Sun 1-5
Friends of the Library Group
Bookmobiles: 1

PALO ALTO

S ACTERRA ENVIRONMENTAL LIBRARY*, 3921 E Bayshore Rd, 94303. SAN 326-1352. Tel: 650-962-9876, Ext 306. FAX: 650-962-8234. E-mail: library@acterra.org. Web Site: www.acterra.org/library/index.html. *Interim Exec Dir,* Debbie Mytels; Tel: 650-962-9876, Ext 302, E-mail: debbiem@acterra.org; *Pub Info Coordr,* Pat Martin; E-mail: patm@acterra.org; Staff 1 (Non-MLS 1)
Founded 1970
Library Holdings: Bk Titles 6,000; Bk Vols 6,500; Per Subs 30
Special Collections: Backpacking & Trails; Birding, bks, per; Energy; Environmental Careers; Environmental Volunteers Coll; Wildlife & Endangered Species Coll
Friends of the Library Group

R FIRST CONGREGATIONAL CHURCH LIBRARY*, 1985 Louis Rd, 94303-3499. SAN 301-1720. Tel: 650-856-6662. FAX: 650-856-6664. Web Site: www.fccpa.org.
Library Holdings: Bk Titles 2,100
Subject Interests: Fiction
Open Mon-Fri 9-3

SR FIRST UNITED METHODIST CHURCH LIBRARY*, 625 Hamilton Ave, 94301. SAN 301-1739. Tel: 650-323-6167. FAX: 650-323-3923. Web Site: www.firstpaloalto.com. *Librn,* Florence Jensen
Founded 1964
Jul 2006-Jun 2007. Mats Exp $4,100, Books $3,500, Per/Ser (Incl. Access Fees) $100, AV Mat $500
Library Holdings: AV Mats 200; CDs 10; DVDs 50; High Interest/Low Vocabulary Bk Vols 400; Large Print Bks 20; Bk Titles 4,000; Bk Vols 5,000; Per Subs 10
Subject Interests: Relig
Wireless access

P PALO ALTO CITY LIBRARY*, 1213 Newell Rd, 94303-2907. (Mail add: PO Box 10250, 94303-0250), SAN 333-5348. Tel: 650-329-2436. FAX: 650-327-2033. TDD: 650-856-6839. E-mail: pa.library@cityofpaloalto.org. Web Site: www.cityofpaloalto/library. *Dir,* Monique le Conge Ziesenhenne; *Asst Dir, Pub Serv,* Cornelia van Aken; Tel: 650-329-2668, E-mail: cornelia.vanaken@cityofpaloalto.org; *Mgr, Circ Serv,* Rose Sebastian; Tel: 650-329-2478, E-mail: rose.sebastian@cityofpaloalto.org; *Mgr, Ref Serv,* Ouida Charles; Tel: 650-329-2620, E-mail: ouida.charles@cityofpaloalto.org; Staff 24 (MLS 20, Non-MLS 4)
Founded 1904. Pop 62,600; Circ 1,414,509
Library Holdings: AV Mats 30,657; Bk Titles 167,008; Bk Vols 240,098; Per Subs 681
Special Collections: Palo Alto Historical Association Files
Subject Interests: Local hist
Automation Activity & Vendor Info: (Acquisitions) SirsiDynix; (Cataloging) SirsiDynix; (Circulation) SirsiDynix; (ILL) SirsiDynix; (OPAC) SirsiDynix; (Serials) SirsiDynix
Database Vendor: Gale Cengage Learning, SirsiDynix
Publications: Hot Off the Shelf (Newsletter)
Open Mon & Thurs 12-8, Tues & Wed 10-8, Fri & Sat 10-6, Sun 1-5
Restriction: Circ limited
Friends of the Library Group
Branches: 4
CHILDREN'S, 1276 Harriet St, 94301, SAN 333 5372. Administration Tel: 650-329-2516. FAX: 650-463-4964. Administration FAX: 650-327-7568. E-mail: librarychildrensservices@cityofpaloalto.org. *Br Mgr,* Jenny Jordan; Tel: 659-463-4961, E-mail: jenny.jordan@cityofpaloalto.org; *Sr Librn,* Cheryl Lee; E-mail: cheryl.lee@cityofpaloalto.org; *Librn,* Susan Rodgers; E-mail: susan.rodgers@cityofpaloalto.org; Staff 7.38 (MLS 3.35, Non-MLS 4.03)
Founded 1940. Pop 4,000; Circ 371,997
Library Holdings: AV Mats 6,428; Bk Vols 40,223
Function: After school storytime, Children's prog, Computers for patron use, E-Reserves, Electronic databases & coll, Free DVD rentals, Holiday prog, Homebound delivery serv, Music CDs, Online cat, Online ref, Online searches, Outreach serv, Photocopying/Printing, Prog for children & young adult, Ref serv available, Story hour, Summer reading prog, Telephone ref, Web catalog
Open Mon & Thurs 12-6, Tues & Wed 10-6, Fri & Sat 10-5, Sun 1-5
Friends of the Library Group
COLLEGE TERRACE, 2300 Wellesley St, 94306, SAN 333-5402. *Circ Mgr,* Rose Sebastian; Tel: 650-329-2478, E-mail: rose.sebastian@cityofpaloalto.org; Staff 2.41 (Non-MLS 2.41)
Founded 1936. Pop 7,000; Circ 67,227
Library Holdings: AV Mats 2,147; Bk Vols 11,728
Function: Bks on CD, Children's prog, Computers for patron use, E-Reserves, Electronic databases & coll, Free DVD rentals, Handicapped accessible, Music CDs, Online cat, Online ref, Online searches, Pub access computers, Story hour, Summer reading prog
Open Tues, Wed, Fri & Sat 10-6
Friends of the Library Group
DOWNTOWN, 270 Forest Ave, 94301, SAN 333-5437. FAX: 650-327-7568. *Circ Mgr,* Rose Sebastian; Tel: 650-329-2478, E-mail: rose.sebastian@cityofpaloalto.org; Staff 3 (Non-MLS 3)
Founded 1971. Pop 8,000; Circ 67,227
Library Holdings: AV Mats 4,091; Bk Vols 11,218
Function: Bks on CD, Children's prog, Computers for patron use, Copy machines, Electronic databases & coll, Free DVD rentals, Handicapped accessible, Music CDs, Online cat, Online ref, Online searches, Prog for adults, Web-catalog, Wheelchair accessible
Open Tues, Wed & Sat 10-6, Thurs 12-6
Friends of the Library Group
MITCHELL PARK, 3700 Middlefield Rd, 94303, SAN 333-5461. FAX: 650-856-7925. *Br Mgr,* RuthAnn Garcia; E-mail: ruthann.garcia@cityofpaloalto.org; *Sr Librn,* Deborah Anthonyson; *Sr Librn,* Melissa Morwood; *Sr Librn,* Mary Ann Young; *Librn,* Dave Irving; *Librn,* Karen Richins
Founded 1958. Circ 507,531
Library Holdings: AV Mats 16,096; Bk Vols 70,793
Function: After school storytime, Bks on CD, Children's prog, Computers for patron use, Copy machines, Electronic databases & coll, Free DVD rentals, Handicapped accessible, Music CDs, Online cat, Online ref, Online searches, Photocopying/Printing, Prog for children & young adult, Story hour, Summer reading prog, Teen prog, Web-catalog, Wheelchair accessible
Special Services for the Deaf - TDD equip
Open Mon & Thurs 12-8, Tues & Wed 10-8, Fri & Sat 10-6, Sun 1-5
Friends of the Library Group

M PALO ALTO MEDICAL FOUNDATION*, Barnett-Hall Library, Ames Bldg, 795 El Camino Real, 94301-2302. SAN 301-178X. Tel: 650-326-8120, Ext 4831. FAX: 650-853-2909. Web Site: www.pamf.org. *Librn,* Debbie Schide
Founded 1950
Library Holdings: Bk Vols 12,107; Per Subs 229
Subject Interests: Clinical med
Publications: Annual Report; Newsletter (Quarterly)
Partic in National Network of Libraries of Medicine; Northern California & Nevada Medical Library Group (NCNMLG); Pacific Southwest Regional Medical Library (PSRML)

C PALO ALTO UNIVERSITY*, Library & Media Center, 1791 Arastradero Rd, 94304. SAN 371-8425. Tel: 650-433-3808. Interlibrary Loan Service Tel: 650-433-3807. Reference Tel: 650-433-3855. FAX: 650-433-3888. E-mail: library-circ@paloaltou.edu. Web Site: www.paloaltou.edu/department/omar-seddiqui-research-library. *Dir, Acad Tech, Univ Librn,* Scott Hines; E-mail: shines@paloaltou.edu; *Head, Tech Serv, ILL & Circ,* Mary Anderson; Tel: 650-433-3816, E-mail: mwood@paloaltou.edu; Staff 4 (MLS 2, Non-MLS 2)
Founded 1975. Enrl 1,000; Fac 100; Highest Degree: Doctorate
Library Holdings: DVDs 500; e-books 150,000; e-journals 19,500; Bk Titles 155,000; Bk Vols 5,000; Per Subs 19,500; Videos 2,500
Subject Interests: Psychiat, Psychol
Automation Activity & Vendor Info: (Acquisitions) OCLC WorldShare Interlibrary Loan; (Cataloging) OCLC WorldShare Interlibrary Loan; (Circulation) OCLC WorldShare Interlibrary Loan; (Course Reserve) Docutek; (ILL) OCLC ILLiad; (OPAC) OCLC WorldShare Interlibrary Loan; (Serials) OCLC WorldShare Interlibrary Loan
Database Vendor: Alexander Street Press, American Psychological Association (APA), ebrary, EBSCOhost, Elsevier, IBISWorld, LexisNexis, OCLC WorldShare Interlibrary Loan, OCLC Worldshare Management Services, Oxford Online, ProQuest, ScienceDirect, Springer-Verlag, Wiley
Wireless access
Function: ILL available, Res libr
Partic in Asn of Mental Health Librn (AMHL); Northern & Central California Psychology Libraries; Northern California & Nevada Medical Library Group (NCNMLG); Statewide California Electronic Library Consortium (SCELC)
Restriction: Private libr

S PARC, A XEROX COMPANY*, Information Center, 3333 Coyote Hill Rd, 94304-1314. SAN 301-1844. Tel: 650-812-4042. E-mail: library@parc.com. *Mgr,* Katherine Jarvis; Tel: 650-812-4903; Staff 1 (MLS 1)
Founded 1971
Library Holdings: e-books 100; e-journals 150; Bk Titles 10,000; Per Subs 200
Subject Interests: Computer sci, Eng, Mat sci, Psychol
Automation Activity & Vendor Info: (Cataloging) OCLC; (Circulation) Livelink for Libraries; (OPAC) Livelink for Libraries
Wireless access
Restriction: Access at librarian's discretion

C SOFIA UNIVERSITY LIBRARY*, 1069 E Meadow Circle, 94303. SAN 326-4483. Tel: 650-493-4430, Ext 221. Interlibrary Loan Service Tel: 650-493-4430, Ext 253. Administration Tel: 650-493-4430, Ext 223. FAX: 650-852-9780. E-mail: refdesk@sofia.edu. Web Site: www.sofia.edu/library. *Libr Dir,* Katrina Rahn; E-mail: katrina.rahn@sofia.edu; *Cataloger/Ref Librn,* Linda Magnusson; Tel: 650-493-4430, Ext 263, E-mail: linda.magnusson@sofia.edu; *Ref Librn,* Lucy Erman; Tel: 650-493-4430, Ext 251, E-mail: lucy.erman@sofia.edu; *Cat Spec,* Bing Zuo-Dittmer; Tel: 650-493-4430, Ext 302, E-mail: bing.zuo-dittmer@sofia.edu; *Circ Tech,* Yoko Noda; E-mail: yoko.noda@sofia.edu; *ILL Tech,* Sharon Hamrick; E-mail: sharon.hamrick@sofia.edu; Staff 6 (MLS 3, Non-MLS 3)
Founded 1981. Enrl 500; Fac 150; Highest Degree: Doctorate
Library Holdings: AV Mats 1,000; CDs 240; DVDs 500; e-books 80,000; e-journals 3,000; Bk Titles 15,000; Per Subs 169
Special Collections: Collected Works of C G Jung; Complete Psychological Works of Sigmund Freud; Spirituality (Classics of Western Spirituality Coll)

Subject Interests: Psychol, Relig
Automation Activity & Vendor Info: (Cataloging) EOS International; (Circulation) EOS International; (ILL) OCLC; (OPAC) EOS International; (Serials) EBSCO Online
Database Vendor: American Psychological Association (APA), Annual Reviews, ebrary, EBSCOhost, ProQuest, PubMed, Sage, Springer-Verlag
Wireless access
Partic in Califa; Northern & Central California Psychology Libraries; Northern California & Nevada Medical Library Group (NCNMLG); Statewide California Electronic Library Consortium (SCELC)
Open Mon-Thurs 9-9, Fri 9-5, Sat 10-4, Sun 12-6
Restriction: Pub use on premises
Friends of the Library Group

M STANFORD HEALTH LIBRARY*, 211 Quarry Rd, Ste 201, 94304. SAN 374-5376. Tel: 650-725-8400. Toll Free Tel: 800-295-5177. FAX: 650-725-1444. E-mail: healthlibrary@stanfordmed.org. Web Site: healthlibrary.stanford.edu. *Chief Librn,* Nancy Dickenson; Staff 5 (MLS 3, Non-MLS 2)
Founded 1989
Library Holdings: AV Mats 1,000; e-books 1,000; Bk Titles 8,000; Per Subs 40
Subject Interests: Consumer health, Med
Automation Activity & Vendor Info: (Cataloging) Inmagic, Inc.; (OPAC) Inmagic, Inc.
Open Mon, Wed, Fri & Sat 10-6, Thurs 10-9
Branches:
STANFORD COMPREHENSIVE CANCER CENTER, 875 Blake Wilbur Dr, Stanford, 94305. Tel: 650-736-1713. FAX: 650-736-7157. *Librn,* Gillian Kumagai; E-mail: gkumagai@stanfordmed.org
Library Holdings: Bk Titles 1,000
Subject Interests: Cancer, Surgery
Open Mon-Fri 9-5
STANFORD HOSPITAL, E303 Stanford Hospital, 300 Pasteur Dr, 94305. Tel: 650-725-8100. FAX: 650-725-8102. *Librn,* Carmen Huddleston; E-mail: chuddleston@stanfordmed.org
Library Holdings: Bk Titles 1,100
Open Mon-Fri 9-5

L WILSON, SONSINI, GOODRICH & ROSATI*, Library, 650 Page Mill Rd, 94304. SAN 372-2988. Tel: 650-493-9300. FAX: 650-493-6811. *Mgr, Res Librn,* Leiza D MacMorris
Library Holdings: Bk Vols 40,000; Per Subs 300
Open Mon-Fri 9-5

PARLIER

G UNITED STATES DEPARTMENT OF AGRICULTURE*, Agricultural Research Service-Horticultural Crops Research Laboratory, 9611 S Riverbend Ave, 93648-9757. SAN 300-7685. Tel: 559-596-2728. Web Site: fresno.ars.usda.gov/hcrl/hcrlhome.htm.
Library Holdings: Bk Vols 4,000
Subject Interests: Entomology
Publications: Pamphlets; reports

PASADENA

C ART CENTER COLLEGE OF DESIGN*, James Lemont Fogg Memorial Library, 1700 Lida St, 91103. SAN 301-1895. Tel: 626-396-2231. Circulation Tel: 626-396-2233. Reference Tel: 626-396-2237. FAX: 626-568-0428. E-mail: library@artcenter.edu. Web Site: www.artcenter.edu/library. *Librn,* Simone Fujita; E-mail: simone.fujita@artcenter.edu; *Evening Librn,* Robert Lundquist; E-mail: robert.lundquist@artcenter.edu; *Pub Serv Librn,* Rachel Julius; *Ref Serv Librn,* Claudia Michelle Betty; E-mail: c.betty@artcenter.edu; *Libr Syst Adminr,* Jennifer Faist; Tel: 626-396-2236, E-mail: jennifer.faist@artcenter.edu; *Acq,* George Porcari; E-mail: george.porcari@artcenter.edu; *Tech Serv,* Gina Solares; Tel: 626-396-2230, E-mail: gina.solares@artcenter.edu; Staff 11 (MLS 5, Non-MLS 6)
Founded 1930. Enrl 1,700; Fac 300; Highest Degree: Master
Library Holdings: DVDs 2,000; Electronic Media & Resources 14; Bk Titles 86,000; Bk Vols 100,000; Per Subs 400; Spec Interest Per Sub 400; Videos 6,000
Special Collections: College Archives; Melinda Fassett Welles, PhD, Children's Illustrated Books
Subject Interests: Advertising, Art, Films & filmmaking, Graphic design, Photog, Product design, Transportation
Automation Activity & Vendor Info: (Cataloging) Innovative Interfaces, Inc; (Circulation) Innovative Interfaces, Inc; (Course Reserve) Innovative Interfaces, Inc; (OPAC) Innovative Interfaces, Inc; (Serials) Innovative Interfaces, Inc
Database Vendor: Baker & Taylor, Checkpoint Systems, Inc, Corbis, Coutts Information Service, CredoReference, Discovery Education, EBSCO Information Services, H W Wilson, Hoovers, Innovative Interfaces, Inc, JSTOR, Luna Imaging/Insight, Material ConneXion, McGraw-Hill, Newsbank, OCLC FirstSearch, OCLC WorldShare Interlibrary Loan, Project MUSE, ProQuest, Safari Books Online, Wilson - Wilson Web
Wireless access
Partic in OCLC Online Computer Library Center, Inc
Open Mon-Thurs 8am-10pm, Fri 8-5, Sat 9-5
Restriction: Not open to pub, Open to students, fac & staff

S AVERY RESEARCH CENTER*, 2900 Bradley St, 91107-1599. SAN 301-1909. Tel: 626-398-2500, Ext 2567. FAX: 626-398-2540. *In Charge,* Amy Henry
Founded 1968
Library Holdings: Bk Vols 5,000; Per Subs 140
Special Collections: Patents Coll
Subject Interests: Films & filmmaking
Database Vendor: Dialog
Function: ILL available
Restriction: Staff use only

C CALIFORNIA INSTITUTE OF TECHNOLOGY*, Caltech Library System 1-32, 1200 E California Blvd, M/C 1-32, 91125-3200. SAN 333-5704. Tel: 626-395-3404. FAX: 626-792-7540. E-mail: library@caltech.edu. Web Site: www.library.caltech.edu. *Univ Librn,* Kimberly Douglas; Tel: 626-395-6416, E-mail: kdouglas@library.caltech.edu; *Adminr, Libr Operations,* Robin Izon; Tel: 626-395-6411, E-mail: rizon@library.caltech.edu; *Head, Archives & Spec Coll,* Shelley Erwin; Tel: 626-395-3149, Ext 2702, E-mail: cerwin@caltech.edu; *Mgr,* Judith Brott; Tel: 626-395-6834, E-mail: brott@library.caltech.edu; *Access & Fulfillment Serv Mgr,* David McCaslin; Tel: 626-395-6412, E-mail: david@library.caltech.edu; *Metadata Serv Mgr,* Laura Smart; Tel: 626-395-6149, E-mail: laura@library.caltech.edu; Staff 18 (MLS 12, Non-MLS 6)
Founded 1891. Enrl 2,100; Fac 400; Highest Degree: Doctorate
Library Holdings: Bk Vols 548,752; Per Subs 3,144
Special Collections: NACA/NASA Technical Reports. Oral History; State Document Depository; US Document Depository
Subject Interests: Eng, Hist of sci, Soc sci & issues
Automation Activity & Vendor Info: (Acquisitions) Innovative Interfaces, Inc; (Cataloging) Innovative Interfaces, Inc; (Circulation) Innovative Interfaces, Inc; (Serials) Innovative Interfaces, Inc
Publications: CLS Guide to SciSearch Services; CLS Online Resources; CLS Rules of Access
Open Mon-Fri 8-5
Friends of the Library Group
Departmental Libraries:
ASTROPHYSICS, 1201 E California Blvd, M/C 105-24, 91125, SAN 333-5763. Tel: 626-395-4008. *Librn,* Kimberly Douglas
Library Holdings: Bk Vols 12,000; Per Subs 35
Automation Activity & Vendor Info: (Cataloging) Innovative Interfaces, Inc; (Circulation) Innovative Interfaces, Inc; (OPAC) Innovative Interfaces, Inc
Open Mon-Fri 8-5
EARTHQUAKE ENGINEERING RESEARCH, Sherman Fairchild Library, 200 E California Blvd, M/C 1-43, 91125, SAN 333-5852. Tel: 626-395-3409. FAX: 626-568-2719. Web Site: libguides.caltech.edu/EarthquakeEngineering. *Librn,* George Porter; E-mail: george@library.caltech.edu
Library Holdings: Bk Vols 15,000; Per Subs 25
Publications: Earthquake Engineering Abstracts; Quakeline
Open Mon-Fri 1:30-4
SHERMAN FAIRCHILD LIBRARY OF ENGINEERING & APPLIED SCIENCE, Fairchild Library I-43, 91125, SAN 376-8961. Tel: 626-395-3404. FAX: 626-431-2681. *Eng Librn,* George Porter
Founded 1997
Library Holdings: Bk Vols 75,000
Database Vendor: Innovative Interfaces, Inc
Open Mon-Fri 8-5

S CALIFORNIA INSTITUTE OF TECHNOLOGY*, Jet Propulsion Laboratory Library, Archives & Records Section, 4800 Oak Grove Dr, MS 111-113, 91109-8099. SAN 301-195X. Tel: 818-354-3007. Circulation Tel: 818-354-3840. Interlibrary Loan Service Tel: 818-354-9258. Reference Tel: 818-354-4200. FAX: 818-393-6752. E-mail: library@jpl.nasa.gov. Web Site: beacon.jpl.nasa.gov. *Mgr, Libr & Archives,* Robert Powers; Tel: 818-354-9263, E-mail: robert.a.powers@jpl.nasa.gov; *Rec Mgr,* Susan Hendrickson; Staff 21 (MLS 11, Non-MLS 10)
Founded 1948
Library Holdings: Bk Titles 40,977; Bk Vols 84,827; Per Subs 1,030
Special Collections: JPL Archives. Oral History
Subject Interests: Aerospace, Astronomy, Astrophysics, Bus & mgt, Eng, Phys sci
Automation Activity & Vendor Info: (Acquisitions) OCLC; (Cataloging) OCLC; (Circulation) OCLC; (OPAC) OCLC; (Serials) OCLC
Function: Archival coll, ILL available, Ref & res, Web-catalog
Partic in OCLC Online Computer Library Center, Inc
Restriction: Not open to pub

SR FIRST UNITED METHODIST CHURCH LIBRARY*, 500 E Colorado Blvd, 91101. SAN 373-0344. Tel: 626-796-0157. FAX: 626-568-1615. E-mail: library@fumcpasadena.org. Web Site: www.fumcpasadena.org. *Librn,* Ruth McPherson
Library Holdings: Bk Vols 5,000
Subject Interests: Relig
Restriction: Mem only

CR FULLER THEOLOGICAL SEMINARY*, David Allan Hubbard Library, 135 N Oakland Ave, 91182. SAN 301-1933. Tel: 626-584-5218. Administration Tel: 626-584-5219. FAX: 626-584-5613. Web Site: www.fuller.edu/academics/library.aspx. *Asst Provost,* Michael Murray; *Circ Librn,* Genalyn McNeil; *Database Mgr, Syst Coordr,* Daniela Matei
Founded 1948. Enrl 1,704; Fac 93; Highest Degree: Doctorate
Library Holdings: Bk Vols 227,000; Per Subs 960
Subject Interests: Biblical studies, Church hist, Feminism, Philos, Psychol, Relig, Theol
Database Vendor: SirsiDynix
Wireless access
Partic in Metronet; OCLC Online Computer Library Center, Inc
Open Mon-Sat 9am-11pm
Friends of the Library Group

M HUNTINGTON MEMORIAL HOSPITAL*, Health Sciences Library, 100 W California Blvd, 91105-3010. (Mail add: PO Box 7013, 91109-7013), SAN 301-1941. Tel: 626-397-5161. FAX: 626-397-2908. E-mail: library@huntingtonhospital.com. Web Site: www.huntingtonhospital.com. *Mgr,* Sherrill Olsen; *Ref Serv,* Jeya Thangarajah; *Ref Serv,* Louisa Verma; Staff 3 (MLS 3)
Library Holdings: Bk Vols 800; Per Subs 600
Special Collections: Medical & Paramedical Texts, bks, journals, AV
Subject Interests: Allied health, Nursing
Automation Activity & Vendor Info: (Acquisitions) Marcive, Inc; (Cataloging) EOS International; (Circulation) EOS International; (OPAC) EOS International; (Serials) EBSCO Online
Database Vendor: EBSCO Information Services, Elsevier, EOS International, Gale Cengage Learning, Marcive, Inc, McGraw-Hill, MD Consult, Micromedex, Natural Standard, OVID Technologies, PubMed, RefWorks, ScienceDirect, UpToDate
Wireless access
Partic in Docline; National Network of Libraries of Medicine
Open Mon-Fri 8-4
Restriction: Badge access after hrs, Mem only
Friends of the Library Group

S NATIONAL ASSOCIATION FOR HISPANIC ELDERLY LIBRARY*, 234 E Colorado Blvd, Ste 300, 91101. Tel: 626-564-1988. FAX: 626-564-2659. Web Site: www.anppm.org. *Pres,* Dr Carmela G Lacayo; *Librn,* Therese Grenier
Library Holdings: Bk Titles 4,200; Per Subs 77
Open Mon-Fri 9-5
Friends of the Library Group

S OBSERVATORIES OF THE CARNEGIE INSTITUTION OF WASHINGTON*, Hale Library, 813 Santa Barbara St, 91101. SAN 371-0297. Tel: 626-304-0228. FAX: 626-795-8136. Web Site: www.ociw.edu. *Librn,* John Grula; Staff 1 (MLS 1)
Founded 1904
Library Holdings: Bk Titles 4,660; Bk Vols 31,498; Per Subs 28
Subject Interests: Astronomy, Astrophysics
Function: Res libr
Restriction: Open by appt only, Restricted access

S PACIFIC ASIA MUSEUM LIBRARY*, 46 N Los Robles Ave, 91101-2009. SAN 326-2413. Tel: 626-449-2742, Ext 124. FAX: 626-449-2754. E-mail: library@pacificasiamuseum.org. Web Site: www.pacificasiamuseum.org. *Librn,* Sarah McKay; Staff 1 (MLS 1)
Founded 1986
Jan 2012-Jan 2013 Income $720. Mats Exp $993, Books $635, Per/Ser (Incl. Access Fees) $358
Library Holdings: Bk Vols 9,000; Per Subs 6
Special Collections: India (Paul Sherbert Coll)
Subject Interests: Asian art & culture, Pac art & culture
Open Wed & Fri 12-4

C PACIFIC OAKS COLLEGE*, Andrew Norman Library, 55 Eureka St, 91103. SAN 301-1976. Tel: 626-529-8451. Toll Free Tel: 800-684-0500. E-mail: library@pacificoaks.edu. Web Site: po.librarypass.org, www.pacificoaks.edu/library. *Campus Librn,* Kelsey Vukic; Tel: 626-529-8453, E-mail: kvukic@pacificoaks.edu. Subject Specialists: *Info sci,* Kelsey Vukic
Founded 1946. Enrl 1,100; Fac 40; Highest Degree: Master
Library Holdings: AV Mats 420; e-books 100; Electronic Media & Resources 250; Bk Titles 5,000; Videos 300
Automation Activity & Vendor Info: (Cataloging) EOS International; (Circulation) EOS International; (ILL) OCLC; (OPAC) EOS International
Database Vendor: ebrary, EBSCOhost, OCLC FirstSearch, OCLC WorldShare Interlibrary Loan, ProQuest
Open Mon-Thurs 10-7, Fri 10-6, Sat & Sun 10-3
Restriction: Access at librarian's discretion

S PARSONS CORP*, Technical Library, 100 W Walnut, 91124. SAN 320-5789. Tel: 626-440-3998. FAX: 626-440-2630. Web Site: www.parsons.com. *Mgr,* Claire Hammond
Founded 1949
Library Holdings: Bk Vols 10,000
Special Collections: Company Project Reports; Published Articles
Subject Interests: Aviation, Transportation
Publications: TIPS (monthly newsletter)

J PASADENA CITY COLLEGE LIBRARY*, Shatford Library, 1570 E Colorado Blvd, 91106-2003. SAN 301-1992. Tel: 626-585-7360. Circulation Tel: 626-585-7174. Interlibrary Loan Service Tel: 626-585-7835. Information Services Tel: 626-585-7221. FAX: 626-585-7913. Web Site: www.pasadena.edu/library. *Dir,* Position Currently Open
Founded 1924. Enrl 28,000; Fac 1,102; Highest Degree: Associate
Library Holdings: Bk Titles 103,532; Bk Vols 135,666; Per Subs 350
Subject Interests: Educ, Hist, Local hist
Automation Activity & Vendor Info: (Cataloging) Ex Libris Group; (Circulation) Ex Libris Group; (Course Reserve) Ex Libris Group
Database Vendor: OCLC FirstSearch
Function: Archival coll, AV serv, Handicapped accessible, ILL available, Magnifiers for reading, Online searches, Photocopying/Printing, Ref serv available, Telephone ref, Wheelchair accessible
Open Mon-Thurs 7:30am-9:30pm, Fri 7:30-4:30, Sat 9-2
Restriction: Open to students, fac & staff, Residents only

S PASADENA MUSEUM OF HISTORY, Research Library & Archives, 470 W Walnut St, 91103-3594. SAN 301-200X. Tel: 626-577-1660. Reference Tel: 626-577-1660, Ext 13. FAX: 626-577-1662. E-mail: research@pasadenahistory.org. Web Site: www.pasadenahistory.org. *Dir of Coll,* Laura Verlaque; Staff 0.5 (Non-MLS 0.5)
Founded 1924
Library Holdings: Bk Titles 1,800; Bk Vols 2,000
Special Collections: Fenyes-Curtin-Paloheimo Family Archives; Giddings-Hollingsworth Family Coll; J Allen Hawkins Photo Coll; Pasadena Star-News Photo Archive; Sylvanus Marston Coll; Tournament of Roses. Oral History
Subject Interests: African-Am hist, Archit, Local hist, Maps, Real estate
Function: Archival coll, Photocopying/Printing, Res libr
Publications: A Southern California Paradise; Historic Pasadena (Lund); Pasadena Photographs & Photographers 1880-1920; Pasadena's Super Athletes; Walter Raymond, A Gentleman of the Old School
Open Thurs-Sun 1-4
Restriction: Non-circulating, Open to pub for ref only

P PASADENA PUBLIC LIBRARY*, 285 E Walnut St, 91101. SAN 333-6212. Tel: 626-744-4066. Interlibrary Loan Service Tel: 626-744-4223. FAX: 626-585-8396. TDD: 626-564-2837. Web Site: www.cityofpasadena.net/library. *Dir, Info Serv,* Jan Sanders; Tel: 626 744-3867, E-mail: jsanders@cityofpasadena.net; *IT Dir,* Bryan Sands; *Principal Librn,* Susan Gegenhuber; *Principal Librn,* Beth Walker
Founded 1882. Pop 146,166; Circ 1,589,247
Jul 2006-Jun 2007. Mats Exp $929,252
Library Holdings: Bk Vols 710,566; Per Subs 1,145
Special Collections: US Document Depository
Automation Activity & Vendor Info: (Acquisitions) SirsiDynix; (Cataloging) SirsiDynix; (Circulation) SirsiDynix; (OPAC) SirsiDynix
Wireless access
Function: Adult literacy prog, Homebound delivery serv, Photocopying/Printing, Prog for children & young adult, Ref serv available, Summer reading prog, Telephone ref
Partic in Southern California Library Cooperative
Open Mon-Thurs 9-9, Fri & Sat 9-6, Sun 1-5
Friends of the Library Group
Branches: 9
ALLENDALE, 1130 S Marengo Ave, 91106, SAN 333-6247. Tel: 626-744-7260.
Pop 8,760; Circ 65,289
Library Holdings: Bk Vols 41,418
Open Mon-Thurs & Sat 10-6
HASTINGS, 3325 E Orange Grove Blvd, 91107, SAN 333-6271. Tel: 626-744-7262. FAX: 626-440-0222. *Librn,* Thelma Watson
Pop 19,860; Circ 210,275
Library Holdings: Bk Vols 64,069
Open Mon-Thurs 10-9, Fri 10-6

HILL AVENUE, 55 S Hill Ave, 91106, SAN 333-6301. Tel: 626-744-7264. FAX: 626-440-0183. *Actg Librn,* Shauna Redmond
Pop 22,572; Circ 83,514
Library Holdings: Bk Vols 41,859
Special Collections: Asian languages & subjects
Open Mon-Thurs & Sat 10-6

LA PINTORESCA, 1355 N Raymond Ave, 91103, SAN 333-6360. Tel: 626-744-7268. Web Site: www.ci.pasadena.ca.us/library/lapintoresca.asp. *Librn,* Elizabeth Brooks
Pop 33,291; Circ 77,010
Library Holdings: Bk Vols 56,861
Subject Interests: African-Am hist, Arts, Career, Cookery, Music, Spanish lang
Open Mon-Thurs 10-7, Fri 10-6

LAMANDA PARK, 140 S Altadena Dr, 91107, SAN 333-6336. Tel: 626-744-7266. Web Site: www.ci.pasadena.ca.us/library/lamanda.asp. *Librn,* Christine Reeder
Founded 1967. Pop 5,621; Circ 77,264
Library Holdings: Bk Vols 51,846
Subject Interests: Juv, Mysteries, Popular fiction
Open Mon-Thurs & Sat 10-6

LINDA VISTA, 1281 Bryant St, 91103, SAN 333-6395. Tel: 626-744-7278. Web Site: www.ci.pasadena.ca.us/library/lindavista.asp. *Librn,* Robin Reidy
Founded 1957. Pop 5,447; Circ 48,957
Library Holdings: Bk Vols 28,976
Subject Interests: Biographies, Cooking, Gardening, Travel
Open Mon-Thurs & Sat 10-6
Friends of the Library Group

SAN RAFAEL, 1240 Nithsdale Rd, 91105, SAN 333-6425. Tel: 626-744-7270. FAX: 626-440-0160. Web Site: www.ci.pasadena.ca.us/library/sanrafael.asp.
Founded 1957. Pop 5,201; Circ 58,101
Library Holdings: Bk Vols 37,555
Subject Interests: Art, Best sellers, Biographies, Travel
Open Mon-Thurs & Sat 10-6

SANTA CATALINA, 999 E Washington Blvd, 91104, SAN 333-645X. Tel: 626-744-7272. Web Site: www.ci.pasadena.ca.us/library/santacat.asp. *Librn,* Barbara Martin
Founded 1930. Pop 20,270; Circ 95,128
Library Holdings: Bk Vols 48,589
Special Collections: Armenian language and subjects
Open Mon-Thurs & Sat 10-6

VILLA PARKE COMMUNITY CENTER, 363 E Villa St, 91101, SAN 374-8103. Tel: 626-744-6510. Web Site: www.ci.pasadena.ca.us/library/villaparke.asp. *Librn,* Rosa Martin
Founded 1992. Circ 24,353
Open Mon-Fri 10-6

S RIGHT TO LIFE LEAGUE OF SOUTHERN CALIFORNIA LIBRARY*, 1028 N Lake Ave, Ste 207, 91104. SAN 370-4327. Tel: 626-398-6100. FAX: 626-398-6101. E-mail: info@rtllsc.org. Web Site: rtllsc.org.
Founded 1969
Subject Interests: Abortion, Abstinence educ, Euthanasia, Genetic eng, Human experimentation, Infanticide, Pop control, Pre-natal develop, Sex educ
Function: AV serv, Res libr
Open Mon-Fri 9-5

L US COURT OF APPEALS, NINTH CIRCUIT LIBRARY*, 125 S Grand Ave, 91105. SAN 323-7680. Tel: 626-229-7190. FAX: 626-229-7460. *Librn,* Joy M Shoemaker; Staff 3 (MLS 2, Non-MLS 1)
Founded 1985
Library Holdings: Bk Titles 2,020; Bk Vols 26,000; Per Subs 30
Subject Interests: Law
Wireless access

PASO ROBLES

P PASO ROBLES PUBLIC LIBRARY*, 1000 Spring St, 93446-2207. SAN 301-2069. Tel: 805-237-3870. FAX: 805-238-3665. Web Site: www.prcity.com. *Libr Mgr,* Julie Dahlen; E-mail: jdahlen@prcity.com; *Adult Serv,* Karen Christiansen; *Ch Serv,* Kris Bell; *Ref,* Barbara Bilyeu
Founded 1903. Pop 27,200; Circ 222,936
Jul 2005-Jun 2006 Income $1,602,300, State $93,306, City $1,443,101, Federal $2,838, Locally Generated Income $63,055. Mats Exp $54,909, Books $39,927, Per/Ser (Incl. Access Fees) $4,877, AV Mat $8,156, Electronic Ref Mat (Incl. Access Fees) $1,949. Sal $546,952 (Prof $301,900)
Library Holdings: AV Mats 7,548; Bk Vols 56,070; Per Subs 120; Videos 4,459
Special Collections: Paso Robles Newspapers from 1892, micro
Mem of Black Gold Cooperative Library System
Open Mon-Fri 10-8, Sat 10-5
Friends of the Library Group

PATTON

PATTON STATE HOSPITAL

M PATIENTS LIBRARY*, 3102 E Highland Ave, 92369, SAN 320-1600. Tel: 909-425-6039. FAX: 909-425-6162. *Sr Librn,* Frederick Brenion; Staff 1 (MLS 1)
Library Holdings: Bk Titles 10,300; Bk Vols 13,000; Per Subs 50

M STAFF LIBRARY*, 3102 E Highland Ave, 92369, SAN 320-1619. Tel: 909-425-7484. FAX: 909-425-6053. *Librn,* Angela Stoner; Staff 1 (MLS 1)
Founded 1941
Library Holdings: Bk Titles 3,300; Per Subs 130
Subject Interests: Psychiat
Automation Activity & Vendor Info: (Acquisitions) Sydney; (Cataloging) Sydney; (Circulation) Sydney; (Course Reserve) Sydney; (ILL) Sydney; (Media Booking) Sydney; (OPAC) Sydney; (Serials) Sydney
Database Vendor: OVID Technologies
Function: Ref serv available
Partic in Medical Library Group of Southern California & Arizona (MLGSCA); San Bernardino, Inyo, Riverside Counties United Library Services
Restriction: Open by appt only

PETALUMA

S INSTITUTE OF NOETIC SCIENCES LIBRARY*, 625 Second St, Ste 200, 94952-9524. SAN 327-5590. Tel: 707-775-3500. FAX: 707-781-7420. Web Site: www.noetic.org. *Librn,* Charlene Farrell; *Operations Mgr,* Tiffany Mitchell
Library Holdings: Bk Vols 3,000
Wireless access
Restriction: Staff use only

PICO RIVERA

S ARMENIAN NUMISMATIC SOCIETY RESEARCH LIBRARY*, 8511 Beverly Park Pl, 90660-1920. SAN 374-4825. Tel: 562-695-0380. E-mail: armnumsoc@aol.com. Web Site: www.armnumsoc.org. *Librn,* W Gewenian; *Asst Librn,* Y T Nercessian
Founded 1971
Oct 2012-Sept 2013. Mats Exp $10,000
Library Holdings: Bk Titles 5,000; Per Subs 10
Subject Interests: Numismatics
Restriction: Not open to pub

PITTSBURG

J LOS MEDANOS COLLEGE LIBRARY*, 2700 E Leland Rd, 94565. Tel: 925-439-2181. Circulation Tel: 925-439-2181, Ext 3320. Reference Tel: 925-439-2181, Ext 3275. Web Site: www.losmedanos.edu/lmc_library/default.htm. *Dir,* Christina Goff; *Librn,* Edwin Bolds; Tel: 925-439-2181, Ext 3219, E-mail: ebolds@losmedanos.edu; *Librn,* April Corioso; Tel: 925-439-2181, Ext 3385, E-mail: acorioso@losmedanos.edu; *Librn,* Linda Simpson; Tel: 925-439-2181, Ext 3396, E-mail: lsimpson@losmedanos.edu
Library Holdings: Bk Vols 17,000
Wireless access
Open Mon-Thurs 7:45am-8:45pm, Fri 7:45-2:45, Sat 10-2

PLACENTIA

P PLACENTIA LIBRARY DISTRICT*, 411 E Chapman Ave, 92870. SAN 301-1488. Tel: 714-528-1906. FAX: 714-528-8236. E-mail: reference@placentialibrary.org. Web Site: www.placentialibrary.org. *Dir,* Jeanette Contreras; E-mail: jcontreras@placentialibrary.org; *Ch,* Lori Worden; *Circ Supvr,* Fernando Maldonado; Staff 13.5 (MLS 5.25, Non-MLS 8.25)
Founded 1919. Pop 54,980; Circ 211,285
Library Holdings: Audiobooks 1,388; CDs 2,002; DVDs 5,935; Large Print Bks 966; Bk Vols 95,515; Per Subs 112
Special Collections: Placentia Local History Coll
Automation Activity & Vendor Info: (Circulation) SirsiDynix
Wireless access
Function: Adult bk club, Adult literacy prog, Art exhibits, AV serv, Bilingual assistance for Spanish patrons, Bks on CD, Children's prog, Computer training, Computers for patron use, Copy machines, Digital talking bks, Electronic databases & coll, Exhibits, Free DVD rentals, Handicapped accessible, Homework prog, ILL available, Music CDs, Online cat, Outside serv via phone, mail, e-mail & web, Passport agency, Photocopying/Printing, Preschool outreach, Prog for adults, Prog for children & young adult, Pub access computers, Ref serv in person, Summer reading prog, Telephone ref, Web-catalog, Wheelchair accessible, Workshops
Partic in Southern California Library Cooperative

Open Mon-Thurs 9-9, Sat 9-5, Sun 1-5
Friends of the Library Group

PLACERVILLE

GL EL DORADO COUNTY LAW LIBRARY, 550 Main St, Ste A, 95667. SAN 301-2123. Tel: 530-626-1932. E-mail: edlawlibrary@gmail.com. Web Site: eldoradocountylawlibrary.org. *Dir/Adminr,* Linda Fox. Subject Specialists: *Legal res,* Linda Fox; Staff 1 (Non-MLS 1)
Pop 182,404
Jul 2013-Jun 2014 Income $117,042, State $111,703, County $536, Locally Generated Income $4,803. Mats Exp $61,594, Books $31,895, Electronic Ref Mat (Incl. Access Fees) $29,699. Sal $43,139 (Prof $32,524)
Library Holdings: Bk Titles 9,200
Special Collections: CA & FED Legal Materials
Subject Interests: Legal
Database Vendor: EBSCOhost, Westlaw
Wireless access
Function: Computers for patron use, Copy machines, Electronic databases & coll, Pub access computers, Scanner, Workshops
Open Mon-Fri 8-12 & 1-4

P EL DORADO COUNTY LIBRARY, 345 Fair Lane, 95667. SAN 333-6484. Tel: 530-621-5540. FAX: 530-622-3911. E-mail: lib-pl@eldoradolibrary.org. Web Site: www.eldoradolibrary.org. *Dir,* Jeanne Amos; Tel: 530-621-5546, E-mail: jeanne.amos@eldoradolibrary.org; Staff 14.1 (MLS 3.5, Non-MLS 10.6)
Founded 1906. Pop 62,448; Circ 291,731
Jul 2012-Jun 2013 Income (Main Library and Branch(s)) $3,222,553, State $205,610, Federal $14,736, County $2,698,135, Other $304,072. Mats Exp $286,187, Books $158,941, Per/Ser (Incl. Access Fees) $18,546, Other Print Mats $47,588, Electronic Ref Mat (Incl. Access Fees) $61,112. Sal $1,641,237
Library Holdings: Audiobooks 5,262; DVDs 4,277; e-books 2,952; Bk Titles 210,114; Bk Vols 123,062; Per Subs 454
Subject Interests: Calif
Automation Activity & Vendor Info: (Acquisitions) SirsiDynix; (Cataloging) SirsiDynix; (Circulation) SirsiDynix; (OPAC) SirsiDynix
Database Vendor: EBSCO Auto Repair Reference, EBSCOhost, Gale Cengage Learning, LearningExpress, Overdrive, Inc, World Book Online
Wireless access
Function: ILL available
Mem of NorthNet Library System
Open Tues & Wed 12-7, Thurs-Sat 10-5
Friends of the Library Group
Branches: 5
CAMERON PARK BRANCH, 2500 Country Club Dr, Cameron Park, 95682, SAN 374-6852. Tel: 530-621-5500. FAX: 530-672-1346. E-mail: lib-cp@eldoradolibrary.org. *Mgr,* Nancy Owen-Hazard; Staff 4.8 (Non-MLS 4.8)
Pop 31,092; Circ 153,987
Library Holdings: Audiobooks 3,038; DVDs 2,780; Bk Vols 57,209
Open Mon, Wed & Fri 10-5, Tues & Thurs 12-7
Friends of the Library Group
EL DORADO HILLS BRANCH, 7455 Silva Valley Pkwy, El Dorado Hills, 95762, SAN 333-6514. Tel: 916-358-3500. FAX: 916-933-7089. E-mail: lib-edh@eldoradolibrary.org. *Br Mgr,* Carolyn Brooks; Staff 6.55 (MLS 1.8, Non-MLS 4.75)
Pop 28,735; Circ 213,465
Library Holdings: Audiobooks 3,592; DVDs 3,802; Bk Vols 63,153
Open Mon & Sat 1-5, Tues & Wed 12-7, Thurs & Fri 10-5
Friends of the Library Group
GEORGETOWN BRANCH, 6680 Orleans St, Georgetown, 95634. (Mail add: PO Box 55, Georgetown, 95634-0055), SAN 333-6549. Tel: 530-333-4724. FAX: 530-333-4724. E-mail: lib-gt@eldoradolibrary.org. *Mgr,* Jillian Firth; Staff 1.45 (Non-MLS 1.45)
Pop 8,188; Circ 32,135
Library Holdings: Audiobooks 1,085; DVDs 2,470; Bk Vols 18,411
Open Tues & Wed Noon-7, Thurs 10-5, Fri 1-5, Sat 10-3
Friends of the Library Group
POLLOCK PINES BRANCH, 6210 Pony Express Trail, Pollock Pines, 95726. (Mail add: PO Box 757, Pollock Pines, 95726-0757), SAN 333-6603. Tel: 530-644-2498. FAX: 530-644-2498. E-mail: lib-pp@eldoradolibrary.org. *Mgr,* Wendy Smith; Staff 0.85 (Non-MLS 0.85)
Pop 19,037; Circ 23,001
Library Holdings: Audiobooks 869; DVDs 962; Bk Vols 15,896
Special Services for the Blind - Audio mat; Bks & mags in Braille, on rec, tape & cassette; Bks available with recordings; Bks on cassette; Bks on CD; Large print bks; Lending of low vision aids; Magnifiers
Open Tues 12-7, Wed & Thurs 10-5
Friends of the Library Group
SOUTH LAKE TAHOE BRANCH, 1000 Rufus Allen Blvd, South Lake Tahoe, 96150, SAN 333-6573. Tel: 530-573-3185. FAX: 530-544-8954. E-mail: lib-slt@eldoradolibrary.org. *Mgr,* Katharine Miller; E-mail: katharine.miller@eldoradolibrary.org; Staff 6.35 (MLS 1, Non-MLS 5.35)
Library Holdings: Audiobooks 3,008; DVDs 3,187; Bk Vols 56,928
Open Tues & Wed 10-8, Thurs-Sat 10-5
Friends of the Library Group
Bookmobiles: 1. Bk titles 2,500

PLEASANT HILL

P CONTRA COSTA COUNTY LIBRARY*, Library Administration, 1750 Oak Park Blvd, 94523-4497. SAN 333-6662. Tel: 925-646-6434. Interlibrary Loan Service Tel: 925-927-3224. Administration Tel: 925-646-6423. FAX: 925-646-6461. Reference FAX: 925-646-6030. E-mail: libadmin@ccclib.org. Web Site: www.ccclib.org. *County Librn,* Barbara Flynn; *Dep County Librn, Pub Serv,* Gail McPartland; *Dep County Librn, Support Serv,* Cathy Sanford; *Sr Commun Libr Mgr,* Kathy Middleton; *Circ Mgr,* Linda Barbero; *Mgr, Coll Develop/Tech Serv,* Elliot Warren; *Human Res Mgr,* Beth Kilian. Subject Specialists: *Support serv,* Cathy Sanford; *Pub serv,* Kathy Middleton; Staff 165 (MLS 58, Non-MLS 107)
Founded 1913. Pop 902,200; Circ 4,736,101
Library Holdings: AV Mats 158,971; Bk Vols 1,291,051; Per Subs 1,981
Special Collections: California Hist Coll; Contra Costa Hist Coll; Food Technology (Vincent Davi Coll). State Document Depository; US Document Depository
Automation Activity & Vendor Info: (Acquisitions) TLC (The Library Corporation); (Cataloging) TLC (The Library Corporation); (Circulation) TLC (The Library Corporation); (OPAC) TLC (The Library Corporation); (Serials) TLC (The Library Corporation)
Database Vendor: Baker & Taylor, BWI, EBSCOhost, Gale Cengage Learning, Newsbank, OCLC FirstSearch, TLC (The Library Corporation)
Wireless access
Function: Adult literacy prog, Govt ref serv, Handicapped accessible, Homebound delivery serv, ILL available, Photocopying/Printing, Prog for adults, Prog for children & young adult, Ref serv available, Summer reading prog
Mem of Bay Area Library & Information System
Special Services for the Blind - Closed circuit radio for broadcast serv; Talking bks & player equip
Open Mon-Fri 8-5
Friends of the Library Group
Branches: 26
ANTIOCH COMMUNITY LIBRARY, 501 W 18th St, Antioch, 94509-2292, SAN 333-6697. Tel: 925-757-9224. FAX: 925-427-8540. *Actg Commun Libr Mgr,* Deanna Leachman
Pop 102,113; Circ 214,591
Library Holdings: Bk Vols 64,333
Open Mon & Tues 12-8, Wed & Thurs 10-5, Sat 12-5
Friends of the Library Group
BAY POINT LIBRARY, 205 Pacifica Ave, Bay Point, 94565, SAN 377-6654. Tel: 925 458 9597. *In Charge,* Darcel Jones
Pop 22,074; Circ 11,976
Library Holdings: Bk Vols 8,706
Open Mon & Fri 2:30 6, Tues & Thurs 2:30-8
Friends of the Library Group
BRENTWOOD LIBRARY, 104 Oak St, Brentwood, 94513-1359, SAN 333-6727. Tel: 925-516-5290. *Sr Commun Libr Mgr,* Liz Fuller
Pop 56,492; Circ 161,593
Library Holdings: Bk Vols 45,996
Open Mon-Thurs 10-8, Fri & Sat 10-6
Friends of the Library Group
CLAYTON LIBRARY, 6125 Clayton Rd, Clayton, 94517, SAN 377-6670. Tel: 925-673-0659. FAX: 925-673-0359. *Commun Libr Mgr,* Karen Hansen-Smith; Staff 4 (MLS 2, Non-MLS 2)
Pop 11,398; Circ 222,073
Library Holdings: Bk Vols 63,457
Open Mon & Wed 1-9, Tues, Thurs & Sat 10-6, Sun 1-5
Friends of the Library Group
CONCORD LIBRARY, 2900 Salvio St, Concord, 94519-2597, SAN 333-6786. Tel: 925-646-5455. FAX: 925-646-5453. *Sr Commun Libr Mgr,* Bill Kolb
Circ 289,307
Library Holdings: Bk Vols 79,858
Open Mon & Thurs 12-9, Tues & Wed 10-6, Fri & Sat 10-5, Sun 1-5
Friends of the Library Group
CROCKETT LIBRARY, 991 Loring Ave, Crockett, 94525-1168, SAN 333-6816. Tel: 510-787-2345. FAX: 510-787-7275. *In Charge,* Liz Watts
Pop 3,443; Circ 7,240
Library Holdings: Bk Vols 5,449
Open Mon, Wed & Fri 11-5, Sat 10-4
Friends of the Library Group

DANVILLE LIBRARY, 400 Front St, Danville, 94526-3465, SAN 333-7235. Tel: 925-837-4889. FAX: 925-831-1299. *Sr Commun Libr Mgr,* Seng Lovan
Library Holdings: Bk Vols 81,690
Open Mon-Thurs 10-8, Fri & Sat 10-6, Sun 1-5
Friends of the Library Group

DOUGHERTY STATION LIBRARY, 17017 Bollinger Canyon Rd, San Ramon, 94582. Tel: 925-973-3380. *Actg Sr Commun Libr Mgr,* Nancy Kreiser
Library Holdings: Bk Vols 57,349
Open Mon & Thurs 10-8, Tues & Wed 12-8, Fri & Sat 10-5

EL CERRITO LIBRARY, 6510 Stockton Ave, El Cerrito, 94530-3189, SAN 333-6840. Tel: 510-526-7512. FAX: 510-526-6375. *Commun Libr Mgr,* Liz Ruhland
Pop 26,751; Circ 110,645
Library Holdings: Bk Vols 33,476
Open Mon & Tues 12-8, Thurs 10-6, Fri 1-5, Sat 10-5
Friends of the Library Group

EL SOBRANTE BRANCH, 4191 Appian Way, El Sobrante, 94803-2298, SAN 333-6875. Tel: 510-374-3991. FAX: 510-222-4137. *Sr Commun Libr Mgr,* Ian Richards; Staff 9 (MLS 4, Non-MLS 5)
Founded 1961
Library Holdings: Bk Vols 30,037
Database Vendor: Facts on File, Gale Cengage Learning, Overdrive, Inc, Safari Books Online, World Book Online
Function: Adult bk club, Children's prog, Computers for patron use, Copy machines, Electronic databases & coll, Free DVD rentals, Large print keyboards, Magnifiers for reading
Open Mon & Thurs 12-8, Tues 10-6, Fri 1-5, Sat 10-5
Friends of the Library Group

HERCULES LIBRARY, 109 Civic Dr, Hercules, 94547. Tel: 510-245-2420. *Sr Commun Libr Mgr,* Alison McKee
Library Holdings: Bk Vols 56,277
Open Mon & Tues 1-9, Wed, Thurs & Sat 10-6

KENSINGTON LIBRARY, 61 Arlington Ave, Kensington, 94707-1098, SAN 333-6905. Tel: 510-524-3043. FAX: 510-528-2567. *Commun Libr Mgr,* Laura Martinengo
Pop 4,975; Circ 75,780
Library Holdings: Bk Vols 25,934
Open Mon & Tues 12-8, Thurs 10-6, Fri 1-5, Sat 10-5
Friends of the Library Group

LAFAYETTE LIBRARY, 3491 Mount Diablo Blvd, Lafayette, 94549-4594, SAN 333-693X. Tel: 925-385-2280. *Sr Commun Libr Mgr,* Vickie Sciacca
Library Holdings: Bk Vols 72,461
Open Mon-Thurs 10-8, Fri & Sat 10-5, Sun 1-5
Friends of the Library Group

MARTINEZ LIBRARY, 740 Court St, Martinez, 94553-1218, SAN 333-6964. Tel: 925-646-9900. Web Site: ccclib.org/locations/martinez.html. *Sr Commun Libr Mgr,* Karen Hansen-Smith; Staff 2.5 (MLS 2, Non-MLS 0.5)
Founded 1941
Library Holdings: Bk Vols 29,485
Special Collections: John Muir Coll; Shell Community Environmental Impact Reports
Function: Bi-weekly Writer's Group
Open Mon 12-8, Tues 10-8, Wed & Fri 12-5, Sat 10-5
Restriction: Access for corporate affiliates
Friends of the Library Group

MORAGA LIBRARY, 1500 Saint Mary's Rd, Moraga, 94556-2099, SAN 333-6999. Tel: 925-376-6852. FAX: 925-376-3034. *Actg Sr Commun Libr Mgr,* Melanie McCallum
Library Holdings: Bk Vols 50,216
Open Tues & Thurs 12-8, Wed 10-6, Fri 1-5, Sat 10-5
Friends of the Library Group

OAKLEY BRANCH, 1050 Neroly Rd, Oakley, 94561-3843, SAN 333-7022. Tel: 925-625-2400. FAX: 925-625-8398. *Commun Libr Mgr,* Jenna Skinner
Library Holdings: Bk Vols 31,665
Open Tues & Wed 10-9, Thurs 2-9, Fri 2-6, Sat 10-6
Friends of the Library Group

ORINDA LIBRARY, 26 Orinda Way, Orinda, 94563-2555, SAN 333-7057. Tel: 925-254-2184. FAX: 925-253-8629. *Sr Commun Libr Mgr,* Beth Grishman
Library Holdings: Bk Vols 67,988
Open Mon-Thurs 10-8, Fri & Sat 10-6, Sun 1-5
Friends of the Library Group

PINOLE LIBRARY, 2935 Pinole Valley Rd, Pinole, 94564-1494, SAN 333-7111. Tel: 510-758-2741. FAX: 510-758-2745. *Sr Commun Libr Mgr,* Ian Richards
Library Holdings: Bk Vols 36,826
Open Mon 10-6, Wed 2-8, Fri & Sat 12-5
Friends of the Library Group

PITTSBURG LIBRARY, 80 Power Ave, Pittsburg, 94565-3842, SAN 333-7146. Tel: 925-427-8390. FAX: 925-427-8137. *Commun Libr Mgr,* Chris Brown
Library Holdings: Bk Vols 39,226
Open Tues 12-8, Wed 10-6, Thurs 1-8, Fri & Sat 11-5
Friends of the Library Group

PLEASANT HILL LIBRARY, 1750 Oak Park Blvd, 94523-4497, SAN 333-6751. Tel: 925-646-6434. FAX: 925-646-6040. *Circ Mgr,* Linda Barbero
Pop 39,650; Circ 518,646
Library Holdings: Bk Vols 153,449
Open Tues 1-8, Wed & Thurs 11-6, Fri & Sat 10-5
Friends of the Library Group

PREWETT LIBRARY, 4703 Lone Tree Way, Antioch, 94531. Tel: 925-776-3060. *Libr Asst,* Courtney Diputado
Library Holdings: Bk Vols 5,958
Open Tues 10-7, Wed & Thurs 12-8, Fri & Sat 12-5

RODEO COMMUNITY LIBRARY, 220 Pacific Ave, Rodeo, 94572-1118, SAN 333-7170. Tel: 510-799-2606. FAX: 510-799-3349. *In Charge,* Position Currently Open
Library Holdings: Bk Vols 7,873
Open Mon & Sat 12-5, Tues & Thurs 1-7
Friends of the Library Group

SAN PABLO LIBRARY, 2300 El Portal Dr, Ste D, San Pablo, 94806-4452, SAN 371-3350. Tel: 510-374-3998. FAX: 510-374-3225. *Commun Libr Mgr,* Chela Lucas
Library Holdings: Bk Vols 30,011
Open Mon & Tues 12-8, Wed 10-6, Fri & Sun 1-5, Sat 10-5
Friends of the Library Group

SAN RAMON LIBRARY, 100 Montgomery St, San Ramon, 94583-4707, SAN 333-7200. Tel: 925-973-2850. FAX: 925-866-6720. *Actg Sr Commun Libr Mgr,* Nancy Kreiser
Library Holdings: Bk Vols 73,843
Open Mon-Thurs 10-8, Fri & Sat 10-5, Sun 1-5
Friends of the Library Group

WALNUT CREEK LIBRARY, 1644 N Broadway, Walnut Creek, 94596-4297, SAN 333-726X. Tel: 925-977-3340. FAX: 925-646-6048. *Sr Commun Libr Mgr,* Carolina Gick
Library Holdings: Bk Vols 72,160
Open Mon-Thurs 10-8, Fri & Sat 10-6
Friends of the Library Group

YGNACIO VALLEY LIBRARY, 2661 Oak Grove Rd, Walnut Creek, 94598-3627, SAN 333-7294. Tel: 925-938-1481. FAX: 925-646-6026. *Sr Commun Libr Mgr,* Carolina Gick; Staff 2.5 (MLS 2.5)
Pop 23,338; Circ 348,680
Library Holdings: Bk Vols 65,634
Function: Adult bk club, Art exhibits, Audiobks via web, Bks on CD, Children's prog, Computers for patron use, e-mail serv, Exhibits, Free DVD rentals, Handicapped accessible, ILL available, Music CDs, Photocopying/Printing, Prog for adults, Prog for children & young adult, Pub access computers, Story hour, Summer reading prog, Wheelchair accessible
Open Mon-Thurs 10-8, Fri & Sat 10-6
Friends of the Library Group

S CONTRA COSTA COUNTY OFFICE OF EDUCATION*, Learning Resource Center, 77 Santa Barbara Rd, 94523. SAN 324-4504. Tel: 925-942-5332. FAX: 925-942-5398. Web Site: www.cccoe.k12.ca.us. *Mgr, Instrul Tech,* Rovina Salinas; E-mail: rsalinas@cccoe.k12.ca.us; Staff 3 (MLS 3)
Founded 1952
Library Holdings: Bk Titles 1,200; Per Subs 33
Special Collections: ERIC; Grant Resources; State-adopted Materials; State-adopted Textbooks
Subject Interests: Educ, Grants, Libr sci
Database Vendor: EBSCOhost, Newsbank
Open Mon-Fri 8-5

J DIABLO VALLEY COLLEGE LIBRARY*, 321 Golf Club Rd, 94523-1576. SAN 301-2131. Tel: 925-685-1230, Ext 2241. Circulation Tel: 925-685-1230, Ext 2441. Reference Tel: 925-685-1230, Ext 2246. FAX: 925-798-3588. Web Site: www.dvc.edu/library. *Interim Dir, Libr Serv,* Andy Kivel; Tel: 925-685-1230, Ext 2237, E-mail: akivel@dvc.edu; *Instrul Serv Librn,* Ruth Sison; Tel: 925-685-1230, Ext 2681, E-mail: rsison@dvc.edu; *Cat, Coll Develop,* Marva DeLoach; Tel: 925-685-1230, Ext 2780, E-mail: mdeloach@dvc.edu; *Electronic Access Librn,* Daniel Kiely; Tel: 925-685-1230, Ext 2393, E-mail: dkiely@dvc.edu; *Ref Serv,* Florence Espiritu; Tel: 925-685-1230, Ext 2239, E-mail: fespiritu@dvc.edu; Staff 13 (MLS 6, Non-MLS 7)
Founded 1950. Enrl 22,022; Fac 767; Highest Degree: Associate
Jul 2008-Jun 2009 Income $559,663. Mats Exp $172,970, Books $79,911, Per/Ser (Incl. Access Fees) $26,376, Micro $905, Electronic Ref Mat (Incl. Access Fees) $65,778. Sal $972,081 (Prof $605,996)
Library Holdings: CDs 367; e-books 18,005; Bk Titles 97,159; Bk Vols 106,517; Per Subs 250

Special Collections: Californiana
Automation Activity & Vendor Info: (Acquisitions) Innovative Interfaces, Inc; (Cataloging) Innovative Interfaces, Inc; (Circulation) Innovative Interfaces, Inc; (Course Reserve) Innovative Interfaces, Inc; (OPAC) Innovative Interfaces, Inc; (Serials) Innovative Interfaces, Inc
Database Vendor: Gale Cengage Learning, ProQuest
Wireless access
Partic in Bay Area Library & Information Network; Community College League of California (CCLC)
Special Services for the Blind - Assistive/Adapted tech devices, equip & products
Open Mon Thurs 8am-9pm, Fri 8-5, Sat 12-4
Friends of the Library Group

C JOHN F KENNEDY UNIVERSITY LIBRARIES*, Robert M Fisher Library, 100 Ellinwood Way, 94523. SAN 301-150X. Tel: 925-969-3100. Reference Tel: 925-969-3109. Toll Free Tel: 800-696-5358. FAX: 925-969-3101. Web Site: library.jfku.edu. *Interim Univ Librn,* Claudia Chester; Tel: 925-969-3108, E-mail: cchester@jfku.edu; Staff 8.7 (MLS 5, Non-MLS 3.7)
Founded 1964. Enrl 1,494; Fac 518; Highest Degree: Doctorate
Jul 2012-Jun 2013 Income (Main Library Only) $483,865. Mats Exp $203,298, Books $45,308, Per/Ser (Incl. Access Fees) $62,402, AV Mat $4,794, Electronic Ref Mat (Incl. Access Fees) $90,794. Sal $383,486 (Prof $279,692)
Library Holdings: AV Mats 2,570; e-books 72,879; e-journals 47,608; Bk Titles 39,749; Bk Vols 60,283; Videos 1,679
Subject Interests: Bus & mgt, Holistic studies, Psychol
Automation Activity & Vendor Info: (Acquisitions) Innovative Interfaces, Inc; (Cataloging) Innovative Interfaces, Inc; (Circulation) Innovative Interfaces, Inc; (Course Reserve) Innovative Interfaces, Inc; (ILL) Innovative Interfaces, Inc; (OPAC) Innovative Interfaces, Inc; (Serials) Innovative Interfaces, Inc
Database Vendor: Alexander Street Press, American Psychological Association (APA), Cambridge Scientific Abstracts, ebrary, EBSCOhost, Elsevier, Gale Cengage Learning, H W Wilson, LexisNexis, McGraw-Hill, Medline, OCLC ArticleFirst, OCLC FirstSearch, OCLC WorldShare Interlibrary Loan, ProQuest, PubMed, Sage, ScienceDirect, SerialsSolutions, Springer-Verlag, Springshare, LLC, Wiley InterScience
Wireless access
Function: Accessibility serv available based on individual needs, Audio & video playback equip for onsite use, Computers for patron use, Copy machines, Distance learning, Doc delivery serv, e-mail & chat, Electronic databases & coll, Free DVD rentals, ILL available, Mail loans to mem, Online cat, Online ref, Orientations, Photocopying/Printing, Ref serv available, Ref serv in person, Spoken cassettes & CDs, Spoken cassettes & DVDs, VHS videos, Web-catalog, Wheelchair accessible
Partic in BayNet Library Association; Califa; Docline; Northern & Central California Psychology Libraries; OCLC Online Computer Library Center, Inc; Statewide California Electronic Library Consortium (SCELC)
Special Services for the Deaf - Bks on deafness & sign lang; Closed caption videos
Special Services for the Blind - Audio mat; Cassette playback machines; Cassettes; Sound rec
Open Mon-Thurs 11-8, Fri 11-5, Sat 10-5
Restriction: Borrowing requests are handled by ILL, Fee for pub use, In-house use for visitors, Open to students, fac, staff & alumni

Departmental Libraries:

BERKELEY CAMPUS LIBRARY, 2956 San Pablo Ave, 2nd Flr, Berkeley, 94702. Tel: 510-649-1008. FAX: 510-645-0910. *Br Librn,* Laraine Hilgers; E-mail: lhilgers@jfku.edu; Staff 1.5 (MLS 0.8, Non-MLS 0.7)
Founded 2003. Highest Degree: Master
Jul 2010-Jun 2011 Income $97,296. Mats Exp $13,362, Books $6,154, Per/Ser (Incl. Access Fees) $4,056, AV Mat $1,576. Sal $81,562 (Prof $51,261)
Library Holdings: AV Mats 57; Bk Titles 6,035; Bk Vols 6,963; Per Subs 46
Subject Interests: Arts, Museology, Psychol
Function: Audio & video playback equip for onsite use, AV serv, Computers for patron use, Copy machines, e-mail serv, Electronic databases & coll, Handicapped accessible, ILL available, Online cat, Orientations, Photocopying/Printing, Pub access computers, Ref serv available, Telephone ref, VHS videos, Web-catalog, Wheelchair accessible
Open Mon-Thurs 12-8:30, Sat 8:30-5
Restriction: Fee for pub use, In-house use for visitors

CL LAW LIBRARY, 100 Ellinwood Way, 94523-4817, SAN 321-4400. Tel: 925-969-3120. *Librn,* Tina Miller; *Librn,* Jane Minor
Highest Degree: Doctorate
Library Holdings: Bk Vols 24,000
Open Mon-Thurs 9:30-9, Fri 9:30-5, Sat 10-5, Sun 1-6

PLEASANTON

P PLEASANTON PUBLIC LIBRARY*, 400 Old Bernal Ave, 94566-7012. SAN 332-124X. Tel: 925-931-3400. FAX: 925-846-8517. E-mail: circadm@cityofpleasantonca.gov. Web Site: www.ci.pleasanton.ca.us/services/library. *Dir,* Julie Farnsworth; Tel: 925-931-3406, E-mail: jfarnsworth@cityofpleasantonca.gov; Staff 11 (MLS 9, Non-MLS 2)
Founded 1999. Pop 71,300; Circ 1,385,211
Jul 2009-Jun 2010 Income $4,253,845, State $68,332, City $4,108,025, Federal $14,251, Locally Generated Income $63,237
Library Holdings: AV Mats 1,260; Bk Titles 105,000; Bk Vols 168,000; Per Subs 329
Special Collections: Pleasanton History Coll. Municipal Document Depository
Automation Activity & Vendor Info: (Acquisitions) Innovative Interfaces, Inc; (Cataloging) Innovative Interfaces, Inc; (Circulation) Innovative Interfaces, Inc; (ILL) Innovative Interfaces, Inc; (OPAC) Innovative Interfaces, Inc; (Serials) Innovative Interfaces, Inc
Database Vendor: Gale Cengage Learning
Wireless access
Function: Adult bk club, Adult literacy prog, Audiobks via web, AV serv, Bk club(s), Bks on cassette, Bks on CD, Children's prog, Computer training, Computers for patron use, Copy machines, Digital talking bks, e-mail & chat, E-Reserves, Electronic databases & coll, Free DVD rentals, Genealogy discussion group, Handicapped accessible, Homebound delivery serv, Jazz prog, Magnifiers for reading, Music CDs, Online cat, Online ref, Online searches, Outside serv via phone, mail, e-mail & web, Photocopying/Printing, Prog for adults, Prog for children & young adult, Pub access computers, Ref & res, Ref serv available, Ref serv in person, Senior computer classes, Senior outreach, Story hour, Summer reading prog, Telephone ref, Web-catalog, Wheelchair accessible
Mem of Bay Area Library & Information System
Special Services for the Deaf - TDD equip
Open Mon-Thurs 10-9, Fri & Sat 10-5, Sun 1-5
Friends of the Library Group

POINT REYES STATION

G US NATIONAL PARK SERVICE*, Point Reyes National Seashore Library & Archives, One Bear Valley Rd, 94956. SAN 323-7168. Tel: 415-464-5125. FAX: 415-464-5229. Web Site: www.nps.gov/pore. *Archivist,* Carola DeRooy; E-mail: carola_derooy@nps.gov
Library Holdings: Bk Vols 1,350
Restriction: Open by appt only

POMONA

C CALIFORNIA STATE POLYTECHNIC UNIVERSITY LIBRARY*, 3801 W Temple Ave, Bldg 15, 91768. SAN 301-2158. Tel: 909-869-5250. Circulation Tel: 909 869 3075. Interlibrary Loan Service Tel: 909-869-3111. Reference Tel: 909-869-3076. Information Services Tel: 909-869-3074. FAX: 909-869-6922. Interlibrary Loan Service FAX: 909-869-4375. E-mail: library@csupomona.edu. Web Site: www.csupomona.edu/~library. *Dean,* Dr Ray Wang; E-mail: rwang@csupomona.edu; *Cat,* Yvonne Zhang; *Doc Delivery,* Isela Gomez; Staff 47 (MLS 12, Non-MLS 35)
Founded 1938. Enrl 19,804; Fac 672; Highest Degree: Master
Library Holdings: AV Mats 10,574; e-books 12,436; e-journals 3,460; Electronic Media & Resources 6,377; Bk Titles 492,551; Bk Vols 760,350; Per Subs 2,384
Special Collections: Poetry Coll; Twentieth Century English & American Literature (First Editions); Wine Coll
Automation Activity & Vendor Info: (Acquisitions) Innovative Interfaces, Inc; (Cataloging) Innovative Interfaces, Inc; (Circulation) Innovative Interfaces, Inc; (Course Reserve) Innovative Interfaces, Inc; (OPAC) Innovative Interfaces, Inc; (Serials) Innovative Interfaces, Inc
Database Vendor: EBSCOhost, Gale Cengage Learning, LexisNexis, OCLC FirstSearch, OVID Technologies, ProQuest, Wilson - Wilson Web
Partic in OCLC Online Computer Library Center, Inc
Open Mon-Thurs 7:30am-10:30pm, Fri 7:30-5, Sat 10-6, Sun 12-9

Departmental Libraries:

COLLEGE OF ENVIRONMENTAL DESIGN LIBRARY, Bldg 7, 3801 W Temple Ave, 91768, SAN 329-0352. Tel: 909-869-2665. Information Services Tel: 909-869-7659. *In Charge,* Christine Johnson
Founded 1975. Enrl 1,150; Highest Degree: Master
Library Holdings: Bk Titles 18,000; Per Subs 152
Special Collections: Architect Craig Elwood Coll, letters, papers, photographs; Architect Raphael Soriano, drawings, letters, papers; Richard Nentra sketches, papers
Open Mon-Fri 8-4

J DEVRY UNIVERSITY*, Pomona Campus Library, 901 Corporate Center Dr, 91768. Tel: 909-868-4201. Web Site: www.pom.devry.edu/campus_library.html. *Dir of Libr Serv,* Nicole Bird; Tel: 909-868-4227, E-mail: nbird@devry.edu; Staff 1 (MLS 1)

Founded 1987
Automation Activity & Vendor Info: (Cataloging) Ex Libris Group; (Circulation) Ex Libris Group; (OPAC) Ex Libris Group
Database Vendor: EBSCOhost, ProQuest
Wireless access
Open Mon-Fri 9-8, Sat 9-5

M LANTERMAN DEVELOPMENTAL CENTER*, Staff Library, Research Bldg, 3530 W Pomona Blvd, 91769. SAN 333-7413. Tel: 909-444-7264. FAX: 909-444-2832. *Head of Libr,* Position Currently Open
Founded 1954
Library Holdings: AV Mats 300; Bks on Deafness & Sign Lang 50; Bk Titles 6,000; Bk Vols 6,020; Per Subs 140; Spec Interest Per Sub 100
Subject Interests: Autism, Mental retardation, Nursing
Function: ILL available
Partic in Inland Empire Med Libr Coop; Medical Library Group of Southern California & Arizona (MLGSCA)
Open Mon-Fri 8-4:30
Restriction: Circulates for staff only

P POMONA PUBLIC LIBRARY*, 625 S Garey Ave, 91766-3322. (Mail add: PO Box 2271, 91769), SAN 301-2174. Tel: 909-620-2043. Circulation Tel: 909-620-2043, Ext 2720, 909-620-2043, Ext 2722. Interlibrary Loan Service Tel: 909-620-2043, Ext 2723. Reference Tel: 909-620-2043, Ext 2701, 909-620-2043, Ext 2702. Administration Tel: 909-620-2473. Automation Services Tel: 909-620-3709. FAX: 909-620-3713. TDD: 909-620-3690. E-mail: library@ci.pomona.ca.us. Web Site: www.pomonalibrary.org. *Dir,* Bruce Guter; Tel: 909-620-2036; Staff 9 (MLS 7, Non-MLS 2)
Founded 1887. Pop 163,683; Circ 182,812
Jul 2009-Jun 2010 Income $2,191,043, State $46,864, City $2,041,362, Locally Generated Income $102,817. Mats Exp $95,230, Books $70,057, Per/Ser (Incl. Access Fees) $6,794, Micro $4,978, Electronic Ref Mat (Incl. Access Fees) $6,593. Sal $1,247,294 (Prof $567,385)
Library Holdings: Audiobooks 9,339; AV Mats 870; Large Print Bks 4,025; Microforms 11,837; Bk Titles 239,388; Bk Vols 287,231; Per Subs 207; Videos 300
Special Collections: Citrus Crate Labels; Cooper Photo Coll; Frasher Coll, photos & postcards; International Doll Coll; Laura Ingalls Wilder Coll, bks, dolls, mss & papers; Pomona Valley History Coll. Oral History
Subject Interests: Local hist, Photog
Automation Activity & Vendor Info: (Acquisitions) TLC (The Library Corporation); (Cataloging) TLC (The Library Corporation); (Circulation) TLC (The Library Corporation); (ILL) OCLC; (OPAC) TLC (The Library Corporation); (Serials) TLC (The Library Corporation)
Database Vendor: Baker & Taylor, Gale Cengage Learning, OCLC WebJunction, OCLC WorldShare Interlibrary Loan, ProQuest, ReferenceUSA, TLC (The Library Corporation)
Wireless access
Function: Adult bk club, Adult literacy prog, Archival coll, Art exhibits, Bilingual assistance for Spanish patrons, Bks on cassette, Bks on CD, Children's prog, Computers for patron use, Copy machines, Electronic databases & coll, Family literacy, Genealogy discussion group, Handicapped accessible, Homework prog, ILL available, Newsp ref libr, Online cat, Orientations, Passport agency, Photocopying/Printing, Preschool outreach, Prog for children & young adult, Pub access computers, Ref serv available, Spoken cassettes & CDs, Story hour, Summer reading prog, Tax forms, Teen prog, Telephone ref, Wheelchair accessible
Partic in OCLC Online Computer Library Center, Inc; Southern California Library Cooperative
Special Services for the Deaf - TDD equip
Special Services for the Blind - Bks on cassette; Bks on CD; Large print bks
Open Mon & Wed 2-7, Tues 10-3, Sat Noon-5
Restriction: Non-resident fee
Friends of the Library Group

M POMONA VALLEY HOSPITAL MEDICAL CENTER*, Medical Library, 1798 N Garey Ave, 91767. SAN 333-7448. Tel: 909-865-9878. FAX: 909-865-9770. *Librn,* Deborah Klein
Founded 1950
Library Holdings: Bk Vols 850; Per Subs 180
Partic in National Network of Libraries of Medicine; Pacific Southwest Regional Medical Library (PSRML)
Open Mon-Thurs 8:30-4:30, Fri 8-12
Restriction: Non-circulating to the pub

CM WESTERN UNIVERSITY OF HEALTH SCIENCES*, Harriet K & Philip Pumerantz Library, 287 E Third St, 91766-1854. (Mail add: 309 E Second St, 91766), SAN 322-8894. Tel: 909-469-5323. Interlibrary Loan Service Tel: 909-469-5320. Reference Tel: 909-469-6124. FAX: 909-469-5486. E-mail: reference@westernu.edu. Web Site: www.westernu.edu/library/index.html. *Dir,* Patricia A Vader; E-mail: pvader@westernu.edu; Staff 16 (MLS 4, Non-MLS 12)
Founded 1977. Enrl 1,923; Highest Degree: Doctorate
Library Holdings: Bk Titles 13,411; Bk Vols 13,541; Per Subs 374
Special Collections: Osteopathic Medicine (includes books and journals)
Subject Interests: Allied health, Nursing, Osteopathic med, Veterinary med
Automation Activity & Vendor Info: (Cataloging) SirsiDynix; (Circulation) SirsiDynix; (Course Reserve) SirsiDynix; (OPAC) SirsiDynix; (Serials) SirsiDynix
Function: ILL available
Partic in Inland Empire Acad Libr Coop (IEALC); Statewide California Electronic Library Consortium (SCELC)
Open Mon-Thurs 7am-11pm, Fri 7-6, Sat & Sun 11-7
Restriction: In-house use for visitors, Open to students, fac & staff, Photo ID required for access

PORTERVILLE

J PORTERVILLE COLLEGE LIBRARY, 100 E College Ave, 93257-5901. SAN 301-2182. Tel: 559-791-2318. FAX: 559-791-2289. Web Site: www.portervillecollege.edu. *Librn,* Lorie Barker; Tel: 559-791-2370, E-mail: lebarker@portervillecollege.edu; Staff 5 (MLS 2, Non-MLS 3)
Founded 1927. Highest Degree: Associate
Special Collections: Anthropology Library; Valley Writers Coll
Automation Activity & Vendor Info: (Cataloging) Follett Software; (Circulation) Follett Software
Database Vendor: EBSCOhost, Gale Cengage Learning, Newsbank, ProQuest
Wireless access
Publications: Library Handbook
Open Mon-Thurs 7am-9pm, Fri 7-Noon

P PORTERVILLE PUBLIC LIBRARY*, 41 W Thurman, 93257-3652. SAN 301-2190. Tel: 559-784-0177. FAX: 559-781-4396. Web Site: www.ci.porterville.ca.us, www.sjvls.org. *Librn,* Position Currently Open; *Ref,* Kathie Poundstone; Staff 6 (Non-MLS 6)
Founded 1904. Pop 34,450
Library Holdings: AV Mats 788; Bk Titles 68,889; Bk Vols 70,000; Per Subs 151
Special Collections: Local History, bks, photos
Mem of San Joaquin Valley Library System
Open Mon-Thurs 9-9, Fri 9-6, Sat 9-5
Friends of the Library Group

QUINCY

C FEATHER RIVER COLLEGE LIBRARY*, 570 Golden Eagle Ave, 95971-9124. SAN 301-2220. Tel: 530-283-0202, Ext 236. FAX: 530-283-4097. E-mail: library@frc.edu. Web Site: library.frc.edu/. *Librn,* Position Currently Open; *Sr Libr Asst,* Dottie Arcangelie; Staff 2 (Non-MLS 2)
Founded 1969. Enrl 1,102; Fac 85; Highest Degree: Associate
Jul 2010-Jun 2011. Mats Exp $43,460, Books $3,188, Per/Ser (Incl. Access Fees) $7,225, Electronic Ref Mat (Incl. Access Fees) $33,047. Sal $191,208 (Prof $109,725)
Library Holdings: Bks on Deafness & Sign Lang 32; DVDs 2,466; e-books 11,000; Bk Vols 21,762; Per Subs 89; Spec Interest Per Sub 13
Special Collections: Oral History
Subject Interests: Bus & mgt, Environ studies, Equine studies, Forestry, Natural sci, Nursing, Rodeos
Automation Activity & Vendor Info: (Cataloging) TLC (The Library Corporation); (Circulation) TLC (The Library Corporation); (OPAC) TLC (The Library Corporation)
Database Vendor: CQ Press, EBSCO Information Services, EBSCOhost, LexisNexis, Newsbank, Oxford Communications, TLC (The Library Corporation)
Wireless access
Special Services for the Deaf - Bks on deafness & sign lang; Closed caption videos; Deaf publ
Special Services for the Blind - Assistive/Adapted tech devices, equip & products; Computer with voice synthesizer for visually impaired persons
Open Mon-Thurs 8am-9pm, Fri 8-4:30

GL PLUMAS COUNTY LAW LIBRARY*, 520 W Main St, Rm 414, 95971. SAN 301-2239. Tel: 530-283-6325. Web Site: www.countyofplumas.com. *Law Librn,* Nancy Stewart
Founded 1905
Library Holdings: Bk Vols 6,150
Subject Interests: Calif, Law
Wireless access
Open Mon & Wed 11-4, Thurs 9-2

P PLUMAS COUNTY LIBRARY*, 445 Jackson St, 95971-9410. SAN 301-2247. Tel: 530-283-6310. FAX: 530-283-3242. Web Site: www.plumascounty.us. *County Librn,* Lynn Sheehy; E-mail:

lynnsheehy@countyofplumas.com; *Tech Serv,* Jeannette Legg; Staff 1.75 (MLS 0.75, Non-MLS 1)
Founded 1916. Pop 24,440; Circ 90,612
Library Holdings: Bk Vols 73,324; Per Subs 220; Talking Bks 805
Special Collections: Local History & Local Mining Colls
Subject Interests: Botany
Automation Activity & Vendor Info: (Cataloging) LibLime; (Circulation) LibLime; (OPAC) LibLime
Database Vendor: Gale Cengage Learning
Wireless access
Function: Bks on cassette, Bks on CD, Computers for patron use, Electronic databases & coll, Family literacy, Free DVD rentals, Handicapped accessible, ILL available, Jail serv, Literacy & newcomer serv, Music CDs, Online cat, OverDrive digital audio bks, Photocopying/Printing, Summer reading prog, Wheelchair accessible
Mem of NorthNet Library System
Special Services for the Blind - Assistive/Adapted tech devices, equip & products; Bks on cassette; Bks on CD; Closed circuit TV; Computer with voice synthesizer for visually impaired persons; Large print bks; Magnifiers; Talking bks; Talking bks & player equip
Open Mon-Wed 11-6, Thurs 11-7, Fri 11-3
Friends of the Library Group
Branches: 3
CHESTER BRANCH, 210 First Ave, Chester, 96020-0429. (Mail add: PO Box 429, Chester, 96020-0429), SAN 377-8142. Tel: 530-258-2742. FAX: 530-258-3725. *Br Mgr,* Wanda Heath-Grunder
Library Holdings: Bk Vols 9,000; Per Subs 32
Automation Activity & Vendor Info: (OPAC) TLC (The Library Corporation)
Database Vendor: Gale Cengage Learning
Open Mon-Wed & Fri 10-1 & 1:30-5:30, Thurs 12-5 & 6-8
Friends of the Library Group
GREENVILLE BRANCH, 204 Ann St, Greenville, 95947. (Mail add: PO Box 635, Greenville, 95947-0635). Tel: 530-284-7416. *Br Mgr,* Andrea Wilson; Staff 1 (Non-MLS 1)
Library Holdings: Bk Vols 10,000; Per Subs 20
Open Mon-Wed 10-1 & 1:30-5:30, Thurs 12-4 & 4:30-7
Friends of the Library Group
PORTOLA BRANCH, 34 Third Ave, Portola, 96122. Tel: 530-832-4241. FAX: 530-832-4241. *Br Mgr,* Linda Hale; Staff 1 (Non-MLS 1)
Library Holdings: Bk Vols 10,000; Per Subs 30
Database Vendor: Gale Cengage Learning
Open Mon-Wed 10-1 & 2-6, Thurs 12-4 & 5-7
Friends of the Library Group

RANCHO CORDOVA

J HEALD COLLEGE*, Learning Resource Center-Rancho Cordova Campus, 2910 Prospect Park Dr, 95670. Tel: 916-638-1616. FAX: 916-414-2676. *Mgr,* Martha Squire; E-mail: martha_squire@heald.edu
Library Holdings: Bk Vols 500
Database Vendor: EBSCOhost
Open Mon-Thurs 7am-10pm, Fri 8-6, Sat 9-1

RANCHO CUCAMONGA

J CHAFFEY COLLEGE LIBRARY*, 5885 Haven Ave, 91737-3002. SAN 300-5623. Tel: 909-652-6800. Circulation Tel: 909-652-6807. Reference Tel: 909-652-6808. FAX: 909-466-2821. E-mail: library@chaffey.edu. Web Site: www.chaffey.edu/library. *Assoc Dean,* Laura Hope; *Bibliog Instr, Ref,* Marie Boyd; *Bibliog Instr, Ref,* Carol Hutte; Staff 4 (MLS 4)
Founded 1916. Enrl 20,500; Fac 270; Highest Degree: Associate
Library Holdings: e-books 20,000; Electronic Media & Resources 20; Bk Vols 80,350; Per Subs 120
Automation Activity & Vendor Info: (Acquisitions) Auto-Graphics, Inc; (Cataloging) Auto-Graphics, Inc; (Circulation) Auto-Graphics, Inc; (Course Reserve) Auto-Graphics, Inc; (OPAC) Auto-Graphics, Inc; (Serials) Auto-Graphics, Inc
Database Vendor: EBSCOhost, Gale Cengage Learning, LexisNexis, SerialsSolutions
Function: Distance learning, Handicapped accessible, Photocopying/Printing, Wheelchair accessible
Partic in California Community College Library Consortium (CCLC); San Bernardino, Inyo, Riverside Counties United Library Services
Open Mon-Thurs 7:30am-8pm, Fri 10-2
Restriction: Open to students, fac & staff

P RANCHO CUCAMONGA PUBLIC LIBRARY, 7368 Archibald Ave, 91730. SAN 376-6756. Tel: 909-477-2720. Circulation Tel: 909-477-2720, Ext 5000. Reference Tel: 909-477-2720, Ext 5008. FAX: 909-477-2721. E-mail: reference@cityofrc.com. Web Site: www.rcpl.lib.ca.us. *Libr Dir,* Robert Karatsu; Tel: 909-477-2720, Ext 5022, E-mail: Robert.Karatsu@cityofrc.us; *Asst Libr Dir,* Michelle Perera; Tel: 909-477-2720, Ext 5055, E-mail: Michelle.Perera@cityofrc.us; *Libr Serv Mgr,* Renee Tobin; Tel: 909-477-2720, Ext 5024, E-mail: Robin.Tobin@cityofrc.us; Staff 64 (MLS 14, Non-MLS 50)
Founded 1994. Pop 168,000; Circ 1,150,000
Library Holdings: AV Mats 9,752; Bks on Deafness & Sign Lang 12; High Interest/Low Vocabulary Bk Vols 1,451; Large Print Bks 2,108; Bk Titles 116,000; Bk Vols 136,924; Per Subs 215; Talking Bks 1,826
Automation Activity & Vendor Info: (Cataloging) SirsiDynix; (Circulation) SirsiDynix; (OPAC) SirsiDynix
Database Vendor: EBSCOhost, Gale Cengage Learning, SirsiDynix
Mem of Inland Library System
Open Mon-Thurs 10-9, Sat 10-5, Sun 1-5
Friends of the Library Group
Bookmobiles: 1. Librn, Jason Daly. Bk Vols 3,500

RANCHO MIRAGE

M EISENHOWER MEDICAL CENTER*, Medical Library, 39000 Bob Hope Dr, 92270. SAN 301-2255. Tel: 760-837-3782. FAX: 760-837-8581. Web Site: www.emc.org. *Exec Dir,* Nancy Arendt; E-mail: narendt@emc.org; Staff 1 (MLS 1)
Founded 1973
Library Holdings: Per Subs 140
Subject Interests: Clinical med
Partic in San Bernardino, Inyo, Riverside Counties United Library Services
Restriction: Staff use only

P RANCHO MIRAGE PUBLIC LIBRARY*, 71-100 Hwy 111, 92270. SAN 375-3549. Tel: 760-341-7323. FAX: 760-341-5213. E-mail: librarian@ranchomiragelibrary.org. Web Site: www.ranchomiragelibrary.org. *Dir,* David Bryant; E-mail: davidb@ranchomiragelibrary.org; *Principal Librn,* Sandy Mathews; E-mail: sandym@ranchomiragelibrary.org; *Sr Librn, Ch Serv,* Ingrid Johnson; E-mail: ingridj@ranchomiragelibrary.org; *Sr Librn, Ref,* Susan Cook; E-mail: susan@ranchomiragelibrary.org; *Supvr, Circ,* Jessie Hernandez; E-mail: jessie@ranchomiragelibrary.org; Staff 12.91 (MLS 9.35, Non-MLS 3.56)
Founded 1994. Pop 21,886; Circ 491,604
Jul 2006-Jun 2007 Income $3,079,808, State $237,031, City $2,659,309, Locally Generated Income $183,468. Mats Exp $404,733, Books $152,677, Per/Ser (Incl. Access Fees) $44,606, AV Mat $128,425, Electronic Ref Mat (Incl. Access Fees) $79,025. Sal $1,105,968
Library Holdings: AV Mats 21,319; CDs 10,600; DVDs 10,719; e-books 68; Bk Vols 84,918; Per Subs 453
Special Collections: Oral History
Subject Interests: Golf, Local authors
Automation Activity & Vendor Info: (Acquisitions) SirsiDynix; (Cataloging) SirsiDynix; (Circulation) SirsiDynix; (ILL) OCLC FirstSearch; (OPAC) SirsiDynix
Database Vendor: Dun & Bradstreet, EBSCO Information Services, EBSCOhost, Electric Library, Facts on File, Gale Cengage Learning, infoUSA, Newsbank, OCLC FirstSearch, OCLC WorldShare Interlibrary Loan, Overdrive, Inc, ProQuest, Standard & Poor's, World Book Online
Wireless access
Function: Art exhibits, Audiobks via web, AV serv, Bks on cassette, Bks on CD, Children's prog, Computer training, Computers for patron use, Copy machines, E-Reserves, Electronic databases & coll, Handicapped accessible, Holiday prog, ILL available, Jazz prog, Mail & tel request accepted, Music CDs, Online cat, Online searches, Outside serv via phone, mail, e-mail & web, OverDrive digital audio bks, Preschool outreach, Prog for adults, Prog for children & young adult, Ref & res, Ref serv available, Spoken cassettes & CDs, Summer reading prog, Tax forms, Telephone ref, VHS videos, Wheelchair accessible
Publications: Bi-Monthly Program & Exhibits Calendar (Newsletter); The Bookworm (Newsletter)
Mem of Inland Library System
Partic in OCLC Online Computer Library Center, Inc; Southern California Library Cooperative
Special Services for the Blind - Bks on cassette; Bks on CD; Cassettes; Large print bks
Open Mon, Tues, Thurs-Sat 9-6, Wed 9-8, Sun (Nov-April) 12-4
Friends of the Library Group

RANCHO PALOS VERDES

CR MARYMOUNT CALIFORNIA UNIVERSITY LIBRARY, 30800 Palos Verdes Dr E, 90275-6299. SAN 301-2263. Tel: 310-377-5501, Ext 260. FAX: 310-377-6223. E-mail: library@marymountpv.edu. Web Site: www.marymountpv.edu/library. *Interim Dir, Libr Serv,* Dr Sharon Valente; *Coll Serv Librn,* Gary Medina; Tel: 310-303-7375, E-mail: gmedina@marymountpv.edu; *Electronic Res & Syst Librn,* Jeffrey Sabol; Staff 4 (MLS 4)
Founded 1932. Enrl 973; Fac 48; Highest Degree: Bachelor
Library Holdings: DVDs 1,077; e-books 75,842; Electronic Media & Resources 20,221; Bk Vols 24,034; Per Subs 107
Automation Activity & Vendor Info: (Cataloging) OCLC; (Circulation) OCLC; (Course Reserve) OCLC; (ILL) OCLC; (OPAC) OCLC

Database Vendor: Alexander Street Press, ARTstor, CQ Press, CredoReference, Dun & Bradstreet, ebrary, EBSCOhost, Gale Cengage Learning, Hoovers, LexisNexis, McGraw-Hill, OCLC CAMIO, OCLC FirstSearch, OCLC Worldshare Management Services, Oxford Online, ProQuest, Springshare, LLC
Wireless access
Publications: Library Guides; Library Newsletter
Partic in Statewide California Electronic Library Consortium (SCELC)
Open Mon-Thurs 8-8, Fri 8-4, Sun 12-6

S THE SALVATION ARMY COLLEGE FOR OFFICER TRAINING AT CRESTMONT*, Elftman Memorial Library, 30840 Hawthorne Blvd, 90275. SAN 301-2271. Tel: 310-377-0481, 310-544-6475. FAX: 310-265-6565. Web Site: www.crestmont.edu/#!library. *Dir of Libr Serv,* Sheila Chatterjee; Staff 3 (MLS 1, Non-MLS 2)
Founded 1923. Enrl 92; Fac 20; Highest Degree: Associate
Oct 2010-Sept 2011. Mats Exp $20,000
Library Holdings: e-journals 1,500; Bk Titles 40,000; Per Subs 100; Spec Interest Per Sub 50
Special Collections: Salvation Army Publications
Subject Interests: Relig
Automation Activity & Vendor Info: (Cataloging) LibraryWorld, Inc; (Circulation) LibraryWorld, Inc
Database Vendor: EBSCOhost
Wireless access
Partic in Christian Library Consortium
Open Mon-Fri (Winter) 8:15am-9pm, Sat 1-5; Mon-Fri (Summer) 8:15-4:15

RED BLUFF

GL TEHAMA COUNTY LAW LIBRARY*, Courthouse, Rm 38, 633 Washington St, 96080. Tel: 530-529-5033. FAX: 530-527-9255. *Librn,* Donna Eirish
Library Holdings: Bk Vols 10,500
Special Collections: City & County Charter & Code Coll
Subject Interests: Fed law, Local law, State law
Open Mon-Fri 10-1

P TEHAMA COUNTY LIBRARY*, 645 Madison St, 96080-3383. SAN 333-7804. Tel: 530-527-0607. FAX: 530-527-1562. Web Site: www.tehamacountylibrary.org. *County Librn,* Sally Ainsworth; Staff 2 (MLS 1, Non-MLS 1)
Founded 1916. Pop 61,774; Circ 103,000
Library Holdings: Bk Titles 114,640; Bk Vols 122,336; Per Subs 45
Special Collections: Tehama County History
Wireless access
Mem of NorthNet Library System
Open Mon & Fri 2-6, Tues 11-8, Wed 2-8, Thurs 11-6
Friends of the Library Group
Branches: 2
CORNING BRANCH, 740 Third St, Corning, 96021-2517, SAN 333-7839. Tel: 530-824-7050. FAX: 530-824-7051. *County Librn,* Sally Ainsworth; Staff 2 (MLS 1, Non-MLS 1)
Open Mon, Thurs & Fri 2-6, Tues 9-1, Wed 4-8
Friends of the Library Group
LOS MOLINOS BRANCH, 7881 Hwy 99E, Los Molinos, 96055-9701. (Mail add: 645 Madison St, 96080), SAN 329-6598. Tel: 530-384-2772. FAX: 530-384-9826. *Librn,* Caryn Brown; Staff 0.4 (Non-MLS 0.4)
Pop 63,100
Open Mon-Thurs 9-1 & 2-6

REDDING

J SHASTA COLLEGE LIBRARY*, 11555 Old Oregon Trail, 96003-7692. (Mail add: PO Box 496006, 96049-6006), SAN 301-2298. Tel: 530-242-7550. Interlibrary Loan Service Tel: 530-242-2343. Reference Tel: 530-242-7551. Web Site: www.shastacollege.edu/library. *Dean, Libr Serv & Educ Tech,* Will Breitbach; E-mail: wbreitbach@shastacollege.edu; *Assoc Dean, Libr Serv,* Position Currently Open; *Syst/Tech Proc Librn,* Cheryl Cruse; Tel: 530-242-2348, E-mail: ccruse@shastacollege.edu; *Ref Librn,* Carolyn Singh; Tel: 530-242-2347, E-mail: csingh@shastacollege.edu; Staff 9.16 (MLS 2.69, Non-MLS 6.47)
Founded 1948. Enrl 7,253; Fac 4; Highest Degree: Associate
Library Holdings: Audiobooks 760; AV Mats 3,232; e-books 27,013; Bk Titles 70,903; Bk Vols 78,750; Per Subs 71
Subject Interests: Local hist
Automation Activity & Vendor Info: (Acquisitions) SirsiDynix; (Cataloging) SirsiDynix; (Circulation) SirsiDynix; (Course Reserve) SirsiDynix; (ILL) SirsiDynix; (Media Booking) SirsiDynix; (OPAC) SirsiDynix; (Serials) SirsiDynix
Database Vendor: Alexander Street Press, ARTstor, Baker & Taylor, CountryWatch, CQ Press, EBSCOhost, Gale Cengage Learning, JSTOR, LearningExpress, Newsbank, OVID Technologies, Oxford Online, ProQuest, SirsiDynix
Wireless access
Mem of NorthNet Library System
Partic in Community College League of California (CCLC); OCLC Online Computer Library Center, Inc
Open Mon-Thurs 7:45-6:45, Fri 7:45-3:45

GL SHASTA COUNTY PUBLIC LAW LIBRARY*, 1500 Court St, Rm B-7, 96001. SAN 370-4246. Tel: 530-245-6243. FAX: 530-245-6966. *Librn,* Mimi Gimblin
Founded 1968
Library Holdings: Bk Titles 9,800; Per Subs 12
Subject Interests: Legal res
Open Mon-Thurs 8-5, Fri 8-2

S SHASTA HISTORICAL SOCIETY*, Research Library, 1449 Market St, 96001. SAN 375-1945. Tel: 530-243-3720. FAX: 530-246-3708. Web Site: www.shastahistorical.org.
Founded 1930
Library Holdings: Microforms 30; Bk Vols 2,000; Spec Interest Per Sub 5; Videos 20
Automation Activity & Vendor Info: (Cataloging) ByWater Solutions; (OPAC) ByWater Solutions
Function: Archival coll, Copy machines, Electronic databases & coll, Exhibits, Magnifiers for reading, Photocopying/Printing, Prog for adults, VHS videos, Web-catalog
Open Mon-Fri 10-4
Restriction: Non-circulating

P SHASTA PUBLIC LIBRARIES*, 1100 Parkview Ave, 96001. SAN 333-8010. Tel: 530-245-7250. Reference Tel: 530-245-7252. Web Site: www.shastalibraries.org. *Dir,* Janice Erickson; Staff 15 (MLS 5, Non-MLS 10)
Founded 1949. Pop 181,483; Circ 262,253
Jul 2005-Jun 2006 Income (Main Library and Branch(s)) $1,402,287, State $69,978, City $265,500, County $837,739, Locally Generated Income $229,070. Mats Exp $42,662, Books $22,962, Per/Ser (Incl. Access Fees) $9,314, Micro $1,671, AV Mat $8,715. Sal $499,084
Library Holdings: AV Mats 7,363; Bk Vols 204,681; Per Subs 249
Special Collections: Californiana Coll. State Document Depository; US Document Depository
Subject Interests: Calif, County hist, Forestry, Parenting, Shasta County Indians
Automation Activity & Vendor Info: (Acquisitions) SirsiDynix; (Circulation) SirsiDynix; (OPAC) SirsiDynix
Database Vendor: Baker & Taylor, BWI, Gale Cengage Learning, OCLC WorldShare Interlibrary Loan, SirsiDynix
Function: Bk club(s), Computer training, Copy machines, ILL available, Magnifiers for reading, Mail & tel request accepted, Music CDs, Prog for children & young adult, Ref serv available, Spoken cassettes & CDs, Spoken cassettes & DVDs, Summer reading prog, Tax forms, Telephone ref, VHS videos
Mem of NorthNet Library System
Partic in RLIN (Research Libraries Information Network)
Special Services for the Deaf - Bks on deafness & sign lang
Special Services for the Blind - Bks on cassette; Bks on CD; Copier with enlargement capabilities; Large print bks; Magnifiers
Open Mon-Thurs 12-6, Sat 9-2
Friends of the Library Group
Branches: 2
ANDERSON BRANCH, 3200 W Center St, Anderson, 96007, SAN 333-8045. Tel: 530-365-7685. FAX: 530-365-7685. *Br Mgr,* Christy Windle; E-mail: christyw@shastalibraries.org
Founded 1950
Open Tues-Thurs 11-7, Fri & Sat 9-5
Friends of the Library Group
BURNEY LIBRARY, 37038 Siskiyou St, Burney, 96013, SAN 333-807X. Tel: 530-335-4317. FAX: 530-335-4317. *Br Head,* Deborah Dean
Founded 1949
Automation Activity & Vendor Info: (Circulation) SirsiDynix; (OPAC) SirsiDynix
Database Vendor: Gale Cengage Learning
Open Mon-Thurs 10-1 & 2-6
Friends of the Library Group

CR SIMPSON UNIVERSITY, Start-Kilgour Memorial Library, 2211 College View Dr, 96003-8606. SAN 301-4665. Tel: 530-226-4117. Interlibrary Loan Service Tel: 530-226-4944. Reference Tel: 530-226-4943. FAX: 530-226-4858. E-mail: library@simpsonu.edu. Web Site: www.simpsonulibrary.org. *Dir, Libr Serv,* Larry L Haight; Tel: 530-226-4110, E-mail: lhaight@simpsonu.edu; *Reader & Digital Serv Librn,* Eric Wheeler; E-mail: ewheeler@simpsonu.edu; *Archivist,* Mairlyne Shamansky; Tel: 530-226-4115, E-mail: mshamansky@simpsonu.edu; Staff 3 (MLS 2, Non-MLS 1)
Founded 1921. Enrl 1,267; Fac 221; Highest Degree: Master

May 2013-Apr 2014 Income $371,530. Mats Exp $122,343, Books $26,139, Per/Ser (Incl. Access Fees) $12,332, AV Mat $1,653, Electronic Ref Mat (Incl. Access Fees) $82,219. Sal $163,151 (Prof $114,288)
Library Holdings: CDs 571; DVDs 2,239; e-books 292,000; Microforms 242,910; Bk Vols 103,800; Per Subs 85
Special Collections: A W Tozer Coll; Christian & Missionary Alliance Denominational History (A B Simpson Coll)
Automation Activity & Vendor Info: (Acquisitions) OCLC; (Cataloging) OCLC; (Circulation) OCLC; (Course Reserve) OCLC; (ILL) OCLC; (OPAC) OCLC WorldShare Interlibrary Loan; (Serials) OCLC
Database Vendor: American Mathematical Society, American Psychological Association (APA), ebrary, EBSCOhost, Gale Cengage Learning, Ingenta, JSTOR, OCLC, OCLC ArticleFirst, OCLC FirstSearch, OCLC WorldShare Interlibrary Loan, OCLC Worldshare Management Services, Oxford Online, ProQuest, PubMed, Sage
Wireless access
Function: Archival coll, Computers for patron use, Copy machines, Distance learning, E-Reserves, Electronic databases & coll, Handicapped accessible, ILL available, Microfiche/film & reading machines, Music CDs, Online cat, Online ref, Online searches, Orientations, Photocopying/Printing, Pub access computers, Ref & res, Tax forms, Web-catalog, Wheelchair accessible
Partic in Christian Library Consortium; Statewide California Electronic Library Consortium (SCELC)
Restriction: Borrowing privileges limited to fac & registered students, In-house use for visitors, Open to students, fac, staff & alumni, Pub use on premises

REDLANDS

R THE RIVER CHRISTIAN REFORMED CHURCH LIBRARY, 459 E Highland Ave, 92373. (Mail add: PO Box 8938, 92375), SAN 301-2301. Tel: 909-798-2221. FAX: 909-798-4133. Web Site: www.therivercrc.com. *Interim Librn,* Roger A Whitman; Tel: 909-793-6801, E-mail: rwhitman@alum.mit.edu
Founded 1957
Library Holdings: Audiobooks 22; CDs 2; DVDs 65; Bk Vols 4,200; Videos 175
Special Collections: Acts of Synod of the Christian Reformed Church of North America
Open Sun 9:30am-11:30am

P A K SMILEY PUBLIC LIBRARY*, 125 W Vine St, 92373. SAN 301-2344. Tel: 909 798 7565. FAX: 909-798-7566. E-mail: admin@akspl.org. Web Site: www.akspl.org. *Dir,* Larry E Burgess; *Adult Serv,* Lorraine Estelle, E-mail: lestelle@akspl.org; *Ch Serv,* Blanca Rodriguez; *ILL,* Anna Pearson; E-mail: reference@akspl.org; *Spec Coll Librn,* Don McCue; Tel: 909-798-7632, E-mail: dmccue@akspl.org; *Tech Serv,* Jean Griffing; *Tech Serv,* Sandra Sanchez; Tel: 909-798-7676, E-mail: ssanchez@akspl.org; Staff 5 (MLS 2, Non-MLS 3)
Founded 1894. Pop 71,926; Circ 264,663
Library Holdings: AV Mats 9,246; DVDs 3,171; e-books 1,540; Large Print Bks 2,480; Bk Titles 113,096; Bk Vols 136,466; Per Subs 237
Special Collections: Californiana, Redlands Heritage, bks & pamphlets, ms, maps, photog; Encountering the Lincoln Scholarly Zareba; Horace Greely, Lincoln & the War for the Union; Lincoln (Watchorn Memorial Shrine), bks, pamphlets, photog, tapes & ephemera; Lincoln Shrine, bks, pamphlets, photos, tapes & ephemera; Powderly, Lincoln & the Shrine; Smiley Family Letters, papers; The Archives of the A K Smiley Public Library; The Lincoln Memorial Shrine Golden Jubilee; The Lincoln Memorial Shrine, Redlands, California; What is Patron Saint's Day?. Oral History; State Document Depository
Subject Interests: Art & archit, Civil War
Automation Activity & Vendor Info: (Cataloging) SirsiDynix; (Circulation) SirsiDynix; (OPAC) SirsiDynix
Database Vendor: SirsiDynix
Publications: A K Smiley Public Library, A Brief History; A Lost Letter Found
Special Services for the Blind - Assistive/Adapted tech devices, equip & products
Open Mon & Tues 9-9, Wed & Thurs 9-7, Fri & Sat 9-5, Sun 1-5
Friends of the Library Group

C UNIVERSITY OF REDLANDS*, George & Verda Armacost Library, 1200 E Colton Ave, 92374-3758. (Mail add: PO Box 3080, 92373), SAN 301-2352. Tel: 909-748-8022. Circulation Tel: 909-748-8876. Reference Tel: 909-748-8878. FAX: 909-335-5392. E-mail: reference@redlands.edu. Web Site: www.redlands.edu/library.xml. *Dir,* Gabriela Sonntag; *Acq Librn, Natural Sci Librn,* Les Canterbury; *Art Librn, Coordr, Electronic Res,* Sanjeet Mann; *Behav Sci Librn, Outreach Librn,* Melissa Cardenas-Dow; *Bus Librn,* Janelle Julagay; *Govt Doc, Humanities Librn,* William Kennedy; *Librn,* Lua Gregory; *Phys Sci Librn,* Paige Mann; *Coordr, Libr Instruction, Ref Librn,* Shana Higgins; *Circ Supvr, ILL,* Sandi Richey; *Tech Serv Supvr,* Trisha Aurelio; *Weekend Supvr,* Kathy Poole; Staff 20 (MLS 9, Non-MLS 11)
Founded 1907. Enrl 4,769; Fac 202; Highest Degree: Doctorate
Jul 2011-Jun 2012. Mats Exp $1,890,239, Books $162,615, Per/Ser (Incl. Access Fees) $190,943, AV Mat $11,611, Electronic Ref Mat (Incl. Access Fees) $244,486. Sal $941,028 (Prof $506,507)
Library Holdings: AV Mats 11,550; Bks on Deafness & Sign Lang 312; Braille Volumes 27; CDs 4,489; DVDs 1,657; e-books 16,844; e-journals 68,040; Microforms 748,962; Music Scores 9,656; Bk Vols 516,398; Per Subs 55,230; Videos 3,439
Special Collections: Californiana & the Great Southwest (Vernon & Helen Farquhar Coll); Harley Farnsworth & Florence Ayscough McNair Far Eastern Library; James Irvine Foundation Map Coll. US Document Depository
Automation Activity & Vendor Info: (Acquisitions) Innovative Interfaces, Inc; (Cataloging) Innovative Interfaces, Inc; (Circulation) Innovative Interfaces, Inc; (Course Reserve) Innovative Interfaces, Inc; (ILL) Innovative Interfaces, Inc; (OPAC) Innovative Interfaces, Inc; (Serials) Innovative Interfaces, Inc
Wireless access
Partic in Inland Empire Acad Libr Coop (IEALC); OCLC Online Computer Library Center, Inc; San Bernardino, Inyo, Riverside Counties United Library Services; Statewide California Electronic Library Consortium (SCELC)

REDONDO BEACH

P REDONDO BEACH PUBLIC LIBRARY*, 303 N Pacific Coast Hwy, 90277. SAN 333-8525. Tel: 310-318-0675. FAX: 310-318-3809. E-mail: rbplweb@redondo.org. Web Site: www.redondo.org/library. *Dir,* Susan Anderson; E-mail: susan.anderson@redondo.org; *Sr Librn,* Erin Schoonover; E-mail: erin.schoonover@redondo.org; *AV,* Steve Fritch; *Tech Serv,* Margaret Menninger; Staff 27.7 (MLS 10, Non-MLS 17.7)
Founded 1908. Pop 67,488; Circ 858,934
Jul 2008-Jun 2009 Income (Main Library and Branch(s)) $3,818,534, State $72,820, City $3,595,094, Federal $5,650, Locally Generated Income $144,970. Mats Exp $346,040, Books $184,980, Per/Ser (Incl. Access Fees) $18,760, AV Mat $64,320, Electronic Ref Mat (Incl. Access Fees) $77,980. Sal $1,471,680
Library Holdings: AV Mats 36,292; Electronic Media & Resources 15; Bk Vols 177,834; Per Subs 280
Automation Activity & Vendor Info: (Acquisitions) SirsiDynix; (Cataloging) SirsiDynix; (Circulation) SirsiDynix; (ILL) OCLC; (OPAC) SirsiDynix
Database Vendor: CQ Press, EBSCOhost, Gale Cengage Learning, infoUSA, Newsbank, OCLC FirstSearch, Overdrive, Inc, ProQuest, ReferenceUSA, SirsiDynix
Wireless access
Partic in Califa; Southern California Library Cooperative
Special Services for the Blind - Reader equip
Open Mon-Thurs 10-8, Fri 10-6, Sat 9-5
Friends of the Library Group
Branches: 1
NORTH BRANCH, 2000 Artesia Blvd, 90278, SAN 333-855X. Tel: 310-318-0677. FAX: 310-374-3768. *Br Mgr,* Erin Schoonover
Library Holdings: Bk Vols 44,000; Per Subs 51
Open Mon Thurs Noon-8, Fri Noon-6, Sat 9-5
Friends of the Library Group

REDWOOD CITY

J CANADA COLLEGE LIBRARY*, Bldg 9, 3rd Flr, 4200 Farm Hill Blvd, 94061-1099. SAN 301-2395. Tel: 650-306-3267. Circulation Tel: 650-306-3485. Reference Tel: 650-306-3480. FAX: 650-306-3434. Web Site: canadacollege.net/library. *Circ,* Paul Gaskins; E-mail: gaskins@smccd.net; *Librn,* Dave Patterson; Tel: 650-306-3383; Staff 5 (MLS 3, Non-MLS 2)
Founded 1968. Enrl 3,000; Fac 100; Highest Degree: Associate
Library Holdings: Bk Vols 60,000; Per Subs 110
Special Collections: Center for the American Musical Library, Archives
Subject Interests: Early childhood educ, Fashion design, Interior design, Radiologic tech
Database Vendor: Gale Cengage Learning, ProQuest, Wilson - Wilson Web
Partic in Coop Libr Agency for Syst & Servs
Open Mon-Thurs 8-9, Fri 8-3, Sat 10-2

M KAISER-PERMANENTE MEDICAL CENTER*, Health Sciences Library, 1150 Veterans Blvd, 94063. SAN 301-2409. Tel: 650-299-2437. FAX: 650-299-2488. *Librn,* Florence Fong
Library Holdings: Bk Vols 1,500
Open Mon-Fri 8:30-5

P REDWOOD CITY PUBLIC LIBRARY*, 1044 Middlefield Rd, 94063-1868. SAN 333-8584. Tel: 650-780-7018. Circulation Tel: 650-780-7020. Administration Tel: 650-780-7061. Information Services Tel:

650-780-7026. FAX: 650-780-7069. Web Site: www.rcpl.info. *Dir,* Derek Wolfgram; *Div Mgr,* Maria Kramer; Staff 19 (MLS 19)
Founded 1865. Pop 70,500; Circ 727,321
Library Holdings: AV Mats 17,735; e-books 418; Bk Titles 205,281; Per Subs 745
Special Collections: State Document Depository; US Document Depository
Automation Activity & Vendor Info: (Circulation) Innovative Interfaces, Inc
Partic in Coop Libr Agency for Syst & Servs
Open Mon-Thurs 10-9, Fri & Sat 10-5, Sun 1-5
Friends of the Library Group
Branches: 2
FAIR OAKS, 2510 Middlefield Rd, 94063-3402, SAN 333-8614. Tel: 650-780-7261. FAX: 650-568-3371. *Mgr,* Elizabeth Meeks
Library Holdings: Bk Vols 15,000
Open Mon-Thurs 10-7, Fri 10-5
Friends of the Library Group
SCHABERG BRANCH, 2140 Euclid Ave, 94061-1327, SAN 333-8649. Tel: 650-780-7010. FAX: 650-568-1702. *Mgr,* Elizabeth Meeks
Library Holdings: Bk Vols 32,000
Open Mon-Thurs 10-7, Fri & Sat 10-5
Friends of the Library Group

L ROPERS, MAJESKI, KOHN & BENTLEY*, Law Library, 1001 Marshall St, 94063. SAN 323-6919. Tel: 650-364-8200. FAX: 650-780-1701. Web Site: www.ropers.com. *Librn,* Carmen Callahan
Library Holdings: Bk Titles 1,800; Bk Vols 10,000; Per Subs 12
Automation Activity & Vendor Info: (Acquisitions) Inmagic, Inc.
Open Mon-Fri 8-6

S SAN MATEO COUNTY HISTORY MUSEUM & ARCHIVES*, 2200 Broadway, 94063. SAN 301-522X. Tel: 650-299-0104. FAX: 650-299-0141. Web Site: www.sanmateocountyhistory.com. *Archivist,* Carol Peterson
Founded 1935
Library Holdings: Bk Vols 1,500
Subject Interests: County hist
Publications: La Peninsula (a journal published 2-3 times a year); News Report (Monthly)
Open Tues-Thurs 10-12 & 12:30-4, Sun 12-4
Restriction: Non-circulating to the pub
Friends of the Library Group

GL SAN MATEO COUNTY LAW LIBRARY*, 710 Hamilton St, 94063. SAN 301-2417. Tel: 650-363-4913. FAX: 650-367-8040. Web Site: www.smcll.org. *Dir,* Karen M Lutke; E-mail: kmlutke@sbcglobal.net; Staff 5 (MLS 1, Non-MLS 4)
Jul 2008-Jun 2009 Income $826,177. Mats Exp $319,373, Books $281,973, Electronic Ref Mat (Incl. Access Fees) $37,400. Sal $182,666
Library Holdings: Bk Titles 1,944; Bk Vols 32,524; Per Subs 3
Special Collections: State Document Depository
Wireless access
Open Mon-Thurs 8-8, Fri 8-5, Sat 12-4

REEDLEY

R FIRST MENNONITE CHURCH LIBRARY*, 1208 L St, 93654. (Mail add: PO Box 111, 93654-0111), SAN 301-2433. Tel: 559-638-2917. FAX: 559-637-8826. E-mail: fmcreedley@juno.com. Web Site: www.fmcreedley.org.
Library Holdings: Bk Vols 2,000
Subject Interests: Bible, Mennonite-Anabaptist theol
Wireless access

J REEDLEY COLLEGE LIBRARY*, 995 N Reed Ave, 93654. SAN 301-2441. Tel: 559-638-0352. FAX: 559-638-0384. Web Site: www.reedleycollege.edu. *Librn,* Wilifred Louise Alire; E-mail: willie.alire@reedleycollege.edu; *Librn,* Stephanie Curry; Tel: 559-638-0362, E-mail: stephanie.curry@reedleycollege.edu; Staff 6 (MLS 2, Non-MLS 4)
Founded 1956. Enrl 6,000; Fac 91
Library Holdings: e-books 4,000; Large Print Bks 100; Bk Titles 3,800; Per Subs 100
Automation Activity & Vendor Info: (Cataloging) SirsiDynix; (Circulation) SirsiDynix
Database Vendor: Gale Cengage Learning, ProQuest, SirsiDynix
Function: Handicapped accessible, ILL available, Photocopying/Printing, Wheelchair accessible
Open Mon-Thurs 7:30-7, Fri 7:30-2

RICHMOND

S CHEVRON INFORMATION TECHNOLOGY COMPANY, DIVISION OF CHEVRON USA, INC*, Chevron Global Library, 100 Chevron Way, Bldg 50 Rm 1212, 94802. SAN 301-2468. Tel: 510-242-4755. Administration Tel: 915-842-1000. FAX: 510-242-5621. E-mail: infomgmt@chevron.com. *Libr Mgr,* Nan M Dubbelde; Staff 12 (MLS 10, Non-MLS 2)
Founded 1908
Subject Interests: Chem, Chem eng, Fuels, Patents, Petroleum
Publications: Library bulletin
Restriction: By permission only, Co libr, Employees only, External users must contact libr

P RICHMOND PUBLIC LIBRARY*, 325 Civic Center Plaza, 94804-9991. SAN 333-8673. Tel: 510-620-6555. FAX: 510-620-6850. TDD: 510-233-2348. Web Site: www.richmondlibrary.org. *Ch Serv,* Kathy Haug; *Media Spec,* Geoffrey Miller; Staff 17 (MLS 17)
Founded 1907. Pop 89,300; Circ 421,979
Library Holdings: AV Mats 1,788; Bk Titles 176,322; Bk Vols 312,030; Per Subs 558
Special Collections: Afro-American History & Literature; California History Coll; Richmond History Coll. Oral History; State Document Depository; US Document Depository
Automation Activity & Vendor Info: (Circulation) Innovative Interfaces, Inc
Publications: Monthly Booklist
Mem of Bay Area Library & Information System
Partic in Coop Libr Agency for Syst & Servs; OCLC Online Computer Library Center, Inc
Special Services for the Deaf - TDD equip; TTY equip; Videos & decoder
Open Mon & Tues 12-8, Wed 10-8, Thurs 10-5, Fri 12-5, Sat 10-5
Friends of the Library Group
Bookmobiles: 1

RIDGECREST

J CERRO COSO COMMUNITY COLLEGE LIBRARY, 3000 College Heights Blvd, 93555-9571. SAN 333-8827. Tel: 760-384-6131. Interlibrary Loan Service Tel: 760-384-6138. FAX: 760-384-6139. E-mail: reference@cerrocoso.edu. Web Site: www.cerrocoso.edu/lrc. *Librn,* Julie Cornett; *Libr Asst II,* Karen Spurlock; E-mail: kspurlock@cerrocoso.edu; *Libr Tech 1,* Becky Parker; E-mail: rebecca.parker@cerrocoso.edu; *Libr Tech II,* Kathryn Lulofs; Tel: 760-384-6137, E-mail: Kathryn.lulofs@cerrocoso.edu; Staff 4 (MLS 1, Non-MLS 3)
Founded 1973. Enrl 4,735; Fac 156
Library Holdings: AV Mats 2,180; CDs 54; DVDs 100; e-books 27,400; Bk Titles 30,000; Bk Vols 32,901; Per Subs 15
Automation Activity & Vendor Info: (Acquisitions) SirsiDynix; (Cataloging) SirsiDynix; (Circulation) SirsiDynix; (Course Reserve) SirsiDynix; (OPAC) SirsiDynix
Database Vendor: Gale Cengage Learning, Newsbank, OCLC FirstSearch, SerialsSolutions
Special Services for the Blind - Braille bks
Open Mon-Thurs 8am-9pm, Fri 8-Noon

S MATURANGO MUSEUM*, Resource Library, 100 E Las Flores Ave, 93555. SAN 375-8184. Tel: 760-375-6900. FAX: 760-375-0479. E-mail: matmus@maturango.org. Web Site: www.maturango.org. *Exec Dir,* Harris Brokke; *Curator of Hist,* Elizabeth Babcock; *Web Adminr,* Janet Westbrook; E-mail: jwest@ridgenet.net
Library Holdings: Bk Titles 2,500
Wireless access
Open Mon-Sun 10-5
Restriction: Non-circulating

RIVERSIDE

CR CALIFORNIA BAPTIST UNIVERSITY*, Annie Gabriel Library, 8432 Magnolia Ave, 92504. SAN 301-2492. Tel: 951-343-4228. Reference Tel: 951-343-4242. Toll Free Tel: 877-228-3615. E-mail: library@calbaptist.edu. Web Site: www.calbaptist.edu/library. *Dir,* Dr Steve Emerson; E-mail: semerson@calbaptist.edu; *Coll Develop Librn,* Elizabeth Flater; Tel: 951-552-8624, Fax: eflater@calbaptist.edu; *Access Serv Mgr,* Patricia Palmer; Tel: 951-343-4331, E-mail: ppalmer@calbaptist.edu; *Cat,* Helen Xu; Tel: 951-343-4354, E-mail: hxu@calbaptist.edu; *Circ,* Keri Murcray; E-mail: kmurcray@calbaptist.edu; *Digital Serv,* Matthew Goddard; Tel: 951-343-4365, E-mail: mgoddard@calbaptist.edu; *Ser,* Dr Barry Parker; E-mail: bparker@calbaptist.edu; *Tech Serv,* Rose Lilley; Tel: 951-343-4353, E-mail: rlilley@calbaptist.edu; Staff 8 (MLS 5, Non-MLS 3)
Founded 1950. Enrl 6,200; Highest Degree: Master
Library Holdings: Bk Vols 220,000; Per Subs 250
Special Collections: Hymnology (P Boyd Smith Coll); Nie Wieder Coll; Virginia Hyatt Baptist Coll; Wallace Coll. Oral History
Subject Interests: Educ, Fine arts, Holocaust, Hymnology, Psychol, Relig

Automation Activity & Vendor Info: (Acquisitions) SirsiDynix; (Cataloging) SirsiDynix; (Circulation) SirsiDynix; (ILL) OCLC; (OPAC) SirsiDynix; (Serials) SerialsSolutions
Database Vendor: ebrary, EBSCOhost, Gale Cengage Learning, JSTOR, LexisNexis, OCLC FirstSearch, OCLC WorldShare Interlibrary Loan, OVID Technologies, ProQuest, Springer-Verlag, Springshare, LLC
Wireless access
Function: ILL available, Ref serv available, Wheelchair accessible
Partic in Inland Empire Acad Libr Coop (IEALC); OCLC Online Computer Library Center, Inc; Statewide California Electronic Library Consortium (SCELC)
Open Mon-Thurs 7:45am Midnight, Fri 8-5, Sat 10-6, Sun 4-Midnight

S CALIFORNIA SCHOOL FOR THE DEAF LIBRARY*, 3044 Horace St, 92506. SAN 320-5746. Tel: 951-248-7700. Web Site: www.csdr-cde.ca.gov/. *Libr Supvr,* Erik Lasiewski; Tel: 951-248-7700, Ext 4138
Library Holdings: Bk Vols 13,000
Special Collections: American Annals for the Deaf; Volta Review
Subject Interests: Deaf, Spec educ
Automation Activity & Vendor Info: (Acquisitions) Follett Software
Partic in San Bernardino, Inyo, Riverside Counties United Library Services
Special Services for the Deaf - TTY equip
Open Tues & Thurs 8-3

G CALIFORNIA STATE COURT OF APPEAL*, Fourth Appellate District, Division Two Library, 3389 12th St, 92501. SAN 327-1587. Tel: 951-782-2485. FAX: 909-248-0235. *Librn,* Terry R Lynch; E-mail: terry.lynch@jud.ca.gov
Library Holdings: Bk Vols 30,000

R CALVARY PRESBYTERIAN CHURCH USA LIBRARY*, 4495 Magnolia Ave, 92501. SAN 301-2506. Tel: 951-686-0761. FAX: 951-686-1488. E-mail: church@calvarypresch.com. Web Site: www.calvarypresch.org *Head of Libr,* Dr Dean Kokjer
Library Holdings: Bk Vols 2,000
Open Mon-Thurs 9-5, Fri 9-1:30
Restriction: Mem only

M KAISER-PERMANENTE MEDICAL CENTER*, Health Sciences Library, 10800 Magnolia Ave, 92505. SAN 377-5208. Tel: 951-353-3659. FAX: 951-353-3262. *Librn,* William Paringer; *Libr Tech,* Maria Ramirez
Library Holdings: Bk Vols 1,500
Open Mon-Fri 8-4:30

C LA SIERRA UNIVERSITY LIBRARY, 4500 Riverwalk Pkwy, 92505-3344. SAN 333-8851. Tel: 951-785-2397. Circulation Tel: 951-785-2044. Interlibrary Loan Service Tel: 951-785-2403. Reference Tel: 951-785-2396. FAX: 951-785-2445. Web Site: www.lasierra.edu/library. *Dir,* Kitty Simmons; E-mail: ksimmons@lasierra.edu; *Ref Librn,* Jeffrey De Vries; E-mail: jdevries@lasierra.edu; *Ref Librn,* Hilda Smith; E-mail: hsmith@lasierra.edu; *Ref, Spec Coll Librn,* Chelsi Cannon; E-mail: ccannon@lasierra.edu; *Tech Serv Librn,* Christina Viramontes; E-mail: cviramon@lasierra.edu; Staff 11 (MLS 5, Non-MLS 6)
Founded 1927. Enrl 2,000; Fac 100; Highest Degree: Doctorate
Jul 2012-Jun 2013. Mats Exp $466,522, Books $136,642, Per/Ser (Incl. Access Fees) $143,717, Electronic Ref Mat (Incl. Access Fees) $170,239, Presv $15,924. Sal $837,642
Library Holdings: AV Mats 386,267; e-books 90,939; e-journals 39,067; Bk Vols 216,782; Per Subs 807
Special Collections: Far Eastern Coll; History (W A Scharffenberg Coll); Library of American Civilization, micro; Library of English Literature, micro; Reformation History (William M Landeen Coll); Seventh Day Adventist Coll
Automation Activity & Vendor Info: (Acquisitions) Innovative Interfaces, Inc; (Cataloging) Innovative Interfaces, Inc; (Circulation) Innovative Interfaces, Inc; (ILL) Innovative Interfaces, Inc; (OPAC) Innovative Interfaces, Inc; (Serials) Innovative Interfaces, Inc
Database Vendor: Innovative Interfaces, Inc
Wireless access
Partic in OCLC Online Computer Library Center, Inc; Statewide California Electronic Library Consortium (SCELC)
Open Mon-Thurs 8am-Midnight, Fri 8am-1pm, Sun 1pm-Midnight

J RIVERSIDE COMMUNITY COLLEGE DISTRICT*, Digital Library & Learning Resource Center, 4800 Magnolia Ave, 92506-1299. SAN 301-2530. Tel: 951-222-8651. Reference Tel: 951-222-8652. FAX: 951-328-3679. Web Site: library.rcc.edu. *Dean of Libr,* Cecilia Wong; Tel: 951-222-8038, E-mail: cecilia.wong@rcc.edu; *Librn,* Steve Breaster; *Coll Develop,* Paul Moores; *Network Serv,* Hayley Garcia; *Per,* Linda Urquizu; *Tech Serv,* Rebecca Ng. Subject Specialists: *Bus educ,* Steve Breaster; Staff 8 (MLS 8)
Founded 1919. Enrl 35,170; Fac 830; Highest Degree: Associate
Library Holdings: AV Mats 7,733; Bks on Deafness & Sign Lang 183; Bk Titles 121,346; Bk Vols 153,865; Per Subs 888; Talking Bks 30
Automation Activity & Vendor Info: (Acquisitions) Innovative Interfaces, Inc; (Cataloging) Innovative Interfaces, Inc; (Circulation) Innovative Interfaces, Inc; (Course Reserve) Innovative Interfaces, Inc; (ILL) Innovative Interfaces, Inc; (Media Booking) Innovative Interfaces, Inc; (OPAC) Innovative Interfaces, Inc; (Serials) Innovative Interfaces, Inc
Database Vendor: Gale Cengage Learning, OVID Technologies, ProQuest
Open Mon-Thurs 7:30am-9pm, Fri 7:30-4
Departmental Libraries:
MORENO VALLEY CAMPUS
See Separate Entry in Moreno Valley

GL RIVERSIDE COUNTY LAW LIBRARY*, Victor Miceli Law Library, 3989 Lemon St, 92501-4203. SAN 301-2549. Tel: 951-368-0368. Administration Tel: 951-368-0360. FAX: 951-368-0185. E-mail: lawlibrary.riverside@rclawlibrary.org. Web Site: www.rclawlibrary.org. *Dir,* Position Currently Open; *Assoc Dir,* Elizabeth Manouchehri; Tel: 951-368-0362, E-mail: betsy.manouchehri@rclawlibrary.org; *Pub Serv Librn,* Bret N Christensen; Tel: 951-368-0379, E-mail: bret.christensen@rclawlibrary.org; *Pub Serv Librn,* Daisy Cortes; E-mail: daisy.cortes@rclawlibrary.org; Staff 5 (MLS 4, Non-MLS 1)
Founded 1941
Jul 2006-Jun 2007 Income $2,496,219, County $2,347,351, Locally Generated Income $40,154, Other $108,714. Mats Exp $671,585, Books $3,672, Per/Ser (Incl. Access Fees) $481,061, AV Equip $3,740, Electronic Ref Mat (Incl. Access Fees) $129,895, Presv $1,950. Sal $544,414
Library Holdings: Bk Titles 6,043; Bk Vols 102,782
Special Collections: Municipal Codes. State Document Depository
Automation Activity & Vendor Info: (Acquisitions) SirsiDynix; (Cataloging) SirsiDynix; (Circulation) SirsiDynix; (OPAC) SirsiDynix; (Serials) SirsiDynix
Wireless access
Function: Ref & res
Publications: Bookmark; Brochure; The ABC's of the RCLL (CD)
Partic in SIRCULS
Open Mon-Thurs 8-7, Fri 8-5, Sat 9-1
Restriction: Non-circulating

P RIVERSIDE COUNTY LIBRARY SYSTEM*, 1335 Spruce St, 92507. Tel: 951-955-1158. FAX: 951-955-8916. Web Site: www.rivlib.net. *County Librn,* Barbara Williams; Staff 65.3 (MLS 33.7, Non-MLS 31.6)
Founded 1911. Pop 1,084,811; Circ 3,280,929
Library Holdings: Bk Vols 1,034,429; Per Subs 875
Automation Activity & Vendor Info: (Acquisitions) SirsiDynix; (Cataloging) SirsiDynix; (Circulation) SirsiDynix; (ILL) SirsiDynix; (OPAC) SirsiDynix; (Serials) SirsiDynix
Function: Adult bk club, Adult literacy prog, Art exhibits, Audiobks via web, Bilingual assistance for Spanish patrons, Bk club(s), Bks on cassette, Bks on CD, CD-ROM, Children's prog, Computer training, Computers for patron use, Copy machines, Electronic databases & coll, Exhibits, Family literacy, Free DVD rentals, Games & aids for the handicapped, Handicapped accessible, Holiday prog, Homebound delivery serv, Homework prog, ILL available, Learning ctr, Magnifiers for reading, Mail & tel request accepted, Music CDs, Online cat, Online info literacy tutorials on the web & in blackboard, Online ref, Online searches, Orientations, Outreach serv, Outside serv via phone, mail, e-mail & web, Photocopying/Printing, Preschool outreach, Prog for adults, Prog for children & young adult, Pub access computers, Ref serv available, Ref serv in person, Referrals accepted, Senior computer classes, Senior outreach, Spoken cassettes & CDs, Spoken cassettes & DVDs, Story hour, Summer reading prog, Tax forms, Teen prog, Telephone ref, VHS videos, Web-catalog, Wheelchair accessible, Workshops, Writing prog
Mem of Inland Library System
Open Mon-Fri 8-5
Branches: 33
ANZA LIBRARY, 57430 Mitchell Rd, Anza, 92539. Tel: 951-763-4216. FAX: 951-763-0657. *Br Mgr,* Doreen Nagel
Open Mon & Fri 8-3, Tues-Thurs 8-7, Sat 10-2
CALIMESA LIBRARY, 974 Calimesa Blvd, Calimesa, 92320. Tel: 909-795-9807. FAX: 909-795-3198. *Br Mgr,* Yelena Antonov
Open Tues, Thurs & Fri 10-6, Wed 12-8, Sat 9-5
CANYON LAKE LIBRARY, 31516 Railroad Canyon Rd, Canyon Lake, 92587. Tel: 951-244-9181. FAX: 951-244-7382. *Br Mgr,* Trish Jenkins
Open Mon 10-7, Wed & Fri 10-6, Sat 10-3
CATHEDRAL CITY LIBRARY, 33520 Date Palm Dr, Cathedral City, 92234-4725. Tel: 760-328-4262. FAX: 760-770-9828. *Br Mgr,* Amy Dodson; Tel: 760-770-9050
Open Mon, Tues, Thurs & Sat 10-6, Wed 12-8, Sun 1-5
Friends of the Library Group
COACHELLA LIBRARY, 1538 Seventh St, Coachella, 92236. Tel: 760-398-5148. FAX: 760-398-1068. *Br Mgr,* Miguel Guitron- Rodriguez
Open Mon & Wed 2-6, Tues & Thurs 10-6, Sat 10-5

DESERT HOT SPRINGS LIBRARY, 11691 West Dr, Desert Hot Springs, 92240. Tel: 760-329-5926. FAX: 760-329-3593. Web Site: rivlib.info/desert-hot-springs-library. *Br Mgr,* Sharon Snow
Open Mon-Wed 10-6, Thurs 12-8, Sat 9-3
EASTVALE LIBRARY, 7447 Cleveland Ave, Corona, 92880. Tel: 951-273-1520. FAX: 951-273-9442. *Br Mgr,* Richelle Crews
Open Mon-Thurs 3-8, Fri 3-6, Sat 10-5
EL CERRITO LIBRARY, 7581 Rudell Rd, Corona, 92881. Tel: 951-270-5012. *Br Mgr,* Nancy Reiter
Open Mon-Thurs 3-7, Sat 10-2
GLEN AVON LIBRARY, 9244 Galena St, 92509. Tel: 951-685-8121. FAX: 951-685-7158. *Br Mgr,* Tracie Carignan
Open Mon-Tues 10-8, Wed 12-8, Thurs 12-6, Fri & Sat 10-5, Sun 1-5
HIGHGROVE LIBRARY, 690 W Center St, Highgrove, 92507. Tel: 951-682-1507. FAX: 951-321-4107. *Br Mgr,* Louise Gutierrez
Open Tues & Thurs 10-6, Wed 10-2, Sat 10-3
HOME GARDENS LIBRARY, 3785 Neece St, Corona, 92879. Tel: 951-279-2148. FAX: 951-734-3170. *Br Mgr,* Jan Kuebel
Open Mon & Tues 12-8, Wed & Thurs 10-6, Fri & Sat 10-5, Sun 1-5
IDYLLWILD LIBRARY, 54401 Village Center Dr, Idyllwild, 92549. Tel: 951-659-2300. FAX: 951-659-2453. *Br Mgr,* Shannon Ng
Open Mon & Wed 10-6, Tues 12-8, Thurs 12-5, Sat 10-4
INDIO LIBRARY, 200 Civic Ctr Mall, Indio, 92201. Tel: 760-347-2383. FAX: 760-347-3159. *Br Mgr,* Donna McCune; Tel: 760-347-2385
Open Mon 12-8, Tues-Thurs & Sat 10-6
LA QUINTA LIBRARY, 78-080 Calle Estado, La Quinta, 92253. Tel: 760-564-4767. FAX: 760-771-0237. *Br Mgr,* Beth Foley
Open Tues 10-8, Wed 10-6, Thurs 12-8, Fri 10-4, Sat 10-2, Sun 12-4
LAKE ELSINORE LIBRARY, 600 W Graham, Lake Elsinore, 92530. Tel: 951-674-4517. FAX: 951-245-7715. *Br Mgr,* Vose Thomas; Tel: 951-245-3918
Open Mon, Thurs & Fri 11-6, Tues & Wed 1-8, Sat 10-3
LAKE TAMARISK LIBRARY, 43880 Lake Tamarisk Dr, Desert Center, 92239. (Mail add: PO Box 260, Desert Center, 92239-0260). Tel: 760-227-3273. FAX: 760-227-3273. *Br Mgr,* Veronica Evans
Open Tues & Thurs 10-6, Sat 10-2
LAKESIDE LIBRARY, 32593 Riverside Dr, Lake Elsinore, 92530. Tel: 951-678-7083. FAX: 951-678-7018. *Br Mgr,* Position Currently Open; *Children's Coordr,* Roya Smith; E-mail: roya_lak@riverside.lib.ca.us
Open Mon-Thurs 10-7, Fri 10-5, Sat 10-2, Sun 12-5
MECCA LIBRARY, 91-260 Ave 66, Mecca, 92254. Tel: 760-396-2363. FAX: 760-396-1503. *Br Mgr,* Miguel Guitron-Rodriguez
Open Mon, Tues & Thurs 1-5, Wed 9-5
GRACE MELLMAN COMMUNITY LIBRARY (TEMECULA COUNTY CENTER LIBRARY), 41000 County Center Dr, Temecula, 92591. Tel: 951-600-6262. FAX: 951-600-6265. *Br Mgr,* Emily Gerstbacher; Tel: 909-600-6266
Open Mon 12-9, Tues-Fri 10-6, Sat 10-5, Sun 1-5
MISSION TRAIL LIBRARY, 34303 Mission Trail, Wildomar, 92595. Tel: 951-471-3855. FAX: 951-471-0188. *Br Mgr,* Jennie Jackson
Open Mon 12-8, Tues-Fri 10-6, Sat 10-3
NORCO LIBRARY, 3954 Old Hamner Rd, Norco, 92860. Tel: 951-735-5329. FAX: 951-735-0263. Web Site: www.rivlib.net/rcls/branches/norco.shtml. *Br Mgr,* Luz Wood
Special Collections: Horse Coll, bks, DVDs, mags, v-tapes
Subject Interests: Breeding, Equestrian, Feeding, Horses, Training
Open Mon-Thurs 10-8, Sat 10-4
Friends of the Library Group
NUVIEW LIBRARY, 29990 Lake View Ave, Nuevo, 92567. (Mail add: PO Box 769, Nuevo, 92567-0769). Tel: 951-928-0769. FAX: 951-928-3360. *Br Mgr,* Louise Gutierrez
Open Mon & Fri 10-6, Wed 3-7
PALM DESERT LIBRARY, 73-300 Fred Waring Dr, Palm Desert, 92260. Tel: 760-346-6552. FAX: 760-341-7862. *Br Mgr,* Jeannie Kays
Open Mon-Wed 10-8, Thurs & Sat 10-5, Sun 1-5
PALOMA VALLEY LIBRARY, 31375 Bradley Rd, Menifee, 92584. Tel: 951-301-3682. FAX: 951-301-8423. *Br Mgr,* Cara Larson
Open Mon-Wed 12-7, Thurs 12-5, Sat 10-2
PERRIS LIBRARY, 163 E San Jacinto, Perris, 92570. Tel: 951-657-2358. FAX: 951-657-9849. *Br Mgr,* Sherry Martinez
Open Mon, Thurs & Sat 10-6, Tues & Wed 12-8, Sun 1-5
LOUIS ROBIDOUX LIBRARY, 5840 Mission Blvd, Jurupa Valley, 92509. Tel: 951-682-5485. FAX: 951-682-8641. *Br Mgr,* Laura Mae Leach; E-mail: lauramae.leach@rivlib.net; Staff 3.725 (MLS 1, Non-MLS 2.725)
Founded 1948
Automation Activity & Vendor Info: (Acquisitions) Innovative Interfaces, Inc
Database Vendor: Gale Cengage Learning
Function: Adult bk club, Bilingual assistance for Spanish patrons, Bks on CD, Children's prog, Computer training, Computers for patron use, Copy machines, Electronic databases & coll, Free DVD rentals, ILL available, Music CDs, Online cat, Online ref, OverDrive digital audio bks, Photocopying/Printing, Prog for children & young adult, Pub access computers, Ref serv available, Story hour, Summer reading prog, Tax forms, Teen prog, Telephone ref, Wheelchair accessible
Open Mon-Wed, Fri & Sat 10-6, Thurs 12-8, Sun 1-5
Restriction: ID required to use computers (Ltd hrs), In-house use for visitors
Friends of the Library Group
ROMOLAND LIBRARY, 26000 Briggs Rd, Romoland, 92585. Tel: 951-325-2090. FAX: 951-926-7989. *Br Mgr,* Sandra Silva
Open Mon-Thurs 3-7, Sat 10-2
SAN JACINTO LIBRARY, 500 Idyllwild Dr, San Jacinto, 92583. Tel: 951-654-8635. FAX: 951-487-8069. *Br Mgr,* Tyler Klaas; Staff 1 (MLS 1)
Open Mon & Fri 7:30-6, Tues-Thurs 7:30-7, Sat 9-1
Friends of the Library Group
SUN CITY LIBRARY, 26982 Cherry Hills Blvd, Sun City, 92586. Tel: 951-679-3534. FAX: 951-672-8293. *Br Mgr,* Nancy Smith; Tel: 951-679-8672
Open Mon, Tues & Fri 9-5, Wed 12-6, Thurs 2-8, Sat 9-1, Sun 12-4
TEMECULA PUBLIC LIBRARY, 30600 Pauba Rd, Temecula, 92592. Tel: 951-693-8900. FAX: 951-693-8998. *Br Mgr,* Rosie Vanderhaak
Open Mon-Thurs 10-9, Fri 10-6, Sat 10-5, Sun 1-5
THOUSAND PALMS LIBRARY, 72-715 La Canada Way, Thousand Palms, 92276. Tel: 760-343-1556. FAX: 760-343-0957. *Br Mgr,* Sharon Ballard
Open Mon & Tues 2-6, Wed 10-6, Sat 10-2
VALLE VISTA LIBRARY, 25757 Fairview Ave, Hemet, 92544. Tel: 951-927-2611. FAX: 951-927-7902. *Br Mgr,* Carol Jenson
Open Mon & Wed 10-7, Tues & Thurs 10-6, Fri 10-5, Sat 10-2
WOODCREST LIBRARY, 16625 Krameria, 92504. Tel: 951-789-7324. FAX: 951-789-7321. *Br Mgr,* Connie Rynning
Open Mon-Wed 10-7, Thurs & Sat 10-4, Fri 12-5

P RIVERSIDE PUBLIC LIBRARY*, 3581 Mission Inn Ave, 92501. (Mail add: PO Box 468, 92502-0468), SAN 333-8886. Tel: 951-826-5201. Administration Tel: 951-826-5213. FAX: 951-788-1528. Administration FAX: 951-826-5407. E-mail: rpllibrary@riversideca.gov. Web Site: www.riversideca.gov/library. *Dir,* Tony Kennon; *Admin Serv Mgr,* George Guzman; E-mail: gguzman@riversideca.gov; *Circ Coordr,* Karen Bracken; Staff 73 (MLS 17, Non-MLS 56)
Founded 1888. Pop 291,398; Circ 1,060,244
Library Holdings: AV Mats 36,500; Bk Vols 522,459; Per Subs 997
Special Collections: Black History Coll; Genealogy Coll; Historical Children's Books (Dorothy Daniels Memorial Coll); Local History Coll; Mexican American Coll; Sight Handicapped Coll, bks, cassettes, per
Automation Activity & Vendor Info: (Cataloging) Innovative Interfaces, Inc; (Circulation) Innovative Interfaces, Inc; (ILL) Innovative Interfaces, Inc; (OPAC) Innovative Interfaces, Inc
Database Vendor: 3M Library Systems, ALLDATA Online, Amigos Library Services, Booksite, BWI, Comprise Technologies Inc, EBSCOhost, Grolier Online, Ingram Library Services, Innovative Interfaces, Inc, OCLC WorldShare Interlibrary Loan, ProQuest, ReferenceUSA, ValueLine
Wireless access
Function: Adult literacy prog, Archival coll, Bks on cassette, Bks on CD, Children's prog, Computers for patron use, Copy machines, Digital talking bks, Electronic databases & coll, Handicapped accessible, Home delivery & serv to Sr ctr & nursing homes, Homebound delivery serv, ILL available, Magnifiers for reading, Music CDs, Online cat, Prog for adults, Prog for children & young adult, Pub access computers, Spoken cassettes & CDs, Spoken cassettes & DVDs, Story hour, Summer reading prog, Teen prog, VHS videos
Special Services for the Deaf - Bks on deafness & sign lang; Closed caption videos; Coll on deaf educ; Staff with knowledge of sign lang; TDD equip; TTY equip
Special Services for the Blind - Home delivery serv; Large print bks
Open Mon-Thurs 10-9, Fri & Sat 10-6, Sun 12-5
Friends of the Library Group
Branches: 5
ARLINGTON, 9556 Magnolia, 92503-3698, SAN 333-8916. Tel: 951-689-6612. FAX: 951-689-6612. *Librn,* Charlene Swanson; Staff 1 (MLS 1)
Library Holdings: Bk Vols 50,815
Open Mon-Thurs 10-8, Fri & Sat 10-6
Friends of the Library Group
CASA BLANCA LIBRARY & FAMILY LEARNING CENTER, 2985 Madison St, 92504-4480, SAN 333-8940. Tel: 951-826-2120. FAX: 951-826-2120. *Site Supvr,* Susie Garcia
Library Holdings: Bk Vols 45,681
Open Mon-Thurs 11-9, Fri & Sat 10-6
Friends of the Library Group
EASTSIDE LIBRARY & CYBRARY, 4033-C Chicago Ave, 92507. Tel: 951-684-8347. *Br Mgr,* Miriam Perez; Tel: 951-369-8120, E-mail: mperez@riversideca.gov; Staff 1 (MLS 1)
Library Holdings: Bk Vols 9,920
Open Mon-Thurs 10-8, Fri & Sat 10-6

LA SIERRA, 4600 La Sierra, 92505-2722, SAN 333-9181. Tel: 951-688-7740. FAX: 951-352-7578. *Br Mgr,* Linda Taylor; E-mail: ltaylor@riversideca.gov; Staff 1 (MLS 1)
Library Holdings: Bk Vols 77,925
Open Mon-Thurs 10-9, Fri & Sat 10-6
Friends of the Library Group

MARCY BRANCH, 6927 Magnolia Ave, 92506, SAN 333-9270. Tel: 951-826-2078. *Supvr,* Gail Hendricks
Library Holdings: Bk Vols 42,451
Open Mon-Thurs 9-7, Fri & Sat 9-5
Friends of the Library Group

C UNIVERSITY OF CALIFORNIA, RIVERSIDE LIBRARIES*, 900 University Ave, 92521. (Mail add: PO Box 5900, 92517-5900), SAN 333-9696. Circulation Tel: 951-827-3220, 951-827-3701. Interlibrary Loan Service Tel: 951-827-3234, 951-827-6387. Reference Tel: 951-827-3316, 951-827-4392. Administration Tel: 951-827-3221. Interlibrary Loan Service FAX: 951-827-2820. Administration FAX: 951-827-2255. Web Site: library.ucr.edu. *Univ Librn,* Dr Ruth M Jackson; E-mail: ruth.jackson@ucr.edu; *Assoc Univ Librn, Info Tech & Syst,* Diane Bisom; Tel: 951-827-2080, E-mail: diane.bisom@ucr.edu; *Asst Univ Librn, Admin Serv,* David Rios; Tel: 951-827-4394, E-mail: david.rios@ucr.edu; *Asst Univ Librn, Coll & Scholarly Communications,* Barbara Schader; Tel: 951-827-4614, E-mail: barbara.schader@ucr.edu; *Asst Univ Librn, Res & Instrul Serv,* Ann Frenkel; Tel: 951-827-4824, E-mail: ann.frenkel@ucr.edu; *Head, Access Serv,* Vincent Novoa; Tel: 951-827-7309, E-mail: vincent.novoa@ucr.edu; *Head, Cat & Metadata Serv,* Manuel Urrizola; Tel: 951-827-5051, E-mail: manuel.urrizola@ucr.edu; *Head, Electronic Res & Continuation,* Sharon Scott; Tel: 951-827-2813, E-mail: sharon.scott@ucr.edu; *Head, Fac & Receiving,* Diana Lightfeldt; Tel: 951-827-2849, E-mail: diana.lightfeldt@ucr.edu; *Head, Presv Serv,* Dr Patricia Smith-Hunt; Tel: 951-827-7702, E-mail: patricia.smith-hunt@ucr.edu; *Head, Spec Coll & Archives,* Dr Melissa Conway; Tel: 951-827-3233, E-mail: melissa.conway@ucr.edu; *Head, Syst,* Terry Toy; Tel: 951-827-4319, E-mail: ttoy@ucr.edu; *Interim Head, Coll Develop,* Kuei Chiu; Tel: 951-827-3703, E-mail: kuei.chiu@ucr.edu. Subject Specialists: *Sci,* Barbara Schader; *Asian studies,* Kuei Chiu; Staff 44 (MLS 37, Non-MLS 7)
Founded 1954. Enrl 18,079; Fac 678; Highest Degree: Doctorate
Jul 2005-Jun 2006 Income (Main and Other College/University Libraries) $13,213,566. Mats Exp $6,109,872
Library Holdings: AV Mats 22,873; CDs 8,966; DVDs 4,680; e-books 380,976; Microforms 2,323,133; Bk Titles 2,291,248; Bk Vols 2,955,171; Per Subs 90,153; Videos 6,399
Special Collections: B Traven Coll; Citrus Experiment Station records; Costo Library of the American Indian; Eaton Science Fiction, Fantasy, Horror & Utopian Literature Coll; Heinreich Schenker Coll; Joaquin Nin-Culmell Coll; Local History; Mexican Revolution Photographs; Panama Canal Coll; Paraguayan Coll; Sadakichi Hartmann Coll; Science Fiction Fanzines; Tuskegee Airmen Archive; University Archives; Working Printing Press Coll & Bk Arts. Oral History; State Document Depository; US Document Depository
Automation Activity & Vendor Info: (Acquisitions) Innovative Interfaces, Inc; (Cataloging) Innovative Interfaces, Inc; (Circulation) Innovative Interfaces, Inc; (Course Reserve) Innovative Interfaces, Inc; (ILL) OCLC; (OPAC) Innovative Interfaces, Inc; (Serials) Innovative Interfaces, Inc
Database Vendor: ACM (Association for Computing Machinery), Agricola, Alexander Street Press, American Chemical Society, American Mathematical Society, American Physical Society, American Psychological Association (APA), Annual Reviews, ARTstor, ASCE Research Library, Baker & Taylor, BioOne, Blackwell, Bowker, Cambridge Scientific Abstracts, Checkpoint Systems, Inc, CountryWatch, Coutts Information Service, CQ Press, CRC Press/Taylor & Francis Group, Dialog, Dun & Bradstreet, ebrary, EBSCO Information Services, EBSCOhost, Elsevier, Emerald, Factiva.com, Facts on File, H W Wilson, Haworth Pres Inc, Hoovers, IEEE (Institute of Electrical & Electronics Engineers), Ingenta, Ingram Library Services, Innovative Interfaces, Inc, IOP, ISI Web of Knowledge, JSTOR, Knovel, LexisNexis, Luna Imaging/Insight, Marcive, Inc, Marquis Who's Who, McGraw-Hill, MD Consult, Medline, Mergent Online, Micromedex, Modern Language Association, Natural Standard, Nature Publishing Group, Newsbank, Newsbank-Readex, OCLC ArticleFirst, OCLC FirstSearch, OCLC WorldShare Interlibrary Loan, OCLC-RLG, OneSource, OVID Technologies, Oxford Online, Project MUSE, ProQuest, PubMed, ReferenceUSA, RefWorks, Safari Books Online, Sage, ScienceDirect, Scopus, Springer-Verlag, Standard & Poor's, STAT!Ref (Teton Data Systems), Thomson - Web of Science, ValueLine, WebMD, Westlaw, Wiley, Wiley InterScience, Wilson - Wilson Web, YBP Library Services
Wireless access
Publications: Associates (Online only)
Partic in Association of Research Libraries (ARL); California Digital Library (CDL); OCLC Online Computer Library Center, Inc; San Bernardino, Inyo, Riverside Counties United Library Services

Departmental Libraries:

MULTIMEDIA LIBRARY, Interdisciplinary Bldg South, Rm 2117, 92521. (Mail add: PO Box 5900, 92517-5900). Tel: 951-827-5606. FAX: 951-827-5753. *Contact, Multimedia Libr,* Ann Frenkel; E-mail: ann.frenkel@ucr.edu
Founded 1978
Library Holdings: AV Mats 9,512; CDs 483; DVDs 3,645; Bk Vols 101; Videos 4,017
Open Mon-Thurs 9-6, Fri 8-5

MUSIC LIBRARY, Arts Bldg, Rm 54, 92521. (Mail add: PO Box 5900, 92517-5900). Tel: 951-827-3137. Interlibrary Loan Service Tel: 951-827-3234. FAX: 951-827-3948. Interlibrary Loan Service FAX: 951-827-2820. Web Site: library.ucr.edu/?view=libraries/music. *Mgr,* Caitlin St John; Tel: 951-827-2268, E-mail: caitlins@ucr.edu
Founded 1978
Library Holdings: AV Mats 12,268; CDs 6,911; DVDs 260; Microforms 1,882; Music Scores 50,946; Videos 542
Open Mon-Thurs 8-8, Fri 8-5, Sat & Sun 1-5

RAYMOND L ORBACH SCIENCE LIBRARY, 900 University Ave, 92521. (Mail add: PO Box 5900, 92517-5900). Circulation Tel: 951-827-3701. Administration Tel: 951-827-3238. Administration FAX: 951-827-6378. *Head, Ref & Info Serv,* Dr Lizbeth Langston; Tel: 951-827-3529, E-mail: lizbeth.langston@ucr.edu; Staff 20 (MLS 15, Non-MLS 5)
Founded 1998
Library Holdings: AV Mats 108,866; CDs 41; DVDs 11; Microforms 74,102; Bk Vols 523,903; Videos 20
Open Mon-Thurs 8am-Midnight, Fri 8-5, Sat 10-5, Sun 1pm-Midnight

TOMAS RIVERA LIBRARY, 900 University Ave, 92521. (Mail add: PO Box 5900, 92517-5900).
Founded 1954
Library Holdings: AV Mats 20,222; CDs 1,531; DVDs 764; Microforms 2,246,989; Bk Vols 1,997,182; Videos 1,820

ROCKLIN

J SIERRA JOINT COMMUNITY COLLEGE DISTRICT*, Learning Resource Center, 5000 Rocklin Rd, 95677. SAN 301-2565. Tel: 916-660-7230. Reference Tel: 916-660-7232. FAX: 916-630-4539. E-mail: referencedesk@sierracollege.edu. Web Site: lrc.sierracollege.edu. *Dean,* Brian Haley; *Cat,* Deirdre Campbell; *Coll Develop, Ref Serv,* Tina Sixt; *Ref,* Sandra Montgomery
Founded 1914
Library Holdings: Bk Titles 90,000; Per Subs 189
Special Collections: Rare Book Coll; Realia Coll
Subject Interests: Calif, Mining
Automation Activity & Vendor Info: (Cataloging) Ex Libris Group; (Circulation) Ex Libris Group; (Course Reserve) Ex Libris Group; (OPAC) Ex Libris Group
Database Vendor: CQ Press, EBSCOhost, Elsevier, JSTOR, SerialsSolutions
Wireless access
Friends of the Library Group

ROHNERT PARK

C SONOMA STATE UNIVERSITY LIBRARY*, Jean & Charles Schulz Information Center, 1801 E Cotati Ave, 94928-3609. SAN 301-2573. Tel: 707-664-2397. Circulation Tel: 707-664-2375. FAX: 707-664-2090. Web Site: www.libweb.sonoma.edu. *Dean,* Barbara Butler; E-mail: barbara.butler@sonoma.edu; *Dir, Operations,* Mike Kiraly; E-mail: mike.kiraly@sonoma.edu; *Dir, Tech & Info Serv,* Brandon Dudley; Tel: 707-664-2986, E-mail: brandon.dudley@sonoma.edu; *Circ Mgr,* Julie Dinkins; Tel: 707-664-4077, E-mail: julie.dinkins@sonoma.edu; *Head, Coll Develop, Web Serv,* Paula Hammett; Tel: 707-664-3912, E-mail: paula.hammett@sonoma.edu; *Instrul Serv Librn, Pub Relations,* Karen Brodsky; Tel: 707-664-4240, E-mail: karen.brodsky@sonoma.edu; *Coordr, Access Serv, Coordr, ILL,* Raye Lynn Thomas; Tel: 707-664-2951, E-mail: raye.lynn.thomas@sonoma.edu; *Ref Serv Coordr,* Rick Robinson; Tel: 707-664-4196, E-mail: rick.robinson@sonoma.edu; *Coordr, Tech Serv,* Geoffrey Skinner; Tel: 707-664-3310, Fax: 707-664-2876, E-mail: geoffrey.skinner@sonoma.edu; *Libr Spec,* Sami Lange; E-mail: samantha.lange@sonoma.edu; *Per,* Mary Dolan; Tel: 707-664-2073, E-mail: mary.dolan@sonoma.edu; Staff 11 (MLS 11)
Founded 1961. Enrl 7,500; Fac 300; Highest Degree: Master
Library Holdings: Bk Vols 560,000
Special Collections: Celtic Coll; North Bay Regional Information Center; Small California Press
Automation Activity & Vendor Info: (Acquisitions) Innovative Interfaces, Inc; (Cataloging) Innovative Interfaces, Inc; (Circulation) Innovative Interfaces, Inc; (OPAC) OCLC
Friends of the Library Group

ROLLING HILLS ESTATES

P PALOS VERDES LIBRARY DISTRICT, Peninsula Center Library, 701 Silver Spur Rd, 90274. SAN 333-5550. Tel: 310-377-9584. Circulation Tel: 310-377-9584, Ext 602. Interlibrary Loan Service Tel: 310-377-9584, Ext 239. Reference Tel: 310-377-9584, Ext 601. Administration Tel: 310-377-9584, Ext 245. Automation Services Tel: 310-377-9584, Ext 258. FAX: 310-541-6807. E-mail: info@pvld.org. Web Site: www.pvld.org. *Dir,* Katherine R Gould; Tel: 310-377-9584, Ext 200, E-mail: kgould@pvld.org; *Mgr, Ad Serv,* Sylvia Richardson; Tel: 310-377-9584, Ext 210, E-mail: srichardson@pvld.org; *Mgr, Circ & Customer Serv,* Eve Wittenmyer; Tel: 310-377-9584, Ext 263, E-mail: ewittenmyer@pvld.org; *Mgr, Digital Serv & Mkt,* David Campbell; Tel: 310-377-9584, Ext 284, E-mail: dcampbell@pvld.org; *Mgr, Tech Serv,* Mary Cohen; Tel: 310-377-9584, Ext 242, E-mail: mcohen@pvld.org; *Mgr, Young Readers,* Laura Henry; Tel: 310-377-9584, Ext 206, E-mail: lhenry@pvld.org; Staff 26 (MLS 17, Non-MLS 9)
Founded 1928. Pop 67,500; Circ 988,452
Jul 2014-Jun 2015 Income (Main Library and Branch(s)) $7,445,100, State $20,000, Locally Generated Income $6,728,400, Other $696,700. Mats Exp $520,300, Books $219,400, Per/Ser (Incl. Access Fees) $36,200, Other Print Mats $17,500, Micro $4,500, AV Mat $72,700, Electronic Ref Mat (Incl. Access Fees) $170,000. Sal $5,717,900
Library Holdings: Audiobooks 8,302; CDs 7,335; DVDs 12,275; e-books 14,000; e-journals 13,780; Electronic Media & Resources 3,410; Large Print Bks 6,013; Music Scores 1,118; Bk Vols 224,000; Per Subs 650; Talking Bks 8,302; Videos 12,275
Special Collections: Oral History
Subject Interests: Art, Genealogy, Local hist, Travel
Automation Activity & Vendor Info: (Acquisitions) Innovative Interfaces, Inc - Millenium; (Cataloging) Innovative Interfaces, Inc - Millenium; (Circulation) Innovative Interfaces, Inc - Millenium; (ILL) Innovative Interfaces, Inc - Millenium; (OPAC) Innovative Interfaces, Inc - Millenium; (Serials) Innovative Interfaces, Inc - Millenium
Database Vendor: Baker & Taylor, Brodart, CQ Press, EBSCOhost, Evanced Solutions, Inc, Gale Cengage Learning, Innovative Interfaces, Inc, Library Ideas, LLC, Newsbank, OCLC, OCLC ArticleFirst, OCLC FirstSearch, OCLC WorldShare Interlibrary Loan, Overdrive, Inc, ProQuest, ValueLine
Wireless access
Function: Adult bk club, Art exhibits, Bk club(s), Bks on CD, Chess club, Children's prog, Computers for patron use, Copy machines, Digital talking bks, e-mail & chat, Electronic databases & coll, Fax serv, Handicapped accessible, Holiday prog, Homebound delivery serv, ILL available, Newsp ref libr, Notary serv, Online cat, Online searches, Outside serv via phone, mail, e-mail & web, OverDrive digital audio bks, Passport agency, Photocopying/Printing, Preschool outreach, Prog for adults, Prog for children & young adult, Pub access computers, Ref serv available, Summer reading prog, Tax forms, Telephone ref, Video lending libr, Wheelchair accessible, Workshops
Publications: Friends of the Library Newsletter (Quarterly); Library Update
Partic in Southern California Library Cooperative
Special Services for the Deaf - ADA equip
Special Services for the Blind - Audio mat; Bks on cassette; Bks on CD; Large print bks; Ref serv; Talking bks; Videos on blindness & phys handicaps
Open Mon-Thurs 9-8, Fri 9-6, Sat 10-5, Sun 1-5
Restriction: Vols & interns use only
Friends of the Library Group
Branches: 2
MALAGA COVE, 2400 Via Campesina, Palos Verdes Estates, 90274-3662, SAN 333-5585. Tel: 310-377-9584, Ext 551. FAX: 310-373-7594. *Br Mgr,* Eve Wittenmyer; Tel: 310-377-9584, Ext 263, E-mail: ewittenmyer@pvld.org; Staff 5 (MLS 1, Non-MLS 4)
Automation Activity & Vendor Info: (ILL) OCLC ILLiad
Open Mon-Sat 10-5
Friends of the Library Group
MIRALESTE, 29089 Palos Verdes Dr E, Rancho Palos Verdes, 90275, SAN 333-5615. Tel: 310-377-9584, Ext 452. FAX: 310-547-4067. *Br Mgr,* Eve Wittenmyer; E-mail: ewittenmyer@pvld.org; Staff 2 (MLS 2)
Library Holdings: Bk Titles 38,500; Bk Vols 40,687
Open Mon-Fri 11-6, Sat 10-5
Friends of the Library Group

ROSEMEAD

J DON BOSCO TECHNICAL INSTITUTE*, Lee Memorial Library, 1151 San Gabriel Blvd, 91770. SAN 301-2581. Tel: 626-940-2000. FAX: 626-940-2001. E-mail: generalinfo@boscotech.edu. Web Site: www.boscotech.edu. *Librn,* Position Currently Open
Founded 1957
Library Holdings: Bk Titles 7,500; Bk Vols 9,500; Per Subs 30
Subject Interests: Art, Relig
Automation Activity & Vendor Info: (Cataloging) Follett Software; (Circulation) Follett Software
Open Mon-Fri 7:30-5
Friends of the Library Group

ROSEVILLE

J HEALD COLLEGE*, Learning Resource Center-Roseville Campus, Seven Sierra Gate Plaza, 95678. Tel: 916-789-8600. FAX: 916-789-8616. Web Site: www.heald.edu. *Mgr,* Ade Galvan; E-mail: ade_galvan@heald.edu
Library Holdings: Bk Vols 500
Database Vendor: EBSCOhost
Open Mon-Thurs 7am-11pm, Fri 8-8, Sat 9-1

P ROSEVILLE PUBLIC LIBRARY*, 225 Taylor St, 95678-2681. SAN 333-9815. Tel: 916-774-5221. FAX: 916-773-5594. E-mail: library@roseville.ca.us. Web Site: www.roseville.ca.us/library. *City Librn,* Dianne Bish; *Sr Libr Supvr,* Rachel Delgadillo; *Libr Supvr-Popular Libr,* Joan Goff; *Circ,* Bonnie Davis; *Tech Serv,* Lisa Dale; Staff 24 (MLS 6, Non-MLS 18)
Founded 1912. Pop 95,000
Library Holdings: Bk Titles 109,000; Bk Vols 159,000; Per Subs 474
Special Collections: Local History, photogs. Oral History
Subject Interests: Railroads
Automation Activity & Vendor Info: (Acquisitions) SirsiDynix; (Cataloging) SirsiDynix; (Circulation) SirsiDynix; (OPAC) SirsiDynix
Database Vendor: EBSCOhost, Gale Cengage Learning, OCLC FirstSearch, ProQuest
Wireless access
Open Mon-Thurs 10-8 (10-7 Summer), Fri & Sat 10-5
Friends of the Library Group
Branches: 1
MAIDU, 1530 Maidu Dr, 95661, SAN 333-984X. Tel: 916-774-5900. FAX: 916-773-0972.
Founded 1990. Pop 11,000
Library Holdings: Bk Vols 48,365; Per Subs 116
Open Mon-Thurs 10-8 (10-7 Summer), Fri & Sat 10-5
Friends of the Library Group
Bookmobiles: 1

M SUTTER ROSEVILLE MEDICAL CENTER LIBRARY*, One Medical Plaza, 95661-3037. SAN 301-2603. Tel: 916-781-1580. FAX: 916-781-1582. *Med Librn,* Heidi J Mortensen; E-mail: MortenH@sutterhealth.org; Staff 1 (MLS 1)
Founded 1968
Library Holdings: Bk Titles 1,000; Per Subs 140
Special Collections: Medical Coll
Subject Interests: Surgery
Function: Health sci info serv, ILL available, Online searches, Photocopying/Printing, Ref serv available, Telephone ref, Wheelchair accessible
Publications: Book Lists; Library Brochure
Partic in Medical Library Association (MLA); Northern California & Nevada Medical Library Group (NCNMLG)
Open Mon-Fri 8-5
Restriction: Circulates for staff only, In-house use for visitors, Non-circulating coll, Open to pub for ref only, Pub use on premises

SACRAMENTO

J AMERICAN RIVER COLLEGE LIBRARY*, 4700 College Oak Dr, 95841. SAN 333-9874. Tel: 916-484-8455. Reference Tel: 916-484-8458. Administration Tel: 916-484-8408. FAX: 916-484-8018, 916-484-8657. Web Site: www.arc.losrios.edu/library. *Assoc VPres, Instruction & Learning Res,* David Redfield; *Ref Serv,* Dan Crump; *Ref Serv,* Connie Ferrara; *Ref Serv,* Sarah Lehmann; *Ref Serv,* David McCusker; *Ref Serv,* Deborah Ondricka; *Ref Serv,* Linda Shoemake; *Ref Serv,* Tim Sturm; *Tech Serv,* Kathy Champion; Staff 14 (MLS 7, Non-MLS 7)
Founded 1955. Enrl 31,675; Highest Degree: Associate
Library Holdings: AV Mats 6,409; Bk Titles 66,078; Bk Vols 75,976; Per Subs 411
Automation Activity & Vendor Info: (Acquisitions) Innovative Interfaces, Inc; (Cataloging) Innovative Interfaces, Inc; (Circulation) Innovative Interfaces, Inc; (Course Reserve) Innovative Interfaces, Inc; (ILL) Innovative Interfaces, Inc; (Media Booking) Innovative Interfaces, Inc; (OPAC) Innovative Interfaces, Inc; (Serials) Innovative Interfaces, Inc
Wireless access
Partic in OCLC Online Computer Library Center, Inc
Open Mon-Thurs 7:30am-10pm, Fri 7:30-5, Sat 9-3

SR BETHANY PRESBYTERIAN CHURCH LIBRARY*, 5625 24th St, 95822. SAN 301-262X. Tel: 916-428-5281. FAX: 916-428-3716. E-mail: office@bethpres.com. Web Site: www.bethpres.com.
Library Holdings: Bk Vols 1,000

Open Mon-Fri 9-3:30
Restriction: Mem only

GL CALIFORNIA COURT OF APPEAL THIRD APPELLATE DISTRICT LIBRARY*, Robert K Puglia Library, 914 Capitol Mall, Ste 501A, Mosk Library & Courts Bldg, 95814. SAN 301-2700. Tel: 916-654-0209. Administration Tel: 916-653-0207. Administration FAX: 916-653-0322. Web Site: www.courts.ca.gov/3dca.htm. *Librn,* Holly Lakatos; E-mail: holly.lakatos@jud.ca.gov; Staff 1 (MLS 1)
Founded 1906
Library Holdings: Bk Titles 1,500; Bk Vols 25,000; Per Subs 50
Special Collections: Robert K Puglia Papers
Subject Interests: Judiciary, Law
Automation Activity & Vendor Info: (OPAC) LibraryWorld, Inc
Function: Govt ref serv
Restriction: Authorized personnel only, By permission only, Non-circulating to the pub

S CALIFORNIA DEPARTMENT OF CORRECTIONS LIBRARY SYSTEM*, c/o The Office of Correctional Education, 1515 S St, 95814-7243. SAN 371-8026. Tel: 916-322-6063. FAX: 916-324-1416. Web Site: www.cdcr.ca.gov. *Supvr,* Troy Fennel; Tel: 916-324-7504, E-mail: troy.fennel@cdcr.ca.gov; Staff 141 (MLS 74, Non-MLS 67)
Library Holdings: Bk Vols 469,838; Per Subs 1,660
Partic in 49-99 Cooperative Library System

Branches:

AVENAL STATE PRISON, One Kings Way, Avenal, 93204. (Mail add: PO Box 8, Avenal, 93204-0008), SAN 371-8034. Tel: 559-386-0587, Ext 6644. *Tech Asst,* Susanne Killen
Library Holdings: Bk Vols 30,000
Restriction: Staff & inmates only

CALIFORNIA CORRECTIONAL CENTER, 711-045 Center Rd, Susanville, 96127. (Mail add: PO Box 790, Susanville, 96130-0790), SAN 371-8042. Tel: 530-257-2181, Ext 4198. FAX: 530-252-3020. *Sr Librn,* Doug Olson; Staff 3 (MLS 3)
Library Holdings: Bk Vols 11,218
Automation Activity & Vendor Info: (Cataloging) Follett Software; (Circulation) Follett Software; (OPAC) Follett Software
Open Tues-Sat 8-2:30

CALIFORNIA CORRECTIONAL INSTITUTION, 24900 Hwy 202, Tehachapi, 93561. (Mail add: PO Box 1031, Tehachapi, 93581-1031), SAN 301-6544. Tel: 661-822-4402. FAX: 661-823-3358, 661-823-5016. *Sr Librn,* Doug Jockinson; *Tech Asst,* Leah Valenzuela; Staff 6 (MLS 1, Non-MLS 5)
Library Holdings: Bk Vols 5,500; Per Subs 15
Subject Interests: Law

CALIFORNIA INSTITUTION FOR MEN, 14901 S Central Ave, Chino, 91710. (Mail add: PO Box 128, Chino, 91708-0128), SAN 300-6654. Tel: 909-597-1821, Ext 4350, 909-597-1821, Ext 4368. FAX: 909-606-7012. *Sr Librn,* Brian Maughan; *Sr Librn,* Christopher Maughan
Library Holdings: Bk Vols 15,000
Restriction: Staff & inmates only

CALIFORNIA INSTITUTION FOR WOMEN, 16756 Chino-Corona Rd, Corona, 92880. (Mail add: PO Box 6000, Corona, 92878-6000), SAN 300-7723. Tel: 909-597-1771. FAX: 909-606-4936. *Sr Librn,* Tom Herrera; Tel: 909-597-1771, Ext 6488
Founded 1952
Library Holdings: Bk Titles 30,000; Per Subs 24
Subject Interests: Women studies
Open Mon, Wed & Fri 8-4, Tues & Thurs 12-8
Friends of the Library Group

CALIFORNIA MEDICAL FACILITY, 1600 California Dr, Vacaville, 95696. (Mail add: PO Box 2000, Vacaville, 95696-2000), SAN 335-2056. Tel: 707-448-6841, Ext 2603. FAX: 707-449-6541. *Sr Librn,* Yaoming Cheng; *Librn,* Leo Sanchez; Staff 2 (MLS 2)
Founded 1955
Open Mon-Sun 8-4

CALIFORNIA MEN'S COLONY-EAST, Hwy 1 Drawer B, San Luis Obispo, 93409. (Mail add: PO Box 8101, San Luis Obispo, 93409), SAN 301-5122. Tel: 805-547-7900, Ext 4197. *Sr Librn,* Steve Robertson; Staff 1 (MLS 1)
Founded 1961
Library Holdings: Bk Vols 25,000; Per Subs 125
Subject Interests: Law

CALIFORNIA MEN'S COLONY-WEST, Hwy 1, San Luis Obispo, 93409. Tel: 805-547-7900, Ext 7185. FAX: 805-547-7792. *Sr Librn,* Patrick Moloney
Library Holdings: Bk Vols 25,000; Per Subs 65
Automation Activity & Vendor Info: (Cataloging) Winnebago Software Co; (Circulation) Winnebago Software Co; (OPAC) Winnebago Software Co
Open Mon-Fri 8-8, Sat & Sun 8-4

CALIFORNIA STATE PRISON, CORCORAN, 4001 King Ave, Corcoran, 93212. (Mail add: PO Box 8800, Corcoran, 93212-8800), SAN 371-8050. Tel: 559-992-8800, Ext 5560. FAX: 559-992-7354. *Sr Librn,* Richard Rosenthal
Open Mon-Fri 7:30-3:30

CALIFORNIA STATE PRISON, LOS ANGELES COUNTY, 44750 60th St W, Lancaster, 93536-7620, SAN 375-5819. Tel: 661-729-2000, Ext 5610. FAX: 661-729-6993. *Sr Librn,* Linda Rowe; Staff 1 (MLS 1)
Jul 2005-Jun 2006. Mats Exp $16,000
Library Holdings: Bk Vols 27,000
Database Vendor: LexisNexis
Function: Legal assistance to inmates
Restriction: Staff & inmates only

CALIFORNIA STATE PRISON, SACRAMENTO INMATE LIBRARY, 100 Prison Rd, Represa, 95671. (Mail add: PO Box 290002, Represa, 95671-0002), SAN 371-8069. Tel: 916-985-8610, Ext 6605. FAX: 916-294-3128. *Sr Law Librn,* Arno Nappi; E-mail: arno.nappi@cdcr.ca.gov. Subject Specialists: *Criminal law,* Arno Nappi; Staff 4 (MLS 3, Non-MLS 1)
Library Holdings: Bk Vols 28,000
Automation Activity & Vendor Info: (Cataloging) Book Systems; (Circulation) Book Systems
Database Vendor: LexisNexis
Function: Adult bk club, Adult literacy prog, Copy machines, Doc delivery serv, Govt ref serv, Handicapped accessible, ILL available, Legal assistance to inmates, Literacy & newcomer serv, Magazines, Magnifiers for reading, Photocopying/Printing, Provide serv for the mentally ill, Ref serv available
Restriction: Residents only

CALIFORNIA STATE PRISON-SOLANO, 2100 Peabody Rd, Vacaville, 95696. (Mail add: PO Box 4000, Vacaville, 95696-4000), SAN 375-5789. Tel: 707-451-0182. FAX: 707-454-3244. *Sr Librn,* Helene Kosher

CALIFORNIA SUBSTANCE ABUSE TREATMENT, 900 Quebec Ave, Corcoran, 93212. (Mail add: PO Box 7100, Corcoran, 93212-7100), SAN 377-8002. Tel: 559-992-7100. FAX: 559-992-7182. *Supvr,* Rod Rollins; Staff 5 (MLS 1, Non-MLS 4)
Library Holdings: Bk Titles 40,000; Bk Vols 50,000; Per Subs 72
Subject Interests: Law ref bks
Special Services for the Blind - Extensive large print coll; Talking bks

CALIPATRIA STATE PRISON, 7018 Blair Rd, Calipatria, 92233. (Mail add: PO Box 5001, Calipatria, 92233-5001), SAN 371-8085. Tel: 760-348-7000, Ext 7612. FAX: 760-348-6041. *Actg Sr Librn,* Jeff Schaller
Library Holdings: Bk Vols 20,000
Open Mon-Sun 8:45-4:15

CENTINELA STATE PRISON, 2302 Brown Rd, Imperial, 92251. (Mail add: PO Box 731, Imperial, 92251-0731), SAN 375-5827. Tel: 760-337-7900, Ext 6356. FAX: 760-337-7631. *Libr Tech,* Patricia Estes
Library Holdings: Bk Vols 35,000
Database Vendor: Westlaw
Open Mon-Fri 8:30-3:30

CENTRAL CALIFORNIA WOMEN'S FACILITY, 23370 Rd 22, Chowchilla, 93610. (Mail add: PO Box 1501, Chowchilla, 93610-1501), SAN 371-8093. Tel: 559-665-5531. FAX: 559-665-6037. *Librn,* Phil Renteria
Library Holdings: Bk Vols 25,000

CORRECTIONAL TRAINING FACILITY, Hwy 101 N, Soledad, 93960. (Mail add: PO Box 686, Soledad, 93960-0686), SAN 301-6137. Tel: 831-678-3951. FAX: 831-678-5910. *Librn,* Robin Cauntay; *Librn,* Timothy Crawford; *Librn,* Julie Stenner
Open Mon-Fri 8-4

RICHARD J DONOVAN CORRECTIONAL FACILITY AT ROCK MOUNTAIN, 480 Alta Rd, San Diego, 92179, SAN 371-814X. Tel: 619-661-6500. FAX: 619-661-7875. *Sr Librn,* Ralph Blahnik; Tel: 619-661-6500, Ext 5590, E-mail: Ralph.Blahnik@cdcr.ca.gov; *Librn,* David J Powell; E-mail: DavidJ.Powell@cdcr.ca.gov; *Librn,* Kathleen Sterling; Tel: 619-661-6500, Ext 6400, E-mail: Kathleen.Sterling@cdcr.ca.gov; Staff 6 (MLS 3, Non-MLS 3)
Library Holdings: Bk Titles 40,000; Per Subs 30
Database Vendor: LexisNexis
Function: Accessibility serv available based on individual needs, Adult literacy prog, Audio & video playback equip for onsite use, BA reader (adult literacy), Bilingual assistance for Spanish patrons, Bks on cassette, Bks on CD, Computers for patron use, Copy machines, Digital talking bks, Distance learning, Electronic databases & coll, Learning ctr, Legal assistance to inmates, Life-long learning prog for all ages, Literacy & newcomer serv, Magazines, Magnifiers for reading, Microfiche/film & reading machines, Notary serv, Online ref, Online searches, Photocopying/Printing, Prog for adults, Provide serv for the mentally ill, Ref serv in person, Satellite serv, Scanner, Serves mentally handicapped consumers, Spanish lang bks, Wheelchair accessible
Restriction: Not open to pub

FOLSOM STATE PRISON, 300 Prison Rd, Represa, 95671. (Mail add: PO Box 71, Represa, 95671-4071), SAN 371-8077. Tel: 916-985-2561. FAX: 916-608-3130. *Sr Librn,* Robert Morris
Library Holdings: Bk Vols 28,000
Subject Interests: African-Am, Law, Literacy, Mental health, Spanish lang

HIGH DESERT STATE PRISON, 475-750 Rice Canyon Rd, Susanville, 96127, SAN 375-5835. Tel: 530-251-5100, Ext 6449. FAX: 530-251-5036. *Sr Librn,* Doug Olson
Founded 1995
Library Holdings: Bk Vols 3,000
Function: Legal assistance to inmates

IRONWOOD STATE PRISON LIBRARY-CENTRAL LIBRARY, 19005 Wiley's Well Rd, Blythe, 92225. (Mail add: PO Box 2229, Blythe, 92226-2229), SAN 375-5843. Tel: 760-921-3000, Ext 5623. Administration Tel: 760-921-3000. FAX: 760-921-7526. *Sr Librn,* Carey Ochs; Staff 6 (MLS 2, Non-MLS 4)
Founded 1994
Jul 2013-Jun 2014. Mats Exp $13,800, Books $10,000, Per/Ser (Incl. Access Fees) $3,800
Library Holdings: Audiobooks 54; Bks on Deafness & Sign Lang 7; CDs 57; High Interest/Low Vocabulary Bk Vols 1,760; Large Print Bks 975; Bk Titles 52,000; Bk Vols 54,000; Per Subs 4; Videos 284
Function: Adult literacy prog, Bilingual assistance for Spanish patrons, Bks on cassette, Computers for patron use, Copy machines, Digital talking bks, Distance learning, Handicapped accessible, Homework prog, ILL available, Jail serv, Literacy & newcomer serv, Magnifiers for reading, Newsp ref libr, Notary serv, Photocopying/Printing
Restriction: Access at librarian's discretion, Authorized patrons, Circ to mem only, Inmate patrons, facility staff & vols direct access. All others through ILL only, Not open to pub, Open to authorized patrons, Staff & inmates only

MULE CREEK STATE PRISON, 4001 Hwy 104, Ione, 95640. (Mail add: PO Box 409099, Ione, 95640-9099), SAN 371-8115. Tel: 209-274-4911, Ext 6510. FAX: 209-274-5904. *Sr Librn,* Carlos Morales; Staff 4 (MLS 1, Non-MLS 3)
Library Holdings: Bk Titles 14,000; Per Subs 11
Restriction: Staff & inmates only

NORTH KERN STATE PRISON, 2737 W Cecil Ave, Delano, 93215. (Mail add: PO Box 567, Delano, 93216-0567), SAN 375-5851. Tel: 661-721-2345. *Sr Librn,* Raul Contreras
Founded 1993
Library Holdings: High Interest/Low Vocabulary Bk Vols 500; Bk Vols 24,000; Per Subs 22
Subject Interests: Fed law, State law
Function: For res purposes
Special Services for the Blind - Bks on cassette; Closed circuit TV magnifier

PELICAN BAY STATE PRISON, 5905 Lake Earl Dr, Crescent City, 95532. (Mail add: PO Box 7000, Crescent City, 95531-7000), SAN 371-8131. Tel: 707-465-1000, Ext 7455. FAX: 707-465-9120. *Librn,* Liz McCumsey
Library Holdings: Bk Vols 10,000
Automation Activity & Vendor Info: (Cataloging) Follett Software; (Circulation) Follett Software

PLEASANT VALLEY STATE PRISON, 24863 W Jayne Ave, Coalinga, 93210. (Mail add: PO Box 8500, Coalinga, 93210-1135), SAN 375-586X. Tel: 559-935-4900, Ext 6165. *Sr Librn,* Brandy Buenafe; *Librn,* B Baker; Tel: 559-935-4900, Ext 6565; Staff 2 (MLS 2)
Library Holdings: Bk Vols 44,244; Per Subs 54
Special Services for the Blind - Reader equip
Open Mon-Fri 8-4

SALINAS VALLEY STATE PRISON, 31625 Hwy 101, Soledad, 93960. (Mail add: PO Box 1020, Soledad, 93960-1020), SAN 375-5878. Tel: 831-678-5500, Ext 6793. FAX: 831-678-5569. *Librn,* Position Currently Open

SAN QUENTIN STATE PRISON LIBRARY, 100 Main St, San Quentin, 94964, SAN 334-8695. Tel: 415-454-1460, Ext 3384. FAX: 415-455-5049. *Sr Librn,* Tom Brobst; *Sr Librn,* Doug Jeffrey; *Librn,* John Cornell; Staff 3 (MLS 3)
Library Holdings: Bk Vols 40,000; Per Subs 50
Automation Activity & Vendor Info: (Acquisitions) A-G Canada Ltd; (Cataloging) LiBRARYSOFT; (Circulation) LiBRARYSOFT; (OPAC) LiBRARYSOFT
Open Mon 10-8, Tues-Fri 7am-9pm, Sat 7-3

VALLEY STATE PRISON FOR WOMEN, 21633 Ave 24, Chowchilla, 93610. (Mail add: PO Box 92, Chowchilla, 93610-0092), SAN 375-5886. Tel: 559-665-6100, Ext 6066. *Sr Librn,* Diane Johnson; *Librn,* Robert Oldfield
Library Holdings: Bk Vols 48,000
Automation Activity & Vendor Info: (Cataloging) Follett Software; (Circulation) Follett Software
Open Mon-Thurs 8am-8:30pm, Fri 8-3

WASCO STATE PRISON, 701 Scofield Ave, Wasco, 93280. (Mail add: PO Box 8800, Wasco, 93280-8800), SAN 371-8158. Tel: 661-758-8400, Ext 5672. FAX: 661-758-7049.
Library Holdings: Bk Vols 44,000
Open Mon-Fri 8:30-3:30

CALIFORNIA DEPARTMENT OF JUSTICE

GL ATTORNEY GENERAL'S LAW LIBRARY*, 1300 I St, 95814. (Mail add: PO Box 944255, 94244-2550), SAN 309-8184. Tel: 916-324-5312. FAX: 916-323-5342. *Principal Librn,* Marguerite Beveridge; E-mail: marguerite.beveridge@doj.ca.gov; Staff 7 (MLS 7)
Library Holdings: Bk Vols 25,000
Subject Interests: Calif law
Automation Activity & Vendor Info: (Cataloging) Inmagic, Inc.

G CCI FORENSIC LIBRARY*, 4949 Broadway, Rm A-107, 95820, SAN 371-6554. Tel: 916-227-3575. FAX: 916-454-5433. *Supv Librn,* Jawadi Waheed; E-mail: waheed.jawadi@doj.ca.gov; Staff 2 (MLS 1, Non-MLS 1)
Founded 1987
Library Holdings: Bk Vols 8,000; Per Subs 13
Subject Interests: Criminal justice, Forensic sci
Database Vendor: Dialog, EBSCOhost, LexisNexis
Partic in Docline; Northern California & Nevada Medical Library Group (NCNMLG)
Restriction: Not open to pub, Staff use only

G CALIFORNIA ENERGY COMMISSION LIBRARY, 1516 Ninth St, MS10, 95814-5512. SAN 320-5754. Tel: 916-654-4292. FAX: 916-654-4046. E-mail: library@energy.ca.gov. Web Site: www.energy.ca.gov/asd/library. *Supv Librn,* Karen Kasuba; E-mail: karen.kasuba@energy.ca.gov; Staff 2 (MLS 2)
Founded 1975
Library Holdings: Bk Vols 18,000; Per Subs 100
Special Collections: California Energy Commission Publications
Subject Interests: Energy, Environment
Automation Activity & Vendor Info: (Acquisitions) SydneyPlus; (Cataloging) SydneyPlus; (Circulation) SydneyPlus; (ILL) OCLC; (OPAC) SydneyPlus; (Serials) SydneyPlus
Database Vendor: Dialog, EBSCOhost, IEEE (Institute of Electrical & Electronics Engineers), JSTOR, LexisNexis, OCLC FirstSearch, ScienceDirect
Wireless access
Function: Doc delivery serv, Electronic databases & coll, Govt ref serv, Online cat
Partic in OCLC Online Computer Library Center, Inc
Open Mon-Fri 8:30-4:30
Restriction: Circulates for staff only

S CALIFORNIA ENVIRONMENTAL PROTECTION AGENCY PUBLIC LIBRARY*, 1001 I St, 95812. SAN 320-1627. Tel: 916-327-0635. E-mail: calepalibrary@arb.ca.gov. Web Site: www.calepa.ca.gov/library. *Sr Librn,* Gwen Chen; E-mail: gchen@dtsc.ca.gov; *Info Syst Analyst,* Kelly Thomas; Tel: 916-322-8598; Staff 3 (MLS 1, Non-MLS 2)
Founded 1976
Library Holdings: Bk Titles 13,500; Per Subs 600
Special Collections: Air Pollution Technical Information Center, rpts & micro
Subject Interests: Air pollution
Wireless access

Branches:

DEPARTMENT OF TOXIC SUBSTANCES CONTROL - TECHNICAL REFERENCE, 1001 I St, 95814. (Mail add: PO Box 806, 95812-0806), SAN 372-3038. Tel: 916-324-5898. FAX: 916-327-4494. *Sr Librn,* Gwen Chen; E-mail: gchen@dtsc.ca.gov
Library Holdings: Bk Vols 7,000; Per Subs 76
Subject Interests: Hazardous waste
Automation Activity & Vendor Info: (Cataloging) EOS International; (Circulation) EOS International; (Serials) EOS International
Open Mon-Fri 8-4

S CALIFORNIA HIGHWAY PATROL*, Headquarters Library, 601 N Seventh St, 95811. (Mail add: PO Box 942898, 94298-0001), SAN 320-5762. Tel: 916-657-7220. Web Site: www.chp.ca.gov. *Librn,* Mary Guido
Library Holdings: Bk Vols 2,525; Per Subs 75
Special Collections: Codes, Federal Register, Reports & Studies
Restriction: Open by appt only

G CALIFORNIA STATE ARCHIVES*, 1020 O St, 95814. SAN 326-5706. Tel: 916-653-7715. Reference Tel: 916-653-2246. FAX: 916-653-7363. Administration FAX: 916-653-7134. E-mail: archivesweb@sos.ca.gov. Web Site: www.sos.ca.gov. *State Archivist,* Nancy Zimmelman Lenoil; Staff 25 (MLS 13, Non-MLS 12)
Founded 1850

Special Collections: California State History & Government. Oral History
Database Vendor: Eloquent Systems Inc
Wireless access
Function: Archival coll, Exhibits, Mail & tel request accepted, Online cat, Photocopying/Printing, Pub access computers, Ref & res, Ref serv in person, Telephone ref
Open Mon-Fri 9:30-4
Restriction: Closed stack, Non-circulating, Not a lending libr
Friends of the Library Group

GL CALIFORNIA STATE BOARD OF EQUALIZATION*, Law Library, 450 N St, 95814. SAN 301-2697. Tel: 916-445-7356. FAX: 916-323-3387. *Librn,* Lisa Ben-Reuven
Library Holdings: Bk Titles 2,000
Special Collections: State Taxation
Database Vendor: LexisNexis
Restriction: Open by appt only

G CALIFORNIA STATE DEPARTMENT OF CORPORATIONS LIBRARY*, 1515 K St, Ste 200, 95814. SAN 321-6438. Tel: 916-324-9600. FAX: 916-445-7975. *Mgr,* Marilyn Stevens; E-mail: mstevens@corp.ca.gov; Staff 1 (MLS 1)
Library Holdings: Bk Titles 3,500; Bk Vols 12,000; Per Subs 100
Subject Interests: Corporate securities
Restriction: Staff use only

G CALIFORNIA STATE DEPARTMENT OF FOOD & AGRICULTURE*, Plant Test Diagnostic Library, 3294 Meadowview Rd, 95832-1448. Tel: 916-262-1157. FAX: 916-262-1191. Web Site: www.cdfa.ca.gov. *Librn,* Ramona Randolph
Library Holdings: Bk Vols 30,000; Per Subs 300
Restriction: Open to govt employees only

GL CALIFORNIA STATE DEPARTMENT OF TRANSPORTATION*, Law Library, 1120 N St, Rm 1315, 95812. (Mail add: PO Box 1438, MS 57, 95812-1438), SAN 333-9998. Tel: 916-654-2630. FAX: 916-654-6128. *Law Librn,* Amanda Sambrano; E-mail: amanda.sambrano@dot.ca.gov; Staff 3 (MLS 1, Non-MLS 2)
Library Holdings: Bk Vols 15,000; Per Subs 179
Subject Interests: Construction law, Contract law, Eminent domain, Environ law, Real property
Database Vendor: LexisNexis
Partic in Westlaw
Restriction: Not open to pub

GL CALIFORNIA STATE DEPARTMENT OF WATER RESOURCES*, Law Library, 1416 Ninth St, Rm 1118-13, 95814. (Mail add: PO Box 942836, 94236-0001), SAN 371-5590. Tel: 916-651-0822. FAX: 916-653-0952. *Librn,* Pam Ryan; E-mail: pryan@water.ca.gov; Staff 2 (MLS 1, Non-MLS 1)
Founded 1966
Library Holdings: Bk Vols 20,000; Per Subs 30
Subject Interests: Law
Database Vendor: Westlaw
Restriction: Not open to pub, Staff use only

GL CALIFORNIA STATE LEGISLATIVE COUNSEL*, Law Library, 925 L St, Lower Level, 95814-3772. SAN 301-2727. Tel: 916-341-8036. E-mail: lcb.library@lc.ca.gov. Web Site: www.leginfo.ca.gov. *Supv Librn,* Dragomir Cosanici; Staff 6 (MLS 2, Non-MLS 4)
Founded 1951
Library Holdings: Bk Vols 45,000; Per Subs 152
Special Collections: Legal Coll
Subject Interests: Legislation
Automation Activity & Vendor Info: (Cataloging) Inmagic, Inc.
Open Mon-Fri 8:30-5

P CALIFORNIA STATE LIBRARY, 900 N St, 95814. (Mail add: PO Box 942837, 94237-0001), SAN 334-0058. Tel: 916-654-0261. FAX: 916-323-9768. TDD: 916-653-0692. E-mail: cslinfo@library.ca.gov. Web Site: www.library.ca.gov. *State Librn,* Greg Lucas; E-mail: Greg.Lucas@library.ca.gov; *Dep State Librn,* Gerald Maginnity; E-mail: Gerald.Maginnity@library.ca.gov
Founded 1850
Special Collections: State Document Depository; US Document Depository
Subject Interests: Calif, Educ, Genealogy, Govt publ, Hist, Law
Automation Activity & Vendor Info: (Acquisitions) Ex Libris Group; (Cataloging) Ex Libris Group; (Circulation) Ex Libris Group; (Media Booking) Ex Libris Group; (OPAC) Ex Libris Group; (Serials) Ex Libris Group
Database Vendor: EBSCOhost, Gale Cengage Learning, HeinOnline, LexisNexis, Mergent Online, Newsbank, Newsbank-Readex, ProQuest, Safari Books Online
Wireless access
Publications: BTBL News (Newsletter); California Library Directory; California Library Laws; California Library Statistics (Library statistics & report); California State Publications; Studies in the News (Current awareness service)
Partic in Califa; OCLC Online Computer Library Center, Inc
Special Services for the Deaf - TDD equip
Special Services for the Blind - Assistive/Adapted tech devices, equip & products; Bks & mags in Braille, on rec, tape & cassette; Cassette playback machines; Closed circuit TV
Open Mon-Fri 9:30-4
Friends of the Library Group
Branches: 1

P BRAILLE & TALKING BOOK LIBRARY, 900 N St, 95814. (Mail add: PO Box 942837, 94237-0001), SAN 301-2735. Tel: 916-654-0640. Toll Free Tel: 800-952-5666. FAX: 916-654-1119. E-mail: btbl@library.ca.gov. Web Site: www.btbl.ca.gov. *Dir,* Mike Marlin; E-mail: mmarlin@library.ca.gov; *Librn,* Mary Jane Kayes; Staff 18 (MLS 2, Non-MLS 16)
Founded 1904
Library Holdings: Audiobooks 73,000; Braille Volumes 7,000; Bk Titles 100,000; Per Subs 70
Special Collections: Blindness & Other Disabilities Reference Material
Automation Activity & Vendor Info: (Circulation) SirsiDynix
Publications: Borrower's Handbook; BTBL Recorded Books on California
Special Services for the Blind - Braille bks
Open Mon-Fri 9:30-4

S CALIFORNIA STATE RAILROAD MUSEUM LIBRARY*, 113 I St, 95814. (Mail add: 111 I St, 95814), SAN 321-6470. Tel: 916-323-8073. FAX: 916-327-5655. E-mail: rrmuseumlibrary@parks.ca.gov. Web Site: www.californiastaterailroadmuseum.org. *Dir of Coll,* Ellen Louise Halteman; Tel: 916-323-2158, E-mail: ehalteman@parks.ca.gov; *Librn,* Cara J Randall; Tel: 916-445-3492, E-mail: crandall@parks.ca.gov; *Archivist,* Kathryn Santos; Tel: 916-322-0375; Staff 3 (MLS 3)
Founded 1981
Library Holdings: Bk Vols 10,000; Per Subs 80
Special Collections: Baldwin Locomotive Works Engine Specification Books, 1869-1938, micro; Corporate Records (Central Pacific, Southern Pacific & Western Pacific Railroads), ms; Correspondence & Business Records (Collis P Huntington Papers, 1856-1901), micro; Drawings & Specifications (Lima Locomotive Works); Railroad Equipment (Pullman Company), glass plate negatives, Railroad History (Gerald M Best, Grahame H Hardy, Gilbert H Kneiss, Stanley F Merritt & Louis L Stein Jr Colls), artifacts, bks, ephemera, ms; Railroad History (Railway & Locomotive Historical Society), artifacts, bks, ms; Railroad History, negatives, photog
Automation Activity & Vendor Info: (Cataloging) Inmagic, Inc.; (OPAC) Inmagic, Inc.
Database Vendor: OCLC FirstSearch
Function: Archival coll, Ref serv available
Publications: Pullman Company Negative Collection Guide; Research & Restoration Reports for CSRM Locomotive & Cars
Open Tues-Sat 1-5
Restriction: Non-circulating coll, Not a lending libr, Open to pub for ref only

C CALIFORNIA STATE UNIVERSITY, SACRAMENTO LIBRARY, 2000 State University Dr E, 95819-6039. SAN 301-2751. Tel: 916-278-6708. Interlibrary Loan Service Tel: 916-278-6395. Reference Tel: 916-278-5672. FAX: 916-278-5917. Interlibrary Loan Service FAX: 916-278-7089. Web Site: library.csus.edu. *Dean, Univ Libr,* Amy Kautzman; *Head, Bibliog Serv,* Charlotte Xanders; Tel: 916-278-5451, E-mail: xanders@csus.edu; *Head, Acq,* Jennifer Ware; Tel: 916-278-7223, E-mail: jdware@csus.edu; *Head, Spec Coll & Archives,* Sheila O'Neill; Tel: 916-278-5469, E-mail: oneills@csus.edu; *Head, User Serv,* Mary Reddick; Tel: 916-278-4045, E-mail: mreddick@csus.edu; *Curator, Tsakopoulos Hellenic Coll,* George Paganelis; Tel: 916-278-4361, E-mail: paganelis@csus.edu; Staff 83 (MLS 32, Non-MLS 51)
Founded 1947. Enrl 27,932; Fac 1,573; Highest Degree: Master
Library Holdings: e-books 3,737; Bk Titles 909,682; Bk Vols 1,327,983; Per Subs 3,143; Videos 14,494
Special Collections: Archives & Special Colls; Congressman John Moss Papers; Dissent & Social Change Coll; Florin Japanese American Citizens League Oral History Project; Japanese American Archival Coll; Tsakopoulos Hellenic Coll. Oral History; State Document Depository; US Document Depository
Subject Interests: Bus, Educ, Eng, Humanities
Automation Activity & Vendor Info: (Acquisitions) Innovative Interfaces, Inc; (Cataloging) Innovative Interfaces, Inc; (Circulation) Innovative Interfaces, Inc; (Course Reserve) Innovative Interfaces, Inc; (OPAC) Innovative Interfaces, Inc; (Serials) Innovative Interfaces, Inc

Database Vendor: Dialog, Gale Cengage Learning, Innovative Interfaces, Inc, LexisNexis, Newsbank, OCLC FirstSearch, ProQuest
Wireless access
Function: Archival coll, Art exhibits, AV serv, CD-ROM, Distance learning, Doc delivery serv, ILL available, Music CDs, Online searches, Outside serv via phone, mail, e-mail & web, Photocopying/Printing, Ref serv available, Telephone ref, VHS videos, Wheelchair accessible
Special Services for the Deaf - Staff with knowledge of sign lang; TDD equip
Restriction: Authorized patrons
Friends of the Library Group

J COSUMNES RIVER COLLEGE LIBRARY*, Library & Learning Resources Center, 8401 Center Pkwy, 95823. SAN 301-2778. Tel: 916-691-7266. Reference Tel: 916-691-7265. FAX: 916-691-7349. Web Site: www.crc.losrios.edu/Student_Services/Library.htm. *Dean of Libr,* Stephen McGloughlin; Tel: 916-691-7589; *Pub Serv Librn,* Andi Adkins Pogue; Tel: 916-691-7904, E-mail: adkinsa@crc.losrios.edu; *Access Serv & Syst, Pub Serv,* Mark Ford; Tel: 916-691-7628, E-mail: fordm@crc.losrios.edu; *Instruction & Outreach, Pub Serv,* Emily Bond; Tel: 916-691-7249, E-mail: bonde@crc.losrios.edu; *Instruction & Outreach, Pub Serv,* Rochelle Perez; Tel: 916-691-7629, E-mail: perezr@crc.losrios.edu. Subject Specialists: *Hist,* Mark Ford; Staff 10.6 (MLS 5.6, Non-MLS 5)
Founded 1970. Enrl 16,124; Fac 670; Highest Degree: Associate
Library Holdings: Bks on Deafness & Sign Lang 100; e-books 15,141; High Interest/Low Vocabulary Bk Vols 300; Bk Titles 59,157; Bk Vols 72,856; Per Subs 123; Spec Interest Per Sub 25; Videos 1,705
Special Collections: California History, examples of fine printing; Campus Oral History
Automation Activity & Vendor Info: (Acquisitions) Innovative Interfaces, Inc; (Cataloging) Innovative Interfaces, Inc; (Circulation) Innovative Interfaces, Inc; (Course Reserve) Innovative Interfaces, Inc; (ILL) OCLC Connexion; (OPAC) Innovative Interfaces, Inc; (Serials) Innovative Interfaces, Inc
Database Vendor: EBSCOhost, Gale Cengage Learning, JSTOR, Newsbank, ProQuest, PubMed, SerialsSolutions
Wireless access
Publications: Library Lines & the Learning Resources (Newsletter)
Mem of NorthNet Library System
Partic in Coop Libr Agency for Syst & Servs; OCLC Online Computer Library Center, Inc
Special Services for the Blind - Braille equip
Open Mon-Thurs 8-8
Restriction: Open to students, fac & staff

GM DEPARTMENT OF HEALTH CARE SERVICES*, Substance Use Disorders Resource Center Library, Substance Use Disorder, Prevention, Treatment & Recovery Services Div, 1700 K St, 1st Flr, 95811-4037. (Mail add: MS 2623, PO Box 997413, 95899-7413), SAN 328-5014. Tel: 916-327-3728. Toll Free Tel: 800-879-2772. FAX: 916-323-1270. TDD: 916-445-1942. E-mail: ResourceCenter@dhcs.ca.gov. Web Site: www.dhcs.ca.gov. *Librn,* Brenda Lopez; E-mail: brenda.lopez@dhcs,ca.gov; Staff 2 (Non-MLS 2)
Jul 2005-Jun 2006. Mats Exp $26,500, Books $1,425, Per/Ser (Incl. Access Fees) $18,868, AV Mat $6,207
Library Holdings: AV Mats 726; Bk Titles 4,176; Bk Vols 4,831; Per Subs 40
Subject Interests: Alcohol & drugs, Prevention & treatment of alcohol, tobacco & other drugs, Tobacco
Automation Activity & Vendor Info: (Cataloging) LibraryWorld, Inc; (Circulation) LibraryWorld, Inc; (Serials) LibraryWorld, Inc
Function: Ref serv available
Open Mon-Fri 8-5

S ICF CONSULTING INC*, ICF International, 630 K St, Ste 400, 95814. SAN 329-2843. Tel: 916-737-3000. FAX: 916-737-3030. E-mail: library@icfi.com. *Coop Librn,* Thomas Herndon; E-mail: thomas.herndon@icfi.com; *Libr Mgr,* Sharon Hoepker; E-mail: sharon.hoepker@icfi.com; Staff 2 (MLS 2)
Library Holdings: AV Mats 250; CDs 100; Bk Vols 30,000
Subject Interests: Biol, Botany, Econ analysis, Energy, Eng, Environ, Health, Planning, Toxicology, Water res
Automation Activity & Vendor Info: (Acquisitions) Inmagic, Inc.; (Cataloging) Inmagic, Inc.; (Circulation) Inmagic, Inc.; (ILL) OCLC FirstSearch; (OPAC) Inmagic, Inc.; (Serials) Inmagic, Inc.
Database Vendor: Dialog, EBSCOhost, Factiva.com, LexisNexis
Wireless access
Function: ILL available
Partic in Dialog Corp; LexisNexis
Restriction: Open by appt only

M KAISER-PERMANENTE MEDICAL CENTER*, Health Sciences Library, 2025 Morse Ave, 95825. SAN 324-508X. Tel: 916-973-6944. FAX: 916-973-6999. *Libr Mgr,* Peggy Makie; Staff 2 (MLS 1, Non-MLS 1)
Founded 1965
Library Holdings: Bk Titles 700; Per Subs 25
Subject Interests: Clinical med
Partic in National Network of Libraries of Medicine

S SACRAMENTO AREA COUNCIL OF GOVERNMENTS LIBRARY*, 1415 L St, Ste 300, 95814. SAN 327-1684. Tel: 916-321-9000. FAX: 916-321-9551. E-mail: infocenter@sacog.org. Web Site: www.sacog.org. *Demographer,* Tina Glover; Staff 1 (Non-MLS 1)
Library Holdings: Bk Titles 4,168; Per Subs 85
Special Collections: Census Data
Subject Interests: Transportation planning
Publications: New Library Acquisitions (Monthly); SACOG Publications
Open Mon-Fri 8-12 & 1-4

J SACRAMENTO CITY COLLEGE*, Learning Resources Division Library, 3835 Freeport Blvd, 95822. SAN 301-2824. Tel: 916-558-2253. FAX: 916-558-2114. Web Site: www.scc.losrios.edu/~library. *Dean,* Dr Rhonda Rios Kravitz; *Acq Librn,* Catherine Chenu-Campbell
Founded 1916. Enrl 24,000
Library Holdings: Bk Vols 68,894; Per Subs 410
Partic in OCLC Online Computer Library Center, Inc
Friends of the Library Group

GL SACRAMENTO COUNTY PUBLIC LAW LIBRARY*, 609 Ninth St, 95814-2403. SAN 301-2832. Tel: 916-874-6011. Circulation Tel: 916-874-8541. Interlibrary Loan Service Tel: 916-874-6012. FAX: 916-244-0699. Circulation FAX: 916-874-7050. Reference FAX: 916-874-7059. Automation Services FAX: 916-874-7053. Web Site: www.saclaw.org. *Dir,* Coral Henning; Tel: 916-874-6013, E-mail: CHenning@saclaw.org; *Asst Dir,* Kelly Browne; E-mail: KBrowne@saclaw.org; *Asst Dir, Support Serv,* Jean Willis; E-mail: JWillis@saclaw.org; Staff 18 (MLS 9, Non-MLS 9)
Founded 1891
Library Holdings: AV Mats 576; Electronic Media & Resources 165; Bk Titles 6,450; Bk Vols 53,000; Per Subs 2,250
Automation Activity & Vendor Info: (Acquisitions) SirsiDynix; (Cataloging) SirsiDynix; (Circulation) SirsiDynix; (OPAC) SirsiDynix; (Serials) SirsiDynix
Wireless access
Function: AV serv, Govt ref serv, Handicapped accessible, ILL available, Magnifiers for reading, Photocopying/Printing, Wheelchair accessible
Publications: Annual Report; Pathfinders (Reference guide)
Partic in RLIN (Research Libraries Information Network); Southside Virginia Library Network
Special Services for the Blind - Computer with voice synthesizer for visually impaired persons
Open Mon 8-8, Tues-Thurs 9-7, Fri 8-5, Sat 10-3

P SACRAMENTO PUBLIC LIBRARY*, 828 I St, 95814. SAN 334-0112. Tel: 916-264-2700. Circulation Tel: 916-264-2789. Reference Tel: 916-264-2920. Toll Free Tel: 800-561-4636. FAX: 916-264-2755. TDD: 916-264-2998. Web Site: www.saclibrary.org. *Libr Dir,* Rivkah K Sass; E-mail: director@saclibrary.org; *Dep Libr Dir,* Denise M Davis; E-mail: deputydirector@saclibrary.org; *Br Serv Mgr,* Mary Mijares; *Mgr, Info Tech,* Gerry Calderon; E-mail: it@saclibrary.org; *Literacy Coordr,* Stephanie Allen
Founded 1857. Pop 1,335,969; Circ 6,806,754
Library Holdings: Bk Titles 485,921; Bk Vols 2,100,251
Special Collections: Art; Californiana; City & County; City Planning & Urban Development; Genealogical; History of Printing. State Document Depository; US Document Depository
Subject Interests: Art & archit, Bus & mgt, Genealogy, Music
Automation Activity & Vendor Info: (Acquisitions) Innovative Interfaces, Inc; (Cataloging) Innovative Interfaces, Inc; (Circulation) Innovative Interfaces, Inc; (OPAC) Innovative Interfaces, Inc; (Serials) Innovative Interfaces, Inc
Wireless access
Publications: Library News
Mem of Mountain-Valley Library System
Special Services for the Deaf - TDD equip
Open Mon & Wed-Fri 10-6, Tues 10-8, Sat 10-5
Friends of the Library Group
Branches: 28
ARCADE COMMUNITY LIBRARY, 2443 Marconi Ave, 95821, SAN 334-0147.
Founded 1941
Open Tues & Wed 10-8, Thurs 10-6, Fri 1-6, Sat 10-5
Friends of the Library Group
ARDEN-DIMICK COMMUNITY LIBRARY, 891 Watt Ave, 95864, SAN 334-0171.
Founded 1949

Open Tues 10-6, Wed & Thurs 10-8, Fri 1-6, Sat 10-5
Friends of the Library Group
CARMICHAEL REGIONAL LIBRARY, 5605 Marconi Ave, Carmichael, 95608, SAN 334-0201.
Special Collections: California
Open Tues & Wed 11-8, Thurs 10-6, Fri 1-5, Sat 10-5, Sun 12-5
Friends of the Library Group
COLONIAL HEIGHTS COMMUNITY LIBRARY, 4799 Stockton Blvd, 95820, SAN 329-5958.
Founded 1989
Open Tues 12-8, Wed & Thurs 10-6, Fri 1-6, Sat 10-5
Friends of the Library Group
BELLE COOLEDGE COMMUNITY LIBRARY, 5600 S Land Park Dr, 95822, SAN 334-0260.
Founded 1958
Open Tues 12-8, Wed & Thurs 10-6, Fri 1-6, Sat 10-5
Friends of the Library Group
COURTLAND COMMUNITY OPERATED NEIGHBORHOOD LIBRARY, 170 Primasing Ave, Courtland, 95615. (Mail add: PO Box 536, Courtland, 95615-0536), SAN 374-714X.
Founded 1993
Open Tues-Fri 1-6, Sat 12-5
Friends of the Library Group
DEL PASO HEIGHTS LIBRARY, 920 Grand Ave, 95838, SAN 334-0325.
Founded 1913
Special Collections: African-American Coll
Open Tues-Thurs 10-6, Fri 1-6, Sat 10-5
Friends of the Library Group
ELK GROVE COMMUNITY LIBRARY, 8900 Elk Grove Blvd, Elk Grove, 95624, SAN 334-035X.
Founded 1908. Pop 64,000
Library Holdings: Bk Titles 21,000
Open Tues & Wed 10-8, Thurs 10-6, Fri 1-6, Sat 10-5
Friends of the Library Group
FAIR OAKS-ORANGEVALE COMMUNITY LIBRARY, 11601 Fair Oaks Blvd, Fair Oaks, 95628, SAN 334-0384.
Founded 1909
Open Tues & Wed 10-8, Thurs 10-6, Fri 1-6, Sat 10-5
Friends of the Library Group
FRANKLIN COMMUNITY LIBRARY, 10055 Franklin High Rd, Elk Grove, 95757.
Founded 2002
Open Tues & Thurs 10-8, Wed 10-6, Fri 1-6, Sat 10-5
GALT NEIGHBORHOOD LIBRARY, 1000 Caroline Ave, Galt, 95632, SAN 334-0473.
Founded 1908
Open Tues 12-8, Wed & Thurs 10-6, Fri 1-6, Sat 10-5
Friends of the Library Group
ISLETON NEIGHBORHOOD LIBRARY, 412 Union St, Isleton, 95641. (Mail add: PO Box 517, Isleton, 95641-0517), SAN 374-7158.
Founded 1915
Open Tues-Fri 1-6, Sat 1-5
Friends of the Library Group
MARTIN LUTHER KING JR REGIONAL LIBRARY, 7340 24th St Bypass, 95822, SAN 334-0597.
Founded 1970
Special Collections: Martin Luther King Jr Coll; Samuel C Pannell African-American Coll
Open Tues & Wed 10-6, Thurs 12-8, Fri 1-6, Sat 10-5
Friends of the Library Group
E K MCCLATCHY NEIGHBORHOOD LIBRARY, 2112 22nd St, 95818, SAN 334-0627.
Founded 1940
Open Tues & Thurs 10-6, Wed 12-8, Fri 1-6, Sat 10-5
Friends of the Library Group
MCKINLEY NEIGHBORHOOD LIBRARY, 601 Alhambra Blvd, 95816, SAN 334-0651.
Founded 1936
Open Tues 12-8, Wed & Thurs 10-6, Fri 1-6, Sat 10-5
Friends of the Library Group
NORTH HIGHLANDS/ANTELOPE LIBRARY, 4235 Antelope Rd, Antelope, 95843, SAN 334-0686.
Founded 2000
Open Tues & Wed 10-8, Thurs 10-6, Fri 1-6, Sat 10-5
Friends of the Library Group
NORTH NATOMAS LIBRARY, 4660 Via Ingoglia, 95835-4600.
Founded 2004
Open Tues & Thurs 12-8, Wed 10-6, Fri 1-6, Sat 10-5
NORTH SACRAMENTO-HAGGINWOOD NEIGHBORHOOD LIBRARY, 2109 Del Paso Blvd, 95815, SAN 334-0716.
Founded 1987
Open Tues & Thurs 12-6, Wed 12-8, Fri 1-6, Sat 10-5
Friends of the Library Group
ORANGEVALE NEIGHBORHOOD LIBRARY, 8820 Greenback Lane, No L, Orangevale, 95662, SAN 374-7166.
Founded 1912
Open Tues 12-8, Wed & Thurs 10-6, Fri 1-6, Sat 10-5
RANCHO CORDOVA COMMUNITY LIBRARY, 9845 Folsom Blvd, 95827, SAN 334-0775.
Founded 1959
Open Tues & Wed 10-8, Thurs 10-6, Fri 1-6, Sat 10-5
Friends of the Library Group
RIO LINDA NEIGHBORHOOD LIBRARY, 631 L St, Rio Linda, 95673, SAN 334-0805.
Founded 1968
Function: Adult literacy prog, Audiobks via web, Bks on cassette, Bks on CD, CD-ROM, Children's prog, Computers for patron use, Copy machines, Digital talking bks, Electronic databases & coll, Free DVD rentals, Handicapped accessible, ILL available, Music CDs, Online cat, Online ref, Online searches, OverDrive digital audio bks, Photocopying/Printing, Prog for children & young adult, Pub access computers, Spoken cassettes & CDs, Spoken cassettes & DVDs, Story hour, Summer reading prog, Tax forms, Teen prog, VHS videos, Web-catalog
Open Tues 12-8, Wed & Thurs 10-6, Fri 1-6, Sat 10-5
Friends of the Library Group
SACRAMENTO ROOM, 828 I St, 95814, SAN 334-0236.
Founded 1857
Special Collections: Sacramento Authors & Printing History. State Document Depository
Subject Interests: Art, Local hist, Music
Open Tues 1-8, Wed & Thurs 1-6, Sat & Sun 1-5
SOUTH NATOMAS COMMUNITY LIBRARY, 2901 Truxel Rd, 95833, SAN 374-7174.
Founded 2001
Open Tues & Thurs 10-6, Wed 12-8, Fri 1-6, Sat 10-5
Friends of the Library Group
SOUTHGATE COMMUNITY LIBRARY, 6132 66th Ave, 95823, SAN 334-083X.
Founded 1975. Pop 75,000
Open Tues & Wed 10-8, Thurs 10-6, Fri 1-6, Sat 10-5
Friends of the Library Group
SYLVAN OAKS COMMUNITY LIBRARY, 6700 Auburn Blvd, Citrus Heights, 95621, SAN 334-0864.
Founded 1919
Open Tues-Thurs 10-8, Fri 1-6, Sat 10-5
Friends of the Library Group
VALLEY HI-NORTH LAGUNA LIBRARY, 7400 Imagination Pkwy, 95823.
Founded 2001
Open Tues 12-8, Wed & Thurs 10-6, Fri 1-6, Sat 10-5
WALNUT GROVE NEIGHBORHOOD LIBRARY, 14177 Market St, Walnut Grove, 95690. (Mail add: PO Box 40, Walnut Grove, 95690-0040), SAN 334-0899.
Founded 1919
Open Tues-Fri & 1-6, Sat 12-5
Friends of the Library Group
ROBBIE WATERS POCKET-GREENHAVEN, 7335 Gloria Dr, 95831. *Librn,* Brendle Wells
Library Holdings: Bk Vols 52,000
Open Tues & Thurs 10-6, Wed 12-8, Fri 1-6, Sat 10-5
Bookmobiles: 3

S SEARCH GROUP, INC LIBRARY*, 7311 Greenhaven Dr, Ste 145, 95831. SAN 370-4262. Tel: 916-392-2550. FAX: 916-392-8440. Web Site: www.search.org. *Mgr,* Twyla Cunningham Putt. Subject Specialists: *Criminal justice, Policy, Statistics,* Twyla Cunningham Putt
Library Holdings: Bk Titles 250; Per Subs 24
Subject Interests: Criminal justice, Law enforcement

S SIERRA RESEARCH LIBRARY*, 1801 J St, 95814. Tel: 916-444-6666. FAX: 916-444-8373. E-mail: library@sierraresearch.com. Web Site: www.sierraresearch.com. *Librn,* Gabriel C McAuliffe; E-mail: gmcauliffe@sierraresearch.com
Library Holdings: Bk Titles 24,000; Per Subs 12
Restriction: Staff use only

A UNITED STATES ARMY*, Corps of Engineers Sacramento District Technical Information Center, 1325 J St, Ste 820, 95814-2922. SAN 334-0929. Tel: 916-557-6660. Interlibrary Loan Service Tel: 202-761-4853. FAX: 916-557-7091. E-mail: library@usace.army.mil. Web Site: www.spk.usace.army.mil. *Tech Serv,* Frances Sweeney; E-mail: Frances.J.Sweeney@usace.army.mil
Founded 1945
Library Holdings: Bk Titles 5,500; Per Subs 15
Subject Interests: Eng, Geol
Publications: Library Bulletin; News & New Books in the District Library

G US DEPARTMENT OF THE INTERIOR, BUREAU OF RECLAMATION*, Mid-Pacific Regional Library, 2800 Cottage Way, Rm W-1825, 95825-1898. SAN 301-2867. Tel: 916-978-5593. FAX: 916-978-5599. *Regional Librn,* Alba Scott; E-mail: ascott@usbr.gov; Staff 2 (MLS 2)
Founded 1946
Library Holdings: Bk Titles 18,000; Bk Vols 21,000; Per Subs 120
Special Collections: Project Histories - Mid-Pacific Region BOR; San Joaquin Valley Drainage Program
Subject Interests: Water res

CM UNIVERSITY OF CALIFORNIA, DAVIS, F William Blaisdell Medical Library, 4610 X St, 95817. SAN 301-2875. Tel: 916-734-3529. Interlibrary Loan Service Tel: 916-734-3533. FAX: 916-734-7418. E-mail: bmlref@ucdavis.edu. Web Site: www.lib.ucdavis.edu/hsl. *Dept Head,* Beth Callahan
Founded 1929
Special Collections: Bioethics Coll; Birth Defects Coll; Civil War Medicine
Subject Interests: Clinical med, Nursing
Wireless access
Partic in Docline; National Network of Libraries of Medicine

CL UNIVERSITY OF THE PACIFIC - MCGEORGE SCHOOL OF LAW*, Gordon D Schaber Law Library, 3282 Fifth Ave, 95817. SAN 301-2883. Tel: 916-739-7131. Interlibrary Loan Service Tel: 916-739-7240. Reference Tel: 916-739-7164. FAX: 916-739-7273. Web Site: www.mcgeorge.edu.
Founded 1924. Enrl 1,091; Fac 85; Highest Degree: Doctorate
Library Holdings: Bk Titles 119,470; Bk Vols 508,873; Per Subs 4,492
Special Collections: State Document Depository; US Document Depository
Automation Activity & Vendor Info: (Acquisitions) Innovative Interfaces, Inc; (Cataloging) Innovative Interfaces, Inc; (Circulation) Innovative Interfaces, Inc; (Course Reserve) Innovative Interfaces, Inc; (OPAC) Innovative Interfaces, Inc; (Serials) Innovative Interfaces, Inc
Wireless access
Partic in RLIN (Research Libraries Information Network); Westlaw
Open Mon-Thurs 7:30am-Midnight, Fri 7:30am-11pm, Sat 10-10, Sun 10am-Midnight

L WEINTRAUB, GENSHLEA, CHEDIAK & SPROUL*, Law Library, 400 Capitol Mall, Ste 1100, 95814. SAN 372-302X. Tel: 916-558-6000. FAX: 916-446-1611. Web Site: www.weintraub.com. *Librn,* Liana Chen-Knapp
Library Holdings: Bk Vols 10,000; Per Subs 52
Open Mon-Fri 8:30-5
Restriction: Staff use only

SAINT HELENA

P SAINT HELENA PUBLIC LIBRARY*, George & Elsie Wood Public Library, 1492 Library Lane, 94574-1143. SAN 301-2891. Tel: 707-963-5244. Circulation Tel: 707-963-5244, Ext 102. Administration Tel: 707-967-2805. Information Services Tel: 707-963-5244, Ext 103. FAX: 707-963-5264. E-mail: admin@shpl.org. Web Site: www.shpl.org. *Dir,* Larry Hlavsa; E-mail: larry@shpl.org; *Ch Serv,* Leslie Stanton; E-mail: leslie@shpl.org; *Info Serv,* Allie LaCentra; E-mail: allie@shpl.org; *Tech Serv,* Bobbie Vierra; E-mail: bobbie@shpl.org; Staff 10 (MLS 5, Non-MLS 5)
Founded 1892. Pop 6,225; Circ 254,247
Library Holdings: AV Mats 35,390; CDs 2,241; DVDs 2,279; e-books 4,600; Large Print Bks 1,877; Bk Vols 92,499; Per Subs 132; Spec Interest Per Sub 50; Talking Bks 3,159; Videos 6,141
Special Collections: Napa Valley Wine Library. Oral History
Subject Interests: Wine, Wine hist
Automation Activity & Vendor Info: (Acquisitions) TLC (The Library Corporation); (Circulation) TLC (The Library Corporation); (OPAC) TLC (The Library Corporation)
Database Vendor: TLC (The Library Corporation)
Function: Art exhibits, AV serv, ILL available, Music CDs, Newsp ref libr, Photocopying/Printing, Prog for adults, Prog for children & young adult, Ref serv available, Summer reading prog, VHS videos, Workshops
Publications: Napa Valley Wine Library Report (Quarterly)
Mem of NorthNet Library System
Partic in Solano Napa & Partners Library Consortium (SNAP)
Open Mon & Wed 12-9, Tues, Thurs & Fri 10-6, Sat 10-4, Sun 1-5
Friends of the Library Group

SALINAS

J HARTNELL COLLEGE LIBRARY*, 411 Central Ave, 93901. SAN 301-2913. Tel: 831-755-6872. Reference Tel: 831-759-6078. FAX: 831-759-6084. Web Site: www.hartnell.edu. *Head Librn,* Peggy Mayfield; Tel: 831-755-6898, E-mail: mmayfield@hartnell.edu; Staff 11 (MLS 3, Non-MLS 8)
Founded 1936. Fac 147
Library Holdings: Bk Titles 60,000; Per Subs 257
Special Collections: Ornithology (O P Silliman Memorial Library of Natural History), bks, ser
Automation Activity & Vendor Info: (Acquisitions) Ex Libris Group; (Media Booking) Ex Libris Group; (OPAC) Ex Libris Group; (Serials) Ex Libris Group
Database Vendor: EBSCOhost, OCLC FirstSearch, ProQuest
Wireless access
Partic in Monterey Bay Area Cooperative Library System; OCLC Online Computer Library Center, Inc
Open Mon-Thurs 8am-9pm, Fri 8-4

J HEALD COLLEGE*, Learning Resource Center-Salinas Campus, 1450 N Main St, 93906. Tel: 831-443-1700. FAX: 831-444-4601. Web Site: www.heald.edu. *Mgr,* Candi Prado
Library Holdings: AV Mats 10; Bk Vols 300; Per Subs 12
Database Vendor: EBSCOhost
Open Mon-Thurs 7:30am-10pm, Fri 7:30am-8pm, Sat 9-1

GL MONTEREY COUNTY LAW LIBRARY*, Federal Office Bldg, Ste 144, 100 W Alisal, 93901. SAN 301-293X. Tel: 831-755-5046. FAX: 831-422-9593. Web Site: www.mtrylawlib1.com. *Libr Dir,* Christopher Cobb; E-mail: christophercobb11@gmail.com; *Asst Librn,* Melissa Foster
Jul 2005-Jun 2006 Income (Main Library and Branch(s)) $205,000, State $200,000, Locally Generated Income $5,000. Sal $65,000
Library Holdings: Bk Vols 15,058
Special Collections: California Legal
Wireless access
Function: For res purposes
Open Mon-Fri 8:30-4:30
Branches:
MONTEREY BRANCH, Monterey County Court House, 1200 Aguajito Rd, Rm 202, Monterey, 93940, SAN 377-015X. Tel: 831-647-7746. FAX: 831-372-6036. *Libr Dir,* Christopher Cobb; *Asst Librn,* Melissa Foster
Library Holdings: Bk Vols 15,536
Database Vendor: LexisNexis, Westlaw
Function: For res purposes
Open Mon-Fri 8:30-4:30

P SALINAS PUBLIC LIBRARY, John Steinbeck Library, 350 Lincoln Ave, 93901. SAN 334-1496. Tel: 831-758-7311. Administration Tel: 831-758-7314. FAX: 831-758-7336. Web Site: www.salinaspubliclibrary.org/john-steinbeck-library. *Libr Dir,* Cynthia Bojorquez; Staff 6 (MLS 5, Non-MLS 1)
Founded 1909. Pop 152,677
Library Holdings: AV Mats 14,902; Bk Vols 204,665; Per Subs 271
Special Collections: John Steinbeck Coll
Automation Activity & Vendor Info: (Acquisitions) SirsiDynix; (Cataloging) SirsiDynix; (Circulation) SirsiDynix; (OPAC) SirsiDynix; (Serials) SirsiDynix
Database Vendor: OCLC FirstSearch
Wireless access
Function: Adult literacy prog, Audio & video playback equip for onsite use, CD-ROM, Digital talking bks, Homework prog, Magnifiers for reading, Music CDs, Online searches, Outside serv via phone, mail, e-mail & web, Photocopying/Printing, Spoken cassettes & CDs, Spoken cassettes & DVDs, Telephone ref, VHS videos
Partic in Monterey Bay Area Cooperative Library System
Open Mon, Fri & Sat 10-6, Tues 10-8, Wed 12-6, Thurs 12-8, Sun 1-6
Friends of the Library Group
Branches: 2
CESAR CHAVEZ LIBRARY, 615 Williams Rd, 93905, SAN 334-1526. Tel: 831-758-7345. FAX: 831-758-9172. Web Site: www.salinaspubliclibrary.org/ceasar-chavez-library. *Librn,* Don Gardner; Staff 2 (MLS 2)
Pop 52,000; Circ 75,000
Library Holdings: Bk Vols 55,000; Per Subs 86
Special Collections: Chicano Cultural Resource Center
Open Mon, Fri & Sat 10-6, Tues & Thurs 12-8, Sun 1-6
Friends of the Library Group
EL GABILAN, 1400 N Main St, 93906, SAN 334-1550. Tel: 831-758-7302. FAX: 831-442-0817. *Br Mgr,* Anthony Lacono; Staff 2 (MLS 1, Non-MLS 1)
Pop 55,000; Circ 124,000
Library Holdings: Bk Vols 54,000; Per Subs 55
Open Mon, Fri & Sat 10-6, Tues & Thurs 12-8, Wed 12-6, Sun 1-6
Friends of the Library Group

SAN ANDREAS

L CALAVERAS COUNTY LAW LIBRARY, Government Center, 891 Mountain Ranch Rd, 95249. SAN 326-0526. Tel: 209-754-6314. *Librn,* Mike Ibold; Staff 0.2 (Non-MLS 0.2)
Jul 2011-Jun 2012 Income $27,991. Mats Exp $27,232. Sal $1,694

Library Holdings: Bk Vols 8,900
Wireless access
Open Mon-Fri 8-5
Restriction: Restricted borrowing privileges

P CALAVERAS COUNTY LIBRARY*, 891 Mountain Ranch Rd, 95249. (Mail add: 1299 Gold Hunter Rd, 95249), SAN 301-2956. Tel: 209-754-6510. FAX: 209-754-6512. E-mail: publiclibrary@co.calaveras.ca.us. Web Site: www.calaveraslibrary.com. *County Librn,* Maurie Hoekstra; Tel: 209-754-6701, E-mail: mhoekstra@co.calaveras.ca.us; *Cat,* Raydine Willis; *Circ,* Elizabeth Castor; *ILL,* Elizabeth Martin; *Tech Serv,* Lynn Cuneo
Founded 1939. Pop 43,350; Circ 50,797
Library Holdings: Bk Vols 50,418; Per Subs 90
Subject Interests: Local hist, Mining
Automation Activity & Vendor Info: (Cataloging) SirsiDynix; (Circulation) SirsiDynix; (ILL) OCLC FirstSearch; (OPAC) SirsiDynix
Partic in 49-99 Cooperative Library System; OCLC Online Computer Library Center, Inc
Open Mon 1-5, Tues, Wed & Fri 9-5, Thurs 12-8
Friends of the Library Group
Branches: 7
ANGELS CAMP BRANCH, 426 N Main St, Angels Camp, 95222. (Mail add: PO Box 456, Angels Camp, 95222-0456), SAN 324-2382. Tel: 209-736-2198. *County Librn,* Maurie Hoekstra; E-mail: mhoekstra@co.calaveras.ca.us
Circ 12,401
Library Holdings: Bk Vols 9,464
Open Tues & Fri 10-2, Wed & Thurs 10-5
Friends of the Library Group
ARNOLD BRANCH, 1065 Blagen Rd, Arnold, 95223. (Mail add: PO Box 788, Arnold, 95223-0788), SAN 324-2390. Tel: 209-795-1009. *Br Mgr,* Fran Devlin; E-mail: fdevlin@gmail.com
Circ 17,883
Library Holdings: Bk Vols 6,897
Special Collections: Verna Johnston Nature Coll
Subject Interests: Ecology, Environment, Geol, Global warming, Indigenous people, Nature, Plants
Open Tues-Sat 10-4
Friends of the Library Group
COPPEROPOLIS BRANCH, 90 Copper Cove Dr, Unit C, Copperopolis, 95228. Tel: 209-785-0920. *Br Mgr,* Valerie Dean
Founded 1998. Pop 2,363; Circ 9,574
Library Holdings: Bk Vols 5,530
Database Vendor: SirsiDynix
Open Tues-Thurs 11-5:30, Fri 10-1
Friends of the Library Group
MOKELUMNE HILL BRANCH, 8328 Main St, Mokelumne Hill, 95245. (Mail add: PO Box 282, Mokelumne Hill, 95245-0282). Tel: 209-286-0507. *Br Mgr,* Brenda Nasser
Founded 1999. Pop 1,557; Circ 3,371
Library Holdings: Bk Vols 4,855
Database Vendor: SirsiDynix
Open Tues-Thurs 1:30-6, Fri 9-1:30
Friends of the Library Group
MURPHYS BRANCH, 480 Park Lane, Murphys, 95247. (Mail add: PO Box 702, Murphys, 95247-0702), SAN 324-2412. Tel: 209-728-3036. *Libr Asst,* Christine Sellman
Circ 8,605
Library Holdings: Bk Vols 5,878
Open Tues-Sat 11-4:30
Friends of the Library Group
VALLEY SPRINGS BRANCH, 240 Pine St, Valley Springs, 95252, SAN 324-2447. Tel: 209-772-1318. *Br Mgr,* Ailene Garrido
Circ 22,576
Library Holdings: Bk Vols 17,091
Open Mon-Thurs 1-5:30, Fri 1-4
Friends of the Library Group
WEST POINT BRANCH, 291 Main St, Ste B, West Point, 95255. (Mail add: PO Box 195, West Point, 95255-0195), SAN 324-2455. Tel: 209-293-7020. *Br Mgr,* Geri Auston
Circ 2,493
Library Holdings: Bk Vols 4,292
Open Wed & Thurs 11-5:30, Fri 10-3
Friends of the Library Group

SAN ANSELMO

P SAN ANSELMO PUBLIC LIBRARY*, 110 Tunstead Ave, 94960-2617. SAN 301-2972. Tel: 415-258-4656. FAX: 415-258-4666. Web Site: sananselmolibrary.org/about. *Town Librn,* Linda M Kenton; E-mail: lkenton@townofsananselmo.org; Staff 6 (MLS 3, Non-MLS 3)
Founded 1915. Pop 12,450; Circ 117,996
Library Holdings: AV Mats 2,500; e-books 3,939; Bk Vols 47,525; Per Subs 100
Special Collections: San Anselmo Historical Museum Coll
Database Vendor: Innovative Interfaces, Inc
Wireless access
Mem of NorthNet Library System
Partic in Marin Automated Resources & Information Network (MARINet)
Open Mon 10-8, Tues, Thurs, Fri & Sat 10-5, Wed 12-8
Friends of the Library Group

SAN BERNARDINO

C ART INSTITUTE OF CALIFORNIA - INLAND EMPIRE LIBRARY*, 674 Brier Rd, First Flr, 92408. Tel: 909-915-2146. Web Site: www.aicaielibrary.info. *Librn,* Denise Westcott
Library Holdings: Bk Vols 12,000; Per Subs 120
Database Vendor: EBSCOhost, ProQuest
Open Mon-Thurs 7:30am-9pm, Fri 7:30-5, Sat 9:30-4

C CALIFORNIA STATE UNIVERSITY, SAN BERNARDINO*, John M Pfau Library, 5500 University Pkwy, 92407-2318. SAN 301-2980. Tel: 909-537-5084, 909-537-5092. Circulation Tel: 909-537-5090. Interlibrary Loan Service Tel: 909-537-5093. Reference Tel: 909-537-5091. Administration Tel: 909-537-5102. Automation Services Tel: 909-537-5116. FAX: 909-537-7048. Interlibrary Loan Service FAX: 909-537-5906. Web Site: www.lib.csusb.edu. *Dean & Univ Librn,* Cesar Caballero; E-mail: ccaballe@csusb.edu; *Head, Circ,* Denise Gipson-Perry; E-mail: dgipson@csusb.edu; *Head, ILL,* Lee Bayer; Tel: 909-537-3498, E-mail: lbayer@csusb.edu; *Head, Libr Info Tech,* Jonathan Smith; Tel: 909-537-3492, E-mail: jsmith@csusb.edu; *Head, Pub Serv,* Les Kong; Tel: 909-537-5111, E-mail: lkong@csusb.edu; *Coord, Coll Develop,* Lisa Bartle; Tel: 909-537-5104, E-mail: lbartle@csusb.edu; *Coordr of Ref Serv,* Brent Singleton; Tel: 909-537-5083, E-mail: bsinglet@csusb.edu; *Coordr, Electronic Res, Ser,* Stacy Magedaz; Tel: 909-537-5103, E-mail: magedanz@csusb.edu; *Coordr, Instruction,* Barbara Quarton; Tel: 909-537-7553, E-mail: bquarton@csusb.edu; *Coordr, Spec Coll, Govt Doc,* Jill Vassilakos-Long; Tel: 909-537-7541, E-mail: jvlong@csusb.edu; *Ref Librn,* Bonnie Petry; Tel: 909-537-5114, E-mail: bpetry@csusb.edu; *Ref Librn,* Xiwen Zhang; Tel: 909-537-5106, E-mail: xzhang@csusb.edu; *Principal Cataloger,* Eva Sorrell; Tel: 909-537-7392, E-mail: esorrell@csusb.edu; Staff 12 (MLS 12)
Founded 1963. Enrl 14,000; Fac 400; Highest Degree: Master
Library Holdings: CDs 1,563; DVDs 1,001; e-books 10,000; e-journals 21,000; Bk Titles 750,000
Database Vendor: EBSCOhost, Gale Cengage Learning, LexisNexis, OCLC FirstSearch, Wilson - Wilson Web
Publications: Pfau Library (Newsletter)
Partic in Info Globe; Inland Empire Acad Libr Coop (IEALC); San Bernardino, Inyo, Riverside Counties United Library Services
Open Mon-Thurs 8am-10pm, Fri 8-5, Sat 9-2, Sun 1-5
Friends of the Library Group

P CITY OF SAN BERNARDINO LIBRARY SERVICES*, Norman F Feldheym Central Library, 555 W Sixth St, 92410-3001. SAN 334-2425. Tel: 909-381-8215. Circulation Tel: 909 381 8201. Reference Tel: 909-381-8226. FAX: 909-381-8229. *Interim Dir,* Edward Erjavek; *Acq of New Ser/Per, Tech Serv,* Ellen Lanto; *Automation Librn,* Ginny Evans-Perry; *Ch Serv,* Mary Chartier; *Doc, Per,* Gerald Linxwiler; *ILL,* Rosemary DuBois; *Purchasing,* Aurora Mendoza; Staff 11 (MLS 11)
Founded 1891. Pop 189,800; Circ 569,867
Library Holdings: Bk Vols 219,367; Per Subs 489
Special Collections: California History (California Coll)
Automation Activity & Vendor Info: (Circulation) TLC (The Library Corporation); (OPAC) TLC (The Library Corporation)
Mem of Inland Library System
Partic in OCLC Online Computer Library Center, Inc; San Bernardino, Inyo, Riverside Counties United Library Services
Friends of the Library Group
Branches: 3
DOROTHY INGHRAM BRANCH, 1505 W Highland Ave, 92411, SAN 334-2484. Tel: 909-887-4494. FAX: 909-887-6594. *Br Mgr,* Debra Bemben
Pop 15,000; Circ 54,020
Library Holdings: Bk Vols 15,000
Special Collections: Black History Coll
Open Mon-Wed 10-8, Thurs-Sat 10-6
Friends of the Library Group
HOWARD M ROWE BRANCH, 108 E Marshall Blvd, 92404, SAN 334-2514. Tel: 909-883-3411. FAX: 909-882-4941. *Br Mgr,* Janet Conway
Pop 60,000; Circ 165,103
Library Holdings: Bk Vols 41,080
Open Mon & Tues 3-8, Wed & Thurs 10-3
Friends of the Library Group

PAUL VILLASENOR BRANCH, 525 N Mount Vernon Ave, 90411, SAN 334-2549. Tel: 909-383-5156. FAX: 909-381-1766. *Br Mgr,* Rosemary Dubois; E-mail: duboisrose@sbpl.org
Pop 12,500; Circ 36,085
Library Holdings: Bk Vols 22,299
Special Collections: Bilingual Material; Spanish language material
Open Mon & Tues 3-8, Wed & Thurs 10-3

M COMMUNITY HOSPITAL OF SAN BERNARDINO*, Medical Library, 1805 Medical Center Dr, 92411-1288. SAN 324-5071. Tel: 909-887-6333, Ext 1488. FAX: 909-806-1062. Web Site: www.chsb.org. *In Charge,* Janice Castro
Library Holdings: Bk Titles 700; Per Subs 80
Partic in Dialog Corp; Nat Libr of Med, Coop Libr Agency for Systems & Servs
Restriction: Staff use only

P INLAND LIBRARY SYSTEM*, 555 W Sixth St, 92140. SAN 301-231X. Tel: 909-381-8257. FAX: 909-888-3171. E-mail: ils@inlandlib.org. Web Site: www.inlandlib.org. *Dir,* Vera Skop; Tel: 909-381-8257, E-mail: vskop@inlandlib.org; *Libr Asst,* Linda Andersen; E-mail: ils@inlandlib.org; Staff 1 (MLS 1)
Founded 1966
Jul 2012-Jun 2013 Income $250,000, State $201,075, Locally Generated Income $23,603, Other $25,322. Sal $50,000
Library Holdings: Bk Titles 375
Wireless access
Member Libraries: Banning Library District; Beaumont Library District; City of San Bernardino Library Services; Colton Public Library; Corona Public Library; Hemet Public Library; Inyo County Free Library; Moreno Valley Public Library; Murrieta Public Library; Ontario City Library; Palm Springs Public Library; Palo Verde Valley Library District; Rancho Cucamonga Public Library; Rancho Mirage Public Library; Riverside County Library System; Upland Public Library
Partic in OCLC Online Computer Library Center, Inc
Restriction: Mem organizations only
Friends of the Library Group

GL LAW LIBRARY FOR SAN BERNARDINO COUNTY*, 402 North D St, 92401. SAN 334-1585. Tel: 909-885-3020. Web Site: www.sblawlibrary.org. *Dir,* Lawrence R Meyer; E-mail: larrym@sblawlibrary.org; Staff 9 (MLS 2, Non-MLS 7)
Founded 1891
Library Holdings: Bk Vols 104,683
Special Collections: American Law & Foreign Law. State Document Depository; US Document Depository
Database Vendor: LexisNexis, Westlaw
Open Mon-Thurs 8:30-7, Fri 8:30-5, Sat 9-3
Restriction: Non-circulating coll
Branches:
HIGH DESERT, 15455 Seneca Rd, Victorville, 92392-2226, SAN 373-8477. Tel: 760-243-2044.
Automation Activity & Vendor Info: (Acquisitions) OCLC; (Cataloging) OCLC
Open Mon-Fri 9-1:30 & 2-5
Restriction: Non-circulating
WEST END BRANCH, 8401 N Haven Ave, Rancho Cucamonga, 91730-3893, SAN 328-2899. Tel: 909-944-5106. *Br Mgr,* Ed Butler
Library Holdings: Bk Titles 9,236; Per Subs 12
Special Collections: California Legal Materials, Primary Authority & Treatises. State Document Depository
Automation Activity & Vendor Info: (OPAC) Auto-Graphics, Inc
Database Vendor: LexisNexis, Westlaw
Open Mon-Fri 8:30-1:15 & 2-5
Restriction: Non-circulating

M SAINT BERNARDINE MEDICAL CENTER*, Medical Library, 2101 N Waterman Ave, 92404. SAN 320-3662. Tel: 909-883-8711. FAX: 909-881-7171. Web Site: www.chw.edu. *Librn,* Kathy Crumpacker; E-mail: kcrumpacker@chw.edu; Staff 1 (MLS 1)
Founded 1964
Library Holdings: Bk Titles 1,500; Bk Vols 5,400; Per Subs 64
Subject Interests: Allied health, Med, Nursing
Partic in Inland Empire Med Libr Coop

P SAN BERNARDINO COUNTY LIBRARY*, Administration, 777 E Rialto Ave, 92415-0035. SAN 334-164X. Tel: 909-387-2220. Administration Tel: 909-387-5721. FAX: 909-387-5724. Web Site: www.sbclib.org. *County Librn,* Leonard X Hernandez; E-mail: lhernandez@lib.sbcounty.gov; *Libr Serv Mgr,* Steven Raughley
Founded 1914. Pop 1,207,667; Circ 2,460,991
Open Mon-Fri 8-5
Branches: 32
ADELANTO BRANCH, 11497 Bartlett, Adelanto, 92301, SAN 334-1674. Tel: 760-246-5661. FAX: 760-246-4157. *Br Mgr,* Rebecca Hooton
Founded 1921
Jul 2005-Jun 2006. Mats Exp $17,275. Sal $90,233
Library Holdings: Bk Vols 21,630
Open Mon-Wed 11-7, Thurs 10-6, Sat 9-5
Friends of the Library Group
BAKER FAMILY LEARNING CENTER, 2818 N Macy St, Muscoy, 92407. Tel: 909-887-5167. *Supvr,* Yuridia Frausto
Founded 2013
Open Mon-Wed 11-7
BARSTOW BRANCH, 304 E Buena Vista St, Barstow, 92311-2806, SAN 334-1739. Tel: 760-256-4850. FAX: 760-256-4852. *Br Mgr,* David Cribbs
Founded 1914
Jul 2005-Jun 2006. Mats Exp $32,469. Sal $195,647
Library Holdings: Bk Vols 34,882
Open Mon-Wed 11-7, Thurs 10-6, Sat 9-5
Friends of the Library Group
NEWTON T BASS BRANCH, 14901 Dale Evans Pkwy, Apple Valley, 92307, SAN 334-1704. Tel: 760-247-2022. FAX: 760-247-7099. *Br Mgr,* Cheri Cervantes
Founded 1949
Jul 2005-Jun 2006. Mats Exp $71,727. Sal $489,440
Library Holdings: Bk Vols 71,286
Open Mon-Wed 11-7, Thurs 10-6, Sat 9-5
Friends of the Library Group
BIG BEAR LAKE BRANCH, 41930 Garstin Dr, Big Bear Lake, 92315. (Mail add: PO Box 1809, Big Bear Lake, 92315-1809), SAN 334-1763. Tel: 909-866-5571. FAX: 909-866-4382. *Br Mgr,* Sheryl Thomas
Founded 1915
Jul 2005-Jun 2006. Mats Exp $23,558. Sal $225,688
Library Holdings: Bk Vols 40,011
Open Mon-Wed 11-7, Thurs 10-6, Sat 9-5
Friends of the Library Group
BLOOMINGTON BRANCH, 993 West Valley Blvd, Ste 102, Bloomington, 92316, SAN 334-1798. Tel: 909-820-0533. *Br Mgr,* Erika Jennings
Founded 1914
Jul 2005-Jun 2006. Mats Exp $17,509. Sal $92,275
Library Holdings: Bk Vols 17,678
Open Mon-Wed 11-7, Thurs 10-6, Sat 9-5
Friends of the Library Group
CAL AERO PRESERVE ACADEMY BRANCH, 15850 Main St, Chino, 91708. Tel: 909-606-2173. *Br Mgr,* Shauna Berenson
Open Mon-Thurs 3:30-8, Sat 10-5
CARTER BRANCH, 2630 N Linden Ave, Rialto, 92377. Tel: 909-854-4100, Ext 28148. *Br Mgr,* Dolores Vicuna
Open Mon-Thurs 3-8, Sat 9-5
CHINO BRANCH, 13180 Central Ave, Chino, 91710, SAN 334-1828. Tel: 909-465-5280. FAX: 909-465-5240. *Br Mgr,* Caryn Valdiserri
Founded 1915
Jul 2005-Jun 2006. Mats Exp $53,408. Sal $301,080
Library Holdings: Bk Vols 59,475
Open Mon-Wed 11-7, Thurs & Fri 10-6, Sat 9-5
Friends of the Library Group
CRESTLINE BRANCH, 24105 Lake Gregory Dr, Crestline, 92325-1087, SAN 334-1852. Tel: 909-338-3294. FAX: 909-338-0964. *Br Mgr,* Jake Zylman
Founded 1919
Jul 2005-Jun 2006. Mats Exp $19,481. Sal $96,648
Library Holdings: Bk Vols 18,458
Open Mon-Wed 11-7, Thurs 10-6, Sat 9-5
Friends of the Library Group
GRAND TERRACE BRANCH, 22795 Barton Rd, Grand Terrace, 92313, SAN 325-4453. Tel: 909-783-0147. FAX: 909-783-1913. *Br Mgr,* Lisa Llewellyn
Founded 1985
Jul 2005-Jun 2006. Mats Exp $21,447. Sal $112,533
Library Holdings: Bk Vols 24,771
Open Mon-Wed 11-7, Thurs & Fri 10-6, Sat 9-5
Friends of the Library Group
HESPERIA BRANCH, 9650 Seventh Ave, Hesperia, 92345, SAN 334-1976. Tel: 760-244-4898. FAX: 760-244-1530. *Br Mgr,* Chelsea Lyons
Founded 1970
Jul 2005-Jun 2006. Mats Exp $198,281. Sal $277,661
Library Holdings: Bk Vols 78,553
Open Mon-Thurs 10-8, Fri 10-6, Sat 9-5, Sun 1-5
Friends of the Library Group
JANICE HORST BRANCH, 33103 Old Woman Springs Rd, Lucerne Valley, 92356, SAN 334-2093. Tel: 760-248-7521. FAX: 760-248-1131. *Br Mgr,* Natalie Griffith
Founded 1914

Jul 2005-Jun 2006. Mats Exp $18,406. Sal $113,893
Library Holdings: Bk Vols 20,620
Open Mon-Wed 11-7, Thurs 10-6, Sat 9-5
Friends of the Library Group
JOSHUA TREE BRANCH, 6465 Park Blvd, Joshua Tree, 92252, SAN 334-200X. Tel: 760-366-8615. FAX: 760-366-8615. *Br Mgr,* Penny Mason
Founded 1945
Jul 2005-Jun 2006. Mats Exp $13,672. Sal $45,669
Library Holdings: Bk Vols 17,560
Open Mon-Wed 11-7, Thurs 10-6, Sat 9-5
Friends of the Library Group
KAISER BRANCH, 11155 Almond Ave, Fontana, 92337. Tel: 909-357-5900, Ext 8029. FAX: 909-428-8494. *Interim Libr Supvr,* David Martinez
Founded 2000
Jul 2005-Jun 2006. Mats Exp $14,330. Sal $121,362
Library Holdings: Bk Vols 29,123
Open Mon-Thurs 3-8, Sat 9-5
Friends of the Library Group
LAKE ARROWHEAD, 27235 Hwy 189, Blue Jay, 92317, SAN 334-2034. Tel: 909-337-3118. FAX: 909-337-2287. *Regional Mgr,* Mike Jimenez
Founded 1924
Jul 2005-Jun 2006. Mats Exp $35,112. Sal $228,164
Library Holdings: Bk Vols 26,284
Open Mon-Wed 11-7, Thurs 10-6, Sat 9-5
Friends of the Library Group
FONTANA LEWIS LIBRARY & TECHNOLOGY CENTER, 8437 Sierra Ave, Fontana, 92335-3892. Tel: 909-574-4500. *Br Mgr,* Michael Jimenez
Open Mon-Thurs 10-9, Fri & Sat 10-6, Sun 12-5
LOMA LINDA BRANCH, 25581 Barton Rd, Loma Linda, 92354, SAN 334-2069. Tel: 909-796-8621. FAX: 909-796-4221. *Br Mgr,* Stan Sewell
Founded 1967
Jul 2005-Jun 2006. Mats Exp $38,979. Sal $210,972
Library Holdings: Bk Vols 42,866
Open Mon-Wed 11-7, Thurs 10-6, Sun 9-5
Friends of the Library Group
MENTONE SENIOR CENTER & LIBRARY, 1331 Opal Ave, Mentone, 92359, SAN 334-2123. Tel: 909-794-0327. FAX: 909-794-8394. *Br Mgr,* Erin Salser
Founded 1939
Jul 2005-Jun 2006. Mats Exp $12,962. Sal $69,353
Library Holdings: Bk Vols 15,965
Open Mon-Wed 11-7, Thurs 10-6, Sat 9-5
Friends of the Library Group
MONTCLAIR BRANCH, 9955 Fremont Ave, Montclair, 91763, SAN 334-2158. Tel: 909-624-4671. FAX: 909-621-1261. *Br Mgr,* Edward Diggins
Founded 1952
Jul 2005-Jun 2006. Mats Exp $28,348. Sal $361,864
Library Holdings: Bk Vols 37,347
Open Mon-Wed 11-7, Thurs & Fri 10-6, Sat 9-5
Friends of the Library Group
NEEDLES BRANCH, 1111 Bailey Ave, Needles, 92363, SAN 334 2182. Tel: 760-326-9255. FAX: 760-326-9238. *Br Mgr,* Joan Meis Wilson
Founded 1917
Jul 2005-Jun 2006. Mats Exp $13,839. Sal $134,198
Library Holdings: Bk Vols 20,951
Open Mon-Wed 11-7, Thurs 10-6, Sat 9-5
Friends of the Library Group
PHELAN MEMORIAL LIBRARY, 9800 Clovis Rd, Phelan, 92371. (Mail add: PO Box 292688, Phelan, 92329). Tel: 760-868-3053. FAX: 760-868-1386. *Br Mgr,* Andrea Anderson
Founded 2002
Jul 2005-Jun 2006. Mats Exp $18,770. Sal $72,097
Library Holdings: Bk Vols 27,174
Open Mon-Wed 11-7, Thurs 10-6, Sat 9-5
Friends of the Library Group
SAM J RACADIO LIBRARY & ENVIRONMENTAL LEARNING CENTER, 7863 Central Ave, Highland, 92346-4107, SAN 334-1917. Tel: 909-425-4700. FAX: 909-425-4710. *Br Mgr,* Judy Sbardellati
Founded 1914
Jul 2005-Jun 2006. Mats Exp $185,106. Sal $503,833
Library Holdings: Bk Vols 68,593
Open Mon-Wed 10-8, Thurs & Fri 10-6, Sat 9-5
Friends of the Library Group
RIALTO BRANCH, 251 W First St, Rialto, 92376, SAN 334-2212. Tel: 909-875-0144. FAX: 909-875-2801. *Br Mgr,* Ayesha Razo
Founded 1914
Jul 2005-Jun 2006. Mats Exp $53,421. Sal $348,669
Library Holdings: Bk Vols 46,880
Open Mon-Wed 11-7, Thurs & Fri 10-6, Sat 9-5
Friends of the Library Group
RUNNING SPRINGS BRANCH, 2677 Whispering Pines Dr, Running Springs, 92382, SAN 334-2247. Tel: 909-867-3604. *Br Mgr,* Frederick Malcomb
Founded 1938
Jul 2005-Jun 2006. Mats Exp $14,851. Sal $89,456
Library Holdings: Bk Vols 9,337
Open Mon-Wed 11-7, Thurs 10-6, Sat 9-5
Friends of the Library Group
SUMMIT BRANCH LIBRARY, 15551 Summit Ave, Fontana, 92336, SAN 334-1941. Tel: 909-357-5950, Ext 3024. *Supvr,* Shelia Panattoni
Founded 1914
Jul 2005-Jun 2006. Mats Exp $193,225. Sal $464,327
Library Holdings: Bk Vols 27,395
Open Mon-Thurs 3-8, Sat 9-5
Friends of the Library Group
JAMES S THALMAN BRANCH, 14020 City Center Dr, Chino Hills, 91709-5442, SAN 373-5885. Tel: 909-590-5380. FAX: 909-591-5267. *Br Mgr,* Shauna Berenson
Founded 1992
Jul 2005-Jun 2006. Mats Exp $72,260. Sal $354,891
Library Holdings: Bk Vols 75,161
Open Mon-Thurs 10-8, Fri 10-6, Sat 9-5, Sun 1-5
Friends of the Library Group
TRONA BRANCH, 82805 Mountain View St, Trona, 93562, SAN 334-2271. Tel: 760-372-5847. FAX: 760-372-5847. *Br Mgr,* Stacy Cliff
Founded 1915
Jul 2005-Jun 2006. Mats Exp $9,755. Sal $112,437
Library Holdings: Bk Vols 9,356
Open Mon-Wed 11-7, Thurs 10-6, Sat 9-5
Friends of the Library Group
TWENTYNINE PALMS BRANCH, 6078 Adobe Rd, Twentynine Palms, 92277, SAN 334-2301. Tel: 760-367-9519. FAX: 760-361-0703. *Br Mgr,* Debbie Medina
Founded 1928
Jul 2005-Jun 2006. Mats Exp $28,328. Sal $189,013
Library Holdings: Bk Vols 27,299
Open Mon-Wed 11-7, Thurs 10-6, Sat 9-5
Friends of the Library Group
WRIGHTWOOD BRANCH, 6011 Pine St, Wrightwood, 92397-1962, SAN 334-2344. Tel: 760-249-4577. FAX: 760-249-3263. *Supvr,* Robin Cornett
Founded 1981
Jul 2005-Jun 2006. Mats Exp $14,260. Sal $86,451
Library Holdings: Bk Vols 14,752
Open Mon-Wed 11-7, Thurs 10-6, Sat 9-5
Friends of the Library Group
YUCAIPA BRANCH, 12040 Fifth St, Yucaipa, 92399, SAN 334-2360. Tel: 909-790-3146. FAX: 909-790-3151. *Br Mgr,* Alicia Mesa
Founded 1914
Jul 2005-Jun 2006. Mats Exp $43,111. Sal $340,977
Library Holdings: Bk Vols 44,830
Open Mon-Wed 11-7, Thurs & Fri 10-6, Sat 9-5
Friends of the Library Group
YUCCA VALLEY BRANCH, 57098 Twentynine Palms Hwy, Yucca Valley, 92284, SAN 334-2395. Tel: 760-228-5455. FAX: 760-228-5459. *Br Mgr,* Danielle Fox
Founded 1946
Jul 2005-Jun 2006. Mats Exp $42,354. Sal $282,065
Library Holdings: Bk Vols 44,432
Open Mon-Wed 11-7, Thurs 10-6, Sat 9-5
Friends of the Library Group

J SAN BERNARDINO VALLEY COLLEGE LIBRARY*, 701 S Mount Vernon Ave, 92410. SAN 301-3022. Tel: 909-384-4448. Reference Tel: 909-384-8289. Administration Tel: 909-384-8684. Web Site: library.valleycollege.edu. *Dean, Libr & Learning Support Serv,* Marie Mestas; Tel: 909-384-8576, E-mail: mmestas@valleycollege.edu; *Librn,* Virginia Evans-Perry; Tel: 909-384-8699, E-mail: gperry@valleycollege.edu; *Librn,* Dr Celia Huston; Tel: 909-384-8574, E-mail: cmckinl@valleycollege.edu; *Librn,* Patricia A Wall; Tel: 909-384-8577, E-mail: pwall@valleycollege.edu; *Circ Supvr,* Angelita Gideon; Tel: 909-384-8567, E-mail: agideon@valleycollege.edu. Subject Specialists: *English lit, Hist,* Marie Mestas; Staff 10 (MLS 3, Non-MLS 7)
Founded 1928. Enrl 13,000; Highest Degree: Associate
Library Holdings: Bk Vols 101,043; Per Subs 305
Special Collections: Local History, California & The West. State Document Depository; US Document Depository
Subject Interests: Humanities, Native Am culture, Native Am hist
Automation Activity & Vendor Info: (Acquisitions) Innovative Interfaces, Inc; (Cataloging) Innovative Interfaces, Inc; (Circulation) Innovative Interfaces, Inc; (Course Reserve) Innovative Interfaces, Inc; (ILL) Innovative Interfaces, Inc; (OPAC) Innovative Interfaces, Inc; (Serials) Innovative Interfaces, Inc
Database Vendor: Baker & Taylor, EBSCO Information Services, EBSCOhost, Ingram Library Services, Innovative Interfaces, Inc, ProQuest
Wireless access

Function: Art exhibits, Audio & video playback equip for onsite use, AV serv, Bilingual assistance for Spanish patrons, Bk club(s), Bks on CD, CD-ROM, Computers for patron use, Copy machines, Distance learning, e-mail & chat, e-mail serv, Electronic databases & coll, Exhibits, Handicapped accessible, ILL available, Magnifiers for reading, Online cat, Online info literacy tutorials on the web & in blackboard, Online ref, Online searches, Orientations, Outreach serv, Outside serv via phone, mail, e-mail & web, Photocopying/Printing, Ref & res, Ref serv available, Ref serv in person, Scanner, Tax forms, Telephone ref, Wheelchair accessible
Partic in SIRCULS
Special Services for the Deaf - ADA equip; Assisted listening device; Assistive tech
Special Services for the Blind - Assistive/Adapted tech devices, equip & products
Open Mon-Thurs 8-8, Fri 8-12
Restriction: Authorized patrons, Authorized scholars by appt, Borrowing privileges limited to fac & registered students, Limited access for the pub, Non-circulating of rare bks, Restricted borrowing privileges

SAN BRUNO

M KRAMES HEALTH SCIENCES LIBRARY*, Krames Health & Safety, 1100 Grundy Lane, 94066. SAN 370-1670. Tel: 650-244-4333. Interlibrary Loan Service Tel: 650-244-4532. FAX: 650-244-4345. E-mail: info@kramesstaywell.com. Web Site: www.kramesstaywell.com. *Libr Mgr,* Craig Cruz; E-mail: craig.cruz@krames.com; Staff 3 (MLS 2, Non-MLS 1)
Founded 1975
Library Holdings: Bk Titles 3,000; Per Subs 400
Function: Archival coll, Doc delivery serv, For res purposes, Govt ref serv, ILL available, Res libr
Restriction: Access at librarian's discretion, By permission only, Circulates for staff only, Internal circ only, Not open to pub

G THE NATIONAL ARCHIVES AT SAN FRANCISCO*, 1000 Commodore Dr, 94066-2350. SAN 301-3030. Tel: 650-238-3501. FAX: 650-238-3510. E-mail: sanbruno.archives@nara.gov. Web Site: www.archives.gov/pacific/san-francisco/index.html. *Dir,* Dr Marcy Goldstein; Staff 11 (MLS 1, Non-MLS 10)
Founded 1969
Library Holdings: Microforms 60,000
Special Collections: Archival Holdings, 1850-1980, architectural drawings, maps, photos, textual doc; Bureau of Indian Affairs, California & Nevada, 1859-1960, doc, micro; Bureau of Land Management, 1853-1960, doc, micro; Chinese Immigration Records, 1882-1955, doc; Department of Energy, 1915-1970, doc; Government of American Samoa, 1900-1966, doc; National Park Service, 1910-1969, doc; San Francisco Mint, 1853-1960, doc; United States Army Corps of Engineers, 1853-1976, doc; United States Attorneys (San Francisco), 1913-1971, doc; United States Census, 1790-1930, micro; United States Committee on Fair Employment Practice, 1941-1946, doc; United States Court of Appeals for Ninth Circuit, 1891-1969, doc; United States District Court, Eastern District of California, 1900-1973, doc; United States District Court, Hawaii, 1900-1968, doc; United States District Court, Nevada (Reno/Carson City), 1865-1963, doc, micro; United States District Courts for Northern District of California, 1851-1972, doc, micro; United States Forest Service, 1870-1970, doc; United States National War Labor Board, 1942-1947; United States Naval Shipyards (Mare Island, Pearl Harbor & San Francisco), 1854-1965, doc; United States Penitentiary at Alcatraz, 1934-1964, doc
Subject Interests: Asian-Am studies, Genealogy, Immigration, Labor, Land, Maritime, Native Am, Natural res, Naturalization, Naval hist, World War II
Function: Archival coll, Copy machines, For res purposes, Govt ref serv, Handicapped accessible, Magnifiers for reading, Photocopying/Printing, Telephone ref, Wheelchair accessible, Workshops
Publications: A Guide to Records of Asian Americans & Pacific Islanders at NARA's Pacific Region (San Francisco); Chinese Immigration & Chinese in the United States: Records in the Regional Archives of the National Archives & Records Administration; Guide to Records in the National Archives-Pacific Sierra Region; Records in the National Archives-Pacific Sierra Region for Study of Science, Technology, Natural Resources & the Environment; Records in the National Archives-Pacific Sierra Region for the Study of Ethnic History; Records in the National Archives-Pacific Sierra Region for the Study of Labor & Business History
Partic in Cooperative Information Network
Open Mon, Tues, Thurs & Fri 7:30-4, Wed 7:30-5:30
Restriction: Non-circulating coll, Not a lending libr, Open to pub for ref only, Pub ref by request, Pub use on premises

P SAN BRUNO PUBLIC LIBRARY*, 701 Angus Ave W, 94066-3490. SAN 301-3049. Tel: 650-616-7078. FAX: 650-876-0848. E-mail: sbpl@plsinfo.org. Web Site: www.sanbrunolibrary.org. *Dir,* Terry Jackson; *Asst Dir,* John Alita; *Coll & Ref Serv Mgr,* Tim Wallace; *Ch Serv,* Barbara Bruxvoort; Staff 11 (MLS 6, Non-MLS 5)
Founded 1916. Pop 40,850; Circ 352,498
Library Holdings: Bk Vols 120,000
Special Collections: San Bruno Historical Pictures. Oral History
Automation Activity & Vendor Info: (OPAC) Innovative Interfaces, Inc - Millenium
Wireless access
Function: Adult bk club, Audiobks via web, Bilingual assistance for Spanish patrons, Bks on cassette, Bks on CD, CD-ROM, Children's prog, Computers for patron use, Copy machines, e-mail & chat, E-Reserves, Electronic databases & coll, Fax serv, Free DVD rentals, Games & aids for the handicapped, Homebound delivery serv, ILL available, Music CDs, Online cat, Online ref, Photocopying/Printing, Prog for adults, Prog for children & young adult, Pub access computers, Ref serv in person, Spoken cassettes & CDs, Story hour, Summer reading prog, Tax forms, Teen prog, VHS videos, Web-catalog
Open Mon-Thurs 10-9, Fri 10-6, Sat 10-5
Friends of the Library Group

J SKYLINE COLLEGE LIBRARY*, 3300 College Dr, 94066-1698. SAN 301-3057. Tel: 650-738-4311. FAX: 650-738-4149. Web Site: www.skylinecollege.net/library. *Dir,* Thomas Hewitt; *Ref,* Eric Brenner; Staff 3 (MLS 3)
Founded 1969. Enrl 6,455; Fac 156
Library Holdings: Bk Titles 50,000; Per Subs 240
Subject Interests: Feminism
Partic in OCLC Online Computer Library Center, Inc
Open Mon-Thurs 8am-10pm, Fri 8-4, Sat (Sept-May) 10-2

SAN DIEGO

C ALLIANT INTERNATIONAL UNIVERSITY*, Walter Library - San Diego Campus, 10455 Pomerado Rd, 92131-1799. SAN 301-357X. Tel: 858-635-4511. Interlibrary Loan Service Tel: 858-635-4605. Reference Tel: 858-635-4510. FAX: 858-635-4599. E-mail: library@alliant.edu, wlibrary@alliant.edu. Web Site: library.alliant.edu. *Dir of Libr Serv, Univ Librn,* Scott Zimmer; Tel: 858-635-4553, E-mail: szimmer@alliant.edu; *Librn/Irvine Location,* Erin Schmidt; Tel: 949-812-7454, E-mail: eschmidt@alliant.edu; *Operations Librn,* Melinda DeWitt; Tel: 858-635-4692, E-mail: mdewitt@alliant.edu; *Ref & Assessment Librn,* Deborah Fleming; Tel: 858-635-4474, E-mail: dfleming@alliant.edu; *Electronic Res Coordr,* Heather Parker; Tel: 858-635-4693, E-mail: hparker@alliant.edu; *Ref & Instrul Serv, Instr Coordr,* Mary Kennedy; Tel: 858-635-4677, E-mail: mkennedy@alliant.edu; *ILL Tech,* Kanjana Boes; E-mail: kboes@alliant.edu; Staff 9 (MLS 5, Non-MLS 4)
Founded 1952. Enrl 1,521; Fac 75; Highest Degree: Doctorate
Jul 2010-Jun 2011. Mats Exp $160,411, Books $4,049, Per/Ser (Incl. Access Fees) $52,735, Other Print Mats $100,321, AV Mat $3,306. Sal $304,981
Library Holdings: DVDs 225; e-books 148,595; Bk Vols 68,108; Per Subs 123; Videos 598
Subject Interests: Bus, Educ, Intl relations, Psychol
Automation Activity & Vendor Info: (Acquisitions) Innovative Interfaces, Inc - Millenium; (Cataloging) Innovative Interfaces, Inc - Millenium; (Circulation) Innovative Interfaces, Inc - Millenium; (Course Reserve) Innovative Interfaces, Inc - Millenium; (ILL) Innovative Interfaces, Inc - Millenium; (Media Booking) Innovative Interfaces, Inc - Millenium; (OPAC) Innovative Interfaces, Inc - Millenium; (Serials) Innovative Interfaces, Inc - Millenium
Database Vendor: Alexander Street Press, Annual Reviews, Blackwell, ebrary, EBSCOhost, Elsevier, Emerald, Haworth Pres Inc, ISI Web of Knowledge, JSTOR, LexisNexis, Medline, OCLC WorldShare Interlibrary Loan, OVID Technologies, ProQuest, Sage, ScienceDirect, Wiley InterScience, YBP Library Services
Wireless access
Partic in Link+; Statewide California Electronic Library Consortium (SCELC)
Open Mon-Thurs 8am-10pm, Fri 8-6, Sat 10-6, Sun 12-8
Restriction: Borrowing privileges limited to fac & registered students
Friends of the Library Group

GL CALIFORNIA COURT OF APPEAL*, Fourth Appellate District-Division One Law Library, 750 B St, Ste 300, 92101-8173. SAN 301-312X. Tel: 619-744-0760. FAX: 619-645-2495. Web Site: www.courts.ca.gov/4dca. *Librn,* Ruth Gervais; Staff 1 (MLS 1)
Founded 1929
Library Holdings: Bk Vols 45,000
Subject Interests: State law
Partic in Dialog Corp; Westlaw
Restriction: Staff use only

GL CALIFORNIA DEPARTMENT OF JUSTICE LIBRARY*, 110 West A St, Ste 1311, 92101. SAN 301-3138. *Head of Libr,* Position Currently Open; *Libr Tech,* Norma Santa Cruz; Staff 2 (MLS 1, Non-MLS 1)
Founded 1972
Library Holdings: Bk Titles 26,000; Per Subs 50
Automation Activity & Vendor Info: (Cataloging) Inmagic, Inc.; (Serials) Inmagic, Inc.

Database Vendor: LexisNexis, Westlaw
Publications: Newsletter
Restriction: Staff use only

CL CALIFORNIA WESTERN SCHOOL OF LAW LIBRARY*, 290 Cedar St, 92101. (Mail add: 225 Cedar St, 92101), SAN 301-3162. Tel: 619-525-1418. Interlibrary Loan Service Tel: 619-525-1426. Reference Tel: 619-525-1419. Administration Tel: 619-525-1421. FAX: 619-685-2918. Web Site: www.cwsl.edu/library. *Dir of Libr,* Phyllis Marion; Tel: 619-525-1429, E-mail: pmarion@cwsl.edu; *Asst Dir, Tech & Admin Serv,* Amy Moberly; E-mail: amoberly@cwsl.edu; *Asst Dir, Pub Serv,* Barbara Glennan; Tel: 619-525-1499, E-mail: bglennan@cwsl.edu; *Acq & Budget Control Librn,* Ian R Kipnes; Tel: 619-515-1512, E-mail: ikipnes@cwsl.edu; *Evening/Weekend Ref Librn,* Bill Bookheim; Tel: 619-515-1584, E-mail: bbookheim@cwsl.edu; *Foreign & Intl Law Ref Librn,* Bobbi Weaver; Tel: 619-525-1497, E-mail: bweaver@cwsl.edu; *Ref Librn,* Brandon Baker, II; Tel: 619-525-1425, E-mail: bbaker@cwsl.edu; *ILL & Distance Libr Serv Spec, Reserves,* Linda Weathers; E-mail: lweathers@cwsl.edu. Subject Specialists: *Foreign law, Intl law,* Bobbi Weaver; Staff 8 (MLS 8)
Founded 1958. Fac 52; Highest Degree: Doctorate
Aug 2012-Jul 2013 Income $1,553,192. Mats Exp $1,020,767, Books $63,937, Per/Ser (Incl. Access Fees) $605,467, Micro $1,007, AV Mat $1,148, Electronic Ref Mat (Incl. Access Fees) $334,451, Presv $14,757
Library Holdings: AV Mats 751; CDs 151; DVDs 568; Bk Titles 60,178; Bk Vols 355,814; Per Subs 5,771
Special Collections: Congressional Information Service (US Congress Coll), micro; US Supreme Court Records & Briefs, micro. State Document Depository
Subject Interests: Law
Automation Activity & Vendor Info: (Acquisitions) Innovative Interfaces, Inc; (Cataloging) Innovative Interfaces, Inc; (Circulation) Innovative Interfaces, Inc; (Course Reserve) Innovative Interfaces, Inc; (ILL) OCLC; (OPAC) Innovative Interfaces, Inc; (Serials) Innovative Interfaces, Inc
Database Vendor: Baker & Taylor, Blackwell, Bloomberg, Bowker, Cassidy Cataloguing Services, Inc, CQ Press, EBSCOhost, Elsevier, Gale Cengage Learning, H W Wilson, HeinOnline, Innovative Interfaces, Inc, JSTOR, LexisNexis, Loislaw, Marcive, Inc, Nature Publishing Group, OCLC FirstSearch, OCLC WorldShare Interlibrary Loan, Oxford Online, ProQuest, Sage, Westlaw, Wiley InterScience, Wilson - Wilson Web, YBP Library Services
Wireless access
Function: Computers for patron use, Copy machines, Electronic databases & coll, Free DVD rentals, Handicapped accessible, ILL available, Online cat, Photocopying/Printing, VHS videos
Partic in Law Library Microform Consortium (LLMC); New England Law Library Consortium, Inc; OCLC Online Computer Library Center, Inc; Statewide California Electronic Library Consortium (SCELC)
Open Mon-Fri 7am-11pm, Sat & Sun 8am-11pm
Restriction: Borrowing privileges limited to fac & registered students, Circ privileges for students & alumni only, In-house use for visitors, Not open to pub

C COLEMAN COLLEGE LIBRARY, 8888 Balba Ave, 92123. SAN 321-5350. Tel: 619-465 3990. *Librn,* Manny Bernad; E-mail: mbernad@coleman.edu; Staff 1 (MLS 1)
Highest Degree: Master
Library Holdings: Bk Titles 37,548; Bk Vols 40,050
Subject Interests: Computers
Automation Activity & Vendor Info: (Cataloging) EOS International; (Circulation) EOS International; (Course Reserve) EOS International; (OPAC) EOS International; (Serials) EOS International
Publications: Library Guides
Open Mon-Thurs 9-9

S CUBIC DEFENSE APPLICATIONS, INC*, Technical Library, 9333 Balboa Ave, 92123. (Mail add: PO Box 85587, 92186-5587), SAN 301-3189. Tel: 858-277-6780. FAX: 858-505-1542. *Librn,* Diane Rosine; Tel: 858-505-2280; Staff 1 (MLS 1)
Founded 1952
Library Holdings: Bk Titles 6,000; Per Subs 320
Subject Interests: Aeronaut, Communications, Computer sci, Electronic eng, Electronics, Math, Mgt, Physics, Radar
Automation Activity & Vendor Info: (Acquisitions) Inmagic, Inc.; (Cataloging) Inmagic, Inc.; (Circulation) Inmagic, Inc.; (OPAC) Inmagic, Inc.; (Serials) Inmagic, Inc.
Database Vendor: Dialog, LexisNexis
Partic in Dialog Corp; Sci & Tech Info Network
Restriction: Open by appt only

J FASHION INSTITUTE OF DESIGN & MERCHANDISING*, Resource & Research Center, 350 Tenth Ave, 3rd Flr, 92101. SAN 370-2197. Tel: 619-235-2049. Web Site: www.fidm.com. *Head Librn,* Beverlee S Cabral; E-mail: bcabral@fidm.com; Staff 3 (MLS 1, Non-MLS 2)
Founded 1969. Enrl 3,000; Highest Degree: Bachelor
Library Holdings: Bk Vols 7,000; Per Subs 120
Automation Activity & Vendor Info: (Acquisitions) Gateway; (Cataloging) Gateway; (Circulation) Gateway; (Course Reserve) Gateway; (ILL) Gateway; (OPAC) Gateway; (Serials) Gateway
Database Vendor: EBSCOhost, Gale Cengage Learning, LexisNexis, ProQuest
Function: For res purposes, ILL available, Ref serv available
Restriction: Not open to pub, Open to students, fac & staff

R FIRST PRESBYTERIAN CHURCH OF SAN DIEGO LIBRARY*, 320 Date St, 92101-3219. SAN 301-3219. Tel: 619-232-7513. FAX: 619-232-8469. Web Site: www.fpcsd.org.
Founded 1940
Library Holdings: Bk Titles 2,000; Per Subs 6
Open Mon-Fri 8:30-12:15 & 1-4

L HIGGS, FLETCHER & MACK LLP*, Law Library, 401 West A St, Ste 2600, 92101-7913. SAN 301-3243. Tel: 619-236-1551. FAX: 619-696-1410. Web Site: www.higgslaw.com. *Libr Serv Coordr,* Position Currently Open
Founded 1939
Library Holdings: Bk Vols 12,000
Partic in American Association of Law Libraries (AALL)
Open Mon-Fri 8-5:30

S HUBBS-SEA WORLD RESEARCH INSTITUTE*, 2595 Ingraham St, 92109. SAN 326-4084. Tel: 619-226-3870. FAX: 619-226-3944. Web Site: www.hswri.org.
Library Holdings: Bk Vols 620; Per Subs 30
Restriction: Not open to pub

M KAISER-PERMANENTE MEDICAL CENTER*, Health Sciences Library, 4647 Zion Ave, 92120. SAN 301-3294. Tel: 619-528-7323. FAX: 619-528-3444. *Librn,* Paul Francis Bielman; Staff 3 (MLS 1, Non-MLS 2)
Founded 1967
Library Holdings: Bk Titles 6,500; Per Subs 100
Subject Interests: Med, Nursing
Restriction: Hospital staff & commun, In-house use for visitors

L LATHAM & WATKINS*, Law Library, 600 W Broadway, Ste 1800, 92101. SAN 371-1021. Tel: 619-236-1234. Reference Tel: 619-236-2975. FAX: 619-696-7419. *Info Res Mgr,* Brent Naritomi; Tel: 619-236-2872; *Ref Librn,* Melinda Briggs; E-mail: melinda.briggs@lw.com; *Info Res Tech,* Heidrun Perez; Tel: 619-238-2834; Staff 4 (MLS 4)
Founded 1982
Library Holdings: Bk Titles 1,000; Bk Vols 2,700
Database Vendor: Dialog, LexisNexis, OCLC FirstSearch, Westlaw
Open Mon-Fri 8-5

A MARINE CORPS RECRUIT DEPOT LIBRARY*, 3800 Chosin Ave, Bldg 7 W, 92140-5196. Tel: 619-524-1849. FAX: 619-524-8243. *Supvry Librn,* Dan Cisco; Tel: 619-524-1850; Staff 6 (MLS 1, Non-MLS 5)
Founded 1927
Library Holdings: CDs 1,245; DVDs 2,638; Bk Vols 31,173; Per Subs 72
Special Collections: Marine Corps Professional Reading Program
Subject Interests: Marine Corps
Automation Activity & Vendor Info: (Circulation) SIRSI WorkFlows
Database Vendor: ProQuest
Wireless access
Function: Audiobks via web, Bks on CD, Children's prog, Computers for patron use, Copy machines, Distance learning, e-mail serv, Electronic databases & coll, Holiday prog, Literacy & newcomer serv, Newsp ref libr, Online cat, Online searches, Orientations, Outreach serv, Photocopying/Printing, Prog for adults, Prog for children & young adult, Ref & res, Ref serv available, Scanner, Spoken cassettes & CDs, Story hour, Summer reading prog, Tax forms
Open Mon-Fri 8:30-6, Sat 8:30-5, Sun 1-5
Restriction: Mil, family mem, retirees, Civil Serv personnel NAF only

S MARITIME MUSEUM OF SAN DIEGO*, The MacMullen Library & Research Archives, 1492 N Harbor Dr, 92101. SAN 371-5604. Tel: 619-234-9153, Ext 118. FAX: 619-234-8345. E-mail: librarian@sdmaritime.org. Web Site: www.sdmaritime.com. *Coll Mgr,* Dr Kevin Sheehan; Staff 1 (Non-MLS 1)
Founded 1977
Library Holdings: Bk Titles 7,500; Bk Vols 7,800; Per Subs 15
Special Collections: Maritime Historical Technical & Commercial Magazines; Maritime History Coll, ephemera, flms, hist docs, photos, postcards, scrapbks, videos; Museum Ship Archives (Star of India, Berkeley, Medea, Pilot, Butcher Boy & Californian); Passenger Ship Memorabilia; Ship & Boat Plans & Blueprints; Ships' Logs. Oral History
Subject Interests: Nautical, Pacific Ocean
Function: For res purposes

Restriction: Pub use on premises
Friends of the Library Group

S MINGEI INTERNATIONAL MUSEUM*, Frances Hamilton White Art Reference Library, 1439 El Prado, 92101-1617. SAN 373-1359. Tel: 619-239-0003, Ext 132. FAX: 619-239-0605. E-mail: library@mingei.org. Web Site: www.mingei.org/education/library. *Libr Mgr,* Kristi Ehrig-Burgess
Library Holdings: Bk Vols 9,000; Videos 200
Special Collections: Chinese Textiles; Florence Temko Paper Coll; Indonesian Coll; Japanese Ceramics; Meiers Mexico Coll; V'Ann Cornelius Origami Book Coll
Subject Interests: Baskets, Ceramics, Clay, Folk art, Glass, Metals, Sculpture, Textiles, Wood
Restriction: Mem only, Not a lending libr, Open to others by appt

S NATIONAL STEEL & SHIPBUILDING CO*, Engineering Library, 7470 Mission Valley Rd, 92108. SAN 301-3383. Tel: 619-544-8644. FAX: 619-544-3543. Web Site: www.nassco.com. *Tech Serv Librn,* Kathy M Baker
Library Holdings: Bk Vols 3,000

C NATIONAL UNIVERSITY LIBRARY*, 9393 Lightwave Ave, 92123-1447. SAN 301-3391. Tel: 858-541-7900. Interlibrary Loan Service Tel: 858-541-7909. Automation Services Tel: 858-541-7911. Toll Free Tel: 800-628-8648, Ext 7900. FAX: 858-541-7994. Interlibrary Loan Service FAX: 858-541-7986, 858-541-7993. Administration FAX: 858-541-7991. E-mail: refdesk@nu.edu. Web Site: library.nu.edu. *Dir, Libr Serv,* Anne Marie Secord; Tel: 858-541-7913, E-mail: asecord@nu.edu; *Assoc Dir, Assessment & Tech Serv,* Ed Jones; Tel: 858-541-7920, E-mail: ejones@nu.edu; *Assoc Dir, Coll & Acces Serv,* Betty Kellogg; Tel: 858-541-7944, E-mail: bkellogg@nu.edu; *Assoc Dir, Instruction, Outreach & Info Serv,* Robin Lockerby; Tel: 858-541-7945, E-mail: rlock@nu.edu; *Assoc Dir, Multimedia Serv,* Phil Oels; Tel: 858-541-7942, E-mail: poels@nu.edu; *Supvr, Access Serv,* Patrick Pemberton; E-mail: ppembert@nu.edu; *Acq, Supvr,* Rose Elkins; Tel: 858-541-7918, Fax: 858-541-7997, E-mail: relkins@nu.edu. Subject Specialists: *Communications, Media,* Phil Oels; Staff 17 (MLS 14, Non-MLS 3)
Founded 1975. Enrl 17,011; Fac 3,114; Highest Degree: Master
Jul 2010-Jun 2011. Mats Exp $2,016,871, Books $395,713, Per/Ser (Incl. Access Fees) $290,384, Micro $37,253, AV Mat $65,503, Electronic Ref Mat (Incl. Access Fees) $1,228,018. Sal $1,596,171
Library Holdings: AV Mats 19,091; Bks on Deafness & Sign Lang 373; CDs 574; DVDs 3,955; e-books 154,750; e-journals 36,801; Electronic Media & Resources 3,040; Microforms 412,000; Bk Titles 158,163; Bk Vols 218,729; Per Subs 1,035; Videos 5,780
Special Collections: Adult Learners
Automation Activity & Vendor Info: (Acquisitions) SirsiDynix; (Cataloging) SirsiDynix; (Circulation) SirsiDynix; (Course Reserve) SirsiDynix; (ILL) OCLC; (Media Booking) Dymaxion; (OPAC) SirsiDynix; (Serials) SirsiDynix
Database Vendor: ABC-CLIO, Alexander Street Press, American Psychological Association (APA), Backstage Library Works, Baker & Taylor, Cambridge Scientific Abstracts, Checkpoint Systems, Inc, Children's Literature Comprehensive Database Company (CLCD), Cinahl, College Source, CQ Press, CRC Press/Taylor & Francis Group, CredoReference, Dun & Bradstreet, Ebooks Corporation, ebrary, EBSCO Information Services, EBSCOhost, Elsevier, Emerald, Ex Libris Group, Gale Cengage Learning, IEEE (Institute of Electrical & Electronics Engineers), infoUSA, Ingram Library Services, ISI Web of Knowledge, JSTOR, LearningExpress, LexisNexis, Medianet, Medline, Mergent Online, OCLC, OVID Technologies, Oxford Online, Project MUSE, ProQuest, PubMed, ReferenceUSA, Safari Books Online, Sage, ScienceDirect, SerialsSolutions, SirsiDynix, Springer-Verlag, Springshare, LLC, Standard & Poor's, Thomson - Web of Science, YBP Library Services
Wireless access
Function: Computers for patron use, Doc delivery serv, Electronic databases & coll, Exhibits, ILL available, Mail & tel request accepted, Online cat, Online info literacy tutorials on the web & in blackboard, Online ref, Outreach serv, Outside serv via phone, mail, e-mail & web, Ref serv available, Ref serv in person, Web-catalog
Partic in Statewide California Electronic Library Consortium (SCELC)
Special Services for the Deaf - Assisted listening device; Assistive tech; Bks on deafness & sign lang; Closed caption videos; Coll on deaf educ
Special Services for the Blind - Ednalite Hi-Vision scope
Open Mon-Thurs 10-10, Fri 10-6, Sat 8:30-5, Sun 10-5
Restriction: Circ privileges for students & alumni only, Open to pub for ref only, Open to students, fac & staff, Pub use on premises

C POINT LOMA NAZARENE UNIVERSITY, Ryan Library, 3900 Lomaland Dr, 92106-2899. SAN 301-3405. Tel: 619-849-2355. Circulation Tel: 619-849-2312. Interlibrary Loan Service Tel: 619-849-2262. Reference Tel: 619-849-2337. Administration Tel: 619-849-2338. FAX: 619-222-0711. E-mail: reflib@pointloma.edu. Web Site: www.pointloma.edu/RyanLibrary. *Dir,* Frank Quinn; E-mail: frankquinn@pointloma.edu; *Cat, Syst Coordr,* Anne Elizabeth Powell; *Bibliog Instr, Online Serv, Ref,* Douglas Fruehling; *Bibliog Instr, Online Serv, Ref,* Denise Nelson; *Bibliog Instr, Online Serv, Ref,* Beryl Pagan; Staff 11 (MLS 6, Non-MLS 5)
Founded 1902. Enrl 3,445; Highest Degree: Master
Library Holdings: Bk Vols 165,000; Per Subs 613
Special Collections: Armenian-Wesleyan Theological Library; Religion (Holiness Authors)
Subject Interests: Relig
Automation Activity & Vendor Info: (OPAC) Innovative Interfaces, Inc
Wireless access
Partic in Coop Libr Agency for Syst & Servs; OCLC Online Computer Library Center, Inc; Southern California Theological Library Association (SCATLA); Statewide California Electronic Library Consortium (SCELC)

M RADY CHILDREN'S HOSPITAL - SAN DIEGO*, Health Sciences Library, 3020 Children's Way, Mailcode 5043, 92123-4282. SAN 325-0369. Tel: 858-966-7474. FAX: 858-966-4934. E-mail: library@rchsd.org. Web Site: www.rchsd.org. *Med Librn,* Charlotte McClamma; E-mail: cmcclamma@rchsd.org; Staff 1 (MLS 1)
Founded 1955
Jul 2009-Jun 2010 Income $192,775. Mats Exp $50,000, Per/Ser (Incl. Access Fees) $18,000, Electronic Ref Mat (Incl. Access Fees) $32,000. Sal $69,900
Library Holdings: AV Mats 291; CDs 54; Bk Titles 2,744; Bk Vols 1,379; Per Subs 237
Subject Interests: Pediatrics
Automation Activity & Vendor Info: (Cataloging) Innovative Interfaces, Inc; (Circulation) Innovative Interfaces, Inc; (OPAC) Innovative Interfaces, Inc; (Serials) Innovative Interfaces, Inc
Partic in Medical Library Association (MLA); Medical Library Group of Southern California & Arizona (MLGSCA); National Network of Libraries of Medicine
Open Mon-Fri 8-4:30

S SAN DIEGO AERO-SPACE MUSEUM, INC*, N Paul Whittier Historical Aviation Library, 2001 Pan American Plaza, Balboa Park, 92101-1636. SAN 321-2653. Tel: 619-234-8291, Ext 125. FAX: 619-233-4526. E-mail: dseracini@sdasm.org. Web Site: www.sandiegoairandspace.org. *Libr Dir,* Katrina Pescador; Tel: 619-234-8291, Ext 123, E-mail: kpescador@sdasm.org; *Librn,* Pamela Gay; Tel: 619-234-8291, Ext 126, E-mail: pgay@sdasm.org; *Archivist,* Alan Renga; Staff 2 (MLS 2)
Founded 1978
Library Holdings: Bk Titles 24,000; Bk Vols 24,500; Per Subs 18
Special Collections: Air Mail Pioneers (Edwin Cooper Coll); Convair Corporate Files; Ed Heinemann Coll; Flying Cars (T P Hall Coll); Flying Wings Engineering (Wilhelm F Schult Coll); Frank T Courtney, Early Birds; George E A Hallett, Adm Marc Mitscher, John J Montgomery, Waldo D Waterman; Gliding & Soaring (Waldo Waterman Coll); John & Helen Sloan (Fokker); Ray Fife & Tex LaGrone Coll; RH Fleet Coll (Consolidated); Ryan Aeronautical Libr Coll
Subject Interests: Aerospace, Aviation, Mil aircraft
Function: Archival coll, For res purposes, Photocopying/Printing, Res libr, Telephone ref
Restriction: Non-circulating to the pub, Open by appt only, Open to others by appt, Open to researchers by request, Restricted borrowing privileges, Staff & prof res

J SAN DIEGO CITY COLLEGE*, Learning Resource Center, 1313 Park Blvd, 92101-4712. SAN 301-3421. Tel: 619-388-3421. FAX: 619-388-3410. Web Site: www.sdcity.edu. *Head Librn,* Cecilia Cheung; Tel: 619-388-3873; *Instrul Serv Librn,* Carol Withers; *Ref,* Jose Salgado; Staff 6 (MLS 6)
Founded 1916. Enrl 13,280; Fac 295
Library Holdings: Bk Vols 70,000; Per Subs 225
Automation Activity & Vendor Info: (Cataloging) SirsiDynix; (Circulation) SirsiDynix
Open Mon-Thurs 8am-9:50pm, Fri 8-4:20, Sat 10-2
Friends of the Library Group

P SAN DIEGO COUNTY LIBRARY*, 5560 Overland Ave, Ste 110, 92123. Tel: 858-694-2415. Circulation Tel: 858-505-6353. Interlibrary Loan Service Tel: 858-694-2484. Reference Tel: 619-588-3715, 760-643-5130. FAX: 858-495-5981. Web Site: www.sdcl.org. *Dir,* Jose A Aponte; Tel: 858-694-2389, Fax: 858-495-5658, E-mail: jose.aponte@sdcounty.ca.gov; *Dep Dir,* Susan Moore; Tel: 858-694-2448, E-mail: susan.moore@sdcounty.ca.gov; *Dep Dir,* Donna Ohr; E-mail: donna.ohr@sdcounty.ca.gov; *Principal Librn, Prog Serv,* Angelica Fortin; Tel: 858-694-2370, E-mail: angelica.fortin@sdcounty.ca.gov; *Principal Librn, Tech Serv,* Robin Isicson; Tel: 858-694-2446, E-mail: robin.isicson@sdcounty.ca.gov; Staff 316 (MLS 75, Non-MLS 241)
Founded 1913. Pop 1,091,536; Circ 10,788,181
Jul 2009-Jun 2010 Income (Main Library and Branch(s)) $33,722,859, State $558,085, Federal $24,247, Locally Generated Income $31,389,395,

Other $1,751,132. Mats Exp $2,996,157, Books $1,308,718, Per/Ser (Incl. Access Fees) $163,967, AV Mat $1,443,781, Electronic Ref Mat (Incl. Access Fees) $79,691. Sal $13,473,763 (Prof $6,021,299)
Library Holdings: Audiobooks 46,807; AV Mats 303,463; CDs 50,150; DVDs 149,459; e-books 3,611; Large Print Bks 30,647; Microforms 9,234; Bk Titles 369,365; Bk Vols 1,270,103; Per Subs 2,969; Videos 8,478
Special Collections: African Languages; Arabic; Armenian; Cantonese; French; German; Greek; Hebrew; Hindi; Hmong; Italian; Japanese; Korean; Laotian; Mandarin; Miao; Mon-Khmer, Cambodian; Pashto; Persian; Portuguese; Punjabi; Russian; Scandinavian Languages; Spanish; Tagalog; Thai; Urdu; Vietnamese
Automation Activity & Vendor Info: (Acquisitions) Innovative Interfaces, Inc - Millenium; (Cataloging) Innovative Interfaces, Inc - Millenium; (Circulation) Innovative Interfaces, Inc - Millenium; (ILL) Innovative Interfaces, Inc - Millenium; (Media Booking) Innovative Interfaces, Inc - Millenium; (OPAC) Innovative Interfaces, Inc - Millenium
Database Vendor: ABC-CLIO, EBSCO Information Services, EBSCOhost, Gale Cengage Learning, infoUSA, Innovative Interfaces, Inc, Innovative Interfaces, Inc, Newsbank, OCLC FirstSearch, OCLC WebJunction, OCLC WorldShare Interlibrary Loan, Overdrive, Inc, ProQuest, TumbleBookLibrary, World Book Online
Wireless access
Publications: Library Calendar of Events (Monthly); Library Services Brochures; Library User's Guide
Partic in Serra Cooperative Library System
Special Services for the Blind - Assistive/Adapted tech devices, equip & products
Friends of the Library Group

Branches: 33

ALPINE BRANCH, 2130 Arnold Way, Alpine, 91901, SAN 334-2603. Tel: 619-445-4221. FAX: 619-445-4856. *Br Mgr,* Elisabeth Newbold; E-mail: elisabeth.newbold@sdcounty.ca.gov
Pop 15,588; Circ 112,999
Library Holdings: Bk Vols 22,554
Open Tues & Thurs 9:30-8, Wed 9:30-6, Fri & Sat 9:30-5
Friends of the Library Group

BONITA-SUNNYSIDE BRANCH, 4375 Bonita Rd, Bonita, 91902-2698, SAN 334-2638. Tel: 619-475-4642. FAX: 619-475-4366. *Br Mgr,* Marisa Lowe; Tel: 619-475-3867, E-mail: marisa.lowe@sdcounty.ca.gov
Pop 14,294; Circ 294,010
Library Holdings: Bk Vols 44,103
Open Mon & Tues 9:30-8, Wed & Thurs 9:30-6, Fri & Sat 9:30-5, Sun 12-5
Friends of the Library Group

BORREGO SPRINGS BRANCH, 587 Palm Canyon Dr, Ste 125, Borrego Springs, 92004. (Mail add: PO Box 685, Borrego Springs, 92004-0685), SAN 334-2662. Tel: 760-767-5761. FAX: 760-767-3619. *Br Mgr,* Eric Robinson; E-mail: Eric.Robinson@sdcounty.ca.gov
Pop 4,971; Circ 47,777
Library Holdings: Bk Vols 13,876
Open Tues & Thurs 9-6, Wed 12-8, Fri & Sat 9-5
Friends of the Library Group

CAMPO-MORENA VILLAGE BRANCH, 31356 Hwy 94, Campo, 91906-3112. (Mail add: PO Box 97, Campo, 91906-0097), SAN 334-2697. Tel: 619-478-5945. FAX: 619-478-2446. *Br Mgr,* Keith Davis; E-mail: Keith.Davis@sdcounty.ca.gov
Pop 3,710; Circ 46,700
Library Holdings: Bk Vols 13,819
Open Tues & Wed 9-6, Thurs 12-8, Fri 9-5, Sat 9-4
Friends of the Library Group

CARDIFF BRANCH, 2081 Newcastle Ave, Cardiff, 92007-1724, SAN 334-3480. Tel: 760-753-4027. FAX: 760-753-4267. *Br Mgr,* Gabriel Aguirre; E-mail: gabriel.aguirre@sdcounty.ca.gov
Pop 17,291; Circ 123,972
Library Holdings: Bk Vols 31,231
Open Mon & Tues 9:30-6, Wed & Thurs 9:30-8, Fri & Sat 9:30-5
Friends of the Library Group

CASA DE ORO, 9805 Campo Rd, No 180, Spring Valley, 91977-1477, SAN 334-2727. Tel: 619-463-3236. FAX: 619-463-8670. *Br Mgr,* Allyson O'Brien; E-mail: allyson.obrien@sdcounty.ca.gov
Pop 23,634; Circ 136,056
Library Holdings: Bk Vols 36,374
Open Mon & Wed 9:30-6, Tues & Thurs 9:30-8, Fri & Sat 9:30-5
Friends of the Library Group

CREST, 105 Juanita Lane, El Cajon, 92021-4399, SAN 334-2786. Tel: 619-442-7083. FAX: 619-442-4972. *Br Mgr,* Paula Soltero; E-mail: Paula.Soltero@sdcounty.ca.gov
Pop 7,954; Circ 30,653
Library Holdings: Bk Vols 12,998
Open Tues 12-8, Wed & Thurs 9:30-6, Fri 9:30-5, Sat 9:30-3

DEL MAR BRANCH, 1309 Camino del Mar, Del Mar, 92014-2693, SAN 334-2816. Tel: 858-755-1666. FAX: 858-755-8734. *Br Mgr,* Polly Cipparrone; E-mail: Polly.Cipparrone@sdcounty.ca.gov
Pop 4,780; Circ 140,089
Library Holdings: Bk Vols 32,184
Open Tues 9:30-6, Wed & Thurs 9:30-8, Fri & Sat 9:30-5, Sun 12-5
Friends of the Library Group

DESCANSO BRANCH, 9545 River Dr, Descanso, 91916. (Mail add: PO Box 185, Descanso, 91916-0185), SAN 334-2840. Tel: 619-445-5279. FAX: 619-445-4891. *Br Mgr,* Christine Buckmaster; E-mail: Christine.Buckmaster@sdcounty.ca.gov
Pop 2,877; Circ 38,917
Library Holdings: Bk Vols 11,715
Open Tues & Wed 9-6, Thurs 12-8, Fri 9-5, Sat 9-4
Friends of the Library Group

EL CAJON BRANCH, 201 E Douglas, El Cajon, 92020, SAN 334-2875. Tel: 619-588-3718. Reference Tel: 619-588-3706, 619-588-3715. FAX: 619-588-3701. *Br Mgr,* Hildie Kraus; Tel: 619-588-3708, E-mail: hildie.kraus@sdcounty.ca.gov
Pop 103,860; Circ 713,517
Library Holdings: Bk Vols 127,495
Open Mon-Thurs 9:30-8, Fri & Sat 9:30-5, Sun 12-5
Friends of the Library Group

ENCINITAS BRANCH, 540 Cornish Dr, Encinitas, 92024-4599, SAN 334-2905. Tel: 760-753-7376. FAX: 760-753-0582. *Br Mgr,* Sheila Crssby; Tel: 760-634-6451, E-mail: Sheila.Crosby@sdcounty.ca.gov
Pop 47,093; Circ 632,659
Library Holdings: Bk Vols 90,272
Open Mon-Thurs 9:30-8, Fri & Sat 9:30-5, Sun 12-5
Friends of the Library Group

FALLBROOK BRANCH, 113 S Main Ave, Fallbrook, 92028, SAN 334-293X. Tel: 760-728-2373. FAX: 760-728-4731. *Br Mgr,* Margo Smart; E-mail: Margo.Smart@sdcounty.ca.gov
Pop 49,961; Circ 404,064
Library Holdings: Bk Vols 53,208
Open Mon, Wed, Fri & Sat 9:30-6, Tues & Thurs 9:30-8, Sun 12-5
Friends of the Library Group

FLETCHER HILLS, 576 Garfield Ave, El Cajon, 92020-2792, SAN 334-2964. Tel: 619-466-1132. FAX: 619-466-4682. *Br Mgr,* Rebekah Sanders; E-mail: Rebekah.Sanders@sdcounty.ca.gov
Pop 16,364; Circ 102,427
Library Holdings: Bk Vols 24,457
Open Tues & Thurs 9:30-6, Wed 12-8, Fri & Sat 9:30-5
Friends of the Library Group

4S RANCH, 10433 Reserve Dr, 92127. Tel: 858-673-4697. FAX: 858-673-1629. *Br Mgr,* June Zhou; E-mail: june.zhou@sdcounty.ca.gov
Pop 13,309; Circ 365,513
Library Holdings: Bk Vols 46,955
Open Mon & Thurs 9:30-6, Tues & Wed 9:30-8, Fri & Sat 9:30-5
Friends of the Library Group

IMPERIAL BEACH BRANCH, 810 Imperial Beach Blvd, Imperial Beach, 91932-2798, SAN 334-2999. Tel: 619-424-6981. FAX: 619-424-8749. *Br Mgr,* June Engel; E-mail: june.engel@sdcounty.ca.gov
Pop 28,351; Circ 180,560
Library Holdings: Bk Vols 34,767
Open Mon & Wed 9:30-8, Tues & Thurs 9:30-6, Fri & Sat 9:30-5
Friends of the Library Group

JACUMBA BRANCH, 44605 Old Hwy 80, Jacumba, 91934, SAN 334-3022. Tel: 619-766-4608. FAX: 619-766-9206. *Br Mgr,* Sarah Misquez; E-mail: Sarah.Misquez@sdcounty.ca.gov
Pop 2,053; Circ 40,879
Library Holdings: Bk Vols 10,867
Open Tues 12-8, Wed & Thurs 9-6, Fri 9-5, Sat 9-4
Friends of the Library Group

JULIAN BRANCH, 1850 Hwy 78, Julian, 92036. (Mail add: PO Box 909, Julian, 92036-0909), SAN 334-3057. Tel: 760-765-0370. FAX: 760-765-2748. *Br Mgr,* Colleen Baker; E-mail: colleen.baker@sdcounty.ca.gov
Pop 4,275; Circ 99,942
Library Holdings: Bk Vols 28,474
Open Tues 9-8, Wed & Thurs 9-6, Fri & Sat 9-5
Friends of the Library Group

LA MESA BRANCH, 8074 Allison Ave, La Mesa, 91941-5001, SAN 334-3111. Tel: 619-469-2151. FAX: 619-697-3751. *Br Mgr,* Heather Pisani-Kristl; E-mail: Heather.Pisani-Kristl@sdcounty.ca.gov
Pop 59,544; Circ 711,643
Library Holdings: Bk Vols 90,918
Open Mon-Thurs 9:30-8, Fri & Sat 9:30-5, Sun 12-5
Friends of the Library Group

LAKESIDE BRANCH, 9839 Vine St, Lakeside, 92040-3199, SAN 334-3081. Tel: 619-443-1811. FAX: 619-443-8002. *Br Mgr,* Marisa Lowe; E-mail: Marisa.Lowe@sdcounty.ca.gov
Pop 54,906; Circ 215,872
Library Holdings: Bk Vols 47,377
Open Mon & Thurs 9:30-6, Tue & Wed 9:30-8, Fri & Sat 9:30-5
Friends of the Library Group

LEMON GROVE BRANCH, 3001 School Lane, Lemon Grove, 91945, SAN 334-3146. Tel: 619-463-9819. FAX: 619-463-8069. *Br Mgr,* Amanda Heller; E-mail: Amanda.Heller@sdcounty.ca.gov
Pop 30,691; Circ 157,754

Library Holdings: Bk Vols 49,134
Open Mon 9:30-6, Tues & Wed 9:30-8, Fri & Sat 9:30-5
Friends of the Library Group

LINCOLN ACRES, 2725 Granger Ave, National City, 91950-0168, SAN 334-3170. Tel: 619-475-9880. FAX: 619-475-4382. *Br Mgr,* Jose Ocadiz; E-mail: jose.ocadiz@sdcounty.ca.gov
Pop 2,097; Circ 28,652
Library Holdings: Bk Vols 10,068
Open Tues 12-8, Wed & Thurs 9:30-6, Fri & Sat 9:30-5
Friends of the Library Group

PINE VALLEY BRANCH, 28804 Old Hwy 80, Pine Valley, 91962. (Mail add: PO Box 580, Pine Valley, 91962-0580), SAN 334-3200. Tel: 619-473-8022. FAX: 619-473-9638. *Br Mgr,* Sherry Markham; E-mail: sherry.markham@sdcounty.ca.gov
Pop 2,797; Circ 50,856
Library Holdings: Bk Vols 11,222
Open Tues 12-8, Wed & Thurs 9-6, Fri 9-5, Sat 9-4
Friends of the Library Group

POTRERO BRANCH, 24883 Potrero Valley Rd, Potrero, 91963-0051. (Mail add: PO Box 70, Potrero, 91963-0070), SAN 334-3235. Tel: 619-478-5978. FAX: 619-478-2695. *Br Mgr,* Candy Bonner; E-mail: candy.bonner@sdcounty.ca.gov
Pop 228; Circ 61,098
Library Holdings: Bk Vols 16,795
Open Tues & Thurs 9-6, Wed 12-8, Fri 9-5, Sat 9-4
Friends of the Library Group

POWAY BRANCH, 13137 Poway Rd, Poway, 92064-4687, SAN 334-326X. Tel: 858-513-2900. FAX: 858-513-2922. *Br Mgr,* Penny Taylor; E-mail: Penny.Taylor@sdcounty.ca.gov
Pop 51,391; Circ 638,494
Library Holdings: Bk Vols 121,457
Open Mon-Thurs 9:30-8, Fri & Sat 9:30-5, Sun 12-5
Friends of the Library Group

RAMONA BRANCH, 1275 Main St, Ramona, 92065, SAN 334-3294. Tel: 760-738-2434. FAX: 760-738-2475. *Br Mgr,* Eleanor Slade; E-mail: eleanor.slade@sdcounty.ca.gov
Pop 35,904; Circ 178,060
Library Holdings: Bk Vols 42,116
Open Mon & Wed 9:30-6, Tues & Thurs 9:30-8, Fri & Sat 9:30-5
Friends of the Library Group

RANCHO SAN DIEGO, 11555 Via Rancho San Diego, El Cajon, 92019. Tel: 619-660-5370. FAX: 619-660-6327. *Br Mgr,* Brenna Ring; E-mail: brenna.ring@sdcounty.ca.gov
Founded 2002. Pop 47,956; Circ 390,868
Library Holdings: Bk Vols 68,984
Open Mon & Wed 9:30-6, Tues & Thurs 9:30-8, Fri & Sat 9:30-5, Sun 12-5
Friends of the Library Group

RANCHO SANTA FE BRANCH, 17040 Avenida de Acacias, Rancho Santa Fe, 92067. (Mail add: PO Box 115, Rancho Santa Fe, 92067-0115), SAN 334-3324. Tel: 858-756-2512. FAX: 858-756-3485. *Br Mgr,* Jo Moeller; E-mail: josephine.moeller@sdcounty.ca.gov
Pop 13,424; Circ 85,187
Library Holdings: Bk Vols 39,623
Open Mon-Sat 9-5
Friends of the Library Group

SAN MARCOS BRANCH, Two Civic Center Dr, San Marcos, 92069-2949, SAN 334-3359. Tel: 760-891-3000. FAX: 760-891-3015. *Br Mgr,* Ruth Ketchum; Tel: 760-891-3008, E-mail: Ruth.Ketchum@sdcounty.ca.gov
Pop 113,292; Circ 667,137
Library Holdings: Bk Vols 92,576
Open Mon-Thurs 9:30-8, Fri & Sat 9:30-5, Sun 12-5
Friends of the Library Group

SANTEE BRANCH, 9225 Carlton Hills Blvd, No 17, Santee, 92071-3192, SAN 334-3383. Tel: 619-448-1863. FAX: 619-448-1497. *Br Mgr,* Cheryl Cosart; E-mail: Cheryl.Cosart@sdcounty.ca.gov
Pop 58,909; Circ 403,073
Library Holdings: Bk Vols 66,941
Open Mon-Thurs 9:30-8, Fri & Sat 9:30-5, Sun 12-5
Friends of the Library Group

SOLANA BEACH BRANCH, 157 Stevens Ave, Solana Beach, 92075-1873, SAN 334-3413. Tel: 858-755-1404. FAX: 858-755-9327. *Br Mgr,* Pat Tirona; E-mail: Pat.Tirona@sdcounty.ca.gov
Pop 14,546; Circ 276,309
Library Holdings: Bk Vols 67,472
Open Mon & Thurs (Winter) 7:30-6, Tues & Wed 7:30-8, Fri 7:30-5, Sat 9:30-5; Mon & Thurs (Summer) 9:30-6, Tues & Wed 9:30-8, Fri & Sat 9:30-5
Friends of the Library Group

SPRING VALLEY BRANCH, 836 Kempton St, Spring Valley, 91977, SAN 334-3448. Tel: 619-463-3006. FAX: 619-463-8917. *Br Mgr,* Jennifer Teitelbaum; E-mail: Jennifer.Teitelbaum@sdcounty.ca.gov
Pop 36,810; Circ 183,904
Library Holdings: Bk Vols 45,036
Open Mon & Tues 9:30-8, Wed & Thurs 9:30-6, Fri & Sat 9:30-5
Friends of the Library Group

VALLEY CENTER BRANCH, 29200 Cole Grade Rd, Valley Center, 92082-5880, SAN 334-3472. Tel: 760-749-1305. FAX: 760-749-1764. *Br Mgr,* Rebecca Lynn; E-mail: Rebecca.Lynn@sdcounty.ca.gov
Pop 15,236; Circ 176,570
Library Holdings: Bk Vols 49,437
Open Mon-Thurs 9:30-8, Fri & Sat 9:30-5
Friends of the Library Group

VISTA BRANCH, 700 Eucalyptus Ave, Vista, 92084-6245, SAN 334-3502. Tel: 760-643-5100. FAX: 760-643-5127. *Br Mgr,* Cecilia Rincon; Tel: 760-643-5117, E-mail: Cecilia.Rincon@sdcounty.ca.gov
Pop 109,618; Circ 792,750
Library Holdings: Bk Vols 152,495
Open Mon-Thurs 9:30-8, Fri & Sat 9:30-5, Sun 12-5
Friends of the Library Group

Bookmobiles: 2. Circ Servs Mgr, Bertha Huertero. Bk titles 7,500

S SAN DIEGO FAMILY HISTORY CENTER*, Family History Center, 4195 Camino Del Rio S, 92108. SAN 329-2118. Tel: 619-584-7668. FAX: 619-584-1225. *Dir,* M Lopez
Founded 1966
Library Holdings: Bk Vols 13,000
Special Services for the Deaf - Staff with knowledge of sign lang
Open Tues, Fri & Sat 10-3, Wed & Thurs 10-9

S SAN DIEGO HISTORY CENTER*, Balboa Park, 1649 El Prado, Ste 3, 92101. SAN 301-3448. Tel: 619-232-6203. Information Services Tel: 619-232-6203, Ext 117. FAX: 619-232-1059. Web Site: www.sandiegohistory.org. *Dir, Photog Coll,* Chris Travers; Tel: 619-232-6203, Ext 116, E-mail: chris.travers@sandiegohistory.org; *Archivist,* Jane Kenealy; E-mail: jane.kenealy@sandiegohistory.org; *Photo Archivist,* Carol Myers; Tel: 616-232-6203, Ext 127, E-mail: carol.myers@sandiegohistory.org; *Asst Archivist,* Lauren Rasmussen; Tel: 619-232-6203, Ext 123, E-mail: Lrasmussen@sandiegohistory.org. Subject Specialists: *Photog,* Chris Travers; *Hist,* Jane Kenealy; *Photog,* Carol Myers; *Hist,* Lauren Rasmussen; Staff 3 (Non-MLS 3)
Founded 1929
Library Holdings: Bk Titles 10,000; Per Subs 30
Special Collections: Architectural Drawings; Booth Historical Photograph Coll; City, County & Superior Court Public Records; Ephemera Coll; Institute of History Coll; Manuscript Coll; Map Coll; Oral History Coll; Scrapbook Coll. Oral History
Subject Interests: Local hist
Automation Activity & Vendor Info: (Cataloging) Sydney; (OPAC) Sydney
Function: Photocopying/Printing, Ref serv available, Res libr, Wheelchair accessible
Publications: Guide to the Architectural Records Collection (2003) (Research guide); Guide to the Photograph Collection (1998) (Research guide); Guide to the Public Records Collection (Research guide); Journal of San Diego History
Open Wed-Sat 9:30-1
Restriction: Non-circulating, Not a lending libr, Open to pub for ref only, Photo ID required for access

GL SAN DIEGO LAW LIBRARY*, 1105 Front St, 92101-3904. SAN 301-343X. Tel: 619-531-3900. FAX: 619-238-7716. Web Site: www.sdcpll.org. *Dir of Libr,* John Adkins; Tel: 619-531-3904, E-mail: jadkins@sdlawlibrary.org; Staff 30 (MLS 8, Non-MLS 22)
Founded 1891
Library Holdings: Bk Vols 221,975; Per Subs 298
Special Collections: California Appellate Court Briefs since 1895; California Supreme Court Briefs 1895; Local Legal History
Automation Activity & Vendor Info: (Cataloging) Innovative Interfaces, Inc; (Circulation) Innovative Interfaces, Inc
Database Vendor: Innovative Interfaces, Inc
Publications: Guide to Collections & Services; Newsletters
Partic in Coop Libr Agency for Syst & Servs; Dialog Corp; Lexis, OCLC Online Computer Libr Ctr, Inc; Westlaw
Open Mon-Thurs 8-6, Fri 8-5, Sat 10-5

Branches:

EAST COUNTY, 250 E Main, El Cajon, 92020-3941, SAN 321-9364. Tel: 619-441-4451. FAX: 619-441-0235. *Librn,* Carolyn Dulude
Library Holdings: Bk Vols 10,754
Open Mon-Fri 9-4

NORTH COUNTY, 325 S Melrose, Ste 300, Vista, 92081-6697, SAN 321-4117. Tel: 760-940-4386. FAX: 760-724-7694. *Librn,* Joan Allen-Hart; *Librn,* Pat Brown
Library Holdings: Bk Vols 20,176
Open Mon-Fri 8-5
Friends of the Library Group

SOUTH BAY, 500 Third Ave, Chula Vista, 91910-5617, SAN 321-4109. Tel: 619-691-4929. FAX: 619-427-7521. *Librn,* Rita Wagstaff
Library Holdings: Bk Vols 16,071
Open Mon-Fri 9-4

J SAN DIEGO MESA COLLEGE LIBRARY*, 7250 Mesa College Dr, 92111-4998. SAN 301-3456. Tel: 619-388-2695. Circulation Tel: 619-388-2696. Reference Tel: 619-388-2660. Administration Tel: 619-388-2799. FAX: 619-388-2922. Web Site: www.sdmesa.sdccd.net/library. *Chairperson,* Jack Forman; Tel: 619-388-2546, E-mail: jforman@sdccd.edu; *Instrul Serv Librn,* Val Ontell; Tel: 619-388-2549, E-mail: vontell@sdccd.edu; *AV Spec,* Jill Baker; Tel: 619-388-2655, E-mail: jibaker@sdccd.edu; *Coll Develop,* Devin Milner; Tel: 619-388-2547, E-mail: dmilner@sdccd.edu; *Online Serv,* Alison Steinberg; Tel: 619-388-2938, E-mail: asteinbe@sdccd.edu; *Per,* Jean Smith; Tel: 619-388-2550, E-mail: jesmith@sdccd.edu; *Tech Serv,* Roger Olson; Tel: 619-388-2548, E-mail: rolson@sdccd.edu; Staff 7 (MLS 7)
Founded 1963. Enrl 23,000; Fac 774; Highest Degree: Associate
Jul 2006-Jun 2007. Mats Exp $181,000, Books $105,000, Per/Ser (Incl. Access Fees) $50,000, Micro $10,000, AV Mat $16,000. Sal $1,711,597
Library Holdings: e-books 20,000; Bk Titles 112,000; Per Subs 250
Special Collections: Career Coll; ESL; Oversize Books
Automation Activity & Vendor Info: (Cataloging) SirsiDynix; (Circulation) SirsiDynix; (Course Reserve) SirsiDynix; (ILL) OCLC; (OPAC) SirsiDynix; (Serials) SirsiDynix
Database Vendor: EBSCOhost, ProQuest
Function: Art exhibits, Audio & video playback equip for onsite use, Computer training, Computers for patron use, Copy machines, Electronic databases & coll, Learning ctr, Online cat, Online info literacy tutorials on the web & in blackboard, Online ref, Online searches, Orientations, Photocopying/Printing, Tax forms, Telephone ref, Wheelchair accessible
Partic in San Diego Greater Metro Area Libr & Info Agency Coun
Open Mon-Thurs 7am-10pm, Fri 7-5, Sat 8-3
Restriction: Borrowing privileges limited to fac & registered students

J SAN DIEGO MIRAMAR COLLEGE*, Learning Resource Center, 10440 Black Mountain Rd, 92126-2999. SAN 301-3359. Tel: 619-388-7310. Reference Tel: 619-388-7316. FAX: 619-388-7918. Web Site: www.miramarcollege.net/library.asp. *Librn,* Mary K Hart; Tel: 619-388-7614, E-mail: mhart@sdccd.edu; *Librn,* Eric M Mosier; Tel: 619-388-7622, E-mail: emosier@sdccd.net; Staff 13 (MLS 5, Non-MLS 8)
Founded 1973. Enrl 11,105; Highest Degree: Associate
Library Holdings: e-books 8,437; Bk Vols 23,295; Per Subs 65
Special Collections: Law Library
Subject Interests: Automotive, Diesel, Emergency med, Fire sci, Law, Transportation
Automation Activity & Vendor Info: (Acquisitions) SirsiDynix; (Cataloging) SirsiDynix; (Circulation) SirsiDynix; (Course Reserve) SirsiDynix; (OPAC) SirsiDynix; (Serials) SirsiDynix
Database Vendor: Gale Cengage Learning, ProQuest, SirsiDynix
Partic in OCLC Online Computer Library Center, Inc

S SAN DIEGO MODEL RAILROAD MUSEUM*, Erwin Welsch Memorial Research Library, 1649 El Prado, 92101. SAN 374-5651. Tel: 619-696-0199. FAX: 619-696-0239. E-mail: library@sdmrm.org. Web Site: www.sdmrm.org. *Exec Dir,* Anthony Ridenour; *Librn,* James F Helt. Subject Specialists: *Railroad hist,* James F Helt; Staff 3 (Non-MLS 3)
Founded 1994
Library Holdings: Audiobooks 10; AV Mats 1,968; CDs 28; DVDs 256; Electronic Media & Resources 102; Bk Vols 4,168; Spec Interest Per Sub 921; Videos 1,274
Special Collections: Railroads Coll
Subject Interests: Railroads
Automation Activity & Vendor Info: (Acquisitions) LibraryWorld, Inc; (Cataloging) LibraryWorld, Inc
Database Vendor: LibraryWorld, Inc
Wireless access
Function: Archival coll, Audio & video playback equip for onsite use, CD-ROM, Copy machines, Electronic databases & coll, For res purposes, Free DVD rentals, Mail & tel request accepted, Online cat, Online ref, Online searches, Res libr, Scanner, VHS videos, Video lending libr
Open Tues-Fri 11-4, Sat & Sun 11-5
Restriction: Non-circulating, Not a lending libr, Open to pub for ref only, Ref only
Friends of the Library Group

S SAN DIEGO MUSEUM OF ART LIBRARY*, 1450 El Prado, 92101. (Mail add: PO Box 122107, 92112-2107), SAN 301-3464. Tel: 619-696-1958. FAX: 619-232-9367. E-mail: library@sdmart.org. Web Site: www.sdmart.org. *Mgr,* Dr James Grebl; Tel: 619-696-1959; *Asst Mgr,* Nancy G Emerson; E-mail: nemerson@sdmart.org; Staff 2 (Non-MLS 2)
Founded 1926
Library Holdings: Bk Vols 30,000; Per Subs 85
Special Collections: Books & Catalogues in Subject Area of Indian Miniature Painting (Binney Coll); Exhibition & Auction Catalogues Coll
Subject Interests: Art
Automation Activity & Vendor Info: (Cataloging) EOS International; (Circulation) EOS International; (OPAC) EOS International; (Serials) EOS International
Partic in OCLC Online Computer Library Center, Inc
Restriction: Authorized scholars by appt, Circulates for staff only

S SAN DIEGO MUSEUM OF MAN*, Scientific Library, Balboa Park, 1350 El Prado, 92101. SAN 301-3472. Tel: 619-239-2001. FAX: 619-239-2749. E-mail: museumofman@museumofman.org. Web Site: www.museumofman.org/scientific-library. *Chief Exec Officer,* Micah Parzen; Tel: 619-239-2001, Ext 14, E-mail: mparzen@museumofman.org
Founded 1915
Library Holdings: Bk Vols 33,000; Per Subs 300
Subject Interests: Anthrop, Archaeology, Egypt, Ethnology
Restriction: Open by appt only

S SAN DIEGO NATURAL HISTORY MUSEUM*, Research Library, Balboa Park, 1788 El Prado, 92101. (Mail add: PO Box 121390, 92112-1390), SAN 301-3480. Tel: 619-255-0225. FAX: 619-232-0248. E-mail: library@sdnhm.org. Web Site: www.sdnhm.org/research/library/index.html. *Dir,* Margaret Dykens; Staff 1 (MLS 1)
Founded 1874
Library Holdings: Bk Vols 56,000
Special Collections: Bird Paintings (Sutton & Brooks Coll); Geology & Paleontology (Anthony W Vodges Coll); Herpetology (Laurence Klauber Coll); Photo Archives; Wild Flower Paintings (Valentien Coll)
Subject Interests: Botany, Entomology, Herpetology, Mammals, Ornithology, Paleontology
Automation Activity & Vendor Info: (OPAC) LibraryWorld, Inc
Publications: Occasional Papers; Proceedings; Transactions & Memoirs superseded by Proceedings of the San Diego Society of Natural History 1990
Restriction: Open by appt only

P SAN DIEGO PUBLIC LIBRARY, Central Library, 330 Park Blvd, MS 17, 92101. SAN 334-3650. Tel: 619-236-5800. Interlibrary Loan Service Tel: 619-236-5823. FAX: 619-238-6639. E-mail: ereference@sandiego.gov, weblibrary@sandiego.gov. Web Site: www.sandiegolibrary.org. *Supv Librn,* Cynthia Shutler
Founded 1882. Pop 58,830; Circ 560,696
Library Holdings: Audiobooks 6,898; AV Mats 61,183; Bks on Deafness & Sign Lang 342; Braille Volumes 172; CDs 35,794; DVDs 18,998; e-books 56,052; Electronic Media & Resources 53; Large Print Bks 5,743; Microforms 214; Music Scores 23,693; Bk Titles 837,121; Bk Vols 1,049,909; Per Subs 2,463; Talking Bks 2; Videos 23,624
Special Collections: Society for American Baseball Research Coll (bks). State Document Depository; US Document Depository
Automation Activity & Vendor Info: (Acquisitions) SirsiDynix; (Cataloging) SirsiDynix; (Circulation) SirsiDynix; (OPAC) SirsiDynix
Database Vendor: Baker & Taylor, EBSCO Information Services, Facts on File, Gale Cengage Learning, JSTOR, Marcive, Inc, OCLC FirstSearch, Overdrive, Inc, Oxford Online, ProQuest, ReferenceUSA, Standard & Poor's, World Book Online
Wireless access
Function: Adult literacy prog, Art exhibits, Audiobks via web, Bilingual assistance for Spanish patrons, Bks on cassette, Bks on CD, Bus archives, CD-ROM, Children's prog, Citizenship assistance, Computer training, Computers for patron use, Copy machines, Digital talking bks, E-Reserves, Electronic databases & coll, Family literacy, Free DVD rentals, Games & aids for the handicapped, Govt ref serv, Handicapped accessible, Homebound delivery serv, Homework prog, ILL available, Large print keyboards, Libr develop, Magnifiers for reading, Music CDs, Newsp ref libr, Online cat, Online info literacy tutorials on the web & in blackboard, Online searches, OverDrive digital audio bks, Photocopying/Printing, Prog for adults, Prog for children & young adult, Pub access computers, Ref serv available, Spoken cassettes & CDs, Spoken cassettes & DVDs, Summer reading prog, Tax forms, Teen prog, Telephone ref, VHS videos, Web-catalog, Wheelchair accessible
Partic in Serra Cooperative Library System
Open Mon & Wed 12-8, Tues, Thurs & Fri 9:30-5:30, Sat 9:30-2:30, Sun 1-5
Friends of the Library Group
Branches: 35
ALLIED GARDENS/BENJAMIN, 5188 Zion St, 92120, SAN 334-374X. Tel: 619-533-3970. FAX: 619-533-3971. *Librn III,* Arianne Lee
Founded 1965. Pop 14,052; Circ 79,615
Library Holdings: Audiobooks 1,624; AV Mats 6,510; Bks on Deafness & Sign Lang 25; CDs 2,911; DVDs 3,069; Large Print Bks 598; Music Scores 15; Bk Titles 27,262; Bk Vols 28,614; Per Subs 91; Videos 3,340
Automation Activity & Vendor Info: (Course Reserve) SirsiDynix; (ILL) SirsiDynix; (Media Booking) SirsiDynix; (Serials) SirsiDynix

Open Mon, Thurs & Fri 9:30-5:30, Tues & Wed 12:30-8, Sat 9:30-2:30
Friends of the Library Group
BALBOA, 4255 Mt Abernathy Ave, 92117-5098, SAN 334-3685. Tel: 858-573-1390. FAX: 858-573-1391. *Librn IV,* Anna Gomez
Founded 1971. Pop 37,431; Circ 116,394
Library Holdings: Audiobooks 1,676; AV Mats 8,843; Bks on Deafness & Sign Lang 71; CDs 3,273; DVDs 4,100; Large Print Bks 394; Music Scores 30; Bk Titles 37,716; Bk Vols 41,110; Per Subs 91; Videos 5,264
Open Mon 12:30-5:30, Tues & Wed 12:30-8, Thurs & Fri 9:30-5:30, Sat 9:30-2:30
Friends of the Library Group
CARMEL MOUNTAIN RANCH, 12095 World Trade Dr, 92128, SAN 377-6808. Tel: 858-538-8181. FAX: 858-674-7372. *Librn IV,* Janet Yeager
Founded 1997. Pop 25,645; Circ 180,177
Library Holdings: Audiobooks 2,130; AV Mats 12,323; Bks on Deafness & Sign Lang 46; CDs 5,060; DVDs 6,070; Large Print Bks 407; Music Scores 29; Bk Titles 44,276; Bk Vols 50,605; Per Subs 73; Videos 6,856
Open Mon, Thurs & Fri 9:30-5:30, Tues & Wed 12:30-8, Sat 9:30-2:30
Friends of the Library Group
CARMEL VALLEY, 3919 Townsgate Dr, 92130, SAN 373-9228. Tel: 858-552-1668. FAX: 858-552-1672. *Librn IV,* Brenda Wegener
Founded 1993. Pop 36,707; Circ 339,573
Library Holdings: Audiobooks 4,420; AV Mats 18,281; Bks on Deafness & Sign Lang 55; CDs 7,986; DVDs 8,332; Large Print Bks 847; Music Scores 96; Bk Titles 70,476; Bk Vols 80,249; Per Subs 167; Videos 9,503
Open Mon, Thurs & Fri 9:30-5:30, Tues & Wed 12:30-8, Sat 9:30-2:30
Restriction: Authorized patrons
Friends of the Library Group
CITY HEIGHTS/WEINGART, 3795 Fairmount Ave, 92105, SAN 334-3839. Tel: 619-641-6100. FAX: 619-640-8902. TDD: 619-640-3842. *Librn IV,* Joseph Miesner
Founded 1998. Pop 55,909; Circ 130,244
Library Holdings: Audiobooks 1,368; AV Mats 15,626; Bks on Deafness & Sign Lang 40; CDs 2,665; DVDs 9,719; Large Print Bks 54; Music Scores 20; Bk Titles 48,450; Bk Vols 55,502; Per Subs 118; Talking Bks 1; Videos 12,410
Special Services for the Deaf - TDD equip
Open Mon, Thurs & Fri 9:30-5:30, Tues & Wed 12:30-8, Sat 9:30-2:30, Sun 1-5
Friends of the Library Group
CLAIREMONT, 2920 Burgener Blvd, 92110-1027, SAN 334-3774. Tel: 858-581-9935. FAX: 858-581-9936. *Librn III,* Glenn Risolo
Founded 1958. Pop 22,879; Circ 99,876
Library Holdings: Audiobooks 1,745; AV Mats 8,049; Bks on Deafness & Sign Lang 31; CDs 3,445; DVDs 3,985; Large Print Bks 609; Music Scores 8; Bk Titles 31,514; Bk Vols 33,281; Per Subs 106; Videos 4,396
Open Mon, Thurs & Fri 9:30-5:30, Tues & Wed 12:30-8, Sat 9:30-2:30
Friends of the Library Group
COLLEGE-ROLANDO, 6600 Montezuma Rd, 92115-2828, SAN 334-3804. Tel: 619-533-3902. FAX: 619-337-0027. *Br Mgr, Librn III,* Sara King
Founded 1955. Pop 49,646; Circ 104,134
Library Holdings: Audiobooks 1,948; AV Mats 12,435; Bks on Deafness & Sign Lang 43; CDs 4,253; DVDs 7,262; Large Print Bks 735; Music Scores 44; Bk Titles 44,942; Bk Vols 48,013; Per Subs 114; Videos 7,964
Open Mon, Thurs & Fri 9:30-5:30, Tues & Wed 12:30-8, Sat 9:30-2:30
Friends of the Library Group
KENSINGTON-NORMAL HEIGHTS, 4121 Adams Ave, 92116, SAN 334-4010. Tel: 619-533-3974. FAX: 619-533-3975. *Br Mgr,* Lynne Russo
Founded 1954. Pop 24,202; Circ 85,519
Library Holdings: Audiobooks 1,111; AV Mats 7,315; Bks on Deafness & Sign Lang 23; CDs 2,619; DVDs 3,876; Large Print Bks 174; Music Scores 38; Bk Titles 21,909; Bk Vols 23,565; Per Subs 65; Videos 4,498
Open Mon, Thurs & Fri 9:30-5:30, Tues & Wed 12:30-8, Sat 9:30-2:30
Friends of the Library Group
LA JOLLA/RIFORD, 7555 Draper Ave, La Jolla, 92037-4802, SAN 334-3863. Tel: 858-552-1657. FAX: 858-551-0519. *Br Mgr,* Shaun Briley
Founded 1989. Pop 28,002; Circ 179,409
Library Holdings: Audiobooks 3,756; AV Mats 18,116; Bks on Deafness & Sign Lang 64; CDs 7,823; DVDs 7,396; Large Print Bks 819; Music Scores 74; Bk Titles 89,135; Bk Vols 96,129; Per Subs 257; Videos 8,931
Special Services for the Deaf - TDD equip
Open Mon, Thurs & Fri 9:30-5:30, Tues & Wed 12-8, Sat 9:30-2:30, Sun 1-5
Friends of the Library Group
LINDA VISTA, 2160 Ulric St, 92111-6628, SAN 334-3898. Tel: 858-573-1399. FAX: 858-573-1398. *Br Mgr, Librn IV,* Jeff Davis
Founded 1987. Pop 30,285; Circ 125,091
Library Holdings: Audiobooks 1,662; AV Mats 16,036; Bks on Deafness & Sign Lang 30; CDs 5,093; DVDs 7,500; Large Print Bks 370; Music Scores 47; Bk Titles 43,357; Bk Vols 47,964; Per Subs 199; Videos 10,396
Open Mon, Thurs & Fri 9:30-5:30, Tues & Wed 12:30-8, Sat 9:30-2:30
Friends of the Library Group
LOGAN HEIGHTS, 567 S 28th St, 92113-2498, SAN 334-3928. Tel: 619-533-3968. FAX: 619-238-0387. *Librn IV,* Eileen Labrador
Founded 1927. Pop 28,113; Circ 80,755
Library Holdings: Audiobooks 1,447; AV Mats 12,138; Bks on Deafness & Sign Lang 48; CDs 4,374; DVDs 7,048; Large Print Bks 511; Music Scores 47; Bk Titles 58,591; Bk Vols 68,104; Per Subs 136; Videos 7,631
Open Mon, Thurs & Fri 9:30-5:30, Tues & Wed 12:30-8, Sat 9:30-2:30
Friends of the Library Group
MIRA MESA, 8405 New Salem St, 92126-2398, SAN 334-3952. Tel: 858-538-8165. FAX: 858-695-2624. TDD: 858-271-7313. *Br Mgr,* Barbara Schwartz
Founded 1994. Pop 77,790; Circ 274,969
Library Holdings: Audiobooks 2,479; AV Mats 18,280; Bks on Deafness & Sign Lang 71; CDs 6,043; DVDs 9,618; Large Print Bks 1,079; Music Scores 115; Bk Titles 71,153; Bk Vols 83,375; Per Subs 199; Videos 11,739
Special Services for the Deaf - TDD equip
Open Mon 12:30-5:30, Tues & Wed 12:30-8, Thurs & Fri 9:30-5:30, Sat 9:30-2:30, Sun 1-5
Friends of the Library Group
MISSION HILLS, 925 W Washington St, 92103-1895, SAN 334-3987. Tel: 619-692-4910. FAX: 619-692-4911. *Br Mgr, Librn III,* Stephen Wheeler
Founded 1961. Pop 19,676; Circ 126,396
Library Holdings: Audiobooks 1,986; AV Mats 9,855; Bks on Deafness & Sign Lang 36; CDs 4,298; DVDs 4,879; Large Print Bks 404; Music Scores 16; Bk Titles 33,992; Bk Vols 35,723; Per Subs 99; Talking Bks 1; Videos 5,098
Open Mon, Thurs & Fri 9:30-5:30, Tues & Wed 12:30-8, Sat 9:30-2:30
Friends of the Library Group
MISSION VALLEY, 2123 Fenton Pkwy, 92108. Tel: 858-573-5007. *Br Mgr,* Karen Reilly
Founded 2002. Pop 14,698; Circ 165,349
Library Holdings: Audiobooks 3,339; AV Mats 16,749; Bks on Deafness & Sign Lang 59; CDs 6,522; DVDs 6,390; Large Print Bks 1,178; Music Scores 102; Bk Titles 62,454; Bk Vols 68,914; Per Subs 112; Videos 8,711
Special Services for the Deaf - TDD equip
Open Mon 12:30-5:30, Tues & Wed 12-8, Thurs & Fri 9:30-5:30, Sat 9:30-2:30
Friends of the Library Group
MOUNTAIN VIEW-BECKWOURTH, 721 San Pasqual St, 92113-1839, SAN 334-3715. Tel: 619-527-3404. FAX: 619-527-3408. Web Site: www.sandiego.gov/public-library. *Librn III,* Anne Defazio
Founded 1976. Pop 45,524; Circ 50,450
Library Holdings: Audiobooks 491; AV Mats 5,828; Bks on Deafness & Sign Lang 39; CDs 1,586; DVDs 3,312; Large Print Bks 22; Music Scores 36; Bk Titles 39,226; Bk Vols 43,906; Per Subs 129; Videos 4,100
Open Mon, Thurs & Fri 9:30-5:30, Tues & Wed 12:30-8, Sat 9:30-2:30
Friends of the Library Group
NORTH CLAIREMONT, 4616 Clairemont Dr, 92117-2701, SAN 334-4045. Tel: 858-581-9931. FAX: 858-273-0032. *Br Mgr,* Eileen Hauser
Founded 1962. Pop 24,132; Circ 106,626
Library Holdings: Audiobooks 1,708; AV Mats 9,368; Bks on Deafness & Sign Lang 42; CDs 3,869; DVDs 4,818; Large Print Bks 775; Music Scores 17; Bk Titles 31,003; Bk Vols 32,899; Per Subs 99; Videos 5,279
Open Mon, Thurs & Fri 9:30-5:30, Tues & Wed 12:30-8, Sat 9:30-2:30
Friends of the Library Group
NORTH PARK, 3795 31st St, 92104. (Mail add: 3795 Park Blvd, 92104-3720), SAN 334-407X. Tel: 619-533-3972. FAX: 619-533-3973. TDD: 619-283-0758. *Br Mgr,* Bill Sannwald
Founded 1959. Pop 39,457; Circ 141,811
Library Holdings: Audiobooks 2,210; AV Mats 14,874; Bks on Deafness & Sign Lang 38; CDs 4,936; DVDs 7,966; Large Print Bks 713; Music Scores 49; Bk Titles 48,206; Bk Vols 51,801; Per Subs 173; Talking Bks 1; Videos 9,540
Special Services for the Deaf - TDD equip
Open Mon, Thurs & Fri 9:30-5:30, Tues & Wed 12:30-8, Sat 9:30-2:30
Friends of the Library Group
NORTH UNIVERSITY COMMUNITY, 8820 Judicial Dr, 92122-4684. Tel: 858-581-9637. FAX: 858-450-0028. *Br Mgr,* Michelle Ruiz
Founded 2007. Pop 48,721; Circ 252,827
Library Holdings: Audiobooks 2,032; AV Mats 12,069; Bks on Deafness & Sign Lang 45; CDs 4,776; DVDs 7,140; Large Print Bks 892; Music Scores 75; Bk Titles 54,901; Bk Vols 64,068; Per Subs 147; Talking Bks 1; Videos 7,212
Special Services for the Deaf - TDD equip

Open Mon 12:30-5:30, Tues & Wed 12:30-8, Thurs & Fri 9:30-5:30, Sat 9:30-2:30
Friends of the Library Group
OAK PARK, 2802 54th St, 92105-4941, SAN 334-410X. Tel: 619-527-3406. FAX: 619-527-3410. *Br Mgr,* Mark Davis
Founded 1969. Pop 33,290; Circ 54,182
Library Holdings: Audiobooks 1,044; AV Mats 8,019; Bks on Deafness & Sign Lang 18; CDs 2,681; DVDs 4,414; Large Print Bks 366; Music Scores 30; Bk Titles 31,177; Bk Vols 34,041; Per Subs 93; Videos 5,093
Open Mon, Thurs & Fri 9:30-5:30, Tues & Wed 12-8, Sat 9:30-2:30
Friends of the Library Group
OCEAN BEACH, 4801 Santa Monica Ave, 92107-2810, SAN 334-4134. Tel: 619-531-1532. FAX: 619-531-1530. *Br Mgr,* Matthew Beatty
Founded 1927. Pop 26,359; Circ 73,189
Library Holdings: Audiobooks 1,546; AV Mats 9,907; Bks on Deafness & Sign Lang 37; CDs 3,621; DVDs 5,216; Large Print Bks 460; Music Scores 45; Bk Titles 32,678; Bk Vols 34,592; Per Subs 105; Videos 6,021
Open Mon, Thurs & Fri 9:30-5:30, Tues & Wed 12-8, Sat 9:30-2:30
Friends of the Library Group
OTAY MESA-NESTOR, 3003 Coronado Ave, 92154-1521, SAN 334-4169. Tel: 619-424-0474. FAX: 619-424-3124. TDD: 619-424-5537. *Br Mgr,* Coco Rios
Founded 1986. Pop 63,945; Circ 89,517
Library Holdings: Audiobooks 1,559; AV Mats 13,996; Bks on Deafness & Sign Lang 45; CDs 3,432; DVDs 8,604; Large Print Bks 454; Music Scores 27; Bk Titles 51,160; Bk Vols 57,363; Per Subs 148; Talking Bks 1; Videos 9,992
Special Services for the Deaf - TDD equip
Open Mon, Thurs & Fri 9:30-5:30, Tues & Wed 12:30-8, Sat 9:30-2:30
Friends of the Library Group
PACIFIC BEACH/TAYLOR, 4275 Cass St, 92109-3194, SAN 334-4193. Tel: 858-581-9934. FAX: 858-270-8408. *Br Mgr,* Christina Wainwright
Founded 1997. Pop 47,365; Circ 169,029
Library Holdings: Audiobooks 3,323; AV Mats 17,123; Bks on Deafness & Sign Lang 53; CDs 6,610; DVDs 8,357; Large Print Bks 1,307; Music Scores 53; Bk Titles 60,440; Bk Vols 65,148; Per Subs 148; Talking Bks 1; Videos 9,843
Open Mon, Thurs & Fri 9:30-5:30, Tues & Wed 12:30-8, Sat 9:30-2:30
Friends of the Library Group
PARADISE HILLS, 5922 Rancho Hills Dr, 92139-3137, SAN 334-4223. Tel: 619-527-3461. FAX: 619-527-3446. *Br Mgr,* Zar Shain
Founded 1964. Pop 35,082; Circ 43,208
Library Holdings: Audiobooks 975; AV Mats 6,490; Bks on Deafness & Sign Lang 24; CDs 1,938; DVDs 3,634; Large Print Bks 225; Music Scores 27; Bk Titles 25,675; Bk Vols 27,386; Per Subs 87; Videos 4,243
Open Mon, Thurs & Fri 9:30-5:30, Tues & Wed 12:30-8, Sat 9:30-2:30
Friends of the Library Group
POINT LOMA/HERVEY, 3701 Voltaire St, 92107-1606, SAN 334-4258. Tel: 619-531-1539. FAX: 619-758-0934. *Br Mgr,* Christine Gonzalez
Founded 1959. Pop 36,580; Circ 195,578
Library Holdings: Audiobooks 3,420; AV Mats 12,891; Bks on Deafness & Sign Lang 45; CDs 4,270; DVDs 5,906; Large Print Bks 3,388; Music Scores 53; Bk Titles 61,954; Bk Vols 68,533; Per Subs 189; Videos 7,372
Special Services for the Deaf - TDD equip
Open Mon, Thurs & Fri 9:30-5:30, Tues & Wed 12:30-8, Sat 9:30-2:30, Sun 1-5
Friends of the Library Group
RANCHO BERNARDO, 17110 Bernardo Center Dr, 92128-2540, SAN 334-4282. Tel: 858-538-8163. FAX: 858-487-3751. *Br Mgr,* Patricia Jenkins
Founded 1996. Pop 26,527; Circ 289,697
Library Holdings: Audiobooks 4,177; AV Mats 15,813; Bks on Deafness & Sign Lang 65; CDs 7,255; DVDs 5,737; Large Print Bks 3,211; Music Scores 87; Bk Titles 71,341; Bk Vols 79,000; Per Subs 206; Videos 7,502
Special Services for the Deaf - TDD equip
Open Mon, Thurs & Fri 9:30-5:30, Tues & Wed 12:30-8, Sat 9:30-2:30, Sun 1-5
Friends of the Library Group
RANCHO PENASQUITOS, 13330 Salmon River Rd, 92129-2640, SAN 322-5577. Tel: 858-538-8159. FAX: 858-538-8160. *Br Mgr, Librn IV,* Adrianne Peterson
Founded 1992. Pop 81,110; Circ 265,049
Library Holdings: Audiobooks 3,506; AV Mats 16,408; Bks on Deafness & Sign Lang 63; Braille Volumes 1; CDs 6,585; DVDs 7,787; Large Print Bks 589; Music Scores 67; Bk Titles 60,262; Bk Vols 67,680; Per Subs 131; Videos 9,166
Open Mon, Thurs & Fri 9:30-5:30, Tues & Wed 12:30-8, Sat 9:30-2:30
Friends of the Library Group
SAN CARLOS, 7265 Jackson Dr, 92119-2314, SAN 334-4312. Tel: 619-527-3430. FAX: 619-527-3433. *Br Mgr,* Rita Glick
Founded 1972. Pop 33,229; Circ 150,983
Library Holdings: Audiobooks 2,527; AV Mats 10,464; Bks on Deafness & Sign Lang 34; CDs 4,637; DVDs 5,086; Large Print Bks 795; Music Scores 54; Bk Titles 46,174; Bk Vols 49,590; Per Subs 102; Talking Bks 1; Videos 5,432
Open Mon, Thurs & Fri 9:30-5:30, Tues & Wed 12:30-8, Sat 9:30-2:30
Friends of the Library Group
SAN YSIDRO, 101 W San Ysidro Blvd, 92173-2516, SAN 334-4347. Tel: 619-424-0475. FAX: 619-424-0477. *Br Mgr,* Adolfo Ocampo
Founded 1924. Pop 39,937; Circ 47,793
Library Holdings: Audiobooks 646; AV Mats 6,836; Bks on Deafness & Sign Lang 29; CDs 1,628; DVDs 3,848; Large Print Bks 24; Music Scores 23; Bk Titles 32,135; Bk Vols 35,734; Per Subs 193; Videos 4,941
Open Mon, Thurs & Fri 9:30-5:30, Tues & Wed 12:30-8, Sat 9:30-2:30
SCRIPPS MIRAMAR RANCH, 10301 Scripps Lake Dr, 92131-1026, SAN 328-7904. Tel: 858-538-8158. FAX: 858-538-8154. *Br Mgr,* Trevor Jones
Founded 1986. Pop 39,859; Circ 196,956
Library Holdings: Audiobooks 2,566; AV Mats 10,319; Bks on Deafness & Sign Lang 49; CDs 4,791; DVDs 4,238; Large Print Bks 321; Music Scores 76; Bk Titles 72,701; Bk Vols 79,302; Per Subs 158; Videos 4,997
Open Mon, Thurs & Fri 9:30-5:30, Tues & Wed 12:30-8, Sat 9:30-2:30
Friends of the Library Group
SERRA MESA-KEARNY MESA, 9005 Aero Dr, 92123-2312, SAN 334-4371. Tel: 858-573-1396. FAX: 858-569-4007. *Br Mgr,* David Ege
Founded 2006. Pop 26,316; Circ 153,166
Library Holdings: Audiobooks 1,892; AV Mats 10,658; Bks on Deafness & Sign Lang 49; CDs 4,201; DVDs 4,356; Large Print Bks 780; Music Scores 30; Bk Titles 48,331; Bk Vols 53,724; Per Subs 141; Videos 5,966
Special Services for the Deaf - TDD equip
Open Mon, Thurs & Fri 9:30-5:30, Tues & Wed 12:30-8, Sat 9:30-2:30, Sun 1-5
Friends of the Library Group
SKYLINE HILLS, 480 S Meadowbrook Dr, 92114-7701, SAN 334-4401. Tel: 619-527-3485. FAX: 619-527-3484. *Br Mgr,* Kelly Pepo
Founded 1969. Pop 23,007; Circ 39,310
Library Holdings: Audiobooks 1,004; AV Mats 8,130; Bks on Deafness & Sign Lang 37; CDs 2,874; DVDs 4,032; Large Print Bks 222; Music Scores 29; Bk Titles 34,267; Bk Vols 36,612; Per Subs 79; Videos 4,889
Open Mon 12:30-5:30, Tues & Wed 12:30-8, Thurs & Fri 9:30-5:30, Sat 9:30-2:30
Friends of the Library Group
TIERRASANTA, 4985 La Cuenta Dr, 92124-2601, SAN 334-4428. Tel: 858-573-1384. FAX: 858-573-1385. *Br Mgr,* Judy Cunninghum
Founded 1984. Pop 31,378; Circ 129,822
Library Holdings: Audiobooks 2,740; AV Mats 9,705; Bks on Deafness & Sign Lang 55; CDs 4,172; DVDs 4,019; Large Print Bks 323; Music Scores 30; Bk Titles 44,717; Bk Vols 49,473; Per Subs 134; Talking Bks 1; Videos 4,979
Open Mon, Thurs & Fri 9:30-5:30, Tues & Wed 12:30-8, Sat 9:30-2:30
Friends of the Library Group
UNIVERSITY COMMUNITY, 4155 Governor Dr, 92122-2501, SAN 334-4460. Tel: 858-552-1655. FAX: 858-552-1654. *Br Mgr,* Sharon Thomerson
Founded 1978. Pop 14,006; Circ 156,328
Library Holdings: Audiobooks 2,803; AV Mats 12,250; Bks on Deafness & Sign Lang 40; CDs 4,927; DVDs 6,009; Large Print Bks 750; Music Scores 47; Bk Titles 51,247; Bk Vols 55,809; Per Subs 213; Videos 6,795
Open Mon, Thurs & Fri 9:30-5:30, Tues & Wed 12:30-8, Sat 9:30-2:30
Friends of the Library Group
UNIVERSITY HEIGHTS, 4193 Park Blvd, 92103-2510, SAN 334-4436. Tel: 619-692-4912. FAX: 619-692-4913. *Br Mgr, Librn III,* Kim Schmidt
Founded 1966. Pop 19,495; Circ 124,346
Library Holdings: Audiobooks 1,529; AV Mats 10,532; Bks on Deafness & Sign Lang 31; CDs 4,750; DVDs 4,824; Large Print Bks 497; Music Scores 18; Bk Titles 27,218; Bk Vols 28,684; Per Subs 114; Videos 5,553
Open Mon, Thurs & Fri 9:30-5:30, Tues & Wed 12:30-8, Sat 9:30-2:30
Friends of the Library Group
VALENCIA PARK/MALCOLM X, 5148 Market St, 92114-4899, SAN 334-4495. Tel: 619-527-3405. FAX: 619-527-5456. *Br Mgr, Librn IV,* Leslie McNabb
Founded 1996. Pop 33,426; Circ 70,509
Library Holdings: Audiobooks 1,133; AV Mats 11,640; Bks on Deafness & Sign Lang 51; CDs 2,959; DVDs 7,281; Large Print Bks 243; Music Scores 53; Bk Titles 59,687; Bk Vols 68,095; Per Subs 130; Videos 8,411
Open Mon, Thurs & Fri 9:30-5:30, Tues & Wed 12:30-8, Sat 9:30-2:30, Sun 1-5
Friends of the Library Group

C SAN DIEGO STATE UNIVERSITY LIBRARY & INFORMATION ACCESS*, 5500 Campanile Dr, 92182-8050. SAN 334-4525. Tel: 619-594-6728. Circulation Tel: 619-594-6793. Interlibrary Loan Service Tel: 619-594-6730. Administration Tel: 619-594-6014. FAX: 619-594-3270. Circulation FAX: 619-594-0742. Interlibrary Loan Service FAX: 619-265-0414. Administration FAX: 619-594-2700. Web Site: library.sdsu.edu. *Dean of Libr,* Dr Gale S Etschmaier; *Assoc Dean,* Patrick McCarthy; *Dir, Access Serv & Human Res,* Sara Baird; Tel: 619-594-2530; *Dir, Libr Info Technologies & Digital Initiatives,* Mark Figueroa; Tel: 619-594-2945; *Head, Circ & Course Reserves,* Joan Goodwin; Tel: 619-594-6759; *Head, Coll Mgt,* Charles Weston; Tel: 619-594-6988; *Head, Coll Presv,* Jennifer Anderson; Tel: 619-594-4962; *Head, Ref Serv,* Linda Salem; Tel: 619-594-5148; *Head, Ser,* Julie Su; Tel: 619-594-0904; *Outreach Librn,* Gloria L Rhodes; Tel: 619-594-1169; *Supvr, ILL,* Darlene Nowak; Tel: 619-594-6908, E-mail: ill@rohan.sdsu.edu; *Supvr, Media Ctr,* Michael Lapins; Tel: 619-594-8241; *Fac Coordr,* Maureen Dotson; Tel: 619-594-4472; *Mkt & Communications Spec,* Roberta Niederjohn; Tel: 619-594-4991; *Info Literacy,* Pamela Jackson; Tel: 619-594-3809; *Spec Coll & Univ Archives,* Rob Ray; Tel: 619-594-4303, Fax: 619-594-0466. Subject Specialists: *Eng,* Charles Weston; *Children's lit, Educ,* Linda Salem; *Asian studies,* Julie Su; *Africana studies,* Gloria L Rhodes; *Film, Television, Theatre,* Pamela Jackson; Staff 76 (MLS 28, Non-MLS 48)
Founded 1897. Enrl 32,936; Fac 2,163; Highest Degree: Doctorate
Library Holdings: AV Mats 12,060; e-books 108,647; e-journals 12,365; Bk Titles 1,102,167; Bk Vols 1,649,455; Per Subs 4,177
Special Collections: 20th Century San Diego History; Adams Postcard Coll; Astronomy & History of Astronomy (Ernst Zinner Coll); Bookbinding (Wallace A Pearce Coll); Chesterfield Coll; Early Botanical Works Coll; H L Mencken Coll; History of Biology (Norland Coll); JFK Coll; Jiddu Krishnamurti Coll; Modern Rare Editions (Paul L Pfaff Coll); Music Scores (Vincent Meads Coll); Orchidology (Reginald S Davies Coll); San Diego State University Archives; Science Fiction (Chater Coll). Oral History; State Document Depository; US Document Depository
Automation Activity & Vendor Info: (Course Reserve) Docutek; (OPAC) Innovative Interfaces, Inc
Wireless access
Publications: The Dome (Newsletter)
Partic in OCLC Online Computer Library Center, Inc; San Diego Greater Metro Area Libr & Info Agency Coun
Special Services for the Deaf - Bks on deafness & sign lang; Spec interest per; Staff with knowledge of sign lang; TTY equip
Friends of the Library Group

S SCOTTISH RITE MASONIC LIBRARY*, 1895 Camino del Rio S, 92108. SAN 301-3499. Tel: 619-293-4888. FAX: 619-297-2751. *In Charge,* Robert Norris
Founded 1974
Library Holdings: Bk Vols 4,000; Per Subs 20
Special Collections: Taped Lectures (Masonic & related subjects)
Publications: Newsletter (Monthly)
Open Mon-Fri 6pm-9pm

M SCRIPPS MERCY HOSPITAL MEDICAL LIBRARY*, Melisa Reasner McGuire Health Sciences Library, 4077 Fifth Ave, MER-36, 92103-2180. SAN 301-3340. Tel: 619-260-7024. FAX: 619-260-7262. E-mail: library.mercy@scrippshealth.org. *Mgr,* Michaele Robinson; E-mail: robinson.micki@scrippshealth.org; *Med Librn,* Sondhaya Sritongsook; E-mail: sritongsook.sondhaya@scrippshealth.org; Staff 3 (MLS 2, Non-MLS 1)
Founded 1937
Oct 2009-Sept 2010 Income $437,182. Mats Exp $243,385. Sal $179,947
Library Holdings: AV Mats 250; e-books 150; e-journals 500; Bk Titles 4,000; Bk Vols 4,300; Per Subs 150
Subject Interests: Archives, Clinical med, Nursing, Psychiat
Automation Activity & Vendor Info: (Cataloging) EOS International; (Circulation) EOS International; (OPAC) EOS International; (Serials) EOS International
Database Vendor: 3M Library Systems, Baker & Taylor, Dialog, DynaMed, EBSCOhost, EOS International, Majors, MD Consult, Medline, Micromedex, OCLC FirstSearch, OVID Technologies, PubMed, UpToDate, Wiley InterScience
Function: Archival coll, Computers for patron use, Copy machines, ILL available, Online cat, Online searches
Partic in Medical Library Group of Southern California & Arizona (MLGSCA); National Network of Libraries of Medicine; OCLC Online Computer Library Center, Inc
Open Mon-Fri 8-5
Restriction: Badge access after hrs, In-house use for visitors, Open to staff, patients & family mem

S SEA WORLD LIBRARY*, 500 Sea World Dr, 92109-7995. SAN 301-3502. Tel: 619-226-3834. FAX: 619-226-3634. Web Site: www.seaworld.com, www.seaworld.org. *Dir,* Joy Wolf
Founded 1972
Library Holdings: Bk Titles 800; Per Subs 25
Special Collections: Children's Marine Life Titles
Subject Interests: Ichthyology, Mammals, Oceanography
Special Services for the Deaf - TDD equip

L SELTZER, CAPLAN, MCMAHON, VITEK*, Law Library, 750 B St, Ste 2100, 92101. SAN 372-3011. Tel: 619-685-3009. FAX: 619-615-0315. Web Site: www.scmv.com. *Dir, Libr Serv,* Patricia Rusheen
Library Holdings: CDs 50; Electronic Media & Resources 15; Bk Vols 4,500; Per Subs 30
Database Vendor: Westlaw
Wireless access
Restriction: Staff use only

L SEMPRA ENERGY*, Law Library, 101 Ash St, 92101-3017. SAN 300-9947. Tel: 619-696-2034.
Library Holdings: Bk Vols 18,000; Per Subs 600
Restriction: Not open to pub

M SHARP HEALTHCARE*, Sharp Memorial Hospital Medical Library, 7901 Frost St, 92123. SAN 301-3529. Tel: 858-939-3242. FAX: 858-939-3248. *Coll Develop, Head of Libr,* Laura Stubblefield; E-mail: laura.stubblefield@sharp.com; *Asst Librn,* Dolly Bucsit; *Asst Librn,* Amy Sharpe
Founded 1970
Library Holdings: Bk Vols 1,100; Per Subs 250
Subject Interests: Health sci, Med, Nursing
Automation Activity & Vendor Info: (Cataloging) EOS International; (Circulation) EOS International; (OPAC) EOS International; (Serials) EOS International
Partic in Dialog Corp

S UNION-TRIBUNE PUBLISHING CO LIBRARY*, 350 Camino de la Reina, 92108. (Mail add: PO Box 120191, 92112-0191), SAN 301-3561. Tel: 619-299-3131. Web Site: www.uniontrib.com. *Mgr,* Sharon Stewart Reeves; *Res,* Merrie Monteagudo; Staff 15 (MLS 3, Non-MLS 12)
Founded 1945
Library Holdings: Bk Titles 3,100; Bk Vols 4,000; Per Subs 50
Subject Interests: Current events, Hist
Open Mon-Fri 9am-10pm, Sat & Sun 3-9

GL UNITED STATES COURTS LIBRARY*, 940 Front St, Rm 3185, 92101-8920. SAN 372-3003. Tel: 619-557-5066. FAX: 619-557-5077. *Librn,* Valerie A Railey; *Libr Tech,* Cynthia Kokocinski; Tel: 619-557-5387; Staff 2 (MLS 1, Non-MLS 1)
Library Holdings: Bk Vols 52,000
Special Collections: Law Library
Subject Interests: Conflicts, Fed procedure, Foreign law, Immigration, Intl law
Function: Ref & res
Partic in OCLC Online Computer Library Center, Inc
Open Mon-Fri 8:30-4:30
Restriction: Authorized patrons

S US NATIONAL PARK SERVICE*, Cabrillo National Monument Library, 1800 Cabrillo Memorial Dr, 92106-3601. Tel: 619-557-5450. FAX: 619-226-6311. TDD: 619-222-8211. Web Site: www.nps.gov/cabr. *Coll Mgr,* Robert Munson; Tel: 619-523-4574, E-mail: robert_munson@nps.gov. Subject Specialists: *Hist,* Robert Munson
Founded 1913
Library Holdings: Bk Vols 2,700; Per Subs 20
Special Collections: Archives-Park Records & Manuscripts
Function: Archival coll, Bus archives, For res purposes, Ref serv available, Res libr
Special Services for the Deaf - TDD equip
Open Mon-Sun 9-5:15
Restriction: Circulates for staff only, In-house use for visitors, Open to pub with supv only, Ref only to non-staff

UNITED STATES NAVY

A THE COMMAND LIBRARY*, Fleet Anti-Sub Warfare Training Ctr, 32444 Echo Lane, Ste 100, 92147-5199, SAN 334-4703. Tel: 619-524-1908. FAX: 619-524-6875.
Founded 1967
Library Holdings: Bk Titles 3,100; Bk Vols 18,000; Per Subs 30
Open Mon-Fri 7-4

A NAVAL BASE CORONADO LIBRARY*, MWR Base Library, 2478 Munda Rd, 92155-5396, SAN 334-4797. Tel: 619-437-3026. FAX: 619-437-3891. *Mgr,* Barbara Siemer
Founded 1944
Library Holdings: AV Mats 1,000; Bk Vols 22,000; Per Subs 124; Talking Bks 900

Special Collections: Special Warfare Coll
Automation Activity & Vendor Info: (Cataloging) EOS International; (Circulation) EOS International; (OPAC) EOS International

AM NAVAL MEDICAL CENTER*, Library Bldg 5-2, Naval Medical Ctr, 92134-5200, SAN 334-4940. Tel: 619-532-7950. FAX: 619-532-9293. Web Site: library.hosted.exlibrisgroup.com/medical.html. *Dir, Libr Serv,* Kathy Parker; Staff 7 (MLS 3, Non-MLS 4)
Founded 1922
Library Holdings: e-books 8,000; e-journals 12,000; Bk Vols 20,000; Per Subs 350
Special Collections: Layman Health Information
Subject Interests: Dentistry, Med, Nursing
Automation Activity & Vendor Info: (Acquisitions) Ex Libris Group; (Cataloging) Ex Libris Group; (Circulation) Ex Libris Group; (OPAC) Ex Libris Group; (Serials) Ex Libris Group
Partic in Consortium of Naval Libraries (CNL); Fedlink; Medical Library Association (MLA); Medical Library Group of Southern California & Arizona (MLGSCA); National Network of Libraries of Medicine; OCLC Online Computer Library Center, Inc

AM NAVAL HEALTH RESEARCH CENTER, WILKINS BIOMEDICAL LIBRARY*, Gate 4, Barracks Bldg 333, Rm 101, McClelland & Patterson Rds, 92152. (Mail add: 140 Sylvester Rd, 92106-3521), SAN 334-4916. Tel: 619-553-8426. FAX: 619-553-0213. *Librn,* Donna Dutton; Tel: 619-767-4614, E-mail: donna.dutton.ctr@med.navy.mil; *Libr Tech,* Betty Croft; E-mail: betty.croft@med.navy.mil; Staff 3 (MLS 1, Non-MLS 2)
Founded 1959
Library Holdings: Bk Titles 5,550; Per Subs 230
Special Collections: Prisoner of War Studies Publications; United States Naval Medical Bulletin, 1907-1949
Subject Interests: Biochem, Immunology, Med, Mil hist, Psychiat, Psychol, Sociol, Statistics
Automation Activity & Vendor Info: (Acquisitions) SirsiDynix; (Cataloging) SirsiDynix; (Circulation) SirsiDynix; (OPAC) SirsiDynix; (Serials) SirsiDynix
Database Vendor: EBSCOhost, OCLC WorldShare Interlibrary Loan, OVID Technologies, PubMed, SerialsSolutions, SirsiDynix, Thomson - Web of Science, Westlaw
Partic in Medical Library Group of Southern California & Arizona (MLGSCA)
Publications: Journal Holdings List; New Acquisitions List
Open Mon-Fri 7-4:30
Restriction: Not open to pub, Staff use only

A SPAWAR SYSTEMS CENTER SAN DIEGO TECHNICAL LIBRARY*, Code 84300, 53560 Hull St, 92152-5001, SAN 334-4851. Tel: 619-553-4890. FAX: 619-553-4893. E-mail: ssc_pac_library@navy.mil. *Dir,* Barbara Busch; E-mail: bbusch@spawar.navy.mil. Subject Specialists: *Eng, Phys sci,* Barbara Busch; Staff 6 (MLS 1, Non-MLS 5)
Founded 1949
Library Holdings: Bk Titles 60,000; Bk Vols 225,000; Per Subs 700
Special Collections: National Defense Research Committee Coll, University of California Division of War Research; Navy Radio & Sound Laboratory Reports
Subject Interests: Computer sci, Electronics, Eng, Marine biol, Math, Ocean eng, Physics
Automation Activity & Vendor Info: (OPAC) SirsiDynix
Database Vendor: Cambridge Scientific Abstracts, OCLC FirstSearch, SirsiDynix
Function: Govt ref serv
Partic in OCLC Online Computer Library Center, Inc
Publications: Periodical Holdings
Restriction: Not open to pub, Open to govt employees only, Open to researchers by request, Photo ID required for access, Restricted access

UNIVERSITY OF SAN DIEGO

C HELEN K & JAMES S COPLEY LIBRARY*, 5998 Alcala Park, 92110, SAN 334-5181. Circulation Tel: 619-260-4799. Interlibrary Loan Service Tel: 619-260-2364. Reference Tel: 619-260-4765. Administration Tel: 619-260-2370. FAX: 619-260-4617. Web Site: marian.sandiego.edu. *Univ Librn,* Edward D Starkey; E-mail: estarkey@sandiego.edu; *Assoc Univ Librn,* Steve Staninger; E-mail: sstan@sandiego.edu; *Outreach Librn,* Jade Winn; E-mail: jade@sandiego.edu; *Head, Access Serv,* Bill Hall; E-mail: billhall@sandiego.edu; *Head, Acq,* Jacqueline Sabanos; E-mail: jsabanos@sandiego.edu; *Head, Cat,* Margit Smith; E-mail: mjps@sandiego.edu; *Electronic Res,* Michael Epstein; E-mail: epstein@sandiego.edu; *ILL,* Alex Moran; E-mail: moran1@sandiego.edu; *Ref Serv,* Alma Ortega; E-mail: alma@sandiego.edu; *Ref Serv,* Tamara Shaw; E-mail: tshaw@sandiego.edu; *Sci,* Amy Besnoy; E-mail: abesnoy@sandiego.edu; *Spec Coll & Archives Librn,* Diane Maher; E-mail: diane@sandiego.edu; *Syst Coordr,* Michael O'Brien; E-mail: michaelo@sandiego.edu. Subject Specialists: *Humanities, Philos, Relig,* Edward D Starkey; *Bus, Polit sci,* Steve Staninger; *Educ, Nursing, Psychol,* Jade Winn; *Ethnic studies,* Alma Ortega; *Communications, Lit,* Tamara Shaw; *Sciences,* Amy Besnoy; *Arts,* Diane Maher; Staff 12 (MLS 10, Non-MLS 2)
Founded 1949. Enrl 7,200; Fac 300; Highest Degree: Doctorate
Library Holdings: Bk Titles 325,000; Bk Vols 500,000; Per Subs 2,200
Subject Interests: Catholicism, Hist, Lit, Philos, Relig
Automation Activity & Vendor Info: (Acquisitions) Innovative Interfaces, Inc; (Cataloging) Innovative Interfaces, Inc; (Circulation) Innovative Interfaces, Inc; (ILL) Innovative Interfaces, Inc; (Media Booking) Innovative Interfaces, Inc; (OPAC) Innovative Interfaces, Inc; (Serials) Innovative Interfaces, Inc
Database Vendor: Dialog, EBSCOhost, Factiva.com, Gale Cengage Learning, Innovative Interfaces, Inc, JSTOR, LexisNexis, OCLC FirstSearch, OCLC WorldShare Interlibrary Loan, OVID Technologies, ProQuest, SerialsSolutions
Partic in San Diego Library Circuit; Statewide California Electronic Library Consortium (SCELC)
Friends of the Library Group

CL KATHERINE M & GEORGE M PARDEE JR LEGAL RESEARCH CENTER, 5998 Alcala Park, 92110-2492, SAN 334-5211. Tel: 619-260-4542. Reference Tel: 619-260-4612. Administration Tel: 619-260-4600, Ext 4337. Automation Services Tel: 619-260-4759. FAX: 619-260-4616. Web Site: www.sandiego.edu/law/lrc. *Assoc Dean, Libr & Info Serv,* Karl Gruben; Tel: 619-260-6846, E-mail: kgruben@sandiego.edu; *Assoc Dir,* L Ruth Levor; Tel: 619-260-4604, E-mail: rlevor@sandiego.edu; *Head, Circ,* Inna Muradyan; Tel: 619-260-7479, E-mail: innam@sandiego.edu; *Head, Pub Serv,* Lihosit Judith; Tel: 619-260-4766, E-mail: jlihosit@sandiego.edu; *Head, Tech Serv,* Harry Loren Stamper; Tel: 619-260-4543, E-mail: stamper@sandiego.edu; *Acq Librn,* Jason Curtis; Tel: 619-260-2875, E-mail: curtis@sandiego.edu; *Coll Develop Librn,* Brent Bernau; Tel: 619-260-7557, E-mail: bbernau@sandiego.edu; *Electronic Serv Librn,* Anna Russell; E-mail: russell@sandiego.edu; *Fac Serv & Outreach Librn, Law Ref Librn,* Jane Larrington; Tel: 619-260-4752, E-mail: jlarrington@sandiego.edu; *Law Ref Librn,* Michele Knapp; Tel: 619-260-4532; *Law Ref Librn/Foreign & Intl Spec,* Melissa Fung; Tel: 619-260-4734. Subject Specialists: *Oral hist,* L Ruth Levor; *Linguistics,* Harry Loren Stamper; *Govt doc, Tax,* Michele Knapp; *Foreign law, Intl law,* Melissa Fung; Staff 11 (MLS 10, Non-MLS 1)
Founded 1954. Enrl 992; Fac 60; Highest Degree: Doctorate
Library Holdings: DVDs 94; Bk Titles 1,128,920; Per Subs 4,760; Videos 379
Special Collections: State Document Depository; UN Document Depository; US Document Depository
Automation Activity & Vendor Info: (Acquisitions) Innovative Interfaces, Inc; (Cataloging) Innovative Interfaces, Inc; (Circulation) Innovative Interfaces, Inc; (Course Reserve) Innovative Interfaces, Inc; (ILL) Innovative Interfaces, Inc; (OPAC) Innovative Interfaces, Inc; (Serials) Innovative Interfaces, Inc
Database Vendor: EBSCOhost, Gale Cengage Learning, Innovative Interfaces, Inc, LexisNexis, OCLC FirstSearch
Function: Archival coll, CD-ROM, Computer training, Computers for patron use, Copy machines, Doc delivery serv, E-Reserves, Free DVD rentals, Govt ref serv, Handicapped accessible, ILL available, Online cat, Online searches, Ref serv available, Scanner, Tax forms, Telephone ref, Video lending libr, Web-catalog, Wheelchair accessible
Partic in San Diego Circuit
Publications: Guide Series (Research guide); Information Series; Patron Guide (Library handbook)
Open Mon-Thurs 7am-Midnight, Fri & Sat 8am-10pm, Sun 8am-Midnight
Restriction: Circ limited
Friends of the Library Group

S URS CORP, Reference Library, 4225 Executive Sq, Ste 1600, 92037. SAN 321-3838. Tel: 858-812-9292. Toll Free Tel: 800-697-1550. FAX: 858-812-9293. Web Site: www.urscorp.com. *Librn,* Margo LaCerte; E-mail: margo.lacerte@urs.com
Founded 1959
Library Holdings: Bk Vols 3,500; Per Subs 85
Subject Interests: Environ law, Geol, Geotech eng, Groundwater, Hazardous waste
Publications: Acquisitions List (Bi-monthly)

GM VA SAN DIEGO HEALTHCARE SYSTEM MEDICAL LIBRARY*, 3350 La Jolla Village Dr, 92161. SAN 301-3588. Tel: 858-552-8585. FAX: 858-552-7537. *Chief Librn,* Deborah Batey; E-mail: deborah.batey@med.va.gov; Staff 2 (MLS 2)
Founded 1972
Library Holdings: Bk Vols 4,400
Subject Interests: Dentistry, Internal med, Nursing, Post-traumatic stress, Psychiat
Automation Activity & Vendor Info: (Cataloging) Innovative Interfaces, Inc; (Circulation) Innovative Interfaces, Inc; (Serials) EOS International
Database Vendor: Elsevier, Micromedex, OVID Technologies, PubMed, SerialsSolutions, Swets Information Services, UpToDate
Partic in Dept of Vet Affairs Libr Network; National Network of Libraries of Medicine

Open Mon-Fri 8-4
Restriction: Non-circulating to the pub

SAN DIMAS

CR LIFE PACIFIC COLLEGE LIBRARY*, 1100 W Covina Blvd, 91773-3203. SAN 300-9467. Tel: 909-706-3009. FAX: 909-599-6690. E-mail: library@lifepacific.edu. Web Site: www.lifepacific.edu/library. *Librn,* Gary Merriman; Tel: 909-706-3008, E-mail: gmerriman@lifepacific.edu. Subject Specialists: *Bible, Theol,* Gary Merriman; Staff 2 (MLS 1, Non-MLS 1)
Founded 1923. Enrl 500; Fac 24; Highest Degree: Master
Library Holdings: e-books 1,500; Bk Vols 40,000; Per Subs 130
Special Collections: Archive of International Church of the Foursquare Gospel
Subject Interests: Educ, Relig
Automation Activity & Vendor Info: (Cataloging) Follett Software; (Circulation) Follett Software; (OPAC) Follett Software
Database Vendor: ProQuest
Wireless access
Open Mon-Thurs 7:30am-10:30pm, Fri 7:30-5, Sat 11-5, Sun 3-9

SAN FRANCISCO

C ACADEMY OF ART UNIVERSITY LIBRARY, 180 New Montogomery, 6th Flr, 94105. (Mail add: 79 New Montgomery St, 94105), SAN 372-6452. Tel: 415-274-2270. Circulation Tel: 415-618-3842. FAX: 415-618-3981. E-mail: library@academyart.edu. Web Site: library.academyart.edu. *Dir,* Audrey Ferrie; E-mail: aferrie@academyart.edu; *Asst Dir,* Hope Johnson; Tel: 415-618-3894, E-mail: hopejohnson@academyart.edu; Staff 10 (MLS 4, Non-MLS 6)
Founded 1977. Enrl 11,500; Fac 1,000; Highest Degree: Master
Library Holdings: DVDs 2,500; e-books 4,000; Bk Titles 38,000; Bk Vols 48,000; Per Subs 275; Videos 2,000
Special Collections: Art & Applied Art, bks, slides, videos, cd-rom
Subject Interests: Visual arts
Automation Activity & Vendor Info: (Acquisitions) Innovative Interfaces, Inc - Millenium; (Cataloging) Innovative Interfaces, Inc - Millenium; (Circulation) Innovative Interfaces, Inc - Millenium; (Course Reserve) Innovative Interfaces, Inc - Millenium; (OPAC) Innovative Interfaces, Inc - Millenium; (Serials) Innovative Interfaces, Inc - Millenium
Database Vendor: 3M Library Systems, Backstage Library Works, ebrary, EBSCO Information Services, Ingram Library Services, Innovative Interfaces, Inc, Luna Imaging/Insight, ProQuest
Wireless access
Open Mon-Thurs 10-10, Fri 10-6, Sat & Sun 12-6

C ALLIANT INTERNATIONAL UNIVERSITY*, Hurwich Library San - Francisco Campus, One Beach St, Ste 100, 94133. SAN 300-6085. Tel: 415-955-2131. Interlibrary Loan Service Tel: 415-955-2158. Reference Tel: 415-955-2068. FAX: 415-955-2180. E-mail: library@alliant.edu. Web Site: library.alliant.edu. *Libr Dir,* Joseph Tally; Tel: 415-955-2157, E-mail: jtally@alliant.edu; *Librn/Ref & Res, Acq, Cat,* Brian Seguin; E-mail: bseguin@alliant.edu; *Libr Syst Mgr,* Nancy Slanger; Tel: 415-955-2155, E-mail: nslanger@alliant.edu; Staff 5 (MLS 3, Non-MLS 2)
Founded 1969. Enrl 1,034; Fac 67; Highest Degree: Doctorate
Jul 2010-Jun 2011. Mats Exp $74,326, Books $6,709, Per/Ser (Incl. Access Fees) $26,601, Other Print Mats $37,298, AV Mat $1,197, Presv $2,521. Sal $181,266
Library Holdings: DVDs 91; Bk Vols 27,185; Per Subs 71; Videos 610
Special Collections: Education Coll; Psychological Assessment Coll
Automation Activity & Vendor Info: (Acquisitions) Innovative Interfaces, Inc - Millenium; (Cataloging) Innovative Interfaces, Inc - Millenium; (Circulation) Innovative Interfaces, Inc - Millenium; (Course Reserve) Innovative Interfaces, Inc - Millenium; (ILL) Innovative Interfaces, Inc - Millenium; (Media Booking) Innovative Interfaces, Inc - Millenium; (OPAC) Innovative Interfaces, Inc - Millenium; (Serials) Innovative Interfaces, Inc - Millenium
Database Vendor: Alexander Street Press, American Psychological Association (APA), Annual Reviews, Blackwell, ebrary, EBSCOhost, Elsevier, Emerald, Haworth Pres Inc, Innovative Interfaces, Inc, ISI Web of Knowledge, JSTOR, LexisNexis, Medline, OCLC WorldShare Interlibrary Loan, ProQuest, Sage, ScienceDirect, Springer-Verlag, Wiley InterScience
Wireless access
Partic in Link+; Northern & Central California Psychology Libraries; Statewide California Electronic Library Consortium (SCELC)
Open Mon-Thurs 8:30am-9pm, Fri 8:30-5, Sat & Sun 11-5
Restriction: Borrowing privileges limited to fac & registered students

M AMERICAN ACADEMY OF OPHTHALMOLOGY LIBRARY*, 655 Beach St, 94109. (Mail add: PO Box 7424, 94120-7424), SAN 374-8995. Tel: 415-561-8500. FAX: 415-561-8533. E-mail: library@aao.org. Web Site: www.aao.org. *Librn,* Jessica Ravetto; E-mail: jravetto@aao.org; Staff 1 (MLS 1)
Restriction: Staff use only

L ARNOLD & PORTER LLP LAW LIBRARY*, Three Embarcadero Ctr, 7th Flr, 94111-4024. SAN 327-5760. Tel: 415-434-1600. FAX: 415-217-5910. Web Site: www.arnoldporter.com, www.hrice.com.
Library Holdings: Bk Vols 13,000
Subject Interests: Law

C ART INSTITUTES OF CALIFORNIA, SAN FRANCISCO, Jamie A MacInnis Memorial Library, 1170 Market St, 94102-4908. SAN 378-3782. Tel: 415-276-4010. Toll Free Tel: 888-493-3261. FAX: 415-863-1121. E-mail: aicasflibrary@aii.edu. Web Site: aii.campusguides.com/aicasf, new.artinstitutes.edu/san-francisco. *Librn,* Erica Watson; E-mail: eawatson@aii.edu; Staff 1 (MLS 1)
Founded 1997
Library Holdings: DVDs 3,000; Bk Vols 10,000; Per Subs 120
Automation Activity & Vendor Info: (OPAC) Ex Libris Group
Database Vendor: ProQuest
Open Mon-Thurs 7:30am-9pm, Fri 7:30-5, Sat 11-4

S ASTRONOMICAL SOCIETY OF THE PACIFIC LIBRARY*, 390 Ashton Ave, 94112. SAN 325-6677. Tel: 415-337-1100. FAX: 415-337-5205. E-mail: membership@astrosociety.org. Web Site: www.astrosociety.org. *Exec Dir,* Jim Manning; E-mail: jmanning@astrosociety.org
Founded 1889
Library Holdings: Bk Titles 1,600; Per Subs 20
Special Collections: People & Objects in Astronomy, Photo Archive
Subject Interests: Astronomy, Hist of sci, Space sci
Publications: Bibliographies; Journals; Newsletter
Restriction: Open by appt only

L BINGHAM MCCUTCHEN LLP*, Law Library, Three Embarcadero Ctr, 94111. SAN 301-4274. Tel: 415-393-2560. FAX: 415-393-2286. Web Site: www.bingham.com. *Libr Mgr,* Lorre Mason; *Ref Serv,* Lynne Palmer
Library Holdings: Bk Vols 30,000
Database Vendor: LexisNexis, Westlaw
Open Mon-Fri 9-5

S THE BOOK CLUB OF CALIFORNIA*, 312 Sutter St, Ste 500, 94108-4320. SAN 326-6249. Tel: 415-781-7532. Toll Free Tel: 800-869-7656. FAX: 415-781-7537. E-mail: library@bccbooks.org. Web Site: www.bccbooks.org. *Exec Dir,* Jennifer Sime; E-mail: jennifer@bccbooks.org; *Librn,* Henry Snyder
Founded 1912
Library Holdings: Bk Vols 8,300
Special Collections: Printing History. Oral History
Subject Interests: Bk arts, Western hist
Automation Activity & Vendor Info: (Cataloging) EOS International
Publications: Keepsake (Annual); Newsletter (Quarterly); Press Books (Annual)
Restriction: Mem only

S CALIFORNIA ACADEMY OF SCIENCES LIBRARY*, Golden Gate Park, 55 Music Concourse Dr, 94118. SAN 301-3774. Tel: 415-379-5484. Interlibrary Loan Service Tel: 415-379-5493. FAX: 415-379-5729. E-mail: library@calacademy.org. Web Site: research.calacademy.org/library. *Archivist, Digital Coll Librn,* Danielle Castronovo; *User Serv Librn,* Rebecca A Morin; Tel: 415-379-5495, E-mail: rmorin@calacademy.org; *ILL, Libr Asst,* Kelly Jensen; *Tech Serv,* David Acheson; Tel: 415-379-5496, E-mail: dacheson@calacademy.org; *Tech Serv,* Stella Tang; Tel: 415-379-5492, E-mail: stang@calacademy.org; Staff 4.7 (MLS 3.4, Non-MLS 1.3)
Founded 1853
Jul 2006-Jun 2007. Mats Exp $169,098, Books $24,648, Per/Ser (Incl. Access Fees) $132,959, AV Mat $600, Electronic Ref Mat (Incl. Access Fees) $10,891. Sal $115,584 (Prof $110,900)
Library Holdings: CDs 100; DVDs 300; e-journals 900; Bk Vols 250,000; Per Subs 1,400; Videos 500
Special Collections: Academy Archives; Natural History Image Clippings Files; Natural History Photography Coll. Oral History
Subject Interests: Anthrop, Astronomy, Botany, Entomology, Geog, Geol, Herpetology, Ichthyology, Marine biol, Museology, Natural hist, Ornithology, Paleontology, Zoology
Automation Activity & Vendor Info: (Acquisitions) Ex Libris Group; (Cataloging) Ex Libris Group; (Circulation) Ex Libris Group; (ILL) OCLC Online; (OPAC) Ex Libris Group; (Serials) Ex Libris Group
Database Vendor: BioOne, EBSCOhost, JSTOR, OCLC FirstSearch, ProQuest
Function: Ref serv available, Res libr, Telephone ref
Publications: Accessions List (Quarterly)
Partic in Bay Area Library & Information Network; OCLC Online Computer Library Center, Inc
Restriction: Non-circulating to the pub, Open by appt only

S CALIFORNIA HISTORICAL SOCIETY*, North Baker Research Library, 678 Mission St, 94105. SAN 320-1635. Tel: 415-357-1848, Ext 20. FAX: 415-357-1850. E-mail: info@calhistory.org. Web Site: www.californiahistoricalsociety.org. *Dir, Libr & Archives,* Mary Morganti; *Archivist,* Wendy Welker; Staff 6 (MLS 6)
Founded 1922
Library Holdings: Bk Titles 36,000; Bk Vols 57,000; Spec Interest Per Sub 80
Special Collections: Ephemera Coll; Manuscript & Archival Coll; Photograph Coll; Taylor & Taylor (S F) Archives; Western Printing & Publishing (Edward C Kemble Coll)
Subject Interests: Calif, Hist, Maps, Rare bks
Function: Ref serv available, Res libr
Partic in Melvyl; RLIN (Research Libraries Information Network)
Open Wed-Fri Noon-5
Restriction: Not a lending libr

C CALIFORNIA INSTITUTE OF INTEGRAL STUDIES*, Laurance S Rockefeller Library, 1453 Mission St, 2nd Flr, 94103. SAN 320-6025. Tel: 415-575-6180. Interlibrary Loan Service Tel: 415-575-6193. Reference Tel: 415-575-6186. FAX: 415-575-1264. E-mail: library@ciis.edu. Web Site: library.ciis.edu. *Libr Dir,* Noah Lowenstein; Tel: 415-755-6181, E-mail: nlowensteinn@ciis.edu; *Pub Serv Librn, Ref Librn,* Marion Severy; Tel: 415-575-6183, E-mail: msevery@ciis.edu; *Ref Librn,* Joan Eahr; Tel: 415-575-6182, E-mail: ejoan@ciis.edu; *Ref Librn, Syst Librn,* Kelly Sundin; Tel: 415-575-6187, E-mail: ksundin@ciis.edu; *Archives Coordr,* Bahman Shirazi; Tel: 415-575-6253, E-mail: bshirazi@ciis.edu; Staff 8 (MLS 3, Non-MLS 5)
Founded 1968. Enrl 1,000; Fac 76; Highest Degree: Doctorate
Library Holdings: AV Mats 600; e-books 22,000; Bk Vols 35,000; Per Subs 200
Special Collections: Heritage Coll (Alan Watts, Frederic Spiegelberg, Haridas Chaudhuri); Institute Authors Coll; Langley-Porter Psychology Coll
Subject Interests: Comparative relig, Cultural studies, E-W relations, Philos, Psychol, Spirituality, Women
Automation Activity & Vendor Info: (Cataloging) ByWater Solutions; (Circulation) ByWater Solutions; (Course Reserve) Docutek; (ILL) OCLC ILLiad; (OPAC) ByWater Solutions
Database Vendor: American Psychological Association (APA), Cinahl, ebrary, EBSCOhost, Medline, OCLC FirstSearch, OCLC WorldShare Interlibrary Loan, Oxford Online, ProQuest, PubMed, RefWorks, Wiley InterScience
Function: Archival coll, Audio & video playback equip for onsite use, ILL available, Online cat, Online ref, Ref serv available
Partic in Northern & Central California Psychology Libraries; Statewide California Electronic Library Consortium (SCELC)
Open Mon-Fri 10-7, Sat & Sun 1-6
Restriction: Circ privileges for students & alumni only

CM CALIFORNIA PACIFIC MEDICAL CENTER*, Health Sciences Library, 2395 Sacramento St, 94115-2328. (Mail add: PO Box 7999, 94120-7999), SAN 301-4851. Tel: 415-600-3240. FAX: 415-600-6597. E-mail: cpmclib@sutterhealth.org. Web Site: www.cpmc.org/professionals/hslibrary. *Dir,* Anne Shew; E-mail: shewa@sutterhealth.org; Staff 6 (MLS 2, Non-MLS 4)
Founded 1912. Enrl 415; Fac 115
Library Holdings: Bk Titles 11,000; Per Subs 50
Subject Interests: Dentistry, Med
Automation Activity & Vendor Info: (Cataloging) EOS International; (Circulation) EOS International; (OPAC) EOS International; (Serials) EOS International
Database Vendor: Brodart, Checkpoint Systems, Inc, Dialog, EBSCO Information Services, EBSCOhost, Elsevier, Ingenta, Lexi-Comp, Marcive, Inc, MD Consult, Medlib, Medline, Nature Publishing Group, OVID Technologies, PubMed, Sage, ScienceDirect, Springer-Verlag, UpToDate
Wireless access
Function: ILL available
Partic in Asn for Vision Sci Librns; Northern California & Nevada Medical Library Group (NCNMLG); San Francisco Biomedical Library Network
Open Mon-Thurs 8am-11pm, Fri 8-6, Sat 9-5, Sun 1:30-9:30
Restriction: Private libr

G CALIFORNIA STATE LIBRARY, Sutro Library, J Paul Leonard Library-Sutro Library, 1630 Holloway Ave, 5th Flr, 94132. SAN 301-4754. Tel: 415-469-6100. FAX: 415-469-6172. E-mail: sutro@library.ca.gov. Web Site: www.library.ca.gov. Staff 4 (MLS 2, Non-MLS 2)
Founded 1913
Library Holdings: Bk Vols 250,000
Special Collections: Adolph Sutro's original coll containing rare bks & ms dating from the 13th through 18th Centuries; Includes Sir Joseph Banks ms coll, Hebraica, Orientalia, Mexicana, English pamphlets, Shakespeare's first folio & British ms from same period; Rivers & Harbours coll of nineteenth Britain & Natural Hist bks
Subject Interests: Genealogy & family histories for 49 states
Automation Activity & Vendor Info: (Circulation) SirsiDynix
Database Vendor: OCLC FirstSearch
Wireless access
Open Mon-Fri 10-5
Restriction: Non-circulating of rare bks

L CARROLL, BURDICK & MCDONOUGH*, Law Library, 44 Montgomery St, Ste 400, 94104. SAN 372-2996. Tel: 415-989-5900. FAX: 415-989-0932. Web Site: www.cbmlaw.com. *Head Librn,* Caren Doyle
Library Holdings: Bk Vols 10,000
Automation Activity & Vendor Info: (Cataloging) TLC (The Library Corporation); (Circulation) TLC (The Library Corporation)
Database Vendor: LexisNexis, Westlaw
Partic in OCLC Online Computer Library Center, Inc
Restriction: Staff use only

J CITY COLLEGE OF SAN FRANCISCO*, Rosenberg Library, 50 Phelan Ave, 94112. SAN 301-388X. Tel: 415-452-5454. Circulation Tel: 415-452-5433. Interlibrary Loan Service Tel: 415-452-5562. Reference Tel: 415-452-5541, 415-452-5543. Automation Services Tel: 415-452-5500. FAX: 415-452-5588. Administration FAX: 415-452-5488. Automation Services FAX: 415-452-5478. Web Site: www.ccsf.edu/NEW/en/library.html. *Dept Head,* Charles Fracchia; E-mail: cfracchi@ccsf.edu; *Acq Librn,* Joao Barretto; E-mail: jbarrett@ccsf.edu; *AV Coordr,* Sirous Monajami; Tel: 415-452-5469, E-mail: smonajam@ccsf.edu; *Distance Educ, Electronic Serv,* James Lim; Tel: 415-452-5430, E-mail: jlim@ccsf.edu; *Media Serv,* Alexander Valentine; Tel: 415-452-5426, E-mail: avalenti@ccsf.edu; *Per,* Karen Chan; Tel: 415-452-4354, E-mail: ychan@ccsf.edu; Staff 28 (MLS 28)
Founded 1935. Enrl 35,541; Fac 1,840; Highest Degree: Associate
Jul 2005-Jun 2006. Mats Exp $198,932, Books $55,238, Per/Ser (Incl. Access Fees) $66,022, Micro $46,261, Electronic Ref Mat (Incl. Access Fees) $31,411. Sal $5,472,440 (Prof $1,996,197)
Library Holdings: CDs 127; DVDs 85; e-books 512; Bk Titles 140,868; Bk Vols 178,811; Per Subs 677; Videos 138
Special Collections: Hotel-Restaurant (Alice Statler Coll), bks, microflm, reels
Automation Activity & Vendor Info: (Acquisitions) Innovative Interfaces, Inc; (Cataloging) Innovative Interfaces, Inc; (Circulation) Innovative Interfaces, Inc, (OPAC) Innovative Interfaces, Inc
Database Vendor: Gale Cengage Learning
Wireless access
Publications: Library Tips
Partic in Bay Area Library & Information Network; Coop Libr Agency for Syst & Servs; OCLC Online Computer Library Center, Inc
Open Mon-Thurs 7:30am-7:45pm, Fri 7:45-2:45, Sat 10-1:45
Friends of the Library Group

S THE HENRY WILSON COIL LIBRARY & MUSEUM OF FREEMASONRY*, 1111 California St, 94108. SAN 301-4088. Tel: 415-776-7000. FAX: 415-776-0483. Web Site: www.freemason.org, www.masonicheritage.org. *Coll Mgr,* Adam Kendall; Tel: 415-292-9137, E-mail: akendall@freemason.org
Founded 1949
Library Holdings: Bk Vols 7,000; Per Subs 6
Special Collections: Annual Proceedings of Masonic Grand Lodge, California 1850-present
Open Mon, Tues & Thurs 10-3, Wed 10-5,

S COMMONWEALTH CLUB OF CALIFORNIA*, Stuart Richardson Ward Library, 595 Market St, 94105. SAN 301-3901. Tel: 415-597-6700. FAX: 415-597-6729. E-mail: club@commonwealthclub.org. Web Site: www.commonwealthclub.org. *In Charge,* Greg Dalton
Founded 1903
Library Holdings: Bk Titles 1,000
Open Mon-Fri 9-5
Restriction: Mem only

L COOLEY GODWARD KRONISH LLP LIBRARY*, 101 California St, 5th Flr, 94111. SAN 301-391X. Tel: 415-693-2000. FAX: 415-693-2222. Web Site: www.cooley.com. *Mgr,* Yvonne Boyer; E-mail: boyery@cooley.com; *Ref,* Margaret Baer; *Tech Serv,* Vera Janour; Staff 3 (MLS 2, Non-MLS 1)
Library Holdings: Bk Vols 20,000
Subject Interests: Law
Automation Activity & Vendor Info: (Cataloging) Softlink America; (OPAC) Softlink America; (Serials) Softlink America
Database Vendor: LexisNexis, Westlaw
Partic in Dialog Corp; Westlaw
Restriction: Staff use only

L COOPER, WHITE & COOPER*, Law Library, 201 California St, 17th Flr, 94111-5002. SAN 372-3917. Tel: 415-433-1900. Interlibrary Loan Service Tel: 415-433-1900, Ext 6269. FAX: 415-433-5530. Web Site: cwclaw.com.

Mgr, Libr Serv, Cindy Beck Weller; E-mail: cweller@cwclaw.com; Staff 1 (MLS 1)
Founded 1896
Library Holdings: Bk Vols 20,000; Per Subs 200
Special Collections: Law
Subject Interests: Construction, Corp law, Employment, Labor, Litigation, Telecommunications law
Automation Activity & Vendor Info: (Acquisitions) Inmagic, Inc.; (Cataloging) Inmagic, Inc.; (ILL) Inmagic, Inc.; (OPAC) Inmagic, Inc.; (Serials) Inmagic, Inc.
Database Vendor: Dialog, Dun & Bradstreet, HeinOnline, Hoovers, Westlaw
Function: Computers for patron use, ILL available, Online cat, Online searches, Ref & res
Partic in Northern Calif Asn of Law Librs
Restriction: Co libr, Employee & client use only

S DEGENKOLB ENGINEERS LIBRARY*, 235 Montgomery St, Ste 500, 94104-2908. SAN 327-6864. Tel: 415-392-6952. FAX: 415-981-3157. Web Site: www.degenkolb.com. *Librn,* Natalia Schoeck
Library Holdings: Bk Vols 5,500
Special Collections: EERC Reports; Technical Papers; Earthquake engineering; California & Worldwide Seismicity
Subject Interests: Earthquake eng, Siesmology
Wireless access
Restriction: Not open to pub

GM DEPARTMENT OF VETERANS AFFAIRS*, Marvin Siperstein Medical Library, Medical Library 142D, 4150 Clement St, 94121. SAN 301-4878. Tel: 415-221-4810, Ext 3302. Interlibrary Loan Service Tel: 415-221-4810, Ext 3304. FAX: 415-750-6919. *Chief Librn,* Anne Ludvik; E-mail: anne.ludvik@va.gov; *ILL Tech,* Nadine Walas
Founded 1949
Library Holdings: Bk Titles 3,500; Bk Vols 3,700; Per Subs 20
Subject Interests: Patient educ
Automation Activity & Vendor Info: (Cataloging) EOS International; (OPAC) EOS International; (Serials) EOS International
Open Mon-Fri 8-4:30

S DOLBY LABORATORIES, INC, Technical Library, 100 Potrero Ave, 94103. SAN 370-2286. Tel: 415-558-0268. FAX: 415-863-1373. E-mail: tlh@dolby.com. Web Site: www.dolby.com. *Managing Librn,* Tamara Horacek; Staff 3 (MLS 1, Non-MLS 2)
Founded 1986
Library Holdings: Bk Vols 5,700; Per Subs 400
Restriction: Open to pub upon request

S FARALLONES MARINE SANCTUARY ASSOCIATION*, Resource Library, Bldg 991, Old Coast Guard Sta, Marine Dr, 94129. SAN 375-2453. Tel: 415-561-6625. FAX: 415-561-6616. Web Site: www.farallones.org. *Dir,* Justin Holl; E-mail: justin.holl@noaa.gov
Founded 1998
Library Holdings: Bk Vols 1,000
Open Wed-Sun 10-4

L FARELLA, BRAUN & MARTEL*, Law Library, 235 Montgomery St, 17th Flr, 94104. SAN 372-297X. Tel: 415-954-4451. FAX: 415-954-4480. Web Site: www.fbm.com. *Librn,* Mary Staats; E-mail: mstaats@fbm.com
Library Holdings: Bk Titles 2,500; Bk Vols 15,000
Wireless access

J FASHION INSTITUTE OF DESIGN & MERCHANDISING LIBRARY*, 55 Stockton St, 5th Flr, 94108-5829. SAN 326-8918. Tel: 415-675-5200. Toll Free Tel: 800-422-3436. FAX: 415-989-5312. Web Site: www.fidm.com. *Libr Dir,* Kathy Bailon; Staff 5 (MLS 1, Non-MLS 4)
Enrl 540
Library Holdings: AV Mats 800; Bk Titles 4,500; Per Subs 150
Special Collections: Costume Study Coll, 1860s to present
Subject Interests: Apparel, Communications, Fashion design, Graphic design, Interior design, Manufacturing, Mkt
Automation Activity & Vendor Info: (Acquisitions) Gateway; (Cataloging) Gateway; (Circulation) Gateway; (Course Reserve) Gateway; (OPAC) Gateway
Database Vendor: EBSCOhost, LexisNexis, ProQuest
Function: For res purposes
Open Mon-Thurs 8-8, Fri 8-5, Sat 9-3
Restriction: Open to students, fac & staff

S FEDERAL RESERVE BANK OF SAN FRANCISCO*, Research Library, 101 Market St, 94105-1579. (Mail add: PO Box 7702, 94120-7702), SAN 301-4029. Tel: 415-974-3216. FAX: 415-974-3429. *Mgr,* Cindy Hill; *Ref/Archives Librn,* Anne Hall; *Tech Serv,* Diane Rosenberger
Library Holdings: Bk Titles 18,000; Bk Vols 35,000; Per Subs 350
Automation Activity & Vendor Info: (Cataloging) Inmagic, Inc.; (Circulation) Inmagic, Inc.
Database Vendor: EBSCOhost, Factiva.com, LexisNexis
Restriction: Open by appt only

S FOUNDATION CENTER-SAN FRANCISCO LIBRARY*, 312 Sutter St, No 606, 94108. SAN 301-4061. Tel: 415-397-0902. FAX: 415-397-7670. Web Site: www.fdncenter.org/sanfrancisco. *Dir,* Janet Camarena; E-mail: jfc@fdncenter.org; Staff 5 (MLS 5)
Founded 1977
Library Holdings: Bk Titles 1,400; Per Subs 50
Special Collections: Foundation Annual Reports; IRS 990-PF; Tax Returns
Publications: This Month in the Foundation Center - San Francisco (Newsletter)
Open Mon 11-6, Tues, Thurs & Fri 10-5, Wed 10-8

C GOLDEN GATE UNIVERSITY*, University Library, 536 Mission St, 94105-2967. SAN 334-5300. Tel: 415-442-7242. Interlibrary Loan Service Tel: 415-442-7256. Reference Tel: 415-442-7244. FAX: 415-543-6779. Web Site: www.ggu.edu/libraries/university-library. *Dir of Libr Serv,* James Krusling; Tel: 415-442-7248, E-mail: jkrusling@ggu.edu; *Head, Access Serv,* Gilles Poitras; *Head, Tech Serv,* Steven Dunlap; *Syst Librn,* Hadi Amjadi
Founded 1851. Enrl 3,813; Fac 100; Highest Degree: Doctorate
Library Holdings: Bk Vols 150,000; Per Subs 370
Publications: The Update
Open Mon-Thurs 10-10, Fri & Sat 10-5, Sun 12-5

Departmental Libraries:

CL SCHOOL OF LAW LIBRARY, 536 Mission St, 94105, SAN 334-5335. Tel: 415-442-6680. FAX: 415-512-9395. Web Site: www.law.ggu.edu/law-library. *Dir,* Michael Daw; Staff 8 (MLS 7, Non-MLS 1)
Founded 1901. Enrl 750; Fac 38
Library Holdings: Bk Vols 275,000; Per Subs 3,424
Special Collections: State Document Depository; US Document Depository
Subject Interests: Anglo-Am law, Calif, Law
Automation Activity & Vendor Info: (Acquisitions) Innovative Interfaces, Inc; (Cataloging) Innovative Interfaces, Inc; (Circulation) Innovative Interfaces, Inc; (Course Reserve) Innovative Interfaces, Inc; (ILL) Innovative Interfaces, Inc; (Media Booking) Innovative Interfaces, Inc; (OPAC) Innovative Interfaces, Inc; (Serials) Innovative Interfaces, Inc
Publications: Guide Series; Information Series
Open Mon-Thurs (Winter) 7:30am-10:30pm, Fri 7:30am-9pm, Sat 10-7, Sun 10am-10:30pm; Mon-Thurs (Summer) 7:30am-10pm, Fri 7:30-7, Sat & Sun 10-6
Restriction: Private libr

L GORDON & REES LLP*, Law Library, 275 Battery St, 20th Flr, 94111. SAN 372-3143. Tel: 415-986-5900. FAX: 415-986-8054. Web Site: www.gordonrees.com. *Librn,* Joanne Dumapay
Library Holdings: Bk Vols 20,000
Subject Interests: Med
Open Mon-Fri 7:45-6

L HANSON BRIDGETT LLP*, Law Library, 425 Market St, 26th Flr, 94105. SAN 372-3429. Tel: 415-995-5855. FAX: 415-541-9366. Web Site: www.hansonbridgett.com. *Librn,* Cathy Hardy; *Ref Librn,* Helen Brobst; *ILL,* Emma Andreoli
Library Holdings: Bk Vols 24,000
Open Mon-Fri 8-5

L HASSARD BONNINGTON*, Law Library, Two Embarcadero Ctr, Ste 1800, 94111. SAN 324-1335. Tel: 415-288-9800. FAX: 415-288-9801. Web Site: www.hassard.com. *Librn,* Diane Rodriguez
Library Holdings: Bk Titles 3,000; Bk Vols 14,000; Per Subs 100
Subject Interests: Med
Open Mon-Fri 9-5

J HEALD COLLEGE*, Learning Resource Center-San Francisco Campus, 875 Howard St, 94103. Tel: 415-808-3000. FAX: 415-808-3006. Web Site: www.heald.edu.
Library Holdings: Bk Vols 1,000; Per Subs 25; Talking Bks 50; Videos 40
Database Vendor: EBSCOhost
Open Mon-Thurs 7am-10pm, Fri 8-8, Sat 10-3

S INSTITUTE FOR ADVANCED STUDY OF HUMAN SEXUALITY*, Research Library, 1523 Franklin St, 94109. SAN 327-5787. Tel: 415-928-1133. FAX: 415-928-8061. E-mail: registrar@iashs.edu. Web Site: www.iashs.edu. *Librn,* Dr Jerry Zientara
Founded 1974

Library Holdings: Bk Titles 300,000; Per Subs 350,000; Videos 100,000
Restriction: Not open to pub

S INSTITUTE FOR CHILDHOOD RESOURCES*, Family Information Center, 268 Bush St, 94104. SAN 324-5128. Tel: 510-540-0111. Web Site: www.drtoy.com. *Dir,* Stevanne Auerbach; E-mail: drtoy@drtoy.com; Staff 4 (MLS 2, Non-MLS 2)
Library Holdings: Bk Titles 5,000; Per Subs 10
Special Collections: Toys
Subject Interests: Child care, Early childhood, Parenting educ
Publications: Choosing Childcare: A Guide for Parents; Dr Toy's Smart Play. Raising a Child with a High PQ (Play Quotient); Toychest: A Sourcebook; Whole Child: A Sourcebook
Restriction: Not open to pub

S INTERNATIONAL LONGSHORE & WAREHOUSE UNION*, Anne Rand Research Library, 1188 Franklin St, 4th Flr, 94109. SAN 301-4177. Tel: 415-775-0533. FAX: 415-775-1302. Web Site: www.ilwu.org. *Librn,* Robin Walker; E-mail: robin.walker@ilwu.org
Founded 1942
Library Holdings: Bk Titles 3,000; Per Subs 125
Open Mon-Fri 9-5

S JAPANESE AMERICAN NATIONAL LIBRARY, 1619 Sutter St, 94109. (Mail add: PO Box 590598, 94159-0598), SAN 374-7751. Tel: 415-567-5006. Web Site: www.janlibrary.org. *Dir,* Karl K Matsushita
Founded 1969
Library Holdings: Bk Vols 35,000; Per Subs 55
Special Collections: Japanese American Redress
Subject Interests: Japanese in Am
Function: Archival coll, Ref serv available, Res libr
Open Mon-Fri 1-5
Restriction: Open to pub for ref only

R JEWISH COMMUNITY LIBRARY*, 1835 Ellis St, 94115. SAN 301-3766. Tel: 415-567-3327. E-mail: library@jewishlearningworks.org. Web Site: www.jewishlearningworks.org/library. *Dir,* Howard Freedman; Tel: 415-567-3327, Ext 705, E-mail: hfreedman@jewishlearningworks.org; *Reader Serv Librn,* Rose Katz; Tel: 415-567-3327, Ext 706, E-mail: rkatz@jewishlearningworks.org
Library Holdings: DVDs 2,000; Bk Vols 35,000; Per Subs 16
Special Collections: Havas Children's Library
Subject Interests: Culture, Jewish hist, Jewish philos, Judaism (religion)
Open Mon & Wed 10-4, Tues 12-6, Thurs 12-8, Sun 12-4
Friends of the Library Group

S JFCS HOLOCAUST CENTER*, Tauber Holocaust Library, 2245 Post St, 94115. SAN 326 064X. Tel: 415-449-3748. FAX: 415-449-3720. E-mail: tauberholocaustlibrary@jfcs.org. Web Site: www.tauberholocaustlibrary.org. *Archivist,* Judy Janec; Tel: 415-777-9060, Ext 206, E-mail: jjanec@hcnc.org; Staff 2 (MLS 1, Non-MLS 1)
Founded 1979
Library Holdings: Bk Vols 13,500
Special Collections: Archives; Historical Pamphlet Coll; Periodicals Coll; Rare Books; Yizkor Book Coll. Oral History
Subject Interests: Genocide, Holocaust, World War II
Wireless access
Function: Ref serv available
Restriction: Non-circulating, Open by appt only

S C G JUNG INSTITUTE OF SAN FRANCISCO*, Virginia Allan Detloff Library, 2040 Gough St, 94109. SAN 372-5928. Tel: 415-771-8055, Ext 207. FAX: 415-771-8926. E-mail: library@sfjung.org. Web Site: www.sfjung.org. *Librn,* Marianne Morgan; E-mail: mmorgan@sfjung.org; *Libr Asst,* Salina Lee; Staff 2 (MLS 1, Non-MLS 1)
Founded 1965
Library Holdings: AV Mats 1,350; CDs 15; DVDs 10; Bk Titles 15,500; Bk Vols 16,000; Per Subs 25; Videos 185
Special Collections: Archive of Historical Jungiana, Audio & Video. Oral History
Subject Interests: Analytical psychol, Art, Jungian psychol, Mythology, Psychol
Automation Activity & Vendor Info: (Acquisitions) Inmagic, Inc.; (Cataloging) Inmagic, Inc.; (OPAC) Inmagic, Inc.; (Serials) Inmagic, Inc.
Function: ILL available, Ref serv available
Partic in Northern & Central California Psychology Libraries
Open Mon-Fri 9-5
Restriction: Staff & mem only, Sub libr

M KAISER-PERMANENTE MEDICAL CENTER*, Health Sciences Library, 2425 Geary Blvd, Mezzanine M150, 94115. SAN 301-4207. Tel: 415-833-2000, 415-833-3837. Administration Tel: 415-833-3835. FAX: 415-833-2200, 415-833-3257. E-mail: sfo.library@kp.org. Web Site: www.kplibraries.libguides.com. *Librn,* Owen Miller; Staff 2 (MLS 1, Non-MLS 1)
Founded 1954
Library Holdings: Bk Titles 3,700; Per Subs 190
Database Vendor: EBSCOhost, Gale Cengage Learning, OVID Technologies
Publications: Journal List; Recent Acquisitions
Partic in Northern California & Nevada Medical Library Group (NCNMLG); San Francisco Biomedical Library Network
Open Mon-Fri 9-Noon

S KAPLAN, MCLAUGHLIN & DIAZ ARCHITECTS LIBRARY*, 222 Vallejo St, 94111. SAN 327-5809. Tel: 415-398-5191. FAX: 415-394-7158. Web Site: www.kmdarchitects.com. *Librn,* Michelle Howard; Staff 1 (MLS 1)
Library Holdings: Bk Titles 5,000; Spec Interest Per Sub 25
Special Collections: Architectural Library
Subject Interests: Archit, Design, Planning
Automation Activity & Vendor Info: (Cataloging) Inmagic, Inc.; (Circulation) Inmagic, Inc.; (OPAC) Inmagic, Inc.; (Serials) Inmagic, Inc.
Restriction: Open by appt only

S KENNEDY-JENKS CONSULTANTS, INC LIBRARY*, 303 Second St, Ste 300 South, 94107. SAN 301-4215. Tel: 415-243-2150. Information Services Tel: 415-243-2531. FAX: 415-896-0999. *Librn,* Cynthia Eastman; Staff 2 (MLS 1, Non-MLS 1)
Library Holdings: Bk Titles 3,500; Bk Vols 3,600; Per Subs 50
Subject Interests: Civil eng, Environ eng, Wastewater treatment
Automation Activity & Vendor Info: (Cataloging) EOS International
Database Vendor: Dialog, EOS International, OCLC FirstSearch, ScienceDirect
Function: Res libr
Restriction: Not open to pub

L LATHAM & WATKINS LLP LIBRARY*, 505 Montgomery St, Ste 1900, 94111. SAN 372-2910. Tel: 415-391-0600. FAX: 415-395-8095. Web Site: www.lw.com. *Librn,* Frank Lee; E-mail: frank.lee@lw.com; Staff 4 (MLS 2, Non-MLS 2)
Library Holdings: Bk Vols 20,000
Partic in OCLC Online Computer Library Center, Inc

S LIGHTHOUSE FOR THE BLIND & VISUALLY IMPAIRED*, Free Lending-Browsing Braille Library, 214 Van Ness Ave, 94102. SAN 301-4606. Tel: 415-431-1481. FAX: 415-863-7568. Web Site: www.lighthouse-sf.org. *Commun Serv Coordr,* Molly Irish; Tel: 415-694-7320, E-mail: mpearson@lighthouse-sf.org
Founded 1949
Library Holdings: Bk Titles 300; Bk Vols 1,200
Special Collections: Braille Codes, Thesaurus, Unabridged Dictionary, World Book
Subject Interests: Fiction, Philos, Relig
Special Services for the Deaf - TTY equip
Open Mon-Fri 8:30-5

L LITTLER MENDELSON LIBRARY*, 650 California St, 20th Flr, 94108-2693. SAN 325-5212. Tel: 415-399-8441. FAX: 415-399-8490. E-mail: info@littler.com. Web Site: www.littler.com. *Mgr,* Lynn Harris; *Librn,* Joanne Block; *Librn,* Yarka Odvarko; *Ref Librn,* Nora Sawyer; Staff 9 (MLS 5, Non-MLS 4)
Founded 1953
Subject Interests: Employment law, Labor law
Automation Activity & Vendor Info: (Acquisitions) Inmagic, Inc.; (Cataloging) Inmagic, Inc.; (Serials) Inmagic, Inc.
Wireless access
Restriction: Not open to pub

S MECHANICS' INSTITUTE LIBRARY*, 57 Post St, 94104-5003. SAN 301-4304. Tel: 415-393-0101. Reference Tel: 415-393-0102. Administration Tel: 415-393-0113. Automation Services Tel: 415-393-0109. FAX: 415-421-4192. E-mail: reference@milibrary.org. Web Site: www.milibrary.org. *Libr Dir,* Deborah Hunt; E-mail: dhunt@milibrary.org; *Head, Tech Serv,* A Craig Jackson; Tel: 415-393-0104, E-mail: acjackson@milibrary.org; *Managing Librn,* Bobbie Monzon; Tel: 415-393-0107, E-mail: bmonzon@milibrary.org; *Mkt & Membership Spec/Ref Librn,* Taryn Edwards; Tel: 415-393-0103, E-mail: tedwards@milibrary.org; *Pub Serv Librn,* Diane Lai; Tel: 415-393-0118, E-mail: dlai@milibrary.org; *Cataloger, Ref Librn,* Erika Schmidt; Tel: 415-393-0115, E-mail: eschmidt@milibrary.org; *Tech Serv Librn,* Matthew Montgomery; E-mail: mmontgomery@milibrary.org; *Web Librn,* Jeremy Snell; Tel: 415-393-0111, E-mail: jsnell@milibrary.org; Staff 15 (MLS 8, Non-MLS 7)
Founded 1854
Library Holdings: AV Mats 7,500; Bk Vols 165,000; Per Subs 500; Talking Bks 2,000

Special Collections: Business; California History Coll; Chess; Finance; Investment; Local Authors
Subject Interests: Fiction, Local hist
Automation Activity & Vendor Info: (Acquisitions) Innovative Interfaces, Inc; (Cataloging) Innovative Interfaces, Inc; (Circulation) Innovative Interfaces, Inc; (OPAC) Innovative Interfaces, Inc; (Serials) Innovative Interfaces, Inc
Database Vendor: Gale Cengage Learning, Hoovers, Innovative Interfaces, Inc, JSTOR, ProQuest, ReferenceUSA, Standard & Poor's, ValueLine
Wireless access
Publications: Newsletter (Bi-annually); This Month @ the Mechanics' (Monthly newsletter)
Partic in Bay Area Library & Information Network

L MILLS LAW LIBRARY*, 220 Montgomery St, Ste 116, 94104. SAN 371-5825. Tel: 415-781-2665. FAX: 415-781-1116. Web Site: www.millslibrary.org. *Librn,* Jacob Koff; *Asst Librn,* Harriet M Kasdan; Staff 2 (MLS 1, Non-MLS 1)
Founded 1987
Library Holdings: Bk Titles 5,000; Bk Vols 20,000; Per Subs 170

S MUSEUM OF RUSSIAN CULTURE, INC LIBRARY*, 2450 Sutter St, 94115. SAN 320-605X. Tel: 415-921-4082. FAX: 415-921-4082. E-mail: contact@mrcsf.org. Web Site: mrcsf.org. *Pres,* Nicholas Koretsky; *VPres,* Georgy Tarala
Founded 1949
Library Holdings: Bk Vols 20,000

S NATIONAL PARK SERVICE*, Golden Gate National Recreation Area Park Archives, Park Archives & Records Ctr, Bldg 667, Presidio of San Francisco, 94129. (Mail add: Fort Mason Bldg 201, 94123), SAN 333-7758. Tel: 415-561-2804. Reference Tel: 415-561-2807. FAX: 415-441-1618. *Supvry Curator,* Susan Ewing Haley; Staff 3 (MLS 3)
Founded 1974
Library Holdings: Bk Titles 8,000; Per Subs 20
Special Collections: History of San Francisco; History of the West; Indian Wars; Korea; Presidio History of San Francisco; US Army History; Vietnam; Women of War; World War I & II. Oral History

L ORRICK, HERRINGTON & SUTCLIFFE LLP*, Law Library, The Orrick Bldg, 405 Howard St, 94105-2669. SAN 301-4398. Tel: 415-773-5700. FAX: 415-773-5759. Web Site: www.orrick.com. *Mgr,* Peg LaFrance; E-mail: mlafrance@orrick.com; Staff 3 (MLS 3)
Founded 1884
Library Holdings: Bk Titles 7,000; Bk Vols 30,000; Per Subs 350
Subject Interests: Calif, Corporate law
Partic in Northern Calif Asn of Law Librs
Restriction: Staff use only

S PACIFIC GAS & ELECTRIC CO*, Energy Resource Center Library, 851 Howard St, 94103. SAN 375-1422. Tel: 415-973-7206. FAX: 415-896-1280. Web Site: www.pge.com/pec/resourcecenter. *In Charge,* Marlene Vogelsang; E-mail: mxv6@pge.com; Staff 1 (MLS 1)
Founded 1991
Library Holdings: Bk Titles 2,000; Per Subs 90
Special Collections: California Energy Commission Documents
Subject Interests: Climate issues, Energy, Energy efficiency, Sustainability
Automation Activity & Vendor Info: (Acquisitions) EOS International; (Cataloging) EOS International; (Circulation) EOS International; (OPAC) EOS International; (Serials) EOS International
Partic in Bay Area Library & Information Network
Restriction: Circ limited

S PESTICIDE ACTION NETWORK NORTH AMERICAN REGIONAL CENTER*, International Information Program, 49 Powell St, Ste 500, 94102. SAN 372-6827. Tel: 415-981-1771. FAX: 415-981-1991. Web Site: www.panna.org/panna. *Librn,* Martha Olson Jarocki
Founded 1988
Library Holdings: Bk Titles 4,000; Per Subs 250
Special Collections: Pesticides, Agriculture & International Development, bks; US Environmental Protection Agency, reports & bd doc
Subject Interests: Agr, Pesticides
Restriction: Open by appt only

L PILLSBURY WINTHROP LLP*, Law Library, 50 Fremont St, 94105. SAN 301-4460. Tel: 415-983-1130. FAX: 415-983-1200. Web Site: www.pillsburywinthrop.com. *Mgr,* Debra Schwarz
Library Holdings: Bk Vols 30,000; Per Subs 500
Open Mon-Fri 8-5:30

M SAINT FRANCIS MEMORIAL HOSPITAL*, Walter F Schaller Memorial Library, 900 Hyde St, 94109. SAN 301-4487. Tel: 415-353-6320. *Libr Serv Mgr,* Maryann Zaremska; E-mail: mzaremsk@chw.edu; Staff 2 (MLS 1, Non-MLS 1)
Founded 1972
Library Holdings: Bk Titles 1,845; Bk Vols 2,000; Per Subs 240
Special Collections: Health & Wellness Resource Center (Consumer Health/Patient Education Coll)
Automation Activity & Vendor Info: (Cataloging) CyberTools for Libraries; (Circulation) CyberTools for Libraries; (OPAC) CyberTools for Libraries; (Serials) CyberTools for Libraries
Database Vendor: EBSCOhost, OVID Technologies
Partic in Docline; Northern California & Nevada Medical Library Group (NCNMLG); San Francisco Biomedical Library Network

M ST MARY'S MEDICAL CENTER, CATHOLIC HEALTHCARE WEST*, Solomon Medical Library, 2235 Hayes St, 4th flr, 94117. (Mail add: 450 Stanyan St, 94117), SAN 301-4517. Tel: 415-750-5795. FAX: 415-750-8149. *Acad Res Coordr/Med Librn,* Janice M Hoobler; E-mail: janice.hoobler@chw.edu; Staff 1 (MLS 1)
Founded 1937
Subject Interests: Med, Orthopedics, Psychiat
Automation Activity & Vendor Info: (Cataloging) Inmagic, Inc.
Partic in Catholic Healthcare W; National Network of Libraries of Medicine; Northern California & Nevada Medical Library Group (NCNMLG); Pacific Southwest Regional Medical Library (PSRML)
Open Mon-Fri 9-5

S SAN FRANCISCO AFRICAN-AMERICAN HISTORICAL & CULTURAL SOCIETY*, Library of San Francisco, 762 Fulton St, 2nd Flr, 94102. SAN 301-3618. Tel: 415-292-6172. FAX: 415-440-4231. Web Site: www.sfblackhistory.org. *Pres,* Al Williams
Founded 1955
Library Holdings: Bk Vols 35,892; Per Subs 10
Publications: A Walking Tour of Black Presence in California during the 19th Century; Ascension - Literary Anthology
Partic in Bay Area Library & Information Network
Friends of the Library Group

C SAN FRANCISCO ART INSTITUTE*, Anne Bremer Memorial Library, 800 Chestnut St, 94133. SAN 301-4533. Tel: 415-749-4562. E-mail: library@sfai.edu. Web Site: www.sfai.edu. *Librn,* Jeff Gunderson; Tel: 415-749-4559; *Librn,* Charles Stephanian; *Cat Spec,* Claudia Marlowe; *Libr Spec,* Rebecca Alexander; Staff 2 (MLS 1, Non-MLS 1)
Founded 1871. Enrl 550; Fac 60; Highest Degree: Master
Library Holdings: Bk Titles 31,000; Bk Vols 34,000; Per Subs 220
Special Collections: California Art, 1871-; History (San Francisco Art Institute), archives, bks, doc, photogs
Subject Interests: Art, Films & filmmaking, Photog
Automation Activity & Vendor Info: (Cataloging) LibraryWorld, Inc; (Circulation) LibraryWorld, Inc; (ILL) OCLC; (OPAC) LibraryWorld, Inc
Database Vendor: ARTstor, H W Wilson
Wireless access
Publications: Hey You!; Read This First (Quarterly)
Restriction: Open to fac, students & qualified researchers

S SAN FRANCISCO BOTANICAL GARDEN SOCIETY AT STRYBING ARBORETUM*, Helen Crocker Russell Library of Horticulture, 1199 Ninth Ave, (Ninth Ave at Lincoln Way), 94122-2384. SAN 301-4738. Tel: 415-661-1316, Ext 303. FAX: 415-661-3539. E-mail: library@sfbotanicalgarden.org. Web Site: www.sfbotanicalgarden.org. *Head Librn,* Barbara M Pitschel; E-mail: bpitschel@sfbotanicalgarden.org; *Assoc Librn,* Jane Glasby; E-mail: jglasby@sfbotanicalgarden.org; *Asst Librn,* Brandy Kuhl; E-mail: bkuhl@sfbotanicalgarden.org; *Libr Tech, Pub Info,* Richard Steger; E-mail: rsteger@sfbotanicalgarden.org. Subject Specialists: *Botany, Hort,* Barbara M Pitschel; *Hort,* Jane Glasby; *Computer application, Gardening,* Brandy Kuhl; Staff 2.5 (MLS 2, Non-MLS 0.5)
Founded 1972
Apr 2007-Mar 2008 Income $222,940, Locally Generated Income $82,550, Parent Institution $140,390. Mats Exp $42,000, Books $13,000, Per/Ser (Incl. Access Fees) $15,000, AV Equip $1,000, Electronic Ref Mat (Incl. Access Fees) $10,000, Presv $3,000. Sal $112,500 (Prof $100,000)
Library Holdings: CDs 100; DVDs 1; Electronic Media & Resources 20; Bk Titles 22,500; Bk Vols 25,000; Per Subs 500; Spec Interest Per Sub 500; Videos 50
Special Collections: Nursery & Seed Catalogs
Subject Interests: Botany, Hort
Automation Activity & Vendor Info: (Cataloging) OCLC; (OPAC) Innovative Interfaces, Inc; (Serials) EBSCO Online
Database Vendor: EBSCOhost, FileMaker, Ingram Library Services, OCLC WorldShare Interlibrary Loan
Function: Art exhibits, Audio & video playback equip for onsite use, Handicapped accessible, ILL available, Orientations, Photocopying/Printing, Prog for children & young adult, Ref serv available, Telephone ref, Wheelchair accessible
Publications: Bibliography Series (Acquisition list)
Partic in CDB-S; Council on Botanical & Horticultural Libraries, Inc (CBHL); OCLC Online Computer Library Center, Inc

Open Mon-Sun 10-4
Restriction: Non-circulating, Open to pub for ref only

S SAN FRANCISCO CAMERAWORK*, Reference Library, 657 Mission St, 2nd Flr, 94105-4104. SAN 328-1140. Tel: 415-512-2020. FAX: 415-512-7109. E-mail: sfcamera@sfcamerawork.org. Web Site: www.sfcamerawork.org. *Mgr,* Chelsea Morse; *Curator,* Chuck Mobley
Founded 1974
Library Holdings: Bk Vols 5,000; Per Subs 50
Special Collections: Artist's bks; Exhibition Catalogues
Subject Interests: Criticism, Hist, Photog
Publications: Camerawork: A Journal of Photographic Arts
Open Tues-Sat 12-5

S SAN FRANCISCO CENTER FOR PSYCHOANALYSIS*, Erik Erikson Library, 2340 Jackson St, 4th Flr, 94115. SAN 301-4622. Tel: 415-563-4477. FAX: 415-563-8406. E-mail: library@sf-cp.org. Web Site: www.sf-cp.org/Library/library.htm. *Dir,* Susanna Bonetti; Staff 1 (Non-MLS 1)
Founded 1950
Library Holdings: AV Mats 582; Electronic Media & Resources 2; Bk Titles 5,600; Per Subs 50
Special Collections: Bernice S Engle Coll; Emmanuel Windholz Coll
Subject Interests: Psychoanalysis
Automation Activity & Vendor Info: (Cataloging) LibraryWorld, Inc; (OPAC) LibraryWorld, Inc; (Serials) LibraryWorld, Inc
Database Vendor: PubMed
Publications: Dialogue
Partic in BayNet Library Association, Northern & Central California Psychology Libraries; Pacific Southwest Regional Medical Library (PSRML)
Friends of the Library Group

S SAN FRANCISCO CHRONICLE LIBRARY*, 901 Mission St, 94103. SAN 301-4541. Tel: 415-777-7843. FAX: 415-896-0668. Web Site: www.sfgate.com/chronicle/. *Dir,* Richard Geiger; Tel: 415-777-6001, E-mail: rgeiger@sfchronicle.com; *Archives Dir,* Bill Van Niekerken; Tel: 415-777-7231, E-mail: bvanniekerken@sfchronicle.com; Staff 6 (MLS 5, Non-MLS 1)
Founded 1879
Library Holdings: Bk Vols 400
Subject Interests: Local hist
Database Vendor: Dialog, EBSCOhost, Factiva.com, Gale Cengage Learning, LexisNexis, Newsbank, ProQuest

S SAN FRANCISCO CONSERVATORY OF MUSIC LIBRARY, 50 Oak St, 94102. SAN 301-4568. Tel: 415-503-6213, 415-503-6253. Information Services Tel: 415-503-6356. FAX: 415-759-3499. Web Site: www.sfcm.edu. *Dir, Libr Serv,* Kevin McLaughlin; E-mail: kmclaughlin@sfcm.edu; *Circ Supvr,* Sarah Bonomo; *Circ Supvr,* Jeff Dittmer; *Circ Supvr,* Sara Hagenbuch; *Archivist,* Tessa Updike; Staff 5 (MLS 2, Non-MLS 3)
Founded 1917
Library Holdings: AV Mats 13,000; Bk Titles 41,000; Bk Vols 75,000; Per Subs 73
Subject Interests: Humanities, Music
Automation Activity & Vendor Info: (Acquisitions) OCLC; (Cataloging) OCLC WorldShare Interlibrary Loan; (Circulation) OCLC WorldShare Interlibrary Loan; (ILL) OCLC WorldShare Interlibrary Loan
Wireless access
Open Mon-Fri 8:30am-10pm
Restriction: Non-circulating to the pub
Friends of the Library Group

M SAN FRANCISCO GENERAL HOSPITAL, Barnett-Briggs Medical Library, 1001 Potrero Ave, Bldg 30, 94110. SAN 301-4584. Tel: 415-206-3114. Interlibrary Loan Service Tel: 415-206-3113. FAX: 415-206-6102. *Dir,* Stephen Kiyoi; E-mail: kioyis@sfghdean.ucsf.edu
Founded 1966
Library Holdings: Bk Titles 18,120; Per Subs 420
Partic in Coop Libr Agency for Syst & Servs; Northern California & Nevada Medical Library Group (NCNMLG); Pacific Southwest Regional Medical Library (PSRML); San Francisco Biomedical Library Network
Open Mon-Fri 8-5

GL SAN FRANCISCO LAW LIBRARY*, 1145 Market St, 4th Flr, 94103. SAN 334-5424. Reference Tel: 415-554-1797. Information Services Tel: 415-554-1772. FAX: 415-893-4020. E-mail: sflawlibrary@sfgov.org. Reference E-mail: sfll.reference@sfgov.org. Web Site: www.sflawlibrary.org. *Dir,* Marcia R Bell; E-mail: marcia.bell@sfgov.org
Founded 1870
Special Collections: Archived Coll (California chapter statutes 1850-present); California Administrative Registers Archive (1945-present); Law Practice Management Coll; Rare Legal Book Coll; San Francisco Municipal Code Archive (SF Charters & previous codes, SF Bldg codes; Self Help Legal Coll; Statutes for all 50 States
Automation Activity & Vendor Info: (Acquisitions) Innovative Interfaces, Inc - Millenium; (Cataloging) Innovative Interfaces, Inc - Millenium; (Circulation) Innovative Interfaces, Inc - Millenium; (ILL) Innovative Interfaces, Inc - Millenium; (OPAC) Innovative Interfaces, Inc - Millenium
Function: Computers for patron use, Copy machines, Doc delivery serv, Electronic databases & coll, Handicapped accessible, Online cat, Pub access computers, Ref serv available
Open Mon-Fri 8:30-5
Restriction: ID required to use computers (Ltd hrs), Non-circulating to the pub, Pub access for legal res only
Branches:
FINANCIAL DISTRICT, Monadnock Bldg, 685 Market St, Ste 420, 94105, SAN 334-5459. Tel: 415-882-9310. FAX: 415-882-9594. *Dir,* Marcia Bell; *Asst Dir,* Mary Hayes
Library Holdings: Bk Vols 45,563; Per Subs 53
Open Mon-Thurs 9-9, Fri & Sat 9-5, Sun 12-4

CL SAN FRANCISCO LAW SCHOOL LIBRARY AT ALLIANT INTERNATIONAL UNIVERSITY*, 20 Haight St, 94102. SAN 301-4592. Tel: 415-626-5550. FAX: 415-626-5584. Web Site: www.sfls.edu. *Dean,* Jane Gamp
Founded 1909
Library Holdings: Bk Vols 21,000
Wireless access
Open Mon-Thurs 9am-9:30pm

S SAN FRANCISCO MARITIME LIBRARY*, Fort Mason Ctr, Bldg E, 3rd Flr, 94123. SAN 301-4363. Tel: 415-561-7030. FAX: 415-556-1624. E-mail: safr_maritime_library@nps.gov. Web Site: www.nps.gov/safr. *Ref Librn,* Gina Bardi; *Tech Serv Librn,* Heather Hernandez; *Coll Mgr,* Keri Koehler; *Llbr Tech,* Debbie Grace, Staff 5 (MLS 2, Non-MLS 3)
Founded 1959
Library Holdings: Bk Vols 75,000; Per Subs 120
Special Collections: Alaska Packers Asn Coll; Barbara Johnson Whaling Coll; Bethlehem Shipbuilding Coll; David W Dickie Coll; Hester Coll; John Lyman Coll; John W Proctor Coll; Mawdeley Coll; Plummer Beaton Coll; Proctor Coll; Reardon Coll. Oral History
Partic in Fedlink; OCLC Online Computer Library Center, Inc
Restriction: Borrowing requests are handled by ILL, Circulates for staff only, Closed stack, Non-circulating of rare bks, Non-circulating to the pub, Off-site coll in storage - retrieval as requested, Open to pub by appt only
Friends of the Library Group

G SAN FRANCISCO MUNICIPAL RAILWAY LIBRARY*, 1145 Market St, Ste 402, 94103-1545. SAN 321-9682. Tel: 415-934-3977. FAX: 415-934-5747. Web Site: www.sfmuni.com. *Librn,* Jerry McGovern; E-mail: jerry.mcgovern@sfmta.com. Subject Specialists: *Transit,* Jerry McGovern; Staff 1 (MLS 1)
Founded 1980
Library Holdings: Bk Titles 5,500; Bk Vols 8,000; Per Subs 50
Special Collections: San Francisco Municipal Railway, charts, doc, maps, plans
Subject Interests: City planning, Transit, Transportation
Automation Activity & Vendor Info: (Cataloging) Inmagic, Inc.; (ILL) OCLC
Database Vendor: OCLC FirstSearch
Function: ILL available
Partic in OCLC Online Computer Library Center, Inc
Open Mon-Fri 1-5

S SAN FRANCISCO MUSEUM OF MODERN ART*, Research Library, Archives & Records Management, 151 Third St, 94103-3107. SAN 301-4614. Tel: 415-357-4120. FAX: 415-357-4038. *Head, Res Libr, Archives & Rec Mgt,* Barbara C Rominski; Tel: 415-357-4121, E-mail: brominski@sfmoma.org; Staff 4 (MLS 2, Non-MLS 2)
Founded 1935
Library Holdings: Bk Titles 80,000; Per Subs 2,000
Special Collections: Kurenboh Japanese Photography Book Coll; Margery Mann Photography Book Coll; Sidney Tillim Photography Book Coll
Subject Interests: Contemporary art, Modern art
Wireless access
Function: Copy machines
Restriction: Circulates for staff only, Closed stack, Open to pub by appt only

P SAN FRANCISCO PUBLIC LIBRARY*, 100 Larkin St, 94102-4733. SAN 334-5483. Tel: 415-557-4400. Interlibrary Loan Service Tel: 415-557-4406. Administration Tel: 415-557-4236. FAX: 415-557-4424. E-mail: info@sfpl.org. Web Site: www.sfpl.org. *City Librn,* Luis Herrera; E-mail: lherrera@sfpl.org; *Dep City Librn,* Position Currently Open; *Chief of Main Libr,* Karen Strauss; Tel: 415-557-4200, E-mail: kstrauss@sfpl.org; *Chief, Coll & Tech Serv,* Laura Lent; Tel: 415-557-4220, E-mail:

llent@sfpl.org; *Chief Info Officer,* Michael Liang; Tel: 415-557-4340, E-mail: mliang@sfpl.org; *Dir, Ch Serv,* Toni Bernardi; Tel: 415-557-4270, E-mail: tbernardi@sfpl.org; *Mgr, Youth Serv,* Megan Ishler Anderson; Staff 679 (MLS 205, Non-MLS 474)
Founded 1878. Pop 812,538; Circ 10,854,725
Jul 2011-Jun 2012 Income (Main Library and Branch(s)) $92,190,623, State $122,275, City $89,545,041, Federal $33,017, Other $2,490,290. Mats Exp $9,733,733, Books $5,403,131, Per/Ser (Incl. Access Fees) $538,355, AV Mat $1,992,159, Electronic Ref Mat (Incl. Access Fees) $1,800,088. Sal $64,414,576
Library Holdings: AV Mats 380,196; e-books 85,305; Bk Vols 2,325,853; Per Subs 9,692
Special Collections: Calligraphy (Richard Harrison Coll); Chinese Language & Interest (Chinatown Branch); Eric Hoffer Manuscripts; Fine Printing & Binding (Kuhl); Gay & Lesbian Archives; History of Printing & Development of the Book (Robert Grabhorn Coll); San Francisco Coll; San Francisco Newspaper Morgues; Science Fiction & Fantasy (McComas Coll); Spanish Language & Interest (Mission Branch); Wit & Humor (Schmulowitz Coll). State Document Depository; US Document Depository
Automation Activity & Vendor Info: (Acquisitions) Innovative Interfaces, Inc; (Cataloging) Innovative Interfaces, Inc; (Circulation) Innovative Interfaces, Inc; (OPAC) Innovative Interfaces, Inc; (Serials) Innovative Interfaces, Inc
Wireless access
Mem of Pacific Library Partnership (PLP)
Special Services for the Deaf - Spec interest per; Staff with knowledge of sign lang; TTY equip
Friends of the Library Group
Branches: 27
ANZA BRANCH LIBRARY, 550 37th Ave, 94121-2691, SAN 334-5548. Tel: 415-355-5717. *Br Mgr,* Regan Gong
Open Mon 12-6, Tues 10-9, Wed 12-9, Thurs 10-6, Fri & Sat 1-6
Friends of the Library Group
BERNAL HEIGHTS BRANCH LIBRARY, 500 Cortland Ave, 94110-5612, SAN 334-5572. Tel: 415-355-2810. FAX: 415-642-9951. *Br Mgr,* Melissa Gooch
Open Mon & Thurs 10-6, Tues 10-9, Wed 1-9, Fri & Sat 1-6
Friends of the Library Group
EXCELSIOR BRANCH LIBRARY, 4400 Mission St (at Cotter), 94112-1927, SAN 334-5696. Tel: 415-355-2868. FAX: 415-337-4738. *Br Mgr,* Rebecca Alcala
Open Mon 1-9, Tues & Wed 10-9, Thurs & Sat 10-6, Fri 1-6, Sun 1-5
GLEN PARK BRANCH LIBRARY, 2825 Diamond St, 94131-3033, SAN 334-5726. Tel: 415-355-2858. FAX: 415-469-8557. *Br Mgr,* Denise Sanderson
Open Mon & Tues 10-6, Wed 12-8, Thurs 1-7, Fri & Sat 1-6
GOLDEN GATE VALLEY BRANCH LIBRARY, 1801 Green St, 94123-4921, SAN 334-5750. Tel: 415-355-5666. FAX: 415-561-0153. *Br Mgr,* Irene Lee
Open Mon & Tues 10-6, Wed 12-8, Thurs 1-7, Fri & Sat 1-6
Friends of the Library Group
INGLESIDE BRANCH LIBRARY, 1298 Ocean Ave, 94112-1717, SAN 334-5785. Tel: 415-355-2898. FAX: 415-469-7390. *Br Mgr,* Nina Pogosyan
Open Mon & Tues 10-6, Wed 12-8, Thurs 1-7, Fri & Sat 1-6, Sun 1-5
Friends of the Library Group
CHINATOWN/HIM MARK LAI BRANCH LIBRARY, 1135 Powell St, 94108, SAN 334-5637. Tel: 415-355-2888. FAX: 415-274-0277. *Br Mgr,* Lorna Chee
Founded 1921
Open Mon 1-9, Tues & Wed 10-9, Thurs & Sat 10-6, Fri 1-6, Sun 1-5
MARINA BRANCH LIBRARY, 1890 Chestnut St, 94123-2804, SAN 334-5815. Tel: 415-355-2823. FAX: 415-447-9308. *Br Mgr,* Chieko Wealand
Open Mon, Tues & Sat 10-6, Wed & Thurs 1-9, Fri 1-6, Sun 1-5
Friends of the Library Group
MERCED BRANCH LIBRARY, 155 Winston Dr, 94132-2032, SAN 334-584X. Tel: 415-355-2825. FAX: 415-337-8350. *Br Mgr,* Elizabeth Thacker
Open Mon, Thurs & Sat 10-6, Tues 10-9, Wed 1-9, Fri 1-6, Sun 1-5
Friends of the Library Group
EUREKA VALLEY-HARVEY MILK MEMORIAL BRANCH LIBRARY, One Jose Sarria Ct, 94114-1621, SAN 334-5661. Tel: 415-355-5616. FAX: 415-552-2584. *Interim Br Mgr,* Anne Vannuchi
Open Mon 12-6, Tues 10-9, Wed 12-9, Thurs 10-6, Fri & Sat 1-6
Friends of the Library Group
MISSION BAY BRANCH LIBRARY, 960 Fourth St, 94158-1628. Tel: 415-355-2838. FAX: 415-947-0723. *Interim Br Mgr,* Lori Chan
Open Mon Tues & Thurs 10-6 Wed Noon-8 Fri & Sat 1-6 Sun 1-5
Friends of the Library Group
MISSION BRANCH LIBRARY, 300 Bartlett St, 94110, SAN 334-5874. Tel: 415-355-2800. FAX: 415-648-6566. *Br Mgr,* Isabel Delgadillo-Romo
Open Mon 1-9, Tues & Wed 10-9, Thurs & Sat 10-6, Fri 1-6, Sun 1-5
Friends of the Library Group
NOE VALLEY/SALLY BRUNN BRANCH LIBRARY, 451 Jersey St, 94114-3632, SAN 334-5904. Tel: 415-355-5707. FAX: 415-282-8736. *Br Mgr,* Irene Lee
Open Tues 10-9, Wed 1-9, Thurs & Sat 10-6, Fri 1-6, Sun 1-5
Friends of the Library Group
NORTH BEACH BRANCH LIBRARY, 2000 Mason St, 94133-2337, SAN 334-5939. Tel: 415-355-5626. FAX: 415-772-8251. *Br Mgr,* Robert Carlson
Open Mon 12-6, Tues 10-9, Wed 1-9, Thurs 10-6, Fri & Sat 1-6
Friends of the Library Group
OCEAN VIEW BRANCH LIBRARY, 345 Randolph St, 94132-3119, SAN 334-5963. Tel: 415-355-5615. FAX: 415-452-8584. *Br Mgr,* Lise Braden
Open Mon & Tues 10-6, Wed 10-7, Thurs 1-7, Fri & Sat 1-6
Friends of the Library Group
ORTEGA BRANCH LIBRARY, 3223 Ortega St, 94122-4053, SAN 334-5998. Tel: 415-355-5700. FAX: 415-665-5942. *Br Mgr,* Tiffany Lac
Open Mon, Tues & Sat 10-6, Wed & Thurs 1-9, Fri 1-6, Sun 1-5
Friends of the Library Group
PARK BRANCH LIBRARY, 1833 Page St, 94117-1909, SAN 334-6021. Tel: 415-355-5656. FAX: 415-752-2290. *Interim Br Mgr,* Ben Cohen
Open Mon, Thurs & Sat 10-6, Tues 10-9, Wed 1-9, Fri 1-6
Friends of the Library Group
PARKSIDE BRANCH LIBRARY, 1200 Taraval St, 94116-2452, SAN 334-6056. Tel: 415-355-5770. FAX: 415-566-8014. *Br Mgr,* Geraldine Anne Dorman
Open Mon & Fri 1-6, Tues 10-9, Wed 1-9, Thurs & Sat 10-6
Friends of the Library Group
PORTOLA BRANCH LIBRARY, 380 Bacon St (at Goettingen), 94134-1526, SAN 334-6080. Tel: 415-355-5660. FAX: 415-468-1644. *Br Mgr,* Nicole Termini Germain
Open Tues 10-6, Wed 12-8, Thurs 1-7, Fri & Sat 1-6, Sun 1-5
Friends of the Library Group
POTRERO BRANCH LIBRARY, 1616 20th St, 94107-2811, SAN 334-6110. Tel: 415-355-2822. FAX: 415-401-8147. *Br Mgr,* Lia Hillman
Open Tues 10-8, Wed 12-8, Thurs 10-6, Fri & Sat 1-6, Sun 1-5
Friends of the Library Group
PRESIDIO BRANCH LIBRARY, 3150 Sacramento St, 94115-2006, SAN 334-5513. Tel: 415-355-2880. FAX: 415-563-3299. *Interim Br Mgr,* Anne Lane
Open Tues 10-9, Wed 1-9, Thurs & Sat 10-6, Fri 1-6, Sun 1-5
Friends of the Library Group
RICHMOND/SENATOR MILTON MARKS BRANCH LIBRARY, 351 Ninth Ave, 94118-2210, SAN 334-617X. Tel: 415-355-5600. FAX: 415-752-7785. *Br Mgr,* Sharon Wilensky
Open Mon & Sat 10-6, Tues & Wed 10-9, Thurs 1-9, Fri 1-6, Sun 1-5
Friends of the Library Group
SUNSET BRANCH LIBRARY, 1305 18th Ave, 94122-1807, SAN 334-620X. Tel: 415-355-2808. FAX: 415-665-2461. *Br Mgr,* Wing Chan
Open Mon 1-9, Tues & Wed 10-9, Thurs & Sat 10-6, Fri 1-6, Sun 1-5
Friends of the Library Group
VISITACION VALLEY BRANCH LIBRARY, 201 Leland Ave, 94134-2829, SAN 334-6234. Tel: 415-355-2848. FAX: 415-333-1027. *Br Mgr,* Alice Chan
Open Mon & Tues 10-6, Wed 12-7, Thurs 1-7, Fri & Sat 1-6, Sun 1-5
Friends of the Library Group
BAYVIEW-ANNA E WADEN BRANCH LIBRARY, 5075 Third St, 94124-2311, SAN 334-6269. Tel: 415-557-5757. FAX: 415-822-1001. *Br Mgr,* Beverly Hayes
Open Mon, Tues & Sat 10-6, Wed 1-8, Thurs 10-8, Fri 1-6, Sun 1-5
Friends of the Library Group
WEST PORTAL BRANCH LIBRARY, 190 Lenox Way, 94127-1113, SAN 334-6293. Tel: 415-355-2886. FAX: 415-731-3269. *Br Mgr,* Terry Carlson
Founded 1936
Open Mon 1-9, Tues & Wed 10-9, Thurs & Sat 10-6, Fri 1-6, Sun 1-5
Friends of the Library Group
WESTERN ADDITION BRANCH LIBRARY, 1550 Scott St, 94115-3512, SAN 334-6323. Tel: 415-355-5727. FAX: 415-440-4527. *Interim Br Mgr,* Jane Hudson
Open Mon & Wed 1-9, Tues, Thurs & Sat 10-6, Fri 1-6, Sun 1-5
Friends of the Library Group
Bookmobiles: 5

C SAN FRANCISCO STATE UNIVERSITY*, J Paul Leonard Library, 1630 Holloway Ave, 94132-4030. SAN 301-4630. Tel: 415-338-1854. Circulation Tel: 415-338-1552. Interlibrary Loan Service Tel: 415-338-1727. Reference Tel: 415-338-1974. Administration Tel: 415-338-1681. Interlibrary Loan Service FAX: 415-338-6199. Administration FAX: 415-338-1504. E-mail: libref@sfsu.edu. Web Site: www.library.sfsu.edu. *Univ Librn,* Deborah C Masters; E-mail: dmasters@sfsu.edu; *Head, Coll Access & Mgt Serv/Dept Co-Chair,* LaVonne Jacobsen; Tel: 415-338-6953, Fax: 415-338-0534, E-mail: lavonne@sfsu.edu; *Head, Info, Res & Instrul Serv/Dept Co-Chair,* Darlene Tong; Tel: 415-338-2188, E-mail: dtong@sfsu.edu; *Head, Info Tech, Head, Media Serv,* Thoreau Lovell; Tel: 415-338-2285, E-mail: tlovell@sfsu.edu.

Subject Specialists: *Environ studies, Geog, Govt publ,* LaVonne Jacobsen; *Art, Dance, Design,* Darlene Tong; Staff 93 (MLS 28, Non-MLS 65)
Founded 1899. Enrl 28,956; Fac 1,506; Highest Degree: Doctorate
Jul 2009-Jun 2010 Income $7,588,715. Mats Exp $2,829,599. Sal $3,942,854 (Prof $1,697,483)
Library Holdings: e-books 9,613; e-journals 7,960; Microforms 1,613,021; Bk Titles 840,625; Per Subs 2,449
Special Collections: Archer Children's Book Coll; Bay Area TV Archives; Frank V deBellis Coll; Labor Archives & Research Center. State Document Depository; US Document Depository
Subject Interests: Art & archit, Bus & mgt, Econ, Educ, Hist
Automation Activity & Vendor Info: (Acquisitions) Innovative Interfaces, Inc; (Cataloging) Innovative Interfaces, Inc; (Circulation) Innovative Interfaces, Inc; (Course Reserve) Innovative Interfaces, Inc; (ILL) Innovative Interfaces, Inc; (OPAC) Innovative Interfaces, Inc; (Serials) Innovative Interfaces, Inc
Database Vendor: 3M Library Systems, ABC-CLIO, ACM (Association for Computing Machinery), Alexander Street Press, American Chemical Society, American Mathematical Society, American Psychological Association (APA), Annual Reviews, ARTstor, Blackwell, Bowker, Cambridge Scientific Abstracts, Career Guidance Foundation, Checkpoint Systems, Inc, CIOS (Communication Institute for Online Scholarship), College Source, Commonwealth Business Media, CountryWatch, CQ Press, Dun & Bradstreet, EBSCO Information Services, EBSCOhost, Elsevier, Emerald, Ex Libris Group, Factiva.com, Facts on File, Gale Cengage Learning, H W Wilson, Haworth Pres Inc, Hoovers, IEEE (Institute of Electrical & Electronics Engineers), Infotrieve, Innovative Interfaces, Inc, ISI Web of Knowledge, JSTOR, LexisNexis, Mergent Online, Modern Language Association, Newsbank, OCLC FirstSearch, OCLC WorldShare Interlibrary Loan, OCLC-RLG, OVID Technologies, Oxford Online, ProQuest, PubMed, ScienceDirect, Springer-Verlag, Standard & Poor's, Swets Information Services, Wiley, Wilson - Wilson Web, YBP Library Services
Wireless access
Publications: Labor Archives Research Center (Newsletter); Research Guides
Partic in Consortium of Western Univ & Col; Link+; OCLC Online Computer Library Center, Inc; San Francisco Biomedical Library Network
Open Mon-Thurs 8-7, Sat Noon-5
Friends of the Library Group

C SAYBROOK UNIVERSITY LIBRARY*, 747 Front St, Third Flr, 94111-1920. SAN 378-2212. Tel: 415-394-5062. FAX: 415-433-9271. E-mail: library@saybrook.edu. Web Site: www.saybrook.edu. *Dir of Libr Serv,* Noah Lowenstein; E-mail: nlowenstein@saybrook.edu. Subject Specialists: *Philos, Psychol, Sociol,* Noah Lowenstein; Staff 2.75 (MLS 1.75, Non-MLS 1)
Founded 1999. Enrl 600; Fac 40; Highest Degree: Doctorate
Library Holdings: e-books 20,000; e-journals 10,000
Subject Interests: Alternative health, Complementary health, Psychol
Automation Activity & Vendor Info: (Cataloging) Follett Software; (Circulation) Follett Software
Function: Distance learning, ILL available, Workshops
Partic in Northern & Central California Psychology Libraries; Statewide California Electronic Library Consortium (SCELC)

L SEDGWICK LLP LIBRARY*, 333 Bush St, 30th flr, 94104. SAN 327-800X. Tel: 415-781-7900. FAX: 415-781-2635. *Librn,* Position Currently Open
Library Holdings: Bk Titles 1,500; Bk Vols 15,000
Partic in Cooperative Library Association Shared System (CLASS); Northern California Association of Law Libraries; RLIN (Research Libraries Information Network)
Restriction: Staff use only

L SHEARMAN & STERLING LLP*, 4 Embarcadero Ctr, Ste 3800, 94111-5974. SAN 373-1006. Tel: 415-616-1100. FAX: 415-616-1199. *Librn,* Suzanne Glab
Library Holdings: Bk Vols 10,000; Per Subs 50

S SIERRA CLUB*, William E Colby Memorial Library, 85 Second St, 2nd Flr, 94105-3441. SAN 301-4657. Tel: 415-977-5506. FAX: 415-977-5799. E-mail: colby.library@sierraclub.org. Web Site: www.sierraclub.org/library. *Librn,* Ellen Byrne; Staff 1 (Non-MLS 1)
Founded 1892
Library Holdings: Bk Vols 11,000; Per Subs 350
Special Collections: Early International & North American Mountaineering (Sierra Club Mountaineering Coll), bd vols, bks, photog
Subject Interests: Conserv, Natural hist, Pollution
Wireless access
Partic in OCLC Online Computer Library Center, Inc
Restriction: Open by appt only

S SMITH GROUP, INC*, Health Planning & Programming Library, 301 Battery St, 94111-3203. SAN 301-472X. Tel: 415-227-0100. FAX: 415-495-5091. Web Site: www.smpshg.com. *Librn,* Patricia Prestinary
Founded 1967
Library Holdings: Bk Vols 2,500; Per Subs 112
Subject Interests: Archit
Restriction: Not open to pub

S SMITH-KETTLEWELL EYE RESEARCH INSTITUTE LIBRARY*, 2318 Fillmore St, 94115. SAN 327-7038. Tel: 415-345-2000. FAX: 415-345-8455. Web Site: www.ski.org. *Asst Librn,* Position Currently Open
Library Holdings: Bk Vols 400
Restriction: Not open to pub

S STANTEC ARCHITECTURE INC LIBRARY*, 901 Market St, Ste 600, 94103. SAN 325-6375. Tel: 415-882-9500. FAX: 415-882-9523. Web Site: www.stantec.com. *Librn,* Rachel Ginsberg; E-mail: rfg@anshen.com. Subject Specialists: *Archit, Phys environment,* Rachel Ginsberg
Library Holdings: Bk Vols 2,000
Restriction: Staff use only

S THEOSOPHICAL SOCIETY LIBRARY*, 809 Mason St, 94108-2210. SAN 301-4649. Tel: 415-771-8777. Web Site: www.sftslodge.org. *Librn,* Peggy Tahir; *Coll Develop,* Shawn Phillips
Founded 1893
Library Holdings: Bk Titles 4,500; Per Subs 16
Special Collections: History, Metaphysics (San Francisco Occult Archives), bks, doc; Metaphysics (Manly P Hall Lectures), bd mss
Subject Interests: Astrology, Occult, Theosophy

M UCSF MEDICAL CENTER AT MOUNT ZION*, Harris M Fishbon Memorial Library, 1600 Divisadero St, Rm A-116, 94115. SAN 301-4347. Tel: 415-885-7378. Web Site: mountzion.ucsfmedicalcenter.org/library. *Dir,* Gail Sorrough
Library Holdings: Bk Titles 11,000; Per Subs 210
Special Collections: History of Medicine Coll; Psychiatry
Subject Interests: Cardiology, Geriatrics & gerontology, Internal med, Oncology, Orthopedics, Pediatrics, Surgery
Partic in National Network of Libraries of Medicine South Central Region; Northern California & Nevada Medical Library Group (NCNMLG); Pacific Southwest Regional Medical Library (PSRML); San Francisco Biomedical Library Network

GL UNITED STATES COURTS FOR THE NINTH CIRCUIT LIBRARY*, 95 Seventh St, 94103. (Mail add: PO Box 193939, 94119-3939), SAN 301-4789. Tel: 415-556-9500. FAX: 415-556-9927. *Dir,* Eric D Wade; *Dep Dir,* Edward Hosey; *Managing Librn,* Cheryl Blare; *Acq,* Lisa Larribeau; *Cat,* James Moldovan; *Ref,* Deborah Celle; *Ref,* Emily Newman; Staff 18 (MLS 9, Non-MLS 9)
Founded 1891
Library Holdings: Per Subs 2,500
Subject Interests: Law
Automation Activity & Vendor Info: (Acquisitions) SirsiDynix; (Cataloging) SirsiDynix; (OPAC) SirsiDynix; (Serials) SirsiDynix
Partic in OCLC Online Computer Library Center, Inc
Open Mon-Fri 9-5

GL UNITED STATES DISTRICT COURT*, Law Library, 450 Golden Gate Ave, Box 36060, 94102. SAN 301-4800. Tel: 415-436-8130. FAX: 415-436-8134. *Librn,* Susan Wong Caulder; E-mail: susan_wong_caulder@lb9.uscourts.gov; *Asst Librn,* John Milton Hendricks; E-mail: john_hendricks@lb9.uscourts.gov; *Tech Serv,* Loan Le; E-mail: loan_le@lb9.uscourts.gov; Staff 3 (MLS 2, Non-MLS 1)
Founded 1960
Library Holdings: Bk Titles 2,463; Bk Vols 36,773; Per Subs 1,145
Automation Activity & Vendor Info: (Acquisitions) SirsiDynix; (Cataloging) SirsiDynix; (OPAC) SirsiDynix; (Serials) SirsiDynix
Database Vendor: LexisNexis, OCLC FirstSearch, Westlaw
Restriction: Staff use only

G UNITED STATES ENVIRONMENTAL PROTECTION*, Region IX Library, 75 Hawthorne St, 13th Flr, 94105. SAN 301-3979. Tel: 415-947-4406. Toll Free Tel: 866-372-9378. FAX: 415-947-3553. E-mail: library-reg9@epa.gov. Web Site: www2.epa.gov/libraries/region-9-environmental-information-centerlibrary-services. *Libr Mgr,* Deborra Cohen; Staff 3 (MLS 3)
Founded 1970
Library Holdings: Bk Titles 8,000; Per Subs 200
Special Collections: Topographical Maps
Subject Interests: Air pollution, Environ justice, Environ law, Hazardous waste, Pesticides, Sustainability, Water pollution
Function: Doc delivery serv, For res purposes, Govt ref serv, Health sci info serv, ILL available, Online searches, Outside serv via phone, mail, e-mail & web, Photocopying/Printing, Ref serv available, Res libr

Partic in OCLC Online Computer Library Center, Inc
Restriction: Restricted borrowing privileges

CL UNIVERSITY OF CALIFORNIA*, Hastings College of the Law Library, 200 McAllister St, 94102-4978. SAN 301-4835. Tel: 415-565-4757. Circulation Tel: 415-565-4750. Interlibrary Loan Service Tel: 415-565-4765. Reference Tel: 415-565-4751. FAX: 415-581-8849. Interlibrary Loan Service FAX: 415-621-4859. Web Site: www.uchastings.edu/library. *Dir,* Jenni Parrish; E-mail: parrishj@uchastings.edu; *Head, Pub Serv,* Linda Weir; *Head, Tech Serv,* Marlene Bubrick; *Cat,* Grace Takatani; *Circ,* Tony Pelczynski; *Computer Serv, Spec Coll,* Dan Taysom; *Ref,* Charles Marcus; *Ser,* Barbara Roush; Staff 20 (MLS 11, Non-MLS 9)
Founded 1878. Enrl 1,290; Fac 50; Highest Degree: Doctorate
Jul 2006-Jun 2007 Income $3,479,041. Mats Exp $1,608,520. Sal $1,614,067
Library Holdings: Bk Titles 146,442; Bk Vols 438,121; Per Subs 7,857
Special Collections: State Document Depository; US Document Depository
Subject Interests: Criminal law & justice, Law
Automation Activity & Vendor Info: (Acquisitions) Innovative Interfaces, Inc; (Cataloging) Innovative Interfaces, Inc; (Circulation) Innovative Interfaces, Inc; (ILL) OCLC; (OPAC) Innovative Interfaces, Inc; (Serials) Innovative Interfaces, Inc
Database Vendor: Dialog, Gale Cengage Learning, HeinOnline, Innovative Interfaces, Inc, LexisNexis, OCLC FirstSearch, ProQuest, Westlaw
Wireless access
Open Mon-Fri 8-6
Restriction: Circ limited, Open to students, fac & staff

CM UNIVERSITY OF CALIFORNIA SAN FRANCISCO*, Library & Center for Knowledge Management, 530 Parnassus Ave, 94143-0840. SAN 301-4843. Tel: 415-476-8293. Information Services Tel: 415-476-2336. Web Site: www.library.ucsf.edu. *Asst Vice Chancellor, Univ Librn,* Karen Butter; E-mail: karen.butter@ucsf.edu; *Dir, Digital Libr & Coll,* Julia Kochi; Tel: 415-502-7539, E-mail: julia.kochi@ucsf.edu; *Dir, Learning Tech & Educ Serv,* Gail Persily; Tel: 415-476-3766, E-mail: gail.persily@ucsf.edu; *Dir, Finance & Operations,* Jim Munson; Tel: 415-476-8060, E-mail: james.munson@ucsf.edu; *Asst Dir, Scholarly Communications & Coll,* Anneliese Taylor; Tel: 415-476-8415, E-mail: anneliese.taylor@ucsf.edu; *Educ & Info Serv,* Peggy Tahir; Tel: 415-476-5765, E-mail: peggy.tahir@ucsf.edu; Staff 68 (MLS 14, Non-MLS 54)
Founded 1873. Enrl 3,664; Fac 4,278; Highest Degree: Doctorate
Jul 2008-Jun 2009. Mats Exp $2,003,158. Sal $4,644,624
Library Holdings: e-books 14,987; e-journals 13,068; Bk Vols 817,724; Per Subs 570
Special Collections: California Medicine (special concentration in communicable diseases, high altitude physiology, industrial/organizational medicine); East Asian Medicine; History of Health Sciences; Japanese Woodblock Print Coll; Legacy Tobacco Documents Library; University Archives
Subject Interests: Health sci, Life sci, Tobacco
Automation Activity & Vendor Info: (Acquisitions) Innovative Interfaces, Inc - Millenium; (Cataloging) Innovative Interfaces, Inc - Millenium; (Circulation) Innovative Interfaces, Inc - Millenium; (OPAC) Innovative Interfaces, Inc - Millenium; (Serials) Innovative Interfaces, Inc - Millenium
Wireless access
Function: Archival coll, Distance learning, Doc delivery serv, For res purposes, ILL available, Libr develop, Photocopying/Printing, Prof lending libr, Ref serv available, Res libr, Telephone ref
Partic in California Digital Library (CDL); National Network of Libraries of Medicine Pacific Southwest Region; OCLC Online Computer Library Center, Inc
Open Mon-Thurs 7:45am-10pm, Fri 7:45am-8pm, Sat 10-6, Sun Noon-10
Friends of the Library Group

Departmental Libraries:

MISSION BAY FAMRI LIBRARY, William J Rutter Conference Ctr, Rm 150, 1675 Owens St, 94143-2119. Tel: 415-514-4060. Web Site: www.library.ucsf.edu/locations/missionbay. *Univ Librn,* Karen Butter; *Mgr, Pub Serv,* Peggy Tahir; Tel: 415-476-5765, E-mail: peggy.tahir@ucsf.edu; *Supvr, Access Serv,* Andy Panado; E-mail: andres.panado@ucsf.edu
Highest Degree: Doctorate
Library Holdings: Bk Vols 1,400; Per Subs 18
Subject Interests: Health sci, Life sci
Function: Distance learning, Doc delivery serv, For res purposes, ILL available, Libr develop, Photocopying/Printing, Prof lending libr, Ref serv available, Res libr, Telephone ref

C UNIVERSITY OF SAN FRANCISCO*, Richard A Gleeson Library-Charles & Nancy Geschke Resource Center, 2130 Fulton St, 94117-1080. SAN 334-6471. Tel: 415-422-6167. Circulation Tel: 415-422-2660. Interlibrary Loan Service Tel: 415-422-5385. Reference Tel: 415-422-2039. FAX: 415-422-5949. Interlibrary Loan Service FAX: 415-422-2233. Web Site: www.usfca.edu/library. *Dean,* Tyrone Cannon; E-mail: cannont@usfca.edu; *Head, Access Serv,* Shawn Calhoun; Tel: 415-422-2048, E-mail: calhouns@usfca.edu; *Head, Acq,* Kathy Woo; Tel: 415-422-6417, E-mail: woo@usfca.edu; *Head, Cat,* Eric Ewen; Tel: 415-422-5361, E-mail: ewene@usfca.edu; *Head, Res Serv & Coll,* Locke Morrisey; Tel: 412-422-5399, E-mail: morrisey@usfca.edu; *Head, Syst,* Karen Johnson; Tel: 415-422-2759, E-mail: johnsonka@usfca.edu; *Admin Serv,* Carmen Fernandez-Baybay; Tel: 415-422-2035, E-mail: fernandezc@usfca.edu; *Archivist,* Michael SJ Kotlanger; Tel: 415-422-5932, E-mail: kotlanger@usfca.edu; *Cat,* Deborah Benrubi; Tel: 415-422-5672, E-mail: benrubi@usfca.edu; *Cat,* Benjamin Watson; Tel: 415-422-5633, E-mail: watsonb@usfca.edu; *Govt Doc,* Carol Spector; Tel: 415-422-2040, E-mail: csspector@usfca.edu; *ILL,* Joseph Campi; *Per,* Debbie Malone; Tel: 415-422-5352, E-mail: maloned@usfca.edu; *Rare Bks,* John Hawk; Tel: 415-422-2036, E-mail: hawkj@usfca.edu; *Ref & Instrul Serv, Instr Coordr,* Joe Garity; Tel: 415-422-5386, E-mail: garity@usfca.edu; *Ref Serv,* Sherise Kimura; Tel: 415-422-5379, E-mail: kimura@usfca.edu; *Ref Serv,* Vicki Rosen; Tel: 415-422-5387, E-mail: rosen@usfca.edu; *Ref Serv,* Penny Scott; Tel: 415-422-5389, E-mail: plscott@usfca.edu; *Ref Serv,* Randy Souther; Tel: 415-422-5388, E-mail: southerr@usfca.edu; Staff 42 (MLS 20, Non-MLS 22)
Founded 1855. Enrl 8,568; Fac 861; Highest Degree: Doctorate
Jun 2005-May 2006 Income $5,500,394, Parent Institution $4,994,073, Other $506,321. Mats Exp $1,775,994, Books $411,164, Per/Ser (Incl. Access Fees) $720,870, Micro $22,449, AV Mat $5,182, Electronic Ref Mat (Incl. Access Fees) $585,851, Presv $30,478. Sal $1,913,862 (Prof $1,109,525)
Library Holdings: AV Mats 1,754; Bks on Deafness & Sign Lang 364; CDs 900; DVDs 269; e-books 27,633; e-journals 920; Bk Titles 546,148; Bk Vols 709,993; Per Subs 2,104; Talking Bks 445; Videos 1,309
Special Collections: 1890's English Literature; A E & Lawrence Housman; Book Club of California; Carrollton; Charles Carroll; Eric Gill; Fine Printing; Grabhorn Press; John Henry Nash; Recusant Literature; Richard Le Gallienne; Robert Graves; Sir Thomas More & Contemporaries; Victor Hammer. State Document Depository; US Document Depository
Automation Activity & Vendor Info: (Acquisitions) Innovative Interfaces, Inc; (Cataloging) Innovative Interfaces, Inc; (Circulation) Innovative Interfaces, Inc; (ILL) Innovative Interfaces, Inc; (OPAC) Innovative Interfaces, Inc; (Serials) Innovative Interfaces, Inc
Database Vendor: 3M Library Systems, ABC-CLIO, ACM (Association for Computing Machinery), American Chemical Society, American Mathematical Society, American Psychological Association (APA), Annual Reviews, BioOne, Blackwell, Bowker, Cambridge Scientific Abstracts, Career Guidance Foundation, CIOS (Communication Institute for Online Scholarship), CQ Press, Dialog, Dun & Bradstreet, ebrary, EBSCO Information Services, EBSCOhost, Elsevier, Emerald, Facts on File, Gale Cengage Learning, Gallup, Greenwood Publishing Group, H W Wilson, Haworth Pres Inc, IEEE (Institute of Electrical & Electronics Engineers), infoUSA, Innovative Interfaces, Inc, Innovative Interfaces, Inc, IOP, JSTOR, LexisNexis, Marcive, Inc, McGraw-Hill, Medianet, Mergent Online, Modern Language Association, Nature Publishing Group, Newsbank, OCLC FirstSearch, OneSource, OVID Technologies, Oxford Online, ProQuest, PubMed, ReferenceUSA, Safari Books Online, SBRnet (Sports Business Research Network), ScienceDirect, SerialsSolutions, Springer-Verlag, Standard & Poor's, STAT!Ref (Teton Data Systems), STN International, Swets Information Services, TDNet, TLC (The Library Corporation), ValueLine, Wiley, Wilson - Wilson Web, YBP Library Services
Wireless access
Function: Archival coll, Art exhibits, Distance learning, Doc delivery serv, Govt ref serv, ILL available, Music CDs, Online searches, Orientations, Photocopying/Printing, Ref serv available, Workshops
Partic in Association of Jesuit Colleges & Universities (AJCU); Association of Research Libraries (ARL); Coop Libr Agency for Syst & Servs; OCLC Online Computer Library Center, Inc; San Francisco Biomedical Library Network; Southern Calif Electronic Libr Consortium
Open Mon-Thurs 8am-Midnight, Fri 8-8, Sat 10-8, Sun Noon-Midnight
Restriction: Limited access for the pub, Private libr
Friends of the Library Group

Departmental Libraries:

CL ZIEF LAW LIBRARY, 2101 Fulton St, 94117-1004. (Mail add: 2130 Fulton St, 94117-1080), SAN 334-6536. Tel: 415-422-6679. FAX: 415-422-2345. Web Site: www.usfca.edu/law_library/. *Head, Tech Serv, Interim Dir,* Shannon S Burchard; E-mail: burchards@usfca.edu; *Cat,* Mehry Samadi; *Ref,* Lee Ryan; *Ref,* John Shafer; Staff 6 (MLS 6)
Founded 1912. Enrl 640; Fac 30; Highest Degree: Master
Jun 2005-May 2006. Mats Exp $1,297,054, Books $110,441, Per/Ser (Incl. Access Fees) $901,720, Electronic Ref Mat (Incl. Access Fees) $197,151, Presv $6,437. Sal $1,155,392 (Prof $507,443)
Library Holdings: Bk Titles 36,379; Bk Vols 354,849; Per Subs 3,293
Restriction: Restricted access

S WELLS FARGO BANK LIBRARY, Historical Research Library, 420 Montgomery St, MAC-A0101-106, 94163. SAN 334-6595. Tel: 415-396-4157. FAX: 415-975-7430.
Library Holdings: Bk Vols 8,000; Per Subs 15
Special Collections: California Gold Rush & Mining; Californiana; History of Banking & Finance; San Francisco History; Staging & Western Transportation; Wells Fargo & Co History
Restriction: Open by appt only, Researchers by appt only

S WINE INSTITUTE LIBRARY*, 425 Market St, Ste 1000, 94105. SAN 301-4886. Tel: 415-512-0151. FAX: 415-543-5882. E-mail: wilib@wineinstitute.org. Web Site: www.wineinstitute.org. *Librn,* Position Currently Open
Founded 1934
Library Holdings: Bk Vols 3,100; Per Subs 150
Special Collections: California Wine Industry. Oral History
Subject Interests: Wine
Restriction: Not open to pub

S ALAN WOFSY FINE ARTS REFERENCE LIBRARY*, Wittenborn Art Books Library, 1109 Geary Blvd, 94109. SAN 374-8979. Tel: 415-292-6500. FAX: 415-292-6594. E-mail: order@art-books.com. Web Site: www.art-books.com. *Dir,* Mark Hyman; E-mail: editeur@earthlink.net; *Coll Develop,* Buzzard Cohen; *Curator,* Adior Butler
Founded 1969
Library Holdings: Bk Titles 1,000
Subject Interests: Art

SAN JACINTO

J MOUNT SAN JACINTO COLLEGE, Milo P Johnson Library, 1499 N State St, 92583-2399. SAN 301-4924. Tel: 951-487-6752. FAX: 951-654-8387. Web Site: www.msjc.edu/sjclibrary. *Librn,* Laura Walker; Tel: 951-487-3450, E-mail: awalker@msjc.edu; *Assoc Librn,* Ross Valenzuela; *Assoc Librn,* Laura Winningham; *Circ Supvr,* Vali Reese; E-mail: vali.reese@msjc.edu; *Tech Serv Coordr,* Robert Pipes; Tel: 951-487-3453
Founded 1963. Enrl 2,930; Highest Degree: Associate
Library Holdings: Bk Titles 34,202; Per Subs 325
Automation Activity & Vendor Info: (Cataloging) SirsiDynix; (Circulation) SirsiDynix; (OPAC) SirsiDynix
Database Vendor: SirsiDynix
Partic in Inland Empire Acad Libr Coop (IEALC); San Bernardino, Inyo, Riverside Counties United Library Services
Open Mon-Thurs 8-8, Fri 8-Noon
Departmental Libraries:
MENIFEE VALLEY, 28237 La Piedra, Menifee Valley, 92584, SAN 378-2085. Tel: 951-639-5455. Interlibrary Loan Service Tel: 951-639-5456. Reference Tel: 951-639-5450. FAX: 951-672-0874. Web Site: www.msjc.edu/mvclibrary. *Librn,* Monica Flores; *Librn,* Sherri Moore; *Libr Serv Coordr,* Cheryl Devenney; Staff 7 (MLS 2, Non-MLS 5)
Founded 1991. Enrl 10,000; Fac 2; Highest Degree: Associate
Jul 2012-Jun 2013. Mats Exp $89,290, Books $31,422, Per/Ser (Incl. Access Fees) $6,147, AV Mat $3,700, Electronic Ref Mat (Incl. Access Fees) $48,021
Library Holdings: Audiobooks 61; AV Mats 4,926; CDs 326; DVDs 1,127; e-books 54,116; Bk Titles 19,069; Per Subs 101; Videos 1,109
Automation Activity & Vendor Info: (Cataloging) OCLC; (Circulation) OCLC; (Course Reserve) OCLC; (ILL) OCLC; (OPAC) OCLC WorldShare Interlibrary Loan; (Serials) EBSCO Online
Database Vendor: CQ Press, EBSCO Auto Repair Reference, EBSCOhost, Facts on File, Gale Cengage Learning, LearningExpress, LexisNexis, ProQuest, SerialsSolutions, SirsiDynix
Partic in Inland Empire Acad Libr Coop (IEALC)
Open Mon-Thurs 8-8, Fri 8-4, Sat 9-2

SAN JOSE

L BERLINER COHEN LAW LIBRARY*, Ten Almaden Blvd, 11th Flr, 95113-2233. SAN 372-3186. Tel: 408-286-5800. FAX: 408-998-5388. *Law Librn,* Gayle Hittle; Tel: 408-938-2458, E-mail: gayle.hittle@berliner.com; Staff 1 (MLS 1)
Library Holdings: Bk Vols 7,000
Subject Interests: Calif, Fed law, Law

J EVERGREEN VALLEY COLLEGE LIBRARY*, 3095 Yerba Buena Rd, 95135. SAN 320-166X. Tel: 408-270-6433. Reference Tel: 408-274-7900, Ext 6661. FAX: 408-532-1925. TDD: 408-531-8512. E-mail: librarian@evc.edu. Web Site: www.evc.edu/library. *Dean,* Mark Gonzales; Tel: 408-223-6792; *Librn,* Shelley Blackman; Tel: 408-274-7900, Ext 6660, E-mail: shelley.blackman@evc.edu; *Librn,* Lorena Mata; Tel: 408-274-7900, Ext 6743, E-mail: lorena.mata@evc.edu; Staff 8 (MLS 2, Non-MLS 6)
Founded 1975. Fac 282; Highest Degree: Associate
Library Holdings: Bk Titles 49,187; Bk Vols 53,568; Per Subs 58
Special Collections: Oral History
Automation Activity & Vendor Info: (Acquisitions) Innovative Interfaces, Inc; (Circulation) Innovative Interfaces, Inc; (OPAC) Innovative Interfaces, Inc
Database Vendor: Gale Cengage Learning
Wireless access
Function: Ref serv available
Special Services for the Deaf - TDD equip
Special Services for the Blind - Reader equip
Open Mon-Thurs (Winter) 8-8, Fri 9-3, Sat 10-2; Mon-Thurs (Summer) 10-3
Restriction: Open to students, fac & staff

S HISTORY SAN JOSE RESEARCH LIBRARY & ARCHIVES, 1650 Senter Rd, 95112. SAN 323-9519. Tel: 408-521-5025. E-mail: research@historysanjose.org. Web Site: www.historysanjose.org. *Curator, Archives & Libr,* Catherine Mills; E-mail: cmills@historysanjose.org; Staff 2 (MLS 2)
Founded 1970
Special Collections: Early Electronics (Perham Coll); New Almaden Mines Coll; San Jose Pueblo Records, early local govt rec, maps; Santa Clara Valley Historical Photos; Sempervirens Club Coll
Subject Interests: Local hist, San Jose, Santa Clara Valley
Wireless access
Function: 24/7 Online cat, Archival coll
Restriction: Non-circulating, Open by appt only

L HOPKINS & CARLEY LIBRARY*, PO Box 1469, 95109-1469. SAN 329-4919. Tel: 408-286-9800. FAX: 408-998-4790. Web Site: www.hopkinscarley.com. *Librn,* Paul Reavis; E-mail: preavis@hopkinscarley.com
Library Holdings: Bk Vols 3,000; Per Subs 75
Open Mon-Fri 8-5

CL LINCOLN LAW SCHOOL OF SAN JOSE*, James F Boccardo Law Library, One N First St, 95113. SAN 301-424X. Tel: 408-977-7227. FAX: 408-977-7228. Web Site: www.lincolnlaw.sj.edu.
Founded 1919. Enrl 150; Fac 25; Highest Degree: Doctorate
Library Holdings: Bk Vols 12,000; Per Subs 15
Automation Activity & Vendor Info: (OPAC) LibraryWorld, Inc
Database Vendor: Westlaw
Wireless access
Open Mon-Thurs 10-10, Sat 10-5

C THE NATIONAL HISPANIC UNIVERSITY LIBRARY, 14271 Story Rd, 95127-3823. SAN 327-7135. Tel: 408-273-2730. FAX: 408-254-1369. E-mail: libstaff@nhu.edu. Web Site: library.nhu.edu. *Dir of Libr Serv,* Gabriela Nocito, Tel. 408-273-2731, E-mail: gabriela.nocito@nhu.edu; Staff 4 (MLS 2, Non-MLS 2)
Founded 1985. Enrl 700; Fac 30; Highest Degree: Master
Library Holdings: AV Mats 500; Bk Titles 13,000; Bk Vols 16,000; Per Subs 20
Subject Interests: Mexican-Am hist & culture
Automation Activity & Vendor Info: (Acquisitions) EOS International; (Cataloging) EOS International; (Circulation) EOS International; (Course Reserve) EOS International; (ILL) OCLC FirstSearch; (OPAC) EOS International; (Serials) EOS International
Database Vendor: ABC-CLIO, Alexander Street Press, CountryWatch, CQ Press, ebrary, EBSCOhost, Gale Cengage Learning, OCLC FirstSearch, ProQuest, Sage, SerialsSolutions, Wilson - Wilson Web, YBP Library Services
Wireless access
Function: Electronic databases & coll, Photocopying/Printing, Ref serv available
Partic in BayNet Library Association; Statewide California Electronic Library Consortium (SCELC)
Restriction: Borrowing privileges limited to fac & registered students, Students only

M O'CONNOR HOSPITAL MEDICAL LIBRARY*, Jorge Franco Medical Library, Bldg 53, 2105 Forest Ave, Rm 221, 95128. SAN 370-7490. Tel: 408-947-2647. FAX: 408-947-3428. E-mail: ochmedlib@dochs.org. Web Site: www.ochlibrary.org. *Med Librn,* Suzie Bahmanyar; E-mail: suziebahmanyar@dochs.org; Staff 1 (MLS 1)
Founded 1985
Library Holdings: e-books 1,000; e-journals 500; Bk Titles 1,500; Per Subs 140
Database Vendor: EBSCO Information Services, Elsevier, LibraryWorld, Inc, McGraw-Hill, MD Consult, Natural Standard, OVID Technologies, PubMed, UpToDate
Wireless access
Function: Computers for patron use, Doc delivery serv, Electronic databases & coll, Handicapped accessible, Online cat, Online searches

Open Mon-Thurs 9-6
Restriction: Open to staff, patients & family mem

CM PALMER COLLEGE OF CHIROPRACTIC-WEST CAMPUS LIBRARY*, 90 E Tasman Dr, 95134. SAN 326-4602. Tel: 408-944-6142. FAX: 408-944-6181. Web Site: www.palmer.edu. *Circ,* Wendy Kubow; E-mail: kubow_w@palmer.edu; Staff 4 (MLS 1, Non-MLS 3)
Founded 1978. Enrl 600; Fac 52; Highest Degree: Doctorate
Library Holdings: Bk Titles 14,000; Bk Vols 15,000; Per Subs 140
Special Collections: Chiropractic Archives, bks
Subject Interests: Chiropractic med
Automation Activity & Vendor Info: (Acquisitions) EOS International; (Cataloging) EOS International; (Circulation) EOS International
Publications: Newsletter
Partic in Coop Libr Agency for Syst & Servs; OCLC Online Computer Library Center, Inc
Open Mon-Thurs 7:30am-11pm, Fri 7:30-5, Sat 10-5, Sun 12-5

S PARENTS HELPING PARENTS LIBRARY, Family Resource Center, 1400 Parkmoor Ave, Ste 100, 95126. SAN 372-8439. Tel: 408-727-5775, Ext 110. Toll Free Tel: 855-727-5775. FAX: 408-286-1116. Web Site: www.php.com. *Librn,* Judy Bower; E-mail: judy@php.com; Staff 1 (Non-MLS 1)
Founded 1981
Library Holdings: Bks on Deafness & Sign Lang 51; CDs 49; DVDs 400; Bk Titles 3,662; Videos 486
Subject Interests: Disability, Parenting
Wireless access
Special Services for the Deaf - Videos & decoder
Open Mon-Fri 10-4

S PRATT & WHITNEY*, CSD Library-Space Propulsion Operations, 600 Metcalf Rd, 95138-9602. SAN 301-6463. Tel: 408-776-4957. Interlibrary Loan Service Tel: 408-776-4673. Reference Tel: 408-776-4452. FAX: 408-776-5995. *Librn,* Karen S Schaffer
Founded 1960
Library Holdings: AV Mats 96; Bk Titles 19,580; Per Subs 100
Subject Interests: Organic chem
Publications: Guide to the CSD Library
Partic in Dialog Corp
Restriction: Staff use only

M REGIONAL MEDICAL CENTER OF SAN JOSE*, Ismael Medical Library, 225 N Jackson Ave, 95116-1603. SAN 322-8797. Tel: 408-259-5000, Ext 2230. FAX: 408-272-6458. *Librn,* Nancy Firchow; Staff 1 (MLS 1)
Library Holdings: Bks on Deafness & Sign Lang 10; Bk Vols 2,000; Per Subs 150
Subject Interests: Med
Publications: Journal List (Semi-yearly); List of Holdings (Yearly)

S ROSICRUCIAN ORDER, AMORC*, Rosicrucian Research Library, Rosicrucian Park, 1342 Naglee Ave, 95191. SAN 301-4983. Tel: 408-947-3600. FAX: 408-947-3677. E-mail: librarian@rosicrucian.org. Web Site: www.rosicrucian.org. *Exec Dir,* Julie Scott; E-mail: gmo@rosicrucian.org
Founded 1939
Library Holdings: Bk Vols 16,000; Per Subs 21
Subject Interests: Alchemy, Egypt, Esoteric studies, Mysticism, Rosicrucians, Spirituality
Function: For res purposes, Ref serv available, Res libr
Publications: Rosicrucian Indexes
Restriction: Non-circulating, Open to pub for ref only
Friends of the Library Group

J SAN JOSE CITY COLLEGE LIBRARY*, Cesar E Chavez Library, 2100 Moorpark Ave, 95128-2799. SAN 301-5009. Tel: 408-288-3775. Reference Tel: 408-298-2181, Ext 3899. FAX: 408-293-4728. TDD: 408-993-0354. E-mail: sjcc.library@sjcc.edu. Web Site: www.sjcc.edu/library. *Librn, Outreach Serv Librn, Pub Serv,* Joseph King; Tel: 408-298-2181, Ext 3115, E-mail: joseph.king@sjcc.edu; *Cat, Librn, Tech Serv,* Robert Wing; Tel: 408-298-2181, Ext 3945, E-mail: robert.wing@sjcc.edu; *Coordr, Per/Databases, Acq,* Linda Meyer; Tel: 408-298-2181, Ext 3944, E-mail: linda.meyer@sjcc.edu; Staff 3 (MLS 3)
Founded 1921. Enrl 12,100; Fac 350; Highest Degree: Associate
Library Holdings: Bk Titles 66,090; Per Subs 90
Automation Activity & Vendor Info: (Acquisitions) Innovative Interfaces, Inc; (Cataloging) Innovative Interfaces, Inc; (Circulation) Innovative Interfaces, Inc; (Course Reserve) Innovative Interfaces, Inc; (ILL) OCLC; (Media Booking) Innovative Interfaces, Inc; (OPAC) Innovative Interfaces, Inc; (Serials) Innovative Interfaces, Inc
Database Vendor: ABC-CLIO, Facts on File, Gale Cengage Learning, LexisNexis
Wireless access
Publications: Information Sheets; Resource Guides

S SAN JOSE MERCURY NEWS LIBRARY*, 750 Ridder Park Dr, 95190. SAN 301-5025. Tel: 408-920-5346. FAX: 408-271-3799. Web Site: www.mercurynews.com. *Dir,* Leigh Poitinger; Staff 2 (MLS 2)
Founded 1928
Library Holdings: Bk Vols 2,000; Per Subs 40
Special Collections: Newspaper Clippings & Photos
Function: Bus archives, Newsp ref libr, Res libr
Restriction: Co libr

S SAN JOSE MUSEUM OF ART LIBRARY*, 110 S Market St, 95113. SAN 321-6454. Tel: 408-271-6840. FAX: 408-294-2977. E-mail: info@sjmusart.org. Web Site: www.sanjosemuseumofart.org. *Librn,* Gloria Turk; Staff 1 (MLS 1)
Founded 1978
Library Holdings: Bk Vols 3,200; Per Subs 12
Special Collections: Children's Art Books Coll
Subject Interests: Art
Restriction: Staff use only

P SAN JOSE PUBLIC LIBRARY*, Dr Martin Luther King Jr Library, 150 E San Fernando St, 95112-3580. SAN 334-6773. Tel: 408-808-2000. Interlibrary Loan Service Tel: 408-808-2076. Reference Tel: 408-808-2100. Administration Tel: 408-808-2355. Administration FAX: 408-808-2133. TDD: 408-808-2130. E-mail: admin.sjpl@sjlibrary.org. Web Site: www.sjlibrary.org. *Dir,* Jill Bourne; *Asst Dir,* Heidi Dolamore; *Sr Librn, Innovation,* Ruth Barefoot; Tel: 408-808-2131, E-mail: ruth.barefoot@sjlibrary.org; *Sr LIbrn, King Pub Ref & Res Unit,* Judith Gregg; Tel: 408-808-2195, Fax: 408-808-2395, E-mail: judith.gregg@sjlibrary.org; *Sr Librn, Prog & Youth Serv,* Angie Miraflor; Tel: 408-808-2188, Fax: 408-808-2004, E-mail: angie.miraflor@sjlibrary.org; *Sr Librn, Tech Serv,* Kristi Bell; Tel: 408-808-2468, Fax: 408-808-2423, E-mail: kristi.bell@sjlibrary.org; *Actg Sr Librn, Calif Rm & Web Team,* Margaret Yamasaki; Tel: 408-808-2135, E-mail: margaret.yamasaki@sjlibrary.org; *Div Mgr,* Katie DuPraw; Tel: 408-808-2192, E-mail: katie.dupraw@sjlibrary.org; *Actg Div Mgr,* Sandra Stewart; Tel: 408-808-2186, E-mail: sandra.stewart@sjlibrary.org; *Admin Officer,* Neil Rufino; Tel: 408-808-2152, E-mail: neil.rufino@sjlibrary.org; *IT Serv,* Howard Yeilding; Tel: 408-808-2420, Fax: 408-808-2401, E-mail: howard.yeilding@sjlibrary.org; Staff 86.6 (MLS 86.1, Non-MLS 0.5)
Founded 1872. Pop 984,299; Circ 10,702,251
Jul 2012-Jun 2013 Income (Main Library and Branch(s)) $37,576,020, City $28,929,488, Federal $107,838, Locally Generated Income $8,113,436, Other $425,258. Mats Exp $2,905,700, Books $3,394,164, Per/Ser (Incl. Access Fees) $178,417, Micro $8,156, AV Mat $1,421,628, Electronic Ref Mat (Incl. Access Fees) $470,143. Sal $26,011,231 (Prof $6,467,541)
Library Holdings: AV Mats 364,356; CDs 65,497; DVDs 255,745; e-books 41,041; Bk Titles 390,862; Bk Vols 1,700,765; Per Subs 578; Talking Bks 42,281; Videos 515
Special Collections: Aging-Handicapped; California Room; Mexican-American Literature & Spanish Language; Vietnamese Language Coll
Subject Interests: Bus & mgt, Chinese lang, Music
Automation Activity & Vendor Info: (Acquisitions) Innovative Interfaces, Inc; (Cataloging) Innovative Interfaces, Inc; (Circulation) Innovative Interfaces, Inc; (OPAC) Innovative Interfaces, Inc; (Serials) Innovative Interfaces, Inc
Database Vendor: Dialog, EBSCOhost, Gale Cengage Learning, OCLC FirstSearch, SirsiDynix, Wilson - Wilson Web
Wireless access
Friends of the Library Group
Branches: 22
ALMADEN, 6445 Camden Ave, 95120. Tel: 408-808-3040. Administration Tel: 408-997-1042. FAX: 408-997-1212. *Sr Librn,* Ruth Barefoot
Pop 228,121; Circ 672,528
Library Holdings: Bk Vols 98,408
Open Wed 11-8, Thurs-Sat 10-6
Friends of the Library Group
ALVISO BRANCH, 5050 N First St, Alviso, 95002, SAN 334-6838. Tel: 408-263-3626. Administration Tel: 408-586-7618. FAX: 408-956-9435. *Sr Librn,* Keye Luke
Pop 62,598; Circ 189,123
Library Holdings: Bk Vols 33,094
Open Wed 11-8, Thurs-Sat 10-6
Friends of the Library Group
BASCOM LIBRARY, 1000 S Bascom Ave, 95128. Tel: 408-808-3077. Administration Tel: 408-279-4221. FAX: 408-286-3951. E-mail: bamail@sjlibrary.org. *Sr Librn,* Vidya Kilambi
Pop 49,660; Circ 132,847
Library Holdings: Bk Vols 63,351
Open Wed 11-8, Thurs-Sat 10-6
Friends of the Library Group

BERRYESSA, 3355 Noble Ave, 95132-3198, SAN 334-6862. Tel: 408-808-3050. Administration Tel: 408-923-3336. FAX: 408-923-3222. *Sr Librn,* Candice Tran
Pop 320,741; Circ 1,067,070
Library Holdings: Bk Vols 123,512
Open Wed 11-8, Thurs-Sat 10-6
Friends of the Library Group

BIBLIOTECA LATINOAMERICANA BRANCH, 921 S First St, 95110-2939, SAN 334-6897. Tel: 408-294-1237. Administration Tel: 408-278-1116. FAX: 408-297-4278. *Sr Librn,* Kim Nguyen
Pop 90,749; Circ 102,476
Library Holdings: Bk Vols 52,790
Subject Interests: Spanish (Lang)
Open Mon & Thurs 10-6, Tues & Wed 11-8
Friends of the Library Group

CALABAZAS, 1230 Blaney Ave, 95129-3799, SAN 334-6927. Tel: 408-808-3066. Administration Tel: 408-278-1116. FAX: 408-297-4278. *Sr Librn,* Pam Crider
Pop 16,257; Circ 30,461
Library Holdings: Bk Vols 65,282
Open Mon & Thurs 10-6, Tues & Wed 11-8
Friends of the Library Group

CAMBRIAN, 1780 Hillsdale Ave, 95124-3199, SAN 334-6951. Tel: 408-808-3080. Administration Tel: 408-264-1889. FAX: 408-264-1894. *Sr Librn,* Ruth Barefoot
Pop 221,359; Circ 613,407
Library Holdings: Bk Vols 113,427
Open Mon & Thurs 10-6, Tues & Wed 11-8
Friends of the Library Group

DR ROBERTO CRUZ - ALUM ROCK, 3090 Alum Rock Ave, 95127. Tel: 408-808-3090. Administration Tel: 408-929-0130. FAX: 408-928-5628. *Sr Librn,* Maddy Walton-Hadlock
Pop 243,256; Circ 327,023
Library Holdings: Bk Vols 81,098
Open Mon & Thurs 10-6, Tues & Wed 11-8
Friends of the Library Group

EAST SAN JOSE CARNEGIE, 1102 E Santa Clara St, 95116-2246, SAN 334-6986. Tel: 408-808-3075. Administration Tel: 408-287-3224. FAX: 408-288-9750. *Sr Librn,* Kim Nguyen
Pop 81,804; Circ 125,172
Library Holdings: Bk Vols 37,634
Open Wed 11-8, Thurs-Sat 10-6
Friends of the Library Group

EDENVALE, 101 Branham Lane E, 95111. Tel: 408-808-3036. Administration Tel: 408-224-9834. FAX: 408-224-9836. *Sr Librn,* Joan Bowlby
Pop 189,266; Circ 455,451
Library Holdings: Bk Vols 69,086
Open Mon & Thurs 10-6, Tues & Wed 11-8
Friends of the Library Group

EDUCATIONAL PARK, 1772 Educational Park Dr, 95133-1703, SAN 334-701X. Tel: 408-808-3073. Administration Tel: 408-937-1861. FAX: 408-254-4278. *Sr Librn,* Ben Lundholm
Pop 22,531; Circ 56,334
Library Holdings: Bk Vols 69,086
Friends of the Library Group

JOYCE ELLINGTON BRANCH, 491 E Empire St, 95112-3308, SAN 334-7044. Tel: 408-808-3043. Administration Tel: 408-998-8054. FAX: 408-286-0664. *Sr Librn,* Keye Luke
Pop 107,489; Circ 159,654
Library Holdings: Bk Vols 53,035
Open Mon & Thurs 10-6, Tues & Wed 11-8
Friends of the Library Group

EVERGREEN, 2635 Aborn Rd, 95121-1294, SAN 334-7079. Tel: 408-808-3060. Administration Tel: 408-238-0384. FAX: 408-238-0584. *Sr Librn,* Candice Tran
Pop 278,251; Circ 1,026,066
Library Holdings: Bk Vols 118,611
Open Mon, Thurs & Sat 10-6, Tues & Wed 11-8
Friends of the Library Group

HILLVIEW, 1600 Hopkins Dr, 95122-1199, SAN 334-7109. Tel: 408-808-3033. Administration Tel: 408-729-9516. FAX: 408-729-9518. *Sr Librn,* Ben Lundholm
Pop 158,523; Circ 268,868
Library Holdings: Bk Vols 58,779
Open Wed 11-8, Thurs-Sat 10-6
Friends of the Library Group

PEARL AVENUE, 4270 Pearl Ave, 95136-1899, SAN 334-7133. Tel: 408-808-3053. Administration Tel: 408-723-6935. FAX: 408-723-6930. *Sr Librn,* Gayleen Thomas
Pop 151,040; Circ 377,164
Library Holdings: Bk Vols 65,841
Open Wed 11-8, Thurs-Sat 10-6
Friends of the Library Group

ROSE GARDEN, 1580 Naglee Ave, 95126-2094, SAN 334-7168. Tel: 408-808-3070. Administration Tel: 408-999-0240. FAX: 408-999-0909. *Sr Librn,* Jean Herriges
Founded 1960. Pop 149,440; Circ 249,795
Library Holdings: Bk Vols 64,115
Open Mon & Thurs 10-6, Tues & Wed 11-8
Friends of the Library Group

SANTA TERESA, 290 International Circle, 95119-1132, SAN 334-7176. Tel: 408-808-3068. Administration Tel: 408-365-5785. FAX: 408-365-5787. *Sr Librn,* Joan Bowlby
Pop 205,861; Circ 764,155
Library Holdings: Bk Vols 104,301
Open Wed 11-8, Thurs-Sat 10-6
Friends of the Library Group

SEVENTREES, 3590 Cas Dr, 95111-2499, SAN 334-7192. Tel: 408-808-3056. Administration Tel: 408-629-3362. FAX: 408-629-3394. *Sr Librn,* Michelle Amores
Pop 73,357; Circ 167,033
Library Holdings: Bk Vols 57,076
Open Wed 11-8, Thurs-Sat 10-6
Friends of the Library Group

TULLY COMMUNITY, 880 Tully Rd, 95111. Tel: 408-808-3030. Administration Tel: 408-977-1441. FAX: 408-977-3113. *Sr Librn,* Michelle Amores; E-mail: michelle.amores@sjlibrary.org
Pop 293,735; Circ 704,947
Library Holdings: Bk Vols 89,181
Open Mon & Thurs 10-6, Tues & Wed 11-8
Friends of the Library Group

VINELAND, 1450 Blossom Hill Rd, 95118, SAN 334-6803. Tel: 408-808-3000. Administration Tel: 408-808-3029. FAX: 408-978-1080. *Sr Librn,* Gayleen Thomas
Pop 157,208; Circ 421,823
Library Holdings: Bk Vols 96,309
Open Mon & Thurs 10-6, Tues & Wed 11-8
Friends of the Library Group

WEST VALLEY, 1243 San Tomas Aquino Rd, 95117-3399, SAN 334-7222. Tel: 408-244-4747. Administration Tel: 408-247-1117. FAX: 408-984-3736. *Sr Librn,* Pam Crider
Pop 220,254; Circ 740,849
Library Holdings: Bk Vols 103,192
Open Wed 11-8, Thurs-Sat 10-6
Friends of the Library Group

WILLOW GLEN, 1157 Minnesota Ave, 95125-3324, SAN 334-7257. Tel: 408-808-3045. Administration Tel: 408-947-7849. FAX: 408-947-8901. *Sr Librn,* Jean Herriges
Pop 136,020; Circ 328,149
Library Holdings: Bk Vols 61,803
Open Wed 11-8, Thurs-Sat 10-6
Friends of the Library Group

C SAN JOSE STATE UNIVERSITY*, King Library, One Washington Sq, 95192-0028. SAN 301-5033. Tel: 408-808-2419. Circulation Tel: 408-808-2304. Interlibrary Loan Service Tel: 408-808-2076. Reference Tel: 408-808-2100. FAX: 408-808-2141. TDD: 408-808-2130. Web Site: www.sjlibrary.org/. *Dean, Univ Libr,* Ruth Kifer; E-mail: ruth.kifer@sjsu.edu; *Assoc Dean, Digital Futures, Tech Serv & IT,* John Wenzler; Tel: 408-808-2065, E-mail: john.wenzler@sjsu.edu; *Interim Assoc Dean,* Mary Nino; Tel: 408-808-2008, E-mail: mary.nino@sjsu.edu; *Dir, Admin Serv,* Luann Budd; Tel: 408-808-2050, E-mail: luann.budd@sjsu.edu; *Dir, Libr Develop,* Marianne Quarre Dean; Tel: 408-924-1474, E-mail: marianne.dean@sjsu.edu; *Dir, Spec Coll,* Danelle Moon; Tel: 408-808-2061, E-mail: danelle.moon@sjsu.edu; *Head, Access Serv,* Julie Kowalewski-Ward; Tel: 408-808-2343, E-mail: julie.kowalewski-ward@sjsu.edu; *Head of Doc Delivery,* Danny Soares; Tel: 408-808-2078, E-mail: danny.soares@sjsu.edu; *Head, Tech Serv,* Rae Ann Stahl; Tel: 408-808-2467, E-mail: raeann.stahl@sjsu.edu; *Co-Unit Head, Ref,* Marci Hunsaker; Tel: 408-808-2094, E-mail: marci.hunsaker@sjsu.edu; *Coordr, Coll Develop,* Susan Kendall; Tel: 408-808-2039, E-mail: susan.kendall@sjsu.edu; *Coordr, Info Literacy & Distance Educ,* Christina Peterson; Tel: 408-808-2099, E-mail: tina.peterson@sjsu.edu; *Cultural Heritage Ctr Librn,* Kathryn Blackmer Reyes; Tel: 408-808-2097, E-mail: kathryn.blackmerreyes@sjsu.edu; *Digital Repository & Scholarly Communications Librn,* Celia Bakke; Tel: 408-808-2469, E-mail: celia.bakke@sjsu.edu; Staff 78 (MLS 33, Non-MLS 45)
Founded 1857. Enrl 32,100; Fac 2,224; Highest Degree: Master
Library Holdings: CDs 24,489; DVDs 11,901; e-books 54,535; e-journals 77,092; Bk Titles 1,020,297; Bk Vols 1,351,494; Per Subs 448
Special Collections: Beethoven Studies; Gay/Lesbian Community in San Jose 1975-2000 (Ted Sahl Archives); John C Gordon Coll of Photography (Santa Clara Valley/San Jose Area 1920-1940); John Steinbeck Coll; World War II Diplomatic & Military History. State Document Depository; US Document Depository
Automation Activity & Vendor Info: (Acquisitions) Innovative Interfaces, Inc; (Cataloging) Innovative Interfaces, Inc; (Circulation) Innovative

Interfaces, Inc; (Course Reserve) Innovative Interfaces, Inc; (ILL) Innovative Interfaces, Inc; (Media Booking) Innovative Interfaces, Inc; (OPAC) Innovative Interfaces, Inc; (Serials) Innovative Interfaces, Inc
Database Vendor: EBSCOhost, Elsevier, Gale Cengage Learning, Innovative Interfaces, Inc, LexisNexis, OVID Technologies, ProQuest, Wilson - Wilson Web
Wireless access
Partic in OCLC Online Computer Library Center, Inc

GL SANTA CLARA COUNTY LAW LIBRARY*, 360 N First St, 95113. SAN 301-505X. Tel: 408-299-3568. FAX: 408-286-9283. Web Site: www.sccll.org. *Circ, Ref,* Elaine Taranto; Staff 3 (Non-MLS 3)
Founded 1874
Library Holdings: Bk Vols 70,000; Per Subs 200
Special Collections: State Document Depository
Open Mon-Thurs 8-7, Fri 8-5, Sat 9-4
Friends of the Library Group

S SANTA CLARA COUNTY OFFICE OF EDUCATION*, Learning Multimedia Center, 1290 Ridder Park Dr, Mail Code 232, 95131. SAN 329-8140. Tel: 408-453-6800. FAX: 408-453-6815. Web Site: www.sccoe.org/depts/library. *Coordr,* Peter Doering; E-mail: peter_doering@sccoe.org; Staff 5 (MLS 2, Non-MLS 3)
Library Holdings: Bk Vols 15,000; Per Subs 152
Subject Interests: Educ mat for professionals
Automation Activity & Vendor Info: (OPAC) SirsiDynix
Database Vendor: SirsiDynix

M SANTA CLARA VALLEY MEDICAL CENTER*, Milton J Chatton Medical Library, 751 S Bascom Ave, Rm 2E063, 95128. SAN 334-7702. Tel: 408-885-5650. FAX: 408-885-5655. E-mail: medical.library@hhs.sccgov.org. Web Site: scvhh.sirsi.net. *Med Librn,* Hella Bluhm-Stieber; Tel: 408-885-5654, E-mail: hella.bluhm-stieber@hhs.sccgov.org; *Med Librn,* Connie Kwan; Tel: 408-885-5651, E-mail: connie.kwan@hhs.sccgov.org; *Libr Asst,* Vaughn Flaming; Tel: 408-885-5652, E-mail: vaughn.flaming@hhs.sccgov.org; Staff 1.5 (MLS 1, Non-MLS 0.5)
Founded 1930
Library Holdings: AV Mats 1,120; DVDs 50; e-books 2,000; e-journals 1,000; Microforms 100; Bk Titles 4,000; Per Subs 400; Spec Interest Per Sub 16; Talking Bks 100; Videos 100
Subject Interests: Head injury, Med, Nursing, Pub health, Spinal cord injury
Automation Activity & Vendor Info: (Acquisitions) SirsiDynix; (Cataloging) SIRSI WorkFlows; (Circulation) SIRSI WorkFlows; (ILL) SERHOLD; (OPAC) SirsiDynix; (Serials) SIRSI WorkFlows
Database Vendor: EBSCOhost, McGraw-Hill, Medline, Micromedex, OVID Technologies, PubMed, ScienceDirect, SerialsSolutions, SirsiDynix, Springer-Verlag, Swets Information Services
Wireless access
Function: Audio & video playback equip for onsite use, Bks on cassette, Bks on CD, Computers for patron use, Copy machines, Doc delivery serv, e-mail & chat, e-mail serv, Electronic databases & coll, Handicapped accessible, ILL available, Microfiche/film & reading machines, Online cat, Ref serv available, Scanner, Wheelchair accessible
Partic in Docline; Med Libr Consortium of Santa Clara County; US National Library of Medicine
Open Mon-Fri 8-1
Restriction: Hospital staff & commun, Med & nursing staff, patients & families, Med staff & students, Open to pub for ref & circ; with some limitations, Open to staff, patients & family mem

G SANTA CLARA VALLEY WATER DISTRICT LIBRARY, 1020 Blossom Hill Rd, 95123. (Mail add: 5750 Almaden Expressway, 95118), SAN 375-5533. Tel: 408-630-2360, 408-630-3748. FAX: 408-979-5693. Web Site: www.valleywater.org. *Librn,* Robert J Teeter; E-mail: bteeter@valleywater.org; Staff 1 (MLS 1)
Library Holdings: Bk Titles 20,000; Per Subs 200
Subject Interests: Eng, Environment, Pub admin, Water
Database Vendor: Dialog, ebrary, EBSCO Information Services, OCLC
Wireless access
Partic in OCLC Online Computer Library Center, Inc
Restriction: Circ limited, In-house use for visitors

L UNITED STATES DISTRICT COURT LIBRARY*, 280 S First St, 95113. SAN 372-3127. Tel: 408-535-5323. FAX: 408-535-5322. *Librn,* Lee Van Duzer
Library Holdings: Bk Vols 20,000; Per Subs 20
Partic in OCLC Online Computer Library Center, Inc
Restriction: Not open to pub

SAN JUAN BAUTISTA

P SAN JUAN BAUTISTA CITY LIBRARY*, Carl Martin Luck Memorial Library, 801 Second St, 95045. (Mail add: PO Box 1420, 95045-1420), SAN 301-5068. Tel: 831-623-4687. FAX: 831-623-4701. E-mail: library@san-juan-bautista.ca.us. Web Site: www.san-juan-bautista.ca.us/cityLibrary.htm. *Libr Asst,* Dee Dee Hanania; *Tech Asst,* Connie Sepulveda; Staff 2 (Non-MLS 2)
Founded 1896. Pop 1,796; Circ 4,800
Library Holdings: CDs 100; DVDs 150; Large Print Bks 200; Music Scores 100; Bk Vols 9,716; Videos 400
Automation Activity & Vendor Info: (Cataloging) Follett Software
Partic in Monterey Bay Area Cooperative Library System
Open Mon, Wed & Fri 1-5, Tues & Thurs 1-7, Sat 9-1
Friends of the Library Group

SAN JUAN CAPISTRANO

M QUEST DIAGNOSTICS, INC*, Corporate Medical Library, 33608 Ortega Hwy, 92690-6130. SAN 301-6846. Tel: 949-728-4689. FAX: 949-728-4047. Web Site: www.questdiagnostics.com. *Libr Serv Mgr,* Liz Liu; Staff 1 (MLS 1)
Founded 2000
Library Holdings: Bk Titles 800; Per Subs 180
Subject Interests: Clinical labs, Endocrinology, Genetics, Oncology, Pathology, Toxicology
Function: For res purposes
Restriction: Not open to pub, Private libr

SAN LEANDRO

S PORTUGUESE UNION OF THE STATE OF CALIFORNIA*, J A Freitas Library, 1120 E 14th St, 94577. SAN 301-5092. Tel: 510-351-4972. Administration Tel: 510-483-7676. FAX: 510-483-5015. Web Site: www.mypfsa.org/library. *Dir,* Timothy L Borges; E-mail: timothy.borges@mypfsa.org
Founded 1967
Library Holdings: Bk Titles 12,000
Special Collections: Portuguese Newspapers of California 1880s
Open Mon-Fri 9-4:30

P SAN LEANDRO PUBLIC LIBRARY*, 300 Estudillo Ave, 94577. SAN 334-7761. Tel: 510-577-3970. Administration Tel: 510-577-3980. Automation Services Tel: 510-577-3977. Information Services Tel: 510-577-3971. FAX: 510-577-3967. Web Site: www.sanleandrolibrary.org. *Dir,* David R Bohne; Tel: 510-577-3940, E-mail: dbohne@ci.san-leandro.ca.us; *Libr Serv Mgr,* Nancy Fong; Tel: 510-577-3947, E-mail: nfong@ci.san-leandro.ca.us; *Support Serv Mgr,* Theresa Mallon; Tel: 510-577-3942, E-mail: tmallon@ci.san-leandro.ca.us; *Sr Librn,* William Sherwood; Tel: 510-577-7964, E-mail: bsherwood@ci.san-leandro.ca.us; *Sr Librn, Ch Serv,* Kelly Keefer; Tel: 510-577-3954, E-mail: kkeefer@ci.san-leandro.ca.us; *Sr Librn, Tech Serv,* Therese Dunn; Tel: 510-577-3958, E-mail: tdunn@ci.san-leandro.ca.us; Staff 80 (MLS 16, Non-MLS 64)
Founded 1906. Pop 83,183; Circ 961,462
Jul 2009-Jun 2010 Income (Main Library and Branch(s)) $4,949,827, State $30,110, City $4,840,616, Other $43,000. Mats Exp $401,041, Books $315,125, Per/Ser (Incl. Access Fees) $11,000, Micro $4,916, AV Mat $40,000, Electronic Ref Mat (Incl. Access Fees) $30,000. Sal $2,014,326
Library Holdings: AV Mats 26,536; e-books 5; Bk Vols 306,395; Per Subs 473
Special Collections: Californiana. US Document Depository
Automation Activity & Vendor Info: (Acquisitions) Horizon; (Cataloging) Horizon; (Circulation) Horizon; (OPAC) Horizon; (Serials) Horizon
Database Vendor: 3M Library Systems, Baker & Taylor, Brodart, BWI, Civica, EBSCOhost, Facts on File, Gale Cengage Learning, Newsbank, OCLC WorldShare Interlibrary Loan, SirsiDynix, TLC (The Library Corporation), TumbleBookLibrary
Wireless access
Function: Adult literacy prog, Archival coll, Bks on CD, Children's prog, Computers for patron use, Copy machines, Digital talking bks, Electronic databases & coll, Govt ref serv, Handicapped accessible, Holiday prog, Large print keyboards, Magnifiers for reading, Music CDs, Newsp ref libr, Online searches, Photocopying/Printing, Prog for adults, Prog for children & young adult, Ref serv available, Story hour, Summer reading prog, Teen prog, Wheelchair accessible, Workshops
Special Services for the Deaf - TTY equip
Special Services for the Blind - Computer with voice synthesizer for visually impaired persons
Friends of the Library Group

Branches: 3
MANOR, 1307 Manor Blvd, 94579-1501, SAN 334-7850. Tel: 510-577-7970. Reference Tel: 510-577-7971. *Sr Librn,* William Sherwood; E-mail: bsherwood@ci.san-leandro.ca.us; Staff 2 (MLS 1, Non-MLS 1)
Founded 1971. Pop 15,038; Circ 91,933
Library Holdings: Bk Vols 42,873
Function: Bk club(s), Bks on CD, Children's prog, Computers for patron use, Copy machines, Free DVD rentals, Holiday prog, Music CDs, Prog for children & young adult, Story hour, Summer reading prog
MULFORD-MARINA, 13699 Aurora Dr, 94577-4036, SAN 334-7885. Tel: 510-357-7976. *Sr Libr Asst,* Hollis Lesur; E-mail: hlesur@ci.san-leandro.ca.us
Founded 1975
Library Holdings: Bk Vols 17,881
Friends of the Library Group
SOUTH, 14799 E 14th St, 94578-2818, SAN 334-7915. Tel: 510-577-7980. *Sr Libr Asst,* Hollis Lesur; E-mail: hlesur@ci.san-leandro.ca.us
Founded 1966
Library Holdings: Bk Vols 15,050

SAN LUIS OBISPO

P BLACK GOLD COOPERATIVE LIBRARY SYSTEM*, 3437 Empresa Dr, Ste C, 93401. SAN 301-5114. Tel: 805-543-6082. Administration FAX: 805-543-9487. Web Site: www.blackgold.org. *Exec Dir,* Maureen Theobald; Tel. 805-543-1093, E mail: mtheobald@blackgold.org; Staff 7 (MLS 2, Non-MLS 5)
Founded 1963. Pop 1,780,000; Circ 4,560,000
Automation Activity & Vendor Info: (Acquisitions) Innovative Interfaces, Inc; (Cataloging) Innovative Interfaces, Inc; (Circulation) Innovative Interfaces, Inc; (ILL) Innovative Interfaces, Inc; (OPAC) Innovative Interfaces, Inc; (Serials) Innovative Interfaces, Inc
Database Vendor: Overdrive, Inc
Member Libraries: Blanchard-Santa Paula Public Library District; Lompoc Public Library; Paso Robles Public Library; San Luis Obispo County Library; Santa Barbara Public Library; Santa Maria Public Library
Open Mon-Fri 8-5

C CALIFORNIA POLYTECHNIC STATE UNIVERSITY*, Robert E Kennedy Library, One Grand Ave, 93407. SAN 301 5130. Tel: 805-756-5760. Interlibrary Loan Service Tel: 805-756-1222. Reference Tel: 805-756-2649. FAX: 805-756-2346. Circulation E-mail: library@calpoly.edu. Web Site: lib.calpoly.edu. *Univ Librn,* Anna K Gold; Tel: 805-756-2345, E-mail: akgold@calpoly.edu; *Assoc Univ Librn,* Sarah F Cohen; Tel: 805-756-2622, E-mail: sfcohen@calpoly.edu; *Dir, Info Res & Archives,* Tim Strawn; Tel: 805-756-1485, E-mail: tstrawn@calpoly.edu; *Dir, Libr Info Tech,* Dale Kohler; Tel: 805-756-1922, E-mail: dkohler@calpoly.edu; Staff 43 (MLS 11.5, Non-MLS 31.5)
Founded 1901. Enrl 17,000; Fac 1,294; Highest Degree: Master
Jul 2010-Jun 2011 Income $7,117,000. Mats Exp $1,593,000. Sal $4,183,000
Library Holdings: e-books 5,000, e-journals 36,000; Bk Titles 640,000; Bk Vols 800,500; Per Subs 800; Videos 1,900
Special Collections: California Promotional & Travel Literature; Fairs & Expositions; Healy Newspaper Coll; Hearst Castle Architectural Drawings; John Henry Nash Coll; Josephine Miles Coll; Julia Morgan Coll; Local History; Upton Sinclair Coll; William F Cody Coll; William McDill Railroad Coll. State Document Depository; US Document Depository
Subject Interests: Agr, Archit, Graphic arts
Automation Activity & Vendor Info: (Acquisitions) Innovative Interfaces, Inc; (Cataloging) Innovative Interfaces, Inc; (Circulation) Innovative Interfaces, Inc; (ILL) OCLC ILLiad; (OPAC) Innovative Interfaces, Inc; (Serials) Innovative Interfaces, Inc
Database Vendor: 3M Library Systems, ACM (Association for Computing Machinery), Agricola, American Chemical Society, American Psychological Association (APA), ARTstor, Factiva.com, H W Wilson, IEEE (Institute of Electrical & Electronics Engineers), JSTOR, LexisNexis, Marcive, Inc, Modern Language Association, Project MUSE, ProQuest, Safari Books Online, Sage, ScienceDirect, SerialsSolutions, Thomson - Web of Science
Wireless access
Function: Art exhibits, Audio & video playback equip for onsite use, Computers for patron use, Copy machines, E-Reserves, Electronic databases & coll, Exhibits, Handicapped accessible, ILL available, Online info literacy tutorials on the web & in blackboard, Photocopying/Printing, Ref serv available, Senior outreach, Tax forms, Telephone ref
Partic in OCLC Online Computer Library Center, Inc
Special Services for the Deaf - Assistive tech; Closed caption videos
Special Services for the Blind - Accessible computers; Assistive/Adapted tech devices, equip & products; Audio mat; Dragon Naturally Speaking software
Open Mon-Fri (Winter) 8-5; Mon-Thurs (Summer) 7-7, Fri 7-5
Restriction: 24-hr pass syst for students only, Borrowing privileges limited to fac & registered students, Borrowing requests are handled by ILL, Open to pub for ref & circ; with some limitations, Open to students, fac & staff

J CUESTA COLLEGE LIBRARY*, Hwy 1, 93401. (Mail add: PO Box 8106, 93403-8106), SAN 301-5149. Tel: 805-546-3155. Interlibrary Loan Service Tel: 805-546-3100, Ext 2469. Reference Tel: 805-546-3157. Administration Tel: 805-546-3159. FAX: 805-546-3109. Web Site: library.cuesta.edu. *Libr Dir,* Mark Stengel; E-mail: mark_stengel@cuesta.edu; *IT Librn,* Kevin Bontenbal; Tel: 805-546-3117, E-mail: kbontenb@cuesta.edu; *Cat, Metadata Librn,* Carina Love; Tel: 805-546-3100, Ext 2688, E-mail: clove@cuesta.edu; Staff 14.43 (MLS 6, Non-MLS 8.43)
Founded 1965. Enrl 9,061; Fac 558; Highest Degree: Associate
Jul 2010-Jun 2011 Income $1,129,518, Parent Institution $1,107,540, Other $21,978. Mats Exp $94,183, Books $16,517, Per/Ser (Incl. Access Fees) $13,524, Manu Arch $289, AV Mat $1,186, Electronic Ref Mat (Incl. Access Fees) $53,827. Sal $837,058 (Prof $484,302)
Library Holdings: Audiobooks 113; AV Mats 1,848; Bks on Deafness & Sign Lang 182; CDs 399; DVDs 226; e-books 12,915; e-journals 38; Electronic Media & Resources 9; High Interest/Low Vocabulary Bk Vols 906; Large Print Bks 14; Microforms 6,541; Bk Titles 60,386; Bk Vols 73,318; Per Subs 255; Videos 1,331
Special Collections: Blythe History Coll; Health Coll; Morro Bay Coll; Professional Development Coll
Automation Activity & Vendor Info: (Cataloging) SirsiDynix; (Circulation) SirsiDynix; (Course Reserve) SirsiDynix; (OPAC) SirsiDynix; (Serials) SirsiDynix
Database Vendor: CountryWatch, EBSCOhost, Gale Cengage Learning, Newsbank, ProQuest
Wireless access
Function: ILL available
Publications: Library Research Workbook
Partic in Amigos Library Services, Inc; Gold Coast Library Network; OCLC Online Computer Library Center, Inc
Open Mon-Thurs 8-8, Fri 8-4, Sat 2-6
Friends of the Library Group

GL SAN LUIS OBISPO COUNTY LAW LIBRARY*, County Government Ctr, Rm 125, 1050 Monterey St, 93408. SAN 301-5157. Tel: 805-781-5855. FAX: 805-781-4172. E-mail: lawlibrarian@slocll.org. Web Site: www.slocll.org. *Librn,* Barry Lewis; Staff 1 (MLS 1)
Founded 1896
Jul 2006-Jun 2007 Income $204,883, Locally Generated Income $14,709, Other $190,171. Mats Exp $177,430, Books $93,027, Electronic Ref Mat (Incl. Access Fees) $15,588. Sal $54,527 (Prof $42,900)
Library Holdings: Bk Vols 14,076; Per Subs 60
Special Collections: State Document Depository
Subject Interests: Calif
Database Vendor: LexisNexis, Westlaw
Publications: Shepard's Online
Open Mon-Fri 8:30-4:30, Sat 10-3
Restriction: Non-circulating

P SAN LUIS OBISPO COUNTY LIBRARY, 995 Palm St, 93401. (Mail add: PO Box 8107, 94303-8107), SAN 334-794X. Tel: 805-781-5774. FAX: 805-781-1320. E-mail: webteam@slolibrary.org. Web Site: www.slolibrary.org. *Dir,* Christopher Barnickel; Tel: 805-781-5990; *Libr Mgr,* Kristine Tardiff; Tel: 805-781-5783, E-mail: katardiff@co.slo.ca.us; *Chief Financial Officer,* John Culpepper; Tel: 805-781-5776, E-mail: jculpepper@co.slo.ca.us; Staff 14.6 (MLS 6.5, Non-MLS 8.1)
Founded 1919. Pop 240,480; Circ 2,432,510
Library Holdings: AV Mats 78,094; e-books 3,058; Electronic Media & Resources 14; Bk Vols 348,954; Per Subs 709
Special Collections: History of San Luis Obispo County (especially Hearst Family)
Subject Interests: Local hist
Automation Activity & Vendor Info: (Acquisitions) Innovative Interfaces, Inc; (Cataloging) Innovative Interfaces, Inc; (Circulation) Innovative Interfaces, Inc; (ILL) Innovative Interfaces, Inc; (OPAC) Innovative Interfaces, Inc
Database Vendor: ALLDATA Online, Gale Cengage Learning, infoUSA, LearningExpress, OCLC FirstSearch, Overdrive, Inc, ReferenceUSA, TumbleBookLibrary, ValueLine
Wireless access
Mem of Black Gold Cooperative Library System
Open Tues 10-8, Wed-Sat 10-5
Friends of the Library Group
Branches: 14
ARROYO GRANDE BRANCH, 800 W Branch St, Arroyo Grande, 93420, SAN 334-7974. Tel: 805-473-7161. FAX: 805-473-7173. E-mail: osstaff@slolibrary.org. *Librn,* Rosalyn Pierini; Staff 11 (MLS 3, Non-MLS 8)

Open Tues 10-7, Wed-Sat 10-5
Friends of the Library Group
ATASCADERO BRANCH, 6850 Morro Rd, Atascadero, 93422, SAN 334-8008. Tel: 805-461-6161. FAX: 805-461-6045. E-mail: oastaff@slolibrary.org. *Libr Mgr,* Kay Rader; Staff 9.2 (MLS 3, Non-MLS 6.2)
Open Tues & Thurs-Sat 10-5, Wed 10-8
Friends of the Library Group
CAMBRIA BRANCH, 900 Main St, Cambria, 93428, SAN 334-8032. Tel: 805-927-4336. FAX: 805-927-3524. E-mail: ocstaff@slolibrary.org. *Librn,* Joen Kommer; Staff 4 (MLS 1, Non-MLS 3)
Open Tues-Fri 11-5, Sat 11-4
Friends of the Library Group
CAYUCOS BRANCH, 310 B St, Cayucos, 93430, SAN 334-8067. Tel: 805-995-3312. FAX: 805-995-0573. E-mail: oustaff@slolibrary.org. *Librn,* Shera Hill; Staff 0.5 (Non-MLS 0.5)
Open Tues 1-6, Wed & Thurs 12-5
Friends of the Library Group
CRESTON BRANCH, 6290 Adams, Creston, 93432, SAN 334-8091. Tel: 805-237-3010. E-mail: otstaff@slolibrary.org. *Librn,* Kathleen Saffell; Staff 0.5 (Non-MLS 0.5)
Open Tues 2-7, Wed & Thurs 1-6
Friends of the Library Group
LOS OSOS BRANCH, 2075 Palisades Ave, Los Osos, 93402, SAN 334-8423. Tel: 805-528-1862. FAX: 805-528-7835. E-mail: oystaff@slolibrary.org. *Libr Mgr,* Joseph Laurenzi; Staff 6.75 (MLS 1, Non-MLS 5.75)
Open Tues, Thurs & Fri 10-5, Wed 10-8, Sat 11-4
Friends of the Library Group
MORRO BAY BRANCH, 625 Harbor St, Morro Bay, 93442. Tel: 805-772-6394. FAX: 805-772-6396. E-mail: omstaff@slolibrary.org. *Librn,* Jackie Kinsey; Staff 7 (MLS 1, Non-MLS 6)
Open Tues & Wed 10-7, Thurs & Fri 10-5, Sat 10-4
NIPOMO BRANCH, 918 W Tefft, Nipomo, 93444, SAN 334-8210. Tel: 805-929-3994. FAX: 805-929-5476. E-mail: onstaff@slolibrary.org. *Librn,* Lesley Corbus; Staff 4 (MLS 1, Non-MLS 3)
Open Tues 11-6, Wed-Sat 11-5
Friends of the Library Group
OCEANO BRANCH, 1551 17th St, Oceano, 93445. Tel: 805-474-7478. FAX: 805-474-7479. E-mail: oestaff@slolibrary.org. *Libr Mgr,* Vicki Cyr
Open Tues, Thurs & Fri 12-5
SAN MIGUEL BRANCH, 254 13th St, San Miguel, 93451, SAN 334-827X. Tel: 805-467-3224. E-mail: ogstaff@slolibrary.org. *Libr Mgr,* Judy Brown; Staff 0.5 (Non-MLS 0.5)
Open Tues 12-4, Wed 11-4, Thurs 12-6
Friends of the Library Group
SANTA MARGARITA BRANCH, 9630 Murphy Ave, Santa Margarita, 93453, SAN 334-830X. Tel: 805-438-5622. FAX: 805-438-4879. E-mail: orstaff@slolibrary.org. *Librn,* Debra Jurey; Staff 0.8 (Non-MLS 0.8)
Open Tues-Thurs 12-6
Friends of the Library Group
SHANDON BRANCH, 240 E Centre St, Shandon, 93461, SAN 334-8334. Tel: 805-237-3009. FAX: 805-237-3022. E-mail: ohstaff@slolibrary.org. *Librn,* Maureen Vestal; Staff 0.35 (Non-MLS 0.35)
Open Thurs 12-5, Sat 11-4
SHELL BEACH BRANCH, 230 Leeward Ave, Shell Beach, 93449, SAN 334-8369. Tel: 805-773-2263. FAX: 805-773-2891. E-mail: olstaff@slolibrary.org. *Librn,* Kate McClure; Staff 0.5 (MLS 0.5)
Open Tues, Wed & Fri 12-5
Friends of the Library Group
SIMMLER BRANCH, 13080 Soda Lake Rd, Simmler, 93453, SAN 334-8393. Tel: 805-475-2603. FAX: 805-475-2759. E-mail: oistaff@slolibrary.org. *Librn,* Maureen Vestal; Staff 0.15 (Non-MLS 0.15)
Open Wed 12-5
Bookmobiles: 1

SAN MARCOS

C CALIFORNIA STATE UNIVERSITY, San Marcos Library, 333 S Twin Oaks Valley Rd, 92096-0001. SAN 323-911X. Tel: 760-750-4340. Circulation Tel: 760-750-4348. Interlibrary Loan Service Tel: 760-750-4345. Reference Tel: 760-750-4391. FAX: 760-750-3287. TDD: 760-750-3163. Web Site: library.csusm.edu. *Dean of Libr,* Jennifer Fabbi; Tel: 760-750-4350; *Behav Sci & Nursing Librn,* Yvonne N Meulemans; *Bus Librn,* Ann M Fiegen; *Educ Librn,* Antonia Olivas; *Humanities & Govt Doc Librn,* Judith A Downie; *Outreach Librn,* Melanie Chu; *Soc Sci Librn,* Allison Carr; *Coordr, Cat,* Kit Herlihy; Tel: 760-750-4357, E-mail: kherlihy@csusm.edu; *Coordr, Coll Develop,* Hua Yi; Tel: 760-750-4368, E-mail: hyi@csusm.edu; *Coordr, Info Tech,* Susan M Thompson; Tel: 760-750-4373, E-mail: sthompsn@csusm.edu; *Coordr, Instruction, Coordr, Ref (Info Serv),* Gabriela Sonntag; Tel: 760-750-4356, E-mail: gsg@csusm.edu; *Coordr, Pub Serv,* Jacqueline M Borin; Tel: 760-750-4336, E-mail: jborin@csusm.edu. Subject Specialists: *Nursing, Sci,* Yvonne N Meulemans; *Bus, Econ,* Ann M Fiegen; *Educ,* Antonia Olivas; *Humanities,* Judith A Downie; *Multicultural,* Melanie Chu; *Soc sci,* Allison Carr; Staff 43 (MLS 15, Non-MLS 28)
Founded 1989. Enrl 7,900; Fac 302; Highest Degree: Master
Jul 2006-Jun 2007 Income $3,874,566. Mats Exp $621,718, Books $125,780, Per/Ser (Incl. Access Fees) $136,229, Micro $29,211, AV Equip $1,800, AV Mat $35,000, Electronic Ref Mat (Incl. Access Fees) $293,321, Presv $377. Sal $2,252,425 (Prof $1,020,597)
Library Holdings: AV Mats 10,290; CDs 3,132; e-books 28,832; e-journals 19,515; Bk Titles 192,450; Bk Vols 268,952; Per Subs 665
Special Collections: Barahona Center for Books in Spanish, bks for children & young adults. State Document Depository; US Document Depository
Automation Activity & Vendor Info: (Acquisitions) Innovative Interfaces, Inc; (Cataloging) Innovative Interfaces, Inc; (Circulation) Innovative Interfaces, Inc; (Course Reserve) Docutek; (ILL) OCLC ILLiad; (Media Booking) Innovative Interfaces, Inc; (OPAC) Innovative Interfaces, Inc; (Serials) Innovative Interfaces, Inc
Database Vendor: ACM (Association for Computing Machinery), American Chemical Society, American Mathematical Society, American Psychological Association (APA), BioOne, Blackwell, Bowker, CIOS (Communication Institute for Online Scholarship), College Source, CountryWatch, CQ Press, EBSCOhost, Elsevier, Emerald, Factiva.com, Innovative Interfaces, Inc, JSTOR, LexisNexis, Mergent Online, Modern Language Association, OCLC FirstSearch, OCLC WorldShare Interlibrary Loan, Oxford Online, Project MUSE, ProQuest, Safari Books Online, ScienceDirect, Springer-Verlag, Swets Information Services, Wiley
Wireless access
Partic in San Diego Circuit
Special Services for the Deaf - Assistive tech
Special Services for the Blind - Assistive/Adapted tech devices, equip & products
Open Mon-Thurs 7am-9pm, Fri 8-5, Sat & Sun 10-5

J PALOMAR COLLEGE LIBRARY - MEDIA CENTER*, 1140 W Mission Rd, 92069-1487. SAN 334-8482. Tel: 760-744-1150, Ext 2848. FAX: 760-761-3500. TDD: 760-736-0246. E-mail: library@palomar.edu. Web Site: www.palomar.edu/library. *Dir,* Linda Morrow; E-mail: lmorrow@palomar.edu; *Cat Librn,* Byung Kang; *Ser Librn,* Tamera Weintraub; Staff 5 (MLS 5)
Founded 1946. Enrl 22,926; Fac 350
Library Holdings: Bk Titles 108,400; Per Subs 900
Special Collections: California History Coll; Early California & Iowa Frontier, newsp on microfilm; Iceland; Indians of North America; World War I Posters. Oral History
Subject Interests: Art & archit, Ethnic studies
Automation Activity & Vendor Info: (Acquisitions) SirsiDynix; (Cataloging) SirsiDynix; (Circulation) SirsiDynix; (Serials) SirsiDynix
Function: Handicapped accessible
Publications: A Guide to the Palomar College Library; Aging in the 1980s; Controversial Issues; Faculty in Print; Grants Bibliog; Library Self Help Bulletins
Partic in BRS; Coop Libr Agency for Syst & Servs; Dialog Corp; OCLC Online Computer Library Center, Inc; San Diego Greater Metro Area Libr & Info Agency Coun
Special Services for the Deaf - TDD equip; Videos & decoder

SAN MARINO

P CROWELL PUBLIC LIBRARY, 1890 Huntington Dr, 91108-2595. SAN 301-5173. Tel: 626-300-0777. FAX: 626-284-0766. E-mail: crowellPL@cityofsanmarino.org. Web Site: www.sanmarinopl.org. *City Librn,* Irene McDermott; Tel: 626-300-0775, E-mail: imcdermott@cityofsanmarino.org; *Librn,* Denise Dobbs; Tel: 626-300-0777, Ext 541, E-mail: ddobbs@cityofsanmarino.org; *Circ Mgr, Librn,* Jeff Plumley; Tel: 626-300-0777, Ext 534, E-mail: jplumley@cityofsanmarino.org; *Ref Librn,* Rex Mayreis; Tel: 626-300-0777, Ext 542, E-mail: rmayreis@cityofsanmarino.org; *Youth Serv Librn,* Tera Forrest; Tel: 626-300-0777, Ext 524, E-mail: tforrest@cityofsanmarino.org; Staff 5 (MLS 5)
Founded 1953
Library Holdings: Bk Vols 90,000; Per Subs 200
Subject Interests: Art & archit, Calif, Travel
Automation Activity & Vendor Info: (Acquisitions) LibLime; (Cataloging) LibLime; (Circulation) LibLime; (ILL) OCLC FirstSearch; (OPAC) LibLime; (Serials) LibLime
Database Vendor: Progressive Technology Federal Systems, Inc (PTFS)
Wireless access
Partic in Southern California Library Cooperative
Open Mon-Thurs 10-9, Sat 10-5, Sun 1-5
Friends of the Library Group

S HENRY E HUNTINGTON LIBRARY & ART GALLERY*, 1151 Oxford Rd, 91108. SAN 301-5165. Tel: 626-405-2100. FAX: 626-449-5720. E-mail: publicInformation@huntington.org. Web Site: www.huntington.org. *Libr Dir,* David S Zeidberg; E-mail: dzeidberg@huntington.org; *Asst Libr*

Dir, Donna Stromberg; E-mail: dstromberg@huntington.org; *Cat Librn,* Gayle Richardson; Staff 65 (MLS 31, Non-MLS 34)
Founded 1919
Library Holdings: Bk Titles 686,154; Per Subs 600
Special Collections: 19th Century Americana; 19th Century England Coll; 20th Century American Literature & Letters; 20th Century British Literature; American Photography, History, Prints, Printmaking & Design; American Sheet Music; Colonial & Early Federal Americana; Early Hispanic Americana; Early Modern England Coll; Incunabula; Medieval Manuscript Coll; Restoration & 18th Century England Coll; Western Americana
Automation Activity & Vendor Info: (Acquisitions) Innovative Interfaces, Inc; (Cataloging) Innovative Interfaces, Inc; (OPAC) Innovative Interfaces, Inc; (Serials) Innovative Interfaces, Inc
Wireless access
Function: Res libr
Publications: Guide to American Historical Manuscripts in the Huntington Library; Guide to British Historical Manuscripts in the Huntington Library; Guide to Literary Manuscripts in the Huntington Library; Guide to Medieval & Renaissance Manuscripts; The Huntington Library (Quarterly)
Restriction: Not open to pub, Restricted access

SAN MATEO

J COLLEGE OF SAN MATEO LIBRARY*, Bldg 9, 1700 W Hillsdale Blvd, 94402-3795. SAN 301-5181. Tel: 650-574-6100. Circulation Tel: 650-574-6548. Reference Tel: 650-574-6232. FAX: 650-574-6497. E-mail: csmlibrary@smccd.net. Web Site: collegeofsanmateo.edu/library. *Dir, Libr & Learning Serv,* Lorrita E Ford; Tel: 650-574-6569, E-mail: fordl@smccd.edu; *Ref & Instrul Serv Librn,* Teresa M Morris; Tel: 650-574-6579, E-mail: morrist@smccd.edu; Staff 8 (MLS 3, Non-MLS 5)
Founded 1923. Enrl 13,800; Fac 300
Library Holdings: Bk Titles 91,761; Bk Vols 130,000; Per Subs 251
Special Collections: American History (LAC, Library of American Civilization)
Subject Interests: Art & archit, Ethnic studies, Feminism, Music, Natural sci, Nursing, Soc sci & issues
Automation Activity & Vendor Info: (Acquisitions) Innovative Interfaces, Inc; (Cataloging) Innovative Interfaces, Inc; (Circulation) Innovative Interfaces, Inc; (Course Reserve) Innovative Interfaces, Inc; (ILL) OCLC Connexion; (OPAC) Innovative Interfaces, Inc
Database Vendor: ARTstor, Comprise Technologies Inc, CQ Press, EBSCOhost, Gale Cengage Learning, Grolier Online, LexisNexis, McGraw-Hill, Oxford Online, ProQuest, Safari Books Online, SerialsSolutions
Wireless access
Partic in Califa
Special Services for the Deaf - Assistive tech; TTY equip
Special Services for the Blind - Assistive/Adapted tech devices, equip & products; Closed circuit TV; Computer with voice synthesizer for visually impaired persons; Reader equip; ZoomText magnification & reading software
Open Mon-Thurs (Winter) 7:45-7, Fri 7:45-3, Sat 11-2; Mon-Thurs (Summer) 9-7

S INTERNATIONAL DATA CORP LIBRARY*, 155 Bovet Rd, Ste 800, 94402. SAN 329-0581. Tel: 650-653-7000. FAX: 650-653-7077. Web Site: www.idc.com. *Mgr,* Laura Brisbee; E-mail: lbrisbee@idc.com; Staff 2 (MLS 1, Non-MLS 1)
Library Holdings: Bk Vols 2,400; Per Subs 250
Subject Interests: Computer sci, Finance
Database Vendor: EBSCOhost
Publications: Happenings; Industry News; Library News; Quote Alert; Reference Highlights
Partic in Dialog Corp; Dow Jones News Retrieval; OCLC Online Computer Library Center, Inc
Restriction: Employee & client use only

R PENINSULA TEMPLE BETH EL LIBRARY*, 1700 Alameda de Las Pulgas, 94403. SAN 301-5203. Tel: 650-341-7701. FAX: 650-570-7183. Web Site: www.templebethel.org. *Librn,* Stephanie Hoffman
Library Holdings: Bk Vols 5,500
Subject Interests: Judaica (lit or hist of Jews)

G SAN MATEO COUNTY*, Medical Library, 222 W 39th Ave, 94403. SAN 301-5211. Tel: 650-573-2520. FAX: 650-573-3510. E-mail: info@smhealth.org. *Librn,* Mark Q Constantz
Founded 1967
Library Holdings: Bk Vols 3,000; Per Subs 100
Subject Interests: Geriatrics & gerontology, Psychiat, Pub health
Partic in National Network of Libraries of Medicine

P SAN MATEO COUNTY LIBRARY, Library Administration, 125 Lessingia Ct, 94402-4000. SAN 331-4979. Tel: 650-312-5258. FAX: 650-312-5382. Web Site: www.smcl.org. *Dir of Libr Serv,* Anne-Marie Despain; Tel: 650-312-5245, E-mail: despain@smcl.org; *Dep Dir, Libr Serv,* Tom Fortin; Tel: 650-312-5256, E-mail: fortin@smcl.org; *Libr Serv Mgr,* Nicole Pasini; Tel: 650-312-5251, E-mail: pasini@smcl.org; *Libr Serv Mgr,* Carine Risley; Tel: 650-312-5312, E-mail: risley@smcl.org; *Libr Serv Mgr,* Sandy Wee; Tel: 650-312-5276, E-mail: wee@smcl.org
Founded 1915. Pop 276,000; Circ 3,211,000
Wireless access
Partic in OCLC Online Computer Library Center, Inc; Peninsula Libraries Automated Network
Friends of the Library Group
Branches: 12
ATHERTON LIBRARY, Two Dinkelspiel Station Lane, Atherton, 94027, SAN 331-5002. Tel: 650-328-2422. FAX: 650-328-4138. Web Site: www.smcl.org/en/content/atherton. *Libr Serv Mgr,* Nicole Pasini; E-mail: pasini@smcl.org
Circ 84,140
Friends of the Library Group
BELMONT LIBRARY, 1110 Alameda de las Pulgas, Belmont, 94002. Tel: 650-591-8286. FAX: 650-591-2763. Web Site: www.smcl.org/en/content/belmont. *Mgr,* Kathleen Beasley; E-mail: beasley@smcl.org
Circ 501,200
Friends of the Library Group
BRISBANE LIBRARY, 250 Visitacion Ave, Brisbane, 94005, SAN 331-5061. Tel: 415-467-2060. FAX: 415-467-4824. Web Site: www.smcl.org/en/content/brisbane. *Libr Serv Mgr,* Nicole Pasini; E-mail: pasini@smcl.org
Circ 61,050
Friends of the Library Group
EAST PALO ALTO LIBRARY, 2415 University Ave, East Palo Alto, 94303, SAN 331-5096. Tel: 650-321-7712. FAX: 650-326-8961. Web Site: www.smcl.org/en/content/east-palo-alto. *Br Mgr,* Dolly Goyal; E-mail: goyal@smcl.org
Circ 98,240
FOSTER CITY LIBRARY, 1000 E Hillsdale Blvd, Foster City, 94404, SAN 331-5126. Tel: 650-574-4842. FAX: 650-572-1875. Web Site: www.smcl.org/en/content/foster-city. *Libr Serv Mgr,* Anna Koch; E-mail: koch@smcl.org
Circ 785,820
Friends of the Library Group
HALF MOON BAY LIBRARY, 620 Correas St, Half Moon Bay, 94019, SAN 331-5150. Tel: 650-726-2316. FAX: 650-726-9282. *Mgr,* Annie Malley; E-mail: malley@smcl.org
Circ 296,430
Friends of the Library Group
MILLBRAE LIBRARY, One Library Ave, Millbrae, 94030, SAN 331-5185. Tel: 650-697-7607. FAX: 650-692-4747. Web Site: www.smcl.org/en/content/millbrae. *Mgr,* Thom Ball; E-mail: ball@smcl.org
Circ 501,350
Friends of the Library Group
PACIFICA SANCHEZ LIBRARY, 1111 Terra Nova Blvd, Pacifica, 94044, SAN 331-5304. Tel: 650-359-3397. FAX: 650-359-3808. Web Site: www.smcl.org/en/content/pacifica-sanchez. *Mgr,* Julie Finklang; E-mail: finklang@smcl.org
Circ 293,200
Friends of the Library Group
PACIFICA SHARP PARK LIBRARY, 104 Hilton Way, Pacifica, 94044, SAN 331-5215. Tel: 650-355-5196. FAX: 650-355-6658. Web Site: www.smcl.org/en/content/pacifica-sharp-park. *Mgr,* Julie Finklang; E-mail: finklang@smcl.org
Circ 293,200
Friends of the Library Group
PORTOLA VALLEY LIBRARY, 765 Portola Rd, Portola Valley, 94028, SAN 331-524X. Tel: 650-851-0560. FAX: 650-851-8365. Web Site: www.smcl.org/en/content/portola-valley. *Libr Serv Mgr,* Nicole Pasini; E-mail: pasini@smcl.org
Circ 86,100
Friends of the Library Group
SAN CARLOS LIBRARY, 610 Elm St, San Carlos, 94070, SAN 331-5274. Tel: 650-591-0341. FAX: 650-591-1585. Web Site: www.smcl.org/en/content/san-carlos. *Mgr,* Chet Mulawka; E-mail: mulawka@smcl.org
Circ 341,680
Friends of the Library Group
WOODSIDE LIBRARY, 3140 Woodside Rd, Woodside, 94062, SAN 331-5339. Tel: 650-851-0147. FAX: 650-851-2695. Web Site: www.smcl.org/en/content/woodside. *Libr Serv Mgr,* Nicole Pasini; E-mail: pasini@smcl.org
Circ 101,990
Friends of the Library Group
Bookmobiles: 1

P SAN MATEO PUBLIC LIBRARY*, 1100 Park Ave, 94403-7108. SAN 334-8571. Tel: 650-522-7802. Circulation Tel: 650-522-7833. Interlibrary Loan Service Tel: 650-522-7811. Reference Tel: 650-522-7818. FAX: 650-522-7801. Web Site: www.smplibrary.org. *City Librn,* Benjamin Ocon; Tel: 650-522-7808, E-mail: bocon@cityofsanmateo.org; *ILL,* Sonja Moss; E-mail: smoss@cityofsanmateo.org; *Ref,* Linda Lubovich; Staff 12 (MLS 12)
Founded 1899. Pop 94,200; Circ 642,498
Library Holdings: Bk Vols 280,000; Per Subs 794
Special Collections: Californiana, maps. State Document Depository
Subject Interests: Calif, Music
Automation Activity & Vendor Info: (Circulation) SirsiDynix
Publications: Annual Report; Business Reference (Bibliographies)
Partic in Coop Libr Agency for Syst & Servs
Friends of the Library Group
Branches: 2
HILLSDALE, 205 W Hillsdale Blvd, 94403-4217, SAN 334-8601. Tel: 650-522-7880. Circulation Tel: 650-522-7882. Reference Tel: 650-522-7885. FAX: 650-522-7881. *Br Coordr,* Linda Janok
Library Holdings: Bk Vols 46,903
MARINA, 1530 Susan Ct, 94403-1193, SAN 334-8660. Tel: 650-522-7890. Circulation Tel: 650-522-7892. Reference Tel: 650-522-7893. FAX: 650-522-7891.
Founded 1966
Library Holdings: Large Print Bks 200; Bk Vols 32,431; Videos 8,000

SAN PABLO

J CONTRA COSTA COLLEGE LIBRARY*, 2600 Mission Bell Dr, 94806-3195. SAN 301-5262. Tel: 510-235-7800, Ext 4318. Reference Tel: 510-235-7800, Ext 4450. FAX: 510-234-8161. Web Site: www.contracosta.edu/library. *Librn,* Andrew Kuo; Tel: 510-235-7800, Ext 4449, E-mail: akuo@contracosta.edu; *Coordr,* Ellen Geringer; Tel: 510-235-7800, Ext 4457, E-mail: egeringer@contracosta.edu; *Bibliog Instr,* Judith Flum; Tel: 510-235-7800, Ext 4445, E-mail: jflum@contracosta.edu; Staff 6.9 (MLS 3.1, Non-MLS 3.8)
Founded 1950. Enrl 7,277; Fac 176; Highest Degree: Associate
Library Holdings: Audiobooks 143; Bks on Deafness & Sign Lang 28; CDs 198; DVDs 323; e-books 8,862; High Interest/Low Vocabulary Bk Vols 636; Microforms 6,881; Bk Titles 47,756; Bk Vols 50,000; Per Subs 90; Videos 1,215
Special Collections: Ethnic Studies Coll
Automation Activity & Vendor Info: (Cataloging) Innovative Interfaces, Inc; (Circulation) Innovative Interfaces, Inc; (Course Reserve) Innovative Interfaces, Inc; (OPAC) Innovative Interfaces, Inc
Database Vendor: Alexander Street Press, CountryWatch, CQ Press, EBSCOhost, Facts on File, Gale Cengage Learning, McGraw-Hill, ProQuest
Wireless access
Partic in California Community College Library Consortium (CCLC)
Special Services for the Deaf - Bks on deafness & sign lang; Closed caption videos; High interest/low vocabulary bks; Videos & decoder
Special Services for the Blind - Internet workstation with adaptive software; ZoomText magnification & reading software
Open Mon-Thurs 9-7:45, Fri & Sat 10am-1:45pm
Friends of the Library Group

SAN PEDRO

S VIRGINIA REID MOORE MARINE RESEARCH LIBRARY*, Cabrillo Marine Aquarium Library, 3720 Stephen White Dr, 90731. SAN 301-5270. Tel: 310-548-7562. FAX: 310-548-2649. TDD: 310-548-2052. Web Site: www.cabrilloaq.org. *Dir,* Mike Schaadt; Tel: 310-548-7562, Ext 230, E-mail: mike.schaadt@lacity.org; Staff 5 (MLS 1, Non-MLS 4)
Founded 1935
Library Holdings: Bk Titles 2,500; Per Subs 25; Spec Interest Per Sub 20
Subject Interests: Calif, Ecology, Marine biol
Function: Online searches, Orientations, Outside serv via phone, mail, e-mail & web, Photocopying/Printing, Prog for adults, Ref & res, Res libr, VHS videos, Wheelchair accessible
Restriction: Circulates for staff only, Non-circulating coll
Friends of the Library Group

M PROVIDENCE LITTLE COMPANY OF MARY SAN PEDRO HOSPITAL*, Medical Library, 1300 W Seventh St, 90732. SAN 301-5297. Tel: 310-832-3311. *Med Librn,* Mary Osborne; Tel: 310-543-5911, E-mail: mary.osborne@providence.org; Staff 1 (MLS 1)
Founded 1940
Library Holdings: Bk Vols 2,000; Per Subs 30
Subject Interests: Med, Nursing
Database Vendor: PubMed
Open Tues 8-5

SAN RAFAEL

SR DOMINICAN SISTERS-CONGREGATION OF THE HOLY NAME ARCHIVES*, 1520 Grand Ave, 94901-2236. SAN 370-2057. Tel: 415-257-4947. FAX: 415-453-8367. E-mail: patcorrop@att.net. Web Site: www.sanrafaelop.org. *Archivist,* Sister Billie Olin
Library Holdings: Bk Vols 400
Subject Interests: Hist of the congregation
Open Mon-Thurs 10-4:30

CR DOMINICAN UNIVERSITY OF CALIFORNIA, Archbishop Alemany Library, 50 Acacia Ave, 94901-2298. SAN 301-5319. Tel: 415-485-3251. Reference Tel: 415-485-3252. FAX: 415-459-2309. E-mail: circdesk@dominican.edu, ref@dominican.edu. Web Site: www.dominican.edu/academics/resources/library. *Univ Librn/Libr Dir,* Gary Gorka; E-mail: gary.gorka@dominican.edu; *Assoc Dir,* Amy Gilbert; E-mail: amy.gilbert@dominican.edu; *Head, Access Serv,* Ethan Annis; Tel: 415-482-1837, E-mail: ethan.annis@dominican.edu; *Head, Acq,* Lisa Wendell; Tel: 415-257-0168, E-mail: lisa.wendell@dominican.edu; *Ref & Instruction Librn,* Michael Pujals; E-mail: michael.pujals@dominican.edu; *Ref & Instruction Librn, Univ Archivist,* Annie Reid; Tel: 415-257-0169, E-mail: anne.reid@dominican.edu; *Ref & Instruction Librn,* Suzanne Roybal; E-mail: suzanne.roybal@dominican.edu; *Sr Librn,* Alan Schut; Tel: 415-458-3703, E-mail: alan.schut@dominican.edu; *ILL Mgr,* Ken Fish; E-mail: kenneth.fish@dominican.edu; *Supvr, Access Serv,* A J Real; E-mail: real.adolfo@dominican.edu; Staff 10 (MLS 7, Non-MLS 3)
Founded 1890. Enrl 1,900; Fac 70; Highest Degree: Master
Library Holdings: AV Mats 396; e-books 50,000; Electronic Media & Resources 40,000; Bk Titles 91,799; Per Subs 100
Special Collections: Ansel Adams Photographic Coll
Automation Activity & Vendor Info: (Acquisitions) Baker & Taylor; (Cataloging) Innovative Interfaces, Inc; (Circulation) Innovative Interfaces, Inc; (ILL) OCLC FirstSearch; (OPAC) Innovative Interfaces, Inc
Database Vendor: Alexander Street Press, ARTstor, CountryWatch, CredoReference, ebrary, EBSCO Discovery Service, EBSCOhost, Elsevier, Gale Cengage Learning, JSTOR, LexisNexis, McGraw-Hill, Mergent Online, OCLC FirstSearch, OneSource, Overdrive, Inc, Oxford Online, ProQuest, ReferenceUSA, RefWorks, Sage, Springer-Verlag, Springshare, LLC, Thomson - Web of Science, Wiley
Wireless access
Partic in Northern & Central California Psychology Libraries; Statewide California Electronic Library Consortium (SCELC)
Open Mon-Thurs 8am-Midnight, Fri 8am-10pm, Sat 9-9, Sun 2-Midnight

M KAISER-PERMANENTE MEDICAL CENTER*, Health Sciences Library, 99 Montecillo Rd, 94903. Tel: 415-444-2058. FAX: 415-444-2492. *Librn,* Carrie Walsh; E-mail: carrie.walsh@kp.org; Staff 2 (MLS 1, Non-MLS 1)
Library Holdings: Bk Titles 1,200

S LUCASFILM RESEARCH LIBRARY*, PO Box 2009, 94912. SAN 327-7305. Tel: 415-662-1912. E-mail: rlibs@lucasfilm.com. *Res,* Jo Donaldson; *Res,* Robyn Stanley; *Res,* Carol Moen Wing; Staff 3 (MLS 3)
Founded 1978
Library Holdings: Bk Vols 20,000; Per Subs 100
Special Collections: Paramount Studios Library; Universal Studios Library
Function: Ref serv available
Restriction: Co libr

P MARIN COUNTY FREE LIBRARY*, 3501 Civic Center Dr, Rm 414, 94903-4177. SAN 334-8784. Tel: 415-499-3220. FAX: 415-499-3726. E-mail: library@co.marin.ca.us. Web Site: www.marinlibrary.org. *Dir,* Position Currently Open; Staff 89 (MLS 31, Non-MLS 58)
Founded 1926. Pop 138,898; Circ 1,420,286
Library Holdings: AV Mats 51,885; e-books 9,043; Bk Vols 416,127
Special Collections: CA Indian Library Coll; Frank Lloyd Wright Coll; San Quentin Prison Coll. Oral History
Wireless access
Function: Adult literacy prog, Archival coll, Art exhibits, Handicapped accessible, Home delivery & serv to Sr ctr & nursing homes, Homebound delivery serv, ILL available, Magnifiers for reading, Music CDs, Prog for adults, Prog for children & young adult, Ref serv available, Spoken cassettes & CDs, Summer reading prog, Telephone ref, VHS videos, Wheelchair accessible
Mem of NorthNet Library System
Partic in Marin Automated Resources & Information Network (MARINet)
Friends of the Library Group
Branches: 10
BOLINAS BRANCH, Wharf Rd, Bolinas, 94924. (Mail add: PO Box 10, Bolinas, 94924-0010), SAN 334-8806. Tel: 415-868-1171. *Sr Librn,* Ann Taylor
Pop 1,630; Circ 24,492
Library Holdings: Bk Vols 9,982
Friends of the Library Group

CIVIC CENTER BRANCH, 3501 Civic Center Dr, Rm 427, 94903-4177, SAN 334-8814. Tel: 415-499-6056. Circulation Tel: 415-499-6057. Reference Tel: 415-499-6058. *Sr Librn,* Damon Hill
Pop 20,999; Circ 198,638
Library Holdings: Bk Vols 100,096
Special Collections: Oral History
Subject Interests: Archit, Calif, Local hist
Friends of the Library Group

CORTE MADERA BRANCH, 707 Meadowsweet, Corte Madera, 94925-1717, SAN 334-8849. Tel: 415-924-4844. Circulation Tel: 415-924-3515. Reference Tel: 415-924-6444. *Sr Librn,* Nancy Davis
Pop 18,895; Circ 334,530
Library Holdings: Bk Vols 88,813
Open Mon-Thurs 10-9, Sat 10-5, Sun 12-5
Friends of the Library Group

FAIRFAX BRANCH, 2097 Sir Francis Drake Blvd, Fairfax, 94930-1198, SAN 334-8873. Tel: 415-453-8092. Circulation Tel: 415-453-8151. Reference Tel: 415-457-5629. *Br Mgr,* Margaret Miles; E-mail: MMiles@co.marin.ca.us
Pop 9,619; Circ 250,051
Library Holdings: Bk Vols 81,632
Open Mon-Thurs 10-9, Sat 10-6
Friends of the Library Group

INVERNESS BRANCH, 15 Park Ave, Inverness, 94937. (Mail add: PO Box 160, Inverness, 94937-0160), SAN 334-8822. Tel: 415-669-1288. *Sr Librn,* Ann Taylor
Pop 1,596; Circ 14,654
Library Holdings: Bk Vols 7,527
Open Mon 3-6 & 7-9, Tues & Wed 10-1 & 2-6, Fri 3-6, Sat 10-1
Friends of the Library Group

MARIN CITY BRANCH, 164 Donahue, Marin City, 94965, SAN 334-8830. Tel: 415-332-6159. Circulation Tel: 415-332-6158. Reference Tel: 415-332-6157. *Br Mgr,* Julie Magnus; E-mail: jmagnus@marincounty.org
Pop 15,186; Circ 41,002
Library Holdings: Bk Vols 22,824
Open Mon & Tues 1-9, Wed & Thurs 10-6, Sat 10-5, Sun 12-5
Friends of the Library Group

NOVATO BRANCH, 1720 Novato Blvd, Novato, 94947, SAN 334-8903. Tel: 415-898-4623. Circulation Tel: 415-897-1141. Reference Tel: 415-897-1142. *Sr Librn,* Donna Mettier
Pop 39,205; Circ 405,538
Library Holdings: Bk Vols 106,342
Open Mon-Thurs 10-9, Sat 10-5, Sun 12-5
Friends of the Library Group

POINT REYES STATION BRANCH, 11431 State Rte 1, Point Reyes Station, 94956. (Mail add: PO Box 1330, Point Reyes Station, 94956-1330), SAN 334-8857. Tel: 415-663-8375. *Sr Librn,* Ann Taylor
Pop 4,681; Circ 30,570
Library Holdings: Bk Vols 15,809
Open Mon 10-6, Tues & Thurs 2-9, Fri & Sat 10-2
Friends of the Library Group

SOUTH NOVATO BRANCH, Six Hamilton Landing, Ste 140A, Novato, 94949. Tel: 415 506 3164. *Librn,* Helen Romero
Pop 21,966; Circ 62,972
Library Holdings: Bk Vols 18,222
Open Tues & Thurs 1-8, Wed & Sat 11-5
Friends of the Library Group

STINSON BEACH BRANCH, 3521 Shoreline Hwy, Stinson Beach, 94970. (Mail add: PO Box 578, Stinson Beach, 94970-0578), SAN 334-8881. Tel: 415-868-0252. FAX: 415-868-2041. *Br Mgr,* Bonny White
Pop 1,295; Circ 13,000
Library Holdings: Bk Vols 13,241
Open Mon & Fri 10-1 & 2-6, Tues 1-5 & 6-9, Sat 10-1 & 2-5
Friends of the Library Group

Bookmobiles: 1

GL MARIN COUNTY LAW LIBRARY*, 20 N San Pedro Rd, Ste 2015, 94903. SAN 301-5327. Tel: 415-499-6356. FAX: 415-507-2048. Web Site: lawlibmc&sonic.net, marinlawlibrary.com. *Dir,* Suzan B Sharpley; Tel: 415-499-6357, Fax: 415-499-6837; *Assoc Dir,* Position Currently Open; Staff 3 (Non-MLS 3)
Founded 1891
Library Holdings: Bk Vols 28,700; Per Subs 66
Special Collections: Continuing Education of the Bar Coll
Wireless access
Open Mon & Fri 8:30-5, Tues-Thurs 8:30am-9pm, Sat & Sun 12-5

S MARIN HISTORY MUSEUM LIBRARY, 1125 B St, 94901. SAN 327-6546. Tel: 415-454-8538. FAX: 415-454-6137. Web Site: www.marinhistory.org. *Dir,* Jean Zerruda; E-mail: jean@marinhistory.org; *Librn,* Jocelyn Moss; E-mail: jocelyn@marinhistory.org
Founded 1935
Library Holdings: Bk Vols 1,000
Special Collections: Bound Newspapers (1868-present); Land Grants Coll. Oral History
Subject Interests: Genealogy, Local hist
Function: Archival coll, Photocopying/Printing, Ref serv available
Publications: Marin People (3 vols)
Restriction: Open by appt only

P SAN RAFAEL PUBLIC LIBRARY*, 1100 E St, 94901-1900. SAN 301-5335. Tel: 415-485-3323. Reference Tel: 415-485-3321. Administration Tel: 415-485-3319. FAX: 415-485-3112. Reference FAX: 415-485-3403. E-mail: library@cityofsanrafael.org. Web Site: srpubliclibrary.org. *Dir,* Sarah Houghton; *Asst Dir,* Vanessa Christman; *Adult Serv Supvr,* Pam Klein; *Children's Serv Supvr,* Hollie Stanaland; *Circ Supvr,* Lashalle Lyons; Staff 22 (MLS 10, Non-MLS 12)
Founded 1887. Pop 60,000; Circ 400,000
Library Holdings: AV Mats 2,811; Large Print Bks 2,646; Bk Titles 120,000; Bk Vols 128,000; Per Subs 302; Talking Bks 2,039
Special Collections: California Coll
Subject Interests: Art & archit
Automation Activity & Vendor Info: (Cataloging) Innovative Interfaces, Inc; (Circulation) Innovative Interfaces, Inc; (OPAC) Innovative Interfaces, Inc; (Serials) Innovative Interfaces, Inc
Function: After school storytime, Archival coll, Audiobks via web, Bilingual assistance for Spanish patrons, Bk club(s), Bks on CD, Children's prog, Computer training, Computers for patron use, Copy machines, Digital talking bks, Electronic databases & coll, Free DVD rentals, Holiday prog, Home delivery & serv to Sr ctr & nursing homes, Homebound delivery serv, Homework prog, ILL available, Mail & tel request accepted, Music CDs, Online cat, Online info literacy tutorials on the web & in blackboard, Online searches, Outreach serv, Outside serv via phone, mail, e-mail & web, OverDrive digital audio bks, Photocopying/Printing, Preschool outreach, Preschool reading prog, Prog for adults, Prog for children & young adult, Pub access computers, Ref & res, Ref serv available, Ref serv in person, Referrals accepted, Scanner, Senior outreach, Spanish lang bks, Story hour, Summer reading prog, Tax forms, Teen prog, Telephone ref, Web-catalog, Wheelchair accessible, Workshops
Mem of NorthNet Library System
Partic in Marin Automated Resources & Information Network (MARINet)
Open Mon 1-8, Tues-Thurs 10-8, Fri & Sat 10-5, Sun 1-5
Friends of the Library Group
Branches: 1
PICKLEWEED LIBRARY, 50 Canal St, 94901. Tel: 415-485-3483. *Libr Supvr,* Irene Morales
Open Tues & Wed 1-8, Thurs 11-8, Fri & Sat 11-5

SAN SIMEON

S HEARST SAN SIMEON STATE HISTORICAL MONUMENT*, Hearst Castle Staff Library, 750 Hearst Castle Rd, 93452-9741. Tel: 805-927-2076. Toll Free Tel: 800-444-4445. FAX: 805-927-2117. TDD: 800-274-7275. Web Site: www.hearstcastle.org. *Coordr,* Ty Smith; *Staff Librn,* Jill Urquhart
Library Holdings: AV Mats 17; CDs 300; DVDs 200; Bk Vols 3,579; Spec Interest Per Sub 6; Videos 427
Special Collections: Oral History
Restriction: Not open to pub, Staff use only

SANTA ANA

P OC PUBLIC LIBRARIES, Administrative Headquarters, 1501 E St Andrew Pl, 92705-4048. SAN 333-4023. Tel: 714-566-3000. FAX: 714-566-3042. Web Site: www.ocpl.org. *County Librn,* Helen Fried; E-mail: helen.fried@occr.ocgov.com; *Coll Develop Mgr,* Shirley N Quan; E-mail: shirley.quan@occr.ocgov.com; Staff 206 (MLS 126, Non-MLS 80)
Founded 1921. Pop 1,426,100
Library Holdings: AV Mats 4,689; Bk Vols 2,500,000; Per Subs 5,070; Talking Bks 2,860
Subject Interests: Bus, Chinese lang, Japanese (Lang), Korean (Lang), Popular music, Spanish (Lang)
Automation Activity & Vendor Info: (Acquisitions) SirsiDynix; (Cataloging) SirsiDynix; (Circulation) SirsiDynix; (OPAC) SirsiDynix; (Serials) SirsiDynix
Database Vendor: Gale Cengage Learning, OCLC FirstSearch, ProQuest
Wireless access
Partic in Southern California Library Cooperative
Open Mon-Fri 8-5
Friends of the Library Group
Branches: 33
ALISO VIEJO BRANCH, One Journey, Aliso Viejo, 92656-3333, SAN 378-2506. Tel: 949-360-1730. FAX: 949-360-1728.
Library Holdings: AV Mats 830; Bk Vols 61,112; Per Subs 57
Special Services for the Blind - Low vision equip; Optolec clearview video magnifier
Open Mon-Thurs 10-9, Fri & Sat 10-5, Sun 12-5
Friends of the Library Group

BREA BRANCH, One Civic Center Circle, Brea, 92821-5784, SAN 333-4058. Tel: 714-671-1722. FAX: 714-990-0581.
Library Holdings: AV Mats 652; Bk Titles 72,422; Bk Vols 75,153; Per Subs 78
Subject Interests: Spanish (Lang)
Open Mon & Thurs 10-6, Tues & Wed 12-8, Fri & Sat 10-5
Friends of the Library Group

CHAPMAN, 9182 Chapman Ave, Garden Grove, 92841-2590, SAN 333-4082. Tel: 714-539-2115.
Library Holdings: AV Mats 380; Bk Titles 51,017; Bk Vols 53,147; Per Subs 61
Open Mon & Tues 12-8, Wed & Thurs 10-6, Sat 10-5
Friends of the Library Group

COSTA MESA TECHNOLOGY, 2263 Fairview Rd, Ste A, Costa Mesa, 92627. Tel: 714-754-4431. FAX: 714-754-6615.
Open Tues-Thurs 1-9, Fri & Sat 10-5
Friends of the Library Group

CYPRESS BRANCH, 5331 Orange Ave, Cypress, 90630-2985, SAN 333-4147. Tel: 714-826-0350. FAX: 714-828-1103.
Library Holdings: AV Mats 1,141; Bk Titles 97,001; Bk Vols 104,088; Per Subs 93
Subject Interests: Adult lit, Music
Open Mon-Wed 10-9, Thurs 10-6, Sat 10-5, Sun 12-5
Friends of the Library Group

DANA POINT BRANCH, 33841 Niguel Rd, Dana Point, 92629-4010, SAN 333-4171. Tel: 949-496-5517. FAX: 949-240-7650.
Library Holdings: AV Mats 780; Bk Titles 76,209; Bk Vols 81,758; Per Subs 92
Open Mon-Wed 10-9, Thurs 10-6, Fri & Sat 10-5, Sun 12-5
Friends of the Library Group

COSTA MESA/DONALD DUNGAN BRANCH, 1855 Park Ave, Costa Mesa, 92627-2778, SAN 333-4112. Tel: 949-646-8845. FAX: 949-631-3112.
Library Holdings: AV Mats 302; Bk Titles 62,060; Bk Vols 63,001; Per Subs 79
Subject Interests: Spanish (Lang)
Open Mon-Thurs 10-9, Fri & Sat 10-5, Sun 12-5
Friends of the Library Group

EL TORO BRANCH, 24672 Raymond Way, Lake Forest, 92630-4489, SAN 333-4228. Tel: 949-855-8173. FAX: 949-586-7412.
Library Holdings: Bk Titles 111,500; Bk Vols 112,488; Per Subs 101
Special Services for the Blind - Braille & cassettes
Open Mon-Thurs 10-9, Fri & Sat 10-5, Sun 12-5
Friends of the Library Group

FOOTHILL RANCH, 27002 Cabriole, Foothill Ranch, 92610. Tel: 949-855-8072. FAX: 949-855-8518.
Open Mon-Thurs 10-8, Sat 10-5
Friends of the Library Group

FOUNTAIN VALLEY BRANCH, 17635 Los Alamos St, Fountain Valley, 92708-5299, SAN 333-4236. Tel: 714-962-1324.
Library Holdings: AV Mats 560; Bk Titles 82,137; Bk Vols 84,321; Per Subs 88
Special Services for the Blind - Merlin electronic magnifier reader
Open Mon-Wed 10-9, Thurs 10-6, Fri & Sat 10-5
Friends of the Library Group

GARDEN GROVE REGIONAL LIBRARY, 11200 Stanford Ave, Garden Grove, 92840-5398, SAN 333-4260. Tel: 714-530-0711. FAX: 714-530-0961.
Library Holdings: AV Mats 1,280; Bk Titles 154,772; Bk Vols 162,258; Per Subs 133
Subject Interests: Calif, Consumer health, Korean (Lang)
Open Mon-Thurs 10-9, Fri & Sat 10-5, Sun 12-5
Friends of the Library Group

HERITAGE PARK REGIONAL LIBRARY, 14361 Yale Ave, Irvine, 92604-1901, SAN 328-9788. Tel: 949-936-4040.
Founded 1988. Pop 150,000; Circ 500,000
Library Holdings: AV Mats 2,100; Bk Titles 131,156; Bk Vols 133,000; Per Subs 350
Special Services for the Blind - Optolec clearview video magnifier
Open Mon-Thurs 10-9, Fri & Sat 10-5, Sun 12-5
Friends of the Library Group

LA HABRA BRANCH, 221 E La Habra Blvd, La Habra, 90631-5437, SAN 333-4325. Tel: 562-694-0078, 714-526-7728. FAX: 562-691-8043.
Library Holdings: Bk Titles 86,261; Bk Vols 87,473; Per Subs 98
Subject Interests: Spanish (Lang)
Open Mon-Thurs 10-8, Sat 10-5, Sun 12-5
Friends of the Library Group

LA PALMA BRANCH, 7842 Walker St, La Palma, 90623-1721, SAN 333-435X. Tel: 714-523-8585.
Library Holdings: Bk Titles 54,832; Bk Vols 59,951; Per Subs 77
Subject Interests: Japanese (Lang)
Open Mon-Thurs 12-8, Sat 10-5
Friends of the Library Group

LADERA RANCH LIBRARY, 29551 Sienna Pkwy, Ladera Ranch, 92694. Tel: 949-234-5940. *Sr Br Mgr,* Cathie Wilson; Staff 9 (MLS 3, Non-MLS 6)
Founded 2003
Function: Adult literacy prog, After school storytime, Audiobks via web, Bi-weekly Writer's Group, Bks on cassette, Bks on CD, CD-ROM, Children's prog, Computers for patron use, Copy machines, Digital talking bks, e-mail & chat, e-mail serv, E-Reserves, Electronic databases & coll, Free DVD rentals, Handicapped accessible, ILL available, Music CDs, Online cat, Online ref, Online searches, OverDrive digital audio bks, Prog for children & young adult, Pub access computers, Ref & res, Ref serv available, Ref serv in person, Spoken cassettes & CDs, Story hour, Summer reading prog, VHS videos, Wheelchair accessible
Open Mon-Thurs 10-8, Sat 10-5
Restriction: Open to pub for ref & circ; with some limitations
Friends of the Library Group

LAGUNA BEACH BRANCH, 363 Glenneyre St, Laguna Beach, 92651-2310, SAN 333-4295. Tel: 949-497-1733. FAX: 949-497-2876.
Library Holdings: Bk Titles 72,687; Bk Vols 75,496; Per Subs 78
Subject Interests: Art
Open Mon-Wed 10-8, Thurs 10-6, Fri & Sat 10-5
Friends of the Library Group

LAGUNA HILLS TECHNOLOGY, Laguna Hills Community Ctr, 25555 Alicia Pkwy, Laguna Hills, 92653. Tel: 949-707-2699. FAX: 949-707-2698. *Br Mgr,* Alicia Zach; Staff 5 (MLS 2, Non-MLS 3)
Open Mon-Thurs 10-9, Fri & Sat 10-5
Friends of the Library Group

LAGUNA NIGUEL BRANCH, 30341 Crown Valley Pkwy, Laguna Niguel, 92677, SAN 328-9745. Tel: 949-249-5252. FAX: 949-249-5258.
Library Holdings: AV Mats 680; Bk Titles 72,425; Bk Vols 77,190; Per Subs 82
Open Mon-Thurs 10-9, Fri & Sat 10-5, Sun 12-5
Friends of the Library Group

LAGUNA WOODS BRANCH, 24264 El Toro Rd, Laguna Woods, 92637. Tel: 949-639-0500.
Open Mon-Fri 10-4:30
Friends of the Library Group

LOS ALAMITOS-ROSSMOOR, 12700 Montecito Rd, Seal Beach, 90740-2745, SAN 333-4414. Tel: 562-430-1048. Administration Tel: 714-846-3240. FAX: 562-431-2931.
Library Holdings: Bk Titles 74,298; Bk Vols 79,333; Per Subs 91
Open Mon & Tues 12-9, Wed 10-6, Fri & Sat 10-5

MESA VERDE, 2969 Mesa Verde Dr E, Costa Mesa, 92626-3699, SAN 333-4473. Tel: 714-546-5274.
Library Holdings: AV Mats 640; Bk Titles 54,630; Bk Vols 59,204; Per Subs 92
Open Mon-Thurs 10-9, Fri & Sat 10-5, Sun 12-5
Friends of the Library Group

RANCHO SANTA MARGARITA BRANCH, 30902 La Promesa, Rancho Santa Margarita, 92688-2821, SAN 376-2440. Tel: 949-459-6094. FAX: 949-459-8391.
Library Holdings: AV Mats 1,100; Bk Titles 90,270; Bk Vols 102,937; Per Subs 130
Open Mon-Thurs 10-9, Fri & Sat 10-5

TIBOR RUBIN LIBRARY, 11962 Bailey St, Garden Grove, 92845-1104, SAN 333-4775. Tel: 714-897-2594. FAX: 714-895-2761. *Br Mgr,* Dennis McGuire
Library Holdings: Bk Titles 51,542; Bk Vols 53,452; Per Subs 63
Open Mon & Tues 12-8, Wed & Thurs 10-6, Sat 10-5
Friends of the Library Group

SAN CLEMENTE BRANCH, 242 Avenida Del Mar, San Clemente, 92672-4005, SAN 333-4538. Tel: 949-492-3493. *Sr Br Librn,* Karen Wall
Library Holdings: Bks on Deafness & Sign Lang 80; Bk Titles 69,981; Bk Vols 72,590; Per Subs 112
Closed for renovation from June 2014 through June 2015.
Friends of the Library Group

SAN JUAN CAPISTRANO LIBRARY, 31495 El Camino Real, San Juan Capistrano, 92675-2600, SAN 333-4562. Tel: 949-493-1752. FAX: 949-240-7680.
Library Holdings: Bk Titles 79,165; Bk Vols 81,996; Per Subs 103
Subject Interests: Archit, Calif, Spanish (Lang)
Open Mon-Wed 10-8, Thurs 10-6, Sat 10-5, Sun 12-5
Friends of the Library Group

SILVERADO BRANCH, 28192 Silverado Canyon Rd, Silverado, 92676. (Mail add: PO Box 535, Silverado, 92676-0535), SAN 333-4597. Tel: 714-649-2216. FAX: 714-649-2121.
Library Holdings: Bk Titles 14,657; Bk Vols 15,386; Per Subs 35
Open Mon & Wed 1-8, Tues & Thurs 12-6, Sat 10-5
Friends of the Library Group

STANTON BRANCH, 7850 Katella Ave, Stanton, 90680-3195, SAN 333-4651. Tel: 714-898-3302.
Library Holdings: Bk Titles 59,381; Bk Vols 62,040; Per Subs 79
Subject Interests: Spanish (Lang)

Open Mon & Tues 12-8, Wed & Thurs 10-6, Sat 10-5
Friends of the Library Group
TUSTIN BRANCH, 345 E Main St, Tustin, 92780-4491, SAN 333-4686. Tel: 714-544-7725. FAX: 714-832-4279.
Library Holdings: Bk Titles 116,511; Bk Vols 117,004
Open Mon-Thurs 10-9, Fri & Sat 10-5, Sun 12-5
Friends of the Library Group
UNIVERSITY PARK, 4512 Sandburg Way, Irvine, 92612-2794, SAN 333-4716. Tel: 949-786-4001. FAX: 949-857-1029.
Library Holdings: AV Mats 500; Bk Titles 91,399; Bk Vols 91,464; Per Subs 115
Open Mon-Thurs 10-9, Fri & Sat 10-5, Sun 12-5
Friends of the Library Group
VILLA PARK BRANCH, 17865 Santiago Blvd, Villa Park, 92861-4105, SAN 333-4740. Tel: 714-998-0861.
Library Holdings: Bk Titles 19,880; Bk Vols 24,744; Per Subs 42
Open Mon-Thurs 11-7, Sat 10-5
Friends of the Library Group
WESTMINSTER BRANCH, 8180 13th St, Westminster, 92683-8118, SAN 333-4805. Tel: 714-893-5057.
Library Holdings: AV Mats 1,200; Bk Titles 134,707; Bk Vols 140,614; Per Subs 127
Special Collections: Vietnamese Language Coll
Open Mon-Thurs 10-9, Fri & Sat 10-5
Friends of the Library Group
KATIE WHEELER LIBRARY, 13109 Old Myford Rd, Irvine, 92602. Tel: 714-669-8753.
Open Mon-Thurs 10-9, Fri & Sat 10-5, Sun 12-5
Friends of the Library Group
SEAL BEACH-MARY WILSON BRANCH, 707 Electric Ave, Seal Beach, 90740-6196, SAN 333-4449. Tel: 562-431-3584, 714-840-6759. FAX: 562-431-3374.
Library Holdings: Bk Titles 50,871; Bk Vols 54,904; Per Subs 80
Open Mon & Tues 12-8, Wed & Thurs 10-6, Sat 10-5
Friends of the Library Group

GL ORANGE COUNTY PUBLIC LAW LIBRARY, 515 N Flower St, 92703-2354. SAN 334-8997. Tel: 714-834-3397. FAX: 714-834-4375. Web Site: www.ocpll.org. *Dir,* Maryruth Storer; Staff 17 (MLS 6, Non-MLS 11)
Founded 1891
Library Holdings: CDs 1,697; DVDs 31; Bk Vols 374,866; Per Subs 934
Special Collections: California SC (Records & Briefs), 1960-64, 1969-, fiche; USSC (Records & Briefs), 1950, fiche. State Document Depository; US Document Depository
Automation Activity & Vendor Info: (Acquisitions) Innovative Interfaces, Inc; (Cataloging) Innovative Interfaces, Inc; (Circulation) Innovative Interfaces, Inc; (OPAC) Innovative Interfaces, Inc; (Serials) Innovative Interfaces, Inc
Database Vendor: EBSCOhost, HeinOnline, Westlaw
Wireless access
Publications: Acquisition List; Bibliographies; Newsletter
Partic in Law Library Microform Consortium (LLMC); Southern California Library Cooperative
Open Mon-Thurs 8-6, Fri 8-5, Sat 9-5

G ORANGE COUNTY RDMD TECHNICAL LIBRARY*, 300 N Flower St, 92703-5001. (Mail add: PO Box 4048, 97202-4048), SAN 334-8938. Tel: 714-834-3497. FAX: 714-834-5188. *Librn,* Sallie Jones; E-mail: sallie.jones@rdmd.ocgov.com; Staff 1 (Non-MLS 1)
Founded 1963
Library Holdings: Bk Titles 10,000
Special Collections: Flood & Flood Control Photographs, 1919-
Subject Interests: Flood control, Harbors, Local hist, Roads, Transportation
Automation Activity & Vendor Info: (Acquisitions) EOS International; (Cataloging) EOS International; (Circulation) EOS International; (OPAC) EOS International
Partic in Metronet
Restriction: Open by appt only

J SANTA ANA COLLEGE*, Nealley Library, 1530 W 17th St, 92706-3398. SAN 301-5432. Tel: 714-564-6700. Reference Tel: 714-564-6708. FAX: 714-564-6729. Web Site: www.sac.edu/students/library/nealley. *VPres, Acad Affairs,* Carolyn Breeden; Tel: 714-564-6080; *Acq,* Denise Phillips; Staff 8 (MLS 8)
Founded 1915. Enrl 24,035; Fac 329
Library Holdings: Bk Vols 99,500; Per Subs 405
Automation Activity & Vendor Info: (Cataloging) SirsiDynix
Partic in Cooperative Library Association Shared System (CLASS)
Open Mon-Thurs 8-8, Fri 8-4, Sat (Fall & Spring) 9-2
Friends of the Library Group

P SANTA ANA PUBLIC LIBRARY*, 26 Civic Center Plaza, 92701-4010. SAN 334-9055. Tel: 714-647-5250. Interlibrary Loan Service Tel: 714-647-5267. FAX: 714-647-5296. Web Site: www.santa-ana.org/library. *Libr Operations Mgr,* Heather Folmar; Fax: 714-647-5291, E-mail: hfolmar@santa-ana.org; *Principal Librn, Adult Serv,* Patricia Lopez; Tel: 714-647-5325, E-mail: plopez@santa-ana.org; *Principal Librn, Tech & Support,* Lynn Nguyen; Tel: 714-647-5259, E-mail: lnguyen@santa-ana.org; *Principal Librn, YA,* Cheryl Eberly; Tel: 714-647-5288, E-mail: ceberly@santa-ana.org; *Principal Librn, Youth Serv,* Lupita Vega; E-mail: lvega@santa-ana.org. Subject Specialists: *Best sellers, Fiction, Ref bks,* Heather Folmar; Staff 13.5 (MLS 10, Non-MLS 3.5)
Founded 1891. Pop 327,731; Circ 465,638
Jul 2010-Jun 2011 Income (Main Library and Branch(s)) $4,056,480. Mats Exp $499,728, Books $240,077, Per/Ser (Incl. Access Fees) $10,500, AV Mat $39,440, Electronic Ref Mat (Incl. Access Fees) $38,742. Sal $2,111,014
Library Holdings: Audiobooks 9,384; DVDs 13,178; e-books 1,301; Electronic Media & Resources 184; Bk Vols 256,717; Per Subs 46
Special Collections: California History Coll; Hispanic & Asian American Heritage Coll; Santa Ana & Orange County History Coll; Spanish Language Coll, AV, bks; Vietnamese Language Coll, AV. Oral History
Automation Activity & Vendor Info: (Acquisitions) Brodart; (Cataloging) Brodart; (Circulation) TLC (The Library Corporation); (OPAC) TLC (The Library Corporation); (Serials) TLC (The Library Corporation)
Database Vendor: ABC-CLIO, Brodart, Gale Cengage Learning, Greenwood Publishing Group, Newsbank, OCLC FirstSearch, TLC (The Library Corporation), World Book Online
Function: Accelerated reader prog, Adult bk club, After school storytime, Archival coll, Art exhibits, Bilingual assistance for Spanish patrons, Bks on CD, Children's prog, Citizenship assistance, Computer training, Computers for patron use, Copy machines, e-mail serv, E-Reserves, Electronic databases & coll, Exhibits, Handicapped accessible, Homework prog, ILL available, Learning ctr, Literacy & newcomer serv, Magnifiers for reading, Mail & tel request accepted, Microfiche/film & reading machines, Music CDs, Online cat, Online searches, Orientations, Passport agency, Photocopying/Printing, Preschool outreach, Prog for adults, Prog for children & young adult, Pub access computers, Ref serv available, Ref serv in person, Res performed for a fee, Serves mentally handicapped consumers, Spanish lang bks, Spoken cassettes & CDs, Story hour, Summer reading prog, Teen prog, Telephone ref, Wheelchair accessible, Workshops, Writing prog
Open Mon-Thurs 10-9, Fri & Sat 10-6
Restriction: Authorized patrons, ID required to use computers (Ltd hrs), In-house use for visitors, Non-resident fee, Photo ID required for access
Friends of the Library Group
Branches: 1
NEWHOPE LIBRARY LEARNING CENTER, 122 N Newhope, 92703, SAN 334-9098. Tel: 714-647-6992. FAX: 714-554-9633.
Library Holdings: Bk Vols 67,457; Per Subs 15
Automation Activity & Vendor Info: (Acquisitions) TLC (The Library Corporation); (Cataloging) TLC (The Library Corporation)
Open Mon-Thurs 2-7, Sat 10-5

CL TRINITY INTERNATIONAL UNIVERSITY, Law Library & Information Center, 2200 N Grand Ave, 92705-7016. SAN 326-5412. Tel: 714-796-7172. FAX: 714-796-7190. Web Site: www.tiu.edu/law. *Supvr,* Brionica Bryson; E-mail: bbryson@tiu.edu; Staff 1 (Non-MLS 1)
Founded 1980. Enrl 250; Fac 6; Highest Degree: Doctorate
Library Holdings: Bk Vols 50,000; Per Subs 56
Special Collections: Arthur Henry Robertson Coll (int law & human rights), ms, bks; European Commission and Court of Human Rights; Rarisma (15th-18th century classical, legal & apologetic books, including numerous English Reporters)
Subject Interests: Human rights
Automation Activity & Vendor Info: (Acquisitions) ComPanion Corp; (Cataloging) ComPanion Corp; (Circulation) ComPanion Corp; (OPAC) ComPanion Corp; (Serials) ComPanion Corp
Partic in LIBRAS, Inc
Restriction: Non-circulating
Friends of the Library Group

SR TRINITY UNITED PRESBYTERIAN CHURCH LIBRARY*, 13922 Prospect Ave, 92705. SAN 301-5459. Tel: 714-544-7850, Ext 121. FAX: 714-544-6837. Web Site: www.tupcsa.org. *Librn,* Lois Boyer; E-mail: loisb@tupcsa.org
Founded 1955
Library Holdings: Bk Vols 7,000; Per Subs 20
Subject Interests: Theol
Open Mon-Fri 9-5, Sun 8-12:30

M WESTERN MEDICAL CENTER*, Medical Library, 1001 N Tustin Ave, 92705. SAN 301-5440. Tel: 714-953-3484. FAX: 714-953-2388. Web Site: www.westernmedicalcenter.com. *Librn,* Zoha Zabihi
Founded 1968
Library Holdings: Bk Titles 40; Per Subs 160
Subject Interests: Dentistry, Med, Nursing, Surgery

Database Vendor: EBSCOhost
Partic in Docline

SANTA BARBARA

C BROOKS INSTITUTE LIBRARY*, 27 E Cota St, 93101. SAN 301-5475. Tel: 805-690-7627, 805-966-3888. FAX: 805-564-1475. Web Site: www.brooks.edu. *Dir,* Donna Burr; E-mail: donna.burr@brooks.edu; Staff 3 (MLS 1, Non-MLS 2)
Founded 1972. Enrl 650; Highest Degree: Master
Library Holdings: DVDs 50; Bk Titles 8,000; Per Subs 110; Videos 364
Automation Activity & Vendor Info: (Cataloging) EOS International; (Circulation) EOS International
Database Vendor: EOS International, ProQuest
Wireless access
Open Mon-Thurs 9-8, Fri 9-5, Sat 3-8, Sun 1-5

M COTTAGE HEALTH SYSTEM*, David L Reeves Medical Library, 401 W Pueblo St, 93105. (Mail add: PO Box 689, 93102-0689), SAN 301-5548. Tel: 805-569-7240. FAX: 805-569-7588. Web Site: www.cottagehealthsystem.org. *Dir,* Brittney Haliani; *Librn,* Betty Flavell; Staff 2.5 (MLS 1, Non-MLS 1.5)
Founded 1941
Library Holdings: CDs 100; DVDs 50; e-books 200; e-journals 1,500; Bk Titles 300; Per Subs 50; Videos 20
Special Collections: Shared Governance
Subject Interests: Consumer health, Internal med, Med, Surgery
Automation Activity & Vendor Info: (Cataloging) Marcive, Inc; (Circulation) CyberTools for Libraries; (OPAC) CyberTools for Libraries; (Serials) CyberTools for Libraries
Database Vendor: Cinahl, EBSCOhost, Medline, Micromedex, PubMed, Sage, Springer-Verlag, UpToDate
Wireless access
Partic in Docline; National Network of Libraries of Medicine; Pacific Southwest Regional Medical Library (PSRML)
Open Mon-Fri 8-5
Restriction: Circ limited
Friends of the Library Group

C FIELDING GRADUATE UNIVERSITY*, Library Services, 2020 De La Vina St, 93105. SAN 375-6874. Tel: 805-690-4373. Reference Tel: 805-898-2920. E-mail: library@fielding.edu. Web Site: web.fielding.edu/library. *Dir, Libr Serv,* Margaret Connors; E-mail: mmconnors@fielding.edu; *Coordr, Instruction & Ref,* Elizabeth Borghi; Fax: 805-690-4313, E-mail: eborghi@fielding.edu. Subject Specialists: *Bus, Educ, Psychol,* Margaret Connors; Staff 2 (MLS 2)
Founded 1974. Enrl 980; Fac 90; Highest Degree: Doctorate
Jul 2013-Jun 2014 Income $360,990. Mats Exp $180,000
Library Holdings: e-books 88,000; e-journals 42,000
Subject Interests: Educ leadership, Human develop, Media psychol, Organizational develop, Psychol
Automation Activity & Vendor Info: (Serials) SerialsSolutions
Database Vendor: American Psychological Association (APA), Annual Reviews, Blackwell, ebrary, EBSCOhost, Elsevier, Emerald, H W Wilson, ISI Web of Knowledge, JSTOR, LexisNexis, Medline, OCLC FirstSearch, Oxford Online, ProQuest, PubMed, Sage, ScienceDirect, SerialsSolutions, Springshare, LLC, Thomson - Web of Science, Wiley InterScience
Wireless access
Function: ILL available, Online ref, Ref serv available, Res libr
Publications: Fielding Dissertations
Restriction: Authorized patrons

GL MCMAHON LAW LIBRARY OF SANTA BARBARA COUNTY*, County Court House, 93101. SAN 301-5572. Tel: 805-568-2296. FAX: 805-568-2299. Web Site: www.countylawlibrary.org. *Dir,* Raymond MacGregor
Founded 1891
Library Holdings: Bk Titles 35,403; Per Subs 20
Wireless access
Open Mon-Fri 8-5

S SANTA BARBARA BOTANIC GARDEN LIBRARY*, 1212 Mission Canyon Rd, 93105-2199. SAN 301-5556. Tel: 805-682-4726, Ext 103, 805-682-4726, Ext 107. FAX: 805-563-0352. Web Site: www.centralcoastmuseums.org, www.sbbg.org. *Coll Mgr,* Tricia Wardlaw; E-mail: tawardlaw@sbbg.org
Founded 1942
Library Holdings: Bk Vols 15,000; Per Subs 200
Special Collections: Oral History
Subject Interests: Botany, Calif, Hort, Manuscripts
Automation Activity & Vendor Info: (Cataloging) TLC (The Library Corporation); (Circulation) TLC (The Library Corporation); (OPAC) TLC (The Library Corporation)
Partic in Central Coast Museum Consortium; Gold Coast Library Network; OCLC Online Computer Library Center, Inc
Open Tues-Fri 9-4
Restriction: Non-circulating to the pub

J SANTA BARBARA CITY COLLEGE*, Eli Luria Library, 721 Cliff Dr, 93109-2394. SAN 301-5564. Tel: 805-730-4430. Interlibrary Loan Service Tel: 805-965-0581, Ext 2640. Reference Tel: 805-730-4444. FAX: 805-965-0771. TDD: 805-965-8853. Web Site: library.sbcc.edu. *Dir,* Kenley Neufeld; Tel: 805-740-4435, E-mail: neufeld@sbcc.edu; *Coll Develop Librn, Outreach Librn,* Elizabeth Bowman; Tel: 805-965-0581, Ext 2633, E-mail: bowmane@sbcc.edu; *Ref Librn,* Jane Haas; E-mail: haas@sbcc.edu; *Cat, Ref,* Sally Chuah; Tel: 805-965-0581, Ext 2643, E-mail: sschuah@sbcc.edu; *Ref,* M'Liss Garza; Tel: 805-965-0581, Ext 2634, E-mail: garza@sbcc.edu; Staff 10 (MLS 5, Non-MLS 5)
Founded 1909. Enrl 19,000; Fac 450; Highest Degree: Associate
Jul 2010-Jun 2011. Mats Exp $231,742, Books $116,829, Per/Ser (Incl. Access Fees) $114,913. Sal $678,322 (Prof $411,039)
Library Holdings: e-books 22,000; Bk Titles 118,846; Bk Vols 123,522; Per Subs 324
Automation Activity & Vendor Info: (Cataloging) SirsiDynix; (Circulation) SirsiDynix; (Course Reserve) SirsiDynix; (OPAC) SirsiDynix; (Serials) SirsiDynix
Database Vendor: ARTstor, Baker & Taylor, EBSCOhost, Gale Cengage Learning, JSTOR, OCLC FirstSearch, Project MUSE, ProQuest, SirsiDynix, World Book Online
Wireless access
Partic in OCLC Online Computer Library Center, Inc
Special Services for the Blind - Assistive/Adapted tech devices, equip & products; Computer with voice synthesizer for visually impaired persons; Magnifiers
Open Mon-Thurs 7:30am-10pm, Fri 7:30-4:30, Sun 1-9
Friends of the Library Group

S SANTA BARBARA COUNTY GENEALOGICAL SOCIETY, Sahyun Library, 316 Castillo St, 93101-3814. (Mail add: PO Box 1303, Goleta, 93116-1303), SAN 376-0790. Tel: 805-884-9909. E-mail: info@sbgen.org. Web Site: sbgen.org. *Dir,* Kathie Morgan; Tel: 805-682-4456, E-mail: kmorgan226@cox.net; *Librn/Cat,* Don Gill; Tel: 805-967-7236, E-mail: toldrig@hotmail.com
Founded 1972
Library Holdings: AV Mats 6,601; Electronic Media & Resources 504; Bk Titles 8,800; Per Subs 100
Subject Interests: Europe, Genealogy, US
Automation Activity & Vendor Info: (Cataloging) LibraryWorld, Inc
Function: Photocopying/Printing, Res libr
Publications: Ancestors West (Quarterly); Tree Tips (Monthly)
Open Tues, Thurs & Fri 10-4, Sun 1-4
Restriction: Pub use on premises

S SANTA BARBARA HISTORICAL MUSEUM*, Gledhill Library, 136 E De La Guerra St, 93101. SAN 301-5599. Tel: 805-966-1601. FAX: 805-966-1603. *Dir, Res,* Michael E Redmon; E-mail: mredmon@sbhistorical.org; Staff 1 (Non-MLS 1)
Founded 1967
Library Holdings: DVDs 96; Microforms 176; Bk Vols 5,000; Per Subs 20
Special Collections: Oral History
Subject Interests: Genealogy, Local hist
Automation Activity & Vendor Info: (Cataloging) TLC (The Library Corporation)
Function: Telephone ref
Publications: Noticias (Research guide)
Open Tues-Fri 10-4
Restriction: Non-circulating to the pub

S SANTA BARBARA MISSION*, Archive-Library, 2201 Laguna St, 93105. SAN 301-5602. Tel: 805-682-4713, Ext 152. FAX: 805-682-9323. E-mail: research@sbmal.org. Web Site: www.sbmal.org. *Dir,* Lynn Bremer; E-mail: director@sbmal.org
Founded 1786
Library Holdings: Bk Vols 23,000
Special Collections: California Missions (Father Junipero Serra Coll, covers all 21 California missions), docs; Early California (Webb Coll, Smilie Coll, Baer Coll & Wilson Coll), mss, papers, bks & docs; Original Spanish & Mexican Missionary Coll, bks; Spanish & Hispanic American Coll, bks; Spanish & Latin Coll, docs
Publications: Spanish California Revisited (Francis Guest, OFM); The Voyage of the Princesa to Southern California in 1782
Special Services for the Deaf - Bks on deafness & sign lang
Open Tues-Fri 9-4

S SANTA BARBARA MUSEUM OF ART, Constance & George Fearing Library, 1130 State St, 93101. SAN 320-1678. Tel: 805-884-6451. FAX: 805-966-6840. E-mail: library@sbma.net. Web Site: sbma.net. *Librn,* Heather Brodhead; Staff 1 (MLS 1)
Founded 1974
Library Holdings: Bk Vols 20,000; Spec Interest Per Sub 10
Special Collections: Ephemera files; Exhibition Files. Oral History
Subject Interests: Art
Automation Activity & Vendor Info: (Cataloging) OCLC CatExpress; (Circulation) TLC (The Library Corporation); (OPAC) TLC (The Library Corporation)
Database Vendor: TLC (The Library Corporation)
Function: Archival coll, Ref & res, Res libr
Partic in Central Coast Museum Consortium
Open Tues-Thurs 1-5
Restriction: Non-circulating coll

S SANTA BARBARA MUSEUM OF NATURAL HISTORY LIBRARY*, 2559 Puesta del Sol Rd, 93105. SAN 301-5610. Reference Tel: 805-682-4711, Ext 135. Web Site: www.sbnature.org/crc/50.html. *Mus Librn,* Terri Sheridan; Tel: 805-682-4711, Ext 134, E-mail: tsheridan@sbnature2.org; Staff 1 (Non-MLS 1)
Founded 1929
Jan 2008-Dec 2008 Income $100,000. Mats Exp $10,000, Books $2,000, Per/Ser (Incl. Access Fees) $7,000, Other Print Mats $1,000. Sal $55,000 (Prof $42,000)
Library Holdings: Bk Titles 22,000; Bk Vols 40,000; Per Subs 420
Special Collections: Channel Islands Archive; John Peabody Harrington California Indian Archives
Subject Interests: Indians, Natural hist, Systematics, Zoology
Automation Activity & Vendor Info: (Cataloging) TLC (The Library Corporation); (Circulation) TLC (The Library Corporation); (ILL) OCLC; (OPAC) TLC (The Library Corporation)
Database Vendor: OCLC FirstSearch, OCLC WorldShare Interlibrary Loan, TLC (The Library Corporation)
Function: Archival coll, Children's prog, Copy machines, e-mail serv, ILL available, Online cat, Summer reading prog
Partic in Central Coast Museum Consortium; Gold Coast Library Network; OCLC Online Computer Library Center, Inc
Open Mon-Fri 10-5
Restriction: Circ limited, Circulates for staff only, In-house use for visitors, Lending libr only via mail, Non-circulating of rare bks, Open to pub for ref only
Friends of the Library Group

S SANTA BARBARA NEWS PRESS LIBRARY*, 715 Anacapa St, 93101-2203. (Mail add: PO Box 1359, 93102-1359), SAN 327-6104. Tel: 805-564-5200, Ext 251. FAX: 805-966-6258. Web Site: www.newspress.com. *Librn,* Cass Cara
Library Holdings: Bk Vols 15,000
Special Collections: New Press Back Issues, micro

P SANTA BARBARA PUBLIC LIBRARY*, 40 E Anapamu St, 93101-2722. (Mail add: PO Box 1019, 93102-1019), SAN 334-9179. Tel: 805-962-7623. Circulation Tel: 805-962-7653. Interlibrary Loan Service Tel: 805-564-5610. Reference Tel: 805-564-5604. Administration Tel: 805-564-5608. Interlibrary Loan Service FAX: 805-564-5626. Reference FAX: 805-564-5661. Administration FAX: 805-564-5660. Web Site: www.sbplibrary.org. *Dir,* Irene Macias; E-mail: IMacias@SantaBarbaraCA.gov; *Mgr, Libr Serv, Pub Serv,* Myra J Nicholas; Tel: 805-564-5602, E-mail: MNicholas@SantaBarbaraCA.gov; *Mgr, Libr Serv,* Roger Hiles; Tel: 805-564-5611; Staff 115 (MLS 15, Non-MLS 100)
Pop 224,500; Circ 1,585,000
Library Holdings: AV Mats 15,200; Bk Vols 183,000; Per Subs 405
Subject Interests: Local hist
Automation Activity & Vendor Info: (Acquisitions) Innovative Interfaces, Inc; (Circulation) Innovative Interfaces, Inc; (ILL) Innovative Interfaces, Inc; (OPAC) Innovative Interfaces, Inc; (Serials) LS 2000
Database Vendor: Baker & Taylor, EBSCOhost, Gale Cengage Learning, Newsbank, OCLC FirstSearch, ProQuest
Mem of Black Gold Cooperative Library System
Partic in Dialog Corp; OCLC Online Computer Library Center, Inc
Friends of the Library Group
Branches: 8
CARPINTERIA BRANCH, 5141 Carpinteria Ave, Carpinteria, 93013, SAN 334-9209. Tel: 805-684-4314. *Br Mgr,* Tara O'Reilly; Staff 3 (Non-MLS 3)
Friends of the Library Group
CENTRAL LIBRARY, 40 E Anapamu St, 93101-2722. (Mail add: PO Box 1019, 93102-1019). Tel: 805-962-7653. FAX: 805-564-5660. *Dir,* Irene Macias; Staff 63.55 (MLS 9, Non-MLS 54.55)
Founded 1870. Pop 218,613; Circ 1,585,643
Jul 2011-Jun 2012 Income (Main Library and Branch(s)) $5,730,221. Mats Exp $495,086, Books $243,649, Per/Ser (Incl. Access Fees) $24,948, AV Mat $93,257. Sal $2,670,539
Library Holdings: e-books 7,551; Bk Vols 287,489; Videos 22,430
Friends of the Library Group
EASTSIDE, 1102 E Montecito St, 93103, SAN 334-9268. Tel: 805-963-3727. *Librn,* Marivel Zambrano-Esparza; Staff 5 (MLS 1, Non-MLS 4)
Database Vendor: SirsiDynix
Friends of the Library Group
GOLETA BRANCH, 500 N Fairview Ave, Goleta, 93117, SAN 334-9292. Tel: 805-964-7878. E-mail: goletalibrary@gmail.com. *Librn,* Allison Gray; Staff 11 (MLS 2, Non-MLS 9)
Friends of the Library Group
LOS OLIVOS, Grange Hall, 93102. (Mail add: PO Box 306, 93102-0306), SAN 377-7790. *In Charge,* Carey McKinnon; E-mail: cmckinnon@ci.santa-barbara.ca.us
MONTECITO, 1469 E Valley Rd, 93108, SAN 334-9357. Tel: 805-969-5063. *In Charge,* Jody Thomas
Friends of the Library Group
SANTA YNEZ BRANCH, 3598 Sagunto St, Santa Ynez, 93460. (Mail add: PO Box 186, Santa Ynez, 93460-0186). *In Charge,* Carey McKinnon; E-mail: cmckinnon@ci.santa-barbara.ca.us
Open Fri 2-5
SOLVANG BRANCH, 1745 Mission Dr, Solvang, 93463, SAN 334-9411. Tel: 805-688-4214. *In Charge,* Carey McKinnon; E-mail: cmckinnon@ci.santa-barbara.ca.us
Friends of the Library Group
Bookmobiles: 1

S STONEHENGE STUDY GROUP*, Stonehenge Viewpoint Library, 800 Palermo Dr, 93105. SAN 327-6120. Tel: 805-687-6029. E-mail: stonevue@aol.com. *Librn,* Joan L Cyr
Founded 1973
Library Holdings: Bk Vols 5,000
Special Collections: Bob Forrest Coll; Colo Epigraphy photos; Donald L Cyr Coll; Isaac N Vail Coll; Louis K Bell Coll; Paul Karlsson Johnstone Coll
Subject Interests: Archaeology, Astronomy, Geol

R TRINITY EPISCOPAL CHURCH LIBRARY*, 1500 State St, 93101. SAN 301-5645. Tel: 805-965-7419. FAX: 805-965-8840. Web Site: www.trinitysb.org. *Librn,* Lou Smitheram; Staff 3 (MLS 2, Non-MLS 1)
Library Holdings: Bk Vols 2,500
Open Mon-Fri 9-5

C UNIVERSITY OF CALIFORNIA, SANTA BARBARA*, Davidson Library, 93106-9010. SAN 301-5653. Tel: 805-893-2478. Circulation Tel: 805-893-3491. Interlibrary Loan Service Tel: 805-893-3436. Reference Tel: 805-893-3133. Administration Tel: 805-893-2741. Information Services Tel: 805-893-8147. FAX: 805-893-7010. Circulation FAX: 805-893-4334. Interlibrary Loan Service FAX: 805-893-5290. Information Services FAX: 805-893-4676. Web Site: www.library.ucsb.edu. *Univ Librn,* Position Currently Open; *Assoc Univ Librn, Human Res,* Detrice Bankhead; Tel: 805 893 3841, E-mail: bankhead@library.ucsb.edu; *Assoc Univ Librn, Tech Serv,* Brad Eden; Tel: 805-893-4261, E-mail: eden@library.ucsb.edu; *Br Head,* Cathy Chiu; *Head, Coll Develop,* Lucia Snowhill; Tel: 805-893-5383, E-mail: snowhill@library.ucsb.edu; *Head, Ser,* Catherine Nelson; Tel: 805-893-2444, E-mail: nelson@library.ucsb.edu; *Access Serv,* Gary Johnson; Tel: 805-893-3386, E-mail: johnson@library.ucsb.edu; *Art Librn,* Susan Moon; *Info Serv,* Sherry DeDecker; Tel: 805-893-3713, E-mail: dedecker@library.ucsb.edu; *Sci,* Andrea L Duda; Tel: 805-893-2647, E-mail: duda@library.ucsb.edu; *Spec Coll & Archives Librn,* David Tambo; Tel: 805-893-3420, E-mail: tambo@library.ucsb.edu. Subject Specialists: *Area studies, E Asia,* Cathy Chiu; *Arts,* Susan Moon; Staff 172 (MLS 41, Non-MLS 131)
Founded 1909. Enrl 22,417; Fac 963; Highest Degree: Doctorate
Library Holdings: Bk Vols 2,948,999; Per Subs 23,218
Special Collections: 20th Century American & British Writers Coll; American Religions Coll; Art Exhibition Catalog Coll; Balkan History (Nikic Coll); California Ethnic & Multicultural Archive; Conservation in Southern California (Pearl Chase Coll); Evolution (Darwin Coll); Historic Sound Recordings (Todd Coll); History of Printing 19th & 20th Century (Skofield Coll); Humanistic Psychology Archive; Late 19th & 20th Century Trade Catalogs (Romaine Coll); Lincoln, Civil War & American Westward Expansion (Wyles Coll); Lotte Lehmann Archives Coll; Rare Bibles Coll. Oral History; State Document Depository; US Document Depository
Automation Activity & Vendor Info: (Acquisitions) Ex Libris Group; (Cataloging) Ex Libris Group; (Circulation) Ex Libris Group; (Course Reserve) Docutek; (ILL) Fretwell-Downing; (OPAC) Ex Libris Group; (Serials) Ex Libris Group
Database Vendor: Cambridge Scientific Abstracts, EBSCOhost, Gale Cengage Learning, JSTOR, LexisNexis, Newsbank, OCLC WorldShare Interlibrary Loan, OVID Technologies, ProQuest

Wireless access
Partic in Association of Research Libraries (ARL); Center for Research Libraries; OCLC Online Computer Library Center, Inc; OCLC Research Library Partnership
Departmental Libraries:
ARTS LIBRARY, UCSB Library, 93106-9010. Tel: 805-893-2850. FAX: 805-893-5879. Web Site: www.library.ucsb.edu/arts-library. *Head of Libr,* Susan Moon; Tel: 805-893-3613, E-mail: smoon@library.ucsb.edu; *Art Librn,* Chizu Morihara; Tel: 805-893-2766, E-mail: cmorihara@library.ucsb.edu; *Music Librn,* Eunice Schroeder; Tel: 805-893-3612, E-mail: schroede@library.ucsb.edu. Subject Specialists: *Arts,* Chizu Morihara; Staff 10 (MLS 3, Non-MLS 7)
Enrl 21,685; Fac 1,050; Highest Degree: Doctorate
Library Holdings: CDs 13,216; DVDs 1,352; Microforms 10,972; Music Scores 44,213; Bk Vols 320,000; Per Subs 534; Videos 280
Automation Activity & Vendor Info: (OPAC) Ex Libris Group

C WESTMONT COLLEGE*, Roger John Voskuyl Library, 955 La Paz Rd, 93108-1099. SAN 301-5661. Tel: 805-565-6000, 805-565-6147. Interlibrary Loan Service Tel: 805-565-6142. Reference Tel: 805-565-6146. Administration Tel: 805-565-6182. FAX: 805-565-6220. Web Site: www.library.westmont.edu. *Dir,* Debra M Quast; E-mail: dquast@westmont.edu; *Assoc Dir, Electronic Res Librn,* Claudia Scott; E-mail: cscott@westmont.edu; *Instrul Serv Librn,* Savannah L Kelly; E-mail: skelly@westmont.edu; *Outreach & Res Serv Librn,* Robin D Lang; E-mail: rlang@westmont.edu; *Col Archivist, Ref & Instruction Librn,* Diane Ziliotto; E-mail: dziliotto@westmont.edu; *Tech Serv Librn,* Mary Louge; Tel: 805-565-6144, E-mail: mlouge@westmont.edu; *ILL Mgr,* Richard Burnweit; E-mail: burnweit@westmont.edu; *Acq & Ser Coordr,* Danielle Willard; E-mail: dwillard@westmont.edu; *Circ Coordr,* Ruth Angelos; E-mail: rangel@westmont.edu; Staff 7 (MLS 6, Non-MLS 1)
Founded 1940. Enrl 1,200; Fac 64; Highest Degree: Bachelor
Library Holdings: Audiobooks 9,983; DVDs 1,764; e-books 50,000; e-journals 2,529; Electronic Media & Resources 143,263; Microforms 15,590; Bk Titles 106,411; Bk Vols 226,657; Per Subs 270
Automation Activity & Vendor Info: (Acquisitions) OCLC; (Cataloging) OCLC; (Circulation) OCLC; (Course Reserve) OCLC; (ILL) OCLC; (OPAC) OCLC; (Serials) OCLC
Database Vendor: OCLC WorldShare Interlibrary Loan, OCLC Worldshare Management Services
Wireless access
Partic in OCLC Online Computer Library Center, Inc; Statewide California Electronic Library Consortium (SCELC)

SANTA CLARA

S GENERAL DYNAMICS ADVANCED INFORMATION SYSTEMS*, AIS Library, 2305 Mission College Blvd, Ste 101, 95054. SAN 301-0880. Tel: 650-966-2003, 650-966-3860. FAX: 650-966-2449. Web Site: www.gd-ais.com. *Mgr, Libr Serv,* Susan Gammon; E-mail: sue.gammon@gd.ais.com; Staff 2 (MLS 1, Non-MLS 1)
Founded 1953
Library Holdings: Bk Titles 7,000; Per Subs 450
Subject Interests: Aerospace, Electronics
Automation Activity & Vendor Info: (Cataloging) EOS International; (Circulation) EOS International; (OPAC) EOS International; (Serials) EOS International
Database Vendor: Dialog, Jane's, LexisNexis, OCLC WorldShare Interlibrary Loan
Partic in Bay Area Library & Information Network; Califa
Open Mon-Fri 7:30-5:15
Restriction: By permission only, Employees only, Restricted loan policy

J MISSION COLLEGE LIBRARY*, 3000 Mission College Blvd, 95054-1897. SAN 301-5742. Tel: 408-855-5150. Reference Tel: 408-855-5151. Administration Tel: 408-855-5152. FAX: 408-855-5462. Web Site: www.missioncollege.org/lib/default.html. *Dean & Dir, Libr Serv,* Timothy Karas; Tel: 408-855-5164, E-mail: tim.karas@wvm.edu; *Coll Develop Librn,* Pat Hernas; Tel: 408-855-5167, E-mail: pat.hernas@wvm.edu; *Electronic Res Librn,* Michele Speck; Tel: 408-855-5169, E-mail: michele.speck@wvm.edu; *Pub Serv Librn,* Cathy Cox; Tel: 408-855-5165, E-mail: cathy.cox@wvm.edu; *Dept Chair, Ref & Instruction,* Elaine Wong; Tel: 408-855-5162, E-mail: elaine.wong@wvm.edu; Staff 12 (MLS 6, Non-MLS 6)
Founded 1975. Enrl 10,500; Fac 325; Highest Degree: Associate
Library Holdings: Audiobooks 794; AV Mats 2,682; e-books 12,617; Microforms 55,000; Bk Titles 48,975; Bk Vols 69,144; Per Subs 160
Special Collections: Asian American Coll
Subject Interests: Allied health, Fire sci
Automation Activity & Vendor Info: (Acquisitions) Innovative Interfaces, Inc; (Cataloging) Innovative Interfaces, Inc; (Circulation) Innovative Interfaces, Inc; (Course Reserve) Innovative Interfaces, Inc; (OPAC) Innovative Interfaces, Inc
Database Vendor: ARTstor, CountryWatch, CQ Press, Gale Cengage Learning, Innovative Interfaces, Inc, LexisNexis, ProQuest, SerialsSolutions
Wireless access
Partic in Califa
Special Services for the Deaf - Assistive tech; Bks on deafness & sign lang; Closed caption videos
Special Services for the Blind - Assistive/Adapted tech devices, equip & products; Computer with voice synthesizer for visually impaired persons
Open Mon-Thurs 9-8:30, Fri 10:30-3:30, Sat 10-3

S NIELSEN ENGINEERING & RESEARCH, INC LIBRARY, 900 Lafayette St, Ste 600, 95050. SAN 301-0902. Tel: 408-454-5246. E-mail: lib@nearinc.com. Web Site: www.nearinc.com. *Coop Librn,* Celeste L Welch; Staff 1 (MLS 1)
Founded 1966
Library Holdings: Bk Vols 1,000; Per Subs 30
Automation Activity & Vendor Info: (Cataloging) Inmagic, Inc.
Function: For res purposes, ILL available, Res libr
Publications: New Accessions List
Restriction: Circ limited, Open by appt only

P SANTA CLARA CITY LIBRARY*, 2635 Homestead Rd, 95051. SAN 301-5750. Tel: 408-615-2900. Circulation Tel: 408-615-2970. Administration Tel: 408-615-2930. FAX: 408-247-9657. Reference FAX: 408-246-9581. TDD: 408-246-2507. E-mail: library@santaclaraca.gov. Web Site: www.library.santaclaraca.gov. *Asst City Librn,* Julie Passalacqua; E-mail: jpassalacqua@santaclaraca.gov; *Adult Serv Mgr,* Trish Taylor; Tel: 408-615-2902, E-mail: ttaylor@santaclaraca.gov; *Coll Serv Mgr,* Position Currently Open; *Support Serv Div Mgr,* Lee Hagan; Tel: 408-615-2961, E-mail: lhagan@ci.santa-clara.ca.us; *Youth & Extn Serv Div Mgr,* Susan Baier; Tel: 408-615-2921, E-mail: sbaier@santaclaraca.gov; *Coordr, Cat, Tech Serv,* Mary Jo Bosteels; Tel: 408-615-2941, E-mail: mjbosteels@santaclaraca.gov; *Coordr, Info Tech,* John Schlosser; Tel: 408-615-2948, E-mail: jschlosser@santaclaraca.gov; *Coordr, Local Hist & Genealogy,* Mary Hanel; Tel: 408-615-2909, E-mail: mhanel@santaclaraca.gov; *Coordr, Ref Serv-Adult,* Jane Botsford; Tel: 408-615-2907, E-mail: jbotsford@santaclaraca.gov; *Coordr, Youth Serv,* Erin Ulrich; Tel: 408-615-2918, E-mail: eulrich@santaclaraca.gov; *Circ Serv Supvr,* Carolyn Parham; Tel: 408-615-2973, E-mail: cparham@santaclaraca.gov; *Supvr, Literacy Serv,* Shanti Bhaskaran; Tel: 408-615-2957, E-mail: sbhaskaran@santaclaraca.gov; *Supvr, Per,* Paulette Kondos; Tel: 408-615-2985, E-mail: pkondos@santaclaraca.gov. Subject Specialists: *Genealogy, Local hist,* Mary Hanel; *Literacy,* Shanti Bhaskaran; Staff 18.4 (MLS 15.4, Non-MLS 3)
Founded 1904. Pop 117,242; Circ 2,647,837
Jul 2008-Jun 2009 Income (Main Library and Branch(s)) $7,679,427, State $327,767, City $7,271,630, Other $80,030. Mats Exp $765,062, Per/Ser (Incl. Access Fees) $70,955, Other Print Mats $469,258, AV Mat $141,660, Electronic Ref Mat (Incl. Access Fees) $83,189. Sal $4,262,436
Library Holdings: AV Mats 50,586; e-books 2,951; Bk Titles 373,226; Per Subs 610
Special Collections: Adult New Reader Coll; Audiovisual Coll, bks on tape, CDs, DVDs, music CDs; Business Reference Coll; Children's Picture Books; Consumer Health Information (Kaiser Permanente Health & Wellness Coll); Large Print Coll; Local History/Genealogy Coll
Subject Interests: Bus, Local hist
Automation Activity & Vendor Info: (Acquisitions) Innovative Interfaces, Inc; (Cataloging) OCLC; (Circulation) Innovative Interfaces, Inc; (OPAC) Innovative Interfaces, Inc; (Serials) Innovative Interfaces, Inc
Database Vendor: EBSCOhost, LearningExpress, OCLC WorldShare Interlibrary Loan, ReferenceUSA, ValueLine
Wireless access
Function: Audiobks via web, BA reader (adult literacy), Bks on cassette, Bks on CD, CD-ROM, Children's prog, Computer training, Computers for patron use, Copy machines, Digital talking bks, e-mail serv, Electronic databases & coll, Family literacy, Free DVD rentals, Handicapped accessible, Health sci info serv, Homebound delivery serv, Magnifiers for reading, Music CDs, Online cat, Online searches, OverDrive digital audio bks, Photocopying/Printing, Preschool outreach, Prog for adults, Prog for children & young adult, Ref serv available, Senior outreach, Story hour, Summer reading prog, Teen prog, Telephone ref, VHS videos, Video lending libr, Web-catalog, Wheelchair accessible
Special Services for the Deaf - Assisted listening device; Assistive tech; Bks on deafness & sign lang; Closed caption videos; High interest/low vocabulary bks; TDD equip
Special Services for the Blind - Audio mat; Bks on cassette; Bks on CD; Closed circuit TV; Computer with voice synthesizer for visually impaired persons; Home delivery serv; Large print bks; Magnifiers; PC for handicapped; Reader equip; Screen enlargement software for people with visual disabilities
Open Mon & Tues 9-9, Wed 12-9, Thurs-Sat 9-6, Sun 1-5
Friends of the Library Group
Branches: 1
MISSION LIBRARY FAMILY READING CENTER, 1098 Lexington St, 95050, SAN 371-358X. Tel: 408-615-2964. FAX: 408-249-2486. E-mail: readsantaclara@ci.santa-clara.ca.us. *Br Mgr, Head, Literacy,* Shanti Bhaskaran; Tel: 408-615-2957; Staff 1 (Non-MLS 1)

Library Holdings: Bk Vols 20,868
Open Mon & Wed 10-9, Tues, Thurs & Fri 10-6
Friends of the Library Group

C SANTA CLARA UNIVERSITY*, Michel Orradre Library, 500 El Camino Real, 95053-0500. SAN 334-9470. Tel: 408-554-6830. Circulation Tel: 408-554-5020. Reference Tel: 408-554-4658. FAX: 408-554-6827. Web Site: www.scu.edu/library. *Dir,* Position Currently Open; *Assoc Librn,* Susan Boyd; *Assoc Librn,* Paul Neuhaus; *Assoc Librn,* Anthony Raymond; Tel: 408-554-5430, E-mail: araymond@scu.edu; *Assoc Librn,* Michal Strutin; *Librn,* George Carlson; Tel: 408-554-5436, E-mail: gcarlson@scu.edu; *Librn,* Leanna Goodwater; *Librn,* Gail Gradowski; Staff 36 (MLS 13, Non-MLS 23)
Founded 1851. Enrl 7,359; Highest Degree: Doctorate
Library Holdings: Bk Vols 3,787; Per Subs 2,630
Special Collections: California: Denise Levertov & Jose Antonio Villareal; Labor Relations in California. State Document Depository
Automation Activity & Vendor Info: (Acquisitions) Innovative Interfaces, Inc; (Cataloging) Innovative Interfaces, Inc; (Circulation) Innovative Interfaces, Inc; (Course Reserve) Docutek; (ILL) Innovative Interfaces, Inc; (OPAC) Innovative Interfaces, Inc; (Serials) Innovative Interfaces, Inc
Database Vendor: Dialog, EBSCOhost, Gale Cengage Learning, Innovative Interfaces, Inc, LexisNexis, OCLC FirstSearch, OVID Technologies
Partic in Golden Gateway Library Network; OCLC Online Computer Library Center, Inc; Southern Calif Electronic Libr Consortium; Statewide California Electronic Library Consortium (SCELC)

Departmental Libraries:

ARCHIVES, 500 El Camino Real, 95053-0500. Tel: 408-554-4117. FAX: 408-554-5179. E-mail: amcmahon@scu.edu. Web Site: www.scu.edu/archives. *Archivist,* Anne McMahon; Staff 1 (Non-MLS 1)
Special Collections: Alaska (Bernard R Hubbard, S J Coll), ms, photog, Botany (George Schoener Coll); Early Aviation (John J Montgomery), ms, photog; Local History

CL EDWIN A HEAFEY LAW LIBRARY, School of Law, 500 El Camino Real, 95053-0430, SAN 334-9500. Tel: 408-554-4451. Circulation Tel: 408-554-4072. Interlibrary Loan Service Tel: 408-554-5133. Reference Tel: 408-554-4452. FAX: 408-554-5318. Web Site: law.scu.edu/library. *Dir, Law Libr,* Mary D Hood; Tel: 408-554-2732, E-mail: mhood@scu.edu; *Dir, Pub Serv,* Prano Amjadi; Tel: 408-554-5320, E-mail: pamjadi@scu.edu; *Dir, Tech Serv,* Whitney Alexander; Tel: 408-554-2733, E-mail: walexander@scu.edu; *Access Serv Librn,* Thomas Deguzman; Tel: 408-554-5327, E-mail: tdeguzman@scu.edu; *Cat Librn,* Marilyn Dreyer; Tel: 408-554-5307, E-mail: mdreyer@scu.edu; *Sr Ref Librn,* Ellen Platt; Tel: 408-554-5139, E-mail: eplatt@scu.edu; Staff 22 (MLS 9, Non-MLS 13)
Founded 1912. Enrl 926; Fac 37; Highest Degree: Master
Library Holdings: AV Mats 5,135; Bk Titles 38,247; Bk Vols 169,192; Per Subs 4,153
Special Collections: Proceedings of the House Judiciary Committee on the Watergate Hearings
Automation Activity & Vendor Info: (Course Reserve) Innovative Interfaces, Inc
Database Vendor: JSTOR, Westlaw, Wilson - Wilson Web
Partic in Jesuit Law Libr Consortium; RLIN (Research Libraries Information Network); S Bay Area Ref Network
Publications: Heafey Headnotes (Newsletter)
Open Mon-Thurs 8am-Midnight, Fri 8am-10pm, Sat & Sun (Fall & Spring) 9am-Midnight

S TRITON MUSEUM OF ART LIBRARY*, 1505 Warburton Ave, 95050. SAN 301-5793. Tel: 408-247-3754. FAX: 408-247-3796. Web Site: www.tritonmuseum.org. *Exec Dir,* George Rivera; Tel: 408-247-3754, Ext 11, E-mail: tritongeorge@aol.com
Founded 1968
Library Holdings: Bk Vols 1,600
Subject Interests: Art, Art hist
Restriction: Open by appt only

SANTA CLARITA

CR ROBERT L POWELL LIBRARY (THE MASTER'S COLLEGE)*, 21726 W Placerita Canyon Rd, 91321-1200. SAN 301-0996. Tel: 661-259-3540. Toll Free Tel: 800-568-6248. FAX: 661-362-2719. *Dir,* John W Stone; *Cat Mgr,* Peg Westphalen; *Ref Librn,* Janet L Tillman. Subject Specialists: *Theol,* John W Stone; *Liberal arts,* Janet L Tillman; Staff 7 (MLS 4, Non-MLS 3)
Founded 1927. Enrl 1,000; Fac 134; Highest Degree: Master
Library Holdings: e-books 60,000; e-journals 30,000; Bk Titles 133,000; Bk Vols 161,000; Per Subs 123
Subject Interests: Biblical studies
Automation Activity & Vendor Info: (Acquisitions) Ex Libris Group; (Cataloging) Ex Libris Group; (Circulation) Ex Libris Group; (Course Reserve) Ex Libris Group; (OPAC) Ex Libris Group; (Serials) Ex Libris Group
Database Vendor: 3M Library Systems, ABC-CLIO, Annual Reviews, BCR: Christian Periodical Index, CQ Press, ebrary, EBSCOhost, Ex Libris Group, Gale Cengage Learning, LexisNexis, OCLC FirstSearch, OCLC WorldShare Interlibrary Loan, Oxford Online, ProQuest
Wireless access
Function: ILL available
Partic in Southern Calif Electronic Libr Consortium; Southern Calif Interlibr Loan Network
Open Mon-Thurs 7:30am-Midnight, Fri 7:30-5, Sat 12-10, Sun 7:30pm-Midnight

P SANTA CLARITA PUBLIC LIBRARY*, Canyon Country Jo Anne Darcy Library, 18601 Soledad Canyon Rd, 91351. SAN 332-4605. Tel: 661-259-0750. E-mail: info@santaclaritalibrary.com. Web Site: www.santaclaritalibrary.com. *City Librn,* Ed Kieczykowski; E-mail: ekieczykowski@santaclaritalibrary.com; *Br Mgr,* Carla Mason; *Coordr, Youth Serv,* Kelly Behle
Founded 2001. Circ 381,424
Library Holdings: Bk Vols 91,530; Per Subs 75
Wireless access
Open Mon-Thurs 9-8, Fri 10-6, Sat 10-5, Sun 1-5
Friends of the Library Group

Branches: 2

OLD TOWN NEWHALL LIBRARY, 24500 Main St, 91321, SAN 332-6047. Tel: 661-259-0750. FAX: 661-254-5760. *Br Mgr,* Erin Christmas
Founded 1957. Pop 36,393; Circ 385,404
Library Holdings: Bk Vols 50,854; Per Subs 35
Open Mon-Thurs 9-8, Fri 10-6, Sat 10-5, Sun 1-5
Friends of the Library Group

VALENCIA LIBRARY, 23743 W Valencia Blvd, 91355, SAN 332-6675. Tel: 661-259-0750. FAX: 661-298-7137. *Br Mgr,* Nancy Kerr; Tel: 661-259-8332, E-mail: nkerr@santaclaritalibrary.com
Founded 1972. Circ 713,699
Open Mon-Thurs 10-9, Fri 10-6, Sat 10-5, Sun 1-5
Friends of the Library Group

SANTA CRUZ

S MUSEUM OF ART & HISTORY LIBRARY*, 705 Front St, 95060-4508. SAN 371-7860. Tel: 831-429-1964. FAX: 831-429-1954. E-mail: archives@santacruzmah.org. Web Site: www.santacruzmah.org. *Archivist,* Marla Nova; Tel: 831-429-1964, Ext 17, E-mail: marla@santacruzmah.org; Staff 1 (MLS 1)
Library Holdings: Bk Titles 2,000
Special Collections: Evergreen Cemetery Records. Oral History
Subject Interests: Local hist
Publications: Santa Cruz County History (Journal)

G NATIONAL MARINE FISHERIES SERVICE*, SWFSC Santa Cruz Library, 110 Shaffer Rd, 95060-5730. SAN 301-6617. Tel: 831-420-3962. FAX: 831-420-3978. *Librn,* Kit Johnston; Staff 1 (MLS 1)
Founded 1962
Library Holdings: Per Subs 120, Videos 15
Subject Interests: Fisheries
Function: For res purposes, ILL available
Partic in Fedlink; OCLC Online Computer Library Center, Inc; OCLC-LVIS
Restriction: Open to others by appt, Staff use only

P SANTA CRUZ CITY-COUNTY LIBRARY SYSTEM*, Headquarters, 117 Union St, 95060-3873. SAN 334-9659. Tel: 831-427-7706. FAX: 831-427-7720. Web Site: www.santacruzpl.org. *Dir of Libr,* Teresa Landers; Tel: 831-427-7706, Ext 7612, E-mail: landerst@santacruzpl.org
Wireless access
Partic in Monterey Bay Area Cooperative Library System
Special Services for the Deaf - TTY equip
Friends of the Library Group

Branches: 9

APTOS BRANCH, 7695 Soquel Dr, Aptos, 95003-3899, SAN 334-9683. Tel: 831-427-7702. FAX: 831-427-7722. *In Charge,* David Addison; Tel: 831-427-7702, Ext 7671
Open Mon-Thurs 11-7, Sat 11-5

BOULDER CREEK BRANCH, 13390 W Park Ave, Boulder Creek, 95006-9301, SAN 334-9772. Tel: 831-427-7703. FAX: 831-427-7723. *In Charge,* Cathy Landis; Tel: 831-427-7700, Ext 7688
Open Tues-Thurs 11-6, Fri & Sat 12-5

CAPITOLA BRANCH, 2005 Wharf Rd, Capitola, 95010-2002, SAN 378-0694. Tel: 831-427-7705. FAX: 831-427-7725. *In Charge,* Melanee Barash; Tel: 831-427-7706, Ext 7672

DOWNTOWN, 224 Church St, 95060-3873, SAN 322-5666. Tel: 831-427-7707. FAX: 831-427-7701. *Mgr,* Richard Eberle; Tel: 831-427-7706, Ext 7717, E-mail: eberler@santacruzpl.org
Open Mon-Thurs 10-7, Sat 10-5, Sun 1-5

FELTON BRANCH, 6299 Gushee St, Felton, 95018-9140. (Mail add: PO Box 56, Felton, 95018-0056), SAN 334-9861. Tel: 831-427-7708. FAX: 831-427-7728. *In Charge,* Jason McCluskey; Tel: 831-427-7700, Ext 7693
Open Tues & Wed 10-6, Thurs & Fri 11-5, Sat 11-6
Friends of the Library Group

GARFIELD PARK, 705 Woodrow Ave, 95060, SAN 334-9926. Tel: 831-427-7709. FAX: 831-427-7729. *In Charge,* Catherine Workman; Tel: 831-427-7700, Ext 7736
Open Mon, Wed & Fri 1-5, Tues & Thurs 2-6

LA SELVA BEACH BRANCH, 316 Estrella, La Selva Beach, 95076, SAN 334-9950. Tel: 831-427-7710. *In Charge,* Galina Wells; Tel: 831-427-7700, Ext 7733
Open Tues & Thurs 10-5, Wed 1-6, Fri & Sat 1-5

LIVE OAK, 2380 Portola Dr, 95062. Tel: 831-427-7711. FAX: 831-427-7718. *Br Mgr,* Paula Contreras; Tel: 831-427-7706, Ext 7677
Library Holdings: Bk Vols 53,535
Open Mon & Wed 11-7, Tues 1-7, Thurs & Sun 1-5

SCOTTS VALLEY BRANCH, 251 Kings Valley Rd, Scotts Valley, 95066, SAN 334-9985. Tel: 831-427-7712. FAX: 831-427-7719. *In Charge,* Linda Gault; Tel: 831-427-7700, Ext 7678
Open Mon-Thurs 11-7, Fri & Sat 11-5

Bookmobiles: 1

L SANTA CRUZ COUNTY LAW LIBRARY*, 701 Ocean St, Rm 070, 95060. SAN 301-5815. Tel: 831-420-2205. FAX: 831-457-2255. E-mail: scclawlib@yahoo.com. Web Site: www.lawlibrary.org. *Librn,* Renee J Fleming; Staff 2 (MLS 1, Non-MLS 1)
Founded 1896
Jul 2011-Jun 2012 Income $215,016, Locally Generated Income $25,145, Other $189,871. Mats Exp $271,829. Sal $176,411 (Prof $72,779)
Library Holdings: CDs 132; Bk Vols 12,000
Subject Interests: Law
Database Vendor: EBSCOhost, LexisNexis, Westlaw
Wireless access
Function: e-mail serv, Fax serv, Handicapped accessible, ILL available, Mail & tel request accepted
Partic in Pacer
Open Mon-Thurs 8-4, Fri 8-Noon
Restriction: Circ limited

C UNIVERSITY OF CALIFORNIA, University Library, 1156 High St, 95064. SAN 335-0045. Tel: 831-459-2076. Interlibrary Loan Service Tel: 831-459-2234. FAX: 831-459-8206. Web Site: library.ucsc.edu. *Univ Librn,* Elizabeth Cowell; E-mail: mcowell@ucsc.edu; *Assoc Dir, Digital Libr & Assessment,* Robin Chandler; E-mail: rlchandl@ucsc.edu; *Head, Assessment & Planning,* Greg Careaga; Tel: 831-459-3687, E-mail: gcareaga@ucsc.edu; *Head, Digital Initiatives,* Sue Chesley Perry; Tel: 831-459-5590, E-mail: chesley@ucsc.edu; *Head, Res Support Serv,* Kerry Scott; Tel: 831-459-2802, E-mail: scottk@ucsc.edu; *Head, Spec Coll,* Elizabeth Remak-Honnef; Tel: 831-459-2459, E-mail: remak@ucsc.edu; *Head, Tech Serv,* Marcia Barrett; Tel: 831-459-5166, E-mail: barrett@ucsc.edu; *Head User Serv & Resource Sharing,* Sarah Troy; Tel: 831-459-3878, E-mail: saraht@ucsc.edu; *Librn,* Christine Caldwell; Tel: 831-459-1287, E-mail: caldwell@ucsc.edu; *Librn,* Frank Gravier; Tel: 831-459-3319, E-mail: gravier@ucsc.edu; *Librn,* Christy Hightower; Tel: 831-459-4708, E-mail: christyh@ucsc.edu; *Librn,* Ann Hubble; Tel: 831-459-4974, E-mail: ahubble@ucsc.edu; *Librn,* Annette Marines; Tel: 831-459-3255, E-mail: amarines@ucsc.edu; *Librn,* Deborah Murphy; Tel: 831-459-3253, E-mail: damurphy@ucsc.edu; *Assoc Librn,* Rachel Jaffe; Tel: 831-502-7291, E-mail: jaffer@ucsc.edu; *Assoc Librn,* Ken Lyons; Tel: 831-459-2593, E-mail: kbplyons@ucsc.edu; *Assoc Librn,* Nicholas Meriwether; Tel: 831-502-7526, E-mail: nicholas@ucsc.edu; *Assoc Librn,* Lucia Orlando; Tel: 831-459-1279, E-mail: luciao@ucsc.edu; *Asst Librn,* Mary deVries; Tel: 831-459-3815, E-mail: mdevries@ucsc.edu; *Asst Librn,* Kate Dundon; Tel: 831-459-4425, E-mail: dundon@ucsc.edu; *Asst Librn,* Annie Tang; Tel: 831-459-5113, E-mail: atang10@ucsc.edu; *Asst Librn,* Jessica Waggoner; Tel: 831-459-5654, E-mail: jspencer@ucsc.edu. Subject Specialists: *Arts, Humanities,* Kerry Scott; *Eng, Sci,* Christine Caldwell; *Arts, Humanities,* Frank Gravier; *Eng, Sci,* Christy Hightower; *Eng, Sci,* Ann Hubble; *Soc sci,* Annette Marines; *Arts, Humanities,* Deborah Murphy; *Arts, Humanities,* Ken Lyons; *Spec coll,* Nicholas Meriwether; *Soc sci,* Lucia Orlando; *Spec coll,* Mary deVries; *Spec coll,* Kate Dundon; *Spec coll,* Annie Tang; Staff 65 (MLS 20, Non-MLS 45)
Founded 1965. Enrl 16,543; Fac 619; Highest Degree: Doctorate
Jul 2013-Jun 2014 Income $10,499,949, State $10,038,907, Other $461,042. Mats Exp $3,067,262, Books $369,216, Per/Ser (Incl. Access Fees) $469,088, Other Print Mats $6,613, Electronic Ref Mat (Incl. Access Fees) $2,184,461, Presv $37,884. Sal $4,623,094 (Prof $4,189,925)
Library Holdings: Bk Vols 2,365,077; Per Subs 56,506
Special Collections: Grateful Dead Archive; Gregory Bateson Coll; Kenneth Patchen Archive; Lime Kiln Press Archive; Mary Lea Shane Archives of the Lick Observatory; Robert Heinlein Archive; Santa Cruz County History Coll; Strouse Coll of Thomas Carlyle; Trianon Press Archive; Turtle Island Press Archive. Oral History; US Document Depository
Automation Activity & Vendor Info: (Acquisitions) Innovative Interfaces, Inc; (Cataloging) Innovative Interfaces, Inc; (Circulation) Innovative Interfaces, Inc; (ILL) OCLC; (Media Booking) Innovative Interfaces, Inc; (OPAC) Innovative Interfaces, Inc; (Serials) Innovative Interfaces, Inc
Database Vendor: OCLC FirstSearch
Wireless access
Function: Archival coll, AV serv, Doc delivery serv, For res purposes, Govt ref serv, Handicapped accessible, Homebound delivery serv, ILL available, Large print keyboards, Libr develop, Newsp ref libr, Photocopying/Printing, Ref serv available, Res libr, Telephone ref, Wheelchair accessible
Publications: Catalog of South Pacific Collection (1978); Catalog of the Carlyle Coll (1980); Norman & Charlotte Strouse Lectures on Carlyle & His Era (Series)
Partic in Monterey Bay Area Cooperative Library System
Special Services for the Deaf - TTY equip
Restriction: Circ limited, In-house use for visitors, Open to students, fac & staff, Restricted borrowing privileges, Restricted loan policy
Friends of the Library Group

SANTA FE SPRINGS

P SANTA FE SPRINGS CITY LIBRARY*, 11700 E Telegraph Rd, 90670-3600. SAN 301-5831. Tel: 562-868-7738. Administration Tel: 562-868-7738, Ext 7801. FAX: 562-929-3680. E-mail: library@santafesprings.org. Web Site: www.santafesprings.org/depts/community_serv/library/default.asp. *Dir of Libr Serv,* Hilary Gordon Keith; E-mail: hilarykeith@santafesprings.org; *Coordr,* Jerry Edwards; *Librn II,* Position Currently Open; *AV, Outreach Serv Librn,* Joyce Ryan; *Youth Serv,* Shannon Dailey. Subject Specialists: *Literacy,* Jerry Edwards; Staff 29 (MLS 4, Non-MLS 25)
Founded 1961. Pop 18,000; Circ 146,000
Library Holdings: Bk Vols 87,500; Per Subs 225
Automation Activity & Vendor Info: (Acquisitions) SirsiDynix; (Cataloging) SirsiDynix; (Circulation) SirsiDynix; (ILL) OCLC; (OPAC) SirsiDynix; (Serials) SirsiDynix
Database Vendor: Gale Cengage Learning
Wireless access
Partic in Southern California Library Cooperative
Friends of the Library Group
Branches: 2
NIETO BRANCH LIBRARY STATION, 9255 Pioneer Blvd, 90670. Tel: 562-692-0261. E-mail: library@santafesprings.org. Web Site: www.santafesprings.org/libindex.htm. *Dir,* Monica Penninger
Library Holdings: Bk Vols 500; Per Subs 15
BETTY WILSON CENTER LIBRARY STATION, 11641 Florence Ave, 90670. Tel: 562-929-7431. E-mail: library@santafesprings.org. Web Site: www.santafesprings.org/libindex.htm. *Dir,* Monica Penninger
Library Holdings: Bk Vols 300

SANTA MARIA

J ALLAN HANCOCK COLLEGE*, Library & Learning Resources, 800 S College Dr, 93454. SAN 301-584X. Tel: 805-922-6966, Ext 3224. Interlibrary Loan Service Tel: 805-922-6966, Ext 3242. Reference Tel: 805-922-6966, Ext 3322. Administration Tel: 805-922-6966, Ext 3215. FAX: 805-922-3763. E-mail: library@hancockcollege.edu. Web Site: www.hancockcollege.edu. *Dir,* Nancy Meddings; Tel: 805-922-6966, Ext 3475, E-mail: nmeddings@hancockcollege.edu; *Librn,* Kathy Headtke; Tel: 805-922-6966, Ext 5474, Fax: 805-735-1554, E-mail: kheadtke@hancockcollege.edu; *Librn,* Leslie Mosson; Tel: 805-922-6966, Ext 3758, E-mail: lmosson@hancockcollege.edu; *Acq,* Mildred Carpenter; Tel: 805-922-6966, Ext 3637, E-mail: mcarpenter@hancockcollege.edu; *Media Serv,* Anna Rice; E-mail: arice@hancockcollege.edu; *Media Serv,* Geraldine Valdiviezo; E-mail: gvaldiviezo@hancockcollege.edu; Staff 3 (MLS 3)
Founded 1920. Enrl 10,000; Fac 141; Highest Degree: Associate
Library Holdings: Bk Titles 50,000; Bk Vols 70,000; Per Subs 334
Special Collections: Theatre
Automation Activity & Vendor Info: (Cataloging) Ex Libris Group; (Circulation) Ex Libris Group; (OPAC) Ex Libris Group
Wireless access
Partic in Gold Coast Library Network
Friends of the Library Group

GL SANTA BARBARA COUNTY LAW LIBRARY, Santa Maria Branch, 312 E Cook St, 93454. SAN 301-5858. Tel: 805-346-7548. FAX: 805-346-7692. E-mail: info@countylawlibrary.org. Web Site: www.countylawlibrary.org. *Dir,* Ray MacGregor; Staff 8 (Non-MLS 8)
Jul 2008-Jun 2009 Income $483,218. Mats Exp $445,307. Sal $171,384
Library Holdings: Bk Titles 48,963
Subject Interests: Fed law, State law
Database Vendor: LexisNexis, Westlaw

Wireless access
Open Mon-Fri 8-12 & 1-4:30
Restriction: Access at librarian's discretion, Circ limited

P SANTA MARIA PUBLIC LIBRARY*, 421 S McClelland St, 93454-5116. SAN 335-0134. Tel: 805-925-0994. FAX: 805-922-2330. E-mail: libraryreference@ci.santa-maria.ca.us. Web Site: www.ci.santa-maria.ca.us/210.shtml. *City Librn,* Mary Housel; E-mail: mhousel@ci.santa-maria.ca.us; Staff 11 (MLS 7, Non-MLS 4)
Founded 1909. Pop 143,379; Circ 479,960
Jul 2011-Jun 2012 Income (Main Library and Branch(s)) $2,476,674, State $3,743, City $2,250,302, Other $222,629. Mats Exp $162,467, Books $111,343, Per/Ser (Incl. Access Fees) $17,232, AV Mat $25,462, Electronic Ref Mat (Incl. Access Fees) $8,430
Library Holdings: AV Mats 31,819; e-books 6,085; Bk Vols 196,562; Per Subs 398
Special Collections: State Document Depository
Subject Interests: Careers, Genealogy, Local hist
Automation Activity & Vendor Info: (Acquisitions) Innovative Interfaces, Inc; (Cataloging) Innovative Interfaces, Inc; (Circulation) Innovative Interfaces, Inc; (ILL) Innovative Interfaces, Inc; (OPAC) Innovative Interfaces, Inc
Database Vendor: Gale Cengage Learning, Overdrive, Inc, ProQuest, ReferenceUSA
Wireless access
Mem of Black Gold Cooperative Library System
Partic in Gold Coast Library Network
Open Mon-Wed Noon-8, Thurs-Sat 10-6
Friends of the Library Group
Branches: 3
CUYAMA BRANCH, 4689 Hwy 166, Cuyama, 93254, SAN 335-0169. Tel: 661-766-2490.
Founded 1970. Pop 1,328; Circ 3,046
Library Holdings: Bk Vols 8,622
Open Mon 2-6, Wed 3-7, Fri 3-6
GUADALUPE BRANCH, 4719 W Main St, Unit D, Guadalupe, 93434, SAN 335-0193. Tel: 805-343-1405.
Founded 1988. Pop 7,132; Circ 12,704
Library Holdings: Bk Vols 12,595
Database Vendor: Gale Cengage Learning, Innovative Interfaces, Inc
Mem of Black Gold Cooperative Library System
Open Mon-Fri 12:30-6, Sat 11-3:30
Friends of the Library Group
ORCUTT BRANCH, 175 S Broadway, Orcutt, 93455, SAN 335-0258. Tel: 805-937-6483.
Founded 1980. Pop 34,642; Circ 69,095
Library Holdings: Bk Vols 24,981
Open Mon-Thurs 11-6, Sat 10-2
Friends of the Library Group

SANTA MONICA

L BRYAN CAVE LLP*, Law Library, 120 Broadway, Ste 300, 90401. SAN 327-6287. Tel: 310-576-2100. FAX: 310-576-2200. *Mgr, Libr Serv,* Karen Lasnick; E-mail: klasnick@bryancave.com; *Res Librn,* Karol Howard; E-mail: karol.howard@bryancave.com
Library Holdings: Bk Vols 60,000
Subject Interests: Corporate law, Intellectual property, Intl trade, Labor, Litigation, Real estate, Securities law
Database Vendor: LexisNexis, Westlaw
Restriction: Private libr

S RAND CORPORATION LIBRARY*, 1776 Main St, M1LIB, 90407. SAN 301-5912. Tel: 310-393-0411, Ext 7788. FAX: 310-451-7029. E-mail: library@rand.org. Web Site: www.rand.org. *Dir,* Lucy S Wegner; Tel: 310-393-0411, Ext 6940, E-mail: lwegner@rand.org; *Assoc Dir,* Susan Scheiberg; E-mail: susanls@rand.org; *Head, Metadata & Taxonomy,* Lori Emadi; E-mail: emadi@rand.org; *Head, Ref,* Roberta Shanman; E-mail: roberta@rand.org; *Br Mgr,* Gail Kouril; Tel: 703-413-1100, E-mail: gkouril@rand.org; Staff 22 (MLS 10, Non-MLS 12)
Founded 1948
Special Collections: RAND Corporate Archives; RAND Publications Archive
Subject Interests: Behav sci, Civil justice, Criminal justice, Econ, Educ, Environment, Intl relations, Labor, Mil sci, Pub safety, Sci tech, Terrorism, Transportation
Automation Activity & Vendor Info: (Cataloging) EOS International; (Circulation) EOS International; (Course Reserve) EOS International; (ILL) OCLC ILLiad; (OPAC) EOS International; (Serials) EOS International
Database Vendor: Altarama Systems & Services, Cambridge Scientific Abstracts, CountryWatch, EBSCOhost, Elsevier, Emerald, Gallup, HeinOnline, ISI Web of Knowledge, Jane's, JSTOR, LexisNexis, Marcive, Inc, OCLC FirstSearch, OCLC WorldShare Interlibrary Loan, OVID Technologies, ProQuest, PubMed, Sage, ScienceDirect, SerialsSolutions, SirsiDynix, Springshare, LLC, TDNet, Thomson - Web of Science
Wireless access
Function: Bus archives
Partic in OCLC Online Computer Library Center, Inc; Statewide California Electronic Library Consortium (SCELC)
Restriction: Authorized scholars by appt, Employees only, In-house use for visitors, Internal use only, Not open to pub

J SANTA MONICA COLLEGE LIBRARY*, 1900 Pico Blvd, 90405-1628. SAN 301-5939. Tel: 310-434-4334, 310-434-4692. Reference Tel: 310-434-4254. FAX: 310-434-4387. Web Site: library.smc.edu. *Dean,* Mona Martin; *Syst Librn,* Steve Hunt; *Bibliog Instr,* Carol Womack; *Ref,* Brenda Antrim; *Ref,* Anne Powers; *Ref Serv,* Eleanor Singleton; *Tech Serv,* Patricia Burson; Staff 7 (MLS 7)
Founded 1929. Fac 300
Library Holdings: Bk Titles 98,000; Bk Vols 105,000; Per Subs 475
Partic in OCLC Online Computer Library Center, Inc
Open Mon-Thurs 8am-9:45pm, Fri 8-3:45, Sat 11-4:45

P SANTA MONICA PUBLIC LIBRARY, 601 Santa Monica Blvd, 90401. SAN 335-0282. Tel: 310-458-8600. Circulation Tel: 310-458-8614. Reference Tel: 310-434-2608. Administration Tel: 310-458-8606. FAX: 310-394-8951. Reference FAX: 310-458-6980. TDD: 310-395-8499. Web Site: www.smpl.org. *City Librn,* Maria Taesil Hudson Carpenter; Tel: 310-458-8611, E-mail: maria.carpenter@smgov.net; *Asst City Librn,* Claudia Fishler; Tel: 310-458-8607, E-mail: claudia.fishler@smgov.net; *Principal Librn, Info Mgt,* Diane Bednarski; Tel: 310-458-8625, E-mail: diane.bednarski@smgov.net; *Principal Librn, Pub & Br Serv,* Susan Annett; Tel: 310-458-8640, E-mail: susan.annett@smgov.net; *Principal Librn, Ref,* Wright Rix; Tel: 310-458-8271, E-mail: wright.rix@smgov.net; Staff 41 (MLS 39, Non-MLS 2)
Founded 1890. Pop 92,185; Circ 1,757,971
Jul 2012-Jun 2013 Income (Main Library and Branch(s)) $11,966,621, City $11,451,906, Federal $19,000, Locally Generated Income $488,054, Other $7,661. Mats Exp $1,101,000, Books $558,420, Per/Ser (Incl. Access Fees) $104,600, AV Mat $276,240, Electronic Ref Mat (Incl. Access Fees) $155,740, Presv $6,000. Sal $6,483,619
Library Holdings: AV Mats 73,000; e-books 4,485; Electronic Media & Resources 29; Bk Titles 279,000; Bk Vols 348,000; Per Subs 774
Special Collections: Santa Monica History & Biography Coll, card file & photog
Automation Activity & Vendor Info: (Acquisitions) Innovative Interfaces, Inc; (Cataloging) Innovative Interfaces, Inc; (Circulation) Innovative Interfaces, Inc; (ILL) OCLC WorldShare Interlibrary Loan; (OPAC) BiblioCommons; (Serials) Innovative Interfaces, Inc
Database Vendor: EBSCOhost, Facts on File, Foundation Center, Gale Cengage Learning, McGraw-Hill, OCLC FirstSearch, OCLC WorldShare Interlibrary Loan, Overdrive, Inc, Oxford Online, ProQuest, ReferenceUSA, World Book Online
Wireless access
Function: 24/7 Online cat, Adult bk club, Audiobks via web, Bilingual assistance for Spanish patrons, Bk club(s), Bks on CD, Children's prog, Computer training, Computers for patron use, Copy machines, e-mail & chat, Electronic databases & coll, Free DVD rentals, Handicapped accessible, Homebound delivery serv, ILL available, Large print keyboards, Magazines, Mango lang, Microfiche/film & reading machines, Music CDs, Online cat, Online searches, OverDrive digital audio bks, Photocopying/Printing, Prog for adults, Prog for children & young adult, Pub access computers, Ref serv available, Senior computer classes, Spanish lang bks, Story hour, Study rm, Summer reading prog, Teen prog, Telephone ref, Wheelchair accessible
Partic in Southern California Library Cooperative
Special Services for the Deaf - Assisted listening device
Special Services for the Blind - Magnifiers
Open Mon-Thurs 10-9, Fri & Sat 10-5:30, Sun 1-5
Restriction: Non-resident fee
Friends of the Library Group
Branches: 4
FAIRVIEW, 2101 Ocean Park Blvd, 90405-5013, SAN 335-0312. Tel: 310-458-8681. FAX: 310-450-5749. *Br Mgr,* Erica Cuyugan
Library Holdings: Bk Vols 54,916
Open Mon-Thurs Noon-9, Fri Noon-5:30, Sat 10-5:30
Friends of the Library Group
MONTANA AVENUE, 1704 Montana Ave, 90403-1908, SAN 335-0347. Tel: 310-458-8682. FAX: 310-829-6391. *Br Mgr,* Shana Sojoyner; Staff 2 (MLS 2)
Library Holdings: Bk Vols 46,870
Open Mon-Thurs Noon-9, Fri Noon-5:30, Sat 10-5:30
Friends of the Library Group
OCEAN PARK, 2601 Main St, 90405-4001, SAN 335-0371. Tel: 310-458-8683. FAX: 310-399-6739. *Br Mgr,* Karen Reitz; Staff 2 (MLS 2)
Library Holdings: Bk Vols 33,237
Open Mon-Thurs Noon-9, Fri Noon-5:30, Sat 10-5:30
Friends of the Library Group

PICO BRANCH LIBRARY, 2201 Pico Blvd, 90405. Tel: 310-458-8684. FAX: 424-280-7830. *Br Mgr,* Cecilia Tovar
Library Holdings: Bk Titles 27,140
Open Mon-Thurs 12-9, Fri 12-5:30, Sat 10-5:30

M SHACKNOVE - SAINT JOHN'S MEDICAL STAFF LIBRARY*, 2200 Santa Monica Blvd, 90404. SAN 301-5920. Tel: 310-582-7141. FAX: 310-582-7353. *Librn,* Gina Worthington; E-mail: worthingtong@jwci.org; Staff 1 (Non-MLS 1)
Founded 1952
Library Holdings: Bk Vols 300; Per Subs 200
Subject Interests: Allied health, Med, Nursing
Restriction: Staff use only

SANTA PAULA

P BLANCHARD-SANTA PAULA PUBLIC LIBRARY DISTRICT*, Blanchard Community Library, 119 N Eighth St, 93060-2709. SAN 301-5963. Tel: 805-525-3615. Administration Tel: 805-525-2394. FAX: 805-933-2324. Web Site: www.rain.org/~stapaula. *District Librn,* Daniel O Robles; E-mail: drobles@blackgold.org; *Adult Ref Librn, Adult Serv,* George Buddy Flick; E-mail: gbflick@yahoo.com; *ILL,* Sue Leonard; *Ch Serv, YA Serv,* Ilene Gavenman; E-mail: igavenman@blackgold.org; *Literacy Serv,* Kathryn Bornhauser; Tel: 805-525-2384, E-mail: flairlit@hotmail.com; *Tech Serv,* Andrea Robles; E-mail: adr_51@hotmail.com. Subject Specialists: *Literacy,* Kathryn Bornhauser; Staff 3 (MLS 2, Non-MLS 1)
Founded 1909. Pop 34,000; Circ 79,000
Jul 2009-Jun 2010 Income $749,527, State $38,655, Provincial $39,640, County $639,894, Locally Generated Income $15,211, Other $16,127. Mats Exp $19,894, Books $4,500, Per/Ser (Incl. Access Fees) $2,785, AV Mat $174, Electronic Ref Mat (Incl. Access Fees) $12,435. Sal $483,533 (Prof $124,548)
Library Holdings: AV Mats 1,873; Bks on Deafness & Sign Lang 12; CDs 520; DVDs 500; Large Print Bks 1,276; Music Scores 37; Bk Vols 88,000; Per Subs 75; Videos 1,400
Special Collections: Spanish/Bilingual (Preciado Coll)
Subject Interests: Local authors, Local hist
Automation Activity & Vendor Info: (Acquisitions) Innovative Interfaces, Inc; (Cataloging) Innovative Interfaces, Inc; (Circulation) Innovative Interfaces, Inc; (ILL) Innovative Interfaces, Inc; (OPAC) Innovative Interfaces, Inc; (Serials) Innovative Interfaces, Inc
Database Vendor: Overdrive, Inc
Wireless access
Function: Accelerated reader prog, Adult literacy prog, Art exhibits, Audiobks via web, BA reader (adult literacy), Bilingual assistance for Spanish patrons, Bks on cassette, Bks on CD, Children's prog, Computer training, Computers for patron use, Copy machines, Digital talking bks, Electronic databases & coll, Exhibits, Family literacy, Free DVD rentals, Handicapped accessible, Holiday prog, Homebound delivery serv, Homework prog, ILL available, Literacy & newcomer serv, Magnifiers for reading, Mail & tel request accepted, Online cat, Online ref, Online searches, OverDrive digital audio bks, Photocopying/Printing, Prof lending libr, Prog for adults, Prog for children & young adult, Ref & res, Ref serv available, Ref serv in person, Story hour, Summer reading prog, Tax forms, Teen prog, Telephone ref, VHS videos, Video lending libr, Web-catalog, Wheelchair accessible
Mem of Black Gold Cooperative Library System
Open Mon, Tues & Thurs 12-8, Wed 10-6, Sat 10-2
Restriction: Open to pub for ref & circ; with some limitations, Open to students, Pub ref by request, Pub use on premises
Friends of the Library Group

C THOMAS AQUINAS COLLEGE*, Saint Bernardine Library, 10000 N Ojai Rd, 93060-9980. SAN 321-4621. Tel: 805-525-4417. Circulation Tel: 805-525-4419, Ext 5948. Toll Free Tel: 800-634-9797. FAX: 805-525-9342. Web Site: www.thomasaquinas.edu. *Librn,* V A Jatulis; E-mail: vjatulis@thomasaquinas.edu; Staff 1 (MLS 1)
Founded 1971. Enrl 375; Fac 50; Highest Degree: Bachelor
Library Holdings: AV Mats 5,540; Bk Vols 69,000; Per Subs 69; Talking Bks 400
Subject Interests: Humanities, Philos, Theol
Automation Activity & Vendor Info: (Serials) EBSCO Online
Wireless access
Open Mon-Thurs 8am-10:45pm, Fri 8-7, Sat 1-5, Sun 1-10:45
Restriction: Open to fac, students & qualified researchers

SANTA ROSA

P MOUNTAIN-VALLEY LIBRARY SYSTEM*, 55 E St, 95404-4728. SAN 301-2808. Tel: 707-544-0142. Toll Free Tel: 800-479-6733. FAX: 707-544-8411. E-mail: nbclsadm@sonic.net. Web Site: www.mvls.org. *Exec Dir,* Linda Crowe; E-mail: crowe@plsinfo.org; *Asst Dir,* Patty Hector; Staff 2 (MLS 1.5, Non-MLS 0.5)
Founded 1969. Pop 2,200,000
Member Libraries: Colusa County Free Library; Lincoln Public Library; Sacramento Public Library; Sutter County Free Library; Yuba County Library

J SANTA ROSA JUNIOR COLLEGE*, Frank P Doyle Library, 1501 Mendocino Ave, 95401. SAN 301-6005. Tel: 707-527-4261 (Media Servs), 707-527-4391. Circulation Tel: 707-527-4550. Interlibrary Loan Service Tel: 707-527-4554. Reference Tel: 707-527-4548. FAX: 707-527-4545. Interlibrary Loan Service FAX: 707-521-6070. Reference FAX: 707-521-6093. Web Site: www.santarosa.edu/library. *Dean III, Learning Res & Educ Tech,* Dr W Cherry Li-Bugg; Tel: 707-527-4392, E-mail: wli-bugg@santarosa.edu; *Dept Chair, Librn,* Nancy Persons; Tel: 707-521-6902, E-mail: npersons@santarosa.edu; *Librn,* Karen Petersen; Tel: 707-778-3972, E-mail: kpetersen@santarosa.edu; *Librn,* Phyllis Usina; Tel: 707-778-4773, E-mail: pusina@santarosa.edu; *Electronic Serv Librn,* Alicia Virtue; Tel: 707-527-4773, E-mail: avirtue@santarosa.edu; *Ref Librn,* Will Baty; Tel: 707-524-1664, E-mail: wbaty@santarosa.edu; *Ref Librn,* Micca Gray; *Ref Librn,* Molly Matheson; Tel: 707-778-4162, E-mail: mmatheson@santarosa.edu; *Ref Librn,* Andrea Proehl; Tel: 707-527-4904, E-mail: aproehl@santarosa.edu; *Tech Serv Librn,* Paula Burks; *Mgr, Libr Media Serv,* Russ Bowden; Staff 10 (MLS 10)
Founded 1918
Library Holdings: Bk Vols 129,197; Per Subs 356
Subject Interests: Computer sci, Dentistry, Hort, Nutrition, Patents
Automation Activity & Vendor Info: (Acquisitions) Ex Libris Group; (Cataloging) Ex Libris Group; (Circulation) Ex Libris Group; (Course Reserve) Ex Libris Group; (ILL) Ex Libris Group; (Media Booking) Ex Libris Group; (OPAC) Ex Libris Group; (Serials) Ex Libris Group
Database Vendor: ARTstor, Baker & Taylor, FileMaker, Gale Cengage Learning, InfoWorks Technology, ProQuest, SerialsSolutions, Wilson - Wilson Web
Wireless access
Mem of NorthNet Library System
Partic in Coop Libr Agency for Syst & Servs; OCLC Online Computer Library Center, Inc
Open Mon-Thurs 7:45am-10pm, Fri 7:45-5, Sat 12-5
Restriction: Borrowing privileges limited to fac & registered students
Friends of the Library Group

S SANTA ROSA PRESS DEMOCRAT*, News Research Center, 427 Mendocino Ave, 95401-6385. (Mail add: PO Box 910, 95402-0910), SAN 325-0512. Tel: 707-526-8520. FAX: 707-521-5330. *Res,* Janet Balicki; Staff 5 (MLS 2, Non-MLS 3)
Founded 1950
Special Collections: Glossy Photographs (In-house Photography Coll); Newspaper Clippings (Subject & Biographical Info Coll); Rare Local Photographs
Subject Interests: Local hist

GL SONOMA COUNTY LAW LIBRARY*, Hall of Justice, Rm 213-J, 600 Administration Dr, 95403-2879. SAN 301-6013. Tel: 707-565-2668. FAX: 707-565-1126. Web Site: www.sonomacountylawlibrary.org. *Dir,* Kim Tucker; E-mail: ktucker@sonoma-county.org
Founded 1891
Library Holdings: Bk Vols 29,000
Publications: List of Holdings; Union List of Legal Periodicals in Sonoma County
Open Mon-Thurs 8-5, Fri 8-4

P SONOMA COUNTY LIBRARY*, 211 E St, 95404. SAN 335-0401. Tel: 707-545-0831. FAX: 707-575-0437. Administration FAX: 707-525-9563. TDD: 707-575-1206. Web Site: www.sonomalibrary.org. *Interim Co-Dir, Mat Mgt Mgr,* Jaime Anderson; E-mail: janderson@sonoma.lib.ca.us; *Coll Mgr, Interim Co-Dir,* David Dodd; *Dir,* Position Currently Open; *Human Res Mgr,* Patrick Preston; *Mrg, Admin Serv,* Elissa Alfano; E-mail: ealfano@sonoma.lib.ca.us; *Pub Serv Mgr,* Kiyo Okazaki; E-mail: kiyo@sonoma.lib.ca.us; Staff 128.32 (MLS 54.5, Non-MLS 73.82)
Founded 1965. Pop 481,785; Circ 263,554
Jul 2010-Jun 2011 Income (Main Library and Branch(s)) $15,329,137, State $433,092, Federal $16,813, Locally Generated Income $14,083,870, Other $795,362. Mats Exp $15,683,124, Books $546,468, Electronic Ref Mat (Incl. Access Fees) $199,456. Sal $7,832,574
Library Holdings: AV Mats 21,347; Bk Vols 721,629; Per Subs 1,758
Special Collections: Sonoma County History; Sonoma County Wine Library. State Document Depository; US Document Depository
Automation Activity & Vendor Info: (Acquisitions) Horizon; (Cataloging) Horizon; (Circulation) Horizon; (ILL) SirsiDynix; (OPAC) SirsiDynix; (Serials) Horizon
Database Vendor: Dialog, EBSCOhost, Gale Cengage Learning, OCLC FirstSearch
Wireless access
Function: Adult bk club, Adult literacy prog, After school storytime, Art exhibits, Audiobks via web, Children's prog, Copy machines, E-Reserves,

Family literacy, ILL available, Photocopying/Printing, Prog for adults, Prog for children & young adult, Summer reading prog, Tax forms
Mem of NorthNet Library System
Special Services for the Deaf - TDD equip
Open Tues, Thurs, Fri 10-6, Wed 10-8, Sat 10-4, Sun 2-6
Friends of the Library Group
Branches: 13
CENTRAL LIBRARY, 211 E St, 95404, SAN 376-8988. Tel: 707-545-0831. FAX: 707-575-0437. *Br Mgr,* Tracy Gray; Tel: 707-545-0831, Ext 1527, E-mail: tgray@sonoma.lib.ca.us
Library Holdings: Bk Vols 173,919
Open Tues, Thurs, & Fri 10-6, Wed 10-8, Sat 10-4, Sun 2-6
Friends of the Library Group
CLOVERDALE REGIONAL, 401 N Cloverdale Blvd, Cloverdale, 95425, SAN 376-8996. Tel: 707-894-5271. FAX: 707-894-1861. *Br Mgr,* Lucinda Wilson; E-mail: lwilson@sonoma.lib.ca.us; Staff 5 (MLS 2, Non-MLS 3)
Library Holdings: Bk Titles 21,603
Open Tues, Thurs & Fri 10-6, Wed 10-8, Sat 10-4
Friends of the Library Group
FORESTVILLE BRANCH, 7050 Covey Rd, Forestville, 95436, SAN 376-9097. Tel: 707-887-7654. FAX: 707-887-7654. *Br Mgr,* Bonnie Smith; E-mail: bsmith@sonoma.lib.ca.us; Staff 1 (Non-MLS 1)
Library Holdings: Bk Titles 4,152
Open Tues-Fri 3-6:30
Friends of the Library Group
GUERNEVILLE REGIONAL, 14107 Armstrong Woods Rd, Guerneville, 95446, SAN 376-9003. Tel: 707-869-9004. FAX: 707-869-1267. *Mgr,* Mairi Barsky
Library Holdings: Bk Titles 23,063
Open Tues, Thurs & Fri 10-6, Wed 10-8, Sat 10-4
Friends of the Library Group
HEALDSBURG REGIONAL, 139 Piper St, Healdsburg, 95448, SAN 376-9011. Tel: 707-433-3772. Circulation Tel: 707-433-3772, Ext 10. Reference Tel: 707-433-3772, Ext 15. FAX: 707-433-7946. *Br Mgr,* Bo Simons; E-mail: bsimons@sonoma.lib.ca.us; Staff 7 (MLS 4, Non-MLS 3)
Library Holdings: Bk Titles 44,377
Special Collections: Sonoma County Wine Library
Open Tues, Thurs & Fri 10-6, Wed 10-8, Sat 10-4
Friends of the Library Group
OCCIDENTAL BRANCH, 73 Main St, Occidental, 95465, SAN 376-9100. Tel: 707-874-3080. *Br Mgr,* Nancy Sampson
Library Holdings: Bk Titles 2,394
Open Tues, Wed & Sat 12-5
Friends of the Library Group
PETALUMA REGIONAL, 100 Fairgrounds Dr, Petaluma, 94952, SAN 376-902X. Tel: 707-763-9801. FAX: 707-763-0288. E-mail: petaluma@sonoma.lib.ca.us. *Br Mgr,* Joe Cochrane
Library Holdings: Bk Titles 87,809
Special Collections: Petaluma History Room
Open Tues, Thurs & Fri 10-6, Wed 10-8, Sat 10-4
Friends of the Library Group
ROHNERT PARK-COTATI REGIONAL LIBRARY, 6250 Lynne Conde Way, Rohnert Park, 94928, SAN 376-9038. Tel: 707-584-9121. FAX: 707-584-8561. Web Site: sonomalibrary.org/locations/rohnert-park-cotati-regional-library. *Br Mgr,* Nancy Lynn Kleban; E-mail: nkleban@sonoma.lib.ca.us
Library Holdings: Bk Titles 80,595
Open Tues, Thurs & Fri 10-6, Wed 10-8, Sat 10-4
Friends of the Library Group
SANTA ROSA NORTHWEST REGIONAL, 150 Coddingtown Ctr, 95401, SAN 376-9046. Tel: 707-546-2265. FAX: 707-546-2510. *Mgr,* Nixon Kathy; E-mail: knixon@sonoma.lib.ca.us
Library Holdings: Bk Titles 36,918
Open Tues, Thurs & Fri 10-6, Wed 10-8, Sat 10-4
Friends of the Library Group
SANTA ROSA RINCON VALLEY REGIONAL, 6959 Montecito Blvd, 95409, SAN 376-9054. Tel: 707-537-0162. FAX: 707-537-0174. *Mgr,* Jennifer Duran; E-mail: jduran@sonoma.lib.ca.us
Library Holdings: Bk Titles 48,229
Open Tues, Thurs & Fri 10-6, Wed 10-8, Sat 10-4
Friends of the Library Group
SEBASTOPOL REGIONAL, 7140 Bodega Ave, Sebastopol, 95472, SAN 376-9062. Tel: 707-823-7691. FAX: 707-823-7172. *Br Mgr,* Matthew Rose; E-mail: mrose@sonoma.lib.ca.us; Staff 7 (MLS 3, Non-MLS 4)
Library Holdings: Bk Titles 49,346
Special Collections: Municipal Document Depository
Database Vendor: EBSCOhost, Gale Cengage Learning
Open Tues, Thurs & Fri 10-6, Wed 10-8, Sat 10-4
Friends of the Library Group
SONOMA VALLEY REGIONAL, 755 W Napa St, Sonoma, 95476, SAN 376-9070. Tel: 707-996-5217. FAX: 707-996-5918. *Br Mgr,* Lisa Musgrove; E-mail: lmusgrove@sonoma.lib.ca.us; Staff 3 (MLS 3)
Library Holdings: Bk Titles 39,091
Open Tues, Thurs & Fri 10-6, Wed 10-8, Sat 10-4
Friends of the Library Group
WINDSOR REGIONAL, 9291 Old Redwood Hwy, No 100, Windsor, 95492, SAN 376-9089. Tel: 707-838-1020. FAX: 707-838-8329. *Mgr,* Bill Coolidge; E-mail: bcoolidge@sonoma.lib.ca.us; Staff 6 (MLS 2, Non-MLS 4)
Founded 1996
Library Holdings: Bk Titles 33,374
Open Tues, Thurs & Fri 10-6, Wed 10-8, Sat 10-4
Friends of the Library Group

M SUTTER MEDICAL CENTER OF SANTA ROSA*, Medical Library, 3325 Chanate Rd, 95404-1794. SAN 301-5971. Tel: 707-576-4675. FAX: 707-576-4321. *Librn,* Ronald Schultz
Jan 2005-Dec 2005. Mats Exp $49,843, Books $15,000, Per/Ser (Incl. Access Fees) $30,000. Sal $80,340
Library Holdings: Bk Titles 3,000; Per Subs 75
Subject Interests: Hist of med
Partic in N Bay Health Sci Libr Consortium; Northern California & Nevada Medical Library Group (NCNMLG); Pacific SW Regional Libr Syst
Open Mon-Fri 7-3:30

SANTA YNEZ

S SANTA YNEZ VALLEY HISTORICAL SOCIETY*, Ellen Gleason Library, 3596 Sagunto St, 93460. (Mail add: PO Box 181, 93460), SAN 328-3364. Tel: 805-688-7889. FAX: 805-688-1109. E-mail: syvm@verizon.net. Web Site: www.santaynezmuseum.org. *Exec Dir,* Chris Bashforth; *Curator,* John Crockett
Library Holdings: Bk Titles 1,500
Subject Interests: Calif, Chumash Indian, Local hist, Santa Ynez Valley
Function: Res libr
Open Fri 2-4

SARATOGA

J WEST VALLEY COMMUNITY COLLEGE LIBRARY*, 14000 Fruitvale Ave, 95070-5698. SAN 301-6021. Tel: 408-741-2021. Interlibrary Loan Service Tel: 408-741-2028. Reference Tel: 408-741-2029. FAX: 408-741-2134. Web Site: www.westvalley.edu/library/. *Dean of Instruction,* Celine Pinet; Tel: 408-741-2140, E-mail: celine_pinet@westvalley.edu; *Acq Librn,* Yanghee Kim; Tel: 408-741-2484, E-mail: yanghee_kim@westvalley.edu; *Automation Librn, Web Coordr,* Bill Proudfoot; Tel: 408-741-2559, E-mail: bill_proudfoot@westvalley.edu; *Tech Serv Librn,* Betsy Sandford; Tel: 408-741-2478, E-mail: betsy_sandford@westvalley.edu; *Info Literacy,* Maryanne Mills; Tel: 408-741-4661, E-mail: maryanne_mills@westvalley.edu; *Instruction & Outreach,* Rachel Sandoval; Tel: 408-741-2479, E-mail: rachel_sandoval@westvalley.edu; Staff 15 (MLS 6, Non-MLS 9)
Founded 1964. Enrl 10,505; Fac 443; Highest Degree: Associate
Library Holdings: AV Mats 18,268; CDs 200; e-books 400; Bk Titles 81,500; Bk Vols 101,000; Per Subs 164; Talking Bks 2,200
Automation Activity & Vendor Info: (Acquisitions) Innovative Interfaces, Inc; (Cataloging) Innovative Interfaces, Inc; (Circulation) Innovative Interfaces, Inc; (Course Reserve) Innovative Interfaces, Inc; (ILL) Innovative Interfaces, Inc; (OPAC) Innovative Interfaces, Inc
Database Vendor: CountryWatch, CQ Press, Facts on File, ProQuest, Wilson - Wilson Web
Wireless access
Partic in OCLC Online Computer Library Center, Inc
Special Services for the Deaf - Bks on deafness & sign lang; Closed caption videos; Videos & decoder
Special Services for the Blind - Aids for in-house use; Audio mat; Bks on cassette; Bks on CD; Cassette playback machines; Closed circuit TV; Closed circuit TV magnifier; Computer with voice synthesizer for visually impaired persons; Low vision equip; Magnifiers; PC for handicapped; Screen enlargement software for people with visual disabilities; Screen reader software; Talking bks; ZoomText magnification & reading software
Open Mon-Thurs 8-7:30, Fri 8-Noon, Sat Noon-4

SAUSALITO

P SAUSALITO PUBLIC LIBRARY*, 420 Litho St, 94965-1933. SAN 301-603X. Tel: 415-289-4121. Administration Tel: 415-289-4123. FAX: 415-331-7943. Web Site: www.ci.sausalito.ca.us/library. *Coll Develop, Librn,* Mary Richardson; *Librn,* Augie Webb; Staff 3 (MLS 3)
Founded 1906. Pop 7,325; Circ 89,000
Jul 2006-Jun 2007 Income $593,233. Mats Exp $80,000, Books $64,000, Per/Ser (Incl. Access Fees) $10,000, Micro $400, AV Mat $4,400, Presv $1,200. Sal $461,783
Library Holdings: CDs 950; DVDs 611; Bk Vols 61,000; Per Subs 185
Subject Interests: Boating, Boats, Local hist
Automation Activity & Vendor Info: (Acquisitions) Innovative Interfaces, Inc; (Cataloging) Brodart; (Circulation) Innovative Interfaces, Inc; (OPAC) Innovative Interfaces, Inc

Database Vendor: Innovative Interfaces, Inc
Mem of NorthNet Library System
Partic in Marin Automated Resources & Information Network (MARINet)
Open Mon-Thurs 10-9, Fri & Sat 10-5, Sun 12-5
Friends of the Library Group

SEASIDE

C CALIFORNIA STATE UNIVERSITY - MONTEREY BAY*, Tanimura & Antle Family Memorial Library, 100 Campus Ctr, 93955-8001. SAN 378-2530. Tel: 831-582-3733. Interlibrary Loan Service Tel: 831-582-3870. Reference Tel: 831-582-3872. FAX: 831-582-3875. E-mail: library_reference@csumb.edu. Web Site: library.csumb.edu. *Dir,* Bill Robnett; Tel: 831-582-4448, E-mail: brobnett@csumb.edu; *Ref & Instruction Librn,* Sarah Dahlen; Tel: 831-582-4432, E-mail: sdahlen@csumb.edu; *Ref & Instrul Tech Librn,* Jacqui Grallo; Tel: 831-582-3142, E-mail: jgrallo@csumb.edu; *Coordr of Ref Serv,* Janie B Silveria; Tel: 831-582-3727, E-mail: jsilveria@csumb.edu; *Coordr, Coll Develop,* Eddy Hogan; Tel: 831-582-3794, E-mail: ehogan@csumb.edu; *Coordr, Libr Instruction,* Pam Baker; Tel: 831-582-3887, E-mail: pbaker@csumb.edu; *Electronic Res Coordr,* Kathlene Hanson; Tel: 831-582-3883, E-mail: khanson@csumb.edu; *Tech Coordr,* Steve Watkins; Tel: 831-582-3793, E-mail: swatkins@csumb.edu; Staff 15.18 (MLS 8.18, Non-MLS 7)
Founded 1995. Enrl 6,000; Fac 7; Highest Degree: Master
Jul 2011-Jun 2012 Income $1,400,594. Mats Exp $287,640, Books $104,567, Per/Ser (Incl. Access Fees) $50,727, AV Mat $4,866, Electronic Ref Mat (Incl. Access Fees) $113,279, Presv $14,201. Sal $1,027,432 (Prof $661,626)
Library Holdings: AV Mats 3,085; e-books 73,595; e-journals 50,386; Microforms 175; Bk Vols 87,595; Per Subs 50,542; Videos 2,828
Special Collections: Environmental Clean-up (Ford Ord Reuse Coll)
Automation Activity & Vendor Info: (Acquisitions) Ex Libris Group; (Cataloging) Ex Libris Group; (Circulation) Ex Libris Group; (Course Reserve) Ex Libris Group; (ILL) OCLC ILLiad; (OPAC) Ex Libris Group; (Serials) Ex Libris Group
Database Vendor: Agricola, Alexander Street Press, American Psychological Association (APA), Annual Reviews, Backstage Library Works, CountryWatch, EBSCOhost, Elsevier, Factiva.com, Gale Cengage Learning, JSTOR, LexisNexis, Marcive, Inc, Modern Language Association, Newsbank, OCLC FirstSearch, OCLC WorldShare Interlibrary Loan, OVID Technologies, Project MUSE, ProQuest, Safari Books Online, ScienceDirect, SerialsSolutions, Tech Logic, Wiley, Wiley InterScience, YBP Library Services
Wireless access
Function: Distance learning, Doc delivery serv, e-mail & chat, e-mail serv, Electronic databases & coll, Handicapped accessible, Learning ctr, Microfiche/film & reading machines, Online cat, Online info literacy tutorials on the web & in blackboard, Online ref, Telephone ref, Web-catalog, Wheelchair accessible
Partic in Monterey Bay Area Cooperative Library System
Open Mon-Thurs 8am-Midnight, Fri 8-5, Sat 10-5, Sun 2-Midnight

SEPULVEDA

GM VA GREATER LOS ANGELES HEALTH CARE CENTER SEPULVEDA CAMPUS*, Library Service (142D), Bldg 22, 16111 Plummer St, 91343. SAN 301-6072. Tel: 818-891-7711, Ext 9253. FAX: 818-895-9553. *Libr Tech,* Shirley Oles
Founded 1955
Library Holdings: Bk Vols 7,000
Open Mon-Fri 8-4:30

SIERRA MADRE

P SIERRA MADRE PUBLIC LIBRARY, 440 W Sierra Madre Blvd, 91024-2399. SAN 301-6102. Tel: 626-355-7186, 626-355-7187. E-mail: ref@cityofsierramadre.com. Web Site: www.cityofsierramadre.com/departments/library. *Dir,* Carolyn Thomas; Staff 6 (MLS 3, Non-MLS 3)
Founded 1887. Pop 10,850
Library Holdings: Bk Vols 59,500; Per Subs 99; Videos 1,612
Special Collections: Sierra Madre Historical Archives
Automation Activity & Vendor Info: (Acquisitions) Innovative Interfaces, Inc; (Cataloging) Innovative Interfaces, Inc; (Circulation) Innovative Interfaces, Inc; (ILL) OCLC WorldShare Interlibrary Loan; (OPAC) Innovative Interfaces, Inc
Database Vendor: Baker & Taylor, Bowker, Comprise Technologies Inc, EBSCOhost, Evanced Solutions, Inc, Gale Cengage Learning, infoUSA, Innovative Interfaces, Inc, OCLC, OCLC FirstSearch, OCLC WebJunction, OCLC WorldShare Interlibrary Loan, Overdrive, Inc, ProQuest
Wireless access
Function: 24/7 Online cat, Adult bk club, Archival coll, Audiobks via web, Bks on CD, Children's prog, Computers for patron use, Copy machines, Electronic databases & coll, Home delivery & serv to Sr ctr & nursing homes, Homebound delivery serv, ILL available, Magazines, Magnifiers for reading, Microfiche/film & reading machines, Music CDs, Online cat, OverDrive digital audio bks, Photocopying/Printing, Prog for adults, Prog for children & young adult, Pub access computers, Ref & res, Scanner, Story hour, Summer reading prog, Tax forms, Teen prog, Telephone ref
Partic in Southern California Library Cooperative
Special Services for the Blind - Bks on cassette; Bks on CD; Copier with enlargement capabilities; Extensive large print coll; Large print bks; Magnifiers
Open Mon & Wed 11-8, Thurs & Fri 12-6, Sat 10-6
Friends of the Library Group

SIGNAL HILL

P SIGNAL HILL PUBLIC LIBRARY, 1770 E Hill St, 90755. SAN 301-6110. Tel: 562-989-7323. Administration Tel: 562-989-7324. FAX: 562-989-7392. E-mail: Library2@cityofsignalhill.org. *Dir,* Charles Hughes; E-mail: chughes@cityofsignalhill.org; Staff 1 (Non-MLS 1)
Founded 1928. Pop 11,089; Circ 44,024
Jul 2005-Jun 2006 Income $300,218, State $4,300, City $289,918, Locally Generated Income $6,000. Mats Exp $43,956, Books $31,667, Per/Ser (Incl. Access Fees) $2,790, AV Mat $3,591, Electronic Ref Mat (Incl. Access Fees) $2,908, Presv $3,000. Sal $161,925 (Prof $69,000)
Library Holdings: AV Mats 1,093; DVDs 300; Large Print Bks 200; Bk Titles 24,052; Bk Vols 24,400; Per Subs 60; Talking Bks 121; Videos 400
Subject Interests: Local hist
Automation Activity & Vendor Info: (Cataloging) Follett Software; (Circulation) Follett Software; (OPAC) Follett Software
Database Vendor: Gale Cengage Learning
Wireless access
Partic in Califa; Southern California Library Cooperative
Open Mon, Tues & Thurs 12-8, Wed, Fri & Sat 10-5
Friends of the Library Group

SIMI VALLEY

S NATIONAL ARCHIVES & RECORDS ADMINISTRATION, Ronald Reagan Presidential Library & Museum, 40 Presidential Dr, 93065. SAN 373-0956. Tel: 805-577-4000. Toll Free Tel: 800-410-8354. FAX: 805-577-4074. E-mail: reagan.library@nara.gov. Web Site: www.reaganlibrary.gov. *Dep Dir,* Michael Duggan; Tel: 805-577-4016; Staff 9 (MLS 3, Non-MLS 6)
Founded 1991
Library Holdings: Bk Titles 2,000; Bk Vols 2,700; Per Subs 12
Special Collections: American Presidency, Ronald Reagan; Politics & Government, 1964-1989
Subject Interests: Am hist, Political hist of the US, Presidents (US)
Automation Activity & Vendor Info: (Cataloging) Inmagic, Inc.
Wireless access
Function: Archival coll
Restriction: Closed stack, Non-circulating, Not a lending libr, Secured area only open to authorized personnel
Friends of the Library Group

S SIMI VALLEY HISTORICAL SOCIETY & MUSEUM*, 137 Strathearn Pl, 93065-1605. SAN 370-4238. Tel: 805-526-6453. FAX: 805-526-6462. E-mail: simimuseum@sbcglobal.net. Web Site: www.simihistory.com. *City Historian, Dir,* Patricia Havens
Publications: Simi Valley, A Journey Through Time (Local historical information)
Open Tues-Fri 9-2
Restriction: Non-circulating

M SIMI VALLEY HOSPITAL & HEALTH CARES SERVICES*, Medical Library, 2975 N Sycamore Dr, 93065. SAN 320-1694. Tel: 805-955-6900. FAX: 805-955-6063. *Dir,* Vicki Vandertorn
Founded 1965
Library Holdings: Bk Titles 480
Subject Interests: Med
Function: Ref serv available
Restriction: Med staff only

SONORA

J COLUMBIA COLLEGE LIBRARY*, 11600 Columbia College Dr, 95370-8581. SAN 300-6794. Tel: 209-588-5119. FAX: 209-588-5121. Web Site: www.gocolumbia.edu/library. *Librn,* Wendy Griffiths-Bender; Tel: 209-588-5179; *Circ, Ref,* Nancy Brooks; Tel: 209-588-5248; *Tech Serv,* Shelley Muniz; Tel: 209-588-5238; Staff 1 (MLS 1)
Founded 1968. Enrl 3,656; Fac 168
Special Collections: History of the Mother Lode, ephemera, bk, maps, micro, per. Oral History
Subject Interests: Forestry
Publications: Mother Lode History (Bibliography)

Partic in 49-99 Cooperative Library System; Central Association of Libraries; OCLC Online Computer Library Center, Inc
Open Mon-Thurs 7:45am-8pm, Fri 7:45-4:30

P TUOLUMNE COUNTY FREE LIBRARY*, 480 Greenley Rd, 95370-5956. SAN 301-6145. Tel: 209-533-5507. FAX: 209-533-0936. E-mail: libref@co.tuolumne.ca.us. *County Librn, Tech Serv,* Margaret Durgin; E-mail: mdurgin@co.tuolumne.ca.us; *Literacy Serv, Outreach Serv, Youth Serv,* Lynn McCormick; *Admin Serv,* Anita Simpson; E-mail: asimpson@co.tuolumne.ca.us; Staff 8 (MLS 2, Non-MLS 6)
Founded 1917. Pop 55,400; Circ 185,949
Library Holdings: Bk Titles 71,000; Bk Vols 96,000; Per Subs 135
Automation Activity & Vendor Info: (Acquisitions) SirsiDynix; (Cataloging) SirsiDynix; (Circulation) SirsiDynix; (OPAC) SirsiDynix
Database Vendor: Newsbank, OCLC WorldShare Interlibrary Loan, ProQuest, SirsiDynix
Partic in 49-99 Cooperative Library System; OCLC Online Computer Library Center, Inc
Open Tues-Sat 10-6
Friends of the Library Group
Branches: 3
GROVELAND BRANCH, 18990 Hwy 120, Groveland, 95321. Tel: 209-962-6144. FAX: 209-962-5178. *Br Mgr,* Michalene Martin
Library Holdings: Large Print Bks 200; Bk Vols 7,000; Per Subs 50; Talking Bks 380; Videos 450
Open Tues-Thurs 1-6, Fri & Sat 10-2
Friends of the Library Group
TUOLUMNE CITY BRANCH, 18636 Main St, Tuolumne, 95379. (Mail add: PO Box 1077, Tuolumne, 95379-1077). Tel: 209-928-3612. *In Charge,* Trisha Davis
Library Holdings: Bk Vols 4,400
Open Tues-Thurs 2-6, Fri & Sat 10-2
TWAIN HARTE BRANCH, 18701 Tiffeni Rd, Ste 1F, Twain Harte, 95383. (Mail add: PO Box 666, Twain Harte, 95383-0666). Tel: 209-586-4501. *In Charge,* Sharyn Alomia
Library Holdings: Bk Vols 3,800; Per Subs 10
Open Tues-Thurs 1-5, Fri & Sat 10-2
Bookmobiles: 1. Bk titles 1,000

S TUOLUMNE COUNTY GENEALOGICAL SOCIETY LIBRARY*, 158 W Bradford Ave, 95370-4920. (Mail add: PO Box 3956, 95370-3956), SAN 322-6956. Tel: 209-532-1317. E-mail: tcgsonline@yahoo.com. Web Site: www.tcgsonline.org. *Libr Dir,* Lori East; *Asst Libr Dir,* Kristine Childress; *Asst Libr Dir,* Betty Sparagna
Founded 1979
Library Holdings: Bk Vols 1,200; Per Subs 10
Special Collections: Books & Periodicals for Most States; Records for Some Surrounding Counties; Tuolumne County, California Records: Cemetery, Census, Church, Family Histories, Obituaries, School, Vital Records, Voter Registers
Subject Interests: Local family hist
Function: Res libr
Publications: 1890 Great Register, Tuolumne Country (Index to educational materials); CH Burden Undertaking Co Records, 1890-1943 (Index to educational materials); Gold Digger Golden Roots of the Mother Lode (Newsletter); Gold Rush Tales; Index to the History of Tuolumne County (Index to educational materials); Index to the Miners' & Business Mens' Directory (Index to educational materials); Tuolumne County Marriages, 1850-1900 (Index to educational materials)
Open Tues & Thurs 10-4, Sat 10-3:30
Restriction: Pub use on premises, Restricted borrowing privileges

SOUTH EL MONTE

S AMERICAN SOCIETY OF MILITARY HISTORY MUSEUM*, Tankland Library, 1918 Rosemead Blvd, 91733. SAN 328-039X. Tel: 626-442-1776. FAX: 626-443-1776. E-mail: tankland@aol.com. Web Site: www.tankland.com. *Librn,* Stephanie Chavez; *Tech Serv Librn,* John Palmer; E-mail: writing2009@gmail.com; Staff 5 (MLS 2, Non-MLS 3)
Founded 1962
Library Holdings: Bk Titles 25,000
Special Collections: Tankland Coll
Subject Interests: Hist, Mil, Presv
Wireless access
Restriction: Non-circulating, Researchers by appt only, Restricted access

SOUTH LAKE TAHOE

J LAKE TAHOE COMMUNITY COLLEGE*, Library-Media Services, One College Dr, 96150. SAN 301-617X. Tel: 530-541-4660, Ext 232. FAX: 530-541-7852. Web Site: library.ltcc.edu. *Dir,* Lisa Foley; E-mail: foley@ltcc.edu; Staff 2 (MLS 2)
Founded 1976
Library Holdings: Bk Titles 43,000; Per Subs 25
Automation Activity & Vendor Info: (Circulation) OCLC; (OPAC) OCLC
Database Vendor: EBSCOhost, Gale Cengage Learning, Newsbank
Open Mon-Thurs 8-7, Fri 11-4

SOUTH PASADENA

P SOUTH PASADENA PUBLIC LIBRARY, 1100 Oxley St, 91030-3198. SAN 301-6188. Tel: 626-403-7333. Circulation Tel: 626-403-7340. Reference Tel: 626-403-7350. Administration Tel: 626-403-7330. FAX: 626-403-7331. *Dir, Libr, Arts & Culture,* Steven Warren Fjeldsted; E-mail: rdesk@southpasadenaca.gov; Staff 20.5 (MLS 6.5, Non-MLS 14)
Founded 1895. Pop 25,800; Circ 450,000
Jul 2014-Jun 2015 Income $1,537,832. Mats Exp $138,000. Sal $1,157,232 (Prof $550,000)
Library Holdings: AV Mats 4,784; CDs 5,000; DVDs 2,000; High Interest/Low Vocabulary Bk Vols 300; Large Print Bks 1,000; Bk Vols 125,000; Per Subs 400
Special Collections: Plays
Subject Interests: Art, Drama, Local hist
Automation Activity & Vendor Info: (Acquisitions) SirsiDynix; (Cataloging) SirsiDynix; (Circulation) SirsiDynix; (OPAC) SirsiDynix
Database Vendor: Baker & Taylor, BWI, Gale Cengage Learning, Newsbank, OCLC WorldShare Interlibrary Loan, ProQuest, SirsiDynix
Wireless access
Function: Bilingual assistance for Spanish patrons, Bks on cassette, Bks on CD, CD-ROM, Children's prog, Computers for patron use, Copy machines, e-mail serv, E-Reserves, Electronic databases & coll, Free DVD rentals, Holiday prog, Homebound delivery serv, Homework prog, ILL available, Music CDs, Online ref, Preschool outreach, Prog for adults, Prog for children & young adult, Ref serv available, Spoken cassettes & CDs, Spoken cassettes & DVDs, Tax forms, Telephone ref, VHS videos, Wheelchair accessible
Publications: South Pasadena: A Centennial History, 1888-1988; Stories from Home: South Pasadena, CA; The South Pasadena Public Library: A History 1895-1982
Partic in OCLC Online Computer Library Center, Inc
Open Mon-Wed 11-9, Thurs & Fri 10-6, Sat 10-5, Sun 1-5
Restriction: Circ to mem only
Friends of the Library Group

SOUTH SAN FRANCISCO

M KAISER PERMANENTE HEALTH SCIENCES LIBRARY*, 1200 El Camino Real, 94080. SAN 320-1708. Tel: 650-742-2540. FAX: 650-742-2239. *Mgr, Libr Serv,* Rebecca Bayrer; Staff 1 (MLS 1)
Founded 1973
Library Holdings: e-books 100; e-journals 4,000; Bk Titles 700
Subject Interests: Health sci, Med, Nursing
Wireless access
Open Mon-Fri 9-5

P SOUTH SAN FRANCISCO PUBLIC LIBRARY*, 840 W Orange Ave, 94080-3125. SAN 335-0495. Tel: 650-829-3860. Administration Tel: 650-829-3863. FAX: 650-829-3866. E-mail: ssfpladm@plsinfo.org. Web Site: www.ssf.net/library. *Dir,* Valerie Sommer; Tel: 650-829-3872, E-mail: sommer@plsinfo.org; *Asst Dir,* Cheryl K Grantano; Tel: 650-829-3876, E-mail: grantano@plsinfo.org; *Head, Ref,* Banny Rucker; Tel: 650-829-3867, E-mail: rucker@plsinfo.org; Staff 20 (MLS 12, Non-MLS 8)
Founded 1916. Pop 64,067; Circ 723,592
Jul 2010-Jun 2011 Income (Main Library and Branch(s)) $4,879,124, State $233,951, City $4,077,163, Federal $76,592, Locally Generated Income $491,418. Mats Exp $247,014, Books $120,755, Per/Ser (Incl. Access Fees) $18,000, AV Mat $91,727, Electronic Ref Mat (Incl. Access Fees) $16,532. Sal $3,260,912
Library Holdings: Audiobooks 13,105; AV Mats 20,852; DVDs 20,314; e-books 7,945; e-journals 6,431; Electronic Media & Resources 25; Bk Vols 172,755; Per Subs 223
Special Collections: South San Francisco Coll. Oral History
Subject Interests: Local hist
Automation Activity & Vendor Info: (Cataloging) Innovative Interfaces, Inc; (Circulation) Innovative Interfaces, Inc; (ILL) OCLC; (OPAC) Innovative Interfaces, Inc
Database Vendor: Gale Cengage Learning, Safari Books Online, TumbleBookLibrary
Wireless access
Function: Homebound delivery serv, Homework prog, ILL available, Large print keyboards, Learning ctr, Magnifiers for reading, Music CDs, Online cat, OverDrive digital audio bks, Photocopying/Printing, Preschool outreach, Prog for adults, Prog for children & young adult, Pub access computers, Ref & res, Ref serv available, Ref serv in person, Spoken cassettes & CDs, Story hour, Summer reading prog, Tax forms, Teen prog, Telephone ref, Web-catalog, Wheelchair accessible, Workshops
Special Services for the Deaf - Video relay serv
Special Services for the Blind - Reader equip

Open Mon & Tues 10-8, Wed & Thurs 12-8, Fri & Sat 10-5, Sun 2-5
Friends of the Library Group
Branches: 1
GRAND AVENUE, 306 Walnut Ave, 94080-2700, SAN 335-0525. Tel: 650-877-8530. FAX: 650-829-6615. *Br Mgr,* Pam Waldrep; E-mail: waldrep@plsinfo.org; Staff 2 (MLS 2)
Founded 1916
Library Holdings: Bk Vols 48,040
Special Collections: Local History Coll; Spanish Language Coll, bks, DVDs, mags, music CDs
Function: Bilingual assistance for Spanish patrons, Bks on cassette, Bks on CD, Children's prog, Computers for patron use, Copy machines, Electronic databases & coll, Free DVD rentals, Handicapped accessible, ILL available, Music CDs, Online cat, Online ref, Outside serv via phone, mail, e-mail & web, Photocopying/Printing, Prog for adults, Prog for children & young adult, Pub access computers, Ref & res, Ref serv available, Spoken cassettes & CDs, Spoken cassettes & DVDs, Story hour, Summer reading prog, Tax forms, Teen prog, Telephone ref, VHS videos, Web-catalog, Wheelchair accessible
Open Mon, Tues & Thurs 10-6, Wed 12-8
Friends of the Library Group

STANFORD

S CENTER FOR ADVANCED STUDY IN THE BEHAVIORAL SCIENCES LIBRARY*, 75 Alta Rd, 94305. SAN 301-6196. Tel: 650-736-0100. E-mail: library@casbs.stanford.edu. Web Site: www.casbs.org. *Info Officer,* Tricia N Soto; *Asst Librn,* Amanda Thomas
Founded 1954
Library Holdings: e-journals 50; Bk Vols 3,500; Per Subs 35
Special Collections: Ralph Tyler Coll
Subject Interests: Anthrop, Hist, Philos, Polit sci, Psychiat, Sociol
Publications: Annual Reports; The Ralph W Tyler Collection, 1954-1979 & 1954-1994
Partic in Dialog Corp; RLIN (Research Libraries Information Network)
Open Mon-Fri 8-5

C STANFORD UNIVERSITY LIBRARIES, Cecil H Green Library, 557 Escondido Mall, 94305-6004. SAN 335-055X. Tel: 650-725-1064. Interlibrary Loan Service Tel: 650-725-1278. E-mail: infocenter@stanford.edu. Web Site: www.stanford.edu. *Dir, Acad Info Res, Univ Librn,* Michael A Keller; Tel: 650-723-5553; *Assoc Univ Librn, Eng & Sci,* Dr Robert Schwarzwalder; *Assoc Univ Librn, Tech Serv,* Catherine Tierney; *Asst Univ Librn for Coll Develop, Humanities & Soc Sci,* Dr Zachary Baker; *Dir, Acad Computing Serv,* Richard Holeton; *Dir, Communications & Develop,* Gabrielle Karampelas; *Dir, Human Res,* Catalina Rodriguez; *Budget Officer,* Susan Horsfall
Founded 1919. Enrl 15,666; Fac 1,903; Highest Degree: Doctorate
Library Holdings: e-books 1,130,723; Music Scores 92,484; Bk Vols 6,474,233; Per Subs 436,966; Videos 58,505
Special Collections: American (Joyce Carol Thomas Coll); Archives & Professional Papers (Lourdes Portillo & Lynn Hershmann Coll); Artwork & Documentation Related to the Execution of the Stanford Memorial Church Mosaics by the Venetian Company A Salviati & Co; California (Borel Coll); Chicano (Ester M Hernandez Coll & Rolando Hinojosa-Smith Coll), ms; Children's Literature (Schofield Coll); Doug Menuez & Ira Nowinski Colls, photog; Engineering Mechanics (Timoshenko Coll); English & American Literature of the 19th & 20th Centuries (Felton Coll); Gunst Memorial Library (Book Arts), bks, ms; Hebraica & Judaica (Taube/Baron Coll & Samson Copenhagen Coll), bks, ms; History (Elmer E Robinson Coll); History of Science (Barchas, Brasch & Dudley Coll); Hopkins Transportation Library; Irish Literature (Healy Coll), bks, ms; Latin America (Jose Guadalupe Posada, Taller de Grafica Popular & Felipe Ehernberg Coll); Memorial Library of Music, bks, ms; Oscar I Norwich Coll, maps; Slavic (Andrei Voznesenskii Coll); Stanford Professor Emeritus Marjorie Perloff Papers; Tel Aviv (Eliasaf Robison Coll), 1909-1948; Theatre Coll. State Document Depository; UN Document Depository; US Document Depository
Subject Interests: Archit, Art, Bus & mgt, Computer sci, Educ, Hist, Law, Lit, Marine biol, Math, Med, Music, Natural sci, Physics, Soc sci & issues
Wireless access
Publications: A Vast & Useful Art: The Gustave Gimon Collection on French Political Economy; Catching the Light: Remembering Wallace Stegner; Contemporary Polish Book Art; Felipe Ehrenberg: A Neologist's Art & Archive; First Drafts, Last Drafts: Forty Years of the Creative Writing Program at Stanford; Ira Nowinski: The Photographer as Witness; Johannes Lebek: The Artist as a Witness of His Time; John Steinbeck: From Salinas to Stockholm; Jose Guadalupe Posada & the Taller de Gafica Popular: Mexican Popular Prints; Matt Phillips: The Magic in His Prints; Momentary Bliss: An American Memoir; Ordeal by Piton: Writings from the Golden Age of Yosemite Climbing; The Barchas Collection at Stanford University, History of Science & Ideas; The Heart Unguarded: William Abrahams; The Rediscovery of Africa 1400-1900: Antique Maps & Rare Images; The William Saroyan Collection at Stanford
Partic in Coop Libr Agency for Syst & Servs; Northeast Research Libraries Consortium (NERL); OCLC Online Computer Library Center, Inc; Pacific Neighborhood Consortium (PNC); Pacific Rim Digital Library Alliance (PRDLA)
Departmental Libraries:
ART & ARCHITECTURE LIBRARY, 102 Cummings Art Bldg, Main Flr, 94305-2018, SAN 335-0614. Tel: 650-723-3408, 650-725-1037. FAX: 650-725-0140. E-mail: artlibrary@stanford.edu. *Head Librn,* Peter Blank
Library Holdings: Bk Vols 181,864; Per Subs 457
BRANNER EARTH SCIENCES & MAP COLLECTIONS, Mitchell Bldg, 2nd Flr, 94305-2174. Tel: 650-723-2746, 650-725-1103. FAX: 650-725-2534. E-mail: brannerlibrary@stanford.edu. Web Site: library.stanford.edu/branner. *Head Librn,* Julie Sweetkind-Singer; Tel: 650-725-1102
Library Holdings: Bk Vols 143,115; Per Subs 1,892
Special Collections: Geothermal Engineering Coll; GIS Maps; State Geological Survey, open-file rpts
Subject Interests: Geochemistry, Geol, Petroleum eng
CL ROBERT CROWN LAW LIBRARY, Stanford Law School, 559 Nathan Abbott Way, 94305-8610, SAN 335-1068. Tel: 650-723-2477. Interlibrary Loan Service Tel: 650-723-1932. Reference Tel: 650-725-0800. FAX: 650-723-1933. E-mail: reference@law.stanford.edu. Web Site: www.law.stanford.edu/library. *Dir,* Paul Lomio
Founded 1897. Highest Degree: Doctorate
Library Holdings: Bk Vols 429,662; Per Subs 6,922
Subject Interests: Law
CUBBERLEY EDUCATION LIBRARY, Education Bldg, Rm 202-205, 94305-3096. Tel: 650-723-2121. FAX: 650-736-0536. E-mail: cubberley@stanford.edu. *Curator, Educ Res, Head of Libr,* Kathy Kerns
Library Holdings: Bk Vols 92,293; Per Subs 1,077
EAST ASIA LIBRARY, 560 Escondido Mall, 94305-6004. Tel: 650-725-3435. FAX: 650-724-2028. E-mail: eastasialibrary@stanford.edu. *Dir,* Dongfang Shao
Library Holdings: Bk Vols 686,905; Per Subs 4,883
Special Collections: Chinese Coll, bks, govt doc (pre-1949), microfilm reels, per, ser, statistical rpts; East Asia Library (EAL), Stanford's Primary East Asian-Language Coll; Japanese Coll, 1920's-1940's, ser; Korean Coll, bks, ser
Subject Interests: Chinese, Defense, Econ, Educ, Humanities, Japanese, Korean (Lang), Lang, Law, Lit, Politics, Pub finance, Sci tech, Soc sci, Sociol, Statistics
ENGINEERING LIBRARY, Terman Engineering Ctr, 2nd Flr, 94305-4029. Tel: 650-723-0001. FAX: 650-725-1096. E-mail: englibrary@stanford.edu. *Head, Eng Libr,* Helen Josephine
Library Holdings: Bk Vols 16,458; Per Subs 91
Special Collections: Timoshenko Coll
CM FALCONER BIOLOGY LIBRARY, Herrin Hall, 3rd Flr, 94305-5020. Tel: 650-723-1528. FAX: 650-725-7712. *Bibliographer, Head Librn,* Michael Newman
Library Holdings: Bk Vols 108,575; Per Subs 439
Subject Interests: Biochem, Biophysics, Cell biol, Developmental biol, Genetics, Molecular biol, Neurobiol, Pop biol
Partic in National Network of Libraries of Medicine South Central Region
GRADUATE SCHOOL OF BUSINESS LIBRARY, Knight Management Ctr, 655 Knight Way, 94305-7298, SAN 335-1009. Tel: 650-725-2055. FAX: 650-723-0281. E-mail: library@gsb.stanford.edu. Web Site: www.gsb.stanford.edu/library. *Dir,* Kathy Long
Founded 1933. Highest Degree: Doctorate
Subject Interests: Bus & mgt, Econ
HOOVER INSTITUTION ON WAR, REVOLUTION & PEACE LIBRARY, 94305-6004. Tel: 650-723-1754. FAX: 650-723-1687. *Librn,* Paul Thomas
Founded 1919
Library Holdings: Bk Vols 916,036; Per Subs 13
Special Collections: Hoover Institution Archives; Western Language Coll
Publications: Guide to Hoover Institution Archives (Hoover Institution Press, 1980); The Library Catalogs of the Hoover Institution on War, Revolution & Peace (G K Hall, 1969-77); The Library of the Hoover Institution on War, Revolution & Peace (Hoover Institution Press, 1985)
CM LANE MEDICAL LIBRARY, Stanford University Medical Ctr, 300 Pasteur Dr, Rm L109, 94305-5123, SAN 335-1033. Tel: 650-723-6831. Circulation Tel: 650-723-6691. Interlibrary Loan Service Tel: 650-725-4584. FAX: 650-725-7471. Web Site: www.lane.stanford.edu. *Assoc Dean, Knowledge Mgt, Dir,* Heidi Heilemann; E-mail: heidih@stanford.edu
Founded 1906. Highest Degree: Doctorate
Library Holdings: e-books 14,356; e-journals 9,003; Bk Vols 381,368; Per Subs 16,547
Special Collections: Fleischmann Learning Coll; History of Medicine Coll
Subject Interests: Biomed sci, Med, Nursing, Pub health
Automation Activity & Vendor Info: (Acquisitions) Ex Libris Group; (Cataloging) Ex Libris Group; (Circulation) Ex Libris Group; (Course

Reserve) Ex Libris Group; (OPAC) Ex Libris Group; (Serials) Ex Libris Group
Database Vendor: Cinahl, LexisNexis, Medline, PubMed, UpToDate
Supports Stanford University Medical Center, which includes the School of Medicine, Stanford Hospitals & Clinics & Lucile Packard Children's Hospital

MATHEMATICS & STATISTICS, Falconer Biology Library, 393 Serra Mall, Herrin Hall, 3rd Flr, 94305-2125. E-mail: mathstatlibrary@stanford.edu. *Bibliographer, Head Librn,* Michael L Newman; Tel: 650-723-1110, E-mail: mnewman@stanford.edu
Library Holdings: Bk Vols 108,979; Per Subs 209
Special Collections: Collected Works of Prominent Mathematicians; Computer Books Online; Electronic Journals; Online Reference Coll, MathSciNet (Mathematical Reviews), INSPEC (incl Computer & Control Abstracts) & Current Index to Statistics; Stanford Theses; Technical Reports in Computer Science
Subject Interests: Computer sci, Math, Statistics

HAROLD A MILLER MARINE BIOLOGY LIBRARY, Hopkins Marine Sta, Pacific Grove, 93950-3094, SAN 371-1501. Tel: 831-655-6228, 831-655-6229. FAX: 831-373-7859. *Bibliographer, Head Librn,* Joseph G Wible; E-mail: wible@stanford.edu
Library Holdings: Bk Vols 44,266
Subject Interests: Marine biol

MUSIC LIBRARY, Braun Music Ctr, 541 Lasuen Mall, 94305-3076. Tel: 650-723-1211. Reference Tel: 650-723-1212. FAX: 650-725-1145. E-mail: muslibcirc@stanford.edu. *Head Librn,* Jerry McBride
Library Holdings: Bk Vols 136,081
Special Collections: Kronos Quartet Coll; Lully Archive, a Repository of Primary Sources on Microfilm of the Music of Jean-Baptiste Lully; Women's Philharmonic Coll
Subject Interests: Historical musicology, Western art music

SLAC NATIONAL ACCELERATOR LABORATORY RESEARCH LIBRARY, 2575 Sand Hill Rd, MS82, Menlo Park, 94025, SAN 335-1092. Tel: 650-926-2411. E-mail: library@slac.stanford.edu. Web Site: www-group.slac.stanford.edu/library. *Mgr,* Jean Marie Deken; Staff 2 (MLS 2)
Founded 1962
Library Holdings: Bk Vols 18,509
Special Collections: High-energy Physics Archives; SLAC Archives & History Office; SPIRES-HEP Databases
Function: Res libr
Partic in Unix-Spires

STANFORD AUXILIARY LIBRARY, 691 Pampas Lane, 94305. Tel: 650-723-9201. *Interim Head, Access Serv,* Regina Wallen
Library Holdings: Bk Vols 2,100,833

SWAIN LIBRARY OF CHEMISTRY & CHEMICAL ENGINEERING, Organic Chemistry Bldg, 364 Lomita Dr, 94305-5080. Tel: 650-723-9237. FAX: 650-725-2274. E-mail: swainlibrary@stanford.edu. *Bibliographer, Head Librn,* Grace Baysinger
Library Holdings: Bk Vols 40,000; Per Subs 300

STOCKTON

CALIFORNIA YOUTH AUTHORITY

S N A CHADERJIAN YOUTH CORRECTIONAL FACILITY LIBRARY*, 7650 S Newcastle Rd, 95213. (Mail add: PO Box 213014, 95213-9014). Tel: 209-944-6444, Ext 6755. FAX: 209-944-6167. *Head Librn,* Tammy Fishman
Library Holdings: Bk Vols 5,837
Open Mon-Fri 8-4

S O H CLOSE YOUTH CORRECTIONAL FACILITY LIBRARY*, 7650 S Newcastle Rd, 95213-9001. (Mail add: PO Box 213001, 95213-9001). Tel: 209-944-6346. FAX: 209-944-6136. *Sr Librn,* Jonathan Frye
Library Holdings: Bk Vols 10,000
Open Mon-Fri 8-3

R CHRISTIAN LIFE COLLEGE LIBRARY*, Hogue Library, 9023 West Lane, 95210. SAN 301-6323. Tel: 209-476-7840. Toll Free Tel: 800-326-9495. FAX: 209-476-7868. E-mail: info@clc.edu. Web Site: www.clc.edu. *Librn,* Sherry Kinney
Founded 1955
Library Holdings: Bk Vols 18,000; Per Subs 50
Open Mon, Tues, Thurs & Fri 8am-9pm, Wed 11-9, Sat 10-4

S HAGGIN MUSEUM*, Petzinger Library, 1201 N Pershing Ave, 95203-1699. SAN 301-6234. Tel: 209-940-6324. FAX: 209-940-6304. E-mail: archive@hagginmuseum.org. Web Site: www.hagginmuseum.org. *Curator,* Kylee D Denning
Founded 1949
Library Holdings: Bk Titles 7,000; Per Subs 15
Special Collections: California History Coll; Holt Manufacturing Company History Coll; James Ben Ali Haggin Family Records; Joseph Christian Leyendecker Coll; Ralph Yardley Drawings; San Joaquin Society of California Pioneers Coll; Stephens Bros Boat Builders Archive; Stockton Industrial Archive; Stockton/San Joaquin County History Coll; Valentines Coll
Subject Interests: Art Ref, Local hist
Wireless access
Function: Archival coll, Ref serv available
Restriction: Authorized scholars by appt, Non-circulating

J HEALD COLLEGE*, Learning Resource Center-Stockton Campus, 1605 E March Lane, 95210. Tel: 209-473-5200. FAX: 209-473-5287. E-mail: stc_lrc@heald.edu. Web Site: www.heald.edu. *Mgr,* Chris Frymire; E-mail: chris_frymire@heald.edu; *Coordr,* Caleb Holt; E-mail: caleb_holt@heald.edu; *Coordr,* Meg Jordan; E-mail: megann_jordan@heald.edu; *Coordr,* Annalyn Vosoughi; E-mail: annalyn_vosoughi@heald.edu
Highest Degree: Associate
Library Holdings: Bk Vols 1,500; Per Subs 40
Database Vendor: EBSCOhost
Function: Learning ctr
Open Mon-Thurs 7am-10pm, Fri 7-6, Sat 10-2
Restriction: Open to pub with supv only, Open to students, fac, staff & alumni

C HUMPHREYS COLLEGE LIBRARY*, 6650 Inglewood Ave, 95207. SAN 301-6226. Tel: 209-478-0800. FAX: 209-478-8721. Web Site: www.humphreys.edu. *Librn,* Dr Stanislav Perkner; Tel: 209-235-2933, E-mail: sperkner@humphreys.edu; Staff 1 (MLS 1)
Founded 1896
Library Holdings: Bk Vols 24,922; Per Subs 113
Subject Interests: Bus, Criminal justice, Educ, Law
Database Vendor: EBSCOhost, LexisNexis, OCLC FirstSearch, ProQuest, Westlaw, Wilson - Wilson Web
Wireless access
Partic in Statewide California Electronic Library Consortium (SCELC)
Open Mon-Fri 8am-10pm, Sat 8-5, Sun 8-3

S THE RECORD LIBRARY*, 530 E Market St, 95202. (Mail add: PO Box 900, 95201-0900), SAN 301-6285. Tel: 209-546-8286. FAX: 209-547-8186. E-mail: library@recordnet.com. Web Site: www.recordnet.com. *Admin Supvr,* Paula Allard; Tel: 209-546-8271; Staff 1 (Non-MLS 1)
Founded 1960
Function: Newsp ref libr
Restriction: Not open to pub

M SAINT JOSEPH'S MEDICAL CENTER LIBRARY*, 1800 N California St, 95213. SAN 320-6076. Tel: 209-467-6332. FAX: 209-461-5098. *Librn,* Position Currently Open; *Asst Librn,* Christine Reyes
Library Holdings: Bk Titles 1,200; Per Subs 140
Subject Interests: Human relations, Med, Nursing

GL SAN JOAQUIN COUNTY LAW LIBRARY*, Kress Legal Center, 20 N Sutter St, 95202. SAN 301-6242. Tel: 209-468-3920. FAX: 209-468-9968. *Dir,* Barbara M Zaruba; Staff 3 (MLS 1, Non-MLS 2)
Library Holdings: Bk Vols 30,000
Special Collections: State Document Depository
Automation Activity & Vendor Info: (Acquisitions) LibraryWorld, Inc; (Cataloging) LibraryWorld, Inc; (OPAC) LibraryWorld, Inc; (Serials) LibraryWorld, Inc
Database Vendor: LexisNexis, Westlaw
Wireless access
Open Mon-Fri 8-5

J SAN JOAQUIN DELTA COLLEGE*, Goleman Library, 5151 Pacific Ave, 95207-6370. SAN 301-6250. Tel: 209-954-5139. Circulation Tel: 209-954-5143. Interlibrary Loan Service Tel: 209-954-5148. Reference Tel: 209-954-5145. FAX: 209-954-5691. E-mail: library@deltacollege.edu. Web Site: www.deltacollege.edu/dept/library. *Dean, Libr Serv,* Joe Gonzales; *Archivist, Pub Serv,* Linda Peabody; Tel: 209-954-5147, E-mail: lpeabody@deltacollege.edu; *Automation Librn, Tech Serv,* Steve Schermerhorn; Tel: 209-954-5152, E-mail: sschermerhorn@deltacollege.edu; *Bibliog Instr,* Dr Jun Wang; Tel: 209-954-5146, E-mail: jwang@deltacollege.edu; *Coll Develop,* Nancy Mangum; Tel: 209-954-5862, E-mail: nmangum@deltacollege.edu; Staff 16 (MLS 6, Non-MLS 10)
Founded 1948. Enrl 18,836; Fac 565; Highest Degree: Associate
Jul 2005-Jun 2006. Mats Exp $317,314, Books $100,000, Per/Ser (Incl. Access Fees) $62,520, Micro $14,495, AV Mat $17,600, Electronic Ref Mat (Incl. Access Fees) $12,364, Presv $1,335
Library Holdings: AV Mats 6,696; Bks on Deafness & Sign Lang 136; e-books 7,212; High Interest/Low Vocabulary Bk Vols 61; Large Print Bks 14; Bk Titles 82,999; Bk Vols 95,966; Per Subs 528; Talking Bks 1,607
Automation Activity & Vendor Info: (Acquisitions) SirsiDynix; (Cataloging) SirsiDynix; (Circulation) SirsiDynix; (Course Reserve) SirsiDynix; (ILL) SirsiDynix; (OPAC) SirsiDynix
Database Vendor: OCLC FirstSearch

Publications: Handbook for Instructors; Instructor of Record Handbook; Library Handbook; Library Research Workbook; Library Skills Workbook
Partic in Central Association of Libraries; Coop Libr Agency for Syst & Servs; OCLC Online Computer Library Center, Inc
Friends of the Library Group

P STOCKTON-SAN JOAQUIN COUNTY PUBLIC LIBRARY*, 605 N El Dorado St, 95202. SAN 335-1122. Tel: 209-937-8362. Circulation Tel: 209-937-8416. Reference Tel: 209-937-8221. FAX: 209-937-8683. E-mail: library@ci.stockton.ca.us. Web Site: www.stockton.lib.ca.us. *Dir, Commun Serv,* Position Currently Open; *City Librn/Dep Dir, Commun Serv,* Chris Freeman; Tel: 209-937-8364, E-mail: chris.freeman@stocktongov.com; *Supv Librn,* Susan Johnston; Tel: 209-937-8312, E-mail: susan.johnston@stocktongov.com; *Supv Librn-City Br,* Peaches Ehrich; Tel: 209-937-8261, Fax: 209-937-8547, E-mail: peaches.ehrich@stocktongov.com; *Supv Librn-County Br,* Debra Furtado; Tel: 209-456-8677, E-mail: debra.furtado@stocktongov.com; Staff 51 (MLS 21, Non-MLS 30)
Founded 1880. Pop 620,000; Circ 1,675,548
Library Holdings: AV Mats 88,501; Bk Vols 868,068; Per Subs 1,090; Talking Bks 678
Special Collections: Career Center; Local History; Online Community Info Database; Picture Book Subject Index; Southeast Asian Languages; Spanish Language; Stockton & San Joaquin County History; Stockton Record Index. US Document Depository
Automation Activity & Vendor Info: (Acquisitions) SirsiDynix; (Cataloging) SirsiDynix; (Circulation) SirsiDynix; (ILL) SirsiDynix; (OPAC) SirsiDynix; (Serials) SirsiDynix
Wireless access
Function: Adult bk club, Adult literacy prog, Audiobks via web, Bilingual assistance for Spanish patrons, Bk club(s), Bks on cassette, Bks on CD, Children's prog, Computer training, Computers for patron use, Copy machines, e-mail & chat, Electronic databases & coll, Free DVD rentals, Handicapped accessible, Homebound delivery serv, Homework prog, ILL available, Music CDs, Outreach serv, OverDrive digital audio bks, Photocopying/Printing, Prog for adults, Prog for children & young adult, Pub access computers, Ref serv in person, Story hour, Summer reading prog, Tax forms, Teen prog, Telephone ref, VHS videos, Wheelchair accessible
Publications: Annual Report; Let's Connect (Newsletter)
Partic in 49-99 Cooperative Library System
Special Services for the Deaf - Closed caption videos
Special Services for the Blind - Assistive/Adapted tech devices, equip & products; BiFolkal kits; Bks on cassette; Bks on CD; Large print bks; Magnifiers
Open Mon, Tues & Thurs 10-6, Wed 1-6, Fri 10-5
Restriction: ID required to use computers (Ltd hrs)
Friends of the Library Group
Branches: 11
MAYA ANGELOU BRANCH, 2324 Pock Lane, 95205, SAN 335-1270. FAX: 209-937-7702. *Librn,* Janice Bailey; Tel: 209-937-7701, E-mail: alex.bailey@stocktongov.com; Staff 2 (MLS 1, Non-MLS 1)
Pop 19,165; Circ 61,380
Library Holdings: Bk Vols 56,913
Friends of the Library Group
ESCALON BRANCH, 1540 Second St, Escalon, 95320, SAN 335-1157. FAX: 209-838-2032. *Librn,* Jamie Turner; Tel: 209-838-2494, E-mail: jamie.turner@stocktongov.com; Staff 2 (MLS 1, Non-MLS 1)
Pop 13,320; Circ 43,570
Library Holdings: Bk Vols 53,785
Friends of the Library Group
LATHROP BRANCH, 450 Spartan Way, Lathrop, 95330. FAX: 209-858-5239. *Librn,* Suzanne Sutterfield; E-mail: suzanne.sutterfield@stocktongov.com; Staff 1 (MLS 1)
Pop 14,702; Circ 21,531
Library Holdings: Bk Titles 2,500
LINDEN BRANCH, 19059 E Main St, Linden, 95236, SAN 335-136X. FAX: 209-887-2075. *Librn,* Jennifer Fontanilla; E-mail: jennifer.fontanilla@stocktongov.com; Staff 1 (MLS 1)
Pop 16,783; Circ 24,238
Library Holdings: Bk Vols 14,743
Friends of the Library Group
MANTECA BRANCH, 320 W Center St, Manteca, 95336, SAN 335-1211. Toll Free Tel: 866-805-7323. FAX: 209-825-2394. *Librn,* Anne Stevens; E-mail: anne.stevens@stocktongov.com; Staff 6 (MLS 3, Non-MLS 3)
Pop 75,172; Circ 221,096
Library Holdings: Bk Vols 136,000
Friends of the Library Group
MOUNTAIN HOUSE BRANCH, 250 E Main St, Mountain House, 95391. Tel: 209-937-8221. Administration Tel: 209-937-8362. Toll Free Tel: 866-805-7323. *Br Librn,* Kathleen Buffleben; Tel: 209-831-5661, Fax: 209-831-5665; Staff 2 (MLS 1, Non-MLS 1)
Pop 16,787; Circ 83,614
Open Mon 3-8, Tues 2-7, Wed 1-6, Thurs 10-3, Fri-Sun 12-5
RIPON BRANCH, 333 W Main St, Ripon, 95336, SAN 335-1246. Tel: 209-599-3326. FAX: 209-599-5530. *Librn,* Melinda Kopp; E-mail: melinda.kopp@ci.stockton.ca.us; Staff 3 (MLS 1, Non-MLS 2)
Pop 16,688; Circ 77,990
Library Holdings: Bk Vols 60,034
Friends of the Library Group
THORNTON BRANCH, 26341 N Thornton Rd, Thornton, 95686. (Mail add: PO Box 158, Thornton, 95686), SAN 335-1394. Toll Free Tel: 866-805-7323. *Br Mgr,* Mark Rodriguez; E-mail: mark.rodriguez@ci.stockton.ca.us; Staff 1 (MLS 1)
Pop 10,313; Circ 10,652
Library Holdings: Bk Vols 18,481
TRACY BRANCH, 20 E Eaton Ave, Tracy, 95376, SAN 335-1335. FAX: 209-831-4252. *Librn,* Merrilee Chapman; E-mail: merrilee.chapman@stocktongov.com; Staff 6 (MLS 2, Non-MLS 4)
Pop 89,466; Circ 296,392
Library Holdings: Bk Vols 162,890
Special Collections: Kiersh Memorial Music Coll; Tugel Memorial Natural History
Friends of the Library Group
MARGARET K TROKE BRANCH, 502 W Benjamin Holt Dr, 95207, SAN 335-1300. FAX: 209-937-7721. *Librn,* Bill Walker; Staff 8 (MLS 3, Non-MLS 5)
Pop 182,009; Circ 376,139
Library Holdings: Bk Vols 183,941
Open Tues & Thurs 10-6, Wed 1-6, Fri & Sat 11-5
Friends of the Library Group
WESTON RANCH BRANCH, 1453 W French Camp Rd, 95206. Administration Tel: 209-937-8362. Toll Free Tel: 866-805-7323. FAX: 209-937-8660. Administration FAX: 209-937-8683. *Librn,* Christine Lum; Tel: 209-937-8540, E-mail: christine.lum@stocktongov.com; Staff 2 (MLS 1, Non-MLS 1)
Library Holdings: Bk Vols 30,691
Bookmobiles: 2

C UNIVERSITY OF THE PACIFIC LIBRARY*, 3601 Pacific Ave, 95211. SAN 335-1459. Tel: 209-946-2434. Interlibrary Loan Service Tel: 209-946-2196. Reference Tel: 209-946-2433. FAX: 209-946-2805. Web Site: library.pacific.edu. *Interim Dean,* Lynn Beck; E-mail: lbeck@pacific.edu; *Asst Dean,* Ginger Trow; Tel: 209-946-2939, E-mail: vtrow@pacific.edu; *Ref Librn,* Lorrie Knight; Staff 9 (MLS 9)
Founded 1851. Enrl 4,627; Fac 310; Highest Degree: Doctorate
Jan 2006-Dec 2006. Mats Exp $931,000. Sal $1,096,700
Library Holdings: AV Mats 9,100; Bk Titles 373,750; Per Subs 1,826
Special Collections: Dave Brubeck Coll; Folk Dance (Lawton Harris), rec; John Muir Papers; Methodist History (Fry Research Library). Oral History
Automation Activity & Vendor Info: (Acquisitions) Ex Libris Group; (Cataloging) Ex Libris Group; (Circulation) Ex Libris Group; (Course Reserve) Docutek; (ILL) OCLC ILLiad; (OPAC) Ex Libris Group; (Serials) Ex Libris Group
Wireless access
Publications: Speaking Volumes (Newsletter)
Partic in OCLC Western Service Center; Statewide California Electronic Library Consortium (SCELC)
Open Mon-Thurs 7:30am-12:45am, Fri 7:30-5:45, Sat Noon-6:45, Sun Noon-12:45am
Friends of the Library Group
Departmental Libraries:
CM HEALTH SCIENCES, School of Pharmacy Bldg, 3601 Pacific Ave, 95211, SAN 335-1602. Tel: 209-946-2940. FAX: 209-946-2041.
Subject Interests: Chem, Phys therapy
HOLT-ATHERTON DEPARTMENT OF SPECIAL COLLECTIONS, 3601 Pacific Ave, 95211. Tel: 209-946-2404.
Subject Interests: Calif, Western Americana

SUN VALLEY

SR THE MASTER'S SEMINARY LIBRARY*, 13248 Roscoe Blvd, 91352. SAN 323-620X. Tel: 818-909-5634. Administration Tel: 818-909-5643. FAX: 818-909-5680. Web Site: www.tms.edu. *Dir of Libr,* Dennis M Swanson; E-mail: dswanson@tms.edu; *Head, Pub Serv,* Lauren Garber; *Acq Librn,* Michael Busch; *Cat Librn,* Anna Lois Kroll; *Per,* Linda Pettegrew; Staff 5 (MLS 3, Non-MLS 2)
Founded 1986. Enrl 370; Fac 19; Highest Degree: Doctorate
Library Holdings: DVDs 500; e-journals 26; Bk Titles 125,000; Bk Vols 175,000; Per Subs 650; Videos 500
Subject Interests: Archaeology, Biblical studies, Church hist, Theol
Automation Activity & Vendor Info: (Acquisitions) Ex Libris Group; (Cataloging) Ex Libris Group; (Circulation) Ex Libris Group; (ILL) OCLC; (OPAC) Ex Libris Group; (Serials) EBSCO Online
Function: Art exhibits, Copy machines, Doc delivery serv, E-Reserves, Electronic databases & coll, ILL available, Online searches, Workshops
Partic in OCLC Online Computer Library Center, Inc

Open Mon-Thurs (Winter) 8am-10pm, Fri & Sat 9-5, Sun 12:30-5:30; Mon-Sat (Summer) 9-5
Restriction: Authorized patrons

SUNNYVALE

C COGSWELL POLYTECHNICAL COLLEGE LIBRARY*, 1175 Bordeaux Dr, 94089. SAN 301-3898. Tel: 408-541-0100. Circulation Tel: 408-498-5144. FAX: 408-747-0764. E-mail: library@cogswell.edu. Web Site: www.cogswell.edu. *Librn,* Position Currently Open
Founded 1887. Enrl 300; Fac 50; Highest Degree: Bachelor
Library Holdings: Bk Titles 13,000; Per Subs 80
Automation Activity & Vendor Info: (Cataloging) LibraryWorld, Inc; (Circulation) LibraryWorld, Inc
Open Mon-Thurs 9-7:30, Fri 9-5

R ST THOMAS EPISCOPAL CHURCH LIBRARY*, 231 Sunset Ave, 94086-5938. SAN 328-1884. Tel: 408-736-4155. FAX: 408-736-8655. E-mail: office@stthomas-svale.org. Web Site: www.stthomas-svale.org. *Librn,* Carol Campbell; Fax: 408-733-7054, E-mail: resourcecenterecr@sbcglobal.net; Staff 5 (MLS 1, Non-MLS 4)
Founded 1979
Library Holdings: DVDs 500; Large Print Bks 100; Bk Titles 7,000; Per Subs 33
Special Collections: Oral History
Subject Interests: Relig
Automation Activity & Vendor Info: (Acquisitions) Book Systems; (Cataloging) Book Systems; (Circulation) Book Systems; (OPAC) Book Systems
Wireless access
Open Tues-Fri 10-4

P SUNNYVALE PUBLIC LIBRARY*, 665 W Olive Ave, 94086-7622. (Mail add: PO Box 3714, 94088-3714), SAN 301-6455. Tel: 408-730-7300. Interlibrary Loan Service Tel: 408-730-7323. Administration Tel: 408-730-7314. FAX: 408-735-8767. E-mail: library@ci.sunnyvale.ca.us. Web Site: www.sunnyvalelibrary.org. *Dir,* Lisa Rosenblum; E-mail: lrosenblum@ci.sunnyvale.ca.us; *Head, Cat,* Marsha Pollak; *Head, Ch,* Sue Kaplan; *Head, Circ,* Ellen Giarrizzo; *Head, Coll Develop,* Christine Mendoza; *Head, Pub Serv,* Susan Denniston; *Admin Librn,* Steve Sloan; Staff 20.24 (MLS 19.22, Non-MLS 1.02)
Founded 1908. Pop 141,099; Circ 2,524,293
Jul 2009-Jun 2010 Income $7,503,341, State $56,151, City $7,158,288, Federal $20,000, Locally Generated Income $268,902. Mats Exp $602,040. Sal $2,784,490
Library Holdings: e-books 15,866; Bk Vols 222,518; Per Subs 326
Special Collections: Patents & Trademarks (USPTO Depository Library); Sunnyvale Local History Coll
Automation Activity & Vendor Info: (Acquisitions) Innovative Interfaces, Inc; (Cataloging) Innovative Interfaces, Inc; (Circulation) Innovative Interfaces, Inc; (ILL) Innovative Interfaces, Inc; (OPAC) Innovative Interfaces, Inc
Wireless access
Partic in Califa, OCLC Online Computer Library Center, Inc
Friends of the Library Group

S WESTERN PHILATELIC LIBRARY*, Bldg 6, Rm 6, 1500 Partridge Ave, 94087. (Mail add: PO Box 2219, 94087-0219), SAN 324-3524. Tel: 408-733-0336. Web Site: www.fwpl.org. *Pres,* Stuart Leven; E-mail: stulev@ix.netcom.com
Library Holdings: Bk Titles 8,000; Per Subs 50
Subject Interests: Stamp collecting
Automation Activity & Vendor Info: (Cataloging) Inmagic, Inc.
Publications: The Bay Phil
Open Tues & Sat 12-5, Wed 5-9, Fri 9-5 & 7-9
Friends of the Library Group

SUSANVILLE

J LASSEN COMMUNITY COLLEGE LIBRARY*, 478-200 Hwy 139, 96130. (Mail add: PO Box 3000, 96130-3000), SAN 301-6498. Tel: 530-251-8830. FAX: 530-257-8964. Web Site: www.lassencollege.edu/academics/academic-support/library-index. *Dir,* Marita Dimond; E-mail: mdimond@lassencollege.edu; Staff 1 (MLS 1)
Founded 1926. Enrl 1,800; Fac 38; Highest Degree: Associate
Library Holdings: e-books 18,776; Bk Titles 20,000; Per Subs 28
Special Collections: California Coll; Gunsmithing Coll; N American Indian Coll
Subject Interests: Criminal law & justice
Automation Activity & Vendor Info: (Cataloging) TLC (The Library Corporation); (Circulation) TLC (The Library Corporation); (Course Reserve) TLC (The Library Corporation); (OPAC) TLC (The Library Corporation)
Function: Copy machines, Electronic databases & coll, ILL available, Large print keyboards, Magnifiers for reading, Music CDs, Online searches, Outside serv via phone, mail, e-mail & web, Photocopying/Printing, Ref & res, Tax forms, Telephone ref
Mem of NorthNet Library System
Open Mon-Thurs (Fall & Spring) 8-8, Fri 8-4; Mon-Thurs (Summer) 8-6, Fri 8-4

L LASSEN COUNTY LAW LIBRARY*, 2610 Riverside Dr, 96130. Tel: 530-251-8353. *Law Librn,* Nancy Holsey
Library Holdings: Bk Vols 3,500
Open Mon-Fri 8-12 & 1-5

P LASSEN LIBRARY DISTRICT*, 1618 Main St, 96130-4515. SAN 301-6501. Tel: 530-251-8127. Administration Tel: 530-257-8113. FAX: 530-257-8115. E-mail: lassenlibrary@citlink.net. Web Site: www.lassenlibrary.org. *Interim Dir, Libr Mgr,* Jeffrey Hawkins; Staff 10 (MLS 1, Non-MLS 9)
Founded 1995. Pop 36,000; Circ 36,300
Jul 2006-Jun 2007 Income $185,500, State $38,600, County $117,900, Locally Generated Income $25,200, Other $3,800. Mats Exp $4,620, Books $3,600, Per/Ser (Incl. Access Fees) $865, AV Mat $155. Sal $103,000
Library Holdings: CDs 476; DVDs 218; Large Print Bks 874; Bk Titles 40,000; Bk Vols 43,000; Per Subs 101; Talking Bks 725; Videos 2,189
Special Collections: California History Coll. Oral History
Subject Interests: Indians, Local hist
Automation Activity & Vendor Info: (Cataloging) Follett Software; (Circulation) Follett Software; (ILL) OCLC FirstSearch
Database Vendor: Gale Cengage Learning
Wireless access
Mem of NorthNet Library System
Open Tues-Thurs 11-5, Sat 11-3
Friends of the Library Group

SYLMAR

J LOS ANGELES MISSION COLLEGE LIBRARY*, 13356 Eldridge Ave, 91342-3200. SAN 301-360X. Tel: 818-364-7750. Circulation Tel: 818-364-7600, Ext 7106. Reference Tel: 818-364-7600, Ext 7105. FAX: 818-364-7749. E-mail: library@lamission.edu. Web Site: www.lamission.edu/library. *Librn,* Sandy Thomsen; E-mail: thomses@lamission.edu; *Instruction & Ref Librn,* Donna Ayers; *Cat, Tech Serv,* Ed Casson; *Pub Serv, Ref,* David Garza; Staff 4 (MLS 4)
Founded 1975. Enrl 8,500; Fac 57
Library Holdings: Bk Vols 44,000; Per Subs 193
Special Collections: Los Angeles Mission College Archives
Wireless access
Publications: Bibliographies & Study Aids
Partic in Metronet

S ST JUDE MEDICAL LIBRARY & RESOURCE CENTER, Information & Innovation Research Center, Library & Resource Center, 15900 Valley View Ct, 91342. SAN 373-286X. Tel: 818-362-6822, 818-493-3101. Toll Free Tel: 800-423-5611, Ext 3101. E-mail: library@sjm.com. *Mgr,* Sandra Crumlish; E-mail: scrumlish@sjm.com; Staff 1 (Non-MLS 1)
Founded 1990
Library Holdings: Bk Titles 1,000; Per Subs 110
Subject Interests: Cardiology, Neurology
Automation Activity & Vendor Info: (Acquisitions) EOS International; (Cataloging) EOS International; (Circulation) EOS International; (OPAC) EOS International; (Serials) EOS International
Wireless access
Function: Computers for patron use, Copy machines, Doc delivery serv, e-mail serv, Electronic databases & coll, Health sci info serv, Mail & tel request accepted, Mail loans to mem, Online cat, Online ref, Online searches, Orientations, Printer for laptops & handheld devices, Prof lending libr, Ref & res, Res libr, Scanner, Web-catalog, Workshops
Partic in Medical Library Association (MLA); Medical Library Group of Southern California & Arizona (MLGSCA)
Restriction: Access for corporate affiliates

TAFT

J TAFT COLLEGE LIBRARY*, 29 Emmons Park Dr, 93268-2317. SAN 301-6536. Tel: 661-763-7707. FAX: 661-763-7778. Web Site: www.taftcollege.edu/library/library.php. *Res & Instruction Librn,* Terri Smith; Tel: 661-763-7817, E-mail: tsmith@taftcollege.edu; Staff 2 (MLS 2)
Founded 1952. Fac 1; Highest Degree: Associate
Library Holdings: DVDs 1,600; e-books 9,000; Bk Vols 20,000; Per Subs 85
Automation Activity & Vendor Info: (Acquisitions) Ex Libris Group; (Cataloging) Ex Libris Group; (Circulation) Ex Libris Group; (Course Reserve) Ex Libris Group; (OPAC) Ex Libris Group; (Serials) Ex Libris Group
Wireless access
Partic in California Community College Library Consortium (CCLC); Heartland Regional Library Network of the Library of California

Open Mon-Thurs (Fall & Spring) 8-8, Fri 8-5; Mon-Thurs (Summer) 8-8
Friends of the Library Group

TARZANA

J COLUMBIA COLLEGE HOLLYWOOD*, Learning Resource Center, 18618 Oxnard St, 91356. SAN 328-2449. Tel: 818-345-8414. FAX: 818-345-9053. Web Site: www.columbiacollege.edu. *Librn,* Cherice Hall; Tel: 818-401-1027, E-mail: chall@columbiacollege.edu; Staff 5 (MLS 2, Non-MLS 3)
Founded 1952. Enrl 30; Fac 70; Highest Degree: Bachelor
Library Holdings: Bk Titles 12,000; Per Subs 100
Special Collections: Hollywood Museum Coll; Motion Picture & Revision Script Coll, scripts; Society of Motion Picture & Television Engineers, jrnls, 1910-present
Friends of the Library Group

THOUSAND OAKS

S AMGEN INC LIBRARY*, One Amgen Center Dr, 91320. SAN 329-5745. Tel: 805-447-4636. FAX: 805-375-7791. Web Site: www.amgen.com.
Founded 1981
Library Holdings: Bk Titles 5,000; Bk Vols 6,000; Per Subs 500
Automation Activity & Vendor Info: (Cataloging) Ex Libris Group
Database Vendor: OVID Technologies
Partic in Coop Libr Agency for Syst & Servs; Pacific Southwest Regional Medical Library (PSRML)
Restriction: Staff use only

C CALIFORNIA LUTHERAN UNIVERSITY*, Pearson Library, 60 W Olsen Rd, 91360-2787. SAN 301-6560. Tel: 805-493-3250. FAX: 805-493-3842. E-mail: libcirc@clunet.edu. Web Site: www.clunet.edu. *Asst Dir,* Lala Badal; *Cat,* Kristin Hughes; *ILL,* Kathy Horneck; Staff 9 (MLS 4, Non-MLS 5)
Founded 1961. Enrl 2,766; Fac 111; Highest Degree: Master
Library Holdings: Bk Vols 135,000; Per Subs 425
Special Collections: Scandinavian
Subject Interests: Counseling, Marriage, Pacific Islands
Automation Activity & Vendor Info: (Acquisitions) SirsiDynix; (Cataloging) SirsiDynix; (Circulation) SirsiDynix; (OPAC) SirsiDynix; (Serials) SirsiDynix
Database Vendor: LexisNexis, OCLC FirstSearch, ProQuest
Partic in Pac Net

M LOS ROBLES REGIONAL MEDICAL CENTER*, Medical Staff Library, 215 W Janss Rd, 91360. SAN 301-6579. Tel: 805-370-4609. FAX: 805-370-4843. *Libr Tech,* Yvonne Thomas
Library Holdings: Bk Vols 350; Per Subs 55
Subject Interests: Med
Open Mon-Fri 2-6

S ROCKWELL SCIENTIFIC CO, Technical Information Center, 1049 Camino Dos Rios, 91360. SAN 301-6587. Tel: 805-373-4748. *Libr Mgr,* Philip Brenneise; E-mail: philip.brenneise@teledyne.com; Staff 2 (MLS 2)
Founded 1962
Library Holdings: Bk Vols 7,600; Per Subs 4,100
Subject Interests: Electronics, Imaging sci, Mat sci, Optics
Restriction: Co libr

P THOUSAND OAKS LIBRARY*, Grant R Brimhall Library, 1401 E Janss Rd, 91362-2199. SAN 335-2323. Tel: 805-449-2660. FAX: 805-373-6858. Interlibrary Loan Service FAX: 805-495-8485. E-mail: library@toaks.org. Web Site: www.toaks.org/library. *Libr Serv Dir,* Stephen R Brogden; Tel: 805-449-2660, Ext 7300, E-mail: sbrogden@tolibrary.org; *Dep Libr Serv Dir,* Nancy Schram; Tel: 805-449-2660, Ext 7351, E-mail: nschram@tolibrary.org; *Div Mgr,* Chris Hendel; Tel: 805-449-2660, Ext 7367, E-mail: chendel@tolibrary.org; *Div Mgr,* Samantha Yeung; Tel: 805-449-2660, Ext 7332, E-mail: syeung@tolibrary.org; *Circ Serv Supvr,* Eamon McSweeney; Tel: 805-449-2660, Ext 7330, E-mail: emcsween@tolibrary.org; *Prov Libr Serv Supvr,* Charlotte Burrows; Tel: 805-449-2660, Ext 7338, E-mail: cburrows@tolibrary.org; *Prov Libr Serv Supvr,* Darren Jeffery; Tel: 805-449-2660, Ext 7350, E-mail: djeffery@tolibrary.org; Staff 20 (MLS 17, Non-MLS 3)
Founded 1982. Pop 128,000; Circ 1,559,385
Library Holdings: Audiobooks 19,980; AV Mats 32,728; e-books 13,613; Electronic Media & Resources 62; Bk Vols 458,677; Per Subs 614
Special Collections: American Radio Archives; Book Arts; Local History Coll
Subject Interests: Genealogy, Hist of radio, Local hist, TV broadcasting
Automation Activity & Vendor Info: (Acquisitions) Innovative Interfaces, Inc - Millenium; (Cataloging) Innovative Interfaces, Inc - Millenium; (Circulation) Innovative Interfaces, Inc - Millenium; (ILL) OCLC FirstSearch; (OPAC) Innovative Interfaces, Inc; (Serials) Innovative Interfaces, Inc
Database Vendor: Baker & Taylor, BWI, CQ Press, CredoReference, ebrary, EBSCO Auto Repair Reference, EBSCO Information Services, Foundation Center, Gale Cengage Learning, H W Wilson, Ingram Library Services, Innovative Interfaces, Inc, LearningExpress, Marcive, Inc, Newsbank, OCLC FirstSearch, OCLC WorldShare Interlibrary Loan, Overdrive, Inc, ProQuest, ReferenceUSA, Sage, TumbleBookLibrary, Wilson - Wilson Web, World Book Online
Wireless access
Function: Adult bk club, Archival coll, Audio & video playback equip for onsite use, Audiobks via web, AV serv, Bk club(s), Bks on cassette, Bks on CD, Children's prog, Computer training, Computers for patron use, Copy machines, Digital talking bks, Electronic databases & coll, Genealogy discussion group, Handicapped accessible, Homebound delivery serv, Homework prog, ILL available, Magnifiers for reading, Microfiche/film & reading machines, Music CDs, Newsp ref libr, Online cat, Online ref, Orientations, OverDrive digital audio bks, Photocopying/Printing, Prog for adults, Prog for children & young adult, Pub access computers, Ref serv available, Ref serv in person, Senior computer classes, Serves mentally handicapped consumers, Spanish lang bks, Spoken cassettes & CDs, Spoken cassettes & DVDs, Story hour, Summer reading prog, Teen prog, Telephone ref, VHS videos, Video lending libr, Web-catalog, Wheelchair accessible
Publications: Bibliographies; Brochures; Fliers; Pathfinders; Programs
Partic in Southern California Library Cooperative
Open Mon-Thurs 11-8, Fri 10-6, Sat 10-5, Sun 12-5
Friends of the Library Group
Branches: 1
NEWBURY PARK BRANCH, 2331 Borchard Rd, Newbury Park, 91320-3206, SAN 372-5626. Tel: 805-498-2139. FAX: 805-498-7034. *Libr Serv Supvr,* Sherri Smith; Tel: 805-498-8488, Ext 7225; Staff 3.5 (MLS 3.5)
Library Holdings: Bk Vols 87,418
Function: Audiobks via web, Bks on cassette, Bks on CD, Children's prog, Computers for patron use, Copy machines, Digital talking bks, Electronic databases & coll, Free DVD rentals, Handicapped accessible, ILL available, Music CDs, Online cat, Online ref, OverDrive digital audio bks, Photocopying/Printing, Prog for adults, Prog for children & young adult, Pub access computers, Ref serv available, Ref serv in person, Spanish lang bks, Spoken cassettes & CDs, Spoken cassettes & DVDs, Summer reading prog, Teen prog, Telephone ref, VHS videos, Video lending libr, Web-catalog, Wheelchair accessible
Open Mon-Wed 12-8, Thurs & Fri 10-6, Sat 10-5
Friends of the Library Group

TIBURON

P BELVEDERE-TIBURON LIBRARY, 1501 Tiburon Blvd, 94920. Tel: 415-789-2665. Reference Tel: 415-789-2661. Administration Tel: 415-789-2660. FAX: 415-789-2650. E-mail: refdesk@bel-tib-lib.org. Web Site: bel-tib-lib.org, thelibrary.info. *Dir,* Deborah Mazzolini; E-mail: dmazzolini@bel-tib-lib.org; *Asst Dir,* Jacki Dunn; E-mail: jdunn@bel-tib-lib.org; *Ch,* Alicia Bell; E-mail: abell@bel-tib-lib.org; *Ref Librn,* Heather Lamb; E-mail: hlamb@bel-tib-lib.org; *Teen Librn,* Rebecca Jung; E-mail: rjung@bel-tib-lib.org; *Adult Serv,* Joan Garrett; E-mail: jgarrett@bel-tib-lib.org; *Circ,* Jason Duran; E-mail: jduran@bel-tib-lib.org; *Tech Serv,* Patty McDonough; E-mail: pmcdonough@bel-tib-lib.org; Staff 17 (MLS 8, Non-MLS 9)
Founded 1997. Pop 13,048; Circ 340,000
Library Holdings: Audiobooks 2,300; AV Mats 11,500; CDs 6,100; DVDs 6,150; e-books 104,000; e-journals 500; Large Print Bks 1,460; Bk Titles 57,000; Per Subs 400
Automation Activity & Vendor Info: (Acquisitions) Innovative Interfaces, Inc; (Cataloging) Innovative Interfaces, Inc; (Circulation) Innovative Interfaces, Inc; (OPAC) Innovative Interfaces, Inc; (Serials) Innovative Interfaces, Inc
Database Vendor: EBSCOhost, Gale Cengage Learning, Innovative Interfaces, Inc
Wireless access
Mem of NorthNet Library System
Partic in Marin Automated Resources & Information Network (MARINet)
Open Mon 10-6, Tues-Thurs 10-9, Fri & Sat 10-5, Sun 12-5
Friends of the Library Group

TORRANCE

J EL CAMINO COLLEGE, 16007 S Crenshaw Blvd, 90506. SAN 301-6625. Tel: 310-660-3525. Circulation Tel: 310-660-3519. Reference Tel: 310-660-6483. FAX: 310-660-3513. *Dir, Learning Res,* Alice B Grigsby; E-mail: agrigsby@elcamino.edu; *Bibliog Instruction Librn,* Claudia Striepe; *Music Librn,* Don Brown; *Pub Serv Librn,* Mary McMillan; *Ref/Electronic Res Librn,* Moon Ichinaga; *Syst Librn,* Noreth Men; *Tech Serv Librn,* Alice Cornelio; Tel: 310-660-3593, Ext 3522; *Fac Coordr,* Howard Story; *Ref,* Seth Daugherty; Staff 7 (MLS 7)
Founded 1948. Enrl 24,756; Fac 321; Highest Degree: Associate

Library Holdings: Bks on Deafness & Sign Lang 64; High Interest/Low Vocabulary Bk Vols 193; Bk Titles 112,020; Bk Vols 122,063; Per Subs 220
Subject Interests: Japanese (Lang), Music
Automation Activity & Vendor Info: (Acquisitions) Innovative Interfaces, Inc; (Cataloging) Innovative Interfaces, Inc; (Circulation) Innovative Interfaces, Inc; (Course Reserve) Innovative Interfaces, Inc; (ILL) OCLC; (OPAC) Innovative Interfaces, Inc; (Serials) Innovative Interfaces, Inc
Database Vendor: Cinahl, CountryWatch, CQ Press, CredoReference, EBSCOhost, Facts on File, Gale Cengage Learning, ProQuest, SerialsSolutions
Wireless access
Publications: Bibliographies; Lamppost (Quarterly newsletter)

M LOS ANGELES COUNTY HARBOR UCLA MEDICAL CENTER*, A F Parlow Library of Health Sciences, 1000 W Carson St, 90509-2910. SAN 335-1637. Tel: 310-222-2372. FAX: 310-533-5146. E-mail: libref@labiomed.org. Web Site: harborucla.org/library. *Dir,* Mary Ann Berliner; *Asst Dir,* Marilouise Gil-Gomez
Founded 1964
Library Holdings: Bk Titles 37,201; Per Subs 515
Subject Interests: Hospital admin, Med, Nursing, Soc serv (soc work)
Automation Activity & Vendor Info: (OPAC) CyberTools for Libraries; (Serials) CyberTools for Libraries
Function: Prof lending libr
Partic in National Network of Libraries of Medicine
Open Mon-Fri 8-7:30
Restriction: Circulates for staff only, Lending to staff only, Non-circulating to the pub

S MASONRY INSTITUTE OF AMERICA LIBRARY*, 22815 Frampton Ave, 90501-5034. SAN 370-1778. Tel: 310-257-9000. FAX: 310-257-1942. E-mail: info@masonryinstitute.org. Web Site: masonryinstitute.org. *Exec Dir,* John Chrysler
Library Holdings: Bk Vols 2,000; Per Subs 10
Subject Interests: Construction, Earthquakes
Wireless access
Restriction: Open by appt only, Open to pub for ref only

S PHENOMENEX LIBRARY*, 411 Madrid Ave, 90501. SAN 323-4991. Tel: 310-212-0555. FAX: 310-328-7768. Web Site: www.phenomenex.com. *Librn,* Phil Koerner
Library Holdings: Bk Vols 500, Per Subs 15
Subject Interests: Gas chromatography, Gel permeation chromatography, High performance liquid chromatography
Function: Ref serv available

M TORRANCE MEMORIAL MEDICAL CENTER*, Medical Library, 3330 W Lomita Blvd, 90505. SAN 301-6668. Tel: 310-517-4720. *Librn, Online Serv,* Anita N Klecker; Staff 1 (MLS 1)
Founded 1972
Library Holdings: Bk Titles 500, Per Subs 110
Subject Interests: Med, Nursing
Publications: Serials Holding List
Partic in National Network of Libraries of Medicine
Open Mon-Fri 8-4:30
Restriction: Employees only, Staff use only

P TORRANCE PUBLIC LIBRARY*, Katy Geissert Civic Center, 3301 Torrance Blvd, 90503. SAN 335-1696. Tel: 310-618-5950. Circulation Tel: 310-618-5969. Reference Tel: 310-781-7599. FAX: 310-618-5952. Web Site: www.library.torranceca.gov. *City Librn,* Hillary Theyer; E-mail: htheyer@torranceca.gov; *Principal Librn,* Dana Vinke; Tel: 310-618-5974, E-mail: dvinke@torranceca.gov; *Principal Librn, Pub Serv,* Jan Wierzbicki; E-mail: jwierzbicki@torranceca.gov; *Sr Librn, Youth Serv Supvr,* Heather Firchow; Tel: 310-618-5964; Staff 20 (MLS 20)
Founded 1967. Pop 149,111; Circ 1,698,431
Jul 2010-Jun 2011 Income (Main Library and Branch(s)) $7,468,010, State $86,086, City $7,271,924, Other $110,000. Mats Exp $939,496, Books $646,777, Per/Ser (Incl. Access Fees) $171,991, AV Mat $48,900, Electronic Ref Mat (Incl. Access Fees) $71,328, Presv $500. Sal $5,382,559
Library Holdings: AV Mats 36,068; Electronic Media & Resources 16; Microforms 147,840; Bk Vols 512,699; Per Subs 886; Videos 34,738
Special Collections: Oral History; State Document Depository; US Document Depository
Subject Interests: Art & archit, Hist, Radio
Automation Activity & Vendor Info: (Acquisitions) SirsiDynix; (Cataloging) SirsiDynix; (Circulation) SirsiDynix; (OPAC) SirsiDynix; (Serials) SirsiDynix
Database Vendor: EBSCOhost, Gale Cengage Learning, infoUSA, Ingram Library Services, LearningExpress, Newsbank, OCLC-RLG, ProQuest, ReferenceUSA, SirsiDynix, World Book Online
Wireless access
Function: Adult bk club, Adult literacy prog, After school storytime, Archival coll, Art exhibits, AV serv, Bk club(s), Bks on cassette, Bks on CD, Bus archives, CD-ROM, Children's prog, Computers for patron use, Copy machines, Electronic databases & coll, Exhibits, Family literacy, Free DVD rentals, Games & aids for the handicapped, Genealogy discussion group, Govt ref serv, Handicapped accessible, Holiday prog, Home delivery & serv to Sr ctr & nursing homes, Homebound delivery serv, Homework prog, ILL available, Large print keyboards, Literacy & newcomer serv, Magnifiers for reading, Music CDs, Newsp ref libr, Online cat, Online ref, Online searches, Orientations, Outreach serv, Preschool outreach, Prog for adults, Prog for children & young adult, Pub access computers, Ref serv available, Senior outreach, Spoken cassettes & CDs, Spoken cassettes & DVDs, Story hour, Summer reading prog, Teen prog, Telephone ref, VHS videos, Video lending libr, Wheelchair accessible, Workshops
Partic in Southern California Library Cooperative
Special Services for the Deaf - ADA equip; Assistive tech; Bks on deafness & sign lang
Special Services for the Blind - Accessible computers; Assistive/Adapted tech devices, equip & products; Audio mat; Bks & mags in Braille, on rec, tape & cassette; Bks on cassette; Bks on CD; Braille & cassettes; Braille bks; Braille equip; Computer access aids; Descriptive video serv (DVS); Handicapped awareness prog; Home delivery serv; Large print & cassettes; Large print bks; Low vision equip; PC for handicapped; Rental typewriters & computers; Text reader; Videos on blindness & phys handicaps
Open Mon-Thurs 10-9, Fri 10-6, Sat 10-5:30, Sun (Sept-June) 1-5
Friends of the Library Group
Branches: 5
EL RETIRO, 126 Vista Del Parque, Redondo Beach, 90277, SAN 335-1726. Tel: 310-375-0922. *Supv Librn,* Kay Ujimori; E-mail: kujimori@torranceca.gov; Staff 7 (MLS 2, Non-MLS 5)
Library Holdings: Bk Vols 44,000
Open Mon-Thurs 11-8, Sat 10-5
Friends of the Library Group
ISABEL HENDERSON BRANCH, 4805 Emerald St, 90503-2899, SAN 335-1750. Tel: 310-371-2075. FAX: 310-371-5025. *Sr Librn,* Janice Wierzbicki; E-mail: jwierzbicki@torranceca.gov
Library Holdings: Bk Vols 38,931
Open Mon-Thurs 11-8, Sat 10-5
Friends of the Library Group
NORTH TORRANCE, 3604 Artesia Blvd, 90504-3315, SAN 335-1785. Tel: 310-323-7200. FAX: 310-323-9687. *Sr Librn,* Steve Frame; E-mail: sframe@torranceca.gov
Library Holdings: Bk Vols 45,281
Open Mon-Thurs 11-8, Sat 10-5
Friends of the Library Group
SOUTHEAST, 23115 S Arlington Ave, 90501-5816, SAN 335-1815. Tel: 310-530-5044. FAX: 310-530-5181. *Sr Librn,* Patrice Deleget; E-mail: pdeleget@torranceca.gov
Library Holdings: Bk Vols 46,044
Open Mon-Thurs 11-8, Sat 10-5
Friends of the Library Group
WALTERIA, 3815 W 242nd St, 90505-6410, SAN 335-184X. Tel: 310-375-8418. FAX: 310-375-8325. *Sr Librn,* Philip Ross; E-mail: pross@torranceca.gov
Library Holdings: Bk Vols 40,364
Open Mon-Thurs 11-8, Sat 10-5
Friends of the Library Group

TRAVIS AFB

UNITED STATES AIR FORCE
AM DAVID GRANT USAF MEDICAL CENTER LEARNING RESOURCE CENTER, 101 Bodin Circle, 94535-1800, SAN 335-1874. Tel: 707-423-5344. FAX: 707-423-7965. *Info Spec,* Regina Ann Rowell; E-mail: regina.rowell@us.af.mil; Staff 1 (MLS 1)
Library Holdings: AV Mats 645; e-journals 51; Bk Vols 3,000; Per Subs 76
Subject Interests: Dentistry, Hospital admin, Med, Nursing
Automation Activity & Vendor Info: (Cataloging) Horizon; (Circulation) Horizon; (OPAC) Horizon; (Serials) Horizon
Database Vendor: EBSCOhost, Elsevier, Lexi-Comp, MD Consult, Medline, OCLC FirstSearch, OCLC WorldShare Interlibrary Loan, OVID Technologies, PubMed, RefWorks, ScienceDirect, SerialsSolutions, SirsiDynix, STAT!Ref (Teton Data Systems), UpToDate, WT Cox
Function: Computers for patron use, Copy machines, Electronic databases & coll, ILL available, Online cat, Online searches, Orientations, Ref serv available
Partic in Fedlink; National Network of Libraries of Medicine; Sacramento Area Health Sciences Librs
Restriction: Badge access after hrs, Circulates for staff only, In-house use for visitors, Open to staff, patients & family mem
A MITCHELL MEMORIAL LIBRARY-TRAVIS AIR FORCE BASE LIBRARY*, 60 FSS/FSDL, 510 Travis Ave, 94535-2168, SAN 335-1904. Tel: 707-424-3279. Reference Tel: 707-424-5255. FAX:

707-424-3809. Web Site: www.mitchellmemoriallibrary.org. *Dir,* Marie Ludwig; Tel: 707-424-4940; Staff 2 (MLS 2)
Founded 1943
Automation Activity & Vendor Info: (Circulation) SIRSI WorkFlows

TULARE

P TULARE PUBLIC LIBRARY*, 475 North M St, 93274-4142. SAN 301-6684. Tel: 559-685-4500. Circulation Tel: 559-685-4501. Reference Tel: 559-685-4503. FAX: 559-685-2345. Web Site: www.tularepubliclibrary.org. *Interim Libr Mgr,* Michael C Stowell; Tel: 559-685-4506, E-mail: michael.stowell@sjvls.org; *Ad,* Daniel Brunk; Tel: 559-685-4515, E-mail: daniel.brunk@sjvls.org; *Card Serv & Tech,* Heidi Clark; Tel: 559-685-4505, E-mail: heidi.clark@sjvls.org; *Youth Serv,* Melissa Emerson; Tel: 559-685-4507, E-mail: melissa.emerson@sjvls.org; Staff 3 (MLS 3)
Founded 1878. Pop 59,535; Circ 298,547
Jul 2010-Jun 2011 Income $833,912, State $50,552, City $783,360. Mats Exp $65,600, Books $51,300, Per/Ser (Incl. Access Fees) $5,200, Other Print Mats $4,300, Electronic Ref Mat (Incl. Access Fees) $4,800. Sal $476,750
Library Holdings: AV Mats 6,914; CDs 7,408; DVDs 4,205; e-books 279; Bk Vols 82,664; Per Subs 131
Special Collections: Genealogy & Local History Coll
Subject Interests: Art, Hist, Music, Relig
Automation Activity & Vendor Info: (Acquisitions) Horizon; (Cataloging) Horizon; (Circulation) Horizon
Database Vendor: Baker & Taylor, EBSCOhost, OCLC, SirsiDynix
Wireless access
Mem of San Joaquin Valley Library System
Open Tues-Thurs 11-7, Fri & Sat 11-4
Friends of the Library Group

TULELAKE

S NATIONAL PARK SERVICE*, Lava Beds National Monument Research Library, One Indian Well Headquarters, 96134. (Mail add: PO Box 1240, 96134), SAN 370-0046. Tel: 530-667-8113, 530-667-8119. Circulation Tel: 530-667-8117. FAX: 530-667-2737. Web Site: www.nps.gov/labe. *Superintendent,* Dave Kruse; *Coordr,* Anglea Sutton
Library Holdings: Bk Titles 2,500; Bk Vols 2,550
Restriction: Open by appt only

TURLOCK

C CALIFORNIA STATE UNIVERSITY, STANISLAUS, University Library, One University Circle, 95382. SAN 301-6692. Circulation Tel: 209-667-3233, 209-667-3234. Interlibrary Loan Service Tel: 209-667-3236. Reference Tel: 209-664-6558. Administration Tel: 209-667-3232. Information Services Tel: 209-667-3761. Interlibrary Loan Service FAX: 209-664-7081. Administration FAX: 209-667-3164. E-mail: library@library.csustan.edu. Web Site: library.csustan.edu. *Dean of Libr Serv,* Ronald Rodriguez; Tel: 209-667-3607, E-mail: rrodriguez36@csustan.edu; *Acq Librn,* Annie Hor; Tel: 209-667-3709, E-mail: ahor@csustan.edu; *Electronic Res Librn,* John Brandt; Tel: 209-664-6563, E-mail: jbrandt@csustan.edu; *Instruction & User Serv Librn,* Laura French; Tel: 209-664-6557, E-mail: lfrench@csustan.edu; *Ref & Instruction Librn,* Tim Held; Tel: 209-667-6555, E-mail: theld@csustan.edu; *Ref & Instruction Librn,* Maryann Hight; Tel: 209-664-6553, E-mail: mhight@csustan.edu; *Ref & Instruction Librn,* Warren Jacobs; Tel: 209-664-6565, E-mail: wjacobs@csustan.edu; *Web Serv Librn,* Paul Park; Tel: 209-664-6556, E-mail: jpark5@csustan.edu; *Syst Supvr,* Rick Dietz; Tel: 209-667-3605, E-mail: rdietz@csustan.edu; *Admin Support Coordr,* Loretta Blakeley; E-mail: lblakeley@csustan.edu; *ILL Coordr,* Julie Reuben; E-mail: jreuben@csustan.edu; Staff 21 (MLS 8, Non-MLS 13)
Founded 1960. Enrl 8,917; Fac 492; Highest Degree: Doctorate
Jul 2013-Jun 2014 Income $2,553,060, Locally Generated Income $15,907, Parent Institution $2,032,494, Other $504,659. Mats Exp $642,322, Books $54,380, Per/Ser (Incl. Access Fees) $188,803, Electronic Ref Mat (Incl. Access Fees) $369,039, Presv $30,100. Sal $1,238,225 (Prof $533,261)
Library Holdings: AV Mats 6,095; e-books 8,290; Bk Titles 344,311; Bk Vols 513,565; Per Subs 637
Special Collections: Californiana Coll; Historical Regional Newspaper Coll; Portuguese Culture Photographs; Religious Assyriana Coll; Stanislaus County History Coll; Stanislaus County Photographs; Western US Fine Printing Coll. Oral History; State Document Depository; US Document Depository
Subject Interests: Bus, Liberal arts, Sci, Teacher educ
Automation Activity & Vendor Info: (Acquisitions) Innovative Interfaces, Inc; (Cataloging) Innovative Interfaces, Inc; (Circulation) Innovative Interfaces, Inc; (Course Reserve) Innovative Interfaces, Inc; (ILL) OCLC; (OPAC) Innovative Interfaces, Inc; (Serials) Innovative Interfaces, Inc
Database Vendor: ACM (Association for Computing Machinery), Agricola, American Chemical Society, American Physical Society, Annual Reviews, Cinahl, CountryWatch, CQ Press, CredoReference, ebrary, EBSCOhost, Elsevier, Emerald, Factiva.com, IEEE (Institute of Electrical & Electronics Engineers), Innovative Interfaces, Inc, JSTOR, LexisNexis, Marcive, Inc, Medline, Mergent Online, OCLC, OCLC FirstSearch, OCLC WorldShare Interlibrary Loan, Oxford Online, Project MUSE, ProQuest, PubMed, Safari Books Online, Sage, ScienceDirect, SerialsSolutions, Springer-Verlag, Standard & Poor's, Thomson - Web of Science, ValueLine, Wiley, Wilson - Wilson Web
Wireless access
Partic in OCLC Online Computer Library Center, Inc
Special Services for the Deaf - Assistive tech
Special Services for the Blind - Assistive/Adapted tech devices, equip & products; Closed circuit TV magnifier; Computer with voice synthesizer for visually impaired persons
Open Mon-Thurs 7:45am-Midnight, Fri 7:45-5, Sat 9-5, Sun 11-7

M EMANUEL MEDICAL CENTER LIBRARY*, PO Box 819005, 95381-9005. SAN 301-6706. Tel: 209-667-4200, Ext 5655. FAX: 209-664-5657. *In Charge,* Nadine Neswick
Founded 1971
Library Holdings: Bk Vols 106; Per Subs 21
Partic in N San Joaquin Health Sci Libr Consortium
Restriction: Staff use only

TWENTYNINE PALMS

A UNITED STATES MARINE CORPS*, MCCS Lifelong Learning Library, MCAGCC, Box 788150, 92278-8150. SAN 335-1939. Tel: 760-830-6875. FAX: 760-830-4497. Web Site: www.librarylink.info/29palms. *Librn,* Amy Terrell; Staff 1 (MLS 1)
Founded 1957
Library Holdings: DVDs 4,038; Bk Vols 30,535; Per Subs 73
Subject Interests: Mil hist
Automation Activity & Vendor Info: (Acquisitions) SirsiDynix; (Cataloging) SirsiDynix; (Circulation) SirsiDynix; (ILL) SirsiDynix
Database Vendor: SirsiDynix
Open Mon-Fri 8:30-8, Sat & Sun 10-6
Restriction: Mil, family mem, retirees, Civil Serv personnel NAF only

S UNITED STATES NATIONAL PARK SERVICE*, Joshua Tree National Park Research Library, 74485 National Park Dr, 92277. SAN 371-7879. Tel: 760-367-5571. FAX: 760-367-5588. *In Charge,* Melanie Spoo; E-mail: melanie_spoo@nps.gov
Founded 1994
Library Holdings: Bk Vols 4,000
Special Collections: Early Archeology/Anthropology volumes, William H Campbell Library
Subject Interests: Local hist, Local natural hist, Planning doc
Function: Ref serv available
Restriction: Not a lending libr

UKIAH

G BUREAU OF LAND MANAGEMENT*, Ukiah Field Office Library, 2550 N State St, 95482-3023. SAN 301-6730. Tel: 707-468-4000. FAX: 707-468-4027. Web Site: www.ca.blm.gov/ukiah. *In Charge,* Amber LeLoup
Library Holdings: Bk Vols 2,500
Restriction: Staff use only

J MENDOCINO COLLEGE LIBRARY*, 1000 Hensley Creek Rd, 95482-7821. SAN 301-6749. Tel: 707-468-3053. Circulation Tel: 707-468-3158. Interlibrary Loan Service Tel: 707-468-3052. Reference Tel: 707-468-3245. Automation Services Tel: 707-468-3054. FAX: 707-468-3056. Web Site: www.mendocino.cc.ca.us. *Head Librn,* John Koetzner; E-mail: jkoetzner@mendocino.edu; *Ref Librn,* Toni Sousa; E-mail: tsouda@mendocino.edu; *Ref Librn,* Sandy Spencer; E-mail: sspencer@mendocino.edu; *Ref Librn,* George Spinas; E-mail: gspinas@mendocino.edu; *Ref Librn,* Eliza Wingate; E-mail: ewingate@mendocino.edu; *Cat, ILL,* Hope Patterson; E-mail: hpatterson@mendocino.edu; *Circ,* K J Todd; E-mail: ktodd@mendocino.edu; *Instrul Tech,* David Bushway; E-mail: dbushway@mendocino.edu; Staff 3 (Non-MLS 3)
Founded 1973. Fac 200; Highest Degree: Associate
Library Holdings: Bk Vols 30,000; Per Subs 177
Automation Activity & Vendor Info: (Circulation) Follett Software; (OPAC) Follett Software
Database Vendor: EBSCOhost, ProQuest
Partic in OCLC Online Computer Library Center, Inc
Restriction: Non-circulating to the pub

S MENDOCINO COUNTY HISTORICAL SOCIETY, Held-Poage Historical Research Library, 603 W Perkins St, 95482-4726. SAN 301-6757. Tel: 707-462-6969. E-mail: mchs@pacific.net. Web Site: mchs.pacificsites.com. *Dir,* Dr Paul Poulos; E-mail: pwpoulos@comcast.net; Staff 8 (Non-MLS 8)
Founded 1976

Library Holdings: Bk Titles 4,500; Per Subs 200
Special Collections: Americana (Estelle Beard Coll); California Indians; Civil War (William P Held Coll); Mendocino County
Subject Interests: Genealogy
Publications: Newsletter (Quarterly)
Open Wed-Fri 1-4

GL MENDOCINO COUNTY LAW LIBRARY*, Courthouse, Rm 307, 100 N State St, 95482. SAN 301-6765. Tel: 707-463-4201. FAX: 707-468-3459. E-mail: lawlib@pacific.net. Web Site: www.pacificsites.com/~lawlib. *Dir,* Dan Hibshman
Library Holdings: Bk Vols 8,000

P MENDOCINO COUNTY LIBRARY DISTRICT*, 105 N Main St, 95482. SAN 335-1963. Interlibrary Loan Service Tel: 707-463-2513. Reference Tel: 707-463-4493. Administration Tel: 707-467-2590. E-mail: mendoref@co.mendocino.ca.us. Web Site: www.mendolibrary.org. *County Librn,* Mindy Kittay; E-mail: kittaym@co.mendocino.ca.us; Staff 11 (MLS 4, Non-MLS 7)
Founded 1964. Pop 90,000; Circ 398,794
Library Holdings: Bk Titles 93,000; Bk Vols 159,500; Per Subs 110
Special Collections: Native Americans of Mendocino County
Subject Interests: Art, Fishing, Forestry, Genealogy, Indians, Logging, Wines
Automation Activity & Vendor Info: (Cataloging) Horizon; (Circulation) Horizon; (ILL) OCLC; (OPAC) Horizon
Database Vendor: EBSCOhost, Gale Cengage Learning, SirsiDynix
Wireless access
Mem of NorthNet Library System
Partic in OCLC Online Computer Library Center, Inc
Open Tues & Thurs 10-6, Wed 12-8, Sat 10-5
Friends of the Library Group
Branches: 5
COAST COMMUNITY, 225 Main St, Point Arena, 95468. (Mail add: PO Box 808, Point Arena, 95468-0808), SAN 376-8139. Tel: 707-882-3114. FAX: 707-882-3114. *Libr Assoc,* Julia Larke; Staff 1 (Non-MLS 1)
Founded 1985. Pop 7,000; Circ 9,557
Library Holdings: Bk Vols 12,999
Publications: Redwood Coast Review
Open Mon & Fri 12-6, Tues 10-6, Wed 10-8, Thurs 12-8, Sat 12-3
Friends of the Library Group
FORT BRAGG BRANCH, 499 Laurel St, Fort Bragg, 95437, SAN 335-1998. Tel: 707-964-2020. FAX: 707-961-2623. *Br Mgr,* Judith Kayser
Pop 18,000; Circ 93,869
Library Holdings: Bk Titles 34,669; Per Subs 70
Open Tues & Sat 10-5, Wed 12-8
Friends of the Library Group
ROUND VALLEY, 23925 Howard St, Covelo, 95428. (Mail add: PO Box 620, Covelo, 95428), SAN 372-7858. Tel: 707-983-6736. *Libr Assoc,* Rachel Borum; Tel: 707-983-6738; Staff 1 (Non-MLS 1)
Founded 1990. Pop 2,300; Circ 10,560
Library Holdings: Bk Vols 10,782
Open Mon-Fri 10-5
Friends of the Library Group
UKIAH MAIN LIBRARY, 105 N Main St, 95482. Tel: 707-463-4491. FAX: 707-463-5472. *Br Librn,* Eliza Wingate; Tel: 707-463-4493, Fax: 707-463-5470, E-mail: wingatee@co.mendocino.ca.us; Staff 1 (MLS 1)
WILLITS BRANCH, 390 E Commercial St, Willits, 95490, SAN 335-2021. Tel: 707-459-5908. FAX: 707-459-7819. *Br Mgr,* Donna Kerr; Staff 1 (MLS 1)
Founded 1972
Library Holdings: Bk Vols 34,000
Special Collections: Calif History Coll; Western Americana Coll
Automation Activity & Vendor Info: (Circulation) Horizon
Open Tues 10-8, Wed & Thurs 10-6, Fri & Sat 10-5
Friends of the Library Group
Bookmobiles: 1

UPLAND

R FIRST PRESBYTERIAN CHURCH LIBRARY*, 869 N Euclid Ave, 91786. SAN 301-6781. Tel: 909-982-8811. FAX: 909-985-8014. *Librn,* Annette Davidson
Library Holdings: Bk Vols 500
Wireless access
Restriction: Mem only

M SAN ANTONIO COMMUNITY HOSPITAL*, Weber Memorial Library, 999 San Bernardino Rd, 91786. SAN 327-4152. Tel: 909-920-4972. FAX: 909-931-0102. *Librn,* Ardis Weiss
Library Holdings: Bk Vols 4,800; Per Subs 250
Partic in Inland Empire Med Libr Coop
Open Mon-Fri 8-4:30

P UPLAND PUBLIC LIBRARY*, 450 N Euclid Ave, 91786-4732. SAN 301-679X. Tel: 909-931-4200. Interlibrary Loan Service Tel: 909-931-4225. Administration Tel: 909-931-4203. Information Services Tel: 909-931-4205. FAX: 909-931-4209. Web Site: www.ci.upland.ca.us/asp/site/library/about/general/index.asp. *Dir,* Roberta Knighten; *Principal Librn,* Maria Sunio; *Principal Librn,* Shawn Townsend; *Youth Serv Librn,* Ann-Marie Biden; Tel: 909-931-4215, E-mail: ambiden@ci.upland.ca.us; Staff 20 (MLS 4, Non-MLS 16)
Founded 1913. Pop 75,035; Circ 309,471
Jul 2008-Jun 2009 Income $2,026,908, State $72,122, Locally Generated Income $1,858,110, Other $96,676. Mats Exp $167,697, Books $109,860, Per/Ser (Incl. Access Fees) $15,862, Other Print Mats $1,120, AV Mat $4,118, Electronic Ref Mat (Incl. Access Fees) $36,737. Sal $1,433,018
Library Holdings: AV Mats 7,241; CDs 1,916; DVDs 1,680; e-books 2,125; Large Print Bks 1,514; Bk Titles 157,390; Bk Vols 159,927; Per Subs 220; Talking Bks 1,941; Videos 1,626
Special Collections: Local History Coll. Oral History
Automation Activity & Vendor Info: (Acquisitions) SirsiDynix; (Cataloging) SirsiDynix; (Circulation) SirsiDynix; (ILL) OCLC; (OPAC) SirsiDynix
Database Vendor: EBSCOhost, Gale Cengage Learning, Ingram Library Services, LearningExpress, Newsbank, OCLC FirstSearch, Overdrive, Inc, ProQuest, ReferenceUSA, SirsiDynix
Wireless access
Function: Adult literacy prog, Homebound delivery serv, ILL available, Magnifiers for reading, Photocopying/Printing, Prog for adults, Prog for children & young adult, Ref serv available, Summer reading prog, Wheelchair accessible
Mem of Inland Library System
Partic in Califa; San Bernardino, Inyo, Riverside Counties United Library Services
Special Services for the Blind - Talking bks
Open Mon & Tues 10-8, Wed & Thurs 10-6, Sat 10-4, Sun 1-5
Friends of the Library Group
Bookmobiles: 1. Libr Clerk, Jamie Murray. Bk Vols 2,212

VALENCIA

C CALIFORNIA INSTITUTE OF THE ARTS, Division of Library & Information Resources, 24700 McBean Pkwy, 91355. SAN 301-6803. Tel: 661-253-7885. Reference Tel: 661-291-3024. Automation Services Tel: 661-253-7888. FAX: 661-254-4561. E-mail: libref@calarts.edu. Web Site: calarts.edu/library. *Dean,* Jeff Gatten; E-mail: jgatten@calarts.edu; *Assoc Dean,* Susan Lowenberg; E-mail: susan@calarts.edu; *Access Serv Librn,* Lavinia Welch; E-mail: lwelch@calarts.edu; *Performing Arts Librn,* Kathy Carbone; Tel: 661-253-7882, E-mail: kcarbone@calarts.edu; *Ref, Outreach & Instruction Librn,* Brena Smith; E-mail: bsmith@calarts.edu; *Visual Arts Librn,* Karen Baxter; Tel: 661-253-7880, E-mail: kbaxter@calarts.edu. Subject Specialists: *Performing arts,* Kathy Carbone; *Visual arts,* Karen Baxter; Staff 13 (MLS 6, Non-MLS 7)
Founded 1968. Enrl 1,480; Fac 237; Highest Degree: Doctorate
Jul 2013-Jun 2014. Mats Exp $243,880, Books $90,075, Per/Ser (Incl. Access Fees) $35,275, AV Mat $37,287, Electronic Ref Mat (Incl. Access Fees) $80,251, Presv $992. Sal $820,785 (Prof $427,803)
Library Holdings: AV Mats 33,536; e-books 151,694; e-journals 10,659; Microforms 5,632; Music Scores 26,565; Bk Titles 135,659, Per Subs 240
Special Collections: Artists Books; Film History Coll; MCA Coll; Viola Hegyi Swisher Dance Coll
Subject Interests: Art, Dance, Film, Music, Theatre, Writing
Automation Activity & Vendor Info: (Acquisitions) OCLC WorldShare Interlibrary Loan; (Cataloging) OCLC Connexion; (Circulation) OCLC WorldShare Interlibrary Loan; (Course Reserve) OCLC WorldShare Interlibrary Loan; (ILL) OCLC; (OPAC) OCLC WorldShare Interlibrary Loan; (Serials) OCLC Connexion
Database Vendor: Alexander Street Press, ARTstor, EBSCOhost, Gale Cengage Learning, JSTOR, LexisNexis, OCLC FirstSearch, Project MUSE, ProQuest
Wireless access
Function: Archival coll, Audio & video playback equip for onsite use, AV serv, Copy machines, Electronic databases & coll, Fax serv, ILL available, Music CDs, Online cat, Photocopying/Printing, Ref serv available, Scanner, VHS videos
Partic in Statewide California Electronic Library Consortium (SCELC)
Open Mon-Thurs 9am-Midnight, Fri 9-9, Sat 1-5, Sun 1pm-Midnight
Restriction: Borrowing requests are handled by ILL, Circ limited, In-house use for visitors

VALLEJO

C THE CALIFORNIA MARITIME ACADEMY LIBRARY*, 200 Maritime Academy Dr, 94590. SAN 301-682X. Tel: 707-654-1090. Administration Tel: 707-654-1093. Automation Services Tel: 707-654-1092. Information Services Tel: 707-654-1098. FAX: 707-654-1094. E-mail: library@csum.edu. Web Site: library.csum.edu. *Dean of Libr,* Richard Robison; E-mail: rrobison@csum.edu; *Instruction Coordr, Librn,* Michele

Van Hoeck; Tel: 707-654-1097, E-mail: MVanHoeck@csum.edu; *Instruction & Outreach Librn,* Margot Hanson; Tel: 707-654-1091, E-mail: mhanson@csum.edu; *Cat, Tech Serv & Syst Librn,* Mark Stackpole; E-mail: mstackpole@csum.edu; *Coordr, Campus Hist Coll, Pub Serv,* Larry Stevens; Tel: 707-654-1089, E-mail: lstevens@csum.edu; *Pub Serv, Ser/ILL,* Jennifer Haupt; E-mail: jhaupt@csum.edu. Subject Specialists: *Bus, Gen,* Richard Robison; *Gen,* Michele Van Hoeck; *Gen,* Margot Hanson; *Maritime, Music, Theatre,* Mark Stackpole; *Gen,* Larry Stevens; *Gen,* Jennifer Haupt; Staff 6 (MLS 4, Non-MLS 2)
Founded 1929. Enrl 1,025; Fac 82; Highest Degree: Master
Library Holdings: Bk Titles 38,000; Bk Vols 40,000; Per Subs 276; Spec Interest Per Sub 112
Special Collections: Cal Maritime Academy Historical Archives; Cal Maritime Academy Oral History Project. Oral History
Subject Interests: Electrical eng, Intl studies, Logistics, Marine eng, Marine tech, Marine transportation, Maritime law
Automation Activity & Vendor Info: (Cataloging) Innovative Interfaces, Inc; (Circulation) Innovative Interfaces, Inc; (Course Reserve) Innovative Interfaces, Inc; (ILL) OCLC; (OPAC) Innovative Interfaces, Inc
Database Vendor: CountryWatch, CQ Press, EBSCOhost, Elsevier, Gale Cengage Learning, Grolier Online, H W Wilson, IEEE (Institute of Electrical & Electronics Engineers), JSTOR, LexisNexis, OCLC FirstSearch, Project MUSE, ProQuest, Safari Books Online, Sage, ScienceDirect, Springshare, LLC, Wiley, YBP Library Services
Wireless access
Function: Archival coll, For res purposes, ILL available, Photocopying/Printing, Ref serv available, Referrals accepted, Res libr
Partic in Link+; OCLC Online Computer Library Center, Inc
Open Mon-Thurs 8am-10pm, Fri 8-4:30, Sat 10:30-4:30, Sun 2-10
Restriction: Circ limited, Open to students, fac & staff, Pub use on premises

S VALLEJO NAVAL & HISTORICAL MUSEUM*, 734 Marin St, 94590. SAN 326-5048. Tel: 707-643-0077. FAX: 707-643-2443. E-mail: valmuse@pacbell.net. Web Site: www.vallejomuseum.org. *Librn,* Arlene Valdez
Founded 1974
Library Holdings: AV Mats 100; Bk Titles 5,200; Per Subs 10
Special Collections: Municipal Document Depository; Oral History
Subject Interests: Archives, Local hist, Maritime hist
Function: Res libr
Open Tues 10-3
Restriction: Non-circulating

VALLEY GLEN

J LOS ANGELES VALLEY COLLEGE LIBRARY*, 5800 Fulton Ave, 91401-4096. SAN 301-6900. Tel: 818-947-2425. Circulation Tel: 818-947-2756. Reference Tel: 818-947-2763, 818-947-2764. FAX: 818-947-2751. Web Site: www.lavc.edu/library/library.html. *Dept Chair,* Dora Esten; Tel: 818-947-2761, E-mail: estende@lavc.edu; *Librn,* Mrs Xiaoyang Liu Behlendorf; Tel: 818-947-2762, E-mail: behlenxl@lavc.edu; *Librn,* Dana Lubow; Tel: 818-947-2766, E-mail: lubowdn@lavc.edu. Subject Specialists: *Cataloging,* Dora Esten; *Bibliog instruction,* Mrs Xiaoyang Liu Behlendorf; *Bibliog instruction,* Dana Lubow; Staff 3 (MLS 3)
Founded 1949. Enrl 18,300; Fac 320; Highest Degree: Associate
Library Holdings: e-books 18,075; Bk Titles 105,926; Bk Vols 129,083; Per Subs 106
Subject Interests: Art & archit, Ethnic studies, Humanities, Relig, Soc sci
Automation Activity & Vendor Info: (Cataloging) SirsiDynix; (Circulation) SirsiDynix; (Course Reserve) SirsiDynix; (ILL) SirsiDynix; (OPAC) SirsiDynix; (Serials) SirsiDynix
Database Vendor: Bowker, CountryWatch, CQ Press, Gale Cengage Learning, LexisNexis, McGraw-Hill, ProQuest, Safari Books Online, SirsiDynix
Wireless access
Open Mon-Thurs 8-7, Fri 9-1
Friends of the Library Group

VAN NUYS

S INTERNATIONAL STAMP COLLECTORS SOCIETY LIBRARY*, PO Box 854, 91408-0854. SAN 325-528X. Tel: 818-997-6496. *Exec Dir,* Israel Bick; *Librn,* Lorraine Pollak
Founded 1970
Library Holdings: Bk Titles 500; Per Subs 25

M VALLEY PRESBYTERIAN HOSPITAL*, Richard O Myers Library, 15107 Vanowen St, 91405-9102. SAN 301-6935. Tel: 818-902-2973. FAX: 818-902-3990.
Library Holdings: Bk Titles 1,550; Per Subs 365
Partic in Docline
Open Mon, Wed & Fri 9-12:30 & 1-4
Restriction: Staff use only

VANDENBERG AFB

A UNITED STATES AIR FORCE*, 30th Space Wing Technical Library, F4D 3FA-30 SVX/SVMG, 100 Community Loop, 93437-5223. SAN 335-217X. Tel: 805-606-1110, Ext 69745. FAX: 805-734-8232, Ext 58941. *Dir,* Christianne McLaughlin
Library Holdings: Per Subs 480
Subject Interests: Computer sci, Eng, Fuel, Optics, Radar
Publications: Monthly Acquisitions; Periodicals
Partic in Coop Libr Agency for Syst & Servs; Dialog Corp; OCLC Online Computer Library Center, Inc

VENTURA

C BROOKS INSTITUTE LIBRARY*, 5301 N Ventura Ave, 93001. Tel: 805-585-8000. *Dir,* Donna Burr; Staff 2 (MLS 1, Non-MLS 1)
Founded 2002. Enrl 1,500; Highest Degree: Master
Library Holdings: AV Mats 200; DVDs 800; Bk Vols 5,500

S THE CHURCH OF JESUS CHRIST OF LATTER-DAY SAINTS*, Family History Center Ventura Stake, 76 Saint Paul Dr, 93003. SAN 329-1790. Tel: 805-643-5607. *Dir,* Joan Beem; *Librn,* Rosemarie Salmon; Staff 6 (MLS 1, Non-MLS 5)
Founded 1978
Library Holdings: Bk Vols 1,000
Special Collections: IGI Ancestral File; Social Security Death Index
Open Tues & Thurs 10-8, Wed 10-5, Sat 10-2

S FUGRO WEST*, Ventura Library, 4820 McGrath St, Ste 100, 93003. SAN 320-3689. Tel: 805-650-7000. FAX: 805-650-7010. Web Site: www.fugroconsultants.com.
Library Holdings: Bk Vols 7,900; Per Subs 162
Subject Interests: Geophysics
Open Mon-Fri 8-5:30

S MUSEUM OF VENTURA COUNTY, Historical Research Library, 100 E Main St, 93001. SAN 301-6994. Tel: 805-653-0323, Ext 320. FAX: 805-653-5267. E-mail: library@venturamuseum.org. Web Site: www.venturamuseum.org. *Libr Dir,* Charles Nelson Johnson; Staff 1 (MLS 1)
Founded 1913
Library Holdings: Bk Titles 5,000; Per Subs 16
Special Collections: California Ventura County History, 1871-1935, bks, newsp, photos; Newspapers, 1850-1935; Oral History (400+); Ventura County Historical Society Quarterlies, 1955-Present. Oral History
Publications: Journal of Ventura County History; Ventura County Historical Society (Quarterly)
Member Libraries: Ventura County Library
Partic in Central Coast Museum Consortium
Open Tues-Fri 11-5
Restriction: Non-circulating

J VENTURA COLLEGE*, Evelyn & Howard Boroughs Library, 4667 Telegraph Rd, 93003-3889. SAN 301-6986. Tel: 805-654-6482. FAX: 805-648-8900. Web Site: www.venturacollege.edu/library. *Dean,* Dr Diane Moore; Tel: 805-654-6468, E-mail: dianem@vcccd.net; *Assoc Librn,* Harmony Rodriguez; Tel: 805-654-6400, Ext 3257, E-mail: hrodriguez@vcccd.edu; *Assoc Librn,* Peter H Sezzi; Tel: 805-654-6400, Ext 3258, E-mail: psezzi@vcccd.edu; *Learning Res Supvr,* Sandra Hajas; Tel: 805-654-6400, Ext 3124, E-mail: shajas@vcccd.edu; Staff 6 (MLS 2, Non-MLS 4)
Founded 1925. Enrl 11,695; Fac 530; Highest Degree: Associate
Library Holdings: Bk Titles 54,061; Bk Vols 66,357; Per Subs 494
Subject Interests: Art, Costume, Ethnic studies, Feminism
Automation Activity & Vendor Info: (Cataloging) TLC (The Library Corporation); (Circulation) TLC (The Library Corporation); (OPAC) TLC (The Library Corporation)
Database Vendor: ARTstor, EBSCOhost, Facts on File, Gale Cengage Learning, JSTOR, ProQuest
Function: ILL available
Partic in Coop Libr Agency for Syst & Servs
Open Mon-Thurs 7:30am-9pm, Fri 7:30-4, Sat 9-3
Friends of the Library Group

GL VENTURA COUNTY LAW LIBRARY*, 800 S Victoria Ave, 93009-2020. SAN 301-7001. Tel: 805-642-8982. FAX: 805-642-7177. E-mail: vcll@rain.org. Web Site: www.vencolawlib.org. *Librn,* Jane G Meyer; Staff 5 (MLS 1, Non-MLS 4)
Founded 1891
Library Holdings: Bk Vols 81,292; Per Subs 328
Special Collections: Law Coll
Database Vendor: EOS International, LexisNexis, Westlaw
Wireless access

P VENTURA COUNTY LIBRARY*, 5600 Everglades St, Ste A, 93003. SAN 335-220X. Tel: 805-677-7150. Interlibrary Loan Service Tel: 805-677-7169. Reference Tel: 805-648-2716. Automation Services Tel: 805 701-1317. FAX: 805-677-7173. Interlibrary Loan Service FAX: 805-677-7169. TDD: 805-656-1313. Web Site: www.vencolibrary.org. *Dir,* Jackie Griffin; Tel: 805-677-7153, E-mail: jackie.griffin@ventura.org; *East Region & Adult Serv Mgr,* Dale Redfield; Tel: 805-677-7158, E-mail: dale.redfield@ventura.org; *Support Serv Mgr,* Mark Lager; E-mail: mark.lager@ventura.org; *Tech Serv Mgr,* Sandy Schmitz; Tel: 805-677-7170, E-mail: sandy.schmitz@ventura.org; *West Region & Youth Serv Mgr,* Lori Karns; Tel: 805-677-7156, E-mail: lori.karns@ventura.org; *Adult Literacy Coordr,* Carol Chapman; Tel: 805-677-7159, E-mail: carol.chapman@ventura.org; *ILL,* Liz Romero; E-mail: liz.romero@ventura.org; *Webmaster,* Barbara Eales; Tel: 805-218-5360, E-mail: barbara.eales@ventura.org; Staff 28 (MLS 13, Non-MLS 15)
Founded 1915. Pop 371,033; Circ 1,398,645
Jul 2010-Jun 2011 Income (Main Library and Branch(s)) $9,978,834, State $260,899, Federal $91,569, County $8,312,637, Other $1,313,729. Mats Exp $1,296,360, Books $781,405, Per/Ser (Incl. Access Fees) $45,481, Other Print Mats $117,557, Electronic Ref Mat (Incl. Access Fees) $351,917. Sal $5,882,837
Library Holdings: Audiobooks 21,554; DVDs 28,437; e-books 5,975; Electronic Media & Resources 47; Bk Vols 629,346; Per Subs 613
Special Collections: Local History (Ventura County Coll)
Automation Activity & Vendor Info: (Acquisitions) Baker & Taylor; (Cataloging) SirsiDynix; (Circulation) SirsiDynix; (ILL) OCLC; (OPAC) SirsiDynix; (Serials) SirsiDynix
Database Vendor: Baker & Taylor, EBSCOhost, Gale Cengage Learning, LearningExpress, Newsbank, OCLC WorldShare Interlibrary Loan, Overdrive, Inc, ProQuest, ReferenceUSA, SirsiDynix, Tech Logic, TumbleBookLibrary, World Book Online
Wireless access
Partic in Southern California Library Cooperative
Friends of the Library Group
Branches: 12
AVENUE LIBRARY, 606 N Ventura Ave, 93001, SAN 335-2234. Tel: 805-643-6393. FAX: 805-648-3791. *Supvr,* Laura Paine; Staff 1.4 (Non-MLS 1.4)
Founded 1963. Pop 14,659; Circ 16,882
Library Holdings: Bk Vols 20,710
Open Mon 11-1 & 2-6, Tues & Thurs 2-6, Wed 12-6, Sat 10-3
Friends of the Library Group
FILLMORE LIBRARY, 502 Second St, Fillmore, 93015, SAN 335-2382. Tel: 805-524-3355. FAX: 808-524-4636. *Supvr,* Cathy Krushell; Staff 1.96 (Non-MLS 1.96)
Founded 1916. Pop 16,666; Circ 38,198
Library Holdings: Bk Vols 30,195
Open Mon & Tues 2-7, Wed 10-5, Thurs-Sat 12-5
Friends of the Library Group
E P FOSTER LIBRARY, 651 E Main St, 93001, SAN 335-2412. Tel: 805-648-2715. FAX: 805-648-3696. *Sr City Librn,* Mary Stewart; Tel: 805-641-4414; Staff 14 (MLS 2, Non-MLS 12)
Founded 1921. Pop 83,493; Circ 277,823
Library Holdings: Bk Vols 179,606
Open Mon-Thurs 10-8, Fri & Sat 10-5, Sun 1-5
Friends of the Library Group
MEINERS OAKS LIBRARY, 114 N Padre Juan Ave, Meiners Oaks, 93023, SAN 335-2447. Tel: 805-646-4804. FAX: 805-646-8007. *Supvr,* Deborah Fletcher; Staff 0.7 (Non-MLS 0.7)
Founded 1958. Pop 6,834; Circ 11,518
Library Holdings: Bk Vols 16,749
Open Mon & Tues 10-1 & 2-6, Wed & Thurs 1-6
Friends of the Library Group
OAK PARK LIBRARY, 899 N Kanan Rd, Oak Park, 91377, SAN 335-2528. Tel: 818-889-2239. FAX: 818-706-9746. *Librn Spec,* Laurie Dunning; Staff 3.5 (MLS 1, Non-MLS 2.5)
Founded 1981. Pop 14,111; Circ 50,748
Library Holdings: Bk Vols 32,291
Open Mon & Tues 2-8, Wed & Thurs 10-6, Fri & Sat 10-5
Friends of the Library Group
OAK VIEW LIBRARY, 555 Mahoney Ave, Oak View, 93022, SAN 335-2536. Tel: 805-649-1523. FAX: 805-649-5591. *Supvr,* Sharon Dykstra; Staff 0.67 (Non-MLS 0.67)
Founded 1945. Pop 10,518; Circ 10,669
Library Holdings: Bk Vols 18,762
Open Mon-Thurs 1-6, Sat 10-2
Friends of the Library Group
OJAI LIBRARY, 111 E Ojai Ave, Ojai, 93023, SAN 335-2560. Tel: 805-646-1639. FAX: 805-646-4693. *City Librn,* Mary Lynch; *Youth Serv,* Julie Albright; Staff 7 (MLS 4, Non-MLS 3)
Founded 1916. Pop 11,251; Circ 115,252
Library Holdings: Bk Vols 39,429
Open Mon-Thurs 10-8, Fri-Sun 12-5
Friends of the Library Group
PIRU LIBRARY, 3811 Center St, Piru, 93040, SAN 329-7527. Tel: 805-521-1753. FAX: 805-521-0729. *Supvr,* Cindy Escoto; Staff 0.4 (Non-MLS 0.4)
Founded 1916. Pop 2,822; Circ 13,691
Library Holdings: Bk Vols 14,627
Open Mon-Wed & Fri 3-7, Thurs 1-5, Sat 10-2
RAY D PRUETER LIBRARY, 510 Park Ave, Port Hueneme, 93041, SAN 335-2595. Tel: 805-486-5460. FAX: 805-487-9190. *City Librn,* Bernadette McDowell; *Youth Serv,* Susan Mikula; Staff 5.2 (MLS 2, Non-MLS 3.2)
Founded 1936. Pop 26,674; Circ 75,711
Library Holdings: Bk Vols 66,255
Open Mon 10-7, Tues & Wed 10-6, Thurs-Sat 12-5
Friends of the Library Group
SATICOY LIBRARY, 11426 Violeta St, Saticoy, 93004, SAN 376-2084. Tel: 805-647-5736. FAX: 805-672-0406. *Supvr,* Russell Stevens; Staff 0.7 (Non-MLS 0.7)
Founded 1919. Pop 17,505; Circ 23,918
Library Holdings: Bk Vols 17,424
Open Mon-Thurs 1-6, Sat 10-2
Friends of the Library Group
SIMI VALLEY LIBRARY, 2969 Tapo Canyon Rd, Simi Valley, 93063, SAN 335-265X. Tel: 805-526-1735. FAX: 805-526-1738. *Dir,* Heather Cousin; *Sr City Librn,* Sandi Banks; *Youth Serv,* Chris Culver; Staff 13 (MLS 2, Non-MLS 11)
Founded 1916. Pop 152,437; Circ 413,525
Library Holdings: Bk Vols 142,479
Open Mon-Thurs 10-8, Fri & Sun 1-5, Sat 10-5
Friends of the Library Group
ALBERT H SOLIZ LIBRARY, 2820 Jourdan St, Oxnard, 93036, SAN 335-2358. Tel: 805-485-4515. FAX: 805-604-7966. *Supvr,* Humberto Tello; Staff 1.3 (Non-MLS 1.3)
Founded 1962. Pop 14,063; Circ 14,209
Library Holdings: Bk Vols 14,902
Open Mon, Tues & Fri 2-6, Wed 10-1 & 2-6, Thurs 2-7
Friends of the Library Group

S VENTURA COUNTY MEDICAL CENTER*, Lillian Smolt Memorial Library, 3291 Loma Vista Rd, 93003. SAN 301-6978. Tel: 805-652-6030. FAX: 805-652-6158. *Librn,* Janet Parker; E-mail: Janet.Parker@ventura.org
Library Holdings: Bk Vols 1,200; Per Subs 150
Open Mon-Fri 9-3
Restriction: Med staff only

VERNON

P VERNON PUBLIC LIBRARY*, 4305 Santa Fe Ave, 90058-0805. SAN 301-701X. Tel: 323-583-8811. FAX: 323-826-1438.
Pop 95
Library Holdings: Bk Vols 1,112
Open Mon-Thurs 3:30-5:30

VICTORVILLE

J VICTOR VALLEY COMMUNITY COLLEGE LIBRARY*, 18422 Bear Valley Rd, 92395-5850. SAN 301-7028. Tel: 760 245 4271, Ext 2262. FAX: 760-245-4373. Web Site: www.vvc.edu/library/. *Librn,* John Akins; *Librn,* Fran Elgin; *Librn,* Leslie Huiner
Founded 1961
Library Holdings: Bk Titles 50,000; Bk Vols 54,000; Per Subs 330
Special Collections: Mojave Desert
Wireless access
Partic in Community College League of California (CCLC); Inland Empire Acad Libr Coop (IEALC); OCLC Online Computer Library Center, Inc
Friends of the Library Group

VISALIA

J COLLEGE OF THE SEQUOIAS LIBRARY*, 915 S Mooney Blvd, 93277. SAN 301-7036. Tel: 559-730-3824. FAX: 559-737-4835. Web Site: www.cos.edu/library. *Dir,* Cathy Lewis; *Tech Librn,* Linda Yamakawa; Staff 5 (MLS 5)
Founded 1926. Enrl 10,000; Fac 384
Library Holdings: Bk Vols 84,000; Per Subs 300
Automation Activity & Vendor Info: (Cataloging) Innovative Interfaces, Inc - Millenium; (Circulation) Innovative Interfaces, Inc - Millenium; (OPAC) Innovative Interfaces, Inc - Millenium
Partic in Area Wide Library Network
Open Mon-Thurs 7:30am-8pm, Fri 7:30-Noon

M KAWEAH DELTA HEALTH CARE DISTRICT LIBRARY*, 400 W Mineral King Ave, 93291-6263. SAN 320-6084. Tel: 559-624-2000. FAX: 559-635-4051. *Librn,* Karen Bontekoe; E-mail: kbonteko@kdhcd.org
Subject Interests: Clinical med, Hospital admin, Nursing
Partic in National Network of Libraries of Medicine

P TULARE COUNTY LIBRARY*, Main Library, 200 W Oak Ave, 93291-4993. SAN 335-2749. Tel: 559-713-2700. Circulation Tel: 559-713-2711, 559-713-2712. Reference Tel: 559-713-2703. FAX: 559-737-4586. E-mail: questions@tularecountylibrary.org. Web Site: www.tularecountylibrary.org. *County Librn,* Jeff Scott; *Dep County Librn,* Mike Drake; Staff 38 (MLS 5, Non-MLS 33)
Founded 1910. Pop 146,023; Circ 391,030
Jul 2011-Jun 2012 Income (Main Library and Branch(s)) $3,762,000, State $14,000, Federal $28,000, County $3,560,000, Locally Generated Income $160,000. Mats Exp $540,000, Books $330,000, AV Mat $60,000, Electronic Ref Mat (Incl. Access Fees) $150,000. Sal $1,318,200
Library Holdings: AV Mats 8,000; DVDs 4,500; e-books 6,893; Electronic Media & Resources 12; Bk Titles 154,356; Bk Vols 285,915; Per Subs 448; Talking Bks 3,500; Videos 4,500
Special Collections: History of Sequoia & Kings National Parks (George W Stewart Coll); Los Angeles Times 1989-2003, micro; The Years 1941-1946 in Tulare County; Tulare County Directory 1888-1950, micro; Tulare County History Coll; Visalia Times Delta: 1859-present, micro (weekly & daily). Oral History
Automation Activity & Vendor Info: (Acquisitions) Horizon; (Cataloging) Horizon; (Circulation) Horizon; (OPAC) Horizon
Database Vendor: 3M Library Systems, EBSCO Auto Repair Reference, EBSCO Information Services, EBSCOhost, Gale Cengage Learning, infoUSA, OCLC WorldShare Interlibrary Loan
Wireless access
Function: Adult literacy prog, Archival coll, BA reader (adult literacy), Bilingual assistance for Spanish patrons, Computer training, Electronic databases & coll, ILL available, Music CDs, Prog for children & young adult, Ref serv available, Spoken cassettes & CDs, Spoken cassettes & DVDs, Summer reading prog, Tax forms, VCDs, VHS videos, Web-catalog
Mem of San Joaquin Valley Library System
Partic in AWLNET; OCLC Online Computer Library Center, Inc
Special Services for the Deaf - ADA equip; Assisted listening device; Bks on deafness & sign lang; Sorenson video relay syst
Special Services for the Blind - Talking bk & rec for the blind cat; Talking bks; Talking bks & player equip
Open Tues-Thurs 9-8, Fri 12-6, Sat 9-5
Friends of the Library Group

Branches: 14

ALPAUGH BRANCH, 3816 Ave 54, Alpaugh, 93201. (Mail add: PO Box 69, Alpaugh, 93201-0069), SAN 335-2773. Tel: 559-949-8355. FAX: 559-949-8225. *Br Mgr,* Position Currently Open; Staff 1 (Non-MLS 1)
Founded 1910. Pop 800
Library Holdings: Bk Vols 8,187
Open Tues & Wed 10-1 & 2-6

DINUBA BRANCH, 150 South I St, Dinuba, 93618, SAN 335-2838. Tel: 559-591-5828. FAX: 559-591-5886. *Br Mgr,* Aurelia Rosales; Staff 1 (Non-MLS 1)
Founded 1910. Pop 19,297
Library Holdings: Bk Vols 31,931
Open Tues & Thurs 11-5 & 6-8, Wed & Fri 9-1 & 2-6
Friends of the Library Group

EARLIMART BRANCH, 780 E Washington St, Earlimart, 93219. (Mail add: PO Box 12153, Earlimart, 93219-2153), SAN 335-2897. Tel: 661-849-2525. FAX: 661-849-1517. *Br Mgr,* Position Currently Open
Founded 1914. Pop 7,020
Library Holdings: Bk Vols 10,603

EXETER BRANCH, 230 E Chestnut, Exeter, 93221, SAN 335-2927. Tel: 559-592-5361. FAX: 559-592-4452. *Br Mgr,* Marjorie Fly; Staff 1 (Non-MLS 1)
Founded 1910. Pop 10,160
Library Holdings: Bk Vols 25,305
Open Tues & Wed 11-5 & 6-8, Thurs & Fri 9-1 & 2-6
Friends of the Library Group

IVANHOE BRANCH, 15964 Heather, Ivanhoe, 93235, SAN 335-3044. Tel: 559-798-1264. FAX: 559-798-5634. *Br Mgr,* Amber Beach; Staff 1 (Non-MLS 1)
Founded 1925. Pop 4,474
Library Holdings: Bk Vols 8,495

LINDSAY BRANCH, 157 N Mirage St, Lindsay, 93247, SAN 335-3079. Tel: 559-562-3021. FAX: 559-562-5066. *Br Mgr,* Brenda Biesterfeld; Staff 1 (Non-MLS 1)
Founded 1910. Pop 10,860
Library Holdings: Bk Vols 22,888
Open Tues & Thurs 11-5 & 6-8, Wed & Fri 9-1 & 2-6
Friends of the Library Group

OROSI BRANCH, 12646 Ave 416, Orosi, 93647, SAN 335-3133. Tel: 559-519-5830. FAX: 559-528-9156. *Br Mgr,* Augustina Ortiz; Staff 1 (Non-MLS 1)
Founded 1911. Pop 7,744
Library Holdings: Bk Vols 10,751
Open Wed-Fri 9-1 & 2-6
Friends of the Library Group

PIXLEY BRANCH, 300 N School, PO Box K, Pixley, 93256, SAN 335-3192. Tel: 559-757-3880. *Librn,* Marilyn Maynard; Staff 1 (Non-MLS 1)
Founded 1913. Pop 2,586
Library Holdings: Bk Vols 16,340
Open Mon & Wed 9:30-5, Tues & Thurs 9:30-8, Fri 9:30-3:30, Sat 10-2

SPRINGVILLE BRANCH, 35800 Hwy 190, Springville, 93265. (Mail add: PO Box 459, Springville, 93265-0257), SAN 335-3257. Tel: 559-539-2624. FAX: 559-539-6307. *Br Mgr,* Donna Ellis; Staff 1 (Non-MLS 1)
Founded 1928. Pop 1,109
Library Holdings: Bk Vols 8,509
Open Thurs 11-5 & 6-8, Fri & Sat 9-1 & 2-5
Friends of the Library Group

STRATHMORE BRANCH, 19646 Rd 230, Strathmore, 93267-9608. (Mail add: PO Box 595, Strathmore, 93267-0595), SAN 335-3281. Tel: 559-568-1087. FAX: 559-568-0633. *Br Mgr,* Donna Ellis; Staff 1 (Non-MLS 1)
Founded 1911. Pop 2,584
Library Holdings: Bk Vols 12,635
Open Tues & Wed 9-1 & 2-6
Friends of the Library Group

TERRA BELLA BRANCH, 23825 Ave 92, Terra Bella, 93270-9756. (Mail add: PO Box 442, Terra Bella, 93270-0442), SAN 335-3311. Tel: 559-535-5583.
Founded 1912. Pop 3,780
Library Holdings: Bk Vols 8,947
Open Mon-Thurs 8:30-11:30 & 12-2:30

THREE RIVERS BRANCH, 42052 Eggers Dr, Three Rivers, 93271-9774. (Mail add: PO Box 216, Three Rivers, 93271-0216), SAN 335-3346. Tel: 559-561-4564. FAX: 559-561-7318. *Br Mgr,* Sonja Hoogeveen; Staff 1 (Non-MLS 1)
Founded 1910. Pop 2,248
Library Holdings: Bk Vols 17,055
Open Tues & Thurs 12-5 & 6-8, Wed & Fri 10-1 & 2-6
Friends of the Library Group

TIPTON BRANCH, 221 N Evans Rd, Tipton, 93272, SAN 335-3370. Tel: 559-752-4236. FAX: 559-752-7307. *Br Mgr,* Donald Cotta; Staff 1 (Non-MLS 1)
Founded 1912. Pop 1,790
Library Holdings: Bk Vols 8,023
Open Thurs & Fri 9-1 & 2-6

WOODLAKE BRANCH, 400 W Whitney Ave, Woodlake, 93286, SAN 335-346X. Tel: 559-564-8424. FAX: 559-564-6725. *Br Mgr,* Rosendo Navarro; Staff 1 (Non-MLS 1)
Founded 1911. Pop 7,336
Library Holdings: Bk Vols 11,797
Open Wed-Fri 9-1 & 2-6

G TULARE COUNTY OFFICE OF EDUCATION*, Educational Resource Services, 7000 Doe Ave, Ste A, 93291. SAN 301-7044. Tel: 559-651-3031. FAX: 559-651-1012. Web Site: www.erslibrary.org. *Prog Mgr,* Elainea Scott; Tel: 559-651-3042, E-mail: escott@tcoe.org; *Tech Spec,* Steve Woods; E-mail: stevew@tcoe.org; Staff 12 (MLS 2, Non-MLS 10)
Founded 1927
Library Holdings: Bk Titles 100,000; Bk Vols 250,000; Per Subs 50
Special Collections: Instructional Materials Display Center of Textbooks & Media
Special Services for the Deaf - Captioned film dep
Open Mon-Thurs (Winter) 8-7, Fri 8-5, Sat 10-2:30; Mon-Fri (Summer) 7:30-5:30

GL TULARE COUNTY PUBLIC LAW LIBRARY, 221 S Mooney Blvd, Rm 1, County Courthouse, 93291-4544. SAN 301-7052. Tel: 559-636-4600. E-mail: lawlibrary@co.tulare.ca.us. Web Site: www.tularecounty.ca.gov/lawlibrary. *Dir,* Anne R Bernardo; E-mail: abernard@co.tulare.ca.us; Staff 2 (Non-MLS 2)
Founded 1891
Jul 2013-Jun 2014 Income $336,462, Locally Generated Income $30,938, Other $305,524. Mats Exp $329,517, Books $148,681, Per/Ser (Incl. Access Fees) $1,293, Electronic Ref Mat (Incl. Access Fees) $37,443. Sal $96,359 (Prof $49,677)
Library Holdings: CDs 19; DVDs 7; e-books 8,479; Electronic Media & Resources 7,432; Bk Titles 1,673; Bk Vols 17,145; Per Subs 73; Videos 2
Subject Interests: Legal
Automation Activity & Vendor Info: (Cataloging) ComPanion Corp; (OPAC) ComPanion Corp
Database Vendor: EBSCOhost, HeinOnline, LexisNexis, OCLC FirstSearch, Westlaw
Wireless access
Function: Copy machines, e-mail & chat, Electronic databases & coll, Fax serv, Handicapped accessible, Online cat, Pub access computers, Ref serv available, Web-catalog
Partic in Heartland Regional Library Network of the Library of California

Open Mon-Fri 8-5
Restriction: Non-circulating, Not a lending libr, Pub use on premises

WALNUT

J MT SAN ANTONIO COLLEGE LIBRARY*, 1100 N Grand Ave, 91789. SAN 301-7079. Tel: 909-274-4260. Reference Tel: 909-274-4289. Administration Tel: 909-274-5659. FAX: 909-468-4011. Web Site: www.mtsac.edu/instruction/learning/library. *Dean, Libr & Learning Res,* Meghan Chen; *Electronic Ref Librn,* Paul Kittle; *Automation Syst Coordr,* LeAnn Garrett; *Bibliog Instr,* Deb Distante; *Bibliog Instr,* Pauline Swartz; *Ref Serv,* Emily Woolery; Staff 16 (MLS 6, Non-MLS 10)
Founded 1946. Highest Degree: Associate
Library Holdings: e-books 8,500; Bk Titles 68,985; Per Subs 342
Automation Activity & Vendor Info: (Acquisitions) SirsiDynix; (Cataloging) SirsiDynix; (Circulation) SirsiDynix; (Course Reserve) SirsiDynix; (Media Booking) SirsiDynix; (OPAC) SirsiDynix; (Serials) SirsiDynix
Wireless access
Partic in Inland Empire Acad Libr Coop (IEALC)
Open Mon-Thurs 7:30am-9:30pm, Fri 7:30-4:30, Sat 9-4
Restriction: Staff use only, Students only

WALNUT CREEK

S CONTRA COSTA TIMES NEWS RESEARCH DEPARTMENT*, 2640 Shadelands Dr, 94598. SAN 324-4245. Tel: 925-943-8353. FAX: 925-943-8362. Web Site: www.contracostatimes.com. *Librn,* Camille Donaldson; *Librn,* Veronica Martinez; Tel: 510-208-6420; Staff 2 (Non-MLS 2)
Founded 1978
Library Holdings: Bk Titles 480; Bk Vols 500; Per Subs 10
Special Collections: Contra Costa Times, clippings, micro
Database Vendor: Checkpoint Systems, Inc, LexisNexis
Publications: Orientation Handbook
Restriction: Staff use only

M JOHN MUIR HEALTH MEDICAL LIBRARY*, 1601 Ygnacio Valley Rd, 94598-3237. SAN 326-5110. Tel: 925-947-5231. FAX: 925-947-3237. Web Site: www.johnmuirhealth.com. *Librn,* Helen M Doughty; E-mail: helen.doughty@johnmuirhealth.com; Staff 1 (MLS 1)
Library Holdings: Bk Vols 3,750
Subject Interests: Hist of med
Function: Res libr
Partic in National Network of Libraries of Medicine Pacific Northwest Region
Restriction: Not open to pub

S SHADELANDS RANCH HISTORICAL MUSEUM*, Shadelands History Room Library, 2660 Ygnacio Valley Rd, 94598. SAN 301-7117. Tel: 925-935-7871. FAX: 925-935-7885. E-mail: wcshadelands@sbcglobal.net. Web Site: www.ci.walnut-creek.ca.us/wchs.html. *Librn,* Audrey Veregge
Founded 1972
Library Holdings: Bk Titles 500
Special Collections: Albert Johnson Business Papers; Hutchinson Family Photos; James P Howe Coll, papers; Joseph Reddeford Walker & Family, photog; Local Newspaper Coll: Walnut Creek Independent, Walnut Creek Sentinel, Walnut Kernel Newspaper 1932-1967; Rogers Hotel, photog; Seely Family Letters; Seely-Hodges Family Letters; Shadelands Ranch Business Documents; Walnut Creek (Robert Thain Coll), photog; Walnut Creek City Documents. Oral History
Subject Interests: Calif
Restriction: Open by appt only

WATSONVILLE

P WATSONVILLE PUBLIC LIBRARY*, 275 Main St, Ste 100, 95076. SAN 301-7133. Tel: 831-768-3400. FAX: 831-763-4015. TDD: 831-763-4076. Web Site: www.watsonvillelibrary.org. *Dir,* Carol Heitzig; E-mail: cheitzig@ci.watsonville.ca.us; *Principal Librn,* Dody Anderson; E-mail: danderson@ci.watsonville.ca.us; *Res Librn,* Susan Renison; E-mail: srenison@ci.watsonville.ca.us; *Circ Mgr,* Alicia Martinez; E-mail: amartine@ci.watsonville.ca.us; *Ch Serv,* Susan Nilsson; E-mail: snilsson@ci.watsonville.ca.us; *YA Serv,* Hannah Clement. Subject Specialists: *Agr hist,* Susan Renison; Staff 9 (MLS 8, Non-MLS 1)
Founded 1895. Pop 55,646; Circ 317,837
Library Holdings: Bk Titles 111,425; Per Subs 304
Subject Interests: Spanish (Lang)
Automation Activity & Vendor Info: (Acquisitions) Innovative Interfaces, Inc; (Cataloging) Innovative Interfaces, Inc; (Circulation) Innovative Interfaces, Inc; (ILL) Innovative Interfaces, Inc; (Media Booking) Innovative Interfaces, Inc; (OPAC) Innovative Interfaces, Inc; (Serials) Innovative Interfaces, Inc
Database Vendor: ALLDATA Online, Amigos Library Services, College Source, Facts on File, LearningExpress, Newsbank, OCLC FirstSearch, OCLC WorldShare Interlibrary Loan
Wireless access
Function: Bilingual assistance for Spanish patrons, Bks on cassette, Bks on CD, Children's prog, Computer training, Computers for patron use, Copy machines, e-mail serv, Electronic databases & coll, Family literacy, Handicapped accessible, Holiday prog, Homebound delivery serv, Homework prog, ILL available, Large print keyboards, Magnifiers for reading, Mus passes, Music CDs, Online cat, Online ref, Online searches, Photocopying/Printing, Preschool outreach, Prog for adults, Prog for children & young adult, Senior computer classes, Summer reading prog, Tax forms, Teen prog, Telephone ref, VHS videos, Video lending libr, Web-catalog, Wheelchair accessible, Workshops, Writing prog
Partic in Monterey Bay Area Cooperative Library System
Special Services for the Deaf - TDD equip
Friends of the Library Group
Branches: 1
FREEDOM BRANCH, 2021 Freedom Blvd, Freedom, 95019. Tel: 831-768-3420. FAX: 831-763-4143. *Br Mgr,* Heather Geddes
Pop 6,480; Circ 59,079
Library Holdings: Bk Titles 14,405
Open Tues-Thurs 10-8, Fri & Sat 10-6
Friends of the Library Group

WEAVERVILLE

GL TRINITY COUNTY LAW LIBRARY*, Courthouse, 11 Court St, 96093. (Mail add: PO Box 1258, 96093-1258), SAN 328-6665. Tel: 530-623-1369. *Librn,* Donna Regnani
Open Mon-Fri 8-12 & 1-5

P TRINITY COUNTY LIBRARY*, 211 N Main St, 96093. (Mail add: PO Box 1226, 96093-1226), SAN 301-7141. Tel: 530-623-1373. FAX: 530-623-4427. E-mail: librarian@trinitycounty.org. Web Site: library.trinitycounty.org. *Head Librn,* Oresta Esquibel; E-mail: oesquibel@trinitycounty.org; Staff 1 (MLS 1)
Founded 1916. Pop 13,020; Circ 50,483
Library Holdings: Per Subs 38
Special Collections: Trinity County History; Trinity River Basin Coll
Automation Activity & Vendor Info: (Cataloging) TLC (The Library Corporation)
Mem of NorthNet Library System
Open Mon-Thurs 1-6
Friends of the Library Group
Branches: 2
HAYFORK BRANCH, Hympom Rd, Hayfork, 96041. (Mail add: PO Box 700, Hayfork, 96041-0700), SAN 329-3599. Tel: 530-628-5427. FAX: 530-628-5304. *Libr Asst,* Nancy Ferguson; Staff 2 (Non-MLS 2)
Open Mon & Wed 12-4, Tues & Thurs 10-2
Friends of the Library Group
TRINITY CENTER BRANCH, Scott Museum Bldg, 540-B Airport Rd, Trinity Center, 96091. (Mail add: PO Box 27, Trinity Center, 96091), SAN 370-4386. Tel: 530-266-3242. *Libr Asst,* Mary Keese
Friends of the Library Group

WEED

J COLLEGE OF THE SISKIYOUS LIBRARY*, 800 College Ave, 96094. SAN 301-715X. Tel: 530-938-5331. Toll Free Tel: 888-397-4339, Ext 5331. FAX: 530-938-5226. E-mail: library@siskiyous.edu. Web Site: www.siskiyous.edu/library. *Asst Dean, Learning Res,* Nancy Shepard; E-mail: shepard@siskiyous.edu; Staff 2.3 (MLS 0.5, Non-MLS 1.8)
Founded 1957. Enrl 4,587; Fac 153; Highest Degree: Associate
Library Holdings: e-books 21,000; Bk Vols 39,000; Per Subs 60
Special Collections: Mount Shasta, California, Coll
Subject Interests: Local hist
Automation Activity & Vendor Info: (Circulation) SirsiDynix; (OPAC) SirsiDynix
Database Vendor: EBSCOhost, OCLC FirstSearch
Wireless access
Mem of NorthNet Library System
Open Mon-Thurs 8-5, Fri 8-2

WEST HOLLYWOOD

S CENTER FOR EARLY EDUCATION LIBRARY*, 563 N Alfred St, 90048-2512. SAN 300-9041. Tel: 323-651-0707. FAX: 323-651-0860. Web Site: www.centerforearlyeducation.org. *Librn,* Lucy Rafael; Staff 1 (MLS 1)
Founded 1965
Library Holdings: Bk Titles 21,813; Bk Vols 22,294; Per Subs 92
Subject Interests: Child develop, Children's lit, Educ, Parenting
Automation Activity & Vendor Info: (Acquisitions) Follett Software; (Cataloging) Follett Software; (Circulation) Follett Software; (Media Booking) Follett Software; (OPAC) Follett Software

Database Vendor: ebrary, EBSCOhost, Gale Cengage Learning, ProQuest
Restriction: Open by appt only, Open to pub upon request

WESTCHESTER

C OTIS COLLEGE OF ART & DESIGN LIBRARY*, Millard Sheets Library, 9045 Lincoln Blvd, 90045. SAN 300-9793. Tel: 310-665-6800, Ext 6930. FAX: 310-665-6998. Web Site: www.otis.edu/life_otis/library/index.html. *Dir,* Sue Maberry; *Cat Librn,* Cathy Chambers; E-mail: cathcham@otis.edu; *Librn,* Heather Cleary; E-mail: hcleary@otis.edu; *Libr Syst Adminr, Programming,* Matthew Ballard; *Circ Mgr,* Sheldon Forbes; E-mail: sforbes@otis.edu; *Mgr, Per,* Ian Henderson; *Coordr,* Kathleen Forrest; Staff 3 (MLS 2, Non-MLS 1)
Founded 1917. Enrl 960; Fac 100; Highest Degree: Master
Library Holdings: Bk Vols 30,000; Per Subs 139
Special Collections: Artists bks
Subject Interests: Fashion, Fine arts, Photog
Partic in RLIN (Research Libraries Information Network)
Restriction: Open by appt only

WHITTIER

M PRESBYTERIAN INTERCOMMUNITY HOSPITAL*, Medical Library, 12401 E Washington Blvd, 90602. SAN 301-7184. Tel: 562-698-0811, Ext 2583. FAX: 562-698-9002. *Librn,* Lucinda Allshouse
Library Holdings: Bk Titles 600; Per Subs 165
Partic in National Network of Libraries of Medicine; Pacific Southwest Regional Medical Library (PSRML)
Open Mon-Fri 8-5
Restriction: Staff use only

J RIO HONDO COMMUNITY COLLEGE LIBRARY*, 3600 Workman Mill Rd, 90601. SAN 301-7192. Tel: 562-908-3417. Circulation Tel: 562-692-0921, Ext 3416. Interlibrary Loan Service Tel: 562-908-3416. Reference Tel: 562-908-3484. FAX: 562-463-4642. E-mail: library@riohondo.edu. Web Site: library.riohondo.edu. *Librn,* Robin Babou; E-mail: rbabou@riohondo.edu; *Librn,* Jan Coe; E-mail: jcoe@riohondo.edu; *Librn,* Adele Enright; E-mail: aenright@riohondo.edu; *Librn,* Judy Sevilla-Marzona; E-mail: jsevilla@riohondo.edu; *Librn,* Stephanie Wells; E-mail: swells@riohondo.edu; Staff 27 (MLS 14, Non-MLS 13)
Founded 1965. Enrl 18,497; Fac 559; Highest Degree: Associate
Library Holdings: AV Mats 2,498; DVDs 95; Music Scores 183; Bk Titles 74,856; Bk Vols 83,844; Per Subs 176; Videos 1,120
Subject Interests: Archit, Fire tech, Theatre arts
Automation Activity & Vendor Info: (Acquisitions) SirsiDynix; (Cataloging) SirsiDynix; (Circulation) SirsiDynix; (Course Reserve) SirsiDynix; (Media Booking) SirsiDynix; (OPAC) SirsiDynix; (Serials) SirsiDynix
Database Vendor: Gale Cengage Learning, ProQuest
Function: ILL available, Ref serv available
Partic in Southern California Library Cooperative
Special Services for the Deaf - Assistive tech; Closed caption videos
Special Services for the Blind - Closed circuit TV; Ref serv; Scanner for conversion & translation of mats
Open Mon-Thurs 7:30am-9pm, Fri 7:30-1, Sat 9-1
Restriction: Borrowing privileges limited to fac & registered students

CM SOUTHERN CALIFORNIA UNIVERSITY OF HEALTH SCIENCES*, Learning Resource Center, 16200 E Amber Valley Dr, 90604-4098. (Mail add: PO Box 1166, 90609-1166), SAN 300-7898. Tel: 562-902-3368. Toll Free Tel: 800-221-5222. FAX: 562-902-3323. Web Site: www.scuhs.edu. *In Charge,* Valerie Fernandez; Tel: 562-947-8755, Ext 367, E-mail: valeriefernandez@scuhs.edu; *Circ,* Linda Horat; E-mail: lindahorat@scuhs.edu
Founded 1911. Enrl 1,000
Library Holdings: Bk Titles 10,387; Bk Vols 24,925; Per Subs 222
Special Collections: Chiropractic History; Nutrition & Natural Therapeutics
Subject Interests: Anatomy, Chiropractic med, Neurology, Nutrition, Osteopathology, Phys therapy, Physiology, Sports
Automation Activity & Vendor Info: (Acquisitions) Ex Libris Group; (Cataloging) Ex Libris Group; (Circulation) Ex Libris Group; (Serials) Ex Libris Group
Database Vendor: EBSCOhost, OVID Technologies, ProQuest
Partic in Chiropractic Libr Consortium; CLS; Medical Library Group of Southern California & Arizona (MLGSCA)

WHITTIER COLLEGE

C FAIRCHILD AERIAL PHOTOGRAPHY COLLECTION*, Fairchild Collection, Whittier College, 90608. Tel: 562-907-4220. FAX: 562-693-6117. E-mail: fairchild@whittier.edu. Web Site: web.whittier.edu/fairchild/home.html. *Dir,* Stephanie Breaux
Founded 1965
Special Collections: Aerial Photography Coll 1927-1966
Function: Archival coll
Partic in Nat Cartographic Info Ctr
Restriction: Non-circulating, Not a lending libr, Open by appt only

C MEDIA CENTER*, 13406 Philadelphia St, 90601-4413. (Mail add: PO Box 634, 90608-0634), SAN 335-3559. Tel: 562-907-4267. FAX: 562-907-4922. Web Site: www.whittier.edu. *Dir,* Richard Cheatham; Tel: 562-907-4846, E-mail: rcheatham@whittier.edu
Founded 1971
Subject Interests: Educ, Environ studies, Ethnic studies, Feminism, Hist
Open Mon-Fri 8-5

C BONNIE BELL WARDMAN LIBRARY*, 7031 Founders Hill Rd, 90608-9984, SAN 335-3524. Tel: 562-907-4247. Circulation Tel: 562-907-4693. Reference Tel: 562-907-4692. Administration Tel: 562-907-4245. Automation Services Tel: 562-907-4235. FAX: 562-698-7168. Web Site: web.whittier.edu/academic/library. *Interim Dir,* Mary Ellen Vick; E-mail: mvick@whittier.edu; *Syst Mgr,* Paul Hong; *Media Coordr,* Terry McGonagle; *Cat Librn,* Mike Garabedian; *Ser Librn,* Joe Dmohowski; Tel: 562-907-4246, E-mail: jdmohowski@whittier.edu; *Acq,* Steven Musser; *Instructional Technologist,* Kathy Filatreau; *Tech Serv,* Cindy Bessler; Staff 4 (MLS 4)
Founded 1901. Enrl 1,330; Fac 103; Highest Degree: Master
Jul 2005-Jun 2006 Income $1,067,819. Mats Exp $491,914, Books $128,860, Per/Ser (Incl. Access Fees) $251,667, Electronic Ref Mat (Incl. Access Fees) $93,548, Presv $17,839. Sal $459,791 (Prof $319,851)
Library Holdings: AV Mats 43; CDs 194; e-books 2,294; e-journals 10,239; Bk Vols 302,490; Per Subs 715; Talking Bks 12; Videos 44
Special Collections: Jan de Hartog Coll, bks, mss; Jessamyn West Coll, bks, mss; John Greenleaf Whittier Coll; Richard M Nixon Coll; Society of Friends (Clifford & Susan Johnson Library of Quaker Literature), bks, micro, pamphlets. State Document Depository; US Document Depository
Automation Activity & Vendor Info: (Acquisitions) Innovative Interfaces, Inc; (Cataloging) Innovative Interfaces, Inc; (Circulation) Innovative Interfaces, Inc; (Course Reserve) Innovative Interfaces, Inc; (ILL) Innovative Interfaces, Inc; (Media Booking) Innovative Interfaces, Inc; (OPAC) Innovative Interfaces, Inc; (Serials) Innovative Interfaces, Inc
Database Vendor: Cambridge Scientific Abstracts, Gale Cengage Learning, Innovative Interfaces, Inc, JSTOR, LexisNexis, Newsbank, OCLC FirstSearch, OCLC WorldShare Interlibrary Loan, Wilson - Wilson Web
Function: Copy machines, Govt ref serv, Handicapped accessible, Ref serv available
Partic in OCLC Online Computer Library Center, Inc; Statewide California Electronic Library Consortium (SCELC)
Open Mon-Thurs 8am-11pm, Fri 8-5, Sat 10-5, Sun Noon-11pm

P WHITTIER PUBLIC LIBRARY*, 7344 S Washington Ave, 90602. SAN 335-3583. Tel: 562-567-9900. FAX: 562-567-2880. E-mail: lib@whittierpl.org. Web Site: www.whittierpl.org. *Dir,* Paymaneh Maghsoudi; *Mgr, Libr Serv,* Deborah Shulkatis; E-mail: dshulkatis@whittierlibrary.org; *Mgr, Libr Serv,* Bonnie Weber; E-mail: bweber@whittierlibrary.org; *Acq,* Venus Snell; *ILL,* Joan Roche; *Media Spec,* Vivian Vellanoweth; *Ref,* Ruth Lynch; Staff 14 (MLS 14)
Founded 1900. Pop 83,000; Circ 636,930
Library Holdings: Bk Vols 251,991
Special Collections: Margaret Fulmer Peace Coll; Whittier Hills Archives; Whittier History. State Document Depository
Automation Activity & Vendor Info: (Circulation) SirsiDynix
Database Vendor: EBSCOhost, Gale Cengage Learning, Newsbank, ProQuest, ReferenceUSA
Wireless access
Partic in Southern California Library Cooperative
Open Mon-Wed 10-9, Thurs & Fri 10-6, Sat 10-5
Friends of the Library Group
Branches: 1
WHITTWOOD BRANCH, 10537 Santa Gertrudes Ave, 90603-2760, SAN 335-3613. Tel: 562-567-9950. FAX: 562-567-2881. *Libr Serv Mgr,* Deborah Shulkatis; *Ch Serv,* Patti Beck; Staff 7.5 (MLS 3.5, Non-MLS 4)
Circ 192,148
Library Holdings: Bk Titles 47,196; Bk Vols 66,413; Per Subs 90
Database Vendor: SirsiDynix
Open Mon & Tues 12-9, Wed-Fri 10-6, Sat 10-5
Friends of the Library Group

WILLOWS

P WILLOWS PUBLIC LIBRARY*, 201 N Lassen St, 95988-3010. SAN 301-7214. Tel: 530-934-5156. FAX: 530-934-2225. *Libr Dir,* Sandie Hobbs; E-mail: shobbs@cityofwillows.org; *Cataloger, Libr Tech,* Cha Mee Yang; E-mail: cyang@cityofwillows.org; Staff 2 (Non-MLS 2)
Founded 1906. Pop 14,152; Circ 51,781
Library Holdings: Bk Vols 62,276; Per Subs 100; Talking Bks 1,387
Special Collections: Californiana Coll

Subject Interests: Local hist
Automation Activity & Vendor Info: (Acquisitions) TLC (The Library Corporation); (Cataloging) TLC (The Library Corporation); (Circulation) TLC (The Library Corporation)
Database Vendor: OCLC WorldShare Interlibrary Loan, TLC (The Library Corporation)
Wireless access
Mem of NorthNet Library System
Partic in Cooperative Library Association Shared System (CLASS); RLIN (Research Libraries Information Network)
Open Tues-Thurs 11-7, Fri & Sat 11-5
Friends of the Library Group
Branches: 2
BAYLISS, 7830 Rd 39, Glenn, 95943, SAN 376-2599. Tel: 530-934-2287. *Br Coordr,* Linda Peelle-Haddeman
Founded 1914. Pop 1,020
Library Holdings: Bk Vols 3,581; Per Subs 15
Open Tues 10-6
Friends of the Library Group
ELK CREEK BRANCH, 455 Elm St, Elk Creek, 95939. Tel: 530-968-5238. *Br Mgr,* Evelyn Hayward; Staff 0.2 (Non-MLS 0.2)
Pop 1,515
Library Holdings: Bk Vols 2,603; Per Subs 11
Open Wed & Sat 11-3
Friends of the Library Group

WILMINGTON

J LOS ANGELES HARBOR COLLEGE*, Camille L Baxter Learning Resource Center, 1111 Figueroa Pl, 90744-2397. SAN 301-7222. Tel: 310-233-4480. FAX: 310-233-4689. *Cat, Chair, Ref Serv,* Jonathon Lee; Tel: 310-233-4475, E-mail: leeja@lahc.edu; *Acq, Instrul Serv Librn, Ref Serv,* Ibtesam Dessouky; Tel: 310-233-4473, E-mail: dessouia@lahc.edu; *Acq of New Ser/Per, Ref Serv,* Marian Locascio; Tel: 310-233-4481; Staff 3 (MLS 3)
Founded 1949. Enrl 10,192; Fac 381; Highest Degree: Associate
Library Holdings: e-books 14,920; Bk Vols 86,989; Per Subs 168
Special Collections: Los Angeles Harbor Area History (Los Angeles Harbor College Historical Project), clippings, photogs. Oral History
Automation Activity & Vendor Info: (Acquisitions) EOS International; (Cataloging) SirsiDynix; (Circulation) SirsiDynix; (Course Reserve) SirsiDynix; (ILL) SirsiDynix; (OPAC) SirsiDynix
Database Vendor: CQ Press, EBSCOhost, Gale Cengage Learning, JSTOR, LearningExpress, McGraw-Hill, ProQuest, SirsiDynix
Wireless access
Function: ILL available, Photocopying/Printing, Ref serv available
Partic in California Community College Library Consortium (CCLC)
Special Services for the Blind - Assistive/Adapted tech devices, equip & products; Computer with voice synthesizer for visually impaired persons
Open Mon-Thurs 8am-8:30pm, Fri 8-2, Sat 9-3
Friends of the Library Group

WOODLAND

P WOODLAND PUBLIC LIBRARY*, 250 First St, 95695-3411. SAN 301-7249. Tel: 530-661-5980. Circulation Tel: 530-661-5981. Reference Tel: 530-661-5982. FAX: 530-666 5408. Web Site: www.cityofwoodland.org/library. *Libr Serv Dir,* Greta Galindo; *Ch Serv,* Patricia Lakie; *Ref Serv,* Carol Beckham; *Ref Serv,* Roberta Boegel; *Ref Serv,* Carol Davis; Staff 5 (MLS 5)
Founded 1892. Pop 53,000; Circ 217,527
Jul 2005-Jun 2006 Income $1,600,000, State $140,000, City $1,400,000, Federal $3,500, Other $55,000. Mats Exp $195,000, Books $135,000, Other Print Mats $10,000, Micro $2,000, AV Mat $33,000, Electronic Ref Mat (Incl. Access Fees) $15,000. Sal $980,000
Library Holdings: AV Mats 6,200; CDs 2,343; DVDs 1,952; Large Print Bks 2,482; Bk Vols 82,000; Per Subs 189; Talking Bks 2,508; Videos 1,331
Automation Activity & Vendor Info: (Cataloging) Innovative Interfaces, Inc; (Circulation) Innovative Interfaces, Inc; (ILL) OCLC; (OPAC) Innovative Interfaces, Inc
Database Vendor: Innovative Interfaces, Inc
Wireless access
Partic in OCLC Online Computer Library Center, Inc
Open Mon-Thurs 9-7, Sat 12-4
Friends of the Library Group

GL YOLO COUNTY LAW LIBRARY*, 204 Fourth St, Ste A, 95695. SAN 301-7257. Tel: 530-666-8918. FAX: 530-666-8618. E-mail: law.library@yolocounty.org. Web Site: www.yolocounty.org/org/library/law.htm. *Libr Dir,* Kathryn Bates Turner
Founded 1895
Library Holdings: CDs 35; Bk Titles 13,400; Bk Vols 17,201
Database Vendor: HeinOnline, Innovative Interfaces, Inc, Westlaw
Function: Computers for patron use, Copy machines, Electronic databases & coll, Web-catalog
Open Mon-Fri 9:30-3:30

P YOLO COUNTY LIBRARY*, 226 Buckeye St, 95695-2600. SAN 335-3648. Tel: 530-666-8005. FAX: 530-666-8006. Web Site: www.yolocountylibrary.org. *County Librn,* Patricia Wong; E-mail: patty.wong@yolocounty.org; *Asst County Librn,* Elizabeth Gray; Tel: 530-666-8084, E-mail: elizabeth.gray@yolocounty.org; *Bus Mgr,* Chris Crist; E-mail: chris.crist@yolocounty.org; *Ch Serv,* Peggy Rollins; Tel: 530-757-5597, Fax: 530-757-5590, E-mail: peggy.rollins@yolocounty.org; *Tech Serv,* Kim Sheppard; Tel: 530-666-8085, E-mail: kim.sheppard@yolocounty.org; Staff 33.95 (MLS 14.85, Non-MLS 19.1)
Founded 1910. Pop 146,487; Circ 1,145,645
Jul 2011-Jun 2012 Income (Main Library and Branch(s)) $4,287,777, State $2,383, City $275,000, Federal $3,100, County $132,069, Locally Generated Income $885,685, Other $2,989,540. Mats Exp $636,333, Books $383,645, Per/Ser (Incl. Access Fees) $37,446, AV Mat $85,019, Electronic Ref Mat (Incl. Access Fees) $88,924, Presv $41,299. Sal $1,744,824 (Prof $929,662)
Library Holdings: Audiobooks 20,406; AV Mats 33,251; CDs 9,825; DVDs 23,119; Bk Vols 334,644; Per Subs 282; Talking Bks 8,401
Special Collections: Geography (Beulah Hughes Coll); Russian Language Coll; Spanish Language Coll; Yolo County History Coll
Automation Activity & Vendor Info: (Acquisitions) Innovative Interfaces, Inc - Millenium; (Cataloging) Innovative Interfaces, Inc; (Circulation) Innovative Interfaces, Inc; (ILL) Innovative Interfaces, Inc; (OPAC) Innovative Interfaces, Inc
Database Vendor: Baker & Taylor, EBSCO Information Services, Facts on File, Gale Cengage Learning, Grolier Online, H W Wilson, infoUSA, Ingram Library Services, Innovative Interfaces, Inc, LexisNexis, McGraw-Hill, Newsbank, OCLC, OCLC FirstSearch, OCLC WorldShare Interlibrary Loan, Overdrive, Inc, ReferenceUSA
Wireless access
Mem of NorthNet Library System
Friends of the Library Group
Branches: 7
CLARKSBURG BRANCH, 52915 Netherlands Ave, Clarksburg, 95612-5007. (Mail add: PO Box 229, Clarksburg, 95612-0229), SAN 335-3672. Tel: 916-744-1755. FAX: 916-744-1755. *Br Serv Mgr,* Rebecca Frame
Founded 1911
Library Holdings: Audiobooks 79; AV Mats 900; CDs 391; Bk Vols 16,308; Per Subs 40
Database Vendor: Bowker, LearningExpress
Open Tues & Thurs 9:30-12 & 1-7:30, Wed 5:30-7:30, Sat 9.30-1
Friends of the Library Group
DAVIS BRANCH, 315 E 14th St, Davis, 95616, SAN 335-3702. Tel: 530-757-5593. Circulation Tel: 530-757-5592. FAX: 530-757-5590. *Librn,* Jay Johnstone; *Ch Serv,* Peggy Rollins; *Ref,* Position Currently Open; *YA Serv,* Deatra Cohen
Library Holdings: Audiobooks 2,458; CDs 5,701; DVDs 11,243; Bk Vols 144,351; Per Subs 239
Database Vendor: Bowker, LearningExpress
Open Mon 1-9, Tues-Thurs 10-9, Fri & Sat 10-5:30, Sun 1-5
Friends of the Library Group
ESPARTO BRANCH, 17065 Yolo Ave, Esparto, 95627, SAN 335-3737. Tel: 530-787-3426. FAX: 530-787-4874. *Librn,* Malinda Baker
Library Holdings: Audiobooks 256; CDs 732; DVDs 1,805; Bk Vols 22,284; Per Subs 80
Database Vendor: Booklist Online, Bowker
Open Mon 1-8, Tues & Wed 8:30-12 & 1-8, Thurs 10-12 & 1-8, Fri 1-5, Sat 10-2
Friends of the Library Group
KNIGHTS LANDING BRANCH, 42351 Third St, Knights Landing, 95645. (Mail add: PO Box 517, Knights Landing, 95645-0517), SAN 335-3761. Tel: 530-735-6593. FAX: 530-735-6593. *Librn,* Nora Gortze
Library Holdings: Audiobooks 166; CDs 362; DVDs 1,299; Bk Vols 9,449; Per Subs 46
Database Vendor: Bowker, LearningExpress
Open Mon 1-6, Wed 10-12 & 1-6
Friends of the Library Group
ARTHUR F TURNER COMMUNITY LIBRARY, 1212 Merkley Ave, West Sacramento, 95691, SAN 335-3796. Tel: 916-375-6465. FAX: 916-371-5612. *Br Mgr 1,* Rachel Wolf; Tel: 916-375-6464, E-mail: rachel.wolf@yolocounty.org
Library Holdings: Audiobooks 994; CDs 1,523; DVDs 4,461; Bk Vols 45,313; Per Subs 101
Database Vendor: Booklist Online, Bowker, LearningExpress
Open Mon 12-8, Tues-Thurs 11-8, Fri & Sat 10-5:30, Sun 1-5
Friends of the Library Group

WINTERS BRANCH, 708 Railroad Ave, Winters, 95694, SAN 335-3826. Tel: 530-795-4955. FAX: 530-795-4955. *Librn,* Toni Mendieta; Tel: 530-795-3177, Fax: 530-795-3132
Library Holdings: Audiobooks 520; CDs 914; DVDs 2,361; Bk Vols 21,086; Per Subs 137
Database Vendor: Booklist Online, Bowker, LearningExpress
Open Mon & Wed (Winter) 8-6, Tues & Thurs 8-8, Fri 8-4, Sat 1-5; Mon (Summer) 12-6, Tues 10-8, Wed 10-6, Thurs 12-8, Sat 1-5
Friends of the Library Group

YOLO BRANCH, 37750 Sacramento St, Yolo, 95697. (Mail add: PO Box 447, Yolo, 95697-0447), SAN 335-3850. Tel: 530-662-2363. FAX: 530-662-2363. *Librn,* Nora Gortze
Library Holdings: Audiobooks 29; CDs 202; DVDs 777; Bk Vols 4,565; Per Subs 12
Database Vendor: Booklist Online, Bowker, infoUSA
Open Tues 1-5:30, Thurs 10-12 & 1-5:30

WOODLAND HILLS

J LOS ANGELES PIERCE COLLEGE LIBRARY, 6201 Winnetka Ave, 91371. SAN 301-7281. Tel: 818-719-6409. Reference Tel: 818-710-2833. E-mail: library@piercecollege.edu. Web Site: libguides.piercecollege.edu/content.php?pid=442777. *Dir, Ref,* Paula Paggi; Tel: 818-710-2843, E-mail: paggipm@piercecollege.edu; *Cat & Ref Librn,* Michael Habata; Tel: 818-710-2834, E-mail: habatamh@piercecollege.edu; *Ref/Bibliog Instruction Librn,* Marisa Diehl; Tel: 818-710-4267, E-mail: diehlme@piercecollege.edu; *Tech & Instruction Librn,* Clay Gediman; Tel: 818-710-4268, E-mail: gedimac@piercecollege.edu; *Ref Serv, Syst Librn,* Lauren Valdes; Tel: 818-710-4442, E-mail: valdesle@piercecollege.edu; Staff 10 (MLS 5, Non-MLS 5)
Founded 1947. Enrl 20,000; Fac 350; Highest Degree: Associate
Library Holdings: e-books 70,000; e-journals 20,000; Bk Titles 80,000; Bk Vols 100,000; Per Subs 30
Subject Interests: Agr
Automation Activity & Vendor Info: (Cataloging) SirsiDynix; (Circulation) SirsiDynix; (Course Reserve) SirsiDynix; (ILL) SirsiDynix; (OPAC) SirsiDynix
Database Vendor: EBSCOhost, Gale Cengage Learning, JSTOR, ProQuest
Wireless access
Open Mon-Thurs 8-7:30, Fri 9-3

SR WOODLAND HILLS PRESBYTERIAN CHURCH*, Norman E Nygaard Library, 5751 Platt Ave, 91367. SAN 328-3585. Tel: 818-346-7894. FAX: 818-346-7826. *In Charge,* Bob Thomson
Library Holdings: Bk Titles 1,000
Open Mon-Fri 8:30-4:30

YORBA LINDA

S RICHARD NIXON LIBRARY & BIRTHPLACE*, 18001 Yorba Linda Blvd, 92886. SAN 375-9636. Tel: 714-993-5075. Web Site: www.nixonlibraryfoundation.org. *Dir,* Timothy Naftali; *Archivist,* Greg Cumming; *Archivist,* Kirstin Julian; *Archivist,* Meghan Lee
Library Holdings: Bk Titles 3,000
Special Collections: American Political History 1946-1994; Richard Nixon
Function: Archival coll
Restriction: Non-circulating

P YORBA LINDA PUBLIC LIBRARY*, 18181 Imperial Hwy, 92886-3437. SAN 301-7303. Tel: 714-777-2873. FAX: 714-777-0640. TDD: 714-777-4812. E-mail: ylpl@ylpl.lib.ca.us. Web Site: www.ylpl.lib.ca.us. *Dir,* Melinda Steep; Tel: 714-777-2466, E-mail: melinda@ylpl.lib.ca.us; *Adult Serv Mgr,* Carrie Lixey; E-mail: carriel@ylpl.lib.ca.us; *Circ & Tech Serv Mgr,* Diane Standefer; E-mail: dianest@ylpl.lib.ca.us; *Info & Tech Serv Mgr,* Jon Legree; E-mail: jon@ylpl.lib.ca.us; *Mgr, Ch Serv,* Lucy Salvado; E-mail: lucys@ylpl.lib.ca.us; Staff 10 (MLS 8, Non-MLS 2)
Founded 1913. Pop 64,855; Circ 845,592
Library Holdings: AV Mats 24,076; Bk Vols 137,160; Per Subs 177
Special Collections: Oral History
Subject Interests: Local hist
Automation Activity & Vendor Info: (Acquisitions) SirsiDynix; (Cataloging) Brodart; (Circulation) SirsiDynix; (OPAC) SirsiDynix; (Serials) SirsiDynix
Database Vendor: Baker & Taylor, Brodart, EBSCO Auto Repair Reference, EBSCOhost, Facts on File, Gale Cengage Learning, Grolier Online, infoUSA, Newsbank, ProQuest, ReferenceUSA, SirsiDynix, World Book Online
Wireless access
Publications: California Missions; Yorba Legacy
Partic in Southern California Library Cooperative
Special Services for the Deaf - TDD equip
Open Mon-Thurs 9-9, Fri & Sat 9-5
Friends of the Library Group

YOSEMITE

G YOSEMITE NATIONAL PARK SERVICE*, Research Library, Museum Bldg, PO Box 577, 95389-0577. SAN 301-7311. Tel: 209-372-0280. FAX: 209-372-0255. *Librn,* Position Currently Open; Staff 1 (Non-MLS 1)
Founded 1923
Library Holdings: Bk Titles 12,000; Per Subs 60
Subject Interests: Hist

YOUNTVILLE

S LINCOLN MEMORIAL LIBRARY*, 240 California Dr, 94599-1445. (Mail add: PO Box 1200, 94599-1297), SAN 335-3885. Tel: 707-944-4915. Circulation Tel: 707-944-4916. *Sr Librn,* Carole DeBell; Tel: 707-944-4792, E-mail: carole.debell@cdva.ca.gov; *Acq,* Ann Snow; E-mail: ann.snow@cdva.ca.gov; Staff 2 (MLS 1, Non-MLS 1)
Founded 1886
Library Holdings: Large Print Bks 10,000; Bk Titles 35,000; Per Subs 62; Talking Bks 970
Subject Interests: World War I, World War II

M VETERANS HOME OF CALIFORNIA*, William K Murphy Health Sciences Memorial Library, 250 California Dr, 94599-1446. (Mail add: PO Box 1200, 94599-1297), SAN 335-394X. Tel: 707-944-4600. Reference Tel: 707-944-4792. *Sr Librn,* Carole DeBell; E-mail: carole.debell@cdva.ca.gov. Subject Specialists: *Geriatrics, Gerontology,* Carole DeBell; Staff 1 (MLS 1)
Library Holdings: Bk Titles 400; Per Subs 125
Subject Interests: Geriatrics & gerontology

YREKA

S SISKIYOU COUNTY MUSEUM LIBRARY*, 910 S Main St, 96097. SAN 328-3658. Tel: 530-842-3836. FAX: 530-842-3166. E-mail: hismus@att.net. *Dir,* Mike Hendryx
Founded 1950
Library Holdings: Bk Vols 1,000; Per Subs 12
Special Collections: Bancroft History, complete set; Local newspapers 1917-1980
Subject Interests: Local hist
Restriction: Open by appt only

GL SISKIYOU COUNTY PUBLIC LAW LIBRARY*, Courthouse, 311 Fourth St, 96097. (Mail add: PO Box 1026, 96097-1026), SAN 301-732X. Tel: 530-842-8390. FAX: 530-842-8339. *Dir,* Gina M DeRose Bell; E-mail: gderose@siskiyou.courts.ca.gov. Subject Specialists: *Law,* Gina M DeRose Bell; Staff 20 (Non-MLS 20)
Founded 1891. Pop 45,000
Library Holdings: CDs 50; Electronic Media & Resources 4; Bk Vols 6,000
Database Vendor: HeinOnline, Westlaw
Wireless access
Function: CD-ROM, Computers for patron use, Copy machines, Electronic databases & coll, ILL available, Orientations, Photocopying/Printing, Pub access computers
Open Mon-Fri 8-5
Restriction: Access at librarian's discretion, Open to pub for ref & circ; with some limitations

P SISKIYOU COUNTY PUBLIC LIBRARY*, 719 Fourth St, 96097. SAN 335-3974. Tel: 530-841-4175. Interlibrary Loan Service Tel: 530-841-4176. FAX: 530-842-7001. E-mail: library@co.siskiyou.ca.us. Web Site: www.siskiyoulibrary.info. *County Librn,* Michael Perry; E-mail: mperry@co.siskiyou.ca.us; Staff 4 (MLS 1, Non-MLS 3)
Founded 1915. Pop 45,000; Circ 130,000
Library Holdings: Bk Titles 110,000; Bk Vols 140,000; Per Subs 260
Subject Interests: Calif, Genealogy, Local Native Am, Mining
Automation Activity & Vendor Info: (Acquisitions) ByWater Solutions; (Cataloging) ByWater Solutions; (Circulation) ByWater Solutions; (ILL) OCLC FirstSearch; (OPAC) ByWater Solutions
Database Vendor: Gale Cengage Learning, HeinOnline, infoUSA, ReferenceUSA, Westlaw
Wireless access
Function: Adult literacy prog, Bks on CD, Computers for patron use, Copy machines, ILL available, Music CDs, Online cat, Pub access computers, Summer reading prog, Tax forms
Mem of NorthNet Library System
Special Services for the Blind - Bks on CD; Extensive large print coll; Large print bks
Friends of the Library Group
Branches: 11

DORRIS BRANCH, 800 Third St, Dorris, 96023. (Mail add: PO Box 649, Dorris, 96023-0649), SAN 335-4008. Tel: 530-397-4932. FAX: 530-397-4932. *Br Mgr,* Julie Mitchell; Staff 0.1 (Non-MLS 0.1)
Library Holdings: Bk Titles 4,977

Open Tues 10-4, Thurs 1-6
Friends of the Library Group
DUNSMUIR BRANCH, 5714 Dunsmuir Ave, Dunsmuir, 96025, SAN 335-4032. Tel: 530-235-2035. FAX: 530-235-0243. E-mail: dunsmuirlib@yahoo.com. *Br Asst,* Karen O'Quinn
Library Holdings: Bk Titles 11,628
Open Tues & Thurs 1-6, Wed 1-8, Sat 10-2
Friends of the Library Group
ETNA BRANCH, 121 Collier Way, Etna, 96027-0130, SAN 335-4067. Tel: 530-467-3661. *Br Adminr,* Rick Perkins
Library Holdings: Bk Titles 10,423
Open Mon-Thurs 12-5:30, Fri 12-4
Friends of the Library Group
FORT JONES BRANCH, 119 Sixty E, Fort Jones, 96032-0446. (Mail add: PO Box 632, Fort Jones, 96032-0632), SAN 335-4091. Tel: 530-468-2383. *Br Coordr,* Teresa Johnson
Library Holdings: Bk Titles 7,236
Open Tues & Wed 12:30-5:30, Thurs 1-6, Fri 12:30-5:30
Friends of the Library Group
HAPPY CAMP BRANCH, 143 Buckhorn Rd, Happy Camp, 96039. (Mail add: PO Box 317, Happy Camp, 96039-0317), SAN 335-4121. Tel: 530-493-2964. E-mail: happycamplibrary@yahoo.com. *Br Coordr,* Dorothy LaHue
Library Holdings: Bk Titles 7,878
Open Mon & Tues 2-5:30, Wed & Thurs 1:30-5:30
Friends of the Library Group
MCCLOUD BRANCH, 300 E Colombero Dr, McCloud, 96057. (Mail add: PO Box 425, McCloud, 96057-0425), SAN 335-4156. Tel: 530-964-2169. *Libr Asst,* Debbi Freeze
Library Holdings: Bk Titles 8,927
Open Mon & Thurs 12-4
Friends of the Library Group
MONTAGUE BRANCH, City Hall, 230 S 13th St, Montague, 96064. (Mail add: PO Box 466, Montague, 96064-0466), SAN 335-4164. Tel: 530-459-5473. *Br Mgr,* Becky Sims
Library Holdings: Bk Titles 3,912
Special Services for the Deaf - Bks on deafness & sign lang
Special Services for the Blind - Bks on cassette; Bks on CD; Large print bks
Open Mon-Thurs & Sat 1-5
Friends of the Library Group
MOUNT SHASTA BRANCH, 515 E Alma St, Mount Shasta, 96067, SAN 335-4180. Tel: 530-926-2031. FAX: 530-926-2031. *Librn,* Terry Thompson; *Borrower Serv Librn,* Annie Farris
Library Holdings: Bk Titles 17,251
Open Mon & Thurs 1-6, Tues 12-6, Wed 1-8, Fri & Sat 1-5
Friends of the Library Group
SCOTT BAR BRANCH, 27233 Scott River Rd, Scott Bar, 96085-9998. Tel: 530 496 3248. *Br Coordr,* Genetta Clark
Library Holdings: Bk Vols 400
Open Mon-Fri 8-4:30, Sat 11-1
TULELAKE BRANCH, 451 Main St, Tulelake, 96134-9527. (Mail add: PO Box 1072, Tulelake, 96134-1072), SAN 335-4199. Tel: 530-667-2291. *Br Coordr,* Lorraine Fine
Library Holdings: Bk Titles 8,968
Open Mon & Tues 9-1 & 2-5, Wed 10-1 & 2-5
WEED BRANCH, 780 S Davis St, Weed, 96094, SAN 335-4210. Tel: 530-938-4769. *Br Mgr,* Shelley Green
Library Holdings: Bk Titles 8,984
Open Wed-Fri 1-6

YUBA CITY

P SUTTER COUNTY FREE LIBRARY*, 750 Forbes Ave, 95991-3891. SAN 335-4245. Tel: 530-822-7137. FAX: 530-671-6539. E-mail: suttlibr@yahoo.com. Web Site: www.saclibrary.org. *Dir,* Roxanna Parker; Staff 3 (MLS 3)
Founded 1917. Pop 62,500; Circ 240,970
Library Holdings: Bk Titles 88,000; Bk Vols 98,000; Per Subs 159
Special Collections: Sutter County History Coll
Mem of Mountain-Valley Library System
Friends of the Library Group
Branches: 4
BARBER, 10321 Live Oak Blvd, Live Oak, 95953, SAN 335-427X. Tel: 530-695-2021. *Librn,* Arlene Wheeler
Circ 6,358
Library Holdings: Bk Vols 15,000
Open Mon-Thurs 1-5, Fri 9-1
Friends of the Library Group
BROWNS, 1248 Pacific Ave, Rio Oso, 95674, SAN 335-430X. Tel: 530-633-2170. *Libr Tech,* Ruth Dodds
Circ 11,516
Library Holdings: Bk Vols 6,043
Open Mon & Wed-Fri 8:30-12:30, Tues 2-6
Friends of the Library Group
PLEASANT GROVE BRANCH, 3075 Howsley Rd, Pleasant Grove, 95668-9723, SAN 335-4369. Tel: 916-655-3484. *Libr Tech,* Sandy Capell
Circ 4,090
Library Holdings: Bk Vols 5,237
Open Tues & Thurs 8-4:30
SUTTER BRANCH, 2147 California St, Sutter, 95982. (Mail add: PO Box 747, Sutter, 95982-0747), SAN 335-4393. Tel: 530-755-0485. *Libr Tech,* Karen Crocker
Circ 6,045
Library Holdings: Bk Vols 8,717
Open Mon-Fri 1-5

YUCAIPA

J CRAFTON HILLS COLLEGE LIBRARY*, 11711 Sand Canyon Rd, 92399. SAN 301-7338. Tel: 909-389-3323, 909-794-2161. FAX: 909-794-9524. Web Site: www.craftonhills.edu. *Chief Librn,* Laura Winningham; E-mail: lwinningham@craftonhills.edu; *Librn,* Catherine Hendrickson; *Librn,* Sam Job; Tel: 909-389-3322, E-mail: sejob@craftonhills.edu; Staff 6 (MLS 3, Non-MLS 3)
Founded 1972. Enrl 5,500; Fac 76, Highest Degree: Associate
Library Holdings: Bk Vols 50,000; Per Subs 500
Automation Activity & Vendor Info: (Cataloging) Innovative Interfaces, Inc; (Circulation) Innovative Interfaces, Inc; (Course Reserve) Innovative Interfaces, Inc; (ILL) Innovative Interfaces, Inc; (Media Booking) Innovative Interfaces, Inc; (OPAC) Innovative Interfaces, Inc; (Serials) Innovative Interfaces, Inc
Database Vendor: ProQuest
Partic in Inland Empire Acad Libr Coop (IEALC); San Bernardino, Inyo, Riverside Counties United Library Services
Open Mon-Thurs 8am-9pm, Fri 8-4

COLORADO

Date of Statistics: 2013
Population, 2010 U.S. Census: 5,029,196
Population Served by Public Libraries: 5,166,948
Total Volumes in Public Libraries: 10,806,153 (print books)
Volumes Per Capita: 2.09
Total Public Library Circulation: 65,658,037
Circulation Per Capita: 12.7
Total Public Library Income: $259,111,301 (local operating income)
Source of Income: Mainly public funds from property tax
2013 Regional Library Service Systems: $1,000,000
2013 Federal Library Services & Technology Act: $2,641,979
Total Public Library Expenditures: $256,406,030 (operating expenditures)
Expenditure Per Capita: $49.62

AGUILAR

P AGUILAR PUBLIC LIBRARY*, 146 W Main St, 81020. (Mail add: PO Box 578, 81020-0578), SAN 301-7346. Tel: 719-941-4426. Web Site: aguilarco.com/aguilar-public-library. *Libr Dir,* Linn G Baker; E-mail: aglibaker12@gmail.com; Staff 1 (Non-MLS 1)
Founded 1942. Pop 700; Circ 1,400
Library Holdings: Large Print Bks 250; Bk Vols 6,000; Talking Bks 200
Special Collections: Colorado Coll; Southwest Coll
Wireless access
Partic in Colorado Library Consortium
Open Thurs-Sat 10-2
Friends of the Library Group

AKRON

P AKRON PUBLIC LIBRARY*, 302 Main, 80720-1437. SAN 301-7354. Tel: 970-345-6818.
Founded 1921. Pop 4,800; Circ 8,339
Library Holdings: Bk Vols 7,000; Talking Bks 300; Videos 300
Special Collections: Washington County History. Oral History
Automation Activity & Vendor Info: (Cataloging) SirsiDynix; (Circulation) SirsiDynix; (OPAC) SirsiDynix
Open Mon & Wed-Fri 9-2:30 & 3-5:30, Sat 9-1
Friends of the Library Group

S USDA AGRICULTURAL RESEARCH SERVICE*, Central Great Plains Research Station Library, 40335 County Rd GG, 80720. SAN 370-2499. Tel: 970-345-2259. FAX: 970-345-2088. Web Site: www.akron.ars.usda.gov. *Res,* Merle F Vigil; E-mail: merle.vigil@ars.usda.gov. Subject Specialists: *Agronomy,* Merle F Vigil
Founded 1949
Library Holdings: Bk Vols 300; Per Subs 10
Open Mon-Fri 7:30-4:15
Restriction: Open to pub for ref only

ALAMOSA

C ADAMS STATE UNIVERSITY*, Nielsen Library, 208 Edgemont Ave, 81101-2373. SAN 301-7362. Tel: 719-587-7781. Interlibrary Loan Service Tel: 719-587-7174. Reference Tel: 719-587-7879. Administration Tel: 719-587-7820. Automation Services Tel: 719-587-7581. FAX: 719-587-7590. TDD: 719-587-8041. E-mail: asclib@adams.edu. Web Site: www.library.adams.edu. *Dir,* David Goetzman; E-mail: degoetzm@adams.edu; *Instruction & Ref Librn,* Lynee Sanute; *Res Sharing Librn,* Rosanna Ensley; Tel: 719-587-7187, E-mail: rensley@adams.edu; *Ser & Electronic Res Librn,* Nicole LeBoeuf; Tel: 719-587-7173, E-mail: nicoleleboeuf@adams.edu; *Tech Serv Librn,* Mary Walsh; E-mail: mwalsh@adams.edu. Subject Specialists: *Govt, Hist,* Rosanna Ensley; *Bus, Sci,* Nicole LeBoeuf; *Nursing,* Mary Walsh; Staff 8 (MLS 6, Non-MLS 2)
Founded 1925. Enrl 93; Fac 102; Highest Degree: Master
Jul 2012-Jun 2013. Mats Exp $267,500, Books $48,000, Per/Ser (Incl. Access Fees) $106,000, AV Mat $2,000, Electronic Ref Mat (Incl. Access Fees) $97,500, Presv $2,200. Sal $425,952 (Prof $392,652)
Library Holdings: AV Mats 2,602; DVDs 2,683; e-journals 19,000; Microforms 25,056; Bk Titles 110,041; Bk Vols 125,288; Per Subs 362
Special Collections: Colorado Room. US Document Depository
Automation Activity & Vendor Info: (Acquisitions) Baker & Taylor; (Cataloging) OCLC Online; (Circulation) Innovative Interfaces, Inc; (ILL) OCLC; (OPAC) Innovative Interfaces, Inc; (Serials) Innovative Interfaces, Inc
Database Vendor: Baker & Taylor, EBSCOhost, Innovative Interfaces, Inc, LexisNexis, OCLC FirstSearch
Wireless access
Function: Archival coll, Distance learning, For res purposes, Handicapped accessible, Homebound delivery serv, ILL available, Online searches, Photocopying/Printing, Ref serv available, Telephone ref, Wheelchair accessible
Partic in Marmot Libr Network
Special Services for the Deaf - TDD equip; TTY equip
Open Mon-Thurs 8am-11pm, Fri 8-5, Sat 1-6, Sun 1-11
Restriction: Use of others with permission of librn

P ALAMOSA PUBLIC LIBRARY, 300 Hunt Ave, 81101. SAN 301-7370. Tel: 719-589-6592. FAX: 719-589-3786. E-mail: librarian@alamosalibrary.org. Web Site: www.alamosalibrary.org. *Dir,* Heinz Bergann; Tel: 719-587-2524, Fax: 719-587-3541, E-mail: hbergann@ci.alamosa.co.us; *Libr Mgr,* Salai Taylor; Tel: 719-587-2543, E-mail: librarian@alamosalibrary.org; *Ch,* Becky Steenburg; Tel: 719-587-2550, E-mail: children@alamosalibrary.org; *Support Librn,* Melissa Martinson; Tel: 719-587-2541, E-mail: patrons@alamosalibrary.org; *Libr Tech - ILL,* Sheryl Benson; Tel: 719-587-2538, E-mail: ill@alamosalibrary.org; *Cat Tech,* Rose Strand; Tel: 719-587-2539, E-mail: materials@alamosalibrary.org; *Libr Tech-Mats,* Patty Martinez; Tel: 719-587-2542, E-mail: pmartinez@ci.alamosa.co.us. Subject Specialists: *Juv,* Becky Steenburg; Staff 2.625 (Non-MLS 2.625)
Founded 1908. Pop 8,888; Circ 134,174
Jan 2014-Dec 2014 Income $330,629, State $3,000, City $296,581, Locally Generated Income $31,048. Mats Exp $54,296, Books $32,335, Per/Ser (Incl. Access Fees) $3,064, AV Mat $10,839, Electronic Ref Mat (Incl. Access Fees) $8,058. Sal $170,289 (Prof $89,000)
Library Holdings: Audiobooks 2,174; AV Mats 479; e-books 2,589; Electronic Media & Resources 9; Bk Vols 45,577; Per Subs 112; Videos 6,653
Subject Interests: Colorado, Genealogy, Parenting, Spanish (Lang)
Automation Activity & Vendor Info: (Acquisitions) Baker & Taylor; (Cataloging) LibLime Koha; (Circulation) LibLime Koha; (ILL) Fretwell-Downing; (OPAC) LibLime Koha
Database Vendor: 3M Library Systems, Gale Cengage Learning, OCLC FirstSearch, ProQuest, TumbleBookLibrary, WT Cox
Wireless access
Function: Art exhibits, AV serv, Bk club(s), Bks on cassette, Bks on CD, Computer training, Computers for patron use, Copy machines, Electronic

databases & coll, Fax serv, Free DVD rentals, Handicapped accessible, Home delivery & serv to Sr ctr & nursing homes, Homebound delivery serv, Homework prog, ILL available, Large print keyboards, Mail & tel request accepted, Music CDs, Online cat, Online searches, Outreach serv, Photocopying/Printing, Prog for adults, Prog for children & young adult, Pub access computers, Ref serv available, Scanner, Spoken cassettes & CDs, Story hour, Summer reading prog, Tax forms, VHS videos, Video lending libr, Web-catalog, Wheelchair accessible, Workshops
Partic in Colorado Library Consortium
Special Services for the Deaf - ADA equip; Assistive tech; Closed caption videos; Sign lang interpreter upon request for prog; Staff with knowledge of sign lang
Special Services for the Blind - Accessible computers; Audio mat; Bks on cassette; Bks on CD; Braille bks; Cassettes; Computer access aids; Computer with voice synthesizer for visually impaired persons; Dragon Naturally Speaking software; Internet workstation with adaptive software; Large print & cassettes; Large print bks; Large screen computer & software; PC for handicapped; Talking bk serv referral; Talking bks; Talking bks & player equip
Open Mon-Thurs 9-8, Fri & Sat 9-5, Sun 1-5
Restriction: Non-circulating coll
Friends of the Library Group

ASPEN

S ASPEN HISTORICAL SOCIETY ARCHIVES, 620 W Bleeker St, 81611. SAN 328-5073. Tel: 970-925-3721. FAX: 970-925-5347. E-mail: info@aspenhistory.org. Web Site: www.aspenhistory.org. *Dir,* Kelly Murphy; Tel: 970-925-3721, Ext 101, E-mail: director@aspenhistory.org; *Curator of Coll,* Lisa Hancock; Tel: 970-925-3721, Ext 110, E-mail: curator@aspenhistory.org
Library Holdings: Bk Titles 800
Special Collections: Oral History
Open Tues-Fri 9-4

S THE ASPEN INSTITUTE*, Clarke Library, 1000 N Third St, 81611-1361. SAN 301-7397. Tel: 970-925-7010. FAX: 970-925-4188. Web Site: www.aspeninstitute.org. *In Charge,* Nancy Thorpe; E-mail: nancy.thorpe@aspeninstitute.org
Founded 1963
Library Holdings: Bk Vols 4,000
Open Mon-Fri 9-4:30

P PITKIN COUNTY LIBRARY*, 120 N Mill St, 81611. SAN 301-7400. Tel: 970-925-4025. FAX: 970-925-3935. Web Site: www.pitcolib.org. *Dir,* Kathleen Chandler; *Asst Dir,* Jocelyn Durrance; *Ch Serv,* Susan S Keenan; *ILL,* Helen Palmer; *Music,* David V Gollon; *Tech Serv,* Carol McArdell; Staff 4 (MLS 4)
Founded 1940. Pop 11,500; Circ 79,512
Library Holdings: Large Print Bks 300; Bk Titles 120,000; Per Subs 250
Special Collections: Aspen Newspapers, 1888-present, microfilm; Music, rec & scores
Automation Activity & Vendor Info: (Circulation) Innovative Interfaces, Inc
Partic in Marmot Libr Network
Open Mon-Thurs 10-9, Fri & Sat 10-6, Sun 12-6
Friends of the Library Group

AULT

P NORTHERN PLAINS PUBLIC LIBRARY*, 216 Second St, 80610. (Mail add: PO Box 147, 80610-0147), SAN 301-7419. Tel: 970-834-1259. FAX: 970-834-1259. E-mail: northernplains@gmail.com. *Dir,* Karen Haberman
Founded 1926. Pop 4,800; Circ 34,403
Library Holdings: DVDs 242; Large Print Bks 728; Bk Vols 34,790; Per Subs 70; Talking Bks 124; Videos 1,400
Special Collections: Oral History
Automation Activity & Vendor Info: (Cataloging) SirsiDynix; (Circulation) SirsiDynix; (OPAC) SirsiDynix
Wireless access
Mem of High Plains Library District
Open Mon-Fri 9-7, Sat 9-Noon
Friends of the Library Group

AURORA

S AURORA HISTORY MUSEUM LIBRARY, 15051 E Alameda Pkwy, 80012. Tel: 303-739-6660. FAX: 303-739-6657. Web Site: www.auroramuseum.org. *Curator,* Jennifer Cronk; E-mail: jcronk@auroragov.org
Founded 1979
Library Holdings: Bk Vols 750
Special Collections: Local Directories (1930-1960); Local Newspapers (Aurora Democrat, Advocate, Sun & Sentinel on microfilm); Newspaper Photos (Aurora Sun & Aurora Advocate, 1950-Present)
Subject Interests: Area hist
Function: Ref serv available, Res libr
Restriction: Open by appt only

P AURORA PUBLIC LIBRARY, Administration - Department of Library & Cultural Services, 14949 E Alameda Pkwy, 80012. SAN 335-4458. Tel: 303-739-6600. Circulation Tel: 303-739-6628. Interlibrary Loan Service Tel: 303-739-6618. Reference Tel: 303-739-6630. Administration Tel: 303-739-6640. FAX: 303-739-6579. Circulation FAX: 303-739-6569. Interlibrary Loan Service FAX: 303-739-6638. Administration FAX: 303-739-6586. TDD: 303-739-6571. Web Site: auroralibrary.org, www.auroragov.org. *Dir, Libr & Cultural Serv,* Patti Bateman; Tel: 303-739-6594; *Syst Support Coordr,* Tina Jayroe; Tel: 303-739-6622, E-mail: tjayroe@auroragov.org; Staff 61 (MLS 14, Non-MLS 47)
Founded 1929. Pop 335,000; Circ 801,649
Jan 2011-Dec 2011 Income (Main Library and Branch(s)) $3,252,000, City $2,600,000, Other $652,000. Mats Exp $270,000. Sal $2,497,874
Library Holdings: Bk Vols 269,986
Subject Interests: Spanish (Lang)
Automation Activity & Vendor Info: (Acquisitions) Innovative Interfaces, Inc; (Cataloging) Innovative Interfaces, Inc; (Circulation) Innovative Interfaces, Inc; (ILL) Innovative Interfaces, Inc; (OPAC) Innovative Interfaces, Inc; (Serials) Innovative Interfaces, Inc
Wireless access
Function: 24/7 Online cat, Adult bk club, Adult literacy prog, Bilingual assistance for Spanish patrons, Bk club(s), Bks on CD, Computer training, Computers for patron use, Copy machines, Digital talking bks, e-mail serv, Electronic databases & coll, Fax serv, Free DVD rentals, Genealogy discussion group, Handicapped accessible, ILL available, Life-long learning prog for all ages, Magazines, Mango lang, Microfiche/film & reading machines, Movies, Mus passes, Music CDs, Online cat, Online ref, Online searches, Outreach serv, OverDrive digital audio bks, Photocopying/Printing, Preschool outreach, Prog for adults, Prog for children & young adult, Pub access computers, Ref serv available, Scanner, Spanish lang bks, Story hour, Study rm, Summer & winter reading prog, Telephone ref, Wheelchair accessible
Publications: Annual Report; Aurora Public Library "Five Year Strategic Plan"; Aurora Public Library Qtrly brochure: "The Resource"; Library News Online
Special Services for the Blind - Bks on CD; Large print & cassettes; Talking bk serv referral
Open Mon-Fri 8-5
Friends of the Library Group
Branches: 6
CENTRAL, 14949 E Alameda Pkwy, 80012. *Supvr,* Ryan Ewers; Tel: 303-739-6625, E-mail: rewers@auroragov.org
Open Mon-Thurs 9-9, Sat 10-6, Sun 12:30-6
COLFAX & CHAMBERS PC CENTER, 15200 E Colfax Ave, 80012. Tel: 303-739-1959. *Libr Supvr,* Betsy Baxendale; Staff 1 (Non-MLS 1)
Circ 1,397
Automation Activity & Vendor Info: (Circulation) Innovative Interfaces, Inc - Millenium; (OPAC) Innovative Interfaces, Inc - Millenium
Function: 24/7 Online cat, Computer training, Computers for patron use, Online cat, OverDrive digital audio bks, Pub access computers, Ref serv in person, Scanner, Story hour, Summer & winter reading prog
Open Mon, Tues & Thurs-Sat 10-6, Wed 11-6, Sun 11-5
Friends of the Library Group
HOFFMAN PC CENTER, 1298 Peoria St, 80011. Tel: 303-739-1572. *Libr Asst,* Tyler Walton; Staff 1 (Non-MLS 1)
Circ 1,679
Automation Activity & Vendor Info: (Serials) Innovative Interfaces, Inc - Millenium
Function: 24/7 Online cat, Audiobks via web, Bilingual assistance for Spanish patrons, Bks on CD, Children's prog, Computer training, Computers for patron use, Copy machines, Electronic databases & coll, Handicapped accessible, ILL available, Learning ctr, Magazines, OverDrive digital audio bks, Prog for children & young adult, Pub access computers, Spanish lang bks, Story hour, Study rm, Summer & winter reading prog, Teen prog, Telephone ref
Open Mon 11-7, Tues-Sat 10-6
Friends of the Library Group
MARTIN LUTHER KING JR LIBRARY, 9898 E Colfax Ave, 80010, SAN 335-4547. Tel: 303-739-1940. FAX: 303-739-1944. *Supvr, N Region Libr,* Betsy Baxendale; E-mail: bbaxenda@auroragov.org; Staff 6 (MLS 1, Non-MLS 5)
Circ 172,742
Special Collections: John & Edna Mosely African American Culture Coll
Function: 24/7 Electronic res, 24/7 Online cat, Accelerated reader prog, Audiobks via web, Computer training, Computers for patron use, Copy machines, Homework prog, ILL available, Learning ctr, Magazines, Movies, Music CDs, Outreach serv, Photocopying/Printing, Preschool outreach, Preschool reading prog, Prog for children & young adult, Pub access computers, Ref serv available, Ref serv in person, Spanish lang

bks, Spoken cassettes & CDs, Story hour, Study rm, Summer reading prog, Telephone ref, Web-catalog, Wheelchair accessible
Open Tues 11-7, Wed-Sat 10-6
Friends of the Library Group

MISSION VEIJO BRANCH, 15324 E Hampden Circle, 80015, SAN 335-4571. Tel: 303-326-8600. *Libr Serv Coordr,* Pam Szot; Tel: 303-326-8604, E-mail: pszot@auroragov.org; Staff 1 (MLS 1)
Database Vendor: Innovative Interfaces, Inc
Open Tues-Sat 10-6
Friends of the Library Group

TALLYNS REACH, 23911 E Arapahoe Rd, 80016. Tel: 303-627-3050. FAX: 303-627-3060. *Supvr, S Region Libr,* Pam Szot; E-mail: pszot@auroragov.org
Database Vendor: Innovative Interfaces, Inc

J COMMUNITY COLLEGE OF AURORA*, 16000 E Centretech Pkwy, 80011-9036. Tel: 303-360-4700. FAX: 303-360-4824. E-mail: library@ccaurora.edu. Web Site: www.ccaurora.edu/students/library. *Dir of Libr Serv,* Joanna Primus; E-mail: joanna.primus@ccaurora.edu; Staff 2 (MLS 1, Non-MLS 1)
Founded 1983. Enrl 4,801; Fac 33; Highest Degree: Associate
Library Holdings: Bk Vols 7,206; Videos 1,000
Automation Activity & Vendor Info: (Cataloging) LibLime Koha; (Circulation) LibLime Koha; (OPAC) LibLime Koha; (Serials) LibLime Koha
Open Mon-Thurs 7:30am-8pm, Fri 7:30-5, Sat 9-1

C EVEREST COLLEGE LIBRARY, Aurora Campus, 14280 E Jewell Ave, Ste 100, 80012-5692. SAN 377-4686. Tel: 303-745-6244. *Librn,* Anna Andrews; Staff 1 (MLS 1)
Enrl 230; Highest Degree: Associate
Library Holdings: Bk Titles 2,709; Per Subs 26
Automation Activity & Vendor Info: (Cataloging) LibraryWorld, Inc; (OPAC) LibraryWorld, Inc
Database Vendor: ebrary, EBSCOhost, Westlaw
Wireless access
Partic in Libr & Info Resources Network (LIRN); Lyrasis
Open Mon-Thurs 9-8, Fri 9-6:30

G UNITED STATES DEPARTMENT OF JUSTICE*, The Robert J Kutak Memorial Library, National Institute of Corrections Information Center, 11900 E Cornell Ave, Unit C, 80014. SAN 323-6579. Toll Free Tel: 800-877-1461. TDD: 202-724-3156. *Prog Mgr,* Joshua Stengel; Tel: 303-338-6643, Fax: 303-338-6601
Library Holdings: Bk Titles 20,000; Per Subs 200
Subject Interests: Corrections, Prisons
Wireless access
Special Services for the Deaf - TDD equip
Open Mon-Fri 7:30-5:30

CM UNIVERSITY OF COLORADO DENVER*, Health Sciences Library, 12950 E Montview Blvd, 80045. (Mail add: PO Box 6508, Campus Box A003, 80045), SAN 335-7600. Tel: 303-724-2152. FAX: 303-724-2166. Web Site: www.hsclibrary.uchsc.edu. *Dir,* Jerry Perry; E-mail: jerry.perry@ucdenver.edu; *Dep Dir,* Melissa De Santis; E-mail: melissa.desantis@ucdenver.edu; *Planning & Projects Dir,* Rick Forsman; E-mail: rick.forsman@ucdenver.edu; *Head, Access Serv,* Douglas Stehle; E-mail: douglas.stehle@ucdenver.edu; *Acq Librn,* Sally MacGowan; E-mail: sally.macgowan@ucdenver.edu; *Cat Librn,* Emily Epstein; E-mail: emily.epstein@ucdenver.edu; *Educ Librn,* Lynne Fox; E-mail: lynne.fox@ucdenver.edu; Staff 17 (MLS 17)
Founded 1924. Enrl 2,000; Fac 17; Highest Degree: Doctorate
Library Holdings: AV Mats 4,956; Bk Titles 102,337; Bk Vols 106,987; Per Subs 5,581
Special Collections: Indigenous Medicine Coll
Subject Interests: Med
Automation Activity & Vendor Info: (Acquisitions) Innovative Interfaces, Inc; (Cataloging) Innovative Interfaces, Inc; (Circulation) Innovative Interfaces, Inc; (Course Reserve) Innovative Interfaces, Inc; (ILL) Innovative Interfaces, Inc; (Media Booking) Innovative Interfaces, Inc; (OPAC) Innovative Interfaces, Inc; (Serials) Innovative Interfaces, Inc
Partic in Dialog Corp; National Network of Libraries of Medicine; OCLC Online Computer Library Center, Inc
Open Mon-Thurs 7am-10pm, Fri 7-6, Sat & Sun 10-6
Restriction: Open to students, fac & staff

BAILEY

P PARK COUNTY PUBLIC LIBRARIES, Bailey Branch, 350 Bulldogger Rd, 80421-2379. SAN 335-4636. Tel: 303-838-5539. Administration Tel: 719-836-4299. FAX: 303-838-2351. Administration FAX: 719-836-0863. E-mail: baileylib@parkco.us. Web Site: parkcounty.colibraries.org/libraries/bailey-public-library. *Mgr,* Pat Sohmer; E-mail: psohmer@parkco.us; *Br Mgr,* Bonnie Bickel; Staff 1 (MLS 1)
Founded 1966. Circ 64,000
Library Holdings: Large Print Bks 150; Bk Titles 45,000; Per Subs 35; Talking Bks 1,600; Videos 3,000
Automation Activity & Vendor Info: (Acquisitions) SirsiDynix; (Cataloging) SirsiDynix; (Circulation) SirsiDynix; (Course Reserve) SirsiDynix; (ILL) SirsiDynix; (Media Booking) SirsiDynix; (OPAC) SirsiDynix; (Serials) SirsiDynix
Wireless access
Open Mon, Tues, Thurs & Fri 10-5, Wed 11-6, Sat 10-4
Friends of the Library Group
Branches: 3

FAIRPLAY BRANCH, 418 Main St, Fairplay, 80440. (Mail add: PO Box 592, Fairplay, 80440-0592). Tel: 719-836-4297. FAX: 719-836-0863. E-mail: fairplaylib@parkco.us. Web Site: parkcounty.colibraries.org/libraries/fairplay-public-library. *Br Librn,* Nancy Wood; Staff 2 (MLS 1, Non-MLS 1)
Open Mon-Sat 11-5
Friends of the Library Group

GUFFEY BRANCH, 1625B Park County Rd 102, Guffey, 80820. (Mail add: PO Box 33, Guffey, 80820-0033). Tel: 719-689-9280. FAX: 719-689-9280. E-mail: guffeylib@parkco.us. Web Site: parkcounty.colibraries.org/libraries/guffey-public-library. *Librn,* Chris Brown; *Librn,* Julie Taylor; Staff 2 (MLS 1, Non-MLS 1)
Open Tues-Thurs 1-5, Sat 10-2
Friends of the Library Group

LAKE GEORGE BRANCH, 37900 Hwy 24, Lake George, 80827. Tel: 719-748-3812. FAX: 719-748-3812. E-mail: lakegeorgelib@parkco.us. *Br Librn,* Kim Plutt; Staff 1 (Non-MLS 1)
Pop 3,000
Open Mon-Thurs 12-4:30, Sat 10-2
Friends of the Library Group

BASALT

P BASALT REGIONAL LIBRARY DISTRICT*, 14 Midland Ave, 81621-8305. SAN 320-1724. Tel: 970-927-4311. FAX: 970-927-1351. Web Site: www.basaltrld.org. *Dir,* Barbara Milnor; E-mail: bmilnor@basaltlibrary.org; *Assoc Dir,* Chris Cook; E-mail: chris.cook@basaltlibrary.org; *Youth Serv Dir,* Nicole Scheiblberg; *Ch,* Linda Slaybaugh
Founded 1976. Pop 10,900; Circ 45,126
Library Holdings: Bk Vols 34,134; Per Subs 61
Special Collections: Oral History
Subject Interests: Colorado
Automation Activity & Vendor Info: (Circulation) Innovative Interfaces, Inc; (OPAC) Innovative Interfaces, Inc
Partic in Marmot Libr Network
Open Mon-Thurs 10-7, Fri & Sat 10-5, Sun 12-5
Friends of the Library Group

BAYFIELD

P PINE RIVER PUBLIC LIBRARY DISTRICT*, 395 Bayfield Center Dr, 81122. (Mail add: PO Box 227, 81122-0227), SAN 301-746X. Tel: 970-884-2222. FAX: 970-884-7155. E-mail: librarian@prlibrary.org. Web Site: www.prlibrary.org. *Dir,* Amy Dodson; E-mail: amy@prlibrary.org; *Develop Dir,* Judy Poe; E-mail: judy@prlibrary.org; *Pub Relations Dir & Ad,* Karen Lemke; E-mail: karen@prlibrary.org; *Circ Mgr,* Sven Skoglund; E-mail: sven@prlibrary.org; *Children's Serv Coordr,* Elizabeth VonTauffkirchen; E-mail: elizabeth@prlibrary.org; *Teen Serv Coordr,* Becky Van Den Berg; E-mail: becky@prlibrary.org; Staff 5.9 (MLS 1, Non-MLS 4.9)
Founded 1934. Pop 7,400
Library Holdings: Bk Titles 28,000; Bk Vols 30,000
Automation Activity & Vendor Info: (Cataloging) Innovative Interfaces, Inc - Millenium; (Circulation) Innovative Interfaces, Inc - Millenium; (OPAC) Innovative Interfaces, Inc - Millenium
Database Vendor: EBSCOhost, Ingram Library Services, Innovative Interfaces, Inc, Overdrive, Inc, WT Cox
Wireless access
Function: Adult bk club, Art exhibits, Audio & video playback equip for onsite use, Audiobks via web, Bk club(s), Bks on CD, Children's prog, Computer training, Computers for patron use, Copy machines, e-mail & chat, Equip loans & repairs, Exhibits, Free DVD rentals, Holiday prog, ILL available, Mail & tel request accepted, Music CDs, Newsp ref libr, Online searches, Orientations, Outside serv via phone, mail, e-mail & web, OverDrive digital audio bks, Photocopying/Printing, Preschool outreach, Prog for adults, Prog for children & young adult, Pub access computers, Ref serv available, Referrals accepted, Story hour, Summer reading prog, Telephone ref, Web-catalog, Wheelchair accessible, Workshops, Writing prog
Open Mon-Fri 9-7, Sat 9-5, Sun 1-5
Friends of the Library Group

BERTHOUD

P BERTHOUD PUBLIC LIBRARY*, 236 Welch Ave, 80513. (Mail add: PO Box 1259, 80513-2259), SAN 301-7478. Tel: 970-532-2757. FAX: 970-532-4372. Web Site: www.berthoudlibrary.org. *Dir,* Mark Killie; *Supvr, Circ,* Pam Androulidakis; Staff 4 (MLS 1, Non-MLS 3)
Founded 1931. Pop 11,000; Circ 50,834
Library Holdings: AV Mats 1,000; High Interest/Low Vocabulary Bk Vols 100; Large Print Bks 500; Bk Titles 28,000; Bk Vols 28,400; Per Subs 30; Talking Bks 529
Special Collections: Berthoud Bulletin, microfilm; Xeriscape Materials
Automation Activity & Vendor Info: (Cataloging) Follett Software; (Circulation) Follett Software; (OPAC) Follett Software
Partic in Colorado Library Consortium
Open Mon & Tues 10-8, Wed & Thurs 10-6, Fri 12-5, Sat 10-3
Friends of the Library Group

BLACK HAWK

P GILPIN COUNTY PUBLIC LIBRARY DISTRICT*, 15131 Hwy 119, 80422. SAN 378-0163. Tel: 303-582-5777. Administration Tel: 303-582-0161. FAX: 303-582-3938. E-mail: gilpinlib@co.gilpin.co.us. Web Site: www.gilpinlibrary.org. *Dir,* Lawrence Grieco; E-mail: lgrieco@co.gilpin.co.us; *Cat,* Crystal Morris; *Ch Serv,* Robert Avrett, III; *Libr Tech,* George Blevins; E-mail: gblevins@co.gilpin.co.us; Staff 6 (MLS 1, Non-MLS 5)
Founded 1978. Pop 4,800; Circ 25,000
Jan 2009-Dec 2009 Income $287,425. Mats Exp $15,500, Books $14,000, Per/Ser (Incl. Access Fees) $1,500. Sal $148,965 (Prof $63,000)
Library Holdings: CDs 68; DVDs 213; Large Print Bks 252; Bk Vols 26,331; Per Subs 50; Videos 1,479
Subject Interests: Colorado, County hist, State hist
Automation Activity & Vendor Info: (Cataloging) Follett Software; (Circulation) Follett Software
Database Vendor: OCLC FirstSearch
Wireless access
Function: Adult bk club, Adult literacy prog, Archival coll, Art exhibits, Audio & video playback equip for onsite use, Bk club(s), Bks on cassette, Bks on CD, CD-ROM, Children's prog, Computer training, Computers for patron use, Copy machines, e-mail serv, E-Reserves, Free DVD rentals, Handicapped accessible, Holiday prog, Homebound delivery serv, ILL available, Notary serv, Online cat, Online ref, Online searches, Orientations
Partic in Colorado Library Consortium
Open Tues & Thurs 9-8, Wed & Fri 9-6, Sat 9-4
Friends of the Library Group

BOULDER

M BOULDER COMMUNITY HOSPITAL*, Medical Library, N Broadway & 1100 Balsam Ave, 80301. (Mail add: PO Box 9019, 80301-9019), SAN 301-7508. Tel: 303-440-2091. FAX: 303-938-3483. E-mail: medlib@bch.org. *Librn,* Peg Fletcher; Staff 2 (MLS 1, Non-MLS 1)
Founded 1922
Library Holdings: e-journals 659; Bk Vols 425; Per Subs 30
Subject Interests: Med, Nursing
Database Vendor: EBSCOhost, MD Consult, OVID Technologies
Wireless access
Partic in Colorado Council of Medical Librarians; Medical Library Association (MLA); Mid Continental Med Libr Asn
Open Mon, Wed & Fri 8-Noon, Tues & Thurs 12-4

S BOULDER COUNTY CORRECTIONS LIBRARY*, 3200 Airport Rd, 80301. SAN 377-0788. Tel: 303-441-4686. FAX: 303-441-4608. Web Site: www.co.boulder.co.us/sheriff. *Dir,* Erin E Thompson; E-mail: ethompson@bouldercounty.org; Staff 1 (MLS 1)
Library Holdings: Bk Titles 4,500; Bk Vols 5,000; Per Subs 15
Open Mon-Fri 7-3

P BOULDER PUBLIC LIBRARY*, 1001 Arapahoe Rd, 80302. SAN 335-4695. Tel: 303-441-3100. FAX: 303-442-1808. Web Site: www.boulderlibrary.org. *Libr & Arts Dir,* Valerie Maginnis; *Dep Libr Dir,* Jennifer Miles; *Coll Mgr, Mgr, Ref Serv,* Melinda Mattingly; *Tech Serv Mgr,* Terri Lewis; *Ch Serv, Teen Serv,* Mary Jane Holland; Staff 76.95 (MLS 16.5, Non-MLS 60.45)
Pop 103,600; Circ 1,040,413
Jan 2010-Dec 2010 Income (Main Library and Branch(s)) $6,948,448, City $6,785,848, Other $162,600. Mats Exp $761,409, Books $352,643, AV Mat $104,909, Electronic Ref Mat (Incl. Access Fees) $269,824. Sal $4,840,306
Library Holdings: Audiobooks 7,984; CDs 13,983; DVDs 13,460; e-books 56,441; Electronic Media & Resources 2,512; Bk Vols 310,246; Per Subs 447
Special Collections: Boulder Arts Resource Coll; Children's Literature Reference; Local History; Municipal Government. Oral History
Automation Activity & Vendor Info: (Acquisitions) Innovative Interfaces, Inc; (Cataloging) Innovative Interfaces, Inc; (Circulation) Innovative Interfaces, Inc; (OPAC) Innovative Interfaces, Inc
Database Vendor: ABC-CLIO, Alexander Street Press, ALLDATA Online, EBSCOhost, Gale Cengage Learning, Innovative Interfaces, Inc, Newsbank, OCLC FirstSearch, SerialsSolutions, Springshare, LLC, Wilson - Wilson Web
Wireless access
Function: Adult bk club, Adult literacy prog, Art exhibits, Audiobks via web, Bk club(s), Bks on CD, Bus archives, Children's prog, Citizenship assistance, Computers for patron use, Copy machines, Digital talking bks, E-Reserves, Electronic databases & coll, Exhibits, Family literacy, Free DVD rentals, Handicapped accessible, Home delivery & serv to Sr ctr & nursing homes, Homebound delivery serv, ILL available, Jail serv, Literacy & newcomer serv, Notary serv, Online cat, Online ref, Online searches, Outreach serv, OverDrive digital audio bks, Photocopying/Printing, Printer for laptops & handheld devices, Prog for adults, Prog for children & young adult, Pub access computers, Ref serv in person, Story hour, Summer reading prog, Teen prog, Web-catalog, Wheelchair accessible
Publications: BookLook (Children's publication); Boulder Municipal Government 1871-1946, 1965-1974, 1975-1979 & 1980-1984; Colorado Business; Colorado History; Taking Care of Business (Newsletter); Word (Young Adult Magazine)
Partic in Flatirons Library Consortium
Open Mon-Thurs 10-9, Fri & Sat 10-6, Sun 12-6
Branches: 3
CARNEGIE BRANCH FOR LOCAL HISTORY, 1125 Pine St, 80302-4024, SAN 335-4709. Tel: 303-441-3110. FAX: 720-406-7452. Web Site: www.boulderlibrary.org/carnegie. *Br Mgr,* Wendy Hall; Tel: 303-441-4096, E-mail: hallw@boulderlibrary.org; Staff 4 (MLS 1, Non-MLS 3)
Founded 1983. Pop 90,000
Special Collections: Boulder Historical Society Photograph Coll; Digitized OPAC Images; Maria Rogers Oral History Program. Oral History
Subject Interests: Boulder County & Boulder
Function: Archival coll, Audio & video playback equip for onsite use, Genealogy discussion group, Newsp ref libr, Online searches, Outside serv via phone, mail, e-mail & web, Pub access computers, Ref serv available
Open Mon-Fri 10-5, Sat 10-3
Friends of the Library Group
MEADOWS, 4800 Baseline Rd, Ste C112, 80303-2678, SAN 323-9381. Tel: 303-441-4390. Administration Tel: 303-441-4169. Web Site: boulderlibrary.org. *Mgr,* Donna Klopf; E-mail: klopfd@boulderlibrary.org
Library Holdings: Bk Vols 30,000; Per Subs 33
Function: Art exhibits, Children's prog, Citizenship assistance, Computer training, Computers for patron use, Copy machines, Electronic databases & coll, Free DVD rentals, Handicapped accessible, Home delivery & serv to Sr ctr & nursing homes, Homebound delivery serv, ILL available, Literacy & newcomer serv, Music CDs, Online cat, Online ref, Online searches, OverDrive digital audio bks, Prog for adults, Prog for children & young adult, Pub access computers, Ref serv available, Serves mentally handicapped consumers, Story hour, Tax forms, Wheelchair accessible
Open Mon-Wed 10-9, Fri & Sat 10-6, Sun 1-5
GEORGE F REYNOLDS BRANCH, 3595 Table Mesa Dr, 80305. (Mail add: PO Drawer H, 80306-1326), SAN 335-4725. Tel: 303-441-3120. FAX: 303-441-4094. *Mgr,* Linda Cumming
Library Holdings: Bk Vols 25,000; Per Subs 30
Open Tues-Thurs 10-9, Fri & Sat 10-6, Sun 1-5

R FIRST UNITED METHODIST CHURCH LIBRARY, 1421 Spruce, 80302. SAN 301-7516. Tel: 303-442-3770. FAX: 303-442-4752. E-mail: office@fumcboulder.org. Web Site: www.fumcboulder.org. *Librn,* Nancy Moore
Founded 1952
Library Holdings: Bk Vols 2,940
Subject Interests: Educ, Psychol, Relig, Soc sci & issues
Wireless access
Open Tues 9:30am-11:30am, Sun 9-Noon

M MENTAL HEALTH CENTER LIBRARY*, 1333 Iris Ave, 80304-2296. SAN 325-2132. Tel: 303-443-8500, Ext 273. FAX: 303-449-6029. Web Site: www.mhcbbc.org. *Librn,* Marilyn Fowler; E-mail: mfowler@mhcbbc.org
Library Holdings: Bk Titles 3,000; Per Subs 30
Subject Interests: Psychiat, Psychol, Res
Publications: Annual Report
Restriction: Vols & interns use only

C NAROPA UNIVERSITY LIBRARY*, Allen Ginsberg Library, 2130 Arapahoe Ave, 80302. SAN 320-443X. Tel: 303-546-3507. Interlibrary Loan Service Tel: 303-246-4668. FAX: 303-245-4636. E-mail:

library@naropa.edu. Web Site: library.naropa.edu. *Dir,* Nicholas Weiss; Tel: 305-546-3505, E-mail: nweiss@naropa.edu; Staff 4 (MLS 2, Non-MLS 2)
Founded 1974. Enrl 1,100; Highest Degree: Master
Library Holdings: AV Mats 2,300; e-books 1,676; Bk Vols 27,500; Per Subs 131
Special Collections: Naropa University Recordings; Small Press & Chapbook Coll; Tibetan Coll
Subject Interests: Buddhism, Poetry, Psychol, Tibetan (Lang), Traditional Eastern arts
Wireless access
Function: Archival coll, Audio & video playback equip for onsite use, AV serv, Distance learning, For res purposes, Handicapped accessible, ILL available, Music CDs, Online searches, Orientations, Photocopying/Printing, Ref serv available, Spoken cassettes & CDs, Telephone ref, VHS videos
Partic in OCLC Online Computer Library Center, Inc
Open Mon-Thurs 9-9, Fri 9-5, Sat & Sun 1-5

G NATIONAL CENTER FOR ATMOSPHERIC RESEARCH LIBRARY*, 1850 Table Mesa Dr, 80305. (Mail add: PO Box 3000, 80307-3000), SAN 335-4784. Tel: 303-497-1180. Interlibrary Loan Service Tel: 303-497-1177. FAX: 303-497-1170. E-mail: ncarref@ucar.edu. Web Site: www.ucar.edu/library. *Libr Dir,* Mary Marlino; Tel: 303-497-8350, E-mail: marlino@ucar.edu; *Mgr, Libr Operations,* Terry Murray; Tel: 303-497-1178, E-mail: tmurray@ucar.edu
Founded 1962
Library Holdings: e-journals 400; Per Subs 563
Special Collections: Meteorological Atlases; Meteorological Data
Subject Interests: Chem, Computer sci, Electrical eng, Electronics, Math, Mechanical eng, Meteorology, Oceanography, Physics
Automation Activity & Vendor Info: (Acquisitions) SirsiDynix; (Cataloging) SirsiDynix; (Circulation) SirsiDynix; (OPAC) SirsiDynix; (Serials) SirsiDynix
Database Vendor: Cambridge Scientific Abstracts, IEEE (Institute of Electrical & Electronics Engineers), JSTOR, Newsbank, OCLC FirstSearch, ScienceDirect, SirsiDynix, Thomson - Web of Science
Wireless access
Partic in Colorado Library Consortium; OCLC Online Computer Library Center, Inc

L NATIONAL INDIAN LAW LIBRARY*, Native Americans Rights Fund, 1522 Broadway, 80302-6217. SAN 321-8007. Tel: 303-447-8760. FAX: 303-443-7776. Web Site: www.narf.org/nill/index.htm. *Libr Dir,* David Selden; E-mail: dselden@narf.org; *Asst Law Librn,* Anne Lucke; E-mail: alucke@narf.org; Staff 1 (MLS 1)
Founded 1972
Oct 2013-Sept 2014. Mats Exp $51,000, Books $5,000, Per/Ser (Incl. Access Fees) $40,000, Electronic Ref Mat (Incl. Access Fees) $6,000. Sal $220,000
Library Holdings: AV Mats 60; Bk Titles 8,000; Per Subs 80
Special Collections: Federal Indian Law (National Indian Law Repository), legal briefs, pleadings, legal opinions, rulings, treatises, studies, articles, reports & legislative mat; Tribal Codes & Constitutions; Tribal Court Cases
Automation Activity & Vendor Info: (Acquisitions) Inmagic, Inc.; (Cataloging) Inmagic, Inc.; (Circulation) Inmagic, Inc.; (OPAC) Inmagic, Inc.; (Serials) Inmagic, Inc.
Partic in OCLC Online Computer Library Center, Inc
Open Mon-Fri 9-5
Restriction: Open to pub for ref only
Friends of the Library Group

G US DEPARTMENT OF COMMERCE, Boulder Laboratories Library, 325 Broadway MC5, 80305-3328. SAN 335-4814. Tel: 303-497-3271. Interlibrary Loan Service Tel: 303-497-5569. FAX: 303-497-3890. E-mail: boulderlabs.main.library@noaa.gov. Web Site: library.bldrdoc.gov. *Actg Dir,* Joan Segal; Tel: 303-497-5550, E-mail: joan.s.segal@noaa.gov; *Ref & ILL Librn,* Mike Robinson; Tel: 303-497-5569, E-mail: mike.robinson@noaa.gov; *Ref/Outreach Librn,* Aric Villarreal; *Tech Serv Librn,* Sara Martin; *Cat Tech,* Diann Cullen; *Circ Tech,* Laura Kistner; *ILL Tech,* F T Bronzan; Staff 8 (MLS 4, Non-MLS 4)
Founded 1954
Oct 2014-Sept 2015
Library Holdings: Bk Titles 42,910; Per Subs 575
Special Collections: Boulder Laboratory Research Agencies Technical Reports; NOAA, NIST & NTIA Scientific Publications
Subject Interests: Astrophysics, Atmospheric sci, Chem, Chem eng, Eng, Geophysics, Mat sci, Math, Measurement sci, Optics, Physics, Solar physics, Statistics, Telecommunications sci
Automation Activity & Vendor Info: (Acquisitions) OCLC; (Cataloging) OCLC; (Circulation) OCLC; (ILL) OCLC; (OPAC) OCLC; (Serials) OCLC
Database Vendor: Cambridge Scientific Abstracts, ebrary, IEEE (Institute of Electrical & Electronics Engineers), ISI Web of Knowledge, JSTOR, OCLC WorldShare Interlibrary Loan, ProQuest, ScienceDirect, Thomson - Web of Science
Function: 24/7 Electronic res, 24/7 Online cat, Archival coll, Doc delivery serv, e-mail serv, Electronic databases & coll, ILL available, Online searches, Outreach serv, Photocopying/Printing, Ref & res, Scanner, Wheelchair accessible
Publications: Library Brochure (Brochure); Library Liaison Newsletter (Newsletter); Library Notes (Current awareness service)
Partic in Fedlink; OCLC Online Computer Library Center, Inc
Restriction: Badge access after hrs, Borrowing requests are handled by ILL, Circulates for staff only, External users must contact libr, Open to pub for ref only, Open to pub upon request, Photo ID required for access, Pub use on premises

C UNIVERSITY OF COLORADO BOULDER, University Libraries, 1720 Pleasant St, 184 UCB, 80309-0184. SAN 335-4903. Tel: 303-492-7511. Circulation Tel: 303-492-7477. Interlibrary Loan Service Tel: 303-492-1617. Reference Tel: 303-492-7521. Administration Tel: 303-492-8684. Automation Services Tel: 303-492-0487. Information Services Tel: 303-492-8705. FAX: 303-492-3340. Interlibrary Loan Service FAX: 303-492-4560. Reference FAX: 303-492-0935. Administration FAX: 303-492-1881. E-mail: reflib@colorado.edu. Web Site: ucblibraries.colorado.edu. *Dean, Dir of Libr,* James F Williams, II; Tel: 303-492-7512, E-mail: james.williams@colorado.edu; *Sr Assoc Dean,* Leslie J Reynolds; Tel: 303-492-6252, E-mail: leslie.reynolds@colorado.edu; *Assoc Dean,* Position Currently Open; *Dir of Circ,* Brice Austin; Tel: 303-492-3975, E-mail: brice.austin@colorado.edu; *Dir, Metadata Serv,* Paul Moeller; Tel: 303-735-0492, E-mail: paul.moeller@colorado.edu; *Dir, Archives,* Bruce P Montgomery; Tel: 303-492-7242, Fax: 303-492-3960, E-mail: bruce.montgomery@colorado.edu; *Dir, Arts & Humanities,* Jennifer Knievel; Tel: 303-492-8887, E-mail: jennifer.knievel@colorado.edu; *Dir, Libr Info Tech,* Debra Weiss; Tel: 303-492-3965, E-mail: debra.weiss@colorado.edu; *Dir, Scholarly Res Develop,* Yem Fong; Tel: 303-492-4414, Fax: 303-492-8775, E-mail: judith.fong@colorado.edu; *Dir, Sci,* Jack Maness; Tel: 303-492-4545, E-mail: jack.maness@colorado.edu; *Dir, Soc Sci,* Eugene Hayworth; Tel: 303-492-5383, E-mail: eugene.hayworth@colorado.edu; *Dir, Spec Coll,* Deborah Hollis; Tel: 303-492-3910, E-mail: deborah.hollis@colorado.edu; *Head, Acq,* Position Currently Open; *Head, Bus Libr,* Jennifer Gerke; Tel: 303-735-6804, E-mail: jennifer.gerke@colorado.edu; *Head, Coll Develop & Assessment,* Gabrielle Wiersma; Tel: 303-492-4316, E-mail: gabrielle.wiersma@colorado.edu; *Head, Earth Sci & Map Libr,* Kathryn Lage; Tel: 303-735-4917, E-mail: katie.lage@colorado.edu; *Head, Govt Info,* Margaret Jobe; Tel: 303-492-8834, E-mail: margaret.jobe@colorado.edu; *Head, Monographic & Spec Mat Cat Unit,* Position Currently Open; *Head Music Libr,* Laurie Sampsel; Tel: 303-492-3929; *Prog & Communications Librn,* Deborah Fink; Tel: 303-492-8302, E-mail: deborah.fink@colorado.edu; *Interim Presv Mgr,* Lauren Stapleton; Tel: 303-492-6914, E-mail: lauren.stapleton@colorado.edu; Staff 159 (MLS 66, Non-MLS 93)
Founded 1876. Enrl 30,000; Fac 1,250; Highest Degree: Doctorate
Jul 2014-Jun 2015. Mats Exp $10,860,815
Library Holdings: AV Mats 95,000; Microforms 7,043,254; Bk Vols 5,031,188; Per Subs 62,126
Special Collections: Ira Wolff Coll; Juvenile Literature (Epstein & Block Colls); Mountaineering (John J Jerome Hart Coll); Scuba Photobook Coll; Tippit Photobook Coll; Women Poets of the Romantic Period. State Document Depository; UN Document Depository; US Document Depository
Subject Interests: Environmentalism, Justice, Labor, Peace, Politics, Western Americana
Automation Activity & Vendor Info: (Acquisitions) Innovative Interfaces, Inc; (Cataloging) Innovative Interfaces, Inc; (Circulation) Innovative Interfaces, Inc; (Course Reserve) Innovative Interfaces, Inc; (OPAC) Innovative Interfaces, Inc; (Serials) Innovative Interfaces, Inc
Wireless access
Function: Art exhibits, e-mail serv, E-Reserves, Electronic databases & coll, Govt ref serv, ILL available, Mail & tel request accepted, Online cat, Online ref, Outreach serv, Photocopying/Printing, Pub access computers, Ref & res, Tax forms, Telephone ref
Partic in Association of Research Libraries (ARL); Center for Research Libraries; Colorado Alliance of Research Libraries; Greater Western Library Alliance; OCLC Online Computer Library Center, Inc
Friends of the Library Group

Departmental Libraries:

ARCHIVES, 1720 Pleasant St, 80309. (Mail add: UCB 184, University of Colorado Boulder, 80309-0184). Tel: 303-492-7242. Circulation Tel: 303-492-7477. FAX: 303-492-3340. Circulation FAX: 303-492-4560. E-mail: arv@colorado.edu. *Prof & Fac Dir, Archives & Spec Coll,* Bruce P Montgomery; Tel: 303-492-7394, E-mail: bruce.montgomery@colorado.edu; *Archives Project Mgr,* Dr Stephanie Yuhas; Tel: 303-492-3797, E-mail: stephanie.yuhas@colorado.edu; *Archivist,* Arnold R Bradley; *Archivist,* David M Hayes. Subject Specialists: *Human rights, Labor, Politics,* Bruce P Montgomery; *Philos, Relig studies,* Dr Stephanie Yuhas; *English lit, Film,* Arnold R Bradley;

Civil rights, US Navy Japanese/oriental lang sch in WWII, Western Am, David M Hayes; Staff 11 (MLS 3, Non-MLS 8)
Subject Interests: Environment, Film, Jewish studies, Labor, Western Americana

GEMMILL LIBRARY OF ENGINEERING, MATHEMATICS & PHYSICS, Mathematics Bldg, Rm 135, 184 UCB, 80309-0184, SAN 335-5020. Tel: 303-492-5396. FAX: 303-492-6488. E-mail: engref@colorado.edu. Web Site: ucblibraries.colorado.edu/engineering. *Head, Eng, Match & Physics Libr,* Megan Bresnahan; Tel: 303-492-4679, E-mail: megan.bresnahan@colorado.edu. Subject Specialists: *Computer sci, Math,* Megan Bresnahan; Staff 5 (MLS 2, Non-MLS 3)
Special Collections: Engineering Societies Coll, conference, journal & rpt publs; Standards Coll, incl ANSI & ASTM
Subject Interests: Applied sci, Computer sci, Eng, Math, Physics
Friends of the Library Group

GOVERNMENT INFORMATION, Norlin Library, 1720 Pleasant St, 80309. (Mail add: University Libraries Govt Information, 184 UCB, 80309-0184), SAN 372-5375. Tel: 303-492-8834. FAX: 303-492-1881. E-mail: govpubs@colorado.edu. Web Site: ucblibraries.colorado.edu/govpubs/index.htm. *Head, Govt Info,* Peggy Jobe; Tel: 303-492-4682, E-mail: margaret.jobe@colorado.edu. Subject Specialists: *Fed docs, Tech rpts,* Peggy Jobe; Staff 7 (MLS 4, Non-MLS 3)
Fac 2
Library Holdings: Microforms 5,127,166; Bk Vols 1,838,237
Special Collections: European Union Depository; Technical Reports (NITS, DOD, DIE, & NASA). State Document Depository; UN Document Depository; US Document Depository
Subject Interests: Govt info
Restriction: Borrowing requests are handled by ILL, Non-circulating of rare bks, Off-site coll in storage - retrieval as requested
Friends of the Library Group

INSTITUTE OF ARCTIC & ALPINE RESEARCH INFORMATION CENTER, 1560 30th St, UCB 450, 80309-0450, SAN 335-5144. Tel: 303-492-1867, 303-492-6387. FAX: 303-492-6388. Web Site: instaar.colorado.edu/other/info_center. *Mgr,* Shelly Sommer; E-mail: shelly.sommer@colorado.edu
Library Holdings: Bk Vols 6,700; Per Subs 240
Subject Interests: Climate, Environ sci, Geophysics, Polar regions
Automation Activity & Vendor Info: (Cataloging) Inmagic, Inc.
Publications: Arctic & Alpine Research (Quarterly); Occasional Papers
Restriction: In-house use for visitors, Internal circ only

JERRY CRAIL JOHNSON EARTH SCIENCES & MAP LIBRARY, 2200 Colorado Ave, 184 UCB, 80309-0184. (Mail add: 184 UCB, University Libraries, University of Colorado Boulder, 80309), SAN 335-4997. Tel: 303-492-6133. FAX: 303-735-4879. E-mail: maplib@colorado.edu. Web Site: ucblibraries.colorado.edu/earthsciences/index.htm, ucblibraries.colorado.edu/map/index.htm. *Head, Earth Sci & Map Libr,* Kathryn Lage; Tel: 303-735-4917, E-mail: katie.lage@colorado.edu. Subject Specialists: *Environ studies, Geol, Maps,* Kathryn Lage; Staff 7 (MLS 4, Non-MLS 3)
Founded 1998. Highest Degree: Doctorate
Library Holdings: Bk Vols 47,000; Per Subs 350
Special Collections: US Document Depository
Subject Interests: Atmospheric sci, Cartography, Geochemistry, Geog, Geol, Geophysics, GIS, Maps, Mineral, Mineralogy, Oceanography, Paleontology, Phys geog
Friends of the Library Group

NATURAL HAZARD CENTER LIBRARY, Institute of Behavioral Science Bldg, 1440 15th St, 80302. (Mail add: 483 UCB, 80309-0483). Tel: 303-492-5787, 303-492-6818. FAX: 303-492-2151. E-mail: hazctr@colorado.edu. Web Site: www.colorado.edu/hazards. *Libr Mgr,* Wanda Headley; E-mail: wanda.headley@colorado.edu
Founded 1977
Library Holdings: AV Mats 330; Bk Vols 35,000; Per Subs 21
Function: Ref serv available
Restriction: Open by appt only

SPECIAL COLLECTIONS, 1720 Pleasant St, 184 UCB, 80309-0184. Tel: 303-492-4414. Circulation Tel: 303-492-7477. FAX: 303-492-3340. E-mail: spc@colorado.edu. Web Site: ucblibraries.colorado.edu/specialcollections/. *Fac Dir, Spec Coll Dept,* Deborah R Hollis; Tel: 303-492-3910, E-mail: deborah.hollis@colorado.edu; *Instr,* Amanda H Brown; E-mail: amanda.h.brown@colorado.edu; *Libr Tech III,* Chris Levine; Tel: 303-492-0381, E-mail: christine.levine@colorado.edu; *Libr Tech III,* Greg Robl; Tel: 303-492-3907, E-mail: gregory.robl@colorado.edu; *Res & Teaching Assoc,* Susan Guinn-Chipman; Tel: 303-492-5739, E-mail: susan.guinn-chipman@colorado.edu. Subject Specialists: *Hist of photog,* Amanda H Brown; *British hist,* Susan Guinn-Chipman
Subject Interests: Am & British lit, Artists bks, Hist of photog, Mountaineering

HOWARD B WALTZ MUSIC LIBRARY, Imig Music Bldg, N250, 1720 Pleasant St, 184 UCB, 80309-0184, SAN 335-5098. Tel: 303-492-8093. FAX: 303-735-0100. E-mail: mus@colorado.edu. Web Site: ucblibraries.colorado.edu/music/index.htm. *Fac Dir,* Laurie Sampsel; Tel: 303-492-3929, E-mail: laurie.sampsel@colorado.edu; Staff 6 (MLS 2, Non-MLS 4)
Library Holdings: AV Mats 55,000; DVDs 800; Music Scores 60,407; Bk Vols 74,033; Per Subs 300; Videos 811
Special Collections: 18th Century Comic Opera; American Music Research Center; California Mission Music; Early New England Singing Schools; Limpkin Folk Song; Moravian Music; Music of Colorado Composers; Popular Sheet Music
Friends of the Library Group

WILLIAM M WHITE BUSINESS LIBRARY, Koelbel Bldg, Leeds College of Business, 80309. (Mail add: Business Library, 184 UCB, 80309-0184), SAN 335-4962. Tel: 303-492-3194, 303-492-8367. FAX: 303-735-0333. Web Site: ucblibraries.colorado.edu/business/index.htm. *Head of Libr,* Jennifer Gerke; Tel: 303-735-6804, E-mail: jennifer.gerke@colorado.edu; *Bus Ref & Instruction Librn,* Matthew Brower; Tel: 303-492-7156, E-mail: matthew.brower@colorado.edu; *Bus Ref & Instruction Librn,* Natalia Tingle; Tel: 303-492-3034, E-mail: natalia.tingle@colorado.edu; Staff 6 (MLS 3, Non-MLS 3)
Founded 1970
Library Holdings: CDs 200; DVDs 25; Bk Vols 80,000; Per Subs 660
Subject Interests: Acctg, Finance, Mgt, Mkt, Real estate, Tax, Transportation
Friends of the Library Group

CL THE WILLIAM A WISE LAW LIBRARY, 2450 Kittredge Loop Dr, 402 UCB, 80309-0402, SAN 335-5055. Tel: 303-492-7534. Reference Tel: 303-492-3522. Administration Tel: 303-492-4945. FAX: 303-492-2707. E-mail: lawlib@colorado.edu. Web Site: lawpac.colorado.edu. *Dir,* Susan Nevelow Mart; Tel: 303-492-1233, E-mail: susan.mart@colorado.edu; *Assoc Dir, Head, Tech Serv,* Georgia K Briscoe; Tel: 303-492-7312, E-mail: georgia.bricsoe@colorado.edu; *Assoc Dir, Head, Pub Serv,* Robert Linz; E-mail: robert.linz@colorado.edu; *Asst Dir, Fac Serv,* Jane Thompson; Tel: 303-492-2705, E-mail: jane.thompson@colorado.edu; *Head, Ref,* Alan Pannell; Tel: 303-735-1867, E-mail: alan.pannell@colorado.edu; *Cat Librn,* Karen Selden; Tel: 303-492-7535, E-mail: karen.selden@colorado.edu; *Ref Librn,* Alicia Brillon; Tel: 303-492-2704, E-mail: alicia.brillon@colorado.edu; *Tech Serv Librn,* Yumin Jiang; Tel: 303-492-2706, E-mail: yumin.jiang@colorado.edu; Staff 20 (MLS 8, Non-MLS 12)
Founded 1892. Enrl 535; Fac 44; Highest Degree: Doctorate
Jul 2008-Jun 2009. Mats Exp $1,429,000, Books $170,000, Per/Ser (Incl. Access Fees) $935,000, Electronic Ref Mat (Incl. Access Fees) $310,000, Presv $14,000. Sal $1,003,000 (Prof $633,000)
Library Holdings: Bk Titles 210,000; Bk Vols 700,000
Special Collections: Commonwealth & Foreign Law. US Document Depository
Subject Interests: Constitutional law, Environ law, Intl law, Native Am law
Automation Activity & Vendor Info: (Acquisitions) Innovative Interfaces, Inc; (Cataloging) Innovative Interfaces, Inc; (Circulation) Innovative Interfaces, Inc; (Course Reserve) Innovative Interfaces, Inc; (ILL) Innovative Interfaces, Inc; (OPAC) Innovative Interfaces, Inc; (Serials) Innovative Interfaces, Inc
Database Vendor: Bowker, Cassidy Cataloguing Services, Inc, EBSCOhost, Gale Cengage Learning, H W Wilson, HeinOnline, Innovative Interfaces, Inc, Innovative Interfaces, Inc, JSTOR, LexisNexis, Loislaw, OCLC FirstSearch, OCLC WorldShare Interlibrary Loan, Oxford Online, ProQuest, SerialsSolutions, Westlaw, Wilson - Wilson Web
Partic in Colorado Alliance of Research Libraries; Colorado Library Consortium; OCLC Online Computer Library Center, Inc
Special Services for the Deaf - Assistive tech
Special Services for the Blind - Assistive/Adapted tech devices, equip & products

S WORLD DATA CENTER GLACIOLOGY, BOULDER*, NSIDC Information Center, CIRES, UCB 449, 1540 30th St, 80309-0449. SAN 335-4873. Tel: 303-492-4004, 303-492-5774. FAX: 303-492-2468. E-mail: nsidc@kryos.colorado.edu. Web Site: www.nsidc.org/noaa/library.html. *Head Librn, Tech Serv,* Gloria Hicks; E-mail: ghicks@nsidc.org; *Head, Archives, Librn,* Allaina Howard; E-mail: allaina.howard@nsidc.org; Staff 2 (MLS 2)
Founded 1957
Library Holdings: Bk Vols 6,000; Per Subs 90
Publications: Glaciological Data; New Accessions List
Restriction: Internal circ only, Staff & prof res
Friends of the Library Group

BROOMFIELD

P MAMIE DOUD EISENHOWER PUBLIC LIBRARY*, Broomfield Public, Three Community Park Rd, 80020-3781. SAN 301-7575. Tel: 720-887-2300. Circulation Tel: 720-887-2301. Interlibrary Loan Service Tel: 720-887-2361. Reference Tel: 720-887-2350. Administration Tel: 720-887-2357. FAX: 720-887-1384. E-mail: info@broomfield.org. Web

Site: www.broomfieldlibrary.org, www.ci.broomfield.co.us/library. *Dir,* Depp Roberta; Tel: 720-887-2355; *Mgr, Ch Serv,* Lesley Clayton; Tel: 720-887-2318, E-mail: lclayton@ci.broomfield.co.us; *Circ Mgr,* Jean Patterson; Tel: 720-887-2306, E-mail: jpatterson@ci.broomfield.co.us; *Mgr, Ref Serv,* Susan Simmons; Tel: 720-887-2367; *Tech Serv Mgr,* Barbara Thorne; Tel: 720-887-2326, E-mail: bthorne@ci.broomfield.co.us; *Mgr, YA Serv,* Gigi Yang; Tel: 720-887-2366, E-mail: gyang@ci.broomfield.co.us; *ILL,* Barbara Livsey; E-mail: blivsey@ci.broomfield.co.us; Staff 10 (MLS 9, Non-MLS 1)
Founded 1960. Pop 47,378; Circ 502,390
Jan 2006-Dec 2006 Income $1,875,700, City $1,786,200, Other $77,500. Mats Exp $246,100, Books $172,000, Per/Ser (Incl. Access Fees) $12,600, AV Equip $1,000, AV Mat $20,800, Electronic Ref Mat (Incl. Access Fees) $39,700. Sal $1,437,000
Library Holdings: AV Mats 13,000; Bk Vols 144,250; Per Subs 248
Special Collections: Mamie Doud Eisenhower Coll. US Document Depository
Automation Activity & Vendor Info: (Cataloging) Innovative Interfaces, Inc; (Circulation) Innovative Interfaces, Inc; (Course Reserve) Innovative Interfaces, Inc; (ILL) Innovative Interfaces, Inc; (Media Booking) Innovative Interfaces, Inc; (OPAC) Innovative Interfaces, Inc; (Serials) Innovative Interfaces, Inc
Database Vendor: 3M Library Systems, Baker & Taylor, BWI, Comprise Technologies Inc, EBSCOhost, Gale Cengage Learning, Grolier Online, Newsbank, OCLC FirstSearch, ProQuest, ReferenceUSA, TLC (The Library Corporation), Wilson - Wilson Web
Function: Adult bk club, Adult literacy prog, Electronic databases & coll, Govt ref serv, Handicapped accessible, Homebound delivery serv, ILL available, Magnifiers for reading, Online ref, Photocopying/Printing, Prog for adults, Prog for children & young adult, Ref serv available, Spoken cassettes & CDs, Summer reading prog, Telephone ref, VHS videos
Partic in Colorado Alliance of Research Libraries; Colorado Library Consortium
Special Services for the Deaf - Staff with knowledge of sign lang; TTY equip
Special Services for the Blind - Large print bks; Talking bks
Open Mon-Thurs 9-9, Fri & Sat 9-5, Sun 1-5
Friends of the Library Group

BRUSH

P EAST MORGAN COUNTY LIBRARY DISTRICT*, 500 Clayton St, 80723-2110. SAN 301-7583. Tel: 970-842-4596. FAX: 970-842-2450. E-mail: emclcontact@gmail.com. Web Site: emcl.info. *Dir,* Deborah S Johnson; *Asst Dir,* Elizabeth Jarrell; Staff 9 (MLS 1, Non-MLS 8)
Founded 1915. Pop 7,985; Circ 87,529
Jan 2010-Dec 2010 Income $92,690, City $1,500, County $54,690, Other $36,500. Mats Exp $42,330, Books $31,600, Per/Ser (Incl. Access Fees) $2,200, AV Mat $7,250, Electronic Ref Mat (Incl. Access Fees) $1,280. Sal $139,300 (Prof $47,000)
Library Holdings: Audiobooks 900; Bks on Deafness & Sign Lang 23; Braille Volumes 2; CDs 175; DVDs 100; High Interest/Low Vocabulary Bk Vols 266; Large Print Bks 1,150; Bk Titles 27,000; Bk Vols 28,800; Per Subs 60; Videos 929
Special Collections: HOSPES. Oral History
Subject Interests: Colorado, Gen, Local hist
Automation Activity & Vendor Info: (Acquisitions) Innovative Interfaces, Inc; (Cataloging) Innovative Interfaces, Inc; (Circulation) Innovative Interfaces, Inc; (ILL) Innovative Interfaces, Inc; (OPAC) Innovative Interfaces, Inc
Database Vendor: EBSCOhost, OCLC FirstSearch, SirsiDynix
Wireless access
Function: After school storytime, Bks on cassette, Bks on CD, Computer training, Computers for patron use, Copy machines, e-mail & chat, Fax serv, Free DVD rentals, Genealogy discussion group, Home delivery & serv to Sr ctr & nursing homes, Homebound delivery serv, ILL available, Online cat, Preschool outreach, Prog for adults, Prog for children & young adult, Pub access computers, Story hour, Summer reading prog, Tax forms, Teen prog, VHS videos, Wheelchair accessible
Publications: Friends (Quarterly newsletter); Friends Brochure (Annual); Newspaper Column (Newsletter)
Special Services for the Deaf - ADA equip; Bks on deafness & sign lang
Special Services for the Blind - Audio mat; Recorded bks
Open Mon-Thurs 9-8, Fri & Sat 10-5
Friends of the Library Group

BUENA VISTA

S BUENA VISTA CORRECTIONAL COMPLEX LIBRARY*, 15125 Hwys 24 & 285, 81211. (Mail add: PO Box 2017, 81211-2017), SAN 301-7605. Tel: 719-395-7254. *Libr Tech,* Patti Clarke; E-mail: patti.clarke@doc.state.co.us; *Libr Tech,* Sandra Horrocks; E-mail: sandra.horrocks@doc.state.co.us; Staff 4 (MLS 1, Non-MLS 3)
Library Holdings: Bk Titles 10,050; Bk Vols 10,097
Special Collections: Law Coll
Automation Activity & Vendor Info: (Cataloging) EOS International; (Circulation) EOS International
Function: AV serv, ILL available, Magnifiers for reading, Photocopying/Printing, Ref serv available
Partic in Cooperating Libraries in Consortium
Restriction: Not open to pub, Residents only

P BUENA VISTA PUBLIC LIBRARY*, 131 Linderman Ave, 81211-9184. (Mail add: PO Box 2019, 81211-2019), SAN 301-7591. Tel: 719-395-8700. FAX: 719-395-6426. Web Site: www2.youseemore.com/buenavista. *Dir,* Gail Nottingham; E-mail: gnottingham@buenavistalibrary.org
Founded 1898
Library Holdings: AV Mats 1,243; Large Print Bks 585; Bk Titles 20,500; Bk Vols 21,000; Per Subs 85; Talking Bks 929
Database Vendor: EBSCOhost
Special Services for the Blind - Bks on cassette; Bks on CD; Descriptive video serv (DVS); Large print bks; Magnifiers; Talking bks
Open Mon-Fri 9-7, Sat 9-4
Friends of the Library Group

S COLORADO DEPARTMENT OF CORRECTIONS, Buena Vista Minimum Center Library, PO Box 2005, 81211-2005. Tel: 719-395-2404, Ext 3177. FAX: 719-395-7362. *In Charge,* Patti Clarke; E-mail: patti.clarke@state.co.us
Library Holdings: Bk Vols 5,820; Per Subs 25
Automation Activity & Vendor Info: (Cataloging) EOS International; (Circulation) EOS International

BURLINGTON

P BURLINGTON PUBLIC LIBRARY*, 321 14th St, 80807-1607. SAN 301-7613. Tel: 719-346-8109. FAX: 719-346-8672. *Dir,* Della Yersin; E-mail: dyersin@hotmail.com
Founded 1921. Pop 3,500; Circ 31,000
Library Holdings: Bk Vols 22,000; Per Subs 35
Automation Activity & Vendor Info: (Cataloging) SirsiDynix; (Circulation) SirsiDynix; (OPAC) SirsiDynix
Mem of Lakeshores Library System
Partic in Library Connection, Inc; Merrimack Valley Library Consortium; OCLC
Open Mon-Fri 10-6, Sat 10-2

CANON CITY

P CANON CITY PUBLIC LIBRARY*, 516 Macon Ave, 81212-3380. SAN 301-7621. Tel: 719-269-9020. FAX: 719-269-9031. E-mail: ccpl@canoncity.org. Web Site: ccpl.lib.co.us. *Dir,* Suzanne Lasha; Staff 3 (MLS 3)
Founded 1886
Library Holdings: Bk Titles 68,900; Bk Vols 69,300; Per Subs 130
Special Collections: Local History Coll
Automation Activity & Vendor Info: (Cataloging) Auto-Graphics, Inc; (Circulation) Auto-Graphics, Inc; (OPAC) Auto-Graphics, Inc
Database Vendor: EBSCOhost, OCLC FirstSearch
Wireless access
Partic in Colorado Library Consortium
Open Mon-Thurs 10-7, Fri & Sat 10-5
Friends of the Library Group

COLORADO DEPARTMENT OF CORRECTIONS

S ARROWHEAD CORRECTIONAL CENTER LIBRARY*, US Hwy 50, Evans Blvd, 81215. (Mail add: CMC, PO Box 300, 81215-0300), SAN 373-6369. Tel: 719-269-5601, Ext 3923. FAX: 719-269-5650. Web Site: www.doc.state.co.us. *Libr Tech,* Kristi Lloyd; E-mail: kristi.lloyd@doc.state.co.us; Staff 1 (MLS 1)
Founded 1991
Library Holdings: Bk Titles 10,000; Per Subs 35
Automation Activity & Vendor Info: (Cataloging) EOS International; (Circulation) EOS International; (OPAC) EOS International
Special Services for the Deaf - Bks on deafness & sign lang; High interest/low vocabulary bks
Open Mon 5:30pm-7:30pm, Tues & Thurs 1-3:30 & 5:30-7:30, Wed 8:30am-10:30am, Fri 1-3:30, Sat 2:30-3:30

S CENTENNIAL CORRECTIONAL FACILITY LIBRARY*, PO Box 600, 81215-0600, SAN 301-763X. Tel: 719-269-5546. FAX: 719-269-5545. *Librn,* Jean Frost; E-mail: jean.frost@doc.state.co.us; *Tech Serv,* Diana Reese; E-mail: diana.reese@doc.state.co.us; Staff 8 (MLS 8)
Library Holdings: Bk Vols 8,000; Per Subs 28
Automation Activity & Vendor Info: (Acquisitions) EOS International; (Cataloging) EOS International; (Circulation) EOS International; (Course Reserve) EOS International; (ILL) EOS International; (OPAC) EOS International; (Serials) EOS International
Open Mon & Wed-Fri 7-4, Tues 7-9

S COLORADO STATE PENITENTIARY LIBRARY*, PO Box 777, 81215-0777, SAN 377-080X. Tel: 719-269-5268. FAX: 719-269-5125. Web Site: www.doc.state.co.us. *Librn,* Wendy Rowlands
Library Holdings: Bk Vols 11,500
Automation Activity & Vendor Info: (Cataloging) EOS International; (Circulation) EOS International; (OPAC) EOS International
Open Mon-Sun 7-4

S FOUR MILE CORRECTIONAL CENTER LIBRARY*, CMC - FMCC, PO Box 300, 81215. Tel: 719-269-5601, Ext 3339. FAX: 719-269-5364. Web Site: www.doc.state.co.us. *Libr Tech II,* Nancy Pettit
Library Holdings: Bk Vols 10,000; Per Subs 25
Automation Activity & Vendor Info: (Cataloging) EOS International; (Circulation) EOS International; (OPAC) EOS International
Open Tues, Sat & Sun 1-3:30, Mon, Wed & Fri 5:30-7:30pm, Thurs 9:30-10:30am

S FREMONT CORRECTIONAL FACILITY LIBRARY*, US Hwy 50, Evans Blvd, 81215. (Mail add: PO Box 999, 81215-0999), SAN 322-7316. Tel: 719-269-5002, Ext 3566. FAX: 719-269-5048. Web Site: www.doc.state.co.us. *Mgr,* Linda Lewis; E-mail: linda.lewis@state.co.us; Staff 3 (MLS 1, Non-MLS 2)
Founded 1957
Library Holdings: Bk Vols 18,000; Per Subs 52
Automation Activity & Vendor Info: (Cataloging) EOS International; (Circulation) EOS International; (OPAC) EOS International
Function: ILL available
Open Mon-Thurs 8am-8:30pm, Fri-Sun 8-3:30

S SKYLINE CORRECTIONAL CENTER LIBRARY*, PO Box 300, 81215, SAN 325-3635. Tel: 719-269-5420, Ext 3351. FAX: 719-269-5404. Web Site: www.doc.state.co.us. *Libr Tech II,* Nina Aldrich; E-mail: nina.aldrich@doc.state.co.us
Library Holdings: Bk Vols 3,500; Per Subs 23
Automation Activity & Vendor Info: (Cataloging) EOS International; (Circulation) EOS International; (OPAC) EOS International
Open Mon & Fri 7-4, Tues-Thurs 1-8, Sat & Sun 1-2

S COLORADO TERRITORIAL CORRECTIONAL FACILITY LIBRARY*, PO Box 1010, 81215-1010. SAN 370-7660. Tel: 719-275-4181, Ext 3167. FAX: 719-269-4115. *Librn,* Linda Hyatt
Founded 1985
Library Holdings: Bk Titles 11,000; Bk Vols 12,971; Per Subs 42
Subject Interests: Poetry
Partic in Arkansas Valley Regional Library Service System

CASTLE ROCK

P DOUGLAS COUNTY LIBRARIES, 100 S Wilcox, 80104. SAN 335-5268. Tel: 303-791-7323. FAX: 303-688-7655. Web Site: www.douglascountylibraries.org. *Dir,* Bob Pasicznyuk; Tel: 303-688-7654, E-mail: bpasicznyuk@dclibraries.org; *Assoc Dir, Br Serv,* Sheila Kerber; Tel: 303-688-7657, E-mail: skerber@dclibraries.org; *Assoc Dir, Community Relations,* Amber DeBerry; Tel: 303-688-7641, E-mail: adeberry@dclibraries.org; *Assoc Dir, Finance,* Karen Gargan; Tel: 303-688-7623, E-mail: kgargan@dclibraries.org; *Assoc Dir, Human Res,* Art Glover; Tel: 303-688-7631, E-mail: aglover@dclibraries.org; *Assoc Dir, Info Tech,* Monique Sendze; Tel: 303-688-7617, E-mail: msendze@dclibraries.org; *Assoc Dir, Support Serv,* Rochelle Logan; Tel: 303-688-7603, E-mail: rlogan@dclibraries.org; Staff 199 (MLS 49, Non-MLS 150)
Founded 1966. Pop 280,000; Circ 8,000,000
Jan 2005-Dec 2005 Income (Main Library and Branch(s)) $15,042,119, Locally Generated Income $14,465,236, Other $576,883. Mats Exp $2,342,442, Books $1,367,980, Per/Ser (Incl. Access Fees) $59,338, AV Mat $716,572, Electronic Ref Mat (Incl. Access Fees) $198,552. Sal $7,081,345
Library Holdings: AV Mats 51,741; e-books 550; Bk Vols 540,455; Per Subs 1,203; Talking Bks 41,457
Special Collections: Local History; Newspapers of Douglas County 1881-1992, micro; Photographs. State Document Depository
Automation Activity & Vendor Info: (Cataloging) SirsiDynix; (Circulation) SirsiDynix; (OPAC) SirsiDynix
Database Vendor: EBSCOhost, Gale Cengage Learning, OCLC FirstSearch, ProQuest
Wireless access
Function: Adult bk club, Adult literacy prog, Archival coll, Art exhibits, Audio & video playback equip for onsite use, AV serv, Bk club(s), Bks on CD, Bus archives, CD-ROM, Chess club, Children's prog, Citizenship assistance, Computers for patron use, Copy machines, Digital talking bks, Electronic databases & coll, Family literacy, Fax serv, Free DVD rentals, Handicapped accessible, Homebound delivery serv, Homework prog, ILL available, Literacy & newcomer serv, Magnifiers for reading, Music CDs, Online cat, Online ref, Online searches, Outside serv via phone, mail, e-mail & web, OverDrive digital audio bks, Photocopying/Printing, Prog for adults, Prog for children & young adult, Pub access computers, Ref serv in person, Spoken cassettes & CDs, Spoken cassettes & DVDs, Story hour, Summer reading prog, Telephone ref, Web-catalog, Wheelchair accessible, Workshops
Special Services for the Deaf - TTY equip
Open Mon-Thurs 9-9, Fri & Sat 9-5, Sun 12-5
Branches: 6
HIGHLANDS RANCH LIBRARY, 9292 Ridgeline Blvd, Highlands Ranch, 80129, SAN 371-9510. Tel: 303-791-7323. FAX: 720-348-9510. *Br Mgr,* Sheila Kerber
Library Holdings: Bk Titles 100,000; Bk Vols 138,336; Per Subs 150
Open Mon-Thurs 9-9, Fri & Sat 9-5, Sun 12-5
LONE TREE LIBRARY, 8827 Lone Tree Pkwy, Lone Tree, 80124-8961, SAN 335-5357. Tel: 303-791-7323. FAX: 303-799-4275. *Br Mgr,* Aspen Walker
Library Holdings: Bk Vols 60,000
LOUVIERS LIBRARY, 7885 Louviers Blvd, Louviers, 80131. (Mail add: PO Box 282, Louviers, 80131-0282), SAN 335-5292. Tel: 303-791-7323. FAX: 303-791-7323. *Mgr,* Leslie Good
Library Holdings: Bk Vols 5,949
Open Tues & Thurs 3-8, Sat 9-Noon
PHILIP S MILLER LIBRARY, 100 S Wilcox St, 80104-2726, SAN 370-4955. Tel: 303-791-7323. FAX: 303-688-7615. *Br Mgr,* Leslie Good
Library Holdings: Bk Titles 150,000
Subject Interests: Local hist
Open Mon-Thurs 9-9, Fri & Sat 9-5, Sun 12-5
PARKER LIBRARY, 10851 S Crossroads Dr, Parker, 80134-9081, SAN 335-5322. Tel: 303-791-7323. FAX: 303-841-7892. *Br Mgr,* Amy Long; Tel: 303-841-6344
Library Holdings: Bk Titles 130,000; Per Subs 150
Open Mon-Thurs 9-9, Fri & Sat 9-5, Sun 12-5
ROXBOROUGH, 8357 N Rampart Range Rd, Ste 200, Littleton, 80125. Tel: 303-791-7323. *Mgr,* Sheila Kerber; *Circ,* Leslie Good; *Coll Spec,* Becky Spilver
Library Holdings: Bk Vols 23,000
Open Mon-Thurs 9-9, Fri & Sat 9-5, Sun 12-5

CENTENNIAL

SR GOLDEN GATE BAPTIST THEOLOGICAL SEMINARY LIBRARY*, Rocky Mountain Campus, 7393 S Alton Way, 80112-2302. Tel: 303-779-6431. FAX: 303-779-6432. E-mail: rmc-info@ggbts.edu. *Regional Campus Librn,* Barbara Russo; E-mail: BarbaraRusso@ggbts.edu
Library Holdings: Bk Vols 15,000
Open Mon 11-7, Tues 10-5

CHEYENNE WELLS

P CHEYENNE WELLS PUBLIC LIBRARY*, 151 S First St W, 80810. (Mail add: PO Box 939, 80810-0939). Tel: 719-767-5138. FAX: 719-767-5379. Web Site: www.cwpl.org. *Dir,* Lynne Stutz; *Circ Mgr,* Vicki Henderson
Pop 1,500; Circ 13,135
Library Holdings: AV Mats 300; Bk Titles 10,000; Per Subs 15
Automation Activity & Vendor Info: (Cataloging) Follett Software; (Circulation) Follett Software; (OPAC) Follett Software
Open Mon & Fri 9-5, Tues-Thurs 9-6, Sat 10-12
Friends of the Library Group

COLORADO SPRINGS

S AMERICAN NUMISMATIC ASSOCIATION LIBRARY*, Dwight N Manley Numismatic Library, 818 N Cascade Ave, 80903-3279. SAN 301-7664. Tel: 719-482-9821. Toll Free Tel: 800-367-9723. FAX: 719-634-4085. E-mail: library@money.org. Web Site: www.money.org. *Libr Dir,* RyAnne Scott; Tel: 719-482-9867, E-mail: scott@money.org; *Libr Mgr,* Amanda Harvey; E-mail: harvey@money.org; Staff 3 (Non-MLS 3)
Founded 1891
Library Holdings: Bks-By-Mail 70,016; CDs 36; DVDs 464; Bk Titles 71,250; Bk Vols 108,386; Per Subs 100; Videos 371
Special Collections: Arthur Braddan Coole Library of Oriental Numismatics
Subject Interests: Numismatics
Publications: The Numismatist
Open Tues-Sat 10:30-5

S CHEYENNE MOUNTAIN ZOOLOGICAL PARK LIBRARY*, 4250 Cheyenne Mountain Zoo Rd, 80906. SAN 328-2317. Tel: 719-633-9925. FAX: 719-633-2254. Web Site: www.cmzoo.org. *Educ Curator,* Nicole Mantz; Tel: 719-633-9925, Ext 116, E-mail: nmantz@cmzoo.org
Founded 1926
Library Holdings: Bk Vols 3,000
Subject Interests: Ecology, Environment, Zoology
Restriction: Open by appt only

C COLORADO COLLEGE*, Charles Leaming Tutt Library, 1021 N Cascade Ave, 80903-3252. SAN 301-7680. Tel: 719-389-6658. Interlibrary Loan Service Tel: 719-389-6664. Reference Tel: 719-389-6662. Administration

Tel: 719-389-6670. FAX: 719-389-6082. Web Site: www.coloradocollege.edu/library. *Dir,* Carol Dickerson; *Spec Coll Librn,* Jessy Randall; *Syst Librn,* Carol Ou; *Coordr, Circ,* Mike McEvers; *Bibliog Serv,* Gwen Gregory; *Circ,* Debra Hoke; *ILL,* Diane Broderson; *Ref Serv,* Lisa Lister
Founded 1874. Enrl 1,998
Library Holdings: AV Mats 22,712; e-journals 3,761; Bk Titles 501,234; Per Subs 1,346
Special Collections: Autographs of the British Poets (Alice Bemis Taylor Coll); Chess Books (Alfred R Justice Coll); Colorado College Archives, Colorado Springs, files of early newspapers, also bks, clippings & pamphlets & mss relating to development of Colorado Springs; Colorado Imprints; Dickens (Carruthers Coll); Edmund van Diest Papers; Helen Hunt Jackson Papers; Hendee Coll of Lincolniana; Rare Books (Coll of mss & early printed leaves, Incunabula, drawings & prints from the Romanesque period to the Renaissance); Southwestern United States; United States Relocation Center, Granada, Colorado; Western Americana. US Document Depository
Automation Activity & Vendor Info: (Acquisitions) Innovative Interfaces, Inc; (Cataloging) Innovative Interfaces, Inc; (Circulation) Innovative Interfaces, Inc; (OPAC) Innovative Interfaces, Inc; (Serials) Innovative Interfaces, Inc
Wireless access
Publications: The Chronicle (Newsletter)
Partic in OCLC Online Computer Library Center, Inc
Open Mon-Thurs (Sept-May) 7:45am-Midnight, Fri 7:45am-10pm, Sat 10-10, Sun 10am-Midnight; Mon-Thurs (June-Aug) 8am-9pm, Fri 8-5, Sat 10-5, Sun 12-9

S COLORADO SPRINGS FINE ARTS CENTER LIBRARY*, 30 W Dale St, 80903. SAN 301-7702. Tel: 719-477-4341. FAX: 719-634-0570.
Founded 1936
Library Holdings: Bk Vols 31,000; Per Subs 20
Special Collections: 20th Century American Art; Anthropology & Art of the Southwest (Taylor Museum Coll), bks, series, pamphlets
Automation Activity & Vendor Info: (Cataloging) OCLC
Wireless access
Restriction: Circulates for staff only, Limited access for the pub

S COLORADO SPRINGS PIONEERS MUSEUM*, Starsmore Center for Local History Library, 215 S Tejon St, 80903. SAN 301-7818. Tel: 719-385-5650. FAX: 719-385-5645. E-mail: sclh@ci.colospgs.co.us. Web Site: cspm.org. *Archivist,* Leah Davis-Witherow; E-mail: lwitherow@springsgov.com
Founded 1938
Library Holdings: Bk Titles 9,000; Per Subs 25
Special Collections: Colorado Springs/Pikes Peak Region; Frederick Stehr Glass Plate Negative Coll; Harry L Standley Photograph Coll; Helen Hunt Jackson Coll; Nellie Burget Miller Coll; Southwest (Francis W Cragin Coll), mss; Virginia & Gilbert McClurg Coll, mss; Western US Coll, photogs; William J Palmer Coll; Winfield Scott Stratton Coll. Oral History
Subject Interests: Colorado
Open Tues-Sat 10-4
Restriction: Not a lending libr

C COLORADO TECHNICAL UNIVERSITY LIBRARY*, 4435 N Chestnut, 80907. SAN 322-7456. Tel: 719-590-6708. FAX: 719-590-6818. Web Site: careered.libguides.com/ctu/librarysite. *Librn,* Nicole Hulet; E-mail: nhulet@coloradotech.edu; Staff 3 (MLS 1, Non-MLS 2)
Enrl 1,800; Highest Degree: Doctorate
Library Holdings: Bk Titles 30,000; Bk Vols 38,000
Special Collections: Dissertations & Thesis
Subject Interests: Careers, Computer sci, Electrical eng
Automation Activity & Vendor Info: (Cataloging) EOS International; (Circulation) EOS International; (ILL) OCLC; (Media Booking) EOS International; (OPAC) EOS International
Database Vendor: EBSCOhost, Elsevier, IEEE (Institute of Electrical & Electronics Engineers), McGraw-Hill, ProQuest
Open Mon-Thurs 9-9, Fri 9-6, Sat 9-5, Sun 12-5

S DEPARTMENT OF HUMAN SERVICES-YOUTH CORRECTIONS*, Zebulon Pike Youth Service Center Library, 1417 W Rio Grande, 80906-1297. Tel: 719-329-6931. FAX: 719-633-5302. *Principal,* Idelle Kness
Library Holdings: Bk Vols 1,200
Open Mon-Fri 9-12

R THE DIOCESE OF COLORADO SPRINGS*, Resource Center Library, 228 N Cascade Ave, 80903. Tel: 719-636-2345, Ext 6446. FAX: 719-866-6453. E-mail: info@diocs.org.
Library Holdings: AV Mats 1,500; DVDs 30; Bk Titles 6,000; Per Subs 20; Videos 1,500
Subject Interests: Catechism, Catholic Church
Automation Activity & Vendor Info: (Acquisitions) L4U Library Software; (Cataloging) L4U Library Software; (Circulation) L4U Library Software; (Course Reserve) L4U Library Software; (ILL) L4U Library Software; (Media Booking) L4U Library Software; (OPAC) L4U Library Software; (Serials) L4U Library Software
Open Mon-Fri 8-3

GL EL PASO COUNTY BAR ASSOCIATION LAW LIBRARY*, Penrose Library, 20 N Cascade Ave, 80903. SAN 301-7710, Tel: 719-531-6333. Web Site: ppld.org/aboutyourlibrary/services/lawlibrary/default.asp. *Law Librn,* Esti Shay; E-mail: eshay@ppld.org; Staff 2 (MLS 1, Non-MLS 1)
Founded 1955
Library Holdings: Bk Titles 803; Bk Vols 22,000
Automation Activity & Vendor Info: (Circulation) SirsiDynix; (OPAC) SirsiDynix
Database Vendor: Westlaw
Open Mon-Fri 7am-10am

J EVEREST COLLEGE LIBRARY*, 1815 Jet Wing Dr, 80916. SAN 326-4394. Tel: 719-638-6580. FAX: 719-638-6818. Web Site: everestlibrary.pbwiki.com. *Librn,* Matthew McNulty; E-mail: mmcnulty@cci.edu; Staff 1 (MLS 1)
Enrl 400; Highest Degree: Associate
Jul 2006-Jun 2007 Income $26,702. Mats Exp $26,702, Books $5,800, Per/Ser (Incl. Access Fees) $4,000, AV Mat $3,000, Electronic Ref Mat (Incl. Access Fees) $13,902
Library Holdings: AV Mats 470; Bk Vols 3,899; Per Subs 68
Subject Interests: Bus & mgt, Computer sci, Criminal justice, Legal, Nat security
Automation Activity & Vendor Info: (Acquisitions) LibraryWorld, Inc; (Cataloging) LibraryWorld, Inc; (Circulation) LibraryWorld, Inc
Database Vendor: Gale Cengage Learning, Loislaw, ProQuest
Function: Distance learning, Ref serv available, Telephone ref
Open Mon-Thurs 7:30am-10pm, Fri 7:30-5, Sat 9-1

R FIRST CONGREGATIONAL CHURCH-UNITED CHURCH OF CHRIST*, Gregg Memorial Library, 20 E Saint Vrain St, 80903. SAN 301-7729. Tel: 719-635-3549. FAX: 719-633-4715. Web Site: www.fcucc.org. *Chair,* Karol Finch
Founded 1935
Library Holdings: Bk Vols 2,000
Open Mon-Fri 9-4

R FIRST PRESBYTERIAN CHURCH*, John C Gardner Memorial Library, 219 E Bijou St, 80903. SAN 301-7737. Tel: 719-884-6121. FAX: 719-884-6200. Web Site: www.first-pres.org. *Actg Adminr,* Janet M Wilcox; Staff 32 (MLS 2, Non-MLS 30)
Founded 1945
Library Holdings: CDs 55; DVDs 53; Bk Titles 9,981; Bk Vols 10,551; Per Subs 17; Videos 317
Automation Activity & Vendor Info: (Acquisitions) Follett Software; (Cataloging) Follett Software; (Circulation) Follett Software; (OPAC) Follett Software
Wireless access
Open Mon-Fri 10-2, Sun 9-1

R HOLY APOSTLES CATHOLIC CHURCH LIBRARY*, 4925 N Carefree Circle, 80917. Tel: 719-597-4249. FAX: 719-591-1816. E-mail: haccoffice@holyapostlescc.org. Web Site: www.holyapostlescc.org. *Librn,* Elaine Tourville
Founded 1975
Library Holdings: CDs 83; DVDs 24; Music Scores 40; Bk Titles 5,000; Talking Bks 10; Videos 650
Special Collections: Historical Fiction
Wireless access
Open Sun 7:30-1

M MEMORIAL HOSPITAL*, Health Sciences Library, 1400 E Boulder, Rm 2406, 80909-5599. SAN 301-7761. Tel: 719-365-5182. FAX: 719-365-2642. Web Site: www.memorialhospital.com. *Mgr,* Char Longwell; E-mail: chartroose@yahoo.com; Staff 1 (MLS 1)
Founded 1950
Library Holdings: Bk Titles 3,500; Bk Vols 4,000; Per Subs 200
Special Collections: Historical Medical Works Coll; Rare Book Coll
Subject Interests: Cardiology, Nursing, Obstetrics & gynecology, Pediatrics, Surgery
Automation Activity & Vendor Info: (Cataloging) EBSCO Online; (Circulation) EBSCO Online
Wireless access
Partic in Capital District Library Council; Health Sciences Libraries of New Hampshire & Vermont; Midcontinental Regional Med Libr Program; National Network of Libraries of Medicine Greater Midwest Region; North Atlantic Health Sciences Libraries, Inc; OCLC Online Computer Library Center, Inc
Open Mon-Fri 8:30-5

S NATIONAL ARCHIVES OF THE CHRISTIAN & MISSIONARY ALLIANCE*, Albert B Simpson Historical Library, 8595 Explorer Dr, 80920-1012. (Mail add: PO Box 35000, 80935-3500), SAN 329-8671. Tel: 719-599-5999. FAX: 719-599-8234. E-mail: archives@cmalliance.org. Web Site: archives.cmalliance.org. *Managing Archivist,* Jen L Rohde; Tel: 719-265-2105, E-mail: rohdej@cmalliance.org; *Asst Archivist,* Bruce Armstrong; Tel: 719-265-2172, E-mail: armstrongb@cmalliance.org; Staff 2 (Non-MLS 2)
Library Holdings: Bk Vols 3,000
Special Collections: The Christian & Missionary Alliance Magazine, 1880 to present (also on microfilm). Oral History
Wireless access
Open Mon-Thurs 8-4

CR NAZARENE BIBLE COLLEGE*, Trimble Library, 1111 Academy, Park Loop, 80910-3717. SAN 301-777X. Tel: 719-884-5000, Ext 5071. FAX: 719-884-5119. E-mail: library@nbc.edu. Web Site: www.nbc.edu. *Dir,* Ann M Attig; E-mail: amattig@nbc.edu; Staff 1 (MLS 1)
Founded 1967. Enrl 831; Fac 75; Highest Degree: Bachelor
Special Collections: Wesleyana Coll
Subject Interests: Biblical studies, Theol
Wireless access

M PENROSE-ST FRANCIS HEALTH SERVICES*, Webb Memorial Library, 2222 N Nevada Ave, 80907-0736. (Mail add: PO Box 7021, 80933-7021), SAN 301-7788. Tel: 719-776-5288. FAX: 719-776-5028. Web Site: www.webblibrary.org. *Librn, Mgr,* Casey Welch; Staff 1 (MLS 1)
Founded 1959
Library Holdings: Bk Vols 2,000; Per Subs 200
Special Collections: History of Medicine Coll
Subject Interests: Consumer health, Med
Database Vendor: EBSCOhost, OVID Technologies
Partic in Midcontinental Regional Med Libr Program; OCLC Online Computer Library Center, Inc

J PIKES PEAK COMMUNITY COLLEGE LIBRARY*, 5675 S Academy Blvd, C7, 80906-5498. SAN 301-780X. Circulation Tel: 719-502-2400. Reference Tel: 719-502-3410. Web Site: www.ppcc.edu/library. *Dir of Libr,* Carole Olds; Tel: 719-502-3249, E-mail: carole.olds@ppcc.edu; *Head, Circ Serv,* Susan Dodson; E-mail: susan.dodson@ppcc.edu; *Head, Ref Serv,* Graydon Miller; Tel: 719-502-3389, E-mail: graydon.miller@ppcc.edu; *Head, Tech Serv,* Patricia Stockwell; Tel: 719-502-3238, E-mail: patricia.stockwell@ppcc.edu; Staff 11.5 (MLS 4.5, Non-MLS 7)
Founded 1969. Fac 600; Highest Degree: Associate
Library Holdings: e-books 4,803; Bk Vols 41,888; Per Subs 160
Special Collections: PPCC Archives
Automation Activity & Vendor Info: (Cataloging) Auto-Graphics, Inc; (Circulation) Auto-Graphics, Inc; (ILL) OCLC; (OPAC) Auto-Graphics, Inc; (Serials) SerialsSolutions
Database Vendor: ARTstor, Cinahl, CQ Press, CredoReference, EBSCOhost, Gale Cengage Learning, H W Wilson, JSTOR, OCLC FirstSearch, SerialsSolutions
Wireless access
Function: Archival coll, Bks on CD, Computers for patron use, Copy machines, Electronic databases & coll, Free DVD rentals, Handicapped accessible, ILL available, Music CDs, Online cat, Online ref, Online searches, Orientations, Outside serv via phone, mail, e-mail & web, Ref serv available, Wheelchair accessible
Open Mon-Thurs 7:30am-8pm, Fri 8-5, Sat 9-2
Restriction: Open to pub for ref & circ; with some limitations, Open to students, fac & staff
Departmental Libraries:
RAMPART RANGE CAMPUS, 11195 Hwy 83, Box R-7, 80921-3602. Tel: 719-502-2440. Reference Tel: 719-502-3430. FAX: 719-502-3431. *Managing Librn,* Helen Casias; E-mail: helen.casias@ppcc.edu
Founded 1998
Library Holdings: e-books 4,803; Bk Vols 9,000
Automation Activity & Vendor Info: (Cataloging) Auto-Graphics, Inc; (Circulation) Auto-Graphics, Inc; (OPAC) Auto-Graphics, Inc
Open Mon-Thurs 7:30am-8pm, Fri 7:30-5

P PIKES PEAK LIBRARY DISTRICT*, 20 N Cascade Ave, 80903. (Mail add: PO Box 1579, 80901-1579), SAN 335-5381. Tel: 719-531-6333. Web Site: www.ppld.org. *Exec Dir,* Position Currently Open; *Assoc Dir, Pub Serv,* Sydne Dean; *Assoc Dir, Support Serv & HR,* John Courtney; *Chief, Financial & Bus Officer,* Michael Varnet; *Commun Engagement & Outreach Officer,* Dee Sabol; *Found & Develop Officer,* Dolores Fowler; *Tech & Virtual Serv Officer,* Carolyn Coulter; Staff 41.74 (MLS 41.74)
Founded 1885. Pop 585,158; Circ 8,839,963
Jan 2012-Dec 2012 Income (Main Library and Branch(s)) $26,878,375. Mats Exp $3,947,732. Sal $10,902,147
Library Holdings: AV Mats 208,204; CDs 41,442; DVDs 113,205; e-books 34,042; Bk Vols 841,364; Per Subs 2,513
Special Collections: Oral History
Subject Interests: Genealogy, Local hist
Automation Activity & Vendor Info: (Acquisitions) SIRSI WorkFlows; (Cataloging) SIRSI WorkFlows; (Circulation) SIRSI WorkFlows; (OPAC) SIRSI-iBistro
Wireless access
Function: ILL available
Special Services for the Deaf - Bks on deafness & sign lang; High interest/low vocabulary bks; Spec interest per; Staff with knowledge of sign lang
Friends of the Library Group
Branches: 14
BRIARGATE LIBRARY, 9475 Briar Village Point, 80920. Tel: 719-260-6882. *Mgr,* Debbi Mikash
Open Mon-Thurs 9-9, Fri & Sat 10-6, Sun 1-5
CHEYENNE MOUNTAIN LIBRARY, 1785 S Eighth St, 80905, SAN 335-5411. Tel: 719-633-6278. *Libr Mgr,* Lynne Proctor
Open Mon-Thurs 9-9, Fri & Sat 10-6
Friends of the Library Group
EAST LIBRARY, 5550 N Union Blvd, 80918, SAN 335-5446. Tel: 719-531-6333. FAX: 719-528-5289. *Assoc Dir,* Sydne Dean
Open Mon-Thurs 9-9, Fri & Sat 10-6, Sun 1-5
Friends of the Library Group
FOUNTAIN LIBRARY, 230 S Main St, Fountain, 80817, SAN 335-5608. Tel: 719-382-5347. *Libr Mgr,* Rebecca Cruz
Open Mon-Thurs 9-9, Fri & Sat 10-6
Friends of the Library Group
HIGH PRAIRIE LIBRARY, 7035 Old Meridian Rd, Falcon, 80831. Tel: 719-260-3650. *Mgr,* Janet Cox
Open Mon & Tues 9-8, Wed & Thurs 9-6, Fri & Sat 10-6
RUTH HOLLEY LIBRARY, 685 N Murray Blvd, 80915, SAN 329-6350. Tel: 719-597-5377. *Libr Mgr,* Janet Cox
Open Mon-Thurs 9-9, Fri & Sat 10-6
Friends of the Library Group
MANITOU SPRINGS PUBLIC LIBRARY, 701 Manitou Ave, Manitou Springs, 80829-1887, SAN 301-9853. Tel: 719-685-5206. FAX: 719-685-1169. Web Site: www.ppld.org/manitou-springs-library. *Mgr,* Margaret Morris; E-mail: mmorris@ppld.org; Staff 4 (MLS 2, Non-MLS 2)
Founded 1910. Pop 5,000; Circ 28,000
Special Collections: Colo History Coll, bks & clippings; Large Print Coll
Automation Activity & Vendor Info: (Acquisitions) SirsiDynix; (Cataloging) SirsiDynix; (Circulation) SirsiDynix; (OPAC) SirsiDynix
Database Vendor: OVID Technologies, SirsiDynix
Open Mon-Thurs 10-7, Fri & Sat 10-6
Friends of the Library Group
MONUMENT LIBRARY, 1706 Lake Woodmoor Dr, Monument, 80132-9074. (Mail add: PO Box 1688, Monument, 80132-1688), SAN 335-5535. Tel: 719-488-2370. *Libr Mgr,* Jean Harris
Open Mon-Thurs 9-9, Fri & Sat 10-6, Sun 1-5
Friends of the Library Group
OLD COLORADO CITY LIBRARY, 2418 W Pikes Peak Ave, 80904, SAN 335-556X. Tel: 719-634-1698. *Libr Mgr,* Jocelyne Sansing
Open Mon-Thurs 9-9, Fri & Sat 10-6
Friends of the Library Group
PALMER LAKE LIBRARY, 66 Lower Glenway, Palmer Lake, 80133, SAN 335-5594. Tel: 719-481-2587. *Libr Mgr,* Jean Harris
Open Tues-Fri 10-6, Sat 10-2
Friends of the Library Group
PENROSE LIBRARY, 20 N Cascade Ave, 80903, SAN 329-6334. Tel: 719-531-6333. *Assoc Dir,* Sydne Dean
Subject Interests: Genealogy, Local hist
Open Mon-Thurs 9-9, Fri & Sat 10-6, Sun 1-5
Friends of the Library Group
ROCKRIMMON LIBRARY, 832 Village Center Dr, 80919, SAN 370-4505. Tel: 719-593-8000. *Libr Mgr,* Lynne Proctor
Open Mon-Thurs 9-9, Fri & Sat 10-6
Friends of the Library Group
SAND CREEK LIBRARY, 1821 S Academy Blvd, 80916, SAN 329-6377. Tel: 719-597-7070. *Libr Mgr,* Rebecca Cruz
Open Mon-Thurs 9-9, Fri & Sat 10-6, Sun 1-5
Friends of the Library Group
UTE PASS LIBRARY, 8010 Severy, Cascade, 80809, SAN 335-5624. Tel: 719-684-9342. *Libr Mgr,* Jocelyne Sansing
Open Mon & Tues 1-7, Wed-Sat 10-4
Friends of the Library Group
Bookmobiles: 2

C UNIVERSITY OF COLORADO COLORADO SPRINGS*, Kraemer Family Library, 1420 Austin Bluffs Pkwy, 80918. SAN 301-7850. Tel: 719-255-3286. Circulation Tel: 719-255-3296. Interlibrary Loan Service Tel: 719-255-3285. Reference Tel: 719-255-3295. Administration Tel: 719-255-3068. FAX: 719-528-5227. E-mail: refdesk@uccs.edu. Web Site: www.uccs.edu/library. *Prof & Dean,* Dr Teri R Switzer; Tel: 719-255-3115, E-mail: tswitzer@uccs.edu; *Assoc Dean,* Christina Martinez; Tel:

719-255-3287, E-mail: cmartine@uccs.edu; *Head, Coll Mgt,* Rhonda Glazier; Tel: 719-255-3291, E-mail: rglazier@uccs.edu; Staff 21.5 (MLS 10, Non-MLS 11.5)
Founded 1965. Enrl 10,200; Fac 762; Highest Degree: Doctorate
Jul 2012-Jun 2013. Mats Exp $1,180,136, Books $65,912, Per/Ser (Incl. Access Fees) $501,455, AV Mat $31,770, Electronic Ref Mat (Incl. Access Fees) $114,860, Presv $8,440. Sal $1,249,324 (Prof $588,679)
Library Holdings: AV Mats 9,459; e-books 49,526; e-journals 33,000; Electronic Media & Resources 256; Microforms 743,216; Bk Titles 290,454; Bk Vols 337,477; Per Subs 550
Special Collections: UCCS Archives. State Document Depository; US Document Depository
Subject Interests: Bus, Educ, Electrical eng, Nursing, Psychol
Automation Activity & Vendor Info: (Acquisitions) Innovative Interfaces, Inc; (Cataloging) Innovative Interfaces, Inc; (Circulation) Innovative Interfaces, Inc; (Course Reserve) Innovative Interfaces, Inc; (ILL) Innovative Interfaces, Inc; (OPAC) Innovative Interfaces, Inc; (Serials) Innovative Interfaces, Inc
Database Vendor: 3M Library Systems, ABC-CLIO, ACM (Association for Computing Machinery), Alexander Street Press, American Chemical Society, American Mathematical Society, American Physical Society, American Psychological Association (APA), Annual Reviews, ARTstor, Atlas Systems, Baker & Taylor, BioOne, Cambridge Scientific Abstracts, Children's Literature Comprehensive Database Company (CLCD), Cinahl, College Source, CQ Press, EBSCOhost, Elsevier, Emerald, Factiva.com, Gale Cengage Learning, H W Wilson, Haworth Pres Inc, Hoovers, IEEE (Institute of Electrical & Electronics Engineers), infoUSA, Ingenta, Innovative Interfaces, Inc, IOP, ISI Web of Knowledge, JSTOR, Knovel, LexisNexis, Nature Publishing Group, OCLC FirstSearch, OCLC WorldShare Interlibrary Loan, OVID Technologies, Oxford Online, Project MUSE, ProQuest, PubMed, ReferenceUSA, Sage, ScienceDirect, Scopus, SerialsSolutions, Springer-Verlag, Springshare, LLC, Thomson - Web of Science, Wiley, Wilson - Wilson Web, YBP Library Services
Wireless access
Partic in Colorado Alliance of Research Libraries; OCLC Online Computer Library Center, Inc
Open Mon-Thurs 7:30am-Midnight, Fri 7:30am-8pm, Sat 10-8, Sun 11am-Midnight

S WESTERN MUSEUM OF MINING & INDUSTRY LIBRARY*, 225 N Gate Blvd, I-25 Exit 156, 80921. SAN 326-3371. Tel: 719-488-0880. FAX: 719-488-9261. Web Site: www.wmmi.org. *Dir,* Dr Richard A Sauers; E-mail: rsauers@wmmi.org
Library Holdings: Bk Titles 10,000; Per Subs 8
Subject Interests: Mining
Publications: Annual Report; Newsletter (Quarterly)
Restriction: Open to others by appt
Friends of the Library Group

CORTEZ

P CORTEZ PUBLIC LIBRARY*, 202 N Park, 81321-3300. SAN 301-7869. Tel: 970-565-8117. FAX: 970-565-8720. Web Site: www.cityofcortez.com. *Dir,* Joanie Howland; *ILL,* Margaret O'Brien; Staff 5 (MLS 1, Non-MLS 4)
Founded 1932. Pop 22,000; Circ 143,000
Library Holdings: CDs 400; DVDs 100; Large Print Bks 2,000; Bk Titles 65,000; Per Subs 65; Videos 4,000
Special Collections: Oral History
Automation Activity & Vendor Info: (Cataloging) Follett Software; (Circulation) Follett Software
Function: Copy machines
Partic in Colorado Library Consortium
Open Mon-Thurs 10-7, Fri & Sat 10-4
Friends of the Library Group

S CROW CANYON ARCHAEOLOGICAL CENTER*, Florence C Listen Research Library, 23390 County Rd K, 81321. SAN 377-0958. Tel: 970-565-8975. FAX: 970-565-4859. Web Site: www.crowcanyon.org. *Dir, Res,* Scott Ortman; *Librn,* Jamie Merewether; E-mail: jmerewether@crowcanyon.org
Library Holdings: Bk Titles 5,000
Open Mon-Fri 9-5
Restriction: Non-circulating

CRAIG

G BUREAU OF LAND MANAGEMENT*, Little Snake Field Office Library, 455 Emerson St, 81625-1129. SAN 301-7877. Tel: 970-826-5000. FAX: 970-826-5002. Web Site: www.blm.gov. *Librn,* Marie Andrews; E-mail: marie_andrews@co.blm.gov
Library Holdings: Bk Titles 1,000
Restriction: Not open to pub

P MOFFAT COUNTY LIBRARIES*, 570 Green St, 81625-3027. SAN 301-7885. Tel: 970-824-5116. FAX: 970-824-2867. E-mail: moffatlib@moffat.lib.co.us. *Dir,* Sherry Sampson; E-mail: ssampson@moffat.lib.co.us; Staff 12 (MLS 1, Non-MLS 11)
Founded 1911. Pop 13,000
Jan 2006-Dec 2006 Income $624,500. Mats Exp $40,015, Books $40,000, Per/Ser (Incl. Access Fees) $15. Sal $495,628 (Prof $63,000)
Library Holdings: Bk Titles 75,000; Per Subs 73
Special Collections: Local History Coll. Oral History
Automation Activity & Vendor Info: (Cataloging) Follett Software; (Circulation) Follett Software; (OPAC) Follett Software
Partic in Colorado Library Consortium
Open Mon & Tues 10:30-7, Wed-Fri 9:30-5:30, Sat 11-5:30
Friends of the Library Group

CREEDE

P MINERAL COUNTY REGIONAL LIBRARY*, 308 La Garita Ave, 81130. (Mail add: PO Box 429, 81130-0429), SAN 376-2831. Tel: 719-658-2313. FAX: 719-658-2942. *Librn,* Frances Kolisch; E-mail: frances@creedek12.net
Pop 952; Circ 14,000
Library Holdings: Bk Vols 10,700; Per Subs 26
Open Mon-Thurs 8-4

CRIPPLE CREEK

P FRANKLIN FERGUSON MEMORIAL LIBRARY*, 410 N B St, 80813. (Mail add: PO Box 975, 80813), SAN 301-7893. Tel: 719-689-2800. FAX: 719-689-3187. *Dir,* Mike McDonald; *Asst Librn,* Nancy Fromm; Staff 1 (MLS 1)
Founded 1976. Pop 1,500; Circ 22,764
Jan 2006-Dec 2006 Income $67,956. Mats Exp $11,250, Books $7,700, Per/Ser (Incl. Access Fees) $600, Micro $500, AV Equip $1,200, AV Mat $600, Electronic Ref Mat (Incl. Access Fees) $450, Presv $200. Sal $25,335
Library Holdings: DVDs 120; Bk Titles 22,528; Bk Vols 23,011; Per Subs 33; Talking Bks 165; Videos 1,654
Special Collections: Colorado History; Local history
Subject Interests: Hist
Open Mon-Thurs (Winter) 8-7, Fri 10-2; Mon-Thurs (Summer) 9-5, Fri 9-3

CROOK

P CROOK COMMUNITY LIBRARY*, Fourth St, 80726. (Mail add: PO Box 205, 80726-0205), SAN 301-7907. Tel: 970-886-2833. *Librn,* Elna Hamilton
Founded 1928. Circ 3,055
Library Holdings: Bk Titles 9,000
Partic in Colorado Library Consortium
Open Tues 2-4
Bookmobiles: 1

CROWLEY

S COLORADO DEPARTMENT OF CORRECTIONS*, Arkansas Valley Correctional Facility Library, 12750 Hwy 96, Lane 13, 81034. SAN 376-5768. Tel: 719-267-3520, Ext 3251. FAX: 719-267-5024. *Regional Librn,* Renee Robbins; Tel: 303-307-2226, E-mail: Renee.Robbins@state.co.us; *Librn,* Linda Sue Hollis; E-mail: linda.hollis@state.co.us; *Asst Librn,* Position Currently Open; Staff 3 (MLS 2, Non-MLS 1)
Library Holdings: CDs 600; High Interest/Low Vocabulary Bk Vols 50; Large Print Bks 76; Bk Vols 15,702; Per Subs 49; Talking Bks 27; Videos 317
Automation Activity & Vendor Info: (Cataloging) EOS International; (Circulation) EOS International; (OPAC) EOS International
Function: ILL available, Music CDs, Online searches, Ref serv available, VHS videos
Open Mon & Sun 12:30-9, Tues & Thurs 8am-9pm, Fri & Sat 8-4
Restriction: Authorized patrons

DACONO

P DACONO PUBLIC LIBRARY*, 512 Cherry St, 80514-9382. (Mail add: PO Box 186, 80514-0186), SAN 372-8021. Tel: 303-833-2317, Ext 129. Administration Tel: 303-833-2317, Ext 120. FAX: 303-833-5528. *Librn,* Amy Bruno; Staff 1 (MLS 1)
Founded 1978. Pop 2,228; Circ 5,002
Library Holdings: Bk Vols 7,500; Per Subs 10
Open Mon 10-3, Tues & Wed 4-8, Thurs 11-1, Fri 10-3

DEL NORTE

P DEL NORTE PUBLIC LIBRARY*, 790 Grand Ave, 81132. SAN 301-7915. Tel: 719-657-2633. FAX: 719-657-2633. *Dir,* Kathy Gilliam; E-mail: kathy.gilliam@amigo.net
Founded 1899. Pop 10,770
Library Holdings: Bk Vols 25,000; Per Subs 50
Special Collections: Local Newspaper, 1923-present
Automation Activity & Vendor Info: (Cataloging) Follett Software; (Circulation) Follett Software
Partic in Colorado Library Consortium
Open Mon-Wed & Fri 1-5, Thurs 10-8
Friends of the Library Group

DELTA

S COLORADO DEPARTMENT OF CORRECTIONS*, Delta Correctional Center Library, 4102 Sawmill Mesa Rd, 81416. SAN 376-5784. Tel: 970-874-7614, Ext 2950, 970-874-7614, Ext 2955. FAX: 970-874-5810, 970-874-5890. Web Site: www.doc.state.co.us. *Librn,* Patricia Vigil
Library Holdings: AV Mats 779; Bk Titles 9,500; Per Subs 32; Talking Bks 75
Automation Activity & Vendor Info: (Cataloging) EOS International; (Circulation) EOS International
Restriction: Not open to pub

DENVER

M AORN CENTER FOR LIBRARY SERVICES & ARCHIVES*, 2170 S Parker Rd, Ste 400, 80231-5711. SAN 301-7982. Tel: 303-755-6304, Ext 314. Toll Free Tel: 800-755-2676, Ext 314. FAX: 303-368-4460. E-mail: library@aorn.org. Web Site: www.aorn.org. *Dir,* Position Currently Open; Staff 3 (MLS 2, Non-MLS 1)
Founded 1972
Library Holdings: AV Mats 300; Bk Titles 4,500; Bk Vols 5,000; Per Subs 400
Special Collections: AORN Publications; Archives; Thesis Coll
Subject Interests: Health sci, Med, Nursing
Automation Activity & Vendor Info: (Cataloging) Innovative Interfaces, Inc; (Circulation) Innovative Interfaces, Inc; (ILL) OCLC; (OPAC) Innovative Interfaces, Inc; (Serials) Innovative Interfaces, Inc
Database Vendor: OVID Technologies
Partic in Colorado Council of Medical Librarians; National Network of Libraries of Medicine Midcontinental Region

R AUGUSTANA LUTHERAN CHURCH LIBRARY*, 5000 E Alameda Ave, 80246. SAN 301-7990. Tel: 303-388-4678. FAX: 303-388-1338. E-mail: info@augustanadenver.org. Web Site: www.augustanadenver.org. *Librn,* Linda Crowe
Founded 1963
Library Holdings: Bk Titles 5,000; Bk Vols 5,308

C AURARIA LIBRARY*, 1100 Lawrence St, 80204-2095. SAN 335-5802. Tel: 303-556-2740. Interlibrary Loan Service Tel: 303-556-4498. Reference Tel: 303-556-2585. Information Services Tel: 303-556-2639. FAX: 303-556-3528. Web Site: library.auraria.edu. *Univ Librn/Libr Dir,* Mary M Somerville; Tel: 303-556-4587, E-mail: mary.somerville@ucdenver.edu; *Assoc Dir, Admin Serv,* Marical Farner; Tel: 303-556-3525, E-mail: marical.farner@ucdenver.edu; *Assoc Dir, Educ, Res & Info Serv,* Cynthia Hashert; Tel: 303-556-5256, E-mail: cynthia.hashert@ucdenver.edu; *Assoc Dir, Tech Serv,* Denise Pan; Tel: 303-556-4762, E-mail: denise.pan@ucdenver.edu; *Assoc Dir, Tech Strategy & Learning Spaces,* Margaret Brown-Sica; Tel: 303-556-6762, E-mail: margaret.brown-sica@ucdenver.edu; *Head, Res & Instruction,* Liz Cooper; Tel: 303-552-3953, E-mail: elizabeth.cooper@ucdenver.edu; *Digital Initiatives, Head, Spec Coll,* Matthew Mariner; Tel: 303-556-5817, E-mail: matthew.mariner@ucdenver.edu; *Acq & Assessments Librn,* Leslie Williams; Tel: 303-556-5807, E-mail: leslie.williams@ucdenver.edu; *Coll Develop & Res Librn,* Thomas J Beck; Tel: 303-556-8371, E-mail: thomas.j.beck@ucdenver.edu; *Coll Develop & Res Librn,* Ellen Metter; Tel: 303-556-4516, E-mail: ellen.metter@ucdenver.edu; *Coll Develop Librn,* Linda Tietjen; Tel: 303-556-4298, E-mail: linda.tietjen@ucdenver.edu; *Coll Develop, Res & Instruction Librn,* Nikki McCaslin; Tel: 303-556-3390, E-mail: nikki.mccaslin@ucdenver.edu; *Disability Serv Librn,* Judith Valdez; Tel: 303-556-4999, E-mail: judith.valdez@ucdenver.edu; *Electronic Access/Sci & Eng Coll Develop Librn,* Elaine Jurries; Tel: 303-556-2622, E-mail: elaine.jurries@ucdenver.edu; *E-Res Cat Librn,* Vera Gao; Tel: 303-556-5269, E-mail: vera.gao@ucdenver.edu; *Res & Instruction Librn,* Eric Baker; Tel: 303-556-8192, E-mail: eric.baker@ucdenver.edu; *Res & Instruction Librn,* Lorrie Evans; Tel: 303-556-6776, E-mail: lorrie.evans@ucdenver.edu; *Res & Instruction Librn,* Karen Sobel; Tel: 303-352-3640, E-mail: karen.sobel@ucdenver.edu; *Res & Instruction Librn,* Diane Turner; Tel: 303-556-2719, E-mail: diane.turner@ucdenver.edu; *Scholarly Communications Librn,* Ellen Greenblatt; Tel: 303-556-6704, E-mail: ellen.greenblatt@ucdenver.edu; *Scholarly Initiatives Librn,* Jeffrey Beall; Tel: 303-556-5936, E-mail: jeffrey.beall@ucdenver.edu; *Sci Res & Instruction Librn,* Ignacio Ferrer-Vincent; Tel: 303-556-4919, E-mail: ignacio.ferrer-vinent@ucdenver.edu; *Soc Sci Coll Develop Librn,* Orlando Archibeque; Tel: 303-556-3482, E-mail: orlando.archibeque@ucdenver.edu; *Archivist, Spec Coll Librn,* Rosemary Evetts; Tel: 303-556-3530, E-mail: rosemary.evetts@ucdenver.edu; *User Support/Sci & Eng Coll Develop Librn,* Gayle Bradbeer; Tel: 303-556-2791, E-mail: gayle.bradbeer@ucdenver.edu; *Mgr, Info Tech,* Niraj Chaudhary; Tel: 303-556-4351, E-mail: niraj.chaudhary@ucdenver.edu. Subject Specialists: *Prof studies,* Thomas J Beck; *Art & archit,* Linda Tietjen; *Soc sci,* Lorrie Evans; Staff 53 (MLS 24, Non-MLS 29)
Founded 1976. Enrl 44,616; Fac 2,214; Highest Degree: Doctorate
Jul 2008-Jun 2009 Income $7,144,415. Mats Exp $2,668,940. Sal $3,865,982 (Prof $1,644,977)
Library Holdings: AV Mats 17,735; e-books 170,915; e-journals 46,985; Bk Titles 825,191; Bk Vols 905,630; Per Subs 1,474; Talking Bks 918; Videos 12,562
Special Collections: Amache Japanese-American Internment Center; Civil Liberties in Colorado; Colorado Railroads; Higher Education (Auraria Higher Education Center Archives); Literature & Literary Criticism (Donald Sutherland Coll); State & Local Policy (Seasongood Library, National Municipal League, Conservative Think Tanks); Women's History Coll. State Document Depository; US Document Depository
Subject Interests: Archit
Automation Activity & Vendor Info: (Acquisitions) Innovative Interfaces, Inc; (Cataloging) Innovative Interfaces, Inc; (Circulation) Innovative Interfaces, Inc; (Course Reserve) Docutek; (Media Booking) Innovative Interfaces, Inc; (OPAC) Innovative Interfaces, Inc; (Serials) Innovative Interfaces, Inc
Wireless access
Partic in Colorado Alliance of Research Libraries; OCLC Online Computer Library Center, Inc
Special Services for the Deaf - TTY equip
Special Services for the Blind - VisualTek equip
Friends of the Library Group

G BUREAU OF LAND MANAGEMENT LIBRARY*, Denver Federal Center, Bldg 50, Sixth & Kipling, 80225. (Mail add: PO Box 25047, 80225-0047), SAN 335-5926. Tel: 303-236-6650. Administration Tel: 303-236-6647. FAX: 303-236-4810. E-mail: blm_library@blm.gov. Web Site: www.blm.gov/nstc/library/library.html. *Lead Librn,* Barbara Klassen; E-mail: barbara_klassen@blm.gov; *Libr Tech,* Deborah Harnke; Tel: 303-236-6648, E-mail: dharnke@blm.gov; Staff 1 (Non-MLS 1)
Founded 1971
Library Holdings: Bk Titles 40,000; Per Subs 150
Special Collections: Aerial Photography Archive; Bureau of Land Management Publications; Cadastral Survey Plats & Field Notes, micro
Automation Activity & Vendor Info: (Cataloging) EOS International; (Circulation) EOS International; (OPAC) EOS International; (Serials) EOS International
Database Vendor: EOS International
Partic in Fedlink
Open Mon-Fri 8-4:30

SR CARDINAL STAFFORD LIBRARY, St John Vianney Seminary Library, 1300 S Steele St, 80210-2526. SAN 301-8741. Tel: 303-715-3146. FAX: 303-715-2007. *Libr Dir,* Stephen Sweeney; Tel: 303-715-3192, E-mail: stephen.sweeney@archden.org; *Cat Librn, Ser,* Lyn Cotton; Tel: 303-715-3228, E-mail: lyn.cotton@archden.org; *Circ Librn,* Tamara Conley; E-mail: tamara.conley@archden.org; Staff 3 (MLS 1, Non-MLS 2)
Founded 1907. Enrl 120; Fac 27; Highest Degree: Master
Library Holdings: Bk Vols 150,000; Per Subs 300
Special Collections: Anglican Studies; Hispanic Pastoral Ministry
Subject Interests: Philos, Theol
Automation Activity & Vendor Info: (Acquisitions) SirsiDynix; (Cataloging) SirsiDynix; (Circulation) SirsiDynix; (Course Reserve) SirsiDynix; (ILL) OCLC; (OPAC) SirsiDynix; (Serials) SirsiDynix
Database Vendor: EBSCO Auto Repair Reference, EBSCO Discovery Service, EBSCOhost, OCLC ArticleFirst, OCLC FirstSearch, OCLC WorldShare Interlibrary Loan, OCLC Worldshare Management Services, SirsiDynix
Wireless access
Partic in OCLC Online Computer Library Center, Inc
Open Mon-Fri 10-4
Friends of the Library Group
Branches:
ARCHIVES OF THE CATHOLIC ARCHDIOCESE OF DENVER, 1300 S Steele St, 80210. Tel: 303-520-9986. *Archivist,* Karyl Klein; E-mail: karyl.klein@archden.org
Special Collections: Catholic Church of Colorado, Archbishops papers, photogs, Sacramental recs; Denver Catholic Register, microfilm
Function: Archival coll
Restriction: By permission only, Open by appt only, Private libr

CHILDREN'S HOSPITAL COLORADO

M CLINICAL & RESEARCH LIBRARY, 13123 E 16th Ave, B180, Aurora, 80045, SAN 326-3185. Tel: 720-777-6400. FAX: 720-777-7152. E-mail: library@childrenscolorado.org. *Mgr,* Kristen Desanto; Staff 2.5 (MLS 2, Non-MLS 0.5)
Automation Activity & Vendor Info: (Acquisitions) OCLC; (Cataloging) OCLC; (Circulation) OCLC; (ILL) OCLC; (OPAC) OCLC; (Serials) OCLC
Database Vendor: DynaMed, EBSCOhost, Elsevier, Lexi-Comp, MD Consult, Medline, OCLC FirstSearch, OCLC WorldShare Interlibrary Loan, OVID Technologies, PubMed
Open Mon-Thurs 7:30-5:30, Fri 7:30-4
Restriction: Staff use only

M FAMILY HEALTH LIBRARY, 13123 E 16th Ave, Aurora, 80045, SAN 378-1739. Tel: 720-777-6378. FAX: 720-777-7121. E-mail: familylibrary@childrenscolorado.org. *Librn,* Zelda Hawkins
Library Holdings: Bk Titles 3,000; Bk Vols 3,150; Per Subs 25
Automation Activity & Vendor Info: (Acquisitions) OCLC WorldShare Interlibrary Loan; (Cataloging) OCLC WorldShare Interlibrary Loan
Open Mon-Fri 9-3:30

S COLORADO AGENCY FOR JEWISH EDUCATION LIBRARY*, 300 S Dahlia St, Ste 101, 80246. SAN 377-9041. Tel: 303-321-3191, Ext 220. FAX: 303-321-5436. Web Site: www.caje-co.org. *Exec Dir,* Phyllis Adler; E-mail: padler@caje-co.org
Founded 1974
Library Holdings: AV Mats 700; Bk Vols 10,000; Per Subs 20
Special Collections: Children's Judaica Library; Judaic teacher materials; Video coll
Subject Interests: Educ, Holocaust, Judaica, Spec educ
Automation Activity & Vendor Info: (Cataloging) Follett Software; (Circulation) Follett Software
Wireless access
Partic in Asn of Jewish Librs; Colorado Library Consortium
Open Mon-Thurs 9-3, Fri 9-1
Friends of the Library Group

S COLORADO DEPARTMENT OF CORRECTIONS*, Denver Women's Correctional Facility Library, 3600 Havana St, 80239. Tel: 303-307-2500, Ext 3608. FAX: 303-307-2674. *Librn,* Position Currently Open; *Librn II,* Adrienne Breznau; E-mail: adrienne.breznau@state.co.us; Staff 3 (MLS 1, Non-MLS 2)
Founded 1999
Library Holdings: Bk Vols 10,000; Per Subs 40

G COLORADO DEPARTMENT OF TRANSPORTATION LIBRARY*, Shumate Bldg, 4201 E Arkansas Ave, 80222. SAN 301-8164. Tel: 303-757-9972. Web Site: www.coloradodot.info/library/materials-from-our-library. *Librn,* Joan Pinamont; E-mail: joan.pinamont@state.co.us; Staff 1 (MLS 1)
Founded 1949
Library Holdings: AV Mats 170; Bk Titles 17,000; Per Subs 12; Talking Bks 40
Subject Interests: Environ documentation, Safety, Transportation

G COLORADO DIVISION OF STATE ARCHIVES & PUBLIC RECORDS LIBRARY*, 1313 Sherman St, Rm 1B20, 80203-2236. SAN 373-8175. Tel: 303-866-4900. Toll Free Tel: 800-305-3442 (CO only). FAX: 303-866-2257. E-mail: archives@state.co.us. Web Site: www.colorado.gov/dpa/doit/archives. *State Archivist,* Terry Ketelsen; Staff 6 (MLS 6)
Founded 1943
Special Collections: Colorado Public Officials; Records of Territory & State of Colorado, flm original docs, vols. Oral History
Restriction: Staff use only
Friends of the Library Group

G COLORADO JOINT LEGISLATIVE COUNCIL*, Joint Legislative Library, State Capitol Bldg, Rm 048, 200 E Colfax Ave, 80203-1784. SAN 375-4510. Tel: 303-866-4011. FAX: 303-866-2167. *Mgr, Libr Serv,* Molly Otto; E-mail: molly.otto@state.co.us; *Librn,* Gay Roesch; Tel: 303-866-4799, E-mail: gay.roesch@state.co.us; Staff 2 (MLS 2)
Founded 1973
Library Holdings: CDs 379; DVDs 14; e-journals 7; Electronic Media & Resources 78; Bk Titles 7,650; Bk Vols 15,500; Per Subs 37; Videos 46
Special Collections: Bills; Colorado General Assembly Materials; Fiscal Notes; Interim Committee Reports
Automation Activity & Vendor Info: (Acquisitions) NOTEbookS Library Automation; (Cataloging) NOTEbookS Library Automation; (Circulation) NOTEbookS Library Automation; (Serials) NOTEbookS Library Automation
Database Vendor: LexisNexis, OCLC FirstSearch, OCLC WorldShare Interlibrary Loan
Partic in Colorado Library Consortium
Restriction: Non-circulating to the pub

M COLORADO MENTAL HEALTH INSTITUTE AT FORT LOGAN, Medical Library, 3520 W Oxford Ave, 80236. SAN 301-8385. Tel: 303-866-7844. FAX: 303-866-7090. *Dir, Libr Serv,* Kate Elder; E-mail: kate.elder@state.co.us; Staff 1 (MLS 1)
Founded 1961
Library Holdings: Bk Vols 3,000; Per Subs 150
Subject Interests: Mental health, Nursing, Psychiat, Psychol, Soc sci & issues
Function: ILL available
Publications: The Supplement (Newsletter)
Partic in Asn of Mental Health Librn (AMHL); Colorado Council of Medical Librarians
Open Mon-Fri 8-4:30
Restriction: Circulates for staff only, In-house use for visitors

G COLORADO STATE DEPARTMENT OF NATURAL RESOURCES*, Colorado Water Conservation Board Library, 1580 Logan St, Ste 600, 80203. (Mail add: 1313 Sherman St, Rm 721, 80203), SAN 335-6043. Tel: 303-866-3441. FAX: 303-866-4474. Web Site: www.cwcb.state.co.us. *Librn,* Christian Lyons; Tel: 303-866-3549
Library Holdings: Bk Titles 5,000
Restriction: Staff use only

P COLORADO STATE LIBRARY, 201 E Colfax Ave, Rm 309, 80203-1799. SAN 335-6108. Tel: 303-866-6900. FAX: 303-866-6940. Web Site: www.coloradostatelibrary.org. *Dir, Libr Develop,* Sharon Morris; Tel: 303-866-6730, E-mail: morris_s@cde.state.co.us; *Dir, Networking & Res Sharing,* Regan Harper; Tel: 303-866-6907, E-mail: harper_r@cde.state.co.us; *Dir, Res Serv,* Nicolle Steffen; Tel: 303-866-6927, E-mail: steffen_n@cde.state.co.us; *Dir, State Publ & Talking Bk Libr,* Debbi MacLeod; Tel: 303-866-6994, E-mail: macleod_d@cde.state.co.us; *Asst Commissioner,* Eugene Hainer; E-mail: hainer_g@cde.state.co.us; *Coordr, Institutional Libr,* Diane Walden; Tel: 303-866-6341, E-mail: walden_d@cde.state.co.us; *Fiscal Officer, LSTA Coordr,* Jean Heilig; Tel: 303-866-6731, E-mail: heilig_j@cde.state.co.us; Staff 22 (MLS 21, Non-MLS 1)
Founded 1876
Jul 2010-Jun 2011 Income $4,212,965, State $118,479, Federal $2,915,938, Parent Institution $1,178,548, Mats Exp $72,000, Books $28,000, Per/Ser (Incl. Access Fees) $4,000, Other Print Mats $1,000, AV Equip $15,000, Electronic Ref Mat (Incl. Access Fees) $24,000
Library Holdings: Braille Volumes 2,900; Large Print Bks 11,500; Bk Vols 21,000; Per Subs 25; Talking Bks 48,600; Videos 240
Special Collections: State Publications Coll; Talking Book Library, tapes, vols. State Document Depository
Subject Interests: Educ, Libr & info sci
Automation Activity & Vendor Info: (Cataloging) OCLC; (ILL) OCLC; (OPAC) Innovative Interfaces, Inc; (Serials) Innovative Interfaces, Inc
Database Vendor: EBSCOhost, Gale Cengage Learning, OCLC FirstSearch
Function: Digital talking bks, Electronic databases & coll, Libr develop
Publications: Annual Report; Fast Facts Research Summaries; Getting Ready for Kindergarten; Long Range Plan; Public Library Standards; Reading Tips for Parents; Standards for Adult Correctional Institutions; Statistical Summaries by Type of Library; The Impact of School Library Media Centers on Academic Achievement
Partic in OCLC Online Computer Library Center, Inc
Special Services for the Blind - Aids for in-house use; Assistive/Adapted tech devices, equip & products; Audio mat; Bks & mags in Braille, on rec, tape & cassette; Bks available with recordings; Bks on cassette; Braille bks; Braille equip; Descriptive video serv (DVS)
Open Mon-Fri 8-5
Friends of the Library Group
Branches: 1
COLORADO TALKING BOOK LIBRARY
See Separate Entry

GL COLORADO SUPREME COURT LIBRARY*, 101 W Colfax Ave, Ste A, 80202. SAN 301-8180. Tel: 303-837-3720. FAX: 303-864-4510. E-mail: library@judicial.state.co.us. *Head Librn,* Dan Cordova; Staff 3 (MLS 3)
Founded 1874
Library Holdings: Bk Vols 80,000; Per Subs 300
Subject Interests: Law
Automation Activity & Vendor Info: (Acquisitions) SirsiDynix; (Cataloging) SirsiDynix; (Circulation) SirsiDynix; (ILL) SirsiDynix; (OPAC) SirsiDynix; (Serials) SirsiDynix
Database Vendor: Westlaw
Partic in OCLC Online Computer Library Center, Inc
Open Mon-Fri 8-5

P COLORADO TALKING BOOK LIBRARY*, 180 Sheridan Blvd, 80226. SAN 301-8172. Tel: 303-727-9277. Toll Free Tel: 800-685-2136 (Colo only). FAX: 303-727-9281. E-mail: ctbl.info@cde.state.co.us. Web Site: www.cde.state.co.us/ctbl. *Dir,* Debbi MacLeod; E-mail: macleod_d@cde.state.co.us; Staff 13 (MLS 1, Non-MLS 12)
Founded 1931
Library Holdings: Braille Volumes 14,064; Large Print Bks 20,784; Bk Titles 71,861; Per Subs 3; Talking Bks 453,197; Videos 577
Special Collections: Blindness & Other Handicaps, ref mat; Spanish Language, cassettes; Volunteer Produced Books & Magazines
Automation Activity & Vendor Info: (Acquisitions) Keystone Systems, Inc (KLAS); (Cataloging) Keystone Systems, Inc (KLAS); (Circulation) Keystone Systems, Inc (KLAS); (OPAC) Keystone Systems, Inc (KLAS)
Wireless access
Function: Audiobks via web, Computers for patron use, Digital talking bks, Equip loans & repairs, Handicapped accessible, Home delivery & serv to Sr ctr & nursing homes, Large print keyboards, Magnifiers for reading, Mail & tel request accepted, Online cat, Outreach serv, Summer reading prog, Web-Braille, Web-catalog, Wheelchair accessible
Publications: CTBL News (Newsletter)
Partic in Colorado Library Consortium
Special Services for the Blind - Accessible computers; Bks & mags in Braille, on rec, tape & cassette; Bks available with recordings; Bks on flash-memory cartridges; Braille alphabet card; Braille bks; Braille equip; Cassette playback machines; Cassettes; Children's Braille; Closed circuit TV magnifier; Computer with voice synthesizer for visually impaired persons; Descriptive video serv (DVS); Digital talking bk; Digital talking bk machines; Extensive large print coll; Free checkout of audio mat; Handicapped awareness prog; Home delivery serv; Large print bks; Large screen computer & software; Local mags & bks recorded; Machine repair; Magnifiers; Mags & bk reproduction/duplication; Newsletter (in large print, Braille or on cassette); Newsline for the Blind; Production of talking bks; Screen reader software; Soundproof reading booth; Spanish Braille mags & bks; Talking bks; Talking bks & player equip; Tel Pioneers equip repair group; Variable speed audiotape players; Videos on blindness & phys handicaps; Volunteer serv; Web-Braille; ZoomText magnification & reading software
Restriction: Not open to pub
Friends of the Library Group

SR CONGREGATION EMANUEL LIBRARY*, Brenner Library, 51 Grape St, 80220. SAN 378-3790. Tel: 303-388-4013. FAX: 303-388-6328. Web Site: www.congregationemanuel.com. *Librn,* Rita Dahlke; Staff 1 (Non-MLS 1)
Library Holdings: AV Mats 600; Large Print Bks 25; Bk Titles 7,000; Bk Vols 10,000; Per Subs 30; Talking Bks 40
Automation Activity & Vendor Info: (Cataloging) Follett Software; (Circulation) Follett Software
Open Mon & Tues 9-3, Wed 4-8, Sun 8:45-1

L DAVIS, GRAHAM & STUBBS LLP*, Law Library, 1550 17th St, Ste 500, 80202. SAN 301-8229. Tel: 303-892-7306. FAX: 303-893-1379. Web Site: www.dgslaw.com. *Mgr,* Andrea Hamilton; E-mail: andrea.hamilton@dgslaw.com; Staff 4 (MLS 2, Non-MLS 2)
Library Holdings: e-journals 2,700; Bk Vols 24,000; Per Subs 300
Restriction: Staff use only

S DENVER ACADEMY LIBRARY*, 4400 E Iliff Ave, 80222. SAN 377-9068. Tel: 303-777-5870. FAX: 303-777-5893. Web Site: www.denveracademy.org. *Librn,* Jolene Gutierrez; E-mail: jgutierrez@denveracademy.org; Staff 1 (MLS 1)
Library Holdings: DVDs 100; Bk Titles 11,500; Per Subs 25; Talking Bks 100; Videos 200
Partic in Colo Educ Media Asn; Colo Independent Sch Librs; Colo Libr Asn; Colorado Library Consortium
Open Mon-Fri 7:45-4:15

S DENVER ART MUSEUM LIBRARY*, 414 14th St, 80204-2788. (Mail add: 100 W 14th Ave Pkwy, 80204-2788), SAN 301-8245. Tel: 720-913-0100. FAX: 720-913-0001. Web Site: library/denverartmuseum.org/D6000. *Cat Librn, Mgr,* Susan Ferrer-Vinent; E-mail: sferrer-vinent@denverartmuseum.org; Staff 1 (MLS 1)
Founded 1935
Library Holdings: Bk Titles 30,000
Special Collections: Douglas Coll of Native Arts
Automation Activity & Vendor Info: (Acquisitions) EOS International; (Cataloging) EOS International; (Circulation) EOS International; (OPAC) EOS International
Database Vendor: EOS International, JSTOR
Wireless access
Partic in OCLC Online Computer Library Center, Inc
Restriction: Open to pub by appt only

S DENVER BOTANIC GARDENS*, Helen Fowler Library, 909 York St, 80206-3799. Tel: 720-865-3570. E-mail: library@botanicgardens.org. Web Site: www.botanicgardens.org. *Cat Librn,* Rory O'Connor; E-mail: o'connor@botanicgardens.org; Staff 2 (MLS 2)
Founded 1947
Library Holdings: Bk Titles 24,000; Bk Vols 30,000; Per Subs 400
Special Collections: Waring House Book Room
Subject Interests: Botany, Hort
Automation Activity & Vendor Info: (Acquisitions) EOS International
Partic in Colorado Library Consortium

S DENVER MUSEUM OF NATURE & SCIENCE, Alfred M Bailey Library & Archives, 2001 Colorado Blvd, 80205-5798. SAN 301-8288. Tel: 303-370-6362. FAX: 303-331-6492. E-mail: archives@dmns.org, library@dmns.org. Web Site: www.dmns.org/science/bailey-library-and-archives. *Dept Chair, Librn,* Brent Wagner; E-mail: brent.wagner@dmns.org; *Archivist,* Sam Schiller; Tel: 303-370-6089, E-mail: samuel.schiller@dmns.org; *Image Archivist,* Rene' M Payne; Tel: 303-370-8250, E-mail: rene.payne@dmns.org; Staff 3 (MLS 3)
Founded 1900
Library Holdings: e-journals 126; Bk Vols 53,000; Spec Interest Per Sub 144; Videos 190
Special Collections: Image Archives; Institutional Archives for Museum; Rare Books
Subject Interests: Anthrop, Archaeology, Entomology, Geol, Mus studies, Ornithology, Paleontology, Space sci, Zoology
Automation Activity & Vendor Info: (Cataloging) EOS International; (Circulation) EOS International; (ILL) OCLC; (OPAC) EOS International; (Serials) EOS International
Database Vendor: BioOne, EBSCOhost, JSTOR, Luna Imaging/Insight, OCLC FirstSearch, OCLC WorldShare Interlibrary Loan
Wireless access
Function: Bus archives, Copy machines, Doc delivery serv, e-mail serv, Handicapped accessible, ILL available, Online cat, Online ref, Online searches, Photocopying/Printing, Ref serv available, Scanner, Telephone ref, VHS videos, Web-catalog, Wheelchair accessible
Publications: Annual Report of the Denver Museum of Nature & Science; Denver Museum of Nature & Science Annals (Periodical); DMNS Members' Newsletter (Bi-monthly)
Partic in Access Colo Libr Info Network (ACLIN)
Restriction: Authorized scholars by appt, Staff use only

P DENVER PUBLIC LIBRARY*, Ten W 14th Ave Pkwy, 80204-2731. SAN 335-6167. Tel: 720-865-1111. Circulation Tel: 720-865-1325. Interlibrary Loan Service Tel: 720-865-1718. Reference Tel: 720-865-1363. Automation Services Tel: 720-865-2006. FAX: 720-865-2087. Web Site: www.denverlibrary.org. *City Librn,* Shirley Amore; *Dir, Admin Serv,* Letty Icolari; *Dir, Coll & Tech,* Michelle Jeske; *Dir, Commun Relations,* Diane Lapierre; *Dir, Finance & Planning,* Richard Sosa; *Dir, Pub Serv,* Susan Kotarba; E-mail: skotarba@denverlibrary.org; *Mgr, Bks & Borrowing,* Jennifer J Hoffman; Tel: 720-865-2034, Fax: 720-865-1477, E-mail: jhoffman@denverlibrary.org; *Mgr, Coll Serv,* Rachel Fewell; *IT Mgr, Network Serv,* Kateri Abeyta; *Mgr, Ref Serv,* Genine Plunkett; Tel: 720-865-1345, Fax: 720-865-1481, E-mail: gplunket@denverlibrary.org; *Mgr, Spec Coll,* Jim Kroll; Tel: 720-865-1820, Fax: 720-865-1880, E-mail: jkroll@denverlibrary.org; *Mgr, Website & ILL,* Stacey Watson. Subject Specialists: *Western hist,* Jim Kroll; Staff 85 (MLS 85)
Founded 1889. Pop 592,052; Circ 9,776,905
Jan 2008-Dec 2008 Income (Main Library and Branch(s)) $33,646,281, City $31,396,600, Other $2,249,681. Mats Exp $4,823,315, Books $2,482,299, Per/Ser (Incl. Access Fees) $265,274, AV Mat $1,646,342, Electronic Ref Mat (Incl. Access Fees) $429,400. Sal $24,155,571
Library Holdings: Audiobooks 57,458; e-books 21,120; e-journals 72; Music Scores 84,587; Bk Vols 1,986,162; Per Subs 4,392; Videos 230,138
Special Collections: Aeronautics (Ross-Barrett Historical Aeronautical); Conservation Coll; Eugene Field; Fine Printing (Douglas); Mountaineering Coll; Napoleon, bks, ms; Original Western Art Coll; Western History Coll; World War II 10th Mountain Division. US Document Depository
Subject Interests: Aeronaut, Art & archit, Bus & mgt, Environ studies, Genealogy, Hist, Music, Natural sci
Automation Activity & Vendor Info: (Acquisitions) TLC (The Library Corporation); (Cataloging) OCLC; (Circulation) TLC (The Library Corporation); (ILL) OCLC; (OPAC) TLC (The Library Corporation)
Wireless access
Function: Audiobks via web, Bilingual assistance for Spanish patrons, Computer training, Computers for patron use, Exhibits, Preschool outreach, Prog for adults, Prog for children & young adult, Pub access computers, Ref serv in person
Publications: Dewey's Dispatch (Monthly newsletter); Fresh City Life (Newsletter)
Special Services for the Deaf - TTY equip
Open Mon & Tues 10-8, Wed-Fri 10-6, Sat 9-5, Sun 1-5
Friends of the Library Group

Branches: 22
ATHMAR PARK, 1055 S Tejon St, 80223, SAN 335-6469. Tel: 303-935-0721. FAX: 303-934-9388. *Br Mgr,* Cori Jackamore; *Sr Librn,* Kristen Monroe
Open Mon & Fri 10-6, Wed 12-8, Sat 8-5
BEAR VALLEY, 5171 W Dartmouth, 80236-2006, SAN 335-6493. Tel: 303-935-0616. FAX: 303-934-9403. *Br Mgr,* Gwendolyn Crenshaw; *Sr Librn,* Diane Apperson
Open Mon, Tues Wed & Fri 10-6, Thurs 12-8, Sat 9-5
BLAIR-CALDWELL AFRICAN AMERICAN RESEARCH LIBRARY, 2401 Welton St, 80205-3015, SAN 328-6908. Tel: 720-865-2401. FAX: 720-865-2418. *Sr Spec Coll & Commun Res Mgr,* Terry Nelson; *Western Hist & Genealogy Mgr,* Jim Kroll; *Sr Librn,* Danny Walker
Founded 2003
Special Collections: African American History Coll. Oral History
Open Mon 10-8, Wed & Fri 10-6, Sat 9-5
BYERS, 675 Santa Fe Dr, 80204-4426, SAN 335-6523. Tel: 303-571-1665. FAX: 303-572-4787. *Br Mgr,* Leslie Williams
Open Mon-Thurs 10-6
DECKER, 1501 S Logan, 80210-2632, SAN 335-6612. Tel: 303-733-7584. FAX: 303-733-8665. *Br Mgr,* Cori Jackamore; *Sr Librn,* Judy Stovall
Open Mon 12-8, Wed & Thurs 10-6, Sat 9-5
EUGENE FIELD, 810 S University Blvd, 80209-4725, SAN 335-6647. Tel: 303-777-2301. FAX: 303-722-7331. TDD: 303-733-7435. *Br Mgr,* Cori Jackamore; *Sr Librn,* Ed Kutz
Open Mon, Tues & Fri 10-6, Thurs 12-8, Sat 9-5
FORD-WARREN BRANCH, 2825 High St, 80205-4545, SAN 335-6671. Tel: 720-865-0920. FAX: 720-865-0925. *Br Mgr,* Pilar Castro-Reino; *Sr Librn,* Megan Kinney
Open Tues & Wed 12-8, Thurs 10-6, Sat 9-5
HADLEY, 1890 S Grove St, 80219-4618, SAN 335-6701. Tel: 303-935-4267. FAX: 303-934-1294. *Br Mgr,* Pilar Castro-Reino
Open Mon & Tues 12-8, Wed & Thurs 10-6, Sat 9-5
HAMPDEN, 9755 E Girard Ave, 80231-5003, SAN 335-6736. Tel: 303-750-3885. FAX: 303-751-4878. TDD: 303-671-0905. *Br Mgr,* Pilar Castro-Reino; *Sr Librn,* Becky Russell
Open Mon & Thurs 10-6, Tues & Wed 12-8, Sat 9-5
MONTBELLO, 12955 Albrook Dr, 80239-4704, SAN 335-6795. Tel: 303-373-0767. FAX: 303-371-3542. *Br Mgr,* Pilar Castro-Reino; *Sr Librn,* Rachel Fewell
Open Mon & Tues 12-8, Wed-Fri 10-6, Sat 9-5
PARK HILL, 4705 Montview Blvd, 80207-3760, SAN 335-685X. Tel: 303-331-4063. FAX: 303-388-2335. *Br Mgr,* Cori Jackamore; *Sr Librn,* Kit Cusker
Open Mon, Thurs & Fri 10-6, Tues 12-8, Sat 9-5
VALDEZ PERRY BRANCH, 4690 Vine St, 80216-2823, SAN 376-1088. Tel: 303-295-4302. FAX: 303-295-4307. *Sr Librn,* Joan Vigil
Open Mon, Wed & Fri 10-6, Sat 9-5
PAULINE ROBINSON BRANCH, 5575 E 33rd Ave, 80207-2027, SAN 376-107X. Tel: 303-370-1530. FAX: 303-370-1541. *Mgr, Ch Serv,* Carol Edwards; Tel: 720-865-1307, Fax: 720-865-1470, E-mail: cedwards@denverlibrary.org; *Sr Librn, Youth Serv,* Taliah Abdullah; E-mail: tabdull@denverlibrary.org; Staff 4 (MLS 1, Non-MLS 3)
Founded 1995
Automation Activity & Vendor Info: (Acquisitions) CARL.Solution (TLC); (Circulation) CARL.Solution (TLC)
Function: Adult bk club, After school storytime, Bilingual assistance for Spanish patrons, Bks on cassette, Bks on CD, CD-ROM, Children's prog, Copy machines, Free DVD rentals, Homework prog, ILL available, Music CDs, Outreach serv, Preschool outreach, Prog for children & young adult, Pub access computers, Ref serv available, Ref serv in person, Spoken cassettes & CDs, Summer reading prog, VHS videos
Open Mon 12-8, Tues-Fri 10-6, Sat 9-5
ROSS-BARNUM BRANCH, 3570 W First Ave, 80219-1346, SAN 335-6884. Tel: 303-935-1891. FAX: 303-934-9324. *Br Mgr,* Pilar Castro-Reino; *Sr Librn,* Lou Petterchak
Open Tues & Fri 10-6, Wed & Thurs 12-8, Sat 9-5
ROSS-BROADWAY, 33 E Bayaud Ave, 80209-1503, SAN 335-6914. Tel: 303-777-4845. FAX: 303-733-8601. *Br Mgr,* Gwendolyn Crenshaw; *Sr Librn,* Peggy Combs
Open Mon & Tues 12-8, Wed 10-6, Sat 9-5
ROSS-CHERRY CREEK, 305 Milwaukee St, 80206-4329, SAN 335-6949. Tel: 303-331-4016. FAX: 303-331-3860. TDD: 303-331-5773. *Br Mgr,* Gwendolyn Crenshaw; *Sr Librn,* Brent Wagner
Open Mon & Fri 10-6, Tues & Wed 12-8, Sat 9-5
ROSS-UNIVERSITY HILLS, 4310 E Amherst Ave, 80222-6703, SAN 335-6973. Tel: 303-757-2714. FAX: 303-692-5606. *Br Mgr,* Gwendolyn Crenshaw; *Sr Librn,* Christine Satriano
Open Mon, Wed & Thurs 12-8, Tues & Fri 10-6, Sat 9-5
SCHLESSMAN, 100 Poplar St, 80220-4522, SAN 335-6825. Tel: 720-865-0000. FAX: 720-865-0047. TDD: 720-865-0045. *Br Mgr,* Gwendolyn Crenshaw; *Sr Librn,* Jenny LaPerriere
Founded 2002
Open Mon 12-8, Tues & Thurs 10-6, Sat 9-5, Sun 1-5
SMILEY, 4501 W 46th Ave, 80212-2582, SAN 335-7007. Tel: 303-477-3622. FAX: 303-455-5613. *Br Mgr,* Gwendolyn Crenshaw
Open Tues & Wed 12-8, Thurs 10-6, Sat 9-5
VIRGINIA VILLAGE, 1500 S Dahlia St, 80222, SAN 335-7031. Tel: 303-757-6662. FAX: 303-692-0721. TDD: 303-504-5790. *Br Mgr,* Cori Jackamore; *Sr Librn,* Martha Garbison
Open Mon, Tues & Fri 10-6, Wed 12-8, Sat 9-5
WESTWOOD, 1000 S Lowell Blvd, 80219-3339, SAN 328-6886. Tel: 303-936-8808. FAX: 303-937-4454. *Br Mgr,* Susan Kotarba; *Sr Librn,* Ann Schwab
WOODBURY, 3265 Federal Blvd, 80211-3211, SAN 335-7066. Tel: 720-865-0930. FAX: 720-865-0933. *Br Mgr,* Pilar Castro-Reino; *Sr Librn,* Lisa Murillo
Open Mon, Wed & Fri 10-6, Tues & Thurs 12-8, Sat 9-5
Bookmobiles: 2. Mgr, Bks & Borrowing, Jennifer Hoffman. Bk Titles 10,000

S DEPARTMENT OF HUMAN SERVICES-YOUTH CORRECTIONS*, Gilliam Youth Services Center Library, 2844 Downing St, 80205. SAN 378-0570. Tel: 303-291-8950. FAX: 303-291-8990. *Educ Dir,* Dave Debus
Library Holdings: Bk Titles 1,000

GM DEPARTMENT OF VETERANS AFFAIRS*, Medical Center Library, 1055 Clermont St, 80220. SAN 301-8873. Tel: 303-393-4644. FAX: 303-393-2829. *Chief, Quality Management & Educ,* Marilyn Lynn; Staff 1 (MLS 1)
Oct 2005-Sept 2006 Income $94,000
Library Holdings: Bk Titles 2,600; Per Subs 350
Subject Interests: Allied health, Med, Nursing, Patient health educ
Automation Activity & Vendor Info: (Cataloging) Innovative Interfaces, Inc; (Circulation) Innovative Interfaces, Inc
Database Vendor: OVID Technologies, ProQuest
Restriction: Non-circulating to the pub

C EDUCATION MANAGEMENT CORPORATION, Art Institute of Colorado Library, 1200 Lincoln St, 4th Flr, 80203-2114. Tel: 303-824-4789. Administration Tel: 303-824-4787. FAX: 303-824-4890. E-mail: aiclibrary@edmc.edu. Web Site: aii.campusguides.com/aiclibrary. *Libr Dir,* Martha Neth
Founded 1975. Enrl 2,100; Highest Degree: Bachelor
Library Holdings: AV Mats 250; CDs 200; DVDs 1,400; Bk Titles 21,000; Bk Vols 28,000; Per Subs 212; Videos 600
Automation Activity & Vendor Info: (Cataloging) Ex Libris Group; (Circulation) Ex Libris Group; (OPAC) Ex Libris Group
Database Vendor: Baker & Taylor, Checkpoint Systems, Inc, CredoReference, ebrary, EBSCO Information Services, H W Wilson, Mergent Online, MITINET, Inc, ProQuest, ReferenceUSA
Wireless access
Open Mon-Thurs 7am-10pm, Fri 7-6, Sat 10-4

M EXEMPLA-SAINT JOSEPH HOSPITAL*, Medical Library, 1835 Franklin St, 80218-1191. SAN 301-8733. Tel: 303-837-7375. Interlibrary Loan Service Tel: 303-837-6896. Administration Tel: 303-837-7848. FAX: 303-837-7977. Web Site: www.exempla.org. *Mgr, Libr Serv,* Margaret Bandy; *Ref Serv,* Joyce Condon, Staff 4 (MLS 3, Non MLS 1)
Founded 1965
Library Holdings: e-journals 1,100; Bk Titles 3,000; Per Subs 215
Subject Interests: Med, Nursing
Automation Activity & Vendor Info: (Cataloging) Innovative Interfaces, Inc; (Circulation) Innovative Interfaces, Inc; (ILL) OCLC; (OPAC) Innovative Interfaces, Inc
Database Vendor: Dialog, EBSCOhost, Gale Cengage Learning, OCLC FirstSearch, OCLC WorldShare Interlibrary Loan, OVID Technologies, SerialsSolutions, Wilson - Wilson Web
Wireless access
Function: Health sci info serv, ILL available, Online searches, Ref serv available
Partic in Colorado Council of Medical Librarians
Open Mon-Fri 8-4:30
Restriction: Circulates for staff only, In-house use for visitors, Pub use on premises

L FAEGRE BAKER DANIELS*, Law Library, 3200 Wells Fargo Ctr, 1700 Lincoln St, 80203. Tel: 303-607-3500. FAX: 303-607-3600. Web Site: www.faegre.com. *Res Librn,* Amy Summer; Tel: 303-607-3648
Library Holdings: Bk Vols 10,000
Automation Activity & Vendor Info: (Acquisitions) SydneyPlus
Restriction: Staff use only

M HEALTH ONE PRESBYTERIAN-SAINT LUKE'S MEDICAL CENTER*, Denver Medical Library, 1719 E 19th Ave, 80218-1281. SAN 335-721X. Tel: 303-839-6670. FAX: 303-869-1643. E-mail: info@denvermedlib.org. Web Site: www.denvermedlib.org. *Dir,* Sharon Martin; E-mail: sharon.martin@healthonecares.com; *Librn,* A Fletcher; *Librn,* Nancy Peterson; *Coordr,* Doug Stackhouse; Staff 5 (MLS 3, Non-MLS 2)

Founded 1893
Library Holdings: Bk Vols 56,000; Per Subs 425
Subject Interests: Allied health, Cardiology, Geriatrics & gerontology, Neonatology, Obstetrics & gynecology, Pediatrics
Automation Activity & Vendor Info: (Cataloging) Innovative Interfaces, Inc; (Circulation) Innovative Interfaces, Inc; (ILL) OCLC; (OPAC) Innovative Interfaces, Inc; (Serials) Innovative Interfaces, Inc
Database Vendor: Gale Cengage Learning, OCLC FirstSearch, OVID Technologies
Function: ILL available
Partic in Colorado Council of Medical Librarians
Restriction: Private libr, Staff & mem only

S HISTORY COLORADO*, Stephen H Hart Library & Research Center, 1200 Broadway, 80203-2109. SAN 301-8083. Tel: 303-866-2305. Administration Tel: 303-866-4600. FAX: 303-866-2796. E-mail: cosearch@state.co.us. Web Site: www.historycolorado.org. *Dir,* Laura Ruttum Senturia; Staff 4.6 (MLS 4, Non-MLS 0.6)
Founded 1879
Library Holdings: Microforms 25,000; Bk Vols 22,000; Per Subs 491
Special Collections: Aultman Studio Photo Coll; Colorado Newspapers; Colorado Photographs; Denver & Rio Grande Railroads; H A W Tabor Coll, ms; W H Jackson Coll, ms, photog
Subject Interests: Colorado, Hist, Mining, Railroads, Soc hist
Wireless access
Function: Online cat, Res libr, Workshops
Partic in OCLC Online Computer Library Center, Inc
Restriction: Closed stack, Non-circulating

L HOLLAND & HART*, Law Library, 555 17th St, Ste 3200, 80201-3950. (Mail add: PO Box 8749, 80201-8749), SAN 301-8458. Tel: 303-295-8091. FAX: 303-295-8261. *Dir,* Holly Pinto; E-mail: hlpinto@hollandhart.com; *Electronic Res,* Tamara Tureson; Staff 7 (MLS 5, Non-MLS 2)
Founded 1948
Library Holdings: Bk Titles 15,000
Automation Activity & Vendor Info: (Acquisitions) EOS International; (Circulation) EOS International
Wireless access
Restriction: Staff use only

CR ILIFF SCHOOL OF THEOLOGY*, Ira J Taylor Library, 2201 S University Blvd, 80210. SAN 301-8474. Tel: 303-765-3173. Circulation Tel: 303-765-3172. Reference Tel: 303-765-3179. FAX: 303-777-0164. Web Site: library.iliff.edu. *Dir,* Dr Debbie Creamer; E-mail: dcreamer@iliff.edu; *Emerging Tech Librn,* Mary Olson; E-mail: molson@iliff.edu; *Circ,* Katie Fisher; E-mail: kfisher@iliff.edu; *Ref Serv,* Laura Harris; E-mail: lharris@iliff.edu; *Tech Serv,* Alice Runis; E-mail: arunis@iliff.edu. Subject Specialists: *Theol,* Dr Debbie Creamer; Staff 5.5 (MLS 4.5, Non-MLS 1)
Founded 1892. Enrl 267; Fac 24; Highest Degree: Doctorate
Library Holdings: Bk Vols 211,000; Per Subs 660
Special Collections: Hymnody (Van Pelt Hymnal Coll); Local Methodism (Archives of Iliff School of Theology & Rocky Mountain Conference of the United Methodist Church); Methodistica
Subject Interests: Relig
Automation Activity & Vendor Info: (Acquisitions) SirsiDynix; (Cataloging) SirsiDynix; (Circulation) SirsiDynix; (Course Reserve) SirsiDynix; (ILL) OCLC; (OPAC) SirsiDynix; (Serials) SirsiDynix
Partic in OCLC Online Computer Library Center, Inc
Open Mon-Thurs 8am-9pm, Fri 9-4:30, Sat 10-3, Sun 2-6

C JOHNSON & WALES UNIVERSITY*, Denver Campus Library, College of Business, 7150 Montview Blvd, 80220. Tel: 303-256-9345. Reference Tel: 303-256-9518. FAX: 303-256-9459. E-mail: denvercampuslibrary@jwu.edu. Web Site: library.jwu.edu/denver. *Dir,* Lori Micho; Tel: 303-256-9353; *Librn,* Amanda Samland; Tel: 303-256-9378; *Librn,* Merrie Valliant; *Circ Supvr,* Brad Kottke; Tel: 303-256-9519; Staff 4 (MLS 4)
Founded 2000. Enrl 1,450; Highest Degree: Bachelor
Library Holdings: AV Mats 1,400; Bk Titles 33,600; Per Subs 186
Special Collections: Leadership Library
Subject Interests: Bus, Criminal justice, Culinary arts, Hospitality
Automation Activity & Vendor Info: (Acquisitions) Innovative Interfaces, Inc - Millenium; (Cataloging) Innovative Interfaces, Inc - Millenium; (Circulation) Innovative Interfaces, Inc - Millenium; (Course Reserve) Innovative Interfaces, Inc - Millenium; (OPAC) Innovative Interfaces, Inc - Millenium; (Serials) Innovative Interfaces, Inc
Database Vendor: Brodart, EBSCOhost, Gale Cengage Learning, IBISWorld, Innovative Interfaces, Inc, LexisNexis, Plunkett Research, Ltd, SerialsSolutions, YBP Library Services
Wireless access
Open Mon-Wed 8am-11pm, Thurs 8-7, Fri 8-4, Sat 11-4, Sun 11-11

L MORRISON & FOERSTER LLP*, Law Library, 5200 Republic Plaza Bldg, 370 17th St, 80202. SAN 328-5863. Tel: 303-592-2259. FAX: 303-592-1510. Web Site: www.mofo.com. *Mgr,* Pamela K Lewis; E-mail: pklewis@mofo.com; Staff 2 (MLS 1, Non-MLS 1)
Library Holdings: Bk Vols 4,700; Per Subs 25
Restriction: Not open to pub

G NATIONAL ARCHIVES & RECORDS ADMINISTRATION*, Rocky Mountain Region, Denver Federal Ctr, Bldg 48, W Sixth Ave & Kipling St, 80225-0307. (Mail add: PO Box 25307, 80225-0307). Tel: 303-407-5740. FAX: 303-407-5707. E-mail: denver.archives@nara.gov. Web Site: www.archives.gov/facilities/co/denver.html. *Regional Dir,* Barbara Voss; Tel: 303-407-5701; *Regional Archives Dir,* Eileen Bolger; *Dir, Fed Rec Ctr,* Genola Smith; *Dir, Rec Mgt,* Mark Ferguson; *Adminr,* Julie Newhouse
Special Collections: Colorado Naturalizations, microfilm; Federal Population Censuses for All States, 1790-1930, microfilm; Indian Censuses, microfilm; Pension & Bounty Land Warrant Applications, microfilm; Revolutionary War Records, microfilm; Utah Polygamy Prosecution Case Files, microfilm
Subject Interests: Indian hist, Land reclamation econ, Mining
Open Mon-Fri 7:30am-3:45pm

M NATIONAL JEWISH HEALTH*, Gerald Tucker Memorial Medical Library, 1400 Jackson St, 80206-2762. SAN 301-861X. Tel: 303-398-1482. FAX: 303-270-2149. E-mail: library@njhealth.org. Web Site: library.nationaljewish.org. *Libr Serv Dir,* Shandra Protzko; Tel: 303-398-1483, E-mail: protzkoS@NJHealth.org; Staff 4 (MLS 2, Non-MLS 2)
Founded 1935
Library Holdings: e-books 120; e-journals 4,000; Bk Titles 3,000; Per Subs 300
Special Collections: Patient & Consumer Health Information
Subject Interests: Allergies, Immunology, Molecular biol, Respiratory med
Automation Activity & Vendor Info: (Acquisitions) Innovative Interfaces, Inc; (Cataloging) Innovative Interfaces, Inc; (Circulation) Innovative Interfaces, Inc; (Course Reserve) Innovative Interfaces, Inc; (OPAC) Innovative Interfaces, Inc; (Serials) Innovative Interfaces, Inc
Database Vendor: Dialog, OCLC FirstSearch, OVID Technologies
Partic in Colorado Council of Medical Librarians; Colorado Library Consortium

S NATIONAL THEATRE CONSERVATORY*, The Jones Library, 1101 13th St, 80204. SAN 377-9084. Tel: 303-446-4869. Circulation Tel: 303-893-4000, Ext 2313. FAX: 303-825-2117. Web Site: www.dcpa.org. *Dir,* Linda M Eller; E-mail: eller@dcpa.org; Staff 1 (MLS 1)
Founded 1991
Jul 2005-Jun 2006. Mats Exp $10,000, Books $7,000, Per/Ser (Incl. Access Fees) $1,000, AV Mat $2,000
Library Holdings: AV Mats 2,000; Bk Titles 35,000; Per Subs 15
Special Collections: Denver Center Theater Company Production Documents; Playbills; Vinyl Records
Subject Interests: Musical theatre, Performance
Automation Activity & Vendor Info: (Cataloging) Follett Software; (Circulation) Follett Software
Partic in Colo Libr Asn; Colorado Library Consortium; Theatre Libr Asn
Open Mon-Fri 9-5:30

M NORTH SUBURBAN MEDICAL CENTER LIBRARY*, c/o Denver Medical Library, 1719 E 19th Ave, 80218. (Mail add: 9191 Grant St, Thornton, 80229-4361), SAN 377-8797. Tel: 303-450-3568, 303-839-6670. FAX: 303-450-4504.
Library Holdings: Bk Titles 350; Per Subs 23
Partic in Cnt Colo Libr Syst; Colorado Council of Medical Librarians; Medical Library Association (MLA); Mid Continental Med Libr Asn
Restriction: Staff use only

M PORTER ADVENTIST HOSPITAL, Harley E Rice Memorial Medical Library, 2525 S Downing St, 80210-5817. SAN 301-8636. Tel: 303-778-5656. FAX: 303-778-5608. E-mail: porterlibrary@centura.org. Web Site: www.centura.org. *Med Librn,* Loren Hackett; *Librn,* Janet Williams; Staff 3 (MLS 1, Non-MLS 2)
Founded 1980
Library Holdings: Bk Titles 2,500; Per Subs 250
Subject Interests: Med, Nursing
Partic in BRS; Colorado Council of Medical Librarians; OCLC Online Computer Library Center, Inc
Open Mon-Fri 8-4

C REGIS UNIVERSITY*, Dayton Memorial Library, 3333 Regis Blvd, 80221-1099. SAN 301-8660. Tel: 303-458-4030. FAX: 303-964-5497. Web Site: www.regis.edu. *Dean,* Ivan Gaetz; *Access Serv,* Mary Sponsel; *Archivist,* Elizabeth Cook; *Circ,* Caren Clark; *Distance Educ,* Tom Riedel; *Electronic Serv,* Diana Sweany; *Media Librn,* Andrew Dorfman; *Ref Serv,*

John Schmitt; *Slide Librn,* Ann James-Herron; *Tech Serv,* Janet Lee; Staff 31 (MLS 15, Non-MLS 16)
Founded 1877. Enrl 16,800; Fac 400; Highest Degree: Doctorate
Library Holdings: AV Mats 100,000; e-books 10,000; Bk Titles 250,000; Bk Vols 300,000; Per Subs 25,000
Special Collections: Archives of Loretto Heights College; Archives of Regis College; Early 18th Century Religious Coll, pamphlets (American); Political Campaign Memorabilia; Western Jesuitica Coll. US Document Depository
Subject Interests: Bus, Liberal arts, Mgt, Relig
Automation Activity & Vendor Info: (Acquisitions) Innovative Interfaces, Inc; (Cataloging) Innovative Interfaces, Inc; (Circulation) Innovative Interfaces, Inc; (Course Reserve) Innovative Interfaces, Inc; (ILL) OCLC ILLiad; (Media Booking) Innovative Interfaces, Inc; (OPAC) Innovative Interfaces, Inc; (Serials) SerialsSolutions
Publications: Check It Out!
Partic in Colorado Academic Library Consortium (CALC); Colorado Alliance of Research Libraries; OCLC Online Computer Library Center, Inc
Special Services for the Blind - Computer with voice synthesizer for visually impaired persons

L ROTHGERBER, JOHNSON & LYONS*, Law Library, One Tabor Ctr, Ste 3000, 1200 17th St, 80202. SAN 372-3240. Tel: 303-623-9000. FAX: 303-623-9222. Web Site: www.rothgerber.com. *Librn,* Dianne Kulesa; E-mail: dkulesa@rothgerber.com
Library Holdings: Bk Vols 6,000; Per Subs 50

SR SAINT JOHN'S CATHEDRAL LIBRARY*, 1350 Washington St, 80203. SAN 375-3468. Tel: 303-831-7115. FAX: 303-831-7119. E-mail: info@sjcathedral.org. Web Site: www.sjc.den.org. *Librn,* Joyce L White; Tel: 303-744-0813; Staff 4 (MLS 1, Non-MLS 3)
Founded 1950
Library Holdings: Large Print Bks 25; Bk Vols 5,000; Per Subs 28; Spec Interest Per Sub 23
Special Collections: Old Prayer Books (BCP)
Subject Interests: Church hist, Theol
Partic in OCLC Online Computer Library Center, Inc

C TEIKYO LORETTO HEIGHTS UNIVERSITY LIBRARY*, 3001 S Federal Blvd, 80236. SAN 373-594X. Tel: 303-937-4246. FAX: 303-937-4224. Web Site: www.tlhu.edu. *Dir,* Larry Grieco; Tel: 303-937-4042, E-mail: lgrieco@co.gilpin.co.us; Staff 4 (MLS 2, Non-MLS 2)
Founded 1989. Enrl 303; Fac 14; Highest Degree: Bachelor
Library Holdings: Bk Titles 115,000; Bk Vols 118,000; Per Subs 60
Special Collections: East Asian Coll
Automation Activity & Vendor Info: (Acquisitions) TLC (The Library Corporation); (Circulation) TLC (The Library Corporation); (Serials) TLC (The Library Corporation)
Database Vendor: OCLC FirstSearch, TLC (The Library Corporation), Wilson - Wilson Web
Partic in Colorado Alliance of Research Libraries; Colorado Library Consortium
Open Mon-Thurs 10:30-7, Fri 8-4

GL US COURTS LIBRARY*, Tenth Circuit Court of Appeals, Byron Rogers Courthouse, 1929 Stout St, Rm 430, 80294. SAN 301-8822. Tel: 303-844-3591. FAX: 303-335-2669. E-mail: library@ca10.uscourts.gov. *Dir,* Madeline R Cohen; *Mgr,* Susan Elder; *Br Mgr,* Pat Hummel; *Br Mgr,* Meg Martin; *Br Mgr,* Leslie McGuire; *Br Mgr,* Gregory Townsend; *Br Tech,* Amber Bell; *Br Tech,* Lynda Miller; *Acq,* Donna Stegner; *Ref,* Wendy Lamar; *Ref,* Amy Levine; *Tech Serv,* Ruthann Rehnborg; Staff 23 (MLS 10, Non-MLS 13)
Founded 1929
Library Holdings: Bk Vols 36,000
Subject Interests: Law
Automation Activity & Vendor Info: (Acquisitions) SirsiDynix; (Cataloging) SirsiDynix; (Circulation) SirsiDynix
Database Vendor: LexisNexis, Westlaw
Open Mon-Fri 8-4:30
Restriction: Circulates for staff only

G UNITED STATES DEPARTMENT OF THE INTERIOR, Bureau of Reclamation Library, Denver Fed Ctr, Sixth Ave & Kipling St, Bldg 67, 80225. (Mail add: PO Box 25007, 80225-0007), SAN 335-7392. Tel: 303-445-2072. Interlibrary Loan Service Tel: 303-445-2064. Reference Tel: 303-445-2061. FAX: 303-445-6303. E-mail: library@usbr.gov. Web Site: www.usbr.gov/library. *Mgr,* Dianne Powell; E-mail: dpowell@usbr.gov; Staff 4 (MLS 2, Non-MLS 2)
Founded 1945
Library Holdings: Bk Titles 100,000; Per Subs 100
Special Collections: Construction Specifications
Subject Interests: Construction
Automation Activity & Vendor Info: (Acquisitions) EOS International; (Cataloging) EOS International; (Circulation) EOS International; (ILL) OCLC; (OPAC) EOS International; (Serials) EOS International
Database Vendor: Dialog, OCLC FirstSearch
Function: Govt ref serv
Open Mon-Fri 7:30-4

G UNITED STATES ENVIRONMENTAL PROTECTION*, Region 8 Technical Library, 1595 Wynkoop St, 2nd Flr, 80202-1129. (Mail add: 1595 Wynkoop St, 80C-L, 80202-1129), SAN 301-8334. Tel: 303-312-7226. Toll Free Tel: 800-227-8917. FAX: 303-312-7061. E-mail: library-reg8@epa.gov. Web Site: www2.epa.gov/libraries/region-8-technical-library-services. *Supvry Librn,* Lydia Frederick; Tel: 303-312-6743, E-mail: frederick.lydia@epa.gov; *ILL Librn,* Marcus Elmore; Tel: 303-312-6119, E-mail: elmore.marcus@epa.gov; *Ref Librn,* Dedre Henderson; Tel: 303-312-6745, E-mail: henderson.dedre@epa.gov; Staff 3 (MLS 3)
Founded 1973
Library Holdings: Bk Titles 100,000; Per Subs 50
Subject Interests: Air pollution, Environment, Mining, Water pollution, Wetlands
Wireless access
Function: Computers for patron use, Doc delivery serv, Govt ref serv, ILL available, Microfiche/film & reading machines, Online cat, Pub access computers, Ref & res
Open Mon-Fri 8-4
Restriction: Borrowing requests are handled by ILL, Photo ID required for access, Pub use on premises

G UNITED STATES ENVIRONMENTAL PROTECTION NATIONAL ENFORCEMENT INVESTIGATIONS CENTER, Environmental Forensics Library, Denver Federal Ctr, Bldg 25, Door W-2, 80225. (Mail add: PO Box 25227, 80225-0227), SAN 329-0786. Administration Tel: 303-462-9350. FAX: 303-462-9354. E-mail: neic-library@epamail.epa.gov. Web Site: www.epa.gov/libraries/neic.html. *Librn,* Nancy B Greer; E-mail: greer.nancy@epa.gov; Staff 1 (MLS 1)
Founded 1976
Library Holdings: Bk Titles 7,000; Per Subs 42
Special Collections: EPA Methods Coll
Subject Interests: Analytical chem, Environ law, Indust chem
Database Vendor: OCLC WorldShare Interlibrary Loan
Function: ILL available, Mail & tel request accepted, Online cat, Res libr
Partic in Fedlink
Restriction: Open to pub by appt only

G UNITED STATES GEOLOGICAL SURVEY LIBRARY*, Bldg 20, Rm C2002, Denver Federal Ctr, 80225. (Mail add: PO Box 25046, Stop 914, 80225-0046), SAN 320-1260. Tel: 303-236-1000. Circulation Tel: 303-236-1015. Toll Free Tel: 888-275-8747. FAX: 303-236-0015. Circulation FAX: 303-236-1013. TDD: 303-236-0098. Web Site: library.usgs.gov. Staff 8 (MLS 5, Non-MLS 3)
Founded 1948
Library Holdings: CDs 2,200; e-books 800; e-journals 1,000; Bk Titles 230,000
Special Collections: USGS Geological Division Field Records, USGS Historical Photographs
Subject Interests: Earth sci
Partic in OCLC Online Computer Library Center, Inc
Open Mon-Fri 8-4

C UNIVERSITY OF DENVER*, Penrose Library, 2150 E Evans Ave, 80208-2007. SAN 335-766X. Tel: 303-871-3441. Circulation Tel: 303-871-3707. Interlibrary Loan Service Tel: 303-871-3150. Reference Tel: 303-871-2905. Administration Tel: 303-871-2007. FAX: 303-871-2290. Interlibrary Loan Service FAX: 303-871-3446. Web Site: library.du.edu. *Dean, Libr Dir,* Nancy Allen; E-mail: nancy.allen@du.edu; *Mgr, Libr Tech Serv,* Dave Bishoff; Tel: 303-871-2604, E-mail: david.bishoff@du.edu; *Rare Bks, Spec Coll Librn,* Steven Fisher; *Cat,* Betty Meagher; *Coll Develop,* Michael Levine-Clark; *Online Serv,* Esther Gil; *Ref,* Chris Brown; *Ref,* Carrie Forbes; *Ref,* Peggy Keeran; *Ref,* Joe Kraus; *Ref,* Michael Levine-Clark; Staff 19 (MLS 19)
Founded 1864. Enrl 7,390; Fac 424; Highest Degree: Doctorate
Library Holdings: Bk Vols 909,100; Per Subs 5,540
Special Collections: Ira M Beck Memorial Archives; Levette J Davidson Folklore Coll; Margaret Husted Culinary Coll; Papers of Congressman Wayne Aspinall; Papers of Senator Peter Dominick. US Document Depository
Automation Activity & Vendor Info: (Acquisitions) Innovative Interfaces, Inc; (Cataloging) Innovative Interfaces, Inc; (Circulation) Innovative Interfaces, Inc; (Serials) Innovative Interfaces, Inc
Partic in Colorado Alliance of Research Libraries; OCLC Online Computer Library Center, Inc
Friends of the Library Group

Departmental Libraries:
MUSIC LIBRARY, 2344 E Iliff Ave, 80208, SAN 301-8199. Tel: 303-871-6421. FAX: 303-871-6886. *Head Music Libr, Prof,* Dr Suzanne Moulton-Gertig; E-mail: suzanne.moulton-gertig@du.edu. Subject Specialists: *Harp lit, Musicology,* Dr Suzanne Moulton-Gertig
Founded 1985
Library Holdings: Bk Titles 15,860; Per Subs 27

CL WESTMINSTER LAW LIBRARY, 2255 E Evans Ave, 80208, SAN 335-7694. Tel: 303-871-6188. Interlibrary Loan Service Tel: 303-871-6191. Reference Tel: 303-871-6206. FAX: 303-871-6999. E-mail: refdesk@law.du.edu. Web Site: www.law.du.edu/library. *Interim Dir,* Sylvia Hall-Ellis; *Interim Asst Dir, Outreach & Instrul Coordr,* Stacey Bowers; *Fac Serv Librn,* Diane Burkhardt; *Foreign, Comparative & Intl Law Librn,* Joan Policastri; *Ref Librn,* Catharine Cott; *Ref Librn,* Sheila Green; *Ref Serv Coordr,* Patty Wellinger; *Coll Mgt,* Gary Alexander; E-mail: galexand@law.du.edu; *ILL,* Nancy Sensel; Staff 12.5 (MLS 7.5, Non-MLS 5)
Founded 1892. Enrl 1,000
Library Holdings: Bk Vols 420,007
Special Collections: Colorado Legislative Council Reports; Howard Jenkins Coll; Sturm College of Law Coll. US Document Depository
Automation Activity & Vendor Info: (Acquisitions) Innovative Interfaces, Inc; (Cataloging) Innovative Interfaces, Inc; (Circulation) Innovative Interfaces, Inc
Partic in Desert States Law Library Consortium; New England Law Library Consortium, Inc; OCLC Online Computer Library Center, Inc
Publications: Hearsay Blog (Newsletter)
Restriction: Circ limited

S WASHINGTON GROUP INTERNATIONAL*, Technical Information Center, 7800 E Union Ave, Ste 100, 80237. SAN 327-3288. Tel: 303-843-2256. FAX: 303-843-2208. Web Site: www.wgint.com. *Info Res Spec,* Kathy Jackson; Tel: 303-843-3536, E-mail: kathy.jackson@wgint.com
Library Holdings: Bk Titles 3,000; Bk Vols 5,000; Per Subs 10
Subject Interests: Chem eng, Mechanical eng
Open Mon-Fri 7:30-3:30
Restriction: Co libr, Employee & client use only, No access to competitors

C WESTWOOD COLLEGE OF TECHNOLOGY*, South Campus Library, 3150 S Sheridan Blvd, 80227-5548. Tel: 303-367-5016. Web Site: www.westwood.edu. *Mgr,* Jessica King; E-mail: jking@westwood.edu; Staff 1 (MLS 1)
Founded 1999
Library Holdings: AV Mats 100; Bk Vols 900; Per Subs 50
Automation Activity & Vendor Info: (Cataloging) Surpass; (Circulation) Surpass; (OPAC) Surpass
Database Vendor: EBSCOhost, LexisNexis
Open Mon-Thurs 9-8, Fri 9-1

DOLORES

S ANASAZI HERITAGE CENTER LIBRARY*, 27501 Hwy 184, 81323. Tel: 970-882-5600. FAX: 970-882-7035. Web Site: www.co.blm.gov/ahc.
Library Holdings: AV Mats 60; CDs 6; DVDs 14; Bk Vols 6,000; Per Subs 9; Videos 210
Subject Interests: Anasazi, Archaeology, Four Corners tribes
Function: Wheelchair accessible
Open Mon-Fri 9-4
Friends of the Library Group

P DOLORES LIBRARY DISTRICT*, 1002 Railroad Ave, 81323. (Mail add: PO Box 847, 81323-0847), SAN 301-892X. Tel: 970-882-4127. FAX: 970-882-2224. E-mail: library@fone.net. Web Site: www.doloreslibrary.org. *Dir,* Carole Arnold; E-mail: carole@fone.net; Staff 6 (Non-MLS 6)
Founded 1956. Pop 8,000; Circ 25,000
Jan 2008-Dec 2008 Income $289,050, Locally Generated Income $274,000, Other $15,050. Mats Exp $20,000, Books $15,000, Per/Ser (Incl. Access Fees) $1,000, AV Mat $4,000. Sal $107,000
Library Holdings: Audiobooks 2,000; CDs 25; DVDs 230; e-books 1; Large Print Bks 220; Bk Titles 22,000; Per Subs 30; Videos 560
Special Collections: Archeology 200; Railroad Coll; Spanish (Children's Dual-Language Books). Oral History
Subject Interests: Colorado, Local hist
Automation Activity & Vendor Info: (Acquisitions) LibLime; (Cataloging) LibLime; (Circulation) LibLime; (Course Reserve) LibLime; (ILL) Fretwell-Downing; (Serials) Horizon
Database Vendor: EBSCOhost, Gale Cengage Learning, OCLC FirstSearch, OCLC WorldShare Interlibrary Loan, SirsiDynix
Wireless access
Function: Adult bk club, After school storytime, Art exhibits, Audiobks via web, Bks on cassette, Bks on CD, Children's prog, Computer training, Computers for patron use, Copy machines, Digital talking bks, Doc delivery serv, Electronic databases & coll, Exhibits, Fax serv, Handicapped accessible, Holiday prog, ILL available, Magnifiers for reading, Music CDs, Online cat, Online ref, Online searches, Photocopying/Printing, Prog for adults, Prog for children & young adult, Pub access computers, Scanner, Story hour, Summer reading prog, Tax forms, Teen prog, VHS videos, Video lending libr, Web-catalog, Wheelchair accessible
Publications: Book List
Partic in OCLC Online Computer Library Center, Inc
Special Services for the Blind - Talking bks
Open Mon-Wed 9-6, Thurs 9-7, Fri 9-4, Sat 9-3
Friends of the Library Group

DOVE CREEK

P DOLORES COUNTY PUBLIC LIBRARY*, 425N Main St, 81324. (Mail add: PO Box 578, 81324-0578), SAN 376-2823. Tel: 970-677-2389. FAX: 970-677-2389. Web Site: www.dolorescounty.k12.co.us. *Dir,* Laurie Ernst; E-mail: lernst@dolorescounty.k12.co.us
Founded 1970. Pop 1,700
Library Holdings: Large Print Bks 30; Bk Titles 16,000; Talking Bks 185
Automation Activity & Vendor Info: (Cataloging) Follett Software; (Circulation) Follett Software
Partic in Access Colo Libr Info Network (ACLIN); Colorado Library Consortium
Special Services for the Blind - Bks on cassette
Open Mon-Thurs (Winter) 7:30-5; Mon & Wed (Summer) 12-5, Tues & Thurs 10-4
Friends of the Library Group
Branches: 2
CAHONE READING CENTER, Cahone Recreation Ctr, Cahone, 81320. Tel: 970-562-4626. *Librn,* Shirley Davis
Library Holdings: Bk Titles 1,375
Open Tues & Thurs 11-1
RICO PUBLIC, Two N Commercial St, Rico, 81332. (Mail add: PO Box 69, Rico, 81332-0069). Tel: 970-967-2103. FAX: 970-967-2103. *Librn,* Susan Robertson
Library Holdings: Bk Titles 3,200
Open Wed & Fri 1-7
Friends of the Library Group

DURANGO

P DURANGO PUBLIC LIBRARY*, 1900 E Third Ave, 81301. SAN 301-8938. Tel: 970-375-3380. Interlibrary Loan Service Tel: 970-375-3394. Reference Tel: 970-375-2105. Administration Tel: 970-375-3381. Automation Services Tel: 970-375-3382. FAX: 970-375-3398. E-mail: reference@ci.durango.co.us. Web Site: www.durangopubliclibrary.org. *Dir of Libr Serv,* Andy White; E-mail: whitema@ci.durango.co.us; *Adult/YA Librn Supvr,* Abby Lambert; Tel: 970-375-3387, E-mail: lambertaj@ci.durango.co.us; *Ch Librn Supvr,* Rita Curtis; Tel: 970-375-3385, E-mail: curtisrd@ci.durango.co.us; *Tech Serv & Syst Librn Supvr,* Donna Arment; Tel: 970-375-3386, E-mail: armentdl@ci.durango.co.us; Staff 20 (MLS 6, Non-MLS 14)
Founded 1889. Pop 50,766; Circ 258,723
Jan 2008-Dec 2008 Income $1,611,553, City $759,977, County $851,576. Mats Exp $171,330, Books $116,135, Per/Ser (Incl. Access Fees) $10,415, Micro $500, AV Mat $23,675, Electronic Ref Mat (Incl. Access Fees) $20,605. Sal $1,077,409
Library Holdings: Audiobooks 2,704; CDs 2,252; e-books 2,167; Bk Vols 85,831; Per Subs 204; Videos 4,107
Special Collections: Archaeology (Helen Sloan Daniels); Local History, photogs; Southwestern US History (Helen Sloan Daniels)
Automation Activity & Vendor Info: (Acquisitions) Innovative Interfaces, Inc; (Cataloging) Innovative Interfaces, Inc; (Circulation) Innovative Interfaces, Inc
Wireless access
Open Mon-Wed 9-8, Thurs 10-5:30, Fri & Sat 9-5:30
Friends of the Library Group
Branches: 1
FORT LEWIS MESA, 11274 Hwy 140, Hesperus, 81326, SAN 321-9313. Tel: 970-588-3331. *Br Mgr,* Laurel Penwell
Library Holdings: Bk Vols 3,200
Open Mon-Thurs 2-7

C FORT LEWIS COLLEGE LIBRARY*, John F Reed Library, 1000 Rim Dr, 81301-3999. SAN 301-8946. Tel: 970-247-7250. Circulation Tel: 970-247-7270. Interlibrary Loan Service Tel: 970-247-7233. Reference Tel: 970-247-7551. FAX: 970-247-7149. Web Site: library.fortlewis.edu. *Libr Dir,* Astrid Oliver; E-mail: oliver_a@fortlewis.edu; *Coll Mgt Librn,* Pam Arbeeny; *Info Serv Librn,* Minna Sellers; *Ref Librn,* Tina Evans; *Ref & Instruction Librn,* Mimi Wheatwind; *SW Ctr Librn,* Jen Pack; *Syst Librn,* Brian Slone; *Tech Serv Librn,* Lloyd Chittenden; Staff 15 (MLS 7, Non-MLS 8)
Founded 1911. Enrl 3,900; Fac 300; Highest Degree: Bachelor
Library Holdings: e-journals 17,151; Bk Titles 198,645; Per Subs 845
Automation Activity & Vendor Info: (Acquisitions) Innovative Interfaces, Inc; (Cataloging) Innovative Interfaces, Inc; (Circulation) Innovative

Interfaces, Inc; (OPAC) Innovative Interfaces, Inc; (Serials) Innovative Interfaces, Inc
Wireless access
Partic in Access Colo Libr Info Network (ACLIN)
Open Mon-Thurs 7:30am-10pm, Fri 7:30-5, Sat 1-5, Sun 1-10
Friends of the Library Group

EADS

P KIOWA COUNTY PUBLIC LIBRARY DISTRICT, 1305 Goff St, 81036. (Mail add: PO Box 790, 81036-0790), SAN 301-8962. Tel: 719-438-5581. FAX: 719-438-6581. E-mail: kcpld.eads@gmail.com. *Dir,* Charlene Blakeley; Staff 2 (Non-MLS 2)
Founded 1939. Pop 1,800; Circ 8,789
Library Holdings: Large Print Bks 75; Bk Vols 8,000; Per Subs 20; Talking Bks 100
Wireless access
Function: ILL available
Special Services for the Blind - Cassettes; Copier with enlargement capabilities; Large print bks; PC for handicapped; Talking bks; Videos on blindness & phys handicaps
Open Mon-Fri 8-4:30

EAGLE

P EAGLE VALLEY LIBRARY DISTRICT*, Eagle Public Library, 600 Broadway, 81631. (Mail add: PO Box 240, 81631-0240), SAN 335-7724. Tel: 970-328-8800. FAX: 970-328-6901. Web Site: www.evld.org. *Dir,* Charlyn Canada; *Asst Dir,* Anne Johnson; E-mail: ajohnson@marmot.org; Staff 21 (MLS 4, Non-MLS 17)
Founded 1993. Pop 45,000; Circ 152,163
Library Holdings: AV Mats 5,508; CDs 816; DVDs 3,036; Bk Vols 44,901; Per Subs 228
Special Collections: Colorado Coll; Eagle County Hist Coll
Automation Activity & Vendor Info: (Cataloging) Innovative Interfaces, Inc; (Circulation) Innovative Interfaces, Inc; (ILL) OCLC; (OPAC) Innovative Interfaces, Inc; (Serials) Innovative Interfaces, Inc
Wireless access
Partic in Marmot Libr Network; OCLC Online Computer Library Center, Inc
Open Mon-Thurs 10-8, Fri & Sat 10-5, Sun 1-5
Friends of the Library Group
Branches: 2
AVON PUBLIC LIBRARY, 200 Benchmark Rd, Avon, 81620. (Mail add: PO Box 977, Avon, 81620-0977), SAN 335-7740. Tel: 970-949 6797. FAX: 970-949-0233. *Br Mgr,* Kim Saalfeld
Library Holdings: AV Mats 8,052; CDs 1,339; DVDs 4,297; Bk Vols 59,910; Per Subs 265
Open Mon-Thurs 10-8, Fri & Sat 10-5, Sun 1-5
Friends of the Library Group
GYPSUM PUBLIC LIBRARY, 48 Lundgren Blvd, Gypsum, 81637. (Mail add: PO Box 979, Gypsum, 81637-0979), SAN 377-7227. Tel: 970-524-5080. FAX: 970-524-5082. *Br Mgr,* Rebecca Brackett
Library Holdings: AV Mats 3,183; CDs 383; DVDs 891; Bk Vols 23,915; Per Subs 64; Videos 1,303
Open Mon 10-8, Tues-Thurs 10-6
Friends of the Library Group

EATON

P EATON PUBLIC LIBRARY, 132 Maple Ave, 80615-3441. SAN 301-8970. Tel: 970-454-2189. FAX: 970-454-2958. Web Site: www.eatonco.org/library.htm. *Dir,* Jerome W Krois; E-mail: jkrois@highplains.us; Staff 3.8 (MLS 1, Non-MLS 2.8)
Founded 1901. Pop 5,000; Circ 79,220
Jan 2013-Dec 2013 Income $817,066. Mats Exp $26,746, Books $12,485, Per/Ser (Incl. Access Fees) $1,894, AV Mat $12,367. Sal $160,476 (Prof $55,852)
Library Holdings: Audiobooks 1,626; CDs 400; DVDs 2,493; Large Print Bks 630; Bk Vols 24,416; Per Subs 25; Videos 625
Automation Activity & Vendor Info: (Acquisitions) Horizon; (Cataloging) Horizon; (Circulation) Horizon; (ILL) OCLC ILLiad; (OPAC) SirsiDynix
Wireless access
Function: 24/7 Electronic res, 24/7 Online cat, Adult bk club, After school storytime, Bks on CD, Children's prog, Computer training, Computers for patron use, Copy machines, Doc delivery serv, e-mail serv, E-Reserves, Family literacy, Free DVD rentals, Handicapped accessible, ILL available, Magazines, Mango lang, Online cat, OverDrive digital audio bks, Photocopying/Printing, Preschool reading prog, Pub access computers, Scanner, Tax forms
Mem of High Plains Library District
Open Mon-Thurs 9-7, Fri 9-6 & Sat 10-5
Friends of the Library Group

ELIZABETH

P ELBERT COUNTY LIBRARY DISTRICT*, 651 W Beverly St, 80107-7560. SAN 335-8534. Tel: 303-646-3416. FAX: 303-646-0315. Web Site: www.elbertcountylibrary.org. *Dir,* Kari Baumann
Founded 1937. Pop 22,000
Subject Interests: Agr, Antiques, Local hist
Automation Activity & Vendor Info: (Cataloging) SirsiDynix; (Circulation) SirsiDynix
Database Vendor: SirsiDynix
Friends of the Library Group
Branches: 4
ELBERT BRANCH, 24489 Main St, Elbert, 80106. (Mail add: PO Box 38, Elbert, 80106-0038). Tel: 303-648-3533. FAX: 303-648-3853. *Br Mgr,* Sue Dischner
Open Mon 10-3, Tues-Thurs 4:30-7, Sat 10-3
ELIZABETH BRANCH, 651 W Beverly St, 80107. Tel: 303-646-3416. FAX: 303-646-9217. E-mail: elizabeth@elbertcountylibrary.org. *Br Mgr,* Jan Gabehart
Open Mon-Thurs 9-7, Fri & Sat 9-5
Friends of the Library Group
KIOWA BRANCH, 331 Comanche, Kiowa, 80117. (Mail add: PO Box 538, Kiowa, 80117-0538). Tel: 303-621-2111. FAX: 303-621-2754. *Br Mgr,* Sue Dischner; E-mail: sdischner@elbertcountylibrary.org
Open Mon-Thurs 10-6, Fri 9-5, Sat 9-2
SIMLA BRANCH, 504 Washington, Simla, 80835. (Mail add: PO Box 245, Simla, 80835), SAN 335-8593. Tel: 719-541-2573. FAX: 719-541-2152. *Br Mgr,* Shanna Engler
Open Mon-Fri 9-7, Sat 10-2
Friends of the Library Group

ENGLEWOOD

S THE AMERICAN HUMANE ASSOCIATION*, Children's Services Library, 63 Inverness Dr E, 80112-5117. SAN 323-6307. Tel: 303-792-9900. FAX: 303-792-5333. E-mail: info@americanhumane.org. Web Site: www.americanhumane.org. *Ch Serv,* Jesse Rainey
Founded 1986
Library Holdings: Bk Titles 3,000; Per Subs 100
Subject Interests: Child abuse
Automation Activity & Vendor Info: (Cataloging) Inmagic, Inc.
Publications: Child Protection Leader (quarterly); Protecting Children (journal)

P ARAPAHOE LIBRARY DISTRICT*, 12855 E Adam Aircraft Circle, 80112. SAN 335-9042. Tel: 303-542-7279. FAX: 303-798-2485. Web Site: www.arapahoelibraries.org. *Exec Dir,* Nicolle Ingui Davies; *Dir, Human Res,* Ted Fleagle; Staff 60 (MLS 60)
Founded 1966. Pop 202,000; Circ 4,510,000
Library Holdings: AV Mats 79,281; Large Print Bks 6,802; Bk Titles 225,971; Bk Vols 477,298; Per Subs 1,691; Talking Bks 25,047
Publications: By the Book (Newsletter); Community Information Guide
Open Mon-Fri 9-5
Friends of the Library Group
Branches: 8
CASTLEWOOD XPRESS LIBRARY, 6739 S Uinta St, Centennial, 80112, SAN 335-9190. *Mgr,* Daisy Grice
Library Holdings: Bk Titles 70,000; Bk Vols 71,000
Open Mon-Thurs 9-9, Fri & Sat 9-5, Sun 1-5
Friends of the Library Group
DAVIES PUBLIC LIBRARY, 303 Third Ave, Deer Trail, 80105, SAN 335-9131. Tel: 303-769-4310. *Mgr,* Cynthia Kiyotake
Library Holdings: Bk Titles 21,000
Open Mon & Wed 9-8, Tues, Thurs & Fri 9-5, Sat 9-Noon
Friends of the Library Group
KELVER PUBLIC LIBRARY, 404 E Front St, Byers, 80103, SAN 335-9077. *Mgr,* Cynthia Kiyotake
Library Holdings: Bk Titles 28,000
Open Mon, Wed & Fri 8-5, Tues & Thurs 8-8, Sat 9-5
Friends of the Library Group
KOELBEL PUBLIC LIBRARY, 5955 S Holly St, Centennial, 80121, SAN 335-9107. *Mgr,* Daisy Grice
Library Holdings: Bk Titles 179,000
Open Mon-Thurs 9-9, Fri & Sat 9-5, Sun 1-5
Friends of the Library Group
MAY PUBLIC LIBRARY, 1471 S Parker Rd, Denver, 80231. *Mgr,* Holly Whelan
Open Mon-Thurs 9-9, Fri & Sat 9-5, Sun 1-5
SHERIDAN PUBLIC LIBRARY, 3425 W Oxford Ave, Sheridan, 80236, SAN 335-9166. *Mgr,* Cynthia Kiyotake
Library Holdings: Bk Titles 30,000; Per Subs 50
Open Mon-Thurs 9-8, Fri & Sat 9-5
Friends of the Library Group

SMOKY HILL PUBLIC LIBRARY, 5430 S Biscay Circle, Centennial, 80015, SAN 335-9174. FAX: 303-690-4572. *Mgr,* Holly Whelan; Staff 30 (MLS 4, Non-MLS 26)
Library Holdings: Bk Titles 85,000; Per Subs 117
Database Vendor: Innovative Interfaces, Inc
Open Mon-Thurs 9-9, Fri & Sat 9-5, Sun 1-5
Friends of the Library Group

SOUTHGLENN PUBLIC LIBRARY, 6972 S Vine St, Centennial, 80122-3270, SAN 373-5753. *Mgr,* Daisy Grice
Library Holdings: Bk Titles 55,000
Open Mon-Thurs 10-9, Fri & Sat 10-7, Sun 12-6
Bookmobiles: 1

S DEPARTMENT OF HUMAN SERVICES-YOUTH CORRECTIONS*, Marvin W Foote Youth Services Center Library, 13500 E Fremont Pl, 80112. Tel: 303-768-7529, 303-768-7566. FAX: 303-768-7525. Web Site: www.cdhs.state.co.us. *Head Librn,* Nadine McAlister; E-mail: nadine.mcalister@state.co.us
Library Holdings: Bk Vols 4,000; Per Subs 12
Open Mon-Fri 8-4

P ENGLEWOOD PUBLIC LIBRARY*, 1000 Englewood Pkwy, 80110. SAN 301-9012. Tel: 303-762-2560. Circulation Tel: 303-762-2550. Interlibrary Loan Service Tel: 303-762-2565. Reference Tel: 303-762-2555. Administration Tel: 303-762-2572. FAX: 303-783-6890. Circulation TDD: 303-762-2548. Reference TDD: 303-762-2549. Web Site: www.englewoodgov.org. *Dir,* Dorothy Hargrove; Staff 16 (MLS 8, Non-MLS 8)
Founded 1920. Pop 32,500; Circ 197,729
Jan 2008-Dec 2008 Income $1,334,313. Mats Exp $248,692. Sal $919,183
Library Holdings: AV Mats 7,505; Bk Vols 105,108; Per Subs 310
Special Collections: Englewood Local History Coll, docs, newsp & photogs
Automation Activity & Vendor Info: (Acquisitions) SirsiDynix; (Cataloging) SirsiDynix; (Circulation) SirsiDynix; (OPAC) SirsiDynix
Database Vendor: College Source, CQ Press, EBSCO Information Services, EBSCOhost, Gale Cengage Learning, LearningExpress, Newsbank, OCLC FirstSearch, ProQuest, ReferenceUSA, SirsiDynix, World Book Online
Wireless access
Open Mon-Thurs 10:30-8:30, Fri & Sat 10:30-5, Sun 1-5
Friends of the Library Group

R FIRST PLYMOUTH CONGREGATIONAL CHURCH LIBRARY*, 3501 S Colorado Blvd, 80113. SAN 301-9020. Tel: 303-762-0616. FAX: 303-789-2783. Web Site: www.firstplymouthchurch.org.
Library Holdings: Bk Vols 3,000
Open Mon-Fri 8:30-4:30, Sun 8-Noon

S NATIONAL STROKE ASSOCIATION LIBRARY*, 9707 E Easter Lane, 80112-3747. SAN 372-7610. Tel: 303-649-9299. Interlibrary Loan Service Toll Free Tel: 800-787-6537. FAX: 303-649-1328. TDD: 303-771-1887. Web Site: www.stroke.org.
Library Holdings: Bk Titles 100; Per Subs 10
Subject Interests: Stroke
Special Services for the Deaf - TDD equip

M SWEDISH MEDICAL CENTER LIBRARY*, Medical Library, 501 E Hampden Ave, 80113. SAN 301-9047. Tel: 303-788-6617. FAX: 303-788-6840. E-mail: smclibrary@healthonecares.com. *Med Librn,* W Robin Waters; Tel: 303-788-6669, E-mail: robin.waters@healthonecares.com. Subject Specialists: *Med,* W Robin Waters; Staff 0.8 (MLS 0.8)
Founded 1967
Library Holdings: e-journals 300; Bk Titles 500; Bk Vols 3,500; Per Subs 110
Subject Interests: Med, Neurology, Nursing, Traumatic brain injury
Automation Activity & Vendor Info: (Cataloging) OCLC; (Circulation) Innovative Interfaces, Inc - Millenium; (OPAC) Innovative Interfaces, Inc - Millenium; (Serials) SerialsSolutions
Database Vendor: EBSCOhost, Elsevier, Innovative Interfaces, Inc, Medline, Micromedex, OCLC FirstSearch, OCLC WorldShare Interlibrary Loan, ScienceDirect, SerialsSolutions, STAT!Ref (Teton Data Systems), UpToDate, Wiley InterScience
Wireless access
Partic in Access Colo Libr Info Network (ACLIN); Colorado Council of Medical Librarians; Impulse; Medical Library Association (MLA)
Restriction: Employee & client use only

ESTES PARK

P ESTES PARK PUBLIC LIBRARY*, 335 E Elkhorn Ave, 80517. (Mail add: PO Box 1687, 80517-1687), SAN 301-9055. Tel: 970-586-8116. FAX: 970-586-0189. Web Site: www.estesvalleylibrary.org. *Dir,* Claudine Perrault; E-mail: cperrault@estesvalleylibrary.org; *Head, Circ,* Peggy Moore; *Adult Serv Supvr,* Kurtis Kelly; Staff 17 (MLS 1, Non-MLS 16)
Founded 1922. Pop 12,615; Circ 134,743
Library Holdings: AV Mats 4,000; Large Print Bks 1,000; Bk Titles 50,000; Bk Vols 61,000; Per Subs 200
Special Collections: Oral History
Subject Interests: Local hist
Automation Activity & Vendor Info: (Cataloging) TLC (The Library Corporation); (Circulation) TLC (The Library Corporation); (OPAC) TLC (The Library Corporation)
Wireless access
Special Services for the Blind - Bks on cassette; Bks on CD; Talking bks
Open Mon-Thurs 10-9, Fri & Sat 10-5, Sun 1-5
Friends of the Library Group

FLAGLER

P FLAGLER COMMUNITY LIBRARY*, 311 Main Ave, 80815-9237. (Mail add: PO Box 364, 80815-0364), SAN 301-9071. Tel: 719-765-4310. FAX: 719-765-4498. E-mail: flibrary@esrta.com. *Librn,* Vivian Schaal
Founded 1920. Pop 2,325; Circ 5,013
Library Holdings: Bk Titles 7,500
Special Collections: Hal Borland Coll; Page History Room, American History
Database Vendor: LibLime
Wireless access
Mem of High Plains Regional Library Service System
Open Mon-Fri 9-4
Bookmobiles: 1

FLEMING

P FLEMING COMMUNITY LIBRARY*, 506 N Fremont Ave, 80728. SAN 301-908X. Tel: 970-265-2022. Web Site: www.flemingschools.org. *Libr Dir,* Linda Conn; Staff 2 (MLS 1, Non-MLS 1)
Pop 500; Circ 12,998
Library Holdings: Audiobooks 688; Bk Titles 12,831; Per Subs 35
Automation Activity & Vendor Info: (Cataloging) Follett Software; (Circulation) Follett Software
Wireless access
Partic in Cooperating Libraries in Consortium
Special Services for the Deaf - ADA equip; Closed caption videos
Special Services for the Blind - Accessible computers; PC for handicapped
Open Mon 1-5, Tues-Fri 8-5
Friends of the Library Group

FLORENCE

P JOHN C FREMONT LIBRARY DISTRICT*, 130 Church Ave, 81226. SAN 301-9098. Tel: 719-784-4649. FAX: 719-784-3764. Web Site: florencecolibrary.org. *Dir,* Tabitha Selakovich; E-mail: Tabby.Selakovich@JCFLD.org; *Asst Libr Dir,* Cid Larson; E-mail: cidlarson@gmail.com; *Adult Prog,* Natalia Gray; *Youth Serv,* Robin Hohn; Staff 4 (Non-MLS 4)
Founded 1908. Pop 6,000; Circ 12,000
Library Holdings: Bks on Deafness & Sign Lang 10; CDs 150; DVDs 250; High Interest/Low Vocabulary Bk Vols 100; Large Print Bks 150; Bk Titles 12,000; Bk Vols 24,000; Per Subs 24; Talking Bks 200; Videos 150
Wireless access
Function: Adult bk club, Art exhibits, Bks on CD, Children's prog, Computers for patron use, Copy machines, Digital talking bks, Fax serv, Free DVD rentals, Handicapped accessible, Home delivery & serv to Sr ctr & nursing homes, Homebound delivery serv, ILL available, Large print keyboards, Music CDs, Notary serv, Online cat, Online ref, Online searches, Photocopying/Printing, Printer for laptops & handheld devices, Prog for adults, Prog for children & young adult, Pub access computers, Scanner, Spanish lang bks, Story hour, Summer reading prog, Tax forms, Teen prog, Wheelchair accessible
Special Services for the Deaf - Bks on deafness & sign lang
Special Services for the Blind - Bks on CD; Digital talking bk; Home delivery serv; Large print bks; Large print bks & talking machines; Recorded bks; Talking bk & rec for the blind cat; Talking bks
Open Mon-Thurs 10-7, Fri 10-5, Sat 10-2
Friends of the Library Group

FORT CARSON

UNITED STATES ARMY

A GRANT LIBRARY*, 1637 Flint St, 80913-4105, SAN 335-7813. Tel: 719-526-2350. Circulation Tel: 719-526-2842. Interlibrary Loan Service Tel: 719-526-8142. FAX: 719-524-0070. Web Site: peregrine.usafa.af.mil/grant.html. *Actg Dir,* Kevin Patrick Bokay; Tel: 719-526-8144, E-mail: kevin.bokay@us.army.mil; *Circ Mgr,* Cassandra Osuji; E-mail: cassandra.osuji@carson.army.mil; *Libr Tech,* Marie Acfalle; E-mail: marie.acfalle@carson.army.mil; *Libr Tech,* Viviana Barron; E-mail: viviana.barron@carson.army.mil; *Tech Serv Mgr,* Nadine

Salmons; Tel: 719-526-8140, E-mail: nadine.salmons@carson.army.mil; Staff 9 (MLS 2, Non-MLS 7)
Founded 1942
Library Holdings: AV Mats 4,849; Bk Titles 51,000; Per Subs 200
Special Collections: Colorado; Military Arts & Sciences
Database Vendor: SirsiDynix
Function: Audio & video playback equip for onsite use, Handicapped accessible, ILL available, Orientations, Outside serv via phone, mail, e-mail & web, Photocopying/Printing, Prog for children & young adult, Ref & res, Ref serv available, Res libr, Senior computer classes, Spoken cassettes & CDs, Spoken cassettes & DVDs, Summer reading prog, Tax forms, VCDs, VHS videos, Video lending libr
Open Mon-Thurs 11-8, Fri 11-5, Sat & Sun 10-6
Restriction: Circ to mil employees only

AM LANE MEDICAL LIBRARY - EVANS ARMY COMMUNITY HOSPITAL, 1650 Cochrane Circle, 80913-4604, SAN 335-7848. Tel: 719-526-7285. FAX: 719-526-7113. E-mail: usarmy.carson.medcom-each.list.library@mail.mil. *Librn,* Janet Klieman; Staff 1 (MLS 1)
Founded 1952
Library Holdings: Bk Vols 2,400; Per Subs 120
Special Collections: Consumer's Coll
Subject Interests: Dentistry, Med, Mental health, Nursing, Orthopedics, Phys therapy, Veterinary med
Automation Activity & Vendor Info: (Acquisitions) Ex Libris Group; (Cataloging) Ex Libris Group; (Circulation) Ex Libris Group; (Course Reserve) Ex Libris Group; (ILL) Ex Libris Group; (Media Booking) Ex Libris Group; (OPAC) Ex Libris Group; (Serials) Ex Libris Group
Partic in Dialog Corp; OCLC Online Computer Library Center, Inc
Publications: Patients Health
Open Mon-Fri 7-4

FORT COLLINS

S COLORADO DIVISION OF WILDLIFE*, Research Center Library, 317 W Prospect Rd, 80526-2097. SAN 301-9101. Tel: 970-472-4353. FAX: 970-472-4457. *Res Librn,* Kay Horton Knudsen
Founded 1967
Subject Interests: Environ studies, Wildlife, Zoology
Publications: Division Reports; Special Reports; Technical Publications
Partic in Colorado Library Consortium
Restriction: Restricted access

C COLORADO STATE UNIVERSITY LIBRARIES, Morgan Library, 1201 Center Avenue Mall, 80523-. (Mail add: 1019 Campus Delivery, 80523-1019), SAN 335-7872. Tel: 970-491-1838. Circulation Tel: 970-491-1842. Interlibrary Loan Service Tel: 970-491-1868. Reference Tel: 970-491-1841. FAX: 970-491-1195. Web Site: lib.colostate.edu. *Dean of Libr, VPres, Info Tech,* Dr Patrick Burns; E-mail: patrick.burns@colostate.edu; *Asst Dean, Digital Libr & ePublishing Serv,* Dawn Paschal; E-mail: dawn.paschal@colostate.edu; *Asst Dean, Res Delivery Serv,* Tom Moothart; E-mail: tom.moothart@colostate.edu; *Asst Dean, Scholarly Communications,* Meg Brown-Sica; Tel: 970-491-7105, E-mail: meg.brown-sica@colostate.edu; *Dir of Develop,* Bruce Hallmark; *Dir, Acad Computing & Networking Serv,* Scott Baily; E-mail: scott.baily@colostate.edu; *Coordr, Acq/Metadata,* Nancy Hunter; *Coordr, Archives,* Janet Bishop; *Coordr, Coll Mgt,* Allison Level; *Coordr, Col Liaisons,* Position Currently Open; *Coordr, Digital Coll Serv,* Diane Lunde; *Coordr, ILL,* Cristi MacWaters; *Coordr, Onsite Serv,* Amy Hoseth; Staff 23 (MLS 23)
Founded 1870. Enrl 30,000; Fac 1,700; Highest Degree: Doctorate
Library Holdings: Bk Vols 1,897,005; Per Subs 21,263
Special Collections: Germans From Russia; International Poster Coll; Vietnam War Fiction; Warren & Genevieve Garst Photographic Coll; Water Resources Archive, a-tapes, docs, maps, photos. State Document Depository; US Document Depository
Subject Interests: Agr, Eng, Natural res
Automation Activity & Vendor Info: (Acquisitions) Innovative Interfaces, Inc; (Cataloging) Innovative Interfaces, Inc; (Circulation) Innovative Interfaces, Inc; (OPAC) Innovative Interfaces, Inc; (Serials) Innovative Interfaces, Inc
Database Vendor: Ex Libris Group
Wireless access
Publications: Stay Connected
Partic in Association of Research Libraries (ARL); Coalition for Networked Information (CNI); Colorado Alliance of Research Libraries; Greater Western Library Alliance; Lyrasis; OCLC Online Computer Library Center, Inc
Friends of the Library Group

Departmental Libraries:

CM VETERINARY MEDICAL CENTER, 300 West Drake Rd, 80523-1620. Tel: 970-297-1213. FAX: 970-297-4141. E-mail: library-dl-vet-library@mail.colostate.edu. Web Site: lib.colostate.edu/branches/vet.html. *Libr Mgr,* Dennis Sylvain; E-mail: dennis.sylvain@colostate.edu. Subject Specialists: *Veterinary med,* Dennis Sylvain
Library Holdings: Bk Titles 5,500; Bk Vols 12,000; Per Subs 162

J FRONT RANGE COMMUNITY COLLEGE*, Harmony Library, 4616 S Shields, 80526. SAN 301-9144. Tel: 970-204-8206. Circulation Tel: 970-204-8401. FAX: 970-204-8444. Web Site: www.frontrange.edu. *Librn,* Annie Fox; Tel: 970-204-8207, E-mail: annie.fox@frontrange.edu; Staff 1 (MLS 1)
Founded 1989. Enrl 5,102; Fac 60; Highest Degree: Associate
Library Holdings: AV Mats 1,000; e-books 6,000; Bk Vols 11,000; Per Subs 100
Subject Interests: Nursing, Veterinary tech
Automation Activity & Vendor Info: (Cataloging) Innovative Interfaces, Inc; (Circulation) Innovative Interfaces, Inc; (Course Reserve) Innovative Interfaces, Inc; (OPAC) Innovative Interfaces, Inc
Database Vendor: EBSCOhost, Gale Cengage Learning, OCLC FirstSearch, ProQuest, SirsiDynix
Wireless access
Open Mon-Thurs 8:30-8, Fri 8:30-6, Sat 10-5, Sun 1-5
Friends of the Library Group

G NATIONAL FOREST SERVICE LIBRARY, 240 W Prospect Rd, 80526. SAN 316-8964. Tel: 970-498-1207. Interlibrary Loan Service Tel: 970-498-1205. FAX: 970-498-1059. E-mail: fslibrary@fs.fed.us. Web Site: fsinfo.fs.fed.us/cgi-bin/gw/chameleon. *Dir,* Carol A Ayer; Tel: 970-498-1310, E-mail: cayer@fs.fed.us; *Librn,* Laura Bojanowski; Tel: 970-498-1284, E-mail: lbojanowski@fs.fed.us; *Librn,* Erin Wescott; Tel: 608-231-9357, E-mail: ewescott@fs.fed.us; *Tech Info Spec,* Sally Dunphy; Tel: 970-498-1268, E-mail: sdunphy@fs.fed.us; *Tech Info Spec,* Sara Garetz; Tel: 510-758-7685, E-mail: sgaretz@fs.fed.us; Staff 11 (MLS 7, Non-MLS 4)
Founded 1966
Library Holdings: Bk Vols 375,000; Per Subs 200
Special Collections: Forest Service Reports
Subject Interests: Forestry, Hydrol, Range mgt, Recreation, Silviculture, Watershed, Wildlife
Automation Activity & Vendor Info: (Cataloging) Innovative Interfaces, Inc; (ILL) OCLC; (OPAC) Innovative Interfaces, Inc
Function: Computers for patron use, ILL available, Online cat
Publications: Monthly Alert
Open Mon-Fri 8-4:30
Restriction: Circ limited, Limited access for the pub, Non-circulating coll, Open to pub for ref & circ; with some limitations

P POUDRE RIVER PUBLIC LIBRARY DISTRICT*, Old Town Library, 201 Peterson St, 80524-2990. (Mail add: 301 E Olive St, 80524), SAN 301-9128. Tel: 970-221-6740. FAX: 970-221-6398. Web Site: www.poudrelibraries.org. *Dir,* Holly Carroll; Tel: 970-221-6670, E-mail: hcarroll@poudrelibraries.org; *Dep Dir,* Ken Draves; E-mail: kdraves@poudrelibraries.org; *Libr Mgr,* Jean Bosch; E-mail: jbosch@poudrelibraries.org; *Communications Mgr,* Paula Watson-Lakamp; E-mail: library-pr@poudrelibraries.org; *IT Mgr,* Carol Gyger; E-mail: cgyger@poudrelibraries.org; *Coll,* Tova Aragon; E-mail: tdaragon@poudrelibraries.org; Staff 68 (MLS 18, Non-MLS 50)
Founded 1900. Pop 177,000; Circ 3,000,000
Library Holdings: Audiobooks 13,981; AV Mats 628,760; e-books 60,534; Electronic Media & Resources 60; Bk Titles 1,404,497; Per Subs 632
Special Collections: Local History Archive. Municipal Document Depository; Oral History
Subject Interests: Historic maps, Local hist
Automation Activity & Vendor Info: (Acquisitions) Innovative Interfaces, Inc; (Cataloging) Innovative Interfaces, Inc; (Circulation) Innovative Interfaces, Inc; (Course Reserve) Innovative Interfaces, Inc; (ILL) Innovative Interfaces, Inc; (Media Booking) Innovative Interfaces, Inc; (OPAC) Innovative Interfaces, Inc; (Serials) Innovative Interfaces, Inc
Database Vendor: Baker & Taylor, BWI, EBSCOhost, Gale Cengage Learning, OCLC FirstSearch, Overdrive, Inc, ProQuest, Wilson - Wilson Web
Wireless access
Function: Adult bk club, Adult literacy prog, After school storytime, Bilingual assistance for Spanish patrons, Bks on CD, Bus archives, Chess club, Children's prog, Computer training, Computers for patron use, Copy machines, Digital talking bks, E-Reserves, Family literacy, Free DVD rentals, Genealogy discussion group, Govt ref serv, Handicapped accessible, Holiday prog, Homebound delivery serv, ILL available, Music CDs, Online ref, Online searches, Outreach serv, OverDrive digital audio bks, Preschool outreach, Prof lending libr, Prog for adults, Prog for children & young adult, Pub access computers, Ref serv in person, Spoken cassettes & DVDs, Story hour, Summer reading prog, Teen prog, Telephone ref, Wheelchair accessible, Workshops, Writing prog
Special Services for the Deaf - TDD equip; TTY equip

Special Services for the Blind - Accessible computers; Bks on CD; Bks on flash-memory cartridges; Copier with enlargement capabilities; Large print bks; Large screen computer & software; Playaways (bks on MP3)
Open Mon-Thurs 9:30-9, Fri 10-6, Sat 10-5, Sun 1-5
Friends of the Library Group
Branches: 2
COUNCIL TREE LIBRARY, 2733 Council Tree Ave, Ste 200, 80525. Tel: 970-221-6740. *Mgr,* Currie Meyer; E-mail: cmeyer@poudrelibraries.org
Open Mon-Sat 10-9, Sun 12-6
Friends of the Library Group
HARMONY LIBRARY, 4616 S Shields St, 80526-3812. (Mail add: 301 E Olive St, 80524), SAN 378-1054. Tel: 970-221-6740. FAX: 970-204-8444. *Br Mgr,* Ken Draves; E-mail: kdraves@poudrelibraries.org

G UNITED STATES DEPARTMENT OF AGRICULTURE*, National Wildlife Research Center Library, USDA/APHIS/WS, 4101 LaPorte Ave, 80521-2154. SAN 335-7422. Tel: 970-266-6016. Circulation Tel: 970-266-6015. Interlibrary Loan Service Tel: 970-266-6230. FAX: 970-266-6010. E-mail: nwrc@usda.gov. Web Site: www.aphis.usda.gov/wildlife_damage/nwrc. *Librn,* Laurie Paulik; E-mail: laurie.a.paulik@aphis.usda.gov. Subject Specialists: *Wildlife mgt,* Laurie Paulik; Staff 3 (MLS 2, Non-MLS 1)
Founded 1967
Library Holdings: Bk Titles 5,000; Per Subs 50
Special Collections: Author Reprints Coll; Predator Coll; United States Fish & Wildlife Service Publications; Wildlife Management Dissertations & Theses including foreign titles
Subject Interests: Chem, Invasive species, Pesticides, Toxicology, Vertebrate biol, Wildlife diseases
Automation Activity & Vendor Info: (Cataloging) EOS International; (ILL) OCLC; (OPAC) EOS International; (Serials) EOS International
Database Vendor: Agricola, BioOne, Dialog, JSTOR, OCLC FirstSearch, OVID Technologies, PubMed, ScienceDirect, Scopus, STN International, WT Cox
Function: Res libr
Publications: Annual Publications List
Partic in Fedlink

G US GEOLOGICAL SURVEY*, Fort Collins Science Center Library, 2150 Centre Ave, Bldg C, 80526-8118. SAN 375-653X. Tel: 970-226-9403. FAX: 970-226-9230. E-mail: fort_library_requests@usgs.gov. *Librn,* Megan Frank; Staff 1 (MLS 1)
Founded 1978
Library Holdings: Bk Titles 12,000; Bk Vols 14,000; Per Subs 89
Subject Interests: Biol, Ecology, Fisheries, Wildlife
Automation Activity & Vendor Info: (Cataloging) EOS International; (Circulation) EOS International; (OPAC) EOS International; (Serials) EOS International
Function: For res purposes
Partic in Fedlink; OCLC Online Computer Library Center, Inc
Open Mon-Fri 7:45-4:30

FORT LUPTON

P FORT LUPTON PUBLIC & SCHOOL LIBRARY*, 425 S Denver Ave, 80621-1303. SAN 301-9187. Tel: 303-857-7180. FAX: 303-857-7190. Web Site: www.ftluptolibrary.org. *Chief Librn,* Janice Fisher-Giles; E-mail: jfisher-giles@ftlupton.k12.co.us; Staff 7 (MLS 3, Non-MLS 4)
Founded 1978
Library Holdings: Bk Titles 43,000; Bk Vols 45,500; Per Subs 108
Automation Activity & Vendor Info: (Cataloging) SirsiDynix; (Circulation) SirsiDynix; (OPAC) SirsiDynix
Mem of High Plains Library District
Partic in Cooperating Libraries in Consortium
Open Mon-Thurs 7:30am-8pm, Fri 7:30-5, Sat 9-4

FORT MORGAN

P FORT MORGAN PUBLIC LIBRARY*, 414 Main St, 80701. (Mail add: PO Box 100, 80701-0100), SAN 301-9209. Tel: 970-542-4000. FAX: 970-542-4013. Web Site: www.cityoffortmorgan.com/index.aspx?nid=99. *Dir of Libr Serv,* Jody Hungenberg; Tel: 970-542-4002, E-mail: jhungenberg@cityoffortmorgan.com; *Ch,* Katie Holmburg; Tel: 970-542-4005, E-mail: kholmburg@cityoffortmorgan.com; *Tech Coordr,* Lanny Page; Tel: 970-542-4003, E-mail: lpage@cityoffortmorgan.com; *Libr Asst II,* Josie Diaz; Tel: 970-542-4008, E-mail: lpage@cityoffortmorgan.com; Staff 7 (MLS 1, Non-MLS 6)
Founded 1893. Pop 27,200; Circ 112,000
Jan 2013-Dec 2013 Income $635,000. Mats Exp $17,000. Sal $330,000
Library Holdings: Bk Vols 42,500; Per Subs 101
Special Collections: Cecil J Osborne Coll; Lute Johnson Coll; USGS Maps. Oral History
Subject Interests: Western hist
Automation Activity & Vendor Info: (Cataloging) Innovative Interfaces, Inc; (Circulation) Innovative Interfaces, Inc; (OPAC) Innovative Interfaces, Inc; (Serials) EBSCO Online
Wireless access
Function: ILL available
Publications: Page to Page (Newsletter)
Partic in Colorado Library Consortium
Special Services for the Deaf - Closed caption videos
Open Mon 9-6, Tues-Thurs 9-8, Fri & Sat 9-5
Friends of the Library Group

J MORGAN COMMUNITY COLLEGE LIBRARY*, 920 Barlow Rd, 80701-4399. SAN 301-9217. Tel: 970-542-3185. Interlibrary Loan Service Tel: 970-542-3186. Toll Free Tel: 800-622-0216. FAX: 970-542-3114. TDD: 970-542-3145. Web Site: www.morgancc.edu. *Dir,* April Amack; Tel: 970-542-3187, E-mail: april.amack@morgancc.edu; Staff 3 (MLS 2, Non-MLS 1)
Founded 1972. Fac 93
Library Holdings: Bk Vols 10,000
Automation Activity & Vendor Info: (Acquisitions) Auto-Graphics, Inc; (Cataloging) Auto-Graphics, Inc; (Circulation) Auto-Graphics, Inc; (OPAC) Auto-Graphics, Inc
Wireless access
Open Mon-Thurs 8-7, Fri 8-3

FOWLER

P FOWLER PUBLIC LIBRARY*, 400 Sixth St, 81039. SAN 301-9225. Tel: 719-263-4472. FAX: 719-224-1101. E-mail: library@fowlercolorado.com. *Librn,* Marybeth McCuistion
Founded 1891. Pop 1,570; Circ 13,600
Library Holdings: Bk Titles 8,000; Bk Vols 8,500
Wireless access
Open Mon-Sat 12-6
Friends of the Library Group

FRISCO

P SUMMIT COUNTY LIBRARY*, 0037 Peak One Dr, 80443. (Mail add: PO Box 770, 80443-0770), SAN 335-7937. Tel: 970-668-5555. FAX: 970-668-5556. Web Site: www.co.summit.co.us/library. *Dir,* Joyce Dierauer; Tel: 970-668-4130, E-mail: joyced@co.summit.co.us; *Asst Libr Dir,* Sarah Nordholm; Tel: 970-668-4131, E-mail: sarahn@co.summit.co.us; *ILL,* Becky Astuto; Tel: 970-668-4135, E-mail: beckya@co.summit.co.us; Staff 10.6 (MLS 3, Non-MLS 7.6)
Founded 1962. Pop 29,280; Circ 253,903
Jan 2012-Dec 2012 Income (Main Library and Branch(s)) $1,080,760, County $1,047,814, Other $32,946. Mats Exp $151,418, Books $103,538, Per/Ser (Incl. Access Fees) $12,489, AV Mat $25,329, Electronic Ref Mat (Incl. Access Fees) $10,062. Sal $546,961 (Prof $221,176)
Library Holdings: Audiobooks 6,060; DVDs 7,576; e-books 4,765; Large Print Bks 1,160; Bk Vols 119,642; Per Subs 220; Videos 428
Special Collections: Colorado History (Summit County History); Skiing Coll
Automation Activity & Vendor Info: (Cataloging) Innovative Interfaces, Inc; (Circulation) Innovative Interfaces, Inc; (OPAC) Innovative Interfaces, Inc
Database Vendor: EBSCOhost, Gale Cengage Learning
Wireless access
Function: Audiobks via web, Bks on cassette, Bks on CD, Children's prog, Computers for patron use, Copy machines, Free DVD rentals, Homebound delivery serv, ILL available, Microfiche/film & reading machines, Online cat, Online ref, Online searches, OverDrive digital audio bks, Photocopying/Printing, Preschool reading prog, Prog for adults, Prog for children & young adult, Pub access computers, Ref serv available, Spanish lang bks, Story hour, Summer reading prog, Tax forms, Telephone ref, VHS videos
Partic in Colorado Library Consortium; Marmot Libr Network
Open Mon-Thurs 9-7, Fri & Sat 9-5, Sun 1-5
Friends of the Library Group
Branches: 2
NORTH BRANCH, PO Box 1248, Silverthorne, 80498-1248, SAN 335-7996. Tel: 970-468-5887. FAX: 970-513-0854. *Br Mgr,* Janet Good; Staff 1 (MLS 1)
Open Mon-Thurs 9-6, Fri 9-5, Sat 1-5
Friends of the Library Group
SOUTH BRANCH, 504 Airport Rd, Breckenridge, 80424. (Mail add: PO Box 96, Breckenridge, 80424). Tel: 970-453-6098. FAX: 970-547-9637. *Br Mgr,* Pat Hasenfus; E-mail: path@co.summit.co.us
Open Mon-Thurs 9-6, Fri 9-5, Sat 1-5
Friends of the Library Group

GLENWOOD SPRINGS

J COLORADO MOUNTAIN COLLEGE*, Quigley Library, 3000 County Rd 114, 81601. SAN 335-802X. Tel: 970-947-8271. FAX: 970-947-8288. Web Site: www.coloradomtn.edu/library. *Dir,* Mindy White; Tel: 970-947-8268, E-mail: mwhite@coloradomtn.edu; *Libr Tech,* Brad Baker; *Libr Tech,* Becky Kramer; Staff 1 (MLS 1)
Founded 1968. Enrl 3,200; Fac 70
Library Holdings: CDs 153; DVDs 116; Bk Titles 27,000; Per Subs 150; Talking Bks 445; Videos 536
Special Collections: State Document Depository
Automation Activity & Vendor Info: (Cataloging) Innovative Interfaces, Inc; (Circulation) Innovative Interfaces, Inc; (Course Reserve) Innovative Interfaces, Inc; (OPAC) Innovative Interfaces, Inc; (Serials) Innovative Interfaces, Inc
Wireless access
Partic in Marmot Libr Network
Open Mon-Thurs 8am-10pm, Fri 8-5, Sat 12-5, Sun 12-8

GOLDEN

S AMERICAN ALPINE CLUB LIBRARY*, 710 Tenth St, Ste 15, 80401. SAN 311-5674. Tel: 303-384-0110, Ext 13, 303-384-0112. E-mail: library@americanalpineclub.org. Web Site: www.americanalpineclub.org. *Libr Dir,* Alex Depta; E-mail: adepta@americanalpineclub.org. Subject Specialists: *Conserv, Presv,* Alex Depta; Staff 2 (MLS 2)
Founded 1902
Library Holdings: AV Mats 600; Bks-By-Mail 20,000; Bk Vols 60,000; Per Subs 150
Special Collections: Boyle Himalayan Library; Central Asia Library
Subject Interests: Alps, Antarctic, Archives, Arctic, Glaciology, Himalayas, Maps, Mountaineering, Rare bks
Wireless access
Publications: High Places: The Blog of the American Alpine Club Library (Online only)
Friends of the Library Group

S COLORADO DEPARTMENT OF CORRECTIONS*, Colorado Correctional Center Library, 15445 S Golden Rd, 80401. (Mail add: PO Box 4020, 80401-0020), SAN 377-2594. Tel: 303-273-1635. FAX: 303-279-4407. Web Site: www.doc.state.co.us.
Library Holdings: Bk Vols 4,980; Per Subs 42
Open Mon-Thurs & Sun 12-8:30

S COLORADO RAILROAD HISTORICAL FOUNDATION, INC*, Robert W Richardson Railroad Library, 17155 W 44th Ave, 80403-1621. (Mail add: PO Box 10, 80402-0010), SAN 301-925X. Tel: 303-279-4591. Toll Free Tel: 800-365-6263. FAX: 303-279-4229. E-mail: library@crrm.org. Web Site: www.coloradorailroadmuseum.org. *Librn & Archivist,* Kathy McCardwell; E-mail: kathy@crrm.org; Staff 0.5 (MLS 0.5)
Founded 1959
Library Holdings: CDs 500; Bk Titles 10,000; Spec Interest Per Sub 50; Videos 100
Special Collections: Photograph Coll; Railroad History; Railroad Mechanical & Operating Instructions; Railroadiana Coll, maps, drawings & blueprints
Subject Interests: Railroads, Colo & Am W
Wireless access
Function: Archival coll, Microfiche/film & reading machines, Ref & res
Publications: Journal of Colorado Railroad Museum Library
Open Tues-Sat 11-3
Restriction: Open to pub for ref only

C COLORADO SCHOOL OF MINES*, Arthur Lakes Library, 1400 Illinois St, 80401-1887. SAN 301-9268. Tel: 303-273-3690. Circulation Tel: 303-273-3022. Interlibrary Loan Service Tel: 303-273-3899. Reference Tel: 303-273-3694. FAX: 303-273-3199. Web Site: library.mines.edu. *Dir,* Joanne V Lerud-Heck; E-mail: jlerud@mines.edu; *Head, Ref,* Lisa Dunn; Tel: 303-273-3687, E-mail: ldunn@mines.edu; *Acq Librn,* Heather Whitehead; Tel: 303-273-3540, E-mail: hwhitehe@mines.edu; *Cataloger/Ref Librn,* Christine Baker; Tel: 303-273-3446, E-mail: chbaker@mines.edu; *Govt Pub Librn,* Lisa Nickum; Tel: 303-273-3695, E-mail: lnickum@mines.edu; *Maps Librn,* Christopher J J Thiry; Tel: 303-273-3697, E-mail: cthiry@mines.edu; *Monograph Cat Librn,* Pamela Blome; Tel: 303-273-3691, E-mail: pblome@mines.edu; *Pub Serv Librn,* Patricia Andersen; Tel: 303-273-3652, E-mail: panderse@mines.edu; *Ref Librn,* Megan Tomeo; Tel: 303-273-3689, E-mail: mtomeo@mines.edu; *Syst Librn,* Laura Guy; Tel: 303-384-2355, E-mail: lguy@mines.edu. Subject Specialists: *Geol,* Joanne V Lerud-Heck; *Geol,* Lisa Dunn; Staff 20 (MLS 10, Non-MLS 10)
Founded 1874. Enrl 4,488; Fac 191; Highest Degree: Doctorate
Library Holdings: AV Mats 306; e-books 12,000; e-journals 25,407; Microforms 273,444; Bk Titles 192,128; Per Subs 600
Special Collections: Colorado & Mining History Coll; Energy, Environmental & Public Policy Coll. State Document Depository; US Document Depository
Subject Interests: Chem, Energy, Eng, Environ studies, Geol, Geophysics, Metallurgy, Mining, Petroleum eng, Physics
Automation Activity & Vendor Info: (Cataloging) Ex Libris Group; (Circulation) Ex Libris Group; (Course Reserve) Ex Libris Group; (ILL) Clio; (Media Booking) Ex Libris Group; (OPAC) Ex Libris Group; (Serials) Ex Libris Group
Database Vendor: American Chemical Society, American Mathematical Society, American Physical Society, ASCE Research Library, Cambridge Scientific Abstracts, EBSCO Information Services, EBSCOhost, Elsevier, Gale Cengage Learning, IEEE (Institute of Electrical & Electronics Engineers), IHS, IOP, JSTOR, Knovel, LexisNexis, McGraw-Hill, Medline, OCLC FirstSearch, OCLC WorldShare Interlibrary Loan, ProQuest, ScienceDirect, Springer-Verlag, Thomson - Web of Science, Wiley InterScience, Wilson - Wilson Web
Wireless access
Publications: Inside Arthur Lakes (Newsletter)
Partic in Colorado Alliance of Research Libraries; Colorado Library Consortium
Special Services for the Blind - Accessible computers
Open Mon-Thurs 7:30am-Midnight, Fri 7:30-6, Sat 9-5, Sun 11am-Midnight
Restriction: Badge access after hrs

S DEPARTMENT OF HUMAN SERVICES-YOUTH CORRECTIONS*, Lookout Mountain Youth Services Center Library, MSCD Lab School Library, 2901 Ford St, 80401-1117. Tel: 303-273-2767. FAX: 303-273-2638. *Librn,* Position Currently Open
Library Holdings: Bk Vols 8,000; Per Subs 15
Automation Activity & Vendor Info: (Cataloging) Follett Software; (Circulation) Follett Software
Open Mon-Fri 7:30-1

S FOOTHILLS ART CENTER*, Mary S Robinson Art Library, 809 15th St, 80401. SAN 301-9292. Tel: 303-279-3922. FAX: 303-279-3996. E-mail: info@foothillsartcenter.org. Web Site: www.foothillsartcenter.org. *Exec Dir,* Mary Ellen Williams; E-mail: maryellen@foothillsartcenter.org; *Curator,* Marianne Lorenz; E-mail: marianne@foothillsartcenter.org
Library Holdings: Bk Vols 1,130
Subject Interests: Art, Poetry
Open Tues-Sat 10-5, Sun 12-5

G NATIONAL RENEWABLE ENERGY LABORATORY LIBRARY*, 15013 Denver West Pkwy, 80401-3305. SAN 321-5644. Tel: 303-275-4215. FAX: 303-275-4222. E-mail: library@nrel.gov. *Mgr, Libr Serv,* Annette Berger; Tel: 303-275-3023, E-mail: al.berger@nrel.gov; *Librn, NREL Nat Wind Tech Ctr,* Tami Sandberg; Tel: 303-384-6963, E-mail: tami.sandberg@nrel.gov; *Librn, Syst & Tech Planning,* Jason Youngstrom; Tel: 303-275-4026, E-mail: jason.youngstrom@nrel.gov; *Coll Develop,* Judy Oberg; Tel: 303-275-4022, E-mail: judy.oberg@nrel.gov; *Doc Delivery, ILL,* Suzette Cohn; Tel: 303-275-4034, E-mail: suzette.cohn@nrel.gov; Staff 9 (MLS 6, Non-MLS 3)
Founded 1977
Subject Interests: Alternative fuels, Biomass energy, Energy efficiency, Energy policy, Photovoltaic cells, Renewable energy, Solar energy, Wave energy, Wind energy
Automation Activity & Vendor Info: (ILL) OCLC ILLiad; (OPAC) SirsiDynix; (Serials) SerialsSolutions
Wireless access
Open Mon-Fri 8-5

GRANBY

P GRAND COUNTY LIBRARY DISTRICT*, 225 E Jasper Ave, 80446. (Mail add: PO Box 1050, 80446-1050), SAN 335-8054. Tel: 970-887-2149. FAX: 970-887-3851. E-mail: granlib@gcld.org. Web Site: www.gcld.org. *Dir,* Stephanie Ralph; Staff 24 (MLS 1, Non-MLS 23)
Founded 1933. Pop 12,909; Circ 188,759
Library Holdings: AV Mats 7,773; Bk Vols 74,500; Per Subs 100
Subject Interests: Colorado
Automation Activity & Vendor Info: (Acquisitions) Innovative Interfaces, Inc; (Cataloging) Innovative Interfaces, Inc; (Circulation) Innovative Interfaces, Inc
Open Mon-Wed & Fri 10-6, Thurs 12-8, Sat 10-4
Friends of the Library Group
Branches: 5
FRASER VALLEY BRANCH, 241 Norgren Rd, Fraser, 80442. (Mail add: PO Box 160, Fraser, 80442-0421), SAN 335-8089. Tel: 970-726-5689. FAX: 970-726-9226. E-mail: fvlib@gcld.org. Web Site: www.gcld.org/fraservalley.htm. *Br Mgr,* Jeanette McQuade; E-mail: jmcquade@gcld.org; Staff 5 (Non-MLS 5)
Pop 14,584; Circ 79,900

Library Holdings: AV Mats 2,895; Large Print Bks 39; Bk Titles 21,449; Per Subs 60
Special Collections: Foreign Language, Lithuanian Coll
Open Mon-Tues 10-6, Wed-Thurs 10-7, Fri-Sat 10-3
Friends of the Library Group

GRANBY BRANCH, 55 Zero St, 80446. (Mail add: PO Box 1049, 80446-1049), SAN 335-8119. Tel: 970-887-2149. FAX: 970-887-3851. *Br Librn,* Linda Cumming; Staff 4 (Non-MLS 4)
Pop 14,489; Circ 38,500
Library Holdings: AV Mats 1,434; Large Print Bks 70; Bk Titles 10,000; Bk Vols 10,500; Per Subs 30
Special Collections: Local Newspaper, micro
Open Mon-Fri 11-7, Sat 11-4
Friends of the Library Group

HOT SULPHUR SPRINGS BRANCH, 105 Moffat, Hot Sulphur Springs, 80451. (Mail add: PO Box 336, Hot Sulphur Springs, 80451-0336), SAN 335-8143. Tel: 970-725-3942. FAX: 970-725-0570. E-mail: hsslib@gcld.org. Web Site: www.gcld.org/hss.htm. *Librn,* Lynn Shirley; Staff 2 (Non-MLS 2)
Pop 13,509
Library Holdings: AV Mats 792; Bk Titles 10,000; Per Subs 50
Special Collections: Crafts Coll
Automation Activity & Vendor Info: (Acquisitions) Innovative Interfaces, Inc
Publications: Newsletter (Bi-monthly)
Open Tues & Thurs-Sat 10-3, Wed 12-7
Friends of the Library Group

JUNIPER LIBRARY AT GRAND LAKE, 316 Garfield St, Grand Lake, 80447. (Mail add: PO Box 506, Grand Lake, 80447-0506), SAN 329-613X. Tel: 970-627-8353. FAX: 970-627-0929. E-mail: junilib@gcld.org. Web Site: www.gcld.org/juniper.htm. *Br Librn,* Sue Luton; Staff 2 (Non-MLS 2)
Pop 13,909; Circ 19,880
Library Holdings: AV Mats 1,454; Large Print Bks 50; Bk Titles 11,000; Per Subs 75
Subject Interests: Local hist
Open Tues & Fri 11-6, Wed & Thurs 11-7, Sat 11-5
Friends of the Library Group

KREMMLING BRANCH, 300 S Eighth St, Kremmling, 80459. (Mail add: PO Box 1240, Kremmling, 80459-1240), SAN 335-8178. Tel: 970-724-9228. FAX: 970-724-3419. E-mail: kremlib@gcld.org. Web Site: www.gcld.org/kremmling.htm. *Br Librn,* Emily Pedersen; E-mail: epedersen@gcld.org; Staff 3 (Non-MLS 3)
Pop 14,540; Circ 38,678
Library Holdings: AV Mats 1,207; Large Print Bks 65; Bk Titles 15,000; Bk Vols 15,017; Per Subs 30
Open Mon & Wed-Fri 10-6, Tues 10-8, Sat 10-2
Friends of the Library Group

GRAND JUNCTION

C COLORADO MESA UNIVERSITY*, Tomlinson Library, 1200 College Pl, 81501. (Mail add: 1200 North Ave, 81501), SAN 301-9365. Tel: 970-248-1862. Circulation Tel: 970-248-1244. Interlibrary Loan Service Tel: 970-248-1844. Reference Tel: 970-248-1860. Administration Tel: 970-248-1406. FAX: 970-248-1930. TDD: 970-248-1805. E-mail: libref@coloradomesa.edu. Web Site: www.coloradomesa.edu/cmulibrary. *Dir,* Dr Sarah L Cron; Tel: 970-248-1846, E-mail: slcron@coloradomesa.edu; *Head, Pub Serv,* Sylvia Rael; Tel: 970-248-1029, E-mail: srael@mesastate.edu; *Archives & Spec Coll Librn,* Aimee Brown; Tel: 970-248-1864, E-mail: aimbrown@mesastate.edu; *Instrul Serv Librn,* Barbara Borst; Tel: 970-248-1872, E-mail: bborst@mesastate.edu; *Tech Serv Adminr,* James Walker; Tel: 970-248-1863, E-mail: jwalker@mesastate.edu; *Acq,* Judy Maki; Tel: 970-248-1436, E-mail: jmaki@coloradomesa.edu; *ILL,* Rebecca Bernal; E-mail: bbernal@mesastate.edu; Staff 16 (MLS 8, Non-MLS 8)
Founded 1925. Enrl 8,844; Fac 402; Highest Degree: Master
Jul 2008-Jun 2009. Mats Exp $494,688. Sal $1,027,653
Library Holdings: AV Mats 19,149; CDs 3,247; DVDs 608; e-books 31,085; e-journals 14,800; Bk Vols 402,412; Per Subs 2,004
Special Collections: Ethridge Indian Pottery Coll; Mesa College Archives; Walter Walker Memorial Coll; Wayne Aspinall Coll
Automation Activity & Vendor Info: (Acquisitions) Innovative Interfaces, Inc; (Cataloging) Innovative Interfaces, Inc; (Circulation) Innovative Interfaces, Inc; (Course Reserve) Innovative Interfaces, Inc; (OPAC) Innovative Interfaces, Inc; (Serials) Innovative Interfaces, Inc
Wireless access
Special Services for the Deaf - Closed caption videos; TDD equip
Special Services for the Blind - Accessible computers; Assistive/Adapted tech devices, equip & products; Audio mat; Bks on cassette; Bks on CD; Computer with voice synthesizer for visually impaired persons; Dragon Naturally Speaking software; Internet workstation with adaptive software; Screen reader software; Sound rec; Sub-lending agent for Braille Inst Libr; VisualTek equip
Open Mon-Thurs 7:30am-11pm, Fri 7:30-5, Sat 10-5, Sun 1-11
Friends of the Library Group

M COMMUNITY HOSPITAL*, Medical & Consumer Health Library, 2021 N 12th St, 81501. Tel: 970-256-6209. FAX: 970-256-6526. Web Site: www.gjhosp.org. *Dir,* Janet Nelson
Library Holdings: Bk Titles 2,000; Per Subs 60
Automation Activity & Vendor Info: (Cataloging) CyberTools for Libraries; (Circulation) CyberTools for Libraries; (OPAC) CyberTools for Libraries
Open Mon, Wed & Fri 10-3, Tues & Thurs 10-7

GM DEPARTMENT OF VETERANS AFFAIRS*, Medical Center Libraries, 2121 North Ave, 81501-6428. SAN 301-9403. Tel: 970-242-0731, Ext 2254. FAX: 970-244-1309. *Librn,* Lynn Bragdon
Founded 1951
Library Holdings: AV Mats 550; Large Print Bks 100; Bk Vols 4,300; Per Subs 160
Subject Interests: Patient health educ
Partic in National Network of Libraries of Medicine
Open Mon-Fri 8-4:30
Restriction: Non-circulating to the pub

P MESA COUNTY PUBLIC LIBRARY DISTRICT*, 443 North 6th St, 81501. SAN 335-8208. Tel: 970-243-4442. Administration Tel: 970-683-2434. Administration FAX: 970-243-4744. TDD: 970-241-0500. Web Site: mesacountylibraries.org, www.mcpld.org. *Dir,* Joseph Sanchez; E-mail: jsanchez@mcpld.org; *Dir, Human Res,* Barbara Burr; *Pub Serv Dir,* Shana Wade; E-mail: swade@mcpld.org; Staff 72 (MLS 11, Non-MLS 61)
Founded 1967. Pop 147,083; Circ 1,392,070
Library Holdings: Bk Titles 215,000; Bk Vols 270,092; Per Subs 425
Special Collections: Regional History Coll
Automation Activity & Vendor Info: (Cataloging) Innovative Interfaces, Inc; (Circulation) Innovative Interfaces, Inc
Wireless access
Partic in Marmot Libr Network
Special Services for the Deaf - ADA equip
Special Services for the Blind - Accessible computers
Open Mon-Thurs 9-8, Fri 9-6, Sat 9-5, Sun 1-5
Friends of the Library Group
Branches: 7

CLIFTON BRANCH, 590 32 Rd, Ste F, Clifton, 81520-7608, SAN 335-8232. Tel: 970-434-6936. *Br Mgr,* Wynell Webster
Library Holdings: Bk Vols 13,000
Open Mon-Fri 9-6, Sat 9-4
Friends of the Library Group

COLLBRAN BRANCH, 111 Main St, Collbran, 81624-9900. (Mail add: PO Box 88, Collbran, 81624-0088), SAN 335-8267. Tel: 970-487-3545. FAX: 970-487-3716. *Br Mgr,* Sharon Jordan
Library Holdings: Bk Titles 7,000
Open Tues, Thurs & Fri 10-12 & 1-6, Sat 9-1
Friends of the Library Group

DEBEQUE JOINT BRANCH, 730 Minter Ave, DeBeque, 81630. (Mail add: PO Box 70, Debeque, 81630), SAN 335-8291. Tel: 970-283-8625. *Br Mgr,* Barbara Cook
Library Holdings: Bk Titles 8,184; Bk Vols 8,424
Open Mon-Thurs 3-7
Friends of the Library Group

FRUITA BRANCH, 324 N Coulson, Fruita, 81521, SAN 335-8321. Tel: 970-858-7703. *Br Mgr,* Giselle Smith
Open Mon 10-8, Tues-Thurs 9-7, Fri 9-6, Sat 9-4
Friends of the Library Group

GATEWAY BRANCH, 42700 Hwy No 141, Gateway, 81522. (Mail add: PO Box 387, Gateway, 81522-0387), SAN 335-833X. Tel: 970-931-2428. FAX: 970-931-2428. *Br Mgr,* Janey Raney
Library Holdings: Bk Titles 2,859
Open Wed-Fri 1-5, Sat 9-1

ORCHARD MESA, 2736 Unaweep Ave, 81503, SAN 375-0531. Tel: 970-243-0181. FAX: 970-241-9762. *Br Mgr,* Shanna Engler
Library Holdings: Bk Titles 14,000
Open Mon-Thurs 3:30-7:30

PALISADE BRANCH, 711 Iowa St, Palisade, 81526. (Mail add: PO Box 189, Palisade, 81526-0189), SAN 335-8356. Tel: 970-464-7557. FAX: 970-464-7904. *Br Mgr,* Karen Maheux
Library Holdings: Bk Titles 14,529
Open Tues-Fri 9-6, Sat 9-4
Friends of the Library Group

S MUSEUM OF WESTERN COLORADO*, Loyd Files Research Library, 462 Ute Ave, 81501. (Mail add: PO Box 20000, 81502-5020), SAN 301-9381. Tel: 970-242-0971, Ext 209. FAX: 970-242-3960. Web Site: www.wcmuseum.org/museum.htm. *Curator, Librn,* Michael Menard; E-mail: mmenard@westcomuseum.org; *Asst Librn,* Anita Caldwell
Founded 1965

Library Holdings: Bk Titles 6,000; Per Subs 14
Special Collections: Al Look Papers; Grand Junction Fire Department Coll; Local History (Western Colorado, Mesa County, Grand Junction); Mesa County Genealogical Society; Mesa County Historical Society Coll; Mesa County Newspapers, hardcopy, micro; Mesa County Oral History Coll, tapes (2400 hrs); Quahada Chapter Colorado Archaeological Society; Warren Kiefer Railroad Coll (1940-present)
Subject Interests: Archaeology, Paleontology, Railroads
Function: Archival coll
Publications: Museum Times (Newsletter)
Mem of Pathfinder Regional Library System
Restriction: Non-circulating, Open by appt only, Open to pub for ref only
Friends of the Library Group

M ST MARY'S HOSPITAL*, Dr E H Munro Library, 2635 N Seventh St, 81502. (Mail add: PO Box 1628, 81502-1628), SAN 301-9373. Tel: 970-298-2171. FAX: 970-298-7509.
Founded 1945
Library Holdings: Bk Titles 1,900; Per Subs 45
Automation Activity & Vendor Info: (Cataloging) EOS International; (Circulation) EOS International; (OPAC) EOS International; (Serials) EOS International
Database Vendor: EBSCOhost, OVID Technologies
Wireless access
Partic in Colorado Council of Medical Librarians; Medical Library Association (MLA); Midcontinental Regional Med Libr Program

GREELEY

J AIMS COMMUNITY COLLEGE*, Kiefer Library, College Ctr, 5401 W 20th St, 750.1, 80634-3002. (Mail add: PO Box 69, 80632-0069), SAN 301-942X. Tel: 970-339-6237. Circulation Tel: 970-339-6227. Reference Tel: 970-339-6569. Toll Free Tel: 800-301-5388, Ext 6227. FAX: 970-506-6937. Web Site: www.aims.edu/kieferlibrary/index.html. *Lead Librn,* Ellen Wills; Tel: 970-339-6347, E-mail: ellen.willis@aims.edu; *Bibliog Instr, Pub Serv,* Paul Jackson; Tel: 970-339-6618, E-mail: paul.jackson@aims.edu; *Bibliog Instr, Pub Serv,* Carol Satersmoen; Tel: 970-339-6589, E-mail: carol.satersmoen@aims.edu; Staff 5 (MLS 4, Non-MLS 1)
Founded 1970. Enrl 4,242; Fac 326; Highest Degree: Associate
Library Holdings: Bk Titles 37,000; Bk Vols 42,000; Per Subs 200
Special Collections: Aims Community College Archives
Automation Activity & Vendor Info: (Cataloging) TLC (The Library Corporation); (Circulation) TLC (The Library Corporation); (Course Reserve) Docutek; (ILL) OCLC; (OPAC) TLC (The Library Corporation); (Serials) TLC (The Library Corporation)
Database Vendor: EBSCOhost, Gale Cengage Learning, LexisNexis, OCLC FirstSearch, OCLC WorldShare Interlibrary Loan, ProQuest, TLC (The Library Corporation)
Wireless access
Function: Handicapped accessible, ILL available, Online searches, Orientations, Outside serv via phone, mail, e-mail & web, Photocopying/Printing, Prof lending libr, Ref serv available, Telephone ref, VHS videos, Wheelchair accessible
Partic in CCLINK; CLA; Cooperating Libraries in Consortium; OCLC Online Computer Library Center, Inc
Open Mon-Thurs 7:30-10, Fri 7:30-5

S DEPARTMENT OF HUMAN SERVICES-YOUTH CORRECTIONS*, Platte Valley Youth Services Center Library, 2200 O St, 80631-9503. Tel: 970-304-6277. FAX: 970-304-6274. Web Site: www.cdhs.state.co.us. *Librn,* Susan Eastin; E-mail: seastin@greeleyschools.org
Library Holdings: Bk Vols 6,000; Per Subs 22
Automation Activity & Vendor Info: (Cataloging) Mandarin Library Automation; (Circulation) Mandarin Library Automation
Open Mon-Fri 8:30-3

R FIRST CONGREGATIONAL CHURCH LIBRARY*, 2101 16th St, 80631. SAN 301-9438. Tel: 970-353-0828. FAX: 970-353-8447. Web Site: www.firstconggreeley.com. *Adult Serv,* Peggy Koplitz; *Adult Serv,* Norma Lord; *Ch Serv,* Phyllis Sandstedt
Library Holdings: Bk Vols 1,600
Subject Interests: Relig
Open Mon-Fri 9-4

P HIGH PLAINS LIBRARY DISTRICT, 2650 W 29th St, 80631. SAN 301-9489. Tel: 970-506-8550. Administration Tel: 970-506-8599. Toll Free Tel: 888-861-7323. FAX: 970-506-8551. Web Site: www.mylibrary.us. *Exec Dir,* Janine Reid; Tel: 970-506-8563, E-mail: jreid@highplains.us; *Assoc Dir, Pub Serv,* Elena Rosenfeld; Tel: 970-506-8567, E-mail: erosenfeld@highplains.us; Staff 50 (MLS 33, Non-MLS 17)
Founded 1931. Pop 282,963; Circ 2,824,595
Jan 2014-Dec 2014 Income (Main Library and Branch(s)) $23,399,897, County $23,040,609, Locally Generated Income $359,288. Mats Exp $1,789,777, Books $829,577, Per/Ser (Incl. Access Fees) $55,000, AV Mat $548,000, Electronic Ref Mat (Incl. Access Fees) $357,200. Sal $8,030,803
Library Holdings: Audiobooks 33,954; AV Mats 33; CDs 18,272; DVDs 76,628; e-books 25,148; Electronic Media & Resources 96; Large Print Bks 27,822; Bk Vols 661,354; Per Subs 1,076; Videos 1,994
Special Collections: Small Business & Non-Profit
Subject Interests: Colorado, Genealogy
Automation Activity & Vendor Info: (Acquisitions) Innovative Interfaces, Inc; (Cataloging) Innovative Interfaces, Inc; (Circulation) Innovative Interfaces, Inc; (ILL) OCLC; (OPAC) Innovative Interfaces, Inc; (Serials) Innovative Interfaces, Inc
Database Vendor: ABC-CLIO, ALLDATA Online, American Physical Society, Baker & Taylor, EBSCOhost, Foundation Center, Gale Cengage Learning, LearningExpress, McGraw-Hill, Mergent Online, Newsbank, OCLC FirstSearch, OCLC WorldShare Interlibrary Loan, Overdrive, Inc, Oxford Online, ProQuest, TumbleBookLibrary, World Book Online
Wireless access
Member Libraries: Eaton Public Library; Fort Lupton Public & School Library; Glenn A Jones Memorial Library; Northern Plains Public Library; Platteville Public Library
Partic in Colorado Library Consortium
Branches: 7
CARBON VALLEY REGIONAL LIBRARY, Seven Park Ave, Firestone, 80504, SAN 371-3601. Tel: 720-685-5105. FAX: 720-685-5101. *Br Mgr,* Marjorie Elwood; E-mail: melwood@highplains.us
Open Mon-Thurs 9-8, Fri & Sat 10-5, Sun 1-5
Friends of the Library Group
CENTENNIAL PARK, 2227 23rd Ave, 80634-6632, SAN 372-4891. Tel: 970-506-8600. FAX: 970-506-8601. *Libr Mgr,* Laura Burnett; Tel: 970-506-8626, E-mail: lburnett@highplains.us
Open Mon-Thurs 9-9, Fri & Sat 10-5, Sun 1-5
ERIE COMMUNITY LIBRARY, 400 Powers St, Erie, 80516. Tel: 720-685-5200. FAX: 720-685-5201. *Br Mgr,* Tony Brewer; Tel: 720-685-5202, E-mail: tbrewer@highplains.us
Open Mon-Thurs 10-8, Fri & Sat 10-5, Sun 1-5
FARR REGIONAL LIBRARY, 1939 61st Ave, 80634. Tel: 970-506-8500. FAX: 970-506-8551. *Br Mgr,* Charlene Parker; Tel: 970-506-8528, E-mail: cparker@highplains.us
Open Mon-Thurs 9-9, Fri 10-8, Sat 10-6, Sun 1-5
KERSEY LIBRARY, 413 First St, Kersey, 80644. Tel: 970-584-3244. FAX: 970-584-3944. *Br Mgr,* Sue Schmidt; E-mail: sschmidt@highplains.us
Open Mon-Thurs 1-7, Fri & Sat 10-2
LINCOLN PARK, 919 Seventh St, Ste 100, 80631, SAN 301-9462. Tel: 970-506-8460. FAX: 970-506-8461. *Br Mgr,* Cindy Osborne; Tel: 970-506-8480, E-mail: cosborne@highplains.us
Special Collections: Colorado History bks, per & oral hist tapes; Greeley & Weld County, bks, per, oral hist tapes; History of Germans from Russia (German-Russian Coll), bk, pamphlets, flm, genealogy, maps
Open Mon-Thurs 9-8, Fri & Sat 10-5, Sun 1-5
RIVERSIDE LIBRARY & CULTURAL CENTER, 3700 Golden St, Evans, 80620. *Libr Mgr,* Sue Schmidt; E-mail: sschmidt@highplains.us
Open Mon-Thurs 9-8, Fri & Sat 10-5, Sun 1-5
Bookmobiles: 2. Mgr, Rita Kadavy

S MUTUAL UFO NETWORK, INC*, MUFON Library, 2619 W 11th St Rd, Ste 21, 80634. SAN 329-1626. Toll Free Tel: 888-817-2220. Toll Free FAX: 970-352-5365. E-mail: hq@mufon.com. Web Site: www.mufon.com. *Exec Dir,* Clifford Clift; Staff 1 (Non-MLS 1)
Founded 1969
Library Holdings: Bk Titles 300; Per Subs 65
Special Collections: Unidentified Flying Objects, bks, flms
Publications: MUFON UFO Journal (Monthly)
Restriction: Open by appt only

M NORTH COLORADO MEDICAL CENTER*, Medical Library, 1801 16th St, 80631-5199. Tel: 970-350-6471. Administration Tel: 970-352-4121. FAX: 970-350-6475. Web Site: www.bannerhealth.com. *Librn,* Carmen Urich
Library Holdings: Bk Titles 3,000; Per Subs 120
Restriction: Staff use only
Branches:
WELLSPRING COMMUNITY HEALTH LIBRARY, 1801 16th St, 80631. Tel: 970-350-6074. Web Site: www.bannerhealth.com/wellspringlibrary. *Librn,* Maggie Shawcross; Fax: 970-392-2450, E-mail: maggie.shawcross@bannerhealth.com
Special Collections: Community Health Coll
Open Mon-Fri 9-4

C UNIVERSITY OF NORTHERN COLORADO LIBRARIES, James A Michener Library & Skinner Music Library, 501 20th St, 80639. SAN 335-8380. Tel: 970-351-2601. Interlibrary Loan Service Tel: 970-351-2671. Reference Tel: 970-351-2562. Automation Services Tel: 970-351-4357. FAX: 970-351-2963. Interlibrary Loan Service FAX: 970-351-2540. Web Site: library.unco.edu. *Dean,* Helen Reed; E-mail: helen.reed@unco.edu;

Assoc Dean, Joan Lamborn; E-mail: joan.lamborn@unco.edu; *Head, Archival Serv,* Jay Trask; Tel: 970-351-2322, E-mail: jay.trask@unco.edu; *Head, Instrul Serv,* Andrea Falcone; Tel: 970-351-3043, E-mail: andrea.falcone@unco.edu; *Head, Res Serv,* Annie Epperson; Tel: 970-351-1535, E-mail: annie.epperson@unco.edu; *Music Librn,* Stephen Luttmann; Tel: 970-351-2281, E-mail: stephen.luttmann@unco.edu; *Tech Serv Mgr,* Jessica Hayden; Tel: 970-351-2183, E-mail: jessica.hayden@unco.edu; *Tech Serv Mgr,* Jennifer Leffler; Tel: 970-351-1543, E-mail: jennifer.leffler@unco.edu; *Coordr, Libr Tech & Assessment,* Gregory Heald; E-mail: gregory.heald@unco.edu; *Govt Doc,* Mark Anderson; Tel: 970-351-1474, E-mail: mark.anderson@unco.edu; Staff 19.57 (MLS 19.57)
Founded 1889. Enrl 10,132; Fac 764; Highest Degree: Doctorate
Jul 2013-Jun 2014 Income $6,508,315, State $5,233,455, Locally Generated Income $89,741, Other $1,185,119. Mats Exp $2,762,653, Books $569,920, Per/Ser (Incl. Access Fees) $151,592, Other Print Mats $17,032, AV Mat $65,825, Electronic Ref Mat (Incl. Access Fees) $1,942,487, Presv $15,797. Sal $2,433,575 (Prof $1,332,400)
Library Holdings: CDs 31,140; DVDs 11,354; e-books 60,828; e-journals 56,901; Music Scores 58,288; Bk Vols 1,166,761; Per Subs 505; Videos 1,600
Special Collections: Connie Willis Coll; James A Michener Special Coll; University Archives. US Document Depository
Subject Interests: Bus, Educ, Music
Automation Activity & Vendor Info: (Acquisitions) Innovative Interfaces, Inc; (Cataloging) Innovative Interfaces, Inc; (Circulation) Innovative Interfaces, Inc; (Course Reserve) Innovative Interfaces, Inc; (Media Booking) Innovative Interfaces, Inc; (OPAC) Innovative Interfaces, Inc; (Serials) Innovative Interfaces, Inc
Database Vendor: Alexander Street Press, American Chemical Society, American Mathematical Society, American Psychological Association (APA), ARTstor, Bowker, CQ Press, CRC Press/Taylor & Francis Group, CredoReference, ebrary, EBSCOhost, Elsevier, Emerald, Gale Cengage Learning, IBISWorld, Innovative Interfaces, Inc, ISI Web of Knowledge, JSTOR, LexisNexis, Marcive, Inc, Marquis Who's Who, Mergent Online, Newsbank-Readex, OCLC FirstSearch, OCLC WorldShare Interlibrary Loan, Oxford Online, Project MUSE, ProQuest, PubMed, ReferenceUSA, Safari Books Online, Sage, SBRnet (Sports Business Research Network), ScienceDirect, SerialsSolutions, Springer-Verlag, Springshare, LLC, Thomson - Web of Science, UpToDate, Wiley, YBP Library Services
Wireless access
Publications: Library Letters (Newsletter)
Partic in Colorado Alliance of Research Libraries; Minitex Library Information Network; OCLC Online Computer Library Center, Inc
Open Mon-Fri 7:30am-Midnight, Sat 10-6, Sun Noon-Midnight
Friends of the Library Group

GUNNISON

P GUNNISON PUBLIC LIBRARY OF THE GUNNISON COUNTY LIBRARY DISTRICT*, Ann Zugelder Library, 307 N Wisconsin, 81230-2627. SAN 335-847X. Tel: 970-641-3485. Administration Tel: 970-641-7903. FAX: 970-641-4653. E-mail: gcpl@marmot.org. Web Site: www.gunnisoncountylibraries.org. *Dir,* Nancy Trimm; E-mail: ntrimm@marmot.org; *Asst Dir,* Laurel Bain; *Coordr, Ch & Youth Serv,* Kym Mcnamara
Founded 1939. Pop 15,000
Library Holdings: Bk Titles 40,000; Per Subs 70
Special Collections: Western History Coll. Oral History
Automation Activity & Vendor Info: (Cataloging) Innovative Interfaces, Inc
Wireless access
Open Mon, Wed & Fri 10-5:30, Tues & Thurs 10-8, Sat 10-4
Friends of the Library Group
Branches: 1
CRESTED BUTTE LIBRARY, 507 Maroon Ave, Crested Butte, 81224. (Mail add: PO Box 489, Crested Butte, 81224-0489), SAN 335-850X. Tel: 970-349-6535. FAX: 970-349-0348. *Br Mgr,* Debra Reich; Fax: 970-641-4653, E-mail: dreich@marmot.org; Staff 3 (Non-MLS 3)
Library Holdings: Bk Titles 11,000; Per Subs 76
Database Vendor: OCLC FirstSearch
Open Mon, Wed & Fri 10-6, Tues & Thurs 10-7, Sat 10-2
Friends of the Library Group

C WESTERN STATE COLLEGE*, Leslie J Savage Library, 600 N Adams St, 81231. SAN 301-9497. Tel: 970-943-2053. Circulation Tel: 970-943-2103. Interlibrary Loan Service Tel: 970-943-2054. FAX: 970-943-2042. Web Site: www.western.edu/lib/Welcome.html. *Dir,* Nancy Gauss; Tel: 970-943-2898, E-mail: ngauss@western.edu; *Head, Access Serv,* Eric Escalante; E-mail: eescalante@western.edu; *Info Literacy Librn,* Larry Sheret; E-mail: lsheret@western.edu; *Pub Serv Librn,* Patrick Muckleroy; Tel: 970-943-2054, E-mail: pmuckleroy@western.edu; *Pub Serv Librn, Ref,* Tiffanie Wick; Tel: 970-943-2103, E-mail: twick@western.edu; *Tech Serv Librn,* Shannon Eagles; Tel: 970-943-2399, E-mail: seagles@western.edu; Staff 7 (MLS 4, Non-MLS 3)
Founded 1901. Enrl 2,300; Fac 118; Highest Degree: Bachelor
Library Holdings: CDs 624; DVDs 291; Bk Titles 113,191; Per Subs 428; Videos 2,298
Special Collections: Colorado History (Western Americana); Western Colorado Newspapers, micro. State Document Depository; US Document Depository
Automation Activity & Vendor Info: (Acquisitions) Innovative Interfaces, Inc; (Cataloging) Innovative Interfaces, Inc; (Circulation) Innovative Interfaces, Inc; (Course Reserve) Innovative Interfaces, Inc; (ILL) OCLC; (OPAC) Innovative Interfaces, Inc; (Serials) Innovative Interfaces, Inc
Database Vendor: Cambridge Scientific Abstracts, EBSCOhost, LexisNexis, OCLC FirstSearch, OCLC WorldShare Interlibrary Loan, Wilson - Wilson Web
Partic in Dialog Corp; OCLC Online Computer Library Center, Inc
Open Mon-Thurs 7:30am-10pm, Fri 7:30-6, Sat 10-6, Sun 1-10

HAXTUN

P HAXTUN PUBLIC LIBRARY*, 141 S Colorado Ave, 80731-2711. (Mail add: PO Box 446, 80731-0446), SAN 301-9500. Tel: 970-774-6106. FAX: 970-774-6288. E-mail: townlibr@pctelcom.coop. *Dir,* Vickie Freemyer
Founded 1925. Pop 1,000; Circ 16,500
Library Holdings: AV Mats 150; Large Print Bks 250; Bk Titles 8,000; Bk Vols 8,500
Subject Interests: Agr, Art & archit, Bus & mgt, Econ, Educ
Automation Activity & Vendor Info: (Circulation) Follett Software
Special Services for the Blind - Talking bks
Open Mon, Wed & Fri 9-1, Tues & Thurs 12-4:30
Friends of the Library Group

HAYDEN

P WEST ROUTT LIBRARY DISTRICT*, Hayden Public Library, 201 E Jefferson Ave, 81639. (Mail add: PO Box 1813, 81639-1813), SAN 336-0008. Tel: 970-276-3777. FAX: 970-276-3778. *Dir,* Anna Lash; E-mail: alashhpl@gmail.com
Founded 1930. Pop 2,600
Library Holdings: Bks on Deafness & Sign Lang 15; Large Print Bks 200; Bk Titles 30,000; Per Subs 57; Talking Bks 1,223
Automation Activity & Vendor Info: (Cataloging) Follett Software; (Circulation) Follett Software
Open Mon, Tues, Thurs & Fri 10-6, Wed 10-7, Sat 10-4

HOLLY

P HOLLY PUBLIC LIBRARY*, 302 S Main, 81047-9149. (Mail add: PO Box 706, 81047-0706), SAN 301-9527. Tel: 719-537-6520. FAX: 719-537-6621. *Dir,* Nolamae S Ice; Staff 1 (Non-MLS 1)
Founded 1911. Pop 993; Circ 4,715
Jan 2009-Dec 2009 Income $5,353, City $2,818, Locally Generated Income $2,000, Other $535. Mats Exp $1,127, Books $1,002, AV Mat $125. Sal $143,247
Library Holdings: DVDs 36; Bk Titles 6,030; Bk Vols 6,530; Videos 306
Partic in Arkansas Valley Regional Library Service System
Open Tues-Fri 2-5

HOLYOKE

P HEGINBOTHAM LIBRARY*, 539 S Baxter St, 80734-1497. SAN 301-9535. Tel: 970-854-2597. FAX: 970-854-2636. *Dir,* Laura Roth
Founded 1920. Pop 2,000; Circ 25,004
Library Holdings: Bk Vols 12,500; Per Subs 40
Automation Activity & Vendor Info: (Cataloging) SirsiDynix; (Circulation) SirsiDynix; (OPAC) SirsiDynix
Partic in Colorado Library Consortium
Open Mon, Wed & Fri 12-5, Tues & Thurs 12-6, Sat 9-1
Friends of the Library Group

HOT SULPHUR SPRINGS

S GRAND COUNTY HISTORICAL ASSOCIATION LIBRARY*, 110 E Byers Ave, 80451. (Mail add: PO Box 165, 80451-0165), SAN 372-5731. Tel: 970-725-3939. FAX: 970-725-0129. E-mail: gcha@rkymtnhi.com. Web Site: grandcountymuseum.com. *Dir,* Tim Nicklas
Library Holdings: Bk Vols 200
Special Collections: Oral History
Publications: Grand County Historical Association Journal
Open Tues-Sat 10-5, Sun 1-5
Friends of the Library Group

HOTCHKISS

P DELTA COUNTY LIBRARIES*, Administrative Office, 149 E Main St, 81419. (Mail add: PO Box 858, Delta, 81416). Administration Tel: 970-872-4204. Web Site: www.deltalibraries.org. *Dir,* Annette Choszczyk; *Asst Dir,* Rhonda Duclo; E-mail: rduclo@sopris.net

Branches: 5
CEDAREDGE PUBLIC, 180 SW Sixth Ave, Cedaredge, 81413. (Mail add: PO Box 548, Cedaredge, 81413-0548), SAN 335-5683. Tel: 970-399-7674. FAX: 970-856-3170. Web Site: www.deltalibraries.org/cedaredge. *Regional Mgr,* Lea Hart; E-mail: lhart@deltalibraries.org
Founded 1911
Library Holdings: AV Mats 2,195; Large Print Bks 1,052; Bk Vols 16,677; Per Subs 45
Special Services for the Deaf - ADA equip
Special Services for the Blind - Assistive/Adapted tech devices, equip & products
Open Tues, Thurs & Fri 10-6, Wed 12-7, Sat 10-2
Friends of the Library Group
CRAWFORD PUBLIC, 545 Hwy 92, Crawford, 81415, SAN 335-5713. Tel: 970-921-3500. FAX: 970-921-4500. Web Site: www.deltalibraries.org/crawford. *Mgr,* Kit Stephenson; E-mail: kstephenson@deltalibraries.org
Founded 1981
Library Holdings: AV Mats 2,181; Bk Vols 12,381
Subject Interests: Civil War, Quilting
Open Tues, Wed & Fri 12-6, Thurs 10-6, Sat 12-4
Friends of the Library Group
DELTA PUBLIC LIBRARY, 211 W Sixth St, Delta, 81416, SAN 335-5659. Tel: 970-874-9630. FAX: 970-874-8605. *Regional Mgr,* Lea Hart; E-mail: lhart@deltalibraries.org; Staff 1 (MLS 1)
Founded 1911
Library Holdings: AV Mats 2,771; Large Print Bks 402; Bk Vols 25,595; Per Subs 185
Special Collections: Western Colorado History
Automation Activity & Vendor Info: (Acquisitions) SirsiDynix; (Cataloging) SirsiDynix; (Circulation) SirsiDynix; (ILL) ADLiB; (OPAC) SirsiDynix; (Serials) SirsiDynix
Database Vendor: EBSCOhost
Partic in Cooperating Libraries in Consortium
Special Services for the Deaf - ADA equip; Bks on deafness & sign lang
Special Services for the Blind - Accessible computers; Audio mat; Bks available with recordings; Bks on cassette; Bks on CD; Computer with voice synthesizer for visually impaired persons; Copier with enlargement capabilities; Internet workstation with adaptive software; Large print bks; Large screen computer & software; PC for handicapped; Talking bks
Open Mon 10-7, Tues-Thurs 10-6, Sat 10-3
Friends of the Library Group
HOTCHKISS PUBLIC, 149 E Mian St, 81419. (Mail add: PO Box 540, 81419), SAN 335-5748. Tel: 970-872-4153. FAX: 970-872-3834. Web Site: www.deltalibraries.org/hotchkiss. *Mgr,* Kit Stephenson
Founded 1909
Library Holdings: AV Mats 1,500; Large Print Bks 600; Bk Vols 15,356; Per Subs 40
Subject Interests: Art
Open Mon, Tues & Thurs 10-6, Wed 10-7
PAONIA PUBLIC, Two Third St, Paonia, 81428, SAN 335-5772. Tel: 970-527-3470. FAX: 970-527-3871. Web Site: www.deltalibraries.org/paonia. *Mgr,* Kit Stephenson; E-mail: kstephenson@deltalibraries.org
Founded 1932
Library Holdings: AV Mats 1,995; Large Print Bks 603; Bk Vols 20,184; Per Subs 85
Subject Interests: Hist
Open Mon & Wed-Fri 10-6, Tues 10-7, Sat 10-2
Friends of the Library Group

HUDSON

P HUDSON PUBLIC LIBRARY*, 555 Main St, 80642. (Mail add: PO Box 188, 80642-0188), SAN 301-9543. Tel: 303-536-4550. FAX: 303-536-4404. *Dir,* Teresa Redden
Founded 1951. Pop 3,200; Circ 5,925
Library Holdings: Bk Vols 10,000
Automation Activity & Vendor Info: (Cataloging) SirsiDynix; (Circulation) SirsiDynix; (OPAC) SirsiDynix
Open Mon, Tues, Thurs & Fri 10-6, Wed 10-7, Sat 9-12

HUGO

P HUGO PUBLIC LIBRARY*, 522 Second Ave, 80821. (Mail add: PO Box 429, 80821-0429), SAN 301-9551. Tel: 719-743-2325. *Dir,* Dora Mae Vassios
Founded 1921. Pop 880; Circ 8,206
Library Holdings: Bk Vols 7,500
Open Mon 3-6, Tues-Fri 2-5

IDAHO SPRINGS

P IDAHO SPRINGS PUBLIC LIBRARY*, 219 14th Ave, 80452. (Mail add: PO Box 1509, 80452-1509), SAN 301-956X. Tel: 303-567-2020. FAX: 303-567-2020. E-mail: ispl@clearcreeklibrary.org. *Dir,* Sue Lathrop; Tel: 303-569-2403, E-mail: director@clearcreeklibrary.org; Staff 5 (MLS 1, Non-MLS 4)
Founded 1904. Pop 4,500; Circ 7,000
Library Holdings: Bk Titles 25,000; Bk Vols 19,000; Per Subs 106
Special Collections: Local Newspaper (1888-present), micro
Subject Interests: Colorado, Mineralogy
Automation Activity & Vendor Info: (Cataloging) Follett Software; (Circulation) Follett Software; (OPAC) Follett Software
Function: ILL available
Open Mon & Wed 10-7, Tues & Thurs 10-6, Fri & Sat 10-5
Restriction: Residents only

IGNACIO

P IGNACIO COMMUNITY LIBRARY*, 470 Goddard Ave, 81137. (Mail add: PO Box 886, 81137-0886), SAN 371-8522. Tel: 970-563-9287. FAX: 970-563-9296. E-mail: generaldelivery@ignaciolibrary.org. Web Site: ignacio.colibraries.org. *Dir,* Leslee Shell; Tel: 970-563-9287, Ext 4, E-mail: lshell@ignaciolibrary.org; *Librn,* Marcia Vining; Tel: 970-563-9287, Ext 2, E-mail: mvining@ignaciolibrary.org; *Fac Mgr, Network Coordr,* Dixie Cook; Tel: 970-563-9287, Ext 6, E-mail: dcook@ignaciolibrary.org; Staff 6.5 (MLS 2, Non-MLS 4.5)
Founded 1991. Pop 5,500
Library Holdings: Bk Titles 20,000; Per Subs 18
Special Collections: Elbert Floyd Civil War Coll; Lincoln Coll
Automation Activity & Vendor Info: (Cataloging) SirsiDynix; (Circulation) SirsiDynix
Wireless access
Function: Computer training, Computers for patron use, Copy machines, E-Reserves, Fax serv, Free DVD rentals, Handicapped accessible, ILL available, Mail & tel request accepted, Online cat, Photocopying/Printing, Prog for adults, Prog for children & young adult, Pub access computers, Ref serv available, Story hour, Summer reading prog, Tax forms, VHS videos, Web-catalog, Wheelchair accessible
Open Mon-Thurs 9-7, Fri 9-5, Sat 9-4
Friends of the Library Group

JOHNSTOWN

P GLENN A JONES MEMORIAL LIBRARY*, 400 S Parish Ave, 80534. SAN 301-9578. Tel: 970-587-2459. FAX: 970-587-2352. *Dir,* Pat Betz; *Asst Dir,* Jill Schraeder; Staff 1 (Non-MLS 1)
Founded 1965. Pop 4,000; Circ 31,000
Library Holdings: Bk Vols 25,000; Per Subs 25
Special Collections: MacArthur Foundation Video Coll. Oral History
Automation Activity & Vendor Info: (Cataloging) SirsiDynix; (Circulation) SirsiDynix; (OPAC) SirsiDynix
Database Vendor: EBSCOhost
Publications: What's New at Library, Johnstown Breeze 1969-present (Weekly column)
Mem of High Plains Library District
Partic in Colorado Library Consortium
Open Mon, Tues & Fri 9-5, Wed & Thurs 9-8, Sat 9-1

JULESBURG

P JULESBURG PUBLIC LIBRARY*, 320 Cedar St, 80737-1545. SAN 301-9586. Tel: 970-474-2608. FAX: 970-474-2787. *Dir,* Tina Stone
Founded 1922. Pop 1,576; Circ 10,994
Library Holdings: Bk Titles 8,000
Subject Interests: Hist, Natural sci
Automation Activity & Vendor Info: (Acquisitions) SirsiDynix; (Cataloging) SirsiDynix; (Circulation) SirsiDynix
Mem of High Plains Regional Library Service System
Open Mon-Fri 9-12 & 1-5, Sat 9-12
Friends of the Library Group

LA JARA

P CONEJOS COUNTY LIBRARY*, PO Box 63, 81140-0063. SAN 376-2815. Tel: 719-274-5858. FAX: 719-274-5858. *Dir,* Maria De Herrera
Library Holdings: Bk Titles 19,000; Bk Vols 19,500; Per Subs 37
Automation Activity & Vendor Info: (Acquisitions) Follett Software
Open Mon & Thurs 8:30-4:30, Tues & Wed 8:30-7:30, Fri 8:30-3:30, Sat 9-4:30
Friends of the Library Group

LA JUNTA

S KOSHARE INDIAN MUSEUM LIBRARY*, 115 W 18th St, 81050. (Mail add: PO Box 580, 81050-0580), SAN 321-2394. Tel: 719-384-4411. FAX: 719-384-8836. Web Site: www.koshare.org. *Dir,* Susie Sarlo; E-mail: susie.sarlo@ojc.edu; Staff 2 (Non-MLS 2)
Founded 1950
Library Holdings: Bk Titles 4,000
Special Collections: Oral History
Open Mon-Sun 12-5
Restriction: Non-circulating

J OTERO JUNIOR COLLEGE, Wheeler Library, 20 Pinon Ave, 81050-3347. SAN 301-9594. Tel: 719-384-6882. Administration Tel: 719-384-6946. E-mail: wheelerlibrary@ojc.edu. Web Site: libguides.ojc.edu. *Dir,* Sue Keefer; E-mail: Sue.Keefer@ojc.edu; Staff 2 (MLS 1, Non-MLS 1)
Founded 1941. Enrl 540; Fac 38; Highest Degree: Associate
Jul 2013-Jun 2014 Income $58,620, State $3,000, Parent Institution $55,620. Mats Exp $22,870, Books $4,500, Per/Ser (Incl. Access Fees) $5,425, Electronic Ref Mat (Incl. Access Fees) $12,945. Sal $46,703
Library Holdings: AV Mats 134; Bks on Deafness & Sign Lang 3; CDs 481; DVDs 302; e-books 8,126; Electronic Media & Resources 2,800; Microforms 3; Bk Titles 6,129; Bk Vols 7,874; Per Subs 261; Videos 134
Special Collections: Southwest Coll
Automation Activity & Vendor Info: (Acquisitions) Auto-Graphics, Inc; (Cataloging) Auto-Graphics, Inc; (Circulation) Auto-Graphics, Inc; (Course Reserve) Auto-Graphics, Inc; (OPAC) Auto-Graphics, Inc; (Serials) Auto-Graphics, Inc
Database Vendor: CredoReference, EBSCO Auto Repair Reference, EBSCOhost, Gale Cengage Learning, LearningExpress, OCLC FirstSearch, Oxford Online, ProQuest, PubMed, Wilson - Wilson Web, WT Cox
Wireless access
Function: 24/7 Electronic res, 24/7 Online cat
Partic in Colorado Library Consortium
Special Services for the Deaf - ADA equip; Assisted listening device; Assistive tech; Bks on deafness & sign lang; Closed caption videos
Special Services for the Blind - Assistive/Adapted tech devices, equip & products
Open Mon-Thurs 7:30am-10pm, Fri 7:30-4, Sun (Sept-May) 5pm-10pm

S UNITED STATES NATIONAL PARK SERVICE*, Bent's Old Fort National Historic Site Library, 35110 Hwy 194 E, 81050. SAN 374-7956. Tel: 719-383-5010. FAX: 719-383-2129.
Library Holdings: Bk Vols 1,500

P WOODRUFF MEMORIAL LIBRARY*, City Library of La Junta, 522 Colorado Ave, 81050-2308. (Mail add: PO Box 479, 81050-0479), SAN 301-9608. Tel: 719-384-4612. FAX: 719-383-2514. *Dir,* Sandra Messick; Staff 11 (MLS 1, Non-MLS 10)
Founded 1888. Pop 11,500; Circ 94,000
Library Holdings: Bk Titles 37,000; Bk Vols 45,000; Per Subs 191
Special Collections: Affiliate Dat Center-1990 Census; Area Newspaper Coll. Oral History
Subject Interests: Local hist
Automation Activity & Vendor Info: (Cataloging) Follett Software; (Circulation) Follett Software; (OPAC) Follett Software
Function: Handicapped accessible, ILL available, Magnifiers for reading, Newsp ref libr, Online searches, Photocopying/Printing, Prog for adults, Prog for children & young adult, Ref serv available, Summer reading prog, Telephone ref, Wheelchair accessible
Publications: Centennial Brochure, 1988; Otero County Centennial Brochure, 1989
Open Mon-Thurs 10-8, Fri 10-5, Sat & Sun 1-5
Friends of the Library Group

LA VETA

P LA VETA REGIONAL LIBRARY DISTRICT*, La Veta Public Library, 310 S Main St, 81055. (Mail add: PO Box 28, 81055-0028), SAN 301-9616. Tel: 719-742-3572. Web Site: www.laveta.lib.co.us.
Founded 1974. Pop 1,299; Circ 53,053
Library Holdings: Bk Vols 18,000
Special Collections: History (Colorado Coll), large print
Function: Art exhibits, Bi-weekly Writer's Group, CD-ROM, Homebound delivery serv, ILL available, Photocopying/Printing, Prog for adults, Prog for children & young adult, Summer reading prog, VHS videos
Open Mon & Wed 10-8:30, Tues & Thurs-Sat 10-5:30
Friends of the Library Group
Bookmobiles: 1

LAFAYETTE

P LAFAYETTE PUBLIC LIBRARY, 775 W Baseline Rd, 80026. SAN 301-9624. Tel: 303-665-5200. FAX: 303-665-8936. E-mail: library@cityoflafayette.com. Web Site: www.cityoflafayette.com/library. *Dir,* Betsy Stroomer; Staff 8 (MLS 6, Non-MLS 2)
Founded 1923. Pop 25,000; Circ 377,000
Jan 2010-Dec 2010 Income $1,073,087, City $964,228, Locally Generated Income $108,859. Mats Exp $111,916, Books $77,726, Per/Ser (Incl. Access Fees) $7,448, AV Mat $18,960, Electronic Ref Mat (Incl. Access Fees) $7,782. Sal $625,936
Library Holdings: Audiobooks 4,479; CDs 4,215; DVDs 3,777; e-books 1,537; Electronic Media & Resources 35; Bk Titles 96,739; Per Subs 228
Special Collections: Local History Coll; Spanish Language
Automation Activity & Vendor Info: (Acquisitions) SirsiDynix; (Cataloging) SirsiDynix; (Circulation) SirsiDynix; (OPAC) SirsiDynix
Database Vendor: EBSCOhost, Facts on File, LearningExpress, OCLC FirstSearch, SirsiDynix
Wireless access
Function: 24/7 Online cat, Activity rm, Adult bk club, Archival coll, Art exhibits, Audiobks via web, Bilingual assistance for Spanish patrons, Bk club(s), Bks on CD, Children's prog, Computer training, Computers for patron use, Copy machines, E-Reserves, Electronic databases & coll, eReaders, Exhibits, Family literacy, Free DVD rentals, Handicapped accessible, Holiday prog, Homebound delivery serv, Homework prog, ILL available, Jazz prog, Large print keyboards, Magazines, Magnifiers for reading, Mail & tel request accepted, Microfiche/film & reading machines, Music CDs, Online cat, Online searches, Outreach serv, Outside serv via phone, mail, e-mail & web, OverDrive digital audio bks, Photocopying/Printing, Preschool outreach, Preschool reading prog, Prog for adults, Prog for children & young adult, Pub access computers, Ref serv available, Scanner, Senior outreach, Serves mentally handicapped consumers, Spanish lang bks, Story hour, Study rm, Summer reading prog, Tax forms, Teen prog, Telephone ref, Wheelchair accessible, Workshops
Partic in Colorado Library Consortium
Open Mon-Thurs 10-8, Fri & Sat 10-5, Sun 1-5
Friends of the Library Group

LAKE CITY

P HINSDALE COUNTY LIBRARY DISTRICT*, Lake City Public Library, 221 Silver St, 81235. (Mail add: PO Box 607, 81235-0607), SAN 376-284X. Tel: 970-944-2615. FAX: 970-944-4102. *Dir,* Elaine Gray; E-mail: elaineg@lakecityschool.org; *Asst Librn,* Taffy Bolger
Circ 2,007
Library Holdings: Bk Vols 11,550; Per Subs 44; Talking Bks 320; Videos 645
Open Mon-Fri 1-5, Sat 10-1
Friends of the Library Group

LAKEWOOD

C COLORADO CHRISTIAN UNIVERSITY*, Clifton Fowler Library, 8787 W Alameda Ave, 80226. SAN 301-8679. Tel: 303-963-3250. FAX: 303-963-3251. Web Site: www.ccu.edu/library. *Dir,* Gayle Gunderson; E-mail: ggunderson@ccu.edu; Staff 4 (MLS 4)
Founded 1974. Enrl 950; Fac 42; Highest Degree: Master
Library Holdings: Bk Titles 160,000; Per Subs 175
Subject Interests: Educ, Humanities, Music, Relig
Automation Activity & Vendor Info: (Cataloging) Innovative Interfaces, Inc - Millenium; (Circulation) Innovative Interfaces, Inc - Millenium; (Course Reserve) Innovative Interfaces, Inc - Millenium; (ILL) OCLC FirstSearch; (OPAC) Innovative Interfaces, Inc - Millenium
Database Vendor: Alexander Street Press, EBSCOhost, ProQuest
Wireless access
Partic in Colorado Library Consortium
Open Mon-Wed 7:30am-Midnight, Thurs 7:30am-10pm, Fri 8-6, Sat 10-6, Sun 2-Midnight

S HEALTH & LEARNING RESOURCE CENTER AT RMC HEALTH, 7525 W 10th Ave, 80214. SAN 377-8754. Tel: 303-239-8633. Toll Free Tel: 888-251-4772 (Colo only). FAX: 303-239-8428. E-mail: trc@rmc.org. Web Site: trc.rmc.org. Staff 3 (MLS 2, Non-MLS 1)
Founded 1994. Pop 1,200; Circ 5,000
Subject Interests: Commun develop & planning, Consumer health info, Health educ, Substance abuse prevention & treatment
Wireless access
Function: 24/7 Electronic res, 24/7 Online cat, CD-ROM, Computers for patron use, Doc delivery serv, Electronic databases & coll, ILL available, Mail loans to mem, Movies, Online cat, Prof lending libr, Ref serv available, Ref serv in person, VHS videos
Partic in Automation System Colorado Consortium; Colorado Library Consortium; National Network of Libraries of Medicine Midcontinental Region
Open Mon & Wed-Fri 7:30-4:30, Tues 11:30-4:30

P JEFFERSON COUNTY PUBLIC LIBRARY*, 10200 W 20th Ave, 80215. SAN 335-8623. Tel: 303-232-7114. Reference Tel: 303-232-9507. FAX: 303-275-2202. Web Site: jefferson.lib.co.us. *Exec Dir,* Pam Nissler; *Dep Exec Dir,* Anne Cress; Tel: 303-275-6170, E-mail: acress@jefferson.lib.co.us; *Actg Dir, Libr Serv,* Cindy Phillips; *Dir, Admin Serv,* Patricia Correia; Tel: 303-275-2206, E-mail: pcorreia@jefferson.lib.co.us; Staff 226 (MLS 56, Non-MLS 170)
Founded 1952. Pop 515,200; Circ 3,137,585
Library Holdings: AV Mats 101,000; e-books 2,594; Bk Titles 329,881; Bk Vols 1,200,000; Per Subs 4,357
Special Collections: Jefferson County Archives Coll. State Document Depository; US Document Depository
Subject Interests: Art, Colorado, Consumer health, Folk music, Law, Railroads
Automation Activity & Vendor Info: (Cataloging) Innovative Interfaces, Inc; (Circulation) Innovative Interfaces, Inc; (OPAC) Innovative Interfaces, Inc
Database Vendor: EBSCOhost, Gale Cengage Learning, Innovative Interfaces, Inc, LexisNexis, OCLC FirstSearch, Wilson - Wilson Web
Publications: Exploring Your Library (Newsletter)
Special Services for the Deaf - TDD equip
Open Mon-Fri 8-5
Friends of the Library Group
Branches: 10
ARVADA LIBRARY, 7525 W 57th Ave, Arvada, 80002, SAN 335-8658. Tel: 303-235-5275. *Libr Mgr,* Larry Domingues
Open Tues-Thurs 10-9, Fri & Sat 10-5, Sun 12-5
Friends of the Library Group
BELMAR, 555 S Alison Pkwy, 80226. TDD: 720-963-6647. *Mgr,* Marjorie Elwood
Open Mon-Thurs 10-9, Fri & Sat 10-5, Sun 12-5
Friends of the Library Group
COLUMBINE, 7706 W Bowles Ave, Littleton, 80123, SAN 335-8682. *Br Mgr,* Caroll Mannino
Open Tues-Thurs 10-9, Fri & Sat 10-5, Sun 12-5
Friends of the Library Group
CONIFER PUBLIC, 10441 Hwy 73, Conifer, 80433, SAN 376-9119. Tel: 303-982-5310. *Mgr,* Adrianne Peterson
Open Tues-Thurs 3-9, Sat 10-5, Sun 12-5
Friends of the Library Group
EDGEWATER BRANCH, 5843 W 25th Ave, Edgewater, 80214, SAN 335-8771. *Mgr,* Adrianne Peterson
Open Tues 10-5, Wed & Thurs 1-7, Fri & Sat 1-5
Friends of the Library Group
EVERGREEN BRANCH, 5000 State Hwy 73, Evergreen, 80439, SAN 335-8801. *Mgr,* Priscilla Winter
Open Tues-Thurs 10-9, Fri & Sat 10-5, Sun 12-5
Friends of the Library Group
GOLDEN LIBRARY, 1019 Tenth St, Golden, 80401, SAN 335-8836. *Mgr,* Peg Hooper
Founded 1914
Open Tues-Thurs 10-9, Fri & Sat 10-5, Sun 12-5
Friends of the Library Group
LAKEWOOD LIBRARY, 10200 W 20th Ave, 80215, SAN 335-8860. *Mgr,* Tricia Lee
Open Tues-Thurs 10-9, Fri & Sat 10-5, Sun 12-5
Friends of the Library Group
STANDLEY LAKE LIBRARY, 8485 Kipling St, Arvada, 80005, SAN 371-4918. *Mgr,* Susan McGowan
Founded 1992
Open Tues-Thurs 10-9, Fri & Sat 10-5, Sun 12-5
Friends of the Library Group
WHEAT RIDGE LIBRARY, 5475 W 32nd Ave, Wheat Ridge, 80212. *Mgr,* Adrianne Peterson
Open Tues-Thurs 11-7, Sat 11-5, Sun 12-5
Bookmobiles: 1. Supvr, Richard Allen

S LAKEWOOD'S HERITAGE CENTER LIBRARY*, 801 S Yarrow St, 80226. SAN 374-9258. Tel: 303-987-7850. Reference Tel: 303-987-7853. FAX: 303-987-7851. Web Site: www.lakewood.org. *Curator,* Win Ferrill; Staff 4 (Non-MLS 4)
Founded 1976
Library Holdings: Bk Vols 2,500
Special Collections: Oral History
Subject Interests: Local hist, Native Am
Restriction: Non-circulating, Open by appt only

G NATIONAL PARK SERVICE LIBRARY*, Denver Service Center, 12795 W Alameda Pkwy, 80228. (Mail add: PO Box 25287, Denver, 80225-0287), SAN 301-9667. Tel: 303-969-2534. FAX: 303-969-2557. E-mail: DSC_director@nps.gov. Web Site: www.nps.gov/dsc. *Librn,* Carol Simpson; E-mail: Carol_Simpson@nps.gov; Staff 1 (MLS 1)
Founded 1971
Library Holdings: Bk Titles 30,000; Per Subs 120
Subject Interests: Architect, Construction, Ecology, Hist, Landscape archit, Planning
Automation Activity & Vendor Info: (Cataloging) Ex Libris Group
Partic in OCLC Online Computer Library Center, Inc
Open Mon-Fri 8-4:30
Restriction: Open to pub for ref only

J RED ROCKS COMMUNITY COLLEGE*, Marvin Buckels Library, 13300 W Sixth Ave, 80228-1255. SAN 301-9276. Tel: 303-914-6740. FAX: 303-914-6741. E-mail: library@rrcc.edu. Web Site: www.rrcc.edu/library. *Dir of Libr Serv,* Position Currently Open
Founded 1969. Enrl 4,000; Fac 65; Highest Degree: Associate
Library Holdings: AV Mats 4,500; Bk Titles 38,000; Bk Vols 50,000; Per Subs 320
Automation Activity & Vendor Info: (Cataloging) TLC (The Library Corporation); (Circulation) TLC (The Library Corporation); (OPAC) TLC (The Library Corporation); (Serials) TLC (The Library Corporation)
Database Vendor: OCLC FirstSearch, TLC (The Library Corporation)

C ROCKY MOUNTAIN COLLEGE OF ART & DESIGN LIBRARY, 1600 Pierce St, 80214. SAN 377-9017. Tel: 303-753-6046, 303-753-6046, Ext 22405. FAX: 303-759-4970. Web Site: www.rmcad.edu. *Dir,* Hugh Thurlow; E-mail: hthurlow@rmcad.edu; Staff 6 (MLS 1, Non-MLS 5)
Founded 1962. Enrl 700; Fac 150; Highest Degree: Master
Library Holdings: DVDs 3,200; e-books 185,000; e-journals 25; Electronic Media & Resources 10; Bk Titles 15,500; Per Subs 45
Automation Activity & Vendor Info: (Cataloging) Follett Software; (Circulation) Follett Software; (OPAC) Follett Software
Database Vendor: EBSCOhost, JSTOR, OCLC, ProQuest, WT Cox
Wireless access
Open Mon-Thurs 7:45am-10pm, Fri 7:45-6, Sat 9-5
Restriction: Private libr
Friends of the Library Group

LAMAR

J LAMAR COMMUNITY COLLEGE LIBRARY*, Bowman Bldg, 2401 S Main St, 81052-3999. SAN 301-9691. Tel: 719-336-1541. FAX: 719-336-2448. Web Site: www.lamarcc.edu. *Libr Tech,* Ellen Lovell; E-mail: ellen.lovell@lamarcc.edu
Founded 1937. Enrl 609; Fac 44
Library Holdings: CDs 50; Bk Vols 15,000; Per Subs 60
Special Collections: Colorado Coll; Professional Instructor's Coll
Subject Interests: Cosmetology, Educ, Horse training mgt, Nursing
Automation Activity & Vendor Info: (Cataloging) Follett Software; (Circulation) Follett Software
Publications: Online media catalog
Open Mon-Thurs 8-8, Fri 8-5

P LAMAR PUBLIC LIBRARY*, 102 E Parmenter St, 81052-3239. SAN 301-9705. Tel: 719-336-4632. FAX: 719-336-1294. Web Site: lamarlibrary.colibraries.org. *Dir,* Debbie A Reynolds; E-mail: debbie.reynolds@ci.lamar.co.us; *Acq Librn,* Shandra Esquviel; *Outreach Serv Librn,* Sheri Eirhart; Staff 5 (MLS 1, Non-MLS 4)
Founded 1906. Pop 8,000; Circ 90,000
Library Holdings: AV Mats 1,638; Bks on Deafness & Sign Lang 15, Large Print Bks 1,452; Bk Vols 45,200; Per Subs 70; Talking Bks 1,583
Special Collections: Colorado History Coll
Subject Interests: Spanish (Lang)
Special Services for the Blind - Talking bks
Open Mon-Thurs 9-7, Fri 9-5, Sat 9-4
Friends of the Library Group

LAS ANIMAS

P LAS ANIMAS - BENT COUNTY PUBLIC LIBRARY*, 306 Fifth St, 81054. SAN 301-9713. Tel: 719-456-0111. FAX: 719-456-0112. E-mail: bent.library@bentco.lib.co.us. *Dir,* Paula Shane; *Librn,* Erin Hogue; Staff 1 (MLS 1)
Founded 1922. Pop 6,100; Circ 22,251
Library Holdings: Audiobooks 634; CDs 9; DVDs 19; Bk Titles 13,347; Per Subs 7; Videos 896
Special Collections: Bent County Coll & Llewellyn Thompson Coll
Automation Activity & Vendor Info: (Acquisitions) A-G Canada Ltd; (Cataloging) A-G Canada Ltd; (Circulation) A-G Canada Ltd; (Course Reserve) A-G Canada Ltd; (ILL) A-G Canada Ltd; (Media Booking) A-G Canada Ltd; (OPAC) A-G Canada Ltd; (Serials) A-G Canada Ltd
Database Vendor: EBSCOhost
Wireless access
Function: CD-ROM, Govt ref serv, Handicapped accessible, ILL available, Online searches, Photocopying/Printing, Prog for children & young adult, Ref serv available, Spoken cassettes & CDs, Summer reading prog, Telephone ref, VHS videos, Video lending libr, Wheelchair accessible
Partic in Colorado Library Consortium
Open Mon 12-5, Tues 10-5, Wed & Thurs 10-6, Sat 9-2

Restriction: Authorized patrons
Friends of the Library Group

LEADVILLE

J COLORADO MOUNTAIN COLLEGE, Timberline Campus Library, 901 S US Hwy 24, 80461. SAN 378-4541. Tel: 719-486-4249. Interlibrary Loan Service Tel: 719-486-4283. FAX: 719-486-3212. Web Site: library.coloradomtn.edu/timberline. *Libr Dir,* Christine Whittington; Tel: 719-486-4248, E-mail: cawhittington@coloradomtn.edu; Staff 1 (MLS 1)
Founded 1967. Enrl 287; Highest Degree: Associate
Jul 2013-Jun 2014 Income $105,617. Mats Exp $13,600, Books $7,000, Per/Ser (Incl. Access Fees) $4,500, AV Mat $1,500, Presv $600. Sal $127,000 (Prof $61,044)
Library Holdings: AV Mats 763; Bks on Deafness & Sign Lang 20; Bk Titles 15,400; Bk Vols 17,000; Per Subs 61
Special Collections: Documents relating to EPA California Gulch Superfund Site (Lake County, Colorado)
Automation Activity & Vendor Info: (Circulation) Innovative Interfaces, Inc; (OPAC) Innovative Interfaces, Inc
Wireless access
Partic in Marmot Libr Network
Open Mon-Thurs 8am-9pm, Fri 8-5, Sat 1-5, Sun 1-8

P LAKE COUNTY PUBLIC LIBRARY*, 1115 Harrison Ave, 80461-3398. SAN 335-8984. Tel: 719-486-0569. FAX: 719-486-3544. Web Site: www.leadvillepubliclibrary.com. *Dir,* Nancy S McCain; *Tech Coordr,* Shirley Crawford; *Ch Serv,* Robin Deister; *Ch Serv,* Glenda Dunn; *Circ, ILL,* Debbie Cisneros; Staff 4 (MLS 1, Non-MLS 3)
Founded 1897. Pop 9,000; Circ 36,530
Library Holdings: AV Mats 769; Bk Titles 22,700; Bk Vols 23,235; Per Subs 95
Special Collections: Early Newspapers, micro, memorabilia; Local History (Colorado Mountain History Coll), bks, photos, pamphlets. Oral History
Automation Activity & Vendor Info: (Cataloging) Follett Software; (Circulation) Follett Software
Open Mon & Wed 10-8, Tues & Thurs 10-5, Fri & Sat 1-5, Sun (Sept-May) 1-5

LIMON

COLORADO DEPARTMENT OF CORRECTIONS

S LIMON CORRECTIONAL FACILITY-LAW LIBRARY*, 49030 State Hwy 71, 80826. Tel: 719-775-9221, Ext 3238. E-mail: lcflib@plains.net. *Librn,* Lanny Shelley
Library Holdings: Bk Vols 500
Open Mon-Fri 8-4

S LIMON CORRECTIONAL FACILITY LIBRARY-GENERAL, 49030 State Hwy 71, 80826. Tel: 719-775-9221, Ext 3240. FAX: 719-775-7676. Web Site: www.doc.state.co.us. *Libr Tech,* Phyllis Wilson; E-mail: phyllis.wilson@state.co.us
Library Holdings: Bk Vols 12,000; Per Subs 55
Automation Activity & Vendor Info: (Cataloging) EOS International; (Circulation) EOS International

P LIMON MEMORIAL PUBLIC LIBRARY*, 205 E Ave, 80828. (Mail add: PO Box 236, 80828-0236), SAN 301-973X. Tel: 719-775-2163. FAX: 719-775-8808. E-mail: limonlibrary@hotmail.com. *Dir,* Lucille Reimer; *Librn,* Emily Magnin
Founded 1948. Circ 18,000
Library Holdings: Bk Vols 11,000; Per Subs 38
Special Collections: Eastern Colorado History Coll; Historical Picture Coll; Local Historical Audio Coll
Automation Activity & Vendor Info: (Acquisitions) SirsiDynix; (Cataloging) SirsiDynix; (Circulation) SirsiDynix
Special Services for the Deaf - Bks on deafness & sign lang; High interest/low vocabulary bks; Spec interest per
Open Mon-Fri 9-5

LITTLETON

J ARAPAHOE COMMUNITY COLLEGE*, Weber Center for Learning Resources, 5900 S Santa Fe Dr, 80160. SAN 301-9748. Circulation Tel: 303-797-5090. Reference Tel: 303-797-5726. E-mail: librarians@arapahoe.edu. Web Site: www.arapahoe.edu/student-resources/library. *Dir,* Lisa Grabowski; Tel: 303-797-5746, E-mail: lisa.grabowski@arapahoe.edu; *Pub Serv Librn,* Casey Lansinger; Tel: 303-797-5729, E-mail: casey.lansinger@arapahoe.edu; *Ref Librn,* Lindsay Roberts; E-mail: lindsay.roberts@arapahoe.edu; *Ref/Archives Librn,* Ann Priestman; Tel: 303-797-5731, E-mail: ann.priestman@arapahoe.edu; Staff 6 (MLS 4, Non-MLS 2)
Founded 1966. Enrl 6,400; Fac 96; Highest Degree: Associate
Jul 2012-Jun 2013. Mats Exp $125,500, Books $61,736, Per/Ser (Incl. Access Fees) $20,012, Other Print Mats $50, AV Mat $8,863, Electronic Ref Mat (Incl. Access Fees) $34,837. Sal $235,000 (Prof $161,000)
Library Holdings: AV Mats 1,812; e-books 160; Bk Vols 53,000; Per Subs 195
Subject Interests: Law
Automation Activity & Vendor Info: (Cataloging) TLC (The Library Corporation); (Circulation) TLC (The Library Corporation); (OPAC) TLC (The Library Corporation)
Database Vendor: EBSCOhost, Newsbank, OCLC FirstSearch, OCLC WorldShare Interlibrary Loan, ProQuest
Wireless access
Publications: Film & Video Tape Catalog; Serials Listing
Partic in Colorado Library Consortium
Open Mon-Thurs 7:30am-9pm, Fri 7:30-5, Sat 9-2

P EDWIN A BEMIS PUBLIC LIBRARY*, Littleton Public Library, 6014 S Datura St, 80120-2636. SAN 301-9756. Tel: 303-795-3961. FAX: 303-795-3996. TDD: 303-795-3913. E-mail: bemislib@earthlink.net. Web Site: www.littletongov.org/bemis. *Dir,* Tim Nimz; E-mail: tnimz@littletongov.org; *Dep Dir,* Phyllis Larison; E-mail: plarison@littletongov.org; *Circ Supvr,* Allyson Brown; E-mail: abrown1@littletongov.org; *Ch Serv,* Val Fetters; E-mail: vfetters@littletongov.org; *ILL,* Barbara Stoelb; E-mail: bstoelb@littletongov.org; *Tech Serv,* Robin Trehaeven; E-mail: rtrehaeven@littletongov.org; *Teen Serv,* Mark Decker; E-mail: mdecker@littletongov.org; Staff 19 (MLS 7, Non-MLS 12)
Founded 1897. Pop 48,000; Circ 538,678
Special Collections: Braille Books for Children, Adults, Teens; Colorado & Western History Coll
Subject Interests: Genealogy
Automation Activity & Vendor Info: (Acquisitions) SirsiDynix; (Cataloging) OCLC; (Circulation) SirsiDynix; (OPAC) SirsiDynix; (Serials) SirsiDynix
Wireless access
Special Services for the Deaf - High interest/low vocabulary bks; Sign lang interpreter upon request for prog; TTY equip
Special Services for the Blind - ZoomText magnification & reading software
Open Mon-Thurs 9-9, Fri & Sat 9-5, Sun 1-5
Friends of the Library Group

R DENVER SEMINARY*, Carey S Thomas Library, 6399 S Santa Fe Dr, 80120-2912. SAN 301-9004. Tel: 303-762-6962. Reference Tel: 303-762-6961. FAX: 303-762-6950. E-mail: library@denverseminary.edu. Web Site: www.denverseminary.edu/resources/our-library. *Libr Dir,* Keith Wells; Tel: 303-762-6963, E-mail: keith.wells@denverseminary.edu; *Libr Syst & Operations Dir,* Nadine Ginkel; Tel: 303-762-6955, E-mail: nadine.ginkel@denverseminary.edu; Staff 10 (MLS 4, Non-MLS 6)
Founded 1950. Enrl 875; Fac 25; Highest Degree: Doctorate
Library Holdings: Bk Titles 170,000; Per Subs 550
Subject Interests: Biblical studies, Theol
Automation Activity & Vendor Info: (Acquisitions) SirsiDynix; (Cataloging) SirsiDynix; (Circulation) SirsiDynix; (OPAC) SirsiDynix
Database Vendor: EBSCOhost, OCLC FirstSearch, SirsiDynix
Wireless access
Function: Telephone ref
Partic in OCLC Online Computer Library Center, Inc
Open Mon-Thurs 7:30am-10:30pm, Fri 7:30-6:30, Sat 9:30-5
Restriction: Circ to mem only

S FEDERAL CORRECTIONAL INSTITUTION LIBRARY*, 9595 W Quincy Ave, 80123. SAN 377-8770. Tel: 303-985-1566, Ext 1216. FAX: 303-763-2599. *Librn,* Jason Gunther; E-mail: jgunther@bop.gov
Library Holdings: Bk Titles 6,000; Per Subs 17
Open Mon-Fri 7-3:30

S LITTLETON HISTORICAL MUSEUM RESEARCH CENTER*, 6028 S Gallup, 80120. SAN 301-9764. Tel: 303-795-3950. FAX: 303-730-9818. Web Site: www.littletongov.org/museum. *Dir,* Timothy Nimz; *Curator, Dep Dir,* Lorena Donohue; E-mail: ldonohue@littletongov.org; Staff 1 (Non-MLS 1)
Founded 1969
Library Holdings: Bk Vols 800; Per Subs 10
Special Collections: Early Exploration Maps; Littleton History Coll, bks, doc, micro, photog
Restriction: Open by appt only
Friends of the Library Group

S LOCKHEED MARTIN SPACE SYSTEMS CO*, Library Information Center, 12257 S Wadsworth Blvd, 80125. (Mail add: PO Box 179, MS B9565, Denver, 80201), SAN 301-8547. Tel: 303-977-5532. FAX: 303-977-6412. *Librn,* Mark Merwin; E-mail: mark.merwin@lmco.com; Staff 3 (MLS 2, Non-MLS 1)

Founded 1955
Library Holdings: Bk Titles 19,000; Per Subs 150
Subject Interests: Aerospace sci, Electronics
Automation Activity & Vendor Info: (Circulation) Livelink for Libraries
Partic in BRS; Dialog Corp; DROLS; NASA Libraries Information System-NASA Galaxie
Restriction: Staff use only

LONGMONT

P LONGMONT PUBLIC LIBRARY*, 409 Fourth Ave, 80501-6006. SAN 301-9780. Tel. 303-651-8470. Circulation Tel: 303-651-8476 Interlibrary Loan Service Tel: 303-651-8772. Reference Tel: 303-651-8472, 303-651-8473. Administration Tel: 303-651-8475. Automation Services Tel: 303-651-8614. FAX: 303-651-8911. Interlibrary Loan Service FAX: 303-774-4363. Reference FAX: 303-774-4365. Web Site: www.ci.longmont.co.us/library.htm. *Dir,* Judith Anderson; E-mail: judith.anderson@ci.longmont.co.us; *Head, Adult Serv,* Bob Nyboer; Tel: 303-651-8471, E-mail: bob.nyboer@ci.longmont.co.us; *Head, Tech Serv,* Steve Kenworthy; *Circ Serv Mgr,* Jennifer Marks; Tel: 303-651-8474, E-mail: jennifer.marks@ci.longmont.co.us; *Ch Serv,* Elektra Greer; Tel: 303-651-8781, E-mail: elektra.greer@ci.longmont.co.us; Staff 20 (MLS 12, Non-MLS 8)
Founded 1871. Pop 80,000; Circ 1,100,000
Library Holdings: Bk Titles 260,000; Bk Vols 360,000; Per Subs 400
Special Collections: Local Newspaper Coll, to 1878, index/microfilm
Subject Interests: Automotive, Bus, Career, Consumer, Spanish
Automation Activity & Vendor Info: (Acquisitions) SirsiDynix; (Cataloging) SirsiDynix; (Circulation) SirsiDynix; (ILL) OCLC; (OPAC) SirsiDynix; (Serials) SirsiDynix
Partic in Horizon Users Group
Open Mon-Thurs (Winter) 10-9, Fri & Sat 9-5, Sun 1-5; Mon-Thurs (Summer) 9-9, Fri & Sat 9-5
Friends of the Library Group

LOUISVILLE

P LOUISVILLE PUBLIC LIBRARY*, 951 Spruce St, 80027. SAN 301-9810. Tel: 303-335-4849. FAX: 303-335-4833. Web Site: www.louisville-library.org. *Dir,* Beth Barrett; E-mail: bethb@louisvilleco.gov; *Acq, Librn I,* Ann Stoffel; E-mail: anns@louisvilleco.gov; *Adult Serv, Librn I,* Sean Lamborne; E-mail: seanl@louisvilleco.gov; *Cataloger, Librn I,* Michele Kolman-Weber; E-mail: michelew@louisvilleco.gov; *Ch, Librn I,* Kristen Bodine; E-mail: kristenb@louisvilleco.gov; *Librn I,* Sandra Richmond; *Circ Supvr,* Lisa Merly; E-mail. lisam@louisvilleco.gov; *Supvr, Pub Serv,* Aimee Schumm; E-mail: aimees@louisvilleco.gov; *Teen Serv Coordr, Librn I,* Kriska Daltonhurst; E-mail: kriskad@louisvilleco.gov; *Ch Serv,* Adrienne Gass; E-mail: adrienneg@louisvilleco.gov; Staff 17.5 (MLS 6.75, Non-MLS 10.75)
Founded 1925. Pop 31,000; Circ 545,999
Jan 2011-Dec 2011 Income $1,239,080, City $1,212,140, Other $26,940. Mats Exp $146,000, Books $76,000, Per/Ser (Incl. Access Fees) $11,000, AV Mat $24,000, Electronic Ref Mat (Incl. Access Fees) $35,000. Sal $770,150
Library Holdings: Audiobooks 2,668; AV Mats 8,000; e-books 6,483; Electronic Media & Resources 7,790; Bk Vols 76,274; Per Subs 183
Special Collections: Louisville History
Automation Activity & Vendor Info: (Acquisitions) Innovative Interfaces, Inc - Millenium; (Cataloging) Innovative Interfaces, Inc - Millenium; (Circulation) Innovative Interfaces, Inc - Millenium; (ILL) Innovative Interfaces, Inc - Millenium; (OPAC) Innovative Interfaces, Inc - Millenium
Database Vendor: ABC-CLIO, EBSCOhost, Gale Cengage Learning, infoUSA, Newsbank, OCLC FirstSearch, OCLC WorldShare Interlibrary Loan, ProQuest, ReferenceUSA
Wireless access
Function: Adult bk club, After school storytime, Art exhibits, Bks on CD, Children's prog, Computer training, Computers for patron use, Copy machines, Electronic databases & coll, Exhibits, Family literacy, Free DVD rentals, Handicapped accessible, Holiday prog, Home delivery & serv to Sr ctr & nursing homes, Homebound delivery serv, Homework prog, ILL available, Learning ctr, Mail & tel request accepted, Music CDs, Newsp ref libr, Online cat, Online ref, Online searches, Outreach serv, OverDrive digital audio bks, Photocopying/Printing, Preschool outreach, Preschool reading prog, Prog for adults, Prog for children & young adult, Pub access computers, Ref serv available, Ref serv in person, Scanner, Spanish lang bks, Story hour, Summer & winter reading prog, Summer reading prog, Teen prog, Wheelchair accessible, Winter reading prog, Workshops
Open Mon-Thurs 10-8, Fri & Sat 10-6, Sun 1-5
Friends of the Library Group

LOVELAND

P LOVELAND PUBLIC LIBRARY*, 300 N Adams Ave, 80537-5754. SAN 301-9837. Tel: 970-962-2665. Circulation Tel: 970-962-2586. Reference Tel: 970-962-2402. FAX: 970-962-2905. TDD: 970-962-2407. Web Site: www.lovelandpubliclibrary.org. *Dir,* Marcia Lewis; *Media Coordr,* Shane Adamson; Tel: 970-962-2598, E-mail: adamss1@ci.loveland.co.us; *Ch Serv,* Dawn Middleton; Tel: 970-962-2587, E-mail: middld@ci.loveland.co.us; *Ref,* Carol Hammang; Tel: 970-962-2589, E-mail: hammac@ci.loveland.co.us; Staff 46 (MLS 7, Non-MLS 39)
Founded 1905. Pop 66,250; Circ 872,870
Jan 2009-Dec 2009 Income $2,837,874, City $2,684,750, Federal $9,998, Locally Generated Income $143,126. Mats Exp $232,567, Books $159,748, AV Mat $23,679, Electronic Ref Mat (Incl. Access Fees) $49,140. Sal $1,436,120 (Prof $698,219)
Library Holdings: AV Mats 23,403; High Interest/Low Vocabulary Bk Vols 1,500; Bk Titles 137,915; Bk Vols 150,000; Per Subs 304; Talking Bks 2,102
Special Collections: Loveland History Coll; Western Americana Books Coll. Oral History
Automation Activity & Vendor Info: (Acquisitions) Innovative Interfaces, Inc; (Cataloging) Innovative Interfaces, Inc; (Circulation) Innovative Interfaces, Inc; (ILL) Innovative Interfaces, Inc; (OPAC) Innovative Interfaces, Inc; (Serials) Innovative Interfaces, Inc
Database Vendor: ALLDATA Online, EBSCOhost, infoUSA, OCLC FirstSearch, OCLC WorldShare Interlibrary Loan, Overdrive, Inc, ProQuest, ReferenceUSA, ValueLine
Wireless access
Function: Adult bk club, After school storytime, Archival coll, Art exhibits, Audio & video playback equip for onsite use, Audiobks via web, AV serv, Bk club(s), Bks on cassette, Bks on CD, Bus archives, Children's prog, Computer training, Computers for patron use, Copy machines, Digital talking bks, e-mail & chat, e-mail serv, E-Reserves, Electronic databases & coll, Exhibits, Fax serv, Free DVD rentals, Genealogy discussion group, Handicapped accessible, Holiday prog, Home delivery & serv to Sr ctr & nursing homes, Homebound delivery serv, ILL available, Instruction & testing, Magnifiers for reading, Music CDs, Newsp ref libr, Notary serv, Online cat, Online info literacy tutorials on the web & in blackboard, Online ref, Online searches, Outreach serv, Outside serv via phone, mail, e-mail & web, OverDrive digital audio bks, Photocopying/Printing, Prog for adults, Prog for children & young adult, Pub access computers, Ref serv available, Ref serv in person, Referrals accepted, Scanner, Senior computer classes, Senior outreach, Spoken cassettes & CDs, Spoken cassettes & DVDs, Story hour, Summer reading prog, Tax forms, Teen prog, Telephone ref, VHS videos, Video lending libr, Web-catalog, Wheelchair accessible, Workshops, Writing prog
Publications: Through Zethyl's Eyes: A Loveland History (Local historical information)
Partic in Cooperating Libraries in Consortium
Special Services for the Deaf - TDD equip
Special Services for the Blind - Descriptive video serv (DVS)
Open Mon-Thurs 9-8, Fri & Sat 9-6, Sun 1-5
Restriction: Badge access after hrs, In-house use for visitors, Non-circulating coll
Friends of the Library Group

M MCKEE MEDICAL CENTER*, Wellspring Health & Resource Library, 2000 Boise Ave, 80538-0830. Tel: 970-635-4048. FAX: 970 593 6006. Web Site: www.bannerhealth.com. *Librn,* Alice Ylarraz
Library Holdings: Bk Vols 3,000
Subject Interests: Consumer health
Open Mon-Fri 10-4

LYONS

P LYONS DEPOT LIBRARY*, 430 Fifth Ave, 80540. (Mail add: PO Box 49, 80540-0049), SAN 377-9858. Tel: 303-823-5165. FAX: 303-823-9532. *Dir,* Merlyn Williams; Staff 2 (Non-MLS 2)
Founded 1977. Pop 3,500; Circ 19,620
Library Holdings: AV Mats 1,700; Bk Titles 15,023; Per Subs 63
Special Collections: Local History Coll; Oral Video Archives. Oral History
Partic in Colorado Library Consortium
Open Mon 10:30-7:30, Tues & Wed 10:30-6:30, Fri & Sat 10:30-3:30
Friends of the Library Group

MANCOS

P MANCOS PUBLIC LIBRARY*, 211 W First St, 81328. (Mail add: PO Box 158, 81328-0158), SAN 301-9845. Tel: 970-533-7600. FAX: 970-533-7289. Web Site: www.mancoslibrary.org/. *Dir,* Patsy Smith; *Tech Mgr,* Victoria Peterson; Staff 3 (Non-MLS 3)
Founded 1946. Pop 3,500; Circ 22,336
Library Holdings: Bk Titles 12,000; Bk Vols 35,000; Per Subs 12
Special Collections: Southwest Coll
Automation Activity & Vendor Info: (Cataloging) Follett Software
Wireless access
Open Mon-Thurs 10-7, Fri 10-5, Sat 10-3
Friends of the Library Group

MEEKER

P MEEKER REGIONAL LIBRARY DISTRICT*, 490 Main St, 81641. SAN 301-987X. Tel: 970-878-5911. FAX: 970-878-5495. E-mail: meekerlibrary@yahoo.com. *Libr Dir,* Mike Bartlett; Staff 2 (MLS 1, Non-MLS 1)
Founded 1913. Pop 2,400; Circ 27,000
Automation Activity & Vendor Info: (Acquisitions) Book Systems; (Cataloging) Book Systems; (Circulation) Book Systems; (OPAC) Book Systems
Wireless access
Function: Adult bk club, Bks on cassette, Bks on CD, CD-ROM, Children's prog, Copy machines, e-mail & chat, Fax serv, Free DVD rentals, ILL available, Instruction & testing, Magnifiers for reading, Music CDs, Online cat, Photocopying/Printing, Prog for adults, Ref serv in person, Scanner, Serves mentally handicapped consumers, Spoken cassettes & CDs, Story hour, Summer reading prog, Tax forms, Telephone ref, VHS videos, Web-catalog
Open Mon, Wed & Fri 9:30-5:30, Tues & Thurs 9:30-9, Sat 9:30-2
Friends of the Library Group

MODEL

S COLORADO DEPARTMENT OF CORRECTIONS*, Trinidad Correctional Facility Library, 21000 Hwy 350, 81059. Tel: 719-845-3212. Administration FAX: 719-845-3237. Web Site: www.doc.state.co.us. *Libr Tech,* Miriam Westbrook
Founded 2002
Library Holdings: Bk Titles 6,200; Per Subs 35
Automation Activity & Vendor Info: (Cataloging) EOS International; (Circulation) EOS International; (OPAC) EOS International
Open Mon & Sun 9-11 & 1-4, Tues-Thurs 9-11, 1-4 & 6-8, Fri & Sat 1-4 & 6-8

MONTE VISTA

P CARNEGIE PUBLIC LIBRARY*, 120 Jefferson St, 81144-1797. SAN 301-9896. Tel: 719-852-3931. FAX: 719-852-0821. E-mail: mvcarnegie@yahoo.com. Web Site: www.montevistalibrary.org. *Dir,* Carol Lee Dugan; *Asst Dir,* Becky Gossard
Founded 1918. Pop 10,000; Circ 41,245
Jan 2007-Dec 2007 Income $128,000. Mats Exp $34,000. Sal $90,000
Library Holdings: Large Print Bks 250; Bk Vols 26,400; Talking Bks 300; Videos 400
Special Collections: Colorado History Coll; County Newspapers, microflm; Spanish Language Coll
Automation Activity & Vendor Info: (Circulation) Follett Software
Wireless access
Open Mon, Wed & Fri 10-5:30, Tues & Thurs 10-9, Sat 10-4
Friends of the Library Group
Branches: 1
SOUTH FORK BRANCH, 0031 Mall St, South Fork, 81154, SAN 320-0833. Tel: 719-873-5079. FAX: 719-873-5192. E-mail: sfbcarnegie@yahoo.com. *Dir,* Carol Lee Dugan; Fax: 719-852-0821, E-mail: cldugan@amigo.net; *Libr Tech,* Melanie Dawn Hart
Library Holdings: Audiobooks 335; CDs 239; DVDs 208; e-books 2,605; Large Print Bks 641; Music Scores 91; Bk Titles 19,000; Videos 487
Open Mon-Wed & Fri 10-5, Thurs 10-9, Sat 10-4
Friends of the Library Group

MONTROSE

P MONTROSE REGIONAL LIBRARY DISTRICT*, 320 S Second St, 81401-3909. SAN 335-9255. Tel: 970-249-9656. FAX: 970-240-1901. Web Site: www.montroselibrary.org. *Dir,* Paul H Paladino; E-mail: ppaladino@montroselibrary.org; *Head, Circ,* Pam Hollier; E-mail: phollier@montroselibrary.org; *Ch Serv,* Janet Oslund; E-mail: joslund@montroselibrary.org; *Ref,* Tania Hajjar; E-mail: thajjar@montroselibrary.org; Staff 22 (MLS 7, Non-MLS 15)
Founded 1969. Pop 40,536; Circ 305,205
Library Holdings: Audiobooks 3,650; DVDs 6,024; Bk Vols 76,284; Per Subs 211
Special Collections: Genealogy; Local History
Automation Activity & Vendor Info: (Cataloging) SirsiDynix; (Circulation) SirsiDynix; (ILL) SirsiDynix; (OPAC) SirsiDynix; (Serials) SirsiDynix
Wireless access
Function: Adult bk club, Adult literacy prog, Art exhibits, Bilingual assistance for Spanish patrons, Bks on CD, Children's prog, Computers for patron use, Copy machines, Electronic databases & coll, Free DVD rentals, Handicapped accessible, Holiday prog, ILL available, Large print keyboards, Music CDs, Online cat, Online searches, Orientations, Outreach serv, Photocopying/Printing, Preschool outreach, Prof lending libr, Prog for adults, Prog for children & young adult, Pub access computers, Ref serv available, Ref serv in person, Scanner, Senior outreach, Story hour, Summer reading prog, Tax forms, Teen prog, Telephone ref, VHS videos, Wheelchair accessible
Open Mon-Thurs 10-8, Fri 10-6, Sat 10-5, Sun 1-5
Friends of the Library Group
Branches: 2
NATURITA BRANCH, 107 W First Ave, Naturita, 81422. (Mail add: PO Box 466, Naturita, 81422-0466), SAN 335-928X. Tel: 970-865-2848. FAX: 970-865-2157. *Coordr,* Susan Rice; E-mail: srice@montroselibrary.org; *Circ,* Betty Stephens; Staff 2 (Non-MLS 2)
Library Holdings: Bk Vols 8,000
Friends of the Library Group
PARADOX BRANCH, 21501 Six Mile Rd, Paradox, 81429. (Mail add: PO Box 419, Paradox, 81429-0419), SAN 335-9344. Tel: 970-859-7236. FAX: 970-859-7235. E-mail: library@paradoxvalleyschool.org. *Br Coordr,* Raquel Schultz; Staff 2 (Non-MLS 2)
Library Holdings: Bk Vols 8,823; Per Subs 8
Function: Accelerated reader prog, Bks on cassette, Computers for patron use, Copy machines, Fax serv, Handicapped accessible, ILL available, Online searches, Photocopying/Printing, Prog for children & young adult, Pub access computers, Scanner, Spoken cassettes & CDs, Spoken cassettes & DVDs, Summer reading prog, VHS videos, Video lending libr, Wheelchair accessible, Workshops
Open Mon 12:30-7, Wed & Fri 12:30-5
Friends of the Library Group
Bookmobiles: 1. Coordr, Jeri Gilham. Bk titles 2,000

NEDERLAND

P NEDERLAND COMMUNITY LIBRARY, 200 Hwy 72 N, 80466. (Mail add: PO Box 836, 80466-0836). Tel: 303-258-1101. E-mail: nederlandlibrary@gmail.com. Web Site: www.nedlib.org. *Dir,* Neli Van Buskirk; *Asst Dir,* Geneva Mixon; E-mail: genevam.ncl@gmail.com
Library Holdings: Bk Titles 13,400; Per Subs 52
Automation Activity & Vendor Info: (Acquisitions) Horizon; (Cataloging) SirsiDynix; (Circulation) SirsiDynix; (OPAC) SirsiDynix
Wireless access
Open Mon-Thurs 10-7, Fri 10-5, Sat 10-4

NEW CASTLE

P GARFIELD COUNTY PUBLIC LIBRARY SYSTEM*, 402 W Main, 81647. (Mail add: PO Box 320, 81647-0320), SAN 335-9433. Tel: 970-984-2347. FAX: 970-984-2487. Web Site: www.garfieldlibraries.org. *Dir,* Anne Moore; *Acq Librn,* Amy Shipley; Staff 30 (MLS 2, Non-MLS 28)
Founded 1938. Pop 37,627; Circ 226,229
Library Holdings: Bk Vols 157,420; Per Subs 292
Special Collections: Oral History
Subject Interests: Agr, Alternative sources (energy), Art, Colorado
Automation Activity & Vendor Info: (Acquisitions) Innovative Interfaces, Inc; (Cataloging) Innovative Interfaces, Inc; (Circulation) Innovative Interfaces, Inc; (Course Reserve) Innovative Interfaces, Inc; (ILL) Innovative Interfaces, Inc; (Media Booking) Innovative Interfaces, Inc; (OPAC) Innovative Interfaces, Inc; (Serials) Innovative Interfaces, Inc
Database Vendor: TLC (The Library Corporation)
Open Mon-Fri 9-5
Friends of the Library Group
Branches: 6
GORDON COOPER BRANCH, 76 S Fourth St, Carbondale, 81623-2014, SAN 335-9468. Tel: 970-963-2889. FAX: 970-963-8573. *Br Mgr,* Marilyn Murphy
Library Holdings: Bk Titles 21,000
Friends of the Library Group
GLENWOOD SPRINGS BRANCH, 413 Ninth St, Glenwood Springs, 81601-3607, SAN 335-9492. Tel: 970-945-5958. FAX: 970-945-7723. *Librn,* Pat Conway
Library Holdings: Bk Vols 29,527
Friends of the Library Group
NEW CASTLE BRANCH, 402 W Main, 81647. (Mail add: PO Box 320, 81647-0320), SAN 373-5249. Tel: 970-984-2346. FAX: 970-984-2081. *Br Mgr,* Ann Honchell
Library Holdings: Bk Vols 53,173
Friends of the Library Group
PARACHUTE BRANCH, 244 Grand Valley Way, Parachute, 81635-9608, SAN 335-9506. Tel: 970-285-9870. FAX: 970-285-7477. *Br Mgr,* Holly Klinzman
Library Holdings: Bk Vols 14,131
Friends of the Library Group
RIFLE BRANCH, 107 E Second St, Rifle, 81650-2313, SAN 335-9522. Tel: 970-625-3471. FAX: 970-625-3549. *Br Mgr,* Judy Martens
Library Holdings: Bk Vols 24,431
Friends of the Library Group

SILT BRANCH, PO Box 10, Silt, 81652-0010, SAN 335-9530. Tel: 970-876-5500. FAX: 970-876-5921. *Librn,* Janine Rose
Library Holdings: Bk Vols 15,147
Friends of the Library Group

NORWOOD

P SAN MIGUEL LIBRARY DISTRICT 2*, Norwood Public Library, 1110 Lucerne St, 81423. (Mail add: PO Box 127, 81423-0127), SAN 376-2858. Tel: 970-327-4833. FAX: 970-327-4129. Web Site: www.norwoodlibrary.com. *Dir,* Barbara Youngblood; E-mail: barbaray_45@hotmail.com
Library Holdings: AV Mats 1,258; Bk Titles 11,752; Per Subs 18; Talking Bks 631
Automation Activity & Vendor Info: (Cataloging) Mandarin Library Automation; (Circulation) Mandarin Library Automation; (OPAC) Mandarin Library Automation
Open Mon, Wed, Fri & Sat 11-5, Tues & Thurs 11-8
Friends of the Library Group

NUCLA

P NUCLA PUBLIC LIBRARY*, 544 Main St, 81424. (Mail add: PO Box 129, 81424-0129), SAN 301-9942. Tel: 970-864-2166. FAX: 970-864-2123. Web Site; nuclapl.colibraries.org. *Dir,* Kathryn Redd
Pop 750; Circ 6,500
Library Holdings: CDs 250; DVDs 250; Bk Vols 6,500; Per Subs 20; Talking Bks 400; Videos 150
Wireless access
Partic in Colorado Library Consortium
Open Tues & Thurs (Winter) 1-5, Wed 3-7, Fri & Sat 10-2; Tues & Thurs-Sat (Summer) 10-6, Wed 2-7
Friends of the Library Group

OAK CREEK

P SOUTH ROUTT LIBRARY DISTRICT*, Oak Creek Public Library, 227 Dodge Ave, 80467. (Mail add: PO Box 896, 80467-0896), SAN 336-0032. Tel: 970-736-8371. FAX: 970-736-8371. E-mail: southroutlibrarydistrict@yahoo.com. *Dir,* Barry Bertollini
Library Holdings: Bk Titles 7,000; Per Subs 25
Automation Activity & Vendor Info: (Acquisitions) Book Systems; (Circulation) Book Systems; (OPAC) Book Systems
Open Mon & Wed 10-7, Tues 3-7, Fri 10-5, Sat 10-1:30
Friends of the Library Group
Branches: 1
YAMPA PUBLIC LIBRARY, 310 Main St, Yampa, 80483. (Mail add: PO Box 10, Yampa, 80483-0010), SAN 302-0398. Tel: 970-638-4654. FAX: 970-638-4654. *Librn,* Debbie Curtis
Founded 1934
Library Holdings: DVDs 400; Bk Titles 6,000; Per Subs 25
Special Collections: Local History Coll; Old Western Novels
Open Mon & Tues 10-5, Wed 10-4, Thurs 3-7, Sat 10-2

ORDWAY

P COMBINED COMMUNITY LIBRARY*, 1007 Main St, 81063-1316. SAN 301-9969. Tel: 719-267-3823. Web Site: combinedcommunity.colibraries.org. *Dir,* Theresa Hartley
Circ 4,154
Library Holdings: Bk Titles 27,000
Open Mon, Wed & Thurs 10-12 & 1-7, Fri 10-4, Sun 12-4
Friends of the Library Group

OVID

P OVID PUBLIC LIBRARY*, 400 Main St, 80744-9500. (Mail add: PO Box 245, 80744-0245), SAN 301-9993, *Librn,* Gloria Kinnison; Staff 4.375 (Non-MLS 4.375)
Founded 1927. Pop 350
Jul 2009-Jun 2010 Income $2,000, Locally Generated Income $900. Mats Exp $1,800
Library Holdings: Audiobooks 63; Large Print Bks 500; Bk Titles 4,460; Bk Vols 5,050; Talking Bks 200
Open Tues 2-5, Thurs 3-5

PAGOSA SPRINGS

P RUBY M SISSON MEMORIAL LIBRARY*, Upper San Juan Library District, 811 San Juan St, 81147. (Mail add: PO Box 849, 81147-0849), SAN 302-0002. Tel: 970-264-2209. FAX: 970-264-4764. E-mail: ruby@pagosalibrary.org. Web Site: pagosa.colibraries.org. *Dir,* Jacqueline Welch; *Ad,* Meg Wempe; *Youth Serv Librn,* Kristine MacNeill; Staff 6.1 (Non-MLS 6.1)
Founded 1985. Pop 10,000; Circ 70,000
Jan 2006-Dec 2006 Income $655,450
Library Holdings: Bk Titles 28,500; Per Subs 70
Special Collections: Chimney Rock Coll; Hershey Coll (Southwest Literature); Southwest Coll
Automation Activity & Vendor Info: (Cataloging) SirsiDynix; (Circulation) SirsiDynix; (OPAC) SirsiDynix
Database Vendor: EBSCOhost, OCLC FirstSearch, OCLC WebJunction, OCLC WorldShare Interlibrary Loan, SirsiDynix, WebMD
Wireless access
Special Services for the Blind - Bks on cassette; Large print bks
Open Mon-Wed 8:30-6, Thurs 8:30-7:30, Fri 8:30-5, Sat 9-3
Friends of the Library Group

PENROSE

P PENROSE COMMUNITY LIBRARY*, 35 Seventh Ave, 81240-0318. SAN 376-4966. Tel: 719-372-6017. Circulation Tel: 719-372-6017, Ext 23. Administration Tel: 719-372-6017, Ext 20. FAX: 719-372-6018. Web Site: penrose.colibraries.org. *Dir,* Kristi Lindsey
Founded 1992. Pop 5,000
Jan 2010-Dec 2010 Income $200,000, Locally Generated Income $178,000, Other $22,000. Mats Exp $21,500, Books $17,000, Per/Ser (Incl. Access Fees) $500, AV Mat $4,000. Sal $118,000
Library Holdings: Audiobooks 510; CDs 147; Bk Vols 15,127; Per Subs 27; Videos 2,592
Automation Activity & Vendor Info: (Cataloging) Follett Software; (Circulation) Follett Software; (OPAC) Follett Software
Wireless access
Partic in Colorado Library Consortium
Open Mon & Wed 10-8, Tues, Thurs & Fri 10-6, Sat 10-2
Friends of the Library Group

PETERSON AFB

A UNITED STATES AIR FORCE*, Peterson Air Force Base Library FL2500, 21 SVS/SVMG, 201 W Stewart Ave, Bldg 1171, 80914-1600. SAN 335-976X. Tel: 719-556-7463. FAX: 719-556-6752. *Dir,* Kathleen Kucharski; E-mail: kathy.kucharski@peterson.af.mil; Staff 6 (MLS 2, Non-MLS 4)
Founded 1950
Library Holdings: Large Print Bks 50; Bk Titles 32,000; Bk Vols 35,000; Per Subs 150
Subject Interests: Aeronaut, Bus & mgt, Mil hist, Space sci
Open Mon-Thurs 10-7, Fri 10-5, Sat 9-5
Restriction: Open to govt employees only

PINE GROVE

P PINE PUBLIC LIBRARY*, 16720 Pine Valley Rd, 80470. SAN 378-018X. Tel: 303-838-6093. FAX: 303-838-6093.
Library Holdings: Bk Titles 10,000
Open Tues & Thurs 3-6, Sat 10-2

PLATTEVILLE

P PLATTEVILLE PUBLIC LIBRARY*, 504 Marion Ave, 80651. (Mail add: PO Box 567, 80651-0567), SAN 302-0010. Tel: 970-785-2231. FAX: 970-785-0708. *Dir,* Dianne Norgren; *Asst Librn,* Donna Galusha; Staff 3 (Non-MLS 3)
Founded 1932. Pop 2,500; Circ 30,000
Library Holdings: DVDs 100; Large Print Bks 500; Bk Titles 24,000; Per Subs 25; Talking Bks 1,100; Videos 400
Subject Interests: State hist, World War II
Automation Activity & Vendor Info: (Circulation) Horizon
Mem of High Plains Library District
Open Mon, Tues & Fri 10-6, Wed & Thurs 10-8, Sat 10-2
Friends of the Library Group

PUEBLO

COLORADO DEPARTMENT OF CORRECTIONS

S LAVISTA CORRECTIONAL FACILITY LIBRARY*, 1401 W 17th St, 81003. (Mail add: PO Box 3, 81002-0003). Tel: 719-544-4800, Ext 3721. FAX: 719-583-5909. *Libr Tech II,* Kristy Scott; E-mail: kristy.scott@doc.state.co.us; Staff 3 (MLS 1, Non-MLS 2)
Automation Activity & Vendor Info: (Cataloging) EOS International; (Circulation) EOS International

S SAN CARLOS CORRECTIONAL FACILITY LIBRARY*, 1410 W 13th St, 81003-1961, SAN 376-5792. Tel: 719-544-4800, Ext 3346. FAX: 719-583-5510. *Libr Tech,* Beth Masterson
Library Holdings: Bk Titles 4,500; Per Subs 28
Automation Activity & Vendor Info: (Cataloging) EOS International; (Circulation) EOS International; (OPAC) EOS International

S YOUTH OFFENDER SERVICES*, PO Box 35010, 81003. Tel: 719-544-4800, Ext 3507. FAX: 719-583-5909. *Librn,* Elina Shneyder; *Libr Tech,* Sue Lutz; E-mail: susan.lutz@doc.state.co.us
Automation Activity & Vendor Info: (Cataloging) EOS International; (Circulation) EOS International; (OPAC) EOS International
Function: ILL available, Photocopying/Printing
Open Mon-Wed 7am-8pm, Thurs & Fri 7-4, Sat & Sun 7:30-4
Restriction: Private libr

GM COLORADO MENTAL HEALTH INSTITUTE OF PUEBLO*, Hospital Community Library, 1600 W 24th St, 81003. SAN 335-9794. Tel: 719-546-4197. Administration Tel: 719-546-4678. FAX: 719-546-4484. *Librn,* Sharon Foote; Staff 2 (MLS 1, Non-MLS 1)
Library Holdings: Audiobooks 150; DVDs 400; Large Print Bks 124; Bk Titles 960; Bk Vols 10,945; Per Subs 52; Videos 300
Automation Activity & Vendor Info: (Cataloging) Follett Software; (Circulation) Follett Software
Open Mon-Thurs 8-3:30, Fri 8-12
Restriction: Staff & patient use

C COLORADO STATE UNIVERSITY*, 2200 Bonforte Blvd, 81001-4901. SAN 302-0053. Tel: 719-549-2361. Circulation Tel: 719-549-2386. Interlibrary Loan Service Tel: 719-549-2362. Reference Tel: 719-549-2333. FAX: 719-549-2738. Web Site: library.colostate-pueblo.edu. *Dean of Libr Serv,* Rhonda Gonzales; *Dept Chair, Head, Pub Serv,* Sandy Hudock; Tel: 719-549-2527; *Dept Chair, Head, Info Mgt,* Karen Pardue; Tel: 719-549-2326; *Access Serv Librn,* Margaret Kleszynski; *Acq/ERM Librn,* Maria Hugger; *Outreach & Instruction Librn,* Julie Fronmueller; *Instruction Coordr,* Kevin Seeber; Tel: 719-549-2363; *Archivist,* Bev Allen; Tel: 719-549-2475; *Cat,* Shahrzad Khosrowpour; Staff 9 (MLS 9)
Founded 1933. Enrl 5,000; Fac 185; Highest Degree: Master
Library Holdings: AV Mats 12,990; CDs 2,553; DVDs 9,953; e-books 9,185; e-journals 8,408; Bk Vols 272,243; Per Subs 4,479
Special Collections: Colorado Chicano Movement Archives; University Archives; US Western History, pamphlets, bks. US Document Depository
Automation Activity & Vendor Info: (Acquisitions) Innovative Interfaces, Inc - Millenium; (Cataloging) Innovative Interfaces, Inc - Millenium; (Circulation) Innovative Interfaces, Inc - Millenium; (Course Reserve) Innovative Interfaces, Inc - Millenium; (ILL) Clio; (OPAC) Innovative Interfaces, Inc - Millenium; (Serials) Innovative Interfaces, Inc - Millenium
Database Vendor: Alexander Street Press, American Chemical Society, American Mathematical Society, Blackwell, CQ Press, EBSCOhost, Ex Libris Group, Gale Cengage Learning, H W Wilson, IEEE (Institute of Electrical & Electronics Engineers), Innovative Interfaces, Inc, ISI Web of Knowledge, JSTOR, Knovel, LexisNexis, Marcive, Inc, Mergent Online, Modern Language Association, Nature Publishing Group, OCLC, OVID Technologies, ProQuest, PubMed, ScienceDirect, Springer-Verlag, ValueLine, YBP Library Services
Wireless access
Open Mon-Thurs 7am-11pm, Fri 7-6, Sat 10-6, Sun 1-11

S DEPARTMENT OF HUMAN SERVICES-YOUTH CORRECTIONS*, Pueblo Youth Services Center Library, 1406 W 17th St, 81003-1929. Tel: 719-546-4928. FAX: 719-546-4917. *Librn,* Connie Espinosa; Tel: 719-546-4934, E-mail: connie.espinosa@state.co.us
Library Holdings: Bk Vols 500; Per Subs 13
Open Mon-Fri 8-4

S PUEBLO CHIEFTAIN NEWSPAPER LIBRARY*, 825 W Sixth St, 81003-2313. (Mail add: PO Box 36, 81002-0036), SAN 323-570X. Tel: 719-404-2774, 719-544-3520, Ext 491. E-mail: library@chieftain.com. Web Site: www.chieftain.com. *Librn,* Margie Strescino
Library Holdings: Bk Titles 9,500
Special Collections: The Pueblo Chieftain 1868 to present; The Star Journal 1946-1984
Open Mon-Thurs 3:30-8

P PUEBLO CITY-COUNTY LIBRARY DISTRICT, Robert Hoag Rawlings Public Library, 100 E Abriendo Ave, 81004-4290. SAN 335-9859. Tel: 719-562-5600. FAX: 719-562-5610. TDD: 719-553-0236. Web Site: www.pueblolibrary.org. *Exec Dir,* Jon Walker; Tel: 719-562-5625, E-mail: jon.walker@pueblolibrary.org; *Dir, Pub Serv,* Michael Cox; Tel: 719-562-5627, E-mail: michael.cox@pueblolibrary.org; *Human Res Dir,* Sara Rose; Tel: 719-562-5632, E-mail: sara.rose@pueblolibrary.org; *IT Dir,* Charles Hutchins; Tel: 719-562-5622, E-mail: charles.hutchins@pueblolibrary.org; *Commun Relations Mgr,* Midori Clark; Tel: 719-562-5605, E-mail: midori.clark@pueblolibrary.org; *Customer Serv Mgr,* Andrew Bregar; Tel: 719-562-5621, E-mail: andrew.bregar.barnett@pueblolibrary.org; *Ref & Readers Advisory Mgr,* Carol Rooney; Tel: 719-562-5624, E-mail: carol.rooney@pueblolibrary.org; *Spec Coll & Mus Serv Mgr,* Maria Tucker; Tel: 719-562-5626, E-mail: maria.tucker@pueblolibrary.org; *Chief Financial Officer,* Chris Brogan; Tel: 719-562-5652, E-mail: chris.brogan@pueblolibrary.org; *Tech Serv,* Teresa Valenti; Tel: 719-562-5629, E-mail: teresa.valenti@pueblolibrary.org; *Youth Serv Mgr,* Janina Goodwin; Tel: 719-562-5618, E-mail: janina.goodwin@pueblolibrary.org. Subject Specialists: *Govt doc,* Carol Rooney; *Genealogy, Hist, Mus,* Maria Tucker; Staff 88 (MLS 21, Non-MLS 67)
Founded 1891. Pop 156,737; Circ 1,278,881
Jan 2008-Dec 2008 Income (Main Library and Branch(s)) $7,752,696, City $7,060,911, Locally Generated Income $277,918, Other $413,867. Mats Exp $879,593. Sal $3,393,100
Library Holdings: AV Mats 9,285; CDs 3,019; DVDs 13,357; e-journals 19,286; Electronic Media & Resources 63; Large Print Bks 8,153; Bk Titles 189,839; Bk Vols 553,091
Special Collections: Business (Frank I Lamb Memorial Coll); Southeastern Colorado Coll, photogs; Western-American History (Western Research Coll). Oral History; State Document Depository; US Document Depository
Subject Interests: Genealogy, Hispanic studies, Local hist
Automation Activity & Vendor Info: (Acquisitions) SirsiDynix; (Cataloging) SirsiDynix; (Circulation) SirsiDynix; (ILL) OCLC WorldShare Interlibrary Loan; (OPAC) SirsiDynix; (Serials) SirsiDynix
Database Vendor: Alexander Street Press, EBSCO Information Services, Facts on File, Gale Cengage Learning, infoUSA, LearningExpress, Loislaw, OCLC FirstSearch, Oxford Online, ProQuest, SirsiDynix, ValueLine
Wireless access
Publications: Calendar of Events (Monthly); InfoZone (Newsletter)
Partic in Colorado Library Consortium
Special Services for the Deaf - Assisted listening device; TDD equip
Special Services for the Blind - Accessible computers; Assistive/Adapted tech devices, equip & products; Audio mat; BiFolkal kits; Bks on CD; Closed circuit TV magnifier; Dragon Naturally Speaking software; Large print bks; Playaways (bks on MP3); ZoomText magnification & reading software
Open Mon-Thurs 9-9, Fri & Sat 9-6, Sun 1-5
Friends of the Library Group
Branches: 6
FRANK & MARIE BARKMAN BRANCH, 1300 Jerry Murphy Rd, 81001-1862, SAN 335-9883. Tel: 719-562-5600. E-mail: bark.ref@pueblolibrary.org. *Br Mgr,* Jill Deulen; Tel: 719-562-5683, E-mail: jill.deulen@pueblolibrary.org; Staff 8 (MLS 2, Non-MLS 6)
Founded 1990
Library Holdings: Audiobooks 3,023; DVDs 3,449; Large Print Bks 1,501; Bk Titles 40,000; Bk Vols 63,729
Open Mon-Thurs 9-9, Fri & Sat 9-6
Friends of the Library Group
TOM L & ANNA MARIE GIODONE LIBRARY, 24655 US Hwy 50 E, 81006. Tel: 719-553-0360. Administration Tel: 719-553-0365. *Libr Mgr,* Kayci Barnett
GREENHORN VALLEY LIBRARY, 4801 Cibola Dr, Colorado City, 81019. Tel: 719-553-0350. *Libr Mgr,* Amy Martin; Tel: 719-553-0355, E-mail: amy.martin@pueblolibrary.org
FRANK I LAMB BRANCH, 2525 S Pueblo Blvd, 81005-2700, SAN 322-5801. Tel: 719-562-5670. FAX: 719-562-5675. ; Staff 6 (MLS 2, Non-MLS 4)
Founded 1984. Circ 186,135
Open Mon-Thurs 9-9, Fri & Sat 9-6
Friends of the Library Group
PUEBLO WEST LIBRARY, 298 S Joe Martinez Blvd, Pueblo West, 81007-2740, SAN 377-6360. Tel: 719-562-5660. FAX: 719-562-5665. *Libr Mgr,* Cindy Shimizu; Tel: 719-562-5662, Fax: 719-562-5663, E-mail: cindy.shimizu@pueblolibrary.org; Staff 9 (MLS 4, Non-MLS 5)
Founded 1997. Circ 186,135
Open Mon-Thurs 9-9, Fri & Sat 9-6
Friends of the Library Group
PATRICK A LUCERO LIBRARY, 1315 E Seven St, 81001. Tel: 719-652-5600. *Br Mgr,* Diann Logie; E-mail: diann.logie@pueblolibrary.org
Open Mon-Thurs 10-7, Fri & Sat 10-6

J PUEBLO COMMUNITY COLLEGE LIBRARY, 900 W Orman Ave, 81004-1430. SAN 325-2264. Tel: 719-549-3308. FAX: 719-549-3309. Web Site: www.pueblocc.edu/campusresources/library. *Dir, Libr Serv,* W Jeanne Gardner; E-mail: Jeanne.Gardner@pueblocc.edu; *Circ Serv,* Christina McGrath; *Circ Serv,* Effie Romero; *Tech Serv,* Tracy Overton; Staff 4 (MLS 1, Non-MLS 3)
Founded 1979. Enrl 12,876; Fac 112; Highest Degree: Associate
Jul 2013-Jun 2014. Mats Exp $45,741, Books $2,233, Per/Ser (Incl. Access Fees) $29,763, Other Print Mats $6,770, AV Mat $3,106, Electronic Ref Mat (Incl. Access Fees) $3,869
Library Holdings: AV Mats 343; Braille Volumes 1; CDs 428; DVDs 4,996; e-books 20,213; e-journals 8,908; Electronic Media & Resources 30; Microforms 115; Bk Titles 18,484; Bk Vols 19,119; Per Subs 40; Talking Bks 1; Videos 150
Special Collections: College Archives
Subject Interests: Criminal justice, Dental hygiene, Respiratory therapy
Automation Activity & Vendor Info: (Acquisitions) Auto-Graphics, Inc; (Cataloging) OCLC; (Circulation) Auto-Graphics, Inc; (OPAC) Auto-Graphics, Inc; (Serials) Auto-Graphics, Inc

Database Vendor: Auto-Graphics, Inc, ebrary, EBSCOhost, Loislaw, Oxford Online, Sage, STAT!Ref (Teton Data Systems)
Wireless access
Function: Archival coll, Distance learning, ILL available, Online cat, Orientations, Ref serv available
Partic in Colorado Library Consortium; Lyrasis
Special Services for the Deaf - ADA equip; Bks on deafness & sign lang; Closed caption videos
Special Services for the Blind - Digital talking bk machines
Open Mon-Thurs 8-8, Fri 8-4, Sat 10-2, Sun 1-4
Restriction: Open to pub for ref & circ; with some limitations, Open to students, fac & staff, Photo ID required for access

M SAINT MARY CORWIN MEDICAL CENTER*, Finney Memorial Library, 1008 Minnequa Ave, 81004-9988. SAN 302-0045. Tel: 719-560-5598. FAX: 719-560-4018. Web Site: www.stmarycorwin.org. *Dir, Pub Relations,* Rochelle Kelly DeVargas; E-mail: rochellekellydevargas@centura.org; *Asst Librn,* Amanda Marez; E-mail: amandamarez@centura.org
Founded 1818
Library Holdings: Bk Titles 600; Per Subs 100
Subject Interests: Cardiology, Internal med, Nursing, Obstetrics & gynecology, Oncology, Pediatrics, Surgery
Partic in Arkansas Valley Regional Library Service System
Branches:
M DORCY CANCER CENTER RESOURCE LIBRARY, 1008 Minnequa Ave, 81004. Tel: 719-557-4000. Toll Free Tel: 800-228-4039. *Dir, Mkt & Communications,* Rochelle Kelly DeVargas; E-mail: rochellekellydevargas@centura.org
Special Collections: Cancer Resources
Open Mon-Thurs 8:30-2:30

RANGELY

J COLORADO NORTHWESTERN COMMUNITY COLLEGE LIBRARY*, 500 Kennedy Dr, CNCC-Box 29, 81648. SAN 302-0061. Tel: 970-675-3334, 970-675-3576. Toll Free Tel: 800-562-1105, Ext 334. FAX: 970-675-3267. Toll Free FAX: 800-562-1105. Web Site: www.cncc.edu. *Acq Mgr, Interim Librn,* Leana J Cox; E-mail: leana.cox@cncc.edu; Staff 1 (Non-MLS 1)
Founded 1962. Enrl 350; Fac 43; Highest Degree: Associate
Library Holdings: AV Mats 360; Bks on Deafness & Sign Lang 22; CDs 120; DVDs 870; e-books 774; High Interest/Low Vocabulary Bk Vols 632; Large Print Bks 120; Bk Titles 21,356; Bk Vols 27,935; Per Subs 109; Talking Bks 936; Videos 2,210
Special Collections: Colorado History Coll
Subject Interests: Drama, Native Am, Rare bks
Automation Activity & Vendor Info: (Cataloging) Follett Software; (Circulation) Follett Software; (Serials) Follett Software
Database Vendor: EBSCOhost, LexisNexis, OCLC FirstSearch, ProQuest, Wilson - Wilson Web
Function: Spoken cassettes & CDs, VCDs, VHS videos, Wheelchair accessible, Workshops
Partic in Capitol Area Library Consortium; Cooperating Libraries in Consortium; Western Colorado Academic Library Consortium (WCALC)
Open Mon-Thurs 7:30am-9:30pm, Fri 8-5, Sat 1-5, Sun 1-10
Friends of the Library Group

P RANGELY REGIONAL LIBRARY, 109 E Main, 81648-2737. SAN 302-007X. Tel: 970-675-8811. FAX: 970-675-8844. *Dir,* Amorette Hawkins; Staff 4 (Non-MLS 4)
Founded 1960. Pop 2,400; Circ 17,700
Library Holdings: Bk Titles 20,000; Bk Vols 23,000; Per Subs 25
Automation Activity & Vendor Info: (Cataloging) Follett Software; (Circulation) Follett Software
Wireless access
Open Mon & Wed-Fri 10-6, Tues 10-8, Sat 10-3

RED FEATHER LAKES

P RED FEATHER LAKES COMMUNITY LIBRARY*, 71 Firehouse Lane, 80545. (Mail add: PO Box 123, 80545-0123). Tel: 970-881-2664. FAX: 970-881-2836. E-mail: redfeatherlibrary@gmail.com. Web Site: redfeather.colibraries.org. *Libr Dir,* Creed Kidd; *Pub Serv Librn,* Jeanette Heath; *Pub Serv Librn,* Darlene Kilpatrick
Founded 1969. Pop 5,000
Library Holdings: AV Mats 500; Large Print Bks 300; Bk Vols 13,000; Per Subs 20; Talking Bks 1,500; Videos 400
Automation Activity & Vendor Info: (Cataloging) SirsiDynix; (Circulation) SirsiDynix; (OPAC) SirsiDynix
Wireless access
Function: Adult bk club, Art exhibits, Bi-weekly Writer's Group, Bks on cassette, Bks on CD, Children's prog, Computer training, Computers for patron use, Copy machines, Fax serv, Free DVD rentals, Holiday prog, ILL available, Magnifiers for reading, Music CDs, Online cat, Photocopying/Printing, Prog for adults, Prog for children & young adult, Pub access computers, Ref & res, Story hour, Summer reading prog, Tax forms, Teen prog, Workshops, Writing prog
Open Tues-Sat 10-6
Friends of the Library Group

RIDGWAY

P RIDGWAY PUBLIC LIBRARY*, 300 Charles St, 81432. Tel: 970-626-5252. FAX: 970-626-5252. E-mail: library@ouraynet.com. Web Site: www1.youseemore.com/ridgwayPL. *Dir,* Kristen Moberg
Pop 2,350
Library Holdings: AV Mats 500; Bk Titles 15,000
Open Mon, Tues & Thurs 10-6, Wed 10-7, Fri 10-5, Sat & Sun 10-3
Friends of the Library Group

RIFLE

S COLORADO DEPARTMENT OF CORRECTIONS*, Rifle Correctional Center Library, 0200 County Rd 219, 81650. SAN 327-7666. Tel: 970-625-1700, Ext 3064. FAX: 970-625-7565. Web Site: www.doc.state.co.us. *Libr Tech,* Edd Carter
Library Holdings: AV Mats 300; Bk Titles 5,200; Per Subs 24
Automation Activity & Vendor Info: (Cataloging) EOS International; (Circulation) EOS International
Open Mon-Wed & Sun 1-4 & 6-8, Thurs & Sat 9-11 & 1-4, Fri 9-11, 1-4 & 6-8

ROCKY FORD

P ROCKY FORD PUBLIC LIBRARY*, 400 S Tenth St, 81067. SAN 302-0096. Tel: 719-254-6641. FAX: 719-254-6647. E-mail: rflib@rockyford.lib.co.us. Web Site: rockyford.colibraries.org. *Dir,* Sheila Henry; Staff 4 (MLS 1, Non-MLS 3)
Founded 1905. Pop 5,000; Circ 20,000
Library Holdings: CDs 531; Large Print Bks 1,272; Bk Titles 21,000; Bk Vols 18,000; Per Subs 4; Talking Bks 460; Videos 517
Automation Activity & Vendor Info: (Cataloging) Auto-Graphics, Inc; (Circulation) Auto-Graphics, Inc; (OPAC) Auto-Graphics, Inc
Database Vendor: EBSCO Auto Repair Reference, EBSCO Information Services, EBSCOhost, LearningExpress, Newsbank
Wireless access
Function: Homebound delivery serv, ILL available, Magnifiers for reading, Music CDs, Online cat, Photocopying/Printing, Preschool outreach, Prog for adults, Prog for children & young adult, Scanner, Senior outreach, Story hour, Summer reading prog, Tax forms, VHS videos, Web-catalog, Wheelchair accessible
Special Services for the Deaf - Assisted listening device; Closed caption videos; Video & TTY relay via computer
Special Services for the Blind - Audio mat; Bks available with recordings; Bks on cassette; Bks on CD; Cassette playback machines; Cassettes; Closed circuit TV; Copier with enlargement capabilities; Home delivery serv; Integrated libr/media serv; Large print & cassettes; Large print bks; Large screen computer & software; Large type calculator; Low vision equip; Magnifiers
Open Mon-Fri 10-6, Sat 10-2
Friends of the Library Group

SAGUACHE

P SAGUACHE COUNTY PUBLIC LIBRARY*, 702 Pitkin Ave, 81149. (Mail add: PO Box 448, 81149-0448), SAN 335-9913. Tel: 719-655-2551. Administration Tel: 719-655-2231. FAX: 719-655-2579. Web Site: www.slv.org/saguachelibrary. *Dir,* Carla Mondragon; E-mail: cjean_mond@hotmail.com
Founded 1950. Pop 600; Circ 16,000
Library Holdings: Bk Titles 20,000; Per Subs 52
Special Collections: American History & Memorials; Bicentennial History; Colorado & Southwest History; Cookbooks; Juvenile; Saguache & Saguache County; Southwest Fiction & Nonfiction
Subject Interests: Am hist, Colorado
Automation Activity & Vendor Info: (Cataloging) SirsiDynix; (Circulation) SirsiDynix; (Course Reserve) Horizon; (OPAC) SirsiDynix
Partic in Colorado Library Consortium
Open Mon & Wed 10-5:30, Tues & Thurs 10-5:30 & 7-9, Fri 1-5, Sat 9-1
Friends of the Library Group

SALIDA

P SALIDA REGIONAL LIBRARY*, 405 E St, 81201. SAN 302-010X. Tel: 719-539-4826. Web Site: www.salidalibrary.org. *Dir,* Jeff Donlan; E-mail: jdonlan@salidalibrary.org; *Cat, Computer Serv,* Vic Mabus; E-mail: vmabus@salidalibrary.org; *Ch Serv,* Becky Nelson; E-mail: bnelson@salidalibrary.org; Staff 13 (Non-MLS 13)
Founded 1908. Pop 9,000; Circ 196,372
Jan 2010-Dec 2010 Income $697,708. Mats Exp $156,521. Sal $263,810

Library Holdings: Audiobooks 3,514; Bk Vols 57,645; Per Subs 205; Videos 5,273
Special Collections: Local History Coll; Sheet Music Coll
Automation Activity & Vendor Info: (Acquisitions) SirsiDynix; (Cataloging) SirsiDynix; (Circulation) SirsiDynix; (OPAC) SirsiDynix; (Serials) SirsiDynix
Wireless access
Publications: Library Information (Brochure)
Open Mon-Fri 9-8:30, Sat 9-5:30, Sun 1-5

SAN LUIS

P COSTILLA COUNTY LIBRARY*, 418 Gasper St, 81152. (Mail add: PO Box 351, 81152-0351), SAN 302-0118. Tel: 719-672-3309. FAX: 719-672-3309. Web Site: www.costilla-county.com/library.html. *Dir,* Sherry Fischer
Founded 1972. Pop 3,660
Jan 2007-Dec 2007 Income (Main Library and Branch(s)) $35,200, County $35,000, Locally Generated Income $200. Mats Exp $700, Books $400, Per/Ser (Incl. Access Fees) $100, Electronic Ref Mat (Incl. Access Fees) $200. Sal $43,680
Library Holdings: CDs 5; DVDs 5; Bk Titles 10,000; Per Subs 4; Videos 20
Special Collections: Bilingual (Children; Bilingual-Bicultural); Literature (Adult Spanish Book); Minority Studies (Southwest Chicano); Solar Energy Coll. Oral History
Partic in Colorado Library Consortium
Open Mon-Thurs 8-5, Fri 8-4:30
Branches: 1
BLANCA-FT GARLAND BRANCH, 17591 E Hwy 160, Blanca, 81123. (Mail add: PO Box 310, Blanca, 81123-0310). Tel: 719-379-3945. FAX: 719-379-3945. *Asst Dir,* Paula Harrison
Founded 2007
Library Holdings: CDs 10; DVDs 10; Large Print Bks 20; Bk Titles 5,000; Videos 20
Open Mon-Wed 10-5, Thurs 10-6

SECURITY

P SECURITY PUBLIC LIBRARY*, 715 Aspen Dr, 80911-1807. SAN 302-0126. Tel: 719-391-3191. Circulation Tel: 719-391-3196. Reference Tel: 719-391-3195. FAX: 719-392-7641. Web Site: www.securitypubliclibrary.org. *Libr Dir,* Susan Schmitz-Garrett; Tel: 710-390-2814, E-mail: garretts@wsd3.k12.co.us; *Head, Pub Serv,* Barbara Janssen; Tel: 719-391-3190, E-mail: janssenb@wsd3.k12.co.us; *Ref Librn,* Ines Cardo; *Children's Mgr,* Molly Reimers; Staff 5 (MLS 2, Non-MLS 3)
Founded 1961. Pop 45,000; Circ 209,302
Library Holdings: AV Mats 3,527; CDs 979; DVDs 4,284; Large Print Bks 2,000; Bk Vols 59,500; Per Subs 135; Talking Bks 2,103
Subject Interests: Colorado
Automation Activity & Vendor Info: (Cataloging) SirsiDynix; (Circulation) SirsiDynix; (OPAC) SirsiDynix
Publications: Newsletter (Monthly)
Open Mon-Thurs 10-8, Fri & Sat 9-5
Friends of the Library Group

SILVERTON

P SILVERTON PUBLIC LIBRARY*, 1111 Reese, 81433. (Mail add: PO Box 68, 81433-0068), SAN 302-0142. Tel: 970-387-5770. FAX: 970-387-0217. *Dir,* Jackie Kerwin; E-mail: jkerwin@silverton.co.us
Founded 1901. Pop 800; Circ 8,700
Library Holdings: AV Mats 60; Bk Titles 10,000; Per Subs 21
Subject Interests: Local hist
Automation Activity & Vendor Info: (Cataloging) LibLime Koha; (Circulation) LibLime Koha; (OPAC) LibLime Koha
Open Tues-Thurs 11-8, Fri & Sat 10-5
Friends of the Library Group

SPRINGFIELD

P BACA COUNTY PUBLIC LIBRARY*, 1260 Main, Ste 1, 81073-1542. SAN 302-0169. Tel: 719-523-6962. FAX: 719-523-6962. Web Site: www.springfield.colorado.com/library.html. *Dir,* Beulah Collins
Founded 1925. Pop 4,514; Circ 9,996
Library Holdings: AV Mats 252; Bk Vols 10,283; Per Subs 40
Open Mon-Fri 10-5
Friends of the Library Group
Branches: 2
TWO BUTTES BRANCH, Main St, Two Buttes, 81084. (Mail add: PO Box 52, Two Buttes, 81084-0052). *Dir,* Beaulah Collins
Pop 50
Library Holdings: Bk Vols 2,000
Open Fri 10-2
WALSH BRANCH, 400 N Colorado St, Walsh, 81090. (Mail add: PO Box 201, Walsh, 81090-0201). Tel: 719-324-5349. FAX: 719-324-5349. *Librn,* Hebbard Janice
Library Holdings: Bk Vols 5,000; Per Subs 16
Open Mon-Wed 1:30-5:30

STEAMBOAT SPRINGS

J COLORADO MOUNTAIN COLLEGE*, Alpine Campus Library, 1330 Bob Adams Dr, 80487. SAN 324-654X. Tel: 970-870-4445. FAX: 970-870-4490. E-mail: steamboatcampuslibrary@coloradomtn.edu. Web Site: library.coloradomtn.edu. *Dir,* Kevin Williams; Tel: 970-870-4493; *Librn,* Tracey Hughes; Tel: 970-870-4451; *ILL,* Kristin Weber; Tel: 970-870-4449; Staff 3 (MLS 2, Non-MLS 1)
Founded 1983. Highest Degree: Bachelor
Special Collections: Colorado State Documents. State Document Depository
Subject Interests: Bus, Resort mgt, Ski bus, Sustainability
Database Vendor: ProQuest
Wireless access
Open Mon-Thurs (Winter) 9-9, Fri 9-5, Sat 12-5, Sun 1-9; Mon-Thurs (Summer) 9-8, Fri 9-5, Sun 1-8

P BUD WERNER MEMORIAL LIBRARY*, 1289 Lincoln Ave, 80487. SAN 335-9972. Tel: 970-879-0240. FAX: 970-879-3476. Web Site: www.steamboatlibrary.org. *Dir,* Christine Painter; E-mail: cpainter@steamboatlibrary.org; *Head, Circ,* Michelle Dover; *Ref Librn,* Jackie Kuusinen; *ILL,* Fran Caparrelli; *ILL,* Mical Hutson; *Youth Serv,* Sarah Kostin; Staff 15 (MLS 3, Non-MLS 12)
Founded 1967. Pop 15,040; Circ 234,260
Library Holdings: Large Print Bks 431; Bk Titles 62,500; Bk Vols 72,695; Per Subs 250; Talking Bks 4,321; Videos 3,542
Special Collections: Ski History Coll; Western Coll
Automation Activity & Vendor Info: (Cataloging) Innovative Interfaces, Inc; (Circulation) Innovative Interfaces, Inc; (OPAC) Innovative Interfaces, Inc
Partic in Marmot Libr Network; OCLC Online Computer Library Center, Inc
Open Mon-Thurs 9-8, Fri 9-6, Sat 9-5, Sun 12-5

STERLING

S COLORADO DEPARTMENT OF CORRECTIONS*, Sterling Correctional Facility Library-West Side, 12101 Hwy 61, 80751. (Mail add: PO Box 6000, 80751-6000). Tel: 970-521-5010, Ext 3404. FAX: 970-521-8905. Web Site: www.doc.state.co.us. *Dir,* Samantha Leif; E-mail: samantha.leif@state.co.us; *Libr Tech II,* Edna Edelen; E-mail: edna.edelen@state.co.us
Library Holdings: Bk Vols 18,500; Per Subs 50
Automation Activity & Vendor Info: (Cataloging) EOS International; (Circulation) EOS International; (OPAC) EOS International
Open Mon & Tues 1:45-4 & 6:30-8:30, Wed-Fri 9-11 & 1:45-3:45, Sat 9am-11am, Sun 1:45-4
Branches:
STERLING CORRECTIONAL FACILITY LIBRARY-EAST SIDE, 12101 Hwy 61, 80751. (Mail add: PO Box 6000, 80751). Tel: 970-521-5010, Ext 3827. FAX: 970-521-8905. *Dir,* Samantha Leif; E-mail: samantha.leif@state.co.us; *Libr Tech II,* Edna Edelen; E-mail: edna.edelen@state.co.us
Library Holdings: Bk Vols 14,000; Per Subs 50
Open Mon & Tues 1:45-4 & 6:30-8:45, Wed-Fri 8:30-10:30 & 1:45-4, Sat 1:45-4, Sun 6:30pm-8:30pm

J NORTHEASTERN JUNIOR COLLEGE*, Monahan Library, 100 College Ave, 80751-2399. SAN 302-0177. Tel: 970-521-6612. Automation Services Tel: 970-521-6613. FAX: 970-521-6759. Web Site: www.njc.edu/library. *Libr Tech,* Leslie Rosa; E-mail: leslie.rosa@njc.edu; Staff 6 (MLS 1, Non-MLS 5)
Founded 1941. Enrl 1,500; Fac 95; Highest Degree: Associate
Jul 2012-Jun 2013 Income $150,000. Mats Exp $75,090. Sal $241,198
Subject Interests: Colorado
Automation Activity & Vendor Info: (Cataloging) Auto-Graphics, Inc; (Circulation) Auto-Graphics, Inc; (OPAC) Auto-Graphics, Inc
Database Vendor: EBSCOhost
Wireless access
Open Mon-Thurs 7:45am-9pm, Fri 7:45-5, Sun 5pm-9pm

P STERLING PUBLIC LIBRARY*, 420 N Fifth St, 80751-3363. (Mail add: PO Box 4000, 80751-4000), SAN 302-0185. Tel: 970-522-2023. FAX: 970-522-2657. E-mail: library@sterlingcolo.com. Web Site: sterling.polarislibrary.com. *Librn,* Sandy VanDusen; Staff 1 (MLS 1)
Founded 1918. Pop 18,000; Circ 103,000
Library Holdings: Bk Titles 57,000; Per Subs 125
Special Collections: Aviation Coll; Western History (Otto C Unfug Coll & T M Rogers Coll). State Document Depository

Automation Activity & Vendor Info: (Cataloging) Innovative Interfaces, Inc; (Circulation) Innovative Interfaces, Inc; (Serials) Innovative Interfaces, Inc
Wireless access
Mem of South Central Kansas Library System
Friends of the Library Group

STRATTON

P STRATTON PUBLIC LIBRARY, 331 New York Ave, 80836-1128. SAN 302-0193. Tel: 719-348-5922. FAX: 719-348-5922. E-mail: strattonlibrary@yahoo.com. *Head Librn,* Janice Salmans; Staff 0.5 (Non-MLS 0.5)
Pop 500; Circ 7,250
Library Holdings: Bk Vols 5,000
Automation Activity & Vendor Info: (Cataloging) Koha; (Circulation) Koha
Wireless access

TELLURIDE

P WILKINSON PUBLIC LIBRARY*, 100 W Pacific Ave, 81435-2189. (Mail add: PO Box 2189, 81435), SAN 302-0215. Tel: 970-728-4519. FAX: 970-728-3340. E-mail: askus@telluridelibrary.org. Web Site: www.telluridelibrary.org. *Dir,* Sarah Landeryou; *Ref Librn,* Alison Farnham; *Syst & Tech Serv Librn,* Amy Sieving; Staff 9 (MLS 7, Non-MLS 2)
Founded 1975. Pop 6,300; Circ 250,000
Jan 2010-Dec 2010 Income $2,615,658. Mats Exp $323,500, Books $163,900, Per/Ser (Incl. Access Fees) $10,000, Other Print Mats $14,300, AV Mat $87,100, Electronic Ref Mat (Incl. Access Fees) $48,200. Sal $1,160,375
Special Collections: Books about Film; Classic Movie Video Coll
Automation Activity & Vendor Info: (Acquisitions) Innovative Interfaces, Inc - Millenium; (Cataloging) Innovative Interfaces, Inc - Millenium; (Circulation) Innovative Interfaces, Inc - Millenium; (OPAC) Innovative Interfaces, Inc
Database Vendor: 3M Library Systems, Baker & Taylor, Booksite, BWI, CQ Press, Dun & Bradstreet, EBSCO Auto Repair Reference, EBSCO Information Services, EBSCOhost, Gale Cengage Learning, Grolier Online, Ingram Library Services, Innovative Interfaces, Inc, OCLC FirstSearch, OCLC WorldShare Interlibrary Loan, Overdrive, Inc, ProQuest
Wireless access
Partic in Marmot Libr Network
Open Mon-Thurs 10-8, Fri & Sat 10-6, Sun 12-5
Friends of the Library Group

THORNTON

P ANYTHINK LIBRARIES*, 5877 E 120th Ave, 80602. SAN 335-9557. Tel: 303-288-2001. FAX: 303-451-0190. E-mail: ithink@anythinklibraries.org. Web Site: www.anythinklibraries.org. *Dir,* Pam Sandlian Smith; E mail: psmith@anythinklibraries.org; *Dir, Human Res,* Susan Dobbs; E-mail: sdobbs@anythinklibraries.org; *Family Libr Serv Dir,* Lynda Freas; *Financial Dir,* Mindy Kittay; *Pub Serv Dir,* Ronnie Storey-Ewoldt; *Coll Develop Mgr,* Logan Macdonald; *Communications Mgr,* Stacie Ledden; *IT Mgr,* Matt Hamilton; *Develop Officer,* Mahala Evans; Staff 84 (MLS 8, Non-MLS 76)
Founded 1953. Pop 283,787; Circ 727,170
Jan 2005-Dec 2005 Income (Main Library and Branch(s)) $4,170,386, County $4,019,019, Locally Generated Income $151,367. Mats Exp $434,467, Books $301,426, Per/Ser (Incl. Access Fees) $21,609, AV Mat $45,557, Electronic Ref Mat (Incl. Access Fees) $65,875. Sal $2,199,772 (Prof $413,523)
Library Holdings: AV Mats 20,825; Bks on Deafness & Sign Lang 200; CDs 6,447; DVDs 1,424; High Interest/Low Vocabulary Bk Vols 846; Large Print Bks 6,026; Bk Titles 131,242; Bk Vols 287,236; Per Subs 678; Talking Bks 7,841; Videos 6,907
Special Collections: Community Health Resource Center
Automation Activity & Vendor Info: (Acquisitions) Horizon; (Cataloging) Horizon; (Circulation) Horizon; (OPAC) SirsiDynix
Database Vendor: EBSCOhost, Gale Cengage Learning, Newsbank, OCLC FirstSearch, OCLC WorldShare Interlibrary Loan, ProQuest, SirsiDynix
Function: Adult literacy prog, AV serv, Home delivery & serv to Sr ctr & nursing homes, Homebound delivery serv, ILL available, Photocopying/Printing, Prog for children & young adult, Ref serv available, Summer reading prog, Telephone ref
Special Services for the Deaf - Adult & family literacy prog; Bks on deafness & sign lang; Closed caption videos; High interest/low vocabulary bks; TDD equip
Special Services for the Blind - Assistive/Adapted tech devices, equip & products; Audio mat; Bks on cassette; Bks on CD; Copier with enlargement capabilities; Extensive large print coll; Home delivery serv; Large print bks; Talking bks
Open Mon-Fri 8-5:30
Friends of the Library Group
Branches: 7
ANYTHINK BENNETT, 495 Seventh St, Bennett, 80102, SAN 335-9581. Tel: 303-405-3231. FAX: 303-644-5419. *Br Mgr,* Sharon Hall
Library Holdings: AV Mats 914; CDs 304; Large Print Bks 174; Bk Vols 21,449; Per Subs 44; Talking Bks 600; Videos 342
Open Tues-Sat 10-6
ANYTHINK BRIGHTON, 327 E Bridge St, Brighton, 80601, SAN 335-9611. Tel: 303-405-3230. *Br Mgr,* Dara Schmidt
Library Holdings: AV Mats 4,878; CDs 1,288; DVDs 250; Large Print Bks 760; Bk Vols 56,801; Per Subs 107; Talking Bks 1,400; Videos 1,688
Open Mon-Thurs 9:30-8:30, Fri & Sat 9:30-5:30
ANYTHINK COMMERCE CITY, 7185 Monaco St, Commerce City, 80022, SAN 335-9646. Tel: 303-287-0063. FAX: 303-289-6313. *Br Mgr,* Deborah Hogue
Library Holdings: AV Mats 3,555; CDs 1,081; DVDs 296; Large Print Bks 458; Bk Vols 37,023; Per Subs 79; Talking Bks 1,450; Videos 1,288
Open Mon, Wed & Sat 9:30-5:30, Tues & Thurs 11-7
ANYTHINK HURON STREET, 9417 Huron St, 80260, SAN 335-9670. Tel: 303-452-7534. FAX: 303-450-2578. *Br Mgr,* Sandra Sebbas
Library Holdings: AV Mats 4,523; CDs 1,418; DVDs 434; Large Print Bks 1,043; Bk Vols 68,940; Per Subs 177; Videos 1,213
Open Mon-Thurs 9:30-8:30, Fri & Sat 9:30-5:30
ANYTHINK PERL MACK, 7611 Hilltop Circle, Denver, 80221, SAN 335-9700. Tel: 303-428-3576. FAX: 303-428-1358. *Br Mgr,* Annette Martinez
Library Holdings: AV Mats 2,561; CDs 903; DVDs 178; Large Print Bks 765; Bk Vols 38,256; Per Subs 144; Talking Bks 1,050; Videos 831
Open Mon & Wed 11-7, Tues, Thurs & Fri 9:30-5:30
ANYTHINK WASHINGTON STREET, 8992 Washington St, 80229, SAN 335-9735. Tel: 303-287-2514. FAX: 303-286-8467. *Br Mgr,* Kathy Totten
Library Holdings: AV Mats 2,829; CDs 1,101; DVDs 213; Large Print Bks 888; Bk Vols 42,415; Per Subs 100; Talking Bks 1,050; Videos 921
Subject Interests: Colorado
Open Mon, Wed & Fri 9:30-5:30, Tues & Thurs 11-7
ANYTHINK WRIGHT FARMS, 5877 E 120th Ave, 80602. Tel: 303-405-3200. *Br Mgr,* Sandra Jones
Open Mon-Thurs 9:30-8:30, Fri & Sat 9:30-5:30
Bookmobiles: 1

C EVEREST COLLEGE LIBRARY, Thornton Campus, 9065 Grant St, 80229. SAN 377-466X. Tel: 303-457-2757. *Librn,* Anna Andrews; Staff 1 (MLS 1)
Founded 1895. Enrl 260; Fac 25; Highest Degree: Associate
Library Holdings: Bk Vols 1,086; Per Subs 26
Automation Activity & Vendor Info: (OPAC) LibraryWorld, Inc
Database Vendor: cbrary, LibraryWorld, Inc, Westlaw
Wireless access
Partic in Libr & Info Resources Network (LIRN); Lyrasis
Open Mon-Thurs 8-8, Fri 8-5

TOPONAS

P TOPONAS PUBLIC LIBRARY*, 33650 Hwy 134, 80479. (Mail add: PO Box C, 80479-0249). Tel: 970-638-4436. *Dir,* Mary Jean Perry
Founded 1978. Pop 50
Library Holdings: CDs 25; DVDs 100; Bk Vols 2,500; Per Subs 30; Spec Interest Per Sub 4; Videos 100
Special Collections: Oral History
Subject Interests: Colorado, Local hist

TOWAOC

S UTE MOUNTAIN TRIBAL LIBRARY*, Education Ctr, 450 Sunset, 81334. (Mail add: PO Box CC, 81334-0048). Tel: 970-564-5348. FAX: 970-564-5342. *Dir,* Martina King
Library Holdings: AV Mats 500; Bk Vols 10,000; Per Subs 15; Talking Bks 200
Special Collections: Ute History
Automation Activity & Vendor Info: (Cataloging) Follett Software; (Circulation) Follett Software; (OPAC) Follett Software
Database Vendor: EBSCOhost, OCLC FirstSearch
Open Mon-Thurs 8-6:30, Fri 8-5

TRINIDAD

P CARNEGIE PUBLIC LIBRARY*, 202 N Animas St, 81082. SAN 302-0223. Tel: 719-846-6841, 719-846-7517. FAX: 719-846-0885. E-mail: trinidadpubliclibrary@msn.com. Web Site: www.carnegiepubliclibrary.org. *Dir,* Jane Besel; *Cat,* Position Currently Open; *ILL,* Shawna Nall; Staff 1 (Non-MLS 1)
Founded 1882. Pop 10,000; Circ 45,000

Library Holdings: Audiobooks 1,699; AV Mats 3; DVDs 520; Large Print Bks 1,148; Bk Vols 34,000; Videos 609
Special Collections: Genealogy; Local History
Automation Activity & Vendor Info: (Cataloging) Auto-Graphics, Inc; (Circulation) Auto-Graphics, Inc; (OPAC) Auto-Graphics, Inc
Database Vendor: Auto-Graphics, Inc
Wireless access
Function: Res performed for a fee
Partic in Colorado Library Consortium
Special Services for the Blind - Digital talking bk machines
Open Mon 9-7, Tues-Fri 9-5, Sat 9-3
Restriction: ID required to use computers (Ltd hrs)
Friends of the Library Group

J TRINIDAD STATE JUNIOR COLLEGE*, Samuel Freudenthal Memorial Library, 600 Prospect St, 81082. SAN 302-0231. Tel: 719-846-5593. Web Site: www.trinidadstate.edu/students/library. *Mgr, Libr Res,* Patrick Rivera; E-mail: patrick.rivera@trinidadstate.edu; Staff 1 (MLS 1)
Founded 1925. Enrl 2,009; Fac 127
Library Holdings: Bk Titles 52,000; Per Subs 154
Subject Interests: Gunsmithing, Law enforcement, Local hist, Nursing
Partic in Colo Libr Asn; Colorado Alliance of Research Libraries

USAF ACADEMY

C UNITED STATES AIR FORCE ACADEMY LIBRARIES*, McDermott Library, 2354 Fairchild Dr, Ste 3A10, 80840-6214. SAN 336-0067. Tel: 719-333-4406. Circulation Tel: 719-333-4664. Interlibrary Loan Service Tel: 719-333-4793. Reference Tel: 719-333-4749. Administration Tel: 719-333-2590. Automation Services Tel: 719-333-3660. FAX: 719-333-4754. Interlibrary Loan Service FAX: 719-333-2999. Reference FAX: 719-333-1478. Web Site: afac.sdp.sirsi.net, www.usafa.edu/df/dflib. *Libr Dir,* Dr Edward A Scott; E-mail: edward.scott@usafa.edu; *Assoc Dir,* Steven E Maffeo; E-mail: steven.maffeo@usafa.edu; *Head, Acq,* David A Schaffter; Tel: 719-333-4654, E-mail: david.schaffter@usafa.edu; *Head, Cat,* Lizbeth A Jones; Tel: 719-333-4783, E-mail: lizbeth.jones@usafa.edu; *Head, Circ,* John J Ortega; E-mail: john.ortega@usafa.edu; *Head, Electronic Syst,* M Douglas Johnson; E-mail: douglas.johnson@usafa.edu; *Head, Ref,* Robert W Humes; E-mail: robert.humes@usafa.edu; *Govt Doc, Ref Librn,* Sharon E Johnson; Tel: 719-333-2223, E-mail: sharon.johnson@usafa.edu; *Archivist, Curator, Spec Coll,* Dr Mary Elizabeth Ruwell; Tel: 719-333-6919, E-mail: mary.ruwell@usafa.edu; Staff 16 (MLS 15, Non-MLS 1)
Founded 1955. Enrl 4,100; Fac 520; Highest Degree: Bachelor
Oct 2010-Sept 2011 Income (Main Library Only) $4,847,229. Mats Exp $1,679,862, Books $446,043, Per/Ser (Incl. Access Fees) $526,096, Micro $19,428, AV Mat $10,279, Electronic Ref Mat (Incl. Access Fees) $651,016, Presv $27,000. Sal $2,238,729
Library Holdings: AV Mats 3,640; CDs 1,255; DVDs 939; e-books 150,000; e-journals 100,000; Microforms 759,000; Bk Vols 530,000; Per Subs 998; Videos 5,086
Special Collections: Colonel Richard Gimbel Aeronautical History Coll (Books, prints, & realia from 2700 BCE to the beginning of powered flight); Stalag Luft III Coll (Books, manuscripts, photographs, realia); US Air Force Academy Archives. Oral History; US Document Depository
Subject Interests: Aviation, Mil hist
Automation Activity & Vendor Info: (Acquisitions) SirsiDynix; (Cataloging) SirsiDynix; (Circulation) SirsiDynix; (Course Reserve) SirsiDynix; (ILL) SirsiDynix; (OPAC) SirsiDynix; (Serials) SirsiDynix
Database Vendor: ABC-CLIO, ACM (Association for Computing Machinery), American Chemical Society, American Mathematical Society, Annual Reviews, Bowker, College Source, CountryWatch, EBSCO Auto Repair Reference, EBSCOhost, Gale Cengage Learning, IEEE (Institute of Electrical & Electronics Engineers), IOP, ISI Web of Knowledge, JSTOR, LexisNexis, Marcive, Inc, Medline, Modern Language Association, Newsbank, OCLC WorldShare Interlibrary Loan, Oxford Online, Project MUSE, ProQuest, PubMed, ReferenceUSA, SerialsSolutions, SirsiDynix, ValueLine
Wireless access
Publications: Special Bibliography Series
Partic in Fedlink; MECC/LWG
Open Mon-Thurs 7am-10:30pm, Fri 7-5, Sat 9-5, Sun 2-10:30; Mon-Fri (Summer) 7-5
Restriction: Limited access based on advanced application, Secured area only open to authorized personnel
Friends of the Library Group
Departmental Libraries:
BASE LIBRARY (10SVS/SVMG), 5136 Red Tail Dr, Ste H103, 80840-2600, SAN 336-0091. Tel: 719-333-3198, 719-333-4665. FAX: 719-333-9491. *Libr Dir,* Position Currently Open
Founded 1955
Library Holdings: Bk Vols 31,000; Per Subs 102
Function: Online searches, Photocopying/Printing, Prog for children & young adult, Ref serv available, Summer reading prog
Open Mon-Thurs 8-6:30, Fri 8-5, Sat 9-2
Restriction: Employees & their associates, Not open to pub, Restricted access

VAIL

S COLORADO SKI MUSEUM-SKI HALL OF FAME*, Library & Research Center, 231 S Frontage Rd E, 81657-3616. (Mail add: PO Box 1976, 81658-1976), SAN 371-8263. Tel: 970-476-1876. Toll Free Tel: 800-950-7410. FAX: 970-476-1879. Web Site: www.skimuseum.net. *Curator,* Justin Henderson
Founded 1990
Library Holdings: Bk Titles 500; Per Subs 300
Special Collections: Oral History
Open Tues-Sun 10-5

P TOWN OF VAIL PUBLIC LIBRARY, 292 W Meadow Dr, 81657. SAN 302-024X. Tel: 970-479-2184. Circulation Tel: 970-479-2191. Reference Tel: 970-479-2187. Administration Tel: 970-479-2194. FAX: 970-479-2192. E-mail: libinfo@vailgov.com. Web Site: vaillibrary.com. *Dir,* Lori Ann Barnes; E-mail: lbarnes@vailgov.com; *Librn II,* Jo Norris; Tel: 970-479-2195, E-mail: jnorris@vailgov.com; *Ch Serv,* Cricket Pylman; Tel: 970-479-2179, E-mail: cpylman@vailgov.com; *Circ Serv,* Liz Willhoff; Tel: 970-479-2190, E-mail: lwillhoff@vailgov.com; *Circ & User Serv,* Alison Harakal; Tel: 970-479-2331, E-mail: aharakal@vailgov.com; *Tech Serv,* Liz Schramm; E-mail: lschramm@vailgov.com; *Ref & Info Spec,* Kathleen Winfield; Tel: 970-479-2182, E-mail: kwinfield@vailgov.com; Staff 8 (MLS 2, Non-MLS 6)
Founded 1972. Pop 4,150; Circ 89,116
Jan 2009-Dec 2009 Income $867,556, City $825,745, Locally Generated Income $41,811. Mats Exp $139,369, Books $57,053, Per/Ser (Incl. Access Fees) $15,556, AV Mat $38,678, Electronic Ref Mat (Incl. Access Fees) $28,082. Sal $406,951 (Prof $78,624)
Library Holdings: Audiobooks 3,553; AV Mats 13,143; CDs 970; DVDs 5,576; e-books 10,011; e-journals 7; Electronic Media & Resources 50; Bk Titles 37,782; Per Subs 306
Special Collections: Municipal Document Depository; Oral History
Automation Activity & Vendor Info: (Cataloging) Innovative Interfaces, Inc; (Circulation) Innovative Interfaces, Inc; (ILL) Innovative Interfaces, Inc; (OPAC) Innovative Interfaces, Inc
Database Vendor: Checkpoint Systems, Inc, EBSCOhost, Ingram Library Services
Wireless access
Partic in Colorado Alliance of Research Libraries; Marmot Libr Network
Open Mon-Thurs 10-8, Fri-Sun 11-6

VICTOR

P VICTOR PUBLIC LIBRARY, 124 S Third St, 80860. (Mail add: PO Box 5, 80860-0005), SAN 302-0258. Tel: 719-689-2011. FAX: 719-689-3157. *Librn,* Belinda Brown
Circ 15,000
Library Holdings: Bk Vols 10,000
Special Collections: Colorado Local History Coll
Automation Activity & Vendor Info: (Cataloging) Follett Software; (Circulation) Follett Software

WALDEN

P JACKSON COUNTY PUBLIC LIBRARY*, 412 Fourth St, 80480. (Mail add: PO Box 398, 80480-0398), SAN 302-0266. Tel: 970-723-4602. FAX: 970-723-4602. *Dir,* Kathy Humrich; E-mail: kkhjcpl@yahoo.com
Founded 1954. Pop 1,577; Circ 17,423
Library Holdings: AV Mats 766; Bk Titles 16,472; Bk Vols 17,077; Per Subs 51
Special Collections: Local History Coll
Automation Activity & Vendor Info: (Cataloging) Follett Software; (Circulation) Follett Software
Partic in Evergreen Indiana Consortium; Midwest Collaborative for Library Services (MCLS)
Open Mon 1-9, Tues & Thurs 1-6, Wed 10-6, Fri 9:30-4:30
Friends of the Library Group

WALSENBURG

P SPANISH PEAKS LIBRARY DISTRICT*, 415 Walsen Ave, 81089. SAN 302-0274. Tel: 719-738-2774. FAX: 719-738-2468. E-mail: librarian@spld.org. Web Site: www.spld.org. *Dir,* Monica Anne Birrer; E-mail: mbirrer@spld.org; *Asst Dir, Network Adminr,* John M Thomas; E-mail: jthomas@spld.org; *Tech Serv,* Beth Harper; E-mail: bharper@spld.org; *Youth Serv,* Dianne Hanisch; E-mail: dhanisch@spld.org; Staff 1.5 (MLS 1, Non-MLS 0.5)
Founded 1906. Pop 5,403; Circ 24,746
Jan 2009-Dec 2009 Income $236,344, Federal $5,919, Locally Generated Income $158,997, Other $71,428. Mats Exp $17,486, Books $9,643,

Per/Ser (Incl. Access Fees) $1,640, AV Mat $2,833, Electronic Ref Mat (Incl. Access Fees) $3,370. Sal $120,000 (Prof $31,200)
Library Holdings: Audiobooks 1,518; AV Mats 1,398; CDs 446; Electronic Media & Resources 44; Bk Vols 20,303; Per Subs 62
Automation Activity & Vendor Info: (Cataloging) Insignia Software; (Circulation) Insignia Software; (ILL) Insignia Software; (OPAC) Insignia Software; (Serials) Insignia Software
Database Vendor: BWI, EBSCO Auto Repair Reference, EBSCOhost, Gale Cengage Learning, Ingram Library Services, LearningExpress, OCLC FirstSearch, OCLC WorldShare Interlibrary Loan
Wireless access
Function: Audio & video playback equip for onsite use, Audiobks via web, Bilingual assistance for Spanish patrons, Bks on cassette, Bks on CD, CD-ROM, Chess club, Children's prog, Computer training, Computers for patron use, Copy machines, Digital talking bks, e-mail & chat, Electronic databases & coll, Exhibits, Fax serv, Free DVD rentals, Handicapped accessible, Holiday prog, Homework prog, ILL available, Mail & tel request accepted, Music CDs, Online cat, Online ref, Orientations, Outside serv via phone, mail, e-mail & web, Photocopying/Printing, Preschool outreach, Prog for adults, Prog for children & young adult, Pub access computers, Ref serv in person, Scanner, Senior computer classes, Spoken cassettes & CDs, Spoken cassettes & DVDs, Story hour, Summer reading prog, Tax forms, Teen prog, Telephone ref, VHS videos, Wheelchair accessible
Partic in Colorado Library Consortium
Special Services for the Blind - Audio mat; Bks on cassette; Bks on CD; Cassettes; Copier with enlargement capabilities; Digital talking bk; Extensive large print coll; Large print & cassettes; Large print bks; Recorded bks; Ref serv; Sound rec; Talking bk serv referral
Open Mon, Wed & Fri 10-6, Tues & Thurs 10-7, Sat 10-4
Friends of the Library Group

WELLINGTON

P WELLINGTON PUBLIC LIBRARY*, 3800 Wilson Ave, 80549. (Mail add: PO Box 416, 80549-0416), SAN 370-6710. Tel: 970-568-3040. FAX: 970-568-9713. Web Site: wellington.colibraries.org. *Dir,* Kathy Bornhoft; E-mail: wpldir@gmail.com; *Asst Dir,* Kim Keiss; Staff 3 (MLS 1, Non-MLS 2)
Founded 1980. Pop 4,500; Circ 48,000
Jan 2010-Dec 2010 Income $205,000. Mats Exp $22,950, Books $17,000, Per/Ser (Incl. Access Fees) $700, AV Mat $3,850, Electronic Ref Mat (Incl. Access Fees) $1,400. Sal $116,301 (Prof $45,000)
Library Holdings: Audiobooks 1,200; AV Mats 190; Bks on Deafness & Sign Lang 25; CDs 175; DVDs 600; Large Print Bks 150; Bk Titles 24,000; Per Subs 40; Videos 500
Special Collections: Local History Coll. Oral History
Database Vendor: EBSCOhost, LearningExpress, LibLime
Wireless access
Function: Adult bk club, Bks on CD, Children's prog, Computers for patron use, Copy machines, E-Reserves, Electronic databases & coll, Fax serv, Free DVD rentals, Handicapped accessible, ILL available, Mail & tel request accepted, Music CDs, Photocopying/Printing, Prog for children & young adult, Pub access computers, Story hour, Summer reading prog, VHS videos, Video lending libr, Web-catalog, Wheelchair accessible
Special Services for the Deaf - Closed caption videos
Special Services for the Blind - Bks on cassette; Bks on CD; Copier with enlargement capabilities; Large print bks
Open Mon, Tues & Thurs 10-6, Wed 10-8, Fri 10-3:30, Sat 10-1
Friends of the Library Group

WESTCLIFFE

P WEST CUSTER COUNTY LIBRARY DISTRICT*, 209 Main St, 81252. (Mail add: PO Box 689, 81252-0689), SAN 302-0290. Tel: 719-783-9138. FAX: 719-783-2155. E-mail: wccld@hotmail.com. Web Site: westcliffe.colibraries.org. *Dir,* Marty Frick; *Asst Dir,* Claudia Cole; Staff 1 (MLS 1)
Founded 1930. Pop 4,611; Circ 43,500
Library Holdings: Bk Vols 12,214; Per Subs 18
Special Collections: Local History Coll
Automation Activity & Vendor Info: (Cataloging) Follett Software; (Circulation) Follett Software
Wireless access
Open Tues-Fri 10-5:30, Sat 10-2
Friends of the Library Group

WESTMINSTER

C DEVRY UNIVERSITY*, Westminster Campus Library, 1870 W 122nd Ave, 80234. Tel: 303-280-7620. Web Site: www.wes.devry.edu/academics_library.html. *Dir,* Morganne Wagoner-Perry; Tel: 303-280-7621, E-mail: mwagoner@devry.edu
Founded 2003
Library Holdings: Bk Vols 12,000; Per Subs 50
Automation Activity & Vendor Info: (Acquisitions) Ex Libris Group; (Cataloging) Ex Libris Group; (Circulation) Ex Libris Group; (OPAC) Ex Libris Group; (Serials) Ex Libris Group
Database Vendor: ProQuest
Wireless access
Open Mon-Thurs 8am-9pm, Fri 8-8, Sat 9-1

J FRONT RANGE COMMUNITY COLLEGE*, College Hill Library, 3705 W 112th Ave, 80031-2140. (Mail add: 3645 W 112th Ave, Campus 12, 80031), SAN 302-0312. Tel: 303-404-5555. Circulation Tel: 303-404-5504. Interlibrary Loan Service Tel: 303-404-5501. Reference Tel: 303-404-5143. Automation Services Tel: 303-658-2645. FAX: 303-404-5144. Web Site: www.frontrange.edu/library/wc. *Dir,* Position Currently Open; *Ref & Instruction Librn,* Position Currently Open; *Coll Develop, Tech Serv Mgr,* Ann Marie Obarski; Tel: 303-404-5505, E-mail: annmarie.obarski@frontrange.edu; *Circ Supvr,* David Wittke; Tel: 303-404-5372, E-mail: david.wittke@frontrange.edu; *Coordr, Instruction & Ref,* Courtney Bruch; Tel: 303-404-5133, E-mail: courtney.bruch@frontrange.edu; *Circ,* Melanie Heinz; Tel: 303-404-5587, E-mail: melanie.heinz@frontrange.edu; *Circ, Tech Serv,* Karpagam Rajagopal; E-mail: Karpagam.Rajagopal@frontrange.edu; Staff 6.75 (MLS 3.75, Non-MLS 3)
Founded 1968. Highest Degree: Associate
Library Holdings: Bk Titles 39,715; Bk Vols 44,764; Per Subs 57
Automation Activity & Vendor Info: (Acquisitions) SirsiDynix; (Cataloging) SirsiDynix; (Circulation) SirsiDynix; (Course Reserve) SirsiDynix; (ILL) OCLC; (OPAC) SirsiDynix; (Serials) SirsiDynix
Database Vendor: Career Guidance Foundation, Cinahl, CQ Press, CredoReference, EBSCOhost, Gale Cengage Learning, OCLC WorldShare Interlibrary Loan, Oxford Online, ReferenceUSA, SerialsSolutions, SirsiDynix, Springshare, LLC
Wireless access
Partic in Colorado Library Consortium; OCLC Online Computer Library Center, Inc
Open Mon-Thurs 9-8, Fri 10-5, Sat & Sun 1-5

P WESTMINSTER PUBLIC LIBRARY*, College Hill Library, 3705 W 112th Ave, 80031. SAN 375-409X. Tel: 303-404-5555. Circulation Tel: 303-658-2601. Information Services Tel: 303-658-2603. FAX: 303-404-5135. Web Site: www.westminster.lib.co.us. *Libr Serv Mgr,* Kate Skarbek; Tel: 303-658-2640, E-mail: kskarbek@cityofwestminster.us; *Libr Supvr,* Antonia Gaona; Tel: 303-658-2610, E-mail: agaona@cityofwestminster.us; *Teen Librn,* Hollie Brosseau; Tel: 303-658-2606, E-mail: hbrossea@cityofwestminster.us; *Adult Serv Coordr,* Christine Johnson; Tel: 303-658-2620, E-mail: cajohnso@cityofwestminster.us; *Automation Syst Coordr,* Veronica Smith; Tel: 303-658-2645, E-mail: vsmith@cityofwestminster.us; *Coordr, Youth Serv,* Vicky Sisto; Tel: 303-658-2614, E-mail: vsisto@cityofwestminster.us; Staff 13.1 (MLS 13.1)
Founded 1951. Pop 109,353; Circ 1,100,848
Library Holdings: Bk Vols 221,000; Per Subs 300
Automation Activity & Vendor Info: (Acquisitions) SirsiDynix; (Cataloging) SirsiDynix; (Circulation) SirsiDynix; (Serials) SirsiDynix
Partic in Colorado Library Consortium
Open Mon-Thurs 9-8, Fri 9-5, Sat & Sun 1-5
Friends of the Library Group

WETMORE

P WETMORE COMMUNITY LIBRARY*, 95 County Rd 393, 81253. (Mail add: PO Box 18, 81253-0018). Tel: 719-784-6669. FAX: 719-784-2301. E-mail: wetmorecommunitylibrary@yahoo.com. *Dir,* Nan Davenport; Staff 1 (Non-MLS 1)
Pop 900; Circ 5,200
Library Holdings: AV Mats 180; CDs 60; DVDs 80; Large Print Bks 60; Bk Vols 6,758; Talking Bks 164; Videos 626
Automation Activity & Vendor Info: (Cataloging) Follett Software; (Circulation) Follett Software; (OPAC) Follett Software
Database Vendor: LibLime
Wireless access
Function: Digital talking bks, ILL available, Music CDs, Online searches, Photocopying/Printing, Prog for adults, Prog for children & young adult, Spoken cassettes & CDs, Summer reading prog, VHS videos
Open Mon & Tues 4-7, Wed 2-6, Thurs 11-3, Sat 12-3
Restriction: By permission only

WHEAT RIDGE

M EXEMPLA LUTHERAN MEDICAL CENTER*, Medical Library, 8300 W 38th Ave, 80033-8270. SAN 302-0339. Tel: 303-425-8662. FAX: 303-467-8794. *Mgr, Libr Serv,* Karen Wells; E-mail: wellsk@exempla.org
Subject Interests: Bus & mgt, Consumer health, Med, Nursing, Surgery
Partic in Colorado Council of Medical Librarians; Dialog Corp; OCLC Online Computer Library Center, Inc; RML

S WHEAT RIDGE HISTORICAL SOCIETY LIBRARY*, 4610 Robb St, 80033. (Mail add: PO Box 1833, 80034-1833), SAN 371-8751. Tel: 303-467-0023. Web Site: www.wheatridgehistoricalsociety.org/Joomla. *Pres,* Charlotte Whetsel; *Presv Spec,* Claudia Worth; E-mail: cworth1234@aol.com
Founded 1974
Library Holdings: CDs 150; Bk Titles 500; Bk Vols 1,000; Per Subs 300
Special Collections: Crochet Books 1880-1950; Early Agricultural Books (Carnations, Dahlias, Trees); Early Movie Magazine (1929-1940); Early News Papers (1913-1916); Maps of Co Denver Metro,etc; School Coll, ms, vf; Victorian Toys (Including Doll House); Wheat Ridge, Jefferson County & Colorado History Coll. Municipal Document Depository; Oral History
Function: Res libr
Publications: Guide to Collections
Open Fri 10-3

WINDSOR

P WINDSOR-SEVERANCE LIBRARY*, 720 Third St, 80550-5109. SAN 302-0355. Tel: 970-686-5603. FAX: 970-686-2502. Web Site: www.clearviewlibrary.org. *Dir,* Ann Kling; Tel: 970-686-5603, Ext 302, E-mail: director@myclearview.info; *Asst Dir,* Diane Montgomery; Tel: 970-686-5603, Ext 303, E-mail: diane@myclearview.info; *Outreach & Children's Serv,* Ally Godina; E-mail: ally@myclearview.info; *Tech Serv,* Shari Thompson; E-mail: shari@myclearview.info
Founded 1922. Circ 138,504
Library Holdings: Bk Vols 65,000; Per Subs 60
Automation Activity & Vendor Info: (Cataloging) TLC (The Library Corporation); (Circulation) TLC (The Library Corporation); (OPAC) TLC (The Library Corporation)
Partic in Colorado Library Consortium
Open Mon-Fri 9-8, Sat 9-5, Sun 1-5
Friends of the Library Group

WOODLAND PARK

P RAMPART LIBRARY DISTRICT*, Woodland Park Public Library, 218 E Midland, 80863. (Mail add: PO Box 336, 80866-0336), SAN 302-0363. Tel: 719-687-9281. FAX: 719-687-6631. Web Site: rampart.colibraries.org. *Dir,* Anne Knowles; E-mail: annek@rampartlibrarydistrict.org
Founded 1966. Pop 18,000; Circ 160,000
Library Holdings: Bk Vols 56,000; Per Subs 140
Subject Interests: Local hist
Automation Activity & Vendor Info: (Cataloging) SirsiDynix; (Circulation) SirsiDynix; (OPAC) SirsiDynix
Database Vendor: EBSCOhost, Gale Cengage Learning, OCLC FirstSearch, OCLC WorldShare Interlibrary Loan, ProQuest
Partic in Automation System Colorado Consortium
Open Tues-Thurs 10-7, Fri 10-6, Sat 10-4, Sun 1-4
Friends of the Library Group
Branches: 1
FLORISSANT PUBLIC LIBRARY, 334 Circle Dr, Florissant, 80816. (Mail add: PO Box 252, Florissant, 80816-0252), SAN 320-9687. Tel: 719-748-3939. FAX: 719-748-1237. *Br Mgr,* Polly Roberts; E-mail: pollyr@rampartlibrarydistrict.org
Open Mon & Wed-Fri 10-5, Sat 10-2
Friends of the Library Group

WRAY

P WRAY PUBLIC LIBRARY*, 621 Blake St, 80758-1619. SAN 302-038X. Tel: 970-332-4744. FAX: 970-332-4784. *Dir,* Shara Berghuis
Founded 1913. Circ 31,000
Library Holdings: Bk Titles 16,000; Per Subs 46
Automation Activity & Vendor Info: (Cataloging) Follett Software; (Circulation) Follett Software
Open Mon-Fri 10-5, Sat 9-1

YUMA

P YUMA PUBLIC LIBRARY*, 114 W Third Ave, 80759-2402. SAN 302-0401. Tel: 970-848-2368. FAX: 970-848-0423. *Dir,* Susan Evans; *Asst Dir,* Carla Peterson
Founded 1924. Pop 3,500; Circ 24,600
Jan 2005-Dec 2005. Mats Exp $10,750, Books $8,750, Per/Ser (Incl. Access Fees) $2,000. Sal $56,655
Library Holdings: CDs 114; Bk Titles 15,220; Per Subs 43; Talking Bks 1,450; Videos 228
Automation Activity & Vendor Info: (Acquisitions) SirsiDynix; (Cataloging) SirsiDynix; (Circulation) SirsiDynix
Function: CD-ROM, Copy machines, Genealogy discussion group, Home delivery & serv to Sr ctr & nursing homes, Homebound delivery serv, ILL available, Music CDs, Photocopying/Printing, Prog for children & young adult, Spoken cassettes & CDs, Summer reading prog, Tax forms, VHS videos
Open Mon-Fri 9-6, Sat 9-1

CONNECTICUT

Date of Statistics: FY 2014
Population, 2010 U.S. Census: 3,574,097
Population, 2013 (est.): 3,596,080
Population Served by Public Libraries: 3,590,080
Total Volumes in Public Libraries: 13,785,164
Volumes Per Capita: 3.83
Total Public Library Circulation: 29,591,535
Circulation Per Capita: 8.23
Source of Income: Local taxes: 86%; Other: 14%
Grants-in-Aid to Public Libraries: $203.569
Federal LSTA FY 2014: $2,038,047
Connecticard: $1,000,000
State Grants Public Library Construction (FY 2014): $2,835,943
State aid: $1,200 to each of 165 principal public libraries plus equalization and incentive grants
Connecticard: Half of total annual appropriation is distributed to all participating libraries on a transaction basis; other half distributed to libraries with net plus transactions ($1,000,000)
Total Public Library Expenditures: $192,323,530
Operating Expenditures Per Capita: $53.48
Number of Bookmobiles in State: 5

ABINGTON

P ABINGTON SOCIAL LIBRARY*, 536 Hampton Rd, 06230. (Mail add: PO Box 73, Pomfret Center, 06259), SAN 302-041X. Tel: 860-974-0415. FAX: 860-974-3950. Web Site: www.abingtonsociallibrary.org. *Libr Dir,* Bonnie Duncan
Founded 1793. Pop 3,000
Library Holdings: Bk Titles 12,500
Special Collections: 1700 Mss coll; primary sermons
Wireless access
Open Mon, Wed & Thurs 5-8, Sat 10-12

ANDOVER

P ANDOVER PUBLIC LIBRARY*, 355 Rte 6, 06232. (Mail add: PO Box 117, 06232-0117), SAN 302-0428. Tel: 860-742-7428. FAX: 860-742-7428. E-mail: andoverctpubliclibrary@yahoo.com. Web Site: www.andoverctlibrary.org. *Dir, Librn,* Amy E Orlomoski; *Ch Serv,* Cathy Campen; Staff 1.75 (MLS 0.75, Non-MLS 1)
Founded 1896. Pop 2,700; Circ 21,000
Library Holdings: Bk Titles 18,355; Per Subs 15
Automation Activity & Vendor Info: (Cataloging) Auto-Graphics, Inc; (Circulation) Auto-Graphics, Inc; (OPAC) Auto-Graphics, Inc
Wireless access
Open Mon 10-1 & 3-8, Tues & Thurs 3-8, Wed 10-8, Fri 10-1 & 3-6, Sat 10-4
Friends of the Library Group

ANSONIA

P ANSONIA LIBRARY*, 53 S Cliff St, 06401-1909. SAN 302-0436. Tel: 203-734-6275. FAX: 203-732-4551. Web Site: www.biblio.org/ansonia. *Dir,* Joyce Ceccarelli; *Asst Dir,* Mary Ann Capone; *Ch,* Janet Fitol; *ILL Librn,* Constance Yeager; *Cataloger,* Maureen Levine; Staff 5 (MLS 1, Non-MLS 4)
Founded 1896. Pop 18,744; Circ 89,965
Jul 2006-Jun 2007 Income $574,323, State $2,659, City $490,382, Other $81,282. Mats Exp $63,644, Books $45,267, Per/Ser (Incl. Access Fees) $6,727, AV Mat $6,500, Electronic Ref Mat (Incl. Access Fees) $5,150. Sal $335,790
Library Holdings: AV Mats 3,337; CDs 892; e-books 115; Bk Vols 83,707; Per Subs 144; Talking Bks 592; Videos 1,826
Special Collections: Daughters of American Revolution
Subject Interests: Local hist
Automation Activity & Vendor Info: (Cataloging) SirsiDynix; (Circulation) SirsiDynix; (OPAC) SirsiDynix; (Serials) SirsiDynix
Database Vendor: SirsiDynix
Partic in Bibliomation Inc; Connecticut Library Consortium
Open Mon-Thurs 10-8, Fri 10-4, Sat 10-2

ASHFORD

P BABCOCK LIBRARY*, 25 Pompey Hollow Rd, 06278. SAN 323-6455. Tel: 860-487-4420. FAX: 860-487-4438. Web Site: www.babcocklibrary.org. *Dir,* Ginny Moses; E-mail: gmoses@babcocklibrary.org; Staff 8 (MLS 1, Non-MLS 7)
Founded 1866. Pop 4,000; Circ 30,000
Jul 2006-Jun 2007 Income $149,000
Library Holdings: Bks on Deafness & Sign Lang 75; Large Print Bks 352; Bk Vols 25,000; Per Subs 65; Talking Bks 135
Subject Interests: Genealogy, Local hist
Automation Activity & Vendor Info: (Cataloging) Follett Software; (Circulation) Follett Software; (ILL) Auto-Graphics, Inc; (OPAC) Follett Software
Function: Photocopying/Printing, Prog for adults, Prog for children & young adult, Summer reading prog
Open Mon, Tues & Fri 10-6, Wed 10-8, Sat 9-2
Friends of the Library Group

AVON

P AVON FREE PUBLIC LIBRARY*, 281 Country Club Rd, 06001. SAN 302-0452. Tel: 860-673-9712. FAX: 860-675-6364. TDD: 860-673-3431. E-mail: avonref@avonctlibrary.info. Web Site: www.avonctlibrary.info. *Dir,* Position Currently Open; *Ch,* Karen McNulty; E-mail: kmcnulty@avonctlibrary.info; *Circ Mgr, Pub Serv Mgr,* Tina Panik; E-mail: tpan@avonctlibrary.info; *Coll Mgr, Tech Serv,* Julie Styles; E-mail: jstyles@avonctlibrary.info; Staff 34 (MLS 14, Non-MLS 20)
Founded 1798. Pop 17,800; Circ 318,033
Jul 2006-Jun 2007 Income $1,461,252, State $6,671, City $1,237,152, Locally Generated Income $28,608, Other $188,821. Mats Exp $145,265, Books $85,500, Per/Ser (Incl. Access Fees) $13,179, AV Mat $11,700, Electronic Ref Mat (Incl. Access Fees) $34,886. Sal $721,627
Library Holdings: AV Mats 10,773; CDs 2,275; DVDs 2,112; Electronic Media & Resources 12; Large Print Bks 1,600; Bk Titles 80,174; Bk Vols 79,138; Per Subs 274; Talking Bks 2,420; Videos 3,675
Subject Interests: Local hist
Automation Activity & Vendor Info: (Cataloging) SirsiDynix; (Circulation) SirsiDynix; (ILL) SirsiDynix; (OPAC) SirsiDynix
Database Vendor: CQ Press, EBSCOhost, Gale Cengage Learning, LearningExpress, OCLC FirstSearch, ProQuest, ReferenceUSA, ValueLine, Wilson - Wilson Web
Wireless access
Publications: Friends (Newsletter)
Partic in Library Connection, Inc
Special Services for the Deaf - TDD equip
Open Mon, Tues & Thurs 10-8:30, Wed 10-6, Fri & Sat 10-5, Sun (Oct-May) 1-5
Friends of the Library Group

BALTIC

P SPRAGUE PUBLIC LIBRARY*, 76 Main St, 06330-1320. SAN 376-5334. Tel: 860-822-3012. FAX: 860-822-3013. E-mail: spraguepublic.library@gmail.com. Web Site: sites.google.com/site/spraguepubliclibrary2, www.ctsprague.org. *Dir,* Christine Kolar; Staff 2 (MLS 1, Non-MLS 1)
Pop 2,975
Library Holdings: AV Mats 575; Bk Vols 90,000; Talking Bks 213
Subject Interests: Genealogy, Local hist, Native Am lit
Automation Activity & Vendor Info: (Cataloging) Follett Software; (Circulation) Follett Software; (OPAC) Follett Software
Wireless access
Function: Telephone ref
Publications: Our Town (Newsletter)
Open Mon & Tues 2-7, Wed & Thurs 9-7, Sat 9-2
Friends of the Library Group

BEACON FALLS

P BEACON FALLS PUBLIC LIBRARY*, Ten Maple Ave, 06403. SAN 302-0460. Tel: 203-729-1441. FAX: 203-729-4927. E-mail: beaconfallslibrary@yahoo.com. Web Site: bflib.org. *Head Librn,* Marsha Durley; E-mail: marsha@bflib.org; Staff 2 (MLS 0.75, Non-MLS 1.25)
Founded 1957. Pop 5,246; Circ 26,500
Library Holdings: AV Mats 1,317; Bks on Deafness & Sign Lang 3; CDs 125; DVDs 700; e-books 18; Large Print Bks 60; Bk Vols 11,613; Talking Bks 151; Videos 564
Automation Activity & Vendor Info: (Acquisitions) Follett Software; (Cataloging) Follett Software; (Circulation) Follett Software; (ILL) Auto-Graphics, Inc; (OPAC) Follett Software
Database Vendor: Baker & Taylor
Wireless access
Function: Adult bk club, Bks on cassette, Bks on CD, Children's prog, Computer training, Computers for patron use, Copy machines, Electronic databases & coll, Fax serv, Free DVD rentals, Handicapped accessible, Holiday prog, Homebound delivery serv, ILL available, Mail & tel request accepted, Mus passes, Music CDs, Online cat, Online ref, Photocopying/Printing, Prog for adults, Prog for children & young adult, Pub access computers, Scanner, Spoken cassettes & CDs, Spoken cassettes & DVDs, Story hour, Summer reading prog, Tax forms, Telephone ref, VHS videos, Web-catalog, Workshops
Partic in Connecticut Library Consortium
Special Services for the Blind - Assistive/Adapted tech devices, equip & products; Bks on cassette; Bks on CD; Large print bks
Open Mon, Wed & Fri 10-5:30, Tues & Thurs 12:30-8, Sat (Sept-June) 9-1
Friends of the Library Group

BERLIN

P BERLIN FREE LIBRARY*, 834 Worthington Ridge, 06037-3203. (Mail add: PO Box 8187, 06037-8187), SAN 302-0479. Tel: 860-828-3344. *Librn,* Marcia Trotta; *Ch Serv,* Colleen Kim; *Ch Serv,* Lisa Turgeon
Pop 17,800
Library Holdings: Bk Vols 17,500; Per Subs 15
Open Mon 2:30-5 & 7-8:30, Wed 9-11:30 & 7-8:30, Fri 2:30-5

P BERLIN-PECK MEMORIAL LIBRARY*, 234 Kensington Rd, 06037. SAN 302-2005. Tel: 860-828-7125. FAX: 860-829-1848. E-mail: illbpml@libraryconnection.info. Web Site: www.berlinpeck.lib.ct.us. *Dir,* Helen Aveline; *Asst Dir, Ch Serv,* Position Currently Open; *Head, Cat, Ref Serv,* Andrew J Fal; Staff 11.5 (MLS 4.5, Non-MLS 7)
Founded 1829. Pop 20,450; Circ 217,000
Jul 2007-Jun 2008 Income $964,487. Mats Exp $151,700, Books $92,000, Per/Ser (Incl. Access Fees) $4,500, AV Mat $13,000, Electronic Ref Mat (Incl. Access Fees) $42,000, Presv $200. Sal $536,906
Library Holdings: AV Mats 11,286; Bk Titles 106,000; Per Subs 135
Special Collections: Oral History
Subject Interests: Local hist
Automation Activity & Vendor Info: (Cataloging) SirsiDynix; (Circulation) SirsiDynix; (ILL) SirsiDynix; (OPAC) SirsiDynix
Database Vendor: Alexander Street Press, BWI, EBSCO Auto Repair Reference, Facts on File, infoUSA, Newsbank, SirsiDynix
Wireless access
Partic in Library Connection, Inc; OCLC Online Computer Library Center, Inc
Open Mon-Thurs 10-8, Fri 10-5, Sat (Sept-June) 10-4
Friends of the Library Group

BETHANY

P CLARK MEMORIAL LIBRARY*, 538 Amity Rd, 06524-3015. SAN 302-0495. Tel: 203-393-2103. *Dir,* Sarah Shepherd; *Ch,* Dorothy Esparo; *Librn,* Jean Johnson
Founded 1930. Pop 4,600; Circ 50,400
Library Holdings: Bk Vols 36,000
Automation Activity & Vendor Info: (Cataloging) Follett Software; (Circulation) Follett Software; (OPAC) Follett Software
Open Mon-Thurs 2-8, Fri 2-6, Sat (Sept-June) 10-2
Friends of the Library Group

BETHEL

P BETHEL PUBLIC LIBRARY*, 189 Greenwood Ave, 06801-2598. SAN 302-0509. Tel: 203-794-8756. Circulation Tel: 203-794-8756, Ext 3. Interlibrary Loan Service Tel: 203-794-8756, Ext 0. Reference Tel: 203-794-8756, Ext 4. Administration Tel: 203-794-8756, Ext 6. FAX: 203-794-8761. E-mail: adult@bethellibrary.org. Web Site: www.bethellibrary.org. *Dir,* Lynn M Rosato; *Adult Serv,* Barbara Van Achterberg; *Ch Serv,* Joanne Grumman; *YA Serv,* Amy Schumann; Staff 22 (MLS 4, Non-MLS 18)
Founded 1909. Pop 18,000; Circ 143,000
Library Holdings: AV Mats 4,146; High Interest/Low Vocabulary Bk Vols 75; Bk Vols 92,975; Per Subs 209; Talking Bks 2,155
Subject Interests: Local hist
Automation Activity & Vendor Info: (Acquisitions) SirsiDynix; (Cataloging) SirsiDynix; (Circulation) SirsiDynix; (OPAC) SirsiDynix; (Serials) SirsiDynix
Database Vendor: EBSCOhost, Gale Cengage Learning
Publications: Newsletter (Bi-monthly)
Open Mon, Wed & Thurs 9:30-8, Tues, Fri & Sat 9:30-5
Friends of the Library Group

BETHLEHEM

SR ABBEY OF REGINA LAUDIS LIBRARY*, Flanders Rd, 06751. SAN 302-0517. Tel: 203-266-7727. E-mail: rllibrary@sbcglobal.net. Web Site: www.abbeyofreginalaudis.com. *Librn,* Mother Lucia Kuppens; Staff 3 (MLS 1, Non-MLS 2)
Founded 1947
Library Holdings: Bk Vols 24,100; Per Subs 12
Special Collections: Art & Art History (Lauren Ford Coll); English Monastic History (Hope Emily Allen Coll); Gregorian Chant (Rev Thomas F Dennehy Coll); Literature (Heinrich Brunning & Lloyd B Holsapple Coll); Medieval Mystics; Patristics (Sources Chretiennes, Migne & Corpus Christianorum); Sacred Music (T F Dennehy Coll); Social Science (Sage Coll)
Subject Interests: Art & archit, Church hist, Ecumenism, Judaism (religion), Liturgy, Near East, Theol
Restriction: Not open to pub

P BETHLEHEM PUBLIC LIBRARY*, 32 Main St S, 06751. (Mail add: PO Box 99, 06751-0099), SAN 302-0525. Tel: 203-266-7792. FAX: 203-266-7792. Web Site: ci.bethlehem.ct.us/. *Dir,* Anne Small; E-mail: blib96@sbcglobal.net
Founded 1857. Pop 3,540; Circ 225,461
Library Holdings: CDs 550; DVDs 50; Large Print Bks 550; Bk Vols 29,976; Per Subs 33; Talking Bks 730; Videos 644
Special Collections: Oral History
Subject Interests: Local hist
Wireless access
Open Mon & Wed 10-8:30, Tues & Thurs 10-5, Fri & Sat 10-2
Friends of the Library Group

BLOOMFIELD

S CIGNA CO LIBRARY*, 900 Cottage Grove Rd, 06002. SAN 302-0541. Tel: 860-226-3257. FAX: 860-226-5128. *Mgr,* Sarah Polirer; *Info Spec,* Evelyn Green; *Info Spec,* Nicholas Sacco; Tel: 860-226-4327; Staff 3 (MLS 3)
Founded 1922
Subject Interests: Bus & mgt, Econ, Healthcare, Investing, Law
Function: Online searches, Ref & res, Ref serv available
Partic in Connecticut Library Consortium; OCLC Online Computer Library Center, Inc
Restriction: Access for corporate affiliates, Employees only, Internal use only, Not open to pub

P PROSSER PUBLIC LIBRARY*, One Tunxis Ave, 06002-2476. SAN 336-0245. Tel: 860-243-9721. FAX: 860-242-1629. Web Site: www.prosserlibrary.info. *Dir,* Beverly Lambert; E-mail: blambert2@mac.com; *Ref Librn,* Carol Lennig; *Ch Serv,* Linda Gabianelli; Staff 10 (MLS 10)
Founded 1901. Pop 19,070; Circ 292,883
Library Holdings: Bk Titles 81,742; Bk Vols 96,000; Per Subs 183
Automation Activity & Vendor Info: (Acquisitions) SirsiDynix; (Cataloging) SirsiDynix; (Circulation) SirsiDynix; (ILL) SirsiDynix; (OPAC) SirsiDynix
Publications: Monthly Calendar; Newsletter
Partic in Connecticut Library Consortium; Lyrasis

Open Mon-Thurs 10-8, Fri 10-6, Sat 10-5
Friends of the Library Group
Branches: 1
WINTONBURY, 1015 Blue Hills Ave, 06002. Tel: 860-242-0041. *Librn,* Claudia Wright
Open Tues & Thurs 1-8, Wed, Fri & Sat 10-5

CR ST THOMAS SEMINARY & ARCHDIOCESAN CENTER*, Archbishop O'Brien Library, 467 Bloomfield Ave, 06002. SAN 302-0576. Tel: 860-242-5573, Ext 2609. Administration Tel: 860-242-5573, Ext 2608. FAX: 860-242-4886, Library. Web Site: www.stseminary.org/obrienlibrary.htm. *Dir, Libr Serv,* Karen Lesiak; E-mail: klesiak@stseminary.org; *Asst Librn,* Rody Bazzano; Staff 2 (MLS 1, Non-MLS 1)
Founded 1928. Enrl 100; Fac 6
Jul 2010-Jun 2011 Income $12,500. Mats Exp $10,000. Sal $65,000
Library Holdings: AV Mats 2,500; Bk Titles 26,000; Bk Vols 30,000; Per Subs 87; Talking Bks 100
Special Collections: 15th-17th Century Religious Coll, docs, mss, rare bks; 18th-19th Century Catholic Americana; Bibles
Subject Interests: Catholicism, Philos, Theol
Automation Activity & Vendor Info: (Acquisitions) Auto-Graphics, Inc; (Cataloging) Auto-Graphics, Inc; (Circulation) Follett Software; (Course Reserve) Follett Software; (ILL) Auto-Graphics, Inc; (Media Booking) Baker & Taylor; (OPAC) Follett Software; (Serials) Auto-Graphics, Inc
Database Vendor: Auto-Graphics, Inc, EBSCOhost, OCLC WorldShare Interlibrary Loan, ProQuest
Wireless access
Function: ILL available, Res libr
Publications: Word & Spirit (Newsletter)
Special Services for the Deaf - Closed caption videos
Special Services for the Blind - Audio mat; Bks on cassette; Bks on CD; Copier with enlargement capabilities; Large print bks; Magnifiers; Recorded bks; Ref serv; Scanner for conversion & translation of mats
Open Mon, Tues, Thurs & Fri 9:30-5, Wed 9:30-6

BOLTON

P BENTLEY MEMORIAL LIBRARY*, 206 Bolton Center Rd, 06043. SAN 302-0584. Tel: 860-646-7349. FAX: 860-649-9059. E-mail: bentley@biblio.org. *Dir,* Elizabeth E Thornton; Staff 5 (MLS 1, Non-MLS 4)
Founded 1915. Pop 5,000; Circ 45,562
Library Holdings: Bk Vols 43,000; Per Subs 120
Special Collections: Dolls from around the World (Private Coll)
Automation Activity & Vendor Info: (Cataloging) Horizon; (Circulation) Horizon
Open Mon-Thurs 10-8, Sat 10-3
Friends of the Library Group

BRANFORD

P JAMES BLACKSTONE MEMORIAL LIBRARY*, 758 Main St, 06405-3697. SAN 302-0592. Tel: 203-488-1441. FAX: 203-481-6077. Reference FAX: 203-488-1260. E-mail: library@blackstone.lioninc.org. Web Site: www.blackstonelibrary.org. *Dir,* Karen Jensen; E-mail: kjensen@blackstonelibrary.org; *Assoc Librn, Access Serv,* Deirdre Santora; E-mail: dsantora@blackstone.lioninc.org; *Assoc Librn, Youth Serv,* Carly Rencsko; E-mail: crencsko@blackstone.lioninc.org; *Assoc Librn, Pub Serv,* Barbara Cangiano; E-mail: bcangian@blackstone.lioninc.org; *Assoc Librn, Tech Serv,* Gennett Grinnell; E-mail: ggrinnell@blackstone.lioninc.org; Staff 6 (MLS 6)
Founded 1896. Pop 28,683; Circ 202,957
Jul 2010-Jun 2011 Income $1,267,773, State $2,400, City $1,109,373, Locally Generated Income $151,000, Other $5,000. Mats Exp $100,000, Books $95,000, AV Mat $5,000. Sal $725,448 (Prof $48,256)
Library Holdings: Audiobooks 1,563; AV Mats 203; CDs 1,176; DVDs 4,168; Electronic Media & Resources 63; Bk Vols 76,753; Per Subs 138; Videos 1,138
Subject Interests: Genealogy, Local hist
Automation Activity & Vendor Info: (Cataloging) Innovative Interfaces, Inc; (Circulation) Innovative Interfaces, Inc; (Course Reserve) Innovative Interfaces, Inc; (ILL) Innovative Interfaces, Inc; (OPAC) Innovative Interfaces, Inc
Database Vendor: Baker & Taylor, Innovative Interfaces, Inc, OCLC WebJunction, ReferenceUSA, Wilson - Wilson Web
Wireless access
Publications: Constant Contact (Online only); Marble Columns (Newsletter)
Partic in Libraries Online, Inc
Special Services for the Deaf - Assistive tech
Special Services for the Blind - Assistive/Adapted tech devices, equip & products
Open Mon-Thurs 9-8, Fri & Sat 9-5, Sun 1-4
Friends of the Library Group

BRIDGEPORT

M BRIDGEPORT HOSPITAL*, Reeves Health Sciences Library, 267 Grant St, 06610-2870. (Mail add: PO Box 5000, 06610-0120), SAN 302-0622. Tel: 203-384-3254. FAX: 203-384-3107.
Library Holdings: e-books 84; Bk Titles 3,500; Bk Vols 4,400; Per Subs 300
Subject Interests: Health sci
Automation Activity & Vendor Info: (Cataloging) EOS International
Partic in Conn Asn of Health Scis Librs
Open Mon-Fri 8-4:30

P BRIDGEPORT PUBLIC LIBRARY*, 925 Broad St, 06604. SAN 336-0334. Tel: 203-576-7403. Circulation Tel: 203-576-7400. Reference Tel: 203-576-7406. Administration Tel: 203-576-7777. Information Services Tel: 203-576-7404. FAX: 203-576-8255. Reference FAX: 203-576-7044. Administration FAX: 203 333-0253. TDD: 203-576-7405. Web Site: www.bridgeportpubliclibrary.org. *City Librn,* Scott Hughes; E-mail: shughes@bridgeportpubliclibrary.org; *Head, Circ,* Angela Guglielmo; Tel: 203-576-7419, E-mail: aguglielmo@bridgeportpubliclibrary.org; *Head, Historical Coll,* Mary Witkowski; Tel: 203-576-7417, E-mail: mwitkowski@bridgeportpubliclibrary.org; *Ch,* Bina Williams; Tel: 203-576-7408; *Children & Teen Librn,* Jane Flynn; E-mail: jflynn@bridgeportpubliclibrary.org; *Commun Relations Librn,* Michael Bielawa; Tel: 203-576-7413, E-mail: mbielawa@bridgeportpubliclibrary.org; *Hist Coll Librn,* Elizabeth Van Tuyl; *Info Serv Librn,* Ron Fontaine; *Info Serv Librn,* Steve Kwasnik; *Info Serv Librn,* Herb Lazration; *Info Serv Librn,* John Soltis; *Tech Coordr,* Sylvia Boyd; Tel: 203-576-8284, E-mail: sboyd@bridgeportpubliclibrary.org; Staff 87 (MLS 31, Non-MLS 56)
Founded 1881. Pop 139,529; Circ 443,010
Library Holdings: AV Mats 40,075; Bk Vols 514,960
Special Collections: P T Barnum Circus. Oral History; State Document Depository; US Document Depository
Subject Interests: Art & archit, Bus & mgt, Lit, Local hist
Automation Activity & Vendor Info: (Acquisitions) SirsiDynix; (Cataloging) SirsiDynix; (Circulation) SirsiDynix; (OPAC) SirsiDynix; (Serials) SirsiDynix
Database Vendor: Dialog, Gale Cengage Learning, OCLC FirstSearch, SirsiDynix, Wilson - Wilson Web
Special Services for the Deaf - TDD equip
Open Tues 12-8, Wed & Thurs 10-6, Fri & Sat 10-5
Friends of the Library Group
Branches: 4
BLACK ROCK. Tel: 203-576-7427. *Librn,* Tina Geoffino
Library Holdings: Bk Vols 17,897
Friends of the Library Group
NEWFIELD, 1230 Stratford Ave, 06607, SAN 336-0423. Tel: 203-576-7828. *Head Librn,* Michael Bielawa
Library Holdings: Bk Vols 15,000
Open Mon & Fri 12-5, Tues & Thurs 10-6, Wed 12-8
Friends of the Library Group
NORTH, 3455 Madison Ave, 06606, SAN 336-0458. Tel: 203-576-7423. FAX: 203-576-7752. *Br Head,* Paula Keegan; Tel: 203-576-8021, E-mail: pkeegan@bridgeportpubliclibrary.org; *Librn,* Lucy Boland
Library Holdings: Bk Vols 50,000
Open Mon & Wed 1-9, Tues & Thurs 10-6, Sat 9-5
Friends of the Library Group
OLD MILL GREEN, 1677-81 E Main St, 06608, SAN 336-0393. Tel: 203-576-7634. E-mail: oldmillgreen@bridgeportpubliclibrary.org. *Br Head,* Sharon Breslow; Staff 4.5 (MLS 2, Non-MLS 2.5)
Library Holdings: Bk Vols 34,000
Subject Interests: Spanish lang
Open Mon 10-6, Tues-Thurs 10-8, Fri & Sat 10-5
Friends of the Library Group

R CONGREGATION B'NAI ISRAEL LIBRARY*, 2710 Park Ave, 06604. SAN 302-0649. Tel: 203-336-1858. FAX: 203-367-7889. Web Site: www.congregationbnaiisrael.org.
Founded 1960
Library Holdings: Bk Vols 2,000
Subject Interests: Judaica (lit or hist of Jews)
Open Mon-Thurs (Winter) 9-5, Fri 9-4:30; Mon-Thurs (Summer) 9-4:30, Fri 9-4

J HOUSATONIC COMMUNITY COLLEGE LIBRARY*, 900 Lafayette Blvd, 06604. SAN 302-0657. Tel: 203-332-5070. FAX: 203-332-5252. Web Site: www.hcc.commnet.edu/library. *Dir,* Shelley Strohm; Tel: 203-332-5072, E-mail: sstrohm@hcc.commnet.edu; *Librn,* Omaa Chukwurah; Tel: 203-332-5179, E-mail: ochukwurah@hcc.commnet.edu; *Media Serv Tech,* Doug Alton; Tel: 203-332-5077, E-mail: dalton@hcc.commnet.edu; *Media Serv Librn,* Lois McCracken; Tel: 203-332-5076, E-mail: lmccracken@hcc.commnet.edu; *Pub Serv Librn,* Peter Everett; Tel: 203-332-5074, E-mail: peverett@hcc.commnet.edu; *Syst*

Librn, Qiming Han; Tel: 203-332-5073, E-mail: qhan@hcc.commnet.edu; *Libr Assoc,* Jennifer Falasco; Staff 8 (MLS 6, Non-MLS 2)
Founded 1967. Enrl 4,500; Fac 83; Highest Degree: Associate
Library Holdings: AV Mats 6,300; Bk Vols 42,500; Per Subs 170
Automation Activity & Vendor Info: (Cataloging) Ex Libris Group; (Circulation) Ex Libris Group; (Course Reserve) Ex Libris Group
Partic in Lyrasis; OCLC Online Computer Library Center, Inc
Special Services for the Blind - Magnifiers
Open Mon-Thurs 8:30am-9pm, Fri 8:30-4, Sat 8:30-2:30, Sun 1-5

C UNIVERSITY OF BRIDGEPORT, Wahlstrom Library, 126 Park Ave, 06604-5620. SAN 302-0711. Tel: 203-576-4745. Interlibrary Loan Service Tel: 203-576-4522. Reference Tel: 203-576-4747. FAX: 203-576-4791. E-mail: reference@bridgeport.edu. Web Site: www.bridgeport.edu/academics/magnus-wahlstrom-library/. *Univ Librn,* Deborah Dulepski; Tel: 203-576-2388, E-mail: ddulepsk@bridgeport.edu; *Digital Content Librn,* Matthew Sherman; Tel: 203-576-4528, E-mail: msherman@bridgeport.edu; *Evening/Weekend Librn, Tech Serv,* Dale Outhouse; E-mail: douthouse@bridgeport.edu; *Health Sci Librn,* Rebecca Dowgiert; E-mail: rdowgier@bridgeport.edu; *Instruction/Info Lit Librn,* Matthew Schirano; E-mail: mschiran@bridgeport.edu. Subject Specialists: *Computer sci, Eng, Mass communications,* Deborah Dulepski; Staff 8 (MLS 6, Non-MLS 2)
Founded 1927. Highest Degree: Doctorate
Jul 2013-Jun 2014. Mats Exp $1,248,556, Per/Ser (Incl. Access Fees) $446,737, AV Equip $80,000. Sal $671,693
Automation Activity & Vendor Info: (Serials) Ex Libris Group
Database Vendor: 3M Library Systems, ABC-CLIO, ACM (Association for Computing Machinery), American Chemical Society, American Mathematical Society, American Physical Society, Baker & Taylor, Blackwell, Cinahl, CQ Press, ebrary, EBSCO Information Services, EBSCOhost, Elsevier, Ex Libris Group, Faulkner Information Services, Gale Cengage Learning, Greenwood Publishing Group, Hoovers, IEEE (Institute of Electrical & Electronics Engineers), Ingenta, JSTOR, Lexi-Comp, Material ConneXion, McGraw-Hill, MD Consult, Natural Standard, OCLC, OCLC FirstSearch, OCLC WorldShare Interlibrary Loan, OVID Technologies, ProQuest, PubMed, ScienceDirect, Scopus, Springer-Verlag, UpToDate, Westlaw, Wiley
Wireless access
Function: Ref serv available
Partic in Council of Connecticut Academic Library Directors (CCALD); OCLC-LVIS
Restriction: Badge access after hrs, Borrowing privileges limited to fac & registered students, Borrowing requests are handled by ILL, Restricted borrowing privileges

BRIDGEWATER

P BRIDGEWATER LIBRARY ASSOCIATION*, Burnham Library, 62 Main St S, 06752-9998. (Mail add: PO Box 430, 06752-0430), SAN 302-0738. Tel: 860-354-6937. FAX: 860-354-4583. E-mail: staff@burnhamlibrary.org. Web Site: www.burnhamlibrary.org. *Dir,* Sandra Neary; *Asst Librn,* Jean Archiere; Staff 2 (Non-MLS 2)
Founded 1926. Pop 1,895; Circ 25,619
Library Holdings: CDs 61; DVDs 127; Large Print Bks 390; Bk Titles 32,100; Per Subs 55; Talking Bks 679; Videos 575
Special Collections: Bridgewater Authors; Civil War Letters; Van Wyck Brooks
Automation Activity & Vendor Info: (Acquisitions) Auto-Graphics, Inc; (Cataloging) Auto-Graphics, Inc; (Circulation) Auto-Graphics, Inc; (ILL) Auto-Graphics, Inc; (OPAC) Auto-Graphics, Inc; (Serials) Auto-Graphics, Inc
Database Vendor: Gale Cengage Learning
Function: Art exhibits, Audio & video playback equip for onsite use, AV serv, CD-ROM, Handicapped accessible, Homebound delivery serv, ILL available, Music CDs, Photocopying/Printing, Prog for adults, Prog for children & young adult, Ref serv available, Summer reading prog, VHS videos, Wheelchair accessible, Workshops
Publications: Friends of the Library Events Postcard (Quarterly)
Special Services for the Blind - Extensive large print coll; Home delivery serv; Large print bks
Open Tues 1-5, Wed 9-6, Thurs 9-5, Sat 9-1
Friends of the Library Group

BRISTOL

S AMERICAN CLOCK & WATCH MUSEUM, INC*, Edward Ingraham Library, 100 Maple St, 06010-5092. SAN 302-0746. Tel: 860-583-6070. FAX: 860-583-1862. Web Site: www.clockmuseum.org. *Curator,* Chris H Bailey
Founded 1952
Library Holdings: Bk Vols 2,000
Subject Interests: Clock historical, Watch
Restriction: Non-circulating

M BRISTOL HOSPITAL & HEALTH CARE GROUP*, Library Services Department, 41 Brewster Rd, 06011. (Mail add: PO Box 977, 06011-0977). Tel: 860-585-3239. E-mail: info@bristolhospital.org. Web Site: www.bristolhospital.org. *Dir,* Marilyn Pitman; Staff 3 (MLS 2, Non-MLS 1)
Library Holdings: Bk Titles 1,300; Per Subs 180
Partic in Basic Health Sciences Library Network; Conn Asn of Health Scis Librs; Lyrasis; National Network of Libraries of Medicine
Open Mon-Fri 8-2

P BRISTOL PUBLIC LIBRARY*, Five High St, 06010. SAN 336-0571. Tel: 860-584-7787. FAX: 860-584-7696. E-mail: liblab@ci.bristol.ct.us. Web Site: www.bristollib.com. *Dir,* Francine Petosa; *Supvr, Ch Serv,* Valerie Toner; *Circ Supvr,* Floyd Wyche; *Ref Supvr,* Beth Stavola
Founded 1892. Pop 60,790; Circ 296,315
Library Holdings: Bk Vols 142,000; Per Subs 328
Special Collections: Local & State History Coll
Subject Interests: Agr, Art & archit, Educ, Environ studies, Music
Automation Activity & Vendor Info: (Acquisitions) SirsiDynix; (Cataloging) SirsiDynix; (Circulation) SirsiDynix; (Course Reserve) SirsiDynix; (ILL) SirsiDynix; (Media Booking) SirsiDynix; (OPAC) SirsiDynix; (Serials) SirsiDynix
Database Vendor: Gale Cengage Learning, ReferenceUSA
Special Services for the Blind - Bks on cassette; Bks on CD; Home delivery serv; Large print bks
Open Mon-Thurs 8:30-8, Fri & Sat 8:30-5
Friends of the Library Group
Branches: 1
MANROSS MEMORIAL, 260 Central St, Forestville, 06010, SAN 336-0601. Tel: 860-584-7790. *Br Supvr,* Deborah Prozzo
Library Holdings: Bk Vols 45,000
Open Mon-Thurs 10-8, Fri & Sat 9-5
Friends of the Library Group

BROAD BROOK

P BROAD BROOK PUBLIC LIBRARY*, 81 Main St, 06016. (Mail add: 44 Broad Brook Rd, 06016). Tel: 860-623-1334. FAX: 860-627-0493. *Librn,* Mary White
Library Holdings: Bk Titles 9,000; Bk Vols 11,000
Open Wed 1-7, Sat 10-2

BROOKFIELD

P THE BROOKFIELD LIBRARY*, 182 Whisconier Rd, 06804. SAN 302-0762. Tel: 203-775-6241. FAX: 203-740-7723. Web Site: www.brookfieldlibrary.org. *Dir,* Anita Barney; E-mail: abarney@brookfieldlibrary.org; *Adult Serv, Asst Dir,* Katherine Van Leeuwen; E-mail: kvanlee@brookfieldlibrary.org; *Ch Serv, Commun Serv,* Mary Proudfoot; E-mail: mproud@brookfieldlibrary.org; *ILL, Ref Serv,* Elizabeth Oedel; E-mail: eoedel@brookfieldlibrary.org; *Tech Serv, Teen Serv,* Jennifer Doyon; E-mail: jdoyon@brookfieldlibrary.org; Staff 7.25 (MLS 3.25, Non-MLS 4)
Founded 1951. Pop 16,700; Circ 156,000
Jul 2012-Jun 2013 Income $613,019, State $2,500, City $589,519, Locally Generated Income $21,000. Mats Exp $75,000. Sal $449,369
Library Holdings: Bk Vols 64,000; Per Subs 60
Automation Activity & Vendor Info: (Acquisitions) Evergreen; (Cataloging) Evergreen; (Circulation) Evergreen; (ILL) Bibliomation Inc; (OPAC) Evergreen
Database Vendor: Bibliomation Inc, EBSCOhost, Ingram Library Services, OCLC, Overdrive, Inc, WT Cox
Wireless access
Function: Adult bk club, Audiobks via web, AV serv, Bk club(s), Bks on CD, Children's prog, Computer training, Computers for patron use, Copy machines, e-mail & chat, Electronic databases & coll, Fax serv, Free DVD rentals, Handicapped accessible, Holiday prog, Home delivery & serv to Sr ctr & nursing homes, Homebound delivery serv, ILL available, Jazz prog, Mail & tel request accepted, Microfiche/film & reading machines, Mus passes, Music CDs, Notary serv, Online cat, Outside serv via phone, mail, e-mail & web, OverDrive digital audio bks, Photocopying/Printing, Printer for laptops & handheld devices, Prog for adults, Prog for children & young adult, Pub access computers, Ref & res, Scanner, Story hour, Summer & winter reading prog, Summer reading prog, Tax forms, Teen prog, Telephone ref, Web-catalog, Wheelchair accessible, Workshops
Publications: The Brookfield Library E-Newsletter (Monthly newsletter)
Partic in Connecticut Library Consortium
Open Mon, Wed, Fri & Sat 10-5, Tues & Thurs 11-8
Friends of the Library Group

BROOKLYN

P BROOKLYN TOWN LIBRARY ASSOCIATION*, Ten Canterbury Rd, 06234. (Mail add: PO Box 357, 06234-0357), SAN 302-0770. Tel: 860-774-0649. FAX: 860-774-0649. *Librn,* Catherine Tucker
Pop 6,600; Circ 15,070

Library Holdings: Bk Vols 18,000
Subject Interests: Local hist
Partic in Connecticut Library Consortium
Open Mon & Wed 2-8, Tues & Sat 11-5, Thurs & Fri 2-5
Friends of the Library Group

BURLINGTON

P BURLINGTON PUBLIC LIBRARY*, 34 Library Lane, 06013. SAN 302-0789. Tel: 860-673-3331. FAX: 860-673-0897. E-mail: bpl@libraryconnection.info. Web Site: www.burlingtonctlibrary.info. *Libr Dir,* Marie Spratlin Hasskarl; *Asst Dir,* Diana Rudzinski; *Sr Libr Asst,* Wendy Cunningham; *Libr Asst,* Tamara Christensen; *Libr Asst,* Sara LoPresti; *Ch Serv,* Laurie Meheran; *Youth Serv,* Sheila McCallum; Staff 3 (MLS 3)
Founded 1896. Pop 8,300
Library Holdings: Bk Vols 57,000
Subject Interests: Local hist
Automation Activity & Vendor Info: (Circulation) SirsiDynix; (OPAC) SirsiDynix
Wireless access
Function: Handicapped accessible, ILL available, Photocopying/Printing, Prog for children & young adult, Summer reading prog
Open Mon-Thurs 10-8, Fri & Sat 10-5
Friends of the Library Group

CANAAN

P DOUGLAS LIBRARY*, 108 Main St, 06018. (Mail add: PO Box 608, North Canaan, 06018), SAN 302-0797. Tel: 860-824-7863. FAX: 860-824-7863. E-mail: douglaslibrary@comcast.net. *Libr Dir,* Norma DeMay; *Asst Librn,* Pam Farzan; Staff 2 (Non-MLS 2)
Founded 1821. Pop 3,000; Circ 20,694
Jul 2008-Jun 2009 Income $102,900, City $58,875, Locally Generated Income $28,642. Mats Exp $12,750, Books $9,750, Other Print Mats $1,500, AV Mat $1,500. Sal $68,900
Library Holdings: Audiobooks 969; CDs 500; DVDs 726; Bk Vols 17,702; Per Subs 60
Automation Activity & Vendor Info: (Acquisitions) Follett Software; (Cataloging) Follett Software; (Circulation) Follett Software; (OPAC) Follett Software
Wireless access
Function: Adult bk club, Adult literacy prog, Art exhibits, Bk club(s), Bks on cassette, Bks on CD, Children's prog, Computers for patron use, Copy machines, Electronic databases & coll, Exhibits, Fax serv, Free DVD rentals, Holiday prog, Home delivery & serv to Sr ctr & nursing homes, Homebound delivery serv, ILL available, Mus passes, Music CDs, Online ref, Outreach serv, Photocopying/Printing, Preschool outreach, Prog for adults, Prog for children & young adult, Pub access computers, Spoken cassettes & CDs, Spoken cassettes & DVDs, Story hour, Summer reading prog, VHS videos, Video lending libr, Wheelchair accessible, Workshops
Partic in Region I Coop Libr Servs Unit
Open Mon 1:30-8, Wed & Fri 10-8, Sat 10-1
Friends of the Library Group

CANTERBURY

P CANTERBURY PUBLIC LIBRARY*, One Municipal Dr, 06331-1453. SAN 376-3234. Tel: 860-546-9022. FAX: 860-546-1142. E-mail: canterburypublic@yahoo.com. Web Site: canterburylibrary.org. *Libr Dir,* Marion Sheehan; *Ref & Ad Serv Librn,* Marilyn Kitlas; *Prog Coordr,* Kathleen Hart; *Web Coordr,* Kara Berglund; *ILL,* Bobbi Ann Orlomoski; Staff 1 (Non-MLS 1)
Founded 1925. Pop 5,060; Circ 45,125
Jul 2012-Jun 2013 Income $149,271, State $3,455, City $117,559, Locally Generated Income $3,098. Mats Exp $37,540, Books $14,589. Sal $94,151 (Prof $36,400)
Library Holdings: AV Mats 683; DVDs 1,836; e-books 162; Bk Titles 16,781; Per Subs 26
Automation Activity & Vendor Info: (Acquisitions) Baker & Taylor; (Cataloging) Auto-Graphics, Inc; (Circulation) Auto-Graphics, Inc; (ILL) Auto-Graphics, Inc; (OPAC) Auto-Graphics, Inc
Database Vendor: EBSCOhost, Evanced Solutions, Inc, WT Cox
Wireless access
Function: Adult bk club, Audiobks via web, Bk club(s), Bks on CD, Children's prog, Computer training, Computers for patron use, Copy machines, E-Reserves, Electronic databases & coll, Fax serv, Free DVD rentals, Handicapped accessible, Home delivery & serv to Sr ctr & nursing homes, Homebound delivery serv, ILL available, Magnifiers for reading, Mail & tel request accepted, Mus passes, Music CDs, Online cat, Outside serv via phone, mail, e-mail & web, Photocopying/Printing, Preschool outreach, Preschool reading prog, Prog for adults, Prog for children & young adult, Pub access computers, Ref serv available, Senior computer classes, Senior outreach, Serves mentally handicapped consumers, Spoken cassettes & CDs, Spoken cassettes & DVDs, Story hour, Summer reading prog, Tax forms, Teen prog, Telephone ref, Web-catalog, Wheelchair accessible
Partic in Connecticut Library Consortium
Special Services for the Deaf - Pocket talkers
Special Services for the Blind - Closed circuit TV magnifier
Open Mon-Wed 10-7, Thurs 10-8, Sat 10-2
Friends of the Library Group

S CONNECTICUT COMMISSION ON CULTURE & TOURISM*, Prudence Crandall Museum Library, One S Canterbury Rd, Rte 14 & 169, 06331. (Mail add: PO Box 58, 06331-0058), SAN 325-0431. Tel: 860-546-7800. FAX: 860-546-7803. *Curator,* Kazimiera Kozlowski; E-mail: Kaz.Kozlowski@ct.gov
Founded 1983
Library Holdings: Bk Vols 600
Subject Interests: African-Am hist

CANTON

P CANTON PUBLIC LIBRARY*, 40 Dyer Ave, 06019. SAN 302-0878. Tel: 860-693-5800. FAX: 860-693-5804. Web Site: www.cantonpubliclibrary.org. *Dir,* Robert Simon; E-mail: rsimon@cantonpubliclibrary.org; *Ch,* Cheryl Donahue; *Ref Serv,* Beth Van Ness; *Tech Serv,* Win Purrington; *Circ,* Norma Ignatowicz
Pop 8,453
Jul 2006-Jun 2007 Income $444,250. Mats Exp $50,925. Sal $329,000
Library Holdings: Bk Vols 60,000
Subject Interests: Connecticut, Local hist
Automation Activity & Vendor Info: (Cataloging) SirsiDynix; (Circulation) SirsiDynix; (OPAC) SirsiDynix
Partic in Metronet
Open Mon-Thurs 10-8, Fri & Sat 10-5, Sun (Nov-March) 1-4
Friends of the Library Group

CENTRAL VILLAGE

P CENTRAL VILLAGE PUBLIC LIBRARY*, 51 Black Hill Rd, 06332. (Mail add: PO Box 158, 06332-0158), SAN 376-3250. Tel: 860-564-7753. FAX: 860-564-2738. E-mail: cntrl.vllge.pub.lib@snet.net. *Dir,* Shirley DeFosse
Pop 15
Library Holdings: Audiobooks 322; CDs 50; DVDs 257; Large Print Bks 200; Bk Titles 13,000; Per Subs 12; Videos 107
Special Collections: State of Connecticut Books & Information Coll
Automation Activity & Vendor Info: (Acquisitions) Auto-Graphics, Inc; (Cataloging) Follett Software; (Circulation) Follett Software
Wireless access
Function: Wheelchair accessible
Partic in Connecticut Library Consortium
Open Mon & Fri 11-5, Tues 1-5, Thurs 12-5
Friends of the Library Group

CHAPLIN

P CHAPLIN PUBLIC LIBRARY*, 130 Chaplin St, 06235-2302. SAN 302-0819. Tel: 860 455 9424. FAX: 860-455-0515. E-mail: chaplinlibrary@yahoo.com. *Librn,* Geraldine Helmer
Founded 1911. Pop 1,900
Library Holdings: Bk Vols 12,000; Per Subs 40
Subject Interests: Local hist
Partic in Connecticut Library Consortium
Open Mon 1-6, Wed 2-8, Fri 2-6, Sat 10-5

CHESHIRE

P CHESHIRE PUBLIC LIBRARY*, 104 Main St, 06410-2499. SAN 302-0827. Tel: 203-272-2245. Reference Tel: 203-272-2245, Ext 3007. FAX: 203-272-7714. Circulation E-mail: circ@cheshirelibrary.org. Interlibrary Loan Service E-mail: ill@cheshirelibrary.org. Web Site: cheshirelibrary.com. *Dir,* Ramona Burkey; E-mail: rburkey@cheshirelibrary.org; *Dep Dir,* Deborah Rutter; E-mail: drutter@cheshirelibrary.org; *Asst Libr Dir,* Mary Dattilo; E-mail: mdattilo@cheshirelibrary.org; *Head, Ch,* Susan Hartley; E-mail: shartley@cheshirelibrary.org; *Head, Circ,* Noureen Hakim; E-mail: nhakim@cheshirelibrary.org; *Head, Ref,* William Basel; E-mail: bbasel@cheshirelibrary.org; *Head, Tech Serv,* Gail Roberts; E-mail: groberts@cheshirelibrary.org; Staff 30 (MLS 12, Non-MLS 18)
Founded 1892. Pop 28,883; Circ 424,041
Jul 2013-Jun 2014 Income $1,595,951, State $19,000, City $1,536,951, Locally Generated Income $40,000. Mats Exp $184,000, Books $129,000, Per/Ser (Incl. Access Fees) $14,000, AV Mat $25,000, Electronic Ref Mat (Incl. Access Fees) $16,000. Sal $1,315,140
Library Holdings: CDs 12,124; DVDs 10,283; e-books 11,092; Bk Vols 102,063; Per Subs 265
Subject Interests: Genealogy

Automation Activity & Vendor Info: (Cataloging) Innovative Interfaces, Inc; (Circulation) Innovative Interfaces, Inc; (OPAC) Innovative Interfaces, Inc; (Serials) Innovative Interfaces, Inc
Database Vendor: EBSCOhost, Newsbank, ReferenceUSA
Wireless access
Function: Adult literacy prog, After school storytime, Art exhibits, Audiobks via web, AV serv, Bk club(s), Bks on cassette, Bks on CD, Children's prog, Computer training, Computers for patron use, Copy machines, Digital talking bks, e-mail serv, E-Reserves, Electronic databases & coll, Exhibits, Family literacy, Free DVD rentals, Handicapped accessible, Holiday prog, Home delivery & serv to Sr ctr & nursing homes, Homebound delivery serv, ILL available, Magnifiers for reading, Mail & tel request accepted, Mus passes, Music CDs, Online cat, Online ref, Online searches, Outreach serv, OverDrive digital audio bks, Preschool outreach, Prog for adults, Prog for children & young adult, Pub access computers, Spoken cassettes & CDs, Spoken cassettes & DVDs, Story hour, Summer reading prog, Tax forms, Teen prog, Telephone ref, VHS videos, Web-catalog, Wheelchair accessible
Partic in Library Connection, Inc
Open Mon-Thurs 9:30-9, Fri 9:30-5, Sat (Sept-June) 9:30-5
Friends of the Library Group

S CONNECTICUT CORRECTIONAL INSTITUTION*, Cheshire Library, 900 Highland Ave, 06410. Tel: 203-250-2600, Ext 2124. FAX: 203-250-2707. *Librn,* Mark Sosnowski
Library Holdings: Bk Titles 1,800; Bk Vols 2,000; Per Subs 30
Open Mon-Fri 7:30-4

CHESTER

P CHESTER PUBLIC LIBRARY*, 21 W Main St, 06412. (Mail add: PO Box 310, 06412-0310), SAN 302-0843. Tel: 860-526-0018. E-mail: chesterctlibrary@yahoo.com. *Dir,* Linda Fox; *Asst Librn, ILL,* Pam Larson; *Asst Librn,* Patricia Petrus; *Circ Asst,* Leigh Basilone. Subject Specialists: *Children's prog,* Patricia Petrus
Founded 1789. Pop 3,700; Circ 32,120
Library Holdings: AV Mats 800; Large Print Bks 100; Bk Vols 17,700; Per Subs 63
Subject Interests: Local hist
Automation Activity & Vendor Info: (Cataloging) Auto-Graphics, Inc; (Circulation) Auto-Graphics, Inc; (OPAC) Auto-Graphics, Inc
Function: Ref serv available
Open Mon 10-8, Tues 2-6, Wed & Fri 10-6, Thurs 2-8, Sat 10-2
Friends of the Library Group

CLINTON

P HENRY CARTER HULL LIBRARY, INC, Ten Killingworth Tpk, 06413. SAN 302-0851. Tel: 860-669-2342. FAX: 860-669-8318. E-mail: askus@hchlibrary.org. Web Site: www.hchlibrary.org. *Dir,* Maribeth Breen; E-mail: Maribeth@hchlibrary.org; *Ref & Tech Librn,* Lisa Gugliotti; E-mail: Lisa@hchlibrary.org; *YA Librn,* Cathleen Cole; E-mail: cathleen@hchlibrary.org; *Adult Prog/Ref,* Elizabeth Tucker; E-mail: Elizabeth@hchlibrary.org; *Ch Serv,* Kara Gilbert; E-mail: Kara@hchlibrary.org; *ILL,* Beth Taddonio; E-mail: Beth@hchlibrary.org; Staff 5 (MLS 5)
Founded 1925. Pop 13,500
Library Holdings: Bk Vols 84,000; Per Subs 130
Automation Activity & Vendor Info: (Cataloging) ByWater Solutions; (Circulation) ByWater Solutions
Wireless access
Publications: H C Hull Library News
Open Mon 12-8, Tues-Thurs 9-8, Fri 9-5, Sat 10-4
Friends of the Library Group

COLCHESTER

P CRAGIN MEMORIAL LIBRARY*, Eight Linwood Ave, Rte 16, 06415. SAN 302-086X. Tel: 860-537-5752. FAX: 860-537-4559. Web Site: colchesterct.gov/library, craginlibrary.org. *Libr Dir,* Kate Byroade; E-mail: kbyroade@colchesterct.gov; *Asst Dir,* Antoinette Charest; E-mail: acharest@colchesterct.gov; *Head, Children's/Youth Serv,* Karen Giugno; Tel: 860-537-7201, E-mail: kgiugno@colchesterct.gov; *Head, Circ,* Vickie Lynch; E-mail: vlynch@colchesterct.gov; *Cataloger,* Joann Koch; E-mail: jkoch@colchesterct.gov; *Ch Asst,* Joann MacDonald; E-mail: jmacdonald@colchesterct.gov; *Libr Asst,* Travis Feder; *Libr Asst,* Samantha Partney; *Libr Asst,* Kris Patterson; *Libr Asst,* Liz Perez-Balesky; *Libr Asst,* Lindsay Riordan; *Prog Asst,* Elaine Alexander; E-mail: ealexander@colchesterct.gov; Staff 6.6 (MLS 1.875, Non-MLS 4.725)
Founded 1905. Pop 17,000; Circ 157,358
Library Holdings: Bks on Deafness & Sign Lang 10; CDs 600; Bk Titles 39,000; Bk Vols 55,000; Per Subs 160
Special Collections: Local History Coll
Wireless access
Function: After school storytime, Bks on CD, Children's prog, Computers for patron use, Copy machines, Fax serv, Handicapped accessible, Home delivery & serv to Sr ctr & nursing homes, ILL available, Magnifiers for reading, Mus passes, Music CDs, OverDrive digital audio bks, Photocopying/Printing, Preschool outreach, Preschool reading prog, Prog for adults, Prog for children & young adult, Pub access computers, Story hour, Summer reading prog, Tax forms, Wheelchair accessible
Partic in Connecticut Library Consortium; Library Connection, Inc
Special Services for the Blind - Home delivery serv
Open Mon, Wed & Thurs 10-8, Tues 10-5, Fri & Sat 10-4
Friends of the Library Group
Bookmobiles: 1

COLLINSVILLE

S CANTON HISTORICAL SOCIETY LIBRARY*, 11 Front St, 06019. SAN 329-8418. Tel: 860-693-2793. E-mail: cantonmuseum@sbcglobal.net. Web Site: www.cantonmuseum.org. *Curator,* Kathleen Woolman; Tel: 860-693-8893
Library Holdings: Bk Vols 400
Special Collections: Local Census, 1790-1930; Samuel W Collins & the Collins Company Coll, 1826-1966. Oral History
Subject Interests: Local hist
Function: Res libr
Restriction: Open by appt only, Open to pub for ref only

COLUMBIA

P SAXTON B LITTLE FREE LIBRARY, INC*, 319 Rte 87, 06237-1143. SAN 302-0886. Tel: 860-228-0350. FAX: 860-228-1569. E-mail: staff@columbiactlibrary.org. Web Site: www.columbiactlibrary.org. *Dir,* Su Epstein; *Adult Serv,* Caitlyn Orlomoski; *Ch,* Megan Quigley; Staff 4 (MLS 1, Non-MLS 3)
Founded 1883. Pop 5,406; Circ 63,352
Library Holdings: AV Mats 3,605; Bk Vols 41,000; Per Subs 110
Special Collections: Oral History
Subject Interests: Local hist
Automation Activity & Vendor Info: (Acquisitions) Auto-Graphics, Inc; (Cataloging) Auto-Graphics, Inc; (Circulation) Auto-Graphics, Inc; (Course Reserve) Auto-Graphics, Inc; (ILL) Auto-Graphics, Inc; (Media Booking) Auto-Graphics, Inc; (OPAC) Auto-Graphics, Inc; (Serials) Auto-Graphics, Inc
Publications: Friends (Newsletter)
Open Mon, Fri & Sat 10-5, Tues, Wed & Thurs 10-8
Friends of the Library Group

CORNWALL

P CORNWALL FREE LIBRARY*, 30 Pine St, 06753. (Mail add: PO Box 126, 06753-0126), SAN 302-0908. Tel: 860-672-6874. FAX: 860-672-6398. E-mail: cornwalllibrary@biblio.org, Web Site: www.biblio.org/cornwall. *Dir,* Amy Worthington-Cady; *Ch Serv,* Amy Buck; Staff 2 (Non-MLS 2)
Pop 1,443; Circ 19,500
Library Holdings: Bk Vols 26,000; Per Subs 50
Automation Activity & Vendor Info: (Cataloging) SirsiDynix; (Circulation) SirsiDynix
Open Tues, Thurs & Fri 10-5, Wed 12-7, Sat 10-2
Friends of the Library Group

COS COB

S GREENWICH HISTORICAL SOCIETY*, William E Finch Jr Library & Archives, Bush-Holley Historic Site, 39 Strickland Rd, 06807. SAN 302-0924. Tel: 203-869-6899. FAX: 203-861-9720. E-mail: admin@greenwichhistory.org. Web Site: greenwichhistory.org. *Archivist,* Christopher Shields; E-mail: cshields@greenwichhistory.org; *Curator,* Karen L Frederick; E-mail: curator@greenwichhistory.org; Staff 2 (MLS 1, Non-MLS 1)
Founded 1931
Library Holdings: Bk Vols 3,500
Special Collections: Anya Seton Papers; Greenwich Family History Coll; Holley/MacRae Family Papers; Photograph Coll; Postcard Coll; Real Estate Company Records
Subject Interests: Am Impressionism, Archit, Decorative art, Genealogy, Local hist, State hist
Function: Archival coll, For res purposes, Handicapped accessible, Photocopying/Printing, Ref serv available, Telephone ref
Publications: Annual Report of the Historical Society of the Town of Greenwich; Building Greenwich: Architectural & Design, 1640 to the Present; Post (Newsletter)
Open Wed 10-4
Restriction: Non-circulating

COVENTRY

P BOOTH & DIMOCK MEMORIAL LIBRARY*, 1134 Main St, 06238. SAN 302-0932. Tel: 860-742-7606. FAX: 860-742-7491. Web Site: www.CoventryPL.org. *Dir,* Sharon Pacholski; E-mail: spacholski@coventryct.org; Staff 3 (MLS 1, Non-MLS 2)
Founded 1880. Pop 12,215; Circ 96,000
Jul 2009-Jun 2010 Income $372,556. Mats Exp $38,450, Books $29,250, Per/Ser (Incl. Access Fees) $2,950, AV Mat $5,900, Electronic Ref Mat (Incl. Access Fees) $350. Sal $225,000
Library Holdings: Bk Titles 55,000; Per Subs 75; Talking Bks 2,400; Videos 2,300
Automation Activity & Vendor Info: (Cataloging) Auto-Graphics, Inc; (Circulation) Auto-Graphics, Inc; (ILL) Auto-Graphics, Inc; (OPAC) Auto-Graphics, Inc
Wireless access
Publications: Daily Dragon (Online only); Library Lingo (Newsletter)
Open Tues & Thurs 10-8, Wed 1-8, Fri 1-6, Sat 10-3

CROMWELL

P CROMWELL BELDEN PUBLIC LIBRARY*, 39 West St, 06416. SAN 302-0959. Tel: 860-632-3460. FAX: 860-632-3484. Web Site: cromwellct.com/library. *Dir,* Eileen Branciforte; *Asst Dir, Ch Serv,* Lois Meltzer; *Adult Serv,* Terry Crescimanno
Founded 1888
Library Holdings: Electronic Media & Resources 15; Bk Vols 52,025; Per Subs 150; Talking Bks 2,375; Videos 3,250
Subject Interests: Local hist
Automation Activity & Vendor Info: (Cataloging) SirsiDynix; (Circulation) SirsiDynix
Partic in Connecticut Library Consortium; Library Connection, Inc
Open Mon, Tues & Thurs 10-8, Wed 1-8, Fri & Sat 10-5
Friends of the Library Group

C HOLY APOSTLES COLLEGE & SEMINARY LIBRARY*, 33 Prospect Hill Rd, 06416-2005. SAN 302-0967. Tel: 860-632-3009. FAX: 860-632-3090. E-mail: library@holyapostles.edu. Web Site: www.holyapostles.edu. *Dir,* Clare Adamo; Staff 3 (MLS 1, Non-MLS 2)
Founded 1957. Enrl 150; Fac 29; Highest Degree: Master
Library Holdings: Bk Titles 60,000; Per Subs 220
Special Collections: Papal Documents; USCCB Documents
Subject Interests: Bioethics, Philos, Theol
Automation Activity & Vendor Info: (Cataloging) OCLC; (OPAC) Auto-Graphics, Inc
Database Vendor: EBSCO Information Services, Gale Cengage Learning, OCLC WorldShare Interlibrary Loan
Wireless access
Partic in Connecticut Library Consortium; OCLC Online Computer Library Center, Inc
Friends of the Library Group

DANBURY

M DANBURY HOSPITAL*, Health Sciences Library, 24 Hospital Ave, 06810. SAN 302-0991. Tel: 203-797-7419. FAX: 203-731-8662. *Mgr,* Amanda Pomeroy
Founded 1956
Library Holdings: Bk Vols 3,000; Per Subs 300
Subject Interests: Allied health, Hospital admin, Med, Nursing
Automation Activity & Vendor Info: (Cataloging) CyberTools for Libraries
Wireless access
Open Mon-Fri 8-5

S DANBURY MUSEUM & HISTORICAL SOCIETY*, Research Library & Archives, 43 Main St, 06810. SAN 302-1025. Tel: 203-743-5200. FAX: 203-743-1131. E-mail: info@danburymuseum.org, research@danburymuseum.org. Web Site: www.danburymuseum.org/danburymuseum/Research.html. *Exec Dir,* Brigid Guertin; E-mail: bguertin@danburymuseum.org; *Res Spec,* Diane Hassan; E-mail: dhassan@danburymuseum.org; Staff 2 (Non-MLS 2)
Founded 1947
Library Holdings: Bk Vols 600
Special Collections: DAR Lineage Books; Hat Life Magazine Coll; Hatting Industry (Charles Ives Coll)
Subject Interests: Antiques, Genealogy, Local hist
Wireless access
Function: For res purposes
Restriction: Non-circulating to the pub, Open by appt only
Friends of the Library Group

P DANBURY PUBLIC LIBRARY*, 170 Main St, 06810. SAN 302-1017. Tel: 203-797-4505. Interlibrary Loan Service Tel: 203-797-4690. Administration Tel: 203-797-4512. Information Services Tel: 203-797-4527. FAX: 203-797-4501. Administration FAX: 203-796-1677. Information Services FAX: 203-796-1518. Web Site: danburylibrary.org. *Dir,* Lambert Shell; E-mail: lshell@danburylibrary.org; *Asst Dir,* Katie Ventura; E-mail: kventura@danburylibrary.org; Staff 30 (MLS 14, Non-MLS 16)
Founded 1869. Pop 79,226; Circ 622,356
Jul 2009-Jun 2010 Income $2,101,806, State $32,132, City $1,982,455, Locally Generated Income $87,219. Sal $1,524,541
Library Holdings: AV Mats 19,896; e-books 4,146; Bk Vols 99,912; Per Subs 336
Special Collections: State Document Depository
Subject Interests: Local hist
Automation Activity & Vendor Info: (Acquisitions) Innovative Interfaces, Inc; (Cataloging) Innovative Interfaces, Inc; (Circulation) Innovative Interfaces, Inc; (Course Reserve) Innovative Interfaces, Inc; (ILL) Innovative Interfaces, Inc; (Media Booking) Innovative Interfaces, Inc; (OPAC) Innovative Interfaces, Inc; (Serials) Innovative Interfaces, Inc
Database Vendor: Innovative Interfaces, Inc
Wireless access
Open Mon-Thurs 10-7, Fri & Sat 10-5, Sun 1-5
Friends of the Library Group

S FEDERAL CORRECTIONAL INSTITUTION*, Department of Justice Centralized Library, 33 1/2 Pembroke Sta, 06811. SAN 302-1033. Tel: 203-743-6471, Ext 5410. FAX: 203-312-5138.
Founded 1979
Library Holdings: Bk Vols 2,000; Per Subs 25
Special Collections: World War I & II Coll
Open Mon-Fri 7:30-4

P LONG RIDGE LIBRARY*, 191 Long Ridge Rd, 06810-8463. (Mail add: Seven Wicks Manor Dr, 06810), SAN 321-6578. Tel: 203-748-1011. *Librn,* Barbara Fulton; Tel: 203-748-7520
Founded 1919. Pop 78,000
Jan 2011-Dec 2011 Income $4,600
Library Holdings: CDs 25; DVDs 50; Bk Titles 2,100; Bk Vols 2,300; Talking Bks 85; Videos 102
Special Collections: Oral History
Subject Interests: Historic bldg
Open Wed 5-7, Sat 10-4
Friends of the Library Group

C WESTERN CONNECTICUT STATE UNIVERSITY, Ruth A Haas Library, 181 White St, 06810. SAN 302-1076. Tel: 203-837-9100. FAX: 203-837-9108. Web Site: library.wcsu.edu. *Dir, Libr Serv,* Veronica Kenausis; Tel: 203-837-9109, E-mail: kenausisv@wcsu.edu; *Access Serv Librn,* Russell Gladstone; Tel: 203-837-9102, E-mail: gladstoner@wcsu.edu; *Acq Librn,* Xiao Hua Yang; Tel: 203-837-9105, Fax: 203-837-9103, E-mail: yangx@wcsu.edu; *Archives & Spec Coll Librn,* Brian Stevens; *Cat Librn,* Alesia Sczabo; *Educ Librn, Pub Serv,* Tom Schnicdel; *Instruction Librn,* Joan Reitz; Tel: 203-837-8308, E-mail: reitzj@wcsu.edu; *Ref Librn,* Vijay Nair; Tel: 203-837-9116, E-mail: nairj@wcsu.edu; *Ser Librn,* Jennifer O'Brien; *Doc Delivery, ILL,* Joanne Elpern; Tel: 203-837-9114, E-mail: elpernj@wcsu.edu; *Syst,* Brian Kennison; Tel: 203-837-8847, E-mail: kennisonb@wcsu.edu; *Tech Serv,* Teresa Saunders; Tel: 203-837-9106, E-mail: saunderst@wcsu.edu; Staff 10 (MLS 10)
Founded 1905. Enrl 5,080; Fac 181; Highest Degree: Doctorate
Library Holdings: AV Mats 8,315; Bk Titles 105,000; Bk Vols 200,000; Per Subs 700
Special Collections: Fairfield County & Connecticut History (Connecticut Room), bks, doc; Music Education, bks, rec; Teacher Educ (Curriculum Room). US Document Depository
Subject Interests: Local hist
Automation Activity & Vendor Info: (Acquisitions) Innovative Interfaces, Inc; (Cataloging) Innovative Interfaces, Inc; (Circulation) Innovative Interfaces, Inc; (ILL) OCLC ILLiad
Database Vendor: EBSCOhost, JSTOR, OCLC FirstSearch, ReferenceUSA
Wireless access
Publications: Library Guide
Partic in BRS; Dialog Corp; OCLC Online Computer Library Center, Inc
Open Mon-Thurs 8am-11pm, Fri 8-4, Sat 10-6, Sun 2-10

Departmental Libraries:

ROBERT S YOUNG BUSINESS LIBRARY, 181 White St, 06810-6885. Tel: 203-837-9139. FAX: 203-837-9135. Web Site: library.wcsu.edu. *Librn,* Joanne Raider; E-mail: raiderj@wcsu.edu; *Bus Librn,* Xiao Mei Gong; E-mail: gongx@wcsu.edu; *Bus Librn,* Mary Kay Loomis; E-mail: loomism@wcsu.edu; Staff 2 (MLS 2)
Founded 1982
Library Holdings: Bk Vols 6,000; Per Subs 125
Database Vendor: EBSCOhost, LexisNexis, Westlaw
Open Mon-Thurs 9-9, Fri 9-4, Sat 11-4, Sun 2-7

DANIELSON

P KILLINGLY PUBLIC LIBRARY*, 25 Westcott Rd, 06239. SAN 302-1092. Tel: 860-779-5383. FAX: 860-779-1823. Web Site: www.killinglypubliclibrary.org. *Dir,* Peter Ciparelli; *Adult Serv,* Laura Zipkin; E-mail: lzipkin@biblio.org; *Ref,* Karen Wall; Staff 13 (MLS 4, Non-MLS 9)
Founded 1903. Pop 17,428; Circ 105,209
Jul 2011-Jun 2012 Income $728,000. Mats Exp $671,110
Special Collections: Local History (Windham County Coll)
Automation Activity & Vendor Info: (Cataloging) Evergreen; (Circulation) Evergreen; (OPAC) Evergreen; (Serials) Evergreen
Database Vendor: Bibliomation Inc, EBSCOhost
Wireless access
Partic in Bibliomation Inc; Connecticut Library Consortium; OPEN
Open Mon & Fri 9:30-5:30, Tues & Thurs 9:30-7, Sat 9:30-3:30
Friends of the Library Group

J QUINEBAUG VALLEY COMMUNITY COLLEGE LIBRARY, 742 Upper Maple St, 06239. SAN 302-1106. Tel: 860-932-4007. FAX: 860-932-4308. E-mail: library@qvcc.edu. Web Site: www.qvcc.edu/library. *Dir of Libr Serv,* Sharon Moore; Tel: 860-932-4131, E-mail: smoore@qvcc.edu; *Ref & Instruction Librn,* M'lyn Hines; Tel: 860-932-4056, E-mail: mhines@qvcc.edu; *Syst Librn,* Michael Lynch; Tel: 860-932-4119, E-mail: mlynch@qvcc.edu; *Libr Assoc II,* Cheryl White; Tel: 860-932-4171, E-mail: cwhite@qvcc.edu; Staff 4 (MLS 3, Non-MLS 1)
Founded 1971. Enrl 2,000; Highest Degree: Associate
Library Holdings: DVDs 2,500; e-books 200,000; e-journals 40,000; Bk Titles 28,000; Bk Vols 30,000; Per Subs 125
Automation Activity & Vendor Info: (Acquisitions) Ex Libris Group; (Cataloging) Ex Libris Group; (Circulation) Ex Libris Group; (Course Reserve) Ex Libris Group; (ILL) OCLC; (Media Booking) Ex Libris Group; (OPAC) Ex Libris Group; (Serials) EBSCO Online
Database Vendor: American Chemical Society, ARTstor, Auto-Graphics, Inc, CredoReference, ebrary, EBSCOhost, Elsevier, Gale Cengage Learning, ProQuest, Springer-Verlag
Wireless access
Partic in Council of Connecticut Academic Library Directors (CCALD); Westchester Academic Library Directors Organization (WALDO)
Open Mon-Thurs 9-8:30, Fri 9-2

DARIEN

S DARIEN HISTORICAL SOCIETY, INC LIBRARY*, 45 Old Kings Hwy N, 06820. SAN 302-1114. Tel: 203-655-9233. FAX: 203-656-3892. E-mail: darien-historical@sbcglobal.net. Web Site: historical.darien.org. *Exec Dir,* Judith Groppa
Founded 1953
Library Holdings: Bk Vols 1,600; Per Subs 10
Subject Interests: Decorative art, Genealogy, Local hist, New England

P DARIEN LIBRARY*, 1441 Post Rd, 06820-5419. SAN 302-1122. Tel: 203-655-1234. Circulation Tel: 203-669-5239. Administration Tel: 203-669-5220. Information Services Tel: 203-669-5236. FAX: 203-655-1547. E-mail: askus@darienlibrary.org. Web Site: www.darienlibrary.org. *Dir,* Alan Kirk Gray; Tel: 203-669-5224, E-mail: akgray@darienlibrary.org; *Asst Dir, Innovation & UX,* John Blyberg; Tel: 203-669-5222, E-mail: jblyberg@darienlibrary.org; Staff 28.8 (MLS 12.2, Non-MLS 16.6)
Founded 1894. Pop 19,607; Circ 783,521
Jul 2009-Jun 2010 Income $97,385,260, State $62,800, City $3,061,349, Locally Generated Income $94,261,111. Mats Exp $464,924, Books $204,093, Per/Ser (Incl. Access Fees) $31,130, AV Mat $107,681, Electronic Ref Mat (Incl. Access Fees) $122,020. Sal $1,967,510
Library Holdings: Audiobooks 3,378; CDs 5,679; DVDs 11,598; e-journals 7,877; Electronic Media & Resources 36; Large Print Bks 2,500; Bk Vols 115,034; Per Subs 259; Talking Bks 4,813
Subject Interests: Genealogy, Lit, Local hist, Travel
Automation Activity & Vendor Info: (Circulation) Innovative Interfaces, Inc; (ILL) OCLC
Database Vendor: Baker & Taylor, EBSCOhost, Gale Cengage Learning, OCLC FirstSearch, Overdrive, Inc, ProQuest
Wireless access
Function: Adult bk club, After school storytime, Art exhibits, Audio & video playback equip for onsite use, Audiobks via web, Bk club(s), Bk reviews (Group), Bks on CD, CD-ROM, Children's prog, Computer training, Computers for patron use, Copy machines, e-mail & chat, e-mail serv, E-Reserves, Electronic databases & coll, Equip loans & repairs, Exhibits, Fax serv, Free DVD rentals, Games & aids for the handicapped, Genealogy discussion group, Handicapped accessible, Health sci info serv, Holiday prog, Home delivery & serv to Sr ctr & nursing homes, Homebound delivery serv, Homework prog, ILL available, Large print keyboards, Magnifiers for reading, Mail & tel request accepted, Music CDs, Notary serv, Online cat, Online ref, Online searches, Outreach serv, OverDrive digital audio bks, Photocopying/Printing, Preschool outreach, Prog for adults, Prog for children & young adult, Provide serv for the mentally ill, Pub access computers, Ref serv available, Ref serv in person, Scanner, Senior computer classes, Senior outreach, Story hour, Summer & winter reading prog, Summer reading prog, Tax forms, Teen prog, Telephone ref, Wheelchair accessible
Partic in Connecticut Library Consortium
Open Mon-Thurs 9-9, Fri 9-6, Sat 9-5, Sun 1-5
Friends of the Library Group

S ZOTOS INTERNATIONAL LIBRARY*, 100 Tokeneke Rd, 06820-1005. SAN 320-6149. Tel: 203-656-7700, 203-656-7805. FAX: 203-656-7963. *Res Librn,* Sue Pickard
Founded 1932
Library Holdings: Bk Titles 5,300; Per Subs 30
Subject Interests: Cosmetics industry, Toiletries
Publications: Newsletters
Partic in Dialog Corp
Restriction: Staff use only

DEEP RIVER

P DEEP RIVER PUBLIC LIBRARY*, 150 Main St, 06417. SAN 302-1157. Tel: 860-526-6039. FAX: 860-526-6040. Web Site: www.deepriverct.com. *Dir,* Ann Paietta; E-mail: apaietta@att.net; Staff 1 (MLS 1)
Founded 1900. Pop 4,600; Circ 69,051
Library Holdings: Bk Titles 3,100; Per Subs 100
Automation Activity & Vendor Info: (Cataloging) Winnebago Software Co; (Circulation) Winnebago Software Co; (OPAC) Winnebago Software Co; (Serials) Winnebago Software Co
Wireless access
Function: Art exhibits, Bk club(s), Computer training, Computers for patron use, Copy machines, Exhibits, Family literacy, Free DVD rentals, Handicapped accessible, Holiday prog, Home delivery & serv to Sr ctr & nursing homes, Homebound delivery serv, ILL available, Mus passes, Music CDs, Preschool reading prog, Prog for adults, Prog for children & young adult, Senior computer classes, Tax forms, Wheelchair accessible, Workshops
Partic in Connecticut Library Consortium; ReQuest OPAC Catalog
Open Mon 1-8, Tues, Thurs & Fri 10-6, Wed 12:30-8, Sat 10-5
Friends of the Library Group

DERBY

P DERBY NECK LIBRARY*, 307 Hawthorne Ave, 06418-1199. SAN 302-1165. Tel: 203-734-1492. FAX: 203-732-2913. E-mail: derbynecklibrary@yahoo.com. Web Site: www.derbynecklibrary.org. *Head Librn,* Ian Parsells; E-mail: headlibrarian@biblio.org; *Youth Serv Librn,* Kathleen Gordon; Staff 4 (MLS 2, Non-MLS 2)
Founded 1897. Pop 12,500; Circ 49,581
Library Holdings: Audiobooks 1,485; CDs 1,092; DVDs 2,992; e-books 86; Large Print Bks 2,850; Bk Vols 52,962; Per Subs 130; Videos 2,402
Subject Interests: Cooking, Fiction, Irish, Local hist, Poetry, Urban affairs
Automation Activity & Vendor Info: (Acquisitions) Bibliomation Inc; (Cataloging) Evergreen; (Circulation) Evergreen; (ILL) Evergreen; (OPAC) Evergreen; (Serials) Evergreen
Database Vendor: Bibliomation Inc, Gale Cengage Learning
Wireless access
Function: Audio & video playback equip for onsite use, Audiobks via web, Bilingual assistance for Spanish patrons, Bk club(s), Bks on CD, Children's prog, Computer training, Computers for patron use, Copy machines, Electronic databases & coll, Fax serv, Free DVD rentals, Genealogy discussion group, Handicapped accessible, Holiday prog, Mail & tel request accepted, Mus passes, Music CDs, Online cat, OverDrive digital audio bks, Preschool outreach, Prog for adults, Prog for children & young adult, Pub access computers, Ref serv available, Ref serv in person, Res libr, Scanner, Senior computer classes, Spoken cassettes & CDs, Spoken cassettes & DVDs, Story hour, Summer reading prog, Tax forms, Teen prog, Telephone ref, VHS videos, Web-catalog, Wheelchair accessible, Workshops, Writing prog
Open Mon-Thurs 10-8, Sat & Sun 1-5
Friends of the Library Group

P DERBY PUBLIC LIBRARY*, Harcourt Wood Memorial Library, 313 Elizabeth St, 06418. SAN 302-1173. Tel: 203-736-1482. FAX: 203-736-1419. TDD: 800-842-9710. Web Site: www.derbypubliclibrary.org. *Dir,* Cathy Williams; E-mail: cwilliams@biblio.org; *Head, Circ,* Kathy Wilson; *Ch Serv,* Susan Sherman; E-mail: ssherman@biblio.org; *Hist Coll Librn,* Steven Zavednak; E-mail: szavednak@biblio.org; *Tech Librn,* Terence O'Keefe; E-mail: tokeefe@biblio.org; Staff 4 (MLS 1, Non-MLS 3)
Founded 1902. Pop 12,520; Circ 45,000
Library Holdings: DVDs 1,975; Bk Vols 47,044; Per Subs 97; Talking Bks 1,040
Special Collections: Family Place; Parent's Place

Subject Interests: Career, Compact discs, Employment, Finance, Genealogy, Hist, Lit, Literacy, Local hist, Sheet music
Automation Activity & Vendor Info: (Acquisitions) Bibliomation Inc; (Cataloging) Bibliomation Inc; (Circulation) Bibliomation Inc; (Course Reserve) Bibliomation Inc; (ILL) Bibliomation Inc; (OPAC) Bibliomation Inc; (Serials) Bibliomation Inc
Database Vendor: EBSCOhost
Publications: Derby Public Library Newsletter
Special Services for the Deaf - Closed caption videos; TDD equip
Special Services for the Blind - Bks on cassette; Large print bks; Magnifiers
Open Mon-Wed 9-8, Thurs 9-6, Fri 9-5, Sat (Sept-June) 9-2
Friends of the Library Group

M GRIFFIN HOSPITAL*, Health Resource Center, 130 Division St, 06418. SAN 371-5264. Tel: 203-732-7399. FAX: 203-732-1390. E-mail: griflib@griffinhealth.org. *Coordr,* Kerry Dennigan; Staff 2 (MLS 1, Non-MLS 1)
Founded 1994
Library Holdings: Bk Titles 1,000; Per Subs 250
Subject Interests: Consumer health
Partic in Conn Asn of Health Scis Librs
Open Mon, Tues & Fri 9-5, Wed & Thurs 9-8, Sat 11-3

DURHAM

P DURHAM PUBLIC LIBRARY*, Seven Maple Ave, 06422. SAN 302-1181. Tel: 860-349-9544. FAX: 860-349-1897. Web Site: www.durhamlibrary.org. *Dir,* Trish Connolly; E-mail: tconnolly@durhamlibrary.org; *Asst Dir,* Cynthia Shirshac; E-mail: cshirshac@durhamlibrary.org; *Head, Ch,* Christine Michaud; *Head, YA,* Karyn Gardiner; Staff 8 (MLS 4, Non-MLS 4)
Founded 1894. Pop 7,200; Circ 210,000
Jul 2008-Jun 2009 Income $474,424. Mats Exp $52,000, Books $37,000, Per/Ser (Incl. Access Fees) $3,000, AV Mat $11,500. Sal $298,661
Library Holdings: Audiobooks 600; CDs 590; DVDs 3,200; Large Print Bks 1,200; Bk Vols 58,989; Per Subs 75; Videos 500
Subject Interests: Local hist
Automation Activity & Vendor Info: (Acquisitions) Innovative Interfaces, Inc; (Cataloging) Innovative Interfaces, Inc; (Circulation) Innovative Interfaces, Inc; (ILL) Innovative Interfaces, Inc; (OPAC) Innovative Interfaces, Inc
Wireless access
Partic in Libraries Online, Inc
Open Mon-Thurs 10-9, Fri & Sat 10-5
Friends of the Library Group

EAST BERLIN

P EAST BERLIN LIBRARY ASSOCIATION*, 80 Main St, 06023. (Mail add: PO Box 334, 06023-0334), SAN 302-119X. Tel: 860-828-3123. *Librn,* Janice Jacobs
Circ 6,000
Library Holdings: Bk Vols 6,900; Per Subs 15
Open Mon & Thurs 3-5 & 6:30-8:30

EAST GRANBY

P EAST GRANBY PUBLIC LIBRARY*, 24 Center St, 06026. (Mail add: PO Box G, 06026-0470), SAN 302-1203. Tel: 860-653-3002. FAX: 860-653-3936. E-mail: eastgranbylibrary@egpl.org. Web Site: www.egpl.org. *Dir,* Lisa Salazar; E-mail: lsalazar@egpl.org; Staff 9 (MLS 1, Non-MLS 8)
Founded 1922. Pop 4,500; Circ 33,990
Library Holdings: Bk Vols 30,000; Per Subs 28
Subject Interests: Careers, Consumer info, Educ, Local hist
Automation Activity & Vendor Info: (Circulation) Follett Software
Publications: Literally Speaking
Partic in Connecticut Library Consortium
Open Mon-Thurs 10-8, Sat 9:30-1:30
Friends of the Library Group

EAST HADDAM

S GOODSPEED OPERA HOUSE FOUNDATION*, The Scherer Library of Musical Theatre, 20 Norwich Rd, 06423-1344. (Mail add: PO Box A, 06423-0281), SAN 370-6044. Tel: 860-873-8664, Ext 745. FAX: 860-873-2329. Web Site: www.goodspeed.org/education-library/library. *Educ & Libr Dir,* Joshua S Ritter; E-mail: jritter@goodspeed.org; *Educ & Libr Asst,* Christine Hopkins; Tel: 860-873-8664, Ext 373, E-mail: chopkins@goodspeed.org; Staff 2 (Non-MLS 2)
Founded 1979
Special Collections: Goodspeed Opera House Archives (Historical information on the Goodspeed Opera House, as well as libretti, scores, videos, orchestrations, & memorabilia from productions); Music Theatre International Libretti & Scores (A complete coll of libretti & scores from musicals licensed by Music Theatre International); The Carol & Frank Tuit Record Coll (An extensive coll of music by George Gershwin on tape, vinyl & acetate, including rare recordings); The Crowley-Stoll Coll (Memorabilia & audio & video recordings covering a wide range of 20th & 21st Century musical theatre with special thanks to Alex Membreno); The Josef Weinberger Coll (An extensive coll of libretti & scores donated by Josef Weinberger, London); The Judge David I Harfeld Coll (An extensive coll of vinyl recordings, cds, memorabilia, photographs, news clippings, reviews, & videos); The Michael Kuchwara Coll (Plays, scores, libretti, playbills & books established in his memory by his family & friends); The National Broadcasting Company (NBC) Sheet Music Library (Extensive coll of sheet music, which contains more than 30,000 titles dating back to the turn of the century, used in the heyday of radio & the early days of live television); The Patricia Hoag Simon Coll (Interviews with associates of Joshua Logan & taped seminars at Marymount Manhattan College from 1987 to 2010 with such individuals as Arthur Laurents, Harold Prince, Stephen Sondheim, & Chita Rivera. The coll was compiled by Patricia Hoag Simon, MFA; Associate Professor of Theatre; Marymount Manhattan College); The Rodgers & Hammerstein Organization Libretti & Scores (A complete coll of libretti from musicals licensed by The Rodgers & Hammerstein Organization)
Subject Interests: Musical theatre
Automation Activity & Vendor Info: (Acquisitions) ByWater Solutions; (Cataloging) ByWater Solutions; (Circulation) ByWater Solutions; (OPAC) ByWater Solutions
Wireless access
Function: Archival coll
Restriction: Access at librarian's discretion, Circulates for staff only, Internal circ only, Non-circulating, Open by appt only, Open to pub by appt only, Open to pub with supv only, Open to students, fac & staff, Private libr
Friends of the Library Group

P RATHBUN FREE MEMORIAL LIBRARY*, 36 Main St, 06423. (Mail add: PO Box G, 06423), SAN 302-122X. Tel: 860-873-8210. FAX: 860-873-3601. Web Site: www.rathbun.lioninc.org. *Dir,* Kelly Marszycky
Founded 1935. Circ 59,604
Library Holdings: Bk Vols 23,000; Per Subs 68
Special Collections: East Haddam History Coll, clippings, micro
Open Mon & Wed 10-5, Tues & Thurs 10-8, Sat 10-2
Friends of the Library Group

EAST HAMPTON

P EAST HAMPTON PUBLIC LIBRARY*, 105 Main St, 06424. SAN 302-1238. Tel. 860-267-6621. FAX: 860-267-4427. E-mail: ehplct@hotmail.com. Web Site: www.easthamptonct.org. *Dir,* Susan Berescik; *Ch Serv,* Kathleen Sands; Staff 13 (MLS 2, Non-MLS 11)
Founded 1898. Pop 12,300; Circ 118,958
Jul 2007-Jun 2008 Income $385,164. Mats Exp $385,164. Sal $247,481 (Prof $102,336)
Library Holdings: AV Mats 7,843; Bk Vols 53,439; Per Subs 85
Subject Interests: Local hist
Automation Activity & Vendor Info: (Cataloging) Auto-Graphics, Inc; (Circulation) Auto-Graphics, Inc; (ILL) Auto-Graphics, Inc; (OPAC) Auto-Graphics, Inc
Database Vendor: Bowker
Wireless access
Function: Bk club(s), Bks on cassette, Bks on CD, Children's prog, Computers for patron use, Copy machines, Digital talking bks, E-Reserves, Electronic databases & coll, Handicapped accessible, Holiday prog, Home delivery & serv to Sr ctr & nursing homes, ILL available, Mus passes, Music CDs, Photocopying/Printing, Preschool outreach, Prog for adults, Prog for children & young adult
Open Mon-Wed 10-8, Thurs-Sat 10-5
Friends of the Library Group

EAST HARTFORD

S CONNECTICUT SOCIETY OF GENEALOGISTS, INC LIBRARY*, 175 Maple St, 06118-2364. (Mail add: PO Box 435, Glastonbury, 06033-0435), SAN 372-6525. Tel: 860-569-0002. FAX: 860-569-0339. E-mail: csginc@csginc.org. Web Site: www.csginc.org. *In Charge,* Stephanie Hyland; Staff 1 (Non-MLS 1)
Founded 1968
Library Holdings: Bk Titles 5,000
Wireless access
Open Mon-Fri 9:30-4

P EAST HARTFORD PUBLIC LIBRARY, Raymond Memorial Library, 840 Main St, 06108. SAN 336-0636. Tel: 860-289-6429. FAX: 860-291-9166. Web Site: easthartfordct.gov/library. *Dir,* Susan Hansen
Founded 1879. Pop 59,000; Circ 250,000
Library Holdings: Bk Vols 290,000; Per Subs 400
Special Collections: Aviation Coll; Tobacco Coll

Automation Activity & Vendor Info: (Cataloging) Innovative Interfaces, Inc; (Circulation) Innovative Interfaces, Inc; (OPAC) Innovative Interfaces, Inc
Wireless access
Open Mon-Thurs 9-8, Fri & Sat 9-5
Friends of the Library Group

EAST HAVEN

P HAGAMAN MEMORIAL LIBRARY, 227 Main St, 06512-3003. SAN 302-1262. Tel: 203-468-3890. FAX: 203-468-3892. *Dir,* Bruce George; *Head, Ref,* Fawn Gillespie; *Circ Mgr,* Darleen Hood; *Ch,* Sascha Gardiner; *Commun Serv Librn,* Cynthia Gwiazda; Staff 22 (MLS 6, Non-MLS 16)
Founded 1909. Pop 27,969; Circ 125,957
Jul 2013-Jun 2014 Income $820,000. Mats Exp $48,000. Sal $425,000
Library Holdings: AV Mats 5,377; CDs 855; DVDs 1,216; Large Print Bks 3,096; Bk Vols 66,642; Per Subs 133; Talking Bks 2,040; Videos 3,213
Automation Activity & Vendor Info: (Cataloging) Innovative Interfaces, Inc; (Circulation) Innovative Interfaces, Inc; (OPAC) Innovative Interfaces, Inc
Function: Homebound delivery serv, ILL available, Magnifiers for reading
Partic in Library Exchange Aids Patrons
Special Services for the Blind - Closed circuit TV magnifier
Open Mon, Fri & Sat 10-5, Tues, Wed & Thurs 10-8
Friends of the Library Group

S THE SHORE LINE TROLLEY MUSEUM LIBRARY*, 17 River St, 06512. SAN 302-1254. Tel: 203-467-6927. FAX: 203-467-7635. Web Site: www.bera.org. *Mgr,* Geo Boucher; *Curator,* Michael H Schreiber
Library Holdings: Bk Vols 4,000
Special Collections: Technical & Social History of the Street Railway & Electric Railway Industry, equip, blueprints, doc, trade journals & photos
Open Sat & Sun 10-5

EAST WINDSOR

S CONNECTICUT ELECTRIC RAILWAY ASSOCIATION, INC*, Connecticut Trolley Museum Library, 58 North Rd, 06088-0360. (Mail add: PO Box 360, 06088-0360), SAN 326-3983. Tel: 860-627-6540. FAX: 860-627-6510. E-mail: information@ceraweb.org. Web Site: www.ct-trolley.org. *Pres,* Galen Semprebon
Founded 1940
Library Holdings: Bk Vols 3,000; Spec Interest Per Sub 1,200
Special Collections: Historic Connecticut Trolley Companies; Historic Material Including Pictures, Book/Literature
Restriction: Open by appt only

P LIBRARY ASSOCIATION OF WAREHOUSE POINT*, 107 Main St, 06088. SAN 302-4091. Tel: 860-623-5482. FAX: 860-627-6823. Web Site: www.warehousepointlibrary.info. *Dir,* Vincent Bologna; Staff 1 (MLS 1)
Founded 1811. Pop 9,100; Circ 37,218
Library Holdings: Bk Titles 35,000; Per Subs 85
Automation Activity & Vendor Info: (Cataloging) SirsiDynix; (Circulation) SirsiDynix; (OPAC) SirsiDynix
Partic in Connecticut Library Consortium
Open Mon & Tues 10-8, Wed-Fri 10-5, Sat 10-3
Friends of the Library Group

EAST WOODSTOCK

P EAST WOODSTOCK LIBRARY ASSOCIATION, May Memorial Library, 15 Prospect St, 06244. (Mail add: PO Box 14, 06244-0014), SAN 323-7249. Tel: 860-928-0284. E-mail: maymemoriallibrary@sbcglobal.net. *Librn,* Mary M Weaver; Staff 1 (Non-MLS 1)
Founded 1930. Pop 6,000; Circ 8,000
Jul 2008-Jun 2009 Income $18,000. Mats Exp $3,500, Books $3,000, AV Mat $500
Library Holdings: Audiobooks 100; DVDs 100; Bk Titles 8,216
Wireless access
Partic in Connecticut Library Consortium
Open Wed & Fri 1-5, Sat 10-12

EASTFORD

P EASTFORD PUBLIC LIBRARY*, Ivy Glenn Memorial Bldg, 179 Eastford Rd, 06242. SAN 302-1270. Tel: 860-974-0125. FAX: 860-974-0125. Web Site: www.townofeastford.org. *Librn,* Susan Shead; *Asst Librn,* Marcia Day; Staff 1 (MLS 1)
Founded 1896
Library Holdings: Bk Titles 14,000
Wireless access
Partic in Connecticut Library Consortium
Open Mon & Thurs 3-8, Tues 10-8, Sat 9-1

EASTON

P EASTON PUBLIC LIBRARY*, 691 Morehouse Rd, 06612. (Mail add: PO Box 2, 06612-0002), SAN 302-1289. Tel: 203-261-0134. FAX: 203-261-0708. E-mail: epl@eastonlibrary.org. Web Site: www.eastonlibrary.org. *Dir,* Bernadette Baldino; *Asst Dir,* Lisa B Forman; Staff 8 (MLS 2, Non-MLS 6)
Founded 1934. Pop 72,000; Circ 104,800
Library Holdings: Bk Vols 52,596
Automation Activity & Vendor Info: (Cataloging) Follett Software; (Circulation) Follett Software; (OPAC) Follett Software
Database Vendor: EBSCOhost
Partic in Connecticut Library Consortium
Open Mon & Fri 10-5, Tues & Wed 10-8, Thurs 10-6, Sat 10-3
Friends of the Library Group

ELLINGTON

P HALL MEMORIAL LIBRARY*, 93 Main St, 06029. (Mail add: PO Box 280, 06029), SAN 302-1297. Tel: 860-870-3160. FAX: 860-870-3163. E-mail: hallmlib@biblio.org. Web Site: www.biblio.org/ellington/hall.htm. *Dir,* Susan J Phillips; *Ch Serv,* Patricia W Grundman
Founded 1903. Pop 12,000; Circ 91,986
Library Holdings: Bk Titles 35,500; Bk Vols 47,000; Per Subs 150
Special Collections: Ellington History, docs, pamphlets
Automation Activity & Vendor Info: (Cataloging) SirsiDynix; (Circulation) SirsiDynix
Partic in Connecticut Library Consortium
Open Mon-Thurs 10-8, Fri & Sat 10-5
Friends of the Library Group

ENFIELD

J ASNUNTUCK COMMUNITY COLLEGE LIBRARY*, 170 Elm St, 06082-0068. SAN 302-1300. Tel: 860-253-3174. Reference Tel: 860-253-3170. FAX: 860-253-3176. E-mail: as-lrcref@acc.commnet.edu. Web Site: www.asnuntuck.edu/library. *Dir of Libr Serv,* Matthew Hall; Tel: 860-253-3171, E-mail: mhall@asnuntuck.edu; *Evening Librn,* Lindsay Roberts; E-mail: lroberts@asnuntuck.edu; *Info Literacy Librn,* Angelina Hinojosa; E-mail: ahinojosa@asnuntuck.edu; *Syst Librn,* Qiong Zou; Tel: 860-253-3172, E-mail: qzou@asnuntuck.edu; Staff 4 (MLS 4)
Founded 1972. Enrl 1,000; Highest Degree: Associate
Library Holdings: Bks on Deafness & Sign Lang 40; CDs 200; DVDs 300; e-books 1,000; e-journals 10,000; Bk Vols 30,000; Per Subs 100; Videos 700
Special Collections: Copernicus Coll (Polish History & Culture); Literacy Volunteers
Automation Activity & Vendor Info: (Cataloging) OCLC Connexion; (Circulation) Ex Libris Group; (Course Reserve) Ex Libris Group; (ILL) OCLC FirstSearch; (OPAC) Ex Libris Group; (Serials) OCLC Connexion
Database Vendor: EBSCOhost, Gale Cengage Learning, OCLC FirstSearch
Wireless access
Partic in Connecticut Library Consortium; Lyrasis
Special Services for the Deaf - TTY equip
Special Services for the Blind - Assistive/Adapted tech devices, equip & products; Closed circuit TV; Reader equip; ZoomText magnification & reading software
Open Mon-Thurs 8:30-8:30, Fri 8:30-2

S CONNECTICUT CORRECTIONAL INSTITUTION*, Enfield-Medium Library, 289 Shaker Rd, 06083. (Mail add: PO Box 1500, 06082-1500), SAN 371-5760. Tel: 860-763-7383. FAX: 860-763-7350. *Librn,* Edwin Wilmot; Staff 6 (MLS 1, Non-MLS 5)
Library Holdings: Bk Titles 10,000; Per Subs 30
Special Collections: Law - Connecticut, Federal & State

P ENFIELD PUBLIC LIBRARY*, Central Library, 104 Middle Rd, 06082. SAN 336-0784. Tel: 860-763-7510. FAX: 860-763-7514. Web Site: www.enfieldpubliclibrary.org. *Dir,* Henry Dutcher; E-mail: hdutcher@enfield.org; *Asst Dir,* Mary Palomba; E-mail: mpalomba@enfield.org; *Ch Serv,* Suzanne Lott; *Ch Serv,* Ellen Phillips; *Circ,* Yvonne Wollenberg; *ILL,* Eleanor Varnet; *Pub Serv,* Lisa Sprague; *Ref,* Cheryl Beturne; E-mail: cbeturne@enfield.org; *Tech Serv,* Phyllis Gleeson; Staff 29 (MLS 5, Non-MLS 24)
Founded 1874. Pop 45,567; Circ 337,483
Library Holdings: AV Mats 8,844; Bk Titles 130,529; Per Subs 275
Special Collections: Local History/Shaker History (Enfield Centennial Coll), bks
Automation Activity & Vendor Info: (Cataloging) SirsiDynix; (Circulation) SirsiDynix; (OPAC) SirsiDynix
Database Vendor: EBSCOhost, SirsiDynix
Partic in Connecticut Library Consortium; Library Connection, Inc
Open Mon-Fri 9-9, Sat 9-5
Friends of the Library Group

Branches: 1
PEARL STREET, 159 Pearl St, 06082. Tel: 860-253-6433. FAX: 860-253-6433. *Br Coordr,* Colleen Santanella; E-mail: csantanella@enfield.org; Staff 2 (Non-MLS 2)
Circ 15,735
Library Holdings: AV Mats 465; Bk Titles 9,357; Per Subs 30
Open Mon-Thurs 10-8, Fri 12-6, Sat 10-2
Friends of the Library Group

S CARL ROBINSON CORRECTIONAL INSTITUTION LIBRARY*, 285 Shaker Rd, 06083. (Mail add: PO Box 1400, 06083-1400), SAN 324-4466. Tel: 860-763-6230. FAX: 860-763-6345. *Librn,* Nafi Donat; Staff 1 (MLS 1)
Founded 1985
Library Holdings: Bk Vols 30,000; Per Subs 58
Open Mon, Thurs & Fri 8-4, Tues & Wed 12-8

S WILLARD-CYBULSKI CORRECTIONAL INSTITUTION LIBRARY*, 391 Shaker Rd, 06082. Tel: 860-763-6190, 860-763-6193, 860-763-6590. FAX: 860-763-6517. *Librn,* Gay Maiolo
Library Holdings: Bk Vols 10,000; Per Subs 15
Automation Activity & Vendor Info: (Cataloging) LiBRARYSOFT; (Circulation) LiBRARYSOFT
Open Mon & Wed-Fri 7-3:30, Tues 12-8

ESSEX

S CONNECTICUT RIVER MUSEUM*, Stevens Library, 67 Main St, 06426. Tel: 860-767-8269. FAX: 860-767-7028. Web Site: www.ctrivermuseum.org. *Curator,* Amy Trout; E-mail: atrout@ctrivermuseum.org; Staff 1 (Non-MLS 1)
Library Holdings: Bk Vols 2,000
Special Collections: Manuscript Coll Relating to Connecticut River Maritime Individuals, corresp, personal papers; Papers Related to Capt Nathaniel B Palmer & the Discovery of Antarctica; River Industries Business Records; River Related Vessels, accounts, journals & logs; West Indies Documents, Summary Registers & Enrollments from Middletown Customs District
Subject Interests: Local hist, Maritime hist
Function: Ref serv available
Restriction: Closed stack

P ESSEX LIBRARY ASSOCIATION, INC*, 33 West Ave, 06426-1196. SAN 302-1327. Tel: 860-767-1560. FAX: 860-767-2500. Web Site: www.essexlib.org. *Dir,* Richard Conroy; E mail: rconroy@essexlib.org; *Head, Adult Serv,* Ann Thompson; E-mail: athompson@essexlib.org; *Head, Children's & Young Adult Serv,* Jessica Branciforte; E-mail: jbranciforte@essexlib.org; *Adult Prog & Serv,* Jenny Tripp; E-mail: jtripp@essexlib.org; *Adult Serv,* Anita Amos; E-mail: aamos@essexlib.org; *Adult Serv, ILL,* Anna Cierocki; E-mail: acierocki@essexlib.org; *Cataloger,* Marjorie Ruschau; E-mail: mruschau@essexlib.org; Staff 7 (MLS 4, Non MLS 3)
Founded 1889. Pop 6,500; Circ 70,000
Library Holdings: Bk Titles 27,000
Subject Interests: Gardening, Sailing
Automation Activity & Vendor Info: (Cataloging) Innovative Interfaces, Inc; (Circulation) Innovative Interfaces, Inc; (ILL) Innovative Interfaces, Inc; (OPAC) Innovative Interfaces, Inc
Database Vendor: Gale Cengage Learning
Wireless access
Function: Adult bk club, Art exhibits, Audiobks via web, AV serv, Bk club(s), Bks on CD, Children's prog, Computer training, Computers for patron use, Copy machines, E-Reserves, Electronic databases & coll, Equip loans & repairs, Exhibits, Free DVD rentals, Govt ref serv, Handicapped accessible, Home delivery & serv to Sr ctr & nursing homes, Homebound delivery serv, ILL available, Mus passes, Music CDs, Online cat, Outreach serv, OverDrive digital audio bks, Prog for adults, Prog for children & young adult, Pub access computers, Ref serv in person, Senior computer classes, Senior outreach, Story hour, Summer reading prog, Tax forms, Teen prog, Telephone ref, Writing prog
Publications: Ex Libris (Newsletter)
Partic in Libraries Online, Inc
Open Mon, Wed & Fri 10-5, Tues & Thurs 10-8, Sat 10-2
Friends of the Library Group

FAIRFIELD

S FAIRFIELD MUSEUM & HISTORY CENTER, Library & Special Collections, 370 Beach Rd, 06824. SAN 302-1335. Tel: 203-259-1598, Ext 106. FAX: 203-255-2716. E-mail: library@fairfieldhs.org. Web Site: www.fairfieldhistory.org. *Libr Dir,* Dr Elizabeth Rose; Staff 1 (MLS 1)
Founded 1903
Library Holdings: Bk Titles 10,000; Per Subs 18
Special Collections: Manuscript Coll, account bks, architectural rec, bus & family papers, city directories, diaries, ephemera, glass slides, local church & cemetery rec, local organization rec, photog, sch & town rec, scrapbks, shipping logs, VF. Municipal Document Depository; Oral History
Subject Interests: Decorative art, Genealogy, Local hist
Automation Activity & Vendor Info: (Cataloging) SIRSI WorkFlows; (OPAC) SIRSI WorkFlows
Wireless access
Function: Archival coll, Online cat, Photocopying/Printing, Ref serv available, Res libr
Partic in Connecticut Library Consortium
Open Wed-Fri 10-4, Sat & Sun 12-4
Restriction: Non-circulating

P FAIRFIELD PUBLIC LIBRARY*, 1080 Old Post Rd, 06824. SAN 336-0873. Tel: 203-256-3155. Reference Tel: 203-256-3160. Administration FAX: 203-256-3198. Web Site: www.fairfieldpubliclibrary.org. *Town Librn,* Karen Ronald; Tel: 203-256-3158, E-mail: kronald@fplct.org; *Dep Town Librn-Br Serv,* Nancy Coriaty; Tel: 203-255-7307, E-mail: ncoriaty@fplct.org; *Asst Dir, Admin Serv,* Dawn La Valle; Tel: 203-256-3154, E-mail: dlavalle@fplct.org; *Ch Serv Librn,* Barbara Hawkins; *IT Librn,* Jim Swift; *Ref Serv Librn,* Valerie Fredericks; *Tech Serv Librn,* Marilyn Rice; *Teen Librn,* Nicole Scherer; Staff 29 (MLS 17, Non-MLS 12)
Founded 1877. Pop 58,400; Circ 1,004,417
Library Holdings: AV Mats 41,168; e-books 272; Bk Vols 298,599; Per Subs 672
Automation Activity & Vendor Info: (Acquisitions) SirsiDynix; (Cataloging) SirsiDynix; (Circulation) SirsiDynix; (OPAC) SirsiDynix; (Serials) SirsiDynix
Wireless access
Partic in LibraryLinkNJ, The New Jersey Library Cooperative
Open Mon-Thurs 9-9, Fri 9-6, Sat 10-4, Sun 1-5
Friends of the Library Group
Branches: 1
FAIRFIELD WOODS, 1147 Fairfield Woods Rd, 06825, SAN 336-0903. Tel: 203-255-7310. Reference Tel: 203-255-7308. FAX: 203-255-7311. *Dep Town Librn,* Nancy Coriaty; E-mail: ncoriaty@fplct.org
Library Holdings: Bk Vols 67,387; Per Subs 154
Open Mon-Thurs 9-8, Fri 9-6, Sat 9-5, Sun 9-1
Friends of the Library Group

C FAIRFIELD UNIVERSITY, DiMenna-Nyselius Library, 1073 N Benson Rd, 06430-5195. SAN 302-1343. Tel: 203-254-4044. Circulation Tel: 203-254-4000, Ext 2188. Interlibrary Loan Service Tel: 203-254-4000, Ext 2135. Reference Tel: 203-254-4000, Ext 2178. FAX: 203-254-4135. E-mail: reference@fairfield.edu.
Founded 1948. Enrl 5,091; Fac 280; Highest Degree: Doctorate
Jul 2013-Jun 2014 Income $1,576,110. Mats Exp $1,576,110, Books $196,000, Per/Ser (Incl. Access Fees) $587,633, Manu Arch $262, AV Mat $18,309, Electronic Ref Mat (Incl. Access Fees) $565,293
Library Holdings: AV Mats 157,810; CDs 4,211; DVDs 6,553; e-books 545,077; e-journals 70,000; Electronic Media & Resources 170; Microforms 110,693; Bk Vols 373,404; Per Subs 443; Videos 4,383
Automation Activity & Vendor Info: (Acquisitions) Innovative Interfaces, Inc - Millenium; (Cataloging) Innovative Interfaces, Inc - Millenium; (Circulation) Innovative Interfaces, Inc - Millenium; (Course Reserve) Innovative Interfaces, Inc - Millenium; (ILL) Innovative Interfaces, Inc - Millenium; (OPAC) Innovative Interfaces, Inc - Millenium; (Serials) Innovative Interfaces, Inc - Millenium
Database Vendor: ABC-CLIO, Alexander Street Press, American Psychological Association (APA), ARTstor, Baker & Taylor, Blackwell, Bowker, Ebooks Corporation, ebrary, EBSCOhost, Gale Cengage Learning, H W Wilson, Innovative Interfaces, Inc, ISI Web of Knowledge, JSTOR, LexisNexis, Marquis Who's Who, OCLC FirstSearch, OCLC WorldShare Interlibrary Loan, Project MUSE, ProQuest, Sage, SerialsSolutions, ValueLine, Westlaw, Wilson - Wilson Web, YBP Library Services
Wireless access
Function: Audio & video playback equip for onsite use, Computers for patron use, Copy machines, Doc delivery serv, e-mail & chat, E-Reserves, Electronic databases & coll, Exhibits, Online cat
Partic in Association of Jesuit Colleges & Universities (AJCU); Coun of Conn Acad Libr Dirs; Lyrasis

C SACRED HEART UNIVERSITY, Ryan-Matura Library, 5151 Park Ave, 06825-1000. SAN 302-069X. Tel: 203-371-7702. Interlibrary Loan Service Tel: 203-371-7705. Reference Tel: 203-371-7726. Administration Tel: 203-371-7700. Automation Services Tel: 203-365-4854. FAX: 203-374-9968. Interlibrary Loan Service FAX: 203-371-7833. E-mail: circulation@sacredheart.edu. Web Site: library.sacredheart.edu. *Univ Librn,* P Gavin Ferriby, PhD; Tel: 203-396-8283, E-mail: ferribyp@sacredheart.edu; *Dir, Digital Libr Tech & Serv,* Xiaohua Li; E-mail: lix@sacredheart.edu; *Head, Info Literacy Programs,* Elizabeth Knapik; Tel: 203-365-4816, E-mail: kanpike@sacredheart.edu; *Dept Head, Tech Serv,* Bonnie Figgatt; Tel: 203-371-7749, E-mail: figgattb@sacredheart.edu; *Health Sci Librn,* Jeff Orrico; Tel: 203-365-4841,

E-mail: orricoj@sacredheart.edu; *Soc Sci Librn,* Robert H Berry; Tel: 203-365-4842, E-mail: berryr@sacredheart.edu; *Coll Develop,* Nancy Del Vecchio; Tel: 203-371-7701, E-mail: delvecchion@sacredheart.edu; *Ref,* Kimberly Macomber; Tel: 203-371-7746, E-mail: macomberk@sacredheart.edu. Subject Specialists: *Sci,* Bonnie Figgatt; *Hist, Polit sci,* Robert H Berry; *Humanities,* Nancy Del Vecchio; *Educ,* Kimberly Macomber; Staff 13 (MLS 12, Non-MLS 1)
Founded 1967. Highest Degree: Doctorate
Jul 2013-Jun 2014. Mats Exp $642,074, Books $21,248, Per/Ser (Incl. Access Fees) $170,612, Micro $7,918, Electronic Ref Mat (Incl. Access Fees) $437,192, Presv $5,104. Sal $928,098 (Prof $680,208)
Library Holdings: DVDs 1,249; e-books 121,464; e-journals 46,704; Microforms 223,059; Bk Vols 126,290
Special Collections: Art (MacDonald Coll); Christian-Jewish Understanding Coll; Humanities (Behuncik Coll); Humanities (Rycenga Coll); Marian Coll, bks, dvd's, videos
Subject Interests: Bus mgt, Psychol, Relig
Automation Activity & Vendor Info: (Acquisitions) Innovative Interfaces, Inc; (Cataloging) Innovative Interfaces, Inc; (Circulation) Innovative Interfaces, Inc; (Course Reserve) Innovative Interfaces, Inc; (ILL) Innovative Interfaces, Inc; (Media Booking) Innovative Interfaces, Inc; (OPAC) Innovative Interfaces, Inc; (Serials) Innovative Interfaces, Inc
Database Vendor: BioOne, CredoReference, ebrary, EBSCOhost, JSTOR, Mergent Online, OCLC FirstSearch, OVID Technologies, Project MUSE, ProQuest, Westlaw, Wilson - Wilson Web
Wireless access
Partic in OCLC Online Computer Library Center, Inc
Open Mon-Thurs 8am-3am, Fri 8am-9pm, Sat 10-9, Sun 12pm-3am

FALLS VILLAGE

P DAVID M HUNT LIBRARY*, 63 Main St, 06031. (Mail add: PO Box 217, 06031-0217), SAN 324-5152. Tel: 860-824-7424. *Dir,* Erica Joncyk; *Asst Dir,* Karen Lindquist; *Ch,* Rita Delgado; *Asst Librn,* Akke Jasmine deVlas
Founded 1891. Pop 1,080; Circ 24,067
Jul 2010-Jun 2011 Income $132,000. Mats Exp $9,700, Books $7,800, Other Print Mats $1,900. Sal $66,027
Library Holdings: Audiobooks 297; CDs 154; DVDs 544; Large Print Bks 140; Bk Titles 23,333; Per Subs 48; Videos 175
Subject Interests: Local hist
Automation Activity & Vendor Info: (Circulation) Bibliomation Inc; (Course Reserve) Bibliomation Inc; (ILL) Best-Seller, Inc; (OPAC) Bibliomation Inc
Database Vendor: Overdrive, Inc
Wireless access
Open Tues (Winter) 10-5, Wed 2-5, Thurs 10-8, Sat 10-2; Tues (Summer) 10-6, Wed 2-6, Thurs 10-8, Sat 10-2
Friends of the Library Group

FARMINGTON

P THE FARMINGTON LIBRARY, Six Monteith Dr, 06032. SAN 336-0938. Tel: 860-673-6791. FAX: 860-675-7148.
Founded 1901. Pop 25,361; Circ 433,259
Library Holdings: Bk Vols 190,000; Per Subs 375
Special Collections: Oral History
Automation Activity & Vendor Info: (Circulation) SirsiDynix; (OPAC) SirsiDynix
Wireless access
Partic in Connecticut Library Consortium
Open Mon-Thurs 9-9, Fri & Sat 9-5
Friends of the Library Group
Branches: 1
BARNEY BRANCH, 71 Main St, 06032, SAN 336-0962. Tel: 860-673-6791. *Dir, Children's & Br Serv,* Sarah Kline-Morgan; Staff 1 (MLS 1)
Library Holdings: Bk Vols 30,000
Open Mon-Thurs & Sat 9-5
Friends of the Library Group

M HARTFORD MEDICAL SOCIETY*, Historical Library, University of Connecticut Health Center, 263 Farmington Ave, 06032. (Mail add: PO Box 4003, 06032-4003), SAN 302-1823. Tel: 860-679-3200. FAX: 860-679-1230. Web Site: library.uchc.edu/hms. *Librn,* Jennifer Miglus; E-mail: miglus@uchc.edu
Founded 1846
Library Holdings: Bk Titles 6,000; Bk Vols 34,300; Per Subs 10
Special Collections: Gershom Bulkeley, ms; Hartford Imprints; History of Anesthesia; History of Medicine; Steiner Coll
Subject Interests: Med
Wireless access
Partic in Connecticut Library Consortium
Open Mon-Fri 9-4

L LEVY & DRONEY*, Law Library, 74 Batterson Park Rd, 06032. SAN 372-3372. Tel: 860-676-3000. FAX: 860-676-3200. Web Site: www.ldlaw.com. *Librn,* Patty Mackiewicz; E-mail: pmack@ldlaw.com
Library Holdings: Bk Vols 15,000
Database Vendor: LexisNexis
Open Mon-Fri 8:30-5

J TUNXIS COMMUNITY COLLEGE LIBRARY*, 271 Scott Swamp Rd, 06032. SAN 302-1416. Tel: 860-255-3800. Interlibrary Loan Service Tel: 860-255-3803. Reference Tel: 860-255-3801. Administration Tel: 860-255-3805. FAX: 860-255-3808. Web Site: www.tunxis.edu/library. *Dir of Libr Serv,* Dr Lisa Lavoie; Tel: 860-255-3786, E-mail: LLavoie@tunxis.edu; Staff 11 (MLS 8, Non-MLS 3)
Founded 1970. Enrl 4,740; Fac 305; Highest Degree: Associate
Jul 2010-Jun 2011. Mats Exp $195,390, Books $71,451, Per/Ser (Incl. Access Fees) $20,014, Other Print Mats $250, AV Mat $15,878, Electronic Ref Mat (Incl. Access Fees) $56,173. Sal $699,795 (Prof $545,924)
Library Holdings: Audiobooks 773; AV Mats 86; Bks on Deafness & Sign Lang 17; CDs 523; DVDs 4,561; e-books 592; Bk Vols 57,084; Per Subs 192; Videos 88
Special Collections: American Literature Coll; Art Coll; Criminal Justice Coll
Subject Interests: Criminal justice, Dental assisting, Dental hygiene, Fine arts, Lit, Photog
Automation Activity & Vendor Info: (Acquisitions) Ex Libris Group; (Cataloging) Ex Libris Group; (Circulation) Ex Libris Group; (Course Reserve) Ex Libris Group; (ILL) OCLC FirstSearch; (OPAC) Ex Libris Group; (Serials) Ex Libris Group
Database Vendor: Alexander Street Press, American Psychological Association (APA), CQ Press, CredoReference, ebrary, EBSCOhost, Ex Libris Group, Facts on File, Gale Cengage Learning, Hoovers, LexisNexis, McGraw-Hill, Medline, Newsbank, OCLC FirstSearch, ProQuest, PubMed, SerialsSolutions, Springshare, LLC, Westlaw
Wireless access
Function: Audio & video playback equip for onsite use, Bks on CD, Computers for patron use, Copy machines, Electronic databases & coll, Handicapped accessible, ILL available, Mus passes, Music CDs, Online cat, Online ref, Online searches, Photocopying/Printing, Pub access computers, Ref serv available, Ref serv in person, Tax forms, Wheelchair accessible
Partic in Connecticut Library Consortium; OCLC Online Computer Library Center, Inc
Open Mon-Thurs 8am-9pm, Fri 8-4, Sat 9-2

CM UNIVERSITY OF CONNECTICUT HEALTH CENTER*, Lyman Maynard Stowe Library, 263 Farmington Ave, 06034. (Mail add: PO Box 4003, 06034-4003), SAN 302-1424. Tel: 860-679-3808. Interlibrary Loan Service Tel: 860-679-2940. Reference Tel: 860-679-2942. Administration Tel: 860-679-2840. Information Services Tel: 860-679-4053. FAX: 860-679-4046. Reference FAX: 860-679-1068. E-mail: library@nso.uchc.edu. Web Site: library.uchc.edu. *Dir,* Evelyn B Morgen; Fax: 860-679-1230, E-mail: emorgen@uchc.edu; *Admin Officer,* Mary Petruzzi; Fax: 860-679-1230, E-mail: petruzzi@nso.uchc.edu; *Bibliog Instr, Ref,* Hongjie Wang; E-mail: wang@nso.uchc.edu; *Circ, ILL,* Jacqueline Lewis; Tel: 860-679-2941, E-mail: jlewis@nso.uchc.edu; *Network Serv,* Sheryl Bai; Tel: 860-679-8371, E-mail: bai@nso.uchc.edu; *Tech Serv,* Lorna Wright; Tel: 860-679-4058, E-mail: wright@nso.uchc.edu; Staff 29 (MLS 15, Non-MLS 14)
Founded 1965. Enrl 1,624; Fac 533; Highest Degree: Doctorate
Library Holdings: AV Mats 1,646; Bk Vols 39,498; Per Subs 1,760
Special Collections: Hartford Medical Society Library Coll; History of Medicine Coll
Subject Interests: Dentistry, Med, Nursing
Automation Activity & Vendor Info: (Acquisitions) Ex Libris Group; (Cataloging) Ex Libris Group; (Circulation) Ex Libris Group; (Course Reserve) Ex Libris Group; (ILL) Ex Libris Group; (OPAC) Ex Libris Group; (Serials) Ex Libris Group
Database Vendor: DynaMed, Elsevier, Gale Cengage Learning, Micromedex, OVID Technologies
Wireless access
Function: ILL available, Outside serv via phone, mail, e-mail & web, Photocopying/Printing, Ref serv available
Open Mon-Thurs 7am-11pm, Fri 7-7, Sat 9-5, Sun Noon-10
Restriction: Circulates for staff only

S THE STANLEY WHITMAN HOUSE LIBRARY*, 37 High St, 06032. Tel: 860-677-9222. FAX: 860-677-7758. Web Site: www.stanleywhitman.org. *Exec Dir,* Lisa Johnson; E-mail: lisa@stanleywhitman.org
Library Holdings: Bk Vols 1,500
Special Collections: 18th Century Farmington Coll, archival docs; Photographs & Slides, Early 1900s; Solomon Whitman, Esq Private Subscription Coll
Subject Interests: Bibles, Genealogy, Philos
Function: Ref serv available

Publications: Newsletter
Restriction: Open by appt only

GALES FERRY

SR ST DAVID EPISCOPAL CHURCH LIBRARY*, Corner Rte 12 & Rte 214, 06335. (Mail add: PO Box 296, 06335-0296), SAN 372-5162. Tel: 860-464-6516. FAX: 860-464-6446. E-mail: stdavidsgf@aol.com. Web Site: members.aol.com/sdweb2.
Founded 1968
Library Holdings: Bk Titles 2,700
Open Mon-Fri 9-5, Sun 8-12

GLASTONBURY

P EAST GLASTONBURY PUBLIC LIBRARY*, 1389 Neipsic Rd, 06033. SAN 324-279X. Tel: 860-633-5637.
Founded 1960. Pop 32,000; Circ 12,088
Jul 2011-Jun 2012 Income $19,750, City $7,500, Locally Generated Income $5,700, Other $6,550. Mats Exp $6,080, Books $5,500, Per/Ser (Incl. Access Fees) $580
Library Holdings: Bk Vols 14,000; Per Subs 40
Open Mon 1-4 & 7-9, Tues 9-4 (1-4 July & Aug), Thurs 9-4 & 7-9
Friends of the Library Group

P WELLES-TURNER MEMORIAL LIBRARY*, 2407 Main St, 06033. SAN 302-1440. Tel: 860-652-7719. Reference Tel: 860-652-7720. Administration Tel: 860-652-7717. FAX: 860-652-7721. Web Site: www.wtmlib.com. *Dir,* Barbara J Bailey; *Adult Serv,* Sue Jensen; Tel: 860-652-7730, E-mail: jensen@glasct.org; *Ch Serv,* Renee Pease; Tel: 860-652-7725, E-mail: pease@glasct.org; *Coll Develop,* Elizabeth Twarkins; Tel: 860-652-7727, E-mail: twarkins@glasct.org; *Outreach Serv Librn,* Carole Noble; Tel: 860-652-7718, E-mail: noble@glasct.org; *Ref,* Sally Ruef; E-mail: ruef@glasct.org; *YA Serv,* Miriam Neiman; E-mail: neiman@glasct.org; Staff 23 (MLS 9, Non-MLS 14)
Founded 1865. Pop 32,575; Circ 552,403
Library Holdings: Bk Vols 136,525; Per Subs 312
Subject Interests: Gardening, Local hist, Parenting
Automation Activity & Vendor Info: (Cataloging) SirsiDynix; (Circulation) SirsiDynix; (OPAC) SirsiDynix; (Serials) SirsiDynix
Database Vendor: Baker & Taylor, EBSCOhost, ProQuest, ReferenceUSA
Wireless access
Function: Handicapped accessible, Homebound delivery serv, ILL available, Online searches, Prog for adults, Prog for children & young adult, Ref serv available, Spoken cassettes & CDs, Spoken cassettes & DVDs, Summer reading prog, Telephone ref, VHS videos, Wheelchair accessible
Partic in Cap Region Libr Coun
Special Services for the Deaf - Bks on deafness & sign lang; Closed caption videos
Special Services for the Blind - Videos on blindness & phys handicaps
Open Mon, Tues & Thurs 9-9, Wed 12-9, Fri 9-6, Sat 9-5, Sun (Sept-May) 1-5
Friends of the Library Group

GOSHEN

S GOSHEN HISTORICAL SOCIETY LIBRARY*, 21 Old Middle Rd, 06756-2001. (Mail add: PO Box 457, 06756-0457), SAN 302-1459. Tel: 860-491-9610. Administration Tel: 860-491-3129. Web Site: www.goshenhistoricalct.org. *Curator, Pres,* Henrietta C Horvay; Tel: 860-491-3129; *Asst Curator,* Walter M Horvay
Founded 1955
Library Holdings: Bk Vols 1,000
Special Collections: Furniture; Glass; Natural Science; Pewter; Tools; Toys. Oral History
Subject Interests: Local hist
Open Tues (April-Nov) 10-Noon
Friends of the Library Group

P GOSHEN PUBLIC LIBRARY*, 42 North St, 06756-1509. (Mail add: PO Box 180, 06756-0180), SAN 376-2726. Tel: 860-491-3234. FAX: 860-491-0100. Web Site: www.goshenpublib.org. *Dir,* Lynn Steinmayer; Staff 1 (MLS 1)
Founded 1901. Pop 3,000
Library Holdings: Bk Titles 25,921; Per Subs 29
Automation Activity & Vendor Info: (Acquisitions) Auto-Graphics, Inc; (Cataloging) Auto-Graphics, Inc; (Circulation) Auto-Graphics, Inc; (OPAC) Auto-Graphics, Inc; (Serials) Auto-Graphics, Inc
Wireless access
Partic in Midwest Collaborative for Library Services (MCLS)
Open Mon & Tues 10-8, Wed-Fri 10-6, Sat (Sept-June) 10-3, (July & Aug) 9-12
Friends of the Library Group

GRANBY

P GRANBY PUBLIC LIBRARY*, 15 N Granby Rd, 06035. SAN 302-1467. Tel: 860-844-5275. FAX: 860-653-0241. *Dir, Libr Serv,* Kathleen Marszycki; *Ch,* Joan Beatson; Staff 2 (MLS 2)
Founded 1869. Pop 9,629
Library Holdings: Bk Vols 55,035; Per Subs 251
Automation Activity & Vendor Info: (Cataloging) Auto-Graphics, Inc; (Circulation) Auto-Graphics, Inc
Database Vendor: Gale Cengage Learning, Wilson - Wilson Web
Open Mon & Wed Noon-8, Tues & Thurs 9-6, Fri & Sat 9-1
Friends of the Library Group
Branches: 1
FREDERICK H COSSITT LIBRARY, 388 N Granby Rd, North Granby, 06060. (Mail add: PO Box 98, North Granby, 06060), SAN 374-3594. Tel: 860-653-8958. FAX: 860-653-8958. E-mail: cossittlib@granby-ct.gov. *Br Librn,* Lynn Stewart; Staff 4 (Non-MLS 4)
Founded 1890
Open Tues & Thurs 10-12 & 3-8, Sat 12-5
Friends of the Library Group

S SALMON BROOK HISTORICAL SOCIETY, Genealogy & Research Library, 208 Salmon Brook St, 06035-2402. (Mail add: PO Box 840, 06035-0840), SAN 302-1475. Tel: 860-653-9713. Web Site: www.salmonbrookhistorical.org. *Librn,* Carol Laun. Subject Specialists: *Archives, Genealogy, Local hist,* Carol Laun
Founded 1975
Library Holdings: Bk Titles 1,000
Special Collections: American History (State 19th Century Newspapers); Connecticut History, doc; Granby Town Records (1786-1853); Home Guard, doc; Local Document Colls, account bks, bus papers, deeds, letters
Subject Interests: Genealogy
Publications: Collections 1979, 1980, 1987, 1989, 1995, 1999
Restriction: In-house use for visitors, Internal use only, Non-circulating, Not a lending libr, Open by appt only, Open to pub with supv only, Pub use on premises

SR SOUTH CONGREGATIONAL CHURCH*, Ethel L Austin Library, 242 Salmon Brook St, 06035. SAN 302-1483. Tel: 860-653-7289. FAX: 860-653-7952. Web Site: www.southchurchgranby.org. *Librn,* Position Currently Open
Library Holdings: Bk Vols 2,600
Subject Interests: Psychol, Theol

GREENWICH

M GREENWICH HOSPITAL*, Sackler Medical Library, Five Perryridge Rd, 06830. SAN 302-1521. Tel: 203-863-3285. Interlibrary Loan Service Tel: 203-863-3284. FAX: 203-863-4664. Web Site: www.greenhosp.org/library.asp. *Dir, Libr Serv,* Katherine Stemmer Frumento; E-mail: katherinef@greenhosp.org; Staff 2 (MLS 1, Non-MLS 1)
Founded 1965
Oct 2005-Sept 2006. Mats Exp $105,000, Books $30,000, Per/Ser (Incl. Access Fees) $70,000, Presv $5,000
Library Holdings: Bk Vols 1,500; Per Subs 225
Subject Interests: Nursing
Database Vendor: EBSCOhost, OVID Technologies
Function: Ref serv available
Partic in Basic Health Sciences Library Network; Conn Asn of Health Scis Librs; North Atlantic Health Sciences Libraries, Inc
Open Mon-Fri 9-4:30
Restriction: Non-circulating to the pub, Staff use only

P GREENWICH LIBRARY*, 101 W Putnam Ave, 06830-5387. SAN 336-1144. Tel: 203-622-7956. Circulation Tel: 203-625-6524. Interlibrary Loan Service Tel: 203-622-7944. Reference Tel: 203-622-7910. Administration Tel: 203-622-7960. FAX: 203-622-7959. Interlibrary Loan Service FAX: 203-622-7939. Reference FAX: 203-625-6556. Administration FAX: 203-625-6555. Information Services FAX: 203-622-6556. Web Site: www.greenwichlibrary.org. *Dir,* Barbara Ormerod-Glynn; Tel: 203-622-7961, E-mail: bglynn@greenwichlibrary.org; *Dep Dir,* Position Currently Open; *Mgr, Info Serv,* Wynne Delmhorst; Tel: 203-622-7921, E-mail: wdelmhorst@greenwichlibrary.org; *IT Mgr,* John Yoke; Tel: 203-622-7955, E-mail: jyoke@greenwichlibrary.org; *Mgr, Lending Serv,* Moira Danehy; *Pub Relations Mgr,* Kate Petrov; Tel: 203-625-6550, E-mail: kpetrov@greenwichlibrary.org; *Mgr, Res Mgt,* Marcia Fosnot; Tel: 203-622-7926, E-mail: mfosnot@greenwichlibrary.org; Staff 66 (MLS 27, Non-MLS 39)
Founded 1878. Pop 61,871; Circ 1,484,619
Jul 2005-Jun 2006. Mats Exp $1,245,941, Books $638,481, Per/Ser (Incl. Access Fees) $219,173, AV Mat $204,610, Electronic Ref Mat (Incl. Access Fees) $183,677

Library Holdings: AV Mats 6,922; CDs 41,070; DVDs 14,287; e-books 8,228; Electronic Media & Resources 94; Bk Vols 361,227; Per Subs 739; Videos 14,078
Special Collections: Oral History
Subject Interests: Local hist
Automation Activity & Vendor Info: (Acquisitions) Innovative Interfaces, Inc; (Circulation) Innovative Interfaces, Inc; (ILL) OCLC; (OPAC) Innovative Interfaces, Inc; (Serials) Innovative Interfaces, Inc
Database Vendor: Bloomberg, Dun & Bradstreet, EBSCOhost, Factiva.com, Gale Cengage Learning, Hoovers, Mergent Online, OCLC FirstSearch, ProQuest, Standard & Poor's, ValueLine
Wireless access
Function: Adult bk club, Art exhibits, Audio & video playback equip for onsite use, Audiobks via web, Bk club(s), Bks on CD, Bus archives, Children's prog, Computer training, Computers for patron use, Copy machines, E-Reserves, Electronic databases & coll, Exhibits, Free DVD rentals, Handicapped accessible, Home delivery & serv to Sr ctr & nursing homes, ILL available, Instruction & testing, Jazz prog, Learning ctr, Magnifiers for reading, Music CDs, Newsp ref libr, Online cat, OverDrive digital audio bks, Photocopying/Printing, Preschool outreach, Prog for adults, Prog for children & young adult, Pub access computers, Ref & res, Ref serv available, Ref serv in person, Senior computer classes, Senior outreach, Spoken cassettes & CDs, Spoken cassettes & DVDs, Story hour, Summer reading prog, Tax forms, Teen prog, Telephone ref, Web-catalog, Wheelchair accessible, Workshops
Partic in Lyrasis
Special Services for the Deaf - ADA equip; Bks on deafness & sign lang; Coll on deaf educ; Sign lang interpreter upon request for prog; Staff with knowledge of sign lang; TTY equip
Special Services for the Blind - Accessible computers; Aids for in-house use; Assistive/Adapted tech devices, equip & products; Audio mat; Bks available with recordings; Bks on cassette; Bks on CD; Braille bks; Children's Braille; Closed circuit TV magnifier; Computer access aids; Computer with voice synthesizer for visually impaired persons; Copier with enlargement capabilities; Handicapped awareness prog; Home delivery serv; Internet workstation with adaptive software; Large print & cassettes; Large print bks; Lending of low vision aids; Low vision equip; Magnifiers; Networked computers with assistive software; Talking bk serv referral; ZoomText magnification & reading software
Open Mon-Fri 9-9, Sat 9-5, Sun 1-5
Friends of the Library Group

Branches: 2

COS COB BRANCH, Five Sinawoy Rd, Cos Cob, 06807-2701, SAN 336-1209. Tel: 203-622-6883. FAX: 203-661-5315. *Br Mgr,* Wendy Silver; E-mail: wsilver@greenwichlibrary.org; Staff 4 (MLS 1, Non-MLS 3)
Founded 1930
Library Holdings: Bk Vols 41,424
Special Services for the Deaf - TTY equip
Special Services for the Blind - Reader equip
Open Mon 12-8, Tues-Sat 9-5
Friends of the Library Group

BYRAM SHUBERT BRANCH, 21 Mead Ave, 06830-6812, SAN 336-1179. Tel: 203-531-0426. FAX: 203-531-0789. *Br Mgr,* Miguel Garcia-Colon; E-mail: mcolon@greenwichlibrary.org; Staff 4 (MLS 1, Non-MLS 3)
Library Holdings: Bk Vols 26,927
Special Collections: Byram Historical Vertical File. Oral History
Special Services for the Deaf - TTY equip
Special Services for the Blind - Reader equip
Open Mon, Wed, Fri & Sat 9-5, Tues 10-6, Thurs 12-8
Friends of the Library Group

Bookmobiles: 1. Mgr, Lending Serv, Elaine Tai-Lauria

GROTON

P BILL MEMORIAL LIBRARY*, 240 Monument St, 06340. SAN 302-1556. Tel: 860-445-0392. FAX: 860-449-8971. E-mail: info@billmemorial.org. Web Site: www.billmemorial.org. *Dir,* Hali R Keeler; E-mail: hkeeler@billmemorial.org; *Ch Serv,* Mary-Jane Carle; *ILL,* Marsha Dietrich; Staff 5 (MLS 1, Non-MLS 4)
Founded 1890
Library Holdings: Bk Vols 21,000
Subject Interests: Genealogy, Local hist
Automation Activity & Vendor Info: (Cataloging) Auto-Graphics, Inc; (Circulation) Auto-Graphics, Inc; (ILL) Auto-Graphics, Inc; (OPAC) Auto-Graphics, Inc
Wireless access
Function: Handicapped accessible, Homebound delivery serv, ILL available, Prog for adults, Prog for children & young adult, Summer reading prog
Partic in Connecticut Library Consortium
Open Mon & Thurs 10-9, Tues & Wed 10-5, Sat 10-3
Friends of the Library Group

S GENERAL DYNAMICS CORP*, Electric Boat Company Library, 75 Eastern Point Rd, Dept 455, 06340. SAN 302-1564. Tel: 860-433-3481. FAX: 860-433-0647. *Librn, Project Coordr,* Theresa Morales; E-mail: tmorales@gdeb.com
Founded 1955
Library Holdings: Bk Titles 8,000; Bk Vols 12,000; Per Subs 450
Subject Interests: Oceanography
Open Mon-Fri 7-4

P GROTON PUBLIC LIBRARY*, 52 Newtown Rd, 06340. SAN 302-1572. Tel: 860-441-6750. FAX: 860-448-0363. E-mail: reference@grotonpl.org. Web Site: www.grotonpl.org. *Dir of Libr Serv,* Betty Anne Reiter; E-mail: breiter@groton-ct.gov; *Ch,* Kimmerle Balentine; E-mail: kbalentine@groton-ct.gov; *Ch,* Tracy Torres; E-mail: ttorres@groton-ct.gov; *Ref Librn,* Barbara Clark-Greene; E-mail: bclarkgreene@groton-ct.gov; *Ref Librn, Ser,* Sarah B Freeland; E-mail: sfreeland@groton-ct.gov; *ILL, Ref Librn,* Judy Kelmelis; E-mail: jkelmelis@groton-ct.gov; *Ref Librn,* Jean Schweid; E-mail: jschweid@groton-ct.gov; *Ref Librn,* Michael Spellmon; E-mail: mspellmon@groton-ct.gov; *YA Librn,* Anne S Campbell; E-mail: acampbell@groton-ct.gov; *Mgr, Circ & Tech Serv,* Cynthia R Wright; E-mail: cwright@groton-ct.gov; *Mgr, Pub Serv,* Jennifer Miele; E-mail: jmiele@groton-ct.gov; *Circ Supvr,* Linda Wallace; E-mail: lwallace@groton-ct.gov; *Municipal Video Spec,* Shawn P Greeley; E-mail: sgreeley@groton-ct.gov. Subject Specialists: *Local hist,* Barbara Clark-Greene; *Genealogy,* Michael Spellmon; Staff 25.7 (MLS 10.3, Non-MLS 15.4)
Founded 1959. Pop 39,551; Circ 368,587
Special Collections: Local Doc Dep. State Document Depository
Subject Interests: Genealogy, Local hist
Wireless access
Function: Archival coll, Audiobks via web, Bks on cassette, Bks on CD, CD-ROM, Children's prog, Computer training, Computers for patron use, Copy machines, Digital talking bks, Electronic databases & coll, Fax serv, Free DVD rentals, Handicapped accessible, Home delivery & serv to Sr ctr & nursing homes, Homebound delivery serv, ILL available, Microfiche/film & reading machines, Mus passes, Music CDs, Online cat, Online ref, Outreach serv, OverDrive digital audio bks, Photocopying/Printing, Prog for adults, Prog for children & young adult, Pub access computers, Scanner, Spoken cassettes & CDs, Spoken cassettes & DVDs, Story hour, Summer reading prog, Tax forms, Teen prog, Telephone ref, Winter reading prog
Partic in Central & Western Massachusetts Automated Resource Sharing
Open Mon-Thurs 9-9, Fri 9-5:30, Sat 9-5, Sun (Sept-May) 1-5
Friends of the Library Group

UNITED STATES NAVY

A BASE LIBRARY*, Naval Submarine Base New London, Bldg 164, 06349. (Mail add: PO Box 15, 06349-5015), SAN 336-1233. Tel: 860-694-2578, 860-694-3723. FAX: 860-694-2578. Web Site: www.navy.mil/nwr. *Dir,* Tammy-Jo Ferdula; E-mail: tammyjo.ferdula@navy.mil; *YA Serv,* Marie Jennings; E-mail: marie.jennings@navy.mil; Staff 2 (MLS 1, Non-MLS 1)
Founded 1942
Library Holdings: CDs 100; DVDs 300; Bk Titles 20,000; Per Subs 60; Talking Bks 100; Videos 700
Special Collections: CNO Suggested Navy Reading List Coll
Automation Activity & Vendor Info: (Cataloging) Follett Software; (Circulation) Follett Software; (OPAC) Follett Software
Partic in OCLC Online Computer Library Center, Inc
Open Mon-Thurs 11-6, Fri & Sat 10:30-5:30

A HISTORIC SHIP NAUTILUS-SUBMARINE FORCE LIBRARY & ARCHIVES*, One Crystal Lake Rd, 06340-2464. (Mail add: Naval Submarine Base NLON, 06349-5571), SAN 336-1292. Tel: 860-694-3558. FAX: 860-694-4150. *Librn,* Wendy S Gulley
Library Holdings: Bk Vols 7,600
Special Collections: Copies of World War II Patrol Reports-US; Histories of General Dynamics-Electric Boat (1915-1964) & Naval Submarine Base, Groton (1868-); John P Holland & Simon Lake Papers; Photograph Coll; Scrapbook Binders on all US Submarines; Submarines & Related Topics; Submarines & their Inventors Prior to 1900
Automation Activity & Vendor Info: (Cataloging) Surpass; (OPAC) Surpass
Database Vendor: Surpass
Function: Archival coll, For res purposes, Res libr
Restriction: Closed stack, Non-circulating, Not a lending libr, Open by appt only

C UNIVERSITY OF CONNECTICUT AT AVERY POINT LIBRARY*, 1084 Shennecossett Rd, 06340-6097. SAN 302-1599. Tel: 860-405-9146. FAX: 860-405-9150. *Librn,* Jan E Heckman; E-mail: jan.heckman@uconn.edu; *Librn,* Beth Rumery; Tel: 860-405-9148, E-mail: elizabeth.rumery@uconn.edu; Staff 1 (MLS 1)
Founded 1967. Enrl 800; Fac 50; Highest Degree: Doctorate
Library Holdings: Bk Vols 40,100; Per Subs 120

Special Collections: Dredging Data; Hydrographic Charts (East Coast) 1832-1876; Literature of the Sea. US Document Depository
Automation Activity & Vendor Info: (Acquisitions) Ex Libris Group; (Cataloging) Ex Libris Group; (Circulation) Ex Libris Group; (Course Reserve) Ex Libris Group; (OPAC) Ex Libris Group
Database Vendor: Cambridge Scientific Abstracts, EBSCOhost, Gale Cengage Learning, JSTOR, LexisNexis, OCLC FirstSearch, OCLC WorldShare Interlibrary Loan, ProQuest
Partic in Lyrasis

GUILFORD

P GUILFORD FREE LIBRARY*, 67 Park St, 06437. SAN 302-1602. Tel: 203-453-8282. FAX: 203-453-8288. Web Site: www.guilfordfreelibrary.org. *Dir,* Sandra Ruoff; E-mail: sruoff@guilfordfreelibrary.org; *Asst Dir,* Stephanie Johnson; E-mail: sjohnson@guilfordfreelibrary.org; *Ch Serv,* Suellen Heinrich; E-mail: sheinrich@guilfordfreelibrary.org; *Ref,* Patty Baldwin; E-mail: pbaldwin@guilfordfreelibrary.org; Staff 7 (MLS 7)
Founded 1888. Pop 20,000; Circ 250,000
Library Holdings: Bk Titles 112,000; Bk Vols 117,000; Per Subs 209
Special Collections: Guilford History & Genealogy; Spanish Language Books. Oral History
Subject Interests: Poetry
Automation Activity & Vendor Info: (Acquisitions) Innovative Interfaces, Inc; (Cataloging) Innovative Interfaces, Inc; (Circulation) Innovative Interfaces, Inc; (Course Reserve) Innovative Interfaces, Inc; (ILL) Innovative Interfaces, Inc; (Media Booking) Innovative Interfaces, Inc; (OPAC) Innovative Interfaces, Inc; (Serials) Innovative Interfaces, Inc
Publications: Steiner's History of Guilford & Madison
Partic in Connecticut Library Consortium; Libraries Online, Inc
Open Mon-Thurs 9-8, Fri 9-6, Sat 9-5, Sun (Oct-Apr) 1-4
Friends of the Library Group

S HENRY WHITFIELD STATE MUSEUM RESEARCH LIBRARY*, 248 Old Whitfield St, 06437-3459. Tel: 203-453-2457. FAX: 203-453-7544. E-mail: whitfieldmuseum@ct.gov. Web Site: www.cultureandtourism.org/cct/cwp/view.asp?a=2127&q=302248. *Curator,* Michael McBride
Founded 1899
Library Holdings: Bk Vols 450
Special Collections: 17th-19th Century History Coll, incl ledgers, town records, Grand Army of the Republic mat & maps
Subject Interests: 17th Century hist, Genealogy, Local hist, State hist
Function: Ref serv available
Restriction: Non circulating coll, Open by appt only

HADDAM

P BRAINERD MEMORIAL LIBRARY*, 920 Saybrook Rd, 06438. SAN 302-1610. Tel: 860-345-2204. FAX: 860-345-7735. E-mail: library@brainerdlibrary.lioninc.org. Web Site: www.brainerdlibrary.lioninc.org. *Dir,* Cynthia Muhlbach; E-mail: cmuhlbach@brainerdlibrary.lioninc.org; Staff 12 (MLS 5, Non-MLS 7)
Founded 1908. Pop 8,346
Jul 2011-Jun 2012 Income $403,768, State $2,239, City $332,896, Locally Generated Income $68,633. Mats Exp $46,350, Books $26,141, AV Mat $20,209. Sal $233,701
Library Holdings: AV Mats 8,895; Bk Vols 38,421; Per Subs 58
Special Collections: Genealogy & Haddam History Coll
Automation Activity & Vendor Info: (Cataloging) Innovative Interfaces, Inc; (Circulation) Innovative Interfaces, Inc; (ILL) Auto-Graphics, Inc; (OPAC) Innovative Interfaces, Inc
Wireless access
Function: Bks on CD, Children's prog, Computer training, Computers for patron use, Copy machines, Fax serv, Free DVD rentals, Handicapped accessible, Home delivery & serv to Sr ctr & nursing homes, Homebound delivery serv, ILL available, Mus passes, Music CDs, Online cat, OverDrive digital audio bks, Photocopying/Printing, Preschool outreach, Prog for adults, Prog for children & young adult, Pub access computers, Ref serv available, Story hour, Summer reading prog, Tax forms, Web-catalog, Wheelchair accessible
Partic in Libraries Online, Inc
Open Tues-Thurs (Winter) 10-8, Fri 10-6, Sat 10-3; Tues-Thurs (Summer) 10-8, Fri 10-4, Sat 10-1
Friends of the Library Group

HAMDEN

R CONGREGATION MISHKAN ISRAEL LIBRARY*, 785 Ridge Rd, 06517. SAN 302-1629. Tel: 203-288-3877. FAX: 203-248-2148. *Librn,* Linda K Cohen
Founded 1840
Library Holdings: Bk Titles 4,000; Per Subs 6
Special Collections: Archives of Congregation (founded 1840); Rabbi Robert E Goldburg Coll
Subject Interests: Judaica (lit or hist of Jews)

P HAMDEN PUBLIC LIBRARY, Miller Memorial Central Library, 2901 Dixwell Ave, 06518-3135. SAN 336-1357. Tel: 203-287-2686. Circulation Tel: 203-287-2682. Reference Tel: 203-287-2680. FAX: 203-287-2685. Web Site: www.hamdenlibrary.org. *Dir,* Marian Amodeo; E-mail: mamodeo@hamdenlibrary.org; *Asst Dir,* Nancy McNicol; Tel: 203-287-2686, Ext 11, E-mail: nmcnicol@hamdenlibrary.org; *Head, Ch,* Nancy McLaughlin; Tel: 203-230-3770, E-mail: nancymcl@hamdenlibrary.org; *Head, Circ,* Janet Perrotti; E-mail: jperrotti@hamdenlibrary.org; *Head, Tech Serv,* Jessica Dans; E-mail: jdans@hamdenlibrary.org; *Coll Develop, Pub Serv,* Irene Nolan; E-mail: inolan@hamdenlibrary.org; Staff 32 (MLS 13, Non-MLS 19)
Founded 1944. Pop 58,180; Circ 451,874
Jul 2013-Jun 2014 Income (Main Library and Branch(s)) $1,783,544, State $7,840, City $1,762,704, Other $13,000. Mats Exp $240,000, Books $175,805, Per/Ser (Incl. Access Fees) $13,500, AV Mat $10,000, Electronic Ref Mat (Incl. Access Fees) $40,695. Sal $143,403
Library Holdings: AV Mats 21,101; Bk Vols 200,000; Per Subs 231
Special Collections: ADA Coll; Business Resource Center; Hamden History Coll; Job Resource Center; Literacy Coll
Automation Activity & Vendor Info: (Acquisitions) Innovative Interfaces, Inc - Millenium; (Cataloging) Innovative Interfaces, Inc - Millenium; (Circulation) Innovative Interfaces, Inc - Millenium; (OPAC) Innovative Interfaces, Inc - Millenium
Database Vendor: Medline
Wireless access
Function: Adult bk club, Art exhibits, Bks on cassette, Bks on CD, Children's prog, Computers for patron use, Copy machines, E-Reserves, Electronic databases & coll, Free DVD rentals, Games & aids for the handicapped, Handicapped accessible, Holiday prog, Homebound delivery serv, ILL available, Magnifiers for reading, Mail & tel request accepted, Mus passes, Music CDs, Online cat, Online ref, Outreach serv, Outside serv via phone, mail, e-mail & web, Prog for adults, Prog for children & young adult, Pub access computers, Spoken cassettes & CDs, Story hour, Summer reading prog, Tax forms, Telephone ref, VHS videos
Open Mon-Wed 10-9, Thurs-Sat 10-5:30
Friends of the Library Group
Branches: 2
BRUNDAGE COMMUNITY, 91 Circular Ave, 06514, SAN 336-1381. Tel: 203-287-2675. FAX: 203-287-2675. *Br Mgr,* Sandra Bartell; E-mail: sbartell@hamdenlibrary.org; Staff 2 (MLS 1, Non-MLS 1)
Special Collections: Spanish Language Coll
Open Mon, Tues, Thurs & Fri 10-12 & 1-5:30
Friends of the Library Group
WHITNEYVILLE, 125 Carleton St, 06517, SAN 336-1446. Tel: 203-287-2677. FAX: 203-287-2677. *Br Mgr,* Maureen Armstrong; E-mail: marmstrong@hamdenlibrary.org; Staff 2 (MLS 1, Non-MLS 1)
Open Mon, Tues, Thurs & Fri 10-12:30 & 1-6
Friends of the Library Group

C PAIER COLLEGE OF ART, INC LIBRARY, 20 Gorham Ave, 06514-3902. SAN 324-2803. Tel: 203-287-3023. FAX: 203-287-3021. E-mail: paierartlibrary@snet.net. Web Site: www.paierart.com. *Librn, Tech Serv,* Beth R Harris; Staff 1 (MLS 1)
Enrl 285; Fac 40; Highest Degree: Bachelor
Library Holdings: Bk Vols 13,000
Special Collections: Picture Reference File
Subject Interests: Fine arts, Lit, Photog, Tech arts
Automation Activity & Vendor Info: (OPAC) Follett Software
Wireless access
Publications: ARLIS (Newsletter)

C QUINNIPIAC UNIVERSITY*, Arnold Bernhard Library, 275 Mount Carmel Ave, 06518. SAN 302-1645. Tel: 203-582-8634. Reference Tel: 203-582-8633. FAX: 203-582-3451. Web Site: www.quinnipiac.edu. *Univ Librn,* Robert Joven; Tel: 203-582-8631, E-mail: robert.joven@quinnipiac.edu; *Cat,* Susan O'Brien; Tel: 203-582-8918, E-mail: susan.pfister@quinnipiac.edu; *Coll Mgt,* June DeGennaro; Tel: 203-582-8944, E-mail: june.degennaro@quinnipiac.edu; *Electronic Res,* Linda Hawkes; Tel: 203-582-8946, E-mail: linda.hawkes@quinnipiac.edu; *ILL,* Frances Kelly; Tel: 203-582-8635, E-mail: frances.kelly@quinnipiac.edu; *Ref,* Janet L Valeski; Tel: 203-582-8943, E-mail: janet.valeski@quinnipiac.edu; Staff 24 (MLS 14, Non-MLS 10)
Founded 1929. Enrl 5,000; Fac 5; Highest Degree: Doctorate
Library Holdings: Bk Titles 140,000; Bk Vols 167,000; Per Subs 900
Special Collections: Albert Schweitzer Related; Great Hunger (Irish Famine)
Subject Interests: Holocaust
Automation Activity & Vendor Info: (Acquisitions) Innovative Interfaces, Inc; (Cataloging) Innovative Interfaces, Inc; (Circulation) Innovative Interfaces, Inc; (OPAC) Innovative Interfaces, Inc
Database Vendor: EBSCOhost, Gale Cengage Learning, OCLC FirstSearch, ProQuest
Function: ILL available

Partic in Coun of Conn Acad Libr Dirs; Lyrasis
Open Mon-Thurs 8am-Midnight, Fri 8-6, Sat 9-6, Sun Noon-Midnight
Restriction: Circ limited

J SACRED HEART ACADEMY*, Mary & James Dimeo Library, c/o Sacred Heart Academy, 265 Benham St, 06514. SAN 302-1637. Tel: 203-288-2309. FAX: 203-230-9680. Web Site: sha-excelsior.org. *Librn,* Maureen Hayes; *Asst Librn,* Karen Reidy; E-mail: kreidy@sha-excelsior.org
Founded 1946. Enrl 480; Fac 46; Highest Degree: Doctorate
Library Holdings: Bk Vols 40,000; Per Subs 100
Automation Activity & Vendor Info: (Cataloging) Follett Software; (Circulation) Follett Software; (OPAC) Follett Software

R TEMPLE BETH SHOLOM*, Esther Swinkin Memorial Library, 1809 Whitney Ave, 06517. SAN 302-1653. Tel: 203-288-7748. FAX: 203-288-0582. E-mail: library@tbshamden.com. Web Site: www.tbshamden.com. *Librn,* Michael Brooks
Founded 1960
Library Holdings: Bk Titles 1,500; Videos 75
Subject Interests: Holocaust

HAMPTON

P FLETCHER MEMORIAL LIBRARY*, 257 Main St, 06247. (Mail add: PO Box 6, 06247), SAN 302-1661. Tel: 860-455-1086. E-mail: postmaster@fletchermemorial.org. *Dir,* Jill Tofferi; *Ref Librn,* Ginger Palmer
Pop 1,350; Circ 12,000
Library Holdings: Bk Vols 20,000
Partic in Connecticut Library Consortium
Open Mon 9-12, Tues 6-8, Wed 2-8, Thurs 9-12 & 6-8, Sat 10-5

HARTFORD

L AETNA*, Law Library, 151 Farmington Ave-RC61, 06156. SAN 336-156X,
Founded 1975
Subject Interests: Corporate law, Health law
Wireless access
Function: Res libr
Restriction: Staff use only, Use of others with permission of librn

J CAPITAL COMMUNITY COLLEGE LIBRARY*, 950 Main St, 06103. SAN 302-1777. Tel: 860-906-5027. Administration Tel: 860-906-5021. FAX: 860-906-5255. Web Site: www.ccc.commnet.edu/library. *Dir,* Carl Antonucci; Staff 5 (MLS 4, Non-MLS 1)
Founded 1967
Library Holdings: AV Mats 4,500; e-books 5,478; Bk Vols 45,000; Per Subs 362
Automation Activity & Vendor Info: (Acquisitions) Ex Libris Group; (Cataloging) Ex Libris Group; (Circulation) Ex Libris Group; (Course Reserve) Ex Libris Group; (OPAC) Ex Libris Group
Wireless access
Publications: Guide to Research; Library Workbook
Partic in Connecticut Library Consortium; OCLC Online Computer Library Center, Inc
Open Mon-Thurs 8:30-8, Fri 8:30-4:30, Sat 10-2

S CONNECTICUT HISTORICAL SOCIETY RESEARCH CENTER*, One Elizabeth St, 06105. SAN 302-1696. Tel: 860-236-5621. Reference Tel: 860-236-5621, Ext 230. FAX: 860-236-2664. E-mail: libchs@chs.org. Web Site: www.chs.org. *Head, Res Ctr,* Diana McCain; Tel: 860-236-5621, Ext 213, E-mail: diana_mccain@chs.org; *Archivist,* Barbara Austen; Tel: 860-236-5621, Ext 251, E-mail: barbara_austen@chs.org; Staff 2 (MLS 2)
Founded 1825
Library Holdings: Bk Vols 125,000; Per Subs 200
Special Collections: Connecticut Imprints; Historical Manuscripts; Juvenile (Bates & Caroline Hewins Coll); Sermons
Subject Interests: Children's lit, Connecticut, Genealogy, Local hist, New England, Relig
Automation Activity & Vendor Info: (Acquisitions) Ex Libris Group; (Cataloging) Ex Libris Group; (Circulation) Ex Libris Group; (OPAC) Ex Libris Group; (Serials) Ex Libris Group
Wireless access
Function: Archival coll, Online cat, Online ref, Photocopying/Printing, Telephone ref, Wheelchair accessible
Partic in OCLC Online Computer Library Center, Inc; ReQuest OPAC Catalog
Open Thurs 12-5, Fri & Sat 9-5
Restriction: Closed stack, Fee for pub use, Non-circulating coll, Photo ID required for access

GL CONNECTICUT JUDICIAL BRANCH LAW LIBRARIES*, Administrative Office, 90 Washington St, Third Flr, 06106. Tel: 860-706-5145. FAX: 860-706-5086. Web Site: www.jud.ct.gov/lawlib. *Dep Dir,* Ann Doherty; E-mail: ann.doherty@jud.ct.gov; *Supv Law Librn,* Jeffrey Dowd; E-mail: jeffrey.dowd@jud.ct.gov; *Supv Law Librn,* Claudia Jalowka; E-mail: claudia.beth.jalowka@jud.ct.gov
Partic in New England Law Library Consortium, Inc
Branches:
BRIDGEPORT LAW LIBRARY, Bridgeport Courthouse, 1061 Main St, Bridgeport, 06604, SAN 336-1802. Tel: 203-579-7244. FAX: 203-579-7298. *Librn,* Mary Ann Krivick; E-mail: maryann.krivick@jud.ct.gov; *Librn,* Karen Yeltema; E-mail: karen.yeltema@jud.ct.gov
Library Holdings: Bk Vols 38,000; Per Subs 92
Automation Activity & Vendor Info: (Cataloging) Auto-Graphics, Inc; (Circulation) Auto-Graphics, Inc
Open Mon-Fri 9-5
DANBURY LAW LIBRARY, Danbury Courthouse, 146 White St, Danbury, 06810, SAN 302-1009. Tel: 203-207-8625. FAX: 203-207-8627. *Librn,* Linda Mellick; E-mail: linda.mellick@jud.ct.gov; Staff 2 (MLS 1, Non-MLS 1)
Library Holdings: Bk Titles 400; Bk Vols 28,000; Per Subs 30
Special Collections: Connecticut Legislative Histories; Historical Information (Connecticut Law)
Subject Interests: Connecticut, Law
Open Mon-Fri 9-5
HARTFORD LAW LIBRARY, Hartford Courthouse, 95 Washington St, 06106, SAN 336-1837. Tel: 860-548-2866. FAX: 860-548-2868. *Librn,* Catherine Mazur; E-mail: Catherine.Mazur@jud.ct.gov
Library Holdings: Bk Vols 40,000
Automation Activity & Vendor Info: (Cataloging) Auto-Graphics, Inc; (Circulation) Auto-Graphics, Inc
Database Vendor: LexisNexis, Westlaw
Open Mon-Fri 9-5
LITCHFIELD LAW LIBRARY, Litchfield Courthouse, 15 West St, Litchfield, 06759-3501. Tel: 860-567-0598. FAX: 860-567-4533. *Librn,* Louise Tucker; E-mail: louise.tucker@jud.ct.gov; Staff 1 (MLS 1)
Library Holdings: Bk Vols 15,000
Special Collections: Law - primary & secondary sources with a concentration on Connecticut materials
Automation Activity & Vendor Info: (OPAC) Auto-Graphics, Inc
Open Mon-Fri 9-5
MIDDLETOWN LAW LIBRARY, Middletown Courthouse, One Court St, Middletown, 06457. Tel: 860-343-6560. FAX: 860-343-6568. *Librn,* Bonnie Gallagher; E-mail: bonnie.gallagher@jud.ct.gov; *Librn,* Lori Sulmasy; E-mail: lori.sulmasy@jud.ct.go
Open Mon-Fri 9-5
NEW BRITAIN LAW LIBRARY, New Britain Courthouse, 20 Franklin Sq, New Britain, 06051. Tel: 860-515-5110. FAX: 860-515-5111. *Librn,* George Booth; E-mail: george.booth@jud.ct.gov; *Librn,* Christopher Roy; E-mail: christopher.roy@jud.ct.gov
Open Mon-Fri 9-5
NEW HAVEN LAW LIBRARY, New Haven Courthouse, 235 Church St, New Haven, 06510, SAN 336-1926. Tel: 203-503-6828. FAX: 203-789-6499. *Librn,* Ann Doherty; E-mail: ann.doherty@jud.ct.gov
Library Holdings: Bk Vols 55,000; Per Subs 75
Automation Activity & Vendor Info: (Cataloging) Auto-Graphics, Inc
Open Mon-Fri 9-5
NEW LONDON LAW LIBRARY, New London Courthouse, 108 Valley St, New London, 06320. Tel: 860-442-7561. FAX: 860-442-9416. *Librn,* Peter Jenkins; E-mail: peter.jenkins@jud.ct.gov
Open Mon-Fri 9-5
PUTNAM LAW LIBRARY, Putnam Courthouse, 155 Church St, Putnam, 06260, SAN 336-1985. Tel: 860-928-3716. FAX: 860-963-7531. *Librn,* Donna R Izbicki; E-mail: donna.izbicki@jud.ct.gov; Staff 1 (MLS 1)
Library Holdings: Bk Vols 17,500
Open Mon-Fri 9-5
ROCKVILLE LAW LIBRARY, Rockville Courthouse, 69 Brooklyn St, Rockville, 06066, SAN 336-2019. Tel: 860-896-4955. FAX: 860-875-3213. *Librn,* Roseann Canny; E-mail: roseann.canny@jud.ct.gov
Library Holdings: Bk Vols 25,000
Automation Activity & Vendor Info: (Cataloging) Auto-Graphics, Inc; (OPAC) Auto-Graphics, Inc
Open Mon-Fri 9-5
STAMFORD LAW LIBRARY, Stamford Courthouse, 123 Hoyt St, Stamford, 06905, SAN 336-2043. Tel: 203-965-5250. FAX: 203-965-5784. *Law Librn,* Michael Beetham; Tel: 203-965-4521, E-mail: michael.beetham@jud.ct.gov; *Law Librn,* Pamela Kaufman; Tel: 203-965-5377, E-mail: pamela.kaufman@jud.ct.gov; Staff 2 (MLS 2)
Library Holdings: Microforms 129,806; Bk Vols 38,954; Per Subs 19
Automation Activity & Vendor Info: (Cataloging) Auto-Graphics, Inc; (OPAC) Auto-Graphics, Inc
Database Vendor: LexisNexis, Westlaw
Open Mon-Fri 9-5

WATERBURY LAW LIBRARY, Waterbury Courthouse, 300 Grand St, Waterbury, 06702, SAN 375-7528. Tel: 203-591-3338. FAX: 203-596-4137. *Supv Law Librn,* Mary Fuller; E-mail: mary.fuller@jud.ct.gov; *Librn,* Kathleen Koller; E-mail: kathleen.koller@jud.ct.gov; Staff 2 (MLS 2)
Jul 2009-Jun 2010. Mats Exp $180,000. Sal $241,433 (Prof $202,092)
Library Holdings: Bk Vols 40,000; Per Subs 35
Automation Activity & Vendor Info: (Cataloging) Auto-Graphics, Inc; (OPAC) Auto-Graphics, Inc
Open Mon-Fri 9-5

S CONNECTICUT LEGISLATIVE LIBRARY*, Legislative Office Bldg, Rm 5400, 300 Capitol Ave, 06106-1591. SAN 372-3844. Tel: 860-240-8888. FAX: 860-240-8881. E-mail: library@cga.ct.gov. *Librn,* Jennifer Bernier; *Librn,* Carrie Rose; Staff 4 (MLS 3, Non-MLS 1)
Library Holdings: Bk Vols 10,000
Wireless access
Restriction: Non-circulating

P CONNECTICUT STATE LIBRARY, 231 Capitol Ave, 06106. SAN 336-1594. Tel: 860-757-6500. Circulation Tel: 860-757-6530. Interlibrary Loan Service Tel: 860-757-6590. Administration Tel: 860-757-6510. Toll Free Tel: 866-886-4478. FAX: 860-757-6503. Interlibrary Loan Service FAX: 860-757-6559. Web Site: www.ctstatelibrary.org. *State Librn,* Kendall Wiggin; E-mail: kendall.wiggin@ct.gov; *Dir, Libr Develop,* Dawn La Valle; Tel: 860-757-6665, E-mail: dawn.lavalle@ct.gov; *Presv Librn,* Jane Cullinane; Tel: 860-757-6525; *Ser Librn,* Carol Trinchitella; Tel: 860-757-6562; *Cat Mgr,* Stephen Slovasky; Tel: 860-757-6546; *Coll Serv Mgr,* Diane Pizzo; *Children's & Youth Serv,* Linda Williams; Staff 124 (MLS 48, Non-MLS 76)
Founded 1854
Jul 2013-Jun 2014 Income (Main Library and Branch(s)) $17,603,154, State $13,248,004, Federal $1,931,653, Other $2,423,497. Mats Exp $825,954, Books $18,659, Per/Ser (Incl. Access Fees) $424,760, Manu Arch $1,005, Electronic Ref Mat (Incl. Access Fees) $342,168, Presv $39,362. Sal $6,173,239 (Prof $3,394,103)
Library Holdings: AV Mats 595; Bks on Deafness & Sign Lang 151; DVDs 1,213; e-journals 70,410; Electronic Media & Resources 86; Bk Vols 1,338,809; Per Subs 8,821; Videos 276
Special Collections: Archives & Historical Manuscripts; Cemetery Inscriptions; Census Records; Charter of 1662; Church, Town & Vital Records; Colt Firearms; Connecticut Aerial Photographic Surveys; Connecticut Shelf Clock Coll; Fraternal Orders; Governor's Portraits; Law Coll; Legislative Transcripts; Maps; Medals & Coins; Military Records & War Posters Coll; Newspapers; Old Houses of Connecticut Coll; State & Local History Coll; State Statutes. State Document Depository; US Document Depository
Subject Interests: Genealogy, Govt, Law, Legislation, Pub policy, State hist
Automation Activity & Vendor Info: (Acquisitions) Innovative Interfaces, Inc; (Cataloging) Innovative Interfaces, Inc; (Circulation) Innovative Interfaces, Inc; (ILL) OCLC; (OPAC) Innovative Interfaces, Inc; (Serials) Innovative Interfaces, Inc
Database Vendor: 3M Library Systems, Baker & Taylor, Blackwell, Booklist Online, Brodart, BWI, Cambridge Scientific Abstracts, Checkpoint Systems, Inc, CQ Press, CRC Press/Taylor & Francis Group, EBSCO Information Services, Emerald, Facts on File, Gale Cengage Learning, H W Wilson, Haworth Pres Inc, HeinOnline, infoUSA, Ingenta, Innovative Interfaces, Inc, JSTOR, LexisNexis, Newsbank, OCLC ArticleFirst, OCLC FirstSearch, OCLC WebJunction, OCLC WorldShare Interlibrary Loan, Oxford Online, Paratext, ProQuest, PubMed, ReferenceUSA, Sage, SerialsSolutions, Springer-Verlag, Westlaw, Wilson - Wilson Web
Wireless access
Function: Archival coll, Computers for patron use, Electronic databases & coll, Govt ref serv, Ref & res
Publications: Checklist of Connecticut State Documents; Connecticut Union List of Serials; The Connector; The CONNservator
Partic in CONSULS (Connecticut State University Library System)
Special Services for the Deaf - Bks on deafness & sign lang
Open Tues-Fri 9-5, Sat 9-2
Restriction: Circ limited
Branches: 3
LIBRARY FOR THE BLIND & PHYSICALLY HANDICAPPED
See Separate Entry in Rocky Hill
MIDDLETOWN LIBRARY SERVICE CENTER, 786 S Main St, Middletown, 06457, SAN 336-1683. Tel: 860-704-2200. FAX: 860-704-2228. *Dir,* Position Currently Open; *LSTA Coordr,* Maria Bernier; Tel: 860-704-2204, E-mail: maria.bernier@ct.gov; Staff 4 (MLS 2, Non-MLS 2)
Founded 1955
Library Holdings: Audiobooks 4,461; CDs 1,169; DVDs 35; Large Print Bks 14,408; Bk Vols 51,879; Per Subs 2
Subject Interests: Librarianship
Automation Activity & Vendor Info: (Circulation) Innovative Interfaces, Inc - Millenium; (OPAC) Innovative Interfaces, Inc - Millenium
Function: Workshops
Restriction: Open only to librarians
WILLIMANTIC LIBRARY SERVICE CENTER, 1320 Main St, Ste 25, Willimantic, 06226-1944, SAN 302-4504. Tel: 860-456-1717. Toll Free Tel: 800-253-7944. FAX: 860-423-5874. *Dir,* Susan Draper Cormier; Tel: 860-456-1717, Ext 301, E-mail: susan.cormier@ct.gov; Staff 2 (MLS 2)
Library Holdings: Bk Titles 70,977; Bk Vols 86,732; Per Subs 12
Function: ILL available, Prof lending libr, Wheelchair accessible, Workshops
Restriction: Not open to pub

M HARTFORD HOSPITAL*, Robinson Health Sciences Library, ERC Bldg-3, 80 Seymour St, 06102. (Mail add: PO Box 5037, 06102-5037), SAN 336-2108. Tel: 860-545-2230. Interlibrary Loan Service Tel: 860-545-5085. FAX: 860-545-2572. E-mail: hh.library@hhchealth.org. Web Site: www.harthosp.org/hsl. *Dir,* Shirley Gronholm; Tel: 860-545-2420, E-mail: Shirley.Gronholm@hhchealth.org; *Sr Librn, Computer & Web-Based Res,* Sheila Hayes; Tel: 860-972-2416, E-mail: Sheila.Hayes@hhchealth.org; *Clinical Librn,* Lisa Carter; Tel: 860-545-2425, E-mail: Lisa.Carter@hhchealth.org; *Clinical Librn, Pediatrics,* Linda Kaczmarczyk; Tel: 860-545-2422, E-mail: Linda.Kaczmarczyk@hhchealth.org; *Clinical Librn, Surgery,* Ellen MacNaughton; Tel: 860-545-2424, E-mail: Ellen.MacNaughton@hhchealth.org; *Librn,* Katarzyna (Kathy) Woznica; Tel: 860-545-5096, E-mail: Katarzyna.Woznica@hhchealth.org. Subject Specialists: *Allied health, Nursing,* Lisa Carter; *Pediatrics,* Linda Kaczmarczyk; *Surgery,* Ellen MacNaughton; Staff 11 (MLS 6, Non-MLS 5)
Founded 1855
Library Holdings: e-books 350; e-journals 2,000; Bk Titles 30,875; Per Subs 343
Special Collections: History of Nursing (Foley Coll), archives, bks
Subject Interests: Allied health, Clinical med, Hospital admin, Nursing
Automation Activity & Vendor Info: (Acquisitions) Ex Libris Group; (Cataloging) Ex Libris Group; (Circulation) EOS International; (OPAC) EOS International; (Serials) EOS International
Database Vendor: Agricola, American Psychological Association (APA), Cinahl, EBSCO Information Services, EBSCOhost, EOS International, Ingenta, Lexi-Comp, Majors, McGraw-Hill, MD Consult, Medline, Natural Standard, OCLC WorldShare Interlibrary Loan, OVID Technologies, PubMed, ScienceDirect, STAT!Ref (Teton Data Systems), UpToDate
Wireless access
Function: Computers for patron use, Copy machines, Doc delivery serv, Electronic databases & coll, ILL available, Online cat, Photocopying/Printing, Web-catalog
Partic in Capital Area Health Consortium; Conn Asn of Health Scis Librs; Medical Library Association (MLA), National Network of Libraries of Medicine; North Atlantic Health Sciences Libraries, Inc; OCLC Online Computer Library Center, Inc
Restriction: Badge access after hrs, Borrowing requests are handled by ILL, Hospital employees & physicians only, Med & health res only, Med & nursing staff, patients & families, Not open to pub, Open to fac, students & qualified researchers, Open to hospital affiliates only, Private libr, Prof mat only
Branches:
INSTITUTE OF LIVING MEDICAL LIBRARY, Research Bldg 3, 200 Retreat Ave, 06106-5037, SAN 302-1866. Tel: 860-545-7147. FAX: 860-545-7275. *Librn,* Elizabeth Fishe; E-mail: Betty.Fishe@hhchealth.org. Subject Specialists: *Neurology, Psychiat, Psychol,* Elizabeth Fishe; Staff 1 (MLS 1)
Library Holdings: e-books 250; e-journals 2,000; Bk Titles 10,000; Per Subs 150
Subject Interests: Psychiat, Psychol
Automation Activity & Vendor Info: (Acquisitions) EOS International; (Cataloging) EOS International; (Circulation) EOS International; (OPAC) EOS International; (Serials) EOS International
Database Vendor: American Psychological Association (APA), Cinahl, EBSCO Information Services, EBSCOhost, EOS International, Lexi-Comp, Majors, McGraw-Hill, MD Consult, Medline, OCLC WorldShare Interlibrary Loan, OVID Technologies, PubMed, STAT!Ref (Teton Data Systems), UpToDate
Function: Computers for patron use, Copy machines, Doc delivery serv, ILL available, Online cat, Photocopying/Printing
Open Tues-Thurs 8:30-5
Restriction: Hospital employees & physicians only, In-house use for visitors, Med & nursing staff, patients & families, Med staff & students, Open to hospital affiliates only, Private libr

P HARTFORD PUBLIC LIBRARY*, 500 Main St, 06103-3075. SAN 336-2280. Tel: 860-695-6300. Circulation Tel: 860-695-6290. Interlibrary Loan Service Tel: 860-695-6286. Reference Tel: 860-695-6295. Administration Tel: 860-695-6280. Automation Services Tel: 860-695-6315.

FAX: 860-722-6900. Interlibrary Loan Service FAX: 860-722-6889. TDD: 860-722-6890. E-mail: reference@hplct.org. Web Site: www.hplct.org. *Chief Exec Officer,* Matt Poland; E-mail: mpoland@hplct.org; *Chief Develop Officer,* Mary Crean; Tel: 860-695-6360, E-mail: mcrean@hplct.org; *Chief, Pub Serv,* Mary Billings; *Assoc Librn, Adult Learning Serv,* Mary Albro; Tel: 860-695-6284, E-mail: malbro@hplct.org; *Assoc Librn, Commun Develop & Civic Serv,* Richard Frieder; Tel: 860-695-6365, E-mail: rfrieder@hplct.org; *Assoc Librn, Info Tech Serv,* Irene Iwan; Tel: 860-695-6350, E-mail: iiwan@hplct.org; *Assoc Librn, Neighborhood Libr Serv,* Anwar Ahmad; Tel: 860-695-7523, Fax: 860-722-6906, E-mail: aahmad@hplct.org; *Assoc Librn, Youth Serv,* Debra Perry; Tel: 860-695-6333, Fax: 860-722-6897, E-mail: dcperry@hplct.org; Staff 38 (MLS 17, Non-MLS 21)
Founded 1774. Pop 121,578; Circ 498,542
Jul 2009-Jun 2010 Income (Main Library and Branch(s)) $9,043,236, City $7,915,000, Federal $307,548, Locally Generated Income $820,688. Mats Exp $600,000, Books $355,000, Per/Ser (Incl. Access Fees) $68,000, AV Mat $177,000. Sal $7,186,747
Special Collections: Chamber Music Parts (Helen Rice Memorial Coll); Foundation Center Cooperating Coll; Hartford Coll; Outstanding Children's Books (Caroline M Hewins Coll); Patent & Trademark Coll. Oral History
Subject Interests: Art, Bus & mgt, Econ, Educ, Hist, Literary criticism, Music
Automation Activity & Vendor Info: (Acquisitions) Innovative Interfaces, Inc; (Cataloging) Innovative Interfaces, Inc; (Circulation) Innovative Interfaces, Inc; (OPAC) Innovative Interfaces, Inc; (Serials) Innovative Interfaces, Inc
Wireless access
Function: Adult literacy prog, Art exhibits, Audio & video playback equip for onsite use, Bilingual assistance for Spanish patrons, Bk club(s), Bks on cassette, Bks on CD, Children's prog, Citizenship assistance, Computer training, Computers for patron use, Copy machines, Doc delivery serv, e-mail serv, Electronic databases & coll, Exhibits, Family literacy, Fax serv, Free DVD rentals, Govt ref serv, Handicapped accessible, Health sci info serv, Home delivery & serv to Sr ctr & nursing homes, ILL available, Jazz prog, Learning ctr, Libr develop, Magnifiers for reading, Mus passes, Music CDs, Online cat, Online searches, Outreach serv, Outside serv via phone, mail, e-mail & web, Passport agency, Photocopying/Printing, Preschool outreach, Prog for adults, Prog for children & young adult, Pub access computers, Ref serv available, Res performed for a fee, Story hour, Summer reading prog, Tax forms, Teen prog, Telephone ref, Visual arts prog, Wheelchair accessible, Workshops
Publications: Program Guide (Bi-monthly); Readings (Quarterly)
Special Services for the Deaf - Assistive tech; Bks on deafness & sign lang; TDD equip; TTY equip
Special Services for the Blind - Assistive/Adapted tech devices, equip & products; Bks on cassette; Bks on CD; Computer with voice synthesizer for visually impaired persons; Large print bks; Magnifiers; PC for handicapped; ZoomText magnification & reading software
Open Mon-Thurs 10-8, Sat 10-5, Sun (Nov-April) 1-5
Branches: 9
ALBANY, 1250 Albany Ave, 06112, SAN 336-2310. Tel: 860-695-7380. Administration Tel: 860-695-7381. FAX: 860-722-6902. *Cluster Coordr,* Celestia Simmons; E-mail: csimmons@hplct.org; Staff 2 (MLS 1, Non-MLS 1)
Founded 1926. Circ 19,333
Library Holdings: Bk Vols 23,610
Open Mon & Wed 12-6, Tues & Thurs 12-8, Fri & Sat 12-5
BARBOUR, 281 Barbour St, 06120, SAN 336-2345. Tel: 860-695-7400. Administration Tel: 860-695-7401. FAX: 860-722-6881. *Asst Commun Librn,* Jose Santiago; E-mail: jsantiago@hplct.org; Staff 2 (Non-MLS 2)
Founded 1927. Circ 17,068
Library Holdings: Bk Vols 20,503
Open Mon, Tues & Thurs 12:30-5:30, Wed 12:30-7:30, Fri & Sat 12:30-5
BLUE HILLS, 649 Blue Hills Ave, 06112, SAN 336-237X. Tel: 860-695-7420. Administration Tel: 860-695-7422. FAX: 860-722-6907. *Asst Commun Librn,* Linda Kurylowski; E-mail: lkurylowski@hplct.org; Staff 2 (Non-MLS 2)
Founded 1949. Circ 20,723
Library Holdings: Bk Vols 14,931
Open Mon, Wed & Thurs 12:30-5:30, Tues 12:30-7:30, Fri & Sat 12:30-5
CAMP FIELD, 30 Campfield Ave, 06114, SAN 336-240X. Tel: 860-695-7440. Administration Tel: 860-695-7442. FAX: 860-722-6874. *Asst Commun Librn,* Patricia Knapp; E-mail: pknapp@hplct.org; Staff 2 (Non-MLS 2)
Founded 1916. Circ 37,176
Library Holdings: Bk Vols 22,653
Open Mon-Wed 12:30-5:30, Thurs 12:30-7:30, Fri & Sat 12:30-5
DWIGHT BRANCH, Seven New Park Ave, 06106, SAN 336-2434. Tel: 860-695-7462. Administration Tel: 860-695-7461. FAX: 860-722-6884. *Asst Commun Librn,* Ivelisse Ortiz; E-mail: iortiz@hplct.org; Staff 2 (Non-MLS 2)
Founded 1907. Circ 34,463
Library Holdings: Bk Vols 15,170
Open Mon, Tues & Thurs 12:30-5:30, Wed 12:30-7:30, Fri 12:30-5
GOODWIN BRANCH, 460 New Britain Ave, 06106, SAN 336-2469. Tel: 860-695-7480. Administration Tel: 860-695-7483. FAX: 860-722-6887. *Cluster Coordr,* Irene Blean; E-mail: iblean@hplct.org; Staff 2 (MLS 1, Non-MLS 1)
Founded 1941. Circ 34,583
Library Holdings: Bk Vols 17,211
Open Mon, Wed & Thurs 12:30-5:30, Tues 12:30-7:30, Fri & Sat 12:30-5
PARK, 744 Park St, 06106, SAN 336-2523. Tel: 860-695-7500. Administration Tel: 860-695-7501. FAX: 860-722-6878. *Asst Commun Librn,* Leticia Cotto-Hilliman; E-mail: lcotto-hilliman@hplct.org; Staff 2 (Non-MLS 2)
Founded 1928. Circ 20,757
Library Holdings: Bk Vols 29,292
Open Mon 12:30-7:30, Tues-Thurs 12:30-5:30, Fri 12:30-5
ROPKINS BRANCH, 1750 Main St, 06120, SAN 336-2558. Tel: 860-695-7520. Administration Tel: 860-695-7523. FAX: 860-722-6906. *Cluster Coordr,* Irene Blean; E-mail: iblean@hplct.org; Staff 2 (MLS 1, Non-MLS 1)
Founded 1995. Circ 17,212
Library Holdings: Bk Vols 20,921
Open Mon, Tues & Thurs 12:30-5:30, Wed 12:30-7:30, Fri 12:30-5
MARK TWAIN BRANCH, 55 Forest St, 06105, SAN 336-2493. Tel: 860-695-7541. Administration Tel: 860-695-7542. FAX: 860-722-8134. *Asst Commun Librn,* Michelle McFarland; Staff 2 (Non-MLS 2)
Founded 1930. Circ 32,800
Library Holdings: Bk Vols 21,611
Open Mon 12:30-7:30, Tues-Thurs 12:30-5:30, Fri & Sat 12:30-5
Bookmobiles: 1

R HARTFORD SEMINARY LIBRARY, 77 Sherman St, 06105-2260. SAN 302-1831. Tel: 860-509-9561. Interlibrary Loan Service Tel: 860-509-9500. Administration Tel: 860-509-9560. FAX: 860-509-9509. E-mail: library@hartsem.edu. Web Site: www.hartsem.edu/current-students/library. *Dir,* Dr Steven P Blackburn; E-mail: sblackburn@hartsem.edu. Subject Specialists: *Arabic lang, Christian-Muslim relations, Studies in Islam,* Dr Steven P Blackburn; Staff 5 (MLS 2, Non-MLS 3)
Founded 1834. Enrl 120; Fac 16; Highest Degree: Doctorate
Jul 2013-Jun 2014 Income $217,362, Locally Generated Income $69,400, Parent Institution $147,962. Mats Exp $56,972, Books $8,943, Per/Ser (Incl. Access Fees) $25,266, Other Print Mats $1,182, Electronic Ref Mat (Incl. Access Fees) $21,581. Sal $142,562
Library Holdings: CDs 47; DVDs 110; e-books 7,500; e-journals 73; Microforms 6,660; Bk Titles 67,052; Bk Vols 68,192; Per Subs 308; Videos 405
Special Collections: Arabian Nights (multiple languages); Macdonald Coll (Arabic/Islamic studies)
Automation Activity & Vendor Info: (Acquisitions) EOS International; (Cataloging) OCLC Connexion; (Circulation) EOS International; (Course Reserve) EOS International; (ILL) Clio; (OPAC) EOS International; (Serials) EOS International
Database Vendor: EBSCO Information Services, EBSCOhost, Gale Cengage Learning, OCLC ArticleFirst, OCLC FirstSearch, OCLC WorldShare Interlibrary Loan, ProQuest
Wireless access
Function: 24/7 Online cat, Archival coll, CD-ROM, Computers for patron use, Copy machines, Doc delivery serv, e-mail serv, E-Reserves, Electronic databases & coll, Free DVD rentals, Handicapped accessible, ILL available, Microfiche/film & reading machines, Online cat, Orientations, Photocopying/Printing, Printer for laptops & handheld devices, Pub access computers, Ref serv available, Ref serv in person, Spanish lang bks, Spoken cassettes & CDs, Study rm, Telephone ref, VHS videos, Video lending libr, Wheelchair accessible
Partic in Lyrasis; OCLC Online Computer Library Center, Inc
Open Mon-Thurs 9am-10pm, Fri 9-5, Sat 8:30-5
Restriction: Non-circulating of rare bks

S HARTFORD STEAM BOILER INSPECTION & INSURANCE CO, Virtual Information Center, One State St, 9th Flr, 06102. (Mail add: PO Box 5024, 06102), SAN 324-4423. Tel: 860-722-5486. FAX: 860-722-5530. Web Site: www.hsb.com. *Mgr,* Peter S Moon; E-mail: peter_moon@hsb.com; Staff 1 (MLS 1)
Founded 1988
Library Holdings: AV Mats 625; Bk Titles 15,700; Per Subs 25
Special Collections: ASME Boiler & Pressure Vessel Code
Subject Interests: Eng, Ins
Automation Activity & Vendor Info: (Acquisitions) Baker & Taylor; (Cataloging) LibraryWorld, Inc; (Circulation) LibraryWorld, Inc; (OPAC) LibraryWorld, Inc
Database Vendor: EBSCO Information Services, LexisNexis, STN International
Partic in Connecticut Library Consortium
Restriction: Co libr, Open by appt only

L MURTHA CULLINA LLP LIBRARY*, City Pl, 06103. SAN 371-6503. Tel: 860-240-6092. FAX: 860-240-6150. Web Site: www.murthalaw.com. *Librn,* Judith Vanotta; Staff 3 (MLS 3)
Library Holdings: Bk Titles 10,000; Per Subs 300
Automation Activity & Vendor Info: (Cataloging) Inmagic, Inc.; (Circulation) Inmagic, Inc.
Publications: Acquisition List; Handbook
Open Mon-Fri 9-5

L PULLMAN & COMLEY*, Law Library, 90 Statehouse Sq, Flr 13, 06103-3711. SAN 372-3380. Tel: 860-525 6645. FAX: 860-424-4370. *Librn,* Dottie McCaughtry
Library Holdings: Bk Vols 5,000

S ROBINSON & COLE LLP LIBRARY*, 280 Trumbull St, 06103-3597. SAN 326-1557. Tel: 860-275-8200. FAX: 860-275-8299. *Libr Serv Mgr,* Nancy Marcove; Staff 3 (MLS 2, Non-MLS 1)
Library Holdings: Bk Titles 8,500; Bk Vols 31,000; Per Subs 222
Open Mon-Fri 9-5
Restriction: Staff use only

M SAINT FRANCIS HOSPITAL & MEDICAL CENTER*, Health Sciences Library, 114 Woodland St, 06105. SAN 336-2582. Tel: 860-714-4773. FAX: 860-714-8022. E-mail: library@stfranciscare.org. *Dir,* Joseph M Pallis; Tel: 860-714-4883, E-mail: jpallis@stfranciscare.org; Staff 3 (MLS 2, Non-MLS 1)
Library Holdings: Bk Vols 5,000; Per Subs 600
Special Collections: Hospital Archives
Automation Activity & Vendor Info: (Acquisitions) Ex Libris Group; (Cataloging) Ex Libris Group; (Circulation) Ex Libris Group; (OPAC) Ex Libris Group; (Serials) Ex Libris Group
Database Vendor: EBSCOhost, Elsevier, MD Consult, OVID Technologies, PubMed, Sage, ScienceDirect, STAT!Ref (Teton Data Systems), Wiley InterScience
Wireless access
Publications: Library Notes
Partic in Conn Asn of Health Scis Librs; Lyrasis; Medical Library Association (MLA); North Atlantic Health Sciences Libraries, Inc; OCLC Online Computer Library Center, Inc
Open Mon-Fri 7:30-5

S HARRIET BEECHER STOWE CENTER LIBRARY*, 77 Forest St, 06105-3296. SAN 336-2647. Tel: 860-522-9258, Ext 313. FAX: 860-522-9259. E-mail: info@stowecenter.org. Web Site: www.harrietbeecherstowe.org. *Coll Mgr,* Beth Burguess; Staff 1 (Non-MLS 1)
Founded 1965
Library Holdings: Bk Vols 15,000; Per Subs 40
Special Collections: Conservancy photo survey & data sheets on Hartford; Harriet Beecher Stowe Coll; Lyman Beecher Family Coll, photogs; Warner Family Coll; William H Gillette Coll
Subject Interests: 19th Century Am decorative arts, 19th Century women's hist, African-Am hist
Wireless access
Partic in OCLC Online Computer Library Center, Inc
Restriction: Open by appt only

C TRINITY COLLEGE LIBRARY*, 300 Summit St, 06106. SAN 336-2701. Tel: 860-297-2255. Circulation Tel: 860-297-5184. Interlibrary Loan Service Tel: 860-297-2242. Reference Tel: 860-297-2252. FAX: 860-297-2251. Web Site: www.trincoll.edu/depts/library/. *Col Librn,* Richard S Ross; Tel: 860-297-2258; *Head Librn, Coll, Res & Instruction,* Doris Kammradt; Tel: 860-297-5352; *Head Librn, Tech Serv,* Thomas Zaharevich; Tel: 860-297-2244; *Access Serv,* Alice Angelo; Tel: 860-297-2247; *Acq,* Yuksel Serindag; Tel: 860-297-2249; *Archivist,* Peter Knapp; Tel: 860-297-2269; *ILL,* Mary Curry; *Music & Media Librn,* Amy Harrell; Tel: 860-297-2193; *Ref Serv,* Patricia Bunker; Tel: 860-297-2254; *Res & Instrul Serv Librn,* Erin Valentino; Tel: 860-297-5211; *Ser,* Jennifer van Sickle; Tel: 860-297-2250; *Visual Res,* Nancy Smith; Tel: 860-297-4061. Subject Specialists: *Music, Performing arts,* Amy Harrell; Staff 34.5 (MLS 20, Non-MLS 14.5)
Founded 1823. Enrl 2,151; Fac 196; Highest Degree: Master
Jul 2007-Jun 2008. Mats Exp $1,560,666, Books $586,067, Per/Ser (Incl. Access Fees) $900,966, AV Mat $33,379, Presv $40,254. Sal $1,573,631 (Prof $1,165,158)
Library Holdings: AV Mats 101,249; CDs 8,256; DVDs 1,816; e-books 54,066; e-journals 17,038; Microforms 381,055; Bk Vols 904,988; Per Subs 1,407; Videos 5,098
Special Collections: American Indian Coll; Americana; Bibliography & History of Printing; Charles Dudley Warner Coll, mss; Charles Nodier Coll; Civil War Coll; Cruikshank Coll; Early American Education Textbooks (Henry Barnard Coll); Early American Sheet Music & Periodicals; Early Voyages & Discoveries; Edna St Vincent Millay Coll; Edwin Arlington Robinson Coll; Folklore Coll; Horology Coll; Incunabula (Trumbull-Prime Coll); Philology Coll; Private Press Books; Psalm & Hymn Books; Robert Frost Coll; Slavery Coll; Walter de la Mare Coll; Witchcraft Coll; World War I Coll. US Document Depository
Subject Interests: Educ, Hist, Music
Automation Activity & Vendor Info: (Acquisitions) Ex Libris Group; (Cataloging) Ex Libris Group; (Circulation) Ex Libris Group; (Course Reserve) Ex Libris Group; (OPAC) Ex Libris Group; (Serials) Ex Libris Group
Database Vendor: EBSCOhost, Gale Cengage Learning, OCLC FirstSearch
Wireless access
Publications: Exhibition Catalogs; Gatherings; Ornithology Books in the Library of Trinity College, Hartford 1983
Partic in Connecticut Library Consortium; CTW Library Consortium; Greater Hartford Consortium for Higher Educ
Friends of the Library Group

Departmental Libraries:

WATKINSON LIBRARY, 300 Summit St, 06106. Tel: 860-297-2268. *Head Librn,* Jeffrey H Kaimowitz; Staff 3 (MLS 3)
Subject Interests: Abolitionism, Am Indians (Lang), Americana, Bibliographies, Bk illustr, Botany, British hist, Civil War, Cultural hist, Early printing, Educ, Hist, Natural hist, Ornithology, Popular music, Printing hist, Sacred music, Slavery, Travel, Voyages
Friends of the Library Group

SR UNITED CHURCH OF CHRIST*, Connecticut Conference Archives, 125 Sherman St, 06105. SAN 325-7665. Tel: 860-233-5564. FAX: 860-231-8111. Web Site: ctucc.org. *Archivist,* Dr Evans Sealand; E-mail: evanss@ctucc.org
Library Holdings: Bk Vols 5,000
Special Collections: Church Records, doc; Early Americana; Missionary Papers
Open Tues & Thurs 9-2

CL UNIVERSITY OF CONNECTICUT*, School of Law Library, 39 Elizabeth St, 06105-2287. SAN 336-5492. Tel: 860-570-5200. Reference Tel: 860-570-5068. Administration Tel: 860-570-5109. Information Services Tel: 860-570-5158. FAX: 860-570-5104. Administration FAX: 860-570-5109. TDD: 860-570-5063. Web Site: law.uconn.edu/library. *Assoc Dean of Libr & Tech,* Darcy Kirk; E-mail: darcy.kirk@law.uconn.edu; *Dir, Libr Serv,* Jocelyn Kennedy; Tel: 860-570-5098, E-mail: jocelyn.kennedy@law.uconn.edu; *Dir, Info Tech Serv,* Jessica de Perio Wittman; Tel: 860-570-5059, E-mail: jessica.deperio@law.uconn.edu; *Head, Ref Serv,* Catherine Dunn; Tel: 860-570-5071, E-mail: catherine.dunn@law.uconn.edu. Subject Specialists: *Advan legal res, Higher educ law,* Darcy Kirk; *Advan legal res,* Jocelyn Kennedy; *Educ tech,* Jessica de Perio Wittman; *Advan legal res,* Catherine Dunn; Staff 13.5 (MLS 8.5, Non-MLS 5)
Founded 1921. Enrl 704; Fac 54; Highest Degree: Doctorate
Library Holdings: Bk Titles 190,364; Bk Vols 553,811
Subject Interests: Law
Automation Activity & Vendor Info: (Acquisitions) Innovative Interfaces, Inc; (Cataloging) Innovative Interfaces, Inc; (Circulation) Innovative Interfaces, Inc; (Course Reserve) Innovative Interfaces, Inc; (OPAC) Innovative Interfaces, Inc; (Serials) Innovative Interfaces, Inc
Database Vendor: Innovative Interfaces, Inc, LexisNexis, OCLC FirstSearch
Wireless access
Function: Accessibility serv available based on individual needs, Copy machines, e-mail & chat, Electronic databases & coll, Handicapped accessible, ILL available, Microfiche/film & reading machines, Online cat, Online searches, Ref serv available, Ref serv in person, Scanner, Telephone ref
Partic in OCLC Online Computer Library Center, Inc
Special Services for the Deaf - TDD equip
Restriction: Borrowing privileges limited to fac & registered students, Circ limited, Non-circulating to the pub, Pub ref by request, Pub use on premises

S WADSWORTH ATHENEUM*, Auerbach Art Library, 600 Main St, 06103. SAN 302-1955. Tel: 860-278-2670, Ext 3115. FAX: 860-527-0803. Web Site: www.wadsworthatheneum.org. *Librn,* John Teahan; E-mail: john.teahan@wadsworthatheneum.org
Founded 1934
Library Holdings: Bk Vols 47,000; Per Subs 90
Special Collections: Art (Watkinson Coll); Bookplates (Baker Coll)
Subject Interests: Costume design, Decorative art, Fine arts, Local hist, Museology, Photog
Automation Activity & Vendor Info: (Cataloging) TLC (The Library Corporation)
Open Wed & Thurs 11-5
Restriction: Non-circulating to the pub, Open to pub for ref only
Friends of the Library Group

HARWINTON

P HARWINTON PUBLIC LIBRARY*, 80 Bentley Dr, 06791. SAN 302-198X. Tel: 860-485-9113. FAX: 860-485-2713. E-mail: staff@harwintonpl.org. Web Site: www.harwintonpl.org. *Librn,* Stasia Motuzick; *Ch Serv,* Heather Baker; Staff 5 (MLS 2, Non-MLS 3)
Founded 1909. Pop 5,000; Circ 21,000
Library Holdings: CDs 409; DVDs 119; Large Print Bks 300; Bk Vols 30,000; Per Subs 75; Talking Bks 1,270; Videos 1,294
Subject Interests: Local hist
Automation Activity & Vendor Info: (Acquisitions) Follett Software; (Cataloging) Follett Software; (Circulation) Follett Software
Open Mon & Wed 1-8:30, Tues & Thurs 9:30-5, Fri 1-5, Sat 9:30-3 (9:30-1 Summer)
Friends of the Library Group

HEBRON

P DOUGLAS LIBRARY OF HEBRON, 22 Main St, 06248. SAN 302-1998. Tel: 860-228-9312. FAX: 860-228-4372. Web Site: douglaslibrary.org. *Dir,* Amanda Brouwer; E-mail: abrouwer@hebronct.com; Staff 7 (MLS 2, Non-MLS 5)
Founded 1899. Pop 9,500
Jul 2013-Jun 2014 Income $365,000. Mats Exp $40,000. Sal $202,000
Library Holdings: AV Mats 6,000; Bk Vols 39,000
Subject Interests: Genealogy
Automation Activity & Vendor Info: (Cataloging) OCLC; (Circulation) Evergreen; (OPAC) Evergreen
Wireless access
Function: Handicapped accessible, ILL available, Photocopying/Printing, Prog for children & young adult, Summer reading prog, Wheelchair accessible
Publications: Our Town's Heritage (by John Sibun)
Open Mon & Wed (Sept-June) 12-8, Tues & Thurs 10-8, Fri 12-6, Sat 10-3
Friends of the Library Group

IVORYTON

P IVORYTON LIBRARY ASSOCIATION*, 106 Main St, 06442. (Mail add: PO Box 515, 06442-0515), SAN 324-2811. Tel: 860-767-1252. E-mail: staff@ivoryton.com. Web Site: www.ivoryton.com. *Dir,* Elizabeth Alvord; *Ch Serv,* Elizabeth Bartlett; E-mail: ebartlett@ivoryton.com
Founded 1871. Pop 1,500; Circ 12,000
Library Holdings: Bk Titles 8,000; Per Subs 30
Special Collections: Oral History
Automation Activity & Vendor Info: (Cataloging) SirsiDynix; (Circulation) SirsiDynix; (OPAC) SirsiDynix
Wireless access
Open Tues & Thurs 10-6, Wed 10-8, Fri 2-6, Sat 9-Noon, Sun 1-4

JEWETT CITY

P SLATER LIBRARY*, 26 Main St, 06351. SAN 376-2629. Tel: 860-376-0024. FAX: 860-376-0024. Web Site: www.geocities.com/slaterlibrary/slater.html. *Dir,* Meg Vantine; E-mail: mvantine_slaterlibrary@yahoo.com; *Ch Serv,* Kathy Choiniere; E-mail: kchoiniere_slaterlibrary@yahoo.com; Staff 9 (Non-MLS 9)
Founded 1882. Pop 14,000; Circ 35,000
Jul 2005-Jun 2006 Income $120,000. Mats Exp $14,000, Books $11,000, Per/Ser (Incl. Access Fees) $1,400, AV Equip $600, AV Mat $350, Electronic Ref Mat (Incl. Access Fees) $650. Sal $61,000 (Prof $23,000)
Library Holdings: AV Mats 1,000; Large Print Bks 445; Bk Titles 21,000; Per Subs 50
Automation Activity & Vendor Info: (Serials) EBSCO Online
Database Vendor: ProQuest
Partic in Connecticut Library Consortium; SLiMs
Open Mon-Thurs 12-7, Fri 12-5, Sat 10-2
Friends of the Library Group

KENT

P KENT LIBRARY ASSOCIATION*, Kent Memorial Library, 32 N Main St, 06757-0127. (Mail add: PO Box 127, 06757-0127), SAN 302-2013. Tel: 860-927-3761. FAX: 860-927-1427. E-mail: kmlinfo@biblio.org. Web Site: www.kentmemoriallibrary.org.
Founded 1915. Pop 2,960; Circ 36,073
Library Holdings: Audiobooks 1,042; AV Mats 1,052; Bk Vols 25,548; Per Subs 25
Automation Activity & Vendor Info: (Cataloging) Evergreen; (Circulation) Evergreen
Wireless access
Partic in Bibliomation Inc; Connecticut Library Consortium
Open Mon-Fri 10-5:30, Sat 10-4

KILLINGWORTH

P KILLINGWORTH LIBRARY ASSOCIATION*, 301 Rte 81, 06419-1218. (Mail add: PO Box 725, 06419-0725), SAN 302-2021. Tel: 860-663-2000. FAX: 860-663-2783. E-mail: mail@killingworthlibrary.org. Web Site: www.killingworthlibrary.org. *Head Librn,* Tammy Eustis; Staff 5 (MLS 3, Non-MLS 2)
Founded 1964. Pop 6,381; Circ 69,053
Library Holdings: AV Mats 3,176; CDs 323; DVDs 1,047; Large Print Bks 738; Bk Titles 32,200; Bk Vols 33,600; Per Subs 94; Talking Bks 1,097; Videos 1,032
Special Collections: Business Resource Center; Early Literacy Resource; Education Resources; Listening Center
Automation Activity & Vendor Info: (Acquisitions) Auto-Graphics, Inc; (Cataloging) Auto-Graphics, Inc; (Circulation) Auto-Graphics, Inc; (ILL) Auto-Graphics, Inc; (OPAC) Auto-Graphics, Inc; (Serials) Auto-Graphics, Inc
Database Vendor: Auto-Graphics, Inc, Gale Cengage Learning, Grolier Online, Newsbank, ProQuest, Wilson - Wilson Web
Wireless access
Function: Art exhibits, Bk club(s), Bks on CD, Children's prog, Computer training, Computers for patron use, Copy machines, e-mail serv, E-Reserves, Electronic databases & coll, Exhibits, Free DVD rentals, Handicapped accessible, ILL available, Magnifiers for reading, Mail & tel request accepted, Mus passes, Music CDs, Online cat, Online ref, Online searches, Photocopying/Printing, Preschool outreach, Prog for adults, Prog for children & young adult, Pub access computers, Ref & res, Ref serv available, Ref serv in person, Senior computer classes, Spoken cassettes & CDs, Story hour, Summer & winter reading prog, Tax forms, Telephone ref, VHS videos, Wheelchair accessible
Open Mon, Wed, Fri & Sat 10-4:30, Tues & Thurs 10-8

LEBANON

P JONATHAN TRUMBULL LIBRARY*, 580 Exeter Rd, 06249. (Mail add: PO Box 145, 06249-0145), SAN 302-203X. Tel: 860-642-2020, 860-642-7763. FAX: 860-642-4880. E-mail: librarian@lebanonctlibrary.org. Web Site: www.lebanonctlibrary.org. *Dir,* Julie Culp; E-mail: jculp@lebanonctlibrary.org; *Ch Serv,* Linda Slate; E-mail: lslate@lebanonctlibrary.org; Staff 3 (MLS 1, Non-MLS 2)
Founded 1896. Pop 7,250; Circ 50,000
Library Holdings: Bk Titles 40,000; Bk Vols 42,000; Per Subs 40
Automation Activity & Vendor Info: (Cataloging) Follett Software; (Circulation) Follett Software; (OPAC) Follett Software
Wireless access
Function: Adult bk club, CD-ROM, Computer training, Digital talking bks, E-Reserves, Fax serv, ILL available, Magnifiers for reading, Online searches, Photocopying/Printing, Prog for adults, Prog for children & young adult, Ref serv available, Summer reading prog, Tax forms, Telephone ref, VHS videos
Open Mon 9-5, Tues & Thurs 1-8, Sat 9-2
Friends of the Library Group

LEDYARD

P LEDYARD PUBLIC LIBRARIES, Bill Library, 718 Colonel Ledyard Hwy, 06339. (Mail add: PO Box 225, 06339-0225), SAN 302-2048. Tel: 860-464-9912. Administration Tel: 860 464-9917. FAX: 860-464-9927. E-mail: bill-lib@ledyard.lioninc.org. Web Site: www.ledyard.lioninc.org. *Dir,* Gale F Bradbury; E-mail: bradbury@ledyard.lioninc.org; *Sr Asst Librn,* Marty Hubbard; E-mail: mhubbard@ledyard.lioninc.org; *Asst Librn,* Mary Ellen Osborne; Tel: 860-464-6943, E-mail: mosborne@ledyard.lioninc.org
Founded 1863. Pop 15,149; Circ 159,701
Jul 2005-Jun 2006 Income (Main Library and Branch(s)) $541,278, State $1,953, City $520,294, Locally Generated Income $19,031. Mats Exp $70,490, Books $52,003, Per/Ser (Incl. Access Fees) $6,974, Micro $1,370, AV Mat $9,663, Electronic Ref Mat (Incl. Access Fees) $480. Sal $365,245 (Prof $56,722)
Library Holdings: CDs 2,186; Bk Titles 72,876; Bk Vols 85,225; Per Subs 178; Videos 2,116
Special Collections: Oral History
Subject Interests: Local hist
Automation Activity & Vendor Info: (Acquisitions) Innovative Interfaces, Inc; (Cataloging) Innovative Interfaces, Inc; (Circulation) Innovative Interfaces, Inc; (OPAC) Innovative Interfaces, Inc
Database Vendor: EBSCOhost
Wireless access
Publications: Books & Beyond (Newsletter)
Partic in Connecticut Library Consortium; Libraries Online, Inc
Open Mon-Thurs 9-9, Fri & Sat 9-5
Friends of the Library Group

Branches: 1
GALES FERRY LIBRARY, 18 Hurlbutt Rd, Gales Ferry, 06335. (Mail add: PO Box 225, 06339). Tel: 860-464-6943. E-mail: gf-lib@ledyard.lioninc.org. *Asst Librn,* Mary Ellen Osborne; E-mail: mosborne@ledyard.lioninc.org
Open Mon-Thurs 9-8, Fri & Sat 9-5

LITCHFIELD

S LITCHFIELD HISTORICAL SOCIETY*, H J Ingraham Memorial Research Library, Seven South St, 06759-0385. (Mail add: PO Box 385, 06759-0385), SAN 302-2056. Tel: 860-567-4501. FAX: 860-567-3565. E-mail: lhsoc@snet.net. *Dir,* Catherine Fields
Founded 1856
Library Holdings: Bk Titles 6,150; Bk Vols 8,000; Per Subs 11
Special Collections: American History; Litchfield Female Academy Coll (1792-1833); Litchfield Law Coll (1784-1833); Local Economic History (Account Bk (571) Coll); Local History (Litchfield Newspaper)
Subject Interests: Local hist
Open Tues-Fri 9-12 & 1-4
Friends of the Library Group

P OLIVER WOLCOTT LIBRARY*, Litchfield Public Library, 160 South St, 06759-0187. (Mail add: PO Box 187, 06759-0187), SAN 302-2064. Tel: 860-567-8030. FAX: 860-567-4784. E-mail: owlibrary@owlibrary.org. Web Site: www.owlibrary.org. *Dir,* Ann Marie White; E-mail: awhite@owlibrary.org; *Ch,* Lisa Shaia; E-mail: lshaia@owlibrary.org; *Ad,* Audra MacLaren; E-mail: amaclaren@owlibary.org; Staff 10 (MLS 3, Non-MLS 7)
Founded 1862. Pop 8,747; Circ 145,155
Jul 2011-Jun 2012 Income $721,683, City $312,069, Locally Generated Income $248,031, Other $116,515. Mats Exp $75,316. Sal $339,597
Library Holdings: Bk Vols 50,000; Per Subs 99
Special Collections: Oral History
Subject Interests: Local hist
Automation Activity & Vendor Info: (Cataloging) Evergreen; (Circulation) Evergreen
Database Vendor: Bibliomation Inc, EBSCOhost, Gale Cengage Learning, TLC (The Library Corporation)
Wireless access
Function: Holiday prog, Home delivery & serv to Sr ctr & nursing homes, ILL available, Magnifiers for reading, Mus passes, Music CDs, Outreach serv, Preschool outreach, Preschool reading prog, Prog for adults, Prog for children & young adult, Pub access computers, Summer reading prog, Tax forms
Publications: E_news (Online only); Owl News (Newsletter)
Partic in Bibliomation Inc; Connecticut Library Consortium
Open Mon 12-5, Tues & Thurs 10-9, Wed & Fri 10-5, Sat 9-2, Sun 11-3
Friends of the Library Group

LYME

P LYME PUBLIC LIBRARY*, 482 Hamburg Rd, 06371-3110. SAN 302-2072. Tel: 860-434-2272. FAX: 860-434-9972. E-mail: staff@lymepl.org. Web Site: www.lymepl.org. *Dir,* Theresa R Conley; E-mail: tconley@lymepl.org; *Ch Serv,* Barbara L Carlson; E-mail: bcarlson@lymepl.org; *Circ,* LynnAnn Baldi; *Circ,* Catherine Stebbins; *Circ,* Kathy Varady; Staff 4 (MLS 1, Non-MLS 3)
Founded 1913. Pop 2,099; Circ 15,287
Jul 2012-Jun 2013 Income $195,917, State $1,522, City $138,775, Locally Generated Income $9,470, Other $46,150. Mats Exp $22,554, Books $17,820, Per/Ser (Incl. Access Fees) $2,261, AV Mat $2,473. Sal $101,261
Library Holdings: Audiobooks 778; CDs 321; DVDs 1,210; Large Print Bks 434; Bk Vols 23,997; Per Subs 65; Videos 568
Special Collections: Dominick Dunne Video Coll; Dot Orr Cookbook Coll; Tucky Jewett Garden Book Coll
Automation Activity & Vendor Info: (Cataloging) Auto-Graphics, Inc; (Circulation) Auto-Graphics, Inc; (ILL) Auto-Graphics, Inc; (OPAC) Auto-Graphics, Inc
Wireless access
Function: Adult bk club, Bks on CD, Computers for patron use, Copy machines, E-Reserves, Fax serv, ILL available, Mus passes, Music CDs, Online cat, OverDrive digital audio bks, Photocopying/Printing, Preschool reading prog, Prog for adults, Prog for children & young adult, Pub access computers, Ref serv available, Tax forms, VHS videos
Partic in Connecticut Library Consortium
Open Tues & Thurs 10-8, Wed & Fri 10-5, Sat 10-4
Friends of the Library Group

MADISON

P E C SCRANTON MEMORIAL LIBRARY*, 801 Boston Post Rd, 06443. SAN 302-2080. Tel: 203-245-7365. FAX: 203-245-7821. E-mail: scrantonlibrary@madisonct.org. Web Site: www.scrantonlibrary.org. *Dir,* Beth Crowley; *Asst Dir,* Marcia Sokolnicki; *Ch Serv,* Jane Ash; Tel: 203-245-8722, Ext 15; *Info & Tech Serv,* Anne O'Connor; *ILL,* Clara Flath; *YA Serv,* Katie Fargo; Staff 18 (MLS 6, Non-MLS 12)
Founded 1900. Pop 18,719; Circ 300,374
Library Holdings: AV Mats 13,679; Large Print Bks 1,740; Bk Vols 101,115; Per Subs 215
Automation Activity & Vendor Info: (Cataloging) Innovative Interfaces, Inc; (Circulation) Innovative Interfaces, Inc; (Course Reserve) Innovative Interfaces, Inc; (ILL) Innovative Interfaces, Inc; (OPAC) Innovative Interfaces, Inc; (Serials) Innovative Interfaces, Inc
Database Vendor: Baker & Taylor, Booksite, Brodart, EBSCO Information Services, Facts on File, infoUSA, Innovative Interfaces, Inc, Overdrive, Inc, ProQuest, ReferenceUSA, World Book Online
Wireless access
Partic in Libraries Online, Inc
Open Mon-Thurs (Sept-June) 9-9, Fri 9-5:30, Sat 9-5, Sun 1-4; Mon-Thurs (June-Sept) 9-9, Fri 9-5:30, Sat 9-12
Friends of the Library Group

MANCHESTER

M EASTERN CONNECTICUT HEALTH NETWORK*, Medical Library, 71 Haynes St, 06040-4188. SAN 302-2110. Tel: 860-647-6853. FAX: 860-647-6443. Web Site: www.echnlibrary.org. *Dir,* Jeannine Cyr Gluck; E-mail: jgluck@echn.org; *Libr Supvr-Popular Libr,* Kimberly Person; E-mail: kperson@echn.org; *Med Librn,* Ellen Francoline; E-mail: francoline@echn.org
Founded 1948
Library Holdings: Bk Titles 1,000; Per Subs 300
Subject Interests: Allied health, Nursing
Automation Activity & Vendor Info: (Cataloging) CyberTools for Libraries
Database Vendor: Gale Cengage Learning, Medianet, PubMed, STAT!Ref (Teton Data Systems)
Open Mon-Fri 8-4
Friends of the Library Group

S FUSS & O'NEILL INC, 146 Hartford Rd, 06040-5992. Tel: 860-646-2469, Ext 5367. FAX: 860-533-5143. Web Site: www.fando.com. *Librn,* Laurice Klemarczyk; E-mail: lklemarczyk@fando.com; Staff 1 (MLS 1)
Founded 1989
Library Holdings: Bk Titles 6,500; Bk Vols 7,000; Per Subs 170
Subject Interests: Civil eng, Environ eng
Automation Activity & Vendor Info: (OPAC) Inmagic, Inc.
Database Vendor: Dialog
Partic in Connecticut Library Consortium
Restriction: Not open to pub

J MANCHESTER COMMUNITY COLLEGE LIBRARY*, Great Path, 06040. (Mail add: PO Box 1046, MS No 15, 06045-1046), SAN 302-2102. Tel: 860-512-2880. Interlibrary Loan Service Tel: 860-512-2886. Reference Tel: 860-512-2883. FAX: 860-512-2871. Web Site: www.mcc.commnet.edu/library. *Dir, Libr Serv,* Randy Fournier; Tel: 860-512-2872, E-mail: rfournier@mcc.commnet.edu; *Acq & Cat,* Diana Paris; Tel: 860-512-2879, E-mail: dparis@mcc.commnet.edu; *Acq & Cat,* Zhijiang Zhang; Tel: 860-512-2875, E-mail: zzhang@mcc.commnet.edu; *Circ,* Donna Brice; Tel: 860-512-2878, E-mail: dbrice@mcc.commnet.edu; *Circ, ILL,* Christi Geisinger; E-mail: cgeisinger@mcc.commnet.edu; *Per,* Melissa Rivera; Tel: 860-512-2884, E-mail: mrivera@mcc.commnet.edu; *Ref Serv,* Evelyn Angry-Smith; Tel: 860-512-2874, E-mail: eangry-smith@mcc.commnet.edu; *Ref Serv,* Paula Cook; Tel: 860-512-2877, E-mail: pcook1@mcc.commnet.edu; *Ref Serv,* Patricia Ronalter; Tel: 860-512-2876, E-mail: pronalter@mcc.commnet.edu; Staff 9 (MLS 4, Non-MLS 5)
Founded 1963. Enrl 4,681; Fac 201; Highest Degree: Associate
Library Holdings: Audiobooks 235; CDs 2,245; DVDs 3,245; Bk Titles 62,028; Per Subs 450
Automation Activity & Vendor Info: (Cataloging) Ex Libris Group; (Circulation) Ex Libris Group; (ILL) OCLC; (OPAC) Ex Libris Group
Wireless access
Partic in Connecticut Library Consortium; Dialog Corp; OCLC Online Computer Library Center, Inc
Open Mon-Thurs 8am-9pm, Fri 8-4:30, Sat 10-4, Sun 12-4

P MANCHESTER PUBLIC LIBRARY, Mary Cheney Library, 586 Main St, 06040. SAN 302-2129. Tel: 860-643-2471. Reference Tel: 860-645-0821. FAX: 860-643-9453. Web Site: library.townofmanchester.org. *Dir,* Douglas McDonough; E-mail: dmcdonough@manchesterct.gov; *Head, Cat & Circ,* Jessica Sweetland; E-mail: jsweetland@manchesterct.gov; *Asst Dir, Head, Ch,* Norma Nevers; E-mail: nnevers@manchesterct.gov; *Head, Ref,* Kathy Lee; E-mail: klee@manchesterct.gov; *Br Mgr,* Hong Chen; Tel: 860-643-6892, E-mail: hchen@manchesterct.gov; Staff 22 (MLS 13, Non-MLS 9)
Founded 1871. Pop 58,241; Circ 802,101
Jul 2013-Jun 2014 Income (Main Library and Branch(s)) $3,076,521, State $34,000, City $2,977,521, Locally Generated Income $65,000. Mats Exp

$3,050,000, Books $260,000, Per/Ser (Incl. Access Fees) $9,000, AV Mat $31,000, Electronic Ref Mat (Incl. Access Fees) $9,000. Sal $1,727,000 (Prof $898,000)
Library Holdings: Audiobooks 9,500; CDs 5,000; DVDs 19,000; e-books 7,500; e-journals 70; Large Print Bks 4,000; Bk Vols 180,000; Per Subs 255
Automation Activity & Vendor Info: (Cataloging) Innovative Interfaces, Inc; (Circulation) Innovative Interfaces, Inc; (OPAC) Innovative Interfaces, Inc
Wireless access
Partic in Library Connection, Inc
Open Mon-Thurs 9-9, Fri & Sat 9-5, Sun (Winter) 1-5
Friends of the Library Group
Branches: 1
WHITON BRANCH, 100 N Main St, 06040, SAN 371-3571. Tel: 860-643-6892. FAX: 860-533-1251. *Librn II,* Hong Chen; Staff 4 (MLS 2, Non-MLS 2)
Library Holdings: Audiobooks 600; CDs 1,000; DVDs 1,600; e-books 6,500; Bk Titles 30,000; Per Subs 68
Open Mon-Thurs 10-8:30, Fri & Sat 9-5
Bookmobiles: 1

MANSFIELD CENTER

P MANSFIELD PUBLIC LIBRARY*, 54 Warrenville Rd, 06250. SAN 302-2137. Tel: 860-423-2501. FAX: 860-423-9856. E-mail: mansfield@biblio.org. Web Site: mansfieldpubliclibraryct.org. *Dir,* Leslie McDonough; E-mail: mcdonoughlb@mansfieldct.org; *Librn, Adult Serv,* Peggy McCarthy; E-mail: mccarthyml@mansfieldct.org; *Ch,* Judy Stoughton; E-mail: stoughtonj@mansfieldct.org; *YA Librn,* Emily Tinnel; E-mail: tinnelew@!mansfieldct.org; Staff 3 (MLS 3)
Founded 1906. Pop 18,000; Circ 250,000
Library Holdings: Bk Vols 80,000
Automation Activity & Vendor Info: (Circulation) Horizon; (OPAC) Horizon; (Serials) Horizon
Open Mon & Wed 10-5, Tues & Thurs 10-8, Fri & Sat 9-5
Friends of the Library Group

MARLBOROUGH

P RICHMOND MEMORIAL LIBRARY*, 15 School Dr, 06447-1582. (Mail add: PO Box 387, 06447-0387), SAN 302-2145. Tel: 860-295-6210. FAX: 860-295-6212. Web Site: www.richmondlibrary.info. *Dir,* Nancy M Wood; Staff 10 (MLS 3, Non-MLS 7)
Founded 1924. Pop 6,005; Circ 121,165
Jul 2011-Jun 2012 Income $3,636,230, State $7,003, City $301,023, Locally Generated Income $55,204, Other $32,730. Mats Exp $66,944, Books $28,338, Per/Ser (Incl. Access Fees) $3,293, AV Mat $11,445, Electronic Ref Mat (Incl. Access Fees) $23,868. Sal $214,809
Library Holdings: AV Mats 3,821; Bks on Deafness & Sign Lang 20; DVDs 4,687; e-books 8,036; Large Print Bks 175; Bk Vols 37,887; Per Subs 81
Automation Activity & Vendor Info: (Acquisitions) SirsiDynix; (Cataloging) SirsiDynix; (Circulation) SirsiDynix; (ILL) SirsiDynix; (OPAC) SirsiDynix
Database Vendor: EBSCOhost
Wireless access
Partic in Library Connection, Inc
Open Mon-Thurs 10-8, Fri 10-6, Sat 10-4
Friends of the Library Group

MASHANTUCKET

S MASHANTUCKET PEQUOT MUSEUM & RESEARCH CENTER*, Information Resources, 110 Pequot Trail, 06338. (Mail add: PO Box 3180, 06338-3180), SAN 376-5814. Tel: 860-396-6897. FAX: 860-396-6874. E-mail: reference@pequotmuseum.org. Web Site: www.mpmrc.org. *Dir,* Betsy Bahr Peterson; Tel: 860-396-6858, E-mail: bpeterson@pequotmuseum.org; Staff 2 (MLS 1, Non-MLS 1)
Founded 1998
Library Holdings: Bk Titles 40,000; Per Subs 810
Special Collections: Native American Research Library for Children; Popular Culture & Ephemera with Native American Themes; Tribal Archives
Subject Interests: Native Am culture, Native Am hist
Automation Activity & Vendor Info: (Acquisitions) Ex Libris Group; (Cataloging) Ex Libris Group; (Circulation) Ex Libris Group; (Media Booking) Ex Libris Group; (OPAC) Ex Libris Group; (Serials) Ex Libris Group
Database Vendor: OCLC FirstSearch
Wireless access
Open Wed-Sat 1-5
Restriction: Non-circulating coll

MERIDEN

SR EPISCOPAL DIOCESE OF CONNECTICUT, Diocesan Library & Archives, The Commons, 290 Pratt St, 06450. SAN 325-7541. Tel: 203-639-3501, Ext 135. Administration Tel: 203-639-3501. FAX: 203-235-1008. Web Site: www.episcopalct.org, www.episcopalct.org/staff/archives. *Archivist,* Margaret Smith; E-mail: mbsmith@episcopalct.org. Subject Specialists: *Episcopal church,* Margaret Smith; Staff 1 (MLS 1)
Founded 1784
Special Collections: Bishop Samuel Seabury's Papers; Colonial Connecticut Church Records; Letters & papers of early Anglican missionaries in USA
Subject Interests: Relig
Function: Archival coll
Open Mon-Thurs 9-5
Restriction: Access at librarian's discretion, Non-circulating, Researchers by appt only

P MERIDEN PUBLIC LIBRARY*, 105 Miller St, 06450. SAN 302-217X. Tel: 203-238-2344, 203-238-2346. Administration Tel: 203-630-6352. FAX: 203-238-3647. Administration FAX: 203-238-6950. Web Site: www.meridenlibrary.org. *Dir,* Karen Roesler; E-mail: kroesler@meridenct.gov; *Head, Bibliog Serv,* Rebecca Hagstrom; Tel: 203-630-6350, E-mail: bhagstom@meridenct.gov; *Head, Ch,* Kathie Matsil; Tel: 203-630-6347, E-mail: kmatsil@meridenct.gov; *Head, Circ, Pub Serv Coordr,* Michelle Baker; Tel: 203-630-6351, E-mail: mbaker@meridenct.gov; *Cat & Ref Librn,* Susan O'Brien; *Ch,* Gretchen Durley; E-mail: gdurley@meridenct.gov; *Commun Serv Librn,* Alexis Burgess; Tel: 203-630-6349, E-mail: aburgess@meridenct.gov; *Ref Librn,* Janis Franco; E-mail: jfranco@meridenct.gov; *Coordr, ILL, Ref Librn,* Laura Hartwig; Tel: 203-238-2347, E-mail: lhartwig@meridenct.gov; *Ref Librn, Teen Serv,* Melissa Murphy; *Coll Develop Mgr,* Rebecca Starr; E-mail: bstarr@ci.meriden.ct.us. Subject Specialists: *Genealogy, Local hist,* Janis Franco; Staff 12.5 (MLS 12.5)
Founded 1903. Pop 60,868; Circ 232,000
Jul 2011-Jun 2012 Income $2,687,277, State $2,369, City $2,572,023, Locally Generated Income $25,809. Mats Exp $163,984, Books $110,657, AV Mat $25,605, Electronic Ref Mat (Incl. Access Fees) $27,722. Sal $1,560,285 (Prof $835,120)
Library Holdings: AV Mats 16,707; Bk Vols 234,635; Per Subs 137
Special Collections: Silver Industry Coll. Oral History
Subject Interests: Local hist
Automation Activity & Vendor Info: (Acquisitions) Innovative Interfaces, Inc; (Cataloging) Innovative Interfaces, Inc; (Circulation) Innovative Interfaces, Inc; (ILL) Innovative Interfaces, Inc; (OPAC) Innovative Interfaces, Inc
Database Vendor: Baker & Taylor, EBSCOhost, Gale Cengage Learning, Innovative Interfaces, Inc, LearningExpress, Newsbank, Overdrive, Inc, WT Cox
Wireless access
Function: Adult bk club, Audiobks via web, Bi-weekly Writer's Group, Bks on CD, Chess club, Children's prog, Computer training, Computers for patron use, Copy machines, Doc delivery serv, E-Reserves, Exhibits, Fax serv, Free DVD rentals, Handicapped accessible, Home delivery & serv to Sr ctr & nursing homes, Homebound delivery serv, ILL available, Large print keyboards, Magnifiers for reading, Microfiche/film & reading machines, Mus passes, Music CDs, Notary serv, Online ref, Online searches, Outreach serv, OverDrive digital audio bks, Preschool outreach, Preschool reading prog, Prog for adults, Prog for children & young adult, Pub access computers, Scanner, Spanish lang bks, Web-catalog, Wheelchair accessible
Publications: Friends of the Library Newsletter (Monthly); MPL Newsletter (Monthly)
Partic in Libraries Online, Inc
Special Services for the Deaf - ADA equip; Bks on deafness & sign lang; Closed caption videos
Special Services for the Blind - Accessible computers; Audio mat; Bks available with recordings; Bks on cassette; Bks on CD; Computer with voice synthesizer for visually impaired persons; Copier with enlargement capabilities; Internet workstation with adaptive software; Large print bks; Magnifiers; ZoomText magnification & reading software
Open Mon-Wed 9:30-8:30, Thurs-Sat 9:30-5
Restriction: Residents only
Friends of the Library Group
Bookmobiles: 1. In Charge, Alexis Burgess

MIDDLE HADDAM

P MIDDLE HADDAM PUBLIC LIBRARY*, Two Knowles Landing, 06456. (Mail add: PO Box 221, 06456-0221), SAN 302-2196. Tel: 860-267-9093. E-mail: middle.haddam.lib@snet.net. *Librn,* Melissa Coury
Founded 1909. Pop 600; Circ 5,650
Library Holdings: Bk Vols 12,000
Subject Interests: Antiques, Gardening, Local hist

Publications: 80 Years of Progress
Open Tues & Fri 3-7, Sat 12-4

MIDDLEBURY

S CHEMTURA CORP, Information Services-Library, 199 Benson Rd, 06749. SAN 302-2218. Tel: 203-573-4508. FAX: 203-573-2890. *Mgr,* Patricia Ann Harmon; E-mail: ann.harmon@chemtura.com; Staff 1 (MLS 1)
Founded 1914
Library Holdings: e-journals 10; Bk Vols 15,000; Per Subs 25
Special Collections: Encyclopedia of Polymer Science & Engineering; Kirk-Othmer Encyclopedia of Chemical-Technology; Organic Chemistry (Houben-Weyl-Methoden Coll)
Subject Interests: Chem, Eng, Plastics
Automation Activity & Vendor Info: (ILL) OCLC FirstSearch
Database Vendor: EBSCOhost, IHS, Knovel, LexisNexis, STN International
Wireless access
Partic in Connecticut Library Consortium
Restriction: Employees only

P MIDDLEBURY PUBLIC LIBRARY*, 30 Crest Rd, 06762. SAN 302-220X. Tel: 203-758-2634. FAX: 203-577-4164. Web Site: www.middleburypubliclibrary.org. *Dir,* Jane O Gallagher; *Asst Dir,* Janice LeDuc; Staff 8 (MLS 3, Non-MLS 5)
Founded 1794. Pop 7,400; Circ 106,000
Library Holdings: Bk Vols 65,000; Per Subs 90
Automation Activity & Vendor Info: (Acquisitions) Evergreen; (Cataloging) Evergreen; (Circulation) Evergreen; (OPAC) SirsiDynix
Database Vendor: EBSCOhost
Wireless access
Publications: Newsletter (Monthly)
Open Mon & Fri 10-5, Tues-Thurs 10-8
Friends of the Library Group

MIDDLEFIELD

P LEVI E COE LIBRARY, 414 Main St, 06455-1207. (Mail add: PO Box 458, 06455-0458), SAN 302-2226. Tel: 860-349-3857. FAX: 860-349-2131. E-mail: levicoelibrary@gmail.com. Web Site: www.leviecoe.com. *Dir,* Jessica Lobner; Staff 4 (MLS 1, Non-MLS 3)
Founded 1893. Pop 4,200; Circ 37,892
Library Holdings: AV Mats 1,000; Large Print Bks 200; Bk Vols 25,000; Per Subs 60; Talking Bks 225
Automation Activity & Vendor Info: (Cataloging) Auto-Graphics, Inc; (Circulation) Auto-Graphics, Inc; (OPAC) Auto-Graphics, Inc
Wireless access
Open Mon-Thurs 10-7, Sat (Sept-May) 10-2

MIDDLETOWN

CONNECTICUT VALLEY HOSPITAL
M HALLOCK MEDICAL LIBRARY*, Page Hall, Silver St, 06457. (Mail add: PO Box 351, 06457-7023), SAN 302-2234. Tel: 860-262-5059. FAX: 860-262-5049. *Librn,* Mary Conlon; E-mail: mary.conlon@po.state.ct.us; *Librn,* Pauline A Kruk, E-mail: pauline.kruk@po.state.ct.us; Staff 2 (MLS 2)
Founded 1950
Library Holdings: Bk Titles 10,000; Per Subs 75
Subject Interests: Mental health, Psychiat, Psychol
Database Vendor: EBSCOhost, OCLC FirstSearch
Function: ILL available
Partic in Basic Health Sciences Library Network; Conn Asn of Health Scis Librs; Lyrasis; OCLC Online Computer Library Center, Inc
Publications: Health Source; Psych Lit
Restriction: Open by appt only, Staff use only

M WILLIS ROYLE LIBRARY*, Silver St, 06457. (Mail add: PO Box 351, 06457), SAN 324-3303. Tel: 860-262-5520. FAX: 860-262-5049. *Med Librn,* Kandace Yuen; E-mail: kandace.yuen@ct.gov; Staff 2 (MLS 2)
Founded 1980
Library Holdings: AV Mats 1,000; Large Print Bks 50; Bk Titles 4,000; Bk Vols 5,000; Per Subs 40; Talking Bks 100
Special Collections: Daily Living Skills; Entertainment videos; High interest - low reading level materials; Large Print; Music Cassettes & CD's; Spanish Language
Subject Interests: Addictions, Commun living, Fiction, Mental health, Psychol, Soc sci
Automation Activity & Vendor Info: (Cataloging) Follett Software; (Circulation) Follett Software; (Serials) EBSCO Online
Database Vendor: EBSCOhost
Function: ILL available
Restriction: Open by appt only, Residents only

S GODFREY MEMORIAL LIBRARY*, 134 Newfield St, 06457-2534. SAN 302-2242. Tel: 860-346-4375. FAX: 860-347-9874. E-mail: library@godfrey.org. Web Site: www.godfrey.org. *Dir,* Richard E Black; *Admin Librn,* Christine LeFoll; *Librn,* Sharon Dahlmeyer; *Ref Librn,* Kerstin (Kris) Lindner; *Acq, Ser,* Nancy Thurrott
Founded 1950
Library Holdings: Bk Vols 35,000
Subject Interests: Genealogy, Hist
Automation Activity & Vendor Info: (Acquisitions) Surpass; (Cataloging) Surpass; (ILL) OCLC
Database Vendor: Gale Cengage Learning, OCLC FirstSearch, OCLC WorldShare Interlibrary Loan, ReferenceUSA
Wireless access
Function: Genealogy discussion group, Online ref, Online searches
Publications: The Godfrey Update (Newsletter)
Open Mon 9-8, Tues-Fri 9-4, Sat 9-1
Restriction: Not a lending libr, Pub use on premises
Friends of the Library Group

J MIDDLESEX COMMUNITY COLLEGE*, Jean Burr Smith Library, 100 Training Hill Rd, 06457-4889. SAN 302-2250. Tel: 860-343-5830. FAX: 860-343-5874. E-mail: mx-library@mxcc.commnet.edu. Web Site: www.mxcc.commnet.edu/library. *Dir,* Lan Liu; Tel: 860-343-5833, E-mail: lliu@mxcc.commnet.edu; *Librn,* Joy Hansen; Tel: 860-343-5832, E-mail: jhansen@mxcc.commnet.edu; *Syst Librn,* Tamara Ottum; Tel: 860-343-5835, E-mail: jyang@mxcc.commnet.edu; *ILL,* Alma Zyko; Tel: 860-343-5834, E-mail: azyko@mxcc.commnet.edu; *Ref Serv,* Anne Paluck; Tel: 860-343-5831, E-mail: apaluck@mxcc.commnet.edu; *Libr Asst,* Gayle Esidore; Tel: 860-343-5829, E-mail: gesidore@mxcc.commnet.edu; Staff 5.6 (MLS 3.6, Non-MLS 2)
Founded 1966. Enrl 2,963; Fac 45; Highest Degree: Associate
Library Holdings: Audiobooks 183; CDs 239; DVDs 1,529; e-books 25,292; e-journals 25,874; Microforms 6,180; Bk Titles 40,631; Bk Vols 44,038; Per Subs 151; Videos 860
Automation Activity & Vendor Info: (Acquisitions) Ex Libris Group; (Cataloging) Ex Libris Group; (Circulation) Ex Libris Group; (Course Reserve) Ex Libris Group; (ILL) OCLC; (OPAC) Ex Libris Group; (Serials) Ex Libris Group
Database Vendor: Baker & Taylor, Brodart, CredoReference, ebrary, EBSCOhost, Elsevier, Ex Libris Group, Gale Cengage Learning, Greenwood Publishing Group, LexisNexis, ProQuest, SerialsSolutions, Westlaw, Wilson - Wilson Web
Wireless access
Partic in Connecticut Library Consortium
Special Services for the Deaf - Accessible learning ctr; ADA equip; Assistive tech; Closed caption videos
Open Mon-Thurs (Spring) 8:30-8, Fri 8:30-4:30, Sat 8:30-1:30; Mon-Thurs (Summer & Winter) 8:30-6, Fri 8:30-4:30

S MIDDLESEX COUNTY HISTORICAL SOCIETY LIBRARY*, 151 Main St, 06457-3423. SAN 326-159X. Tel: 860-346-0746. FAX: 860-346-0746. E-mail: middlesexhistory@wesleyan.edu. Web Site: middlesexhistory.org. *Dir,* Deborah Shapiro; Staff 1 (Non-MLS 1)
Founded 1901
Special Collections: Genealogy (African-American Coll), bks, ms; Genealogy (Frank Farnsworth Starr Coll), bks, ms; Local History Coll; Town Coll
Open Tues-Thurs 10-3, Fri 10-12

M MIDDLESEX HOSPITAL*, Tremaine Library, 28 Crescent St, 06457-7005. SAN 302-2269. Tel: 860-358-6286. FAX: 860-358-6115. E-mail: library@midhosp.org. Web Site: www.midhosp.org. *Dir,* Nancy Goodwin; Staff 3 (MLS 3)
Founded 1972
Library Holdings: e-books 50; e-journals 1,000; Bk Titles 2,000; Per Subs 90
Subject Interests: Med, Nursing
Automation Activity & Vendor Info: (Cataloging) CyberTools for Libraries; (Circulation) CyberTools for Libraries
Database Vendor: EBSCOhost, MD Consult, Micromedex, Natural Standard, PubMed, UpToDate
Wireless access
Partic in Conn Asn of Health Scis Librs; Docline; Regional Med Libr Network

P RUSSELL LIBRARY*, 123 Broad St, 06457. SAN 302-2277. Tel: 860-347-2528. Reference Tel: 860-347-2520. Administration Tel: 860-347-0196. Administration FAX: 860-347-6690. Web Site: www.russelllibrary.org. *Dir,* Arthur S Meyers; Tel: 860-347-2528, Ext 141, E-mail: ameyers@russell.lioninc.org; *Asst Dir,* Vincent Juliano; Tel: 860-347-2528, Ext 144, E-mail: vjuliano@russell.lioninc.org; *Head, Ch,* Kathryn Robinson; Tel: 860-347-2528, Ext 148; *Head, Circ,* Brandie Doyle; *Head, Media Serv,* Gail Thompson-Allen; Tel: 860-347-2528, Ext 132; *Head, Ref (Info Serv),* Jason Neely; Tel: 860-347-2528, Ext 123, E-mail: jneely@russell.lioninc.org; *Head, Tech Serv,* Debra Barbari; Tel: 860-347-2528, Ext 151; *Asst Head, Ch Serv,* Kate Bond; Tel: 860-347-2528, Ext 161, E-mail: kbond@russell.lioninc.org; *Asst Head, Ref*

(Info Serv), Catherine Ahern; E-mail: cahern@russell.lioninc.org; *Asst Head, Tech Serv,* Paula Soares; Tel: 860-347-2528, Ext 155, E-mail: psoares@russell.lioninc.org; *Ch Serv,* Ken Kruse; *Ch Serv,* Laura Larson; *Ref,* Valerie Grate; *Ref,* Julia Lee; *Ref,* Denise Mackey-Russo; *Circ Asst,* Christy Billings; Tel: 860-347-2528, Ext 159, E-mail: cbillings@russell.lioninc.org; *Circ Asst,* Karen Carey; Tel: 860-347-2528, Ext 158, E-mail: kcarey@russell.lioninc.org. Subject Specialists: *Cataloging,* Paula Soares; Staff 41 (MLS 20, Non-MLS 21)
Founded 1875. Pop 47,749; Circ 585,351
Library Holdings: AV Mats 33,093; Bk Vols 168,390; Per Subs 253
Special Collections: Adult Basic Education (ABE); Literacy Materials. State Document Depository
Subject Interests: Genealogy, Local hist
Automation Activity & Vendor Info: (Acquisitions) Innovative Interfaces, Inc; (Cataloging) Innovative Interfaces, Inc; (Circulation) Innovative Interfaces, Inc; (OPAC) Innovative Interfaces, Inc
Database Vendor: EBSCO Information Services, Foundation Center, Newsbank, ProQuest, ReferenceUSA, World Book Online
Wireless access
Function: Adult literacy prog, Art exhibits, Bk club(s), Bks on CD, Children's prog, Computer training, Computers for patron use, Copy machines, Digital talking bks, Electronic databases & coll, Fax serv, Free DVD rentals, Handicapped accessible, Home delivery & serv to Sr ctr & nursing homes, Homebound delivery serv, ILL available, Instruction & testing, Magnifiers for reading, Mus passes, Music CDs, Online ref, Online searches, Outreach serv, OverDrive digital audio bks, Photocopying/Printing, Preschool outreach, Prog for adults, Prog for children & young adult, Pub access computers, Ref & res, Ref serv in person, Scanner, Senior computer classes, Senior outreach, Story hour, Summer & winter reading prog, Tax forms, Teen prog, Telephone ref, Web-catalog, Wheelchair accessible, Workshops, Writing prog
Publications: Russell Reminder (Monthly bulletin)
Partic in Libraries Online, Inc
Special Services for the Deaf - Assistive tech; Closed caption videos
Special Services for the Blind - Assistive/Adapted tech devices, equip & products; Bks on cassette; Bks on CD; Closed circuit TV magnifier; Computer with voice synthesizer for visually impaired persons; Large print bks; Magnifiers
Open Mon-Thurs (Sept-April) 9-8:30, Fri 9-6, Sat 9-5, Sun 1-4; Mon-Thurs (May-Aug) 9-8:30, Fri 9-6, Sat 9-1
Friends of the Library Group

S STATE EDUCATION RESOURCE CENTER LIBRARY*, 25 Industrial Park Rd, 06457-1516. SAN 324-5497. Tel: 860-632-1485. FAX: 860-632-0438. E-mail: library@ctserc.org. Web Site: www.ctserc.org. *Asst Dir, Libr Serv,* Carol Sullivan; Tel: 860-632-1485, Ext 341; *Head Librn,* Donna-Lee Rulli; Tel: 860-632-1485, Ext 219; *Assoc Librn,* Diana Whitehill; Tel: 860-632-1485, Ext 271; *Asst Librn,* Susan Cohan-Chase; Tel: 860-632-1485, Ext 218; *Asst Librn,* Renee Thompson; Tel: 860-632-1485, Ext 213; Staff 7 (Non-MLS 7)
Founded 1969
Library Holdings: Bks on Deafness & Sign Lang 123; CDs 230; DVDs 225; High Interest/Low Vocabulary Bk Vols 45; Bk Titles 9,200; Per Subs 200; Spec Interest Per Sub 200; Videos 285
Subject Interests: Children's lit, Disability, Family
Automation Activity & Vendor Info: (Cataloging) Auto-Graphics, Inc; (Circulation) Auto-Graphics, Inc
Database Vendor: Auto-Graphics, Inc, EBSCOhost, Sage, ScienceDirect, Springshare, LLC
Wireless access
Function: Res libr
Publications: Bibliographies; How to do Research in Special Education; Newsletter; Test List
Open Mon & Fri (Sept-May) 8:30-4:30, Tues-Thurs 8:30-7, Sat 9-1

C WESLEYAN UNIVERSITY, Olin Memorial Library, 252 Church St, 06459-3199. SAN 336-2825. Tel: 860-685-3844. FAX: 860-685-2661. Web Site: www.wesleyan.edu/libr. *Interim Univ Librn,* Diane Klare; Tel: 860-685-3867, E-mail: dklare@wesleyan.edu; *Dir, Spec Coll & Archives,* Suzy Taraba; *Doc Librn,* Erhard Konerding; *Coord, Coll Develop,* Aaron Sandoval; *Ser, E-Res,* Helen Aiello; Staff 16 (MLS 16)
Founded 1831. Enrl 3,205; Fac 340; Highest Degree: Doctorate
Special Collections: US Document Depository
Automation Activity & Vendor Info: (Acquisitions) Ex Libris Group; (Cataloging) Ex Libris Group; (Circulation) Ex Libris Group; (Course Reserve) Ex Libris Group; (ILL) OCLC ILLiad; (OPAC) Ex Libris Group; (Serials) Ex Libris Group
Publications: Numerous Guides & Pathfinders
Partic in CTW Library Consortium; Lyrasis
Friends of the Library Group
Departmental Libraries:
ART LIBRARY, 301 High St, 06459-3199. Tel: 860-685-3327. *Librn,* Susanne Javorski
Library Holdings: Bk Vols 24,000
Subject Interests: Art, Art hist
SCIENCE, 262 Church St, 06459-3199. Tel: 860-685-2860. *Librn,* Position Currently Open
Enrl 3,247
Subject Interests: Astronomy, Biol, Chem, Geol, Math, Physics
SCORES & RECORDINGS COLLECTION, 252 Church St, 06459-3199. Tel: 860-685-3898. *Librn,* Alec McLane
Special Collections: World Music Archives

G WHITING FORENSIC INSTITUTE LIBRARY*, 70 O'Brien Dr, 06457. (Mail add: PO Box 70, 06457-0070), SAN 326-0097. Tel: 860-262-5400, Ext 2522, 860-262-5469. FAX: 860-262-5470. *Librn,* Timothy E Sweeney
Founded 1970
Library Holdings: Bk Vols 1,100; Per Subs 50
Automation Activity & Vendor Info: (ILL) OCLC
Partic in Conn Asn of Health Scis Librs; Inter-Conn Orgn
Open Mon-Fri 8:30-4

MILFORD

P MILFORD PUBLIC LIBRARY, 57 New Haven Ave, 06460. SAN 336-2973. Tel: 203-783-3290. Circulation Tel: 203-783-3304. Reference Tel: 203-783-3292. Administration Tel: 203-783-3291. Automation Services Tel: 203-783-3307. FAX: 203-877-1072. Web Site: www.ci.milford.ct.us/milford-public-library. *Dir,* Christine Angeli; Tel: 203-783-3399, E-mail: cangeli@ci.milford.ct.us; *Asst Dir, Head, Tech Serv,* Nancy Abbey; E-mail: nabbey@ci.milford.ct.us; *Info Syst Librn,* Fred Danowski; E-mail: fdanowski@ci.milford.ct.us; *Ch Serv,* Suzanne Harrison-Thomas; Tel: 203-783-3312, E-mail: sthomas@ci.milford.ct.us; *Circ,* Maria Teresa Battad; E-mail: mtbattad@ci.milford.ct.us; *Media Spec,* Position Currently Open; *Ref Serv,* Monica Slomski; Staff 6.88 (MLS 5.94, Non-MLS 0.94)
Founded 1895. Pop 53,600; Circ 284,215
Jul 2013-Jun 2014. Mats Exp $120,000. Sal $850,000
Library Holdings: AV Mats 10,591; CDs 2,665; DVDs 2,275; Large Print Bks 2,352; Bk Vols 101,777; Per Subs 216
Special Collections: Milford & Connecticut History & Genealogy
Automation Activity & Vendor Info: (Acquisitions) SirsiDynix; (Cataloging) SirsiDynix; (Circulation) SirsiDynix; (OPAC) SirsiDynix; (Serials) SirsiDynix
Database Vendor: SirsiDynix
Wireless access
Open Mon-Wed 10-8:30, Thurs & Sat 10-5, Fri 1-5
Friends of the Library Group

G US DEPARTMENT OF COMMERCE, NATIONAL OCEANIC & ATMOSPHERIC ADMINISTRATION*, National Marine Fisheries Service, Milford Laboratory Library, 212 Rogers Ave, 06460. SAN 302-2307. Tel: 203-882-6509. Administration Tel: 203-882-6500. FAX: 203-882-6517. Administration FAX: 203-882-6570. Web Site: www.mi.nmfs.gov.
Library Holdings: Bk Vols 2,800; Per Subs 15
Special Collections: Food & Agriculture Organization of the United Nations, fisheries items; NOAA Documents; United States Bureau of Fisheries
Function: Res libr
Partic in Dialog Corp
Open Mon-Fri 8-4:30

MONROE

P EDITH WHEELER MEMORIAL LIBRARY*, 733 Monroe Tpk, 06468. SAN 302-2315. Tel: 203-452-2850. FAX: 203-261-3359. E-mail: reference@ewml.org. Web Site: www.ewml.org. *Dir,* Margaret Borchers; *Adult & Teen Serv,* Lorna Rhyins; *Ch Serv,* Michelle Turbak; Staff 23 (MLS 4, Non-MLS 19)
Founded 1954. Pop 20,000; Circ 176,269
Special Collections: Environmental Resources Information Center; Loveland Newspaper Clippings of Monroe History
Automation Activity & Vendor Info: (Cataloging) SirsiDynix; (Circulation) SirsiDynix; (ILL) SirsiDynix; (OPAC) SirsiDynix; (Serials) SirsiDynix
Wireless access
Partic in Bibliomation Inc
Open Mon-Wed 10-8, Thurs & Fri 10-5, Sat 10-4
Friends of the Library Group

MOODUS

P EAST HADDAM FREE PUBLIC LIBRARY*, 18 Plains Rd, 06469. (Mail add: PO Box 372, 06469-0372), SAN 302-1211. Tel: 860-873-8248. FAX: 860-873-1269. E-mail: staff@ehfpl.org. Web Site: www.ehfpl.org. *Dir,* Michael Gilroy; E-mail: mgilroy@ehfpl.org; Staff 6 (MLS 1, Non-MLS 5)
Founded 1888. Pop 8,880; Circ 2,153
Library Holdings: AV Mats 897; Large Print Bks 289; Bk Vols 18,785; Per Subs 67; Videos 1,214
Subject Interests: Genealogy

Automation Activity & Vendor Info: (Acquisitions) Auto-Graphics, Inc; (Cataloging) Auto-Graphics, Inc; (Circulation) Auto-Graphics, Inc; (Course Reserve) Auto-Graphics, Inc; (ILL) Auto-Graphics, Inc; (Media Booking) Auto-Graphics, Inc; (OPAC) Auto-Graphics, Inc; (Serials) Auto-Graphics, Inc
Wireless access
Function: Homebound delivery serv
Open Mon & Wed 10-8, Tues, Thurs & Fri 12-6, Sat 9-1
Restriction: Non-circulating coll
Friends of the Library Group

MOOSUP

P ALDRICH FREE PUBLIC LIBRARY*, 299 Main St, 06354. SAN 302-2331. Tel: 860-564-8760. FAX: 860-564-8491. E-mail: info@aldrichlibrary.org. *Dir,* Jean Jakoboski; *Asst Dir, ILL Librn,* Bonnie Theriault; *Asst Librn,* Marge Hawley; *Asst Librn,* Arlene Sweet; Staff 5 (Non-MLS 5)
Founded 1896. Pop 15,000; Circ 20,439
Jul 2005-Jun 2006 Income $41,295. Mats Exp $1,697, Books $1,254, Per/Ser (Incl. Access Fees) $443. Sal $19,579
Library Holdings: Bk Titles 26,500; Per Subs 32
Automation Activity & Vendor Info: (Circulation) Follett Software
Wireless access
Open Mon, Wed & Fri 2-7:30, Tues & Sat 9-12:30

MORRIS

P MORRIS PUBLIC LIBRARY*, Four North St, 06763-1415. (Mail add: PO Box 85, 06763-0085), SAN 302-234X. Tel: 860-567-7440. FAX: 860-567-7432. E-mail: mplib@optonline.net. *Dir,* Helen Wasti; Staff 5 (MLS 1, Non-MLS 4)
Founded 1900. Pop 2,000; Circ 21,251
Library Holdings: Bk Titles 13,975; Per Subs 30; Talking Bks 343; Videos 468
Open Tues 10-8, Wed-Fri 1-8, Sat 10-3

MYSTIC

P MYSTIC & NOANK LIBRARY, INC*, 40 Library St, 06355. SAN 302-2358. Tel: 860-536-7721. Interlibrary Loan Service Tel: 860-536-3019. FAX: 860-536-2350. E-mail: mnl@juno.com. Web Site: www.mysticnoanklibrary.com. *Dir,* Lois W Hiller; *Adult Serv, Coll Develop,* Kate Nelson; *Ch Serv,* Roberta Donahue; Staff 4 (MLS 3, Non-MLS 1)
Founded 1893. Pop 15,000; Circ 83,000
Oct 2007-Sept 2008 Income $480,545, State $16,469, City $281,500, Locally Generated Income $104,483, Parent Institution $78,093. Mats Exp $41,213, Books $22,236, Per/Ser (Incl. Access Fees) $4,670, AV Mat $7,552, Electronic Ref Mat (Incl. Access Fees) $6,755. Sal $249,093
Library Holdings: Audiobooks 1,664; DVDs 1,016; e-books 2,715; Bk Vols 44,746; Per Subs 134; Videos 1,331
Subject Interests: Genealogy, Local hist
Automation Activity & Vendor Info: (Cataloging) SirsiDynix; (Circulation) SirsiDynix
Wireless access
Publications: Annual Report
Partic in Connecticut Library Consortium
Open Mon-Wed 10-9, Thurs-Sat 10-5
Friends of the Library Group

S MYSTIC SEAPORT MUSEUM*, G W Blunt White Library, 75 Greenmanville Ave, 06355-0990. (Mail add: PO Box 6000, 06355-6000), SAN 302-2366. Tel: 860-572-5367. Web Site: library.mysticseaport.org. *Dir of Libr,* Paul J O'Pecko; *Cat,* Susan M Filupeit
Founded 1929
Library Holdings: Bk Titles 40,000; Bk Vols 70,000; Per Subs 404
Special Collections: American Maritime Studies, ms. Oral History
Partic in Connecticut Library Consortium; Lyrasis
Open Wed 2-5, Thurs 10-5, Fri 10-3
Friends of the Library Group

NAUGATUCK

P HOWARD WHITTEMORE MEMORIAL LIBRARY*, 243 Church St, 06770-4198. SAN 336-3090. Tel: 203-729-4591. FAX: 203-723-1820. Web Site: www.whittemorelibrary.org. *Dir,* Jocelyn Miller; Staff 2 (MLS 2)
Founded 1894. Pop 31,862; Circ 83,696
Jul 2011-Jun 2012 Income $796,856, State $1,297, City $577,000, Locally Generated Income $112,634, Other $105,925. Mats Exp $20,949, Books $19,260, Other Print Mats $1,689. Sal $414,443 (Prof $81,627)
Library Holdings: Audiobooks 615; CDs 300; DVDs 1,535; Electronic Media & Resources 31; Bk Vols 62,154; Per Subs 56; Videos 400
Subject Interests: Art & archit, Connecticut, Local hist
Automation Activity & Vendor Info: (Acquisitions) Bibliomation Inc; (Cataloging) Bibliomation Inc; (Circulation) Bibliomation Inc; (OPAC) Bibliomation Inc
Wireless access
Partic in Connecticut Library Consortium
Open Mon Noon-6, Tues & Wed 10-8, Thurs 10-6, Fri 10-4, Sat 10-2
Friends of the Library Group

NEW BRITAIN

C CENTRAL CONNECTICUT STATE UNIVERSITY, Elihu Burritt Library, 1615 Stanley St, 06050. SAN 302-2382. Tel: 860-832-2097. Circulation Tel: 860-832-2055. Interlibrary Loan Service Tel: 860-832-3408. Reference Tel: 860-832-2060. FAX: 860-832-3409. Administration FAX: 860-832-2118. Web Site: library.ccsu.edu. *Libr Dir,* Carl Antonucci; E-mail: antonucci@ccsu.edu; *Head, Access Serv & ILL,* Kim Farrington; Tel: 860-832-3403, E-mail: farringtonk@ccsu.edu; *Head, Acq, Ser & Electronic Res Librn,* Kristin D'Amato; Tel: 860-832-2074, E-mail: damatok@ccsu.edu; *Head, Info Syst,* Dana Hanford; Tel: 860-832-2058, E-mail: hanfordd@ccsu.edu; *Head, Ref & Instruction,* Susan Slaga-Metiver; Tel: 860-832-2095, E-mail: slagas@ccsu.edu; *Head, Spec Coll,* Ewa Wolynska; Tel: 860-832-2086, E-mail: wolynska@ccsu.edu; *Assoc Head, Ref,* Richard Churchill; Tel: 860-832-2066, E-mail: churchill@ccsu.edu; *Acq Librn,* Kristina Edwards; Tel: 860-832-2073, E-mail: kedwards@ccsu.edu; *Assessment Librn, Ref & Instruction,* Martha Kruy; Tel: 860-832-2063, E-mail: mkruy@ccsu.edu; *Digital Librn,* Sharon Clapp; Tel: 860-832-2059, E-mail: sclapp@ccsu.edu; *Outreach & Spec Coll Librn, Univ Archivist,* Renata Vickrey; Tel: 860-832-2085, E-mail: vickreyr@ccsu.edu; *Syst Librn,* Edward Iglesias; Tel: 860-832-2082, E-mail: edward.iglesias@ccsu.edu; *Asst Cat Librn,* Steven Bernstein; Tel: 860-832-2079, E-mail: bernsteinstj@ccsu.edu; *Bibliog Instruction/Ref,* Nick Tomaiuolo; Tel: 860-832-2068, E-mail: tomaiuolon@ccsu.edu. Subject Specialists: *Cataloging,* Dana Hanford; *Govt doc,* Richard Churchill; *Govt doc,* Martha Kruy; Staff 16 (MLS 16)
Founded 1849. Enrl 9,539; Fac 434; Highest Degree: Doctorate
Library Holdings: AV Mats 11,203; CDs 4,037; DVDs 1,854; e-books 433; e-journals 64,644; Bk Vols 733,377; Per Subs 1,592
Special Collections: Bruce Rogers Coll; Daniel Webster Coll; Elihu Burritt Coll, bks, ms; Frederic W Goudy Coll; GLBTQ Archives; John J Woodcock Lemon Law Archives; Polish Heritage Coll; Walter Hart Blumenthal Coll; William A O'Neill Gubernatorial Records & Oral History Interviews; World's Fairs Coll. US Document Depository
Subject Interests: Educ, Humanities
Automation Activity & Vendor Info: (Acquisitions) Innovative Interfaces, Inc; (Cataloging) Innovative Interfaces, Inc; (Circulation) Innovative Interfaces, Inc; (Course Reserve) Innovative Interfaces, Inc; (OPAC) Innovative Interfaces, Inc; (Serials) Innovative Interfaces, Inc
Database Vendor: ACM (Association for Computing Machinery), Alexander Street Press, American Chemical Society, American Mathematical Society, American Physical Society, American Psychological Association (APA), Annual Reviews, Bowker, Coutts Information Service, CQ Press, CredoReference, Dialog, EBSCOhost, Elsevier, Emerald, Ex Libris Group, Gale Cengage Learning, IEEE (Institute of Electrical & Electronics Engineers), Ingenta, Innovative Interfaces, Inc, IOP, ISI Web of Knowledge, JSTOR, LexisNexis, Luna Imaging/Insight, Medline, Mergent Online, Modern Language Association, Newsbank, OCLC FirstSearch, OCLC WorldShare Interlibrary Loan, OVID Technologies, Oxford Online, Paratext, Project MUSE, ProQuest, PubMed, RefWorks, Safari Books Online, Sage, ScienceDirect, Springshare, LLC, ValueLine, Wiley InterScience, WT Cox
Wireless access
Publications: CCSU Library (Newsletter)
Partic in Connecticut Library Consortium; Hartford Consortium For Higher Education; Lyrasis; OCLC Online Computer Library Center, Inc; Westchester Academic Library Directors Organization (WALDO)

S NEW BRITAIN MUSEUM OF AMERICAN ART LIBRARY*, 56 Lexington St, 06052. SAN 371-232X. Tel: 860-229-0257. FAX: 860-229-3445. E-mail: nbmaa@nbmaa.org. Web Site: www.nbmaa.org. *Dir,* Douglas Hyland; *Coll Mgr,* James Kopp
Founded 1903
Library Holdings: Bk Vols 4,000
Function: Ref serv available
Open Tues, Wed & Fri 11-5, Thurs 11-8, Sat 10-5, Sun 12-5
Restriction: Open by appt only

P NEW BRITAIN PUBLIC LIBRARY*, 20 High St, 06051-4226. SAN 336-3155. Tel: 860-224-3155. FAX: 860-223-6729. Administration FAX: 860-826-5191. Web Site: www.nbpl.info. *Dir,* Patricia Rutkowkski; Tel: 860-224-3155, Ext 113; *Head, Adult Serv,* Pat Watson; E-mail: pwatson@nbpl.info; *Head, Ch,* Amy Litke; E-mail: alitke@nbpl.info; *Head, Tech Serv,* Barbara Morse; E-mail: bmorse@nbpl.info; *Teen Librn,* Katherine Chacon; Staff 47 (MLS 14, Non-MLS 33)
Founded 1858. Pop 71,832; Circ 406,067
Library Holdings: Bk Vols 229,245; Per Subs 297

Special Collections: Elihu Burritt, bks, mss, pamphlets; Materials in other Languages, Polish & Spanish
Subject Interests: Local hist
Automation Activity & Vendor Info: (Circulation) SirsiDynix
Publications: Monthly Calendar
Partic in Connecticut Library Consortium
Open Mon-Thurs 9-9, Fri & Sat 9-5
Friends of the Library Group
Branches: 1
JEFFERSON, 140 Horse Plain Rd, 06053, SAN 336-321X. Tel: 860-225-4700. FAX: 860-832-9521. *Br Mgr,* Kathi Holly
Library Holdings: Bk Vols 16,500
Open Mon & Tues 9-6, Wed & Thurs 9-5, Fri 9-3
Friends of the Library Group

S POLISH GENEALOGICAL SOCIETY OF CONNECTICUT INC*, Archive & Resource Center, Eight Lyle Rd, 06053-2104. SAN 370-6974. Tel: 860-223-5596. E-mail: pgsctne@yahoo.com. Web Site: www.pgsctne.org. *Archivist, Dir,* Jonathan D Shea; Staff 1 (MLS 1)
Founded 1984
Library Holdings: CDs 10; Bk Vols 3,000; Per Subs 15
Special Collections: Cartography Coll; Cemetery Inscriptions; Marriage & Immigrant Origins Databases; Polish & Lithuanian Telephone Directories; Polish Diocesan Church Directories; Polish-American Church Histories
Friends of the Library Group

NEW CANAAN

S NEW CANAAN HISTORICAL SOCIETY LIBRARY*, 13 Oenoke Ridge, 06840. SAN 302-2420. Tel: 203-966-1776. FAX: 203-972-5917. E-mail: newcanaan.historical@gmail.com. Web Site: www.nchistory.org. *Exec Dir,* Janet Lindstrom
Founded 1889
Library Holdings: Bk Titles 6,000; Per Subs 30
Special Collections: Historical Society Biographical & Genealogical Index, 1640-present, filecards; Historical Society Newspaper File & Subject Index, 1868-present, bd vols, microfilm; Hoyt Nursery Coll; Noyes Family; Paul Prindle FASG (Weed Coll); Price & Lee New Canaan Darien Directories, original to 1903 & current; Silliman Coll
Subject Interests: Art & archit, Costume design, Genealogy
Wireless access
Publications: A Child's Walking Tour of New Canaan; A Guide to God's Acre; A New Canaan Private in the Civil War (Letters of Justus M Silliman, 17th Connecticut Volunteers); Annuals; John Rogers & the Rogers Groups; Mary J Kelley & the Little Red Schoolhouse; My Impressions of the Hour - The Diary of an Early New Canaan Teacher; New Canaan; New Canaan, Texture of a Community, 1950-2000; Philip Johnson in New Canaan; The Hanford Silliman House; The Merritt Parkway; Wampum to Wall Street
Open Tues-Fri 9:30-4:30, Sat 9:30-12:30
Restriction: Open to pub for ref only

P NEW CANAAN LIBRARY*, 151 Main St, 06840. SAN 302-2439. Tel: 203-594-5000. Circulation Tel: 203-594-5001. Information Services Tel: 203-594-5003. FAX: 203-594-5026. Toll Free FAX: 866-245-6033. E-mail: onlineref@newcanaanlibrary.org. Web Site: newcanaanlibrary.org. *Exec Dir,* Lisa Oldham; Tel: 203-594-5005, E-mail: loldham@newcanaanlibrary.org; *Dir, Admin & Finance,* Anne Romanello; Tel: 203-594-5020, E-mail: aromanello@newcanaanlibrary.org; *Dir, Coll & Serv,* Lauren Phillips; E-mail: lphillips@newcanaanlibrary.org; *Prog Dir,* Susan LaPerla; E-mail: slaperla@newcanaanlibrary.org; *Head, Ch,* Rose Marie Zaharek; E-mail: rzaharek@newcanaanlibrary.org; *Head, Circ,* Maria Livoti; E-mail: mlivoti@newcanaanlibrary.org; *Head, Info Serv, Head, Reader Serv,* Laurie Iffland; E-mail: liffland@newcanaanlibrary.org; *Head, Info Tech,* Jeff Zaino; E-mail: jzaino@newcanaanlibrary.org; *Teen Serv Librn,* Cheryl Capitani; E-mail: capitani@newcanaanlibrary.org
Founded 1877. Pop 19,395; Circ 478,791
Library Holdings: AV Mats 25,000; Bk Vols 157,200; Per Subs 345
Special Collections: Broadcast Journalism (Richard Salant Room with Eric Sevareid Coll); European Art, 476-1900 (Arturo Alfandari Coll); Gardening/Landscaping (Susan McDaniel Coll); Howard Schless Medieval Coll; Nature (Alice A & Helen C Bristow Coll); World War II (Chester Hansen Coll)
Subject Interests: Art & archit, Natural sci, Popular
Automation Activity & Vendor Info: (Acquisitions) Innovative Interfaces, Inc; (Cataloging) OCLC; (Circulation) Innovative Interfaces, Inc; (Course Reserve) Innovative Interfaces, Inc; (ILL) Innovative Interfaces, Inc; (Media Booking) Innovative Interfaces, Inc; (OPAC) Innovative Interfaces, Inc; (Serials) Innovative Interfaces, Inc
Database Vendor: Innovative Interfaces, Inc
Wireless access
Publications: Beyond the Best Seller (Monthly bulletin); New Canaan Library News (Newsletter)
Special Services for the Blind - Closed circuit TV magnifier; Reader equip
Open Mon-Thurs 9-8, Fri & Sat 9-5, Sun 12-5
Friends of the Library Group

M SILVER HILL HOSPITAL*, Medical Research Library, 208 Valley Rd, 06840. Tel: 203-966-3561, Ext 2270. FAX: 203-801-2388. Web Site: www.silverhillhospital.com. *Dir,* Anne Marie Romano
Library Holdings: Bk Titles 1,110; Per Subs 157
Open Mon-Fri 9-5, Sat 11-3

NEW FAIRFIELD

P NEW FAIRFIELD FREE PUBLIC LIBRARY, Two Brush Hill Rd, 06812. SAN 302-2463. Tel: 203-312-5679. FAX: 203-312-5685. E-mail: nfl@newfairfieldlibrary.org. Web Site: www.newfairfieldlibrary.org. *Dir,* Linda Fox; E-mail: lfox@newfairfieldlibrary.org; Staff 3 (MLS 3)
Founded 1897. Pop 14,338
Library Holdings: Audiobooks 2,324; CDs 600; DVDs 4,733; Electronic Media & Resources 7; Large Print Bks 837; Bk Vols 39,627; Per Subs 175; Videos 518
Special Collections: Census Records
Subject Interests: Local hist
Automation Activity & Vendor Info: (Acquisitions) Auto-Graphics, Inc; (Cataloging) Auto-Graphics, Inc; (Circulation) Auto-Graphics, Inc; (ILL) Auto-Graphics, Inc; (OPAC) Auto-Graphics, Inc; (Serials) Auto-Graphics, Inc
Database Vendor: OCLC, Overdrive, Inc, WebClarity Software Inc
Wireless access
Function: 24/7 Online cat, Audiobks via web, Bks on cassette, Bks on CD, Children's prog, Computers for patron use, Copy machines, Electronic databases & coll, Fax serv, Genealogy discussion group, Homebound delivery serv, ILL available, Magazines, Microfiche/film & reading machines, Movies, Mus passes, Music CDs, Online cat, Online searches, OverDrive digital audio bks, Photocopying/Printing, Preschool outreach, Prog for adults, Prog for children & young adult, Pub access computers, Ref serv available, Ref serv in person, Scanner, Spoken cassettes & CDs, Story hour, Summer reading prog, Tax forms
Special Services for the Blind - Bks on cassette; Bks on CD; Cassettes; Home delivery serv; Large print & cassettes; Large print bks
Open Mon & Wed 10-8, Tues, Thurs & Sat 10-5, Fri 1-8, Sun (Oct-April) 1-4
Friends of the Library Group

NEW HARTFORD

P BAKERVILLE LIBRARY*, Six Maple Hollow Rd, 06057. SAN 302-2471. Tel: 860-482-8806. FAX: 860-482-8806. Web Site: www.bakervillelibrary.org. *Librn,* Julie LaSata
Founded 1949. Pop 5,810
Library Holdings: Bk Titles 14,500; Per Subs 39
Special Collections: Bicentennial of the Constitution Bookshelf
Subject Interests: Agr, Art, Gardening
Automation Activity & Vendor Info: (Cataloging) Follett Software; (Circulation) Follett Software
Publications: Friends of Bakerville Library (Newsletter)
Partic in Region I Coop Libr Servs Unit
Open Mon & Wed-Fri 2-6, Tues 2-8, Sat 9-2
Friends of the Library Group

P LICIA & MASON BEEKLEY COMMUNITY LIBRARY*, Ten Central Ave, 06057. (Mail add: PO Box 247, 06057), SAN 302-248X. Tel: 860-379-7235. FAX: 860-379-5806. E-mail: staff@beekleylibrary.org. Web Site: www.beekleylibrary.org. *Dir,* Andrea Gaedeke; *Asst Dir,* Karin Schneider; *Ch,* Ericka Bajrami; *Acq of New Ser/Per, ILL,* Lisa Bequillard; *Libr Asst,* Peggy Grohs; *Libr Asst,* David MacHenry; Staff 4 (Non-MLS 4)
Founded 1906. Pop 6,700
Jul 2009-Jun 2010 Income $318,000, State $7,765, City $214,000, Locally Generated Income $49,500, Other $46,735. Mats Exp $36,500. Sal $166,952 (Prof $46,251)
Library Holdings: Audiobooks 799; CDs 2,181; DVDs 3,700; Large Print Bks 681; Bk Titles 48,225; Bk Vols 49,362; Per Subs 63; Videos 278
Automation Activity & Vendor Info: (Acquisitions) Follett Software; (Cataloging) Follett Software; (Circulation) Follett Software; (Serials) Follett Software
Database Vendor: Gale Cengage Learning, Newsbank
Wireless access
Function: Audio & video playback equip for onsite use, Bks on cassette, Bks on CD, Children's prog, Computers for patron use, Copy machines, e-mail serv, Family literacy, Fax serv, For res purposes, Free DVD rentals, Handicapped accessible, Home delivery & serv to Sr ctr & nursing homes, Homebound delivery serv, ILL available, Instruction & testing, Large print keyboards, Magnifiers for reading, Mus passes, Music CDs, Online cat, Online searches, Photocopying/Printing, Prog for adults, Prog for children & young adult, Pub access computers, Ref serv available, Referrals accepted, Spoken cassettes & CDs, Story hour, Summer reading prog, Tax forms, Telephone ref, VHS videos, Web-catalog, Wheelchair accessible

Publications: Program Brochures (Library handbook)
Special Services for the Deaf - Closed caption videos
Special Services for the Blind - Assistive/Adapted tech devices, equip & products; Bks on cassette; Bks on CD; Cassette playback machines; Closed circuit TV magnifier; Large print bks; Magnifiers; Talking bks
Open Mon 12-6, Tues & Thurs 10-8, Wed & Fri 10-6, Sat 9-3 (9-12 Summer)
Friends of the Library Group

NEW HAVEN

CR ALBERTUS MAGNUS COLLEGE LIBRARY*, Rosary Hall, 700 Prospect St, 06511. SAN 302-2498. Tel: 203-773-8594. Reference Tel: 203-773-8511. FAX: 203-773-8588. Web Site: www.albertus.edu/student-resources/library. *Dir,* Anne Leeney-Panagrossi; E-mail: apanagrossi@albertus.edu; *Assoc Dir, Tech Serv Librn,* Joanne Day; E-mail: jday@albertus.edu; *Head, Ref,* John McCann; E-mail: jmccann@albertus.edu; *Acq & Access Serv Librn,* Eileen Bujalski; E-mail: ebujalski@albertus.edu; *ILL/Ser & Media Coordr,* Patricia Dawson; E-mail: padawson@albertus.edu; Staff 10 (MLS 5, Non-MLS 5)
Founded 1925. Enrl 2,157; Highest Degree: Master
Library Holdings: Bk Vols 103,994; Per Subs 588
Special Collections: Donald Grant Mitchell Coll; Louis Imogen Guiney Coll; Samuel Flagg Bemis Coll
Automation Activity & Vendor Info: (Acquisitions) Ex Libris Group; (Cataloging) Ex Libris Group; (Circulation) Ex Libris Group; (OPAC) Ex Libris Group; (Serials) Ex Libris Group
Partic in Lyrasis
Open Mon-Thurs 8:30am-11pm, Fri 8:30am-9pm, Sat 10-6, Sun 1-11

G THE CONNECTICUT AGRICULTURAL EXPERIMENT STATION*, Thomas B Osborne Library, 123 Huntington St, 06511-2000. (Mail add: PO Box 1106, 06504-1106), SAN 302-2528. Tel: 203-974-8447. Administration Tel: 203-974-8500. Toll Free Tel: 877-855-2237 (CT only). FAX: 203-974-8502. Web Site: www.ct.gov/caes. *Info Officer,* Vickie Marie Bomba-Lewandoski; E-mail: vickie.bomba-lewandoski@ct.gov
Founded 1875
Library Holdings: Bk Vols 11,000; Per Subs 500
Subject Interests: Analytical chem, Biochem, Climatology, Ecology, Entomology, Environ studies, Forestry, Genetics, Hort, Plant pathology, Tobacco
Automation Activity & Vendor Info: (OPAC) Follett Software

J GATEWAY COMMUNITY COLLEGE LIBRARY & LEARNING COMMONS*, 20 Church St, 06510. SAN 302-2617. Tel: 203-285-2057. FAX: 203-285-2055. E-mail: library@gatewayct.edu. Web Site: www.gatewayct.edu/library-home. *Dir, Libr Serv,* Dr Clara Ogbaa; Tel: 203-285-2058, E-mail: cogbaa@gwcc.commnet.edu; *Head, Ref,* Martha Lipowski; Tel: 203-285-2053, E-mail: mlipowski@gwcc.commnet.edu; *Cataloger/Ref Librn,* Michael Cifferelli; Tel: 203-285-2052, E-mail: mcifferelli@gwcc.commmnet.edu; *Emerging Tech Librn,* Jainxin Yang; Tel: 203-285-2158, E-mail: jyang@gwcc.commnet.edu; *Mkt Librn, Outreach Librn,* Shauna DeStefano; Tel: 203-285-2059, E-mail: sdestefano@gwcc.commnet.edu; *Coordr, Info Literacy,* Todd Hampton; Tel: 203-285-2615, E-mail: thampton@gwcc.commnet.edu; Staff 7 (MLS 6, Non-MLS 1)
Founded 1968. Enrl 3,690; Highest Degree: Associate
Library Holdings: Bk Vols 53,000; Per Subs 350
Automation Activity & Vendor Info: (Acquisitions) Ex Libris Group; (Cataloging) Ex Libris Group; (Circulation) Ex Libris Group; (Course Reserve) Ex Libris Group; (ILL) OCLC; (OPAC) Ex Libris Group; (Serials) Ex Libris Group
Database Vendor: ABC-CLIO, CountryWatch, ebrary, EBSCOhost, Facts on File, Gale Cengage Learning, H W Wilson, LexisNexis, Micromedex, OVID Technologies, Oxford Online, ProQuest, Springshare, LLC, Wilson - Wilson Web
Wireless access
Partic in Connecticut Library Consortium
Open Mon-Thurs 8-8, Fri 8-5, Sat 8-Noon
Departmental Libraries:
NORTH HAVEN CAMPUS, 88 Bassett Rd, North Haven, 06473, SAN 377-7650. Tel: 203-285-2340. FAX: 203-285-2342. *Dir,* Michele Cone
Open Mon-Thurs 8-8, Fri 8-3

S KNIGHTS OF COLUMBUS SUPREME COUNCIL ARCHIVES*, One State St, 06511-6702. SAN 372-6126. Tel: 203-752-4578. FAX: 203-865-0351. Web Site: www.kofcmuseum.org/en/archives/index.html. *Archivist, Librn,* Susan H Brosnan; E-mail: susan.brosnan@kofc.org; Staff 1 (MLS 1)
Founded 1882
Special Collections: Catholic Church, articles, bks; Christopher Columbus Coll, articles, bks; Knights of Columbus, archival mat, bks
Restriction: Open by appt only

P NEW HAVEN FREE PUBLIC LIBRARY*, 133 Elm St, 06510. SAN 336-3244. Tel: 203-946-8130. FAX: 203-946-8140. TDD: 203-946-6200. Web Site: www.cityofnewhaven.com/library. *City Librn & Exec Dir,* Martha Brogran; E-mail: mbrogan@nhfpl.org; *Dep Dir,* Cathleen DeNigris; E-mail: cdenigris@nhfpl.org; *Pub Serv Adminr, Adult Serv,* Brad Bullis; *Pub Serv Adminr, Youth Serv,* Xia Feng; Tel: 203-946-2279, E-mail: xia.feng@nhfpl.org; Staff 72 (MLS 47, Non-MLS 25)
Founded 1887. Pop 126,000; Circ 200,000
Library Holdings: Bk Vols 640,000; Per Subs 350
Automation Activity & Vendor Info: (Cataloging) Innovative Interfaces, Inc; (Circulation) Innovative Interfaces, Inc
Database Vendor: PubMed, ReferenceUSA
Open Mon 12-8, Tues-Thurs 10-8, Fri 12-5, Sat 10-5
Friends of the Library Group
Branches: 4
FAIR HAVEN, 182 Grand Ave, 06513, SAN 336-3368. Tel: 203-946-8115. *Librn,* Betsy Goldberg
Library Holdings: Bk Vols 25,140
Open Mon, Tues & Thurs (Winter) 10-6, Wed 12-8, Sat 1-5; Mon, Tues & Thurs (Summer) 10-6, Wed 12-8, Fri 1-5
Friends of the Library Group
MITCHELL, 37 Harrison St, 06515, SAN 336-3422. Tel: 203-946-8117. *Librn,* Diane Carvalho
Library Holdings: Bk Vols 51,000
Open Mon, Tues & Thurs (Winter) 10-6, Wed 12-8, Sat 1-5; Mon, Tues & Thurs (Summer) 10-6, Wed 12-8, Fri 1-5
Friends of the Library Group
STETSON BRANCH, 200 Dixwell Ave, 06511, SAN 336-3457. Tel: 203-946-8119. FAX: 203-946-6782. *Br Mgr,* Diane Brown-Petteway; Staff 4 (MLS 2, Non-MLS 2)
Function: ILL available
Open Mon, Tues & Thurs (Winter) 10-6, Wed 12-8, Sat 1-5; Mon, Tues & Thurs (Summer) 10-6, Wed 12-8, Fri 1-5
Friends of the Library Group
SEYMOUR WILSON BRANCH, 303 Washington St, 06511. Tel: 203-946-2226. FAX: 203-946-6540. *In Charge,* Nancy Moscoso-Guzman
Library Holdings: Bk Vols 30,000
Open Mon, Tues & Thurs (Winter) 10-6, Wed 12-8, Sat 1-5; Mon, Tues & Thurs (Summer) 10-6, Wed 12-8, Fri 1-5

S NEW HAVEN MUSEUM & HISTORICAL SOCIETY, Whitney Library, 114 Whitney Ave, 06510-1025. SAN 302-2579. Tel: 203-562-4183. FAX: 203-562-2002. Web Site: newhavenmuseum.org. *Actg Librn,* Betsy Goldberg; *Res Librn,* Frances H Skelton; *Ref Serv,* Bonnie L Campbell; Staff 1 (MLS 1)
Founded 1863
Library Holdings: Bk Vols 30,000; Per Subs 20
Special Collections: Genealogy (Lewis, Sedgwick & Sperry Family Colls), mss; Local History (business, civic & religious organizations)
Subject Interests: Genealogy
Wireless access
Publications: A Guide to the Manuscripts & Archives in the Whitney Library of the New Haven Colony Historical Society; The Seton Guide to Business & Industrial Holdings in the Whitney Library
Open Tues-Fri 10-5, Sat 12-5
Friends of the Library Group

S PLANNED PARENTHOOD OF SOUTHERN NEW ENGLAND*, 345 Whitney Ave, 06511-2384. SAN 376-1932. Tel: 203-865-5158. FAX: 203-752-2914. Web Site: www.ppsne.org. *Librn,* Sarah Pigg
Library Holdings: Bk Vols 4,600

C SOUTHERN CONNECTICUT STATE UNIVERSITY*, Hilton C Buley Library, 501 Crescent St, 06515. SAN 302-2625. Tel: 203-392-5750. Circulation Tel: 203-392-5756. Interlibrary Loan Service Tel: 203-392-7009. Reference Tel: 203-392-5732. Administration Tel: 203-392-5742. Automation Services Tel: 203-392-5734. FAX: 203-392-5775. Administration FAX: 203-392-5740. Web Site: www.library.southernct.edu. *Dir,* Christina Baum; E-mail: baumc1@southernct.edu; *Spec Coll Librn,* Paul Holmer; Tel: 203-392-5746, E-mail: holmerp1@southernct.edu; *Access Serv,* Shirley Cavanagh; Tel: 203-392-5768, E-mail: cavanaghs1@southernct.edu; *Per,* Edward Hoyer; Tel: 203-392-5731, E-mail: hoyere1@southernct.edu; *Ref,* Winnie Shyam; Tel: 203-392-5762, E-mail: shyamw1@southernct.edu; *Tech Serv,* Cindy Schofield-Bodt; Tel: 203-392-5778, E-mail: schofieldbc1@southernct.edu; Staff 23 (MLS 20, Non-MLS 3)
Founded 1895. Enrl 12,143; Fac 541; Highest Degree: Doctorate
Library Holdings: Bk Titles 400,000; Bk Vols 600,000; Per Subs 1,450
Special Collections: Children's Books (Caroline Sherwin Bailey Historical Coll), early Am textbks; Connecticut books, pamphlets, photogs, maps (Connecticut Room). US Document Depository
Subject Interests: Educ, Info sci, Libr sci, Women's studies
Automation Activity & Vendor Info: (Acquisitions) Innovative Interfaces, Inc; (Cataloging) Innovative Interfaces, Inc; (Circulation) Innovative

Interfaces, Inc; (ILL) Innovative Interfaces, Inc; (OPAC) Innovative Interfaces, Inc; (Serials) Innovative Interfaces, Inc
Database Vendor: ABC-CLIO, Alexander Street Press, Amigos Library Services, ARTstor, Bowker, Cambridge Scientific Abstracts, CIOS (Communication Institute for Online Scholarship), CQ Press, EBSCOhost, Gale Cengage Learning, infoUSA, JSTOR, LexisNexis, Mergent Online, OCLC FirstSearch, OVID Technologies, Oxford Online, ProQuest, ValueLine, Westlaw
Wireless access
Publications: Buley Bulletin (Newsletter)
Partic in Lyrasis
Open Mon-Thurs 8am-11pm, Fri 8-4:30, Sat 9-5, Sun 1-9

L WIGGIN & DANA LLP*, Wiggin & Dana Information Center, 265 Church St, 06510. (Mail add: PO Box 1832, 06508-1832). Tel: 203-498-4400. FAX: 203-782-2889. Web Site: www.wiggin.com. *Dir,* Ana Oman; E-mail: aoman@wiggin.com; *Head, Tech Serv,* Linda Abbott; E-mail: labbott@wiggin.com; *Ref Serv,* Doug Apicella; E-mail: dapicella@wiggin.com; Staff 7 (MLS 5, Non-MLS 2)
Library Holdings: Bk Vols 17,000
Subject Interests: Law
Automation Activity & Vendor Info: (Acquisitions) SirsiDynix; (Cataloging) SirsiDynix; (Circulation) SirsiDynix; (OPAC) SirsiDynix; (Serials) SirsiDynix
Database Vendor: LexisNexis, Westlaw
Partic in Dialog Corp; Dow Jones News Retrieval; Westlaw
Open Mon-Fri 9-5

C YALE UNIVERSITY LIBRARY*, 120 High St, 06520. (Mail add: PO Box 208240, 06520-8240), SAN 336-3546. Circulation Tel: 203-432-2798. Interlibrary Loan Service Tel: 203-432-1789. Reference Tel: 203-432-1775. Administration Tel: 203-432-1810. Circulation FAX: 203-432-9486. Interlibrary Loan Service FAX: 203-432-2257. Administration FAX: 203-432-1294. E-mail: smlref@yale.edu. Web Site: www.library.yale.edu. *Univ Librn,* Susan Gibbons; Staff 233 (MLS 158, Non-MLS 75)
Founded 1701. Enrl 17,046; Fac 1,736; Highest Degree: Doctorate
Library Holdings: Bk Vols 12,025,695; Per Subs 76,022
Special Collections: Beinecke Rare Book & Manuscript Library; Manuscript & Archives, see also School & Department Libraries
Automation Activity & Vendor Info: (Acquisitions) Ex Libris Group; (Cataloging) Ex Libris Group; (Circulation) Ex Libris Group; (Course Reserve) Ex Libris Group; (OPAC) Ex Libris Group; (Serials) Ex Libris Group
Partic in Northeast Research Libraries Consortium (NERL); OCLC Online Computer Library Center, Inc
Friends of the Library Group

Departmental Libraries:

AMERICAN ORIENTAL SOCIETY, 329 Sterling Memorial Library, 06520, SAN 336-3635. Tel: 203-432-2455. FAX: 203-432-4087. Web Site: www.umich.edu/~aos. *Curator,* Stanley Insler; E-mail: stanley.insler@yale.edu
Library Holdings: Bk Vols 22,774; Per Subs 250
Subject Interests: Hist, Lang arts, Lit
Partic in RLIN (Research Libraries Information Network)
Publications: American Oriental Series (89 vols); Journal of the American Oriental Society
Open Mon-Fri 10-3

ASTRONOMY, J W Gibbs Lab, Rm 217, 260 Whitney Ave, 06511-8903. (Mail add: PO Box 208101, 06520-8101), SAN 336-4356. Tel: 203-432-3033. FAX: 203-432-5048. Web Site: www.astro.yale.edu. *In Charge,* Kim Monocchi
Library Holdings: Bk Vols 38,000
Special Collections: Astronomy Slides; Domestic & Foreign Observatory Publications
Subject Interests: Astronomy, Astrophysics, Math, Physics
Friends of the Library Group

BABYLONIAN COLLECTION, 130 Wall St, 06520, SAN 336-3724. Tel: 203-432-1837. E-mail: babylonian.collection@yale.edu. Web Site: www.babylonian-collection.yale.edu. *Curator,* Benjamin R Foster; *Curator,* Ulla Kasten; Staff 3 (MLS 1, Non-MLS 2)
Founded 1911
Library Holdings: AV Mats 10,000; Bk Titles 12,000; Bk Vols 20,000; Per Subs 42
Special Collections: Cuneiform Tablets & Cylinder Seals
Subject Interests: Ancient & Near Eastern studies, Ancient hist, Archaeology, Art hist, Lit
Function: 24/7 Online cat
Partic in RLIN (Research Libraries Information Network)
Publications: Catalogue of the Babylonian Collections at Yale (Collection catalog)
Restriction: Non-circulating
Friends of the Library Group

BEINECKE RARE BOOK & MANUSCRIPT LIBRARY, 121 Wall St, 06511. (Mail add: PO Box 208240, 06520-8240), SAN 336-3759. Tel: 203-432-2977. FAX: 203-432-4047. Web Site: beinecke.library.yale.edu. *Dir,* Edwin Schroeder; Tel: 203-432-2959, E-mail: edwin.schroeder@yale.edu; *Head, Access Serv,* Stephen Jones; Tel: 203-432-7962, E-mail: stephen.jones@yale.edu; *Head, Tech Serv,* Matthew Beacom; Tel: 202-432-4947, E-mail: matthew.beacom@yale.edu; *Head, Tech & Digital Assets,* Raymond Frohlich; E-mail: raymond.frohlich@yale.edu; *Asst Head, Access Serv,* Moira Fitzgerald; Tel: 203-432-2973, E-mail: moira.fitzgerald@yale.edu; *Res Serv Librn,* Elizabeth Frengel; Tel: 203-432-6436, E-mail: elizabeth.frengel@yale.edu; Staff 52 (MLS 29, Non-MLS 23)
Founded 1963
Library Holdings: Bk Vols 575,092
Special Collections: Aldus Manutius; Arthus Davison Ficke; Asch; Barrett Clark; Barrie; Baskerville; Baskin; Boccaccio; Boswell; Browning; Bruce Rogers; Bryon; Buchan; Burney; Cabell; Carlyle; Coleridge; Conrad; Cooper; D H Lawrence; David Low; Defoe; Dickens; Dorothy Richardson; Dryden; Edith Wharton; Edmund Wilson; Eleanor Wylie; Erza Stiles; Ezra Pound; F T Marinetti; Fielding; Garrick; George Eliot; George MacDonald; George Moore; Gertrude Stein; Gissing; Goethe; Hardy; Herman Hagedorn; Hermann Broch; Hilda Doolittle; Hogg; Hutchins & Neith Boyce Hapgood; James Gates Percival; James Purdy; James Weldon Johnson; Jean Giono; Joel Barlow; John Gould Fletcher; John Hersey; Jonathan Edwards; Joseph Ireland; Joyce; Katherine Dreier; Kipling; Kurt & Helen Wolff; Landor; Langston Hughes; Leo Stein; Leonie Adams; Mabel Luhan; MacLeish; Maria Edgeworth; Marquand; Marsden Hartley; Masefield; Matthew Arnold; Mencken; Meredith; Milosz; Milton; Muriel Draper; Norman Douglas; Norman MacLeod; O'Neill; Paul Horgan; Paul Leicester Ford; Pope; Rachel Carson; Rebecca West; Richard Wright; Rilke; Robert Nathan; Robert Penn Warren; Robinson Jeffers; Ruskin; S V Benet; Samuel Johnson; Samuel Richardson; Shakespeare; Sheridan; Sinclair Lewis; Sir Thomas More; Sir Winston Churchill; Spenser; Spinelli Family; Stevenson; Stieglitz; Swinburne; Tennyson; Thackeray; Theatre Guild; Thomas Mann; Tocqueville; Toklas; Trollope; Van Vechten; Vardis Fisher; W R Benet; Walter Crane; Walton; Washington Irving; Whitman; Wilder; William Beckford; William Carlos Williams; William McFee; Wordsworth
Subject Interests: Alchemy, Children's lit, European hist, Hist of sci, Judaica (lit or hist of Jews), Latin Am, Lit, Music, Theol, Travel
Partic in RLIN (Research Libraries Information Network)
Publications: The Yale University Library Gazette
Open Mon-Thurs 9-7, Fri 9-5, Sat 12-5
Friends of the Library Group

CENTER FOR SCIENCE & SOCIAL SCIENCE INFORMATION, Kline Biology Tower, Concourse Level, 219 Prospect St, 06520. (Mail add: PO Box 208111, 06520-8111), SAN 336-447X. Tel: 203-432-3300. Reference Tel: 203-432-3301. Administration Tel: 203-432-3303, 203-432-3304. FAX: 203-432-8979. E-mail: csssi@yale.edu. Web Site: csssi.yale.edu. *Dir,* Jill Parchuck; *Librn,* Carla Heister. Subject Specialists: *Govt info, Polit sci,* Jill Parchuck; *Environ studies, Forestry,* Carla Heister; Staff 16 (MLS 7, Non-MLS 9)
Highest Degree: Doctorate
Library Holdings: Bk Vols 100,000
Special Collections: Economic Growth Center Coll; Roper Center Archive; Social Science Data Archive
Subject Interests: Econ, Finance, Intl relations, Polit sci, Psychol, Sociol
Automation Activity & Vendor Info: (ILL) Ex Libris Group
Database Vendor: EBSCOhost, LexisNexis, OCLC FirstSearch, OVID Technologies
Function: Doc delivery serv, ILL available, Ref serv available, Res libr, Telephone ref
Open Mon-Thurs (Winter) 8:30am-11pm, Fri 8:30-7, Sat 12-8, Sun 1-11
Restriction: Open to fac, students & qualified researchers, Open to pub for ref only

CLASSICS, Phelps Hall, 344 College St, 5th Flr, 06511. (Mail add: PO Box 208266, 06520-8266), SAN 336-3813. Tel: 203-432-0854. Web Site: www.library.yale.edu/arts/classics.html. *Classics Librn,* Colin McCaffrey. Subject Specialists: *Ancient philos, Classics,* Colin McCaffrey; Staff 1 (MLS 1)
Founded 1892. Highest Degree: Doctorate
Library Holdings: Bk Vols 27,000
Subject Interests: Ancient hist, Classics, Greek, Latin, Philology
Function: Specialized serv in classical studies
Open Mon-Fri 8:30-5

THE WILLIAM ROBERTSON COE ORNITHOLOGY LIBRARY, Environmental Science Ctr, Rm 151, 21 Sachem St, 06520-8118. (Mail add: 170 Whitney Ave, 06511), SAN 336-4380. Tel: 203-436-4892. E-mail: ornithology.library@yale.edu. Web Site: www.peabody.yale.edu/collections/vz/orn_library.html. *Librn,* Jorge De Leon
Founded 1890
Library Holdings: Bk Vols 4,000; Per Subs 300
Database Vendor: EBSCO Information Services
Open Tues 4-7, Fri 1-5
Restriction: Non-circulating

CM HARVEY CUSHING/JOHN HAY WHITNEY MEDICAL LIBRARY, Sterling Hall of Medicine, 333 Cedar St, 06510. (Mail add: PO Box 208014, 06520-8014), SAN 336-4291. Tel: 203-785-5352. Circulation Tel: 203-785-5354. Information Services Tel: 203-737-4065. FAX: 203-785-5636. E-mail: medcirc@yale.edu, medref@yale.edu. Web Site: library.medicine.yale.edu. *Interim Dir,* John Gallagher; Tel: 202-785-5356, E-mail: john.gallagher@yale.edu; *Head, Coll Develop & Mgt,* Nathan Rupp; Tel: 203-785-2883, E-mail: nathan.rupp@yale.edu; *Curric Support Librn,* Judy Spak; Tel: 203-737-2961, E-mail: judy.spak@yale.edu; *Educ Serv Librn,* Jan Glover; Tel: 203-737-2962, E-mail: jan.glover@yale.edu; *Instrul Design Librn,* Lei Wang; Tel: 203-785-6485, E-mail: lei.wang@yale.edu; *Ref Librn,* Lynn Sette; Tel: 203-737-2963, E-mail: lynn.sette@yale.edu; *Web Serv Librn,* Andy Hickner; Tel: 203-785-3969, E-mail: andrew.hickner@yale.edu; *Mgr, Libr Syst,* Arthur Belanger; Tel: 203-785-6928, E-mail: arthur.belanger@yale.edu; Staff 41 (MLS 17, Non-MLS 24)
Founded 1814. Enrl 975; Fac 1,304; Highest Degree: Doctorate
Library Holdings: Bk Vols 433,240; Per Subs 2,483
Special Collections: Early Ichthyology (George Milton Smith Coll), bks & per; History of Medicine, Medical Prints & Drawings (Clements C Fry Coll); Weights & Measures (Edward Clark Streeter Coll), artifacts
Subject Interests: Med, Nursing
Database Vendor: EBSCOhost, OVID Technologies, Wilson - Wilson Web
Partic in National Network of Libraries of Medicine; RLIN (Research Libraries Information Network)
Publications: Connections
Open Mon-Thurs 8am-2am, Fri 8am-10pm, Sat 10-10, Sun 9:30am-2am
Friends of the Library Group

DIVINITY SCHOOL LIBRARY, 409 Prospect St, 06511-2108, SAN 336-3902. Tel: 203-432-5290. Circulation Tel: 203-432-5274. Reference Tel: 203-432-6374. FAX: 203-432-3906. E-mail: divinity.library@yale.edu. Web Site: www.library.yale.edu/div/. *Dir, Ministry Res Ctr,* Carolyn Hardin Engelhardt; Tel: 203-432-5319, E-mail: carolynhardin.engelhardt@yale.edu; *Acq Mgr,* Mary Ellen Barbarito; Tel: 203-432-5294, E-mail: mary.barbarito@yale.edu; *Circ & ILL Mgr,* Susan Burdick; Tel: 203-432-5288, E-mail: susan.burdick@yale.edu; *Librn,* Paul F Stuehrenberg; Tel: 203-432-5292, E-mail: paul.stuehrenberg@yale.edu; *Ref & Instrul Serv Librn,* Suzanne Estelle-Holmer; E-mail: suzanne.estelle-holmer@yale.edu; *Res & Electronic Serv Librn,* Amy Limpitlaw; E-mail: amy.limpitlaw@yale.edu; *Ser & Presv Librn,* Christine Pesch; Tel: 203-432-5295, E-mail: christine.pesch@yale.edu; *Spec Coll Librn/Curator, Day Missions Coll, Syst Mgr,* Martha Lund Smalley; Tel: 203-432-5289, E-mail: martha.smalley@yale.edu; *Asst Divinity Librn, Tech Serv,* Eric Friede; Tel: 203-432-6372; Staff 8.5 (MLS 5, Non-MLS 3.5)
Founded 1932. Enrl 367; Fac 34; Highest Degree: Master
Library Holdings: Bk Vols 510,000; Per Subs 1,700
Special Collections: American Home Missionary Society; China Missions; Day Historical Library of Foreign Missions; Ghana Archives of the Basel Mission; Historical Sermons Coll; International Missionary Council & Conference of British Missionary Societies; Jansenism; John R Mott Papers; Kenneth Scott Latourette Papers; Liston Pope Coll of Christian Social Ethics; Methodist Missionary Society; Mircofilm/Fiche Coll-Council for World Mission; Missions Pamphlets; Religious Education Association Archives; Student Volunteer Movement Archives; The United Board for Christian Higher Education in Asia Archives; World Student Christian Federation Archives
Automation Activity & Vendor Info: (Acquisitions) Ex Libris Group
Open Mon-Thurs (Sept-May) 8:30am-11pm, Fri & Sat 8:30-5, Sun 2-11
Friends of the Library Group

GEOLOGY, 210 Whitney Ave, Rm 328, 06511, SAN 336-4054. Tel: 203-432-3157. Web Site: web.library.yale.edu/building/geology-library. *Libr Support Serv Asst,* Robert Heister; Tel: 203-432-3157, E-mail: robert.heister@yale.edu; Staff 2 (Non-MLS 2)
Library Holdings: Bk Vols 113,840; Per Subs 1,395
Subject Interests: Geochemistry, Geol, Geophysics, Meteorology, Oceanography, Paleontology
Open Mon-Fri 8:30-5

IRVING S GILMORE MUSIC LIBRARY, 120 High St, 06520. (Mail add: 130 Wall St, PO Box 208240, 06520-8240), SAN 336-4321. Tel: 203-432-0492. Circulation Tel: 203-432-0496. Reference Tel: 203-432-0497. FAX: 203-432-7339. E-mail: musiclibrary@yale.edu. Web Site: web.library.yale.edu/music. *Andrew W Mellon Found Music Librn,* Ruthann Boles McTyre; Tel: 203-432-0495, E-mail: ruthann.mctyre@yale.edu; *Asst Librn, Tech Serv,* Helen Bartlett; *Pub Serv Librn,* Suzanne Eggleston Lovejoy; Staff 11 (MLS 5, Non-MLS 6)
Founded 1917
Library Holdings: Bk Vols 139,606
Special Collections: 19th Century American Hymn Tunes Coll; Alec Templeton Papers; Benny Goodman Papers; Carl Ruggles Papers; Charles Ives Papers; David Kraehenbuehl Papers; David Stanley Smith Papers; Deems Taylor Papers; E Robert Schmitz/Pro Musica Society Papers; Franz Schreker Coll; German Theoretical Literature 16th-18th Centuries; Harold Rome Papers; Henry Gilbert Papers; Hershey Kay Papers; Horatio Parker Papers; J Rosamund Johnson Papers; John Kirkpatrick Papers; Karl Weigl Papers; Kay Swift Papers; Kurt Weill & Lotte Lenya Papers; Lehman Engel Papers; Leo Ornstein Coll; Leo Ornstein Papers; Leroy Anderson Papers; Lowell Mason Coll; Mel Powell Papers; Miscellaneous Manuscripts; Newell Jenkins/Clarion Society Papers; Paul Bekker Coll; Paul Hindemith Coll; Quincy Porter Papers; Ralph Kirkpatrick Coll; Robert Shaw Papers; Seymour Shifrin Papers; Stanley Dance Coll; Thomas de Hartmann Coll; Virgil Thomson Coll; Vladimir Horowitz Coll
Partic in OCLC Online Computer Library Center, Inc
Open Mon-Thurs 8:30am-9pm, Fri 8:30-5, Sat 10-5, Sun 1-9
Friends of the Library Group

CL LILLIAN GOLDMAN LIBRARY YALE LAW SCHOOL, 127 Wall St, 06511. (Mail add: PO Box 208215, 06520-8215), SAN 336-4232. Tel: 203-432-1600. Circulation Tel: 203-432-1608. Interlibrary Loan Service Tel: 203-432-1640. Reference Tel: 203-432-1606. FAX: 203-432-2112. Web Site: www.yale.edu/law.library. *Dir,* S Blair Kauffman; *Assoc Librn, Admin,* Teresa Miguel-Stearns; Tel: 203-432-8023, E-mail: teresa.miguel@yale.edu; *Coll Librn,* Fred Shapiro; *Foreign & Intl Law Librn,* Ryan Harrington; Tel: 203-432-7371, E-mail: ryan.harrington@yale.edu; *Ref Librn,* Margaret Chisholm; *Ref Librn,* Jason Eiseman; *Ref Librn,* Evelyn Ma; *Acq, Ser,* Anne Myers; *Circ,* Julian Aiken; *ILL,* Alison Burke; *Principal Cataloger,* Susan Karpuk; *Rare Bks,* Mike Widener; *Ref,* Sarah Ryan; *Ref,* Michael VanderHeijden; *Ref,* John Nann; *Ref Serv,* Julie Krishnaswami; *Tech Serv,* Scott Matheson; Staff 17 (MLS 17)
Founded 1834. Enrl 600; Fac 50; Highest Degree: Doctorate
Library Holdings: Bk Vols 1,000,000
Special Collections: American Statute Law (Cole Coll); Blackstone Coll; International Law; Italian Medieval Statutes; Roman Law (Wheeler Coll)
Automation Activity & Vendor Info: (Acquisitions) Innovative Interfaces, Inc; (Cataloging) Innovative Interfaces, Inc; (Circulation) Innovative Interfaces, Inc; (Course Reserve) Innovative Interfaces, Inc; (ILL) Innovative Interfaces, Inc; (Media Booking) Innovative Interfaces, Inc; (OPAC) Innovative Interfaces, Inc; (Serials) Innovative Interfaces, Inc
Partic in RLIN (Research Libraries Information Network)
Open Mon-Fri (Winter) 8:30am-10pm, Sat 10-5, Sun 12-10; Mon-Fri (Summer) 8:30-5, Sat 10-5

GOVERNMENT DOCUMENTS & INFORMATION CENTER, 38 Mansfield St, 06511. (Mail add: PO Box 208294, 06520-8294), SAN 336-433X. Tel: 203-432-3209. Administration Tel: 203-432-3310. FAX: 203-432-3214. E-mail: govdoc@yale.edu. Web Site: www.library.yale.edu/govdocs/. *Govt Doc,* Julie Linden; *Govt Doc,* Sandra K Peterson; Tel: 203-432-3212. Subject Specialists: *US Federal docs,* Julie Linden; *Intl docs,* Sandra K Peterson; Staff 4 (MLS 1, Non-MLS 3)
Special Collections: Access UN; Canadian Research Index; CIS Unpublished US House of Representatives Hearings, 1833-1964, index & microfiche; CIS US Congressional Committee Prints, through 1969; CIS US Senate Executive Documents; CIS US Senate Unpublished Hearings, 1824-1972 Index Coll, micro; CIS US Serial Set Index; CRS Major Studies; Declassified Documents Reference System, micro; Digital Serial Set (Readex); FAO Comprehensive Coll, 1978-1996, micro; FAO, European Union; Foreign Broadcast Information Service Daily Reports, 1946-1996; Index & Microfiche Coll; Index to Foreign Broadcast Information Service Daily Reports, StatCAN & Statistical Universe; Index to International Statistics, 1986-present, microfiche; Issue Briefs, micro; Joint Publications Research Services Translations, 1953-1996; Lexis-Nexis Congressional; Microfiche Coll; Nondepository Coll from the American Statistics Index & CIS Index to Publications of the US Congress; Presidential Executive Orders; Proclamations 1789-1964 Index; Readex United Nations Documents & Publications, 1946-present, microfiche; Reports 1817-1969 (not in serial set); World News Connection (online). Can & Prov; UN Document Depository; US Document Depository
Subject Interests: Am hist, Econ, US Congress
Function: Govt ref serv, Telephone ref
Open Mon 8:30-7:45, Tues-Fri 8:30-4:45, Sat 1-5
Restriction: Non-circulating

ROBERT B HAAS FAMILY ARTS LIBRARY, Loria Ctr, 180 York St, 06520. (Mail add: PO Box 208318, 06520-8318), SAN 336-3694. Tel: 203-432-2645. FAX: 203-432-0549. E-mail: art.library@yale.edu. Web Site: library.yale.edu/arts. *Dir,* Allen Townsend; Tel: 203-432-2642, E-mail: allen.townsend@yale.edu; *Asst Dir, Access Serv,* Holly Hatheway; E-mail: holly.hatheway@yale.edu; *Asst Dir, Spec Coll,* Jae Rossman; Tel: 203-432-1712, E-mail: jae.rossman@yale.edu; Staff 9 (MLS 3, Non-MLS 6)
Special Collections: Arts Library Locked Case Coll; Arts of the Book; Faber Birren Coll on Color
Subject Interests: Archit, Art hist, Graphic arts, Painting, Photog, Sculpture
Partic in RLIN (Research Libraries Information Network)
Open Mon-Thurs 8:30am-11pm, Fri 8:30-5, Sat 10-6, Sun 2-11

KLINE SCIENCE LIBRARY, 219 Prospect St, 06511-2106. (Mail add: PO Box 208111, 06520-8111), SAN 336-4208. Tel: 203-432-3439. FAX: 203-432-3441. *Dir,* David Stern
Founded 1966
Special Collections: Bryology & Lichenology (Evans Coll); Various 19th Century Expeditions Reports
Subject Interests: Biol, Chem, Conserv, Oceanography, Physics
Partic in RLIN (Research Libraries Information Network)
Publications: Science Imprint (Newsletter)
Open Mon-Thurs (Winter) 8:30-7:45, Fri 8:30-4:45, Sat 10-6:45, Sun 12-7:45; Mon-Thurs (Summer) 8:30-8, Fri 8:30-5, Sat 10-5, Sun 1-8

LIBRARY SHELVING FACILITY, 147 Leeder Hill Rd, Hamden, 06518. Tel: 203-432-9140. FAX: 203-432-9139. *Mgr,* Michael DiMassa; E-mail: michael.dimassa@yale.edu; Staff 2 (Non-MLS 2)
Library Holdings: Bk Titles 2,500,000
Special Collections: Less frequently used research materials from all Yale University Library coll

MATHEMATICS, Leete Oliver Memorial Hall, 12 Hillhouse Ave, 06511. (Mail add: PO Box 208283, 06520-8283), SAN 336-4267. Tel: 203-432-4179. FAX: 203-432-7316. Web Site: www.library.yale.edu/science.
Library Holdings: Bk Vols 21,000; Per Subs 331
Subject Interests: Math
Open Mon-Fri 8:30-5

REFERENCE LIBRARY, YALE CENTER FOR BRITISH ART, 1080 Chapel St, 06520. (Mail add: PO Box 208280, 06520-8280), SAN 336-3783. Tel: 203-432-2818. Reference FAX: 203-432-7180. E-mail: ycba.reference@yale.edu. Web Site: britishart.yale.edu, britishart.yale.edu/about-us/departments/reference-library-and-archives. *Chief Librn,* Kraig Binkowski; Tel: 203-432-2846, E-mail: kraig.binkowski@yale.edu; *Asst Librn,* Elizabeth Morris; Tel: 203-432-2848, E-mail: elizabeth.morris@yale.edu; *Sr Libr Asst,* Lori Misura; Tel: 203-432-7689, E-mail: lori.misura@yale.edu; *Sr Archivist,* Rachel Chatalbash; Tel: 203-432-8395, E-mail: rachel.chatalbash@yale.edu; *Sr Cataloger/Libr Asst,* Grace Bright; E-mail: grace.bright@yale.edu; Staff 6 (MLS 3, Non-MLS 3)
Founded 1977
Library Holdings: Bk Vols 40,000; Per Subs 75
Special Collections: British Art Photograph Archive; Jennings Album of Historical English Portraits; Sotheby & Christie Catalogs on British Art
Subject Interests: Archit, Art, Hist, Lit, Performing arts
Function: Ref serv available, Res libr
Partic in OCLC Online Computer Library Center, Inc
Open Tues & Thurs-Sat 10-4:30, Wed 10-8, Sun 12-4:30; Tues-Fri (Summer) 10-4:30
Restriction: Non-circulating

STERLING CHEMISTRY LIBRARY, 225 Prospect St, 06511-8499. (Mail add: PO Box 208107, 06520-8107), SAN 336-4216. Tel: 203-432-3960. FAX: 203-432-3049. Web Site: www.library.yale.edu/science. *Librn,* David Stern; Staff 1 (Non-MLS 1)
Library Holdings: Bk Vols 18,123; Per Subs 144
Subject Interests: Biochem, Chem, Inorganic chem, Organic chem, Phys chem
Automation Activity & Vendor Info: (Acquisitions) Ex Libris Group; (Cataloging) Ex Libris Group; (Circulation) Ex Libris Group; (OPAC) Ex Libris Group; (Serials) Ex Libris Group

STERLING MEMORIAL LIBRARY, 120 High St, 06520, SAN 336-3600. Tel: 203-432-2798. Interlibrary Loan Service Tel: 203-432-1789. Reference Tel: 203-432-1775. Administration Tel: 203-432-1810. FAX: 203-432-1294. Circulation FAX: 203-432-9486. Interlibrary Loan Service FAX: 203-432-2257. *Univ Librn,* Frank M Turner; *Head, Access Serv,* Bradly Warren; Tel: 203-432-3597, E-mail: brad.warren@yale.edu; *Head, Cat,* Richard E Garcia; Tel: 203-432-6406, E-mail: richard.garcia@yale.edu; *Head, Presv,* Roberta Pilette; Tel: 203-432-1714, Fax: 203-432-9900, E-mail: roberta.pilette@yale.edu; *Head, Res Serv & Coll,* Alan C Solomon; Tel: 203-432-1778, Fax: 203-432-8527, E-mail: alan.solomon@yale.edu; *Interim Head, Acq,* Eric Friede; Tel: 203-432-8373, E-mail: eric.friede@yale.edu; *Spec Coll Librn, Arts of the Bk,* Jae J Rossman; Tel: 203-432-1712, E-mail: jae.rossman@yale.edu
Founded 1932
Library Holdings: Bk Vols 3,000,000
Special Collections: American Musical Theater, Civic Repertory Theater & Theater Guild; Antebellum American South & Civil War; Arts of the Book; Babylonian Tablets; Bibliography; Bookplates; British Economic Tracts; Canadian History & Literature (including French Canadian literature); Classical Archaeology; Congregationalism; Connecticut & New England History; Contemporary Medical & Health Care Policy; Economic History; Ethnic (Black) Arts & Letters; Family History; Forestry & Ecology; Futurism; German Literature; Greek & Latin Classics; Historical Sound Recordings; Historiography; Individuals: Henry Ward Beecher Family, Berkeley, Chester Bowles, Edmund Burke, Aaron Burr Family, John Collier (1884-1968), Jerome Frank, Franklin, Gay, Goldsmith, Heine, Edward M House, Ellsworth Huntington, Josephus Flavius, Juvenal, Lafayette, Max Lerner, Lincoln, Lindbergh Family (restricted), Walter Lippman, Malinowski, Marcus Aurelius, O C Marsh, J S Mill, Jedediah & Samuel F B Morse Family, Napoleon, Ouspensky, Philo Judaeus, C Rhodes, Richelieu, Shaw, Silliman Family, Henry L Stimson, Anson Phelps Stokes, Harold Phelps Stokes, Rose Pastor Stokes, William Graham Sumner, Tacitus, Mabel Loomis Todd, Ernst Toller, John Trumbull, Twain, Eli Whitney. Subjects of Special Strength - American & English Literature & History; Italian Literature & Travel; Journalism & Political Writing, 20th Century; Judaica; Latin America; Legal Thought; Maps & Atlases; Modern African History; Naval History; Near East, including Arabic & Sanskrit; Newspapers; Oxford; Printing History; Scandinavia; Science & Technology, 19th Century; Slavic; Social Sciences; Southeast Asia; Sporting Books; United States Colonial & Progressive Period, Religious History & Contemporary Reform Movements; Urban & Regional Planning; World War I & II Diplomacy; Yale University

LEWIS WALPOLE LIBRARY, 154 Main St, Farmington, 06032. (Mail add: PO Box 1408, Farmington, 06034), SAN 336-4526. Tel: 860-677-2140. FAX: 860-677-6369. E-mail: walpole@yale.edu. Web Site: www.library.yale.edu/walpole. *Exec Dir, Librn,* Margaret K Powell; Tel: 860-284-5025, E-mail: margaret.powell@yale.edu; *Head, Pub Serv,* Susan Odell Walker; E-mail: susan.walker@yale.edu; *Head, Tech Serv,* Ellen Cordes; E-mail: ellen.cordes@yale.edu; *Mgr, Digital Assets & Info Tech,* George Ouellette; *Conservator,* Laura O'Brien Miller; E-mail: laura.miller@yale.edu; *Curator,* Cynthia Roman; E-mail: cynthia.roman@yale.edu. Subject Specialists: *Drawings, Paintings, Prints,* Cynthia Roman; Staff 11.5 (MLS 5, Non-MLS 6.5)
Library Holdings: Bk Vols 35,000; Per Subs 32
Special Collections: British 18th Century Prints & Drawings; Charles Hanbury Williams (1708-1759) Coll, ms; Horace Walpole (1717-1797) Coll, bks, ms, prints & drawings, fine & decorative arts; William Hogarth (1696-1764) Coll, prints
Subject Interests: 18th Century Britain
Function: Archival coll, Res libr
Restriction: Non-circulating, Open by appt only

S YOUNG MEN'S INSTITUTE LIBRARY*, 847 Chapel St, 06510. SAN 302-2633. Tel: 203-562-4045. *Head Librn,* Rebecca McGaffin; *Asst Librn,* Victoria Pacileo
Founded 1826
Library Holdings: Bk Vols 29,500
Open Mon-Fri 10-3
Restriction: Mem only, Private libr

NEW LONDON

S LYMAN ALLYN ART MUSEUM LIBRARY*, 625 Williams St, 06320-4130. SAN 302-2641. Tel: 860-443-2545. FAX: 860-442-1280. E-mail: info@lymanallyn.org. Web Site: www.lymanallyn.org. *Dir,* Samuel Quigley; Tel: 860-443-2545, Ext 113, E-mail: quigley@lymanallyn.org; *Registrar,* Jane LeGrow; Tel: 860-443-2545, Ext 126, E-mail: legrow@lymanallyn.org
Founded 1931
Library Holdings: Bk Vols 4,500; Per Subs 15
Special Collections: Art Exhibition Catalogs
Subject Interests: Art hist, Decorative art, Fine arts, Local hist
Function: Ref & res
Open Tues-Sat 10-5, Sun 1-5
Restriction: Not a lending libr

C CONNECTICUT COLLEGE*, Charles E Shain Library, 270 Mohegan Ave, 06320-4196. SAN 336-4534. Tel: 860-439-2650. Circulation Tel: 860-439-2662. Interlibrary Loan Service Tel: 860-439-2667. Reference Tel: 860-439-2655. FAX: 860-439-2871. E-mail: libref@conncoll.edu. Web Site: www.conncoll.edu/is. *Librn of the Col, VPres for Info Serv,* W Lee Hisle; E-mail: wlhis@conncoll.edu; *Dir, Info Res,* Beth Hansen; Tel: 860-439-2681; *Dir, Instrul Tech,* Chris Penniman; Tel: 860-439-2381; *Dir, Linda Lear Ctr for Spec Coll & Archives,* Benjamin Panciera; Tel: 860-439-2654; *Dir, Res Support & Instruction,* Caroline Kent; Tel: 860-439-2444; *Access Serv Librn,* Benjamin Peck; *Archives & Spec Coll Librn,* Nova Seals; Tel: 860-439-2686; *Res Support & Instruction Librn,* Kathleen Gehring; Tel: 860-439-5225; *Res Support & Instruction Librn,* Ashley Hanson; Tel: 860-439-2653; *Res Support & Instruction Librn,* W James MacDonald; Tel: 860-439-2656; *Coordr, Spec Projects, Res Support & Instruction Librn,* Amanda Watson; Tel: 860-439-2272; *Ser & Electronic Res Librn,* Melodie Hamilton; Tel: 860-439-2669; *Tech Serv & Syst Librn,* Joseph Frawley; Tel: 860-439-2670; *Visual Res Librn,* Mark Braunstein; Tel: 860-439-2729; *Acq, Supvr,* Lorraine McKinney; Tel: 860-439-2641; *ILL Supvr,* Emily Aylward; *Sr Media Serv Tech,* David Baratko; Tel: 860-439-2693. Subject Specialists: *Govt doc,* W James MacDonald; Staff 27 (MLS 14, Non-MLS 13)
Founded 1911. Enrl 1,866; Fac 169; Highest Degree: Master
Library Holdings: e-journals 6,675; Bk Vols 525,944; Per Subs 1,325
Special Collections: 19th & 20th Century Children's Literature (Helen O Gildersleeve Coll); John Masefield (Charles H Simmons Coll); Linda Lear & Rachel Carson Coll; Louis Schaeffer-Eugene O'Neill Coll; New London

County History Coll; Poetry (William Meredith Coll); Printing History (Carl & Alma Weiss Coll); Susanne K Langer Coll; William Meredith & Blanche McCrary Boyd Papers; Wyman Ballad Coll. State Document Depository; US Document Depository
Subject Interests: Art, Chinese lang, Dance, Hist, Humanities, Japanese (Lang), Judaica (lit or hist of Jews), Natural sci, Soc sci & issues
Automation Activity & Vendor Info: (Acquisitions) Ex Libris Group; (Cataloging) Ex Libris Group; (Circulation) Ex Libris Group; (Course Reserve) Ex Libris Group; (ILL) OCLC ILLiad; (OPAC) Ex Libris Group; (Serials) Ex Libris Group
Database Vendor: Alexander Street Press, ARTstor, Cambridge Scientific Abstracts, ebrary, EBSCOhost, Elsevier MDL, Gale Cengage Learning, ISI Web of Knowledge, JSTOR, LexisNexis, Newsbank, OCLC FirstSearch, OCLC WorldShare Interlibrary Loan, OVID Technologies, ProQuest, ScienceDirect, Wilson - Wilson Web
Wireless access
Publications: Friends (Newsletter); Inside Information (Newsletter)
Partic in Connecticut Library Consortium; CTW Library Consortium; Lyrasis; OCLC Online Computer Library Center, Inc; Westchester Academic Library Directors Organization (WALDO)
Open Mon-Thurs 8am-2am, Fri & Sat 8am-10pm, Sun 10am-2am
Friends of the Library Group

Departmental Libraries:

GREER MUSIC LIBRARY, 270 Mohegan Ave, Box 5234, 06320-4196. Tel: 860-439-2711. FAX: 860-439-2871. Web Site: conncoll.libguides.com/greer. *Music Librn,* Carolyn A Johnson; *Libr Asst,* June Ingram; Staff 2 (MLS 1, Non-MLS 1)
Highest Degree: Bachelor
Library Holdings: Bk Vols 12,000
Special Collections: Historic Sheet Music Coll, Mid-19th Century-1950; Jazz (Shelley Colls); LP Coll; Opera & Operetta (Hilliar Coll)
Publications: Greer Music Library (Informational brochure)
Friends of the Library Group

M LAWRENCE & MEMORIAL HOSPITAL*, Health Sciences Library, 365 Montauk Ave, 06320. SAN 302-265X. Tel: 860-442-0711, Ext 2238. FAX: 860-271-4302. *Mgr, Libr Serv,* AnnMarie Kaminsky; *Libr Tech,* Susan Massey
Founded 1972
Subject Interests: Nursing
Restriction: Not open to pub

C MITCHELL COLLEGE LIBRARY*, 437 Pequot Ave, 06320-4498. SAN 302-2668. Tel: 860-701-5156. Reference Tel: 860-701-7091. FAX: 860-701-5099. Web Site: campus.mitchell.edu. *Dir, Libr Serv,* Elizabeth Davidson; Tel: 860-701-5155, E-mail: davidson_e@mitchell.edu; *Instrul Tech Consult,* Gina Ewing; Staff 6 (MLS 3, Non-MLS 3)
Founded 1939. Enrl 600; Highest Degree: Bachelor
Library Holdings: Bk Vols 48,500; Per Subs 28
Special Collections: Robert Penn Warren Letters
Subject Interests: Art, Art hist
Automation Activity & Vendor Info: (Acquisitions) Innovative Interfaces, Inc; (Cataloging) Innovative Interfaces, Inc; (Circulation) Innovative Interfaces, Inc; (Course Reserve) Innovative Interfaces, Inc; (ILL) Innovative Interfaces, Inc; (OPAC) Innovative Interfaces, Inc
Database Vendor: EBSCOhost, Gale Cengage Learning, LexisNexis, OCLC FirstSearch, SirsiDynix
Wireless access
Function: For res purposes
Partic in Connecticut Library Consortium; Libraries Online, Inc; Lyrasis
Open Mon-Thurs (Winter) 8am-12:30am, Fri 8-6, Sat 12-5, Sun 12-10; Mon-Fri (Summer) 8:30-5

S NEW LONDON COUNTY HISTORICAL SOCIETY LIBRARY*, 11 Blinman St, 06320. SAN 302-2676. Tel: 860-443-1209. FAX: 860-443-1209. E-mail: info@newlondonhistory.org. Web Site: www.newlondonhistory.org. *Librn,* Tricia Royston; *Res,* Patricia M Schaefer; Staff 1 (MLS 1)
Founded 1870
Library Holdings: Bk Titles 5,000
Special Collections: Newspapers, 1758-present; Whaling Coll, journals, logs, registers. Oral History
Subject Interests: Genealogy, Local hist
Wireless access
Function: Archival coll, For res purposes, Newsp ref libr, Photocopying/Printing, Ref serv available, Res libr, Res performed for a fee, Telephone ref
Publications: Amistad Incident in New London Gazette (Local historical information); Black Roots in Southeastern Connecticut (Reference guide); Diary of Joshua Hempsted (Local historical information); Greetings from New London (Local historical information); History of the Amistad Captives (Local historical information); Life of Venture (Local historical information); Newsletter (Bi-monthly); Tapestry (Local historical information); View From the Sixties (Local historical information)
Open Wed-Fri (June-Sept) 1-4, Sat 10-4
Restriction: Fee for pub use, Not a lending libr, Visitors must make appt to use bks in the libr

P NEW LONDON PUBLIC LIBRARY*, 63 Huntington St, 06320. SAN 302-2684. Tel: 860-447-1411. FAX: 860-443-2083. Web Site: lioninc.org/newlondon. *Exec Dir,* Peter F Ciparelli; E-mail: peterc@lioninc.org; *Head, Adult Serv, Head, Ref,* Tara Samul; E-mail: tsamul@lioninc.org; *Head, Tech Serv,* Lee Clapp; E-mail: lclapp@lioninc.org; Staff 18 (MLS 4, Non-MLS 14)
Founded 1891. Pop 26,583; Circ 167,880
Jul 2007-Jun 2008 Income $719,200, State $3,200, City $608,000, Locally Generated Income $28,000, Other $80,000. Mats Exp $90,500, Books $44,000, Per/Ser (Incl. Access Fees) $7,500, AV Mat $3,000, Electronic Ref Mat (Incl. Access Fees) $36,000. Sal $387,900 (Prof $150,000)
Library Holdings: DVDs 450; Bk Vols 83,000; Per Subs 155; Videos 3,000
Subject Interests: Genealogy, Local hist
Automation Activity & Vendor Info: (Acquisitions) Innovative Interfaces, Inc; (Cataloging) Innovative Interfaces, Inc; (Circulation) Innovative Interfaces, Inc; (ILL) Innovative Interfaces, Inc; (OPAC) Innovative Interfaces, Inc; (Serials) Innovative Interfaces, Inc
Database Vendor: Innovative Interfaces, Inc
Wireless access
Function: ILL available
Publications: Loomings (Quarterly newsletter)
Partic in Libraries Online, Inc
Special Services for the Blind - Closed circuit TV magnifier
Open Mon-Thurs (Sept-May) 9-9, Fri & Sat 9-5, Sun 1-5
Friends of the Library Group

C UNITED STATES COAST GUARD ACADEMY LIBRARY*, 35 Mohegan Ave, 06320-4195. SAN 302-2692. Tel: 860-444-8510. Interlibrary Loan Service Tel: 860-701-6421. Reference Tel: 860-444-8515, 860-444-8676. Administration Tel: 860-444-8517. Automation Services Tel: 860-444-8553. FAX: 860-444-8516. E-mail: libnotification@uscga.edu. Web Site: libguides.uscga.edu. *Libr Dir,* Lucia Maziar; E-mail: lucia.maziar@uscga.edu; *Head, Ref & Instruction,* Richard Everett; E-mail: richard.everett@uscga.edu; *Ref & Instruction Librn,* Trevor Riley; E-mail: trevor.n.riley@uscga.edu; *Tech Serv Librn,* Position Currently Open; Staff 10 (MLS 5, Non-MLS 5)
Founded 1876. Enrl 950; Fac 119; Highest Degree: Bachelor
Oct 2011-Sept 2012. Mats Exp $522,560
Library Holdings: Bk Vols 153,000; Per Subs 522
Subject Interests: Civil eng, Electrical eng, Marine eng, Mechanical eng, Naval archit
Automation Activity & Vendor Info: (Acquisitions) SirsiDynix; (Cataloging) SirsiDynix; (Circulation) SirsiDynix; (Course Reserve) SirsiDynix; (OPAC) SirsiDynix; (Serials) SirsiDynix
Database Vendor: American Chemical Society, American Geophysical Union, ASCE Research Library, CountryWatch, CQ Press, CredoReference, ebrary, EBSCOhost, Elsevier, Gale Cengage Learning, Grolier Online, IEEE (Institute of Electrical & Electronics Engineers), Jane's, JSTOR, Knovel, Oxford Online, ScienceDirect, SerialsSolutions, SirsiDynix, Springer-Verlag, Westlaw, WT Cox
Wireless access
Partic in Fedlink
Open Mon-Fri 7:30am-11pm, Sat & Sun 10am-11pm; Mon-Fri (Summer) 7:30-4:30

NEW MILFORD

P NEW MILFORD PUBLIC LIBRARY, 24 Main St, 06776. SAN 302-2706. Tel: 860-355-1191. Circulation Tel: 860-355-1191, Ext 201. Interlibrary Loan Service Tel: 860-355-1191, Ext 206. Reference Tel: 860-355-1191, Ext 207. Administration Tel: 860-355-1191, Ext 210. Automation Services Tel: 860-355-1191, Ext 211. FAX: 860-350-9579. TDD: 860-350-3418. Web Site: www.newmilfordlibrary.org. *Dir,* Mark P Hasskarl; E-mail: mhasskarl@biblio.org; *Ch Serv Librn,* Sue Ford; Tel: 860-355-1191, Ext 205, E-mail: sford@biblio.org; *Pub Serv Librn,* Sally Tornow; Tel: 860-355-1191, Ext 203, E-mail: stornow@biblio.org; *YA Librn,* Val Fisher; Tel: 860-355-1191, Ext 204, E-mail: vfisher@biblio.org; *Tech Coordr,* Peggy Ganong; E-mail: pganong@biblio.org; Staff 7 (MLS 5, Non-MLS 2)
Founded 1898. Pop 27,972; Circ 252,113
Jul 2013-Jun 2014 Income $1,085,523, State $4,770, City $977,100, Locally Generated Income $33,073, Other $70,580. Mats Exp $206,356, Books $117,763, Per/Ser (Incl. Access Fees) $10,129, Micro $1,080, AV Mat $36,798, Electronic Ref Mat (Incl. Access Fees) $40,586. Sal $599,878 (Prof $347,329)
Library Holdings: Audiobooks 766; CDs 4,973; DVDs 7,392; e-books 1,357; Large Print Bks 1,071; Microforms 338; Bk Vols 88,346; Per Subs 120; Videos 7,475
Special Collections: Connecticut, Local History

Automation Activity & Vendor Info: (Acquisitions) Baker & Taylor; (Cataloging) Evergreen; (Circulation) Evergreen; (ILL) Evergreen; (OPAC) Evergreen
Database Vendor: Baker & Taylor, Bibliomation Inc, EBSCO Auto Repair Reference, EBSCO Information Services, Gale Cengage Learning, LearningExpress, ProQuest, TumbleBookLibrary
Wireless access
Function: 24/7 Electronic res, 24/7 Online cat, Adult bk club, After school storytime, Art exhibits, Audiobks via web, Bks on CD, Children's prog, Computer training, Computers for patron use, Copy machines, Electronic databases & coll, Exhibits, Fax serv, Free DVD rentals, Handicapped accessible, Health sci info serv, ILL available, Magazines, Mango lang, Microfiche/film & reading machines, Movies, Mus passes, Music CDs, Notary serv, Online cat, Photocopying/Printing, Preschool outreach, Printer for laptops & handheld devices, Prog for adults, Prog for children & young adult, Pub access computers, Senior computer classes, Senior outreach, Story hour, Study rm, Summer & winter reading prog, Tax forms, Teen prog, Telephone ref
Publications: New Milford Public Library (Newsletter)
Partic in Bibliomation Inc
Special Services for the Deaf - Bks on deafness & sign lang
Special Services for the Blind - Bks on CD; Copier with enlargement capabilities; Large print bks; Playaways (bks on MP3)
Open Mon-Thurs 10-8, Fri 10-5, Sat 9-5, Sun (Oct-May) 1-5
Friends of the Library Group

NEWINGTON

G CONNDOT LIBRARY & INFORMATION CENTER*, 2800 Berlin Tpk, 06111-4113. SAN 302-4474. Tel: 860-594-3035. FAX: 860-594-3039. *Librn,* Betty Ambler; E-mail: betty.ambler@po.state.ct.us
Founded 1984
Library Holdings: Bk Vols 20,000
Automation Activity & Vendor Info: (Cataloging) OCLC; (ILL) OCLC
Restriction: Employees only

P LUCY ROBBINS WELLES LIBRARY*, 95 Cedar St, 06111-2645. SAN 302-2749. Reference Tel: 860-665-8700. Administration Tel: 860-665-8730. FAX: 860-667-1255. E-mail: refdept@newingtonct.gov. Web Site: www.newingtonct.gov/library. *Libr Dir,* Donna Miller; *Asst Dir,* Lisa Masten; *Head, Ch,* Pat Pierce; Tel: 860-665-8783; *Head, Coll Mgt,* Jeanette Francini; Tel: 860-665-8714; *Head, Commun Serv,* Shirlee-Ann Kober; Tel: 860-665-8707; *Head, Ref Serv,* Diane Durette; Tel: 860-665-8705; *Bus Mgr,* Lynn Caley; Tel: 860-665-8728; *ILL,* Terri Planco; Tel: 860-665-8718; *YA Serv,* Bailey Ortiz; Tel: 860-665-8704; Staff 15.75 (MLS 11, Non-MLS 4.75)
Founded 1752. Pop 29,699; Circ 404,506
Library Holdings: Audiobooks 3,254; DVDs 9,214; Bk Vols 140,654; Per Subs 258
Special Collections: Index of Local Newspaper; Local History Coll
Automation Activity & Vendor Info: (Acquisitions) SirsiDynix; (Cataloging) SirsiDynix; (Circulation) SirsiDynix; (OPAC) SIRSI-iBistro
Database Vendor: Bowker, EBSCOhost, Gale Cengage Learning, Grolier Online, Hoovers, infoUSA, LearningExpress, Overdrive, Inc, ProQuest, ReferenceUSA, SirsiDynix
Wireless access
Publications: Index of Local Newspaper; Newington Business Directory; Newington Information Packet
Partic in Connecticut Library Consortium; OCLC Online Computer Library Center, Inc
Open Mon-Thurs 10-9, Fri & Sat 10-5, Sun (Nov-May) 1-5
Friends of the Library Group

NEWTOWN

P CYRENIUS H BOOTH LIBRARY*, 25 Main St, 06470. SAN 302-2757. Tel: 203-426-4533. Reference Tel: 203 426-8552. Administration Tel: 203-426-1561. FAX: 203-426-2196. Reference FAX: 203-270-4536. E-mail: boothref@chboothlibrary.org, chbooth@biblio.org. Web Site: www.chboothlibrary.org. *Dir,* Brenda McKinley; *Asst Dir,* Beryl Harrison; E-mail: bharrison@chboothlibrary.org; *Head, Ref,* Andy Forsyth; *Ch,* Alana Bennison; Tel: 203-426-3851; *Circ Supvr,* Julie Hunter; *YA Serv,* Kim Weber; Tel: 203-426-4535, E-mail: chbya@chboothlibrary.org; Staff 37 (MLS 7, Non-MLS 30)
Founded 1932. Pop 25,000; Circ 240,000
Library Holdings: Bks on Deafness & Sign Lang 30; High Interest/Low Vocabulary Bk Vols 25; Large Print Bks 400; Bk Vols 130,000; Per Subs 507; Spec Interest Per Sub 36
Special Collections: Arts (Jack Landau Coll); Genealogy (Julia Brush Coll); Sculpture (John Angel Coll)
Subject Interests: Art & archit, Hist
Automation Activity & Vendor Info: (Acquisitions) Evergreen; (Cataloging) Evergreen; (Circulation) Evergreen; (ILL) Evergreen; (OPAC) Evergreen
Wireless access
Function: Archival coll, Homebound delivery serv, ILL available, Large print keyboards, Magnifiers for reading, Photocopying/Printing, Prog for children & young adult, Ref serv available, Summer reading prog, Telephone ref, Wheelchair accessible
Special Services for the Blind - Home delivery serv; Videos on blindness & phys handicaps
Open Mon-Thurs 9:30-8, Fri 11-5, Sat 9:30-5, Sun 12-5
Restriction: Open to pub for ref & circ; with some limitations
Friends of the Library Group

S GARNER CORRECTIONAL INSTITUTION LIBRARY*, 50 Nunnawauk Rd, 06470. Tel: 203-270-2897. FAX: 203-270-1826. *Media Spec,* Mark Aldrich
Library Holdings: Bk Vols 5,000; Per Subs 15
Automation Activity & Vendor Info: (Cataloging) Follett Software; (Circulation) Follett Software; (OPAC) Follett Software
Open Mon-Fri 8:30-10:30 & 1-3

NIANTIC

P EAST LYME PUBLIC LIBRARY, INC*, 39 Society Rd, 06357-1100. SAN 302-279X. Tel: 860-739-6926. FAX: 860-691-0020. E-mail: elpl@ely.lioninc.org. Web Site: www.lioninc.org/eastlyme. *Exec Dir,* William Deakyne; *Asst Dir,* Lisa Timothy; *Cat,* Lydia Main; *Ch Serv,* Randy Haines; *Circ,* Jean Jones; *Circ,* Patricia Reynolds; *Computer Serv, Ref Serv,* Catherine Shields
Founded 1868. Pop 18,118; Circ 161,938
Jul 2005-Jun 2006 Income $910,640, State $3,689, City $817,241, Locally Generated Income $89,710. Mats Exp $120,876, Books $82,533, Per/Ser (Incl. Access Fees) $20,000, Micro $8,434, AV Mat $6,054, Presv $3,855. Sal $509,470
Library Holdings: CDs 671; DVDs 365; Bk Titles 100,000; Bk Vols 103,000; Per Subs 218; Talking Bks 1,224; Videos 2,322
Special Collections: East Lyme Manuscript Coll; The Chadwick Letters; The Comstock Letter; Victor Frank Ridder & Marie Thompson Ridder Music Coll
Subject Interests: Am Indians, Chinese lang, Fr lang, Gardening, Genealogy, Greek, Local hist
Automation Activity & Vendor Info: (Acquisitions) Innovative Interfaces, Inc; (Cataloging) Innovative Interfaces, Inc; (Circulation) Innovative Interfaces, Inc; (ILL) Innovative Interfaces, Inc; (OPAC) Innovative Interfaces, Inc; (Serials) Innovative Interfaces, Inc
Wireless access
Publications: Annual report; Bibliographic & Program Brochures; Dear & Affectionate Wife, the Letters of Charles & Mary Chadwick, 1828-1851
Partic in Connecticut Library Consortium; Libraries Online, Inc
Open Mon-Wed 9-9, Thurs 9-6, Fri 9-5, Sat 10-4, Sun 1-4
Friends of the Library Group

S GATES CORRECTIONAL INSTITUTION LIBRARY*, 131 N Bridebrook Rd, 06357. Tel: 860-691-4772. FAX: 860-691-4769.
Library Holdings: Bk Titles 15,000; Bk Vols 16,000; Per Subs 22
Special Collections: Black Heritage; Spanish Heritage
Open Mon-Wed 8-2:30, Thurs 9-2:30

S YORK CORRECTIONAL INSTITUTION LIBRARY*, 201 W Main St, 06357. SAN 371-7984. Tel: 860-691-6810, 860-691-6814. FAX: 860-691-6864. *Media Spec,* Joe Lea
Library Holdings: Bk Vols 10,000; Per Subs 20
Special Collections: Law
Publications: The Niantic Voice (Newspaper)
Open Mon-Fri 7:30-3:30

NORFOLK

P NORFOLK LIBRARY*, Nine Greenwoods Rd E, 06058-1320. (Mail add: PO Box 605, 06058-0605), SAN 302-2811. Tel: 860-542-5075. FAX: 860-542-1795. E-mail: norfolklibrary@biblio.org. Web Site: www.norfolklibrary.org. *Interim Dir,* Ann Havemeyer; *Ch Serv,* Eileen Fitzgibbons; E-mail: efitzgibbons@biblio.org; *Tech Serv,* Maryann Anderson; E-mail: manderson@biblio.org; Staff 5 (MLS 1, Non-MLS 4)
Founded 1889. Pop 1,800; Circ 27,000
Library Holdings: Bk Titles 30,000
Special Collections: Fishing & Hunting (Barbour Coll)
Publications: The Owl (Newsletter)
Open Mon 10-7, Tues-Fri 10-5, Sat 10-2, Sun 1-4
Friends of the Library Group

NORTH BRANFORD

P NORTH BRANFORD LIBRARY DEPARTMENT*, Atwater Memorial, 1720 Foxon Rd, 06471. (Mail add: PO Box 258, 06471-0258), SAN 336-4623. Tel: 203-315-6020. FAX: 203-315-6021. *Dir,* Robert V Hull; E-mail: rvhull76@yahoo.com
Library Holdings: Bk Vols 60,000; Per Subs 210

Automation Activity & Vendor Info: (Cataloging) Innovative Interfaces, Inc; (Circulation) Innovative Interfaces, Inc; (OPAC) Innovative Interfaces, Inc
Open Mon-Thurs (Winter) 11-8, Fri 9-6, Sat 9-3; Mon-Thurs (Summer) 11-8, Fri 9-6, Sat 9-12
Friends of the Library Group
Branches: 1
EDWARD SMITH BRANCH, Three Old Post Rd, Northford, 06472. (Mail add: PO Box 130, Northford, 06472-0130), SAN 336-4682. Tel: 203-484-0469. FAX: 203-484-6024. *Dir,* Robert Hull; E-mail: rvhull76@yahoo.com
Open Mon-Thurs 11-8, Fri 9-6, Sat 9-3 (9-12 Summer)
Friends of the Library Group

NORTH GROSVENORDALE

P THOMPSON PUBLIC LIBRARY*, 934 Riverside Dr, 06255. (Mail add: PO Box 855, 06255-0855), SAN 336-5131. Tel: 860-923-9779. FAX: 860-923-3705. Web Site: www.thompsonpubliclibrary.org. *Dir,* Alison Boutaugh; E-mail: aboutaugh@thompsonpubliclibrary.org; Staff 10 (MLS 1, Non-MLS 9)
Founded 1902. Pop 9,324; Circ 85,400
Library Holdings: Bk Vols 55,000; Per Subs 97
Subject Interests: Local hist
Automation Activity & Vendor Info: (Acquisitions) Evergreen; (Cataloging) Bibliomation Inc; (Circulation) Evergreen; (OPAC) Evergreen
Wireless access
Function: Adult bk club, Art exhibits, Audiobks via web, Computers for patron use, Copy machines, Handicapped accessible, Homebound delivery serv, Large print keyboards, Magnifiers for reading, Mus passes, Prog for adults, Prog for children & young adult, Scanner, Story hour, Summer reading prog, Tax forms
Open Mon-Thurs 10-8, Fri 10-5, Sat 10-2
Friends of the Library Group

NORTH HAVEN

P NORTH HAVEN MEMORIAL LIBRARY*, 17 Elm St, 06473. SAN 302-2838. Tel: 203-239-5803. FAX: 203-234-2130. Web Site: www.leaplibraries.org/nhaven. *Dir, Libr Serv,* Lois D Baldini; *Asst Dir,* Patricia A Dortenzio; E-mail: pdortenzio@leaplibraries.org; *Ch Serv,* Patricia Laterza; E-mail: platerza@leaplibraries.org; *Ref,* Nancy Haag; E-mail: nhaag@leaplibraries.org; Staff 20 (MLS 7, Non-MLS 13)
Founded 1894
Library Holdings: AV Mats 7,752; Bk Vols 95,387; Per Subs 225
Special Collections: Rotary Job & Career Corner, AV sets, DVD's
Subject Interests: Cassettes, Compact discs
Automation Activity & Vendor Info: (Circulation) Innovative Interfaces, Inc; (OPAC) Innovative Interfaces, Inc
Database Vendor: ProQuest
Function: ILL available
Partic in Library Exchange Aids Patrons
Special Services for the Blind - Large print & cassettes; Reader equip
Open Mon-Thurs (Sept June) 11-9, Sat 10-5
Friends of the Library Group

NORTH STONINGTON

P WHEELER LIBRARY*, 101 Main St, 06359. (Mail add: PO Box 217, 06359-0217), SAN 302-2862. Tel: 860-535-0383. E-mail: wheelerlibrary@hotmail.com. Web Site: www.wheelerlibrary.org. *Dir,* Amy Kennedy
Founded 1900. Pop 111,489
Library Holdings: Bk Vols 32,000; Per Subs 84
Subject Interests: Local hist, World War II
Automation Activity & Vendor Info: (Cataloging) Auto-Graphics, Inc; (Circulation) Auto-Graphics, Inc; (OPAC) Auto-Graphics, Inc
Open Mon, Wed & Fri 10-4, Tues & Thurs 10-8, Sat 9-12
Friends of the Library Group
Bookmobiles: 1

NORTHFIELD

P GILBERT LIBRARY, INC*, 38 Main St, 06778. SAN 302-2870. Tel: 860-283-8176. E-mail: gilbert.library@snet.net. *Librn,* Nancy Gnitzcavich
Founded 1892. Pop 1,000; Circ 8,675
Library Holdings: Bk Titles 8,385; Per Subs 50
Special Collections: Local History, scrapbks
Open Mon, Wed & Fri 2-7

NORWALK

P EAST NORWALK IMPROVEMENT ASSOCIATION LIBRARY*, 51 Van Zant St, 06855. SAN 302-2900. Tel: 203-838-0408. Web Site: www.eastnorwalklibrary.org. *Librn,* Maureen Tovish; E-mail: maureen@eastnorwalklibrary.org
Pop 6,540; Circ 50,941
Library Holdings: Bk Vols 25,000; Per Subs 100
Automation Activity & Vendor Info: (Cataloging) Follett Software; (Circulation) Follett Software
Open Mon-Fri 12:30-5:30, Sat 9:30-5:30

S FINANCIAL ACCOUNTING FOUNDATION LIBRARY*, 401 Merritt 7, 06856-5116. (Mail add: PO Box 5116, 06856-5116), SAN 320-619X. Tel: 203-956-5238. FAX: 203-956-3492. E-mail: library@f-a-f.org. Web Site: www.fasb.org. *Librn,* Charry D Boris; E-mail: cdborris@f-a-f.org; *Assoc Librn,* Miriam A Solomon; E-mail: masolomon@f-a-f.org
Founded 1973
Library Holdings: Bk Vols 5,000; Per Subs 300
Subject Interests: Acctg, Finance
Automation Activity & Vendor Info: (Acquisitions) EOS International; (Cataloging) EOS International; (OPAC) EOS International; (Serials) EOS International
Wireless access
Partic in Connecticut Library Consortium
Restriction: Not open to pub

S NORTHROP GRUMMAN NORDEN SYSTEMS*, Library & Information Services, 10000 Norden Pl, 06854-2807. Tel: 203-852-5886. FAX: 203-852-4579. *Libr Assoc,* Linda Asik
Founded 1943
Library Holdings: Bk Vols 5,000; Per Subs 111
Subject Interests: Bus & mgt, Electrical eng, Electronics, Math
Partic in Dialog Corp
Restriction: Not open to pub
Friends of the Library Group

J NORWALK COMMUNITY COLLEGE*, Baker Library, 188 Richards Ave, 06854-1655. SAN 302-2935. Tel: 203-857-7200. Reference Tel: 203-857-7379. FAX: 203-857-7380. Web Site: www.norwalk.edu/library. *Dir,* Linda Lerman; E-mail: llerman@norwalk.edu; *Ref Librn,* Martha Kruy; Tel: 203-857-7208, E-mail: mkruy@norwalk.edu; *Coordr, Circ,* Liz Pisaretz; E-mail: lpisaretz@norwalk.edu; *Acq, Ref Serv,* Curleen Elliott; E-mail: celliott@norwalk.edu; *Ref,* Gunnar Sahlin; E-mail: gsahlin@norwalk.edu; *Syst, Tech Serv,* Ann Sommers; E-mail: asommers@norwalk.edu. Subject Specialists: *Info literacy,* Martha Kruy; Staff 7 (MLS 5, Non-MLS 2)
Highest Degree: Associate
Library Holdings: AV Mats 21,000; e-books 86,000; e-journals 57,000; Bk Vols 65,000; Per Subs 200
Automation Activity & Vendor Info: (Acquisitions) Ex Libris Group; (Cataloging) Ex Libris Group; (Circulation) Ex Libris Group; (Course Reserve) Ex Libris Group; (ILL) Ex Libris Group; (OPAC) Ex Libris Group; (Serials) Ex Libris Group
Database Vendor: ARTstor, EBSCOhost, Gale Cengage Learning, JSTOR, LexisNexis, OCLC FirstSearch, ProQuest, Westlaw, YBP Library Services
Wireless access
Partic in OCLC Online Computer Library Center, Inc; ReQuest OPAC Catalog
Open Mon-Thurs 8:30-8, Fri-Sun 10-3

M NORWALK HOSPITAL, Wiggans Health Sciences Library, Maple St, 06856. SAN 336-4712. Tel: 203-852-2793. FAX: 203-855-3575. *Dir,* Jill Golrick; Staff 1 (MLS 1)
Founded 1950
Library Holdings: e-books 100; e-journals 500; Bk Titles 1,500; Bk Vols 2,500; Per Subs 150
Subject Interests: Med
Wireless access
Partic in Conn Asn of Health Scis Librs; Health Info Librs of Westchester (HILOW)
Restriction: Badge access after hrs, Circ limited

P NORWALK PUBLIC LIBRARY*, One Belden Ave, 06850. SAN 336-4771. Tel: 203-899-2780. FAX: 203-866-7982. E-mail: informationnpl@norwalkpubliclibrary.org. Web Site: www.norwalkpubliclibrary.org. *Dir,* Christine Bradley; *Asst Dir,* Sherelle Harris; *Ch Serv,* Vicki Oatis; *Tech Serv,* Tom Schadlich; Staff 60 (MLS 20, Non-MLS 40)
Founded 1895. Pop 82,000; Circ 450,000
Jul 2005-Jun 2006 Income (Main Library and Branch(s)) $3,085,125. Mats Exp $492,270, Books $245,006, Per/Ser (Incl. Access Fees) $162,264, AV Mat $45,000, Electronic Ref Mat (Incl. Access Fees) $40,000. Sal $2,239,811 (Prof $871,004)
Library Holdings: AV Mats 28,426; Bk Titles 140,000; Bk Vols 225,000; Per Subs 410
Automation Activity & Vendor Info: (Acquisitions) Innovative Interfaces, Inc; (Cataloging) Innovative Interfaces, Inc; (Circulation) Innovative Interfaces, Inc; (OPAC) Innovative Interfaces, Inc

Open Mon & Wed 9-8:30, Tues, Fri & Sat 9-5:30
Friends of the Library Group
Branches: 1
SOUTH NORWALK BRANCH, Ten Washington St, South Norwalk, 06854, SAN 336-4801. Tel: 203-899-2790. FAX: 203-899-2788. *Librn,* Reginald St Fort; E-mail: rstfort@yahoo.com
Library Holdings: Bk Vols 71,654
Subject Interests: Gen interest
Open Mon & Wed-Fri 9-5:30, Tues 12-8:30

NORWICH

P OTIS LIBRARY*, Two Cliff St, 06360. SAN 302-3044. Tel: 860-889-2365. FAX: 860-886-4744. Web Site: www.otislibrarynorwich.org. *Dir,* Bob Farwell; *Cat,* Nancy Bruckner; *Ch Serv,* Laurie Emerson; *Ref Serv, Ad,* Tara Samuels; Tel: 860-889-2365, Ext 13; Staff 30 (MLS 3, Non-MLS 27)
Founded 1850. Pop 39,500; Circ 200,000
Library Holdings: Bk Vols 99,000; Per Subs 158
Special Collections: Genealogy & Local Hist; Large Print
Subject Interests: Bus & mgt, Careers
Automation Activity & Vendor Info: (Acquisitions) Innovative Interfaces, Inc; (Cataloging) Innovative Interfaces, Inc; (Circulation) Innovative Interfaces, Inc; (Course Reserve) Innovative Interfaces, Inc; (ILL) Innovative Interfaces, Inc; (Media Booking) Innovative Interfaces, Inc; (OPAC) Innovative Interfaces, Inc; (Serials) Innovative Interfaces, Inc
Database Vendor: Gale Cengage Learning
Function: ILL available
Publications: Monthly Activities Calendar
Partic in Connecticut Library Consortium; Libraries Online, Inc
Special Services for the Blind - Bks on cassette; Large print bks
Open Mon-Thurs 9-8, Fri & Sat 9-5, Sun (Oct-Apr) 12-4
Friends of the Library Group

J THREE RIVERS COMMUNITY COLLEGE*, Donald R Welter Library, 574 New London Tpk, 06360-6598. SAN 302-3060. Tel: 860-892-5713. Reference Tel: 860-383-5289. FAX: 860-886-0691. *Dir of Libr Serv,* Mildred Hodge; Tel: 860-892-5727, E-mail: MHodge@trcc.commnet.edu; *Ref & Instruction Librn,* Pam Williams; E-mail: PWilliams@trcc.commnet.edu; Staff 7 (MLS 2, Non-MLS 5)
Founded 1964. Enrl 4,000; Fac 96; Highest Degree: Associate
Library Holdings: AV Mats 2,937; Bk Titles 51,186; Per Subs 420
Special Collections: Local Public Records Room; Nuclear Regulatory Commission Documents
Automation Activity & Vendor Info: (Acquisitions) Ex Libris Group; (Cataloging) Ex Libris Group; (Circulation) Ex Libris Group; (Course Reserve) Ex Libris Group; (ILL) OCLC; (OPAC) Ex Libris Group; (Serials) EBSCO Online
Database Vendor: EBSCOhost, Gale Cengage Learning

OLD GREENWICH

P PERROT MEMORIAL LIBRARY*, 90 Sound Beach Ave, 06870. SAN 302-3095. Tel: 203-637-1066. Reference Tel: 203-637-3870. FAX: 203-698-2620. Web Site: www.perrotlibrary.org. *Dir,* Kevin McCarthy; E-mail: kevinm@perrotlibrary.org; *Asst Dir, Ref,* Linda White; *Dir, Youth Serv,* Kathy Jarombek; Tel: 203-637-8802; *Circ,* Kathy McLennan; *Tech Serv,* Mirja Johanson
Founded 1905. Pop 62,000; Circ 262,163
Jul 2010-Jun 2011 Income $1,508,088
Library Holdings: Bk Vols 70,000
Special Collections: Oral History
Subject Interests: Cooking, Gardening, Sailing
Automation Activity & Vendor Info: (Acquisitions) Innovative Interfaces, Inc; (Cataloging) Innovative Interfaces, Inc; (Circulation) Innovative Interfaces, Inc - Millenium; (OPAC) Innovative Interfaces, Inc
Database Vendor: EBSCOhost, Factiva.com, Gale Cengage Learning, OCLC FirstSearch, ProQuest
Wireless access
Publications: Precis (Newsletter)
Partic in Connecticut Library Consortium; OCLC Online Computer Library Center, Inc
Special Services for the Blind - Closed circuit TV
Open Mon, Wed & Fri 9-6, Tues & Thurs 9-8, Sat 9-5, Sun 1-5

OLD LYME

C LYME ACADEMY COLLEGE OF FINE ARTS, Krieble Library, 84 Lyme St, 06371-2333. Tel: 860-434-5232, Ext 130. FAX: 860-434-2095. E-mail: library@lymefs.newhaven.edu. Web Site: www.lymeacademy.edu/index.php/about/the_krieble_library. *Librn,* Loree Bourgoin; Tel: 860-434-3571, Ext 130, E-mail: lbourgoin@lymefs.newhaven.edu; *Coordr, Access Serv,* Joe Shea; E-mail: jshea@lymefs.newhaven.edu; Staff 2 (MLS 1, Non-MLS 1)
Founded 1991. Enrl 200; Fac 23; Highest Degree: Bachelor
Library Holdings: AV Mats 25,306; Electronic Media & Resources 20; Bk Titles 13,291; Per Subs 79
Subject Interests: Drawing, Fine arts, Painting, Sculpture
Automation Activity & Vendor Info: (Cataloging) Follett Software; (Circulation) Follett Software; (ILL) OCLC; (OPAC) Follett Software
Database Vendor: ARTstor, EBSCOhost, Oxford Online
Wireless access
Partic in Connecticut Library Consortium
Open Mon-Thurs (Spring & Fall) 8am-10pm, Fri 8-5, Sat & Sun 12-5; Mon-Fri (Summer) 9-5
Restriction: Open to pub for ref only, Open to students, fac & staff

S LYME HISTORICAL SOCIETY LIBRARY*, 96 Lyme St, 06371. SAN 302-3109. Tel: 860-434-5542. FAX: 860-434-9778. Web Site: www.florencegriswold.org. *Dir,* Jeff Andersen; E-mail: jeff@flogris.org
Founded 1956
Library Holdings: Bk Titles 700
Special Collections: Art Colony at Old Lyme Archives; History of Lyme & Old Lyme Conn; Papers of Local Families
Subject Interests: Connecticut, Genealogy, Local hist
Restriction: Open by appt only

P OLD LYME*, Phoebe Griffin Noyes Library, Two Library Lane, 06371. SAN 302-3117. Tel: 860-434-1684. Administration Tel: 860-434-1802. FAX: 860-434-9547. Web Site: www.oldlyme.lioninc.org. *Dir,* Mary Fiorelli; E-mail: mfiorell@oldlyme.lioninc.org; *YA Librn,* Susan Parodi; E-mail: sparodi@oldlyme.lioninc.org; *Circ Supvr,* Stephanie Romano; E-mail: sromano@oldlyme.lioninc.org; *Ch Serv,* Ronna Keith; E-mail: rkeith@oldlyme.lioninc.org; *Info Serv,* Linda Alexander; E-mail: lalexander@oldlyme.lioninc.org; *Info Serv, Tech Spec,* Abhar Nauqti; E-mail: anauqti@oldlyme.lioninc.org; Staff 9 (MLS 5, Non-MLS 4)
Founded 1898. Pop 7,525; Circ 74,661
Jul 2010-Jun 2011 Income $626,401, State $3,087, City $255,000, Locally Generated Income $75,274, Parent Institution $188,400. Mats Exp $78,366, Books $50,169, Electronic Ref Mat (Incl. Access Fees) $28,197. Sal $304,796 (Prof $45,000)
Library Holdings: AV Mats 4,190; Electronic Media & Resources 30; Bk Titles 42,155; Per Subs 30
Subject Interests: Genealogy, Local hist
Automation Activity & Vendor Info: (Acquisitions) Innovative Interfaces, Inc; (Cataloging) Innovative Interfaces, Inc; (Circulation) Innovative Interfaces, Inc; (ILL) Auto-Graphics, Inc; (OPAC) Innovative Interfaces, Inc; (Serials) Innovative Interfaces, Inc
Database Vendor: Gale Cengage Learning, OCLC FirstSearch
Wireless access
Publications: More Than Just Books (Newsletter)
Partic in Libraries Online, Inc
Open Mon & Wed 10-7, Tues & Thurs 10-6, Fri 10-5, Sat 10-4
Friends of the Library Group

OLD MYSTIC

S INDIAN & COLONIAL RESEARCH CENTER, INC, Butler Library, 39 Main St Rte 27, 06372. (Mail add: PO Box 525, 06372-0525), SAN 302-3125. Tel: 860-536-9771. E-mail: icrc06372@yahoo.com. Web Site: www.theicrc.org. *Pres,* Kimberly Hatcher-White
Founded 1965
Library Holdings: Bk Vols 3,500
Special Collections: Glass Plate negatives & prints 1890-1920; Local Genealogy; Rare American School Books. Oral History
Subject Interests: Am Indians, Genealogy
Publications: Along Shore; Around the Pond; Two Little Navahos Dip Their Sheep; When the Frogs Begin to Peep

OLD SAYBROOK

P ACTON PUBLIC LIBRARY*, 60 Old Boston Post Rd, 06475-2200. SAN 302-3133. Tel: 860-395-3184. FAX: 860-395-2462. E-mail: actonpubliclibrary@gmail.com. Web Site: www.oldsaybrookct.org/library. *Dir,* Michele Van Epps; *Ref Librn,* Wendy Connal; E-mail: actonref@gmail.com; Staff 17 (MLS 4, Non-MLS 13)
Founded 1873. Pop 10,535; Circ 244,218
Jul 2006-Jun 2007 Income $640,542, State $2,000, City $638,542. Mats Exp $96,983, Books $82,206, Per/Ser (Incl. Access Fees) $7,633, AV Mat $7,144. Sal $429,398 (Prof $219,247)
Library Holdings: CDs 1,023; DVDs 402; Large Print Bks 3,200; Bk Vols 71,180; Per Subs 133; Talking Bks 1,520; Videos 1,440
Subject Interests: Local hist
Automation Activity & Vendor Info: (Cataloging) Follett Software
Wireless access
Function: Adult bk club, Adult literacy prog, Bk club(s), Copy machines, Digital talking bks, Handicapped accessible, Homebound delivery serv, ILL available, Magnifiers for reading, Mail & tel request accepted, Online ref, Orientations, Preschool outreach, Prof lending libr, Prog for adults, Prog for children & young adult, Ref serv available, Satellite serv, Spoken

cassettes & CDs, Summer reading prog, Tax forms, Telephone ref, VHS videos, Video lending libr, Wheelchair accessible
Publications: Old Saybrook Events (Quarterly)
Open Mon-Thurs 10-8:30, Fri & Sat 9-5, Sun (Oct-May) 1-5
Friends of the Library Group

ONECO

P STERLING PUBLIC LIBRARY*, 1183 Plainfield Pike, 06373. (Mail add: PO Box 158, 06373-0158), SAN 323-6226. Tel: 860-564-2692. FAX: 860-564-0789. E-mail: sterlingpublib@ct.metrocast.net. *Chairperson,* Holly J Wood; *Librn,* Rachel Vincent
Founded 1928. Pop 3,400
Library Holdings: CDs 75; DVDs 375; Large Print Bks 150; Bk Titles 21,000; Per Subs 25
Function: ILL available, Photocopying/Printing
Open Tues 10-7:45, Thurs 1-7:45, Sat 10-2:45

ORANGE

P CASE MEMORIAL LIBRARY*, 176 Tyler City Rd, 06477-2498. SAN 302-315X. Tel: 203-891-2170. FAX: 203-891-2190. Web Site: www.lioninc.org. *Dir,* Meryl P Farber; E-mail: mfarber@lioninc.org; *Ch,* Helena Estes; E-mail: hestes@lioninc.org; *Adult Serv, Ref,* Rebecca Harlow; E-mail: rharlow@lioninc.org; *Cat,* Jonathan Wiener; E-mail: jwiener@lioninc.org; *Circ,* Robert Knapik; E-mail: rknapik@lioninc.org; Staff 14 (MLS 5, Non-MLS 9)
Founded 1956. Pop 13,233; Circ 137,000
Library Holdings: AV Mats 12,056; Bk Vols 103,957; Per Subs 143
Subject Interests: Local hist
Automation Activity & Vendor Info: (Acquisitions) Innovative Interfaces, Inc; (Cataloging) Innovative Interfaces, Inc; (Circulation) Innovative Interfaces, Inc; (ILL) Innovative Interfaces, Inc - Millenium; (OPAC) Innovative Interfaces, Inc
Database Vendor: Gale Cengage Learning
Wireless access
Partic in Libraries Online, Inc
Open Mon-Thurs (Winter) 10-8, Fri 10-5, Sat 10-4; Mon & Thurs (Summer) 10-8, Tues & Wed 10-5, Sat 10-4
Friends of the Library Group

OXFORD

P OXFORD PUBLIC LIBRARY*, 486 Oxford Rd, 06478. SAN 302-3176. Tel: 203-888-6944. FAX: 203-888-2666. E-mail: oxlib@yahoo.com. Web Site: www.oxfordlib.org. *Dir,* Dawn Higginson; E-mail: dhigginson@oxfordlib.org; Staff 4.8 (MLS 2.8, Non-MLS 2)
Founded 1883. Pop 12,800; Circ 49,000
Jul 2012-Jun 2013 Income $248,519, State $1,000, City $243,319, Locally Generated Income $4,200. Mats Exp $23,000, Books $19,000, Per/Ser (Incl. Access Fees) $3,000, Electronic Ref Mat (Incl. Access Fees) $1,000. Sal $188,332 (Prof $170,062)
Library Holdings: Bk Vols 30,000; Per Subs 40
Subject Interests: Hist
Automation Activity & Vendor Info: (Acquisitions) Bibliomation Inc; (Cataloging) Evergreen; (Circulation) Evergreen; (OPAC) Evergreen
Database Vendor: Baker & Taylor, Bibliomation Inc, Gale Cengage Learning, Overdrive, Inc
Wireless access
Function: Adult bk club, Art exhibits, Audiobks via web, Bks on cassette, Bks on CD, Computers for patron use, Copy machines, e-mail serv, Free DVD rentals, Handicapped accessible, ILL available, Mus passes, Music CDs, Online cat, OverDrive digital audio bks, Photocopying/Printing, Prog for adults, Prog for children & young adult, Pub access computers, Ref serv available, Spoken cassettes & CDs, Spoken cassettes & DVDs, Story hour, Summer reading prog, Teen prog, VHS videos
Open Mon & Thurs 8-8, Tues, Wed & Fri 8-5
Friends of the Library Group

PLAINVILLE

S CONNECTICUT CLEARINGHOUSE LIBRARY*, 334 Farmington Ave, 06062-1321. SAN 378-3723. Tel: 860-793-9797. Toll Free Tel: 800-232-4424. FAX: 860-793-9813. E-mail: info@ctclearinghouse.org. Web Site: www.ctclearinghouse.org.
Library Holdings: AV Mats 1,600; Bk Titles 3,600
Subject Interests: Mental health, Substance abuse, Wellness
Automation Activity & Vendor Info: (Cataloging) SirsiDynix; (OPAC) SirsiDynix
Open Mon-Wed & Fri 8:30-5, Thurs 8:30-7:30

P PLAINVILLE PUBLIC LIBRARY*, 56 E Main St, 06062. SAN 302-3206. Tel: 860-793-1446. FAX: 860-793-2241. E-mail: plainvillepubliclibrary@gmail.com. Web Site: www.plainvillelibrary.org. *Dir,* Peter F Chase; Staff 4 (MLS 3, Non-MLS 1)
Founded 1894. Pop 16,770; Circ 153,239
Library Holdings: Bk Vols 94,000; Per Subs 164
Automation Activity & Vendor Info: (Cataloging) SirsiDynix; (Circulation) SirsiDynix; (OPAC) SirsiDynix
Wireless access
Partic in Connecticut Library Consortium; SAILS Library Network
Open Mon-Thurs 10-9, Fri & Sat 10-5
Friends of the Library Group

PLYMOUTH

P PLYMOUTH LIBRARY ASSOCIATION*, 692 Main St, 06782. SAN 302-3222. Tel: 860-283-5977. *Librn,* Johannah Synott
Founded 1871. Pop 3,500
Library Holdings: Bk Titles 9,521; Per Subs 16
Special Collections: Local History (Plymouth Coll)
Wireless access
Partic in Region I Coop Libr Servs Unit
Open Mon, Wed & Fri 10-5, Sat 10-2

POMFRET

R CHRIST CHURCH LIBRARY*, 527 Pomfret St, 06258. (Mail add: PO Box 21, 06258-0021). Tel: 860-928-7026. FAX: 860-963-2684. *Librn,* Joy Daentl; *Librn,* Carole Gooder; Staff 1 (Non-MLS 1)
Founded 1988
Library Holdings: Bk Titles 2,000
Function: Prof lending libr
Friends of the Library Group

P POMFRET PUBLIC LIBRARY, 449 Pomfret St, 06258. (Mail add: PO Box 91, 06258-0091), SAN 302-3230. Tel: 860-928-3475. Web Site: www.pomfretlibrary.org. *Dir,* Laurie M Bell; E-mail: lbell@pomfretlibrary.org; *Children's Prog Mgr,* Kristin Lavitt; E-mail: klavitt@pomfretlibrary.org; *Libr Asst,* Jackie Santerren; Staff 1.5 (MLS 0.5, Non-MLS 1)
Founded 1740. Pop 4,000; Circ 12,600
Library Holdings: Bk Vols 22,000; Per Subs 50
Special Collections: Pomfret & Windham County Historical Coll. Oral History
Wireless access
Function: Bk club(s), Copy machines, Fax serv, Handicapped accessible, ILL available, Prog for children & young adult, Summer reading prog
Partic in Connecticut Library Consortium
Special Services for the Blind - Bks on cassette; Bks on CD; Large print bks; Lending of low vision aids
Open Tues 10-7, Thurs 10-5, Fri 2-7, Sat 10-1
Friends of the Library Group

PORTLAND

P PORTLAND LIBRARY, 20 Freestone Ave, 06480. SAN 302-3257. Tel: 860-342-6770. FAX: 860-342-6778. Web Site: www.portlandlibraryct.org. *Dir,* Janet Nocek; E-mail: jnocek@portlandct.org; *Asst Dir,* Anne Calvert; E-mail: acalvert@portlandct.org
Founded 1895. Pop 9,052; Circ 145,000
Library Holdings: Bk Vols 60,000; Per Subs 256
Subject Interests: Local hist
Automation Activity & Vendor Info: (Cataloging) Innovative Interfaces, Inc; (Circulation) SirsiDynix; (OPAC) Innovative Interfaces, Inc
Database Vendor: EBSCOhost, ProQuest
Wireless access
Function: Prog for children & young adult
Partic in Connecticut Library Consortium; Library Connection, Inc
Special Services for the Blind - Audio mat; Bks on cassette; Bks on CD; Large print bks; Magnifiers
Open Mon-Wed 10-8, Thurs 12-8, Fri & Sat 10-5
Friends of the Library Group

PRESTON

P PRESTON PUBLIC LIBRARY*, 389 Rt 2, 06365. SAN 376-3242. Tel: 860-886-1010. FAX: 860-886-4952. E-mail: library@prestonlibrary.org. Web Site: prestonlibrary.org. *Dir,* Denise Bachand; *Asst Dir,* Susan Brosnan. Subject Specialists: *Local genealogy,* Susan Brosnan; Staff 7 (Non-MLS 7)
Founded 1898. Pop 5,500
Jul 2008-Jun 2009 Income $162,000. Mats Exp $162,000
Library Holdings: Bks on Deafness & Sign Lang 50; Large Print Bks 858; Bk Vols 27,000; Per Subs 40; Talking Bks 450; Videos 1,877
Special Collections: Preston Historical Society Coll
Subject Interests: Genealogy
Automation Activity & Vendor Info: (Cataloging) Auto-Graphics, Inc; (Circulation) Auto-Graphics, Inc; (ILL) Auto-Graphics, Inc; (OPAC) Auto-Graphics, Inc
Wireless access

Function: Adult bk club, Bks on cassette, Bks on CD, CD-ROM, Children's prog, Computer training, Computers for patron use, Copy machines, Digital talking bks, E-Reserves, Electronic databases & coll, Fax serv, Free DVD rentals, Handicapped accessible, Homebound delivery serv, ILL available, Large print keyboards, Learning ctr, Magnifiers for reading, Mus passes, Music CDs, Online cat, Photocopying/Printing, Prog for adults, Prog for children & young adult, Pub access computers, Ref serv available, Story hour, Summer reading prog, Tax forms, VHS videos, Wheelchair accessible
Special Services for the Deaf - Assistive tech; Bks on deafness & sign lang; Closed caption videos; TTY equip
Special Services for the Blind - Assistive/Adapted tech devices, equip & products; Closed circuit TV; Dragon Naturally Speaking software; Large print bks; Magnifiers; Reader equip; Talking bks
Open Mon 9-3, Tues-Thurs 9-8, Fri 9-5, Sat 9-1
Friends of the Library Group

PROSPECT

P PROSPECT PUBLIC LIBRARY*, 17 Center St, 06712. SAN 302-3273. Tel: 203-758-3001. FAX: 203-758-0080. E-mail: libraryprospect@yahoo.com. Web Site: www.prospectct.com/library. *Dir,* John Wiehn; *Asst Dir,* Lisa Murno; Staff 4 (MLS 2, Non-MLS 2)
Founded 1904. Pop 8,500; Circ 65,000
Library Holdings: Bk Vols 42,000; Per Subs 42
Special Collections: Large Print-Mysteries
Automation Activity & Vendor Info: (Cataloging) Auto-Graphics, Inc; (Circulation) Auto-Graphics, Inc; (OPAC) Auto-Graphics, Inc
Wireless access
Partic in Connecticut Library Consortium
Open Mon, Wed & Fri 10-5, Tues & Thurs 10-8, Sat 10-3
Friends of the Library Group

PUTNAM

M LAPALME HEALTH SCIENCES LIBRARY*, 320 Pomfret St, 06260. SAN 302-329X. Tel: 860-928-6541, Ext 2596. FAX: 860-928-1398. *Mgr,* Jane Duffany; Staff 1 (Non-MLS 1)
Founded 1973
Library Holdings: Bk Titles 500; Per Subs 65
Partic in Conn Asn of Health Scis Librs
Open Mon-Thurs 8-4:30

P PUTNAM PUBLIC LIBRARY, 225 Kennedy Dr, 06260-1691. SAN 302-3303. Tel: 860-963-6826. FAX: 860-963-6828. E-mail: ppl2252000@yahoo.com. *Dir,* Priscilla Colwell; E-mail: priscilla.colwell@putnamct.us; *Dir of Circ,* Kathleen Raymond; *Asst Dir, Ch,* Tina Aubin; *Ad,* Patricia Jensen; Staff 6.75 (MLS 1.75, Non-MLS 5)
Founded 1884. Pop 9,307; Circ 80,766
Jul 2009-Jun 2010 Income $459,877, State $11,741, City $444,286, Locally Generated Income $750, Other $3,100. Mats Exp $31,316, Books $22,074, Per/Ser (Incl. Access Fees) $4,742, AV Mat $4,500. Sal $220,507
Library Holdings: Bk Vols 38,376; Per Subs 66
Special Collections: Genealogy Coll
Automation Activity & Vendor Info: (Cataloging) Bibliomation Inc; (Circulation) Bibliomation Inc; (ILL) Bibliomation Inc; (OPAC) Bibliomation Inc; (Serials) EBSCO Online
Database Vendor: Gale Cengage Learning
Wireless access
Function: Satellite serv
Partic in Bibliomation Inc
Special Services for the Blind - Bks on cassette; Bks on CD; Large print bks; Low vision equip
Open Mon-Thurs 10:30-8, Fri 10:30-5:30, Sat 10-5
Friends of the Library Group

SR SISTERS OF THE IMMACULATE CONCEPTION CONVENT LIBRARY*, 600 Liberty Hwy, 06260. SAN 302-3311. Tel: 860-928-7955. FAX: 860-928-1930. *Librn,* Ona Strimaitis
Founded 1944
Library Holdings: Bk Vols 15,000; Per Subs 25
Special Collections: Lithuanian Art, paintings, ceramics, wood-carvings, amber & woven art. State Document Depository; UN Document Depository; US Document Depository
Subject Interests: Linguistics
Restriction: Not open to pub

REDDING

P MARK TWAIN LIBRARY*, Rte 53 & Diamond Hill Rd, 06896. (Mail add: PO Box 1009, 06875-1009), SAN 302-332X. Tel: 203-938-2545. FAX: 203-938-4026. E-mail: askus@marktwainlibrary.org. Web Site: marktwainlibrary.org. *Dir,* Beth Dominianni; E-mail: Beth@marktwainlibrary.org; *Asst Dir, Children & Teen Librn,* Mary Hoskinson-Dean; E-mail: mhdean@marktwainlibrary.org; *Ad,* Janet Ivaldi; *ILL Librn,* Maureeen Jones; *Ref Librn,* Jean Taylor; E-mail: jean@marktwainlibrary.org; Staff 5.25 (MLS 2.25, Non-MLS 3)
Founded 1908. Pop 8,572; Circ 96,978
Jun 2005-May 2006 Income $531,871, State $1,990, City $271,259, Locally Generated Income $258,622. Mats Exp $80,887, Books $35,920, Per/Ser (Incl. Access Fees) $19,135, AV Mat $22,832, Electronic Ref Mat (Incl. Access Fees) $1,000. Sal $262,105 (Prof $130,286)
Library Holdings: AV Mats 4,150; Bk Vols 45,162; Per Subs 122
Special Collections: Civil War (Massie Coll); Mark Twain Coll; Redding Land Trust; Religion & Mysticism (Hutchinson Coll)
Automation Activity & Vendor Info: (Cataloging) Follett Software; (Course Reserve) Follett Software; (ILL) Auto-Graphics, Inc; (Serials) Follett Software
Wireless access
Publications: Mark Twain Tatler (Newsletter)
Special Services for the Blind - Bks on CD
Open Mon-Wed, Fri & Sat (Sept-June) 10-5, Thurs 10-8, Sun 12-5

RIDGEFIELD

S ALDRICH MUSEUM OF CONTEMPORARY ARTS LIBRARY*, 258 Main St, 06877. Tel: 203-438-4519. FAX: 203-438-0198. E-mail: general@aldrichart.org. Web Site: www.aldrichart.org. *Dir,* Harry Philbrick
Library Holdings: Bk Titles 200; Per Subs 20
Open Mon-Fri 9-5

P RIDGEFIELD LIBRARY ASSOCIATION INC*, 472 Main St, 06877-4585. SAN 302-3346. Tel: 203-438-2282. Administration Tel: 203-438-6960. FAX: 203-438-4558. Administration FAX: 203-431-9303. Web Site: www.ridgefieldlibrary.org. *Dir,* Christina B Nolan; E-mail: cbnolan@ridgefieldlibrary.org; *Asst Dir,* Mary Rindsleisch; *Adult Serv,* Dorothy Pawlowski; *Ch Serv,* Geri Diorio; E-mail: gadiorio@ridgefieldlibrary.org; *ILL,* Karen Kazzi; E-mail: klkazzi@ridgefieldlibrary.org; *Ref,* Victoria Carlquist; E-mail: vmcarlquist@ridgefieldlibrary.org; Staff 7.5 (MLS 7.5)
Founded 1901. Pop 24,000; Circ 408,557
Jul 2007-Jun 2008 Income $2,133,900, State $4,000, City $1,642,400, Other $487,500. Mats Exp $293,500, Books $200,000, Per/Ser (Incl. Access Fees) $15,000, AV Mat $40,500, Electronic Ref Mat (Incl. Access Fees) $38,000. Sal $1,195,600 (Prof $450,200)
Library Holdings: Bk Titles 106,000; Bk Vols 130,000; Per Subs 240
Special Collections: Ridgefield History, bks, monographs
Subject Interests: Genealogy
Automation Activity & Vendor Info: (Acquisitions) SirsiDynix; (Cataloging) SirsiDynix; (Circulation) SirsiDynix; (OPAC) SirsiDynix; (Serials) SirsiDynix
Function: Adult bk club, Art exhibits, Audiobks via web, Bk club(s), Bks on CD, Children's prog, Computers for patron use, Copy machines, e-mail & chat, Electronic databases & coll, Exhibits, Fax serv, Homebound delivery serv, ILL available, Mus passes, Music CDs, Online ref, Photocopying/Printing, Prog for adults, Prog for children & young adult, Pub access computers, Story hour, Summer reading prog, Tax forms, Telephone ref, Web-catalog
Publications: Newsletter
Special Services for the Blind - Reader equip
Open Mon, Wed & Fri (Sept-June) 10-6, Tues & Thurs 10-9, Sat 9-5, Sun 1-5
Friends of the Library Group

ROCKY HILL

P CORA J BELDEN LIBRARY*, 33 Church St, 06067-1568. SAN 302-3370. Tel: 860-258-7621. Reference Tel: 860-258-7623. E-mail: cora@rockyhillct.gov. Web Site: www.rockyhilllibrary.info. *Dir,* Mary Hogan; E-mail: mhogan@rockyhillct.gov; *Asst Dir, Tech,* Terri Corry; E-mail: tcorry@rockyhillct.gov; *Asst Dir, Prog,* Carole Fisher; E-mail: cfisher@rockyhillct.gov; Staff 14 (MLS 4, Non-MLS 10)
Founded 1794. Pop 17,996; Circ 264,280
Library Holdings: AV Mats 9,930; Large Print Bks 2,361; Bk Titles 61,023; Per Subs 200
Automation Activity & Vendor Info: (Cataloging) SirsiDynix; (Circulation) SirsiDynix; (ILL) OCLC; (OPAC) SirsiDynix
Database Vendor: Overdrive, Inc, ReferenceUSA
Function: ILL available
Publications: Library Window (Newsletter)
Partic in Connecticut Library Consortium; Library Connection, Inc
Special Services for the Deaf - Closed caption videos
Open Mon-Thurs 10-8, Fri & Sat 10-5, Sun 12-5
Friends of the Library Group

S CONNECTICUT HORTICULTURAL SOCIETY LIBRARY*, 2433 Main St, 06067-2539. SAN 321-6748. Tel: 860-529-8713. FAX: 860-563-2217. E-mail: connhort@aol.com. Web Site: www.cthort.org. *Mgr,* Bonnie McLachlan
Founded 1960

Library Holdings: Bk Titles 2,000
Subject Interests: Hort
Open Tues & Thurs 11-4

P CONNECTICUT STATE LIBRARY, Library for the Blind & Physically Handicapped, 198 West St, 06067. SAN 302-1750. Tel: 860-721-2020. Toll Free Tel: 800-842-4516. FAX: 860-721-2056. *Dir,* Gordon Reddick; E-mail: gordon.reddick@ct.gov; Staff 2 (MLS 2)
Founded 1968
Library Holdings: Braille Volumes 12,568; Bk Titles 62,000; Bk Vols 232,472; Talking Bks 219,902
Special Collections: Connecticut Cassettes
Subject Interests: Connecticut, New England
Function: Handicapped accessible, Homebound delivery serv, Mail loans to mem, Web-Braille
Special Services for the Blind - Bks on cassette; Braille bks; Cassette playback machines; Digital talking bk; Digital talking bk machines; Home delivery serv; Talking bks & player equip
Open Mon-Fri 9-3
Restriction: Registered patrons only, Restricted loan policy
Friends of the Library Group

S ROCKY HILL HISTORICAL SOCIETY, INC*, Ethel Miner Cooke Historical & Genealogical Library, 785 Old Main St, 06067-1519. (Mail add: PO Box 185, 06067-0185), SAN 302-3397. Tel: 860-563-6704. E-mail: info@rockyhillhistory.us. Web Site: rockyhillhistory.wordpress.com. *Librn,* Mildred R Sword
Founded 1969
Library Holdings: Bk Titles 700
Special Collections: Oral History
Subject Interests: Local hist
Function: Res libr
Restriction: Open by appt only

ROGERS

S ROGERS CORPORATION*, Global Research Library, One Technology Dr, 06263. (Mail add: PO Box 157, 06263-0157), SAN 302-3400. Tel: 860-779-5726. FAX: 860-779-5760. *Supvr,* Angela Kneeland; Staff 1 (Non-MLS 1)
Founded 1962
Library Holdings: AV Mats 300; CDs 100; e-journals 25; Bk Titles 3,000; Per Subs 300; Spec Interest Per Sub 300; Videos 100
Subject Interests: Adhesives, Chem, Electroluminescence, Liquid crystal films & coatings, Microelectronics, Polymeric mats, Statistical quality control, Thermal mgt of electronics
Automation Activity & Vendor Info: (Cataloging) EOS International; (Circulation) EOS International; (OPAC) EOS International; (Serials) EOS International
Function: Res libr
Partic in Connecticut Library Consortium; Lyrasis
Open Mon-Fri 9-4
Restriction: Access for corporate affiliates, Authorized patrons, Authorized scholars by appt, Co libr

ROWAYTON

P ROWAYTON LIBRARY*, The Association of the Free Library & Reading Room of Rowayton, Inc., 33 Highland Ave, 06853. SAN 302-3419. Tel: 203-838-5038. FAX: 203-523-0438, 928-437-5038. E-mail: library@rowayton.org. Web Site: www.rowayton.org/, www.rowaytonlibrary.org. *Dir,* Cynthia F Johnson; *Tech Serv,* Jonathan Engle; Staff 4 (MLS 1, Non-MLS 3)
Founded 1903. Pop 4,000; Circ 23,473
Library Holdings: Bk Vols 33,000; Per Subs 75
Automation Activity & Vendor Info: (Acquisitions) Bibliomation Inc; (Cataloging) Bibliomation Inc; (Circulation) Bibliomation Inc; (ILL) Auto-Graphics, Inc; (OPAC) Bibliomation Inc; (Serials) Bibliomation Inc
Database Vendor: Bibliomation Inc, LearningExpress
Wireless access
Function: Adult bk club, Bk club(s), Bk reviews (Group), Bks on CD, CD-ROM, Chess club, Children's prog, Computer training, Computers for patron use, Copy machines, Digital talking bks, Electronic databases & coll, Fax serv, Free DVD rentals, Handicapped accessible, Holiday prog, Homework prog, ILL available, Instruction & testing, Jazz prog, Mus passes, Music CDs, Online cat, Online info literacy tutorials on the web & in blackboard, Online ref, Online searches, Orientations, OverDrive digital audio bks, Photocopying/Printing, Preschool outreach, Prog for adults, Prog for children & young adult, Pub access computers, Ref & res, Ref serv available, Scanner, Senior outreach, Spoken cassettes & CDs, Spoken cassettes & DVDs, Story hour, Summer reading prog, Tax forms, Teen prog, Telephone ref, Video lending libr, Web-catalog, Wheelchair accessible, Workshops, Writing prog
Partic in Bibliomation Inc
Special Services for the Deaf - Assisted listening device
Open Mon, Tues, Thurs & Fri 10-5, Wed 10-7, Sat 10-1

ROXBURY

P MINOR MEMORIAL LIBRARY, 23 South St, 06783. (Mail add: PO Box 249, 06783-0249), SAN 374-5791. Tel: 860-350-2181. FAX: 860-350-6882. E-mail: roxbury@biblio.org. Web Site: www.minormemoriallibrary.org. *Dir,* Valerie G Annis; E-mail: vannis@biblio.org; *Coord, Ad Serv,* Betty Synnestvedt; *Coordr, Ch Serv,* Paula Sapse; Staff 6 (MLS 1, Non-MLS 5)
Founded 1896. Pop 2,300; Circ 16,138
Jul 2005-Jun 2006 Income $222,095, State $1,300, City $101,000, Locally Generated Income $119,795. Mats Exp $13,400, Books $8,100, Per/Ser (Incl. Access Fees) $1,000, AV Mat $4,300. Sal $127,890 (Prof $56,235)
Library Holdings: AV Mats 5,792; Electronic Media & Resources 5,454; Large Print Bks 345; Bk Titles 35,737; Per Subs 20; Talking Bks 2,299; Videos 3,493
Special Collections: Hanson Baldwin Coll
Subject Interests: World War II
Automation Activity & Vendor Info: (Cataloging) Evergreen; (Circulation) Evergreen; (OPAC) Evergreen
Wireless access
Publications: Bookmark (Friends)
Partic in Bibliomation Inc
Special Services for the Blind - Assistive/Adapted tech devices, equip & products
Open Mon 12-7, Wed & Fri 10-5, Thurs 12-5, Sat 10-2
Friends of the Library Group

SALEM

P SALEM FREE PUBLIC LIBRARY*, 264 Hartford Rd, 06420. SAN 376-2645. Tel: 860-859-1130. FAX: 860-859-9961. E-mail: salemctlibrary@yahoo.com. Web Site: salemct.gov/pages/salemct_library/index. *Dir,* Jackie I Hemond; E-mail: jives98@hotmail.com; Staff 3 (MLS 1, Non-MLS 2)
Founded 1915. Pop 6,500; Circ 71,500
Jul 2010-Jun 2011 Income $149,150. Sal $85,610 (Prof $43,800)
Library Holdings: Audiobooks 2,065; CDs 620; DVDs 1,840; e-books 24; Large Print Bks 755; Bk Vols 26,000; Per Subs 40; Videos 1,450
Automation Activity & Vendor Info: (Cataloging) Bibliomation Inc; (Circulation) Horizon; (OPAC) Infor Library & Information Solutions
Database Vendor: Bibliomation Inc, Overdrive, Inc
Wireless access
Open Mon-Wed 12-7:30, Thurs 10-7:30, Fri 12-6, Sat 10-4 (10-2 July & Aug)
Friends of the Library Group

SALISBURY

P SCOVILLE MEMORIAL LIBRARY*, 38 Main St, 06068. SAN 302-3443. Tel: 860-435-2838. FAX: 860-435-8136. Web Site: www.scovillelibrary.org. *Dir,* Claudia E Cayne; E-mail: ccayne@biblio.org
Pop 4,131; Circ 59,142
Library Holdings: Bk Vols 35,000; Per Subs 70
Special Collections: Local History (Smith & Bingham Coll)
Automation Activity & Vendor Info: (Acquisitions) SirsiDynix; (Cataloging) SirsiDynix; (Circulation) SirsiDynix; (OPAC) SirsiDynix
Partic in Region I Coop Libr Servs Unit
Open Tues & Thurs 10-7, Wed & Fri 10-5, Sat 10-4 (10-2 July & Aug)

SCOTLAND

P SCOTLAND PUBLIC LIBRARY*, 21 Brook Rd, 06264. (Mail add: PO Box 286, 06264-0286), SAN 302-3451. Tel: 860-423-1492. FAX: 860-423-1526. E-mail: scotlandpubliclibrary@yahoo.com. *Dir,* Mary Geragotelis; Staff 2 (Non-MLS 2)
Pop 1,700; Circ 3,307
Library Holdings: AV Mats 575; Large Print Bks 100; Bk Vols 12,000; Per Subs 30; Videos 900
Wireless access
Partic in Connecticut Library Consortium
Open Tues, Wed & Fri 2:30-7, Thurs 9-12 & 2:30-8, Sat 9-2

SEYMOUR

P SEYMOUR PUBLIC LIBRARY, 46 Church St, 06483. SAN 302-346X. Tel: 203-888-3903. FAX: 203-888-4099. Web Site: www.seymourpubliclibrary.org. *Dir,* Suzanne Garvey; E-mail: sgarvey@biblio.org; *Asst Librn,* Lisa Omlor; E-mail: lomlor@biblio.org; *Ref Librn,* Charlotte Rowell; E-mail: crowell@biblio.org; *Ch Serv,* Ann Szaley; E-mail: aszaley@biblio.org; Staff 5 (MLS 2, Non-MLS 3)
Founded 1892. Pop 15,700; Circ 87,556

Jul 2013-Jun 2014 Income $520,163, City $427,902, Locally Generated Income $92,261. Mats Exp $84,790, Electronic Ref Mat (Incl. Access Fees) $4,200. Sal $300,277
Library Holdings: AV Mats 2,374; e-books 5,000; Bk Vols 76,000; Per Subs 7,000; Talking Bks 1,194; Videos 4,000
Special Collections: Historical Reference Coll
Automation Activity & Vendor Info: (Circulation) Evergreen; (OPAC) Evergreen
Wireless access
Publications: Voices (Newsletter)
Partic in Connecticut Library Consortium
Open Tues & Wed 9-8, Thurs & Fri 9-5:30, Sat 10-4
Friends of the Library Group

SHARON

P HOTCHKISS LIBRARY OF SHARON, INC*, Ten Upper Main St, 06069. SAN 302-3478. Tel: 860-364-5041. FAX: 860-364-6060. E-mail: hotchkisslib@snet.net. *Dir,* Louise Manteuffel
Founded 1893. Pop 2,900; Circ 29,645
Library Holdings: DVDs 30; Large Print Bks 150; Bk Vols 23,000; Per Subs 55; Talking Bks 300; Videos 200
Special Collections: Connecticut Historical Room
Partic in Region I Coop Libr Servs Unit

E SHARON HOSPITAL*, Health Science Library, 50 Hospital Hill Rd, 06069. (Mail add: PO Box 789, 06069), SAN 302-3486. Tel: 860-364-4008. *In Charge,* Bonnie Boodee
Library Holdings: e-books 400; e-journals 90
Partic in Conn Asn of Health Scis Librs; North Atlantic Health Sciences Libraries, Inc; NW Conn Health Sci Libr
Restriction: Staff use only

SHELTON

P PLUMB MEMORIAL LIBRARY*, 65 Wooster St, 06484. SAN 302-3516. Tel: 203-924-1580. FAX: 203-924-8422. Web Site: www.sheltonlibrarysystem.org. *Dir,* C Elspeth Lydon; E-mail: elydon@biblio.org; *Ch,* Barbara Fritsch; Tel: 203-924-9461, E-mail: bfritsch@biblio.org; *Circ Supvr, Tech Serv Supvr,* Karen Lanigan; E-mail: klanigan@biblio.org; Staff 4 (MLS 4)
Founded 1896. Pop 38,000; Circ 277,051
Jul 2011-Jun 2012. Mats Exp $159,651, Books $65,347, Per/Ser (Incl. Access Fees) $11,200, AV Mat $35,631, Electronic Ref Mat (Incl. Access Fees) $37,347. Sal $785,196
Library Holdings: Audiobooks 3,945; CDs 3,015; DVDs 10,523; e-books 2,503; Electronic Media & Resources 43; Large Print Bks 2,412; Bk Vols 131,145; Per Subs 387; Videos 5,025
Subject Interests: Connecticut, Local hist
Automation Activity & Vendor Info: (Cataloging) Evergreen; (Circulation) Evergreen; (ILL) Evergreen; (OPAC) Evergreen
Database Vendor: Booksite, EBSCO Auto Repair Reference, Gale Cengage Learning, LearningExpress, Newsbank, Overdrive, Inc, TumbleBookLibrary
Wireless access
Partic in Bibliomation Inc; Connecticut Library Consortium
Open Mon-Thurs 9-8:30, Fri & Sat 9-4:30
Friends of the Library Group
Branches: 1
HUNTINGTON BRANCH, 41 Church St, 06484-5804, SAN 375-5940. Tel: 203-926-0111. FAX: 203-926-0181.
Founded 1991. Pop 40,000
Automation Activity & Vendor Info: (Circulation) Evergreen
Database Vendor: Bibliomation Inc
Partic in Bibliomation Inc
Open Mon 12-8, Tues-Thurs 10-8, Fri 10-5, Sat 10-3
Friends of the Library Group
Bookmobiles: 1

SHERMAN

P SHERMAN LIBRARY ASSOCIATION*, Rte 37 & 39, 06784. (Mail add: PO Box 40, 06784-0040), SAN 302-3524. Tel: 860-354-2455. FAX: 860-354-7215. E-mail: sl@biblio.org. Web Site: www.biblio.org/sherman. *Dir,* Millie Loeb
Founded 1926. Pop 3,827; Circ 60,000
Library Holdings: Bk Vols 25,000; Per Subs 40
Special Collections: Sherman Authors
Automation Activity & Vendor Info: (Cataloging) Bibliomation Inc; (Circulation) Bibliomation Inc; (ILL) Bibliomation Inc; (OPAC) Bibliomation Inc
Partic in Region I Coop Libr Servs Unit
Open Tues, Wed & Fri 11-6, Thurs 11-7, Sat 10-4

SIMSBURY

S SIMSBURY HISTORICAL SOCIETY ARCHIVES*, Phelps Tavern Museum, 800 Hopmeadow St, 06070. (Mail add: PO Box 2, 06070-0002), SAN 302-3532. Tel: 860-658-2500. FAX: 860-651-4354. E-mail: info@simsburyhistory.org. Web Site: www.simsburyhistory.org. *Archivist,* Stephen E Simon; E-mail: archives@simsburyhistory.org. Subject Specialists: *Early manufacturing, Family papers, Local hist,* Stephen E Simon; Staff 3 (MLS 1, Non-MLS 2)
Founded 1911
Special Collections: Early Fuse Manufacturing Industry (Ensign Bickford Company Coll); Early Republic Period Documents Detailing the Barber Family of Connecticut (Lucius Israel Barber Coll); Family Papers of the Eno & Related Phelps Families (William P Eno Foundation Coll); Photographic Images in Various Media of People & Places Connected to Simsbury; Simsbury Area Persons Family Papers. Oral History
Subject Interests: Local hist
Wireless access
Function: Archival coll, Audio & video playback equip for onsite use, Bus archives, Computers for patron use, e-mail serv, For res purposes, Mail & tel request accepted, Photocopying/Printing, Ref & res, VHS videos
Open Tues-Sat 12-4
Restriction: Closed stack, Non-circulating coll, Photo ID required for access

P SIMSBURY PUBLIC LIBRARY, 725 Hopmeadow St, 06070. SAN 302-3540. Tel: 860-658-7663. FAX: 860-658-6732. Web Site: www.simsburylibrary.info. *Dir,* Lisa Karim; E-mail: lkarim@simsburylibrary.info; *Adult Serv,* Susan Ray; *Ch Serv,* Cheryl Donahue; *Ref,* Celia Roberts; Staff 6 (MLS 6)
Founded 1890. Pop 23,985; Circ 414,000
Library Holdings: Bk Vols 175,000
Subject Interests: Genealogy
Automation Activity & Vendor Info: (Cataloging) Innovative Interfaces, Inc - Sierra; (Circulation) Innovative Interfaces, Inc - Sierra; (OPAC) Innovative Interfaces, Inc - Sierra
Database Vendor: ReferenceUSA
Wireless access
Partic in Connecticut Library Consortium; Dialog Corp
Open Mon-Thurs 9:30-8:30, Fri & Sat 9:30-5:30, Sun 1-5
Friends of the Library Group

SOMERS

S OSBORN CORRECTIONAL INSTITUTION*, Osborn CI Library, 335 Bilton Rd, 06071. (Mail add: PO Box 100, 06071-0100), SAN 302-3559. Tel: 860-566-7500, Ext 5471, 860-566-7500, Ext 5478. FAX: 860-763-3157. *Librn,* Darrell Harrison
Library Holdings: Bk Vols 18,000
Subject Interests: Law
Open Mon-Fri 8-4 & 7-9

P SOMERS PUBLIC LIBRARY*, 51 Ninth District Rd, 06071-0368. SAN 302-3567. Tel: 860-763-3501. FAX: 860-763-1718. E-mail: somerspl@biblio.org. Web Site: www.somersnow-com/library. *Dir,* Francine A Aloisa; *Ch Serv,* Annette Ouellet; *Ref,* Cecelia Becker; Staff 6 (MLS 5, Non-MLS 1)
Founded 1887. Pop 7,600; Circ 87,905
Jul 2005-Jun 2006 Income $352,409. Mats Exp $58,295, Books $47,545, AV Mat $5,850, Electronic Ref Mat (Incl. Access Fees) $4,900. Sal $195,592 (Prof $129,393)
Library Holdings: Bk Vols 46,674; Per Subs 169; Talking Bks 1,066
Subject Interests: Local hist
Automation Activity & Vendor Info: (Acquisitions) SirsiDynix; (Cataloging) SirsiDynix; (Circulation) SirsiDynix; (ILL) Auto-Graphics, Inc; (OPAC) SirsiDynix; (Serials) SirsiDynix
Database Vendor: EBSCOhost, Gale Cengage Learning, ProQuest
Partic in Bibliomation Inc
Open Mon-Thurs 10-8, Fri 10-5, Sat 10-3, Sun 1-5
Friends of the Library Group

SOUTH WINDHAM

P GUILFORD SMITH MEMORIAL LIBRARY*, 17 Main St, 06266-1121. (Mail add: PO Box 159, 06266-0159), SAN 302-3583. Tel: 860-423-5159. FAX: 860-423-5159. Web Site: www.guilfordsmith.org. *Dir,* Afton Elizabeth Seal; E-mail: aseal@biblio.org; Staff 2 (Non-MLS 2)
Founded 1930. Pop 500; Circ 10,000
Jul 2005-Jun 2006 Income $55,520, City $5,000, Federal $5,000, County $5,000, Locally Generated Income $40,000, Other $520. Mats Exp $55,520, Books $47,000, AV Equip $1,000, Electronic Ref Mat (Incl. Access Fees) $4,000. Sal $21,000
Library Holdings: Audiobooks 25; AV Mats 138; Bks on Deafness & Sign Lang 12; CDs 80; DVDs 100; e-books 201; High Interest/Low Vocabulary Bk Vols 225; Large Print Bks 130; Bk Titles 9,969; Per Subs 40

Special Collections: Connecticut History Coll; South Windham History Coll; Windham County History Coll. Oral History
Automation Activity & Vendor Info: (Acquisitions) Baker & Taylor; (Circulation) Bibliomation Inc; (Serials) EBSCO Online
Wireless access
Function: Adult bk club, After school storytime, Audiobks via web, Bk club(s), Bks on cassette, Bks on CD, CD-ROM, Children's prog, Computer training, Computers for patron use, Copy machines, Electronic databases & coll, Fax serv, Free DVD rentals, Genealogy discussion group, Handicapped accessible, Holiday prog, Home delivery & serv to Sr ctr & nursing homes, Homebound delivery serv, Homework prog, ILL available, Mus passes, Music CDs, Photocopying/Printing, Prog for adults, Prog for children & young adult, Pub access computers, Scanner, Story hour, Summer & winter reading prog, Summer reading prog, Tax forms, Teen prog, Wheelchair accessible
Partic in Bibliomation Inc
Open Tues 10-8, Thurs 5-8, Fri 2-6, Sat 10-2
Friends of the Library Group

SOUTH WINDSOR

P SOUTH WINDSOR PUBLIC LIBRARY*, 1550 Sullivan Ave, 06074. SAN 302-3605. Tel: 860-644-1541. FAX: 860-644-7645. TDD: 860-644-7645. Web Site: www.southwindsorlibrary.org. *Dir,* Mary J Etter; E-mail: metter@libraryconnection.info; *Ch Serv,* Sandy Westbrook; *Circ,* Linda Clark; *Coll Develop,* Joseph Pava; Staff 29 (MLS 5, Non-MLS 24)
Founded 1898. Pop 25,000
Library Holdings: Bk Vols 124,000; Per Subs 350
Subject Interests: Local hist
Automation Activity & Vendor Info: (Cataloging) SirsiDynix; (Circulation) SirsiDynix; (ILL) SirsiDynix
Wireless access
Partic in Connecticut Library Consortium; Library Connection, Inc
Open Mon-Thurs 9-9, Fri & Sat 9-4:30, Sun 1-4:30
Friends of the Library Group

P WOOD MEMORIAL LIBRARY*, 783 Main St, 06074. (Mail add: PO Box 131, 06074-0131), SAN 376-2807. Tel: 860-289-1783. E-mail: wood.memorial.lib@snet.net. Web Site: pages.cthome.net/wood.memorial.lib.
Library Holdings: Bk Titles 12,000; Bk Vols 15,000
Subject Interests: Birding, Birds, Local hist
Partic in Connecticut Library Consortium
Open Mon-Thurs 10-8
Friends of the Library Group

SOUTHBURY

P SOUTHBURY PUBLIC LIBRARY*, 100 Poverty Rd, 06488. SAN 302-3613. Tel: 203-262-0626. FAX: 203-262-6734. Web Site: www.southburylibrary.org. *Dir,* Shirley Thorson; E-mail: sthorson@biblio.org; *Asst Dir, Ch Serv,* Joan Stokes; *Head, Circ,* Jacqueline Hoffman; *Head, Ref (Info Serv),* Judith Stark; *Head, Tech Serv,* Judy Von Holtz; Staff 5 (MLS 5)
Founded 1969. Pop 18,567; Circ 212,704
Library Holdings: Bk Vols 89,439; Per Subs 127
Automation Activity & Vendor Info: (Cataloging) SirsiDynix; (Circulation) SirsiDynix; (ILL) SirsiDynix; (OPAC) SirsiDynix
Database Vendor: EBSCOhost
Publications: Monthly calendar
Open Mon, Wed & Fri 9:30-5:30, Tues & Thurs 9:30-9, Sat 9:30-4
Friends of the Library Group

SOUTHINGTON

C LINCOLN COLLEGE OF NEW ENGLAND*, Anthony A Pupillo Library, 2279 Mount Vernon Rd, 06489-1057. SAN 324-282X. Tel: 860-628-4751, Ext 149. FAX: 860-628-6444. Web Site: www.lincolncollegene.edu. *Dir, Libr Serv,* Valeri Wallace; Tel: 860-628-4751, Ext 148, E-mail: wallacev@briarwood.edu; *Asst Librn,* John Clark; Staff 5 (MLS 1, Non-MLS 4)
Founded 1966. Enrl 612; Fac 124; Highest Degree: Bachelor
Jul 2006-Jun 2007 Income $70,000. Mats Exp $70,000, Books $35,000, Per/Ser (Incl. Access Fees) $13,000, AV Mat $2,000, Electronic Ref Mat (Incl. Access Fees) $20,000
Library Holdings: AV Mats 485; Bk Vols 14,000; Per Subs 178
Special Collections: Environmental Special Coll
Subject Interests: Vocational educ
Automation Activity & Vendor Info: (Cataloging) Follett Software; (Circulation) Follett Software; (ILL) Auto-Graphics, Inc; (OPAC) Follett Software; (Serials) Follett Software
Database Vendor: EBSCOhost, Gale Cengage Learning, LexisNexis, OCLC WorldShare Interlibrary Loan, ProQuest, Westlaw, Wilson - Wilson Web
Function: ILL available
Partic in Connecticut Library Consortium
Open Mon-Thurs 8:30am-9:30pm, Fri 8:30-4:30, Sat 10-6, Sun 4-9:30

P SOUTHINGTON PUBLIC LIBRARY & MUSEUM*, 255 Main St, 06489. SAN 302-363X. Tel: 860-628-0947. FAX: 860-628-0488. Web Site: www.southingtonlibrary.org. *Dir,* Susan Smayda; E-mail: smaydas@southington.org; *Acq, Pub Relations,* Jeanne Chmielewski; E-mail: chmielewskij@southington.org; *Adult Serv,* Michael Berube; E-mail: berubem@southington.org; *Adult Serv,* Joanne Cyr; E-mail: cyrj@southington.org; *Adult Serv,* Michelle Lord; E-mail: lordm@southington.org; *Adult Serv,* Sue Meneo; E-mail: meneos@southington.org; *Adult Serv,* Cheryl Nadeau; E-mail: nadeauc@southington.org; *Adult Serv,* Colleen Perone; E-mail: peronec@southington.org; *Cataloger,* Billie Witkovic; E-mail: witkovicb@southington.org; *Ch Serv,* Shelley Holley; E-mail: holleys@southington.org; *Ch Serv,* Lynn Pawloski; E-mail: pawloskil@southington.org; *Ch Serv,* Carla Sheehan; E-mail: sheehanc@southington.org; *Ch Serv,* Cindy Wall; E-mail: wallc@southington.org; *Coll Develop, Tech Serv,* Mark Henne; E-mail: hennem@southington.org; *Info Serv,* Louise Champagne; E-mail: champagnel@southington.org; *Info Serv,* Gene Grass; E-mail: grassg@southington.org; *Info Serv,* Craig Holmes; E-mail: holmes@southington.org; *Info Serv,* Marion Urban; E-mail: urbanm@southington.org; Staff 6 (MLS 6)
Founded 1902. Pop 38,683; Circ 220,237
Library Holdings: Bk Vols 120,000; Per Subs 240
Special Collections: Artifacts, 18-20th Century
Subject Interests: Bus, Local hist, Transition
Automation Activity & Vendor Info: (Cataloging) Innovative Interfaces, Inc; (Circulation) Innovative Interfaces, Inc; (ILL) Innovative Interfaces, Inc; (OPAC) Innovative Interfaces, Inc
Database Vendor: EBSCOhost
Publications: Business Center (Brochure); Character Development (Brochure); Newsletter; Summer Reading Program (Brochure); Transition Center (Brochure)
Partic in Connecticut Library Consortium
Special Services for the Deaf - Closed caption videos
Open Mon-Thurs (Winter) 9-9, Fri & Sat 9-5; Mon-Thurs (Summer) 9-9, Fri 9-5
Friends of the Library Group

SOUTHPORT

P PEQUOT LIBRARY*, 720 Pequot Ave, 06890-1496. SAN 302-3648. Tel: 203-259-0346. FAX: 203-259-5602. Web Site: www.pequotlibrary.com. *Interim Exec Dir,* Martha Gates; Tel: 203-259-0346, Ext 17; *Head Librn,* Robyn Swan Filippone; Tel: 203-259-0346, Ext 16, E-mail: filippone@pequotlibrary.com; *Ref Serv, Ad, Spec Coll Librn,* Danielle Carriera; E-mail: carriera@pequotlibrary.com; *Ch Serv,* Susan Ei; Tel: 203-259-0346, Ext 18, E-mail: sei@pequotlibrary.com; *ILL,* Vicki Hanusovsky; Tel: 203-259-0346, Ext 19, E-mail: hanusovsky@pequotlibrary.com
Founded 1887. Circ 59,352
Library Holdings: Bk Titles 110,000; Per Subs 140
Special Collections: 19th Century Periodicals; Americana; Genealogy & Local History Coll
Automation Activity & Vendor Info: (Circulation) SirsiDynix; (ILL) OCLC Online; (OPAC) SirsiDynix
Publications: Catalogue of the Monroe, Wakeman & Holman Collection of the Pequot Library Southport, Connecticut Deposited in the Yale University Library; Clare Leighton; The Kelmscott Press
Open Mon-Fri 9-6, Sat 9-5 (9-1 July-Aug)

STAFFORD SPRINGS

M JOHNSON MEMORIAL HOSPITAL*, Medical Library, 201 Chestnut Hill Rd, 06076. Tel: 860-684-8166. FAX: 860-684-8129. Web Site: www.johnsonmemorial.com. *Librn,* Brenda Wong; E-mail: brenda.wong@jmhosp.org; Staff 1 (MLS 1)
Library Holdings: Bk Titles 450; Per Subs 38
Database Vendor: Lexi-Comp, UpToDate
Special Services for the Deaf - TTY equip
Open Tues-Fri 8:30-5

P STAFFORD LIBRARY*, Ten Levinthal Run, 06075. SAN 302-3672. Tel: 860-684-2852. FAX: 860-684-2128. E-mail: stafforddesk@biblio.org. Web Site: www.staffordlibrary.org. *Dir,* Christopher Frank; E-mail: cfrank@biblio.org; *Ref & Teen Librn,* Lori-Ellen Smith; E-mail: lsmith@biblio.org; *Tech Serv Coordr,* Adreana Scussel; E-mail: ascussel@biblio.org; *Ch Serv,* Deborah Muska; E-mail: dmuska@biblio.org; Staff 3 (MLS 2, Non-MLS 1)
Founded 1876. Pop 12,000; Circ 83,000
Jul 2006-Jun 2007 Income $428,221, State $2,000, City $319,672, Locally Generated Income $106,549. Mats Exp $58,538. Sal $236,150 (Prof $108,745)

Library Holdings: CDs 305; DVDs 800; Large Print Bks 546; Bk Vols 55,000; Per Subs 100; Videos 2,172
Special Collections: Local History
Automation Activity & Vendor Info: (Acquisitions) Evergreen; (Cataloging) Evergreen; (Circulation) Evergreen; (ILL) Evergreen; (OPAC) Evergreen; (Serials) Evergreen
Database Vendor: Bibliomation Inc, EBSCOhost
Wireless access
Function: Computer training, Copy machines, E-Reserves, Electronic databases & coll, Fax serv, Handicapped accessible, Home delivery & serv to Sr ctr & nursing homes, Homebound delivery serv, Homework prog, ILL available, Online ref, Photocopying/Printing, Prog for adults, Prog for children & young adult, Ref serv available, Senior computer classes, Spoken cassettes & CDs, Summer reading prog, Tax forms, Telephone ref, VHS videos, Wheelchair accessible
Partic in Connecticut Library Consortium
Open Mon-Thurs 10-8, Fri 10-5, Sat (Sept-June) 10-5, Sun (July-Aug) 10-1
Friends of the Library Group

STAMFORD

L CUMMINGS & LOCKWOOD*, Law Library, Six Landmark Sq, 06901. SAN 372-3399. Tel: 203-351-4375. FAX: 203-708-3847. Web Site: www.cl-law.com. *Mgr,* Barbara J Bentley; E-mail: bbentley@cl-law.com; *Libr Asst,* Brenda DellaCava; Staff 2 (MLS 1, Non-MLS 1)
Library Holdings: Bk Vols 20,000
Automation Activity & Vendor Info: (Acquisitions) Inmagic, Inc.; (Cataloging) Inmagic, Inc.; (OPAC) Inmagic, Inc.; (Serials) Inmagic, Inc.
Partic in Connecticut Library Consortium

P THE FERGUSON LIBRARY*, One Public Library Plaza, 96 Broad St, 06904. SAN 336-4925. Tel: 203-964-1000. Circulation Tel: 203-351-8261. Interlibrary Loan Service Tel: 203-351-8266. Reference Tel: 203-351-8221, 203-351-8222. Information Services Tel: 203-351-8231. FAX: 203-357-9098. E-mail: comments@fergusonlibrary.org. Web Site: www.fergusonlibrary.org. *Interim Pres,* Alice Knapp; Tel: 203-351-8201, E-mail: aknapp@fergusonlibrary.org; *Admin Serv Dir,* Nicholas A Bochicchio, Jr; Tel: 203-351-8202, E-mail: nboch@fergusonlibrary.org; *Dir, Develop & Communications,* Avellar Linda; Tel: 203-351-8208, E-mail: linda@fergusonlibrary.org; *IT Dir,* Gary Giannelli; Tel: 203-351-8270, E-mail: gary@fergusonlibrary.org; *Bus Off Mgr,* Marie Giuliano; Tel: 203-351-8210, E-mail: mgiuliano@fergusonlibrary.org; *Circ Supvr,* Alex Lee; Tel: 203-351-8260, E-mail: alee@fergusonlibrary.org; *Adult/Info Serv Coordr,* Elizabeth Joseph; Tel: 203-351-8224, E-mail: ejoseph@fergusonlibrary.org; *Youth Serv Coordr,* Caroline Ward; Tel: 203-351-8240, E-mail: cward@fergusonlibrary.org; Staff 73.85 (MLS 38.85, Non-MLS 35)
Founded 1880. Pop 123,868; Circ 953,298
Jul 2012-Jun 2013 Income $8,387,669, State $3,168, City $7,140,000, Federal $1,500. Mats Exp $8,854,290. Sal $4,579,887
Library Holdings: Bk Titles 459,697
Wireless access
Publications: Ferguson Focus (Newsletter)
Open Mon-Thurs 10-9, Fri 10-6, Sat 10-5, Sun 1-5
Friends of the Library Group
Branches: 3
HARRY BENNETT BRANCH, 115 Vine Rd, 06905, SAN 336-495X. Tel: 203-351-8290. Circulation Tel: 203-351-8291. FAX: 203-968-2728. *Supvr,* Erin Shea; E-mail: eshea@fergusonlibrary.org
Friends of the Library Group
SOUTH END, 34 Woodland Ave, 06902, SAN 336-4941. Tel: 203-351-8280. FAX: 203-969-0797. *Supvr,* Josephine Fulcher-Anderson; Tel: 203-351-8281, E-mail: janderson@fergusonlibrary.org
Friends of the Library Group
WEED MEMORIAL & HOLLANDER, 1143 Hope St, 06907, SAN 336-4984. Tel: 203-351-8284. Circulation Tel: 203-351-8285. FAX: 203-321-7024. *Supvr,* Erin Shea
Friends of the Library Group
Bookmobiles: 1. In Charge, Josephine Fulcher-Anderson

R FIRST CONGREGATIONAL CHURCH LIBRARY*, Walton Pl, 06901. SAN 302-3761. Tel: 203-323-0200. FAX: 203-348-2270. Web Site: www.fccstamford.org. *Chairperson,* Barbara Arata; Tel: 203-323-6511
Founded 1956
Library Holdings: Bk Vols 3,000
Subject Interests: Biblical studies, Children's lit, Church hist, Relig
Wireless access

E PURDUE PHARMA LP, Purdue Library, One Stamford Forum, 201 Tresser Blvd, 06901. SAN 302-296X. Tel: 203-588-7265. FAX: 203-588-6212. *Sr Dir, Libr & Info Serv,* Kathryn Walsh; E-mail: kathy.walsh@pharma.com; *Asst Dir, Libr Operations,* Marianne Cirrito; Tel: 203-588-8498, E-mail: marianne.cirrito@pharma.com; *Asst Dir, Libr Tech,* Cynthia Geremia; Tel: 203-588-7267, E-mail: cynthia.geremia@pharma.com; *Libr Serv Supvr,* Carol Pappolla; E-mail: carol.pappolla@pharma.com; *Info Spec,* Nicole DiNatle; E-mail: nicole.dinatale@pharma.com; Staff 5 (MLS 4, Non-MLS 1)
Founded 1970
Library Holdings: e-books 1,000; e-journals 2,500; Bk Vols 2,000; Per Subs 300; Talking Bks 50
Subject Interests: Bus, Med, Pharmaceuticals
Automation Activity & Vendor Info: (Cataloging) SydneyPlus; (Circulation) SydneyPlus; (OPAC) SydneyPlus; (Serials) SydneyPlus
Database Vendor: Dialog, Factiva.com, STN International
Wireless access
Partic in Connecticut Library Consortium; National Network of Libraries of Medicine
Restriction: Co libr, Internal use only, Not open to pub

C SAINT BASIL COLLEGE LIBRARY*, 39 Clovelly Rd, 06902-3004. (Mail add: 195 Glenbrook Rd, 06902-3099). Tel: 203-327-7899. FAX: 203-967-9948. E-mail: ukrmulrec@optonline.net. Web Site: www.umlsct.org. *Librn,* John Terlecky; E-mail: jmterlecky@aol.com; Staff 5 (MLS 3, Non-MLS 2)
Founded 1933. Enrl 20; Fac 22; Highest Degree: Bachelor
Library Holdings: Bk Vols 131,423; Spec Interest Per Sub 12
Special Collections: Church history & Liturgy of the Ukrainian people
Automation Activity & Vendor Info: (Cataloging) OCLC; (ILL) OCLC
Database Vendor: Baker & Taylor
Wireless access
Partic in Connecticut Library Consortium; Lyrasis
Open Mon-Fri 9-4, Wed 6pm-9pm
Restriction: Private libr

S STAMFORD HISTORICAL SOCIETY LIBRARY*, 1508 High Ridge Rd, 06903-4107. SAN 302-3842. Tel: 203-329-1183. FAX: 203-322-1607. Web Site: www.stamfordhistory.org. *Librn,* Ronald Marcus; Staff 3 (MLS 3)
Founded 1901
Library Holdings: Bk Vols 10,500
Special Collections: 17th-20th Century Americana, Maps & Atlases of Stamford & Fairfield County, Photographic Coll, Stamford Business & Industry, Stamford Government, Stamford Postcard
Subject Interests: Local hist
Open Tues-Sat 12-4

M STAMFORD HOSPITAL*, Health Sciences Library, Shelborne Rd at W Broad, 06904. (Mail add: PO Box 9317, 06904-9317), SAN 324-4202. Tel: 203-325-7523. FAX: 203-276-7109. E-mail: library@stamhealth.org. Web Site: www.stamhealth.org. *Dir,* Guillaume Van Moorsel
Founded 1963
Library Holdings: e-journals 1,200; Bk Vols 2,100; Per Subs 200
Special Collections: Medicine, Allied Health & Nursing Coll
Automation Activity & Vendor Info: (Cataloging) CyberTools for Libraries
Database Vendor: OVID Technologies, PubMed
Partic in Conn Asn of Health Scis Librs; North Atlantic Health Sciences Libraries, Inc
Open Mon-Fri 8-4

C UNIVERSITY OF CONNECTICUT AT STAMFORD*, Jeremy Richard Library, One University Pl, 06901-2315. SAN 302-3877. Tel: 203-251-8500. FAX: 203-251-8501. Web Site: www.lib.uconn.edu. *Dir,* Phara Bayonne; Tel: 203-251-8523, Fax: 203-251-8526, E-mail: phara.bayonne@uconn.edu; *Ref, Regional Campus Libr Dir,* Nancy Dryden; Tel: 203-251-8439, E-mail: nancy.dryden@uconn.edu; *Access Serv,* Nancy Romanello; Tel: 203-251-8518, E-mail: nancy.romanello@uconn.edu; *Circ,* Radha Srikanth; Tel: 203-251-8438, E-mail: radha.srikanth@uconn.edu; *Ref,* Shelley Cudiner; Tel: 203-251-8521, E-mail: shelley.cudiner@uconn.edu. Subject Specialists: *Soc sci,* Phara Bayonne; *Hist, Polit sci,* Radha Srikanth; *Bus, Info, Literacy,* Shelley Cudiner; Staff 4.5 (MLS 3, Non-MLS 1.5)
Founded 1962. Enrl 1,700; Fac 33; Highest Degree: Master
Library Holdings: Bk Vols 90,000; Per Subs 88
Subject Interests: Bus & mgt, Econ, Lit, Soc sci & issues
Automation Activity & Vendor Info: (Acquisitions) Ex Libris Group; (Cataloging) Ex Libris Group; (Circulation) Ex Libris Group; (Course Reserve) Ex Libris Group; (OPAC) Ex Libris Group
Database Vendor: ARTstor, EBSCOhost, Gale Cengage Learning, JSTOR, LexisNexis, OCLC FirstSearch, OCLC WorldShare Interlibrary Loan, ScienceDirect
Wireless access
Partic in Boston Library Consortium, Inc; Lyrasis; Northeast Research Libraries Consortium (NERL)
Open Mon-Thurs 8-8, Fri 9-4:30, Sat 10-4

STONINGTON

P STONINGTON FREE LIBRARY, 20 High St, 06378. (Mail add: PO Box 232, 06378-0232), SAN 302-3907. Tel: 860-535-0658. Administration Tel: 860-535-0268. FAX: 860-535-3945. E-mail: stonlib@stoningtonfreelibrary.org. Web Site: www.stoningtonfreelibrary.org. *Libr Dir,* Margaret Victoria; E-mail: margaretvictoria@stoningtonfreelibrary.org; *Ch Serv,* Maris Frey; E-mail: marisf79@cox.net; Staff 9 (MLS 1, Non-MLS 8)
Founded 1887. Pop 17,903
Jul 2013-Jun 2014 Income $503,413, State $1,503, City $147,000, Locally Generated Income $354,910. Mats Exp $56,644, Books $47,500, Per/Ser (Incl. Access Fees) $4,944, AV Mat $4,200. Sal $264,000 (Prof $63,654)
Library Holdings: Audiobooks 1,450; DVDs 550; e-books 450; e-journals 10; High Interest/Low Vocabulary Bk Vols 95; Large Print Bks 1,075; Bk Titles 38,925; Bk Vols 41,478; Per Subs 64; Videos 100
Subject Interests: Genealogy, Local hist
Automation Activity & Vendor Info: (Cataloging) TLC (The Library Corporation); (Circulation) TLC (The Library Corporation); (OPAC) TLC (The Library Corporation)
Database Vendor: Newsbank, ValueLine
Wireless access
Function: 24/7 Online cat, Audiobks via web, Bks on CD, Children's prog, Computers for patron use, Copy machines, eReaders, Fax serv, Free DVD rentals, Handicapped accessible, ILL available, Magazines, Magnifiers for reading, Mus passes, OverDrive digital audio bks, Photocopying/Printing, Preschool outreach, Preschool reading prog, Prog for adults, Prog for children & young adult, Pub access computers, Scanner, Summer & winter reading prog, Summer reading prog, Tax forms, Web-catalog
Publications: e-Librarian (Monthly); The Librarian (Newsletter)
Partic in Connecticut Library Consortium
Special Services for the Deaf - Bks on deafness & sign lang
Special Services for the Blind - Aids for in-house use; Assistive/Adapted tech devices, equip & products; Audio mat; Bks on cassette; Bks on CD; Cassettes; Closed circuit TV; Computer with voice synthesizer for visually impaired persons; Large print & cassettes; Large print bks; Magnifiers; Talking bks
Open Mon, Tues, Thurs & Fri 10-5, Wed 10-8, Sat 10-3

S STONINGTON HISTORICAL SOCIETY*, Richard W Woolworth Library & Research Center, 40 Palmer St, 06378. (Mail add: PO Box 103, 06378-0103), SAN 326-7989. Tel: 860-535-1131. E-mail: library@stoningtonhistory.org. Web Site: www.stoningtonhistory.org. *Exec Dir,* Mary Beth Baker; Tel: 860-535-8445, E-mail: director@stoningtonhistory.org; *Libr Dir,* Anne C Thacher; E-mail: annelibrary@comcast.net; *Asst Librn,* Scotty Breed; Staff 4 (MLS 1, Non-MLS 3)
Founded 1895
Library Holdings: Bk Vols 3,500
Special Collections: Photographs & Postcards, primarily Stonington Area & People; Stonington Banks
Subject Interests: Genealogy, Local hist
Wireless access
Function: Handicapped accessible, Ref & res
Open Mon & Wed 1-5, Fri (May-Oct) 1-5, Sat 1-4
Restriction: Non-circulating, Not a lending libr

STONY CREEK

P WILLOUGHBY WALLACE MEMORIAL LIBRARY*, 146 Thimble Islands Rd, 06405. SAN 302-3915. Tel: 203-488-8702. FAX: 203-315-3347. Web Site: www.wwml.org. *Dir,* Susan Donovan; *Circ Supvr,* Barbara Welch; *Media Serv,* Alaina Driscoll
Founded 1958. Pop 3,000; Circ 45,000
Library Holdings: Bk Vols 23,000; Per Subs 55
Subject Interests: Art
Automation Activity & Vendor Info: (Cataloging) Innovative Interfaces, Inc; (Circulation) Innovative Interfaces, Inc; (OPAC) Innovative Interfaces, Inc
Open Mon-Thurs (Winter) 10-8, Fri & Sat 10-5, Sun 1-4; Mon-Thurs (Summer) 10-8, Fri & Sat 10-5
Friends of the Library Group

STORRS

S MANSFIELD HISTORICAL SOCIETY*, Edith Mason Library, 954 Storrs Rd, 06268. (Mail add: PO Box 145, 06268), SAN 328-1663. Tel: 860-429-6575. E-mail: mansfield.historical@snet.net. Web Site: www.mansfield-history.org. *Dir,* Ann Galonska; *Librn,* Richard H Schimmelpfeng; Staff 1 (MLS 1)
Library Holdings: Bk Titles 815; Bk Vols 2,804
Special Collections: Photograph Coll. Oral History
Subject Interests: Genealogy, Local hist
Publications: Local History Pamphlets (Annual)
Restriction: Non-circulating to the pub

C UNIVERSITY OF CONNECTICUT LIBRARIES*, 369 Fairfield Rd, 06269-1005. SAN 336-5042. Tel: 860-486-2219. Circulation Tel: 860-486-2518. Interlibrary Loan Service Tel: 860-486-4959. Reference Tel: 860-486-2513. FAX: 860-486-0584. Web Site: www.lib.uconn.edu. *Vice Provost for Libr,* Brinley Franklin; *Univ Archivist,* Betsy Pittman; *Dir, Coll Serv,* Francine DeFranco; *Dir, Libr Info Tech,* Patrick McGlamery; *Dir, Res Serv,* Scott Kennedy; *Coll Develop Mgr,* Peter Allison; *Head, Access Serv,* Barbara Des Rosiers; *Admin Librn,* Deborah Stansbury-Sunday; E-mail: deborah.sunday@uconn.edu; *Spec Coll & Archives Librn,* Tom Wilsted; Staff 112 (MLS 46, Non-MLS 66)
Founded 1881. Enrl 26,629; Fac 1,200; Highest Degree: Doctorate
Library Holdings: Bk Titles 3,168,617; Per Subs 42,059
Special Collections: Alternative Press; American Socialism & Communism; Belgium History (Revolution, 1830-1839); Black Mountain Poets; Bookplates; Charles Olson Coll; Chilean History & Literature; Conneticut History (primarily 1850-, emphasis on business, labor, ethnicity, public affairs); French History (including Paris Commune 1871); French Language & Linguistics; French Renaissance Literature; French Restoration Pamphlets; French Satirical Magazines, 19th Century; Italian History (including Italian Risorgimento, 1815-1870); Italian Risorgionento, 1815-1870; Labor History; Latin America; Little Magazines; Luis Camoens Coll; Madrid History; Medina Coll; Modern German Drama; Napoleonic Period; Paris Commune, 1871; Powys Brothers Coll; Sermons (Connecticut); Spanish Periodicals & Newspapers; University & Historical Archives; William Berkson. Oral History; State Document Depository; US Document Depository
Subject Interests: Children's lit, Latin Am, Maps
Automation Activity & Vendor Info: (Acquisitions) Ex Libris Group; (Cataloging) Ex Libris Group; (Circulation) Ex Libris Group; (Media Booking) Ex Libris Group; (OPAC) Ex Libris Group; (Serials) Ex Libris Group
Database Vendor: Agricola, Baker & Taylor, Cambridge Scientific Abstracts, Dialog, EBSCOhost, Elsevier MDL, Factiva.com, Gale Cengage Learning, JSTOR, LexisNexis, Newsbank, OCLC FirstSearch, OCLC WorldShare Interlibrary Loan, OVID Technologies, ProQuest, PubMed, ScienceDirect, SerialsSolutions, STN International
Publications: Harvest; Journal of the Charles Olson Bibliography Series; University of Connecticut Libraries
Partic in Association of Research Libraries (ARL); Boston Library Consortium, Inc; Center for Research Libraries; Lyrasis; Northeast Research Libraries Consortium (NERL); OCLC Online Computer Library Center, Inc; Scholarly Publ & Acad Resources Coalition
Special Services for the Deaf - Assistive tech
Special Services for the Blind - Assistive/Adapted tech devices, equip & products
Friends of the Library Group

Departmental Libraries:

MUSIC & DRAMATIC ARTS LIBRARY, 1295 Storrs Rd, Unit 1153, 06269-1153. Tel: 860-486-2502. FAX: 860-486-5551. Web Site: music.lib.uconn.edu. *Librn,* Anna Kijas; Tel: 860-486-0519, E-mail: anna.kijas@uconn.edu; Staff 3 (MLS 2, Non-MLS 1)
Highest Degree: Doctorate
Library Holdings: Bk Vols 75,000; Per Subs 150
Automation Activity & Vendor Info: (Cataloging) Follett Software; (Circulation) Follett Software; (OPAC) Follett Software
Open Mon-Thurs 8am-10pm, Fri 8-5, Sat Noon-5, Sun 1-10

PHARMACY, Pharmacy/Biology Bldg, 69 North Eagleville Rd, Rm 228, 06269-3092. Tel: 860-486-2218. FAX: 860-486-4998. Web Site: www.lib.uconn.edu/online/research/speclib/pharmacy/. *Librn,* Sharon Giovenale; Staff 1 (MLS 1)
Highest Degree: Doctorate
Library Holdings: Bk Vols 27,548; Per Subs 50
Subject Interests: Medicinal chem, Pharmaceutical sci, Pharmacology
Friends of the Library Group

HARLEIGH B TRECKER LIBRARY, Greater Hartford Campus, 1800 Asylum Ave, West Hartford, 06117, SAN 336-5506. Tel: 860-570-9024. Reference Tel: 860-570-9032. FAX: 860-570-9036. E-mail: treckref@lib.uconn.edu. *Librn,* Marsha Lee; Tel: 860-570-9030, E-mail: marsha.lee@lib.uconn.edu; *Librn,* Janice Mathews; Tel: 860-570-9105, E-mail: janice.mathews@lib.uconn.edu; *Coordr, Access Serv,* Claudia Lopes; Tel: 860-570-9040, E-mail: claudia.lopes@lib.uconn.edu; *Access Serv,* Steve Bustamante; Tel: 860-570-9031, E-mail: steve.bustamante@lib.uconn.edu. Subject Specialists: *Humanities, Soc work, Undergrad educ,* Marsha Lee; *Soc sci, Urban studies,* Janice Mathews; Staff 4.3 (MLS 3, Non-MLS 1.3)
Founded 1939. Enrl 2,100; Fac 120; Highest Degree: Doctorate
Library Holdings: DVDs 2,400; Bk Titles 50,000; Bk Vols 60,000; Per Subs 18; Spec Interest Per Sub 9; Videos 100
Special Collections: Social Work History Coll, vintage bks & journals
Subject Interests: Soc sci

Automation Activity & Vendor Info: (Acquisitions) Ex Libris Group; (Cataloging) Ex Libris Group; (Circulation) Ex Libris Group; (ILL) OCLC ILLiad; (OPAC) Ex Libris Group; (Serials) SerialsSolutions
Function: Computers for patron use, Copy machines, Electronic databases & coll, Exhibits, Microfiche/film & reading machines, Online cat, Photocopying/Printing, Printer for laptops & handheld devices, Scanner, Study rm
Special Services for the Deaf - Assistive tech
Open Mon-Thurs 9-9, Fri 10-5, Sat 12-5
Restriction: Circ limited, In-house use for visitors, Open to pub for ref & circ; with some limitations

SR EDWINA WHITNEY LIBRARY OF THE STORRS CONGREGATIONAL CHURCH*, Two N Eagleville Rd, 06268. Tel: 860-429-9382. FAX: 860-429-9693. E-mail: info@storrscongchurch.org. Web Site: www.storrscongchurch.org. *Librn,* Janet Atkins; Tel: 860-423-5930
Library Holdings: Bk Titles 4,000

STRATFORD

S STRATFORD HISTORICAL SOCIETY LIBRARY*, 967 Academy Hill, 06615. (Mail add: PO Box 382, 06615-0382), SAN 325-657X. Tel: 203-378-0630. FAX: 203-378-2562. E-mail: judsonhousestfd@aol.com. Web Site: www.stratfordhistoricalsociety.com. *Curator,* Carol Lovell
Founded 1925
Library Holdings: Bk Titles 650
Subject Interests: Local hist
Open Tues & Thurs 9-2:30

P STRATFORD LIBRARY ASSOCIATION*, 2203 Main St, 06615. SAN 302-3931. Tel: 203-385-4161. Circulation Tel: 203-385-4160. Reference Tel: 203-385-4164. Administration Tel: 203-381-4166. Automation Services Tel: 203-381-2076. FAX: 203-381-2079. E-mail: ask@stratfordlibrary.org. Web Site: www.stratfordlibrary.org. *Libr Dir,* Barbara Blosveren; E-mail: bblosveren@stratfordlibrary.org; *Asst Dir,* Sheri Szymanski; Tel: 203-381-2063, E-mail: sszymanski@stratfordlibrary.org; *Head, Info Tech Serv,* Diane Kurtz; E-mail: dkurtz@stratfordlibrary.org; *Head, Adult Serv,* Katie Courcey; E-mail: kcourcey@stratfordlibrary.org; *Head, Ch,* Martha Simpson; Tel: 203-385-4165, E-mail: msimpson@stratfordlibrary.org; *Head, Circ,* Catherine Coda; E-mail: ccoda@stratfordlibrary.org; *Head, Youth Serv,* Lucretia Duwel; Tel: 203-385-4167, E-mail: lduwel@stratfordlibrary.org; *Pub Relations,* Tom Holehan; Tel: 203-385-4162, E-mail: tholehan@stratfordlibrary.org; Staff 28.2 (MLS 12.07, Non-MLS 16.13)
Founded 1886. Pop 51,901; Circ 459,055
Library Holdings: AV Mats 18,292; Electronic Media & Resources 3,891; Bk Vols 150,934; Per Subs 192
Special Collections: ESOL Coll; Leading to Reading Kits; Local History Coll; Raymark EPA Documents
Automation Activity & Vendor Info: (Acquisitions) SirsiDynix; (Cataloging) SirsiDynix; (Circulation) SirsiDynix; (ILL) OCLC; (OPAC) SirsiDynix; (Serials) SirsiDynix
Database Vendor: EBSCO Auto Repair Reference, EBSCO Information Services, EBSCOhost, Gale Cengage Learning, Grolier Online, Ingram Library Services, Library Ideas, LLC, LibraryInsight, Newsbank, OCLC, OCLC FirstSearch, Overdrive, Inc, ReferenceUSA, SirsiDynix, TumbleBookLibrary, World Book Online
Wireless access
Function: Adult bk club, After school storytime, Art exhibits, Audiobks via web, AV serv, Bk club(s), Bks on CD, Children's prog, Computer training, Computers for patron use, Copy machines, Digital talking bks, e-mail serv, Electronic databases & coll, Family literacy, Fax serv, Free DVD rentals, Handicapped accessible, Holiday prog, Homework prog, ILL available, Magnifiers for reading, Mail & tel request accepted, Microfiche/film & reading machines, Mus passes, Music CDs, Online ref, Online searches, Outreach serv, Outside serv via phone, mail, e-mail & web, OverDrive digital audio bks, Photocopying/Printing, Preschool outreach, Preschool reading prog, Printer for laptops & handheld devices, Prof lending libr, Prog for adults, Prog for children & young adult, Pub access computers, Ref serv in person, Referrals accepted, Scanner, Senior outreach, Spanish lang bks, Story hour, Summer & winter reading prog, Tax forms, Teen prog, Telephone ref, Web-catalog, Wheelchair accessible, Workshops
Publications: Annual Report; Monthly Calendar
Partic in Connecticut Library Consortium
Special Services for the Deaf - Assistive tech; Bks on deafness & sign lang; Closed caption videos; High interest/low vocabulary bks
Special Services for the Blind - Assistive/Adapted tech devices, equip & products; Audio mat; Bks on cassette; Bks on CD; Digital talking bk; Large print bks; Low vision equip; Magnifiers; Playaways (bks on MP3); Recorded bks
Open Mon-Thurs 10-8, Fri & Sat 10-5, Sun (Oct-May) 1-5

SUFFIELD

P KENT MEMORIAL LIBRARY*, 50 N Main St (Junction of Rtes 75 & 168), 06078-2117. SAN 302-3958. Tel: 860-668-3896. FAX: 860-668-3895. Web Site: www.suffield-library.org. *Dir,* John Fuchs; *Asst Dir,* Kim Lord; E-mail: kimlord@suffield-library.org; *Cat,* Dorian Taylor; *Ch Serv,* Wendy Taylor; *Circ,* Lois Hayes; *ILL,* Sue Mack; Staff 17 (MLS 3, Non-MLS 14)
Founded 1884. Pop 12,900; Circ 139,882
Jul 2008-Jun 2009 Income $512,968, City $427,468. Mats Exp $56,500, Books $52,000, Per/Ser (Incl. Access Fees) $4,500. Sal $294,720 (Prof $148,484)
Library Holdings: Audiobooks 2,228; AV Mats 327; CDs 3,647; DVDs 4,558; e-books 634; Electronic Media & Resources 18; Large Print Bks 1,114; Microforms 176; Bk Vols 75,106; Per Subs 106; Videos 1,860
Special Collections: Local Suffield History, bks, doc
Automation Activity & Vendor Info: (Acquisitions) SirsiDynix; (Cataloging) SirsiDynix; (Circulation) SirsiDynix; (ILL) SirsiDynix; (OPAC) SirsiDynix; (Serials) SirsiDynix
Database Vendor: Bibliomation Inc, Facts on File
Wireless access
Function: Adult bk club, Archival coll, Art exhibits, Audio & video playback equip for onsite use, Audiobks via web, Bks on CD, CD-ROM, Children's prog, Copy machines, E-Reserves, Electronic databases & coll, Free DVD rentals, Home delivery & serv to Sr ctr & nursing homes, ILL available, Magnifiers for reading, Mail & tel request accepted, Mus passes, Music CDs, Online cat, Online ref, Online searches, Orientations, OverDrive digital audio bks, Photocopying/Printing, Prog for adults, Prog for children & young adult, Pub access computers, Ref serv available, Scanner, Story hour, Summer reading prog, Tax forms, Telephone ref, VHS videos, Web-catalog
Publications: Directory of Suffield Clubs & Organizations
Open Mon-Thurs 10-8:30, Fri & Sat 10-5, Sat (Summer) 10-1
Friends of the Library Group

C LINCOLN COLLEGE LIBRARY*, 1760 Mapleton Ave, 06078-1463. Tel: 860-668-3515. Toll Free Tel: 800-955-0809. FAX: 860-668-7369. Web Site: ichm.edu. *Dir, Libr & Info Serv,* Eileen Rhodes; Staff 5 (MLS 1, Non-MLS 4)
Founded 1990. Enrl 85; Fac 20; Highest Degree: Associate
Library Holdings: Bk Vols 10,000; Per Subs 40
Automation Activity & Vendor Info: (Cataloging) Follett Software; (Circulation) Follett Software; (OPAC) Follett Software
Database Vendor: EBSCOhost, Gale Cengage Learning, Newsbank
Wireless access
Function: ILL available, Photocopying/Printing
Partic in Connecticut Library Consortium
Open Mon-Fri 9-5
Restriction: Open to students, fac & staff, Pub use on premises

TERRYVILLE

S LOCK MUSEUM OF AMERICA, INC LIBRARY*, 230 Main St, 06786-5900. (Mail add: PO Box 104, 06786-0104), SAN 326-2537. Tel: 860-589-6359. FAX: 860-589-6359. Web Site: www.lockmuseumofamerica.org. *Curator,* Thomas Hennessy, Jr
Founded 1972
Library Holdings: Bk Titles 100; Per Subs 500
Special Collections: Lockmaking Research Materials; Patent Indexes, 1790-1977
Open Tues-Fri (May-Oct) 1:30-4

P TERRYVILLE PUBLIC LIBRARY*, 238 Main St, 06786. SAN 302-3974. Tel: 860-582-3121. Reference Tel: 860-583-4467. FAX: 860-585-4068. E-mail: tplstaff@biblio.org. Web Site: www.terryvillepl.info. *Dir,* Lynn White; Staff 12 (MLS 1, Non-MLS 11)
Founded 1895. Pop 11,800; Circ 60,000
Jul 2005-Jun 2006 Income $406,385, State $7,500, City $380,885, Locally Generated Income $7,000, Other $11,000. Mats Exp $65,700, Books $50,000, Per/Ser (Incl. Access Fees) $5,700, Other Print Mats $400, Micro $400, AV Equip $1,000, AV Mat $5,000, Electronic Ref Mat (Incl. Access Fees) $3,000, Presv $100. Sal $227,900 (Prof $52,300)
Library Holdings: Bks on Deafness & Sign Lang 15; High Interest/Low Vocabulary Bk Vols 250; Large Print Bks 1,000; Bk Titles 56,000; Per Subs 101; Talking Bks 800
Special Collections: Career Corner; Terryville-Plymouth Room
Subject Interests: Literacy
Automation Activity & Vendor Info: (Cataloging) CARL.Solution (TLC); (Circulation) CARL.Solution (TLC); (OPAC) CARL.Solution (TLC)
Publications: The Footnote (Newsletter)
Partic in Region I Coop Libr Servs Unit
Open Mon-Wed 10-8, Thurs 10-6, Fri & Sat 10-5
Friends of the Library Group

THOMASTON

P THOMASTON PUBLIC LIBRARY*, 248 Main St, 06787. SAN 302-3990. Tel: 860-283-4339. FAX: 860-283-4330. Web Site: www.biblio.org/thomaston. *Dir,* Debra Radosevich; E-mail: dradosevich@biblio.org; *Asst Librn,* Cindy Killian; *Cat,* Ruth Fields
Founded 1898. Pop 6,276; Circ 70,000
Library Holdings: Bk Vols 50,000; Per Subs 115
Special Collections: Art Techniques (Bradshaw Coll); Career Information; Conklin Coll of the Arts, bks, fs; Connecticut History (Allan C Innes Coll); Innes Coll (J P Seth) Thomaston Centennial (Seth Thomas Clock Company & Family Coll). Oral History
Automation Activity & Vendor Info: (Acquisitions) Horizon; (Cataloging) Horizon; (Circulation) Horizon; (Course Reserve) Horizon; (ILL) Horizon; (OPAC) Horizon; (Serials) Horizon
Publications: Thomaston Public Library Gazette
Open Mon-Thurs 10-8, Fri 10-5, Sat (Sept-June) 10-3
Friends of the Library Group

TOLLAND

S FRENCH-CANADIAN GENEALOGICAL SOCIETY OF CONNECTICUT, INC LIBRARY*, 53 Tolland Green, 06084. (Mail add: PO Box 928, 06084-0928), SAN 326-9698. Tel: 860-872-2597. E-mail: french.canadian@snet.net. Web Site: www.fcgsc.org. *Pres,* Raymond Lamaire; Tel: 860-643-7231; *Dir,* Germaine Hoffman; Tel: 860-623-8721
Founded 1981
Library Holdings: Bk Titles 3,000
Special Collections: Brown New England Coll; Hebert Acadian Coll; Tolland Library Association Genealogical Coll
Subject Interests: Acadian genealogy, Fr Can
Publications: Connecticut Maple Leaf (semi annual)
Partic in Area Libr Serv Authority
Open Mon & Wed 1-5, Sat 9-4, Sun 1-4

P TOLLAND PUBLIC LIBRARY, 21 Tolland Green, 06084. SAN 302-4008. Tel: 860-871-3620. FAX: 860-871-3626. *Dir,* Barbara Pettijohn; E-mail: bpettijohn@tolland.org; *Ch Serv,* Ginny Brousseau; Staff 9 (MLS 2, Non-MLS 7)
Founded 1899. Pop 12,036; Circ 134,969
Library Holdings: Bk Titles 71,568; Per Subs 80
Automation Activity & Vendor Info: (Acquisitions) Bibliomation Inc; (Cataloging) Bibliomation Inc; (Circulation) Bibliomation Inc; (OPAC) Bibliomation Inc
Database Vendor: EBSCOhost
Wireless access
Function: ILL available, Photocopying/Printing
Partic in Connecticut Library Consortium
Open Mon-Thurs 10-8, Fri & Sat 10-5
Friends of the Library Group

TORRINGTON

M CHARLOTTE HUNGERFORD HOSPITAL*, Health Sciences Library, 540 Litchfield, 06790. Tel: 860-496-6689. Administration Tel: 860-496-6340. Administration FAX: 860-482-8627. *VPres,* Dr Mark R Prete; Tel: 860-496-6434, E-mail: mprete@hungerford.org
Library Holdings: Bk Titles 350; Bk Vols 450
Database Vendor: UpToDate
Open Mon-Fri 8-4:30

S TORRINGTON HISTORICAL SOCIETY LIBRARY*, John Thompson Memorial Library, 192 Main St, 06790. SAN 302-4016. Tel: 860-482-8260. E-mail: torringtonhistorical@snet.net. Web Site: www.torringtonhistoricalsociety.org. *Dir,* Mark McEachern; *Archivist, Librn,* Carol Clapp
Founded 1944
Library Holdings: Bk Titles 2,000
Special Collections: CT Journal (1782-1813), newsp; General Archives; Litchfield Enquirer (1842-1941), newsp; Litchfield Monitor (1791-1795), newsp; Torrington Building Co, blueprints; Torrington History; Torrington Register (1874-present)
Subject Interests: Genealogy, Local hist
Restriction: Open by appt only

P TORRINGTON LIBRARY*, 12 Daycoeton Pl, 06790-6399. SAN 302-4024. Tel: 860-489-6684. FAX: 860-482-4664. E-mail: info@torringtonlibrary.org. Web Site: www.torringtonlibrary.org. *Dir,* Karen Worrall
Founded 1864. Pop 35,202; Circ 111,121
Library Holdings: AV Mats 1,400; Large Print Bks 2,826; Bk Vols 54,596; Per Subs 74; Talking Bks 800
Special Collections: Large Print Coll
Automation Activity & Vendor Info: (Cataloging) Follett Software; (Circulation) Follett Software; (ILL) Auto-Graphics, Inc; (OPAC) Follett Software
Publications: The Bookworm (Newsletter)
Partic in Region I Coop Libr Servs Unit
Open Mon, Tues & Fri 10-6, Wed & Thurs 10-8, Sat 10-3

C UNIVERSITY OF CONNECTICUT - TORRINGTON REGIONAL CAMPUS LIBRARY, Julia Brooker Thompson Library, 855 University Dr, 06790. SAN 302-4032. Tel: 860-626-6820. FAX: 860-626-6817. E-mail: torrcl@lib.uconn.edu. Web Site: www.lib.uconn.edu. *Dir/Ref Librn,* Sheila A Lafferty; Tel: 806-626-6841, E-mail: sheila.lafferty@uconn.edu; Staff 1 (MLS 1)
Founded 1965. Highest Degree: Bachelor
Library Holdings: Bk Vols 16,000
Automation Activity & Vendor Info: (Circulation) Ex Libris Group; (Course Reserve) Atlas Systems; (ILL) OCLC WorldShare Interlibrary Loan; (OPAC) Ex Libris Group
Database Vendor: ABC-CLIO, Agricola, Alexander Street Press, American Chemical Society, American Psychological Association (APA), ARTstor, Auto-Graphics, Inc, Cambridge Scientific Abstracts, Cinahl, CQ Press, CRC Press/Taylor & Francis Group, ebrary, EBSCOhost, Elsevier, Factiva.com, Facts on File, Gale Cengage Learning, H W Wilson, HeinOnline, IBISWorld, IEEE (Institute of Electrical & Electronics Engineers), ISI Web of Knowledge, JSTOR, Knovel, LexisNexis, Nature Publishing Group, OCLC FirstSearch, OCLC WorldShare Interlibrary Loan, OVID Technologies, Project MUSE, ProQuest, PubMed, RefWorks, Safari Books Online, Sage, ScienceDirect, Scopus, Springshare, LLC, Westlaw, Wilson - Wilson Web, YBP Library Services
Wireless access
Partic in Boston Library Consortium, Inc
Open Mon-Thurs 9:30-6:30

TRUMBULL

P TRUMBULL LIBRARY*, 33 Quality St, 06611. SAN 336-5190. Tel: 203-452-5197. FAX: 203-452-5125. Web Site: www.trumbullct-library.org. *Dir,* Susan Horton; E-mail: shorton@trumbull-ct.gov; *Assoc Dir, Info Syst,* Mary Rogers; E-mail: mrogers@trumbull-ct.org; *Asst Dir,* Louise Sheehy; *Head, Ch,* Kara Canney; *Head, Ref,* Walter Dembowski; E-mail: mdembowski@trumbull-ct.org; *Circ,* Megan Norrell; E-mail: mnorrell@trumbull-ct.org; Staff 48 (MLS 7, Non-MLS 41)
Founded 1975. Pop 34,857; Circ 367,180
Library Holdings: Bk Vols 172,000; Per Subs 200; Talking Bks 1,700; Videos 11,000
Automation Activity & Vendor Info: (Acquisitions) Horizon; (Cataloging) Horizon; (Circulation) Horizon; (OPAC) Horizon
Open Mon-Thurs 9-8, Fri & Sat 9-5, Sun 1-5
Friends of the Library Group
Branches: 1
FAIRCHILD NICHOLS MEMORIAL, 1718 Huntington Tpk, 06611, SAN 336-5220. Tel: 203-452-5196. *Librn,* Position Currently Open; Staff 6 (MLS 1, Non-MLS 5)
Library Holdings: Bk Vols 34,000
Database Vendor: SirsiDynix
Open Mon & Wed 10-8, Tues & Thurs 10-5, Sat 10-2, Sun (Oct-May) 1-5
Friends of the Library Group

S UNILEVER HPC NA*, Research Laboratories Library, Trumbull Corporate Park, 40 Merritt Blvd, 06611. SAN 302-4059. Tel: 203-377-8300, Ext 4312. *Res Librn,* Mary M Davis; E-mail: mary.m.davis@unilever.com; *Res Librn,* Anne McDermott; E-mail: anne.c.mcdermott@unilever.com
Founded 1959
Library Holdings: Bk Vols 5,000; Per Subs 249
Subject Interests: Chem, Dentistry, Dermatology, Pharmacology
Automation Activity & Vendor Info: (Cataloging) Horizon; (Circulation) Horizon; (OPAC) Horizon; (Serials) Horizon
Wireless access
Partic in Dialog Corp
Open Mon-Fri 8-4:30
Restriction: Employees only

UNCASVILLE

S RADGOWSKI CORRECTIONAL INSTITUTION LIBRARY*, 982 Norwich-New London Tpk, 06382. Tel: 860-848-5070. FAX: 860-848-5097. *Res Coordr,* Ida Kleiner
Library Holdings: Bk Vols 2,800

UNION

P UNION FREE PUBLIC LIBRARY*, 979 Buckley Hwy, 06076. SAN 302-3680. Tel: 860-684-4913. FAX: 860-684-4913. E-mail: littlelibrary979@gmail.com, littlelibrary979@unionctfreepubliclibrary.org.

Web Site: unionctfreepubliclibrary.org. *Libr Dir,* Kathleen M Robertson; E-mail: kmrobertson@unionctfreepubliclibrary.org. Subject Specialists: *Ch,* Kathleen M Robertson; Staff 0.5 (Non-MLS 0.5)
Founded 1894. Pop 755; Circ 6,233
Library Holdings: Bk Titles 11,000; Bk Vols 12,300
Automation Activity & Vendor Info: (Cataloging) Bibliomation Inc; (Circulation) Bibliomation Inc; (ILL) Bibliomation Inc; (OPAC) Bibliomation Inc
Database Vendor: Bibliomation Inc
Wireless access
Function: Family literacy, Fax serv, Free DVD rentals, Holiday prog, Mus passes, Music CDs, Online cat, Online searches, Photocopying/Printing, Prog for adults, Prog for children & young adult, Pub access computers, Ref serv available, Referrals accepted, Scanner, Story hour, Summer reading prog, Teen prog, VHS videos
Partic in Connecticut Library Consortium
Open Mon 1-4, Wed 5-8, Sat 9-1

VERNON

P ROCKVILLE PUBLIC LIBRARY, INC*, George Maxwell Memorial Library, 52 Union St, 06066-3155. (Mail add: PO Box 1320, 06066-1320), SAN 302-4067. Tel: 860-875-5892. Administration Tel: 860-872-4431. FAX: 860-875-9795. E-mail: refnet@biblio.org. Web Site: www.biblio.org/rockville. *Circ Supvr, Co-Dir, Tech Serv Supvr,* Donna R Enman; *Ch Serv,* Shahla Zarinejad; *ILL,* Jan Smith; Staff 1 (MLS 1)
Founded 1893. Pop 29,672; Circ 162,000
Library Holdings: Bk Titles 60,000; Per Subs 90
Subject Interests: Local hist
Automation Activity & Vendor Info: (Cataloging) Horizon; (Circulation) Horizon
Database Vendor: Bibliomation Inc, EBSCOhost
Function: Adult bk club, Bks on cassette, Bks on CD, Children's prog, Computers for patron use, Homebound delivery serv, ILL available, Mus passes, Online cat, Online ref, Photocopying/Printing, Prog for adults, Prog for children & young adult, Pub access computers, Ref serv available, Senior outreach, Spoken cassettes & CDs, Story hour, Summer reading prog, Tax forms, VHS videos, Web-catalog
Partic in Bibliomation Inc
Open Mon-Thurs 10-8, Fri & Sat 10-5
Friends of the Library Group

VOLUNTOWN

P VOLUNTOWN PUBLIC LIBRARY*, 107 Main St, 06384-1820. (Mail add: PO Box 26, 06384-0026), SAN 302-4075. Tel: 860-376-0485. FAX: 860-376-4324. E-mail: vltnlib@yahoo.com. *Dir,* Deborah D Fleet; *Asst Librn,* Sharon Geer; Staff 4 (MLS 1, Non-MLS 3)
Founded 1940. Pop 2,558
Library Holdings: Bk Vols 18,000
Special Collections: Finnish Culture & Language Coll; Parenting/Home Education Coll
Subject Interests: Local hist
Automation Activity & Vendor Info: (Cataloging) Follett Software; (Circulation) Follett Software; (ILL) Auto-Graphics, Inc; (OPAC) Auto-Graphics, Inc
Wireless access
Function: Bi-weekly Writer's Group, Handicapped accessible, Home delivery & serv to Sr ctr & nursing homes, Homebound delivery serv, ILL available, Photocopying/Printing, Prog for children & young adult, Summer reading prog, Telephone ref, Wheelchair accessible
Partic in CLA
Special Services for the Deaf - Bks on deafness & sign lang; Closed caption videos
Special Services for the Blind - Cassettes; Home delivery serv; Large print bks
Open Mon, Wed & Fri 12-4, Tues 10:30 am-7:30pm, Thurs 2-6, Sat 10-1
Friends of the Library Group

WALLINGFORD

M GAYLORD HOSPITAL*, Tremaine Library & Resource Center, PO Box 400, 06492. SAN 328-4697. Tel: 203-741-3328. FAX: 203-284-2892. Web Site: www.gaylord.org. *Coordr,* Lyn Crispino; E-mail: lcrispino@gaylord.org; Staff 1 (MLS 1)
Library Holdings: Bk Vols 1,500; Per Subs 120
Publications: Newsletter
Partic in Basic Health Sciences Library Network; Conn Asn of Health Scis Librs
Open Mon-Fri 8-4:30, Sat & Sun 12-7:30

S WALLINGFORD HISTORICAL SOCIETY INC, LIBRARY*, Samuel Parsons House, 180 S Main St, 06492. (Mail add: PO Box 73, 06492-0073), SAN 326-9981. Tel: 203-294-1996. *Pres,* Raymond Chappell
Founded 1916
Library Holdings: Bk Vols 500
Subject Interests: Local genealogy, Local hist
Function: Res libr
Publications: Wallingford - Images of America Series
Restriction: Open by appt only

P WALLINGFORD PUBLIC LIBRARY*, 200 N Main St, 06492-3791. SAN 336-5255. Tel: 203-265-6754. FAX: 203-269-5698. Web Site: www.wallingford.lioninc.org. *Dir,* Jane Fisher; *Asst Dir,* Amy Humphries; Tel: 203-284-6422, E-mail: amyh@lioninc.org; *Head, Ch,* Sunnie Lovelace; *Head, Circ,* Judy Sgammato; *Head, Innovation & Emerging Tech,* Janet Flewelling; *Head, Tech Serv,* Patricia Johnson; *Head, Teen Serv,* Jennifer Nash; *Ch,* Bonnie Strickland-Naczi; *Commun Serv Librn,* Elizabeth Devlin; *Ref Librn,* David Andrews; Staff 12 (MLS 12)
Founded 1881. Pop 44,680; Circ 646,244
Jul 2008-Jun 2009 Income (Main Library and Branch(s)) $2,869,229, State $4,000, City $2,579,793, Locally Generated Income $80,000, Other $205,436. Mats Exp $280,868, Books $196,778, Per/Ser (Incl. Access Fees) $22,090, Micro $5,000, AV Mat $35,000, Electronic Ref Mat (Incl. Access Fees) $22,000. Sal $1,473,449
Library Holdings: CDs 8,324; DVDs 6,421; Electronic Media & Resources 15; Bk Vols 196,246; Per Subs 320; Talking Bks 4,699; Videos 6,277
Special Collections: Oneida Community, Holocaust
Subject Interests: Local hist
Automation Activity & Vendor Info: (Acquisitions) Innovative Interfaces, Inc; (Cataloging) Innovative Interfaces, Inc; (Circulation) Innovative Interfaces, Inc; (ILL) Innovative Interfaces, Inc; (OPAC) Innovative Interfaces, Inc; (Serials) Innovative Interfaces, Inc
Database Vendor: Baker & Taylor, EBSCO Auto Repair Reference, EBSCOhost, Gale Cengage Learning, Innovative Interfaces, Inc, ReferenceUSA, Wilson - Wilson Web
Wireless access
Function: Mus passes, Music CDs, Online cat, OverDrive digital audio bks, Photocopying/Printing
Publications: WORDS (Newsletter)
Partic in Libraries Online, Inc
Open Mon-Fri 9:30-9, Sat 9:30-5, Sun 1-5
Friends of the Library Group
Branches: 1
YALESVILLE BRANCH, 400 Church St, Yalesville, 06492, SAN 336-528X. Tel: 203-269-3688. *Dir,* Leslie Scherer
Library Holdings: Bk Vols 5,000
Automation Activity & Vendor Info: (Circulation) Innovative Interfaces, Inc - Millenium
Open Tues & Thurs 10-8, Sat 10-2
Friends of the Library Group

WARREN

P WARREN PUBLIC LIBRARY*, 15 Sackett Hill Rd, 06754. SAN 302-4105. Tel: 860-868-2195. E-mail: warrenpl@optonline.net. Web Site: www.warrenctlibrary.org/. *Dir,* Martha Winkel; *Asst Librn,* Barbara Ayres; *Asst Librn,* Bernice Merz; Staff 3 (Non-MLS 3)
Pop 1,400; Circ 7,000; Highest Degree: Bachelor
Library Holdings: Bk Vols 14,000
Wireless access
Function: Audio & video playback equip for onsite use, Bks on cassette, Bks on CD, Children's prog, Computers for patron use, Copy machines, e-mail serv, Free DVD rentals, Homebound delivery serv, ILL available, Literacy & newcomer serv, Mail & tel request accepted, Music CDs, Photocopying/Printing, Preschool outreach, Prog for adults, Prog for children & young adult, Ref serv available
Open Tues 10-7, Thurs & Fri 10-5, Sat 10-1

WASHINGTON

P GUNN MEMORIAL LIBRARY, INC*, Five Wykeham Rd, 06793-1308. (Mail add: PO Box 1273, 06793-0273), SAN 302-4113. Tel: 860-868-7586. FAX: 860-868-7247. E-mail: gunnlib@biblio.org. Web Site: www.gunnlibrary.org. *Dir,* Jean Chapin; *Adult Serv,* Martie Smolka
Founded 1908. Pop 4,000; Circ 66,747
Jul 2009-Jun 2010. Mats Exp $21,300, Books $12,000, Per/Ser (Incl. Access Fees) $4,000, AV Mat $5,000, Electronic Ref Mat (Incl. Access Fees) $300
Library Holdings: Audiobooks 3,764; DVDs 2,197; e-books 204; Bk Vols 50,296; Per Subs 82; Videos 1,811
Subject Interests: Connecticut
Automation Activity & Vendor Info: (Cataloging) Bibliomation Inc; (Circulation) Bibliomation Inc; (OPAC) Bibliomation Inc
Wireless access
Open Mon & Fri 9:30-5, Tues & Thurs 9:30-8, Sat 9:30-3

S THE GUNNERY*, Tisch Family Library, 99 Green Hill Rd, 06793. SAN 326-0054. Tel: 860-868-7334, Ext 224. FAX: 860-868-0859. *Dir,* Susan Rogers; E-mail: rogerss@gunnery.org; *Asst Librn,* Sheila Kahn; Staff 2 (MLS 2)
Library Holdings: Bk Vols 15,000; Per Subs 90
Special Collections: Alumni bks & publications

S INSTITUTE FOR AMERICAN INDIAN STUDIES*, Research & Education Libraries, 38 Curtis Rd, 06793-0260. SAN 321-0359. Tel: 860-868-0518. FAX: 860-868-1649. E-mail: iais@charter.net. Web Site: birdstone.org. *Dir,* Dr Lucianne Lavin, *Coordr,* Lisa Piastuch-Temmen
Founded 1975
Library Holdings: Bk Titles 2,400
Subject Interests: Archaeology, Ethnobotany
Restriction: Open by appt only

WASHINGTON DEPOT

S WASHINGTON ART ASSOCIATION LIBRARY*, Four Bryan Plaza, 06794. Tel: 860-868-2878. Web Site: washingtonart.org. *In Charge,* Materne Delancey
Founded 1952
Library Holdings: Bk Titles 1,600
Open Tues-Sat 10-5, Sun 12-5

WATERBURY

P SILAS BRONSON LIBRARY*, 267 Grand St, 06702-1981. SAN 336-531X. Tel: 203-574-8222. Circulation Tel: 203-574-8206. Reference Tel: 203-574-8225. FAX: 203-574-8055. TDD: 203-574-8226. Web Site: www.bronsonlibrary.org. *Dir,* J Emmett McSweeney; Tel: 203-574-8221; Staff 30 (MLS 15, Non-MLS 15)
Founded 1869. Pop 108,859; Circ 238,806
Library Holdings: AV Mats 16,021; Electronic Media & Resources 20; Bk Vols 256,314; Per Subs 195
Subject Interests: Genealogy, Local hist
Automation Activity & Vendor Info: (Cataloging) Horizon; (Circulation) Horizon; (ILL) Horizon; (OPAC) Horizon; (Serials) Horizon
Database Vendor: EBSCOhost
Wireless access
Function: Adult bk club, AV serv, BA reader (adult literacy), Chess club, Digital talking bks, E-Reserves, Electronic databases & coll, Handicapped accessible, Homebound delivery serv, ILL available, Magnifiers for reading, Mail & tel request accepted, Music CDs, Newsp ref libr, Online searches, Photocopying/Printing, Preschool outreach, Prog for adults, Prog for children & young adult, Ref & res, Ref serv available, Spoken cassettes & CDs, Spoken cassettes & DVDs, Summer reading prog, Telephone ref, VHS videos, Video lending libr, Wheelchair accessible
Publications: Books & Happenings (Newsletter)
Special Services for the Deaf - Bks on deafness & sign lang; Closed caption videos; High interest/low vocabulary bks; TTY equip
Special Services for the Blind - Audio mat; Bks on cassette; Bks on CD; Computer with voice synthesizer for visually impaired persons; Extensive large print coll; Internet workstation with adaptive software; Large print bks; Large screen computer & software; Low vision equip; Magnifiers; Newsletter (in large print, Braille or on cassette); PC for handicapped; Photo duplicator for making large print; Ref serv; Screen enlargement software for people with visual disabilities; Talking bks; Videos on blindness & phys handicaps
Open Mon-Thurs 9-8, Fri 9-5:30, Sat (Sept-May) 10-2
Friends of the Library Group
Branches: 1
BUNKER HILL, 192 Bunker Hill Ave, 06708, SAN 336-5344. Tel: 203-574-8240. *Br Librn,* Hugh Curran
Library Holdings: Bk Vols 7,000
Open Tues 1-8, Thurs 10-5:30, Sat (Sept-May) 10-2

L CARMODY & TORRANCE*, Law Library, 50 Leavenworth St, 06702. SAN 372-3402. Tel: 203-573-1200. FAX: 203-575-2600. E-mail: ahodges@carmodylaw.com. *Librn,* Ann C Hodges
Library Holdings: Bk Vols 12,000; Per Subs 100
Automation Activity & Vendor Info: (Cataloging) EOS International; (Circulation) EOS International
Open Mon-Fri 9-5

S COUNCIL OF GOVERNMENTS OF THE CENTRAL NAUGATUCK VALLEY LIBRARY*, 60 N Main St, 3rd Flr, 06702-1403. SAN 373-0948. Tel: 203-757-0535. FAX: 203-756-7688. E-mail: cogcnv@cogcnv.org. Web Site: www.cogcnv.org. *Exec Dir,* Position Currently Open; *Actg Exec Dir,* Sam Gold; E-mail: sgold@cogcnv.org
Library Holdings: Bk Titles 1,200; Per Subs 20; Spec Interest Per Sub 20
Special Collections: GIS Maps; US Census Data. US Document Depository
Subject Interests: Econ develop, Land use, Solid waste, Transportation, Water
Restriction: Non-circulating, Staff use only

S MACDERMID, INC LIBRARY*, 245 Freight St, 06702. SAN 302-4156. Tel: 203-575-5700. FAX: 203-575-5630. *In Charge,* Eleanor Barkauskas
Library Holdings: Bk Vols 1,500; Per Subs 50
Open Mon-Fri 8-5

S MATTATUCK HISTORICAL SOCIETY LIBRARY*, Mattatuck Museum Library, 144 W Main St, 06702. SAN 302-4172. Tel: 203-753-0381. FAX: 203-756-6283. Web Site: www.mattatuckmuseum.org. *Dir,* Robert Burns; Tel: 203-753-0381, Ext 122; *Curator,* Cynthia Roznoy; Tel: 203-753-0381, Ext 115; *Coll Mgr,* Suzie Fateh-Tehrani; Tel: 203-753-0381, Ext 112
Founded 1877
Library Holdings: Bk Vols 1,500; Per Subs 10
Special Collections: Brass Workers History Project Archives; Connecticut Artists Coll; Decorative Arts; Pictorial History of Waterbury, 1674-1974; Platt Brothers Archives; Waterbury Industrial History Archives
Subject Interests: Local hist
Restriction: Open by appt only

J NAUGATUCK VALLEY COMMUNITY COLLEGE, Max R Traurig Library, 750 Chase Pkwy, 06708. SAN 302-4229. Tel: 203-575-8024. Reference Tel: 203-575-8244. FAX: 203-575-8258. TDD: 203-596-8762. E-mail: library@nvcc.commnet.edu. Web Site: www.nv.edu/academics/library. *Dir,* Jaime Hammond; E-mail: jhammond@nvcc.commnet.edu; *Instrul Serv Librn, Ref,* Liz Frechette; *Ref/Instruction/Tech Serv Librn,* John Leonetti; *Syst Librn, Tech Serv,* Alison Wang; *Circ Supvr,* Elaine Milnor; Staff 5 (MLS 4, Non-MLS 1)
Founded 1964. Enrl 7,000; Fac 120; Highest Degree: Associate
Library Holdings: e-books 26,000; Bk Vols 35,000
Automation Activity & Vendor Info: (Acquisitions) Ex Libris Group; (Cataloging) Ex Libris Group; (Circulation) Ex Libris Group; (Course Reserve) Ex Libris Group; (ILL) Ex Libris Group; (OPAC) Ex Libris Group; (Serials) Ex Libris Group
Database Vendor: 3M Library Systems, CredoReference, ebrary, EBSCOhost, Facts on File, JSTOR, ProQuest, Springshare, LLC, Westlaw
Wireless access
Special Services for the Deaf - TDD equip
Special Services for the Blind - Braille bks; Closed circuit TV magnifier; Computer with voice synthesizer for visually impaired persons; Magnifiers; Reader equip
Open Mon & Tues (Fall & Spring) 8-8, Wed & Thurs 8-6, Fri 8-4, Sat & Sun 10-2
Restriction: Open to pub for ref & circ; with some limitations

C POST UNIVERSITY, Traurig Library & Learning Resources Center, 800 Country Club Rd, 06723-2540. SAN 302-4180. Tel: 203-596-4560. E-mail: library@post.edu. Web Site: www.post.edu/library.shtml. *Dir,* Tracy Ralston; Tel: 203-596-4564, E-mail: Tralston@post.edu; *Info Serv Librn,* Susan Garry; Tel: 203-596-4565; *Ref Librn,* Kelly Marchand; Tel: 203-596-4609; Staff 3 (MLS 3)
Founded 1890. Enrl 5,813; Fac 130; Highest Degree: Master
Jul 2013-Jun 2014. Mats Exp $253,333
Special Collections: Equine Coll. State Document Depository; US Document Depository
Automation Activity & Vendor Info: (OPAC) Auto-Graphics, Inc
Database Vendor: EBSCOhost, LexisNexis, OCLC WorldShare Interlibrary Loan
Wireless access
Function: Computers for patron use, Copy machines, E-mail & chat, Electronic databases & coll, Fax serv, ILL available, Online info literacy tutorials on the web & in blackboard, Online ref, Online searches, Photocopying/Printing, Printer for laptops & handheld devices, Pub access computers, Ref serv available, Telephone ref, Web-catalog
Partic in Connecticut Library Consortium; Lyrasis; OCLC Online Computer Library Center, Inc
Open Mon-Wed (Fall-Spring) 8am-10pm, Thurs 8-8, Fri 8-5:30, Sat 10-4, Sun 2-8; Mon (Summer) 8-5, Tues-Thurs 8-6, Fri 8-4:30, Sat 10-4

M SAINT MARY'S HOSPITAL*, Health Science Library, 56 Franklin St, 06706. Tel: 203-709-6408. FAX: 203-709-7738. *Dir, Libr Serv,* Ellen Sheehan; Staff 1.75 (MLS 1, Non-MLS 0.75)
Library Holdings: e-books 10; e-journals 140; Bk Titles 4,000; Per Subs 360
Automation Activity & Vendor Info: (Circulation) CyberTools for Libraries; (OPAC) CyberTools for Libraries
Partic in Conn Asn of Health Scis Librs
Open Mon-Fri 8-4:30

C UNIVERSITY OF CONNECTICUT*, Waterbury Regional Campus Library, 99 E Main St, 06702-2311. SAN 302-4202. Tel: 203-236-9900. Interlibrary Loan Service Tel: 203-236-9903. Reference Tel: 203-236-9901.

Administration Tel: 203-236-9902, 203-236-9908. FAX: 203-236-9905. Web Site: www.lib.uconn.edu. *Dir,* Shelley Roseman; E-mail: shelley.roseman@uconn.edu; *Librn,* Janet M Swift; E-mail: janet.swift@uconn.edu; *ILL,* Norma Holmquist; E-mail: norma.holmquist@uconn.edu. Subject Specialists: *Undergrad studies,* Janet M Swift; *Bus,* Norma Holmquist; Staff 3 (MLS 3)
Founded 1946
Library Holdings: Bk Vols 35,000; Per Subs 100
Subject Interests: Art
Automation Activity & Vendor Info: (Acquisitions) Ex Libris Group; (Circulation) Ex Libris Group; (Course Reserve) Ex Libris Group; (ILL) OCLC; (OPAC) Ex Libris Group; (Serials) Ex Libris Group
Database Vendor: EBSCOhost, Gale Cengage Learning, OCLC FirstSearch
Partic in Boston Library Consortium, Inc; Connecticut Library Consortium; Lyrasis; New England Law Library Consortium, Inc; OCLC Online Computer Library Center, Inc

M WATERBURY HOSPITAL*, Health Center Library, 64 Robbins St, 06721. SAN 302-4210. Tel: 203-573-6136. FAX: 203-573-6706. E-mail: library@wtbyhosp.org. *Dir,* Linda Spadaccini; *Librn,* Lynn Sabol; Staff 2 (MLS 2)
Library Holdings: Bk Vols 2,000; Per Subs 220
Subject Interests: Med, Nursing
Automation Activity & Vendor Info: (Cataloging) LibraryWorld, Inc; (Circulation) LibraryWorld, Inc; (OPAC) LibraryWorld, Inc
Database Vendor: EBSCOhost, Elsevier, LibraryWorld, Inc, McGraw-Hill, Natural Standard, OCLC WorldShare Interlibrary Loan, OVID Technologies, PubMed, Wiley
Wireless access
Partic in National Network of Libraries of Medicine
Open Mon-Fri 8-4:30

S WATERBURY REPUBLICAN & AMERICAN LIBRARY*, 389 Meadow St, 06702. SAN 324-3583. Tel: 203-574-3636, Ext 1497. FAX: 203-596-9277. *Librn,* Michael C Dooling
Library Holdings: Bk Titles 800; Bk Vols 2,000; Per Subs 20
Special Collections: Local History Books; Local Newspaper Clippings; Local Photo Coll
Subject Interests: NW Conn
Wireless access
Restriction: Open by appt only

WATERFORD

S EUGENE O'NEILL THEATER CENTER*, Liebling-Wood Library, 305 Great Neck Rd, 06385. SAN 302-4237. Tel: 860-443-5378, Ext 227. Administration Tel: 860-443-5378. FAX: 860-443-9653. E-mail: litoffice@theoneill.org. Web Site: www.theoneill.org. *Actg Adminr, Lit Spec/Librn,* Martin Kettling. Subject Specialists: *Drama,* Martin Kettling; Staff 2 (MLS 1, Non-MLS 1)
Founded 1966
Library Holdings: Bk Titles 4,000
Special Collections: Eugene O'Neill Coll; National Critics Institute; National Music Theater Conference Archive; National Playwrights Conference Archive; National Puppetry Conference; National Theatre Institute Library. Oral History
Subject Interests: Develop of performance art, Standard drama & variations
Database Vendor: FileMaker
Wireless access
Function: Prog for children & young adult, Workshops, Writing prog
Restriction: External users must contact libr, In-house use for visitors, Open to fac, students & qualified researchers, Open to pub by appt only
Friends of the Library Group

P WATERFORD PUBLIC LIBRARY*, 49 Rope Ferry Rd, 06385. SAN 302-4245. Tel: 860-444-5805. FAX: 860-437-1685. E-mail: waterfordlibrary@juno.com. Web Site: www.waterfordpubliclibrary.org. *Dir,* Roslyn Rubinstein; *Ch,* Christine Tkaczyx
Founded 1923. Pop 19,100
Library Holdings: CDs 1,000; DVDs 750; Large Print Bks 2,500; Bk Vols 85,000; Per Subs 125; Talking Bks 1,250; Videos 2,000
Special Collections: Travel Coll
Subject Interests: Local hist
Automation Activity & Vendor Info: (Cataloging) SirsiDynix; (Circulation) SirsiDynix; (OPAC) SirsiDynix
Wireless access
Open Mon-Thurs 9-9, Fri 9-5:30, Sat 9-5, Sun 1-5

WATERTOWN

S WATERTOWN HISTORICAL SOCIETY LIBRARY*, 22 De Forest St, 06795. SAN 302-4253. Tel: 860-274-1050. *Pres,* Jeffrey Grenier
Founded 1947
Library Holdings: Bk Vols 1,000
Subject Interests: Genealogy, Local hist
Open Wed 2-4

P WATERTOWN LIBRARY ASSOCIATION*, 470 Main St, 06795. SAN 336-5409. Tel: 860-945-5360. FAX: 860-945-5367. Web Site: www.watertownlibrary.org. *Dir,* Joan K Rintelman; E-mail: joankr@watertownlibrary.org; *Asst Dir,* Dona L Rintelman
Founded 1865. Pop 20,000; Circ 113,657
Library Holdings: Bk Vols 107,000; Per Subs 180
Wireless access
Partic in Region I Coop Libr Servs Unit
Open Tues-Thurs 10-8, Fri 10-5, Sat (Winter) 10-4
Friends of the Library Group
Branches: 1
OAKVILLE BRANCH, 55 Davis St, Oakville, 06779, SAN 336-5433. Tel: 860-945-5368. FAX: 860-945-7199. *Br Mgr,* Donald Stepanek; *Asst Librn,* Lisa Dalton
Founded 1914
Open Tues & Wed 9-5, Thurs 9-1
Friends of the Library Group

WEST CORNWALL

P THE HUGHES MEMORIAL PUBLIC LIBRARY*, 35 Lower River Rd, 06796. (Mail add: PO Box 4, 06796), SAN 324-3753. Tel: 860-672-6374. Circ 5,000
Library Holdings: Bk Titles 16,000
Open Fri 4-7, Sat 9:30-12:30

WEST HARTFORD

R CONGREGATION BETH ISRAEL*, Deborah Library, 701 Farmington Ave, 06119. SAN 372-5820. Tel: 860-233-8215. FAX: 860-523-0223. Web Site: www.cbict.org. *Librn,* Danielle Stordy; E-mail: dstordy@cbict.org; Staff 1 (Non-MLS 1)
Founded 1934
Library Holdings: Bk Titles 15,000
Subject Interests: Judaica
Automation Activity & Vendor Info: (Cataloging) Follett Software; (Circulation) Follett Software
Open Tues, Thurs & Fri 9-2, Sun 9-1
Friends of the Library Group

R EMANUEL SYNAGOGUE LIBRARY*, 160 Mohegan Dr, 06117. SAN 302-4288. Tel: 860-233-2774, 860-236-1275. FAX: 860-231-8890. E-mail: library@emanuelsynagogue.org. Web Site: www.emanuelsynagogue.org.
Library Holdings: Bk Vols 5,200
Restriction: Mem only

R FIRST CHURCH OF CHRIST CONGREGATIONAL*, John P Webster Library, 12 S Main St, 06107. SAN 370-0305. Tel: 860-232-3893. FAX: 860-232-8183. E-mail: jpwebsterdir@snet.net. Web Site: www.jpwlibrary.org. *Dir,* Patricia Malahan; *Asst Dir,* Margaret Morris-Horstman; Staff 3 (MLS 1, Non-MLS 2)
Library Holdings: Bk Vols 10,000; Per Subs 50
Special Collections: The Practice of Parish Ministry
Subject Interests: Relig, Soc issues
Wireless access
Open Mon, Wed & Thurs 9-5, Fri 9-3, Sun 9-12

C SAINT JOSEPH UNIVERSITY*, Pope Pius XII Library, 1678 Asylum Ave, 06117-2791. SAN 302 430X. Tel: 860-232-4571. Circulation Tel: 860-231-5209. Interlibrary Loan Service Tel: 860-231-5750. Reference Tel: 860-231-5435. FAX: 860-523-4356. Web Site: www.usj.edu/academics/library/. *Dir,* Linda Geffner; E-mail: lgeffner@usj.edu; *Pharm Librn,* Catherine Posteraro; Tel: 860-231-5484; *Archivist,* Diana Barnard; Tel: 860-231-5740; *Cat,* Ann Williams; Tel: 860-231-5207; *Circ,* Erin Horanzy; *Circ,* Elizabeth Lesso; *Circ,* Tanya Robillard; *ILL,* Kathleen Kelley; *Ref Serv,* Antoinette Collins; *Ref Serv,* Angelina Hinojosa; *Ref Serv,* Lynne Piacentini; Tel: 860-231-5751; Staff 8 (MLS 6, Non-MLS 2)
Founded 1932. Highest Degree: Master
Automation Activity & Vendor Info: (Cataloging) OCLC; (Circulation) SirsiDynix; (Course Reserve) Docutek; (ILL) OCLC; (OPAC) SirsiDynix; (Serials) SerialsSolutions
Database Vendor: EBSCOhost
Wireless access
Function: Archival coll
Partic in Connecticut Library Consortium; Hartford Consortium For Higher Education; Library Connection, Inc; Lyrasis; OCLC Online Computer Library Center, Inc

C UNIVERSITY OF HARTFORD LIBRARIES*, W H Mortensen Library, 200 Bloomfield Ave, 06117. SAN 302-4318. Tel: 860-768-4264. Interlibrary Loan Service Tel: 860-768-4364. Reference Tel: 860-768-4142. Administration Tel: 860-768-4269. Circulation FAX: 860-768-5298. Administration FAX: 860-768-4274. Web Site: library.hartford.edu. *Dir,* Randi Lynn Ashton-Pritting; E-mail: pritting@hartford.edu; *Head, Ref,* Position Currently Open; *Access Serv, Circ,* Bob Antaramia; *Access Serv, ILL,* Christine Bird; *Ref Serv,* Deborah Fowler; *Tech Serv,* Kristina Edwards; *Tech Serv,* Laurie Haggan; Staff 9 (MLS 2, Non-MLS 7)
Founded 1957. Enrl 6,882; Fac 306; Highest Degree: Doctorate
Library Holdings: Bk Vols 450,000; Per Subs 2,089; Videos 2,000
Special Collections: Black Literature; Judaica (Millie & Irving Bercowetz Family Coll)
Subject Interests: Art, Music
Automation Activity & Vendor Info: (Cataloging) Ex Libris Group; (Circulation) Ex Libris Group; (Course Reserve) Ex Libris Group; (OPAC) Ex Libris Group
Database Vendor: Cambridge Scientific Abstracts, EBSCOhost, Gale Cengage Learning, ProQuest
Wireless access
Publications: Resources (Newsletter)
Partic in Connecticut Library Consortium; Coun of Conn Acad Libr Dirs; Greater Hartford Consortium for Higher Educ; Lyrasis; OCLC Online Computer Library Center, Inc
Special Services for the Blind - Closed circuit TV magnifier
Open Mon-Thurs 8:30am-Midnight, Fri 8:30-6, Sat 10-6, Sun Noon-Midnight
Friends of the Library Group
Departmental Libraries:
MILDRED P ALLEN MEMORIAL, 200 Bloomfield Ave, 06117-0395, SAN 324-3060. Tel: 860-768-4491. Interlibrary Loan Service Tel: 860-768-4364. FAX: 860-768-5295. Web Site: library.hartford.edu/allen.allenhome.html. *Dir,* Linda Solow Blotner; Tel: 860-768-4492, E-mail: blotner@hartford.edu; *Asst Librn,* Brooke Lippy; Tel: 860-768-4404, E-mail: lippy@hartford.edu; *Coordr, Access Serv,* Andrew King; Tel: 860-768-4840, E-mail: anking@hartford.edu; *Pub Serv,* Thomas S Caw; Tel: 860-768-4770, E-mail: caw@hartford.edu; *Tech Serv,* Jennifer Olson; E-mail: jolson@hartford.edu; Staff 6 (MLS 2, Non-MLS 4)
Founded 1938. Enrl 700; Fac 125; Highest Degree: Doctorate
Library Holdings: AV Mats 23,000; Music Scores 38,000; Bk Vols 12,000; Per Subs 211
Special Collections: Kalmen Opperman Clarinet Coll; Stuart Smith Coll, mss, writings & published works
Subject Interests: Music, Performing arts
Automation Activity & Vendor Info: (Acquisitions) Ex Libris Group; (Cataloging) Ex Libris Group; (Circulation) Ex Libris Group; (Course Reserve) Ex Libris Group; (ILL) Ex Libris Group; (OPAC) Ex Libris Group
Partic in OCLC Online Computer Library Center, Inc
Open Mon-Thurs (Fall & Spring) 8:30am-11pm, Fri 8:30-6, Sat 11-5, Sun Noon-11; Mon-Thurs (Summer) 10-8, Fri 10-5, Sat 10-1; Mon-Thurs (Winter) 8:30-6, Fri 8:30-4
Restriction: Non-circulating to the pub

S NOAH WEBSTER HOUSE & WEST HARTFORD HISTORICAL SOCIETY*, 227 S Main St, 06107-3430. SAN 329-160X. Tel: 860-521-5362. Circulation Tel: 860-521-5362, Ext 17. FAX: 860-521-4036. Web Site: www.noahwebsterhouse.org. *Archivist,* Sheila Daley; E-mail: daleys@noahwebsterhouse.org
Founded 1974
Library Holdings: Bk Vols 300; Per Subs 10
Special Collections: 18th Century History, lifestyle, gardening; Lexicography. Oral History
Subject Interests: Decorative art, Hist
Function: Res libr
Partic in W Hartford Libr Syst
Restriction: Non-circulating, Open by appt only

P WEST HARTFORD PUBLIC LIBRARY*, Noah Webster Memorial Library, 20 S Main St, 06107-2432. SAN 336-5522. Tel: 860-561-6950. Circulation Tel: 860-561-6960. Interlibrary Loan Service Tel: 860-561-6968. Reference Tel: 860-561-6990. Administration Tel: 860-561-6970. FAX: 860-561-6976. Web Site: www.westhartfordlibrary.org. *Dir,* Patricia Holloway; *Automated Serv,* Glenn Grube; *Cat,* Karen Polmatier; *Ch Serv,* Carol Waxman; *Circ Serv,* Jacqueline Douglas; *Coll Develop,* Agatha Monahan; *Commun Serv,* Joe Cadieux; *ILL,* Martha Church; *Ref,* Judy Eisenberg; *Teen Serv,* Ann Marie Naples; Staff 29 (MLS 10, Non-MLS 19)
Founded 1897. Pop 64,946; Circ 798,099
Jul 2008-Jun 2009 Income (Main Library and Branch(s)) $3,669,805, State $17,555, City $3,652,250. Mats Exp $428,915, Books $311,004, Per/Ser (Incl. Access Fees) $40,244, AV Mat $77,667. Sal $2,988,851
Library Holdings: Bk Vols 204,371; Per Subs 400
Special Collections: Connecticut Reference Coll; Local History Coll; Noah Webster Coll; West Hartford News, micro
Automation Activity & Vendor Info: (Cataloging) OCLC; (Circulation) SirsiDynix; (ILL) OCLC; (OPAC) SirsiDynix; (Serials) SirsiDynix
Wireless access
Partic in Connecticut Library Consortium; Library Connection, Inc; OCLC Online Computer Library Center, Inc
Special Services for the Deaf - Spec interest per; TTY equip
Friends of the Library Group
Branches: 2
BISHOP'S CORNER, 15 Starkel Rd, 06117, SAN 336-5581. Tel: 860-561-8210. Circulation Tel: 860-561-8211. Reference Tel: 860-561-8212. *Br Mgr,* Susan Hansen; *Ch Serv,* Janet Murphy; *Circ,* Caren Jo Smith
Library Holdings: Bk Vols 45,135
Open Mon & Wed 10-6, Tues & Thurs 1-9, Sat 10-5
Friends of the Library Group
JULIA FAXON BRANCH, 1073 New Britain Ave, 06110, SAN 336-5557. Tel: 860-561-8200. Circulation Tel: 860-561-8201. Reference Tel: 860-561-8202. *Br Mgr,* Marcia Lewis; *Ch Serv,* Jane Breen; *Circ,* Kate Fitzgerald
Library Holdings: Bk Vols 39,448
Special Services for the Deaf - TDD equip
Open Mon & Wed 1-9, Tues & Thurs 10-6, Sat 10-5
Friends of the Library Group

WEST HARTLAND

P HARTLAND PUBLIC LIBRARY*, 61 Center St, 06091. SAN 302-4326. Tel: 860-379-0048. Web Site: www.munic.state.ct.us/hartland/library.htm. *Chairperson,* Timothy Mrowka; E-mail: tmrowka379@aol.com
Founded 1965. Pop 2,058; Circ 3,483
Jul 2005-Jun 2006 Income $6,300, State $1,200, City $5,000, Locally Generated Income $100. Mats Exp $5,564, Books $5,000, AV Mat $480, Electronic Ref Mat (Incl. Access Fees) $84
Library Holdings: AV Mats 155; Large Print Bks 21; Bk Titles 7,732; Bk Vols 8,082; Per Subs 20; Talking Bks 58; Videos 20
Wireless access
Partic in Region I Coop Libr Servs Unit
Open Tues 6pm-8pm, Sat 10-12
Friends of the Library Group

WEST HAVEN

C UNIVERSITY OF NEW HAVEN*, Marvin K Peterson Library, 300 Boston Post Rd, 06516. SAN 302-4342. Tel: 203-932-7190. Circulation Tel: 203-932-7197. Interlibrary Loan Service Tel: 203-932-7194. Reference Tel: 203-932-7189. FAX: 203-932-1469. Web Site: library.newhaven.edu. *Dir,* Hanko H Dobi; Tel: 203-932-7191, E-mail: hdobi@newhaven.edu; *Head, Access Serv,* Christine Edgar; E-mail: edgar@newhaven.edu; *Head, Ref,* Anne O'Connor; E-mail: aoconnor@newhaven.edu; *Head, Tech Serv,* Marion Sachdeva; Tel: 203-932-7193, E-mail: msachdeva@newhaven.edu; *Acq,* Patricia Donnelly; E-mail: pdonnelly@newhaven.edu; *ILL,* Evelina Woodruff; E-mail: ewoodruff@newhaven.edu; *Ser,* Anna Vecchio; Tel: 203-932-7188, E-mail: avecchio@newhaven.edu; Staff 6 (MLS 6)
Founded 1920. Enrl 3,140; Fac 232; Highest Degree: Master
Library Holdings: Bk Vols 300,000; Per Subs 1,000
Special Collections: US Document Depository
Subject Interests: Criminal law & justice, Eng, Forensic sci
Automation Activity & Vendor Info: (Acquisitions) Ex Libris Group; (Cataloging) Ex Libris Group; (Circulation) Ex Libris Group; (Course Reserve) Ex Libris Group; (ILL) OCLC; (OPAC) Ex Libris Group; (Serials) Ex Libris Group
Database Vendor: Dialog, EBSCOhost, Gale Cengage Learning, LexisNexis, OCLC FirstSearch, OVID Technologies, ProQuest
Wireless access
Publications: Friends (Newsletter); Library Guides; Library Newsletter
Partic in Connecticut Library Consortium; Coun of Conn Acad Libr Dirs; Lyrasis
Friends of the Library Group

GM VA CONNECTICUT HEALTH CARE SYSTEM*, Library Service, 950 Campbell Ave, 06516-5247. SAN 302-4350. Tel: 203-932-5711, Ext 2898. FAX: 203-937-3822. *Librn,* Gail Lascola
Founded 1953
Library Holdings: Bk Titles 5,000; Per Subs 298
Database Vendor: OVID Technologies
Partic in Conn Asn of Health Scis Librs
Open Mon-Fri 7:30-4

P WEST HAVEN PUBLIC LIBRARY*, 300 Elm St, 06516-4692. SAN 336-5611. Tel: 203-937-4233. Reference Tel: 203-937-4233, Ext 2. Administration Tel: 203-937-4242. Interlibrary Loan Service FAX: 203-931-7827. TDD: 203-937-4235. Web Site: whpl.lioninc.org. *Dir,* Kathy Giotsas; *Asst Dir,* Claudia Volano; *Head, Circ,* Catherine Bushman; *Head,*

Tech Serv, Coleen Bailie; *Children & Youth Serv Librn,* Bernadette Niedermeier; Staff 36 (MLS 7, Non-MLS 29)
Founded 1906. Pop 51,477; Circ 267,580
Library Holdings: Bk Vols 160,000; Per Subs 303
Subject Interests: Connecticut, Hist
Automation Activity & Vendor Info: (Circulation) Infor Library & Information Solutions
Partic in Connecticut Library Consortium; LEAP
Open Mon-Thurs 9-8, Fri & Sat 9-5
Friends of the Library Group
Branches: 2
ORA B MASON BRANCH, 260 Benham Hill Rd, 06516-6541, SAN 336-5646. Tel: 203-933-9381. FAX: 203-931-7149. *Br Mgr,* Elaine Braithwaite
Library Holdings: Bk Vols 24,829
Open Mon & Wed 9-8, Tues & Thurs 1-8, Fri & Sat 9-5, Sun 1-5
Friends of the Library Group
LOUIS PIANTINO BRANCH, One Forest Rd, 06516-1698, SAN 336-5670. Tel: 203-933-9335. E-mail: lpcirc@westhavenlibrary.org. *Br Mgr,* Ray Woollett
Library Holdings: Bk Vols 30,655
Open Mon & Wed 9-7, Tues & Thurs-Sat 9-5
Friends of the Library Group
Bookmobiles: 1

WESTBROOK

P WESTBROOK PUBLIC LIBRARY*, 61 Goodspeed Dr, 06498. SAN 302-4369. Tel: 860-399-6422. FAX: 860-399-6344. E-mail: westbrook.public.lib@snet.net. Web Site: westbrooklibrary.lioninc.org. *Librn,* Lewis B Daniels, III; Staff 2 (MLS 1, Non-MLS 1)
Founded 1895. Pop 6,938; Circ 49,036
Jul 2011-Jun 2012 Income $375,119, State $1,826, City $364,002, Locally Generated Income $9,291. Mats Exp $47,532, Books $33,047, Per/Ser (Incl. Access Fees) $5,268, AV Equip $1,046, AV Mat $5,771, Electronic Ref Mat (Incl. Access Fees) $2,400. Sal $224,661 (Prof $71,286)
Library Holdings: CDs 1,294; DVDs 1,516; Electronic Media & Resources 4,636; Large Print Bks 670; Bk Titles 46,540; Per Subs 128; Videos 964
Special Collections: Literacy Volunteers Coll
Automation Activity & Vendor Info: (Circulation) Innovative Interfaces, Inc
Wireless access
Publications: Friends of the Library (Monthly newsletter)
Partic in Libraries Online, Inc
Open Tues & Thurs 9-8, Wed, Fri & Sat 9-5
Friends of the Library Group

WESTON

P WESTON PUBLIC LIBRARY*, 56 Norfield Rd, 06883-2225. SAN 302-4385. Tel: 203-222-2665. Interlibrary Loan Service Tel: 203-222-2550. FAX: 203-222-2560. E-mail: westonlibrary@westonct.gov. Web Site: www.westonpubliclibrary.org. *Dir,* Karen Tatarka; Tel: 203-222-2650; *Asst Dir,* Nancy Lincoln; *Ch Serv,* Joy Beckwith; *Tech Asst, ILL,* Karen Bennett
Founded 1963. Pop 10,263; Circ 65,000
Library Holdings: Audiobooks 5,014; AV Mats 5,810; DVDs 3,657; e-books 4,814; Large Print Bks 275; Bk Vols 48,212; Per Subs 124
Automation Activity & Vendor Info: (Circulation) Bibliomation Inc; (OPAC) Bibliomation Inc; (Serials) EBSCO Online
Wireless access
Open Mon, Tues, Thurs & Fri 9-5, Wed 9-8, Sat 10-4, Sun 12-4
Friends of the Library Group

WESTPORT

S WESTPORT HISTORICAL SOCIETY LIBRARY*, 25 Avery Pl, 06880-3215. SAN 302-4458. Tel: 203-222-1424. FAX: 203-221-0981. Web Site: www.westporthistory.org. *Exec Dir,* Susan Gold; Tel: 203-222-1424, Ext 105, E-mail: sgold@westporthistory.org
Library Holdings: Bk Vols 200
Special Collections: Historical Items from 1783 to present
Restriction: Open by appt only, Open to pub for ref only

P THE WESTPORT LIBRARY*, 20 Jesup Rd, 06880. SAN 302-4466. Tel: 203-291-4820. Circulation Tel: 203-291-4800. Interlibrary Loan Service Tel: 203-291-4821. FAX: 203-227-3829. Interlibrary Loan Service FAX: 203-291-4850. Reference FAX: 203-291-4856. E-mail: ref@westportlibrary.org. Web Site: www.westportlibrary.org. *Dir,* Maxine Bleiweis; Tel: 203-291-4801, E-mail: mbleiweis@westportlibrary.org; *Dir of Develop,* Cindy Clark; *Asst Dir & Chief Operating Officer,* Paul Mazzaccaro; *Asst Dir, Innovation & User Experience,* Bill Derry; *Asst Dir, Pub Serv,* Jerome L Myers
Founded 1908. Pop 25,749; Circ 924,058
Library Holdings: Audiobooks 6,546; CDs 6,659; DVDs 18,152; Bk Vols 193,483; Per Subs 323
Special Collections: Picture File, clippings & photos
Subject Interests: Performing arts, Visual arts
Automation Activity & Vendor Info: (Acquisitions) Horizon; (Cataloging) Horizon; (Circulation) Horizon; (ILL) OCLC; (OPAC) Horizon; (Serials) Horizon
Wireless access
Function: Adult bk club, Art exhibits, Audiobks via web, Bk club(s), Bks on CD, Children's prog, Computers for patron use, Copy machines, e-mail & chat, E-Reserves, Electronic databases & coll, Exhibits, Fax serv, Free DVD rentals, Games & aids for the handicapped, Handicapped accessible, Home delivery & serv to Sr ctr & nursing homes, Homebound delivery serv, ILL available, Magnifiers for reading, Mail & tel request accepted, Music CDs, Online cat, Online ref, Online searches, Outside serv via phone, mail, e-mail & web, Prog for adults, Prog for children & young adult, Pub access computers, Ref & res, Ref serv in person, Spoken cassettes & CDs, Spoken cassettes & DVDs, Story hour, Summer reading prog, Teen prog, Telephone ref
Publications: Westport Public Library Annual Report; Westport Public Library Newsletter/Calendar
Special Services for the Deaf - Bks on deafness & sign lang; Closed caption videos
Special Services for the Blind - Bks on cassette; Bks on CD; Closed circuit TV magnifier; Home delivery serv; Large print bks; Magnifiers; Talking bks
Open Mon-Thurs 9-9, Fri 9-6, Sat 9-5, Sun 1-5
Friends of the Library Group

WETHERSFIELD

S WETHERSFIELD HISTORICAL SOCIETY*, Old Academy Library, 150 Main St, 06109. SAN 302-4482. Tel: 860-529-7656. FAX: 860-563-2609. E-mail: society@wethhist.org. Web Site: www.wethhist.org. *Interim Dir,* Melissa Josefiak; *Asst Dir,* Melissa Josefiak
Founded 1932
Library Holdings: Bk Titles 1,500; Bk Vols 2,000
Special Collections: Old manuscripts, deeds, letters, log books, maps, bibles, textbooks & account books; Pamphlet Coll; Photograph Coll
Subject Interests: Archit, Genealogy, Local hist
Open Tues-Fri 10-4

P WETHERSFIELD PUBLIC LIBRARY, 515 Silas Deane Hwy, 06109. SAN 302-4490. Tel: 860-529-2665. FAX: 860-257-2822. E-mail: library@wethersfieldlibrary.org. Web Site: www.wethersfieldlibrary.org. *Dir,* Brook Berry; *Adult Info Serv Mgr,* Pamela Kelly; *Mgr, Ch Serv,* Regina Aleksandravicius; *Mgr, Coll Serv,* Celia Allison
Founded 1893. Pop 26,700; Circ 350,000
Library Holdings: Bk Vols 120,000; Per Subs 250
Automation Activity & Vendor Info: (Cataloging) Innovative Interfaces, Inc; (Circulation) Innovative Interfaces, Inc; (ILL) OCLC WorldShare Interlibrary Loan; (OPAC) Innovative Interfaces, Inc
Database Vendor: Innovative Interfaces, Inc
Partic in Library Connection, Inc
Open Mon, Tues & Thurs 10-9, Wed, Fri & Sat 10-5, Sun (Sept-June) 1-5
Friends of the Library Group

WILLIMANTIC

C EASTERN CONNECTICUT STATE UNIVERSITY, J Eugene Smith Library, 83 Windham St, 06226-2295. SAN 302-4512. Tel: 860-465-4506. Interlibrary Loan Service Tel: 860-465-4462. Reference Tel: 860-465-4699. Administration Tel: 860-465-4397. Toll Free Tel: 877-587-8693. FAX: 860-465-5521. Interlibrary Loan Service FAX: 860-465-4355. Administration FAX: 860-465-5522. Web Site: www.easternct.edu/smithlibrary. *Dir, Libr Serv,* Patricia S Banach; Tel: 860-465-4466, E-mail: banachp@easternct.edu; *Head, Cat,* Kristin M Jacobi; Tel: 860-465-4508, Fax: 860-465-5523, E-mail: jacobikr@easternct.edu; *Head, Coll & e-Res Mgt,* Caroline Davis; Tel: 860-465-5562, E-mail: davisca@easternct.edu; *Head, Pub Serv, Head, Res Serv,* Gregory Robinson; Tel: 860-465-5553, E-mail: robinsong@easternct.edu; *Head, Tech Serv,* Sandy Rosado; Tel: 860-465-4464, Fax: 860-465-5523, E-mail: rosados@easternct.edu; *Acq Librn,* Carolyn Coates; Tel: 860-465-5557, Fax: 860-465-5523, E-mail: coatesc@easternct.edu; *Curric Center Librn,* Hope Marie Cook; Tel: 860-465-4456, Fax: 860-465-5517, E-mail: cookh@easternct.edu; *Ref/Govt Doc Librn,* Janice Wilson; Tel: 860-465-5550, E-mail: wilsonj@easternct.edu; *Ref & Instruction Librn,* Carol Reichardt; Tel: 860-465-5566, E-mail: reichardtc@easternct.edu; *Archivist, Spec Coll Librn,* Tara Hurt; Tel: 860-465-5563, E-mail: hurtt@easternct.edu; *Access Serv Librn,* Tracy Sutherland; E-mail: sutherlandt@easternct.edu; *Syst Librn,* Bruce Johnston; Tel: 860-465-5552, E-mail: johnstonb@easternct.edu; Staff 29 (MLS 13, Non-MLS 16)
Founded 1889. Enrl 5,622; Fac 478; Highest Degree: Master

Jul 2012-Jun 2013. Mats Exp $938,085, Books $287,083, Per/Ser (Incl. Access Fees) $642,068, AV Mat $8,934. Sal $2,110,729 (Prof $1,083,196)
Library Holdings: AV Mats 9,108; e-books 125,000; Electronic Media & Resources 125; Microforms 975,423; Bk Vols 406,087
Special Collections: Carribbean Coll, AV, bks; Connecticut History Coll, bks, pamphlets, per, prints, slides; Vocation (Career Information Center), bks, microfiche, per. Can & Prov; State Document Depository; US Document Depository
Automation Activity & Vendor Info: (Acquisitions) Innovative Interfaces, Inc; (Cataloging) Innovative Interfaces, Inc; (Circulation) Innovative Interfaces, Inc; (Course Reserve) Innovative Interfaces, Inc; (ILL) OCLC ILLiad; (OPAC) Innovative Interfaces, Inc; (Serials) Innovative Interfaces, Inc
Database Vendor: Alexander Street Press, American Chemical Society, American Geophysical Union, Annual Reviews, ARTstor, BioOne, Bowker, CQ Press, EBSCOhost, Elsevier, Facts on File, Gale Cengage Learning, Innovative Interfaces, Inc, JSTOR, LexisNexis, OCLC, OCLC ArticleFirst, OCLC FirstSearch, OCLC WorldShare Interlibrary Loan, OVID Technologies, Oxford Online, Plunkett Research, Ltd, Project MUSE, ProQuest, ReferenceUSA, Sage, ScienceDirect, SerialsSolutions, YBP Library Services
Wireless access
Function: Copy machines, Electronic databases & coll, Fax serv, ILL available, Music CDs, Online cat, Ref serv available
Publications: ECSU Library Newsletter
Partic in Connecticut Library Consortium; CONSULS (Connecticut State University Library System); Lyrasis; OCLC Online Computer Library Center, Inc
Special Services for the Blind - Cassette playback machines; PC for handicapped; Scanner for conversion & translation of mats; Videos on blindness & phys handicaps
Open Mon-Thurs 8-Midnight, Fri 8-6, Sat 10-6, Sun Noon-Midnight

P WILLIMANTIC PUBLIC LIBRARY*, 905 Main St, 06226. (Mail add: PO Box 218, 06226), SAN 302-4520. Tel: 860-465-3079. FAX: 860-465-3083. E-mail: wpldir@biblio.org. Web Site: www.willimanticlibrary.org. *Dir,* Ted Perch; Tel: 860-465-3080, E-mail: wpldir@biblio.org; *Adult Serv,* Julia Graham; Tel: 860-465-2176, E-mail: wplref@biblio.org; *Ch Serv,* Gail Zeiba; Tel: 860-465-3081, E-mail: wplchd@biblio.org; Staff 9 (MLS 3, Non-MLS 6)
Founded 1854. Pop 25,000; Circ 70,000
Library Holdings: Bk Vols 60,000; Per Subs 137
Automation Activity & Vendor Info: (Acquisitions) Bibliomation Inc; (Cataloging) OCLC WorldShare Interlibrary Loan; (Circulation) Evergreen; (ILL) OCLC, (OPAC) Evergreen
Database Vendor: Auto-Graphics, Inc
Wireless access
Function: Computers for patron use, Copy machines, Free DVD rentals, ILL available, Music CDs, Notary serv, Preschool outreach, Prog for children & young adult, Pub access computers, Story hour, Summer reading prog, Wheelchair accessible
Partic in Bibliomation Inc; Connecticut Library Consortium
Open Mon & Wed (Oct-June) 9-6, Tues & Thurs 12-8, Fri 9-5, Sat 10-2; Mon & Wed (Summer) 9-5, Tues & Thurs 12-8, Fri 9-5
Friends of the Library Group

M WINDHAM COMMUNITY MEMORIAL HOSPITAL*, Grant Health Sciences Library, 112 Mansfield Ave, 06226. SAN 325-2809. Tel: 860-456-6807. FAX: 860-456-6883. TDD: 860-456-6877. Web Site: www.wcmh.org. *Librn,* Kate Cheromcha
Founded 1959
Database Vendor: EBSCOhost
Special Services for the Deaf - TDD equip

S WINDHAM TEXTILE & HISTORY MUSEUM*, Dunham Hall Library, 411 Main St, 06226. SAN 375-1856. Tel: 860-456-2178. E-mail: themillmuseum@gmail.com. Web Site: www.millmuseum.org. *Dir,* Jamie Eves; *Coll Mgr,* Rita Allen; Staff 2 (Non-MLS 2)
Founded 1989
Jan 2013-Dec 2013. Mats Exp $1,000
Library Holdings: AV Mats 25; CDs 50; Music Scores 40; Bk Titles 2,000; Videos 50
Special Collections: Mill Blue Prints. Oral History
Subject Interests: Immigration, Textile
Wireless access
Publications: Willimantic, Industry & Community
Open Fri-Sun 10-4
Restriction: Open to pub for ref only

WILLINGTON

P MARY D EDWARDS PUBLIC LIBRARY*, c/o Hall Memorial School, 111 River Rd, Rte 32, 06279. SAN 302-4547. Tel: 860-429-3854. FAX: 860-429-2136. E-mail: m.edwards.pub.libr@snet.net. Web Site: www.willingtonct.org. *Dir,* Roberta S Passardi
Founded 1923. Pop 5,100; Circ 17,379
Library Holdings: Bk Vols 18,000
Open Mon, Wed & Fri 11-5, Tues & Thurs 11-8, Sat 9-3
Friends of the Library Group

WILTON

P WILTON LIBRARY ASSOCIATION*, 137 Old Ridgefield Rd, 06897-3019. SAN 302-4563. Tel: 203-762-3950. Administration Tel: 203-762-7196. FAX: 203-834-1166. E-mail: library@wiltonlibrary.org. Web Site: www.wiltonlibrary.org. *Exec Dir,* Elaine Tai-Lauria; *Asst Dir,* Lauren McLaughlin; E-mail: lmclaughlin@wiltonlibrary.org; *Develop Dir,* Anne Rowlands; E-mail: arowlands@wiltonlibrary.org; *Head, Ch,* Andrea Falkner; E-mail: afalkner@wiltonlibrary.org; *Head, Circ,* Karen Zeibak; E-mail: kzeibak@wiltonlibrary.org; *Head, Network Serv,* Mary Anne Franco; E-mail: mamfranco@wiltonlibrary.org; *Head, Tech Serv,* Carolyn Benjamin; E-mail: cbenjamin@wiltonlibrary.org; *Head, Teen Serv,* Susan Lauricella; E-mail: slauricella@wiltonlibrary.org; *Media Librn,* Melissa Baker; E-mail: mbaker@wiltonlibrary.org; *Prog & Rental Mgr,* Sally Gemmill; E-mail: sgemmill@wiltonlibrary.org; *ILL,* Catherine Steele; E-mail: csteele@wiltonlibrary.org; Staff 58 (MLS 8, Non-MLS 50)
Founded 1895. Pop 17,600
Library Holdings: Audiobooks 5,142; CDs 5,137; DVDs 8,459; Large Print Bks 2,443; Bk Vols 116,687; Per Subs 243
Special Collections: Wilton History Coll
Automation Activity & Vendor Info: (Acquisitions) SirsiDynix; (Cataloging) SirsiDynix; (Circulation) SirsiDynix; (ILL) OCLC; (OPAC) SirsiDynix
Database Vendor: Baker & Taylor, Booklist Online, EBSCOhost, Gale Cengage Learning, ReferenceUSA, SirsiDynix
Wireless access
Publications: Annual Report; librarEmail (Newsletter); Wilton Business Directory Online (Business & organization papers & directories); Wilton Community Organizations Directory; Wilton Obituary Index (Local historical information)
Special Services for the Blind - Bks on cassette; Bks on CD; Closed circuit TV magnifier; Computer with voice synthesizer for visually impaired persons; Home delivery serv; Large print bks; Magnifiers
Open Mon-Thurs (Sept-June) 10-8, Fri 10-6, Sat 10-5, Sun 1-5

WINDHAM

P WINDHAM FREE LIBRARY ASSOCIATION*, Seven Windham Green Rd, 06280. (Mail add: PO Box 168, 06280-0168), SAN 302-4571. Tel: 860-423-0636. FAX: 860-423-0636. Web Site: windhamfreelibrary.org. *Dir, Libr Serv,* Carol Santa Lucia; Staff 3 (Non-MLS 3)
Founded 1896. Pop 23,000
Library Holdings: Bk Titles 9,800; Bk Vols 9,900; Per Subs 51
Subject Interests: Connecticut, Local hist
Wireless access
Open Tues & Thurs 10-12 & 1-7, Wed 1-5, Sat 9-1

WINDSOR

S LIMRA INTERNATIONAL INFOCENTER*, William J Mortimer Library, 300 Day Hill Rd, 06095-4761. (Mail add: PO Box 208, Hartford, 06141-0208), SAN 374-468X. Tel: 860-688-3358. FAX: 860-298-9555. E-mail: infocenter@limra.com. Web Site: www.limra.com. *Dir,* Gail W Buchholz; Staff 2 (Non-MLS 2)
Founded 1926
Library Holdings: Bk Vols 6,000; Per Subs 300
Subject Interests: Market res
Automation Activity & Vendor Info: (Acquisitions) Inmagic, Inc.; (Cataloging) Inmagic, Inc.; (Circulation) Inmagic, Inc.; (ILL) OCLC; (OPAC) Inmagic, Inc.; (Serials) Inmagic, Inc.
Database Vendor: Factiva.com, Swets Information Services
Partic in Connecticut Library Consortium; Lyrasis
Restriction: Open by appt only

S WINDSOR HISTORICAL SOCIETY LIBRARY*, 96 Palisado Ave, 06095. SAN 302-4628. Tel: 860-688-3813. FAX: 860-687-1633. E-mail: info@windsorhistoricalsociety.org. *Dir,* Christine Ermenc; *Librn,* Barbara Goodwin; Staff 1 (MLS 1)
Founded 1925
Library Holdings: Bk Titles 5,000
Special Collections: Church & School Records & Newspapers; Local History, family papers, genealogies, photogs, slides, town histories; Manuscripts & Deeds. Oral History
Wireless access
Restriction: Non-circulating

P WINDSOR PUBLIC LIBRARY*, 323 Broad St, 06095. SAN 336-5700. Tel: 860-285-1910. Reference Tel: 860-285-1918. FAX: 860-285-1889. E-mail: library@townofwindsorct.com. Web Site: www.windsorlibrary.com. *Dir,* Gaye Rizzo; Tel: 860-285-1912, E-mail: rizzo@townofwindsorct.com;

Head, Adult Serv, Leanne Costello; Tel: 860-285-1920, E-mail: costello@townofwindsorct.com; *Head, Ch,* Debbie Roe; *Head, Lending Serv,* Gail Mannion; Tel: 860-285-1923, E-mail: mannion@townofwindsorct.com; *Ref Librn,* Robert Kinney; *Ref Librn, Tech Librn,* Denise Ricotta; Tel: 860-285-1922, E-mail: ricotta@townofwindsorct.com; Staff 9 (MLS 4, Non-MLS 5)
Founded 1888. Pop 27,475; Circ 283,750
Jul 2006-Jun 2007 Income (Main Library and Branch(s)) $1,373,780, State $4,500, City $1,320,440, Other $48,840. Mats Exp $159,837, Books $101,670, AV Mat $15,100, Electronic Ref Mat (Incl. Access Fees) $43,067. Sal $664,456
Library Holdings: AV Mats 17,938; Bk Vols 93,295; Per Subs 212
Special Collections: Career Center; Health Info Ctr; Parenting Ctr; Travel Ctr
Automation Activity & Vendor Info: (Cataloging) OCLC; (Circulation) SirsiDynix; (ILL) OCLC; (OPAC) SirsiDynix
Database Vendor: Gale Cengage Learning, Wilson - Wilson Web
Wireless access
Partic in Connecticut Library Consortium; Library Connection, Inc
Open Mon-Thurs 10-9, Fri & Sat 10-5, Sun 2-5
Friends of the Library Group
Branches: 1
WILSON, 365 Windsor Ave, 06095-4550, SAN 336-576X. Tel: 860-247-8960. *Br Mgr,* Kevin Sullivan; Tel: 860-285-1931, E-mail: sullivan@townofwindsorct.com; Staff 1 (Non-MLS 1)
Open Mon 10-7:30, Tues-Fri 10-5:30, Sat 10-3

WINDSOR LOCKS

S NEW ENGLAND AIR MUSEUM*, John W Ramsay Research Library, Bradley Int Airport, 06096. SAN 302-4636. Tel: 860-623-3305. FAX: 860-627-2820. E-mail: library@neam.org. Web Site: www.neam.org. *Dir,* Robert Foster; *Res Librn,* Carl Stidsen; Staff 17 (MLS 2, Non-MLS 15)
Founded 1960
Library Holdings: DVDs 50; Bk Titles 20,000; Per Subs 105,000; Videos 350
Special Collections: Burnelli Aircraft Coll
Subject Interests: Aviation
Database Vendor: JayWil Software Development, Inc
Wireless access
Function: Res libr
Publications: Newsletter (Quarterly)
Restriction: Non-circulating

P WINDSOR LOCKS PUBLIC LIBRARY*, 28 Main St, 06096. SAN 302-4660. Tel: 860-627-1495. FAX: 860-627-1496. Web Site: www.windsorlockslibrary.org. *Dir,* Gloria Malec; E-mail: gmalec@libraryconnection.info; *Adult Serv,* Eileen Pearce; E-mail: epearce@libraryconnnection.info; *Ch Serv,* Kristin Raiche; E-mail: kraiche@libraryconnection.info; *Tech Serv,* Mary Elizabeth Morrill; E-mail: bmorrill@libraryconnection.info; Staff 3 (MLS 1, Non-MLS 2)
Founded 1907. Pop 12,400; Circ 87,000
Library Holdings: Bk Vols 65,000; Per Subs 70
Special Collections: ESL (English as a Second Language) Coll; Local Interest Coll
Wireless access
Function: Computer training
Partic in Connecticut Library Consortium; Library Connection, Inc
Open Mon-Thurs 10-8:30, Fri & Sat 10-5

WINSTED

P BEARDSLEY & MEMORIAL LIBRARY*, 40 Munro Pl, 06098. SAN 302-4679. Tel: 860-379-6043. FAX: 860-379-3621. E-mail: director@beardsleyandmemorial.org. Web Site: www.beardsleyandmemorial.org. *Dir,* Karin Taylor; Staff 1 (MLS 1)
Founded 1898. Pop 15,616; Circ 1,060,151
Jul 2009-Jun 2010 Income $366,683, State $4,633, City $211,437, Locally Generated Income $99,041, Other $51,572. Mats Exp $38,430, Books $21,948, Per/Ser (Incl. Access Fees) $3,095, Manu Arch $600, Other Print Mats $650, AV Equip $8,000, AV Mat $3,137, Electronic Ref Mat (Incl. Access Fees) $1,000. Sal $143,022 (Prof $46,000)
Library Holdings: Bk Vols 58,115; Per Subs 105
Special Collections: Oral History
Subject Interests: Genealogy, Hist
Automation Activity & Vendor Info: (Cataloging) TLC (The Library Corporation); (Circulation) TLC (The Library Corporation); (ILL) TLC (The Library Corporation); (OPAC) TLC (The Library Corporation); (Serials) TLC (The Library Corporation)
Wireless access
Open Tues-Thurs 10:30-8, Fri 10:30-4, Sat 10-2
Friends of the Library Group

J NORTHWESTERN CONNECTICUT COMMUNITY COLLEGE LIBRARY*, Park Pl E, 06098. SAN 302-4687. Tel: 860-738-6480. FAX: 860-379-4995. E-mail: NW-LibRequests@nwcc.commnet.edu. Web Site: www.nwcc.commnet.edu/library/nccc_library.htm. *Dir, Libr Serv,* James Patterson; E-mail: jpatterson@nwcc.commnet.edu; *Pub Serv, Ref Librn,* Seth Kershner; Tel: 860-738-6481, E-mail: skershner@nwcc.commnet.edu; *ILL,* Andrea Dombrowski; Tel: 860-738-6478, E-mail: adombrowski@nwcc.commnet.edu; *Tech Serv,* Ann Marie Hyres; Tel: 860-738-6479; Staff 5 (MLS 2, Non-MLS 3)
Founded 1965. Enrl 1,632; Fac 30; Highest Degree: Associate
Jul 2006-Jun 2007 Income $78,143. Mats Exp $78,143, Books $22,416, Per/Ser (Incl. Access Fees) $15,775, Electronic Ref Mat (Incl. Access Fees) $24,433. Sal $319,000 (Prof $313,924)
Library Holdings: AV Mats 2,511; Bk Vols 42,569; Per Subs 175
Special Collections: Deaf Education; Historical Jazz, compact discs; World War I & II. State Document Depository
Subject Interests: Art, Deaf, Recreation
Automation Activity & Vendor Info: (Acquisitions) Ex Libris Group; (Cataloging) Ex Libris Group; (Circulation) Ex Libris Group; (Course Reserve) Ex Libris Group; (ILL) OCLC Online; (OPAC) Ex Libris Group; (Serials) Ex Libris Group
Database Vendor: EBSCOhost, Gale Cengage Learning, ProQuest, SerialsSolutions, Wilson - Wilson Web
Function: Audio & video playback equip for onsite use, Bks on cassette, Bks on CD, Computers for patron use, Copy machines, Electronic databases & coll, Instruction & testing, Music CDs, Online cat, Online info literacy tutorials on the web & in blackboard, Online ref, Orientations, Spoken cassettes & CDs, Spoken cassettes & DVDs, VHS videos
Publications: Periodical List
Partic in OCLC Online Computer Library Center, Inc
Special Services for the Deaf - Bks on deafness & sign lang; Closed caption videos; Coll on deaf educ; Deaf publ; TDD equip; TTY equip
Special Services for the Blind - Assistive/Adapted tech devices, equip & products; Bks on cassette; Bks on CD; Internet workstation with adaptive software; Magnifiers; Screen enlargement software for people with visual disabilities; ZoomText magnification & reading software
Open Mon-Wed 8:30-8, Thurs & Fri 8:30-4:30, Sat 9:30-1

S WINCHESTER HISTORICAL SOCIETY LIBRARY*, 225 Prospect St, 06098-1942. (Mail add: PO Box 206, 06098-0206), SAN 370-3029. Tel: 860-379-8433. Reference Tel: 860-379-1677. *Curator, In Charge,* Milly Hudak; E-mail: milly345@sbcglobal.net
Special Collections: 11 Rooms of Victorian Furnishings; Civil War Coll; Fire Department Museum Coll. Oral History
Subject Interests: Local genealogy, Local hist
Restriction: Open by appt only

WOLCOTT

P WOLCOTT PUBLIC LIBRARY*, 469 Boundline Rd, 06716. SAN 302-4695. Tel: 203-879-8110. FAX: 203-879-8109. Web Site: www.wolcottlibrary.org. *Dir,* Candace Barth; E-mail: cbarth@biblio.org; *Asst Dir, Head, Adult Serv,* Suzanne Garvey; E-mail: sgarvey@biblio.org; Staff 9 (MLS 2, Non-MLS 7)
Founded 1828. Pop 17,840; Circ 96,000
Library Holdings: CDs 1,898; DVDs 1,160; Bk Vols 54,417; Per Subs 72; Talking Bks 819; Videos 4,352
Special Collections: Foreign Language Cassettes; Job Resource Center
Automation Activity & Vendor Info: (Acquisitions) Bibliomation Inc; (Cataloging) Bibliomation Inc; (Circulation) Bibliomation Inc; (ILL) Bibliomation Inc; (OPAC) Bibliomation Inc; (Serials) Bibliomation Inc
Database Vendor: Bibliomation Inc, EBSCOhost, Gale Cengage Learning, ProQuest, Wilson - Wilson Web
Partic in Bibliomation Inc; Connecticut Library Consortium
Open Mon-Thurs 10-8, Fri 10-7, Sat 9-4:30, Sun (Sept-May) 1-5
Friends of the Library Group

WOODBRIDGE

P WOODBRIDGE TOWN LIBRARY*, Ten Newton Rd, 06525. SAN 302-4709. Tel: 203-389-3433. Administration Tel: 203-389-3437. Information Services Tel: 203-389-3434. FAX: 203-389-3457. Web Site: www.woodbridge.lioninc.org. *Dir,* Janet Vaill Day; Tel: 203-389-3435, E-mail: jvday@ci.woodbridge.ct.us; *Asst Dir, Head, Tech Serv,* Lynn Serra; Tel: 203-389-3438, E-mail: lserra@lioninc.org; *Head, Ch,* Judy Rabin; Tel: 203-389-3439, E-mail: jrabin@ci.woodbridge.ct.us; *Head, Ref (Info Serv),* Mary G Kelley; E-mail: mkelley@ci.woodbridge.ct.us; *Circ Mgr,* Barbara Wolfer; E-mail: bwolfer@ci.woodbridge.ct.us; Staff 23 (MLS 7, Non-MLS 16)
Founded 1940. Pop 9,775; Circ 162,267
Jul 2008-Jun 2009 Income $750,855, State $16,000, City $722,855, Other $12,000. Mats Exp $78,980, Books $67,940, Per/Ser (Incl. Access Fees) $10,500, Electronic Ref Mat (Incl. Access Fees) $540. Sal $505,644 (Prof $347,393)
Library Holdings: AV Mats 8,976; Bk Titles 77,009; Per Subs 144

Special Collections: Chinese Language Coll
Subject Interests: Russian (Lang), Travel
Automation Activity & Vendor Info: (Acquisitions) Innovative Interfaces, Inc; (Cataloging) Innovative Interfaces, Inc; (Circulation) Innovative Interfaces, Inc; (OPAC) Innovative Interfaces, Inc; (Serials) Innovative Interfaces, Inc
Database Vendor: Innovative Interfaces, Inc, Newsbank
Wireless access
Function: Art exhibits, Bks on CD, CD-ROM, Children's prog, Computers for patron use, Electronic databases & coll, Handicapped accessible, Homebound delivery serv, ILL available, Mus passes, Music CDs, Preschool outreach, Prog for adults, Prog for children & young adult, Pub access computers, Senior outreach, Story hour, Summer reading prog, Tax forms, Teen prog
Publications: At Your Library (Newsletter)
Partic in Libraries Online, Inc
Open Mon-Thurs 10-8, Fri & Sat 10-5
Friends of the Library Group

WOODBURY

S SEABURY SOCIETY FOR THE PRESERVATION OF THE GLEBE HOUSE, INC*, Glebe House Museum Library, 49 Hollow Rd, 06798. (Mail add: PO Box 245, 06798-0245), SAN 374-8618. Tel: 203-263-2855. FAX: 203-263-6726. E-mail: ghmgjg@snet.net. Web Site: www.theglebehouse.org. *Dir,* Sarah Griswold
Founded 1926
Library Holdings: Bk Vols 200
Special Collections: 18th Century Social & Religious History Coll; Museum Archives
Subject Interests: Episcopal church, Gardening
Function: Ref serv available
Restriction: Non-circulating

P WOODBURY PUBLIC LIBRARY*, 269 Main St S, 06798. SAN 302-4717. Tel: 203-263-3502. FAX: 203-263-0571. Web Site: www.woodburylibraryct.org. *Dir,* Patricia Lunn; E-mail: plunn@biblio.org; *Head, Ch,* Ann Bumstead; E-mail: alb@biblio.org; *Ad,* Susan Piel; E-mail: spiel@biblio.org; *Ch,* Bonnie Knapik; E-mail: bknapik@biblio.org; *ILL Librn,* Cheric Dalton; E-mail: woodburyill@biblio.org; *Ref & Tech Librn,* Beth Lovallo; E-mail: blovallo@biblio.org; *Teen Librn,* Marla Martin; E-mail: mmartin@biblio.org; *Tech Serv,* Maura Yerger; E-mail: myerger@biblio.org; Staff 16 (MLS 5, Non-MLS 11)
Founded 1902. Pop 9,765; Circ 136,529
Library Holdings: Bk Vols 100,000; Per Subs 145
Subject Interests: Local hist
Automation Activity & Vendor Info: (Cataloging) Evergreen; (Circulation) Evergreen; (ILL) Evergreen; (OPAC) Evergreen; (Serials) Evergreen
Database Vendor: Bibliomation Inc, EBSCO Auto Repair Reference, EBSCO Information Services, EBSCOhost, Overdrive, Inc
Wireless access
Open Mon, Wed, Fri & Sat 10-5, Tues & Thurs 10-9, Sun (Oct-May) 1-5
Friends of the Library Group

WOODSTOCK

P BRACKEN MEMORIAL LIBRARY*, 57 Academy Rd, 06281. (Mail add: PO Box 355, South Woodstock, 06267-0355), SAN 302-4725. Tel: 860-928-0046. FAX: 860-928-2117. Web Site: www.woodstockacademy.org/library.htm. *Librn,* Deb Sharpe; *Asst Librn,* Michelle Laprade; Staff 1 (MLS 1)
Founded 1926. Pop 5,000; Circ 18,000
Library Holdings: Bk Titles 20,000; Per Subs 60
Automation Activity & Vendor Info: (Cataloging) Follett Software; (Circulation) Follett Software
Partic in Connecticut Library Consortium
Open Mon-Fri 7-5:30, Sat 1-4

P NORTH WOODSTOCK LIBRARY*, 1286 Rte 169, 06281. Tel: 860-928-2629. *Dir,* Priscilla C Cady; Tel: 860-928-2688, E-mail: priscady@gmail.com
Founded 1834. Pop 7,854; Circ 6,117
Jul 2012-Jun 2013. Mats Exp $11,492
Library Holdings: CDs 53; DVDs 168; Bk Vols 11,692; Per Subs 3; Videos 273
Wireless access
Partic in Connecticut Library Consortium
Open Mon 1-5, Thurs 2-5, Sat 1:30-4:30

P WEST WOODSTOCK LIBRARY*, Five Bungay Hill Connector, 06281. SAN 320-6211. Tel: 860-974-0376. *Librn,* Patricia Pelloth
Pop 7,000
Library Holdings: Bk Vols 20,000
Subject Interests: Local hist, State hist
Partic in Connecticut Library Consortium
Open Tues 3-6, Wed 4-7, Thurs 4-6, Sat 10-1
Friends of the Library Group

DELAWARE

Date of Statistics: FY 2014
Population, 2010 U.S. Census: 897,934
Population Served by Public Libraries: 897,934
Total Materials in Public Libraries: 2,612,242
Materials Per Capita: 2.90
Total Public Library Circulation: 5,919,626
Circulation Per Capita: 6.59
Total Public Library Income: $26,555,619
Number of County Systems: 3
Number of Library Outlets: 35
Number of Bookmobiles in State: 2
Grants-in-Aid to Public Libraries:
Federal: $1,025,955
State Aid: $4,296,900

BEAR

P BEAR LIBRARY*, 101 Governor's Pl, 19701. Tel: 302-838-3300. FAX: 302-838-3307. Web Site: www2.nccde.org/libraries/Bear. *Mgr,* Eric Kuhn; Staff 28 (MLS 3, Non-MLS 25)
Founded 1998. Pop 80,000; Circ 645,000
Library Holdings: Bk Vols 98,804; Per Subs 273; Talking Bks 8,392; Videos 7,245
Special Collections: Delawareana
Automation Activity & Vendor Info: (Cataloging) Horizon; (Circulation) Horizon; (OPAC) Horizon; (Serials) Horizon
Database Vendor: EBSCOhost, Gale Cengage Learning, ProQuest
Open Mon-Wed 10-9, Thurs & Sat 10-5, Sun 1-5
Friends of the Library Group

BRIDGEVILLE

P BRIDGEVILLE PUBLIC LIBRARY*, 600 S Cannon St, 19933. SAN 302-4733. Tel: 302-337-7401. FAX: 302-337-3270. Web Site: www.bridgevillelibrary.com. *Dir,* Karen J Johnson; Staff 4 (Non-MLS 4)
Founded 1919. Pop 6,922; Circ 95,680
Jul 2005-Jun 2006 Income $209,704, State $30,275, County $140,804, Locally Generated Income $38,625. Mats Exp $12,605. Sal $112,469
Library Holdings: Bk Vols 25,000; Per Subs 90
Special Collections: Delaware & Eastern Shore; Genealogy Coll
Automation Activity & Vendor Info: (Cataloging) SirsiDynix; (Circulation) SirsiDynix; (OPAC) SirsiDynix
Function: Genealogy discussion group, ILL available, Photocopying/Printing, Prog for children & young adult, Summer reading prog, Telephone ref
Mem of Sussex County Department of Libraries
Open Mon-Fri 10-7, Sat 10-3

CLAYMONT

P CLAYMONT PUBLIC LIBRARY*, 400 Lenape Way, 19703. SAN 302-4741. Tel: 302-798-4164. FAX: 302-798-6329. Web Site: www2.nccde.org/libraries/Claymont. *Mgr,* Beth Kloetzer; Staff 8 (MLS 2, Non-MLS 6)
Founded 1929. Pop 39,000; Circ 166,000
Jul 2007-Jun 2008 Income $595,653, State $107,863, Federal $3,120, County $481,384, Other $3,286
Library Holdings: Audiobooks 4,434; DVDs 4,086; Electronic Media & Resources 210; Per Subs 123
Automation Activity & Vendor Info: (Cataloging) Horizon; (Circulation) Horizon; (Serials) EBSCO Online
Database Vendor: EBSCOhost, ProQuest
Wireless access
Function: Adult bk club, After school storytime, Bks on cassette, Bks on CD, Children's prog, Computers for patron use, Electronic databases & coll, Free DVD rentals, Handicapped accessible, Holiday prog, ILL available, Mail & tel request accepted, Music CDs, Online cat, Orientations, Outreach serv, Photocopying/Printing, Preschool outreach, Prog for adults, Prog for children & young adult, Pub access computers, Ref serv available, Senior outreach, Summer reading prog, Tax forms, Wheelchair accessible, Workshops
Special Services for the Deaf - Closed caption videos
Special Services for the Blind - Audio mat
Open Mon 10-8, Tues & Thurs 12-8, Wed & Sat 10-5
Restriction: Non-resident fee
Friends of the Library Group

DELAWARE CITY

P DELAWARE CITY PUBLIC LIBRARY*, 250 Fifth St, 19706. SAN 302-475X. Tel: 302-834-4148. Web Site: www2.nccde.org/libraries/DelawareCity. *Dir,* Josias Bartram; Staff 1 (MLS 1)
Founded 1973
Library Holdings: Bk Vols 24,000; Per Subs 75
Automation Activity & Vendor Info: (Cataloging) SirsiDynix; (Circulation) SirsiDynix; (OPAC) SirsiDynix; (Serials) SirsiDynix
Open Mon-Thurs 12-8, Sat 11-4, Sun 12-3
Friends of the Library Group

DELMAR

P DELMAR PUBLIC LIBRARY, 101 N Bi-State Blvd, 19940. SAN 302-4784. Tel: 302-846-9894. FAX: 302-846-3408. E-mail: delmar.library@lib.de.us. Web Site: Delmarpubliclibrary.org. *Dir,* Susan Upole; Staff 1 (MLS 1)
Founded 1940. Pop 6,049; Circ 64,297
Library Holdings: Bk Vols 18,791; Per Subs 45
Special Collections: Railroad Coll
Automation Activity & Vendor Info: (Cataloging) SirsiDynix; (Circulation) SirsiDynix; (OPAC) SirsiDynix
Wireless access
Function: Bk club(s), Bks on CD, Children's prog, Computer training, Computers for patron use, Copy machines, Electronic databases & coll, Fax serv, Free DVD rentals, ILL available, Music CDs, Online cat, Online ref, Online searches, Photocopying/Printing, Preschool reading prog, Prog for adults, Prog for children & young adult, Pub access computers, Story hour, Summer reading prog, Teen prog, Telephone ref, Web-catalog
Mem of Sussex County Department of Libraries
Open Mon-Thurs 10-8, Fri 10-5, Sat 10-2
Friends of the Library Group

DOVER

S DELAWARE AGRICULTURAL MUSEUM & VILLAGE LIBRARY-ARCHIVES*, 866 N Du Pont Hwy, 19901. SAN 377-5100. Tel: 302-734-1618. FAX: 302-734-0457. E-mail: damv@verizon.net. Web Site: www.agriculturalmuseum.org.
Founded 1974
Library Holdings: Bk Titles 3,000; Per Subs 36
Special Collections: Oral History

Subject Interests: Agr, Archives
Function: Res libr
Restriction: Not a lending libr

C DELAWARE STATE UNIVERSITY, William C Jason Library, 1200 N Dupont Hwy, 19901-2277. SAN 302-4814. Tel: 302-857-6191. Interlibrary Loan Service Tel: 302-857-7909. Reference Tel: 302-857-6180. Administration Tel: 302-857-6136. FAX: 302-857-6177. E-mail: askref@desu.edu. Web Site: www.desu.edu/library. *Dean, Univ Libr,* Dr Rebecca E Batson; Tel: 302-857-7887, E-mail: rbatson@desu.edu; *Fed Govt Doc Librn,* Christopher P Lemery; Tel: 302-857-6184, E-mail: cplemery@desu.edu; *Ref & Pub Serv Librn,* Rebecca J Montgomery; Tel: 302-857-7886, E-mail: rjmontgomery@desu.edu; *Tech & Syst Librn,* Jean M Charlot; Tel: 302-857-6135, E-mail: jcharlot@desu.edu; *Coordr, Tech Serv,* Beverly D Charlot; Tel: 302-857-6193, E-mail: bcharlot@desu.edu; *Pub Serv, Ref Serv,* Monifa T Carter; Tel: 302-857-7588, E-mail: mtcarter@desu.edu; *Pub Serv, Ref Serv,* Ronald W Davis; Tel: 302-857-6187, E-mail: rdavis@desu.edu; *Pub Serv, Ref Serv,* Rosamond Panda; Tel: 302-857-6197, E-mail: rpanda@desu.edu; *Ser,* Wanda F Nesbit; Tel: 302-857-7883, E-mail: wnesbit@desu.edu. Subject Specialists: *Arts, Humanities, Soc sci,* Christopher P Lemery; *Bus,* Rebecca J Montgomery; *Math, Natural sci, Tech,* Beverly D Charlot; *African-Am coll, Africana studies,* Monifa T Carter; *Agr, Related sci,* Ronald W Davis; *Educ,* Rosamond Panda; *Health, Pub policy,* Wanda F Nesbit; Staff 19 (MLS 9, Non-MLS 10)
Founded 1891. Enrl 4,178; Fac 198; Highest Degree: Doctorate
Jul 2012-Jun 2013 Income $1,845,488. Mats Exp $928,365, Books $38,468, Per/Ser (Incl. Access Fees) $586,878, Electronic Ref Mat (Incl. Access Fees) $300,019, Presv $3,000. Sal $856,091 (Prof $712,156)
Library Holdings: Audiobooks 207; AV Mats 7,019; CDs 763; DVDs 887; e-books 25,229; e-journals 42,765; Electronic Media & Resources 6,062; Large Print Bks 233; Microforms 268,561; Music Scores 124; Bk Titles 240,000; Bk Vols 411,618; Per Subs 1,300
Special Collections: Archival Coll; Delaware Coll; Select Government Depository; Special Rare Books Coll
Subject Interests: African-Am studies, Bus, Curric, Del, Educ, Nursing
Automation Activity & Vendor Info: (Acquisitions) SirsiDynix; (Cataloging) SirsiDynix; (Circulation) SirsiDynix; (Course Reserve) SirsiDynix; (OPAC) SirsiDynix; (Serials) SirsiDynix
Wireless access
Partic in OCLC Online Computer Library Center, Inc; Tri-State College Library Cooperative
Open Mon-Thurs (Winter) 8am-Midnight, Fri 8-5, Sat 12-5, Sun 2-10; Mon-Thurs (Summer) 8am-10pm, Fri 8-5, Sun 2-10

J DELAWARE TECHNICAL & COMMUNITY COLLEGE*, Terry Campus Library, 100 Campus Dr, 19904. SAN 302-4822. Tel: 302-857-1060. E-mail: terry-library@dtcc.edu. Web Site: www.library.dtcc.edu. *Head Librn,* Margaret R Prouse; E-mail: mprouse@dtcc.edu; Staff 2.8 (MLS 1.8, Non-MLS 1)
Founded 1974. Enrl 1,964; Fac 76; Highest Degree: Associate
Jul 2007-Jun 2008. Mats Exp $48,419, Books $40,000, Per/Ser (Incl. Access Fees) $8,419
Library Holdings: AV Mats 461; Bk Vols 15,327; Per Subs 98
Automation Activity & Vendor Info: (Acquisitions) SirsiDynix; (Cataloging) SirsiDynix; (Circulation) SirsiDynix; (Course Reserve) SirsiDynix; (ILL) SirsiDynix; (OPAC) SirsiDynix; (Serials) SirsiDynix
Database Vendor: EBSCOhost, LexisNexis, OCLC FirstSearch, ProQuest
Wireless access
Partic in OCLC Online Computer Library Center, Inc
Open Mon-Thurs 8:15am-9pm, Fri 8:15-4, Sat 9-1
Restriction: Open to students, fac & staff, Restricted pub use

P DOVER PUBLIC LIBRARY*, 35 Lockerman Plaza, 19901. SAN 302-4830. Tel: 302-736-7030. Administration Tel: 302-736-7032. FAX: 302-736-5087. Web Site: www.doverpubliclibrary.org. *Dir,* Margery Cyr; E-mail: margery.cyr@lib.de.us; *Asst Dir, Head, Ch,* Rebecca Norton; *Head, Adult Serv,* Michelle Hughes; *Head, Circ,* Audrey Avery; E-mail: audrey.avery@lib.de.us; *Head, Tech Serv,* David Giglio; E-mail: david.giglio@lib.de.us; *Teen Serv,* Kathy Goff; Staff 24 (MLS 7, Non-MLS 17)
Founded 1885. Pop 65,000; Circ 398,666
Jul 2005-Jun 2006 Income $1,597,509, State $186,127, City $963,582, Federal $50,000, County $392,800, Other $5,000. Mats Exp $158,057, Books $130,294, AV Mat $26,263, Electronic Ref Mat (Incl. Access Fees) $1,500. Sal $607,000 (Prof $292,333)
Library Holdings: Bk Vols 115,000; Per Subs 320
Special Collections: Countywide Reference Center; Delaware & Delmarva Peninsula (Delawareana); Kent County Consumer Health Coll
Database Vendor: EBSCOhost, ProQuest, SirsiDynix, SirsiDynix
Partic in Lyrasis; OCLC Online Computer Library Center, Inc
Open Mon-Thurs 9-9, Fri & Sat 9-5, Sun 1-5
Friends of the Library Group

GL KENT COUNTY LAW LIBRARY*, State Law Library - Kenty County, 38 The Green, Rm 100, 19901. SAN 302-4857. Tel: 302-674-7470. FAX: 302-674-7471. *Law Librn,* Patricia Burris; E-mail: patricia.burris@state.de.us
Library Holdings: Bk Vols 35,000; Per Subs 30
Special Collections: Early & Unusual Law Books
Wireless access
Function: Res libr
Open Mon-Fri 8:30-4:30

P KENT COUNTY PUBLIC LIBRARY*, 497 S Red Haven Ln, 19901. Tel: 302-698-6440. FAX: 302-698-6441. E-mail: KCPL@co.kent.de.us. Web Site: www.co.kent.de.us/kc-library.aspx. *Dir,* Hilary Welliver; Staff 1 (MLS 1)
Founded 1989
Library Holdings: AV Mats 500; Electronic Media & Resources 13; Large Print Bks 400; Bk Vols 18,000; Per Subs 20; Talking Bks 1,000
Automation Activity & Vendor Info: (Cataloging) SirsiDynix; (Circulation) SirsiDynix; (OPAC) SirsiDynix
Function: Doc delivery serv, Handicapped accessible, Homebound delivery serv, ILL available, Photocopying/Printing, Prog for adults, Prog for children & young adult, Summer reading prog
Open Mon-Fri 9-8, Sat & Sun 1-5
Friends of the Library Group
Bookmobiles: 1

P STATE OF DELAWARE*, Delaware Division of Libraries, 121 Martin Luther King Jr Blvd N, 19901. SAN 336-5859. Tel: 302-257-3000. Toll Free Tel: 800-282-8696. FAX: 302-739-6787. Web Site: www.delawarelibraries.org, www.libraries.delaware.gov. *State Librn,* Dr Annie Norman; E-mail: annie.norman@state.de.us; *Dep Dir,* Beth-Ann Ryan; E-mail: beth-ann.ryan@state.de.us; Staff 11 (MLS 11)
Founded 1901
Special Collections: Delaware Heritage Coll
Automation Activity & Vendor Info: (Cataloging) SirsiDynix; (Circulation) SirsiDynix; (ILL) OCLC; (OPAC) SirsiDynix; (Serials) SirsiDynix
Friends of the Library Group
Branches: 1
DELAWARE LIBRARY ACCESS SERVICES, 121 Martin Luther King Blvd N, 19901. Tel: 302-257-3015. Toll Free Tel: 800-282-8676. FAX: 302-739-6787. E-mail: debph@lib.de.us. *Admin Librn,* John Philos; E-mail: john.phillos@state.de.us; Staff 1 (MLS 1)
Founded 1971. Pop 1,500; Circ 54,000
Library Holdings: Bk Titles 36,000; Bk Vols 63,000; Per Subs 10
Automation Activity & Vendor Info: (Circulation) Keystone Systems, Inc (KLAS); (OPAC) Keystone Systems, Inc (KLAS)
Open Mon-Fri 8-4:30
Friends of the Library Group

C WESLEY COLLEGE LIBRARY*, Robert H Parker Library, 120 N State St, 19901. Tel: 302-736-2413. FAX: 302-736-2533. Web Site: www.wesley.edu. *Dir,* Jessica Olin
Founded 1873
Library Holdings: Bk Vols 101,000; Per Subs 300
Special Collections: Delaware Poetry Coll
Subject Interests: Bus, Environ sci, Hist, Lit, Nursing, Polit sci, Psychol, Relig
Automation Activity & Vendor Info: (Cataloging) SirsiDynix; (Circulation) SirsiDynix; (OPAC) SirsiDynix
Database Vendor: EBSCOhost, LexisNexis, OCLC FirstSearch
Function: ILL available, Photocopying/Printing

DOVER AFB

A UNITED STATES AIR FORCE*, Dover Air Force Base Library, 262 Chad St, Rm 208, 19902-7235. SAN 336-5913. Tel: 302-677-3992. FAX: 302-677-5490.
Library Holdings: Bk Vols 38,000; Per Subs 150
Automation Activity & Vendor Info: (Cataloging) SirsiDynix; (Circulation) SirsiDynix
Wireless access
Open Mon-Thurs 10-8, Fri 9:30-5, Sat 9:30-6

FRANKFORD

P FRANKFORD PUBLIC LIBRARY*, Eight Main St, 19945. (Mail add: PO Box 610, 19945-0610), SAN 302-4873. Tel: 302-732-9351. FAX: 302-732-3353. Web Site: www.frankfordlibrary.org. *Dir,* Elizabeth Hamilton
Founded 1930. Pop 7,487; Circ 30,087
Jul 2011-Jun 2012 Income $200,234. Mats Exp $26,429. Sal $100,583 (Prof $28,132)
Library Holdings: AV Mats 750; CDs 855; DVDs 1,942; Bk Vols 12,212; Per Subs 60

Special Collections: Delaware Coll
Automation Activity & Vendor Info: (Cataloging) SirsiDynix; (Circulation) SirsiDynix; (OPAC) SirsiDynix
Function: ILL available
Mem of Sussex County Department of Libraries
Open Mon-Thurs 10-8, Fri & Sat 10-2
Friends of the Library Group

GEORGETOWN

J DELAWARE TECHNICAL & COMMUNITY COLLEGE*, Stephen J Betze Library, 21179 College Dr, 19947. (Mail add: PO Box 630, 19947), SAN 302-4881. Tel: 302-259-6199. FAX: 302-259-6765. E-mail: owens-library@dtcc.edu. Web Site: www.library.dtcc.edu. *Dir,* Dr Shirin Jamasb; E-mail: sjamasb@dtcc.edu; *Evening Librn,* Katy Goff; *Librn,* Mary Sue Drugash; *Librn,* Richard Huffman; *Librn,* Michelle Rumble; *Evening Libr Tech,* Lori Bergey; *Libr Asst,* Aleta Esham; *Libr Spec,* Georgia Ryan; *Sr Libr Tech,* Tami Tucker; *Libr Tech,* Janice Stickels; Staff 10 (MLS 3, Non-MLS 7)
Founded 1967. Enrl 2,928; Fac 250; Highest Degree: Associate
Jul 2005-Jun 2006 Income $245,000. Mats Exp $207,000
Library Holdings: AV Mats 11,850; Bk Titles 51,907; Bk Vols 59,963; Per Subs 467
Special Collections: Delaware History Coll. US Document Depository
Automation Activity & Vendor Info: (Cataloging) SirsiDynix; (Circulation) SirsiDynix; (Course Reserve) SirsiDynix; (ILL) SirsiDynix; (OPAC) SirsiDynix; (Serials) SirsiDynix
Database Vendor: EBSCOhost, LexisNexis, OCLC FirstSearch, ProQuest
Wireless access
Partic in Tri-State College Library Cooperative
Open Mon-Thurs 8am-10pm, Fri 8-4:30, Sat 9-1

P GEORGETOWN PUBLIC LIBRARY*, 123 W Pine St, 19947. SAN 302-489X. Tel: 302-856-7958. E-mail: georgetown.library@lib.de.us. Web Site: www.georgetownpubliclibrary.org. *Dir,* Elaine Fike; Staff 2 (Non-MLS 2)
Circ 41,791
Library Holdings: Audiobooks 1,744; DVDs 852; Bk Vols 26,044; Per Subs 87
Special Collections: Delawareana
Subject Interests: Del, Genealogy, Mysteries
Automation Activity & Vendor Info: (Acquisitions) SirsiDynix; (Cataloging) OCLC CatExpress; (Circulation) SIRSI WorkFlows; (Serials) SIRSI WorkFlows
Database Vendor: EBSCO Information Services, Evanced Solutions, Inc, LearningExpress, LexisNexis, Overdrive, Inc, ProQuest, SirsiDynix, World Book Online
Wireless access
Function: ILL available
Special Services for the Deaf - Assistive tech
Open Mon-Thurs 10-8, Fri 10-5, Sat 10-2
Friends of the Library Group

P SUSSEX COUNTY DEPARTMENT OF LIBRARIES*, 22215 DuPont Blvd, 19947-2809. (Mail add: PO Box 589, 19947-0589), SAN 302-4903. Tel: 302-855-7890. FAX: 302-855-7895. Web Site: www.sussex.lib.de.us. *Dir,* Kathy Graybeal
Founded 1975
Library Holdings: Bk Vols 4,910; Per Subs 42
Special Collections: Eastern Shore Coll
Subject Interests: Libr & info sci
Automation Activity & Vendor Info: (Acquisitions) SirsiDynix; (Cataloging) SirsiDynix; (Circulation) SirsiDynix; (OPAC) SirsiDynix; (Serials) SirsiDynix
Member Libraries: Bridgeville Public Library; Delmar Public Library; Frankford Public Library; Laurel Public Library; Milford Public Library; Millsboro Public Library; Rehoboth Beach Public Library; Seaford Library; Selbyville Public Library
Open Mon-Fri 8:30-4:30
Branches: 3
GREENWOOD PUBLIC, 100 Mill St, Greenwood, 19950. (Mail add: PO Box, Greenwood, 19950). Tel: 302-349-5309. FAX: 302-349-5284. E-mail: greenwood.library@lib.de.us. Web Site: www.greenwood.lib.de.us/. *Dir,* Patricia Brown; E-mail: pbrown@lib.de.us
Library Holdings: Bk Titles 15,000; Per Subs 200
Open Mon, Tues, Thurs & Fri 10-8, Wed 10-5, Sat 10-2
Friends of the Library Group
MILTON PUBLIC, 121 Union St, Milton, 19968, SAN 321-1312. Tel: 302-684-8856. Web Site: www.milton.lib.de.us. *Dir,* Mary Catherine Hopkins; E-mail: milton-director@lib.de.us
Library Holdings: Bk Vols 38,507; Per Subs 294
Open Mon-Fri 10-8, Sat 10-4
Friends of the Library Group
SOUTH COASTAL PUBLIC LIBRARY, 43 Kent Ave, Bethany Beach, 19930. Tel: 302-539-5231. FAX: 302-537-9106. E-mail: southcoastal.library@lib.de.us. Web Site: www.southcoastal.lib.de.us. *Dir,* Susanne Keefe; Staff 3.51 (MLS 2.63, Non-MLS 0.88)
Founded 1978. Pop 13,441; Circ 117,270
Library Holdings: AV Mats 1,016; CDs 648; DVDs 2,200; Large Print Bks 1,385; Music Scores 769; Bk Titles 25,080; Bk Vols 26,361; Per Subs 190; Videos 1,179
Function: Adult bk club, Adult literacy prog, Audiobks via web, Bk club(s), Bk reviews (Group), Bks on cassette, Bks on CD, Children's prog, Computer training, Computers for patron use, Copy machines, Digital talking bks, Electronic databases & coll, Genealogy discussion group, Handicapped accessible, Homebound delivery serv, ILL available, Music CDs, Notary serv, Online cat, Online searches, Photocopying/Printing, Prog for adults, Prog for children & young adult, Pub access computers, Ref serv available, Summer reading prog, Tax forms, Telephone ref, VHS videos, Wheelchair accessible
Open Mon-Thurs 10-8, Fri 1-5, Sat 9-3
Friends of the Library Group
Bookmobiles: 1. Bk vols 10,898

GREENVILLE

S MT CUBA ASTRONOMICAL OBSERVATORY MEMORIAL LIBRARY*, 1610 Hillside Mill Rd, 19807. (Mail add: PO Box 3915, 19807), SAN 326-9787. Tel: 302-654-6407. E-mail: mtcuba@physics.udel.edu. Web Site: mountcuba.org. *Mgr,* Greg Weaver
Founded 1958
Library Holdings: Bk Titles 608
Subject Interests: Astronomy

HARRINGTON

P HARRINGTON PUBLIC LIBRARY*, 110 Center St, 19952. Tel: 302-398-4647. FAX: 302-398-3847. E-mail: harrington.library@lib.de.us. Web Site: harrington.delaware.gov/library. *Dir,* Christine Hayward; *Asst Dir, Youth Serv Librn,* Marleena Young; Staff 3 (Non-MLS 3)
Founded 1979. Pop 11,000
Library Holdings: AV Mats 1,000; Bk Vols 22,000; Per Subs 35; Talking Bks 500
Automation Activity & Vendor Info: (Acquisitions) SirsiDynix; (Cataloging) SirsiDynix; (Circulation) SirsiDynix; (Course Reserve) SirsiDynix; (ILL) SirsiDynix; (Media Booking) SirsiDynix; (OPAC) SirsiDynix; (Serials) SirsiDynix
Function: Adult literacy prog, Handicapped accessible, ILL available, Large print keyboards, Photocopying/Printing, Prog for children & young adult, Ref serv available, Summer reading prog, Telephone ref, Wheelchair accessible
Open Mon, Wed & Fri 10-6, Tues & Thurs 11:30-8, Sat 10-2
Friends of the Library Group

HOCKESSIN

P HOCKESSIN PUBLIC LIBRARY*, 1023 Valley Rd, 19707. SAN 302-4946. Tel: 302-239-5160. FAX: 302-239-1519. Web Site: www2.nccde.org/libraries/Hockessin. *Mgr,* Sue Rekart, Staff 12 (MLS 3, Non-MLS 9)
Founded 1977. Pop 26,795; Circ 490,689
Jul 2005-Jun 2006 Income $1,167,978, State $148,261, County $1,016,190, Other $3,527. Mats Exp $200,000. Sal $405,000
Library Holdings: AV Mats 8,000; Bk Vols 70,700; Per Subs 150
Special Collections: Delaware Coll
Automation Activity & Vendor Info: (Cataloging) SirsiDynix; (Circulation) SirsiDynix; (OPAC) SirsiDynix
Database Vendor: EBSCOhost, Gale Cengage Learning, Newsbank, ProQuest, SirsiDynix
Function: ILL available, Photocopying/Printing
Partic in OCLC Online Computer Library Center, Inc
Open Mon-Wed 10-9, Fri & Sat 10-5, Sun 1-5
Friends of the Library Group

LAUREL

P LAUREL PUBLIC LIBRARY*, 101 E Fourth St, 19956-1567. SAN 302-4954. Tel: 302-875-3184. Web Site: laurel.lib.de.us. *Dir,* Wendy Roberts; Staff 3 (MLS 3)
Founded 1909. Pop 12,500; Circ 107,000
Library Holdings: Bk Vols 51,000; Per Subs 132
Special Collections: Local History (Delaware Coll)
Function: Adult bk club, After school storytime, Archival coll, Art exhibits, Bk club(s), Bks on cassette, Bks on CD, Children's prog, Computers for patron use, Copy machines, Doc delivery serv, Electronic databases & coll, Free DVD rentals, Genealogy discussion group, Handicapped accessible, Holiday prog, ILL available, Music CDs, Online cat, Photocopying/Printing, Prog for adults, Prog for children & young

adult, Pub access computers, Story hour, Summer reading prog, Tax forms, Teen prog, Wheelchair accessible
Mem of Sussex County Department of Libraries
Open Mon-Thurs 10-8, Fri 10-5, Sat 10-2
Friends of the Library Group

LEWES

M BEEBE MEDICAL CENTER*, Health Sciences Library, 424 Savannah Rd, 19958. SAN 336-5948. Tel: 302-645-3100, Ext 5472. FAX: 302-644-2319. *Librn,* Jean Winstead; Staff 1 (MLS 1)
Founded 1921
Library Holdings: Bk Vols 150; Per Subs 40
Subject Interests: Med, Nursing
Partic in Basic Health Sciences Library Network; Consortium for Health Information & Library Services; National Network of Libraries of Medicine
Branches:
MARGARET H ROLLINS NURSING SCHOOL LIBRARY, 424 Savannah Rd, 19958, SAN 336-5972. Tel: 302-645-3100, Ext 5667. FAX: 302-645-3488. *Librn,* Mary Somers; E-mail: msomers@bbhealthcare.org; Staff 1 (MLS 1)
Founded 1921
Library Holdings: DVDs 10; Bk Vols 2,273; Per Subs 3; Videos 70
Subject Interests: Nursing
Restriction: Borrowing privileges limited to fac & registered students

P LEWES PUBLIC LIBRARY*, 111 Adams Ave, 19958. SAN 302-4962. Tel: 302-645-2733. FAX: 302-645-6235. Web Site: www.leweslibrary.org. *Dir,* Ed Goyda; *Asst Dir,* Kristen Gramer; *Ch,* Maureen Miller; *Teen Librn,* Lea Tomer; *Circ Mgr,* Heather Lachmann; *Tech Serv,* Margaret Melson; Staff 9 (MLS 4.5, Non-MLS 4.5)
Founded 1935. Pop 17,073; Circ 184,174
Jul 2012-Jun 2013 Income $493,957, State $77,556, Federal $1,242, County $181,006, Locally Generated Income $234,153. Mats Exp $47,330, Books $35,816, Per/Ser (Incl. Access Fees) $6,408, AV Mat $2,971, Electronic Ref Mat (Incl. Access Fees) $2,135. Sal $321,107
Library Holdings: Audiobooks 1,206; CDs 1,147; DVDs 1,994; Electronic Media & Resources 9; Large Print Bks 2,210; Bk Titles 44,806; Bk Vols 47,653; Per Subs 111; Videos 575
Special Collections: Delaware Coll; Writer's Library
Wireless access
Function: Accelerated reader prog, Adult bk club, Archival coll, Audiobks via web, Bk club(s), Bks on cassette, Bks on CD, Children's prog, Computer training, Computers for patron use, Copy machines, Digital talking bks, Electronic databases & coll, Exhibits, Free DVD rentals, Genealogy discussion group, Handicapped accessible, ILL available, Music CDs, Online cat, Online ref, OverDrive digital audio bks, Photocopying/Printing, Preschool outreach, Preschool reading prog, Prog for adults, Prog for children & young adult, Pub access computers, Senior computer classes, Spanish lang bks, Spoken cassettes & CDs, Story hour, Summer reading prog, Tax forms, Teen prog, Telephone ref, VHS videos, Workshops, Writing prog
Open Mon-Thurs 10-8, Fri 10-5, Sat 10-2
Friends of the Library Group

MIDDLETOWN

P APPOQUINIMINK COMMUNITY LIBRARY*, 651 N Broad St, Ste 101, 19709-6401. SAN 302-4989. Tel: 302-378-5588. FAX: 302-378-5594. Web Site: www2.nccde.org/libraries/Appoquinimink. *Mgr,* Paula Davino
Pop 8,602; Circ 103,074
Library Holdings: AV Mats 3,501; Bk Vols 46,644; Per Subs 128
Automation Activity & Vendor Info: (Cataloging) SirsiDynix; (Circulation) SirsiDynix; (OPAC) SirsiDynix; (Serials) SirsiDynix
Open Mon 10-8, Tues & Wed 12-8, Fri & Sat 10-5
Friends of the Library Group

MILFORD

P MILFORD PUBLIC LIBRARY*, 11 SE Front St, 19963. SAN 302-4997. Tel: 302-422-8996. FAX: 302-422-9269. Web Site: www.milfordpubliclibrary.org. *Dir,* Kay M Hudson; E-mail: kay.hudson@lib.de.us; Staff 16 (Non-MLS 16)
Founded 1882. Pop 18,112; Circ 140,604
Jul 2008-Jun 2009 Income $521,279, State $93,277, County $380,326. Mats Exp $93,277. Sal $288,575
Library Holdings: AV Mats 3,000; Bks on Deafness & Sign Lang 10; CDs 1,200; DVDs 2,480; High Interest/Low Vocabulary Bk Vols 50; Large Print Bks 1,500; Bk Vols 45,000; Per Subs 116; Talking Bks 1,000; Videos 600
Special Collections: Milford Chronicles & Peninsula News from 1886; Quilting Coll
Subject Interests: Del
Automation Activity & Vendor Info: (Acquisitions) SirsiDynix; (Cataloging) SirsiDynix; (Circulation) SirsiDynix; (OPAC) SirsiDynix; (Serials) SirsiDynix
Mem of Sussex County Department of Libraries
Special Services for the Deaf - High interest/low vocabulary bks
Special Services for the Blind - Low vision equip
Open Mon-Fri 9-8, Sat 9-2
Friends of the Library Group

NEW CASTLE

M DELAWARE DIVISION OF SUBSTANCE ABUSE & MENTAL HEALTH*, Medical Library, 1901 N Dupont Hwy, 19720. SAN 302-5039. Tel: 302-255-2789. FAX: 302-255-4458. *Admin Librn,* Jonathan Dunkle
Library Holdings: Bk Vols 300; Per Subs 40
Subject Interests: Nursing, Psychiat, Psychol, Soc serv (soc work)
Partic in Wilmington Area Biomedical Library Consortium (WABLC)
Open Mon-Thurs 8-12 & 1-4:30

§P GARFIELD PARK LENDING LIBRARY, 26 Karlyn Dr, 19720. Tel: 302-571-7312. FAX: 302-571-7490. *Mgr,* Steven Davis
Open Mon-Thurs 9-8, Sat 9-Noon

P NEW CASTLE PUBLIC LIBRARY*, 424 Delaware St, 19720-5099. SAN 302-5047. Tel: 302-328-1995. FAX: 302-328-4412. Web Site: www2.nccde.org/libraries/NewCastle. *Actg Dir,* Julie Kirk; Staff 4 (MLS 2, Non-MLS 2)
Founded 1811. Pop 35,726; Circ 109,629
Library Holdings: CDs 362; DVDs 398; Large Print Bks 249; Bk Titles 38,972; Per Subs 79; Talking Bks 1,590; Videos 713
Special Collections: Delawareana, Original New Castle Library Company Coll
Automation Activity & Vendor Info: (Cataloging) SirsiDynix; (Circulation) SirsiDynix; (OPAC) SirsiDynix
Open Mon & Tues 10-9, Wed & Thurs 2-9, Fri & Sat 10-5
Friends of the Library Group

C WILMINGTON UNIVERSITY LIBRARY, Robert C & Dorothy M Peoples Library, 320 N DuPont Hwy, 19720. SAN 302-5055. Tel: 302-356-6879. Circulation Tel: 302-356-6878. Interlibrary Loan Service Tel: 302-356-6745. Toll Free Tel: 800-451-5724. FAX: 302-328-0914. E-mail: librarycontact@wilmu.edu. Web Site: www.wilmu.edu/library. *Dir of Libr,* James M McCloskey; E-mail: james.m.mccloskey@wilmu.edu; *Asst Dir,* Adrienne M Johnson; E-mail: adrienne.m.johnson@wilmu.edu; *Librn,* Michelle C Reyes; E-mail: michelle.c.reyes@wilmu.edu; *Librn,* Pamela A Shukitt; E-mail: pamela.a.shukitt@wilmu.edu; *Librn,* William L Smith; E-mail: william.l.smith@wilmu.edu; *Instruction Librn,* James Bradley; E-mail: james.a.bradley@wilmu.edu; *Libr Tech II,* Craig S Conrad; *Libr Tech II,* Milo H Gibbons; E-mail: milo.h.gibbons@wilmu.edu; Staff 11.5 (MLS 7.5, Non-MLS 4)
Founded 1968. Enrl 14,000; Fac 7; Highest Degree: Doctorate
Library Holdings: Bk Vols 100,004; Per Subs 500
Subject Interests: Bus mgt, Educ, Leadership, Nursing, Soc sci
Automation Activity & Vendor Info: (Acquisitions) SirsiDynix; (Cataloging) SirsiDynix; (Circulation) SirsiDynix; (Course Reserve) SirsiDynix; (ILL) OCLC ILLiad; (OPAC) SirsiDynix; (Serials) SirsiDynix
Database Vendor: 3M Library Systems, Alexander Street Press, American Psychological Association (APA), Annual Reviews, Cinahl, CredoReference, ebrary, EBSCOhost, JSTOR, LexisNexis, McGraw-Hill, Mergent Online, OCLC FirstSearch, OCLC WorldShare Interlibrary Loan, OVID Technologies, ProQuest, Sage, SBRnet (Sports Business Research Network), SirsiDynix, ValueLine, YBP Library Services
Wireless access
Partic in Lyrasis; OCLC Online Computer Library Center, Inc; OCLC-LVIS; Tri-State College Library Cooperative
Open Mon-Thurs 9am-10pm, Fri 9-8, Sat 9-5, Sun 1-8
Restriction: Non-circulating to the pub

NEWARK

M CHRISTIANA HOSPITAL LIBRARY, Lewis B Flinn Medical Library, John H Ammon Medical Educ Ctr, 4755 Ogletown-Stanton Rd, 19718-0002. SAN 302-539X. Tel: 302-733-1115. FAX: 302-733-1365. Web Site: www.christianacare.org/libraries. *Dir,* Barbara Henry; Tel: 302-733-1151, E-mail: bhenry@christianacare.org; *Assoc Dir,* Sharon Easterby-Gannett; E-mail: seg@christianacare.org; *Ref Librn,* Ene Belleh; E-mail: ebelleh@christianacare.org. Subject Specialists: *Consumer health,* Barbara Henry; Staff 10 (MLS 5, Non-MLS 5)
Founded 1965
Library Holdings: e-books 600; e-journals 1,100; Bk Titles 5,400; Per Subs 30
Subject Interests: Cancer, Clinical med, Consumer health, Preventive med
Automation Activity & Vendor Info: (Cataloging) Marcive, Inc; (Circulation) Softlink America; (OPAC) Softlink America
Database Vendor: McGraw-Hill, OVID Technologies

Wireless access
Function: Doc delivery serv, ILL available, Online searches, Ref serv available
Partic in Lyrasis
Open Mon-Fri 7:30-5
Branches:
GAIL P GILL COMMUNITY HEALTH LIBRARY, 4755 Ogletown-Stanton Rd, 19718. Tel: 302-733-1122. *Commun Health Librn,* Ellen M Justice
Founded 1997
Library Holdings: Bk Titles 900
Subject Interests: Chronic disease, Consumer health, Wellness
Database Vendor: Softlink America
Function: Outside serv via phone, mail, e-mail & web, Pub access computers, Ref serv available
Restriction: Open to pub for ref & circ; with some limitations
HEALTH LIBRARY AT WILMINGTON, 501 W 14th St, Rm 1N69, Wilmington, 19801, SAN 374-4973. Tel: 302-320-2201. *Commun Health Librn,* Ellen M Justice; Staff 2 (MLS 1, Non-MLS 1)
Founded 1971
Library Holdings: Bk Titles 1,000; Per Subs 75
Automation Activity & Vendor Info: (Serials) Basch Subscriptions, Inc
Database Vendor: Softlink America
Restriction: Badge access after hrs, Circulates for staff only, In-house use for visitors
JUNIOR BOARD CANCER RESOURCE LIBRARY, Helen F Graham Cancer Ctr, 4701 Ogletown-Stanton Rd, Rm 1106, 19713. Tel: 302-623-4580. Reference Tel: 302-623-4585. *Commun Health Librn,* Ellen M Justice; Staff 2 (MLS 1, Non-MLS 1)
Founded 2002
Library Holdings: Bk Vols 3,000; Per Subs 40
Automation Activity & Vendor Info: (Serials) Softlink America
Database Vendor: PubMed

J DELAWARE TECHNICAL & COMMUNITY COLLEGE*, Stanton Campus Library, 400 Stanton-Christiana Rd, Rm D 201, 19713-2197. SAN 302-5063. Tel: 302-453-3716. FAX: 302-453-3079. Web Site: www.library.dtcc.edu. *Dir,* Regina Wells; E-mail: rwells@dtcc.edu; *Instruction Librn,* Janet Chin; *ILL,* Karen Dower; *Ref,* Aurelia Simon; Staff 4 (MLS 4)
Founded 1968. Enrl 1,800; Fac 106
Library Holdings: Bk Vols 31,448; Per Subs 364
Subject Interests: Careers, Criminal justice, Fire sci, Nursing, Soc sci & issues
Automation Activity & Vendor Info: (Cataloging) SirsiDynix; (Circulation) SirsiDynix; (Course Reserve) SirsiDynix; (ILL) SirsiDynix; (OPAC) SirsiDynix; (Serials) SirsiDynix
Wireless access
Partic in Wilmington Area Biomedical Library Consortium (WABLC)
Open Mon-Thurs 8am-9pm, Fri 8-4, Sat 9-1

S EDUCATION RESOURCE CENTER*, 16 W Main St, Rm 012, Williard Hall Education Bldg, 19716. Tel: 302-831-2335. FAX: 302-831-8404. Web Site: www.erc.udel.edu. *Dir,* Christine McBride
Founded 1971
Library Holdings: AV Mats 2,000; Bk Vols 41,530; Per Subs 39
Special Collections: Book Examination Site
Subject Interests: Curric related mat for K-12, Young adult bks
Automation Activity & Vendor Info: (Acquisitions) Follett Software; (Cataloging) Follett Software; (Circulation) Follett Software; (Course Reserve) Follett Software; (OPAC) Follett Software; (Serials) Follett Software
Function: ILL available, Photocopying/Printing
Open Mon-Thurs 8:30-8, Fri 8:30-5, Sat 9-1

S INTERNATIONAL READING ASSOCIATION LIBRARY*, Ralph C Staiger Library, 800 Barksdale Rd, 19711. (Mail add: PO Box 8139, 19714-8139), SAN 302-5071. Tel: 302-731-1600, Ext 217. FAX: 302-731-1057. Web Site: www.reading.org. *Exec Dir,* Marcie Post; E-mail: mpost@reading.org; Staff 2 (MLS 1, Non-MLS 1)
Founded 1974
Library Holdings: Bk Titles 4,000; Per Subs 100
Special Collections: Children's Choices Coll; IRA Past President & Historical Readers Coll
Subject Interests: Children's lit, Lang arts, Learning disabilities, Reading
Automation Activity & Vendor Info: (Cataloging) TLC (The Library Corporation); (Circulation) TLC (The Library Corporation)
Function: Res libr
Open Mon-Fri 9-4
Restriction: Non-circulating to the pub

P NEWARK FREE LIBRARY*, 750 Library Ave, 19711-7146. SAN 302-508X. Tel: 302-731-7550. FAX: 302-731-4019. Web Site: www2.nccde.org/libraries/Newark. *Mgr,* Martha Birchenall; Staff 16 (MLS 4, Non-MLS 12)
Founded 1897. Pop 70,160; Circ 617,042
Library Holdings: Bk Vols 106,956; Per Subs 326
Automation Activity & Vendor Info: (Cataloging) SirsiDynix; (Circulation) SirsiDynix; (OPAC) SirsiDynix; (Serials) SirsiDynix
Function: Telephone ref
Special Services for the Deaf - High interest/low vocabulary bks; Spec interest per
Open Mon-Wed & Fri 10-9, Sat 10-5, Sun 1-5
Friends of the Library Group

R NEWARK UNITED METHODIST CHURCH*, Bunting Library, 69 E Main St, 19711-4645. SAN 326-2235. Tel: 302-368-8774. *Librn,* Marietta J Garrett; Tel: 302-738-6741, E-mail: cgarr13@aol.com
Founded 1955
Library Holdings: High Interest/Low Vocabulary Bk Vols 100; Large Print Bks 25; Bk Vols 2,000
Subject Interests: Children's lit, Family, Relig
Open Mon-Fri 8-4, Sun 8-12

S MARGARET S STERCK SCHOOL FOR THE DEAF LIBRARY*, 630 E Chestnut Hill Rd, 19713. SAN 302-5098. Tel: 302-454-2301. FAX: 302-454-3493. TDD: 302-451-1403.
Library Holdings: Bk Vols 10,000
Special Collections: Captioned Filmstrip Coll; Large Print Books for the Visually Impaired; Professional Library of materials on deafness, deaf culture & visual impairment
Subject Interests: Deaf
Special Services for the Deaf - Staff with knowledge of sign lang
Restriction: Staff use only, Students only

C UNIVERSITY OF DELAWARE LIBRARY*, 181 S College Ave, 19717-5267. SAN 336-609X. Tel: 302-831-2231. Interlibrary Loan Service Tel: 302-831-2236. FAX: 302-831-1046. Web Site: www.lib.udel.edu. *Vice Provost & May Morris Univ Librn,* Susan Brynteson; E-mail: susanb@udel.edu; *Assoc Univ Librn, Info Tech & Digital Initiatives,* Gregg Silvis; E-mail: gregg@udel.edu; *Assoc Univ Librn for Serv, Outreach & Assessment,* Sandra Millard; E-mail: skm@udel.edu; *Assoc Univ Librn, Tech Serv & Res Mgt,* M Dina Giambi; E-mail: dinag@udel.edu; *Assoc Univ Librn, Admin Serv,* Paul Anderson, E-mail: pa@udel.edu; *Head, Access Serv,* Nancy Nelson; E-mail: nrnelson@udel.edu; *Head, Acq,* Janet Siar; E-mail: jsiar@udel.edu; *Head, Ctr for Digital Coll,* Mary Durio; E-mail: mdurio@udel.edu; *Head, Coll Develop,* Susan Davi; E-mail: sdavi@udel.edu; *Head, Flm & Video Coll,* Francis Poole; E-mail: fpoole@udel.edu; *Head, Instrul Serv, Head, Ref Serv,* Shirley Branden; E-mail: sbranden@udel.edu; *Head, Libr Data & Server Mgt,* Mark Grabowski; E-mail: elric@udel.edu; *Head, Libr Info Tech User Support,* Justin Wing; E-mail: wingman@udel.edu; *Head, Ms & Archives,* L Rebecca Johnson Melvin; E mail: lrjm@udel.edu; *Head, Metadata Serv,* Deborah Rae, E-mail: drae@udel.edu; *Head, Spec Coll,* Timothy Murray; E-mail: tdm@udel.edu; *Head, Student Multimedia Design Ctr,* Shelly McCoy; E-mail: smccoy@udel.edu, *Mrg, Admin Serv, Mgr, Libr Human Res,* Julie Brewer; E-mail: jbrewer@udel.edu; Staff 58 (MLS 49, Non-MLS 9)
Founded 1743. Enrl 21,489; Fac 1,131; Highest Degree: Doctorate
Jul 2011-Jun 2012. Mats Exp $9,349,319. Sal $8,287,142 (Prof $4,716,809)
Library Holdings: Bk Titles 2,271,488; Bk Vols 3,222,014; Per Subs 42,841
Special Collections: Delaware History & Politics (James C Booth Papers, Senator John Williams Papers, Senator J Allen Frear Jr Papers); History of Papermaking & Contemporary Fine Printing (Bird & Bull Press Archives, Plough Press Archives); Irish Literature; John De Pol Papers; Senatorial Papers of Vice President Joseph R Biden, Jr; Twentieth-Century American Literature (Alice Dunbar-Nelson Papers, Emily Coleman Papers, Louis Untermeyer Papers, John Malcolm Brinnin Papers, Ishmael Reed Papers, Paul Bowles Papers, Donald Justice Papers, Tennessee Williams Coll, Marguerite & Captain Louis Henry Cohn Ernest Hemingway Coll, Ezra Pound Coll, Archives of Pagany); Unidel History of Chemistry Coll; Unidel History of Horticulture & Landscape Architecture Coll; US Patent Coll. US Document Depository
Wireless access
Publications: Collections; Exhibition Catalogs; University of Delaware Library Associates Newsletter
Partic in Association of Research Libraries (ARL); Center for Research Libraries; Chesapeake Information & Research Library Alliance (CIRLA); OCLC Online Computer Library Center, Inc
Special Services for the Deaf - Assistive tech
Special Services for the Blind - Assistive/Adapted tech devices, equip & products
Friends of the Library Group

ODESSA

P CORBIT-CALLOWAY MEMORIAL LIBRARY*, Second & High St, 19730. SAN 302-511X. Tel: 302-378-8838. FAX: 302-378-7803. Web Site: www2.nccde.org/libraries/corbit. *Ch Serv, Dir,* Karen Quinn; Staff 4 (MLS 1, Non-MLS 3)
Founded 1847. Pop 6,100; Circ 34,660
Library Holdings: AV Mats 300; High Interest/Low Vocabulary Bk Vols 500; Large Print Bks 700; Bk Titles 28,000; Bk Vols 35,000; Per Subs 95; Spec Interest Per Sub 65; Talking Bks 150
Special Collections: DelMarva Coll of History & Culture
Automation Activity & Vendor Info: (Circulation) SirsiDynix; (OPAC) SirsiDynix; (Serials) SirsiDynix
Database Vendor: EBSCOhost
Publications: The Face of a Town: The Corbit-Calloway Memorial Library; Yesterday & Today (Histories of eight towns)
Open Mon & Thurs 1-8, Tues & Fri 10-4, Wed 10-8, Sat 9-1
Friends of the Library Group

REHOBOTH BEACH

P REHOBOTH BEACH PUBLIC LIBRARY*, 226 Rehoboth Ave, 19971-2134. SAN 302-5128. Tel: 302-227-8044. FAX: 302-227-0597. Web Site: www.rehobothlibrary.org. *Dir,* Margaret LaFond; *Circ Supvr,* Jessica Porter; Staff 5 (MLS 5)
Founded 1912. Circ 58,239
Library Holdings: Bk Vols 50,000; Per Subs 85
Special Collections: Delaware Coll
Automation Activity & Vendor Info: (Acquisitions) SirsiDynix; (Cataloging) SirsiDynix; (Circulation) SirsiDynix; (OPAC) SirsiDynix
Database Vendor: EBSCOhost, Newsbank, ProQuest
Wireless access
Mem of Sussex County Department of Libraries
Open Mon-Wed 10-8, Thurs & Fri 10-5, Sat 10-3, Sun (Summer) 12-4
Friends of the Library Group

SEAFORD

P SEAFORD LIBRARY*, 402 Porter St Extended, 19973. SAN 302-5136. Tel: 302-629-2524. FAX: 302-629-9181. Web Site: www.seaford.lib.de.us. *Dir,* Jerry Keiser; Staff 9 (MLS 1, Non-MLS 8)
Founded 1902. Pop 25,000; Circ 107,435
Library Holdings: Bk Vols 44,265; Per Subs 120
Special Collections: Classic Cars Coll; Delaware History (Delawareana Coll); Large Print Coll; Parents & Children (Parenting Coll)
Automation Activity & Vendor Info: (Cataloging) SirsiDynix; (Circulation) SirsiDynix; (OPAC) SirsiDynix
Function: ILL available
Mem of Sussex County Department of Libraries
Open Mon-Thurs 9-8, Fri & Sat 9-5
Friends of the Library Group

SELBYVILLE

P SELBYVILLE PUBLIC LIBRARY, 11 Main & McCabe Sts, 19975. (Mail add: PO Box 739, 19975-0739), SAN 302-5144. Tel: 302-436-8195. FAX: 302-436-1508. Web Site: www.selbyvillelibrary.org. *Dir,* Kelly Kline; E-mail: Kelly.Kline@lib.de.us
Pop 3,000
Library Holdings: Bk Vols 21,833; Per Subs 21
Wireless access
Mem of Sussex County Department of Libraries
Open Mon & Thurs 10-8, Tues, Wed & Fri 10-6, Sat 10-2
Friends of the Library Group

SMYRNA

P SMYRNA PUBLIC LIBRARY*, 107 S Main St, 19977. SAN 302-5160. Tel: 302-653-4579. FAX: 302-653-2650. Web Site: www.smyrna.delaware.gov/index.aspx?nid=84. *Dir,* Beverly Hirt; E-mail: Beverly.Hirt@lib.de.us
Founded 1858. Circ 37,895
Library Holdings: CDs 102; DVDs 39; Large Print Bks 515; Bk Titles 19,822; Per Subs 67; Talking Bks 659; Videos 770
Special Collections: Delaware Authors
Subject Interests: Del
Partic in OCLC Online Computer Library Center, Inc
Open Mon, Wed & Fri 8:30-6, Tues & Thurs 10-8, Sat 9-2
Friends of the Library Group

S JAMES T VAUGHN CORRECTIONAL CENTER LAW LIBRARY*, 1181 Paddock Rd, 19977. SAN 302-5152. Tel: 302-653-9261, Ext 2450. FAX: 302-659-6687. *Legal Serv Adminr,* Mike Little; E-mail: michael.little@state.de.us
Founded 1971
Library Holdings: Bk Titles 4,000
Database Vendor: Westlaw

WILMINGTON

P BRANDYWINE HUNDRED LIBRARY*, 1300 Foulk Rd, 19803. SAN 302-5217. Tel: 302-477-3150. FAX: 302-477-4545. Web Site: www2.nccde.org/libraries/BrandyWineHundred. *Mgr,* Jean Kaufman; Staff 31 (MLS 6, Non-MLS 25)
Founded 1959
Library Holdings: Bk Vols 151,725; Per Subs 330
Special Collections: Coin Coll; Delawareana Coll; Holocaust
Automation Activity & Vendor Info: (Acquisitions) SirsiDynix; (Cataloging) SirsiDynix; (Circulation) SirsiDynix; (OPAC) SirsiDynix
Database Vendor: EBSCOhost
Wireless access
Function: Handicapped accessible, ILL available, Outside serv via phone, mail, e-mail & web, Photocopying/Printing, Prog for children & young adult, Ref serv available, Summer reading prog, Telephone ref, Wheelchair accessible
Publications: Friends of the Brandywine Hundred Library (Newsletter)
Open Mon-Wed & Fri 10-9, Sat 10-5, Sun 1-5
Friends of the Library Group

R CONGREGATION BETH EMETH, William, Vitellia & Topkis Library, 300 W Lea Blvd, 19802. SAN 302-5365. Tel: 302-764-2393. FAX: 302-764-2395. Web Site: www.bethemethde.org. *Librn,* Bonnie Silbermann; E-mail: bonnies@aol.com
Library Holdings: Bk Vols 3,000
Subject Interests: Judaica (lit or hist of Jews)
Wireless access
Open Mon-Thurs 9-5, Fri 8:30-4

S DELAWARE ART MUSEUM*, Helen Farr Sloan Library, 2301 Kentmere Pkwy, 19806. SAN 302-5233. Tel: 302-351-8540. Web Site: www.delart.org. *Head Librn,* Rachael DiEleuterio; E-mail: rdieleuterio@delart.org; Staff 1 (MLS 1)
Founded 1912
Library Holdings: Bk Vols 40,000; Per Subs 50
Special Collections: Bancroft Pre-Raphaelite Library, archival rec, bks, cat, mss; Everett Shinn Archives; Frank Schoonover Coll, archives, bks, illus, photog; Gayle Hoskins Coll, memorabilia, photog, complete published works; Howard Pyle Library & Archives, illus, photog, complete published works; Jerome Myers Coll, archival rec, memorabilia; John Sloan Coll, bks, cat, personal papers, photog; N C Wyeth Coll, bks, illus, per; Stanley Arthurs Coll, bks, illus, clippings
Automation Activity & Vendor Info: (Cataloging) Follett Software; (OPAC) Follett Software
Function: Res libr
Restriction: Open by appt only

S DELAWARE HISTORICAL SOCIETY RESEARCH LIBRARY*, 505 N Market St, 19801. SAN 302-5276. Tel: 302-655-7161. FAX: 302-655-7844. E-mail: deinfo@dehistory.org. Web Site: www.dehistory.org. *Chief Exec Officer,* Scott W Loehr; E-mail: sloehr@dehistory.org; *Chief Curator,* Dr Constance Cooper; Tel: 302-295-2385, E-mail: ccooper@dehistory.org; *Curator of Images,* Heather Isbell Schumacher; Tel: 302-295-2386, E-mail: hischumacher@dehistory.org; *Curator, Printed Mat,* Edward Richi; Tel: 302-295-2387, E-mail: research@dehistory.org; Staff 4 (Non-MLS 4)
Founded 1864
Library Holdings: Bk Vols 32,000; Per Subs 73
Special Collections: Ephemera; Manuscripts; Maps; Newspapers; Photographs. Oral History
Subject Interests: Del hist, Genealogy, US hist
Automation Activity & Vendor Info: (Cataloging) Cuadra Associates, Inc; (OPAC) Cuadra Associates, Inc
Wireless access
Publications: Delaware History (Bi-annually)
Open Mon 1-9, Tues & Thurs 9-1, Fri 9-5
Friends of the Library Group

S DELAWARE MUSEUM OF NATURAL HISTORY LIBRARY, 4840 Kennett Pike, 19807. (Mail add: PO Box 3937, 19807-0937), SAN 302-492X. Tel: 302-658-9111. FAX: 302-658-2610. Web Site: www.delmnh.org. *Curator,* Dr Jean Woods; Tel: 302-658-9111, Ext 314, E-mail: jwoods@delmnh.org
Founded 1972
Library Holdings: Bk Vols 10,000; Per Subs 130
Subject Interests: Birds, Mollusks
Function: Res libr
Publications: Nemouria Research Journal
Restriction: Non-circulating, Open by appt only

J DELAWARE TECHNICAL & COMMUNITY COLLEGE*, John Eugene Derrickson Memorial Library, Wilmington Campus, West Bldg, First Flr, 333 Shipley St, 19801. SAN 302-525X. Tel: 302-573-5422. FAX: 302-577-2038. Web Site: www.library.dtcc.edu. *Dir,* Mary Anne Farrell; *Bibliog Instruction Librn,* Paul Page; *Electronic Res Librn,* Laurel Ferris; Staff 4 (MLS 4)
Founded 1973. Enrl 3,000; Fac 125; Highest Degree: Associate
Library Holdings: Bk Vols 36,400; Per Subs 410
Subject Interests: Allied health, Bus & mgt, Computer tech
Automation Activity & Vendor Info: (Acquisitions) SirsiDynix; (Cataloging) SirsiDynix; (Circulation) SirsiDynix; (Course Reserve) SirsiDynix; (ILL) SirsiDynix; (OPAC) SirsiDynix; (Serials) SirsiDynix
Database Vendor: EBSCOhost, OCLC FirstSearch
Partic in Lyrasis; OCLC Online Computer Library Center, Inc
Open Mon-Thurs 8:15am-9pm, Fri 8:15-4:30, Sat 9-1

GM DEPARTMENT OF VETERANS AFFAIRS*, Medical Library, 1601 Kirkwood Hwy, Rm 7090, 19805-4988. SAN 302-5381. Tel: 302-994-2511, Ext 4255, 302-994-2511, Ext 4381. FAX: 302-633-5285. *Libr Mgr,* Jeffrey Garverick; E-mail: jeffrey.garverick@va.gov; Staff 1 (MLS 1)
Founded 1949
Oct 2010-Sept 2011 Income $50,000. Mats Exp $50,000, Books $7,000, Per/Ser (Incl. Access Fees) $9,000, Other Print Mats $1,000, Electronic Ref Mat (Incl. Access Fees) $33,000
Library Holdings: Audiobooks 30; DVDs 10; e-books 100; e-journals 400; Bk Titles 480; Bk Vols 510; Per Subs 19; Videos 20
Subject Interests: Allied health, Dentistry, Med, Nursing, Surgery
Automation Activity & Vendor Info: (Cataloging) EOS International; (Circulation) EOS International; (OPAC) EOS International; (Serials) EBSCO Online
Database Vendor: American Psychological Association (APA), Cinahl, EBSCO Information Services, Elsevier, EOS International, Library Systems & Services (LSSI), MD Consult, Medline, PubMed, SerialsSolutions
Wireless access
Function: ILL available, Photocopying/Printing
Publications: Book List (Bi-monthly); Journal Holdings Listing (Bi-annually)
Partic in Docline; Veterans Affairs Libr Network (VALNET)
Restriction: Employees & their associates, Restricted access

P ELSMERE PUBLIC LIBRARY*, 30 Spruce Ave, 19805. SAN 377-0974. Tel: 302-892-2210. FAX: 302-892-2213. Web Site: www2.nccde.org/libraries/Elsmere. *Mgr,* Beth Kloetzer; Staff 3.5 (MLS 1.5, Non-MLS 2)
Founded 1995. Pop 44,294; Circ 271,992
Jul 2008-Jun 2009 Income $819,607, State $253,138, County $566,337, Locally Generated Income $132. Mats Exp $138,769. Sal $257,738
Library Holdings: Audiobooks 4,824; DVDs 4,693; Electronic Media & Resources 64; Bk Vols 34,521; Per Subs 102
Automation Activity & Vendor Info: (Acquisitions) SirsiDynix; (Cataloging) SirsiDynix; (Circulation) SirsiDynix; (OPAC) SirsiDynix; (Serials) EBSCO Online
Database Vendor: EBSCOhost, Newsbank, ProQuest, ReferenceUSA
Wireless access
Partic in OCLC Online Computer Library Center, Inc; Tipcat
Open Mon 10-8, Tues & Thurs 12-8, Fri & Sat 10-5
Friends of the Library Group

C GOLDEY-BEACOM COLLEGE*, J Wilbur Hirons Library, 4701 Limestone Rd, 19808. SAN 302-5268. Tel: 302-225-6247. FAX: 302-998-6189. E-mail: hirons@gbc.edu. Web Site: www.gbc.edu/library. *Head Librn,* Rusty Michalak; Tel: 303-225-6227, E-mail: michalr@gbc.edu; *Librn,* Bethany Geleskie; E-mail: geleskb@gbc.edu; *Librn,* Alison Wessel; E-mail: wessel@gbc.edu; *Libr Asst,* Sandy McNeal; Staff 4 (MLS 3, Non-MLS 1)
Founded 1969. Enrl 1,800; Fac 85; Highest Degree: Master
Library Holdings: AV Mats 1,320; Bk Titles 40,346; Bk Vols 44,602; Per Subs 1,051
Special Collections: College Archives; Delaware Business
Subject Interests: Bus & mgt
Automation Activity & Vendor Info: (Cataloging) SirsiDynix; (Circulation) SirsiDynix; (OPAC) SirsiDynix
Wireless access
Partic in Lyrasis
Open Mon-Thurs 8:30am-10pm, Fri 8-5, Sat 8-6, Sun 11-5

S HAGLEY MUSEUM & LIBRARY*, 298 Buck Rd E, 19807. (Mail add: PO Box 3630, 19807-0630), SAN 302-4938. Tel: 302-658-2400. FAX: 302-658-0568. Web Site: www.hagley.org. *Dir of Libr Serv,* Erik Rau; *Ref Librn,* Linda Gross; E-mail: lgross@hagley.org; *Curator,* Lynn Catanese; E-mail: lcatanese@hagley.org; *Curator,* Max Moeller; E-mail: mmoeller@hagley.org; *Curator,* Jon M Williams; E-mail: jwilliams@hagley.org. Subject Specialists: *Archives, Manuscripts,* Lynn Catanese; *Prints,* Jon M Williams; Staff 13 (MLS 4, Non-MLS 9)
Founded 1955
Library Holdings: Bk Vols 250,000; Per Subs 259
Special Collections: Chemical history, bks, flm, ms; Dupont Company & Family Papers; Iron & Steel, bks & ms; Pennsylvania Power & Light Coll; Petroleum Bks & ms; Railroad Firms; Reading Railroad Coll, ms; Textile Bks & ms; Trade Catalogs & Journals; World's Fairs & International Expositions
Subject Interests: Bus & mgt, Consumerism, Econ hist, Hist of tech, Indust design, Indust hist
Automation Activity & Vendor Info: (Cataloging) EOS International; (OPAC) EOS International
Wireless access
Function: Res libr
Publications: A Guide to the Manuscripts in the Eleutherian Mills Historical Library (1970) & Supplement (1978); Pennsylvania Power & Light: A Guide to the Records (1985)
Partic in Independent Res Libr Asn; OCLC Research Library Partnership; Philadelphia Area Consortium of Special Collections Libraries
Open Mon-Fri 8:30-4:30
Restriction: Non-circulating to the pub

R IMMANUEL CHURCH LIBRARY*, 2414 Pennsylvania Ave, 19806. Tel: 302-652-3121. FAX: 302-652-1078. E-mail: immanuellibrary@comcast.net. Web Site: www.immanuelchurch.us. *Librn,* Frances Dunkelberger
Founded 1865
Library Holdings: AV Mats 400; DVDs 60; Bk Vols 3,500; Videos 200
Special Collections: Immanuel History, newsclippings
Restriction: Mem only

R INTERFAITH RESOURCE CENTER, 1530 Foulk Rd, 19803. Tel: 302-477-0910. FAX: 302-477-0911. E-mail: resource.ctr1@gmail.com. Web Site: www.interfaithresourcecenter.com. *Exec Dir,* Sister Barbara Jean Brown
Founded 1968
Jan 2013-Dec 2013. Mats Exp $7,600. Sal $28,500 (Prof $28,500)
Library Holdings: AV Mats 2,000; Bk Vols 6,500
Subject Interests: Relig
Wireless access
Open Mon-Thurs 9-4
Restriction: Mem only

P KIRKWOOD LIBRARY*, 6000 Kirkwood Hwy, 19808-4817. SAN 302-5284. Tel: 302-995-7663. FAX: 302-995-7687. Web Site: www2.nccde.org/libraries/Kirkwood. *Mgr,* Steven Davis, Staff 10 (MLS 3, Non-MLS 7)
Founded 1967. Pop 52,702; Circ 418,634
Library Holdings: Bk Vols 85,934; Per Subs 206
Automation Activity & Vendor Info: (Cataloging) SirsiDynix; (Circulation) SirsiDynix; (OPAC) SirsiDynix; (Serials) SirsiDynix
Wireless access
Open Mon-Wed 10-9, Thurs & Sat 10-5, Sun 1-5
Friends of the Library Group

L MORRIS JAMES LLP*, Law Library, 500 Delaware Ave, Ste 1500, 19801-1494. (Mail add: PO Box 2306, 19899-2306), SAN 370-6672. Tel: 302-888-6863. FAX: 302-571-1750. Web Site: www.morrisjames.com. *Librn,* Sandra J Proctor; E-mail: sproctor@morrisjames.com; Staff 2 (MLS 1, Non-MLS 1)
Subject Interests: Bankruptcy, Corp law, Family law, Real estate law, Tax law
Automation Activity & Vendor Info: (Cataloging) Inmagic, Inc.; (Serials) Inmagic, Inc.
Database Vendor: EBSCOhost, LexisNexis, Westlaw
Function: ILL available
Restriction: By permission only

L MORRIS, NICHOLS, ARSHT & TUNNELL, LLP*, Law Library, 1201 N Market St, 19801. (Mail add: PO Box 1347, 19899). Tel: 302-658-9200. FAX: 302-658-3989. Web Site: www.mnat.com. *Librn,* Elizabeth Stack; Tel: 302-351-9240, E-mail: estack@mnat.com; Staff 2 (MLS 1, Non-MLS 1)
Library Holdings: Bk Vols 2,500; Per Subs 25
Subject Interests: Bankruptcy, Corporate law, Intellectual property law, Securities law
Database Vendor: Westlaw
Function: ILL available, Photocopying/Printing
Restriction: Staff use only

GL NEW CASTLE COUNTY LAW LIBRARY*, 500 N King St, Ste 2500, 19801. SAN 302-5322. Tel: 302-255-0847. FAX: 302-255-2223. *Law Librn,* Alda Monsen; E-mail: alda.monsen@state.de.us
Founded 1911
Library Holdings: Bk Vols 25,000

Database Vendor: LexisNexis, Westlaw
Wireless access
Open Mon-Fri 8:30-4:30
Restriction: Non-circulating to the pub

L POTTER ANDERSON & CORROON LLP*, Law Library, Hercules Plaza, 1313 N Market St, 19801. (Mail add: PO Box 951, 19899-0951). Tel: 302-984-6000. FAX: 302-658-1192. Web Site: www.potteranderson.com. *Dir, Libr Serv,* Kathleen H Veith; Tel: 302-984-6195, Fax: 302-778-6195, E-mail: kveith@potteranderson.com; Staff 1 (MLS 1)
Subject Interests: Bankruptcy, Corporate law, Estates, Tax law, Trusts
Database Vendor: Bloomberg, Westlaw, Westlaw Business
Wireless access
Function: ILL available, Photocopying/Printing
Restriction: Staff use only

L RICHARDS, LAYTON & FINGER LIBRARY*, One Rodney Sq, 920 N King St, 19801. SAN 326-9744. Tel: 302-651-7700. FAX: 302-651-7701. Web Site: www.rlf.com. *Libr Mgr,* Robert L Guerrero; Tel: 302-651-7775, E-mail: guerrero@rlf.com; Staff 2 (MLS 1, Non-MLS 1)
Founded 1929
Library Holdings: Bk Vols 14,000; Per Subs 27
Subject Interests: Law
Partic in Westlaw
Restriction: Staff use only

L SKADDEN, ARPS, SLATE, MEAGHER & FLOM LLP LIBRARY*, One Rodney Sq, 7th Flr, 920 N King St, 19801. SAN 329-1073. Tel: 302-651-3224. FAX: 302-651-3001. *Head Librn,* Leslie Corey Leach; Staff 2 (MLS 1, Non-MLS 1)
Founded 1979
Library Holdings: e-books 45; e-journals 30; Bk Titles 850; Bk Vols 9,000; Per Subs 25
Subject Interests: Bankruptcy, Del law, Securities
Automation Activity & Vendor Info: (Acquisitions) EOS International; (Cataloging) OCLC; (Circulation) EOS International; (ILL) EOS International; (OPAC) EOS International; (Serials) EOS International
Database Vendor: EOS International
Wireless access
Restriction: Staff use only

GL UNITED STATES COURT OF APPEALS*, Branch Library, US Courts Library, 5122 Federal Bldg, 844 King St, Unit 43, 19801. SAN 302-5373. Tel: 302-573-5880, 302-573-5881. FAX: 302-573-6430. *Librn,* Michael Hayes; Staff 2 (MLS 1, Non-MLS 1)
Founded 1974
Library Holdings: Bk Vols 14,000; Per Subs 25
Open Mon-Fri 8:30-4:30
Restriction: Non-circulating to the pub

WIDENER UNIVERSITY

CL HARRISBURG CAMPUS LAW LIBRARY, 3800 Vartan Way, Harrisburg, 17110. (Mail add: PO Box 69380, Harrisburg, 17106-9380), SAN 370-3517. Tel: 717-541-3933. FAX: 717-541-3998. Web Site: www.law.widener.edu/LawLibrary. *Dir,* Michael J Slinger; Tel: 302-477-2111, Fax: 302-477-2228, E-mail: mjslinger@widener.edu; *Assoc Dir,* Patricia Fox; Tel: 717-541-3935, E-mail: pfox@widener.edu; *Ref/Emerging Technologies Librn,* Stephanie Engerer; Tel: 717-541-3953, E-mail: sjengerer@widener.edu; *Ref/Tech Serv Librn,* Susan Giusti; Tel: 717-541-3929, E-mail: smgiusti@widener.edu; *Govt Doc, Ref Serv,* Edmund Sonnenberg; Tel: 717-541-3932, E-mail: ejsonnenberg@widener.edu; *Ref Serv,* Brent Johnson; Tel: 717-541-3984, E-mail: bljohnson@widener.edu. Subject Specialists: *State doc,* Brent Johnson; Staff 11 (MLS 6, Non-MLS 5)
Founded 1989
Library Holdings: Bk Titles 28,504; Bk Vols 199,864
Special Collections: US Document Depository
Subject Interests: Pa law, Pub law
Database Vendor: Innovative Interfaces, Inc
Open Mon-Thurs 8am-Midnight, Fri 8am-11pm, Sat 8-8, Sun 10am-Midnight

CL SCHOOL OF LAW LIBRARY, 4601 Concord Pike, 19803. (Mail add: PO Box 7474, 19083), SAN 302-5241. Tel: 302-477-2244. FAX: 302-477-2240. E-mail: law.libref@law.widener.edu. Web Site: law.widener.edu/lawlibrary. *Assoc Dean, Info Serv & Tech, Dir, Legal Info Ctr,* Michael J Slinger; Tel: 302-477-2111, Fax: 302-477-2228, E-mail: mjslinger@widener.edu; *Assoc Dir,* Mary K Marzolla; Tel: 302-477-2157, E-mail: mkmarzolla@widener.edu; *Head, Outreach Serv,* Mary Alice Peeling; *Ref & ILL Librn,* Enza Klotzbucher; Tel: 302-477-2292; *Ref/Electronic Serv Librn,* Janet Lindenmuth; Tel: 302-477-2245; *Ref/Outreach Librn,* Margaret S Adams; Tel: 302-477-2039; *Tech Serv Librn,* Laurie Palumbo; Staff 8 (MLS 8)
Founded 1973. Enrl 1,100; Fac 100; Highest Degree: Doctorate
Library Holdings: Bk Vols 610,000; Per Subs 8,400
Special Collections: US Document Depository
Subject Interests: Corp, Del, Environ law, Health law
Partic in Interlibrary Delivery Service of Pennsylvania; Mid-Atlantic Law Library Cooperative; New England Law Library Consortium, Inc; OCLC Online Computer Library Center, Inc; Tri-State College Library Cooperative

P WILMINGTON PUBLIC LIBRARY*, Tenth & Market St, 19801. (Mail add: PO Box 2303, 19899-2303), SAN 336-6480. Tel: 302-571-7400. Interlibrary Loan Service Tel: 302-571-7421. Reference Tel: 302-571-7416. FAX: 302-654-9132. Web Site: www.wilmlib.org. *Dir,* Larry Manuel; Staff 18 (MLS 9, Non-MLS 9)
Founded 1788. Pop 131,000; Circ 185,463
Library Holdings: AV Mats 26,638; CDs 7,770; DVDs 5,000; Bk Vols 335,329; Per Subs 700; Talking Bks 3,700; Videos 10,168
Special Collections: Delawareana; Periodicals
Automation Activity & Vendor Info: (Acquisitions) SirsiDynix; (Circulation) SirsiDynix; (Media Booking) SirsiDynix
Publications: Institute of the Colonies; So Laudable An Undertaking: Grapevine; Wilmington Library
Open Mon-Wed 9:30-8, Thurs 9:30-5, Fri & Sat 9-5
Friends of the Library Group
Branches: 1
NORTH WILMINGTON, 3400 N Market St, 19802, SAN 377-7383. Tel: 302-761-4290. Reference Tel: 302-761-4292. FAX: 302-761-4291. *Librn,* Cathy Hall; E-mail: cjh16886@yahoo.com
Open Mon-Wed 11:30-8, Thurs 11:30-5, Fri & Sat 11:30-4
Friends of the Library Group

P WOODLAWN LIBRARY*, 2020 W Ninth St, 19805. SAN 336-6545. Tel: 302-571-7425. FAX: 302-571-7320. Web Site: www2.nccde.org/libraries/Woodlawn. *Mgr,* Tanya Moye
Wireless access
Open Mon-Wed 10-9, Thurs & Sat 10-5, Sun 1-5
Friends of the Library Group

WINTERTHUR

S THE WINTERTHUR LIBRARY*, 5105 Kennett Pike, 19735. SAN 302-5411. Tel: 302-888-4681. FAX: 302-888-4870. E-mail: reference@winterthur.org. Web Site: www.winterthur.org. *Dir,* Richard McKinstry; E-mail: ERMcKi@winterthur.org. Subject Specialists: *Manuscripts,* Richard McKinstry; Staff 6 (MLS 5, Non-MLS 1)
Founded 1951
Library Holdings: Bk Vols 100,000; Per Subs 300
Special Collections: Auction Catalogs; Decorative Arts Photographic Coll, VF; Edward Deming Andrews Memorial Shaker Coll, bks, ms, photog; Joseph Downs Coll of Manuscripts & Printed Ephemera, microfiche, ms, photostats; Maxine Waldron Coll; Thelma S Mendsen Coll; Waldron Phoenix Belknap, Jr Research Library of American Painting; Winterthur Archives
Automation Activity & Vendor Info: (Cataloging) Innovative Interfaces, Inc; (Circulation) Innovative Interfaces, Inc; (OPAC) Innovative Interfaces, Inc; (Serials) Innovative Interfaces, Inc
Database Vendor: OCLC
Wireless access
Function: Res libr
Publications: An American Cornucopia; Guide to the Winterthur Library: The Joseph Downs Collection & the Winterthur Archives; Personal Accounts of Events, Travels & Everyday Life in America: An Annotated Bibliography; The Edward Deming Andrews Memorial Shaker Collection; The Winterthur Library Revealed; The Winterthur Museum Library Collection of Printed Books & Periodicals (9 Vol); Trade Catalogues at Winterthur
Partic in Independent Res Libr Asn; OCLC Online Computer Library Center, Inc; Philadelphia Area Consortium of Special Collections Libraries
Open Mon-Fri 8:30-4:30
Restriction: Open to pub for ref only
Friends of the Library Group

DISTRICT OF COLUMBIA

WASHINGTON

S ACADEMY FOR EDUCATIONAL DEVELOPMENT*, Information Services Center, 1825 Connecticut Ave NW, 20009-5721. SAN 328-5480. Tel: 202-884-8000, 202-884-8118. Information Services Tel: 202-884-8761. FAX: 202-884-8491. *Dir,* David Wolfe; *Info Spec,* Juan Carlos Toscano; *Info Assoc,* Lisa Hueneke; Staff 3 (MLS 1, Non-MLS 2)
Founded 1980
Library Holdings: Bk Vols 6,000
Automation Activity & Vendor Info: (OPAC) Inmagic, Inc.
Database Vendor: Dialog, LexisNexis, OCLC FirstSearch
Open Mon-Fri 9-5
Restriction: Co libr

L ADMINISTRATIVE OFFICE OF THE UNITED STATES COURTS LIBRARY, Law Library & Research Room, One Columbus Circle NE, Ste 4-400, 20544. SAN 372-1108. Tel: 202-502-1237. FAX: 202-502-1588. Web Site: www.uscourts.gov/adminoff.html. *Law Librn,* Elizabeth Stroup Endicott; E-mail: elizabeth_endicott@ao.uscourts.gov; Staff 2 (MLS 1, Non-MLS 1)
Library Holdings: e-books 124; e-journals 3,500; Electronic Media & Resources 25; Bk Titles 5,500; Bk Vols 20,700; Per Subs 70
Subject Interests: Admin law, Bankruptcy law & Federal rules, Civil law, Criminal law, US & intl judiciary, US courts
Automation Activity & Vendor Info: (Acquisitions) SIRSI WorkFlows; (Cataloging) OCLC Connexion; (Circulation) SIRSI WorkFlows; (ILL) SIRSI WorkFlows
Database Vendor: CQ Press, Elsevier, HeinOnline, JSTOR, LexisNexis, McGraw-Hill, OCLC FirstSearch, OCLC WorldShare Interlibrary Loan, Oxford Online, Sage, SirsiDynix, Westlaw, Wiley, Wilson - Wilson Web
Partic in Docline; Law Library Microform Consortium (LLMC)
Restriction: External users must contact libr, Not open to pub, Open by appt only

S ADVOCATES FOR YOUTH*, The Mary Lee Tatum Library, 2000 M St NW, Ste 750, 20036. SAN 375-0566. Tel: 202-419-3420. FAX: 202-419-1448. Web Site: www.advocatesforyouth.org. *Librn,* Emily Bridges; Tel: 202-419-3420, Ext 43; Staff 2 (MLS 2)
Library Holdings: Bk Vols 3,000; Per Subs 150
Subject Interests: Behav, Health, Youth
Automation Activity & Vendor Info: (ILL) OCLC
Restriction: Open by appt only

SR AHMADIYYA MOVEMENT IN ISLAM INC*, Muslim Library, 2141 LeRoy Pl NW, 20008. SAN 326-9272. Tel: 202-232-3737. FAX: 202-232-8181. E-mail: info@alislam.org. Web Site: www.alislam.org/library. *Librn,* Zaheer Bajwa
Library Holdings: Bk Titles 500

L AKERMAN SENTERFITT LLP LAW LIBRARY*, 750 9th St NW, Ste 750, 20001. SAN 377-4015. Tel: 202-393-6222. FAX: 202-393-5959. Web Site: www.akerman.com. *Librn,* Linda Fowley
Library Holdings: Bk Vols 2,500; Per Subs 40
Open Mon-Fri 9-5:30

L AKIN, GUMP, STRAUSS, HAUER & FELD LLP*, Law Library, 1333 New Hampshire Ave NW, 20036-1564. SAN 377-3787. Tel: 202-887-4000. FAX: 202-887-4288. E-mail: washdcinfo@akingump.com. Web Site: www.akingump.com. *Librn,* Annette Erbrecht
Library Holdings: Bk Vols 15,000
Partic in DC Soc of Law Librs

S ALEXANDER GRAHAM BELL ASSOCIATION*, Volta Bureau Library, 3417 Volta Pl NW, 20007. SAN 302-5969. Tel: 202-337-5220. FAX: 202-337-8314. E-mail: info@agbell.org. Web Site: www.agbell.org. *Dir of Communications,* Susan Boswell
Founded 1887
Library Holdings: Bk Vols 12,000; Per Subs 20
Special Collections: Hearing (Alexander Graham Bell Coll), mss, correspondence
Subject Interests: Deaf, Speech & hearing
Restriction: Open by appt only

S AMERICAN ASSOCIATION OF STATE HIGHWAY & TRANSPORTATION OFFICIALS LIBRARY*, 444 N Capitol St NW, Ste 249, 20001. SAN 377-1326. Tel: 202-624-8918. FAX: 202-624-5806. E-mail: info@aashto.org. Web Site: www.transportation.org. *Info Res Mgr,* Bob Collen
Library Holdings: Bk Vols 5,000; Per Subs 60
Open Mon-Fri 9-4:30

S AMERICAN BAR ASSOCIATION LIBRARY*, 1050 Connecticut Ave NW, Ste 400, 20036. SAN 326-9116. Tel: 202-662-1011. FAX: 202-662-1032. *Dir, DC Info Serv,* Rhonda J McMillion; Tel: 202-662-1017, E-mail: Rhonda.McMillion@americanbar.org; *Librn,* Jill Sandor; Tel: 202-662-1015, E-mail: jill.sandor@americanbar.org
Library Holdings: Bk Titles 7,350; Per Subs 140
Function: ILL available
Open Mon-Fri 9:30-5:30
Restriction: Borrowing requests are handled by ILL

S AMERICAN CHEMICAL SOCIETY INFORMATION RESOURCE CENTER*, 1155 16th St NW, 20036. SAN 302-5578. Tel: 202-872-4513. Toll Free Tel: 800-227-5556, Ext 4513. FAX: 202 872 6257. E-mail: library@acs.org. Web Site: www.chemistry.org/library/index.html. *Librn,* Moria Smith; E-mail: m_smith@acs.org; *Asst Librn,* Courtney O'Donnell; E-mail: c_odonnell@acs.org. Subject Specialists: *Chem, Phys & life sci,* Moria Smith; *Phys & life sci,* Courtney O'Donnell; Staff 2 (MLS 2)
Founded 1876
Library Holdings: Bk Titles 7,500; Per Subs 250; Spec Interest Per Sub 150

Special Collections: ACS Materials, print & digital photos
Subject Interests: Chem
Automation Activity & Vendor Info: (Acquisitions) Sydney; (Cataloging) Sydney; (Circulation) Sydney; (ILL) OCLC; (OPAC) Sydney; (Serials) EBSCO Online
Database Vendor: Dialog, EBSCOhost, LexisNexis, OCLC FirstSearch, OVID Technologies
Function: Doc delivery serv, For res purposes, Handicapped accessible, ILL available, Photocopying/Printing, Prof lending libr, Ref serv available, Res libr, Wheelchair accessible
Partic in OCLC-LVIS
Open Mon-Fri 8:30-5
Restriction: Circulates for staff only, Open to pub for ref only, Open to pub with supv only

M AMERICAN COLLEGE OF OBSTETRICIANS & GYNECOLOGISTS, Resource Center, 409 12th St SW, 20024-2188. (Mail add: PO Box 96920, 20090-6920), SAN 303-8068. Tel: 202-863-2518. FAX: 202-484-1595. E-mail: resources@acog.org. Web Site: www.acog.org. *Sr Dir,* Mary A Hyde; *Acq/Syst Librn,* Mary Hay Glass; *Spec Coll Librn,* Debra G Scarborough; *Ref Serv,* Jean E Riedlinger; *Ref Serv,* Pamela M Van Hine; Staff 8 (MLS 5, Non-MLS 3)
Founded 1969
Library Holdings: Bk Vols 15,000; Per Subs 450
Special Collections: J Bay Jacobs Library for the History of Medicine in Obstetrics & Gynecology in America; Ralph W Hale MD History Museum. Oral History
Subject Interests: Obstetrics & gynecology
Automation Activity & Vendor Info: (Acquisitions) EOS International; (Cataloging) EOS International; (Circulation) EOS International; (OPAC) EOS International; (Serials) EOS International
Database Vendor: Dialog, EBSCO Information Services, Elsevier, EOS International, Ingenta, JSTOR, Majors, Nature Publishing Group, OCLC FirstSearch, OVID Technologies, PubMed, RefWorks, ScienceDirect, SerialsSolutions, Springer-Verlag, UpToDate, Westlaw, Wiley InterScience
Wireless access
Publications: Bibliographies
Partic in District of Columbia Area Health Science Libraries; Docline

S AMERICAN COUNCIL OF LIFE INSURERS LIBRARY*, Research & Information Center, 101 Constitution Ave NW, 20001. SAN 302-5586. Tel: 202-624-2000. FAX: 202-624-2319. E-mail: library@acli.com. Web Site: www.acli.com. *Librn,* Anna Varnavas; Staff 8 (MLS 7, Non-MLS 1)
Library Holdings: Bk Titles 3,000; Per Subs 1,000
Subject Interests: Benefits, Econ, Statistics
Database Vendor: LexisNexis, Westlaw
Publications: Acquisitions List; Daily Electronic Newsletter
Open Mon-Fri 9-5
Restriction: Access at librarian's discretion, Non-circulating, Not a lending libr

S AMERICAN FEDERATION OF STATE, COUNTY & MUNICIPAL EMPLOYEES*, Information Center, 1625 L St NW, 20036. SAN 328-6460. Tel: 202-429-1060. FAX: 202-223-3255. Web Site: www.afscme.org. *Librn,* William Wilkinson; Staff 4 (MLS 3, Non-MLS 1)
Library Holdings: Bk Vols 7,000; Per Subs 615
Automation Activity & Vendor Info: (Acquisitions) Inmagic, Inc.; (Cataloging) Inmagic, Inc.; (Circulation) Inmagic, Inc.; (OPAC) Inmagic, Inc.; (Serials) Inmagic, Inc.
Database Vendor: Dialog, Dun & Bradstreet, Factiva.com, LexisNexis, Westlaw
Wireless access
Restriction: Staff use only

S AMERICAN FEDERATION OF TEACHERS LIBRARY*, 555 New Jersey Ave NW, 20001-2079. SAN 371-8840. Tel: 202-879-4481. FAX: 202-879-4406. Web Site: www.aft.org. *Librn,* Bernadette Bailey; E-mail: bbailey@aft.org; Staff 2 (MLS 1, Non-MLS 1)
Founded 1916
Library Holdings: Bk Vols 2,000; Per Subs 350
Special Collections: AFT Conventions & Executive Council Minutes, 1916-2006
Subject Interests: Educ, Labor
Open Mon-Fri 8:30-4:30
Restriction: Circulates for staff only, In-house use for visitors, Lending to staff only

M AMERICAN INSTITUTE FOR CANCER RESEARCH LIBRARY*, 1759 R St NW, 20009. SAN 377-3043. Tel: 202-328-7744. Toll Free Tel: 800-843-8114. FAX: 202-328-7226. E-mail: aicrweb@aicr.org. Web Site: www.aicr.org. *Librn,* Steve Krompf; Staff 1 (MLS 1)
Founded 1991
Library Holdings: Bk Vols 400; Per Subs 75
Subject Interests: Cancer, Diet, Health, Nutrition
Automation Activity & Vendor Info: (Cataloging) JayWil Software Development, Inc; (OPAC) JayWil Software Development, Inc; (Serials) JayWil Software Development, Inc
Open Mon-Fri 9-5

L AMERICAN INSURANCE ASSOCIATION*, Law Library, 2101 L St NW, Ste 400, 20037. SAN 311-5852. Tel: 202-828-7100. FAX: 202-293-1219. E-mail: info@aiadc.org. Web Site: www.aiadc.org. *Librn,* Position Currently Open
Library Holdings: Bk Vols 5,000; Per Subs 65
Subject Interests: Auto liability, Environ, Property casualty, Superfund, Workmen's compensation ins
Open Mon-Fri 9-5

S AMERICAN PHARMACISTS ASSOCIATION FOUNDATION LIBRARY*, 1100 15th St NW, Ste 400, 20005. SAN 302-5721. Tel: 202-429-7524. FAX: 202-783-2351. Web Site: www.pharmacist.com. *In Charge,* Gwen Norheim; E-mail: gnorheim@aphanet.org
Founded 1934
Library Holdings: Bk Titles 1,300; Bk Vols 6,000; Per Subs 119
Restriction: Open by appt only

S AMERICAN PSYCHOLOGICAL ASSOCIATION*, Arthur W Melton Library, 750 First St NE, Rm 3012, 20002-4242. SAN 302-5756. Tel: 202-336-5640. Interlibrary Loan Service Tel: 202-336-5642. Toll Free Tel: 800-374-2721, Ext 5640. FAX: 202-336-5643. E-mail: archives@apa.org. Web Site: www.apa.org/archives. *Assoc Archivist, Head Librn,* Rennie Georgieva; Tel: 202-336-5664, E-mail: rgeorgieva@apa.org; *Assoc Librn,* Dan Hanlon; Tel: 202-336-5645, E-mail: dhanlon@apa.org; Staff 4 (MLS 2, Non-MLS 2)
Founded 1970
Library Holdings: AV Mats 116; e-journals 62; Bk Titles 7,120; Per Subs 121
Special Collections: American Psychological Association Archives; American Psychological Association Central Office, Division & State Association Publications; Classic Books in Psychology
Subject Interests: Allied disciplines, Mental health, Psychol
Automation Activity & Vendor Info: (Cataloging) Inmagic, Inc.; (Circulation) Inmagic, Inc.; (ILL) Inmagic, Inc.
Database Vendor: OVID Technologies
Function: Archival coll
Publications: APA Convention Directory; Biography Index
Open Mon-Fri 8:30-4:30

S AMERICAN PUBLIC POWER ASSOCIATION LIBRARY*, 2301 M St NW, 20037-1484. SAN 302-5764. Tel: 202-467-2957. FAX: 202-467-2910. Web Site: www.appanet.org. *Librn,* Mary Rufe; E-mail: mrufe@appanet.org
Founded 1973
Library Holdings: Bk Titles 6,000; Per Subs 200
Subject Interests: Electrical utilities, Energy
Automation Activity & Vendor Info: (Acquisitions) Inmagic, Inc.; (Cataloging) Inmagic, Inc.; (Circulation) Inmagic, Inc.; (Course Reserve) Inmagic, Inc.; (Media Booking) Inmagic, Inc.; (Serials) Inmagic, Inc.
Database Vendor: Factiva.com
Open Mon-Fri 9-5

S AMERICAN PUBLIC TRANSPORTATION ASSOCIATION*, Information Center, 1666 K St NW, Ste 1100, 20005. SAN 371-8654. Tel: 202-496-4889. FAX: 202-496-4326. E-mail: info@apta.com. Web Site: www.apta.com/research/info.
Founded 1915
Library Holdings: Bk Vols 10,000; Per Subs 85
Special Collections: APTA Publications; Fed Transit Agency
Subject Interests: Pub transportation
Automation Activity & Vendor Info: (Cataloging) Inmagic, Inc.
Database Vendor: LexisNexis, OCLC FirstSearch, OVID Technologies
Function: Ref serv available
Publications: Catalog of Member Products & Services (COMPS); Index to Weekly Newspaper; Information Center Brochure; Passenger Transport; Publication Catalog
Restriction: Open by appt only

L AMERICAN SOCIETY OF INTERNATIONAL LAW LIBRARY*, 2223 Massachusetts Ave NW, 20008-2864. SAN 302-5802. Tel: 202-939-6005. FAX: 202-319-1670. Web Site: www.asil.org. *Dir, Info Res,* Kelly Vinopal; E-mail: kvinopal@asil.org
Founded 1960
Library Holdings: Bk Vols 20,000; Per Subs 125
Subject Interests: Intl law, Intl trade
Publications: Guide to Electronic Resources for International Law
Open Mon-Fri 9-4
Friends of the Library Group

S AMERICAN SOCIETY OF LANDSCAPE ARCHITECTS*, Professional Practice Library, 636 I St NW, 20001-3736. SAN 372-6142. Tel: 202-216-2354. FAX: 202-898-1185. E-mail: library@asla.org. Web Site: www.asla.org. *Dir,* Susan Cahill-Aylward; Tel: 202-216-2320, E-mail: scahill@asla.org; Staff 2 (MLS 2)
Library Holdings: Bk Titles 2,100; Per Subs 150
Subject Interests: Environment, Gardening, Gardens, Hist presv, Landscape archit, Landscape design, Landscape hist, Planning, Sustainable agr, Urban planning
Automation Activity & Vendor Info: (Cataloging) Readerware
Database Vendor: OCLC-RLG
Open Mon-Fri 8-4

CL AMERICAN UNIVERSITY*, Pence Law Library, Washington College of Law, 4801 Massachusetts Ave NW, 20016-8182. SAN 336-660X. Tel: 202-274-4300. Circulation Tel: 202-274-4351. Interlibrary Loan Service Tel: 202-274-4327. Reference Tel: 202-274-4352. Administration Tel: 202-274-4375. FAX: 202-274-4365. E-mail: reflib@wcl.american.edu. Web Site: library.wcl.american.edu. *Dean,* Claudio M Grossman; *Assoc Dean, Info,* Billie Jo Kaufman; Tel: 202-274-4374, E-mail: bkaufman@wcl.american.edu; *Access Serv Librn,* Amy Taylor; Tel: 202-274-4324, E-mail: amytaylor@wcl.american.edu; *Acq/Ser Librn,* John A Smith; Tel: 202-274-4354, E-mail: jasmith@wcl.american.edu; *Ref Librn,* John Heywood; Tel: 202-274-4329, E-mail: heywood@american.edu; *Assoc Law Librn, Tech & Metadata Serv,* Christine Dulaney; Tel: 202-274-4345, E-mail: cdulaney@wcl.american.edu; *Assoc Librn, Foreign & Intl Law,* William Ryan; Tel: 202-274-4331, E-mail: wryan@wcl.american.edu; *Assoc Librn, Pub Serv,* Susan Lewis; Tel: 202-274-4330, E-mail: slewis@wcl.american.edu; *Cat,* Sima Mirkin; Tel: 202-274-4344, E-mail: smirkin@wcl.american.edu; *Electronic & Ref Serv,* Ripple Weistling; Tel: 202-274-4382, E-mail: rweistling@wcl.american.edu. Subject Specialists: *Intl law,* John Heywood; *Foreign law, Intl law,* William Ryan; *Environ law,* Ripple Weistling; Staff 22 (MLS 10, Non-MLS 12)
Founded 1896. Enrl 1,750; Fac 80; Highest Degree: Doctorate
May 2011-Apr 2012. Mats Exp $3,800,454, Per/Ser (Incl. Access Fees) $512,314, Electronic Ref Mat (Incl. Access Fees) $415,763
Library Holdings: Bk Titles 243,746; Bk Vols 585,600; Per Subs 6,761
Special Collections: Goodman Coll of Rare Law Books; National Bankruptcy Review Commission. US Document Depository
Automation Activity & Vendor Info: (Acquisitions) Innovative Interfaces, Inc; (Cataloging) Innovative Interfaces, Inc; (Circulation) Innovative Interfaces, Inc; (Course Reserve) Innovative Interfaces, Inc; (ILL) OCLC; (OPAC) Innovative Interfaces, Inc; (Serials) Innovative Interfaces, Inc
Database Vendor: Blackwell, CQ Press, Dialog, EBSCO Discovery Service, EBSCOhost, Gale Cengage Learning, Haworth Pres Inc, HeinOnline, Innovative Interfaces, Inc, JSTOR, LexisNexis, Marcive, Inc, OCLC FirstSearch, OCLC WorldShare Interlibrary Loan, ProQuest, Westlaw, Wilson - Wilson Web, YBP Library Services
Wireless access
Partic in New England Law Library Consortium, Inc; Washington Research Library Consortium
Restriction: Access at librarian's discretion, Vols & interns use only

C AMERICAN UNIVERSITY LIBRARY*, Jack I & Dorothy G Bender Library & Learning Resources Center, 4400 Massachusetts Ave NW, 20016-8046. SAN 336-657X. Tel: 202-885-3237. Circulation Tel: 202-885-3221. Interlibrary Loan Service Tel: 202-885-3282. Reference Tel: 202-885-3260. FAX: 202-885-3226. Web Site: www.american.edu/library. *Univ Librn,* Nancy Davenport; E-mail: davenpor@american.edu; *Dir, Acad Tech,* Michael Piller; Tel: 202-885-3228, E-mail: piller@american.edu; *Dir of Admin Serv,* Michele Mikkelsen; Tel: 202-885-3234, E-mail: mmikkel@american.edu; *Dir, Multimedia Coll & Serv,* Christopher Lewis; Tel: 202-885-3257, E-mail: clewis@american.edu; *Dir, Res, Teaching & Learning,* Gwendolyn Reece; Tel: 202-885-3281, E-mail: greece@american.edu; *Dir, Access Serv,* Robert Kelshian; E-mail: calvin@american.edu; *Dir, AV,* Robert Brownlee; Tel: 202-885-2297; *Assoc Dir, Organizational Develop,* Katherine Simpson; Tel: 202-885-3225, E-mail: mirch@american.edu; *Coll Develop,* Martin Shapiro; Tel: 202-885-3854, E-mail: mshapir@american.edu. Subject Specialists: *Film, Media,* Christopher Lewis; Staff 56.65 (MLS 23.65, Non-MLS 33)
Founded 1893. Enrl 11,720; Fac 825; Highest Degree: Doctorate
Library Holdings: DVDs 1,400; e-books 193,000; e-journals 14,374; Music Scores 13,000; Bk Vols 1,000,000; Per Subs 4,200; Videos 9,300
Special Collections: Asia & the East, Japanese Culture (Spinks Coll); Drew Pearson Coll; Friends of Colombia Archives; John Hickman Coll; Mathematics (Artemas Martin Coll); Papers of the National Commission on the Public Service; Peace Corps Community Archive; Records of the National Peace Corps Association Archives; Theatre Play Bill Coll
Subject Interests: Art, Bus & mgt, Econ, Hist, Humanities, Intl studies, Polit sci
Automation Activity & Vendor Info: (Acquisitions) Ex Libris Group; (Cataloging) Ex Libris Group; (Circulation) Ex Libris Group; (Course Reserve) Atlas Systems; (ILL) OCLC ILLiad; (Media Booking) Ex Libris Group; (OPAC) Ex Libris Group; (Serials) SerialsSolutions
Wireless access
Partic in OCLC Online Computer Library Center, Inc
Open Sat 9-9
Friends of the Library Group

Departmental Libraries:

MUSIC LIBRARY, Katzen Arts Center, Rm 150, 4400 Massachusetts Ave NW, 20016-8046, SAN 336-6634. Tel: 202-885-3264. FAX: 202-885-3226. *Music & Performing Arts Librn,* Nobue Matsuoka; Tel: 202-885-3465; Staff 2 (MLS 1, Non-MLS 1)
Founded 1966
Library Holdings: CDs 10,000; Music Scores 15,000
Partic in OCLC Online Computer Library Center, Inc
Open Mon-Fri 9-8, Sat 11-4

L ANDREWS KURTH LLP LIBRARY*, 1350 I St NW, Ste 1100, 20005. SAN 377-2845. Tel: 202-662-2761. FAX: 202-662-2739. Web Site: www.andrewskurth.com. *Librn,* Martha Birdseye; E-mail: marthabirdseye@andrewskurth.com
Library Holdings: Bk Vols 5,000; Per Subs 75
Wireless access
Open Mon-Fri 9-5:30

L ARENT FOX PLLC LIBRARY*, 1050 Connecticut Ave NW, 20036-5339. SAN 326-9191. Tel: 202-857-6000. Interlibrary Loan Service Tel: 202-857-6297. FAX: 202-857-6395. Web Site: www.arentfox.com. *Librn,* Robert Dickey
Library Holdings: Bk Vols 60,000; Per Subs 400
Database Vendor: LexisNexis, Westlaw
Open Mon-Fri 9-5

S ARMY & NAVY CLUB LIBRARY*, 901 17th St NW, 20006-2503. SAN 302-587X. Tel: 202-628-8400, Ext 386, 202-721-2096. FAX: 202-296-8787. E-mail: library@armynavyclub.org. Web Site: www.armynavyclub.org. *Librn,* Aleksandra M Zajackowski
Founded 1885
Library Holdings: Bk Titles 15,000; Bk Vols 16,000; Per Subs 40
Special Collections: Reginald W Oakie Coll of Civil War Stereographs; Writings of Club Members
Database Vendor: EBSCO Information Services
Wireless access
Open Mon-Thurs 9-5, Fri 9-1

L ARNOLD & PORTER LIBRARY*, 555 12th St NW, 20004-1206. SAN 302-5888. Tel: 202-942-5000. Interlibrary Loan Service Tel: 202-942-5370. Reference Tel: 202-942-5427. FAX: 202-942-5999. Web Site: www.arnoldporter.com. *Librn,* James W Shelar; E-mail: james_shelar@aporter.com; Staff 13 (MLS 6, Non-MLS 7)
Library Holdings: Bk Vols 70,000; Per Subs 350
Subject Interests: Law, Legislation
Automation Activity & Vendor Info: (Acquisitions) EOS International; (Cataloging) EOS International; (Circulation) EOS International; (ILL) EOS International; (OPAC) EOS International; (Serials) EOS International
Database Vendor: LexisNexis, Westlaw
Publications: Miscellaneous Research Guides; Monthly Accessions List
Restriction: Not open to pub

S ASPIRA ASSOCIATION LIBRARY*, 1444 I St NW 8th Flr, Ste 800, 20005. SAN 373-0379. Tel: 202-835-3600. FAX: 202-835-3613. E-mail: info@aspira.org. Web Site: www.aspira.org. *VPres,* Hilda Crespo
Library Holdings: Bk Vols 1,000
Special Collections: Puerto Rican Art & Culture Coll
Open Mon-Fri 9-5

S ASSOCIATION OF GOVERNING BOARDS OF UNIVERSITIES & COLLEGES, Zwingle Resource Center, 1133 20th St NW, Ste 300, 20036. SAN 326-3193. Tel: 202-776-0818. Administration Toll Free Tel: 800-356-6317. FAX: 202-223-7053. Web Site: www.agb.org/zwingle-resource-center. *Dir, Libr Serv,* Pat Wood; E-mail: patw@agb.org; Staff 1.2 (MLS 1.2)
Founded 1975
Library Holdings: Bk Titles 10,000; Per Subs 43
Subject Interests: Govt, Higher educ
Automation Activity & Vendor Info: (OPAC) Inmagic, Inc.
Function: Res libr
Open Mon-Fri 9-4
Restriction: Circulates for staff only, Mem only

L BAACH, ROBINSON & LEWIS LIBRARY*, 1201 F St NW, Ste 500, 20004. SAN 377-4546. Tel: 202-833-8900. FAX: 202-466-5738. Web Site: www.baachrobinson.com. *Fac Mgr,* Thomas D McBride; E-mail: thomas.mcbride@baachrobinson.com
Library Holdings: Bk Vols 5,000; Per Subs 30
Restriction: Open by appt only

L BAKER & HOSTETLER*, Law Library, Washington Sq, Ste 1100, 1050 Connecticut Ave NW, 20036. SAN 377-3019. Tel: 202-861-1500. FAX: 202-861-1783. Web Site: www.bakerlaw.com. *Librn,* Esther Koblenz; Tel: 202-861-1578
Library Holdings: Bk Vols 25,000; Per Subs 50
Database Vendor: LexisNexis, Westlaw
Open Mon-Fri 8-6

L BAKER & MCKENZIE LLP LIBRARY*, 815 Connecticut Ave NW, Ste 900, 20006-4078. SAN 326-2162. Tel: 202-452-7070. FAX: 202-452-7074. Web Site: www.bakernet.com. *Regional Dir,* Leslee Budlong; E-mail: leslee.i.budlong@bakernet.com; *ILL,* Nour Dich; Tel: 202-452-7052; Staff 3 (MLS 1, Non-MLS 2)
Library Holdings: Bk Titles 3,500; Bk Vols 20,000; Per Subs 70
Subject Interests: Corporate law, Intl law, Intl trade, Taxation
Automation Activity & Vendor Info: (Acquisitions) SydneyPlus; (Cataloging) SydneyPlus; (Circulation) SydneyPlus; (Course Reserve) SydneyPlus; (ILL) SydneyPlus; (Media Booking) SydneyPlus; (OPAC) SydneyPlus; (Serials) SydneyPlus
Open Mon-Fri 9-5:30

L BAKER BOTTS LLP*, Law Library, 1299 Pennsylvania Ave NW, 20004-2400. SAN 377-3604. Tel: 202-639-7967. FAX: 202-639-7890. Web Site: www.bakerbotts.com. *Mgr,* Edward O'Rourke; E-mail: edward.orourke@bakerbotts.com; Staff 3 (MLS 2, Non-MLS 1)
Library Holdings: Bk Vols 25,000; Per Subs 250
Automation Activity & Vendor Info: (Cataloging) Inmagic, Inc.; (Circulation) Inmagic, Inc.; (OPAC) Inmagic, Inc.
Database Vendor: Westlaw
Wireless access
Partic in DC Soc of Law Librs
Open Mon-Fri 9-5

L BEVERIDGE & DIAMOND, PC LIBRARY*, 1350 I St NW, Ste 700, 20005-3311. SAN 377-2993. Tel: 202-789-6000. Interlibrary Loan Service Tel: 202-789-6173. FAX: 202-789-6190. *Librn,* Scott Larson
Library Holdings: Bk Vols 10,000; Per Subs 300
Subject Interests: Environ law
Open Mon-Fri 9-5:30

L BLANK ROME LLP*, Law Library, 600 New Hampshire Ave NW, Ste 1200, 20037. SAN 377-1350. Tel: 202-944-3527. FAX: 202-772-5858. Web Site: www.blankrome.com. *Mgr,* Position Currently Open
Library Holdings: Bk Vols 2,500; Per Subs 100
Subject Interests: Maritime law
Restriction: Not open to pub

BOARD OF GOVERNORS OF THE FEDERAL RESERVE SYSTEM

GL LAW LIBRARY*, 20th & C St NW, MS 7, 20551, SAN 336-6723. Tel: 202-452-3040. Interlibrary Loan Service Tel: 202-452-2454. Reference Tel: 202-452-3283. FAX: 202-452-3101. Web Site: www.federalreserve.gov. ; Staff 4 (MLS 3, Non-MLS 1)
Founded 1975
Library Holdings: Bk Vols 30,000; Per Subs 500
Special Collections: Congressional (Legislative History Coll of Banking-Related Statutes of the US), micro. US Document Depository
Subject Interests: Admin law, Banking law
Publications: Current Legislative & Regulatory Activity; Recent Law Journal Articles of Interest; Textual Changes in the Federal Reserve Act
Restriction: Open by appt only

G RESEARCH LIBRARY*, 20th & C St NW, MS 102, 20551, SAN 336-6758. Tel: 202-452-3333. FAX: 202-530-6222. *Chief Librn,* Kristin Vajs; *Lead Librn, Data Contracts,* Christine Black; *Lead Librn, Tech Serv,* Jane Olvera; *Sr Librn, Acq & Per,* Anna Harkins; *Sr Librn, Data Contracts,* Jasmine Griffiths; *Sr Librn, Data Contracts,* Alison Labonte; *Sr Librn, Tech Serv,* Marlene Vikor; *Sr Res Librn,* Krista Box; *Sr Res Librn,* Sian Seldin; *Tech & Acq Librn,* Yin Zhu; Staff 14 (MLS 12, Non-MLS 2)
Founded 1914
Library Holdings: Bk Vols 62,000; Per Subs 1,200
Special Collections: Federal Reserve System; Foreign Central Bank Publications
Subject Interests: Banks & banking, Econ, Finance, Monetary policy
Automation Activity & Vendor Info: (Acquisitions) Innovative Interfaces, Inc; (Cataloging) Innovative Interfaces, Inc; (Circulation) Innovative Interfaces, Inc; (ILL) Innovative Interfaces, Inc; (OPAC) Innovative Interfaces, Inc; (Serials) Innovative Interfaces, Inc
Partic in OCLC Online Computer Library Center, Inc
Publications: Recent Acquisitions
Restriction: Open by appt only
Friends of the Library Group

L BRACEWELL & GIULIANI LLP*, Law Library, 2000 K St NW, Ste 500, 20006-1872. SAN 372-1728. Tel: 202-828-5800, Ext 7660. FAX: 202-223-1225. Web Site: www.bracewellgiuliani.com. *Librn,* Ruth Mendelson
Library Holdings: Bk Vols 10,000; Per Subs 25
Subject Interests: Admin law, Environ law
Automation Activity & Vendor Info: (Acquisitions) Sydney
Partic in OCLC Online Computer Library Center, Inc
Open Mon-Fri 9-5

S BREAD FOR THE WORLD LIBRARY, 425 Third St SW, Ste 1200, 20024. SAN 329-0514. Tel: 202-639-9400. Administration Tel: 202-688-1082. Web Site: www.bread.org. *Librn,* Christine Matthews; E-mail: cmatthews@bread.org; Staff 1 (MLS 1)
Library Holdings: AV Mats 40; Bk Titles 3,000; Per Subs 65
Subject Interests: Agr, Christian perspective, Foreign aid, Gender, Hunger, Immigration, Intl develop, Nutrition, Poverty, Trade, US budget
Automation Activity & Vendor Info: (OPAC) Inmagic, Inc.
Wireless access
Function: For res purposes, ILL available
Restriction: Open by appt only

L BRICKFIELD, BURCHETTE, RITTS & STONE LAW LIBRARY*, 1025 Thomas Jefferson St NW, Ste 800 W, 20007. Tel: 202-342-0800. FAX: 202-342-0807. *Librn,* Kathleen Alvarez; E-mail: kalvarez@bbrslaw.com
Library Holdings: Bk Titles 400
Database Vendor: LexisNexis, Westlaw
Function: Res libr
Restriction: Authorized personnel only, Borrowing requests are handled by ILL, Co libr

S BROOKINGS INSTITUTION LIBRARY*, 1775 Massachusetts Ave NW, 20036. SAN 302-6019. Tel: 202-797-6240. FAX: 202-797-2970. E-mail: circdesk@brookings.edu. Web Site: www.brookings.edu/lib/lib_hp.htm. *Dir,* Cy Behroozi; *Archives, Ref Librn,* Sarah Chilton; *Acq, Per,* John Grunwell; *Cat,* David Bair; *ILL,* Laura Mooney; Staff 6 (MLS 5, Non-MLS 1)
Founded 1927
Library Holdings: Bk Vols 68,000; Per Subs 350
Subject Interests: Econ, Intl relations, Soc sci, Urban policy, US govt
Automation Activity & Vendor Info: (Cataloging) SirsiDynix; (Circulation) SirsiDynix; (OPAC) SirsiDynix
Wireless access
Publications: Acquisitions List
Restriction: Open to pub by appt only

L BRYAN CAVE LAW LIBRARY*, 700 13th St NW, Ste 700, 20005-3960. SAN 377-2977. Tel: 202-508-6055. Reference Tel: 202-508-6115. FAX: 202-508-6200. *Mgr, Libr & Res Serv,* Laura Green; E-mail: laura.green@bryancave.com; *Res Librn,* Sarah C Nagel; Staff 3 (MLS 2, Non-MLS 1)
Library Holdings: Bk Vols 10,000; Per Subs 200
Automation Activity & Vendor Info: (Acquisitions) Inmagic, Inc.; (Cataloging) Inmagic, Inc.; (ILL) Inmagic, Inc.; (Serials) Inmagic, Inc.
Open Mon-Fri 9-6:30

L BUCHANAN INGERSOLL ROONEY PC*, Law Library, 1700 K St NW, Ste 300, 20006-3807. SAN 377-3957. Tel: 202-452-7938. FAX: 202-452-7989. Web Site: www.bipc.com. *Librn,* Matthew B Mahaffie; E-mail: matthew.mahaffie@bipc.com
Automation Activity & Vendor Info: (Cataloging) EOS International
Database Vendor: Westlaw
Restriction: Open to staff only

L CADWALADER, WICKERSHAM & TAFT*, Law Library, 700 Sixth St NW, Ste 300, 20001. SAN 372-1442. Tel: 202-862-2217. Interlibrary Loan Service Tel: 202-862-2289. FAX: 202-862-2400. Web Site: www.cwt.com. *Librn,* Jane Platt-Brown; E-mail: jane.platt-brown@cwt.com; *Asst Librn,* Jacqueline Henderson; E-mail: jacqueline.henderson@cwt.com; *Ref Librn,* Laura Bradley; E-mail: laura.bradley@cwt.com; Staff 2 (MLS 1, Non-MLS 1)
Library Holdings: Bk Vols 9,000; Per Subs 45
Automation Activity & Vendor Info: (Cataloging) SIMA, Inc; (Serials) SIMA, Inc
Database Vendor: Bloomberg, Dun & Bradstreet, HeinOnline, LexisNexis, OneSource, Westlaw, Westlaw Business
Wireless access
Restriction: Staff use only

L CAHILL, GORDON & REINDEL LIBRARY*, 1990 K St NW, Ste 950, 20006. SAN 302-6043. Tel: 202-862-8953. FAX: 202-862-8958. Web Site: www.cahill.com. *Librn,* Michael Bizik; E-mail: bizikm@cgrdc.com
Library Holdings: Bk Vols 3,000; Per Subs 25
Database Vendor: LexisNexis
Partic in Westlaw
Open Mon-Fri 9:30-5:30

L CAPLIN & DRYSDALE LIBRARY*, One Thomas Circle, NW, Ste 1100, 20005. SAN 302-606X. Tel: 202-862-5073. FAX: 202-429-3301. E-mail: library@capdale.com. Web Site: www.caplindrysdale.com. *Mgr, Libr Serv,* Nalini Rajguru; E-mail: nr@capdale.com; *Ref Librn,* Carl Kessler; Tel: 202-862-7835; *Ref Librn,* Mary Lou Ranck; Staff 4 (MLS 3, Non-MLS 1)
Founded 1969
Library Holdings: Bk Titles 4,911; Bk Vols 15,010; Per Subs 50
Automation Activity & Vendor Info: (Acquisitions) Inmagic, Inc.; (Cataloging) Inmagic, Inc.; (OPAC) Inmagic, Inc.; (Serials) Inmagic, Inc.
Database Vendor: LexisNexis, Westlaw
Function: ILL available
Open Mon-Fri 9-5:30

C CAPUCHIN COLLEGE LIBRARY*, 4121 Harewood Rd NE, 20017. SAN 302-6078. Tel: 202-529-2188. FAX: 202-526-6664. *Librn,* Sonia Bernardo; Staff 1 (MLS 1)
Library Holdings: CDs 26; Bk Titles 2,500; Bk Vols 75,000; Per Subs 25
Subject Interests: Catholicism, Theol
Database Vendor: JayWil Software Development, Inc

R THE CARMELITE PROVINCE OF THE MOST PURE HEART OF MARY*, Carmelitana Collection, Whitefriars Hall, 1600 Webster St NE, 20017. Tel: 202-526-1221, Ext 204. E-mail: carmelitanacoll@gmail.com, librarian@carmelitanacollection.com. Web Site: www.carmelitanacollection.com. *Dir,* Fr Patrick Thomas McMahon; *Librn,* Patricia O'Callaghan; Staff 3 (MLS 2, Non-MLS 1)
Founded 1948
Library Holdings: Bk Titles 14,000; Per Subs 32
Special Collections: Carmelite Tradition in Roman Catholic Spirituality (Carmelitana Coll), AV mat, microfilm, rare & modern bks
Wireless access
Function: ILL available
Restriction: Not open to pub, Open by appt only

S CARNEGIE ENDOWMENT FOR INTERNATIONAL PEACE LIBRARY, 1779 Massachusetts Ave NW, 20036. SAN 328-5189. Tel: 202-939-2255. Interlibrary Loan Service Tel: 202-939-2256. FAX: 202-483-4462. E-mail: library@carnegieendowment.org. Web Site: www.carnegieendowment.org/about/library.
Library Holdings: Bk Vols 8,500; Per Subs 200
Subject Interests: Foreign policy
Automation Activity & Vendor Info: (Acquisitions) EOS International; (Cataloging) EOS International; (Circulation) EOS International; (ILL) OCLC; (OPAC) EOS International
Open Mon-Fri 9-5

CARNEGIE INSTITUTION OF WASHINGTON
S DEPARTMENT OF TERRESTRIAL MAGNETISM & GEOPHYSICAL LABORATORY, 5241 Broad Branch Rd NW, 20015-1395, SAN 336-6847. Tel: 202-478-7960. Interlibrary Loan Service Tel: 202-478-7962. FAX: 202-478-8821. E-mail: library@ciw.edu. Web Site: www.library.gl.ciw.edu. *Librn,* Shaun J Hardy; Staff 2 (MLS 1, Non-MLS 1)
Founded 1904
Library Holdings: Bk Titles 10,000; Per Subs 300
Special Collections: Early 20th Century Exploration & Travel; Foreign Dissertations; History of Terrestrial Magnetism; History of Volcanology, Petrology & Physical Chemistry
Subject Interests: Astrobiology, Astrophysics, Crystallography, Geochemistry, Geophysics, Mineralogy, Petrology, Planetary sci
Automation Activity & Vendor Info: (Cataloging) Inmagic, Inc.; (OPAC) Inmagic, Inc.
Database Vendor: American Chemical Society, American Geophysical Union, American Physical Society, Annual Reviews, Dialog, Elsevier, FileMaker, GeoScienceWorld, IOP, Medline, Nature Publishing Group, OCLC, OCLC WorldShare Interlibrary Loan, ProQuest, ScienceDirect, Springer-Verlag, STN International, Thomson - Web of Science, Wiley
Partic in Lyrasis
Publications: Carnegie Institution of Washington Year Book; Carnegie Science (Newsletter)
Open Mon-Fri 9-5 (By appointment only)
Restriction: Open to pub by appt only

C CATHOLIC UNIVERSITY OF AMERICA, John K Mullen of Denver Memorial Library, 620 Michigan Ave NE, 315 Mullen Library, 20064. SAN 336-6871. Tel: 202-319-5055. Circulation Tel: 202-319-5060. Interlibrary Loan Service Tel: 202-319-5063. Reference Tel: 202-319-5070. FAX: 202-319-4735. Interlibrary Loan Service FAX: 202-319-6101. Web Site: libraries.cua.edu. *Univ Librn,* Steve Connaghan; Tel: 202-319-5169, E-mail: connaghan@cua.edu; *Dir, Res & Instruction Serv,* Joan Stahl; Tel: 202-319-6473, E-mail: stahlj@cua.edu; *Dir, Res Mgt & Digital Serv,* Elzbieta Rymsza-Pawlowska; Tel: 202-319-5554; *Bus Mgr,* Mary Mathews; Tel: 202-319-5464, E-mail: mathews@cua.edu; Staff 132 (MLS 30, Non-MLS 102)
Founded 1889. Enrl 6,201; Fac 400; Highest Degree: Doctorate
Apr 2012-May 2013. Mats Exp $3,847,207, Books $439,600, Per/Ser (Incl. Access Fees) $1,803,000, Other Print Mats $110,000, Micro $34,380, AV Mat $3,267, Electronic Ref Mat (Incl. Access Fees) $1,409,960, Presv $47,000. Sal $3,245,160 (Prof $1,675,208)
Library Holdings: Audiobooks 42,687; AV Mats 52,786; DVDs 507; e-books 51,114; e-journals 42,560; Electronic Media & Resources 9,619; Bk Vols 1,444,018; Per Subs 9,720; Spec Interest Per Sub 46; Videos 8,682
Special Collections: Catholic Americana; Celtic Coll; Knights of Malta Coll; Library of Pope Clement XI (Clementine Library); Luso-Brazilian Studies (Oliveira Lima Library); Semitic & Egyptian Languages & Literatures
Subject Interests: Canon law, Church hist, Greek, Immigration, Labor, Latin, Medieval studies, Patristics
Automation Activity & Vendor Info: (Acquisitions) Ex Libris Group; (Cataloging) Ex Libris Group; (Circulation) Ex Libris Group; (Course Reserve) Ex Libris Group; (ILL) Ex Libris Group; (Media Booking) Ex Libris Group; (OPAC) Ex Libris Group; (Serials) Ex Libris Group
Database Vendor: LexisNexis, OCLC FirstSearch, OVID Technologies, ProQuest
Wireless access
Function: Archival coll, Distance learning, Doc delivery serv, Handicapped accessible, ILL available, Magnifiers for reading, Photocopying/Printing, Ref serv available, Res libr, Telephone ref, Wheelchair accessible
Partic in Washington Theological Consortium
Special Services for the Deaf - Bks on deafness & sign lang; TDD equip; TTY equip
Special Services for the Blind - Reader equip
Open Mon-Thurs 8am-11:30pm, Fri 8am-10pm, Sat 9am-10pm, Sun 11am-11:30pm
Restriction: Open to pub for ref & circ; with some limitations, Open to students, fac & staff
Friends of the Library Group

Departmental Libraries:

ENGINEERING-ARCHITECTURE & MATHEMATICS LIBRARY, 016 Crough, 620 Michigan Ave NE, 20064, SAN 336-7177. Tel: 202-319-5167. FAX: 202-319-4485. *Archit & Planning Librn,* Anne Marie Hules; Tel: 202-319-6178, E-mail: hules@cua.edu
Function: ILL available
Open Mon-Thurs 9am-10pm, Fri 9-5, Sat 1-5, Sun 1-10

CL JUDGE KATHRYN J DUFOUR LAW LIBRARY, 3600 John McCormack Rd NE, 20064-8206, SAN 336-6995. Tel: 202-319-5156. Interlibrary Loan Service Tel: 202-319-4458. Reference Tel: 202-319-6284. FAX: 202-319-5581. Web Site: law.cua.edu/library. *Dir,* Stephen Margeton; Tel: 202-319-5116, E-mail: margeton@law.edu; *Assoc Dir,* Elizabeth Edinger; Tel: 202-319-5228, E-mail: edinger@law.edu; *Assoc Dir,* Mary Strouse; Tel: 202-319-5547, E-mail: strouse@law.edu; Staff 22 (MLS 10, Non-MLS 12)
Founded 1898
Library Holdings: Bk Vols 400,000; Per Subs 4,853
Open Mon-Fri (Winter) 7am-11:45pm, Sat & Sun 9am-11:45pm; Mon-Fri (Summer) 9am-10:45pm, Sat & Sun 9-4:45

OLIVEIRA LIMA LIBRARY, 22 Mullen Library, 620 Michigan Ave NE, 20064, SAN 336-7118. Tel: 202-319-5059. FAX: 202-319-4735. Web Site: libraries.cua.edu/limacoll.html. *Asst Curator,* Maria Angela Leal; E-mail: leal@cua.edu
Library Holdings: Bk Vols 59,000
Open Mon-Fri 10-5

MUSIC, 101 Ward Hall, 620 Michigan St, 20064, SAN 336-7053. Tel: 202-319-5424. FAX: 202-319-6280. Web Site: libraries.cua.edu/musicoll.html. *Head Librn,* Maurice Saylor; E-mail: saylor@cua.edu; *Libr Asst,* Thad Garrett; E-mail: garrett@cua.edu
Open Mon-Thurs 9-9, Fri 9-5, Sat 11-5, Sun 1-8

CM NURSING-BIOLOGY LIBRARY, 212 Gowan Hall, 620 Michigan Ave NE, 20064, SAN 336-7088. Tel: 202-319-5411. FAX: 202-319-5410. Web Site: libraries.cua.edu/nurscoll. *Librn,* Linda Todd; Tel: 202-319-6695, E-mail: todd@cua.edu
Founded 1932
Special Collections: Nursing Historical Coll
Subject Interests: Biol, Botany, Nursing
Function: CD-ROM, Doc delivery serv, For res purposes, Handicapped accessible, Homebound delivery serv, ILL available, Newsp ref libr, Online searches, Outside serv via phone, mail, e-mail & web, Photocopying/Printing, Ref serv available, Res libr, Wheelchair accessible
Special Services for the Deaf - Bks on deafness & sign lang; TDD equip; TTY equip
Special Services for the Blind - Reader equip
Open Mon-Thurs 9am-10pm, Fri 9-5, Sat 1-5, Sun 1-10

PHYSICS LIBRARY, 101 Hannan Hall, 620 Michigan Ave NE, 20064. Tel: 202-319-5320. FAX: 202-319-4485. *In Charge,* Min-Jing Chen; Tel: 202-319-5167, E-mail: chenm@cua.edu; *Coordr of Sci Libr,* Kimberly Hoffman

RARE BOOKS SPECIAL COLLECTIONS, 214 Mullen Library, 620 Michigan Ave NE, 20064, SAN 336-6936. Tel: 202-319-5091. FAX: 202-319-4735. Web Site: www.libraries.cua.edu/rarecoll. *Curator,* Lenore Rouse; E-mail: rouse@cua.edu
Function: ILL available
Open Mon-Fri 10-5

REFERENCE & INSTRUCTIONAL SERVICES DIVISION, 124 Mullen Library, 620 Michigan Ave NE, 20064, SAN 336-7142. Tel: 202-319-5070. FAX: 202-319-6054. Web Site: libraries.cua.edu/refcoll.html. *Librn,* Anne Lesher; Tel: 202-319-5068, E-mail: lesher@cua.edu; *Librn,* Mary Agnes Thompson; Tel: 292-319-6421, E-mail: thompsom@cua.edu

CR RELIGIOUS STUDIES-PHILOSOPHY & HUMANITIES LIBRARIES, 312 Mullen Library, 620 Michigan Ave NE, 20064, SAN 336-7150. Tel: 202-319-5088. FAX: 202-319-4735. Web Site: libraries.cua.edu/theocoll.html. *Relig Studies Librn,* Dustin Booher; Tel: 202-319-5091, E-mail: booher@cua.edu; *Coordr, Libr Serv,* Kevin Gunn; Tel: 202-319-5075, E-mail: gunn@cua.edu
Open Mon-Fri 8am-10pm, Sat 9am-10pm, Sun 11-10

CR SEMITICS/ICOR LIBRARY, 18 Mullen Library, 620 Michigan Ave NE, 20064, SAN 336-7207. Tel: 202-319-5084. FAX: 202-319-4735. Web Site: libraries.cua.edu/semicoll.html. *Curator,* Dr Monica Blanchard; E-mail: blanchard@cua.edu
Library Holdings: CDs 35; DVDs 15; Bk Vols 46,950; Per Subs 763
Special Collections: Ostraca & Papyri Colls; Syriac Digital Library Projects, bks, maps, ms, photog & other doc; Syriac Studies Reference Library
Partic in Washington Research Library Consortium
Open Mon-Fri 9-5

M CENTER FOR MOLECULAR NUTRITION & SENSORY DISORDERS, Taste & Smell Clinic Library, 5125 MacArthur Blvd, Ste 20, 20016. SAN 371-8255. Tel: 202-364-4180. Toll Free Tel: 877-697-6355. FAX: 202-364-9727. E-mail: doc@tasteandsmell.com. Web Site: www.tasteandsmell.com. *Chief Librn,* Robert I Henkin
Founded 1975
Library Holdings: Bk Titles 1,000; Per Subs 90; Spec Interest Per Sub 60
Special Collections: Dan Bradley Coll; R I Henkin Coll
Subject Interests: Taste & smell pathology & physiology

S CENTER ON CONSCIENCE & WAR LIBRARY, 1830 Connecticut Ave NW, 20009-5706. SAN 370-7547. Tel: 202-483-2220. FAX: 202-483-1246. E-mail: ccw@centeronconscience.org. Web Site: www.centeronconscience.org.
Founded 1940
Library Holdings: Bk Titles 350; Bk Vols 400; Per Subs 15
Special Collections: Conscientious Objection; Military Service & Conscription; Selective Service System & the Draft
Wireless access
Restriction: Pub use on premises

L CHADBOURNE & PARKE LLP*, Law Library, 1200 New Hampshire Ave NW, Ste 300, 20036. SAN 377-3760. Tel: 202-974-5695. FAX: 202-974-5602. Web Site: www.chadbourne.com. *Librn,* Amy Ratchford
Library Holdings: Bk Vols 10,000; Per Subs 250
Automation Activity & Vendor Info: (Acquisitions) Sydney

S COSMOS CLUB LIBRARY, 2121 Massachusetts Ave NW, 20008. SAN 377-2381. Tel: 202-387-7783, Ext 333, 202-939-1525. FAX: 202-234-6817. Web Site: www.cosmosclub.org. *Librn,* Karen Mark; E-mail: karen@cosmosclub.org; Staff 1 (MLS 1)
Library Holdings: Audiobooks 50; CDs 100; DVDs 10; e-books 15; Bk Titles 9,000; Per Subs 150; Videos 25
Special Collections: Cosmos Club Members Oral History Coll; John Wesley Powell Coll (Powelliana). Oral History
Automation Activity & Vendor Info: (Acquisitions) Inmagic, Inc.; (Cataloging) Inmagic, Inc.; (Circulation) Inmagic, Inc.; (Course Reserve) Inmagic, Inc.; (ILL) Inmagic, Inc.; (Media Booking) Inmagic, Inc.; (OPAC) Inmagic, Inc.; (Serials) Inmagic, Inc.
Wireless access
Function: Archival coll, Bk club(s), Bks on cassette, Bks on CD, Computers for patron use, Online cat, Ref & res, Spoken cassettes & CDs
Partic in DC Libr Asn
Restriction: Circ to mem only, Not a lending libr, Not open to pub, Private libr

S COUNCIL FOR ADVANCEMENT & SUPPORT OF EDUCATION*, CASE Information Center, 1307 New York Ave, Ste 1000, 20005-4701. SAN 302-6256. Tel: 202-328-2273. Web Site: www.case.org. *Dir,* Megan Galaida; Staff 4 (MLS 4)
Founded 1974
Subject Interests: Commun, Fundraising, Mkt
Restriction: Mem only, Open by appt only

L COVINGTON & BURLING LLP, Law Library, One City Center, 850 Tenth St, NW, 20001. SAN 302-6264. Tel: 202-662-6000. Interlibrary Loan Service Tel: 202-662-6158. FAX: 202-778-6658. Web Site: www.cov.com. *Dir, Libr & Info Mgt,* John Harbison; Tel: 202-662-6156, E-mail: jharbison@cov.com; *Asst Librn, Tech Serv & Automation,* Rhea Wilson; Tel: 202-662-6169, E-mail: rwilson@cov.com; *ILL Librn,* Lawrence Simpson Guthrie, II; Fax: 202-778-6658, E-mail: lguthrie@cov.com; Staff 10 (MLS 9, Non-MLS 1)
Founded 1919
Library Holdings: Bk Vols 75,000; Per Subs 200
Special Collections: Food & Drug Library; Legislative History Coll
Subject Interests: Antitrust, Bankruptcy, Drug, Food, Intellectual property, Intl law, Legis, Sports law
Automation Activity & Vendor Info: (Cataloging) EOS International; (Circulation) EOS International; (ILL) OCLC; (Serials) EOS International
Database Vendor: LexisNexis, OCLC FirstSearch, Westlaw
Function: ILL available
Partic in OCLC Online Computer Library Center, Inc
Restriction: Borrowing requests are handled by ILL

G DC COURT OF APPEALS LIBRARY, 430 E St NW, Rm 203, 20001. SAN 374-6143. Tel: 202-879-2767. FAX: 202-879-9912. *Librn,* Letty Limbach; E-mail: llimbach@dcappeals.gov; Staff 1 (MLS 1)
Founded 1977
Library Holdings: Bk Vols 20,000
Wireless access
Restriction: Staff use only

P DC REGIONAL LIBRARY FOR THE BLIND & PHYSICALLY HANDICAPPED*, Adaptive Services Division, Rm 215, 901 G St NW, 20001. SAN 302-6345. Tel: 202-559-5368 (videophone), 202-727-2142. FAX: 202-727-0322. TDD: 877-243-2823 (then 202-727-2255). E-mail: lbph.dcpl@dc.gov. Web Site: www.dclibrary.org/services/lbph. *Head of Libr,* Philip Wong-Cross; E-mail: philip.wong-cross@dc.gov; *Regional Librn,* Venetia V Demson; E-mail: venetia.demson@dc.gov; *Adaptive Tech Librn,* Patrick Timony; E-mail: james.timony@dc.gov; *Librn for Deaf,* Janice Rosen; E-mail: janice.rosen@dc.gov; *Readers' Advisor Librn,* Serena McGuire; E-mail: serena.mcguire@dc.gov; *Coll Mgr,* Michael Wayne; E-mail: michael.wayne@dc.gov; *Adaptive Tech/IT Spec,* Position Currently Open; *Adaptive Tech Training Coordr,* Christopher Corrigan; Tel: 202-727-2143, E-mail: christopher.corrigan@dc.gov; *Circ Coordr,* Rose Asuquo; E-mail: rose.asuquo@dc.gov; Staff 9 (MLS 4, Non-MLS 5)
Founded 1973
Library Holdings: Bks on Deafness & Sign Lang 100; Braille Volumes 200; DVDs 160; Bk Vols 300; Per Subs 50; Talking Bks 200,000; Videos 200
Special Collections: Americans with Disabilities Act Coll; Blindness & Other Disabilities Reference Coll; Deaf Culture & ASL Learning; Friends Group; Services & Agencies for the Handicapped File Coll; Volunteer Tapists; Washington Volunteer Readers for the Blind
Subject Interests: Disabilities, Employment, Rehabilitation
Wireless access
Function: Adult bk club, Audio & video playback equip for onsite use, Audiobks via web, Bk club(s), Children's prog, Computer training, Free DVD rentals, Handicapped accessible, Large print keyboards, Magnifiers for reading, OverDrive digital audio bks, Prog for children & young adult, Pub access computers, Teen prog, Web-Braille, Wheelchair accessible
Publications: Inside the Beltway (Newsletter); Library Services to the Deaf Community (Newsletter)
Special Services for the Deaf - Am sign lang & deaf culture; Assisted listening device; Assistive tech; Bks on deafness & sign lang; Closed caption videos; Coll on deaf educ; Deaf publ; Lecture on deaf culture; Pocket talkers; Sign lang interpreter upon request for prog; Sorenson video relay syst; Spec interest per; Staff with knowledge of sign lang; TTY equip; Video & TTY relay via computer; Video relay serv
Special Services for the Blind - Accessible computers; Assistive/Adapted tech devices, equip & products; Bks & mags in Braille, on rec, tape & cassette; Bks on flash-memory cartridges; Braille alphabet card; Braille bks; Cassette playback machines; Cassettes; Children's Braille; Closed circuit TV magnifier; Computer with voice synthesizer for visually impaired persons; Daisy reader; Descriptive video serv (DVS); Digital talking bk machines; Dragon Naturally Speaking software; Handicapped awareness prog; Home delivery serv; Info on spec aids & appliances; Inspiration software; Internet workstation with adaptive software; Large screen computer & software; Local mags & bks recorded; Low vision equip; Magnifiers; Mags & bk reproduction/duplication; Micro-computer access & training; Networked computers with assistive software; Newsletter (in large print, Braille or on cassette); Newsline for the Blind; Open bk software on pub access PC; Scanner for conversion & translation of mats; Screen enlargement software for people with visual disabilities; Screen reader software; Soundproof reading booth; Talking bks & player equip; Talking calculator; Web-Braille; ZoomText magnification & reading software
Open Mon & Tues 12-9, Wed-Fri 9:30-5:30
Friends of the Library Group

L DEBEVOISE & PLIMPTON*, Law Library, 555 13th St NW, Ste 1100 E, 20004. SAN 377-3523. Tel: 202-383-8055, 202-383-8075. FAX: 202-383-8118. Web Site: www.debevoise.com. *Libr Mgr,* Helen Fiori; E-mail: hefiori@debevoise.com
Library Holdings: Bk Titles 10,000; Bk Vols 15,000; Per Subs 65
Database Vendor: LexisNexis, Westlaw
Open Mon-Fri 9:30-5:30

L DECHERT LLP, Law Library, 1900 K St NW, 20006-1110. SAN 372-3445. Tel: 202-261-7909. FAX: 202-261-3333. Web Site: www.dechert.com. *Librn,* David W Lang; E-mail: david.lang@dechert.com. Subject Specialists: *Securities law,* David W Lang; Staff 1 (MLS 1)
Library Holdings: Bk Vols 5,000; Per Subs 50
Subject Interests: Securities law
Database Vendor: Dialog, LexisNexis, Westlaw
Function: ILL available
Restriction: Not open to pub

M DEPARTMENT OF MENTAL HEALTH, ST ELIZABETHS HOSPITAL*, Frances N Waldrop Health Sciences Library, 1100 Alabama Ave SE, 20032. SAN 373-0395. Tel: 202-299-5997. Interlibrary Loan Service Tel: 202-299-5203. Reference Tel: 202-299-5435. E-mail: seh.library@dc.gov. *Librn,* Velora Jernigan-Pedrick; E-mail: velora.jerniganpedrick@dc.gov; *Libr Tech/Ser & Doc Delivery,* Barbara Brown; E-mail: barbaraj.brown@dc.gov; Staff 2 (MLS 1, Non-MLS 1)
Library Holdings: Bk Vols 12,000
Subject Interests: Mental health, Psychiat, Psychol
Automation Activity & Vendor Info: (Acquisitions) CyberTools for Libraries; (Cataloging) CyberTools for Libraries; (OPAC) CyberTools for Libraries; (Serials) CyberTools for Libraries
Database Vendor: EBSCOhost, OVID Technologies, PubMed
Wireless access
Partic in National Network of Libraries of Medicine Southeastern Atlantic Region
Restriction: Lending to staff only, Researchers by appt only, Staff use only

DEPARTMENT OF VETERANS AFFAIRS
GM CENTRAL OFFICE LIBRARY*, 810 Vermont Ave NW, 20420, SAN 337-2510. Tel: 202-273-8523. FAX: 202-273-9125. *Chief Librn,* Caryl Kazen; E-mail: caryl.kazen@va.gov; *ILL,* Robyn Washington; Tel: 202-273-8520; *Tech Serv,* Position Currently Open; Staff 2 (MLS 2)
Founded 1923
Library Holdings: Bk Vols 7,000; Per Subs 208
Special Collections: US Document Depository
Subject Interests: Med, Mil hist, Veterans
Database Vendor: EBSCOhost, ProQuest
Open Mon-Fri 8-5
GM MEDICAL CENTER LIBRARY*, 50 Irving St NW, 20422, SAN 337-260X. Tel: 202-745-8262. FAX: 202-745-8632.
Library Holdings: Bk Vols 2,171; Per Subs 319
Subject Interests: Clinical med
Partic in National Network of Libraries of Medicine
Open Mon-Fri 8-4:30
GL OFFICE OF THE GENERAL COUNSEL LAW LIBRARY*, 810 Vermont Ave NW, 20420, SAN 337-257X. Tel: 202-273-6558. FAX: 202-273-6645. Web Site: www.va.gov/ogc. *Librn,* Susan Sokoll; E-mail: susan.sokoll@va.gov; Staff 3 (MLS 1, Non-MLS 2)
Library Holdings: Bk Vols 25,120; Per Subs 21
Database Vendor: LexisNexis
Restriction: Not open to pub

L DICKSTEIN SHAPIRO LLP*, Research Services, 1825 Eye St NW, 20006. SAN 377-4783. Tel: 202-420-4999. FAX: 202-420-2201. Web Site: www.dsmo.com. *Mgr, Libr Serv,* Joe Meringolo; *Mgr, Res,* Jim DiNatale; *Legis Librn,* Julia Taylor; *Tech Serv Adminr,* Pam Acree; *ILL,* Kim Perry; *Ref Serv,* Susan Crowley
Library Holdings: Bk Vols 30,000; Per Subs 75
Database Vendor: LexisNexis, Westlaw
Partic in DC Soc of Law Librs
Open Mon-Fri 8:30-6

S DISTANCE EDUCATION & TRAINING COUNCIL*, 1601 18th St NW, Ste 2, 20009. SAN 327-1293. Tel: 202-234-5100. FAX: 202-332-1386. Web Site: www.detc.org. *Exec Dir,* Leah K Matthews; Tel: 202-234-5100, Ext 101, E-mail: leah@detc.org
Founded 1926
Library Holdings: Bk Titles 1,500
Subject Interests: Distance educ
Restriction: Non-circulating to the pub, Open by appt only

S DISTRICT OF COLUMBIA DEPARTMENT OF CORRECTIONS, Correctional Treatment Facility Law Library, 1901 E St SE, 20003. SAN 377-1229. Tel: 202-698-3000, Ext 72263. FAX: 202-698-3301. *Librn,* Danielle Zoller; Staff 2 (MLS 2)
Library Holdings: Bk Titles 8,000; Per Subs 15
Restriction: Not open to pub

P DISTRICT OF COLUMBIA PUBLIC LIBRARY*, 901 G St NW, 20001-4531. SAN 336-9366. Tel: 202-727-1101. Circulation Tel: 202-727-1579. Interlibrary Loan Service Tel: 202-727-1304. Information Services Tel: 202-727-0321, 202-727-0324. FAX: 202-727-1129. TDD: 202-727-2145. Web Site: www.dclibrary.org. *Chief Librn/CEO,* Richard Reyes-Gavilan; E-mail: rrg@dc.gov; *Dir, Communications,* Joi Mecks; E-mail: joilette.mecks@dc.gov; *Dir, Human Res,* Barbara Kirven; E-mail: barbara.kirven@dc.gov; *Dir, Info Tech,* Lami Aromire; *Assoc Dir, Coll,* Elissa Miller; E-mail: elissa.miller@dc.gov; *Coordr, Ch & Youth Serv,* Micki Freeny; *Coordr, Early Literacy Prog & Partnerships,* Gary Romero
Founded 1896. Pop 591,833; Circ 1,781,862
Library Holdings: Audiobooks 37,346; AV Mats 15,853; Bks on Deafness & Sign Lang 285; Braille Volumes 1,189; CDs 37,117; DVDs 137,999; e-books 29,900; Electronic Media & Resources 77; Large Print Bks 14,860; Microforms 4; Music Scores 25,012; Bk Titles 459,023; Bk Vols 1,802,305; Per Subs 2,309; Talking Bks 88,005; Videos 1,454
Special Collections: African-American Studies; Washingtoniana. Oral History; State Document Depository; US Document Depository
Automation Activity & Vendor Info: (Acquisitions) SirsiDynix; (Cataloging) SirsiDynix; (Circulation) SirsiDynix; (OPAC) SirsiDynix
Database Vendor: Gale Cengage Learning, Greenwood Publishing Group, H W Wilson, LearningExpress, ProQuest, ReferenceUSA, Standard & Poor's, World Book Online
Wireless access
Publications: Beyond Words (Newsletter)
Special Services for the Deaf - Am sign lang & deaf culture; Assistive tech; Bks on deafness & sign lang; Deaf publ; Lecture on deaf culture; TTY equip; Video relay serv
Special Services for the Blind - Accessible computers; Assistive/Adapted tech devices, equip & products; Bks on CD; Large print bks; Playaways (bks on MP3); Spec prog; Talking bks
Open Mon-Thurs 9:30-9, Fri & Sat 9:30-5:30, Sun 1-5
Friends of the Library Group
Branches: 22
CHEVY CHASE, 5625 Connecticut Ave NW, 20015, SAN 336-948X. Tel: 202-282-0021. E-mail: chevychaselibrary@dc.gov. *Mgr,* Tracy Myers
Library Holdings: Bk Vols 106,710
Open Mon-Wed 9:30-9, Thurs 1-9, Fri & Sat 9:30-5:30, Sun 1-5
Friends of the Library Group
CLEVELAND PARK, 3310 Connecticut Ave NW, 20008, SAN 336-9544. Tel: 202-282-3080. E-mail: clevelandparklibrary@dc.gov. *Mgr,* Barbara Gauntt
Library Holdings: Bk Vols 98,976
Open Mon-Wed 9:30-9, Thurs 1-9, Fri & Sat 9:30-5:30, Sun 1-5
Friends of the Library Group
GEORGETOWN, 3260 R St NW, 20007, SAN 336-9633. Tel: 202-727-0232. E-mail: georgetownlibrary@dc.gov. *Mgr,* Lucy Thrasher
Library Holdings: Bk Vols 90,408
Subject Interests: Local hist
Open Mon-Wed 9:30-9, Thurs 1-9, Fri & Sat 9:30-5:30, Sun 1-5
Friends of the Library Group
FRANCIS A GREGORY BRANCH, 3660 Alabama Ave SE, 20020, SAN 336-9609. Tel: 202-698-6373. E-mail: francisgregorylibrary@dc.gov. *Mgr,* Betty Smith
Library Holdings: Bk Vols 50,000
Open Mon-Wed 9:30-9, Thurs 1-9, Fri & Sat 9:30-5:30, Sun 1-5
Friends of the Library Group
DOROTHY I HEIGHT/BENNING NEIGHBORHOOD LIBRARY, 3935 Benning Rd NE, 20019, SAN 336-9455. Tel: 202-281-2583, 202-281-2586. Information Services Tel: 202-281-2598. Toll Free Tel: 202-727-4076. E-mail: benninglibrary@dc.gov. Web Site: dclibrary.org/benning. *Br Mgr,* Winnell Morris Montague; E-mail: winnell.montague@dc.gov. Subject Specialists: *Mgt,* Winnell Morris Montague
Library Holdings: Bk Vols 40,000
Open Mon-Wed 9:30-9, Thurs 1-9, Fri & Sat 9:30-5:30, Sun 1-5
Friends of the Library Group
MARTIN LUTHER KING JR MEMORIAL, 901 G St NW, 20001-4531. Tel: 202-727-0321. FAX: 202-727-0321. E-mail: mlkjrlibrary@dc.gov. *Interim Assoc Dir,* Kim Zablub; Staff 91 (MLS 41, Non-MLS 50)
Library Holdings: Bk Vols 875,580
Special Collections: The Black Studies Center; The Children's Illustrator Coll; The District of Columbia Community Archives; Washingtoniana
Special Services for the Deaf - Accessible learning ctr; ADA equip; Assisted listening device; Assistive tech; Bks on deafness & sign lang; Closed caption videos; Coll on deaf educ; Deaf publ; Described encaptioned media prog; Staff with knowledge of sign lang
Special Services for the Blind - Accessible computers; Assistive/Adapted tech devices, equip & products; Bks on cassette; Braille & cassettes; Braille alphabet card; Braille bks; Braille equip; Cassettes; Large print bks; Magnifiers; Newsp on cassette; Reader equip; Recorded bks; Ref in Braille; Talking bks; Volunteer serv

Open Mon-Thurs 9:30-9, Fri & Sat 9:30-5:30, Sun 1-5
Friends of the Library Group

LAMOND RIGGS, 5401 S Dakota Ave NE, 20011, SAN 336-965X. Tel: 202-541-6255. E-mail: lamondriggslibrary@dc.gov. *Interim Mgr,* Rob Schneider
Library Holdings: Bk Vols 50,000
Open Mon-Wed 9:30-9, Thurs 1-9, Fri & Sat 9:30-5:30, Sun 1-5

LIBRARY FOR THE BLIND & PHYSICALLY HANDICAPPED
See Separate Entry DC Regional

WILLIAM O LOCKRIDGE/BELLEVUE, 115 Atlantic St SW, 20032, SAN 336-9994. Tel: 202-243-1185. E-mail: bellevuelibrary@dc.gov. *Mgr,* Marie Perry
Library Holdings: Bk Vols 67,435
Open Mon-Wed 9:30-9, Thurs 1-9, Fri & Sat 9:30-5:30, Sun 1-5
Friends of the Library Group

MOUNT PLEASANT, 3160 16th St NW, 20010, SAN 336-9692. Tel: 202-671-3121. E-mail: mtpleasantlibrary@dc.gov. *Mgr,* Tracy Sumler; Staff 5 (MLS 4, Non-MLS 1)
Founded 1925
Library Holdings: Bk Vols 60,000
Open Mon-Wed 9:30-9, Thurs 1-9, Fri & Sat 9:30-5:30, Sun 1-5
Friends of the Library Group

NORTHEAST NEIGHBORHOOD LIBRARY, 330 Seventh St NE, 20002, SAN 336-9722. Tel: 202-698-0058. E-mail: northeastlibrary@dc.gov. *Actg Mgr,* Russell Martin
Library Holdings: Bk Vols 57,694
Open Mon-Wed 9:30-9, Thurs 1-9, Fri & Sat 9:30-5:30, Sun 1-5
Friends of the Library Group

PALISADES, 4901 V St NW, 20007, SAN 336-9757. Tel: 202-282-3139. E-mail: palisadeslibrary@dc.gov. *Mgr,* Kimberly Knight
Library Holdings: Bk Vols 81,644
Open Mon-Wed 9:30-9, Thurs 1-9, Fri & Sat 9:30-5:30, Sun 1-5
Friends of the Library Group

PARKLANDS-TURNER COMMUNITY, The Shops at Park Village, 1547 Alabama Ave SE, 20032, SAN 337-0178. Tel: 202-645-4532. E-mail: parklandsturnerlibrary@dc.gov. *Mgr,* Robin Imperial
Library Holdings: Bk Vols 40,701
Open Mon-Wed 9:30-9, Thurs 1-9, Fri & Sat 9:30-5:30, Sun 1-5

PETWORTH, 4200 Kansas Ave NW, 20011, SAN 336-9781. Tel: 202-243-1188. E-mail: petworthlibrary@dc.gov. *Mgr,* Jeff Neher
Library Holdings: Bk Vols 73,239
Automation Activity & Vendor Info: (Circulation) SirsiDynix
Open Mon-Wed 9:30-9, Thurs 1-9, Fri & Sat 9:30-5:30, Sun 1-5
Friends of the Library Group

WATHA T DANIEL SHAW INTERIM LIBRARY, 1630 Seventh St NW, 20001. Tel: 202-727-1288. E-mail: wathashawlibrary@dc.gov. *Sr Librn,* Leslie Griffin; Staff 7 (MLS 3, Non-MLS 4)
Special Collections: Graphic Novel Coll
Subject Interests: Adult & young adult prog
Open Mon-Wed 9:30-9, Thurs 1-9, Fri & Sat 9:30-5:30, Sun 1-5
Friends of the Library Group

SOUTHEAST, 403 Seventh St SE, 20003, SAN 336-9811. Tel: 202-698-3377. E-mail: southeastlibrary@dc.gov. *Mgr,* Laura Gonzales
Library Holdings: Bk Vols 77,598
Special Collections: Hist of Eastern Mkt & Capital Hill Communities
Open Mon-Wed 9:30-9, Thurs 1-9, Fri & Sat 9:30-5:30, Sun 1-5
Friends of the Library Group

SOUTHWEST, 900 Wesley Pl SW, 20024, SAN 336-9846. Tel: 202-724-4752. E-mail: southwestlibrary@dc.gov. *Mgr,* Karen Quash
Library Holdings: Bk Vols 70,028
Open Mon-Wed 9:30-9, Thurs 1-9, Fri & Sat 9:30-5:30, Sun 1-5
Friends of the Library Group

TAKOMA PARK, 416 Cedar St NW, 20012, SAN 336-9900. Tel: 202-576-7252. E-mail: takomaparklibrary@dc.gov. *Mgr,* Heather Petsche; E-mail: heather.petsche@dc.gov
Library Holdings: Bk Vols 38,637
Open Mon-Wed 9:30-9, Thurs 1-9, Fri & Sat 9:30-5:30, Sun 1-5
Friends of the Library Group

TENLEY-FRIENDSHIP, 4450 Wisconsin Ave NW, 20016, SAN 336-9935. Tel: 202-727-1488.
Library Holdings: Bk Vols 79,533
Open Mon-Wed 9:30-9, Thurs 1-9, Fri & Sat 9:30-5:30, Sun 1-5
Friends of the Library Group

JUANITA E THORNTON/SHEPHERD PARK NEIGHBORHOOD LIBRARY, 7420 Georgia Ave NW, 20012, SAN 373-5745. Tel: 202-541-6100. E-mail: shepherdparklibrary@dc.gov. *Mgr,* Elizabeth Lang
Library Holdings: Bk Vols 66,942
Open Mon-Wed 9:30-9, Thurs 1-9, Fri & Sat 9:30-5:30, Sun 1-5
Friends of the Library Group

WEST END, 2522 Virginia Ave NW, 20037, SAN 337-0054. Tel: 202-724-8707. E-mail: westendlibrary@dc.gov. *Mgr,* Karen Blackman-Mills
Library Holdings: Bk Vols 71,664
Open Mon-Wed 9:30-9, Thurs 1-9, Fri & Sat 9:30-5:30, Sun 1-5
Friends of the Library Group

WOODRIDGE, 1790 Douglas St NE, 20018, SAN 337-0089. Tel: 202-541-6226. E-mail: woodridgelibrary@dc.gov. *Mgr,* Jeanette Graham
Library Holdings: Bk Vols 87,709
Open Mon-Wed 9:30-9, Thurs 1-9, Fri & Sat 9:30-5:30, Sun 1-5
Friends of the Library Group

GL DISTRICT OF COLUMBIA SUPERIOR COURT JUDGES LIBRARY*, 500 Indiana Ave NW, Rm 5400, 20001-2131. SAN 302-6353. Tel: 202-879-1435. Web Site: www.dccourts.gov. *Librn,* Yousuf Galeel
Library Holdings: Bk Vols 30,000; Per Subs 30
Database Vendor: LexisNexis
Open Mon-Fri 8:30-5

L DLA PIPER US LLP*, Law Library, 500 Eighth St NW, 20004. SAN 372-154X. Tel: 202-799-4000. FAX: 202-799-5000. Web Site: www.dlapiper.com. *Head Librn,* Position Currently Open; *Res Librn,* May Guo; Staff 4 (MLS 2, Non-MLS 2)
Library Holdings: Bk Vols 6,000; Per Subs 50
Special Collections: Government Contracts
Subject Interests: Environ law, Franchises
Database Vendor: LexisNexis, Westlaw
Restriction: Not open to pub

CR DOMINICAN THEOLOGICAL LIBRARY*, Dominican House of Studies Library, 487 Michigan Ave NE, 20017-1585. SAN 302-752X. Tel: 202-495-3821. FAX: 202-495-3873. E-mail: librarian@dhs.edu. Web Site: www.dhs.edu. *Librn,* Fr John Martin Ruiz; *Asst Librn, Tech Serv,* Jennifer Gullickson; *Circ,* Alpha Randolph; E-mail: arandolph@dhs.edu; Staff 4 (MLS 2, Non-MLS 2)
Founded 1905. Enrl 80; Fac 14; Highest Degree: Master
Library Holdings: AV Mats 800; Bk Vols 75,000; Per Subs 450
Special Collections: Dissertations by Dominican Authors; Dominican History, Liturgy & Authors; St Thomas Aquinas Writings
Subject Interests: Philos, Theol, Thomist
Automation Activity & Vendor Info: (Cataloging) Innovative Interfaces, Inc - Millenium; (Circulation) Innovative Interfaces, Inc - Millenium; (Course Reserve) Innovative Interfaces, Inc - Millenium; (ILL) Innovative Interfaces, Inc - Millenium; (Media Booking) Innovative Interfaces, Inc - Millenium; (OPAC) Innovative Interfaces, Inc - Millenium; (Serials) Innovative Interfaces, Inc - Millenium
Wireless access
Function: ILL available
Open Mon-Thurs 8:30-6:30, Fri 8:30-5, Sat 9-12

L DOW LOHNES PLLC*, Law Library, 1200 New Hampshire NW, Ste 800, 20036-6802. SAN 325-643X. Tel: 202-776-2000, 202-776-2650. FAX: 202-776-2222. Web Site: www.dowlohnes.com. *Dir, Libr & Info Serv,* Elinor Russell; Tel: 202-776-2653, E-mail: erussell@dowlohnes.com
Library Holdings: Bk Titles 5,000; Per Subs 30
Automation Activity & Vendor Info: (Acquisitions) Cuadra Associates, Inc; (Cataloging) Cuadra Associates, Inc; (Circulation) Cuadra Associates, Inc; (Serials) Cuadra Associates, Inc
Database Vendor: Dialog, LexisNexis, Westlaw
Wireless access
Open Mon-Fri 9-6

S ECONOMIC POLICY INSTITUTE*, Library Information Center, East Tower, 1333 H St NW, Ste 300, 20005. SAN 374-5481. Tel: 202-775-8810. FAX: 202-775-0819. Web Site: www.epi.org.
Founded 1991
Library Holdings: Bk Titles 4,500; Per Subs 83
Partic in Northern Lights Library Network
Restriction: Open by appt only

S ECONOMICS RESEARCH ASSOCIATES LIBRARY*, 1101 Connecticut Ave NW, Ste 750, 20036. SAN 377-1504. Tel: 202-496-9870. FAX: 202-496-9877. Web Site: www.econres.com. *Coop Librn,* Ruth Behling; Tel: 310-477-9585 (Los Angeles), E-mail: ruth.behling@econres.com
Library Holdings: Bk Vols 1,000; Per Subs 100

S ECONOMISTS INC LIBRARY*, 1200 New Hampshire Ave NW, Ste 400, 20036-6809. SAN 376-3730. Tel: 202-223-4700. FAX: 202-296-7138. E-mail: info@ei.com. Web Site: www.ei.com. *Head Librn,* Zelda Schiffenbauer; E-mail: schiffenbauer.z@ei.com; Staff 1 (MLS 1)
Founded 1981
Library Holdings: Bk Titles 5,000; Per Subs 180
Special Collections: Industrial Organization Coll, bks, per
Subject Interests: Econ
Restriction: Access at librarian's discretion

S EDISON ELECTRIC INSTITUTE*, Information Resources Center, 701 Pennsylvania Ave NW, 3rd Flr, 20004-2696. SAN 302-640X. Tel: 202-508-5623. Interlibrary Loan Service Tel: 202-508-5603. *Info Res Mgr,* Jacqueline Johnson; E-mail: jjohnson@eei.org; Staff 1 (MLS 1)
Founded 1917
Library Holdings: Bk Titles 6,750; Bk Vols 11,000; Per Subs 20
Special Collections: Edison Electric Institute Publications, 1933-present; Electrical World Directory of Electric Utilities, 1912-present; Moodys/Mergent Public Utility Manual, 1928-2007; National Electric Light Association (NELA) Publications, 1917-1933
Subject Interests: Electric power, Energy, Environ studies, Legislation
Automation Activity & Vendor Info: (Cataloging) EOS International; (Circulation) EOS International; (OPAC) EOS International; (Serials) EOS International
Database Vendor: Dialog, EBSCOhost
Wireless access
Restriction: Fee for pub use, Open to pub by appt only

L ELIAS, MATZ, TIERNAN & HERRICK LLP*, 734 15th St NW, 11th Flr, 20005. SAN 377-2284. Tel: 202-347-0300. FAX: 202-347-2172. Web Site: www.emth.com. *Librn,* Kathy Matthews; E-mail: kmatt@emth.com
Library Holdings: Bk Vols 1,000; Per Subs 150
Database Vendor: LexisNexis
Partic in DC Soc of Law Librs
Open Mon-Fri 10-6:30

G ENVIRONMENTAL PROTECTION AGENCY*, Headquarters & Chemical Libraries, West Bldg, Rm 3340, 1301 Constitution Ave NW, 20004. (Mail add: 1200 Pennsylvania Ave NW, MC 3404T, 20460), SAN 302-6450. Tel: 202-566-0556. FAX: 202-566-0574. E-mail: hqchemlibraries@epa.gov. Web Site: www.epa.gov/libraries/hqchem.html. *Supvry Librn,* Kezia Procita; Tel: 202-566-9982, E-mail: procita.kezia@epa.gov
Founded 1971
Special Collections: Emergency Planning Community Right-To-Know Act Coll; Toxic Substances Control Act Coll
Automation Activity & Vendor Info: (Cataloging) OCLC Connexion
Partic in OCLC Online Computer Library Center, Inc
Open Mon-Fri 8:30-4:30

G EXECUTIVE OFFICE OF THE PRESIDENT LIBRARIES*, Library & Research Services, 725 17th St NW, Rm G-007, 20503. SAN 336-7266. Tel: 202-395-4690. FAX: 202-395-6137. *Dir,* Lea Uhre; E-mail: luhre@oa.eop.gov; Staff 13 (MLS 10, Non-MLS 3)
Library Holdings: Bk Vols 100,000; Per Subs 200
Special Collections: Congressional Appropriations Legislation Coll; Federal Budget Documents Coll; Legal Coll; Legislative Histories of Federal Government Reorganization Plans Coll; The Presidency
Subject Interests: Econ, Intl trade, Presidents (US)
Automation Activity & Vendor Info: (Acquisitions) Innovative Interfaces, Inc; (Cataloging) Innovative Interfaces, Inc; (Circulation) Innovative Interfaces, Inc; (OPAC) Innovative Interfaces, Inc; (Serials) Innovative Interfaces, Inc
Database Vendor: Dialog, LexisNexis
Function: Res libr
Partic in Fedlink; OCLC Online Computer Library Center, Inc; Westlaw
Restriction: Circulates for staff only, Not open to pub

G FEDERAL BUREAU OF PRISONS LIBRARY*, 400 First St NW, 3rd Flr, 20534. (Mail add: Bldg 400, 3rd Flr, 320 First St NW, 20534), SAN 302-6507. Tel: 202-307-3029. FAX: 202-307-5756. E-mail: library@bop.gov. Web Site: www.bop.library.net. *Head of Libr,* Denise W Lomax; E-mail: dlomax@bop.gov; Staff 2 (MLS 1, Non-MLS 1)
Founded 1960
Library Holdings: AV Mats 500; Bk Titles 6,000; Bk Vols 7,000; Per Subs 70
Subject Interests: Corrections, Criminal justice, Psychol, Sociol
Automation Activity & Vendor Info: (Cataloging) OCLC; (Circulation) TLC (The Library Corporation); (OPAC) TLC (The Library Corporation); (Serials) TLC (The Library Corporation)
Database Vendor: American Psychological Association (APA), Dialog, EBSCOhost, LexisNexis, Sage, Westlaw
Function: Prof lending libr, Res libr
Publications: Periodical List; Video List
Partic in Fedlink; OCLC Online Computer Library Center, Inc; World Criminal Justice Libr Network

G FEDERAL COMMUNICATIONS COMMISSION LIBRARY*, 445 12th St SW, 20554. SAN 302-6515. Tel: 202-418-0450. FAX: 202-418-2805. E-mail: fcclibrary@fcc.gov. *Dir,* Lisa Leyser
Special Collections: Legislative Histories: Communications Act of 1934 & subsequent Amendments
Subject Interests: Computer sci, Econ, Eng, Law
Wireless access

G FEDERAL DEPOSIT INSURANCE CORP LIBRARY, 550 17th St NW, 20429-0002. SAN 302-6523. Tel: 202-898-3631. FAX: 202-898-3984. E-mail: library@fdic.gov. *Head Librn,* Teresa Neville; E-mail: tneville@fdic.gov; *Chief, Ref Serv,* Len Samowitz; Staff 11 (MLS 8, Non-MLS 3)
Founded 1934
Library Holdings: Bk Titles 13,000; Bk Vols 15,000; Per Subs 200
Special Collections: FDIC Archival Material
Subject Interests: Banks & banking, Econ, Law, Real estate
Database Vendor: EBSCOhost, Factiva.com, HeinOnline, Hoovers, IBISWorld, JSTOR, LexisNexis, Mergent Online, Newsbank, OCLC FirstSearch, ProQuest, Standard & Poor's, Westlaw
Function: ILL available
Partic in OCLC Online Computer Library Center, Inc
Restriction: Open by appt only

GL FEDERAL ELECTION COMMISSION, Law Library, 999 E St NW, Rm 801, 20463. SAN 325-7975. Tel: 202-694-1516. FAX: 202-208-3579. Web Site: www.fec.gov. *Dir,* Leta Holley; E-mail: lholley@fec.gov; Staff 2 (MLS 1, Non-MLS 1)
Library Holdings: Bk Vols 10,000; Per Subs 30
Subject Interests: Law, Polit sci
Automation Activity & Vendor Info: (Acquisitions) Inmagic, Inc.; (Cataloging) OCLC; (Circulation) Inmagic, Inc.; (Serials) Inmagic, Inc.
Database Vendor: Westlaw
Partic in DC Soc of Law Librs; Fedlink
Open Mon-Fri 9-4:30

G FEDERAL JUDICIAL CENTER*, Information Services Office, One Columbus Circle NE, 20002-8003. SAN 325-7991. Tel: 202-502-4153. FAX: 202-502-4077. Web Site: www.fjc.gov. *Librn,* Roger N Karr; Staff 2 (MLS 1, Non-MLS 1)
Library Holdings: AV Mats 4,500; Bk Titles 5,800; Bk Vols 12,000; Per Subs 300
Automation Activity & Vendor Info: (Circulation) NOTEbookS Library Automation; (OPAC) NOTEbookS Library Automation
Function: ILL available, Res libr
Partic in Fedlink; OCLC Online Computer Library Center, Inc
Restriction: Open by appt only

G FEDERAL MARITIME COMMISSION LIBRARY*, 800 N Capitol St NW, 20573. SAN 302-6531. Tel: 202-523-5762. FAX: 202-523-5738. E-mail: libraryinquiries@fmc.gov. Web Site: www.fmc.gov. *Librn,* Charlotte White; E-mail: cwhite@fmc.gov; Staff 1 (MLS 1)
Founded 1961
Library Holdings: Bk Vols 8,700; Per Subs 50
Database Vendor: Westlaw
Open Mon-Fri 8-4:30
Restriction: External users must contact libr

G FEDERAL TRADE COMMISSION LIBRARY*, 600 Pennsylvania Ave NW, Rm 630, 20580. SAN 302-654X. Tel: 202-326-2395. FAX: 202-326-2732. *Dir,* Margie Knott, Staff 3 (MLS 3)
Founded 1914
Library Holdings: AV Mats 175; Bk Vols 117,000, Per Subs 350
Special Collections: Archives; Legislative Histories
Subject Interests: Bus, Consumer protection, Econ, Law
Database Vendor: EBSCOhost, HeinOnline, JSTOR, LexisNexis, ReferenceUSA, Westlaw
Publications: Periodical Holdings List
Partic in OCLC Online Computer Library Center, Inc
Open Mon-Fri 8:30-5

S FEDERATION OF AMERICAN SCIENTISTS LIBRARY*, 1725 Dasales St NW, Ste 600, 20036. SAN 371-1412. Tel: 202-546-3300. FAX: 202-675-1010. E-mail: fas@fas.org. Web Site: www.fas.org.
Library Holdings: Bk Vols 4,000; Per Subs 29
Restriction: Open by appt only

G FEMA/DHS LIBRARY*, 500 C St SW, Rm 123, 20472. SAN 328-0543. Tel: 202-646-3771. FAX: 202-646-4295. Web Site: www.fema.gov. *Head of Libr,* Mercedes Lopez Emperado; E-mail: mercedes.emperado@dhs.gov; *ILL,* Arlett Hodges Leigh; Tel: 202-646-3769, E-mail: arlett.leigh@dhs.gov; Staff 2 (MLS 1, Non-MLS 1)
Founded 1980
Library Holdings: Bk Titles 25,000; Bk Vols 100,000; Per Subs 120
Special Collections: Emergency Preparedness Coll; Freedom of Information Act; Security Management Coll
Database Vendor: Dialog, LexisNexis, OCLC FirstSearch
Function: Telephone ref
Publications: Quarterly Accessions List
Partic in Dialog Corp; OCLC Online Computer Library Center, Inc
Open Mon-Fri 8-4:30

L FINNEGAN, HENDERSON, FARABOW, GARRETT & DUNNER*, Law Library, 901 New York Ave NW, 20001-4413. SAN 370-1166. Tel: 202-408-4290. FAX: 202-408-4400. *Mgr, Libr Serv,* Virginia A McNitt; Tel: 202-408-4372; *Sr Res Librn,* Faith Ottenhoff; Tel: 202-408-4364; *Res Librn,* Javii Austin; Tel: 202-408-4373; *Res Librn,* Sanema Hardrick; Tel: 202-216-5040; Staff 7 (MLS 2, Non-MLS 5)
Library Holdings: Bk Titles 3,483; Bk Vols 12,000; Per Subs 40
Subject Interests: Intellectual property law, Patents, Trademarks
Database Vendor: Dialog, LexisNexis, STN International, Westlaw
Function: Doc delivery serv, Online cat, Online ref, Online searches
Restriction: Private libr

L FOLEY & LARDNER LLP*, Private Law Library, 3000 K St NW, 4th Flr, 20007. SAN 321-7639. Tel: 202-672-5300. FAX: 202-672-5399. Web Site: www.foley.com. *Res Librn,* Robin Evans; E-mail: revans@foley.com; Staff 5 (MLS 2, Non-MLS 3)
Library Holdings: Bk Titles 15,000
Partic in Dialog Corp; Westlaw
Restriction: Not open to pub, Staff use only

S FOLGER SHAKESPEARE LIBRARY, 201 E Capitol St SE, 20003-1094. SAN 302-6558. Tel: 202-544-4600. Reference Tel: 202-675-0311. Information Services Tel: 202-675-0306. FAX: 202-544-4623. Reference FAX: 202-675-0313. E-mail: reference@folger.edu. Web Site: www.folger.edu. *Dir,* Dr Michael Witmore; E-mail: mwitmore@folger.edu; *Head, Acq,* Laura Cofield; E-mail: lcofield@folger.edu; *Head, Coll Info Serv,* Dr Erin Blake; E-mail: eblake@folger.edu; *Head, Conserv,* Renate Mesmer; E-mail: rmesmer@folger.edu; *Head, Photog & Digital Imaging,* Julie Ainsworth; Tel: 202-675-0390, Fax: 202-608-1715, E-mail: jainsworth@folger.edu; *Head, Reader Serv,* Elizabeth Walsh; E-mail: bwalsh@folger.edu; *Assoc Librn, Head, Ref,* Dr Georgianna Ziegler; E-mail: gziegler@folger.edu; *Librn,* Daniel De Simone; E-mail: ddesimone@folger.edu; *Exhibitions Mgr,* Caryn Lazzuri; Tel: 202-675-0709, E-mail: clazzuri@folger.edu; *Curator of Ms,* Dr Heather Wolfe; Tel: 202-675-0325, E-mail: hwolfe@folger.edu; *Curator, Early Modern Bks & Prints,* Caroline Duroselle-Melish; Tel: 202-675-0356. Subject Specialists: *English paleography,* Dr Heather Wolfe
Founded 1932
Library Holdings: Bk Titles 265,000; Per Subs 200
Special Collections: Manuscripts; Shakespeare, playbills, promptbooks; STC/Wing Coll, printed bks
Subject Interests: Art, English lit, Hist, Renaissance, Shakespeare, Theatre
Automation Activity & Vendor Info: (Acquisitions) Ex Libris Group; (Cataloging) Ex Libris Group; (Circulation) Ex Libris Group; (OPAC) Ex Libris Group; (Serials) Ex Libris Group
Wireless access
Publications: Exhibition Catalogues; Folger Library Edition of the Complete Plays of William Shakespeare; Folger Magazine; Shakespeare Quarterly
Partic in OCLC Online Computer Library Center, Inc
Open Mon-Sat 10-5
Friends of the Library Group

S FOUNDATION CENTER-WASHINGTON, DC LIBRARY*, 1627 K St NW, 3rd Flr, 20006. SAN 302-6582. Tel: 202-331-1400. FAX: 202-331-1739. Web Site: foundationcenter.org. *Sr Librn,* Janice Z Rosenberg; Tel: 202-331-1400, Ext 4027, E-mail: jzr@foundationcenter.org; *Dir,* Patricia E Pasqual; Tel: 202-331-1400, Ext 4022, E-mail: pep@foundationcenter.org; Staff 5 (MLS 3, Non-MLS 2)
Founded 1964
Library Holdings: Bk Titles 2,350; Per Subs 60; Videos 50
Special Collections: Foundation IRS Information Returns Coll; Foundation Published Reports
Subject Interests: Philanthropy
Publications: Newsletter
Open Mon & Wed-Fri 10-5, Tues 10-8
Restriction: Circ limited

SR FRANCISCAN MONASTERY LIBRARY*, Commissariat of the Holy Land USA, 1400 Quincy St NE, 20017. SAN 302-6604. Tel: 202-526-6800. FAX: 202-529-9889. Web Site: www.myfranciscan.com. *Archivist/Librn,* Karen L Levenback; E-mail: karen@myfranciscan.com. Subject Specialists: *Relig & fraternal groups,* Karen L Levenback; Staff 2 (MLS 1, Non-MLS 1)
Founded 1900
Library Holdings: Bk Vols 20,000; Per Subs 12
Special Collections: Franciscan Coll; Holy Land Coll; Rare Books. Oral History
Subject Interests: Catholic hist, Franciscan hist, Holy Land & Palestine
Wireless access
Restriction: Access at librarian's discretion, Open by appt only

L FRIED, FRANK, HARRIS, SHRIVER & JACOBSON LLP*, Law Library, 801 17th St NW, Ste 600, 20006. Tel: 202-639-7000. FAX: 202-639-7003. *Libr Mgr,* Janet James; E-mail: janet.james@friedfrank.com; *ILL,* Thomas King; *Res,* Sue Ann Orsini; *Tech Serv,* Leigh Beatson; Staff 4 (MLS 3, Non-MLS 1)
Library Holdings: Bk Titles 5,500; Bk Vols 25,000; Per Subs 300
Automation Activity & Vendor Info: (Cataloging) SirsiDynix; (Circulation) SirsiDynix; (OPAC) SirsiDynix; (Serials) SirsiDynix
Database Vendor: LexisNexis, OCLC FirstSearch, Westlaw
Wireless access
Restriction: Open by appt only

C GALLAUDET UNIVERSITY LIBRARY, 800 Florida Ave NE, 20002-3095. SAN 302-6620. Tel: 202-651-5217. E-mail: library.help@gallaudet.edu. Web Site: library.gallaudet.edu. *Interim Dir, Libr Deaf Coll & Archives,* Michael Olson; E-mail: michael.olson@gallaudet.edu; *Pub Serv Dir,* Sarah Hamrick; Tel: 202-651-5214, E-mail: sarah.hamrick@gallaudet.edu; *Instruction & Ref/Electronic Res Librn,* Elizabeth Henry; E-mail: elizabeth.henry@gallaudet.edu; *Instruction & Ref Librn,* Patrick Oberholtzer; Tel: 202-651-5233, E-mail: patrick.oberholtzer@gallaudet.edu; *Metadata/Cat Librn,* Jamie Smith; E-mail: jamie.smith@gallaudet.edu; *Supvr, Instruction & Ref,* Laura Jacobi; Tel: 202-651-5239, E-mail: laura.jacobi@gallaudet.edu. Subject Specialists: *Deafness,* Michael Olson; *Sci,* Patrick Oberholtzer; *Human relations,* Laura Jacobi; Staff 12 (MLS 5, Non-MLS 7)
Founded 1876. Enrl 1,500; Fac 250; Highest Degree: Doctorate
Special Collections: Archival Materials, artifacts, bks, doc, microfilm, V-tapes; Deaf Coll, bks, V-tapes. Oral History
Subject Interests: Audiology & hearing, Deafness, Institutional memory & hist
Wireless access
Partic in OCLC Online Computer Library Center, Inc; Washington Research Library Consortium
Special Services for the Deaf - ADA equip; Assisted listening device; Bks on deafness & sign lang; Captioned film dep; Closed caption videos; Coll on deaf educ; Deaf publ; Interpreter on staff; Lecture on deaf culture; Pocket talkers; Sorenson video relay syst; Spec interest per; Staff with knowledge of sign lang; TDD equip; TTY equip; Video & TTY relay via computer
Open Mon-Thurs 8am-Midnight, Fri 8-8, Sat 9-5, Sun Noon-Midnight

S GENERAL FEDERATION OF WOMEN'S CLUBS*, Women's History & Resource Center, 1734 N St NW, 20036-2990. SAN 371-8417. Tel: 202-347-3168. FAX: 202-835-0246. E-mail: whrc@gfwc.org. Web Site: www.gfwc.org/whrc.htm. *Exec Dir,* Natasha Kalteis; *Dir,* Gail McCormick; Staff 2 (MLS 1, Non-MLS 1)
Founded 1984
Library Holdings: AV Mats 250; Bk Titles 1,500
Special Collections: Art & Artifacts Coll; GH Coll on UN Decade for Women, bks, mss; Women's History & Volunteerism (General Federation of Women's Clubs Archives), doc. Oral History
Subject Interests: Women's hist
Wireless access
Open Mon-Fri 9-5
Friends of the Library Group

C THE GEORGE WASHINGTON UNIVERSITY, Melvin Gelman Library, 2130 H St NW, Ste 201, 20052. SAN 336-741X. Tel: 202-994-6455. Circulation Tel: 202-994-6840. Interlibrary Loan Service Tel: 202-994-7128. Reference Tel: 202-994-6048. FAX: 202-994-6464. Interlibrary Loan Service FAX: 202-994-1340. Web Site: www.gwu.edu/gelman. *Univ Librn, Vice Provost for Libr,* Geneva Henry; *Assoc Univ Librn, Res & User Serv,* Debbie Bezanson; *Assoc Univ Librn, Spec Coll,* Elisabeth Kaplan; *Assoc Univ Librn, Digital Initiatives & Content Mgt,* Karim Boughida; Staff 76 (MLS 35, Non-MLS 41)
Founded 1821. Enrl 25,116; Fac 1,111; Highest Degree: Doctorate
Jul 2012-Jun 2013. Mats Exp $5,915,027, Books $996,077, Per/Ser (Incl. Access Fees) $3,584,937. Sal $6,342,921 (Prof $3,300,933)
Library Holdings: e-books 475,153; Bk Titles 1,706,288; Bk Vols 2,226,421
Special Collections: Africana Research Center (Walter Fauntroy Papers, John A Wilson Papers); American Labor History (International Brotherhood of Teamsters, National Education Association, American Association of University Professors); Art & Design Coll from the Corcoran; I Edward Kiev Judaica Coll; Media & Journalism (Jack Anderson Papers, Mutual Broadcasting System Records); Middle East Institute Rare Book Coll; University Archives (University Historical Material, Freeman-Watts Coll, Janet Travell Papers, Mount Vernon Seminary & College Coll); Washington Area & Holy Land (Map Coll); Washingtoniana (Washington Writers' Archive, PNC-Riggs Coll, C&O Canal Association, DC City Councilmember Papers, Metro History Coll). US Document Depository
Subject Interests: Art hist, Asian studies, Bus & mgt, Educ, Eng, European studies, Intl affairs, Polit sci, Slavic studies
Automation Activity & Vendor Info: (Acquisitions) Ex Libris Group; (Cataloging) Ex Libris Group; (Circulation) Ex Libris Group; (Course

Reserve) Ex Libris Group; (ILL) OCLC; (Media Booking) Ex Libris Group; (OPAC) Ex Libris Group; (Serials) Ex Libris Group
Database Vendor: EBSCOhost, Gale Cengage Learning, LexisNexis, OCLC FirstSearch, OVID Technologies, ProQuest
Wireless access
Publications: Gelman Exposed! (Newsletter)
Partic in Northeast Research Libraries Consortium (NERL); Washington Research Library Consortium
Special Services for the Blind - Accessible computers; Assistive/Adapted tech devices, equip & products; Braille equip; Handicapped awareness prog
Friends of the Library Group

Departmental Libraries:

CL JACOB BURNS LAW LIBRARY, 716 20th St NW, 20052, SAN 336-7444. Tel: 202-994-6648. Interlibrary Loan Service Tel: 202-994-4156. Reference Tel: 202-994-6647. FAX: 202-994-2874. Interlibrary Loan Service FAX: 202-994-0433. Web Site: www.law.gwu.edu/burns. *Assoc Dean & Dir,* Scott B Pagel; Tel: 202-994-7337, Fax: 202-994-1430, E-mail: spagel@law.gwu.edu; *Asst Dir, Admin,* Leslie A Lee; Tel: 202-994-2385, E-mail: llee@law.gwu.edu; *Asst Dir, Info Syst,* Nicole Harris; Tel: 202-994-4225, E-mail: nharris@law.gwu.edu; *Asst Dir, Pub Serv,* Deborah Norwood; Tel: 202-994-7338, E-mail: dnorwood@law.gwu.edu; *Asst Dir, Tech Serv,* Virginia Bryant; Tel: 202-994-1378, E-mail: vbryant@law.gwu.edu; *Head, Acq,* Trina Robinson; Tel: 202-994-8550, E-mail: trrobinson@law.gwu.edu; *Head, Coll Serv,* Iris M Lee; Tel: 202-994-2733, E-mail: ilee@law.gwu.edu; *Head, Doc Serv,* Lesliediana Jones; Tel: 202-994-9017, E-mail: ljones@law.gwu.edu; *Head, Info Serv,* Larry Ross; Tel: 202-994-0057, E-mail: lross@law.gwu.edu; *Head, Ref,* Germaine Leahy; Tel: 202-994-8551, E-mail: gleahy@law.gwu.edu; *Head, Ser,* Susan Chinoransky; Tel: 202-994-8902, E-mail: schinoransky@law.gwu.edu; *Bibliographer, Rare Bks,* Jennie C Meade; Tel: 202-994-6857, E-mail: jmeade@law.gwu.edu. Subject Specialists: *Info serv,* Nicole Harris; *Media,* Larry Ross; *Environ law,* Germaine Leahy; Staff 42 (MLS 22, Non-MLS 20)
Founded 1865. Enrl 1,749; Fac 97; Highest Degree: Doctorate
Library Holdings: Bk Titles 379,988; Bk Vols 677,379; Per Subs 5,006
Special Collections: Early French Law (French Coll)
Subject Interests: Environ law, Fr law, Intellectual property law, Intl law, Law, Legal hist
Automation Activity & Vendor Info: (Acquisitions) Innovative Interfaces, Inc; (Cataloging) Innovative Interfaces, Inc; (Circulation) Innovative Interfaces, Inc; (OPAC) Innovative Interfaces, Inc; (Serials) Innovative Interfaces, Inc
Database Vendor: Innovative Interfaces, Inc
Partic in Washington Research Library Consortium
Publications: A Legal Miscellanea (Newsletter); Basic Legal Research Guide Series (Research guide); Guide to the Law Library (Library handbook); Specialized Legal Research Guide Series (Research guide); The French Collection (Collection catalog)
Friends of the Library Group

ECKLES LIBRARY, 2100 Foxhall Rd NW, 20007-1199, SAN 302-6973. Tel: 202-242-6620. Reference Tel: 202-242-6666. FAX: 202-242-6632. E-mail: eckles@gwu.edu. Web Site: www.gwu.edu/gelman/eckles. *Interim Dir,* Zachary W Elder; Tel. 202-242-6621, E-mail: elder@gwu.edu; *Ref & Coll Develop Librn,* David Killian; Tel: 202-242-6623, E-mail: dkillian@gwu.edu; *Ref & Instruction Librn,* Bill Gillis; Tel: 202-242-8290, E-mail: gillis@gwu.edu; *Coordr, Outreach Serv,* Jessica A Matthews; Tel: 202-242-8294, E-mail: jorsulak@gwu.edu; *Info Tech, Pub Serv Spec,* Gary Williams; Tel: 202-242-6631, E-mail: garywil@gwu.edu; Staff 5 (MLS 4, Non-MLS 1)
Founded 1875. Enrl 700; Fac 35; Highest Degree: Doctorate
Library Holdings: Bk Titles 53,779; Bk Vols 63,406; Per Subs 154
Special Collections: Les Dames d'Escoffier Culinary Book Coll; Walter Beach Archives of the American Political Science Association
Subject Interests: Art, Art hist, Interior design, Women's studies

CM PAUL HIMMELFARB HEALTH SCIENCES LIBRARY, 2300 I St NW, 20037, SAN 336-7479. Tel: 202-994-2850. Interlibrary Loan Service Tel: 202-994-2860. FAX: 202-994-4343. Web Site: www.gwumc.edu/library. *Dir,* Anne Linton; Tel: 202-994-1826, E-mail: alinton@gwu.edu; *Assoc Dir, Coll & Acces Serv,* Kathe Obrig; Tel: 202-994-8906; *Assoc Dir, Pub Serv/Instruction,* Alexandra Gomes; Tel: 202-994-1825; Staff 14 (MLS 14)
Founded 1857. Enrl 1,000; Fac 400; Highest Degree: Doctorate
Library Holdings: e-journals 1,500; Bk Titles 27,000; Per Subs 500
Special Collections: Interviews with George Washington University VIPs from 1930-50's. Oral History
Automation Activity & Vendor Info: (Circulation) SirsiDynix; (Serials) SirsiDynix
Partic in OCLC Online Computer Library Center, Inc
Publications: Information Interface

VIRGINIA SCIENCE & TECHNOLOGY CAMPUS LIBRARY, 44983 Knoll Sq, Ste 179, Ashburn, 20147-2604, SAN 371-9642. Tel: 703-726-8230. FAX: 703-726-8237. E-mail: virginia@gwu.edu. Web Site: library.gwu.edu/virginia. *Ref & Instruction Librn,* Dorinne Banks; E-mail: dbanks@gwu.edu. Subject Specialists: *Higher educ,* Dorinne Banks; Staff 3 (MLS 1, Non-MLS 2)
Founded 1991. Enrl 555; Highest Degree: Doctorate
Library Holdings: Bk Titles 3,379; Bk Vols 3,458; Per Subs 61
Special Collections: Foundation Center Funding Information Network (Foundation Center database assistance available by appointment)
Subject Interests: Computer sci, Eng sci, Environ sci, Higher educ, Nursing, Pharmacogenomics, Physics, Transportation eng, Transportation safety
Function: Computers for patron use, Distance learning, Doc delivery serv, E-Reserves, Electronic databases & coll, Homebound delivery serv, ILL available, Ref serv available, Res libr, Scanner, Telephone ref, Workshops
Open Tues 11-3, Wed-Fri 9-7, Sat 9-5
Restriction: Limited access for the pub, Open to qualified scholars, Open to researchers by request, Photo ID required for access, Pub use on premises, Restricted pub use

C GEORGETOWN UNIVERSITY*, Joseph Mark Lauinger Library, 37th & N St NW, 20057-1174. SAN 336-7533. Tel: 202-687-7425. Circulation Tel: 202-687-7607. Interlibrary Loan Service Tel: 202-687-7428. Reference Tel: 202-687-7452. FAX: 202-687-7501. Interlibrary Loan Service FAX: 202-687-1215. Web Site: www.library.georgetown.edu. *Univ Librn,* Artemis Kirk; E-mail: agk3@georgetown.edu; *Assoc Univ Librn, Digital Serv & Tech Planning,* Shu-Chen Tsung; Tel: 202-687-7429, E-mail: tsungs@georgetown.edu; *Assoc Univ Librn, Scholarly Resources & Serv,* Position Currently Open; *Dir, Finance & Operations,* Phyllis Barrow; Tel: 202-687-7454, E-mail: barrowp@georgetown.edu; *Dir, Personnel & Staff Develop,* Deirdre Francis; Tel: 202-687-3980, E-mail: df235@georgetown.edu; *Dir, Planning & Assessment,* Stephanie Clark; Tel: 202-687-1601, E-mail: sc486@georgetown.edu; *Head, Access Serv,* Deborah Cook; Tel: 202-687-7461, E-mail: dac42@georgetown.edu; *Head, Coll Develop,* David Marshall; Tel: 202-687-7616, E-mail: marshald@georgetown.edu; *Head, Copyright & Digital Rights Mgt,* Joan Cheverie; Tel: 202-687-1870, E-mail: cheverij@georgetown.edu; *Head, Info Tech,* David Gewirtz; Tel: 202-687-7385, E-mail: dg287@georgetown.edu; *Head, Metadata Serv,* Susan Leister; Tel: 202-687-1557, E-mail: sel44@georgetown.edu; *Head, New Media Ctr,* Beth Marhanka; Tel: 202-687-7534, E-mail: marhankb@georgetown.edu; *Head, Res & Instruction,* William Wheeler; Tel: 202-687-6818, E-mail: wjw27@georgetown.edu; *Head, Spec Coll Res Ctr,* John Buchtel; Tel: 202-687-7475, E-mail: jb593@georgetown.edu; *Head, Woodstock Theol Ctr Libr,* Fr Leon Hooper; Tel: 202-687-4250, E-mail: jlh3@georgetown.edu; *Metadata Librn,* Wei Zhang; Staff 104 (MLS 34, Non MLS 70)
Founded 1789. Enrl 15,300; Fac 1,270; Highest Degree: Doctorate
Library Holdings: Bk Vols 2,326,901; Per Subs 47,969
Special Collections: Archives of Dag Hammarskjold College; Archives of Maryland Province, Society of Jesus; Archives of the American Political Science Association; Archives of Woodstock College; Catholic History; Diplomacy & Foreign Affairs; Political Science; United States-American & English Literature; University Archives; Woodstock Theological Library Coll. US Document Depository
Automation Activity & Vendor Info: (Acquisitions) Innovative Interfaces, Inc; (Cataloging) Innovative Interfaces, Inc; (Circulation) Innovative Interfaces, Inc; (Course Reserve) Innovative Interfaces, Inc; (ILL) OCLC; (OPAC) Innovative Interfaces, Inc; (Serials) Innovative Interfaces, Inc
Wireless access
Publications: Library Associates (Newsletter); Special Collections at Georgetown, A Descriptive Catalog
Partic in Chesapeake Information & Research Library Alliance (CIRLA); OCLC Online Computer Library Center, Inc
Restriction: Photo ID required for access
Friends of the Library Group

Departmental Libraries:

BLOMMER SCIENCE LIBRARY, 302 Reiss Science Bldg, Box 571230, 20057-1230. Tel: 202-687-5651. Circulation Tel: 202-687-5687. FAX: 202-687-5897. Web Site: www.library.georgetown.edu/blommer/. *Dept Head,* Gwen Owens; Tel: 202-687-5685, E-mail: owensg@georgetown.edu; Staff 4.5 (MLS 2, Non-MLS 2.5)
Open Mon-Thurs (Winter) 8:30am-11pm, Fri 8:30-6, Sat 11-7, Sun Noon-11; Mon-Thurs (Summer) 8:30am-9pm, Fri 8:30-6, Sat 10-5:30, Sun Noon-8

CM DAHLGREN MEMORIAL LIBRARY, Preclinical Science Bldg GM-7, 3900 Reservoir Rd NW, 20007. (Mail add: PO Box 571420, 20057-1420), SAN 336-7568. Tel: 202-687-1448. Interlibrary Loan Service Tel: 202-687-1029. Administration Tel: 202-687-1187. FAX: 202-687-1862. E-mail: dmlreference@georgetown.edu. Web Site: dml.georgetown.edu. *Assoc Dean, Knowledge Mgt & Dir,* Jett McCann; E-mail: jm594@georgetown.edu; *Sr Assoc Dir/Biomedical Informationist,* Douglas Varner; Tel: 202-687-1328, E-mail: dlv2@georgetown.edu; *Assoc Dir, Res & Access Mgt,* Linda Van Keuren; Tel: 202-687-1168, E-mail: lav30@georgetown.edu; *Assoc Dir, Info Serv,* Laurie Davidson; Tel: 202-687-7708, E-mail: lwd7@georgetown.edu; *Assoc Dir, Libr Computing Serv,* Taffy McKeon; Tel: 202-687-1537, E-mail: ktm4@georgetown.edu; *Digital Info Serv Mgr,* C Scott Dorris; Tel:

202-687-2942, E-mail: csd24@georgetown.edu; *Hospital Informationist/Hospital Outreach Librn,* Jonathan Hartmann; Tel: 202-687-1308, E-mail: jth52@georgetown.edu; *Interdisciplinary Res Support Librn,* Grant Connors; Tel: 202-687-2914, E-mail: gc275@georgetown.edu; *Med Illustration/Digital Imaging & Graphics Mgr,* David Klemm; Tel: 202-687-1148, E-mail: klemmd@georgetown.edu; *Educ Serv Coordr,* Sarah Cantrell; Tel: 202-687-8874, E-mail: sec62@georgetown.edu; *Fac Coordr,* Brandon Hudson; E-mail: bsh26@georgetown.edu; *Info Serv Coordr,* Meghan Wallace; Tel: 202-687-1173, E-mail: maw55@georgetown.edu; *ILL Coordr,* Eugennie Buckley; E-mail: buckleye@georgetown.edu; *Coordr of Res Serv,* Michele Malloy; Tel: 202-687-1783, E-mail: mlm236@georgetown.edu; *Curric Support Spec,* Dr Taeyeol Park; Tel: 202-687-5089, E-mail: tp3@georgetown.edu; Staff 12 (MLS 9, Non-MLS 3)

Founded 1912. Highest Degree: Doctorate

Library Holdings: e-books 1,500; e-journals 5,400; Bk Vols 6,000; Per Subs 10

Function: Computers for patron use, Doc delivery serv, e-mail & chat, Electronic databases & coll, Health sci info serv

Partic in Washington Research Library Consortium

Restriction: Badge access after hrs, Borrowing privileges limited to fac & registered students, Circ limited, Open to students, fac & staff, Restricted pub use

CM MATERNAL & CHILD HEALTH LIBRARY, 2115 Wisconsin Ave NW, Ste 601, 20007. (Mail add: PO Box 571272, 20057-1272), SAN 371-7402. Tel: 202-784-9770. Toll Free Tel: 877-624-1935. FAX: 202-784-9777. E-mail: mchgroup@georgetown.edu. Web Site: www.mchlibrary.info. *Dir, Libr Serv,* Olivia K Pickett; E-mail: opickett@ncemch.org; Staff 5 (MLS 3, Non-MLS 2)

Founded 1982

Library Holdings: Bk Vols 29,000; Per Subs 40

Special Collections: Final Reports of Projects Funded by US Maternal & Child Health Bureau; Hiscock Coll of EPSDT Program; US Children's Bureau Coll, 1912-1969, micro, publs

Subject Interests: Adolescent health, Child health, Infant health, Nutrition, Oral health, Pub health, Women's health

Open Mon-Fri 8:30-5

CL GEORGETOWN LAW LIBRARY (JOHN WOLFF & EDWARD BENNETT WILLIAMS LIBRARIES), 111 G St NW, 20001, SAN 336-7592. Circulation Tel: 202-662-4194 (Wolff Library), 202-662-9131 (Williams Library). Interlibrary Loan Service Tel: 202-662-9152. Reference Tel: 202-662-4195 (Wolff Library), 202-662-9140 (Williams Library). Administration Tel: 202-662-9160. FAX: 202-662-9168. E-mail: intlref@law.georgetown.edu. Web Site: www.ll.georgetown.edu. *Dir of Libr,* Michelle Wu; E-mail: mmw84@law.georgetown.edu; *Head, Access Serv,* Craig Lelansky; *Head, Acq, Ser & Coll Care,* Position Currently Open; *Head, Cat & Metadata Serv,* Yan Liao; *Head, Digital Initiatives & Spec Coll,* Leah Prescott; *Head, Electronic Res & Serv,* Roger Skalbeck; *Head, Ref,* Christine Ciambella; *Head, Res Serv,* Thanh Nguyen; *Assoc Law Librn, Intl & Foreign Law,* Marylin Raisch; *Asst Intl & Foreign Law Librn,* Mabel Shaw; *Electronic Coll Librn,* Smita Parkhe; *Electronic Res & Serv Librn,* Matthew Zimmerman; *Foreign & Intl Ref Librn,* Heather Casey; *Instrul Tech Librn,* Jill Smith; *Ref Librn,* Barbara Monroe; *Ref Librn,* Carla Wale; *Ref Librn,* Jason Zarin; *Res Serv Librn,* Esther Cho; *Res Serv Librn,* Morgan Stoddard; *Spec Coll Librn,* Hannah Miller; *Spec Projects,* Jennifer Davitt; Staff 54 (MLS 28, Non-MLS 26)

Founded 1870

Library Holdings: Bk Titles 800,000; Bk Vols 1,000,000

Special Collections: US Document Depository

Subject Interests: Intl law

Automation Activity & Vendor Info: (Acquisitions) Innovative Interfaces, Inc; (Cataloging) Innovative Interfaces, Inc; (Circulation) Innovative Interfaces, Inc; (Course Reserve) Innovative Interfaces, Inc; (ILL) Innovative Interfaces, Inc; (Media Booking) Innovative Interfaces, Inc; (OPAC) Innovative Interfaces, Inc; (Serials) Innovative Interfaces, Inc

Database Vendor: LexisNexis, Westlaw

Partic in OCLC Online Computer Library Center, Inc

Publications: Friends of the Library (Newsletter); Guides

Open Mon-Fri 8am-Midnight, Sat 9am-10pm, Sun 10am-Midnight

Restriction: Restricted access

Friends of the Library Group

S GERMAN HISTORICAL INSTITUTE LIBRARY, 1607 New Hampshire Ave NW, 20009-2562. SAN 323-8350. Tel: 202-387-3355. FAX: 202-483-3430. E-mail: library@ghi-dc.org. Web Site: www.ghi-dc.org. *Head Librn,* Evi Hartmann; E-mail: hartmann@ghi-dc.org; Staff 3 (MLS 1, Non-MLS 2)

Founded 1987

Library Holdings: DVDs 100; e-journals 94; Bk Vols 50,000; Per Subs 220; Videos 30

Subject Interests: German hist, German-Am relations

Wireless access

Open Mon-Thurs 9-5, Fri 9-4

Restriction: In-house use for visitors

Friends of the Library Group

S GERONTOLOGICAL SOCIETY OF AMERICA*, Association for Gerontology in Higher Education Resource Library, 1220 L St NW, No 901, 20005. SAN 371-5620. Tel: 202-289-9806. FAX: 202-289-9824. E-mail: info@aghe.org. Web Site: www.aghe.org. *Dir,* Angela Baker; Tel: 202-289-9806, Ext 125, E-mail: abaker@aghe.org

Library Holdings: Bk Titles 2,500

Restriction: Open by appt only

GL GOVERNMENT PRINTING OFFICE*, Office of General Counsel Law Library, 732 N Capitol NW, Rm C-818, MS GCL, 20401. SAN 377-2012. Tel: 202-512-0064. FAX: 202-512-0076. *Librn,* Suzanne Campbell

Library Holdings: Bk Vols 2,000; Per Subs 100

Database Vendor: LexisNexis, Westlaw

Open Mon-Fri 9:30-6

M ATIN GUHA, MD MEDICAL LIBRARY*, Providence Hospital, 1150 Varnum St NE, 20017. SAN 302-7554. Tel: 202-269-7144. Interlibrary Loan Service Tel: 202-269-7143. FAX: 202-269-7142. *Dir,* RoseMarie Leone Winiewicz; E-mail: rleone@provhosp.org; Staff 3 (MLS 1, Non-MLS 2)

Library Holdings: Bk Vols 505; Per Subs 150

Subject Interests: Hospital admin, Med, Nursing

Partic in National Network of Libraries of Medicine

Open Mon-Fri 8-5

Restriction: Hospital employees & physicians only, Not open to pub

S HILLWOOD ESTATE, MUSEUM & GARDENS*, 4155 Linnean Ave NW, 20008. SAN 374-6011. Tel: 202-243-3953. FAX: 202-966-7846. Web Site: www.hillwoodmuseum.org/resources/library.html. *Head Librn,* Kristen Regina; E-mail: kregina@hillwoodmuseum.org; *Asst Librn,* Position Currently Open; Staff 2 (MLS 2)

Founded 1966

Library Holdings: Bk Titles 35,000; Per Subs 30

Special Collections: 18th Century French Decorative Arts; Imperial Russian Decorative Arts

Automation Activity & Vendor Info: (Acquisitions) Inmagic, Inc.; (OPAC) Inmagic, Inc.

Database Vendor: JSTOR, OCLC FirstSearch, Oxford Online

Wireless access

Restriction: Open by appt only

L HOLLAND & KNIGHT LAW LIBRARY*, 2099 Pennsylvania Ave NW, Ste 100, 20006. SAN 370-7636. Tel: 202-955-3000. FAX: 202-955-5564. Web Site: hklaw.com. *Head Librn,* Dominique Cain; Staff 3 (MLS 2, Non-MLS 1)

Library Holdings: Bk Vols 3,000; Per Subs 40

Subject Interests: Aviation, Construction, Housing, Real estate, Securities

Restriction: Open by appt only

C HOWARD UNIVERSITY LIBRARIES, Founders Library, 500 Howard Pl NW, 20059. Interlibrary Loan Service Tel: 202-806-5716, 202-806-7132. Reference Tel: 202-806-7250, 202-806-7446. Administration Tel: 202-806-7234. Information Services Tel: 202-806-7443. Interlibrary Loan Service FAX: 202-806-4622. Administration FAX: 202-806-5903. Web Site: www.howard.edu/library. *Dir,* Dr Howard Dodson; E-mail: howard.dodson@howard.edu; *Assoc Dir, Univ Archivist,* Dr Clifford L Muse, Jr; Tel: 202-806-7498, E-mail: cmuse@howard.edu; *Assoc Dir,* Dr Arthuree McLaughlin Wright; E-mail: arwright@howard.edu; *Asst Dir,* Carrie M Hackney; Tel: 202-806-0768, E-mail: chackney@howard.edu; *Curator, Interim Chief Librn,* Joellen ElBashir; Tel: 202-806-4261, E-mail: jelbashir@howard.edu; *Fac Adminr & Head, Multimedia Serv,* Errol Watkis; Tel: 202-806-4091, E-mail: ewatkis@howard.edu; *Head, Access Serv & Soc Work Librn,* Leida Torres; Tel: 202-806-7213, E-mail: leida.torres@howard.edu; *Head, Acq & Ser,* Alliah V Humber; Tel: 202-884-1535, E-mail: ahumber@howard.edu; *Head, Metadata & Res Description Serv,* Dr Andrew Sulavik; Tel: 202-806-4224, E-mail: andrew.sulavik@howard.edu; *Head, Ref & Instruction,* Celia C Daniel; E-mail: ccdaniel@howard.edu; *Bus Librn,* Tommy Waters; Tel: 202-806-1599, E-mail: tommy.waters@howard.edu; *First Year Experience Librn & Educ Liaison,* Niketha O McKenzie; Tel: 202-806-7301, E-mail: niketha.mckenzie@howard.edu; *Metada Cataloger,* Sean Varner; Tel: 202-884-1503, E-mail: sean.varner@howard.edu; *Pub Relations & Communications Spec,* D Kamili Anderson; Tel: 202-806-7237, E-mail: kamili.anderson@howard.edu. Subject Specialists: *Relig,* Carrie M Hackney; *Soc work,* Leida Torres; *Art,* Alliah V Humber; *Classics, Philos, Theol,* Dr Andrew Sulavik; *African-Am studies, Eng,* Celia C Daniel; *Bus, Polit sci,* Tommy Waters; *Educ,* Niketha O McKenzie; *Music,* Sean Varner; Staff 27 (MLS 17, Non-MLS 10)

Founded 1939. Enrl 8,941; Fac 1,024; Highest Degree: Doctorate

Jul 2012-Jun 2013 Income (Main and Other College/University Libraries) $5,875,762. Mats Exp $2,955,862. Sal $2,889,900

Library Holdings: Bk Vols 2,402,648
Special Collections: Channing Pollock Theatre Coll; Moorland Spingarn Research Center (African Diaspora)
Subject Interests: Humanities, Soc sci, STEM
Automation Activity & Vendor Info: (Acquisitions) SerialsSolutions; (Cataloging) OCLC; (Serials) SerialsSolutions
Database Vendor: ABC-CLIO, Alexander Street Press, American Mathematical Society, American Psychological Association (APA), Annual Reviews, BioOne, CQ Press, CRC Press/Taylor & Francis Group, CredoReference, Dun & Bradstreet, ebrary, EBSCOhost, Elsevier, Emerald, Ex Libris Group, Foundation Center, Gale Cengage Learning, Greenwood Publishing Group, IEEE (Institute of Electrical & Electronics Engineers), IOP, JSTOR, LexisNexis, Marcive, Inc, Mergent Online, Nature Publishing Group, OCLC, Project MUSE, ProQuest, RefWorks, Sage, ScienceDirect, Scopus, SerialsSolutions, Springer-Verlag, Springshare, LLC, Standard & Poor's, Swets Information Services, Wiley InterScience, YBP Library Services
Wireless access
Function: Archival coll, AV serv, Computers for patron use, Copy machines, Doc delivery serv, e-mail & chat, E-Reserves, Electronic databases & coll, Handicapped accessible, ILL available, Mail & tel request accepted, Microfiche/film & reading machines, Notary serv, Online cat, Online info literacy tutorials on the web & in blackboard, Online ref, Online searches, Orientations, Outreach serv, Outside serv via phone, mail, e-mail & web, Photocopying/Printing, Pub access computers, Ref & res, Ref serv available, Ref serv in person, Referrals accepted, Res libr, Workshops
Restriction: 24-hr pass syst for students only
Friends of the Library Group

Departmental Libraries:

ARCHITECTURE, 2366 Sixth St NW, 20059, SAN 336-7835. Tel: 202-806-7774. FAX: 202-806-4441. *Curator,* Alliah Humber; Tel: 202-806-7773, E-mail: ahumber@howard.edu; Staff 2 (Non-MLS 2)
Founded 1971. Enrl 180; Fac 19; Highest Degree: Bachelor
Library Holdings: Bk Vols 33,876; Per Subs 62
Subject Interests: Archit, Bldg construction, Design, Environ planning, Interior design, Landscape archit, Urban planning
Function: Res libr
Open Mon-Thurs 8:30-6, Fri 8:30-5

BUSINESS, 2600 Sixth St NW, 20059, SAN 336-786X. Tel: 202-806-1561. FAX: 202-797-6393. *Asst Dir,* Lucille Smiley; Tel: 202-806-1560; Staff 5 (MLS 1, Non-MLS 4)
Founded 1970. Enrl 1,366; Fac 80; Highest Degree: Doctorate
Library Holdings: Bk Vols 94,331; Per Subs 1,100
Subject Interests: Acctg, Electronic commerce, Finance, Housing, Info syst, Mgt, Mkt, Real estate
Open Mon-Fri 8:30-5
Restriction: Open to students, fac & staff, Restricted pub use

DEPARTMENT OF AFRO-AMERICAN STUDIES RESOURCE CENTER, 500 Howard Pl NW, Rm 300, 20059, SAN 336-8076. Tel: 202-806-7242. FAX: 202-986-0538. *Dir,* E Ethelbert Miller; E-mail: emiller@howard.edu
Founded 1969
Library Holdings: Bk Vols 32,000
Subject Interests: African-Am studies, Lit
Open Mon-Fri 9-4:30

CR DIVINITY, 1400 Shepherd St NE, 20017, SAN 336-7924. Tel: 202-806-0760. Interlibrary Loan Service Tel: 202-806-5716. FAX: 202-806-0711. *Head Librn,* Carrie Hackney; Tel: 202-806-0768, E-mail: chackney@howard.edu; Staff 3 (MLS 1, Non-MLS 2)
Founded 1935. Enrl 286; Fac 14; Highest Degree: Doctorate
Library Holdings: Bk Vols 121,000; Per Subs 240
Special Collections: African Heritage Coll
Subject Interests: Biblical studies, Church hist, Ethics, Pastoral counseling, World relig
Automation Activity & Vendor Info: (Acquisitions) Innovative Interfaces, Inc; (Cataloging) Innovative Interfaces, Inc; (Circulation) Innovative Interfaces, Inc; (Course Reserve) Innovative Interfaces, Inc; (ILL) Innovative Interfaces, Inc; (Media Booking) Innovative Interfaces, Inc; (OPAC) Innovative Interfaces, Inc; (Serials) Innovative Interfaces, Inc
Open Mon-Thurs 8:30-10, Fri & Sat 8:30-5
Friends of the Library Group

CL LAW LIBRARY, 2929 Van Ness St NW, 20008, SAN 336-8106. Tel: 202-806-8045. Interlibrary Loan Service Tel: 202-806-8207. Reference Tel: 202-806-8208. FAX: 202-806-8400. Web Site: www.law.howard.edu/library/. *Dir,* Rhea Ballard-Thrower; Tel: 202-806-8047, E-mail: rballard@law.howard.edu; *Asst Dir, Pub Serv,* Eileen Santos; Tel: 202-806-8301, Fax: 202-806-8590, E-mail: esantos@law.howard.edu; *Asst Dir, Tech Serv,* Ruth Owopetu; Tel: 202-806-8036, E-mail: rowopetu@law.howard.edu; *Acq Librn,* Kwei Hung; Tel: 202-806-8051, E-mail: khung@law.howard.edu; *ILL,* Felicia Ayanbiola; E-mail: fayanbiola@law.howard.edu; Staff 9 (MLS 8, Non-MLS 1)
Founded 1868. Enrl 450; Fac 36; Highest Degree: Doctorate
Library Holdings: Bk Titles 28,500; Bk Vols 253,000; Per Subs 621
Special Collections: Indritz Papers
Subject Interests: Civil rights
Partic in Consortium of Southeastern Law Libraries; District of Columbia Area Health Science Libraries; Washington Research Library Consortium
Special Services for the Blind - Braille equip
Open Mon-Fri 7am-11pm, Sat 9-9, Sun 11-11
Restriction: Non-circulating to the pub

MOORLAND-SPINGARN RESEARCH CENTER, 500 Howard Pl NW, 20059, SAN 336-8130. Tel: 202-806-7240. Reference Tel: 202-806-4237. FAX: 202-806-6405. *Dir,* Position Currently Open
Founded 1914
Library Holdings: Bk Vols 200,000; Per Subs 632
Special Collections: Africa; Afro-American & Afro-Latin Authors (Spingarn Coll); Arthur B Spingarn Music Coll, sheet music; Civil Rights (Ralph J Bunche Oral History Coll), tapes; Journalism (Documentary Series on the Black Press), tapes; Mary O'H Williamson Photograph Coll; Rose McClendon-Carl Van Vechten Photograph Coll. Oral History
Subject Interests: Africa, African-Am, Caribbean, S Am
Open Mon & Wed 9-1 & 2-4:45, Fri 9-1 & 2-4:30
Restriction: Non-circulating
Friends of the Library Group

SOCIAL WORK, 601 Howard Pl NW, 20059, SAN 336-7959. Tel: 202-806-7316. *Head Librn,* Carrie Hackney; Staff 3 (MLS 1, Non-MLS 2)
Library Holdings: Bk Vols 40,000; Per Subs 344
Subject Interests: Hist, Philos, Soc work mat
Open Mon-Thurs (Fall-Spring) 8:30am-10pm, Fri 8:30-5, Sat & Sun 1-6; Mon-Fri (Summer) 8:30-5

CM LOUIS STOKES HEALTH SCIENCES LIBRARY, 501 W St NW, 20059, SAN 336-7711. Tel: 202-884-1500. Circulation Tel: 202-884-1520. Interlibrary Loan Service Tel: 202-884-1503. Reference Tel: 202-884-1522. Administration Tel: 202-884-1732. FAX: 202-884-1733. Circulation FAX: 202-884-1506. Web Site: hsl.howard.edu. *Exec Dir,* Cynthia L Henderson; E-mail: cynthia.henderson@howard.edu; *Dir, Operations,* Toni Yancey; Tel: 202-884-1526, E-mail: toni.yancey@howard.edu; Staff 15 (MLS 8, Non-MLS 7)
Founded 1927. Highest Degree: Doctorate
Library Holdings: Bk Vols 100,000; Per Subs 350
Special Collections: Allied Health & Pharmacy; Biographical Files on Blacks in Medicine, Dentistry & Nursing; Local History (Howard University, Colleges of Medicine, Dentistry & Nursing)
Partic in National Network of Libraries of Medicine Southeastern Atlantic Region
Open Mon Thurs 8am-Midnight, Fri 8-5, Sat 9-5, Sun Noon-Midnight

L HUGHES, HUBBARD & REED LLP LIBRARY, 1775 I St NW, Ste 600, 20006-2401. SAN 375-0213. Tel: 202-721-4600. FAX: 202-721-4646. Web Site: www.hugheshubbard.com. *Librn,* Tina Ramoy; E-mail: tinasr@hotmail.com
Library Holdings: Bk Vols 5,000; Per Subs 10
Wireless access
Restriction: Staff & mem only

G JOHN T HUGHES LIBRARY*, Defense Intelligence Agency, (MCA-4), Bldg 6000, Bolling Air Force Base, 20340-5100. SAN 374-597X. Circulation Tel: 202-231-2935. Interlibrary Loan Service Tel: 202-231-3839. Administration Tel: 202-231-3777. Automation Services Tel: 202-231-3863. Information Services Tel: 202-231-3836. Circulation FAX: 202-231-3838. *Dir,* Position Currently Open; Staff 9 (MLS 6, Non-MLS 3)
Founded 1992
Library Holdings: Audiobooks 375; CDs 450; DVDs 1,000; e-journals 456; Bk Titles 83,789; Bk Vols 97,989; Per Subs 854; Talking Bks 975; Videos 1,500
Special Collections: Diaries & Personal Papers of Ambassador Vernon A Walters
Automation Activity & Vendor Info: (Cataloging) Ex Libris Group; (Circulation) Ex Libris Group; (Course Reserve) Ex Libris Group; (ILL) Ex Libris Group; (OPAC) Ex Libris Group; (Serials) Ex Libris Group
Database Vendor: 3M Library Systems, Bowker, Dialog, EBSCO Information Services, EBSCOhost, Ex Libris Group, Gale Cengage Learning, H W Wilson, Jane's, JSTOR, LexisNexis, OCLC FirstSearch, OCLC WorldShare Interlibrary Loan, ProQuest, Wilson - Wilson Web
Function: ILL available
Publications: Guide to Library Services
Partic in Fedlink
Restriction: Restricted access

S THE HUMANE SOCIETY OF THE UNITED STATES LIBRARY*, 2100 L St NW, 20037. SAN 376-1975. Tel: 202-452-1100. FAX: 202-258-3078. Web Site: www.hsus.org.
Library Holdings: Bk Vols 4,000; Per Subs 200
Subject Interests: Animal welfare

S INSTITUTE OF INTERNATIONAL FINANCE LIBRARY*, 1333 H St NW, Ste 800E, 20005-4770. SAN 329-1634. Tel: 202-857-3600. FAX: 202-775-1430. E-mail: info@iif.com. Web Site: www.iif.com. *Librn,* Charlotte Hannagan
Library Holdings: Bk Titles 2,000; Per Subs 450
Database Vendor: Factiva.com
Restriction: Staff use only

S INSTITUTE OF TRANSPORTATION ENGINEERS*, Traffic Calming Library, 1099 14th St NW, Ste 300W, 20005-3438. SAN 377-4112. Tel: 202-289-0222, Ext 120. FAX: 202-289-7722. E-mail: ite_staff@ite.org. Web Site: www.ite.org. *Info Serv Mgr,* Zach Pleasant; E-mail: zpleasant@ite.org
Library Holdings: CDs 150; Bk Titles 2,000; Videos 100
Open Mon-Fri 8:30-4:30

S INTER-AMERICAN DEVELOPMENT BANK LIBRARY*, Felipe Herrera Library, 1300 New York Ave NW, Stop W-0102, 20577. SAN 336-8165. Tel: 202-623-3211. FAX: 202-623-3183. E-mail: library@iadb.org. Web Site: www.iadb.org/lib. *Chief, Libr Serv,* Norma Palomino; Tel: 202-623-3918, E-mail: npalomino@iadb.org; *Syst/Electronic Info Res Librn,* Rodrigo Calloni; Tel: 202-623-2952, E-mail: rcalloni@iadb.org; Staff 5 (MLS 2, Non-MLS 3)
Founded 1960
Library Holdings: Bk Titles 100,000; Per Subs 1,500
Special Collections: International Documents Coll (UN, OECD, World Bank, FAO, etc); Latin American & Caribbean History
Subject Interests: Latin Am & Caribbean soc & econ develop
Automation Activity & Vendor Info: (Acquisitions) Ex Libris Group; (Cataloging) Ex Libris Group; (Circulation) Ex Libris Group; (ILL) OCLC ILLiad; (OPAC) Ex Libris Group; (Serials) Ex Libris Group
Database Vendor: Baker & Taylor, Blackwell, Cambridge Scientific Abstracts, Checkpoint Systems, Inc, Dialog, EBSCO Information Services, EBSCOhost, Ex Libris Group, JSTOR, LexisNexis, OCLC, OCLC FirstSearch, OCLC WorldShare Interlibrary Loan, Oxford Online, ProQuest, ScienceDirect
Wireless access
Function: Ref & res, Web-catalog
Partic in OCLC Online Computer Library Center, Inc
Open Mon-Fri 10-5
Restriction: Borrowing requests are handled by ILL, Internal circ only, Non-circulating to the pub, Res pass required for non-affiliated visitors

S INTERNATIONAL CENTER FOR RESEARCH ON WOMEN LIBRARY, 1120 20th St NW, Ste 500 N, 20036. SAN 326-2847. Tel: 202-742-1226, 202-797-0007. FAX: 202-797-0020. E-mail: library@icrw.org. Web Site: www.icrw.org. *Sr Info Res Spec,* Laurie Calhoun; E-mail: lcalhoun@icrw.org; Staff 1 (MLS 1)
Founded 1976
Library Holdings: Bk Titles 12,700; Per Subs 20
Subject Interests: Gender studies, HIV-AIDS, Intl develop
Wireless access
Function: ILL available, Res libr
Partic in Association of Population/Family Planning Libraries & Information Centers-International (APLIC-I)
Restriction: Employees & their associates, In-house use for visitors, Open by appt only, Open to researchers by request

S INTERNATIONAL FOOD POLICY RESEARCH INSTITUTE LIBRARY*, 2033 K St NW, 20006-1002. SAN 302-6817. Tel: 202-862-5600, 202-862-5614. Reference Tel: 202-862-5616. FAX: 202-467-4439. E-mail: ifpri-library@cgiar.org. Web Site: www.ifpri.org. *Head Librn,* Luz Alvare; E-mail: l.alvare@cgiar.org; Staff 2 (MLS 2)
Founded 1975
Library Holdings: Bk Vols 8,200; Per Subs 129
Subject Interests: Developing countries, Environment, Food admin, Intl trade, Nutrition
Database Vendor: OCLC FirstSearch
Wireless access
Publications: New Acquisitions List
Restriction: Open by appt only

C INTERNATIONAL GRADUATE UNIVERSITY LIBRARY*, Capitol Hill Campus, 1325 D St SE, 22003. SAN 320-2704. Tel: 202-544-1555. FAX: 202-547-8819. E-mail: igu@internationalgraduateuniversity.org. Web Site: www.internationalgraduateuniversity.org. *Dir,* Dr Jean Boak
Founded 1967. Enrl 120
Library Holdings: Bk Vols 23,000
Special Collections: American History & Government; District of Columbia Court of Appeals & District of Columbia Law Documents (Judge Godfrey Munter Coll); Government Procurement (Paul H Gantt Coll)
Subject Interests: Behav sci, Develop planning, Environ mgt, Govt, Govt procurement, Origins of democracy, Polit sci, Res mgt

L IVINS, PHILIPS & BARKER LIBRARY*, 1700 Pennsylvania Ave NW, Ste 600, 20006. SAN 377-4635. Tel: 202-393-7600. FAX: 202-347-4256. Web Site: www.ipbtax.com. *Librn,* Jeffrey Freilich; E-mail: jefff@ipbtax.com
Library Holdings: Bk Vols 3,000; Per Subs 25
Subject Interests: Employee benefits, Tax
Database Vendor: LexisNexis, Westlaw
Open Mon-Fri 8:30-5

S JAPAN-AMERICAN SOCIETY OF WASHINGTON DC LIBRARY*, 1819 L St NW, Level 1B, 20036. SAN 375-7773. Tel: 202-833-2210. FAX: 202-833-2456. E-mail: jaswdc@us-japan.org. Web Site: www.us-japan.org/dc. *Pres,* John Malott
Library Holdings: Bk Titles 1,000; Per Subs 10
Subject Interests: Japanese studies

C JOHNS HOPKINS UNIVERSITY LIBRARIES*, Washington Library Resource Center, 1717 Massachusetts Ave, 20036. Tel: 202-452-0714. E-mail: washrocklibraries@jhu.edu. *Mgr,* Sharon Morris; E-mail: smorris@jhu.edu

C JOHNS HOPKINS UNIVERSITY SCHOOL OF ADVANCED INTERNATIONAL STUDIES*, Sydney R & Elsa W Mason Library, 1740 Massachusetts Ave NW, 20036. SAN 302-6868. Tel: 202-663-5900. Interlibrary Loan Service Tel: 202-663-5908. Reference Tel: 202-663-5901. Administration Tel: 202-663-5905. FAX: 202-663-5916. E-mail: saislibrary@jhu.edu. Web Site: www.sais-jhu.edu/library. *Dir,* Sheila Thalhimer; E-mail: sthalhimer@jhu.edu; *Circ Mgr,* Dina Herbert; *Electronic Res,* Stephen A Sears; Tel: 202-663-5907, E-mail: sasears@jhu.edu; *Reader Serv,* Linda Carlson; Tel: 202-663-5903, E-mail: lcarlson@jhu.edu; *Tech Serv,* Jennifer Kusmik; Tel: 202-663-5958, E-mail: jkusmik@jhu.edu; Staff 15 (MLS 5, Non-MLS 10)
Founded 1943. Enrl 550; Fac 100; Highest Degree: Doctorate
Library Holdings: Bk Titles 70,000; Bk Vols 110,000; Per Subs 950
Automation Activity & Vendor Info: (Acquisitions) SirsiDynix; (Cataloging) SirsiDynix; (Circulation) SirsiDynix; (Course Reserve) Docutek; (ILL) OCLC ILLiad; (OPAC) SirsiDynix
Database Vendor: Cambridge Scientific Abstracts, EBSCOhost, JSTOR, LexisNexis, Newsbank, OCLC FirstSearch, OCLC WorldShare Interlibrary Loan, OVID Technologies, ProQuest, ScienceDirect, Westlaw, Wilson - Wilson Web
Wireless access
Partic in OCLC Online Computer Library Center, Inc
Restriction: Not open to pub

S JOINT WORLD BANK-INTERNATIONAL MONETARY FUND LIBRARY*, 700 19th St NW, 20431. SAN 321-9062. Tel: 202-623-7054. FAX: 202-623-6417. E-mail: jlibrary@worldbank.org. Web Site: jolis.worldbankimflib.org. *Dep Div Chief,* Karen Eggert; Staff 32 (MLS 21, Non-MLS 11)
Founded 1946
Library Holdings: e-books 3,000; e-journals 3,000; Bk Titles 149,332; Per Subs 593
Special Collections: Bretton Woods Coll
Subject Interests: Banking, Econ develop, Intl econ, Intl finance, Money
Publications: A Basic Collection for Central Bank Libraries (1984); Blueprint: Bibliolist Updates in Print (Monthly); Economics & Finance Indexes: Index to Periodical Articles, 1947-1971 (1972, 4 vol); First Supplement, 1972-1974; IntlEc: Index to International Economics, Development & Finance, 1981-1991; Second Supplement, 1975-1977; The Developing Areas, a Classified Bibliography of the Joint Bank-Fund Library (1975, 3 vols)
Restriction: Staff use only

L JONES DAY*, Law Library, 51 Louisiana Ave NW, 20001-2113. SAN 372-3232. Tel: 202-879-3939, 202-879-3953. FAX: 202-626-1700. Web Site: www.jonesday.com. *Librn,* Cameron Gowan
Library Holdings: Bk Vols 10,000

L K&L GATES LLP*, Law Library, 1601 K St NW, L-3, 20006. SAN 372-1485. Tel: 202-661-3715. Interlibrary Loan Service Tel: 202-778-9165. FAX: 202-778-9100. Web Site: www.klgates.com. *Libr Mgr,* Walker Chaffin; Tel: 202-778-9162, E-mail: walker.chaffin@klgates.com; *Law Librn,* Gretchen W Asmuth; E-mail: gretchen.asmuth@klgates.com; *ILL/Doc Delivery Serv,* Jason Harrington; *Ref Serv,* Justin Resti; Tel: 202-778-9169; Staff 6 (MLS 2, Non-MLS 4)
Founded 1973
Library Holdings: Bk Titles 6,000; Bk Vols 10,000; Per Subs 250
Subject Interests: Banking, Investment mgt, Maritime law, Taxation, Trial practice
Automation Activity & Vendor Info: (Acquisitions) SIRSI WorkFlows; (Cataloging) SydneyPlus; (OPAC) SIRSI-iLink; (Serials) SIRSI WorkFlows

Database Vendor: Bloomberg, CQ Press, Dialog, Dun & Bradstreet, GalleryWatch, HeinOnline, Hoovers, IEEE (Institute of Electrical & Electronics Engineers), LexisNexis, Mergent Online, OCLC FirstSearch, Westlaw, Westlaw Business
Wireless access
Function: CD-ROM, Computer training, Computers for patron use, Copy machines, Doc delivery serv, Electronic databases & coll, ILL available, Notary serv, Online cat, Online ref, Online searches, Orientations, Ref & res, Telephone ref
Restriction: Employee & client use only, External users must contact libr

L KATTEN MUCHIN ROSENMAN LLP*, Law Library, 2900 K St NW, Ste 200, 20007. SAN 372-3879. Tel: 202-625-3500. FAX: 202-298-7570. Web Site: www.kattenlaw.com. *Librn,* Lourie Russell; E-mail: lourie.russell@kattenlaw.com
Founded 1974
Library Holdings: Bk Vols 10,000; Per Subs 100
Subject Interests: Corporate, Real estate
Automation Activity & Vendor Info: (Cataloging) EOS International; (Circulation) EOS International; (Serials) EOS International
Database Vendor: Westlaw
Partic in OCLC Online Computer Library Center, Inc
Open Mon-Fri 8-5

L KING & SPALDING*, Law Library, 1700 Pennsylvania Ave NW, Ste 200, 20006-4706. SAN 320-4340. Tel: 202-737-0500. FAX: 202-626-3737. E-mail: kingspalding@kslaw.com. Web Site: www.kslaw.com. *Librn,* Sara Uehlein
Library Holdings: Bk Vols 10,000
Restriction: Staff use only

L KIRKLAND & ELLIS LLP LIBRARY*, 655 15th St NW, Ste 1200, 20005-5793. SAN 302-6892. Tel: 202-879-5000, 202-879-5113. FAX: 202-879-5200. *Librn,* Ansley Calhoun; Staff 8 (MLS 3, Non-MLS 5)
Founded 1951
Library Holdings: Bk Titles 6,500; Bk Vols 10,000; Per Subs 100
Subject Interests: Law, Legislation
Wireless access
Open Mon-Fri 9-5:30

L KIRKPATRICK & LOCKHART, PRESTON, GATES, ELLIS*, Law Library, 1601 K St NW, 20006-1600. SAN 371-0319. Tel: 202-778-9000 (main), 202-778-9160. FAX: 202-778-9100. Web Site: www.klgates.com. *Libr Mgr,* Walker Chaffin; E-mail: walker.chaffin@klgates.com; *Law Librn,* Gretchen Asmuth
Library Holdings: Bk Vols 11,000; Per Subs 350
Subject Interests: Securities
Database Vendor: Dialog, LexisNexis, Westlaw
Open Mon-Fri 9-5:30
Restriction: Staff use only

S KUTAK & ROCK LIBRARY*, 1101 Connecticut Ave NW, Ste 1000, 20036. SAN 370-1476. Tel: 202-828-2400. FAX: 202-828-2488. *Librn,* Position Currently Open
Library Holdings: Bk Vols 2,500; Per Subs 200
Special Collections: Security Exchange Commission (microfiche)
Partic in Dialog Corp; Westlaw
Restriction: Open by appt only

S LEAGUE OF ARAB STATES*, Arab Information Center, 1100 17th St NW, Ste 602, 20036-3602. SAN 325-741X. Tel: 202-265-3210. FAX: 202-331-1525. E-mail: arableague@aol.com. *In Charge,* Dr Hussein Hassouna
Library Holdings: Bk Vols 1,000; Per Subs 12
Restriction: Staff use only

P LIBRARY OF CONGRESS*, 101 Independence Ave SE, 20540. SAN 336-8343. Tel: 202-707-5000. Interlibrary Loan Service Tel: 202-707-5444. FAX: 202-707-1925. Web Site: www.loc.gov. *Librn of Congress,* Dr James H Billington; Tel: 202-707-5205; *Dep Librn,* Robert Dizard; *Head, Ref,* Carolyn Larson; *Assoc Librn, Libr Serv,* Roberta I Shaffer; *Assoc Librn, Strategic Initiatives,* Laura Campbell
Founded 1800
Library Holdings: Large Print Bks 11,500; Bk Vols 31,000,000
Special Collections: Gutenberg Bible; Manuscripts of Eminent Americans; Papers of the first 23 Presidents
Automation Activity & Vendor Info: (Acquisitions) Ex Libris Group; (Cataloging) Ex Libris Group; (Circulation) Ex Libris Group; (OPAC) Ex Libris Group; (Serials) Ex Libris Group
Wireless access
Publications: Library of Congress Information Bulletin (biweekly); The Gazette (weekly staff newsp)
Partic in Association of Research Libraries (ARL); OCLC Online Computer Library Center, Inc; OCLC Research Library Partnership
Special Services for the Deaf - Spec interest per; Staff with knowledge of sign lang; TTY equip
Special Services for the Blind - Reader equip
Open Mon-Fri 8-4:30
Friends of the Library Group
Branches: 12
ACQUISITIONS & BIBLIOGRAPHIC ACCESS, Madison Memorial Bldg, LM Rm 642, 101 Independence Ave SE, 20540. Tel: 202-707-5325. FAX: 202-707-6269. *Dir,* Beacher Wiggins; E-mail: bwig@loc.gov
Open Mon-Fri 8-5
AFRICAN & MIDDLE EASTERN DIVISION, Jefferson Bldg, Rm 220, 101 Independence Ave SE, 20540-4820, SAN 336-870X. Tel: 202-707-7937. FAX: 202-252-3180. E-mail: amed@loc.gov. Web Site: www.loc.gov/rr/amed. *Chief,* Mary Jane Deeb
Library Holdings: Bk Vols 600,000
Special Collections: African Coll, mainly Sub-Saharan Africa; African Language & Literature Files, pamphlets, per, unpubl res papers; Biblical Subjects, Response Literature & Sociopolitical Conditions in Israel; Hebraic Coll, vols in Hebrew, Yiddish, Judeo-Arabic, Judeo-Persian, Ladino, Aramaic, Syriac, Samaritan, Amharic & cognate langs; Near East Coll, vols in Arabic, Armenian, Persian, Turkish & related langs
Open Mon-Fri 8:30-5
AMERICAN FOLKLIFE CENTER, Library of Congress Thomas Jefferson Bldg, G53, 101 Independence Ave SE, 20540-4610, SAN 336-8521. Tel: 202-707-5510. FAX: 202-707-2076. E-mail: folklife@loc.gov. Web Site: www.loc.gov/folklife. *Dir,* Elizabeth Peterson; E-mail: epet@loc.gov; *Head, Archives,* Nicole Saylor
Library Holdings: AV Mats 300,000; Bk Vols 3,000; Per Subs 1,000
Special Collections: Alan Lomax Coll; Field Documentary Recordings Dating Back to 1890, cylinders, discs, wires & tapes; Folk Related Books & Periodicals, Dissertations, Field Notes, Tape Transcriptions, etc; Manuscripts; Photographs; Veterans History Project
Subject Interests: Cultural anthrop, Ethnomusicology, Folk music, Folklore, Oral hist
Publications: Folklife Center News (Newsletter)
Open Mon-Fri 8:30-5
ASIAN DIVISION, Jefferson Bldg, Rm 149, 20540-4810, SAN 336-8858. Tel: 202-707-3766, 202-707-5426. Web Site: www.loc.gov/rr/asian. *Div Chief,* Dongfang Shao; Tel: 202-707-5919
Library Holdings: Bk Vols 3,000,000; Per Subs 14,900
Special Collections: Ch'ing (1644-1911) Period & Local History (Chinese Coll); Economics, History & Literature (Japanese Coll); Modern History & Social Sciences (Korean Coll); People's Republic of China Periodicals & Local Newspapers; Science Technology & Social Sciences (Government, Learned Society & University Periodicals); Southern Asia Literature
Open Mon-Fri 8:30-5
MANUSCRIPT DIVISION, James Madison Memorial Bldg, Rms 101-102, 101 Independence Ave SE, 20540, SAN 336-8734. Reference Tel: 202-707-5387. Administration Tel: 202-707-5383. Reference FAX: 202-707-7791. Administration FAX: 202-707-6336. Web Site: www.loc.gov/rr/mss. *Chief Librn,* James H Hutson; Staff 33 (MLS 13, Non-MLS 20)
Special Collections: Harkness Coll (Mexican & Peruvian); Lincolniana (Herndon-Weik Coll); Papers of Henry H Arnold, Newton D Baker, Nathaniel P Banks, Clara Barton, Alexander Graham Bell, Albert J Beveridge, Nicholas Biddle, Gutzon Borglum, Huntington Cairns, Truman Capote, Andrew Carnegie, Caleb Cushing, Charlotte S Cushman, Jo Davidson, William O Douglas, Frederick Douglass, James A Farley, Peter Force, Felix Frankfurter, Benjamin Franklin, Daniel Chester French, Sigmund Freud, Arnold Gesell, Lillian Gish, Alexander Hamilton, John Hay, Benjamin W Huebsch, Henry Kissinger, Clare Boothe Luce, Archibald MacLeish, Thurgood Marshall, Margaret Mead, Edna St Vincent Millay, Ogden Mills, William (Billy) Mitchell, S F B Morse, Louise Chandler Moulton, Reinhold Niebuhr, J Robert Oppenheimer, George S Patton Jr, John J Pershing, Gifford Pinchot, Whitelaw Reid, Elihu Root, Carl Schurz, William T Sherman, Carl Spaatz, Arthur B Spingarn, Edwin M Stanton, Robert A Taft, Melvin Tolson, Joseph M Toner, Earl Warren, Booker T Washington, Daniel Webster, Caspar W Weinberger, Gideon Welles, James McNeill Whistler, William Allen White, Walt Whitman, Harvey W Wiley, Roy Wilkins, Owen Wister, Wilbur & Orville Wright; Records of the Virginia Company of London, the American Colonization Society, the League of Women Voters, American Council of Learned Societies, the National Association for the Advancement of Colored People, the National Urban League & Russian Orthodox-Greek Catholic Church in Alaska; Reproductions of Manuscripts in European Archives that relate to American History
Subject Interests: Am hist
Function: Archival coll, Copy machines, e-mail serv, Electronic databases & coll, ILL available, Online cat, Outside serv via phone, mail, e-mail & web, Photocopying/Printing, Ref serv in person
Open Mon-Sat 8:30-5

Restriction: Authorized patrons, Borrowing requests are handled by ILL, Circ limited, Closed stack, Off-site coll in storage - retrieval as requested, Photo ID required for access, Registered patrons only, Restricted loan policy

MOTION PICTURE, BROADCASTING & RECORDED SOUND DIVISION, Packard Campus for Audio-Visual Conservation, 19053 Mount Pony Rd, Culpeper, 22701-7551. Tel: 202-707-5840. FAX: 202-707-0857. Web Site: www.loc.gov/avconservation. *Div Chief,* Gregory Lukow; E-mail: gluk@loc.gov

Library Holdings: AV Mats 4,900,000

Special Collections: Armed Forces Radio & Television Service Coll; Berliner Coll; Early Films Dating from 1894 (emphasis on American films, 1912-1942); Edison Laboratories Coll; George Kleine Coll (1898-1926); German, Japanese & Italian Film (received through transfer from other government agencies); House of Representatives Debates; John Secrist Coll; Mary Pickford Coll (1909-1931); National Broadcasting Company Coll; OWI Coll; Paper Print Coll of Early Film (1894-1915), deposited for copyright, converted to projectable flm; Raymond Swing Coll; Retrospective Acquisition Program (in cooperation with the American Film Institute); Selected Films & Television Programs (1942-present); Theodore Roosevelt Memorial Association Coll; US Marine Corps Combat Records

Open Mon-Fri 8:30-5

NATIONAL LIBRARY SERVICE FOR THE BLIND & PHYSICALLY HANDICAPPED, 1291 Taylor St NW, 20542, SAN 336-8610. Tel: 202-707-5100. FAX: 202-707-0712. TDD: 202-707-0744. E-mail: nls@loc.gov. Web Site: www.loc.gov/nls. *Dir,* Karen Keninger

Publications: Braille Book Review (Bi-monthly); Musical Mainstream (Periodical); News (Newsletter); Talking Book Topics (Bi-monthly); Update (Newsletter)

Special Services for the Blind - Audio mat; Bks & mags in Braille, on rec, tape & cassette; Bks on flash-memory cartridges; Digital talking bk machines; Music instrul cassettes; Musical scores in Braille & large print; Production of talking bks; Ref serv; Web-Braille

Open Mon-Fri 8-4:30

PRESERVATION DIRECTORATE, 101 Independence Ave, 20540-4530. Tel: 202-707-5213. Web Site: www.loc.gov/preservation. *Dir,* Mark Sweeney; Tel: 202-707-2958, E-mail: mswe@loc.gov

Open Mon-Fri 8:30-6

PRINTS & PHOTOGRAPHS DIVISION, Madison Bldg, Rm LM337, 101 Independence Ave SE, 20540-4730, SAN 336-8882. Tel: 202-707-6394. FAX: 202-707-6647. Web Site: www.loc.gov/rr/print. *Div Chief,* Helena Zinkham; E-mail: hzin@loc.gov

Library Holdings: Bk Vols 14,000,000

Special Collections: 19th century American historical & popular prints especially from Currier & Ives; American, French & British Satirical Prints from the 18th & 19th Centuries; among the 80,000 American & Foreign Posters are the Art Nouveau Posters, German Posters from 1914-1945, the Yander Coll of Political Propaganda Posters, 1965-1989 & Fine Arts Posters from the 1860's to the present; Architectural Colls include the Historic American Buildings Survey; Captured World War II Photographs of the Third Reich; Carnegie Survey of the Architecture of the South, & original documentary drawings & photographs. Outstanding graphic art collections include fine prints from the 15th century to the present, especially chiaroscuro woodcuts, extensive holdings of the graphic art of Joseph Pennell & James McNeil Whistler, American fine prints from 1900 to the 1980s & contemporary graphics from Eastern Europe; Civil War drawings by Edwin Forbes, A R Waud & others; Civil War, Portraits, The American Scene (Mathew S Brady & the Brady-Handy Coll); Daguerreotypes; Detroit Publishing Company Archive of Views, Events & Americana, 1898-1914; Erwin Evans Smith Coll of the American Cowboy; Geographic Coll; George Grantham Bain Coll of News Photographs, 1898-1926; Herbert E French Coll, 1910-1935, news photogs; Historic Native American, US News & World Report News Photo Coll; Matson Coll of the Near East, 1898-1946; Photographic Survey of America by Farm Security Administration & the Office of War Information, 1935-1945; Pictorial Archives of Early American Architecture; Professional & Personal Coll of Alexander Graham Bell & His Family; the Cabinet of American Illustration; the Caroline & Erwin Swann Coll of Caricature & Cartoon; The Historic American Engineering Record; The Seagram County Courthouse Archives; Toni Frissell Coll of Personalities, Fashion & World War II; Uriah Hunt Painter Coll of Early Kodak snapshots; Washingtoniana; Work of such noted photographers as Roger Fenton, Arnold Genthe, Frances Benjamin Johnston, F Holland Day, the Photo-Secessionist group & Lewis Hine

Open Mon-Fri 8:30-5

RARE BOOK & SPECIAL COLLECTIONS DIVISION, Thomas Jefferson Bldg, LJ239, 20540, SAN 336-8912. Tel: 202-707-3448. FAX: 202-707-4142. Web Site: www.loc.gov/rr/rarebook. *Div Chief,* Mark G Dimunation; E-mail: mdim@loc.gov

Library Holdings: Bk Vols 900,000

Special Collections: Aeronautics & Ballooning; American Imprints, 1640-1800; Americana (Marian S Carson Coll); Americana Almanacs, 1646-1900; Americana Extremism; Anarchism; Bacon-Shakespeare Controversy & Cryptography (George Fabyan Coll); Benjamin Franklin, books by, about, printed by & part of personal library; Bibles; Books designed by Bruce Rogers; Books from Peter Force's Library; Bound Pamphlets Coll (including Colls formed in the 18th & 19th centuries by Ebenezer Hazard, William Duane, Jacob Bailey Moore, Oliver Wolcott & Israel Thorndike); Broadsides, 15th century to present; Bulgarian Renaissance Imprints; Children's Books (Frank Hogan Coll); Colls of the Printed Output of Individual Publishers, some received as archival sets from the publishers (Armed Forces Editions, Big Little Books, Bollingen Coll, Franklin Book Program, Little Blue Books, Stone & Kimball, Dell Paperbacks); Confederate States of America Coll, 1860-65; Copyright Records, 1790-1870; Copyright Title-Pages; Daniel Murray Coll of Pamphlets by Negro Authors; Dime Novels, 1860-1910; Documents of the First 14 Congresses; Don Quixote (Leonard Kebler Coll); Early American Architecture; Early English Plays (Francis Longe Coll); Early Printing, 1501-1520; English Printing, 1478-1640; Frederic W Goudy's Library; Gastronomy & Cookery (Kathleen Golden Bitting & Elizabeth Pennell Colls); Genealogical Manuscripts of Charles Edward Banks; Hans & Hanni Kraus Sir Francis Drake Coll; Harrison Elliott Coll of Paperiana; Hawaiian Coll; Henry James Coll; Hunting Library of Theodore Roosevelt; Jean Hersholt Colls of Hans Christian Andersen, Sinclair Lewis & Hugh Walpole; John Boyd Thacher Coll (incunabula, discovery of the Americas, history of the French Revolution, autographs of European notables); John Davis Batchelder Coll of First Editions & Association Copies; Joseph Meredith Toner of Medicine Coll & 19th Century Local History; Justice Oliver Wendell Holmes' Library; Lessing J Rosenwald Coll of Incunabula, Illustrated Books & Rare Books; Lincolniana (Alfred Whital Stern Coll); Magic & the Occult (Harry Houdini & McManus-Young Colls); Manuscript Plays received as Copyright Deposits; Martin Luther Coll; Medieval & Renaissance Manuscripts; Miniature Books; Otto H Vollbehr Coll of Incunabula & 16th-18th Century Continental Title Pages & Printers' Marks; Personal Library of Henry Harrisse; Playbills; Private Press Books; Reformation Coll; Rudyard Kipling (Admiral Lloyd H Chandler, William M Carpenter & H Dunscombe Colt Colls); Russian Imperial Coll; Shakers; Sigmund Freud Coll, including books from Freud's library; Spanish-American Imprints, 1543-1820; Third Reich Coll; Thomas Jefferson's Library; Wagner-Camp Coll; Walt Whitman (Carolyn Wells Houghton, Charles Feinberg & Thomas B Harned Colls); Woman Suffrage (Susan B Anthony's Library, Carrie Chapman Catt & National American Woman Suffrage Association Coll); Woodrow Wilson's Library; Yudin Coll of Early Russian Books

Open Mon-Fri 8:30-5

SCIENCE, TECHNOLOGY & BUSINESS DIVISION, John Adams Bldg, Rm LA508, Second St & Independence Ave SE, 20540-4750, SAN 374-4329. Tel: 202-707-5664. Reference Tel: 202-707-1205, 202-707-5639. FAX: 202-707-1925. Web Site: www.loc.gov/rr/scitech. *Div Chief,* Ronald Bluestone

Library Holdings: Bk Vols 3,750,000

Special Collections: American National Standards; British, Chinese, French, German & Japanese Colls; OSRD Reports on World War II Research & Development (Department of Energy, Department of Defense, National Aeronautics & Space Administration & National Technical Information Service)

Open Mon, Wed & Thurs 8:30am-9:30pm, Tues, Fri & Sat 8:30-5

SERIAL & GOVERNMENT PUBLICATIONS DIVISION, Madison Bldg, LM-133, 20540-4760, SAN 336-8947. Tel: 202-707-5690, 202-707-5691. FAX: 202-707-6128. Web Site: www.loc.gov/rr/news. *Div Chief,* J Mark Sweeney; Tel: 202-707-2958, E-mail: mswe@loc.gov; Staff 43 (MLS 15, Non-MLS 28)

Founded 1800

Library Holdings: Per Subs 50,000

Special Collections: Comics (over 6000 titles, totaling more than 100,000); largest comic coll in the United States; Early American Newspapers (1704-1820); Federal Advisory Committee Coll (consists of approximately 200,000 documents); Historic Events; Newspaper Coll; Serials of International Organizations; United Nations Document Coll; United States & Foreign Government Serials

Open Mon, Wed & Thurs 8:30am-9:30pm, Tues, Fri & Sat 8:30-5

L MANATT, PHELPS & PHILLIPS LLP*, Law Library, 700 12th St NW, Ste 1100, 20005-4075. SAN 377-287X. Tel: 202-585-6500, 202-585-6680. Interlibrary Loan Service Tel: 202-585-6681. FAX: 202-585-6600. Web Site: www.manatt.com. *ILL,* Patrick Eugene; E-mail: peugene@manatt.com; Staff 3 (MLS 1, Non-MLS 2)

Founded 1965

Library Holdings: Per Subs 300

Subject Interests: General law, Litigation

Automation Activity & Vendor Info: (Acquisitions) SirsiDynix; (Cataloging) SirsiDynix; (Circulation) SirsiDynix; (OPAC) SirsiDynix

Database Vendor: LexisNexis, Westlaw

Open Mon-Fri 9:30-6

CR MARIST COLLEGE LIBRARY*, 815 Varnum St NE, 20017-2199. SAN 302-6922. Tel: 202-529-2821. *Librn,* Paul Osmanski
Founded 1898
Library Holdings: Bk Titles 4,355; Bk Vols 5,444; Per Subs 47
Subject Interests: Philos, Theol
Restriction: Not open to pub, Open to students, fac & staff

S MATHEMATICA POLICY RESEARCH, INC LIBRARY*, 1100 First St NE, 12Flr, 20002-4221. SAN 377-1210. Tel: 202-484-4692. FAX: 202-863-1763. Web Site: www.mathematica-mpr.com. *Librn,* Sally Henderson; Staff 3 (MLS 2, Non-MLS 1)
Library Holdings: Bk Vols 14,750; Per Subs 300
Subject Interests: Health sci
Restriction: Not open to pub, Staff use only

S MAYER, BROWN, ROWE & MAW LIBRARY*, 1909 K St NW, Ste 1200, 20006-1101. SAN 329-8868. Tel: 202-263-3000, 202-263-3100, 202-263-3314. FAX: 202-263-3300. Web Site: www.mayerbrownrowe.com. *Librn,* Barbara Fisher; Staff 5 (MLS 3, Non-MLS 2)
Library Holdings: Bk Vols 5,000
Subject Interests: Law, Litigation
Database Vendor: LexisNexis
Open Mon-Fri 9-5

S MCCLATCHY WASHINGTON BUREAU LIBRARY*, 700 12th St NW, Ste 1000, 20005. SAN 325-1616. Tel: 202-383-6032. Web Site: www.mcclatchydc.com. *Librn,* Tish Wells; E-mail: twells@mcclatchydc.com
Founded 1977
Library Holdings: Bk Titles 100; Per Subs 50
Subject Interests: Govt, Intl relations
Database Vendor: Factiva.com, LexisNexis
Restriction: Staff use only

L MCKENNA LONG & ALDRIDGE LLP*, Law Library, 1900 K St NW, 20006. SAN 372-137X. Tel: 202-496-7579. FAX: 202-496-7756. *Bus Intelligence Librn,* Elizabeth Sullivan; E-mail: esullivan@mckennalong.com; *Sr Res Librn,* Deborah Vergara; Tel: 202-496-7125, E-mail: dvergara@mckennalong.com; *Res Librn,* Douglas Malerba; Tel: 202-496-7791, E-mail: dmalerba@mckennalong.com; Staff 6 (MLS 5, Non-MLS 1)
Library Holdings: Bk Vols 30,000; Per Subs 210
Subject Interests: Environ law, Govt contracts, Litigation
Automation Activity & Vendor Info: (Cataloging) Softlink America; (OPAC) Softlink America; (Serials) Softlink America
Function: ILL available
Partic in OCLC Online Computer Library Center, Inc
Restriction: Not open to pub

L MCMANUS DARDEN & FELSEN LLP*, 1155 15th St NW, Ste 810, 20005. Tel: 202-296-9260. FAX: 202-659-3732. *Adminr,* Amber Broha; E-mail: abroha@mcmanus-darden.com
Library Holdings: Bk Titles 234
Restriction: Not a lending libr

S METROPOLITAN CLUB OF THE CITY OF WASHINGTON LIBRARY*, 1700 H St, NW, 20006. Tel: 202-835-2556. Administration FAX: 202-835-2582. E-mail: library@metroclub.org. Web Site: www.metroclub.org. *Dir, Libr & Archives,* Michael J Higgins; *Libr Tech,* Robin W Higgins; E-mail: RHiggins@metroclub.org; Staff 1 (MLS 1)
Founded 1863
Library Holdings: Audiobooks 200; Bk Vols 18,000; Per Subs 90
Special Collections: Club Member Publications; Metropolitan Club Archives
Automation Activity & Vendor Info: (Cataloging) Inmagic, Inc.; (Circulation) Inmagic, Inc.; (OPAC) Inmagic, Inc.
Publications: An Annotated Guide to New Books in the Library (Monthly bulletin)
Restriction: Authorized patrons

S MIDDLE EAST INSTITUTE, The Oman Library, 1761 N St NW, 20036. SAN 302-6949. Tel: 202-785-0183. FAX: 202-331-8861. E-mail: library@mideasti.org. Web Site: www.mideasti.org/library. *Libr Dir,* Amal Morsy; E-mail: amorsy@mei.edu; Staff 1 (MLS 1)
Founded 1946
Library Holdings: AV Mats 100; e-books 500; Bk Vols 20,000, Per Subs 300
Special Collections: 18th & 19th Century travel accounts of the Middle East
Subject Interests: Africa, Archit, Caucasus, Cent Asia, Islam, Middle East, N Africa, Political
Automation Activity & Vendor Info: (Cataloging) Inmagic, Inc.; (Circulation) Inmagic, Inc.; (OPAC) Inmagic, Inc.; (Serials) Inmagic, Inc.
Partic in OCLC Online Computer Library Center, Inc
Open Mon-Thurs 10-6, Fri 10-5

L MIGRANT LEGAL ACTION PROGRAM LIBRARY*, 1001 Connecticut Ave NW, Ste 915, 20036. SAN 373-0980. Tel: 202-775-7780. FAX: 202-775-7784. E-mail: mlap@mlap.org. Web Site: www.mlap.org. *Exec Dir,* Roger C Rosenthal
Library Holdings: Bk Vols 500
Subject Interests: Farming, Rural
Restriction: Staff use only

L MILLER & CHEVALIER, Law Library, 655 15th St NW, Ste 900, 20005-5701. SAN 372-1361. Tel: 202-626-6094. FAX: 202-626-5801. Web Site: www.millerchevalier.com. *Librn,* Carol Gruenburg; E-mail: cgruenburg@milchev.com; *Asst Librn,* Karen Polk
Automation Activity & Vendor Info: (Cataloging) SIMA, Inc; (Circulation) SIMA, Inc; (OPAC) SIMA, Inc
Database Vendor: Dialog, LexisNexis, Westlaw
Open Mon-Fri 8:30-5:30

L MORGAN LEWIS & BOCHIUS LLP*, Law Library, 1111 Pennsylvania Ave NW, 20004-2541. SAN 302-6957. Tel: 202-739-6424. FAX: 202-739-3001. Web Site: www.morganlewis.com. *Dir, Libr Serv,* Barbara Folensbee-Moore; Tel: 202-739-5131; Staff 9 (MLS 4, Non-MLS 5)
Library Holdings: Bk Titles 11,000; Bk Vols 45,000; Per Subs 750
Subject Interests: Employment, Environ law, Finance, Intellectual property, Labor, Law, US Congress
Automation Activity & Vendor Info: (Cataloging) Innovative Interfaces, Inc
Database Vendor: Dialog, Gale Cengage Learning, LexisNexis, OCLC FirstSearch, Westlaw
Publications: ML&B Library Bulletin
Partic in Dialog Corp; OCLC Online Computer Library Center, Inc
Restriction: Not open to pub

L MORRIS, MANNING & MARTIN LIBRARY LLP*, 1333 H St NW, Ste 820, 20005. SAN 377-4368. Tel: 202-408-5153. FAX: 202-408-5146. Web Site: www.mmmlaw.com. *In Charge,* Heather Boos
Library Holdings: Bk Vols 100
Subject Interests: Antitrust, Ins law
Open Mon-Fri 9-5:30

R MOUNT VERNON PLACE UNITED METHODIST CHURCH LIBRARY*, 900 Massachusetts Ave NW, 20001-4396. SAN 302-6981. Tel: 202-347-9620. FAX: 202-347-9217. Web Site: www.mvpumc.org.
Founded 1855
Library Holdings: Bk Titles 1,750
Subject Interests: Biblical studies, Counseling, Drama, Fiction, Hist, Poetry, Psychol, Recreation
Open Mon-Fri 9-4:30, Sun 9-2

G NASA HEADQUARTERS LIBRARY, Dr T Keith Glennan Memorial Library, 300 E St SW, Rm 1W53, 20546. SAN 302-699X. Tel: 202-358-0168. Interlibrary Loan Service Tel: 202-358-2259. FAX: 202-358-3251. E-mail: library@hq.nasa.gov. Web Site: www.hq.nasa.gov/office/hqlibrary. *Mgr,* Richard Spencer; Tel: 202-358-0172; *Ref Librn,* Lee Shapiro; Tel: 202-358-0171; Staff 4 (MLS 4)
Founded 1958
Library Holdings: DVDs 60; Bk Titles 16,000; Per Subs 100; Videos 100
Special Collections: NACA Documents; NASA Documents
Subject Interests: Aerospace sci
Automation Activity & Vendor Info: (Cataloging) OCLC; (ILL) OCLC
Publications: Alerts
Partic in OCLC Online Computer Library Center, Inc
Open Mon-Fri 7:30-5
Restriction: Circ to mem only, Open to pub for ref only

S THE NATIONAL ACADEMIES, George E Brown Jr Library/Research Center, 500 Fifth St NW, Keck 304, 20001-2721. SAN 302-7023. Tel: 202-334-2125. Interlibrary Loan Service Tel: 202-334-1309. FAX: 202-334-1651. E-mail: research@nas.edu. Web Site: nas.edu/researchcenter/index.html. *Mgr,* Victoria Harriston; *Sr Librn,* Daniel Bearss; E-mail: dbearss@nas.edu; *Sr Librn,* Colleen Willis; *Res Librn,* Ellen Kimmel; *Res Librn,* Rebecca Morgan; *Libr Asst,* Genevia Chamblee; Staff 6 (MLS 5, Non-MLS 1)
Founded 1945
Library Holdings: e-books 80,000; Bk Vols 35,000
Special Collections: National Academy of Sciences Reports Archives
Subject Interests: Educ, Eng, Global affairs, Med, Policy, Sci, Soc sci
Automation Activity & Vendor Info: (Acquisitions) OCLC WorldShare Interlibrary Loan; (Cataloging) OCLC WorldShare Interlibrary Loan; (Circulation) OCLC WorldShare Interlibrary Loan; (ILL) OCLC ILLiad; (OPAC) OCLC; (Serials) OCLC

Database Vendor: Agricola, American Chemical Society, American Geophysical Union, American Physical Society, American Psychological Association (APA), ebrary, EBSCOhost, Elsevier, HeinOnline, IEEE (Institute of Electrical & Electronics Engineers), Ingenta, ISI Web of Knowledge, JSTOR, LexisNexis, Medline, Nature Publishing Group, OCLC, OCLC WorldShare Interlibrary Loan, OCLC Worldshare Management Services, OVID Technologies, ProQuest, PubMed, Sage, ScienceDirect, Scopus, Springer-Verlag, Thomson - Web of Science, Wiley InterScience
Wireless access
Function: Res libr
Partic in National Network of Libraries of Medicine; OCLC Online Computer Library Center, Inc
Restriction: Authorized scholars by appt, Borrowing requests are handled by ILL, Circ limited, External users must contact libr, In-house use for visitors, Open by appt only, Visitors must make appt to use bks in the libr

Branches:

TRANSPORTATION RESEARCH BOARD LIBRARY, 500 Fifth St NW, 20001, SAN 302-7015. Tel: 202-334-2989. E-mail: trblibrary@nas.edu. Web Site: www.trb.org/Library. *Mgr, Info Serv,* Lisa Loyo; Tel: 202-334-2990, E-mail: lloyo@nas.edu; *Sr Librn,* Aryeh Cohen; E-mail: hcohen@nas.edu; *Database Librn,* William McLeod; E-mail: wmcleod@nas.edu; *Sr Abstractor/Indexer,* Janet Daly; E-mail: jdaly@nas.edu; Staff 4 (MLS 4)
Founded 1946
Library Holdings: Bk Titles 17,000; Per Subs 575
Special Collections: Highway Research Board & Transportation Research Board Publications; Marine Board; Strategic Highway Research Program (SHRP & SHRP2) Publications
Subject Interests: Civil eng, Transportation
Automation Activity & Vendor Info: (Acquisitions) EOS International; (Cataloging) EOS International; (Circulation) EOS International; (ILL) OCLC; (OPAC) EOS International; (Serials) EOS International
Partic in OCLC Online Computer Library Center, Inc
Open Mon-Fri 8:30-5

S NATIONAL ACADEMY OF SOCIAL INSURANCE LIBRARY*, 1776 Massachusetts Ave NW, Ste 615, 20036. SAN 374-9959. Tel: 202-452-8097. FAX: 202-452-8111. E-mail: nasi@nasi.org. Web Site: www.nasi.org. *Exec VPres,* Pamela Larson
Library Holdings: Bk Titles 3,000; Per Subs 12
Subject Interests: Soc ins progs
Function: For res purposes
Restriction: Mem only

S NATIONAL CENTER FOR VICTIMS OF CRIME LIBRARY*, 2000 M St NW, Ste 480, 20036. SAN 372-4107. Tel: 202-467-8700. FAX: 202-467-8701. Web Site: www.ncvc.org. *Pub Policy Dir,* Susan Howley; Tel: 202-467-8722
Founded 1985
Library Holdings: Bk Titles 4,500; Per Subs 50
Special Collections: Victimization & Victim Services & Assistance
Automation Activity & Vendor Info: (Acquisitions) Inmagic, Inc.; (Cataloging) Inmagic, Inc.; (Circulation) Inmagic, Inc.; (Serials) Inmagic, Inc.
Partic in OCLC Online Computer Library Center, Inc

S NATIONAL ECONOMIC RESEARCH ASSOCIATES, INC LIBRARY*, 1255 23rd St NW, Ste 600, 20037. SAN 302-7171. Tel: 202-466-3510. FAX: 202-466-9285. Web Site: www.nera.com. *Info Spec,* Barbara Eames
Founded 1965
Library Holdings: Bk Vols 6,000; Per Subs 25
Subject Interests: Econ, Energy
Database Vendor: LexisNexis, OVID Technologies
Publications: Library Letter (Monthly)
Partic in Vutext

S NATIONAL ENDOWMENT FOR DEMOCRACY LIBRARY*, Democracy Resource Center, 1025 F St NW, Ste 800, 20004. SAN 377-4554. Tel: 202-378-9700. FAX: 202-378-9407. E-mail: drc@ned.org. Web Site: www.ned.org, www.ned.org/research/democracy-resource-center. *Dir,* Allen Overland; E-mail: allen@ned.org; *Sr Librn,* Tim Myers; E-mail: tim@ned.org; *Sr Electronic Res Librn,* Position Currently Open; *Archivist/Librn,* Anna Yevropina; E-mail: anna@ned.org; *Electronic Res Librn,* Morgan Grimes; E-mail: morgang@ned.org; *Libr Asst,* Emily Vaughan; E-mail: emilyv@ned.org. Subject Specialists: *Knowledge mgt,* Morgan Grimes; Staff 5 (MLS 4, Non-MLS 1)
Founded 1994
Library Holdings: DVDs 300; Electronic Media & Resources 4,000; Bk Vols 20,000; Per Subs 300
Subject Interests: Govt, Intl affairs, Politics
Automation Activity & Vendor Info: (Acquisitions) OCLC WorldShare Interlibrary Loan; (Cataloging) OCLC WorldShare Interlibrary Loan; (Circulation) OCLC WorldShare Interlibrary Loan; (ILL) OCLC WorldShare Interlibrary Loan; (OPAC) OCLC WorldShare Interlibrary Loan; (Serials) OCLC WorldShare Interlibrary Loan
Partic in OCLC Online Computer Library Center, Inc
Open Mon-Fri 9-5

G NATIONAL ENDOWMENT FOR THE HUMANITIES LIBRARY, NEH Library, 4th Flr, 400 Seventh St SW, 20506. SAN 325-9854. Tel: 202-606-8244. FAX: 202-606-8457. E-mail: library@neh.gov. *Tech Info Spec,* Donna McClish; Staff 1 (Non-MLS 1)
Founded 1965
Library Holdings: Bk Vols 11,000
Partic in OCLC Online Computer Library Center, Inc
Open Mon-Fri 8:30-4:45

S NATIONAL GALLERY OF ART LIBRARY*, Fourth St & Constitution Ave NW, 20565. (Mail add: 2000B S Club Dr, Door 7, Landover, 20785-3230), SAN 302-7228. Tel: 202-842-6511. Circulation Tel: 202-842-6516. Interlibrary Loan Service Tel: 202-842-6512. Administration Tel: 202-842-6505. FAX: 202-789-3068. Web Site: www.nga.gov/resources/dldesc.htm. *Head, Reader Serv,* Lamia Doumato; Tel: 202-842-6510, E-mail: l-doumato@nga.gov; *Exec Librn,* Neal Turtell; *Admin Librn,* Roger Lawson; *Automation Syst Coordr,* Karen Cassedy; *Image Coll,* Gregory Most; *Ref,* John Hagood; E-mail: library@nga.gov; *Tech Serv,* Anna Rachwald; Staff 42 (MLS 18, Non-MLS 24)
Founded 1941
Library Holdings: Bk Titles 370,000; Bk Vols 400,000; Per Subs 958
Special Collections: Art Exhibition Catalogs; Art Sales Records; Artists Book Coll; Leonardo da Vinci Coll; Museum & Private Art Coll; Photographic Archives of European & American Art
Subject Interests: Archit, Graphic arts, Paintings, Sculpture
Automation Activity & Vendor Info: (Acquisitions) Ex Libris Group; (Cataloging) Ex Libris Group; (Circulation) Ex Libris Group; (ILL) OCLC; (OPAC) Ex Libris Group; (Serials) Ex Libris Group
Database Vendor: JSTOR, OCLC FirstSearch, OCLC WorldShare Interlibrary Loan, Wilson - Wilson Web
Publications: Annotated Bibliography of Microforms (1991); Guide to the National Gallery of Art Library (1994); Guide to the National Gallery of Art Photo Archives (2002); The Patricia G England Collection of Fine Press & Artists' Books (2000)
Partic in Fedlink; OCLC Online Computer Library Center, Inc; OCLC Research Library Partnership
Open Mon 12-4:30, Tues-Fri 10-4:30

Branches:

DEPARTMENT OF EDUCATION RESOURCES, Fourth St & Constitution Ave NW, 20565. (Mail add: 2000B S Club Dr, Landover, 20785), SAN 329-9686. Tel: 202-842-6280. FAX: 202-842-6935. E-mail: edresources@nga.gov. Web Site: www.nga.gov/education/classroom/loanfinder. *Head, Dept of Educ Res,* Leo J Kasun
Library Holdings: AV Mats 140; CDs 10; DVDs 22; Electronic Media & Resources 2; Bk Titles 43; Videos 63
Subject Interests: Educ
Open Mon-Fri 9-5

S NATIONAL GEOGRAPHIC SOCIETY LIBRARY*, 1146 16th St NW, 20036. (Mail add: 1145 17th St NW, 20036), SAN 336-9129. Tel: 202-857-7783. Interlibrary Loan Service Tel: 202-857-7786. FAX: 202-429-5731. E-mail: library@ngs.org. Web Site: www.nationalgeographic.com. *Dir, Libr & Info Serv,* Barbara Ferry; Staff 18 (MLS 14, Non-MLS 4)
Founded 1920
Library Holdings: Bk Vols 48,000; Per Subs 129
Special Collections: Hakluyt Society Publications
Subject Interests: Geog, Natural hist, Travel, Voyages
Automation Activity & Vendor Info: (Acquisitions) Innovative Interfaces, Inc; (Cataloging) Innovative Interfaces, Inc; (Circulation) Innovative Interfaces, Inc; (ILL) OCLC; (OPAC) Innovative Interfaces, Inc; (Serials) Innovative Interfaces, Inc
Database Vendor: Blackwell, Dialog, Dun & Bradstreet, Gale Cengage Learning, Hoovers, Ingenta, JSTOR, LexisNexis, OCLC FirstSearch, Oxford Online, ProQuest, SerialsSolutions, World Book Online
Function: Archival coll, Bks on CD, Computer training, Computers for patron use, Copy machines, Doc delivery serv, Newsp ref libr, Online cat, Online ref, Online searches, Orientations, Ref & res, Telephone ref, Web-catalog
Publications: Annual Report; Earth Current; Research Guides to the Internet (pathfinders); Staff Brochure; Staff Searches on Demand; Visitor Brochure
Partic in OCLC Online Computer Library Center, Inc
Restriction: Access for corporate affiliates, Authorized scholars by appt, Circulates for staff only, Open to pub by appt only, Photo ID required for access, Use of others with permission of librn

Branches:

IMAGE COLLECTION, 1145 17th St NW, 20036. Tel: 202-857-7493. FAX: 202-429-5776. *Dir,* Barbara Penford Ferry; Staff 32 (MLS 26, Non-MLS 6)
Founded 1919
Special Collections: Antarctic (Herbert G Ponting Coll), photog; China (Joseph F Rock Coll), photog; Machu; Mount Katmai, Alaska (Robert F Griggs Coll), photog; NASA Space Probes; Picchu, Peru (Hiram Bingham Coll), photog; Polar Expeditions (Robert E Peary Coll), photog; Skylab Missions (Skylab Coll), color; Space Coll, negatives, prints & transparencies; Transparencies, Prints & Negatives; Wildlife (Georg Shiras III Coll), photog; Yukon (Bradford Washburn Coll), photog
Subject Interests: Geog
Restriction: Open to pub by appt only

NATIONAL GEOGRAPHIC DIGITAL MOTION, 1145 17th St NW, 20036. Tel: 202-857-7000, 202-857-7695. FAX: 202-429-5755. Web Site: www.ngdigitalmotion.com. *VPres,* Jocelyn Shearer; Staff 11 (MLS 4, Non-MLS 7)
Special Collections: National Geographic Television & Educational Films, 16mm color out-takes
Subject Interests: Animals, behavior of, Geog, Recreation, Transportation

A NATIONAL GUARD MEMORIAL LIBRARY*, One Massachusetts Ave NW, 20001. SAN 326-1786. Tel: 202-408-5890, 202-789-0031. FAX: 202-682-9358. Web Site: ngef.org. *Dir, Archives,* Anne Armstrong; E-mail: anne.armstrong@ngaus.org; Staff 1 (MLS 1)
Library Holdings: Bk Vols 4,000; Per Subs 1
Special Collections: Air National Guard and Army National Guard Photos; National Guard Association Archives; State Guard Histories, bks, correspondence, clippings. Oral History
Open Mon-Fri 9-4

GL NATIONAL INSTITUTE OF JUSTICE*, Online Research & Information Center, 810 Seventh St NW, Rm 6304, 20531. SAN 377-4228. Tel: 202-307-6742. FAX: 202-307-6742. Web Site: www.ojp.usdoj.gov. *Coordr,* James Fort; E-mail: james.fort@usdoj.gov
Library Holdings: Bk Vols 500; Per Subs 30
Database Vendor: EBSCOhost, OCLC FirstSearch
Open Mon-Fri 8:30-5

S NATIONAL LABOR RELATIONS BOARD LIBRARY*, 1099 14th St NW, Ste 8000, 20570-0001. SAN 302-7260. Tel: 202-273-3720. FAX: 202-273-2906. Web Site: www.nlrb.gov. *Chief Librn,* Andrew Martin; E-mail: andrew.martin@nlrb.gov; Staff 9 (MLS 3, Non-MLS 6)
Library Holdings: Bk Vols 37,000; Per Subs 30
Special Collections: Publications By or About National Labor Relations Board, National Labor Relations Act, Labor; Relations Act of 1947 & Landrum-Griffin Act, Title VII
Subject Interests: Bus, Employment law, Labor, Law
Automation Activity & Vendor Info: (Cataloging) EOS International; (Circulation) EOS International; (Serials) EOS International
Publications: New Books & Current Labor Articles
Partic in OCLC Online Computer Library Center, Inc
Open Mon-Fri 9-4

G NATIONAL LIBRARY OF EDUCATION*, 400 Maryland Ave SW, BE-101, 20202-5523. SAN 336-9242. Tel: 202-205-5015. Circulation Tel: 202-205-4945, 202-205-5012. Interlibrary Loan Service Tel: 202-260-0194. Reference Tel: 202-205-5019. Administration Tel: 202-219-1012. Toll Free Tel: 800-424-1616. FAX: 202-260-7364, 202-401-0547. Administration FAX: 202-219-2198. TDD: 202-205-7561. E-mail: library@ed.gov. Web Site: www.ed.gov/NLE. *Dir,* Pamela Tripp-Melby; Tel: 202-453-6536, E-mail: Pamela.Tripp-Melby@ed.gov
Founded 1994
Oct 2013-Sept 2014 Income $2,000,000
Library Holdings: Bk Vols 100,000; Per Subs 682
Special Collections: ERIC (Educational Resources Information Center), 1966-2003, micro; Rare Books Coll; US Department of Education Historical Coll. US Document Depository
Subject Interests: Educ policy, Educ psychol, Educ res, Educ statistics, Soc sci res methodology
Automation Activity & Vendor Info: (Acquisitions) SIRSI-iBistro; (Cataloging) SIRSI-iBistro; (Circulation) SIRSI-iBistro; (ILL) OCLC; (OPAC) SIRSI-iBistro; (Serials) SIRSI-iBistro
Database Vendor: American Psychological Association (APA), Checkpoint Systems, Inc, CQ Press, Dialog, ebrary, EBSCOhost, Elsevier, Gale Cengage Learning, H W Wilson, Haworth Pres Inc, HeinOnline, Infotrieve, Ingenta, JSTOR, LexisNexis, Nature Publishing Group, OCLC, OCLC FirstSearch, OCLC WorldShare Interlibrary Loan, Paratext, ProQuest, RefWorks, Scopus, SerialsSolutions, SirsiDynix, Springshare, LLC, Swets Information Services, TDNet, Westlaw, Wilson - Wilson Web, YBP Library Services
Wireless access
Function: Archival coll, e-mail serv, Govt ref serv, ILL available, Orientations, Photocopying/Printing, Ref & res, Telephone ref
Partic in Coalition for Networked Information (CNI); Fedlink; OCLC Online Computer Library Center, Inc
Special Services for the Deaf - TTY equip
Open Mon-Fri 9-5
Restriction: Non-circulating to the pub, Photo ID required for access

S NATIONAL MUSEUM OF AMERICAN JEWISH MILITARY HISTORY LIBRARY*, 1811 R St NW, 20009. SAN 377-1172. Tel: 202-265-6280. FAX: 202-234-5662. E-mail: nmajmh@nmajmh.org. Web Site: www.nmajmh.org. *Dir, Operations,* Larry Richardson
Library Holdings: Bk Vols 22,000
Open Mon-Fri 9-5

S NATIONAL MUSEUM OF WOMEN IN THE ARTS*, Library & Research Center, 1250 New York Ave NW, 20005-3920. Tel: 202-783-7365. FAX: 202-393-3234. E-mail: library@nmwa.org. Web Site: www.nmwa.org. *Dir,* Susan Fisher Sterling; Tel: 202-266-2806; Staff 3 (MLS 2, Non-MLS 1)
Founded 1982
Library Holdings: Bk Titles 18,000; Bk Vols 18,500; Per Subs 50
Special Collections: Archives on Women Artists; Artists' Books Coll; Irene Rice Pereira Library
Automation Activity & Vendor Info: (Acquisitions) Ex Libris Group; (Cataloging) Ex Libris Group; (Circulation) Ex Libris Group; (OPAC) Ex Libris Group; (Serials) Ex Libris Group
Restriction: Open by appt only
Friends of the Library Group

R THE NATIONAL PRESBYTERIAN CHURCH & CENTER*, William Smith Culbertson Memorial Library, Administration Bldg, 4101 Nebraska Ave NW, 20016-2793. SAN 302-7317. Tel: 202-537-7529. Administration Tel: 202-537-0800. FAX: 202-686-0031. E-mail: library@nationalpres.org. Web Site: www.nationalpres.org. *Dir, Libr & Archives,* J Theodore Anderson
Founded 1969
Jan 2012-Dec 2012 Income $76,000, Locally Generated Income $70,000, Parent Institution $6,000. Mats Exp $12,650, Books $5,000, Per/Ser (Incl. Access Fees) $650, Manu Arch $1,000, Other Print Mats $2,000, AV Mat $500, Electronic Ref Mat (Incl. Access Fees) $500, Presv $3,000. Sal $30,000
Library Holdings: AV Mats 3,900; Bks on Deafness & Sign Lang 100; Braille Volumes 125; DVDs 100; Bk Titles 18,000; Per Subs 42; Spec Interest Per Sub 30; Talking Bks 200; Videos 1,400
Special Collections: Chambers Theology Coll; Chapman Memorial Archives. Oral History
Subject Interests: Children's lit, Hist, Music, Relig, Theol
Automation Activity & Vendor Info: (Acquisitions) Surpass; (Cataloging) Surpass; (Circulation) Surpass; (Course Reserve) Surpass; (Media Booking) Surpass; (OPAC) Surpass; (Serials) Surpass
Database Vendor: FileMaker, Surpass
Wireless access
Publications: Current Awareness Bulletin; New Book Lists; Reading for Special Days
Partic in Church & Synagogue Libr Asn
Open Mon-Fri 8:30-4, Sun 8-1
Friends of the Library Group

S NATIONAL PRESS CLUB*, Eric Friedheim Library, 529 14th St NW, 13th Flr, 20045. SAN 326-128X. Tel: 202-662-7523. FAX: 202-879-6725. E-mail: info@press.org. Web Site: www.press.org/library. *Dir,* Julie Schoo; Tel: 202-662-7507; *Archivist,* Marlene Justsen; Tel: 202-662-7598; *Res Librn,* Beth Shankle; Tel: 202-662-7509; Staff 5 (MLS 2, Non-MLS 3)
Founded 1908
Library Holdings: Bk Vols 3,000
Special Collections: Hammond Photographs (John Hay Hammond Coll); NPC Cartoon Coll, original art & political cartoons; Sigma Delta Chi DC Chapter, docs; Washington Press Club Archives
Subject Interests: Current news
Open Mon-Fri 9-6
Friends of the Library Group

S NATIONAL REFERENCE CENTER FOR BIOETHICS LITERATURE*, Kennedy Institute of Ethics, Georgetown University, 37th & O St NW, 20057. (Mail add: Georgetown University, Box 571212, 20057-1212), SAN 336-8289. Tel: 202-687-3885. Toll Free Tel: 800-633-3849, 888-246-3849. FAX: 202-687-6770. E-mail: bioethics@georgetown.edu. Web Site: bioethics.georgetown.edu/. *Dir,* Doris Goldstein; *Ref,* Martina Darragh; *Ref,* Kathleen A Schroeder; Staff 13 (MLS 9, Non-MLS 4)
Founded 1973
Library Holdings: Bk Vols 28,000; Per Subs 500
Special Collections: Archives Colls of Federal Bioethics & Human Experimentation Commissions; Archives National Bioethics Advisory

Commission (NBAC); Curriculum Development Clearinghouse for Bioethics (Syllubus Exchange Coll); Kampelman Coll of Jewish Ethics; Shriver Coll of Christian Ethics
Function: Doc delivery serv, Photocopying/Printing
Publications: Bibliography of Bioethics (published by Kennedy Institute beginning with vol 10); Bioethics: A Guide to Information Sources; New Titles in Bioethics; Scope Notes
Partic in National Network of Libraries of Medicine; OCLC Online Computer Library Center, Inc
Restriction: Open to pub for ref only

S NATIONAL RESTAURANT ASSOCIATION*, Information Services & Library, 1200 17th St NW, 20036. SAN 303-9862. Tel: 202-331-5960. Toll Free Tel: 800-424-5156. FAX: 202-331-5950. Web Site: www.restaurant.org. *Sr Dir,* Myra Engers Weinberg; E-mail: mweinberg@restaurant.org; Staff 4 (MLS 4)
Founded 1975
Library Holdings: Bk Titles 3,500; Per Subs 100
Special Collections: Association Archives; Restaurant/Foodservice Management Coll
Subject Interests: Food indust & trade, Restaurant mgt

S NATIONAL RIGHT TO LIFE LIBRARY*, 512 Tenth St NW, 20004. SAN 371-8689. Tel: 202-626-8800, Ext 129. FAX: 202-393-0745. E-mail: NRLC@nrlc.org. Web Site: www.nrlc.org. *Adminr,* Joe Landrum
Library Holdings: Bk Titles 1,000; Per Subs 30
Special Collections: Abortion; Euthanasia; Infanticide

NATIONAL SOCIETY OF THE DAUGHTERS OF THE AMERICAN REVOLUTION

S DAR LIBRARY, 1776 D St NW, 20006-5303, SAN 302-7368. Tel: 202-879-3229. Reference Tel: 202-777-2366. FAX: 202-879-3227. E-mail: library@dar.org. Web Site: www.dar.org. *Coll Develop, Dir,* Eric G Grundset; *Asst Dir,* Position Currently Open; *Tech Serv,* Bertha Mutz; Staff 16 (MLS 3, Non-MLS 13)
Founded 1896
Mar 2014-Jan 2014 Income $1,120,000, Locally Generated Income $120,000, Parent Institution $1,000,000. Mats Exp $47,000, Books $30,000, Per/Ser (Incl. Access Fees) $15,000, Micro $2,000. Sal $800,000 (Prof $200,000)
Library Holdings: CDs 700; Bk Titles 175,000; Bk Vols 230,000; Per Subs 1,100
Special Collections: American Indians Coll; Minority Participants in the American Revolution (African American & American Indian Patriots); Women's History Coll
Subject Interests: Genealogy, State hist, US hist
Automation Activity & Vendor Info: (Acquisitions) TLC (The Library Corporation); (Cataloging) TLC (The Library Corporation); (Circulation) TLC (The Library Corporation); (OPAC) TLC (The Library Corporation); (Serials) TLC (The Library Corporation)
Database Vendor: ABC-CLIO, JSTOR, Newsbank, ProQuest
Function: CD-ROM, Computers for patron use, Copy machines, Microfiche/film & reading machines, Online ref, Orientations, Pub access computers, Ref serv available, Ref serv in person, Telephone ref, Workshops
Publications: America's women in the Revolutionary Era (Bibliographies); Forgotten Patriots: African American & American Indian Patriots in the Revolutionary War: Service (Reference guide); Georgia in the American Revolution (Research guide); New York in the American Revolution (Research guide); Rhode Island in the American Revolution (Research guide); South Carolina in the American Revolution (Research guide); Virginia in the American Revolution (Research guide)
Special Services for the Deaf - Sorenson video relay syst; Staff with knowledge of sign lang
Special Services for the Blind - Closed circuit TV magnifier
Open Mon-Fri 8:30-4, Sat 9-5
Restriction: Non-circulating, Open to pub for ref only, Open to students
Friends of the Library Group

S MUSEUM REFERENCE LIBRARY*, 1776 D St NW, 20006, SAN 321-2262. Tel: 202-879-3241. FAX: 202-628-0820. E-mail: museum@dar.org. Web Site: www.dar.org/museum. *Dir,* Heidi Campbell-Shoaf; Staff 10 (Non-MLS 10)
Founded 1970
Library Holdings: Bk Vols 3,000; Per Subs 30
Subject Interests: Decorative art
Function: For res purposes
Open Mon-Fri 9:30-4, Sat 9-5

A NAVAL HISTORY & HERITAGE*, Navy Department Library, 805 Kidder-Breese St SE, 20374-5060. SAN 337-1670. Tel: 202-433-4132. FAX: 202-433-9553. Web Site: www.history.navy.mil/library. *Libr Dir,* Glenn E Helm; *Cat Librn,* Dr Young Park; *Ref Librn,* James Allen Knechtmann; Tel: 202-433-7837; *Libr Tech,* Linda Edwards; *Tech Info Spec/Fed Dep Libr,* Tonya Simpson; E-mail: tonya.simpson@navy.mil; *Tech Info Spec/Libr Syst,* Davis Elliott. Subject Specialists: *Hist of Indochina/Vietnam war, Mil hist, Naval hist,* Glenn E Helm; *Mil naval hist,* James Allen Knechtmann; Staff 7 (MLS 3, Non-MLS 4)
Founded 1800
Library Holdings: Bk Titles 102,000; Per Subs 375
Special Collections: Administrative Histories of World War II Coll; Cruise Books; Cryptologic Documents; Dissertations on Naval & Military History; Navy Officer Registers; Rare Books & Manuscripts; US Navy Shipbuilding Contracts. US Document Depository
Subject Interests: Maritime hist, Naval hist
Automation Activity & Vendor Info: (Cataloging) EOS International; (Circulation) EOS International; (ILL) OCLC Online; (OPAC) EOS International; (Serials) EOS International
Database Vendor: OCLC FirstSearch
Function: Ref serv available
Publications: Accessions List; Subject Bibliographies
Partic in Dialog Corp; OCLC Online Computer Library Center, Inc
Open Mon-Fri 9-4
Restriction: Open to pub for ref & circ; with some limitations

G NAVAL RESEARCH LABORATORY*, Ruth H Hooker Research Library, 4555 Overlook Ave SW, Code 5596, 20375-5334. SAN 302-7392. Tel: 202-767-2357. FAX: 202-767-3352. E-mail: ref@library.nrl.navy.mil. Web Site: infoweb.nrl.navy.mil. *Chief Librn,* Suzanne Ryder; *Acq,* Rosette Risell; Staff 22 (MLS 6, Non-MLS 16)
Library Holdings: Bk Vols 46,000; Per Subs 2,506
Subject Interests: Atmospheric sci, Biomolecular sci, Chem, Computer sci, Electronics sci & tech, Info tech, Mat sci, Nanotechnologies, Ocean sci, Optical sci, Physics, Radar
Automation Activity & Vendor Info: (Cataloging) SirsiDynix; (Circulation) SirsiDynix; (ILL) OCLC; (Serials) SirsiDynix
Partic in Consortium of Naval Libraries (CNL); National Research Library Alliance (NRLA)

S NEW YORK TIMES*, Washington Bureau Library, 1627 I St NW, 20006. SAN 302-7422. Tel: 202-862-0300. FAX: 202-862-0428. Web Site: nytimes.com.
Founded 1932
Library Holdings: Bk Titles 4,500; Per Subs 30
Subject Interests: Fed govt, Politics
Database Vendor: Dialog, Factiva.com, LexisNexis
Partic in NY Times Info Bank
Restriction: Not open to pub, Staff use only

S THE NEWSPAPER GUILD-CWA*, Heywood Broun Memorial Library, 501 Third St NW, 6th Flr, 20001-2760. SAN 302-7430. Tel: 202-434-7177. FAX: 202-434-1472. Web Site: www.newsguild.org.
Founded 1957
Library Holdings: Bk Vols 900; Per Subs 50
Special Collections: Works of Heywood Broun
Restriction: By permission only, Private libr

L NIXON PEABODY LLP*, Law Library, 401 Ninth St NW, Ste 900, 20004. SAN 371-5582. Tel: 202-585-8000, Ext 8320. FAX: 202-585-8080. *Dir, Libr & Res Serv,* Sara G Eakes; E-mail: seakes@nixonpeabody.com; *Librn,* Beverly Miller; *Librn,* Michael Willens; Staff 3 (MLS 3)
Library Holdings: Bk Titles 1,500; Bk Vols 5,000; Per Subs 250
Automation Activity & Vendor Info: (Cataloging) SydneyPlus; (Circulation) SydneyPlus; (OPAC) SydneyPlus; (Serials) SydneyPlus
Database Vendor: Dialog, LexisNexis, Westlaw
Restriction: Not open to pub

§L NOSSAMAN LLP LIBRARY, Washington, 1666 K Street NW, Ste 500, 20006,

S NPR LIBRARY, 1111 N Capitol St NE, 20002. SAN 326-2189. Reference Tel: 202-513-2350. Administration Tel: 202-513-2355. E-mail: library@npr.org. Web Site: www.npr.org. *Chief Librn,* Laura Soto-Barra; E-mail: lsotobarra@npr.org; *Librn,* Katie Daugert; *Librn,* Jane Gilvin; *Librn,* Robert Goldstein; *Librn,* Sarah Knight; *Librn,* Candice Kortkamp; *Librn,* Ayda Pourasad; *Librn,* Camille Salas; *Product Develop Mgr,* Hannah Sommers; *Res & Operations Mgr,* Mary Glendinning; Staff 10 (MLS 9, Non-MLS 1)
Founded 1971
Special Collections: NPR content 1971 - today, different formats; Spoken Word & Music, CDs, files
Database Vendor: Bloomberg, EBSCO Discovery Service, EBSCO Information Services, Factiva.com, Facts on File, Gale Cengage Learning, H W Wilson, LexisNexis, Newsbank, Oxford Online, ProQuest
Wireless access
Function: Archival coll, Computer training, e-mail serv, Electronic databases & coll, For res purposes, Music CDs, Online cat, Online ref, Online searches, Orientations, Outreach serv, Ref & res, Spoken cassettes & DVDs

Open Mon-Sun 9-6
Restriction: Employees only

S NUCLEAR ENERGY INSTITUTE LIBRARY*, 1776 I St NW, Ste 400, 20006-3708. SAN 302-5926. Tel: 202-739-8135. FAX: 202-533-0152. Web Site: www.nei.org. *Librn,* Martha Parks Gow; E-mail: mpg@nei.org; Staff 1 (MLS 1)
Founded 1954
Library Holdings: Bk Titles 10,000; Per Subs 250
Subject Interests: Energy, Environ studies, Nuclear energy, Radiation
Automation Activity & Vendor Info: (Cataloging) EOS International; (Circulation) EOS International; (OPAC) EOS International
Database Vendor: EBSCO Information Services, EOS International, Ingenta, LexisNexis, OCLC WorldShare Interlibrary Loan, Westlaw
Wireless access
Restriction: Researchers by appt only, Staff & mem only

L O'MELVENY & MYERS LLP*, Law Library, 1625 Eye St NW, 20006. SAN 372-3208. Tel: 202-383-5300. Reference Tel: 202-383-5347. FAX: 202-383-5414. Web Site: www.omm.com. *Mgr,* Debra Fisher; E-mail: dfisher@omm.com; *Sr Res Librn,* Martha Cocker; Staff 5 (MLS 3, Non-MLS 2)
Special Collections: In-house Legislative History Coll
Subject Interests: Antitrust, Employee benefits, Employment law, Estate planning, Financial institutions, Intellectual property, Intl trade, Labor law, Litigation, Mergers, Telecommunication
Automation Activity & Vendor Info: (Acquisitions) OCLC; (Cataloging) OCLC; (Circulation) OCLC; (Course Reserve) OCLC Online; (OPAC) OCLC
Restriction: Open by appt only

S ORGANIZATION FOR ECONOMIC COOPERATION & DEVELOPMENT*, Washington Center, 2001 L St NW, Ste 650, 20036-4922. SAN 320-1341. Tel: 202-785-6323. FAX: 202-785-0350. E-mail: washington.contact@oecd.org. Web Site: www.oecdwash.org. *Pub Serv,* Kathleen DeBoer; Tel: 202-822-3866, E-mail: kathleen.deboer@oecd.org
Founded 1966
Library Holdings: Bk Vols 3,800; Per Subs 22
Special Collections: Economics (OECD), bks, doc, electronic publication (CD-Rom & diskettes)
Subject Interests: Agr, Econ, Educ, Energy, Environment, Intl law, Pub mgt, Sci tech, Transportation
Publications: OECD Recent Publications
Open Mon-Fri 9-5

S ORGANIZATION OF AMERICAN STATES*, Columbus Memorial Library, 19th & Constitution Ave NW, 20006-4499. SAN 302-7465. Tel: 202-458-6041. Interlibrary Loan Service Tel: 202-458-6037. FAX: 202-458-3914. Web Site: www.oas.org. *Chief Librn,* Beverly Wharton-Lake; Tel: 202-458-3849, E-mail: bwhartonlake@oas.org; *Cat,* Jean Craigwell; Tel: 202-458-6172, E-mail: jcraigwell@oas.org; *Doc,* Rene L Gutierrez; Tel: 202-458-6233, E-mail: rgutierrez@oas.org; *Ref,* Stella Villagran; E-mail: svillagran@oas.org. Subject Specialists: *Archives, Rec mgt,* Beverly Wharton-Lake; Staff 10 (MLS 4, Non-MLS 6)
Founded 1890
Library Holdings: Bk Vols 500,000; Per Subs 2,679
Special Collections: Democracy; Drugs; Historical Photographs; Human Rights Coll; Inter-American System; International Orgns; Latin America, Caribbean, Canada & the US; Sustainable Development; Trade; Women in the Americas. UN Document Depository
Database Vendor: LexisNexis, OCLC FirstSearch
Publications: Guide to the Columbus Memorial Library; Hipolito Unanue Bibliographic Servs; Indice Analitico de Documentos Oficiales; Information & Documentation Series; List of Recently Catalogued Books; Lista General de Documentos Oficiales; OAS Records Management Handbook; OAS Records Management Manual; Periodical Articles of Interest
Open Mon-Thurs 9:30-4:30, Fri 1:30-4:30
Restriction: Non-circulating to the pub
Friends of the Library Group

G OSHA, Technical Data Center, 200 Constitution Ave NW, Rm N-2625, 20210-2001. SAN 323-9233. Tel: 202-693-2350. FAX: 202-693-1648. E-mail: technicaldatacenter@dol.gov. *Dir,* Michelle Walker; *Tech Info Spec,* Sandy Lewis; E-mail: lewis.sandra@dol.gov; Staff 1 (MLS 1)
Library Holdings: Bk Titles 6,000; Bk Vols 12,500; Per Subs 206
Special Collections: OSHA Rulemaking Records
Subject Interests: Eng, Med, Occupational safety
Database Vendor: Bloomberg, ebrary, IHS, OCLC, OCLC WorldShare Interlibrary Loan, PubMed, ReferenceUSA, RefWorks, SirsiDynix
Function: ILL available
Partic in Docline; Fedlink; OCLC Online Computer Library Center, Inc

Open Mon-Fri 8:15-4:45
Restriction: Non-circulating to the pub

G OVERSEAS PRIVATE INVESTMENT CORP LIBRARY*, 1100 New York Ave NW, 11th Flr, 20527. SAN 302-7473. Tel: 202-336-8566. Interlibrary Loan Service Tel: 202-336-8568. FAX: 202-408-9860. Web Site: www.opic.gov. *Mgr, Libr Serv,* Ellen Lytton; E-mail: elytt@opic.gov; Staff 4 (MLS 3, Non-MLS 1)
Founded 1974
Library Holdings: Bk Titles 12,000; Per Subs 150
Special Collections: Country File; Foreign Assistance & International Development (Legislative History Coll)
Subject Interests: Econ, Finance
Automation Activity & Vendor Info: (Acquisitions) SirsiDynix; (Cataloging) SirsiDynix; (Circulation) SirsiDynix; (OPAC) SirsiDynix; (Serials) SirsiDynix
Partic in Fedlink; OCLC Online Computer Library Center, Inc
Restriction: Open by appt only

S PAN AMERICAN HEALTH ORGANIZATION HEADQUARTERS LIBRARY*, 525 23rd St NW, 20037. SAN 302-749X. Tel: 202-974-3160, 202-974-3734. E-mail: libraryhq@paho.org. Web Site: www.paho.org. *Chief, Libr Serv,* Elaine Santos. Subject Specialists: *Pub health,* Elaine Santos; Staff 5 (MLS 3, Non-MLS 2)
Founded 1926
Library Holdings: Bk Titles 50,000; Per Subs 30
Special Collections: Pan American Health Organization/World Health Organization Documents
Subject Interests: Pub health
Automation Activity & Vendor Info: (Cataloging) SirsiDynix; (OPAC) SirsiDynix
Wireless access
Restriction: Open by appt only

L PATTON & BOGGS LLP*, Law Library, 2550 M St NW, 8th Flr, 20037. SAN 376-0669. Tel: 202-457-6000. FAX: 202-457-6315. Web Site: www.pattonboggs.com. *Librn,* Kevin McCall
Library Holdings: Bk Titles 3,500; Bk Vols 20,000; Per Subs 200
Database Vendor: Dialog, LexisNexis, Westlaw
Open Mon-Fri 9-5:30

S PENSION BENEFIT GUARANTY CORPORATION*, Corporate Library, 1200 K St NW, Ste 360, 20005-4026. SAN 320-135X. Tel: 202-326-4000, Ext 3091. FAX: 202-326-4011. E-mail: librarystaff2@pbgc.gov. *Libr Mgr,* Judith M Weiss; E-mail: weiss.judith@pbgc.gov; *Ref Librn,* Ann Wakefield; Tel: 202-326-4000, Ext 3550, E-mail: wakefield.ann@pbgc.gov; *Tech Info Spec,* Lynn Artabane; Tel: 202-326-4000, Ext 6061, E-mail: artabane.lynn@pbgc.gov; *Libr Tech,* M Eva Salvetti; Tel: 202-326-4000, Ext 3242, E-mail: salvetti.maria@pbgc.gov; Staff 4 (MLS 2, Non-MLS 2)
Founded 1976
Library Holdings: Bk Vols 12,000; Per Subs 65
Subject Interests: Bankruptcy, Pensions
Restriction: Open to pub by appt only

S PEW CHARITABLE TRUSTS LIBRARY, 901 E St, 20004. SAN 374-5430. Tel: 215-575-9050. Administration Tel: 215-575-4920. FAX: 215-575-4939. E-mail: library@pewtrusts.org. *Mgr, Res Serv,* Melanie Sciochetti; E-mail: msciochetti@pewtrusts.org; *Res Librn,* Melissa Jordan; Tel: 202-540-6611, E-mail: mjordan@pewtrusts.org. Subject Specialists: *Legal res,* Melissa Jordan; Staff 2 (MLS 2)
Founded 1989
Jul 2013-Jun 2014. Mats Exp $238,000, Books $13,000, Per/Ser (Incl. Access Fees) $80,000, Electronic Ref Mat (Incl. Access Fees) $145,000
Special Collections: Internal Digital Documents Coll. Oral History
Subject Interests: Philanthropy
Automation Activity & Vendor Info: (Acquisitions) EOS International; (Cataloging) EOS International; (Circulation) EOS International; (OPAC) EOS International; (Serials) EOS International
Database Vendor: EBSCOhost, Factiva.com, Foundation Center, HeinOnline, JSTOR, LexisNexis, OCLC, ProQuest
Wireless access
Restriction: Not open to pub

S THE PHILLIPS COLLECTION LIBRARY*, 1600 21st St NW, 20009-1090. SAN 321-2297. Tel: 202-387-2151, Ext 212. FAX: 202-387-2436. Web Site: www.phillipscollection.org. *Librn,* Karen Schneider; E-mail: kschneider@phillipscollection.org; Staff 1 (Non-MLS 1)
Founded 1976
Library Holdings: Bk Vols 8,000; Per Subs 10
Special Collections: 19th & 20th Century European & American Artists, monographs; Duncan Phillips Coll, mss; Exhibition Catalogues; History of American Art Museums & Collecting; Phillips Coll Artists, monographs
Restriction: Open by appt only

S POLISH LIBRARY*, 1503 21st St NW, 20036. SAN 375-9237. Tel: 202-466-2665. E-mail: mailbox@polishlibrary.org. Web Site: www.polishlibrary.org. *Pres,* Anna Firsowicz
Founded 1991
Library Holdings: AV Mats 250; Bk Titles 7,000
Special Collections: Polish Culture, History, Literature, Magazines & Newspapers
Open Tues 7pm-9:30pm, Sat 11-2
Friends of the Library Group

S POPULATION ACTION INTERNATIONAL LIBRARY*, 1300 19th St NW, Ste 200, 20036-1624. SAN 320-1368. Tel: 202-557-3400. FAX: 202-728-4177. Web Site: www.populationaction.org. *Dir, Strategic Knowledge,* Mary Panke
Library Holdings: Bk Titles 6,000; Per Subs 30
Subject Interests: Ecology, Reproductive health
Automation Activity & Vendor Info: (Cataloging) Inmagic, Inc.; (Circulation) Inmagic, Inc.; (OPAC) Inmagic, Inc.
Open Mon-Fri 9-5
Restriction: Staff use only

S POPULATION REFERENCE BUREAU LIBRARY*, 1875 Connecticut Ave NW, Ste 520, 20009-5728. SAN 302-7538. Toll Free Tel: 800-877-9881. FAX: 202-328-3937. E-mail: popref@prb.org. Web Site: www.prb.org. *Librn,* Ellen Carnevale
Founded 1960
Library Holdings: Bk Titles 5,000; Per Subs 50
Special Collections: Demographic & Health Surveys; International Statistical Publications; United Nations Publications; United States Census Materials; United States Vital Statistics; World Bank Publications
Subject Interests: Aging, Demography, Environment, Health, Migration, Pop policy, Pop studies, Women's studies
Database Vendor: JSTOR, LexisNexis
Function: For res purposes, ILL available, Photocopying/Printing
Partic in Association of Population/Family Planning Libraries & Information Centers-International (APLIC-I)
Restriction: Non-circulating to the pub, Open to pub upon request, Pub ref by request

L PORTER, WRIGHT, MORRIS & ARTHUR LLP, Law Library, 1900 K St NW, Ste 1110, 20006. SAN 377-4279. Tel: 202-778-3000, 202-778-3044. Toll Free Tel: 800-456-7962. FAX: 202-778-3063. Web Site: www.porterwright.com. *Librn,* Robert Oszakiewski; E-mail: roszakiewski@porterwright.com
Library Holdings: Bk Vols 2,000; Per Subs 8
Open Mon-Fri 9-6

L PROSKAUER ROSE LLP LIBRARY*, 1001 Pennsylvania Ave NW, Ste 400 S, 20004-2533. SAN 377-4473. Tel: 202-416-6823. FAX: 202-416-6899. *Librn,* Carla Evans; E-mail: cevans@proskauer.com; Staff 2 (MLS 1, Non-MLS 1)
Library Holdings: Bk Vols 5,000; Per Subs 40
Restriction: Open to pub by appt only

S PUBLIC CITIZEN LIBRARY*, 215 Pennsylvania Ave SE, 3rd Flr, 20003. SAN 325-8580. Tel: 202-546-4996. FAX: 202-547-7392. Web Site: www.citizen.org.
Library Holdings: Bk Titles 1,000; Per Subs 20
Subject Interests: Consumer
Open Mon-Fri 9-6

L REED SMITH LLP*, Law Library, 1301 K St NW, Ste 1100, E Tower, 20005-3317. SAN 325-8564. Tel: 202-414-9200. Interlibrary Loan Service Tel: 202-414-9415. FAX: 202-414-9299. Web Site: www.reedsmith.com. *Librn,* Lorraine DeSouza; *Legis Librn,* Karen Burris; *Ref Serv,* Amy Denniston
Library Holdings: Bk Vols 21,041; Per Subs 250
Automation Activity & Vendor Info: (Acquisitions) SirsiDynix
Open Mon-Fri 8:30-6

S REPUBLICAN NATIONAL COMMITTEE LIBRARY*, 310 First St SE, 20003. SAN 302-7600. Tel: 202-863-8815. FAX: 202-863-8744. Web Site: www.rnc.org. *Res Analyst,* Courtney Sanders
Library Holdings: Bk Titles 1,500; Per Subs 10
Special Collections: Convention Proceedings
Subject Interests: Govt
Restriction: Staff use only

S RESOURCES FOR THE FUTURE INC LIBRARY*, 1616 P St NW, Rm B-6, 20036-1400. SAN 374-471X. Tel: 202-328-5089. FAX: 202-939-3460. Web Site: www.rff.org. *Librn,* Christopher B Clotworthy; E-mail: clotworthy@rff.org; Staff 1 (MLS 1)
Founded 1985
Library Holdings: Bk Titles 5,500; Per Subs 180
Subject Interests: Environ policy
Restriction: Open by appt only

R SAINT PAUL'S COLLEGE LIBRARY, 3015 Fourth St NE, 20017. SAN 302-7643. Tel: 202-269-2545. FAX: 202-269-2507. *Librn,* Denise Eggers; E-mail: librariancsp@aol.com; Staff 1 (MLS 1)
Founded 1889
Library Holdings: Bk Titles 40,000; Bk Vols 45,000; Per Subs 59
Special Collections: 17th & 18th Century Works; Isaac T Hecker Archival Coll; Paulist Fathers Archive
Subject Interests: Catholicism, Ecumenism, Spirituality, Theol
Partic in Washington Theological Consortium
Restriction: Open to researchers by request

SR ST PAUL'S EPISCOPAL CHURCH*, Thomas Bray Library, Rock Creek Church Rd & Webster St NW, 20011. SAN 372-591X. Tel: 202-726-2080. FAX: 202-726-1084. Web Site: www.rockcreekparish.org. *Librn,* Anne Greenwood
Library Holdings: Bk Titles 700
Subject Interests: Christian relig
Open Mon-Fri 9-5

S SCOTTISH RITE LIBRARY*, 1733 16th St NW, 20009-3103. SAN 302-7686. Tel: 202-232-3579. FAX: 202-464-0487. E-mail: info@culturaltourismdc.org. Web Site: www.scottishrite.org. *Curator, Librn,* Joan K Sansbury; Tel: 202-777-3139, E-mail: jsansbury@scottishrite.org; *Asst Librn,* Larissa Watkins; Tel: 202-777-3127, E-mail: lwatkins@scottishrite.org
Founded 1881
Library Holdings: Bk Vols 193,000
Special Collections: Abraham Lincoln Coll; Goethe Coll; J Edgar Hoover Coll; Masonic Coll; Panama Canal (Thatcher Coll); Robert Burns Coll
Subject Interests: Freemasonry, Hist
Automation Activity & Vendor Info: (Cataloging) SirsiDynix
Wireless access
Open Mon-Thurs 8-5
Friends of the Library Group

S SEYFARTH SHAW*, Washington Branch Office Library, 975 F St NW, 20004. SAN 302-7694. Tel: 202-828-3559, 202-828-5345. FAX: 202-828-5393. *Librn,* Susan Ryan; E-mail: sryan@seyfarth.com; Staff 2 (MLS 1, Non-MLS 1)
Founded 1978
Library Holdings: Bk Vols 11,000; Per Subs 150
Subject Interests: Construction, Employment law, Labor law, Law
Automation Activity & Vendor Info: (Cataloging) OCLC
Database Vendor: LexisNexis, OCLC FirstSearch, Westlaw
Function: ILL available
Partic in OCLC Online Computer Library Center, Inc
Open Mon-Fri 9-5

L SHEARMAN & STERLING LIBRARY*, 801 Pennsylvania Ave NW, Ste 900, 20004-2634. SAN 373-0972. Tel: 202-508-8055. FAX: 202-508-8100. Web Site: www.shearman.com. *Head Librn,* Jill Sidford; *Res,* Eleanor Gonzalez; E-mail: eleanor.gonzalez@shearman.com; Staff 6 (MLS 3, Non-MLS 3)
Library Holdings: Bk Vols 10,000; Per Subs 70
Subject Interests: Antitrust, Corporate, Intl trade, Litigation, Securities
Restriction: Open by appt only

R SHILOH BAPTIST CHURCH*, Susie E Miles Library, 1510 Ninth St NW, 20001. SAN 302-7716. Tel: 202-232-4288. Administration Tel: 202-232-4200. FAX: 202-234-6235. Web Site: shilohbaptist.org. *Librn,* Vera Hunter
Founded 1959
Library Holdings: Bk Titles 4,000; Per Subs 17
Subject Interests: Relig
Restriction: Open by appt only

M SIBLEY MEMORIAL HOSPITAL, Medical Library, 5255 Loughboro Rd NW, 20016. SAN 329-5184. Tel: 202-537-4110. *Librn,* Yelena Suprunova; Staff 1 (MLS 1)
Library Holdings: Bk Titles 2,500; Per Subs 100
Subject Interests: Med, Nursing
Partic in District of Columbia Area Health Science Libraries

L SIDLEY AUSTIN LLP*, Law Library, 1501 K St NW, 20005. SAN 371-6317. Tel: 202-736-8525. Interlibrary Loan Service Tel: 202-736-8505. FAX: 202-736-8711. *Dir,* Jeffrey V Bosh; E-mail: jbosh@sidley.com; *Circ,* Hang Ngo; *ILL,* Wyman L Colona, Jr; *Ref,* Ellen Kreis; *Ref Serv,* Jennifer Butler; Staff 3 (MLS 3)
Library Holdings: Bk Vols 25,000; Per Subs 300
Special Collections: Legislative Histories

Partic in OCLC Online Computer Library Center, Inc
Open Mon-Fri 9-5

L SKADDEN, ARPS, SLATE, MEAGHER & FLOM LLP*, Law Library, 1440 New York Ave NW, 20005. SAN 372-1434. Tel: 202-371-7760. FAX: 202-393-5760. Web Site: www.skadden.com. *Librn,* Margaret M Heath
Library Holdings: Bk Vols 30,000; Per Subs 400
Subject Interests: Energy, Intl trade, Litigation, Mergers, Securities, Tax
Open Mon-Fri 9:30-5:30

S SMITHSONIAN LIBRARIES*, Nat Museum of Natural Hist, Rm 22, MRC154, Tenth St & Constitution Ave NW, 20002. (Mail add: PO Box 37012, 20013-7012), SAN 337-0321. Tel: 202-633-2240. Interlibrary Loan Service Tel: 202-633-1245. FAX: 202-633-4315. Interlibrary Loan Service FAX: 202-633-4317. E-mail: libmail@si.edu. Web Site: www.library.si.edu. *Dir of Libr,* Nancy E Gwinn; E-mail: gwinnn@si.edu; *Dep Dir,* Mary Augusta Thomas; E-mail: thomasm@si.edu; *Assoc Dir, Digital Serv, Prog Dir, Biodiversity Heritage Libr,* Martin Kalfatovic; Tel: 202-633-1705, E-mail: kalfatovicm@si.edu; *Admin Officer,* Kathy Hill; Tel: 202-633-1945, Fax: 202-633-7367, E-mail: hillka@si.edu; Staff 112 (MLS 60, Non-MLS 52)
Founded 1846
Library Holdings: Bk Vols 1,587,735
Special Collections: History of Science & Technology; Natural History, Trade Literature
Subject Interests: African art, Am art, Am cultural hist, Asian art, Aviation hist, Ethnology, Mus studies, Natural hist, Sci tech, Trade
Automation Activity & Vendor Info: (Acquisitions) SirsiDynix; (Cataloging) SirsiDynix; (Circulation) SirsiDynix; (ILL) OCLC ILLiad; (OPAC) SirsiDynix; (Serials) SirsiDynix
Database Vendor: Dialog, JSTOR, LexisNexis, OCLC WorldShare Interlibrary Loan, ProQuest, ScienceDirect, SirsiDynix
Publications: Information (Newsletter)
Partic in Association of Research Libraries (ARL); Chesapeake Information & Research Library Alliance (CIRLA); Metropolitan New York Library Council; OCLC Online Computer Library Center, Inc
Restriction: Open to others by appt

Branches:

S ANACOSTIA COMMUNITY MUSEUM LIBRARY, 1901 Fort Pl SE, MRC 520, 20020-0520. (Mail add: PO Box 37012, 20013-7012), SAN 302-5845. Tel: 202-633-4862. FAX: 202-610-3374. E-mail: libmail@si.edu. Web Site: www.sil.si.edu/libraries/anacostia.
Library Holdings: Bk Vols 5,581
Subject Interests: Abolitionism, African, African-Am, Local hist, Slavery
Publications: Newsletter
Restriction: Open by appt only

BOTANY & HORTICULTURE LIBRARY, Nat Museum of Natural Hist, Rm W422, MRC 154, Tenth St & Constitution Ave NW, 20560. (Mail add: PO Box 37012, 20013-7012), SAN 374-8073. Tel: 202-633-1685. Interlibrary Loan Service Tel: 202-633-1245. FAX: 202-357-1896. Interlibrary Loan Service FAX: 202-786-2443. Web Site: www.sil.si.edu/libraries/bothort. *Librn,* Robin Everly; Tel: 202-633-2146, E-mail: everlyr@si.edu
Library Holdings: Bk Vols 51,313
Special Collections: Agrostology (Hitchcock-Chase Coll); Algology (Dawson Coll); General Botany (John Donnell Smith Coll)
Subject Interests: Botany, Hort
Restriction: Open to pub by appt only

COOPER-HEWITT, NATIONAL DESIGN MUSEUM LIBRARY, Two E 91st St, 3rd Flr, New York City, 10128, SAN 312-0651. Tel: 212-849-8330. FAX: 212-849-8339. Web Site: www.sil.si.edu/libraries/chm. *Librn,* Jennifer Cohlman; Tel: 212-848-8333, E-mail: cohlmanj@si.edu; *Librn,* Stephen H Van Dyk; Tel: 212-849-8335, E-mail: vandyks@si.edu; *Ref Librn,* Elizabeth Broman; Tel: 212-633-8336, E-mail: bromane@si.edu; Staff 2 (MLS 2)
Library Holdings: Bk Vols 71,166
Special Collections: American & Foreign Auction Catalogs; Donald Deskey Archive; Henry Dreyfuss Archive; Ladislav Sutnar Archive; Pop-Up Book Coll; Therese Bonney Photographs; World's Fair Coll, 1844-1964
Subject Interests: Archit, Decorative art, Decorative design, Interior design, Rare bks, Textiles
Restriction: Open by appt only
Friends of the Library Group

JOSEPH F CULLMAN 3RD, LIBRARY OF NATURAL HISTORY, Nat Museum of Natural Hist, Rm CE-G15, MRC 154, Tenth St & Constitution Ave NW, 20560. (Mail add: PO Box 37012, 20013-7012). Tel: 202-633-1184. Interlibrary Loan Service Tel: 202-633-1177. FAX: 202-633-0219. Web Site: www.sil.si.edu/libraries/cullman. *Curator, Natural Hist Rare Bks,* Leslie K Overstreet; Tel: 202-633-1176, E-mail: overstreetl@si.edu; *Libr Tech,* Daria Wingreen-Mason; E-mail: wingreend@si.edu; Staff 2 (MLS 1, Non-MLS 1)
Library Holdings: Bk Vols 6,560
Special Collections: James Smithson Library; Natural History & Natural Sciences Coll
Subject Interests: Anthrop, Botany, Hist of mus & sci coll, Hort, Mineral sci, Paleontology, Voyages, Zoology
Restriction: Open by appt only

THE VINE DELORIA, JR LIBRARY, NATIONAL MUSEUM OF THE AMERICAN INDIAN, Cultural Resource Ctr, MRC 538, 4220 Silver Hill Rd, Suitland, 20746-0537. Tel: 301-238-1376. FAX: 301-238-3038. Web Site: library.si.edu/libraries/american-indian. *Librn,* Elayne Silversmith; E-mail: silversmithe@si.edu; *ILL Librn,* Harriet Gray; Tel: 202-633-1241, E-mail: grayh@si.edu; Staff 2 (MLS 1, Non-MLS 1)
Library Holdings: Bk Vols 12,000
Automation Activity & Vendor Info: (Cataloging) SirsiDynix; (Circulation) SirsiDynix; (OPAC) SirsiDynix
Database Vendor: Dialog, OCLC FirstSearch, ProQuest, Wilson - Wilson Web
Function: Res libr
Restriction: Open to pub by appt only

THE DIBNER LIBRARY OF THE HISTORY OF SCIENCE & TECHNOLOGY, Nat Museum of American Hist, Rm 1041, MRC 672, 12th St & Constitution Ave NW, 20560-0672. (Mail add: PO Box 37012, 20013-7012), SAN 375-5266. Tel: 202-633-3872. Interlibrary Loan Service Tel: 202-633-3871. E-mail: dibnerlibrary@si.edu. Web Site: www.sil.si.edu/libraries/dibner. *Curator, Head, Spec Coll,* Lilla Vekerdy; E-mail: vekerdyl@si.edu; *Tech Info Spec,* Kirsten Van Der Veen; E-mail: vanderveenk@si.edu; Staff 2 (MLS 1, Non-MLS 1)
Library Holdings: Bk Vols 29,711
Special Collections: A G Bell & Joseph Henry Coll; Burndy Library Donation; Comegys Library; Wetmore Bequest; World's Fair Coll
Subject Interests: Applied arts, Astronomy, Eng, Natural hist, Phys sci, Tech
Publications: Dibner Library Lecture (Annual); Heralds of Science; Manuscripts of the Dibner Collection
Restriction: Open by appt only

FREER GALLERY OF ART & ARTHUR M SACKLER GALLERY LIBRARY, Arthur M Sackler Gallery, Rm 2057, MRC 707, 1050 Independence Ave NW, 20560. (Mail add: PO Box 37012, 20013-7012), SAN 337-047X. Tel: 202-633-0477. FAX: 202-786-2936. Web Site: www.asia.si.edu/research/library.asp. *Head Librn,* Reiko Yoshimura; Tel: 202-633-0481, E-mail: yoshire@si.edu; *Librn,* Kathryn Phillips; Tel: 202-633-0478, E-mail: phillka@si.edu; *Librn,* Yue Shu; Tel: 202-633-0479, E-mail: shuyuex@si.edu; *Librn,* Mike Smith; Tel: 202-633-0480, E-mail: smithmi@si.edu; Staff 3 (MLS 3)
Founded 1923
Library Holdings: Bk Vols 86,804
Special Collections: Charles Lang Freer Coll, archives; Herzfeld Coll, archives; James M Whistler & His Contemporaries
Subject Interests: Arts, Asia, E Asian, Far East, Near East, S Asia, SE Asia
Automation Activity & Vendor Info: (OPAC) Innovative Interfaces, Inc
Open Mon-Fri 10-5
Restriction: Non-circulating to the pub

HIRSHHORN MUSEUM & SCULPTURE GARDEN LIBRARY, Seventh St & Independence Ave SW, Rm 427, MRC 361, 20560. (Mail add: PO Box 37012, 20013-7012), SAN 337-050X. Tel: 202-633-2773. Interlibrary Loan Service Tel: 202-633-2775. FAX: 202-633-8796. E-mail: hmsglibmail@si.edu. Web Site: www.hirshhorn.si.edu. *Librn,* Anna Brooke; Tel: 202-633-2774, E-mail: brookea@si.edu; Staff 2 (MLS 1, Non-MLS 1)
Founded 1969
Library Holdings: Bk Vols 67,353
Special Collections: Press Books, photogs, slides
Subject Interests: 19th Century, 20th Century, Memorabilia, Painting, Sculpture
Restriction: Open by appt only

MUSEUM STUDIES & REFERENCE LIBRARY, Nat Museum of Natural Hist, Tenth St & Constitution Ave NW, Rm EC 1st Flr, MRC 154, 20560. (Mail add: PO Box 37012, 20013-7012), SAN 337-0356. Tel: 202-633-1680. Interlibrary Loan Service Tel: 202-633-1245. E-mail: libmail@si.edu. *Librn,* Martha Rosen; E-mail: RosenM@si.edu; Staff 1 (MLS 1)
Library Holdings: Bk Vols 25,964
Special Collections: Smithsoniana (Publications by & about the Smithsonian Institution)
Subject Interests: Museology
Automation Activity & Vendor Info: (Cataloging) SirsiDynix; (Circulation) SirsiDynix; (OPAC) SirsiDynix
Database Vendor: Dialog, OCLC WorldShare Interlibrary Loan, OVID Technologies, ProQuest, PubMed, SirsiDynix
Restriction: Open by appt only

MUSEUM SUPPORT CENTER LIBRARY, Smithsonian Museum Support Center, Rm C-2000, MRC 534, 4210 Silver Hill Rd, Suitland, 20746-2863, SAN 376-9348. Tel: 301-238-1030. Web Site: library.si.edu/libraries/museum-support-center. *Librn,* Carrie Smith; Tel:

301-238-1026, E-mail: smithc@si.edu; *Libr Tech,* Sharad Shah; E-mail: shahs@si.edu; Staff 2 (MLS 2)
Library Holdings: Bk Vols 25,647
Subject Interests: Art conserv, Mat & conserv sci, Object conserv, Restoration
Automation Activity & Vendor Info: (OPAC) SirsiDynix
Function: Audio & video playback equip for onsite use
Restriction: Open by appt only

NATIONAL AIR & SPACE MUSEUM LIBRARY, National Air & Space Museum, Rm 3100, MRC 314, Sixth St & Independence Ave SW, 20560-0314. (Mail add: PO Box 37012, 20013-7012), SAN 337-0534. Tel: 202-633-2320. FAX: 202-786-2835. Web Site: www.sil.si.edu/libraries/nasm. *Librn,* William Baxter; Tel: 202-633-2324, E-mail: baxterw@si.edu; Staff 4 (MLS 1, Non-MLS 3)
Library Holdings: Bk Titles 44,000
Special Collections: Aerospace (Bella Landauer Sheet Music & Children's Book Coll); Aerospace (Institute of Aeronautical Sciences Historical Coll), bk, per, photog; Ballooning (William A M Burden Coll), bks, per; Rare & Scarce Aeronautica & Astronautica (Ramsey Room)
Subject Interests: Aeronaut, Astronautics, Astronomy, Astrophysics, Earth sci, Planetary sci
Restriction: Open to pub by appt only

NATIONAL MUSEUM OF AMERICAN HISTORY LIBRARY, NMAH Rm 5016, MRC 630, 14th & Constitution Ave NW, 20560. (Mail add: PO Box 37012, 20013-7012), SAN 337-0593. Tel: 202-633-3865. Interlibrary Loan Service Tel: 202-633-3863. FAX: 202-633-3427. Web Site: smithsonianlibraries.si.edu. *Head Librn,* Bill Baxter; Tel: 202-633-2067, E-mail: baxterw@si.edu; *Ref Librn,* Paul McCutcheon; Tel: 202-633-3859, E-mail: mccutcheonp@si.edu; *Ref Librn,* Jim Roan; Tel: 202-633-3860, E-mail: roanj@si.edu
Founded 1958
Library Holdings: Bk Vols 468,857
Special Collections: Exhibitions & Expositions; History of Science & Technology; Radioana; Trade Literature
Subject Interests: Am hist, Culture, Decorative art, Graphic arts, Mil hist, Numismatics, Photog, Textiles
Restriction: Open to pub by appt only

NATIONAL MUSEUM OF NATURAL HISTORY LIBRARY, Tenth St & Constitution Ave NW, 1st Flr, MRC 154, 20013-0712. (Mail add: PO Box 37012, 20013-7012), SAN 337-0623. Tel: 202-633-1680. Interlibrary Loan Service Tel: 202-633-1245. FAX: 202-357-1896. Interlibrary Loan Service FAX: 202-786-2443. Web Site: www.sil.si.edu/libraries/nmnh. *Librn,* Ann Juneau; Tel: 202-633-4939, E-mail: juneaua@si.edu; *Librn,* Martha Rosen; Tel: 202-633-1674, E-mail: rosenm@si.edu; *Ref Serv,* Polly Lasker; Tel: 202-633-1702, E-mail: laskerp@si.edu; *Libr Tech,* Richard Greene; Tel: 202-633-1672, E-mail: greener@si.edu; *Libr Tech,* Ronald Lindsey; Tel: 202-633-1673, E-mail: lindseyr@si.edu; Staff 9 (MLS 5, Non-MLS 4)
Library Holdings: Bk Vols 129,544
Special Collections: Entomology (Casey Coleoptera Coll); Foraminifera (Cushman Coll); Invertebrate Zoology (Wilson Copepoda Coll); Meteorites (Paneth Coll)
Subject Interests: Botany, Ecology, Entomology, Evolution, Geol, Oceanography, Zoology
Open Mon-Fri 8:45-5:15

NATIONAL POSTAL MUSEUM LIBRARY, Two Massachusetts Ave NE, MRC 570, 20560-0570. (Mail add: PO Box 37012, 20013-7012), SAN 375-5258. Tel: 202-633-5544. FAX: 202-633-9371. Web Site: www.sil.si.edu/libraries/npm/. *Librn,* Paul McCutcheon; E-mail: mccutcheonp@si.edu; Staff 1 (MLS 1)
Library Holdings: Bk Vols 22,190
Special Collections: Postal History (Thaddeus Hyatt Postcard & Clipping Files); Sydnor Zip-Code File; US Post Office Department Files
Subject Interests: Philately
Restriction: Open by appt only

NATIONAL ZOOLOGICAL PARK LIBRARY, Nat Zoological Park, Education Bldg Visitor Ctr, MRC 551, 3000 Block of Connecticut Ave NW, 20008-0551. (Mail add: PO Box 37012, 20013-7012), SAN 337-0712. Tel: 202-673-1030. FAX: 202-673-4900. E-mail: nzplibrary@si.edu. Web Site: www.sil.si.edu/libraries/nzp. *Librn,* Polly Lasker; Tel: 202-633-1702, E-mail: laskerp@si.edu; Staff 1 (MLS 1)
Library Holdings: Bk Vols 13,871
Subject Interests: Animal husbandry, Animals, behavior of, Clinical med, Pathology, Veterinary med, Wildlife
Restriction: Open by appt only

JOHN WESLEY POWELL LIBRARY OF ANTHROPOLOGY, Nat Museum of Natural Hist, Rm 331, MRC 112, Tenth St & Constitution Ave NW, 20560-0112. (Mail add: PO Box 37012, 20013-7012), SAN 374-8081. Tel: 202-633-1640. Interlibrary Loan Service Tel: 202-633-1245. FAX: 202-357-1896. Interlibrary Loan Service FAX: 202-786-2443. Web Site: www.sil.si.edu/libraries/anth/. *Librn,* Margaret R Dittemore; Tel: 202-633-1638, E-mail: dittemorem@si.edu; *Librn,* James Haug; Tel: 202-633-1641, E-mail: haugj@si.edu; Staff 3 (MLS 2, Non-MLS 1)
Library Holdings: Bk Vols 84,223
Special Collections: Asian Cultural History (Echols Coll); Bureau of American Ethnology Library Coll; Mesoamerican Codices; Native American Languages/Linguistics; Physical Anthropology (Hrdlicka Coll)
Subject Interests: Anthrop, Archaeology
Restriction: Open by appt only

WARREN M ROBBINS LIBRARY, NATIONAL MUSEUM OF AFRICAN ART, National Museum of African Art, 950 Independence Ave SW, Rm 2138, MRC 708, 20560. (Mail add: PO Box 37012, 20013-7012), SAN 302-637X. Tel: 202-633-4680. FAX: 202-357-4879. Web Site: www.sil.si.edu/libraries/nmafa. *Librn,* Janet L Stanley; Tel: 202-633-4681, E-mail: stanleyj@si.edu; *Libr Tech,* Karen Brown; Tel: 202-633-4682, E-mail: brownkf@si.edu; Staff 1 (MLS 1)
Library Holdings: Bk Vols 30,076
Subject Interests: Africa, Archeology, Art, Folklore, Hist, Mat culture, Music, Relig
Restriction: Open to pub by appt only

SMITHSONIAN AMERICAN ART MUSEUM/NATIONAL PORTRAIT GALLERY LIBRARY, Victor Bldg, Rm 2100, MRC 975, 750 Ninth St NW, 20560. (Mail add: PO Box 37012, 20013-7012), SAN 337-0569. Tel: 202-633-8230. Reference Tel: 202-633-8240. FAX: 202-633-8232. Web Site: library.si.edu/libraries/american-art-portrait-gallery. *Head Librn,* Douglas Litts; E-mail: littsd@si.edu; *Ref Librn,* Anne Evenhaugen; Tel: 202-633-8227, E-mail: evenhaugena@si.edu; Staff 5 (MLS 2, Non-MLS 3)
Founded 1964
Library Holdings: Bk Vols 135,834
Special Collections: California Art & Artists (Ferdinand Perret Art Reference Library), scrapbks; Mallet Library of Art Reproductions
Subject Interests: 20th Century art, Am art, Biog, Hist, Portraiture
Automation Activity & Vendor Info: (Circulation) SirsiDynix
Partic in Dialog Corp; Wilsonline
Publications: Brochure
Open Mon-Fri 10-12 & 1-5

SMITHSONIAN ENVIRONMENTAL RESEARCH CENTER LIBRARY, 647 Contees Wharf Rd, Edgewater, 21037. (Mail add: PO Box 28, Edgewater, 21037-0028), SAN 307-0174. Tel: 443-482-2273. FAX: 443-482-2286. Web Site: library.si.edu/libraries/environmental-research-center. *Librn,* Susan Zwicker; Tel: 202-633-1675, E-mail: zwickers@si.edu; Staff 1 (Non-MLS 1)
Founded 1977
Library Holdings: Bk Vols 12,500
Subject Interests: Ecology, Environ mgt, Land use
Restriction: Open to pub by appt only

L SNR DENTON LLP LIBRARY*, 1301 K St NW, Ste 600E, 20005. SAN 370-5714. Tel: 202-408-6452. FAX: 202-408-6399. Web Site: www.snrdenton.com. *Sr Res Analyst,* Ann Green; E-mail: ann.green@snrdenton.com; Staff 2 (MLS 2)
Founded 1986
Library Holdings: Bk Titles 1,000; Bk Vols 15,000; Per Subs 25
Restriction: Not open to pub

S SOCIETY OF THE CINCINNATI LIBRARY, 2118 Massachusetts Ave NW, 20008. SAN 302-7767. Tel: 202-785-2040, Ext 411. FAX: 202-785-0729. E-mail: library@societyofthecincinnati.org. Web Site: www.societyofthecincinnati.org. *Libr Dir,* Ellen Clark; *Res Serv Librn,* Rachel Jirka; *Archivist,* Valerie Sallis; *Cat,* E K Hong; Staff 4 (MLS 4)
Founded 1783
Library Holdings: Bk Titles 45,000; Per Subs 100
Special Collections: 18th Century, American Revolution, Art of War & Military History, engravings, maps, ms, prints, rare bks; Archives of the Society of the Cincinnati
Function: Archival coll, Exhibits, Online cat
Publications: Cincinnati Fourteen; Exhibit Catalogs; George Rogers Clark Lectures
Partic in OCLC Online Computer Library Center, Inc
Restriction: Open by appt only

L SPIEGEL & MCDIARMID LLP, Law Library, 1875 Eye St NW, Ste 700, 20006. SAN 372-1744. Tel: 202-879-4055. FAX: 202-393-2866. E-mail: library@spiegelmcd.com. Web Site: www.spiegelmcd.com. *Librn,* Jeffrey J Berns; E-mail: jeff.berns@spiegelmcd.com; Staff 1 (MLS 1)
Founded 1967
Library Holdings: e-books 430; Bk Titles 4,300; Bk Vols 9,000; Per Subs 140; Videos 70
Subject Interests: Admin law, Energy law, Environ law, Telecommunications law
Automation Activity & Vendor Info: (Cataloging) Inmagic, Inc.; (OPAC) Inmagic, Inc.; (Serials) Inmagic, Inc.
Database Vendor: HeinOnline, LexisNexis, OCLC FirstSearch, Westlaw
Wireless access
Publications: Library Blog (Newsletter)
Open Mon-Fri 9-5:30

L SQUIRE, SANDERS & DEMPSEY LIBRARY*, 1201 Pennsylvania Ave NW, Ste 500, 20044. (Mail add: PO Box 407, 20044-0407), SAN 377-3817. Tel: 202-626-6708. Interlibrary Loan Service Tel: 202-626-6704. Reference Tel: 202-626-6853. FAX: 202-626-6780. Web Site: www.ssd.com. *Managing Librn,* Scott Bailey; E-mail: sbailey@ssd.com; *Ref Serv,* Kristin Humphreys; E-mail: khumphreys@ssd.com; Staff 4 (MLS 1, Non-MLS 3)
Library Holdings: Bk Vols 15,000; Per Subs 60

S STATE SERVICES ORGANIZATION LIBRARY*, Hall of the States, Ste 237, 444 North Capital St NW, 20001. SAN 320-1376. Tel: 202-624-5485. Web Site: www.sso.org. *Libr Dir,* Charles W Walton; E-mail: cwalton@sso.org; Staff 1 (MLS 1)
Founded 1977
Library Holdings: Bk Titles 1,000; Bk Vols 2,000; Per Subs 200
Subject Interests: Congress/State relations, Educ, Energy, Environ, Healthcare, Tech, Transportation
Automation Activity & Vendor Info: (Cataloging) Inmagic, Inc.; (Circulation) Inmagic, Inc.; (OPAC) Inmagic, Inc.; (Serials) Inmagic, Inc.
Database Vendor: EBSCOhost, LexisNexis, Westlaw
Wireless access
Publications: State-Federal Relations Index
Restriction: Open to pub for ref only

L STEPTOE & JOHNSON LIBRARY*, 1330 Connecticut Ave NW, 20036. SAN 302-7805. Tel: 202-828-3620. FAX: 202-429-3902. *Dir,* Ellen Brondfield; Tel: 202-429-6429, E-mail: ebrondfield@steptoe.com; Staff 9 (MLS 8, Non-MLS 1)
Founded 1972
Library Holdings: Bk Vols 60,000
Subject Interests: Law, Legislation
Partic in OCLC Online Computer Library Center, Inc

L STERNE, KESSLER, GOLDSTEIN & FOX LIBRARY*, 1100 New York Ave NW, 8th Flr, 20005-3934. SAN 371-7666. Tel: 202-371-2600. Interlibrary Loan Service Tel: 202-772-8808. FAX: 202-371-2540. E-mail: info@skgf.com. Web Site: www.skgf.com. *Libr Mgr,* Kelley M Martin; E-mail: kmartin@skgf.com; Staff 2 (MLS 1, Non-MLS 1)
Library Holdings: Bk Titles 10,000

C STRAYER UNIVERSITY*, Wilkes Library, 1133 15th St NW, 20005. SAN 302-7813. Tel: 202-419-0483. FAX: 202-419-1463. Web Site: icampus.strayer.edu/lrc/about. *Dir,* David Moulton; Tel: 202-833-0542, E-mail: dam@strayer.edu
Founded 1965. Highest Degree: Master
Library Holdings: e-books 68,000; Bk Vols 100,000; Per Subs 600
Subject Interests: Acctg, Bus admin, Criminal justice, Educ, Health serv admin, Info syst, Mkt, Pub admin
Automation Activity & Vendor Info: (Cataloging) SirsiDynix; (Circulation) SirsiDynix; (OPAC) SirsiDynix
Database Vendor: ACM (Association for Computing Machinery), CQ Press, CredoReference, EBSCOhost, Faulkner Information Services, LexisNexis, Loislaw, Mergent Online, Oxford Online, ProQuest
Partic in Lyrasis; OCLC Online Computer Library Center, Inc

L SULLIVAN & CROMWELL LLP*, Law Library, 1701 Pennsylvania Ave NW, 20006-5805. SAN 372-1477. Tel: 202-956-7538. FAX: 202-293-6330. Web Site: www.sullcrom.com. *Librn,* Denise Noller
Library Holdings: Bk Vols 8,000; Per Subs 25

GL SUPREME COURT OF THE UNITED STATES LIBRARY*, One First St NE, 20543. (Mail add: 3035 V St NE, 20018), SAN 302-7848. Tel: 202-479-3037. FAX: 202-479-3477. *Librn,* Linda Maslow; *Coll Mgr,* David Graham; *Tech Coordr,* Reginald Gerig; *Tech Serv,* Diane Simpson; Staff 29 (MLS 16, Non-MLS 13)
Founded 1887
Library Holdings: Bk Vols 500,000; Per Subs 5,500
Special Collections: Supreme Court Legislative Coll
Subject Interests: Law
Automation Activity & Vendor Info: (OPAC) Innovative Interfaces, Inc
Database Vendor: Dialog, Gale Cengage Learning, HeinOnline, JSTOR, LexisNexis, PubMed, Westlaw, Wilson - Wilson Web
Function: For res purposes
Partic in Law Library Microform Consortium (LLMC)
Open Mon-Fri 9-4:30
Restriction: Private libr

G SURFACE TRANSPORTATION BOARD LIBRARY*, 395 E St SW, 20024. SAN 302-6841. Tel: 202-245-0406. FAX: 202-245-0462. Web Site: www.stb.dot.gov. *Librn,* Christine L Glaab; E-mail: glaabc@stb.dot.gov; Staff 1 (MLS 1)
Founded 1894
Library Holdings: Bk Vols 10,000; Per Subs 10
Special Collections: Congressional Materials; Transportation in the US, doc, rare bks; US & Canada Regulatory Commissions, rpts
Subject Interests: Admin law, Statistics, Transportation
Automation Activity & Vendor Info: (Cataloging) Inmagic, Inc.
Database Vendor: EBSCOhost, LexisNexis
Restriction: Open to pub for ref only

L SUTHERLAND, ASBILL & BRENNAN LLP LIBRARY*, 1275 Pennsylvania Ave NW, 6th Flr, 20004-2415. SAN 302-7856. Tel: 202-383-0100. Interlibrary Loan Service Tel: 202-383-0450. FAX: 202-637-3593. Web Site: www.sablaw.com. *Mgr, Libr Serv,* Sara T Stephens; E-mail: sstephens@sablaw.com; Staff 5 (MLS 2, Non-MLS 3)
Library Holdings: Bk Vols 30,000
Special Collections: Energy, Insurance, Patents, Tax & Trademarks Coll; Tax Legislative Histories Coll
Subject Interests: Corporate securities, Energy, Intellectual property, Tax
Database Vendor: LexisNexis, OCLC FirstSearch
Function: ILL available

R TEMPLE SINAI LIBRARY*, 3100 Military Rd NW, 20015. SAN 302-7872. Tel: 202-363-6394. FAX: 202-363-6396. Web Site: www.templesinaidc.org. *Librn,* Ruth Polk
Founded 1955
Library Holdings: Bk Vols 6,000; Per Subs 30
Special Collections: Bill Rabin Art Coll; Children's Literature (Lisa Sanders Ressell Coll); Comparative Religion (Celia Freedman Coll); Hebrew Texts
Subject Interests: Biblical studies, Holocaust, Jewish hist & lit, Judaica, Philos, Relig
Publications: Selected Bibliographies on Judaica
Open Tues & Thurs 9-4, Wed 4-6, Sun Noon-1pm

S TEXTILE MUSEUM*, Arthur D Jenkins Library, 2320 S St NW, 20008-4088. SAN 302-7880. Tel: 202-667-0441, Ext 31. FAX: 202-483-0994. Web Site: www.textilemuseum.org.
Founded 1926
Library Holdings: Bk Titles 20,000; Per Subs 144
Special Collections: Cultural History of the Americas, Asia, Africa, the Middle East & the Pacific Rim; History of Rugs, Textiles, Costume
Subject Interests: Costume design, Textile hist, Textile tech
Publications: Annual Bibliography of Textile Literature; Textile Museum Journal
Open Wed-Fri 10-2, Sat 10-4
Restriction: Not a lending libr

L THOMPSON COBURN LIBRARY*, DC Branch, 1909 K St NW, Ste 600, 20006. SAN 377-4449. Tel: 202-585-6900. FAX: 202-585-6969. Web Site: www.thompsoncoburn.com. *Legis Librn,* Charlotte Osborn-Bensaada; E-mail: cbensaada@thompsoncoburn.com

S TRANSAFRICA FORUM*, Arthur R Ashe Jr Foreign Policy Library, 1629 K St NW, Ste 1100, 20006. SAN 377-4600. Tel: 202-223-1960. FAX: 202-223-1966. E-mail: info@transafricaforum.org. Web Site: www.transafricaforum.org. *Exec Dir,* Nicole Lee; *Dir of Outreach,* Mwiza Munthali
Library Holdings: Bk Vols 5,000; Per Subs 100
Open Mon-Fri 9-5

C TRINITY UNIVERSITY*, Sister Helen Sheehan Library, 125 Michigan Ave NE, 20017. SAN 302-7929. Tel: 202-884-9350. Interlibrary Loan Service Tel: 202-884-9357. FAX: 202-884-9241. E-mail: trinitylibrary@trinitydc.edu. Web Site: library.trinitydc.edu. *Dir,* Kaye Gaspen; *Coordr of Libr Tech,* Shirley Butler; Tel: 202-884-9353, E-mail: butlers@trinitydc.edu; *ILL, Monograms & Journals Acq,* Jacob Berg; E-mail: bergj@trinitydc.edu; *Ref,* Ashley Ryan; Staff 3 (MLS 2, Non-MLS 1)
Founded 1897. Enrl 1,600; Fac 100; Highest Degree: Master
Subject Interests: Hist, Lit, Women's studies
Automation Activity & Vendor Info: (Acquisitions) Ex Libris Group; (Cataloging) Ex Libris Group; (Circulation) Ex Libris Group; (ILL) OCLC; (OPAC) Ex Libris Group; (Serials) Ex Libris Group
Database Vendor: EBSCOhost, Gale Cengage Learning, ISI Web of Knowledge, JSTOR, LexisNexis, OCLC WorldShare Interlibrary Loan, ProQuest, PubMed
Wireless access
Function: Copy machines, Distance learning, Doc delivery serv, e-mail serv, Electronic databases & coll, Handicapped accessible, Homework prog, ILL available, Libr develop, Online ref, Online searches, Outside serv via phone, mail, e-mail & web, Photocopying/Printing, Ref & res, Ref serv available, Telephone ref, VHS videos, Video lending libr, Wheelchair accessible, Workshops
Partic in OCLC Online Computer Library Center, Inc

S UKRAINIAN CONGRESS COMMITTEE OF AMERICA LIBRARY*, 311 Massachusetts Ave NE, 20002. SAN 375-6386. Tel: 202-547-0018. FAX: 202-543-5502. E-mail: unis@ucca.org. Web Site: www.ucca.org. *Pres,* Michael Sawkiw
Library Holdings: Bk Titles 4,000; Per Subs 12
Subject Interests: Soviet studies, Ukrainian culture, Ukrainian hist
Restriction: Open by appt only

S UNITED FOOD & COMMERCIAL WORKERS INTERNATIONAL UNION LIBRARY*, 1775 K St NW, 20006. SAN 337-0208. Tel: 202-223-3111. FAX: 202-466-1562. Web Site: www.ufcw.org.
Founded 1974
Library Holdings: Bk Vols 2,000; Per Subs 750
Subject Interests: Bus & mgt, Econ, Retailing
Partic in Dialog Corp
Restriction: Open by appt only

S UNITED NATIONS INFORMATION CENTER*, 1775 K St NW, Ste 400, 20006. SAN 302-7937. Tel: 202-331-8670. FAX: 202-331-9191. E-mail: unicdc@unic.org. Web Site: www.unicwash.org. *Librn, Pub Info,* Liam Murphy
Founded 1946
Library Holdings: Bk Titles 2,000; Bk Vols 3,000; Per Subs 10
Special Collections: Film Library; United Nations Chronicles & Publications; United Nations Official Reports. UN Document Depository
Subject Interests: Econ, Energy, Finance, Human rights, Intl law, Soc sci & issues, United Nations
Restriction: Open by appt only

G UNITED STATES AGENCY FOR INTERNATIONAL DEVELOPMENT*, USAID Library, 1300 Pennsylvania Ave NW, Rm M01-010, 20523-1000. SAN 302-5497. Tel: 202-712-0579. FAX: 202-216-3515. E-mail: ksc@usaid.gov. Web Site: www.usaid.gov/km. *Sr Librn,* Karen White; *Electronic Res Librn,* Nellie Kamau; E-mail: nkamau@usaid.gov; *Syst & Cat Librn,* Sean Crumley; *ILL,* Mike Trufanow; E-mail: ksc@usaid.gov; *Learning Res Ctr Spec,* Fatmata McCormack; E-mail: fmccormack@usaid.gov; *Tech Serv,* April Knepp; E-mail: aknepp@usaid.gov; Staff 6 (MLS 5, Non-MLS 1)
Founded 1967
Library Holdings: DVDs 500; e-journals 200; Bk Vols 12,000; Per Subs 200
Automation Activity & Vendor Info: (Acquisitions) SirsiDynix; (Cataloging) SirsiDynix; (Circulation) SirsiDynix; (ILL) OCLC; (Serials) SirsiDynix
Database Vendor: Cinahl, Dialog, Dun & Bradstreet, EBSCO - WebFeat, EBSCOhost, Elsevier, Factiva.com, Gale Cengage Learning, Hoovers, LexisNexis, Medline, OCLC FirstSearch, PubMed, ScienceDirect, SerialsSolutions, SirsiDynix
Wireless access
Publications: DEC Express (Acquisition list); KSC E-Monitor (Newsletter); New This Month (Acquisition list)
Partic in OCLC Online Computer Library Center, Inc
Restriction: Authorized scholars by appt
Friends of the Library Group

UNITED STATES AIR FORCE

A ANDREWS AIR FORCE BASE LIBRARY FL4425*, 89 SVS/SVMG, Brookley & D St, Bldg 1642, Andrews AFB, 20762, SAN 337-0836. Tel: 301-981-6454. FAX: 301-981-4231. *Dir,* Anette Powell; Tel: 301-981-1637, E-mail: anette.powell@andrews.af.mil; Staff 5 (MLS 1, Non-MLS 4)
Library Holdings: Bk Vols 30,714; Per Subs 140
Special Collections: Air War College; Children's Coll
Subject Interests: Bus & mgt, Intl relations, Polit sci
Automation Activity & Vendor Info: (Cataloging) SirsiDynix; (Circulation) SirsiDynix; (ILL) OCLC; (OPAC) SirsiDynix
Open Mon 9-8, Tues, Wed & Fri 9-6, Thurs 11-8

A BOLLING AIR FORCE BASE LIBRARY*, FL 7054 HQ 11 MSG/SVMG, 410 Tinker St Bolling AFB, 20032-0703, SAN 337-0895. Tel: 202-767-5578. FAX: 202-404-8526. *Dir,* Shirley Foster; E-mail: shirley.foster@afncr.af.mil
Founded 1931
Library Holdings: Bk Vols 28,090; Per Subs 33
Subject Interests: Mil hist
Automation Activity & Vendor Info: (Cataloging) Softlink America; (Circulation) Softlink America; (OPAC) Softlink America
Database Vendor: EBSCOhost, OCLC FirstSearch
Restriction: Not open to pub

S UNITED STATES BOTANIC GARDEN LIBRARY*, 245 First St SW, 20024. SAN 374-7689. Tel: 202-226-8333. FAX: 202-225-1561. E-mail: usbg@aoc.gov. Web Site: www.usbg.gov. *In Charge,* Ari Novy
Library Holdings: Bk Vols 1,200; Per Subs 10
Subject Interests: Botany, Hort, Landscape design
Restriction: Open by appt only

G UNITED STATES COMMISSION ON CIVIL RIGHTS*, National Clearinghouse Library, 624 Ninth St NW, Ste 600, 20425. SAN 302-7953. Tel: 202-376-8110. FAX: 202-376-7597. TDD: 202-376-8116. Web Site: www.usccr.gov. *Libr Tech,* Vanessa Williamson
Founded 1957
Library Holdings: Per Subs 95
Special Collections: Civil Rights (US Commission on Civil Rights Coll); Federal Register, micro
Subject Interests: Aging, Civil rights, Educ, Handicaps
Automation Activity & Vendor Info: (Cataloging) OCLC; (ILL) OCLC
Database Vendor: EBSCOhost, OCLC FirstSearch, OCLC WorldShare Interlibrary Loan, Westlaw
Partic in OCLC Online Computer Library Center, Inc
Special Services for the Deaf - TDD equip
Open Mon-Fri 10-4
Restriction: Restricted pub use

SR UNITED STATES CONFERENCE OF CATHOLIC BISHOPS*, Department of Communications Library & Archives, 3211 Fourth St NE, 20017-1194. SAN 371-6341. Tel: 202-541-3286. Web Site: www.catholicnews.com, www.usccb.org. *Mgr, Info & Archive Serv,* Katherine Nuss; E-mail: knuss@usccb.org; Staff 1 (MLS 1)
Founded 1920
Library Holdings: Bk Vols 3,500; Per Subs 20
Special Collections: Catholic News Service; NCWC American Bishops, bks & pamphlets; United States Conference of Catholic Bishops Publications, bks & pamphlets
Subject Interests: Church hist, Human rights, Theol
Wireless access
Function: Archival coll, Ref & res
Restriction: Non-circulating coll, Not a lending libr, Open by appt only

GL UNITED STATES COURT OF APPEALS FOR THE ARMED FORCES LIBRARY*, 450 E St NW, 20442-0001. SAN 302-7988. Tel: 202-761-1466. *Law Librn,* Agnes Kiang; *Libr Tech,* Hyecha Carroll; Staff 2 (MLS 1, Non-MLS 1)
Founded 1951
Library Holdings: Bk Vols 20,000; Per Subs 40
Subject Interests: Criminal law, Mil justice
Function: For res purposes, ILL available
Restriction: By permission only

GL UNITED STATES COURT OF APPEALS FOR THE DISTRICT OF COLUMBIA*, Judges' Library, US Court House, 333 Constitution Ave NW, Rm 5518, 20001. SAN 302-7961. Tel: 202-216-7396. Web Site: www.cadc.uscourts.gov. *Circuit Librn,* Patricia Michalowskij; Tel: 202-216-7400; *Dep Circuit Librn,* Terri Santella
Library Holdings: Bk Vols 90,000; Per Subs 160
Automation Activity & Vendor Info: (Acquisitions) SirsiDynix; (Cataloging) SirsiDynix; (Circulation) SirsiDynix; (ILL) SirsiDynix; (Serials) SirsiDynix
Partic in OCLC Online Computer Library Center, Inc; Westlaw

G US CUSTOMS & BORDER PROTECTION INFORMATION RESOURCES CENTER (IRC), CBP Library, 90 K St NE, 20229. Tel: 202-325-0130. Circulation Tel: 202-325-0172. Interlibrary Loan Service Tel: 202-325-0171. FAX: 202-325-0170. E-mail: cbp.library@dhs.gov. *Libr Dir,* Linda Cullen; *Cat/Syst Librn,* Tamara L B Wilson; *Legal Ref Librn,* Mary Ann Keeling; *Ref/Bus Librn,* Carolina Menendez-Llosa; *IT Spec,* Salvin Dave; *ILL, Libr Tech-Mats,* Mark Hempstead; *Mgt & Prog Analyst,* Sandra McCoy-Lewis. Subject Specialists: *Law, Legal res,* Mary Ann Keeling; *Taxonomy,* Carolina Menendez-Llosa; *Web design,* Salvin Dave; Staff 7 (MLS 4, Non-MLS 3)
Founded 1975
Special Collections: Anti-Terrorism Coll
Subject Interests: Bus & mgt, Intl trade, Law enforcement
Automation Activity & Vendor Info: (Acquisitions) EOS International; (Cataloging) EOS International; (Circulation) EOS International; (Course Reserve) EOS International; (ILL) EOS International; (OPAC) EOS International; (Serials) EOS International
Database Vendor: Dun & Bradstreet, EBSCOhost, Gale Cengage Learning, HeinOnline, LexisNexis, OCLC, Swets Information Services, ValueLine, Westlaw
Function: ILL available
Partic in Fedlink; OCLC Online Computer Library Center, Inc
Restriction: Access at librarian's discretion

UNITED STATES DEPARTMENT OF AGRICULTURE

G ECONOMIC RESEARCH SERVICE RESOURCE CENTER*, 1800 M St, Rm N-3050, 20036, SAN 321-270X. Tel: 202-694-5065. FAX: 202-694-5689. *Dir, Ref,* Marilynn Graham; E-mail: mgraham@ers.usda.gov

Founded 1978
Library Holdings: Bk Vols 2,000; Per Subs 250
Special Collections: ERS/ESCS Publications on micro, incl staff rpts
Subject Interests: Agr econ
Partic in OCLC Online Computer Library Center, Inc
Restriction: Open by appt only

GL UNITED STATES DEPARTMENT OF COMMERCE, Law Library, 1401 Constitution Ave NW, Rm 1894, 20230. SAN 337-1042. Tel: 202-482-1154. FAX: 202-482-0221. E-mail: research@doc.gov. Web Site: library.doc.gov.
Founded 1913
Library Holdings: Bk Vols 60,000; Per Subs 25
Automation Activity & Vendor Info: (Cataloging) SirsiDynix
Wireless access
Partic in Dialog Corp; OCLC Online Computer Library Center, Inc
Restriction: Open by appt only

G US DEPARTMENT OF DEFENSE*, National Defense University Library, Fort McNair, Marshall Hall, 20319-5066. (Mail add: Bldg 62, Marshall Hall, 300 Fifth Ave, 20319-5066), SAN 302-7163. Tel: 202-685-3511. Interlibrary Loan Service Tel: 202-685-3968. Reference Tel: 202-685-3954, 202-685-3964. Automation Services Tel: 202-685-2384. FAX: 202-685-3733. Web Site: www.merln.ndu.edu, www.ndu.edu/library. *Dir,* Meg Tulloch; Tel: 202-685-3948, E-mail: tullochh@ndu.edu; *Chief, Info Archit Div,* Patricia Alderman; E-mail: aldermanp@ndu.edu; *Chief, Res & Info Serv,* Rosemary Marlowe-Dziuk; E-mail: marlowe-dziukr@ndu.edu; *MERLN Librn,* Julie Arrighetti; Tel: 202-685-3470, E-mail: arrighettij@ndu.edu; *Spec Coll & Archives Librn,* Susan K Lemke; Tel: 202-685-3957, E-mail: lemkes@ndu.edu. Subject Specialists: *Nat security, Mil-indust,* Rosemary Marlowe-Dziuk; *Mil hist,* Susan K Lemke; Staff 30 (MLS 18, Non-MLS 12)
Founded 1976. Enrl 4,500; Fac 261; Highest Degree: Master
Library Holdings: e-journals 18,000; Electronic Media & Resources 75; Bk Titles 320,000; Bk Vols 675,000; Per Subs 1,200
Special Collections: Archives of the Hudson Institute; Conduct of the Persian Gulf War; Correspondence of Bernard Baruch & Julius A Krug; Ft McNair History, including photographs & materials of the Lincoln assassination; Library & Papers of Dr Ralph L Powell (China); Library of Hoffman Nickerson (military history); Mallahan World War I Coll; Military Classics, including the early editions of Marshal de Saxe; NDU Academic & Institutional Archives; Personal Papers (Restricted) of Generals Frank S Besson Jr, John Galvin, Andreu J Goodpaster, George Joulwan, Lyman L Lemnitzer, Colin Powell, John Shalikashvili, Maxwell D Taylor; Speeches on Industrial Mobilization & Papers of J Carlton Ward Jr; Working Papers for the Presidential Commission on Women in the Combat. US Document Depository
Subject Interests: Intl relations, Logistics, Mil hist, Nat security, Polit sci
Automation Activity & Vendor Info: (Acquisitions) SirsiDynix; (Cataloging) SirsiDynix; (Circulation) SirsiDynix; (Course Reserve) SirsiDynix; (ILL) OCLC; (OPAC) SirsiDynix; (Serials) SirsiDynix
Database Vendor: Baker & Taylor, Blackwell, Dialog, EBSCOhost, Gale Cengage Learning, ISI Web of Knowledge, Jane's, JSTOR, LexisNexis, OCLC FirstSearch, OCLC WorldShare Interlibrary Loan, ProQuest, SirsiDynix, Wilson - Wilson Web
Function: Archival coll, Art exhibits, Computer training, Distance learning, e-mail serv, E-Reserves, Electronic databases & coll, Govt ref serv, ILL available, Online info literacy tutorials on the web & in blackboard, Online ref, Online searches, Orientations, Outside serv via phone, mail, e-mail & web, Ref & res, Ref serv available, Telephone ref
Publications: Military Policy Awareness Links (Current awareness service); Subject Bibliographies
Partic in Fedlink
Restriction: Not open to pub, Open to students, fac & staff

S US DEPARTMENT OF DEFENSE ARMED FORCES PEST MANAGEMENT BOARD*, Information Services Division, Walter Reed Army Medical Ctr, Forest Glen Section, 20307-5001. SAN 370-2561. Tel: 301-295-7476. FAX: 301-295-7473. Web Site: www.afpmb.org. *Chief Librn,* Dr Richard G Robbins; Tel: 301-295-8309, E-mail: richard.robbins@osd.mil. Subject Specialists: *Med entomology, Parasitology,* Dr Richard G Robbins; Staff 9 (MLS 9)
Library Holdings: Bk Titles 1,550; Bk Vols 2,000; Per Subs 261
Subject Interests: Med entomology, Natural res, Parasitology, Pest control, Pub health
Database Vendor: Dialog, OVID Technologies
Function: Ref serv available
Publications: Disease Vector Ecology Profiles; Technical Guides
Open Mon-Fri 6-6

G UNITED STATES DEPARTMENT OF DEFENSE, WASHINGTON HEADQUARTERS SERVICES*, The Pentagon Library, 1155 Defense Pentagon, 20301-1155. SAN 337-1611. Circulation Tel: 703-695-1992. Reference Tel: 703-695-1997. FAX: 703-695-3999. Web Site: www.whs.mil/library. *Dir,* David Suiter; E-mail: david.suiter@whs.mil; Staff 21 (MLS 9, Non-MLS 12)
Founded 1944
Special Collections: DoD/DA Regulatory Publications & Manuals; Law Coll; Legislative Histories Relating to DoD Issues; Military Arts & Sciences Coll; Military History Coll; Regulatory Publications
Subject Interests: Foreign affairs, Intl relations, Mil hist (US), Mil sci
Automation Activity & Vendor Info: (Cataloging) EOS International; (Circulation) EOS International
Database Vendor: CQ Press, EBSCOhost, EOS International, Gale Cengage Learning, Jane's, JSTOR, LexisNexis, Medline, OCLC WorldShare Interlibrary Loan, ProQuest, PubMed, Wilson - Wilson Web
Partic in Fedlink
Open Mon-Fri 7:30-4

UNITED STATES DEPARTMENT OF ENERGY

G ENERGY LIBRARY*, MA-90, Rm 1G-033/FORS, 1000 Independence Ave SW, 20585, SAN 337-1107. Tel: 202-586-6021. FAX: 202-586-0573. E-mail: forrestal.library@hq.doe.gov. Web Site: energy.gov/oe/information-center/library. *In Charge,* Courtney Byrd
Founded 1948
Special Collections: Atomic Energy Commission, Department of Energy, Energy Research & Development Administration, Federal Energy Administration Reports, micro; International Atomic Energy Agency Publications; National Technical Information Services Selected Research in Microfiche Service for Energy
Subject Interests: Bus conserv, Eng, Hist of energy, Statistics energy
Automation Activity & Vendor Info: (Cataloging) TLC (The Library Corporation); (Circulation) TLC (The Library Corporation); (ILL) OCLC; (OPAC) TLC (The Library Corporation)
Partic in OCLC Online Computer Library Center, Inc
Friends of the Library Group

G UNITED STATES DEPARTMENT OF HEALTH & HUMAN SERVICES*, Office of the General Counsel, Law Library, Rm 4541, Cohen Bldg, 330 Independence Ave SW, 20201. SAN 377-399X. Tel: 202-619-0190. FAX: 202-619-3719. E-mail: law.library@hhs.gov. *Legal Info Mgr,* Susan Marie Panasik; E-mail: susan.panasik@hhs.gov; *Ref Librn,* Daniel Beam; Tel: 202-619-2700, E-mail: dan.beam@hhs.gov; *Libr Tech,* Luan Tang; E-mail: luan.tang@hhs.gov. Subject Specialists: *Law,* Daniel Beam; Staff 3 (MLS 2, Non-MLS 1)
Founded 1989
Library Holdings: Bk Vols 10,000; Per Subs 20
Subject Interests: Admin law, Health law
Database Vendor: LexisNexis, Westlaw
Wireless access
Open Mon-Fri 9-5:30
Restriction: Circ limited

G UNITED STATES DEPARTMENT OF HOUSING & URBAN DEVELOPMENT*, HUD Library, 451 Seventh St SW, Rm 8141, 20410. SAN 302-802X. Tel: 202-708-2370. FAX: 202-708-1485. E-mail: webmanager@hud.gov. Web Site: www.hud.gov. *Dir,* Robin Lewis
Founded 1934
Library Holdings: Bk Vols 680,000; Per Subs 2,200
Special Collections: Comprehensive Housing Affordability Strategy Reports; Housing in the 70's Background Papers; Management Evaluation Reports
Subject Interests: Am housing, Archit, Bldg construction, Bldg tech, Commun develop, Econ, Environ, Fed govt, Homelessness, Law, Local govt, Metrop area problems, Regional data, Regional planning, Sociologic data, State govt, Urban land use
Publications: Library Periodicals List: internal distribution; Recent Library Acquisitions
Partic in Fedlink
Open Mon-Fri 8-4

GL UNITED STATES DEPARTMENT OF JUSTICE*, Justice Libraries, 950 Pennsylvania Ave, Ste 5313, 20530. SAN 337-1190. Tel: 202-514-2133. Interlibrary Loan Service Tel: 202-514-3695. Reference Tel: 202-514-3775. FAX: 202-514-3546. TDD: 202-353-0304. Web Site: www.usdoj.gov. *Dir,* Blane K Dessy; Staff 78 (MLS 35, Non-MLS 43)
Founded 1831
Library Holdings: Bk Titles 85,000; Bk Vols 300,000; Per Subs 1,700
Special Collections: American, Canadian & British Law; Department of Justice Publications; United States Supreme Court Records & Briefs
Subject Interests: Antitrust, Civil, Civil rights, Criminal, Environment, Natural res, Tax
Automation Activity & Vendor Info: (Acquisitions) Ex Libris Group; (Cataloging) OCLC; (Circulation) SirsiDynix; (OPAC) SirsiDynix; (Serials) SirsiDynix
Partic in OCLC Online Computer Library Center, Inc
Special Services for the Deaf - TDD equip
Restriction: Open by appt only

G UNITED STATES DEPARTMENT OF LABOR*, Wirtz Labor Library, 200 Constitution Ave NW, Rm N-2445, 20210. SAN 337-1344. Tel: 202-693-6600. FAX: 202-693-6644. E-mail: library@dol.gov. Web Site: library.dol.gov. *Dir,* Catherine Breitenbach; Staff 11 (MLS 5, Non-MLS 6)
Founded 1917
Library Holdings: e-journals 4,500; Bk Titles 140,000; Per Subs 4,500
Special Collections: Labor Unions, doc, mat
Subject Interests: Econ, Labor
Database Vendor: EBSCO Information Services, ProQuest, Westlaw
Special Services for the Deaf - ADA equip; Am sign lang & deaf culture; Assisted listening device
Special Services for the Blind - Aids for in-house use
Open Mon-Fri 8:15-4:45
Restriction: Fee for pub use

G UNITED STATES DEPARTMENT OF STATE*, Ralph J Bunche Library, 2201 C St NW, Rm 3239, 20520-2442. SAN 302-8038. Tel: 202-647-1099. FAX: 202-647-2971. E-mail: library@state.gov. Web Site: www.state.gov/m/a/ls. *Chief Librn,* Howard Hugh; *Ref Librn,* Linda Schweizer; *Ref Librn,* Joan Sherer; *Ser Librn,* David Schaffler; *Info Res,* Ned Kraft; Tel: 202-647-2196; *Info Serv,* Fran Perros; Tel: 202-647-0451; Staff 29 (MLS 17, Non-MLS 12)
Founded 1789
Library Holdings: e-books 7,000; e-journals 8,136; Electronic Media & Resources 51; Bk Vols 400,000; Per Subs 800
Special Collections: Department of State Publications; Diplomatic Lists
Subject Interests: Diplomatic hist, Foreign affairs, Intl law
Automation Activity & Vendor Info: (Cataloging) Ex Libris Group; (Circulation) Ex Libris Group; (OPAC) Ex Libris Group
Database Vendor: CountryWatch, Dialog, Dun & Bradstreet, ebrary, Factiva.com, Gale Cengage Learning, GalleryWatch, HeinOnline, LexisNexis, OCLC FirstSearch, OCLC WorldShare Interlibrary Loan, SerialsSolutions, Swets Information Services, Westlaw
Publications: Acquisitions List (Monthly)
Restriction: Open by appt only

G UNITED STATES DEPARTMENT OF THE INTERIOR LIBRARY*, 1849 C St NW, MS 1151, 20240. SAN 302-8046. Tel: 202-208-5815. FAX: 202-208-6773. E-mail: library@ios.doi.gov. Web Site: www.doi.gov/library. *Libr Dir,* George Franchois; Tel: 202-208-3796, E-mail: george_franchois@ios.doi.gov; *Head, Ref Serv,* Jennifer Klang; Tel: 202-208-3396, E-mail: jennifer_klang@ios.doi.gov; *Law Librn,* Maureen Booth; Tel: 202-208-3686, E-mail: maureen_booth@ios.doi.gov; *ILL, Ref Librn,* Shyamalika Ghoshal; Tel: 202-208-3309, E-mail: shyamalika_ghoshal@ios.doi.gov; *Tech Serv Mgr,* Judy Din; Tel: 202-208-3402, E-mail: judy_din@ios.doi.gov. Subject Specialists: *Hist,* George Franchois; Staff 8 (MLS 7, Non-MLS 1)
Founded 1949
Library Holdings: Bk Vols 950,000; Per Subs 1,000
Special Collections: Conservation & Natural Resources; Dept of the Interior; Rare Book Coll. US Document Depository
Subject Interests: Am hist, Energy, Land mgt, Mining, Natural res, Nature, Parks, Recreation, Wildlife
Automation Activity & Vendor Info: (Acquisitions) SirsiDynix; (Cataloging) SirsiDynix; (Circulation) SirsiDynix; (Serials) SirsiDynix
Partic in OCLC Online Computer Library Center, Inc
Open Mon-Fri 7:45-5

UNITED STATES DEPARTMENT OF THE NAVY

AL NAVY GENERAL COUNSEL LAW LIBRARY*, Bldg 36, Rm 213, 720 Kennon St SE, 20374, SAN 337-1948. Tel: 202-685-6944. FAX: 202-685-6959.
Founded 1949
Library Holdings: Bk Vols 30,000
Special Collections: Law & Legislation (Legislative Histories)
Function: ILL available

A OFFICE OF NAVAL INTELLIGENCE RESEARCH LIBRARY*, 4251 Suitland Rd, 20395-5720, SAN 337-1859. Tel: 301-669-4386. FAX: 301-669-4282. *Chief Librn,* Magen Dane; Tel: 301-669-3116, E-mail: mdane@nmic.navy.mil; Staff 9 (MLS 2, Non-MLS 7)
Library Holdings: Bk Vols 10,000; Per Subs 1,000
Subject Interests: Maritime
Partic in OCLC Online Computer Library Center, Inc

UNITED STATES DEPARTMENT OF TRANSPORTATION

GL FEDERAL HIGHWAY ADMINISTRATION-CHIEF COUNSEL'S LAW LIBRARY*, 1200 New Jersry Ave SE, Rm E84-464, 20590, SAN 323-8725. Tel: 202-366-1387. FAX: 202-366-1380. Web Site: www.fhwa.dot.gov. *Librn,* Shelia Taylor; Staff 4 (MLS 1, Non-MLS 3)
Library Holdings: Bk Vols 500
Special Collections: Highway Legislative Histories (1893-present)
Database Vendor: LexisNexis, Westlaw
Partic in CQ Washington Alert
Publications: Federal Laws & Materials Relating to the Federal Highway Administration

G NATIONAL HIGHWAY TRAFFIC SAFETY ADMINISTRATION-TECHNICAL INFORMATION SERVICES*, NPO-400, 1200 New Jersey Ave SE, 20590, SAN 302-7252. Information Services Toll Free Tel: 800-424-9393. FAX: 202-493-2833. E-mail: tis@nhtsa.dot.gov. Web Site: www.nhtsa.dot.gov/. *Dir,* Kevin Mahoney; E-mail: kevin.mahoney@dot.gov; *Lead, Info Spec/Analyst,* Shirlene D Ball; E-mail: shirlene.ball@dot.gov; *Info Spec,* Theresa Gordon; E-mail: theresa.gordon@dot.gov; *Info Spec,* Derrick Lewis; E-mail: derrick.lewis@dot.gov; Staff 5 (MLS 1, Non-MLS 4)
Founded 1967
Library Holdings: CDs 450; Electronic Media & Resources 15,000; Bk Vols 100; Per Subs 30
Special Collections: Automotive Safety (Research & Test Reports of National Highway Traffic Safety Administration); Defect Investigation Files Coll; Record of Rulemaking Activity of National Highway Traffic Safety Administration
Function: For res purposes, ILL available, Online searches, Photocopying/Printing, Telephone ref
Partic in TRIS File
Open Mon-Fri 9:30-4

S UNITED STATES EQUAL EMPLOYMENT OPPORTUNITY COMMISSION LIBRARY, 131 M St NE, Rm 4SW16N, 20507. SAN 302-8070. Tel: 202-663-4630. FAX: 202-663-4629. TDD: 202-663-4641. *Dir,* Position Currently Open; *Sr Res Librn, Team Leader,* Holly Wilson; E-mail: holly.wilson@eeoc.gov; *Res Librn,* Linda Hutchinson; Tel: 202-663-4902, E-mail: linda.hutchinson@eeoc.gov; *Res Librn,* Felicia Maynard; Tel: 202-663-4631, E-mail: felicia.maynard@eeoc.gov; Staff 5 (MLS 4, Non-MLS 1)
Founded 1966
Special Collections: EEOC (Agency) Archives
Subject Interests: Civil rights, Employment, Labor
Publications: What's New in the Library? (Newsletter)
Partic in OCLC Online Computer Library Center, Inc
Special Services for the Deaf - TDD equip

G UNITED STATES GOVERNMENT ACCOUNTABILITY OFFICE*, Library Services, 441 G St NW, Rm 6H19, 20548. SAN 337-2154. E-mail: gaolibrary@gao.gov. *Libr Mgr,* Mark Ziomek; Tel: 202-512-2396, E-mail: ziomekm@gao.gov; Staff 7 (MLS 7)
Founded 1972
Special Collections: US Document Depository
Subject Interests: Acctg, Auditing, Econ, Law, Soc serv (soc work)
Automation Activity & Vendor Info: (OPAC) Innovative Interfaces, Inc
Partic in OCLC Online Computer Library Center, Inc
Restriction: Access at librarian's discretion, Authorized patrons, Borrowing requests are handled by ILL, Circulates for staff only, Open by appt only, Photo ID required for access, Use of others with permission of librn

G UNITED STATES HOLOCAUST MEMORIAL MUSEUM LIBRARY*, 100 Raoul Wallenberg Pl SW, 20024. SAN 376-2009. Tel: 202-479-9717. FAX: 202-479-9726. E-mail: library@ushmm.org. Web Site: www.ushmm.org/research/library. *Dir,* Position Currently Open; *Syst Librn,* Ron Coleman; *Cat,* Amy Alderfer; *Cat,* Holly Vorhies; *Libr Tech,* Steven Kanaley; *Ref Serv,* Vincent Slatt; Staff 6 (MLS 5, Non-MLS 1)
Founded 1993
Library Holdings: CDs 500; DVDs 400; Bk Titles 62,000; Bk Vols 80,000; Per Subs 100; Videos 800
Special Collections: Memorial Books
Subject Interests: Holocaust
Automation Activity & Vendor Info: (OPAC) Ex Libris Group
Database Vendor: EBSCOhost, JSTOR, OCLC FirstSearch, OVID Technologies, Project MUSE, ProQuest
Wireless access
Function: Res libr

G UNITED STATES HOUSE OF REPRESENTATIVES LIBRARY*, Cannon House Office Bldg, B-106, Legislative Resource Ctr, 20515-6606. SAN 302-8100. Tel: 202-226-5200. FAX: 202-226-4874. E-mail: info.clerkweb@mail.house.gov. Web Site: library.clerk.house.gov. *Librn,* Rae Ellen Best; Staff 9 (MLS 4, Non-MLS 5)
Founded 1792
Library Holdings: Bk Vols 150,000
Open Mon-Fri 9-6
Restriction: Non-circulating, Open to pub for ref only

G UNITED STATES INSTITUTE OF PEACE*, Jeannette Rankin Library Program, 2301 Constitution Ave NW, 20037. SAN 370-9973. Tel: 202-429-4742, 202-457-1700. E-mail: library@usip.org. Web Site: www.usip.org/publications-tools/usip-library. *Knowledge Mgr,* Ellen H Ensel; Tel: 202-429-3895; *Knowledge Mgt Spec,* Gretchen Sauvey; E-mail: gsauvey@usip.org; Staff 2 (MLS 2)

Library Holdings: Bk Vols 12,000; Per Subs 150
Subject Interests: Diplomacy, Mediation
Automation Activity & Vendor Info: (OPAC) Innovative Interfaces, Inc - Millenium
Wireless access
Partic in OCLC Online Computer Library Center, Inc
Open Mon-Fri 9-5:30

UNITED STATES INTERNATIONAL TRADE COMMISSION
GL LAW LIBRARY*, 500 E St SW, Rm 614, 20436, SAN 337-2219. Tel: 202-205-3287. FAX: 202-205-3111. *Librn,* Maureen Bryant; E-mail: maureen.bryant@usitc.gov; Staff 1 (MLS 1)
Founded 1972
Library Holdings: Bk Vols 10,000
Special Collections: Legislative Histories dealing with Trade & Tariff Acts
Subject Interests: Anti-dumping, Countervailing duties, Imports, Intellectual property, Tariffs, US trade law
Automation Activity & Vendor Info: (Cataloging) OCLC
Publications: Bibliography of Law Journal Articles on Statutes Administered by the United States International Trade Commission & Related Subjects
Restriction: Borrowing requests are handled by ILL, External users must contact libr

G NATIONAL LIBRARY OF INTERNATIONAL TRADE*, 500 E St SW, Rm 300, 20436, SAN 337-2189. Tel: 202-205-2630. FAX: 202-205-2316. Web Site: www.usitc.gov. ; Staff 8 (MLS 5, Non-MLS 3)
Founded 1916
Library Holdings: Bk Vols 40,000; Per Subs 2,500
Subject Interests: Agr products, Econ, Electronics, Energy, Forest products, Intl trade, Machinery manufacturers, Misc manufacturers, Textiles, Transportation
Partic in OCLC Online Computer Library Center, Inc
Open Mon-Fri 9-5
Restriction: Open to pub for ref only
Friends of the Library Group

A UNITED STATES MARINE BAND*, Music Library, Marine Barracks Annex & Band Support Facility, Seventh & L Sts SE, 20003. (Mail add: Eighth & I Sts SE, 20390-5000), SAN 302-8135. Tel: 202-433-4298. FAX: 202-433-2221. Web Site: www.marineband.usmc.mil. *Chief Librn,* Jane Cross
Founded 1798
Library Holdings: Music Scores 50,000; Bk Vols 1,000; Per Subs 25
Special Collections: Band Music; Dance Band; Historical & Program Files; Instrumental Ensembles; John Philip Sousa Coll; Marine Band Archives & Historical Coll, mss, photogs; Military & Wind Music; Orchestra Music; Piano Sheet Music; Reference Books & Scores
Restriction: Open by appt only

G UNITED STATES MERIT SYSTEMS PROTECTION BOARD LIBRARY*, 1615 M St NW, 20419. SAN 328-3488. Tel: 202-653-7200. FAX: 202-653-6182. Web Site: www.mspb.gov. *Librn,* Darryl Aaron; E-mail: darryl.aaron@mspb.gov; Staff 1 (MLS 1)
Library Holdings: Per Subs 20
Wireless access
Function: Archival coll, Govt ref serv, ILL available, Ref & res
Partic in Westlaw
Restriction: Open by appt only

G UNITED STATES NATIONAL ARBORETUM LIBRARY*, 3501 New York Ave NE, 20002-1958. SAN 326-6680. Tel: 202-245-4538. FAX: 202-245-4575. Web Site: www.usna.usda.gov. *Librn,* Position Currently Open
Founded 1964
Library Holdings: Bk Titles 10,000; Per Subs 140
Special Collections: Bonsai & Related Arts Coll; Mary Cokely Wood Ikebana Coll; US Department of Agriculture Plant Exploration Trips
Subject Interests: Botany, Gardening, Hort
Automation Activity & Vendor Info: (Cataloging) Ex Libris Group; (OPAC) Ex Libris Group
Function: For res purposes, Govt ref serv
Restriction: Access at librarian's discretion, Circulates for staff only

S US NATIONAL PARK SERVICE*, Frederick Douglass NHS Library, 1411 W St SE, 20020. SAN 370-291X. Tel: 202-426-5961. FAX: 202-426-0880. TDD: 202-426-1452. Web Site: www.cr.nps.gov/csd/exhibits/douglass. *Curator,* Cathy Ingram
Founded 1962
Library Holdings: Bk Vols 2,000
Special Collections: Cartes-de-visite; Lantern Slides; Photographic Prints Coll
Special Services for the Deaf - TTY equip

G UNITED STATES NAVAL OBSERVATORY, James Melville Gilliss Library, 3450 Massachusetts Ave NW, 20392-5420. SAN 302-8143. Tel: 202-762-1463. FAX: 202-762-1516. Web Site: www.usno.navy.mil/usno/library. *Dir,* Sally Bosken; E-mail: sally.bosken@navy.mil; Staff 2 (MLS 2)
Founded 1830
Library Holdings: Bk Vols 85,000; Per Subs 60
Special Collections: Astronomy, Mathematics, Physics & Navigation (Pre-19th Century Books)
Automation Activity & Vendor Info: (OPAC) Inmagic, Inc.
Partic in Fedlink; OCLC Online Computer Library Center, Inc; OCLC-LVIS
Open Mon-Fri 8-4

G UNITED STATES POSTAL SERVICE LIBRARY*, 475 L'Enfant Plaza SW, Rm 11800, 20260-1540. SAN 302-816X. Tel: 202-268-2074. FAX: 202-268-4423. *Ref Librn,* Raymond Plante; Tel: 202-268-2906
Founded 1955
Library Holdings: Bk Titles 50,000; Bk Vols 115,000
Special Collections: Congressional Reports (US Congressional Serial Document Set)
Subject Interests: Data proc, Econ, Human resources, Law, Mkt
Open Mon-Fri 8:30-12:30 & 1:30-5

G UNITED STATES SECURITIES & EXCHANGE COMMISSION LIBRARY*, 100 F St NE, Rm 1500, 20549-0002. SAN 302-8178. Tel: 202-551-5450. FAX: 202-772-9326. E-mail: library@sec.gov. *Dir,* Sheryl Rosenthal; Staff 9 (MLS 6, Non-MLS 3)
Founded 1934
Library Holdings: Bk Vols 62,000; Per Subs 425
Special Collections: Legislative Histories of Statutes Administered by Agency
Subject Interests: Acctg, Bus, Econ, Finance, Securities laws & regulations
Publications: Library Information Bulletin; Periodical Holdings
Partic in OCLC Online Computer Library Center, Inc
Open Mon-Fri 9-5:30
Friends of the Library Group

G UNITED STATES SENATE LIBRARY*, SRB-15 Senate Russell Bldg, 20510-7112. SAN 302-8186. Tel: 202-224-7106. FAX: 202-224-0879. TDD: 202-228-1269. *Head, Ref,* Kimberly Ferguson; *Librn,* Leona Faust; *Sr Ref Librn,* Zoe Davis; *Sr Ref Librn,* Nancy Kervin; *Sr Ref Librn,* Annie Young; *Cat Supvr,* Betsy Moon; *Cat,* Carmelita De Castro; *Cat,* Hannah Moyer; *Coll Develop,* Jean Keleher; *Ref,* Megan Dunn; *Ref,* Tamara Elliott; *Ref,* Brian McLaughlin; *Ref,* Natalie Sager; Staff 20 (MLS 17, Non-MLS 3)
Founded 1871
Library Holdings: Bk Vols 200,000; Per Subs 115
Special Collections: Bills & Resolutions, bk, micro; Congressional Hearings, bk, micro; Congressional Record, bk, micro; Serial Set, bk, micro. US Document Depository
Automation Activity & Vendor Info: (Acquisitions) TLC (The Library Corporation); (Cataloging) TLC (The Library Corporation), (Circulation) TLC (The Library Corporation); (OPAC) TLC (The Library Corporation); (Serials) TLC (The Library Corporation)
Publications: Presidential Vetoes
Partic in Dialog Corp; OCLC Online Computer Library Center, Inc; Westlaw
Special Services for the Deaf - TDD equip

L UNITED STATES SENTENCING COMMISSION LIBRARY*, One Columbus Circle NE, Ste 2-500 S Lobby, 20002-8002. SAN 372-3097. Tel: 202-502-4500. FAX: 202-502-4699. Web Site: www.ussc.gov. *Head Librn,* Linda Baltrusch
Library Holdings: Bk Vols 10,000
Partic in OCLC Online Computer Library Center, Inc

GL UNITED STATES TAX COURT LIBRARY*, 400 Second St NW, 20217. SAN 302-8194. Tel: 202-521-4585. FAX: 202-521-4574. E-mail: tclib@ustaxcourt.gov. Web Site: www.ustaxcourt.gov. *Librn,* Tania Andreeff; Staff 6 (MLS 2, Non-MLS 4)
Founded 1924
Library Holdings: Bk Titles 36,000; Per Subs 1,500
Special Collections: Tax Laws
Automation Activity & Vendor Info: (Acquisitions) SIMA, Inc; (Cataloging) OCLC Connexion
Database Vendor: 3M Library Systems, LexisNexis, OCLC FirstSearch, OCLC WorldShare Interlibrary Loan, Westlaw
Function: ILL available
Publications: Monthly Bulletin
Partic in OCLC Online Computer Library Center, Inc; Westlaw
Restriction: Not open to pub

UNIVERSITY OF THE DISTRICT OF COLUMBIA

CL DAVID A CLARKE SCHOOL OF LAW, CHARLES N & HILDA H M MASON LAW LIBRARY*, Bldg 39, Rm B-16, 4200 Connecticut Ave NW, 20008, SAN 371-9952. Tel: 202-274-7310. FAX: 202-274-7311. E-mail: lawlibrary@udc.edu. Web Site: catalog.law.udc.edu, www.law.udc.edu. *Dir,* Vinenc Feliu; Tel: 202-274-7354, E-mail: vfeliu@udc.edu; *Assoc Dir, Pub Serv,* Helen Frazer; Tel: 202-274-7356, E-mail: hfrazer@udc.edu; *Asst Dir, Tech Serv,* Han Ouyang; Tel: 202-274-7358, E-mail: houyang@udc.edu; *Acq Librn,* John Jensen; Tel: 202-274-5214, E-mail: jjensen@udc.edu; *Cat Librn,* Yasmin Morais; *Circ Librn,* Gail Mathapo; Tel: 202-274-7357, E-mail: gmathapo@udc.edu; *Emerging Tech Librn,* Brittany Kolonay; *Network Adminr,* Lewis Perry; *Ser Tech,* Kim Walker; *Ser Tech,* Marvin Williams; *Tech Support,* Lachelle Cooper; Staff 7 (MLS 7)
Founded 1987. Enrl 280; Fac 20
Library Holdings: Bk Vols 255,000
Automation Activity & Vendor Info: (Acquisitions) Innovative Interfaces, Inc
Publications: Guide
Open Mon-Fri 8am-11:30pm, Sat 10-10, Sun Noon-11:30

C LEARNING RESOURCES DIVISION*, 4200 Connecticut Ave NW, 20008, SAN 337-2391. Tel: 202-274-6370. Circulation Tel: 202-274-6009. Interlibrary Loan Service Tel: 202-274-6011. Reference Tel: 202-274-6122. FAX: 202-274-6012. Web Site: www.lrdudc.wrlc.org. *Dean of Libr,* Albert J Casciero; E-mail: casciero@wrlc.org; *Electronic Serv Librn,* Michael Fitzgerald; *Info Literacy Librn,* Rachel Jorgensen; *Ref Librn,* John Page; E-mail: jpage@wrlc.org; *Ref/Archives Librn,* Christopher Anglim; *Acq,* Gemma Park; *Electronic Ref Librn,* Lindsay Sarin; Staff 28 (MLS 10, Non-MLS 18)
Founded 1976. Enrl 5,200; Fac 211; Highest Degree: Master
Library Holdings: Bk Vols 549,678; Per Subs 594
Subject Interests: Educ, Health sci, Humanities
Partic in Washington Research Library Consortium
Publications: Access; Learning Link; Learning Resources Division Annual Report
Special Services for the Blind - Scanner for conversion & translation of mats

S URBAN LAND INSTITUTE*, Information Center, 1025 Thomas Jefferson St NW, Ste 500W, 20007. SAN 302-8216. Tel: 202-624-7137. FAX: 202-624-7140. Web Site: www.uli.org. *Librn,* Joan Campbell; E-mail: jec@uli.org
Founded 1936
Library Holdings: Bk Vols 10,000; Per Subs 275
Subject Interests: Real estate
Restriction: Open by appt only

G US ARCHITECTURAL & TRANSPORTATION BARRIERS COMPLIANCE BOARD*, Technical Resources Library, 1331 F St NW, Ste 1000, 20004-1111. SAN 325-9811. Tel: 202-272-0080. Toll Free Tel: 800-872-2253. FAX: 202-272-0081. TDD: 202-272-0082, 800-993-2822. E-mail: info@access-board.gov. Web Site: www.access-board.gov. *Librn,* Forrest Pecht
Library Holdings: Bk Vols 5,300; Per Subs 50
Special Collections: State, Local & Model Code on Accessibility
Special Services for the Deaf - TTY equip
Restriction: Open by appt only

S US ENGLISH*, Mary Cavitt Memorial Library, 1747 Pennsylvania Ave NW, Ste 1050, 20006-2712. SAN 328-6509. Tel: 202-833-0100. Toll Free Tel: 800-787-8216. FAX: 202-833-0108. E-mail: info@usenglish.org. Web Site: usenglish.org. *Chmn,* Mauro E Mujica
Library Holdings: Bk Titles 1,200; Per Subs 15

S US NEWS & WORLD REPORT*, Library & Information Services, 1050 Thomas Jefferson St NW, 20007-1196. SAN 302-8224. Tel: 202-955-2350. FAX: 202-955-2685. E-mail: reference@usnews.com. Web Site: www.usnews.com.
Library Holdings: Bk Vols 7,500; Per Subs 100
Special Collections: Government Documents Coll, VF
Subject Interests: Current events, Govt, Hist, Polit sci
Publications: U.S. News Index

S VALVE MANUFACTURERS ASSOCIATION OF AMERICA*, Crawford Library, 1050 17th St NW, Ste 280, 20036. SAN 328-3682. Tel: 202-331-8105. FAX: 202-296-0378. Web Site: www.vma.org. *Pres,* William S Sandler
Founded 1982
Library Holdings: Bk Titles 300
Publications: Valve Magazine

L VAN NESS FELDMAN LIBRARY*, 1050 Thomas Jefferson St NW, 20007. SAN 371-8948. Tel: 202-298-1800. FAX: 202-338-2416. Web Site: www.vnf.com. *Librn,* George Bernard Kirlin; E-mail: gbk@vnf.com; Staff 3 (MLS 2, Non-MLS 1)
Founded 1976
Library Holdings: Bk Titles 12,000; Bk Vols 35,000; Per Subs 250
Subject Interests: Energy
Automation Activity & Vendor Info: (Cataloging) Inmagic, Inc.
Open Mon-Fri 9-6

L VENABLE LLP LIBRARY*, Washington, DC Office, 575 Seventh St, NW, 20004-1601. SAN 325-3902. Tel: 202-344-4612. Reference Tel: 202-344-8325. FAX: 202-344-8300. *Admin Serv Librn,* David Konieczko; Tel: 202-344-8377, E-mail: dkonieczko@venable.com; *Admin Serv,* Demetria Clark; Tel: 202-344-4942, E-mail: dclark@venable.com; Staff 6 (MLS 5, Non-MLS 1)
Founded 1981
Library Holdings: Bk Vols 27,500; Per Subs 50
Subject Interests: Banks & banking, Corporate law, Drug laws, Energy, Environ law, Estates, Govt, Intl trade, Labor, Litigation, Patents, Real estate law, Securities, Taxation, Trademarks, Trusts
Automation Activity & Vendor Info: (Cataloging) Sydney; (Circulation) Sydney; (OPAC) Sydney; (Serials) Sydney
Partic in CourtLink; Dialog Corp; Dun & Bradstreet Info Servs; LexisNexis; LivEdgar; Westlaw

L VORYS, SATER, SEYMOUR & PEASE LIBRARY*, 1909 K St, 20036-5109. SAN 377-3930. Tel: 202-467-8800. FAX: 202-467-8900. Web Site: www.vssp.com. *Librn,* Mick Baugh
Library Holdings: Bk Titles 1,000; Per Subs 40

R WASHINGTON HEBREW CONGREGATION LIBRARIES*, 3935 Macomb St NW, 20016-3741. SAN 302-8259. Tel: 301-354-3212. FAX: 301-354-3200. E-mail: eshare@whctemple.org. Web Site: whclibrary.follettdestiny.com. *Librn,* Ellen Share; E-mail: eshare@whctemple.org; Staff 2 (MLS 1, Non-MLS 1)
Library Holdings: Bk Vols 15,000
Subject Interests: Biblical studies, Holocaust, Jewish hist & lit
Automation Activity & Vendor Info: (Cataloging) Follett Software; (Circulation) Follett Software
Wireless access
Friends of the Library Group

M WASHINGTON HOSPITAL CENTER*, William B Glew MD Health Sciences Library, 110 Irving St NW, Rm 2A-21, 20010-2975. SAN 302-8267. Tel: 202-877-6221. FAX: 202-877-6757. E-mail: libraryreferenceservices@medstar.net. Web Site: www.whcenter.org. *Dir,* Lynne Siemers; Staff 9 (MLS 5, Non-MLS 4)
Founded 1958
Library Holdings: Bk Titles 10,000; Bk Vols 29,800; Per Subs 700
Subject Interests: Med, Nursing
Automation Activity & Vendor Info: (Cataloging) SirsiDynix; (Circulation) SirsiDynix; (OPAC) SirsiDynix; (Serials) SirsiDynix
Publications: Annual Report; Newsletter
Partic in National Network of Libraries of Medicine; OCLC Online Computer Library Center, Inc
Friends of the Library Group

G WASHINGTON METROPOLITAN AREA TRANSIT AUTHORITY*, General Counsel's Office Law Library, 600 Fifth St NW, 20001. SAN 377-3914. Tel: 202-962-1012. FAX: 202-962-2550. Web Site: www.wmata.com. *Librn,* Jeanette Richmond
Library Holdings: Bk Vols 7,000; Per Subs 50

S WASHINGTON NATIONAL CATHEDRAL*, Cathedral Rare Book Library, Massachusetts & Wisconsin Aves NW, 20016-5098. SAN 371-1129. Tel: 202-537-6200. Web Site: www.nationalcathedral.org. *Coll Coordr,* Anna Alston Donnelly
Library Holdings: Bk Vols 9,000; Per Subs 21
Restriction: Not open to pub

S THE WASHINGTON POST*, News Research Center, 1150 15th St NW, 20071. SAN 302-8275. Tel: 202-334-7341. FAX: 202-728-3130. Web Site: www.washingtonpost.com. *Dir,* Lucy Shackelford; *Librn,* Mrs Eddy Palanzo
Founded 1933
Library Holdings: Bk Vols 5,000; Per Subs 40
Publications: News Research Bulletin; Reference Guides
Restriction: Not open to pub

S THE WASHINGTON TIMES CORP*, The World & I Magazine Library & Research Department, The Library/Research Dept, 3600 New York Ave NE, 20002-1947. SAN 323-6773. Tel: 202-636-3334. FAX: 202-636-3323. E-mail: education@worldandi.com. Web Site: www.worldandi.com. *Mgr,* Diane M Falk
Founded 1986

Library Holdings: AV Mats 100; Bk Titles 5,000; Per Subs 125; Spec Interest Per Sub 100
Special Collections: International Conference on the Unity of the Science Papers, bd docs; International Federation for World Peace; Literary Federation for World Peace; Professors World Peace Academy Conference Papers, bd docs; Summit Council for Former Heads of State; Unification Movement Archives & Current Information, bks, bulletins, journals, newsletters; Women's Federation for World Peace; World Media Conference; Youth Federation for World Peace
Subject Interests: Art, Film, Fine arts, Hist, Lit, Music, Performing arts, Philos, Politics, Relig
Function: Res libr
Restriction: Open to staff only
Friends of the Library Group

L WEIL, GOTSHAL & MANGES LLP*, Law Library, 1300 Eye St NW, Ste 900, 20005. SAN 372-1132. Tel: 202-682-7117. Interlibrary Loan Service Tel: 202-682-7118. FAX: 202-682-7297. Web Site: www.weil.com. *Libr Mgr,* DiAnne T Moore
Library Holdings: Bk Vols 30,000
Subject Interests: Banking, Corporate, Environ law, Intl trade, Litigation, Securities, Tax

L WEINER, BRODSKY, SIDMAN & KIDER PC*, Law Library, 1300 19th St NW, 5th Flr, 20036. SAN 372-1736. Tel: 202-628-2000. FAX: 202-628-2011. Web Site: www.wbsk.com.
Founded 1992
Library Holdings: Bk Vols 6,500; Per Subs 40
Function: ILL available
Open Mon-Fri 9-6

R WESLEY THEOLOGICAL SEMINARY LIBRARY*, 4500 Massachusetts Ave NW, 20016-5690. SAN 302-8313. Tel: 202-885-8695. Reference Tel: 202-885-8696. FAX: 202-885-8691. E-mail: library@wesleyseminary.edu. Web Site: library.wesleyseminary.edu. *Dir,* William D Faupel; Tel: 202-885-8960, E-mail: bfaupel@wesleyseminary.edu; *Info Serv Librn,* James Estes; E-mail: jestes@wesleyseminary.edu; *Circ Supvr,* Christina Fairman; E-mail: cfairman@wesleyseminary.edu; *Acq,* Jonathan Andrew Klenklen; Tel: 202-885-8692, E-mail: aklenklen@wesleyseminary.edu; *Tech Serv,* Hope Cooper; Tel: 202-885-8658, E-mail: hcooper@wesleyseminary.edu; Staff 5 (MLS 4, Non-MLS 1)
Founded 1882. Enrl 630; Fac 38; Highest Degree: Doctorate
Library Holdings: Bk Vols 171,500; Per Subs 600
Special Collections: Early American Methodism Coll; Methodist Protestant Church Coll
Subject Interests: Relig, Theol
Automation Activity & Vendor Info: (Acquisitions) Ex Libris Group; (Cataloging) Ex Libris Group; (Circulation) Ex Libris Group; (Course Reserve) Ex Libris Group; (ILL) OCLC WorldShare Interlibrary Loan; (OPAC) Ex Libris Group; (Serials) Ex Libris Group
Database Vendor: Baker & Taylor, EBSCOhost, OCLC WorldShare Interlibrary Loan, Tech Logic, YBP Library Services
Wireless access
Partic in Washington Theological Consortium
Open Mon-Fri 8am 10:30pm, Sat 9 6

L WHITE & CASE LLP*, Law Library, 701 13th St NW, 20005-3807. SAN 372-1469. Tel: 202-626-6475. FAX: 202-639-9355. Web Site: www.whitecase.com. *Librn,* Richard Cousins; *Asst Librn,* Roshni Santiago
Library Holdings: Bk Vols 11,000; Per Subs 40
Subject Interests: Intl law
Database Vendor: LexisNexis, Westlaw
Partic in OCLC Online Computer Library Center, Inc
Open Mon-Fri 9-5

SR WHITEFRIARS HALL*, Order of Carmelites Library, 600 Webster St NE, 20017. SAN 371-8662. Tel: 202-526-1221, Ext 201. FAX: 202-526-9217. E-mail: library@whitefriarshall.org. Web Site: www.loc.gov/rr/main/religion.wfh.html. *Librn,* Fr Patrick McMahon; Staff 1 (Non-MLS 1)
Founded 1948
Library Holdings: Bk Vols 50,000; Per Subs 60
Special Collections: Whitefriars Hall (Theology)
Restriction: Open to pub by appt only, Open to students, fac & staff

L WILEY REIN LLC LIBRARY*, 1776 K St NW, 20006. SAN 377-3833. Tel: 202-719-7000. FAX: 202-719-7049. Web Site: www.wileyrein.com.
Library Holdings: Bk Vols 25,000; Per Subs 200
Wireless access
Restriction: Not open to pub

L WILKINSON BARKER KNAUER LLP LIBRARY, 2300 N St NW, Ste 700, 20037. Tel: 202-383-3420. FAX: 202-783-5851. Web Site: www.wbklaw.com. *Librn,* Louis C Abramovitz; E-mail: labramovitz@wbklaw.com. Subject Specialists: *Communications law, Regulation, Telecommunications law,* Louis C Abramovitz; Staff 1 (MLS 1)
Library Holdings: Bk Titles 900; Bk Vols 5,000; Per Subs 35
Wireless access
Function: ILL available
Restriction: Access at librarian's discretion, Circ limited, Not open to pub

L WILLIAMS & CONNOLLY LIBRARY, 725 12th St NW, 20005. SAN 302-833X. Tel: 202-434-5303. FAX: 202-434-5029. *Dir, Libr Serv,* Caitlin Lietzan; Tel: 202-434-5306, E-mail: clietzan@wc.com; *Head, Res Serv,* Tony Minerva; Tel: 202-434-5310, E-mail: aminerva@wc.com; *Head, Tech Serv,* Andrea Bender; Tel: 202-434-5319, E-mail: abender@wc.com; *ILL Librn, Res,* Shannon O'Connell; E-mail: soconnell@wc.com; *Legis/Res Librn,* Alicia Julian; Tel: 202-434-5312, E-mail: ajulian@wc.com; *Res Librn,* Matt Foley; Tel: 202-434-5308, E-mail: mfoley@wc.com; *ILL,* Patti Hennessy; Tel: 202-434-5302, E-mail: phennessy@wc.com; *Tech Serv,* Shannah Andrews; Tel: 202-434-5376, E-mail: sandrews@wc.com; Staff 13 (MLS 5, Non-MLS 8)
Founded 1970
Library Holdings: Bk Vols 75,000; Per Subs 300
Subject Interests: Law
Automation Activity & Vendor Info: (Acquisitions) Softlink America; (Cataloging) Softlink America; (Circulation) Softlink America; (ILL) Softlink America; (OPAC) Softlink America; (Serials) Softlink America
Database Vendor: Bloomberg, Dialog, Dun & Bradstreet, LexisNexis, OCLC FirstSearch, Westlaw
Wireless access
Partic in OCLC Online Computer Library Center, Inc

L WILMER, CUTLER, HALE & DORR LIBRARY*, 1875 Pennsylvnia Ave NW, 20006. SAN 302-8348. Tel: 202-663-6771. FAX: 202-663-6363. Web Site: www.wilmerhale.com. *Dir,* Lynn Oser; Staff 18 (MLS 13, Non-MLS 5)
Founded 1963
Library Holdings: Bk Vols 55,750
Subject Interests: Antitrust law, Banks & banking, Legislation, Securities
Database Vendor: LexisNexis, Westlaw
Partic in Dialog Corp; Dow Jones News Retrieval; Westlaw
Open Mon-Fri 8-7

S WOODROW WILSON INTERNATIONAL CENTER FOR SCHOLARS LIBRARY*, 1300 Pennsylvania Ave NW, 20004-3027. SAN 302-7732. Tel: 202-691-4150. Interlibrary Loan Service Tel: 202 691-4197. FAX: 202-691-4001. Web Site: www.wilsoncenter.org. *Librn,* Janet Spikes; E-mail: janet.spikes@wilsoncenter.org; Staff 3 (MLS 1, Non-MLS 2)
Founded 1970
Library Holdings: Bk Titles 8,000; Bk Vols 12,000; Per Subs 250
Subject Interests: Russia
Database Vendor: EBSCOhost
Restriction: Open by appt only
Branches:
KENNAN INSTITUTE FOR ADVANCED RUSSIAN STUDIES LIBRARY, 1300 Pennsylvania Ave NW, 20004-3027. Tel: 202-691-4150. *Librn,* Janet Spikes, Tel: 202-691-4198, E-mail: janet.spikes@wilsoncenter.org; Staff 3 (MLS 1, Non-MLS 2)
Founded 1975
Library Holdings: Bk Titles 8,000; Bk Vols 10,000; Per Subs 50
Subject Interests: Hist, Literary criticism, Soviet studies
Restriction: Open by appt only

L WINSTON & STRAWN LLP LIBRARY*, 1700 K St NW, 20006. SAN 372-3089. Interlibrary Loan Service Tel: 202-282-5844. Reference Tel: 202-282-5273, 202-282-5485. Administration Tel: 202-282-5843. Administration FAX: 202-282-5100. E-mail: dclib11@winston.com. Web Site: www.winston.com. *Dir of Libr Serv,* Deborah A Miller; Tel: 704-350-7795, E-mail: dmiller@winston.com; Staff 3 (Non-MLS 3)
Library Holdings: Bk Vols 5,500; Per Subs 90
Wireless access
Partic in Illinois Library & Information Network
Restriction: Lending libr only via mail, Not open to pub

SR WOODSTOCK THEOLOGICAL CENTER LIBRARY*, Georgetown University, Lauinger Library, PO Box 571170, 20057-1170. SAN 322-8568. Tel: 202-687-7513. FAX: 202-687-7473. E-mail: jlh3@georgetown.edu. Web Site: woodstock.georgetown.edu/library/index.htm. *Dir,* J Leon Hooper; Tel: 202-687-4250, E-mail: jlh3@georgetown.edu; *Circ Supvr,* Susan Karp; E-mail: karps@georgetown.edu; *Tech Serv,* Paul S Osmanski; Tel: 202-687-7473; *Spec Coll Cataloger,* Amy Phillips; E-mail: aep49@georgetown.edu; Staff 4 (MLS 3, Non-MLS 1)
Founded 1869
Library Holdings: Microforms 325; Bk Vols 210,000; Per Subs 747

Special Collections: 16th-19th Century Counter-Reformational Coll; Palestinian Antiquities (Halpern Coll), engravings; Theology & Jesuitica (Joques, Shrub Oak & Parsons Coll)
Subject Interests: Relig, Scriptures, Theol
Automation Activity & Vendor Info: (Cataloging) Innovative Interfaces, Inc; (OPAC) Innovative Interfaces, Inc - Millenium
Wireless access
Partic in Washington Research Library Consortium; Washington Theological Consortium
Open Mon-Thurs 9-8, Fri 9-5

S THE WORLD BANK GROUP LIBRARY*, 1818 H St NW, MSN MC-C3-220, 20433. SAN 377-4619. Tel: 202-473-2000, 202-473-8670. FAX: 202-522-1160. E-mail: wbglibrary@worldbank.org. Web Site: www.jolis.worldbankimflib.org/external.htm. *Mgr,* Marion Richards
Library Holdings: Bk Vols 85,000; Per Subs 525
Open Mon-Fri 9-5:30

S WORLD RESOURCES INSTITUTE*, Library & Information Center, Ten G St NE, Ste 800, 20002. Tel: 202-729-7602. FAX: 202-729-7610. E-mail: library@wri.org. Web Site: www.wri.org/about/library. *Libr Mgr,* Mary Maguire; E-mail: mmaguire@wri.org; *Librn,* Julia Hussey; Staff 4 (MLS 2, Non-MLS 2)
Founded 1982
Library Holdings: Bk Titles 10,000; Per Subs 250
Automation Activity & Vendor Info: (Circulation) Inmagic, Inc.
Database Vendor: Dialog, EBSCOhost, LexisNexis, OCLC FirstSearch
Restriction: Open by appt only

S WORLD WILDLIFE FUND-US INFORMATION RESOURCE CENTER*, 1250 24th St NW, 20037-1125. SAN 302-623X. Tel: 202-778-9636. FAX: 202-331-8836. E-mail: library@wwfus.org. Web Site: www.worldwildlife.org. *Librn,* Dawn McCleskey; Staff 1 (MLS 1)
Founded 1949
Library Holdings: Bk Titles 5,000; Bk Vols 6,000; Per Subs 50
Special Collections: WWF Publications Archive
Subject Interests: Conserv, Ecology
Automation Activity & Vendor Info: (Cataloging) Softlink America; (Circulation) Softlink America; (ILL) Softlink America
Database Vendor: LexisNexis
Function: For res purposes, ILL available
Partic in OCLC Online Computer Library Center, Inc
Open Mon-Fri 9-5
Restriction: Circulates for staff only, In-house use for visitors, Pub use on premises

L WRIGHT & TALISMAN PC*, Law Library, 1200 G St NW, Ste 600, 20005-3802. SAN 370-1174. Tel: 202-393-1200. FAX: 202-393-1240. Web Site: www.wrightlaw.com. *In Charge,* Sarah Gordon
Library Holdings: Per Subs 37
Wireless access
Restriction: Staff use only

FLORIDA

Date of Statistics: FY 2013
Population, 2010 U.S. Census: 18,801,310
Population, 2013: 19,526,504
Population Served by Public Libraries: 19,483,498
Total Public Library Circulation: 125,886,799
Total Public Library Income (incl. Grants-in-Aid): $496,426,103
Source of Income: Public 95.39%; Local 90.47%; State 4.5%; Federal 0.42%; Other 4.61%
Expenditures Per Capita: $25.84
Number of County Systems: 39
Regional Systems: 8 Multi-County Systems covering 28 counties
Counties Served: 67
Number of Bookmobiles in State: 27
Grants-in-Aid to Public Libraries: $21,300,000
Formula for Apportionment of State Aid: Legally established county, municipality or multi-county libraries receive grants based on local support; additional funds are provided to 32 poorest counties and to multi-county systems

ALTAMONTE SPRINGS

P ALTAMONTE SPRINGS CITY LIBRARY*, 281 N Maitland Ave, 32701. SAN 302-8380. Tel: 407-571-8830. FAX: 407-571-8834. Web Site: www.altamonte.org. *Dir,* Diana Long; E-mail: DLLong@altamonte.org; *Ch Serv,* Fazana Baksh; *YA Serv,* Chris Druhan; Staff 5 (MLS 1, Non-MLS 4)
Founded 1959. Pop 42,000; Circ 47,730
Library Holdings: Bk Vols 36,000; Per Subs 24
Special Collections: Local Historical Coll
Subject Interests: Fla
Automation Activity & Vendor Info: (Acquisitions) Mandarin Library Automation; (Cataloging) Mandarin Library Automation; (Circulation) Mandarin Library Automation
Open Mon-Thurs 10-7, Fri & Sat 10-4

J CITY COLLEGE, Altamonte Springs Library, 177 Montgomery Rd, 32714-3129. Tel: 407-831-9816. FAX: 407-831-1147. Web Site: www.citycollege.edu. *Librn,* Sonjia McSween; E-mail: smcsween@citycollege.edu; Staff 1 (MLS 1)
Founded 1996. Enrl 300; Highest Degree: Associate
Library Holdings: e-books 14,000; e-journals 1,000; Bk Vols 2,000; Per Subs 50; Spec Interest Per Sub 25
Database Vendor: Gale Cengage Learning, OCLC FirstSearch, ProQuest, Westlaw
Wireless access
Partic in Florida Library Information Network; Lyrasis; Tampa Bay Library Consortium, Inc
Open Mon-Thurs 8am-10pm, Fri 8-5

S INSTITUTE OF INTERNAL AUDITORS LIBRARY*, 247 Maitland Ave, 32701-4201. SAN 302-8399. Tel: 407-937-1362. Information Services Tel: 407-937-1100. FAX: 407-937-1101. Web Site: www.theiia.org. *In Charge,* Lisa Krist; E-mail: lisa.krist@theiia.org
Founded 1941
Library Holdings: Bk Vols 1,000; Per Subs 52
Special Collections: Institute of Internal Auditors publications
Subject Interests: Acctg, Bus & mgt, Data proc
Restriction: Staff use only

APALACHICOLA

P APALACHICOLA MUNICIPAL LIBRARY*, 74 Sixth St, Gorrie Square, 32320. SAN 370-4610. Tel: 850-653-8436. E-mail: apalachlib@gtcom.net. *Dir,* Ann Sizemore
Library Holdings: Bk Titles 15,000
Open Mon 10-5, Tues, Thurs & Fri 10-12 & 2-5, Wed 10-12

APOPKA

C MID FLORIDA RESEARCH & EDUCATION CENTER LIBRARY*, 2725 S Binion Rd, 32703-8504. SAN 322-9009. Tel: 407-884-2034, Ext 140. FAX: 407-814-6186. Web Site: www.mrec.ifas.ufl.edu. *Librn,* Kathy Phillips
Library Holdings: Bk Vols 5,000
Subject Interests: Agr
Open Mon-Fri 9-5

C UNIVERSITY OF FLORIDA*, Mid-Florida Research & Education Center, 2725 Binion Rd, 32703-8504. SAN 323-715X. Tel: 407-884-2034. FAX: 407-814-6186. Web Site: www.mrec.ifas.ufl.edu.
Library Holdings: Bk Vols 12,000; Per Subs 132
Open Mon-Fri 7:30-5

ARCADIA

P DESOTO COUNTY LIBRARY*, 125 N Hillsborough Ave, 34266. SAN 302-8402. Tel: 863-993-4851. Web Site: www.myhlc.org. *Dir,* Linda Waters; E-mail: linda.w@myhlc.org
Founded 1963. Pop 23,865; Circ 167,811
Library Holdings: Bk Vols 59,000; Per Subs 63
Automation Activity & Vendor Info: (Cataloging) Innovative Interfaces, Inc; (Circulation) Innovative Interfaces, Inc
Wireless access
Open Tues-Fri 9-6, Sat 9-2:30
Friends of the Library Group

AUBURNDALE

P AUBURNDALE PUBLIC LIBRARY*, 100 W Bridgers Ave, 33823. SAN 302-8437. Tel: 863-965-5548. FAX: 863-965-5554. Web Site: www.auburndalefl.com/Library/Home/citylibrary.asp. *Librn,* Holmes Kristal; E-mail: kholmes@auburndalefl.com; *Ch,* Yvonne Williams; E-mail: ywilliams@auburndalefl.com
Founded 1951. Pop 10,000; Circ 62,000
Library Holdings: Bk Titles 46,000; Per Subs 72
Open Mon-Fri 10-7, Sat 9-5

AVE MARIA

CR CANIZARO LIBRARY AT AVE MARIA UNIVERSITY, 5251 Donahue St, 34142. Tel: 239-280-2557. E-mail: library@avemaria.edu. Web Site: www.avemaria.edu/majorsprograms/library. *Dir of Libr Serv,* Jennifer Nodes; Tel: 239-348-4710, E-mail: jennifer.nodes@avemaria.edu; *Head, Pub Serv,* Sarah DeVille; Tel: 239-280-2422, E-mail: sarah.deville@avemaria.edu; *Head, Tech Serv,* Susan Mansfield; Tel: 239-280-1687, E-mail: susan.mansfield@avemaria.edu; *Libr Assoc,* Carianne Svoboda-Wilson; Tel: 239-280-2428, E-mail: carianne.svoboda-wilson@avemaria.edu; Staff 6 (MLS 3, Non-MLS 3)
Founded 2003. Enrl 1,080; Fac 60; Highest Degree: Doctorate
Jul 2008-Jun 2009 Income $841,295. Mats Exp $841,295, Books $102,000, Per/Ser (Incl. Access Fees) $48,000, AV Mat $6,420, Electronic Ref Mat (Incl. Access Fees) $69,600, Presv $7,200. Sal $437,478 (Prof $220,000)
Library Holdings: CDs 700; DVDs 1,400; e-books 2,000; Electronic Media & Resources 80; Music Scores 1,000; Bk Titles 160,000; Bk Vols 190,000; Per Subs 280; Videos 200

Special Collections: Catholic Americana; Natural Family Planning Archives
Automation Activity & Vendor Info: (Acquisitions) Baker & Taylor; (Cataloging) OCLC Connexion; (Circulation) OCLC; (Course Reserve) OCLC; (ILL) OCLC; (OPAC) OCLC; (Serials) OCLC
Database Vendor: ARTstor, EBSCOhost, JSTOR, LexisNexis, OCLC ArticleFirst, OCLC FirstSearch, OCLC WorldShare Interlibrary Loan, Project MUSE, ScienceDirect, YBP Library Services
Wireless access
Function: Audio & video playback equip for onsite use, Copy machines, Exhibits, ILL available, Instruction & testing, Music CDs, Online cat, Online ref, Ref serv available, Scanner
Publications: Lanthorn (Newsletter)
Partic in Southwest Florida Library Network
Open Mon-Thurs 8am-1am, Fri 8-8, Sat 9-8, Sun 1pm-1am
Restriction: 24-hr pass syst for students only, Authorized scholars by appt, In-house use for visitors, Open to students, fac & staff

AVON PARK

P AVON PARK PUBLIC LIBRARY*, 100 N Museum Ave, 33825. SAN 302-8453. Tel: 863-452-3803. FAX: 863-452-3809. Web Site: www.myhlc.org. *Librn,* Mary Beth Isaacson; E-mail: marybeth@myhlc.org
Pop 8,200
Library Holdings: Bk Vols 70,000
Special Collections: Large Print Coll
Automation Activity & Vendor Info: (Cataloging) Innovative Interfaces, Inc; (Circulation) Innovative Interfaces, Inc; (OPAC) Innovative Interfaces, Inc
Wireless access
Mem of Highlands County Library System
Open Tues 10:30-6:30, Wed-Sat 9:30-5:30
Friends of the Library Group

J SOUTH FLORIDA STATE COLLEGE LIBRARY*, 600 W College Dr, 33825-9356. SAN 302-847X. Tel: 863-784-7306. Reference Tel: 863-784-7304. FAX: 863-452-6042. E-mail: sfsc-library@southflorida.edu. Web Site: www.southflorida.edu/student/resources/library. *Dean, Acad Support,* Dr Michael McLeod; Tel: 863-453-6661, E-mail: mcleodm@southflorida.edu; *Chair, Libr Serv,* Lena Phelps; Tel: 863-784-7303, E-mail: phelpsl@southflorida.edu; *Librn,* Position Currently Open; *Librn,* Claire Miller; Tel: 863-784-7305, E-mail: millerc@southflorida.edu; Staff 2 (MLS 2)
Founded 1966. Enrl 2,500; Fac 68; Highest Degree: Bachelor
Jul 2008-Jun 2009. Mats Exp $33,012, Books $18,730, Per/Ser (Incl. Access Fees) $8,459, AV Mat $2,581, Electronic Ref Mat (Incl. Access Fees) $3,242. Sal $212,276 (Prof $107,598)
Library Holdings: AV Mats 1,753; e-books 3,224; Bk Titles 40,870; Bk Vols 46,141; Per Subs 60
Automation Activity & Vendor Info: (Acquisitions) Ex Libris Group; (Cataloging) Ex Libris Group; (Circulation) Ex Libris Group; (Course Reserve) Ex Libris Group; (ILL) Ex Libris Group; (Media Booking) Ex Libris Group; (OPAC) Ex Libris Group; (Serials) Ex Libris Group
Database Vendor: ABC-CLIO, ARTstor, CQ Press, ebrary, EBSCOhost, Ex Libris Group, Facts on File, Gale Cengage Learning, Greenwood Publishing Group, Hoovers, JSTOR, Medline, Micromedex, Newsbank, OCLC CAMIO, OCLC WorldShare Interlibrary Loan, Oxford Online, ProQuest, Sage, Springshare, LLC
Wireless access
Partic in Tampa Bay Library Consortium, Inc

BABSON PARK

C WEBBER INTERNATIONAL UNIVERSITY*, Grace & Roger Babson Learning Center, 1201 State Rd 17, 33827. (Mail add: PO Box 97, 33827-0097), SAN 302-8496. Tel: 863-638-2937. E-mail: library@webber.edu. Web Site: www.webber.edu/Babson%20Library/Library.aspx. *Dir, Head Librn,* Sue Dunning; *Info Spec,* Stephanie Lucas; Staff 2 (MLS 1, Non-MLS 1)
Founded 1927. Enrl 630; Highest Degree: Master
Library Holdings: DVDs 120; Electronic Media & Resources 15; Bk Titles 3,220; Bk Vols 3,850; Per Subs 10
Special Collections: Civil War Coll
Subject Interests: Bus & mgt, Econ
Automation Activity & Vendor Info: (Cataloging) Book Systems; (Circulation) Book Systems; (OPAC) Book Systems
Database Vendor: Bowker, EBSCOhost, Facts on File, Gale Cengage Learning, Grolier Online, LexisNexis, ProQuest
Wireless access
Function: Computers for patron use, Electronic databases & coll
Open Mon-Thurs 9am-10pm, Fri 9-5, Sun 6pm-11pm; Mon-Thurs (Summer) 9-5
Restriction: Borrowing privileges limited to fac & registered students

BARTOW

P BARTOW PUBLIC LIBRARY*, 2150 S Broadway Ave, 33830. SAN 302-850X. Tel: 863-534-0131. FAX: 863-534-0913. E-mail: bartowpubliclibrary@gmail.com. Web Site: www.pclc.lib.fl.us/bartow. *Dir,* Roxanne Tovrea; E-mail: roxanne.tovrea@mypclc.info; *Cat,* Barbara Stampfl; *Ref Serv,* Melissa Mohler; *Youth Serv,* Melissa Causey; Staff 5 (MLS 4, Non-MLS 1)
Founded 1897. Pop 17,000; Circ 161,000
Library Holdings: DVDs 1,700; Bk Titles 57,000; Per Subs 122
Automation Activity & Vendor Info: (Acquisitions) SirsiDynix; (Cataloging) SirsiDynix; (Circulation) SirsiDynix
Function: Adult bk club, After school storytime, Art exhibits, Audiobks via web, AV serv, Bk club(s), Bks on cassette, Bks on CD, Children's prog, Computer training, Computers for patron use, Copy machines, Distance learning, e-mail serv, Electronic databases & coll, Exhibits, Fax serv, Free DVD rentals, Handicapped accessible, Holiday prog, Homebound delivery serv, ILL available, Mail & tel request accepted, Mail loans to mem, Music CDs, Notary serv, Online cat, Online searches, Photocopying/Printing, Preschool outreach, Prog for adults, Prog for children & young adult, Pub access computers, Ref serv in person, Spoken cassettes & CDs, Spoken cassettes & DVDs, Story hour, Summer reading prog, Tax forms, Teen prog, Telephone ref, VHS videos, Video lending libr, Wheelchair accessible
Partic in Polk County Libr Coop; Tampa Bay Library Consortium, Inc
Open Mon-Thurs 9-8, Fri & Sat 9-5
Restriction: 24-hr pass syst for students only
Friends of the Library Group

S FLORIDA INSTITUTE OF PHOSPHATE RESEARCH*, FIPR Library & Info Clearinghouse, 1855 W Main St, 33830-4338. SAN 324-5594. Tel: 863-534-7160. FAX: 863-534-7165. Web Site: www.fipr.state.fl.us. *Dir,* Gary R Albarelli; E-mail: galbarel@mail.usf.edu; Staff 3 (MLS 2, Non-MLS 1)
Founded 1980
Library Holdings: Bk Titles 7,800; Per Subs 110
Subject Interests: Beneficiation, Environ incl radon, Phosphate mining, Reclamation
Automation Activity & Vendor Info: (Circulation) Follett Software; (OPAC) Follett Software
Publications: Annual Report
Partic in Dialog Corp; Lyrasis; OCLC Online Computer Library Center, Inc; Tampa Bay Library Consortium, Inc
Open Mon-Fri 8:30-5

S POLK COUNTY HISTORICAL & GENEALOGICAL LIBRARY*, Historic Courthouse, 100 E Main St, 33830. SAN 302-8526. Tel: 863-534-4380. FAX: 863-534-4382. Web Site: library.mypclc.org/historical. *Librn,* Gladys Roberts; E-mail: gladys.roberts@mypclc.info
Founded 1940
Library Holdings: Bk Titles 12,800; Per Subs 40
Special Collections: Genealogy & History of the Southeastern US
Automation Activity & Vendor Info: (Cataloging) SirsiDynix
Wireless access
Open Tues-Sat 9-5
Restriction: Open to pub for ref only

GL POLK COUNTY LAW LIBRARY, Justice Steven H Grimes Law Library, Courthouse, Rm 3076, 255 N Broadway, 33830. SAN 302-8534. Tel: 863-534-4013. Administration Tel: 863-534-4016. FAX: 863-534-7443. *Dir,* Amanda Horton; E-mail: ahorton@jud10.flcourts.org
Founded 1956
Library Holdings: Bk Vols 25,000; Per Subs 60
Automation Activity & Vendor Info: (Cataloging) Follett Software; (Circulation) Follett Software
Database Vendor: LexisNexis, Westlaw
Open Mon-Fri 8:30-5
Restriction: Non-circulating to the pub

BAY PINES

GM BAY PINES VETERANS AFFAIRS HEALTHCARE SYSTEM*, 10000 Bay Pines Blvd, 33744. (Mail add: PO Box 5005, 33744-5005), SAN 302-8542. Tel: 727-398-9366. FAX: 727-398-9367. Staff 6 (MLS 2, Non-MLS 4)
Founded 1930
Library Holdings: AV Mats 3,000; e-journals 25; Bk Titles 6,900; Bk Vols 7,000; Per Subs 400
Subject Interests: Allied health, Consumer health, Geriatrics & gerontology, Med, Nursing
Automation Activity & Vendor Info: (Cataloging) OCLC; (Circulation) Follett Software; (Serials) SerialsSolutions
Database Vendor: Dialog, EBSCOhost, Elsevier MDL, Micromedex, OVID Technologies, PubMed

Function: Audio & video playback equip for onsite use, Computers for patron use, Copy machines, Digital talking bks, Doc delivery serv, e-mail serv, Electronic databases & coll, Health sci info serv, ILL available, Online searches, Scanner, VHS videos, Wheelchair accessible
Publications: Library Service (Newsletter)
Partic in Medical Library Association (MLA); Tampa Bay Library Consortium, Inc; Tampa Bay Medical Library Network
Special Services for the Deaf - ADA equip; Closed caption videos
Special Services for the Blind - Audio mat; BiFolkal kits; Bks & mags in Braille, on rec, tape & cassette
Open Mon-Thurs 7-4:30, Fri 7-1:30
Restriction: Circulates for staff only, In-house use for visitors

BELLE GLADE

J PALM BEACH STATE COLLEGE*, Belle Glade-Campus Library/Learning Resource Center, 1977 College Dr, Mail Sta 43, 33430. SAN 302-8577. Tel: 561-993-1150. FAX: 561-993-1157. Web Site: www.palmbeachstate.edu/LLRC.xml. *Librn,* Hadi Sheikhnia; Tel: 561-993-1131; *Libr Tech 1,* Halimeh Shatara; Tel: 561-993-1155, E-mail: shatarah@palmbeachstate.edu; Staff 2 (MLS 2)
Highest Degree: Associate
Library Holdings: Bk Vols 11,000; Per Subs 82
Automation Activity & Vendor Info: (Cataloging) Ex Libris Group; (Circulation) Ex Libris Group; (Course Reserve) Ex Libris Group; (OPAC) Ex Libris Group; (Serials) Ex Libris Group
Open Mon-Thurs 8-8, Fri & Sat 8-12

C UNIVERSITY OF FLORIDA*, Everglades Research & Education Center, 3200 E Palm Beach Rd, 33430. SAN 302-8585. Tel: 561-993-1517. FAX: 561-993-1582. Web Site: erec.ifas.ufl.edu. *Librn,* Kathleen Krawchuk
Founded 1926
Library Holdings: Bk Titles 12,000; Per Subs 100
Subject Interests: Agr, Turfgrass, Water quality
Wireless access
Publications: Journal Series; Research Reports
Open Mon-Fri 8-5

BEVERLY HILLS

P CITRUS COUNTY LIBRARY SYSTEM*, Administrative Offices, 425 W Roosevelt Blvd, 34465-4281. SAN 328-8633. Tel: 352-746-9077. FAX: 352-746-9493. TDD: 352-249-1292. E-mail: suggestions@citruslibraries.org. Web Site: www.cclib.org, www.citruslibraries.org. *Dir, Libr Serv,* Eric C Head; *Acq Librn,* Deborah McElvey; *Communications Facilitator,* Teddianne Goshorn; Staff 14 (MLS 5, Non-MLS 9)
Founded 1987. Pop 140,031; Circ 704,746
Library Holdings: Audiobooks 9,364; AV Mats 21,080; Bks on Deafness & Sign Lang 105; Braille Volumes 37; CDs 6,049; DVDs 8,939; e-books 8,258; High Interest/Low Vocabulary Bk Vols 536; Large Print Bks 11,728; Bk Titles 147,981; Bk Vols 211,922; Per Subs 165; Videos 1,777
Automation Activity & Vendor Info: (Cataloging) SirsiDynix; (Circulation) SirsiDynix; (OPAC) SirsiDynix
Wireless access
Function: Adult bk club, Adult literacy prog, Art exhibits, Audio & video playback equip for onsite use, Bk club(s), Bks on cassette, Bks on CD, CD-ROM, Chess club, Children's prog, Citizenship assistance, Computer training, Computers for patron use, Copy machines, Digital talking bks, e-mail & chat, Electronic databases & coll, Family literacy, Free DVD rentals, Genealogy discussion group, Govt ref serv, Handicapped accessible, Holiday prog, Home delivery & serv to Sr ctr & nursing homes, Homebound delivery serv, ILL available, Instruction & testing, Literacy & newcomer serv, Magnifiers for reading, Mail & tel request accepted, Microfiche/film & reading machines, Music CDs, Online cat, Online ref, Outreach serv, OverDrive digital audio bks, Photocopying/Printing, Preschool outreach, Preschool reading prog, Prog for adults, Prog for children & young adult, Pub access computers, Ref & res, Ref serv available, Ref serv in person, Scanner, Senior computer classes, Senior outreach, Serves mentally handicapped consumers, Spanish lang bks, Spoken cassettes & CDs, Spoken cassettes & DVDs, Story hour, Summer & winter reading prog, Tax forms, Telephone ref, VHS videos, Video lending libr, Web-catalog, Wheelchair accessible
Open Mon-Fri 8-5
Friends of the Library Group
Branches: 5
CENTRAL RIDGE, 425 W Roosevelt Blvd, 34465-4281, SAN 337-8780. Tel: 352-746-6622. FAX: 352-746-4170. TDD: 352-249-1293. *Br Mgr, Pub Serv,* Kim Slocomb
Open Mon-Thurs 10-7, Fri & Sat 10-5
Friends of the Library Group
COASTAL REGION, 8619 W Crystal St, Crystal River, 34428-4468, SAN 337-8608. Tel: 352-795-3716. FAX: 352-795-3103. TDD: 352-794-4191. *Circ Supvr,* Donna Russell
Open Mon-Thurs 10-7, Fri & Sat 10-5
Friends of the Library Group
FLORAL CITY PUBLIC, 8360 E Orange Ave, Floral City, 34436-3200, SAN 337-8667. Tel: 352-726-3671. FAX: 352-726-1159. TDD: 352-344-0614. *Circ Supvr,* TerriAnne Caraluzzo
Open Tues & Thurs 10-8, Wed & Fri 10-5, Sat 10-4
Friends of the Library Group
HOMOSASSA PUBLIC, 4100 S Grandmarch Ave, Homosassa, 34446-1120, SAN 337-8721. Tel: 352-628-5626. FAX: 352-628-3011. TDD: 352-628-6751. *Mgr, Ref Serv,* Susan Mutschler
Open Mon-Thurs 10-8, Fri & Sat 10-5
Friends of the Library Group
LAKES REGION, 1511 Druid Rd, Inverness, 34452-4507, SAN 337-8756. Tel: 352-726-2357. FAX: 352-726-2814. TDD: 352-344-1871. *Mgr, Programming & Youth Serv,* Karen Slaska
Open Mon-Thurs 10-8, Fri & Sat 10-5
Friends of the Library Group

BLOUNTSTOWN

P CALHOUN COUNTY PUBLIC LIBRARY*, 17731 NE Pear St, 32424. SAN 370-4688. Tel: 850-674-8773. FAX: 850-674-2843. *Dir,* Rita Maupin; E-mail: maupinr@yahoo.com; *Br Coordr, Circ,* Phyllis Cauley; *Tech Serv,* Karen Bryant
Library Holdings: Bk Vols 30,705; Per Subs 10
Automation Activity & Vendor Info: (Acquisitions) SirsiDynix; (Cataloging) SirsiDynix; (Circulation) SirsiDynix; (OPAC) SirsiDynix
Partic in Panhandle Library Access Network
Open Mon & Thurs 9:30-7, Tues & Wed 9:30-5:30, Sat 9-3
Branches: 4
ALTHA BRANCH, PO Box 241, Altha, 32421, SAN 370-4696. Tel: 850-762-8280. FAX: 850-762-4547. *Librn,* Lavaine Williams
Library Holdings: AV Mats 83; Large Print Bks 292; Bk Titles 2,447; Bk Vols 4,952; Videos 221
Open Mon-Thurs 2-5, Sat 9-12
HUGH CREEK PARK, 11442 SE CR 69, 32424. Tel: 850-674-3334. FAX: 850-674-3334. *Br Mgr,* Dolly Boyd
Library Holdings: Bk Vols 900
Open Mon-Thurs 2-5, Sat 9-12
KINARD BRANCH, 5416 SW State Rd 73, Kinard, 32449, SAN 370-470X. Tel: 850-639-5125. FAX: 850-639-5125. *Librn,* Nancy Newsome
Library Holdings: AV Mats 18; Large Print Bks 175; Bk Titles 1,814; Bk Vols 4,501; Videos 47
Open Mon-Thurs 2-5, Sat 9-12
SHELTON'S PARK, 25008 NW State Rd 73, Altha, 32421, SAN 377-8355. Tel: 850-762-3992. FAX: 850-762-3992 (call first). *Librn,* Alice McCardle
Library Holdings: Bk Titles 908
Open Mon-Thurs 2-5, Sat 9-12

BOCA RATON

M BOCA RATON COMMUNITY HOSPITAL*, Medical Staff Library, 800 Meadows Rd, 33486. SAN 324-5632. Tel: 561-955-4088. FAX: 561-955-4825. Web Site: www.brch.com. *Med Librn,* Rana Dole; E-mail: rdole@brch.com; Staff 1 (MLS 1)
Founded 1969
Library Holdings: Bk Titles 4,800; Per Subs 125
Partic in Fla Health Sci Libr Asn; National Network of Libraries of Medicine
Open Mon-Fri 7:30-4:30

P BOCA RATON PUBLIC LIBRARY, Downtown Library, 400 NW Boca Raton Blvd, 33432-3798. SAN 302-8593. Tel: 561-393-7852. Circulation Tel: 561-367-7019. Reference Tel: 561-393-7906. FAX: 561-393-7823. TDD: 561-347-0149. Web Site: www.bocalibrary.org. *Mgr, Libr Serv,* Ann Nappa; Tel: 561-393-7916, E-mail: anappa@myboca.us; Staff 55 (MLS 5, Non-MLS 50)
Founded 1938. Pop 70,000; Circ 675,000
Library Holdings: AV Mats 35,337; Bks on Deafness & Sign Lang 100; High Interest/Low Vocabulary Bk Vols 625; Large Print Bks 4,921; Bk Titles 113,116; Bk Vols 150,746; Per Subs 188; Talking Bks 3,143
Special Collections: Florida Coll
Automation Activity & Vendor Info: (Acquisitions) Innovative Interfaces, Inc; (Cataloging) Innovative Interfaces, Inc; (Circulation) Innovative Interfaces, Inc; (ILL) Innovative Interfaces, Inc; (OPAC) Innovative Interfaces, Inc; (Serials) Innovative Interfaces, Inc
Database Vendor: ebrary, EBSCOhost, Gale Cengage Learning, Grolier Online, infoUSA, LearningExpress, Newsbank, OCLC FirstSearch, OCLC WorldShare Interlibrary Loan, ProQuest, ReferenceUSA
Wireless access

Function: Adult bk club, Adult literacy prog, Bks on cassette, Bks on CD, CD-ROM, Children's prog, Copy machines, Electronic databases & coll, ILL available
Special Services for the Deaf - Closed caption videos; High interest/low vocabulary bks; TDD equip
Special Services for the Blind - Bks on cassette; Bks on CD
Open Mon-Thurs 9-9, Fri & Sat 9-6, Sun Noon-6
Friends of the Library Group
Branches: 1
SPANISH RIVER LIBRARY, 1501 NW Spanish River Blvd, 33431. Tel: 561-393-7852. *Mgr, Libr Serv,* Ann Nappa; E-mail: anappa@myboca.us
Open Mon-Thurs 9-9, Fri & Sat 9-6, Sun Noon-6

S CRC PRESS INC LIBRARY*, 6000 Broken Sound Pkwy NW, Ste 300, 33487. SAN 302-8615. Tel: 561-994-0555. FAX: 561-998-9784. Web Site: crcpress.com. *In Charge,* Evelyn Elias; E-mail: evelyn.elias@taylorandfrancis.com
Founded 1967
Library Holdings: Bk Titles 9,200
Restriction: Staff use only

C EVERGLADES UNIVERSITY, 5002 T-REX Ave, Ste 100, 33431. Tel: 561-912-1211. Toll Free Tel: 888-772-6077. FAX: 561-912-1191. Web Site: www.evergladesuniversity.edu/library. *Dir of Libr Serv,* Karen Gelover; E-mail: kgelover@evergladesuniversity.edu; Staff 3 (MLS 3)
Highest Degree: Master
Database Vendor: ebrary, EBSCOhost, LexisNexis, Natural Standard, Westlaw
Wireless access
Partic in Library & Information Resources Network (LIRN); SEFLIN - Southeast Florida Library Information Network, Inc
Open Mon, Tues & Thurs 8:30am-9pm, Wed 10-7, Sat 8:30-5

C FLORIDA ATLANTIC UNIVERSITY, S E Wimberly Library, 777 Glades Rd, 33431. (Mail add: PO Box 3092, 33431-0992), SAN 337-2693. Tel: 561-297-6762. Circulation Tel: 561-297-6911. Interlibrary Loan Service Tel: 561-297-0563. Reference Tel: 561-297-3785. Automation Services Tel: 561-297-3789. Information Services Tel: 561-297-3770. FAX: 561-297-2189. Interlibrary Loan Service FAX: 561-297-2232. E-mail: lyref@fau.edu. Web Site: www.fau.edu/library. *Dean of Libr,* William Miller; Tel: 561-297-3717, E-mail: miller@fau.edu; *Assoc Dean,* Rita Pellen; Tel: 561-297-3781, E-mail: pellen@fau.edu; *Asst Dean, Pub Serv,* Dawn M Smith; Tel: 561-297-1029, E-mail: dsmith@fau.edu; *Asst Dean, Syst,* Amy Kornblau; E-mail: kornblau@fau.edu; *Asst Dean, Tech Serv,* Janice E Donahue; Tel: 561-297-2767, E-mail: donahue@fau.edu; *Head, Monographic Organization,* Maria A Berenbaum; Tel: 561-297-2134, E-mail: mberenba@fau.edu; *Head of Ref & Instrul Serv,* Kenneth Frankel; Tel: 561-297-0079, E-mail: frankel@fau.edu; *Head, Ser Mgt & Acq,* Deb Hoban; Tel: 561-297-3778, E-mail: dhoban@fau.edu; *Head, Access Serv,* Steven Matthew; Tel: 561-297-4027, E-mail: matthew@fau.edu; *Head, Coll Develop,* Maris Hayashi; Tel: 561-297-4317, E-mail: mhayashi@fau.edu; *Ser,* Teresa Abaid; Tel: 561-297-1091, E-mail: abaid@fau.edu; Staff 35 (MLS 35)
Founded 1961. Enrl 30,750; Fac 877; Highest Degree: Doctorate
Jul 2013-Jun 2014. Mats Exp $3,265,519, Books $242,199, Per/Ser (Incl. Access Fees) $22,230, AV Mat $28,784, Electronic Ref Mat (Incl. Access Fees) $2,795,433, Presv $7,136
Library Holdings: CDs 8,186; DVDs 8,881; e-books 582,016; e-journals 59,721; Bk Vols 1,170,585; Per Subs 719; Videos 8,554
Special Collections: Arlyn Austin Katims Civil War Coll; Clarke Family Papers; Harold L Glasser Coll; Jaffe Books as Aesthetic Objects; K Frank Korf Papers; Marvin & Sybil Weiner Spirit of America Coll; Marvin Kemery Letters; Print Music Coll; Recorded Sound Archives; Theodore Pratt Papers; University Archives; Virginia Snyder Coll; Walter Wadepuhl Papers. State Document Depository; US Document Depository
Subject Interests: Am hist, Art, Eng, Ethnic studies, Film studies, Music, Nursing, Women's studies
Automation Activity & Vendor Info: (Acquisitions) Ex Libris Group; (Cataloging) Ex Libris Group; (Circulation) Ex Libris Group; (Course Reserve) Ex Libris Group; (ILL) OCLC; (OPAC) Ex Libris Group; (Serials) Ex Libris Group
Database Vendor: ABC-CLIO, ACM (Association for Computing Machinery), Alexander Street Press, American Chemical Society, American Geophysical Union, American Mathematical Society, American Physical Society, American Psychological Association (APA), Annual Reviews, ARTstor, ASCE Research Library, BioOne, Bowker, Cambridge Scientific Abstracts, Community of Science (COS), CQ Press, ebrary, EBSCOhost, Elsevier, Emerald, Ex Libris Group, Facts on File, Gale Cengage Learning, Greenwood Publishing Group, Hoovers, IBISWorld, IEEE (Institute of Electrical & Electronics Engineers), IOP, ISI Web of Knowledge, JSTOR, LexisNexis, Marcive, Inc, Medline, Mergent Online, Modern Language Association, Nature Publishing Group, Newsbank, Newsbank-Readex, OVID Technologies, Oxford Online, Paratext, Plunkett Research, Ltd, Project MUSE, ProQuest, PubMed, RefWorks, Sage, SBRnet (Sports Business Research Network), ScienceDirect, SerialsSolutions, Springer-Verlag, Springshare, LLC, Standard & Poor's, Thomson - Web of Science, ValueLine, Westlaw, Wiley InterScience, YBP Library Services
Wireless access
Partic in Lyrasis
Open Mon-Thurs 7:40am-2am, Fri 7:40-6, Sat 10:30- 6, Sun Noon-2am
Friends of the Library Group

C LYNN UNIVERSITY LIBRARY*, 3601 N Military Trail, 33431-5598. SAN 302-8607. Tel: 561-237-7254. Reference Tel: 561-237-7058. FAX: 561-237-7074. Web Site: www.lynn.edu/library. *Dir,* Charles L Kuhn; Tel: 561-237-7067, Fax: 561-237-7065, E-mail: ckuhn@lynn.edu; *Coll Develop Librn,* Melissa Johnson; Tel: 561-237-7056, E-mail: mmjohnson@lynn.edu; *Bibliog Instr,* Leecy Barnett; Tel: 561-237-7072, E-mail: lbarnett@lynn.edu; *Cat,* Sally Seaman; Tel: 561-237-7073, E-mail: sseaman@lynn.edu; *Circ,* Matthew Roos; Tel: 561-237-7066, E-mail: mroos@lynn.edu; *Info Tech,* Becky Rose; Tel: 561-237-7060, E-mail: rrose@lynn.edu; *ILL,* Judy Alsdorf; Tel: 561-237-7055, E-mail: jalsdorf@lynn.edu; *Music,* Tuskasa Cherkaoui; Tel: 561-237-7214, E-mail: tcherkaoui@lynn.edu; Staff 8 (MLS 7, Non-MLS 1)
Founded 1963. Enrl 2,500; Fac 85; Highest Degree: Doctorate
Jul 2005-Jun 2006 Income $750,000. Mats Exp $306,000, Books $155,000, Per/Ser (Incl. Access Fees) $38,000, AV Mat $20,000, Electronic Ref Mat (Incl. Access Fees) $93,000. Sal $400,000
Library Holdings: AV Mats 4,000; Bk Vols 100,000; Per Subs 350
Subject Interests: Bus & mgt, Humanities, Intl commun, Leadership
Automation Activity & Vendor Info: (Acquisitions) Mandarin Library Automation; (Cataloging) Mandarin Library Automation; (Circulation) Mandarin Library Automation; (Course Reserve) Mandarin Library Automation; (OPAC) Mandarin Library Automation; (Serials) Mandarin Library Automation
Database Vendor: EBSCOhost, Gale Cengage Learning, LexisNexis, OCLC FirstSearch, ProQuest, SerialsSolutions, Westlaw
Wireless access

J PALM BEACH STATE COLLEGE*, South Campus-Media Center, 3000 St Lucie Ave, 33431-6415. Tel: 561-862-4800. FAX: 561-862-4805. Web Site: www.palmbeachstate.edu/south/media. *Media Coordr,* Willie Ford; E-mail: fordw@palmbeachstate.edu
Library Holdings: AV Mats 3,000
Automation Activity & Vendor Info: (Cataloging) Ex Libris Group; (Circulation) Ex Libris Group; (OPAC) Ex Libris Group
Open Mon-Thurs 8-8, Fri 8-2

BONIFAY

P HOLMES COUNTY PUBLIC LIBRARY*, 303 N J Harvey Etheridge, 32425. SAN 376-2718. Tel: 850-547-3573. FAX: 850-547-2801. E-mail: hcpl32425@yahoo.com. *Dir,* Susan Harris; E-mail: director@myhcpl.org; *Asst Dir,* Ann Leavins; *Cat,* Patti Wilson; *Ch Serv,* Joan Biddle; *Circ,* Monette French; *ILL,* Lillian Payne; *Tech Serv,* Don Rhodes; Staff 4 (Non-MLS 4)
Founded 1973. Pop 19,564; Circ 29,689
Library Holdings: Large Print Bks 2,000; Bk Titles 19,053; Per Subs 36; Talking Bks 1,509; Videos 1,420
Automation Activity & Vendor Info: (Cataloging) SirsiDynix; (Circulation) SIRSI WorkFlows; (ILL) SIRSI WorkFlows
Database Vendor: Gale Cengage Learning, LearningExpress
Wireless access
Function: Computers for patron use, ILL available, Prog for children & young adult
Open Tues-Fri 8-5, Sat 8-12
Friends of the Library Group

BOYNTON BEACH

M BETHESDA HEALTH - BETHESDA HOSPITAL EAST, Robert E Raborn Medical Library, 2815 S Seacrest Blvd, 33435-7934. SAN 302-864X. Tel: 561-737-7733, Ext 4439. FAX: 561-735-7080. Web Site: www.bethesdaweb.com. *Med Librn,* RoseMarie Lonergan; E-mail: RLonergan@BHinc.org
Founded 1967
Library Holdings: Bk Vols 3,500; Per Subs 35
Special Collections: NCME Tapes
Wireless access
Restriction: Not open to pub

P BOYNTON BEACH CITY LIBRARY*, 208 S Seacrest Blvd, 33435. SAN 302-8658. Tel: 561-742-6390. Administration Tel: 561-742-6380. FAX: 561-742-6381. E-mail: boyntonref@gmail.com. Web Site: www.boyntonlibrary.org. *Libr Dir,* Craig B Clark; E-mail: clarkc@bbfl.us; *Asst Libr Dir,* Anne Watts; E-mail: wattsa@bbfl.us; *Head, Customer Serv,* Joseph Green; E-mail: greenjh@bbfl.us; *Customer Serv Mgr, Head, Tech Serv,* Ellen Mancuso; E-mail: mancusoe@boyntonlibrary.org; *Head, Tech,* Michael Naughton; E-mail: naughtonm@bbfl.us; *Cat Librn,* Gloria Rooney;

E-mail: grooney@boyntonlibrary.org; *Ref Librn,* Patricia Mooar; E-mail: mooarp@boyntonlibrary.org; *Teen Librn,* Lisa Kreutter; E-mail: kreutterl@bbfl.us; *Youth Serv Librn,* Cheryl Fishman; E-mail: fishmanc@bbfl.us; *Archivist,* Janet De Vries; E-mail: devriesj@bbfl.us; Staff 37 (MLS 9, Non-MLS 28)
Founded 1961. Pop 65,000; Circ 300,488
Library Holdings: Bk Titles 120,000; Bk Vols 129,200; Per Subs 200
Special Collections: Florida Coll; History & Archives (local history). Oral History
Subject Interests: Gardening, Investing, Songbooks
Automation Activity & Vendor Info: (Acquisitions) SIRSI Unicorn; (Cataloging) SIRSI Unicorn; (Circulation) SIRSI Unicorn; (OPAC) SIRSI-iBistro
Database Vendor: ALLDATA Online, Gale Cengage Learning, ProQuest, ValueLine
Partic in Coop Authority for Libr Automation; Library Cooperative of the Palm Beaches
Special Services for the Deaf - TDD equip
Open Mon-Thurs 9-8:30, Sat 9-5
Friends of the Library Group

R ST VINCENT DE PAUL REGIONAL SEMINARY LIBRARY*, 10701 S Military Trail, 33436-4811. SAN 302-8666. Tel: 561-732-4424, Ext 174. FAX: 561-737-2205. Web Site: www.svdp.edu. *Dir, Libr Serv,* Arthur G Quinn; E-mail: aquinn@svdp.edu; *Tech Serv,* Cynthia Krueger; E-mail: ckrueger@svdp.edu. Subject Specialists: *Theol,* Arthur G Quinn; Staff 2 (MLS 2)
Founded 1963. Enrl 125; Fac 19; Highest Degree: Master
Jul 2012-Jun 2013. Mats Exp $71,540, Books $27,309, Per/Ser (Incl. Access Fees) $31,948, Micro $442, AV Equip $2,100, Electronic Ref Mat (Incl. Access Fees) $5,525, Presv $4,216. Sal $88,602
Library Holdings: AV Mats 2,291; e-books 15; Electronic Media & Resources 31; Microforms 721; Bk Titles 64,730; Bk Vols 71,079; Per Subs 295
Special Collections: Loeb Series; Sources Chretiennes Series
Subject Interests: Latin Am, Philos, Theol
Automation Activity & Vendor Info: (Cataloging) EOS International; (Circulation) EOS International; (Course Reserve) EOS International; (OPAC) EOS International; (Serials) EOS International
Database Vendor: EBSCOhost, EOS International, OCLC FirstSearch
Wireless access
Function: Res libr
Open Mon-Fri 8am 11pm, Sat & Sun 10am-11pm

BRADENTON

S ART CENTER MANATEE*, McKelvey Memorial Library, 209 Ninth St W, 34205. SAN 302-8674. Tel: 941-746-2862. FAX: 941-746-2319. E-mail: acm@artcentermanatee.org. Web Site: www.artcentermanatee.org. *Exec Dir,* Diane Shelly
Founded 1955
Library Holdings: Bk Titles 1,400; Bk Vols 1,500; Videos 50
Restriction: Mem only

L MANATEE COUNTY LAW LIBRARY*, Manatee County Judicial Ctr, Rm 1101, 1051 Manatee Ave W, 34205. SAN 302-8682. Tel: 941-741-4090. FAX: 941-741-4085. *Librn,* Audrey Russo; Staff 1 (Non-MLS 1)
Oct 2009-Sept 2010. Mats Exp $101,000, Books $100,000, AV Equip $1,000. Sal $60,363
Library Holdings: CDs 68; Bk Vols 16,000
Database Vendor: Westlaw
Wireless access
Open Mon-Fri 8:30-5

P MANATEE COUNTY PUBLIC LIBRARY SYSTEM, 1301 Barcarrota Blvd W, 34205-7522. SAN 337-2723. Tel: 941-748-5555. Circulation Tel: 941-748-5555, Ext 6321. Interlibrary Loan Service Tel: 941-748-5555, Ext 6333. Administration Tel: 941-748-5555, Ext 6303. Information Services Tel: 941-748-5555, Ext 6311. FAX: 941-749-7191. E-mail: reference@mymanatee.org. Web Site: www.mymanatee.org/library. *Head Cataloger,* Sandra Clowes; Tel: 941-748-5555, Ext 6331, E-mail: sandra.clowes@mymanatee.org; *Mgr, Libr Serv,* Ava Ehde; Tel: 941-748-5555, Ext 6301, E-mail: ava.ehde@mymanatee.org; *Operations Mgr,* Kevin S. Beach; Tel: 941-748-5555, Ext 6325, E-mail: kevin.beach@mymanatee.org; *Supvr, Ad Serv,* Ericka Dow; E-mail: ericka.dow@mymanatee.org; *Supvr, Circ,* Linda Sell; E-mail: linda.sell@mymanatee.org; *Supvr, Coll Develop,* Mark Wylie; Fax: 941-742-5893, E-mail: mark.wylie@mymanatee.org; *Automation Coordr, Info Tech,* Rob Taylor; Tel: 941-748-5555, Ext 6330, E-mail: rob.taylor@mymanatee.org; *Prog Coordr,* Jyna Scheeren; Tel: 941-748-5555, Ext 6308, E-mail: jyna.scheeren@mymanatee.org; *Coordr, Youth Serv,* Chris O'Hara; Tel: 941-748-5555, Ext 6319, E-mail: chris.ohara@mymanatee.org; Staff 63 (MLS 30, Non-MLS 33)
Founded 1964. Pop 334,680; Circ 3,166,210
Library Holdings: Bk Vols 470,567; Per Subs 300
Special Collections: Digitized Archival Negatives. Oral History; US Document Depository
Subject Interests: Fla, Genealogy, Local hist, Spanish lang mat
Automation Activity & Vendor Info: (Acquisitions) SirsiDynix; (Cataloging) SirsiDynix; (Circulation) SirsiDynix; (OPAC) SirsiDynix; (Serials) SirsiDynix
Database Vendor: 3M Library Systems, Baker & Taylor, EBSCO Auto Repair Reference, EBSCOhost, Gale Cengage Learning, LearningExpress, Library Ideas, LLC, Newsbank, OCLC FirstSearch, OCLC WorldShare Interlibrary Loan, Overdrive, Inc, ProQuest, ReferenceUSA, SirsiDynix, ValueLine
Wireless access
Function: 24/7 Electronic res, 24/7 Online cat, Accelerated reader prog, After school storytime, Archival coll, Art exhibits, Audio & video playback equip for onsite use, Audiobks via web, AV serv, Bilingual assistance for Spanish patrons, Bk club(s), Bks on CD, Children's prog, Computer training, Computers for patron use, Copy machines, e-mail serv, Electronic databases & coll, Equip loans & repairs, Exhibits, Family literacy, Free DVD rentals, Govt ref serv, Handicapped accessible, ILL available, Magazines, Magnifiers for reading, Mango lang, Microfiche/film & reading machines, Music CDs, Online cat, Online ref, Online searches, Outreach serv, OverDrive digital audio bks, Photocopying/Printing, Preschool outreach, Prog for adults, Prog for children & young adult, Pub access computers, Ref & res, Ref serv available, Ref serv in person, Res libr, Serves mentally handicapped consumers, Spanish lang bks, Spoken cassettes & CDs, Story hour, Study rm, Summer reading prog, Tax forms, Teen prog, Telephone ref, VCDs, VHS videos
Publications: Friends & Foundation (Newsletter)
Partic in Tampa Bay Library Consortium, Inc
Special Services for the Deaf - Staff with knowledge of sign lang
Special Services for the Blind - Talking bks
Open Mon 10-8, Tues 10-6, Wed 12-8, Thurs & Fri 9-5, Sat 11-5
Restriction: Non-resident fee
Friends of the Library Group
Branches: 5
BRADEN RIVER, 4915 53rd Ave E, 34203, SAN 371-3709. Tel: 941-727-6079. FAX: 941-727-6059. *Br Mgr,* Cathryn Laird; Staff 8 (MLS 3, Non-MLS 5)
Library Holdings: Bk Vols 84,787
Open Wed & Fri 10-6, Tues 10-8, Thurs 12-8, Sat 10-5
Friends of the Library Group
ISLAND BRANCH, 5701 Marina Dr, Holmes Beach, 34217-1516, SAN 337-2758. Tel: 941-778-6341. FAX: 941-749-7184. *Supvr,* Inez Tamanaha; Tel: 941-778-6341, Ext 6373, E-mail: inez.tamanaha@mymanatee.org; Staff 6 (MLS 2, Non-MLS 4)
Open Tues & Thurs-Sat 9-5, Wed 12-8
Friends of the Library Group
PALMETTO BRANCH, 923 Sixth St W, Palmetto, 34221, SAN 337-2812. Tel: 941-722-3333. FAX: 941-749-7193. *Br Mgr,* Yoshira Castro; Staff 7 (MLS 3, Non-MLS 4)
Open Mon, Wed, Fri & Sat 9-5, Thurs 9-8
Friends of the Library Group
ROCKY BLUFF, 7016 US Hwy 301 N, Ellenton, 34222, SAN 374-5244. Tel. 941-723-4821. FAX: 941 723 4825. *Br Mgr,* Brenda Booth; Staff 4 (MLS 1, Non-MLS 3)
Open Tues, Thurs & Fri 10-6, Wed 12-8, Sat 10-5
Friends of the Library Group
SOUTH MANATEE COUNTY, 6081 26th St N, 34207, SAN 337-2847. Tel: 941-755-3892. FAX: 941-751-7098. *Br Mgr,* Zenobia Giles; Tel: 941-727-6081, E-mail: zenobia.giles@mymanatee.org; Staff 8 (MLS 3, Non-MLS 5)
Open Mon & Tues 9-8, Wed-Sat 9-5
Friends of the Library Group

J STATE COLLEGE OF FLORIDA MANATEE-SARASOTA LIBRARY, 5840 26th St W, 34207. SAN 302-8690. Tel: 941-752-5305. Interlibrary Loan Service Tel: 941-752-5657. Reference Tel: 941-752-5304. Administration Tel: 941-752-5306. FAX: 941-752-5308. E-mail: reference@scf.edu. Web Site: www.scf.edu. *Dir, Libr Serv,* Tracy Elliott; Tel: 941-752-5399, E-mail: elliott@scf.edu; *Digital Presence Librn,* Rhonda Kitchens; Tel: 941-408-1431, E-mail: kitcher@scf.edu; *Evening Librn,* Kirsten Beauchamp; E-mail: beauck@scf.edu; *Info Literacy Librn,* Mark Marino; Tel: 941-752-5317, E-mail: marinom@scf.edu; *Supvr, Access Serv,* Meg Hawkins; E-mail: hawkinm@scf.edu; *Libr Supvr, Digital Initiatives,* Dana Bowker; Tel: 941-408-1434, E-mail: bowkerd@scf.edu; *Acq, Tech Serv Supvr,* Judy Born; Tel: 941-752-5262, E-mail: bornj@scf.edu. Subject Specialists: *Knowledge mgt,* Dana Bowker; Staff 8 (MLS 8)
Founded 1958. Enrl 11,500; Fac 650; Highest Degree: Bachelor
Jul 2007-Jun 2008. Mats Exp $191,100, Books $95,500, Per/Ser (Incl. Access Fees) $68,600, AV Mat $9,500, Electronic Ref Mat (Incl. Access Fees) $17,500. Sal $599,800 (Prof $396,800)

Library Holdings: AV Mats 4,098; e-books 9,502; Bk Vols 66,000; Per Subs 355
Subject Interests: Lit, Nursing
Automation Activity & Vendor Info: (Acquisitions) Ex Libris Group; (Cataloging) Ex Libris Group; (Circulation) Ex Libris Group; (ILL) OCLC; (OPAC) Ex Libris Group; (Serials) Ex Libris Group
Database Vendor: CQ Press, EBSCOhost, Gale Cengage Learning, H W Wilson, JSTOR, OCLC FirstSearch, OCLC WorldShare Interlibrary Loan, Oxford Online, ProQuest, Westlaw
Wireless access
Function: 24/7 Electronic res, 24/7 Online cat, Archival coll, Bk reviews (Group), Computer training, Computers for patron use, Copy machines, Digital talking bks, Distance learning, Doc delivery serv, e-mail & chat, E-Reserves, Electronic databases & coll, eReaders, Exhibits, Health sci info serv, Life-long learning prog for all ages, Movies, Online info literacy tutorials on the web & in blackboard, Online ref, Online searches, Orientations, Outreach serv, Outside serv via phone, mail, e-mail & web, OverDrive digital audio bks, Photocopying/Printing, Ref & res, Ref serv available, Ref serv in person, Study rm, Video lending libr, Web-catalog, Wheelchair accessible, Workshops
Partic in Tampa Bay Library Consortium, Inc
Open Mon-Thurs 7:45am-9pm, Sun 5pm-9pm
Restriction: 24-hr pass syst for students only, Access at librarian's discretion, Access for corporate affiliates, Authorized patrons

Departmental Libraries:

VENICE CAMPUS, 8000 S Tamiami Trail, Venice, 34293, SAN 371-3660. Tel: 941-408-1435. FAX: 941-486-2687. *Libr Supvr,* Dana Bowker; Tel: 941-408-1434; *Digital Presence Librn,* Rhonda Kitchens; E-mail: kitcher@scf.edu; Staff 4 (MLS 2, Non-MLS 2)
Library Holdings: AV Mats 2,964; e-books 9,502; Bk Vols 27,916; Per Subs 137
Open Mon-Thurs 8:30-8, Fri 8:30-2

BRADENTON BEACH

P TINGLEY MEMORIAL LIBRARY, Bradenton Beach Public Library, 111 Second St N, 34217-2465. SAN 375-3360. Tel: 941-779-1208. Web Site: cityofbradentonbeach.com. *Librn,* Eveann Adams; Staff 26 (MLS 1, Non-MLS 25)
Founded 1959
Oct 2013-Sept 2014. Mats Exp $7,000
Library Holdings: Audiobooks 200; CDs 200; DVDs 600; Large Print Bks 400; Bk Vols 8,000; Per Subs 20; Videos 20
Special Collections: Municipal Document Depository
Subject Interests: Fla
Database Vendor: Baker & Taylor
Function: Art exhibits, Bk club(s), Bks on cassette, Bks on CD, Computers for patron use, Copy machines, Fax serv, Handicapped accessible, Photocopying/Printing, Pub access computers, Spoken cassettes & CDs, Spoken cassettes & DVDs, VHS videos, Video lending libr, Wheelchair accessible
Open Tues-Sat 10-3

BRONSON

P LEVY COUNTY PUBLIC LIBRARY SYSTEM*, 612 E Hathaway Ave, 32621. (Mail add: PO Box 1210, 32621-1210). Tel: 352-486-5552. FAX: 352-486-5553. Web Site: www.levy.lib.fl.us. *Dir,* Lisa Brasher
Library Holdings: Bk Vols 75,950
Automation Activity & Vendor Info: (Acquisitions) SirsiDynix; (Cataloging) SirsiDynix; (Circulation) SirsiDynix
Database Vendor: SirsiDynix
Wireless access
Open Mon-Fri 8-5

Branches: 5

BRONSON PUBLIC, 600 Gilbert St, 32621. Tel: 352-486-2015. FAX: 352-486-2015. *Br Mgr,* Sandy Moseley; E-mail: smoseley@neflin.org
Automation Activity & Vendor Info: (Acquisitions) Auto-Graphics, Inc; (Cataloging) Auto-Graphics, Inc; (Circulation) Auto-Graphics, Inc
Database Vendor: Auto-Graphics, Inc
Partic in Northeast Florida Library Information Network
Open Mon 10-3, Tues & Thurs 1-8, Wed 12-5, Fri 11-4, Sat 10-3
Friends of the Library Group

LUTHER CALLAWAY PUBLIC, 104 NE Third St, Chiefland, 32626-0937, SAN 374-4523. Tel: 352-493-2758. FAX: 352-493-2758. *Librn,* Sue Ann Burkhardt; E-mail: sburkhardt@neflin.org
Open Mon, Wed & Fri 10-5, Tues & Thurs 1-8, Sat 10-3
Friends of the Library Group

CEDAR KEY PUBLIC, 460 Second St, Cedar Key, 32625. (Mail add: PO Box 550, Cedar Key, 32625-0550), SAN 337-8543. Tel: 352-543-5777. FAX: 352-543-5777. *Librn,* Molly Jubitz; E-mail: mjubitz@neflin.org
Open Mon, Wed & Thurs 10-4, Tues 4-8, Sat 10-1
Friends of the Library Group

AF KNOTTS PUBLIC, 11 56th St, Yankeetown, 34498, SAN 374-454X. Tel: 352-447-4212. FAX: 352-447-4212. *Librn,* L Cohan; E-mail: lcohan@neflin.org
Open Tues 3-8, Wed & Thurs 9-5, Sat 9-1
Friends of the Library Group

WILLISTON PUBLIC, Ten SE First St, Williston, 32696-2671. (Mail add: PO Box 373, Williston, 32696), SAN 337-8845. Tel: 352-528-2313. FAX: 352-528-2313. *Librn,* Michelle Traylor; E-mail: mtraylor@neflin.org
Open Mon-1-7, Tues 1-5, Wed & Thurs 9-4, Sat 10-3

BROOKSVILLE

P HERNANDO COUNTY PUBLIC LIBRARY SYSTEM*, Lykes Memorial Library, 238 Howell Ave, 34601. SAN 337-2871. Tel: 352-754-4043. Reference Tel: 352-754-4042. FAX: 352-754-4044. TDD: 352-592-5608. Web Site: www.hernandocountylibrary.us. *Libr Serv Dir,* Adam Brooks; *Youth Serv Librn,* Justin King; *Coll Mgr,* Lauren Rouhana; *Br Serv Coordr,* Susan Kiley; Staff 57 (MLS 12, Non-MLS 45)
Founded 1926. Circ 595,714
Oct 2011-Sept 2012 Income (Main Library and Branch(s)) $533,676, County $864,558. Mats Exp $303,851, Books $224,158, AV Mat $25,536, Electronic Ref Mat (Incl. Access Fees) $54,157. Sal $1,583,556
Library Holdings: Audiobooks 6,813; AV Mats 9,317; e-books 8,916; Electronic Media & Resources 61; Bk Titles 184,163; Per Subs 457
Subject Interests: Fla
Automation Activity & Vendor Info: (Cataloging) ByWater Solutions; (Circulation) ByWater Solutions
Database Vendor: Baker & Taylor, Brodart, Gale Cengage Learning, infoUSA, LearningExpress, OVID Technologies, ProQuest
Wireless access
Function: Adult bk club, Audiobks via web, Bks on cassette, Bks on CD, Children's prog, Computer training, Computers for patron use, Copy machines, Handicapped accessible, Holiday prog, ILL available, Jail serv, Mail & tel request accepted, Music CDs, Online ref, OverDrive digital audio bks, Prog for adults, Prog for children & young adult, Ref & res, Ref serv available, Tax forms, Teen prog, Telephone ref, VHS videos, Web-catalog, Wheelchair accessible
Partic in Florida Library Information Network; Tampa Bay Library Consortium, Inc
Special Services for the Deaf - Closed caption videos
Special Services for the Blind - Audio mat; Bks on cassette; Bks on CD
Open Mon-Thurs 10-7, Fri 10-5
Friends of the Library Group

Branches: 4

EAST HERNANDO, 6457 Windemere Rd, 34602, SAN 373-806X. Tel: 352-754-4043. FAX: 352-754-4445. *Libr Serv Supvr,* Daniel Velez-Rubio
Open Tues-Thurs 10-7, Fri & Sat 10-5
Friends of the Library Group

ISTACHATTA LIBRARY STATION, 16257 Lingle Rd, Istachatta, 34601. Tel: 352-540-4304. *Br Serv Coordr,* Susan Kiley
Open Wed 1-4:30
Friends of the Library Group

SPRING HILL BRANCH, 9220 Spring Hill Dr, Spring Hill, 34608, SAN 337-2995. Tel: 352-754-4043. FAX: 352-688-5038. *Libr Serv Supvr,* Colleen Ludington
Open Tues-Thurs 10-7, Fri & Sat 10-5
Friends of the Library Group

WEST HERNANDO, 6335 Blackbird Ave, 34613, SAN 325-4429. Tel: 352-754-4043. Reference Tel: 352-540-6392. FAX: 352-592-5609. *Br Serv Coordr,* Susan Kiley
Open Mon-Thurs 10-7, Fri 10-5
Friends of the Library Group

J PASCO-HERNANDO COMMUNITY COLLEGE-NORTH CAMPUS*, Alfred A McKethan Library, 11415 Ponce de Leon Blvd, 34601-8698. SAN 302-8720. Tel: 352-797-5006. FAX: 352-797-5080. Web Site: www.phcc.edu. *Assoc Dir,* Melanie Cooksey
Founded 1974
Library Holdings: Bk Vols 17,000; Per Subs 100
Automation Activity & Vendor Info: (Cataloging) Ex Libris Group; (Circulation) Ex Libris Group; (Course Reserve) Ex Libris Group; (ILL) OCLC; (OPAC) Ex Libris Group; (Serials) Ex Libris Group
Open Mon-Thurs 8am-9pm, Fri 8-4:30

G SOUTHWEST FLORIDA WATER MANAGEMENT DISTRICT LIBRARY*, 2379 Broad St, 34604-6899. SAN 302-8739. Tel: 352-796-7211, Ext 4051. Toll Free Tel: 800-423-1476, Ext 4051. FAX: 352-797-5807. Web Site: www.swfwmd.state.fl.us. *Librn,* Valerie Jordan; E-mail: valerie.jordan@watermatters.org; Staff 2 (MLS 1, Non-MLS 1)
Founded 1961
Library Holdings: Bk Vols 7,500; Per Subs 30
Subject Interests: Ecology, Eng
Automation Activity & Vendor Info: (Cataloging) Inmagic, Inc.
Database Vendor: Dialog

Publications: Monthly List of New Acquisitions
Partic in Dialog Corp

BUSHNELL

P BUSHNELL PUBLIC LIBRARY*, 402 N Florida St, 33513. SAN 376-2998. Tel: 352-569-1790. FAX: 352-569-1791.
Library Holdings: Bk Vols 6,565; Per Subs 15
Automation Activity & Vendor Info: (Cataloging) SirsiDynix; (Circulation) SirsiDynix; (OPAC) SirsiDynix
Wireless access
Open Mon-Wed & Fri 9-6, Thurs 9-8, Sat 9-2
Friends of the Library Group

CAPE CANAVERAL

P CAPE CANAVERAL PUBLIC LIBRARY*, 201 Polk Ave, 32920-3067. SAN 302-8755. Tel: 321-868-1101. FAX: 321-868-1103. Web Site: www.brev.org. *Dir,* Jennifer Morrison; E-mail: jmorrison@brev.org; *Ref,* Dorothy Livingstone; E-mail: dlivingstone@brev.org; *Youth Serv,* Cara Redington; E-mail: credington@brev.org; Staff 3 (MLS 2, Non-MLS 1)
Founded 1966
Library Holdings: Bk Vols 44,191; Per Subs 82
Mem of Brevard County Library System
Open Mon 12-8, Tues-Fri 9-5, Sat 10-2
Friends of the Library Group

CASSELBERRY

P SEMINOLE COUNTY PUBLIC LIBRARY SYSTEM, 215 N Oxford Rd, 32707. SAN 338-0645. Tel: 407-665-1505. FAX: 407-665-1510. Web Site: www.seminolecountyfl.gov/libraries. *Libr Serv Mgr,* Christine Patten; Tel: 407-665-1501, E-mail: cpatten@seminolecountyfl.gov; *Libr Res Mgr - Coll Develop, Tech Serv,* Denise Tate; Tel: 407-665-1507, E-mail: dtatc@seminolecountyfl.gov; *Pub Serv Res Mgr,* Virginia Howerton; Tel: 407-665-1545, E-mail: vhowerton@seminolecountyfl.gov; Staff 71 (MLS 29, Non-MLS 42)
Founded 1987. Pop 422,718; Circ 1,778,006
Library Holdings: AV Mats 27,364; Electronic Media & Resources 23,831; Bk Titles 212,892; Bk Vols 551,889; Per Subs 198
Automation Activity & Vendor Info: (Acquisitions) SIRSI WorkFlows; (Cataloging) SIRSI WorkFlows; (Circulation) SIRSI WorkFlows; (OPAC) SirsiDynix; (Serials) SIRSI WorkFlows
Database Vendor: Baker & Taylor, Brodart, Gale Cengage Learning, Ingram Library Services, LearningExpress, OCLC, OCLC ArticleFirst, OCLC FirstSearch, Overdrive, Inc, ProQuest, ReferenceUSA, SirsiDynix, TumbleBookLibrary, WT Cox
Wireless access
Function: 24/7 Electronic res, 24/7 Online cat, Adult bk club, Bks on CD, Chess club, Children's prog, Computer training, Computers for patron use, Copy machines, e-mail & chat, Electronic databases & coll, eReaders, Free DVD rentals, Handicapped accessible, Home delivery & serv to Sr ctr & nursing homes, Homebound delivery serv, Magazines, Online cat, OverDrive digital audio bks, Photocopying/Printing, Prog for adults, Prog for children & young adult, Pub access computers, Ref serv available, Ref serv in person, Spanish lang bks, Story hour, Summer reading prog, Tax forms, Telephone ref
Open Mon-Thurs 9-8, Sat 9-5, Sun 1-5
Friends of the Library Group
Branches: 5
EAST BRANCH, 310 Division St, Oviedo, 32765, SAN 328-8978. Tel: 407-665-1580. FAX: 407-665-1585. *Br Mgr,* Barbara McCullough; Tel: 407-665-1561, E-mail: bmccullough@seminolecountyfl.gov
NORTH BRANCH, 150 N Palmetto Ave, Sanford, 32771, SAN 338-067X. Tel: 407-665-1630. FAX: 407-665-1615. *Br Mgr,* Barbara McCullough; Tel: 407-665-1621, E-mail: bmccullough@seminolecountyfl.gov
NORTHWEST BRANCH, 580 Greenway Blvd, Lake Mary, 32746, SAN 328-8994. Tel: 407-665-1650. FAX: 407-665-1645. *Br Mgr,* Sara Gonzalez; Tel: 407-665-1641, E-mail: sgonzalez@seminolecountyfl.gov
JEAN RHEIN CENTRAL LIBRARY, 215 N Oxford Rd, 32707, SAN 338-070X. Tel: 407-665-1530. FAX: 407-665-1511. *Br Mgr,* Barbara Piel; Tel: 407-665-1520, E-mail: bpiel@seminolecountyfl.gov
WEST, 245 Hunt Club Blvd N, Longwood, 32779, SAN 328-901X. Tel: 407-665-1680. FAX: 407-665-1675. *Br Mgr,* Sara Gonzalez; Tel: 407-665-1671, E-mail: sgonzalez@seminolecountyfl.gov

CHATTAHOOCHEE

M FLORIDA STATE HOSPITAL, Library Services, Main Library Bldg 1260, 32324. (Mail add: PO Box 1000, 32324-1000), SAN 302-881X. Tel: 850-663-7671. FAX: 850-663-7303. *Dir, Libr Serv,* Loretta Bramlett; E-mail: loretta_bramlett@dcf.state.fl.us. Subject Specialists: *Mental illness,* Loretta Bramlett; Staff 2 (MLS 2)
Library Holdings: Bk Titles 35,000; Per Subs 22
Subject Interests: Law, Music, Psychol, Relig
Open Mon-Fri 8-4

CHIPLEY

P WASHINGTON COUNTY LIBRARY*, 1444 Jackson Ave, 32428. SAN 376-5016. Tel: 850-638-1314. FAX: 850-638-9499. Web Site: www.pplcs.org. *Dir,* Linda Norton; *Br Mgr,* Barbara Russell; *Youth Serv,* Sandy Locke
Library Holdings: Bk Vols 150,000
Automation Activity & Vendor Info: (Acquisitions) SirsiDynix; (Cataloging) SirsiDynix; (Circulation) SirsiDynix
Open Mon-Fri 9-6, Sat 9-12
Friends of the Library Group
Branches: 2
SAM MITCHELL PUBLIC LIBRARY, 3731 Roche Ave, Vernon, 32462, SAN 376-8287. Tel: 850-535-1208. FAX: 850-535-1208. *Mgr,* Dorothy Pichardo
Open Tues, Thurs & Fri 9-6, Sat 9-12
WAUSAU PUBLIC LIBRARY, Town Hall, 1607 Second Ave, Wausau, 32463, SAN 376-8295. Tel: 850-638-2532. FAX: 850-638-2532. *Mgr,* Susan Cook
Open Tues 9:30-4, Thurs & Fri 1-6

CITRUS SPRINGS

P CITRUS SPRINGS MEMORIAL LIBRARY*, 1826 W Country Club Blvd, 34434. SAN 376-3005. Tel: 352-489-2313. Web Site: www.library.citrussprings.org. *Pres,* Virginia Buelke
Library Holdings: AV Mats 600; Bk Vols 14,000; Talking Bks 124
Open Mon, Wed & Fri 10-4, Sat (Sept-May) 10-1

CLEARWATER

C CLEARWATER CHRISTIAN COLLEGE*, Easter Library, 3400 Gulf-to-Bay Blvd, 33759-4595. SAN 302-8828. Tel: 727-726-1153, Ext 218. FAX: 727-723-8566. Web Site: libguides.clearwater.edu/easterlibrary. *Dir,* Elizabeth Werner; *Librn,* Vanessa Slagle; Staff 4 (MLS 3, Non-MLS 1)
Founded 1966. Enrl 582; Fac 54; Highest Degree: Bachelor
Jul 2005-Jun 2006. Mats Exp $46,550, Books $27,000, Per/Ser (Incl. Access Fees) $16,000, AV Mat $3,550
Library Holdings: AV Mats 7,900; CDs 375; DVDs 108; e-books 3,700; Music Scores 4,200; Bk Vols 101,000; Per Subs 5,351; Videos 1,175
Subject Interests: Am hist, British hist, Native Am, Relig
Automation Activity & Vendor Info: (Cataloging) OCLC Connexion; (Circulation) LibLime; (Course Reserve) LibLime; (ILL) OCLC FirstSearch; (OPAC) LibLime
Database Vendor: EBSCO Information Services, EBSCOhost, LibLime, OCLC FirstSearch, OCLC WorldShare Interlibrary Loan, ProQuest
Wireless access
Partic in Asn of Christian Librs; Lyrasis; OCLC Online Computer Library Center, Inc; Tampa Bay Library Consortium, Inc
Special Services for the Blind - Accessible computers; Aids for in-house use
Open Mon-Thurs (Fall & Spring) 7:30am-10pm, Sat 1-5; Mon-Fri (Summer) 8-4:30

S CLEARWATER MARINE AQUARIUM LIBRARY*, 249 Windward Passage, 33767. SAN 377-3086. Tel: 727-441-1790, Ext 222. Toll Free Tel: 888-239-9414. FAX: 727-442-9466. Web Site: www.cmaquarium.org. *Exec Dir,* Dale Schmidt
Founded 1972
Library Holdings: Bk Vols 3,000
Restriction: Not a lending libr

P CLEARWATER PUBLIC LIBRARY SYSTEM*, 100 N Osceola Ave, 33755. SAN 337-3053. Tel: 727-562-4970. FAX: 727-562-4977. Web Site: www.myclearwater.com/cpl. *Dir,* Barbara Pickell; Tel: 727-562-4971, E-mail: barbara.pickell@myclearwater.com; *Asst Dir,* Jennifer Obermaier; Tel: 727-562-4973, E-mail: jennifer.obermaier@myclearwater.com; *Financial Serv Adminr,* Paula Chaplinsky; E-mail: paula.chaplinsky@myclearwater.com; *Head, Circ,* Position Currently Open; *Head, Ref (Info Serv),* David Stoner; E-mail: David.stoner@myclearwater.com; *Head, Youth Serv,* Mercedes Bleattler; E-mail: mercedes.bleattler@myclearwater.com; *Ref Librn,* Daise Castillo; E-mail: daise.castillo@myclearwater.com; *Ref Librn,* Renee Gould; E-mail: renee.hochberg-gould@myclearwater.com; *Ref Librn,* Mary Frances Kirkpatrick; E-mail: mary.kirkpatrick@myclearwater.com; *Ref Librn,* Christa Smith; E-mail: Christa.smith@myclearwater.com; *Youth Serv Librn,* Jessica Pollock; E-mail: jessica.pollock@myclearwater.com; *Asst Circ Mgr,* Kayla Grant; E-mail: kayla.grant@myclearwater.com; *Automation Syst Coordr,* Kent Walker; E-mail: kent.walker@myclearwater.com; *Asst Automation Coordr,* Glen Slawsky; E-mail: glen.slawsky@myclearwater.com; *Acq,* Laura Dann; E-mail: laura.dann@myclearwater.com; *Adult Prog/Ref,* Jan Nickols; E-mail: jan.nickols@myclearwater.com; *Cat,* Rebecca Wogoman; E-mail: rebecca.wogoman@myclearwater.com; *Coll Develop,* Bonnie Potters;

E-mail: bonnie.potters@myclearwater.com; *Govt Doc,* Michelle Arnold; E-mail: michelle.arnold@myclearwater.com; *Ref,* Marsha McGrath; E-mail: marsha.mcgrath@myclearwater.com; *Ref, Ser,* Edward Tumber; E-mail: edward.tumber@myclearwater.com; *Youth Serv,* Joanne Howard; E-mail: joanne.howard@myclearwater.com; *Youth Serv,* David Lane; E-mail: david.lane@myclearwater.com; Staff 20.5 (MLS 18.5, Non-MLS 2)
Founded 1916. Pop 107,000
Library Holdings: AV Mats 20,415; Bk Vols 229,556; Per Subs 427
Special Collections: US Document Depository
Automation Activity & Vendor Info: (Acquisitions) Innovative Interfaces, Inc; (Cataloging) Innovative Interfaces, Inc; (Circulation) Innovative Interfaces, Inc; (OPAC) Innovative Interfaces, Inc; (Serials) Innovative Interfaces, Inc
Database Vendor: 3M Library Systems, Evanced Solutions, Inc, Gale Cengage Learning
Wireless access
Function: Adult bk club, Archival coll, Audiobks via web, Bk club(s), Bks on CD, Children's prog, Computer training, Computers for patron use, Copy machines, Digital talking bks, e-mail serv, E-Reserves, Electronic databases & coll, Exhibits, Free DVD rentals, Govt ref serv, Handicapped accessible, Mail & tel request accepted, Microfiche/film & reading machines, Music CDs, Online cat, Online searches, OverDrive digital audio bks, Photocopying/Printing, Preschool outreach, Preschool reading prog, Prog for adults, Prog for children & young adult, Pub access computers, Ref & res, Ref serv available, Ref serv in person, Spanish lang bks, Story hour, Summer reading prog, Tax forms, Teen prog, Telephone ref, Web-catalog, Wheelchair accessible
Mem of Pinellas Public Libr Coop
Partic in Tampa Bay Library Consortium, Inc
Special Services for the Blind - ABE/GED & braille classes for the visually impaired & print handicapped
Open Mon-Thurs 10-7, Fri-Sun 12-5
Friends of the Library Group

Branches: 4

BEACH, 69 Bay Esplanade, 33767, SAN 337-3088. Tel: 727-562-4970. *Br Librn,* Joyce Kirchoffer; E-mail: joyce.kirchoffer@myclearwater.com; Staff 1 (Non-MLS 1)
Founded 1961
Open Mon-Fri 1-5
Friends of the Library Group

COUNTRYSIDE, 2741 State Rd 580, 33761, SAN 329-6741. Tel: 727-562-4970. *Br Mgr,* Tracey Reed; E-mail: tracey.reed@myclearwater.com; *Ch Serv,* Julie Hudson; E-mail: julie.hudson@myclearwater.com; *Circ,* Jennifer Mortell; E-mail: jennifer.mortell@myclearwater.com; *Ref Serv,* Jennifer Hambacher; E-mail: Jennifer.hambacher@myclearwater.com; *Ref Serv,* Carmen Heidt; E-mail: carmen.heidt@myclearwater.com; *Ref Serv,* Nicole Kennedy; E-mail: Nicole.kennedy@myclearwater.com; Staff 6 (MLS 6)
Founded 1988
Open Mon-Thurs 10-7, Sat & Sun 12-5
Friends of the Library Group

EAST, 2251 Drew St, 33765, SAN 326-8586. Tel: 727-562-4970. *Br Mgr, Ref Serv,* Tereasa Roose; E-mail: tereasa.roose@myclearwater.com; *Ch Serv,* Valerie Mathre; E-mail: valerie.mathre@myclearwater.com; *Circ,* Jennifer Tudor; E-mail: jennifer.tudor@myclearwater.com; *Ref,* April Troyer; E-mail: april.troyer@myclearwater.com; *Ref Serv,* Adriana Topel; E-mail: adriana.topel@myclearwater.com; *Youth Serv,* Marcela Estavez; E-mail: marcela.estavez@myclearwater.com; Staff 6 (MLS 6)
Founded 1985
Open Mon-Thurs 10-7, Fri & Sat 12-5
Friends of the Library Group

NORTH GREENWOOD, 905 N Martin Luther King Jr Ave, 33755, SAN 337-3142. Tel: 727-562-4970. *Br Mgr,* Rachel Robledo; E-mail: rachel.robledo@myclearwater.com; Staff 1 (MLS 1)
Founded 1950
Special Collections: African-American Coll; Christine Wigfall Morris African American Coll
Open Mon-Thurs 10-7, Fri 12-5
Friends of the Library Group

R FIRST UNITED METHODIST CHURCH*, Clearwater United Church Library, 411 Turner St, 33756. SAN 372-7955. Tel: 727-446-5955. FAX: 727-447-1308. Web Site: www.fumc-clw.com. *Librn,* Karma Schaefer; Staff 6 (MLS 1, Non-MLS 5)
Library Holdings: Bk Titles 3,000; Bk Vols 4,391
Special Collections: John Wesley's Works & Books
Subject Interests: Church hist, Fiction

M MORTON PLANT MEASE HEALTH CARE*, Medical Library, 300 Pinellas St, 33756. (Mail add: PO Box 210, 33756-0210), SAN 322-7219. Tel: 727-462-7889. FAX: 727-461-8755. E-mail: medical.library@baycare.org. *Mgr, Libr Serv,* Karen L Roth; Staff 2 (MLS 1, Non-MLS 1)
Founded 1955
Library Holdings: Bk Vols 2,500; Per Subs 200
Subject Interests: Allied health, Med, Nursing
Automation Activity & Vendor Info: (Cataloging) EOS International; (Circulation) EOS International; (OPAC) EOS International; (Serials) EOS International
Database Vendor: EBSCOhost, Natural Standard, ProQuest, PubMed, STAT!Ref (Teton Data Systems), TDNet, UpToDate, Wiley
Wireless access
Partic in National Network of Libraries of Medicine; Tampa Bay Medical Library Network

GL PINELLAS COUNTY LAW LIBRARY*, Clearwater, 324 S Ft Harrison Ave, 33756-5165. SAN 302-8852. Tel: 727-464-3411. FAX: 727-464-4571. Web Site: www.jud6.org/lawlibraries. *Libr Dir,* Donna L Haverkamp; E-mail: dhaverka@jud6.org; Staff 1 (Non-MLS 1)
Founded 1950
Library Holdings: Bk Vols 34,000
Special Collections: Laws of Florida
Database Vendor: LexisNexis, Westlaw
Wireless access
Open Mon-Fri 8:30-4:30

P PINELLAS TALKING BOOK LIBRARY*, 1330 Cleveland St, 33755-5103. Tel: 727-441-9958. FAX: 727-441-9068. TDD: 727-441-3168. Web Site: www.pplc.us/tbl. *Head Librn,* Marilyn Stevenson
Library Holdings: Talking Bks 69,000
Automation Activity & Vendor Info: (Cataloging) Keystone Systems, Inc (KLAS); (Circulation) Keystone Systems, Inc (KLAS); (OPAC) Keystone Systems, Inc (KLAS)
Partic in Tampa Bay Library Consortium, Inc
Open Mon-Fri 9-4:30
Friends of the Library Group

CLEWISTON

P HENDRY COUNTY LIBRARY SYSTEM*, Clewiston Public Library (Headquarters), 120 W Osceola Ave, 33440. SAN 302-8895. Tel: 863-983-1493. FAX: 863-983-9194. Web Site: www.hendrylibraries.org. *Dir,* Eric Tommerdahl
Founded 1962. Pop 10,000; Circ 39,366
Library Holdings: Bk Vols 71,385; Per Subs 152
Automation Activity & Vendor Info: (Cataloging) TLC (The Library Corporation); (Circulation) TLC (The Library Corporation); (OPAC) TLC (The Library Corporation)
Open Mon & Wed 9-8, Tues, Thurs & Fri 9-5
Friends of the Library Group

Branches: 2

BARRON LIBRARY, 461 N Main St, Labelle, 33935. (Mail add: PO Box 785, Labelle, 33935-0785), SAN 302-9948. Tel: 863-675-0833. FAX: 863-675-7544. *Librn,* Karen Hildebrand
Pop 8,000; Circ 40,000
Library Holdings: Bk Vols 24,126; Per Subs 25
Open Mon & Thurs 10-5 & 7-9, Tues, Wed & Fri 10-5, Sat 10-1
Friends of the Library Group

HARLEM LIBRARY, 1010 J Harlem Academy Ave, 33440. Tel: 863-902-3322. FAX: 863-902-3323. *Librn,* Florida Thomas; E-mail: fthomas@hendryfla.net
Library Holdings: Bk Vols 11,000
Open Mon-Thurs 12-6, Fri 12-5
Friends of the Library Group

COCOA

P BREVARD COUNTY LIBRARY SYSTEM*, 308 Forrest Ave, 2nd Flr, 32922-7781. SAN 303-0393. Tel: 321-633-1801. FAX: 321-633-1798. Web Site: www.mylibrary.com. *Dir, Libr Serv,* Catherine Schweinsberg; E-mail: cschweinsberg@brev.org; *Tech Serv,* Becky Slack; Tel: 321-633-1785, E-mail: bslack@brev.org
Founded 1972. Pop 460,977; Circ 5,132,773
Oct 2008-Sept 2009 Income $36,004,244, State $536,080, County $17,734,082, Locally Generated Income $17,734,082. Sal $8,371,000
Library Holdings: Bk Vols 1,254,063; Per Subs 2,357; Talking Bks 34,534; Videos 110,381
Automation Activity & Vendor Info: (Circulation) TLC (The Library Corporation)
Wireless access
Member Libraries: Cape Canaveral Public Library; Central Brevard Library & Reference Center; Cocoa Beach Public Library; Dr Martin Luther King Jr Library; Eau Gallie Public Library; Franklin T Degroodt Library; Melbourne Beach Public Library; Merritt Island Public Library; Mims/Scottsmoor Public Library; Palm Bay Public Library; Port St John Public Library; Satellite Beach Public Library; South Mainland Library; Suntree/Viera Public Library; Titusville Public Library; West Melbourne Public Library
Partic in Cent Fla Libr Consortium
Special Services for the Blind - Talking bks

Open Mon-Thurs 9-9, Fri 9-6, Sat 9-5, Sun 1-5
Friends of the Library Group
Bookmobiles: 1. Libr Supvr, Tammy Moon

P CENTRAL BREVARD LIBRARY & REFERENCE CENTER*, 308 Forrest Ave, 32922. SAN 302-8909. Tel: 321-633-1792. Circulation Tel: 321-633-1793. Administration Tel: 321-635-7845. FAX: 321-633-1806. Administration FAX: 321-633-1964. Web Site: www.brev.org. *Dir,* Catherine Schweinsberg; E-mail: cschweinsberg@brev.org; *Head, Ref,* Diane Vosatka; E-mail: dvosatka@brev.org; *Ch Serv,* Cynthia Clendenning; Tel: 321 633 1795, E-mail: cridolf@brev.org; Staff 14 (MLS 5, Non-MLS 9)
Founded 1895. Pop 450,000; Circ 439,161
Library Holdings: AV Mats 11,336; DVDs 5,992; Bk Vols 162,112; Per Subs 364; Talking Bks 60,718
Special Collections: Municipal Document Depository; State Document Depository; US Document Depository
Subject Interests: Fla, Genealogy
Automation Activity & Vendor Info: (OPAC) TLC (The Library Corporation); (Serials) Brodart
Database Vendor: Baker & Taylor, Gale Cengage Learning, OCLC FirstSearch
Wireless access
Mem of Brevard County Library System
Partic in Cent Fla Libr Consortium
Special Services for the Blind - Closed circuit TV; Reader equip; Talking bks
Open Mon, Wed, Fri & Sat 9-5, Tues & Thurs 9-8, Sun 1-5
Friends of the Library Group

C EASTERN FLORIDA STATE COLLEGE, Cocoa Campus Joint Use Library, 1519 Clearlake Rd, 32922. SAN 337-3266. Tel: 321-433-7804. Circulation Tel: 321-433-7250. Interlibrary Loan Service Tel: 321-433-7262. FAX: 321-433-7678. E-mail: libraryb@brevardcc.edu. Web Site: www.brevardcc.edu/library. *Cat Librn,* MacArthur Karen; Tel: 321-433-7266; *Ref Serv/eRes,* Karen Simpson; Tel: 321-433-7264; *Acq, Ser,* Michelle Rezeau; Tel: 321-433-7189; *Circ/eRes,* Jill Simser; Tel: 321-433-7252; *ILL,* Gina Rippins; Staff 30 (MLS 11, Non-MLS 19)
Founded 1960. Highest Degree: Associate
Library Holdings: e-books 60,000; Electronic Media & Resources 80; Bk Vols 196,700; Per Subs 1,300
Automation Activity & Vendor Info: (Acquisitions) Ex Libris Group; (Cataloging) Ex Libris Group; (Circulation) Ex Libris Group; (Course Reserve) Ex Libris Group; (OPAC) Ex Libris Group; (Serials) Ex Libris Group
Database Vendor: EBSCOhost, Gale Cengage Learning, Newsbank, OCLC FirstSearch, OCLC WorldShare Interlibrary Loan, ProQuest, Westlaw, Wilson - Wilson Web
Function: Audio & video playback equip for onsite use, Doc delivery serv, ILL available, Ref serv available, Telephone ref
Partic in Lyrasis; Northeast Florida Library Information Network
Open Mon-Thurs 8-8, Fri 9-1

S FLORIDA HISTORICAL SOCIETY*, Library of Florida History, 435 Brevard Ave, 32922. SAN 338-196X. Tel: 321-690-1971, Ext 211. FAX: 321-690-4388. E-mail: tebeaulib@aol.com. Web Site: www.florida-historical-soc.org. *Exec Dir,* Lewis N Wynne; Staff 2 (MLS 1, Non-MLS 1)
Founded 1856
Library Holdings: Bk Vols 7,000; Per Subs 75
Subject Interests: State hist
Publications: Florida Historical (Quarterly); The Society Report
Open Tues-Sat 10-5
Friends of the Library Group

P PORT ST JOHN PUBLIC LIBRARY*, 6500 Carole Ave, 32927. SAN 376-5105. Tel: 321-633-1867. FAX: 321-633-1869. Web Site: www.brev.org. *Dir,* Mike Perini; E-mail: mperini@brev.org
Library Holdings: Bk Vols 45,000; Per Subs 79
Automation Activity & Vendor Info: (Cataloging) TLC (The Library Corporation); (Circulation) TLC (The Library Corporation); (OPAC) TLC (The Library Corporation)
Database Vendor: EBSCOhost, OCLC FirstSearch
Mem of Brevard County Library System
Open Mon, Tues & Fri 9-5, Wed 12-8, Thurs 10-6
Friends of the Library Group

COCOA BEACH

P COCOA BEACH PUBLIC LIBRARY*, 550 N Brevard Ave, 32931. SAN 302-8917. Tel: 321-868-1104. FAX: 321-868-1107. Web Site: www.brev.org, www.cocoabeachpubliclibrary.org. *Dir,* Ray Dickinson; *Adult Prog Serv Dir,* Margot Gould; *Circ,* Teresa Boleman; *Ref,* Gwen Birck; *Tech Serv,* Lynn Fischer; *Youth Serv,* Cindy Heinig; Staff 3 (MLS 3)
Founded 1955. Pop 20,000; Circ 286,488
Library Holdings: AV Mats 23,819; Bk Vols 106,714; Per Subs 221
Special Collections: Cocoa Beach Artists, oil, watercolor, batik & bronze
Subject Interests: Fiction, Fla
Automation Activity & Vendor Info: (Cataloging) TLC (The Library Corporation); (Circulation) TLC (The Library Corporation); (OPAC) TLC (The Library Corporation)
Wireless access
Publications: Footnotes (Newsletter)
Mem of Brevard County Library System
Open Mon, Thurs & Fri 10-6, Tues & Wed 9-8, Sat 9-5, Sun 1-5
Friends of the Library Group

COLEMAN

P COLEMAN PUBLIC LIBRARY*, 712 Central Ave, 33521-0456. (Mail add: PO Box 425, 33521-0456), SAN 376-2793. Tel: 352-748-4598. FAX: 352-748-5384. *Librn,* June Gibson
Library Holdings: Bk Titles 5,659; Per Subs 30
Automation Activity & Vendor Info: (Cataloging) SirsiDynix; (Circulation) SirsiDynix
Open Mon-Thurs 11-6, Fri 2-6, Sat 10-2

CORAL GABLES

M DOCTOR'S HOSPITAL, BAPTIST HEALTH*, Medical Library, 5000 University Dr, 33146. SAN 324-6388. Tel: 305-669-2360. FAX: 305-669-2456. E-mail: library@baptisthealth.net. Web Site: www.baptisthealth.net. *Dir,* Diane Rourke; E-mail: dianer@baptisthealth.net
Founded 1954
Library Holdings: Bk Vols 500
Special Collections: Oral History
Partic in Lyrasis

R TEMPLE JUDEA*, Mel Harrison Memorial Library, 5500 Granada Blvd, 33146. SAN 302-8941. Tel: 305-667-5657. FAX: 305-665-5834. Web Site: www.judeagables.org. *Librn,* Phyllis Robarts; Staff 1 (MLS 1)
Library Holdings: Bk Vols 5,000
Special Collections: Judaica Coll & Holocaust Coll
Automation Activity & Vendor Info: (Cataloging) Follett Software; (Circulation) Follett Software; (OPAC) Follett Software
Open Mon-Thurs 9-5, Fri 9-4
Restriction: Mem only, Staff use only

CL UNIVERSITY OF MIAMI*, School of Law Library, 1311 Miller Dr, 33146. (Mail add: PO Box 248087, 33124-0247), SAN 337-338X. Tel: 305-284-2251. Circulation Tel: 305-284-3563. Reference Tel: 305-284-3585. FAX: 305-284-3554. Web Site: law.miami.edu/library. *Dir,* Sally H Wise; Tel: 305-284-2755, E-mail: swise@law.miami.edu; *Assoc Dir,* Robin Schard; *Head, Acq & Coll Develop,* Helen Wohl; *Head, Ref,* Pam Lucken; *Circ Librn,* William Latham; *Electronic Res/Spec Formats Cat Librn,* Calmer Chattoo; *Ref & Instrul Serv Librn,* Nick Harrell; *Ref/Fac Serv Librn,* Barbara Brandon; *Ref/Publ Librn,* Virginia Templeton; *Foreign & Intl Law Librn, Ref Librn,* Bianca Anderson; *Syst Librn,* Emerita Cuesta; *Adjunct Cat Librn,* Renee Meyer; *Adjunct Ref Librn,* Carlos Espinosa; *Adjunct Ref Librn,* Patricia Partdo; Staff 12 (MLS 11, Non-MLS 1)
Highest Degree: Doctorate
Automation Activity & Vendor Info: (Acquisitions) Innovative Interfaces, Inc; (Cataloging) Innovative Interfaces, Inc; (Circulation) Innovative Interfaces, Inc; (Course Reserve) Innovative Interfaces, Inc; (ILL) OCLC; (OPAC) Innovative Interfaces, Inc; (Serials) Innovative Interfaces, Inc
Wireless access
Publications: Law Library Research Guides
Partic in Lyrasis
Open Mon-Thurs 7am-Midnight, Fri 7am-10pm, Sat 9am-10pm, Sun 9am-Midnight

C UNIVERSITY OF MIAMI LIBRARIES*, Otto G Richter Library, 1300 Memorial Dr, 33146. (Mail add: PO Box 248214, 33124-0320), SAN 337-3290. Tel: 305-284-3233. Interlibrary Loan Service Tel: 305-284-6102. Reference Tel: 305-284-4722. FAX: 305-284-4027. Web Site: www.library.miami.edu. *Dean of Libr,* Charles D Eckman; E-mail: ceckman@miami.edu; *Dir, Info Mgt & Syst,* Cheryl Gowing; E-mail: cgowing@miami.edu; *Head, Monographic Ordering & Database Maintenance,* Carmen Civieta-Gaskell; *Head, Educ & Outreach,* Anna Stoute; E-mail: astoute@miami.edu; Staff 38 (MLS 38)
Founded 1926. Enrl 14,685; Fac 1,865; Highest Degree: Doctorate
Library Holdings: Bk Vols 3,000,000; Per Subs 70,000
Special Collections: Amigos of the University of Miami Library Cuban Heritage Coll; Floridiana; Latin American (especially Cuban, Caribbean & Colombian); Marine & Atomospheric Sciences. State Document Depository; US Document Depository

Automation Activity & Vendor Info: (Acquisitions) Innovative Interfaces, Inc; (Cataloging) Innovative Interfaces, Inc; (Circulation) Innovative Interfaces, Inc
Database Vendor: EBSCOhost, Innovative Interfaces, Inc
Publications: Context (Friends of the Library Newsletter)
Partic in Association of Southeastern Research Libraries; Lyrasis; OCLC Online Computer Library Center, Inc
Open Mon-Thurs 7:30am-2am, Fri 7:30am-10pm, Sat 9am-10pm, Sun 9am-2am
Friends of the Library Group
Departmental Libraries:
PAUL BUISSON ARCHITECTURE LIBRARY, 1223 Dickison Dr, Bldg 48, 33146. Tel: 305-284-5282. FAX: 305-284-1894. Web Site: www.arc.miami.edu/school/facilities/library.html. *Head, Archit Libr,* Gilda Santana; E-mail: gsantana@miami.edu
Library Holdings: Bk Vols 5,000
Open Mon-Fri 9-8:30
MARTA & AUSTIN WEEKS MUSIC LIBRARY, PO Box 248165, 33124-7610. Tel: 305-284-2429. FAX: 305-284-1041. Web Site: www.library.miami.edu/musiclib. *Head Music Libr,* Nancy C Zavac; E-mail: nzavac@miami.edu; Staff 8 (MLS 2, Non-MLS 6)
Library Holdings: CDs 22,000; DVDs 1,060; Music Scores 75,000; Bk Titles 24,200; Per Subs 130; Videos 1,133
Special Collections: Larry Taylor-Billy Matthews Musical Theater Archive Coll, CDs, LPs, playbills, scores, scripts
Open Mon-Thurs 8:30am-11pm, Fri 8:30-6, Sat 10-6, Sun 12-11
Restriction: Open to pub for ref only

CRAWFORDVILLE

P WAKULLA COUNTY PUBLIC LIBRARY*, 4330 Crawfordville Hwy, 32327. (Mail add: PO Box 1300, 32326-1300), SAN 320-4685. Tel: 850-926-7415. FAX: 850-926-4513. TDD: 850-926-1201. Web Site: www.wakullalibrary.org. *Dir,* Doug Jones; *Cat,* Tristan Mor; *Circ, ILL,* Clarissa Wilkerson; *Youth Serv,* Leilania Nichols; Staff 5 (MLS 1, Non-MLS 4)
Founded 1972. Pop 22,500; Circ 57,000
Library Holdings: Bk Titles 30,000; Per Subs 18
Special Collections: Florida & Local History (The Elizabeth Smith Coll), bks, publications; Hi Lo Literary Coll. Oral History
Automation Activity & Vendor Info: (Circulation) SirsiDynix; (OPAC) SirsiDynix
Database Vendor: EBSCOhost, OCLC FirstSearch
Mem of Wilderness Coast Public Libraries
Partic in Panhandle Library Access Network
Open Wed & Fri 9-6, Tues & Thurs 9-8, Sat 9-1
Friends of the Library Group

CRESTVIEW

P ROBERT L F SIKES PUBLIC LIBRARY*, Crestview Public Library, 1445 Commerce Dr, 32539. SAN 302-8976. Tel: 850-682-4432. FAX: 850-689-4788. Web Site: www.cityofcrestview.org/library.php. *Dir,* Jean Lewis; E-mail: jlewis@okaloosa.lib.fl.us; *Cat Librn,* Marie Garcia; E-mail: mgarcia@okaloosa.lib.fl.us; *Ref Librn,* Sandra Dreaden; E-mail: sdreaden@okaloosa.lib.fl.us; *Youth Serv Librn,* Heather Nitzel; E-mail: hnitzel@okaloosa.lib.fl.us; Staff 10 (MLS 2, Non-MLS 8)
Founded 1976. Pop 85,000; Circ 205,000
Library Holdings: CDs 2,900; DVDs 4,200; e-books 400; Large Print Bks 2,000; Bk Vols 48,000; Per Subs 60; Videos 600
Automation Activity & Vendor Info: (Cataloging) SirsiDynix; (Circulation) SirsiDynix; (ILL) OCLC FirstSearch; (OPAC) SirsiDynix
Database Vendor: Gale Cengage Learning, ProQuest
Wireless access
Partic in Okaloosa County Public Library Cooperative
Open Mon & Tues 10-8, Wed & Thurs 10-6, Fri 8:30-4:30, Sat 10-4
Friends of the Library Group

CROSS CITY

P DIXIE COUNTY PUBLIC LIBRARY*, 16328 SE Hwy 19, 32628. SAN 337-680X. Tel: 352-498-1219. FAX: 352-498-1408. Web Site: www.3rivers.lib.fl.us, www.neflin.org. *Mgr,* Cindy Bellot; *Asst Mgr,* Patti Driggers
Library Holdings: Bk Vols 7,000; Per Subs 25
Automation Activity & Vendor Info: (Cataloging) SirsiDynix; (Circulation) SirsiDynix
Open Mon-Fri 9-5:30, Sat 9-11
Friends of the Library Group

DADE CITY

J PASCO-HERNANDO COMMUNITY COLLEGE-EAST CAMPUS*, Charles E Conger Library, 36727 Blanton Rd, 33523-7599. SAN 302-900X. Tel: 352-518-1307. FAX: 352-518-1350. Web Site: www.phcc.edu. *Dir of Libr,* Charles R Rodgers
Founded 1972. Enrl 2,800; Highest Degree: Associate
Library Holdings: Bk Titles 19,000; Bk Vols 24,000; Per Subs 110
Subject Interests: Agr, Data proc, Law enforcement, Nursing, Paramedics
Automation Activity & Vendor Info: (Cataloging) Ex Libris Group; (Circulation) Ex Libris Group; (Course Reserve) Ex Libris Group; (ILL) OCLC; (OPAC) Ex Libris Group; (Serials) Ex Libris Group
Partic in Tampa Bay Library Consortium, Inc
Open Mon-Thurs 8am-9pm, Fri 8-4:30

DANIA BEACH

S IGFA FISHING HALL OF FAME & MUSEUM*, E K Harry Library of Fishes, 300 Gulf Stream Way, 33004. SAN 325-8823. Tel: 954-927-2628. FAX: 954-924-4299. Web Site: www.igfa.org. *Librn,* G Morchower; Staff 1 (MLS 1)
Founded 1973
Library Holdings: AV Mats 2,200; Bk Vols 15,000; Per Subs 150
Special Collections: Art; Historical Photos; Stamps

DAVIE

C BROWARD COLLEGE, University/College Library, 3501 SW Davie Rd, 33314. SAN 337-3959. Tel: 954-201-6648. Circulation Tel: 954-201-6649. Interlibrary Loan Service Tel: 954-201-6658. Administration Tel: 954-201-6480. FAX: 954-201-6490. Web Site: ucl.broward.edu. *Assoc Dean, Dean of Libr, LRC & Campus Tech, Libr Instruction,* Alice Murillo; E-mail: amurillo@broward.edu; *Archives,* Andrew Dutka; *Automation Serv,* Dennis Levine; *Coll Develop, Ref,* Michelle Apps; *ILL,* Grushenska Elusta; *Tech Serv,* Jan Rothhaar; Staff 11.5 (MLS 11.5)
Founded 1960. Enrl 21,000; Fac 375; Highest Degree: Bachelor
Library Holdings: AV Mats 3,795; CDs 898; e-books 8,632; Microforms 1,471; Bk Titles 239,420; Bk Vols 276,105; Per Subs 195
Automation Activity & Vendor Info: (Acquisitions) Ex Libris Group; (Cataloging) Ex Libris Group; (Circulation) Ex Libris Group; (Course Reserve) Ex Libris Group; (ILL) Ex Libris Group; (OPAC) Ex Libris Group; (Serials) Ex Libris Group
Wireless access
Partic in Lyrasis; SEFLIN - Southeast Florida Library Information Network, Inc
Open Mon-Thurs 7:30am-10pm, Fri 7:30-5, Sat 9-5, Sun 2-10
Departmental Libraries:
NORTH CAMPUS LIBRARY LRC, 1100 Coconut Creek Blvd, Coconut Creek, 33066, SAN 321-1878. Tel: 954-201-2600. FAX: 954-201-2650. *Head of Libr,* Debbie Passalacqua; Staff 2 (MLS 2)
Library Holdings: Bk Vols 225,000
Open Mon-Thurs 7:30am-9pm, Fri 7:30-4, Sat 9-5, Sun 1-5
SOUTH CAMPUS LIBRARY LRC, 7300 Hollywood, Pembroke Pines, 33024, SAN 321-1886. Tel: 954-201-8827. FAX: 954-201-0282. Web Site: www.browardlibrary.org. *Dean,* Terri Justice; E-mail: tjustice@broward.edu; *Librn,* Chris Casper; E-mail: ccasper@broward.edu
Library Holdings: Bk Titles 155,000; Per Subs 850
Automation Activity & Vendor Info: (Cataloging) TLC (The Library Corporation); (Circulation) TLC (The Library Corporation)
Open Mon-Thurs 7:30am-9:30pm, Fri 7:30-4, Sat 9-5, Sun 1-5

C TRINITY INTERNATIONAL UNIVERSITY*, Florida Regional Center Library, 8190 W State Rd 84, 33324-4611. SAN 303-0628. Tel: 954-382-6561. FAX: 954-382-6421. Web Site: www.tiu.edu/florida/library. *Libr Dir, Res Coordr,* Verna E Thomas; E-mail: vthomas@tiu.edu; Staff 1 (MLS 1)
Founded 1949. Enrl 672; Fac 65; Highest Degree: Master
Library Holdings: Bk Titles 6,500
Subject Interests: Bus, Educ, Psychol, Relig
Database Vendor: EBSCOhost, Gale Cengage Learning, LexisNexis, ProQuest
Wireless access
Partic in SEFLIN - Southeast Florida Library Information Network, Inc
Open Mon, Tues, Thurs & Fri 1-10, Sat 8:30-2:30

DAYTONA BEACH

C BETHUNE-COOKMAN COLLEGE*, Carl S Swisher Library & Learning Resource Center, 640 Mary McLeod Bethune Blvd, 32114. SAN 302-9018. Tel: 386-481-2186. FAX: 386-481-2182. Web Site: www.cookman.edu/subpages/about_library.asp. *Libr Dir,* Tasha Lucas-Youmans; Tel: 368-481-2118, E-mail: youmanst@cookman.edu; *Evening Ref Librn,* Andre Jansons; E-mail: jansonsa@cookman.edu; *Ref Librn,* Joseph A Campbell; E-mail: campbelj@cookman.edu; *Archivist,* Angelo Salvo; E-mail: salvoa@cookman.edu; *Info Tech,* Jason Hubbard; E-mail: hubbardj@cookman.edu
Founded 1904. Enrl 3,090; Fac 147; Highest Degree: Master
Library Holdings: Bk Vols 175,483; Per Subs 770
Special Collections: Africa & the Negro, bk, micro; Archival (Mary McLeod Bethune & others); Art (Peter Turcheon); Attica Coll; Children's

Coll; Rosewood Exhibit. Oral History; State Document Depository; US Document Depository
Automation Activity & Vendor Info: (Cataloging) TLC (The Library Corporation); (Circulation) TLC (The Library Corporation); (OPAC) TLC (The Library Corporation)
Database Vendor: Baker & Taylor, ebrary, EBSCOhost, JSTOR, LexisNexis, Newsbank, OCLC FirstSearch, OCLC WorldShare Interlibrary Loan, ProQuest, TLC (The Library Corporation), Westlaw
Wireless access
Publications: Annual Library Report; Faculty Library Manual; Nonprint Media Newsletter
Partic in Lyrasis; OCLC Online Computer Library Center, Inc
Open Mon-Thurs 8am-Midnight, Fri 8-5, Sat 9-5, Sun 3pm-Midnight; Mon-Fri (Summer) 8am-10pm, Sat 10-2

P BUREAU OF BRAILLE & TALKING BOOKS LIBRARY*, 421 Platt St, 32114-2804. SAN 302-9042. Tel: 386-239-6000. Toll Free Tel: 800-226-6075. FAX: 386-239-6069. *Bur Chief,* Susan Roberts; E-mail: susan.roberts@dbs.fldoe.org; *Adminr,* Phyllis Vaughn; Staff 32 (MLS 5, Non-MLS 27)
Founded 1950. Pop 39,126; Circ 1,627,173
Jul 2005-Jun 2006 Income $1,200,000
Library Holdings: Bk Titles 72,347; Bk Vols 2,400,000
Special Collections: Floridiana, braille & audio cassette; Womyn's Braille Press, braille & audio cassette
Automation Activity & Vendor Info: (Cataloging) Keystone Systems, Inc (KLAS); (Circulation) Keystone Systems, Inc (KLAS); (OPAC) Keystone Systems, Inc (KLAS)
Wireless access
Publications: Bi-Monthly Patron Oriented Newsletter for Adults, Children & Young Adults (in large print, braille & cassette); Subject Bibliographies (in large print, braille & cassette)
Special Services for the Blind - Braille bks; Videos on blindness & phys handicaps
Open Mon-Fri 8-5
Friends of the Library Group

C DAYTONA BEACH COLLEGE LIBRARY*, Mary Karl Memorial Learning Resources Center, 1200 W International Speedway Blvd, 32114. (Mail add: PO Box 2811, 32120-2811), SAN 302-9026. Tel: 386-506-3055. Reference Tel: 386-506-3518. FAX: 386-506-3008. *Assoc VPres & Dean,* Michelle McCraney; E-mail: mccranm@daytonastate.edu; *Head Librn,* Mercedes Clement; Tel: 386-506-3440, E-mail: clemenm@daytonastate.edu; *Head, Circ,* Katheleene Bryan; Tel: 386-506-3521, E-mail: bryank@daytonastate.edu; *Head, Ref,* Fred Harden; Tel: 386-506-3608, E-mail: hardenf@daytonastate.edu; *Head, Tech Serv,* Dustin Weeks; Tel: 386-506-3593, E-mail: weeksd@daytonastate.edu; *Br Head,* Christina Hastie; Tel: 386-785-2017, E-mail: hastiec@daytonastate.edu; *Res Librn,* Rachel Owens; Tel: 386-506-3842, E-mail: owensr@daytonastate.edu
Enrl 14,000; Highest Degree: Bachelor
Library Holdings: Bk Titles 75,500; Bk Vols 100,000; Per Subs 752
Automation Activity & Vendor Info: (Cataloging) Ex Libris Group; (Circulation) Ex Libris Group; (Course Reserve) Ex Libris Group; (ILL) Ex Libris Group; (OPAC) Ex Libris Group; (Serials) Ex Libris Group
Wireless access
Partic in Lyrasis; Tampa Bay Library Consortium, Inc
Open Mon-Thurs 7:30am-10pm, Fri 7:30-5, Sat 8-4, Sun 1-9

C EMBRY-RIDDLE AERONAUTICAL UNIVERSITY*, Hunt Library, 600 S Clyde Morris Blvd, 32114-3900. SAN 302-9034. Tel: 386-226-6595. Circulation Tel: 386-226-6592. Interlibrary Loan Service Tel: 386-323-8774. Reference Tel: 386-226-6604. Administration Tel: 386-226-6933. Toll Free Tel: 800-678-9428. E-mail: library@erau.edu. Web Site: library.erau.edu/daytona/index.html. *Libr Dir,* Anne Marie Casey; Tel: 386-226-6593, E-mail: caseya3@erau.edu; *Assoc Dir, Access Serv,* Melanie West; Tel: 386-226-6591, E-mail: melanie.west@erau.edu; *Assoc Dir, Budget & Planning,* Jane Deighan; Tel: 386-226-6589, E-mail: jane.deighan@erau.edu; *Assoc Dir, Electronic/Tech Libr Serv,* Suzanne Sprague; Tel: 386-226-6932, E-mail: suzanne.sprague@erau.edu; *Assoc Dir, Res/Worldwide Libr Serv,* Kathleen Citro; Tel: 386-226-6596, E-mail: kathleen.citro@erau.edu; *ILL Librn,* Elizabeth Sterthaus; E-mail: elizabeth.sterthaus@erau.edu; Staff 33 (MLS 19, Non-MLS 14)
Founded 1965. Enrl 6,844; Fac 392; Highest Degree: Doctorate
Jul 2013-Jun 2014. Mats Exp $902,977, Books $191,000, Per/Ser (Incl. Access Fees) $325,000, AV Mat $9,000, Electronic Ref Mat (Incl. Access Fees) $377,977. Sal $1,795,930
Library Holdings: AV Mats 5,337; e-books 5,666; Microforms 308,127; Bk Titles 52,425; Bk Vols 76,569; Per Subs 1,039
Special Collections: Aviation History & Aeronautical Engineering Coll, bks, doc, per; FAA, NTSB & NASA Documents
Subject Interests: Aeronautical eng, Aerospace eng, Aviation
Automation Activity & Vendor Info: (Acquisitions) Ex Libris Group; (Cataloging) Ex Libris Group; (Circulation) Ex Libris Group; (Course Reserve) Ex Libris Group; (ILL) Clio; (Media Booking) Ex Libris Group; (OPAC) Ex Libris Group; (Serials) Ex Libris Group
Database Vendor: ACM (Association for Computing Machinery), Alexander Street Press, American Mathematical Society, American Psychological Association (APA), Annual Reviews, ASCE Research Library, Blackwell, Bowker, Career Guidance Foundation, CISTI Source, College Source, Coutts Information Service, CQ Press, CRC Press/Taylor & Francis Group, CredoReference, ebrary, EBSCO Information Services, EBSCOhost, Elsevier, Emerald, Ex Libris Group, Facts on File, Gale Cengage Learning, Haworth Pres Inc, HeinOnline, IEEE (Institute of Electrical & Electronics Engineers), IHS, Ingenta, Ingram Library Services, ISI Web of Knowledge, Jane's, JSTOR, LexisNexis, McGraw-Hill, Mergent Online, Modern Language Association, Nature Publishing Group, Newsbank, OCLC, ProQuest, RefWorks, Sage, ScienceDirect, Scopus, SerialsSolutions, Springshare, LLC, Standard & Poor's, Thomson - Web of Science, ValueLine
Wireless access
Partic in Florida Library Information Network; Independent Cols & Univs of Fla; Lyrasis; OCLC Online Computer Library Center, Inc
Special Services for the Deaf - Assistive tech
Open Mon-Thurs 7:15am-Midnight, Fri 7:15-6, Sat 12-6, Sun Noon-Midnight

S MUSEUM OF ARTS & SCIENCES*, Margaret & John Wilkinson Library, 352 S Nova Rd, 32114. SAN 302-9093. Tel: 386-255-0285. FAX: 386-255-5040. Web Site: www.moas.org. *Chief Curator,* Cynthia Duval; E-mail: cduval@moas.org; Staff 46 (MLS 28, Non-MLS 18)
Founded 1956
Library Holdings: Bk Vols 5,000
Special Collections: American Art; Florida history books, periodicals & manuscripts; Lucy Shepard Bequest; Natural history; Ornithology Coll; Rare Cuban books (General Fulgencio Batista Coll); World Art. Oral History
Subject Interests: Art, Astronomy, Cuba, Fla, Natural hist
Function: Ref serv available
Partic in Lee County

GL VOLUSIA COUNTY LAW LIBRARY*, Courthouse Annex, Rm 208, 125 E Orange Ave, 32114. SAN 302-9107. Tel: 386-257-6041. FAX: 386-257-6052. *Librn,* Deborah Patterson
Library Holdings: Bk Vols 25,000
Open Mon-Fri 8:30-4:30

P VOLUSIA COUNTY PUBLIC LIBRARY*, 1290 Indian Lake Rd, 32124. SAN 337-3444. Tel: 386-248-1745. Circulation Tel: 386-257-6036. Reference Tel: 386-257-6037. FAX: 386-248-1746. TDD: 386-255-3765. Web Site: www.vcpl.lib.fl.us. *Dir,* Lucinda Colee; *Tech Coordr,* Anne Powers; *Coll Develop,* Janet Dudding; *ILL,* Esther Jones; *Tech Serv,* Pia Andersen; Staff 23 (MLS 6, Non-MLS 17)
Founded 1961. Pop 456,000; Circ 3,274,066
Library Holdings: e-books 31,118; Bk Vols 859,415; Per Subs 1,380; Talking Bks 71,118; Videos 123,813
Special Collections: Genealogy Coll. US Document Depository
Subject Interests: Genealogy
Automation Activity & Vendor Info: (Circulation) Infor Library & Information Solutions; (OPAC) Infor Library & Information Solutions
Wireless access
Publications: Annual Report; Happenings (Monthly newsletter)
Partic in Lyrasis
Special Services for the Deaf - Bks on deafness & sign lang; High interest/low vocabulary bks; Staff with knowledge of sign lang
Open Mon-Fri 8-4:30
Friends of the Library Group
Branches: 13
DAYTONA BEACH REGIONAL, City Island, 32114. SAN 337-3533. Tel: 386-257-6036. FAX: 386-257-6026. *Regional Librn,* Brook White; Staff 21 (MLS 8, Non-MLS 13)
Open Mon-Thurs 9-7, Fri 9-5, Sat 9-3, Sun 1-5
Friends of the Library Group
DEBARY PUBLIC, 200 N Charles R Beall Blvd, DeBary, 32713. SAN 337-3568. Tel: 386-668-3835. FAX: 386-668-3837. *Head of Libr,* Sheri Brumback; Staff 5 (MLS 2, Non-MLS 3)
Open Mon & Fri 10-5, Tues-Thurs 10-8, Sat 9-5
Friends of the Library Group
DELAND AREA PUBLIC, 130 E Howry Ave, DeLand, 32724. SAN 337-3592. Tel: 386-822-6430. FAX: 386-822-6435. *Regional Librn,* Kathleen Mann; Staff 19 (MLS 9, Non-MLS 10)
Special Services for the Deaf - TDD equip
Open Mon-Thurs 9:30-7:30, Fri & Sat 10-5, Sun 1-5
Friends of the Library Group
DELTONA REGIONAL, 2150 Eustace Ave, Deltona, 32725. SAN 337-3622. Tel: 386-789-7207. FAX: 386-789-7211. *Regional Librn,* Melissa Reynolds; Staff 18 (MLS 8, Non-MLS 10)
Founded 1976

Open Mon-Thurs 9:30-7:30, Fri & Sat 10-5, Sun 1-5
Friends of the Library Group
JOHN H DICKERSON HERITAGE, 411 S Keech St, 32114, SAN 337-3509. Tel: 386-239-6478. *Head of Libr,* Inez Jeffers; Staff 4 (MLS 1, Non-MLS 3)
Founded 1977
Open Mon, Wed & Thurs 10-6, Tues 10-7, Fri & Sat 10-5
Friends of the Library Group
EDGEWATER PUBLIC, 103 Indian River Blvd, Edgewater, 32132, SAN 337-3681. Tel: 386-424-2916. FAX: 386-424-2918. *Head of Libr,* Kristen Bennett; Staff 6 (MLS 3, Non-MLS 3)
Open Mon & Wed 9:30-6, Tues & Thurs 9:30-7:30, Fri & Sat 9:30-5
Friends of the Library Group
LAKE HELEN PUBLIC, 221 N Euclid Ave, Lake Helen, 32744, SAN 337-3746. Tel: 386-228-1152. FAX: 386-228-1154. *Head of Libr,* Pam Swanto; Staff 2 (Non-MLS 2)
Open Tues 11:30-7:30, Wed-Sat 9-5
Friends of the Library Group
NEW SMYRNA BEACH PUBLIC, 1001 S Dixie Freeway, New Smyrna Beach, 32168, SAN 337-3479. Tel: 386-424-2910. FAX: 386-424-2913. *Regional Librn,* Walter Jubinsky; Staff 14 (MLS 5, Non-MLS 9)
Open Mon-Thurs 9:30-7:30, Fri & Sat 10-5, Sun 1-5
Friends of the Library Group
OAK HILL PUBLIC, 125 E Halifax Ave, Oak Hill, 32759, SAN 337-3770. Tel: 386-345-5510. FAX: 386-345-5510. *Head of Libr,* Linda Rutty; Staff 1 (Non-MLS 1)
Open Tues & Thurs 10-5, Wed & Fri 1-5, Sat 9-1
Friends of the Library Group
ORANGE CITY PUBLIC, 148 Albertus Way, Orange City, 32763, SAN 337-3657. Tel: 386-775-5270. *Head of Libr,* Ruth Knockel; Staff 2 (Non-MLS 2)
Open Mon-Thurs 10-6, Fri & Sat 9-5
Friends of the Library Group
ORMOND BEACH PUBLIC, 30 S Beach St, Ormond Beach, 32174, SAN 337-3789. Tel: 386-676-4191. FAX: 386-676-4194. *Regional Librn,* Suzan Howes; Staff 19 (MLS 7, Non-MLS 12)
Open Mon-Thurs 9-7, Fri 9-5, Sat 9-3, Sun 1-5
Friends of the Library Group
PIERSON PUBLIC, 115 N Volusia Ave, Pierson, 32180, SAN 378-0090. Tel: 386-749-6930. *Head of Libr,* Pat Sowell; Staff 2 (MLS 1, Non-MLS 1)
Open Mon & Fri 10-12 & 1-5, Tues-Thurs 11-2 & 3-7
PORT ORANGE PUBLIC, 1005 City Center Circle, Port Orange, 32119, SAN 322-6174. Tel: 386-322-5152. FAX: 386-322-5155. *Regional Librn,* Jane Weimer; Staff 17 (MLS 7, Non-MLS 10)
Open Mon-Thurs 9-7, Fri 9-5, Sat 9-3, Sun 1-5
Friends of the Library Group

DE FUNIAK SPRINGS

P WALTON COUNTY PUBLIC LIBRARY SYSTEM*, Walton-DeFuniak Library, Three Circle Dr, 32435-2542. SAN 302-9115. Tel: 850-892-3624. FAX: 850-892-4438. E-mail: dfslibrary@co.walton.fl.us. Web Site: www.youseemore.com/walton. *Dir,* Dan Owens; E-mail: owedan@co.walton.fl.us; Staff 15 (MLS 3, Non-MLS 12)
Founded 1886. Pop 40,571; Circ 123,109
Library Holdings: AV Mats 314; High Interest/Low Vocabulary Bk Vols 200; Large Print Bks 800; Bk Titles 87,000; Per Subs 60; Talking Bks 517
Special Collections: Antique Record Player; Armor Coll; Shell Coll
Automation Activity & Vendor Info: (Acquisitions) TLC (The Library Corporation); (Cataloging) TLC (The Library Corporation); (Circulation) TLC (The Library Corporation); (OPAC) TLC (The Library Corporation)
Database Vendor: OCLC FirstSearch, ProQuest
Wireless access
Function: ILL available, Photocopying/Printing
Open Mon & Wed-Sat 9-5, Tues 9-8
Restriction: Internal use only
Friends of the Library Group
Branches: 3
COASTAL, 437 Greenway Trail, Santa Rosa Beach, 32459-5589, SAN 328-641X. Tel: 850-267-2809. FAX: 850-267-9452. *Librn,* Linda Thompson; Staff 5 (MLS 1, Non-MLS 4)
Founded 1986
Open Mon 10-6, Tues-Sat 9-5
Friends of the Library Group
FREEPORT PUBLIC, 76 Hwy 20 W, Freeport, 32439, SAN 328-6436. Tel: 850-835-2040. FAX: 850-835-2154. *Br Mgr,* Mary Balint; Staff 3 (MLS 1, Non-MLS 2)
Founded 1986
Open Mon-Wed, Fri & Sat 9-5, Thurs 9-8
Friends of the Library Group
NORTH WALTON COUNTY - GLADYS N MILTON MEMORIAL, 261 Flowersview Blvd, Laurel Hill, 32567. Tel: 850-834-5383. FAX: 850-834-5487. *In Charge,* Debra Hogans; Staff 2 (Non-MLS 2)
Open Mon & Tues, Thurs-Sat 9-5
Bookmobiles: 1

DELAND

C STETSON UNIVERSITY*, duPont-Ball Library, 421 N Woodland Blvd, Unit 8418, 32723. SAN 337-3835. Tel: 386-822-7175. Interlibrary Loan Service Tel: 386-822-7183. Reference Tel: 386-747-9028. Interlibrary Loan Service FAX: 386-822-7199. Administration FAX: 386-740-3626. Web Site: www.stetson.edu/library. *Dean, Libr & Digital Learning Res,* Susan M Ryan; Tel: 386-822-7181, E-mail: sryan@stetson.edu; *Assoc Dean,* Debora Dinkins; Tel: 386-822-7179, E-mail: ddinkins@stetson.edu; *Head, Pub Serv,* M Jason Martin; Tel: 386-822-7178, E-mail: jmartin2@stetson.edu; *Govt Doc & Res Librn,* Barbara Costello; Tel: 386-822-7185, E-mail: bcostell@stetson.edu; *Learning & Info Literacy Librn,* Rosalie Flowers; Tel: 386-822-7190, E-mail: rflowers@stetson.edu; *Music & Res Librn,* Jean Wald; Tel: 386-822-8958, E-mail: jwald@stetson.edu; *Res Librn,* Sims D Kline; Tel: 386-822-7176, E-mail: skline@stetson.edu; *Cat,* Laura Kirkland; Tel: 386-822-4027, E-mail: lkirklan@stetson.edu; *Circ,* Catherine Ervin; Tel: 386-822-7187, E-mail: cervin@stetson.edu; *ILL,* Susan Derryberry; Tel: 386-822-4034, E-mail: sconnell@stetson.edu; Staff 10.5 (MLS 8.5, Non-MLS 2)
Founded 1883. Enrl 3,961; Fac 381; Highest Degree: Master
Jul 2012-Jun 2013 Income $1,891,994. Mats Exp $713,947, Books $46,867, Per/Ser (Incl. Access Fees) $304,747, Other Print Mats $7,240, AV Mat $12,204, Electronic Ref Mat (Incl. Access Fees) $328,189, Presv $1,790. Sal $963,863 (Prof $620,461)
Library Holdings: AV Mats 18,883; CDs 10,223; DVDs 2,982; e-books 111,468; e-journals 78,699; Electronic Media & Resources 32,144; Microforms 195,448; Music Scores 18,274; Bk Titles 211,159; Bk Vols 243,547; Per Subs 725; Videos 4,410
Special Collections: Congressman E Clay Shaw Congressional Papers; Goverment Documents Coll; Juvenile Literature (Greenlaw Coll); Senator J Maxwell Cleland Memorabilia; University Archives. State Document Depository; US Document Depository
Subject Interests: Bus, Educ, Humanities, Lit, Music, Relig, Russia
Automation Activity & Vendor Info: (Acquisitions) SirsiDynix; (Cataloging) SirsiDynix; (Circulation) SirsiDynix; (Course Reserve) SirsiDynix; (OPAC) SirsiDynix; (Serials) SirsiDynix
Database Vendor: ABC-CLIO, ACM (Association for Computing Machinery), Agricola, Alexander Street Press, American Chemical Society, American Mathematical Society, American Psychological Association (APA), Annual Reviews, ARTstor, Bowker, Checkpoint Systems, Inc, College Source, CQ Press, CredoReference, Dialog, ebrary, EBSCOhost, Elsevier, Gale Cengage Learning, H W Wilson, HeinOnline, Hoovers, Ingenta, Ingram Library Services, ISI Web of Knowledge, JSTOR, LexisNexis, Marquis Who's Who, Modern Language Association, Newsbank, OCLC ArticleFirst, OCLC FirstSearch, OCLC WorldShare Interlibrary Loan, Oxford Online, Project MUSE, ProQuest, PubMed, Sage, ScienceDirect, SirsiDynix, Springer-Verlag, Standard & Poor's, STN International, ValueLine, Westlaw, Wilson - Wilson Web
Wireless access
Publications: Faculty Review (Annual); Library Brochure (Annual); Newsletter (Bi-annually)
Partic in Independent Cols & Univs of Fla; Lyrasis; Northeast Florida Library Information Network
Open Mon-Thurs 8am-1am, Fri 8-5, Sat 11-5, Sun 11am-1am
Restriction: Access at librarian's discretion

DELRAY BEACH

P DELRAY BEACH PUBLIC LIBRARY*, 100 W Atlantic Ave, 33444. SAN 302-9174. Tel: 561-266-0194. Reference Tel: 561-266-0196. Administration Tel: 561-266-0799. FAX: 561-266-9757. E-mail: info.delraylibrary@gmail.com. Web Site: www.delraylibrary.org. *Dir,* Alan Kornblau; *Asst Dir, Syst Coordr,* Mykal Banta; Tel: 561-266-0198, E-mail: mykal.banta@delraylibrary.org; *Asst Dir, Finance/Admin,* Karen Evanson; Tel: 561-266-9489, E-mail: karen.evanson@delraylibrary.org; *Head, Ref,* Christopher Leary; Tel: 561-819-6406, E-mail: christopher.leary@delraylibrary.org; *Ref Librn,* Kathleen Hensman; Tel: 561-819-6404, E-mail: kathleen.hensman@delraylibrary.org; *Ref Librn, YA Librn,* Loanis Menendez-Cuesta; Tel: 561-819-6299, E-mail: loanis.menendez@delraylibrary.og; *Ref Librn,* Brian Smith; Tel: 561-819-6405, E-mail: brian.smith@delraylibrary.org; *Ch Serv,* Lynda Hunter; Tel: 561-266-0197, E-mail: lynda.hunter@delraylibrary.org; *Tech Serv,* Linda Otis; E-mail: linda.otis@delraylibrary.org; Staff 9 (MLS 5, Non-MLS 4)
Founded 1939. Pop 62,040; Circ 257,950
Library Holdings: AV Mats 9,276; Bk Vols 250,000; Per Subs 350
Subject Interests: Fla
Automation Activity & Vendor Info: (Circulation) SirsiDynix; (OPAC) SirsiDynix

Database Vendor: Booklist Online, Gale Cengage Learning, OCLC FirstSearch
Wireless access
Function: Adult bk club, After school storytime, Art exhibits, AV serv, Bilingual assistance for Spanish patrons, Bk club(s), Bk reviews (Group), Bks on cassette, Bks on CD, CD-ROM, Children's prog, Computer training, Computers for patron use, Copy machines, e-mail serv, Electronic databases & coll, Handicapped accessible, Holiday prog, Homework prog, ILL available, Instruction & testing, Literacy & newcomer serv, Magnifiers for reading, Music CDs, Online cat, Online searches, Outreach serv, Outside serv via phone, mail, e-mail & web, Photocopying/Printing, Prog for adults, Prog for children & young adult, Pub access computers, Ref & res, Ref serv available, Ref serv in person, Senior computer classes, Story hour, Summer & winter reading prog, Summer reading prog, Tax forms, Teen prog, Telephone ref, VHS videos, Video lending libr, Web-catalog, Wheelchair accessible, Workshops, Writing prog
Publications: Newsletter (Bi-monthly)
Partic in Coop Authority for Libr Automation; Library Cooperative of the Palm Beaches
Open Mon-Wed 9-8, Thurs-Sat 9-5, Sun (Sept-May) 1-5

S MORIKAMI MUSEUM*, Colonel Donald B Gordon Memorial Library, 4000 Morikami Park Rd, 33446. SAN 322-8770. Tel: 561-495-0233, Ext 217. FAX: 561-499-2557. Web Site: www.morikami.org. *Curator of Coll,* Veljko Dujin; E-mail: VDujin@pbcgov.org; Staff 1 (Non-MLS 1)
Founded 1977
Library Holdings: Bk Titles 6,500; Bk Vols 7,000; Spec Interest Per Sub 8
Special Collections: Japanese culture, language, people
Subject Interests: Japanese (Lang), Japanese culture
Function: For res purposes
Open Tues-Sun 10-5
Restriction: Non-circulating to the pub

L SOUTH COUNTY LAW LIBRARY*, 200 W Atlantic Ave, 33444. SAN 373-0409. Tel: 561-274-1440. *Librn,* Sara Jones
Library Holdings: Bk Vols 4,500
Partic in Westlaw
Open Mon-Fri 8-4:30

DESTIN

P DESTIN LIBRARY*, 150 Sibert Ave, 32541-1523. Tel: 850-837-8572. FAX: 850-837-5248. E-mail: library@cityofdestin.com. Web Site: www.cityofdestin.com/library.html. *Dir,* Jurate S Burns; E-mail: jburns@cityofdestin.com; *Circ,* Kitti Capps; E-mail: kcapps@cityofdestin.com; *Ref Serv, Youth Serv,* Will Rogers, Jr; E-mail: wrogers@cityofdestin.com; *Tech Serv,* Sandra Kelly; E-mail: skelly@okaloosa.lib.fl.us; Staff 9 (MLS 2, Non-MLS 7)
Founded 1940. Pop 12,600; Circ 69,907
Oct 2011-Sept 2012 Income $366,548, City $287,002, County $59,968, Locally Generated Income $19,578. Mats Exp $37,900, Books $27,000, Per/Ser (Incl. Access Fees) $1,900, AV Mat $6,000, Electronic Ref Mat (Incl. Access Fees) $3,000. Sal $298,722 (Prof $65,000)
Library Holdings: Audiobooks 1,739; DVDs 2,349; e-books 1,500; Electronic Media & Resources 2; Large Print Bks 2,500; Bk Titles 31,000; Bk Vols 36,000; Per Subs 40; Videos 40
Special Collections: Florida Coll, bks, ms; Library of America Coll; Sea Life Coll, art, artifacts, bks, films, ms
Subject Interests: Rare bks
Automation Activity & Vendor Info: (Acquisitions) SirsiDynix; (Cataloging) SirsiDynix; (Circulation) SirsiDynix; (Course Reserve) SirsiDynix; (OPAC) SirsiDynix
Database Vendor: EBSCOhost, Gale Cengage Learning, SirsiDynix
Wireless access
Function: Accelerated reader prog, Adult bk club, Adult literacy prog, Art exhibits, Bk club(s), Bks on cassette, Bks on CD, Children's prog, Computer training, Computers for patron use, Copy machines, e-mail serv, E-Reserves, Electronic databases & coll, Free DVD rentals, Handicapped accessible, Holiday prog, ILL available, Magnifiers for reading, Mail & tel request accepted, Online cat, Photocopying/Printing, Prog for adults, Pub access computers, Ref & res, Ref serv available, Referrals accepted, Senior computer classes, Senior outreach, Story hour, Video lending libr, Wheelchair accessible
Partic in Okaloosa County Public Library Cooperative; Panhandle Library Access Network
Open Mon 9-5, Tues & Thurs 9-8, Wed 1-5, Fri 9-6, Sat 9-1
Restriction: Non-resident fee
Friends of the Library Group

DUNDEE

P DUNDEE PUBLIC LIBRARY, 202 E Main St, 33838. Tel: 863-439-9424. Administration Tel: 863-439-9425. FAX: 863-439-9426. Web Site: townofdundee.com/our-community/libraries. *Interim Dir,* Julie Feagle; E-mail: jfeagle@townofdundee.com; *Ch Serv,* Mary Ann Podbielski; *Circ,* Kaliayh Monroe; *Circ,* Eileen Young; Staff 3 (MLS 1, Non-MLS 2)
Founded 1990. Pop 3,000; Circ 3,500
Library Holdings: AV Mats 200; High Interest/Low Vocabulary Bk Vols 350; Large Print Bks 400; Bk Titles 12,000; Per Subs 11; Talking Bks 30; Videos 200
Special Collections: Home School Coll
Subject Interests: Fla, Spanish
Automation Activity & Vendor Info: (Acquisitions) SirsiDynix; (Cataloging) SirsiDynix; (Circulation) SirsiDynix; (ILL) OCLC; (OPAC) SirsiDynix
Wireless access
Function: Audio & video playback equip for onsite use, Handicapped accessible, ILL available, Online searches, Photocopying/Printing, Prog for adults, Prog for children & young adult, Ref serv available, Spoken cassettes & CDs, Summer reading prog, Telephone ref, VHS videos, Wheelchair accessible
Partic in Polk County Libr Coop
Special Services for the Deaf - Bks on deafness & sign lang
Special Services for the Blind - Bks on CD
Open Mon-Fri 10-6, Sat 9-1
Friends of the Library Group

DUNEDIN

P DUNEDIN PUBLIC LIBRARY*, 223 Douglas Ave, 34698. SAN 302-9182. Tel: 727-298-3080. Circulation Tel: 727-298-3080, Ext 249. Reference Tel: 727-298-3080, Ext 253. FAX: 727-298-3088. Web Site: www.dunedingov.com. *Dir,* Phyllis Gorshe; Tel: 727-298-3080, Ext 226, E-mail: pgorshe@dunedinfl.net; *Adult Serv,* Elizabeth White; Tel: 727-298-3080, Ext 224, E-mail: ewhite@dunedinfl.net; *Circ,* Kirtley Luney; Tel: 727-298-3080, Ext 248, E-mail: kluney@dunedinfl.net; *Info Serv,* Kathy Smuz; Tel: 727-298-3080, Ext 222, E-mail: ksmuz@dunedinfl.net; *Tech Serv,* Doreen Chonko; Tel: 727-298-3080, Ext 237; *Youth Serv,* Olivia Wilson; Tel: 727-298-3080, Ext 238, E-mail: owilson@dunedinfl.net; Staff 24 (MLS 11, Non-MLS 13)
Founded 1895. Pop 35,000; Circ 473,683
Oct 2011-Sept 2012. Mats Exp $240,000
Library Holdings: Bk Titles 98,000; Bk Vols 109,000; Per Subs 198
Special Collections: Multimedia
Automation Activity & Vendor Info: (Acquisitions) Innovative Interfaces, Inc; (Cataloging) Innovative Interfaces, Inc; (Circulation) Innovative Interfaces, Inc; (ILL) Innovative Interfaces, Inc; (OPAC) Innovative Interfaces, Inc; (Serials) Innovative Interfaces, Inc
Wireless access
Function: Adult bk club, Bks on CD, CD-ROM, Computers for patron use, Homebound delivery serv, ILL available, Photocopying/Printing, Prog for children & young adult, Summer reading prog, Wheelchair accessible
Publications: Friends (Newsletter)
Mem of Pinellas Public Libr Coop
Partic in Tampa Bay Library Consortium, Inc
Open Mon-Wed 9:30-8, Thurs & Fri 9:30-6, Sat 9:30-5, Sun 1-5
Friends of the Library Group

EAGLE LAKE

P EAGLE LAKE PUBLIC LIBRARY*, 75 N Seventh St, 33839-3430. (Mail add: PO Box 129, 33839-0129), SAN 370-4718. Tel: 863-293-2914. FAX: 863-292-0210. Web Site: www.pclc.lib.fl.us/location/eagle_lake/info. *Dir,* Ruth Waltonbaugh; E-mail: ruthw@mypclc.org
Library Holdings: AV Mats 250; CDs 10; DVDs 45; Large Print Bks 169; Bk Vols 7,500; Videos 301
Automation Activity & Vendor Info: (Cataloging) SirsiDynix; (Circulation) SirsiDynix
Database Vendor: SirsiDynix
Wireless access
Partic in Polk County Libr Coop
Open Mon-Fri 9-5

EASTPOINT

P FRANKLIN COUNTY PUBLIC LIBRARY*, Point Mall, 29 Island Dr, 32328-3265. (Mail add: PO Box 722, 32328-0722), SAN 377-2888. Tel: 850-670-8151. FAX: 850-670-8151. *Dir,* Anne Birchwell
Library Holdings: Bk Vols 30,000; Per Subs 12
Automation Activity & Vendor Info: (Cataloging) SirsiDynix; (Circulation) SirsiDynix; (OPAC) SirsiDynix
Open Tues-Thurs 12-6, Fri 10-7
Friends of the Library Group
Branches: 1
CARRABELLE BRANCH, 311 Saint James Ave, Carrabelle, 32322. (Mail add: PO Box 722, 32328-0722), SAN 376-7604. Tel: 850-697-2366. FAX: 850-697-4562. *Br Mgr,* Position Currently Open
Open Tues 11-7, Wed & Thurs 8-6, Fri 9-5, Sat 10-2
Friends of the Library Group

EGLIN AFB

AIR FORCE RESEARCH LABORATORY
A MUNITIONS DIRECTORATE TECHNICAL LIBRARY*, 203 W Eglin Blvd, Ste 300, 32542-6843, SAN 377-3108. Tel: 850-882-5586. FAX: 850-882-4476. *Info Spec,* Cheryl Mack; E-mail: cheryl.mack@eglin.af.mil; Staff 5 (MLS 1, Non-MLS 4)
Library Holdings: Bk Titles 10,000; Bk Vols 12,000; Per Subs 200
Subject Interests: Aerospace, Chem, Math, Physics
Automation Activity & Vendor Info: (Cataloging) EOS International; (Circulation) EOS International; (ILL) OCLC; (OPAC) EOS International; (Serials) EOS International
Database Vendor: American Chemical Society, EBSCOhost, Elsevier, EOS International, IEEE (Institute of Electrical & Electronics Engineers), Knovel, OCLC ArticleFirst, OCLC FirstSearch, OCLC WorldShare Interlibrary Loan, Overdrive, Inc, ProQuest, PubMed, SerialsSolutions, Springer-Verlag, Wiley
Function: Computers for patron use, Copy machines, e-mail serv, Electronic databases & coll, Govt ref serv, Handicapped accessible, ILL available, Online cat, Online ref, Online searches, Orientations, Outside serv via phone, mail, e-mail & web, Photocopying/Printing, Scanner, Web-catalog
Partic in Fedlink; Panhandle Library Access Network
Restriction: Govt use only, Open to mil & govt employees only, Photo ID required for access

A TECHNICAL LIBRARY*, 203 W Eglin Blvd, Ste 300, 32542-6843, SAN 337-3924. Tel: 850-882-3212, 850-882-5586. FAX: 850-882-3214. *Dir,* Cheryl Mack; Tel: 850-882-6849, E-mail: cheryl.mack@eglin.af.mil; *Ref Librn,* Eleanor Baudouin; E-mail: eleanor.baudouin@eglin.af.mil; *Info Spec,* Christi Rountree; E-mail: christina.rountree.ctr@eglin.af.mil; Staff 5 (MLS 1, Non-MLS 4)
Founded 1955
Library Holdings: e-journals 440; Electronic Media & Resources 64; Large Print Bks 488; Bk Titles 10,000; Per Subs 450
Subject Interests: Aeronaut, Biol, Chem, Electronics, Math, Physics
Automation Activity & Vendor Info: (Acquisitions) EOS International; (Cataloging) EOS International; (Circulation) EOS International; (OPAC) EOS International; (Serials) EOS International
Function: Computers for patron use, Copy machines, Doc delivery serv, e-mail & chat, e-mail serv, Electronic databases & coll, Fax serv, Govt ref serv, Online cat, Online ref, Online searches, Photocopying/Printing, Ref serv available, Ref serv in person, Scanner, Telephone ref, Web-catalog
Partic in Fedlink; OCLC-LVIS; Panhandle Library Access Network
Open Mon-Fri 7-4
Restriction: Not open to pub, Restricted access, Secured area only open to authorized personnel

A UNITED STATES AIR FORCE*, Eglin Air Force Base Library, 305 W F St, Bldg 278, 32542-6842. SAN 337-386X. Tel: 850-882-5016. Interlibrary Loan Service Tel: 850-882-3462. Administration Tel: 850-882-5088. FAX: 850-882-2621. Web Site: www.youseemore.com/eglin. *Dir,* Vicky Stever; E-mail: stever@eglin.af.mil; *Libr Tech, Mkt,* Dorothee Bennett; Tel: 850-882-3462, E-mail: dorothee.bennett@eglin.af.mil; *Syst Adminr,* Jesus Rodriguez; E-mail: jesus.rodriguez@eglin.af.mil; Staff 8 (MLS 1, Non-MLS 7)
Founded 1942
Library Holdings: CDs 1,900; DVDs 1,600; e-books 8,000; Electronic Media & Resources 15; Large Print Bks 258; Bk Titles 40,086; Bk Vols 43,087; Per Subs 198; Talking Bks 1,200; Videos 1,800
Subject Interests: Aeronaut, Bus & mgt, Mil hist
Automation Activity & Vendor Info: (Cataloging) TLC (The Library Corporation); (Circulation) TLC (The Library Corporation); (ILL) TLC (The Library Corporation); (OPAC) TLC (The Library Corporation); (Serials) TLC (The Library Corporation)
Database Vendor: Gale Cengage Learning, Newsbank, OCLC FirstSearch, ProQuest
Wireless access
Function: Copy machines, Doc delivery serv, Handicapped accessible, ILL available, Orientations, Prog for adults, Prog for children & young adult, Ref serv available, Senior computer classes, Spoken cassettes & CDs, Summer reading prog, Tax forms, Telephone ref, VHS videos, Wheelchair accessible
Publications: Periodicals Holding List (Accession list)
Partic in Fedlink; OCLC Online Computer Library Center, Inc; Panhandle Library Access Network
Open Mon-Thurs 9-8, Sat & Sun 10-4
Restriction: Not open to pub

ENGLEWOOD

P ELSIE QUIRK PUBLIC LIBRARY OF ENGLEWOOD*, 100 W Dearborn St, 34223-3309. SAN 302-9190. Tel: 941-861-1200. Circulation Tel: 941-861-1225. Reference Tel: 941-861-1210. Administration Tel: 941-861-1205. TDD: 941-475-9705. Web Site: www.sclibs.net. *Mgr,* Jennifer M Perry; E-mail: jperry@scgov.net; *Coordr,* Michele Strickland; Tel: 941-861-1215, E-mail: mstrickland@scgov.net; *Ref Serv,* Toni Hopper; Tel: 941-861-1211, E-mail: thopper@scgov.net; *Youth Serv,* Cris Walton; Tel: 941-861-1214, E-mail: cwalton@scgov.net; Staff 11 (MLS 4, Non-MLS 7)
Founded 1962. Pop 28,000; Circ 221,464
Special Collections: Englewood History Information
Automation Activity & Vendor Info: (Acquisitions) Baker & Taylor; (Cataloging) Innovative Interfaces, Inc - Millenium; (Circulation) Innovative Interfaces, Inc - Millenium; (OPAC) Innovative Interfaces, Inc - Millenium
Wireless access
Function: Adult bk club, Audiobks via web, Bi-weekly Writer's Group, Bk club(s), Bks on cassette, Bks on CD, Children's prog, Computer training, Computers for patron use, Copy machines, Digital talking bks, E-Reserves, Electronic databases & coll, Family literacy, Free DVD rentals, Genealogy discussion group, Handicapped accessible, Literacy & newcomer serv, Music CDs, Newsp ref libr, Online cat, Online ref, Online searches, Outreach serv, OverDrive digital audio bks, Photocopying/Printing, Prog for adults, Prog for children & young adult, Pub access computers, Ref serv available, Spoken cassettes & CDs, Spoken cassettes & DVDs, Story hour, Summer reading prog, Tax forms, Teen prog, VHS videos, Wheelchair accessible
Mem of Sarasota County Library System
Partic in Tampa Bay Library Consortium, Inc
Special Services for the Deaf - TTY equip
Special Services for the Blind - Accessible computers; Assistive/Adapted tech devices, equip & products; Bks on cassette; Bks on CD
Open Mon & Wed 10-8, Tues & Thurs-Sat 10-5
Friends of the Library Group

EUSTIS

P EUSTIS MEMORIAL LIBRARY*, 120 N Center St, 32726. SAN 302-9212. Tel: 352-357-5686. Circulation Tel: 352-357-5003. Reference Tel: 352-357-6110. FAX: 352-357-5450. E-mail: EMLContact@eustis.org. Web Site: www.eustismemoriallibrary.org. *Dir,* Marlene V Blye; E-mail: blyem@ci.eustis.fl.us; *Circ Supvr,* Celeste Bringard; *Tech Serv Supvr,* Jennifer Codding; *Adult/Ref Serv,* Nancy Flint; *Ch Serv,* Lauren McLaughlin; Tel: 352-357-0896; Staff 5 (MLS 5)
Founded 1902. Pop 19,129; Circ 118,000
Library Holdings: Audiobooks 1,725; CDs 1,505; DVDs 3,767; e-books 1,051; Bk Vols 100,048; Per Subs 152; Talking Bks 1,929; Videos 603
Special Collections: Florida Coll
Automation Activity & Vendor Info: (Cataloging) SirsiDynix; (Circulation) SirsiDynix; (OPAC) SirsiDynix
Wireless access
Function: Handicapped accessible, Homebound delivery serv, ILL available, Magnifiers for reading, Online searches, Spoken cassettes & CDs, Summer reading prog, VHS videos, Video lending libr, Wheelchair accessible
Partic in Tampa Bay Library Consortium, Inc
Special Services for the Blind - Bks on cassette; Bks on CD
Open Mon & Thurs 9-8, Tues, Wed & Fri 9-6, Sat 9-1
Restriction: Non-resident fee

FERNANDINA BEACH

P NASSAU COUNTY PUBLIC LIBRARY SYSTEM*, Fernandina Beach Branch, 25 N Fourth St, 32034-4123. Tel: 904-277-7365. Interlibrary Loan Service Tel: 904-548-4467. Information Services Tel: 904-548-4870. FAX: 904-277-7366. Interlibrary Loan Service FAX: 904-548-4426. E-mail: libraryinfo@nassaucountyfl.com. Web Site: nassaureads.com. *Dir, Pub Libr Serv,* Dawn S Bostwick; Tel: 904-548-4862, E-mail: dbostwick@nassaucountyfl.com; *Asst Dir,* Janet W Loveless; Tel: 904-548-4857, E-mail: jloveless@nassaucountyfl.com; *Dir, Info Tech,* Mark Johnson; Tel: 904-491-7393, E-mail: mjohnson@nassaucountyfl.com; *Youth Serv Librn,* Michelle Forde; Tel: 904-548-4858, E-mail: mforde@nassaucountyfl.com; *Cat,* Jeanne Marshall; Tel: 904-548-4865, E-mail: jmarshall@nassaucountyfl.com; *Cat,* Elaine Strickland; Tel: 904-548-4860, E-mail: estrickland@nassaucountyfl.com; *ILL,* Patricia Thirsk; Tel: 904-548-4465, Fax: 904-548-4426, E-mail: pthirsk@nassaucountyfl.com; Staff 10 (MLS 4, Non-MLS 6)
Founded 1966. Pop 68,188; Circ 176,912
Oct 2009-Sept 2010 Income (Main Library Only) $774,880, State $229,410, City $51,667, Federal $16,592, County $521,325, Locally Generated Income $24,145. Mats Exp $62,112, Per/Ser (Incl. Access Fees) $8,600. Sal $436,324
Library Holdings: Bk Titles 80,000; Bk Vols 166,000; Per Subs 95
Special Collections: AIGS; Genealogy & Local History (Permanent loan from Amelia Island Genealogical Society)
Automation Activity & Vendor Info: (Acquisitions) SirsiDynix; (Cataloging) SirsiDynix; (Circulation) SirsiDynix; (ILL) OCLC; (OPAC) SirsiDynix

Database Vendor: Gale Cengage Learning, LearningExpress, OCLC FirstSearch, ProQuest
Wireless access
Function: Bk club(s), Bks on CD, Computers for patron use, Copy machines, e-mail & chat, Free DVD rentals, Govt ref serv, Handicapped accessible, Holiday prog, ILL available, Music CDs, Online cat, Online ref, Orientations, OverDrive digital audio bks, Photocopying/Printing, Preschool outreach, Prog for adults, Prog for children & young adult, Pub access computers, Summer reading prog, Telephone ref
Partic in Florida Library Information Network; Northeast Florida Library Information Network; OCLC Online Computer Library Center, Inc
Open Mon & Thurs 10-8, Tues, Wed, Fri & Sat 10-6
Restriction: Non-resident fee
Friends of the Library Group
Branches: 4
BRYCEVILLE BRANCH, 7280 Motes Rd, Bryceville, 32009. Tel: 904-266-9813. FAX: 904-266-2271. *Libr Asst,* Susan McKenney; E-mail: smckenney@nassaucountyfl.com; Staff 1 (Non-MLS 1)
Founded 2003. Circ 7,749
Oct 2009-Sept 2010 Income County $93,493. Mats Exp $10,280, Per/Ser (Incl. Access Fees) $250. Sal $46,777
Library Holdings: Bk Vols 8,000; Per Subs 10
Automation Activity & Vendor Info: (Acquisitions) SirsiDynix; (Cataloging) SIRSI WorkFlows; (Circulation) SIRSI WorkFlows; (OPAC) SIRSI-iBistro
Database Vendor: Gale Cengage Learning, OCLC FirstSearch, ProQuest
Function: Bks on CD, Children's prog, Computers for patron use, Copy machines, e-mail serv, Electronic databases & coll, Free DVD rentals, Govt ref serv, Holiday prog, ILL available, Online cat, Online ref, Orientations, OverDrive digital audio bks, Photocopying/Printing, Pub access computers, Summer reading prog, Tax forms, Telephone ref
Partic in Northeast Florida Library Information Network; OCLC Online Computer Library Center, Inc
Open Tues, Wed & Sat 10-6, Thurs Noon-8
Restriction: Non-resident fee
Friends of the Library Group
CALLAHAN BRANCH, 450077 State Rd 200, Callahan, 32011-3767. Tel: 904-879-3434. *Libr Mgr,* Alison McCarty; E-mail: amccarty@nassaucountyfl.com; *Circ,* Heather Griffin; E-mail: hgriffin@nassaucountyfl.com; Staff 2 (MLS 1, Non-MLS 1)
Founded 1985. Circ 52,587
Oct 2009-Sept 2010 Income $200,841, County $200,841. Mats Exp $33,704. Sal $77,625
Library Holdings: Bk Vols 45,000; Per Subs 3
Automation Activity & Vendor Info: (Circulation) SIRSI WorkFlows; (ILL) OCLC; (OPAC) SIRSI-iBistro
Database Vendor: Gale Cengage Learning, LearningExpress, OCLC FirstSearch, ProQuest
Function: Bk club(s), Bks on CD, Children's prog, Computers for patron use, Copy machines, Free DVD rentals, Govt ref serv, Holiday prog, ILL available, Music CDs, Online cat, Orientations, OverDrive digital audio bks, Photocopying/Printing, Prog for adults, Pub access computers, Summer reading prog, Tax forms
Open Mon & Wed-Fri 10-6, Tues Noon-8
Restriction: Non-resident fee
Friends of the Library Group
HILLIARD BRANCH, 15821 CR 108, Hilliard, 32046. Tel: 904-845-2495. FAX: 904-845-2449. *Br Mgr,* Rosemary Szczygiel; Tel: 904-548-4866, E-mail: rszczygiel@nassaucountyfl.com; *Circ,* Sandra Drury; E-mail: sdrury@nassaucountyfl.com. Subject Specialists: *Creative writing,* Rosemary Szczygiel; Staff 2 (MLS 1, Non-MLS 1)
Founded 1994. Circ 30,040
Oct 2009-Sept 2010 Income $168,132. Mats Exp $29,330, Per/Ser (Incl. Access Fees) $1,425. Sal $76,600
Library Holdings: Bk Vols 40,000; Per Subs 30
Automation Activity & Vendor Info: (Circulation) SIRSI WorkFlows; (ILL) OCLC; (OPAC) SIRSI-iBistro
Function: Bks on cassette, Bks on CD, Children's prog, Computers for patron use, Copy machines, Free DVD rentals, Govt ref serv, Holiday prog, ILL available, Music CDs, Online cat, Orientations, OverDrive digital audio bks, Photocopying/Printing, Prog for adults, Pub access computers, Summer reading prog, Tax forms
Partic in Northeast Florida Library Information Network; OCLC Online Computer Library Center, Inc
Open Mon-Wed & Fri 10-6, Thurs 12-8
Restriction: Non-resident fee
Friends of the Library Group
YULEE BRANCH, 76346 William Burgess Blvd, Yulee, 32097. Tel: 904-548-4467. FAX: 904-548-4426. *Libr Mgr,* Susan McKinney; Staff 2 (MLS 1, Non-MLS 1)
Founded 2001. Circ 17,365
Oct 2009-Sept 2010 Income $121,530. Mats Exp $8,700. Sal $80,172
Library Holdings: Bk Vols 12,000; Per Subs 2
Automation Activity & Vendor Info: (Circulation) SIRSI WorkFlows; (OPAC) SIRSI-iBistro
Function: Bks on CD, Children's prog, Computers for patron use, Copy machines, e-mail & chat, Free DVD rentals, Govt ref serv, Holiday prog, ILL available, Online cat, Orientations, OverDrive digital audio bks, Photocopying/Printing, Prog for adults, Pub access computers, Summer reading prog, Tax forms
Open Mon-Thurs 8am-9pm, Fri 8-3
Restriction: Non-resident fee
Friends of the Library Group

FLAGLER BEACH

P FLAGLER BEACH LIBRARY*, 315 S Seventh St, 32136-3524. (Mail add: PO Box 449, 32136-0449), SAN 370-4629. Tel: 386-517-2030. FAX: 386-517-2234. Web Site: www.cityofflaglerbeach.com. *Head Librn,* Ruth E Young; E-mail: ryoung@cityofflaglerbeach.com; Staff 1 (Non-MLS 1)
Library Holdings: Audiobooks 350; Bks on Deafness & Sign Lang 15; DVDs 600; Large Print Bks 500; Music Scores 250; Bk Titles 26,000; Per Subs 65; Talking Bks 350
Wireless access
Special Services for the Blind - Bks on cassette
Open Tues 1-7, Wed-Fri 10-5, Sat 10-2

FORT LAUDERDALE

C ART INSTITUTE OF FORT LAUDERDALE*, Meinhardt Memorial Library, 1600 SE 17th St, 3rd Flr, 33316. (Mail add: 1799 SE 17th St, 33316), SAN 377-8053. Tel: 954-308-2631. Toll Free Tel: 800-275-7603. FAX: 954-463-3393. E-mail: aifl_library@aii.edu. Web Site: www.aifllibrary.com. *Librn,* Pam Reagan; Staff 2 (MLS 1, Non-MLS 1)
Enrl 2,700; Highest Degree: Bachelor
Library Holdings: Bk Titles 22,000; Bk Vols 26,000; Per Subs 315
Automation Activity & Vendor Info: (Circulation) Ex Libris Group; (OPAC) Ex Libris Group
Function: ILL available
Partic in Lyrasis; OCLC Online Computer Library Center, Inc
Restriction: Non-circulating to the pub

P BROWARD COUNTY DIVISION OF LIBRARIES*, Main Library, 100 S Andrews Ave, 33301. SAN 337-3983. Tel: 954-357-7444. Circulation Tel: 954-357-7407. Interlibrary Loan Service Tel: 954-357-7442. Reference Tel: 954-357-7428. Administration Tel: 954-357-7397. Automation Services Tel: 954-357-8620. FAX: 954-357-5733. TDD: 954-357-7528. E-mail: answer@browardlibrary.org. Web Site: www.broward.org/library. *Dir, Libr Div,* Skye Patrick; Tel: 954-357-7559, E-mail: spatrick@broward.org; *Asst Dir,* Position Currently Open; *Assoc Dir, Pub Serv,* Laura Connors; Tel: 954-357-6592, E-mail: lconnors@broward.org; *Regional Libr Mgr,* Cindy Shulman; Tel: 954-357-7417, E-mail: cshulman@broward.org; Staff 744 (MLS 206, Non-MLS 538)
Founded 1974. Pop 1,759,591; Circ 10,530,000
Oct 2011-Sept 2012 Income (Main Library and Branch(s)) $63,478,691, State $1,350,000, County $58,788,710, Other $3,339,981. Mats Exp $6,252,863, Books $3,391,718, Per/Ser (Incl. Access Fees) $411,059, AV Mat $1,874,975, Electronic Ref Mat (Incl. Access Fees) $575,111. Sal $46,223,653
Library Holdings: Audiobooks 102,134; AV Mats 2,524; Bks-By-Mail 2,134; Bks on Deafness & Sign Lang 284, Braille Volumes 407; CDs 187,617; DVDs 399,553; e-books 65,871; Electronic Media & Resources 392; High Interest/Low Vocabulary Bk Vols 1,664; Large Print Bks 101,532; Microforms 22,750; Music Scores 7,417; Bk Titles 377,631; Bk Vols 2,632,730; Per Subs 2,850; Talking Bks 52,536; Videos 51,225
Special Collections: African-American Research Library; Bienes Rare Books Coll; Florida Diagnostic & Learning Resource System; Judaica (Isaac Mayer Wise Coll); Music Scores; Small Business Resource Center
Subject Interests: Fla, Genealogy, Intl trade, Patents
Automation Activity & Vendor Info: (Acquisitions) CARL.Solution (TLC); (Cataloging) CARL.Solution (TLC); (Circulation) CARL.Solution (TLC); (ILL) OCLC WorldShare Interlibrary Loan; (Serials) CARL.Solution (TLC)
Database Vendor: Gale Cengage Learning, OCLC FirstSearch
Wireless access
Publications: Connections (Monthly); WPA Museum Extension Project 1935-1943 (Bienes Museum of the Modern Book 2009)
Partic in Lyrasis; OCLC Online Computer Library Center, Inc
Special Services for the Deaf - Assisted listening device; Bks on deafness & sign lang; Closed caption videos; Spec interest per; Staff with knowledge of sign lang; TTY equip
Special Services for the Blind - Braille bks; Closed circuit TV; Large print bks; Magnifiers; Talking bks; Videos on blindness & phys handicaps
Open Mon, Thurs & Fri 10-6, Tues & Wed 12-8
Friends of the Library Group
Branches: 42
AFRICAN-AMERICAN RESEARCH LIBRARY & CULTURAL CENTER, 2650 Sistrunk Blvd, 33311, SAN 337-4378. Tel: 954-357-6282. FAX: 954-357-6257. *Regional Libr Mgr,* Elaina Norlin; Tel: 954-357-6149, E-mail: enorlin@broward.org; *Asst Regional Libr*

Mgr, Essie DeNoms; Tel: 954-357-5979, E-mail: edenoms@broward.org; Staff 45 (MLS 14, Non-MLS 31)
Founded 2002. Circ 81,647
Special Collections: Black Heritage Coll
Open Mon & Wed 12-8, Tues & Thurs-Sun 10-6
Friends of the Library Group

BEACH BRANCH, 221 Pompano Beach Blvd, Pompano Beach, 33062, SAN 373-5192. Tel: 954-357-7830. FAX: 954-357-4908. *Br Mgr,* Coleen Thorson; E-mail: cthorson@broward.org; Staff 3 (MLS 1, Non-MLS 2)
Founded 1991. Circ 52,154
Open Mon-Fri 10-6
Friends of the Library Group

BOOKS BY MAIL, 100 S Andrews Ave, 1st Flr, 33301, SAN 378-0678. Tel: 954-357-5757. *Libr Spec,* Elouise Player; E-mail: eplayer@broward.org; Staff 1 (Non-MLS 1)
Circ 21,471
Open Mon, Thurs & Fri 10-6, Tues & Wed 12-8

BROWARD COUNTY HISTORICAL COMMISSION LIBRARY, 301 SW 13th Ave, 33312, SAN 302-9247. Tel: 954-357-5553. FAX: 954-357-5522. Web Site: www.co.broward.fl.us/history.htm. *Mgr,* Peggy Davis; Tel: 954-357-6379, E-mail: pdavis@broward.org
Founded 1972
Library Holdings: Bk Titles 1,601
Special Collections: Cooper Kirk Coll; Judge Nance Coll, Rare bks. Oral History
Subject Interests: Local hist
Function: Res libr
Publications: Broward Legacy
Open Mon-Fri 8:30-4:30
Restriction: Non-circulating

TYRONE BRYANT BRANCH, 2230 NW 21st Ave, 33311, SAN 337-4327. Tel: 954-357-8210. FAX: 954-357-8216. *Br Mgr,* Michael Bryant; E-mail: mbryant@broward.org; Staff 4 (MLS 1, Non-MLS 3)
Founded 1980. Circ 24,387
Open Mon & Thurs 12-8, Tues, Wed & Sat 10-6
Friends of the Library Group

CARVER RANCHES, 4735 SW 18th St, West Park, 33023, SAN 337-4025. Tel: 954-357-6245. FAX: 954-357-6316. *Br Mgr,* Tanisha Jones; E-mail: tcjones@broward.org; Staff 7 (MLS 1, Non-MLS 6)
Founded 1982. Circ 1,878
Open Mon & Wed 12-8, Tues, Thurs & Sat 10-6
Friends of the Library Group

CYBRARY CENTER, 100 S Andrews Ave, 1st & 7th Flr, 33301, SAN 378-0988. Tel: 954-357-7485. FAX: 954-357-7792. *Libr II,* Bill Forbes; E-mail: wforbes@broward.org; Staff 6 (MLS 1, Non-MLS 5)
Open Mon, Thurs & Fri 10-6, Tues & Wed 12-8

DAVIE-COOPER CITY BRANCH, 4600 SW 82nd Ave, Davie, 33328, SAN 337-4068. Tel: 954-357-6399. FAX: 954-357-6058. *Br Mgr,* Position Currently Open; Staff 7 (MLS 3, Non-MLS 4)
Circ 211,125
Open Mon & Tues 12-8, Wed, Thurs & Sat 10-6
Friends of the Library Group

DANIA BEACH-PAUL DEMAIO LIBRARY, One Park Ave E, Dania Beach, 33004, SAN 337-4076. Tel: 954-357-7073. FAX: 954-357-7069. *Br Mgr,* Tim Bain; E-mail: tbain@broward.org; Staff 9 (MLS 2, Non-MLS 7)
Founded 1979. Circ 122,346
Open Mon & Thurs 12-8, Tues, Wed & Sat 10-6
Friends of the Library Group

FORT LAUDERDALE BRANCH, 1300 E Sunrise Blvd, 33304, SAN 337-4106. Tel: 954-357-7890. FAX: 954-357-7868. *Br Mgr,* Mary Lou Galvin; E-mail: mgalvin@broward.org; Staff 5 (MLS 1, Non-MLS 4)
Circ 85,750
Open Mon & Fri 10-6
Friends of the Library Group

FOSTER PARK COMMUNITY CENTER MICRO-LIBRARY, 609 NW 6th Ave, Hallandale Beach, 33009. Tel: 954-455-0310. *Librn,* Robert Gold; E-mail: rgold@broward.org; Staff 1 (MLS 1)
Open Mon & Tues 10-1, Wed & Thurs 5-8, Fri 10-1 & 5-8, Sun 10-6

GALT OCEAN MILE READING CENTER, 3403 Galt Ocean Dr, 33308, SAN 373-5206. Tel: 954-357-7840. FAX: 954-357-7854. *Br Mgr,* Marlene Barnes; Staff 5 (MLS 1, Non-MLS 4)
Circ 89,769
Open Mon, Tues, Fri & Sat 10-6, Thurs 12-8
Friends of the Library Group

HALLANDALE BEACH BRANCH, 300 S Federal Hwy, Hallandale, 33009, SAN 337-4130. Tel: 954-357-6380. FAX: 954-357-5324. *Br Mgr,* Eric Gomez; E-mail: ergomez@broward.org; Staff 12 (MLS 4, Non-MLS 8)
Circ 223,265
Open Mon & Tues 12-8, Wed, Thurs & Sat 10-6
Friends of the Library Group

HOLLYWOOD BRANCH, 2600 Hollywood Blvd, Hollywood, 33020, SAN 337-4165. Tel: 954-357-7760. FAX: 954-357-6582. *Br Mgr,* Carol Russo; E-mail: crusso@broward.org; Staff 17 (MLS 7, Non-MLS 10)
Circ 211,534
Open Mon-Wed 10-8, Thurs-Sat 10-6
Friends of the Library Group

IMPERIAL POINT BRANCH, 5985 N Federal Hwy, 33308, SAN 328-9036. Tel: 954-357-6530. FAX: 954-357-6694. *Br Mgr,* Jill Sears; E-mail: jsears@broward.org; Staff 9 (MLS 3, Non-MLS 6)
Circ 132,932
Open Mon, Thurs & Sat 10-6, Tues & Wed 12-8
Friends of the Library Group

LAUDERDALE LAKES BRANCH/EDUCATIONAL & CULTURAL CENTER, 3580 W Oakland Park Blvd, Lauderdale Lakes, 33311, SAN 337-419X. Tel: 954-357-8650. FAX: 954-357-8653. *Br Mgr,* Michelle Powell; E-mail: mpowell@broward.org; Staff 6 (MLS 3, Non-MLS 3)
Circ 61,446
Open Mon-Thurs & Sat 10-6
Friends of the Library Group

LAUDERHILL MALL BRANCH, 4257 NW 12th St, Lauderhill, 33313, SAN 337-422X. Tel: 954-357-7833. FAX: 954-357-7837. *Br Mgr,* Mary-Alice Gage; E-mail: mgage@broward.org; Staff 6 (MLS 3, Non-MLS 3)
Circ 33,484
Open Mon & Wed 12-8, Tues, Thurs & Sat 10-6
Friends of the Library Group

LAUDERHILL TOWNE CENTRE LIBRARY, 6399 W Oakland Park Blvd, Lauderhill, 33313, SAN 337-4238. Tel: 954-357-6406. FAX: 954-357-6479. *Br Mgr,* Rose-Marie Gulley; E-mail: rgulley@broward.org; Staff 12 (MLS 3, Non-MLS 9)
Circ 172,154
Open Mon & Tues 12-8, Wed, Thurs & Sat 10-6
Friends of the Library Group

THE LITTLE GREEN LIBRARY, 1033 NW 6th St, Ste 102, 33311. Tel: 954-712-0441. *Librn,* Robert Gold; E-mail: rgold@broward.org; Staff 1 (MLS 1)
Special Collections: Recycling
Open Mon-Fri 9-2

MIRAMAR BRANCH LIBRARY & EDUCATION CENTER, 2050 Civic Center Pl, Miramar, 33025. Tel: 954-357-8090. FAX: 954-357-8564. *Br Mgr,* Chris Marhenke; Tel: 954-357-8201, E-mail: cmarhenke@broward.org
Open Mon-Wed 10-8, Thurs-Sat 10-6
Friends of the Library Group

JAN MORAN COLLIER CITY LEARNING LIBRARY, 2800 NW Ninth Ct, Pompano Beach, 33069-2149, SAN 337-4033. Tel: 954-357-7670. FAX: 954-357-8630. *Br Mgr,* Debra Floyd; E-mail: dfloyd@broward.org. Subject Specialists: *Literacy,* Debra Floyd; Staff 9 (MLS 2, Non-MLS 7)
Founded 1985. Circ 13,551
Special Collections: Adult Literacy Coll
Subject Interests: Family literacy
Function: Adult bk club, Adult literacy prog, Children's prog, Citizenship assistance, Computer training, Computers for patron use, Copy machines, Electronic databases & coll, Family literacy, Homework prog, Learning ctr, Literacy & newcomer serv, Magnifiers for reading, Music CDs, OverDrive digital audio bks, Photocopying/Printing, Preschool outreach, Prog for adults, Prog for children & young adult, Pub access computers, Ref serv available, Scanner, Story hour, Summer reading prog, Teen prog, Telephone ref, Wheelchair accessible, Workshops
Open Mon & Wed 12-8, Tues, Thurs & Fri 10-6
Restriction: 24-hr pass syst for students only
Friends of the Library Group

NORTH LAUDERDALE SARANIERO BRANCH, 6901 Kimberly Blvd, North Lauderdale, 33068, SAN 337-4262. Tel: 954-357-6660. FAX: 954-357-6663. *Br Mgr,* Joan Hinton; E-mail: jhinton@broward.org; Staff 16 (MLS 5, Non-MLS 11)
Circ 77,136
Open Mon & Tues 12-8, Wed, Thurs & Sat 10-6
Friends of the Library Group

NORTH REGIONAL-BROWARD COLLEGE LIBRARY, 1100 Coconut Creek Blvd, Coconut Creek, 33066, SAN 373-5214. Tel: 954-201-2600. FAX: 954-201-2650. *Regional Libr Mgr,* Marty Onieal; Tel: 954-201-2605, E-mail: monieal@broward.org; *Asst Regional Libr Mgr,* Ronnie Kowal; Tel: 954-201-2607, E-mail: rkowal@broward.org; Staff 56 (MLS 19, Non-MLS 37)
Circ 135,640
Open Mon-Thurs 7:30am-8pm, Fri 7:30-4, Sat & Sun 10-6
Friends of the Library Group

NORTHWEST BRANCH, 1580 NW Third Ave, Pompano Beach, 33060, SAN 373-5222. Tel: 954-357-6599. FAX: 954-357-6625. *Br Mgr,* Rhonda Walker; E-mail: rwalker@broward.org; Staff 11 (MLS 3, Non-MLS 8)
Circ 17,801

Open Mon & Wed 12-8, Tues, Thurs & Sat 10-6
Friends of the Library Group
NORTHWEST REGIONAL, 3151 University Dr, Coral Springs, 33065. Tel: 954-357-7990. FAX: 954-357-7864. *Regional Libr Mgr,* Marty Onieal; Tel: 954-357-8045, E-mail: monieal@broward.org; *Asst Regional Libr Mgr,* Position Currently Open; Staff 66 (MLS 19, Non-MLS 47)
Circ 813,273
Special Services for the Blind - Large print bks; Talking bks
Open Mon-Wed 10-8, Thurs-Sun 10-6
Friends of the Library Group
HOLLYWOOD BEACH-BERNICE P OSTER READING CENTER, 1301 S Ocean Dr, Hollywood, 33019, SAN 374-8049. Tel: 954-357-4798. FAX: 954-357-4791. *Br Mgr,* Gerard Jackson; E-mail: gjackson@broward.org; Staff 4 (Non-MLS 4)
Circ 58,485
Open Mon-Fri 10-6
Friends of the Library Group
SUNRISE DAN PEARL BRANCH, 10500 W Oakland Park Blvd, Sunrise, 33351, SAN 375-605X. Tel: 954-357-7440. FAX: 954-357-7445. *Br Mgr,* Ann Miller; E-mail: amiller@broward.org; Staff 15 (MLS 6, Non-MLS 9)
Circ 257,315
Open Mon, Thurs & Sat 10-6, Tues & Wed 12-8
Friends of the Library Group
POMPANO BEACH BRANCH, 1213 E Atlantic Blvd, Pompano Beach, 33060, SAN 373-5230. Tel: 954-357-7595. FAX: 954-357-7656. *Br Mgr,* Rita Talchik; E-mail: rtalchik@broward.org; Staff 14 (MLS 3, Non-MLS 11)
Circ 155,046
Open Mon & Wed 12-8, Tues, Fri & Sat 10-6
Friends of the Library Group
RIVERLAND BRANCH, 2710 W Davie Blvd, 33312, SAN 337-4319. Tel: 954-357-7455. FAX: 954-357-7493. *Br Mgr,* Rita Lipof; E-mail: rlipof@broward.org; Staff 7 (MLS 3, Non-MLS 4)
Circ 94,267
Open Mon & Thurs 12-8, Tues, Wed & Sat 10-6
Friends of the Library Group
ALVIN SHERMAN LIBRARY, RESEARCH & INFORMATION TECHNOLOGY CENTER AT NOVA SOUTHEASTERN UNIVERSITY, 3100 Ray Ferrero Jr Blvd, 33314, SAN 378-0651. Tel: 954-262-4601. FAX: 954-262-3805. *Pub Libr Serv,* Anne Leon; E-mail: aleon@nsu.nova.edu; Staff 4 (Non-MLS 4)
Circ 240,645
Open Mon-Thurs 7:30am-11pm, Fri 7:30am-9pm, Sat 8-8, Sun 11am-11:30pm
Friends of the Library Group
CENTURY PLAZA LEON SLATIN BRANCH, 1856A W Hillsboro Blvd, Deerfield Beach, 33442, SAN 337-405X. Tel: 954-357-7740. FAX: 954-357-8597. *Br Mgr,* William Fritz; E-mail: wfritz@broward.org; Staff 9 (MLS 2, Non-MLS 7)
Founded 1982. Circ 203,727
Open Mon-Wed, Fri & Sat 10-6
Friends of the Library Group
SOUTH REGIONAL - BROWARD COLLEGE LIBRARY, 7300 Pines Blvd, Pembroke Pines, 33024, SAN 337-4343. Tel: 954-201-8825. FAX: 954-964-0282. *Regional Libr Mgr,* Valrie Simpson; Tel: 954-201-8834, E-mail: vsimpson@broward.org; *Asst Regional Libr Mgr,* Marcia Ward; Tel: 954-201-8840, E-mail: mward@broward.org; Staff 56 (MLS 18, Non-MLS 38)
Circ 586,694
Special Services for the Deaf - TDD equip
Open Mon-Thurs 7:30am-8pm, Fri 7:30-4, Sat & Sun 10-6
Friends of the Library Group
SOUTHWEST REGIONAL, 16835 Sheridan St, Pembroke Pines, 33331. Tel: 954-357-6580. FAX: 954-357-7150. *Regional Libr Mgr,* Valrie Simpson; E-mail: vsimpson@broward.org; *Asst Regional Libr Mgr,* Lisa Manners; Tel: 954-357-7074, E-mail: lmanners@broward.org; Staff 70 (MLS 26, Non-MLS 44)
Founded 2000. Circ 783,118
Special Services for the Blind - Large print bks; Talking bks
Open Mon-Wed 10-8, Thurs-Sun 10-6
Friends of the Library Group
STIRLING ROAD BRANCH, 3151 Stirling Rd, Hollywood, 33312-6526. Tel: 954-357-7550. FAX: 954-357-7404. *Br Mgr,* Neil Pollack; E-mail: npollack@broward.org; Staff 12 (MLS 4, Non-MLS 8)
Founded 2003. Circ 321,031
Open Mon, Fri & Sat 10-6, Tues & Thurs 12-8
Friends of the Library Group
P TALKING BOOK LIBRARY, 100 S Andrews Ave, 33301, SAN 337-4017. Tel: 954-357-7555. FAX: 954-357-7413. TDD: 954-357-7528. E-mail: talkingbooks@broward.org. *Librn II,* Wayne Draper; E-mail: wdraper@broward.org; Staff 6 (MLS 1, Non-MLS 5)
Founded 1977. Circ 146,841
Special Services for the Blind - Closed circuit TV; Magnifiers; Talking bks & player equip
Open Mon, Thurs & Fri 10-6, Tues & Wed 12-8
TAMARAC BRANCH, 8701 W Commercial Blvd, Tamarac, 33351, SAN 337-4424. Tel: 954-765-1500. FAX: 954-765-1550. *Br Mgr,* Linda Kamin; E-mail: lkamin@broward.org; Staff 29 (MLS 10, Non-MLS 19)
Founded 2003. Circ 559,128
Open Mon-Wed 10-8, Thurs-Sat 10-6
Friends of the Library Group
WEST REGIONAL, 8601 W Broward Blvd, Plantation, 33324, SAN 337-4416. Tel: 954-765-1560. FAX: 954-765-1536. *Regional Libr Mgr,* Ellen Lindenfeld; Tel: 954-765-1596, E-mail: elindenf@broward.org; *Asst Regional Libr Mgr,* Marlene Widrich; Tel: 954-765-1619, E-mail: mwidrich@broward.org; Staff 48 (MLS 15, Non-MLS 33)
Circ 603,546
Special Services for the Deaf - TDD equip
Open Mon & Tues 12-8, Wed-Sun 10-6
Friends of the Library Group
WESTON BRANCH, 4205 Bonaventure Blvd, Weston, 33332, SAN 374-8065. Tel: 954-357-5420. FAX: 954-357-7891. *Br Mgr,* Eileen McNally; E-mail: emcnally@broward.org; Staff 5 (MLS 2, Non-MLS 3)
Circ 13,586
Open Mon-Wed 10-8, Thurs-Sat 10-6
Friends of the Library Group
DEERFIELD BEACH-PERCY WHITE BRANCH, 837 E Hillsboro Blvd, Deerfield Beach, 33441, SAN 337-4084. Tel: 954-357-7680. FAX: 954-357-7735. *Br Mgr,* Elizabeth Lambert; E-mail: elambert@broward.org; Staff 9 (MLS 3, Non-MLS 6)
Circ 161,817
Open Mon, Wed & Sat 10-6, Tues & Thurs 12-8
Friends of the Library Group
YOUNG AT ART MUSEUM & BROWARD COUNTY LIBRARY, 751 SW 121st Ave, Davie, 33325. Tel: 954-357-5437. FAX: 954-357-5799. *Actg Br Mgr,* Angel Vaccaro; E-mail: ajenkins@broward.org; Staff 9 (MLS 2, Non-MLS 7)
Library Holdings: CDs 307,757; DVDs 475,796; e-books 115,810; Bk Titles 2,764,321; Per Subs 2,850
Open Mon-Sat 10-6, Sun 11-6
Friends of the Library Group
MARGATE-CATHARINE YOUNG BRANCH, 5810 Park Dr, Margate, 33063, SAN 337-4246. Tel: 954-357-7500. FAX: 954-357-7523. *Br Mgr,* Susan Hodos; E-mail: shodos@broward.org; Staff 10 (MLS 3, Non-MLS 7)
Circ 117,968
Special Services for the Blind - Talking bks
Open Mon, Wed & Sat 10-6, Tues & Thurs 12-8
Friends of the Library Group
PEMBROKE PINES BRANCH-WALTER C YOUNG RESOURCE CENTER, 955 NW 129th Ave, Pembroke Pines, 33028. Tel: 954-357-6750. FAX: 954-357-6718. *Br Mgr,* Alicia McHugh; E-mail: amchugh@broward.org; Staff 20 (MLS 5, Non-MLS 15)
Circ 295,689
Subject Interests: Middle sch
Open Mon & Wed 8-8, Tues, Thurs & Fri 8-4
Friends of the Library Group

J CITY COLLEGE LIBRARY - FORT LAUDERDALE*, 2000 W Commercial Blvd, Ste 200, 33309-3001. Tel: 954-492-5353, Ext 2239. FAX: 954-491-1965. Web Site: www.citycollege.edu. *Dir,* Sharon Neubauer; E-mail: sneubauer@citycollege.edu; *Libr Asst,* Gabrielle Gramazio; Staff 2 (MLS 1, Non-MLS 1)
Highest Degree: Bachelor
Library Holdings: AV Mats 102; DVDs 102; Bk Titles 2,055; Per Subs 71
Wireless access
Open Mon-Thurs 8am-10pm, Fri 8-5, Sat 9-1

S FLORIDA DIAGNOSTIC & LEARNING RESOURCE SYSTEM*, Media Center, Main Library, 4th Flr, 100 S Andrews Ave, 33301. SAN 377-354X. Tel: 754-321-1700. FAX: 954-357-7507. Web Site: www.broward.org/library. *Coordr,* Spring Raulerson; E-mail: sraulers@browardlibrary.org; *Res,* Sandy Pollack; Tel: 954-357-7177, E-mail: spollack@browardlibrary.org
Library Holdings: Bk Titles 3,500; Bk Vols 4,900; Per Subs 55
Open Mon-Sat 9-5
Friends of the Library Group

S FORT LAUDERDALE HISTORICAL SOCIETY*, Hoch Heritage Center, 219 SW Second Ave, 33301. SAN 325-853X. Tel: 954-463-4431. Reference Tel: 954-463-4431, Ext 11. FAX: 954-523-6228. E-mail: info@fortlauderdalehistorycenter.org. Web Site: www.fortlauderdalehistorycenter.org/research_main.html, www.oldfortlauderdale.org. *Dir, Res,* Merrilyn Rathbun; Tel: 954-463-4431, Ext 11, E-mail: research@fortlauderdalehistorycenter.org; *Coll Mgr,*

Christopher Barfield; Tel: 954-463-4431, Ext 20, E-mail: collections@fortlauderdalehistorycenter.org; Staff 2 (Non-MLS 2)
Founded 1962
Library Holdings: Bk Titles 3,000; Bk Vols 3,500
Special Collections: Architectural Drawings; Manuscript & Subject Coll; Photograph Coll. Oral History
Subject Interests: Local hist, Maps
Function: Archival coll, Photocopying/Printing
Publications: Businesses That Built Fort Lauderdale (Local historical information); New River Innsider (Newsletter)
Partic in Fla Soc of Archivists
Open Mon-Fri 10-4
Restriction: Access at librarian's discretion, Circ limited, In-house use for visitors, Not a lending libr, Pub use on premises

L GREENSPOON MARDER*, Law Library, 200 E Broward Blvd, 33301. (Mail add: PO Box 1500, 33302-1500), SAN 327-781X. Tel: 954-764-6660. FAX: 954-764-4996. E-mail: info@gmlaw.com. Web Site: www.gmlaw.com. *Librn,* Christine Skrytek; Staff 2 (MLS 1, Non-MLS 1)
Library Holdings: Bk Vols 10,000; Per Subs 25
Partic in S Fla Law Libr Asn

J ITT TECHNICAL INSTITUTE*, Learning Resource Center, 3401 S University Dr, 33328. Tel: 954-476-9300, Ext 141. Toll Free Tel: 800-488-7797. Web Site: www.itt-tech.edu. *Dir,* Julia Lewis-Spann
Library Holdings: Bk Vols 1,700; Per Subs 26
Automation Activity & Vendor Info: (Cataloging) Follett Software; (Circulation) Follett Software; (OPAC) Follett Software
Open Mon-Fri 9-9, Sat 9-2

C KEISER UNIVERSITY LIBRARY SYSTEM*, 1500 NW 49th St, 33309. SAN 373-1294. Tel: 954-351-4035. FAX: 954-351-4051. Web Site: www.keiserlibrary.com. *Assoc Vice Chancellor, Univ Libr Syst,* Benjamin Williams; E-mail: ben@keiseruniversity.edu; *Daytona Beach Campus Libr Dir,* Gwenyth Adamson; E-mail: gadamson@keiseruniversity.edu; *Ft Lauderdale Campus Libr Dir,* Nicholas Blaga; E-mail: nblaga@keiseruniversity.edu; *Ft Myers Campus Libr Dir,* Mary Thompson; E-mail: mthompson@keiseruniversity.edu; *Jacksonville Campus Libr Dir,* Patricia Lynn Mayfield; E-mail: lmayfield@keiseruniversity.edu; *Lakeland Campus Libr Dir,* Karyn Zelbovitz; E-mail: kzelbovitz@keiseruniversity.edu; *Miami Campus Libr Dir,* Henry Georget; E-mail: hgeorget@keiseruniversity.edu; *Melbourne Campus Libr Dir,* Richard Shea; E-mail: rshea@keiseruniversity.edu; *Orlando Campus Libr Dir,* Jennifer Carless; E-mail: jcarless@keiseruniversity.edu; *Pembroke Pines Campus Libr Dir,* Bonnie Marshak; E-mail: bmarshak@keiseruniveristy.edu; *Port St Lucie Campus Libr Dir,* Justin Rogers; E-mail: jrogers@keiseruniversity.edu; *Sarasota Campus Libr Dir,* Abby Chasky; E-mail: achasky@keiseruniversity.edu; *Tallahassee Campus Libr Dir,* Lifeng Yu; E-mail: lifengy@keiseruniversity.edu; *Tampa Campus Libr Dir,* Debra Bogart; E-mail: dbogart@keiseruniversity.edu; *W Palm Beach Campus Libr Dir,* Laura Hagmaier; E-mail: lhagmaier@keiseruniversity.edu; *Chief Librn, Port St Lucie Campus Col of Golf,* Dawn Tagblom; E-mail: dtagblom@keiseruniversity.edu; *Head, Circ,* Fay Cottoy; E-mail: fcottoy@keiseruniversity.edu; *Librn, Daytona Beach Campus,* Diane Scot; E-mail: dscot@keiseruniversity.edu; *Librn, Ft Lauderdale Campus,* Rebecca Rodriguez; E-mail: rguillen@keiseruniversity.edu; *Librn, Jacksonville Campus,* Deborah Williams; E-mail: dewilliams@keiseruniversity.edu; *Librn, Melbourne Campus,* Kellie Sparks; E-mail: ksparks@keiseruniversity.edu; *Librn, Orlando Campus,* Cynthia Jewett; *Librn, Pembroke Pines Campus,* Timothy Guillen; E-mail: tguillen@keiseruniversity.edu; *Librn, Sarasota Campus,* Julia Hagar; E-mail: jhagar@keiseruniversity.edu; *Librn, Tallahassee Campus,* Emily Douglas; E-mail: edouglas@keiseruniversity.edu; *Librn, Tampa Campus,* Marilene Riemer; E-mail: mriemer@keiseruniversity.edu. Subject Specialists: *Humanities,* Benjamin Williams; Staff 29 (MLS 26, Non-MLS 3)
Founded 1976. Enrl 15,000; Highest Degree: Doctorate
Library Holdings: Bk Titles 65,755; Bk Vols 85,212
Database Vendor: Auto-Graphics, Inc, Bowker, CredoReference, EBSCO Information Services, EBSCOhost, Gale Cengage Learning, H W Wilson, Medline, ProQuest, Westlaw
Wireless access
Function: Bk club(s), Computers for patron use, Copy machines, Electronic databases & coll, Fax serv, Free DVD rentals, Online info literacy tutorials on the web & in blackboard, Online ref, Online searches, Photocopying/Printing, Pub access computers, Ref serv available, Ref serv in person, Telephone ref, Web-catalog
Publications: Bibliographies; New Books; Student Manuals; Style Sheets
Partic in Library & Information Resources Network (LIRN); Northeast Florida Library Information Network; Panhandle Library Access Network; SEFLIN - Southeast Florida Library Information Network, Inc; Tampa Bay Library Consortium, Inc
Library System serves Keiser University, Everglades University, Southeastern College & Southeastern Institute

Open Mon-Thurs 7:30am-9:30pm, Fri 7:30-6, Sat 8-5
Restriction: Open to pub for ref & circ; with some limitations

S MOTOROLA TECHNICAL & BUSINESS LIBRARY*, 8000 W Sunrise Blvd, 33322. SAN 328-5502. Tel: 954-723-5049. FAX: 954-723-4466. Web Site: www.motorola.com. *Librn,* Kim Searer
Library Holdings: Bk Titles 3,000; Per Subs 100
Subject Interests: Eng
Automation Activity & Vendor Info: (Cataloging) SirsiDynix; (Circulation) SirsiDynix
Restriction: Not open to pub

CM NOVA SOUTHEASTERN UNIVERSITY*, Health Professions Division Library, 3200 S University Dr, 33328. SAN 373-420X. Tel: 954-262-3106. FAX: 954-262-1821. Web Site: www.nova.edu/cwis/hpdlibrary/. *Exec Dir,* Kaye Robertson; *Dir, Tech Serv,* Todd Puccio; *Ref Librn,* Bonnie DiGiallonardo; *Ref Librn,* Lynne Joshi; *Ref Librn,* Courtney Mlinar. Subject Specialists: *Allied health, Nursing,* Bonnie DiGiallonardo; *Med sci, Osteopathic med,* Lynne Joshi; *Dental med, Optometry, Pharm,* Courtney Mlinar; Staff 23 (MLS 5, Non-MLS 18)
Founded 1979. Enrl 4,692; Highest Degree: Doctorate
Library Holdings: e-books 201; e-journals 1,969; Electronic Media & Resources 38; Bk Titles 23,790; Bk Vols 70,381; Per Subs 3,388
Subject Interests: Audiology, Dentistry, Nursing, Occupational therapy, Optometry, Osteopathic med, Pharmacology, Phys therapy
Automation Activity & Vendor Info: (Acquisitions) Innovative Interfaces, Inc; (Cataloging) Innovative Interfaces, Inc; (Circulation) Innovative Interfaces, Inc; (Course Reserve) Innovative Interfaces, Inc
Database Vendor: 3M Library Systems, American Psychological Association (APA), Annual Reviews, Cinahl, EBSCOhost, Elsevier, ISI Web of Knowledge, MD Consult, Micromedex, Nature Publishing Group, OCLC FirstSearch, OCLC WorldShare Interlibrary Loan, OVID Technologies, ProQuest, PubMed, Sage, STAT!Ref (Teton Data Systems), UpToDate, Wiley
Wireless access
Function: Online cat, Online ref
Partic in Docline; Fla Health Sci Libr Asn; Lyrasis; Miami Health Sciences Library Consortium; OCLC Online Computer Library Center, Inc
Open Mon-Thurs 7:30am-Midnight, Fri 7:30am-9pm, Sat 10-10, Sun 10am-Midnight
Restriction: Badge access after hrs, Borrowing privileges limited to fac & registered students, Circ privileges for students & alumni only, Open to pub for ref only, Open to students, fac, staff & alumni, Prof mat only, Restricted borrowing privileges

C NOVA SOUTHEASTERN UNIVERSITY LIBRARIES*, Alvin Sherman Library, Research & Information Technology Center, 3100 Ray Ferrero Jr Blvd, 33314. SAN 337-4432. Tel: 954-262-4600. Circulation Tel: 954-262-4601. Interlibrary Loan Service Tel: 954-262-4619, 954-262-4660. Reference Tel: 954-262-4613. Administration Tel: 954-262-4545, 954-262-4546. Toll Free Tel: 800-541-6682. FAX: 954-262-3805. Circulation FAX: 954-262-4038. Interlibrary Loan Service FAX: 954-262-3944. Reference FAX: 954-262-6830. Administration FAX: 954-262-3225. Web Site: www.nova.edu/library. *Univ Librn, VPres for Info Serv,* Lydia Acosta; E-mail: lacosta@nsu.nova.edu; *Asst Univ Librn, Head of Doc Delivery,* Jim Hutchens; Tel: 954-262-4648, E-mail: jamesh@nsu.nova.edu; *Dir,* Harriett MacDougall; E-mail: harriett@nova.edu; *Univ Archivist,* Bob Bogorff; Tel: 954-262-4641, E-mail: bogorff@nsu.nova.edu; *Head, Circ,* Constantinos Andreou; Tel: 954-262-4682, E-mail: constant@nsu.nova.edu; *Head, Coll Develop,* Lia Hemphill; Tel: 954-262-4633, E-mail: lia@nova.edu; *Head, Distance & Instrul Libr Serv,* Johanna Tunon; Tel: 954-262-4608, E-mail: tunon@nsu.nova.edu; *Head, Ref,* Nora Quinlan; Tel: 954-262-4637, E-mail: nora@nsu.nova.edu; *Head, Tech Serv,* Susi Seiler; Tel: 954-262-4665, E-mail: seilersu@nsu.nova.edu; Staff 93 (MLS 41, Non-MLS 52)
Founded 1966. Enrl 23,522; Fac 2,154; Highest Degree: Doctorate
Library Holdings: AV Mats 23,738; Bks on Deafness & Sign Lang 2,091; e-books 17,972; e-journals 20,572; High Interest/Low Vocabulary Bk Vols 200; Large Print Bks 119; Bk Vols 405,449; Per Subs 2,442
Special Collections: Microforms. Oral History
Automation Activity & Vendor Info: (Acquisitions) Innovative Interfaces, Inc; (Cataloging) Innovative Interfaces, Inc; (Circulation) Innovative Interfaces, Inc; (Course Reserve) Innovative Interfaces, Inc; (ILL) Innovative Interfaces, Inc; (Media Booking) Innovative Interfaces, Inc; (OPAC) Innovative Interfaces, Inc; (Serials) Innovative Interfaces, Inc
Database Vendor: ABC-CLIO, ACM (Association for Computing Machinery), Alexander Street Press, American Psychological Association (APA), Baker & Taylor, Blackwell, Bowker, BWI, Cambridge Scientific Abstracts, Checkpoint Systems, Inc, Coutts Information Service, CQ Press, CredoReference, Dun & Bradstreet, EBSCO Information Services, EBSCOhost, Elsevier, Emerald, Gale Cengage Learning, Greenwood Publishing Group, Grolier Online, H W Wilson, Haworth Pres Inc, Hoovers, IEEE (Institute of Electrical & Electronics Engineers), ISI Web of Knowledge, JSTOR, LearningExpress, LexisNexis, Mergent Online, Modern Language Association, Newsbank, OCLC FirstSearch, OCLC

WorldShare Interlibrary Loan, OVID Technologies, Oxford Online, ProQuest, ReferenceUSA, RefWorks, Springer-Verlag, Standard & Poor's, STAT!Ref (Teton Data Systems), Swets Information Services, ValueLine, Wiley, Wilson - Wilson Web, YBP Library Services
Wireless access
Publications: Tidings (Newsletter)
Partic in Consortium of Southeastern Law Libraries; Florida Library Information Network; Independent Cols & Univs of Fla; SEFLIN - Southeast Florida Library Information Network, Inc
Open Mon-Thurs 7:30am-11pm, Fri 7:30am-9pm, Sat 8-8, Sun 11am-11:30pm
Friends of the Library Group
Departmental Libraries:

CL SHEPARD BROAD LAW CENTER LIBRARY, 3305 College Ave, 33314, SAN 337-4491. Tel: 954-262-6100. Circulation Tel: 954-262-6202. Reference Tel: 954-262-6201. Administration Tel: 954-262-6211. Administration FAX: 954-262-3839. E-mail: referencedesk@nsu.law.nova.edu. Web Site: www.nsulaw.nova.edu. *Dir, Tech & Info Serv,* Eric Young; *Dep Dir,* Becka Rich; *Assoc Dir, Ref & Outreach,* Carol Yecies; *Assoc Dir, Tech Serv,* Mary P Smith; *Acq,* Stephanie Hess; *Cat,* Rosann Auchstetter. Subject Specialists: *Law,* Eric Young; *Law,* Becka Rich
Founded 1974. Enrl 830
Library Holdings: Bk Vols 360,067; Per Subs 5,466
Special Collections: UN Document Depository; US Document Depository
Automation Activity & Vendor Info: (Acquisitions) Innovative Interfaces, Inc; (Cataloging) Innovative Interfaces, Inc; (Circulation) Innovative Interfaces, Inc; (Course Reserve) Innovative Interfaces, Inc; (ILL) OCLC FirstSearch; (OPAC) Innovative Interfaces, Inc
Partic in OCLC
Publications: Book Docket (Monthly); Tydbytes (Quarterly)
Open Mon-Thurs 8am-Midnight, Fri 8am-10pm, Sat 9-9, Sun 10am-Midnight

HEALTH PROFESSIONS DIVISION LIBRARY
See Separate Entry

NORTH MIAMI CAMPUS, FGSEHS Tech Bldg, 1750 NE 167th St, North Miami Beach, 33162-3017. Tel: 954-262-8423. Toll Free Tel: 800-541-6682. FAX: 954-262-3219. *Br Mgr,* Laura Lucio Ramirez; E-mail: lucio@nova.edu
Library Holdings: Bk Vols 5,000
Function: Distance learning, Doc delivery serv, ILL available, Ref serv available
Open Mon-Thurs 8:30-6, Fri 10-6

OCEANOGRAPHIC CENTER LIBRARY, 8000 N Ocean Dr, Dania Beach, 33004, SAN 337-4580. Tel: 954-262-3643, 954-262-3681. Toll Free Tel: 800-541-6882, Ext 23643. FAX: 954-262-4021. E-mail: oclibrary@nova.edu. Web Site: nova.campusguides.com/oclibrary. *Ref Librn II,* Jaime Goldman; E-mail: hjaime@nova.edu. Subject Specialists: *Marine sci,* Jaime Goldman; Staff 2 (MLS 2)
Founded 1970. Enrl 253; Fac 16; Highest Degree: Doctorate
Library Holdings: AV Mats 130; e-journals 64; Bk Vols 15,291; Per Subs 37
Open Mon & Tues 8:30-8, Wed & Thurs 8:30-6:30, Fri 8:30-4:30, Sat 10-6
Restriction: Borrowing privileges limited to fac & registered students

S STONEWALL NATIONAL MUSEUM & ARCHIVES, Stonewall Library, 1300 E Sunrise Blvd, 33304. Tel: 954-763-8565. FAX: 866-929-5694. Web Site: www.stonewallnationalmuseum.org/library. *Exec Dir,* David Jobin; *Chief Librn,* Robert Lee
Library Holdings: CDs 1,000; Bk Titles 20,000; Per Subs 60
Automation Activity & Vendor Info: (Cataloging) Inmagic, Inc.; (Circulation) Inmagic, Inc.
Open Mon-Fri 11-8, Sat 10-5

GL LAMAR WARREN LAW LIBRARY OF BROWARD COUNTY*, 1800 Broward County Judicial Complex, 201 SE Sixth St, 33301. SAN 302-9255. Tel: 954-831-6226. *Dir,* Arleen Elies; Staff 3 (MLS 1, Non-MLS 2)
Founded 1956
Library Holdings: Bk Vols 30,000
Special Collections: Retrospective Florida Law Coll
Database Vendor: LexisNexis, Main Library Systems, OCLC WorldShare Interlibrary Loan, Westlaw
Wireless access
Special Services for the Blind - Reader equip

FORT MEADE

P FORT MEADE PUBLIC LIBRARY*, 75 E Broadway, 33841-2998. SAN 302-9328. Tel: 863-285-8287. FAX: 863-285-8093. *Librn,* Kay Jackson; *Asst Librn, ILL,* June Gillis
Pop 5,457; Circ 21,361
Oct 2012-Sept 2013 Income $225,765. Mats Exp $30,574. Sal $161,966
Library Holdings: CDs 900; Bk Vols 33,402; Per Subs 38
Special Collections: Fort Meade History
Automation Activity & Vendor Info: (Cataloging) SirsiDynix; (Circulation) SirsiDynix; (OPAC) SirsiDynix
Partic in Polk County Libr Coop
Open Mon & Wed (Winter) 9-5 & 7-9, Tues, Thurs & Fri 9-5, Sat 9-12; Mon (Summer) 9-5 & 7-9, Tues-Fri 9-5

FORT MYERS

J EDISON STATE COLLEGE*, Richard H Rush Library - Lee Campus, 8099 College Pkwy SW, Bldg J, 33919. (Mail add: PO Box 60210, 33906-6210), SAN 302-9336. Tel: 239-489-9300. Circulation Tel: 239-489-9220. Reference Tel: 239-489-9279. FAX: 239-489-9095. Web Site: www.edison.edu/learningresources. *District Dir,* Mary B Faulkner; Tel: 239-489-9032, E-mail: mfaulkner@edison.edu; *Acq,* Cindy Campbell; Tel: 239-433-8026, E-mail: ccampbell@edison.edu; *Circ,* Peggy Phetterplace; Tel: 239-489-9299, E-mail: pphetterplace@edison.edu; *ILL,* Donna Malaschak; Tel: 239-489-9376, E-mail: dmalaschak@edison.edu; *Ref,* Jane V Charles; E-mail: jcharles@edison.edu; *Ref,* Frank Dowd; Tel: 239-489-9449, E-mail: fdowd@edison.edu; *Ref,* William Shuluk; Tel: 239-489-9356, Fax: 239-489-9465, E-mail: wshuluk@edison.edu; Staff 18.5 (MLS 6.5, Non-MLS 12)
Founded 1962. Enrl 11,000; Fac 200; Highest Degree: Bachelor
Library Holdings: Electronic Media & Resources 25; Bk Titles 75,000; Per Subs 250
Database Vendor: EBSCOhost, Gale Cengage Learning, LexisNexis, OCLC FirstSearch, ProQuest, Westlaw, Wilson - Wilson Web
Publications: User's Brochure
Partic in Florida Asn of Commun Col
Open Mon-Thurs 7:30-9, Fri 7:30-4, Sat & Sun 10-6

C FLORIDA GULF COAST UNIVERSITY LIBRARY*, 10501 FGCU Blvd S, 33965-6501. SAN 377-6719. Circulation Tel: 239-590-7610. Reference Tel: 239-590-7630. Administration Tel: 239-590-7600. Administration FAX: 239-590-7609. TDD: 239-590-7618. Web Site: library.fgcu.edu. *Dean of Libr Serv, Univ Librn,* Dr Kathleen Miller; Tel: 239-590-7605, E-mail: kmiller@fgcu.edu; *Univ Librn, E-Res,* Anjana Bhatt; Tel: 239-590-7634, E-mail: abhatt@fgcu.edu; *Assoc Dir,* Dr Barbara Stites; Tel: 239-590-7602, E-mail: bstites@fgcu.edu; *Asst Dir, Coll Mgt & Tech Serv,* Rebecca Donlan; Tel: 239-590-7641, E-mail: rdonlan@fgcu.edu; *Asst Dir, Libr Bus Serv,* Donna Vazquez; Tel: 239-590-7603, E-mail: devazque@fgcu.edu; *Asst Dir, Libr Computing & Tech Syst,* Mario Bernardo; Tel: 239-590-7621, E-mail: mbernard@fgcu.edu; *Head, Ref, Res & Instruction,* Kay Oistad; Tel: 239-590-7604, E-mail: koistad@fgcu.edu; *Digital Serv Librn,* Melissa Minds VandeBurgt; Tel: 239-590-7658, E-mail: mvandeburgt@fgcu.edu; *First Year Experience & Outreach Librn,* Heather Snapp; Tel: 239-745-4224, E-mail: hsnapp@fgcu.edu; *Info Literacy Librn,* Anna Carlin; Tel: 239-590-7663, E-mail: acarlin@fgcu.edu; *Web Develop Librn,* Danielle Rosenthal; Tel: 239-590-7633, E-mail: drosenth@fgcu.edu; *Tech Serv Supvr,* Catherine Gardiner; Tel: 239-590-7640, E-mail: cgardine@fgcu.edu. Subject Specialists: *Bus, Hospitality mgt, Resort mgt,* Kay Oistad; *Archives, Spec coll,* Melissa Minds VandeBurgt; *Anthrop, Communication, Philos,* Anna Carlin; *Eng, Sci,* Danielle Rosenthal; Staff 36.5 (MLS 16, Non-MLS 20.5)
Founded 1997. Enrl 12,000; Fac 14; Highest Degree: Doctorate
Jul 2011-Jun 2012 Income $3,227,180. Mats Exp $1,215,827. Sal $1,651,536
Library Holdings: AV Mats 16,324; e-books 33,552; Per Subs 6,585; Videos 4,880
Automation Activity & Vendor Info: (Acquisitions) Ex Libris Group; (Cataloging) Ex Libris Group; (Circulation) Ex Libris Group; (ILL) OCLC ILLiad; (OPAC) Ex Libris Group; (Serials) SerialsSolutions
Database Vendor: ABC-CLIO, Agricola, Alexander Street Press, American Psychological Association (APA), ARTstor, Blackwell, Cambridge Scientific Abstracts, Dialog, Dun & Bradstreet, EBSCOhost, Elsevier, Gale Cengage Learning, H W Wilson, JSTOR, LexisNexis, Newsbank, OCLC FirstSearch, OCLC WorldShare Interlibrary Loan, OVID Technologies, Oxford Online, ProQuest, RefWorks, Sage, ScienceDirect, SerialsSolutions, Springer-Verlag, Springshare, LLC, Standard & Poor's, Westlaw, Wiley InterScience, Wilson - Wilson Web, YBP Library Services
Wireless access
Partic in Fla Ctr for Libr Automation; ISI; Lyrasis; Southwest Florida Library Network
Special Services for the Deaf - TTY equip
Open Mon-Thurs 8am-11pm, Fri & Sat 8-6, Sun 1-11

GL LEE COUNTY LAW LIBRARY*, Lynn Gerald Law Library, Lee County Justice Ctr, 1700 Monroe St, 33901. SAN 302-9352. Tel: 239-533-9195. FAX: 239-485-2598. *Law Librn,* Guyatri Sharon Radoopersad; E-mail: gradoopersad@ca.cjis20.org
Founded 1959
Library Holdings: Bk Vols 1,800
Wireless access
Open Mon-Fri 8:30-5

P LEE COUNTY LIBRARY SYSTEM*, 2345 Union St, 33901-3917. SAN 337-4610. Tel: 239-533-4800. Interlibrary Loan Service Tel: 239-533-4199. Reference Tel: 239-479-4636. FAX: 239-485-1100. Interlibrary Loan Service FAX: 239-485-1121. Automation Services FAX: 239-485-1102. E-mail: lcls@leegov.com. Web Site: library.leegov.com. *Dir,* Sheldon Kaye; Tel: 239-533-4830, E-mail: skaye@leegov.com; *Dep Dir,* Terri Crawford; Tel: 239-533-4832, E-mail: tcrawford@leegov.com; *Mgr, Automation & Continuing Educ,* Mindi Simon; Tel: 239-533-4810, E-mail: msimon@leegov.com; *Fiscal Mgr,* Sue Lange; Tel: 239-533-4820, E-mail: slange@leegov.com; *Pub Serv Mgr,* Marilyn Graham; Tel: 239-533-4807, E-mail: mgraham@leegov.com; *Tech Serv Mgr,* Deb Czarnik; Tel: 239-533-4180, E-mail: dczarnik@leegov.com; *Sr Librn/e-Br Mgr,* Keith Belton; Tel: 239-533-4813, E-mail: kbelton@leegov.com; *Sr Librn, Tel Ref,* Amy Krueger; E-mail: akrueger@leegov.com; *Adult Coll Develop Officer,* Diana Dearing; Tel: 239-533-4179, E-mail: ddearing@leegov.com; *ILL,* Eileen Downing; Tel: 239-533-4185, E-mail: edowning@leegov.com; *Youth & Multicultural Coll Develop,* Diane Lettieri; E-mail: dlettieri@leegov.com; Staff 227.5 (MLS 74, Non-MLS 153.5)
Founded 1964. Pop 613,546; Circ 5,500,000
Oct 2008-Sept 2009 Income $37,626,994, State $1,164,282, County $31,649,549, Locally Generated Income $4,813,163. Mats Exp $4,589,139, Books $2,698,436, AV Mat $1,500,096, Electronic Ref Mat (Incl. Access Fees) $390,607. Sal $13,088,175
Library Holdings: Audiobooks 45,467; AV Mats 260,727; Bks-By-Mail 5,283; CDs 41,035; DVDs 163,117; e-books 65,058; e-journals 13,545; Electronic Media & Resources 22,553; Large Print Bks 64,642; Bk Vols 1,213,797
Special Collections: Florida Coll
Subject Interests: African-Am, Genealogy, Spanish lang
Automation Activity & Vendor Info: (Acquisitions) Innovative Interfaces, Inc; (Cataloging) Innovative Interfaces, Inc; (Circulation) Innovative Interfaces, Inc; (ILL) OCLC; (OPAC) Innovative Interfaces, Inc; (Serials) Innovative Interfaces, Inc
Wireless access
Function: Adult bk club, Bk club(s), Bks on cassette, Bks on CD, Chess club, Children's prog, Computers for patron use, Copy machines, Digital talking bks, e-mail & chat, E-Reserves, Electronic databases & coll, Exhibits, Free DVD rentals, Games & aids for the handicapped, Handicapped accessible, Home delivery & serv to Sr ctr & nursing homes, Homebound delivery serv, ILL available, Instruction & testing, Libr develop, Literacy & newcomer serv, Magnifiers for reading, Mail & tel request accepted, Music CDs, Online cat, Online ref, Outreach serv, OverDrive digital audio bks, Photocopying/Printing, Preschool outreach, Prog for adults, Prog for children & young adult, Pub access computers, Ref & res, Ref serv in person, Senior outreach, Spoken cassettes & CDs, Spoken cassettes & DVDs, Story hour, Summer reading prog, Tax forms, Teen prog, Telephone ref, Web-catalog, Wheelchair accessible
Partic in Southwest Florida Library Network
Special Services for the Deaf - Assistive tech; TTY equip
Special Services for the Blind - Assistive/Adapted tech devices, equip & products; Closed circuit TV; Descriptive video serv (DVS); Magnifiers; Talking bks
Open Mon-Wed 9-8, Thurs 9-6, Fri & Sat 9-5
Restriction: Borrowing requests are handled by ILL, Non-resident fee
Friends of the Library Group
Branches: 14
BONITA SPRINGS PUBLIC, 26876 Pine Ave, Bonita Springs, 34135-5009, SAN 302-8631. Tel: 239-533-4860. TDD: 239-992-1043. *Sr Librn,* Maureen Pollock; E-mail: mpollock@leegov.com; Staff 10.5 (MLS 2, Non-MLS 8.5)
Special Collections: Geneology Coll
Special Services for the Deaf - TTY equip
Open Mon, Wed & Fri 10-6, Tues & Thurs 10-8, Sat 9-5
Friends of the Library Group
CAPE CORAL-LEE COUNTY PUBLIC, 921 SW 39th Terrace, Cape Coral, 33914-5721, SAN 337-467X. Tel: 239-533-4500. TDD: 239-485-1141. *Principal Librn,* Tori Hersh; E-mail: thersh@leegov.com; Staff 23.5 (MLS 8, Non-MLS 15.5)
Special Services for the Deaf - TTY equip
Open Mon-Wed 9-8, Thurs 9-6, Fri & Sat 9-5
Friends of the Library Group
CAPTIVA MEMORIAL LIBRARY, 11560 Chapin Lane, Captiva, 33924. (Mail add: PO Box 99, Captiva, 33924-0099), SAN 302-8801. Tel: 239-533-4890. FAX: 239-485-1150. *Sr Librn,* Ann E Bradley; E-mail: abradley@leegov.com; Staff 3 (MLS 1, Non-MLS 2)
Library Holdings: Bk Vols 23,000
Special Services for the Deaf - Pocket talkers
Special Services for the Blind - Closed circuit TV magnifier
Open Tues, Thurs & Fri 10-6, Wed 12-8, Sat 9-5
Friends of the Library Group
DUNBAR JUPITER HAMMON PUBLIC LIBRARY, 3095 Blount St, 33916-2032, SAN 337-4734. Tel: 239-334-3602. FAX: 239-334-7940. TDD: 239-334-2272. *Sr Librn,* Jubilee Brainerd; E-mail: jbrainerd@leegov.com; Staff 4 (MLS 1, Non-MLS 3)
Library Holdings: AV Mats 3,052; Large Print Bks 448; Bk Vols 44,473; Per Subs 112; Talking Bks 826
Special Collections: African-American Literature Coll
Special Services for the Deaf - TTY equip
Open Tues & Thurs 12-8, Wed & Fri 10-6, Sat 9-5
Friends of the Library Group
EAST COUNTY REGIONAL, 881 Gunnery Rd N, Lehigh Acres, 33971. Tel: 239-533-4200. Circulation Tel: 239-533-4240. Interlibrary Loan Service Tel: 239-533-4199. Reference Tel: 239-533-4250. TDD: 239-485-1126. *Principal Librn, Regional Mgr,* Jacqueline Fling; Tel: 239-533-4205, E-mail: jfling@leegov.com; *Head, Ref, Sr Librn,* Dora Schilling; Tel: 239-533-4206, E-mail: dschilling@leegov.com; *Head, Youth Serv, Sr Librn,* Lynn Hourigan; Tel: 239-533-4231, E-mail: lhourigan@leegov.com; *Librn,* Sarah Brown; Tel: 239-533-4213, E-mail: sbrown3@leegov.com; *Librn,* Alyssa Diekman; Tel: 239-533-4212, E-mail: adiekman@leegov.com; *Librn,* Lynn Wetzel; Tel: 239-533-4216, E-mail: lwetzel@leegov.com; Staff 25 (MLS 7, Non-MLS 18)
Circ 55,320
Library Holdings: Bk Titles 168,500; Per Subs 60
Subject Interests: Fla
Open Mon-Wed 9-8, Thurs 9-6, Fri & Sat 9-5
Friends of the Library Group
FORT MYERS-LEE COUNTY PUBLIC, 2050 Central Ave, 33901-3917, SAN 302-9344. Tel: 239-479-4636. FAX: 239-479-4634. *Principal Librn,* Madeleine Plummer; Tel: 941-479-4632; Staff 24 (MLS 10, Non-MLS 14)
Pop 58,708
Library Holdings: Bk Vols 171,359; Per Subs 524
Special Collections: Florida History Coll. State Document Depository
Subject Interests: Genealogy
Special Services for the Deaf - TTY equip
Open Mon-Thurs 9-9, Fri & Sat 9-6
Friends of the Library Group
LAKES REGIONAL, 15290 Bass Rd, 33919, SAN 372-0233. Tel: 239-533-4000. FAX: 239-533-4040. TDD: 239-533-4087. *Principal Librn,* Joanne Fischer; E-mail: jfischer@leegov.com; Staff 35 (MLS 9, Non-MLS 26)
Library Holdings: Bk Vols 186,500
Special Services for the Deaf - TTY equip
Open Mon-Thurs 9-9, Fri & Sat 9-6
Friends of the Library Group
NORTH FORT MYERS PUBLIC, 2001 N Tamiami Trail NE, North Fort Myers, 33903-2802, SAN 337-4823. Tel: 239-997-0320. FAX: 239-656-7949. TDD: 239-656-7950. *Sr Librn,* Maryellen Woodside; E-mail: mwoodsid@leegov.com; Staff 12 (MLS 4, Non-MLS 8)
Library Holdings: Bk Vols 69,049
Special Services for the Deaf - TTY equip
Open Mon, Wed & Fri 10-6, Tues & Thurs 10-8, Sat 9-5
Friends of the Library Group
OUTREACH SERVICES, 21100 Three Oaks Pkwy, Estero, 33928, SAN 374-406X. Tel: 239-390-3234. Toll Free Tel: 800-660-6420. FAX: 239-498-6424. TDD: 239-498-6425. *Actg Literacy Contact, Mgr, Outreach Serv, Principal Librn,* Kathy Mayo; E-mail: kmayo@leegov.com; *Sr Libr Assoc,* Susan Roseberry; Tel: 239-390-3231, E-mail: sroseberry@leegov.com; *Libr Assoc/Bks-By-Mail Coordr,* Lisa Cooke; Tel: 239-390-3232, E-mail: lcooke@leegov.com; Staff 5 (MLS 1, Non-MLS 4)
Circ 52,764
Oct 2007-Sept 2008. Mats Exp $117,913
Library Holdings: Audiobooks 438; Bks-By-Mail 5,076; CDs 123; DVDs 1,506; Large Print Bks 4,700; Bk Vols 24,516; Videos 102
Special Collections: Adult Learner & ESL Coll
Function: Writing prog
Publications: The Mailbag (Newsletter)
Special Services for the Deaf - TTY equip
PINE ISLAND PUBLIC LIBRARY, 10700 Russell Rd NW, Bokeelia, 33922-3110, SAN 337-4858. Tel: 239-461-3188. FAX: 239-283-7711. TDD: 239-283-4343. *Sr Librn,* Randy Briggs; E-mail: rbriggs@leegov.com; Staff 6 (MLS 1, Non-MLS 5)
Library Holdings: Bk Vols 42,145
Special Services for the Deaf - TTY equip
Open Tues, Thurs & Fri 10-6, Wed 12-8, Sat 9-5
Friends of the Library Group
PROCESSING CENTER, 881 Gunnery Rd N, Ste 2, Lehigh Acres, 33971-1246, SAN 372-0217. Tel: 239-461-7380. FAX: 239-461-7373. *Adult Coll Develop Librn,* Diana Dearing; Tel: 239-461-7382, E-mail: ddearing@leegov.com; *Coll Develop Librn,* Diane Lettieri; Tel: 239-461-7317, E-mail: dlettier@leegov.com; *Mgr, Tech Serv & Coll Mgt,* Deb Czarnik; Tel: 239-461-7381, E-mail: dczarnik@leegov.com; *Cat Supvr,* Carol Bell; Tel: 239-461-7327, E-mail: cbell@leegov.com; *Coordr, Acq,* Diane Millott; Tel: 239-461-7387, E-mail: dmillott@leegov.com; *ILL/Doc Delivery Serv,* Eileen Downing; Tel: 239-461-7322, E-mail: edowning@leegov.com. Subject Specialists: *Juv, Multilingual,* Diane Lettieri; Staff 26 (MLS 6, Non-MLS 20)
Special Collections: State Document Depository

Subject Interests: Fla, Genealogy
Automation Activity & Vendor Info: (ILL) OCLC FirstSearch; (OPAC) Innovative Interfaces, Inc
Database Vendor: 3M Library Systems, ABC-CLIO, ALLDATA Online, Backstage Library Works, Baker & Taylor, Booksite, Bowker, Brodart, BWI, Children's Literature Comprehensive Database Company (CLCD), EBSCOhost, Electric Library, Facts on File, Gale Cengage Learning, Greenwood Publishing Group, Grolier Online, H W Wilson, Newsbank, OCLC FirstSearch, OCLC WorldShare Interlibrary Loan, Overdrive, Inc, ProQuest, ReferenceUSA, SerialsSolutions, Wilson - Wilson Web
Function: ILL available
Partic in Lyrasis
Open Mon-Fri 8-5
Restriction: Access for corporate affiliates

RIVERDALE BRANCH, 2421 Buckingham Rd, 33905, SAN 372-0225. Tel: 239-461-3130. FAX: 239-694-6146. TDD: 239-694-5887. *Sr Librn,* Sharon Hamman; E-mail: shamman@leegov.com; Staff 1 (MLS 1)
Founded 1991. Pop 21,000; Circ 90,000
Library Holdings: AV Mats 4,300; Large Print Bks 884; Bk Titles 46,000; Per Subs 108
Special Services for the Deaf - TTY equip
Open Tues & Thurs 12-8, Wed & Fri 10-6, Sat 9-5
Friends of the Library Group

SOUTH COUNTY REGIONAL, 21100 Three Oaks Pkwy, Estero, 33928-3020, SAN 376-9453. Tel: 239-533-4400. FAX: 239-485-1130. TDD: 239-485-1131. *Principal Librn,* Elizabeth Nitch; Tel: 239-533-4402, E-mail: enitch@leegov.com; Staff 20 (MLS 7, Non-MLS 13)
Founded 1996. Pop 31,781; Circ 606,293
Library Holdings: AV Mats 21,559; Large Print Bks 6,903; Bk Vols 159,831; Per Subs 116; Talking Bks 4,154
Special Collections: Science & Technology Coll
Special Services for the Deaf - TTY equip
Open Mon-Thurs 9-9, Fri & Sat 9-6
Friends of the Library Group

P TALKING BOOKS, 13240 N Cleveland Ave, North Fort Myers, 33903-4855, SAN 372-0241. Tel: 239-995-2665. Toll Free Tel: 800-854-8195. FAX: 239-995-1681. *Librn,* Karin McLeish-Delgado; E-mail: kmcleish@leegov.com; Staff 3 (Non-MLS 3)
Library Holdings: AV Mats 509; Bk Vols 29,681
Special Services for the Deaf - Assistive tech; TTY equip
Special Services for the Blind - Closed circuit TV; Descriptive video serv (DVS); Magnifiers; Talking bks
Open Mon-Fri 8:30-5
Bookmobiles: 1. Outreach Servs, Maria Palacio. Bk titles 19,262

M LEE MEMORIAL HEALTH SYSTEM LIBRARY*, PO Box 2218, 33902-2218. Tel: 239-334-5410. FAX: 239-332-6422. Web Site: www.leememorial.org/medlibrary. *Librn,* Narges Ahmadi, E-mail: narges.ahmadi@leememorial.org; *Libr Assoc,* Madlyn Blom; Staff 1 (MLS 1)
Library Holdings: e-journals 1,800; Bk Titles 6,000; Per Subs 115
Open Mon-Fri 7:30-4

C SOUTHERN TECHNICAL COLLEGE, Learning Resource Center, (Formerly Southwest Florida College), 1685 Medical Lane, 33907. Tel: 239-939-4766. FAX: 239-936-4040. Web Site: www.southerntech.edu/. *Libr Dir,* Dana Thimons; Staff 2 (MLS 1, Non-MLS 1)
Automation Activity & Vendor Info: (Acquisitions) LibraryWorld, Inc; (Cataloging) LibraryWorld, Inc; (Circulation) LibraryWorld, Inc; (ILL) OCLC; (Serials) LibraryWorld, Inc
Database Vendor: ebrary, Gale Cengage Learning, ProQuest, Westlaw
Wireless access
Open Mon-Fri 8am-9pm, Sat 9-5

Departmental Libraries:

LEARNING RESOURCE CENTER, TAMPA BRANCH, 3910 Riga Blvd, Tampa, 33619. Tel: 813-630-4401. FAX: 813-630-4272. *Libr Dir,* Cynthia Dixson; Staff 1 (MLS 1)
Highest Degree: Bachelor

S SOUTHWEST FLORIDA REGIONAL PLANNING COUNCIL LIBRARY*, 1926 Victoria Ave, 33901. Tel: 239-338-2550, Ext 217. FAX: 239-338-2560. Web Site: www.swfrpc.org. *Info Spec,* Rebekah Harp; E-mail: rharp@swfrpc.org
Founded 1973
Library Holdings: Bk Vols 6,000; Per Subs 50
Special Collections: US Document Depository
Subject Interests: Environ sci, Land use, Planning, Transportation, US census
Function: For res purposes, Photocopying/Printing, Ref serv available
Partic in Southwest Florida Library Network
Open Mon-Fri 8-5
Restriction: In-house use for visitors, Non-circulating, Not a lending libr, Restricted loan policy

FORT MYERS BEACH

P FORT MYERS BEACH PUBLIC LIBRARY*, 2755 Estero Blvd, 33931. SAN 302-9379. Tel: 239-765-8162. Reference Tel: 239-765-8163. Administration Tel: 239-463-9691. FAX: 239-463-8776. TDD: 239-463-7482. Web Site: www.fmb.lib.fl.us. *Dir,* Dr Leroy Hommerding; *Cataloger,* John Lukow; Staff 12 (MLS 3, Non-MLS 9)
Founded 1955. Pop 16,500; Circ 110,944
Library Holdings: AV Mats 10,100; Bk Titles 81,000; Per Subs 173
Special Collections: Florida Coll
Automation Activity & Vendor Info: (Cataloging) TLC (The Library Corporation)
Database Vendor: ProQuest
Partic in Southwest Florida Library Network
Open Mon & Wed 9-8, Tues, Thurs & Fri 9-5, Sat 9-1
Friends of the Library Group

FORT PIERCE

C FLORIDA ATLANTIC UNIVERSITY*, Harbor Branch Oceanographic Institute Library, 5600 US 1 N, 34946. SAN 302-9387. Tel: 772-242-2201. FAX: 772-242-2348. Web Site: www.hboi.edu. *Assoc Univ Librn,* Carla Ruth Robinson; E-mail: crobins@hboi.fau.edu; Staff 1 (MLS 1)
Founded 1975
Library Holdings: Bk Vols 30,000
Subject Interests: Aquaculture, Marine drug discovery, Ocean eng, Ocean exploration, Ocean health
Automation Activity & Vendor Info: (Acquisitions) Mandarin Library Automation; (Cataloging) Mandarin Library Automation; (Circulation) Mandarin Library Automation; (Course Reserve) Mandarin Library Automation; (OPAC) Mandarin Library Automation
Wireless access
Publications: Acquisitions List; Publications List
Partic in SEFLIN - Southeast Florida Library Information Network, Inc

C INDIAN RIVER STATE COLLEGE, Miley Library, 3209 Virginia Ave, 34981-5599. SAN 302-9395. Tel: 772-462-7600. FAX: 772-462-4780. E-mail: library@irsc.edu. Web Site: www.irsc.edu. *Dean, Learning Res,* Dr Patricia C Profeta; Tel: 772-462-7590, E-mail: pprofeta@irsc.edu; *Emerging Tech Librn,* Mia Tignor; Tel: 772-462-7124, E-mail: mtignor@irsc.edu; *Ref/Outreach Librn,* Alexis Carlson; Tel: 772-462-7194, E-mail: acarlson@irsc.edu; *Ref/Outreach Librn,* Daniel Hood; Tel: 772-462-7587, E-mail: dhood@irsc.edu; Staff 6 (MLS 4, Non-MLS 2)
Founded 1960. Fac 167; Highest Degree: Bachelor
Library Holdings: e-books 108,000; Bk Vols 81,000; Per Subs 200
Special Collections: Florida; Instructional Effectiveness. US Document Depository
Automation Activity & Vendor Info: (Cataloging) Ex Libris Group; (Circulation) Ex Libris Group; (ILL) OCLC Online; (OPAC) Ex Libris Group
Database Vendor: EBSCOhost, Gale Cengage Learning, OCLC FirstSearch, OCLC WorldShare Interlibrary Loan, ProQuest, PubMed, Westlaw
Wireless access
Partic in OCLC Online Computer Library Center, Inc
Open Mon-Thurs (Fall & Spring) 7:45am-9pm, Fri 7:45-5, Sun 1-5; Mon-Thurs (Summer) 7am-8pm

Departmental Libraries:

BRACKETT LIBRARY - MUELLER CAMPUS, Indian River State College, Mueller Campus, 6155 College Lane, Vero Beach, 32966. Tel: 772-226-2544. Reference Tel: 772-226-4565. FAX: 772-226-2542. *Ref Librn,* Marta Kendrick; E-mail: mkendric@irsc.edu; Staff 1 (MLS 1)
Founded 2009
Open Mon, Thurs & Fri 9-5, Tues & Wed Noon-8

DIXON HENDRY CAMPUS LIBRARY, 2229 NW Ninth Ave, Okeechobee, 34972. Tel: 863-763-8017. *Emerging Tech Librn,* Mia Tignor; Tel: 863-462-7124, E-mail: mtignor@irsc.edu; *Ref/Outreach Librn,* Dan Hood; Tel: 863-462-7587, E-mail: dhood@irsc.edu; *Ref/Outreach Librn,* Alexis Carlson; Tel: 863-462-7194, E-mail: acarlson@irsc.edu
Library Holdings: Bk Vols 500
Open Mon-Thurs 8-8, Fri 8-2

KEN PRUITT CAMPUS LIBRARY, 500 NW California Blvd, Port Saint Lucie, 34986. Tel: 772-336-6380. FAX: 772-873-3409.
Library Holdings: Bk Vols 12,000; Per Subs 50
Open Mon-Thurs 9-9, Fri 9-5, Sat & Sun 1-5

P SAINT LUCIE COUNTY LIBRARY SYSTEM*, Fort Pierce Branch, 101 Melody Lane, 34950-4402. SAN 337-4912. Tel: 772-462-1615. Circulation Tel: 772-462-1616, 772-462-1617. Interlibrary Loan Service Tel: 772-462-1964. Reference Tel: 772-462-2187, 772-462-2188. FAX: 772-462-2750. TDD: 772-462-1619. Web Site: www.st-lucie.lib.fl.us. *Dir,* Susan Jacob; *Mgr, Info Sys,* Dr Edward Werner; Tel: 772-462-1802, E-mail: ewerner@co.st-lucie.fl.us; *Cat,* Frances Frazer; Tel: 772-462-2193; *Ch Serv,* Gicele Perna; Tel: 772-462-2812, E-mail: pernag@co.st-lucie.fl.us; *Pub*

Serv, Marilyn Mittleman; Tel: 772-462-1607, E-mail: mittlemm@co.st-lucie.fl.us; Staff 18.5 (MLS 10.5, Non-MLS 8)
Founded 1953. Pop 282,000; Circ 658,000
Library Holdings: AV Mats 5,054; Bk Titles 171,719; Bk Vols 306,332; Per Subs 737
Special Collections: Black History; Florida Coll, bks
Subject Interests: Bus & mgt, Genealogy, Local hist, Soc sci & issues
Automation Activity & Vendor Info: (Acquisitions) SirsiDynix; (Circulation) SirsiDynix; (OPAC) SirsiDynix
Database Vendor: EBSCOhost, OCLC FirstSearch
Partic in Tampa Bay Library Consortium, Inc
Open Mon-Wed 8-8:30, Thurs & Fri 9-6, Sat 9-5, Sun 1-5
Restriction: 24-hr pass syst for students only
Friends of the Library Group
Branches: 4
ZORA NEALE HURSTON BRANCH, 3008 Avenue D, 34947, SAN 328-6398. Tel: 772-462-2154. FAX: 772-462-2844.
Founded 1991
Library Holdings: Bk Vols 25,500
Special Collections: Zora Neale Hurston Coll
Open Tues & Thurs 10-7, Sat 9-5
LAKEWOOD PARK, 7605 Santa Barbara Dr, 34951, SAN 322-6239. Tel: 772-462-6870. FAX: 772-462-6874. *Br Head,* Carol Shroyer; Staff 2 (MLS 1, Non-MLS 1)
Founded 1989
Library Holdings: Bk Vols 50,500
Special Services for the Deaf - TDD equip
Open Tues & Thurs 9-5:30, Wed 12-8, Fri & Sat 9-5
Friends of the Library Group
MORNINGSIDE BRANCH, 2410 Morningside Blvd, Port Saint Lucie, 34952, SAN 372-7904. Tel: 772-337-5632. FAX: 772-337-5631. *Br Mgr,* Mary Beth Pickney; Staff 3 (MLS 1, Non-MLS 2)
Founded 1993
Library Holdings: Bk Vols 48,000
Partic in Tampa Bay Library Consortium, Inc
Open Mon-Wed 9-8:30, Thurs 9-6, Fri & Sat 9-5, Sun 1-5
Friends of the Library Group
PORT SAINT LUCIE BRANCH, 180 SW Prima Vista Blvd, Port Saint Lucie, 34983, SAN 337-4947. Tel: 772-871-5450. FAX: 772-871-5454. *Br Mgr,* Mark Freed; E-mail: freedm@stlucieco.org; Staff 2 (MLS 1, Non-MLS 1)
Founded 1970
Library Holdings: Bk Vols 48,500
Special Services for the Deaf - TDD equip
Open Wed 10-6, Fri 9-5

G SAINT LUCIE COUNTY REGIONAL HISTORY CENTER, Research Library, 414 Seaway Dr, 34949. SAN 327-3113. Tel: 772-462-1795, 772-462-1891. FAX: 772-462-1877. Web Site: www.stlucieco.gov/history. *Registrar,* Harry Quatraro
Founded 1968
Library Holdings: CDs 30; Bk Vols 1,500; Videos 75
Subject Interests: Fla hist
Restriction: Open to pub by appt only

GL RUPERT J SMITH LAW LIBRARY OF SAINT LUCIE COUNTY*, Saint Lucie County Law Library, 218 S Second St, Courthouse Addition, Rm 102, 34950. SAN 302-9409. Tel: 772-462-2370. FAX: 772-462-2145. Web Site: www.rjslawlibrary.org. *Librn,* Nora J Everlove; *Librn,* Merrilyn Phillips
Library Holdings: Bk Vols 15,000
Open Mon-Fri 8:30-12 & 1-4:30
Friends of the Library Group

C UNIVERSITY OF FLORIDA, Indian River Research & Education Center, 2199 S Rock Rd, 34945-3138. SAN 325-3503. Tel: 772-468-3922. FAX: 772-468-5668. Web Site: www.irrec.ifas.ufl.edu. *Dir,* Peter J Stoffella; E-mail: pjs@ufl.edu; *Assoc Dir,* Charles A Powell; E-mail: capowell@ufl.edu
Founded 1960
Library Holdings: Bk Titles 500; Bk Vols 525; Per Subs 20
Wireless access
Open Mon-Fri 8-5

FORT WALTON BEACH

P FORT WALTON BEACH LIBRARY, 185 Miracle Strip Pkwy SE, 32548. SAN 302-9417. Tel: 850-833-9590. FAX: 850-833-9659. E-mail: fwblibr@fwb.org. Web Site: www.fwb.org/library. *Dir,* Patricia Gould; *Adult Serv,* Jennifer Kepple; *Ch Serv,* Nancy Cardinal; Staff 7.5 (MLS 1, Non-MLS 6.5)
Founded 1954. Pop 25,000; Circ 118,368
Library Holdings: AV Mats 4,656; Bk Vols 62,000; Per Subs 184
Special Collections: Daily News Archives, microfilm back to 1915
Automation Activity & Vendor Info: (Cataloging) SirsiDynix; (Circulation) SirsiDynix
Database Vendor: ProQuest
Wireless access
Partic in Lyrasis; Okaloosa County Public Library Cooperative; Panhandle Library Access Network
Open Mon & Tues 9-8, Wed & Thurs 9-6, Fri 10-5, Sat 10-4

S INDIAN TEMPLE MOUND MUSEUM LIBRARY*, 139 Miracle Strip Pkwy SE, 32548. SAN 373-0417. Tel: 850-833-9595. FAX: 850-833-9675. Web Site: www.fwb.org. *Mgr,* Gail Meyer; E-mail: gmeyer@fwb.org
Founded 1970
Library Holdings: Bk Vols 2,500; Per Subs 25
Subject Interests: Archaeology, Local hist
Function: For res purposes
Open Mon-Fri Noon-4:30, Sat 10-4:30
Restriction: Not a lending libr

C UNIVERSITY OF WEST FLORIDA*, Fort Walton Beach Campus Library, 1170 Martin Luther King Jr Blvd, 32547. Tel: 850-863-6578. Web Site: libguides.uwf.edu/EmeraldCoast. *Librn,* Paul Williford; Tel: 850-863-6577, E-mail: williford@uwf.edu
Library Holdings: Bk Vols 30,000
Wireless access
Open Mon-Thurs 8am-9pm, Fri 8-5, Sat 1-5

FROSTPROOF

P LATT MAXCY MEMORIAL LIBRARY*, 15 N Magnolia Ave, 33843. SAN 329-143X. Tel: 863-635-7857. FAX: 863-635-8502. Web Site: www.mypclc.org/library/latt-maxcy-memorial-library. *Dir,* Melissa Hadden; E-mail: Missy.Hadden@mypclc.org; *Circ,* Shirley A Richardson; E-mail: richars@mypclc.org; *YA Serv,* Kellie D Wilbanks; E-mail: kelliew@mypclc.org; Staff 4 (Non-MLS 4)
Founded 1922. Pop 2,800; Circ 38,217
Library Holdings: Bk Titles 33,000; Bk Vols 35,478; Per Subs 41
Special Collections: Florida Coll, large print bks; Spanish Coll, vertical file
Automation Activity & Vendor Info: (Cataloging) TLC (The Library Corporation); (Circulation) TLC (The Library Corporation); (OPAC) TLC (The Library Corporation)
Database Vendor: EBSCOhost, OCLC FirstSearch
Function: ILL available
Partic in Polk County Libr Coop; Tampa Bay Library Consortium, Inc
Special Services for the Deaf - Bks on deafness & sign lang
Special Services for the Blind - Bks on cassette
Open Mon & Thurs 8:30-8, Tues, Wed & Fri 8:30-5, Sat 9-12
Friends of the Library Group

FRUITLAND PARK

P FRUITLAND PARK LIBRARY*, 205 W Berckman St, 34731. (Mail add: 506 W Berckman St, 34731), SAN 302-9433. Tel: 352-360-6561. FAX: 352-360-6691. Web Site: www.lakeline.lib.fl.us. *Dir,* Jo-Ann Glendinning; Staff 5 (Non-MLS 5)
Founded 1936
Library Holdings: Bk Vols 37,000; Per Subs 35
Automation Activity & Vendor Info: (Acquisitions) SIRSI WorkFlows; (Cataloging) SirsiDynix; (Circulation) SirsiDynix
Wireless access
Mem of Lake County Library System
Open Mon 9-7, Tues & Thurs 9-5, Wed & Fri 9-6, Sat 10-1
Friends of the Library Group

GAINESVILLE

P ALACHUA COUNTY LIBRARY DISTRICT, Headquarters Library, 401 E University Ave, 32601-5453. SAN 337-503X. Tel: 352-334-3900. Circulation Tel: 352-334-3950. Interlibrary Loan Service Tel: 352-334-3938. Reference Tel: 352-334-3934, 352-334-3939. Administration Tel: 352-334-3910. Automation Services Tel: 352-334-3998. FAX: 352-334-3918. Circulation FAX: 352-334-3948. Automation Services FAX: 352-334-1252. Web Site: www.aclib.us. *Dir,* Shaney T Livingston; E-mail: slivingston@aclib.us; *Div Dir, Admin Serv,* Vivian M Alexander; Tel: 352-334-0158, E-mail: valexander@aclib.us; *Div Dir, Pub Serv,* Christine Culp; Tel: 352-334-3922, E-mail: cculp@aclib.us; *Admin Serv Adminr,* Darrell E Elmore; Tel: 352-334-3914, E-mail: delmore@aclib.us; *Auromated Serv Adminr,* Clinton McNair; Tel: 352-334-3995, Fax: 352-334-1252, E-mail: cmcnair@aclib.us; *Fac/Safety Serv Adminr,* Daniel Whitcraft; Tel: 352-334-3915, E-mail: dwhitcraft@aclib.us; *Financial Serv Adminr,* Diana A Sanchez; Tel: 352-334-3913, E-mail: dsanchez@aclib.us; *Pub Serv Adminr,* Suzi Blaze; Tel: 352-334-3968, E-mail: sblaze@aclib.us; *Pub Serv Adminr,* Phillis Filer; Tel: 352-334-3957, E-mail: pfiler@aclib.us; *Tech Serv Adminr,* Tracy Babiasz; Tel: 352-334-3960, Fax: 352-334-3999, E-mail: tbabiasz@aclib.us; *Adult Serv Sr Libr Mgr,* Joyce West; Tel: 352-334-3930, E-mail: jwest@aclib.us; *Circ Serv Sr Libr Mgr,* Renee

Patterson; Tel: 352-334-1258, E-mail: rpatterson@aclib.us; *E-Br Mgr,* Otto Pleil-Muete; Tel: 352-334-3936, E-mail: opleil@aclib.us; *Outreach Serv Mgr,* David Fuller; Tel: 352-334-3991, Fax: 352-334-3994, E-mail: dfuller@aclib.us; *Pub Relations Mgr,* Nickie Kortus; Tel: 352-334-3909, E-mail: nkortus@aclib.us; *Youth Serv Sr Libr Mgr,* Erin Phemester; Tel: 352-334-3947, Fax: 352-334-1256, E-mail: ephemester@aclib.us; *Literacy Coordr,* Theresa Sterling; Tel: 352-334-3929, E-mail: tsterling@aclib.us; Staff 59.5 (MLS 57.5, Non-MLS 2)

Founded 1906. Pop 250,730; Circ 3,562,732

Oct 2013-Sept 2014 Income (Main Library and Branch(s)) $15,842,336, State $441,324, County $14,788,821, Locally Generated Income $44,641, Other $567,550. Mats Exp $1,837,198, Books $615,059, Per/Ser (Incl. Access Fees) $124,608, Micro $4,000, AV Mat $874,784, Electronic Ref Mat (Incl. Access Fees) $218,747. Sal $10,491,953 (Prof $4,685,938)

Library Holdings: Audiobooks 24,432; AV Mats 176,287; Bks-By-Mail 2,520; Bks on Deafness & Sign Lang 529; Braille Volumes 255; CDs 37,645; DVDs 109,660; e-books 62,263; Electronic Media & Resources 81,676; High Interest/Low Vocabulary Bk Vols 7,122; Large Print Bks 18,538; Microforms 818; Bk Titles 259,531; Bk Vols 557,730; Per Subs 1,415; Spec Interest Per Sub 70; Videos 4,308

Special Collections: Digital Heritage Coll; Genealogy Coll; Local Government Documents (Gainesville, Alachua County, North Central Florida), bd doc, microfilm & minutes; Local History (Alachua County/Gainesville), a-tapes, index to local newsp, maps, pamphlets, photog & v-tapes; Snuggle Up Coll; Spanish Language Materials. Municipal Document Depository

Subject Interests: Genealogy

Automation Activity & Vendor Info: (Acquisitions) Innovative Interfaces, Inc; (Cataloging) Innovative Interfaces, Inc; (Circulation) Innovative Interfaces, Inc; (ILL) OCLC ILLiad; (OPAC) Innovative Interfaces, Inc; (Serials) Innovative Interfaces, Inc

Database Vendor: EBSCO Auto Repair Reference, EBSCO Information Services, EBSCOhost, Facts on File, Foundation Center, Gale Cengage Learning, Grolier Online, LearningExpress, Newsbank, Overdrive, Inc, Oxford Online, ProQuest, ReferenceUSA, Safari Books Online, ValueLine, Westlaw, World Book Online

Wireless access

Function: 24/7 Electronic res, 24/7 Online cat, Accelerated reader prog, Adult bk club, Adult literacy prog, After school storytime, Archival coll, Art exhibits, Audio & video playback equip for onsite use, Audiobks via web, Bilingual assistance for Spanish patrons, Bk club(s), Bk reviews (Group), Bks on cassette, Bks on CD, Children's prog, Computer training, Computers for patron use, Copy machines, Doc delivery serv, e-mail & chat, e-mail serv, E-Reserves, Electronic databases & coll, Exhibits, Family literacy, Free DVD rentals, Games & aids for the handicapped, Govt ref serv, Handicapped accessible, Holiday prog, Home delivery & serv to Sr ctr & nursing homes, Homebound delivery serv, Homework prog, ILL available, Jail serv, Life-long learning prog for all ages, Literacy & newcomer serv, Magnifiers for reading, Mail & tel request accepted, Movies, Music CDs, Newsp ref libr, Online cat, Online ref, Online searches, Orientations, Outreach serv, Outside serv via phone, mail, e-mail & web, OverDrive digital audio bks, Photocopying/Printing, Preschool outreach, Prog for adults, Prog for children & young adult, Pub access computers, Ref serv available, Ref serv in person, Senior computer classes, Senior outreach, Serves mentally handicapped consumers, Spanish lang bks, Spoken cassettes & CDs, Spoken cassettes & DVDs, Story hour, Study rm, Summer reading prog, Tax forms, Teen prog, Telephone ref, VHS videos, Web-catalog, Wheelchair accessible, Workshops

Partic in Northeast Florida Library Information Network; PAL Library Cooperative

Special Services for the Deaf - ADA equip; Am sign lang & deaf culture; Assistive tech; Bks on deafness & sign lang; Closed caption videos; High interest/low vocabulary bks; Lecture on deaf culture; Sign lang interpreter upon request for prog; Staff with knowledge of sign lang; Video & TTY relay via computer

Special Services for the Blind - Accessible computers; Aids for in-house use; Assistive/Adapted tech devices, equip & products; Audio mat; BiFolkal kits; Bks & mags in Braille, on rec, tape & cassette; Bks available with recordings; Bks on cassette; Bks on CD; Braille bks; Children's Braille; Copier with enlargement capabilities; Descriptive video serv (DVS); Extensive large print coll; Free checkout of audio mat; Home delivery serv; Info on spec aids & appliances; Internet workstation with adaptive software; Large print & cassettes; Large print bks; Large print bks & talking machines; Large screen computer & software; Low vision equip; Magnifiers; Playaways (bks on MP3); Recorded bks; Ref serv; Screen enlargement software for people with visual disabilities; Sound rec; Talking bk & rec for the blind cat; Talking bk serv referral; Talking bks; Talking bks & player equip; Videos on blindness & phys handicaps; ZoomText magnification & reading software

Open Mon-Thurs 9:30-9, Fri 9:30-6, Sat 9:30-5, Sun 1-5

Restriction: Non-resident fee

Friends of the Library Group

Branches: 12

ALACHUA BRANCH, 14913 NW 140 St, Alachua, 32615. (Mail add: PO Box 550, Alachua, 32616), SAN 337-5048. Tel: 386-462-2592. FAX: 386-462-5537. *Libr Mgr,* Ross Woodbridge; E-mail: rwoodbridge@aclib.us
Open Mon-Thurs 11-7, Fri & Sat 11-5, Sun 1-5
Friends of the Library Group

ARCHER BRANCH, 13266 SW State Rd 45, Archer, 32618-5524. (Mail add: PO Box 920, Archer, 32618-0920), SAN 373-5680. Tel: 352-495-3367. FAX: 352-495-3061. *Libr Mgr,* Jodie Patterson; E-mail: jpatterson@aclib.us
Open Mon-Thurs 10 7, Sun 1-5
Friends of the Library Group

CONE PARK BRANCH, 2841-A E University Ave, 32641. Tel: 352-334-0720. FAX: 352-334-0310. *Libr Mgr,* Jennifer Johnson; E-mail: jjohnson@aclib.us
Open Mon-Thurs 10-6, Fri & Sat 10-5
Friends of the Library Group

HAWTHORNE BRANCH, 6640 SE 221 St, Hawthorne, 32640-3815. (Mail add: PO Box 1179, Hawthorne, 32640-1179), SAN 337-5064. Tel: 352-481-1920. FAX: 352-481-1921. *Libr Mgr,* Keith Harmon; E-mail: kharmon@aclib.us
Open Mon-Thurs 10-7, Fri-Sun 1-5
Friends of the Library Group

HIGH SPRINGS BRANCH, 135 NW First Ave, High Springs, 32643-1001, SAN 337-5099. Tel: 386-454-2515. FAX: 386-454-3439. *Libr Mgr,* Beth Noll; E-mail: bnoll@acld.us
Open Mon, Wed & Fri 10-5, Tues & Thurs 10-8, Sat 10-2, Sun 1-5
Friends of the Library Group

LIBRARY PARTNERSHIP: A NEIGHBORHOOD RESOURCE CENTER, 1130 NE 16th Ave, 32601. Tel: 352-334-0165. FAX: 352-334-0167. *Libr Mgr,* Anita Jenkins; E-mail: ajenkins@aclib.us
Open Mon & Tues 9-6, Wed & Thurs 11-7, Fri 9-5, Sat 10-3
Friends of the Library Group

MICANOPY BRANCH, Micanopy Town Hall, 706 NE Cholokka Blvd, Micanopy, 32667-4113. (Mail add: PO Box 200, Micanopy, 32667-0200), SAN 337-5129. Tel: 352-466-3122. FAX: 352-466-3124. *Libr Mgr,* Elizabeth Allerton; E-mail: eallerton@aclib.us
Open Mon 11-7, Tues-Thurs 1-7, Sun 1-5
Friends of the Library Group

MILLHOPPER BRANCH, 3145 NW 43rd St, 32606-6107, SAN 373-5664. Tel: 352-334-1272. FAX: 352-334-1280. *Sr Libr Mgr,* Emily Young; E-mail: eyoung@aclib.us
Open Mon-Thurs 9:30-8:30, Fri & Sat 9:30-5, Sun 1-5
Friends of the Library Group

NEWBERRY BRANCH, 110 S Seaboard Dr, Newberry, 32669. (Mail add: PO Box 1288, Newberry, 32669-1288), SAN 373-5699. Tel: 352-472-1135. FAX: 352-472-1136. *Libr Mgr,* Marlin Day; E-mail: mday@aclib.us
Open Mon-Thurs 10-8, Fri & Sat 10-5, Sun 1-5
Friends of the Library Group

SHERIFF'S DEPARTMENT OF THE JAIL, 3333 NE 39th Ave, 32609-2699. (Mail add: 401 E University Ave, 32601), SAN 328-9672. Tel: 352 334 3991. FAX: 352-334-3994. *Outreach Serv Mgr,* David Fuller; Fax: 352-334-3904, E-mail: dfuller@aclib.us
Restriction: Not open to pub
Friends of the Library Group

TOWER ROAD BRANCH, 3020 SW 75th St, 32608, SAN 373-5672. Tel: 352-333-2840. FAX: 352-333-2846. *Sr Libr Mgr,* Lauren Brosnihan; E-mail: lbrosnihan@aclib.us
Open Mon-Thurs 9:30-8:30, Fri & Sat 9:30-5, Sun 1-5
Friends of the Library Group

WALDO BRANCH, 14257 Cole St, Waldo, 32694. (Mail add: PO Box 960, Waldo, 32694-0960), SAN 376-9178. Tel: 352-468-3298. FAX: 352-468-3299. *Libr Mgr,* Bruce Stewart; E-mail: bstewart@aclib.us
Open Mon-Thurs 12:30-7, Sun 1-5
Friends of the Library Group

Bookmobiles: 2

S CENTER FOR APPLICATIONS OF PSYCHOLOGICAL TYPE*, Isabel Briggs Myers Memorial Library, 2815 NW 13th St, Ste 401, 32609. SAN 325-1683. Tel: 352-375-0160. FAX: 352-378-0503. E-mail: library@capt.org. Web Site: www.capt.org. *Res Librn,* Logan Abbitt; Staff 1 (MLS 1)

Founded 1975

Library Holdings: AV Mats 1,499; Bk Vols 1,680; Per Subs 11

Special Collections: Articles & Papers; Conference Proceedings; Dissertations & Theses

Subject Interests: Jungian psychol

Open Mon-Fri 9-5

Restriction: Not a lending libr

J CITY COLLEGE-GAINESVILLE LIBRARY*, 2400 SW 13th St, 32608. Tel: 352-335-4000, Ext 29. FAX: 352-335-4303. *Br Librn,* Tina Worthen; E-mail: tworthen@citycollege.edu
Highest Degree: Bachelor
Library Holdings: Bk Vols 6,600; Per Subs 15
Automation Activity & Vendor Info: (Cataloging) OCLC CatExpress; (Circulation) Follett Software
Database Vendor: Gale Cengage Learning, ProQuest, Westlaw
Wireless access
Function: ILL available, Online cat
Partic in Lyrasis; Northeast Florida Library Information Network
Open Mon-Thurs 9-9, Fri 9-5
Restriction: Borrowing privileges limited to fac & registered students

FIRST UNITED METHODIST CHURCH
R EPWORTH LIBRARY & SUSANNAH WESLEY MEDIA CENTER*, 419 NE First St, 32601, SAN 302-9476. Tel: 352-372-8523. FAX: 352-372-2524. Web Site: www.fumcgnv.org. *In Charge,* Pat Jennings
Founded 1950
Library Holdings: Large Print Bks 25; Bk Vols 3,500
Subject Interests: Theol
Open Mon-Thurs 1-4:30, Sun 8:30-12
R LAURA KNIGHT CHILDREN'S LIBRARY*, 419 NE First St, 32601, SAN 320-9628. Tel: 352-372-8523. FAX: 352-372-2524. *In Charge,* Joan Van Winkle
Founded 1978
Library Holdings: Bk Vols 630
Open Mon-Thurs 1-4:30

G FLORIDA DEPARTMENT OF AGRICULTURE & CONSUMER SERVICES*, Division of Plant Industry Library, 1911 SW 34th St, 32608. (Mail add: PO Box 147100, 32614-7100), SAN 302-9484. Tel: 352-395-4720. FAX: 352-395-4614. E-mail: dpi-library@freshfromflorida.com. Web Site: www.neflin.org/dpi. *Librn,* Beverly Pope; E-mail: beverly.pope@freshfromflorida.com; *Asst Librn,* Alice Sanders; Staff 2 (MLS 1, Non-MLS 1)
Founded 1915
Library Holdings: Bk Titles 17,000; Per Subs 300
Subject Interests: Entomology
Automation Activity & Vendor Info: (Cataloging) NOTIS
Open Mon-Fri 8-5

S GAINESVILLE CORRECTIONAL INSTITUTION LIBRARY*, 2845 NE 39th Ave, 32609. SAN 377-2322. Tel: 352-955-2001, Ext 2816. FAX: 352-334-1675.
Library Holdings: Bk Titles 6,000; Per Subs 40
Open Tues-Sat 9-5

GL JOHN A H MURPHREE LAW LIBRARY*, Alachua County Courthouse, Rm 413, 201 E University Ave, 32601. Tel: 352-374-3659. FAX: 352-381-0136. Web Site: circuit8.org/library. *Mgr,* Beverly Carter; Staff 1 (Non-MLS 1)
Founded 1957
Library Holdings: Bk Vols 10,000
Automation Activity & Vendor Info: (Circulation) SirsiDynix
Database Vendor: Westlaw
Open Mon-Fri 8-1:30 & 2:30-5
Restriction: Non-circulating, Open to pub for ref only

J SANTA FE COMMUNITY COLLEGE*, Lawrence W Tyree Library, 3000 NW 83rd St, Bldg Y-100, 32606. SAN 337-4971. Tel: 352-395-5406. Circulation Tel: 352-395-5412. Interlibrary Loan Service Tel: 352-395-5771. Reference Tel: 352-395-5409. Administration Tel: 352-381-3638. FAX: 352-395-5102. Administration FAX: 352-395-7326. E-mail: library@sfcollege.edu. *Dir,* Myra Sterrett; E-mail: myra.sterrett@sfcollege.edu; *Ref Librn,* Nance Lempinen-Leedy; *Ref Librn,* Diana Matthews; *Ref Librn,* Jenna Miller; Tel: 352-395-5329, E-mail: jenna.miller@fscc.edu; *Ref Librn,* Scott Tarbox; Tel: 352-395-5233, E-mail: scott.tarbox@sfcollege.edu; *Ref Librn,* Ramona Miller-Ridlon; Tel: 352-381-3637, E-mail: ramona.miller-ridlon@sfcollege.edu; *Tech Serv Librn,* Trenita White; E-mail: trenita.white@sfcollege.edu; *Circ Supvr,* Peter Sokol; Tel: 352-395-5411, E-mail: peter.sokol@sfcollege.edu; *Evening Circ Supvr,* Mike Muhlhauser; E-mail: mike.muhlhauser@sfcollege.edu; *Coll Mgt,* John Reames; *Libr Spec,* Kim Hankins; Tel: 352-395-5415, E-mail: kim.hankins@sfcollege.edu; *Support Serv,* Tom Holland; Tel: 352-395-5103, E-mail: tom.holland@sfcollege.edu; *Support Serv,* Jimmy Mercer; Staff 13 (MLS 7, Non-MLS 6)
Founded 1966. Enrl 14,000; Fac 300; Highest Degree: Associate
Library Holdings: Bk Vols 86,470; Per Subs 435
Automation Activity & Vendor Info: (Acquisitions) Ex Libris Group; (Cataloging) Ex Libris Group; (Circulation) Ex Libris Group; (OPAC) Ex Libris Group; (Serials) Ex Libris Group
Wireless access
Partic in Northeast Florida Library Information Network
Open Mon-Thurs 7am-10pm, Fri 7-4:30, Sat Noon-6, Sun Noon-8

GM UNITED STATES DEPARTMENT OF VETERANS AFFAIRS*, Gainesville VA Medical Center, 1601 SW Archer Rd, 32608-1197. SAN 302-9506. Tel: 352-376-1611, Ext 6313. FAX: 352-374-6148. *Chief Librn,* Marylyn Gresser; *Asst Librn,* Marsha White
Founded 1967
Library Holdings: Bk Titles 7,000; Per Subs 350
Automation Activity & Vendor Info: (Circulation) EOS International
Partic in Veterans Affairs Libr Network (VALNET)
Open Mon-Fri 8-4:30
Restriction: Staff use only

C UNIVERSITY OF FLORIDA LIBRARIES, George A Smathers Libraries, 535 Library W, 32611-7000. (Mail add: PO Box 117000, 32611-7000), SAN 337-5153. Tel: 352-273-2505. Circulation Tel: 352-273-2525. Interlibrary Loan Service Tel: 352-273-2535. Reference Tel: 352-273-2665. FAX: 352-392-7251. Interlibrary Loan Service FAX: 352-392-7598. Web Site: www.uflib.ufl.edu. *Dean, Univ Libr,* Judith C Russell; E-mail: jcrussell@ufl.edu; *Assoc Dean, Dir, Health Sci Ctr Libr,* Cecilia Botero; Tel: 352-273-8400, Fax: 352-392-2565, E-mail: cecbote@ufl.edu; *Dir of Develop,* Katie Boudreau; E-mail: boudreau@ufl.edu; *Assoc Dean, Digital Serv & Shared Coll,* Ben F Walker; Tel: 352-273-2545, E-mail: benwalk@uflib.ufl.edu; *Assoc Dean, Scholarly Res & Serv,* Patrick J Reakes; E-mail: pjr@uflib.ufl.edu; *Asst Dean, Admin & Fac Affairs,* Brian W Keith; Tel: 352-273-2595, Fax: 352-392-4538, E-mail: bwkeith@ufl.edu; *Regional Dep Librn,* Jan Swanbeck; Tel: 352-273-0374, E-mail: janswan@uflib.ufl.edu; *Chair, Marston Sci Libr,* Val Minson; Tel: 352-273-2880, E-mail: vdavis@ufl.edu; *Chair, Spec & Area Studies Coll,* Haven Hawley; Tel: 352-273-2765, E-mail: ehh@ufl.edu; *Interim Chair, Libr West/Humanities & Soc Sci Libr,* Jana Ronan; Tel: 352-273-2623, Fax: 352-392-8118, E-mail: jronan@ufl.edu; *Digital Coll Curator,* Chelsea Dinsmore; Tel: 352-273-0369, Fax: 352-846-3702, E-mail: chedins@uflib.ufl.edu; *Head, Access Support,* Michele Crump; Tel: 352-273-2717, Fax: 352-392-6540, E-mail: mcrump@uflib.ufl.edu; *Head, Acq & Licensing,* Steven Carrico; Tel: 352-273-2700, Fax: 352-392-4788, E-mail: stecarr@uflib.ufl.edu; *Head, Archit & Fine Arts Libr,* Ann Lindell; Tel: 352-273-2805, Fax: 352-846-2747, E-mail: annlind@uflib.ufl.edu; *Head, Cat & Metadata Serv,* Betsy Simpson; Tel: 352-273-2730, Fax: 352-392-7365, E-mail: betsys@uflib.ufl.edu; *Head, Educ Libr,* Rachael Elrod; Tel: 352-273-2627, Fax: 352-392-4789, E-mail: relrod@ufl.edu; *Head, Fac & Security,* Peter Miller; Tel: 352-273-2578, Fax: 352-392-4507, E-mail: petmill@uflib.ufl.edu; *Head, Map & Imagery Libr,* Carol McAuliffe; Tel: 352-273-2825, Fax: 352-392-4787, E-mail: carolmc@uflib.ufl.edu; *Grants Mgr,* Bess de Farber; Tel: 352-273-2519, E-mail: besdefa@uflib.ufl.edu; *ILL Coordr,* Melanie Davis; Tel: 352-273-2522, E-mail: davism@ufl.edu; Staff 265 (MLS 80, Non-MLS 185)
Founded 1853. Enrl 50,000; Fac 4,000; Highest Degree: Doctorate
Library Holdings: Microforms 8,100,000; Bk Vols 5,800,000
Special Collections: African Studies Coll; Architecture Archives; Archives and Manuscripts; Asian Studies Coll; Baldwin-Historical Children's Literature; Harold & Mary Jean Hanson Rare Book Coll; Latin American and Caribbean Coll; Map & Imagery Library; P K Yonge Library of Florida History; Popular Culture; Price Library of Judaica; University Archives. State Document Depository; UN Document Depository; US Document Depository
Subject Interests: Archit, Educ, Fine arts, Humanities, Journalism, Sciences
Automation Activity & Vendor Info: (Acquisitions) Ex Libris Group; (Cataloging) Ex Libris Group; (Circulation) Ex Libris Group; (Course Reserve) Docutek; (ILL) OCLC ILLiad; (OPAC) Ex Libris Group; (Serials) Ex Libris Group
Wireless access
Function: Res libr
Publications: Chapter One
Partic in Association of Research Libraries (ARL)
Special Services for the Deaf - Assisted listening device
Friends of the Library Group

GRACEVILLE

CR THE BAPTIST COLLEGE OF FLORIDA, Ida J McMillan Library, 5400 College Dr, 32440-1833. SAN 302-9514. Tel: 850-263-3261, Ext 424. Circulation Tel: 800-328-2660, Ext 424. FAX: 850-263-5704. E-mail: library@baptistcollege.edu. Web Site: www.baptistcollege.edu. *Dir, Libr Serv,* John Shaffett; Tel: 800-328-2660, Ext 449, E-mail: jeshaffett@baptistcollege.edu; Staff 2 (MLS 2)
Founded 1943. Highest Degree: Master
Library Holdings: Bk Vols 72,222; Per Subs 327
Special Collections: Baptist Coll; College Archives
Subject Interests: Educ, Humanities, Leadership, Music, Psychol, Relig
Automation Activity & Vendor Info: (Cataloging) OCLC; (OPAC) TLC (The Library Corporation)

Wireless access
Partic in OCLC Online Computer Library Center, Inc; Panhandle Library Access Network
Open Mon, Tues & Thurs 7:30am-10:30pm, Wed & Fri 7:30-4:30, Sat 10-4

GULF BREEZE

G UNITED STATES ENVIRONMENTAL PROTECTION, Gulf Ecology Division Library, One Sabine Island Dr, 32561-5299. SAN 302-9530. Tel: 850-934-9318. FAX: 850-934-2409. Web Site: www.epa.gov/ged/bld42_dw.htm. *Librn III,* Sonya M Doten; E-mail: doten.sonya@epa.gov; Staff 0.8 (MLS 0.8)
Founded 1967
Library Holdings: Bk Titles 6,457; Per Subs 43
Special Collections: Environmental Issues-Northwest Florida
Subject Interests: Environ analysis (water), Estuarine biol, Water pollution
Database Vendor: BioOne, Dialog, JSTOR, OCLC FirstSearch, ScienceDirect, Springer-Verlag, WT Cox
Function: ILL available
Publications: Laboratory Publications Bibliography; Periodicals List
Partic in OCLC Online Computer Library Center, Inc; Panhandle Library Access Network
Restriction: Open by appt only

GULFPORT

P GULFPORT PUBLIC LIBRARY*, 5501 28th Ave S, 33707. SAN 302-9549. Tel: 727-893-1074. Reference Tel: 727-893-1073. FAX: 727-893-1072. E-mail: gulfport@tblc.org. Web Site: tblc.org/gpl/. *Dir,* Catherine Smith; Tel: 727-893-1075, E-mail: smithki@tblc.org; *Pub Serv,* Karen Aust; E-mail: kaust@ci.gulfport.fl.us; *Pub Serv,* Thomas Bourke; E-mail: tbourke@ci.gulfport.fl.us; *Tech Serv,* Carol Parker; Tel: 727-893-1076, E-mail: parkerc@tblc.org; *Youth Serv,* Patricia Brinkley; Staff 14 (MLS 5, Non-MLS 9)
Founded 1935. Pop 12,000; Circ 115,894
Library Holdings: Bk Vols 70,000; Per Subs 100
Special Collections: Russian Books (popular)
Automation Activity & Vendor Info: (Cataloging) Innovative Interfaces, Inc; (Circulation) Innovative Interfaces, Inc; (OPAC) Innovative Interfaces, Inc
Database Vendor: SirsiDynix
Mem of Pinellas Public Libr Coop
Partic in Florida Library Information Network; Tampa Bay Library Consortium, Inc
Open Mon-Thurs 9-8, Fri 9-9, Sat 9-5
Friends of the Library Group

CL STETSON UNIVERSITY COLLEGE OF LAW LIBRARY*, 1401 61st St S, 33707. SAN 338-0580. Tel: 727-562-7820. Reference Tel: 727-562-7821. FAX: 727-345-8973. Web Site: library.law.stetson.edu. *Dir,* Rebecca S Trammell; E-mail: rtrammel@law.stetson.edu; *Assoc Dir, Head, Pub Serv,* Pamela Burdett; Tel: 727-562-7824, E-mail: burdett@law.stetson.edu; *Asst Dir, Head, Pub Serv,* Earlene Kuester; Tel: 727-562-7826, E-mail: kuester@law.stetson.edu; Staff 16 (MLS 6, Non-MLS 10)
Founded 1901. Enrl 895; Fac 45; Highest Degree: Master
Library Holdings: Bk Titles 120,248; Bk Vols 398,443; Per Subs 4,061
Special Collections: US Document Depository
Automation Activity & Vendor Info: (Acquisitions) Innovative Interfaces, Inc; (Cataloging) Innovative Interfaces, Inc; (Circulation) Innovative Interfaces, Inc; (OPAC) Innovative Interfaces, Inc; (Serials) Innovative Interfaces, Inc
Database Vendor: Gale Cengage Learning, LexisNexis, OCLC FirstSearch, ProQuest
Partic in Consortium of Southeastern Law Libraries; OCLC Online Computer Library Center, Inc; Tampa Bay Library Consortium, Inc

HAINES CITY

P HAINES CITY PUBLIC LIBRARY, 111 N Sixth St, 33844. SAN 302-9557. Tel: 863-421-3633. *Dir,* Mary Ellin Barrett; E-mail: mbarrett@hainescity.com; *Libr Spec I,* John Shaw; E-mail: jshaw@hainescity.com; Staff 6 (MLS 1, Non-MLS 5)
Founded 1920. Pop 18,780
Library Holdings: Bk Titles 53,000; Per Subs 35
Special Collections: Florida Coll
Automation Activity & Vendor Info: (Cataloging) SirsiDynix; (Circulation) SirsiDynix; (ILL) OCLC FirstSearch
Wireless access
Partic in Polk County Libr Coop
Open Mon-Fri 10-6, Sat 10-1

HAVANA

S NORTHWEST FLORIDA WATER MANAGEMENT DISTRICT*, Library & Information Center, 81 Water Management Dr, 32333. SAN 374-8405. Tel: 850-539-5999. FAX: 850-539-2777. Web Site: www.nwfwmd.state.fl.us. *Librn,* Lucinda Scott; E-mail: lucinda.scott@nwfwmd.state.fl.us
Library Holdings: Bk Titles 100; Per Subs 50
Special Collections: Archives of Northwest Florida Water Management District; Environmental Reports; USGS Coll
Function: Res libr
Open Mon-Fri 8-5
Restriction: Non-circulating

HIALEAH

P HIALEAH PUBLIC LIBRARIES*, John F Kennedy Library, 190 W 49th St, 33012-3798. SAN 337-5633. Tel: 305-821-2700. FAX: 305-818-9144. E-mail: jfklib@hialeahfl.gov. Web Site: www.hialeahfl.gov/library. *Dir,* Grisel Torralbas; Staff 14 (MLS 7, Non-MLS 7)
Founded 1928. Pop 220,000; Circ 160,000
Library Holdings: AV Mats 13,000; e-books 13,700; Bk Titles 140,000; Bk Vols 163,300; Per Subs 200
Subject Interests: Art & archit, Bus & mgt, Fla, Music, Sci tech, Spanish
Automation Activity & Vendor Info: (Cataloging) SirsiDynix; (Circulation) SirsiDynix; (OPAC) SirsiDynix
Database Vendor: Newsbank
Wireless access
Function: After school storytime, Bilingual assistance for Spanish patrons, Children's prog, Citizenship assistance, Computer training, Computers for patron use, Copy machines, Electronic databases & coll, Fax serv, ILL available, Prog for adults, Prog for children & young adult, Senior computer classes, Telephone ref, Workshops
Publications: Que Pasa Hialeah (Newsletter)
Open Mon-Thurs Noon-8, Sat 9-5
Friends of the Library Group
Branches: 5
CURTIS E-LIBARY, 501 E Fourth Ave, 33010, SAN 337-5668. Tel: 305-883-6950. FAX: 305-883-6951. *In Charge,* Position Currently Open
Open Tues & Thurs 3-8
NORTH HIALEAH E-LIBRARY, 7400 W Tenth Ave, 33014. Tel: 305-816-4470. FAX: 305-816-4473. *In Charge,* Position Currently Open
Open Mon & Wed 3-8
WALKER E-LIBRARY, 800 W 29th St, 33012. Tel: 305-883-6317.
Open Mon & Wed 3-8
WEST HIALEAH E-LIBRARY, 7400 W 24th Ave, 33016. Tel: 305-698-3615. FAX: 305-698-3616. *In Charge,* Position Currently Open
Open Mon-Thurs 3-8:45, Sat 11-4:45
WILDE E-LIBRARY, 5400 W 18th Ave, 33012. Tel: 305-818-9766. *In Charge,* Position Currently Open
Open Tues & Thurs 3-8

HIGHLAND BEACH

P HIGHLAND BEACH LIBRARY*, 3618 S Ocean Blvd, 33487. SAN 376-4990. Tel: 561-278-5455. FAX: 561-278-0156. Web Site: www.ci.highland-beach.fl.us/index.aspx?nid=114. *Dir,* Mari Suarez; E-mail: msuarez@highlandbeachlibrary.org; Staff 4 (MLS 1, Non-MLS 3)
Founded 1986
Oct 2006-Sept 2007. Mats Exp $60,000
Library Holdings: CDs 900; DVDs 3,350; Bk Titles 29,000; Per Subs 90; Talking Bks 800
Special Collections: Florida Coll
Database Vendor: Gale Cengage Learning
Open Mon-Thurs 10-8, Fri 10-4, Sat 10-1
Friends of the Library Group

HOBE SOUND

CR HOBE SOUND BIBLE COLLEGE LIBRARY*, 11440 SE Gomez Ave, 33455-3378. (Mail add: PO Box 1065, 33475-1065), SAN 302-9603. Tel: 772-545-1400, Ext 1078. FAX: 772-545-1422. Web Site: www.hsbc.edu/library. *Librn,* William Snider; Staff 2 (MLS 1, Non-MLS 1)
Founded 1960. Enrl 144; Fac 24; Highest Degree: Doctorate
Library Holdings: Bk Vols 33,400; Per Subs 220
Special Collections: Child Evangelism Coll
Subject Interests: Humanities, Music
Automation Activity & Vendor Info: (Circulation) Follett Software
Open Mon, Tues & Thurs 8-4:45 & 6:30-9:30, Wed & Fri 8-4:45, Sat 1-4:45 & 7-9

HOLLYWOOD

M MEMORIAL HEALTHCARE SYSTEM*, Memorial Regional Hospital Knowledge Services Library, 3501 Johnson St, 33021. SAN 302-962X. Tel: 954-985-5840. FAX: 954-967-2951. Web Site: www.mhs.net. *Librn,* Sally E Haff; E-mail: shaff@mhs.net; Staff 1 (MLS 1)
Founded 1963
Library Holdings: Bk Titles 300; Per Subs 90
Subject Interests: Allied health, Clinical med, Nursing
Partic in Miami Health Sciences Library Consortium
Restriction: Clients only, Med staff only, Non-circulating

R TEMPLE BETH EL*, Billie Davis Rodenberg Memorial Library, 1351 S 14th Ave, 33020-6499. SAN 302-9638. Tel: 954-920-8225. FAX: 954-920-7026.
Founded 1962
Library Holdings: Bk Titles 5,500
Subject Interests: Judaica (lit or hist of Jews)
Wireless access

HOMESTEAD

C MIAMI DADE COLLEGE*, Homestead Campus Library, 500 College Terrace, Bldg D, Rm D-206, 33030-6609. Tel: 305-237-5057. FAX: 305-237-5084. Web Site: www.mdc.edu/homestead/library. *Assoc Dir, Learning Res,* Lindsey Schriftman; E-mail: lschrift@mdc.edu
Library Holdings: Bk Titles 20,000; Per Subs 150
Automation Activity & Vendor Info: (Acquisitions) Ex Libris Group; (Cataloging) Ex Libris Group; (Circulation) Ex Libris Group; (Course Reserve) Ex Libris Group; (ILL) Ex Libris Group; (Media Booking) Ex Libris Group; (OPAC) Ex Libris Group; (Serials) Ex Libris Group
Open Mon-Thurs 7:30am-9pm, Fri 7:30-5, Sat 8-1

C UNIVERSITY OF FLORIDA, TROPICAL RESEARCH & EDUCATION CENTER*, Institute of Food & Agricultural Sciences Library, 18905 SW 280th St, 33031. SAN 302-9662. Tel: 305-246-6340. FAX: 305-246-7003. Web Site: trec.ifas.ufl.edu. *In Charge,* Bessy Torres
Library Holdings: Bk Vols 4,000; Per Subs 71
Open Mon-Fri 8-5

HOWEY IN THE HILLS

P MARIANNE BECK MEMORIAL LIBRARY*, Howey-in-the-Hills Library, 112 W Central Ave, 34737. Tel: 352-324-0254. FAX: 352-324-1115. E-mail: howeylibrary@howey.org. *Dir,* Tara Hall
Library Holdings: Audiobooks 100; DVDs 500; e-books 40; Large Print Bks 200; Bk Titles 12,000
Mem of Lake County Library System
Open Mon & Fri 12-5, Tues & Thurs 12-7, Wed 9-5, Sat 9-12

HUDSON

P PASCO COUNTY LIBRARY SYSTEM*, 8012 Library Rd, 34667. SAN 324-8003. Tel: 727-861-3020. Reference Tel: 727-861-3040. Automation Services Tel: 727-834-3635. Toll Free Tel: 800-368-2411, Ext 3020. FAX: 727-861-3025. Automation Services FAX: 727-834-3335. Web Site: pascolibraries.org. *Libr Adminr,* Nancy Fredericks; E-mail: nancyfredericks@pascolibraries.org; Staff 33 (MLS 33)
Founded 1980. Pop 435,425; Circ 2,000,000
Library Holdings: e-books 18,281; Bk Titles 174,970; Bk Vols 625,359; Per Subs 1,684; Videos 18,016
Subject Interests: Fla
Automation Activity & Vendor Info: (Acquisitions) TLC (The Library Corporation); (Cataloging) TLC (The Library Corporation); (Circulation) TLC (The Library Corporation); (OPAC) TLC (The Library Corporation); (Serials) TLC (The Library Corporation)
Database Vendor: Gale Cengage Learning, infoUSA, Newsbank, OCLC FirstSearch, OCLC WorldShare Interlibrary Loan
Wireless access
Function: AV serv, CD-ROM, ILL available, Magnifiers for reading, Newsp ref libr, Online searches, Outside serv via phone, mail, e-mail & web, Photocopying/Printing, Prog for adults, Prog for children & young adult, Ref serv available, Satellite serv, Spoken cassettes & CDs, Summer reading prog, Telephone ref, VHS videos
Publications: Friends of Pasco County Newsletter; LIB (Newsletter)
Member Libraries: Zephyrhills Public Library
Partic in Lyrasis; Tampa Bay Library Consortium, Inc
Special Services for the Deaf - Assisted listening device; Closed caption videos; Sign lang interpreter upon request for prog; Staff with knowledge of sign lang; TDD equip
Special Services for the Blind - Audio mat; Bks on cassette; Bks on CD; Large print bks; Magnifiers
Open Mon-Fri 8-5
Friends of the Library Group

Branches: 7

CENTENNIAL PARK, 5740 Moog Rd, Holiday, 34690, SAN 370-3622. Tel: 727-834-3204. FAX: 727-834-3225. *Mgr,* Sandra Abini; *Librn I,* Linda Rothstein; Staff 2 (MLS 2)
Founded 1986. Pop 25,906; Circ 233,298
Library Holdings: Bk Titles 62,456
Function: AV serv, ILL available, Online searches, Prog for adults, Prog for children & young adult, Ref serv available, Spoken cassettes & CDs, Summer reading prog, VHS videos
Special Services for the Deaf - TDD equip
Open Tues 10-8, Wed & Thurs 11-6, Fri 11-5, Sat 11-4
Friends of the Library Group

HUGH EMBRY BRANCH, 14215 Fourth St, Dade City, 33523, SAN 302-8992. Tel: 352-567-3576. FAX: 352-521-6670. TDD: 352-523-0902. *Br Mgr,* Angelo Liranzo; E-mail: angelol@pascolibraries.org; Staff 1 (MLS 1)
Founded 1904. Pop 19,131; Circ 153,855
Library Holdings: Bk Titles 54,586
Function: AV serv, CD-ROM, ILL available, Online searches, Photocopying/Printing, Prog for adults, Prog for children & young adult, Ref serv available, Spoken cassettes & CDs, Summer reading prog, VHS videos
Special Services for the Deaf - TDD equip; TTY equip
Open Tues 10-6, Wed 11-8, Thurs 11-6, Fri 11-5, Sat 11-4
Friends of the Library Group

HUDSON REGIONAL, 8012 Library Rd, 34667, SAN 370-6257. Tel: 727-861-3040. FAX: 727-861-3025. TDD: 727-861-3024. *Actg Br Mgr,* Sue Griffiths; Staff 10 (MLS 10)
Founded 1990. Pop 45,402; Circ 445,073
Library Holdings: Bk Titles 93,472
Function: CD-ROM, Homebound delivery serv, ILL available, Magnifiers for reading, Online searches, Outside serv via phone, mail, e-mail & web, Photocopying/Printing, Prog for adults, Prog for children & young adult, Ref serv available, Spoken cassettes & CDs, Summer reading prog, VHS videos
Special Services for the Deaf - TDD equip; TTY equip
Special Services for the Blind - Audio mat; BiFolkal kits; Bks on cassette; Bks on CD; Large print bks; Talking bks
Open Tues 10-8, Wed & Thurs 11-6, Fri 11-5, Sat 11-4
Friends of the Library Group

LAND O' LAKES BRANCH, 2818 Collier Pkwy, Land O' Lakes, 34639, SAN 370-6265. Tel: 813-929-1214. FAX: 813-929-1235. TDD: 813-949-3746. *Br Mgr,* Kathleen Rothstein; Staff 12 (MLS 3, Non-MLS 9)
Founded 1991. Pop 30,064; Circ 269,438
Library Holdings: Bk Titles 67,695
Function: AV serv, ILL available, Online searches, Photocopying/Printing, Prog for adults, Prog for children & young adult, Ref serv available, Spoken cassettes & CDs, Summer reading prog, VHS videos
Special Services for the Deaf - TDD equip
Open Tues 10-8, Wed & Thurs 10-6, Fri & Sat 10-5
Friends of the Library Group

NEW RIVER, 34043 State Rd 54, Zephyrhills, 33543, SAN 371-3687. Tel: 813-788-6375. FAX: 813-788-6977. TDD: 813-780-8054. *Br Mgr,* Lisa Morgan; Staff 2 (MLS 2)
Founded 1991. Pop 26,103; Circ 249,115
Library Holdings: Bk Titles 63,596
Function: AV serv, CD-ROM, ILL available, Online searches, Photocopying/Printing, Prog for adults, Prog for children & young adult, Ref serv available, Spoken cassettes & CDs, Summer reading prog, VHS videos
Special Services for the Deaf - TDD equip
Open Tues 10-6, Wed 11-6, Thurs 11-8, Fri 11-5, Sat 11-4
Friends of the Library Group

REGENCY PARK, 9701 Little Rd, New Port Richey, 34654, SAN 370-6273. Tel: 727-861-3049. FAX: 727-861-3011. TDD: 727-943-8085. *Coordr,* Margaret Griffith; Staff 3 (MLS 3)
Founded 1990. Pop 37,945; Circ 261,266
Library Holdings: Bk Titles 69,655
Function: AV serv, CD-ROM, ILL available, Online searches, Photocopying/Printing, Prog for adults, Prog for children & young adult, Ref serv available, Spoken cassettes & CDs, Summer reading prog, VHS videos
Special Services for the Deaf - TDD equip
Open Tues 10-6, Wed 11-6, Thurs 11-8, Fri 11-5, Sat 11-4
Friends of the Library Group

SOUTH HOLIDAY BRANCH, 4649 Mile Stretch Rd, Holiday, 34690, SAN 371-3695. Tel: 727-834-3331. FAX: 727-942-6740. TDD: 727-834-3370, 727-946-8085. *Mgr,* Dave Mather; Staff 2 (MLS 2)
Pop 18,326; Circ 168,502
Library Holdings: Bk Titles 47,827
Function: AV serv, CD-ROM, ILL available, Online searches, Prog for adults, Prog for children & young adult, Ref serv available, Spoken cassettes & CDs, Summer reading prog, VHS videos

Special Services for the Deaf - TDD equip
Open Tues 10-6, Wed 11-8, Thurs 11-6, Fri 11-5, Sat 11-4
Friends of the Library Group

HURLBURT FIELD

A UNITED STATES AIR FORCE, Hurlburt Field Base Library, Base Library, 443 Cody Ave, 32544. SAN 337-3894. Tel: 850-884-6947. FAX: 850-884-6050. Web Site: commandolibrary.com. *Actg Dir,* Lilly B Woods; E-mail: lilly.woods@hurlburt.af.mil; Staff 8 (MLS 1, Non-MLS 7)
Founded 1955
Library Holdings: Bk Vols 28,000, Per Subs 60
Special Collections: Special Operations (Military)
Automation Activity & Vendor Info: (OPAC) SirsiDynix
Wireless access
Function: Doc delivery serv, ILL available, Online searches, Photocopying/Printing, Prof lending libr, Prog for adults, Prog for children & young adult, Ref serv available, Summer reading prog, Telephone ref
Publications: Selected Resources on Special Operations
Partic in Panhandle Library Access Network
Restriction: Restricted access, Restricted borrowing privileges

INDIANTOWN

S MARTIN CORRECTIONAL INSTITUTION LIBRARY*, 1150 SW Allapattah Rd, 34956-4310. SAN 377-290X. Tel: 772-597-3705, Ext 224. FAX: 772-597-4529. *Librn,* Linda Ampol; E-mail: ampol.linda@mail.dc.state.fl.us
Library Holdings: Bk Vols 19,152; Per Subs 79
Special Collections: Major Law Coll
Open Mon-Thurs & Sat 8:30-11 & 12:30-3:30, Fri 12:30-3:30

JACKSONVILLE

S CUMMER MUSEUM OF ART LIBRARY, 829 Riverside Ave, 32204. SAN 326-5846. Tel: 904-356-6857. FAX: 904-353-4101. Web Site: www.cummer.org.
Founded 1961
Library Holdings: Bk Vols 15,000; Per Subs 43
Special Collections: European Porcelains
Subject Interests: Art hist
Restriction: Non-circulating to the pub

GL DUVAL COUNTY LAW LIBRARY*, 501 W Adams St, Rm 2291, 32202. SAN 302-9719. Tel: 904-255-1150. FAX: 904-255-1164. *Dir,* Bud Maurer; E-mail: bmaurer@coj.net; Staff 8 (MLS 1, Non-MLS 7)
Founded 1939
Library Holdings: Bk Vols 47,000
Subject Interests: Fla, Law
Automation Activity & Vendor Info: (Cataloging) LibraryWorld, Inc; (Circulation) LibraryWorld, Inc
Database Vendor: HeinOnline, LexisNexis, Westlaw
Wireless access
Open Mon-Thurs 8-6, Fri 8-5

C THE EDWARD WATERS COLLEGE LIBRARY*, 1658 Kings Rd, 32209-6199. SAN 302-9727. Tel: 904-470-8080. Reference Tel: 904-470-8081. FAX: 904-470-8032. Web Site: www.ewc.edu/index.php/library. *Dir, Libr Serv,* Carmella Martin; E-mail: carmella.martin0906@ewc.edu; *Circ Librn,* Michael A Wolfe; Tel: 904-470-8086, E-mail: michael.wol0911@ewc.edu; *Ref Librn,* Juanita E Brown; Tel: 904-470-8082, E-mail: juanita.brown@ewc.edu
Founded 1945. Enrl 1,300; Fac 49; Highest Degree: Bachelor
Library Holdings: AV Mats 2,900; Bk Titles 65,798; Per Subs 150
Special Collections: Afro-American
Function: AV serv, Handicapped accessible, ILL available, Photocopying/Printing, Ref serv available, Wheelchair accessible
Publications: Library Newsletter
Open Mon-Thurs 8am-9pm, Fri 8-5, Sat 9-3, Sun 2-6

C EVEREST UNIVERSITY*, Jacksonville Library, 8226 Phillips Hwy, 32256. Tel: 904-731-4949. FAX: 904-731-0599. *Dir,* Kevin Dobyns
Library Holdings: Bk Vols 4,000
Open Mon-Thurs 9-9, Fri 9-5, Sat 9-1

CL FLORIDA COASTAL SCHOOL OF LAW*, Library & Technology Center, 8787 Baypine Rd, 32256. SAN 378-4266. Tel: 904-680-7600. Interlibrary Loan Service Tel: 904-680-7611. Reference Tel: 904-680-7612. Administration Tel: 904-680-7604. FAX: 904-680-7677. Web Site: www.fcsl.edu/library/index.asp. *Dir,* Alma Nickell Singleton; Tel: 904-680-7601, E-mail: nsingleton@fcsl.edu; *Assoc Dir,* Martha Smith; Tel: 904-680-7602, E-mail: msmith@fcsl.edu; *Assoc Dir, Pub Serv,* Colleen Manning; Tel: 904-680-7615, E-mail: cmanning@fcsl.edu; *Circ Librn,* Ryan Saltz; Tel: 904-680-7663, E-mail: rsaltz@fcsl.edu; *Ref Librn,* Karen Kronenberg; Tel: 904-256-1112, E-mail: kkronenberg@fcsl.edu; *Ref Librn,* Lisa Parisi; Tel: 904-680-7642, E-mail: lparisi@fcsl.edu; *Syst Librn,* Judy Meirose; Tel: 904-680-7603, E-mail: jmeirose@fcsl.edu; *Circ Mgr,* Meredith Evans; Tel: 904-680-7608, E-mail: mevans@fcsl.edu; *Acq,* Position Currently Open; *Cat,* Thomas Latuszek; Tel: 904-680-7637, E-mail: tlatuszek@fcsl.edu; Staff 7 (MLS 7)
Founded 1996. Enrl 1,000; Fac 42; Highest Degree: Doctorate
Library Holdings: AV Mats 191; Bk Titles 21,566; Bk Vols 139,432; Per Subs 3,139
Automation Activity & Vendor Info: (Acquisitions) Innovative Interfaces, Inc; (Cataloging) Innovative Interfaces, Inc; (Circulation) Innovative Interfaces, Inc; (Course Reserve) Innovative Interfaces, Inc; (OPAC) Innovative Interfaces, Inc; (Serials) Innovative Interfaces, Inc
Function: ILL available, Ref serv available
Partic in Lyrasis; Northeast Florida Library Information Network
Restriction: Not open to pub

C FLORIDA STATE COLLEGE AT JACKSONVILLE, Kent Campus Library & Learning Commons, 3939 Roosevelt Blvd, C-100, 32205. SAN 337-5846. Tel: 904-381-3522. Reference Tel: 904-381-3545. FAX: 904-381-3579. Web Site: www.fscj.edu/library. *Assoc Dean,* Victoria McGlone; E-mail: victoria.mcglone@fscj.edu; Staff 1 (MLS 1)
Founded 1966
Wireless access
Partic in Florida Library Information Network; Northeast Florida Library Information Network
Open Mon-Thurs 7:30am-9pm, Fri & Sat 8-3
Friends of the Library Group

Departmental Libraries:

DEERWOOD CENTER LIBRARY, 9911 Old Baymeadows Rd, 32256. Tel: 904-997-2562. FAX: 904-997-2571. Web Site: www.fscj.edu. *Head Librn,* Jametoria Burton; Tel: 904-997-2563, E-mail: jburton@fscj.edu; Staff 2 (MLS 1, Non-MLS 1)
Founded 2000. Enrl 9,337; Highest Degree: Associate
Library Holdings: Bk Titles 13,709; Per Subs 120
Automation Activity & Vendor Info: (ILL) Ex Libris Group; (Media Booking) Ex Libris Group; (Serials) Ex Libris Group
Database Vendor: Factiva.com, Gale Cengage Learning, JSTOR, Newsbank, OCLC WorldShare Interlibrary Loan, ProQuest, Wilson - Wilson Web
Function: ILL available
Partic in LINCC
Open Mon-Thurs 8-8, Fri 8-1, Sat 9-1

DOWNTOWN CAMPUS, 101 W State St, Bldg A, Rm A-2102, 32202-3056. SAN 337-5811. Tel: 904-633-8368. Reference Tel: 904-633-8169. FAX: 904-633-8328. *Mgr,* Jennifer R Grey; Tel: 904-632-3305, E-mail: jennifer.grey@fscj.edu; *Librn,* Sheri Brown; Tel: 904-633-8414, E-mail: sheri.a.brown@fscj.edu
Library Holdings: Bk Vols 50,000; Per Subs 285
Open Mon-Thurs 8-7:30, Fri 8-3, Sat 9-3

NASSAU CENTER LIBRARY, 76346 William Burgess Blvd, Yulee, 32097. Tel: 904-548-4468. FAX: 904-548-4427. *Mgr,* Catherine Hodges; E-mail: chodges@fscj.edu

NORTH CAMPUS, 4501 Capper Rd, 32218-4499. SAN 337-5870. Tel: 904-766-6717. Interlibrary Loan Service Tel: 904-766-6634. Reference Tel: 904-766-6714. Administration Tel: 904-766-6765. FAX: 904-766-6640. *Interim Assoc Dean,* Youlana Henry; *Assoc Dean, Libr & Learning Commons,* Position Currently Open; *Librn,* Mary Dumbleton; *Librn,* Victoria Mary McGlone; Tel: 904-766-6714, E-mail: vmcglone@fccj.edu; Staff 3 (MLS 3)
Enrl 7,700; Highest Degree: Bachelor
Library Holdings: Bk Vols 38,000; Per Subs 325
Open Mon-Thurs 7:30am-10pm, Fri 7:30-5, Sat 8-4

SOUTH CAMPUS, 11901 Beach Blvd, 32246-6624. SAN 337-5781. Tel: 904-646-2173. Circulation Tel: 904-646-2174. FAX: 904-646-2155. *Libr Mgr,* Charlotte Clements; *Dir, Learning Serv,* Denise Norris; E-mail: dnorris@fccj.edu; *Librn,* Barbara Markham
Library Holdings: AV Mats 7,200; Bk Vols 79,531; Per Subs 523
Open Mon-Thurs 7:30am-9pm, Fri 7:30-5, Sat 9-5, Sun 1-5

J ITT TECHNICAL INSTITUTE, Learning Resource Center, 7011 A C Skinner Pkwy, Ste 140, 32256. Tel: 904-573-9100, Ext 135. Toll Free Tel: 800-318-1264. FAX: 904-573-0512. Web Site: www.itt-tech.edu. *Librn,* Tristan Denmark; Tel: 904-674-2867, E-mail: tdenmark@itt-tech.edu; Staff 2 (MLS 1, Non-MLS 1)
Founded 1991. Enrl 600; Fac 30; Highest Degree: Bachelor
Library Holdings: AV Mats 2,000; e-books 20,000; Bk Vols 7,000; Per Subs 45
Automation Activity & Vendor Info: (Cataloging) Follett Software; (Circulation) Follett Software
Wireless access
Partic in Fla Libr Asn; Northeast Florida Library Information Network
Open Mon-Fri 8am-10:30pm, Sat 8-2

P JACKSONVILLE PUBLIC LIBRARY*, 303 N Laura St, 32202-3505. SAN 337-5935. Tel: 904-630-2665. Circulation Tel: 904-630-1984. Interlibrary Loan Service Tel: 904-630-2986. Reference Tel: 904-630-1962, 904-630-2793. Administration Tel: 904-630-1994. FAX: 904-630-2431. Interlibrary Loan Service FAX: 904-630-2734. Administration FAX: 904-630-1343. TDD: 904-630-2740. E-mail: libdir@coj.net. Web Site: jaxpubliclibrary.org. *Dir,* Barbara A B Gubbin; *Dep Dir,* Carolyn Williams; Tel: 904-630-1636, E-mail: cshehee@coj.net; *Dep Dir, Admin & Finance,* Mark Merritt; Tel: 904-630-1171, Fax: 904-630-2450, E-mail: MMerritt@coj.net; *Asst Dir, Commun Relations & Mkt,* Kathy Lussier; Tel: 904-630-7595, E-mail: klussier@coj.net; *Asst Dir, Fac,* Eric Lawrence; Tel: 904-630-7561, Fax: 904-630-2066; *Asst Dir, Pub Serv,* Julie McNeil; Tel: 904-630-1181, Fax: 904-630-1435, E-mail: jmcneil@coj.net; *Asst Dir, Support Serv,* Gretchen Mitchell; Tel: 904-630-1666, Fax: 904-630-1435, E-mail: gmitch@coj.net; *Bibliog Syst & Access Mgr,* Lynn Jacobson; Tel: 904-630-1318, E-mail: jacobson@coj.net; *Fac Mgr,* Position Currently Open; *Mgr, E-Serv & Digital Access,* Karen Walker; Tel: 904-630-1155, E-mail: kwalker@coj.net; *Mgr, Strategic Initiatives,* Richard Mott; Tel: 904-630-2407, E-mail: rmott@coj.net; *Mgr, Youth Serv & Commun Outreach,* Laura Minnich; Tel: 904-630-2434, E-mail: lminnich@coj.net; *Tech Syst Adminr,* Lisa Peterson; Tel: 904-630-1167, E-mail: lpeterson@coj.net; Staff 359 (MLS 133, Non-MLS 226)
Founded 1903. Pop 879,602; Circ 8,396,991
Oct 2012-Sept 2013 Income (Main Library and Branch(s)) $36,429,569, State $1,071,161, Federal $86,374, County $34,567,052, Locally Generated Income $595,630, Other $109,352. Mats Exp $3,831,346, Books $2,380,062, Per/Ser (Incl. Access Fees) $88,612, Other Print Mats $3,176, Micro $4,222, AV Equip $22,579, AV Mat $386,537, Electronic Ref Mat (Incl. Access Fees) $944,618, Presv $1,540. Sal $11,716,689 (Prof $11,599,926)
Library Holdings: AV Mats 493,208; CDs 224,667; DVDs 231,501; e-books 28,492; Electronic Media & Resources 47,300; Bk Vols 2,500,375; Per Subs 2,826; Talking Bks 79,033; Videos 37,040
Special Collections: African-American Coll; Delius Coll, mss,music, secondary sources; Digital Library Coll; Florida Coll; Genealogy Coll, Southeast Region; Holocaust Coll; Lewis Ansbacher Map Coll; Nonprofit Resources. State Document Depository; US Document Depository
Automation Activity & Vendor Info: (Acquisitions) SirsiDynix; (Cataloging) SirsiDynix; (Circulation) SirsiDynix; (ILL) OCLC; (OPAC) SirsiDynix; (Serials) SirsiDynix
Database Vendor: ABC-CLIO, EBSCO Auto Repair Reference, EBSCOhost, Foundation Center, Gale Cengage Learning, Mergent Online, Newsbank, Overdrive, Inc, ProQuest, SerialsSolutions, SirsiDynix, TumbleBookLibrary, World Book Online
Wireless access
Function: Adult bk club, Adult literacy prog, After school storytime, Art exhibits, Audiobks via web, Bilingual assistance for Spanish patrons, Bk club(s), Bks on cassette, Bks on CD, Children's prog, Citizenship assistance, Computer training, Computers for patron use, Copy machines, e-mail serv, E-Reserves, Electronic databases & coll, Exhibits, Free DVD rentals, Govt ref serv, Handicapped accessible, Holiday prog, Homework prog, ILL available, Learning ctr, Literacy & newcomer serv, Microfiche/film & reading machines, Music CDs, Newsp ref libr, Online ref, Online searches, Outreach serv, OverDrive digital audio bks, Photocopying/Printing, Preschool outreach, Prog for adults, Prog for children & young adult, Pub access computers, Ref serv available, Spanish lang bks, Spoken cassettes & CDs, Spoken cassettes & DVDs, Summer reading prog, Tax forms, Teen prog, Telephone ref, VHS videos, Video lending libr, Web-catalog, Wheelchair accessible
Publications: All About E-Services (Brochure); Annual Report (Annual report); Center for Adult Learning (Brochure); Discovery Awaits Online (Brochure); E-newsletter (Monthly newsletter); Find a Job, Start a Business (Brochure); GET CARDED (Brochure); Jean Ribault Mural (Brochure); Quarterly Update (Quarterly); Special Collections (Brochure); The Conference Center (Brochure); Traveling Tales (Brochure); Youth Services for Educators (Brochure); Youth Services for Parents & Caregivers (Brochure)
Partic in Fla Computer Catalogue of Monographic Holdings; Lyrasis; Northeast Florida Library Information Network; OCLC Online Computer Library Center, Inc; Urban Libraries Council (ULC)
Special Services for the Deaf - Closed caption videos
Special Services for the Blind - Talking bks
Friends of the Library Group
Branches: 21
ARGYLE BRANCH, 7973 Old Middleburg Rd S, 32222-1817. Tel: 904-573-3164. FAX: 904-573-3162. *Br Mgr,* Amber Holley; Staff 8 (MLS 3, Non-MLS 5)
Circ 345,233
Library Holdings: Bk Vols 60,381
Open Mon & Tues 12-9, Wed-Sat 10-6
BEACHES BRANCH, 600 Third St, Neptune Beach, 32266-5014, SAN 337-6087. Tel: 904-241-1141. FAX: 904-241-4965. *Br Mgr,* Pat Doyle; Staff 15 (MLS 5, Non-MLS 10)
Circ 597,806
Library Holdings: Bk Vols 134,501
Special Collections: Joe Gill Business Coll
Open Mon-Thurs 10-9, Fri & Sat 10-6, Sun 1-6
Friends of the Library Group
BRADHAM-BROOKS NORTHWEST BRANCH, 1755 Edgewood Ave W, 32208-7206, SAN 371-4748. Tel: 904-765-5402. FAX: 904-768-7609. *Br Mgr,* Sara Radovic; Staff 9 (MLS 3, Non-MLS 6)
Circ 146,305
Library Holdings: Bk Vols 92,695
Open Mon & Thurs Noon-9, Tue, Wed, Fri & Sat, 10-6
Friends of the Library Group
BRENTWOOD BRANCH, 3725 Pearl St, 32206-6401, SAN 337-6141. Tel: 904-630-0924. FAX: 904-630-0441. *Br Mgr,* Marshelle Berry; Staff 4 (MLS 1, Non-MLS 3)
Circ 67,832
Library Holdings: Bk Vols 16,911
Open Mon-Thurs & Sat 10-6
RAIFORD A BROWN EASTSIDE BRANCH, 1390 Harrison St, 32206-5324, SAN 337-6028. Tel: 904-630-5466. FAX: 904-630-5463. *Br Mgr,* Marshelle Berry; Staff 2 (Non-MLS 2)
Circ 39,984
Library Holdings: Bk Vols 13,089
Open Mon-Thurs & Sat 10-6
DALLAS JAMES GRAHAM BRANCH, 2304 N Myrtle Ave, 32209-5099, SAN 337-5994. Tel: 904-630-0922. FAX: 904-630-0439. *Br Mgr,* Daniel Kibler; Staff 6 (MLS 2, Non-MLS 4)
Circ 76,090
Library Holdings: Bk Vols 35,891
Open Mon & Tues 12-8, Wed-Sat 10-6
HIGHLANDS BRANCH, 1826 Dunn Ave, 32218-4712, SAN 325-416X. Tel: 904-757-7702. FAX: 904-696-4328. *Br Mgr,* Donna Thomas; Staff 15 (MLS 5, Non-MLS 10)
Circ 439,687
Library Holdings: Bk Vols 153,090
Open Mon-Thurs 10-9, Fri & Sat 10-6, Sun 1-6
Friends of the Library Group
MANDARIN BRANCH, 3330 Kori Rd, 32257-5454, SAN 328-7254. Tel: 904-262-5201. FAX: 904-292-1029. *Br Mgr,* Lynne Baldwin; Staff 16 (MLS 6, Non-MLS 10)
Circ 638,616
Library Holdings: Bk Vols 150,073
Open Mon-Thurs 10-9, Fri & Sat 10-6
MAXVILLE BRANCH, 8375 Maxville Rd, 32234-2748. Tel: 904-289-7563. FAX: 904-289-9285. *Br Mgr,* Jane Harris
Circ 52,546
Library Holdings: Bk Vols 27,884
Open Mon 11-8, Tues-Thurs & Sat 10-6
MURRAY HILL BRANCH, 918 Edgewood Ave S, 32205-5341, SAN 337-6117. Tel: 904-384-2665. FAX: 904-381-1104. *Br Mgr,* Michael Sullivan; Staff 7 (MLS 2, Non-MLS 5)
Circ 148,022
Library Holdings: Bk Vols 45,584
Open Mon & Tues 12-9, Wed-Sat 10-6
PABLO CREEK REGIONAL, 13295 Beach Blvd, 32246-7259. Tel: 904-992-7101. FAX: 904-992-3987. *Br Mgr,* Bob Silkett; Staff 18 (MLS 6, Non-MLS 12)
Circ 955,508
Library Holdings: Bk Vols 160,129
Open Mon-Thurs 10-9, Fri & Sat 10-6
REGENCY SQUARE BRANCH, 9900 Regency Square Blvd, 32225-6539. Tel: 904-726-5142. FAX: 904-726-5153. TDD: 904-726-5152. *Br Mgr,* Sally Doherty; Staff 16 (MLS 6, Non-MLS 10)
Circ 639,892
Library Holdings: Bk Vols 140,058
Special Services for the Deaf - TDD equip
Open Mon-Thurs 10-9, Fri & Sat 10-6
SAN MARCO BRANCH, 1513 LaSalle St, 32207-8653, SAN 337-6206. Tel: 904-858-2907. FAX: 904-306-2182. *Br Mgr,* Pam Thompson; Staff 8 (MLS 3, Non-MLS 5)
Circ 291,012
Library Holdings: Bk Vols 64,841
Open Mon & Tues 12-9, Wed-Sat 10-6
Friends of the Library Group
SOUTH MANDARIN BRANCH, 12125 San Jose Blvd, 32223-2636. Tel: 904-288-6385. FAX: 904-288-6399. *Br Mgr,* Ed Murray; Staff 16 (MLS 6, Non-MLS 10)
Circ 647,739
Library Holdings: Bk Vols 100,955
Open Mon-Thurs 10-9, Fri & Sat 10-6, Sun 1-6
SOUTHEAST REGIONAL, 10599 Deerwood Park Blvd, 32256-0507, SAN 377-6204. Tel: 904-996-0325. FAX: 904-996-0340. *Br Mgr,* Michael Sullivan; Staff 17 (MLS 7, Non-MLS 10)
Circ 909,786
Library Holdings: Bk Vols 210,259
Open Mon-Thurs 10-9, Fri & Sat 10-6

P TALKING BOOKS FOR THE BLIND & PHYSICALLY HANDICAPPED, 303 N Laura St, Conference Level, 32202, SAN 375-5770. Tel: 904-630-1999. *Talking Bks Libr Mgr,* Jonathan Reynolds; Staff 3 (MLS 2, Non-MLS 1)
Founded 1974. Circ 169,490
Library Holdings: AV Mats 3,326; DVDs 648; e-books 19,703; e-journals 48; Per Subs 5; Talking Bks 79,033; Videos 1,769
Function: Writing prog
Mem of Reaching Across Illinois Library System (RAILS)
Special Services for the Blind - Assistive/Adapted tech devices, equip & products; Computer with voice synthesizer for visually impaired persons
Open Mon-Fri 9-5

UNIVERSITY PARK BRANCH, 3435 University Blvd N, 32277-2464. Tel: 904-630-1265. FAX: 904-744-6892. *Br Mgr,* Michael Rouse; Staff 12 (MLS 4, Non-MLS 8)
Circ 392,515
Library Holdings: Bk Vols 83,748
Open Mon & Tues 12-9, Wed-Sat 10-6

CHARLES WEBB WESCONNETT REGIONAL, 6887 103rd St, 32210-6897, SAN 337-6230. Tel: 904-778-7305. FAX: 904-777-2262. *Br Mgr,* Marshelle Berry; Staff 15 (MLS 5, Non-MLS 10)
Circ 548,784
Library Holdings: Bk Vols 141,143
Open Mon-Thurs 10-9, Fri & Sat 10-6, Sun 1-6

WEST REGIONAL, 1425 Chaffee Rd S, 32221-1119. Tel: 904-693-1448. FAX: 904-693-1470. *Br Mgr,* Jane Harris; Staff 18 (MLS 5, Non-MLS 13)
Circ 651,499
Library Holdings: Bk Vols 189,782
Open Mon-Thurs 10-9, Fri & Sat 10-6

WESTBROOK BRANCH, 2809 Commonwealth Ave, 32254-2599, SAN 337-596X. Tel: 904-384-7424. FAX: 904-381-1107. *Br Mgr,* Marshelle Berry; Staff 7 (MLS 2, Non-MLS 5)
Founded 1959. Circ 64,998
Library Holdings: Bk Vols 15,563
Open Mon-Thurs & Sat 10-6

WILLOWBRANCH BRANCH, 2875 Park St, 32205-8099, SAN 337-6265. Tel: 904-381-8490. FAX: 904-381-8495. *Br Mgr,* Donna Carroll; Staff 7 (MLS 2, Non-MLS 5)
Circ 218,714
Library Holdings: Bk Vols 43,882
Open Mon, Tues, Fri & Sat 10-6, Wed & Thurs 12-9
Friends of the Library Group

C JACKSONVILLE UNIVERSITY*, Carl S Swisher Library, 2800 University Blvd N, 32211-3394. SAN 302-976X. Tel: 904-256-7267. Circulation Tel: 904-256-7277. Interlibrary Loan Service Tel: 904-256-7275. Reference Tel: 904-256-7263. FAX: 904-256-7259. Circulation FAX: 904-256-7191. Web Site: www.ju.edu/library. *Libr Dir,* David M Jones; E-mail: djones1@ju.edu; *Electronic Res, Ref Librn,* Damon DeBorde; Tel: 904-256-7269, E-mail: ddebord@ju.edu; *Acq, Cat,* Paula McIntyre; Tel: 904-256-7265, E-mail: pmcinty@ju.edu; *Circ Serv, Per,* Linda Matyas; Tel: 904-256-7274, E-mail: lmatyas@ju.edu; *Libr Instruction, Ref Serv,* Anna Large; Tel: 904-256-7263, E-mail: alarge@ju.edu; Staff 13 (MLS 5, Non-MLS 8)
Founded 1934. Enrl 3,400; Fac 242; Highest Degree: Master
Jul 2009-Jun 2010 Income $812,491, Locally Generated Income $12,956. Mats Exp $271,328, Books $32,514, Per/Ser (Incl. Access Fees) $76,698, AV Mat $4,127, Electronic Ref Mat (Incl. Access Fees) $117,637, Presv $1,285. Sal $418,919 (Prof $261,378)
Library Holdings: Bks on Deafness & Sign Lang 114; CDs 6,051; DVDs 801; e-books 68,972; e-journals 51,959; Electronic Media & Resources 2,571; Music Scores 9,197; Bk Vols 273,986; Per Subs 350; Videos 616
Special Collections: Delius Coll; Jacksonville Historical Society Archives; Jacksonville University Archives; Rare Books. State Document Depository; US Document Depository
Subject Interests: Bus, Educ, Fine arts, Liberal arts, Nursing, Orthodontics
Automation Activity & Vendor Info: (Acquisitions) Ex Libris Group; (Cataloging) Ex Libris Group; (Circulation) Ex Libris Group; (Course Reserve) Ex Libris Group; (ILL) OCLC WorldShare Interlibrary Loan; (OPAC) Ex Libris Group; (Serials) EBSCO Online
Database Vendor: Dun & Bradstreet, EBSCOhost, Elsevier MDL, infoUSA, LexisNexis, McGraw-Hill, OCLC FirstSearch, ProQuest, Standard & Poor's
Wireless access
Function: Telephone ref
Partic in Florida Library Information Network; Lyrasis; Northeast Florida Library Information Network; OCLC Online Computer Library Center, Inc
Open Mon-Thurs 7:30am-11pm, Fri 8-6, Sat 10-5, Sun 2-11
Friends of the Library Group

C JONES COLLEGE*, James V Forrestal Library, 5353 Arlington Expressway, Rm 311, 32211. SAN 302-9778. Tel: 904-743-1122, Ext 101. FAX: 904-743-4446. Web Site: www.jones.edu. *Dir,* Evelyn Brown; E-mail: ebrown@jones.edu; Staff 3 (MLS 1, Non-MLS 2)
Founded 1967. Enrl 1,400; Fac 45; Highest Degree: Doctorate
Jan 2005-Dec 2005 Income Parent Institution $30,000. Mats Exp $30,000, Books $12,500, Per/Ser (Incl. Access Fees) $3,500, Other Print Mats $500, AV Equip $1,000, AV Mat $2,500, Electronic Ref Mat (Incl. Access Fees) $10,000
Library Holdings: AV Mats 1,679; Large Print Bks 50; Bk Titles 6,498; Bk Vols 10,647; Per Subs 45; Spec Interest Per Sub 39
Subject Interests: Allied health, Bus & mgt, Law
Automation Activity & Vendor Info: (Cataloging) Thomson ISI ResearchSoft; (Circulation) Thomson ISI ResearchSoft
Database Vendor: EBSCOhost, OCLC FirstSearch, ProQuest
Function: Audio & video playback equip for onsite use, CD-ROM, Copy machines, Distance learning, Electronic databases & coll, Online ref, Online searches, Orientations, Photocopying/Printing, Ref serv available, VHS videos
Partic in Northeast Florida Library Information Network
Open Mon-Thurs 8:30-8, Fri 8-1
Restriction: Open to students, fac & staff

R RIVERSIDE PRESBYTERIAN CHURCH*, Jean Miller Memorial Library, 849 Park St, 32204. SAN 302-9816. Tel: 904-355-4585. FAX: 904-355-4508. Web Site: www.rpcjax.org. *Librn,* Arden Brugger; Staff 1 (MLS 1)
Founded 1946
Library Holdings: Bk Vols 3,167
Function: Archival coll
Restriction: In-house use for visitors, Mem only

M SAINT VINCENT'S MEDICAL CENTER*, Doctors Library, One Shircliff Way, 32204. SAN 302-9832. Tel: 904-308-8165. FAX: 904-308-2976. *Med Librn,* Deborah Lawless; Staff 1 (MLS 1)
Library Holdings: Bk Titles 1,000; Bk Vols 1,500; Per Subs 125
Database Vendor: OVID Technologies
Wireless access
Function: ILL available
Restriction: Not open to pub

CR TRINITY BAPTIST COLLEGE LIBRARY*, 800 Hammond Blvd, 32221-1342. Tel: 904-596-2508. Administration Tel: 904-596-2507. FAX: 904-596-2531. *Dir,* John Lucy; E-mail: jlucy@tbc.edu; *Asst Librn,* Janice Claxton; E-mail: jclaxton@tbc.edu; Staff 2 (MLS 1, Non-MLS 1)
Founded 1974. Enrl 469; Fac 41; Highest Degree: Master
Jul 2005-Jun 2006. Mats Exp $34,700, Books $23,000, Per/Ser (Incl. Access Fees) $4,500, Electronic Ref Mat (Incl. Access Fees) $6,200, Presv $1,000
Library Holdings: Bks on Deafness & Sign Lang 50; CDs 185; DVDs 240; e-books 365; Music Scores 50; Bk Vols 35,000; Per Subs 120; Videos 690
Subject Interests: Baptist hist, Educ, Relig
Automation Activity & Vendor Info: (Acquisitions) A-G Canada Ltd; (Cataloging) Book Systems; (Circulation) Follett Software; (OPAC) Follett Software
Database Vendor: Electric Library, Gale Cengage Learning, ProQuest
Wireless access
Partic in Library & Information Resources Network (LIRN); Northeast Florida Library Information Network

M UNITED MEDICAL TECHNOLOGIES CORP*, Medical Cybernetics Foundation Library, 3804 Arrow Lakes Dr S, 32257. SAN 372-6282. Tel: 904-288-8832. *Librn,* Bob Frost
Founded 1986
Library Holdings: Bk Titles 4,000; Per Subs 4,000

A UNITED STATES ARMY*, Corps of Engineers Technical Library, 701 San Marco Blvd, Rm 430-W, 32207. (Mail add: PO Box 4970, 32232-0019), SAN 337-629X. Tel: 904-232-3643. FAX: 904-232-1838. *Librn,* Oriana B Armstrong; E-mail: oriana.b.armstrong@usace.army.mil; Staff 1 (MLS 1)
Founded 1978
Library Holdings: Bk Vols 27,000; Per Subs 400
Special Collections: Cross Florida Barge Canal Study
Subject Interests: Civil eng, Construction, Eng, Recreation, Sci tech
Automation Activity & Vendor Info: (Cataloging) OCLC; (ILL) OCLC
Database Vendor: OCLC FirstSearch
Partic in Dialog Corp; Legislate; LePac; OCLC Online Computer Library Center, Inc
Open Mon-Fri 6:30am-3pm

AM UNITED STATES NAVY*, Naval Hospital Library, 2080 Child St, 32214. SAN 337-6389. Tel: 904-542-7300. FAX: 904-542-7093. *Librn,* Bettye W Stilley
Library Holdings: Bk Titles 600; Per Subs 50
Subject Interests: Med
Restriction: Staff use only

M UNIVERSITY OF FLORIDA HEALTH SCIENCE CENTER-JACKSONVILLE*, Borland Health Sciences Library, 653-1 W Eighth St, 32209-6511. SAN 302-9751. Tel: 904-244-3240. FAX: 904-244-3191. Web Site: www.borland.ufl.edu. *Dir,* Kathleen Moeller; *Tech Serv,* Marina Salcedo; E-mail: msalcedo@ufl.edu; Staff 5 (MLS 3, Non-MLS 2)
Founded 1961
Library Holdings: Bk Vols 6,000; Per Subs 560
Special Collections: Florida Public Health History
Subject Interests: Allied health, Dentistry, Med, Nursing
Wireless access
Open Mon-Thurs 8-7, Fri 8-5

C UNIVERSITY OF NORTH FLORIDA*, Thomas G Carpenter Library, Bldg 12-Library, One UNF Dr, 32224-2645. SAN 320-9385. Tel: 904-620-2616. Circulation Tel: 904-620-2615. Administration Tel: 904-620-2553. FAX: 904-620-2719. Interlibrary Loan Service FAX: 904-620-2613. Web Site: www.unf.edu/library. *Dean of Libr,* Dr Shirley Hallblade; Tel: 904-620-2587, E-mail: shirley.hallblade@unf.edu; *Assoc Dean of Libr,* Kathleen F Cohen; Tel: 904-620-2599, E-mail: kcohen@unf.edu; *Dir, Libr Syst & Tech,* Michael Kucsak; Tel: 904-620-2552, E-mail: michael.kucsak@unf.edu; *Dir, Pub Serv,* Laurel Crump; Tel: 904-620-2247, E-mail: laurel.crump@unf.edu; *Head, Access Serv,* Robb Waltner; Tel: 904-620-1515, E-mail: rwaltner@unf.edu; *Head, Cat,* Jeffrey T Bowen; Tel: 904-620-1502, E-mail: j.t.bowen@unf.edu; *Head, Ref,* Sarah M Philips; Tel: 904-620-1530, E-mail: sphilips@unf.edu; *Head, Ser,* Victoria Stanton; Tel: 904-620-1512, E-mail: vstanton@unf.edu; *Govt Doc,* Courtenay McLeland; Tel: 904-620-1529, E-mail: d.c.mcleland@unf.edu; *Spec Coll & Archives Librn,* Eileen Brady; Tel: 904-620-1533, E-mail: ebrady@unf.edu; Staff 46.5 (MLS 21, Non-MLS 25.5)
Founded 1970. Enrl 16,000; Fac 540; Highest Degree: Doctorate
Jul 2007-Jun 2008 Income $4,452,394. Mats Exp $1,525,484, Books $156,209, Per/Ser (Incl. Access Fees) $1,337,696, AV Mat $5,913, Presv $25,666. Sal $2,115,318 (Prof $1,277,359)
Library Holdings: AV Mats 30,718; CDs 13,544; DVDs 782; Music Scores 486; Bk Titles 511,858; Bk Vols 813,389; Per Subs 2,350; Videos 7,977
Special Collections: Arthur N Sollee Papers; Eartha White Memorial Coll, memorabilia, photog; Senator Jack E Mathews Papers; University Archives
Subject Interests: Bus & mgt, Econ, Educ, Nursing
Automation Activity & Vendor Info: (Acquisitions) Ex Libris Group; (Cataloging) Ex Libris Group; (Circulation) Ex Libris Group; (Course Reserve) Ex Libris Group; (ILL) OCLC ILLiad; (OPAC) Ex Libris Group; (Serials) Ex Libris Group
Database Vendor: Cambridge Scientific Abstracts, Gale Cengage Learning, JSTOR, LexisNexis, Newsbank, OCLC FirstSearch, OCLC WorldShare Interlibrary Loan, ProQuest, ScienceDirect, SerialsSolutions, Westlaw, Wiley, Wilson - Wilson Web
Wireless access
Publications: Annual Report
Partic in Lyrasis; Northeast Florida Library Information Network; OCLC Online Computer Library Center, Inc
Special Services for the Deaf - TDD equip
Restriction: Open to fac, students & qualified researchers

JUPITER

C FLORIDA ATLANTIC UNIVERSITY*, John D MacArthur Campus Library, 5353 Parkside Dr, 33458. SAN 371-375X. Tel: 561-799-8530. FAX: 561-799-8587. Web Site: www.library.fau.edu/npb/npb.htm. *Dean, Univ Libr,* Dr William Miller; Tel: 561-297-3760; *Dir,* Ethan J Allen, Jr; Tel: 561-799-8030, E-mail: eallen@fau.edu; Staff 6 (MLS 2, Non-MLS 4)
Founded 1972. Enrl 1,300; Fac 77; Highest Degree: Doctorate
Library Holdings: DVDs 3,000; Bk Vols 80,000; Per Subs 19; Videos 336
Special Collections: Children's Books; Senior Theses
Automation Activity & Vendor Info: (Acquisitions) Ex Libris Group; (Cataloging) Ex Libris Group; (Circulation) Ex Libris Group; (Course Reserve) Ex Libris Group; (ILL) OCLC ILLiad; (OPAC) Ex Libris Group; (Serials) Ex Libris Group
Database Vendor: ABC-CLIO, ACM (Association for Computing Machinery), Agricola, Alexander Street Press, American Chemical Society, American Mathematical Society, American Physical Society, American Psychological Association (APA), Amigos Library Services, ARTstor, ASCE Research Library, BioOne, Bowker, Cambridge Scientific Abstracts, Checkpoint Systems, Inc, Cinahl, Community of Science (COS), CountryWatch, CQ Press, CRC Press/Taylor & Francis Group, Dun & Bradstreet, EBSCOhost, Elsevier, Emerald, Ex Libris Group, Facts on File, Gale Cengage Learning, Gallup, Greenwood Publishing Group, H W Wilson, Haworth Pres Inc, Hoovers, IEEE (Institute of Electrical & Electronics Engineers), infoUSA, Ingenta, ISI Web of Knowledge, JSTOR, LexisNexis, LGB & Associates, Inc, Medline, Mergent Online, Modern Language Association, Newsbank, Newsbank-Readex, OCLC ArticleFirst, OCLC FirstSearch, OCLC WorldShare Interlibrary Loan, OVID Technologies, Oxford Online, Plunkett Research, Ltd, Project MUSE, ProQuest, PubMed, RefWorks, Safari Books Online, Sage, SBRnet (Sports Business Research Network), ScienceDirect, SerialsSolutions, Springer-Verlag, Standard & Poor's, ValueLine, Westlaw, Wiley InterScience, Wilson - Wilson Web, YBP Library Services
Wireless access
Function: Audio & video playback equip for onsite use, Bks on CD, CD-ROM, Computers for patron use, Copy machines, Digital talking bks, Doc delivery serv, Electronic databases & coll, Exhibits, For res purposes, Handicapped accessible, ILL available, Music CDs, Online info literacy tutorials on the web & in blackboard, Online searches, Orientations, Photocopying/Printing, Pub access computers, Ref & res, Scanner, Telephone ref, Video lending libr, Web-catalog, Wheelchair accessible
Partic in Fla Ctr for Libr Automation; Lyrasis
Special Services for the Blind - Reader equip
Restriction: Open to fac, students & qualified researchers, Open to pub for ref & circ; with some limitations

KENNEDY SPACE CENTER

G NASA, John F Kennedy Space Center Library, 32899. SAN 302-9905. Tel: 321-867-3600. FAX: 321-867-4534. E-mail: ksc-dl-library@mail.nasa.gov. *Chief Librn,* Bennett Wight; *Acq,* Deborah Guelzow; *Archivist,* Elaine Liston; *Doc,* Lori Uffner
Founded 1962
Library Holdings: Bk Titles 18,000; Per Subs 900
Special Collections: Archives Coll; Kennedy Space Center History Coll, photog
Subject Interests: Aerospace sci
Automation Activity & Vendor Info: (Cataloging) SirsiDynix; (Circulation) SirsiDynix; (ILL) OCLC
Publications: Chronology of KSC & Related Events (Annual); Index for the Space Transportation System; Index of KSC Specifications & Standards; Index to Spaceport News (official Space Center newspaper)
Partic in Aerospace Res Info Network; Cent Fla Libr Consortium; Florida Library Information Network; NASA Libraries Information System-NASA Galaxie
Restriction: Open by appt only

KEY WEST

J FLORIDA KEYS COMMUNITY COLLEGE LIBRARY*, Bldg A, 2nd Fl, 5901 College Rd, 33040. SAN 302-9913. Tel: 305-809-3194. Administration Tel: 305-809-3501. FAX: 305-292-5162. E-mail: library@fkcc.edu. Web Site: library.fkcc.edu. *Dir of Libr,* Juana Careaga; Tel: 305-809-3501, E-mail: juana.careaga@fkcc.edu; *Librn,* Beverly Westermeyer; Staff 5 (MLS 2, Non-MLS 3)
Founded 1965. Enrl 259; Fac 36
Library Holdings: AV Mats 2,865; Bk Titles 29,769; Bk Vols 32,746; Per Subs 163
Automation Activity & Vendor Info: (Acquisitions) Ex Libris Group; (Cataloging) Ex Libris Group; (Circulation) Ex Libris Group; (Course Reserve) Ex Libris Group; (ILL) OCLC; (Media Booking) Ex Libris Group; (OPAC) Ex Libris Group; (Serials) Ex Libris Group
Wireless access
Partic in Lyrasis; Southwest Florida Library Network
Open Mon 8:30-9, Tues-Thurs 8:30-8:30, Fri & Sat 8:30-4
Friends of the Library Group

P MONROE COUNTY PUBLIC LIBRARY*, 700 Fleming St, 33040. SAN 337-6443. Tel: 305-292-3595. FAX: 305-295-3368. Web Site: www.keyslibraries.org. *Dir of Libr,* Norma Kula; Tel: 305-853-7349, Fax: 305-451-4536, E-mail: kula-norma@monroecounty-fl.gov; *HQ Adminr,* Position Currently Open; *Libr Adminr,* Anne Layton Rice; Tel: 305-292-3594, E-mail: rice-anne@monroecounty-fl.gov; *Ch,* Nancy Howanitz; E-mail: howanitz-nancy@monroecounty-fl.gov; *Historian,* Tom Hambright; E-mail: hambright-tom@monroecounty-fl.gov; *Circ,* Kris Neihouse; E-mail: neihouse-kris@monroecounty-fl.gov; *Ref Serv,* Robin Henderson; E-mail: henderson-robin@monroecounty-fl.gov; *Tech Serv,* Juana Careaga; Tel: 305-809-5263, E-mail: careaga-juana@monroecounty-fl.gov. Subject Specialists: *Fla Keys hist,* Tom Hambright; Staff 13 (MLS 6, Non-MLS 7)
Founded 1892. Pop 76,000; Circ 392,524
Library Holdings: Bk Vols 183,757; Per Subs 120
Subject Interests: Local hist
Automation Activity & Vendor Info: (Acquisitions) Innovative Interfaces, Inc; (Cataloging) Innovative Interfaces, Inc; (Circulation) Innovative Interfaces, Inc; (ILL) OCLC FirstSearch; (OPAC) Innovative Interfaces, Inc
Database Vendor: Gale Cengage Learning, LearningExpress
Wireless access
Function: Adult bk club, Archival coll, Audiobks via web, Bilingual assistance for Spanish patrons, Bk club(s), Bks on cassette, Bks on CD, Children's prog, Computer training, Computers for patron use, Copy machines, Digital talking bks, Electronic databases & coll, Exhibits, Free DVD rentals, Handicapped accessible, Holiday prog, ILL available, Mail & tel request accepted, Music CDs, Online cat, Online ref, Outside serv via

phone, mail, e-mail & web, OverDrive digital audio bks, Photocopying/Printing, Preschool outreach, Prog for adults, Prog for children & young adult, Pub access computers, Ref serv available, Ref serv in person, Senior outreach, Spanish lang bks, Spoken cassettes & CDs, Spoken cassettes & DVDs, Story hour, Summer reading prog, Tax forms, Teen prog, Telephone ref, Wheelchair accessible
Open Mon, Tues, Thurs & Fri 9:30-6, Wed 9:30-8, Sat 10-6
Friends of the Library Group
Branches: 4
BIG PINE KEY BRANCH, 213 Key Deer Blvd, Big Pine Key, 33043, SAN 376-9143. Tel: 305-872-0992. FAX: 305-289-6304. *Br Mgr,* Stephen Chambers; E-mail: chambers-stephen@monroecounty-fl.gov; Staff 1 (MLS 1)
Open Tues 12-8, Wed-Sat 10-6
Friends of the Library Group
GEORGE DOLEZAL - MARATHON BRANCH, 3251 Overseas Hwy, Marathon, 33050, SAN 337-6532. Tel: 305-743-5156. FAX: 305-289-6093. *Br Mgr,* Gloria Goodman; E-mail: goodman-gloria@monroecounty-fl.gov
Open Mon & Wed 10-8, Tues & Thurs-Sat 10-6
Friends of the Library Group
KEY LARGO BRANCH, Tradewinds Shopping Ctr, 101485 Overseas Hwy, Key Largo, 33037, SAN 337-6508. Tel: 305-451-2396. FAX: 305-853-7311. *Br Mgr,* Paulette Sullivan; E-mail: sullivan-paulette@monroecounty-fl.gov
Open Mon & Wed 10-8, Tues & Thurs-Sat 10-6
Friends of the Library Group
HELEN WADLEY BRANCH, PO Box 1129, Islamorada, 33036-1129, SAN 337-6478. Tel: 305-664-4645. FAX: 305-853-7312. *Br Mgr,* Kathy Ebert; E-mail: ebert-kathy@monroecounty-fl.gov
Open Wed-Fri 9:30-6, Tues 9:30-8, Sat 10-6
Friends of the Library Group

KISSIMMEE

CR JOHNSON UNIVERSITY FLORIDA LIBRARY, 1011 Bill Beck Blvd, 34744. Tel: 407-569-1386. E-mail: LibraryFL@JohnsonU.edu. Web Site: JohnsonU.edu/Florida/Student-Life/Campus-Services/Library-Resources.aspx. *Assoc Librn,* Linda Stark; Tel: 407-569-1318, Fax: 321-206-2007, E-mail: lstark@johnsonu.edu; *Libr Support Serv Asst,* Marla Black; E-mail: mblack@JohnsonU.edu; Staff 1 (MLS 1)
Founded 1976. Enrl 300; Fac 1; Highest Degree: Bachelor
Library Holdings: Audiobooks 20; AV Mats 19,383; Bks on Deafness & Sign Lang 5; Braille Volumes 30; CDs 640; DVDs 204; e-books 209,900; e-journals 35,000; Electronic Media & Resources 369; Microforms 23,969; Bk Titles 33,629; Bk Vols 51,509; Per Subs 131; Spec Interest Per Sub 19; Videos 1,376
Special Collections: Fayetta Storm Davis Restoration Coll; Robert E Reeves Missions Coll
Subject Interests: Missions, Restoration movement
Automation Activity & Vendor Info: (Cataloging) Mandarin Library Automation; (Circulation) Mandarin Library Automation; (ILL) OCLC WorldShare Interlibrary Loan; (OPAC) Mandarin Library Automation
Database Vendor: ABC-CLIO, Bowker, CredoReference, EBSCOhost, Electric Library, Gale Cengage Learning, H W Wilson, MITINET, Inc, OCLC ArticleFirst, OCLC FirstSearch, OCLC WorldShare Interlibrary Loan, ProQuest
Wireless access
Function: Handicapped accessible, Wheelchair accessible
Partic in Christian Library Consortium; Libr & Info Resources Network (LIRN); Tampa Bay Library Consortium, Inc
Restriction: In-house use for visitors

P OSCEOLA LIBRARY SYSTEM*, Hart Memorial Central Library & Ray Shanks Law Library, 211 E Dakin Ave, 34741. SAN 323-5947. Tel: 407-742-8888. FAX: 407-742-8897. E-mail: thelibrary@osceolalibrary.org. Web Site: www.osceolalibrary.org.
Founded 1989. Pop 275,000; Circ 1,266,573
Automation Activity & Vendor Info: (Acquisitions) SirsiDynix; (Cataloging) OCLC Online; (Circulation) SirsiDynix; (ILL) OCLC Online; (OPAC) SirsiDynix
Database Vendor: Baker & Taylor, BWI, Checkpoint Systems, Inc, Dialog, EBSCOhost, Gale Cengage Learning, Grolier Online, infoUSA, Ingram Library Services, Newsbank, OCLC FirstSearch, OCLC WorldShare Interlibrary Loan, ProQuest, ReferenceUSA, SirsiDynix, Westlaw
Wireless access
Special Services for the Deaf - TDD equip
Open Mon-Thurs 9-9, Fri & Sat 9-6, Sun 12-6
Friends of the Library Group
Branches: 5
BUENAVENTURA LAKES BRANCH, 405 Buenaventura Blvd, 34743, SAN 376-9224. Tel: 407-742-8888. *Libr Dir,* Denise Galarraga; E-mail: Denise.Galarraga@osceolalibrary.org
Open Mon-Thurs 9-9, Fri & Sat 9-6, Sun 12-6
Friends of the Library Group
KENANSVILLE BRANCH, 1154 S Canoe Creek Rd, Kenansville, 34739. Tel: 407-742-8888.
Open Tues, Thurs & Fri 3-7, Wed & Sat 10-2 & 3-7
Friends of the Library Group
POINCIANA BRANCH, 101 N Doverplum Ave, 34758. Tel: 407-742 8888.
Open Mon-Thurs 9-9, Fri & Sat 9-6, Sun 12-6
Friends of the Library Group
VETERANS MEMORIAL LIBRARY-ST CLOUD, 810 13th St, Saint Cloud, 34769, SAN 376-2688. Tel: 407-742-8888.
Open Mon-Thurs 9-9, Fri & Sat 9-6, Sun 12-6
Friends of the Library Group
WEST OSCEOLA BRANCH, Water Tower Shoppes, 21 Blake Blvd, Celebration, 34747. Tel: 407-742-8888.
Open Mon-Sat 10-7
Friends of the Library Group

C VALENCIA COLLEGE*, Osceola Campus Library, 1800 Denn John Lane, 34744. SAN 376-8309. Tel: 407-582-4155. Reference Tel: 407-582-4154. Web Site: valenciacollege.edu/library. *Librn,* Sarah Dockray; Tel: 407-582-4156, E-mail: sdockray@valenciacollege.edu; *Libr Spec,* Marcie Rhodes; Tel: 407-582-4153, E-mail: mrhodes@valenciacollege.edu; Staff 10 (MLS 5, Non-MLS 5)
Founded 1967. Fac 3
Library Holdings: Bk Titles 27,000; Per Subs 80
Automation Activity & Vendor Info: (Acquisitions) Ex Libris Group; (Cataloging) Ex Libris Group; (Circulation) Ex Libris Group; (Course Reserve) Ex Libris Group; (ILL) Ex Libris Group; (Media Booking) Ex Libris Group; (OPAC) Ex Libris Group; (Serials) Ex Libris Group
Wireless access
Function: Copy machines, Electronic databases & coll, Free DVD rentals, Handicapped accessible, ILL available, Instruction & testing, Magnifiers for reading, Online cat, Online info literacy tutorials on the web & in blackboard, Photocopying/Printing, Ref serv available, Scanner, Telephone ref, Wheelchair accessible
Partic in Tampa Bay Library Consortium, Inc
Open Mon-Thurs 7am-10pm, Fri 7-5 (7-Noon Summer), Sat 8-Noon
Restriction: Borrowing privileges limited to fac & registered students, ID required to use computers (Ltd hrs)

LADY LAKE

P LADY LAKE PUBLIC LIBRARY, 225 W Guava St, 32159. SAN 376-2661. Tel: 352-753-2957. FAX: 352-753-3361. Web Site: ladylakelibrary.com. *Dir,* Beth Maciejewski; E-mail: bmaciejewski@lakeline.lib.fl.us, *Admin Coordr,* Mary Ellen Petrucelli; E-mail: mpetrucelli@lakeline.lib.fl.us; *Prog & Youth Coordr,* Thom Mazak; E-mail: ladylakelibrary@yahoo.com, *Circ/Acq,* Beth Gobeil; E-mail: bgobeil@lakeline.lib.fl.us; *Ref Asst,* Lori Sadler; E-mail: lsadler@lakeline.lib.fl.us. Subject Specialists: *Computer art, Youth,* Thom Mazak; Staff 7 (MLS 1, Non-MLS 6)
Founded 1992. Pop 30,000; Circ 117,000
Library Holdings: Bk Titles 46,000; Per Subs 77
Subject Interests: Civil War, Collectibles, Fla, Gardening
Automation Activity & Vendor Info: (Acquisitions) SirsiDynix; (Cataloging) SirsiDynix; (Circulation) SirsiDynix; (OPAC) SirsiDynix; (Serials) SirsiDynix
Database Vendor: SirsiDynix
Wireless access
Mem of Lake County Library System
Partic in Tampa Bay Library Consortium, Inc
Special Services for the Blind - Talking bks
Open Mon & Wed 9-7, Tues & Thurs 9-6, Fri 9-5, Sat 9-12
Friends of the Library Group

LAKE ALFRED

S CITRUS RESEARCH & EDUCATION CENTER*, 700 Experiment Station Rd, 33850-2299. SAN 302-9964. Tel: 863-956-1151. FAX: 863-956-4631. Web Site: www.crec.ifas.ufl.edu. *Librn,* Jennifer Dawson
Founded 1947
Library Holdings: Bk Titles 6,980; Bk Vols 8,350; Per Subs 50
Wireless access
Function: For res purposes, Ref serv available, Res libr
Open Mon-Fri 8-5
Friends of the Library Group

P LAKE ALFRED PUBLIC LIBRARY*, 245 N Seminole Ave, 33850. SAN 302-9956. Tel: 863-291-5378. FAX: 863-965-6386. Web Site: laatla.webs.com/welcome.htm. *Dir,* Linda Hitchcock; E-mail: lhitchcock@mylakealfred.com; *Asst Dir,* Kimberly Walker; E-mail: kwalker@mylakealfred.com; *Ch Serv,* Mamie Carr; E-mail: mcarr@mylakealfred.com; Staff 3 (MLS 1, Non-MLS 2)
Founded 1973. Pop 4,000; Circ 14,000
Library Holdings: Bk Vols 24,000; Per Subs 20
Subject Interests: Fla
Automation Activity & Vendor Info: (Cataloging) Horizon; (Circulation) Horizon
Wireless access
Function: Photocopying/Printing, Prog for children & young adult, Summer reading prog
Partic in Polk County Libr Coop
Open Mon-Fri 9-6, Sat 9-3
Friends of the Library Group

LAKE BUTLER

P NEW RIVER PUBLIC LIBRARY COOPERATIVE, 110 N Lake Ave, 32054. SAN 377-8800. Tel: 386-496-2526. FAX: 386-496-3394. E-mail: newriver@neflin.org. Web Site: www.newriver.lib.fl.us. Staff 5 (MLS 1, Non-MLS 4)
Founded 1996. Pop 70,000
Library Holdings: Bk Titles 152,000; Per Subs 200
Automation Activity & Vendor Info: (Cataloging) SirsiDynix; (Circulation) SirsiDynix; (OPAC) SirsiDynix
Wireless access
Member Libraries: Bradford County Public Library; Emily Taber Public Library; Union County Public Library
Partic in Northeast Florida Library Information Network
Open Mon-Fri 8-4
Bookmobiles: 1. Bk vols 5,000

P UNION COUNTY PUBLIC LIBRARY*, 175 W Main St, 32054-1639. SAN 323-7516. Tel: 386-496-3432. FAX: 386-496-1285. Web Site: union.newriver.lib.fl.us. *Dir,* Mary C Brown; E-mail: marycb@neflin.org; *Youth Serv,* Dianne Hannon
Founded 1989. Pop 14,200
Oct 2005-Sept 2006 Income $180,000, State $95,000, County $85,000. Mats Exp $25,000, Books $20,000, Per/Ser (Incl. Access Fees) $1,500, AV Mat $3,500. Sal $86,000
Library Holdings: Bk Vols 30,000; Per Subs 35
Subject Interests: Local hist
Automation Activity & Vendor Info: (Circulation) SirsiDynix
Mem of New River Public Library Cooperative
Partic in Evergreen Indiana Consortium
Open Mon & Wed-Fri 9-6, Tues 9-8, Sat 9-3
Friends of the Library Group

LAKE CITY

P COLUMBIA COUNTY PUBLIC LIBRARY, 308 NW Columbia Ave, 32055. SAN 323-7761. Tel: 386-758-2101. Administration Tel: 386-758-1018. FAX: 386-758-2135. TDD: 386-758-1016. Web Site: www.ccpl.sirsi.net. *Dir,* Deborah J Paulson; *Asst Dir,* Katrina Evans; *Outreach Serv Librn, Youth Serv,* Stephanie Tyson; *Br Mgr, Main Libr,* Zulima Martinez; Staff 6 (MLS 4, Non-MLS 2)
Founded 1959. Pop 67,966; Circ 323,613
Library Holdings: Bk Vols 119,000; Per Subs 206
Automation Activity & Vendor Info: (Acquisitions) SirsiDynix; (Cataloging) SirsiDynix; (Circulation) SirsiDynix; (OPAC) SirsiDynix; (Serials) SirsiDynix
Wireless access
Publications: Friends Newsletter; Various Bibliographies
Open Mon & Tues 9-9, Wed-Fri 9-6, Sat & Sun 1-5
Friends of the Library Group
Branches: 2
FORT WHITE BRANCH, 17700 SW State Rd 47, Fort White, 32038, SAN 376-821X. Tel: 386-497-1108. FAX: 386-497-2066. *Br Mgr,* Patti Street
Open Mon & Wed 11-6, Tues & Thurs 11-7, Fri & Sat 11-5
Friends of the Library Group
WEST BRANCH, 435 NW Hall of Fame Dr, 32055. Tel: 386-758-1321. *Br Mgr,* Barbara Gray
Open Tues 10-8, Wed & Thurs 10-6, Fri & Sat 10-5

J FLORIDA GATEWAY COLLEGE*, Wilson S Rivers Library & Media Center, 149 SE College Pl, 32025-2006. SAN 302-9980. Tel: 386-754-4337. Circulation Tel: 386-754-4401. Reference Tel: 386-754-4391. FAX: 386-754-4837. Reference FAX: 386-754-4891. Web Site: www.fgc.edu. *Exec Dir,* Jim Morris; *Dir, Libr Serv,* Christine Boatright; E-mail: christine.boatright@fgc.edu; *Coordr, Libr Res,* Patricia Morris; E-mail: patricia.morris@fgc.edu; *Libr Tech 1,* Karen Thomas; Tel: 386-754-4339, E-mail: karen.thomas@fgc.edu; *Libr Tech 1,* Lynnda White; Tel: 386-754-4400, E-mail: lynnda.white@fgc.edu; *Libr Tech II,* Jo Ann Bailey; Tel: 386-754-4338, E-mail: joann.bailey@fgc.edu. Subject Specialists: *Hist, Polit sci,* Jim Morris; Staff 5 (MLS 2, Non-MLS 3)
Founded 1962. Enrl 3,361; Fac 68; Highest Degree: Bachelor
Jul 2011-Jun 2012 Income $256,216. Mats Exp $167,431, Books $56,040, Per/Ser (Incl. Access Fees) $14,296, AV Mat $56,217, Electronic Ref Mat (Incl. Access Fees) $40,253, Presv $625. Sal $197,948
Library Holdings: e-books 56,217; Bk Titles 100,028
Subject Interests: Allied health, Art, Water res
Automation Activity & Vendor Info: (Acquisitions) GRCI; (Cataloging) Ex Libris Group; (Circulation) Ex Libris Group; (Course Reserve) Ex Libris Group; (ILL) Ex Libris Group; (OPAC) Ex Libris Group; (Serials) Ex Libris Group
Database Vendor: ARTstor, CQ Press, CredoReference, EBSCOhost, Facts on File, Gale Cengage Learning, Greenwood Publishing Group, H W Wilson, OCLC FirstSearch, Oxford Online, ProQuest
Wireless access
Publications: Annual Report; Orientation Brochures; Student Handbook
Partic in LINCC; Northeast Florida Library Information Network
Open Mon-Thurs (Fall-Spring) 7:30-7:30, Fri 7:30-4:30; Mon-Thurs (Summer) 7:30-6:30

GM NORTH FLORIDA/SOUTH GEORGIA VETERANS HEALTH SYSTEM*, VA Medical Center Library, 619 S Marion Ave, 32025. SAN 302-9999. Tel: 386-755-3016, Ext 2232. FAX: 386-758-3218. *Chief Librn,* Marylyn Gresser; Tel: 352-376-1611, Ext 6312, Fax: 352-374-6148; Staff 2 (Non-MLS 2)
Founded 1955
Library Holdings: AV Mats 1,154; e-journals 220; Large Print Bks 188; Bk Vols 8,342; Per Subs 614; Spec Interest Per Sub 55; Talking Bks 50
Subject Interests: Med sci, Patient health educ
Automation Activity & Vendor Info: (Cataloging) EOS International; (Circulation) EOS International
Function: ILL available, Referrals accepted
Publications: Acquisitions Bulletin; Periodical Holdings
Partic in Northeast Florida Library Information Network
Open Mon-Fri 8-4:30

LAKE MARY

J ITT TECHNICAL INSTITUTE*, Learning Resource Center, 1400 S International Pkwy, 32746. Tel: 407-936-0600, 407-936-0600, Ext 572. FAX: 407-936-0512. *Librn,* Brian Calhoun; Tel: 407-936-0572
Founded 1982. Enrl 300; Fac 30; Highest Degree: Bachelor
Library Holdings: Bk Vols 2,500
Wireless access
Open Mon-Thurs 7:30am-9pm, Fri 7:30-6, Sat 8:30-3

LAKE PANASOFFKEE

P PANASOFFKEE COMMUNITY LIBRARY*, 1500 County Rd 459, 33538. SAN 376-2742. Tel: 352-689-4567. FAX: 352-569-1941. *Br Supvr,* Judith Lee
Library Holdings: Bk Titles 15,200; Per Subs 40
Automation Activity & Vendor Info: (Cataloging) Innovative Interfaces, Inc; (Circulation) Innovative Interfaces, Inc
Wireless access
Mem of Sumter County Library System
Open Mon & Wed-Fri 9-6, Tues 9-8, Sat 9-4
Friends of the Library Group

LAKE PARK

P LAKE PARK PUBLIC LIBRARY, 529 Park Ave, 33403. SAN 303-0008. Tel: 561-881-3330. Web Site: www.lakepark-fl.gov. *Dir,* Karen H Mahnk; Tel: 561-881-3331, E-mail: kmahnk@lakeparkflorida.gov; *Librn,* Amy Natale; Tel: 561-881-3337, E-mail: anatale@lakeparkflorida.gov; Staff 6 (MLS 2, Non-MLS 4)
Pop 11,452; Circ 37,683
Library Holdings: Bk Titles 33,000; Per Subs 70
Subject Interests: Fla
Automation Activity & Vendor Info: (Acquisitions) SIRSI WorkFlows; (Cataloging) SIRSI-iBistro; (Circulation) SirsiDynix; (OPAC) SirsiDynix
Wireless access
Publications: E-blast (Periodical); Lake Park Library (Newsletter)
Partic in Coop Authority for Libr Automation; Library Cooperative of the Palm Beaches
Open Mon 9-5, Tues-Thurs 9-8, Fri 9-4, Sat 10-4
Friends of the Library Group

LAKE PLACID

P LAKE PLACID MEMORIAL LIBRARY*, 205 W Interlake Blvd, 33852. SAN 376-5008. Tel: 863-699-3705. FAX: 863-699-3713. Web Site: www.myhlc.org. *Librn,* Kresta Harris; Staff 1 (MLS 1)
Founded 1929. Pop 19,500; Circ 98,000
Library Holdings: AV Mats 5,000; Bk Vols 49,000; Per Subs 30
Subject Interests: Genealogy
Automation Activity & Vendor Info: (Circulation) Innovative Interfaces, Inc; (ILL) OCLC FirstSearch; (OPAC) Innovative Interfaces, Inc; (Serials) EBSCO Online
Database Vendor: EBSCOhost, OCLC FirstSearch
Wireless access
Function: AV serv, CD-ROM, Digital talking bks, Handicapped accessible, ILL available, Magnifiers for reading, Music CDs, Photocopying/Printing, Prog for adults, Prog for children & young adult, Ref serv available, Spoken cassettes & CDs, Summer reading prog, Telephone ref, VHS videos, Wheelchair accessible
Mem of Highlands County Library System
Partic in Tampa Bay Library Consortium, Inc
Open Mon-Wed 9-5:30, Thurs 10-7, Fri 9-3, Sat 9-12
Friends of the Library Group

LAKE WALES

S BOK TOWER GARDENS, Anton Brees Carillon Library, 1151 Tower Blvd, 33853-3412. SAN 371-7933. Tel: 863-734-1227. FAX: 863-676-6770. E-mail: library@boktower.org. Web Site: www.boktower.org. *Librn,* Joy Banks; Staff 2 (MLS 2)
Founded 1968
Library Holdings: AV Mats 179; CDs 1,455; Music Scores 2,988; Bk Vols 3,030; Per Subs 20
Special Collections: Personal Archives
Automation Activity & Vendor Info: (Cataloging) Mandarin Library Automation; (OPAC) Mandarin Library Automation
Database Vendor: OCLC, OCLC FirstSearch
Wireless access
Function: Archival coll, Audio & video playback equip for onsite use, Online cat, Ref serv available
Restriction: Access at librarian's discretion, Authorized scholars by appt, Limited access based on advanced application, Limited access for the pub, Non-circulating, Not a lending libr, Open by appt only

P LAKE WALES PUBLIC LIBRARY*, 290 Cypress Garden Lane, 33853. SAN 303-0032. Tel: 863-678-4004. FAX: 863-678-4051. E-mail: library@cityoflakewales.com. Web Site: www.cityoflakewales.com/library. *Dir,* Tina M Peak; E-mail: peakt@cityoflakewales.com; *Circ Librn,* Jodi Adam; E-mail: jadam@cityoflakewales.com; *Bks by Mail Supvr, Libr Spec,* Carolyn Avirett; Tel: 863-679-4441, E-mail: cavirett@cityoflakewales.com; *Circ Supvr, Libr Spec,* Melissa Mayer; *Libr Spec, Teen Coordr,* Dawn Copple; E-mail: dcopple@cityoflakewales.com; *Coll Develop, ILL, Ref,* Marcia Loveman; E-mail: mloveman@cityoflakewales.com; *Tech Serv,* Marie Zero; E-mail: mzero@cityoflakewales.com; *Youth Serv,* Kara Wiseman; E-mail: kwiseman@cityoflakewales.com; Staff 14 (MLS 5, Non MLS 9)
Founded 1919. Pop 16,000; Circ 235,000
Library Holdings: Audiobooks 4,500; Bks on Deafness & Sign Lang 20; CDs 3,800; DVDs 7,000; e-books 3,500; Electronic Media & Resources 10; High Interest/Low Vocabulary Bk Vols 200; Large Print Bks 18,000; Microforms 50; Bk Titles 86,000; Per Subs 182; Spec Interest Per Sub 10; Talking Bks 3,350
Special Collections: Florida; Local History Archives. Oral History
Subject Interests: Bus, Careers, Fla, Genealogy, Spanish (Lang)
Automation Activity & Vendor Info: (Acquisitions) SirsiDynix; (Cataloging) SirsiDynix; (Circulation) SirsiDynix; (OPAC) SirsiDynix; (Serials) SirsiDynix
Database Vendor: Backstage Library Works, Booklist Online, EBSCO Auto Repair Reference, EBSCOhost, Gale Cengage Learning, Overdrive, Inc, ProQuest, Wilson - Wilson Web, World Book Online
Wireless access
Function: Adult bk club, Archival coll, Art exhibits, Audiobks via web, Bks on CD, Chess club, Children's prog, Computer training, Computers for patron use, Copy machines, e-mail & chat, E-Reserves, Electronic databases & coll, Exhibits, Fax serv, Free DVD rentals, Handicapped accessible, Home delivery & serv to Sr ctr & nursing homes, Homebound delivery serv, ILL available, Magnifiers for reading, Mail & tel request accepted, Mail loans to mem, Microfiche/film & reading machines, Music CDs, Online cat, Online ref, Online searches, OverDrive digital audio bks, Photocopying/Printing, Preschool outreach, Preschool reading prog, Printer for laptops & handheld devices, Prog for adults, Prog for children & young adult, Pub access computers, Ref serv available, Ref serv in person, Senior computer classes, Senior outreach, Spanish lang bks, Story hour, Summer & winter reading prog, Summer reading prog, Tax forms, Teen prog, Telephone ref, Wheelchair accessible, Workshops, Writing prog
Publications: America Libraries; Booklist; Library Journal
Partic in Fla Libr Asn; Polk County Libr Coop; Tampa Bay Library Consortium, Inc
Open Mon, Tues & Thurs 9-6:30, Wed & Fri 9-5:30, Sat 9-3
Friends of the Library Group

C WARNER UNIVERSITY, Pontious Learning Resource Center, 13895 Hwy 27, 33859. SAN 303-0040. Tel: 863-638-7674. Circulation Tel: 863-638-7235. Reference Tel: 863-638-7666. FAX: 863-638-7675. E-mail: researchhelp@warner.edu. Web Site: www.warner.edu/lrc. *Libr Dir,* Sherill Lynn Harriger; E-mail: sherill.harriger@warner.edu; *Head, Access Serv,* Mary Thorsen; Tel: 863-638-7586, E-mail: mary.thoresen@warner.edu; *Instrul Serv Librn,* Virginia Ann Schnarre; Tel: 863-638-7620, E-mail: virginia.schnarre@warner.edu; *Coordr, Distance Libr Serv,* Amy Beatty; Tel: 863-638-7619, E-mail: amy.beatty@warner.edu. Subject Specialists: *Hist,* Virginia Ann Schnarre; Staff 4 (MLS 3, Non-MLS 1)
Founded 1967. Enrl 1,100; Highest Degree: Master
Library Holdings: Audiobooks 1; AV Mats 2,407; DVDs 943; e-books 216,188; e-journals 30,420; Microforms 67; Bk Titles 73,831; Per Subs 225; Videos 453
Subject Interests: Educ, Liberal arts, Music, Recreation, Relig, Soc sci & issues
Automation Activity & Vendor Info: (Acquisitions) Book Systems; (Cataloging) Book Systems; (Circulation) Book Systems; (OPAC) Book Systems
Database Vendor: ABC-CLIO, Agricola, Bowker, CredoReference, ebrary, EBSCOhost, Facts on File, Gale Cengage Learning, JSTOR, LexisNexis, ProQuest
Wireless access
Partic in Christian Library Consortium; Independent Cols & Univs of Fla; Library & Information Resources Network (LIRN); Lyrasis; Tampa Bay Library Consortium, Inc
Special Services for the Blind - Accessible computers
Open Mon-Thurs 7:30am-10pm, Fri 7:30-5, Sat 12-4, Sun 6pm-10pm
Restriction: Authorized patrons, Non-circulating of rare bks, Open to students, fac & staff, Restricted pub use

LAKE WORTH

P LAKE WORTH PUBLIC LIBRARY*, 15 North M St, 33460. SAN 303-0059. Tel: 561-533-7354. FAX: 561-586-1651. E-mail: lwlibrary@lakeworth.org. Web Site: www.lakeworth.org. *Libr Serv Mgr,* Vickie Joslin; Staff 8.5 (MLS 1, Non-MLS 7.5)
Founded 1912. Pop 34,500; Circ 125,000
Library Holdings: Audiobooks 500; CDs 450; DVDs 800; e-books 14,000; Bk Titles 55,400; Bk Vols 60,000; Per Subs 102; Videos 150
Special Collections: Lake Worth History (Florida Coll), clipping, micro; Large Print Books Coll
Automation Activity & Vendor Info: (Cataloging) Innovative Interfaces, Inc; (Circulation) Innovative Interfaces, Inc; (OPAC) Innovative Interfaces, Inc
Wireless access
Function: After school storytime, Bks on CD, Children's prog, Computers for patron use, Copy machines, E-Reserves, ILL available, Magnifiers for reading, Music CDs, Online cat, Pub access computers, Ref serv available, Story hour, Summer reading prog, Tax forms, Teen prog
Partic in Library Cooperative of the Palm Beaches
Open Mon-Wed 9:30-8, Thurs-Sat 9:30-5
Friends of the Library Group

J PALM BEACH STATE COLLEGE*, Harold C Manor Library, 4200 Congress Ave, Mail Sta 17, 33461. SAN 337-6591. Tel: 561-868-3800. Circulation Tel: 561-868-3710. Reference Tel: 561-868-3713. FAX: 561-868-3708. Web Site: www.palmbeachstate.edu/. *Dir, Libr Serv,* Brian C Kelley; Tel: 561-868-3706, E-mail: kelleyb@palmbeachstate.edu; *Ref,* Doug Cornwell; *ILL,* Penny Brown; *Media Spec,* Bill Buntin; *Per,* Patricia Alvarez; *Pub Serv,* Estaline Rogers; *Ref,* Connie Tuisku; *Ref Serv,* Rob Krull; *Tech Serv,* Kenneth Myers; Staff 9 (MLS 9)
Founded 1933. Enrl 16,016; Fac 247
Library Holdings: e-books 18,000; e-journals 19,000; Bk Titles 161,121; Bk Vols 210,567; Per Subs 1,863; Videos 6,500
Special Collections: Finnish Coll
Subject Interests: Civil War
Automation Activity & Vendor Info: (Acquisitions) Ex Libris Group; (Cataloging) Ex Libris Group; (Circulation) Ex Libris Group; (Course Reserve) Ex Libris Group; (ILL) Ex Libris Group; (OPAC) Ex Libris Group; (Serials) Ex Libris Group
Database Vendor: Baker & Taylor, Checkpoint Systems, Inc, EBSCOhost, Gale Cengage Learning, JSTOR, LexisNexis, Medianet, Newsbank, OCLC FirstSearch, OCLC WorldShare Interlibrary Loan, ProQuest, PubMed, SerialsSolutions, TLC (The Library Corporation), WebMD, Wilson - Wilson Web
Wireless access
Partic in Lyrasis; OCLC Online Computer Library Center, Inc; SEFLIN - Southeast Florida Library Information Network, Inc
Open Mon-Thurs 7:30am-9pm, Fri 7:30-5, Sat 10-3

LAKELAND

C EVEREST UNIVERSITY, Lakeland Campus Library, 995 E Memorial Blvd, Ste 110, 33801. SAN 376-9615. Tel: 863-274-7031. *Dir,* Betty Martinez; E-mail: bettym@cci.edu; Staff 1 (MLS 1)
Enrl 350; Highest Degree: Bachelor
Library Holdings: Bk Titles 9,000; Bk Vols 10,000; Per Subs 90
Automation Activity & Vendor Info: (Circulation) Follett Software; (OPAC) Follett Software
Database Vendor: ebrary, EBSCO Information Services, Gale Cengage Learning, OCLC FirstSearch, Westlaw
Wireless access
Function: 24/7 Electronic res, Computers for patron use, Copy machines, Electronic databases & coll, Magazines, Outside serv via phone, mail, e-mail & web, Spoken cassettes & DVDs, VHS videos
Partic in Lyrasis; Tampa Bay Library Consortium, Inc
Open Mon-Fri 8-8, Sat 9-3
Restriction: Borrowing privileges limited to fac & registered students, ID required to use computers (Ltd hrs), Limited access for the pub

C FLORIDA SOUTHERN COLLEGE, Roux Library, 111 Lake Hollingsworth Dr, 33801-5698. SAN 303-0067. Tel: 863-680-4164. FAX: 863-680-4126. E-mail: circ@flsouthern.edu. Web Site: www.flsouthern.edu/library. *Libr Dir,* Randall M MacDonald; Tel: 863-680-4165, E-mail: rmacdonald1@flsouthern.edu; *Cat/Metadata Librn,* Bonita Pollock; Tel: 863-680-4736, E-mail: bpollock@flsouthern.edu; *Electronic Res Librn,* Eridan J Thompson; Tel: 863-616-6450, E-mail: ethompson@flsouthern.edu; *Instrul Serv Librn,* Cathy Jones; Tel: 863-616-6451, E-mail: cjones@flsouthern.edu; *Instrul Serv Librn,* Kimberly Nordon; Tel: 863-680-4496, E-mail: knordon@flsouthern.edu; *Res Sharing Librn,* Nora E Galbraith; Tel: 863-616-6454, E-mail: ngalbraith@flsouthern.edu; *Circ Supvr,* Donna Kahelin; Tel: 863-616-6453, E-mail: dkahelin@flsouthern.edu; *Col Archivist,* Position Currently Open; *Archives, Tech,* Jeffrey Zines; Tel: 863-616-6487, E-mail: jzines2@flsouthern.edu; *Circ Asst,* Gloria C Aycrigg; Tel: 863-616-6452, E-mail: gloaycrigg@flsouthern.edu; *Tech Serv Asst,* Position Currently Open; Staff 11 (MLS 6, Non-MLS 5)
Founded 1885. Enrl 2,339; Fac 115; Highest Degree: Doctorate
Jun 2006-May 2007. Mats Exp $413,043, Books $92,665, Per/Ser (Incl. Access Fees) $203,759, AV Mat $11,973, Electronic Ref Mat (Incl. Access Fees) $104,646
Library Holdings: AV Mats 15,610; CDs 4,310; DVDs 1,550; e-books 27,000; Music Scores 1,192; Bk Vols 182,000; Per Subs 680; Videos 2,755
Special Collections: Andy Ireland Coll; Florida United Methodist History Coll; Frank Lloyd Wright Coll; James A Haley Coll
Automation Activity & Vendor Info: (Acquisitions) Innovative Interfaces, Inc; (Cataloging) Innovative Interfaces, Inc; (Circulation) Innovative Interfaces, Inc; (Course Reserve) Innovative Interfaces, Inc; (ILL) OCLC; (OPAC) Innovative Interfaces, Inc; (Serials) Innovative Interfaces, Inc
Database Vendor: American Chemical Society, American Mathematical Society, ARTstor, BioOne, College Source, CQ Press, CredoReference, ebrary, EBSCO Discovery Service, EBSCOhost, Elsevier, Foundation Center, Gale Cengage Learning, IBISWorld, Innovative Interfaces, Inc, JSTOR, LexisNexis, Mergent Online, Micromedex, OCLC, OCLC FirstSearch, OCLC WorldShare Interlibrary Loan, OVID Technologies, ProQuest, Sage, ScienceDirect, Springer-Verlag, Springshare, LLC, ValueLine, Wiley
Wireless access
Partic in Lyrasis; Tampa Bay Library Consortium, Inc; Westchester Academic Library Directors Organization (WALDO)
Open Mon-Thurs 7:30am-11pm, Fri & Sat 8-5, Sun Noon-11pm

P LAKELAND PUBLIC LIBRARY*, 100 Lake Morton Dr, 33801-5375. SAN 337-6621. Tel: 863-834-4280. FAX: 863-834-4293. E-mail: publiclibrary@lakelandgov.net. Web Site: www.lakelandgov.net/library. *City Librn,* Lisa Lilyquist; E-mail: lisa.lilyquist@lakelandgov.net; *Asst Dir,* Rivanne Chasteen-Futch; E-mail: rivanne.chasteen-futch@lakelandgov.net; *Ad,* Brenda Patterson; *Computer Serv Librn,* David Gonzalez; *Spec Coll Librn,* Kevin Logan; *Tech Serv Librn,* Janice Crawford; *Youth Serv Librn,* Jeannine Davis; *Circ, Librn Supvr,* Christina Hielscher; *Ref,* Varrick Nunez; Tel: 863-834-4265, E-mail: varrick.nunez@lakelandgov.net; Staff 13 (MLS 7, Non-MLS 6)
Founded 1927. Circ 999,203
Oct 2009-Sept 2010 Income (Main Library and Branch(s)) $3,482,504, City $2,328,547, County $1,153,957. Mats Exp $498,354. Sal $2,368,409
Library Holdings: Bk Vols 275,000; Per Subs 220
Special Collections: Lakeland Chapter DAR; Lakeland Coll; Lakeland Photographs; Polk County Citrus Labels
Subject Interests: Local hist
Automation Activity & Vendor Info: (Cataloging) SirsiDynix; (Circulation) SirsiDynix; (OPAC) SirsiDynix
Database Vendor: SirsiDynix
Wireless access
Function: Adult bk club, Archival coll, Audiobks via web, AV serv, Bks on CD, Children's prog, Computer training, Computers for patron use, Copy machines, Electronic databases & coll, Free DVD rentals, ILL available, Music CDs, Notary serv, Online cat, OverDrive digital audio bks, Photocopying/Printing, Prog for adults, Tax forms
Publications: Friends of the Library (Newsletter)
Partic in Lyrasis; OCLC Online Computer Library Center, Inc; Polk County Libr Coop; Tampa Bay Library Consortium, Inc
Open Mon-Thurs 9-9, Fri & Sat 9-5, Sun 1:30-5
Friends of the Library Group
Branches: 1
LARRY R JACKSON BRANCH, 1700 N Florida Ave, 33805, SAN 337-6656. Tel: 863-834-4288. FAX: 863-834-4327. *Librn Supvr,* Henry Simmons; *Circ,* Renee Kane; Staff 9 (MLS 1, Non-MLS 8)
Founded 1995
Function: Prog for children & young adult, Summer reading prog
Open Mon, Tues & Thurs 9-8, Wed, Fri & Sat 9-5
Friends of the Library Group
Bookmobiles: 1. Librn, Robin Newman. Titles 3,000

M LAKELAND REGIONAL MEDICAL CENTER*, Medical Library, 1324 Lakeland Hills Blvd, 33805. (Mail add: PO Box 95448, 33804-5448), SAN 325-8920. Tel: 863-687-1176. FAX: 863-687-1488. E-mail: medlibdesk@lrmc.com. *Librn/Mgr,* Jan Booker; E-mail: jan.booker@lrmc.com; Staff 5 (Non-MLS 5)
Library Holdings: Audiobooks 100; CDs 100; DVDs 20; Bk Titles 1,000; Per Subs 175; Videos 100
Special Collections: Leadership Development
Database Vendor: EBSCOhost, OVID Technologies
Partic in SEND; Tampa Bay Medical Library Network

S POLK MUSEUM OF ART*, Penfield Library, 800 E Palmetto St, 33801-5529. SAN 303-0075. Tel: 863-688-7743. FAX: 863-688-2611. Web Site: www.polkmuseumofart.org. *Curator,* Adam Justice; Tel: 863-688-7743, Ext 241, E-mail: ajustice@polkmuseumofart.org; Staff 1 (Non-MLS 1)
Founded 1966
Library Holdings: Bk Vols 2,000; Per Subs 20
Special Collections: Florida Contemporary Artists
Subject Interests: Archit, Art, Craft, Exhibition catalogs
Function: For res purposes
Restriction: Non-circulating, Open by appt only

GL SECOND DISTRICT COURT OF APPEAL*, Law Library, 1005 E Memorial Blvd, 33801. (Mail add: PO Box 327, 33802), SAN 325-8416. Tel: 863-499-2290. FAX: 863-499-2277. *Librn,* Position Currently Open
Library Holdings: Bk Vols 21,000

CR SOUTHEASTERN UNIVERSITY*, Steelman Library, 1000 Longfellow Blvd, 33801. SAN 303-0083. Tel: 863-667-5089. Circulation Tel: 863-667-5059. Reference Tel: 863-667-5060, 863-667-5897. FAX: 863-669-4160. Web Site: www.seu.edu/library. *Dean of Libr Serv,* Grace Veach; E-mail: gveach@seu.edu; *Head, Circ, Head, ILL,* Kathy Kempa; E-mail: kfkempa@seuniversity.edu; *Head, Ref,* Amy Harris; *Head, Ser, Ref Librn,* Glenn Pearl; E-mail: gapearl@seuniversity.edu; *Head, Tech Serv,* Joanna Hause; Tel: 863-667-5062, E-mail: jhause@seuniversity.edu; *Distance & Off-Campus Serv, Electronic Res,* Richard W Felver; Tel: 863-667-5949, E-mail: rwfelver@seuniversity.edu. Subject Specialists: *English, Music,* Grace Veach; *English,* Amy Harris; *Communication, Relig,* Glenn Pearl; *Behav & soc sci, Hist, Relig,* Joanna Hause; *Bus, Music,* Richard W Felver; Staff 11.5 (MLS 4.5, Non-MLS 7)
Founded 1935. Enrl 2,725; Fac 99; Highest Degree: Master
Library Holdings: Bk Vols 95,000; Per Subs 600
Special Collections: Amy Bullock Coll; Curriculum Lab, children's mat & textbks
Subject Interests: Biol, Bus, Communications, Educ, Math, Music, Pentecostal, Psychol, Relig
Automation Activity & Vendor Info: (Acquisitions) LibLime; (Cataloging) LibLime; (Circulation) LibLime; (Course Reserve) LibLime; (ILL) OCLC; (OPAC) LibLime; (Serials) EBSCO Online
Database Vendor: ABC-CLIO, Alexander Street Press, CIOS (Communication Institute for Online Scholarship), CredoReference, EBSCOhost, Greenwood Publishing Group, H W Wilson, JSTOR, LexisNexis, McGraw-Hill, Modern Language Association, OCLC WorldShare Interlibrary Loan, ProQuest, SBRnet (Sports Business Research Network), SerialsSolutions, ValueLine, Wilson - Wilson Web, World Book Online
Wireless access
Function: Distance learning, ILL available, Photocopying/Printing, Ref serv available
Partic in Independent Cols & Univs of Fla; Tampa Bay Library Consortium, Inc; Westchester Academic Library Directors Organization (WALDO)
Restriction: Open to students, fac & staff

LANTANA

A G HOLLEY STATE HOSPITAL

M BENJAMIN L BROCK MEDICAL LIBRARY*, 1199 W Lantana Rd, 33462. (Mail add: PO Box 3084, 33465-3084), SAN 322-8215. Tel: 561-582-5666. FAX: 561-540-3710. Web Site: www.agholley.com. *Librn,* Markesha Burgess
Library Holdings: Bk Titles 200; Per Subs 10
Special Collections: Oral History
Restriction: Staff use only

M PATIENTS LIBRARY*, 1199 W Lantana Rd, 33465, SAN 303-0105. Tel: 561-582-5666, Ext 3799. FAX. 561-540-3753. *Librn,* Tim Thompson
Library Holdings: Bk Titles 9,800

P LANTANA PUBLIC LIBRARY, 205 W Ocean Ave, 33462. SAN 303-0113. Tel: 561-540-5740. FAX: 561-540-5742. E-mail: lib.lantana@gmail.com. Web Site: www.lantanalibrary.org/. *Dir,* Sidney A Patchett; E-mail: sidpatchett@yahoo.com; Staff 1 (MLS 1)
Founded 1947. Pop 10,300
Oct 2014-Sept 2015. Mats Exp $108,000, Books $20,000, Per/Ser (Incl. Access Fees) $85,000, Electronic Ref Mat (Incl. Access Fees) $3,000
Library Holdings: e-books 1,300; e-books 1,300; e-journals 28; e-journals 28; Large Print Bks 1,000; Large Print Bks 1,000; Bk Titles 20,000; Bk Titles 20,000; Bk Vols 23,000; Per Subs 58
Special Collections: Linehan Coll (Books & slides on Florida & Lantana history)
Automation Activity & Vendor Info: (Cataloging) ByWater Solutions; (Circulation) ByWater Solutions; (OPAC) ByWater Solutions
Database Vendor: ByWater Solutions, Gale Cengage Learning, Overdrive, Inc, World Book Online
Wireless access
Function: 24/7 Online cat, Adult bk club
Partic in Library Cooperative of the Palm Beaches
Open Mon & Thurs 10-8, Tues, Wed & Fri 10-6, Sat (Sept-May)10-2
Friends of the Library Group

LARGO

C EVEREST UNIVERSITY*, Largo Campus Library, 1199 E Bay Dr, 33770. SAN 324-7937. Tel: 727-725-2688. FAX: 727-796-3722. *Dean,* Christina Degenhardt; *Librn,* Candice Pascual
Library Holdings: e-books 4,000; Bk Titles 5,000
Wireless access
Open Mon-Wed 8-8, Thurs 7am-10pm, Fri 8-5, Sat 9-1

P LARGO PUBLIC LIBRARY*, 120 Central Park Dr, 33771. SAN 303-0156. Tel: 727-587-6715. Interlibrary Loan Service Tel: 727-587-6748. FAX: 727-586-7353. Circulation FAX: 727-586-7345. TDD: 727-587-6778. Web Site: www.asklargo.com. *Dir,* Casey McPhee; Tel: 727-587-6715, Ext 2511, E-mail: librarydirector@largo.com; *Ch Serv,* Mercedes Bleattler; *Ref,* Olga Koz; *Tech Serv,* Osmera Euemduan; Staff 10 (MLS 9, Non-MLS 1)
Founded 1916. Pop 68,244; Circ 713,488
Oct 2005-Sept 2006. Mats Exp $297,000
Library Holdings: Bk Vols 231,000; Per Subs 198
Subject Interests: Arts & crafts, Genealogy, Local hist
Automation Activity & Vendor Info: (Cataloging) SirsiDynix; (Circulation) SirsiDynix; (OPAC) SirsiDynix
Special Services for the Deaf - Bks on deafness & sign lang; High interest/low vocabulary bks
Open Mon-Thurs 9:30-9, Fri & Sat 9:30-5, Sun 1-5
Friends of the Library Group

G PINELLAS COUNTY GOVERNMENT*, Heritage Village Archives & Library, 11909 125th St N, 33774. SAN 372-6053. Tel: 727-582-2127. FAX: 727-582-2211. E-mail: heritagevillage@pinellascounty.org. Web Site: www.pinellascounty.org/heritage/archives_library.htm. *Operations Mgr,* Ellen Babb; E-mail: ebabb@pinellascounty.org; Staff 1 (MLS 1)
Founded 1961
Library Holdings: Bk Vols 3,500; Per Subs 10
Special Collections: Pinellas County History, photog, postcards
Function: Archival coll
Restriction: Lending limited to county residents, Open by appt only

LECANTO

J COLLEGE OF CENTRAL FLORIDA LEARNING RESOURCES CENTER*, Citrus Campus Library, 3800 S Lecanto Hwy, C2-202, 34461. Tel: 352-249-1205. FAX: 352-249-1212. TDD: 352-249-1201. E-mail: citruslb@cf.edu. Web Site: www.cf.edu, www.cf.edu/departments/lrc.htm. *Mgr,* Edith Ramlow; E-mail: ramlowe@cf.edu; *Sr Libr Tech,* Pat Booth; E-mail: boothp@cf.edu; Staff 3 (MLS 1.5, Non-MLS 1.5)
Founded 1996. Enrl 9,500; Highest Degree: Bachelor
Library Holdings: Bk Vols 9,000
Special Collections: Florida & Ecological Sciences (David E Walker Environmental Sciences Coll)
Automation Activity & Vendor Info: (Acquisitions) Ex Libris Group; (Cataloging) Ex Libris Group; (Circulation) Ex Libris Group; (Course Reserve) Ex Libris Group; (ILL) OCLC FirstSearch; (OPAC) Ex Libris Group; (Serials) Ex Libris Group
Wireless access
Function: Audio & video playback equip for onsite use, Computers for patron use, Copy machines, ILL available, Magnifiers for reading, Online cat
Partic in Northeast Florida Library Information Network
Open Mon-Thurs (Aug-April) 8am-9pm, Fri 8-4:30; Mon-Thurs (May-July) 8-6
Restriction: Borrowing privileges limited to fac & registered students, Borrowing requests are handled by ILL, External users must contact libr

LEESBURG

C BEACON COLLEGE LIBRARY*, 105 E Main St, 34748. Tel: 352-638-9707. Web Site: beaconcollege.edu. *Dir, Libr Res,* Tiffany Reitz; E-mail: treitz@beaconcollege.edu; Staff 2 (MLS 1, Non-MLS 1)
Founded 1995. Enrl 190; Fac 27; Highest Degree: Bachelor
Library Holdings: AV Mats 211; e-books 154,000; e-journals 30,876; Bk Titles 19,000; Per Subs 50; Spec Interest Per Sub 18; Videos 1,186
Subject Interests: Learning disabilities
Automation Activity & Vendor Info: (Cataloging) TLC (The Library Corporation); (Circulation) TLC (The Library Corporation); (ILL) TLC (The Library Corporation); (OPAC) TLC (The Library Corporation); (Serials) TLC (The Library Corporation)
Database Vendor: American Psychological Association (APA), EBSCOhost, Electric Library, JSTOR, Newsbank, OCLC CAMIO, OCLC FirstSearch, OCLC WebJunction, OCLC WorldShare Interlibrary Loan, ProQuest, SerialsSolutions
Wireless access
Partic in Florida Library Information Network; Tampa Bay Library Consortium, Inc
Restriction: Borrowing requests are handled by ILL, Open to students, fac & staff

C LAKE-SUMTER STATE COLLEGE LIBRARY, 9501 US Hwy 441, 34788-8751. SAN 303-0164. Tel: 352-365-3563. Web Site: www.lssc.edu/library. *Dir, Libr Serv,* Denise English; E-mail: englishd@lssc.edu; *Access Serv,* Kevin Arms; E-mail: armsk@lssc.edu; *Acq, Coll Develop,* James Cason; Tel: 352-435-5030, E-mail: casonj@lssc.edu; *Cat, ILL,* David Goff; Tel: 352-365-3527, E-mail: goffd@lssc.edu, *Govt Doc, Ser,* Nora Rackley; Tel: 352-365-3586, E-mail: rackleyn@lssc.edu; Staff 5 (MLS 5)
Founded 1962. Enrl 6,042; Fac 87; Highest Degree: Associate
Library Holdings: AV Mats 1,481; e-books 222,832; Bk Vols 70,870; Per Subs 117
Special Collections: US Document Depository
Automation Activity & Vendor Info: (Acquisitions) Ex Libris Group; (Cataloging) Ex Libris Group; (Circulation) Ex Libris Group; (Course Reserve) Ex Libris Group; (ILL) Ex Libris Group; (OPAC) Ex Libris Group; (Serials) Ex Libris Group
Partic in Lyrasis; OCLC Online Computer Library Center, Inc; Tampa Bay Library Consortium, Inc
Open Mon-Thurs 7:45am-9pm, Fri 7:45-4:30, Sat 10-3

P LEESBURG PUBLIC LIBRARY*, 100 E Main St, 34748. SAN 337-6680. Tel: 352-728-9790. FAX: 352-326-6635. E-mail: librarian@leesburgflorida.gov. Web Site: www.leesburgflorida.gov/library. *Libr Dir,* Lucy B Gangone; E-mail: lucy.gangone@leesburgflorida.gov; *Ad,* Dusty Matthews; E-mail: dusty.matthews@leesburgflorida.gov; *Ad,* Roberta Rowold; E-mail: roberta.rowold@leesburgflorida.gov; *Ad,* Tom Wilcox; E-mail: tom.wilcox@leesburgflorida.gov; *Teen Librn,* Julia Hutchins; E-mail: Julia.Hutchins@leesburgflorida.gov; *Support Serv Mgr,* Cathy Haines; E-mail: cathy.haines@leesburgflorida.gov; *Adult Serv Supvr,* Carol Anderson; E-mail: carol.anderson@leesburgflorida.gov; *Circ Supvr,* Claudia Procko; E-mail: claudia.procko@leesburgflorida.gov; *Youth Serv Supvr,* Alicisa Nelson; E-mail: alicisa.nelson@leesburgflorida.gov. Subject Specialists: *Genealogy, Local hist,* Tom Wilcox; *Genealogy, Local hist,* Carol Anderson; Staff 10.5 (MLS 7.5, Non-MLS 3)
Founded 1883. Pop 70,000; Circ 352,084
Oct 2012-Sept 2013 Income $1,419,301, City $1,097,632, County $292,072, Locally Generated Income $29,597. Mats Exp $150,039, Books $88,297, AV Mat $45,675, Electronic Ref Mat (Incl. Access Fees) $16,067. Sal $952,189
Library Holdings: AV Mats 664; DVDs 3,702; e-books 1,412; Large Print Bks 7,183; Bk Titles 19,491; Bk Vols 135,523
Special Collections: Genealogy & Local History
Subject Interests: Genealogy, Local hist
Automation Activity & Vendor Info: (Acquisitions) OCLC; (Cataloging) SirsiDynix; (Circulation) SirsiDynix; (OPAC) SirsiDynix; (Serials) SirsiDynix
Database Vendor: Comprise Technologies Inc, EBSCOhost, OCLC WorldShare Interlibrary Loan, ProQuest, WT Cox

Wireless access
Mem of Lake County Library System
Open Mon-Thurs 9-8, Sat 9-5
Friends of the Library Group

LIGHTHOUSE POINT

P LIGHTHOUSE POINT LIBRARY*, 2200 NE 38th St, 33064-3913. SAN 303-0180. Tel: 954-946-6398. FAX: 954-781-1950. Web Site: lighthousepointlibrary.com. *Dir,* Christy Keyes; E-mail: ckeyes@lighthousepointlibrary.com; *Circ Serv,* Rosemary Wilson; E-mail: rwilson@lighthousepointlibrary.com; Staff 4 (MLS 1, Non-MLS 3)
Founded 1965. Pop 10,767
Oct 2008-Sept 2009 Income $382,878, State $9,944, City $367,861, Federal $5,073. Mats Exp $68,400, Books $52,000, Per/Ser (Incl. Access Fees) $4,400, Electronic Ref Mat (Incl. Access Fees) $12,000. Sal $204,277 (Prof $89,683)
Library Holdings: AV Mats 2,216; Bks on Deafness & Sign Lang 15; High Interest/Low Vocabulary Bk Vols 60; Large Print Bks 3,707; Bk Titles 33,280; Bk Vols 32,251; Per Subs 143; Talking Bks 715
Subject Interests: Fla
Automation Activity & Vendor Info: (Cataloging) Follett Software; (Circulation) Follett Software; (ILL) OCLC FirstSearch; (OPAC) Follett Software
Database Vendor: OVID Technologies
Wireless access
Partic in SEFLIN - Southeast Florida Library Information Network, Inc
Open Mon & Wed 9-6, Tues & Thurs 9-8, Fri 9-5, Sat 9-1
Friends of the Library Group

LIVE OAK

P SUWANNEE RIVER REGIONAL LIBRARY*, 1848 Ohio Ave S, Dr Martin Luther King Jr Ave S, 32064-4517. SAN 337-6745. Tel: 386-362-2317. Administration Tel: 386-362-5779. FAX: 386-364-6071. Web Site: www.neflin.org/srrl. *Dir,* John D Hales, Jr; Tel: 386-362-5779, E-mail: dhales@neflin.org; *Youth Serv Mgr,* Marlene Mitchell; Tel: 386-364-3480; *Adult Serv, Pub Serv,* Linda Sanderson; *ILL,* Paulette Hankerson; Tel: 386-205-1531; *Tech Serv,* Sherry Millington; Tel: 386-364-3482; Staff 1 (Non-MLS 1)
Founded 1958. Pop 68,140; Circ 331,297
Oct 2005-Sept 2006 Income (Main Library and Branch(s)) $2,036,453, State $1,070,945, County $963,078, Other $2,430. Mats Exp $267,278, Books $207,278, AV Mat $39,000, Electronic Ref Mat (Incl. Access Fees) $21,000. Sal $1,153,491
Library Holdings: Bk Titles 71,401; Bk Vols 160,787; Per Subs 507
Automation Activity & Vendor Info: (Acquisitions) SirsiDynix; (Cataloging) SirsiDynix; (Circulation) SirsiDynix; (OPAC) SirsiDynix
Partic in Lyrasis; Northeast Florida Library Information Network
Special Services for the Deaf - TDD equip
Open Mon & Thurs 8:30-8, Tues, Wed & Fri 8:30-5:30, Sat 8:30-4
Friends of the Library Group
Branches: 7
BRANFORD PUBLIC LIBRARY, 703 NW Suwannee Ave, Branford, 32008-3279. (Mail add: PO Box 580, Branford, 32008-3279), SAN 337-677X. Tel: 386-935-1556. FAX: 386-935-6351. *Mgr,* Shirley Clark
Open Mon 8:30-8, Tues-Fri 8:30-5:30, Sat 8:30-4
Friends of the Library Group
GREENVILLE PUBLIC LIBRARY, 312 SW Church Ave, Greenville, 32331. (Mail add: PO Box 279, Greenville, 32331-0278), SAN 337-6834. Tel: 850-948-2529. FAX: 850-948-5220. E-mail: greenville@neflin.org. *Br Mgr,* Kerry Cohen; Staff 2 (MLS 1, Non-MLS 1)
Open Mon-Fri 9-12:30 & 1:30-5:30
JASPER PUBLIC LIBRARY, 311 Hatley St NE, Jasper, 32052, SAN 337-6869. Tel: 386-792-2285. FAX: 386-792-1966. *Mgr,* Barbara Jones
Open Mon 9-8, Tues-Fri 9-5:30, Sat 9-12:30
JENNINGS PUBLIC LIBRARY, 1322 Plum St, Jennings, 32053-2221. (Mail add: PO Box 30, Jennings, 32053-0030). Tel: 386-938-1143. FAX: 386-938-1153. E-mail: jennings@neflin.org. *Mgr,* Barbara McClain
Library Holdings: Bk Vols 11,000; Per Subs 47
Open Mon, Wed, Thurs & Fri 1-6, Tues 10-6
LEE PUBLIC LIBRARY, 190 SE County Rd 255, Lee, 32059-0040. (Mail add: PO Box 40, Lee, 32059-0040), SAN 377-0508. Tel: 850-971-5665. FAX: 850-971-4333. *Mgr,* Linda Swann
Open Mon-Wed & Fri 10-12:30 & 1:30-5:30, Sat 9-1
MADISON PUBLIC LIBRARY, 378 NW College Loop, Madison, 32340-1446, SAN 337-6958. Tel: 850-973-6814. FAX: 850-973-8322.
Open Mon-Fri 9-5:30, Sat 8:30-4
WHITE SPRINGS PUBLIC LIBRARY, 12797 Roberts St, White Springs, 32096. (Mail add: PO Box 660, White Springs, 32096-0660), SAN 377-6689. Tel: 386-397-1389. FAX: 386-397-4460. *Mgr,* Tracy Woodard
Founded 1997
Library Holdings: Bk Vols 3,300
Open Mon-Wed & Fri 1-6, Thurs 10-6

LONGBOAT KEY

S LONGBOAT LIBRARY, INC*, 555 Bay Isles Rd, 34228-3102. SAN 324-7104. Tel: 941-383-2011. *Pres,* Amy Roth; Tel: 941-387-0504
Founded 1957. Pop 15,000
Library Holdings: Bk Vols 15,100
Open Mon-Fri 9-4, Sat 9-12:30
Restriction: Mem only

LYNN HAVEN

P LYNN HAVEN PUBLIC LIBRARY*, 901 Ohio Ave, 32444. SAN 376-2734. Tel: 850-265-2781. FAX: 850-265-7311. E-mail: library@cityoflynnhaven.com. Web Site: www.lynnhavenlibrary.com. *Mgr,* Sue Wiles; *Cat,* Alice Fritze; *Ch Serv,* Candie Smith; *ILL,* Jill Snipes; Staff 4 (Non-MLS 4)
Pop 18,000
Library Holdings: Audiobooks 701; Large Print Bks 1,503; Bk Titles 25,810; Bk Vols 27,325; Per Subs 38
Automation Activity & Vendor Info: (Cataloging) TLC (The Library Corporation); (Circulation) TLC (The Library Corporation); (ILL) OCLC FirstSearch; (OPAC) TLC (The Library Corporation)
Database Vendor: Gale Cengage Learning, OCLC FirstSearch, TLC (The Library Corporation)
Wireless access
Open Mon & Fri 9-5, Tues & Thurs 12-8, Wed 1-5, Sat 10-3

MACCLENNY

P EMILY TABER PUBLIC LIBRARY*, 14 McIver Ave W, 32063. SAN 377-8789. Tel: 904-259-6464. Web Site: taber.newriver.lib.fl.us. *Dir,* April Teel
Founded 1961. Pop 22,000
Library Holdings: Bk Titles 35,041; Bk Vols 36,383; Per Subs 85
Automation Activity & Vendor Info: (Cataloging) SirsiDynix; (Circulation) SirsiDynix
Mem of New River Public Library Cooperative
Partic in Northeast Florida Library Information Network
Open Mon, Wed & Fri 12-5, Tues & Thurs 10:30-7, Sat 10-2
Friends of the Library Group

MACDILL AFB

A UNITED STATES AIR FORCE*, MacDill Air Force Base Library FL4814, 8102 Condor St, 33621-5408. SAN 337-7105. Tel: 813-828-3607. Reference Tel: 813-828-0440. FAX: 813-828-4416. E-mail: 6svslibrary@macdill.af.mil. Web Site: amccrooms.sirsi.net. *Dir,* Kathleen M Brady; Tel: 813-828-0424, E-mail: kathleen.brady@us.af.mil; Staff 7 (MLS 1, Non-MLS 6)
Founded 1940
Library Holdings: Bk Titles 19,000; Bk Vols 21,000; Per Subs 129
Subject Interests: Middle East, Mil hist
Automation Activity & Vendor Info: (Acquisitions) SirsiDynix; (Cataloging) SirsiDynix; (Circulation) SirsiDynix; (OPAC) SIRSI Unicorn
Database Vendor: EBSCO - WebFeat, EBSCOhost, Gale Cengage Learning, OCLC FirstSearch, Overdrive, Inc, Wilson - Wilson Web
Wireless access
Function: Accelerated reader prog, After school storytime, Audio & video playback equip for onsite use, Bks on CD, Children's prog, Computers for patron use, Copy machines, Doc delivery serv, Electronic databases & coll, Exhibits, Fax serv, Free DVD rentals, Handicapped accessible, Holiday prog, ILL available, Music CDs, Online cat, Online searches, Orientations, OverDrive digital audio bks, Photocopying/Printing, Preschool outreach, Prog for children & young adult, Ref serv in person, Scanner, Senior outreach, Spoken cassettes & CDs, Story hour, Summer reading prog, Tax forms, Teen prog
Publications: Bibliographies
Partic in OCLC Online Computer Library Center, Inc; Tampa Bay Library Consortium, Inc
Restriction: Not open to pub, Open to authorized patrons

MADEIRA BEACH

P GULF BEACHES PUBLIC LIBRARY*, 200 Municipal Dr, 33708. SAN 303-0229. Tel: 727-391-2828. FAX: 727-399-2840. Web Site: www.tblc.org/gulfbeaches. *Dir,* Jan L Horah; *Head, Circ,* Stanley Silverstine; *ILL, Ref Serv, Ch,* Harriet Thompkins; *Tech Serv,* Pat Ludwick
Founded 1952. Pop 16,900; Circ 165,000
Library Holdings: Bk Vols 70,000; Per Subs 127
Special Collections: Florida Coll
Automation Activity & Vendor Info: (Cataloging) Innovative Interfaces, Inc; (Circulation) Innovative Interfaces, Inc
Mem of Pinellas Public Libr Coop
Partic in Tampa Bay Library Consortium, Inc
Open Mon, Wed & Fri 10-6, Tues & Thurs 10-9, Sat 10-5
Friends of the Library Group

MADISON

J NORTH FLORIDA COMMUNITY COLLEGE LIBRARY*, Marshall W Hamilton Library, 325 NW Turner Davis Dr, 32340-1699. SAN 303-0237. Tel: 850-973-1624. E-mail: library@nfcc.edu. Web Site: www.nfcc.edu/library. *Dir,* Kay Hogan; Tel: 850-973-9422; *Ref,* Kathy Sale; Tel: 850-973-9452; Staff 2 (MLS 2)
Founded 1958. Enrl 1,700; Fac 33; Highest Degree: Associate
Library Holdings: AV Mats 3,688; Bks on Deafness & Sign Lang 85; CDs 117; DVDs 191; e-books 34,920; Bk Titles 32,000; Bk Vols 35,475; Per Subs 222; Videos 2,541
Special Collections: Florida Coll; Madison History Coll
Automation Activity & Vendor Info: (Acquisitions) Ex Libris Group; (Cataloging) Ex Libris Group; (Circulation) Ex Libris Group; (OPAC) Ex Libris Group; (Serials) Ex Libris Group
Partic in Florida Library Information Network; Lyrasis; Northeast Florida Library Information Network
Special Services for the Deaf - TDD equip
Special Services for the Blind - Magnifiers
Open Mon-Thurs 8-7, Fri 8-4:30

MAITLAND

P MAITLAND PUBLIC LIBRARY, 501 S Maitland Ave, 32751-5672. SAN 303-0261. Tel: 407-647-7700. Web Site: www.maitlandpubliclibrary.org. *Dir,* Ellen Schellhause; E-mail: eschellhause@maitlandpl.org; *E-Serv Librn,* Position Currently Open; *Pub Serv Librn,* Position Currently Open; *Mgr, Pub Serv,* Stacie Larson; E-mail: slarson@maitlandpl.org; *Circ,* Veronica Dailey; *Youth Serv,* Mary Daniels; E-mail: mdaniels@maitlandpl.org; Staff 17 (MLS 6, Non-MLS 11)
Founded 1896. Pop 16,919; Circ 193,640
Library Holdings: Bk Vols 69,185; Per Subs 57
Special Collections: Natural History & Environment (Audubon Coll)
Automation Activity & Vendor Info: (Circulation) SirsiDynix
Database Vendor: SirsiDynix
Wireless access
Function: 24/7 Electronic res, 24/7 Online cat, Adult bk club, Art exhibits, Bk club(s), Bks on CD, Children's prog, Computers for patron use, Copy machines, Digital talking bks, e-mail & chat, Electronic databases & coll, Fax serv, Magazines, Movies, Music CDs, Online cat, Online ref, OverDrive digital audio bks, Photocopying/Printing, Prog for adults, Prog for children & young adult, Story hour, Summer reading prog, Writing prog
Publications: Directors Newsletter
Partic in Tampa Bay Library Consortium, Inc
Open Mon-Thurs 10-9, Fri & Sat 10-6, Sun 1-6
Restriction: Authorized scholars by appt
Friends of the Library Group

MANALAPAN

§P J TURNER MOORE MEMORIAL LIBRARY, 1330 Lands End Rd, 33462. Tel: 561-383-2541, 561-588-7577. E-mail: librarian@manalapan.org. *Dir,* Lisa Petersen
Founded 1970
Open Tues & Thurs-Sat (Oct 31 to May 1) 9-Noon

MARIANNA

C CHIPOLA COLLEGE LIBRARY*, 3094 Indian Circle, 32446. SAN 303-0288. Tel: 850-718-2274. FAX: 850-718-2349. Web Site: www.chipola.edu/library. *Dir, Libr & Distance Learning,* Lou Kind; Tel: 850-718-2295, E-mail: kindl@chipola.edu; *Coordr, Cat & Ref,* Renee Hopkins; Tel: 850-718-2372, E-mail: hopkinsr@chipola.edu; *Circ Coordr,* Jane Stephens; Tel: 850-718-2279, E-mail: stephensj@chipola.edu; *Acq, ILL,* Nell Donaldson; Tel: 850-718-2273, E-mail: donaldsonn@chipola.edu; Staff 5 (MLS 3, Non-MLS 2)
Founded 1948. Enrl 1,300; Highest Degree: Bachelor
Library Holdings: Bk Titles 33,500; Bk Vols 35,000; Per Subs 220
Special Collections: Florida Coll
Automation Activity & Vendor Info: (Cataloging) SirsiDynix; (Circulation) SirsiDynix; (Course Reserve) SirsiDynix; (ILL) SirsiDynix; (OPAC) SirsiDynix; (Serials) SirsiDynix
Database Vendor: EBSCOhost, Gale Cengage Learning, Sage
Wireless access
Function: ILL available
Partic in Florida Library Information Network; Lyrasis; OCLC Online Computer Library Center, Inc; Panhandle Library Access Network
Open Mon-Thurs 7:30-6, Fri 7:30-4

P JACKSON COUNTY PUBLIC LIBRARY SYSTEM*, 2929 Green St, 32446. SAN 303-0296. Tel: 850-482-9631. FAX: 850-482-9632. Web Site: www.pplcs.org. *Dir,* Jo-Ann Rountree; *Asst Dir,* Stanley Littleton; *Ch Serv,* Lynn Lowenthal; *ILL,* Doris Green; *Tech Serv,* Alan Barber
Founded 1977. Pop 43,000
Library Holdings: Bk Vols 78,000; Per Subs 192
Special Collections: Genealogy Coll; Local History Coll
Automation Activity & Vendor Info: (Cataloging) SirsiDynix; (Circulation) SirsiDynix
Partic in Lyrasis; Panhandle Library Access Network
Open Mon-Thurs 9-8, Fri 9-6, Sat 9-3
Friends of the Library Group
Branches: 1
GRACEVILLE BRANCH, 5314 Brown St, Graceville, 32440. Tel: 850-263-3659. FAX: 850-263-3652. *Br Mgr,* Luci Fowler
Library Holdings: Bk Vols 3,526
Open Tues-Sat 9-5

S SUNLAND TRAINING CENTER*, Ellen A Thiel Library, 3700 Williams Dr, 32446. SAN 303-030X. Tel: 850-482-9378. FAX: 850-482-9236. *Librn,* Clifford Butler
Founded 1962
Library Holdings: Bk Titles 1,975; Bk Vols 2,000; Per Subs 11
Special Collections: Audio-Visual Coll of General Interest for the Mentally Retarded
Partic in Fla ILL Network
Special Services for the Deaf - High interest/low vocabulary bks; Staff with knowledge of sign lang
Open Mon-Fri 8-4:30

MARY ESTHER

P MARY ESTHER PUBLIC LIBRARY*, 100 Hollywood Blvd W, 32569-1957. SAN 303-0318. Tel: 850-243-5731. FAX: 850-243-4931. Web Site: www.readokaloosa.org. *Dir,* Sheila Ortyl; E-mail: sortyl@okaloosa.lib.fl.us; *Asst Dir,* Debbie Lamb
Founded 1974. Pop 6,000
Library Holdings: Bk Vols 25,000; Per Subs 30; Talking Bks 600
Automation Activity & Vendor Info: (Acquisitions) SirsiDynix; (Cataloging) SirsiDynix; (Circulation) SirsiDynix
Partic in Okaloosa County Public Library Cooperative
Open Mon 12-6, Tues & Thurs 9-8, Wed & Fri 9-6, Sat 9-5
Friends of the Library Group

MAYO

P LAFAYETTE COUNTY PUBLIC LIBRARY*, 120 NE Crawford St, 32066. (Mail add: PO Box 418, 32066-0418), SAN 337-6982. Tel: 386-294-1021. FAX: 386-294-3396. E-mail: lafayette@neflin.org. Web Site: www.3rivers.lib.fl.us. *Mgr,* Cindy Tysall
Library Holdings: Bk Vols 12,500; Per Subs 45
Automation Activity & Vendor Info: (Cataloging) LibLime; (Circulation) LibLime
Wireless access
Partic in Three Rivers Regional Library Service System
Open Mon-Fri 8:30-5:30

MELBOURNE

J EASTERN FLORIDA STATE COLLEGE, Melbourne Campus Library, (Formerly Brevard Community College), Philip F Nohrr Learning Resource Ctr, 3865 N Wickham Rd, 32935-2399. SAN 303-0326. Tel: 321-433-5575. Toll Free Tel: 888-747-2802. Web Site: www.easternflorida.edu/library. *Ref,* Ken Lemhouse; Staff 2 (MLS 2)
Founded 1968
Library Holdings: Bk Titles 48,000; Per Subs 225
Automation Activity & Vendor Info: (Acquisitions) Ex Libris Group; (Cataloging) Ex Libris Group; (Circulation) Ex Libris Group; (Course Reserve) Ex Libris Group; (Media Booking) Ex Libris Group; (OPAC) Ex Libris Group; (Serials) Ex Libris Group
Wireless access
Open Mon-Thurs 8-8, Fri 9-1

P EAU GALLIE PUBLIC LIBRARY*, 1521 Pineapple Ave, 32935-6594. SAN 303-0342. Tel: 321-255-4304. FAX: 321-255-4323. Web Site: www.brev.org. *Dir,* Jenny Morrison; *Ref & ILL Librn,* Elanya K Bairefoot; *Ch Serv,* Mary Jessica Sibayan; Staff 6.2 (MLS 4, Non-MLS 2.2)
Founded 1939. Pop 47,000; Circ 245,075
Oct 2007-Sept 2008 Income $1,041,175, Locally Generated Income $47,702, Parent Institution $993,473. Mats Exp $120,886, Books $101,061, Per/Ser (Incl. Access Fees) $9,100, AV Mat $10,725. Sal $775,698 (Prof $268,228)
Library Holdings: AV Mats 7,585; Bk Vols 72,957; Per Subs 213
Automation Activity & Vendor Info: (Cataloging) TLC (The Library Corporation); (Circulation) TLC (The Library Corporation); (OPAC) TLC (The Library Corporation)
Database Vendor: TLC (The Library Corporation)
Wireless access
Function: Adult bk club, Bks on cassette, Bks on CD, Children's prog, Computers for patron use, Copy machines, Free DVD rentals, Handicapped accessible, Holiday prog, ILL available, Music CDs, Online cat, Online ref,

Photocopying/Printing, Preschool outreach, Prog for adults, Prog for children & young adult, Pub access computers, Ref serv in person, Spoken cassettes & CDs, Spoken cassettes & DVDs, Story hour, Summer reading prog, Telephone ref, VHS videos, Video lending libr, Wheelchair accessible
Mem of Brevard County Library System
Open Mon & Wed-Fri 9-5, Sun Noon-8
Friends of the Library Group

C EVEREST UNIVERSITY*, Melbourne Campus Library, 2401 N Harbor City Blvd, 32935. SAN 375-5371. Tel: 321-253-2929, Ext 176. FAX: 321-255-2017. Web Site: www.fmulibraries.net. *Librn,* Gloria Semeroz
Highest Degree: Bachelor
Library Holdings: Bk Titles 4,087; Per Subs 60
Automation Activity & Vendor Info: (Cataloging) Follett Software; (Circulation) Follett Software; (OPAC) Follett Software
Partic in Tampa Bay Library Consortium, Inc
Open Mon & Fri 10-8, Tues-Thurs 9-9, Sat 9-12:30

C FLORIDA INSTITUTE OF TECHNOLOGY*, Evans Library, 150 W University Blvd, 32901-6988. SAN 337-713X. Tel: 321-674-8021. Interlibrary Loan Service Tel: 321-674-7539. FAX: 321-724-2559. *Dean of Libr,* Dr Celine Lang; Tel: 321-674-7111, E-mail: celine@fit.edu; *Dir, Admin Serv,* Tom McFarland; E-mail: mcfarlan@fit.edu; *Dir, Info Res & Serv,* Wendy Helmstetter; E-mail: whelmste@fit.edu; *Dir, Instrul Serv,* Kathy Turner; E-mail: kturner@fit.edu; *Syst Librn,* Rodd Newcombe; E-mail: rnewcomb@fit.edu; *Mgr, Info Tech,* Travis Jones; E-mail: jonest@fit.edu; *Mgr, User Serv,* Scott Blackwell; E-mail: blackwel@fit.edu; *Coll Mgt,* Suzanne Jones; E-mail: sjones@fit.edu; *Coll Develop,* Debra Wooldridge; E-mail: dwooldri@fit.edu; *ILL,* Tori Smith; E-mail: tosmith@fit.edu; Staff 11 (MLS 11)
Founded 1958. Enrl 4,683; Fac 265; Highest Degree: Doctorate
Library Holdings: Bk Vols 419,274; Per Subs 17,148
Special Collections: Dr Jerome Penn Keuper Coll; Edwin A Link Coll (Ocean Related Personal Papers, electronic archives); General John Bruce Medaris Coll (Personal Papers & Memorabilia); University Archives. US Document Depository
Subject Interests: Aeronaut, Eng, Marine & environ syst, Psychol
Automation Activity & Vendor Info: (Acquisitions) SirsiDynix; (Cataloging) SirsiDynix; (Circulation) SirsiDynix; (Serials) SirsiDynix
Wireless access
Partic in Cent Fla Libr Consortium; OCLC Online Computer Library Center, Inc
Special Services for the Blind - VisualTek equip
Friends of the Library Group

S FLORIDA TODAY NEWSPAPER LIBRARY*, One Gannett Plaza, 32940. SAN 324-4512. Tel: 321-242-3500. FAX: 321-242-6620. Web Site: www.floridatoday.com. *In Charge,* Christina LaFortune; E-mail: clafortune@floridatoday.com; Staff 1 (MLS 1)
Founded 1966
Library Holdings: Bk Titles 200
Special Collections: Newspaper 1917-Present
Publications: Library Clips (Quarterly)
Restriction: Staff use only

P DR MARTIN LUTHER KING JR LIBRARY*, 955 E University Blvd, 32901. SAN 376-2750. Tel: 321-952-4511. FAX: 321-952-4512. Web Site: www.brev.org. *Dir,* Estella Edwards; E-mail: eedwards@brev.org; *Ref,* Janice Murray; E-mail: jmurray@brev.org
Library Holdings: Audiobooks 850; CDs 1,189; DVDs 3,031; Bk Vols 21,275; Per Subs 53
Automation Activity & Vendor Info: (Cataloging) Infor Library & Information Solutions; (Circulation) Infor Library & Information Solutions; (OPAC) Infor Library & Information Solutions
Wireless access
Mem of Brevard County Library System
Open Mon & Fri 9-5, Tues & Thurs 12-8
Friends of the Library Group

P MELBOURNE PUBLIC LIBRARY*, 540 E Fee Ave, 32901. SAN 303-0377. Tel: 321-952-4514. FAX: 321-952-4518. Web Site: www.brev.org. *Dir,* Geraldine Prieth; *Ch Serv,* Lucinda Dann; *Ref Serv, Ad,* Mauri Baumann; *Tech Serv,* Cindy Peterson; Staff 5 (MLS 5)
Founded 1918. Pop 66,970; Circ 459,601
Library Holdings: Bk Vols 107,513; Per Subs 298
Special Collections: Florida Coll; Genealogy Coll; Investing Coll
Automation Activity & Vendor Info: (Cataloging) Infor Library & Information Solutions; (Circulation) Infor Library & Information Solutions; (OPAC) Infor Library & Information Solutions
Wireless access
Open Mon, Wed, Thurs & Fri 9-5, Tues 9-8, Sun 1-5
Friends of the Library Group

P SUNTREE/VIERA PUBLIC LIBRARY*, 902 Jordan Blass Dr, 32940. Tel: 321-255-4404. FAX: 321-255-4406. Reference FAX: 321-253-6640. Web Site: www.brev.org. *Dir,* Mary Scholtz; E-mail: mscholtz@brev.org; *Ref Serv,* Cindy Leist; E-mail: cleist@brev.org
Circ 222,000
Library Holdings: AV Mats 1,500; CDs 1,300; DVDs 1,227; Large Print Bks 3,500; Bk Titles 50,000; Per Subs 91; Talking Bks 1,250; Videos 1,227
Automation Activity & Vendor Info: (Cataloging) Infor Library & Information Solutions; (Circulation) Infor Library & Information Solutions
Mem of Brevard County Library System
Open Mon-Thurs 9-8, Fri & Sat 9-5, Sun 1-5
Friends of the Library Group

MELBOURNE BEACH

P MELBOURNE BEACH PUBLIC LIBRARY*, 324 Ocean Ave, 32951. Tel: 321-956-5642. FAX: 321-953-6942. Web Site: www.brev.org. *Dir,* Cynthia Leist; *Ch Serv,* Dianne Leary; *Circ,* Susan Nigh; *Ref Serv,* Irma Fordham; Staff 4 (MLS 2, Non-MLS 2)
Founded 2002
Library Holdings: Bk Vols 53,000; Per Subs 65
Automation Activity & Vendor Info: (Cataloging) Infor Library & Information Solutions; (Circulation) Infor Library & Information Solutions; (OPAC) Infor Library & Information Solutions
Wireless access
Mem of Brevard County Library System
Open Mon & Thurs 10-6, Tues 12-8, Wed & Fri 9-5, Sat 10-2
Friends of the Library Group

MERRITT ISLAND

P MERRITT ISLAND PUBLIC LIBRARY*, 1195 N Courtenay Pkwy, 32953-4596. SAN 303-0407. Tel: 321-455-1369. *Dir,* Jeff Thompson
Founded 1965. Pop 36,090; Circ 316,681
Library Holdings: Bk Titles 101,000; Per Subs 200
Automation Activity & Vendor Info: (Circulation) Infor Library & Information Solutions; (OPAC) Infor Library & Information Solutions
Function: Archival coll, AV serv, For res purposes, Homebound delivery serv, ILL available, Magnifiers for reading, Newsp ref libr, Online searches, Photocopying/Printing, Prog for children & young adult, Ref serv available, Telephone ref, Wheelchair accessible
Mem of Brevard County Library System
Open Mon-Thurs 9-9, Fri & Sat 9-5

MIAMI

L BAKER & MCKENZIE*, Law Library, 1111 Brickell Ave, Ste 1700, 33131. SAN 372-1337. Tel: 305-789-8951. FAX: 305-789-8953. Web Site: www.bakerinfo.com. *Librn,* Clem Noble
Library Holdings: Bk Vols 5,000; Per Subs 75
Automation Activity & Vendor Info: (Cataloging) SydneyPlus
Restriction: Staff use only

M BAPTIST HOSPITAL OF MIAMI*, Jaffee Medical Library, 8900 N Kendall Dr, 33176. SAN 303-0423. Tel: 786-596-6506. FAX: 786-596-5910. E-mail: library@baptisthealth.net. Web Site: www.baptisthealth.net. *Dir,* Diane Rourke; E-mail: dianer@baptisthealth.net; *Online Serv,* Devica Samsundar; E-mail: devica@baptisthealth.net; Staff 2 (MLS 2)
Founded 1966
Library Holdings: e-journals 900; Bk Titles 600; Per Subs 50
Special Collections: Antique Surgical Instruments
Subject Interests: Allied health, Consumer health, Hist of med, Hospital admin, Med, Nursing
Automation Activity & Vendor Info: (Cataloging) CyberTools for Libraries; (Circulation) CyberTools for Libraries; (OPAC) CyberTools for Libraries; (Serials) EBSCO Online
Database Vendor: EBSCO Information Services, OVID Technologies
Publications: Newsletter
Partic in Docline; Miami Health Sciences Library Consortium; National Network of Libraries of Medicine; SE-Atlantic Regional Med Libr Servs
Restriction: Non-circulating to the pub

CR BARRY UNIVERSITY*, Monsignor William Barry Memorial Library, 11300 NE Second Ave, 33161. SAN 303-0806. Tel: 305-899-3760. FAX: 305-899-4792. Web Site: www.barry.edu/libraryservices. *Dir of Libr Serv,* Tom Messner; Tel: 305-899-4062, E-mail: tmessner@mail.barry.edu; *Asst Dir, Tech Serv,* Marietta DeWinter; Tel: 305-899-4813; *Sr Ref Librn,* Philip M O'Neill; Tel: 305-899-3762, E-mail: poneill@mail.barry.edu; *Ref Librn,* Pamela Beagle; *Ref Librn,* Maria Gonzalez; Tel: 305-899-3761, E-mail: magonzalez@mail.barry.edu; *Ref Librn,* Merlene Nembhard; Tel: 305-899-4051, E-mail: mnembhard@mail.barry.edu; *Ref Librn,* Frances O'Dell, Sr; Tel: 305-899-2977, E-mail: fodell@mail.barry.edu; *Mgr, Archives & Spec Coll,* Ximena Valdivia; Tel: 305-899-3027, E-mail: xvaldivia@mail.barry.edu; *Coll Develop Mgr,* William Patrick Morrissey;

Tel: 305-899-3755, E-mail: wmorrissey@mail.barry.edu; *Mgr, Pub Serv,* Rodrigo Castro; Tel: 305-899-3768, E-mail: rcastro@mail.barry.edu; *Supvr, Ser,* Cathy Pyle; *Acq,* Maureen Lama; *Archivist,* Katherine L Fleming; *ILL,* Marvilean Brown; *ILL,* Marcia Dixon. Subject Specialists: *Bus, Soc work,* Tom Messner; *Fine arts,* Marietta DeWinter; *Hist of philosophy, Polit sci, Theol,* Philip M O'Neill; *Med sci, Nursing, Podiatry,* Pamela Beagle; *Adult educ, Continuing educ, Fine arts,* Maria Gonzalez; *Computer sci, Math, Psychol,* Merlene Nembhard; *Educ, English,* Frances O'Dell, Sr; *Archives,* Ximena Valdivia; Staff 12 (MLS 12)
Founded 1940. Enrl 8,112; Fac 255; Highest Degree: Doctorate
Library Holdings: Bk Titles 800,000; Bk Vols 980,000; Per Subs 1,200
Special Collections: Atonement Coll
Subject Interests: Catholicism
Automation Activity & Vendor Info: (Acquisitions) Innovative Interfaces, Inc - Millenium; (Cataloging) Innovative Interfaces, Inc - Millenium; (Circulation) Innovative Interfaces, Inc - Millenium; (Course Reserve) Innovative Interfaces, Inc - Millenium; (ILL) Innovative Interfaces, Inc - Millenium; (OPAC) Innovative Interfaces, Inc - Millenium; (Serials) Innovative Interfaces, Inc - Millenium
Database Vendor: American Chemical Society, American Psychological Association (APA), Baker & Taylor, BioOne, Checkpoint Systems, Inc, CQ Press, CRC Press/Taylor & Francis Group, EBSCOhost, Elsevier, Emerald, Gale Cengage Learning, HeinOnline, Hoovers, Innovative Interfaces, Inc, ISI Web of Knowledge, JSTOR, LexisNexis, Mergent Online, Modern Language Association, Newsbank, OCLC, OCLC FirstSearch, OCLC WorldShare Interlibrary Loan, OVID Technologies, Oxford Online, ProQuest, PubMed, Sage, ScienceDirect, SerialsSolutions, Springer-Verlag, Standard & Poor's, UpToDate, ValueLine, Westlaw, Wiley InterScience
Wireless access
Partic in Lyrasis; SEFLIN - Southeast Florida Library Information Network, Inc
Open Mon-Thurs 7:30am-Midnight, Fri 7:30am-10pm, Sat 9am-10pm, Sun 12-Midnight

R BETH DAVID CONGREGATION*, Harry Simons Library, 2625 SW Third Ave, 33129. SAN 303-0431. Tel: 305-854-3911. FAX: 305-285-5841. E-mail: info@bethdavid.com. Web Site: www.bethdavid.com. *Chairperson,* Lillian Beer; *Librn,* Saresta Rowland
Founded 1962
Library Holdings: Bk Vols 7,000
Subject Interests: Biol, Children's lit, Educ, Fiction, Hist, Relig
Restriction: Mem only, Students only

C CARLOS ALBIZU UNIVERSITY LIBRARY*, 2173 NW 99 Ave, 33172. SAN 375-3565. Tel: 305-593-1223, Ext 131. FAX: 305-593-8318. Web Site: www.mia.albizu.edu/web/albizu_library.asp. *Librn,* Mary Bishop; E-mail: mbishop@albizu.edu; *Libr Serv Mgr,* Juan Zaragoza; E-mail: jzaragoza@albizu.edu, *Asst Librn,* Yamilka Gonzalez; E-mail: ygonzalez@albizu.edu; *Acq,* Bernadette Corneliuson; E-mail: bcorneliuson@albizu.edu; Staff 4 (MLS 1, Non-MLS 3)
Enrl 850; Fac 80; Highest Degree: Doctorate
Library Holdings: Bks on Deafness & Sign Lang 21; Bk Titles 19,298; Bk Vols 25,824; Per Subs 399
Subject Interests: Bus, Cross-cultural studies, Psychol
Automation Activity & Vendor Info: (Cataloging) Follett Software; (Circulation) Follett Software; (OPAC) Follett Software
Wireless access
Publications: Library Report
Partic in Florida Library Information Network; Lyrasis
Open Mon-Fri 10-9, Sat 9-3

R CENTER FOR THE ADVANCEMENT OF JEWISH EDUCATION*, Adler Shinensky Library, 4200 Biscayne Blvd, 33137-3279. SAN 303-0458. Tel: 305-576-4030, Ext 154. FAX: 305-576-0307. Web Site: www.caje-miami.org. *In Charge,* Allsion DiGiacomo; Staff 4 (MLS 1, Non-MLS 3)
Founded 1948
Library Holdings: Bk Titles 55,000; Per Subs 70
Special Collections: Hebrew Reference; Holocaust (Educational Resource Center Coll), bk, flm, fs, a-tapes, CD-ROM
Subject Interests: Archaeology, Biblical studies, Holocaust, Israel, Jewish hist & lit
Automation Activity & Vendor Info: (Acquisitions) Follett Software; (Cataloging) Follett Software; (Circulation) Follett Software; (ILL) Follett Software; (Serials) Follett Software
Publications: Chanukah Rappings; Ecology in the Bible; Joy of the Shabbat; Soviet Russian Jewry; Wandering through Jewish Miami
Restriction: Open by appt only

J CITY COLLEGE - MIAMI LIBRARY*, 9300 S Dadeland Blvd, Ste PH, 33156. Tel: 305-666-9242. FAX: 305-666-9243. Web Site: www.citycollege.edu. *Exec Dir,* Carlos Arce
Highest Degree: Bachelor
Library Holdings: Bk Vols 2,000; Per Subs 50; Spec Interest Per Sub 20; Videos 400
Special Collections: Florida Legal Coll
Automation Activity & Vendor Info: (Cataloging) Winnebago Software Co
Partic in OCLC Online Computer Library Center, Inc
Open Mon-Thurs 8am-9:30pm, Fri 8-5, Sat 9-1

S FAIRCHILD TROPICAL BOTANIC GARDEN*, Montgomery Library, 11935 Old Cutler Rd, 33156. SAN 303-0504. Tel: 305-667-1651, Ext 3424. FAX: 305-669-4074. Web Site: www.fairchildgarden.org. *Librn,* Nancy Korber; E-mail: library@fairchildgarden.org; Staff 1 (MLS 1)
Founded 1941
Library Holdings: Bk Vols 16,000; Per Subs 60
Special Collections: David Fairchild Coll, papers & photos; Florida Botanists
Subject Interests: Botany, Hort
Automation Activity & Vendor Info: (OPAC) CyberTools for Libraries
Function: Archival coll, For res purposes
Restriction: Not a lending libr, Open by appt only

C FLORIDA INTERNATIONAL UNIVERSITY*, Steven & Dorothea Green Library, 11200 SW Eighth St, 33199. SAN 337-7199. Tel: 305-348-2461. Circulation Tel: 305-348-2451. Interlibrary Loan Service Tel: 305-348-4054. Reference Tel: 305-348-2470. Automation Services Tel: 305-348-3127. FAX: 305-348-3408. Interlibrary Loan Service FAX: 305-348-6055. Reference FAX: 305-348-6579. TDD: 305-348-1295. Web Site: library.fiu.edu. *Dean, Univ Libr,* Laura Probst; E-mail: probstl@fiu.edu; *Assoc Dean, Admin Operations & Budget,* Ana Mendoza; Tel: 305-348-1900, E-mail: ana.mendoza@fiu.edu; *Assoc Dean, Tech & Digital Serv,* Dr Bryan Cooper; Tel: 305-348-2982, Fax: 305-348-0122, E-mail: lbcooper@fiu.edu; *Assoc Dean, Pub Serv,* Dr Consuella Askew; Tel: 305-348-2463, E-mail: consuella.askew@fiu.edu; *Head of GIS Ctr,* Jennifer Fu; Tel: 305-348-3138, Fax: 305-348-6445, E-mail: fujen@fiu.edu; *Head, Res Develop,* Rita Cauce; Tel: 305-348-0547, Fax: 305-348-1798, E-mail: rita.cauce@fiu.edu; *Head, Cat,* Sue Wartzok; Tel: 305-348-6269, Fax: 305-348-1798, E-mail: swartzok@fiu.edu; *Head, Spec Coll, Univ Archivist,* Vicki Silvera; Tel: 305-348-3136, Fax: 305-348-4739, E-mail: silverav@fiu.edu; *Head, Syst,* George Fray; Tel: 305-348-2488, Fax: 305-348-6450, E-mail: frayg@fiu.edu; *Bibliog Instr, Ref Serv,* Stephanie Brenenson; Tel: 305-348-1843, E-mail: brenenso@fiu.edu; *Coll Officer,* Valerie E Boulos; Tel: 305-348-6447, Fax: 305 348-0122, E-mail: edwardsv@fiu.edu. Subject Specialists: *Admin, Fr opera, Musicology,* Laura Probst; *Budgeting, Human resources,* Ana Mendoza; *Admin, Automation, Digitization,* Dr Bryan Cooper; *Higher educ, Leadership, Mgt,* Dr Consuella Askew; *Archives, Caribbean area, Latin Am,* Vicki Silvera; *Info literacy,* Stephanie Brenenson; *Electronic res,* Valerie E Boulos; Staff 40 (MLS 26, Non-MLS 14)
Founded 1972. Enrl 33,540; Fac 891; Highest Degree: Doctorate
Jul 2010-Jun 2011 Income $10,501,410. Mats Exp $5,231,848, Books $631,744, Per/Ser (Incl. Access Fees) $3,100,956, Micro $22,502, AV Mat $30,423, Electronic Ref Mat (Incl. Access Fees) $1,034,686, Presv $43,548. Sal $4,412,132 (Prof $1,753,455)
Library Holdings: Audiobooks 1,061; AV Mats 48,540; e-books 122,297; e-journals 87,257; Electronic Media & Resources 85,681; Microforms 2,843,669; Bk Vols 1,379,635; Per Subs 1,531; Videos 15,950
Special Collections: Diaz-Ayala Music Coll; European Documentation Center; Geological Survey Maps; Latin American & Caribbean Coll; Urban & Regional Documents. State Document Depository; UN Document Depository; US Document Depository
Automation Activity & Vendor Info: (Acquisitions) Ex Libris Group; (Cataloging) Ex Libris Group; (Circulation) Ex Libris Group; (Course Reserve) Ex Libris Group; (ILL) OCLC ILLiad; (OPAC) Ex Libris Group; (Serials) Ex Libris Group
Database Vendor: Baker & Taylor, BWI, Cambridge Scientific Abstracts, EBSCOhost, Gale Cengage Learning, Grolier Online, Haworth Pres Inc, ISI Web of Knowledge, JSTOR, LexisNexis, Newsbank, OCLC FirstSearch, OCLC WorldShare Interlibrary Loan, OVID Technologies, ProQuest, PubMed, ScienceDirect, SirsiDynix, Westlaw, Wiley, Wilson - Wilson Web
Wireless access
Function: Archival coll, Art exhibits, Audio & video playback equip for onsite use, AV serv, Bilingual assistance for Spanish patrons, Bks on cassette, Bks on CD, Computers for patron use, Copy machines, Digital talking bks, Distance learning, Doc delivery serv, e-mail serv, E-Reserves, Electronic databases & coll, Govt ref serv, Handicapped accessible, Health sci info serv, ILL available, Large print keyboards, Music CDs, Newsp ref libr, Online cat, Online info literacy tutorials on the web & in blackboard, Online ref, Online searches, Orientations, Outside serv via phone, mail, e-mail & web, Photocopying/Printing, Pub access computers, Ref serv available, Scanner, Spoken cassettes & CDs, Tax forms, Telephone ref, VHS videos, Video lending libr, Web-catalog
Partic in Association of Southeastern Research Libraries; Center for Research Libraries; Florida Library Information Network; Lyrasis; SEFLIN - Southeast Florida Library Information Network, Inc

Special Services for the Deaf - TDD equip
Special Services for the Blind - Computer with voice synthesizer for visually impaired persons
Open Mon-Thurs 7:30am-1am, Fri 7:30am-10pm, Sat 8-8, Sun 10am-1am

L GREENBERG TRAURIG LLP*, Research Center Law Library, 333 SE Second Ave, Ste 4400, 33131. (Mail add: Doral Concourse, 8400 NW 36th St, Ste 400, Doral, 33166), SAN 328-0705. Tel: 305-579-0500. FAX: 305-579-0717. Administration FAX: 305-755-0904. *Supvr,* Denise Mason; Staff 13 (MLS 3, Non-MLS 10)
Founded 1975
Library Holdings: Bk Titles 8,000; Bk Vols 20,000; Per Subs 450
Function: Doc delivery serv, For res purposes, ILL available, Online searches, Ref serv available, Telephone ref
Restriction: Access at librarian's discretion

L HOLLAND & KNIGHT LLP, Law Library, 701 Brickell Ave, Ste 3300, 33131. SAN 372-1329. Tel: 305-789-7420. FAX: 305-789-7799. *Libr Mgr,* Elizabeth Chifari; E-mail: elizabeth.chifari@hklaw.com; Staff 1 (MLS 1)
Library Holdings: Bk Vols 10,000; Per Subs 75

M MERCY HOSPITAL LIBRARY SERVICES*, 3663 S Miami Ave, 33133. SAN 303-0601. Tel: 305-285-2160. FAX: 305-285-2128. *Librn,* Jean Garrison; E-mail: jgarrison@mercymiami.org; Staff 1 (Non-MLS 1)
Founded 1951
Library Holdings: e-books 118; e-journals 1,500; Bk Titles 500; Per Subs 25
Partic in Miami Health Sciences Library Consortium
Restriction: Staff use only

M MIAMI CHILDREN'S HOSPITAL MEDICAL LIBRARY*, 3100 SW 62nd Ave, 33155-3009. SAN 328-1329. Tel: 305-666-6511, Ext 4470. FAX: 305-284-1145. Web Site: www.mch.com. *Dir,* Roumiana Katzarkov; E-mail: roumiana@mch.com; *Coordr, ILL,* Miriam Ruiz; E-mail: mperez@mch.com; Staff 3 (MLS 1, Non-MLS 2)
Library Holdings: e-books 65; e-journals 400; Bk Vols 3,700; Per Subs 150
Subject Interests: Pediatrics
Automation Activity & Vendor Info: (Cataloging) EOS International; (Circulation) EOS International; (OPAC) EOS International; (Serials) EOS International
Database Vendor: EBSCOhost, Majors, OVID Technologies
Partic in Docline; Miami Health Sciences Library Consortium
Restriction: Employees only

MIAMI DADE COLLEGE

C KENDALL CAMPUS LIBRARY*, 11011 SW 104th St, 33176-3393, SAN 337-7253. Tel: 305-237-0996, 305-237-2015, 305-237-2291. Interlibrary Loan Service Tel: 305-237-2783. Reference Tel: 305-237-2292. FAX: 305-237-2923. Interlibrary Loan Service FAX: 305-237-2864. Administration FAX: 305-237-0302. Web Site: www.mdc.edu/kendall/library. *Dir,* Eric Dominicis; *Asst Dir,* Jennifer Diptee; *Librn,* Barbara Feldman-Joy; *Librn,* Laurie Hime; *Librn,* Steven Kronen; *Librn,* David Picca; *Librn,* Jennifer Saxton; Staff 23.79 (MLS 7.86, Non-MLS 15.93)
Founded 1965. Enrl 63,092; Fac 204; Highest Degree: Bachelor
Jul 2006-Jun 2007. Mats Exp $215,985, Books $95,955, Per/Ser (Incl. Access Fees) $46,230, Other Print Mats $12,000, Micro $33,800, AV Mat $2,100, Electronic Ref Mat (Incl. Access Fees) $25,400, Presv $500. Sal $846,764 (Prof $470,846)
Library Holdings: Bk Titles 126,194; Bk Vols 139,798; Per Subs 431
Special Collections: Archival Coll
Automation Activity & Vendor Info: (Acquisitions) Ex Libris Group; (Cataloging) LAC Group; (Circulation) Ex Libris Group; (OPAC) Ex Libris Group
Publications: Kendall Campus Library Fact Sheet
Open Mon-Thurs 7am-10pm, Fri 7-6, Sat 10-4

CM MEDICAL CENTER CAMPUS LIBRARY & INFORMATION RESOURCE CENTER*, 950 NW 20th St, 33127, SAN 337-7318. Tel: 305-237-4129. FAX: 305-237-4301. *Dir,* Elisa Abella; Tel: 305-237-4498, E-mail: elisa.abella@mdc.edu; *Asst Dir,* Ivan Toledo; Tel: 305-237-4325; *Librn,* Carla Clark; Tel: 305-237-4342; Staff 3 (MLS 3)
Founded 1975. Enrl 41,000; Fac 100
Library Holdings: Bk Titles 11,000; Bk Vols 12,000; Per Subs 96
Subject Interests: Allied health, Nursing
Partic in SE Fla Educ Consortium
Open Mon-Thurs 7:30am-9pm, Fri 7:30-5, Sat 9-4

C NORTH CAMPUS LEARNING RESOURCES*, 11380 NW 27th Ave, 33167, SAN 337-7229. Tel: 305-237-1142. Reference Tel: 305-237-1183. FAX: 305-237-8276. Web Site: www.mdc.edu/north/library. *Dir,* Estrella Iglesias; Tel: 305-237-1471; *Assoc Dir,* Dr Sara Alegria; Tel: 305-237-1777; *ILL,* Devi Singh; Staff 7 (MLS 7)
Founded 1960. Enrl 25,000; Fac 350; Highest Degree: Bachelor
Library Holdings: Bk Titles 107,760; Bk Vols 130,000; Per Subs 650
Partic in Lyrasis; Miami Health Sciences Library Consortium

C WOLFSON CAMPUS LIBRARY*, 300 NE Second Ave, 33132, SAN 337-7288. Tel: 305-237-3144. Interlibrary Loan Service Tel: 305-237-3454. Reference Tel: 305-237-3451. Web Site: www.mdc.edu/main/library. *Dir, Learning Res,* Zoila De Yurre Fatemian; Tel: 305-237-7454, E-mail: zdeyurre@mdc.edu; *Assoc Dir, Learning Res,* Katia Nunez; Tel: 305-237-7385, E-mail: knunez1@mdc.edu; *Librn,* Adria Leal; Tel: 305-237-3449, E-mail: aleal2@mdc.edu; Staff 11 (MLS 5, Non-MLS 6)
Founded 1972
Library Holdings: AV Mats 3,821; Bk Vols 45,015; Per Subs 170; Talking Bks 236
Automation Activity & Vendor Info: (Cataloging) Ex Libris Group; (Circulation) Ex Libris Group; (OPAC) Ex Libris Group; (Serials) Ex Libris Group
Open Mon-Thurs 7:30am-9pm, Fri 7:30-5, Sat 8-1

L MIAMI-DADE COUNTY LAW LIBRARY*, County Courthouse, Rm 321A, 73 W Flagler St, 33130. SAN 303-0466. Tel: 305-349-7548. FAX: 305-349-7552. E-mail: refdesk@mdcll.org. Web Site: www.mdcll.org. *Dir,* Johanna Porpiglia; Staff 14 (MLS 7, Non-MLS 7)
Founded 1937
Library Holdings: Bk Vols 127,270; Per Subs 30
Subject Interests: State law
Automation Activity & Vendor Info: (Acquisitions) Inmagic, Inc.; (Cataloging) Inmagic, Inc.; (Serials) Inmagic, Inc.
Database Vendor: LexisNexis, Westlaw
Wireless access
Partic in Westlaw
Restriction: Pub use on premises

P MIAMI-DADE PUBLIC LIBRARY SYSTEM*, Main Library, 101 W Flagler St, 33130-1523. SAN 337-7342. Tel: 305-375-5184. FAX: 305-375-3048. TDD: 305-375-2878. Web Site: www.mdpls.org. *Dir,* Position Currently Open; *Asst Dir,* Suzet Alvarez-Cleary; Tel: 305-375-5034, E-mail: suzeta@miamidade.gov; *Asst Dir,* Lucrece Louisdhon-Louinis; Tel: 305-375-5501, E-mail: louisdhonl@mdpls.org; *Asst Dir,* Sylvia Mora-Ona; Tel: 305-375-5005, E-mail: moras@mdpls.org; *Asst Dir,* William Urbizu; Tel: 305-375-5016, E-mail: urbizub@mdpls.org; *Asst Dir, Outreach, Communications & Prog,* Gia Arbogast; *Circ & Main Libr Adminr,* Sue Cvejanovich; Tel: 305-375-3555, E-mail: cvejanovichs@mdpls.org; *Coll Mgmt & Tech Serv Adminr,* Position Currently Open; *Govt Doc Librn,* Min Shaheen; Tel: 305-375-5575, E-mail: shaheenm@mdpls.org; *ILL Librn,* Charles Whittaker; Tel: 305-375-4068, E-mail: whittakerc@mdpls.org; *Access Serv Mgr,* Diana De Hernandez; Tel: 305-375-8321, E-mail: hernandezd@mdpls.org; *Ch Mgr,* Elizabeth Pearson; Tel: 305-375-5021, E-mail: pearsone@mdpls.org; *Fine Arts Dept Mgr,* Kelly Rodriguez; Tel: 305-375-5015, E-mail: rodriguezk@mdpls.org; *First Flr Ref Mgr,* Jennifer Dewsnap-Shipley; Tel: 305-375-5231, E-mail: dewsnapj@mdpls.org; *Fla/Genealogy Dept Mgr,* Robert Klein; Tel: 305-375-5023, E-mail: kleinr@mdpls.org; *Lang Dept Mgr,* Jorge Gonzalez; Tel: 305-375-5579, E-mail: gonzalezj@mdpls.org; *Second Flr Ref Mgr,* Candy Granda; Tel: 305-375-1031, E-mail: grandac@mdpls.org; *Soc Sci Dept Mgr,* Mary Garcia; E-mail: garciam@mdpls.org; *Urban Affairs Dept Mgr,* Julio Granda; E-mail: grandaj@mdpls.org. Subject Specialists: *Govt doc,* Min Shaheen; *Fla,* Charles Whittaker; *Fine arts,* Kelly Rodriguez; *Bus, Per, Sci,* Jennifer Dewsnap-Shipley; *Fla, Genealogy,* Robert Klein; *Fine arts, Humanities, Soc sci,* Candy Granda; *Humanities, Soc sci,* Mary Garcia; *Urban affairs,* Julio Granda; Staff 218 (MLS 200, Non-MLS 18)
Founded 1971. Pop 2,121,798; Circ 8,132,818
Oct 2010-Sept 2011 Income (Main Library and Branch(s)) $49,632,356, State $1,655,348, County $46,022,927, Other $1,954,081. Mats Exp $1,599,999, Books $687,241, Per/Ser (Incl. Access Fees) $97,838, Other Print Mats $58,247, Micro $3,825, AV Mat $244,593, Electronic Ref Mat (Incl. Access Fees) $508,255. Sal $40,637,228 (Prof $15,447,692)
Library Holdings: Audiobooks 53,133; AV Mats 25,328; Bks on Deafness & Sign Lang 1,152; Braille Volumes 432; CDs 23,575; DVDs 158,360; e-books 4,850; Electronic Media & Resources 3,789; High Interest/Low Vocabulary Bk Vols 899; Large Print Bks 52,795; Microforms 66,751; Music Scores 28,893; Bk Titles 621,509; Bk Vols 2,588,195; Per Subs 1,265; Videos 30,099
Special Collections: Florida Room (books, clippings, photos,rare books); Foundations Center Regional Coll; Patent. State Document Depository; US Document Depository
Subject Interests: Fla, Intl, Latin Am, Patents, Spanish lang
Automation Activity & Vendor Info: (Acquisitions) Innovative Interfaces, Inc; (Cataloging) Innovative Interfaces, Inc; (Circulation) Innovative Interfaces, Inc; (OPAC) Innovative Interfaces, Inc; (Serials) Innovative Interfaces, Inc
Database Vendor: Alexander Street Press, Baker & Taylor, Brodart, BWI, EBSCO - WebFeat, EBSCO Auto Repair Reference, EBSCO Information Services, EBSCOhost, Gale Cengage Learning, Grolier Online, infoUSA, LearningExpress, Newsbank, OCLC FirstSearch, OCLC WorldShare Interlibrary Loan, Overdrive, Inc, ProQuest, ReferenceUSA,

SerialsSolutions, TumbleBookLibrary, ValueLine, World Book Online, WT Cox
Wireless access
Publications: Guide to Services; Library Happenings (Newsletter); Long Range Plan; Schedule of Programs (Monthly)
Partic in SEFLIN - Southeast Florida Library Information Network, Inc
Special Services for the Deaf - Staff with knowledge of sign lang; TDD equip
Special Services for the Blind - Talking bks
Open Mon-Sat 10-6
Friends of the Library Group
Branches: 50
ALLAPATTAH, 1799 NW 35th St, 33142-5421, SAN 337-7407. Tel: 305-638-6086. FAX: 305-638-6782.
Open Mon-Thurs & Sat 10-6
ARCOLA LAKES BRANCH, 8240 NW 7 Ave, 33150. Tel: 305-694-2707. FAX: 305-693-6236.
Open Mon, Tues & Sat 10-6, Wed & Thurs 12-8
CALIFORNIA CLUB, 850 Ives Dairy Rd, 33179. Tel: 305-770-3155. FAX: 305-770-3157.
Open Mon, Fri & Sat 10-6, Tues & Wed 12-8
CIVIC CENTER PORTA KIOSK, Metrorail Civic Center Sta, 1501 NW 12th Ave, 33136. (Mail add: 227 22nd St, Miami Beach, 33139), SAN 377-7138. Tel: 305-324-0291. FAX: 305-545-3370.
Open Mon-Fri 6-10 & 2-6
COCONUT GROVE BRANCH, 2875 McFarlane Rd, Coconut Grove, 33133, SAN 337-7431. Tel: 305-442-8695. FAX: 305-567-9421.
Open Mon, Wed, Thurs & Sat 10-6, Tues 12-8
CONCORD, 3882 SW 112th Ave, 33165. Tel: 305-207-1344. FAX: 305-207-1474.
Open Mon, Wed, Thurs & Sat 10-6, Tues 12-8
CONNECTIONS, 2455 NW 183 St, 33056. Tel: 305-474-7251. FAX: 305-474-7258.
Open Mon-Fri 8:30-5
CORAL GABLES BRANCH, 3443 Segovia St, Coral Gables, 33134, SAN 337-7466. Tel: 305-442-8706. FAX: 305-529-2763.
Open Mon & Thurs-Sat 10-6, Tues & Wed 1-9
CORAL REEF, 9211 Coral Reef Dr, 33157, SAN 337-7474. Tel: 305-233-8324. FAX: 305-378-1166.
Open Mon, Fri & Sat 10-6, Tues & Wed 1-9
COUNTRY WALK, 15433 SW 137th Ave, 33177. Tel: 786-293-4577. FAX: 786-293-4582.
Open Mon, Tues, Thurs & Sat 10-6, Wed 12-8
CULMER OVERTOWN, 350 NW 13th St, 33136, SAN 337-7490. Tel: 305-579-5322. FAX: 305-372-7734.
Open Mon-Thurs & Sat 10-6
DORAL BRANCH, 10785 NW 58th St, Doral, 33178. Tel: 305-716-9598. FAX: 305-418-2746.
Open Mon, Tues, Thurs & Sat 10-6, Wed 12-8
EDISON CENTER, 531 NW 62nd St, 33150, SAN 337-7520. Tel: 305-757-0668. FAX: 305-757-3975.
Open Mon-Thurs & Sat 10-6
FAIRLAWN, 6376 SW Eighth St, 33144, SAN 337-7555. Tel: 305-261-1571. FAX: 305-264-1716.
Open Mon & Thurs-Sat 10-6, Tues 12-8
GOLDEN GLADES, 100 NE 166 St, 33162. Tel: 305-787-1544. FAX: 305-787-8297.
Open Mon, Thurs & Sat 10-6, Tues & Wed 12-8
HIALEAH GARDENS BRANCH, 11300 NW 87th Ct, Ste 112-114, Hialeah Gardens, 33018. Tel: 305-820-8520. FAX: 305-820-8577.
Open Mon-Wed & Sat 10-6, Thurs 12-8
HISPANIC, 1398 SW First St, 33135, SAN 337-761X. Tel: 305-643-8574. FAX: 305-643-8578.
Subject Interests: Latin Am, Spanish (Lang)
Open Mon, Tues, Thurs & Sat 10-6, Wed 12-8
HOMESTEAD BRANCH, 700 N Homestead Blvd, Homestead, 33030, SAN 337-7644. Tel: 305-246-0168. FAX: 305-248-7817.
Open Mon, Thurs & Sat 10-6, Tues & Wed 1-9
INTERNATIONAL MALL, 10315 NW 12 St, 33172. Tel: 305-594-2514. FAX: 305-418-2746.
Open Mon, Fri & Sat 10-6, Tues & Wed 12-8
KENDALE LAKES, 15205 SW 88 St, 33196. Tel: 305-388-0326. FAX: 305-388-2259.
Open Mon, Fri & Sat 10-6, Wed & Thurs 1-9
KENDALL, 9101 SW 97th Ave, 33176, SAN 337-7679. Tel: 305-279-0520. FAX: 305-270-2983.
Open Mon, Thurs & Sat 10-6, Tues & Wed 1-9
KEY BISCAYNE BRANCH, 299 Crandon Blvd, Key Biscayne, 33149, SAN 322-5941. Tel: 305-361-6134. FAX: 305-365-0496.
Open Mon & Thurs-Sat 9:30-6, Tues & Wed 9:30-9
LAKES OF THE MEADOW, 4284 SW 152nd Ave, 33185. Tel: 305-222-2149. FAX: 305-222-2146.
Open Mon, Tues, Thurs & Sat 10-6, Wed 12-8
LEMON CITY, 430 NE 61st St, 33137, SAN 337-7709. Tel: 305-757-0662. FAX: 305-757-5747.
Founded 1894
Open Mon-Wed & Fri-Sat 10-6
LITTLE RIVER, 160 NE 79th St, 33138, SAN 337-7733. Tel: 305-751-8689. FAX: 305-757-5237.
Open Mon-Thurs & Sat 10-6
MIAMI BEACH REGIONAL BRANCH, 227 22nd St, Miami Beach, 33139, SAN 328-6452. Tel: 305-535-4219. FAX: 305-535-4224.
Open Mon & Tues 1-9, Wed-Sat 10-6
MIAMI LAKES BRANCH, 6699 Windmill Gate Rd, Miami Lakes, 33014, SAN 337-775X. Tel: 305-822-6520. FAX: 305-364-0802.
Open Mon, Thurs & Sat 10-6, Tues & Wed 1-9
MIAMI SPRINGS BRANCH, 401 Westward Dr, Miami Springs, 33166, SAN 337-7768. Tel: 305-805-3811. FAX: 305-805-1611.
Open Mon, Wed, Thurs & Sat 10-6, Tues 12-8
MODEL CITY, 2211 NW 54th St, 33142, SAN 337-7792. Tel: 305-636-2233. FAX: 305-638-6828.
Open Mon-Fri 10-6
NARANJA, 14850 SW 280 St, 33032. Tel: 305-242-2290. FAX: 305-242-2297.
Open Mon, Fri & Sat 10-6, Tues & Thurs 12-8
NORTH CENTRAL, 9590 NW 27th Ave, 33147, SAN 371-3431. Tel: 305-693-4541. FAX: 305-694-0315.
Open Mon, Tues, Fri & Sat 10-6, Thurs 12-8
NORTH DADE REGIONAL, 2455 NW 183rd St, 33056, SAN 337-7822. Tel: 305-625-6424. FAX: 305-628-3854.
Special Collections: Schomburg Clipping & Index File
Open Mon & Thurs-Sat 10-6, Tues & Wed 1-9
NORTH SHORE, 7501 Collins Ave, Miami Beach, 33141, SAN 328-6479. Tel: 305-864-5392. FAX: 305-861-2032.
Open Mon, Tues, Thurs & Sat 10-6, Wed 12-8
NORTHEAST, 19200 W Country Club Dr, 33180, SAN 337-7857. Tel: 305-931-5512. FAX: 305-931-5515.
Open Mon-Fri 9-5
OPA-LOCKA, 780 Fisherman St, Ste 140, Opa-Locka, 33054. Tel: 305-688-1134. FAX: 305-769-4045.
Open Mon-Thurs & Sat 10-6
PALM SPRINGS NORTH BRANCH, 17601 NW 78th Ave, Palm Springs North, 33015. Tel: 305-820-8564. FAX: 305-557-2173.
Open Mon, Tues, Fri & Sat 10-6, Wed 12-8
PALMETTO BAY, 17641 Old Cutler Rd, 33157. Tel: 305-232-1771. FAX: 305-232-1706.
Open Mon, Fri & Sat 10-6, Tues & Wed 12-8
PINECREST, 5835 SW 111 St, Pinecrest, 33156. Tel: 305-668-4571. FAX: 305-668-4480.
Open Mon, Tues & Sat 10-6, Wed & Thurs 1-9
SHENANDOAH, 2111 SW 19th St, 33145, SAN 337-7881. Tel: 305-250-4688. FAX: 305-250-4687.
Open Mon, Wed, Thurs & Sat 10-6, Tues 12-8
SOUTH DADE REGIONAL, 10750 SW 211th St, 33189, SAN 337-7911. Tel: 305-233-8140. FAX: 305-233-4419.
Open Mon, Tues, Fri & Sat 10-6, Wed & Thurs 1-9
SOUTH MIAMI BRANCH, 6000 Sunset Dr, South Miami, 33143, SAN 337-7946. Tel: 305-667-6121. FAX: 305-661-6558.
Open Mon, Fri & Sat 10-6, Tues & Wed 1-9
SOUTH SHORE, 131 Alton Rd, Miami Beach, 33139, SAN 328-6495. Tel: 305-535-4223. FAX: 305-535-4225.
Open Mon, Tues, Thurs & Sat 10-6, Wed 12-8
SUNNY ISLES BEACH BRANCH, 18070 Collins Ave, Sunny Isles Beach, 33160. Tel: 305-682-0726. FAX: 305-682-0781.
Open Mon, Tues & Sat 10-6, Wed & Thurs 12-8
SUNSET, 10855 SW 72 St, No 13, 33173. Tel: 305-270-6368. FAX: 305-273-6074.
Open Mon, Thurs & Sat 10-6, Tues & Wed 12-8
P TALKING BOOKS, 2455 NW 183rd St, 33056, SAN 337-7377. Tel: 305-751-8687. Toll Free Tel: 800-451-9544. FAX: 305-757-8401.
Special Collections: Blindness & Other Handicaps Reference Material; Spanish Language Coll, cassettes
Open Mon-Fri 8:30-5
TAMIAMI, 13250-52 SW 8 St, 33184. Tel: 305-223-4758. FAX: 305-480-8571.
Open Mon-Wed & Sat 10-6, Thurs 12-8
VIRRICK PARK, 3255 Plaza St, Coconut Grove, 33133. Tel: 305-442-7872. FAX: 305-442-7876.
Open Mon, Fri & Sat 10-6, Wed & Thurs 12-8
WEST DADE REGIONAL, 9445 Coral Way, 33165, SAN 337-7970. Tel: 305-553-1134. FAX: 305-226-5343.
Open Mon, Tues, Fri & Sat 10-6, Wed & Thurs 1-9
WEST FLAGLER, 5050 W Flagler St, 33134, SAN 337-8004. Tel: 305-442-8710. FAX: 305-445-5495.
Open Mon, Wed, Thurs & Sat 10-6, Tues 12-8

WEST KENDALL REGIONAL, 10201 Hammocks Blvd, 33196, SAN 371-3016. Tel: 305-385-7135. FAX: 305-385-5285.
Open Mon & Thurs-Sat 10-6, Tues & Wed 1-9
Bookmobiles: 2

S THE MIAMI HERALD*, Information Center, One Herald Plaza, 33132. SAN 303-0636. Tel: 305-376-3402, 305-376-3434. FAX: 305-376-4424, 305-995-8183. Web Site: www.herald.com. *Dir, Info Serv,* Monika Leal; Tel: 305-376-3665, E-mail: mleal@miamiherald.com; *Licensing & Copyright Ed,* Fernanda Rocha; Tel: 305-376-3737, E-mail: frocha@miamiherald.com
Founded 1940
Library Holdings: Bk Vols 2,500; Per Subs 70
Special Collections: Newspaper clippings: Mia-Herald & News 1940-1982
Partic in Dialog Corp; Dow Jones News Retrieval
Restriction: Open by appt only
Friends of the Library Group

C MIAMI INTERNATIONAL UNIVERSITY OF ART & DESIGN LIBRARY*, 1501 Biscayne Blvd, Ste 100, 33132-1418. SAN 375-3220. Tel: 305-428-5674. Toll Free Tel: 800-225-9023, Ext 5674. FAX: 305-374-7946. Web Site: www.aimiu.artinstitutes.edu. *Dir, Libr Serv,* Lori Kelly; Staff 2 (MLS 2)
Founded 1967. Enrl 1,600; Fac 115; Highest Degree: Master
Jul 2005-Jun 2006. Mats Exp $65,000
Library Holdings: Bk Titles 25,000; Per Subs 211
Special Collections: History of Costume Coll; Vogue Magazine, 1947-present
Subject Interests: Animation, Fashion, Film, Graphic design, Interior design, Visual arts
Automation Activity & Vendor Info: (Cataloging) OCLC; (Circulation) Follett Software
Wireless access
Function: Res libr
Publications: TWIS
Partic in Library & Information Resources Network (LIRN); SEFLIN - Southeast Florida Library Information Network, Inc
Open Mon-Thurs 7:30am-9:30pm, Fri 7:30-6, Sat 10-5
Restriction: Open to students, fac & staff

GM MIAMI VA HEALTHCARE SYSTEM, Medical Library, 1201 NW 16th St, 33125-1693. SAN 337-8128. Tel: 305-575-3187. Toll Free Tel: 888-276-1785, Ext 3187. FAX: 305-575-3118. E-mail: vhamialibrary@va.gov. *Supvr,* Monica Bamio-Aparicio; E-mail: monica.bamio-aparicio@va.gov; *ILL, Libr Tech,* Christine A Kittler; E-mail: christine.kittler@va.gov; Staff 2 (Non-MLS 2)
Founded 1947
Library Holdings: Bk Titles 3; Per Subs 200
Automation Activity & Vendor Info: (Cataloging) CyberTools for Libraries; (Circulation) CyberTools for Libraries
Database Vendor: CyberTools for Libraries, DynaMed, EBSCOhost, LexisNexis, OCLC FirstSearch, OCLC WorldShare Interlibrary Loan, OVID Technologies, PubMed, STAT!Ref (Teton Data Systems), UpToDate, WebMD
Partic in Veterans Affairs Library Network (VALNET)
Special Services for the Deaf - TTY equip
Open Mon-Fri 7-4:30

P MICCOSUKEE COMMUNITY LIBRARY*, Tamiami Sta, 33144. (Mail add: PO Box 440021, 33144-0021), SAN 377-3140. Tel: 305-223-8380, Ext 2248. FAX: 305-223-1011. Web Site: www.miccosukee.com. *Librn,* Sharon Logan
Library Holdings: Bk Vols 25,000; Per Subs 35
Restriction: Mem only
Friends of the Library Group

L MORGAN, LEWIS & BOCKIUS LLP*, Law Library, 200 S Biscayne Blvd, Ste 5300, 33131. SAN 372-1310. Tel: 305-415-3000. FAX: 305-415-3001. Web Site: www.morganlewis.com.
Library Holdings: Bk Vols 1,500; Per Subs 20
Partic in OCLC Online Computer Library Center, Inc
Restriction: Staff use only

G NATIONAL MARINE FISHERIES SERVICE*, Southeast Fisheries Science Center Library, 75 Virginia Beach Dr, 33149. SAN 303-0660. Tel: 305-361-4229. FAX: 305-365-4104. Web Site: www.sefsc.noaa.gov. *Librn,* Maria Bello
Founded 1965
Library Holdings: Bk Titles 5,000; Per Subs 180
Special Collections: Fish, Fish Eggs, Larvae, Systematics & Scallops, reprints & micro
Subject Interests: Ecology, Environ studies, Marine biol
Partic in Dialog Corp; OCLC Online Computer Library Center, Inc

G NATIONAL OCEANIC & ATMOSPHERIC ADMINISTRATION*, Miami Regional Library, 4301 Rickenbacker Causeway, 33149. SAN 377-7405. Tel: 305-361-4428. FAX: 305-361-4448. E-mail: aoml.library@noaa.gov. Web Site: www.aoml.noaa.gov/general/lib/. *Regional Librn,* Linda Pikula; E-mail: linda.pikula@noaa.gov; *Librn,* Gloria Aversano; Tel: 305-229-4406; *Librn,* Ashley Jefferson; Tel: 305-361-4429, E-mail: ashley.jefferson@noaa.gov. Subject Specialists: *Atmospheric sci, Marine sci,* Linda Pikula; *Atmospheric sci,* Gloria Aversano; *Marine sci,* Ashley Jefferson; Staff 3 (MLS 3)
Library Holdings: Microforms 60,000; Bk Vols 20,776; Per Subs 190
Special Collections: Oceanography
Subject Interests: Atmospheric, Earth, Geoscience
Automation Activity & Vendor Info: (Cataloging) SirsiDynix; (Circulation) SirsiDynix
Function: ILL available, Ref & res
Restriction: Non-circulating, Open to pub by appt only

M NORTH SHORE MEDICAL CENTER*, Medical Library, 1100 NW 95th St, 33150. SAN 375-1643. Tel: 305-694-3640. FAX: 305-694-4810. Web Site: www.northshoremedical.com. *Educ Coordr,* Douchelle Wiley
Library Holdings: Bk Vols 350
Restriction: Med staff & students

R SAINT JOHN VIANNEY COLLEGE*, Seminary Library, 2900 SW 87th Ave, 33165. SAN 303-0687. Tel: 305-223-4561. FAX: 305-223-0650. *Dir,* Maria Rodriguez; E-mail: rodriguez@sjvcs.edu; Staff 3 (MLS 2, Non-MLS 1)
Founded 1960. Enrl 55; Fac 20; Highest Degree: Bachelor
Library Holdings: Bk Titles 44,451; Bk Vols 52,802; Per Subs 155
Special Collections: Philosophy & Literature Bi-lingual Coll
Subject Interests: Philos, Relig, Theol
Automation Activity & Vendor Info: (Acquisitions) Follett Software; (Cataloging) Follett Software; (Circulation) Follett Software
Open Mon, Tues, Thurs & Fri 8:30-4:30, Wed 8:30am-9pm
Restriction: Open to pub with supv only

M SOUTH MIAMI HOSPITAL*, Health Sciences Library, 6200 SW 73rd St, 33143. SAN 328-1035. Tel: 786-662-8219. FAX: 786-662-5124. E-mail: library@baptisthealth.net. Web Site: www.baptisthealth.net. *Dir,* Diane Rourke; E-mail: dianer@baptisthealth.net; *Online Serv,* Devica Samsundar; E-mail: devica@baptisthealth.net; Staff 2 (MLS 1, Non-MLS 1)
Founded 1977
Library Holdings: e-books 60; e-journals 900; Bk Titles 800; Per Subs 160
Subject Interests: Allied health, Med, Nursing
Automation Activity & Vendor Info: (Cataloging) CyberTools for Libraries; (Circulation) CyberTools for Libraries; (ILL) CyberTools for Libraries; (OPAC) CyberTools for Libraries; (Serials) CyberTools for Libraries
Database Vendor: OVID Technologies
Publications: Library Letter
Partic in Miami Health Sciences Library Consortium
Open Mon-Fri 8:30-5

L SQUIRE SANDERS & DEMPSEY LLC LIBRARY*, 200 S Biscayne Blvd, Ste 4000, 33131. SAN 327-0939. Tel: 305-577-2932. FAX: 305-577-7001. Web Site: www.steelhector.com/library_banner.htm. *Dir, Libr Serv,* Sid Kaskey
Library Holdings: Bk Vols 30,000; Per Subs 700
Restriction: Not open to pub

L STEARNS, WEAVER, MILLER, WEISSLER, ALHADEFF & SITTERSON*, Law Library, 2200 Museum Tower, 150 W Flagler St, 33130. SAN 372-1345. Tel: 305-789-3251. FAX: 305-789-3395. Web Site: www.stearnsweaver.com. *Dir of Libr Serv,* Jeanne S Korman; E-mail: jkorman@stearnsweaver.com; *Libr Asst,* Kathryn G Rodriguez; Tel: 305-789-3225, E-mail: krodriguez@stearnsweaver.com; Staff 2 (MLS 1, Non-MLS 1)
Library Holdings: Bk Vols 15,000; Per Subs 186
Subject Interests: Banking, Bankruptcy, Corp law, Employment, Labor, Real estate, State law
Automation Activity & Vendor Info: (Acquisitions) Inmagic, Inc.; (Cataloging) Inmagic, Inc.; (Circulation) Inmagic, Inc.; (OPAC) Inmagic, Inc.; (Serials) Inmagic, Inc.
Database Vendor: Westlaw
Restriction: Not open to pub

S SURVIVAL RESEARCH FOUNDATION LIBRARY*, 1000 Island Blvd, Ste 512, 33160. SAN 329-1960. Tel: 305-936-1408. E-mail: s5rf@aol.com. *Librn,* Joyce Berger
Founded 1980
Library Holdings: Bk Titles 350

Special Collections: Aristocracy of the Dead; Encyclopedia of Parapsychology & Psychical Research; Evidence of Life After Death; Journals of the American Society for Psychical Research; Journals of the Society for Psychical Research; Lives & Letters in American Parapsychology; Religion & Parapsychology
Subject Interests: Relig
Special Services for the Blind - Talking bks

GL THIRD DISTRICT COURT OF APPEALS*, Law Library, 2001 SW 117th Ave, 33175. SAN 303-0555. Tel: 305-229-3200. *Librn,* Joanne Sargent
Founded 1957
Library Holdings: Bk Vols 25,000; Per Subs 65
Partic in Westlaw
Open Mon-Fri 8-5

G UNITED STATES NATIONAL OCEANIC & ATMOSPHERIC ADMINISTRATION*, NOAA Miami Regional Library at AOML, 4301 Rickenbacker Causeway, 33149-1097. SAN 303-0679. Tel: 305-361-4428, 305-361-4429. FAX: 305-361-4448. Web Site: www.aoml.noaa.gov/general/lib. *Regional Dir,* Linda L Pikula; *Librn,* Bossarte Randy; E-mail: pikula@aoml.noaa.gov
Founded 1972
Library Holdings: Bk Titles 22,000; Per Subs 240
Special Collections: US Coast & Geodetic Survey Report 1851-1928
Subject Interests: Math, Ocean eng, Oceanography
Automation Activity & Vendor Info: (Acquisitions) SirsiDynix; (Cataloging) SirsiDynix; (Circulation) SirsiDynix
Publications: Acquisitions Monthly; Database listing; Serials catalog
Partic in BRS; Dialog Corp; OCLC Online Computer Library Center, Inc
Open Mon-Fri 9-5
Branches:
NATIONAL HURRICANE CENTER/TROPICAL PREDICTION CENTER LIBRARY, 11691 SW 17 St, 33165-2149, SAN 302-8933. Tel: 305-229-4406. FAX: 305-553-9879. Web Site: www.aoml.noaa.gov/general/lib/lib1/nhclib/index/htm. *Regional Dir,* Linda Pikula; *Librn,* Gloria Aversano
Founded 1956
Library Holdings: Bk Vols 9,000; Per Subs 50
Special Collections: Technical Reports Coll; Tropical Typhoons & Cyclones
Subject Interests: Meteorology
Automation Activity & Vendor Info: (Acquisitions) SirsiDynix; (Cataloging) SirsiDynix; (Circulation) SirsiDynix
Partic in BRS; Dialog Corp; OCLC Online Computer Library Center, Inc
Publications: Acquisitions; Database listing; Newsletter; Serials listing
Open Tues-Thurs 9-5
Restriction: Open to pub for ref only

C UNIVERSITY OF MIAMI, Rosenstiel School of Marine & Atmospheric Science Library, 4600 Rickenbacker Causeway, 33149-1098. SAN 337-8039. Tel: 305-421-4060. FAX: 305-361-9306. E-mail: libcirc@rsmas.miami.edu. Web Site: www.rsmas.miami.edu/support/lib. *Dir,* Elizabeth Fish; Tel: 305-421-4021, E-mail: efish@rsmas.miami.edu; *Asst Librn,* Angela Clark; Tel: 305-421-4020, E-mail: aclark@rsmas.miami.edu. Subject Specialists: *Atmospheric sci, Marine sci, Ocean sci,* Angela Clark; Staff 4 (MLS 2, Non-MLS 2)
Founded 1943. Highest Degree: Doctorate
Library Holdings: Bk Vols 70,151; Per Subs 765
Special Collections: Expedition reports; Marine & Atmospheric Atlases; Nautical Charts
Subject Interests: Atmospheric sci, Marine sci
Automation Activity & Vendor Info: (Acquisitions) EBSCO Online; (ILL) OCLC FirstSearch; (OPAC) Innovative Interfaces, Inc; (Serials) EBSCO Online
Database Vendor: Agricola, Baker & Taylor, Cambridge Scientific Abstracts, EBSCOhost, Elsevier MDL, Innovative Interfaces, Inc, JSTOR, Newsbank, OCLC FirstSearch, OCLC WorldShare Interlibrary Loan, ProQuest, PubMed, ScienceDirect, SerialsSolutions, Wilson - Wilson Web
Wireless access
Publications: Serials list
Partic in OCLC Online Computer Library Center, Inc
Open Mon-Thurs 8:30am-9pm, Fri 8:30-5, Sat 1-5, Sun 1-9
Restriction: Restricted borrowing privileges
Departmental Libraries:
LOUIS CALDER MEMORIAL LIBRARY, Miller School of Medicine, 1601 NW Tenth Ave, 33136. (Mail add: PO Box 016950 (R950), 33101), SAN 337-8063. Tel: 305-243-6403. Interlibrary Loan Service Tel: 305-243-6749. Reference Tel: 305-243-6648. Administration Tel: 305-243-6441. FAX: 305-325-8853. Interlibrary Loan Service FAX: 305-243-9698. Reference FAX: 305-325-9670. Web Site: calder.med.miami.edu. *Dir of Libr Operations,* JoAnn Van Schaik; *Dep Dir,* Kimberly Loper; Tel: 305-243-6424, E-mail: kloper@med.miami.edu; *Asst Dir, ILL,* Jian-Min Xiong; Tel: 305-243-6749, E-mail: jxiong@med.miami.edu; *Sr Ref Librn,* Yanira Garcia-Barcena; Tel: 305-243-5439, E-mail: ygarcia@med.miami.edu; *Mgr, Acq & Ser,* Amalia de la Vega; Tel: 305-243-6901, E-mail: adelavega@med.miami.edu; *Metadata & Spec Coll Librn,* Erica Powell; Tel: 305-243-6931, E-mail: epowell@med.miami.edu; Staff 11 (MLS 11)
Founded 1952. Enrl 1,018; Fac 1,193; Highest Degree: Doctorate
Library Holdings: AV Mats 3,000; e-books 450; e-journals 13,000; Bk Titles 61,000; Bk Vols 133,000; Per Subs 1,159
Special Collections: Florida Coll; Floridiana, bks, pamphlets; History of Medicine Archives & Faculty Publications
Partic in Consortium of Southern Biomedical Libraries; Miami Health Sciences Library Consortium; OCLC Online Computer Library Center, Inc
Publications: Biennial Report; Calder Communications (Newsletter)
Open Mon-Thurs 7:30am-Midnight, Fri 7:30am-8pm, Sat 8-8, Sun Noon-Midnight
Friends of the Library Group
MARY & EDWARD NORTON LIBRARY OF OPHTHALMOLOGY, Bascom Palmer Eye Inst, 900 NW 17th St, 33136, SAN 337-8098. Tel: 305-326-6078. FAX: 305-326-6066. Web Site: www.bascompalmer.org. *Supvr,* Cynthia Birch
Founded 1962
Library Holdings: Bk Vols 18,000; Per Subs 230
Special Collections: AV Coll; Historical Coll
Subject Interests: Ophthalmology
Open Mon-Fri 9-5

M UNIVERSITY OF MIAMI HOSPITAL LIBRARY*, 1400 NW 12th Ave, 33136. SAN 377-2985. Tel: 305-325-5737. FAX: 305-325-5736. *Librn,* Jenny Garcia-Barcena; E-mail: ygarcia6@med.miami.edu
Library Holdings: Bk Titles 300
Subject Interests: Med, Nursing
Function: Res libr
Partic in Miami Health Sciences Library Consortium
Open Mon-Fri 8:30-Noon
Restriction: Non-circulating

S UP FRONT, INC*, Drug Information Library, 12360 SW 132nd St, Ste 215, 33186. SAN 324-637X. Tel: 786-242-8222. FAX: 786-242-8759. E-mail: upfrontin@aol.com. *Exec Dir,* James Hall
Founded 1973
Library Holdings: Bk Titles 2,700
Subject Interests: Drug info, Drug related topics
Restriction: Open by appt only

L WALTON, LANTAFF, SCHROEDER & CARSON*, Law Library, 9350 S Dixie Hwy, 10th Flr, 33156. SAN 325-8572. Tel: 305-671-1300. FAX: 305-670-7065. Web Site: www.waltonlantaff.com. *In Charge,* Leticia Coleman
Library Holdings: Bk Vols 5,000
Restriction: Staff use only

MIAMI BEACH

M MOUNT SINAI MEDICAL CENTER*, Medical Library, 4300 Alton Rd, 33140. SAN 303-0768. Tel: 305-674-2840. FAX: 305 674 2843. Web Site: www.msmc.com. Staff 2 (MLS 1, Non-MLS 1)
Founded 1946
Library Holdings: Bk Vols 15,000; Per Subs 300
Automation Activity & Vendor Info: (Cataloging) Surpass; (Circulation) Surpass
Partic in Miami Health Sciences Library Consortium
Restriction: Staff use only

R TEMPLE BETH SHOLOM LIBRARY*, 4144 Chase Ave, 33140. SAN 303-0784. Tel: 305-538-7231. FAX: 305-531-5428. Web Site: www.tbsmb.org.
Founded 1949
Library Holdings: Bk Titles 5,049; Per Subs 63
Special Collections: Holocaust Literature
Subject Interests: Current events, Holocaust, Judaica (lit or hist of Jews)
Open Mon-Thurs 9-7, Fri 9-4
Friends of the Library Group

MIAMI GARDENS

C FLORIDA MEMORIAL UNIVERSITY*, Nathan W Collier Library, 15800 NW 42nd Ave, 33054. SAN 303-0539. Tel: 305-626-3640. Reference Tel: 305-626-3647. FAX: 305-626-3625. E-mail: libref@fmuniv.edu. Web Site: www.fmuniv.edu/library. *Interim Dir,* Jauquinda Sturdivant; Tel: 305-626-3641, E-mail: jauquinda.sturdivant@fmuniv.edu. Subject Specialists: *Bus,* Jauquinda Sturdivant; Staff 11 (MLS 5, Non-MLS 6)
Founded 1879. Enrl 1,500; Fac 70; Highest Degree: Master
Library Holdings: Bk Vols 131,000; Per Subs 715

Special Collections: Archives Coll; Florida Coll, bks, mats; Laban C Connor Black Coll; Theological, Pastoral & Sermonic Materials (Reverend I C Mickins Coll)
Subject Interests: Soc sci & issues
Automation Activity & Vendor Info: (Cataloging) Innovative Interfaces, Inc; (Circulation) Innovative Interfaces, Inc; (OPAC) Innovative Interfaces, Inc
Database Vendor: EBSCOhost, JSTOR, LexisNexis, Medline, ProQuest, World Book Online
Function: Ref serv available
Publications: Handbook; Newsletter
Partic in Independent Cols & Univs of Fla; SEFLIN - Southeast Florida Library Information Network, Inc
Open Mon-Thurs 8am-Midnight, Fri 8-5, Sat 10-6, Sun 1-11

C ST THOMAS UNIVERSITY LIBRARY*, 16401 NW 37th Ave, 33054. SAN 321-5415. Tel: 305-628-6667. Reference Tel: 305-628-6668. FAX: 305-628-6666. Web Site: www.stu.edu/library. *Dir, Libr Serv,* Bryan Cooper; Tel: 305-474-6814, E-mail: bcooper@stu.edu; *Admin Serv,* Marta Gutierrez; Tel: 305-628-6672, E-mail: mgutierr@stu.edu; *Acq,* Isabel Medina Pascu; Tel: 305-628-6769, E-mail: imedina@stu.edu; *Archivist,* Margaret Elliston; Tel: 305-648-6669, E-mail: mellisto@stu.edu; *Cat,* Olga Urrea; Tel: 305-474-6863, E-mail: ourrea@stu.edu; *Circ,* Orly Garcia; E-mail: ogarcia@stu.edu; *ILL, Ref Serv,* Mary Monaco; Tel: 305-628-6671, E-mail: mmonaco@stu.edu; *Media Spec,* Wolfgang Riesterer; Tel: 305-628-6733, E-mail: wolfgang@stu.edu; *Ref Serv,* Lawrence Treadwell, IV; Tel: 305-474-6860, E-mail: ltreadwell@stu.edu; *Ser,* Rosario M Cruz; Tel: 305-474-6862, E-mail: rcruz@stu.edu; *Tech Serv,* Pedro Figueredo; Tel: 305-474-6861, E-mail: pfigueredo@stu.edu; Staff 11 (MLS 5, Non-MLS 6)
Founded 1962. Enrl 2,100; Fac 80; Highest Degree: Doctorate
Library Holdings: Bk Vols 235,000; Per Subs 900
Special Collections: Black Catholic Archives; Dorothy Day Coll; Jackie Gleason Kinescope Archives; Walt Whitman Coll. US Document Depository
Automation Activity & Vendor Info: (Cataloging) Ex Libris Group; (Circulation) Ex Libris Group
Publications: Library Handbook; Library Newsletter
Partic in OCLC Online Computer Library Center, Inc
Open Mon-Thurs 8-11, Fri 8-5, Sat 9-5, Sun 2-10
Departmental Libraries:
CL ALEX A HANNA LAW LIBRARY, 16401 NW 37th Ave, 33054. Tel: 305-623-2330. Circulation Tel: 305-623-2332. Reference Tel: 305-623-2331. FAX: 305-623-2337. Web Site: www.stu.edu/lawlib. *Dir,* Roy Balleste; Tel: 305-623-2341, E-mail: rballeste@stu.edu; *Assoc Dir, Head, Tech Serv,* Sonia Luna-Lamas; Tel: 305-623-2387, E-mail: slamas@stu.edu; *Asst Dir, Head, Pub Serv,* Jacob Hurst; Tel: 305-623-2335, E-mail: jhurst@stu.edu; *Ref/Fac Serv Librn,* Courtney Segota; Tel: 305-623-2339, E-mail: csegota@stu.edu; *Tech Serv Librn,* Iris Garcia; Tel: 305-623-2336, E-mail: lgarcia@stu.edu; *Weekend Ref Librn,* Nina Rose; Tel: 305-623-2378, E-mail: nrose@stu.edu; *Cat,* Danniza Liendo; Tel: 305-623-2313, E-mail: dliendo@stu.edu; *Multimedia,* Amado Lugo; Tel: 305-623-2333, E-mail: alugo@stu.edu; *Ser,* Rosario Cruz; Tel: 305-623-6862, E-mail: rcruz@stu.edu
Library Holdings: Bk Vols 120,000
Automation Activity & Vendor Info: (Acquisitions) Ex Libris Group; (Cataloging) Ex Libris Group; (Circulation) Ex Libris Group; (ILL) Clio; (OPAC) Ex Libris Group; (Serials) Ex Libris Group
Partic in SEFLIN - Southeast Florida Library Information Network, Inc
Open Mon-Thurs 7:30am-Midnight, Fri 7:30am-9pm, Sat 8-7, Sun 10am-Midnight

MIAMI SHORES

P BROCKWAY MEMORIAL LIBRARY, 10021 NE Second Ave, 33138. SAN 303-0814. Tel: 305-758-8107. Web Site: brockwaylibrary.org. *Dir,* Michelle Brown; *Adult Serv,* Francis Walsh; *Children's/Young Adult Serv,* Anne Kelly; Staff 6.13 (MLS 3, Non-MLS 3.13)
Founded 1949. Pop 10,250; Circ 76,060
Library Holdings: Audiobooks 1,980; AV Mats 5,281; DVDs 3,301; e-books 16,000; Electronic Media & Resources 2; Large Print Bks 1,867; Bk Vols 65,000; Per Subs 115
Automation Activity & Vendor Info: (Acquisitions) Baker & Taylor; (Cataloging) Follett Software; (Circulation) Follett Software; (OPAC) Follett Software
Wireless access
Function: Adult bk club, Art exhibits, Bk club(s), Bks on cassette, Bks on CD, Children's prog, Computers for patron use, Copy machines, e-mail serv, Electronic databases & coll, Free DVD rentals, ILL available, Magnifiers for reading, Online cat, Prog for adults, Prog for children & young adult, Pub access computers, Ref & res, Story hour, Summer reading prog, Teen prog, Video lending libr, Web-catalog
Open Mon, Tues & Thurs 9-8, Wed & Fri 9-6, Sat 9-1
Restriction: Circ to mem only

MICCO

P SOUTH MAINLAND LIBRARY*, 7921 Ron Beatty Blvd, 32976. SAN 370-3592. Tel: 772-664-4066. FAX: 772-664-0534. *Dir,* Diane Vosatka; E-mail: dvosatka@brev.org; *Head, Ref, Head, Youth Serv,* Emily Derrough; E-mail: ederrough@brev.org; *Supvr, Circ,* Susan Getter; E-mail: sgetter@brev.org; Staff 8 (MLS 1, Non-MLS 7)
Founded 1987. Circ 250,000
Library Holdings: Audiobooks 2,500; CDs 2,000; DVDs 10,000; Bk Titles 45,000; Per Subs 96; Videos 2,000
Wireless access
Function: Adult bk club, Bk club(s), Bks on CD, Computers for patron use, Copy machines, Electronic databases & coll, Fax serv, Free DVD rentals, Handicapped accessible, Holiday prog, Music CDs, Notary serv, Online cat, OverDrive digital audio bks, Prog for adults, Prog for children & young adult, Pub access computers, Ref serv available
Mem of Brevard County Library System
Special Services for the Deaf - TDD equip
Open Mon & Fri 9-5, Tues & Thurs 12-8, Wed & Sat 10-2
Friends of the Library Group

MILTON

P SANTA ROSA COUNTY LIBRARY SYSTEM*, 6275 Dogwood Dr, 32570. Tel: 850-623-2043. FAX: 850-623-2138. Web Site: www.santarosa.fl.gov/libraries. *Dir,* Linda Hendrix; Staff 6 (MLS 6)
Founded 2006. Pop 117,500; Circ 705,000
Library Holdings: AV Mats 15,000; Bk Vols 125,000; Per Subs 40
Wireless access

MIMS

P MIMS/SCOTTSMOOR PUBLIC LIBRARY*, 3615 Lionel Rd, 32754. Tel: 321-264-5080. FAX: 321-264-5081. Web Site: www.brev.org. *Dir,* Susan E Szymula; E-mail: sszymula@brev.org; *Ch Serv,* Sandra Chafin; *Ref Serv,* Janet Miller
Library Holdings: Bk Vols 33,500; Per Subs 55
Automation Activity & Vendor Info: (Cataloging) Infor Library & Information Solutions; (Circulation) Infor Library & Information Solutions; (OPAC) Infor Library & Information Solutions
Mem of Brevard County Library System
Open Mon 10-6, Wed & Fri 9-5, Thurs Noon-8
Friends of the Library Group

MIRAMAR

C DEVRY UNIVERSITY*, South Florida Library, 2300 SW 145th Ave, 33027-4150. Tel: 954-499-9619. FAX: 954-499-9659. Web Site: www.mir.devry.edu/academics_library.html. *Dir, Libr Serv,* Dr Mary Howrey; E-mail: mhowrey@devry.edu; *Evening/Weekend Librn,* Lucy Osemota; E-mail: losemota@devry.edu; Staff 3.6 (MLS 1.6, Non-MLS 2)
Founded 2002. Enrl 1,100; Fac 50; Highest Degree: Master
Library Holdings: e-books 14,000; Bk Titles 16,500; Per Subs 150
Automation Activity & Vendor Info: (Acquisitions) Ex Libris Group; (Cataloging) Ex Libris Group; (Circulation) Ex Libris Group; (ILL) OCLC; (OPAC) Ex Libris Group
Database Vendor: CQ Press, EBSCOhost, Facts on File, Faulkner Information Services, Hoovers, LexisNexis, OCLC FirstSearch, ProQuest
Partic in Lyrasis
Open Mon-Thurs 8am-9pm, Fri 8-5, Sat 9-4
Friends of the Library Group

MONTICELLO

P JEFFERSON COUNTY PUBLIC LIBRARY*, R J Bailar Public Library, 375 S Water St, 32344. SAN 303-0830. Tel: 850-342-0205, 850-342-0206. FAX: 850-342-0207. Web Site: jcpl.wildernesscoast.org. *Dir,* Kitty Brooks; E-mail: kbrooks@jeffersoncountyfl.gov; *Cat,* Natalie Binder
Founded 1984. Pop 15,000
Library Holdings: Bk Vols 35,000; Per Subs 52
Special Collections: Florida Coll; Keyston Genealogy Library; Literacy, Prof, Equipment
Automation Activity & Vendor Info: (Cataloging) LibLime; (Circulation) LibLime
Wireless access
Mem of Wilderness Coast Public Libraries
Open Mon, Wed & Fri 9-5:30, Tues & Thurs 9-7:30, Sat 9-3
Friends of the Library Group

P WILDERNESS COAST PUBLIC LIBRARIES*, 1180 W Washington St, 32344. (Mail add: PO Box 551, 32345), SAN 375-3190. Tel: 850-997-7400. Automation Services Tel: 850-926-4571. FAX: 850-997-7403. Automation Services FAX: 850-926-5157. Web Site: www.wildernesscoast.org. *Dir,* Pat Gilleland; E-mail: pat@wildernesscoast.org; Staff 4 (MLS 2, Non-MLS 2)
Founded 1992. Pop 50,218; Circ 161,526

Library Holdings: AV Mats 10,087; e-books 23,572; Electronic Media & Resources 30; Bk Vols 107,210; Per Subs 158
Special Collections: Florida Coll; Jefferson County Elder Black People Recollections. Oral History
Automation Activity & Vendor Info: (Cataloging) OCLC; (Circulation) SirsiDynix; (OPAC) SirsiDynix
Wireless access
Publications: Annual Plan of Service & Budget
Member Libraries: Franklin County Public Library; Jefferson County Public Library; Wakulla County Public Library
Partic in Panhandle Library Access Network
Friends of the Library Group
Bookmobiles: 1. Extension Mgr, Linda Norton. Bk vols 2,500

MONTVERDE

P HELEN LEHMANN MEMORIAL LIBRARY*, Montverde Library, 17435 Fifth St, 34756. Tel: 407-469-3838. FAX: 407-469-2773. Web Site: mylakelibrary.org/libraries/helen_lehmann_memorial_library.aspx. *Dir,* Martha Policke; *Libr Asst,* Beverly Fisher
Library Holdings: Bk Vols 11,000
Wireless access
Mem of Lake County Library System
Open Mon & Wed 10-4, Tues & Thurs 10-6, Fri & Sat 10-2

MOORE HAVEN

P GLADES COUNTY PUBLIC LIBRARY*, 201 Riverside Dr SW, 33471. (Mail add: PO Box 505, 33471), SAN 338-0254. Tel: 863-946-0744. FAX: 863-946-1661. *Librn,* Mary Booher; Staff 2 (Non-MLS 2)
Circ 8,143
Library Holdings: Bk Titles 17,043; Per Subs 60; Talking Bks 519; Videos 255
Special Collections: County History Coll
Open Mon-Fri 9-5

S MOORE HAVEN CORRECTIONAL FACILITY LIBRARY*, 1282 E State Rd 78, 33471. Tel: 863-946-2420. FAX: 863-946-2393. *Librn,* Stankeisha Burchell; Staff 3 (MLS 1, Non-MLS 2)
Founded 1995
Library Holdings: Bk Vols 4,980; Per Subs 16
Open Mon-Sat 8-11:15 & 11:45-4:15

MOUNT DORA

P W T BLAND PUBLIC LIBRARY*, 1995 N Donnelly St, 32757. SAN 303-0849. Tel: 352-735-7180. Reference Tel: 352-735-7180, Ext 3110. FAX: 352-735-0074. *Dir,* Stephanie Haimes; E-mail: haimess@cityofmountdora.com; *Ch Serv, Youth Serv,* Lynn Gonzales; E-mail: gonzalesl@cityofmountdora.com; *Circ,* Doreen Tewksbury; E-mail: tewksburyd@cityofmountdora.com; *Ref Serv,* Gregory Phillips; E-mail: phillipsg@cityofmountdora.com; Staff 12 (MLS 3, Non-MLS 9)
Founded 1905. Circ 150,132
Library Holdings: Bk Titles 60,000; Per Subs 150; Talking Bks 2,187
Special Collections: Florida Coll; Large Print Coll
Automation Activity & Vendor Info: (Cataloging) Horizon; (Circulation) Horizon; (OPAC) Horizon
Mem of Lake County Library System
Partic in Tampa Bay Library Consortium, Inc
Open Mon, Thurs & Fri 9:30-6, Tues & Wed 11-8, Sat 10-1:30
Friends of the Library Group

MULBERRY

P MULBERRY PUBLIC LIBRARY*, 103 E Canal St, 33860. Tel: 863-425-3246. FAX: 863-425-8818. Web Site: www.mypclc.org/libraries/mulberry. *Dir,* Cheri Schisler; Staff 3.5 (MLS 1, Non-MLS 2.5)
Founded 1949. Pop 3,650; Circ 61,000
Library Holdings: CDs 2,100; Bk Titles 19,500
Automation Activity & Vendor Info: (Cataloging) SirsiDynix; (Circulation) SirsiDynix; (ILL) OCLC
Wireless access
Function: Computer training, Copy machines, Electronic databases & coll, Fax serv, Handicapped accessible, Homebound delivery serv, ILL available, Music CDs, Photocopying/Printing, Preschool outreach, Prog for children & young adult, Ref & res, Ref serv available, Senior computer classes, Spoken cassettes & CDs, Spoken cassettes & DVDs, Summer reading prog, Tax forms, VHS videos, Wheelchair accessible
Partic in Polk County Libr Coop
Open Mon-Thurs 9-6, Fri 9-5, Sat 9-2
Friends of the Library Group

NAPLES

S AMERICAN IVY SOCIETY LIBRARY*, PO Box 2123, 34106-2123. SAN 326-5145. Tel: 845-688-5318. FAX: 845-688-5318. E-mail: ivyladysabina@sbcglobal.net. Web Site: www.ivy.org. *Dir, Res,* Russell Windle
Founded 1973
Publications: Between the Vines; The Ivy Journal

CL AVE MARIA SCHOOL OF LAW LIBRARY, 1025 Commons Circle, 34119. Tel: 239-687-5504. Web Site: www.avemarialaw.edu/library. *Head, Pub Serv, Interim Dir,* Ulysses Jaen; Staff 7 (MLS 4, Non-MLS 3)
Founded 2000. Enrl 380; Fac 21; Highest Degree: Doctorate
Library Holdings: Bk Titles 177,204; Bk Vols 200,000; Per Subs 4,501
Special Collections: Canon Law Coll
Automation Activity & Vendor Info: (Acquisitions) Innovative Interfaces, Inc; (Cataloging) Innovative Interfaces, Inc; (Circulation) Innovative Interfaces, Inc; (OPAC) Innovative Interfaces, Inc; (Serials) Innovative Interfaces, Inc
Wireless access
Restriction: Open to students, fac & staff, Pub use on premises

P COLLIER COUNTY PUBLIC LIBRARY*, 2385 Orange Blossom Dr, 34109. Tel: 239-593-0334. Interlibrary Loan Service Tel: 239-261-8208. Reference Tel: 239-263-7768. Administration Tel: 239-593-3511. FAX: 239-254-8167. Web Site: www.collier-library.org. *Dir,* Marilyn Matthes; E-mail: mmatthes@collier-lib.org; *Asst Dir,* Position Currently Open; *Acq,* Carol Travis; *AV,* Blane Halliday; *Ch Serv,* Pamela Moore; *ILL,* Carolann Adams; *Syst Coordr,* Michael Widner; Staff 22 (MLS 22)
Pop 260,000; Circ 2,500,000
Library Holdings: Bk Vols 631,830; Per Subs 1,300
Automation Activity & Vendor Info: (Acquisitions) Innovative Interfaces, Inc; (Cataloging) Innovative Interfaces, Inc; (Circulation) Innovative Interfaces, Inc; (OPAC) Innovative Interfaces, Inc; (Serials) Innovative Interfaces, Inc
Database Vendor: SirsiDynix
Publications: Bibliographies; Calendar (Monthly); Friends of Library (Newsletter)
Partic in Southwest Florida Library Network
Open Mon-Thurs 9-8, Fri & Sat 9-5, Sun 1-5
Friends of the Library Group
Branches: 8
EAST NAPLES BRANCH, 8787 E Tamiami Trail, 34113, SAN 337 8322. Tel: 239-775-5592. FAX: 239-774-5148. *Librn,* Marilyn McKay; Staff 1 (MLS 1)
Open Mon-Thurs 9-8, Fri & Sat 9-5
ESTATES, 1266 Golden Gate Blvd W, 34120, SAN 374-7514. Tel: 239-455-8088. FAX: 239-455-8113. *Librn,* Nina Metzel; Staff 1 (MLS 1)
Open Mon-Thurs 9-8, Fri & Sat 9-5
EVERGLADES BRANCH, City Hall, Everglades City, 34139, SAN 375-0175. Tel: 239-695-2511. FAX: 239-695-2511. *Mgr,* Roberta Stone. Subject Specialists: *Customer serv,* Roberta Stone; Staff 1 (Non-MLS 1)
Open Mon-Thurs 9 5, Fri 9 12
GOLDEN GATE, 2432 Lucerne Rd, 34116, SAN 337-8330. Tel: 239-455-1441. FAX: 239-455-8921. *Librn,* David Chalick; *Ch Serv,* Katherine Hemmat; Staff 2 (MLS 2)
Open Mon-Thurs 9-8, Fri & Sat 9-5
IMMOKALEE BRANCH, 417 N First St, Immokalee, 34142, SAN 337-8365. Tel: 239-657-2882. FAX: 239-657-4901. *Librn,* Tanya Saldivar; Staff 1 (MLS 1)
Open Mon & Thurs 11-7, Tues, Wed & Fri 9-5
MARCO ISLAND BRANCH, 210 S Heathwood Dr, Marco Island, 34145, SAN 337-839X. Tel: 239-394-3272. FAX: 239-394-2383. *Librn,* Gwynn Goodman; Staff 1 (MLS 1)
Open Mon-Thurs 9-8, Fri & Sat 9-5
Friends of the Library Group
NAPLES REGIONAL LIBRARY, 650 Central Ave, 34102, SAN 337-8306. Tel: 239-262-4130. Reference Tel: 239-263-7768. FAX: 239-649-1293. *Br Mgr,* Kay Oistad; *Extn Serv, Outreach Serv Librn,* Marilyn Norris; Tel: 239-261-8208; Staff 27 (MLS 8, Non-MLS 19)
Founded 1957
Open Mon-Thurs 9-8, Fri & Sat 9-5, Sun (Jan-March) 1-5
Friends of the Library Group
VANDERBILT BEACH, 788 Vanderbilt Beach Rd, 34108, SAN 337-8314. Tel: 239-597-8444. FAX: 239-597-3653. *Librn,* Blane Halliday; E-mail: bhalliday@collier-lib.org; Staff 1 (MLS 1)
Open Mon-Thurs 10-7

J EDISON STATE COLLEGE*, Collier County Campus Learning Resources Center, 7007 Lely Cultural Pkwy, 34113-8976. Tel: 239-732-3774. FAX: 239-732-3777. Web Site: www.edison.edu/learningresources. *Dir,* Tony Valenti; E-mail: apvalenti@edison.edu; Staff 5 (MLS 1, Non-MLS 4)
Founded 1992. Enrl 5,000; Fac 45; Highest Degree: Associate
Library Holdings: Bk Titles 10,000; Per Subs 60

Automation Activity & Vendor Info: (Acquisitions) Ex Libris Group; (Cataloging) Ex Libris Group; (Circulation) Ex Libris Group; (Course Reserve) Ex Libris Group; (ILL) Ex Libris Group; (OPAC) Ex Libris Group; (Serials) Ex Libris Group
Database Vendor: OCLC FirstSearch
Open Mon-Thurs 7:30am-9pm, Fri 8-4

C HODGES UNIVERSITY*, Terry P McMahan Library, 2655 Northbrooke Dr, 34119. SAN 374-6240. Tel: 239-598-6109, 239-938-7812. Toll Free Tel: 800-466-8017, Ext 6109. FAX: 239-598-6250, 239-938-7886. Web Site: www.hodges.edu. *Libr Dir,* Gayle Haring; Tel: 800-466-8017, Ext 7811, E-mail: gharing@hodges.edu; Staff 7 (MLS 4, Non-MLS 3)
Founded 1990. Enrl 2,439; Fac 5; Highest Degree: Master
Library Holdings: e-books 1,400; Bk Titles 26,000; Bk Vols 37,400; Per Subs 225; Videos 500
Special Collections: Marco Island, Florida Incorporation Files-Archives; Rare Books College Archives; Travel & Far East Rare Books Coll. US Document Depository
Automation Activity & Vendor Info: (Acquisitions) OCLC WorldShare Interlibrary Loan; (Cataloging) OCLC WorldShare Interlibrary Loan; (Circulation) OCLC WorldShare Interlibrary Loan; (ILL) OCLC WorldShare Interlibrary Loan; (OPAC) OCLC WorldShare Interlibrary Loan
Database Vendor: EBSCOhost, Gale Cengage Learning, LexisNexis, OCLC WorldShare Interlibrary Loan, ProQuest, Westlaw
Wireless access
Publications: Odyssey (Newsletter); Research Guides (Bibliographies)
Partic in Florida Library Information Network; Library & Information Resources Network (LIRN); Lyrasis; Southwest Florida Library Network

M NAPLES COMMUNITY HOSPITAL*, William J Bailey Library, 350 Seventh St N, 34102-5730. (Mail add: PO Box 413029, 34101-3029), SAN 375-4863. Tel: 239-436-5384. FAX: 239-436-5058. Web Site: www.nchmd.org. *Librn,* Annette Campbell; Staff 2 (MLS 1, Non-MLS 1)
Founded 1975
Library Holdings: Bk Titles 2,250; Bk Vols 3,000
Subject Interests: Clinical med
Partic in SEND; Southwest Florida Library Network; Tampa Bay Medical Library Network

S NAPLES DAILY NEWS LIBRARY*, 1100 Immokalee Rd, 34110-4810. SAN 329-3289. Tel: 239-263-4796. FAX: 239-263-4816. Web Site: www.naplesnews.com. *Librn,* Gerald B Johnson
Founded 1970
Library Holdings: Bk Titles 250
Special Collections: Naples Daily News 1923-2001 micro, newsclips, newsphotos
Restriction: Open to pub by appt only, Staff use only

NEW PORT RICHEY

P NEW PORT RICHEY PUBLIC LIBRARY*, 5939 Main St, 34652. SAN 303-0865. Tel: 727-853-1279. FAX: 727-853-1280. Web Site: www.tblc.org/newport. *Dir,* Susan D Dillinger; Tel: 727-853-1263, E-mail: sdillinger@nprlibrary.org; *Coll Develop, Tech Serv,* Richard Kleim; *Info Serv,* Marcia Horton; *Outreach Serv Librn,* Ann Scott; *Youth Serv,* Kristie Casey; Staff 20 (MLS 3, Non-MLS 17)
Founded 1919. Pop 16,177; Circ 172,470
Library Holdings: AV Mats 7,178; e-books 5,920; Bk Vols 86,801; Per Subs 202
Special Collections: Avery Coll; Florida Coll; Genealogy Coll
Automation Activity & Vendor Info: (Cataloging) SirsiDynix; (Circulation) SirsiDynix; (OPAC) SirsiDynix
Database Vendor: EBSCOhost, OCLC FirstSearch, SirsiDynix
Publications: Friends of the New Port Richey Library (Newsletter)
Partic in Sunline; Tampa Bay Library Consortium, Inc
Open Mon & Thurs 10-8, Fri & Sat 10-5
Friends of the Library Group

J PASCO-HERNANDO COMMUNITY COLLEGE*, Alric CT Pottberg Library - West Campus Library, 10230 Ridge Rd, 34654-5199. SAN 337-842X. Tel: 727-816-3418. Circulation Tel: 727-816-3232. Reference Tel: 727-816-3407. FAX: 727-816-3346. Web Site: phcc.edu. *Assoc Dir,* Douglas A Butler; E-mail: butlerd@phcc.edu; Staff 4.5 (MLS 1, Non-MLS 3.5)
Founded 1972. Enrl 4,000; Fac 200; Highest Degree: Associate
Library Holdings: e-books 75,000; Bk Titles 30,000; Per Subs 85
Automation Activity & Vendor Info: (Cataloging) Ex Libris Group; (Circulation) Ex Libris Group; (Course Reserve) Ex Libris Group; (OPAC) Ex Libris Group; (Serials) Ex Libris Group
Partic in Lyrasis; OCLC Online Computer Library Center, Inc; Tampa Bay Library Consortium, Inc
Open Mon-Fri 8am-9pm, Sat 8-4:30, Sun 1-5

NICEVILLE

P NICEVILLE PUBLIC LIBRARY*, 206 N Partin Dr, 32578. SAN 370-4661. Tel: 850-729-4070. Reference Tel: 850-729-4090. FAX: 850-729-4053. E-mail: ncvlibrary@okaloosa.lib.fl.us. Web Site: www.cityofniceville.org/library.html. *Dir,* Sheila K Bishop; Fax: 850-729-4093, E-mail: sbishop@okaloosa.lib.fl.us; *Acq, Tech Serv,* Lee Luton; *ILL, Ref,* Lora Glass; E-mail: lglass@okaloosa.lib.fl.us; *Youth Serv,* Martha Zimmerman; Staff 12 (MLS 1, Non-MLS 11)
Founded 1974
Library Holdings: AV Mats 2,709; Bk Vols 540,627; Per Subs 149; Talking Bks 2,986
Automation Activity & Vendor Info: (Cataloging) SirsiDynix; (Circulation) SirsiDynix; (OPAC) SirsiDynix
Partic in Okaloosa County Public Library Cooperative; Panhandle Library Access Network
Open Tues & Thurs 9-8, Wed & Fri 9-6, Sat 9-2

J NORTHWEST FLORIDA STATE COLLEGE*, Learning Resources Center, 100 College Blvd, 32578. SAN 303-0873. Tel: 850-729-5392. Circulation Tel: 850-729-5318. Reference Tel: 850-729-5395. FAX: 850-729-5295. Interlibrary Loan Service FAX: 850-729-4984. Web Site: lrc.owc.edu. *Dir,* Janice W Henderson; *Access Serv Librn, Circ,* Rhonda Trueman; *Cat/Ref Librn,* Owen E Adams, Jr; *Outreach & Instructional Serv Librn,* Paula Schrader; *AV,* Edward M Livingston; Staff 17.5 (MLS 5.25, Non-MLS 12.25)
Founded 1964. Enrl 4,830; Fac 250; Highest Degree: Bachelor
Jul 2008-Jun 2009 Income $198,084. Mats Exp $210,403
Library Holdings: AV Mats 7,973; e-books 29,767; Electronic Media & Resources 451; Bk Titles 74,354; Bk Vols 106,383; Per Subs 480; Videos 2,246
Special Collections: Florida & Works of Floridians
Automation Activity & Vendor Info: (Acquisitions) Ex Libris Group; (Cataloging) Ex Libris Group; (Circulation) Ex Libris Group; (Course Reserve) Ex Libris Group; (ILL) OCLC; (OPAC) Ex Libris Group; (Serials) Ex Libris Group
Wireless access
Partic in Florida Library Information Network; OCLC Online Computer Library Center, Inc; Panhandle Library Access Network
Open Mon-Thurs 7:30am-9pm, Fri 7:30-5, Sat 9-1

NORTH MIAMI

C FLORIDA INTERNATIONAL UNIVERSITY*, Glenn Hubert Library, 3000 NE 151st St, 33181-3600. SAN 303-089X. Tel: 305-919-5726. Circulation Tel: 305-919-5718. Interlibrary Loan Service Tel: 305-919-5715. Administration Tel: 305-919-5730. FAX: 305-919-5914. Interlibrary Loan Service FAX: 305-949-1591. Information Services FAX: 305-940-6865. Web Site: library.fiu.edu. *Dean of Libr,* Laura Probst; Tel: 305-919-5714, E-mail: probstl@fiu.edu; *Assoc Dean, Pub Serv,* Dr Consuella Askew; E-mail: caskew@fiu.edu; *Head, Cat,* Sue Wartzok; Tel: 305-348-6269, Fax: 305-348-3408, E-mail: swartzok@fiu.edu; *Head, Reader Serv,* Scott Kass; Tel: 305-919-5933, E-mail: kasss@fiu.edu; *Head, Res Develop,* Rita Cauce; Tel: 305-919-4052, E-mail: caucer@fiu.edu; *Distance Learning Librn,* Sarah Hammill; Tel: 305-919-5604, E-mail: hammills@fiu.edu; *Ref Librn,* Lauren Christos; Tel: 305-919-5721, E-mail: christol@fiu.edu; *Ref Librn,* George Pearson; Tel: 305-919-5272, E-mail: pearsong@fiu.edu; *Ref Librn,* Susan Weiss; Tel: 305-919-5725, E-mail: weisss@fiu.edu; *Res Sharing Librn,* Mary Radnor; Tel: 305-919-5764, E-mail: mary.radnor@fiu.edu; *LTA Supvr, Acq,* Ivy Torres; Tel: 305-919-5717, E-mail: torresiv@fiu.edu; *LTA Supvr, Circ,* Jude Cobham; Tel: 305-919-5797, E-mail: cobhamj@fiu.edu; *LTA Supvr, Ser,* Peter Matcau; Tel: 305-919-5716, E-mail: matcaup@fiu.edu; *ILS Coordr/Planning Officer,* Nancy Sun Hershoff; Tel: 305-919-5727, E-mail: sunn@fiu.edu; *Sr LTA, ILL/ICL,* Ana Cabrera-Luna; E-mail: cabreraa@fiu.edu. Subject Specialists: *Admin, Fr opera, Musicology,* Laura Probst; *Assessment, Higher educ,* Dr Consuella Askew; *Cataloging,* Sue Wartzok; *English,* Scott Kass; *Presv,* Rita Cauce; *Distance learning, Diversity,* Sarah Hammill; *English,* Lauren Christos; *Anime, Intl relations, Libr governance,* George Pearson; *Fine arts, Local & urban doc,* Susan Weiss; *Leadership, Mgt,* Nancy Sun Hershoff; Staff 9 (MLS 8, Non-MLS 1)
Founded 1977. Enrl 7,383; Fac 110; Highest Degree: Doctorate
Jul 2010-Jun 2011 Income $1,748,692. Mats Exp $322,618, Books $86,083, Per/Ser (Incl. Access Fees) $151,514, Micro $19,921, AV Mat $28,982, Electronic Ref Mat (Incl. Access Fees) $707, Presv $7,316. Sal $1,310,636 (Prof $491,843)
Library Holdings: AV Mats 7,803; e-books 122,297; e-journals 87,257; Electronic Media & Resources 85,681; Microforms 689,155; Bk Vols 313,103; Per Subs 439; Videos 7,541
Special Collections: Holocaust Oral History Video Coll
Automation Activity & Vendor Info: (Acquisitions) Ex Libris Group; (Cataloging) Ex Libris Group; (Circulation) Ex Libris Group; (Course Reserve) Ex Libris Group; (ILL) OCLC ILLiad; (OPAC) Ex Libris Group; (Serials) Ex Libris Group

Database Vendor: Baker & Taylor, BWI, Cambridge Scientific Abstracts, Dialog, EBSCOhost, Gale Cengage Learning, Grolier Online, Haworth Pres Inc, ISI Web of Knowledge, JSTOR, LexisNexis, Newsbank, OCLC FirstSearch, OCLC WorldShare Interlibrary Loan, OVID Technologies, ProQuest, PubMed, ScienceDirect, SirsiDynix, Westlaw, Wiley, Wilson - Wilson Web
Wireless access
Function: Art exhibits, Audio & video playback equip for onsite use, AV serv, Bks on CD, Bus archives, Computer training, Computers for patron use, Copy machines, Digital talking bks, Distance learning, Doc delivery serv, e-mail serv, E-Reserves, Electronic databases & coll, Equip loans & repairs, Govt ref serv, Handicapped accessible, Health sci info serv, ILL available, Mail & tel request accepted, Music CDs, Notary serv, Online cat, Online info literacy tutorials on the web & in blackboard, Online ref, Online searches, Orientations, Outside serv via phone, mail, e-mail & web, Photocopying/Printing, Prog for adults, Pub access computers, Ref & res, Ref serv available, Referrals accepted, Scanner, Spoken cassettes & CDs, Spoken cassettes & DVDs, Tax forms, Telephone ref, VHS videos, Video lending libr, Web-catalog, Wheelchair accessible, Workshops
Partic in Association of Southeastern Research Libraries; Center for Research Libraries; Florida Center for Library Automation; Lyrasis
Special Services for the Deaf - Assistive tech; Closed caption videos; TDD equip
Special Services for the Blind - Assistive/Adapted tech devices, equip & products; Audio mat; Bks on cassette; Braille equip; Cassette playback machines; Closed caption display syst; Computer with voice synthesizer for visually impaired persons; Reader equip
Open Mon-Thurs 7:30am-1am, Fri 7:30am-10pm, Sat 8-8, Sun 10am-1am
Friends of the Library Group

C JOHNSON & WALES UNIVERSITY*, Florida Campus Library, 1701 NE 127th St, 33181. Tel: 305-892-7043. Web Site: library.jwu.edu/florida. *Dir, Libr Serv,* Nicole Covone; Tel: 305-892-5398; *Librn,* Mary Culhane; *Librn,* Monique Swain; *Libr Assoc,* Kristin Ingman
Founded 1992
Library Holdings: AV Mats 2,000; Bk Vols 12,500; Per Subs 150
Subject Interests: Bus, Culinary arts, Hospitality
Automation Activity & Vendor Info: (Cataloging) Innovative Interfaces, Inc; (Circulation) Innovative Interfaces, Inc; (OPAC) Innovative Interfaces, Inc
Database Vendor: Gale Cengage Learning, LexisNexis
Wireless access
Publications: Speaking Volumes (Monthly newsletter)
Partic in Helin
Open Mon-Thurs 8am-9pm, Fri 9-4, Sat 10-5, Sun 12-8

P NORTH MIAMI PUBLIC LIBRARY*, E May Avil Library, 835 NE 132nd St, 33161. SAN 303-0903. Tel: 305-891-5535. FAX: 305-892-0843. TDD: 305-899-9268. E-mail: library@northmiamifl.gov. Web Site: www.northmiamifl.gov/departments/library/index.asp. *Outreach Serv Librn,* Jennifer Bryant; E-mail: jbryant@northmiamifl.gov; *Tech Serv,* Mary Culhane; E-mail: mculhane@northmiamifl.gov; Staff 5.77 (MLS 2.11, Non-MLS 3.66)
Founded 1949. Pop 59,310; Circ 71,232
Library Holdings: AV Mats 2,653; High Interest/Low Vocabulary Bk Vols 800; Large Print Bks 7,000; Bk Vols 90,445; Per Subs 186; Talking Bks 2,749; Videos 3,806
Special Collections: Art (Smik Memorial Coll); Bicentennial of the US Constitution Coll; Civil War Coll; Filipiniana Coll; Florida Coll; Literacy Coll; Parenting Coll; Stage & Studio Coll
Automation Activity & Vendor Info: (Cataloging) Innovative Interfaces, Inc; (Circulation) Innovative Interfaces, Inc; (OPAC) Innovative Interfaces, Inc
Database Vendor: Gale Cengage Learning
Function: ILL available
Special Services for the Deaf - TDD equip
Special Services for the Blind - Braille equip
Open Mon-Thurs 9:30-9, Fri & Sat 9:30-5, Sun 1-5
Friends of the Library Group

NORTH MIAMI BEACH

P NORTH MIAMI BEACH PUBLIC LIBRARY*, 1601 NE 164th St, 33162-4099. SAN 303-0911. Tel: 305-948-2970. FAX: 305-787-6007. E-mail: nmblib@citynmb.com. Web Site: www.citynmb.com. *Libr Mgr,* Susan Sandness; *Circ,* Maria Ileana Eltus; E-mail: maria.eltus@citynmb.com; *ILL,* George Gibson; E-mail: george.gibson@citynmb.com; *Youth Serv,* Sandra Gordon; E-mail: sandra.gordon@citynmb.com; Staff 4 (MLS 3, Non-MLS 1)
Founded 1961. Pop 44,000; Circ 137,683
Oct 2005-Sept 2006 Income $1,087,627, State $54,254, City $1,033,373. Mats Exp $87,697. Sal $757,540
Library Holdings: AV Mats 8,025; Bk Vols 58,523; Per Subs 200
Subject Interests: Chinese, Creole, Spanish
Automation Activity & Vendor Info: (Acquisitions) SirsiDynix; (Cataloging) SirsiDynix; (Circulation) SirsiDynix; (Course Reserve) SirsiDynix; (OPAC) SirsiDynix
Wireless access
Function: Ref serv available
Open Mon & Wed 9:30-7:50, Tues & Sat 9:30-4:50, Sun 1-4:50

R TEMPLE SINAI OF NORTH DADE*, Hollander-Rachleff Library, 18801 NE 22nd Ave, 33180. SAN 303-092X. Tel: 305-932-9010, 305-932-9011. FAX: 305-932-5153. Web Site: www.tsnd.org. *Media Spec,* Joyce Miller; E mail: joyce.miller@jsamiami.org
Founded 1967
Library Holdings: Bk Titles 7,000
Subject Interests: Children's lit, Jewish hist & lit
Open Mon-Fri 8-3:30
Friends of the Library Group

NORTH PALM BEACH

P NORTH PALM BEACH PUBLIC LIBRARY*, 303 Anchorage Dr, 33408. SAN 303-0938. Tel: 561-841-3383. FAX: 561-848-2874. E-mail: library@village-npb.org. Web Site: www.npblibrary.org. *Dir,* Betty Sammis; E-mail: bsammis@village-npb.org; *Circ,* Lynn Ruiz; *Pub Serv,* Diana Kirby; *Tech Serv,* Sue Holmes; Staff 2 (MLS 2)
Founded 1963. Pop 13,000; Circ 105,500
Oct 2007-Sept 2008 Income $749,896, State $18,000, City $719,996, Locally Generated Income $11,900. Mats Exp $89,987, Books $51,200, Per/Ser (Incl. Access Fees) $4,000, AV Mat $18,000, Electronic Ref Mat (Incl. Access Fees) $16,787. Sal $404,952 (Prof $71,838)
Library Holdings: Audiobooks 941; CDs 991; DVDs 2,179; e-books 166; Large Print Bks 1,091; Bk Vols 28,214; Per Subs 71; Videos 28
Automation Activity & Vendor Info: (Acquisitions) SirsiDynix; (Cataloging) SirsiDynix; (Circulation) SirsiDynix; (OPAC) SIRSI-iBistro; (Serials) SirsiDynix
Database Vendor: ProQuest, ReferenceUSA, SirsiDynix
Wireless access
Partic in Library Cooperative of the Palm Beaches
Open Mon-Thurs 9-7, Fri & Sat 9-5, Sun 1-5
Friends of the Library Group

NORTH PORT

P NORTH PORT PUBLIC LIBRARY, 13800 S Tamiami Trail, 34287-2030. SAN 370-3614. Tel: 941-861-1300. FAX: 941-426-6564. Web Site: www.scgov.net/library. *Mgr,* Carolann Palm-Abramoff; E-mail: cpalmabram@scgov.net; *Asst Mgr,* Janita Wisch; E-mail: jwisch@scgov.net; Staff 12.25 (MLS 6, Non-MLS 6.25)
Founded 1975
Library Holdings: Bk Vols 55,000; Per Subs 122
Automation Activity & Vendor Info: (Cataloging) Innovative Interfaces, Inc; (Circulation) Innovative Interfaces, Inc; (OPAC) Innovative Interfaces, Inc
Database Vendor: Innovative Interfaces, Inc
Wireless access
Mem of Sarasota County Library System
Partic in Tampa Bay Library Consortium, Inc
Special Services for the Deaf - TDD equip
Special Services for the Blind - BC CILS
Open Mon, Thurs, Fri & Sat 10-5, Tues & Wed 10-8
Friends of the Library Group

OAKLAND PARK

P OAKLAND PARK CITY LIBRARY*, 1298 NE 37th St, 33334. SAN 303-0946. Tel: 954-630-4370. Administration Tel: 954-630-4366. Information Services Tel: 954-630-4378. FAX: 954-561-6146. Web Site: www.oaklandparkfl.org. *Libr Mgr,* Heidi Burnett; E-mail: heidib@oaklandparkfl.gov; *Tech Serv Librn,* Kathleen Everall; Tel: 954-630-4373, E-mail: kathleene@oaklandparkfl.gov; *Youth Serv Librn,* Lisa Testa; Tel: 954-630-4372, E-mail: lisat@oaklandparkfl.gov; Staff 7.4 (MLS 3.8, Non-MLS 3.6)
Founded 1963. Pop 42,000; Circ 100,000
Library Holdings: Bk Vols 40,508; Per Subs 125
Special Collections: Urban fiction. Municipal Document Depository
Subject Interests: Fla, Spanish (Lang)
Automation Activity & Vendor Info: (Cataloging) SirsiDynix; (Circulation) SirsiDynix
Wireless access
Function: Accelerated reader prog, Adult bk club, After school storytime, Art exhibits, Bks on CD, CD-ROM, Children's prog, Citizenship assistance, Computer training, Computers for patron use, Copy machines, e-mail & chat, e-mail serv, Exhibits, Free DVD rentals, Handicapped accessible, Holiday prog, ILL available, Music CDs, Newsp ref libr, Online cat, Online searches, Outside serv via phone, mail, e-mail & web, Photocopying/Printing, Preschool outreach, Prog for children & young

adult, Pub access computers, Ref & res, Ref serv available, Ref serv in person, Senior computer classes, Spoken cassettes & CDs, Spoken cassettes & DVDs, Story hour, Summer reading prog, Tax forms, Teen prog, Telephone ref, VHS videos, Web-catalog, Wheelchair accessible
Partic in Lyrasis
Open Mon, Wed, Fri & Sat 9-6, Tues & Thurs Noon-8
Friends of the Library Group

OCALA

S APPLETON MUSEUM OF ART LIBRARY*, 4333 E Silver Springs Blvd, 34470. SAN 373-4218. Tel: 352-291-4455. FAX: 352-291-4460. E-mail: ormej@cf.edu. Web Site: www.appletonmuseum.org.
Library Holdings: Bk Titles 1,648; Per Subs 200
Subject Interests: Art, Art hist
Wireless access
Function: Res libr
Open Tues-Sat 10-5, Sun 12-5
Restriction: Non-circulating

J CENTRAL FLORIDA COMMUNITY COLLEGE*, Learning Resources Center, 3001 SW College Rd, 34474-4415. (Mail add: PO Box 1388, 34474-1388), SAN 303-0954. Tel: 352-237-2111, Ext 1344. FAX: 352-873-5818. E-mail: library@cf.edu. Web Site: www.gocfcc.com. *Dean,* Joanne Bellovin; *Librn,* Susan Bradshaw; *Librn,* Liz Minnerly; *Librn,* Jan Quiros; *Librn,* Pam Williams; *Access Serv,* Jeffrey Williams; Staff 4 (MLS 4)
Founded 1958. Enrl 6,271; Fac 122
Library Holdings: Bk Vols 68,031; Per Subs 318
Special Collections: Equine; Wisdom Traditions; Women's History
Automation Activity & Vendor Info: (Acquisitions) Ex Libris Group; (Cataloging) Ex Libris Group; (Circulation) Ex Libris Group; (Course Reserve) Ex Libris Group; (ILL) OCLC; (OPAC) Ex Libris Group; (Serials) Ex Libris Group
Open Mon-Thurs 7:30am-9pm, Fri 7:30-4:30, Sat 10-5

G MARION CORRECTIONAL INSTITUTION LIBRARY*, 3269 NW 105th St, 34482. (Mail add: PO Box 158, Lowell, 32663-0158), SAN 322-6689. Tel: 352-401-6813. FAX: 352-840-5657. *Librn,* Stephanie Stover; E-mail: stover.stephanie@mail.dc.state.fl.us; Staff 23 (MLS 1, Non-MLS 22)
Founded 1977
Library Holdings: Bks on Deafness & Sign Lang 12; High Interest/Low Vocabulary Bk Vols 300; Bk Titles 20,000; Bk Vols 23,000; Per Subs 40
Special Collections: Major Law Library Coll
Subject Interests: Gen ref
Special Services for the Blind - Bks available with recordings

P MARION COUNTY PUBLIC LIBRARY SYSTEM*, 2720 E Silver Springs Blvd, 34470. SAN 337-8454. Tel: 352-671-8551. Administration Tel: 352-368-4500. FAX: 352-368-4545. TDD: 352-368-4578. Web Site: library.marioncountyfl.org. *Dir,* Julia H Sieg; E-mail: julie.sieg@marioncountyfl.org; *Asst Dir,* Patsy Marsee; *Automation Syst Coordr,* Linda Watson; *Coll Develop,* Linda Porter; *Info Serv,* Roseanne Russo; *ILL, Tech Serv,* Carol Durrence
Founded 1961. Pop 330,000; Circ 1,424,614
Oct 2010-Sept 2011. Mats Exp $500,000
Library Holdings: Bk Vols 561,302; Per Subs 700
Automation Activity & Vendor Info: (Cataloging) SirsiDynix; (Circulation) SirsiDynix
Wireless access
Publications: WORDS (Quarterly)
Partic in Northeast Florida Library Information Network
Friends of the Library Group
Branches: 8
BELLEVIEW PUBLIC LIBRARY, 13145 SE Hwy 484, Belleview, 34420, SAN 337-8489. Tel: 352-438-2500. FAX: 352-438-2502. *Br Supvr,* Lee Schwartz
Open Mon & Tues 10-8, Wed-Sat 10-6
Friends of the Library Group
DUNNELLON PUBLIC LIBRARY, 20351 Robinson Rd, Dunnellon, 34431, SAN 337-8632. Tel: 352-438-2520. FAX: 352-438-2522. *Br Supvr,* Karen Kociemba
Founded 1961
Open Mon, Wed, Fri & Sat 10-6, Tues & Thurs 10-8
Friends of the Library Group
FOREST PUBLIC LIBRARY, 905 S County 314A, Ocklawaha, 32179, SAN 374-4515. Tel: 352-438-2540. FAX: 352-438-2545. *Br Supvr,* Greg Malak
Founded 1987
Open Mon & Tues 10-8, Wed-Sat 10-6
Friends of the Library Group
FORT MCCOY PUBLIC LIBRARY, 14660 NE Hwy 315, Fort McCoy, 32134, SAN 377-7618. Tel: 352-438-2560. FAX: 352-438-2562. *Br Supvr,* Position Currently Open
Founded 1996
Open Mon 11-7, Wed 10-6, Sat 10-4
Friends of the Library Group
FREEDOM PUBLIC LIBRARY, 5870 SW 95 St, 34476. Tel: 352-438-2580. FAX: 352-438-2582. *Br Supvr,* Heather Ogilvie
Open Mon, Wed, Fri & Sat 10-6, Tues & Thurs 10-8
MARION OAKS PUBLIC LIBRARY, 294 Marion Oaks Lane, 34473, SAN 377-7634. Tel: 352-438-2570. FAX: 352-438-2572. *Br Supvr,* Martha Free
Founded 1996
Open Mon & Wed 2-8, Tues, Thurs & Fri 10-6, Sat 10-4
Friends of the Library Group
HEADQUARTERS-OCALA PUBLIC LIBRARY, 2720 E Silver Springs Blvd, 34470. Tel: 352-671-8551. FAX: 352-368-4545. *Dir,* Julia Sieg
Automation Activity & Vendor Info: (Acquisitions) SirsiDynix; (Cataloging) SirsiDynix; (Circulation) SirsiDynix; (OPAC) SirsiDynix; (Serials) SirsiDynix
Database Vendor: EBSCO Auto Repair Reference, Gale Cengage Learning, LearningExpress, Newsbank, ProQuest, Standard & Poor's, TumbleBookLibrary, ValueLine
Open Mon-Thurs 10-8, Fri & Sat 10-6, Sun 1-5
Friends of the Library Group
REDDICK PUBLIC LIBRARY, 15150 NW Gainsville Rd, Reddick, 32686-3221. (Mail add: PO Box 699, Reddick, 32686-0699), SAN 374-4531. Tel: 352-438-2566. FAX: 352-438-2567. *Br Supvr,* Elizabeth Waller
Open Tues 11-7, Thurs 10-6, Sat 10-4
Friends of the Library Group
Bookmobiles: 2

OKEECHOBEE

P OKEECHOBEE COUNTY PUBLIC LIBRARY*, 206 SW 16th St, 34974. SAN 370-3789. Tel: 863-763-3536. FAX: 863-763-5368. Web Site: www.myhlc.org. *Dir,* Kresta L King; E-mail: kresta@myhlc.org; *Cat & Adult Serv,* Marcia DiStefano; *Children's Spec,* Jonette Myers; *Libr Spec I,* Kim Bass; *Libr Spec I,* Matthew Belleville; *Libr Spec I,* Zenda Morris; Staff 8 (MLS 1, Non-MLS 7)
Founded 1967. Pop 40,140; Circ 153,606
Oct 2012-Sept 2013 Income $410,090, State $93,123, County $316,967, Locally Generated Income $4,000. Mats Exp $30,130, Books $25,000, Per/Ser (Incl. Access Fees) $1,000, Micro $130, AV Mat $4,000. Sal $198,000 (Prof $52,000)
Library Holdings: AV Mats 11,859; DVDs 8,916; Electronic Media & Resources 77; Bk Vols 69,134; Per Subs 20
Subject Interests: Fla, Genealogy
Automation Activity & Vendor Info: (Circulation) Innovative Interfaces, Inc
Database Vendor: Baker & Taylor, OCLC FirstSearch
Wireless access
Function: Accelerated reader prog, Accessibility serv available based on individual needs, Adult bk club, After school storytime, Art exhibits, Audiobks via web, Bi-weekly Writer's Group, Bilingual assistance for Spanish patrons, Bk club(s), Bks on cassette, Bks on CD, Children's prog, Computers for patron use, Copy machines, E-Reserves, Electronic databases & coll, Free DVD rentals, Govt ref serv, Handicapped accessible, Holiday prog, ILL available, Libr develop, Magnifiers for reading, Mail & tel request accepted, Microfiche/film & reading machines, Music CDs, Newsp ref libr, Online cat, Online ref, Online searches, Orientations, Outside serv via phone, mail, e-mail & web, OverDrive digital audio bks, Photocopying/Printing, Preschool reading prog, Prog for adults, Prog for children & young adult, Pub access computers, Ref serv available, Ref serv in person, Serves mentally handicapped consumers, Spanish lang bks, Story hour, Summer reading prog, Tax forms, Telephone ref, VHS videos, Web-catalog, Wheelchair accessible
Partic in Tampa Bay Library Consortium, Inc
Open Tues-Thurs 9:30-7, Fri 9:30-6, Sat 9:30-5
Friends of the Library Group

P SEMINOLE TRIBE OF FLORIDA*, Tribal Library System, Rte 6, Box 668, 34974-8912. SAN 323-7842. Tel: 863-763-4236, 863-763-5520. FAX: 863-763-0679. Web Site: www.seminoletribe.com. *Dir,* John Fraser; E-mail: jfraser@semtribe.com; *Asst Dir,* Deborah Johns; E-mail: djohns@semtribe.com; Staff 12 (MLS 7, Non-MLS 5)
Library Holdings: Bk Titles 22,000; Per Subs 25
Special Collections: Seminole Indians of Florida
Partic in Southwest Florida Library Network
Open Mon-Fri 8-5
Friends of the Library Group
Branches: 2
WILLIE FRANK LIBRARY, Big Cypress Reservation, HC 61, Box 46A, Clewiston, 33440, SAN 376-9577. Tel: 863-902-3200, Ext 13124. FAX: 863-902-3223. *Dir,* Barbara Oeffner
Open Mon-Fri 8-5

DOROTHY SCOTT OSCEOLA MEMORIAL, 3100 NW 63rd Ave, Hollywood, 33024, SAN 378-0139. Tel: 954-989-6840, Ext 10521. Administration Tel: 954-966-6300, Ext 10504. FAX: 954-233-9536. Open Mon-Fri 8-5

OLDSMAR

P OLDSMAR LIBRARY*, 400 St Petersburg Dr E, 34677. SAN 323-9454. Tel: 813-749-1178. FAX: 813-854-1881. Web Site: www.tblc.org/opl. *Dir,* Roberta L Weber; E-mail: rweber@ci.oldsmar.fl.us; *Head, Tech Serv,* Jane Lingle; E-mail: jlingle@ci.oldsmar.fl.us; *Ch,* Susan Taylor; E-mail: staylor@ci.oldsmar.fl.us; *Circ, ILL,* Darlene Cadwallader, E-mail: dcadwallader@ci.oldsmar.fl.us; *Ref Serv, Ad,* Claire LeBlanc; E-mail: cleblanc@ci.oldsmar.fl.us; Staff 14 (MLS 4, Non-MLS 10)
Founded 1920. Pop 13,500; Circ 200,000
Library Holdings: AV Mats 8,000; Bk Vols 45,000; Per Subs 90
Automation Activity & Vendor Info: (Circulation) SirsiDynix
Database Vendor: Baker & Taylor, Newsbank, OCLC FirstSearch, OCLC WorldShare Interlibrary Loan, SirsiDynix
Mem of Pinellas Public Libr Coop
Partic in Tampa Bay Library Consortium, Inc
Open Mon-Thurs 9-8, Fri & Sat 9-5
Friends of the Library Group

ORANGE PARK

P CLAY COUNTY PUBLIC LIBRARY SYSTEM*, Headquarters Library, 1895 Town Center Blvd, 32003. (Mail add: PO Box 10109, Fleming Island, 32006-0109). Tel: 904-278-3720. Administration Tel: 904-278-4745. FAX: 904-278-6220. Administration FAX: 904-278-4747. Web Site: ccpl.lib.fl.us. *Dir of Libr,* Position Currently Open; *Asst Dir,* Pat Coffman; *Br Mgr,* Lynn Pinilla
Library Holdings: Bk Vols 267,881
Automation Activity & Vendor Info: (Cataloging) SirsiDynix; (Circulation) SirsiDynix; (OPAC) SirsiDynix
Database Vendor: Infomart
Partic in Florida Library Information Network
Open Mon-Thurs 10-9, Fri & Sat 10-5
Branches: 4
GREEN COVE SPRINGS BRANCH, 403 Ferris St, Green Cove Springs, 32043, SAN 337-5544. Tel: 904-269-6315, 904-284-6315. FAX: 904-284-4053. *Br Mgr,* Jennifer Parker
Founded 1961
Library Holdings: Bk Titles 58,672; Per Subs 189
Subject Interests: Fla, Genealogy
Partic in Lyrasis
Open Mon 10-6, Tues-Thurs 10-9, Fri & Sat 9-5
Friends of the Library Group
KEYSTONE HEIGHTS BRANCH, 175 Oriole, Keystone Heights, 32656. (Mail add: PO Box 710, Keystone Heights, 32656-0710), SAN 337-5579. Tel: 352-473-4286. FAX: 352-473-5123. *Br Mgr,* Margaret Whipple
Library Holdings: Bk Vols 37,194; Per Subs 25
Open Mon & Wed 10-6, Tues & Thurs 1-9, Fri & Sat 9-5
Friends of the Library Group
MIDDLEBURG CLAY-HILL BRANCH, 2245 Aster Ave, Middleburg, 32068, SAN 322-5712. Tel: 904-541-5855. *Br Mgr,* Opal Leino
Library Holdings: Bk Vols 36,141; Per Subs 25
Open Mon 10-6, Tues-Thurs 10-9, Fri & Sat 10-5
Friends of the Library Group
ORANGE PARK PUBLIC LIBRARY, 2054 Plainfield Ave, 32073-5498, SAN 337-5609. Tel: 904-278-4750. FAX: 904-278-3618. *Br Mgr,* Walter Brown
Library Holdings: Bk Vols 83,960
Open Mon-Thurs 10-9, Fri & Sat 10-5
Friends of the Library Group

ORLANDO

C ADVENTIST UNIVERSITY OF HEALTH SCIENCES, R A Williams Library, (Formerly Florida Hospital College of Health Sciences), 671 Winyah Dr, 32803. SAN 303-1063. Tel: 407-303-1851. Interlibrary Loan Service Tel: 407-303-7747. FAX: 407-303-9622. Web Site: library.adu.edu, www.fhchs.edu. *Dir,* Deanna L Flores; Tel: 407-303-7747, Ext 110-9878, E-mail: deanna.flores@adu.edu; *Acq,* Becky Fisher; Tel: 407-303-7747, Ext 110-9882, E-mail: rebecca.fisher@adu.edu; *Cat, Ref,* Mary Rickelman; Tel: 407-303-7747, Ext 110-6046, E-mail: mary.rickelman@adu.edu; *Circ & ILL,* Sylvia Dominguez; Tel: 407-303-7747, Ext 110-9890, E-mail: sylvia.dominguez@adu.edu; Staff 6.5 (MLS 3.5, Non-MLS 3)
Enrl 2,100; Highest Degree: Bachelor
Library Holdings: AV Mats 1,600; Bk Vols 15,585; Per Subs 174
Subject Interests: Health sci, Nursing
Automation Activity & Vendor Info: (OPAC) Book Systems
Database Vendor: Blackwell, EBSCOhost, Electric Library, Elsevier MDL, Gale Cengage Learning, OVID Technologies, ProQuest, PubMed, ScienceDirect
Function: ILL available
Publications: Infolink
Partic in Independent Cols & Univs of Fla; Tampa Bay Medical Library Network
Open Mon-Thurs 8am-9pm, Fri 8-3, Sun 3-9

L AKERMAN SENTERFITT & EIDSON PA*, Law Library, 420 S Orange Ave, Ste 1200, 32801. (Mail add: PO Box 231, 32802-0231), SAN 325-8432. Tel: 407-423-4000. FAX: 407-843-6610. E-mail: info.library@akerman.com. Web Site: www.akerman.com. *Dir,* Linda Fowlie; E-mail: linda.fowlie@akerman.com; *Librn,* Wendy Oliver; E-mail: wendy.oliver@akerman.com; *Librn,* Alexandra Olson; E-mail: alexandra.olson@akerman.com; *Librn,* Mark Plotkin; Tel: 305-374-5600, E-mail: mark.plotkin@akerman.com; *Librn,* Larry Stallings; E-mail: lstallings@akerman.com; Staff 8 (MLS 4, Non-MLS 4)
Founded 1922
Library Holdings: CDs 200; e-books 500; e-journals 10,000; Bk Vols 20,000
Special Collections: Law Coll
Subject Interests: Legis mat
Automation Activity & Vendor Info: (Acquisitions) Inmagic, Inc.; (Cataloging) Inmagic, Inc.; (OPAC) Inmagic, Inc.; (Serials) Inmagic, Inc.
Function: Bus archives, Doc delivery serv, For res purposes, Handicapped accessible, ILL available
Partic in Lyrasis
Restriction: Employees & their associates

C ANA G MENDEZ UNIVERSITY SYSTEM*, Learning Resource Center, 5601 Semoran Blvd, Ste 55, 32822. Tel: 407-207-3363, Ext 1813. FAX: 407-207-3373. Web Site: www.suagm.edu/orlando. *Learning Res Ctr Dir,* Juan Lopez; E-mail: julopez@suagm.edu. Subject Specialists: *Cataloging, Info literacy,* Juan Lopez; Staff 5 (MLS 2, Non-MLS 3)
Founded 2003. Enrl 1,213; Fac 256; Highest Degree: Master
Library Holdings: AV Mats 29; Bk Vols 3,500; Per Subs 35
Automation Activity & Vendor Info: (Cataloging) Ex Libris Group; (Circulation) Ex Libris Group; (Course Reserve) Ex Libris Group; (OPAC) Ex Libris Group
Database Vendor: EBSCOhost, Gale Cengage Learning, Wilson - Wilson Web
Open Mon-Fri 8:30am-10pm, Sat 8-5, Sun 12:30-5

S CENTRAL FLORIDA RECEPTION CENTER*, Main Unit Library, 7000 H C Kelley Rd, 32831. SAN 377-340X. Tel: 407-207-7443. FAX: 407-249-6570.
Library Holdings: Large Print Bks 80; Bk Titles 5,900; Bk Vols 8,800

C DEVRY UNIVERSITY*, Orlando Library, 4000 Millenia Blvd, 32839. Tel: 407-355-4807. FAX: 407-355-4777. Web Site: www.orl.devry.edu/campus_library.html. *Dir,* Dr Candace Keller-Raber; Tel: 407-355-4809, E-mail: ckeller-raber@devry.edu; *Ref,* Dan Kennedy; E-mail: dkennedy@devry.edu
Library Holdings: AV Mats 1,100; e-books 1,200; Bk Titles 12,000; Per Subs 60
Open Mon-Thurs 8-8, Fri 8-6, Sat 9-3

C EVEREST UNIVERSITY*, North Orlando Campus Library, 5421 Diplomat Circle, 32810. SAN 303-0997. Tel: 407-628-5870, Ext 144. FAX: 407-628-1344. Web Site: www.cci.edu. *Librn,* Tamara DuJardin
Enrl 1,600; Fac 98; Highest Degree: Master
Library Holdings: AV Mats 300; e-books 15,000; Bk Titles 6,500; Per Subs 78
Automation Activity & Vendor Info: (Acquisitions) Follett Software; (Cataloging) Follett Software; (Circulation) Follett Software; (Course Reserve) Follett Software; (ILL) OCLC; (OPAC) Follett Software; (Serials) EBSCO Online
Partic in Lyrasis; Tampa Bay Library Consortium, Inc

C EVEREST UNIVERSITY, South Orlando Campus Library, 9200 Southpark Center Loop, 32819. SAN 329-3483. Tel: 407-851-2525, Ext 204. FAX: 407-345-8671. E-mail: everestlibrary@gmail.com. Web Site: www.learningresources.everestuniversity.edu/south-orlando.php. *Libr Dir,* Position Currently Open; *Libr Asst,* Raymond Scarola; Staff 2.5 (MLS 1, Non-MLS 1.5)
Founded 1991. Enrl 980; Fac 85; Highest Degree: Master
Library Holdings: Audiobooks 200; AV Mats 350; Bk Vols 3,750; Per Subs 60
Subject Interests: Acctg, Allied health, Bus, Computer sci, Criminal justice, Info sci, Law, Legal assisting, Mgt, Pharmaceutical tech
Automation Activity & Vendor Info: (Cataloging) LibraryWorld, Inc; (Circulation) LibraryWorld, Inc; (OPAC) LibraryWorld, Inc; (Serials) EBSCO Online
Database Vendor: Baker & Taylor, Bowker, CredoReference, EBSCOhost, H W Wilson, LexisNexis, LibraryWorld, Inc, OCLC, ProQuest, PubMed, Westlaw, YBP Library Services
Wireless access

Function: Bks on cassette, Bks on CD, Computers for patron use, Copy machines, Distance learning, Electronic databases & coll, For res purposes, ILL available, Instruction & testing, Online cat, Online info literacy tutorials on the web & in blackboard, Online ref, Online searches, Orientations, Outreach serv, Photocopying/Printing, VHS videos, Web-catalog
Partic in Library & Information Resources Network (LIRN); Lyrasis; Tampa Bay Library Consortium, Inc
Open Mon-Fri 8:30am-9:30pm
Restriction: Authorized patrons, Borrowing privileges limited to fac & registered students, Open to students, fac & staff

C FLORIDA AGRICULTURAL & MECHANICAL UNIVERSITY*, Law Library, 201 Beggs Ave, 32801. Tel: 407-254-3263. Reference Tel: 407-254-3262. FAX: 407-254-3273. Web Site: www.famu.edu. *Dir,* Grace Mills
Library Holdings: Bk Vols 350,000
Open Mon-Thurs 7am-11pm, Fri 7am-10pm, Sat 8am-9pm, Sun 10-6

M FLORIDA HOSPITAL*, Medical Library, 601 E Rollins, 32803. SAN 303-2515. Tel: 407-303-1860. FAX: 407-303-1786. *Librn,* Ann McDonald; Staff 3 (MLS 2, Non-MLS 1)
Founded 1964
Library Holdings: Bk Titles 3,100; Per Subs 249
Database Vendor: EBSCO Information Services, EBSCOhost, Elsevier, MD Consult, OVID Technologies, ScienceDirect
Wireless access
Open Mon-Thurs 8-4:30, Fri 8-1
Restriction: Badge access after hrs

J FLORIDA TECHNICAL COLLEGE LIBRARY*, 12689 Challenger Pkwy, Ste 130, 32826. Tel: 407-447-7300. FAX: 407-447-7301. Web Site: www.flatech.edu.
Library Holdings: Bk Vols 7,000; Per Subs 100
Automation Activity & Vendor Info: (Acquisitions) Follett Software; (Cataloging) Follett Software; (Circulation) Follett Software; (ILL) Follett Software
Open Mon-Thurs 8-8, Fri 8-5

S THE GAY, LESBIAN, BISEXUAL, & TRANSGENDER COMMUNITY CENTER*, The Center Library, 946 N Mills Ave, 32803. Tel: 407-228-8272. FAX: 407-228-8230. Web Site: www.thecenterorlando.com. *Exec Dir,* Randy Stephens
Library Holdings: DVDs 15; Bk Vols 4,000
Open Mon-Fri 9-6, Sat 12-6, Sun 12-5

L HOLLAND & KNIGHT LLP*, Law Library, 200 S Orange Ave, Ste 2600, 32801. (Mail add: PO Box 1526, 32802-1526), SAN 327-2702. Tel: 407-425-8500. FAX: 407-244-5288. Web Site: www.hklaw.com. *Librn,* Margie Hawkins; Tel: 407-244-1153, E-mail: margie.hawkins@hklaw.com; Staff 2 (MLS 1, Non-MLS 1)
Library Holdings: Bk Vols 25,000; Per Subs 72
Subject Interests: Law
Automation Activity & Vendor Info: (Acquisitions) Inmagic, Inc.; (Cataloging) Inmagic, Inc.; (Circulation) Inmagic, Inc.; (ILL) OCLC; (Serials) Inmagic, Inc.
Database Vendor: OCLC FirstSearch
Partic in Lyrasis; Tampa Bay Library Consortium, Inc
Restriction: Staff use only

S LOCKHEED MARTIN CORP*, Missiles & Fire Control Technical Information Center, 5600 Sand Lake Rd, MP 30, 32819-8907. SAN 377-130X. Tel: 407-356-2051. FAX: 407-356-3665. *Librn,* Patricia Puglisi
Library Holdings: Bk Vols 10,000; Per Subs 100
Open Mon-Fri 7:30-5
Restriction: Staff use only

P ORANGE COUNTY LIBRARY DISTRICT*, Orlando Public Library, 101 E Central Blvd, 32801. SAN 337-8969. Tel: 407-835-7323. Interlibrary Loan Service Tel: 407-835-7426. TDD: 407-835-7641. Web Site: www.ocls.info. *Dir,* Mary Anne Hodel; E-mail: hodel.maryanne@ocls.info; *Asst Dir,* Debbie Moss; E-mail: moss.debbie@ocls.info; *Head, Info Serv,* Eric Atkinson; E-mail: atkinson.eric@ocls.info; *Acq Mgr,* Debra Tour; E-mail: tour.debra@ocls.info; *Commun Relations Adminr,* Tracy Zampaglione; Fax: 407-835-7643, E-mail: zampaglione.tracy@ocls.info; Staff 123 (MLS 58, Non-MLS 65)
Founded 1923. Pop 1,000,000; Circ 13,262,020
Library Holdings: AV Mats 252,000; e-books 21,430; Bk Vols 2,300,000; Per Subs 2,097
Special Collections: Florida Coll; Genealogy (Florida DAR); Walt Disney World Coll. State Document Depository
Automation Activity & Vendor Info: (Acquisitions) Innovative Interfaces, Inc; (Cataloging) Innovative Interfaces, Inc; (Circulation) Innovative Interfaces, Inc; (ILL) OCLC; (OPAC) Innovative Interfaces, Inc; (Serials) Innovative Interfaces, Inc
Database Vendor: Baker & Taylor, Gale Cengage Learning, LexisNexis, Newsbank, OCLC FirstSearch, OCLC WorldShare Interlibrary Loan, ProQuest, Wilson - Wilson Web
Wireless access
Function: AV serv, Bk club(s), Bks on CD, Children's prog, Citizenship assistance, Computer training, Computers for patron use, Copy machines, e-mail & chat, E-Reserves, Electronic databases & coll, Exhibits, Family literacy, Free DVD rentals, Homework prog, Magnifiers for reading, Mail & tel request accepted, Music CDs, Online cat, Online ref, Online searches, Outreach serv, OverDrive digital audio bks, Preschool outreach, Prog for adults, Prog for children & young adult, Pub access computers, Ref & res, Ref serv available, Ref serv in person, Spoken cassettes & CDs, Story hour, Summer reading prog, Telephone ref, Web-catalog, Wheelchair accessible
Partic in Lyrasis; OCLC Online Computer Library Center, Inc
Special Services for the Deaf - Assistive tech; High interest/low vocabulary bks; Staff with knowledge of sign lang; TDD equip; TTY equip
Special Services for the Blind - Aids for in-house use; Assistive/Adapted tech devices, equip & products; Audio mat; Bks on cassette; Bks on CD; Braille bks; Closed circuit TV; Computer with voice synthesizer for visually impaired persons; Copier with enlargement capabilities; Descriptive video serv (DVS); Home delivery serv; Large print bks; Low vision equip; Magnifiers; Talking bk & rec for the blind cat; Talking bks
Friends of the Library Group
Branches: 15
ALAFAYA, 12000 E Colonial Dr, 32826, SAN 337-8993. *Br Mgr,* Danielle King
Library Holdings: Bk Vols 123,962
Open Mon-Thurs 10-9, Fri & Sat 10-5
Friends of the Library Group
EATONVILLE BRANCH, 200 E Kennedy Blvd, Eatonville, 32751. *Br Mgr,* Patrice Florence-Walker
EDGEWATER, 5049 Edgewater Dr, 32810-4743, SAN 329-6210. *Br Mgr,* Kelly Pepo
Library Holdings: Bk Vols 110,000; Per Subs 20
Open Mon-Thurs 10-9, Fri & Sat 10-5
Friends of the Library Group
HERNDON, 4324 E Colonial Dr, 32803, SAN 378-0392. *Br Mgr,* Edward Booker
Library Holdings: Bk Vols 72,262
Open Mon-Thurs 10-9, Fri & Sat 10-5
Friends of the Library Group
HIAWASSEE, 7391 W Colonial Dr, 32818, SAN 371-9855. FAX: 407-521-2461. *Br Mgr,* Ken Gibert
Library Holdings: Bk Vols 113,721
Open Mon-Thurs 10-9, Fri & Sat 10-5
Friends of the Library Group
NORTH ORANGE, 1211 E Semoran Blvd, Apopka, 32703, SAN 337-9116. *Br Mgr,* Tammy Erikstrup
Library Holdings: Bk Vols 109,381
Open Mon-Thurs 10-9, Fri & Sat 10-5
Friends of the Library Group
SOUTH CREEK, 1702 Deerfield Blvd, 32837, SAN 371-9847. *Br Mgr,* Julie Ventura
Library Holdings: Bk Vols 104,350
Open Mon-Thurs 10-9, Fri & Sat 10-5
Friends of the Library Group
SOUTH TRAIL, 4600 S Orange Blossom Trail, 32839, SAN 337-9027. *Br Mgr,* Carolyn McClendon
Library Holdings: Bk Vols 93,909
Open Mon-Thurs 10-7, Fri & Sat 10-5
Friends of the Library Group
SOUTHEAST, 5575 S Semoran Blvd, 32822, SAN 328-6517. *Br Mgr,* Paolo Melillo
Library Holdings: Bk Vols 89,895
Open Mon-Thurs 10-9, Fri & Sat 10-5
Friends of the Library Group
SOUTHWEST, 7255 Della Dr, 32819, SAN 329-6253. *Br Mgr,* Bethany Stone
Library Holdings: Bk Vols 107,592
Open Mon-Thurs 10-9, Fri & Sat 10-5
Friends of the Library Group
P TALKING BOOKS SECTION, 101 E Central Blvd, 32801, SAN 337-8977. Tel: 407-835-7464. FAX: 407-835-7645. *Mgr, Ref Serv,* Donna Bachowski
Partic in Florida Library Information Network
Special Services for the Deaf - TDD equip
Friends of the Library Group
WASHINGTON PARK, 5151 Raleigh St, Ste A, 32811, SAN 337-923X. FAX: 407-521-2468. *Br Mgr,* Patsy Williams
Library Holdings: Bk Vols 51,612
Open Mon-Thurs 10-8, Fri & Sat 10-5
Friends of the Library Group

WEST OAKS, 1821 E Silver Star Rd, Ocoee, 34761. *Br Mgr,* Gregg Gronlund
Library Holdings: Bk Vols 45,179
Friends of the Library Group
WINDERMERE BRANCH, 530 Main St, Windermere, 34786, SAN 371-9871. *Br Mgr,* Leila Higgins
Library Holdings: Bk Vols 49,276
Open Tues-Thurs 10-9, Fri & Sat 10-5
Friends of the Library Group
WINTER GARDEN BRANCH, 805 E Plant St, Winter Garden, 34787, SAN 337-9264. *Br Mgr,* August Calabrese
Library Holdings: Bk Vols 66,026
Open Tues-Thurs 10-9, Fri & Sat 10-5
Friends of the Library Group

S ORANGE COUNTY REGIONAL HISTORY CENTER*, Joseph L Brechner Research Center, 65 E Central Blvd, 32801. SAN 326-1883. Tel: 407-836-8541. FAX: 407-836-8550. Web Site: www.thehistorycenter.org. *Res Librn,* Steven Gataletto; E-mail: Steven.Gataletto@ocfl.net; *Archivist,* Garret B Kremer-Wright; Tel: 407-836-8584, E-mail: garret.kremer-wright@ocfl.net; *Photo Archivist,* Stephanie Gaub; Tel: 407-836-8559, E-mail: stephanie.gaub@ocfl.net; *Curator,* Cynthia Cardona Melendez; Tel: 407-836-8587, E-mail: cynthia.cardona@ocfl.net; Staff 4 (Non-MLS 4)
Library Holdings: Bk Titles 7,000; Bk Vols 8,000; Per Subs 11
Special Collections: Joseph L Brechner Coll. Oral History
Function: Archival coll, For res purposes, Ref serv available, Res libr, Telephone ref
Restriction: Closed stack, Non-circulating to the pub

M ORLANDO HEALTH*, Health Sciences Library, 1414 Kuhl Ave, MP 28, 32806-2134. SAN 328-3895. Tel: 321-841-5454. FAX: 321-843-6825. E-mail: library@orlandohealth.com. Web Site: www.orlandohealth.com. *Syst Librn,* Rebecca Harrington; E-mail: rebecca.harrington@orlandohealth.com; *Ref Serv,* Stephanie Harris; E-mail: stephanie.harris@orlandohealth.com; *Libr Tech,* Tracy Lau; E-mail: tracy.lau@orlandohealth.com; *Libr Tech,* Aidy Silva-Ortiz; E-mail: aidybert.silva-ortiz@orlandohealth.com; Staff 3.5 (MLS 2, Non-MLS 1.5)
Library Holdings: Bk Titles 2,000; Per Subs 375
Subject Interests: Allied health, Med, Nursing
Automation Activity & Vendor Info: (Cataloging) OCLC; (Circulation) LibraryWorld, Inc; (OPAC) LibraryWorld, Inc
Wireless access
Function: Computers for patron use, Copy machines, Doc delivery serv, Electronic databases & coll, ILL available, Online cat
Partic in Tampa Bay Medical Library Network
Restriction: Badge access after hrs, Circulates for staff only, Open to staff only, Photo ID required for access
Branches:
CLIFFORD E GRAESE COMMUNITY HEALTH LIBRARY, 1414 Kuhl Ave, MP 28, 32806. Tel: 321-841-4636. E-mail: graeselibrary@orlandohealth.com. *Librn,* Anne Rosebrock; E-mail: anne.rosebrock@orlandohealth.com. Subject Specialists: *Med,* Anne Rosebrock; Staff 1 (MLS 1)
Library Holdings: AV Mats 144; Bk Titles 555; Per Subs 27
Subject Interests: Chronic disease, Elderly concerns, Fitness, Growth, Health, Nutrition, Obgyn, Pain mgt, Palliative care
Function: Health sci info serv
Open Mon-Fri 8-4:30

S ORLANDO MUSEUM OF ART*, 2416 N Mills Ave, 32803. SAN 329-9708. Tel: 407-896-4231, Ext 222. FAX: 407-896-9920. Web Site: www.omart.org.
Founded 1926
Library Holdings: Bk Vols 5,000; Per Subs 10
Subject Interests: African art, Pre-Columbian art
Publications: Library Corner (bi-monthly column in newsletter)
Open Tues-Fri 10-4, Sat & Sun 12-4

L RUMBERGER, KIRK & CALDWELL PA*, Law Library, 300 S Orange Ave, Ste 1400, 32801. (Mail add: PO Box 1873, 32802-1873), SAN 323-6838. Tel: 407-872-7300. FAX: 407-841-2133. Web Site: www.rumberger.com. *Coordr,* Dennis Herald; E-mail: dherald@rumberger.com; Staff 2 (MLS 1, Non-MLS 1)
Founded 1978
Library Holdings: Bk Titles 2,500; Bk Vols 15,000
Special Collections: Continuing Legal Education Audiovisuals; Engineering & Automotive Technical Publications; Florida Attorney & Judge Vertical Files; Florida Legislative Histories
Subject Interests: Law
Database Vendor: CISTI Source, Infotrieve, LexisNexis, MD Consult, OCLC FirstSearch, PubMed, Westlaw
Wireless access
Publications: Library News (Newsletter)
Partic in Lyrasis; OCLC Online Computer Library Center, Inc
Open Mon-Fri 9-5
Restriction: Access at librarian's discretion

C UNIVERSITY OF CENTRAL FLORIDA LIBRARIES, 12701 Pegasus Dr, 32816. (Mail add: PO Box 162666, 32816-2666), SAN 303-1098. Tel: 407-823-2564. Circulation Tel: 407-823-2580. Interlibrary Loan Service Tel: 407-823-2383. Reference Tel: 407-823-3379. Automation Services Tel: 407-823-3685. Information Services Tel: 407-823-2562. FAX: 407-823-2529. Circulation FAX: 407-823-6327. Interlibrary Loan Service FAX: 407-823-3047. Reference FAX: 407-823-5865. E-mail: libadmin@ucf.edu. Web Site: library.ucf.edu. *Dir of Libr,* Barry B Baker; E-mail: barry.baker@ucf.edu; *Asst Dir, Info Tech & Digital Initiatives,* Selma K Jaskowski; Tel: 407-823-5444, Fax: 407-823-4627, E-mail: selmaj@ucf.edu; *Assoc Dir, Admin Serv,* Frank R Allen; Tel: 407-823-2892, E-mail: frank.allen@ucf.edu; *Assoc Dir, Coll & Tech Serv, Head, Cat,* Mary S Page; Fax: 407-823-6289, E-mail: mary.page@ucf.edu; *Assoc Dir, Communications, Assessment & Pub Relations,* Margaret K Scharf; Tel: 407-823-6193, E-mail: meg@ucf.edu; *Assoc Dir, Info Serv & Scholarly Communication,* Penny M Beile; Tel: 407-823-5488, E-mail: pbeile@ucf.edu; *Head, ILL & Doc Delivery,* Kristine Shrauger; Tel: 407-823-5422, E-mail: kristine.shrauger@ucf.edu; *Head, Acq & Coll Serv,* Michael A Arthur; Tel: 407-882-0143, E-mail: michael.arthur@ucf.edu; *Head, Curric Mat Ctr,* Yolanda Hood; Tel: 407-823-2327, Fax: 407-823-3984, E-mail: yolanda.hood@ucf.edu; *Head, Hospitality (UOF) Libr,* Timothy Bottorrf; Tel: 407-903-8004, Fax: 407-903-8101, E-mail: timothy.bottorff@ucf.edu; *Head, Regional Campus Libr,* Cynthia Kisby; Tel: 407-823-2890, E-mail: cynthia.kisby@ucf.edu; *Head, Res & Info Serv,* Barbara Tierney; E-mail: barbara.tierney@ucf.edu; *Head, Spec Coll & Univ Archives,* Position Currently Open; *Interim Head, Circ,* Buenaventura Basco; Tel: 407-823-2527, E-mail: buenaventura.basco@ucf.edu; Staff 132 (MLS 55, Non-MLS 77)
Founded 1963. Enrl 59,770; Fac 1,965; Highest Degree: Doctorate
Jul 2013-Jun 2014 Income $12,810,845. Mats Exp $6,515,608, Books $1,018,427, Per/Ser (Incl. Access Fees) $3,583,229, AV Mat $41,410, Electronic Ref Mat (Incl. Access Fees) $1,851,315, Presv $21,227. Sal $5,981,821 (Prof $4,303,923)
Library Holdings: AV Mats 46,842; e-books 937,955; e-journals 49,060; Microforms 3,252,185; Bk Titles 2,405,030; Bk Vols 2,422,535; Per Subs 50,677
Special Collections: African American Legacy: The Carol Mundy Coll, 1720-2010; George & Anne Millay Coll, 1959-2006; Harrison "Buzz" Price Papers, 1952-2006; Henry Nehrling Papers, 1886-1970; John L Ducker Personal Papers, 1944-2002; Joy Postle Papers, 1912-2006; Joy Postle Papers, 1912-2006; Lou Frey Papers, 1947-2006; Michael A Spencer Bromeliad Research Coll, 1754-2014; NASA Photographs Coll, 1974-2001; Robert P Foster Coll; Stephen Danks Lodwick Papers, 1964-2002; Susan King Papers & Library; Van Sickle Leftist Pamphlet Coll, 1920s-1970s; William L Bryant West Indies Archaeological Artifacts Coll, 1956-1964. State Document Depository; US Document Depository
Subject Interests: Bio, Chem, Civil eng, Communication sci & disorder, Criminal justice, Educ res, Electrical eng, Indust eng, Math, Mechanical eng, Nursing, Physics, Polit sci, Psychol, Pub admin, Soc work
Automation Activity & Vendor Info: (Acquisitions) Ex Libris Group; (Cataloging) Ex Libris Group; (Circulation) Ex Libris Group; (Course Reserve) Ex Libris Group; (ILL) OCLC ILLiad; (Media Booking) Ex Libris Group; (OPAC) Ex Libris Group; (Serials) Ex Libris Group
Database Vendor: ABC-CLIO, ACM (Association for Computing Machinery), Alexander Street Press, American Chemical Society, American Geophysical Union, American Mathematical Society, American Physical Society, American Psychological Association (APA), Annual Reviews, ARTstor, ASCE Research Library, BioOne, Bowker, Career Guidance Foundation, Children's Literature Comprehensive Database Company (CLCD), Cinahl, College Source, CountryWatch, Coutts Information Service, CQ Press, CRC Press/Taylor & Francis Group, CredoReference, Dun & Bradstreet, DynaMed, Ebooks Corporation, ebrary, EBSCO Discovery Service, EBSCO Information Services, EBSCOhost, Elsevier, Emerald, Ex Libris Group, Gale Cengage Learning, H W Wilson, Haworth Pres Inc, Hoovers, IBISWorld, IEEE (Institute of Electrical & Electronics Engineers), Ingenta, IOP, ISI Web of Knowledge, JSTOR, LexisNexis, Marcive, Inc, Marquis Who's Who, MD Consult, Medline, Mergent Online, Modern Language Association, Natural Standard, Nature Publishing Group, Newsbank-Readex, OCLC FirstSearch, OCLC-RLG, OVID Technologies, Oxford Online, Project MUSE, ProQuest, PubMed, RefWorks, Sage, SBRnet (Sports Business Research Network), ScienceDirect, Springer-Verlag, Standard & Poor's, Thomson - Web of Science, ValueLine, WebMD, Westlaw, Wiley, Wilson - Wilson Web
Wireless access
Function: Res libr
Partic in Association of Southeastern Research Libraries; Center for Research Libraries; Coalition for Networked Information (CNI); Lyrasis;

OCLC Online Computer Library Center, Inc; Scholarly Publ & Acad Resources Coalition
Special Services for the Blind - Computer with voice synthesizer for visually impaired persons; Reader equip; VisualTek equip; ZoomText magnification & reading software

VALENCIA COMMUNITY COLLEGE
C EAST CAMPUS*, 701 N Econlockhatchee Trail, 32825, SAN 329-269X. Tel: 407-582-2467. Circulation Tel: 407-582-2459. Interlibrary Loan Service Tel: 407-582-2461. Reference Tel: 407-582-2456. FAX: 407-582-8914. Web Site: www.valenciacollege.edu/east/. *Dir,* Dr Dennis Weeks; E-mail: dweeks@valenciacollege.edu; *Librn,* Erich Heintzelman; *AV,* Steven Suarez; *Circ,* Maria Moreno; *Computer Serv,* Joshua Chapkin; *ILL, Ref Serv,* Mark Bollenback; *Ref Serv,* Chris Wettstein; Staff 14 (MLS 5, Non-MLS 9)
Founded 1975. Enrl 14,000; Fac 200; Highest Degree: Associate
Library Holdings: Bk Titles 46,360; Bk Vols 57,734; Per Subs 385
Special Collections: College Archives
Automation Activity & Vendor Info: (Acquisitions) Ex Libris Group; (Cataloging) Ex Libris Group; (Circulation) Ex Libris Group; (Course Reserve) Ex Libris Group; (ILL) Ex Libris Group; (OPAC) Ex Libris Group; (Serials) Ex Libris Group
Partic in Cent Fla Libr Consortium; Florida Library Information Network; Lyrasis
Open Mon-Thurs (Winter) 7am-10pm, Fri 7am-9pm, Sat 8-4, Sun 2-8; Mon-Thurs (Summer) 7am-10pm, Fri 7am-12:30pm, Sat 8-2
C RAYMER MAGUIRE JR LEARNING RESOURCES CENTER, WEST CAMPUS*, 1800 S Kirkman Rd, 32811, SAN 303-1012. Tel: 407-582-1210. FAX: 407-582-1686. Web Site: www.valenciacc.edu/library/west. *Dir,* Karen Blondeau; Tel: 407-582-1601; *Coordr, Ref,* Donna J Carver; E-mail: dcarver@valenciacc.edu; *Ref,* Suzanne Johnson; *Ref,* Paulette Smith; *Tech Serv,* Kusum Aneja; Staff 5 (MLS 5)
Founded 1967. Enrl 10,500
Library Holdings: Bk Titles 70,284; Bk Vols 80,500; Per Subs 131
Subject Interests: Educ, Hort, Hotel admin, Nursing
Automation Activity & Vendor Info: (Acquisitions) Ex Libris Group; (Cataloging) Ex Libris Group; (Circulation) Ex Libris Group; (ILL) Ex Libris Group; (OPAC) Ex Libris Group; (Serials) Ex Libris Group
Partic in Cent Fla Libr Consortium; Lyrasis; OCLC Online Computer Library Center, Inc
Publications: Handbook; Instructional Materials in Various Formats; LRC Alert (Bi-annually); Pathfinders
Open Mon-Thurs 7:30am-10pm, Fri 7-5, Sat 9-1, Sun 2-6

OVIEDO

SR REFORMED THEOLOGICAL SEMINARY LIBRARY*, Orlando Campus, 1231 Reformation Dr, 32765. SAN 371-8921. Tel: 407-366-9493, Ext 217. FAX: 407-366-9425. E-mail: library.orlando@rts.edu. Web Site: library.rts.edu. *Dir, Libr Serv,* Dr John R Muether; Tel: 407-366-9493, Ext 234; Staff 3 (MLS 2, Non-MLS 1)
Founded 1989. Enrl 255; Fac 15; Highest Degree: Master
Library Holdings: Bk Vols 100,000; Per Subs 300
Subject Interests: Biblical studies, Church hist, Theol
Automation Activity & Vendor Info: (Cataloging) TLC (The Library Corporation); (Circulation) TLC (The Library Corporation); (ILL) OCLC FirstSearch; (OPAC) TLC (The Library Corporation)
Database Vendor: EBSCO Information Services
Wireless access
Partic in Lyrasis
Open Mon-Fri 8am-10pm, Sat 9-3

J SEMINOLE COMMUNITY COLLEGE*, Oviedo Campus Library, 2505 Lockwood Blvd, 32765-9189. Tel: 407-971-5061. Reference Tel: 407-971-5062. FAX: 407-971-5067. Web Site: www.seminolestate.edu/library/about-us/campuses/oviedo.php. *Campus Librn,* Kellie Diaz; Tel: 407-971-5051, E-mail: diazk@seminolestate.edu
Founded 2001
Library Holdings: AV Mats 159; Bk Titles 12,000; Per Subs 56
Automation Activity & Vendor Info: (Cataloging) Ex Libris Group; (Circulation) Ex Libris Group; (OPAC) Ex Libris Group
Database Vendor: EBSCOhost, LexisNexis, OCLC FirstSearch, ProQuest, Westlaw
Wireless access
Open Mon-Thurs (Winter) 8am-9pm, Fri 8-12; Mon-Thurs (Summer) 8am-9pm
Friends of the Library Group

PALATKA

P PUTNAM COUNTY LIBRARY SYSTEM*, Palatka Public Library, 601 College Rd, 32177-3873. SAN 303-1136. Tel: 386-329-0126. Toll Free Tel: 800-826-1437. FAX: 386-329-1240. Web Site: www.putnam-fl.com/lib. *Dir,* Stephen J Crowley; *Adult Serv, Outreach Serv Librn,* Position Currently Open; *Archivist, Ref Serv, Res,* Darlene Walker; *Ch Serv,* Kathlyeen Brougden; *Circ,* Robin Bellmany; *ILL,* Marian Purifoy; *Tech Serv,* Mary E Dandle; Staff 12 (MLS 2, Non-MLS 10)
Founded 1895. Pop 73,586
Library Holdings: Large Print Bks 2,531; Bk Titles 101,000; Per Subs 275; Talking Bks 1,581
Special Collections: Genealogy (Materials of the Southeast); Putnam County Archives & History Coll. Municipal Document Depository; Oral History
Subject Interests: Genealogy
Automation Activity & Vendor Info: (Acquisitions) TLC (The Library Corporation); (Cataloging) TLC (The Library Corporation); (Circulation) TLC (The Library Corporation); (ILL) OCLC FirstSearch; (OPAC) TLC (The Library Corporation)
Database Vendor: EBSCOhost, Gale Cengage Learning, OCLC FirstSearch, Westlaw
Function: Archival coll, AV serv, BA reader (adult literacy), Home delivery & serv to Sr ctr & nursing homes, Homebound delivery serv, ILL available, Magnifiers for reading, Prog for children & young adult, Ref serv available, Serves mentally handicapped consumers, Summer reading prog
Open Mon & Wed 9-6, Tues & Thurs 9-9, Fri 9-5, Sat 9-1
Branches: 4
BOSTWICK PUBLIC, 125 Tillman St, 32177. Tel: 386-326-2750. FAX: 386-326-2733. E-mail: bostwicklib@putnam-fl.com. *Br Mgr,* Claudia W Wilkinson
Founded 1999
Library Holdings: Large Print Bks 22; Bk Titles 101; Per Subs 15; Talking Bks 36
Function: ILL available, Prog for children & young adult, Summer reading prog
Open Tues 12-6, Wed & Fri 10-3, Thurs 2:30-8, Sat 9-12:30
Friends of the Library Group
CRESCENT CITY PUBLIC LIBRARY, 610 N Summit, Crescent City, 32112-2148, SAN 328-9001. Tel: 386-698-2600. FAX: 386-698-4212. E-mail: crescentcitylib@putnam-fl.com. *Br Mgr,* Adia Smith; Staff 3 (Non-MLS 3)
Founded 1990. Pop 7,022
Library Holdings: Large Print Bks 95; Bk Titles 20,959; Per Subs 43; Talking Bks 178
Function: BA reader (adult literacy), Handicapped accessible, ILL available, Summer reading prog, Telephone ref
Special Services for the Blind - Large screen computer & software
Open Tues 9-5:30, Wed 10-7, Thurs & Fri 9-5, Sat 9-1
Friends of the Library Group
INTERLACHEN PUBLIC LIBRARY, 133 N County Rd 315, Interlachen, 32148. (Mail add: PO Box 260, Interlachen, 32148-0260), SAN 372-7882. Tel: 386-684-1600. FAX: 386-684-1601. E-mail: interlachenlib@putnam-fl.com. *Br Mgr,* Marilyn Meetz; Staff 3 (Non-MLS 3)
Founded 1984
Library Holdings: Large Print Bks 308; Bk Vols 15,914; Per Subs 49; Talking Bks 144
Function: ILL available, Summer reading prog, Telephone ref
Open Tues-Fri 9:30-6, Sat 9-12:30
Friends of the Library Group
MELROSE PUBLIC LIBRARY, 312 Wynnwood Ave, Melrose, 32666, SAN 324-2617. Tel: 352-475-3382. FAX: 352-475-5779. E-mail: melroselib@putnam-fl.com. *Br Mgr,* Sheree Simms; Staff 3 (Non-MLS 3)
Founded 1984
Library Holdings: Large Print Bks 201; Bk Titles 20,395; Per Subs 35; Talking Bks 92
Function: ILL available, Prog for children & young adult, Summer reading prog, Telephone ref
Open Tues-Fri 9:30-6, Sat 9-12:30
Friends of the Library Group

C SAINT JOHNS RIVER STATE COLLEGE*, B C Pearce Learning Resources Center, 5001 St Johns Ave, 32177-3897. SAN 303-1144. Tel: 386-312-4200. Circulation Tel: 386-312-4150. Reference Tel: 386-312-4154. Administration Tel: 386-312-4152. FAX: 386-325-4292. Web Site: www.sjrstate.edu/libraries.html. *Dean of Libr Serv,* Carmen M Cummings; E-mail: carmencummings@sjrstate.edu; *Pub Serv,* Robbie Allen; E-mail: robbieallen@sjrstate.edu; *Pub Serv,* Joyce Smith; E-mail: joycesmith@sjrstate.edu; Staff 14 (MLS 7, Non-MLS 7)
Founded 1958. Highest Degree: Bachelor
Library Holdings: e-books 30,000; Bk Vols 65,000; Per Subs 350
Special Collections: Civil War Coll
Automation Activity & Vendor Info: (Cataloging) Ex Libris Group; (Circulation) Ex Libris Group; (Course Reserve) Ex Libris Group; (ILL) OCLC; (OPAC) Ex Libris Group
Database Vendor: ARTstor, Bowker, CQ Press, EBSCOhost, H W Wilson, Hoovers, Ingram Library Services, JSTOR, Marquis Who's Who, OCLC

FirstSearch, ProQuest, RefWorks, Springer-Verlag, Wilson - Wilson Web, World Book Online, WT Cox
Wireless access
Publications: Civil War Collection Bibliography (Bibliographies); Faculty Handbook (Annual); Library Handbook (Annual)
Partic in Northeast Florida Library Information Network
Special Services for the Deaf - ADA equip; Assistive tech; Closed caption videos
Special Services for the Blind - Newsletter (in large print, Braille or on cassette); Playaways (bks on MP3); Text reader
Open Mon-Thurs (Winter) 8am-9pm, Fri 8-5; Mon-Thurs (Summer) 8-7
Departmental Libraries:
ORANGE PARK CENTER LIBRARY, 283 College Dr, Orange Park, 32065-6751, SAN 374-4558. Tel: 904-276-6830. FAX: 904-276-6796. *Librn,* Dixie Yaeger; Tel: 904-276-6840; *Pub Serv,* Eric Biggs; Tel: 904-276-6831
Open Mon-Thurs (Aug-April) 8am-9pm, Fri 8-5, Sat 12-4; Mon-Thurs (May-July) 8-7, Fri 8-5, Sat 12-4
SAINT AUGUSTINE CENTER LIBRARY, 2990 College Dr, Saint Augustine, 32084, SAN 323-5440. Tel: 904-808-7474. FAX: 904-808-7478. *Librn,* Christina Will; *Pub Serv,* Royce Bass
Library Holdings: Bk Vols 10,000; Per Subs 95
Open Mon-Thurs 8-9, Fri 8-5, Sat 9-1; Mon-Thurs 8-7, Fri 8-5, Sat (Summer) 9-1

G ST JOHN'S RIVER WATER MANAGEMENT DISTRICT*, Scientific Reference Center, 4049 Reid St, 32177. (Mail add: PO Box 1429, 32178-1429), SAN 322-6654. Tel: 386-329-4190. Toll Free Tel: 800-451-7106. *Sci Ref Spec,* Susie Hallowell; E-mail: shallowell@sjrwmd.com; Staff 1 (MLS 1)
Founded 1975
Library Holdings: Bk Titles 20,100; Per Subs 217
Subject Interests: Ecology, Eng, Geol, Hydrol, Water res
Automation Activity & Vendor Info: (Cataloging) EOS International; (OPAC) EOS International
Database Vendor: BioOne, EOS International, Thomson - Web of Science
Wireless access

PALM BAY

P FRANKLIN T DEGROODT LIBRARY, 6475 Minton Rd SW, 32908. SAN 325-0768. Tel: 321-952-6317. Web Site: www.brevardcounty.us/publiclibraries/branches/franklindegroodt/home. *Dir,* Christine Sullivan; E-mail: csullivan@brev.org; *Circ,* Melanie Tibbals; *Tech Serv,* Mara Bailey; *YA Serv,* Amber Down; Staff 26 (MLS 2, Non-MLS 24)
Founded 1992. Pop 90,000
Library Holdings: Bk Vols 68,136; Per Subs 205; Talking Bks 2,144
Automation Activity & Vendor Info: (Cataloging) Infor Library & Information Solutions; (Circulation) Infor Library & Information Solutions; (OPAC) Infor Library & Information Solutions
Wireless access
Mem of Brevard County Library System
Special Services for the Deaf - Bks on deafness & sign lang; High interest/low vocabulary bks, TDD equip
Open Mon, Wed, Fri & Sat 9-5, Tues & Thurs 9-8, Sun 1-5
Friends of the Library Group

J EASTERN FLORIDA STATE COLLEGE, Palm Bay Campus Library, (Formerly Brevard Community College), 250 Community College Pkwy, 32909. SAN 370-7822. Tel: 321-433-5270. Interlibrary Loan Service Tel: 321-433-5262. Reference Tel: 321-433-5275. Administration Tel: 321-433-5260. FAX: 321-433-5309. Web Site: www.easternflorida.edu/library. *Librn,* Deborah F Anderson; E-mail: andersond@easternflorida.edu; *Asst Librn,* Duke Darkwolf; E-mail: darkwolfd@easternflorida.edu; Staff 4 (MLS 2, Non-MLS 2)
Founded 1989. Enrl 3,000; Fac 30; Highest Degree: Associate
Jul 2006-Jun 2007. Mats Exp $60,000, Books $35,420, Per/Ser (Incl. Access Fees) $19,080, AV Mat $5,500
Library Holdings: e-books 30,000; Bk Titles 26,000; Per Subs 129
Automation Activity & Vendor Info: (Acquisitions) Ex Libris Group; (Cataloging) Ex Libris Group; (Circulation) Ex Libris Group; (Course Reserve) Ex Libris Group; (ILL) OCLC; (OPAC) Ex Libris Group; (Serials) Ex Libris Group
Database Vendor: EBSCOhost, Gale Cengage Learning, Newsbank, OCLC FirstSearch, OCLC WorldShare Interlibrary Loan, ProQuest, Wilson - Wilson Web
Wireless access
Partic in Florida Library Information Network; OCLC Online Computer Library Center, Inc; Tampa Bay Library Consortium, Inc
Open Mon-Thurs 7:30am-9pm, Fri 7:30-5, Sat 9-Noon

S HARRIS CORPORATION-GCS, Harris-GCS Engineering Library, Harris Corp-GCS, 1000 Charles J Herbert Drive, MS Bldg 62 Library, 32905. SAN 303-0350. Tel: 321-724-7733. FAX: 321-729-1019. *Head Librn,* Mary B Briand; E-mail: mbrian02@harris.com; Staff 1 (MLS 1)
Founded 1952
Library Holdings: Bk Vols 15,329; Per Subs 150
Subject Interests: Electronics, Eng, Semiconductor devices
Automation Activity & Vendor Info: (Acquisitions) SirsiDynix; (Cataloging) SirsiDynix; (Circulation) SirsiDynix; (ILL) SirsiDynix; (OPAC) SirsiDynix; (Serials) SirsiDynix
Database Vendor: Elsevier, IEEE (Institute of Electrical & Electronics Engineers), IHS, OCLC, SirsiDynix
Function: Archival coll, Doc delivery serv, ILL available, Outside serv via phone, mail, e-mail & web, Photocopying/Printing, Ref serv available, Telephone ref
Publications: IEEE (Periodical)
Partic in Lyrasis
Restriction: Employees only
Friends of the Library Group

P PALM BAY PUBLIC LIBRARY*, 1520 Port Malabar Blvd NE, 32905. SAN 372-7572. Tel: 321-952-4519. FAX: 321-952-4543. Web Site: www.brev.org. *Dir,* Jennifer Morrison; Staff 3 (MLS 1, Non-MLS 2)
Founded 1980
Library Holdings: Bk Vols 37,000; Per Subs 60
Automation Activity & Vendor Info: (Cataloging) Infor Library & Information Solutions; (Circulation) Infor Library & Information Solutions; (OPAC) Infor Library & Information Solutions
Mem of Brevard County Library System
Open Mon, Wed, Fri & Sat 9-5, Tues & Thurs 9-8
Friends of the Library Group

PALM BEACH

S THE SOCIETY OF THE FOUR ARTS*, King Library, Three Four Arts Plaza, 33480. SAN 303-1160. Tel: 561-655-2766. FAX: 561-832-6779. Administration FAX: 561-655-7233. E-mail: kinglibrary@fourarts.org. Web Site: www.fourarts.org. *Libr Dir,* Dr Rachel Schipper; Tel: 561-659-8519, E-mail: rschipper@fourarts.org; Staff 7 (MLS 3, Non-MLS 4)
Founded 1936
Library Holdings: Audiobooks 300; DVDs 2,500; Large Print Bks 600; Bk Vols 60,000; Per Subs 51
Special Collections: Addison Mizner Coll; Jessup Coll
Subject Interests: Fine arts, Paintings
Database Vendor: EBSCOhost
Wireless access
Publications: Library Notes & Booklist
Partic in SEFLIN - Southeast Florida Library Information Network, Inc
Special Services for the Blind - Audio mat
Open Mon-Fri 10-5, Sat (Nov-April) 10-1

PALM BEACH GARDENS

J PALM BEACH STATE COLLEGE*, Eissey Campus Library Learning Resource Center, 3160 PGA Blvd, 33410-2893. SAN 303-2396. Tel: 561-207-5800. FAX: 561-207-5805. Web Site: www.palmbeachstate.edu/LLRC/. *Dir,* David Pena; Tel: 561-207-5810, E-mail: penad@palmbeachstate.edu; *Librn,* Susan Fetterlund; *Circ,* Position Currently Open; *ILL,* Lisa Hogan; *Ref,* Joanne Cameron; Staff 3 (MLS 3)
Founded 1974
Library Holdings: AV Mats 3,050; Bk Titles 34,108; Bk Vols 38,055; Per Subs 198
Partic in Libr Info Network for Commun Cols; Lyrasis; OCLC Online Computer Library Center, Inc
Open Mon-Thurs 7:30am-9:30pm, Fri 7:30-4, Sat 10-3

PALM COAST

P FLAGLER COUNTY PUBLIC LIBRARY*, 2500 Palm Coast Pkwy NW, 32137. SAN 323-7044. Tel: 386-446-6763. FAX: 386-446-6773. Web Site: www.flaglerlibrary.org. *Dir,* Holly Albanese; Tel: 904-446-6764, E-mail: halbanese@flaglercounty.org; *Head, Circ,* Regina McManus; *Br Coordr,* Linda Crego; E-mail: lcrego@flaglercounty.org; *Ch Serv,* Theresa Owen; E-mail: towen@flaglercounty.org; *Ref Serv,* Deidre Jean Wright; E-mail: dwright@flaglercounty.org; *Tech Serv,* Victoria Abreu; E-mail: vabreu@flaglercounty.org; Staff 14 (MLS 3, Non-MLS 11)
Circ 20,649
Library Holdings: Bks on Deafness & Sign Lang 22; High Interest/Low Vocabulary Bk Vols 80; Bk Titles 55,000; Bk Vols 78,000; Per Subs 150
Special Collections: Flagler County Coll; Genealogy Coll; Palm Coast Coll
Automation Activity & Vendor Info: (Cataloging) Follett Software; (Circulation) Follett Software; (OPAC) Follett Software
Database Vendor: Gale Cengage Learning, OCLC FirstSearch
Function: ILL available, Photocopying/Printing
Publications: FOL Newsletter; Library Extra - From the Director
Partic in Northeast Florida Library Information Network
Special Services for the Deaf - Bks on deafness & sign lang; High interest/low vocabulary bks; Staff with knowledge of sign lang

Open Mon-Thurs 9-8, Fri 9-6, Sat 9-5, Sun 1-5
Friends of the Library Group
Branches: 1
BUNNELL BRANCH, 103 E Moody Blvd, Bunnell, 32110. Tel: 386-437-7390. FAX: 386-437-7390. E-mail: bunnell@flaglercounty.org. *Br Mgr,* Linda Crego
Founded 2004
Special Collections: Flagler County Law Library
Open Mon-Fri 9-6
Bookmobiles: 1

PALM HARBOR

P EAST LAKE COMMUNITY LIBRARY, 4125 East Lake Rd, 34685. Tel: 727-773-2665. FAX: 727-773-9583. E-mail: eastlakelibrary@gmail.com. Web Site: www.eastlakelibrary.org. *Dir,* Lois Eannel; Staff 6 (MLS 2, Non-MLS 4)
Founded 1999. Pop 30,000; Circ 157,027
Library Holdings: Audiobooks 2,837; AV Mats 7,500; Bks on Deafness & Sign Lang 143; DVDs 4,791; Bk Vols 38,469; Per Subs 25
Special Collections: Florida Coll
Subject Interests: Fla
Automation Activity & Vendor Info: (Cataloging) Innovative Interfaces, Inc; (Circulation) Innovative Interfaces, Inc
Wireless access
Function: Adult bk club, Adult bk club, Art exhibits, Art exhibits, Audio & video playback equip for onsite use, Audio & video playback equip for onsite use, AV serv, AV serv, Bi-weekly Writer's Group, Bi-weekly Writer's Group, Bk club(s), Bk club(s), Computer training, Computer training, Copy machines, Copy machines, Digital talking bks, Digital talking bks, e-mail serv, e-mail serv, E-Reserves, E-Reserves, Electronic databases & coll, Electronic databases & coll, Handicapped accessible, Handicapped accessible, Home delivery & serv to Sr ctr & nursing homes, Home delivery & serv to Sr ctr & nursing homes, Homebound delivery serv, Homebound delivery serv, Homework prog, Homework prog, ILL available, ILL available, Mail & tel request accepted, Mail & tel request accepted, Mail loans to mem, Mail loans to mem, Music CDs, Music CDs, Online ref, Online ref, Online searches, Online searches, Photocopying/Printing, Photocopying/Printing, Prog for adults, Prog for adults, Prog for children & young adult, Prog for children & young adult, Ref & res, Ref & res, Ref serv available, Ref serv available, Senior computer classes, Senior computer classes, Serves mentally handicapped consumers, Serves mentally handicapped consumers, Spoken cassettes & CDs, Spoken cassettes & CDs, Spoken cassettes & DVDs, Spoken cassettes & DVDs, Summer reading prog, Summer reading prog, Tax forms, Tax forms, Telephone ref, Telephone ref, Wheelchair accessible, Wheelchair accessible, Workshops, Workshops
Mem of Pinellas Public Libr Coop
Partic in Tampa Bay Library Consortium, Inc
Open Mon-Wed 9-8, Thurs 12-8, Fri & Sat 9-5
Friends of the Library Group

P PALM HARBOR LIBRARY*, 2330 Nebraska Ave, 34683. SAN 323-9217. Tel: 727-784-3332. Circulation Tel: 727-784-3332, Ext 209. Interlibrary Loan Service Tel: 727-784-3332, Ext 203. Reference Tel: 727-784-3332, Ext 213. Automation Services Tel: 727-784-3332, Ext 212. Information Services Tel: 727-784-3332, Ext 222. FAX: 727-785-6534. Web Site: www.palmharborlibrary.org. *Dir,* Gene Coppola; *Asst Dir, Youth Serv,* Lois Eannel; *Head, Circ,* Kathy Souers; *Head, Tech Serv,* Nancy Sheffield-Warman; *Automation Syst Coordr,* Dana Dockery; *Ch Serv,* Lois Eannel; Staff 22 (MLS 6, Non-MLS 16)
Founded 1978. Pop 59,000; Circ 371,156
Library Holdings: Bk Vols 215,000; Per Subs 45
Special Collections: Florida Coll; New Readers Literacy Coll; Toys to Go (Adaptive Toys for Special Needs)
Subject Interests: Genealogy, Handcrafts
Function: Adult literacy prog, AV serv, Games & aids for the handicapped, Handicapped accessible, Home delivery & serv to Sr ctr & nursing homes, Homebound delivery serv, ILL available, Large print keyboards, Online searches, Prog for adults, Prog for children & young adult, Ref serv available, Summer reading prog, Telephone ref, Wheelchair accessible, Workshops
Publications: Annual Report; Find Your Roots Genealogy Guide; Friends of the Library Newsletter
Mem of Pinellas Public Libr Coop
Partic in Tampa Bay Library Consortium, Inc
Special Services for the Deaf - Adult & family literacy prog
Special Services for the Blind - Assistive/Adapted tech devices, equip & products
Open Mon-Thurs 10-8, Fri & Sat 10-5
Friends of the Library Group

PALM SPRINGS

P PALM SPRINGS PUBLIC LIBRARY*, 217 Cypress Lane, 33461-1698. SAN 324-0274. Tel: 561-965-2204. FAX: 561-964-2803. Web Site: www.vpslibrary.org. *Dir,* Elena Romeo; E-mail: eromeo@vpslibrary.org; *Ch,* Mary Helen Sakellarios; E-mail: msakellarios@vpslibrary.org; *Circ Supvr,* Patricia Rogers; E-mail: progers@vpslibrary.org; Staff 2 (MLS 2)
Pop 12,894; Circ 69,572
Library Holdings: Bk Titles 46,311; Per Subs 141
Automation Activity & Vendor Info: (Acquisitions) SirsiDynix
Mem of Inland Library System
Partic in Coop Authority for Libr Automation; Library Cooperative of the Palm Beaches
Open Mon-Thurs 9-8:30, Fri & Sat 9-5:30
Friends of the Library Group

PANAMA CITY

C GULF COAST STATE COLLEGE LIBRARY*, 5230 W Hwy 98, 32401. SAN 303-1195. Tel: 850-872-3893. FAX: 850-872-3861. E-mail: library@gulfcoast.edu. Web Site: library.gulfcoast.edu. *Dir,* Lori Driscoll; E-mail: ldriscoll@gulfcoast.edu; *Access Serv Librn,* Wendy Dover; E-mail: wdover@gulfcoast.edu; *Coll Librn,* Sara Duff; E-mail: sduff@gulfcoast.edu; *Emerging Tech Librn,* Wei Cen; E-mail: wcen@gulfcoast.edu; *Instruction Librn,* Connie Head; E-mail: chead@gulfcoast.edu; *Librn, Tech Proc,* John Armstrong; E-mail: jarmstrong@gulfcoast.edu. Subject Specialists: *Soc sci,* Wendy Dover; *Bus, Tech, Visual arts,* Sara Duff; *Health sci, Wellness,* Wei Cen; *Lang, Lit, Pub safety,* Connie Head; *Math, Nat sci,* John Armstrong; Staff 9 (MLS 6, Non-MLS 3)
Founded 1957. Enrl 4,000; Highest Degree: Bachelor
Automation Activity & Vendor Info: (Acquisitions) Ex Libris Group; (Cataloging) Ex Libris Group; (Circulation) Ex Libris Group; (Course Reserve) Ex Libris Group; (ILL) OCLC; (OPAC) Ex Libris Group; (Serials) Ex Libris Group
Wireless access
Partic in Panhandle Library Access Network
Open Mon-Thurs 7:15am-9:30pm, Fri 7:15-4, Sat 9-5

G NATIONAL MARINE FISHERIES SERVICE*, Panama City Laboratory Library, 3500 Delwood Beach Rd, 32408. SAN 303-1209. Tel: 850-234-6541, Ext 227. FAX: 850-235-3559. Web Site: www.sefscpanamalab.noaa.gov/lib.html. *Librn,* Emily Harrell; E-mail: emily.harrell@noaa.gov; Staff 1 (MLS 1)
Founded 1973
Library Holdings: Bk Vols 4,000; Per Subs 400
Special Collections: St Andrew Bay Research
Subject Interests: Marine biol, Oceanography
Function: ILL available
Publications: Reprints list; Serials list
Partic in OCLC Online Computer Library Center, Inc; Panhandle Library Access Network
Open Mon & Wed 8-4:30, Tues 8-2, Thurs 8-2:30, Fri 1-5
Restriction: Limited access for the pub

A NAVAL SURFACE WARFARE CENTER*, Panama City Division Technical Library, 110 Vernon Ave, 32407-7001. SAN 337-9655. Tel: 850-234-4848. FAX: 850-234-4844. *Librn,* Angelia Whatley; E-mail: angelia.whatley@navy.mil; *Acq, Ser,* Nadine Iferd; *Cat, Ref,* Deborah Caldwell; *Cat, Circ,* Valerie Williams; Staff 2 (MLS 1, Non-MLS 1)
Founded 1948
Library Holdings: Bk Titles 16,000; Per Subs 95
Subject Interests: Diving, Hydrodynamics, Underwater acoustics
Automation Activity & Vendor Info: (Cataloging) SirsiDynix; (Circulation) SirsiDynix; (Serials) SirsiDynix
Database Vendor: Dialog, Jane's
Restriction: Not open to pub

P NORTHWEST REGIONAL LIBRARY SYSTEM*, Bay County Public Library, 898 W 11 St, 32401. (Mail add: PO Box 59625, 32412-0625), SAN 337-9353. Tel: 850-522-2100. Interlibrary Loan Service Tel: 850-522-2107. FAX: 850-522-2138. Web Site: www.nwrls.com. *Dir,* Joyce Dannecker; *AV, Librn for the Handicapped,* Vicki Patterson; *Ch Serv,* Sandra Pierce; *Circ,* Ann Robbins; *Genealogy Serv,* Rebecca Saunders; *Ref,* Sheila Bankhead; *Tech Serv,* Theresa Hill; *YA Serv,* Tania Watts; Staff 39.75 (MLS 8, Non-MLS 31.75)
Founded 1942. Pop 167,631; Circ 440,295
Oct 2007-Sept 2008 Income (Main Library and Branch(s)) $2,808,994, State $410,382, City $184,900, County $2,031,170, Other $182,542. Mats Exp $262,446. Sal $1,573,069
Library Holdings: Audiobooks 4,519; Bk Titles 170,151; Bk Vols 187,278; Per Subs 483
Special Collections: Local History Coll; Local Newspaper Coll; Local Photographic Coll

Automation Activity & Vendor Info: (Acquisitions) TLC (The Library Corporation); (Cataloging) TLC (The Library Corporation); (Circulation) TLC (The Library Corporation); (ILL) OCLC WorldShare Interlibrary Loan; (OPAC) TLC (The Library Corporation); (Serials) TLC (The Library Corporation)
Database Vendor: EBSCOhost, Gale Cengage Learning, OCLC FirstSearch, ProQuest, Wilson - Wilson Web
Wireless access
Partic in Panhandle Library Access Network
Open Mon-Wed 9-8, Thurs-Sat 9-5, Sun 1-5
Branches: 6
GULF COUNTY PUBLIC LIBRARY, 110 Library Dr, Port Saint Joe, 32456, SAN 337-9531. Tel: 850-229-8879. FAX: 850-229-8313. *Mgr,* Carl Copeland
Founded 1965
Partic in Panhandle Library Access Network
Open Mon & Tues 10-8, Thurs & Fri 10-6, Sat 10-4
Friends of the Library Group
HARRELL MEMORIAL LIBRARY OF LIBERTY COUNTY, 12818 NW Hwy 12, Bristol, 32321. (Mail add: PO Box 697, Bristol, 32321-0697), SAN 337-9477. Tel: 850-643-2247. FAX: 850-643-2208. *Mgr,* Fonda Tanner
Open Mon 9-7, Tues 9-6, Wed & Thurs 9-5, Sat 9-3
Friends of the Library Group
PARKER PUBLIC LIBRARY, 4710 Second St, Parker, 32404, SAN 370-9329. Tel: 850-871-3092. FAX: 850-874-8978. *Mgr,* Debbie Daniels
Open Mon, Tues, Thurs & Sat 10-5
Friends of the Library Group
SPRINGFIELD PUBLIC LIBRARY, 408 School Ave, Springfield, 32401, SAN 337-9566. Tel: 850-872-7510. FAX: 850-747-5758. *Mgr,* Frances Wittkopf
Open Wed & Fri 9-5, Thurs 9-7, Sat 9-1
Friends of the Library Group
CHARLES WHITEHEAD WEWAHITCHKA PUBLIC LIBRARY, 314 North Second St, Wewahitchka, 32465, SAN 337-9620. Tel: 850-639-2419. FAX: 850-639-3862. *Mgr,* Beulah Harrison
Open Mon & Wed-Fri 10-5, Tues 10-8, Sat 10-2
Friends of the Library Group
ROBERT L YOUNG PUBLIC LIBRARY, 116 S Arnold Rd, Panama City Beach, 32413, SAN 337-9523. Tel: 850-233-5055. FAX: 850-233-5019. *Mgr,* Frank Walker
Open Mon 10-8, Tues-Fri 10-5, Sat 10-4
Friends of the Library Group

PARKLAND

P PARKLAND LIBRARY*, 6620 University Dr, 33067. Tel: 954-757-4200. FAX: 954-753-5223. E-mail: library@cityofparkland.org. Web Site: www.cityofparkland.org. *Librn,* Pat Markey; Staff 8 (MLS 3, Non-MLS 5)
Library Holdings: Audiobooks 1,000; DVDs 3,200; Electronic Media & Resources 25; Large Print Bks 1,000; Bk Vols 40,000; Per Subs 25
Automation Activity & Vendor Info: (Cataloging) Softlink America; (Circulation) Softlink America; (OPAC) Softlink America
Wireless access
Partic in SEFLIN - Southeast Florida Library Information Network, Inc
Open Mon-Thurs 10-7:30, Fri & Sat 10-5
Restriction: Residents only
Friends of the Library Group

PATRICK AFB

UNITED STATES AIR FORCE
A PATRICK AIR FORCE BASE LIBRARY*, Bldg 722B, 842 Falcon Ave, 32925-3439, SAN 337-971X. Tel: 321-494-6881. FAX: 321-494-4190. *Dir,* Marta Demopoulos; Staff 5 (MLS 2, Non-MLS 3)
Founded 1950
Library Holdings: AV Mats 875; CDs 450; DVDs 500; Large Print Bks 300; Bk Vols 40,000; Per Subs 90; Videos 850
Special Collections: CLEP/DANTES Testing Materials; Leadership/Management Coll; Professional Military Education Coll
Subject Interests: Mil hist
Automation Activity & Vendor Info: (Acquisitions) Softlink America; (Cataloging) Softlink America; (Circulation) Softlink America; (ILL) OCLC; (OPAC) Softlink America; (Serials) Softlink America
Database Vendor: EBSCOhost, LexisNexis, Newsbank, OCLC FirstSearch, ProQuest
Partic in Tampa Bay Library Consortium, Inc
Restriction: Authorized patrons, Mil only

PEMBROKE PINES

GM FLORIDA DEPARTMENT OF CHILDREN & FAMILIES*, Geocare Library, 800 E Cypress Dr, 33025-1499. SAN 377-3736. Tel: 954-392-3000. *Librn,* Gwen Henry
Library Holdings: Bk Vols 1,600; Per Subs 10
Wireless access
Special Services for the Blind - Bks on cassette
Restriction: Not open to pub

PENSACOLA

M BAPTIST HOSPITAL*, Medical Library, 1000 W Moreno St, 32501. (Mail add: PO Box 17500, 32501), SAN 337-9744. Tel: 850-434-4877. *Librn,* Elizabeth Richbourg; Staff 1 (MLS 1)
Founded 1951
Library Holdings: Bk Titles 8,000; Per Subs 150
Subject Interests: Clinical med
Restriction: Staff use only

GL ESCAMBIA COUNTY LAW LIBRARY*, 190 Governmental Ctr, 32502. SAN 303-1241. Tel: 850-595-4468. FAX: 850-595-4470. *Librn,* Susan Dobinson
Library Holdings: Bk Vols 27,000; Per Subs 10
Open Mon-Fri 8-5

A NAVAL AIR STATION PENSACOLA LIBRARY*, Station Library, 250 Chambers Ave, Bldg 634, 32508-5217. Tel: 850-452-4362. FAX: 850-452-3961. *Dir,* Judith A Walker; E-mail: judith.walker1@navy.mil; Staff 6 (MLS 1, Non-MLS 5)
Founded 1914
Library Holdings: Bk Titles 11,000; Bk Vols 14,000; Per Subs 65; Talking Bks 2,000; Videos 100
Subject Interests: Aviation, Mil art, Mil sci, Navy hist, US hist
Automation Activity & Vendor Info: (Acquisitions) EOS International; (Cataloging) EOS International; (Circulation) EOS International; (OPAC) EOS International; (Serials) EOS International
Wireless access
Function: Bks on CD, Computers for patron use, Copy machines, Digital talking bks, Electronic databases & coll, Free DVD rentals, Prog for children & young adult, Pub access computers, Ref serv available, Scanner, Summer reading prog, Wheelchair accessible
Open Mon-Fri 8-8, Sat & Sun 12-6

S PENSACOLA MUSEUM OF ART*, Harry Thornton Library, 407 S Jefferson St, 32502-5901. SAN 303-1276. Tel: 850-432-6247. FAX: 850-469-1532. E-mail: info@pensacolamuseumofart.org. Web Site: www.pensacolamuseumofart.org. *Exec Dir,* Maria Butler
Founded 1960
Library Holdings: Bk Titles 300
Subject Interests: Art hist
Open Tues-Fri 10-5, Sat & Sun 12-5

C PENSACOLA STATE COLLEGE, Edward M Chadbourne Library, 1000 College Blvd, 32504-8998. SAN 337-9809. Tel: 850-484-2006. Circulation Tel: 850-484-2002. Administration Tel: 850-484-2013. FAX: 850-484-1991. Circulation FAX: 850-484-2098. Web Site: library.pensacolastate.edu. *District Dept Head of Libr,* LisaMarie Bartusik; Tel: 850-484-2007, E-mail: lbartusik@pensacolastate.edu; *Dir, Tech Serv,* Linda Broyles; Tel: 850-484-1107, E-mail: lbroyles@pensacolastate.edu; *Emerging Tech Librn,* Margaret Henderson; Tel: 850-484-2091, E-mail: mhenderson@pensacolastate.edu; *Ref & Instrul Serv Librn,* Virginia Vail; Tel: 850-484-2084, E-mail: gvail@pensacolastate.edu; *ILL,* Cynthia Koklas; Tel: 850-484-2089, E-mail: ckoklas@pensacolastate.edu; Staff 7 (MLS 7)
Founded 1948. Enrl 35,000; Fac 261; Highest Degree: Associate
Jul 2006-Jun 2007. Mats Exp $234,707, Books $155,680, Per/Ser (Incl. Access Fees) $17,129, Other Print Mats $12,058, AV Mat $37,045, Electronic Ref Mat (Incl. Access Fees) $11,363, Presv $1,432
Library Holdings: AV Mats 4,392; CDs 261; DVDs 1,820; e-books 3,122; High Interest/Low Vocabulary Bk Vols 82; Bk Titles 125,879; Bk Vols 147,853; Per Subs 202; Videos 1,256
Automation Activity & Vendor Info: (Cataloging) Ex Libris Group; (Circulation) Ex Libris Group; (Course Reserve) Ex Libris Group; (OPAC) Ex Libris Group; (Serials) Ex Libris Group
Wireless access
Publications: PJC LRC News (Newsletter)
Partic in Lyrasis; OCLC Online Computer Library Center, Inc; Panhandle Library Access Network
Special Services for the Blind - Assistive/Adapted tech devices, equip & products; VisualTek equip
Open Mon-Thurs 7:30am-8:30pm, Fri 7:30-4, Sun 1-5; Mon-Thurs (Summer) 7am-8:30pm, Sun 1-5
Departmental Libraries:
MILTON CAMPUS, 5988 Hwy 90, Milton, 32583-1798, SAN 337-9833. Tel: 850-484-4450. FAX: 850-484-4453. *Campus Librn,* Charlotte Sweeney; Staff 4 (MLS 1, Non-MLS 3)
Library Holdings: Bk Titles 12,627; Bk Vols 15,822; Per Subs 24
Open Mon, Tues & Thurs 7:30am-8:30pm, Wed & Fri 7:30-4
WARRINGTON CAMPUS, 5555 West Hwy 98, 32507-1097, SAN 337-9868. Tel: 850-484-2252. FAX: 850-484-2355. *Campus Ref & Instrul Serv Librn,* Dorothy Perry; Tel: 850-484-2263, E-mail: dperry@pensacolastate.edu; Staff 3 (MLS 1, Non-MLS 2)

Library Holdings: Bk Titles 27,578; Bk Vols 30,657; Per Subs 82
Open Mon, Tues & Thurs 7:30am-8:30pm, Wed & Fri 7:30-4

M SACRED HEART HEALTH SYSTEM*, Medical Library, 5151 N Ninth Ave, 32504. SAN 337-9892. Tel: 850-416-7109. FAX: 850-416-6864. E-mail: medlib@shhpens.org. *Med Librn,* Jennifer Stewart; Staff 1 (MLS 1)
Founded 1959
Library Holdings: e-books 30; Bk Vols 933
Partic in Docline
Open Mon-Fri 7-3:30
Restriction: Hospital staff & commun

UNITED STATES NAVY

AM MEDICAL LIBRARY, CODE 185*, 6000 W Hwy 98, Code 185, 32512-0003, SAN 338-0025. Tel: 850-505-6635. FAX: 850-505-7063. *In Charge,* Cortiz Stewart; Staff 1 (MLS 1)
Library Holdings: AV Mats 1,864; Bk Vols 1,260; Per Subs 75
Function: Online searches
Partic in DOD-Drols
Open Mon-Fri 7:30-4
Restriction: Authorized patrons, Circulates for staff only

AM NAVAL OPERATIONAL MEDICINE INSTITUTE LIBRARY*, 340 Hulse Rd, 32508-1089. Tel: 850-452-2256. FAX: 850-452-2304. Web Site: www.nomi.med.navy.mil/NAMI/library.htm. *Librn,* Valerie S McCann; E-mail: valerie.mccann@med.navy.mil; Staff 2 (MLS 1, Non-MLS 1)
Founded 1940
Library Holdings: Bk Titles 8,000; Bk Vols 10,000; Per Subs 51
Special Collections: Naval Aerospace Medical Research Laboratory Reports
Database Vendor: Dialog, EBSCOhost, OCLC FirstSearch, OVID Technologies, OVID Technologies
Function: Res libr
Partic in Consortium of Naval Libraries (CNL); Panhandle Library Access Network
Open Mon-Fri 8-4

C UNIVERSITY OF WEST FLORIDA*, John C Pace Library, 11000 University Pkwy, 32514-5750. SAN 303-1306. Tel: 850-474-2492. Circulation Tel: 850-474-2414. Interlibrary Loan Service Tel: 850-474-2411. Reference Tel: 850-474-2424. FAX: 850-474-3338. TDD: 850-474-2190. Web Site: library.uwf.edu. *Dean of Libr,* Robert Dugan; Tel: 850-474-3135, E-mail: hdugan@uwf.edu; *Spec Coll & Archives Librn,* Dean DeBolt; Tel: 850-474-2213, E-mail: ddebolt@uwf.edu; Staff 43 (MLS 15, Non-MLS 28)
Founded 1966. Enrl 10,380; Fac 368; Highest Degree: Doctorate
Jul 2007-Jun 2008 Income $4,214,956, State $50,558, Federal $100,000, Locally Generated Income $11,463, Parent Institution $3,985,009, Other $67,926. Mats Exp $1,233,725, Books $289,065, Per/Ser (Incl. Access Fees) $444,079, Other Print Mats $437, Micro $14,584, AV Mat $33,375, Electronic Ref Mat (Incl. Access Fees) $431,170, Presv $21,015. Sal $1,648,159 (Prof $859,359)
Library Holdings: Audiobooks 410; AV Mats 9,042; Bks on Deafness & Sign Lang 543; CDs 1,304; DVDs 2,003; e-books 90,786; e-journals 3,321; Electronic Media & Resources 333; Microforms 1,162,896; Music Scores 3,959; Bk Titles 497,817; Bk Vols 724,067; Per Subs 5,019; Videos 5,021
Special Collections: Langston Hughes Coll; Panton Leslie & Company Papers; West Florida History, bks, mss, maps, photos. Oral History; State Document Depository; US Document Depository
Automation Activity & Vendor Info: (Acquisitions) Ex Libris Group; (Cataloging) OCLC Connexion; (Circulation) Ex Libris Group; (Course Reserve) Ex Libris Group; (ILL) OCLC ILLiad; (Media Booking) Ex Libris Group; (OPAC) Endeca Technologies, Inc; (Serials) Ex Libris Group
Database Vendor: ACM (Association for Computing Machinery), Agricola, Alexander Street Press, American Chemical Society, ARTstor, Blackwell, Cambridge Scientific Abstracts, Cinahl, CQ Press, DATASTAR Inc, Dialog, ebrary, EBSCOhost, Elsevier, Emerald, Ex Libris Group, Factiva.com, Gale Cengage Learning, H W Wilson, IEEE (Institute of Electrical & Electronics Engineers), Ingram Library Services, JSTOR, LexisNexis, Marcive, Inc, Mergent Online, OCLC FirstSearch, OCLC WebJunction, OCLC WorldShare Interlibrary Loan, Project MUSE, ProQuest, RefWorks, Sage, SBRnet (Sports Business Research Network), ScienceDirect, Springer-Verlag, ValueLine, Westlaw, Wiley InterScience, Wilson - Wilson Web
Wireless access
Partic in Florida Library Information Network; Lyrasis; OCLC Online Computer Library Center, Inc; Panhandle Library Access Network
Special Services for the Deaf - TDD equip
Special Services for the Blind - Braille equip; Computer with voice synthesizer for visually impaired persons; Reader equip; ZoomText magnification & reading software
Open Mon-Thurs 7:30am-10pm, Fri 7:30-6, Sat 10-6, Sun 1-9

S UNIVERSITY OF WEST FLORIDA HISTORIC TRUST, Lelia Abercrombie Historical Resource Center, (Formerly Pensacola Historical Society), 110 E Church St, 32502. (Mail add: PO Box 12866, 32591), SAN 303-1284. Tel: 850-595-5840. Administration Tel: 850-595-5985. FAX: 850-595-5842. Web Site: www.historicpensacola.org. *Chief Operating Officer,* Robert Overton, Jr; Tel: 850-595-5985, Ext 106, E-mail: roverton@uwf.edu; *Archivist,* Jacquelyn T Wilson; Tel: 850-595-5840, Ext 102, E-mail: jwilson2@uwf.edu. Subject Specialists: *Northwest Fla hist,* Jacquelyn T Wilson; Staff 3 (Non-MLS 3)
Founded 1960
Library Holdings: DVDs 3; Bk Titles 5,000; Bk Vols 5,500; Per Subs 20; Spec Interest Per Sub 5
Special Collections: Architecture & Preservation Coll, blueprints, bks, photog, slides, VF; Artifact ID & Dating Coll, bks, pamphlets, VF; Cartography Coll-Southeastern US, Florida & Local Area, Circa 1500-present; Civil War Coll, archival mat, bks, doc & personal papers, pamphlets, photos, VF; Family Histories Coll, archival items; General Florida History, bks, pamphlets; Historic Districts & Pensacola Architectural Review Board File; History of Pensacola & Northwest Florida, archival papers & objects, bks, pamphlets, photos, VF; Museum Studies Coll, bks, VF; Pensacola Genealogy Coll, bks, pamphlets, personal papers, VF; Photograph Coll-Pensacola & Escambia County, Florida, daguerreotypes, digital images, photos, slides, tintypes. Oral History
Subject Interests: Hist presv, Mus mgt, Northwest Fla hist
Wireless access
Function: Archival coll, Computers for patron use, Copy machines, e-mail serv, Handicapped accessible, Mail & tel request accepted, Microfiche/film & reading machines, Photocopying/Printing, Printer for laptops & handheld devices, Scanner, Telephone ref, Wheelchair accessible
Publications: Pensacola History Illustrated: A Journal of Pensacola & West Florida History (Bi-annually); Pensacola History Today (Newsletter)
Open Tues-Fri 10-4
Restriction: Fee for pub use, Free to mem, In-house use for visitors, Not a lending libr, Pub use on premises
Friends of the Library Group

M WEST FLORIDA HOSPITAL*, Medical Library, 8383 N Davis Hwy, 32514. (Mail add: PO Box 18900, 32523-8900), SAN 322-726X. Tel: 850-494-4490. FAX: 850-494-6060. *Librn,* Art Levine; Staff 1 (MLS 1)
Founded 1954
Jan 2007-Dec 2007. Mats Exp $100,000. Sal Prof $30,000
Library Holdings: Bk Titles 1,547; Per Subs 10
Special Collections: Oncology (Chadbourne Coll), bks
Subject Interests: Oncology
Database Vendor: OVID Technologies
Function: Res libr
Partic in Florida Library Information Network; Panhandle Library Access Network
Open Mon, Tues & Thurs 8:30-4:30
Restriction: Staff use only

P WEST FLORIDA PUBLIC LIBRARY*, 200 W Gregory, 32502. SAN 338-0041. Tel: 850-436-5060. Administration FAX: 850-436-5039. Web Site: www.wfrl.lib.fl.us. *Libr Adminr,* Darlene Howell; E-mail: dhowell@ci.pensacola.fl.us; *Genealogy Librn,* William Nelson; Tel: 850-494-7373; *Tech Serv Supvr,* Cindy Birden; *Coordr, Ch Serv,* Rachel Wallace; *AV, Circ,* Mike Lane; *Coll Develop, Talking Bks,* Melissa Thacker; E-mail: mthacker@ci.pensacola.fl.us; *ILL,* Deann Peters; *Ref,* Cynthia Wolfe. Subject Specialists: *Genealogy,* William Nelson; Staff 14 (MLS 12, Non-MLS 2)
Founded 1937. Pop 303,343; Circ 778,052
Oct 2008-Sept 2009 Income (Main Library and Branch(s)) $4,958,412, State $134,712, City $1,346,300, County $3,477,400. Mats Exp $5,184,157, Books $279,198, AV Equip $123,966, AV Mat $148,361, Electronic Ref Mat (Incl. Access Fees) $54,957. Sal $3,326,327 (Prof $31,678)
Library Holdings: Audiobooks 8,956; CDs 3,553; DVDs 10,063; e-books 27,411; Electronic Media & Resources 66; Bk Vols 209,318; Per Subs 450; Talking Bks 22,498; Videos 2,240
Subject Interests: Genealogy, Local hist
Automation Activity & Vendor Info: (Acquisitions) SirsiDynix; (Cataloging) SirsiDynix; (Circulation) SirsiDynix; (OPAC) SirsiDynix; (Serials) SirsiDynix
Database Vendor: EBSCOhost, Gale Cengage Learning, infoUSA, Newsbank, OCLC FirstSearch, ProQuest, ReferenceUSA
Wireless access
Publications: PPL Friends Newsletter (Bi-monthly)
Partic in Panhandle Library Access Network
Special Services for the Blind - Talking bk & rec for the blind cat
Open Mon-Thurs 9-8, Fri & Sat 9-5, Sun 2-7
Friends of the Library Group

Branches: 3
SOUTHWEST BRANCH LIBRARY, 12248 Gulf Beach Hwy, 32507, SAN 378-1410. Tel: 850-453-7780. FAX: 850-453-7782. *Librn,* Melanie Skaggs
Open Tues-Thurs 9-8, Fri & Sat 9-5
LUCIA M TRYON BRANCH LIBRARY, 1200 Langley Ave, 32504, SAN 338-0076. Tel: 850-471-6980. *Mgr,* Position Currently Open
Open Tues-Thurs 9-8, Fri & Sat 9-5
Friends of the Library Group
WEST FLORIDA GENEALOGY BRANCH LIBRARY, 5740 N Ninth Ave, 32504. Tel: 850-494-7373.
Bookmobiles: 1. Bkmobile Operator, Steve Cox. Bk vols 2,830

PERRY

P TAYLOR COUNTY PUBLIC LIBRARY, 403 N Washington St, 32347-2732. SAN 303-1314. Tel: 850-838-3512. FAX: 850-838-3514. E-mail: para.pro@taylorcountygov.com. Web Site: tcplreads.com. *Mgr,* Linda Hawkins
Pop 17,150; Circ 53,923
Library Holdings: Bk Vols 42,000; Per Subs 80
Automation Activity & Vendor Info: (Cataloging) Innovative Interfaces, Inc; (Circulation) Innovative Interfaces, Inc
Mem of Three Rivers Regional Library System
Special Services for the Deaf - Bks on deafness & sign lang; Captioned film dep; High interest/low vocabulary bks
Open Mon-Thurs 9-7, Fri 9-5, Sat 10-2
Friends of the Library Group

PINELLAS PARK

SR GOOD SAMARITAN CHURCH LIBRARY*, 6085 Park Blvd, 33781. SAN 328-4638. Tel: 727-544-8558. FAX: 727-544-8558. E-mail: goodsam-church@tampabay.rr.com. Web Site: www.goodsam-church.org. *Librn,* James D Anderson; Staff 0.5 (MLS 0.5)
Library Holdings: Bk Vols 1,200
Open Sun 11:30-12:15
Restriction: Mem only

G JWB CHILDREN'S SERVICES COUNCIL OF PINELLAS COUNTY RESOURCE CENTER*, Mailande W Holland Library, 6698 68th Ave N, 33781-5015. SAN 326-0801. Tel: 727-547-5670. FAX: 727-547-5689. Web Site: www.jwbpinellas.org. *Librn,* Joyce Sparrow; Tel: 727-547-5671, E-mail: jsparrow@jwbpinellas.org; Staff 1 (MLS 1)
Founded 1976
Oct 2007-Sept 2008. Mats Exp $19,545, Books $3,750, Per/Ser (Incl. Access Fees) $14,170, AV Mat $1,625. Sal $48,194
Library Holdings: DVDs 41; Bk Vols 5,000; Per Subs 67; Videos 1,159
Subject Interests: Grantsmanship, Nonprofit develop, Parenting, Youth develop
Automation Activity & Vendor Info: (Cataloging) Mandarin Library Automation; (Circulation) Mandarin Library Automation; (OPAC) Mandarin Library Automation
Partic in Tampa Bay Library Consortium, Inc
Open Mon-Fri 8-5
Restriction: Lending limited to county residents

P PINELLAS PARK PUBLIC LIBRARY*, 7770 52nd St, 33781. SAN 303-1322. Tel: 727-541-0718. Reference Tel: 727-541-0719. FAX: 727-541-0818. Web Site: www.pinellas-park.com//library. *Dir,* Angela Pietras; *Asst Dir, Coll Mgt,* Vivian Godfrey; *Circ,* Bonnie Vincent; *Ref,* Erin Hollingsworth; *Youth Serv,* Arline Hollingsworth; Staff 6 (MLS 6)
Founded 1948. Pop 48,835; Circ 369,728
Library Holdings: AV Mats 9,184; e-books 36,593; High Interest/Low Vocabulary Bk Vols 225; Large Print Bks 7,005; Bk Vols 111,159; Per Subs 315
Automation Activity & Vendor Info: (Cataloging) SirsiDynix; (Circulation) SirsiDynix; (OPAC) SirsiDynix
Wireless access
Function: ILL available, Ref serv available
Publications: Newsletter
Mem of Pinellas Public Libr Coop
Partic in Tampa Bay Library Consortium, Inc
Special Services for the Deaf - Bks on deafness & sign lang; TDD equip; Video relay serv
Open Mon-Thurs 9-8:30, Fri & Sat 9-5, Sun 1-5
Friends of the Library Group

C SAINT PETERSBURG COLLEGE*, M M Bennett Libraries, 7200 66th St N, 33781. (Mail add: PO Box 13489, Saint Petersburg, 33733-3489), SAN 337-3185. Tel: 727-341-3719. FAX: 727-341-3658. Web Site: www.spcollege.edu. *Dir,* Dr Susan Anderson; Staff 36 (MLS 12, Non-MLS 24)
Founded 1927. Enrl 16,933; Highest Degree: Bachelor
Library Holdings: AV Mats 12,404; Bk Titles 147,771; Bk Vols 224,708; Per Subs 1,510
Special Collections: US Document Depository
Automation Activity & Vendor Info: (Circulation) SirsiDynix
Partic in Tampa Bay Library Consortium, Inc
Open Mon-Thurs 7:30am-9pm, Fri 7:30-4:00, Sat 10-5
Departmental Libraries:
CLEARWATER CAMPUS LIBRARY, 2465 Drew St, Clearwater, 33765, SAN 337-3177. Tel: 727-791-2614. FAX: 727-791-2601. Web Site: www.spcollege.edu/central/libonline. *Head Librn/Prog Dir II,* Kim Wolff; Tel: 727-791-2417, E-mail: wolff.kim@spcollege.edu; *Librn,* Paula Bagwell; Tel: 727-791-2415, E-mail: bagwell.paula@spcollege.edu; *Librn,* Pat Barbier; Tel: 727-791-2603, E-mail: barbierp@spcollege.edu; *Librn,* Antoinette Caraway; Tel: 727-791-2416, E-mail: caraway.antoinette@spcollege.edu; *Librn,* Donna Kelly; Tel: 727-341-3771, E-mail: kelly.donna@spcollege.edu; Staff 4 (MLS 4)
CM HEALTH EDUCATION CENTER, 7200 66th St N, 33781, SAN 370-2014. Tel: 727-341-3657. FAX: 727-341-3658. *Head Librn/Prog Dir,* Hector Perez-Gilbe; E-mail: perezgilbe.hector@spcollege.edu; Staff 4 (MLS 1, Non-MLS 3)
Partic in SEFLIN - Southeast Florida Library Information Network, Inc; Tampa Bay Library Consortium, Inc; Tampa Bay Medical Library Network
PROCESSING CENTER, 6021 142nd Ave N, Clearwater, 33760, SAN 370-2022. Tel: 727-341-3693. FAX: 727-341-3399. *Head Librn/Prod Dir I,* Rebecca Frank; Tel: 727-341-3759, E-mail: frank.rebecca@spcollege.edu; Staff 3 (MLS 1, Non-MLS 2)
SAINT PETERSBURG-GIBBS CAMPUS LIBRARY, 6605 Fifth Ave N, Saint Petersburg, 33710, SAN 338-0432. Tel: 727-341-7198. FAX: 727-341-7188. *Head Librn/Prog Dir II,* Tracy Elliott; Tel: 727-341-7197, E-mail: elliott.tracy@spcollege.edu; *Librn,* Betty Jo Gaston; Tel: 727-341-7179, E-mail: gaston.betty@spcollege.edu; *Librn,* Gail Lancaster; Tel: 727-341-4793, E-mail: lancasterg@spcollege.edu; *Librn,* Chad Mairn; Tel: 727-341-7188, E-mail: mairn.chad@spcollege.edu; Staff 9 (MLS 4, Non-MLS 5)
TARPON SPRINGS CAMPUS LIBRARY, 600 Klosterman Rd, Tarpon Springs, 34689, SAN 370-226X. Tel: 727-712-5728. FAX: 727-712-5706. *Head Librn,* Jorge Perez; E-mail: perez.jorge@spcollege.edu; *Librn,* Mathew Bodie; Tel: 727-712-5240, E-mail: bodie.mathew@spcollege.edu; Staff 4 (MLS 2, Non-MLS 2)
Open Mon-Thurs 7:30am-9pm, Fri 7:30-4, Sat 10-5, Sun 1-5

S TAMPA BAY REGIONAL PLANNING COUNCIL*, Research & Information Center, 4000 Gateway Center Blvd, Ste 100, 33782. SAN 303-1632. Tel: 727-570-5151. FAX: 727-570-5118. Web Site: www.tbrpc.org. Avera Wynne
Library Holdings: Bk Vols 3,000; Per Subs 90
Special Collections: Developments of Regional Impact for Pinellas, Hillsborough, Pasco, and Manatee Counties Coll
Subject Interests: Housing, Planning, Transportation
Open Mon-Fri 8:30-12 & 1-5

PLANT CITY

P BRUTON MEMORIAL LIBRARY*, 302 W McLendon St, 33563. SAN 303-1349. Tel: 813-757-9215. FAX: 813-757-9217. Web Site: www.plantcitygov.com/index.aspx?nid=544. *Dir,* Tonda F Morris; *Circ,* Julie Robinson; *Tech Serv,* Susan Ambrose Miles; Staff 14 (MLS 4, Non-MLS 10)
Founded 1960. Pop 27,000; Circ 254,898
Library Holdings: Bk Vols 118,000; Per Subs 175
Special Collections: Florida History Coll
Automation Activity & Vendor Info: (Cataloging) Horizon; (Circulation) Horizon; (OPAC) Horizon
Publications: Between the Pages (Friends Newsletter)
Partic in Hillsborough County Public Library Cooperative; Tampa Bay Library Consortium, Inc
Open Mon-Thurs 10-9, Fri 10-6, Sat 10-5, Sun 1-5
Friends of the Library Group

PLANTATION

P HELEN B HOFFMAN PLANTATION LIBRARY*, 501 N Fig Tree Lane, 33317. SAN 303-1357. Tel: 954-797-2140. Reference Tel: 954-797-2144. Administration Tel: 954-797-2141. FAX: 954-797-2767. E-mail: library@plantation.org. Web Site: www.plantation.org. *Dir,* Dee Anne Merritt; Staff 5 (MLS 2, Non-MLS 3)
Founded 1963. Pop 89,000
Oct 2006-Sept 2007 Income $25,000
Library Holdings: Bk Vols 70,000
Special Collections: Florida Coll; Large Print Coll; Spanish Coll
Automation Activity & Vendor Info: (Cataloging) Mandarin Library Automation; (Circulation) Mandarin Library Automation; (OPAC) Mandarin Library Automation; (Serials) Mandarin Library Automation
Database Vendor: EBSCOhost

Open Mon-Thurs 12-9, Fri 12-7, Sat 10-5
Restriction: Non-resident fee
Friends of the Library Group

POLK CITY

P POLK CITY COMMUNITY LIBRARY*, 215 S Bougainvillea Ave, 33868. (Mail add: 123 Broadway Blvd, 33868), SAN 377-2705. Tel: 863-984-4340. FAX: 863-965-6385. *Dir,* Mary Ellin Barrett; Staff 1 (Non-MLS 1)
Library Holdings: Bk Vols 10,000; Per Subs 20
Automation Activity & Vendor Info: (Cataloging) SirsiDynix; (Circulation) SirsiDynix; (OPAC) SirsiDynix
Function: ILL available
Partic in Polk County Libr Coop
Open Tues-Sat 10-1 & 2-7

POMPANO

C EVEREST UNIVERSITY*, Pompano Beach Campus Library, 225 N Federal Hwy, 33062. SAN 375-3239. Tel: 954-783-7339, Ext 223. Toll Free Tel: 800-468-0168. FAX: 954-783-9023. Web Site: www.fmulibraries.net. *Dir,* Ella Galbreath; Staff 4 (MLS 1, Non-MLS 3)
Founded 1940. Enrl 2,400; Fac 55; Highest Degree: Master
Library Holdings: Bk Titles 6,000; Per Subs 82
Special Services for the Deaf - Bks on deafness & sign lang; High interest/low vocabulary bks; Spec interest per
Open Mon-Thurs 8am-9pm, Fri 8-7, Sat 8-2

PORT CHARLOTTE

P CHARLOTTE COUNTY LIBRARY SYSTEM, 2050 Forrest Nelson Blvd, 33952. SAN 338-019X. Tel: 941-613-3200. Interlibrary Loan Service Tel: 941-613-3198. FAX: 941-613-3196. Web Site: www.charlottecountyfl.com/library. *Dir,* Anne Shepherd; E-mail: anne.shepherd@charlottefl.com; *Regional Librn,* Evelyn Kennedy; Tel: 941-613-3190, E-mail: evelyn.kennedy@charlottefl.com; Staff 31.5 (MLS 10, Non-MLS 21.5)
Founded 1963. Pop 160,000; Circ 792,548
Oct 2009-Sept 2010 Income (Main Library and Branch(s)) $3,269,500, State $84,600, County $2,772,000, Locally Generated Income $412,900. Mats Exp $385,600, Books $282,300, Per/Ser (Incl. Access Fees) $10,000, AV Mat $70,700, Electronic Ref Mat (Incl. Access Fees) $22,600. Sal $1,688,555 (Prof $704,000)
Library Holdings: Audiobooks 18,149; DVDs 25,146; e-books 12,082; Bk Vols 208,692; Per Subs 329
Special Collections: Florida Coll; Genealogy Coll; Large Print Book Coll; Local Author Coll
Automation Activity & Vendor Info: (Acquisitions) TLC (The Library Corporation); (Cataloging) TLC (The Library Corporation); (Circulation) TLC (The Library Corporation); (OPAC) TLC (The Library Corporation); (Serials) TLC (The Library Corporation)
Wireless access
Function: Adult bk club, Art exhibits, AV serv, Bk club(s), Bks on CD, Children's prog, Computer training, Computers for patron use, Copy machines, e-mail & chat, Electronic databases & coll, Exhibits, Fax serv, Free DVD rentals, Genealogy discussion group, Handicapped accessible, ILL available, Large print keyboards, Magnifiers for reading, Mail & tel request accepted, Music CDs, Notary serv, Online cat, Outside serv via phone, mail, e-mail & web, Photocopying/Printing, Preschool outreach, Prog for adults, Prog for children & young adult, Pub access computers, Ref & res, Ref serv available, Scanner, Senior computer classes, Story hour, Tax forms, Teen prog, Telephone ref, Wheelchair accessible
Publications: Friend's Newsletters; Information pamphlets
Partic in Southwest Florida Library Network
Special Services for the Deaf - ADA equip; Assisted listening device; Closed caption videos; Pocket talkers
Special Services for the Blind - Accessible computers; Assistive/Adapted tech devices, equip & products; Audio mat; Copier with enlargement capabilities; Internet workstation with adaptive software; Large print bks; Screen reader software
Open Mon-Thurs 10-7, Fri & Sat 10-5
Restriction: Non-resident fee
Friends of the Library Group
Branches: 4
ENGLEWOOD CHARLOTTE PUBLIC, 3450 North Access Rd, Englewood, 34224, SAN 338-022X. Tel: 941-681-3736. Circulation Tel: 941-681-3735. FAX: 941-681-3740. *Librn Supvr,* Lynda L Citro; Tel: 941-681-3739, E-mail: lynda.citro@charlottefl.com; Staff 5 (MLS 1, Non-MLS 4)
Circ 68,557
Function: Adult bk club, Bks on CD, Children's prog, Computers for patron use, Copy machines, E-Reserves, Electronic databases & coll, Free DVD rentals, Music CDs, Online cat, Online ref, Photocopying/Printing, Pub access computers, Summer reading prog, Teen prog, Web-catalog
Publications: Friend's Newsletters
Special Services for the Blind - Talking bks
Open Tues-Thurs 10-6, Fri 10-5, Sat 10-2
Restriction: Non-resident fee
Friends of the Library Group
MID-COUNTY REGIONAL LIBRARY, 2050 Forrest Nelson Blvd, 33952, SAN 326-7377. Reference Tel: 941-613-3166. FAX: 941-613-3177. *Supv Librn,* Nicole Langley; E-mail: Nicole.Langley@Charlottefl.com; Staff 18.5 (MLS 6, Non-MLS 12.5)
Founded 2005. Circ 397,052
Special Collections: Genealogy Coll
Function: Art exhibits, Bk club(s), Bks on CD, Children's prog, Computer training, Computers for patron use, Copy machines, Electronic databases & coll, Fax serv, Free DVD rentals, Genealogy discussion group, ILL available, Large print keyboards, Music CDs, Newsp ref libr, Notary serv, Online cat, Online searches, Photocopying/Printing, Prog for adults, Prog for children & young adult, Pub access computers, Ref serv available, Scanner, Senior computer classes, Story hour, Summer reading prog, Tax forms, Teen prog, Telephone ref, Wheelchair accessible
Publications: Newsletters
Open Mon-Thurs 10-7, Fri & Sat 10-5
Restriction: Non-resident fee
Friends of the Library Group
PORT CHARLOTTE PUBLIC, 2280 Aaron St, 33952, SAN 338-0289. Reference Tel: 941-764-5562. FAX: 941-764-5571. *Librn,* Patricia Raisch; Tel: 941-764-5570, E-mail: Patti.Raisch@Charlottefl.com; Staff 4.5 (MLS 1, Non-MLS 3.5)
Circ 100,672
Function: Adult bk club, Bks on CD, Children's prog, Computers for patron use, Copy machines, Electronic databases & coll, Exhibits, Fax serv, Free DVD rentals, Handicapped accessible, ILL available, Magnifiers for reading, Music CDs, Online cat, Photocopying/Printing, Prog for adults, Prog for children & young adult, Summer reading prog, Tax forms, Telephone ref, Wheelchair accessible
Publications: Newsletters
Special Services for the Blind - Talking bks
Open Tues-Thurs 10-6, Fri 10-5
Restriction: Non-resident fee
Friends of the Library Group
PUNTA GORDA PUBLIC, 424 W Henry St, Punta Gorda, 33950, SAN 338-0319. Reference Tel: 941-833-5460. FAX: 941-833-5463. *Librn Supvr,* Alison Layne; Tel: 941-833-5459, E-mail: Alison.Layne@Charlottefl.com; Staff 5 (MLS 1, Non-MLS 4)
Circ 175,971
Special Collections: Florida Coll
Publications: Newsletters
Special Services for the Blind - Talking bks
Open Tues & Wed 10-6, Thurs 10-7, Fri 10-5
Restriction: Non-resident fee
Friends of the Library Group

PUNTA GORDA

J EDISON COLLEGE*, Vernon Peeples Learning Resource Center - Charlotte Campus, 26300 Airport Rd, 33950. Information Services Tel: 941-637-5260. FAX: 941-637-3501. *Dir,* Jamie Reynolds; Tel: 941-637-5644, E-mail: jreynolds@edison.edu; Staff 6 (MLS 3, Non-MLS 3)
Founded 1996. Enrl 1,400; Fac 15; Highest Degree: Associate
Library Holdings: Bk Titles 10,000; Per Subs 90
Automation Activity & Vendor Info: (Acquisitions) Ex Libris Group; (Cataloging) Ex Libris Group; (Circulation) Ex Libris Group; (Course Reserve) Ex Libris Group; (ILL) OCLC; (OPAC) Ex Libris Group; (Serials) Ex Libris Group
Database Vendor: EBSCOhost, Gale Cengage Learning, JSTOR, OCLC FirstSearch, OCLC WorldShare Interlibrary Loan, ProQuest
Partic in Southwest Florida Library Network
Open Mon-Thurs 7:30am-9pm, Fri 7:30-5:30, Sat 8-2

QUINCY

P GADSDEN COUNTY PUBLIC LIBRARY*, 7325 Pat Thomas Pkwy, 32351. SAN 320-4715. Tel: 850-627-7106. FAX: 850-627-7775. Web Site: www.gcpls.org. *Dir,* Jane Mock; *Libr Serv Mgr,* Gail Fairtolth; *Ch Serv,* Kris Odahouski; *ILL,* Ricki Bennett; *Outreach Serv Librn,* Shannon Allen; *Ref,* Jim Elliott; Staff 2 (MLS 2)
Founded 1979. Pop 45,000
Library Holdings: Bk Titles 83,559; Bk Vols 85,000; Per Subs 76
Automation Activity & Vendor Info: (Circulation) TLC (The Library Corporation)
Open Mon, Tues & Thurs-Sat 10-9, Wed 12-9, Sun 1-5
Friends of the Library Group

Branches: 2
CHATTAHOOCHEE PUBLIC LIBRARY, 300 Maple St, Chattahoochee, 32324, SAN 320-5088. Tel: 850-663-2707. FAX: 850-663-4598. *Br Mgr,* Sonia Crawford; *Libr Tech,* Marie Parker
Open Mon-Fri 12-6, Sat 9-12
Friends of the Library Group
HAVANA PUBLIC, 203 E Fifth Ave, Havana, 32333, SAN 320-9954. Tel: 850-539-2844. *Librn,* Virginia Green; *Asst Librn,* Shirron Cannon; *Asst Librn,* Michauna Pugh
Library Holdings: Bk Vols 4,000
Open Mon & Tues 11-8, Wed-Fri 11-6, Sat 9-12
Friends of the Library Group
Bookmobiles: 1

S GADSEN CORRECTIONAL INSTITUTION LIBRARY*, 6044 Greensboro Hwy, 32351-9100. SAN 377-0885. Tel: 850-875-9701, Ext 2261. FAX: 850-875-9710. *Librn,* Gary Kitch
Library Holdings: Bk Vols 12,000; Per Subs 71
Open Mon-Fri 8-11 & 1-5, Sat 8-12

RIVERVIEW

S MERYMAN LIBRARY OF AQUATIC RESEARCH*, 10408 Bloomingdale Ave, 33569. SAN 320-4707. Tel: 813-626-9551. FAX: 813-623-6613. *Coordr,* Mona Francis; Staff 3 (MLS 2, Non-MLS 1)
Founded 1974
Library Holdings: Bk Titles 6,000; Bk Vols 6,500; Per Subs 42
Special Collections: Fish and Aquatic Life, periodicals; Fisheries (Assorted First Issues from 1700's), bks
Subject Interests: Animals, behavior of
Publications: Research papers

RIVIERA BEACH

P RIVIERA BEACH PUBLIC LIBRARY*, 600 W Blue Heron Blvd, 33404-4398. (Mail add: PO Box 11329, 33419-1329), SAN 303-1403. Tel: 561-845-4195. FAX: 561-881-7308. E-mail: library@rivierabch.com. Web Site: www.rivierabch.com. *Dir,* Anne Sutton; *Ch Serv,* Sharmain Arnold
Founded 1950. Pop 30,000; Circ 79,230
Library Holdings: Bk Vols 86,000; Per Subs 126
Special Collections: African-American Studies Coll; Florida Coll
Automation Activity & Vendor Info: (Cataloging) Auto-Graphics, Inc; (Circulation) Auto-Graphics, Inc; (OPAC) Auto-Graphics, Inc
Publications: Cornucopia
Partic in Library Cooperative of the Palm Beaches
Open Mon-Thurs 9:30-8, Fri & Sat 9:30-5
Friends of the Library Group

ROYAL PALM BEACH

C SOUTH UNIVERSITY, West Palm Beach Campus Library, 9801 Belvedere Rd, 33411-3640. SAN 375-3786. Tel: 561-273-6402. Administration Tel: 561-273-6403. FAX: 561-273-6420. Web Site: www.southuniversity.edu/west-palm-beach.aspx. *Libr Dir,* David Bosca; E-mail: dbosca@southuniversity.edu; *Librn,* Laura Balseiro; E-mail: lbalseiro@southuniversity.edu; *Librn,* Dawn Frood; E-mail: dalbuhaisi@southuniversity.edu; Staff 3 (MLS 3)
Enrl 1,000; Fac 75; Highest Degree: Doctorate
Library Holdings: AV Mats 1,783; e-books 300,000; Electronic Media & Resources 95; Bk Titles 17,066; Bk Vols 19,283; Per Subs 36
Subject Interests: Advan practice nursing, Bus, Counseling, Criminal justice, Health sci, Healthcare mgt, Info tech, Legal studies, Nursing, Occupational therapy, Paralegal studies, Phys therapy, Psychol
Automation Activity & Vendor Info: (Acquisitions) Baker & Taylor; (Cataloging) Baker & Taylor; (Circulation) Ex Libris Group; (ILL) OCLC; (OPAC) Ex Libris Group; (Serials) EBSCO Online
Database Vendor: Alexander Street Press, American Chemical Society, American Psychological Association (APA), Baker & Taylor, Bowker, Cinahl, CRC Press/Taylor & Francis Group, CredoReference, ebrary, EBSCOhost, Ex Libris Group, Gale Cengage Learning, Hoovers, LexisNexis, Medline, Mergent Online, Micromedex, Natural Standard, OVID Technologies, ProQuest, PubMed, RefWorks, Sage, ScienceDirect, Thomson - Web of Science, UpToDate, WebMD, Westlaw
Wireless access
Function: Audio & video playback equip for onsite use, Audiobks via web, Bks on CD, CD-ROM, Computer training, Computers for patron use, Copy machines, e-mail & chat, Electronic databases & coll, ILL available, Online cat, Online info literacy tutorials on the web & in blackboard, Online ref, Online searches, Orientations, Outside serv via phone, mail, e-mail & web, Ref & res
Open Mon-Fri 8am-9:30pm, Sat 8:30-4:30
Restriction: Borrowing privileges limited to fac & registered students

SAFETY HARBOR

P SAFETY HARBOR PUBLIC LIBRARY*, 101 Second St N, 34695. SAN 323-7575. Tel: 727-724-1525. FAX: 727-724-1533. TDD: 727-724-1529. Web Site: www.tblc.org/shpl/. *Dir,* Lana Bullian; E-mail: bullial@tblc.org; *Adult Serv, Ref,* Robin Leigh; E-mail: leighr@tblc.org; *Ch Serv, YA Serv,* Mary Kay Smith; E-mail: smithmk@tblc.org; *Circ,* Gail Geraci; E-mail: geracig@tblc.org; *Tech Serv,* Mary Ann DeMeo; E-mail: demeom@tblc.org; Staff 5 (MLS 4, Non-MLS 1)
Founded 1938. Pop 17,300; Circ 276,528
Jan 2005-Dec 2005 Income $421,266. Mats Exp $701,621
Library Holdings: AV Mats 7,881; Bks on Deafness & Sign Lang 1,842; e-books 3,598; High Interest/Low Vocabulary Bk Vols 100; Large Print Bks 1,797; Bk Titles 53,218; Bk Vols 65,000; Per Subs 113; Talking Bks 3,456; Videos 10,163
Special Collections: Books & Videos on Deafness & Sign Language
Subject Interests: Deafness, Sign lang
Automation Activity & Vendor Info: (Acquisitions) SirsiDynix; (Cataloging) SirsiDynix; (Circulation) SirsiDynix; (OPAC) SirsiDynix; (Serials) SirsiDynix
Database Vendor: Gale Cengage Learning, Newsbank, OCLC FirstSearch, OVID Technologies, Wilson - Wilson Web
Mem of Pinellas Public Libr Coop
Partic in Tampa Bay Library Consortium, Inc
Special Services for the Deaf - Adult & family literacy prog; Bks on deafness & sign lang; Captioned film dep; Deaf publ; TDD equip
Open Mon-Thurs 9:30-6, Fri & Sat 9:30-5, Sun 1-5
Friends of the Library Group

SAINT AUGUSTINE

G CASTILLO DE SAN MARCOS & FORT MATANZAS NATIONAL MONUMENTS*, National Monument Library, One S Castillo Dr, 32084-3699. SAN 370-288X. Tel: 904-829-6506, Ext 223. FAX: 904-823-9388. Web Site: www.nps.gov/casa. *Admin Officer,* Lindsey Phillips
Library Holdings: Bk Vols 620
Special Collections: Military History; Stetson Coll
Open Mon-Fri 8-5

C FLAGLER COLLEGE, Proctor Library, 44 Sevilla St, 32084-4302. (Mail add: 74 King St, 32084), SAN 303-1411. Tel: 904-819-6206. Circulation Tel: 904-819-6329. Reference Tel: 904-819-6331. FAX: 904-823-8511. E-mail: library@flagler.edu. Web Site: library.flagler.edu. *Dir of Libr Serv,* Brian Nesselrode; E-mail: bness@flagler.edu; *Access Serv Librn,* Caitlin Baker; E-mail: cbaker1@flagler.edu; *Coll Develop Librn,* Jessie Rutland; E-mail: jrutland@flagler.edu; *Evening/Weekend Ref Librn,* Lisa Barnett; E-mail: lbarnett@flagler.edu; *Evening/Weekend Ref Librn,* Stephen Derrig; E-mail: sderrig@flagler.edu; *Spec Coll Librn,* Katherine Owens; E-mail: kowens@flagler.edu; *Teaching & Learning Librn,* Dr Jack Daniels; E-mail: danielsj@flagler.edu; *Web Serv Librn,* Blake Pridgen; E-mail: bpridgen@flagler.edu; *Archive Spec,* Jolene DuBray; E-mail: JDubray679@flagler.edu; *Circ Spec,* Adam Ehrenberg; E-mail: aehrenberg@flagler.edu; *Circ Spec,* Catherine Norwood; E-mail: cnorwood@flagler.edu; *Cataloger,* Margaret Draskovich; E-mail: mdraskovich@flagler.edu; *ILL Serv,* Peggy Dyess; E-mail: dyesspd@flagler.edu; Staff 9 (MLS 9)
Founded 1968. Enrl 3,242; Fac 236; Highest Degree: Bachelor
Library Holdings: AV Mats 5,578; Bks on Deafness & Sign Lang 909; e-books 178,782; e-journals 31,000; Bk Vols 97,338; Per Subs 177
Special Collections: Deaf Studies Coll
Automation Activity & Vendor Info: (Acquisitions) Ex Libris Group; (Cataloging) Ex Libris Group; (Circulation) Ex Libris Group; (Course Reserve) Ex Libris Group; (ILL) OCLC Connexion; (OPAC) Ex Libris Group; (Serials) Ex Libris Group
Database Vendor: 3M Library Systems, Alexander Street Press, American Psychological Association (APA), Baker & Taylor, Bowker, College Source, CredoReference, ebrary, EBSCO Information Services, EBSCOhost, Ex Libris Group, Facts on File, Gale Cengage Learning, H W Wilson, JSTOR, LexisNexis, Nature Publishing Group, OCLC, OCLC CAMIO, OCLC FirstSearch, OCLC WorldShare Interlibrary Loan, Oxford Online, ProQuest, SBRnet (Sports Business Research Network), Standard & Poor's
Wireless access
Partic in Florida Library Information Network; Independent Cols & Univs of Fla; Lyrasis; Northeast Florida Library Information Network
Open Mon-Thurs 7:30am-Midnight, Fri 7:30am-9pm, Sat 10-5, Sun 11am-Midnight

S SAINT AUGUSTINE HISTORICAL SOCIETY*, Research Library, Six Artillery Lane, 2nd Flr, 32084. (Mail add: 271 Charlotte St, 32084-5099), SAN 303-1438. Tel: 904-825-2333. E-mail: sahslibrary@bellsouth.net. Web Site: www.staugustinehistoricalsociety.org. *Chief Librn,* Robert F Nawrocki; *Asst Librn,* Debby Willis; E-mail: sahslibhelp@bellsouth.net; *Sr Res Librn,*

Charles Tingley; E-mail: sahslibquestion@bellsouth.net; Staff 3 (MLS 1, Non-MLS 2)
Founded 1883
Library Holdings: Microforms 1,200; Bk Titles 8,000; Per Subs 10
Special Collections: Card Calendar of Spanish Documents, 1512-1764; Card Index of St Augustine Residents; Cathedral Parish Records, 1594-1763 & 1784-1882, including Baptisms, Marriages & Burials; Ceiba Mocha Parish, Cuban Archives, 1797-1920, microfilm; Census Records for Northeast Florida, 1784-1920; Colonial Office Records, 1763-1784, British period, microfilm; Court Records for St Johns County, 1812-1960; East Florida Papers on microfilm, 1783-1821; Florida Times Union Newspaper, 1881-1895, microfilm; Maps of Florida & St Augustine (copies), 16th Century to present; Photographs of the St Augustine Area, 19th Century to present; St Augustine Newspapers, 1821 to Present, with gaps; Stetson Coll, 1500's-1817; Various Manuscript Coll. Oral History
Subject Interests: Fla colonial hist, St Augustine, Fla, St Johns County
Automation Activity & Vendor Info: (Cataloging) TLC (The Library Corporation)
Publications: East Florida Gazette (Bi-annually); El Escribano, St Augustine Journal of History (Annual)
Open Tues-Fri 9-4:30
Friends of the Library Group

S SAINT AUGUSTINE PRESERVATION DEPARTMENT LIBRARY*, Government House, PO Box 210, 32085-0210. SAN 303-142X. Tel: 904-825-5033. FAX: 904-825-5096. *Dir,* William R Adams
Founded 1963
Library Holdings: Bk Vols 2,000
Special Collections: Architectural Survey Coll; Historical Maps Coll, copies; Saint Augustine Preservation Projects Coll, VF; Translations & Transcripts of 16th-18th Century Documents
Subject Interests: Archaeology, Local hist

P SAINT JOHNS COUNTY PUBLIC LIBRARY SYSTEM, Southeast Branch Library & Administrative Headquarters, 6670 US 1 South, 32086. SAN 338-0408. Tel: 904-827-6900. Circulation Tel: 904-827-6904. Interlibrary Loan Service Tel: 904-827-6934. Reference Tel: 904-827-6902. Administration Tel: 904-827-6925. Automation Services Tel: 904-827-6924. Circulation FAX: 904-827-6905. Administration FAX: 904-827-6930. Web Site: www.sjcpls.org. *Dir,* Debra Rhodes Gibson; Tel: 904-827-6926, E-mail: dgibson@sjcfl.us; *Tech Serv Adminr,* Jae Bass; E-mail: jbass@sjcfl.us; *Circ Mgr,* Kris Mangus; Tel: 904-827-6916, E-mail: kmangus@sjcfl.us; *Extn Serv Mgr,* Harold George; Tel: 904-827-6928, E-mail: hgeorge@sjcfl.us; *Ch Serv,* Alex Phillips; Tel: 904-827-6912, E-mail: aphillips@sjcfl.us; *ILL,* Karlene Adams; E-mail: kadams@sjcfl.us; *Ref Serv,* Todd Booth; Tel: 904-827-6913, E-mail: tbooth@sjcfl.us; Staff 71.4 (MLS 22.5, Non-MLS 48.9)
Founded 1975. Pop 211,549; Circ 1,704,138
Oct 2013-Sept 2014 Income (Main Library and Branch(s)) $5,655,590, State $145,096, County $5,432,387, Other $78,107. Mats Exp $596,052, Books $418,356, Other Print Mats $145,096, Electronic Ref Mat (Incl. Access Fees) $30,000, Presv $2,600. Sal $3,819,701
Library Holdings: Audiobooks 32,449; e-books 8,555; Electronic Media & Resources 67; Bk Vols 307,268; Per Subs 408; Videos 36,988
Special Collections: Genealogy
Subject Interests: Fla
Automation Activity & Vendor Info: (Acquisitions) SirsiDynix; (Cataloging) SirsiDynix; (Circulation) SirsiDynix; (ILL) OCLC WorldShare Interlibrary Loan; (OPAC) SirsiDynix
Database Vendor: Baker & Taylor, Booksite, Gale Cengage Learning, LearningExpress, OCLC FirstSearch, SirsiDynix, Westlaw, World Book Online, WT Cox
Wireless access
Function: 24/7 Online cat, Adult bk club, Art exhibits, Audiobks via web, Bks on CD, Chess club, Children's prog, Computers for patron use, Copy machines, Electronic databases & coll, Fax serv, Handicapped accessible, Homebound delivery serv, ILL available, Magazines, Music CDs, Notary serv, Online cat, Online ref, Outreach serv, OverDrive digital audio bks, Preschool outreach, Prog for adults, Prog for children & young adult, Pub access computers, Ref serv available, Scanner, Senior outreach, Spanish lang bks, Story hour, Summer reading prog, Tax forms, Teen prog, Telephone ref, Web-catalog
Partic in Lyrasis; Northeast Florida Library Information Network
Special Services for the Deaf - Assistive tech; Bks on deafness & sign lang; Sign lang interpreter upon request for prog; Staff with knowledge of sign lang; Video relay serv
Special Services for the Blind - Assistive/Adapted tech devices, equip & products; BiFolkal kits; Bks on CD; Braille bks; Dragon Naturally Speaking software; Extensive large print coll; Large screen computer & software; Magnifiers; Talking bk serv referral
Open Mon, Tues & Thurs 10-8, Wed & Fri 10-6, Sat 10-5
Friends of the Library Group
Branches: 5
ANASTASIA ISLAND BRANCH, 124 Seagrove Main St, Saint Augustine Beach, 32080. Tel: 904-209-3730. Circulation Tel: 904-209-4074. Reference Tel: 904-209-4075. FAX: 904-209-3735. E-mail: libai@sjcfl.us. *Br Mgr,* Mikki Sampo; Tel: 904-209-3731, E-mail: msampo@sjcfl.us; *Circ Supvr,* Deborah Braden; Tel: 904-209-3734, E-mail: dbraden@sjcfl.us; *Ch Serv,* Nicole Jebbia; Tel: 904-209-3732, E-mail: njebbia@sjcfl.us; Staff 6.325 (MLS 2, Non-MLS 4.325)
Founded 2007. Pop 26,361; Circ 217,649
Open Tues & Thurs 10-8, Wed & Fri 10-6, Sat 10-5
Friends of the Library Group
BARTRAM TRAIL, 60 Davis Pond Blvd, Fruit Cove, 32259-4390, SAN 325-4100. Tel: 904-827-6960. Reference Tel: 904-827-4748. FAX: 904-827-6965. *Br Mgr,* Dan Markus; Tel: 904-827-6961, E-mail: libbt@sjcfl.us; *Circ Supvr,* Melissa Burke; Tel: 904-827-6964, E-mail: mburke@sjcfl.us; *Ch Serv,* Lisa Darenberg; Tel: 904-827-6962, E-mail: ldarenberg@sjcfl.us; *Ref Serv,* Maribeth Wood; Tel: 904-827-6963, E-mail: mwood@sjcfl.us; Staff 10.5 (MLS 4, Non-MLS 6.5)
Founded 1997. Pop 63,386; Circ 363,182
Open Mon, Tues & Thurs 10-8, Wed & Fri 10-6, Sat 10-5
Friends of the Library Group
HASTINGS BRANCH, 6195 S Main St, Hastings, 32145, SAN 338-0416. Tel: 904-827-6970. FAX: 904-692-1255. E-mail: libh@sjcfl.us. *Br Mgr,* Brad Powell; Tel: 904-827-6971, E-mail: bpowell@sjcfl.us; *Ch Serv Librn,* Michelle Kiley; Tel: 904-827-6976, E-mail: mkiley@sjcfl.us; *Circ Supvr,* Terri Beverly; Tel: 904-827-6974, E-mail: tbeverly@sjcfl.us; Staff 5.3 (MLS 2, Non-MLS 3.3)
Founded 1997. Pop 7,352; Circ 85,735
Automation Activity & Vendor Info: (Circulation) Horizon
Open Tues & Thurs 10-7, Wed & Fri 10-6, Sat 10-3
Friends of the Library Group
MAIN BRANCH, 1960 N Ponce de Leon Blvd, 32084. Tel: 904-827-6940. Circulation Tel: 904-827-4707. Reference Tel: 904-827-4702. FAX: 904-827-6945. E-mail: libm@sjcfl.us. *Br Mgr,* Valerie Peischel Mull; Tel: 904-827-6941, E-mail: vpeischel@sjcfl.us; *Ch Serv Librn,* Andy Calvert; Tel: 904-827-6943, E-mail: acalvert@sjcfl.us; *Ref Librn,* Amy Ackerman; Tel: 904-827-6942, E-mail: aackerman@sjcfl.us; *Circ Supvr,* Richard Steinmeyer; Tel: 904-827-6946, E-mail: rsteinmeyer@sjcfl.us; Staff 10 (MLS 3.5, Non-MLS 6.5)
Founded 1977. Pop 47,343; Circ 389,732
Friends of the Library Group
PONTE VEDRA BEACH BRANCH, 101 Library Blvd, Ponte Vedra Beach, 32082, SAN 325-4127. Tel: 904-827-6950. Circulation Tel: 904-827-4762. Reference Tel: 904-827-4766. FAX: 904-827-6955. E-mail: libpv@sjcfl.us. *Br Mgr,* Amy Ring; Tel: 904-827-6951, E-mail: aring@sjcfl.us; *Circ Supvr,* Lidia Wolfcale; Tel: 904-827-6956, E-mail: lwolfcale@sjcfl.us; *Ch Serv,* Anne Crawford; Tel: 904-827-6952, E-mail: acrawford@sjcfl.us; *Ref Serv,* Joan Hakala; Tel: 904-827-6953, E-mail: jhakala@sjcfl.us; Staff 10.825 (MLS 3, Non-MLS 7.825)
Founded 1993. Pop 34,884; Circ 282,332
Open Mon-Wed 10-8, Thurs & Fri 10-6, Sat 10-5
Friends of the Library Group
Bookmobiles: 2

SAINT LEO

C SAINT LEO UNIVERSITY*, Cannon Memorial Library, 33701 State Rd 52, 33574. (Mail add: PO Box 6665, MC2128, 33574-6665), SAN 303-1446. Tel: 352-588-8258. Reference Tel: 352-588-8477. FAX: 352-588-8484. Web Site: www.saintleo.edu. *Dir, Libr Serv,* Brent Short; Tel: 352-588-8260, E-mail: brent.short@saintleo.edu; *Cat Librn,* Rachel Longstaff; Tel: 352-588-8586, E-mail: rachel.longstaff@saintleo.edu; *Digital Res Librn,* Sandy Hawes; Tel: 352-588-8262, E-mail: sandra.hawes@saintleo.edu; *Fac Develop Librn,* Doris Van Kampen; Tel: 352-588-8485, E-mail: doris.vankampen@saintleo.edu; *Fla & Cent Region Librn,* Viki Stoupenos; Tel: 912-352-7970, E-mail: viki.stoupenos@saintleo.edu; *Instruction Prog & Info Literacy Librn,* Elana Karshmer; Tel: 352-588-8412, E-mail: elana.karshmer@saintleo.edu; *Online Librn,* Kerry Vash; Tel: 352-588-8267, E-mail: kerry.vash@saintleo.edu; *Ref & Instrul Outreach Librn,* Carol Ann Moon; Tel: 352-588-8261, E-mail: carol.moon@saintleo.edu; *Ref & Instrul Serv Librn,* Jackie Bryan; Tel: 352-588-7437, E-mail: jacalyn.bryan@saintleo.edu; *Ref Librn,* Mary Anne Gallagher; Tel: 352-588-7867, E-mail: mary.gallagher@saintleo.edu; *Tech Serv Librn,* Elizabeth C Henry; Tel: 352-588-8265, E-mail: elizabeth.henry@saintleo.edu; *Va Region Librn,* Steve Weaver; Tel: 757-766-1468, E-mail: steven.weaver@saintleo.edu; *Circ Supvr,* Aaron Reines; Tel: 352-588-8648, E-mail: aaron.reines@saintleo.edu; *Circ Evening Coordr,* Muriel Clemens; Tel: 352-588-8476, E-mail: muriel.clemens@saintleo.edu; *Online Res Coordr/Ref Librn,* Darla Asher; Tel: 352-588-8475, E-mail: darla.asher@saintleo.edu; *Staff Coordr,* Sonja Fraser; E-mail: sonja.fraser@saintleo.edu; *Acq Asst,* Yuni McGahey; Tel: 352-588-8419, E-mail: yuni.mcgahey@saintleo.edu; *ILL Asst,* Cecelia Bolich; Tel: 352-588-8328, E-mail: cecelia.bolich@saintleo.edu; Staff 16 (MLS 12, Non-MLS 4)

Founded 1959. Enrl 8,376; Fac 70; Highest Degree: Master
Library Holdings: e-books 235,000; Bk Titles 101,311; Bk Vols 111,138; Per Subs 474
Subject Interests: Catholic Church, Humanities, Monasticism, Theol
Automation Activity & Vendor Info: (Acquisitions) Ex Libris Group; (Cataloging) Ex Libris Group; (Circulation) Ex Libris Group; (Course Reserve) Ex Libris Group; (ILL) OCLC; (OPAC) Ex Libris Group; (Serials) Ex Libris Group
Database Vendor: EBSCOhost, Gale Cengage Learning, LexisNexis, Newsbank, OCLC FirstSearch, OCLC WorldShare Interlibrary Loan, ProQuest, Westlaw, Wilson - Wilson Web
Publications: Acquisitions List; Bibliographies; Handbook, Library Guides; Newsletter; Periodicals Lists
Partic in Lyrasis; OCLC Online Computer Library Center, Inc; Tampa Bay Library Consortium, Inc
Open Sun-Thurs 8am-2am, Fri & Sat 8-7

SAINT PETE BEACH

P ST PETE BEACH PUBLIC LIBRARY*, 365 73rd Ave, 33706-1996. SAN 303-1683. Tel: 727-363-9238. FAX: 727-552-1760. Web Site: www.stpetebeach.org/city-departments/public-library.html. *Libr Adminr,* Phyllis Ruscella; E-mail: p.ruscella@stpetebeach.org; *Librn,* Maryjane Hyatt; E-mail: MaryJane@stpetebeach.org; Staff 10 (MLS 2, Non-MLS 8)
Founded 1951. Pop 9,200; Circ 153,406
Oct 2012-Sept 2013 Income $517,978, City $355,841, County $162,137. Mats Exp $57,440. Sal $312,434 (Prof $135,000)
Library Holdings: AV Mats 3,009; DVDs 4,345; e-books 6,647; Bk Titles 50,544; Per Subs 61
Special Collections: Florida Coll; Sister City Coll
Automation Activity & Vendor Info: (Acquisitions) Innovative Interfaces, Inc; (Cataloging) Innovative Interfaces, Inc; (Circulation) Innovative Interfaces, Inc
Wireless access
Mem of Pinellas Public Libr Coop
Open Mon & Wed 10-8, Tues, Thurs & Fri 10-6, Sat 10-2
Friends of the Library Group

SAINT PETERSBURG

M ALL CHILDRENS' HOSPITAL, Medical Library, 501 Sixth Ave S, 33701. SAN 303-1454. Tel: 727-767-4278. FAX: 727-767-8557. E-mail: achedicallibrary@jhmi.edu. *Dir,* Patricia Clark; E-mail: pclark19@jhmi.edu; *Ref Serv,* Pamela Williams; E-mail: pwilli78@jhmi.edu; Staff 2 (MLS 2)
Library Holdings: e-journals 4,000; Bk Titles 900; Per Subs 200
Subject Interests: Cardiology, Med, Neurology, Nursing, Pediatrics
Automation Activity & Vendor Info: (Cataloging) LibraryWorld, Inc; (OPAC) LibraryWorld, Inc; (Serials) LibraryWorld, Inc
Database Vendor: Checkpoint Systems, Inc, Cinahl, DynaMed, EBSCO Information Services, EBSCOhost, Majors, Medline, Nature Publishing Group, OVID Technologies, ProQuest, PubMed, ScienceDirect, STAT!Ref (Teton Data Systems), UpToDate
Wireless access
Function: Doc delivery serv, For res purposes, Health sci info serv, ILL available, Online searches, Ref serv available
Partic in Florida Health Sciences Library Association (FHSLA); SEND; Tampa Bay Medical Library Network
Restriction: Staff & prof res

M BAYFRONT HEALTH ST PETERSBURG, Aucremann Medical Library, 701 Sixth St S, 33701. SAN 303-1462. Tel: 727-893-6751. FAX: 727-893-6819. Web Site: www.bayfront.org. *Mgr,* Julie Hunt; E-mail: julie.hunt2@bayfronthealth.com
Founded 1937
Library Holdings: Bk Vols 1,500; Per Subs 50
Subject Interests: Clinical med, Neurosurgery, Obstetrics & gynecology
Partic in SE-Atlantic Regional Med Libr Servs; Tampa Bay Medical Library Network
Open Mon-Fri 8-5

S SALVADOR DALI FOUNDATION INC, Dali Museum Library, One Dali Blvd, 33701. SAN 322-7421. Tel: 727-823-3767. FAX: 727-894-6068. Web Site: www.salvadordalimuseum.org. *Chief Curator,* Joan R Kropf; E-mail: jkropf@thedali.org; *Librn,* Shaina Buckles; Tel: 727-623-4734, E-mail: sbuckles@thedali.org; Staff 0.5 (MLS 0.5)
Founded 1982
Library Holdings: Bk Titles 4,700; Bk Vols 5,500
Special Collections: Salvador Dali Coll
Subject Interests: Surrealism
Wireless access
Function: Res libr
Publications: Books on Dali: Dali in the Nude; Dali the Passions; Dali, A Panorama; Exhibit Catalogs; Newsletter
Restriction: Authorized scholars by appt, Non-circulating

C ECKERD COLLEGE*, Peter H Armacost Library, 4200 54th Ave S, 33711. SAN 303-1489. Tel: 727-864-8337. Interlibrary Loan Service Tel: 727-864-8475. Administration Tel: 727-864-8336. FAX: 727-864-8997. Web Site: www.eckerd.edu/library. *Dir, Libr Serv,* David W Henderson; E-mail: henderdw@eckerd.edu; *Ser Librn, Tech Serv Supvr,* Jamie Gill; E-mail: gilljw@eckerd.edu; *Ref, Syst Librn,* Beatrice Nichols; E-mail: nicholbf@eckerd.edu; *Electronic Serv, Ref Serv, Web Developer,* Helene Gold; E-mail: goldhe@eckerd.edu; *ILL, Ref Serv,* Yort Watson; E-mail: watsony@eckerd.edu; Staff 12 (MLS 5, Non-MLS 7)
Founded 1959. Enrl 1,608; Fac 124; Highest Degree: Bachelor
Library Holdings: Bk Titles 131,976; Bk Vols 165,085; Per Subs 821
Automation Activity & Vendor Info: (Acquisitions) Ex Libris Group; (Cataloging) Ex Libris Group; (Circulation) Ex Libris Group; (Course Reserve) Ex Libris Group
Database Vendor: Gale Cengage Learning, OCLC FirstSearch, ProQuest, Wilson - Wilson Web
Wireless access
Partic in Florida Library Information Network; Independent Cols & Univs of Fla; Library & Information Resources Network (LIRN); OCLC Online Computer Library Center, Inc; Tampa Bay Library Consortium, Inc
Open Mon-Thurs 8am-1am, Fri 8-5, Sat 10-5, Sun Noon-1am
Friends of the Library Group

G FISH & WILDLIFE RESEARCH INSTITUTE*, Research Information Center, 100 Eighth Ave SE, 33701-5095. SAN 303-1497. Tel: 727-896-8626. FAX: 727-823-0166. Web Site: www.myfwc.com. *Librn,* Jan Boyett; E-mail: jan.boyett@myfwc.com; Staff 3 (MLS 1, Non-MLS 2)
Founded 1955
Library Holdings: Bk Titles 6,500; Per Subs 170
Subject Interests: Biological, Environ studies, Ichthyology, Marine biol
Publications: Florida Marine Research Publications; Memoirs of the Hourglass Cruises; Reprints of Articles in Outside Journals; Technical Reports
Open Mon-Fri 8-5

S MUSEUM OF FINE ARTS*, Reference Library, 255 Beach Dr NE, 33701-3498. SAN 303-156X. Tel: 727-896-2667. FAX: 727-894-4638. Web Site: www.fine-arts.org. *Librn,* Jordana S Weiss; Staff 1 (MLS 1)
Founded 1962
Library Holdings: Bk Titles 27,000; Per Subs 21
Subject Interests: Art & archit, Decorative art
Open Tues-Thurs 10-5
Restriction: Non-circulating

SR PASADENA COMMUNITY UNITED METHODIST CHURCH LIBRARY*, 227 70th St S, 33707. SAN 322-807X. Tel: 727-381-2499. FAX: 727-343-7783. Web Site: www.pasadenacommunitychurch.org.
Library Holdings: Bk Vols 7,208
Subject Interests: Bio, Fiction, Hist, Relig
Restriction: Mem only

R PASADENA PRESBYTERIAN CHURCH LIBRARY*, Maxine Perry Library, 100 Pasadena Ave N, 33710-8315. SAN 303-1578. Tel: 727-345-0148. FAX: 727-347-6836. Web Site: www.pasadenapc.com. *Librn,* Laurie Smith; Staff 1 (Non-MLS 1)
Founded 1960
Library Holdings: Audiobooks 20; CDs 40; DVDs 154; Large Print Bks 20; Bk Titles 4,800; Bk Vols 4,850; Spec Interest Per Sub 2; Videos 159
Special Collections: Christian Children's & Youth Books (Including an Easy Section & Reading-Level Books)
Subject Interests: Bible study, Christian bks, Christian fiction, Christian life
Function: Bks on cassette, Bks on CD, VHS videos, Video lending libr
Open Sun 8:30-Noon

S POYNTER INSTITUTE FOR MEDIA STUDIES*, Eugene Patterson Library, 801 Third St S, 33701. SAN 323-5661. Tel: 727-821-9494. FAX: 727-898-9201. Web Site: www.poynter.org. *Dir,* David Shedden; Tel: 727-821-9494, Ext 252; Staff 4 (MLS 2, Non-MLS 2)
Founded 1985
Library Holdings: Bk Vols 11,000; Per Subs 100
Special Collections: Don Murray Papers; Eugene Patterson Papers; Newsleaders Videotape Oral History Coll. Oral History
Subject Interests: Journalism, Mass communications
Automation Activity & Vendor Info: (Cataloging) EOS International; (Circulation) EOS International
Database Vendor: Dialog, LexisNexis
Function: Res libr
Publications: Bibliography Series
Partic in Tampa Bay Library Consortium, Inc
Restriction: Students only

M SAINT ANTHONY'S HEALTH CARE LIBRARY*, 1200 Seventh Ave N, 33705. SAN 303-1594. Tel: 727-825-1286. FAX: 727-820-7877. *In Charge,* Bianca Lenglet; Staff 1 (Non-MLS 1)
Library Holdings: Bk Vols 2,000
Partic in Tampa Bay Medical Library Network
Restriction: Staff use only

S ST PETERSBURG MUSEUM OF HISTORY LIBRARY*, 335 Second Ave NE, 33701-3501. SAN 303-1608. Tel: 727-894-1052. FAX: 727-823-7276. Web Site: www.museumofhistoryonline.org. *Archivist,* Ann Wikoff
Founded 1922
Library Holdings: Bk Vols 1,020
Special Collections: Baseball Coll 1930-60's; Florida Tourism Materials; Railroad & Early Florida Settlement (Peter Demens Coll); Regional Photgraph Coll; Regional Postcard Coll; St Petersburg Area History (Blocker Coll)
Subject Interests: Aviation, Baseball, Hist of Fla

P SAINT PETERSBURG PUBLIC LIBRARY*, 3745 Ninth Ave N, 33713. SAN 338-0467. Tel: 727-893-7724. FAX: 727-892-5432. TDD: 727-893-7995. Web Site: splibraries.org. *Dir,* Mary Gaines; Tel: 727-893-7268; *Mgr,* Laurel Gustasson; *Mgr, Spec Proj,* Elaine Birkinshaw; *Ref Serv Coordr,* JoAnn Balistreri; *Adult Serv, Circ,* Angela Pictras; *Govt Doc,* Sarah Thogode; *Tech Serv,* Pamela Peterson; *Youth Serv,* Sharon Coppola
Founded 1910. Pop 240,318; Circ 1,051,108
Library Holdings: Bk Vols 435,634; Per Subs 886
Special Collections: Florida History. State Document Depository; US Document Depository
Automation Activity & Vendor Info: (Acquisitions) Innovative Interfaces, Inc; (Cataloging) Innovative Interfaces, Inc; (Circulation) Innovative Interfaces, Inc
Mem of Pinellas Public Libr Coop
Open Mon-Thurs 9-9, Fri & Sat 9-6, Sun 10-6
Friends of the Library Group
Branches: 5
JAMES WELDON JOHNSON BRANCH, 1059 18th Ave S, 33705, SAN 338-0491. Tel: 727-893-7113. FAX: 727-821-4845.
Open Mon-Wed 9-9, Thurs-Sat 9-6
Friends of the Library Group
MIRROR LAKE, 280 Fifth St N, 33701, SAN 338-0521. Tel: 727-893-7268. FAX: 727-821-4975.
Open Mon-Sat 9-6
Friends of the Library Group
NORTH, 861 70th Ave N, 33702, SAN 338-0556. Tel: 727-893-7214. FAX: 727-522-6902. *Asst Librn,* Carol Brooks
Open Mon, Wed, Fri & Sat 9-6, Tues & Thurs 9-9
Friends of the Library Group
SOUTH, 2300 Roy Hanna Dr S, 33712, SAN 338-0564. Tel: 727-893-7244. FAX: 727-864-2470. *Br Mgr,* Sandra Allen
Open Mon, Wed, Fri & Sat 9-6, Tues & Thurs 9-9
Friends of the Library Group
WEST SAINT PETERSBURG COMMUNITY LIBRARY, 750 66th St N, 33710, SAN 323-9195. Tel: 727-341-7199. *Br Mgr,* Dorothy Bell
Open Mon-Thurs 7:30am-9pm, Fri 7:30-4, Sat 10-5
Friends of the Library Group
Bookmobiles: 1

S TIMES PUBLISHING CO*, Tampa Bay Times News Library, 490 First Ave S, 33701-4223. (Mail add: PO Box 1121, 33731-1121), SAN 303-1640. Tel: 727-893-8111. Toll Free Tel: 800-333-7505. FAX: 727-893-8107. Web Site: www.tampabay.com. *Res Editor,* Tim Rozgonyi; E-mail: trozgonyi@tampabay.com; *Res,* Caryn Baird; E-mail: cbaird@tampabay.com; *Res,* Carolyn Edds; E-mail: cedds@tampabay.com; *Res,* John Martin; E-mail: jmartin@tampabay.com; *Res,* Natalie Watson; E-mail: nwatson@tampabay.com; Staff 9 (MLS 5, Non-MLS 4)
Founded 1923
Library Holdings: Bk Titles 3,000
Special Collections: Florida Book Coll; Historic Local Photographs
Partic in Tampa Bay Library Consortium, Inc
Restriction: Staff use only

C UNIVERSITY OF SOUTH FLORIDA SAINT PETERSBURG, Nelson Poynter Memorial Library, 140 Seventh Ave S, POY118, 33701. SAN 303-1667. Tel: 727-873-4401. Circulation Tel: 727-873-4405. Interlibrary Loan Service Tel: 727-873-4549. FAX: 727-873-4196. Web Site: www.lib.usfsp.edu. *Dean of Libr,* Carol Hixson; E-mail: hixson@mail.usf.edu; *Head, Coll & Tech Serv,* Patricia Pettijohn; *Head, Syst & Digital Tech,* Berrie Watson; *Head, Access Serv,* Virginia Champion; Tel: 727-873-4843; *Head, Res & Instruction,* Tina Neville; Tel: 727-873-4081, E-mail: neville@nelson.usf.edu; *Distance Learning/Bus Librn,* Gary Austin; *Librn, Scholarly Support Services & Spec Projects,* Anthony Stamatoplos; *Res & Instruction Librn,* Deborah Henry; *Res & Instruction Librn,* Kaya van Beynen; *Vis Instr Librn,* Camielle Swenson; *Mgr, Libr Operations,* Estevez Marcela; *Coordr, Distance Learning & Instrul Media Serv,* David Brodosi. Subject Specialists: *Marine sci,* Deborah Henry; Staff 12 (MLS 9, Non-MLS 3)
Founded 1968. Enrl 5,500; Fac 166; Highest Degree: Master
Jul 2013-Jun 2014. Mats Exp $87,606, Books $32,334, Per/Ser (Incl. Access Fees) $54,635, AV Mat $498, Presv $139
Library Holdings: Audiobooks 437; AV Mats 15,948; CDs 1,076; DVDs 3,776; Bk Titles 208,370; Bk Vols 214,701; Per Subs 290; Videos 7,069
Special Collections: Florida & Local History Coll; Ichthyology, Natural History & Zoology (Dr John C Briggs Coll); Mark Twain (Dr David Hubbell Coll); Papers of Nelson Poynter, Publisher of the St Petersburg Times; University of South Florida St Petersburg Archives. Oral History
Subject Interests: Bus & mgt, Educ, Humanities, Marine sci, Soc sci
Automation Activity & Vendor Info: (Acquisitions) Ex Libris Group; (Cataloging) Ex Libris Group; (Circulation) Ex Libris Group; (Course Reserve) Ex Libris Group; (ILL) OCLC; (OPAC) Ex Libris Group; (Serials) Ex Libris Group
Wireless access
Function: Archival coll, AV serv, Distance learning, E-Reserves, Electronic databases & coll, Ref & res
Publications: The Library Connection (Newsletter)
Partic in Lyrasis; Tampa Bay Library Consortium, Inc
Restriction: Pub use on premises
Friends of the Library Group

SANFORD

J SEMINOLE COMMUNITY COLLEGE LIBRARY*, 100 Weldon Blvd, 32773-6199. SAN 303-1691. Circulation Tel: 407-328-2295. Interlibrary Loan Service Tel: 407-328-2114. Reference Tel: 407-328-2305. Administration Tel: 407-328-3217. FAX: 407-328-2233. E-mail: library@seminolestate.edu. Web Site: www.seminolestate.edu/Library. *Dean,* Patricia DeSalvo; Tel: 407-328-2136, E-mail: desalvop@seminolestate.edu; *Assoc Dir of Libr,* Linda Sutton; Tel: 407-708-2114, E-mail: suttonl@seminolestate.edu; Staff 35 (MLS 8, Non-MLS 27)
Founded 1966. Enrl 9,500; Fac 275; Highest Degree: Associate
Library Holdings: AV Mats 9,000; Bks on Deafness & Sign Lang 20; High Interest/Low Vocabulary Bk Vols 580; Bk Titles 105,000; Per Subs 400; Talking Bks 102
Automation Activity & Vendor Info: (Acquisitions) Ex Libris Group; (Cataloging) Ex Libris Group; (Circulation) Ex Libris Group; (Course Reserve) Ex Libris Group; (ILL) Ex Libris Group; (Media Booking) Ex Libris Group; (OPAC) Ex Libris Group; (Serials) Ex Libris Group
Database Vendor: OCLC FirstSearch
Partic in Lyrasis; OCLC Online Computer Library Center, Inc; Tampa Bay Library Consortium, Inc
Special Services for the Blind - Assistive/Adapted tech devices, equip & products

SANIBEL

P SANIBEL PUBLIC LIBRARY DISTRICT*, 770 Dunlop Rd, 33957. SAN 303-1705. Tel: 239-472-2483. FAX: 239-472-9524. Web Site: www.sanlib.org. *Dir,* Margaret Mohundro; E-mail: mmohundro@sanlib.org; *Ch,* Barbara Dunkle; *Ref Librn,* Candy Heise; *IT Mgr, Webmaster,* Joanne Wessels; *Coll Develop,* Duane Shaffer; Staff 9 (MLS 4, Non-MLS 5)
Founded 1962. Pop 5,975; Circ 125,428
Library Holdings: AV Mats 3,500; High Interest/Low Vocabulary Bk Vols 10; Bk Titles 58,000; Bk Vols 62,000; Per Subs 226
Special Collections: Oral History
Subject Interests: Fla, Local hist, Paintings
Automation Activity & Vendor Info: (Cataloging) Innovative Interfaces, Inc; (Circulation) Innovative Interfaces, Inc; (OPAC) Innovative Interfaces, Inc
Publications: SPLash
Partic in OCLC Online Computer Library Center, Inc; Southwest Florida Library Network
Open Mon & Thurs 9-8, Tues, Wed, Fri & Sat 9-5
Friends of the Library Group

SARASOTA

C ARGOSY UNIVERSITY*, Sarasota Campus Library, 5250 17th St, 34235. SAN 320-1384. Tel: 941-379-0404, Ext 229. Toll Free Tel: 800-331-5995. FAX: 941-379-9464. *Asst Librn,* Heather Lauer; E-mail: hlauer@argosy.edu; Staff 5 (MLS 1, Non-MLS 4)
Founded 1974. Enrl 2,000; Fac 90; Highest Degree: Doctorate
Sept 2005-Aug 2006 Income $200,000. Mats Exp $135,000, Books $50,000, Per/Ser (Incl. Access Fees) $35,000, AV Equip $25,000, AV Mat $25,000. Sal $45,000
Library Holdings: AV Mats 250; e-books 15,000; e-journals 18,000; Bk Titles 12,000
Special Collections: Marian Hopkins Jung Coll
Subject Interests: Bus & mgt, Educ, Psychol

Automation Activity & Vendor Info: (Acquisitions) Ex Libris Group; (Cataloging) OCLC Connexion; (Circulation) Ex Libris Group; (ILL) OCLC ILLiad; (Media Booking) Ex Libris Group; (OPAC) Ex Libris Group; (Serials) Ex Libris Group
Database Vendor: Baker & Taylor, EBSCOhost, Gale Cengage Learning, OCLC FirstSearch, ProQuest, Wilson - Wilson Web
Function: Distance learning, ILL available, Res libr
Partic in Lyrasis; Tampa Bay Library Consortium, Inc
Restriction: Open to students, fac & staff

P FRUITVILLE PUBLIC LIBRARY*, 100 Coburn Rd, 34240. Tel: 941-861-2500. Circulation Tel: 941-861-2513. Reference Tel: 941-861-2517. FAX: 941-861-2528. TDD: 941-861-2527. Web Site: www.sclibs.net. *Libr Mgr,* Ann Ivey; *Ref Librn,* Peggy Border; *Ref Librn,* Valerie Oakley; *Youth Ref Librn,* Ellen Berk; *Youth Ref Librn,* Barbara Davis; *Youth Ref Librn,* Jennifer Hitchcock; *Youth Ref Librn,* Heather Tweed
Founded 2001
Library Holdings: AV Mats 17,000; Bk Vols 75,000; Per Subs 170; Talking Bks 3,000
Special Collections: Florida Coll; Spanish Language
Subject Interests: Gardening
Automation Activity & Vendor Info: (Acquisitions) Innovative Interfaces, Inc; (Cataloging) Innovative Interfaces, Inc; (Circulation) Innovative Interfaces, Inc; (OPAC) Innovative Interfaces, Inc
Database Vendor: Loislaw, Medline, OCLC ArticleFirst, OCLC WorldShare Interlibrary Loan, ProQuest, ReferenceUSA
Wireless access
Mem of Sarasota County Library System
Special Services for the Deaf - Bks on deafness & sign lang
Special Services for the Blind - Bks on cassette; Bks on CD; Descriptive video serv (DVS); Large print bks; Low vision equip; Talking bk serv referral
Open Mon-Thurs 9-8, Fri & Sat 9-5
Friends of the Library Group

P GULF GATE PUBLIC LIBRARY*, 7112 Curtiss Ave, 34231. Tel: 941-861-1230. FAX: 941-316-1221. Web Site: www.sclibs.net. *Asst Mgr,* Shirley Birkett; Staff 15 (MLS 5, Non-MLS 10)
Library Holdings: Bk Vols 80,000; Per Subs 75
Automation Activity & Vendor Info: (Acquisitions) Innovative Interfaces, Inc; (Cataloging) Innovative Interfaces, Inc; (Circulation) Innovative Interfaces, Inc
Wireless access
Mem of Sarasota County Library System
Open Mon-Wed 10-8, Fri & Sat 10-5
Friends of the Library Group

S MOTE MARINE LABORATORY LIBRARY*, Arthur Vining Davis Library, 1600 Ken Thompson Pkwy, 34236-1096. SAN 303-173X. Tel: 941-388-4441, Ext 333. E-mail: library@mote.org. Web Site: www.mote.org/library. *Dir, Libr & Archives,* Susan M Stover; Staff 1 (MLS 1)
Founded 1978
Library Holdings: DVDs 25; e-books 5,000; e-journals 3,500; Bk Titles 15,000; Bk Vols 17,000; Per Subs 425; Videos 50
Special Collections: Bass Biological Laboratory Papers, 1931-1942 (Biological Research Florida); Charles M Breder, Jr Manuscripts, 1921-1974; Mina Walther Newspaper Columns, 1971-2003 (Nature Articles); Perry W Gilbert, PhD Papers
Subject Interests: Aquaculture, Biomed res, Coral reefs, Ecotoxicology, Fisheries, Marine biol
Database Vendor: Agricola, BioOne, EBSCO Information Services, JSTOR, Medline, OCLC ArticleFirst, OCLC FirstSearch, OCLC WorldShare Interlibrary Loan, PubMed, ScienceDirect, Springer-Verlag
Wireless access
Function: Ref serv available
Publications: Collected Papers of MML; Mote Magazine (Periodical); Mote Technical Reports; Protect Our Reefs Reports
Partic in Florida Library Information Network; Tampa Bay Library Consortium, Inc
Restriction: Open by appt only
Friends of the Library Group

C NEW COLLEGE OF FLORIDA UNIVERSITY OF SOUTH FLORIDA SARASOTA MANATEE, Jane Bancroft Cook Library, 5800 Bay Shore Rd, 34243-2109. SAN 303-1748. Tel: 941-487-4305. Interlibrary Loan Service Tel: 941-487-4410. FAX: 941-487-4307. E-mail: library@ncf.edu. Web Site: www.ncf.edu/library. *Dean of Libr,* Brian Doherty; Tel: 941-487-4401, E-mail: bdoherty@ncf.edu; *Dir, Access & Metadata Services,* Alison Piper; Tel: 941-487-4409, E-mail: apiper@ncf.edu; *Dir, Res, Instruction & Outreach,* Caroline Reed; Tel: 941-487-4568, E-mail: creed@ncf.edu; *Librn & Archivist,* Gail Donovan; Tel: 941-487-4405, E-mail: gdonovan@ncf.edu; *Humanities Librn,* Theresa Burress; Tel: 941-487-4416, E-mail: tburress@ncf.edu; *Sci Librn,* Tammera Race; E-mail: trace@ncf.edu; *Tech Serv Librn,* Sarah Norris; Tel: 941-487-4313, E-mail: snorris@ncf.edu. Subject Specialists: *Humanities,* Theresa Burress; *Sci,* Tammera Race; Staff 19 (MLS 7, Non-MLS 12)
Founded 1962. Enrl 800; Fac 70; Highest Degree: Bachelor
Library Holdings: AV Mats 8,400; CDs 4,951; DVDs 3,449; e-books 169,780; e-journals 22,222; Bk Vols 285,897; Per Subs 855
Special Collections: Helen N Fagin Holocaust Coll. US Document Depository
Automation Activity & Vendor Info: (Acquisitions) Ex Libris Group; (Cataloging) Ex Libris Group; (Circulation) Ex Libris Group; (Course Reserve) Ex Libris Group; (ILL) Ex Libris Group; (OPAC) Ex Libris Group; (Serials) Ex Libris Group
Wireless access
Partic in Tampa Bay Library Consortium, Inc
Open Mon-Thurs 8am-1am, Fri 8-5, Sat 12-5, Sun 1-1

S THE RINGLING ART LIBRARY*, 5401 Bayshore Rd, 34243. SAN 303-1756. Tel: 941-359-5700, Ext 2700. FAX: 941-360-7370. E-mail: library@ringling.org. Web Site: www.ringling.org. Staff 2 (MLS 2)
Founded 1946
Special Collections: A Everett Austin Jr Coll; John Ringling Book Coll; Mrs Potter Palmer Library Coll
Subject Interests: Art, Art hist, Rare bks
Automation Activity & Vendor Info: (Acquisitions) Follett Software; (Cataloging) OCLC Connexion; (Circulation) Follett Software; (ILL) OCLC; (OPAC) Follett Software
Database Vendor: ARTstor, JSTOR, OCLC ArticleFirst, OCLC CAMIO, OCLC FirstSearch, OCLC WorldShare Interlibrary Loan, ProQuest
Wireless access
Function: Instruction & testing
Publications: Rare Books from the Library of the Ringling Museum of Art Sarasota, Florida
Partic in Florida Library Information Network; OCLC Online Computer Library Center, Inc; Tampa Bay Library Consortium, Inc
Open Mon-Fri 1-5
Restriction: Pub use on premises
Friends of the Library Group

C RINGLING COLLEGE OF ART & DESIGN*, Verman Kimbrough Memorial Library, 2700 N Tamiami Trail, 34234. SAN 303-1764. Tel: 941-359-7587. Interlibrary Loan Service Tel: 941-359-7630. FAX: 941-359-7632. E-mail: library@ringling.edu. Web Site: www.lib.ringling.edu. *Dir, Libr Serv,* Kathleen L List; Tel: 941-359-7582, E-mail: klist@ringling.edu; *Image Librn,* Allen Novak; Tel: 941-359-7583, E-mail: anovak@ringling.edu; *Circ,* Tim DeForest; E-mail: tdefores@ringling.edu; *Info & Res Serv,* Sarah Carter; Tel: 941-359-7671, E-mail: scarter2@ringling.edu; *Tech Serv,* Janet K Thomas; Tel: 941-359-7586, E-mail: jthomas@ringling.edu. Subject Specialists: *Art hist,* Sarah Carter; Staff 13 (MLS 4, Non-MLS 9)
Founded 1931. Enrl 1,300; Fac 160. Highest Degree: Bachelor
Jun 2007-May 2008 Income $844,014, Federal $9,750, Locally Generated Income $119,755, Parent Institution $714,509. Mats Exp $203,652, Books $74,732, Per/Ser (Incl. Access Fees) $29,250, AV Mat $45,253, Electronic Ref Mat (Incl. Access Fees) $50,000, Presv $4,417. Sal $469,546
Library Holdings: AV Mats 175,000; CDs 863; DVDs 5,000; e-books 40,200; Electronic Media & Resources 334; Bk Titles 50,427; Bk Vols 55,470; Per Subs 370; Videos 2,500
Special Collections: Artist's Books; Visual Resources Library, digital images, 35mm transparencies
Subject Interests: Art & archit, Computer animation, Digital film, Fine arts, Game art, Graphic design, Illustration, Interior design, Photog
Automation Activity & Vendor Info: (Acquisitions) Ex Libris Group; (Cataloging) Ex Libris Group; (Circulation) Ex Libris Group; (Course Reserve) Ex Libris Group; (ILL) OCLC; (OPAC) Ex Libris Group; (Serials) Ex Libris Group
Database Vendor: 3M Library Systems, ARTstor, Bowker, Cambridge Scientific Abstracts, CredoReference, ebrary, EBSCOhost, Ex Libris Group, Foundation Center, Gale Cengage Learning, H W Wilson, Ingram Library Services, Marquis Who's Who, OCLC WorldShare Interlibrary Loan, Oxford Online, ProQuest, Safari Books Online, Wilson - Wilson Web
Wireless access
Function: Art exhibits, Audio & video playback equip for onsite use, CD-ROM, Computers for patron use, Copy machines, Electronic databases & coll, ILL available, Instruction & testing, Online cat, Ref & res, VHS videos, Video lending libr
Partic in Independent Cols & Univs of Fla; Lyrasis; Tampa Bay Library Consortium, Inc
Special Services for the Deaf - Closed caption videos
Open Mon-Thurs 8am-11pm, Fri 8-6, Sat 12-6, Sun 10am-11pm
Restriction: Open to pub for ref & circ; with some limitations
Friends of the Library Group

S MARIE SELBY BOTANICAL GARDENS RESEARCH LIBRARY*, 811 S Palm Ave, 34236-7726. SAN 371-6457. Tel: 941-366-5731, Ext 248. FAX: 941-366-9807. Web Site: www.selby.org. *Dir,* Bruce Holst; Tel: 941-955-7553, Ext 312, Fax: 941-951-1474, E-mail: bholst@selby.org
Founded 1975
Jul 2006-Jun 2007. Mats Exp $8,350, Books $2,400, Per/Ser (Incl. Access Fees) $4,500, Presv $600
Library Holdings: Bk Titles 6,250; Bk Vols 7,800; Per Subs 307
Special Collections: Early Botanical Reference Microfiche Coll; Rare Botanical Book Coll
Subject Interests: Botany, Conserv, Ecology, Hort, Orchids
Automation Activity & Vendor Info: (Cataloging) ComPanion Corp
Publications: Field Guide to the Mangroves of Florida; Icones; Selbyana; The Nature Trail at Pine View School - Plants of Sarasota County, Florida, Part 1 (Research guide); The Tropical Dispatch (Newsletter)
Open Mon-Fri 1-5
Restriction: Circulates for staff only

P SELBY PUBLIC LIBRARY*, 1331 First St, 34236-4899. SAN 338-0734. Tel: 941-861-1100. Reference Tel: 941-861-1120. FAX: 941-316-1188. TDD: 941-316-1190. E-mail: libraryinfo@scgov.net. *Head of Libr,* Liz Nolan; *Spec Coll Librn,* Vera Neumann-Wood; *Ch Serv,* Marilyn Nykiforuk; *Circ,* Trina Turton; *Ref Serv,* Andrea Ginsky; *YA Serv,* Nadia Ingram; Staff 48 (MLS 17, Non-MLS 31)
Founded 1907. Pop 371,155; Circ 1,922,992
Library Holdings: Bk Titles 100,000; Bk Vols 192,747; Per Subs 372
Special Collections: US Document Depository
Subject Interests: Genealogy
Automation Activity & Vendor Info: (Cataloging) Innovative Interfaces, Inc; (Circulation) Innovative Interfaces, Inc
Wireless access
Mem of Sarasota County Library System
Partic in OCLC Online Computer Library Center, Inc
Special Services for the Deaf - TDD equip
Open Mon-Thurs 10-8, Fri & Sat 10-5
Friends of the Library Group

SATELLITE BEACH

P SATELLITE BEACH PUBLIC LIBRARY*, 751 Jamaica Blvd, 32937. SAN 303-1772. Tel: 321-779-4004. FAX: 321-779-4036. Web Site: www.brev.org. *Dir,* Nancy Grout; *Head, Ref,* Fran Reid; *Circ,* Ellen Noyd; *Youth Serv,* Marlena Harold; Staff 12.35 (MLS 3.5, Non-MLS 8.85)
Founded 1966. Circ 293,000
Library Holdings: Bk Titles 83,000; Per Subs 218
Special Collections: Florida Coll
Automation Activity & Vendor Info: (Circulation) Infor Library & Information Solutions
Mem of Brevard County Library System
Special Services for the Deaf - High interest/low vocabulary bks; TDD equip
Open Mon 9-8, Tue 12-8, Wed-Sat 9-5
Friends of the Library Group

SEBRING

P HIGHLANDS COUNTY LIBRARY SYSTEM*, Sebring Public Library, 319 W Center Ave, 33870-3109. SAN 303-1780. Tel: 863-402-6716. FAX: 863-385-2883. Web Site: www.myhlc.org/hcls. *Dir,* Mary Myers; *Adult Serv,* Michael Pate; *Ch Serv,* Maria Chenique; *ILL,* Carolyn Hesselink; *Tech Serv,* Yvonne Schilling; Staff 5 (MLS 5)
Founded 1926. Pop 95,000; Circ 345,362
Library Holdings: Bk Titles 75,916; Bk Vols 102,477; Per Subs 145
Special Collections: Florida Coll
Automation Activity & Vendor Info: (Circulation) Innovative Interfaces, Inc; (OPAC) Innovative Interfaces, Inc
Member Libraries: Avon Park Public Library; Lake Placid Memorial Library
Open Mon & Tues 9:30-7, Wed-Fri 9:30-5:30, Sat 9:30-Noon
Friends of the Library Group

SEMINOLE

P SEMINOLE COMMUNITY LIBRARY*, 9200 113th St N, 33772. SAN 323-7966. Tel: 727-394-6905. FAX: 727-398-3113. Web Site: www.spcollege.edu/scl. *Dir,* Michael Bryan; E-mail: mbryan@ci.seminole.fl.us; *Asst Dir,* Patricia Bartell; *Coll Develop, Head, Ref,* Ben Fiedler; *Circ Supvr,* Marion Chamberlain; *Supvr, User Serv,* Kimberly Goonis; *ILL, Ref Serv,* Kathy Ogden; *Ref Serv,* Carla Kerns; *Tech Serv,* Patty Halloway; *Tech Serv,* Eileen Shannahan; Staff 7 (MLS 6, Non-MLS 1)
Founded 1959. Pop 9,000; Circ 252,549
Library Holdings: Bk Vols 76,000; Per Subs 128
Special Collections: Parent-Teacher
Automation Activity & Vendor Info: (Acquisitions) Ex Libris Group; (Cataloging) Ex Libris Group; (Circulation) Ex Libris Group
Mem of Pinellas Public Libr Coop
Partic in Lyrasis; Tampa Bay Library Consortium, Inc
Special Services for the Deaf - Bks on deafness & sign lang; Captioned film dep
Open Mon-Thurs 7:30am-9pm, Fri 7:30-4, Sat 10-5, Sun 1-5
Friends of the Library Group

SHALIMAR

P SHALIMAR PUBLIC LIBRARY*, Six Tenth Ave, 32579. Tel: 850-609-1515. *Mgr, Libr Serv,* Alice Brown; *Youth Serv,* Gloria Crews
Library Holdings: Bk Vols 14,000
Open Mon & Wed 12-6, Tues, Thurs & Sat 10-2, Fri 12-4
Friends of the Library Group

SOUTH BAY

S THE GEO GROUP INC*, South Bay Correctional Facility Library, 600 US Hwy 27 S, 33493. Tel: 561-992-9505, Ext 150. Automation Services Tel: 561-829-1907. FAX: 561-992-9551. *Librn,* Victoria Randall
Library Holdings: Bk Vols 4,300; Per Subs 45

STARKE

P BRADFORD COUNTY PUBLIC LIBRARY, 456 W Pratt St, 32091-3396. SAN 303-1802. Tel: 904-368-3911. FAX: 904-964-2164. E-mail: bradford@neflin.org. Web Site: www.bradford-co-fla.org/departments/library. *Dir,* Robert Perone; Tel: 904-368-3920; *Asst Dir, Tech Serv,* Cindy Weeks; E-mail: cweeks@neflin.org; *Circ Supvr,* Lori Butcher; E-mail: lbutcher@neflin.org; *IT & Young Adult Prog,* Terry Carver; E-mail: tcarver@neflin.org; Staff 12 (MLS 2, Non-MLS 10)
Founded 1935. Pop 26,080; Circ 120,000
Library Holdings: Bk Vols 42,000; Per Subs 100
Special Collections: Florida Coll; Genealogy Coll
Automation Activity & Vendor Info: (Cataloging) SirsiDynix; (Circulation) SirsiDynix; (OPAC) SirsiDynix
Database Vendor: OCLC FirstSearch
Mem of New River Public Library Cooperative
Partic in Northeast Florida Library Information Network
Open Mon, Tues & Thurs 8-8, Wed 8-5, Fri 9-5
Friends of the Library Group
Bookmobiles: 1

STUART

P MARTIN COUNTY LIBRARY SYSTEM, Blake Library, 2351 SE Monterey Rd, 34996. SAN 303-1837. Tel: 772-288-5702. Reference Tel: 772-221-1413. Administration Tel: 772-221-1408. Automation Services Tel: 772-219-4969. FAX: 772-219-4959. Circulation FAX: 772-221-1358. TDD: 772-463-3236. Web Site: www.library.martin.fl.us. *Libr Dir,* Jennifer Salas; Tel: 772-221-1410, E-mail: jsalas@martin.fl.us; *Libr Operations & Serv Adminr,* Richard Reilly; Tel: 772-219-4964, E-mail: rreilly@martin.fl.us; *Libr Mgr,* Jamie Rowles; Tel: 772-221-1402, E-mail: jrowles@martin.fl.us; *Literacy, Educ & Outreach Mgr,* Sara Johnson; Tel: 772-219-4908, E-mail: sjohnson@martin.fl.us; *Coll Develop,* Janette Noe; Tel: 772-219-4968, E-mail: jnoe@martin.fl.us; *Fac Planning,* Nicole Lebeau; Tel: 772-221-1404, Fax: 772-221-1404, E-mail: nlebeau@martin.fl.us; Staff 45 (MLS 11, Non-MLS 34)
Founded 1957. Pop 164,806; Circ 381,598
Oct 2012-Sept 2013 Income (Main Library and Branch(s)) $3,702,935, State $78,561, County $3,151,237, Locally Generated Income $473,137. Mats Exp $361,043, Books $140,128, Per/Ser (Incl. Access Fees) $37,611, Micro $7,176, AV Mat $79,187, Electronic Ref Mat (Incl. Access Fees) $96,941. Sal $1,764,794 (Prof $893,454)
Library Holdings: Audiobooks 28,100; AV Mats 62,099; Bks on Deafness & Sign Lang 69; Braille Volumes 8; DVDs 33,999; e-books 4,528; Large Print Bks 13,406; Microforms 2,245; Bk Titles 195,234; Bk Vols 259,676; Per Subs 214
Special Collections: Anne M & Joel L Pearl Cancer Resource Center; Florida Coll; Genealogy Coll
Automation Activity & Vendor Info: (Acquisitions) SirsiDynix; (Cataloging) SirsiDynix; (Circulation) SirsiDynix; (OPAC) SirsiDynix; (Serials) SirsiDynix
Database Vendor: Baker & Taylor, EBSCO Auto Repair Reference, EBSCOhost, Foundation Center, Gale Cengage Learning, Ingram Library Services, LearningExpress, LexisNexis, Library Ideas, LLC, MITINET, Inc, Newsbank, OCLC WorldShare Interlibrary Loan, Overdrive, Inc, ProQuest, ReferenceUSA, SirsiDynix, Standard & Poor's, TumbleBookLibrary
Wireless access
Function: 24/7 Electronic res, 24/7 Online cat, Activity rm, Adult bk club, Adult literacy prog, After school storytime, Alaskana res, Art exhibits, Audiobks via web, BA reader (adult literacy), Bilingual assistance for Spanish patrons, Bk club(s), Bk reviews (Group), Bks on CD, CD-ROM,

Children's prog, Citizenship assistance, Computer training, Computers for patron use, Copy machines, Digital talking bks, e-mail & chat, e-mail serv, E-Reserves, Electronic databases & coll, Equip loans & repairs, Exhibits, Family literacy, Free DVD rentals, Games & aids for the handicapped, Genealogy discussion group, Handicapped accessible, Health sci info serv, Holiday prog, Homework prog, ILL available, Jail serv, Large print keyboards, Learning ctr, Libr develop, Life-long learning prog for all ages, Literacy & newcomer serv, Magazines, Magnifiers for reading, Mail & tel request accepted, Microfiche/film & reading machines, Movies, Mus passes, Music CDs, Newsp ref libr, Online cat, Online info literacy tutorials on the web & in blackboard, Online ref, Online searches, Orientations, Outreach serv, Outside serv via phone, mail, e-mail & web, OverDrive digital audio bks, Photocopying/Printing, Preschool outreach, Preschool reading prog, Prof lending libr, Prog for adults, Prog for children & young adult, Pub access computers, Ref & res, Ref serv available, Ref serv in person, Referrals accepted, Scanner, Senior computer classes, Senior outreach, Serves mentally handicapped consumers, Spanish lang bks, Spoken cassettes & CDs, Spoken cassettes & DVDs, Story hour, Study rm, Summer reading prog, Tax forms, Teen prog, Telephone ref, Video lending libr, Visual arts prog, Wheelchair accessible, Words travel prog, Workshops, Writing prog
Partic in Lyrasis; OCLC Online Computer Library Center, Inc
Special Services for the Deaf - TTY equip
Special Services for the Blind - Magnifiers
Open Mon & Thurs 10-8, Tues, Wed, Fri & Sat 10-5:30
Restriction: Lending limited to county residents
Friends of the Library Group
Branches: 6
PETER & JULIE CUMMINGS LIBRARY, 2551 SW Matheson Ave, Palm City, 34990, SAN 375-5924. Tel: 772-288-2551. FAX: 772-288-5563. *Br Mgr,* Emma Castle
Founded 1995
Open Tues-Thurs & Sat 10-5:30, Fri 12-8
Friends of the Library Group
HOBE SOUND BRANCH, 10595 SE Federal Hwy, Hobe Sound, 33455, SAN 328-6533. Tel: 772-546-2257. FAX: 772-546-3816. *Br Mgr,* Lynn Warner
Founded 1985
Open Mon, Tues & Thurs-Sat 10-5:30, Wed 12-8
Friends of the Library Group
HOKE LIBRARY, 1150 NW Jack Williams Way, Jensen Beach, 34957, SAN 329-5915. Tel: 772-463-2870. FAX: 772-463-2874. *Br Mgr,* Maureen Gallagher
Founded 1986
Open Tues-Thurs & Sat 10-5:30, Fri 12-8
Friends of the Library Group
ELISABETH LAHTI LIBRARY, 15200 SW Adams Ave, Indiantown, 34956, SAN 328-655X. Tel: 772-597-4200. *Br Mgr,* Sandy Henry; E-mail: shenry@martin.fl.us
Founded 1991
Open Tues & Thurs-Sat 10-5:30, Wed 12-8
Friends of the Library Group
MARTIN COUNTY LAW LIBRARY, 100 SE Ocean Blvd, 34994, SAN 371-9146. Tel: 772-221-1427. *In Charge,* Position Currently Open
Open Mon-Fri 9-5
ROBERT MORGADE LIBRARY, Indian River State College, Chastain Campus, 5851 SE Community Dr, 34997. Tel: 772-463-3245. FAX: 772-463-3246. *Br Mgr,* Ann Schreffler
Founded 2001
Open Mon, Tues, Fri & Sat 10-5:30, Wed 12-8, Thurs 10-8
Friends of the Library Group

SUMTERVILLE

P CLARK MAXWELL JR LIBRARY*, 1405 CR 526A, 33585. Tel: 352-568-3074. FAX: 352-568-3376. *Librn,* Dr Richard Morrill; E-mail: morrillR@lssc.edu
Library Holdings: Bk Vols 8,000; Per Subs 50
Automation Activity & Vendor Info: (Cataloging) SirsiDynix; (Circulation) SirsiDynix
Mem of Sumter County Library System
Open Mon-Thurs 9-7, Fri 9-3, Sat 9-1

SURFSIDE

P SURF-BAL-BAY LIBRARY*, 9301 Collins Ave, 33154. SAN 303-1853. Tel: 305-865-2409. Web Site: town.surfside.fl.us. *Librn,* Suzanne McGlynn; E-mail: smcglynn@townofsurfsidefl.gov; Staff 1 (MLS 1)
Founded 1956. Pop 11,500; Circ 47,605
Library Holdings: Bk Vols 26,000; Per Subs 52
Subject Interests: Fla
Open Mon, Wed, Fri & Sat 10-5:30, Tues 1-8

TALLAHASSEE

P LEROY COLLINS LEON COUNTY PUBLIC LIBRARY SYSTEM*, 200 W Park Ave, 32301-7720. SAN 303-2035. Tel: 850-606-2665. FAX: 850-606-2601. Interlibrary Loan Service FAX: 850-606-2606. TDD: 850-606-2603. E-mail: answersquad@leoncountyfl.gov. Web Site: www.leoncountylibrary.org. *Dir,* Cay Hohmeister; E-mail: hohmeisterc@leoncountyfl.gov; *Budget & Coll Develop Mgr,* Linda Barber White; E-mail: barberwhitel@leoncountyfl.gov; *Coll Mgt Mgr,* Christopher Gorsuch; Fax: 850-606-2607, E-mail: gorsuchc@leoncountyfl.gov; *Extn Serv Mgr,* Debra Sears; E-mail: searsd@leoncountyfl.gov; *Operations Mgr,* Donna Cirenza; E-mail: cirenzad@leoncountyfl.gov; *Adult, Tech & Media Serv Coordr,* Mercedes Carey; E-mail: careym@leoncountyfl.gov; *Circ Serv Coordr,* Jennifer Taylor; E-mail: taylorje@leoncountyfl.gov; *Libr Serv Coordr, Bkmobile/Outreach Serv,* Danielle Daguerre; E-mail: daguerred@leoncountyfl.gov; *Youth Serv Coordr,* Mary Douglas; E-mail: douglasm@leoncountyfl.gov; Staff 102 (MLS 34, Non-MLS 68)
Founded 1955. Pop 272,896; Circ 1,942,200
Oct 2011-Sept 2012 Income $6,900,539, State $134,266, Federal $13,652, County $6,752,621. Mats Exp $739,684, Books $493,653, AV Mat $120,105, Electronic Ref Mat (Incl. Access Fees) $125,926. Sal $3,500,678
Library Holdings: Audiobooks 43,269; AV Mats 47,000; CDs 10,017; DVDs 15,763; e-books 27,000; Electronic Media & Resources 64; Bk Vols 608,504; Per Subs 284; Videos 7,770
Automation Activity & Vendor Info: (Acquisitions) SirsiDynix; (Cataloging) SirsiDynix; (Circulation) SirsiDynix
Database Vendor: Gale Cengage Learning, LearningExpress, Newsbank, OCLC FirstSearch, Overdrive, Inc, ProQuest, SirsiDynix, ValueLine, World Book Online
Wireless access
Function: ILL available
Partic in Lyrasis; OCLC Online Computer Library Center, Inc; Panhandle Library Access Network
Special Services for the Deaf - Deaf publ; TDD equip; Videos & decoder
Special Services for the Blind - Reader equip
Open Mon-Thurs 10-9, Fri 10-6, Sat 10-5, Sun 1-6
Friends of the Library Group
Branches: 6
EASTSIDE BRANCH, 1583 Pedrick Rd, 32317. Tel: 850-606-2750.
FORT BRADEN, 16327 Blountstown Hwy, 32310. Tel: 850-606-2900. FAX: 850-606-2901. *Br Mgr,* Teretha Scott; E-mail: scottte@leoncountyfl.gov
Open Tues & Thurs 11-8, Wed & Fri 10-6, Sat 10-4
NORTHEAST BRANCH, THE BRUCE J HOST CENTER, 5513 Thomasville Rd, 32309, SAN 374-6844. Tel: 850-606-2800. FAX: 850-606-2801. *Br Mgr,* Muriel Llewellyn
Open Wed & Fri 10-6, Tues & Thurs 11-8, Sat 10-4
LAKE JACKSON, Huntington Oaks Plaza, 3840-302 N Monroe, 32303, SAN 371-3768. Tel: 850-606-2850. FAX: 850-606-2851. *Br Mgr,* Bart Pisapia; E-mail: pisapiab@leoncountyfl.gov
Special Services for the Deaf - TDD equip
Open Wed & Fri 10-6, Tues & Thurs 11-8, Sat 10-4
DR B L PERRY JR BRANCH, 2817 S Adams St, 32301, SAN 321-9119. Tel: 850-606-2950. FAX: 850-606-2951. TDD: 850-922-2518. *Br Mgr,* Beverly Bass; E-mail: bassb@leoncountyfl.gov
Open Wed & Fri 10-6, Tues & Thurs 11-8, Sat 10-4
Friends of the Library Group
WOODVILLE BRANCH, 8000 Old Woodvile Rd, 32305. Tel: 850-606-2925. *Br Mgr,* Verna Brock
Bookmobiles: 2

S FEDERAL CORRECTIONAL INSTITUTION LIBRARY*, 501 Capital Circle NE, 32301-3572. SAN 303-1861. Tel: 850-878-2173, Ext 1345. FAX: 850-671-6121. *Librn,* Jenny Warfield
Founded 1947
Library Holdings: Bk Vols 11,000; Per Subs 90
Partic in Colorado Library Consortium; Florida Library Information Network
Open Mon-Fri 8-4

GL FIRST DISTRICT COURT OF APPEAL LIBRARY*, 2000 Drayton Dr, 32399. SAN 377-3221. Tel: 850-487-1000. *Librn,* Janet McPherson; E-mail: mcphersj@1dca.org
Library Holdings: Bk Vols 15,000
Open Mon-Fri 8-5

C FLORIDA AGRICULTURAL & MECHANICAL UNIVERSITY LIBRARIES*, Samuel H Coleman Memorial Library, 525 Orr Dr, 32307-4700. (Mail add: 1500 S Martin Luther King Blvd, 32307-4700), SAN 338-0793. Tel: 850-599-3370. Circulation Tel: 850-599-3376. Reference Tel: 850-599-3330. FAX: 850-561-2293. Interlibrary Loan Service FAX: 850 561-2651. Web Site: www.famu.edu/library. *Dean,* Faye Watkins; E-mail: faye.watkins@famu.edu; *Assoc Dean,* Brenda Wright; E-mail: brenda.wright@famu.edu; *Asst Dir, Coll Mgt & Develop,* Position

Currently Open; *Asst Dir, Pub Serv,* Jeneice Smith; E-mail: jeneice.smith@famu.edu; *Head, Acq,* Ernestine Holmes; Tel: 850-599-3314, E-mail: ernestine.holmes@famu.edu; *Head, Ref,* Jean Adams; Tel: 850-599-8576, E-mail: mjean.williamsadams@famu.edu; *Archit Librn,* Kimberly Windham; Tel: 850-599-8770, Fax: 850-599-3436, E-mail: kimberly.windham@famu.edu; *Sci Res Ctr Librn,* Shuchun Liang; Tel: 850-599-3423, Fax: 850-599-3422, E-mail: shuchun.liang@famu.edu; *Access Serv, Govt Doc,* Priscilla B Henry; E-mail: priscilla.henry@famu.edu; *Journalism & Graphic Communication Res,* Karen Southwood; Tel: 850-599-3704, Fax: 850-599-2769, E-mail: karen.southwood@famu.edu; *Spec Coll,* Gloria T Woody; E-mail: gloria.woody@famu.edu. Subject Specialists: *Psychol,* Ernestine Holmes; *Agr, Eng,* Jean Adams; *Archit, Art,* Kimberly Windham; *Environ sci, Health sci,* Shuchun Liang; *Educ,* Priscilla B Henry; *Graphic arts, Journalism,* Karen Southwood; *African-Am culture, African-Am hist,* Gloria T Woody; Staff 52 (MLS 17, Non-MLS 35)
Founded 1887. Enrl 12,051; Fac 596; Highest Degree: Doctorate
Jul 2012-Jun 2013 Income Federal $1,568,948. Mats Exp $2,034,540, Books $698,731, Per/Ser (Incl. Access Fees) $558,105, Other Print Mats $577,442, Micro $4,774, Electronic Ref Mat (Incl. Access Fees) $2,357,418, Presv $23,138. Sal $2,258,211 (Prof $1,011,713)
Library Holdings: AV Mats 76,391; e-books 55,411; e-journals 29,416; Electronic Media & Resources 537; Bk Titles 712,296; Bk Vols 807,308; Per Subs 19,735; Videos 1,228
Special Collections: 1890 Land Grant Publications, clippings & news; Afro-American Culture & History, bks, clippings, magazines; Materials About Florida A&M University (FAMUANA), fac pub minutes, programs, memorabilia, 1890-present clippings, newsp. US Document Depository
Automation Activity & Vendor Info: (Acquisitions) Ex Libris Group; (Cataloging) Ex Libris Group; (Circulation) Ex Libris Group; (Course Reserve) Ex Libris Group; (ILL) Clio; (OPAC) Ex Libris Group; (Serials) Ex Libris Group
Database Vendor: ABC-CLIO, ACM (Association for Computing Machinery), Agricola, Alexander Street Press, American Chemical Society, American Psychological Association (APA), Annual Reviews, Bowker, Cambridge Scientific Abstracts, Checkpoint Systems, Inc, CQ Press, Dun & Bradstreet, EBSCOhost, Elsevier, Ex Libris Group, Gale Cengage Learning, Greenwood Publishing Group, H W Wilson, IEEE (Institute of Electrical & Electronics Engineers), IOP, ISI Web of Knowledge, JSTOR, LexisNexis, Marcive, Inc, McGraw-Hill, Mergent Online, Micromedex, Modern Language Association, Nature Publishing Group, Newsbank, OCLC FirstSearch, OCLC WorldShare Interlibrary Loan, OVID Technologies, Oxford Online, ProQuest, PubMed, RefWorks, ScienceDirect, SerialsSolutions, Springer-Verlag, Standard & Poor's, ValueLine, Westlaw, Wiley, Wilson - Wilson Web
Wireless access
Publications: A Classified Catalogue of the Negro Collection in the Samuel H Coleman Memorial Library; A National Network for the Acquisition, Organization, Processing & Dissemination of Materials By & About Blacks; Instructional Media Film & Video Catalog; Library Handbook
Partic in Fla Ctr for Libr Automation; Florida Library Information Network; Lyrasis; Panhandle Library Access Network
Special Services for the Deaf - Assistive tech; TTY equip
Special Services for the Blind - Accessible computers
Friends of the Library Group

Departmental Libraries:

ARCHITECTURE LIBRARY, 1938 S Martin Luther King Jr Blvd, 32307. Tel: 850-599-8776. FAX: 850-599-3535. Web Site: library.famu.edu/architecturelibrary. *Instr Librn,* Kimberly Windham; Tel: 850-599-8770, E-mail: kimberly.windham@famu.edu
Library Holdings: Bk Vols 24,835; Per Subs 100
Subject Interests: Archit, Eng tech
Automation Activity & Vendor Info: (ILL) Ex Libris Group; (Media Booking) Ex Libris Group
Database Vendor: EBSCO Information Services
Open Mon 8-5, Tues-Thurs 8am-9pm, Fri 8-5, Sun 2-7

GL FLORIDA ATTORNEY GENERAL'S LAW LIBRARY*, Collins Bldg, 107 W Gaines St, Rm 437, 32399-1050. (Mail add: PL-01 The Capitol, 32301), SAN 303-1950. Tel: 850-414-3300. FAX: 850-921-5784. E-mail: library@myfloridalegal.com. *Dir, Libr Serv,* Betsy L Stupski; *Res Asst,* Travis Dudley; Staff 3 (MLS 1, Non-MLS 2)
Subject Interests: Law
Database Vendor: LexisNexis, Westlaw
Function: Ref serv available
Open Mon-Fri 8-5

G FLORIDA AUDITOR GENERAL LIBRARY*, Claude Pepper Bldg, Rm G-78, 111 W Madison St, 32399-1450. Tel: 850-412-2722. FAX: 850-488-6975. Web Site: www.state.fl.us/audgen. *Librn,* Bearnice Keaton
Library Holdings: Bk Titles 4,000; Per Subs 15
Restriction: Staff use only

GL FLORIDA DEPARTMENT OF AGRICULTURE & CONSUMER SERVICES*, Legal Section Library, Mayo Bldg, Rm 520, 407 S Calhoun St, 32399-0800. SAN 326-9396. Tel: 850-245-1000. FAX: 850-245-1001. Web Site: www.doacs.state.fl.us.
Library Holdings: Per Subs 400
Open Mon-Fri 8-5

G FLORIDA DEPARTMENT OF EDUCATION*, Clearinghouse Information Center, 325 W Gaines St, 32399-0400. SAN 377-0907. Tel: 850-245-0983. FAX: 850-245-0987. Web Site: www.firn.edu/doe/commhome. *Dir,* Kathy Dejoie
Library Holdings: Bk Titles 7,000
Automation Activity & Vendor Info: (Cataloging) Inmagic, Inc.; (ILL) Inmagic, Inc.
Open Mon-Fri 7:30-5

G FLORIDA DEPARTMENT OF ELDER AFFAIRS*, Information Clearinghouse, 4040 Esplanade Way, Ste 360, 32399-7000. Tel: 850-414-2000. Toll Free Tel: 800-963-5337. FAX: 850-414-2364. TDD: 800-955-8771. *Librn,* Faye Wilkes
Library Holdings: Bk Vols 3,500; Per Subs 50
Special Collections: Emergency Management (Elder Update Editions)
Subject Interests: Disabled, Spec needs
Open Mon-Fri 9-5

G FLORIDA DEPARTMENT OF ENVIRONMENTAL PROTECTION, Florida Geological Survey Research Library, FSU Campus, 903 W Tennessee St, 32304. SAN 303-1969. Tel: 850-617-0316. FAX: 850-412-0500, 850-617-0341. Web Site: www.dep.state.fl.us/geology/publications/library.htm. *Librn Spec,* Doug Calman; E-mail: doug.calman@dep.state.fl.us. Subject Specialists: *Geol,* Doug Calman; Staff 1 (MLS 1)
Founded 1908
Library Holdings: Bk Vols 33,000; Per Subs 40
Special Collections: Florida Aerial Photographs; Florida Sinkhole Research Institute Archives; Florida Topographic Maps; Photo Archives Coll
Subject Interests: Environ protection, Fla, Geol
Automation Activity & Vendor Info: (Cataloging) OCLC CatExpress; (Circulation) Follett Software; (ILL) OCLC; (OPAC) Follett Software; (Serials) EBSCO Online
Database Vendor: OCLC FirstSearch
Function: Archival coll, For res purposes, Mail & tel request accepted, Online searches, Ref serv available, Scanner, Telephone ref, Wheelchair accessible
Partic in Florida Library Information Network; OCLC-LVIS; Panhandle Library Access Network; Soline
Open Mon-Fri 8:30-11:45 & 12:45-5:30
Restriction: Circulates for staff only, In-house use for visitors, Non-circulating of rare bks, Open to pub for ref only

G FLORIDA DEPARTMENT OF HIGHWAY SAFETY & MOTOR VEHICLES*, Management & Planning Services Library, Neil Kirkman Bldg, Rm A430, 32399-0505. SAN 377-3558. Tel: 850-617-3105. FAX: 850-414-7195. Web Site: www.hsmv.state.fl.us.
Library Holdings: Bk Titles 750; Bk Vols 1,200; Per Subs 100
Open Mon-Fri 8-5

P FLORIDA DEPARTMENT OF STATE, DIVISION OF LIBRARY & INFORMATION SERVICES*, State Library & Archives of Florida, R A Gray Bldg, 500 S Bronough St, 32399-0250. SAN 303-2051. Tel: 850-245-6600. Interlibrary Loan Service Tel: 850-245-6680. Reference Tel: 850-245-6682. FAX: 850-245-6735. Interlibrary Loan Service FAX: 850-245-6744. Reference FAX: 850-487-6651. TDD: 850-922-4085. E-mail: info@dos.myflorida.com. Web Site: info.florida.gov. *State Librn,* Judith A Ring; E-mail: judi.ring@dos.myflorida.com; *Libr Divisional Mgr,* Cathy Moloney; Tel: 850-245-6641, E-mail: cathy.moloney@dos.myflorida.com; *Libr Develop Coordr,* Amy Johnson; Tel: 850-245-6622, E-mail: amy.johnson@dos.myflorida.com; *Access Serv,* Gerard Clark; Tel: 850-245-6639, E-mail: gerard.clark@dos.myflorida.com; *Fla Electronic Libr,* Stephanie Race; Tel: 850-245-6630, E-mail: stephanie.race@dos.myflorida.com; Staff 65 (MLS 33, Non-MLS 32)
Founded 1845. Pop 18,801,310
Special Collections: Florida Coll, bks, mss, maps, memorabilia, per; State Planning Coll, 1970 to present. State Document Depository; US Document Depository
Subject Interests: Educ, Govt, Libr & info sci
Automation Activity & Vendor Info: (Acquisitions) SirsiDynix; (Cataloging) SirsiDynix; (Circulation) SirsiDynix; (ILL) OCLC; (OPAC) SirsiDynix; (Serials) SirsiDynix
Database Vendor: OCLC FirstSearch
Wireless access
Function: Photocopying/Printing
Publications: Florida Library Directory & Statistics

Partic in Association of Southeastern Research Libraries; Florida Library Information Network; Lyrasis
Special Services for the Deaf - ADA equip; TDD equip
Special Services for the Blind - Accessible computers; Braille equip; Computer access aids; Copier with enlargement capabilities; Internet workstation with adaptive software; Magnifiers
Open Mon-Fri 9-4:30
Friends of the Library Group

G FLORIDA DEPARTMENT OF TRANSPORTATION*, Research Management Library, Burns Bldg, 605 Suwannee St, Mail Sta 30, 32399. SAN 303-1985. Tel: 850-414-4615. FAX: 850-414-4696. Web Site: myflorida.com. *Dir,* Richard C Long
Founded 1967
Library Holdings: Bk Vols 15,000; Per Subs 20
Special Collections: Historical DOT Coll; HRD Materials; Transportation Research-Related Reports
Subject Interests: Transportation
Open Mon-Fri 8-5
Restriction: Non-circulating, Not open to pub

G FLORIDA OFFICE OF FINANCIAL REGULATION*, Legal Library, Fletcher Bldg, 101 E Gaines St, Ste 526, 32399-0379. SAN 325-8548. Tel: 850-410-9896. FAX: 850-410-9645. Web Site: www.flofr.com. *Librn,* Mary Howell
Library Holdings: Bk Vols 2,000
Open Mon-Fri 9-5

C FLORIDA STATE UNIVERSITY*, Institute on World War II & the Human Experience Library, Rm 401 BEL, 113 Collegiate Loop, 32306-2200. Tel: 850-644-9033. FAX: 850-644-6402. E-mail: ww2@ww2.fsu.edu. Web Site: www.fsu.edu/~ww2. *Dir,* Dr Kurt Piehler; E-mail: kpiehler@fsu.edu
Founded 1997
Library Holdings: Bk Titles 5,200
Special Collections: World War II Coll: artwork, diaries, journals, letters, maps, memorabilia, military documents, music, personal memoirs, photos, poetry, videos.. Oral History
Subject Interests: World War II
Function: Archival coll
Open Mon-Fri 9-4
Restriction: Open by appt only, Pub use on premises

C FLORIDA STATE UNIVERSITY LIBRARIES*, Robert Manning Strozier Library, Strozier Library Bldg, 116 Honors Way, 32306-2047. Tel: 850-644-2706. Circulation Tel: 850-644-6061. Interlibrary Loan Service Tel: 850-644-4466. Administration Tel: 850-644-5211. Information Services Tel: 850-644-1486. Interlibrary Loan Service FAX: 850-644-4702. Reference FAX: 850-644-1231. Administration FAX: 850-644-5016. Web Site: www.lib.fsu.edu. *Dean,* Julia A Zimmerman; E-mail: jazimmerman@fsu.edu; *Assoc Dean, Spec Coll,* Kathleen McCormick; E-mail: kmccormick@fsu.edu; *Assoc Dean, Admin Serv,* Policia Clyne; *Assoc Dean, Coll Develop,* Roy Ziegler; E-mail: rziegler@fsu.edu; *Assoc Dean, Digital Scholarship & Tech Serv,* Nancy Kellett; E-mail: nkellett@fsu.edu; *Assoc Dean, Pub Serv,* Position Currently Open; *Assoc Dean, Tech Serv,* Amy Weiss; E-mail: akweiss@fsu.edu
Founded 1888. Enrl 39,652; Fac 1,124; Highest Degree: Doctorate
Library Holdings: AV Mats 250,484; e-journals 29,485; Bk Vols 2,889,810; Per Subs 42,076
Special Collections: Carothers Memorial Coll of Bibles & Rare Books; Florida Coll; FSU Archives; Herbal Coll; Lois Lenski Coll; Mildred & Claude Pepper Coll; Napoleon & French Revolution; Press Works (including Kelmscott Press); Rare Books & Manuscripts Coll; Scottish Coll; Shaw Poetry Coll. State Document Depository; UN Document Depository; US Document Depository
Automation Activity & Vendor Info: (Acquisitions) Ex Libris Group; (Cataloging) Ex Libris Group; (Circulation) Ex Libris Group; (ILL) OCLC ILLiad; (Serials) Ex Libris Group
Wireless access
Function: Res libr
Partic in Florida Center for Library Automation; Lyrasis; OCLC Online Computer Library Center, Inc
Special Services for the Deaf - Assistive tech
Special Services for the Blind - Assistive/Adapted tech devices, equip & products
Friends of the Library Group

Departmental Libraries:

WARREN D ALLEN MUSIC LIBRARY, Housewright Music Bldg, 122 N Copeland St, 32306. Tel: 850-644-5028. Interlibrary Loan Service Tel: 850-644-4466. Administration Tel: 850-644-3999. FAX: 850-644-3982. Web Site: music.fsu.edu/library. *Head Librn,* Laura Gayle Green; E-mail: lgreen3@fsu.edu; *Assoc Librn, Head, Cat,* Sarah Cohen; Tel: 850-644-4137, E-mail: shcohen@fsu.edu; *Asst Librn, Head, Coll Develop, Spec Coll,* Sara Nodine; Tel: 850-644-4698, E-mail: snodine@fsu.edu; Staff 7 (MLS 3, Non-MLS 4)
Highest Degree: Doctorate
Library Holdings: Bk Titles 150,000
Database Vendor: Alexander Street Press, Blackwell, EBSCOhost, Gale Cengage Learning, JSTOR, OCLC FirstSearch, OCLC WorldShare Interlibrary Loan, ProQuest
Open Mon-Thurs 8am-10pm, Fri 8-5, Sat 10-6, Sun 1-10

THE CAREER CENTER LIBRARY, Dunlap Success Ctr 1200, 100 S Woodward Ave, 32304. (Mail add: PO Box 3064162, 32306-4162). Tel: 850-644-9779. FAX: 850-644-3273. Web Site: career.fsu.edu/library. *Info Res Spec,* Elizabeth Barwick
Library Holdings: Bk Titles 1,500; Spec Interest Per Sub 25
Open Mon-Fri 9-4

CENTER FOR DEMOGRAPHY & POPULATION HEALTH, 601 Bellamy Bldg, 113 Collegiate Loop, 32306-2240, SAN 338-1218. Tel: 850-644-1762. FAX: 850-644-8818. E-mail: popctr@fsu.edu. Web Site: popcenter.fsu.edu.
Library Holdings: Bk Vols 7,500; Per Subs 15
Special Collections: Charles M Grigg Memorial Coll; Soviet Population Materials (Galina Selegan Coll)
Open Mon-Fri 8-3
Restriction: Open to students, fac & staff

CL COLLEGE OF LAW LIBRARY, 425 W Jefferson St, 32306, SAN 338-1242. Tel: 850-644-4578. Circulation Tel: 850-644-3405. Reference Tel: 850-644-4095. Web Site: www.law.fsu.edu/library. *Dir,* Faye Jones; E-mail: fejones@law.fsu.edu; *Assoc Dir,* Elizabeth Farrell; *Asst Dir, Cat & Ser,* Pat Bingham-Harper; *Asst Dir, Digital Projects,* Jon Lutz; Tel: 850-644-7479, E-mail: jlutz@law.fsu.edu; *Asst Dir, Intl Legal Res,* Margaret Clark; Tel: 850-644-9244, E-mail: maclark@law.fsu.edu; *Asst Dir, Res Serv,* Mary McCormick; Staff 10 (MLS 10)
Founded 1966. Enrl 766; Fac 45; Highest Degree: Doctorate
Jul 2005-Jun 2006 Income $1,876,535. Mats Exp $958,297, Books $72,493, Per/Ser (Incl. Access Fees) $455,366, Micro $35,696, AV Mat $230, Electronic Ref Mat (Incl. Access Fees) $387,320, Presv $7,192. Sal $841,631 (Prof $562,584)
Library Holdings: AV Mats 1,349; Bk Titles 199,619; Bk Vols 510,662; Per Subs 3,580
Special Collections: Works by or about US Supreme Court Justices. US Document Depository
Automation Activity & Vendor Info: (Cataloging) Ex Libris Group; (Circulation) Ex Libris Group; (Course Reserve) Ex Libris Group; (OPAC) Ex Libris Group; (Serials) Ex Libris Group
Database Vendor: LexisNexis, Westlaw
Partic in Lyrasis; OCLC Online Computer Library Center, Inc
Open Mon-Thurs (Fall & Spring) 7:30am-11pm, Fri 7:30am-6, Sat 10-5, Sun 1-10; Mon-Fri (May-Aug) 8-6

CM COLLEGE OF NURSING, LEARNING RESOURCE CENTER, 98 Varsity Way, 32306-4310, SAN 338-1315. Tel: 850-644-1291. FAX: 850-644-7660. Web Site: nursing.fsu.edu. *IT Mgr,* Jamie Marsh; E-mail: jmarsh@nursing.fsu.edu
Library Holdings: Per Subs 425
Special Collections: Nursing History
Subject Interests: Nursing
Automation Activity & Vendor Info: (Circulation) Follett Software
Partic in Center for Research Libraries; Florida Library Information Network; OCLC Research Library Partnership
Open Mon-Thurs 7:30am-8pm, Fri 7:30-5, Sun 12-6

JOHN A DEGEN RESOURCE ROOM, School of Theater, Fine Arts Bldg, 540 W Call St, 32306. Tel: 850-645-7247. *Coordr, Financial & Auxiliary Serv,* Mark Thorp; Tel: 850-644-7259, E-mail: mthorp@admin.fsu.edu
Library Holdings: CDs 430; DVDs 100; Bk Titles 8,500
Special Collections: Historic Playbills Coll
Subject Interests: Theatre
Automation Activity & Vendor Info: (Cataloging) SIRSI WorkFlows; (Circulation) SIRSI WorkFlows; (OPAC) SirsiDynix
Open Mon-Fri 9-6
Restriction: Open to students, fac & staff

CR DEPARTMENT OF RELIGION LIBRARY, 301-B Dodd Hall, 32306-1520. Tel: 850-644-1020. FAX: 850-644-7225. *In Charge,* David Levenson
Open Mon-Fri 8-5
Restriction: Open to students

PAUL A M DIRAC SCIENCE LIBRARY, 110 N Woodward Ave, 32306-4140. Tel: 850-644-5534. FAX: 850-644-0025. *Head Librn,* Rachel Besara; Staff 12 (MLS 4, Non-MLS 8)
Founded 1988
Subject Interests: Applied sci, Pure sci
Open Mon-Thurs & Sun 8am-1am, Fri 8-5, Sat 10-6

FILM SCHOOL RESOURCE & RESEARCH CENTER, 3100 University Center, Bldg A, 32306. Tel: 850-644-0693. FAX: 850-644-2626. *Archivist,* Richard Travis; E-mail: rtravis@film.fsu.edu
Library Holdings: Bk Vols 5,500

Special Collections: Filmmaking & Film Industry, bks, screenplays & trade mag
Restriction: By permission only

GEOPHYSICAL FLUID DYNAMICS INSTITUTE, 18 Keen Bldg, 32306-4360, SAN 338-1188. Tel: 850-644-5594, 850-644-5595. FAX: 850-644-8972. Web Site: www.gfdi.fsu.edu. *Mgr,* Vijaya Challa
Library Holdings: Bk Titles 8,200
Restriction: Not open to pub

HAROLD GOLDSTEIN LIBRARY, 142 Collegiate Loop, 32306. (Mail add: PO Box 3062100, 32306-2100). Tel: 850-644-1803. FAX: 850-644-0460. E-mail: library@cci.fsu.edu. Web Site: goldstein.cci.fsu.edu. *Dir,* Pam Doffek; Tel: 850-644-0461, E-mail: pam.doffek@cci.fsu.edu; *Assoc Dir,* Leila Gibradze; Tel: 850-645-8418, E-mail: leila.gibradze@cci.fsu.edu. Subject Specialists: *Cataloging, Distance learning,* Leila Gibradze; Staff 2 (MLS 2)
Founded 1985. Enrl 2,700; Fac 77; Highest Degree: Doctorate
Jul 2013-Jun 2014 Income $88,500. Mats Exp $89,000, Books $23,000, Per/Ser (Incl. Access Fees) $57,000, Electronic Ref Mat (Incl. Access Fees) $9,000. Sal $88,000
Library Holdings: CDs 50; DVDs 40; e-books 1,700; Bk Vols 82,000; Per Subs 35; Videos 100
Special Collections: Contemporary Award Winning, Multicultural & International Juvenile Literature Coll; Florida & Caribbean Chapter, SLA, Archives; John David Marshall Papers; Joseph Wheeler Papers & Colls; Juvenile Literature Coll; Library & Information Science Coll; Louis Shores Papers; Paul Howard Papers
Subject Interests: Info sci, Info tech, Juv lit, Libr sci
Database Vendor: Children's Literature Comprehensive Database Company (CLCD), Ex Libris Group
Function: Distance learning, Doc delivery serv, e-mail & chat, Electronic databases & coll, Exhibits, ILL available, Online cat, Online ref, Orientations, Ref serv in person, Telephone ref, Wheelchair accessible
Partic in Panhandle Library Access Network
Open Mon-Thurs 7:30am-10pm, Fri 7:30-5, Sat 10-6, Sun 1-6
Restriction: Borrowing privileges limited to fac & registered students, Pub use on premises

HERBARIUM LIBRARY, 100 Biology I, 32306-4370. Tel: 850-644-6278. FAX: 850-644-0481. *Dir,* Dr Austin Mast; E-mail: amast@bio.fsu.edu
Function: Res libr
Restriction: By permission only, Open by appt only, Open to students, fac & staff

LEARNING RESOURCE CENTER, COLLEGE OF EDUCATION, 1301 Stone Bldg, 32306-4450, SAN 338-1161. Tel: 850-644-4553. Web Site: www.coe.fsu.edu. *Dir,* Dina Vyortkina
Library Holdings: Bk Titles 1,000
Open Mon-Thurs 8am-10pm, Fri 8-6
Restriction: Open to students, fac & staff

CM CHARLOTTE EDWARDS MAGUIRE MEDICAL LIBRARY, 1115 W Call St, 32306-4300. Tel: 850-644-3883. Interlibrary Loan Service Tel: 850-644-6683. FAX: 850-644-9942. E-mail: MedLibrary@med.fsu.edu. Web Site: med.fsu.edu/library. *Dir,* Martin Wood; Tel: 850-645-7304, E-mail: martin.wood@med.fsu.edu; *Head, Web Serv,* Suzanne Nagy; Tel: 850-644-7623, E-mail: suzanne.nagy@med.fsu.edu; *Scholarly Communications Librn,* Roxann Mouratidis; Tel: 850-645-9398, E-mail: roxann.mouratidis@med.fsu.edu; *Syst Librn,* Susan Epstein; E-mail: susan.epstein@med.fsu.edu; *Pub Serv,* Robyn Rosasco; Staff 5 (MLS 5)
Founded 2000. Enrl 488; Fac 2,100; Highest Degree: Doctorate
Automation Activity & Vendor Info: (Course Reserve) Ex Libris Group; (ILL) Ex Libris Group; (Serials) SerialsSolutions
Database Vendor: Baker & Taylor, Cambridge Scientific Abstracts, EBSCOhost, Elsevier MDL, Gale Cengage Learning, JSTOR, LexisNexis, OVID Technologies, PubMed, ScienceDirect, SerialsSolutions, Wilson - Wilson Web
Partic in Fla Ctr for Libr Automation
Open Mon-Fri 8-5

RADZINOWICZ CRIMINOLOGY READING ROOM, 201 Hecht House, 32306. Tel: 850-644-9845. *In Charge,* Claire Knox
Restriction: Open to students, fac & staff

M LYNETTE THOMPSON CLASSICS LIBRARY, 205 Dodd Hall, 32306. Tel: 850-644-4259. *Chmn,* Daniel Pullen; E-mail: dpullen@fsu.edu
Library Holdings: Bk Titles 2,300
Subject Interests: Classics, Greek, Latin
Restriction: Open to students, fac & staff of Classics Dept only

GL FLORIDA SUPREME COURT LIBRARY*, 500 S Duval St, 32399-1926. SAN 303-2027. Tel: 850-488-8919. FAX: 850-922-5219. Web Site: library.flcourts.org. *Librn,* Billie Blaine; *Asst Librn, Ref Serv,* Teresa Farley; *Tech Serv,* Jeff Spalding; Staff 3 (MLS 3)
Founded 1845
Library Holdings: Bk Titles 12,157; Bk Vols 114,587; Per Subs 1,476
Special Collections: Florida Supreme Court Historical Society. Oral History; US Document Depository
Automation Activity & Vendor Info: (Cataloging) Innovative Interfaces, Inc; (OPAC) Innovative Interfaces, Inc
Partic in Dialog Corp; Lyrasis; Westlaw
Open Mon-Fri 8-5

L HOPPING, GREEN & SAMS*, Law Library, PO Box 6526, 32314-6526. SAN 372-1795. Tel: 850-222-7500. FAX: 850-224-8551. Web Site: www.hgslaw.com. *Librn,* Marisol Roberts; Staff 1 (MLS 1)
Library Holdings: e-journals 5; Bk Vols 8,000; Per Subs 10; Spec Interest Per Sub 35
Subject Interests: Admin law, Environ law
Restriction: Private libr

S CLAUDE PEPPER LIBRARY*, 636 W Call St, 32306-1123. Tel: 850-644-9305. FAX: 850-644-9350. Web Site: www.claudepeppercenter.fsu.edu. *Interim Dir,* Tom Herndon; Staff 1 (MLS 1)
Library Holdings: Bk Titles 2,500
Open Mon-Fri 9-5

G STATE LIBRARY OF FLORIDA*, Capitol Branch Library, The Capitol, Rm 701, 32399. SAN 303-1993. Tel: 850-245-6612. Web Site: dlis.dos.state.fl.us/leglib. *Librn,* Dan Emerick; Tel: 850-245-6799, E-mail: dan.emerick@dos.myflorida.com; *Archivist,* Delbra McGriff; Tel: 850-245-6726; Staff 2 (MLS 1, Non-MLS 1)
Founded 1949
Library Holdings: Bk Titles 10,000; Bk Vols 22,000; Per Subs 410
Special Collections: Public Administration & Legislative Mats
Automation Activity & Vendor Info: (Cataloging) SirsiDynix; (Circulation) SirsiDynix
Publications: Checklist of Recent Acquisitions (Monthly); Checklist of Recent Legislative Publications (Quarterly); The Florida Legislative Library: Functions, Scope, Procedures (revised as needed)
Partic in Westlaw
Open Mon-Fri 9-4:30

S TALL TIMBERS RESEARCH STATION LIBRARY, 13093 Henry Beadel Dr, 32312-0918. SAN 320-1392. Tel: 850-893-4153, Ext 234. FAX: 850-668-7781. Web Site: www.talltimbers.org. *Librn,* Carol Armstrong Kimball; E-mail: carol@ttrs.org. Subject Specialists: *Conserv, Fire ecology, Land mgt,* Carol Armstrong Kimball; Staff 1.3 (MLS 1, Non-MLS 0.3)
Library Holdings: Bk Titles 9,612; Bk Vols 10,000; Per Subs 120
Special Collections: Tall Timbers On-Line Fire Ecology Database
Subject Interests: Bio, Conserv, Fire ecology, Forestry
Automation Activity & Vendor Info: (Acquisitions) Book Systems; (Cataloging) Book Systems; (Circulation) Book Systems; (OPAC) Book Systems
Wireless access
Function: Res libr
Partic in Panhandle Library Access Network
Restriction: Open by appt only

J TALLAHASSEE COMMUNITY COLLEGE LIBRARY*, 444 Appleyard Dr, 32304-2895. SAN 303-2078. Tel: 850-201-8376. Reference Tel: 850-201-8383. FAX: 850-201-8380. E-mail: library@tcc.fl.edu. Web Site: www.tcc.fl.edu/library. *Dir,* Deborah P Robinson; Tel: 850-201-8396, E-mail: robindeb@tcc.fl.edu; *Fac Librn,* Carol A Chenoweth; Tel: 850-201-6187, E-mail: chenowec@tcc.fl.edu; *Head, Access Serv,* Shelly R Schmucker; Tel: 850-201-6189, E-mail: schmusch@tcc.fl.edu; Staff 7 (Non-MLS 7)
Founded 1966. Enrl 11,200; Fac 490; Highest Degree: Associate
Library Holdings: Bk Titles 95,157; Bk Vols 121,462; Per Subs 782
Special Collections: Florida (Beatrice Shaw Coll)
Subject Interests: Paramedics
Wireless access
Publications: Acquisitions (newsletter); Library Handbook; Library Staff Newsletter
Partic in Panhandle Library Access Network
Open Mon-Thurs (Fall-Spring) 7:30am-9pm, Fri 7:30-5, Sat 10-2; Mon-Thurs (Summer) 7:30am-8pm, Fri 7:30-5

TAMPA

C ARGOSY UNIVERSITY*, Tampa Library, 4401 N Himes Ave, Ste 150, 33614. Tel: 813-393-5322, 813-393-5333. FAX: 813-874-1989. Web Site: www.argosyu.edu/tampa/student_library.asp. *Dir, Libr Serv,* John R Davies; E-mail: jdavies@edmc.edu
Library Holdings: Bk Titles 4,000; Per Subs 90
Database Vendor: EBSCOhost, OCLC FirstSearch
Wireless access
Function: ILL available
Open Mon-Thurs 8:30am-9pm, Fri 8:30-6, Sat 8:30-3
Restriction: Open to students, fac & staff

S CAE USA, INC LIBRARY*, 4908 Tampa West Blvd, 33634. SAN 326-7865. Tel: 813-887-1658. FAX: 813-901-6417. *Librn,* Betsy King; *Asst Librn,* Bridget Diffenderfer; Tel: 813-887-1540; Staff 2 (MLS 2)
Subject Interests: Aeronaut, Eng

L CARLTON FIELDS*, Law Library, 4221 W Boy Scout Blvd, Ste 1000, 33607. (Mail add: PO Box 3239, 33601-3239), SAN 303-2086. Tel: 813-223-7000. FAX: 813-229-4133. Web Site: www.carltonfields.com. *Mgr, Libr Serv,* Terry Psarras; *Acq,* Liz Reichert; *Ref,* Marcia Morelli
Founded 1915
Library Holdings: Bk Vols 30,000; Per Subs 200
Automation Activity & Vendor Info: (Cataloging) Inmagic, Inc.
Database Vendor: LexisNexis, Westlaw
Restriction: Not open to pub

EVEREST UNIVERSITY

C BRANDON CAMPUS LIBRARY, Sabal Business Ctr, 3924 Coconut Palm Dr, 33619, SAN 370-9256. Tel: 813-621-0041. FAX: 813-623-5769. Web Site: learningresources.everestuniversity.edu/brandon.php. *Dir,* Shannon Schane; Tel: 813-744-2554, E-mail: sschane@cci.edu; Staff 2 (MLS 1, Non-MLS 1)
Highest Degree: Master
Library Holdings: Bk Titles 4,500; Per Subs 70
Partic in Tampa Bay Library Consortium, Inc
Open Mon-Thurs 8:30-8:30, Fri 8:30-6, Sat 9-1

C TAMPA CAMPUS LIBRARY-WEST HILLSBOROUGH*, 3319 W Hillsborough Ave, 33614, SAN 302-8879. Tel: 813-879-6000. FAX: 813-875-7764. Web Site: www.tblc.org/tcw. *Librn,* Keri Enterline; Tel: 813-879-6000, Ext 117; Staff 5 (MLS 1, Non-MLS 4)
Enrl 1,300; Fac 75; Highest Degree: Master
Library Holdings: AV Mats 273; Bk Titles 4,106; Bk Vols 4,679; Per Subs 100
Subject Interests: Allied health, Bus, Computer sci, Criminal justice, Paralegal
Automation Activity & Vendor Info: (Acquisitions) Follett Software; (Circulation) Follett Software; (ILL) OCLC; (OPAC) Follett Software
Database Vendor: LexisNexis, OCLC FirstSearch, Westlaw
Partic in Fla Libr Asn; Lyrasis; Tampa Bay Library Consortium, Inc
Publications: Bibliographies; Internal Acquisitions List; Newsletter
Open Mon-Thurs 8am-9pm, Fri 8-7, Sat 9-2

M FLORIDA HOSPITAL-TAMPA*, Medical Library, 3100 E Fletcher Ave, 33613-4688. SAN 324-5616. Tel: 813-615-7236. FAX: 813 615-7854. Web Site: www.elevatinghealthcare.org/locations/tampa, www.uch.org. *Mgr,* Sharon Henrich; E-mail: sharon.henrich@ahss.org; Staff 1 (MLS 1)
Founded 1974
Library Holdings: Bk Titles 1,000; Per Subs 596
Automation Activity & Vendor Info: (Cataloging) TLC (The Library Corporation); (Circulation) TLC (The Library Corporation)
Wireless access
Partic in National Network of Libraries of Medicine; Regional Med Libr - Region 2; Tampa Bay Library Consortium, Inc; Tampa Bay Medical Library Network
Open Mon-Fri 8-4:30

L GRAY-ROBINSON, PA*, Law Library, 201 N Franklin St, Ste 2200, 33602-5822. (Mail add: PO Box 3324, 33601-3324), SAN 373-6598. Tel: 813-273-5000. Reference Tel: 813-273-5294. FAX: 813-273-5145. Web Site: www.gray-robinson.com.
Library Holdings: Bk Titles 3,500; Bk Vols 25,000; Per Subs 75
Open Mon-Fri 8-5:30
Restriction: Staff use only

J HILLSBOROUGH COMMUNITY COLLEGE*, District Library Technical Services, Collaboration Studio, Rm 139, 1602 N 15th St, 33605. SAN 338-1390. Tel: 813-259-6059. Automation Services Tel: 813-259-6058. FAX: 813-253-7510. Web Site: libguides.hccfl.edu/dlts. *Automation Coordr,* Andrea Dufault; E-mail: adufault@hccfl.edu; *Learning Res Coordr,* Jackie del Val; E-mail: jdelval@hccfl.edu; Staff 5 (MLS 2, Non-MLS 3)
Founded 1968. Highest Degree: Associate
Library Holdings: AV Mats 3,653; CDs 1,351; DVDs 5,218; e-books 6,000; Electronic Media & Resources 15,155; Bk Titles 117,067; Per Subs 614
Special Collections: Art Slides; Literary Criticism File; Opthalmology (Stimson Coll)
Subject Interests: Allied health, Music, Nursing
Automation Activity & Vendor Info: (Acquisitions) Ex Libris Group; (Cataloging) Ex Libris Group; (Circulation) Ex Libris Group; (Course Reserve) Ex Libris Group; (ILL) Ex Libris Group; (OPAC) Ex Libris Group; (Serials) Ex Libris Group
Database Vendor: ABC-CLIO, Alexander Street Press, ARTstor, Booklist Online, College Source, ebrary, EBSCOhost, Facts on File, Gale Cengage Learning, Greenwood Publishing Group, H W Wilson, Ingram Library Services, JSTOR, LexisNexis, Newsbank, OCLC ArticleFirst, OCLC FirstSearch, OCLC WorldShare Interlibrary Loan, ProQuest, Sage, Springshare, LLC, Westlaw, Wiley InterScience, Wilson - Wilson Web, WT Cox
Wireless access
Partic in Florida Library Information Network; Lyrasis; Tampa Bay Library Consortium, Inc
Open Mon-Fri 7:30-4:30
Restriction: 24-hr pass syst for students only

Departmental Libraries:

BRANDON CAMPUS LEARNING RESOURCES CENTER, 10414 E Columbus Dr, 33619-9640, SAN 322-8983. Tel: 813-253-7803. Interlibrary Loan Service Tel: 813 253 7847. Reference Tel: 813-253-7886. Web Site: www.hccfl.edu/library/blrc. *Librn,* Jeremy Bullian; *Librn,* Wendy Foley; *Learning Res Coordr,* Laurie Macnicol; Tel: 813-253-7935, E-mail: lmacnicol@hccfl.edu; *AV,* Chris Gunn; *Learning Res Tech,* Marie O'Connell; Staff 5 (MLS 2, Non-MLS 3)
Enrl 1,601; Highest Degree: Associate
Partic in OCLC Online Computer Library Center, Inc
Publications: LRC Newsletter
Open Mon-Thurs 8-8, Fri 8-4:30, Sat 8-2

DALE MABRY CAMPUS LIBRARY, 4001 Tampa Bay Blvd, 33614-7820. (Mail add: PO Box 30030, 33630-3030), SAN 338-1420. Tel: 813-253-7381. FAX: 813-253-7400. Web Site: www.hccfl.edu/library. *Librn,* Jacqueline Cress; E-mail: jcress@hccfl.edu; *Librn,* Vic Harke; E-mail: vharke@hccfl.edu; *AV,* Milan Gumbarevic; Staff 10 (MLS 3, Non-MLS 7)
Founded 1968. Enrl 22,000
Special Collections: Literary Criticism File; Slide Library
Partic in OCLC Online Computer Library Center, Inc
Open Mon-Thurs 8-8, Fri 8-2, Sat 8-3

PLANT CITY CAMPUS LEARNING RESOURCES CENTER, 1206 N Park Rd, Plant City, 33563, SAN 303-1330. Tel: 813-757-2163. FAX: 813-757-2167. Web Site: www.hccfl.edu/library/pclrc. *Librn,* Kristin Heathcock; *Learning Res Coordr,* Michelle Monteleon; Staff 3 (MLS 1, Non-MLS 2)
Enrl 1,200; Fac 20; Highest Degree: Associate
Partic in OCLC Online Computer Library Center, Inc
Open Mon-Thurs 8-8, Fri 8-4:30

YBOR CITY CAMPUS LEARNING RESOURCES CENTER, 1502 E Ninth Ave, 33605. (Mail add: 2112 N 15th St, 33605-3648), SAN 329-5729. Tel: 813-253-7645. Reference Tel: 813-253-7729. FAX: 813-259-6070. Web Site: www.hccfl.edu/yborlibrary. *Librn,* Alicia Ellison; Tel: 813-253-7731, E-mail: aellison@hccfl.edu; *Librn,* Jeneice Sorrentino; Tel: 813-253-7613, E-mail: jsorrentino@hccfl.edu; Staff 6.5 (MLS 2, Non-MLS 4.5)
Partic in OCLC Online Computer Library Center, Inc
Open Mon-Thurs (Winter) 8-8, Fri 8-4:30; Mon-Thurs (Summer) 8-7, Fri 8-4:30

L HOLLAND & KNIGHT LLP*, Library & Research Services, 100 N Tampa St, Ste 4100, 33602. (Mail add: PO Box 1288, 33601-1288), SAN 372-1396. Tel: 813-227-8500. FAX: 813-229-0134. Web Site: www.hklaw.com.
Library Holdings: Bk Vols 30,000
Partic in Florida Library Information Network

S INTERNATIONAL ACADEMY OF DESIGN & TECHNOLOGY*, Learning Resource Center, 5104 Eisenhower Blvd, 33634. SAN 377-3248. Tel: 813-880-8013. FAX: 813-884-9327. *Librn,* Position Currently Open; Staff 2 (MLS 1, Non-MLS 1)
Enrl 2,000; Fac 100; Highest Degree: Bachelor
Library Holdings: Bk Vols 5,000; Per Subs 150
Subject Interests: Animation, Digital production, Fashion design, Graphic design, Interior design, Merchandising, Photog, Rec arts
Wireless access
Partic in Tampa Bay Library Consortium, Inc
Open Mon-Fri 7:30am-10:30pm, Sat 10-2
Restriction: Open to students, fac & staff

J ITT TECHNICAL INSTITUTE*, Learning Resource Center, 4809 Memorial Hwy, 33634. Tel: 813-885-2244. Toll Free Tel: 800-825-2831. FAX: 813-888-6078. *Librn,* Michael Maiers; E-mail: mmaiers@itt-tech.edu
Library Holdings: Bk Vols 14,000
Open Mon-Thurs 9am-9:30pm, Fri 9-9, Sat 9-1

GL JAMES J LUNSFORD (HILLSBOROUGH COUNTY) LAW LIBRARY*, 701 E Twiggs St, 33602. SAN 303-2132. Tel: 813-272-5818. FAX: 813-272-5226. *Dir,* Norma Wise; *Librn,* Donna L Barnes; Staff 4 (MLS 1, Non-MLS 3)
Founded 1937
Library Holdings: Bk Vols 40,000; Per Subs 75
Database Vendor: Westlaw
Open Mon-Thurs 8-8, Fri 8-5, Sat & Sun 12-5

Restriction: Non-circulating
Friends of the Library Group

M H LEE MOFFITT CANCER CENTER & RESEARCH INSTITUTE*, Biomedical Library, 12902 Magnolia Dr, 33612. Tel: 813-745-4673. FAX: 813-745-3084. *Med Librn,* Susan Sharpe; E-mail: susan.sharpe@moffitt.org; Staff 1.5 (MLS 1, Non-MLS 0.5)
Library Holdings: Bk Vols 425; Per Subs 180
Subject Interests: Molecular biol, Oncology
Database Vendor: Dialog
Function: Health sci info serv, ILL available, Res libr
Partic in Tampa Bay Library Consortium, Inc; Tampa Bay Medical Library Network
Open Mon-Fri 10-4
Restriction: Circ limited, Non-circulating coll

S PROVIDENCE HISTORICAL SOCIETY, 3980 Tampa Rd, Ste 207, 34677. SAN 300-1717. Tel: 813-855-4635. FAX: 813-855-2309. *Librn,* Nancy Stewart; Staff 10 (MLS 4, Non-MLS 6)
Founded 1971
Library Holdings: Bk Titles 11,000; Bk Vols 15,000

J REMINGTON COLLEGE, Tampa Campus, 6302 E Dr Martin Luther King Jr Blvd, Ste 400, 33619. SAN 370-5013. Tel: 813-935-5700. FAX: 813-935-7415. Web Site: www.remingtoncollege.edu. *Dir,* Vicki Hamaker; E-mail: vicki.hamaker@remingtoncollege.edu; Staff 1 (MLS 1)
Founded 1948. Enrl 1,000; Fac 41; Highest Degree: Bachelor
Library Holdings: Bk Titles 4,000; Bk Vols 5,000; Per Subs 141
Subject Interests: Bus, Computer, Electronics, Graphic arts, Med asst, Mgt
Automation Activity & Vendor Info: (OPAC) SirsiDynix
Function: Ref serv available, Telephone ref
Partic in Fla Libr Asn; SLA; Sunline; Tampa Bay Library Consortium, Inc
Special Services for the Deaf - Spec interest per
Open Mon-Thurs 8am-9pm

M ST JOSEPH'S BAPTIST HEALTHCARE*, St Joseph's Hospital Library, PO Box 4227, 33677. SAN 322-8223. Tel: 813-870-4659. Interlibrary Loan Service Tel: 813-870-4660. FAX: 813-870-4479. Web Site: www.baycare.org. *In Charge,* Gita Halder; E-mail: gita.halder@baycare.org
Library Holdings: e-journals 20; Bk Vols 800; Per Subs 129
Special Collections: Medicine Coll; Nursing Management Coll
Database Vendor: OVID Technologies
Function: ILL available, Ref serv available
Restriction: Lending to staff only, Mem organizations only

M SHRINERS HOSPITAL FOR CHILDREN*, Professional Library, 12502 USF Pine Dr, 33612-9411. SAN 371-5728. Tel: 813-972-2250, Ext 7608. FAX: 813-975-7125. Web Site: www.shrinershq.org. *Librn,* Claire Keneally; E-mail: ckeneally@shrinenet.org; Staff 1 (MLS 1)
Founded 1985
Library Holdings: Bk Titles 1,500; Bk Vols 5,000; Per Subs 120
Subject Interests: Orthopedics
Partic in Tampa Bay Medical Library Network

S TAMPA BAY HISTORY CENTER*, Hillsborough County Historic Commission Library, 801 Old Water St, 33602. SAN 303-2124. Tel: 813-228-0097. FAX: 813-223-7021. E-mail: info@tampabayhistorycenter.org. Web Site: www.tampabayhistorycenter.org. *Archivist, Asst Curator,* Travis Puterbaugh. Subject Specialists: *Anthrop,* Travis Puterbaugh; Staff 1 (Non-MLS 1)
Founded 1996
Library Holdings: Bk Titles 5,000
Special Collections: Militaria; Robert Hawk Coll; Robert Saunders Papers (NAACP); Spanish-American (Hatton & Memorabilia)
Subject Interests: Fla
Function: Photocopying/Printing
Partic in Tampa Bay Library Consortium, Inc
Open Mon-Fri 10-12 & 1-4
Restriction: Not a lending libr

M TAMPA GENERAL HOSPITAL*, Medical Library, PO Box 1289, 33601-1289. SAN 303-2159. Tel: 813-844-7328. FAX: 813-844-7325. *Librn,* Margaret H Henry; Staff 2 (MLS 1, Non-MLS 1)
Founded 1960
Library Holdings: Bk Titles 2,000; Per Subs 450
Subject Interests: Clinical med
Publications: TGH Library Letter, brochure
Partic in SE-Atlantic Regional Med Libr Servs; Tampa Bay Medical Library Network
Open Mon-Fri 8:30-5

P TAMPA-HILLSBOROUGH COUNTY PUBLIC LIBRARY SYSTEM*, John F Germany Public Library, 900 N Ashley Dr, 33602-3704. SAN 338-1455. Tel: 813-273-3652. FAX: 813-273-3707. TDD: 813-273-3610. E-mail: libraryinformation@hillsboroughcounty.org. Web Site: thpl.org, www.hcplc.org. *Dir of Libr,* Andrew Breidenbaugh; Staff 122.25 (MLS 122.25)
Founded 1915. Pop 1,263,050; Circ 6,584,063
Library Holdings: Bk Vols 2,348,835
Special Collections: State Document Depository; US Document Depository
Subject Interests: Fla, Genealogy, Local hist
Wireless access
Partic in Florida Library Information Network; Hillsborough County Public Library Cooperative
Open Mon-Wed 10-9, Thurs 10-8, Fri & Sat 10-6, Sun 12:30-5
Friends of the Library Group
Branches: 25
C BLYTHE ANDREWS, JR PUBLIC LIBRARY, 2607 E Martin Luther King Blvd, 33610-7770, SAN 370-0917.
Open Mon-Tues 10-8, Wed-Sat 10-6
Friends of the Library Group
BLOOMINGDALE REGIONAL PUBLIC, 1906 Bloomingdale Ave, Valrico, 33594-6204.
Open Mon-Wed 10-9, Thurs 12-8, Fri & Sat 10-6, Sun 12:30-5
Friends of the Library Group
BRANDON REGIONAL LIBRARY, 619 Vonderburg Dr, Brandon, 33511-5972, SAN 338-151X.
Open Mon-Wed 10-9, Thurs 12-8, Fri-Sat 10-6, Sun 12:30-5
Friends of the Library Group
AUSTIN DAVIS PUBLIC LIBRARY, 17808 Wayne Rd, Odessa, 33556, SAN 338-1544.
Open Mon 12-8, Tues 10-8, Wed-Sat 10-6
Friends of the Library Group
EGYPT LAKE PARTNERSHIP LIBRARY, 3403 W Lambright St, 33614-4618.
Open Mon-Wed 2:30-8, Thurs & Fri 2:30-6, Sat 10-6; Mon-Wed (Summer) 1-8, Thurs 1-6, Sat 10-6
CHARLES J FENDIG PUBLIC LIBRARY, 3909 W Neptune St, 33629, SAN 338-1668.
Open Mon 12-9, Tues 10-8, Wed-Sat 10-6
Friends of the Library Group
JIMMIE B KEEL REGIONAL LIBRARY, 2902 W Bearss Ave, 33618-1828, SAN 328-8927.
Open Mon-Wed 10-9, Thurs 12-8, Fri & Sat 10-6, Sun 12:30-5
Friends of the Library Group
LUTZ BRANCH, 101 Lutz Lake Fern Rd W, Lutz, 33548-7220, SAN 338-1609.
Open Mon 12-8, Tues 10-8, Wed-Sat 10-6
Friends of the Library Group
NEW TAMPA REGIONAL LIBRARY, 10001 Cross Creek Blvd, 33647-2581, SAN 377-5798.
Open Mon-Wed 10-9, Thurs 12-8, Fri-Sat 10-6, Sun 12:30-5
Friends of the Library Group
NORTH TAMPA BRANCH, 8916 North Blvd, 33604-1299, SAN 338-1633.
Open Mon & Wed 10-8, Tues 12-8, Thurs-Sat 10-6, Sun 12:30-5
Friends of the Library Group
JAN KAMINIS PLATT REGIONAL LIBRARY, 3910 S Manhattan Ave, 33611-1214.
Open Mon-Wed 10-9, Thurs 12-8, Fri & Sat 10-6, Sun 12:30-5
Friends of the Library Group
PORT TAMPA CITY LIBRARY, 4902 W Commerce St, 33616-2704, SAN 338-1692.
Open Tues & Thurs-Sat 10-6, Wed 12-8
Friends of the Library Group
RIVERVIEW BRANCH, 10509 Riverview Dr, Riverview, 33578-4367, SAN 338-1714.
Open Mon & Tues 10-8, Wed-Sat 10-6
Friends of the Library Group
NORMA & JOSEPH ROBINSON PARTNERSHIP LIBRARY@SULPHUR SPRINGS, 8412 N 13th St, 33604-1842.
Open Mon & Wed 2:30-8, Tues, Thurs & Fri 2:30-6, Sat 10-6; Mon & Wed (Summer) 1-8, Tues & Thurs 1-6, Sat 10-6
RUSKIN BRANCH, 26 Dickman Dr SE, Ruskin, 33570-4313, SAN 338-1722.
Open Mon-Tues & Thurs-Sat 10-6, Wed 12-8
Friends of the Library Group
ROBERT W SAUNDERS SR PUBLIC LIBRARY, 1505 N Nebraska Ave, 33602-2849, SAN 338-1870.
Open Mon-Sat 10-6
Friends of the Library Group
SEFFNER-MANGO BRANCH, 410 N Kingsway Rd, Seffner, 33584-3602.
Open Mon 10-8, Tues 12-8, Wed-Sat 10-6
Friends of the Library Group

SEMINOLE HEIGHTS BRANCH, 4711 Central Ave, 33603-3905, SAN 338-1757.
Open Mon 12-8, Tues 10-8, Wed-Sat 10-6
Friends of the Library Group

SEVENTY-EIGHTH STREET COMMUNITY LIBRARY, 7625 Palm River Rd, 33619-4135, SAN 377-5771.
Open Mon 12-8, Tues 10-8, Wed-Sat 10-6
Friends of the Library Group

SOUTHSHORE REGIONAL LIBRARY, 15816 Beth Shields Way, Ruskin, 33573-4903.
Open Mon-Wed 10-9, Thurs 12-8, Fri & Sat 10-6, Sun 12:30-5
Friends of the Library Group

P TALKING BOOK LIBRARY, 3804 S Manhattan Ave, 33611, SAN 338-148X. Tel: 813-272-6024. TDD: 813-272-6305.
Special Collections: Talking Books Coll
Special Services for the Deaf - TDD equip
Open Mon-Fri 10-5

THONOTOSASSA BRANCH, 10715 Main St, Thonotosassa, 33592-2831, SAN 370-0925.
Open Mon 12-8, Tues-Sat 10-6

TOWN 'N COUNTRY REGIONAL PUBLIC LIBRARY, 7606 Paula Dr, 33615-4116, SAN 338-1811.
Open Mon-Wed 10-9, Thurs 12-8, Fri & Sat 10-6, Sun 12:30-5
Friends of the Library Group

UPPER TAMPA BAY REGIONAL PUBLIC LIBRARY, 11211 Countryway Blvd, 33626-2624.
Open Mon-Wed 10-9, Thurs 12-8, Fri & Sat 10-6, Sun 12:30-5
Friends of the Library Group

WEST TAMPA BRANCH, 2312 W Union St, 33607-3423, SAN 338-1846.
Open Mon-Sat 10-6
Friends of the Library Group

Bookmobiles: 2

S TAMPA MUSEUM OF ART*, Judith Rozier Blanchard Library, 120 W Gasparilla Plaza, 33602. SAN 303-2140. Tel: 813-274-8130. Circulation Tel: 813-259-1729. FAX: 813-274-8732. Web Site: www.tampamuseum.com. *Educ Adminr, Mus Spec,* Michelle Moseley; E-mail: michelle.moseley@tampamuseum.org
Jan 2009-Dec 2009. Mats Exp $5,250, Books $2,250, Per/Ser (Incl. Access Fees) $3,000
Library Holdings: Bk Vols 7,845; Per Subs 19
Special Collections: Greek & Roman Antiquities, bks, corpus vasoreum, elephant folios, journals, offprints, rare bks
Publications: Exhibition Catalogs; Newsletter (Monthly)
Restriction: Not open to pub, Private libr

GM UNITED STATES DEPARTMENT OF VETERANS AFFAIRS*, Willard S Harris Medical Library, Library Service (142D), 13000 Bruce B Downs Blvd, 33612. SAN 303-2183. Tel: 813-972-2000, Ext 6570. Interlibrary Loan Service Tel: 813-972-2000, Ext 6569. FAX: 813-978-5917. E-mail: tamlibrary@med.va.gov. *Chief Librn,* Janet Schneider; Tel: 813-972-7531, E-mail: janet.schneider@va.gov; *Clinical Med Librn,* Laurie Barnett; E-mail: laurie.barnett@va.gov; *Tech Serv Librn,* Dorothy Kelly; Tel: 813-972-2000, Ext 6571, E-mail: dorothy.kelly1@va.gov; Staff 4 (MLS 4)
Founded 1972
Library Holdings: AV Mats 817; Bk Titles 2,506; Per Subs 378
Subject Interests: Med, Nursing
Automation Activity & Vendor Info: (Cataloging) Follett Software; (Circulation) Follett Software; (OPAC) Follett Software
Wireless access
Publications: Medical Library Newsletter
Partic in Tampa Bay Medical Library Network; Veterans Affairs Libr Network (VALNET)
Restriction: Not open to pub

UNIVERSITY OF SOUTH FLORIDA

GM LOUIS DE LA PARTE FLORIDA MENTAL HEALTH INSTITUTE RESEARCH LIBRARY*, 13301 Bruce B Downs Blvd, 33612-3899, SAN 303-2108. Tel: 813-974-4471. FAX: 813-974-7242. *Access Serv, ILL,* Walter Cone; *Coll Develop,* Patricia C Pettijohn; Staff 5 (MLS 3, Non-MLS 2)
Founded 1974
Library Holdings: Bk Titles 30,000; Per Subs 430
Special Collections: AAD/ADHD Coll; De la Parte Institute Archives; Florida State Behavioral Healthcare Policy Coll; Multicultural Coll; Streaming Video Online Training Coll
Subject Interests: AIDS, Autism, Behav studies, Domestic violence, Epidemiology, Fla, Gerontology, Homelessness, Mental health, Mental health of children, Psychol, Soc serv (soc work), Spec educ
Automation Activity & Vendor Info: (Acquisitions) NOTIS; (Cataloging) NOTIS; (Circulation) NOTIS
Database Vendor: Dialog, Gale Cengage Learning, LexisNexis, OCLC FirstSearch, OVID Technologies, ProQuest, TLC (The Library Corporation), Wilson - Wilson Web
Function: Res libr
Partic in Lyrasis; OCLC Online Computer Library Center, Inc; Tampa Bay Medical Library Network
Open Mon-Thurs 8-8, Fri 8-4

CM HINKS & ELAINE SHIMBERG HEALTH SCIENCES LIBRARY, 12901 Bruce B Downs Blvd, MDC 31, 33612, SAN 338-1900. Tel: 813-974-2243. Interlibrary Loan Service Tel: 813-974-2123. Reference Tel: 813-974-2288. Web Site: library.hsc.usf.edu. *Dir,* Rose Bland; Tel: 813-974-2390; *Cat/Ref Librn,* Allison Howard; Tel: 813-974-4752; *Libr Operations Supvr/Access Serv, ILL & Doc Delivery,* Jeff Honker; *Acq,* Clint Cherry; Tel: 813-974-9078; Staff 8 (MLS 6, Non-MLS 2)
Founded 1971. Enrl 1,117, Fac 551, Highest Degree: Doctorate
Library Holdings: Bk Titles 29,863; Per Subs 1,373
Subject Interests: Med, Nursing, Pharm, Pub health
Automation Activity & Vendor Info: (Acquisitions) Ex Libris Group; (Cataloging) Ex Libris Group
Partic in Consortium of Southern Biomedical Libraries; National Network of Libraries of Medicine Southeastern Atlantic Region
Open Mon-Fri 7:30am-11pm, Sat 10-6, Sun Noon-11

C TAMPA CAMPUS LIBRARY*, 4101 USF Apple Dr, LIB122, 33620. (Mail add: 4202 E Fowler Ave, LIB122, 33620-5400). Tel: 813-974-2729. Circulation Tel: 813-974-1611. Interlibrary Loan Service Tel: 813-974-1627. FAX: 813-974-5153. TDD: 813-974-9874. Web Site: www.lib.usf.edu. *Dean,* William A Garrison; Tel: 813-974-1642, E-mail: wgarrison@usf.edu; *Dir, Acad Res,* Todd A Chavez; Tel: 813-974-7905, E-mail: tchavez@usf.edu; *Dir, Acad Serv,* Nancy A Cunningham; Tel: 813-974-0450, E-mail: nancy@usf.edu; *Dir, Admin Serv,* Tom Cetwinski; Tel: 813-974-4592, E-mail: tcetwinski@usf.edu; *Dir, Spec & Digital Coll, Fla Studies Ctr & Holocaust & Genocide Prog,* Dr Mark I Greenberg; Tel: 813-974-4141, E-mail: migreenberg@usf.edu; Staff 73.5 (MLS 37, Non-MLS 36.5)
Founded 1960. Enrl 47,321; Fac 2,349; Highest Degree: Doctorate
Jul 2010-Jun 2011 Income $10,905,473. Mats Exp $6,561,811, Books $1,079,724, Per/Ser (Incl. Access Fees) $3,595,300, Other Print Mats $247,561, Micro $45,917, AV Mat $69,105, Electronic Ref Mat (Incl. Access Fees) $1,513,459, Presv $10,745. Sal $4,088,866 (Prof $2,378,297)
Library Holdings: Audiobooks 16,472; CDs 16,339; DVDs 4,763; e-books 543,452; e-journals 80,112; Electronic Media & Resources 3,125; Microforms 2,894,423; Music Scores 16,717; Bk Vols 2,051,766; Per Subs 82,536; Videos 17,729
Special Collections: 19th Century American Literature (Dobkin Coll); 19th Century American Playscript Coll; 19th Century American Printed Ephemera Coll; 19th Century American Songbook Coll; American Almanac Coll; American Currency (Wollowick Coll); American Juvenile Series Book Coll; American Toybook Coll; Archives & Manuscripts Coll; Bartok Coll; Black Musical Heritage Coll; Cigar Art Coll; Cigar Label Progressive Proof Books (Kane-Greenberg Lithography Coll); Congressman Sam M Gibbons Papers; Dime Novel Coll; Dion Boucicault Theatre Coll; Early American Textbook Coll; Florida (Regional History Coll), bks, journals, maps, ms, photog, postcards; Florida Federal Writers Project Papers; Florida Sheet Music Coll; Floridiana (Hampton Dunn & Tony Pizzo Colls); George Alfred Henty Press Coll, Governor LeRoy Collins Papers, Haldeman-Julius Coll, Miles Hanley Papers; Mosher Press Coll; National Amateur Press Coll; Nations Bank Coll; Piers Anthony Papers; Rare Books Coll; Rare Map Coll, primarily North America, 1524-1900; Records of Tampa Ethnic Mutual Aid Societies; Robert W & Helen Saunders Papers; US Tobacco Museum Coll. Oral History; State Document Depository; US Document Depository
Automation Activity & Vendor Info: (Acquisitions) Ex Libris Group; (Cataloging) Ex Libris Group; (Circulation) Ex Libris Group; (Course Reserve) Blackboard Inc
Database Vendor: EBSCO Information Services, Elsevier, LexisNexis, ProQuest, Springer-Verlag, Thomson - Web of Science
Partic in Association of Southeastern Research Libraries; Center for Research Libraries; Florida Center for Library Automation; Lyrasis
Publications: Library Leads (Newsletter); Library Link (Newsletter)

C UNIVERSITY OF TAMPA*, Macdonald-Kelce Library, 401 W Kennedy Blvd, 33606-1490. SAN 303-2175. Tel: 813-253-6231. FAX: 813-258-7426. Web Site: utopia.ut.edu. *Dir,* Marlyn Pethe; E-mail: mpethe@ut.edu; *Tech Serv Librn,* Laura Rounds; E-mail: lrounds@ut.edu; *Syst Coordr,* Linda Rodriguez; E-mail: lrodriguez@ut.edu; *Coll Develop, Ref,* Art Bagley; E-mail: abagley@ut.edu; *Electronic Res, Ref,* Mickey Wells; E-mail: mwells@ut.edu; *Govt Doc, Ref,* Elizabeth Barron; E-mail: ebarron@ut.edu; *Info Literacy, Ref,* Melisandre Hilliker; E-mail: mhilliker@ut.edu; *Per, Ref,* Shannon Spencer; E-mail: sspencer@ut.edu; *Pub Serv, Ref,* Jeanne Vince; E-mail: jvince@ut.edu; Staff 21 (MLS 9, Non-MLS 12)
Founded 1931. Enrl 6,600; Fac 460; Highest Degree: Master
Library Holdings: AV Mats 1,600; Bk Titles 175,000; Bk Vols 275,000; Per Subs 50,500
Special Collections: Drama (Blanche Yurka Coll), letters, res mat, scrapbks; Florida Military Coll; John Wilkes Booth (Stanley Kimmel Coll),

bks, photog, res mat; Local History Coll; University Archives. US Document Depository
Subject Interests: Bus & mgt, Computer sci, Nursing
Automation Activity & Vendor Info: (Acquisitions) Ex Libris Group; (Cataloging) Ex Libris Group; (Circulation) Ex Libris Group; (Course Reserve) Ex Libris Group; (OPAC) Ex Libris Group; (Serials) Ex Libris Group
Wireless access
Publications: Bibliographies; faculty library handbook, library guide, fact sheet
Partic in Dialog Corp; Florida Library Information Network; Lyrasis; OCLC Online Computer Library Center, Inc; Tampa Bay Library Consortium, Inc
Open Mon-Thurs (Winter) 8am-Midnight, Fri 8-6, Sat 10-6, Sun Noon-Midnight; Mon-Thurs (Summer) 8am-11pm, Sat 10-6, Sun 1-9
Friends of the Library Group

S URS CORP LIBRARY*, 7650 W Courtney Campbell Causeway, 33607-1462. SAN 370-873X. Tel: 813-675-6764. FAX: 813-636-2496. Web Site: www.urscorp.com. *Librn,* Scott Smith; Staff 2 (MLS 1, Non-MLS 1)
Founded 1984
Library Holdings: Bk Titles 3,700; Per Subs 100
Subject Interests: Archit, Civil eng, Construction mgt, Environ sci, Planning, Structural eng
Open Mon-Fri 7:30-4:30
Restriction: Staff use only

TARPON SPRINGS

P TARPON SPRINGS PUBLIC LIBRARY*, 138 E Lemon St, 34689. SAN 303-2221. Tel: 727-943-4922. FAX: 727-943-4926. Web Site: tarponspringslibrary.org. *Dir,* Cari Rupkalvis; *Head, Adult Serv,* Salvatore Miranda; *Head, Tech Serv,* Barbara Aglieri; *Head, Youth Serv,* Joy Herrera; *Ref & ILL Librn,* Irene Marcus; *Circ,* Terrie Olson; Staff 21 (MLS 5, Non-MLS 16)
Founded 1916
Library Holdings: AV Mats 9,664; Bks on Deafness & Sign Lang 60; e-books 3,600; Large Print Bks 5,000; Bk Titles 77,609; Bk Vols 95,982; Per Subs 270; Spec Interest Per Sub 50; Talking Bks 2,009
Subject Interests: Bus, Fla, Greek
Automation Activity & Vendor Info: (Circulation) Innovative Interfaces, Inc; (ILL) OCLC; (OPAC) Innovative Interfaces, Inc; (Serials) Innovative Interfaces, Inc
Database Vendor: EBSCOhost, Gale Cengage Learning, OCLC FirstSearch, ProQuest
Wireless access
Publications: Newsletter
Mem of Pinellas Public Libr Coop
Partic in Tampa Bay Library Consortium, Inc
Open Mon-Wed 10-9, Thurs & Fri 10-6, Sat 10-5
Friends of the Library Group

TAVARES

P CITY OF TAVARES PUBLIC LIBRARY*, 314 N New Hampshire Ave, 32778. SAN 323-651X. Tel: 352-742-6204. Reference Tel: 352-742-6203. FAX: 352-742-6472. Web Site: www.tavares.org. *Dir,* Rosa Rosario; E-mail: rrosario@tavares.org; Staff 11 (MLS 2, Non-MLS 9)
Founded 1959. Pop 10,301; Circ 87,428
Library Holdings: AV Mats 3,756; Bks on Deafness & Sign Lang 28; High Interest/Low Vocabulary Bk Vols 168; Large Print Bks 2,365; Bk Titles 38,000; Bk Vols 44,100; Per Subs 153; Talking Bks 997
Special Collections: Dorothy Young Johnson Dance & Theater Coll; Florida Materials; Large Print Coll
Subject Interests: Dance
Database Vendor: SirsiDynix
Wireless access
Function: Ref serv available
Publications: @ the Library (Newsletter)
Mem of Lake County Library System
Partic in Tampa Bay Library Consortium, Inc
Open Mon & Thurs 10-8, Tues, Wed & Fri 10-6, Sat 10-5
Friends of the Library Group

S LAKE COUNTY HISTORICAL SOCIETY LIBRARY*, 317 W Main St, 32778. (Mail add: PO Box 7800, 32778-7800), SAN 325-1845. Tel: 352-343-9890. FAX: 352-343-9814.
Founded 1954
Library Holdings: Bk Titles 600
Special Collections: Poll Tax Books, 1887-1937
Subject Interests: Maps, Rare bks
Function: Res libr
Publications: Lake County Florida: A Pictorial History
Open Mon-Thurs 9-4

P LAKE COUNTY LIBRARY SYSTEM*, 2401 Woodlea Rd, 32778. (Mail add: PO Box 7800, 32778-7800), SAN 370-4653. Tel: 352-253-6180. Interlibrary Loan Service Tel: 352-253-6155. FAX: 352-253-6184. Web Site: www.mylakelibrary.org. *Libr Serv Mgr,* Tom Merchant; Tel: 352-253-6168, E-mail: tmerchant@lakeline.lib.fl.us; *Asst Libr Serv Mgr,* Charlene Smith; Tel: 352-253-6160, E-mail: cpsmith@lakeline.lib.fl.us; *Asst Libr Serv Mgr/Regional Br Mgr,* Boyd Bruce; Tel: 352-536-2275, E-mail: jbruce@lakeline.lib.fl.us; *Literacy Coordr,* Erika Greene; Tel: 352-253-6183, E-mail: egreene@lakeline.lib.fl.us; *Youth Serv Coordr,* Linda Goff; Tel: 352-253-6169, E-mail: lgoff@lakeline.lib.fl.us; *Tech Serv,* Donna Gray-Williams; Tel: 352-253-6161, E-mail: dgraywms@lakeline.lib.fl.us; Staff 47.5 (MLS 29.5, Non-MLS 18)
Founded 1982. Pop 293,478; Circ 2,113,840
Oct 2008-Sept 2009 Income (Main Library and Branch(s)) $8,123,236, State $239,321, City $2,798,851, Federal $8,983, County $4,936,200, Other $139,881. Mats Exp $890,063. Sal $5,347,451
Library Holdings: Audiobooks 33,399; DVDs 64,117; Bk Vols 547,991; Per Subs 1,549
Special Collections: Florida Environment Coll
Subject Interests: Genealogy
Automation Activity & Vendor Info: (Acquisitions) SirsiDynix; (Cataloging) SirsiDynix; (Circulation) SirsiDynix; (OPAC) SirsiDynix
Database Vendor: EBSCOhost, Gale Cengage Learning, Newsbank, OCLC FirstSearch, ProQuest, ReferenceUSA, Westlaw
Wireless access
Member Libraries: City of Tavares Public Library; Fruitland Park Library; Helen Lehmann Memorial Library; Lady Lake Public Library; Leesburg Public Library; Marianne Beck Memorial Library; Umatilla Public Library; W T Bland Public Library
Partic in OCLC Online Computer Library Center, Inc
Friends of the Library Group
Branches: 6
ASTOR COUNTY LIBRARY, 54905 Alco Rd, Astor, 32102. Tel: 352-759-9913. FAX: 352-759-9923. *Br Mgr,* Pam Goodson; E-mail: pgoodson@lakeline.lib.fl.us
Founded 2002
Open Mon & Wed 9-5, Tues & Thurs 9-8, Sat 9-1
Friends of the Library Group
MARION BAYSINGER MEMORIAL COUNTY LIBRARY, 756 W Broad St, Groveland, 34736, SAN 370-4645. Tel: 352-429-5840. FAX: 352-429-9924. *Br Mgr,* Katherine Spurgeon; E-mail: kspurgeo@lakeline.lib.fl.us
Open Mon & Wed 10-6, Tues & Thurs 10-8, Fri & Sat 10-3
Friends of the Library Group
CAGAN CROSSINGS COMMUNITY LIBRARY, 16729 Cagan Oaks, Clermont, 34714. Tel: 352-243-1840. Toll Free Tel: 877-292-7930. FAX: 352-243-3230. *Regional Br Mgr,* Jane Martin; E-mail: jmartin@lakeline.lib.fl.us
Founded 2000
Open Mon-Thurs 10-7:30, Fri & Sat 10-4
Friends of the Library Group
COOPER MEMORIAL LIBRARY, 2525 Oakley Seaver Dr, Clermont, 34711, SAN 302-8887. Tel: 352-536-2275. FAX: 352-536-2259. *Regional Br Mgr,* Boyd Bruce; *Ref Librn,* Dennis Smolarek; *Youth Serv Librn,* Amy Stultz; *Circ Supvr,* Gary Earl; Tel: 352-536-2262, E-mail: gearl@lakeline.lib.fl.us; Staff 4 (MLS 3, Non-MLS 1)
Founded 1914
Special Collections: Oral History; US Document Depository
Subject Interests: Fla, Genealogy, Local hist
Automation Activity & Vendor Info: (Cataloging) SirsiDynix; (Circulation) SirsiDynix; (OPAC) SirsiDynix
Open Mon-Thurs 9-7, Fri & Sat 9-1
Friends of the Library Group
EAST LAKE COUNTY LIBRARY, 31340 County Rd 437 South, Sorrento, 32776. Tel: 352-383-9980. Toll Free Tel: 866-292-7659. FAX: 352-383-9982. *Br Mgr,* George Dore; E-mail: gdore@lakeline.lib.fl.us
Founded 2000
Open Mon & Tues 10-8, Wed & Thurs 10-6, Fri & Sat 10-3
Friends of the Library Group
PAISLEY COUNTY LIBRARY, 24954 County Rd 42, Paisley, 32767. Tel: 352-669-1001. Toll Free Tel: 866-292-0891. FAX: 352-669-2180. *Br Mgr,* Ron Moore; E-mail: rmoore@lakeline.lib.fl.us
Founded 2001
Open Mon & Wed 9:30-6, Tues & Thurs 9:30-8, Sat 10-2
Friends of the Library Group

TEMPLE TERRACE

C FLORIDA COLLEGE*, Chatlos Library, 119 N Glen Arven Ave, 33617-5578. SAN 303-223X. Tel: 813-988-5131, Ext 210. Interlibrary Loan Service Tel: 813-988-5131, Ext 215. Web Site: www.floridacollege.edu/library. *Dir of Libr,* Wanda D Dickey; Tel: 813-988-5131, Ext 211, E-mail: dickeyw@floridacollege.edu; *Archives, Ser Librn,* Brooke Ward; Tel: 813-988-5131, Ext 212, E-mail:

wardb@floridacolleg.edu; *Cataloger,* Dr James Hodges; E-mail: hodgesj@floridacollege.edu; *ILL,* Jennifer Kearney; Staff 3 (MLS 3)
Founded 1946. Enrl 500; Fac 40; Highest Degree: Bachelor
Library Holdings: CDs 696; e-books 40,000; Bk Titles 122,482; Per Subs 290; Videos 979
Subject Interests: Hist, Music, Relig
Automation Activity & Vendor Info: (Cataloging) OCLC CatExpress; (Circulation) Follett Software; (ILL) OCLC FirstSearch; (OPAC) Follett Software
Database Vendor: Alexander Street Press, EBSCOhost, Newsbank, OCLC FirstSearch, OCLC WorldShare Interlibrary Loan, Wilson - Wilson Web
Wireless access
Partic in Christian Col Libr; Independent Cols & Univs of Fla; Tampa Bay Library Consortium, Inc

P TEMPLE TERRACE PUBLIC LIBRARY, 202 Bullard Pkwy, 33617-5512. SAN 303-2248. Tel: 813-506-6770. Web Site: www.templeterrace.com/library. *Libr Dir,* Armand Ternak; Tel: 813-506-6772, E-mail: aternak@templeterrace.com; Staff 4 (MLS 4)
Founded 1960. Pop 81,570; Circ 482,510
Library Holdings: Bk Titles 82,758; Bk Vols 94,181; Per Subs 90
Wireless access
Partic in Hillsborough County Public Library Cooperative; Tampa Bay Library Consortium, Inc
Open Mon & Wed 10-8, Tues & Thurs 12-8, Fri & Sat 9-5
Friends of the Library Group

THE VILLAGES

P VILLAGES PUBLIC LIBRARY AT BELVEDERE*, 325 Belvedere Blvd, 32162. Tel: 352-689-4690. FAX: 352-689-4691. *Libr Serv Supvr,* Marsha Cournoyer
Library Holdings: Bk Vols 45,000
Automation Activity & Vendor Info: (Cataloging) SirsiDynix; (Circulation) SirsiDynix; (OPAC) SirsiDynix
Mem of Sumter County Library System
Open Mon, Wed & Fri 9-6, Tues & Thurs 9-8, Sat 9-2
Friends of the Library Group

TITUSVILLE

J EASTERN FLORIDA STATE COLLEGE*, Titusville Campus Library, (Formerly Brevard Community College), Dr Frank Elbert Williams Learning Resource Ctr, 1311 N US 1, 32796-2192. SAN 303-2256. Tel: 321-433-5066. Toll Free Tel: 888-747-2802, Ext 5066. FAX: 321-433-5114. Web Site: www.brevardcc.edu/library. *Librn,* Joanne Connell; Staff 2 (MLS 2)
Founded 1973. Enrl 2,000; Fac 18
Library Holdings: Bk Vols 22,000; Per Subs 200
Automation Activity & Vendor Info: (Acquisitions) Ex Libris Group; (Cataloging) Ex Libris Group; (Circulation) Ex Libris Group; (Course Reserve) Ex Libris Group; (ILL) Ex Libris Group; (OPAC) Ex Libris Group; (Serials) Ex Libris Group
Database Vendor: ABC-CLIO, Alexander Street Press, ARTstor, CQ Press, EBSCOhost, Facts on File, Gale Cengage Learning, Greenwood Publishing Group, H W Wilson, Hoovers, JSTOR, Lexi-Comp, Micromedex, Newsbank, OCLC, OCLC ArticleFirst, OCLC CAMIO, OCLC FirstSearch, OCLC WorldShare Interlibrary Loan, Oxford Online, ProQuest, Safari Books Online, Springshare, LLC, Westlaw, Wilson - Wilson Web
Wireless access
Partic in LINCC
Open Mon-Thurs 8-8, Fri 9-1

P TITUSVILLE PUBLIC LIBRARY, 2121 S Hopkins Ave, 32780. SAN 303-2272. Tel: 321-264-5026. FAX: 321-264-5030. Web Site: www.brev.org. *Dir,* Mary Toupin; E-mail: mtoupin@brev.org; *Circ,* Sandy Kump; E-mail: skump@brev.org; *Youth Serv,* Karen Dreschel; E-mail: kdreschel@brev.org; Staff 15.9 (MLS 3, Non-MLS 12.9)
Founded 1906. Pop 45,000; Circ 433,630
Library Holdings: Audiobooks 5,284; Bk Vols 94,990; Per Subs 69
Subject Interests: Genealogy
Automation Activity & Vendor Info: (Cataloging) TLC (The Library Corporation); (Circulation) TLC (The Library Corporation); (OPAC) TLC (The Library Corporation)
Wireless access
Function: Bk club(s), Bks on cassette, Bks on CD, Copy machines, Free DVD rentals, Handicapped accessible, Music CDs, Notary serv, OverDrive digital audio bks, Prog for children & young adult, Pub access computers, Ref serv available, Summer reading prog, Tax forms, Telephone ref
Mem of Brevard County Library System
Special Services for the Deaf - TTY equip
Open Mon & Tues 9-8, Wed-Sat 9-5, Sun 1-5
Friends of the Library Group

TRENTON

P GILCHRIST COUNTY PUBLIC LIBRARY*, 105 NE 11th Ave, 32693-3803. Tel: 352-463-3176. FAX: 352-463-3164. Web Site: www.neflin.org/gilchristcneflin.org. *Mgr,* Wilma Mattucci
Pop 17,000
Library Holdings: Bk Vols 20,000; Per Subs 43
Automation Activity & Vendor Info: (Circulation) SirsiDynix
Partic in Three Rivers Regional Library Service System
Open Mon 9-7, Tues-Fri 9-6
Friends of the Library Group

TRINITY

C TRINITY COLLEGE*, Raymond H Center Library, 2430 Welbilt Blvd, 34655. Tel: 727-376-6911. FAX: 727-376-0781. Web Site: www.trinitycollege.edu. *Dir,* Janet Kuehne; Staff 1 (MLS 1)
Founded 1932. Enrl 200; Fac 6; Highest Degree: Bachelor
Library Holdings: Bk Vols 45,000; Per Subs 100
Special Collections: Theology Books of the 1890s (E C Bragg Coll)
Function: Handicapped accessible, ILL available, Online searches, Orientations, Photocopying/Printing, VHS videos, Wheelchair accessible
Partic in Tampa Bay Library Consortium, Inc
Open Mon-Thurs 7am-10pm, Fri 7-5, Sat 10-5
Restriction: Open to students, fac & staff, Use of others with permission of librn
Friends of the Library Group

TYNDALL AFB

UNITED STATES AIR FORCE

A AIR FORCE RESEARCH LAB, TYNDALL RESEARCH SITE TECHNICAL INFORMATION CENTER, 139 Barnes Dr, Ste 2, 32403-5323, SAN 324-5845. Tel: 850-283-6285. FAX: 850-283-6500. E-mail: tic@tyndall.af.mil. *Chief Librn,* Amber Collins; E-mail: amber.collins@tyndall.af.mil; *Ref Librn,* Mariana Grey; E-mail: mariana.grey.ctr@tyndall.af.mil; Staff 2 (MLS 2)
Founded 1968
Special Collections: Air Base Survivability; Air-Bird Strikes; Aircraft Fire Research Studies; Chemical/Biological Decontamination, especially Military Equipment; Corrosion Control of Military Facilities; Hazardous Materials; Rapid Runway Repair
Subject Interests: Chem eng, Civil eng, Energy, Mat sci, Structural eng
Automation Activity & Vendor Info: (Acquisitions) Mandarin Library Automation; (Cataloging) Mandarin Library Automation; (Circulation) Mandarin Library Automation
Partic in Air Force Res Lab Virtual Libr Team; Fedlink; OCLC Online Computer Library Center, Inc; Panhandle Library Access Network
Publications: Early Alert Services; Periodicals Listing; Tic Talk
Open Mon-Thurs 8-4, Fri 8-3

A TYNDALL AIR FORCE BASE LIBRARY FL4819*, 325 SVS/SVMG/45, 640 Suwanee Rd, Bldg 916, 32403-5531, SAN 338-1994. Tel: 850-283-4287. FAX: 850-283-4994. *Librn,* Position Currently Open
Founded 1982
Oct 2010-Sept 2011 Income $80,000
Library Holdings: Bk Vols 27,000; Per Subs 300
Subject Interests: Aeronaut, Mil hist
Automation Activity & Vendor Info: (Cataloging) SirsiDynix; (Circulation) SirsiDynix; (OPAC) SirsiDynix
Partic in OCLC Online Computer Library Center, Inc; Panhandle Library Access Network
Publications: Substance (Monthly newsletter)
Restriction: Authorized patrons, Authorized personnel only

UMATILLA

P UMATILLA PUBLIC LIBRARY*, 412 Hatfield Dr, 32784-8913. SAN 303-2280. Tel: 352-669-3284. FAX: 352-669-2927. TDD: 352-669-2927. E-mail: the_librarian@umatillalibrary.com. Web Site: umatillalibrary.com. *Dir,* Laurel Gainer; E-mail: lgainer@lakeline.lib.fl.us; *Ch,* Jeanine Ryan; *Circ Supvr,* Sandi Jude
Founded 1917. Circ 67,738
Library Holdings: Bk Vols 32,000; Per Subs 86
Automation Activity & Vendor Info: (Cataloging) Horizon; (Circulation) Horizon
Mem of Lake County Library System
Open Mon 9-8, Tues-Fri 9-5, Sat 9:30-12:30
Friends of the Library Group

VALPARAISO

P VALPARAISO COMMUNITY LIBRARY*, 459 Valparaiso Pkwy, 32580. SAN 303-2299. Tel: 850-729-5406. FAX: 850-729-1120. Web Site: www.vcl.valp.org. *Dir,* David L Weatherford; E-mail: dweatherford@valp.org; *Admin Dir,* Shipley B Alvin; E-mail: tshipley@valp.org; *Cat,* Bonnie Walker-Lowitz; E-mail: blowitz@valp.org;

Circ, Patricia Camizzi; E-mail: pcamizzi@valp.org; *Tech Serv,* Michael L O'Neal; E-mail: moneal@valp.org. Subject Specialists: *Hist,* David L Weatherford; Staff 6 (MLS 2, Non-MLS 4)
Founded 1973. Pop 178,000
Library Holdings: Bk Titles 40,000; Per Subs 50
Subject Interests: Genealogy
Automation Activity & Vendor Info: (Circulation) SirsiDynix
Database Vendor: OCLC FirstSearch, SirsiDynix
Partic in Okaloosa County Public Library Cooperative
Open Mon-Wed 9-8, Thurs 9-6, Fri 9-5
Friends of the Library Group

VENICE

P FRANCES T BOURNE JACARANDA PUBLIC LIBRARY, 4143 Woodmere Park Blvd, 34293. SAN 376-267X. Tel: 941-861-1260. Circulation Tel: 941-861-1280. Reference Tel: 941-861-1270. FAX: 941-486-2725. Web Site: www.sclibs.net. *Libr Mgr,* Taylor Andrea; Tel: 941-861-1277, E-mail: jtaylor@scgov.net; *Asst Mgr,* Mary Louise Fischer; Tel: 941-861-1272, E-mail: mfischer@scgov.net; Staff 12 (MLS 6, Non-MLS 6)
Founded 1994. Pop 35,000; Circ 360,000
Library Holdings: Bk Titles 55,100; Per Subs 188
Special Collections: College & Career Coll; Florida Coll; Reader Development Coll
Automation Activity & Vendor Info: (Acquisitions) Innovative Interfaces, Inc; (Cataloging) Innovative Interfaces, Inc; (Circulation) Innovative Interfaces, Inc; (Course Reserve) Innovative Interfaces, Inc; (ILL) Innovative Interfaces, Inc; (Media Booking) Innovative Interfaces, Inc; (OPAC) Innovative Interfaces, Inc; (Serials) Innovative Interfaces, Inc
Wireless access
Mem of Sarasota County Library System
Partic in Tampa Bay Library Consortium, Inc
Special Services for the Deaf - Assistive tech; Bks on deafness & sign lang; Closed caption videos
Special Services for the Blind - Assistive/Adapted tech devices, equip & products; Children's Braille; Closed circuit TV; Descriptive video serv (DVS); Large print bks; Lending of low vision aids; Magnifiers; Talking bks
Open Mon, Fri & Sat 10-5, Tues-Thurs 10-8, Sun 1-5
Friends of the Library Group

P VENICE PUBLIC LIBRARY*, 300 S Nokomis Ave, 34285-2416. SAN 303-2302. Tel: 941-861-1330. Circulation Tel: 941-861-1331. Reference Tel: 941-861-1347. FAX: 941-486-2345. Web Site: www.sclibs.net. *Libr Mgr,* Ann Hall; Tel: 941-861-1350, E-mail: ahall@scgov.net; *Asst Libr Mgr,* Roland Marcotte; *Ref Serv,* Pat Maurer; *Ref Serv,* Melanie Odom; *Youth Serv,* Joanne Lize; *Libr Asst,* Diane McCauley. Subject Specialists: *Genealogy,* Melanie Odom; Staff 13 (MLS 5, Non-MLS 8)
Founded 1964. Pop 46,441; Circ 465,486
Library Holdings: Bk Vols 110,000; Per Subs 230
Automation Activity & Vendor Info: (Acquisitions) Innovative Interfaces, Inc; (Cataloging) Innovative Interfaces, Inc; (Circulation) Innovative Interfaces, Inc
Wireless access
Publications: Bookbits; FOL Newsletter (Quarterly)
Mem of Sarasota County Library System
Open Mon, Tues & Thurs 10-8, Wed, Fri & Sat 10-5
Friends of the Library Group

VENUS

S ARCHBOLD BIOLOGICAL STATION LIBRARY*, 123 Main Dr, 33960. (Mail add: PO Box 2057, Lake Placid, 33862-2057), SAN 303-0024. Tel: 863-465-2571. FAX: 863-699-1927. Web Site: www.archbold-station.org. *Librn,* Fred E Lohrer; Staff 1 (Non-MLS 1)
Founded 1941
Library Holdings: Bk Vols 7,200; Per Subs 200
Special Collections: Biology of North American Land Tortoise-Gopherus, cataloged reprints; Florida Department of Geology Publications; Florida Natural History
Subject Interests: Agro-ecology, Animal behavior, Conserv biol, Ecology, Entomology, Evolution, Herpetology, Ichthyology, Mammalogy, Ornithology
Automation Activity & Vendor Info: (Cataloging) Innovative Interfaces, Inc
Wireless access
Restriction: Non-circulating, Open by appt only

VERO BEACH

P INDIAN RIVER COUNTY LIBRARY SYSTEM*, 1600 21st St, 32960. SAN 303-2329. Tel: 772-770-5060. FAX: 772-770-5066. E-mail: refdesk@irclibrary.org. Web Site: www.irclibrary.org. *Admin Dir,* Mary D Snyder; *Asst Dir,* Craig Tarry. Subject Specialists: *English, Info sci,* Mary D Snyder; *Art, Psychol,* Craig Tarry; Staff 66.5 (MLS 6, Non-MLS 60.5)
Founded 1915. Pop 126,000; Circ 1,170,561
Library Holdings: AV Mats 49,362; e-books 24,812; Electronic Media & Resources 70; Large Print Bks 40,000; Bk Titles 330,459; Bk Vols 443,277; Per Subs 1,912
Special Collections: Florida Authors; Vero Beach Authors
Subject Interests: Bus, Civil War, Genealogy, Health, Lit, State hist
Automation Activity & Vendor Info: (Acquisitions) Innovative Interfaces, Inc; (Cataloging) Innovative Interfaces, Inc; (Circulation) Innovative Interfaces, Inc; (ILL) OCLC Online; (OPAC) Innovative Interfaces, Inc; (Serials) Innovative Interfaces, Inc
Database Vendor: Baker & Taylor, Bowker, EBSCOhost, Facts on File, Gale Cengage Learning, Newsbank, OCLC FirstSearch, ProQuest, Wilson - Wilson Web
Function: Archival coll
Member Libraries: Indian River County Library System
Partic in Cent Fla Libr Consortium
Special Services for the Deaf - TDD equip
Special Services for the Blind - Bks on cassette
Open Mon-Thurs 10-8, Tues, Wed & Fri 10-5, Sat 10-4, Sun 1-5
Friends of the Library Group
Branches: 2
GIFFORD BRANCH, 4875 43rd Ave, 32967. Tel: 772-794-1005. FAX: 772-569-5563.
Open Mon-Fri 1-5
NORTH INDIAN RIVER COUNTY LIBRARY, 1001 Sebastian Blvd, CR 512, Sebastian, 32958, SAN 370-3584. Tel: 772-589-1355. FAX: 772-388-3697. TDD: 772-581-7654. Web Site: www.sebastianlibrary.com. *Dir,* Mary Synder; E-mail: msynder@irclibrary.org; *YA Librn,* Amanda Atwater; E-mail: aatwater@irclibrary.org; *Ch Serv,* Shirley Wolstenholme; E-mail: swolstenholme@irclibrary.org; *Circ,* Sandra Bachmann; E-mail: sbachmann@irclibrary.org; *Computer Serv,* Daniel Clark; E-mail: daniel@sebastianlibrary.com; *Ref,* Kathleen Bowman; E-mail: kbowman@irclibrary.org; *Tech Serv,* Anne Moutenot; E-mail: amoutenot@irclibrary.org; Staff 6 (MLS 1, Non-MLS 5)
Founded 1983. Pop 47,222; Circ 369,650
Oct 2010-Sept 2011 Income $968,687, County $928,877, Locally Generated Income $14,810, Other $25,000. Mats Exp $74,493, Books $52,512, Per/Ser (Incl. Access Fees) $6,818, AV Mat $12,308, Electronic Ref Mat (Incl. Access Fees) $2,855. Sal $591,390
Library Holdings: Audiobooks 4,080; AV Mats 18,211; Braille Volumes 83; CDs 2,485; DVDs 6,107; Large Print Bks 12,071; Bk Vols 117,236; Per Subs 149; Videos 5,510
Special Collections: Florida Coll
Automation Activity & Vendor Info: (Cataloging) Innovative Interfaces, Inc; (Circulation) Innovative Interfaces, Inc; (OPAC) Innovative Interfaces, Inc
Database Vendor: Baker & Taylor, Bowker, EBSCO Information Services, Facts on File, Gale Cengage Learning, Grolier Online, H W Wilson, infoUSA, Newsbank, OCLC WorldShare Interlibrary Loan, ProQuest, PubMed, ReferenceUSA, Standard & Poor's, ValueLine, Wilson - Wilson Web
Function: Adult bk club, Art exhibits, Audio & video playback equip for onsite use, Bi-weekly Writer's Group, Bks on cassette, Bks on CD, Chess club, Children's prog, Computer training, Computers for patron use, Copy machines, Electronic databases & coll, Exhibits, Fax serv, Free DVD rentals, Homebound delivery serv, ILL available, Music CDs, Notary serv, Online cat, Preschool outreach, Prog for adults, Prog for children & young adult, Pub access computers, Ref serv in person, Scanner, Story hour, Summer reading prog, Tax forms, VHS videos, Wheelchair accessible
Partic in Tampa Bay Library Consortium, Inc
Mem of Indian River County Library System
Special Services for the Deaf - TDD equip
Open Mon-Wed 10-8, Thurs & Fri 10-5, Sat 10-4
Friends of the Library Group

M INDIAN RIVER MEDICAL CENTER*, J C Robertson Memorial Library, 1000 36th St, 32960. SAN 326-2103. Tel: 772-567-4311, Ext 5039. FAX: 772-563-4593. Web Site: www.irmc.com.
Founded 1967
Library Holdings: Bk Titles 816; Per Subs 75
Restriction: Open to staff, patients & family mem

G UNIVERSITY OF FLORIDA*, Florida Medical Entomology Laboratory Library, 200 Ninth St SE, 32962. SAN 303-2310. Tel: 772-778-7200. FAX: 772-778-7205. Web Site: www.fmel.ifas.ufl.edu. *Librn,* Yvonne Reese
Library Holdings: Bk Titles 5,600; Per Subs 105
Subject Interests: Biochem, Biol, Ecology, Entomology, Ornithology, Virology
Restriction: Not open to pub

VIERA

L A MAX BREWER MEMORIAL LAW LIBRARY, Brevard County Law Library, Harry T & Harriette V Moore Justice Ctr, 2825 Judge Fran Jamieson Way, 32940. SAN 324-7627. Tel: 321-617-7295. FAX: 321-617-7303. *Libr Dir,* Annette Melnicove; *Law Librn,* Teresa Cassella; *Law Librn,* Teri Elgin-Smith; Staff 3 (MLS 3)
Founded 1955
Library Holdings: Bk Vols 32,000; Per Subs 20
Automation Activity & Vendor Info: (Cataloging) OCLC
Wireless access
Open Mon-Fri 8-5
Restriction: Non-circulating to the pub

WAUCHULA

P HARDEE COUNTY PUBLIC LIBRARY*, 315 N Sixth Ave, Ste 114, 33873. SAN 303-2337. Tel: 863-773-6438. FAX: 863-767-1091. Web Site: myhlc.org/hardee-county. *Dir,* Diane C Hunt
Circ 15,000
Library Holdings: Bk Titles 45,000; Per Subs 20
Open Mon 9-7, Tues-Fri 9-5:30, Sat 9-12
Friends of the Library Group

WEBSTER

P E C ROWELL PUBLIC LIBRARY*, 85 E Central Ave, 33597-4701. (Mail add: PO Box 1044, 33597-1044). Tel: 352-568-1600. FAX: 352-568-1399. *Librn,* Judy Lee
Library Holdings: Bk Titles 15,000; Bk Vols 17,000; Per Subs 40
Automation Activity & Vendor Info: (Cataloging) SirsiDynix; (Circulation) SirsiDynix
Mem of Sumter County Library System
Open Mon-Fri 9-4:30, Sat 10-12

WELAKA

P WOMEN'S CLUB OF WELAKA LIBRARY*, Hwy 309, 32193. (Mail add: PO Box 154, 32193-0154), SAN 320-4723. Tel: 386-467-9706. *Librn,* Wynn Zarka
Founded 1960. Pop 1,000; Circ 2,100
Library Holdings: Bk Vols 3,000
Subject Interests: Fla
Open Mon-Fri 9-5

WEST MELBOURNE

P WEST MELBOURNE PUBLIC LIBRARY*, 2755 Wingate Blvd, 32904. Tel: 321-952-4508. FAX: 321-952-4510. Web Site: www.brev.org. *Dir,* Marian Hallett Griffin; E-mail: MGriffin@brev.org; *Adult Serv,* Vicki Williams; *Youth Serv,* Wendy Stevenson; Staff 16 (MLS 2, Non-MLS 14)
Founded 1970. Pop 10,000; Circ 140,000
Library Holdings: Bk Vols 68,000; Per Subs 98
Automation Activity & Vendor Info: (Circulation) CARL.Solution (TLC); (OPAC) CARL.Solution (TLC); (Serials) EBSCO Online
Database Vendor: EBSCOhost, OCLC FirstSearch
Wireless access
Mem of Brevard County Library System
Partic in SEFLIN - Southeast Florida Library Information Network, Inc
Open Mon & Wed 12-8, Tues, Thurs, Fri & Sat 9-5
Friends of the Library Group

WEST PALM BEACH

M GOOD SAMARITAN MEDICAL CENTER, Richard S Beinecke Medical Library, 1309 N Flagler Dr, 33401. SAN 303-2361. Tel: 561-650-6315. FAX: 561-671-7428. *Mgr,* Anjana Roy; E-mail: anjana.roy@tenethealth.com; Staff 1 (MLS 1)
Founded 1967
Jan 2014-Dec 2014 Income $65,000. Mats Exp $65,000, Books $15,000, Electronic Ref Mat (Incl. Access Fees) $50,000
Library Holdings: e-books 100; Bk Titles 3,000; Bk Vols 4,000; Per Subs 225
Special Collections: Medicine (Rare Book Coll)
Subject Interests: Hospital admin, Med, Nursing, Surgery
Automation Activity & Vendor Info: (Serials) EBSCO Online
Database Vendor: EBSCOhost, MD Consult
Wireless access
Function: Computers for patron use, Copy machines, Doc delivery serv, e-mail serv, Electronic databases & coll, Fax serv, Health sci info serv, ILL available, Mail & tel request accepted, Online searches, Photocopying/Printing, Ref serv available
Partic in Docline; Miami Health Sciences Library Consortium; North Atlantic Health Sciences Libraries, Inc; SE-Atlantic Regional Med Libr Servs
Restriction: Hospital employees & physicians only, Non-circulating, Not open to pub

S HISTORICAL SOCIETY OF PALM BEACH COUNTY, 300 N Dixie Hwy, 33401. (Mail add: PO Box 4364, 33402-4364), SAN 303-1152. Tel: 561-832-4164. Reference Tel: 561-832-4164, Ext 303. FAX: 561-832-7965. E-mail: archive@historicalsocietypbc.org. *Chief Curator,* Debi Murray; Tel: 561-832-4164, Ext 105, E-mail: dmurray@historicalsocietypbc.org. Subject Specialists: *Fla hist,* Debi Murray; Staff 3 (Non-MLS 3)
Founded 1937
Library Holdings: Bk Vols 4,000
Special Collections: Addison Mizner Coll, architectural drawings, house photog; Boca News Photo Coll; Gustav Maass Coll, architectural drawings; Maurice Fatio, Trainor & Fatio Coll, architectural drawings, house photos; Miami Herald Palm Beach Bureau Photo Coll, 1970-1980; Pioneer Manuscripts; Sam R Quincey Coll, 1945-mid 1970, photos. Oral History
Subject Interests: Hist of Fla
Publications: Guide to the Archives (Archives guide); Palm Beach Life Index (Index to periodicals); The Newsletter; Tustenegee (Online only)
Restriction: Open to pub for ref only

P MANDEL PUBLIC LIBRARY OF WEST PALM BEACH, 411 Clematis St, 33401. SAN 303-2469. Tel: 561-868-7700. Information Services Tel: 561-868-7701. FAX: 561-868-7706. Web Site: www.mycitylibrary.org. *Dir,* Christopher Murray; Tel: 561-868-7717, E-mail: murrayc@mycitylibrary.org; *Asst Dir,* Lisa Hathaway; Tel: 561-868-7787, E-mail: hathawayl@mycitylibrary.org; *Pub Serv Mgr,* Marsha Warfield; Tel: 561-868-7719, E-mail: warfieldm@mycitylibrary.org; *Tech Serv Mgr,* Barbara J Storch; Tel: 561-868-7721, E-mail: storchb@mycitylibrary.org; *Youth Serv Mgr,* Jennifer McQuown; Tel: 561-868-7722, E-mail: mcquownj@mycitylibrary.org; *Supvr, Circ,* Tamara McKenna; Tel: 561-868-7767, E-mail: mckennat@mycitylibrary.org; *Supvr, Coll Develop,* Tina Maura; Tel: 561-868-7765, E-mail: maurat@mycitylibrary.org; *Tech Supvr,* Janice Collins; Tel: 561-868-7798, E-mail: collinsj@mycitylibrary.org; Staff 20.5 (MLS 20.5)
Founded 1894. Pop 99,919; Circ 862,956
Oct 2012-Sept 2013 Income $4,576,764, State $113,172, City $3,812,056, Locally Generated Income $651,536. Mats Exp $398,520, Books $202,887, Per/Ser (Incl. Access Fees) $14,406, AV Mat $127,020, Electronic Ref Mat (Incl. Access Fees) $54,207. Sal $2,570,394
Library Holdings: Audiobooks 6,239; AV Mats 60,441; CDs 17,951; DVDs 42,490; e-books 2,110; Electronic Media & Resources 51; Large Print Bks 3,374; Bk Vols 162,513; Per Subs 318
Special Collections: Florida Coll
Automation Activity & Vendor Info: (Acquisitions) Innovative Interfaces, Inc - Millenium; (Cataloging) Innovative Interfaces, Inc - Millenium; (Circulation) Innovative Interfaces, Inc - Millenium; (ILL) Innovative Interfaces, Inc - Millenium; (OPAC) Innovative Interfaces, Inc - Millenium; (Serials) Innovative Interfaces, Inc - Millenium
Database Vendor: Baker & Taylor, Gale Cengage Learning
Wireless access
Function: Bks on CD, Computers for patron use, e-mail & chat, Electronic databases & coll, Exhibits, Free DVD rentals, Handicapped accessible, Homework prog, ILL available, Life-long learning prog for all ages, Magazines, Magnifiers for reading, Microfiche/film & reading machines, Movies, Music CDs, Online cat, Online ref, Online searches, Outside serv via phone, mail, e-mail & web, Photocopying/Printing, Preschool outreach, Preschool reading prog, Prog for adults, Prog for children & young adult, Pub access computers, Ref & res, Ref serv available, Ref serv in person, Scanner, Spanish lang bks, Story hour, Study rm, Summer reading prog, Tax forms, Teen prog, Telephone ref, Visual arts prog, Web-catalog, Wheelchair accessible, Writing prog
Open Mon-Thurs 9:30-8:30, Fri & Sat 9:30-5, Sun 1-5
Friends of the Library Group

C NORTHWOOD UNIVERSITY*, Dr & Mrs Peter C Cook Library, 2600 N Military Trail, 33409-2911. SAN 329-5648. Tel: 561-478-5537. Circulation Tel: 561-478-5536. Reference Tel: 561-681-7998. FAX: 561-697-3138. E-mail: fl.library@northwood.edu. Web Site: www.northwood.edu. *Dir,* Sue Ann Berard; E-mail: berards@northwood.edu; *Assoc Dir,* Kathleen Olds; Tel: 561-681-7998; Staff 3 (MLS 2, Non-MLS 1)
Founded 1984. Enrl 1,100; Fac 15; Highest Degree: Bachelor
Library Holdings: Bk Vols 20,000; Per Subs 150; Spec Interest Per Sub 100
Subject Interests: Bus
Automation Activity & Vendor Info: (Cataloging) Follett Software; (Circulation) Follett Software; (Course Reserve) Docutek; (Serials) EBSCO Online
Database Vendor: CountryWatch, EBSCOhost, Factiva.com, LexisNexis, ProQuest, SBRnet (Sports Business Research Network), ValueLine
Wireless access

Function: Res libr
Partic in Lyrasis; OCLC Online Computer Library Center, Inc
Restriction: Not open to pub
Friends of the Library Group

CR PALM BEACH ATLANTIC UNIVERSITY, Warren Library, 300 Pembroke Pl, 33401-6503. (Mail add: 901 S Flagler Dr, 33416), SAN 303-237X. Tel: 561-803-2226. Interlibrary Loan Service Tel: 561-803-2228. Reference Tel: 561-803-2227. Information Services Tel: 561-803-2240. FAX: 561-803-2235. E-mail: library_circulationdesk@pba.edu, library_reference@pba.edu. Web Site: library.pba.edu. *Dean of Libr,* Steven Baker; Tel: 561-803-2223, E-mail: steven_baker@pba.edu; *Asst Dean,* Ed Nordine; Tel: 561-803-2232, E-mail: ed_nordine@pba.edu; *Coordr, Access Serv,* Nadine Nance; Tel: 561-803-2231, E-mail: nadine_nance@pba.edu; *Digital Serv,* Chris Lovell; Tel: 561-803-2221, E-mail: christopher_lovell@pba.edu; *Ref Serv,* Cheri L DuMee; Tel: 561-803-2230, E-mail: cheri_dumee@pba.edu; *Ref Serv,* Elizabeth Fairall; Tel: 561-803-2224, E-mail: elizabeth_Fairall@pba.edu; *Ref Serv,* Robert K Triplett; Tel: 561-803-2234, E-mail: bob_triplett@pba.edu; *Ref Serv,* Anthony Verdesca; Tel: 561-803-2238, E-mail: anthony_verdesca@pba.edu; Staff 7 (MLS 6, Non-MLS 1)
Founded 1968. Enrl 3,400; Fac 180; Highest Degree: Doctorate
Automation Activity & Vendor Info: (Acquisitions) Ex Libris Group; (Cataloging) Ex Libris Group; (Circulation) Ex Libris Group; (Course Reserve) Ex Libris Group; (ILL) Ex Libris Group; (OPAC) Ex Libris Group; (Serials) Ex Libris Group
Database Vendor: Alexander Street Press, American Psychological Association (APA), ARTstor, Bowker, Cinahl, CIOS (Communication Institute for Online Scholarship), CredoReference, ebrary, EBSCOhost, Elsevier, Ex Libris Group, Gale Cengage Learning, infoUSA, JSTOR, LexisNexis, Mergent Online, Modern Language Association, OCLC FirstSearch, OCLC WorldShare Interlibrary Loan, OVID Technologies, Project MUSE, ProQuest, PubMed, ReferenceUSA, Safari Books Online, Sage, ScienceDirect, YBP Library Services
Wireless access
Function: Art exhibits, Computers for patron use, Copy machines, e-mail & chat, Electronic databases & coll, Free DVD rentals, Handicapped accessible, ILL available, Magnifiers for reading, Mail & tel request accepted, Music CDs, Online cat, Online ref, Orientations, Outside serv via phone, mail, e-mail & web, Photocopying/Printing, Printer for laptops & handheld devices, Ref serv available, Scanner, Telephone ref, VHS videos, Web-catalog, Wheelchair accessible
Partic in Lyrasis; SEFLIN - Southeast Florida Library Information Network, Inc
Open Mon-Thurs 7:30-Midnight, Fri 7:30-5, Sat 9:30-6, Sun 2-Midnight

GL PALM BEACH COUNTY LAW LIBRARY*, County Courthouse, Rm 12200, 205 N Dixie Hwy, 33401. SAN 303-2388. Tel: 561-355-2928. FAX: 561-355-1654. *Mgr,* Linda Sims
Founded 1947
Library Holdings: Bk Vols 30,000; Per Subs 30
Open Mon-Fri 8-5
Restriction: Non-circulating to the pub

P PALM BEACH COUNTY LIBRARY SYSTEM, 3650 Summit Blvd, 33406-4198. SAN 338-2028. Tel: 561-233-2600. Administration Tel: 561-233-2799. Toll Free Tel: 888-780-4962. FAX: 561-233-2692. Reference FAX: 561-233-2630. Administration FAX: 561-233-2644. TDD: 800-382-0775. E-mail: pbclref@pbclibrary.org. Web Site: www.pbclibrary.org. *Dir,* Douglas Crane; E-mail: craned@pbclibrary.org; *Asst Dir,* Sharon Hill; Tel: 561-233-2725, E-mail: hills@pbclibrary.org; *Outreach Librn,* Wendy Rosenfeld; Tel: 561-649-5500, E-mail: rosenfeldw@pbclibrary.org; *Tech Serv,* Ann Fleming; E-mail: fleminga@pbclibrary.org; Staff 468.875 (MLS 122.3, Non-MLS 346.575)
Founded 1967. Pop 854,813; Circ 9,326,377
Library Holdings: AV Mats 297,757; e-books 35,022; Bk Vols 1,647,532; Per Subs 4,412
Special Collections: Audubon Coll; Florida Coll; Large Print Coll
Automation Activity & Vendor Info: (Cataloging) SirsiDynix; (Circulation) SirsiDynix; (OPAC) SirsiDynix
Wireless access
Function: Adult literacy prog, Health sci info serv, Homebound delivery serv, ILL available, Magnifiers for reading, Online searches, Photocopying/Printing, Prof lending libr, Prog for adults, Prog for children & young adult, Ref serv available, Summer reading prog, Telephone ref, VHS videos, Wheelchair accessible
Publications: Brochures; Happenings (Newsletter); Staff Newsletter
Partic in Library Cooperative of the Palm Beaches; OCLC Online Computer Library Center, Inc; SEFLIN - Southeast Florida Library Information Network, Inc
Special Services for the Deaf - TDD equip; TTY equip
Special Services for the Blind - Talking bks
Open Mon-Thurs 9-9, Fri 9-6, Sat 9-5, Sun 12-5
Friends of the Library Group

Branches: 17
ACREAGE BRANCH, 15801 Orange Blvd, Loxahatchee, 33470. Tel: 561-681-4100. *Br Mgr,* Suvi Morales
Founded 2012
Open Mon-Thurs 10-9, Fri 10-6, Sat 10-5, Sun Noon-5
CLARENCE E ANTHONY BRANCH, 375 SW Second Ave, South Bay, 33493, SAN 375-5894. Tel: 561-992-8393. FAX: 561-996-5925. *Br Mgr,* Phyllis J Lilley; E-mail: lilleyp@pbclibrary.org
Founded 1992
Open Mon & Wed 11-7, Tues & Thurs-Sat 9-5
BELLE GLADE BRANCH, 725 NW Fourth St, Belle Glade, 33430, SAN 302-8550. Tel: 561-996-3453. FAX: 561-996-2304. *Br Mgr,* Phyllis J Lilley; E-mail: lilleyp@pbclibrary.org
Open Mon-Wed 10-8, Thurs-Sat 10-5
GARDENS, 11303 Campus Dr, Palm Beach Gardens, 33410, SAN 377-0486. Tel: 561-626-6133. FAX: 561-626-9688. *Br Mgr,* Carol Roggenstein; E-mail: roggensteinc@pbclibrary.org
Open Mon-Thurs 10-9, Fri 10-6, Sat 10-5, Sun 12-5
GLADES ROAD BRANCH, 20701 95th Ave S, Boca Raton, 33434, SAN 338-2230. Tel: 561-482-4554. FAX: 561-483-9679. *Br Mgr,* Elizabeth Prior; E-mail: priore@pbclibrary.org
Open Mon-Wed 10-8, Thurs-Sat 10-5
GREENACRES BRANCH, 3750 Jog Rd, Greenacres City, 33467, SAN 338-2117. Tel: 561-641-9100. FAX: 561-642-0823. *Br Mgr,* David Scott; E-mail: scottd@pbclibrary.org
Open Mon & Tues 10-8, Wed-Fri 10-6, Sat 10-5
HAGEN RANCH ROAD, 14350 Hagen Ranch Rd, Delray Beach, 33446, SAN 338-2087. Tel: 561-894-7500. FAX: 561-495-5451. *Br Mgr,* Karen Crisco; E-mail: criscok@pbclibrary.org
Open Mon-Wed 9-9, Thurs & Fri 9-6, Sat 9-5, Sun 12-5
JUPITER BRANCH, 705 N Military Trail, Jupiter, 33458, SAN 326-7598. Tel: 561-744-2301. FAX: 561-744-6297. *Br Mgr,* Anne Alsup; E-mail: alsupa@pbclibrary.org
Open Mon-Thurs 10-9, Fri 9-6, Sat 9-5, Sun 12-5
LANTANA ROAD BRANCH, 4020 Lantana Rd, Lake Worth, 33462. Tel: 561-304-4500. *Br Mgr,* Nemoure Nianombeko-Ahmed
Founded 2009
Open Mon-Wed 10-8, Fri 10-6, Sat 10-5, Sun Noon-5
OKEECHOBEE BOULEVARD, 5689 Okeechobee Blvd, 33417, SAN 338-2176. Tel: 561-233-1880. FAX: 561-233-1889. *Br Mgr,* Charles Waugh; E-mail: waughc@pbclibrary.org
Open Mon-Wed 10-8, Thurs-Sat 10-5
PALM BEACH COUNTY LIBRARY ANNEX, 4639 Lake Worth Rd, Greenacres, 33463-3451, SAN 338-2052. Tel: 561-649-5500. Toll Free Tel: 888-780-5151. FAX: 561-649-5402. *Head, Outreach Serv,* Wendy Rosenfeld; E-mail: rosenfeldw@pbclibrary.org; *Head, Tech Serv,* Ann Fleming; E-mail: fleminga@pbclibrary.org
ROYAL PALM BEACH BRANCH, 500 Civic Center Way, Royal Palm Beach, 33411, SAN 338-2249. Tel: 561-790-6030. FAX: 561-790-6036. *Br Mgr,* Deborah McElroy; E-mail: mcelroyd@pbclibrary.org
Open Mon-Wed 10-9, Thurs & Fri 10-6, Sat 10-5
TEQUESTA BRANCH, 461 Old Dixie Hwy N, Tequesta, 33469, SAN 338-2141. Tel: 561-746-5970. *Br Mgr,* Anne Alsup; E-mail: alsupa@pbclibrary.org
Open Mon-Wed 10-8, Thurs-Sat 10-5
WELLINGTON BRANCH, 1951 Royal Fern Dr, Wellington, 33414, SAN 377-6530. Tel: 561-790-6070. FAX: 561-790-6078. *Br Mgr,* Karen Stroly; E-mail: strolyk@pbclibrary.org
Open Mon-Thurs 10-9, Fri 10-6, Sat 10-5, Sun 12-5
WEST BOCA BRANCH, 18685 State Rd 7, Boca Raton, 33498. Tel: 561-470-1600. FAX: 561-451-1437. *Mgr,* Julie Brown; E-mail: brownj@pbclibrary.org
Open Mon-Thurs 10-9, Fri 10-6, Sat 10-5, Sun Noon-5
WEST BOYNTON BRANCH, 9451 Jog Rd, Boynton Beach, 33437, SAN 375-5908. Tel: 561-734-5556. FAX: 561-681-4041. *Br Mgr,* Cindi Permenter; E-mail: permenterc@pbclibrary.org
Open Mon-Thurs 10-9, Fri 10-6, Sat 10-5, Sun 12-5
LOULA V YORK BRANCH, 525 Bacom Point Rd, Pahokee, 33476, SAN 370-0186. Tel: 561-924-5928. FAX: 561-924-2271. *Br Mgr,* Phyllis J Lilley; E-mail: lilleyp@pbclibrary.org
Open Mon & Wed 11-7, Tues & Thurs-Sat 9-5
Bookmobiles: 1. In Charge, Ronald Glass

S SOUTH FLORIDA WATER MANAGEMENT DISTRICT*, Reference Center Library, 3301 Gun Club Rd, 33406. (Mail add: PO Box 24680, 33416-4680), SAN 303-2418. Tel: 561-682-6076. FAX: 561-682-2093. Web Site: www.sfwmd.gov. *Librn,* Rachael Cathcart; Staff 2 (MLS 1, Non-MLS 1)
Founded 1949
Library Holdings: Per Subs 200
Special Collections: Florida Environmental History Coll; Technical Reports & Documents
Subject Interests: Agr, Conserv, Environ eng, Water pollution, Water res
Partic in Dialog Corp; Lyrasis; OCLC Online Computer Library Center, Inc

Open Mon-Fri 8-5
Restriction: Open to pub for ref only

WESTON

C AMERICAN INTERCONTINENTAL UNIVERSITY*, South Florida Library, 2250 N Commerce Pkwy, 33326. Tel: 954-446-6100, Ext 6325. Circulation Tel: 954-446-6325. Reference Tel: 954-446-6108. Administration Tel: 954-446-6147. Toll Free Tel: 866-248-4723, Ext 6325. FAX: 954-660-4147. E-mail: aiufllibrary@aiufl.edu. Web Site: www.aiufl.edu. *Dir, Libr & Info Res,* Sharon R Argov; E-mail: sargov@aiufl.edu; *Librn,* Position Currently Open; Staff 2 (MLS 2)
Founded 1998. Enrl 500; Highest Degree: Master
Library Holdings: Audiobooks 10; AV Mats 1,000; CDs 900; DVDs 350; e-books 40,000; e-journals 10; Electronic Media & Resources 20; Bk Titles 12,000; Bk Vols 15,000; Per Subs 120; Spec Interest Per Sub 100; Videos 400
Automation Activity & Vendor Info: (Acquisitions) TLC (The Library Corporation); (Cataloging) TLC (The Library Corporation); (Circulation) TLC (The Library Corporation); (Course Reserve) TLC (The Library Corporation); (ILL) OCLC CatExpress; (OPAC) TLC (The Library Corporation); (Serials) TLC (The Library Corporation)
Database Vendor: Baker & Taylor, Bowker, Checkpoint Systems, Inc, Cinahl, CredoReference, Dun & Bradstreet, ebrary, EBSCOhost, Electric Library, Gale Cengage Learning, Hoovers, Knovel, LexisNexis, Newsbank, OCLC FirstSearch, OCLC WebJunction, OCLC WorldShare Interlibrary Loan, ProQuest, Safari Books Online, TLC (The Library Corporation), Wilson - Wilson Web
Wireless access
Function: Audio & video playback equip for onsite use, AV serv, Bk club(s), Bks on cassette, CD-ROM, Computers for patron use, Copy machines, Doc delivery serv, E-Reserves, Electronic databases & coll, Handicapped accessible, ILL available, Instruction & testing, Learning ctr, Mail & tel request accepted, Online cat, Online info literacy tutorials on the web & in blackboard, Online ref, Online searches, Orientations, Photocopying/Printing, Pub access computers, Ref & res, Ref serv available, Scanner, Telephone ref, VHS videos, Web-catalog, Wheelchair accessible
Publications: AIU South Florida Literary Journal (Quarterly); Campus Connection (Newsletter)
Partic in Libr & Info Resources Network (LIRN); Lyrasis
Open Mon-Fri 8am-10pm, Sat 8-6
Restriction: Authorized patrons, Borrowing privileges limited to fac & registered students, Borrowing requests are handled by ILL, In-house use for visitors, Open to students, fac, staff & alumni

WEWAHITCHKA

S GULF CORRECTIONAL INSTITUTION LIBRARY, 500 Ike Steel Rd, 32465. SAN 377-2675. Tel: 850-639-1480. FAX: 850-639-1182. *Librn,* Marilyn Mock Stump; E-mail: mock-stump@mail.dc.state.fl.us
Library Holdings: Bk Vols 13,229; Per Subs 72

Branches:

ANNEX BRANCH, 699 Ike Steel Rd, 32465. Tel: 850-639-1780. *Libr Tech,* William Weeks
Library Holdings: Bk Vols 6,558; Per Subs 45

WILDWOOD

P SUMTER COUNTY LIBRARY SYSTEM, 7375 Powell Rd, Ste 150, 34785. Tel: 352-689-4560. FAX: 352-689-4561. Web Site: sumtercountyfl.gov/library. *Libr Single Admin Head,* Leslie Burch; Tel: 352-689-4400, E-mail: leslie.burch@sumtercountyfl.gov
Pop 111,125; Circ 490,000
Library Holdings: Bk Titles 160,429
Automation Activity & Vendor Info: (Acquisitions) Innovative Interfaces, Inc; (Cataloging) Innovative Interfaces, Inc; (Circulation) Innovative Interfaces, Inc
Wireless access
Function: 24/7 Electronic res, 24/7 Online cat, Adult bk club, After school storytime, Audiobks via web, Bks on CD, Children's prog, Computer training, Computers for patron use, Copy machines, E-Reserves, Electronic databases & coll, eReaders, Fax serv, Free DVD rentals, ILL available, Magazines, Mango lang, Music CDs, Outreach serv, OverDrive digital audio bks, Photocopying/Printing, Preschool reading prog, Summer reading prog, Tax forms
Member Libraries: Bushnell Public Library; Clark Maxwell Jr Library; E C Rowell Public Library; Panasoffkee Community Library; Villages Public Library at Belvedere; Villages Public Library at Pinellas Plaza
Open Mon-Fri 8:30-5:30
Friends of the Library Group
Bookmobiles: 1

§P VILLAGES PUBLIC LIBRARY AT PINELLAS PLAZA, 7375 Powell Rd, 34785. Tel: 352-689-4580. FAX: 352-689-4581. *Librn,* Virginia Patrick-Downs
Mem of Sumter County Library System

WILTON MANORS

P RICHARD C SULLIVAN PUBLIC LIBRARY OF WILTON MANORS*, 500 NE 26th St, 33305. SAN 303-2477. Tel: 954-390-2195. FAX: 954-390-2183. Web Site: www.wiltonmanors.com/library. *Dir,* Rick Sterling; E-mail: rsterling@wiltonmanors.com; *Pub Serv,* Cynthia Exterkamp; E-mail: cexterkamp@wiltonmanors.com; *Tech Serv,* Marilyn Jansa; E-mail: mjansa@wiltonmanors.com; Staff 5.4 (MLS 1.9, Non-MLS 3.5)
Founded 1957. Pop 12,895; Circ 46,138
Oct 2006-Sept 2007. Mats Exp $36,578, Books $31,674, AV Mat $4,284, Electronic Ref Mat (Incl. Access Fees) $620. Sal $369,558
Library Holdings: CDs 1,159; DVDs 378; Large Print Bks 554; Bk Vols 23,765; Per Subs 86; Talking Bks 965; Videos 2,342
Special Collections: Florida Coll
Subject Interests: Travel
Automation Activity & Vendor Info: (Cataloging) Follett Software; (Circulation) Follett Software; (OPAC) Follett Software
Database Vendor: Newsbank, World Book Online
Wireless access
Function: Bilingual assistance for Spanish patrons, Bks on cassette, Bks on CD, Children's prog, Computers for patron use, Copy machines, Fax serv, Homebound delivery serv, ILL available, Magnifiers for reading, Music CDs, Online cat, Photocopying/Printing, Preschool outreach, Pub access computers, Story hour, Summer reading prog
Publications: Friends News (Newsletter)
Open Mon, Tues, Thurs & Fri 9:30-5:30, Wed 12-8, Sat 9:30-1
Friends of the Library Group

WINTER HAVEN

C POLK STATE COLLEGE*, James W Dowdy Library, 999 Ave H NE, 33881-4299. SAN 303-2485. Tel: 863-297-1040. FAX: 863-297-1065. Web Site: www.polk.edu/winter-haven-campus-library. *Dir, Learning Res,* Christina Fullerton; Tel: 863-292-3663, E-mail: cfullerton@polk.edu; *Bibliog Serv Librn,* Beverly Chapa; Tel: 863-298-6813, E-mail: bchapa@polk.edu; *Emerging Tech Librn,* Jarrod Jones; *Ref Librn,* Linda Young; Tel: 863-292-3665, E-mail: lyoung@polk.edu; Staff 12 (MLS 5, Non-MLS 7)
Founded 1965. Enrl 6,600; Fac 125; Highest Degree: Associate
Library Holdings: e-books 49,000; Bk Titles 93,000; Per Subs 350; Videos 4,500
Subject Interests: Fla, State hist
Automation Activity & Vendor Info: (Cataloging) Ex Libris Group; (Circulation) Ex Libris Group; (Course Reserve) Ex Libris Group; (ILL) OCLC; (OPAC) Ex Libris Group; (Serials) Ex Libris Group
Database Vendor: Baker & Taylor, EBSCOhost, Gale Cengage Learning, JSTOR, LexisNexis, OCLC FirstSearch, OCLC WorldShare Interlibrary Loan, ProQuest, Wilson - Wilson Web
Wireless access
Partic in Lyrasis; OCLC Online Computer Library Center, Inc; Tampa Bay Library Consortium, Inc
Special Services for the Deaf - Assistive tech; Bks on deafness & sign lang; Closed caption videos; TDD equip
Special Services for the Blind - Assistive/Adapted tech devices, equip & products; Cassette playback machines; Closed circuit TV; Computer with voice synthesizer for visually impaired persons; Low vision equip; ZoomText magnification & reading software
Open Mon-Thurs 7:30am-9pm, Fri 7:30-4, Sat 9-1

Departmental Libraries:

LAKELAND CAMPUS LIBRARY, 3425 Winter Lake Rd, Sta 62, Lakeland, 33803, SAN 374-6771. Tel: 863-297-1042. FAX: 863-297-1064. *Dir, Learning Res, Lakeland,* William C Foege, Jr; E-mail: bfoege@polk.edu; *Librn,* Helen Schmidt; E-mail: hschmidt@polk.edu; *Ref,* Helen Schmidt; E-mail: hschmidt@polk.edu; *Learning Res Asst, Cir/Reserve,* Lynn Heil; *Learning Res Asst, Ser & ILL,* Kristen Jernigan; Staff 6.125 (MLS 3.275, Non-MLS 2.85)
Founded 1988. Enrl 3,120; Highest Degree: Bachelor
Open Mon-Thurs 8am-9pm, Fri 8-4, Sat 9-1

S RIDGE CAREER CENTER LIBRARY*, 7700 State Rd 544, 33881. SAN 377-3264. Tel: 863-419-3060, Ext 4133. FAX: 863-419-3062. Web Site: www.pcsb.k12.fl.us/ridge. *Media Spec,* Linda Minnix
Founded 1979
Library Holdings: Bks on Deafness & Sign Lang 10; High Interest/Low Vocabulary Bk Vols 2,000; Bk Titles 8,500; Per Subs 35
Subject Interests: Career, Vocational
Automation Activity & Vendor Info: (Acquisitions) Brodart; (Circulation) Follett Software; (Serials) EBSCO Online

Restriction: Students only
Friends of the Library Group

M WINTER HAVEN HOSPITAL*, J D Converse Memorial Medical Library, 200 Ave F NE, 33881. SAN 338-2265. Tel: 863-291-6033. FAX: 863-291-6022. *Res Info Spec,* Henry Hasse; E-mail: hank.hasse@winterhavenhospital.org; Staff 1 (Non-MLS 1)
Founded 1950
Library Holdings: e-books 24; e-journals 645; Electronic Media & Resources 2; Bk Titles 700; Per Subs 84; Videos 53
Subject Interests: Consumer health, Ethics, Healthcare mgt, Med, Nursing
Partic in Fla Health Sci Libr Asn; Tampa Bay Medical Library Network
Open Mon-Fri 7:30-4

P WINTER HAVEN PUBLIC LIBRARY*, Kathryn L Smith Memorial, 325 Ave A NW, 33881. SAN 303-2493. Tel: 863-291-5880. FAX: 863-291-5889. Web Site: whpl.mywinterhaven.com. *Libr Dir,* Jane Martin; E-mail: jmartin@mywinterhaven.com; *Pub Serv Librn,* Cori Greear; E-mail: cgreear@mywinterhaven.com; *Ref & Info Serv Librn,* Linda Babli; E-mail: lbabli@mywinterhaven.com; *Youth Serv Librn,* Kristen Barnes; *Building Serv Mgr/Acq,* Pat Wike
Founded 1910. Pop 25,000; Circ 237,414
Library Holdings: Bk Titles 80,000
Automation Activity & Vendor Info: (Acquisitions) SirsiDynix; (Cataloging) SirsiDynix; (Circulation) SirsiDynix
Wireless access
Open Mon & Wed 9-6, Tues & Thurs 10-7, Fri & Sat 9-5
Friends of the Library Group

WINTER PARK

C HERZING COLLEGE LIBRARY*, 1595 S Semoran Blvd, Ste 1501, 32792. Tel: 407-478-0500. FAX: 407-478-0501. Web Site: www.orl.herzing.edu. *Librn,* Michael Taylor
Highest Degree: Bachelor
Library Holdings: AV Mats 320; Bk Vols 4,000; Per Subs 30
Automation Activity & Vendor Info: (Cataloging) Follett Software; (Circulation) Follett Software; (OPAC) Follett Software
Database Vendor: Gale Cengage Learning, ProQuest, Westlaw
Partic in Lyrasis
Open Mon-Thurs 8:30am-9pm, Fri 8:30-5

C ROLLINS COLLEGE, Olin Library, 1000 Holt Ave, Campus Box 2744, 32789-2744. SAN 338-232X. Tel: 407-646-2627. Circulation Tel: 407-646-2521. Interlibrary Loan Service Tel: 407-646-1554. Reference Tel: 407-646-2507. E-mail: askolinlibrary@rollins.edu. Web Site: www.rollins.edu/library. *Dir,* Jonathan Miller; Tel: 407-646-2676, E-mail: jxmiller@rollins.edu; *Digital Serv, Head, Coll,* Jonathan Harwell; Tel: 407-646-2148, E-mail: jharwell@rollins.edu; *Head, Pub Serv,* Dorothy Mays; Tel: 407-646-1533, E-mail: dmays@rollins.edu; *Digital Serv Librn,* Paul Gindlesperger; Tel: 407-691-1372, E-mail: pgrindlesperger@rollins.edu; *Digital Serv Librn,* Nate Hosburgh; Tel: 407-646-1157, E-mail: nhosburgh@rollins.edu; *Emerging Serv Librn,* William Svitavsky; Tel: 407-646-2679, E-mail: wsvitavsky@rollins.edu; *Pub Serv Librn,* Susan Montgomery; Tel: 407-646-2295, E-mail: smontgomery@rollins.edu; *Pub Serv Librn,* Emma Oxford; Tel: 407-646-2683, E-mail: eoxford@rollins.edu; *Electronic Res, Ser Librn,* Erin Gallagher; Tel: 407-691-6431, E-mail: egallagher@rollins.edu; *Archivist,* Wenxian Zhang; Tel: 407-646-2231, E-mail: wzhang@rollins.edu; Staff 9 (MLS 9)
Founded 1885. Enrl 3,290; Fac 192; Highest Degree: Master
Library Holdings: AV Mats 749; CDs 453; DVDs 749; e-books 11,238; Electronic Media & Resources 62; Bk Titles 253,797; Bk Vols 300,783; Per Subs 1,239; Videos 2,023
Special Collections: Constance F Woolson Coll; Floridiana; Hamilton Holt Papers; M P Shiel Coll; Poetry & Letters (Jessie B Rittenhouse Coll); Rollins College Archives; Walt Whitman Coll. US Document Depository
Automation Activity & Vendor Info: (Acquisitions) SirsiDynix; (OPAC) SirsiDynix
Database Vendor: EBSCOhost, JSTOR, LexisNexis, Newsbank, OCLC FirstSearch, OCLC WorldShare Interlibrary Loan, ProQuest, PubMed, SerialsSolutions, STN International, Westlaw, Wilson - Wilson Web
Publications: Olin Info (Newsletter)
Partic in Lyrasis; Tampa Bay Library Consortium, Inc
Open Mon-Thurs 7:45am-12am, Fri 7:45-6, Sat 9-5, Sun 11am-12am

J VALENCIA COMMUNITY COLLEGE*, Winter Park Campus Learning Resources Center, 850 W Morse Blvd, 32789. Tel: 407-582-6814. FAX: 407-582-6014. Web Site: valenciacc.edu/wp/library. *Dir,* Susan Craig; Tel: 407-582-6815; *Librn,* Nuria Curras; *Coordr,* Betsy Hanna; E-mail: bhanna@valenciacc.edu; Staff 7 (MLS 3, Non-MLS 4)
Library Holdings: Bk Vols 18,000
Open Mon-Thurs 8-8, Fri 8-5, Sat 8-12

P WINTER PARK PUBLIC LIBRARY, 460 E New England Ave, 32789. SAN 303-2523. Tel: 407-623-3300. FAX: 407-623-3489. Web Site: www.wppl.org. *Dir,* Shawn G Shaffer; Tel: 407-623-3300, Ext 5, E-mail: sshaffer@wppl.org; *Head, Ch,* Evelyn Malles; Tel: 407-623-3300, Ext 115, E-mail: emalles@wppl.org; *Head, Circ,* Melissa Schneider; Tel: 407-623-3300, Ext 107, E-mail: mschneider@wppl.org; *Head, Ref,* Nicole Heintzelman; Tel: 407-623-3300, Ext 104, E-mail: nheintzelman@wppl.org; *YA Librn,* Lisa Blue; Tel: 407-623-3300, Ext 114, E-mail: lblue@wppl.org; *Archivist,* Barbara White; Tel: 407-623-3300, Ext 106, E-mail: bwhite@wppl.org; *Ch Serv,* Shanna Kuster; Tel: 407-623-3300, Ext 112, E-mail: skuster@wppl.org; *Commun Serv,* Mary Gail Coffee; Tel: 407-623-3486, E-mail: mgcoffee@wppl.org; Staff 17 (MLS 13, Non-MLS 4)
Founded 1885. Pop 27,200; Circ 530,865
Library Holdings: Bk Titles 153,000; Bk Vols 175,000; Per Subs 326
Special Collections: Winter Park History Archive
Automation Activity & Vendor Info: (Circulation) SirsiDynix; (OPAC) SirsiDynix
Wireless access
Publications: Read All About It (Newsletter)
Partic in Tampa Bay Library Consortium, Inc
Open Mon-Thurs 9-9, Fri & Sat 9-5, Sun 1-5
Friends of the Library Group

ZEPHYRHILLS

P ZEPHYRHILLS PUBLIC LIBRARY*, 5347 Eighth St, 33542. SAN 303-2531. Tel: 813-780-0064. FAX: 813-780-0066. E-mail: library@ci.zephyrhills.fl.us. Web Site: www.ci.zephyrhills.fl.us. *Dir,* Vicki S Elkins; *Asst Dir,* Peggy L Panak; *Circ,* Debbie Lopez; *Circ,* Victoria Reeves; Staff 2 (MLS 1, Non-MLS 1)
Founded 1912. Pop 30,000; Circ 120,745
Library Holdings: Audiobooks 761; AV Mats 1,968; Bk Vols 29,000; Per Subs 60
Special Collections: Civil War Coll; World War II Coll
Subject Interests: Civil War, Fla, Gardening
Automation Activity & Vendor Info: (Acquisitions) TLC (The Library Corporation); (Cataloging) TLC (The Library Corporation); (Circulation) TLC (The Library Corporation)
Mem of Pasco County Library System
Open Tues-Fri 9-7, Sat 9-12

GEORGIA

Date of Statistics: FY 2014
Population, 2010 U.S. Census: 9,687,653
Population, 2014 (Governor's Office of Planning & Budget): 10,344,907
Total Volumes in Public Libraries: 16,603,157
Volumes Per Capita: 1.60
Total Public Library Circulation: 39,111,217
Circulation Per Capita: 3.78
Total Public Library Income: $187,361,783
Source of Income: Public Funds, Federal, State & Local
Income Per Capita: $18.11
Expenditures Per Capita: $17.69
Grants-in-Aid to Public Libraries:
Federal Library Services and Technology Act: $4,229,250
State Service Grants: $31,234,480

ACWORTH

J NORTH METRO TECHNICAL COLLEGE/GEORGIA HIGHLANDS COLLEGE LIBRARY*, 5198 Ross Rd, 30102. Tel: 770-975-4054. FAX: 770-975-4284. Web Site: www.northmetrotech.edu/library/index.html. *Librn,* Kate Stirk; E-mail: kstirk@ChattahoocheeTech.edu; Staff 3 (MLS 3)
Founded 1989. Enrl 2,000; Highest Degree: Associate
Library Holdings: CDs 40; DVDs 15; e-books 34,000; e-journals 3,000; Bk Vols 6,000; Per Subs 35; Talking Bks 50; Videos 500
Automation Activity & Vendor Info: (Cataloging) Surpass; (Circulation) Surpass; (OPAC) Surpass
Partic in GALILEO (Georgia Library Learning Online)
Open Mon 8am-9pm, Tues-Thurs 8am-10pm, Fri 8-4

ALBANY

C ALBANY STATE UNIVERSITY*, James Pendergrast Memorial Library, 504 College Dr, 31705-2796. SAN 303-2558. Tel: 229-430-4799. Circulation Tel: 229-430-4805. E-mail: circulation@asurams.edu. Web Site: www.asurams.edu/library. *Dir of Libr Serv,* LaVerne McLaughlin; E-mail: laverne.mclaughlin@asurams.edu
Founded 1903. Enrl 4,024; Fac 300; Highest Degree: Master
Library Holdings: CDs 139; DVDs 10; e-books 27,442; Bk Vols 192,582; Per Subs 323
Special Collections: History & Literature (Black Studies); Library of American Civilization; US Govt Census Data
Automation Activity & Vendor Info: (Acquisitions) Ex Libris Group; (Cataloging) Ex Libris Group; (Circulation) Ex Libris Group; (Course Reserve) Ex Libris Group; (ILL) Ex Libris Group; (Media Booking) Ex Libris Group; (OPAC) Ex Libris Group; (Serials) Ex Libris Group
Publications: New Acquisitions List
Partic in Lyrasis; OCLC Online Computer Library Center, Inc
Open Mon-Thurs 7:30am-11pm, Fri 7:30-7, Sat 10-6, Sun 2-10

J DARTON COLLEGE*, Harold B Wetherbee Library, 2400 Gillionville Rd, 31707. SAN 303-254X. Tel: 229-317-6760. Circulation Tel: 229-317-6766. Interlibrary Loan Service Tel: 229-317-6764. FAX: 229-317-6652. Web Site: www.darton.edu/~dclib/. *Dir,* Mary Washington; Tel: 229-317-6761, E-mail: mary.washington@darton.edu; *Syst Coordr,* Caryl Nemajovsky; Tel: 229-317-6765, E-mail: caryl.nemajovsky@darton.edu; *Electronic Res,* David Fry; Tel: 229-317-6933, E-mail: david.fry@darton.edu; Staff 7 (MLS 3, Non-MLS 4)
Founded 1966. Enrl 5,800; Fac 125; Highest Degree: Associate
Library Holdings: AV Mats 5,182; e-books 27,417; Bk Vols 98,000; Per Subs 247
Subject Interests: Allied health, Nursing
Automation Activity & Vendor Info: (Acquisitions) Ex Libris Group; (Cataloging) Ex Libris Group; (Circulation) Ex Libris Group; (ILL) OCLC; (OPAC) Ex Libris Group
Wireless access
Function: Distance learning, Handicapped accessible, ILL available, Magnifiers for reading, Ref serv available, Wheelchair accessible
Partic in Georgia Online Database; OCLC Online Computer Library Center, Inc
Special Services for the Deaf - Assistive tech
Special Services for the Blind - Assistive/Adapted tech devices, equip & products; Computer with voice synthesizer for visually impaired persons
Open Mon-Thurs 7:30-9, Fri 7:30-5, Sun 2-6

P DOUGHERTY COUNTY PUBLIC LIBRARY*, 300 Pine Ave, 31701-2533. SAN 338-2419. Tel: 229-420-3200. Circulation Tel: 229-420-3201. Reference Tel: 229-420-3210. FAX: 229-420-3215. Web Site: www.docolib.org. *Dir,* Position Currently Open; *Head, Ref,* Patricia Henson; *Finance Mgr,* Sabrina Little; E-mail: little@docolib.org; *Ch Serv,* Erin Hunt; Staff 35 (MLS 7, Non-MLS 28)
Founded 1905. Pop 99,880
Jul 2011-Jun 2012 Income (Main Library and Branch(s)) $2,566,478
Library Holdings: Bk Vols 317,655; Per Subs 118
Subject Interests: Genealogy, Local hist
Automation Activity & Vendor Info: (Cataloging) Evergreen; (Circulation) Evergreen; (ILL) OCLC; (OPAC) Evergreen
Database Vendor: Gale Cengage Learning
Wireless access
Partic in Georgia Online Database; PINES (Public Information Network for Electronic Services)
Open Mon 10-8, Tues-Thurs 10-6, Fri & Sat 10-2, Sun 2-6
Branches: 4
TALLULAH MASSEY BRANCH, 2004 Stratford Dr, 31705, SAN 338-2532. Tel: 229-420-3250. *Br Mgr,* Steve DeJarnette
Open Mon-Sat 9:30-6
NORTHWEST, 2507 Dawson Rd, 31707, SAN 322-7189. Tel: 229-420-3270. *Br Mgr,* Pauline Abbide
Open Mon & Thurs 9:30-9, Tues, Wed, Fri & Sat 9:30-6
SOUTHSIDE, 2114 Habersham Rd, 31705, SAN 370-1085. Tel: 229-420-3260. *Br Mgr,* Patricia Henson
Open Mon-Sat 9:30-6
WESTTOWN, 2124 Waddell Ave, 31707, SAN 371-2982. Tel: 229-420-3280. *Mgr,* Azurinthia Walker
Open Mon-Sat 9:30-6

A UNITED STATES NAVY*, Marine Corps Logistics Base Library, Base Library, Bldg 7122, 814 Radford Blvd, Ste 20311, 31704-0311. SAN 338-2591. Tel: 229-639-5242. FAX: 229-639-5197. *Librn,* Amos Tookes; E-mail: amos.tookes@usmc-mccs.org
Library Holdings: Bk Titles 27,000; Per Subs 60
Open Mon-Thurs 9-6, Fri 9-5

ALPHARETTA

C DEVRY UNIVERSITY*, Alpharetta Library, 2555 Northwinds Pkwy, 30009. Tel: 770-619-3640. Web Site: www.atl.devry.edu/library.html. *Dir,* Position Currently Open
Library Holdings: e-books 11,000; Bk Titles 14,000; Per Subs 70
Database Vendor: EBSCOhost, LexisNexis, ProQuest

Partic in GALILEO (Georgia Library Learning Online)
Open Mon-Thurs 8:30am-9pm, Fri 8:30-6, Sat 10-3
Restriction: Open to students, fac & staff

ALTO

S GEORGIA DEPARTMENT OF CORRECTIONS, OFFICE OF LIBRARY SERVICES*, Arrendale State Prison, 2023 Gainesville Hwy S, 30510. (Mail add: PO Box 709, 30510-0709). Tel: 706-776-4700. FAX: 706-776-4710. Web Site: www.dcor.state.ga.us. *Librn,* Regina Bell
Library Holdings: Bk Vols 10,000
Database Vendor: LexisNexis
Open Mon-Thurs 8-7, Fri 2-7

AMERICUS

C GEORGIA SOUTHWESTERN STATE UNIVERSITY*, James Earl Carter Library, 800 Georgia Southwestern State University Dr, 31709. SAN 303-2582. Tel: 229-931-2259. Circulation Tel: 229-931-2266. FAX: 229-931-2265. E-mail: library@gsw.edu. Web Site: gsw.edu/Library. *Dean of Libr,* Ru Story-Huffman; E-mail: ru.story-huffman@gsw.edu; *Bibliog Database Mgr, Cat Librn,* Lee Ann Dalzell; Tel: 229-931-2258, E-mail: lee.dalzell@gsw.edu; *Coll Develop Librn,* Gretchen Smith; Tel: 229-931-2789, E-mail: gretchen.smith@gsw.edu; *Govt Info Coordr, Ref Librn,* Position Currently Open; *Supvr, Access Serv,* Valarie Anthony; E-mail: valarie.anthony@gsw.edu; Staff 5 (MLS 4, Non-MLS 1)
Founded 1928. Enrl 2,600; Fac 125; Highest Degree: Master
Library Holdings: e-books 27,417; Bk Titles 131,658; Bk Vols 143,557; Per Subs 516
Special Collections: Third World Studies Coll. US Document Depository
Subject Interests: Educ
Automation Activity & Vendor Info: (Acquisitions) Ex Libris Group; (Cataloging) Ex Libris Group; (Circulation) Ex Libris Group; (Course Reserve) Ex Libris Group; (ILL) Ex Libris Group; (OPAC) Ex Libris Group
Partic in GALILEO (Georgia Library Learning Online)
Special Services for the Blind - Reader equip
Open Mon-Thurs 8am-10pm, Fri 8-3, Sat 9-5, Sun 2-10

P LAKE BLACKSHEAR REGIONAL LIBRARY SYSTEM*, 307 E Lamar St, 31709-3633. SAN 338-2621. Tel: 229-924-8091. FAX: 229-928-4445. E-mail: info@lbrls.org. Web Site: www.lbrls.org. *Dir,* Anne M Isbell; E-mail: amisbell@lbrls.org; *Asst Dir,* Rich Hawkins; E-mail: rhawkins@lbrls.org; Staff 4 (MLS 4)
Founded 1878. Pop 68,000; Circ 90,852
Special Collections: Andersonville Prison, bks, photog; Genealogy Coll, bks, microfiche, microfilm; Jimmy Carter Coll, multi-media; Local History Coll, bks, photog
Automation Activity & Vendor Info: (Acquisitions) Evergreen; (Cataloging) Evergreen; (Circulation) Evergreen; (ILL) OCLC; (OPAC) Evergreen
Wireless access
Publications: Index to the Roster of Confederate Soldiers
Partic in Lyrasis
Open Mon 10-6, Tues-Thurs 10-8, Fri & Sat 10-4
Friends of the Library Group
Branches: 5
BYROMVILLE PUBLIC, 452 Main St, Byromville, 31007-2500. (Mail add: PO Box 6, Byromville, 31007-0006), SAN 338-2656. Tel: 478-433-5100. *Mgr,* Virginia Jeter
Open Tues & Thurs 4-6, Sat 10-12
CORDELE-CRISP CARNEGIE, 115 E 11th Ave, Cordele, 31015-4232, SAN 338-2680. Tel: 229-276-1300. FAX: 229-276-1151. *Br Mgr,* Debbie Brogdon
Open Mon & Wed 10-6, Tues & Thurs 10-8, Fri & Sat 10-4
Friends of the Library Group
DOOLY COUNTY, 1200 E Union St, Vienna, 31092-7545, SAN 338-2710. Tel: 229-268-4687. FAX: 229-268-4687. *Mgr,* Vonni Baker-Walker; E-mail: lybaker@lbrls.org
Open Mon 1:30-6, Tues-Thurs 8:30-6, Fri 8:30-4, Sat 8:30-1
ELIZABETH HARRIS LIBRARY, 312 Harman St, Unadilla, 31091. (Mail add: PO Box 930, Unadilla, 31091-0930), SAN 326-8411. Tel: 478-627-9303. FAX: 478-627-9303. *Br Mgr,* Rhonda Bartlett
Open Tues 9-6, Wed & Thurs 9-7, Fri 9-4, Sat 9-12
SCHLEY COUNTY, 54 S Broad St, Ellaville, 31806-3457. (Mail add: PO Box 365, Ellaville, 31806-0365), SAN 338-2745. Tel: 229-937-2004. FAX: 229-937-2004. *Mgr,* Donna Franklin
Open Mon & Fri 10-4:30, Tues & Thurs 10-7, Sat 10-2
Friends of the Library Group
Bookmobiles: 1. Outreach Servs, Jean Deriso

J SOUTH GEORGIA TECHNICAL COLLEGE*, Americus Campus Library, 900 S Georgia Tech Pkwy, 31709. Tel: 229-931-2562. FAX: 229-931-2732. Web Site: www.southgatech.edu. *Dir,* Jerry Stovall; E-mail: jstovall@southgatech.edu; Staff 2 (MLS 1, Non-MLS 1)
Founded 1948. Enrl 1,400; Highest Degree: Associate
Library Holdings: e-journals 27,000; Bk Vols 13,000; Per Subs 105
Automation Activity & Vendor Info: (Cataloging) TLC (The Library Corporation); (Circulation) TLC (The Library Corporation); (OPAC) TLC (The Library Corporation)
Partic in GALILEO (Georgia Library Learning Online)
Open Mon-Thurs 8-8, Fri 8-4

ATHENS

SR ATHENS FIRST UNITED METHODIST CHURCH LIBRARY*, 327 N Lumpkin St, 30601. SAN 303-2604. Tel: 706-543-1442. FAX: 706-546-4797. Web Site: athensfirstumc.org. *Dir,* Cindy Kuhlman
Library Holdings: AV Mats 80; Bk Vols 2,050; Spec Interest Per Sub 3
Special Collections: UMW Holdings
Subject Interests: Local authors

P ATHENS REGIONAL LIBRARY SYSTEM, Athens-Clarke County Library, 2025 Baxter St, 30606-6331. SAN 338-277X. Tel: 706-613-3650. FAX: 706-613-3660. E-mail: contact_us@arlsmail.org. Web Site: www.athenslibrary.org/athens. *Dir,* Kathryn Ames; Staff 46.5 (MLS 10.55, Non-MLS 35.95)
Founded 1936. Pop 225,833; Circ 1,274,466
Special Collections: County Library; Genealogy & Georgia; Genealogy, Daughters of American Revolution
Subject Interests: Local hist, State hist
Wireless access
Partic in Georgia Online Database; OCLC Online Computer Library Center, Inc; PINES (Public Information Network for Electronic Services)
Special Services for the Deaf - Bks on deafness & sign lang; Closed caption videos; High interest/low vocabulary bks
Special Services for the Blind - Aids for in-house use; Computer with voice synthesizer for visually impaired persons
Friends of the Library Group
Branches: 11
BOGART BRANCH, 200 S Burson Ave, Bogart, 30622. (Mail add: PO Box 218, Bogart, 30622), SAN 338-280X. Tel: 770-725-9443. Web Site: www.athenslibrary.org/bogart. *Br Mgr,* Donna Butler
Founded 1940
Open Mon, Wed & Fri 10-6, Tues 12-8, Thurs 12-9
Friends of the Library Group
EAST ATHENS COMMUNITY RESOURCE CENTER, 400 McKinley Dr, 30601. Tel: 706-613-3657. Reference Tel: 706-613-3650, Ext 356. FAX: 706-613-3657. Web Site: www.athenslibrary.org/eastathens. *Br Mgr,* Tonya Sands
Founded 1998
Open Mon-Thurs 2-6
LAVONIA-CARNEGIE BRANCH, 28 Hartwell Rd, Lavonia, 30553. (Mail add: PO Box 237, Lavonia, 30553-0237), SAN 338-2869. Tel: 706-356-4307. Information Services Tel: 706-769-3950. FAX: 706-356-4307. Web Site: www.athenslibrary.org/lavonia. *Br Mgr,* Emma LeCroy
Founded 1904
Open Mon & Wed 10-8, Tues & Fri 10-6, Sat 10-2
Friends of the Library Group
LAY PARK COMMUNITY RESOURCE CENTER, 297 Hoyt St, 30601. (Mail add: 2025 Baxter St, 30606). Tel: 706-613-3667. FAX: 706-613-3667. Web Site: www.athenslibrary.org/laypark. *Br Mgr,* Dorothy Harrison
Founded 1998
Open Mon-Fri 3-7
MADISON COUNTY BRANCH, 1315 Hwy 98 W, Danielsville, 30633. (Mail add: PO Box 38, Danielsville, 30633-0038), SAN 338-2893. Tel: 706-795-5597. FAX: 706-795-0830. Web Site: www.athenslibrary.org/madison. *Br Mgr,* Kim James; *Ch Serv Spec,* Jennifer Ivey; *Computer Spec,* Alisa Claytor
Founded 1935
Automation Activity & Vendor Info: (Acquisitions) Baker & Taylor; (Cataloging) Baker & Taylor; (Circulation) Evergreen; (OPAC) Evergreen
Database Vendor: Baker & Taylor, Booklist Online, Dun & Bradstreet, EBSCO Information Services, EBSCOhost, Facts on File, Gale Cengage Learning, Medline, ValueLine, WebMD, Wilson - Wilson Web
Function: Art exhibits, Audiobks via web, Bks on cassette, Bks on CD, Children's prog, Computer training, Computers for patron use, Copy machines, Digital talking bks, Electronic databases & coll, Exhibits, Fax serv, Free DVD rentals, Handicapped accessible, Holiday prog, Home delivery & serv to Sr ctr & nursing homes, ILL available, Large print keyboards, Music CDs, Online cat, OverDrive digital audio bks, Photocopying/Printing, Prog for children & young adult, Scanner, Senior computer classes, Story hour, Summer reading prog, Tax forms, Teen prog, Telephone ref, VHS videos, Wheelchair accessible
Open Mon, Wed, Fri & Sat 10-6, Tues & Thurs 10-8, Sun 2-6
Friends of the Library Group

NORTHEAST GEORGIA TALKING BOOK CENTER, 2025 Baxter St, 30606-6331, SAN 338-2788. Tel: 706-310-3650. Toll Free Tel: 800-531-2063. FAX: 706-769-3952. E-mail: talkingbooks@athenslibrary.org. Web Site: www.athenslibrary.org/talking-book-center. *Mgr,* Claudia Markov
Founded 1975
Special Collections: Accessibility, Handicapping Conditions, Aids & Appliances for Handicapped (Reference Coll)
Publications: Insight Newsletter (Quarterly)
Open Mon & Wed 10-9, Tues & Thurs-Sat 10-6, Sun 2-6
Restriction: Registered patrons only

OCONEE COUNTY-WATKINSVILLE BRANCH, 1080 Experiment Station Rd, Watkinsville, 30677. (Mail add: PO Box 837, Watkinsville, 30677-0019), SAN 338-2923. Tel: 706-769-3950. FAX: 706-769-3952. Web Site: www.athenslibrary.org/oconee. *Br Mgr,* Rhea Hebert; Tel: 706-769-3951
Founded 1940
Open Mon, Wed, Fri & Sat 10-6, Tues & Thurs 10-9, Sun 2-6
Friends of the Library Group

OGLETHORPE COUNTY BRANCH, 858 Athens Rd, Lexington, 30648. (Mail add: PO Box 100, Lexington, 30648-0100), SAN 338-2958. Tel: 706-743-8817. FAX: 706-743-8817. Web Site: www.athenslibrary.org/oglethorpe. *Br Mgr,* Tiffany Speed
Founded 1940
Open Mon, Wed & Fri 10-6, Tues & Thurs 10-9, Sat 10-2, Sun 2-6
Friends of the Library Group

PINEWOODS LIBRARY & LEARNING CENTER, North Lot G-10, 1465 US Hwy 29 N, 30628. (Mail add: 2025 Baxter St, 30606). Tel: 706-613-3708. FAX: 706-613-3708. Web Site: www.athenslibrary.org/pinewoods. *Br Mgr,* Aida Quinones
Founded 2005
Open Mon-Thurs 1-8, Fri 11-1

ROYSTON BRANCH, 634 Franklin Springs St, Royston, 30662, SAN 338-2982. Tel: 706-245-6748. FAX: 706-245-6748. Web Site: www.athenslibrary.org/royston. *Br Mgr,* Rosie Chitwood
Founded 1920
Open Mon & Fri 10-6, Tues & Thurs 10-8, Sat 10-2
Friends of the Library Group

WINTERVILLE BRANCH, 115 Marigold Lane, Winterville, 30683. (Mail add: PO Box 89, Winterville, 30683-0089), SAN 338-3016. Tel: 706-742-7735. FAX: 706-742-7735. Web Site: www.athenslibrary.org/winterville. *Br Mgr,* Toby Mayfield
Founded 1974
Open Mon, Tues & Thurs 3-7, Wed 9-12, Sat 10-2
Friends of the Library Group

J ATHENS TECHNICAL COLLEGE LIBRARY*, 800 US Hwy 29 N, 30601-1500. SAN 323-5513. Tel: 706-355-5020. Interlibrary Loan Service Tel: 706-355-5164. Administration Tel: 706-355-5019. FAX: 706-355-5162. E-mail: alibrary@athenstech.edu, elibrary@athenstech.edu. Web Site: library.athenstech.edu. *Dir, Libr Serv,* Carol Stanley; E-mail: cstanley@athenstech.edu; *Circ Mgr, Librn, Mgr, Per,* Qian Fang; E-mail: qfang@athenstech.edu; Staff 5 (MLS 3, Non-MLS 2)
Founded 1984. Enrl 9,000; Fac 150; Highest Degree: Associate
Library Holdings: AV Mats 4,250; e-books 120,000; Electronic Media & Resources 310; Bk Titles 37,841; Per Subs 512; Videos 10,000
Special Collections: Allied Health Coll; Technical Education
Automation Activity & Vendor Info: (Acquisitions) SirsiDynix; (Cataloging) SirsiDynix; (Circulation) SirsiDynix; (OPAC) SirsiDynix; (Serials) SirsiDynix
Database Vendor: 3M Library Systems, ALLDATA Online, Cinahl, EBSCO Auto Repair Reference, EBSCO Discovery Service, EBSCOhost, Gale Cengage Learning, LearningExpress, OCLC, OCLC WorldShare Interlibrary Loan, ProQuest, SirsiDynix, Westlaw
Wireless access
Function: Audio & video playback equip for onsite use, CD-ROM, Distance learning, Electronic databases & coll, Handicapped accessible, Health sci info serv, ILL available, Mail & tel request accepted, Orientations, Photocopying/Printing, Ref serv available, Spoken cassettes & CDs, VHS videos, Wheelchair accessible
Partic in Georgia Online Database
Open Mon-Thurs 7:30am-10pm, Fri & Sat 7:30-4
Restriction: Authorized personnel only

Departmental Libraries:

ELBERT COUNTY CAMPUS, 1317 Athens Hwy, Elberton, 30635, SAN 377-7863. Tel: 706-213-2116. FAX: 706-213-2149. *Br Librn, Cat, ILL,* Carol Stanley; Staff 1 (MLS 1)
Founded 1997
Automation Activity & Vendor Info: (Cataloging) OCLC; (ILL) OCLC; (Serials) EBSCO Online
Function: Audio & video playback equip for onsite use, CD-ROM, Distance learning, Electronic databases & coll, Handicapped accessible, Homebound delivery serv, ILL available, Orientations, Photocopying/Printing, Ref serv available, Telephone ref, VHS videos, Wheelchair accessible
Open Mon-Thurs 7:30am-10pm, Fri 7:30-4

GREENE COUNTY CAMPUS, 1051 Athens Tech Dr, Greensboro, 30642. Tel: 706-453-0536. *Support Serv Coordr,* Marjorie Heimer
Automation Activity & Vendor Info: (Cataloging) OCLC; (ILL) OCLC; (Serials) EBSCO Online
Database Vendor: LearningExpress, OCLC WorldShare Interlibrary Loan, SirsiDynix
Function: Audio & video playback equip for onsite use, CD-ROM, Distance learning, Electronic databases & coll, Handicapped accessible, Homebound delivery serv, ILL available, Orientations, Photocopying/Printing, Ref serv available, Telephone ref, VHS videos, Wheelchair accessible
Open Mon-Thurs 7:30am-10pm, Fri 7:30-4

WALTON COUNTY CAMPUS, 212 Bryant Rd, Monroe, 30648. Tel: 770-207-3126. *Support Serv Coordr,* Marjorie Heimer
Automation Activity & Vendor Info: (Cataloging) OCLC; (ILL) OCLC; (Serials) EBSCO Online
Database Vendor: LearningExpress, OCLC WorldShare Interlibrary Loan, SirsiDynix
Function: Audio & video playback equip for onsite use, CD-ROM, Distance learning, Electronic databases & coll, Handicapped accessible, Homebound delivery serv, ILL available, Orientations, Photocopying/Printing, Ref serv available, Telephone ref, VHS videos, Wheelchair accessible
Open Mon-Thurs 7:30am-10pm, Fri 7:30-4

G ENVIRONMENTAL PROTECTION AGENCY*, Ecosystems Research Division - Athens Library, 960 College Station Rd, 30605-2700. SAN 303-2590. Tel: 706-355-8015. FAX: 706-355-8007. *Librn,* Position Currently Open
Founded 1966
Library Holdings: Bk Vols 5,000; Per Subs 113
Subject Interests: Biol, Chem, Eng, Microbiology, Spectroscopy
Open Tues-Thurs 8-4:30

S THE STATE BOTANICAL GARDEN OF GEORGIA LIBRARY*, 2450 S Milledge Ave, 30605. SAN 375-7080. Tel: 706-542-3977. Administration Tel: 706-542-1244. FAX: 706-542-3091. E-mail: garden@uga.edu. *Librn,* Ginny Knappenberger; Staff 3 (MLS 1, Non-MLS 2)
Founded 1990
Library Holdings: Bk Titles 2,000; Per Subs 24
Subject Interests: Botany, Gardening, Hort, Landscape design
Restriction: Open to pub with supv only, Staff & prof res, Use of others with permission of librn

UNIVERSITY OF GEORGIA

CL ALEXANDER CAMPBELL KING LAW LIBRARY*, 225 Herty Dr, 30602-6018, SAN 338-3105. Tel: 706-542-1922. Interlibrary Loan Service Tel: 706-542-6670. Reference Tel: 706-542-6591. Administration Tel: 706-542-8480. FAX: 706-542-5001. Web Site: www.law.uga.edu/library. *Dir,* Carol A Watson; E-mail: cwatson@uga.edu; *Adminr,* Deborah Baker; E-mail: debbb@uga.edu; *Acq Librn,* Wendy Moore; Tel: 706-542-5081, E-mail: wemoore@uga.edu; *Cat Serv Librn,* Suzanne R Graham; Tel: 706-542-5082, Fax: 706-542-5130, E-mail: srgraham@uga.edu; *Fac Serv Librn,* Thomas J Striepe; Tel: 706-542-5077, E-mail: tstriepe@uga.edu; *Foreign & Intl Law Librn,* Anne E Burnett; Tel: 702-542-5298; *IT Librn,* Jason Tubinis; Tel: 706-542-7365; *Spec Coll Librn,* Sharon A Bradley; Tel: 706-542-5083, E-mail: bradleys@uga.edu; *Student Serv Librn,* Maureen Cahill; Tel: 706-542-3825, E-mail: mcahill@uga.edu; Staff 25 (MLS 8, Non-MLS 17)
Founded 1859. Enrl 675; Fac 40
Special Collections: The Louis B Sohn Library on International Studies
Subject Interests: Intl law
Automation Activity & Vendor Info: (Acquisitions) Innovative Interfaces, Inc; (Cataloging) Innovative Interfaces, Inc; (Circulation) Innovative Interfaces, Inc; (Course Reserve) Innovative Interfaces, Inc; (ILL) Innovative Interfaces, Inc; (Media Booking) Innovative Interfaces, Inc; (Serials) Innovative Interfaces, Inc
Database Vendor: Bloomberg, Cassidy Cataloguing Services, Inc, CQ Press, EBSCOhost, Fastcase, Gale Cengage Learning, HeinOnline, Innovative Interfaces, Inc, LexisNexis, Marcive, Inc, OCLC, ProQuest, SerialsSolutions, Westlaw, YBP Library Services
Function: Res libr
Partic in Lyrasis

C OWENS LIBRARY*, School of Environmental Design, G14 Caldwell Hall, 30602. (Mail add: College of Environment & Design, 609 Caldwell Hall, 30602-1845), SAN 377-6220. Tel: 706-542-8292. FAX: 706-542-4485. Web Site: www.sed.uga.edu/facilities/owenslibrary.htm. *Dir,* Rene D Shoemaker, IV; E-mail: rds@uga.edu; Staff 1 (MLS 1)
Library Holdings: Bk Vols 6,000
Subject Interests: Landscape archit, Planning

Automation Activity & Vendor Info: (Cataloging) Inmagic, Inc.; (Circulation) Inmagic, Inc.; (Serials) Inmagic, Inc.
Open Mon-Fri 8:30-6

C UNIVERSITY OF GEORGIA LIBRARIES*, 30602-1641. SAN 338-3075. Tel: 706-542-0621. Circulation Tel: 706-542-3256. Interlibrary Loan Service Tel: 706-542-3274. Reference Tel: 706-542-8460. FAX: 706-542-4144. Web Site: www.libs.uga.edu. *Assoc Provost, Univ Librn,* Toby Graham; E-mail: tgraham@uga.edu; *Head, Coll Develop,* Nan McMurry; Tel: 706-542-8474, E-mail: nmcmurry@uga.edu; Staff 261 (MLS 75, Non-MLS 186)
Founded 1785. Enrl 33,418; Fac 1,832; Highest Degree: Doctorate
Library Holdings: Bk Vols 4,028,611; Per Subs 67,268
Special Collections: Hargrett Rare Book & Manuscript Library; Richard B Russell Library for Political Research & Studies; Walter J Brown Media Archives & Peabody Awards Coll. State Document Depository; UN Document Depository; US Document Depository
Subject Interests: Ecology, Intl relations, Law, Math, Med, Photog
Automation Activity & Vendor Info: (Acquisitions) Ex Libris Group; (Cataloging) Ex Libris Group; (Circulation) Ex Libris Group; (Course Reserve) Ex Libris Group; (ILL) Ex Libris Group; (Media Booking) Ex Libris Group; (OPAC) Ex Libris Group; (Serials) Ex Libris Group
Database Vendor: EBSCOhost, LexisNexis, OCLC FirstSearch, OVID Technologies, ProQuest, Wilson - Wilson Web
Wireless access
Function: Res libr

Departmental Libraries:

SKIDAWAY INSTITUTE OF OCEANOGRAPHY
See Separate Entry in Savannah

ATLANTA

C ACA LIBRARY OF SAVANNAH COLLEGE OF ART & DESIGN, 1600 Peachtree St NW, 30309. SAN 303-2647. Tel: 404-253-3196. FAX: 404-253-3278. E-mail: ref_atl@scad.edu. Web Site: www.scad.edu/life/libraries. *Dir,* Teresa Burk; *Cat,* Jenny Wang; Staff 5 (MLS 4, Non-MLS 1)
Founded 1905. Enrl 1,900; Highest Degree: Master
Library Holdings: Bk Vols 60,000; Per Subs 145
Special Collections: Artists' Books Coll; Rare Book Coll
Subject Interests: Animation, Art, Art hist, Design, Drawing, Film, Liberal arts, Painting, Photog, Printmaking, Sculpture, Video
Automation Activity & Vendor Info: (Cataloging) Innovative Interfaces, Inc - Millenium; (Circulation) Innovative Interfaces, Inc - Millenium; (Course Reserve) Innovative Interfaces, Inc - Millenium; (OPAC) Innovative Interfaces, Inc - Millenium; (Serials) Innovative Interfaces, Inc - Millenium
Database Vendor: Wilson - Wilson Web
Wireless access
Function: Art exhibits, ILL available, Workshops
Partic in Atlanta Regional Council for Higher Education
Restriction: External users must contact libr

L ALSTON & BIRD LAW LIBRARY*, One Atlantic Ctr, 1201 W Peachtree St, 30309-3424. SAN 303-2620. Tel: 404-881-7120. FAX: 404-881-7777. *Librn,* Frances Pughsley; Staff 8 (MLS 6, Non-MLS 2)
Founded 1893
Library Holdings: Bk Titles 5,000
Subject Interests: Antitrust law, Banks & banking, Finance, Labor, Securities
Restriction: Private libr

AMERICAN INTERCONTINENTAL UNIVERSITY
C ATLANTA CAMPUS LIBRARY*, 6600 Peachtree Dunwoody Rd, 30328. Tel: 404-965-6533. E-mail: atllib@aiuniv.edu. Web Site: www.aiuniv.edu/Atlanta/Library. *Dir, Libr & Info Serv,* Heather Dray; Tel: 404-965-6547, E-mail: hdray@aiuniv.edu; Staff 2 (MLS 2)
Founded 1977. Enrl 1,200; Fac 21; Highest Degree: Master
Library Holdings: DVDs 2,500; Bk Vols 6,500; Per Subs 85
Automation Activity & Vendor Info: (Cataloging) TLC (The Library Corporation); (Circulation) TLC (The Library Corporation); (OPAC) TLC (The Library Corporation)
Partic in GALILEO (Georgia Library Learning Online); SEFLIN - Southeast Florida Library Information Network, Inc
Open Mon-Thurs 7am-10pm, Fri 7-5, Sat 9-4

C DUNWOODY CAMPUS-MEDIA CENTER, 6600 Peachtree-Dunwoody Rd, 500 Embassy Row, 30328. Tel: 404-965-6533. Web Site: www.aiuniv.edu. *Dir, IT,* Rahem Gaines; Staff 2 (MLS 2)
Founded 1998. Highest Degree: Master
Library Holdings: e-books 22,000; Bk Vols 3,700; Per Subs 56; Videos 160
Special Collections: Global Culture Coll
Subject Interests: Bus, Criminal justice, Game design, Info tech, Visual communications
Automation Activity & Vendor Info: (Cataloging) TLC (The Library Corporation); (Circulation) TLC (The Library Corporation); (OPAC) TLC (The Library Corporation)
Database Vendor: Factiva.com
Partic in GALILEO (Georgia Library Learning Online)
Open Mon-Thurs 7:30am-10pm, Fri & Sat 9-3

C ARGOSY UNIVERSITY*, Atlanta Library, Bldg 2, Ste 400, 980 Hammond Dr, 30328. SAN 378-1984. Tel: 770-407-1033. Interlibrary Loan Service Tel: 770-407-1087. Information Services Tel: 770-407-1034. FAX: 770-671-0418. *Dir, Libr & Info Serv,* Betts Markle; Tel: 770-407-1047; *Ref Serv Coordr,* David McCullough; E-mail: dmccullough@argosyu.edu; *ILL,* Tyvon Chisum; E-mail: tchisum@argosyu.edu. Subject Specialists: *Educ,* Betts Markle; *Clinical psychol,* David McCullough; Staff 3 (MLS 2, Non-MLS 1)
Founded 1990. Enrl 2,000; Fac 50; Highest Degree: Doctorate
Sept 2005-Aug 2006 Income $450,000. Mats Exp $215,000. Sal $133,000
Library Holdings: AV Mats 400; DVDs 50; e-books 36,000; Bk Titles 6,500; Per Subs 120
Special Collections: Myth, Symbols & Magic (Paul Schenk Coll)
Subject Interests: Bus, Clinical psychol, Educ
Automation Activity & Vendor Info: (Cataloging) OCLC; (Circulation) Ex Libris Group; (Course Reserve) Ex Libris Group; (ILL) OCLC; (OPAC) Ex Libris Group
Database Vendor: EBSCOhost, Gale Cengage Learning, LexisNexis, OCLC FirstSearch, OCLC WorldShare Interlibrary Loan, ProQuest
Wireless access
Function: ILL available, Orientations, Photocopying/Printing, Ref serv available, Telephone ref, VCDs, VHS videos
Partic in Atlanta Health Science Libraries Consortium; Georgetown LIS Health Sci Libr Consortium; Georgia Private Acad Librs Consortium (GPALS); Lyrasis
Open Mon-Fri 8-10, Sat & Sun 8-8
Restriction: Circ limited, Open to pub for ref only, Open to students, fac & staff, Prof mat only

C ART INSTITUTE OF ATLANTA LIBRARY*, 6600 Peachtree-Dunwoody Rd, 100 Embassy Row, 30328-1635. Tel: 770-689-4885. FAX: 770-730-8767. E-mail: aialibrary@aii.edu. Web Site: www.aii.edu. *Dir, Libr Serv,* Lametric Patterson; Staff 6 (MLS 4, Non-MLS 2)
Founded 1949. Enrl 2,642; Highest Degree: Bachelor
Library Holdings: CDs 1,534; DVDs 3,332; Electronic Media & Resources 54; Bk Vols 52,127; Per Subs 185; Videos 325
Special Collections: Bookout Interior Design Coll
Subject Interests: Culinary arts, Design, Digital film, Fashion, Media arts
Automation Activity & Vendor Info: (Cataloging) Ex Libris Group; (Circulation) Ex Libris Group; (ILL) OCLC WorldShare Interlibrary Loan; (OPAC) Ex Libris Group
Database Vendor: 3M Library Systems, Baker & Taylor, EBSCO Information Services, EBSCOhost, Electric Library, Ex Libris Group, H W Wilson, LexisNexis, MITINET, Inc, OCLC WorldShare Interlibrary Loan, Oxford Online, ProQuest, Safari Books Online, Wilson - Wilson Web
Wireless access
Function: Computers for patron use, Copy machines, Electronic databases & coll, Online cat, Ref & res
Partic in GALILEO (Georgia Library Learning Online)
Open Mon-Thurs 7:30am-10pm, Fri 7:30-6, Sat 8:30-5:30, Sun 1-5
Restriction: Access at librarian's discretion, Borrowing privileges limited to fac & registered students, Borrowing requests are handled by ILL, In-house use for visitors, Non-circulating coll, Use of others with permission of librn

S ATLANTA BOTANICAL GARDEN*, Sheffield Botanical Library & Orchid Reference Library, 1345 Piedmont Ave NE, 30309-3366. SAN 374-5597. Tel: 404-591-1546, 404-591-1725. FAX: 404-876-7472. E-mail: info@atlantabotanicalgarden.org. Web Site: www.atlantabotanicalgarden.org. *Librn,* E Marvel; E-mail: emarvel@atlantabotanicalgarden.org; Staff 1 (MLS 1)
Founded 1985
Library Holdings: Bk Titles 8,000; Per Subs 125
Subject Interests: Botany, Hort
Open Tues-Sun (Nov-March) 9-5; Tues-Sun (April-Oct) 9-7

P ATLANTA-FULTON PUBLIC LIBRARY SYSTEM, Central Library & Library System Headquarters, One Margaret Mitchell Sq, 30303-1089. SAN 338-313X. Tel: 404-730-1700, 404-730-1972. Circulation Tel: 404-730-1824. Interlibrary Loan Service Tel: 404-730-1937. Reference Tel: 404-730-4636. FAX: 404-756-6472. TDD: 404-730-1998. Web Site: www.afpls.org. *Interim Dir,* Anne T Haimes; Tel: 404-730-1881, E-mail: anne.haimes@fultoncountyga.gov; Staff 454 (MLS 144, Non-MLS 310)
Founded 1902. Pop 969,033; Circ 2,534,636
Jan 2006-Dec 2006 Income $30,600,000, State $1,200,000, City $1,100,000, County $27,500,000, Other $800,000. Mats Exp $3,700,000
Library Holdings: Bk Titles 600,000; Bk Vols 2,219,609; Per Subs 6,000

Special Collections: Coll on the History of Atlanta, Georgia & the Southeast; Genealogy Coll; Margaret Mitchell Exhibit. Oral History; US Document Depository
Automation Activity & Vendor Info: (Acquisitions) SirsiDynix; (Cataloging) SirsiDynix; (Circulation) SirsiDynix; (Course Reserve) SirsiDynix; (ILL) OCLC WorldShare Interlibrary Loan; (OPAC) SirsiDynix; (Serials) SirsiDynix
Wireless access
Publications: Access (Newsletter)
Special Services for the Deaf - Bks on deafness & sign lang; Captioned film dep; High interest/low vocabulary bks; Spec interest per; TTY equip
Special Services for the Blind - Reader equip
Open Mon 10-5, Tues 10-7, Wed & Thurs 12-6, Fri-Sun 1-5
Friends of the Library Group
Branches: 32

ADAMS PARK BRANCH, 2231 Campbellton Rd SW, 30311, SAN 338-3164. Tel: 404-752-8763. FAX: 404-752-8765. Web Site: www.afplweb.com/adams-park-branch. *Br Mgr,* Tosha Bussey; *YA Serv,* Shirelle Atkins
Library Holdings: Bk Vols 39,704
Open Mon, Fri & Sat 12-6, Tues & Thurs 10-6, Wed 10-8
Friends of the Library Group

ADAMSVILLE-COLLIER HEIGHTS BRANCH, 3424 Martin Luther King Jr Dr, 30331, SAN 338-3288. Tel: 404-699-4206. FAX: 404-699-6380. Web Site: www.afplweb.com/adamsville-collier-branch. *Br Mgr,* Gabrielle Taylor; *Ch,* Emma Laster; E-mail: emma.laster@fultoncountyga.gov
Library Holdings: Bk Vols 49,327
Open Mon 12-8, Tues-Thurs 10-6, Fri & Sat 12-6
Friends of the Library Group

ALPHARETTA BRANCH, 238 Canton St, Alpharetta, 30009, SAN 338-3199. Tel: 770-740-2425. FAX: 770-740-2427. Web Site: www.afplweb.com/alpharetta-branch. *Br Mgr,* Gayle Holloman; *Asst Br Mgr,* Michael Salpeter; *YA Serv,* Amy Alexander
Library Holdings: Bk Vols 78,562
Open Mon & Wed 10-8, Tues & Thurs 10-6, Fri & Sat 11-6
Friends of the Library Group

AUBURN AVENUE RESEARCH LIBRARY ON AFRICAN-AMERICAN CULTURE & HISTORY, 101 Auburn Ave NE, 30303-2503, SAN 375-1465. Tel: 404-730-4001. Reference Tel: 404-730-4001, Ext 100. FAX: 404-730-5879. Web Site: www.afpls.org/aarl. *Principal Librn,* Sharon E Robinson; Tel: 404-730-4001, Ext 210, E-mail: sharone.robinson@fultoncountyga.gov; *Sr Librn,* Okezie Amalaha; Tel: 404-730-4001, Ext 207, E-mail: okezie.amalaha@fultoncountyga.gov; *Mgr, Sr Librn,* Morris Gardner; E-mail: morris.gardner@fultoncountyga.gov; *Sr Librn,* Charmaine Johnson; Tel: 407-730-4001, Ext 104, E-mail: charmaine.johnson@fultoncountyga.gov; *Sr Librn,* Gloria Mims; Tel: 404-730-4001, Ext 108, E-mail: gloria.mims@fultoncountyga.gov; *Librn,* Eleanor Hunter; Tel: 404-730-4001, Ext 107, E-mail: eleanor.hunter@fultoncountyga.gov; *Librn,* Benjamin Scott; Tel: 404-730-4001, Ext 106, E-mail: benjamin.scott@fultoncountyga.gov; *Librn II,* Carolyn Clark; Tel: 404-730-4001, Ext 105, E-mail: carolyn.clark@fultoncountyga.gov; *Librn II,* Colin Dube; Tel: 404-730-4001, Ext 302, E-mail: colin.dube@fultoncountyga.gov; *Archives Mgr,* Kerrie Cotten Williams; Tel: 404 730 4001, Ext 111, E-mail: kerrie.williams@fultoncountyga.gov; *Libr Assoc,* Angela Ahmad; Tel: 404-730-4001, Ext 308, E-mail: angela.ahmad@fultoncountyg; *Libr Assoc,* Willie Mae Collier; E-mail: willie.collier@fultoncountyga.gov; *Libr Assoc,* Anita Martin; E-mail: anita.martin@fultoncountyga.gov; *Libr Assoc,* Alvin R Robinson; *Libr Assoc,* Marquita Gooch; E-mail: marquita.gooch@fultoncountyga.gov; *Rec Doc Spec,* Jerome Huff; E-mail: jerome.huff@fultoncountyga.gov
Founded 1994
Library Holdings: Bk Vols 54,457
Special Collections: Ambassador Andrew Young Papers; Hosea Williams Coll; Weems Photographic Coll
Function: For res purposes
Open Mon 10-6, Tues-Thurs 12-8, Fri & Sat 12-6, Sun 2-6
Restriction: Non-circulating coll
Friends of the Library Group

BOWEN/BANKHEAD BRANCH, 2685 Donald Lee Hollowell Pkwy, NW, 30318, SAN 370-4742. Tel: 404-792-2646. FAX: 404-332-0459. Web Site: www.afplweb.com/bowen-bankhead-branch. *Br Mgr,* Kelley F Flowers; E-mail: kelley.flowers@fultoncountyga.gov
Library Holdings: Bk Vols 14,241
Open Mon 12-7, Tues 10-6, Wed-Sat 12-6, Sun 2-6

BUCKHEAD BRANCH, 269 Buckhead Ave NE, 30305, SAN 338-361X. Tel: 404-814-3500. FAX: 404-814-3503. Web Site: www.afplweb.com/buckhead-branch. *Br Mgr,* Jane Taylor; *Asst Br Mgr, Sr Ref Librn,* Angela Simpson; E-mail: simpson.angela1@fultoncountyga.gov
Library Holdings: Bk Vols 113,608
Open Mon & Tues 10-6, Wed & Thurs 10-8, Fri & Sat 11-6
Friends of the Library Group

CARVER HOMES BRANCH, 215 Lakewood Way, Ste 104, 30315. Tel: 404-635-4012. FAX: 404-635-4016. *Br Mgr,* Beverly Hawes; E-mail: beverly.hawes@fultoncountyga.gov
Library Holdings: Bk Vols 14,131
Open Mon, Thurs, & Fri 12-6, Tues & Wed 10-6, Sat 10-4

CLEVELAND AVENUE BRANCH, 47 Cleveland Ave SW, 30315, SAN 373-9333. Tel: 404-762-4116. FAX: 404-762-4118. Web Site: www.afplweb.com/cleveland-ave-branch. *Br Mgr,* Gloria Dennis; E-mail: gloria.dennis@fultoncountyga.gov; *Ch,* Vanessa Slaton; E-mail: vanessa.slaton@fultoncountyga.gov
Library Holdings: Bk Vols 56,238
Open Mon 10-8, Tues & Thurs 10-6, Wed, Fri & Sat 12-6
Friends of the Library Group

COLLEGE PARK BRANCH, 3647 Main St, College Park, 30337, SAN 338-3253. Tel: 404-762-4060. FAX: 404-762-4062. Web Site: www.afplweb.com/college-park-branch. *Br Mgr,* Bonita McZorn; E-mail: bonita.mczorn@fultoncountyga.gov; *Ch,* Kimara Mason
Open Mon, Fri & Sat 12-6, Tues & Thurs 10-6, Wed 10-8
Friends of the Library Group

PONCE DE LEON BRANCH, 980 Ponce de Leon Ave NE, 30306, SAN 338-3555. Tel: 404-885-7820. FAX: 404-885-7822. Web Site: www.afplweb.com/ponce-branch6. *Br Mgr,* Position Currently Open; *Youth/Young Adult Librn,* Madigan McGillicuddy
Library Holdings: Bk Vols 86,171
Open Mon, Thurs & Sat 10-6, Tues & Wed 10-8, Fri 12-6, Sun 2-6

DOGWOOD BRANCH, 1838 Donald L Hollowell Pkwy NW, 30318, SAN 338-3342. Tel: 404-792-4961. FAX: 404-792-4963. Web Site: www.afplweb.com/dogwood-branch. *Librn,* Debra Perry; E-mail: debra.perry@fultoncountyga.gov; *Ch,* Vincent Chukumah; E-mail: vincent.chukumah@fultoncountyga.gov
Library Holdings: Bk Vols 39,350
Open Mon, Fri & Sat 12-6, Tues 10-8, Wed & Thurs 10-6
Friends of the Library Group

EAST ATLANTA BRANCH, 400 Flat Shoals Ave SE, 30316, SAN 338-3407. Tel: 404-730-5438. FAX: 404-730-5436. Web Site: www.afplweb.com/east-atlanta-branch. *Br Mgr,* Shannon Duffy; *Asst Br Mgr, Ch,* Oscar Gittemeier
Library Holdings: Bk Vols 38,621
Open Mon 10-8, Tues & Wed 10-6, Thurs-Sat 12-6
Friends of the Library Group

EAST POINT BRANCH, 2757 Main St, East Point, 30344, SAN 376-8546. Tel: 404-762-4842. FAX: 404-762-4844. Web Site: www.afplweb.com/east-point-branch. *Br Mgr,* Michael Hickman; E-mail: michael.hickman@fultoncountyga.gov; *Asst Br Mgr,* Derek Wilson; *Ch,* Kaleema Abdurrahman
Library Holdings: Bk Vols 68,331
Open Mon & Tues 10-8, Wed 12-8, Thurs-Sat 12-6, Sun 2-6
Friends of the Library Group

FAIRBURN BRANCH, 60 Valley View Dr, Fairburn, 30213, SAN 338-358X. Tel: 770-306-3138. FAX: 770-306-3140. Web Site: afpls.org/fairburn-branch. *Br Mgr,* Eugene Haston; E-mail: eugene.haston@fultoncountyga.gov; *Asst Br Mgr, Ch,* Evette Bridges; E-mail: evette.bridges@fultoncountyga.gov
Library Holdings: Bk Vols 38,371
Open Mon, Fri & Sat 12-6, Tues 10-8, Wed & Thurs 10-6

P DR ROBERT E FULTON LIBRARY AT OCEE, 5090 Abbotts Bridge Rd, Johns Creek, 30005. Tel: 770-360-8897. *Br Mgr,* Carla Burton; E-mail: carla.burton@fultoncountyga.gov; *Asst Br Mgr, Youth Serv Coordr,* Karen Kennedy; E-mail: karen.kennedy@fultoncountyga.gov; *Ref Librn,* John Offerdahl; E-mail: john.offerdahl@fultoncountyga.gov
Library Holdings: Bk Vols 191,594
Open Mon-Wed 10-8, Thurs-Sat 10-6, Sun 2-6
Friends of the Library Group

GEORGIA HILL BRANCH, 250 Georgia Ave SE, 30312, SAN 338-3466. Tel: 404-730-5427. FAX: 404-730-5429. Web Site: www.afplweb.com/georgia-hill-branch. *Br Mgr,* Position Currently Open; *Ch,* Edna Godfrey; E-mail: edna.godfrey@fultoncountyga.gov
Library Holdings: Bk Vols 31,185
Open Mon & Thurs-Sat 12-6, Tues 10-6, Wed 12-7

HAPEVILLE BRANCH, 525 King Arnold St, Hapeville, 30354, SAN 338-3520. Tel: 404-762-4065. FAX: 404-762-4067. Web Site: www.afplweb.com/hapeville-branch. *Br Mgr,* Position Currently Open; *Ch,* Mary Clarendon Inman
Library Holdings: Bk Vols 32,246
Open Mon 12-7, Tues-Thurs 10-6, Fri & Sat 12-6
Friends of the Library Group

MARTIN LUTHER KING JR BRANCH, 409 John Wesley Dobbs Ave, 30312-1342, SAN 338-3709. Tel: 404-730-1185. FAX: 404-893-6858. Web Site: www.afplweb.com/mlk-branch. *Br Mgr,* Position Currently Open
Library Holdings: Bk Vols 24,764
Function: Children's prog, Computer training, Homework prog, Music CDs, Prog for adults, Pub access computers, VHS videos
Open Mon-Wed 10-6, Thurs-Sat 12-6

KIRKWOOD BRANCH, 11 Kirkwood Rd SE, 30317, SAN 338-3679. Tel: 404-377-6471. FAX: 404-373-5024. Web Site: www.afplweb.com/kirkwood-branch. *Ch,* Leilani McWilliams; E-mail: leilani.mcwilliams@fultoncountyga.gov
Library Holdings: Bk Vols 31,024
Open Mon 10-8, Tues & Wed 10-6, Thurs-Sat 12-6
Friends of the Library Group

MECHANICSVILLE BRANCH, 400 Formwalt St SW, 30312, SAN 338-3377. Tel: 404-730-4779. FAX: 404-730-4778. Web Site: www.afplweb.com/mechanicsville-branch. *Br Mgr,* David Thrash; *Ch,* Denise Barbour
Library Holdings: Bk Vols 36,352
Open Mon 10-8, Tues & Wed 10-6, Thurs-Sat 12-6

NORTHSIDE BRANCH, 3295 Northside Pkwy NW, 30327, SAN 338-3768. Tel: 404-814-3508. FAX: 404-814-3511. Web Site: www.afplweb.com/northside-branch. *Br Mgr,* Howell Williams; E-mail: howell.williams@fultoncountyga.gov; *Asst Br Mgr, Ch,* Swalena Griffin; E-mail: swalena.griffin@fultoncountyga.gov; *Ref Librn,* Sandra Anderson; E-mail: sandra.alexander@fultoncountyga.gov
Library Holdings: Bk Vols 64,861
Open Mon & Tues 10-8, Wed, Thurs & Sat 10-6, Fri 12-6
Friends of the Library Group

OCEE BRANCH, 5090 Abbotts Bridge Rd, Johns Creek, 30005-4601. Tel: 770-360-8897. FAX: 770-360-8892. *Br Mgr,* Carla Burton; E-mail: carla.burton@fultoncountyga.gov; *Asst Br Mgr, Head, Ch,* Marcia Divack; E-mail: marcia.divack@fultoncountyga.gov; *Ch,* Karen Kennedy; E-mail: karen.kennedy@fultoncountyga.gov; *Ref Librn,* John Offerdahl; E-mail: john.offerdahl@fultoncountyga.gov; *YA Serv,* Virginia Cline; E-mail: virginia.cline@fultoncountyga.gov
Library Holdings: Bk Vols 141,000
Open Mon, Tues, Fri & Sat 10-6, Wed & Thurs 10-8, Sun 2-6
Friends of the Library Group

PEACHTREE BRANCH, 1315 Peachtree St NE, 30309, SAN 329-7438. Tel: 404-885-7830. FAX: 404-885-7833. Web Site: afplweb.com/peachtree-branch6. *Br Mgr,* Hensley Roberts; E-mail: hensley.roberts@fultoncountyga.gov
Library Holdings: Bk Vols 55,133
Open Mon & Tues 10-6, Wed 10-8, Thurs-Sat 12-6
Friends of the Library Group

PERRY HOMES BRANCH, 2011 Bolton Rd, 30318, SAN 370-4769. Tel: 404-792-4994. FAX: 404-893-6795. Web Site: www.afplweb.com/perry-homes-branch6. *Br Mgr,* Kysh Clemons
Library Holdings: Bk Vols 14,740
Open Mon & Tues 10-6, Wed, Fri & Sat 12-6, Thurs 12-8

ROSWELL BRANCH, 115 Norcross St, Roswell, 30075, SAN 338-3857. Tel: 770-640-3075. FAX: 770-640-3077. Web Site: www.afplweb.com/roswell-branch6. *Br Mgr,* Position Currently Open; *Asst Br Mgr,* Margaret Bradford; E-mail: margaret.bradford@fultoncountyga.gov; *Ch,* Virginia Collier; *Ch,* Angela Whelchel; E-mail: angela.whelchel@fultoncountyga.gov
Founded 1946
Library Holdings: Bk Vols 125,000
Open Mon & Tues 10-8, Wed-Sat 10-6, Sun 2-6
Friends of the Library Group

SANDY SPRINGS BRANCH, 395 Mount Vernon Hwy NE, Sandy Springs, 30328, SAN 338-3822. Tel: 404-303-6130. FAX: 404-303-6133. Web Site: www.afplweb.com/sandy-springs-branch6. *Br Mgr,* Dorothy Parker; E-mail: dorothy.parker@fultoncountyga.gov; *Adult Ref Librn,* Karen Reynolds; E-mail: karen.reynolds@fultoncountyga.gov; *Ch,* Leah Germon; *Ref Librn,* Ruby Allen; E-mail: ruby.allen@fultoncountyga.gov
Library Holdings: Bk Vols 123,185
Open Mon & Thurs-Sat 10-6, Tues & Wed 10-8, Sun 2-6
Friends of the Library Group

SOUTH FULTON BRANCH, 4055 Flat Shoals Rd, Union City, 30291-1590, SAN 373-9341. Tel: 770-306-3092. FAX: 770-306-3127. Web Site: afplweb.com/south-fulton-branch6. *Actg Br Mgr,* David Thrash; E-mail: david.thrash@fultoncountyga.gov; *Ch,* Cassie Gwyn; E-mail: cassie.gwyn@fultoncountyga.gov; *Ref Librn,* Dinah Baldwin; E-mail: dinah.baldwin@fultoncountyga.gov; *Ref Librn,* Elizabeth Costello; E-mail: elizabeth.costello@fultoncountyga.gov; *Ref Mgr,* Position Currently Open; *YA Serv,* Position Currently Open
Library Holdings: Bk Vols 100,751
Open Mon & Wed 10-8, Tues, Thurs & Fri 10-6, Sat 12-6, Sun 2-6
Friends of the Library Group

SOUTHWEST BRANCH, 3665 Cascade Rd SW, 30331, SAN 370-4777. Tel: 404-699-6363. FAX: 404-699-6381. *Br Mgr,* Eugene Haston; E-mail: eugene.haston@fultoncountyga.gov; *Asst Mgr,* Darlene McDade; E-mail: darlene.mcdade@fultoncountyga.gov; *Ch,* Teffany Edmondson; E-mail: teffany.edmondson@fultoncountyga.gov; *Ch,* Eileen Slough; E-mail: eileen.slough@fultoncountyga.gov; *Ref Librn,* Malik Grohse; E-mail: malik.grohse@fultoncountyga.gov; *Ref Librn,* Valerie Lewis; E-mail: valeire.lewis@fultoncountyga.gov; *Ref Librn,* Martaire Walker; E-mail: martaire.walker@fultoncountyga.gov; *YA Serv,* William Hutchinson, III; E-mail: william.hutchinson@fultoncountyga.gov
Library Holdings: Bk Vols 133,198
Open Mon-Wed 10-8, Thurs-Sat 10-6, Sun 2-6
Friends of the Library Group

STEWART-LAKEWOOD BRANCH, 2893 Lakewood Ave SW, 30315, SAN 338-3881. Tel: 404-762-4054. FAX: 404-762-4056. *Br Mgr,* Position Currently Open; *Ch,* Vicky LaJesse; E-mail: vicky.lajesse@fultoncountyga.gov
Library Holdings: Bk Vols 39,848
Open Mon, Fri & Sat 12-6, Tues & Wed 10-6, Thurs 10-8
Friends of the Library Group

THOMASVILLE HEIGHTS BRANCH, 1700 Thomasville Dr SE, 30315, SAN 370-4785. Tel: 404-624-0620. FAX: 404-624-0622. *Br Mgr,* Belinda Yellock; E-mail: belinda.yellock@fultoncountyga.gov
Library Holdings: Bk Vols 17,570
Open Mon & Wed 11-6, Tues 10-6, Thurs-Sat 12-6

WASHINGTON PARK BRANCH, 1116 Martin Luther King Jr Dr, 30314, SAN 338-3946. Tel: 404-752-8760. FAX: 404-752-8762. *Br Mgr,* Sharon D Washington; E-mail: sharon.washington@fultoncountyga.gov
Library Holdings: Bk Vols 30,923
Open Mon 10-6, Tues & Wed 10-8, Thurs-Sat 12-6

WEST END BRANCH, 525 Peeples St SW, 30310, SAN 338-3911. Tel: 404-752-8740. FAX: 404-752-8742. *Br Mgr,* Rosie Meadows; E-mail: rosie.meadows@fultoncountyga.gov; *Ch,* Cathy Gwyn; E-mail: cathy.gwyn@fultoncountyga.gov
Library Holdings: Bk Vols 31,277
Open Mon 12-8, Tues & Wed 10-6, Thurs 10-8, Fri & Sat 12-6

S ATLANTA HISTORY CENTER, Kenan Research Center, 3101 Andrews Dr NW, 30305. (Mail add: 130 W Paces Ferry Rd, 30305), SAN 303-2655. Tel: 404-814-4000, 404-814-4040. FAX: 404-814-4175. E-mail: reference@atlantahistorycenter.com. Web Site: www.atlantahistorycenter.com. *Librn,* Helen Matthews; Tel: 404-814-4048, E-mail: hmatthews@atlantahistorycenter.com
Founded 1926
Library Holdings: Bk Vols 25,000; Per Subs 90
Special Collections: Cherokee Garden Library; Decorative Art Books; DuBose Civil War Coll; Joel Chandler Harris Coll; Revolutionary War in Georgia; Shillinglaw Cookbook Coll; Shutze Architecture Coll
Subject Interests: Ga, Genealogy
Automation Activity & Vendor Info: (OPAC) Ex Libris Group
Wireless access
Function: Archival coll
Publications: Connections (Newsletter)
Partic in Georgia Online Database; Lyrasis
Open Wed-Sat 10-5
Restriction: Non-circulating

M ATLANTA MEDICAL CENTER*, Fay E Evatt Medical Library, 303 Parkway Dr NE, Box 415, 30312-1212. SAN 338-4217. Tel: 404-265-4603. FAX: 404-265-3559. E-mail: amclibrary1@gmail.com. *Med Librn,* Lisa Block; Tel: 404-265-4605, E-mail: lisa.block@tenethealth.com; Staff 1 (MLS 1)
Founded 1930
Library Holdings: Bk Titles 3,500; Per Subs 398
Special Collections: Archives
Automation Activity & Vendor Info: (Cataloging) CyberTools for Libraries; (Circulation) CyberTools for Libraries; (OPAC) CyberTools for Libraries; (Serials) CyberTools for Libraries
Database Vendor: Elsevier, Majors, McGraw-Hill, MD Consult, OVID Technologies, PubMed, ScienceDirect, Springer-Verlag, STAT!Ref (Teton Data Systems), Swets Information Services, UpToDate, Wiley InterScience
Wireless access
Function: Health sci info serv
Partic in Atlanta Health Science Libraries Consortium; Georgia Health Sciences Library Association (GHSLA)
Open Mon-Fri 8-4
Restriction: Access at librarian's discretion, Authorized patrons, Badge access after hrs, Circulates for staff only, Hospital staff & commun, Lending to staff only, Med & health res only

C ATLANTA METROPOLITAN STATE COLLEGE LIBRARY*, 1630 Metropolitan Pkwy SW, 30310. SAN 303-2663. Tel: 404-756-4010. FAX: 404-756-5613. *Libr Dir,* Robert Quarles; E-mail: rquarles@atlm.edu; *Ref Librn,* Argent Gibson; E-mail: agibson@atlm.edu; Staff 6.5 (MLS 3.5, Non-MLS 3)
Founded 1974. Enrl 2,500; Highest Degree: Bachelor
Library Holdings: Bk Vols 45,000; Per Subs 87
Automation Activity & Vendor Info: (Cataloging) Ex Libris Group; (Circulation) Ex Libris Group; (ILL) Ex Libris Group; (OPAC) Ex Libris Group; (Serials) EBSCO Online
Database Vendor: EBSCOhost, JSTOR, LexisNexis, OCLC WorldShare Interlibrary Loan, ProQuest
Wireless access
Function: ILL available, Newsp ref libr, Online searches, Ref serv available, Wheelchair accessible

Partic in GALILEO (Georgia Library Learning Online); Georgia Online Database; Lyrasis; OCLC Online Computer Library Center, Inc
Open Mon-Thurs 8am-10pm, Fri 8-6, Sat 9-6, Sun 2-6
Restriction: Open to students, fac & staff

G ATLANTA REGIONAL COMMISSION INFORMATION CENTER*, 40 Courtland St NE, 30303. SAN 303-2698. Tel: 404-463-3100. FAX: 404-463-3105. E-mail: infocenter@atlantaregional.com. Web Site: www.atlantaregional.com. *Dir,* Douglas Hooker
Founded 1947
Library Holdings: Bk Titles 850
Special Collections: Atlanta Regional Commission Planning Reports
Subject Interests: Planning, Transportation
Open Mon-Fri 8:30-5

J ATLANTA TECHNICAL COLLEGE*, Library & Media Services, 1560 Metropolitan Pkwy SW, 30310. Tel: 404-225-4595. E-mail: atclibrary@atlantatech.edu. Web Site: www.atlantatech.edu/library. *Dir, Libr Serv,* Tosha Bussey; Tel: 404-225-4596, E-mail: tbussey@atlantatech.edu; *Cat Librn,* Anet Edwards; E-mail: aedwards@atlantatech.edu; *Circ Librn,* Cordelia Riley; E-mail: criley@atlantatech.edu; Staff 4 (MLS 3, Non-MLS 1)
Founded 1967. Enrl 5,066; Highest Degree: Associate
Library Holdings: Audiobooks 20; CDs 300; DVDs 210; e-books 31,300; Bk Titles 12,860; Bk Vols 20,284; Per Subs 170; Videos 414
Special Collections: Paralegal Law Library
Automation Activity & Vendor Info: (Acquisitions) TLC (The Library Corporation); (Cataloging) TLC (The Library Corporation); (Circulation) TLC (The Library Corporation); (Course Reserve) TLC (The Library Corporation); (ILL) OCLC FirstSearch; (OPAC) TLC (The Library Corporation)
Database Vendor: 3M Library Systems, Baker & Taylor, EBSCO Information Services, EBSCOhost, LexisNexis, OCLC WorldShare Interlibrary Loan, ProQuest, TLC (The Library Corporation), Westlaw, YBP Library Services
Wireless access
Partic in GALILEO (Georgia Library Learning Online); Georgia Online Database
Open Mon-Thurs 7:30am-8pm, Fri 7:30-4

C ATLANTA UNIVERSITY CENTER*, Robert W Woodruff Library, 111 James P Brawley Dr SW, 30314. SAN 303-2701. Tel: 404-978-2000. Circulation Tel: 404-978-2097. Interlibrary Loan Service Tel: 404-978-2025. Reference Tel: 404-978-2067. Administration Tel: 404-978-2018. FAX: 404-577-5158. Web Site: www.auctr.edu. *Dir,* Loretta Parham; Tel: 404-978-2061, E-mail: lparham@auctr.edu; *Tech Librn,* Robert Fallen; Tel: 404-978-2058, E-mail: rfallen@auctr.edu; *Archivist,* Karen Jefferson; Tel: 404-978-2045, E-mail: kjefferson@auctr.edu; *Cat,* Buddhwanti Masih; Tel: 404-978-2071, E-mail: bmasih@auctr.edu; *Circ,* William Holt; Tel: 404-978-2048, E-mail: weholt@auctr.edu; Staff 51 (MLS 24, Non-MLS 27)
Founded 1964. Enrl 9,965; Fac 776; Highest Degree: Doctorate
Library Holdings: Bk Vols 400,000; Per Subs 1,419
Special Collections: Abraham Lincoln Coll, memorabilia; Black History & Literature (Cullen-Jackman, Henry P Slaughter & Hoytt Fuller Coll); C Eric Lincoln (African American Coll); Freedman's Aid Society Records; John Henrik Clarke Coll; Music (Cuney-Hare Coll); Southern Regional Council Archival Coll on Race Relations. US Document Depository
Subject Interests: Acctg, African-Am, Art, Chem, Computer sci, Criminal law & justice, Econ, English (Lang), English lit, Hist, Mass communications, Nursing, Physics, Polit sci, Relig, Soc serv (soc work), Sociol, Theol, Zoology
Publications: Index to Theses
Partic in Atlanta Regional Council for Higher Education; Dialog Corp
Open Mon-Thurs (Fall & Spring) 8:30am-Midnight, Fri 8:30-5, Sat 10-6, Sun 2-10; Mon-Thurs (Summer) 7:30am-10pm, Fri 7:30-6, Sat 12-6, Sun 2-10

C BAUDER COLLEGE LIBRARY, 384 Northyards Blvd NW, Ste 400, 30313. Tel: 404-443-1807. Toll Free Tel: 800-986-9710. FAX: 404-237-1619. Web Site: library.bauder.edu. *Head Librn,* Randall James; E-mail: rjames@bauder.edu; Staff 1 (MLS 1)
Founded 1964. Enrl 300; Highest Degree: Bachelor
Library Holdings: Bk Vols 3,000; Per Subs 50
Automation Activity & Vendor Info: (Acquisitions) Baker & Taylor; (Circulation) TLC (The Library Corporation); (OPAC) TLC (The Library Corporation); (Serials) EBSCO Online
Database Vendor: Cinahl, EBSCOhost, LexisNexis, OCLC FirstSearch, OCLC WebJunction, OCLC WorldShare Interlibrary Loan, ProQuest, PubMed, TLC (The Library Corporation), Westlaw
Wireless access
Function: e-mail & chat, Electronic databases & coll, ILL available, Instruction & testing, Online cat, Online info literacy tutorials on the web & in blackboard, Online ref, Online searches, Ref & res, Ref serv in person, Web-catalog, Writing prog
Partic in GALILEO (Georgia Library Learning Online); Georgia Private Acad Librs Consortium (GPALS)
Restriction: Not open to pub

CR BEULAH HEIGHTS UNIVERSITY*, Barth Memorial Library, 892 Berne St SE, 30316. (Mail add: PO Box 18145, 30316-0145), SAN 303-2728. Tel: 404-627-2681. Toll Free Tel: 888-777-2422. FAX: 404-627-0702. Web Site: www.beulah.org. *Dir,* Pradeep Das; E-mail: pradeep.das@beulah.org; Staff 2 (MLS 2)
Founded 1918. Enrl 815; Fac 45; Highest Degree: Master
Jul 2009-Jun 2010 Income $180,000. Mats Exp $25,000, Books $12,000, Per/Ser (Incl. Access Fees) $8,000, Other Print Mats $2,000, AV Equip $3,000. Sal $86,760 (Prof $69,895)
Library Holdings: AV Mats 1,850; Bk Titles 44,320; Bk Vols 48,000; Per Subs 290
Subject Interests: Biblical studies, Bus, Christian educ, Econ, Finance Bus ethics, Intl trade, Leadership, Missions, Relig, Urban studies
Automation Activity & Vendor Info: (Cataloging) Follett Software; (Circulation) Follett Software; (OPAC) Follett Software
Wireless access
Partic in Georgia Online Database; Georgia Private Acad Librs Consortium (GPALS); Lyrasis; OCLC
Restriction: Not open to pub, Open to students

CR CARVER BIBLE COLLEGE LIBRARY*, 3870 Cascade Rd, 30331. SAN 303-2736. Tel: 404-527-4520. FAX: 404-527-4524. Web Site: www.carver.edu. *Librn,* Kimberly Bugg; *Librn,* Tosha L Bussey; E-mail: tbussey@carver.edu; Staff 3 (MLS 1, Non-MLS 2)
Founded 1943. Enrl 153; Fac 14; Highest Degree: Bachelor
Library Holdings: Bk Titles 14,434; Bk Vols 15,812; Per Subs 60
Wireless access
Open Mon-Fri 9am-10pm

G CENTERS FOR DISEASE CONTROL & PREVENTION*, Stephen B Thacker CDC Library, Tom Harkin Global Communications Ctr, Bldg 19, 1st Flr, MS C04, 1600 Clifton Rd NE, 30333. SAN 303-2744. Tel: 404-639-1717. Toll Free Tel: 800-232-4636. FAX: 404-639-1160. E-mail: cdclibrary@cdc.gov. Web Site: www.cdc.gov/library/index.html. *Br Mgr,* Position Currently Open
Founded 1947
Library Holdings: Bk Vols 25,000; Per Subs 1,531
Special Collections: CDC Publications; CDC Thesis Coll; PHS (HHS) Pamphlet Coll
Subject Interests: Biochem, Environ health, Microbiology, Pub health, Toxicology, Virology
Automation Activity & Vendor Info: (Acquisitions) Ex Libris Group; (Cataloging) Ex Libris Group; (Circulation) Ex Libris Group; (ILL) OCLC ILLiad; (OPAC) Ex Libris Group; (Serials) Ex Libris Group
Database Vendor: Dialog, JSTOR, LexisNexis, OCLC FirstSearch, OVID Technologies, ProQuest
Wireless access
Partic in Fedlink
Open Mon-Fri 8-4:30
Restriction: Badge access after hrs

S COURT OF APPEALS ELEVENTH CIRCUIT LIBRARY*, 56 Forsyth St NW, 30303. SAN 327-8107. Tel: 404-335-6500. FAX: 404-335-6510. Web Site: www.ca11.uscourts.gov/library. *Librn,* Elaine Fenton; Staff 9 (MLS 5, Non-MLS 4)
Founded 1981
Library Holdings: Bk Vols 50,000; Per Subs 300
Special Collections: US Document Depository
Subject Interests: Law
Automation Activity & Vendor Info: (Acquisitions) SirsiDynix; (Cataloging) SirsiDynix; (Circulation) SirsiDynix; (Course Reserve) SirsiDynix; (ILL) SirsiDynix; (Media Booking) SirsiDynix; (OPAC) SirsiDynix; (Serials) SirsiDynix
Partic in OCLC Online Computer Library Center, Inc
Open Mon-Fri 8:30-4
Restriction: Circ limited

M CRAWFORD LONG HOSPITAL - EMORY HEALTHCARE*, Medical Library, 550 Peachtree St, 30308-2225. SAN 303-3082. Tel: 404-686-2637. Web Site: www.emoryhealthcare.org. *Interim Librn,* Rosa Dickens
Founded 1942
Special Collections: Performance Improvement Management
Subject Interests: Allied health, Consumer health, Hospital admin, Med, Nursing, Surgery
Automation Activity & Vendor Info: (Acquisitions) SirsiDynix; (Cataloging) SirsiDynix; (Circulation) SirsiDynix; (Course Reserve) SirsiDynix; (OPAC) SirsiDynix; (Serials) SirsiDynix
Database Vendor: OVID Technologies
Function: ILL available

Publications: Annual Report
Partic in Atlantic Health Sci Librs Consortium; Docline
Restriction: Not open to pub, Staff use only

EMORY UNIVERSITY LIBRARIES
GOIZUETA BUSINESS LIBRARY, 540 Asbury Circle, 30322. Tel: 404-727-1641. FAX: 404-727-1012. Web Site: www.business.library.emory.edu. *Exec Dir,* Susan Klopper; E-mail: susan.kloper@emory.edu; *Bus Librn,* Malisa Anderson-Strait; E-mail: malisa.anderson@emory.edu; *Bus Librn,* Ann Cullen; E-mail: ann.cullen@emory.edu; *Bus Librn,* Marilyn Pahr; E-mail: marilyn.pahr@emory.edu; *Bus Librn,* Lee Pasackow; E-mail: lee.pasackow@emory.edu

CR PITTS THEOLOGY LIBRARY, Candler School of Theology, 1531 Dickey Dr, Ste 560, 30322-2810, SAN 338-4063. Tel: 404-727-4166. FAX: 404-727-1219. E-mail: libmpg@emory.edu. Web Site: www.pitts.emory.edu. *Dir,* Dr Matt Patrick Graham; *Ref/Outreach Librn,* Rebekah Bedard; Tel: 404-727-5094, E-mail: rebekah.bedard@emory.edu; *Archivist,* Robert Presutti; *Cat,* Dr Denise Hanusek; *Cat,* Armin Siedlecki; *Per,* Tracy Powell; *Pub Serv, Reader Serv,* Dr Richard Adams. Subject Specialists: *Ancient Near East,* Rebekah Bedard; Staff 7 (MLS 7)
Founded 1914. Highest Degree: Doctorate
Library Holdings: Microforms 121,000; Bk Vols 610,000; Per Subs 1,041
Special Collections: A Christian Sermon; A Selective Bibliography of Recent Acquisitions Spring 1984; An Annotated Bibliograph; Archives & Manuscript Coll; Early Book Coll incl pre-1750 books published outside the US, pre-1820 US Imprints & Incunabula; Early Reformation Imprints; Elisabeth Creutziger, the Magdeburg Enchiridion, 1536 & Reformation Theology; European Theological Dissertations Printed in the 16th-19th Centuries; Kessler Coll comes to Emory; Luther, Bach & the Early Reformation Chorale; Preserving the Traditions of Faith: A History of the Pitts Theology Library; Richard C Kessler Reformation Coll, incl 16th Century vols by Martin Luther; The Politics of Manning's Conversion; Thomas Menton Coll; Warrington-Paine-Pratt Hymnology Coll; Wesleyana Coll, bks & pamphlets, incl First Edition of the Works of John & Charles Wesley
Subject Interests: Relig, Theol
Partic in Lyrasis; RLIN (Research Libraries Information Network)
Friends of the Library Group

CM WOODRUFF HEALTH SCIENCES CENTER LIBRARY*, 1462 Clifton Rd NE, 30322, SAN 338-4187. Tel: 404-727-8727. Reference Tel: 404-727-3760. Administration Tel: 404-727-5820. FAX: 404-727-9821. Web Site: health.library.emory.edu. *Dir,* Sandra G Franklin; E-mail: librsf@emory.edu; *Coordr, Coll Serv,* Bonita Bryan; E-mail: libbrb@emory.edu; *Info Serv Coordr,* Barbara Abu-Zeid; E-mail: babuzei@emory.edu; Staff 12.8 (MLS 12.8)
Founded 1923
Special Collections: History of Medicine in Georgia
Partic in Consortium of Southern Biomedical Libraries; Lyrasis; National Network of Libraries of Medicine Southeastern Atlantic Region
Open Mon-Thurs 8am-Midnight, Fri 8-7, Sat 10-7, Sun Noon-Midnight

C ROBERT W WOODRUFF LIBRARY*, 540 Asbury Circle, 30322-2870, SAN 338-4039. Tel: 404-727-6861. Circulation Tel: 404-727-6873. Reference Tel: 404-727-6875. FAX: 404-727-0805. Web Site: web.library.emory.edu. *Vice Provost & Dir, Univ Libr,* Position Currently Open; *Assoc Vice-Provost,* Xuemao Wang; Tel: 404-727-6861, E-mail: x.wang@emory.edu; *Bus Librn,* Susan Klopper; Tel: 404-727-0177, Fax: 404-727-1641, E-mail: skloppe@emory.edu; *Sr Leader, Content Div,* Lars Meyer; Tel: 404-727-2437, Fax: 404-727-1132, E-mail: lmeyer2@emory.edu; *Sr Leader, Serv Div,* Position Currently Open; *Media Spec, Music,* Joyce Clinkscales; Tel: 404-727-1066, Fax: 404-727-2257, E-mail: libjm01@emory.edu; Staff 212 (MLS 88, Non-MLS 124)
Founded 1915. Enrl 12,059; Fac 718; Highest Degree: Doctorate
Library Holdings: Bk Vols 3,619,813; Per Subs 66,992
Special Collections: 19th Century English Prose Fiction; African-American History & Culture (James Weldon Johnson Coll, Raymond Andrews Family Papers); American & Asian Communism (Theodore Draper & Philip Jaffe Coll), ms, printed mat; Antebellum, Civil War & Post Civil War (Alexander Stephens & Others), ms; British & Irish Literature (W B Yeats, Lady Gregory, Ted Hughes Colls); Confederate Imprints; Early American History (McGregor Coll); Southern Economic History (Charles Herty Papers & Harrold Coll of Business & Family Letters & Records, Georgia 1836-1953), ms; Southern Literary & Journalistic History (Joel Chandler Harris, Henry Grady, Ralph McGill Coll), ms; Wesleyana & Methodist History, ms & printed mat; Yeats & 20th Century Irish Literature. US Document Depository
Automation Activity & Vendor Info: (Acquisitions) Ex Libris Group; (Cataloging) Ex Libris Group; (Circulation) Ex Libris Group; (Course Reserve) Ex Libris Group; (OPAC) Ex Libris Group; (Serials) Ex Libris Group
Database Vendor: EBSCOhost, LexisNexis, OCLC FirstSearch, OVID Technologies, ProQuest
Partic in Association of Research Libraries (ARL); Atlanta Regional Council for Higher Education; Center for Research Libraries; Coalition for Networked Information (CNI); Digital Libr Fedn; Georgia Libr Info Network; Lyrasis
Publications: Imprint (Newsletter); Library Directions
Special Services for the Deaf - TDD equip
Friends of the Library Group

CL EMORY UNIVERSITY SCHOOL OF LAW*, Hugh F MacMillan Law Library, 1301 Clifton Rd, 30322. SAN 338-4128. Tel: 404-727-6823. Circulation Tel: 404-727-6824. Reference Tel: 404-727-0059. FAX: 404-727-2202. E-mail: lawcirch@mail.library.emory.edu. Web Site: library.law.emory.edu. *Asst Prof of Law, Dir, Libr Serv,* Mark Engsberg; E-mail: mark.engsberg@emory.edu; Staff 19 (MLS 10, Non-MLS 9)
Founded 1916
Library Holdings: Bk Titles 139,577; Bk Vols 400,929; Per Subs 4,053
Special Collections: European Union Depository Coll. US Document Depository
Automation Activity & Vendor Info: (Acquisitions) SirsiDynix; (Cataloging) SirsiDynix; (Circulation) SirsiDynix; (OPAC) SirsiDynix; (Serials) SirsiDynix
Database Vendor: Gale Cengage Learning, LexisNexis, OCLC WorldShare Interlibrary Loan, Westlaw
Wireless access
Function: ILL available
Partic in OCLC Online Computer Library Center, Inc
Open Mon-Sun 7:30am-Midnight

S FEDERAL RESERVE BANK OF ATLANTA*, Research Library, 1000 Peachtree St NE, 30309-4470. SAN 303-2841. Tel: 404-498-8867. Interlibrary Loan Service Tel: 404-498-8740. FAX: 404-498-7931. E-mail: library@atl.frb.org. Web Site: www.frbatlanta.org. *Mgr,* Ernie Evangelista; Staff 5 (MLS 3, Non-MLS 2)
Founded 1938
Library Holdings: Bk Titles 11,000; Per Subs 1,800
Special Collections: Federal Reserve Bank & Federal Reserve Board Publications; Southeastern Regional Economics
Subject Interests: Banks & banking, Econ, Finance, Trade
Publications: Monthly Accessions List
Partic in Dialog Corp; Dow Jones News Retrieval; Georgia Online Database
Special Services for the Deaf - TDD equip
Restriction: Open to pub by appt only

S FERNBANK SCIENCE CENTER LIBRARY*, 156 Heaton Park Dr NE, 30307-1398. SAN 303-2795. Tel: 678-874-7116. FAX: 678-874-7110. Web Site: fsc.fernbank.edu/Library.htm. *Librn,* Mary Larsen; Staff 1 (MLS 1)
Founded 1967
Library Holdings: Bk Titles 14,658; Bk Vols 22,000; Per Subs 35
Subject Interests: Astronomy, Botany, Environ studies, Hort, Sci tech
Automation Activity & Vendor Info: (Cataloging) OCLC; (ILL) OCLC
Database Vendor: OCLC FirstSearch
Wireless access
Partic in Lyrasis
Open Mon-Sat 10-5

G FOOD & DRUG ADMINISTRATION*, Southeast Regional Laboratory Library, 60 Eighth St NE, 30309. SAN 372-7149. Tel: 404-253-1160. FAX: 404-253-1206. *Librn,* Regina Arts; Tel: 404-253-1160, Ext 1261
Founded 1991
Library Holdings: Bk Titles 2,000; Per Subs 70
Special Collections: Laboratory Methods (Laboratory Information Bulletins (LIB)); Safety Sheets (Material Safety Data Sheets (MSOS))
Partic in Dialog Corp

S FRIENDS OF GOETHE, INC*, Goethe-Institut Atlanta Library, Colony Sq, Plaza Level, 1197 Peachtree St NE, 30361-2401. SAN 324-136X. Tel: 404-892-2226. FAX: 404-892-3832. E-mail: germaninstitute@bellsouth.net. Web Site: www.goethe.de/atlanta.
Founded 1977
Library Holdings: Bk Titles 8,500; Per Subs 35
Special Collections: German Language Materials
Subject Interests: Geog, German affairs, German art, Hist, Lit
Function: For res purposes, Handicapped accessible
Open Mon-Thurs 10-6, Fri 10-8
Restriction: Mem only
Friends of the Library Group

GL FULTON COUNTY LAW LIBRARY*, Justice Center Tower JCT 7000, 185 Central Ave SW, 30303. SAN 303-2868. Tel: 404-612-4544. FAX: 404-730-4565. Web Site: www.fultoncourt.org/library. *Info Serv, Libr Mgr,* Jeannie Ashley; E-mail: jeannie.ashley@fultoncountyga.gov; *Ref Librn,* Delicia Williamson; E-mail: delicia.williamson@fultoncountyga.gov

Library Holdings: Bk Vols 18,000; Per Subs 20
Wireless access
Open Mon-Fri 8:30-4:30

C GEORGIA INSTITUTE OF TECHNOLOGY LIBRARY, 266 Fourth St NW, 30332-0900. SAN 303-2922. Tel: 404-894-4500. Interlibrary Loan Service Tel: 404-894-4511. Administration Tel: 404-894-4501. FAX: 404-894-6084. TDD: 404-894-0230. Web Site: www.library.gatech.edu. *Dean of Libr, Vice Provost, Learning Excellence,* Catherine Murray-Rust; *Assoc Dean, Res & Learning Serv,* Bruce Henson; *Assoc Dean, Partnerships, Communications & Assessment,* Kathy Tomajko; *Assoc Dean, Scholarly Communications & Access,* Jeff Carrico; *Head, Archives & Rec Mgt,* Jody Thompson; *Head, Coll Develop,* Nancy Simons; *Head, Fac Engagement,* Lori Critz; *Head, Info Delivery,* Katharine Calhoun; *Head, Info Tech & Develop,* Doag Goans; *Head, Pub Serv,* Bing Wang; *Head, Scholarly Communication & Digital Curation,* Susan Parham; *Head, User Experience,* Ameet Doshi; Staff 108 (MLS 36, Non-MLS 72)
Founded 1885. Enrl 21,471; Fac 2,563; Highest Degree: Doctorate
Jul 2013-Jun 2014 Income (Main and Other College/University Libraries) $16,877,082. Mats Exp $7,474,554. Sal $6,472,220 (Prof $2,622,120)
Library Holdings: e-books 272,503; Bk Titles 1,098,890
Special Collections: ASERL Center of Excellence (NASA, USPTO, EPA); Patent & Trademark Resource Center; Technical Reports (National Technical Information Services, NASA, DOE), micro. US Document Depository
Subject Interests: Archit, Bus & mgt, Econ, Eng, Environ studies, Natural sci, Phys sci, Sci tech
Automation Activity & Vendor Info: (Acquisitions) Ex Libris Group; (Cataloging) Ex Libris Group; (Circulation) Ex Libris Group; (Course Reserve) Atlas Systems; (ILL) OCLC ILLiad; (OPAC) Ex Libris Group; (Serials) Ex Libris Group
Database Vendor: ABC-CLIO, ACM (Association for Computing Machinery), American Chemical Society, American Geophysical Union, American Mathematical Society, American Physical Society, American Psychological Association (APA), Annual Reviews, ASCE Research Library, BioOne, Bloomberg, CQ Press, CRC Press/Taylor & Francis Group, CredoReference, Dun & Bradstreet, ebrary, EBSCO Discovery Service, EBSCOhost, Elsevier, Emerald, Ex Libris Group, Factiva.com, Gale Cengage Learning, H W Wilson, Hoovers, IEEE (Institute of Electrical & Electronics Engineers), Ingenta, IOP, ISI Web of Knowledge, JSTOR, Knovel, LexisNexis, Medline, Mergent Online, Nature Publishing Group, OCLC ArticleFirst, Overdrive, Inc, Oxford Online, Project MUSE, ProQuest, PubMed, ReferenceUSA, RefWorks, Safari Books Online, Sage, ScienceDirect, Scopus, Springer-Verlag, Standard & Poor's, Thomson - Web of Science, ValueLine, Wiley, Wiley InterScience, YBP Library Services
Wireless access
Partic in Association of Southeastern Research Libraries; Lyrasis

Departmental Libraries:

COLLEGE OF ARCHITECTURE LIBRARY, 245 Fourth St, Rm 152, 30332-0900, SAN 321-222X. Tel: 404-894-4877. Web Site: www.library.gatech.edu/architect. *Head, Archit Libr,* Cathy Carpenter; Staff 4 (MLS 1, Non-MLS 3)
Subject Interests: Archit, Construction, Design
Open Mon-Thurs 8am-Midnight, Fri 8-6, Sat 9-6, Sun Noon-Midnight

P GEORGIA LIBRARY FOR ACCESSIBLE STATEWIDE SERVICES*, 1800 Century Place, Ste 150, 30345. SAN 303-2949. Tel: 404-756-4619. Administration Tel: 404-756-4476. Toll Free Tel: 800-248-6701. FAX: 404-756-4618. E-mail: glass@georgialibraries.org. Web Site: www.georgialibraries.org/public/glass.html. *Dir,* Pat Herndon; E-mail: pherndon@georgialibraries.org; *Mgr,* Beverly Williams; E-mail: bwilliams@georgialibraries.org; Staff 4 (MLS 1, Non-MLS 3)
Founded 1931. Pop 4,000; Circ 158,628
Library Holdings: Bk Titles 57,000; Bk Vols 300,000; Talking Bks 57,000
Automation Activity & Vendor Info: (Acquisitions) Keystone Systems, Inc (KLAS); (Cataloging) Keystone Systems, Inc (KLAS); (Circulation) Keystone Systems, Inc (KLAS); (Course Reserve) Keystone Systems, Inc (KLAS); (ILL) Keystone Systems, Inc (KLAS); (Media Booking) Keystone Systems, Inc (KLAS); (OPAC) Keystone Systems, Inc (KLAS); (Serials) Keystone Systems, Inc (KLAS)
Partic in Atlanta Health Science Libraries Consortium
Special Services for the Blind - Bks on cassette; Braille bks; Closed circuit TV; Computer with voice synthesizer for visually impaired persons; Local mags & bks recorded; Photo duplicator for making large print
Open Mon-Fri 8-5
Friends of the Library Group

S GEORGIA POWER CO-SOUTHERN CO, Business Information Center-Research Library, 241 Ralph McGill Blvd NE, Bin 10044, 30308. SAN 303-2930. Tel: 404-506-6633. FAX: 404-506-6652. E-mail: bic@southernco.com. *Librn,* Katherine Meadows; *Libr Assoc,* April Jones; Staff 2 (MLS 1, Non-MLS 1)
Founded 1957
Library Holdings: AV Mats 1,000; Bk Vols 7,000; Per Subs 160
Special Collections: Annual Reports; Company History; Energy Materials
Subject Interests: Bus & mgt, Energy
Wireless access
Restriction: Circulates for staff only, Co libr

P GEORGIA PUBLIC LIBRARY SERVICE, Unit of the Board of Regents of the University System of Georgia, 1800 Century Place, Ste 150, 30345-4304. SAN 338-4306. Tel: 404-235-7200. FAX: 404-235-7201. Web Site: www.georgialibraries.org. *State Librn,* Julie Walker; Tel: 404-235-7140, E-mail: lwalker@georgialibraries.org; *Dep State Librn,* Position Currently Open; Staff 16 (MLS 16)
Founded 1897
Library Holdings: Audiobooks 38; DVDs 193; Bk Titles 5,388; Bk Vols 9,694; Per Subs 29; Videos 300
Subject Interests: Libr & info sci
Automation Activity & Vendor Info: (Cataloging) Evergreen; (Circulation) Evergreen; (ILL) OCLC WorldShare Interlibrary Loan; (OPAC) Evergreen
Wireless access
Function: ILL available
Publications: Collection Development Statement; Georgia Public Library Service News (Bi-monthly); Georgia Public Library Statistics (Annual); Georgia Public Library Trustees Handbook; GOLD ILL Procedures Manual: GOLD Serials Manual; Periodicals List
Partic in Association of Southeastern Research Libraries; Georgia Online Database; Lyrasis; OCLC Online Computer Library Center, Inc; Soline
Restriction: Not open to pub

Branches: 1

GEORGIA LIBRARY FOR ACCESSIBLE SERVICES
See Separate Entry

C GEORGIA STATE UNIVERSITY LIBRARY*, 100 Decatur St SE, 30303-3202. SAN 303-2957. Tel: 404-413-2700. Circulation Tel: 404-413-2840. Interlibrary Loan Service Tel: 404-413-2790. Reference Tel: 404-413-2800. FAX: 404-413-2701. Circulation FAX: 404-413-2821. Interlibrary Loan Service FAX: 404-413-2791. E-mail: libcrn@gsu.edu. Web Site: www.library.gsu.edu. *Interim Dean of Libr,* Tammy Sugarman; E-mail: tsugarman@gsu.edu; *Assoc Dean, Coll Mgt,* Tammy Sugarman; Tel: 404-413-2705, E-mail: tsugarman@gsu.edu; *Assoc Dean, Digital Libr Serv & Spec Coll,* Laura Burtle; Tel: 404-413-2706, E-mail: lburtle@gsu.edu; *Assoc Dean, Pub Serv,* Bryan Sinclair; Tel: 404-413-2721, E-mail: bsinclair@gsu.edu; *Head, Digital Libr Serv,* Krista Graham; Tel: 404-413-2752, E-mail: kgraham13@gsu.edu; *Head, Spec Coll & Univ Archives,* Stephen Zietz; Tel: 404-413-2889, Fax: 404-413-2881, E-mail: szietz@gsu.edu; *Head, Tech Serv,* William Walsh; Tel: 404-413-2731, Fax: 404-413-2751, E-mail: wwalsh@gsu.edu; *Admin Officer,* Carmen Newton; Tel: 404-413-2713, E-mail: libcrn@gsu.edu; *Mgr, User Serv & Tech Support,* Denita Hampton; Tel: 404-413-2822, E-mail: dahampton@gsu.edu; *Coordr, Serv - Arts & Humanities,* Leslie Madden; Tel: 404-413-2807, E-mail: lmadden@gsu.edu; *Coordr, Serv - Health & Natural Sci,* Brenna Helmstutler; Tel: 404-413-2859, E-mail: brenna@gsu.edu; *Coordr, Serv - Soc Sci, Bus & Educ,* Laura Carscaddon; Tel: 404-413-2804, E-mail: lcarscaddon1@gsu.edu; *Webmaster,* Cliff J Landis; Tel: 404-413-2772, E-mail: clifflandis@gsu.edu. Subject Specialists: *Finance, Human res,* Carmen Newton; Staff 53 (MLS 46, Non-MLS 7)
Founded 1931. Enrl 32,092; Fac 1,658; Highest Degree: Doctorate
Special Collections: Georgia Government Documentation Project; Georgia Women's Coll; Labor History (Southern Labor Archives); Lane Brothers & Tracy O'Neal (Photographic Coll); Popular Music (Johnny Mercer Coll); Rare Book Coll; University Archives. Oral History; US Document Depository
Automation Activity & Vendor Info: (Acquisitions) Ex Libris Group; (Cataloging) Ex Libris Group; (Circulation) Ex Libris Group; (Course Reserve) Ex Libris Group; (ILL) OCLC ILLiad; (Media Booking) Ex Libris Group; (OPAC) Ex Libris Group; (Serials) Ex Libris Group
Database Vendor: Dialog, EBSCOhost, Gale Cengage Learning, JSTOR, LexisNexis, OCLC FirstSearch, OCLC WorldShare Interlibrary Loan, OVID Technologies, ProQuest, ScienceDirect, TLC (The Library Corporation), Westlaw
Wireless access
Function: Computers for patron use, Copy machines
Partic in Association of Southeastern Research Libraries; Atlanta Regional Council for Higher Education; OCLC Online Computer Library Center, Inc
Open Mon-Thurs 7:30-12, Fri 7:30-6, Sat 12-6, Sun 12-12
Restriction: Badge access after hrs, Circ limited, ID required to use computers (Ltd hrs), In-house use for visitors, Non-circulating to the pub, Open to students, fac, staff & alumni, Photo ID required for access, Restricted pub use

Departmental Libraries:

CL COLLEGE OF LAW LIBRARY, 140 Decatur St, 30302. (Mail add: PO Box 4008, 30302-4008), SAN 324-2684. Tel: 404-651-2478. Interlibrary Loan Service Tel: 404-651-4148. Reference Tel: 404-651-4143. FAX: 404-651-1112. Web Site: law.gsu.edu/library. *Assoc Dean, Libr & Info*

Serv, Nancy Johnson; Tel: 404-651-4140, E-mail: njohnson@gsu.edu; Staff 19 (MLS 7, Non-MLS 12)
Founded 1982. Enrl 600; Fac 40; Highest Degree: Doctorate
Special Collections: US Document Depository
Automation Activity & Vendor Info: (Acquisitions) Ex Libris Group; (Cataloging) Ex Libris Group; (Circulation) Ex Libris Group; (Course Reserve) Ex Libris Group; (OPAC) Ex Libris Group; (Serials) Ex Libris Group
Database Vendor: LexisNexis, Westlaw
Partic in Lyrasis

R GLENN MEMORIAL UNITED METHODIST CHURCH LIBRARY*, 1660 N Decatur Rd NE, 30307-1010. SAN 303-2973. Tel: 404-634-3936. FAX: 404-634-1994. Web Site: www.glennumc.org. *In Charge,* Betty Jo Copelan
Library Holdings: Bk Vols 3,000
Wireless access
Open Mon-Fri 8-5

C HERZING COLLEGE LIBRARY*, 3393 Peachtree Rd, Ste 1003, 30326. Tel: 404-816-4533. FAX: 404-816-5576. Web Site: www.herzing.edu. *Librn,* Eric Murray; E-mail: ericm@atl.herzing.edu; Staff 1 (Non-MLS 1)
Founded 1965. Enrl 350; Highest Degree: Bachelor
Library Holdings: Bk Vols 7,000; Per Subs 60; Videos 45
Automation Activity & Vendor Info: (Cataloging) Follett Software; (Circulation) Follett Software; (OPAC) Follett Software
Database Vendor: Westlaw
Partic in GALILEO (Georgia Library Learning Online); Georgia Private Acad Librs Consortium (GPALS)
Open Mon-Thurs 8am-10pm, Fri 8-5, Sat 9-2

S HIGH MUSEUM OF ART LIBRARY*, 1280 Peachtree St, 30309. SAN 323-8598. Tel: 404-733-4480. Web Site: www.high.org.
Founded 1984
Library Holdings: Bk Titles 12,000; Bk Vols 14,000; Per Subs 35
Special Collections: Artist Files; Auction Catalogs
Subject Interests: Art, Art hist, Decorative art, Folk art, Photog
Automation Activity & Vendor Info: (Acquisitions) Ex Libris Group; (Cataloging) Ex Libris Group; (ILL) OCLC
Partic in Lyrasis; OCLC Online Computer Library Center, Inc
Restriction: Staff use only

CL JOHN MARSHALL LAW SCHOOL*, Law Library, 1422 W Peachtree St NW, 30309. SAN 303-3031. Tel: 404-872-3593. Circulation Tel: 404-872-3593, Ext 118. Interlibrary Loan Service Tel: 404-872-3593, Ext 167. Reference Tel: 404-872-3593, Ext 103, 404-872-3593, Ext 108. FAX: 404-873-3802. Web Site: www.johnmarshall.edu. *Dir,* Michael J Lynch; E-mail: mlynch@johnmarshall.edu; *Acq,* Mark Durbin; Tel: 404-872-3593, Ext 119, E-mail: mdurbin@johnmarshall.edu; *Pub Serv,* Lynne Rhys; E-mail: lrhys-jones@johnmarshall.edu; *Tech Serv,* Morteza Parvin; Tel: 404-872-3593, Ext 167, E-mail: mparvin@johnmarshall.edu; Staff 9 (MLS 5, Non-MLS 4)
Founded 1935. Enrl 200; Fac 15; Highest Degree: Doctorate
Library Holdings: Bk Titles 103,000; Bk Vols 205,000; Per Subs 1,566
Automation Activity & Vendor Info: (ILL) OCLC
Database Vendor: LexisNexis, Westlaw
Partic in Georgia Private Acad Librs Consortium (GPALS); Lyrasis
Open Mon-Fri 8:30am-10pm, Sat 11-7, Sun 1-9
Restriction: Open to fac, students & qualified researchers

L JONES DAY*, Law Library, 1420 Peachtree St NE, 30309. SAN 303-299X. Tel: 404-581-8118. FAX: 404-581-8330. *Librn,* Jane Crawford
Library Holdings: Bk Vols 15,000
Open Mon-Fri 9-5:30

L KILPATRICK STOCKTON*, Law Library, 1100 Peachtree St, Ste 2800, 30309. SAN 303-304X. Tel: 404-815-6261. FAX: 404-815-6555. *Dir,* Robert Stivers; *Ref,* Louise Adams; *Ref,* Kathy Crosslin
Founded 1904
Library Holdings: Bk Vols 30,000
Publications: Recent Acquisitions; Seminar list (Monthly)
Partic in Dialog Corp; Westlaw

L KING & SPALDING*, Law Library, 1180 Peachtree St NE, Flr 17, 30309. SAN 303-3058. Tel: 404-572-4600, Ext 3300. FAX: 404-572-5123. E-mail: lib.helpdesk@kslaw.com. *Dir, Info Resources & Res,* MaryAnne C Fry; *Assoc Dir,* Joan Houghton-Theall; *Mgr,* Michael Matuszek
Library Holdings: Bk Vols 50,000

S KING LIBRARY & ARCHIVES*, 449 Auburn Ave NE, 30312. SAN 303-3066. Tel: 404-526-8983. FAX: 404-526-8914. E-mail: archives@thekingcenter.org. Web Site: www.thekingcenter.org. *Dir,* Cynthia Patterson Lewis; Tel: 404-526-8986, E-mail: clewis@thekingcenter.org; Staff 3 (MLS 1, Non-MLS 2)
Founded 1969
Library Holdings: Bk Vols 5,000; Per Subs 25
Special Collections: Black American History; Civil Rights Movement, 1954-1968, Post 1968; Nonviolence. Oral History
Subject Interests: Civil rights

S LOMA*, Information Center, 2300 Windy Ridge Pkwy, Ste 600, 30339. SAN 303-3074. Tel: 770-984-3722. FAX: 770-984-6422. E-mail: infoctr@loma.org. Web Site: www.loma.org. *Mgr, Res,* Jean C Gora
Founded 1924
Library Holdings: Bk Vols 1,200; Per Subs 300
Publications: Index to Information
Restriction: Mem only, Not open to pub

L MCKENNA LONG & ALDRIDGE LLP*, Law Library, 303 Peachtree St, Ste 5300, 30308. SAN 325-6456. Tel: 404-527-4057. FAX: 404-527-8474. *Librn,* Cindy Adams
Library Holdings: Bk Titles 10,000
Restriction: Not open to pub

C MERCER UNIVERSITY ATLANTA*, Monroe F Swilley Jr Library, 3001 Mercer University Dr, 30341. SAN 303-3104. Tel: 678-547-6280. Circulation Tel: 678-547-6284. Interlibrary Loan Service Tel: 678-547-6291. Reference Tel: 678-547-6282. FAX: 678-547-6270. Interlibrary Loan Service FAX: 678-547-6287. E-mail: swilley_ref@mercer.edu. Web Site: swilley.mercer.edu. *Assoc Dean,* Judith D Brook; Tel: 678-547-6274, E-mail: brook_jd@mercer.edu; *Assoc Dir,* Kim Eccles; Tel: 678-547-6271, E-mail: eccles_kl@mercer.edu; *Archivist,* Arlene Desselles; Tel: 678-547-6283, E-mail: desselles_af@mercer.edu; *Circ,* Louise Lowe; Tel: 678-547-6207, E-mail: lowe_ll@mercer.edu; *Electronic Res,* Florence Tang; Tel: 678-547-6261, E-mail: tang_fy@mercer.edu; *Pub Serv,* Rebecca Engsberg; Tel: 678-547-6402, E-mail: engsberg_rl@mercer.edu; *Pub Serv,* Hannah Knott-Rogers; Tel: 678-547-6272, E-mail: rogers_hk@mercer.edu; *Pub Serv,* Peter Otto; Tel: 678-547-6256, E-mail: otto_pj@mercer.edu; *Pub Serv,* Beth Perry; Tel: 678-547-6435, E-mail: perry_sb@mercer.edu. Subject Specialists: *Bus,* Kim Eccles; *English lang,* Rebecca Engsberg; *Pharm,* Hannah Knott-Rogers; *Educ,* Peter Otto; *Theol,* Beth Perry; Staff 9 (MLS 9)
Founded 1968. Enrl 2,878; Highest Degree: Doctorate
Jul 2009-Jun 2010. Mats Exp $394,972, Books $60,486, Per/Ser (Incl. Access Fees) $214,400, Micro $4,100, AV Mat $3,300, Electronic Ref Mat (Incl. Access Fees) $112,686. Sal $695,192 (Prof $435,773)
Library Holdings: e-journals 4,000; Bk Titles 128,615; Bk Vols 146,872; Per Subs 586
Special Collections: British & American Literature Coll, 18th-19th Century, 1st ed
Subject Interests: Counseling, Educ, Nursing, Pharm, Theol
Automation Activity & Vendor Info: (Acquisitions) Innovative Interfaces, Inc; (Cataloging) Innovative Interfaces, Inc; (Circulation) Innovative Interfaces, Inc; (ILL) Innovative Interfaces, Inc; (OPAC) Innovative Interfaces, Inc; (Serials) Innovative Interfaces, Inc
Database Vendor: 3M Library Systems, American Psychological Association (APA), Annual Reviews, Baker & Taylor, BCR: Christian Periodical Index, Booklist Online, Bowker, Brodart, Children's Literature Comprehensive Database Company (CLCD), Cinahl, Coutts Information Service, CQ Press, DynaMed, ebrary, EBSCO - WebFeat, EBSCO Information Services, EBSCOhost, Elsevier, H W Wilson, HeinOnline, Hoovers, Innovative Interfaces, Inc, ISI Web of Knowledge, JSTOR, LexisNexis, MD Consult, Medline, Mergent Online, Micromedex, Modern Language Association, OCLC FirstSearch, OCLC WebJunction, OCLC WorldShare Interlibrary Loan, OVID Technologies, ProQuest, PubMed, RefWorks, Sage, ScienceDirect, SerialsSolutions, Springer-Verlag, Thomson - Web of Science, ValueLine, Wiley, Wilson - Wilson Web, YBP Library Services
Wireless access
Function: Archival coll, AV serv, Bks on CD, CD-ROM, Computers for patron use, Copy machines, e-mail & chat, E-Reserves, Electronic databases & coll, Exhibits, Handicapped accessible, Health sci info serv, ILL available, Magnifiers for reading, Online cat, Online ref, Online searches, Orientations, Outside serv via phone, mail, e-mail & web, Photocopying/Printing, Pub access computers, Ref serv available, Scanner, Spoken cassettes & CDs, Spoken cassettes & DVDs, Telephone ref, VHS videos, Video lending libr, Web-catalog, Wheelchair accessible, Workshops
Partic in Atlanta Health Science Libraries Consortium; Atlanta Regional Council for Higher Education; Docline; GALILEO (Georgia Library Learning Online); Georgia Interactive Network for Medical Information; Lyrasis; National Network of Libraries of Medicine; OCLC Online Computer Library Center, Inc
Open Mon-Thurs (Winter) 7:30am-10pm, Fri 7:30am-8pm, Sat 9-6, Sun 1-9; Mon-Thurs (Summer) 8am-9pm, Fri 8-6, Sat 9-6, Sun 1-9
Restriction: Open to students, fac & staff, Photo ID required for access, Staff use only, Students only

CM MOREHOUSE SCHOOL OF MEDICINE LIBRARY, 720 Westview Dr SW, 30310-1495. SAN 320-1457. Tel: 404-752-1530. Circulation Tel: 404-752-1536. Interlibrary Loan Service Tel: 404-752-1528. Reference Tel: 404-752-1533. FAX: 404-752-1049. Reference FAX: 404-755-7318. Web Site: www.msm.edu/library.aspx. *Dir,* Joe Swanson, Jr; E-mail: jswanson@msm.edu; *Librn,* Roland Welmaker; Tel: 404-752-1534, E-mail: rwelmaker@msm.edu; *Mgr,* Tara Douglas-Williams; Staff 9 (MLS 3, Non-MLS 6)
Founded 1978. Enrl 500; Highest Degree: Doctorate
Library Holdings: e-books 601; e-journals 9,141; Bk Vols 34,448; Per Subs 355
Subject Interests: Health sci
Automation Activity & Vendor Info: (Cataloging) CyberTools for Libraries; (Circulation) CyberTools for Libraries; (Course Reserve) CyberTools for Libraries; (OPAC) CyberTools for Libraries
Database Vendor: OCLC FirstSearch, OVID Technologies
Wireless access
Function: 24/7 Electronic res, 24/7 Online cat, Computers for patron use, Copy machines, E-Reserves, Exhibits, Fax serv, Handicapped accessible, ILL available, Mail & tel request accepted, Online cat, Online ref, Online searches, Outreach serv, Photocopying/Printing, Printer for laptops & handheld devices, Pub access computers, Ref serv available, Scanner, Study rm, Telephone ref, Web-catalog, Workshops
Publications: Library Guide
Partic in Atlanta Health Science Libraries Consortium; Atlanta Regional Council for Higher Education; Consortium of Southern Biomedical Libraries; Georgia Health Sciences Library Association (GHSLA); Lyrasis
Restriction: 24-hr pass syst for students only

G NATIONAL ARCHIVES & RECORDS ADMINISTRATION*, Jimmy Carter Presidential Library & Museum, 441 Freedom Pkwy, 30307. SAN 328-5650. Tel: 404-865-7100. FAX: 404-865-7102. E-mail: carter.library@nara.gov. Web Site: www.jimmycarterlibrary.gov. *Actg Dir,* David Stanhope; Tel: 404-865-7128, E-mail: david.stanhope@nara.gov; *AV Archivist/Librn,* Polly S Nodine; Tel: 404-865-7125, E-mail: polly.nodine@nara.gov; *Prog & Vols Coordr,* Janet Harris; Tel: 404-865-7114, E-mail: janet.harris@nara.gov; *Admin Officer,* Terryll Lumpkin; Tel: 404-865-7119, E-mail: terryll.lumpkin@nara.gov; *Supvry Archivist,* Sara Saunders; Tel: 404-865-7155, E-mail: sara.saunders@nara.gov; *Curator,* Sylvia Naguib; Tel: 404-865-7123, E-mail: sylvia.naguib@nara.gov; *Educ Spec,* Kahlil Chism; Tel: 404-865-7126, E-mail: kahlil.chism@nara.gov; *Pub Affairs,* Tony Clark; Tel: 404-865-7109, E-mail: tony.clark@nara.gov; *Web Developer,* Sheila Mayo; Tel: 404-865-7120, E-mail: sheila.mayo@nara.gov
Founded 1986
Library Holdings: Bk Titles 6,500; Per Subs 50; Videos 1,550
Special Collections: Presidental Papers of Jimmy Carter
Wireless access
Function: Res libr
Publications: Historical Materials in the Jimmy Carter Library (Online only)
Open Mon-Fri 8:30-4:30
Friends of the Library Group

S NATIONAL FOOTBALL FOUNDATION'S COLLEGE, College Football Hall of Fame Library, 285 Andrew Young International Blvd NW, 30313-1591. (Mail add: 250 Marietta St NW, 30313), SAN 313-5527. Tel: 404-880-4800, 404-880-4822. FAX: 404-657-4200. E-mail: info@cfbhall.com. Web Site: www.cfbhall.com. *Curator, Historian,* Kent Stephens; E-mail: kstephens@cfbhall.com; Staff 4 (MLS 1, Non-MLS 3)
Library Holdings: AV Mats 1,580; CDs 109; Bk Titles 10,100; Bk Vols 12,300; Per Subs 68; Videos 410
Special Collections: Oral History
Subject Interests: Col football hist
Wireless access
Restriction: Open by appt only

M NORTHSIDE HOSPITAL*, Health Resource Center, 1000 Johnson Ferry Rd NE, 30342-1611. SAN 303-3155. Tel: 404-851-6431. FAX: 404-851-6167. *Librn,* Brenda Curry-Wimberly
Founded 1970
Library Holdings: Bk Titles 1,400; Per Subs 235
Subject Interests: Med, Nursing, Obstetrics & gynecology
Wireless access
Partic in Atlanta Health Science Libraries Consortium
Open Mon-Fri 7-4
Friends of the Library Group

C OGLETHORPE UNIVERSITY*, Philip Weltner Library, 4484 Peachtree Rd NE, 30319. SAN 303-3163. Tel: 404-364-8511. FAX: 404-364-8517. Web Site: library.oglethorpe.edu. *Dir,* Anne Salter; E-mail: asalter@oglethorpe.edu; *Cat,* David Stockton; *Ref,* Tricia Clayton; Staff 3 (MLS 3)
Founded 1916. Enrl 920; Fac 48; Highest Degree: Master
Library Holdings: Bk Titles 157,000; Per Subs 745
Special Collections: James E Oglethorpe Coll; Sidney Lanier Coll
Automation Activity & Vendor Info: (Cataloging) Ex Libris Group; (Circulation) Ex Libris Group
Wireless access
Partic in Atlanta Regional Council for Higher Education

L PAUL, HASTINGS, JANOFSKY & WALKER*, Law Library, 600 Peachtree St NE, Ste 2400, 30308. SAN 372-1388. Tel: 404-815-2143. FAX: 404-815-2424.
Library Holdings: Bk Vols 10,000; Per Subs 50
Restriction: Staff use only

R PEACHTREE PRESBYTERIAN CHURCH*, Pattillo Library, 3434 Roswell Rd NW, 30305. SAN 303-3171. Tel: 404-842-5813. FAX: 404-842-5858. Web Site: www.peachtreepres.org. *In Charge,* Meryl Dilcher
Founded 1960
Library Holdings: Bk Vols 10,000
Open Mon-Fri 10-12, Wed 4-6, Sun 8:30-1

M PIEDMONT HEALTHCARE, INC*, Sauls Memorial Library, 1968 Peachtree Rd NW, 30309. SAN 303-318X. Tel: 404-605-3305. FAX: 404-609-6641. E-mail: sauls@piedmont.org. Web Site: www.piedmonthospital.org. *Chief, Libr Serv,* Stacie Waddell; E-mail: stacie.waddell@piedmont.org; *Acq Librn,* Amy Harkness; E-mail: amy.harkness@piedmont.org; *Ser Librn,* Position Currently Open; Staff 4 (MLS 3, Non-MLS 1)
Founded 1934
Library Holdings: CDs 34; DVDs 169; e-books 189; e-journals 500; Bk Titles 4,950; Per Subs 468; Talking Bks 1,004; Videos 115
Special Collections: Consumer Health (Nicholas E Davies Health Information Center); Piedmont Authors Coll
Subject Interests: Consumer health info, Hist of med, Med, Mgt, Nursing
Automation Activity & Vendor Info: (Acquisitions) SydneyPlus; (Cataloging) SydneyPlus; (Circulation) SydneyPlus; (ILL) SydneyPlus; (OPAC) SydneyPlus; (Serials) SydneyPlus
Database Vendor: EBSCO Information Services, EBSCOhost, Majors, Marcive, Inc, MD Consult, Medline, Micromedex, OVID Technologies, ProQuest, PubMed, ScienceDirect, SerialsSolutions, STAT!Ref (Teton Data Systems), UpToDate
Wireless access
Publications: Library Outreach Near & Far: Programs to Staff & Patients of the Piedmont Healthcare System (Periodical)
Partic in Atlanta Health Science Libraries Consortium; Georgia Health Sciences Library Association (GHSLA); Medical Library Association (MLA); Southern Chapter of Med Libr Asn
Open Mon-Fri 7:30-4
Restriction: Circ limited, Hospital staff & commun, Open to pub with supv only, Open to researchers by request, Restricted borrowing privileges, Restricted loan policy, Staff & prof res

L POPE & MCGLAMRY*, Law Library, 3455 Peachtree Rd NE, Ste 925, 30326. SAN 372-1760. Tel: 404-523-7706. FAX: 404-524-1648. E-mail: pmkm@mindspring.com. *Librn,* Ellen Bailey
Library Holdings: Bk Vols 500; Per Subs 100
Partic in OCLC Online Computer Library Center, Inc

S JOHN PORTMAN & ASSOCIATES LIBRARY*, 303 Peachtree St NE, Ste 4600, 30308. SAN 303-3198. Tel: 404-614-5555. FAX: 404-614-5553. Web Site: www.portmanusa.com. *Librn,* Marvin Brewer
Founded 1973
Library Holdings: Bk Titles 2,000; Per Subs 150
Special Collections: Firm's Architectural Drawings from 1953
Subject Interests: Archit, Art, Finance, Interior design, Law, Real estate, Structural eng

L POWELL, GOLDSTEIN LLP*, Law Library & Information Center, 1201 W Peachtree St, 14th Flr, 30309. SAN 327-8980. Tel: 404-572-6696. FAX: 404-572-6999. E-mail: rdesk@pogolaw.com. Web Site: www.pogolaw.com. *Head, Ref,* Rita Treadwell
Library Holdings: Bk Vols 20,000
Open Mon-Fri 7-6
Restriction: Staff use only

CR PSYCHOLOGICAL STUDIES INSTITUTE*, Ruth Holt Library, 2055 Mount Paran Rd NW, 30327. SAN 329-8361. Tel: 404-233-3949, Ext 110. FAX: 404-239-9460. Web Site: www.psy.edu. *Dir of Libr,* John Hughes; E-mail: jhughes@psy.edu; Staff 1 (MLS 1)
Enrl 100; Highest Degree: Master
Library Holdings: Bk Vols 14,000; Per Subs 39
Automation Activity & Vendor Info: (Cataloging) Follett Software
Database Vendor: EBSCOhost, ProQuest
Wireless access

Partic in Georgia Online Database
Open Mon 9-6, Tues-Thurs 9-7, Fri 9-5

L SCHREEDER, WHEELER & FLINT LLP*, Law Library, 1100 Peachtree St NE, Ste 800, 30309-1845. SAN 372-1426. Tel: 404-681-3450. FAX: 404-681-1046. Web Site: www.swfllp.com. *In Charge,* Debbie Wilson
Library Holdings: Bk Vols 5,000; Per Subs 10
Subject Interests: Real estate

L SMITH, CURRIE & HANCOCK LLP*, Law Library, 2700 Marquis One Tower, 245 Peachtree Center Ave NE, 30303-1227. SAN 328-1183. Tel: 404-582-8098. FAX: 404-688-0671. Web Site: www.smithcurrie.com. *Libr Serv Mgr,* Karen Toler; E-mail: ktoler@smithcurrie.com
Library Holdings: Bk Vols 10,000; Per Subs 20
Subject Interests: Construction law, Govt contracts
Wireless access
Restriction: Staff use only

L SMITH, GAMBRELL & RUSSELL*, Law Library, Prominade II, 1230 Peachtree St NE, Ste 3100, 30309. SAN 303-3228. Tel: 404-815-3538. Information Services Tel: 404-815-3618. FAX: 404-685-6838, 404-815-3509. E-mail: library@sgrlaw.com. *Dir,* Sarah Mauldan; Staff 4 (MLS 1, Non-MLS 3)
Founded 1893
Library Holdings: Bk Vols 50,000; Per Subs 100
Database Vendor: LexisNexis
Partic in CT Advantage; Dialog Corp; Dun & Bradstreet Info Servs; Pacer; Thompson Saegis; Westlaw

S SOUTHERN REGIONAL COUNCIL, INC*, Reference Library, 1201 W Peachtree St, Ste 2000, 30309. SAN 329-3785. Tel: 404-817-8597. FAX: 404-817-8791. E-mail: southernregionalcouncil@gmail.com. Web Site: www.southerncouncil.org. *Exec Dir,* Kevin Bronski
Library Holdings: Bk Titles 1,000

S SOUTHERN REGIONAL EDUCATION BOARD LIBRARY*, 592 Tenth St NW, 30318-5776. SAN 303-3236. Tel: 404-875-9211. FAX: 404-872-1477. Web Site: www.sreb.org. *Actg Librn,* Debbie Curtis; Tel: 404-875-9211, Ext 236, E-mail: debbie.curtis@sreb.org; Staff 1 (MLS 1)
Founded 1949
Library Holdings: Bk Vols 19,000; Per Subs 175
Special Collections: Archive of Corporate Materials (SREB-published) to 1948
Subject Interests: Educ policy, Health educ, Regional studies
Database Vendor: EBSCOhost
Restriction: Staff use only

UNITED STATES ENVIRONMENTAL PROTECTION

G REGION 4 LIBRARY*, Atlanta Federal Center, 61 Forsyth St SW, 30303-3104, SAN 303-2809. Tel: 404-562-8190. FAX: 404-562-8114. E-mail: r4-library@epa.gov. *Sr Librn,* Ora Mims Howell; Tel: 404-562-8125; Staff 1 (MLS 1)
Founded 1973
Library Holdings: Bk Titles 24,000; Per Subs 50
Special Collections: EPA Reports; Public Display; Superfund Docket; USGS Reports
Subject Interests: Air pollution, Environ law, Noise pollution, Water pollution
Partic in OCLC Online Computer Library Center, Inc; OLS
Open Mon-Fri 8-4
Friends of the Library Group

G REGION 4 OEA INFORMATION-RESEARCH CENTER*, 61 Forsyth St SW, 30303-3104, SAN 374-7034. Tel: 404-562-9654. FAX: 404-562-9663. *Dir,* Pat Strougal; Staff 1 (MLS 1)
Founded 1992
Library Holdings: Bk Titles 600; Bk Vols 6,200; Videos 75
Special Collections: EPA Guidances
Subject Interests: Environ law
Function: For res purposes, Ref serv available, Telephone ref
Restriction: Circulates for staff only, Not open to pub

AUGUSTA

S AUGUSTA RICHMOND COUNTY HISTORICAL SOCIETY LIBRARY*, c/o Reese Library, Augusta State University, 2500 Walton Way, 30904-2200. SAN 303-3368. Tel: 706-737-1532. FAX: 706-667-4415. Web Site: www.thearches.org/index.html. *Dir,* Judy McAlhany; E-mail: jmcalhan@aug.edu; *Acq, Cat,* Diane Black
Founded 1946
Library Holdings: Bk Titles 2,091; Bk Vols 3,072
Subject Interests: Ga, Genealogy
Publications: An Augusta Scrapbook - Twentieth Century Memories; Augusta: A Pictorial History; Confederate City, Augusta, Georgia; Historical Markers and monuments of Augusta, Richmond County; Journal of Archibald Campbell in His Majesty's Service, 1778; Reminiscences of Augusta Marines; Richmond County History, The Journal of the Society (annual); Summerville: A Pictorial History; The Story of Augusta; Touring Historic Augusta
Open Mon-Fri 9-4

P AUGUSTA-RICHMOND COUNTY PUBLIC LIBRARY*, (Formerly East Central Georgia Regional Library), 823 Telfair St, 30901. SAN 338-4519. Tel: 706-821-2600. FAX: 706-724-6762. E-mail: main@ecgrl.org. Web Site: www.ecgrl.public.lib.ga.us. *Dir,* Darlene Price; E-mail: priced@arcpls.org; *Asst Dir,* Mashell Fashion; Tel: 706-821-2602, E-mail: fashionm@arcpls.org; *Head, Circ Serv,* Jan Alexander; *Head, Pub Serv,* Russell Liner; E-mail: linerr@arcpls.org; *Head, Tech Serv,* Jennie Feinberg; *Outreach Librn,* Kristin Eberhart; *YA Librn,* Kristin Eberhart; *Mgr, Ch Serv,* Position Currently Open; *ILL,* Tonia Owens; *Syst Adminr,* Benjamin Dudley; Staff 58 (MLS 14, Non-MLS 44)
Founded 1848. Pop 338,000; Circ 113,743
Jul 2007-Jun 2008 Income (Main Library and Branch(s)) $5,457,482, State $1,198,789, County $3,848,590, Locally Generated Income $410,103
Library Holdings: Audiobooks 3,952; AV Mats 30,250; CDs 1,728; DVDs 12,162; e-books 2,200; Bk Vols 618,439; Per Subs 188; Talking Bks 33,836; Videos 18,092
Subject Interests: Ga
Automation Activity & Vendor Info: (Cataloging) Evergreen; (Circulation) Evergreen; (OPAC) Evergreen
Database Vendor: EBSCOhost, Gale Cengage Learning, ProQuest, Wilson - Wilson Web
Wireless access
Function: Handicapped accessible, ILL available, Magnifiers for reading, Newsp ref libr, Photocopying/Printing, Prog for children & young adult, Ref serv available, Summer reading prog, Wheelchair accessible
Publications: Library Links (Newsletter); Personal Name Index to the Augusta Chronicle (Index to newspapers)
Partic in PINES (Public Information Network for Electronic Services)
Special Services for the Deaf - TDD equip; TTY equip
Special Services for the Blind - Bks on cassette; Bks on CD; Computer with voice synthesizer for visually impaired persons; Large print bks; Reader equip
Open Mon-Thurs 9-9, Fri & Sat 9-5:30, Sun 2-5:30
Friends of the Library Group
Branches: 6
APPLEBY BRANCH, 2260 Walton Way, 30904, SAN 338-4578. Tel: 706-736-6244. FAX: 706-481-0616. E-mail: appleby@ecgrl.org. *Br Mgr,* Kathy Crosson; Staff 2 (Non-MLS 2)
Founded 1955. Pop 191,236
Library Holdings: DVDs 216; Bk Vols 36,621; Per Subs 44; Talking Bks 381
Function: Photocopying/Printing, Prog for children & young adult, Summer reading prog
Special Services for the Blind - Bks on CD; Computer with voice synthesizer for visually impaired persons; Large print bks; Talking bks
Open Mon 9-7, Tues-Fri 9-5:30, Sat 10-5:30
Friends of the Library Group
DIAMOND LAKES, 101 Diamond Lakes Way, Hephzibah, 30815. Tel: 706-772-2432. FAX: 706-772-2433. E-mail: diamondlakes@arcpls.org.
Founded 2005. Pop 191,236
Library Holdings: DVDs 455; Bk Vols 14,723; Per Subs 70; Talking Bks 110; Videos 355
Database Vendor: OCLC WorldShare Interlibrary Loan, ProQuest
Function: 24/7 Online cat, Adult bk club, Bks on cassette, Bks on CD, Children's prog, Computer training, Computers for patron use, Copy machines, Electronic databases & coll, Free DVD rentals, ILL available, Magazines, Music CDs, Prog for adults, Prog for children & young adult, Pub access computers, Story hour, Summer reading prog, Tax forms
Partic in PINES (Public Information Network for Electronic Services)
Special Services for the Blind - Bks on cassette; Bks on CD; Computer with voice synthesizer for visually impaired persons
Open Mon & Wed 9-7, Tues, Thurs & Fri 9-5:30, Sat 10-5:30
Friends of the Library Group
FRIEDMAN BRANCH, 1447 Jackson Rd, 30909, SAN 328-7882. Tel: 706-736-6758. FAX: 706-737-2034. E-mail: friedman@ecgrl.org. *Br Mgr,* Jenny Fienberg; Staff 3 (MLS 1, Non-MLS 2)
Founded 1986. Pop 191,236; Circ 117,463
Library Holdings: DVDs 362; Bk Vols 43,290; Per Subs 36; Talking Bks 111; Videos 1,000
Database Vendor: OCLC WorldShare Interlibrary Loan, ProQuest
Function: Handicapped accessible, Photocopying/Printing, Prog for children & young adult, Ref serv available, Summer reading prog, Telephone ref
Special Services for the Blind - Bks on cassette; Bks on CD; Computer with voice synthesizer for visually impaired persons; Large print bks
Open Mon & Wed 9-8, Tues, Thurs & Fri 9-5:30, Sat 10-5:30
Friends of the Library Group

JEFF MAXWELL BRANCH, 1927 Lumpkin Rd, 30906, SAN 338-4608. Tel: 706-793-2020. FAX: 706-790-1023. E-mail: maxwell@ecgrl.org. *Br Mgr,* Linda Beck; Staff 3 (MLS 1, Non-MLS 2)
Founded 1973. Pop 191,236; Circ 130,555
Library Holdings: DVDs 1,200; Bk Vols 59,809; Per Subs 37; Videos 500
Function: Handicapped accessible, Photocopying/Printing, Prog for children & young adult, Ref serv available, Summer reading prog, Telephone ref, Wheelchair accessible
Special Services for the Blind - Bks on cassette; Bks on CD; Large print bks
Open Mon, Wed & Fri 9-5:30, Tues & Thurs 9-8, Sat 10-5:30
Friends of the Library Group

TALKING BOOK CENTER, 823 Telfair St, 30901, SAN 338-4543. Tel: 706-821-2625. FAX: 706-724-5403. E-mail: talkbook@ecgrl.org. *Br Mgr,* Audrey Bell; E-mail: bella@ecgrl.org; Staff 4 (Non-MLS 4)
Founded 1981. Circ 82,524
Library Holdings: DVDs 896; Large Print Bks 1,158; Talking Bks 34,641; Videos 7,739
Subject Interests: Blind, Physically handicapped
Function: AV serv
Publications: Augusta Talking Book Center News (Newsletter)
Special Services for the Blind - Talking bks
Open Mon-Thurs 9-7, Fri & Sat 9-5:30
Friends of the Library Group

WALLACE BRANCH, 1237 Laney-Walker Blvd, 30901, SAN 338-4632. Tel: 706-722-6275. FAX: 706-724-0715. E-mail: wallace@ecgrl.org. *Br Mgr,* Paulette Scurry; Staff 2 (Non-MLS 2)
Founded 1959. Pop 191,236; Circ 18,855
Library Holdings: Bk Vols 28,000; Per Subs 39; Talking Bks 22
Database Vendor: OCLC WorldShare Interlibrary Loan, ProQuest
Function: Handicapped accessible, Photocopying/Printing, Prog for children & young adult, Summer reading prog, Wheelchair accessible
Special Services for the Blind - Bks on CD; Computer with voice synthesizer for visually impaired persons
Open Mon & Wed 9-5:30, Tues & Thurs 9-8, Fri & Sat 12:30-5:30
Friends of the Library Group

Bookmobiles: 1. In Charge, Diane Evans

J AUGUSTA TECHNICAL COLLEGE*, Jack B Patrick Information Tech Center, 3200 Augusta Tech Dr, 30906. SAN 326-6605. Tel: 706-771-4165. FAX: 706-771-4169. Web Site: www.augustatech.edu. *Head Librn,* Patricia Brucker; E-mail: pbrucker@augustatech.edu; *Dir, Acad Computing,* Lucretia Parham; E-mail: lparham@augustatech.edu; *Librn,* Bonnie Owen; Staff 9 (MLS 5, Non-MLS 4)
Library Holdings: Bk Titles 100,000; Per Subs 500
Special Collections: US Document Depository
Subject Interests: Electronics
Wireless access
Partic in Lyrasis

CM GEORGIA REGENTS UNIVERSITY, Robert B Greenblatt MD Library, 1459 Laney-Walker Blvd, 30912-0004. (Mail add: 1120 15th St, 30912), SAN 303-3341. Tel: 706-721-3441. Interlibrary Loan Service Tel: 706-721-6374. FAX: 706-721-2018. Interlibrary Loan Service FAX: 706-721-6006. E-mail: libref@gru.edu. Web Site: www.gru.edu/library. *Dir of Libr,* Brenda L Seago, PhD; Tel: 706-721-2856, E-mail: bseago@gru.edu; *Chair, Content Mgt,* Sandra Bandy; Tel: 706-721-0299, E-mail: sbandy@gru.edu; *Chair, Res & Educ Serv,* Kathy Davies; Tel: 706-721-9911, E-mail: kdavies@gru.edu; *ILL, Mgr, Access Serv,* Lisa Workman; Tel: 706-721-6473, E-mail: lworkman@gru.edu; Staff 23 (MLS 9, Non-MLS 14)
Founded 1834. Enrl 8,995; Fac 1,575; Highest Degree: Doctorate
Jul 2012-Jun 2013. Mats Exp $1,485,093. Sal $1,058,903
Library Holdings: AV Mats 1,772; e-books 548; Bk Titles 27,167; Bk Vols 32,285; Per Subs 6,134
Special Collections: 19th Century Library; Greenblatt Archive; Landmarks in Modern Medicine Coll; Medical Artifacts
Subject Interests: Allied health, Dentistry, Med, Nursing
Automation Activity & Vendor Info: (Cataloging) Ex Libris Group; (Circulation) Ex Libris Group; (Course Reserve) Ex Libris Group; (ILL) OCLC ILLiad; (Media Booking) Ex Libris Group; (OPAC) Ex Libris Group; (Serials) Ex Libris Group
Database Vendor: Cinahl, DynaMed, EBSCOhost, Elsevier MDL, ISI Web of Knowledge, LexisNexis, Micromedex, OCLC WorldShare Interlibrary Loan, OVID Technologies, ProQuest, PubMed, ScienceDirect, Thomson - Web of Science, UpToDate, Wiley InterScience
Wireless access
Function: Res libr
Partic in Consortium of Southern Biomedical Libraries; National Network of Libraries of Medicine Southeastern Atlantic Region; OCLC Online Computer Library Center, Inc; Regents Acad Comt on Librs

C GEORGIA REGENTS UNIVERSITY, Reese Library, (Formerly Augusta State University), 2500 Walton Way, 30904-2200. SAN 303-3333. Tel: 706-737-1745. Interlibrary Loan Service Tel: 706-667-4898. Reference Tel: 706-737-1744. FAX: 706-667-4415. E-mail: reference@gru.edu. Web Site: www.gru.edu/library. *Head Librn,* Barbara Mann; E-mail: bmann@gru.edu; Staff 29 (MLS 10, Non-MLS 19)
Founded 1957. Enrl 6,900; Fac 310; Highest Degree: Master
Library Holdings: Bk Vols 497,172; Per Subs 36,124
Special Collections: Cumming Family Papers; Edison Marshall Papers; Local History Coll (Augusta-Richmond County Historical Society). US Document Depository
Automation Activity & Vendor Info: (Cataloging) Ex Libris Group; (Circulation) Ex Libris Group; (Course Reserve) Ex Libris Group; (ILL) OCLC ILLiad; (Media Booking) Ex Libris Group; (OPAC) Ex Libris Group; (Serials) Ex Libris Group
Database Vendor: ABC-CLIO, ACM (Association for Computing Machinery), Alexander Street Press, American Chemical Society, American Psychological Association (APA), ARTstor, Baker & Taylor, BioOne, Cambridge Scientific Abstracts, CredoReference, Ebooks Corporation, EBSCOhost, H W Wilson, JSTOR, LexisNexis, Marcive, Inc, Medline, OCLC WorldShare Interlibrary Loan, Project MUSE, PubMed, SerialsSolutions, Wiley InterScience, Wilson - Wilson Web
Wireless access
Partic in GALILEO (Georgia Library Learning Online); Lyrasis; OCLC Online Computer Library Center, Inc
Special Services for the Deaf - TTY equip

GM CHARLIE NORWOOD VA MEDICAL CENTER LIBRARY*, One Freedom Way, 30904-6285. SAN 303-3384. Tel: 706-733-0188, Ext 2813. Reference Tel: 706-733-0188, Ext 7518. Information Services Tel: 706-733-0188, Ext 2814. FAX: 706-823-3920. *Chief Librn,* Brian Rothwell; Tel: 706-733-0188, Ext 7501; *Med Librn,* Billy Houke; *Libr Tech,* Shirley McCloud; Tel: 706-733-0188, Ext 2820; *Libr Tech,* Linda Young; Staff 2 (MLS 1, Non-MLS 1)
Founded 1937
Library Holdings: Bk Vols 5,226; Per Subs 321
Subject Interests: Geriatrics, Med, Nursing, Psychiat, Psychol, Soc serv (soc work), Surgery
Partic in Veterans Affairs Libr Network (VALNET)
Restriction: Staff use only

C PAINE COLLEGE*, Collins Callaway Library, 1235 15th St, 30901-3105. SAN 303-335X. Tel: 706-821-8308. Administration Tel: 706-821-8253. FAX: 706-821-8698. Web Site: www.paine.edu/library.
Founded 1882. Enrl 900, Highest Degree: Bachelor
Special Collections: African-American Special Coll
Wireless access
Partic in Georgia Private Acad Librs Consortium (GPALS); Lyrasis
Open Mon-Thurs 7:45am-11pm, Fri 7:45-5, Sat 1-5, Sun 4-8
Restriction: In-house use for visitors

BAINBRIDGE

J BAINBRIDGE STATE COLLEGE LIBRARY*, 2500 E Shotwell St, 39819. (Mail add: PO Box 990, 39818-0990), SAN 303-3392. Tel: 229-248-2590. FAX: 229-248-2589. E-mail: library@bainbridge.edu. Web Site: www.bainbridge.edu/bclib/bc_lib_idx.htm. *Dir,* Susan Ralph; E-mail: sralph@bainbridge.edu; *Assoc Librn,* Heather Battenberg; Tel: 229-243-6416, E-mail: heather.battenberg@bainbridge.edu; *Asst Librn, Early County Site,* Michelle Barsom; Tel: 229-724-2220, E-mail: mbarsom@bainbridge.edu; Staff 3 (MLS 3)
Founded 1973. Enrl 3,681; Fac 68; Highest Degree: Associate
Library Holdings: Audiobooks 497; CDs 365; DVDs 727; Music Scores 20; Bk Titles 38,198; Bk Vols 45,366; Per Subs 90
Special Collections: Apollo Lunar Surface EVA Video Coll; Donalson Papers, Maston O'Neal Papers; Walter E Cox Political Archives
Automation Activity & Vendor Info: (Acquisitions) Ex Libris Group; (Cataloging) Ex Libris Group; (Circulation) Ex Libris Group; (Course Reserve) Ex Libris Group; (ILL) OCLC FirstSearch; (OPAC) Ex Libris Group; (Serials) Ex Libris Group
Database Vendor: OCLC FirstSearch
Wireless access
Partic in Georgia Libr Info Network; Georgia Online Database; Lyrasis

P SOUTHWEST GEORGIA REGIONAL LIBRARY, Decatur County - Gilbert H Gragg Library, 301 S Monroe St, 39819. SAN 338-4667. Tel: 229-248-2665. FAX: 229-248-2670. E-mail: librarian@swgrl.org. Web Site: www.swgrl.org. *Dir,* Susan S Whittle; E-mail: swhittle@swgrl.org; *Asst Dir, Tech, Training & Develop,* Catherine Vanstone; E-mail: cvanstone@swgrl.org; *Youth Serv & Commun Relations Librn,* Carole Albyn; E-mail: calbyn@swgrl.org; Staff 19.5 (MLS 3, Non-MLS 16.5)
Founded 1902. Pop 44,008; Circ 221,715
Jul 2013-Jun 2014 Income (Main Library and Branch(s)) $1,217,940, State $426,752, City $1,621, County $719,701, Other $69,866. Mats Exp $74,775, Books $56,516, Per/Ser (Incl. Access Fees) $5,006, AV Mat

$12,803, Electronic Ref Mat (Incl. Access Fees) $450. Sal $582,765 (Prof $209,530)
Library Holdings: AV Mats 15,442; Electronic Media & Resources 3; Bk Vols 171,075; Per Subs 79; Talking Bks 38,609
Special Collections: Andrew Avery Film Coll; E Ashby Woods World War II Coll; Georgia Author Coll; Jack Wingate Hunters & Anglers Coll. Oral History
Subject Interests: Genealogy, Local hist, World War II
Automation Activity & Vendor Info: (Cataloging) Evergreen; (Circulation) Evergreen; (ILL) OCLC; (OPAC) Evergreen
Database Vendor: EBSCOhost, Westlaw
Wireless access
Function: After school storytime, Bk club(s), Bks on CD, Children's prog, Computer training, Computers for patron use, Copy machines, Digital talking bks, Electronic databases & coll, Exhibits, Fax serv, Free DVD rentals, Handicapped accessible, Holiday prog, ILL available, Music CDs, Online cat, Online ref, Outreach serv, Photocopying/Printing, Preschool outreach, Prog for adults, Prog for children & young adult, Pub access computers, Ref serv available, Senior computer classes, Senior outreach, Spoken cassettes & CDs, Story hour, Summer reading prog, Tax forms, Teen prog, VHS videos, Web-catalog, Wheelchair accessible
Publications: Bainbridge Subregional Library & Physically Handicapped of Southwest Georgia (Monthly newsletter); SWGRL Spotlight (Monthly newsletter)
Partic in PINES (Public Information Network for Electronic Services)
Special Services for the Deaf - Assistive tech; TTY equip
Special Services for the Blind - Accessible computers; Assistive/Adapted tech devices, equip & products; Audio mat; Bks & mags in Braille, on rec, tape & cassette; Bks on cassette; Bks on CD; Braille alphabet card; Braille equip; Cassette playback machines; Cassettes; Children's Braille; Digital talking bk; Home delivery serv; Info on spec aids & appliances; Internet workstation with adaptive software; Large print bks; Low vision equip; Magnifiers; Newsletter (in large print, Braille or on cassette); Newsline for the Blind; Recorded bks; Screen reader software; Talking bks; Talking bks & player equip
Open Mon 9-8, Tues, Wed & Fri 9-6, Thurs 9-7, Sat 9-4
Friends of the Library Group
Branches: 3

P BAINBRIDGE SUBREGIONAL LIBRARY FOR THE BLIND & PHYSICALLY HANDICAPPED-TALKING BOOK CENTER, 301 S Monroe St, 39819. Tel: 229-248-2680. Toll Free Tel: 800-795-2680. FAX: 229-248-2670. *Librn,* Susan Whittle; Staff 3 (MLS 1, Non-MLS 2)
Founded 1971
Library Holdings: Talking Bks 38,609
Automation Activity & Vendor Info: (Circulation) Keystone Systems, Inc (KLAS)
Publications: Talking Book Newsletter (Monthly)
Special Services for the Blind - Aids for in-house use; Assistive/Adapted tech devices, equip & products; Bks & mags in Braille, on rec, tape & cassette; Braille equip; Cassette playback machines; Cassettes; Digital talking bk; Digital talking bk machines; Info on spec aids & appliances; Internet workstation with adaptive software; Newsletter (in large print, Braille or on cassette); Newsline for the Blind; Ref serv; Talking bk & rec for the blind cat; Talking bks; Talking bks & player equip

MILLER COUNTY-JAMES W MERRITT JR MEMORIAL LIBRARY, 259 E Main St, Colquitt, 39837, SAN 338-4721. Tel: 229-758-3131. FAX: 229-758-3131. *Br Mgr,* Susan Grimsley
Friends of the Library Group

SEMINOLE COUNTY PUBLIC LIBRARY, 103 W Fourth St, Donalsonville, 39845, SAN 338-4756. Tel: 229-524-2665. FAX: 229-524-8913. *Br Mgr,* Judy Smith
Subject Interests: Genealogy, Local hist

Bookmobiles: 1. Bk Vols 3,751

BARNESVILLE

J GORDON STATE COLLEGE*, Hightower Library, 419 College Dr, 30204. SAN 303-3406. Tel: 678-359-5076. FAX: 678-359-5240. E-mail: library@gordonstate.edu. Web Site: www.gordonstate.edu/library. *Libr Dir,* Dr Sonya S Gaither; *Ref & Instrul Serv Librn,* Beth Pye; *Circ,* Beverly Eskridge; *ILL/Doc Delivery Serv, Ser/ILL,* Brenda Rutherford; E-mail: brendar@gordonstate.edu; *Tech Serv,* Lisa Millican; Staff 7 (MLS 4, Non-MLS 3)
Founded 1939. Enrl 3,800; Fac 96; Highest Degree: Bachelor
Jul 2005-Jun 2006 Income $471,952. Mats Exp $125,947, Books $45,157, Per/Ser (Incl. Access Fees) $10,422, Micro $8,983, AV Equip $575, AV Mat $1,787, Electronic Ref Mat (Incl. Access Fees) $34,101, Presv $24,922. Sal $322,867 (Prof $174,113)
Library Holdings: AV Mats 4,785; e-books 27,417; Bk Vols 102,757; Per Subs 48
Subject Interests: Ga
Automation Activity & Vendor Info: (Acquisitions) Ex Libris Group; (Cataloging) OCLC; (Circulation) Ex Libris Group; (Course Reserve) Ex Libris Group; (ILL) OCLC; (OPAC) Ex Libris Group; (Serials) Ex Libris Group
Database Vendor: Bowker, EBSCOhost, Gale Cengage Learning, LexisNexis, Newsbank, OCLC FirstSearch, OCLC WorldShare Interlibrary Loan, ProQuest, Westlaw
Wireless access
Partic in Lyrasis
Open Mon-Thurs 7:45am-10pm, Fri 7:45-5, Sat 12-4, Sun 2-10

BLAIRSVILLE

J NORTH GEORGIA TECHNICAL COLLEGE LIBRARY*, Blairsville Campus, 121 Meeks Ave, 30512. Tel: 706-439-6320, 706-439-6326. FAX: 706-439-6301. E-mail: library@northgatech.edu. Web Site: www.northgatech.edu/library. *Librn,* Bryant Chris William; E-mail: wbryant@northgatech.edu; Staff 1 (MLS 1)
Founded 1998. Enrl 500; Fac 20; Highest Degree: Associate
Library Holdings: AV Mats 925; CDs 100; e-books 39,000; Bk Titles 5,000; Bk Vols 5,100; Per Subs 50
Automation Activity & Vendor Info: (Cataloging) OCLC CatExpress; (Circulation) SirsiDynix; (OPAC) SirsiDynix
Wireless access
Partic in Lyrasis

BRUNSWICK

J COLLEGE OF COASTAL GEORGIA*, Clara Wood Gould Memorial Library, One College Dr, 31520-3644. SAN 303-3414. Tel: 912-279-5700. Circulation Tel: 912-279-5874. Toll Free Tel: 800-675-7235. Web Site: www.ccga.edu/library. *Dean of Libr,* Debbie Holmes; Tel: 912-279-5787, E-mail: deholmes@ccga.edu; *Pub Serv Librn,* Lynda Kennedy; Tel: 912-279-5782, E-mail: lkennedy@ccga.edu; *Info Serv Spec,* Reid Lorna; E-mail: lreid@ccga.edu; *Pub Serv,* Cary Knapp; Tel: 912-279-5781, E-mail: cknapp@ccga.edu; Staff 9 (MLS 5, Non-MLS 4)
Founded 1961. Enrl 3,200; Fac 54; Highest Degree: Associate
Library Holdings: e-books 53,000; Electronic Media & Resources 150; Bk Titles 48,894; Bk Vols 51,211; Per Subs 250
Special Collections: Coastal Georgia History
Automation Activity & Vendor Info: (Acquisitions) Ex Libris Group; (Cataloging) Ex Libris Group; (Circulation) Ex Libris Group; (ILL) OCLC ILLiad; (Media Booking) Ex Libris Group; (OPAC) Ex Libris Group; (Serials) Ex Libris Group
Database Vendor: Cambridge Scientific Abstracts, EBSCOhost, Gale Cengage Learning, JSTOR, LexisNexis, OCLC FirstSearch, OCLC WorldShare Interlibrary Loan, ProQuest
Wireless access
Function: ILL available
Partic in Lyrasis
Special Services for the Blind - Reader equip
Open Mon-Thurs 8am-10pm, Fri 8-5, Sat 1-5, Sun 1-9
Restriction: Employees & their associates, In-house use for visitors, Non-circulating to the pub, Open to pub for ref only, Open to students, fac & staff
Departmental Libraries:

CAMDEN CENTER LEARNING RESOURCES CENTER, 8001 Lakes Blvd, Kingsland, 31548. Tel: 912-510-3331. *Pub Serv Librn,* John Kissinger; *Pub Serv Asst,* Angela Salmon
Open Mon-Thurs 9-9, Fri 9-4

P MARSHES OF GLYNN LIBRARIES*, Brunswick-Glynn County Library, 208 Gloucester St, 31520-7007. SAN 338-4780. Tel: 912-267-1212. FAX: 912-267-9597. *Dir,* Gerri Mullis; *Libr Mgr,* Lori Lasson; E-mail: llasson@glynncounty.org; Staff 2 (MLS 1, Non-MLS 1)
Founded 1883. Pop 80,000
Special Collections: Brunswick & Glynn County History Coll, maps & photo; Genealogy, Georgia & Southeast United States Coll; Georgia History Coll
Automation Activity & Vendor Info: (Acquisitions) Evergreen; (Cataloging) Evergreen; (Circulation) Evergreen; (ILL) OCLC; (OPAC) Evergreen
Database Vendor: Westlaw
Wireless access
Member Libraries: Saint Simons Public Library; Wayne County Public Library
Open Mon, Wed, Fri & Sat 9:30-5, Tues & Thurs 9:30-8
Friends of the Library Group

BUFORD

S PHILLIPS STATE PRISON*, Law & General Library, 2989 W Rock Quarry Rd, 30519-4198. SAN 371-0971. Tel: 770-932-4500, Ext 4676. FAX: 770-932-4676. *Actg Librn,* Diane Secrist; Staff 2 (MLS 1, Non-MLS 1)
Library Holdings: Bk Vols 8,000; Per Subs 45
Special Services for the Deaf - High interest/low vocabulary bks
Open Mon, Tues, Thurs & Fri 8-3:45
Restriction: Staff & inmates only

CAIRO

P RODDENBERY MEMORIAL LIBRARY*, 320 N Broad St, 39828-2109. SAN 338-4993. Tel: 229-377-3632. FAX: 229-377-7204. Web Site: www.rmlibrary.org. *Dir,* Pamela Grigg; *Assoc Dir,* Janet R Boudet; *Ch,* Teresa Groves
Founded 1939. Pop 24,845; Circ 92,085
Jul 2010-Jun 2011 Income $509,705, State $126,921, City $237,500, County $92,000, Locally Generated Income $23,284, Other $30,000. Mats Exp $101,861, Books $76,115, Per/Ser (Incl. Access Fees) $5,230, AV Equip $2,026, AV Mat $11,000, Electronic Ref Mat (Incl. Access Fees) $7,292, Presv $198. Sal $416,124 (Prof $178,501)
Library Holdings: Audiobooks 869; AV Mats 2,495; Bks on Deafness & Sign Lang 59; CDs 538; DVDs 485; Electronic Media & Resources 157; High Interest/Low Vocabulary Bk Vols 64; Large Print Bks 4,278; Microforms 309; Bk Titles 59,085; Bk Vols 64,419; Per Subs 127; Talking Bks 47; Videos 544
Special Collections: CARE Center - Cancer Awareness Resource Environment; Genealogy Coll. Oral History
Subject Interests: Gardening, Local authors
Automation Activity & Vendor Info: (Cataloging) Evergreen; (Circulation) Evergreen; (ILL) OCLC; (OPAC) Evergreen
Database Vendor: Baker & Taylor, BWI, Facts on File, Gale Cengage Learning, infoUSA, Ingram Library Services, OCLC FirstSearch, OCLC WebJunction, OCLC WorldShare Interlibrary Loan, ProQuest, Westlaw, World Book Online, WT Cox
Wireless access
Function: Adult literacy prog, Audiobks via web, AV serv, Bks on cassette, Bks on CD, CD-ROM, Children's prog, Computers for patron use, Copy machines, E-Reserves, Electronic databases & coll, Fax serv, Free DVD rentals, Genealogy discussion group, Handicapped accessible, Homework prog, ILL available, Instruction & testing, Magnifiers for reading, Mail & tel request accepted, Music CDs, Notary serv, Online searches, Photocopying/Printing, Preschool outreach, Prog for adults, Prog for children & young adult, Pub access computers, Ref serv available, Spoken cassettes & CDs, Story hour, Summer reading prog, Tax forms, Telephone ref, VHS videos, Wheelchair accessible
Publications: Gleanings from Grady County (Local historical information); Grady County Information & Referral Guide (Annual); I Remember Wessie
Partic in Georgia Online Database; PINES (Public Information Network for Electronic Services)
Special Services for the Blind - Large print bks; Magnifiers; Screen enlargement software for people with visual disabilities; Talking bks & player equip; VisualTek equip
Open Mon-Thurs 10-6, Fri 10-3, Sat 10-2
Friends of the Library Group

CAMILLA

P DE SOTO TRAIL REGIONAL LIBRARY*, 145 E Broad St, 31730-1842. SAN 338-5051. Tel: 229-336-8372. FAX: 229-336-9353. Web Site: www.georgialibraries.org/~desoto/. *Dir,* Lisa Rigsby; E-mail: rigsby@desototrail.org; *Asst Dir,* Faye Lewis; E-mail: flewis@desototrail.org; Staff 4 (MLS 4)
Pop 52,915; Circ 220,000
Library Holdings: Bk Vols 50,000; Per Subs 76
Automation Activity & Vendor Info: (Cataloging) SirsiDynix; (Circulation) SirsiDynix
Open Mon, Tues & Thurs 9-7, Wed & Fri 9-5:30, Sat 9-12:30
Branches: 5
BAKER COUNTY, Historical Court House, 100 Main St, Newton, 39870. Tel: 229-734-3025. *Librn,* Tammy Hawkins
Open Mon-Fri 2-5, Sat 10-12
JAKIN BRANCH, 1001 S Pearl St, Jakin, 31761. Tel: 229-793-2825.
MARGARET JONES PUBLIC, 205 E Pope St, Sylvester, 31791, SAN 338-523X. Tel: 229-776-2096. FAX: 229-776-0079. *Br Mgr,* Vicki Young
Open Mon-Fri 9-5:30
LUCY MADDOX MEMORIAL, 11880 Columbia St, Blakely, 39823, SAN 338-5116. Tel: 229-723-3079. FAX: 229-723-6429. *Librn,* Gayle Anderson
Open Mon-Fri 9-5:30, Sat 9-12
PELHAM CARNEGIE BRANCH, 133 Hand Ave W, Pelham, 31779, SAN 338-5140. Tel: 229-294-6030. FAX: 229-294-6030. *Librn,* Wynell Martin
Open Mon-Fri 9-5:30
Bookmobiles: 1

CANTON

P SEQUOYAH REGIONAL LIBRARY SYSTEM, R T Jones Memorial Library, Headquarters, 116 Brown Industrial Pkwy, 30114-2899. SAN 338-5264. Tel: 770-479-3090, Ext 221. Circulation Tel: 770-479-3090, Ext 234. Reference Tel: 770-479-3090, Ext 228. FAX: 770-479-3069. Web Site: www.sequoyahregionallibrary.org. *Dir,* Anita Summers; E-mail: summersa@seqlib.org; *Asst Dir,* Vicki Gazaway; E-mail: gazawayv@seqlib.org; *Fiscal Officer,* Julie Wise; E-mail: wisej@seqlib.org; *Human Res,* Vicki Gazaway; E-mail: gazawayv@seqlib.org; *Mgr, Coll Develop,* Linda Erickson; E-mail: ericksonl@seqlib.org; *Tech Coordr,* Donna Ferguson; E-mail: fergusod@seqlib.org; *Adult Serv,* Lisa Huskey; E-mail: huskeyl@seqlib.org; *Circ,* Rebecca Camp; E-mail: campr@seqlib.org; *Tech Serv,* Christy Southard; E-mail: southac0@seqlib.org; *Youth Serv,* Melanie Pullen; E-mail: mpullen@seqlib.org; Staff 26 (MLS 3, Non-MLS 23)
Founded 1956. Pop 148,800; Circ 974,618
Library Holdings: Bk Vols 333,345
Special Collections: Career Center; Georgia History; Homeschooling Center; Spanish Center
Automation Activity & Vendor Info: (Acquisitions) TLC (The Library Corporation); (Cataloging) TLC (The Library Corporation); (Circulation) TLC (The Library Corporation); (Course Reserve) TLC (The Library Corporation); (ILL) TLC (The Library Corporation); (Media Booking) TLC (The Library Corporation); (OPAC) TLC (The Library Corporation); (Serials) TLC (The Library Corporation)
Database Vendor: EBSCOhost, Gale Cengage Learning, OCLC FirstSearch, Wilson - Wilson Web
Wireless access
Partic in Georgia Libr Info Network; Georgia Online Database; Lyrasis
Open Mon-Thurs 10-6, Fri 1-5, Sat 9-5
Friends of the Library Group
Branches: 7
BALL GROUND PUBLIC, 435 Old Canton Rd, Ball Ground, 30107. Tel: 770-735-2025. FAX: 770-735-6050. *Mgr,* Shirley Clayton
Founded 1997
Library Holdings: Bk Vols 32,378
Open Mon-Fri 10-6, Sun 2-6
Friends of the Library Group
CHEROKEE COUNTY LAW LIBRARY, Cherokee County Justice Ctr, 90 North St, Ste 250, 30114. Tel: 770-720-6358. *Mgr,* Mary Crowley; E-mail: crowleym@seqlib.org; Staff 1 (Non-MLS 1)
Founded 1996
Open Mon-Fri 8-5
Restriction: Non-circulating
GILMER COUNTY PUBLIC, 268 Calvin Jackson Dr, Ellijay, 30540, SAN 338-5299. Tel: 706-635-4528. FAX: 706-635-3528. *Libr Mgr,* Heath Lee; E-mail: leeh@seqlib.org; Staff 1 (MLS 1)
Founded 1940
Special Collections: Genealogy Coll; Local History Coll
Open Mon-Thurs 9-8, Fri & Sat 9-5
Friends of the Library Group
HICKORY FLAT PUBLIC, 2740 E Cherokee Dr, 30115, SAN 374-4108. Tel: 770-345-7565. FAX: 770-345-7660. *Mgr,* Rhonda Broome; E mail: broomer@seqlib.org; Staff 7 (Non-MLS 7)
Founded 1993
Open Mon-Thurs 10-6, Fri 1-5, Sat 9-5
Friends of the Library Group
PICKENS COUNTY PUBLIC, 100 Library Lane, Jasper, 30143, SAN 338-5329. Tel: 706-692-5411. FAX: 706-692-9518. *Mgr,* Emma Ingle; Staff 5 (MLS 1, Non-MLS 4)
Founded 1958
Open Mon-Thurs 9-9, Fri & Sat 9-5, Sun 2-6
Friends of the Library Group
ROSE CREEK PUBLIC, 4476 Towne Lake Pkwy, Woodstock, 30189, SAN 371-3636. Tel: 770-591-1491. FAX: 770-591-1693. *Mgr,* Brenda Biehl; Staff 7 (Non-MLS 7)
Founded 1991
Open Mon-Thurs 10-6, Fri 1-5, Sat 9-5
Friends of the Library Group
WOODSTOCK PUBLIC, 7735 Main St, Woodstock, 30188, SAN 338-5353. Tel: 770-926-5859. FAX: 770-591-8476. *Mgr,* Sue Stephens; Staff 7 (Non-MLS 7)
Founded 1964
Open Mon-Fri 10-6, Sun 2-6
Friends of the Library Group

CARROLLTON

R OAK GROVE BAPTIST CHURCH LIBRARY*, 2829 Oak Grove Church Rd, 30117. SAN 303-3430. Tel: 770-834-7019. FAX: 770-834-8218. *Dir,* Carolyn Johnson; *Asst Librn,* Zelda Loftin
Founded 1967
Library Holdings: Bk Vols 3,500
Subject Interests: Biblical studies, Relig

R TABERNACLE BAPTIST CHURCH LIBRARY*, 150 Tabernacle Dr, 30117. SAN 303-3457. Tel: 770-832-7063. FAX: 770-834-2777. Web Site: www.tabernacle.org. *Librn,* Position Currently Open
Library Holdings: Bk Vols 9,335
Open Wed 6-8, Sun 9-10:30

M TANNER MEDICAL CENTER*, Medical Library, 705 Dixie St, 30117. SAN 303-3465. Tel: 770-836-9540. FAX: 770-836-9870. *Librn,* Carol Arrington; E-mail: carrington@tanner.org
Founded 1972
Library Holdings: Bk Titles 200; Per Subs 20
Subject Interests: Allied health, Med, Nursing
Open Mon-Fri 8-4:30

C UNIVERSITY OF WEST GEORGIA*, Irvine Sullivan Ingram Library, 1601 Maple St, 30118. SAN 303-3473. Tel: 678-839-6498. Circulation Tel: 678-839-6502. Interlibrary Loan Service Tel: 678-839-6354. Reference Tel: 678-839-6495. Information Services Tel: 678-839-6350. FAX: 678-839-6511. Web Site: www.westga.edu/~library. *Dir, Univ Libr,* E Lorene Flanders; E-mail: lflander@westga.edu; *Assoc Dir, Univ Libr,* Chris Huff; E-mail: chuff@westga.edu; *Head, Access Serv,* Carol Goodson; E-mail: cgoodson@westga.edu; *Head, Instrul Serv,* Anne Barnhart; E-mail: barnhart@westga.edu; *Head, Spec Coll,* Suzanne Durham; Tel: 678-839-6361, E-mail: sdurham@westga.edu; *Head, Tech Serv,* Charlie Sicignano; E-mail: charlie@westga.edu; *Circ Mgr,* Chris Carroll; E-mail: ccarroll@westga.edu; *Coll Develop Librn,* Susan A Smith; E-mail: ssmith@westga.edu; *Govt Doc Librn,* Dean Sullivan; E-mail: dsulliva@westga.edu; *Instrul Serv Librn,* Michael Aldrich; *Instrul Serv Librn,* Jean Cook; *Instrul Serv Librn,* Diane Fulkerson; *Instrul Serv Librn,* Shirley Lankford; E-mail: slankfor@westga.edu; *Instrul Serv Librn,* Mary Jane Rootes; *Instrul Serv Librn,* Andrea Stanfield; *Syst Librn,* Position Currently Open; *Coordr of Develop,* Catherine Hendricks; *Govt Doc Assoc,* Laurie Aycock; *ILL Assoc,* Angela Mehaffey; *Sr Cataloger,* Shelley Rogers; E-mail: srogers@westga.edu; *Ser & Electronic Res Cataloger,* Position Currently Open; Staff 32 (MLS 14, Non-MLS 18)
Founded 1933. Enrl 11,252; Fac 551; Highest Degree: Doctorate
Library Holdings: AV Mats 11,634; Bk Vols 534,446; Per Subs 50,000
Special Collections: Georgia's Political Heritage Program Coll (Twentieth Century Georgia Politicians); Humanistic Psychology. US Document Depository
Automation Activity & Vendor Info: (Acquisitions) Ex Libris Group; (Cataloging) Ex Libris Group; (Course Reserve) Docutek; (ILL) OCLC ILLiad
Function: Archival coll, Art exhibits, Audio & video playback equip for onsite use, Computers for patron use, Copy machines, e-mail & chat, E-Reserves, Electronic databases & coll, Exhibits, Govt ref serv, ILL available, Music CDs, Online cat, Online info literacy tutorials on the web & in blackboard, Orientations
Partic in Cent Ga Associated Librs; Lyrasis; N Ga Associated Librs

P WEST GEORGIA REGIONAL LIBRARY*, Neva Lomason Memorial Library, 710 Rome St, 30117. SAN 338-5388. Tel: 770-836-6711. FAX: 770-836-4787. E-mail: refdesk@wgrl.net. Web Site: www.wgrl.net. *Dir,* Roni L Tewksbury; E-mail: roni@wgrl.net; *Librn,* Cary Dunmire; E-mail: cary@wgrl.net; *Cat Librn,* Jennifer Lawley; E-mail: jennifer@wgrl.net; *Spec Projects Librn,* Martha G Goodson; E-mail: martha@wgrl.net; *Coordr,* Laurie Eubanks; E-mail: laurie@wgrl.net; *Acq,* Melissa Gearhart; E-mail: melissa@wgrl.net; Staff 63 (MLS 7, Non-MLS 56)
Founded 1944. Pop 425,000; Circ 1,756,518
Library Holdings: Audiobooks 32,469; DVDs 47,307; Bk Vols 640,274; Per Subs 300
Subject Interests: Decorative art, Genealogy, Local hist
Wireless access
Function: Adult bk club, After school storytime, Art exhibits, Bk club(s), Bks on cassette, Bks on CD, Children's prog, Computer training, Computers for patron use, Copy machines, e-mail serv, Exhibits, Free DVD rentals, Handicapped accessible, Holiday prog, ILL available, Mail & tel request accepted, Music CDs, Online cat, Online ref, Photocopying/Printing, Prog for adults, Prog for children & young adult, Pub access computers, Spoken cassettes & CDs, Story hour, Tax forms, Teen prog, Telephone ref, VHS videos, Wheelchair accessible
Partic in Lyrasis; N Ga Associated Librs; PINES (Public Information Network for Electronic Services)
Special Services for the Blind - Audio mat; Bks available with recordings; Bks on cassette; Bks on CD; Cassettes; Extensive large print coll; Home delivery serv; Large print bks; Ref serv
Open Mon-Thurs 10-7, Fri 9-5:30, Sat 11-3, Sun 2-6
Friends of the Library Group
Branches: 16
BUCHANAN-HARALSON PUBLIC LIBRARY, 145 Courthouse Sq, Buchanan, 30113. Tel: 770-646-3369. FAX: 770-646-1103. *Br Mgr,* Jana Gentry; E-mail: jana@wgrl.net
Founded 2003. Pop 5,000; Circ 15,899
Library Holdings: CDs 302; DVDs 52; Bk Vols 9,000; Per Subs 15; Talking Bks 370; Videos 410
Open Mon-Thurs 11-6, Sat 10-2
Friends of the Library Group
CROSSROADS PUBLIC LIBRARY, 909 Harmony Grove Church Rd, Acworth, 30101. Tel: 770-975-0197. *Br Mgr,* Cherry Waddell; E-mail: cherry@wgrl.net
Open Mon, Tues & Thurs 11-7, Fri & Sat 9-5
DOG RIVER PUBLIC LIBRARY, 6100 Georgia Hwy 5, Douglasville, 30135. Tel: 770-577-5186. *Br Mgr,* Lindy Moore; E-mail: lindy@wgrl.net; Staff 1 (MLS 1)
Open Mon-Thurs 9-8, Fri 9-5:30, Sat 9-5
DOUGLAS COUNTY PUBLIC LIBRARY, 6810 Selman Dr, Douglasville, 30134, SAN 338-5418. Tel: 770-920-7125. FAX: 770-920-3121. Web Site: www.celebratedouglascounty.com. *County Librn,* Kelley Springer
Open Mon-Thurs 9-8, Fri 9-5:30, Sat 9-5, Sun 1-5
Friends of the Library Group
EPHESUS PUBLIC LIBRARY, 200 Rogers St, Roopville, 30170. Tel: 770-854-7323. FAX: 770-854-7326. *Br Mgr,* Donna Alvis; E-mail: donna@wgrl.net
Library Holdings: DVDs 100; Bk Vols 10,000; Per Subs 20; Talking Bks 50
Open Mon-Wed 9-5, Thurs 11-7, Sat 9-1
Friends of the Library Group
HEARD COUNTY PUBLIC LIBRARY, 564 Main St, Franklin, 30217, SAN 338-5477. Tel: 706-675-6501. FAX: 706-675-1065. *Br Mgr,* Leslie Stokes; E-mail: leslie@wgrl.net
Open Mon & Thurs 10-1 & 1:30-7:30, Tues & Fri 9-1 & 1:30-6, Wed 1-6, Sat 9-2
LITHIA SPRINGS PUBLIC LIBRARY, 7100 Junior High Dr, Lithia Springs, 30122, SAN 338-5507. Tel: 770-944-5931. FAX: 770-944-5932. *Br Mgr,* Judy Maples; E-mail: judy@wgrl.net
Open Mon-Thurs 9-8, Fri 9-5:30, Sat 9-5
Friends of the Library Group
MOUNT ZION PUBLIC LIBRARY, 4455 Mount Zion Rd, Mount Zion, 30150. (Mail add: PO Box 597, Mount Zion, 30150-0597). Tel: 770-832-0056, Ext 104. FAX: 770-834-7228. *Br Mgr,* Vicki Sizemore; E-mail: vicki@wgrl.net
Library Holdings: Bk Titles 1,000
Database Vendor: ProQuest
Open Mon-Thurs 9-4:30, Sun 3-5
NEW GEORGIA PUBLIC LIBRARY, 94 Ridge Rd, Dallas, 30157, SAN 377-7278. Tel: 770-459-8163. FAX: 770-459-9343. *Br Mgr,* Kendra Winters; E-mail: Kendra@wgrl.net
Open Mon, Tues & Thurs 11-7, Fri & Sat 9-5
PAULDING COUNTY PUBLIC LIBRARY, 1010 E Memorial Dr, Dallas, 30132, SAN 338-5531. Tel: 770-445-5680. FAX: 770-443-7626. *Br Mgr,* Lynsey James; E-mail: lynsey@wgrl.net
Open Mon, Tues & Thurs 11-7, Fri & Sat 9-5
MAUDE P RAGSDALE PUBLIC LIBRARY, 1815 Hiram-Douglasville Hwy, Hiram, 30141, SAN 375-5134. Tel: 770-439-3964. FAX: 770-943-8720. *Br Mgr,* Bonne Smith; E-mail: bonne@wgrl.net
Open Mon, Tues & Thurs 11-7, Fri & Sat 9-5
WARREN P SEWELL MEMORIAL LIBRARY, 315 Hamilton Ave, Bremen, 30110, SAN 338-5620. Tel: 770-537-3937. FAX: 770-537-1660. *Br Mgr,* Lisa Walton-Cagle; E-mail: lisa@wgrl.net
Open Mon & Wed 10-5:30, Tues & Thurs 12-7, Fri 12-5:30, Sat 10-3
Friends of the Library Group
WARREN P SEWELL MEMORIAL LIBRARY OF BOWDON, 450 West Ave, Bowdon, 30108, SAN 338-5590. Tel: 770-258-8991. FAX: 770-258-8990. *Br Mgr,* Barbara Bridwell; E-mail: barbara@wgrl.net
Open Mon & Tues 9-6, Wed & Sat 9-1, Thurs & Fri 9-5
TALLAPOOSA PUBLIC LIBRARY, 388 Bowden St, Tallapoosa, 30176, SAN 338-5442. Tel: 770-574-3124. FAX: 770-574-3124. *Br Mgr,* Karen Boling; E-mail: karen@wgrl.net
Open Mon, Tues & Fri 10-5, Thurs 10-8, Sat 10-4
Friends of the Library Group
VILLA RICA PUBLIC LIBRARY, 70 Horace Luther Dr, Villa Rica, 30180, SAN 338-5566. Tel: 770-459-7012. FAX: 770-459-7960. *Interim Br Mgr,* Laura Frey; E-mail: laura@wgrl.net
Founded 1969
Automation Activity & Vendor Info: (Circulation) Evergreen
Open Mon-Thurs 9-7, Fri 9-5, Sat 9-2
WHITESBURG PUBLIC LIBRARY, 800 Main St, Whitesburg, 30185. Tel: 770-834-0713. *Br Mgr,* Ruth Fuller; E-mail: ruth@wgrl.net
Library Holdings: Bk Titles 5,000
Automation Activity & Vendor Info: (Cataloging) Evergreen; (Circulation) Evergreen
Open Mon & Thurs 12-8, Tues 12-6, Fri & Sat 12-4, Sun 2-6

CARTERSVILLE

P BARTOW COUNTY PUBLIC LIBRARY SYSTEM*, 429 W Main St, 30120. SAN 324-0800. Tel: 770-382-4203. FAX: 770-386-3056. Web Site: www.bartowlibraryonline.org/. *Dir,* Carmen Melinda Sims; Tel: 770-382-4203, Ext 123, E-mail: carmen@bartowlibrary.org; Staff 20 (MLS 5, Non-MLS 15)
Founded 1981. Pop 79,244; Circ 188,721
Library Holdings: Bk Titles 55,935; Bk Vols 80,763; Per Subs 121
Subject Interests: Local hist
Automation Activity & Vendor Info: (Cataloging) SirsiDynix; (Circulation) SirsiDynix; (OPAC) SirsiDynix
Database Vendor: Wilson - Wilson Web

Function: Photocopying/Printing
Partic in Georgia Online Database; OCLC Online Computer Library Center, Inc
Open Mon-Thurs 9-8, Fri & Sat 9-5
Friends of the Library Group
Branches: 3
ADAIRSVILLE BRANCH, 202 N Main St, Adairsville, 30123. (Mail add: 429 W Main St, 30120), SAN 324-0827. Tel: 770-769-9200. FAX: 770-769-9201. *Br Mgr,* Cynde Suite; E-mail: cynde@bartowlibrary.org
Library Holdings: Bk Vols 17,000
Open Tues, Wed & Fri 10-6, Thurs 12-8
Friends of the Library Group
CARTERSVILLE MAIN STREET, 429 W Main St, 30120, SAN 324-0843. Tel: 770-382-4203. FAX: 770-386-3056. *Fac Mgr,* Joe Byrne
Library Holdings: Bk Vols 55,769
Open Mon-Thurs 9-8, Fri & Sat 9-5
Friends of the Library Group
EMMIE NELSON BRANCH, 108 Covered Bridge Rd SW, 30120. (Mail add: 429 W Main St, 30120), SAN 328-7467. Tel: 770-382-2057. FAX: 770-382-6316. E-mail: euharlee@bartowlibrary.org. *Br Mgr,* Christina Jedziniak
Library Holdings: Bk Vols 9,784
Open Mon & Wed-Fri 10-6, Tues 12-8
Friends of the Library Group

CHESTER

S GEORGIA DEPARTMENT OF CORRECTIONS, OFFICE OF LIBRARY SERVICES*, Dodge State Prison, 2971 Old Bethel Rd, 31012. (Mail add: PO Box 276, 31012-0276). Tel: 478-358-7200. FAX: 478-358-7303. Web Site: www.dcor.state.ga.us. *In Charge,* Tina Sanders
Library Holdings: Bk Vols 10,000
Special Collections: Law Coll
Database Vendor: LexisNexis
Open Mon 8:30-11, 1:30-4 & 6-8, Tues-Thurs 8:30-11 & 1:30-4

CLARKESVILLE

P CLARKESVILLE-HABERSHAM COUNTY LIBRARY*, 178 E Green St, 30523. Tel: 706-754-4413. FAX: 706-754-3479. *Br Mgr,* Delana Hinson; E-mail: dhinson@negeorgialibraries.org; Staff 3 (MLS 1, Non-MLS 2)
Founded 1928
Wireless access
Mem of Northeast Georgia Regional Library System
Open Mon-Thurs 10-6, Fri 10-5, Sat 9-1

J NORTH GEORGIA TECHNICAL COLLEGE LIBRARY*, Clarkesville Campus, 1500 Hwy 197 N, 30523. (Mail add: PO Box 65, 30523-0065), SAN 303-349X. Tel: 706-754-7720. FAX: 706-754-7777. E-mail: library@northgatech.edu. Web Site: www.northgatech.edu/library. *Librn,* Christina Teasley; E-mail: cteasley@northgatech.edu; *Currahee Campus Librn,* Dawn Adams; Tel: 706-779-8104, E-mail: dadams@northgatech.edu; Staff 2 (MLS 2)
Enrl 2,500; Fac 85
Automation Activity & Vendor Info: (Cataloging) SirsiDynix; (Circulation) SirsiDynix; (ILL) OCLC; (OPAC) SirsiDynix
Database Vendor: CredoReference, EBSCO Auto Repair Reference, EBSCOhost, LearningExpress, LexisNexis, Medline, OCLC WorldShare Interlibrary Loan, ProQuest, SirsiDynix, Westlaw
Wireless access

P NORTHEAST GEORGIA REGIONAL LIBRARY SYSTEM, 204 Ellison St, Ste F, 30523. (Mail add: PO Box 2020, 30523-0034), SAN 338-5655. Tel: 706-754-0416. FAX: 706-754-0420. E-mail: webadmin@negeorgialibraries.org. Web Site: www.negeorgialibraries.org. *Dir & Librn,* Delana Knight; E-mail: dknight@negeorgialibraries.org; *ILL/Tech Serv Librn,* Linh Uong; E-mail: luong@negeorgialibraries.org; *Tech & Syst Librn,* Lewis Lucas; E-mail: llucas@negeorgialibraries.org; Staff 4 (MLS 3, Non-MLS 1)
Founded 1951. Pop 118,843
Library Holdings: Audiobooks 7,892; DVDs 4,529; e-books 333; Electronic Media & Resources 1,374; Bk Vols 184,242; Per Subs 166; Videos 14,622
Automation Activity & Vendor Info: (Cataloging) Evergreen; (Circulation) Evergreen; (OPAC) Evergreen
Wireless access
Member Libraries: Clarkesville-Habersham County Library; Cornelia-Habersham County Library; Rabun County Public Library; Toccoa-Stephens County Public Library; White County Public Library
Friends of the Library Group

CLARKSTON

J GEORGIA PERIMETER COLLEGE*, Jim Cherry Learning Resource Center, 555 N Indian Creek Dr, 30021-2396. SAN 324-2560. Tel: 678-891-3635. Interlibrary Loan Service Tel: 678-891-3666. FAX: 404-298-4919. Web Site: www.gpc.edu/~claib/. *Dir,* Eva Lautemann; Tel: 678-891-3633, E-mail: elautema@gpc.edu; *Ref Serv,* Ann Mallard; Tel: 678-891-3634, E-mail: amallard@gpc.edu; *Tech Serv,* Kathy Gallo; Tel: 678-891-3663
Founded 1964. Highest Degree: Associate
Library Holdings: Bk Titles 151,775; Bk Vols 232,671; Per Subs 1,073
Automation Activity & Vendor Info: (Acquisitions) Ex Libris Group; (Cataloging) Ex Libris Group; (Circulation) Ex Libris Group; (Media Booking) Ex Libris Group; (OPAC) Ex Libris Group
Partic in GALILEO (Georgia Library Learning Online); Lyrasis; OCLC Online Computer Library Center, Inc
Open Mon-Thurs 7:45am-10pm, Fri 7:45-4:30, Sat 9-3, Sun 1-5
Departmental Libraries:
DECATUR LEARNING RESOURCES CENTER, 3251 Panthersville Rd, Decatur, 30034, SAN 338-6554. Tel: 678-891-2585. Circulation Tel: 678-891-2591. Reference Tel: 678-891-2592. FAX: 678-891-2866. Web Site: www.gpc.edu/~declib. *Dir,* Regina Beach; Tel: 678-891-2590, E-mail: regina.beach@gpc.edu; Staff 5 (MLS 3, Non-MLS 2)
Founded 1972
Library Holdings: Bk Vols 30,000; Per Subs 120
Automation Activity & Vendor Info: (Cataloging) Ex Libris Group; (Circulation) Ex Libris Group; (Course Reserve) Ex Libris Group; (ILL) OCLC; (OPAC) OCLC
Open Mon-Thurs 7:45am-10pm, Fri 7:45-5, Sat 10-2, Sun 2-6
DUNWOODY CAMPUS LIBRARY, 2101 Womack Rd, Dunwoody, 30338-4497, SAN 320-1465. Tel: 770-274-5085. Reference Tel: 770-274-5100. FAX: 770-274-5090. Web Site: www.gpc.edu/~dunlib. *Dir,* Dr Joseph W Barnes; Tel: 770-274-5084, E-mail: jbarnes@gpc.edu; *Assoc Dir, Coll Develop,* Lora Mirza; Tel: 770-274-5091, E-mail: mmirza@gpc.edu; *Coordr, Educ Initiatives,* Dr Stephen Koplan; Tel: 770-274-5088, E-mail: skoplan@gpc.edu; *Coordr, Nonprint Coll & Exhibits,* Eugenia Abbey; Tel: 770-274-5096, E-mail: eabbey@gpc.edu; *Bibliog Instr,* Peter Bursi; Tel: 770-274-5086, E-mail: pbursi@gpc.edu; *Circ, Info Tech,* Carmel Chaille Brunson; Tel: 770-274-5092, E-mail: cchaille@gpc.edu; *Coll Mgt,* Amy Moore Bursi; Tel: 770-274-5093, E-mail: abursi@gpc.edu; Staff 12.5 (MLS 8, Non-MLS 4.5)
Founded 1964. Enrl 9,000; Highest Degree: Associate
Jul 2008-Jun 2009 Income $1,050,910. Mats Exp $287,440. Sal $742,370 (Prof $389,709)
Library Holdings: Audiobooks 1,000; CDs 873; DVDs 2,500; Bk Titles 79,182; Bk Vols 80,000; Per Subs 100; Videos 47
Database Vendor: ARTstor, Booklist Online, CQ Press, EBSCOhost, Facts on File, Gale Cengage Learning, Greenwood Publishing Group, JSTOR, Oxford Online, Project MUSE, ProQuest, Wilson - Wilson Web
Function: Audio & video playback equip for onsite use, Computers for patron use, Copy machines, Electronic databases & coll, Online cat, Online ref, Telephone ref
Open Mon-Thurs 7:45am-10pm, Fri 7:45-5, Sat 10-3, Sun 2-6
Restriction: Borrowing privileges limited to fac & registered students

CLAXTON

P EVANS COUNTY PUBLIC LIBRARY*, 701 W Main, 30417. SAN 339-2252. Tel: 912-739-1801. FAX: 912-739-0522. *Mgr,* Charlotte DeLoach; Staff 2 (Non-MLS 2)
Pop 10,074; Circ 18,778
Automation Activity & Vendor Info: (Acquisitions) SirsiDynix; (Cataloging) SirsiDynix; (Circulation) SirsiDynix; (ILL) OCLC
Mem of Statesboro Regional Public Libraries
Partic in PINES (Public Information Network for Electronic Services)
Open Mon & Thurs 12-8, Tues & Wed 9-4

CLAYTON

P RABUN COUNTY PUBLIC LIBRARY*, 73 Jo Dotson Circle, 30525. (Mail add: PO Box 330, 30525-0330), SAN 338-568X. Tel: 706-782-3731. FAX: 706-782-6514. *Mgr,* Stephanie Howard
Wireless access
Mem of Northeast Georgia Regional Library System
Open Mon & Tues 9-2, Wed-Fri 9-6, Sat 10-3

CLEVELAND

C TRUETT-MCCONNELL COLLEGE, Cofer Library, 100 Alumni Dr, 30528-9799. SAN 303-3511. Tel: 706-865-2134, Ext 153. Reference Tel: 706-865-2134, Ext 193. Administration Tel: 706-865-2134, Ext 173. FAX: 706-243-4837. E-mail: library@truett.edu. Web Site: truett.edu/coferlibrary. *Dir of Libr Serv,* Teresa P Haymore; E-mail: thaymore@truett.edu; *Ref Serv,* Vonda Henderson; E-mail: vhenderson@truett.edu; Staff 3 (MLS 2, Non-MLS 1)
Founded 1946. Enrl 1,048; Fac 45; Highest Degree: Master
Library Holdings: AV Mats 500; CDs 1,900; DVDs 400; e-books 140,000; e-journals 300; Electronic Media & Resources 3,400; Microforms 40,000; Music Scores 500; Bk Titles 40,000; Bk Vols 42,000; Per Subs 140; Videos 1,900

Special Collections: Baptist History Coll; Religion (George W Truett Coll)
Automation Activity & Vendor Info: (Acquisitions) TLC (The Library Corporation); (Cataloging) TLC (The Library Corporation); (Circulation) TLC (The Library Corporation); (Course Reserve) TLC (The Library Corporation); (ILL) OCLC WorldShare Interlibrary Loan; (OPAC) TLC (The Library Corporation)
Database Vendor: Cinahl, ebrary, EBSCOhost, Gale Cengage Learning, LexisNexis, OCLC WorldShare Interlibrary Loan, ProQuest, TLC (The Library Corporation), Wilson - Wilson Web, WT Cox
Wireless access
Function: Archival coll, AV serv, Bks on cassette, Bks on CD, CD-ROM, Computers for patron use, Copy machines, Digital talking bks, Distance learning, e-mail serv, E-Reserves, Electronic databases & coll, Fax serv, Free DVD rentals, Handicapped accessible, ILL available, Instruction & testing, Laminating, Magazines, Mail & tel request accepted, Microfiche/film & reading machines, Music CDs, Newsp ref libr, Online cat, Online ref, Online searches, Orientations, Photocopying/Printing, Pub access computers, Ref & res, Ref serv available, Ref serv in person, Referrals accepted, Res libr, Scanner, Study rm, Telephone ref, VHS videos, Video lending libr, Web-catalog, Wheelchair accessible
Partic in Association of Christian Librarians; Georgia Private Acad Librs Consortium (GPALS)
Open Mon-Thurs 8am-10pm, Fri 8-4:30, Sun 7pm-10pm

P WHITE COUNTY PUBLIC LIBRARY*, Cleveland Branch, 10 Colonial Dr, 30528. (Mail add: PO Box 657, 30528-0657), SAN 338-571X. Tel: 706-865-5572. FAX: 706-219-3621. *Mgr,* Miriam Hammond
Library Holdings: CDs 276; DVDs 393; Bk Vols 47,481
Wireless access
Mem of Northeast Georgia Regional Library System
Open Mon 9-7, Tues-Fri 9-5, Sat 9-12
Friends of the Library Group
Branches: 1
HELEN BRANCH, 90 Petes Park Rd, Helen, 30545. (Mail add: PO Box 1088, Helen, 30545-1088), SAN 338-5779. Tel: 706-878-2438. FAX: 706-878-1479. *Mgr,* Deborah Kelley
Open Mon, Wed & Fri 9-5, Tues & Thurs 9-6, Sat 10-1

COCHRAN

J MIDDLE GEORGIA COLLEGE*, Roberts Memorial Library, 1100 Second St SE, 31014-1599. SAN 303-352X. Tel: 478-934-3074. Interlibrary Loan Service Tel: 478-934-3071. FAX: 478-934-3378. Web Site: www.mgc.edu. *Dir,* Paul Robards; E-mail: probards@mgc.edu
Founded 1928. Enrl 2,700; Fac 75
Library Holdings: Bk Titles 98,000; Bk Vols 102,000; Per Subs 211
Special Collections: Archives; County Histories; Georgianna Genealogy
Automation Activity & Vendor Info: (Acquisitions) Ex Libris Group; (Cataloging) Ex Libris Group; (Circulation) Ex Libris Group; (Course Reserve) Ex Libris Group; (ILL) OCLC; (OPAC) Ex Libris Group; (Serials) Ex Libris Group
Wireless access
Publications: Library Handbook
Partic in Lyrasis; OCLC Online Computer Library Center, Inc
Open Mon-Thurs 8am-9pm, Fri 8-3, Sun 3-9

COLUMBUS

P CHATTAHOOCHEE VALLEY LIBRARIES*, Columbus Public Library, Headquarters, 3000 Macon Rd, 31906-2201. SAN 338-5868. Tel: 706-243-2669. Circulation Tel: 706-243-2680. Interlibrary Loan Service Tel: 706-243-2683. Reference Tel: 706-243-2687. Administration Tel: 706-243-2670. FAX: 706-243-2710. Interlibrary Loan Service FAX: 706-243-2711. Reference FAX: 706-243-2712. E-mail: reference@cvrls.net. Web Site: www.cvlga.org. *Dir,* Alan Harkness; E-mail: aharkness@cvrls.net; *Dep Dir,* Gabriel Lundeen; Tel: 706-243-2783, E-mail: glundeen@cvrls.net; *Mkt Coordr,* Tiffany Wilson; Tel: 706-243-2673, E-mail: twilson@cvrls.net; *Prog Coordr,* Henry McCoy; Tel: 706-243-2689, E-mail: hmccoy@cvrls.net; Staff 15 (MLS 15)
Founded 1908. Pop 215,952; Circ 702,739
Library Holdings: Bk Vols 327,639; Per Subs 1,100
Special Collections: Genealogy & Local History; Local Newspapers
Automation Activity & Vendor Info: (Acquisitions) Brodart; (Cataloging) Innovative Interfaces, Inc; (Circulation) Innovative Interfaces, Inc; (ILL) OCLC; (OPAC) Innovative Interfaces, Inc; (Serials) Innovative Interfaces, Inc
Database Vendor: 3M Library Systems, Comprise Technologies Inc, CredoReference, Foundation Center, Gale Cengage Learning, LearningExpress, Newsbank-Readex, Overdrive, Inc
Wireless access
Function: Audiobks via web, Bk club(s), Bks on CD, Children's prog, Computer training, Computers for patron use, Copy machines, Electronic databases & coll, Exhibits, Free DVD rentals, Handicapped accessible, Holiday prog, ILL available, Magnifiers for reading, Microfiche/film & reading machines, Music CDs, Online cat, Outreach serv, OverDrive digital audio bks, Photocopying/Printing, Preschool outreach, Prog for adults, Prog for children & young adult, Pub access computers, Ref serv available, Scanner, Senior computer classes, Senior outreach, Spanish lang bks, Story hour, Summer reading prog, Teen prog, Telephone ref, Writing prog
Partic in Lyrasis
Special Services for the Blind - Aids for in-house use; Assistive/Adapted tech devices, equip & products; Audio mat; Bks on cassette; Bks on CD; Braille bks; Cassette playback machines; Cassettes; Children's Braille; Closed circuit TV; Computer with voice synthesizer for visually impaired persons; Handicapped awareness prog; Home delivery serv; Large print bks; Large screen computer & software; Talking bks & player equip; Tel Pioneers equip repair group
Open Mon-Thurs 10-8, Fri & Sat 10-6, Sun 1:30-6
Friends of the Library Group
Branches: 6
CUSSETA-CHATTAHOOCHEE PUBLIC LIBRARY, 262 Broad St, Cusseta, 31805. (Mail add: PO Box 539, Cusseta, 31805-0539), SAN 338-5957. Tel: 706-989-3700. FAX: 706-989-1850. *Br Mgr,* Pam Burgamy; E-mail: pburgamy@cvrls.net; Staff 3 (Non-MLS 3)
Open Mon, Tues & Thurs 10:30-2:30 & 3-7, Fri 9-1, Sat 1-5
Friends of the Library Group
MARION COUNTY PUBLIC LIBRARY, 123 E Fifth Ave, Buena Vista, 31803-2113. (Mail add: PO Box 12, Buena Vista, 31803-0012), SAN 338-6015. Tel: 229-649-6385. FAX: 229-649-6385. *Br Mgr,* Kim Scott; E-mail: kscott@cvrls.net; Staff 4 (Non-MLS 4)
Open Mon, Tues & Fri 9:30-1 & 1:30-6, Wed 2-6, Sat 10-2
Friends of the Library Group
NORTH COLUMBUS BRANCH, 5689 Armour Rd, 31909-4513, SAN 373-9325. Tel: 706-748-2855. FAX: 706-748-2859. *Br Mgr,* Kirsten Edwards; E-mail: kedwards@cvrls.net; Staff 13 (MLS 1, Non-MLS 12)
Open Mon, Tues, Fri & Sat 10-6, Thurs 12-8
Friends of the Library Group
PARKS MEMORIAL PUBLIC LIBRARY, 890 Wall St, Richland, 31825-0112, SAN 338-6104. Tel: 229-887-2103. FAX: 229-887-2103. Web Site: www.cvlga.org/branches/parks. *Br Mgr,* Pepper Grimmett; E-mail: pgrimmett@cvrls.net; Staff 2 (Non-MLS 2)
Open Mon, Tues & Thurs 9:30-1 & 1:30-6, Wed 3-7, Sat 10-2
Friends of the Library Group
SOUTH COLUMBUS BRANCH, 2034 S Lumpkin Rd, 31903-2728, SAN 338-5922. Tel: 706-683-8805. FAX: 706-683-8809. *Br Mgr,* Natalie Couch; E-mail: ncouch@cvrls.net; Staff 7 (MLS 1, Non-MLS 6)
Open Mon, Thurs, Fri & Sat 10-6, Wed 12-8
Friends of the Library Group
MILDRED L TERRY BRANCH, 640 Veterans Pkwy, 31901, SAN 338-5981. Tel: 706-748-2851. FAX: 706-748-2853. *Br Mgr,* Silvia Bunn; Staff 8 (MLS 2, Non-MLS 6)
Open Mon, Wed, Fri & Sat 10-6, Tues 12-8
Friends of the Library Group
Bookmobiles: 2

M COLUMBUS REGIONAL HEALTHCARE SYSTEM*, Simon Schwob Medical Library, 710 Center St, 31902. (Mail add: PO Box 951, 31902-0951), SAN 303-3562. Tel: 706-571-1178. FAX: 706-660-2674. *Librn,* Charmia Carter; Staff 1 (MLS 1)
Founded 1949
Library Holdings: Bk Titles 2,810; Per Subs 222
Subject Interests: Cancer, Geriatrics & gerontology, Med, Neonatology, Nursing, Pediatrics, Trauma
Wireless access
Partic in Atlantic Health Sci Librs Consortium; Docline; Georgia Health Sciences Library Association (GHSLA); Medical Library Association (MLA)
Open Mon-Fri 8-4:30

C COLUMBUS STATE UNIVERSITY LIBRARIES*, Simon Schwob Memorial Library, 4225 University Ave, 31907. SAN 303-3538. Tel: 706-568-2042. Circulation Tel: 706-562-1494. Interlibrary Loan Service Tel: 706-568-2451. Information Services Tel: 706-562-1492, 706-562-1493. FAX: 706-568-2084. Web Site: library.colstate.edu. *Interim Dean, Libr Serv,* Mark C Flynn; Tel: 706-568-2080, E-mail: flynn_mark@columbusstate.edu; *Head, Tech Serv,* Linda T Jones; Tel: 706-565-3556, E-mail: jones_linda6@colstate.edu; *Head, User Serv,* Paula Adams; Tel: 706-565-3616, E-mail: adams_paula@colstate.edu; *Electronic Res & Syst Librn,* Jacqueline Radebaugh; Tel: 706-565-3555, E-mail: radebaugh_jacqueline@colstate.edu; *Govt Doc Librn,* LuMarie Guth; Tel: 706-565-3497, E-mail: guth_lumarie@colstate.edu; *Instruction Librn,* Thomas Ganzevoort; Tel: 706-565-3683, E-mail: ganzevoort_thomas@colstate.edu; *Music Librn,* Roberta C Ford; Tel: 706-641-5047, Fax: 706-649-7261, E-mail: ford_roberta@colstate.edu; *Circ Serv Coordr,* Cynthia F Fears; E-mail: fears_cynthia@colstate.edu; *Coordr, ILL,* Michelle Jones; E-mail: jones_michelle@colstate.edu. Subject Specialists: *Music,* Mark C Flynn; *Anthrop, Psychol, Sociol,* Linda T Jones; *Eng, Foreign lang, Theatre,* Paula Adams; *Computer sci,* Jacqueline Radebaugh; *Bus,* LuMarie Guth; *Art, Communication, Hist,* Thomas

Ganzevoort; *Music,* Roberta C Ford; *Educ,* Michelle Jones; Staff 10 (MLS 8, Non-MLS 2)
Founded 1961. Enrl 8,179; Fac 296; Highest Degree: Doctorate
Jul 2009-Jun 2010 Income (Main and Other College/University Libraries) $1,507,930. Mats Exp $268,342. Sal $920,000 (Prof $609,682)
Library Holdings: AV Mats 11,769; e-journals 4,890; Microforms 1,132,896; Bk Vols 398,432; Per Subs 395
Special Collections: Architectural Drawings; Chattahoochee Valley Historical Coll; Columbus State University Archives. Oral History; US Document Depository
Automation Activity & Vendor Info: (Acquisitions) Ex Libris Group; (Cataloging) Ex Libris Group; (Circulation) Ex Libris Group; (ILL) OCLC; (OPAC) Ex Libris Group; (Serials) Ex Libris Group
Wireless access
Function: Computers for patron use, Copy machines, Distance learning, e-mail serv, Fax serv, Govt ref serv, Handicapped accessible, ILL available, Online cat, Online ref, Photocopying/Printing, Pub access computers, Ref & res, Scanner, Tax forms, VHS videos, Web-catalog, Workshops
Publications: Muscogiana (Local historical information); Simon Says (Newsletter)
Partic in Lyrasis
Special Services for the Blind - Closed circuit TV; Computer with voice synthesizer for visually impaired persons; ZoomText magnification & reading software
Open Mon-Thurs 7:30am-11pm, Fri 7:30-5, Sat 1-6, Sun 2-10
Restriction: Borrowing privileges limited to fac & registered students, In-house use for visitors, Open to pub for ref & circ; with some limitations, Open to students, fac & staff
Friends of the Library Group

Departmental Libraries:

MUSIC LIBRARY, 900 Broadway, 31901-2735. (Mail add: 4225 University Ave, 31907). Tel: 706-641-5045. FAX: 706-649-7261. Web Site: musiclibrary.columbusstate.edu. *Librn,* Roberta C Ford; Staff 3 (MLS 1, Non-MLS 2)
Founded 2001
Open Mon-Thurs (Winter-Spring) 9am-11pm, Fri 9-5, Sun 2-11; Mon-Thurs (Summer) 9-8, Fri 9-5, Sun 2-8
Restriction: Open to pub for ref only

J COLUMBUS TECHNICAL COLLEGE LIBRARY*, 928 Manchester Expressway, 31904-6577. Tel: 706-649-1852. FAX: 706-649-1885. Web Site: www.columbustech.edu. *Dir, Libr & Media Serv,* Stephanie Middleton; E-mail: smiddleton@columbustech.edu; *Assoc Librn,* Alice McCown; *Circ Mgr, ILL,* Evelyn Willis
Founded 1961. Enrl 3,456; Highest Degree: Associate
Library Holdings: AV Mats 50; CDs 22,293; DVDs 22; e-books 52,000; Bk Vols 28,000; Per Subs 255; Videos 654
Automation Activity & Vendor Info: (Cataloging) TLC (The Library Corporation); (Circulation) TLC (The Library Corporation); (OPAC) TLC (The Library Corporation)
Partic in GALILEO (Georgia Library Learning Online)
Open Mon-Thurs 7:30am-9:30pm, Fri 9-1

S GEORGIA DEPARTMENT OF CORRECTIONS, OFFICE OF LIBRARY SERVICES*, Rutledge State Prison, 7175 Manor Rd, 31907. Tel: 706-568-2439. FAX: 706-568-2126. Web Site: www.dcor.state.ga.us.
Library Holdings: Bk Vols 7,000; Per Subs 15
Special Collections: Law Coll
Database Vendor: LexisNexis

M HUGHSTON FOUNDATION LIBRARY*, 6262 Veterans Pkwy, 31909-3540. (Mail add: PO Box 9517, 31908-9517), SAN 370-6400. Tel: 706-494-3390. Administration Tel: 706-494-3365. FAX: 706-494-3379. Web Site: www.hughstonfoundation.org. *Librn,* Dennise Brogdon; E-mail: dbrogdon@hughston.com; Staff 1 (Non-MLS 1)
Library Holdings: Bk Titles 1,200; Per Subs 42
Partic in National Network of Libraries of Medicine

M WEST CENTRAL GEORGIA REGIONAL HOSPITAL LIBRARY*, 3000 Schatulga Rd, 31907-1035. SAN 303-3570. Tel: 706-568-5309. Interlibrary Loan Service Tel: 706-568-5307. FAX: 706-569-3189. E-mail: wcgrh@dhr.state.ga.us.
Founded 1975
Library Holdings: Bk Vols 5,800; Per Subs 110
Special Collections: Georgia Authors
Subject Interests: Alcohol & drugs, Counseling, Nursing, Psychiat, Psychol, Soc serv (soc work)
Publications: brochures; Library Manual; Patient's Basic Guide to Psychotropic Medication; policy statements
Partic in Dept of Human Resource Consortium; SE-Atlantic Regional Med Libr Servs

CONYERS

P CONYERS-ROCKDALE LIBRARY SYSTEM*, Nancy Guinn Memorial Library, 864 Green St, 30012. SAN 372-5995. Tel: 770-388-5040. FAX: 770-388-5043. Web Site: www.rockdale.public.lib.ga.us. *Dir,* Ben Carter; E-mail: bcarter@ckls.org; *Asst Dir,* Stacy L Brown; *Head, Automation,* Steve Thomas; *Tech Serv,* Renee Pike; Staff 7 (MLS 3, Non-MLS 4)
Library Holdings: Bk Vols 100,000; Per Subs 129
Special Collections: Law
Subject Interests: Genealogy
Automation Activity & Vendor Info: (Acquisitions) Evergreen; (Cataloging) Evergreen; (Circulation) Evergreen; (ILL) OCLC; (OPAC) Evergreen; (Serials) Evergreen
Partic in Georgia Online Database; Lyrasis; OCLC Online Computer Library Center, Inc; PINES (Public Information Network for Electronic Services)
Open Mon-Thurs 10-8, Fri & Sat 10-5, Sun 1-5
Friends of the Library Group

CORDELE

J SOUTH GEORGIA TECHNICAL COLLEGE*, Crisp County Campus Library, 402 N Midway Rd, 31015. Tel: 229-271-4071. FAX: 229-271-4050. Web Site: www.southgatech.edu. *Dir,* Jerry Stovall; E-mail: jstovall@southgatech.edu; *Media Spec,* Dianne Trueblood; E-mail: dtrueblood@southgatech.edu
Founded 2000. Highest Degree: Associate
Library Holdings: e-books 27,000; e-journals 27,000; Bk Vols 3,078; Per Subs 20
Automation Activity & Vendor Info: (Cataloging) TLC (The Library Corporation); (Circulation) TLC (The Library Corporation); (OPAC) TLC (The Library Corporation)
Partic in GALILEO (Georgia Library Learning Online)
Open Mon-Thurs 8-8, Fri 8-4

CORNELIA

P CORNELIA-HABERSHAM COUNTY LIBRARY*, 301 Main St N, 30531. SAN 338-5744. Tel: 706-778-2635. FAX: 706-778-2635. *Mgr,* Annabelle Wiley; Staff 4.5 (Non-MLS 4.5)
Founded 1988. Pop 42,000; Circ 78,000
Automation Activity & Vendor Info: (Acquisitions) Evergreen; (Course Reserve) Evergreen; (ILL) Evergreen; (Media Booking) Evergreen; (Serials) Evergreen
Wireless access
Mem of Northeast Georgia Regional Library System
Open Mon-Wed & Fri 9-6, Thurs 9-8, Sat 9-1
Friends of the Library Group

COVINGTON

J GEORGIA PIEDMONT TECHNICAL COLLEGE*, Newton Campus Learning Resource Center, Bldg B, Rm 109, 16200 Alcovy Rd, 30014. Tel: 770-786-9522, Ext 3212, 770-786-9522, Ext 3233. Web Site: libguides.gptc.edu. *Librn,* Caroline Dial; E-mail: dialc@gptc.edu; Staff 2 (MLS 1, Non-MLS 1)
Founded 1997. Highest Degree: Associate
Wireless access
Function: Computers for patron use, Copy machines, e-mail & chat, Electronic databases & coll, Learning ctr, Online ref, Photocopying/Printing, Ref & res, Scanner
Partic in GALILEO (Georgia Library Learning Online)
Open Mon-Thurs 8:30-8

P NEWTON COUNTY LIBRARY SYSTEM*, 7116 Floyd St NE, 30014. SAN 338-6880. Tel: 770-787-3231. Information Services Tel: 705-385-6449. FAX: 770-784-2092. TDD: 770-784-2091. Web Site: www.newtonlibrary.org. *Dir,* Lace Keaton; *Asst Libr Dir,* Courtney Lumpkin; Staff 27 (MLS 4, Non-MLS 23)
Founded 1969. Pop 103,528; Circ 660,102
Jul 2008-Jun 2009 Income $1,618,513, State $329,814, City $6,000, County $1,133,869, Locally Generated Income $146,430, Other $2,400. Mats Exp $299,403
Library Holdings: Audiobooks 11,987; AV Mats 2,217; CDs 2,205; DVDs 6,800; High Interest/Low Vocabulary Bk Vols 1,600; Large Print Bks 7,000; Bk Titles 123,055; Bk Vols 148,000; Per Subs 192; Videos 6,216
Special Collections: Porter Foundation Garden Coll
Subject Interests: Local hist
Automation Activity & Vendor Info: (Cataloging) Evergreen; (Circulation) Evergreen; (ILL) OCLC
Wireless access
Function: ILL available
Publications: Bookworm Notes: Friends of the Library Newsletter
Partic in Georgia Online Database; Lyrasis; PINES (Public Information Network for Electronic Services)

Special Services for the Blind - Computer with voice synthesizer for visually impaired persons
Open Tues & Thurs 10-8, Wed & Fri 10-6, Sat 10-2
Friends of the Library Group

CUMMING

P FORSYTH COUNTY PUBLIC LIBRARY*, Cumming Library & FCPL Headquarters, 585 Dahlonega Rd, 30040-2109. SAN 375-4162. Tel: 770-781-9840. FAX: 770-781-8089. Web Site: www.forsythpl.org. *Dir,* Jon McDaniel; E-mail: mcdanielj@forsythpl.org; *Asst Dir, Mat Mgr,* Carla Beasley; E-mail: beasleyc@forsythpl.org; *Asst Dir, Pub Serv,* Liz Forster; E-mail: forsterl@forsythpl.org; *Asst Dir, Info Tech,* Cheryl Morgan; E-mail: morganc@forsythpl.org; *Asst Dir, Support Serv,* Anna Lyle; E-mail: lylea@forsythpl.org; Staff 84 (MLS 10, Non-MLS 74)
Founded 1956. Pop 139,473; Circ 1,222,144
Library Holdings: AV Mats 32,838; Electronic Media & Resources 22; Large Print Bks 2,232; Bk Vols 226,492; Per Subs 328; Talking Bks 9,614
Automation Activity & Vendor Info: (Acquisitions) SirsiDynix; (Cataloging) SirsiDynix; (Circulation) SirsiDynix; (OPAC) SirsiDynix; (Serials) SirsiDynix
Database Vendor: Baker & Taylor, BWI, EBSCOhost, Gale Cengage Learning, Newsbank, OCLC WorldShare Interlibrary Loan, SirsiDynix
Function: Homebound delivery serv, ILL available, Photocopying/Printing, Prog for children & young adult, Ref serv available, Summer reading prog, Telephone ref, Wheelchair accessible
Open Mon-Thurs 10-8:30, Fri & Sat 10-5:30, Sun 1:30-5:30
Friends of the Library Group
Branches: 1
SHARON FORKS, 2820 Old Atlanta Rd, 30041. Tel: 770-781-9840. *Br Coordr,* Brenda Johnson
Library Holdings: AV Mats 14,231; Large Print Bks 721; Bk Vols 97,907; Per Subs 158; Talking Bks 4,553
Open Mon-Thurs 10-8:30, Fri & Sat 10-5:30, Sun 1:30-5:30

J LANIER TECHNICAL COLLEGE*, Forsyth Campus Library, 7745 Majors Rd, 30041. Tel: 770-781-6895. FAX: 770-781-6988. Web Site: www.laniertech.edu/library. *Dir, Libr Serv,* Beth Hedrick; Tel: 770-531-6379, E-mail: bhedrick@laniertech.edu; *Librn,* Min Su; E-mail: msu@laniertech.edu
Library Holdings: e-books 23,000; Bk Vols 5,000; Per Subs 90
Automation Activity & Vendor Info: (Cataloging) TLC (The Library Corporation); (Circulation) TLC (The Library Corporation); (OPAC) TLC (The Library Corporation)
Partic in GALILEO (Georgia Library Learning Online)
Open Mon-Thurs 8-8, Fri 8-4

CUTHBERT

J ANDREW COLLEGE*, Pitts Library, 501 College St, 39840. SAN 303-3589. Tel: 229-732-5944. FAX: 229-732-5957. Web Site: www.andrewcollege.edu. *Coll Develop, Dir, Libr Serv,* Karan Berryman Pittman; E-mail: karanpittman@andrewcollege.edu; Staff 2.4 (MLS 1, Non-MLS 1.4)
Founded 1854. Enrl 278; Fac 25; Highest Degree: Associate
Library Holdings: AV Mats 6,550; DVDs 84; Microforms 6,500; Bk Vols 34,600; Per Subs 170; Videos 618
Special Collections: Andrew College Archives, bks, doc, ms, pamphlets, pictures
Automation Activity & Vendor Info: (Acquisitions) Ex Libris Group; (Cataloging) Ex Libris Group; (Circulation) Ex Libris Group; (Course Reserve) Ex Libris Group; (ILL) Ex Libris Group; (OPAC) Ex Libris Group; (Serials) EBSCO Online
Wireless access
Function: Archival coll, Computers for patron use, Copy machines, Electronic databases & coll, ILL available, Online cat, Orientations, Photocopying/Printing, Ref & res, Ref serv in person, Web-catalog
Partic in Georgia Online Database; Georgia Private Acad Librs Consortium (GPALS); Lyrasis; OCLC Online Computer Library Center, Inc
Open Mon-Thurs 8:30am-10pm, Fri 8:30-4:30, Sun 5-9

DALTON

C DALTON STATE COLLEGE, Derrell C Roberts Library, 650 College Dr, 30720-3778. SAN 303-3600. Tel: 706-272-4585. Reference Tel: 706-272-4575. FAX: 706-272-4511. Web Site: www.daltonstate.edu/library. *Dir,* Lydia F Knight; E-mail: lknight@daltonstate.edu; *Archives, Cat Librn, Tech Serv Librn,* Lee Ann Cline; E-mail: lcline@daltonstate.edu; *Govt Doc Librn, ILL,* Barbara Jones; E-mail: bjones@daltonstate.edu; *Instrul & Ref Librn,* Melissa Whitesell; E-mail: mwhitesell@daltonstate.edu; *Ref & Instruction Librn,* David Brown; E-mail: dbrown@daltonstate.edu; Staff 9 (MLS 5, Non-MLS 4)
Founded 1967. Enrl 4,239; Fac 5; Highest Degree: Bachelor
Library Holdings: AV Mats 10,434; e-books 176,595; Microforms 217,879; Bk Vols 141,399; Per Subs 255
Special Collections: College Archives; Dalton Room. US Document Depository
Automation Activity & Vendor Info: (Cataloging) Ex Libris Group; (Circulation) Ex Libris Group; (Course Reserve) Ex Libris Group; (ILL) OCLC; (OPAC) Ex Libris Group; (Serials) Ex Libris Group
Database Vendor: American Chemical Society, American Psychological Association (APA), Bowker, Cinahl, CQ Press, ebrary, EBSCO Discovery Service, EBSCOhost, Ex Libris Group, Gale Cengage Learning, Hoovers, JSTOR, LearningExpress, LexisNexis, Medline, Modern Language Association, OCLC, OCLC FirstSearch, OCLC WorldShare Interlibrary Loan, Plunkett Research, Ltd, ProQuest, Springshare, LLC
Wireless access
Function: Computers for patron use, Copy machines, e-mail & chat, Electronic databases & coll, Exhibits, Govt ref serv, Handicapped accessible, ILL available, Magazines, Microfiche/film & reading machines, Newsp ref libr, Online cat, Online ref, Online searches, Outside serv via phone, mail, e-mail & web, Photocopying/Printing, Pub access computers, Ref & res, Ref serv available, Ref serv in person, Scanner, Spanish lang bks, Study rm
Partic in GALILEO (Georgia Library Learning Online); Lyrasis
Open Mon-Thurs 7:30am-8pm, Fri 7:30-5, Sun 1-7
Restriction: Open to students, fac, staff & alumni

M HAMILTON MEDICAL CENTER*, Medical Library, 1200 Memorial Dr, 30720-2529. (Mail add: PO Box 1168, 30722-1168), SAN 374-8650. Tel: 706-272-6056. FAX: 706-272-6094. *Librn,* Sarah Russell; E-mail: srussell@hhcs.org; Staff 1 (Non-MLS 1)
Library Holdings: Bk Vols 2,000; Per Subs 90

P NORTHWEST GEORGIA REGIONAL LIBRARY SYSTEM*, 310 Cappes St, 30720. SAN 338-6139. Tel: 706-876-1360. FAX: 706-272-2977. Web Site: www.ngrl.org. *Dir,* Joe B Forsee; *Dep Dir,* Nick Fogarty; *Asst Dir,* John McPhearson; Staff 5 (MLS 5)
Founded 1924. Pop 197,000; Circ 320,000
Library Holdings: Bk Vols 210,000; Per Subs 65
Special Collections: Georgia Coll; Newspapers, micro
Subject Interests: Genealogy
Automation Activity & Vendor Info: (Acquisitions) SirsiDynix; (Cataloging) SirsiDynix; (Circulation) SirsiDynix; (ILL) OCLC
Wireless access
Partic in Georgia Libr Info Network
Open Mon-Thurs 10-7, Fri & Sat 10-6
Friends of the Library Group
Branches: 2
CALHOUN-GORDON COUNTY LIBRARY, 100 N Park Ave, Calhoun, 30701, SAN 338-6163. Tel: 706-624-1456. FAX: 706-624-1458. *Mgr,* Dianne Cronon; *Asst Librn,* Geneva Bennett
Special Collections: Dr Henry T Malone Coll
Open Mon-Thurs 10-8, Fri 10-6, Sat 10-3, Sun 2-5
Friends of the Library Group
CHATSWORTH-MURRAY COUNTY LIBRARY, 706 Old Dalton-Ellijay Rd, Chatsworth, 30705, SAN 338-6287. Tel: 706-695-4200. FAX: 706-695-7381. *Mgr,* Pat Ausmus
Open Mon-Fri 8-5, Sat 9-Noon
Friends of the Library Group

S WHITFIELD-MURRAY HISTORICAL SOCIETY*, Crown Gardens & Archives, 715 Chattanooga Ave, 30720. (Mail add: PO Box 6180, 30722), SAN 373-4250. Tel: 706-278-0217. E-mail: wmhs@optilink.us. Web Site: www.whitfield-murrayhistoricalsociety.org. *Exec Dir,* Jennifer Detweiler; Staff 1 (MLS 1)
Founded 1976
Library Holdings: Bk Vols 750
Subject Interests: Genealogy, Local hist
Wireless access
Open Tues-Fri 10-5, Sat 9-1

DAVISBORO

S GEORGIA DEPARTMENT OF CORRECTIONS, OFFICE OF LIBRARY SERVICES*, Washington State Prison, 13262 Hwy 24 E, 31018. (Mail add: PO Box 206, 31018-0206). Tel: 478-348-5814. FAX: 478-348-5613. Web Site: www.dcor.state.ga.us. *Librn,* Shatisha Wilson
Library Holdings: Bk Vols 1,500; Per Subs 15; Talking Bks 100; Videos 150
Special Collections: Law Coll
Database Vendor: LexisNexis
Open Mon-Fri 8-3:30

DAWSON

P KINCHAFOONEE REGIONAL LIBRARY SYSTEM*, 913 Forrester Dr SE, 39842-2106. Tel: 229-995-6331. FAX: 229-995-3383. Web Site: www.krlibrary.org. *Dir,* Jean Turn; *Asst Dir,* Mary Diane Medders; E-mail:

meddersd@krlibrary.org; *Bus & Finance Mgr,* Sonji A Harvey; E-mail: harveys@krlibrary.org; Staff 3 (MLS 2, Non-MLS 1)
Founded 1954. Pop 28,253
Subject Interests: Ga
Automation Activity & Vendor Info: (Cataloging) Evergreen
Partic in Lyrasis; PINES (Public Information Network for Electronic Services)
Open Mon-Fri 8-5
Branches: 6
CALHOUN COUNTY LIBRARY, 19379 E Hartford St, Edison, 39846-5626. (Mail add: PO Box 365, Edison, 39846-0365), SAN 338-6341. Tel: 229 835-2012. FAX: 229 835-2012. *Head of Libr,* Dianna Carter; E-mail: dcarter@krlibrary.org; *Mgr,* Babrara Lewis; Staff 2 (Non-MLS 2)
Founded 1989. Pop 4,970; Circ 13,704
Library Holdings: CDs 40; DVDs 116; Bk Titles 11,436; Per Subs 29; Talking Bks 170; Videos 886
Special Collections: Georgia
Subject Interests: Local hist
Partic in PINES (Public Information Network for Electronic Services)
Open Mon-Fri 9-6, Sat 9-2
Friends of the Library Group
CLAY COUNTY LIBRARY, 208 S Hancock St, Fort Gaines, 39851-9506. (Mail add: PO Box 275, Fort Gaines, 39851-0275), SAN 338-6406. Tel: 229-768-2248. FAX: 229-768-2248. *Br Mgr,* Teresa W Reynolds; E-mail: treynolds@krlibrary.org; *Head Librn,* Jean O Turn; E-mail: jturn@krlibrary.org; Staff 2 (MLS 1, Non-MLS 1)
Founded 1988. Pop 3,489; Circ 19,738
Library Holdings: CDs 17; DVDs 172; Bk Titles 15,209; Per Subs 42; Talking Bks 324; Videos 1,113
Special Collections: Georgia
Subject Interests: Local hist
Publications: Clay County History
Open Mon-Sat 9-5
QUITMAN COUNTY LIBRARY, 39 Old School Rd, Georgetown, 39854. (Mail add: PO Box 278, Georgetown, 31754-0278), SAN 338-6074. Tel: 229-334-8972. *Br Mgr,* Beverly Grant; Staff 2 (Non-MLS 2)
Open Mon-Wed 9-1 & 2-6, Fri 10-1 & 2-5
Friends of the Library Group
RANDOLPH COUNTY LIBRARY, 106 Pearl St, Cuthbert, 39840-1474, SAN 338-649X. Tel: 229-732-2566. FAX: 229-732-6824. Web Site: www.krlibrary.org/branches/randolph.html. *Librn,* Dianna Carter; Staff 3 (MLS 1, Non-MLS 2)
Founded 1997. Pop 6,851; Circ 34,720
Library Holdings: CDs 128; DVDs 272; Bk Titles 14,895; Per Subs 31; Talking Bks 59; Videos 796
Special Collections: Georgia; Local history
Subject Interests: Photog
Publications: Monthly Newsletter
Open Mon, Tues, Thurs & Fri 10-6, Sat 10-2
TERRELL COUNTY LIBRARY, 913 Forrester Dr SE, 39842-2106, SAN 370-7865. Tel: 229-995-2902. FAX: 229-995-5989. *Librn,* Gary McNeely; *Bus Mgr,* Pearlie Bishop; E-mail: bishopp@krlibrary.org; Staff 3 (MLS 1, Non-MLS 2)
Founded 1997. Pop 10,720; Circ 29,009
Library Holdings: CDs 35; DVDs 175; e-books 12; Bk Titles 37,984; Per Subs 28; Talking Bks 520; Videos 2,778
Special Collections: Georgia; Local History
Publications: Friends (Newsletter); Terrell County History
Open Mon-Thurs 10-6, Fri & Sat 10-5
Friends of the Library Group
WEBSTER COUNTY LIBRARY, 572 Washington St, Preston, 31824-0316. (Mail add: PO Box 316, Preston, 31824-0316), SAN 338-652X. Tel: 229-828-5740. FAX: 229-828-5740. Web Site: www.krlibrary.org/webster_link.htm. *Br Mgr,* Diane L Holbrook; E-mail: holbrookd@krlibrary.org; *Librn,* Diane Medders; Staff 2 (Non-MLS 2)
Founded 1989. Pop 1,947; Circ 4,993
Library Holdings: DVDs 125; Bk Titles 8,009; Per Subs 17; Videos 507
Partic in PINES (Public Information Network for Electronic Services)
Open Mon-Fri 2:30-5:30

DAWSONVILLE

P CHESTATEE REGIONAL LIBRARY SYSTEM*, 342 Allen St, 30534. SAN 377-6859. Tel: 706-344-3690. FAX: 706-344-3692. E-mail: crls@chestateelibrary.org. Web Site: www.chestateelibrary.org. *Dir,* Claudia Gibson; E-mail: cgibson@chestateelibrary.org; *Asst Dir,* Peggy King; E-mail: pking@chestateelibrary.org; *Coll Mgt Librn,* Tina Jordan; E-mail: tjordan@chestateelibrary.org; *Syst Librn,* Melanie Hogue; E-mail: mhogue@chestateelibrary.org; Staff 15 (MLS 3, Non-MLS 12)
Founded 1953. Pop 56,985; Circ 312,251
Jul 2012-Jun 2013 Income $962,761, State $211,272, County $674,354, Locally Generated Income $77,135. Mats Exp $109,650, Books $75,297, Electronic Ref Mat (Incl. Access Fees) $4,680. Sal $502,137 (Prof $153,763)
Library Holdings: Audiobooks 15,805; e-books 10,127; Bk Titles 106,115; Per Subs 131; Videos 10,661
Automation Activity & Vendor Info: (Cataloging) Evergreen; (Circulation) Evergreen; (OPAC) Evergreen
Wireless access
Function: Adult bk club, After school storytime, Archival coll, Audio & video playback equip for onsite use, AV serv, Bk club(s), Bks on CD, Children's prog, Computer training, Computers for patron use, Copy machines, Digital talking bks, Doc delivery serv, Electronic databases & coll, Family literacy, Fax serv, Free DVD rentals, Homebound delivery serv, ILL available, Instruction & testing, Microfiche/film & reading machines, Music CDs, Newsp ref libr, Notary serv, Online cat, Outside serv via phone, mail, e-mail & web, OverDrive digital audio bks, Photocopying/Printing, Printer for laptops & handheld devices, Prog for adults, Prog for children & young adult, Pub access computers, Ref & res, Ref serv available, Ref serv in person, Satellite serv, Scanner, Spoken cassettes & CDs, Story hour, Summer & winter reading prog, Summer reading prog, Tax forms, Teen prog, Telephone ref, Web-catalog, Wheelchair accessible, Workshops
Publications: Chestatee Highlighter (Newsletter)
Partic in Georgia Online Database
Friends of the Library Group
Branches: 2
DAWSON COUNTY LIBRARY, 342 Allen St, 30534, SAN 374-7336. Tel: 706-344-3690. FAX: 706-344-3691. E-mail: dawson@chestateelibrary.org. *Br Mgr,* Stacey Leonhardt; Tel: 706-344-3690, Ext 21, E-mail: sleonhardt@chestateelibrary.org; Staff 7 (Non-MLS 7)
Founded 1958. Pop 26,368; Circ 145,845
Jul 2012-Jun 2013 Income $390,549, County $357,545, Locally Generated Income $33,347. Mats Exp $51,363. Sal $144,026
Subject Interests: Local hist
Open Mon, Wed & Thurs 10-5:30, Tues 10-7, Fri & Sat 10-3:30
Friends of the Library Group
LUMPKIN COUNTY LIBRARY, 342 Courthouse Hill, Dahlonega, 30533. Tel: 706-864-3668. FAX: 706-864-3937. E-mail: lumpkin@chestateelibrary.org. *Br Mgr,* Tracey Thomaswick; E-mail: tthomaswick@chestateelibrary.org; Staff 8 (Non-MLS 8)
Founded 1917. Pop 30,617; Circ 166,406
Jul 2012-Jun 2013 Income $360,195, County $316,809, Locally Generated Income $43,386. Mats Exp $51,457. Sal $113,698
Subject Interests: Genealogy, Local hist
Open Mon-Wed 11-5:30, Thurs 12:30-7, Fri & Sat 11:30-3:30
Friends of the Library Group

DECATUR

C AGNES SCOTT COLLEGE, McCain Library, 141 E College Ave, 30030-3770. SAN 303-3619. Tel: 404-471-6339. Circulation Tel: 404-471-6094. Interlibrary Loan Service Tel: 404-471-5342. Reference Tel: 404-471-6096. FAX: 404-471-5037. E-mail: library@agnesscott.edu. Web Site: www.agnesscott.edu/library. *Dir,* Elizabeth Leslie Bagley; E-mail: ebagley@agnesscott.edu; *Access Serv/Reserves/Ref Librn,* Erica Hardy; Tel: 404-471-6337, E-mail: ehardy@agnesscott.edu; *User Educ Librn,* Casey Long; Tel: 404-471-6343, E-mail: clong@agnesscott.edu; *Admin Coordr, Archives Mgr,* Marianne Bradley; Tel: 404-471-6090, E-mail: mbradley@agnesscott.edu; *Acq, Automation Syst Coordr, E-Res Licensing,* Resa Harney; Tel: 404-471-6141, E-mail: rharney@agnesscott.edu; *ILL,* Debbie Adams; E-mail: deadams@agnesscott.edu; Staff 9.5 (MLS 4.5, Non-MLS 5)
Founded 1889. Enrl 930; Fac 95; Highest Degree: Bachelor
Jul 2012-Jun 2013. Mats Exp $998,683, Books $43,174, Per/Ser (Incl. Access Fees) $304,306, AV Mat $5,538, Electronic Ref Mat (Incl. Access Fees) $283,455, Presv $1,646. Sal $403,634 (Prof $252,107)
Library Holdings: AV Mats 26,941; CDs 6,146; DVDs 6,261; e-books 75,171; e-journals 5,648; Microforms 33,644; Bk Titles 189,109; Bk Vols 237,914; Per Subs 5,782
Special Collections: Catherine Marshall Papers; Faculty, Student & Alumnae Publications; Frontier Religion; Robert Frost Coll
Subject Interests: Liberal arts, Sciences
Automation Activity & Vendor Info: (Acquisitions) Innovative Interfaces, Inc; (Cataloging) Innovative Interfaces, Inc; (Circulation) Innovative Interfaces, Inc; (Course Reserve) Innovative Interfaces, Inc; (ILL) Innovative Interfaces, Inc; (Media Booking) Innovative Interfaces, Inc; (OPAC) Innovative Interfaces, Inc; (Serials) Innovative Interfaces, Inc
Database Vendor: ABC-CLIO, American Chemical Society, American Psychological Association (APA), Annual Reviews, ARTstor, BioOne, Blackwell, College Source, CountryWatch, CredoReference, ebrary, EBSCO Discovery Service, EBSCOhost, Elsevier, Gale Cengage Learning, H W Wilson, Infotrieve, Innovative Interfaces, Inc, JSTOR, LexisNexis, Medline, Modern Language Association, Nature Publishing Group, OCLC WorldShare Interlibrary Loan, Oxford Online, Project MUSE, ProQuest, PubMed, RefWorks, Sage, ScienceDirect, Scopus, Springer-Verlag, Springshare, LLC, Wiley InterScience, YBP Library Services
Wireless access

Function: 24/7 Electronic res, 24/7 Online cat, Copy machines
Partic in Atlanta Regional Council for Higher Education; GALILEO (Georgia Library Learning Online); Lyrasis; Oberlin Group; OCLC Online Computer Library Center, Inc
Open Mon-Thurs 8am-10:30pm, Fri 8-6, Sat 9-6, Sun 1-10:30; Mon-Thurs (Summer) 8-5:15
Restriction: Badge access after hrs

GM ATLANTA VA MEDICAL CENTER LIBRARY*, 1670 Clairmont Rd, 30033-4004. SAN 303-3678. Tel: 404-321-6111, Ext 7672. FAX: 404-728-7781. Web Site: www.visn7.med.va.gov. *Chief Librn,* Shirley Avin; *Tech Serv,* Keith Edmonds; Staff 1 (Non-MLS 1)
Founded 1945
Library Holdings: Bk Titles 2,000; Per Subs 482
Subject Interests: Health sci, Med
Partic in Atlanta Health Science Libraries Consortium
Open Mon-Fri 8-4:30

R CLAIRMONT PRESBYTERIAN CHURCH LIBRARY*, 1994 Clairmont Rd, 30033. SAN 303-3635. Tel: 404-634-3355. FAX: 404-321-5057. Web Site: www.clairmontpres.org. *Librn,* Kathy Morton; Tel: 404-248-0187
Library Holdings: Bk Vols 2,750
Subject Interests: Fiction, Relig
Open Wed 8am-9pm, Sun 8-12:30

R COLUMBIA THEOLOGICAL SEMINARY*, John Bulow Campbell Library, 701 Columbia Dr, 30030. SAN 303-3643. Tel: 404-687-4549. Interlibrary Loan Service Tel: 404-687-4548. Reference Tel: 404-687-4620. FAX: 404-687-4687. E-mail: ref-desk@ctsnet.edu. Web Site: www.ctsnet.edu/library/libintro.asp. *Dir,* Sara Myers; *Circ,* Mary Martha Riviere; *Pub Serv,* Richard Blake; *Tech Serv,* Tammy Johnson; Staff 7 (MLS 5, Non-MLS 2)
Founded 1828. Enrl 625
Library Holdings: Bk Vols 200,000; Per Subs 862
Subject Interests: Philos, Relig
Automation Activity & Vendor Info: (Acquisitions) SirsiDynix; (Cataloging) SirsiDynix; (Circulation) SirsiDynix; (Course Reserve) SirsiDynix; (ILL) SirsiDynix; (OPAC) SirsiDynix; (Serials) SirsiDynix
Database Vendor: Alexander Street Press, EBSCO - WebFeat, EBSCOhost, Emerald, Gale Cengage Learning, OCLC ArticleFirst, OCLC FirstSearch, OCLC WorldShare Interlibrary Loan, Oxford Online, ProQuest, SirsiDynix
Wireless access
Partic in OCLC Online Computer Library Center, Inc
Restriction: Open to students, fac & staff, Restricted pub use, Use of others with permission of librn

P DEKALB COUNTY PUBLIC LIBRARY, Library Administrative Ctr, 3560 Kensington Rd, 30032. SAN 338-6589. Tel: 404-508-7190. FAX: 404-508-7185. Web Site: www.dekalblibrary.org. *Dir,* Alison Weissinger; E-mail: weissingera@dekalblibrary.org; *Asst Libr Dir,* Nancy Wright; E-mail: wrightn@dekalblibrary.org; *Br Operations Coordr,* George Ford; E-mail: fordg@dekalblibrary.org; *Br Operations Coordr,* Kitty Wilson; E-mail: wilsonk@dekalblibrary.org; *Coordr, Coll Mgt,* Position Currently Open; *ILL,* Joseph Miller; Tel: 404-370-3070, Ext 2016, Fax: 404-370-3073, E-mail: millerjt@dekalblibrary.org; *Tech Serv,* Patricia Dollisch; E-mail: dollischp@dekalblibrary.org; Staff 230.25 (MLS 58.5, Non-MLS 171.75)
Founded 1925. Pop 721,520; Circ 2,916,460
Jul 2013-Jun 2014 Income (Main Library and Branch(s)) $15,567,689, State $1,046,695, City $279,247, Federal $4,675, County $13,230,068, Locally Generated Income $1,000,190, Other $6,814. Mats Exp $930,804, Books $461,783, Per/Ser (Incl. Access Fees) $46,887, Other Print Mats $42,253, Micro $1,750, AV Mat $176,797, Electronic Ref Mat (Incl. Access Fees) $201,334. Sal $11,513,215
Library Holdings: AV Mats 74,063; CDs 42,861; DVDs 31,202; Large Print Bks 6,044; Bk Vols 812,792; Per Subs 1,417
Special Collections: Georgia & DeKalb County History Coll
Automation Activity & Vendor Info: (Acquisitions) SirsiDynix; (Cataloging) SirsiDynix; (Circulation) SirsiDynix; (ILL) OCLC; (OPAC) SirsiDynix
Wireless access
Friends of the Library Group
Branches: 22
BROOKHAVEN BRANCH, 1242 N Druid Hills Rd NE, Atlanta, 30319, SAN 338-6619. Tel: 404-848-7140. FAX: 404-848-7142. Web Site: www.dekalblibrary.org/branches/broo.htm.
Friends of the Library Group
WESLEY CHAPEL-WILLIAM C BROWN BRANCH, 2861 Wesley Chapel Rd, 30034, SAN 370-8012. Tel: 404-286-6980. FAX: 404-286-6985. Web Site: www.dekalblibrary.org/branches/wesl.htm.
Friends of the Library Group
SCOTT CANDLER BRANCH, 1917 Candler Rd, 30032, SAN 338-6643. Tel: 404-286-6986. FAX: 404-286-6989. Web Site: www.dekalblibrary.org/branches/cand.htm.
Friends of the Library Group
CHAMBLEE BRANCH, 4115 Clairmont Rd, Chamblee, 30341, SAN 338-6678. Tel: 770-936-1380. FAX: 770-936-1385. Web Site: www.dekalblibrary.org/branches/cham.htm.
Friends of the Library Group
CLARKSTON BRANCH, 951 N Indian Creek Dr, Clarkston, 30021, SAN 372-0101. Tel: 404-508-7175. FAX: 404-508-7178. TDD: 404-508-7179. Web Site: www.dekalblibrary.org/branches/clar.htm.
Friends of the Library Group
COVINGTON, 3500 Covington Hwy, 30032, SAN 372-0152. Tel: 404-508-7180. FAX: 404-508-7183. Web Site: www.dekalblibrary.org/branches/covi.htm.
Friends of the Library Group
DECATUR LIBRARY, 215 Sycamore St, 30030, SAN 338-6597. Tel: 404-370-3070. FAX: 404-370-3073. Web Site: www.dekalblibrary.org/branches/deca.htm.
Friends of the Library Group
DORAVILLE BRANCH, 3748 Central Ave, Doraville, 30340, SAN 338-6732. Tel: 770-936-3852. FAX: 770-936-3854. Web Site: www.dekalblibrary.org/branches/dora.htm.
Friends of the Library Group
DUNWOODY BRANCH, 5339 Chamblee-Dunwoody Rd, Dunwoody, 30338, SAN 321-4605. Tel: 770-512-4640. FAX: 770-512-4644. Web Site: www.dekalblibrary.org/branches/dunw.htm.
Friends of the Library Group
EMBRY HILLS BRANCH, 3733 Chamblee-Tucker Rd, Chamblee, 30341, SAN 370-7970. Tel: 770-270-8230. FAX: 770-270-8233. Web Site: www.dekalblibrary.org/branches/emhi.htm.
Friends of the Library Group
FLAT SHOALS, 4022 Flat Shoals Pkwy, 30034, SAN 372-011X. Tel: 404-244-4370. FAX: 404-244-4373. Web Site: www.dekalblibrary.org/branches/flat.htm.
Friends of the Library Group
GRESHAM BRANCH, 2418 Gresham Rd, Atlanta, 30316, SAN 372-0128. Tel: 404-244-4374. FAX: 404-244-4376. Web Site: www.dekalblibrary.org/branches/gres.htm.
HAIRSTON CROSSING BRANCH, 4911 Redan Rd, Stone Mountain, 30088, SAN 370-7989. Tel: 404-508-7170. FAX: 404-508-7173. Web Site: www.dekalblibrary.org/branches/hair.htm.
STONE MOUNTAIN-SUE KELLOGG BRANCH, 952 Leon St, Stone Mountain, 30083, SAN 338-6821. Tel: 770-413-2020. FAX: 770-413-2023. Web Site: www.dekalblibrary.org/branches/kell.htm.
Friends of the Library Group
LITHONIA-DAVIDSON BRANCH, 6821 Church St, Lithonia, 30058, SAN 338-6856. Tel: 770-482-3820. FAX: 770-482-3831. Web Site: www.dekalblibrary.org/branches/lith.htm.
Friends of the Library Group
NORTHLAKE-BARBARA LOAR BRANCH, 3772 La Vista Rd, Tucker, 30084, SAN 372-0136. Tel: 404-679-4408. FAX: 404-679-4411. Web Site: www.dekalblibrary.org/branches/nolk.htm.
Friends of the Library Group
REDAN-TROTTI BRANCH, 1569 Wellborn Rd, Redan, 30074, SAN 372-0144. Tel: 770-482-3821. FAX: 770-482-3825. Web Site: www.dekalblibrary.org/branches/reda.htm.
SALEM-PANOLA BRANCH, 5137 Salem Rd, Lithonia, 30038, SAN 370-7997. Tel: 770-987-6900. FAX: 770-987-6903. Web Site: www.dekalblibrary.org/branches/sapa.htm.
Friends of the Library Group
SCOTTDALE-TOBIE GRANT HOMEWORK CENTER, 644 Parkdale Dr, Scottdale, 30079, SAN 338-6767. Tel: 404-508-7174. FAX: 404-508-6904. Web Site: www.dekalblibrary.org/branches/gran.htm.
STONECREST BRANCH, 3123 Klondike Rd, Lithonia, 30038. Tel: 770-482-3828. FAX: 770-482-3832.
TUCKER-REID COFER BRANCH, 5234 LaVista Rd, Tucker, 30084, SAN 338-6708. Tel: 770-270-8234. FAX: 770-270-8237. Web Site: www.dekalblibrary.org/branches/cofe.htm.
Friends of the Library Group
TOCO HILL-AVIS G WILLIAMS BRANCH, 1282 McConnell Dr, 30033, SAN 338-6910. Tel: 404-679-4404. FAX: 404-679-4407. Web Site: www.dekalblibrary.org/branches/will.htm.
Friends of the Library Group

M DEKALB MEDICAL CENTER*, Health Sciences Library, 2701 N Decatur Rd, 30033. SAN 303-3651. Tel: 404-501-5638. FAX: 404-501-1052. *Dir,* Marilyn Barry; *Librn,* Tim Lammers; Staff 3 (MLS 2, Non-MLS 1)
Founded 1974
Library Holdings: Bk Titles 1,200; Per Subs 300
Subject Interests: Allied health, Clinical med, Nursing
Partic in Atlanta Health Science Libraries Consortium; BRS; Georgia Online Database

Open Mon-Fri 8:30-4:30
Restriction: Staff use only

C DEVRY UNIVERSITY*, One West Court Sq, Ste 100, 30030. SAN 303-271X. Tel: 404-270-2702. Circulation Tel: 404-270-2900. Web Site: www.atl.devry.edu/library.html. *Libr Dir,* Tila Kunnapas; E-mail: tkunnapas@devry.edu
Founded 1969. Enrl 3,882
Library Holdings: Bk Vols 23,000; Per Subs 75
Automation Activity & Vendor Info: (Cataloging) Ex Libris Group; (Circulation) Ex Libris Group; (OPAC) Ex Libris Group
Database Vendor: LexisNexis, OCLC FirstSearch, ProQuest
Partic in GALILEO (Georgia Library Learning Online); Lyrasis
Open Mon-Thurs 7:30am-10pm, Fri 7:30-7, Sat 10-4

DEMOREST

C PIEDMONT COLLEGE*, Arrendale Library, 165 Central Ave, 30535. (Mail add: PO Box 40, 30535-0040), SAN 303-3686. Tel: 706-776-0111. FAX: 706-776-3338. E-mail: refdept@piedmont.edu. Web Site: library.piedmont.edu. *Libr Dir,* Bob Glass; *Acq, Cat,* Joseph Dawsey; *Coordr, Off Campus User Serv,* Hugh A Holden; *Coordr, On Campus User Serv,* Janet L Williams; Staff 6 (MLS 4, Non-MLS 2)
Founded 1897. Enrl 2,250; Fac 95; Highest Degree: Master
Library Holdings: Bk Vols 116,000; Per Subs 345
Automation Activity & Vendor Info: (Acquisitions) SirsiDynix; (Cataloging) SirsiDynix; (Circulation) SirsiDynix; (Course Reserve) SirsiDynix; (ILL) SirsiDynix; (Media Booking) SirsiDynix; (OPAC) SirsiDynix; (Serials) SirsiDynix
Database Vendor: EBSCOhost, Gale Cengage Learning, LexisNexis, OCLC FirstSearch, OVID Technologies, ProQuest, SerialsSolutions, SirsiDynix, Wilson - Wilson Web
Wireless access
Partic in GALILEO (Georgia Library Learning Online); Georgia Libr Info Network; Georgia Private Acad Libs Consortium (GPALS); Lyrasis; OCLC Online Computer Library Center, Inc
Open Mon-Thurs 7:45am-11pm, Fri 7:45-4, Sat 10-4, Sun 2-10
Friends of the Library Group

DOUGLAS

P SATILLA REGIONAL LIBRARY*, Douglas/Coffee County Public Library, 200 S Madison Ave, Ste D, 31533. SAN 338-6945. Tel: 912-384-4667. FAX: 912-389-4365. E-mail: douglib@srlsys.org. Web Site: www.srlsys.org. *Dir,* Mark Cole; *Br Mgr,* Lorrinda Johnson; E-mail: johnsonl@srlsys.org; *Circ,* Regina Bennett; *Circ,* Rosa Deen
Founded 1914. Circ 218,275
Library Holdings: Bk Titles 77,329; Per Subs 317; Talking Bks 701
Subject Interests: Genealogy
Partic in Georgia Libr Info Network; Georgia Online Database; Lyrasis
Open Mon-Thurs 8-6, Fri 8-3, Sat 10-3
Branches: 5
AMBROSE PUBLIC LIBRARY, 1070 Cypress Ave, Ambrose, 31512, SAN 376-9550. Tel: 912-359-2536. FAX: 912-359-2536. E-mail: ambrlib@srlsys.org. *Mgr,* Lydia Lott
Circ 3,738
Library Holdings: Bk Titles 4,017
Open Mon-Wed 2:30-7, Thurs 3:15-7
BROXTON PUBLIC LIBRARY, 105 Church St, Broxton, 31519, SAN 338-6953. Tel: 912-359-3887. FAX: 912-359-3887. E-mail: broxlib@srlsys.org. *Mgr,* Annette Ward
Circ 3,477
Library Holdings: Bk Vols 8,413
Open Mon-Wed 1:30-6, Thurs 2:15-6
NICHOLLS PUBLIC LIBRARY, 108 N Liberty St, Nicholls, 31554, SAN 338-7011. Tel: 912-345-2534. FAX: 912-345-2534. E-mail: nichlib@srlsys.org.
Circ 14,532
Library Holdings: Bk Titles 4,885
Open Mon-Wed 1:30-6, Thurs 2:15-6
PEARSON PUBLIC LIBRARY, 202 E Bullard Ave, Pearson, 31642-9277, SAN 338-7038. Tel: 912-422-3500. FAX: 912-422-3500. E-mail: pearlib@srlsys.org. *Mgr,* Jackie Israel
Pop 3,500; Circ 7,398
Library Holdings: Bk Titles 11,924; Talking Bks 11
Open Mon-Wed 1:30-6, Thurs 2:15-6
WILLACOOCHEE PUBLIC LIBRARY, 300 Fleetwood Ave, Willacoochee, 31650-9653, SAN 338-7062. Tel: 912-534-5252. FAX: 912-534-5252. E-mail: willalib@srlsys.org. *Mgr,* Christine Luke
Pop 3,500; Circ 13,515
Library Holdings: Bk Titles 10,993
Open Mon & Thurs 2:15-5:15, Wed 10-12 & 12:30-5:15, Sat 10-12 & 12:30-3
Bookmobiles: 1. Librn, Lorrinda Johnson. Bk Titles 2,645

J SOUTH GEORGIA COLLEGE*, William S Smith Library, 100 W College Park Dr, 31533-5098. SAN 303-3694. Tel: 912-260-4323. Interlibrary Loan Service Tel: 912-260-4335. Administration Tel: 912-260-4234. Information Services Tel: 912-260-4331. FAX: 912-260-4452. Web Site: www.sgc.edu/library. *Dir,* Jacqueline H Vickers; E-mail: jacqueline.vickers@sgsc.edu; Yolanda Crosby; Staff 5.43 (MLS 2, Non-MLS 3.43)
Founded 1906. Enrl 2,213; Highest Degree: Associate
Library Holdings: AV Mats 3,511; Bks on Deafness & Sign Lang 37; DVDs 189; e-books 30,614; Microforms 48,293; Bk Titles 82,545; Bk Vols 94,296; Per Subs 66
Special Collections: US Geological Survey Maps
Automation Activity & Vendor Info: (Cataloging) Ex Libris Group; (Circulation) Ex Libris Group; (OPAC) Ex Libris Group
Wireless access
Partic in Lyrasis
Open Mon-Thurs 7:30am-9pm, Fri 8-Noon, Sun 4-8

J WIREGRASS GEORGIA TECHNICAL COLLEGE, Coffee Campus Library, 706 W Baker Hwy, 31533. Tel: 229-468-2226. FAX: 912-389-4308. Web Site: www.wiregrass.edu/library. *Coordr, Libr & Media Serv,* Patrice Renee' Toomer-Bennett; E-mail: patrice.toomer@wiregrass.edu; Staff 1 (MLS 1)
Founded 2010. Enrl 731; Fac 18; Highest Degree: Associate
Jul 2013-Jun 2014. Mats Exp $10,952, Books $5,959, Per/Ser (Incl. Access Fees) $1,573, AV Mat $1,650, Electronic Ref Mat (Incl. Access Fees) $1,770
Library Holdings: AV Mats 3; CDs 21; DVDs 200; Bk Titles 2,696; Bk Vols 2,972; Per Subs 24; Videos 59
Automation Activity & Vendor Info: (Cataloging) TLC (The Library Corporation); (Circulation) TLC (The Library Corporation); (ILL) OCLC ILLiad; (OPAC) TLC (The Library Corporation)
Database Vendor: Baker & Taylor, CredoReference, EBSCOhost, Gale Cengage Learning, Medline, Micromedex, OCLC, ProQuest, TLC (The Library Corporation), WebMD, Westlaw, YBP Library Services

DUBLIN

P OCONEE REGIONAL LIBRARY*, Laurens County, 801 Bellevue Ave, 31021. (Mail add: PO Box 100, 31040-0100), SAN 338-7097. Tel: 478-272-5710. Toll Free Tel: 800-453-5441. FAX: 478-275-5381. Web Site: www.ocrl.org. *Dir,* Leard Daughety; *Asst Dir,* Chris C Woodburn; *Ch Serv,* Amy Rooks; *Ref Serv,* Christina Protter; Staff 27 (MLS 6, Non-MLS 21)
Founded 1904. Pop 79,516; Circ 334,627
Library Holdings: Bk Vols 92,950; Per Subs 135
Special Collections: Georgia Coll
Subject Interests: Local hist
Database Vendor: EBSCOhost, OCLC FirstSearch, ProQuest, Wilson - Wilson Web
Function: ILL available
Partic in Georgia Online Database; Lyrasis; PINES (Public Information Network for Electronic Services)
Open Mon, Tues & Thurs 9:30-8:30, Wed, Fri & Sat 9:30-6
Friends of the Library Group
Branches: 5
HARLIE FULFORD MEMORIAL, 301 Elm St, Wrightsville, 31096. (Mail add: PO Box 69, Wrightsville, 31096-0069), SAN 338-7127. Tel: 478-864-3940. FAX: 478-864-0626. *Mgr,* Marolyn Fortner
Library Holdings: Bk Vols 12,298; Per Subs 22
Open Mon-Fri 9:30-6
GLASCOCK COUNTY LIBRARY, 738 Railroad Ave, Gibson, 30810. (Mail add: PO Box 128, Gibson, 30810-0128). Tel: 706-598-9837. FAX: 706-598-2670. *Br Mgr,* Betty Cook; Staff 1 (Non-MLS 1)
Founded 2000. Pop 2,547; Circ 11,139
Library Holdings: DVDs 121; Bk Vols 3,596; Per Subs 16; Talking Bks 33; Videos 239
Database Vendor: OCLC WorldShare Interlibrary Loan, ProQuest
Function: Photocopying/Printing, Prog for children & young adult, Summer reading prog
Special Services for the Blind - Bks on cassette; Bks on CD; Computer with voice synthesizer for visually impaired persons
Open Tues 9-7, Wed & Sat 9-1, Thurs & Fri 12-6

P TALKING BOOK CENTER, 801 Bellevue Ave, 31021. (Mail add: PO Box 100, 31040-0100). Tel: 478-275-5382. Toll Free Tel: 800-453-5541. FAX: 478-275-3821. *Mgr,* Wanda Daniel
Publications: Talking Book News (Newsletter)
Special Services for the Blind - Cassette playback machines; Closed circuit TV; Duplicating spec requests; Home delivery serv; Large screen computer & software; Newsletter (in large print, Braille or on cassette); Reader equip; Screen enlargement software for people with visual disabilities; Spanish Braille mags & bks; Talking bks & player equip; Textbks on audio-cassettes; ZoomText magnification & reading software
Open Mon-Fri 9:30-6

TREUTLEN COUNTY, 585 Second St, Soperton, 30457. (Mail add: PO Box 49, Soperton, 30457), SAN 338-7186. Tel: 912-529-6683. FAX: 912-529-6050. *Br Mgr,* Mary Jane Gabriel-Smith; E-mail: mjsmith@ocrl.org
Library Holdings: Bk Vols 14,921; Per Subs 29
Open Mon-Fri 12-6

WASHINGTON COUNTY, 314 S Harris St, Sandersville, 31082-2669. (Mail add: PO Box 268, Sandersville, 31082-0268), SAN 338-7240. Tel: 478-552-7466. FAX: 478-552-6064. *Mgr,* Diane Meeks
Library Holdings: Bk Vols 41,979; Per Subs 91
Open Mon-Fri 9:30-6, Sat 9-3
Friends of the Library Group

DULUTH

S NATIONAL RAILWAY HISTORICAL SOCIETY, ATLANTA CHAPTER*, Southeastern Railway Museum Library, 3595 Peachtree Rd, 30096. (Mail add: PO Box 1267, 30096-1267), SAN 375-0590. Tel: 770-476-2013. Web Site: www.southeasternrailwaymuseum.org, www.srmduluth.org. *Librn,* Nick Whitehouse
Founded 1959
Library Holdings: Bk Vols 2,000; Per Subs 2; Videos 100
Subject Interests: Rail transportation
Open Thurs-Sat 10-5
Friends of the Library Group

EAST POINT

C ATLANTA CHRISTIAN COLLEGE*, James A Burns Memorial Library, 2605 Ben Hill Rd, 30344-1999. SAN 303-3716. Tel: 404-669-2097. FAX: 404-669-4009. Web Site: www.acc.edu. *Dir,* Michael Bain; E-mail: mbain@acc.edu; *Ref,* Jennifer Clotfelter; Staff 2 (MLS 2)
Founded 1937. Enrl 408; Fac 40; Highest Degree: Bachelor
Library Holdings: Bk Titles 45,000; Bk Vols 55,000; Per Subs 210
Special Collections: Alumni Coll; Library of American Civilizatiion (Core Coll)
Automation Activity & Vendor Info: (Cataloging) Follett Software; (Circulation) Follett Software; (OPAC) Follett Software
Open Mon-Thurs (Sept-May) 8am-10pm, Fri 8-5, Sat 12-5

EASTMAN

P OCMULGEE REGIONAL LIBRARY SYSTEM*, Dodge County Library (System Headquarters), 535 Second Ave, 31023. Tel: 478-374-4711. FAX: 478-374-5646. Web Site: www.orls.org. *Dir,* Anne H Bowen; *Dep Dir,* Chris Campbell Woodburn; *Pub Serv Librn,* Heath Lee; *Cat,* Ellen Jones; *Info Tech,* Josh Sheffield; Staff 7 (MLS 5, Non-MLS 2)
Founded 1954. Pop 6,600; Circ 496,344
Library Holdings: Bk Vols 209,584; Per Subs 262
Special Collections: American Indian (Ethlyn P Rolfe Coll); Genealogy (Burch-Harrell-Smallwood Coll)
Subject Interests: Ethnic studies, Local hist, Nat sci, Relig
Automation Activity & Vendor Info: (Acquisitions) Baker & Taylor
Wireless access
Partic in PINES (Public Information Network for Electronic Services)
Open Mon, Wed, Fri & Sat 9-5, Tues & Thurs 9-7
Branches: 5

TESSIE W NORRIS PUBLIC LIBRARY, 315 Third St, Cochran, 31014, SAN 338-7305. Tel: 478-934-2904. FAX: 478-934-0705.
Open Mon-Fri 9-5:30, Sat 9-2
Friends of the Library Group

M E RODEN MEMORIAL LIBRARY, 400 Commerce St, Hawkinsville, 31036, SAN 338-7364. Tel: 478-892-3155. FAX: 478-892-3155.
Open Mon-Fri 10-5:30
Friends of the Library Group

TELFAIR COUNTY LIBRARY, 815 College St, McRae, 31055, SAN 338-7399. Tel: 229-868-2978.
Open Mon 10-7, Tues-Fri 10-5
Friends of the Library Group

WHEELER COUNTY LIBRARY, 315 W Main St, Alamo, 30411, SAN 338-7216. Tel: 912-568-7321. FAX: 912-568-7116.
Open Mon 1-7, Tues-Thurs 10-5, Fri 9-4

WILCOX COUNTY LIBRARY, Historic Courthouse Sq, 104 N Broad St, Abbeville, 31001, SAN 338-7429. Tel: 229-467-2075. FAX: 229-467-2075.
Founded 1936
Open Mon-Fri 1-5

ELBERTON

P ELBERT COUNTY PUBLIC LIBRARY*, 345 Heard St, 30635. SAN 338-7453. Tel: 706-283-5375. Administration Tel: 706-283-9299. FAX: 706-283-5456. *Dir,* Peggy Jane Johnson; *Asst Dir, Ch Serv,* Anne L Grace; E-mail: agrace@elbertcountypl.org; *Circ,* Valencia Thornton; *Tech Serv,* Camilla Bailey; Staff 5 (MLS 2, Non-MLS 3)
Founded 1925. Pop 19,478; Circ 83,987
Library Holdings: AV Mats 1,314; CDs 293; DVDs 241; Bk Vols 72,201; Per Subs 118; Videos 2,623
Automation Activity & Vendor Info: (Acquisitions) SirsiDynix; (Cataloging) SirsiDynix; (Circulation) SirsiDynix
Database Vendor: OCLC FirstSearch, OCLC WorldShare Interlibrary Loan
Wireless access
Function: Home delivery & serv to Sr ctr & nursing homes, ILL available, Mail loans to mem, Online searches, Photocopying/Printing, Prog for children & young adult, Ref serv available, Summer reading prog, Telephone ref
Partic in PINES (Public Information Network for Electronic Services)
Special Services for the Deaf - Bks on deafness & sign lang; Closed caption videos; High interest/low vocabulary bks
Special Services for the Blind - Audio mat; Bks on cassette; Bks on CD; Extensive large print coll; Home delivery serv; Large print bks; Talking bks; Videos on blindness & phys handicaps
Open Mon, Tues & Thurs 10-8, Wed & Fri 10-5, Sat 9-1
Friends of the Library Group
Branches: 1

BOWMAN BRANCH, 21 Prince Ave, Bowman, 30624. Tel: 706-245-0705. E-mail: thebowmanlibrary@yahoo.com. *Libr Mgr,* Angela Pullian; Tel: 706-246-0046
Open Mon-Fri 1:30-5:30
Friends of the Library Group

Bookmobiles: 1

EVANS

P GREATER CLARKS HILL REGIONAL LIBRARY SYSTEM, Columbia County Public Library, 7022 Evans Town Center Blvd, 30809. SAN 373-9406. Tel: 706-863-1946. Circulation Tel: 706-868-3353. Reference Tel: 706-447-7660. Administration Tel: 706-447-7663. FAX: 706-868-3351. Web Site: www.gchrl.org. *Dir & Librn,* Mary Linda Maner; E-mail: mlmaner@columbiacountyga.gov; *Ch,* Natalie Pulley; Tel: 706-447-7664, E-mail: npulley@columbiacountyga.gov; *Circ Mgr,* Kathy Hebert; Tel: 706-447-7662, E-mail: khebert@columbiacountyga.gov; *Ref Mgr,* Natalie Gibson; Tel: 706-447-7671, E-mail: ngibson@columbiacountyga.gov; Staff 11 (MLS 4, Non-MLS 7)
Founded 1982. Pop 122,000; Circ 418,132
Jul 2012-Jun 2013 Income $1,349,900. Mats Exp $560,500. Sal Prof $594,770
Library Holdings: Bk Vols 170,070; Per Subs 120; Talking Bks 250
Database Vendor: OCLC WorldShare Interlibrary Loan, ProQuest
Wireless access
Function: Adult bk club, After school storytime, AV serv, Children's prog, Computer training, Computers for patron use, Copy machines, Digital talking bks, Electronic databases & coll, Fax serv, Free DVD rentals, Handicapped accessible, Holiday prog, Microfiche/film & reading machines, Music CDs, Notary serv, Online cat, OverDrive digital audio bks, Photocopying/Printing, Preschool outreach, Prog for children & young adult, Pub access computers, Senior computer classes, Spanish lang bks, Story hour, Summer reading prog, Tax forms, Teen prog
Special Services for the Blind - Bks on cassette; Bks on CD; Computer with voice synthesizer for visually impaired persons; Large print bks
Open Mon, Tues & Thurs 10-8, Wed, Fri & Sat 10-5, Sun 2-5
Friends of the Library Group
Branches: 7

BURKE COUNTY LIBRARY, 130 Hwy 24 S, Waynesboro, 30830, SAN 373-9422. Tel: 706-554-3277. FAX: 706-554-0313. E-mail: burke@gchrl.org. *Br Mgr,* Elaine Sikes; Staff 3 (Non-MLS 3)
Founded 1959. Pop 23,424; Circ 59,505
Library Holdings: DVDs 2,000; Bk Vols 28,892; Per Subs 49; Talking Bks 59; Videos 2,553
Subject Interests: Local hist
Function: Newsp ref libr, Photocopying/Printing, Prog for children & young adult, Ref serv available, Summer reading prog, Telephone ref
Special Services for the Blind - Bks on cassette; Bks on CD; Computer with voice synthesizer for visually impaired persons; Large print bks
Open Mon 9-8, Tues-Fri 9-6, Sat 9-1
Friends of the Library Group

EUCHEE CREEK LIBRARY, 5907 Euchee Creek Dr, Grovetown, 30813, SAN 374-8162. Tel: 706-556-0594. FAX: 706-556-2585. *Br Mgr,* Keisha Evans; Staff 4 (MLS 1, Non-MLS 3)
Founded 1994. Pop 97,389; Circ 104,915
Library Holdings: Bk Vols 53,000; Per Subs 61; Talking Bks 150; Videos 3,500
Function: Handicapped accessible, Photocopying/Printing, Prog for children & young adult
Special Services for the Blind - Bks on cassette; Bks on CD; Computer with voice synthesizer for visually impaired persons; Large print bks; Text reader
Open Mon & Tues 10-8, Wed-Fri 10-5, Sat 10-4
Friends of the Library Group

HARLEM BRANCH, 375 N Louisville St, Harlem, 30814, SAN 373-9414. Tel: 706-556-9795. FAX: 706-556-2576. E-mail: harlem@columbiacountyga.gov. *Br Mgr,* Amanda Cash; Staff 1 (Non-MLS 1)
Founded 1981. Pop 97,389; Circ 29,588
Library Holdings: Bk Vols 10,680; Per Subs 25; Talking Bks 25; Videos 2,000
Function: Photocopying/Printing, Prog for children & young adult, Summer reading prog
Special Services for the Blind - Bks on cassette; Bks on CD; Large print bks
Open Tues 9 7, Wed & Fri 1 6, Thurs 1 7, Sat 9-1
Friends of the Library Group

LINCOLN COUNTY LIBRARY, 181 N Peachtree, Lincolnton, 30817. (Mail add: PO Box 310, Lincolnton, 30817-0310), SAN 373-9392. Tel: 706-359-4014. FAX: 706-359-1105. E-mail: lcpl@lincolncountyga.gov. *Br Mgr,* Shirley Dawkins; Staff 2 (Non-MLS 2)
Founded 1986. Pop 8,484; Circ 41,804
Library Holdings: DVDs 1,000; Bk Vols 11,712; Per Subs 10; Talking Bks 51; Videos 907
Function: Photocopying/Printing, Summer reading prog
Special Services for the Blind - Bks on cassette; Bks on CD; Computer with voice synthesizer for visually impaired persons
Open Mon & Thurs 9-6, Tues 9-7, Wed, Fri & Sat 9-2
Friends of the Library Group

MIDVILLE BRANCH, 149 Trout St, Midville, 30441. (Mail add: PO Box 428, Midville, 30441-0428), SAN 373-9449. Tel: 478-589-7825. FAX: 478-589-7825. E-mail: midville@gchrl.org. *Br Mgr,* Diane Yoder; Staff 1 (Non-MLS 1)
Founded 1994. Pop 23,424; Circ 3,830
Library Holdings: Bk Vols 5,341; Per Subs 14
Database Vendor: OCLC WorldShare Interlibrary Loan, ProQuest
Function: Online searches, Summer reading prog
Special Services for the Blind - Computer with voice synthesizer for visually impaired persons
Open Mon & Wed 12-6, Fri 10-6
Friends of the Library Group

SARDIS COUNTY LIBRARY, 750 Charles Perry Ave, Sardis, 30456. (Mail add: PO Box 57, Sardis, 30456), SAN 373-9430. Tel: 478-569-4866. FAX: 478-569-9510. E-mail: sardis@gchrl.org. *Br Mgr,* Deborah Tisani; Staff 1 (Non-MLS 1)
Founded 1980. Pop 23,424
Library Holdings: Bk Vols 6,131; Per Subs 10
Database Vendor: OCLC WorldShare Interlibrary Loan, ProQuest
Function: Online searches
Open Mon & Wed 12-6, Fri 10-6
Friends of the Library Group

WARREN COUNTY LIBRARY, Ten Warren St, Warrenton, 30828, SAN 303-4348. Tel: 706-465-2656. FAX: 706-465-2656. *Mgr,* Sue Simons; Staff 2 (Non-MLS 2)
Founded 1988. Pop 6,380; Circ 19,419
Library Holdings: DVDs 1,000; Bk Vols 12,108; Per Subs 17; Talking Bks 125; Videos 425
Database Vendor: OCLC WorldShare Interlibrary Loan
Function: Handicapped accessible, Photocopying/Printing, Summer reading prog
Special Services for the Blind - Bks on cassette; Bks on CD; Computer with voice synthesizer for visually impaired persons
Open Tues 10-8, Wed-Fri 10-6, Sat 9-3
Friends of the Library Group

FAYETTEVILLE

S FAYETTE COUNTY HISTORICAL SOCIETY, INC LIBRARY*, 195 Lee St, 30214-2081. (Mail add: PO Box 421, 30214-0421), SAN 371-6368. Tel: 770-716-6020. FAX: 770-716-9203. E-mail: adminfhs@fayettehistoricalsociety.com. Web Site: www.fayettehistoricalsociety.com. *Pres,* Alice Reeves
Library Holdings: Bk Titles 1,000
Special Collections: Civil War (War of the Rebellion Records Coll & Confederate Veteran Coll); Genealogy (Family History Coll), bks, mss
Open Tues 6pm-9pm, Thurs 10-1, Sat 9-1

FITZGERALD

P FITZGERALD-BEN HILL COUNTY LIBRARY*, 123 N Main St, 31750-2591. SAN 303-3775. Tel: 229-426-5080. FAX: 229-426-5084. E-mail: librarystaff@fbhcl.org. *Dir,* Sandra Hester; E-mail: shester@fbhcl.org; *Asst Dir,* J Sara Paulk; E-mail: spaulk@fbhcl.org; Staff 2 (MLS 2)
Founded 1915. Pop 18,305; Circ 105,610
Library Holdings: Bk Titles 60,000; Per Subs 200
Special Collections: Georgia Room
Subject Interests: Ga, Local hist
Automation Activity & Vendor Info: (Acquisitions) Evergreen; (Cataloging) Evergreen; (Circulation) Evergreen; (OPAC) Evergreen; (Serials) Evergreen
Partic in Georgia Online Database
Open Mon-Thurs 9-8, Fri & Sat 9-6
Friends of the Library Group

J WIREGRASS GEORGIA TECHNICAL COLLEGE, Lewis I Brinson Sr Library - Ben Hill-Irwin Campus Library, 667 Perry House Rd, 31750. Tel: 229-468-2012. FAX: 229-468-2110. Web Site: www.wiregrass.edu/library. *Exec Dir, Libr Serv,* Roger F Smith; E-mail: roger.smith@wiregrass.edu; Staff 1 (MLS 1)
Founded 2006. Enrl 463; Highest Degree: Associate
Jul 2013-Jun 2014. Mats Exp $12,456, Books $6,926, Per/Ser (Incl. Access Fees) $1,200, AV Mat $1,000, Electronic Ref Mat (Incl. Access Fees) $3,330
Library Holdings: DVDs 372; e-books 34,497; Bk Vols 6,485; Per Subs 29; Videos 74
Automation Activity & Vendor Info: (Cataloging) TLC (The Library Corporation); (Circulation) TLC (The Library Corporation); (ILL) OCLC ILLiad; (OPAC) TLC (The Library Corporation)
Database Vendor: 3M Library Systems, Baker & Taylor, CredoReference, EBSCOhost, Gale Cengage Learning, Medline, Micromedex, OCLC, ProQuest, TLC (The Library Corporation), WebMD, Westlaw, YBP Library Services

FOREST PARK

G GEORGIA DEPARTMENT OF TRANSPORTATION*, Roy A Flynt Memorial, Office of Materials & Testing Bldg, 15 Kennedy Dr, 30297. SAN 323-4134. Tel: 404-608-4800. FAX: 404-608-4752. *Librn,* Stardina Wyche; E-mail: swyche@dot.ga.gov
Library Holdings: Bk Vols 18,000; Per Subs 30
Special Collections: Government Publications; Hazardous Waste; TRB Coll
Publications: Annotated Research Bibliography
Open Mon-Fri 7:30-4

FORSYTH

S GEORGIA DEPARTMENT OF CORRECTIONS, OFFICE OF LIBRARY SERVICES*, Burruss Correctional Training Center, 1000 Indian Springs Dr, 31029. (Mail add: PO Box 5849, 31029-5849). Tel: 478-994-7511. FAX: 478-994-7561. Web Site: www.dcor.state.ga.us. *Librn,* Derek Wilder
Library Holdings: Bk Vols 3,000; Per Subs 10; Talking Bks 80
Special Collections: Law Coll
Database Vendor: LexisNexis
Open Mon-Thurs 5pm-9pm, Sat 8-12:30

FORT BENNING

UNITED STATES ARMY

AM MARTIN ARMY COMMUNITY HOSPITAL MEDICAL LIBRARY*, Bldg 9200, Rm 010 MCXB-IL, 7950 Martin Loop, 31905-5637, SAN 338-7682. Tel: 706-544-3533. FAX: 706-544-3215. Web Site: www.martin.amedd.army.mil/medlib.html. *Librn,* Beverly A McMaster; *Libr Tech,* Susan O Waldrop; Staff 2 (MLS 1, Non-MLS 1)
Library Holdings: Per Subs 90
Automation Activity & Vendor Info: (Acquisitions) Ex Libris Group; (Cataloging) Ex Libris Group; (Circulation) Ex Libris Group; (Course Reserve) Ex Libris Group; (ILL) OCLC; (Media Booking) Ex Libris Group; (OPAC) Ex Libris Group; (Serials) Ex Libris Group
Database Vendor: Elsevier, Gale Cengage Learning, OVID Technologies, UpToDate
Function: Health sci info serv, ILL available, Online searches, Photocopying/Printing, Ref serv available
Partic in Army Medical Department - Medical Library & Information Network (AMEDD MEDLI-NET); Docline; Fedlink; OCLC Online Computer Library Center, Inc
Open Mon-Fri 8-4:30

A SAYERS MEMORIAL LIBRARY*, Bldg 93, Wold Ave, 31905, SAN 338-7518. Tel: 706-545-7141. FAX: 706-545-6363. Web Site: www.benningmwr.com. *Dir,* Renolds Trent; Tel: 706-545-8932; *Tech Serv,* Nancy Wahlstrom; Staff 6 (MLS 3, Non-MLS 3)
Founded 1942
Library Holdings: Bk Titles 51,700; Bk Vols 54,900; Per Subs 227
Subject Interests: Bus & mgt, Hist, Music, Polit sci
Partic in Georgia Libr Info Network; Telecommunications Libr Info Network

A USAIS*, Donovan Research Library, Bldg 9230, 8150 Marne Rd, 31905. SAN 338-7666. Tel: 706-545-5661. FAX: 706-545-8590. *Libr Dir,* Erika Loze-Hudson; Tel: 706-545-8591, E-mail: ericka.loze@us.army.mil; Staff 4 (MLS 2, Non-MLS 2)
Founded 1919
Library Holdings: Bk Vols 58,435; Per Subs 84

Special Collections: After Action Reports; Army Unit Histories; Classified Documents; Rare Books; Staff Studies; The Digitized Monograph Coll of Student Papers, WWI forward
Subject Interests: Mil hist
Automation Activity & Vendor Info: (Acquisitions) SirsiDynix; (Cataloging) SirsiDynix; (Circulation) SirsiDynix; (ILL) OCLC; (OPAC) SirsiDynix
Publications: Bibliographies; Library Handbook; Periodical Holdings List
Partic in United States Army Training & Doctrine Command
Open Mon-Fri 8-6
Friends of the Library Group

A WESTERN HEMISPHERE INSTITUTE FOR SECURITY COOPERATION*, John B Amos Library, Bldg 35, 35 Ridgeway Loop, Rm 257, 31905-6245. SAN 329-2150. Tel: 706-545-1247, 706-545-4631. FAX: 706-545-4027. *Tech Serv,* Yamill Collazo; E-mail: yamill.collazo@us.army.mil
Library Holdings: Bk Titles 12,629; Bk Vols 20,000; Per Subs 75
Subject Interests: Latin Am
Open Mon-Fri 8-5:30

FORT GORDON

UNITED STATES ARMY

A CONSUMER HEALTH LIBRARY*, Eisenhower Army Medical Ctr, Rm 3-D-15, 30905, SAN 338-778X. Tel: 706-787-6765. FAX: 706-787-2327. *Librn,* Janet Millar
Founded 1942
Library Holdings: Bk Vols 1,100; Per Subs 400
Restriction: Not open to pub

AM EISENHOWER ARMY MEDICAL CENTER*, Health Sciences Libr, DDEAMC, 30905-5650, SAN 338-7755. Tel: 706-787-6765. FAX: 706-787-2327. *Librn,* Janet Millar
Library Holdings: Bk Vols 16,000; Per Subs 500
Partic in OCLC Online Computer Library Center, Inc
Restriction: Not open to pub

A WOODWORTH CONSOLIDATED LIBRARY/FORT GORDON POST LIBRARY*, 549 Rice Rd, Bldg 33500, 30905-5081, SAN 338-7720. Tel: 706-791-7323. Interlibrary Loan Service Tel: 706-791-3086. Reference Tel: 706-791-2449. Administration Tel: 706-791-6993. FAX: 706-791-3282. Web Site: gordon.army.mil/library. *Libr Dir,* Susanna Joyner; E-mail: susie.joyner@us.army.mil; Staff 13 (MLS 5, Non-MLS 8)
Founded 1950
Special Collections: US Army Signal Corps
Subject Interests: Computer sci
Automation Activity & Vendor Info: (Acquisitions) Innovative Interfaces, Inc - Millenium; (Cataloging) Innovative Interfaces, Inc - Millenium; (Circulation) Innovative Interfaces, Inc - Millenium; (ILL) OCLC WorldShare Interlibrary Loan; (OPAC) Innovative Interfaces, Inc - Millenium; (Serials) Innovative Interfaces, Inc - Millenium
Database Vendor: Innovative Interfaces, Inc
Function: Adult bk club, Art exhibits, Audio & video playback equip for onsite use, Audiobks via web, Bk club(s), Bks on CD, CD-ROM, Chess club, Children's prog, Computer training, Computers for patron use, Copy machines, Digital talking bks, e-mail & chat, e-mail serv, Electronic databases & coll, Exhibits, Free DVD rentals, Govt ref serv, Handicapped accessible, Holiday prog, ILL available, Instruction & testing, Jazz prog, Mail & tel request accepted, Music CDs, Newsp ref libr, Online cat, Online ref, Online searches, Orientations, Outreach serv, OverDrive digital audio bks, Photocopying/Printing, Preschool outreach, Prog for adults, Prog for children & young adult, Pub access computers, Ref & res, Ref serv available, Ref serv in person, Scanner, Spoken cassettes & CDs, Spoken cassettes & DVDs, Story hour, Summer reading prog, Tax forms, Teen prog, Telephone ref, Visual arts prog, Web-catalog, Wheelchair accessible, Workshops, Writing prog
Partic in Fedlink; Georgia Libr Info Network; OCLC Online Computer Library Center, Inc; United States Army Training & Doctrine Command
Open Mon-Thurs 9-8, Sat & Sun 10-6
Restriction: Authorized patrons, Limited access for the pub, Open to mil & govt employees only, Photo ID required for access, Restricted loan policy

FORT OGLETHORPE

S NATIONAL PARK SERVICE*, Chickamauga Chattanooga National Military Park, Thomas Longstreet Library, 3370 Lafayette Rd, 30742. (Mail add: PO Box 2128, 30742-2128), SAN 373-0425. Tel: 706-866-9241. Web Site: www.nps.gov/chch. *Superintendent,* Catherine Cook; *Historian,* James Ogden, III
Founded 1890
Library Holdings: Bk Vols 5,000; Per Subs 10
Special Collections: Chattanooga Campaign, ms
Subject Interests: Civil War
Restriction: Open by appt only

FORT STEWART

UNITED STATES ARMY

A FORT STEWART MAIN POST LIBRARY*, 316 Lindquist Rd, 31314-5126, SAN 338-7879. Tel: 912-767-2260, 912-767-2828. FAX: 912-767-3794. Web Site: www.stewlib3.stewart.army.mil. *Dir,* Faye Couture; *Ref Librn,* Patricia Alcorn; *Tech Serv,* Meriam D Simmons
Founded 1942
Library Holdings: Bk Titles 55,000; Bk Vols 68,000; Per Subs 250
Subject Interests: Mil hist
Automation Activity & Vendor Info: (Acquisitions) Ex Libris Group; (Cataloging) Ex Libris Group; (Circulation) Ex Libris Group; (OPAC) Ex Libris Group
Database Vendor: EBSCOhost, Gale Cengage Learning, OCLC FirstSearch
Partic in Georgia Libr Info Network; News Bank; OCLC Online Computer Library Center, Inc

AM WINN ARMY COMMUNITY HOSPITAL MEDICAL LIBRARY*, 1061 Harman Ave, Ste 2J11B, 31314-5611, SAN 338-7895. Tel: 912-435-6542. FAX: 912-435-5480. *Librn,* Laura Harvell
Library Holdings: Bk Titles 300; Bk Vols 600; Per Subs 36
Subject Interests: Allied health
Restriction: Open by appt only

FORT VALLEY

S AMERICAN CAMELLIA SOCIETY LIBRARY*, 100 Massee Lane, 31030. SAN 326-8578. Tel: 478-967-2358, 478-967-2722. Toll Free Tel: 877-422-6655. FAX: 478-967-2083. E-mail: ask@camellias-acs.org. Web Site: www.camellias-acs.org. *Exec Dir,* Ann Walton
Founded 1945
Library Holdings: Bk Vols 500; Per Subs 10
Restriction: Open by appt only

C FORT VALLEY STATE UNIVERSITY, Henry Alexander Hunt Memorial Library, 1005 State University Dr, 31030-4313. SAN 303-3791. Tel: 478-825-6342. Circulation Tel: 478-825-6753. Interlibrary Loan Service Tel: 478-825-6762. Reference Tel: 478-825-6761. FAX: 478-825-6663, 478-825-6916. Web Site: www.fvsu.edu. *Dir,* Frank Mahitab; E-mail: mahitabf@fvsu.edu; *Head, Ref,* Shaundra Walker; Tel: 478-825-6764, E-mail: walkers01@.fvsu.edu; Staff 12 (MLS 5, Non-MLS 7)
Founded 1925. Enrl 2,466; Fac 161; Highest Degree: Master
Library Holdings: Bk Vols 189,417; Per Subs 805
Special Collections: Materials and books by and about Blacks
Subject Interests: Agr, Art, Econ, Educ, Ethnic studies, Home econ, Sci tech
Automation Activity & Vendor Info: (Acquisitions) Ex Libris Group; (Cataloging) Ex Libris Group; (Circulation) Ex Libris Group; (ILL) Ex Libris Group; (OPAC) Ex Libris Group; (Serials) Ex Libris Group
Wireless access
Publications: LRC Student Handbook; Newsletter; The Info
Partic in Galileo/GIL

P PEACH PUBLIC LIBRARIES*, Thomas Public Library (Syst Hq), 315 Martin Luther King Jr Dr, 31030-4196. SAN 338-7933. Tel: 478-825-1640. FAX: 478-825-2061. Web Site: www.peach.public.lib.ga.us. *Dir,* Billy Tripp; E-mail: trippb@mail.peach.public.lib.ga.us; *Pub Serv Librn,* Andrew Vickers; E-mail: vickersa@mail.peach.public.lib.ga.us; *Circ Mgr,* Maria Zepeda Aguilar; E-mail: aguilarm@mail.peach.public.lib.ga.us; *Acq, Coll Mgt,* Jane Matthews; E-mail: matthewj@mail.peach.public.lib.ga.us; *Children's Spec, Outreach Serv Spec, Youth Spec,* Maira Hernandez; E-mail: hernandezm@mail.peach.public.lib.ga.us; Staff 6 (MLS 2, Non-MLS 4)
Founded 1915. Pop 22,881; Circ 85,849
Jul 2010-Jun 2011 Income (Main Library and Branch(s)) $487,000, State $171,400, County $297,000, Locally Generated Income $18,500. Mats Exp $14,000
Library Holdings: CDs 580; DVDs 1,068; Bk Vols 48,080; Per Subs 25
Subject Interests: Local hist
Open Mon 9:30-7, Tues-Thurs 9:30-5:30, Fri & Sat 9:30-1:30
Friends of the Library Group
Branches: 1
BYRON PUBLIC, 105 W Church St, Byron, 31008. (Mail add: PO Box 1120, Byron, 31008-1120), SAN 338-7968. Tel: 478-956-2200. FAX: 478-956-5688. *Br Mgr,* Susan Halbedel
Library Holdings: Bk Vols 19,639
Open Tues (Winter) 10-8, Wed & Thurs 10-6, Fri & Sat 10-4; Mon-Thurs (Summer) 9-6, Fri 9-1

FRANKLIN SPRINGS

CR EMMANUEL COLLEGE LIBRARY*, 2261 W Main St, 30639. (Mail add: PO Box 69, 30639-0069), SAN 303-3805. Tel: 706-245-7226, Ext 2850. FAX: 706-245-4424. E-mail: eclibrary@ec.edu. Web Site: www.ec.edu/library. *Dir, Libr & Info Serv,* Austina Jordan; E-mail:

ajordan@ec.edu; *Asst Dir,* Deborah Millier; E-mail: dmillier@ec.edu; *Sr Libr Assoc,* Beth Cochran; E-mail: bcochran@ec.edu; Staff 3.5 (MLS 2, Non-MLS 1.5)
Founded 1935. Enrl 715; Fac 52; Highest Degree: Bachelor
Jul 2010-Jun 2011. Mats Exp $70,450, Books $44,250, Per/Ser (Incl. Access Fees) $7,500, Electronic Ref Mat (Incl. Access Fees) $18,700
Library Holdings: AV Mats 2,817; CDs 337; DVDs 15; e-books 43,098; Microforms 6,224; Bk Vols 44,062; Per Subs 99; Videos 1,096
Special Collections: Archive of Emmanuel College
Automation Activity & Vendor Info: (Cataloging) Follett Software; (Circulation) Follett Software; (OPAC) Follett Software
Database Vendor: EBSCOhost, Gale Cengage Learning, ProQuest, WT Cox
Wireless access
Partic in Christian Libr Network; Georgia Private Acad Librs Consortium (GPALS); OCLC-LVIS
Open Mon, Tues & Thurs (Winter) 7:45am-10pm, Wed 7:45-7, Fri 7:45-4, Sat 12-5, Sun 7pm-10pm; Mon-Fri (Summer) 8-4
Restriction: Open to fac, students & qualified researchers, Restricted pub use

GAINESVILLE

C BRENAU UNIVERSITY*, Trustee Library, 625 Academy St NE, 30501-3343. SAN 303-3813. Tel: 770-534-6113. FAX: 770-534-6254. Web Site: library.brenau.edu, www.brenau.edu/library. *Dir,* Marlene Giguere; Tel: 770-538-4722, E-mail: mgiguere@brenau.edu; *Coll Develop Librn,* Lisa Morgan Echols; Tel: 770-538-4723, E-mail: lmorgan@brenau.edu; *Tech Serv,* Robin Mize; Tel: 770-718-5303, E-mail: rmize@brenau.edu; Staff 9 (MLS 6, Non-MLS 3)
Founded 1878. Enrl 2,100; Fac 110; Highest Degree: Master
Library Holdings: CDs 655; DVDs 233; e-books 50,000; Music Scores 1,200; Bk Vols 80,000; Per Subs 180; Videos 1,919
Special Collections: Elson Judaica Coll; Rare Book Gallery (18th & 19th century fiction); Senator Tom Watson Library
Subject Interests: Educ, Music, Nursing
Automation Activity & Vendor Info: (Acquisitions) Ex Libris Group; (Cataloging) Ex Libris Group; (Circulation) Ex Libris Group; (OPAC) Ex Libris Group
Database Vendor: EBSCOhost, Gale Cengage Learning, LexisNexis, OCLC FirstSearch, ProQuest, Wilson - Wilson Web
Wireless access
Function: For res purposes
Publications: Library Handbook
Partic in Atlanta Regional Council for Higher Education; Lyrasis
Open Mon-Thurs 8am-10pm, Fri 8-6:30, Sat 10-6:30, Sun 1-10
Restriction: Circ limited

P HALL COUNTY LIBRARY SYSTEM, Gainesville Branch, 127 Main St NW, 30501-3699. SAN 338-8026. Tel: 770-532-3311. Circulation Tel: 770-532-3311, Ext 110. Interlibrary Loan Service Tel: 770-532-3311, Ext 128. Reference Tel: 770-532-3311, Ext 114. FAX: 770-532-4305. Web Site: www.hallcountylibrary.org. *Libr Dir,* Adrian Mixson; Tel: 770-532-3311, Ext 122, E-mail: amixson@hallcountylibrary.org; *Asst Libr Dir,* Lisa MacKinney; E-mail: lmackinney@hallcountylibrary.org; *Dir, Adult Serv,* Jeanne Hozak; E-mail: jhozak@hallcountylibrary.org; *Dir, Youth Serv,* Adrianne Junius; E-mail: ajunius@hallcountylibrary.org; Staff 59 (MLS 7, Non-MLS 52)
Founded 1997. Pop 203,894; Circ 1,005,688
Jul 2008-Jun 2009 Income $3,086,793, State $325,217, Federal $2,800, County $2,138,847, Locally Generated Income $261,115, Other $294,787. Mats Exp $323,152. Sal $2,178,053 (Prof $752,017)
Library Holdings: Bk Vols 300,449; Per Subs 200
Special Collections: James Longstreet Coll, papers
Subject Interests: Genealogy, Local hist, Spanish
Automation Activity & Vendor Info: (Cataloging) Evergreen; (Circulation) Evergreen; (ILL) OCLC; (OPAC) Evergreen
Database Vendor: 3M Library Systems, Baker & Taylor, BWI, EBSCO Auto Repair Reference, EBSCOhost, Foundation Center, Gale Cengage Learning, infoUSA, Ingram Library Services, Keystone Systems, Inc (KLAS), LearningExpress, McGraw-Hill, Newsbank, OCLC FirstSearch, ProQuest, ReferenceUSA, Standard & Poor's
Wireless access
Publications: e-link (Monthly newsletter); Friends Footnotes (Quarterly); Staff Newsletter (Monthly)
Partic in GALILEO (Georgia Library Learning Online); Lyrasis; OCLC Online Computer Library Center, Inc; PINES (Public Information Network for Electronic Services)
Special Services for the Deaf - ADA equip; Am sign lang & deaf culture; Assisted listening device; Assistive tech; Closed caption videos; Described encaptioned media prog; TDD equip
Special Services for the Blind - Accessible computers; Assistive/Adapted tech devices, equip & products; Audio mat; BiFolkal kits; Bks & mags in Braille, on rec, tape & cassette; Bks available with recordings; Bks on cassette; Bks on CD; Cassette playback machines; Cassettes; Compressed speech equip; Computer access aids; Computer with voice synthesizer for visually impaired persons; Copier with enlargement capabilities; Digital talking bk; Duplicating spec requests; Extensive large print coll; Info on spec aids & appliances; Large print bks; Large screen computer & software; Lending of low vision aids; Low vision equip; Machine repair; Magnifiers; Micro-computer access & training; Networked computers with assistive software; Newsletter (in large print, Braille or on cassette); PC for handicapped; Ref serv; Screen enlargement software for people with visual disabilities; Talking bks; Talking bks & player equip; Text reader; Volunteer serv
Open Mon & Thurs 12-8, Tues & Wed 9-6, Fri 9-5, Sat 9-1
Friends of the Library Group
Branches: 3
BLACKSHEAR PLACE, 2927 Atlanta Hwy, 30507, SAN 370-9264. Tel: 770-532-3311, Ext 151. FAX: 770-287-3653. *Br Mgr,* Veronica Gomez; E-mail: vgomez@hallcountylibrary.org; Staff 8.5 (Non-MLS 8.5)
Circ 191,384
Library Holdings: Bk Vols 66,661; Per Subs 97
Open Mon & Thurs 12-8, Tues & Wed 9-6, Fri 9-5
Friends of the Library Group
MURRAYVILLE BRANCH, 4796 Thompson Bridge Rd, Murrayville, 30507, SAN 374-7352. Tel: 770-532-3311, Ext 171. FAX: 770-503-9298. *Mgr,* Kathy Evans; E-mail: kevans@hallcountylibrary.org; Staff 3 (Non-MLS 3)
Circ 49,613
Library Holdings: Bk Vols 16,796; Per Subs 12
Open Mon & Thurs 12-8 Tues & Wed 9-6, Fri 9-5
Friends of the Library Group
SPOUT SPRINGS BRANCH, 6488 Spout Springs Rd, Flowery Branch, 30542. Tel: 770-532-3311, Ext 191. FAX: 770-965-9501. *Br Mgr,* Angela Glowcheski; Staff 11.5 (MLS 1, Non-MLS 10.5)
Library Holdings: Bk Vols 82,322; Per Subs 38
Open Mon & Thurs 12-8, Tues & Wed 9-6, Fri 9-5

M NORTHEAST GEORGIA HEALTH SYSTEM*, Health Sciences Library, 743 Spring St NE, 30501-3899. SAN 320-9393. Tel: 770-538-7630. FAX: 770-535-3463. E-mail: library@nghs.com. *Outreach Med Librn,* Mandy Bayer; Staff 1 (MLS 1)
Founded 1963
Library Holdings: Bk Titles 500; Per Subs 20
Subject Interests: Allied health, Consumer health, Med, Nursing
Partic in Southeastern Regional Med Libr Program
Open Mon-Fri 8-4:30

GARDEN CITY

S GEORGIA DEPARTMENT OF CORRECTIONS, OFFICE OF LIBRARY SERVICES*, Coastal State Prison, 200 Gulfstream Rd, 31418. (Mail add: PO Box 7150, 31418-7150). Tel: 912 965 6330. FAX: 912 966 6799. Web Site: www.dcor.state.ga.us. *Librn,* Karla Jackson
Library Holdings: Bk Vols 15,000; Per Subs 41
Special Collections: Law Coll
Database Vendor: Westlaw
Open Mon-Thurs 7-3

GLENNVILLE

S GEORGIA DEPARTMENT OF CORRECTIONS, OFFICE OF LIBRARY SERVICES*, Smith State Prison, 9676 Hwy 301 N, 30427. (Mail add: PO Box 726, 30427-0726). Tel: 912-654-5090. FAX: 912-654-5131. Web Site: www.dcor.state.ga.us. *Librn,* Julia Steele
Library Holdings: AV Mats 150; Bk Vols 11,000; Per Subs 40; Talking Bks 10; Videos 300
Special Collections: Law Coll
Database Vendor: LexisNexis
Open Tues & Thurs 7:30am-8pm, Wed 7:30am-11:30am

GLYNCO

G FEDERAL LAW ENFORCEMENT TRAINING CENTER LIBRARY*, Bldg 262, 1131 Chapel Crossing Rd, 31524. SAN 303-3848. Tel: 912-267-2320. *Librn,* Shirley Holcomb; *Librn,* Sharon Tafoya; Staff 3 (MLS 1, Non-MLS 2)
Founded 1975
Library Holdings: Bk Titles 4,000; Bk Vols 40,000
Automation Activity & Vendor Info: (Cataloging) Follett Software
Restriction: Open to students, fac & staff

GRIFFIN

P FLINT RIVER REGIONAL LIBRARY*, 800 Memorial Dr, 30223. SAN 338-8174. Tel: 770-412-4770. Web Site: doc.frrls.net. *Exec Dir,* Carrie C Zeiger; *Head, Tech,* Ceabron D Williams; *Acq Librn,* Natalie Marshall; *Ch,* Marsha Parham; *ILL Librn,* Ann Turner; *Local Hist Librn,* Evans Millican; *Coordr, Pub Serv,* James D Tingen; *Coordr, Tech Serv,* Vicki W Marshall; Staff 14 (MLS 8, Non-MLS 6)

Founded 1949. Pop 257,006; Circ 1,242,562
Library Holdings: Audiobooks 17,746; DVDs 8,958; Bk Vols 506,046; Videos 5,090
Subject Interests: County hist, State hist
Automation Activity & Vendor Info: (Acquisitions) Evergreen; (Cataloging) Evergreen; (Circulation) Evergreen; (OPAC) Evergreen
Wireless access
Function: Adult bk club, Bks on CD, Children's prog, ILL available
Partic in Georgia Online Database; Lyrasis; PINES (Public Information Network for Electronic Services)
Open Mon & Thurs 9-9, Tues, Wed, Fri & Sat 9-6
Branches: 8
BARNESVILLE-LAMAR COUNTY LIBRARY, 401 Thomaston St, Barnesville, 30204, SAN 338-8239. Tel: 770-358-3270. *Br Supvr,* Kelly Hughes
Circ 48,430
Library Holdings: Audiobooks 768; DVDs 636; Bk Vols 39,119; Videos 1,597
Subject Interests: County hist, State hist
Function: ILL available
Open Mon 10-8, Tues, Thurs & Fri 10-5, Wed 1-8, Sat 10-1
Friends of the Library Group
J JOEL EDWARDS PUBLIC LIBRARY, 7077 Hwy 19 S, Zebulon, 30295. (Mail add: PO Box 574, Zebulon, 30295), SAN 338-8573. Tel: 770-567-2014. *Br Supvr,* Pat Robertson
Circ 24,687
Library Holdings: Bk Vols 22,851
Subject Interests: State hist
Open Mon, Wed & Fri 11-5, Tues & Thurs 11-8, Sat 11-3
FAYETTE COUNTY PUBLIC LIBRARY, 1821 Heritage Pkwy, Fayetteville, 30214, SAN 338-8441. Tel: 770-461-8841. Web Site: www.fayettecountyga.gov. *Br Supvr,* Christeen Snell
Circ 354,033
Library Holdings: Audiobooks 7,850; DVDs 2,172; Bk Vols 127,517; Videos 1,941
Special Collections: Margaret Mitchell Coll
Subject Interests: State hist
Open Mon-Thurs 9-9, Fri & Sat 9-6
Friends of the Library Group
GRIFFIN-SPALDING COUNTY LIBRARY, 800 Memorial Dr, 30223, SAN 338-8352. Tel: 770-412-4770. *Exec Dir,* Carrie C Zeiger; *Coordr, Pub Serv,* James D Tingen
Circ 151,098
Library Holdings: Audiobooks 2,098; DVDs 636; Bk Vols 102,509; Videos 1,597
Subject Interests: County hist, State hist
Open Mon & Thurs 9-9, Tues, Wed, Fri & Sat 9-6
JACKSON-BUTTS COUNTY PUBLIC LIBRARY, 436 E College St, Jackson, 30233, SAN 338-8387. Tel: 770-775-7524. *Br Supvr,* Donn V Taylor
Circ 59,836
Library Holdings: Audiobooks 748; DVDs 340; Bk Vols 44,746
Subject Interests: County hist, State hist
Open Mon-Thurs 9-8, Fri & Sat 9-6
Friends of the Library Group
MONROE COUNTY LIBRARY, 62 W Main St, Forsyth, 31029, SAN 338-8476. Tel: 478-994-7025. *Br Supvr,* Marilyn Smith
Circ 43,510
Library Holdings: Audiobooks 594; DVDs 138; Bk Vols 44,703; Videos 65
Subject Interests: County hist, State hist
Open Mon & Tues 9-8, Wed & Thurs 9-6, Fri 9-5, Sat 9-3
Friends of the Library Group
PEACHTREE CITY LIBRARY, 201 Willowbend Rd, Peachtree City, 30269, SAN 338-8565. Tel: 770-631-2520. Web Site: www.peachtree-city.org/library. *Br Supvr,* Jill Prouty
Founded 1973. Circ 478,325
Library Holdings: Audiobooks 5,324; DVDs 6,247; Bk Vols 98,457; Videos 1,141
Subject Interests: Ga
Friends of the Library Group
TYRONE PUBLIC LIBRARY, 143 Commerce Dr, Tyrone, 30290, SAN 338-859X. Tel: 770-487-1565. *Br Coordr,* Julie Digby
Circ 82,643
Library Holdings: Audiobooks 342; DVDs 393; Bk Vols 26,144; Videos 203

J GRIFFIN TECHNICAL COLLEGE LIBRARY*, 501 Varsity Rd, 30223. Tel: 770-412-4755. FAX: 770-229-3006. E-mail: library@sctech.edu. Web Site: library.griffintech.edu. *Dir, Libr & Media,* Kathleen Williams; E-mail: kate.williams@sctech.edu; *Librn,* Sherry Brooks; E-mail: sbrooks@sctech.edu; *Ser,* Jane Busby; Staff 3 (MLS 1, Non-MLS 2)
Founded 1963. Enrl 2,450
Library Holdings: e-books 25,000; Bk Titles 17,518; Bk Vols 18,010; Per Subs 135
Automation Activity & Vendor Info: (Cataloging) Surpass; (Circulation) Surpass; (OPAC) Surpass
Wireless access
Partic in GALILEO (Georgia Library Learning Online)
Open Mon-Thurs 7:30am-9pm, Fri 7:30-4:30, Sat 8:30-1:30

C UNIVERSITY OF GEORGIA LIBRARIES*, Griffin Campus, 1109 Experiment St, 30223-1797. SAN 303-3759. Tel: 770-228-7238. FAX: 770-229-3213. Web Site: www.griffin.uga.edu. *Librn,* Regina W Cannon; E-mail: rwcannon@uga.edu; Staff 1 (MLS 1)
Founded 1888
Library Holdings: Bk Vols 10,000; Per Subs 300
Subject Interests: Agr
Function: ILL available
Partic in Association of Southeastern Research Libraries; Atlanta Regional Council for Higher Education; Center for Research Libraries; OCLC Online Computer Library Center, Inc
Open Mon-Fri 8-5
Restriction: Non-circulating to the pub

GROVETOWN

S GEORGIA DEPARTMENT OF CORRECTIONS, OFFICE OF LIBRARY SERVICES*, Augusta State Medical Prison, 3001 Gordon Hwy, 30813. Tel: 706-855-4882. FAX: 706-855-4924. Web Site: www.dcor.state.ga.us. *Librn,* Saundra Hood
Library Holdings: Audiobooks 127; Bks on Deafness & Sign Lang 2; Bk Vols 21,000; Per Subs 27; Talking Bks 96
Special Collections: Law Coll
Database Vendor: LexisNexis
Open Mon-Thurs 7:45-4, Fri 7:45-3

HARDWICK

GEORGIA DEPARTMENT OF CORRECTIONS, OFFICE OF LIBRARY SERVICES
S BALDWIN STATE PRISON*, Laying Farm Rd, 31034. (Mail add: PO Box 218, 31034-0218). Tel: 478-445-4175. FAX: 478-453-6507. Web Site: www.dcor.state.ga.us. *Librn,* Brandy Bell
Library Holdings: Bk Vols 7,000; Per Subs 15
Special Collections: Law Coll
Database Vendor: LexisNexis
Open Mon-Fri 8-10:30 & 1-3:30
S RIVERS STATE PRISON*, Rivers Lane, 31034. (Mail add: PO Box 1500, 31034-1500). Tel: 478-445-3245. FAX: 478-445-1391. Web Site: www.dcor.state.ga.us.
Library Holdings: Bk Vols 5,450; Per Subs 20
Special Collections: Law Coll
Database Vendor: LexisNexis
Open Mon 8:30-10:30 & 12:30-3, Tues & Thurs 12:30-3:30 & 5-8, Wed & Fri 8:30-10:30

HARTWELL

P HART COUNTY LIBRARY*, 150 Benson St, 30643. SAN 303-3864. Tel: 706-376-4655. FAX: 706-376-1157. E-mail: info@hartcountylibrary.com. Web Site: www.hartcountylibrary.com. *Dir,* Richard Sanders; *Librn,* Pam Bagby; *Circ,* Tharen Vass; Staff 5 (MLS 2, Non-MLS 3)
Founded 1936. Pop 21,500; Circ 162,000
Library Holdings: Bk Vols 52,000; Per Subs 32
Special Collections: History of Hart County, A-tapes. Oral History
Open Mon & Thurs 9-8, Tues, Wed & Fri 9-6, Sat 9-1
Friends of the Library Group

HAWKINSVILLE

S GEORGIA DEPARTMENT OF CORRECTIONS, OFFICE OF LIBRARY SERVICES*, Pulaski State Prison, Rte 2, Upper River Rd, 31036. (Mail add: PO Box 839, 31036-0839). Tel: 478-783-6102. FAX: 478-783-6008. Web Site: www.dcor.state.ga.us. *Librn,* Lychelle Allen
Library Holdings: Bk Vols 3,500; Per Subs 25; Talking Bks 150; Videos 200
Special Collections: Law Coll
Database Vendor: LexisNexis
Open Mon 1:30-8, Tues-Thurs 8:30-4

HELENA

S GEORGIA DEPARTMENT OF CORRECTIONS, OFFICE OF LIBRARY SERVICES*, Telfair State Prison, 210 Longbridge Rd, 31037. (Mail add: PO Box 549, 31037-0549). Tel: 229-868-7721. FAX: 229-868-6509. Web Site: www.dcor.state.ga.us. *Actg Librn,* Terry Green
Library Holdings: Bk Vols 3,000
Special Collections: Law Coll
Database Vendor: LexisNexis

HINESVILLE

J SAVANNAH TECHNICAL COLLEGE*, Liberty County Campus Library, 100 Technology Dr, 31313. Tel: 912-408-3024, Ext 6017. FAX: 912-408-3038. Web Site: www.savannahtech.edu. *Dir, Libr & Info Serv,* James Burch; Tel: 912-443-5874, E-mail: jburch@savannahtech.edu
Founded 1989. Highest Degree: Associate
Library Holdings: e-books 50,000; e-journals 15,000; Bk Vols 3,000; Per Subs 30
Automation Activity & Vendor Info: (Cataloging) TLC (The Library Corporation); (Circulation) TLC (The Library Corporation); (OPAC) TLC (The Library Corporation)
Wireless access
Partic in GALILEO (Georgia Library Learning Online)
Open Mon-Thurs 7:30am-9pm, Fri 7:30-4, Sat 9-1

HOMERVILLE

S HUXFORD GENEALOGICAL SOCIETY INC*, Huxford-Spear Genealogical Library, 20 S College St, 31634. (Mail add: PO Box 595, 31634-0595), SAN 375-7730. Tel: 912-487-2310. FAX: 912-487-3881. E-mail: huxford.spearlibrary@windstream.net, huxford@windstream.net. Web Site: huxford.com. *Libr Dir,* Cathy Wells; Staff 2 (Non-MLS 2)
Founded 1972
Library Holdings: Bk Titles 4,000; Per Subs 1,500
Wireless access
Publications: Pioneers of Wiregrass Georgia (Quarterly)
Open Mon-Fri 9-12 & 1-5

JACKSON

S GEORGIA DEPARTMENT OF CORRECTIONS, OFFICE OF LIBRARY SERVICES*, Georgia Diagnostic & Classification State Prison, Hwy 36 W, 30233. (Mail add: PO Box 3877, 30233-0078). Tel: 770-504-2000. FAX: 770-504-2006. Web Site: www.dcor.state.ga.us. *Librn,* John Young; Tel: 770-504-2125
Library Holdings: Bk Vols 3,000
Special Collections: Law Coll
Database Vendor: LexisNexis

JESUP

J ALTAMAHA TECHNICAL COLLEGE LIBRARY*, 1777 W Cherry St, 31545. Tel: 912-427-1929. FAX: 912-427-1929. Web Site: www.altamahatech.edu/library. *Dir,* Ben Bryson; E-mail: bbryson@altamahatech.edu; Staff 2 (MLS 1, Non-MLS 1)
Highest Degree: Associate
Library Holdings: CDs 25; Bk Vols 9,000; Per Subs 115
Automation Activity & Vendor Info: (Cataloging) TLC (The Library Corporation); (Circulation) TLC (The Library Corporation); (OPAC) TLC (The Library Corporation)
Wireless access
Partic in GALILEO (Georgia Library Learning Online)
Open Mon-Thurs 8-7:30, Fri 8-3

P THREE RIVERS REGIONAL LIBRARY SYSTEM*, Wayne County Library, 759 Sunset Blvd, 31545-4409. SAN 338-4969. Tel: 912-427-2500. FAX: 912-427-0071. *Mgr,* Debbie Turner; E-mail: dturner@trrl.org
Subject Interests: Ga, Gardening, Local hist
Member Libraries: Taylor County Public Library
Open Mon, Tues & Thurs 10-8, Wed & Fri 10-6, Sat 10-2
Friends of the Library Group
Branches: 7
BRANTLEY COUNTY LIBRARY, 133 E Cleveland St, Nahunta, 31553-9470. (Mail add: PO Box 1090, Nahunta, 31553-1090), SAN 338-4837. Tel: 912-462-5454. FAX: 912-462-5329. *Mgr,* Kathy Moody; E-mail: kmoody@trrl.org
Founded 1980
Subject Interests: Local hist
Open Mon-Fri 8:30-5
Friends of the Library Group
CAMDEN COUNTY LIBRARY, 1410 Hwy 40 E, Kingsland, 31548-9380, SAN 338-487X. Tel: 912-729-2040, 912-729-3741. FAX: 912-729-2039. E-mail: camdenlibrary@gmail.com. *Mgr,* Paul Quinn
Open Mon & Wed 10-6, Tues & Thurs 10-8, Fri & Sat 10-5
Friends of the Library Group
CHARLTON COUNTY LIBRARY, 701 Indian Trail, Folkston, 31537, SAN 338-4845. Tel: 912-496-2041. FAX: 912-496-1144. *Mgr,* Barbara Parker; E-mail: bparker@trrl.org
Subject Interests: Local hist
Open Mon-Thurs 10-6, Fri 10-2
IDA HILTON PUBLIC LIBRARY, 1105 North Way, Darien, 31305. (Mail add: PO Box 1227, Darien, 31305-1227), SAN 329-0077. Tel: 912-437-2124. FAX: 912-437-5113. *Libr Mgr,* Rita Wright; E-mail: rwright@trrl.org
Special Collections: Fanny Kemble Coll; Gullah Coll; Sapelo Island Coll
Subject Interests: Genealogy
Open Tues & Thurs 10-7, Wed & Fri 10-4
Friends of the Library Group
HOG HAMMOCK COMMUNITY LIBRARY, 1023 Hillery Ln, Sapelo Island, 31327. (Mail add: PO Box 69, Sapelo Island, 31327-0006). Tel: 912-485-2186, 912-485-2215. FAX: 912-485-2263. *Mgr,* Michele Johnson; E-mail: mjohnson@trrl.org
Library Holdings: Bk Vols 1,000
Open Tues, Wed & Thurs 7pm-8:30pm
LONG COUNTY LIBRARY, 270 S Main St, Ludowici, 31316. (Mail add: PO Box 640, Ludowici, 31316-0640), SAN 338-490X. Tel: 912-545-2521. FAX: 912-545-8887. *Mgr,* Tammy Goober; E-mail: tgoober@trrl.org
Subject Interests: Local hist
Open Mon, Thurs & Fri 10-8, Tues & Sat 10-6, Wed 10-5
ST MARY'S LIBRARY, 100 Herb Bauer Dr, Saint Marys, 31558-3300, SAN 338-4934. Tel: 912-882-4800. FAX: 912-882-2453. *Mgr,* Judy Armantrout; E-mail: jarmantrout@trrl.org
Open Mon-Thurs 10-8, Fri 10-5, Sat 10-1

JONESBORO

P CLAYTON COUNTY LIBRARY SYSTEM*, 865 Battlecreek Rd, 30236. SAN 338-8417. Tel: 770-473-3850. FAX: 770-473-3858. E-mail: branchhq@claytonpl.org. Web Site: www.claytonpl.org. *Dir, Libr Serv,* Rosalind Lett; *Managing Librn,* Veleda Cofield; *Asst Dir, Br Serv,* Flora Hazelton; *Asst Dir, Cent Libr Serv, Asst Dir, Commun Libr Serv,* Cynthia Hunter; *Asst Dir, Info Tech,* Lewis Lucas; *Asst Dir, Tech Serv,* Yvonne Carmicheal; *Asst Dir, Youth Serv,* Janice Arcuria; *Ch Serv, YA Serv, Youth Serv,* Bea Mengel; Staff 62 (MLS 13, Non-MLS 49)
Founded 1941. Pop 287,677; Circ 680,049
Jul 2006-Jun 2007 Income (Main Library and Branch(s)) $3,597,466, State $667,926, Federal $50,645, County $2,860,895, Other $18,000. Mats Exp $608,739, Books $462,231, AV Mat $112,167, Electronic Ref Mat (Incl. Access Fees) $34,341. Sal $2,011,081
Library Holdings: AV Mats 13,128; CDs 1,957; Bk Vols 439,338; Per Subs 184
Special Collections: Clayton County History
Subject Interests: Ga
Automation Activity & Vendor Info: (Acquisitions) Evergreen; (Cataloging) Evergreen; (Circulation) Evergreen; (OPAC) Evergreen
Database Vendor: Dun & Bradstreet, Gale Cengage Learning, LearningExpress, Mergent Online, Newsbank
Wireless access
Function: Chess club, Children's prog, Citizenship assistance, Computers for patron use, Copy machines, E-Reserves, Electronic databases & coll, Family literacy, Homework prog, ILL available, Magnifiers for reading, Photocopying/Printing, Preschool outreach, Prog for adults, Prog for children & young adult, Pub access computers, Spoken cassettes & CDs, Summer reading prog, Tax forms, Teen prog, VHS videos
Publications: Monthly Calendar of Events
Partic in PINES (Public Information Network for Electronic Services)
Special Services for the Blind - Large print bks
Open Mon-Thurs 9-9, Fri 9-6, Sat 9-5, Sun (Sept-May) 1:30-5:30
Friends of the Library Group
Branches: 5
FOREST PARK BRANCH, 696 Main St, Forest Park, 30297, SAN 338-8298. Tel: 404-366-0850. FAX: 404-366-0884. *Br Mgr,* Lydia Bigard
Library Holdings: AV Mats 1,470; Bk Vols 57,865; Per Subs 55
Open Mon & Tues 9-9, Wed-Fri 9-6, Sat 9-5
Friends of the Library Group
JONESBORO BRANCH, 124 Smith St, 30236, SAN 328-8897. Tel: 770-478-7120. FAX: 770-473-3846. *Br Mgr,* Martha Caldwell
Library Holdings: AV Mats 1,582; Bk Vols 61,475; Per Subs 64
Open Mon & Tues 9-9, Wed-Fri 9-6, Sat 9-5
LOVEJOY, 1721 McDonough Rd, Hampton, 30228. Tel: 770-472-8129. FAX: 770-472-8136. *Br Mgr,* Amelia McBride
Library Holdings: AV Mats 1,441; Bk Vols 32,006; Per Subs 68
Open Mon & Tues 9-9, Wed-Fri 9-6, Sat 9-5
Friends of the Library Group
MORROW BRANCH, 6225 Maddox Rd, Morrow, 30260, SAN 338-8506. Tel: 404-366-7749. FAX: 404-363-4569. *Br Mgr,* June Shapiro
Library Holdings: AV Mats 2,223; Bk Vols 67,540; Per Subs 58
Open Mon & Tues 9-9, Wed-Fri 9-6, Sat 9-5
RIVERDALE BRANCH, 420 Valley Hill Rd, Riverdale, 30274, SAN 324-086X. Tel: 770-472-8100. FAX: 770-472-8106. *Br Mgr,* Vivian Chandler
Library Holdings: AV Mats 2,513; Bk Vols 77,679; Per Subs 72
Open Mon & Tues 9-9, Wed-Fri 9-6, Sat 9-5
Friends of the Library Group

KENNESAW

C KENNESAW STATE UNIVERSITY*, Horace W Sturgis Library, 1000 Chastain Rd, 30144. SAN 303-3937. Tel: 770-423-6186. FAX: 770-423-6185. Web Site: www.kennesaw.edu/library/. *Asst VPres, Libr Serv,* Dr David Evans; Tel: 770-423-6194, E-mail: devans@kennesaw.edu; *Libr Dir,* Betty Childres; Tel: 770-423-6199, E-mail: bchildre@kennesaw.edu; *Assoc Libr Dir,* Alan Lebish; Tel: 770-423-6192, E-mail: alebish@kennesaw.edu; *Dir, Digital Commons/Copyright Mgt,* Jon Hansen; Tel: 770-423-6248, E-mail: jhansen@kennesaw.edu; *Asst Dir, Access Serv,* Martha Henry-Croom; Tel: 770-423-6511, E-mail: mcroom@kennesaw.edu; *Asst Dir, Tech Serv,* Barbara Milam; Tel: 770-423-6259, Fax: 770-423-6727, E-mail: bmilam@kennesaw.edu; *Asst Dir, Virtual Res,* Mary Platt; Tel: 770-423-6197, E-mail: mplatt@kennesaw.edu; *Librn/Head, Ref Coll Develop,* Dewi Wilson; Tel: 770-423-6661, E-mail: dwilson@kennesaw.edu; *Librn/ Head, Ser & Acq,* Olga Russov; Tel: 770-423-6189, E-mail: orussov@kennesaw.edu; *Librn/Cat,* Sandra Barclay; Tel: 770-423-4445, E-mail: sbarclay@kennesaw.edu; *Librn/Cat,* Helene Falkinburg; Tel: 770-423-6660, E-mail: hfalkinb@kennesaw.edu; *Govt Doc Librn,* Chris Sharp; Tel: 770-423-6191, E-mail: csharp@kennesaw.edu; *Librn/Grad Libr Instruction,* Cheryl Stiles; Tel: 770-423-6003, E-mail: cstiles@kennesaw.edu; *Librn, Libr Instruction/Outreach,* Rita Spisak; Tel: 770-423-6188, E-mail: rspisak@kennesaw.edu; *Music Librn,* Steve Burton; Tel: 770-499-3167, E-mail: sburton@kennesaw.edu; *Librn, Virtual Serv,* Johnny Woods; Tel: 678-797-2560, E-mail: jwoods16@kennesaw.edu; *Undergrad Libr Instruction,* Ashley Dupuy; Tel: 770-499-3590, E-mail: adupuy@kennesaw.edu; Staff 19 (MLS 19)
Founded 1963. Enrl 23; Fac 1,400; Highest Degree: Doctorate
Jul 2010-Jun 2011. Mats Exp $981,000, Books $200,000, Per/Ser (Incl. Access Fees) $31,000, Electronic Ref Mat (Incl. Access Fees) $750,000. Sal Prof $42,500
Library Holdings: CDs 1,799; DVDs 200; e-books 150,000; e-journals 50,000; Microforms 1,400,000; Music Scores 3,863; Bk Titles 428,492; Bk Vols 630,614; Per Subs 98
Special Collections: Difazio Children's Literature Coll; Robert Stirk Railroad Coll; Teen Literature Coll. US Document Depository
Automation Activity & Vendor Info: (Acquisitions) Ex Libris Group; (Cataloging) Ex Libris Group; (Circulation) Ex Libris Group; (Course Reserve) Ex Libris Group; (ILL) OCLC; (OPAC) Ex Libris Group; (Serials) Ex Libris Group
Database Vendor: ABC-CLIO, ACM (Association for Computing Machinery), Alexander Street Press, American Chemical Society, American Mathematical Society, American Psychological Association (APA), Annual Reviews, ARTstor, Bowker, Cambridge Scientific Abstracts, CQ Press, CredoReference, Dialog, Dun & Bradstreet, EBSCOhost, Emerald, infoUSA, ISI Web of Knowledge, JSTOR, LexisNexis, Mergent Online, Newsbank, OCLC FirstSearch, OCLC WorldShare Interlibrary Loan, OVID Technologies, Oxford Online, Project MUSE, ProQuest, PubMed, RefWorks, Sage, ScienceDirect, Scopus
Wireless access
Partic in Galileo/GIL; Lyrasis
Open Mon-Thurs 7am-Midnight, Fri 7am-8pm, Sat 8-6, Sun 1-10
Friends of the Library Group

S NATIONAL PARK SERVICE, Kennesaw Mountain National Battlefield Park Library, 900 Kennesaw Mountain Dr, 30152. SAN 303-3953. Tel: 770-427-4686. FAX: 770-528-8398. Web Site: www.nps.gov/kemo. *Superintendent,* Nancy Walter
Founded 1935
Library Holdings: Bk Titles 1,000
Special Collections: Atlanta Campaign-1864
Function: Res libr
Restriction: Non-circulating

LA GRANGE

C LA GRANGE COLLEGE*, William & Evelyn Banks Library, 601 Broad St, 30240-2999. SAN 338-8743. Tel: 706-880-8312. FAX: 706-880-8040. Web Site: www.lagrange.edu/library. *Dir,* Loren L Pinkerman; Tel: 706-880-8234, E-mail: lpinkerman@lagrange.edu; *Acq, Ser,* David Wiggins; Tel: 706-880-8233; *Circ,* Lisa Morgan; Tel: 706-880-8012; *Electronic Res,* Mary Lou Dabbs; Tel: 706-880-8027; *Pub Serv, Tech Serv,* Charlene Baxter; Tel: 706-880-8311; *Ref,* Dr Arthur Robinson; Tel: 706-880-8289, E-mail: arobinson@lagrange.edu. Subject Specialists: *Hist, Music, Polit sci,* Loren L Pinkerman; Staff 7 (MLS 4, Non-MLS 3)
Founded 1836. Enrl 1,100; Fac 75; Highest Degree: Master
Library Holdings: AV Mats 7,299; e-books 110,410; Electronic Media & Resources 27; Bk Vols 119,791; Per Subs 704
Automation Activity & Vendor Info: (Cataloging) SirsiDynix; (Circulation) SirsiDynix; (ILL) OCLC; (OPAC) SirsiDynix
Wireless access
Partic in OCLC Online Computer Library Center, Inc
Open Mon-Thurs 8am-11pm, Fri 8-5, Sat 1-5, Sun 2-10
Friends of the Library Group

P TROUP-HARRIS REGIONAL LIBRARY SYSTEM*, La Grange Memorial Library, 115 Alford St, 30240-3041. SAN 338-8808. Tel: 706-882-7784. FAX: 706-883-7342. Web Site: www.thrl.org. *Dir,* Keith Schuermann; *Head, Tech Serv,* Ruth Elaine Rocap; Tel: 706-882-7784, Ext 17, E-mail: rrocap@thclibrary.net; *Ch Serv,* Patricia Gay; Tel: 706-882-7784, Ext 21, E-mail: pgay@thclibrary.net; *Pub Serv,* Pamela Huff; Tel: 706-882-7784, Ext 32, E-mail: phuff@thclibrary.net; Staff 5 (MLS 4, Non-MLS 1)
Founded 1926. Pop 95,000
Jul 2008-Jun 2009 Income (Main Library and Branch(s)) $1,299,579, State $419,534, City $40,000, Federal $1,255, County $733,966, Locally Generated Income $88,370, Other $16,454. Mats Exp $99,787, Books $90,590, Per/Ser (Incl. Access Fees) $4,237, Micro $500, AV Mat $1,760, Electronic Ref Mat (Incl. Access Fees) $2,700. Sal $646,682 (Prof $297,156)
Library Holdings: AV Mats 2,943; High Interest/Low Vocabulary Bk Vols 375; Bk Titles 183,191; Per Subs 158; Talking Bks 1,389
Special Collections: Historic Photograph Coll Online; Troup County Marriage & Deed Records Online. Oral History
Subject Interests: Ga, Spanish (Lang)
Automation Activity & Vendor Info: (Cataloging) OCLC; (Circulation) Evergreen; (ILL) OCLC; (OPAC) Evergreen
Database Vendor: Agricola, Baker & Taylor, Brodart, BWI, Dun & Bradstreet, EBSCOhost, Facts on File, Newsbank, OCLC FirstSearch, OCLC WebJunction, OCLC WorldShare Interlibrary Loan, Overdrive, Inc, ProQuest, ValueLine, WebMD
Wireless access
Function: Accelerated reader prog, Adult bk club, Audio & video playback equip for onsite use, Audiobks via web, BA reader (adult literacy), Bilingual assistance for Spanish patrons, Bk club(s), Bks on cassette, Bks on CD, Children's prog, Computers for patron use, Copy machines, Digital talking bks, Distance learning, E-Reserves, Electronic databases & coll, Free DVD rentals, Handicapped accessible, ILL available, Music CDs, Notary serv, Online cat, Online searches, OverDrive digital audio bks, Photocopying/Printing, Prog for adults, Prog for children & young adult, Pub access computers, Ref serv available, Spoken cassettes & CDs, Spoken cassettes & DVDs, Story hour, Summer reading prog, Tax forms, Teen prog, Telephone ref, VHS videos, Web-catalog, Wheelchair accessible
Publications: Friends of the LaGrange Memorial Library (Newsletter)
Partic in Georgia Online Database
Open Mon & Tues 9-8, Wed-Fri 9-7, Sat 10-5
Friends of the Library Group
Branches: 3
HARRIS COUNTY PUBLIC LIBRARY, 138 N College St, Hamilton, 31811-6031. (Mail add: PO Box 266, Hamilton, 31811-0266), SAN 338-8867. Tel: 706-628-4685. FAX: 706-628-4685. *Br Mgr,* Debbie Marino; E-mail: dmarino@thrl.org; *Asst Br Mgr,* Tonya Williams; Staff 4 (Non-MLS 4)
Founded 1992. Pop 36,000; Circ 63,000
Jul 2012-Jun 2013 Income $212,000. Mats Exp $13,438, Books $10,387, Per/Ser (Incl. Access Fees) $2,200, AV Mat $851. Sal $130,000
Library Holdings: AV Mats 3,200; Bk Titles 27,000; Per Subs 45; Talking Bks 415
Function: Distance learning, ILL available, Online searches, Photocopying/Printing, Satellite serv, Summer reading prog
Open Mon-Wed & Fri 10-6, Thurs 10-8, Sat 10-2
HOGANSVILLE PUBLIC LIBRARY, 600 E Main St, Hogansville, 30230, SAN 338-8891. Tel: 706-637-6230. *Br Mgr,* Pat Guida; Staff 2 (Non-MLS 2)
Founded 1991. Pop 5,000; Circ 12,955
Jul 2008-Jun 2009 Income $79,688, State $3,417, County $76,271. Mats Exp $11,067. Sal $38,638
Library Holdings: AV Mats 1,127; Bk Titles 16,139; Per Subs 40; Talking Bks 240
Function: Handicapped accessible, ILL available, Online searches, Photocopying/Printing, Summer reading prog
Open Mon-Wed & Fri 2-7, Thurs 11-7, Sat 9-12
WILLIAMS MEMORIAL LIBRARY, 47 Mountain Hill Rd, Fortson, 31808. Tel: 706-660-8796. FAX: 706-660-8796. *Mgr,* Debbie Marino; E-mail: dmarino@thclibrary.net
Founded 2004. Pop 5,000; Circ 5,834
Library Holdings: CDs 51; DVDs 161; Bk Vols 6,183; Per Subs 17; Talking Bks 136; Videos 320
Open Mon-Thurs 2-6
Bookmobiles: 1

LAFAYETTE

P CHEROKEE REGIONAL LIBRARY SYSTEM*, La Fayette-Walker County Public Library, 305 S Duke St, 30728-2936. SAN 338-8980. Tel: 706-638-2992. Interlibrary Loan Service Tel: 706-638-2064. Administration Tel: 706-638-8312. Automation Services Tel: 706-638-7557. FAX: 706-638-3979. Administration FAX: 706-638-4028. Web Site:

www.chrl.org. *Asst Dir,* Lecia Eubanks; E-mail: leubanks@chrl.org; *Mgr,* Valinda Oliver; E-mail: loliver@chrl.org; *Bus & Human Res Mgr,* Misty Reyes; E-mail: mreyes@chrl.org; *Acq,* Gayla Brewer; E-mail: gbrewer@chrl.org; *Genealogy Serv,* Betty Johnson; Tel: 706-638-4912, E-mail: bjohnson@chrl.org; Staff 8 (MLS 3, Non-MLS 5)
Founded 1938. Pop 77,757; Circ 84,532
Library Holdings: CDs 339; Bk Vols 67,328; Per Subs 18; Talking Bks 1,244; Videos 1,662
Special Collections: Local History of Dade & Walker Counties (Georgia History), bk, micro, CD
Subject Interests: Ga, Genealogy, Local hist
Automation Activity & Vendor Info: (Acquisitions) SirsiDynix; (Cataloging) SirsiDynix; (Circulation) SirsiDynix; (ILL) SirsiDynix; (OPAC) SirsiDynix; (Serials) SirsiDynix
Function: Doc delivery serv, ILL available, Outside serv via phone, mail, e-mail & web, Photocopying/Printing, Ref serv available, Telephone ref
Partic in PINES (Public Information Network for Electronic Services)
Special Services for the Blind - Closed circuit TV; Computer with voice synthesizer for visually impaired persons; Descriptive video serv (DVS); Magnifiers; Soundproof reading booth; Talking bks
Open Mon & Wed 9-6, Tues & Thurs 9-8, Fri & Sat 9-5
Friends of the Library Group
Branches: 3
CHICKAMAUGA PUBLIC, 306 Cove Rd, Chickamauga, 30707-1410, SAN 338-9073. Tel: 706-375-3004. FAX: 706-375-7034. *Br Mgr,* Bobbie Abernathy; E-mail: babernathy@chrl.org; Staff 4 (Non-MLS 4)
Founded 1966. Circ 46,981
Library Holdings: CDs 306; Bk Vols 29,870; Per Subs 14; Talking Bks 595; Videos 769
Subject Interests: Civil War, Local hist
Function: ILL available, Photocopying/Printing, Ref serv available, Telephone ref
Open Mon & Thurs 9-6, Tues 9-7, Fri & Sat 10-2
Friends of the Library Group
DADE COUNTY PUBLIC LIBRARY, 102 Court St, Trenton, 30752. (Mail add: PO Box 340, Trenton, 30752-0340), SAN 338-9103. Tel: 706-657-7857. FAX: 706-657-7860. *Br Mgr,* Marshana Sharp; E-mail: msharp@chrl.org; Staff 6 (MLS 1, Non-MLS 5)
Founded 1938. Pop 15,541; Circ 52,370
Library Holdings: Bk Vols 32,772; Per Subs 30; Videos 895
Subject Interests: Local hist
Open Mon, Wed & Thurs 9-6, Tues 1-8, Fri 9-5, Sat 9-Noon
Friends of the Library Group
ROSSVILLE PUBLIC, 504 McFarland Ave, Rossville, 30741-1253, SAN 338-9162. Tel: 706-866-1368. FAX: 706-858-9251. *Br Mgr,* Carmella Clark; E-mail: cclark@chrl.org; Staff 4 (Non-MLS 4)
Founded 1944. Circ 81,488
Library Holdings: CDs 211; Bk Vols 36,078; Per Subs 60; Talking Bks 500; Videos 1,211
Subject Interests: Local hist
Function: ILL available, Photocopying/Printing, Ref serv available, Telephone ref
Open Mon-Wed 9-6, Thurs 9-8, Fri 9-5, Sat 9-12
Friends of the Library Group

LAWRENCEVILLE

L GWINNETT COUNTY LAW LIBRARY*, 75 Langley Dr, 30046. SAN 372-1752. Tel: 770-822-8575. FAX: 770-822-8570. Web Site: www.gcll.org. *Dir,* Grace Holloway; Tel: 770-822-8571
Founded 1988
Library Holdings: Bk Vols 13,000; Per Subs 25
Wireless access
Open Mon-Fri 8:30-5

P GWINNETT COUNTY PUBLIC LIBRARY*, 1001 Lawrenceville Hwy NW, 30046-4707. SAN 338-9197. Tel: 770-978-5154. Administration Tel: 770-822-4522. Administration FAX: 770-822-5379. E-mail: askgcpl@gwinnettpl.org. Web Site: ask.gwinnettpl.org, www.gwinnettpl.org. *Exec Dir,* Nancy Stanbery-Kellam; E-mail: nskellam@gwinnettpl.org; *Dep Dir,* Liz Forster; Tel: 770-822-5340, E-mail: lforster@gwinnettpl.org; *Div Dir, Br Serv,* Barbara Spruill; Tel: 678-985-6078, E-mail: bspruill@gwinnettpl.org; *Div Dir, Bus Serv,* Jane Walters; Tel: 770-822-5324, E-mail: jwalters@gwinnettpl.org; *Div Dir, Human Res,* Kim Rodriguez; Tel: 770-822-5331, E-mail: krodriguez@gwinnettpl.org; *Div Dir, Info Tech,* Michael Casey; Tel: 770-822-5334, E-mail: mcasey@gwinnettpl.org; *Div Dir, Mats Mgt,* Deborah George; Tel: 770-822-5330, E-mail: dgeorge@gwinnettpl.org
Founded 1935. Pop 824,941; Circ 7,667,758
Library Holdings: Audiobooks 12,859; Bks on Deafness & Sign Lang 100; DVDs 7,885; e-books 5,171; Electronic Media & Resources 5,430; Large Print Bks 5,823
Special Collections: Gwinnett Authors (Central Coll)
Automation Activity & Vendor Info: (Acquisitions) SirsiDynix; (Cataloging) SirsiDynix; (Circulation) SirsiDynix; (ILL) OCLC FirstSearch; (OPAC) SirsiDynix; (Serials) SirsiDynix
Database Vendor: EBSCOhost, Gale Cengage Learning, OCLC FirstSearch, ProQuest, Wilson - Wilson Web
Wireless access
Special Services for the Deaf - Assistive tech; Bks on deafness & sign lang; Closed caption videos; High interest/low vocabulary bks; TTY equip
Special Services for the Blind - Assistive/Adapted tech devices, equip & products; Computer with voice synthesizer for visually impaired persons
Open Mon 10-6, Tues & Thurs 12-8, Wed & Fri 10-3, Sat & Sun 12-5
Friends of the Library Group
Branches: 15
BUFORD-SUGAR HILL BRANCH, 2100 Buford Hwy, Buford, 30518, SAN 338-9251.
Friends of the Library Group
CENTERVILLE BRANCH, 3025 Bethany Church Rd, Snellville, 30039.
Friends of the Library Group
COLLINS HILL, 455 Camp Perrin Rd, 30043.
Friends of the Library Group
DACULA BRANCH, 265 Dacula Rd, Dacula, 30019.
DULUTH BRANCH, 3480 Duluth Park Lane, Duluth, 30096, SAN 338-9316.
Friends of the Library Group
FIVE FORKS BRANCH, 2780 Five Forks Trickum Rd, 30044, SAN 373-8736.
Friends of the Library Group
GRAYSON BRANCH, 700 Grayson Pkwy, Grayson, 30017.
HAMILTON MILL BRANCH, 3690 Braselton Hwy, Dacula, 30019.
Friends of the Library Group
LAWRENCEVILLE BRANCH, 1001 Lawrenceville Hwy, 30046, SAN 338-9227.
Friends of the Library Group
LILBURN BRANCH, 788 Hillcrest Rd, Lilburn, 30047, SAN 338-9375.
Friends of the Library Group
MOUNTAIN PARK BRANCH, 1210 Pounds Rd SW, Lilburn, 30047, SAN 338-9405.
Friends of the Library Group
NORCROSS BRANCH, 6025 Buford Hwy, Norcross, 30071, SAN 338-943X.
Friends of the Library Group
PEACHTREE CORNERS BRANCH, 5570 Spalding Dr, Norcross, 30092, SAN 329-7039.
Friends of the Library Group
SUWANEE BRANCH, 361 Main St, Suwanee, 30024.
Friends of the Library Group
ELIZABETH H WILLIAMS BRANCH, 2740 Lenora Church Rd, Snellville, 30078, SAN 338-9464. Tel: 770-978-5154.
Friends of the Library Group

J GWINNETT TECHNICAL COLLEGE LIBRARY*, 5150 Sugarloaf Pkwy, 30043. Tel: 770-962-7580, Ext 6270, 770-962-7580, Ext 6388. FAX: 770-962-7985. E-mail: gtclibrary@gwinnetttech.edu. Web Site: www.gwinnetttech.edu.
Founded 1984. Enrl 4,500; Highest Degree: Associate
Library Holdings: AV Mats 1,300; e-books 26,000; e-journals 30; Bk Vols 14,000; Per Subs 182
Automation Activity & Vendor Info: (Cataloging) TLC (The Library Corporation); (Circulation) TLC (The Library Corporation); (OPAC) TLC (The Library Corporation)
Partic in GALILEO (Georgia Library Learning Online)
Open Mon-Thurs 7:30am-8:30pm, Fri 7:30-3:30, Sat 9-1

LEESBURG

S GEORGIA DEPARTMENT OF CORRECTIONS, OFFICE OF LIBRARY SERVICES*, Lee State Prison, 153 Pinewood Rd, 31763. Tel: 229-759-3113. FAX: 229-759-3065. Web Site: www.dcor.state.ga.us. *Librn,* John Daffin
Library Holdings: Bk Vols 3,000; Per Subs 15
Special Collections: Law Coll
Database Vendor: LexisNexis
Open Mon-Fri 7-12

P LEE COUNTY PUBLIC LIBRARY*, 245 Walnut Ave S, 31763-4367. Tel: 229-759-2369. FAX: 229-759-2326. E-mail: reference@leecountylibrary.org. Web Site: www.leecountylibrary.org. *Dir,* Claire Leavy; E-mail: leavy@leecountylibrary.org
Library Holdings: Bk Vols 45,000
Automation Activity & Vendor Info: (Cataloging) Evergreen; (Circulation) Evergreen; (OPAC) Evergreen
Wireless access
Function: AV serv, Photocopying/Printing
Partic in PINES (Public Information Network for Electronic Services)

Open Mon, Wed, Fri & Sat 9-6, Tues & Thurs 9-8, Sun 2-6
Friends of the Library Group
Branches: 2
REDBONE, 104 Thundering Springs Rd, 31763. Tel: 229-903-8871. FAX: 229-903-8872. *Br Mgr,* Leslie Partridge
Open Mon-Thurs 2-8, Fri 2-6, Sat 10-2
Friends of the Library Group
SMITHVILLE BRANCH, 116 Main St, Smithville, 31787. Tel: 229-846-6625. FAX: 229-846-6625. *Br Mgr,* Eva Majors
Library Holdings: Bk Vols 2,500
Open Mon & Wed 3-8, Tues & Thurs 3-6
Friends of the Library Group

LITHONIA

R LUTHER RICE UNIVERSITY & SEMINARY*, Bertha Smith Library, 3038 Evans Mill Rd, 30038. SAN 302-9786. Tel: 770-484-1204. FAX: 770-484-1155. E-mail: library@lru.edu. Web Site: www.lru.edu. *Dir,* Daryl Fletcher; Staff 1 (MLS 1)
Founded 1962
Library Holdings: CDs 129; DVDs 85; e-books 126; e-journals 38; Electronic Media & Resources 28,170; Microforms 249; Bk Titles 58,835; Per Subs 172; Videos 443
Special Collections: Religion (Christian Ministry), dissertations
Subject Interests: Biblical studies, Theol
Database Vendor: EBSCOhost, OCLC, OCLC FirstSearch, OCLC WorldShare Interlibrary Loan
Wireless access
Open Mon-Fri (Summer) 8-5; Mon, Tues & Thurs 8am-9pm, Wed & Fri 8-5, Sat (Winter) 8:30-4:30

LOOKOUT MOUNTAIN

CR COVENANT COLLEGE, Anna Emma Kresge Memorial Library, 14049 Scenic Hwy, 30750. SAN 315-8411. Tel: 706-419-1430. Interlibrary Loan Service Tel: 706-419-1438. Reference Tel: 706-419-1565. Administration Tel: 706-419-1434. FAX: 706-419-3480. Interlibrary Loan Service FAX: 706-419-1435. E-mail: library@covenant.edu. Web Site: library.covenant.edu. *Dir, Libr Serv,* George A Mindeman; E-mail: tad.mindeman@covenant.edu; *ILL & Presv Librn,* Tom Horner; E-mail: tom.horner@covenant.edu; *Res & Ref Librn,* John E Holberg; E-mail: john.holberg@covenant.edu. Subject Specialists: *Am hist,* George A Mindeman; *English lit,* John E Holberg; Staff 6.7 (MLS 3, Non-MLS 3.7)
Founded 1955. Enrl 1,150; Fac 75; Highest Degree: Master
Jul 2013-Jun 2014 Income $744,400. Mats Exp $439,400, Books $95,000, Per/Ser (Incl. Access Fees) $53,000, AV Mat $10,000, Electronic Ref Mat (Incl. Access Fees) $162,000. Sal $305,000 (Prof $175,000)
Library Holdings: AV Mats 6,735; e-books 98,000; Microforms 122,000; Bk Vols 84,687; Per Subs 300
Special Collections: 19th Century Central & Southern Africa (Carroll R Stegall, Jr Coll); East Asian Studies - English Language Resources (Alvin D Coox Coll); John Bunyan Coll; John Hamm Coll, audio recs, bks, scores, video recs; Puritan & 16th Century Protestant Works (Ian Tait Coll)
Automation Activity & Vendor Info: (Acquisitions) OCLC; (Cataloging) OCLC; (Circulation) OCLC; (Course Reserve) Atlas Systems; (ILL) Atlas Systems; (OPAC) OCLC; (Serials) OCLC
Database Vendor: 3M Library Systems, ACM (Association for Computing Machinery), Alexander Street Press, Annual Reviews, Atlas Systems, Baker & Taylor, BCR: Christian Periodical Index, CQ Press, EBSCOhost, JSTOR, LexisNexis, Newsbank-Readex, OCLC, OCLC WorldShare Interlibrary Loan, Project MUSE, ProQuest, Springshare, LLC, WT Cox
Wireless access
Function: Archival coll, Doc delivery serv, ILL available, Ref serv available
Partic in Georgia Private Acad Librs Consortium (GPALS); Lyrasis

LOUISVILLE

P JEFFERSON COUNTY LIBRARY SYSTEM*, 306 E Broad St, 30434. SAN 338-9499. Tel: 478-625-3751. FAX: 478-625-7683. Web Site: www.jefferson.public.lib.ga.us. *Dir,* Patricia Edwards; E-mail: pedwards@mail.jefferson.public.lib.ga.us; *Asst Dir,* Carol Taylor; E-mail: ctaylor@mail.jefferson.public.lib.ga.us; Staff 7.8 (MLS 2, Non-MLS 5.8)
Founded 1953. Pop 16,430; Circ 49,868
Jul 2011-Jun 2012 Income (Main Library and Branch(s)) $361,425, State $124,953, City $52,856, County $157,641, Locally Generated Income $20,975, Other $5,000. Mats Exp $18,000, Books $12,277, Per/Ser (Incl. Access Fees) $2,595, Micro $100, AV Mat $1,486, Electronic Ref Mat (Incl. Access Fees) $385. Sal $245,693 (Prof $114,996)
Library Holdings: Audiobooks 996; Bk Vols 47,726; Per Subs 102; Videos 2,900
Subject Interests: Genealogy, Local hist
Automation Activity & Vendor Info: (Cataloging) Evergreen; (Circulation) Evergreen; (OPAC) Evergreen
Database Vendor: WT Cox
Wireless access
Function: Bks on cassette, Bks on CD, Computers for patron use, Copy machines, e-mail serv, Electronic databases & coll, Fax serv, Handicapped accessible, ILL available, Magnifiers for reading, Microfiche/film & reading machines, Notary serv, Pub access computers, Ref serv in person, Scanner, Tax forms, VHS videos, Wheelchair accessible
Partic in GALILEO (Georgia Library Learning Online); PINES (Public Information Network for Electronic Services)
Open Mon 9-7, Tues-Fri 8:30-5:30, Sat 9-1
Friends of the Library Group
Branches: 2
MCCOLLUM PUBLIC, 405 N Main St, Wrens, 30833-1142, SAN 338-9529. Tel: 706-547-3484. FAX: 706-547-9358. *Mgr,* Wanda McGahee; Staff 1.4 (Non-MLS 1.4)
Special Collections: Local History & Genealogy (Heritage Coll)
Open Mon-Wed & Fri 8:30-5:30, Thurs 8:30-7, Sat 9-1
Friends of the Library Group
WADLEY PUBLIC, 11 W College Ave, Wadley, 30477. (Mail add: PO Box 356, Wadley, 30477-0356). Tel: 478-252-1366. FAX: 478-252-1337. *Mgr,* Kathy Hudson; Staff 1.25 (Non-MLS 1.25)
Open Mon & Wed-Fri 9-5, Tues 9-7, Sat 9-1

LUMPKIN

S HISTORIC WESTVILLE, INC LIBRARY*, 1850 Martin Luther King Jr Dr, 31815. (Mail add: PO Box 1850, 31815-1850), SAN 303-3880. Tel: 229-838-6310. Toll Free Tel: 888-733-1850. FAX: 229-838-4000. Web Site: www.westville.org. *Dir,* Leo J Goodsell; E-mail: leo@westville.org
Founded 1966
Library Holdings: Bk Titles 1,400
Special Collections: African-American Architecture & History Survey of West Georgia; John West Coll; Pre-Columbian Seminars Transcripts
Subject Interests: Decorative art, Ga, Hort
Open Tues-Sat 10-5
Restriction: Not a lending libr

MACON

J CENTRAL GEORGIA TECHNICAL COLLEGE LIBRARY*, Macon Campus, 3300 Macon Tech Dr, 31206-3628. SAN 375-4898. Tel: 478-757-3549. FAX: 478-757-3545. E-mail: library@centralgatech.edu. Web Site: www.centralgatech.edu/library. *Dir of Libr Serv,* W Neil McArthur; Tel: 478-757-3548, E-mail: nmcarthur@centralgatech.edu; *Ref & Instruction Librn,* Allison Repzynski; Tel: 478-757-3547, E-mail: arepzynski@centralgatech.edu; *Librn,* Lyn Young; E-mail: lyoung@centralgatech.edu; *Librn,* Julie Huskey; E-mail: jhuskey@centralgatech.edu; Staff 4.75 (MLS 3, Non-MLS 1.75)
Founded 1993. Enrl 6,000; Fac 200; Highest Degree: Associate
Jul 2013-Jun 2014 Income $230,000
Library Holdings: AV Mats 2,500; e-books 60,000; Bk Vols 20,000; Per Subs 300
Subject Interests: Bus, Educ, Health, Indust, Info tech, Pub serv, Tech, Trade
Automation Activity & Vendor Info: (Cataloging) TLC (The Library Corporation); (Circulation) TLC (The Library Corporation); (ILL) OCLC; (OPAC) TLC (The Library Corporation)
Database Vendor: Cinahl, CredoReference, EBSCO Auto Repair Reference, EBSCOhost, Gale Cengage Learning, Hoovers, LearningExpress, Medline, OCLC WorldShare Interlibrary Loan, ProQuest, Sage, Springshare, LLC, TLC (The Library Corporation), Westlaw
Wireless access
Function: Audio & video playback equip for onsite use, ILL available, Photocopying/Printing, Ref serv available, Telephone ref, Wheelchair accessible
Partic in Soline

C MACON STATE COLLEGE LIBRARY*, 100 College Station Dr, 31206-5144. SAN 303-3902. Tel: 478-471-2709. FAX: 478-471-2869. Web Site: www.maconstate.edu/library. *Dir,* Patricia Borck; Tel: 478-471-2865, E-mail: pat.borck@maconstate.edu; *Asst Dir, Bibliog Instr,* Felicia Haywood; Tel: 478-471-2867, E-mail: felicia.haywood@maconstate.edu; *Cat Librn,* April Renfroe-Warren; Tel: 478-471-2008; *Info Serv, Ref & Instruction Librn,* Robin Grant; Tel: 478-471-2866, E-mail: robin.grant@maconstate.edu; *Online Serv, Tech Serv,* Kathy Adams; Tel: 478-471-2042, E-mail: kathy.adams@maconstate.edu; Staff 10 (MLS 5, Non-MLS 5)
Founded 1968. Enrl 6,615; Fac 194; Highest Degree: Bachelor
Library Holdings: Bk Titles 88,000; Bk Vols 90,000; Per Subs 313
Special Collections: College Archives; Horticulture Coll
Automation Activity & Vendor Info: (Acquisitions) Ex Libris Group; (Cataloging) Ex Libris Group; (Circulation) Ex Libris Group; (Course Reserve) Ex Libris Group; (ILL) Ex Libris Group; (Media Booking) Ex Libris Group; (OPAC) Ex Libris Group; (Serials) Ex Libris Group
Partic in Lyrasis

Special Services for the Blind - Computer with voice synthesizer for visually impaired persons; ZoomText magnification & reading software
Open Mon-Thurs 8am-10pm, Fri 8-Noon, Sun 2-6

S MACON TELEGRAPH LIBRARY*, 120 Broadway, 31208. SAN 371-1390. Tel: 478-744-4411. Toll Free Tel: 800-677-4110. FAX: 478-744-4411. Web Site: www.macon.com.
Library Holdings: Bk Titles 375
Database Vendor: Dialog, LexisNexis

MERCER UNIVERSITY
CL WALTER F GEORGE SCHOOL OF LAW, FURMAN SMITH LAW LIBRARY*, 1021 Georgia Ave, 31201-1001. (Mail add: 1400 Coleman Ave, 31207-0003), SAN 338-9618. Tel: 478-301-2612. Reference Tel: 478-301-2334. FAX: 478-301-2284. Web Site: www.law.mercer.edu/library. *Dir,* Suzanne L Cassidy; E-mail: cassidy_sl@law.mercer.edu; *IT Supvr,* Chris Bombardo; Tel: 478-301-2182; *Asst Librn,* Denise M Gibson; Tel: 478-301-5905; *Assoc Librn,* Ismael Gullon; Tel: 478-301-5904; *Ref,* John M Perkins; Tel: 478-301-2667; *Ref,* James P Walsh; Tel: 478-301-2625; Staff 6 (MLS 6)
Founded 1850. Enrl 432; Fac 25; Highest Degree: Doctorate
Library Holdings: Bk Titles 57,064; Bk Vols 333,000; Per Subs 1,100
Special Collections: Griffin B Bell Papers. US Document Depository
Subject Interests: Law
Automation Activity & Vendor Info: (Acquisitions) Innovative Interfaces, Inc; (Cataloging) Innovative Interfaces, Inc; (Circulation) Innovative Interfaces, Inc; (OPAC) Innovative Interfaces, Inc; (Serials) Innovative Interfaces, Inc
Database Vendor: Gale Cengage Learning, LexisNexis, Westlaw
Partic in Georgia Interactive Network for Medical Information; New England Law Library Consortium, Inc; OCLC Online Computer Library Center, Inc
Open Mon-Thurs 8-8, Fri 8-5, Sat 1-5, Sun 1-8

CM SCHOOL OF MEDICINE, MEDICAL LIBRARY & LRC*, 1550 College St, 31207, SAN 338-9626. Tel: 478-301-2515. Circulation Tel: 478-301-4056. Interlibrary Loan Service Tel: 478-301-2549. Toll Free Tel: 800-425-4246. FAX: 478-301-2051. E-mail: reference.ill@gain.mercer.edu. Web Site: med.mercer.edu/library. *Interim Dir,* Kim K Meeks; Tel: 478-301-2519, E-mail: meeks_k@mercer.edu; Staff 21 (MLS 9, Non-MLS 12)
Founded 1974. Enrl 313; Fac 837; Highest Degree: Doctorate
Special Collections: Southern History of Medicine. Oral History
Subject Interests: Med
Automation Activity & Vendor Info: (Acquisitions) Innovative Interfaces, Inc; (Cataloging) Innovative Interfaces, Inc; (Circulation) Innovative Interfaces, Inc; (Course Reserve) Innovative Interfaces, Inc; (ILL) OCLC ILLiad; (OPAC) Innovative Interfaces, Inc; (Serials) Innovative Interfaces, Inc
Database Vendor: EBSCOhost, Elsevier, Ingenta, ISI Web of Knowledge, MD Consult, OCLC FirstSearch, OCLC WorldShare Interlibrary Loan, OVID Technologies, PubMed, RefWorks, Wiley
Partic in Atlanta Regional Council for Higher Education; Docline; National Network of Libraries of Medicine Southeastern Atlantic Region; OCLC Online Computer Library Center, Inc
Open Mon-Thurs 8am-11pm, Fri 8-6, Sat 10-6, Sun 1-11
Restriction: Non-circulating to the pub, Restricted pub use

C JACK TARVER LIBRARY*, 1300 Edgewood Ave, 31207, SAN 338-9588. Tel: 478-301-2960. Circulation Tel: 478-301-2961. Reference Tel: 478-301-2055. FAX: 478-301-2111. Web Site: tarver.mercer.edu. *Dean of Libr,* Elizabeth D Hammond; *Assoc Dir, Coll Mgt, Assoc Dir, Pub Serv,* Theresa Preuit; *Assoc Dir, Tech Serv, Spec Coll & Archives Librn,* Susan G Broome; Tel: 478-301-2193; *ILL/Circ Supvr, Ref Librn,* Andrew Shuping; Tel: 478-301-2251; *Syst Librn,* Robert Frasier; Tel: 478-301-2027; *Media Librn, Outreach Librn, Ref Librn,* Lee Twombly; Tel: 478-301-2852; *ILL,* Cecilia Williams; Tel: 478-301-2102; *Coordr, Extn Serv,* Position Currently Open; *Coordr, Libr Instruction, Coordr, Ref (Info Serv),* Consuela Cline; Tel: 478 301-5334; *Head, Spec Coll,* Laura Botts; Tel: 478-301-2968; *Acq,* Brenda Medlin; Tel: 478-301-2505; *Ser,* Brenda Mays; Tel: 478-301-2966; Staff 31 (MLS 12, Non-MLS 19)
Founded 1833. Enrl 6,800; Fac 210; Highest Degree: Doctorate
Jul 2006-Jun 2007 Income $2,384,517. Mats Exp $621,336, Books $140,936, Per/Ser (Incl. Access Fees) $215,500, Micro $24,500, AV Mat $2,700, Electronic Ref Mat (Incl. Access Fees) $237,700
Library Holdings: Electronic Media & Resources 200; Bk Titles 210,000; Bk Vols 250,000; Per Subs 4,500; Videos 1,500
Special Collections: Cooperative Baptist Fellowship Archives; Georgia Baptist History & Archives; Mercer University Archives. US Document Depository
Subject Interests: Baptist hist, Baptists, Civil War, Southern culture, Southern hist
Automation Activity & Vendor Info: (Acquisitions) Innovative Interfaces, Inc; (Cataloging) Innovative Interfaces, Inc; (OPAC) Innovative Interfaces, Inc; (Serials) Innovative Interfaces, Inc
Database Vendor: Dialog, EBSCOhost, LexisNexis, OCLC FirstSearch, OVID Technologies, ProQuest
Function: Photocopying/Printing
Partic in Lyrasis

P MIDDLE GEORGIA REGIONAL LIBRARY SYSTEM*, Washington Memorial Library (Main Library), 1180 Washington Ave, 31201-1790. SAN 338-9642. Tel: 478-744-0800, 478-744-0841. FAX: 478-742-3161. Web Site: www.co.bibb.ga.us/library/. *Dir,* Thomas Jones; Tel: 478-744-0850, E-mail: jonest@bibblib.org; *Head, Circ,* Jeanette Gardner; E-mail: gardnerj@bibblib.org; *Head, Pub Serv,* Judy Harrington; Tel: 478-744-0836, E-mail: harringj@bibblib.org; *Head, Tech Serv,* Brian Coker; Tel: 478-744-0813, E-mail: cokerb@bibblib.org; *Ref Librn,* Robin Hudgins; Tel: 478-744-0838, E-mail: hudginsr@bibblib.org; *Ref Librn,* Susan Lemme; Tel: 478-744-0839, E-mail: lemmes@bibblib.org; *Ref Librn,* Catie Tierney; Tel: 478-744-0825, E-mail: tierneyc@bibblib.org; *Acq,* Denita Spikes; Tel: 478-744-0817, E-mail: spikesd@bibblib.org; *Ch Serv,* Sandra French; Tel: 478-744-0859, E-mail: frenchs@bibblib.org; Staff 20 (MLS 20)
Founded 1889. Pop 257,687
Library Holdings: Bk Vols 483,291
Automation Activity & Vendor Info: (ILL) OCLC
Partic in Georgia Online Database; PINES (Public Information Network for Electronic Services)
Open Mon-Thurs 9-9, Fri & Sat 9-6
Friends of the Library Group
Branches: 15
CRAWFORD COUNTY PUBLIC LIBRARY, 340 McCrary St, Roberta, 31078. (Mail add: PO Box 73, Roberta, 31078), SAN 338-9677. Tel: 478-836-4478. FAX: 478-836-4478. *Br Mgr,* Leda Starnes
Library Holdings: Bk Vols 17,143
Open Mon 1-7, Tues-Thurs 10-12 & 1-7
Friends of the Library Group
EAST WILKINSON COUNTY PUBLIC LIBRARY, 154 E Main St, Irwinton, 31042-2602. (Mail add: PO Box 546, Irwinton, 31042-0546), SAN 325-4437. Tel: 478-946-2778. FAX: 478-946-2778. *Br Mgr,* Arlene Bache
Library Holdings: Bk Vols 10,011
Open Mon-Wed 10-6, Thurs Noon-8, Fri 10-5
Friends of the Library Group
GENEALOGICAL & HISTORICAL ROOM & GEORGIA ARCHIVES, 1180 Washington Ave, 31201-1790. (Mail add: PO Box 6334, 31208-6334). Tel: 478-744-0841. FAX: 478-744-0840. *Head of Libr,* Muriel Jackson; Tel: 478-744-0821, E-mail: jacksonm@bibblib.org
Library Holdings: Bk Vols 131,706
Special Collections: African-American; Archives; Business Reference; Genealogy; Georgiana; Local Hist; Telephone indexes
Subject Interests: Bus & mgt, Genealogy, Local hist
Open Mon-Thurs 9-9, Fri & Sat 9-6, Sun 1:30-5:30
Friends of the Library Group
GORDON PUBLIC LIBRARY, 284 Milledgeville Hwy W, Gordon, 31031. (Mail add: PO Box 336, Gordon, 31031-0336), SAN 338-9707. Tel: 478-628-5352. FAX: 478-628-5352. *Br Mgr,* Judy Brown
Library Holdings: Bk Vols 9,304
Open Mon-Fri 10-6
Friends of the Library Group
IDEAL PUBLIC LIBRARY, 605 Tom Watson Ave, Ideal, 31041. (Mail add: PO Box 9, Ideal, 31041-0009), SAN 325-4399. Tel: 478-949-2720. FAX: 478-949-2720. *Br Mgr,* Betty Rainey
Library Holdings: Bk Vols 1,250
Open Mon-Thurs 8-5, Fri 8-4:15
Friends of the Library Group
JONES COUNTY PUBLIC LIBRARY, Railroad Ave, Gray, 31032. (Mail add: PO Box 156, Gray, 31032-0156), SAN 338-9766. Tel: 478-986-6626. FAX: 478-986-6626. *Br Mgr,* Carol Dye
Founded 1936
Library Holdings: Bk Vols 24,425
Open Mon & Wed 10-6, Tues & Thurs 9-7, Fri 9-5
Friends of the Library Group
CHARLES A LANFORD MD LIBRARY, 6504 Houston Rd, 31216-6702, SAN 338-9944. Tel: 478-621-6970. FAX: 478-621-6985. *Librn,* Wanda Stewart; E-mail: stewartw@bibblib.org
Library Holdings: Bk Vols 44,202
Open Mon-Sat 9:30-6
Friends of the Library Group
P LIBRARY FOR THE BLIND & PHYSICALLY HANDICAPPED, Washington Memorial Library, 1180 Washington Ave, 31201-1790, SAN 338-9650. Tel: 478-744-0877. Toll Free Tel: 800-805-7613. *Librn,* James O'Neal; E-mail: onealj@bibblib.org
Founded 1973
Special Services for the Deaf - TDD equip
Open Mon-Fri 9-5
Friends of the Library Group
MARSHALLVILLE PUBLIC LIBRARY, Main St, Marshallville, 31057. (Mail add: PO Box 201, Marshallville, 31057-0201), SAN 338-9790. Tel: 478-967-2413. FAX: 478-967-2413. *Br Mgr,* Leslie Kirsch
Library Holdings: Bk Vols 4,550

Open Mon-Fri 10-12 & 3:30-6:30, Sat 9-2
Friends of the Library Group
MONTEZUMA PUBLIC LIBRARY, 506 N Dooly St, Montezuma, 31063-1308, SAN 338-9820. Tel: 478-472-6095. FAX: 478-472-6095. *Br Mgr,* Lawanna Journey
Library Holdings: Bk Vols 17,441
Open Mon, Wed & Fri 9-5, Tues & Thurs 9-7
Friends of the Library Group
OGLETHORPE PUBLIC LIBRARY, 115 Chatham St, Oglethorpe, 31068-9103. (Mail add: PO Box 425, Oglethorpe, 31068-0425), SAN 338-9855. Tel: 478-472-7116. FAX: 478-472-7116. *Br Mgr,* Gail Detamore
Library Holdings: Bk Vols 4,978
Open Mon-Thurs 9-6, Fri 8-5
Friends of the Library Group
RIVERSIDE BRANCH, Rivergate Shopping Ctr, 110 Holiday Dr N, 31210, SAN 338-991X. Tel: 478-757-8900. FAX: 478-757-1094. *Librn,* Suzy McCullough; E-mail: suzymc@bibblib.org
Library Holdings: Bk Vols 53,124
Open Mon-Fri 9:30-6
Friends of the Library Group
SHURLING BRANCH, Shurlington Plaza, 1769 Shurling Dr, 31211-2152, SAN 338-9979. Tel: 478-744-0875. E-mail: mgrlsh@bibblib.org. *Br Librn,* Melanie C Duncan; Tel: 478-744-0876
Library Holdings: Bk Vols 43,889
Open Mon-Fri 9:30-6
Friends of the Library Group
TWIGGS COUNTY PUBLIC LIBRARY, 101 Ash St, Jeffersonville, 31044. (Mail add: PO Box 305, Jeffersonville, 31044-0305), SAN 338-9731. Tel: 478-945-3814. FAX: 478-945-3814. *Br Mgr,* Joyce Faulk
Library Holdings: Bk Vols 13,653
Open Mon, Wed & Fri 9-5, Tues & Thurs 11-7
Friends of the Library Group
WEST BIBB BRANCH, Northwest Commons, 5580 Thomaston Rd, 31220-8118, SAN 377-6514. Tel: 478-744-0818. FAX: 478-744-0819. *Librn,* Viveca Jackson; E-mail: jacksonv@bibblib.org
Library Holdings: Bk Vols 72,006
Open Mon-Sat 9:30-6
Friends of the Library Group

S NATIONAL PARK SERVICE, Ocmulgee National Monument Library, 1207 Emery Hwy, 31217. SAN 303-3910. Tel: 478-752-8257. FAX: 478-752-8259. Web Site: www.nps.gov/ocmu. *In Charge,* James David
Founded 1936
Library Holdings: Bk Titles 700; Per Subs 15
Subject Interests: Am Indians, Anthrop, Archaeology, Environ studies
Restriction: Staff use only

C WESLEYAN COLLEGE, Willet Memorial Library, 4760 Forsyth Rd, 31210-4462. SAN 303-3929. Tel: 478-757-5200. FAX: 478-757-3898. E-mail: wlibrary@wesleyancollege.edu. Web Site: www.wesleyancollege.edu. *Dir,* Kristina C Peavy; Tel: 478-757-5201, E-mail: kpeavy@wesleyancollege.edu; *Archivist, Pub Serv Librn,* Virginia Blake; Tel: 478-757-5274, E-mail: vblake@wesleyancollege.edu; *Cat, Tech Serv,* Melissa Roberts; Tel: 478-757-5202, E-mail: mroberts@wesleyancollege.edu; Staff 4 (MLS 3, Non-MLS 1)
Founded 1836. Fac 50; Highest Degree: Master
Library Holdings: AV Mats 1,991; CDs 299; DVDs 86; e-books 16,463; Microforms 33,912; Bk Vols 142,337; Per Subs 456; Videos 240
Special Collections: Americana (McGregor Coll); Georgiana (Park Coll)
Automation Activity & Vendor Info: (Acquisitions) OCLC; (Cataloging) OCLC; (Circulation) OCLC; (Course Reserve) OCLC; (ILL) OCLC WorldShare Interlibrary Loan; (OPAC) OCLC
Database Vendor: EBSCOhost, JSTOR, LexisNexis, OCLC FirstSearch, OCLC WorldShare Interlibrary Loan, OCLC Worldshare Management Services, ProQuest, ScienceDirect
Wireless access
Function: Archival coll, Audio & video playback equip for onsite use, Electronic databases & coll, ILL available, Photocopying/Printing, Ref serv available
Partic in GALILEO (Georgia Library Learning Online); Georgia Online Database; Lyrasis
Open Mon-Thurs 8am-Midnight, Fri 8-5, Sat 10:30-5, Sun 2:30-10
Restriction: Open to pub for ref only, Open to students, fac & staff

MADISON

P UNCLE REMUS REGIONAL LIBRARY SYSTEM*, 1121 East Ave, 30650. SAN 339-0063. Tel: 706-342-4974. FAX: 706-342-4510. Web Site: www.uncleremus.org. *Interim Dir,* Steve Schaefer; *Admin Senior Librn,* Cheryl M Rogers; Tel: 706-342-4974, Ext 21, E-mail: cheryl@uncleremus.org; *Acq,* Tamela Thomas; Tel: 706-342-4974, Ext 14, E-mail: tamela@uncleremus.org; *Ref,* Ana Kadhum; Tel: 706-342-4974, Ext 19, E-mail: ana@uncleremus.org; *Tech Serv,* Holly Jarrell; Tel: 706-342-4974, Ext 18, E-mail: holly@uncleremus.org; Staff 34 (MLS 7, Non-MLS 27)
Founded 1952. Pop 162,000; Circ 484,098
Library Holdings: AV Mats 15,737; CDs 1,015; DVDs 1,040; Electronic Media & Resources 41; Bk Titles 75,262; Bk Vols 215,034; Per Subs 126; Talking Bks 8,321; Videos 7,416
Special Collections: Joel Chandler Harris Coll
Subject Interests: Ga, Genealogy
Automation Activity & Vendor Info: (Cataloging) SirsiDynix; (Circulation) SirsiDynix; (OPAC) SirsiDynix
Database Vendor: EBSCOhost, Gale Cengage Learning, Newsbank, OCLC FirstSearch, ProQuest
Wireless access
Partic in GALILEO (Georgia Library Learning Online); Lyrasis; PINES (Public Information Network for Electronic Services)
Friends of the Library Group
Branches: 8
GREENE COUNTY LIBRARY, 610 S Main St, Greensboro, 30642, SAN 339-3038. Tel: 706-453-7276. FAX: 706-453-0500. *Br Mgr,* Jackie Richardson; E-mail: jackie@uncleremus.org
Subject Interests: Ga, Genealogy
Open Mon, Wed, Thurs & Fri 10-6, Tues 10-8, Sat 10-2, Sun 2-5
Friends of the Library Group
HANCOCK COUNTY LIBRARY, 403 E Broad St, Sparta, 31087, SAN 339-0128. Tel: 706-444-5389. FAX: 706-444-6056. E-mail: hancock@uncleremus.org. *Br Mgr,* Karen Meeks; E-mail: karen@uncleremus.org
Subject Interests: Ga, Genealogy
Open Mon-Fri 10-6, Sat 10-4, Sun 2-5
JASPER COUNTY LIBRARY, 319 E Green St, Monticello, 31064, SAN 339-0152. Tel: 706-468-6292. FAX: 706-468-2060. E-mail: jasper@uncleremus.org. Web Site: www.uncleremus.org/jasper.htm. *Br Mgr,* Tamala Alexander; E-mail: tam@uncleremus.org
Subject Interests: Ga, Genealogy
Open Mon-Wed & Fri 10-6, Thurs 10-8, Sat 10-2, Sun 2-6
MONROE - WALTON COUNTY LIBRARY, 217 W Spring St, Monroe, 30655, SAN 339-3577. Tel: 770-267-4630. FAX: 770-267-6682. *Br Mgr,* Jackie Broderick; E-mail: jackie@uncleremus.org; Staff 1 (MLS 1)
Subject Interests: Ga, Genealogy
Friends of the Library Group
MORGAN COUNTY LIBRARY, 1131 East Ave, 30650, SAN 370-0178. Tel: 706-342-1206. FAX: 706-342-0883. E-mail: morgan@uncleremus.org. *Br Mgr,* Miriam Baker; E-mail: miriam@uncleremus.org
Special Collections: Joel Chandler Harris Coll
Subject Interests: Ga, Genealogy
Open Mon-Wed & Fri 10-6, Thurs 10-8, Sat 10-4, Sun 2-6
Friends of the Library Group
O'KELLY MEMORIAL LIBRARY, 363 Conyers Rd, Loganville, 30052, SAN 339-3518. Tel: 770-466-2895. FAX: 770-466-3700. E-mail: okelly@uncleremus.org. *Br Mgr,* Rick Vetsch; E-mail: rick@uncleremus.org
Open Mon-Thurs 10-7, Fri 10-6, Sat 10-5, Sun 2-6
Friends of the Library Group
PUTNAM COUNTY LIBRARY, 309 N Madison Ave, Eatonton, 31024, SAN 339-0098. Tel: 706-485-6768. FAX: 706-485-5896. *Br Mgr,* Joshua Bell; E-mail: joshua@uncleremus.org
Subject Interests: Ga, Genealogy
Open Mon-Wed & Fri 10-6, Thurs 10-8, Sat 10-2, Sun 2-6
W H STANTON MEMORIAL LIBRARY, 1045 W Hightower Trail, Social Circle, 30025. (Mail add: PO Box 566, Social Circle, 30025-0566), SAN 339-3631. Tel: 770-464-2444. FAX: 770-464-1596. E-mail: stanton@uncleremus.org. *Br Mgr,* Janet King; E-mail: janet@uncleremus.org
Subject Interests: Ga, Genealogy
Open Mon, Wed & Fri 10-6, Tues 10-9, Thurs 10-8, Sat 10-4, Sun 2-6

MANCHESTER

P PINE MOUNTAIN REGIONAL LIBRARY*, 218 Perry St NW, 31816-1317. (Mail add: PO Box 709, 31816-0709), SAN 339-0187. Tel: 706-846-3851. FAX: 706-846-8455, 706-846-9632. Web Site: www.pinemtnlibrary.org. *Dir,* Charles B Gee; *Asst Dir,* Cynthia Kilby; *Tech Coordr,* Lorraine Smalley; *Ch Serv,* Terrie Townsend; *Tech Serv,* Bonita Thomas; Staff 21 (MLS 5, Non-MLS 16)
Founded 1938. Pop 65,712; Circ 157,728
Library Holdings: Bk Vols 118,936
Subject Interests: Genealogy, Local hist
Automation Activity & Vendor Info: (Acquisitions) Evergreen; (Cataloging) Evergreen; (Circulation) Evergreen; (ILL) OCLC; (OPAC) Evergreen; (Serials) Evergreen
Partic in PINES (Public Information Network for Electronic Services)
Open Mon-Wed & Fri 8:30-5:30, Thurs 8:30-8:30, Sat 9-1

Branches: 7
BUTLER PUBLIC, 56 W Main St, Butler, 31006-0508. (Mail add: PO Box 508, Butler, 31006-0508), SAN 339-0217. Tel: 478-862-5428. FAX: 478-862-2924. *Mgr,* Johnnie Harris
Open Tues, 10-1 & 2-6, Wed & Fri 2-6, Thurs 2-8, Sat 9-1
GREENVILLE AREA PUBLIC, 2323 Gilbert St, Greenville, 30222-0710. (Mail add: PO Box 710, Greenville, 30222-0710), SAN 339-0241. Tel: 706-672-4004. FAX: 706-672-9223. E-mail: libraryg@pinemtnlibrary.org.
Open Tues-Fri 2-6, Sat 9-12
HIGHTOWER MEMORIAL, 800 W Gordon St, Thomaston, 30286-3417. (Mail add: PO Box 631, Thomaston, 30286-0008), SAN 339-0330. Tel: 706-647-8649. FAX: 706-647-3977. *Br Mgr,* Shirley Fogarty; *Librn,* Cynthia Kilby
Open Mon-Wed & Fri 10-6, Thurs 10-9, Sat 9-1
MANCHESTER PUBLIC, 218 Perry St, 31816-0709, SAN 373-6229. Tel: 706-846-3851. FAX: 706-846-9632. E-mail: librarym@pinemtnlibrary.org. *Mgr,* Diane Rakhshani
Open Mon-Wed & Fri 8:30-5:30, Thurs 8:30-8:30, Sat 9-1
REYNOLDS COMMUNITY, 208 N Winston St, Reynolds, 31076. (Mail add: PO Box 467, Reynolds, 31076-0467), SAN 339-0276. Tel: 478-847-3468. FAX: 478-847-4553. *Mgr,* Melinda Hortman
Open Mon, Tues & Thurs 1-6, Sat 10-2
TALBOT COUNTY, 75 N Jefferson St, Talbotton, 31827-9732. (Mail add: PO Box 477, Talbotton, 31827-0477), SAN 339-0306. Tel: 706-665-3134. FAX: 706-665-8777. *Br Mgr,* Shamona L Willis
Open Tues & Thurs 12-8, Wed 10-6, Fri 12-6, Sat 1-5
YATESVILLE PUBLIC, 77 Childs Ave, Yatesville, 31097-3661. (Mail add: PO Box 87, Yatesville, 31097-0087). Tel: 706-472-3048. FAX: 706-472-3049. *Br Mgr,* Connie Moncrief
Founded 2002
Open Tues & Wed 2-7, Thurs 2-8, Fri 2-6

MARIETTA

J CHATTAHOOCHEE TECHNICAL COLLEGE LIBRARY, 980 S Cobb Dr SE, 30060-3300. (Mail add: 1046 S Cobb Dr, MD202, 30060), SAN 375-4154. Tel: 770-528-4536. FAX: 770-528-4454. Web Site: www.chattahoocheetech.edu/library. *Dir of Libr,* Barbara N Moore; Tel: 770-528-4422, E-mail: bmoore@chattahoocheetech.edu; *Appalachian Campus Librn,* Michael K Miller; Tel: 706-253-4571, E-mail: mmiller@chattahoocheetech.edu; *Canton Campus Librn,* Karen Preslock; Tel: 770-345-1390, E-mail: kpreslock@chattahoocheetech.edu; *Mountain View Campus Librn,* Lauren Barnes; Tel: 770-509-6320, E-mail: lbarnes@chattahoocheetech.edu; *N Metro Campus Librn,* Kate Stirk Sklikas; Tel: 770-975-4054, E-mail: ksklikas@chattahoocheetech.edu; *Paulding Campus Librn,* Janice Levine; Tel: 770-443-3630, Fax: 770-443-3631, E-mail: Janice.Levine@chattahoocheetech.edu; *Syst Librn,* Leigh Hall; Tel: 770-528-6461, E-mail: lhall@chattahoocheetech.edu; *Cataloger,* Don Auensen; Tel: 770-528-6466, E-mail: dauensen@chattahoocheetech.edu; Staff 14 (MLS 8, Non-MLS 6)
Founded 1986. Highest Degree: Associate
Jul 2014-Jun 2015 Income $160,000
Library Holdings: e-books 232,019; Bk Vols 54,236; Per Subs 390
Special Collections: Georgia Topics & Authors
Automation Activity & Vendor Info: (Acquisitions) SirsiDynix; (Cataloging) SirsiDynix; (Circulation) SirsiDynix; (Course Reserve) SirsiDynix; (ILL) OCLC; (OPAC) SirsiDynix
Database Vendor: Baker & Taylor, CredoReference, ebrary, EBSCO Discovery Service, EBSCOhost, Facts on File, Gale Cengage Learning, Hoovers, LexisNexis, Newsbank, OCLC, OCLC WorldShare Interlibrary Loan, OVID Technologies, ProQuest, SirsiDynix, Springshare, LLC, STAT!Ref (Teton Data Systems)
Wireless access
Partic in GALILEO (Georgia Library Learning Online)
Restriction: Borrowing privileges limited to fac & registered students

P COBB COUNTY PUBLIC LIBRARY SYSTEM*, 266 Roswell St, 30060-2004. SAN 339-0365. Tel: 770-528-2320. Interlibrary Loan Service Tel: 770-528-2339. Reference Tel: 770-528-2377. FAX: 770-528-2349. Interlibrary Loan Service FAX: 770-528-2367. Web Site: www.cobbcat.org. *Dir,* Helen Poyer; Tel: 770-528-2324; *Assoc Dir,* Thelma Glover; Tel: 770-528-2335; *Assoc Dir,* Jonathan McKeown; Tel: 770-528-2332; *Assoc Dir,* Jill Tempest; Tel: 770-528-2330; *Asst Head, Coll Develop,* Debra McLaughlin; *Admin Coordr,* Dinah Bonesteel; *Prog Coordr,* Patricia Latch; Tel: 770-528-2342; *Adult Serv,* Suzanne Weaver; *Cat,* Zhang Shelley; Tel: 770-528-2354; *ILL,* Yogini Desai; Staff 44 (MLS 43, Non-MLS 1)
Founded 1958. Pop 679,325; Circ 4,014,576
Library Holdings: Bk Vols 301,464
Special Collections: Georgia Room
Automation Activity & Vendor Info: (Acquisitions) SirsiDynix; (Circulation) SirsiDynix; (ILL) SirsiDynix; (OPAC) SirsiDynix; (Serials) Sydney
Database Vendor: ALLDATA Online, ReferenceUSA, SerialsSolutions, SirsiDynix
Wireless access
Open Mon-Thurs 9-9:30, Fri & Sat 9-6, Sun 1-5
Friends of the Library Group
Branches: 16
ACWORTH BRANCH, 4569 Dallas St, Acworth, 30101, SAN 339-039X. Tel: 770-917-5165. FAX: 770-917-5177. *Mgr,* Susan Harper
Founded 1958. Circ 116,181
Library Holdings: Bk Vols 31,347
Open Mon-Thurs 9-8, Fri & Sat 9-6
Friends of the Library Group
EAST MARIETTA, 2051 Lower Roswell Rd, 30068, SAN 339-042X. Tel: 770-509-2711. FAX: 770-509-2714. E-mail: eastmarb@cobbcat.org. Web Site: www.cobbcat.org/branchemarietta.html. *Br Mgr,* Bruce Thompson; *Ch,* Deborah Feanny; *Ref Librn,* Melissa White
Founded 1967. Circ 183,401
Library Holdings: Bk Vols 58,302
Open Mon-Wed 10-7, Thurs & Fri 11-6, Sat 1-6
Friends of the Library Group
GRITTERS, 880 Shaw Pk Rd, 30066, SAN 339-0489. Tel: 770-528-2524. FAX: 770-528-2533. *Mgr,* Alexandra Beswick
Founded 1958. Circ 162,418
Library Holdings: Bk Vols 44,944
Open Mon-Thurs 9-9, Fri 9-6, Sat 10-6
Friends of the Library Group
KEMP MEMORIAL, 4029 Due West Rd NW, 30064, SAN 370-8039. Tel: 770-528-2527. FAX: 770-528-2592. *Mgr,* Colleen Moses
Founded 1958. Circ 182,864
Library Holdings: Bk Vols 52,460
Open Mon-Thurs 9-9, Fri 9-6, Sat 10-6
Friends of the Library Group
KENNESAW BRANCH, 2250 Lewis St, Kennesaw, 30144, SAN 339-0519. Tel: 770-528-2529. FAX: 770-528-2593. *Mgr,* Jill Tempest
Founded 1958. Circ 252,560
Library Holdings: Bk Vols 53,836
Open Mon-Thurs 9-9, Fri 9-6, Sat 10-6
Friends of the Library Group
MERCHANT'S WALK, 1315 Johnson Ferry Rd, 30068, SAN 339-0551. Tel: 770-509-2730. FAX: 770-509-2733. *Mgr,* Position Currently Open
Founded 1958. Circ 485,869
Library Holdings: Bk Vols 71,078
Open Mon-Thurs 9-9, Fri 9-6, Sat 10-6
Friends of the Library Group
MOUNTAIN VIEW, 3320 Sandy Plains Rd, 30066, SAN 370-8047. Tel: 770-509-2725. FAX: 770-509-2726. *Regional Mgr,* Mike Aiken; *Br Mgr,* Ansie Krige
Founded 1958. Circ 554,749
Library Holdings: Bk Vols 124,236
Open Mon-Thurs 9-9, Fri & Sat 9-6, Sun 1-5
Friends of the Library Group
POWDER SPRINGS BRANCH, 4181 Atlanta St, Bldg 1, Powder Springs, 30127, SAN 339-0578. Tel: 770-439-3600. FAX: 770-439-3620. *Mgr,* Bruce Thompson
Founded 1958. Circ 159,643
Library Holdings: Bk Vols 51,009
Open Mon-Thurs 9-9, Fri 9-6, Sat 10-6
Friends of the Library Group
LEWIS A RAY BRANCH, 4500 Oakdale Rd, Smyrna, 30080, SAN 339-0608. Tel: 770-801-5335. FAX: 770-801-5316. *Mgr,* Mary Holt
Founded 1958. Circ 61,749
Library Holdings: Bk Vols 22,466
Open Mon-Thurs 9-8, Fri & Sat 9-6
Friends of the Library Group
SIBLEY BRANCH LIBRARY, 1539 S Cobb Dr, 30060, SAN 339-0632. Tel: 770-528-2520. FAX: 770-528-2594. *Mgr,* Joseph Buadoo
Founded 1958. Circ 41,781
Library Holdings: Bk Vols 28,403
Open Mon-Thurs 9-8, Fri & Sat 9-6
Friends of the Library Group
SOUTH COBB, 805 Clay Rd, Mableton, 30126, SAN 339-0667. Tel: 678-398-5828. FAX: 678-398-5833. *Br Mgr,* Jo Lahmon; *Regional Mgr,* Vicki Green
Founded 1958. Circ 321,829
Library Holdings: Bk Vols 88,255
Open Mon-Thurs 9-9, Fri & Sat 9-6, Sun 1-5
Friends of the Library Group
STRATTON, 1100 Powder Springs Rd, 30064, SAN 339-0691. Tel: 770-528-2522. FAX: 770-528-2595. *Mgr,* Patricia Ball
Founded 1958. Circ 129,070
Library Holdings: Bk Vols 41,085
Open Mon-Thurs 9-9, Fri 9-6, Sat 10-6
Friends of the Library Group
SWEETWATER VALLEY, 5000 Austell-Powder Springs Rd, Ste 123, Austell, 30106, SAN 339-0721. Tel: 770-819-3290. FAX: 770-819-3293. *Mgr,* Rhonda Lane
Founded 1958. Circ 57,197
Library Holdings: Bk Vols 27,891

Open Mon-Thurs 9-8, Fri & Sat 9-6
Friends of the Library Group
VININGS, 4290 Paces Ferry Rd NW, Atlanta, 30339, SAN 370-8055. Tel: 770-801-5330. FAX: 770-801-5319. *Mgr,* Susan Kendall
Founded 1958. Circ 152,043
Library Holdings: Bk Vols 43,651
Open Mon-Thurs 9-9, Fri 9-6, Sat 10-6
Friends of the Library Group
WEST COBB REGIONAL, 1750 Dennis Kemp Lane, Kennesaw, 30152. Tel: 770-528-4699. FAX: 770-528-4619. *Regional Mgr,* Sherry Blomeley; *Br Mgr,* Steve Powell
Founded 1958. Circ 456,721
Library Holdings: Bk Vols 95,773
Open Mon-Thurs 9-9, Fri & Sat 9-6, Sun 1-5
Friends of the Library Group
HATTIE G WILSON BRANCH, 350 Lemon St, 30060, SAN 339-0454. Tel: 770-528-2526. FAX: 770-528-2591. *Mgr,* Rachell Heard
Circ 55,213
Library Holdings: Bk Vols 19,368
Open Mon-Fri 9:30-6
Friends of the Library Group

CM LIFE UNIVERSITY*, Library & Learning Resource Center, 1269 Barclay Circle, 30060. SAN 370-5730. Tel: 770-426-2688. FAX: 770-426-2745. E-mail: library@life.edu. Web Site: www.life.edu/library. *Dir,* Susan A Stewart; Tel: 770-426-2692, E-mail: sstewart@life.edu; *Asst Dir,* Geetha Sridaran; Tel: 770-426-2691, E-mail: gsridaran@life.edu; *Electronic Res Librn,* Karen Preston; Tel: 770-426-2690, E-mail: kpreston@life.edu; *ILL,* Pam Shadrix; E-mail: pshadrix@life.edu. Subject Specialists: *Sci ref,* Geetha Sridaran; Staff 3 (MLS 3)
Founded 1975. Enrl 2,300; Fac 167; Highest Degree: Doctorate
Jul 2007-Jun 2008. Mats Exp $338,000, Books $150,000, Per/Ser (Incl. Access Fees) $91,000, AV Mat $15,000, Electronic Ref Mat (Incl. Access Fees) $82,000
Library Holdings: Audiobooks 94; AV Mats 10,442; CDs 196; DVDs 239; e-books 23,090; e-journals 33,470; Bk Titles 52,603; Bk Vols 62,424; Per Subs 126; Videos 6,240
Special Collections: Chiropractic Coll
Subject Interests: Biol, Bus, Chiropractic, Computer info, Dietetics, Health sci, Nutrition, Psychol, Sports health sci
Automation Activity & Vendor Info: (Acquisitions) SirsiDynix; (Cataloging) SirsiDynix; (Circulation) SirsiDynix; (OPAC) SirsiDynix; (Serials) SirsiDynix
Database Vendor: EBSCOhost, Elsevier, LexisNexis, MD Consult, OCLC FirstSearch, ProQuest
Wireless access
Function: Archival coll, AV serv, CD-ROM, Computers for patron use, Copy machines, Digital talking bks, Doc delivery serv, Electronic databases & coll, For res purposes, Health sci info serv, ILL available, Online cat, Orientations, Outside serv via phone, mail, e-mail & web, Photocopying/Printing, Ref serv available, Telephone ref, VHS videos, Workshops
Publications: Today's Chiropractic Lifestyle
Partic in Atlanta Health Science Libraries Consortium; Chiropractic Libr Consortium; GALILEO (Georgia Library Learning Online); Georgia Private Acad Librs Consortium (GPALS); OCLC Online Computer Library Center, Inc
Open Mon-Thurs 7am-11:45pm, Fri 7-6:45, Sat 10-6:45, Sun 1:30-11:45
Restriction: In-house use for visitors, Open to students, fac & staff

CR NEW ORLEANS BAPTIST THEOLOGICAL SEMINARY*, North Georgia Campus Library, 1000 Johnson Ferry Rd, Ste C115, 30068. Tel: 770-321-1606. FAX: 770-321-5363. Web Site: www.nobts.edu. *Dir of Libr,* Jeff Griffin; *Librn,* Helen Shin; E-mail: hshin@nobts.edu; Staff 1 (MLS 1)
Founded 1975. Enrl 350; Highest Degree: Doctorate
Library Holdings: Bk Vols 21,000; Per Subs 25
Automation Activity & Vendor Info: (Cataloging) Horizon; (Circulation) Horizon; (OPAC) Horizon
Open Mon-Thurs (Winter) 8-8; Mon-Thurs (Summer) 8-5

C SOUTHERN POLYTECHNIC STATE UNIVERSITY, Lawrence V Johnson Library, 1100 S Marietta Pkwy, 30060-2896. SAN 303-3961. Tel: 678-915-7276. Interlibrary Loan Service Tel: 678-915-7277. Reference Tel: 678-915-7471. FAX: 678-915-4944. Web Site: www.spsu.edu/library/library.html. *Dir,* Dr Nancy Colyar; Tel: 678-915-7306, E-mail: ncolyar@spsu.edu; *Acq, Assoc Dir,* Yongli Ma; Tel: 678-915-7473, E-mail: yma@spsu.edu; *Head, Ref,* Aaron Wimer; E-mail: awimer@spsu.edu; *Syst Librn,* Li Chen; Tel: 678-915-7467, E-mail: lchen@spsu.edu; Staff 9 (MLS 6, Non-MLS 3)
Founded 1948. Enrl 4,000; Fac 120; Highest Degree: Master
Library Holdings: Bk Titles 117,887; Bk Vols 119,780; Per Subs 1,216
Special Collections: American Architectural History; Architectural drawings; Geological Survey; Surveying maps; University archives
Subject Interests: Art & archit, Bus & mgt, Sci tech
Automation Activity & Vendor Info: (Cataloging) Ex Libris Group; (Circulation) Ex Libris Group; (Course Reserve) Ex Libris Group; (ILL) Ex Libris Group; (OPAC) Ex Libris Group; (Serials) Ex Libris Group
Database Vendor: EBSCOhost, Gale Cengage Learning, LexisNexis, OCLC FirstSearch, OVID Technologies, ProQuest, Wilson - Wilson Web
Partic in Georgia Libr Info Network; Georgia Online Database; Lyrasis; SOQUIJ
Open Mon-Thurs 8-10, Fri 8-6, Sat 11-6, Sun 1-8
Friends of the Library Group

M WELLSTAR LIBRARY SERVICES, Health Sciences Library, 677 Church St, 30060. SAN 329-1715. Tel: 770-793-7178. Interlibrary Loan Service Tel: 770-793-7189. FAX: 770-793-7956. E-mail: medical.library@wellstar.org. Web Site: www.wellstar.org. *Supvr, Libr Serv,* Shannon Glover; E-mail: shannon.glover@wellstar.org; *Asst Librn/ILL,* Cedric Clark; E-mail: cedric.clark@wellstar.org; Staff 2 (MLS 2)
Library Holdings: e-books 134; e-journals 3,400; Bk Vols 1,100; Per Subs 148
Subject Interests: Allied health, Med, Nursing
Automation Activity & Vendor Info: (Cataloging) LibraryWorld, Inc; (OPAC) LibraryWorld, Inc; (Serials) Basch Subscriptions, Inc
Database Vendor: Cinahl, EBSCOhost, Elsevier MDL, LibraryWorld, Inc, Majors, Medline, Natural Standard, OVID Technologies, PubMed, ScienceDirect, Springer-Verlag, STAT!Ref (Teton Data Systems), UpToDate
Wireless access
Function: Health sci info serv
Partic in Atlanta Health Science Libraries Consortium; Georgia Health Sciences Library Association (GHSLA); Medical Library Association (MLA); Southern Chapter of Med Libr Asn
Restriction: Authorized personnel only, Badge access after hrs

METTER

P L C ANDERSON MEMORIAL LIBRARY*, 50 S Kennedy St, 30439-4442. SAN 339-2228. Tel: 912-685-2455. FAX: 912-685-4462. *Mgr,* Evelyn McCarthy; Staff 4 (Non-MLS 4)
Pop 9,454; Circ 23,931
Library Holdings: Bk Vols 19,300; Per Subs 30
Automation Activity & Vendor Info: (Acquisitions) SirsiDynix; (Cataloging) SirsiDynix; (Circulation) SirsiDynix; (ILL) OCLC
Mem of Statesboro Regional Public Libraries
Partic in PINES (Public Information Network for Electronic Services)
Open Mon-Fri 10-6
Friends of the Library Group

MILLEDGEVILLE

J CENTRAL GEORGIA TECHNICAL COLLEGE LIBRARY, Milledgeville Campus, 54 Hwy 22 W, 31061. Tel: 478-445-2333. FAX: 478-445-2346. E-mail: library@centralgatech.edu. Web Site: www.centralgatech.edu/library. *Librn,* Stephanie Crane; E-mail: scrane@centralgatech.edu; *Librn,* Carter Nipper; Tel: 478-445-2319, E-mail: cnipper@centralgatech.edu; *Libr Asst,* Teri Garnto; Tel: 478-445-2338, E-mail: tgarnto@centralgatech.edu; Staff 2.75 (MLS 1.75, Non-MLS 1)
Founded 1997. Enrl 800; Highest Degree: Associate
Jul 2010-Jun 2011 Income $35,000
Library Holdings: AV Mats 750; e-books 46,000; Bk Vols 6,000; Per Subs 60
Wireless access

C GEORGIA COLLEGE & STATE UNIVERSITY*, Library & Instructional Technology Center, 320 N Wayne St, 31061-3397. (Mail add: Campus Box 043, 31061), SAN 339-0780. Tel: 478-445-4047. Interlibrary Loan Service Tel: 478-445-0975. Reference Tel: 478-445-0979. FAX: 478-445-6847. Interlibrary Loan Service FAX: 478-445-2946. Web Site: library.gcsu.edu. *Interim Dir,* Nancy Davis Bray; Tel: 478-445-0991, E-mail: nancy.davisbray@gcsu.edu; *Assoc Dir, Tech Serv,* Christine Zuger; Tel: 478-445-0983, E-mail: christine.zuger@gcsu.edu; *Acq Librn,* Ben Davis; *Cat Librn,* Michael Bonnard; *Coll Develop Librn,* William Richards; *Instrul & Ref Librn,* Gary Austin; *Instruction & Ref Librn,* Edward Whatley; *Coordr, Acq, Coordr, Ser,* David Thibodeau; Staff 39 (MLS 14, Non-MLS 25)
Founded 1889. Enrl 6,000; Fac 230; Highest Degree: Master
Library Holdings: e-books 27,441; Bk Titles 196,919; Bk Vols 199,729; Per Subs 415
Special Collections: Branham Cookbook Coll; Flannery O'Conner Coll, bks, mss, per; Georgia College Archives Coll; Georgia College Horology Coll, clocks, watches; Georgia History Coll, bks, mss; Middle Georgia Towns & Cities Coll; US Senator Paul Coverdell Paners Coll. US Document Depository
Subject Interests: Educ, Nursing, Psychol
Automation Activity & Vendor Info: (Acquisitions) Ex Libris Group; (Cataloging) Ex Libris Group; (Circulation) Ex Libris Group; (ILL) OCLC; (Media Booking) Ex Libris Group; (Serials) Ex Libris Group

Wireless access
Partic in Dialog Corp; Georgia Online Database; Lyrasis; OCLC Online Computer Library Center, Inc; Ser Holdings Network
Open Mon-Thurs 7:30am-11pm, Fri 7:30-5, Sat 10-6, Sun 2-11

J GEORGIA MILITARY COLLEGE*, Sibley-Cone Memorial Library, 201 E Greene St, 31061. SAN 303-3988. Tel: 478-445-2718. Reference Tel: 478-445-1422. FAX: 478-445-5592. Web Site: www.gmc.cc.ga.us/. *Dir,* Jane Simpson; E-mail: jsimpson@gmc.cc.ga.us; *Media Spec,* Robbie F Jones; E-mail: rjones@gmc.cc.ga.us; *Ref,* John Hebel; E-mail: jhebel@gmc.cc.ga.us; Staff 3 (MLS 2, Non-MLS 1)
Founded 1879. Enrl 2,773; Fac 75; Highest Degree: Associate
Library Holdings: Bk Titles 31,000; Bk Vols 32,000; Per Subs 150
Subject Interests: Ga, Hist, Local hist
Automation Activity & Vendor Info: (Acquisitions) Mandarin Library Automation; (Cataloging) Mandarin Library Automation; (Circulation) Mandarin Library Automation
Function: Archival coll, ILL available, Photocopying/Printing
Partic in Cent Ga Associated Librs; Georgia Online Database
Open Mon-Thurs 7:45am-9pm, Fri 7:45-4, Sun 6pm-9pm

P TWIN LAKES LIBRARY SYSTEM*, Mary Vinson Memorial Library - Headquarters, 151 S Jefferson St SE, 31061-3419. SAN 339-0004. Tel: 478-452-0677. FAX: 478-452-0680. Web Site: www.tllsga.org. *Dir,* Barry Reese; E-mail: barryreese@tllsga.org; *Asst Dir,* Position Currently Open; *Human Res Mgr,* LaToya Davidson; E-mail: latoyadavidson@tllsga.org; *Ref Librn,* Kell Carpenter; E-mail: kellcarpenter@tllsga.org; Staff 16 (MLS 2, Non-MLS 14)
Founded 1938. Pop 144,000
Library Holdings: Bk Vols 75,000
Subject Interests: Local hist
Wireless access
Open Mon & Tues 9-9, Wed-Fri 9-6, Sat 10-4
Friends of the Library Group
Branches: 1
LAKE SINCLAIR, 3061 N Columbia St, Ste A, 31061. Tel: 478-452-6522. FAX: 478-452-6524. *Mgr,* Beth Miller
Open Mon-Fri 12-6

MOODY AFB

A UNITED STATES AIR FORCE*, Moody Air Force Base Library FL4830, 23 FSS/FSDL, 3010 Robinson Rd, Bldg 328, 31699-1594. SAN 339-0845. Tel: 229-257-3018, 229-257-3539. FAX: 229-257-4119. *Libr Dir,* Jess G Echord; *Tech Serv,* Debbie Caffey; Staff 6 (MLS 1, Non-MLS 5)
Founded 1952
Library Holdings: Bk Vols 40,000; Per Subs 250
Subject Interests: Mil hist
Wireless access
Partic in OCLC Online Computer Library Center, Inc
Open Mon-Thurs 10-8, Fri 10-6, Sat 10-5

MORGAN

S GEORGIA DEPARTMENT OF CORRECTIONS, OFFICE OF LIBRARY SERVICES*, Calhoun State Prison, 27823 Main St, 31766. (Mail add: PO Box 249, 39866-0249). Tel: 229-849-5058. FAX: 229-849-5017. Web Site: www.dcor.state.ga.us. *Librn,* Al Barge
Library Holdings: Bk Vols 4,000; Per Subs 15
Special Collections: Law Coll
Database Vendor: LexisNexis
Open Mon-Thurs 7:30-4

MORROW

C CLAYTON STATE UNIVERSITY, 2000 Clayton State Blvd, 30260. SAN 303-3996. Tel: 678-466-4325. Circulation Tel: 678-466-4331. Interlibrary Loan Service Tel: 678-466-4326. Reference Tel: 678-466-4329. Administration Tel: 678-466-4332. Automation Services Tel: 678-466-4336. Information Services Tel: 678-466-4345. FAX: 678-466-4349. TDD: 678-466-4346. E-mail: reference@clayton.edu. Web Site: www.clayton.edu/library. *Dean of Libr,* Dr Gordon N Baker; Tel: 678-466-4334, E-mail: gordonbaker@clayton.edu; *Assoc Dean, Coll & Res Mgt Chair,* Cathy Jeffrey; E-mail: cathyjeffrey@clayton.edu; *Head, Monographic Cat,* Adam Kubik; Tel: 678-466-4337, E-mail: adamkubik@clayton.edu; *Head of Ref & Instrul Serv,* Joan Taylor; Tel: 678-466-4340, E-mail: JoanTaylor@clayton.edu; *Head, Electronic Res & Serv,* Kara Mullen; Tel: 678-466-4339, E-mail: karamullen@clayton.edu; *Assessment & Mkt Librn,* Erin Nagel; Tel: 678-466-4330, E-mail: erinnagle@clayton.edu; *Electronic Res Librn,* Chris Stotelmyer; Tel: 678-466-4347, E-mail: cstotelmyer@clayton.edu; *Pub Serv Librn/Weekend Coordr,* Thomas Jackson, Jr; Tel: 678-466-4338, E-mail: thomasjacksonjr@clayton.edu; *Ref & Instruction Librn,* Position Currently Open; *Ser Librn,* Laura Herndon; Tel: 678-466-4335, E-mail: lauraherndon@clayton.edu; *Circ Supvr,* Barbara Dantzler; E-mail: barbaradantzler@clayton.edu; *Acq/CatAsst,* Heather Walls; Tel: 678-466-4341, E-mail: heatherwalls@clayton.edu; *ILL & Reserves Asst,* Rhonda Boozer; E-mail: rhondaboozer@clayton.edu; *Univ Archivist,* Rosemary Fischer; Tel: 678-466-4333, E-mail: rosemaryfischer@clayton.edu. Subject Specialists: *Communication arts, Educ, Theatre,* Dr Gordon N Baker; *Computer sci, Math,* Cathy Jeffrey; *Music,* Adam Kubik; *Psychol, Soc sci,* Joan Taylor; *Humanities,* Kara Mullen; *English,* Erin Nagel; *Phys sci,* Chris Stotelmyer; *Interdisciplinary studies,* Thomas Jackson, Jr; *Life sci,* Laura Herndon; *Archives,* Rosemary Fischer; Staff 18 (MLS 12, Non-MLS 6)
Founded 1969. Enrl 7,150; Fac 220; Highest Degree: Master
Library Holdings: CDs 6,493; DVDs 1,236; e-books 27,500, Microforms 280,618; Bk Vols 111,404; Per Subs 750
Special Collections: Civil War (War of the Rebellion); Georgia (Southern History); The Foundation Center's Funding Information Network
Subject Interests: Bus, Educ, Music, Nursing
Automation Activity & Vendor Info: (Acquisitions) Ex Libris Group; (Cataloging) Ex Libris Group; (Circulation) Ex Libris Group; (Course Reserve) Ex Libris Group; (ILL) OCLC; (OPAC) Ex Libris Group; (Serials) Ex Libris Group
Wireless access
Publications: Library Source
Partic in Atlanta Regional Council for Higher Education; Lyrasis; OCLC Online Computer Library Center, Inc
Open Mon-Thurs 8am-10pm, Fri 8-6, Sat 9-6, Sun 1-10

G GEORGIA ARCHIVES*, Reference Library, 5800 Jonesboro Rd, 30260. SAN 303-2884. Tel: 678-364-3710. FAX: 678-364-3856. Web Site: www.georgiaarchives.org. *Asst Dir, Archival Serv,* Kayla Barrett; Tel: 678-364-3781; Staff 8 (MLS 5, Non-MLS 3)
Founded 1918
Library Holdings: Bk Titles 16,426; Bk Vols 20,000; Per Subs 193
Special Collections: County & Family Histories; DAR Coll; Family Charts; Georgia & Eastern United States Genealogy; Georgia History; Georgia Map Coll; Georgia Newspapers; Georgia Photographs; Local Government Records; Official State Records; Private Papers; Surname Card File
Subject Interests: Local genealogy, Local hist
Automation Activity & Vendor Info: (Cataloging) Ex Libris Group; (OPAC) Ex Libris Group
Database Vendor: OCLC FirstSearch
Wireless access
Function: Res libr
Partic in Lyrasis
Open Fri & Sat 8:30-5
Restriction: Non-circulating
Friends of the Library Group

G NATIONAL ARCHIVES & RECORDS ADMINISTRATION, National Archives at Atlanta, 5780 Jonesboro Rd, 30260. SAN 329-8280. Tel: 770-968-2100. FAX: 770-968-2457. E-mail: atlanta.archives@nara.gov. Web Site: archives.gov/atlanta. *Archives Dir,* Rob Richards; Tel: 770-968-2485, E-mail: rob.richards@nara.gov; *Archivist,* Shane Bell; E-mail: shane.bell@nara.gov; *Archivist,* Guy Hall; E-mail: guy.hall@nara.gov; *Archivist,* Maureen E Hill; E-mail: maureen.hill@nara.gov
Special Collections: Archival records of Federal agencies & courts in Alabama, Florida, Georgia, Kentucky, Mississippi, North Carolina, South Carolina & Tennessee
Subject Interests: Arts, Bus, Census, Civil War, Constitutional, Crime, Econ develop, Space, World War I, World War II
Wireless access
Open Mon-Fri 8:30-5
Restriction: Ref only to non-staff
Friends of the Library Group

MOULTRIE

M COLQUITT REGIONAL MEDICAL CENTER*, Health Sciences Library, 3131 S Main St, 31768. (Mail add: PO Box 40, 31776-0040), SAN 372-5936. Tel: 229-890-3460. FAX: 229-891-9345. *Librn,* Susan Leik
Founded 1979
Library Holdings: Bk Vols 800; Per Subs 63
Wireless access
Partic in Georgia Interactive Network for Medical Information
Restriction: Non-circulating to the pub

P MOULTRIE-COLQUITT COUNTY LIBRARY*, 204 Fifth St SE, 31768. (Mail add: PO Box 2828, 31776-2828), SAN 339-087X. Tel: 229-985-6540. FAX: 229-985-0936. Web Site: www.mccls.org. *Dir,* Holly Phillips; *Cat,* Monique Green; *Ch Serv,* Norma S McKellar; *Ref,* Elois Matthews; *Tech Serv,* Carolyn Clark; Staff 12.83 (MLS 2, Non-MLS 10.83)
Founded 1907. Pop 47,620; Circ 117,460
Jul 2010-Jun 2011 Income (Main Library and Branch(s)) $782,427, State $200,761, Federal $2,000, County $472,996, Locally Generated Income

$106,670. Mats Exp $56,281, Books $32,146, Per/Ser (Incl. Access Fees) $5,611, AV Mat $10,798, Electronic Ref Mat (Incl. Access Fees) $7,726
Library Holdings: Audiobooks 1,596; DVDs 228; Large Print Bks 2,094; Microforms 1,295; Bk Vols 124,170; Per Subs 59; Videos 739
Special Collections: Ellen Payne Odom Genealogy Library
Automation Activity & Vendor Info: (Acquisitions) Evergreen; (Cataloging) OCLC Connexion; (Circulation) Evergreen; (ILL) OCLC; (OPAC) Evergreen
Database Vendor: Facts on File, Gale Cengage Learning, World Book Online
Wireless access
Function: Adult bk club, Bks on cassette, Bks on CD, Children's prog, Computer training, Computers for patron use, Copy machines, Electronic databases & coll, Free DVD rentals, Handicapped accessible, ILL available, Magnifiers for reading, Mail & tel request accepted, Online cat, Photocopying/Printing, Prog for children & young adult, Pub access computers, Ref serv available, Summer reading prog, Tax forms, VHS videos, Wheelchair accessible
Partic in Georgia Libr Info Network; PINES (Public Information Network for Electronic Services)
Special Services for the Blind - Closed circuit TV magnifier; Large print bks; Magnifiers; Talking bks
Open Mon & Wed-Sat 8:30-5:30, Tues 8:30-8
Friends of the Library Group
Branches: 1
DOERUN MUNICIPAL LIBRARY, PO Box 427, Doerun, 31744, SAN 339-0993. Tel: 229-782-5507. *Br Mgr,* Patti Suggs; Staff 0.3 (Non-MLS 0.3)
Function: Computers for patron use, Electronic databases & coll, Handicapped accessible, ILL available, Online cat, Pub access computers, Ref serv in person, Summer reading prog, Tax forms, Wheelchair accessible
Open Mon, Tues, Thurs & Fri 2-6
Bookmobiles: 1

J MOULTRIE TECHNICAL COLLEGE LIBRARY*, Veterans Parkway Campus, 800 Veterans Pkwy N, 31788. Tel: 229-217-4159. FAX: 229-891-7010. Web Site: www.moultrietech.edu/library. *Dir of Libr Serv,* Udella Spicer; Tel: 229-891-7020, E-mail: uspicer@moultrietech.edu
Founded 1964. Enrl 2,000; Fac 140; Highest Degree: Associate
Library Holdings: Bk Titles 3,842; Bk Vols 95
Automation Activity & Vendor Info: (Cataloging) TLC (The Library Corporation); (Circulation) TLC (The Library Corporation)
Wireless access
Open Mon-Thurs 8-7, Fri 8-4
Departmental Libraries:
TIFTON CAMPUS, 52 Tech Dr, Tifton, 31794. Tel: 229-391-2623. FAX: 229-391-3717. *Librn,* Priscilla Hunter; E-mail: phunter@moultrietech.edu
Highest Degree: Associate
Library Holdings: Bk Vols 1,760
Open Mon & Wed 8-7:15, Tues 8-6:15, Thurs 2-5

MOUNT BERRY

C BERRY COLLEGE*, Memorial Library, 2277 Martha Berry Hwy, 30149. SAN 339-1086. Tel: 706-236-2221. Circulation Tel: 706-236-1739. Interlibrary Loan Service Tel: 706-233-4056. Administration Tel: 706-236-1740. Interlibrary Loan Service FAX: 706-233-7814. Administration FAX: 706-238-7937. E-mail: library@berry.edu. Web Site: www.berry.edu/library. *Dir,* Sherre N Harrington; Tel: 706-236-2285; *Instrul Serv Librn, Pub Serv,* Martha Reynolds; Tel: 706-236-1705, E-mail: mareynolds@berry.edu; *Ref Librn,* Judy Thompson; Tel: 706-233-4057, E-mail: jthompson@berry.edu; *ILL, Ref Librn,* Xiaojing Zu; E-mail: xzu@berry.edu; *Govt Doc, Ser Librn,* Maureen Morgan; E-mail: mmorgan@berry.edu; *Tech Serv Librn,* Jeremy Worsham; Tel: 706-368-6707; *Archivist,* Michael O'Malley; Tel: 706-238-5886, Fax: 706-238-5917, E-mail: momalley@berry.edu; Staff 13 (MLS 7, Non-MLS 6)
Founded 1926. Enrl 1,769; Fac 167; Highest Degree: Master
Jul 2006-Jun 2007. Mats Exp $711,166, Books $166,549, Per/Ser (Incl. Access Fees) $356,576, AV Mat $16,506, Electronic Ref Mat (Incl. Access Fees) $171,535. Sal $485,070
Library Holdings: AV Mats 3,719; e-books 15,000; e-journals 22,900; Bk Titles 169,807; Bk Vols 176,892; Per Subs 2,100
Special Collections: Institutional Historical Documents (Berry College Archives). Oral History; US Document Depository
Automation Activity & Vendor Info: (Acquisitions) Ex Libris Group; (Cataloging) Ex Libris Group; (Circulation) Ex Libris Group; (Course Reserve) Ex Libris Group; (ILL) OCLC ILLiad; (OPAC) Ex Libris Group; (Serials) Ex Libris Group
Database Vendor: Agricola, ARTstor, Baker & Taylor, Cambridge Scientific Abstracts, Dialog, EBSCOhost, JSTOR, LexisNexis, OCLC FirstSearch, OCLC WorldShare Interlibrary Loan, ProQuest, SerialsSolutions, STN International, Westlaw, Wiley, Wilson - Wilson Web
Wireless access
Function: Art exhibits, Audio & video playback equip for onsite use, AV serv, Bks on CD, Computers for patron use, Copy machines, Digital talking bks, Doc delivery serv, e-mail serv, E-Reserves, Electronic databases & coll, Fax serv, Handicapped accessible, ILL available, Online cat, Online ref, Online searches, Outreach serv, Ref serv available, Scanner, Spoken cassettes & CDs, Spoken cassettes & DVDs, Telephone ref, VHS videos, Wheelchair accessible
Partic in GALILEO (Georgia Library Learning Online); Georgia Private Acad Librs Consortium (GPALS); Lyrasis
Special Services for the Blind - Assistive/Adapted tech devices, equip & products
Restriction: Non-circulating of rare bks

MOUNT VERNON

C BREWTON-PARKER COLLEGE*, Fountain-New Library, 201 David-Eliza Fountain Circle, 30445. (Mail add: PO Box 197, 30445), SAN 303-4003. Tel: 912-583-3235. Interlibrary Loan Service Tel: 912-583-3232. Reference Tel: 912-583-3234. Toll Free Tel: 800-342-1087. FAX: 912-583-3454. Web Site: www.bpc.edu/academics/library/library.htm. *Dir,* Ann C Hughes; Tel: 912-583-3230, E-mail: ahughes@bpc.edu; *Coll Develop Librn,* Stephen Nichols; *Evening Librn,* Steven Richards; Staff 2 (MLS 2)
Founded 1988. Enrl 1,036; Fac 61; Highest Degree: Bachelor
Library Holdings: AV Mats 8,400; Bk Titles 71,000; Bk Vols 81,000; Per Subs 410
Special Collections: Brewton-Parker College Historical Coll
Subject Interests: Christianity, Educ, Music
Automation Activity & Vendor Info: (Acquisitions) SirsiDynix; (Cataloging) SirsiDynix; (Circulation) SirsiDynix; (OPAC) SirsiDynix
Database Vendor: EBSCOhost, LexisNexis, OCLC FirstSearch, ProQuest, SirsiDynix
Wireless access
Publications: Handbook
Open Mon-Thurs 8am-11pm, Fri 8-4, Sat 1-5, Sun 8pm-11pm

S GEORGIA DEPARTMENT OF CORRECTIONS, OFFICE OF LIBRARY SERVICES*, Montgomery State Prison, Hwy 107 S, 30445. (Mail add: PO Box 256, 30445-0256). Tel: 912-583-3600. FAX: 912-583-3667. Web Site: www.dcor.state.ga.us. *Librn,* Kim Hutchson
Library Holdings: Bk Vols 3,400; Per Subs 21; Videos 30
Database Vendor: LexisNexis

NEWNAN

P COWETA PUBLIC LIBRARY SYSTEM*, Central Library, 85 Literary Lane, 30265. Tel: 770-683-2052. FAX: 770-683-0065. Web Site: www.cowetapubliclibrary.org. *Dir,* Jimmy Bass; *Ref Librn,* Joyce S Burns; *Libr Assoc/Ch,* Kristin Rubenstein; *Libr Assoc/Tech Serv,* Miriam Veale; *Libr Assoc/Teen Serv,* Shamika Pearson
Library Holdings: Audiobooks 1,281; CDs 589; DVDs 1,871; Bk Vols 65,325; Per Subs 133
Automation Activity & Vendor Info: (Cataloging) SirsiDynix; (Circulation) SirsiDynix; (OPAC) SirsiDynix
Wireless access
Open Mon-Wed & Fri 10-7, Thurs 10-8, Sat 10-5
Friends of the Library Group
Branches: 3
GRANTVILLE PUBLIC LIBRARY, 100 Park Dr, Grantville, 30220-1708, SAN 373-8752. Tel: 770-683-0535. *Br Mgr,* Marie Vielot; E-mail: mvielot@coweta.ga.us
Founded 1992. Pop 5,000; Circ 1,316
Library Holdings: AV Mats 158; Bk Titles 6,915
Function: ILL available, Online searches, Summer reading prog
Open Mon-Fri 10-5, Sat 10-2
A MITCHELL POWELL JR PUBLIC LIBRARY, 25 Hospital Rd, 30263, SAN 338-8921. Tel: 770-253-3625. FAX: 770-254-7262. TDD: 770-502-1917. *Br Mgr,* Position Currently Open; *Head, Info Serv,* Bill Skelton; Staff 16 (MLS 4, Non-MLS 12)
Founded 1988. Pop 95,000; Circ 306,000
Library Holdings: AV Mats 2,700; Bk Titles 91,000; Per Subs 141; Talking Bks 1,300
Subject Interests: Law
Function: Handicapped accessible, ILL available, Online searches, Photocopying/Printing, Prog for adults, Prog for children & young adult, Summer reading prog, Telephone ref
Special Services for the Deaf - TDD equip
Open Mon-Wed 10-7, Thurs 10-8, Fri 10-6, Sat 10-5
SENOIA AREA PUBLIC LIBRARY, 70 Main St, Senoia, 30276, SAN 338-8832. Tel: 770-599-3537. FAX: 770-599-3537. *Br Mgr,* Marie Vielot; E-mail: mvielot@coweta.ga.us; Staff 2 (Non-MLS 2)
Founded 1974. Pop 10,000; Circ 15,744
Jul 2005-Jun 2006 Income $70,000. Mats Exp $6,537. Sal $28,265
Library Holdings: AV Mats 218; Bk Titles 13,000; Talking Bks 329

Automation Activity & Vendor Info: (OPAC) TLC (The Library Corporation)
Function: ILL available, Online searches, Photocopying/Printing, Prog for children & young adult, Summer reading prog
Open Mon-Wed & Fri 10-6, Thurs 10-8, Sat 10-3

NICHOLLS

S GEORGIA DEPARTMENT OF CORRECTIONS, OFFICE OF LIBRARY SERVICES*, Coffee Correctional Facility (Privatization Unit), 1153 N Liberty St, 31554. (Mail add: PO Box 650, 31554-0650). Tel: 912-345-5058, Ext 2275. FAX: 912-345-5086. Web Site: www.dcor.state.ga.us.
Founded 1998
Library Holdings: Bk Vols 6,100; Per Subs 40
Special Collections: Law Coll
Automation Activity & Vendor Info: (Cataloging) LRMS, Inc (Library Resource Management Systems); (Circulation) LRMS, Inc (Library Resource Management Systems)
Database Vendor: Westlaw
Open Mon, Tues & Thurs 7am-7:30pm, Wed 7-3:30, Fri 7-11:30 & 5:30-7:30, Sat 9:30-3:30

NORCROSS

G SOUTHERN STATES ENERGY BOARD*, Information Center, 6325 Amherst Ct, 30092. SAN 321-5652. Tel: 770-242-7712. FAX: 770-242-0421. Web Site: www.sseb.org. *Managing Dir,* Kathryn A Baskin; E-mail: baskin@sseb.org
Founded 1978
Library Holdings: Bk Titles 6,000; Per Subs 102
Subject Interests: Energy, Environ studies
Publications: Nuclear Waste Articles; Southern Energy Report; Southern Sources; Southern Utility News Briefs
Open Mon-Fri 8-5

OAKWOOD

J LANIER TECHNICAL COLLEGE*, Oakwood Campus Library, 2990 Landrum Education Dr, 30566. Tel: 770-531-6379. Web Site: www.laniertech.edu/library. *Dir, Libr Syst,* Beth Hedrick; E-mail: bhedrick@laniertech.edu
Library Holdings: e-books 23,000; Bk Vols 8,000; Per Subs 139
Automation Activity & Vendor Info: (Cataloging) TLC (The Library Corporation); (Circulation) TLC (The Library Corporation); (OPAC) TLC (The Library Corporation)
Wireless access
Partic in GALILEO (Georgia Library Learning Online)
Open Mon-Thurs 8-8, Fri 8-4

C UNIVERSITY OF NORTH GEORGIA*, 3820 Mundy Mill Rd, 30566. (Mail add: PO Box 1358, Gainesville, 30503), SAN 303-3597. Tel: 678-717-3653, 706-864-1889. Interlibrary Loan Service Tel: 678-717-3662, 706-864-1518. Reference Tel: 706-864-1520. Administration Tel: 678-717-3466. Toll Free Tel: 866-597-0002. FAX: 678-717-3657. E-mail: askus@ung.edu. Web Site: ung.edu/libraries. *Dean of Libr,* Deborah Prosser, PhD; E-mail: deborah.prosser@ung.edu; *Head Librn - Cumming Campus,* Rebecca Rose, Tel: 470-239-3119, E-mail: rebecca.rose@ung.edu; *Head Librn - Gainesville Campus,* Amanda Nash; Tel: 678-717-3825, E-mail: amanda.nash@ung.edu; *Head Librn - Oconee Campus,* Angela Megaw; Tel: 706-310-6305, E-mail: angela.megaw@ung.edu; *Actg Head Librn - Dahlonega Campus,* Barbara Petersohn; Tel: 706-864-1514, E-mail: barbara.petersohn@ung.edu; Staff 28 (MLS 13, Non-MLS 15)
Founded 1873. Enrl 15,000; Fac 825; Highest Degree: Master
Library Holdings: Bk Vols 229,250; Per Subs 580
Special Collections: Curriculum Development; Leadership. US Document Depository
Subject Interests: Mil hist
Automation Activity & Vendor Info: (Acquisitions) Ex Libris Group; (Cataloging) Ex Libris Group; (Circulation) Ex Libris Group; (Course Reserve) Ex Libris Group; (ILL) OCLC ILLiad; (OPAC) Ex Libris Group; (Serials) Ex Libris Group
Wireless access
Partic in Lyrasis
Restriction: Open to pub for ref & circ; with some limitations

OGLETHORPE

S GEORGIA DEPARTMENT OF CORRECTIONS, OFFICE OF LIBRARY SERVICES*, Macon State Prison, Hwy 49 S, 31068. (Mail add: PO Box 426, 31068-0426). Tel: 478-472-3486. FAX: 478-472-3524. Web Site: www.dcor.state.ga.us. *Librn,* Yolanda Green
Library Holdings: Bk Vols 3,000; Per Subs 35; Talking Bks 15
Special Collections: Law Coll
Database Vendor: LexisNexis
Open Mon-Wed 7:30-3:30, Thurs 7:30-11:30, Fri 1:30-3:30

PELHAM

S GEORGIA DEPARTMENT OF CORRECTIONS, OFFICE OF LIBRARY SERVICES*, Autry State Prison, 3178 Mt Zion Church Rd, 31779. (Mail add: PO Box 648, 31779-0648). Tel: 229-294-2940. FAX: 229-294-6691. Web Site: www.dcor.state.ga.us. *Librn,* Samantha Brown
Library Holdings: Bk Vols 1,700; Per Subs 30
Special Collections: Law Coll
Database Vendor: LexisNexis
Open Mon & Wed 7:30-11:30, Tues & Thurs 7:30-3:30

PEMBROKE

P PEMBROKE PUBLIC LIBRARY*, 1018 Camelia Dr, 31321-0430. (Mail add: PO Box 7, 31321-0007), SAN 339-2317. Tel: 912-653-2822. FAX: 912-653-2802. Web Site: pembrokelibrary.info. *Mgr,* Nancy Nubern; E-mail: nancyn@strl.info; Staff 4 (Non-MLS 4)
Pop 12,999; Circ 27,457
Library Holdings: Bk Vols 20,000; Per Subs 32
Wireless access
Mem of Statesboro Regional Public Libraries
Partic in SAILS Library Network
Open Mon-Fri 10-5:30, Sat 10-2
Friends of the Library Group

PENDERGRASS

P PENDERGRASS PUBLIC LIBRARY*, 75 Glenn Gee Rd, 30567-4654. Tel: 706-693-4450. *Libr Mgr,* Renee Martinez
Library Holdings: Bk Vols 5,492
Wireless access
Open Mon, Tues, Thurs & Fri 9-12 & 1-5
Friends of the Library Group

PERRY

P HOUSTON COUNTY PUBLIC LIBRARY SYSTEM*, 1201 Washington Ave, 31069. SAN 339-1140. Tel: 478-987-3050. FAX: 478-987-4572. Web Site: www.houston.public.lib.ga.us. *Dir,* Karen Odom; *Head Librn,* Nancy Granger; *Cat, Tech Serv,* Janet Sayre; *Ch Serv,* Regina Ray; Staff 4 (MLS 4)
Founded 1974. Pop 100,398; Circ 325,081
Library Holdings: Bk Vols 200,000; Per Subs 125
Automation Activity & Vendor Info: (Acquisitions) SirsiDynix; (Cataloging) SirsiDynix; (Circulation) SirsiDynix; (ILL) OCLC
Partic in PINES (Public Information Network for Electronic Services)
Friends of the Library Group
Branches: 3
NOLA BRANTLEY MEMORIAL LIBRARY, 721 Watson Blvd, Warner Robins, 31093, SAN 339-123X. Tel: 478-923-0128. FAX: 478-929-8611. E-mail: wrlibrary@houpl.org. *Br Mgr,* Mark Bohnstedt; Staff 1 (MLS 1)
Founded 1948. Pop 140,000; Circ 238,629
Library Holdings: Bk Titles 90,000; Per Subs 400
Automation Activity & Vendor Info: (Acquisitions) SirsiDynix; (Cataloging) SirsiDynix; (Circulation) SirsiDynix; (Media Booking) SirsiDynix; (OPAC) SirsiDynix; (Serials) SirsiDynix
Open Mon-Fri 10-6, Sat 11-3
Friends of the Library Group
CENTERVILLE BRANCH, 206 Gunn Rd, Centerville, 31028, SAN 339-1175. Tel: 478-953-4500. FAX: 478-953-7850. *Br Mgr,* Nancy Granger; E-mail: ngranger@houpl.org
Open Mon, Wed, Fri & Sat 9-6, Tues & Thurs 9-9
Friends of the Library Group
PERRY BRANCH, 1201 Washington Ave, 31069, SAN 339-1205. Tel: 478-987-3050. FAX: 478-987-4572. *Head Librn,* Nancy Granger
Open Mon & Tues 9-9, Wed-Sat 9-6
Friends of the Library Group

R PERRY UNITED METHODIST CHURCH LIBRARY*, 1002 Carroll St, 31069. (Mail add: PO Box 73, 31069-0073), SAN 303. Tel: 478-987-1852. FAX: 478-988-1428.
Founded 1967
Library Holdings: Bk Vols 4,500
Subject Interests: Hist
Open Mon-Fri 8:30-4:30

QUITMAN

P BROOKS COUNTY PUBLIC LIBRARY*, 404 Barwick Rd, 31643. SAN 303-4062. Tel: 229-263-4412. FAX: 229-263-8002. Web Site: www.brooks.public.lib.ga.us. *Dir,* Laura Harrison
Pop 16,450; Circ 50,000
Library Holdings: Bk Vols 60,000; Per Subs 45
Subject Interests: African-Am, Genealogy

Automation Activity & Vendor Info: (Cataloging) Evergreen; (Circulation) Evergreen
Wireless access
Publications: Library Edition (Friends)
Partic in PINES (Public Information Network for Electronic Services)
Open Mon & Wed-Fri 9-6, Tues 9-8, Sat 9-5
Friends of the Library Group

REIDSVILLE

GEORGIA DEPARTMENT OF CORRECTIONS, OFFICE OF LIBRARY SERVICES

S GEORGIA STATE PRISON*, 300 First Ave S, 30453. Tel: 912-557-7301. FAX: 912-557-7241. Web Site: www.dcor.state.ga.us. *Librn,* Hortense Moody
Library Holdings: Bk Vols 1,500; Per Subs 15
Special Collections: Law Coll
Database Vendor: LexisNexis
Open Mon-Fri 8:30-10:30 & 1-3

S ROGERS STATE PRISON*, 1978 Georgia Hwy 147, 30453. Tel: 912-557-7771. FAX: 912-557-7051. Web Site: www.dcor.state.ga.us. *Librn,* Andre L Bateman; Tel: 912-557-7019, E-mail: dreb8man@yahoo.com
Library Holdings: Bk Vols 14,000; Per Subs 30
Special Collections: Law Coll
Database Vendor: Westlaw
Open Mon-Thurs 8:30-10, 1-3 & 5-7

RICHMOND HILL

P RICHMOND HILL PUBLIC LIBRARY*, 9607 Ford Ave, 31324. (Mail add: PO Box 939, 31324-0939), SAN 339-2341. Tel: 912-756-3580. FAX: 912-756-2976. Web Site: www.strl.info. *Mgr,* Kate Barker; E-mail: kateb@strl.info; Staff 6 (Non-MLS 6)
Pop 15,000; Circ 97,000
Library Holdings: Bk Vols 21,838; Per Subs 25
Automation Activity & Vendor Info: (ILL) OCLC
Wireless access
Function: Pub access computers
Partic in PINES (Public Information Network for Electronic Services)
Open Mon-Thurs 10-7, Fri & Sat 10-5
Friends of the Library Group

RINGGOLD

P CATOOSA COUNTY LIBRARY*, Benton Place, 108 Catoosa Circle, 30736. SAN 338-6198. Tel: 706-965-3600. FAX: 706-965-3608. Web Site: www.catoosacountylibrary.org. *Dir,* Darla Chambliss; E-mail: dpc@catoosacountylibrary.org
Wireless access
Function: Children's prog, Teen prog
Partic in PINES (Public Information Network for Electronic Services)
Open Mon-Thurs 10-8, Fri & Sat 10-6, Sun 1:30-5:30
Friends of the Library Group

ROME

M FLOYD MEDICAL CENTER LIBRARY*, 304 Turner McCall Blvd, 30162. (Mail add: PO Box 233, 30162-0233), SAN 303-4097. Tel: 706-509-5789. *Dir of Educ,* Linda Wilhelm
Library Holdings: Bk Titles 250; Per Subs 15
Subject Interests: Med, Nursing
Partic in Southeastern Regional Med Libr Program
Restriction: Staff use only

J GEORGIA HIGHLANDS COLLEGE LIBRARIES, 3175 Cedartown Hwy SE, 30161. SAN 303-4089. Tel: 706-295-6318. FAX: 706-295-6365. Web Site: www.highlands.edu/library. *Dir of Libr,* Elijah Scott; E-mail: escott@highlands.edu; *Asst Dir,* Susan Vines; *Pub Serv,* Karin Bennedsen; *Pub Serv,* Betsy Clark; *Pub Serv,* Russell Fulmer; *Pub Serv,* Mark Gatesman; *Pub Serv,* Susanna Smith; *Pub Serv,* Bill Vinson; *Tech Serv,* Jeannie Blakely; *Libr Assoc,* Christin Collins; *Libr Assoc,* Sumer Lang; *Libr Asst,* Melissa Jones; Staff 16 (MLS 11, Non-MLS 5)
Founded 1970. Fac 11; Highest Degree: Associate
Library Holdings: e-books 85,000; Bk Vols 70,000; Per Subs 100
Automation Activity & Vendor Info: (Acquisitions) Ex Libris Group; (Cataloging) Ex Libris Group; (Circulation) Ex Libris Group; (Course Reserve) Ex Libris Group; (ILL) OCLC; (OPAC) Ex Libris Group; (Serials) Ex Libris Group
Wireless access
Partic in GALILEO (Georgia Library Learning Online); Galileo/GIL
Open Mon-Thurs 8am-9pm, Fri 8-Noon

J GEORGIA NORTHWESTERN TECHNICAL COLLEGE*, Floyd County Campus Library, Bldg H, Rm 156, One Maurice Culberson Dr, 30161. Tel: 706-295-6845. Interlibrary Loan Service Tel: 678-757-2043. Administration Tel: 706-295-6511. FAX: 706-295-6843. Interlibrary Loan Service FAX: 678-757-1673. Web Site: www.gntc.edu/library. *Dir, Libr Serv,* John Lassiter; *Evening Librn,* John Rivest; E-mail: jrivest@gntc.edu; *Coordr, Cat,* Stephen Meeks; Tel: 706-295-6263, E-mail: smeeks@gntc.edu; Staff 3.5 (MLS 2.5, Non-MLS 1)
Founded 1962. Enrl 6,000; Highest Degree: Associate
Library Holdings: Audiobooks 150; CDs 20; DVDs 2,000; e-books 22,300; Bk Titles 10,000; Bk Vols 12,000; Per Subs 75; Videos 100
Automation Activity & Vendor Info: (Cataloging) Surpass; (Circulation) Surpass; (Course Reserve) Surpass; (ILL) OCLC; (OPAC) Surpass; (Serials) Surpass
Database Vendor: 3M Library Systems, ABC-CLIO, Baker & Taylor, Blackwell, Booklist Online, Bowker, Brodart, Cinahl, CredoReference, EBSCO - WebFeat, EBSCO Auto Repair Reference, EBSCOhost, Elsevier, Facts on File, Gale Cengage Learning, Greenwood Publishing Group, Haworth Pres Inc, infoUSA, Ingram Library Services, LearningExpress, LexisNexis, McGraw-Hill, MD Consult, Medline, Micromedex, Modern Language Association, ProQuest, PubMed, ReferenceUSA, Sage, Springer-Verlag, Surpass, YBP Library Services
Wireless access
Function: Audio & video playback equip for onsite use, AV serv, Bks on CD, CD-ROM, Computers for patron use, Copy machines, e-mail serv, Electronic databases & coll, Fax serv, Free DVD rentals, Handicapped accessible, ILL available, Large print keyboards, Music CDs, Online cat, Orientations, Ref serv in person, Scanner, Wheelchair accessible
Partic in GALILEO (Georgia Library Learning Online); Georgia Interactive Network for Medical Information; Lyrasis
Special Services for the Deaf - Bks on deafness & sign lang; Closed caption videos; Sorenson video relay syst
Special Services for the Blind - Accessible computers; Bks on CD; Copier with enlargement capabilities; Internet workstation with adaptive software; Networked computers with assistive software; Reader equip; Screen enlargement software for people with visual disabilities; Screen reader software
Open Mon-Thurs 7:30am-9pm, Fri 7:30-4

Departmental Libraries:

GORDON COUNTY CAMPUS LIBRARY, Bldg 400, 1151 Hwy 53 Spur, Calhoun, 30701. Tel: 706-378-1718. Administration Tel: 706-295-6511. FAX: 706-624-1107. Administration FAX: 706-295-6843. *Coordr,* Melinda Sams; E-mail: msams@gntc.edu; Staff 0.95 (MLS 0.2, Non-MLS 0.75)
Founded 2003. Enrl 800; Fac 1; Highest Degree: Associate
Library Holdings: AV Mats 1,200; e-books 22,300; Bk Vols 3,300; Per Subs 54
Automation Activity & Vendor Info: (Cataloging) Surpass; (Circulation) Surpass; (Course Reserve) Surpass; (ILL) OCLC; (OPAC) Surpass; (Serials) Surpass
Database Vendor: 3M Library Systems, Baker & Taylor, Blackwell, Booklist Online, Bowker, BWI, Cinahl, CQ Press, CredoReference, Discovery Education, EBSCO - WebFeat, EBSCO Auto Repair Reference, EBSCOhost, Elsevier, Facts on File, Greenwood Publishing Group, H W Wilson, Haworth Pres Inc, IEEE (Institute of Electrical & Electronics Engineers), Ingram Library Services, JSTOR, Keystone Systems, Inc (KLAS), LearningExpress, LexisNexis, McGraw-Hill, MD Consult, Medline, Micromedex, Modern Language Association, Newsbank, OCLC FirstSearch, OCLC WorldShare Interlibrary Loan, Oxford Online, ProQuest, PubMed, ReferenceUSA, Sage, Springer-Verlag, Surpass, Wiley, Wilson - Wilson Web, YBP Library Services
Function: Adult bk club, Audio & video playback equip for onsite use, AV serv, Bks on cassette, Bks on CD, CD-ROM, Computers for patron use, Copy machines, Distance learning, e-mail serv, Electronic databases & coll, Free DVD rentals, Handicapped accessible, ILL available, Music CDs, Newsp ref libr, Online cat, Online searches, Orientations, Outside serv via phone, mail, e-mail & web, Photocopying/Printing, Ref & res, Ref serv available, Scanner, VHS videos, Wheelchair accessible
Partic in GALILEO (Georgia Library Learning Online)
Special Services for the Deaf - Sorenson video relay syst
Open Mon-Thurs 8-8, Fri 7:30am-1pm
Restriction: Borrowing privileges limited to fac & registered students, Limited access for the pub

POLK COUNTY CAMPUS LIBRARY, 466 Brock Rd, Rockmart, 30153. Tel: 678-757-2043. FAX: 678-757-1673. *Coordr,* Position Currently Open; *Evening Mgr,* Kelly Long; *Libr Asst,* Nancy Coley; Staff 0.5 (MLS 0.5)
Founded 2004. Enrl 200; Highest Degree: Associate
Library Holdings: AV Mats 1,000; e-books 22,300; Bk Vols 3,500; Per Subs 45
Automation Activity & Vendor Info: (Cataloging) Surpass; (Circulation) Surpass; (ILL) OCLC; (OPAC) Surpass; (Serials) Surpass
Database Vendor: 3M Library Systems, Agricola, Baker & Taylor, Booklist Online, Bowker, Cinahl, CredoReference, EBSCO - WebFeat, EBSCO Auto Repair Reference, EBSCOhost, Elsevier, Ex Libris Group, Facts on File, Gale Cengage Learning, Greenwood Publishing Group, Infor Library & Information Solutions, Ingram Library Services,

Keystone Systems, Inc (KLAS), LexisNexis, McGraw-Hill, MD Consult, Medline, Micromedex, Newsbank, ProQuest, PubMed, Springer-Verlag, Surpass, YBP Library Services
Function: CD-ROM, Computers for patron use, Copy machines, Distance learning, E-Reserves, Electronic databases & coll, Fax serv, Handicapped accessible, ILL available, Music CDs, Orientations, Photocopying/Printing, Ref & res
Partic in GALILEO (Georgia Library Learning Online)
Special Services for the Deaf - Assistive tech; Closed caption videos; Sorenson video relay syst
Special Services for the Blind - Accessible computers
Open Mon-Thurs 7:30am-8pm, Fri 7:30am-1pm
Restriction: Open to students, fac, staff & alumni, Use of others with permission of librn

WALKER COUNTY CAMPUS LIBRARY, Bldg 500, 265 Bicentennial Trail, Rock Spring, 30739. (Mail add: PO Box 569, Rock Spring, 30739-0569). Tel: 706-764-3533. FAX: 706-764-3567. Web Site: www.gntc.edu. *Librn,* Lydia Hofstetter; Tel: 706-764-3819, E-mail: lhofstetter@gntc.edu; *Coordr,* Pete Bursi; Tel: 706-764-3568, E-mail: pbursi@gntc.edu; Staff 3 (MLS 2, Non-MLS 1)
Founded 1966. Enrl 2,300; Highest Degree: Associate
Library Holdings: CDs 37; e-books 15,000; Bk Vols 13,000; Per Subs 140; Videos 250
Automation Activity & Vendor Info: (Cataloging) Surpass; (Circulation) Surpass; (OPAC) Surpass
Partic in GALILEO (Georgia Library Learning Online)
Open Mon-Thurs 7:30am-9pm, Fri 7:30-4

P SARA HIGHTOWER REGIONAL LIBRARY*, Rome-Floyd County Library, 205 Riverside Pkwy NE, 30161-2922. SAN 339-1264. Tel: 706-236-4600, 706-236-4601. Interlibrary Loan Service Tel: 706-236-4603. Reference Tel: 706-236-4604. Automation Services Tel: 706-236-4621. FAX: 706-236-4605. Automation Services FAX: 706-236-4631. Web Site: www.romelibrary.org. *Dir,* Delana Hickman; Tel: 406-236-4609; Staff 68 (MLS 4, Non-MLS 64)
Founded 1911. Pop 121,327; Circ 760,000
Library Holdings: Per Subs 184
Special Collections: Audio-Visual Materials; Cherokee Indians; Genealogy & Local History; Marshall Forest Coll; Video Studio Coll
Wireless access
Partic in Georgia Online Database
Special Services for the Deaf - Adult & family literacy prog; Assistive tech; Bks on deafness & sign lang; Closed caption videos; TDD equip
Special Services for the Blind - Duplicating spec requests; Home delivery serv; Large print bks; Magnifiers; Newsp on cassette; Reader equip
Open Mon-Thurs 8:30-8:30, Sat 10-5
Friends of the Library Group
Branches: 4

CAVE SPRING BRANCH, 17 Cedartown St, Cave Spring, 30124-2702. (Mail add: PO Box 329, Cave Spring, 30124-0329), SAN 339-1418. Tel: 706-777-3346. FAX: 706-777-0947. Web Site: www.cavespringlibrary.org. *Br Mgr,* Diana Mills; E-mail: dmills@romelibrary.org; Staff 5 (MLS 1, Non-MLS 4)
Pop 2,153
Special Collections: Municipal Document Depository
Automation Activity & Vendor Info: (Acquisitions) Evergreen; (Cataloging) Evergreen; (Circulation) Evergreen; (OPAC) Evergreen
Database Vendor: EBSCOhost
Function: 24/7 Electronic res, 24/7 Online cat, Children's prog, Computer training, Computers for patron use, Copy machines, Digital talking bks, Doc delivery serv, e-mail & chat, e-mail serv, Electronic databases & coll, Home delivery & serv to Sr ctr & nursing homes
Special Services for the Deaf - Bks on deafness & sign lang; Closed caption videos; Sign lang interpreter upon request for prog; Staff with knowledge of sign lang
Open Mon-Fri 12-6
Restriction: Non-resident fee

CEDARTOWN BRANCH, 245 East Ave, City Complex, Cedartown, 30125-3001, SAN 339-1442. Tel: 770-748-5644. FAX: 770-748-4399. Web Site: www.cedartownlibrary.org. *Br Mgr,* Angela Campbell; E-mail: acampbell@cedartownlibrary.org; Staff 2 (MLS 1, Non-MLS 1)
Function: Bks on CD, Children's prog, Computers for patron use, Copy machines, e-mail & chat, E-Reserves, Fax serv, Free DVD rentals, ILL available, Magnifiers for reading, Mail & tel request accepted, Microfiche/film & reading machines, Music CDs, Online cat, OverDrive digital audio bks, Photocopying/Printing, Prog for children & young adult, Pub access computers, Scanner, Spanish lang bks, Story hour, Summer reading prog, Tax forms
Partic in PINES (Public Information Network for Electronic Services)
Open Mon-Thurs 9-6, Fri 9-5, Sat 9-4

P NORTHWEST GEORGIA TALKING BOOK LIBRARY, 205 Riverside Pkwy, 30161-2922, SAN 339-1299. Tel: 706-236-4618. FAX: 706-236-4631. Web Site: www.rome-lpd.org. *Librn for Blind & Physically Handicapped,* Delana Hickman; Staff 3 (MLS 1, Non-MLS 2)
Founded 1975
Special Collections: Juvenile Books in Print & Braille
Publications: Newsletter (Monthly)
Special Services for the Deaf - TDD equip; TTY equip
Special Services for the Blind - Computer with voice synthesizer for visually impaired persons; Newsp on cassette; Production of talking bks; Reader equip; Rec of textbk mat
Open Mon-Fri 8:30-4

ROCKMART BRANCH, Bldg 201, 316 N Piedmont Ave, Rockmart, 30153-2402, SAN 339-1477. Tel: 770-684-3022. FAX: 770-684-7876. Web Site: www.rockmartlibrary.org. *Br Mgr,* Sharon Cleveland; E-mail: scleveland@rockmartlibrary.org; Staff 3 (Non-MLS 3)
Library Holdings: Bk Vols 46,430; Per Subs 32
Open Mon-Fri 9-5, Sat 9-4

C SHORTER COLLEGE*, Livingston Library, 315 Shorter Ave, 30165. SAN 303-4127. Tel: 706-291-2121, Ext 7296. Interlibrary Loan Service Tel: 706-233-7298. Administration Tel: 706-233-7297. Toll Free Tel: 800-868-6980. FAX: 706-236-1512. Web Site: www.shorter.edu. *Dir of Libr,* Deborah Meyer; *ILL,* Bettie Sumner; *Music,* John Rivest; Staff 5 (MLS 5)
Founded 1873. Enrl 2,428; Fac 62; Highest Degree: Master
Library Holdings: Bk Vols 139,488; Per Subs 832
Special Collections: Baptist Convention & Association Minutes; Georgia Baptist History
Subject Interests: Music, Relig
Automation Activity & Vendor Info: (Cataloging) TLC (The Library Corporation); (Circulation) TLC (The Library Corporation); (OPAC) TLC (The Library Corporation)
Publications: Livingston Library Handbook
Partic in Georgia Private Acad Librs Consortium (GPALS); Lyrasis; OCLC Online Computer Library Center, Inc
Open Mon-Thurs 8am-11pm, Fri 8-5, Sat 1-5, Sun 2-11

SAINT SIMONS ISLAND

G FORT FREDERICA NATIONAL MONUMENT LIBRARY*, 6515 Frederica Rd, 31522. SAN 373-4285. Tel: 912-638-3639. FAX: 912-638-3639. Web Site: www.nps.gov/fofr. *Cultural Res Spec,* Denise Spear
Library Holdings: Bk Vols 300
Restriction: Open by appt only

P SAINT SIMONS PUBLIC LIBRARY*, 530A Beachview Dr, 31522. SAN 303-4143. Tel: 912-638-8234. FAX: 912-638-8254. *Libr Mgr,* Jenny Herring
Founded 1937. Pop 14,000; Circ 26,000
Library Holdings: Bk Vols 47,000; Per Subs 30
Wireless access
Mem of Marshes of Glynn Libraries
Partic in PINES (Public Information Network for Electronic Services)
Open Mon, Tues, Thurs & Fri 10-5, Wed 12-7, Sat 10-1
Friends of the Library Group

SR UNITED METHODIST CHURCH - SOUTH GEORGIA CONFERENCE*, Arthur J Moore Methodist Library, Epworth-by-the-Sea, 100 Arthur Moore Dr, 31522. (Mail add: PO Box 24081, 31522-7081), SAN 373-0433. Tel: 912-638-4050. FAX: 912-638-9050. *Dir,* Judi Fergus; *Asst Dir,* Sandra Harris
Library Holdings: Bk Vols 6,000
Wireless access
Open Tues-Sat 10-4
Friends of the Library Group

SANDERSVILLE

S THIELE KAOLIN CO*, Research & Development Library, 520 Kaolin Rd, 31082. (Mail add: PO Box 1056, 31082), SAN 303-4151. Tel: 478-552-3951. FAX: 478-552-4138. *In Charge,* Brittany Raley; E-mail: brittany.raley@thielekaolin.com
Founded 1965
Library Holdings: Bk Vols 1,500; Per Subs 44
Open Mon-Fri 8-5

SAPELO ISLAND

C UNIVERSITY OF GEORGIA*, Marine Institute Library, One Turkey Fountain Way, 31327. SAN 325-0210. Tel: 912-485-2276. FAX: 912-485-2133. E-mail: ugami@uga.edu. *Dir,* Merryl Alber
Founded 1953
Library Holdings: Bk Vols 5,000; Per Subs 65
Wireless access
Publications: Collected Reprint Series

SAVANNAH

C ARMSTRONG ATLANTIC STATE UNIVERSITY*, Lane Library, 11935 Abercorn St, 31419. SAN 303-416X. Tel: 912-344-3027. Reference Tel: 912-344-3026. FAX: 912-344-3457. Web Site: library.armstrong.edu. *Univ Librn,* Doug Frazier; Tel: 912-344-2818, E-mail: doug.frazier@armstrong.edu; *Head, Circ/ILL,* Ann Fuller; *Head, Media Serv,* Richard Horah; *Head, Ref & Instruction,* Judith Garrison; *Head, Tech Serv,* Beth Burnett; *ILL Librn,* Melissa Jackson; *Ref & Instruction Librn,* Jewell Anderson; *Ref & Instruction Librn,* Caroline Hopkinson; *Ref & Instruction Librn,* Kristin Stout; *Asst Tech Serv Librn,* Robert Jones; Staff 20 (MLS 11, Non-MLS 9)
Founded 1935. Enrl 7,000; Fac 260; Highest Degree: Master
Special Collections: Educational Resources Information Center Coll, fiche; First Editions of Conrad Aiken & other Savannah authors; Library of American Civilization, fiche; Library of English Literature, fiche; Savannah Authors; Savannah History
Subject Interests: Ga
Automation Activity & Vendor Info: (Acquisitions) Ex Libris Group; (Cataloging) Ex Libris Group; (Circulation) Ex Libris Group; (Course Reserve) Docutek; (OPAC) Ex Libris Group; (Serials) Ex Libris Group
Database Vendor: ACM (Association for Computing Machinery), American Psychological Association (APA), Bowker, Cambridge Scientific Abstracts, CQ Press, CredoReference, EBSCOhost, Gale Cengage Learning, H W Wilson, ISI Web of Knowledge, JSTOR, LexisNexis, OCLC WorldShare Interlibrary Loan, OVID Technologies, Oxford Online, ProQuest, ScienceDirect, Thomson - Web of Science, Wilson - Wilson Web
Wireless access
Publications: Annual Report; Faculty Guide to Lane Library; Library Guides
Partic in Galileo/GIL; Lyrasis
Open Mon-Thurs 7:30am-11pm, Fri 7:30-5, Sat 10-5, Sun 2-11

S GEORGIA HISTORICAL SOCIETY*, Research Center, 501 Whitaker St, 31401. SAN 303-4186. Tel: 912-651-2128. Administration Tel: 912-651-2125. FAX: 912-651-2831. E-mail: library@georgiahistory.com. Web Site: www.georgiahistory.com. *Dir,* Lynette Stoudt; Tel: 912-651-2125, Ext 134, E-mail: lstoudt@georgiahistory.com
Founded 1839
Library Holdings: Bk Vols 20,000; Per Subs 50
Special Collections: Central Coll of Georgia Railway; Savannah Jewish Archives. Municipal Document Depository
Subject Interests: Civil War, Ga, Genealogy
Automation Activity & Vendor Info: (Acquisitions) EOS International; (Cataloging) EOS International; (OPAC) EOS International
Wireless access
Publications: Georgia Historical Quarterly; Georgia Historical Society Collections; Georgia History Today Newsletter
Partic in OCLC Online Computer Library Center, Inc
Open Wed-Fri 12-5
Restriction: Non-circulating to the pub

S GIRL SCOUTS OF THE USA*, Juliette Gordon Low Birthplace Library, 10 E Oglethorpe Ave, 31401. SAN 377-3965. Tel: 912-233-4501. FAX: 912-233-4659. E-mail: birthplace@girlscouts.org. Web Site: www.juliettegordonlowbirthplace.org. *Dir,* Fran Powell Harold; E-mail: fharold@girlscouts.org; *Prog Mgr, Archival Coll,* Katherine Knapp Keena. Subject Specialists: *Early girl scout hist,* Katherine Knapp Keena
Library Holdings: Bk Vols 550
Special Collections: Gordon Family Archives, letters, papers, photog & scrapbks
Restriction: Open by appt only

P LIVE OAK PUBLIC LIBRARIES*, 2002 Bull St, 31401. SAN 339-1655. Tel: 912-652-3600. Circulation Tel: 912-652-3629. Reference Tel: 912-652-3627. FAX: 912-652-3638. TDD: 912-652-3635. Web Site: www.liveoakpl.org. *Dir,* Christian Kruse; Tel: 912-652-3601, E-mail: krusec@liveoakpl.org; *Develop Dir, Mkt Dir,* Christy Divine; *Financial Dir,* Neal Vickers; E-mail: vickersn@liveoakpl.org; *Asst Dir, Pub Serv,* John Tuggle; E-mail: tugglej@liveoakpl.org; *Asst Dir, Tech, Asst Dir, Tech Serv,* Karen Reichardt; Tel: 912-652-3694, E-mail: kreichardt@liveoakpl.org; *Coll Develop Librn,* Diane Bronson; E-mail: bronsond@liveoakpl.org; Staff 176 (MLS 35, Non-MLS 141)
Founded 1903. Pop 339,150; Circ 1,088,837
Library Holdings: AV Mats 26,589; Large Print Bks 14,124; Bk Titles 161,726; Bk Vols 302,100; Per Subs 1,148; Talking Bks 18,404
Special Collections: Local History (Gamble Coll)
Subject Interests: Genealogy
Automation Activity & Vendor Info: (Acquisitions) SirsiDynix; (Cataloging) SirsiDynix; (Circulation) SirsiDynix; (OPAC) SirsiDynix
Database Vendor: EBSCOhost, OCLC FirstSearch
Wireless access
Partic in OCLC Online Computer Library Center, Inc
Special Services for the Deaf - TDD equip; Videos & decoder
Open Mon & Tues 9-8, Wed-Fri 9-6, Sun 2-6
Friends of the Library Group
Branches: 17
CARNEGIE BRANCH, 537 E Henry St, 31401, SAN 339-168X. Tel: 912-231-9921. FAX: 912-231-9575. *Br Mgr,* Adriene Tillman; Staff 3 (MLS 1, Non-MLS 2)
Library Holdings: Bk Vols 2,098
Subject Interests: African-Am
Open Mon 10-8, Tues-Thurs 10-6, Fri 2-6
FOREST CITY BRANCH, 1501 Stiles Ave, 31415, SAN 339-1701. Tel: 912-238-0614. FAX: 912-236-8879. *Br Mgr,* Tonya Johnson; E-mail: johnsont@liveoakpl.org; Staff 3 (Non-MLS 3)
Library Holdings: Bk Vols 23,439
Open Mon & Tues 10-6, Wed & Sat 2-6, Thurs 2-8
HINESVILLE BRANCH, 236 Memorial Dr, Hinesville, 31313, SAN 339-1833. Tel: 912-368-4003. FAX: 912-369-7148. *Mgr,* Betsy Stow; Staff 15 (MLS 3, Non-MLS 12)
Library Holdings: Bk Vols 53,922
Open Mon-Thurs 9-8, Fri & Sat 9-6
ISLANDS BRANCH, 125 Wilmington Island Rd, 31410, SAN 339-1752. Tel: 912-897-6233. FAX: 912-897-1496. *Br Mgr,* Sandra O'Connell; E-mail: oconnells@liveoakpl.org; Staff 7 (MLS 1, Non-MLS 6)
Library Holdings: Bk Vols 33,586
Open Mon & Tues 10-8, Wed & Thurs 10-6, Fri & Sat 2-6
W W LAW BRANCH, 909 E Bolton St, 31401, SAN 339-1809. Tel: 912-236-8040. FAX: 912-236-8040. *Br Mgr,* Renette Lewis; E-mail: lewisr@liveoakpl.org; Staff 2 (Non-MLS 2)
Library Holdings: Bk Vols 4,632
Open Mon & Wed 9-1 & 2-6, Tues & Thurs 2-6, Fri 9-1
MIDWAY-RICEBORO BRANCH, 1165 Bill Martin Rd, Midway, 31320, SAN 375-5479. Tel: 912-884-5742. FAX: 912-884-5741. *Mgr,* Betsy Stow; Staff 2 (Non-MLS 2)
Library Holdings: Bk Vols 10,000
Open Mon-Thurs 2-7, Sat 12-5
OGLETHORPE MALL BRANCH, Seven Mall Annex, 31406, SAN 339-1892. Tel: 912-925-5432. FAX: 912-925-2031. *Br Mgr,* Coni Coleman; E-mail: colemanc@liveoakpl.org; Staff 16 (MLS 4, Non-MLS 12)
Library Holdings: Bk Vols 81,298
Open Mon & Wed 9-8, Tues, Thurs & Sat 9-6
POOLER BRANCH, 216 S Rogers St, Pooler, 31322, SAN 339-1922. Tel: 912-748-0471. FAX: 912-748-4947. *Br Mgr,* Jeanie Holland; E-mail: hollandj@liveoakpl.org; Staff 6 (MLS 1, Non-MLS 5)
Library Holdings: Bk Vols 32,167
Open Mon & Tues 10-8, Wed & Thurs 10-6, Fri & Sat 2-6
PORT CITY BRANCH, 3501 Houlihan Ave, 31408, SAN 339-1949. Tel: 912-964-8013. FAX: 912-966-5142. *Br Mgr,* Sheila Henderson; E-mail: hendersons@liveoakpl.org; Staff 4 (Non-MLS 4)
Library Holdings: Bk Vols 24,771
Open Mon, Wed & Thurs 12-6, Tues 10-6, Sat 2-6
PORT WENTWORTH BRANCH, 102 Aberfeldy St, Port Wentworth, 31407, SAN 339-1957. Tel: 912-964-0371. FAX: 912-964-0371. *Br Mgr,* Cassie Jones; E-mail: jonesc@liveoakpl.org; Staff 1 (Non-MLS 1)
Library Holdings: Bk Vols 2,104
Open Tues 10-1 & 2-5, Wed-Fri 3-6
RINCON BRANCH, 17th St & Hwy 21, Rincon, 31326. (Mail add: PO Box 1939, Rincon, 31326-1939), SAN 329-6059. Tel: 912-826-2222. FAX: 912-826-6304. *Br Mgr,* Beatrice Saba; E-mail: sabab@liveoakpl.org; Staff 10 (MLS 2, Non-MLS 8)
Library Holdings: Bk Vols 42,448
Open Mon 10-7,Tues 2-6, Wed, Fri & Sat 10-6
SOUTHWEST CHATHAM BRANCH, 14097 Abercorn St, 31419. Tel: 912-925-8305. Circulation Tel: 912-925-8305, Ext 303. Reference Tel: 912-925-8305, Ext 310. *Br Mgr,* Coni Coleman; E-mail: colemanc@liveoakpl.org
Open Tues & Thurs 9-8, Wed & Fri-Sat 9-6, Sun 2-6
SPRINGFIELD BRANCH, 810 Hwy 119 S, Springfield, 31329. (Mail add: PO Box 189, Springfield, 31329), SAN 339-171X. Tel: 912-754-3003. FAX: 912-754-9494. *Br Mgr,* Rayne Highsmith
Library Holdings: Bk Vols 35,315
Open Mon 2-6, Tues 10-7, Wed 10-2, Thurs 10-6
THUNDERBOLT BRANCH, 2708 Mechanics Ave, Thunderbolt, 31404, SAN 339-1981. Tel: 912-354-5864. FAX: 912-354-5534. *Br Mgr,* Cheri Lewis; E-mail: lewisc@liveoakpl.org; Staff 4 (MLS 1, Non-MLS 3)
Library Holdings: Bk Vols 17,299
Open Mon, Wed, Fri & Sat 2-6, Tues & Thurs 11-6
TYBEE ISLAND BRANCH, 403 Butler Ave, Tybee Island, 31328, SAN 339-2015. Tel: 912-786-7733. FAX: 912-786-7734. *Br Mgr,* Laurel Powers; E-mail: powersl@liveoakpl.org; Staff 2 (Non-MLS 2)
Library Holdings: Bk Vols 12,094
Open Mon, Fri & Sat 2-6, Tues 10-8, Wed 10-6

WEST BROAD BRANCH, YMCA Bldg, 1110 May St, 31415. Tel: 912-232-6395. FAX: 912-232-6395. Web Site: www.liveoakpl.org/branches/west-broad-branch.php. *Br Mgr,* Donald Turner
Open Mon & Fri 2-6, Tues-Thurs 10-6

OLA WYETH BRANCH, Four E Bay St, 31401, SAN 339-204X. Tel: 912-232-5488. FAX: 912-232-5488. *Br Mgr,* Kathy Powell; E-mail: powellk@liveoakpl.org; Staff 2 (Non-MLS 2)
Library Holdings: Bk Vols 5,490
Open Mon-Fri 12-3

Bookmobiles: 1

M MEMORIAL HEALTH UNIVERSITY MEDICAL CENTER*, Health Sciences Library, 4700 Waters Ave, 31403. (Mail add: PO Box 23089, 31403-3089), SAN 323-7370. Tel: 912-350-8345. *Mgr,* Jane Bridges; *Tech Serv,* Vanessa Wallace Lonon; Staff 2 (MLS 1, Non-MLS 1)
Library Holdings: Bk Titles 4,200; Per Subs 325
Open Mon-Thurs 7:30-6, Fri 7:30-5
Restriction: Non-circulating

S SAVANNAH MORNING NEWS*, News Research, 1375 Chatham Pkwy, 31405. (Mail add: PO Box 1088, 31402-1088), SAN 303-4208. Tel: 912-652-0319. FAX: 912-525-0795, 912-525-0796. E-mail: research@savannahnow.com. *Head, Res Serv,* Julia C Muller; E-mail: julia.muller@savannahnow.com; Staff 1 (Non-MLS 1)
Library Holdings: Microforms 2,000; Bk Vols 200
Database Vendor: Newsbank, ProQuest
Restriction: Not open to pub

C SAVANNAH STATE UNIVERSITY*, Asa H Gordon Library, 2200 Tompkins Rd, 31404. (Mail add: PO Box 20394, 31404-9705), SAN 303-4216. Tel: 912-356-2183. Interlibrary Loan Service Tel: 912 356-2932. Reference Tel: 912 356-2327. FAX: 912-356-2874. Web Site: www.library/savstate.edu. *Dir,* Mary Jo Fayoyin; Staff 3 (MLS 3)
Founded 1891. Enrl 2,900; Highest Degree: Master
Library Holdings: Bk Vols 189,000; Per Subs 566
Special Collections: Educational Resources Information Center
Subject Interests: African-Am (ethnic)
Automation Activity & Vendor Info: (Acquisitions) Ex Libris Group; (Cataloging) Ex Libris Group; (Circulation) Ex Libris Group; (Serials) EBSCO Online
Wireless access
Function: ILL available
Publications: Bibliographies; Library Handbook
Partic in Lyrasis

J SAVANNAH TECHNICAL COLLEGE*, Savannah Campus Library, 5717 White Bluff Rd, 31405-5521. Tel: 912-443-5870. FAX: 912-443-5875. Web Site: www.savannahtech.edu. *Dir, Libr & Info Serv,* James Burch; Tel: 912-443-5874, E-mail: jburch@savannahtech.edu; Staff 3 (MLS 2, Non-MLS 1)
Founded 1929. Enrl 3,700; Highest Degree: Associate
Library Holdings: e-books 58,000; e-journals 15,000; Bk Vols 33,000; Per Subs 150; Talking Bks 100; Videos 2,800
Automation Activity & Vendor Info: (Cataloging) TLC (The Library Corporation); (Circulation) TLC (The Library Corporation); (OPAC) TLC (The Library Corporation)
Wireless access
Partic in GALILEO (Georgia Library Learning Online)
Open Mon-Thurs 7:30am-9pm, Fri 7:30-4, Sat 9-1

S SKIDAWAY INSTITUTE OF OCEANOGRAPHY LIBRARY*, John F McGowan Library, Ten Ocean Science Circle, 31411-1011. SAN 303-4224. Tel: 912-598-2474. FAX: 912-598-2391. E-mail: library@skio.usg.edu. Web Site: www.skio.usg.edu/resources/library. *Librn,* John Cruickshank; Staff 1 (MLS 1)
Founded 1970
Library Holdings: Bk Titles 4,000; Bk Vols 8,000; Per Subs 110
Subject Interests: Ecology, Geochemistry, Geol, Marine biol, Oceanography
Automation Activity & Vendor Info: (Acquisitions) Ex Libris Group; (Cataloging) Ex Libris Group; (Circulation) Ex Libris Group; (Course Reserve) Ex Libris Group; (ILL) Ex Libris Group; (Media Booking) Ex Libris Group; (OPAC) Ex Libris Group; (Serials) Ex Libris Group
Function: Photocopying/Printing
Publications: Serials Holdings List
Open Mon-Fri 8-4:30

C SOUTH UNIVERSITY LIBRARY*, 709 Mall Blvd, 31406. SAN 322-8800. Tel: 912-201-8047. Interlibrary Loan Service Tel: 912-201-8046. FAX: 912-201-8070. Web Site: inside.southuniversity.edu. *Libr Dir,* Valerie E Yaughn; Staff 3 (MLS 3)
Founded 1975. Enrl 1,200; Fac 95; Highest Degree: Doctorate
Library Holdings: AV Mats 300; DVDs 50; e-books 200,000; e-journals 40; Electronic Media & Resources 75; Bk Vols 41,000; Per Subs 30; Videos 250
Subject Interests: Allied health, Behav sci, Bus, Legal studies, Theol
Automation Activity & Vendor Info: (Acquisitions) Ex Libris Group; (Cataloging) Ex Libris Group; (Circulation) Ex Libris Group; (OPAC) Ex Libris Group; (Serials) Ex Libris Group
Database Vendor: Alexander Street Press, American Chemical Society, American Psychological Association (APA), CRC Press/Taylor & Francis Group, CredoReference, ebrary, EBSCOhost, Ex Libris Group, Gale Cengage Learning, Hoovers, JSTOR, Lexi-Comp, MD Consult, Medline, Micromedex, Natural Standard, OVID Technologies, ProQuest, PubMed, RefWorks, Sage, ScienceDirect, Springshare, LLC, STAT!Ref (Teton Data Systems), Thomson - Web of Science, UpToDate, Westlaw
Wireless access
Function: AV serv, Computers for patron use, Copy machines, Distance learning, e-mail serv, Electronic databases & coll, Handicapped accessible, ILL available, Instruction & testing, Learning ctr, Online cat, Online ref, Orientations, Outside serv via phone, mail, e-mail & web, Photocopying/Printing, Ref & res, Ref serv in person, Telephone ref, VHS videos, Wheelchair accessible
Partic in Docline; Lyrasis
Restriction: Authorized patrons, Borrowing privileges limited to fac & registered students, Open to pub by appt only, Open to students, fac & staff

S TELFAIR MUSEUM OF ART*, Anderson Library/Jepson Center for the Arts, 207 W York St, 31401. SAN 371-1196. Tel: 912-790-8802. FAX: 912-790-8803. Web Site: www.telfair.org. *Chief Curator,* Holly McCullough; E-mail: mcculloughh@telfair.org; *Asst Curator,* Courtney McGowan; Staff 10 (Non-MLS 10)
Founded 1886
Library Holdings: Bk Titles 4,500; Per Subs 25
Subject Interests: 18th Century decorative arts, 19th Century Am lit, 20th Century art, 21st Century fine art, Decorative art
Wireless access
Restriction: Staff use only

SR ABE & ESTHER TENENBAUM LIBRARY*, Nine Lee Blvd, 31405. SAN 329-7365. Tel: 912-352-4737. FAX: 912-352-3477. *In Charge,* Paula Lewis; Staff 1 (Non-MLS 1)
Library Holdings: Bk Vols 2,000
Special Collections: Judaica, bks
Open Mon-Thurs 8:30-5, Fri 8:30-3

S US NATIONAL PARK SERVICE*, Fort Pulaski Monument Library, PO Box 30757, 31410-0757. SAN 370-2901. Tel: 912-786-5787. FAX: 912-786-6023. *In Charge,* June Devisfruto; E-mail: june_devisfruto@nps.gov
Library Holdings: Bk Vols 800; Per Subs 10
Subject Interests: Natural hist
Restriction: Open by appt only

SMYRNA

P SMYRNA PUBLIC LIBRARY, 100 Village Green Circle, 30080-3478. SAN 303-4232. Tel: 770-431-2860. FAX: 770-431-2862. E-mail: reference@smyrnaga.gov. *Dir,* Mary Wallace Moore; E-mail: mwmoore@smyrnaga.gov; *ILL,* Kate Reinecke; E-mail: rkreinecke@smyrnaga.gov; *Tech Serv,* Ruth Hayden; E-mail: rhayden@smyrnaga.gov; *Youth Serv,* Rebecca Power; E-mail: rpower@smyrnaga.gov; Staff 13 (MLS 7, Non-MLS 6)
Founded 1936. Pop 51,271; Circ 220,652
Jul 2010-Jun 2011 Income $624,421. Mats Exp $114,407, Books $85,732, Per/Ser (Incl. Access Fees) $3,421, AV Equip $1,055, AV Mat $6,019, Electronic Ref Mat (Incl. Access Fees) $17,433, Presv $747. Sal $439,981
Library Holdings: Audiobooks 777; AV Mats 15,350; Bks on Deafness & Sign Lang 48; CDs 5,198; DVDs 4,684; e-books 397; High Interest/Low Vocabulary Bk Vols 98; Large Print Bks 2,462; Bk Titles 76,370; Bk Vols 83,190; Per Subs 125; Videos 2,188
Special Collections: Antique Books; Genealogy Coll
Subject Interests: Children's lit, Ga, Genealogy, Law
Automation Activity & Vendor Info: (Acquisitions) Baker & Taylor; (Cataloging) TLC (The Library Corporation); (Circulation) TLC (The Library Corporation); (OPAC) TLC (The Library Corporation); (Serials) TLC (The Library Corporation)
Database Vendor: Booklist Online, EBSCOhost, Gale Cengage Learning, Hoovers, infoUSA, LearningExpress, Medline, Newsbank, OCLC FirstSearch, ProQuest, ReferenceUSA, TLC (The Library Corporation), WebMD
Wireless access
Function: Adult bk club, After school storytime, Art exhibits, Bk club(s), Bks on cassette, Bks on CD, CD-ROM, Chess club, Children's prog, Computer training, Computers for patron use, Copy machines, e-mail serv, E-Reserves, Electronic databases & coll, Exhibits, Free DVD rentals, Handicapped accessible, Holiday prog, ILL available, Instruction & testing,

Magnifiers for reading, Music CDs, Online cat, Online ref, Photocopying/Printing, Prog for adults, Prog for children & young adult, Pub access computers, Ref serv available, Ref serv in person, Spoken cassettes & CDs, Story hour, Summer reading prog, Tax forms, Teen prog, Telephone ref, VHS videos, Web-catalog, Wheelchair accessible, Workshops
Publications: Library Link (Newsletter)
Partic in GALILEO (Georgia Library Learning Online); Lyrasis; N Ga Associated Librs
Special Services for the Deaf - Assisted listening device; Closed caption videos
Special Services for the Blind - Bks on cassette; Bks on CD; Large print & cassettes; Large print bks; Low vision equip; Magnifiers
Open Mon-Thurs 10-8, Fri 10-6, Sat 10-5, Sun 1-6
Restriction: In-house use for visitors, Non-resident fee, Restricted loan policy
Friends of the Library Group

SPARKS

J WIREGRASS GEORGIA TECHNICAL COLLEGE LIBRARY*, Cook County Workforce Development Resource Center, 1676 Elm St, Rm 112, 31647. (Mail add: 4089 Val Tech Rd, Valdosta, 31602). Tel: 229-549-7368. Circulation Tel: 229-259-5177. Administration Tel: 229-259-5178. FAX: 229-549-6286. Circulation FAX: 229-259-5179. E-mail: library@wiregrass.edu. Web Site: www.wiregrass.edu/library. *Librn,* Brandi Woods Johnson; E-mail: brandi.johnson@wiregrass.edu; Staff 1 (MLS 1)
Founded 2005. Enrl 102; Fac 10; Highest Degree: Associate
Library Holdings: CDs 35; DVDs 76; Electronic Media & Resources 100; Bk Vols 731; Per Subs 3; Videos 28
Automation Activity & Vendor Info: (Acquisitions) TLC (The Library Corporation); (Cataloging) TLC (The Library Corporation); (Circulation) TLC (The Library Corporation); (ILL) OCLC ILLiad; (OPAC) TLC (The Library Corporation); (Serials) EBSCO Online
Database Vendor: CredoReference, EBSCO - WebFeat, Medline, Micromedex, ProQuest, TLC (The Library Corporation), WebMD, Westlaw

SPARTA

S GEORGIA DEPARTMENT OF CORRECTIONS, OFFICE OF LIBRARY SERVICES*, Hancock State Prison, 701 Prison Blvd, 31087. (Mail add: PO Box 339, 31087-0339). Tel: 706-444-1026. FAX: 706-444-1137. Web Site: www.dcor.state.ga.us. *Librn,* Nesial Miller
Library Holdings: Bk Vols 1,700; Per Subs 10; Talking Bks 20
Special Collections: Law Coll
Database Vendor: LexisNexis
Open Mon-Thurs 6-4:30

STATESBORO

C GEORGIA SOUTHERN UNIVERSITY, Zach S Henderson Library, 1400 Southern Dr, 30458. (Mail add: PO Box 8074, 30460), SAN 303-4240. Tel: 912-478-5115. Circulation Tel: 912-478-5647. Interlibrary Loan Service Tel: 912-478-5405. Reference Tel: 912-478-5645. FAX: 912-478-0093. Web Site: library.georgiasouthern.edu. *Dean,* Dr W Bede Mitchell; E-mail: wbmitch@georgiasouthern.edu; *Assoc Dean,* Ann Hamilton; *Head, Coll & Res Serv,* Charles A Skewis; Tel: 912-478-5114, E-mail: cskewis@library.georgiasouthern.edu; *Head, Info Serv,* Jocelyn Poole; *Head, Syst,* David Lowder; Tel: 912-478-0161; *Access Serv,* Fred Smith; *Govt Doc,* Lori Gwinett; Tel: 912-478-5117; Staff 54 (MLS 19, Non-MLS 35)
Founded 1906. Enrl 18,429; Fac 823; Highest Degree: Doctorate
Library Holdings: AV Mats 29,759; e-books 53,083; e-journals 47,862; Microforms 896,632; Bk Vols 649,338; Per Subs 426
Special Collections: Commander William M Rigdon Coll, 1940-1950; Congressman Ronald “Bo” Ginn Coll; Geer Coll; Gulver Kidd Coll; McTell Papers (Michael Gray Coll); Zachert Coll of Private Press Books. State Document Depository; US Document Depository
Automation Activity & Vendor Info: (Acquisitions) Ex Libris Group; (Cataloging) Ex Libris Group; (Circulation) Ex Libris Group; (ILL) OCLC; (OPAC) Ex Libris Group; (Serials) Ex Libris Group
Wireless access
Partic in GALILEO (Georgia Library Learning Online); Lyrasis
Friends of the Library Group

J OGEECHEE TECHNICAL COLLEGE LIBRARY*, One Joe Kennedy Blvd, 30458. Tel: 912-871-1886. Administration Tel: 912-871-1606. FAX: 912-486-7003. E-mail: library@ogeecheetech.edu. Web Site: www.ogeecheetech.edu/index.php/current-students/library. *Dean, Libr Serv,* Dr Lynn Futch; E-mail: lfutch@ogeecheetech.edu; *Librn,* Matthew Stembridge; Tel: 912-871-3524; Staff 3 (MLS 2, Non-MLS 1)
Founded 1989. Enrl 1,069; Highest Degree: Associate
Library Holdings: AV Mats 421; e-books 20,851; Bk Vols 4,834; Per Subs 60
Automation Activity & Vendor Info: (Cataloging) OCLC WorldShare Interlibrary Loan; (OPAC) OCLC WorldShare Interlibrary Loan
Database Vendor: EBSCO Auto Repair Reference, EBSCOhost, Gale Cengage Learning, Hoovers, Medline, OCLC FirstSearch, OCLC WorldShare Interlibrary Loan, OCLC Worldshare Management Services, ProQuest, PubMed, Westlaw
Wireless access
Partic in GALILEO (Georgia Library Learning Online)
Open Mon-Thurs 7am-10pm

P STATESBORO REGIONAL PUBLIC LIBRARIES, 124 S Main St, 30458. SAN 339-2198. Tel: 912-764-1341. Reference Tel: 912-764-1337. FAX: 912-764-1350. E-mail: reference@strl.info. Web Site: www.strl.info. *Dir,* Jennifer Durham; E-mail: director@strl.info; *Asst Dir,* Bridgid McCalister; *Head, Tech Serv,* Jim Rickerson; Tel: 912-764-1333; *Local Hist & Genealogy Librn,* Janice Strickland; Tel: 912-764-1340; *Youth Serv,* Elaine McDuffie; Tel: 912-764-1344. Subject Specialists: *Genealogy, Local hist,* Janice Strickland; Staff 4 (MLS 4)
Founded 1937. Pop 156,000; Circ 214,971
Library Holdings: Bk Vols 196,095; Per Subs 303
Special Collections: Genealogy Coll, bks, micro
Automation Activity & Vendor Info: (Acquisitions) Evergreen; (Cataloging) Evergreen; (Circulation) Evergreen; (ILL) OCLC
Database Vendor: OCLC FirstSearch
Wireless access
Function: 24/7 Online cat, Adult literacy prog, Bk club(s), Bks on CD, Children’s prog, Computer training, Computers for patron use, Copy machines, E-Reserves, Family literacy, Fax serv, Free DVD rentals, Home delivery & serv to Sr ctr & nursing homes, Homebound delivery serv, ILL available, Magazines, OverDrive digital audio bks, Photocopying/Printing, Pub access computers, Scanner, Summer reading prog, Tax forms, Telephone ref, Wheelchair accessible
Publications: 1909 Map (Bulloch County Georgia); Genealogy (incl cemetary rec, census, newsp abstracts)
Member Libraries: Evans County Public Library; Franklin Memorial Library; L C Anderson Memorial Library; Pembroke Public Library
Partic in Georgia Libr Info Network; PINES (Public Information Network for Electronic Services)
Open Mon-Thurs 9-8, Fri & Sat 9-6
Friends of the Library Group

SUMMERVILLE

P CHATTOOGA COUNTY LIBRARY*, 360 Farrar Dr, 30747-2016. SAN 338-9049. Tel: 706-857-2553. FAX: 706-857-7841. Web Site: www.chattoogacountylibrary.org. *Dir,* Susan Stephens; E-mail: sstephens@chattoogacountylibrary.org; Staff 9 (MLS 2, Non-MLS 7)
Founded 1941. Pop 25,000; Circ 85,005
Library Holdings: CDs 300; DVDs 200; Bk Vols 40,000; Per Subs 68; Videos 1,200
Automation Activity & Vendor Info: (Cataloging) Evergreen; (Circulation) Evergreen; (OPAC) Evergreen
Member Libraries: Trion Public Library
Partic in PINES (Public Information Network for Electronic Services)
Open Mon, Wed & Fri 10-6, Tues & Thurs 10-8, Sat 10-5
Friends of the Library Group

SWAINSBORO

C EAST GEORGIA STATE COLLEGE LIBRARY*, 131 College Circle, 30401-2699. SAN 303-4259. Tel: 478-289-2083. Interlibrary Loan Service Tel: 478-289-2085. Administration Tel: 478-289-2088. FAX: 478-289-2089. TDD: 478-289-2159. E-mail: library@ega.edu. Web Site: www.ega.edu/academics/library. *Libr Dir,* Amanda McKenzie; E-mail: amckenzie@ega.edu; *Ref Librn,* Debra Fennell; Tel: 478-289-2087, E-mail: dfennell@ega.edu; *Circ Mgr, Libr Assoc, Res Sharing Mgr,* Constance Wade; E-mail: cwade@ega.edu; *Libr Asst,* Tia Morris; Tel: 478-289-2086, E-mail: tnmorris@ega.edu. Subject Specialists: *Ga hist, Gen ref, Genealogy,* Debra Fennell; Staff 4 (MLS 2, Non-MLS 2)
Founded 1973. Enrl 2,944; Fac 103; Highest Degree: Bachelor
Library Holdings: AV Mats 969; e-books 27,000; Bk Titles 35,442; Bk Vols 41,432; Per Subs 133; Videos 1,055
Special Collections: Ehrlich Military History Coll, bks, media items; The Heritage Center (includes Emanual County, GA hist, Swainsboro, GA hist), mats, artifacts
Automation Activity & Vendor Info: (Acquisitions) Ex Libris Group; (Cataloging) Ex Libris Group; (Circulation) Ex Libris Group; (Course Reserve) Ex Libris Group; (ILL) OCLC Connexion; (OPAC) Ex Libris Group; (Serials) Ex Libris Group
Database Vendor: Agricola, American Chemical Society, Cinahl, EBSCO Discovery Service, EBSCOhost, Ex Libris Group, Gale Cengage Learning, ISI Web of Knowledge, LexisNexis, Marcive, Inc, Medline, OCLC FirstSearch, OCLC WorldShare Interlibrary Loan, ProQuest, Springshare, LLC
Wireless access

Function: Archival coll, Art exhibits, Audio & video playback equip for onsite use, Bks on CD, Chess club, Computers for patron use, Copy machines, Doc delivery serv, e-mail & chat, Electronic databases & coll, Exhibits, For res purposes, Free DVD rentals, Handicapped accessible, ILL available, Learning ctr, Microfiche/film & reading machines, Music CDs, Newsp ref libr, Online cat, Online ref, Online searches, Orientations, Photocopying/Printing, Pub access computers, Ref & res, Ref serv available, Ref serv in person, Referrals accepted, Scanner, Spanish lang bks, Telephone ref, VHS videos, Video lending libr, Web-catalog, Wheelchair accessible, Workshops
Partic in GALILEO (Georgia Library Learning Online); Georgia Online Database; Lyrasis; OCLC-LVIS
Special Services for the Deaf - Assistive tech
Open Mon-Thurs 7:45-7:30, Fri 7:45-5
Restriction: Non-circulating of rare bks, Open to pub for ref & circ; with some limitations, Open to students, fac & staff

P FRANKLIN MEMORIAL LIBRARY*, 331 W Main, 30401. SAN 339-2287. Tel: 478-237-7791. FAX: 478-237-3553. *Mgr,* Ann Buxton; Staff 7 (Non-MLS 7)
Pop 21,536; Circ 44,628
Library Holdings: Bk Vols 32,000; Per Subs 45
Automation Activity & Vendor Info: (Acquisitions) SirsiDynix; (Cataloging) SirsiDynix; (Circulation) SirsiDynix; (ILL) OCLC
Mem of Statesboro Regional Public Libraries
Partic in PINES (Public Information Network for Electronic Services)
Open Mon, Wed & Fri 8:30-5:30, Tues & Thurs 8:30-7, Sat 9-1
Friends of the Library Group

J SOUTHEASTERN TECHNICAL COLLEGE LIBRARY*, 346 Kite Rd, 30401. Tel: 478-289-2322. FAX: 478-289-2322. Web Site: library.southeasterntech.edu. *Dir, Libr Serv,* Jane Summey; E-mail: jsummey@southeasterntech.edu; *Librn,* Leah Dasher; *Asst Librn,* Sandra Hall; *Asst Librn,* Kayc Wickstrom; E-mail: kwickstrom@swainsborotech.edu; Staff 1.5 (MLS 1.5)
Founded 1998. Enrl 714; Highest Degree: Associate
Library Holdings: AV Mats 147; CDs 620; e-books 49,646; Bk Titles 9,985; Bk Vols 12,531; Per Subs 80; Videos 865
Automation Activity & Vendor Info: (Cataloging) Surpass; (Circulation) Surpass; (OPAC) Surpass
Function: Audio & video playback equip for onsite use, CD-ROM, Copy machines, Electronic databases & coll, Fax serv, Online ref, Online searches, Orientations, Photocopying/Printing, VHS videos, Wheelchair accessible
Partic in GALILEO (Georgia Library Learning Online)
Open Mon-Thurs 8-8, Fri 8-2:30
Restriction: Open to students, fac & staff

SYLVANIA

P SCREVEN-JENKINS REGIONAL LIBRARY*, 106 S Community Dr, 30467. SAN 339-2376. Tel: 912-564-7526. FAX: 912-564-7580. Web Site: www.sjrls.org. *Regional Libr Dir,* Kathyrn Youles; *Asst Dir,* Sharon L Blank; Staff 7 (MLS 2, Non-MLS 5)
Founded 1951. Pop 24,713; Circ 153,163
Library Holdings: Bk Vols 144,000; Per Subs 86
Subject Interests: Ga, Genealogy, Local hist
Wireless access
Partic in Lyrasis
Open Mon 10-6, Tues-Fri 9-6, Sat 10-5
Friends of the Library Group
Branches: 1
JENKINS COUNTY MEMORIAL LIBRARY, 223 Daniel St, Millen, 30442, SAN 339-2406. Tel: 478-982-4244. FAX: 478-982-2192. *Mgr,* Daina Lloyd
Library Holdings: Bk Vols 25,000; Per Subs 35
Open Mon-Wed & Fri 10:30-6, Sat 10:30-2:30
Friends of the Library Group
Bookmobiles: 1

THOMASTON

J SOUTHERN CRESCENT TECHNICAL COLLEGE LIBRARY - FLINT CAMPUS*, Quad Graphics Library, 1533 Hwy 19 S, 30286. Tel: 706-646-6173, 706-646-6225. FAX: 706-646-6240. E-mail: flintlibrary@sctech.edu. Web Site: www.sctech.edu/libraries. *Dir,* Kathleen Williams; E-mail: kewilliams@sctech.edu; *Outreach Librn,* Teresa Nesbitt; E-mail: tnesbitt@sctech.edu; Staff 2 (MLS 2)
Founded 1963. Enrl 700; Highest Degree: Associate
Library Holdings: AV Mats 350; e-books 16,000; Bk Vols 11,000; Per Subs 93
Automation Activity & Vendor Info: (Cataloging) Surpass; (Circulation) Surpass; (OPAC) Surpass
Wireless access
Publications: Library Newsletter
Partic in GALILEO (Georgia Library Learning Online); Georgia Online Database
Open Mon-Thurs 8-8
Restriction: Open to students, fac & staff

THOMASVILLE

M JOHN D ARCHBOLD MEMORIAL HOSPITAL*, Perkins Library, PO Box 1018, 31799-1018. SAN 303-4267. Tel: 229-228-2063. *Librn,* Susan T Leik
Library Holdings: Bk Titles 150; Per Subs 65
Restriction: Staff use only

J SOUTHWEST GEORGIA TECHNICAL COLLEGE LIBRARY*, 15689 US Hwy 19 N, 31792. Tel: 229-225-3958. FAX: 229-225-3959. E-mail: library@southwestgatech.edu. Web Site: www.southwestgatech.edu/library. *Dir, Libr & Media Serv,* Gail Roberts; E-mail: groberts@southwestgatech.edu; *Librn,* Sue Stephenson; E-mail: sstephenson@southwestgatech.edu; Staff 2 (MLS 2)
Founded 1947. Enrl 1,700; Highest Degree: Associate
Library Holdings: CDs 2,000; DVDs 200; e-books 23,000; e-journals 8,000; Bk Vols 23,000; Per Subs 90; Videos 200
Automation Activity & Vendor Info: (Cataloging) TLC (The Library Corporation); (Circulation) TLC (The Library Corporation); (OPAC) TLC (The Library Corporation)
Partic in GALILEO (Georgia Library Learning Online)
Open Mon-Thurs 7:45am-8pm, Fri 7:45-3:30

P THOMAS COUNTY PUBLIC LIBRARY SYSTEM*, 201 N Madison St, 31792-5414. SAN 373-2967. Tel: 229-225-5252. FAX: 229-225-5258. Web Site: www.tcpls.org. *Dir,* Nancy Tillinghast; E-mail: nancy@tcpls.org; *Circ Mgr,* Alicia Atherton; E-mail: alicia@tcpls.org; *Automation Syst Coordr,* Joseph Moore; E-mail: joseph@tcpls.org; *Cat,* Donna Jones; E-mail: donna@tcpls.org; *Ch Serv,* Amanda Redker; E-mail: amanda@tcpls.org; *ILL,* Angela McGuire; E-mail: angela@tcpls.org; *Ref,* Perida Mitchell; E-mail: perida@tcpls.org; Staff 19 (MLS 1, Non-MLS 18)
Founded 1988. Pop 17,421; Circ 144,092
Jul 2011-Jun 2012 Income (Main Library and Branch(s)) $712,359, State $88,930, County $613,929, Locally Generated Income $9,500. Mats Exp $44,017, Books $31,517, Per/Ser (Incl. Access Fees) $4,000, AV Mat $2,500, Electronic Ref Mat (Incl. Access Fees) $6,000. Sal $552,261 (Prof $68,270)
Library Holdings: Audiobooks 8,811; CDs 8,811; DVDs 19,926; e-books 3,073; Electronic Media & Resources 197; Bk Titles 103,467; Per Subs 63
Special Collections: Black Culture/History (Flipper Coll); Plantation Project for South Georgia; Thomas County, Georgia, a History (Heritage Room Coll), bks, microfilm & oral hist. Oral History
Subject Interests: Art
Automation Activity & Vendor Info: (Acquisitions) Evergreen; (Cataloging) Evergreen; (Circulation) Evergreen
Wireless access
Function: Adult literacy prog, Art exhibits, Audiobks via web, AV serv, Bk club(s), Bks on cassette, Bks on CD, CD-ROM, Children's prog, Citizenship assistance, Computer training, Computers for patron use, Copy machines, e-mail serv, Exhibits, Family literacy, Free DVD rentals, Handicapped accessible, Holiday prog, Home delivery & serv to Sr ctr & nursing homes, Homebound delivery serv, Homework prog, ILL available, Magnifiers for reading, Microfiche/film & reading machines, Music CDs, Newsp ref libr, Online searches, Photocopying/Printing, Preschool outreach, Prog for adults, Prog for children & young adult, Pub access computers, Ref serv available, Ref serv in person, Senior computer classes, Serves mentally handicapped consumers, Spoken cassettes & CDs, Story hour, Summer & winter reading prog, Summer reading prog, Tax forms, Teen prog, Telephone ref, VHS videos, Web-catalog, Wheelchair accessible, Workshops
Publications: Friends (Newsletter)
Partic in Georgia Online Database; Lyrasis
Special Services for the Deaf - Bks on deafness & sign lang; High interest/low vocabulary bks; Spec interest per; TDD equip
Open Mon & Tues 9:30-8, Wed-Fri 9:30-6, Sat 9:30-3:30, Sun 2-5
Restriction: Non-resident fee, Open to students
Friends of the Library Group
Branches: 5
BOSTON CARNEGIE PUBLIC LIBRARY, 250 S Main St, Boston, 31626-3674. (Mail add: PO Box 310, Boston, 31626-0310), SAN 373-2975. Tel: 229-498-5101. FAX: 229-498-5101. *Co-Mgr,* Judy Harrell; E-mail: judyh@tcpls.org; *Co-Mgr,* Suzanne Moore; E-mail: suzanne@tcpls.org; Staff 2 (Non-MLS 2)
Founded 1914. Pop 430; Circ 8,256
Library Holdings: Audiobooks 24; CDs 9; DVDs 3,474; e-books 3,073; Bk Vols 10,646; Per Subs 8; Videos 822
Friends of the Library Group

GLADYS H CLARK MEMORIAL LIBRARY, 1060 NE Railroad St, Ochlocknee, 31773. (Mail add: PO Box 89, Ochlocknee, 31773-0089), SAN 373-5966. Tel: 229-574-5884. FAX: 229-574-5884. *Mgr,* Kristy McCollough; E-mail: kristy@tcpls.org; Staff 2 (Non-MLS 2)
Founded 1946. Pop 379; Circ 5,585
Library Holdings: Audiobooks 42; CDs 67; DVDs 1,635; e-books 3,073; Electronic Media & Resources 165; Bk Vols 33,791; Per Subs 7; Videos 383
Friends of the Library Group

COOLIDGE PUBLIC LIBRARY, 1029 E Verbena St, Coolidge, 31738. (Mail add: PO Box 429, Coolidge, 31738-0429), SAN 373-2983. Tel: 229-346-3463. FAX: 229-346-3463. *Mgr,* Judy Warmack; E-mail: judy@tcpls.org; Staff 2 (Non-MLS 2)
Founded 1993. Pop 463; Circ 7,918
Library Holdings: Audiobooks 44; CDs 11; DVDs 319; e-books 3,073; Electronic Media & Resources 165; Bk Vols 9,094; Videos 274
Friends of the Library Group

MEIGS PUBLIC LIBRARY, 3058 NE Railroad St, Meigs, 31765. (Mail add: PO Box 176, Meigs, 31765-0176), SAN 373-2991. Tel: 229-683-3853. FAX: 229-683-3853. *Mgr,* Joanita Cook; E-mail: nita@tcpls.org; Staff 2 (Non-MLS 2)
Founded 1976. Pop 443; Circ 4,464
Library Holdings: Audiobooks 30; DVDs 418; e-books 3,073; Electronic Media & Resources 165; Bk Vols 7,737; Per Subs 8; Videos 234
Friends of the Library Group

PAVO PUBLIC LIBRARY, 219 E Harris St, Pavo, 31778-2107. (Mail add: PO Box 396, Pavo, 31778-0396), SAN 373-5974. Tel: 229-859-2697. FAX: 229-859-2697. *Mgr,* Pat Smith; E-mail: pat@tcpls.org
Founded 1987. Pop 528; Circ 7,195
Library Holdings: CDs 15; DVDs 359; e-books 3,073; Electronic Media & Resources 165; Bk Vols 9,250; Per Subs 7; Videos 250
Friends of the Library Group

C THOMAS UNIVERSITY LIBRARY*, 1501 Millpond Rd, 31792. SAN 303-4275. Tel: 229-226-1621. FAX: 229-226-1679. *Dir,* Kelly Lynn; *Tech Serv Mgr,* James Gass; Staff 3 (MLS 2, Non-MLS 1)
Founded 1950. Enrl 800; Highest Degree: Master
Library Holdings: Bk Vols 85,000; Per Subs 412
Wireless access
Partic in Georgia Online Database; Lyrasis
Open Mon-Thurs 8am-9pm, Fri 8-Noon, Sat 10-2

TIFTON

C ABRAHAM BALDWIN AGRICULTURAL COLLEGE*, Baldwin Library, ABAC 5, 2808 Moore Hwy, 31793. SAN 303-4283. Tel: 229-391-4990. FAX: 229-391-4991. Web Site: www.abac.edu/academics/baldwin-library. *Dir,* Marie Davis; Tel: 229-391-4988, E-mail: mdavis@abac.edu; *Pub Serv Librn,* Nicholas Hardin; Tel: 229-391-4986, E-mail: nhardin@abac.edu; *Tech Serv Librn,* Stephanie Coney; Tel: 229-391-4987, E-mail: sconey@abac.edu; Staff 3 (MLS 3)
Founded 1908. Enrl 3,300; Fac 82; Highest Degree: Bachelor
Jul 2013-Jun 2014 Income $252,160. Sal $170,665
Library Holdings: AV Mats 2,126; CDs 76; DVDs 50; e-books 17,862; Bk Vols 79,321; Per Subs 132; Videos 1,124
Special Collections: Dorothy King & Betty King Carr Children's Classic Coll; Georgiana Coll
Automation Activity & Vendor Info: (Cataloging) OCLC; (Circulation) Ex Libris Group; (ILL) OCLC; (OPAC) Ex Libris Group
Database Vendor: EBSCOhost, Gale Cengage Learning, LexisNexis, OCLC FirstSearch, OCLC WorldShare Interlibrary Loan, ProQuest
Wireless access
Function: ILL available
Publications: Library+ (Newsletter)
Partic in GALILEO (Georgia Library Learning Online); OCLC Online Computer Library Center, Inc
Open Mon-Thurs 7:30am-9pm, Fri 7:30-3, Sat 2-5, Sun 5pm-9pm
Restriction: Circ limited

P COASTAL PLAIN REGIONAL LIBRARY*, Headquarters, 2014 Chestnut Ave, 31794. SAN 339-2430. Tel: 229-386-3400. FAX: 229-386-7007. Web Site: www.cprl.org. *Regional Dir,* Kathy Griffis; E-mail: kgriffis@cprl.org; *Spec Serv,* Position Currently Open; *Tech Serv,* Todd Roberson; *Youth Serv,* Catherine Wilson; Staff 3 (MLS 3)
Founded 1956. Pop 88,911; Circ 334,936
Library Holdings: AV Mats 7,948; Bk Vols 220,666; Per Subs 186
Automation Activity & Vendor Info: (Acquisitions) Infor Library & Information Solutions; (Cataloging) SirsiDynix; (Circulation) SirsiDynix; (ILL) OCLC Connexion; (OPAC) SirsiDynix
Wireless access
Partic in Georgia Online Database; PINES (Public Information Network for Electronic Services)
Special Services for the Deaf - Assisted listening device; Closed caption videos; TDD equip
Special Services for the Blind - Large print bks; Low vision equip; Magnifiers; Talking bks
Open Mon-Fri 9-6
Branches: 5

COOK COUNTY, 213 E Second St, Adel, 31620, SAN 339-249X. Tel: 229-896-3652. FAX: 229-896-3652. *Br Mgr,* Janice R Dobransky; E-mail: jdobransky@cprl.org
Open Mon 9:30-7, Tues-Fri 9:30-5:30, Sat 9:30-1
Friends of the Library Group

IRWIN COUNTY, 310 S Beech St, Ocilla, 31774, SAN 339-2554. Tel: 229-468-2148. FAX: 229-468-2148. *Br Mgr,* Deborah Moorman
Open Mon-Fri 10-6, Sat 10-1
Friends of the Library Group

CARRIE DORSEY PERRY MEMORIAL, 315 W Marion Ave, Nashville, 31639, SAN 339-2465. Tel: 229-686-2782. FAX: 229-686-2782. *Br Mgr,* Mary Howard Clayton; E-mail: mclayton@cprl.org
Open Mon 9:30-7:30, Tues-Fri 9:30-5:30, Sat 9:30-12:30
Friends of the Library Group

TIFTON-TIFT COUNTY PUBLIC, 163 S Virginia Ave, 31794. (Mail add: One Library Lane, 31794), SAN 339-2619. Tel: 229-386-7148. FAX: 229-386-7205. *Head Librn,* Victoria Horst; E-mail: vhorst@cprl.org
Open Mon, Wed, Fri & Sat 9-6, Tues & Thurs 9-9, Sun 2-5
Friends of the Library Group

TURNER COUNTY-VICTORIA EVANS MEMORIAL, 605 North St, Ashburn, 31714, SAN 339-252X. Tel: 229-567-4027. FAX: 229-567-4027. *Br Mgr,* JoAnne M Brown; E-mail: jbrown@cprl.org
Open Mon & Thurs 9-8, Tues, Wed & Fri 9-6, Sat 9-12

C UNIVERSITY OF GEORGIA COLLEGE OF AGRICULTURAL & ENVIRONMENTAL SCIENCES, Tifton Campus Library, 4601 Research Way, 31793. (Mail add: 2360 Rainwater Rd, 31793-5766), SAN 303-4291. Tel: 912-386-3447. FAX: 912-391-2501. E-mail: librtif@uga.edu. *Librn,* Duncan McClusky; E-mail: mcclusky@uga.edu; Staff 1 (MLS 1)
Founded 1924. Fac 100; Highest Degree: Bachelor
Library Holdings: Bk Titles 7,000; Bk Vols 8,000; Per Subs 60
Subject Interests: Agr, Biol
Wireless access
Open Mon-Fri 8-12 & 1-5

TOCCOA

P TOCCOA-STEPHENS COUNTY PUBLIC LIBRARY*, 121 W Savannah St, PO Box Drawer L, 30577. SAN 338-5809. Tel: 706-886-6082. FAX: 706-886-2134. *Mgr,* Michelle Austin
Wireless access
Mem of Northeast Georgia Regional Library System
Open Mon & Fri (Sept-May) 10-5:30, Tues 10-7, Sat 10-1

TOCCOA FALLS

C TOCCOA FALLS COLLEGE*, Seby Jones Library, PO Box 800749, 30598. SAN 303-4305. Tel: 706-886-6831, Ext 5300. FAX: 706-282-6010. Web Site: www.tfc.edu/library. *Dir,* Patricia Fisher; E-mail: pfisher@tfc.edu; *Acq,* Selina Slate; *Cat,* Jamey Wilkes; *Media Serv,* Heather Samsa; *Ref,* Sara Dodge
Founded 1911. Enrl 900; Fac 50; Highest Degree: Bachelor
Library Holdings: Bk Vols 146,436; Per Subs 299
Special Collections: Religion (R A Forrest Coll-Founder & First President of College)
Subject Interests: Educ, Music, Relig
Automation Activity & Vendor Info: (Cataloging) Follett Software; (Circulation) Follett Software; (ILL) OCLC; (OPAC) Follett Software
Database Vendor: OCLC FirstSearch
Wireless access
Partic in Georgia Online Database; Georgia Private Acad Librs Consortium (GPALS); OCLC Online Computer Library Center, Inc
Open Mon-Thurs 8am-11pm, Fri 8-5, Sat 10am-11pm, Sun 8:30pm-11pm

TRION

S GEORGIA DEPARTMENT OF CORRECTIONS, OFFICE OF LIBRARY SERVICES*, Hays State Prison, 777 Underwood Rd, 30753. (Mail add: PO Box 668, 30753-0668). Tel: 706-857-0400. FAX: 706-857-0551. Web Site: www.dcor.state.ga.us. *Librn,* Carole Farr; Tel: 706-857-0484
Library Holdings: Bk Vols 13,000; Per Subs 150
Special Collections: Law Coll
Database Vendor: LexisNexis
Open Mon-Wed 7:45-9:50, 10-11:30 & 1:45-3:30

P TRION PUBLIC LIBRARY*, 15 Bulldog Blvd, 30753. Tel: 706-734-7594. FAX: 706-734-7504. Web Site: chattoogacountylibrary.org. *Mgr,* Beth Simmons
Library Holdings: CDs 245; DVDs 170; Bk Vols 10,343; Talking Bks 23; Videos 1,096
Automation Activity & Vendor Info: (ILL) OCLC

Mem of Chattooga County Library
Open Mon-Fri 11-6, Sat 10-2
Friends of the Library Group

UNADILLA

S GEORGIA DEPARTMENT OF CORRECTIONS, OFFICE OF LIBRARY SERVICES*, Dooly State Prison, 1412 Plunkett Rd, 31091. (Mail add: PO Box 750, 31091-0750). Tel: 478-627-2000. FAX: 478-627-2140. Web Site: www.dcor.state.ga.us. *Librn,* Texana Royal
Library Holdings: CDs 61; Bk Vols 5,000; Per Subs 24; Talking Bks 100
Special Collections: Law Coll
Database Vendor: LexisNexis
Open Mon & Wed 8-4, Thurs 8-12, Fri 9-12

VALDOSTA

S GEORGIA DEPARTMENT OF CORRECTIONS, OFFICE OF LIBRARY SERVICES*, Valdosta State Prison, PO Box 310, 31603. Tel: 229-333-7900, 229-333-7991. FAX: 229-333-5387. *Librn,* Zebedee Moore
Library Holdings: Bk Vols 10,697; Per Subs 24
Database Vendor: LexisNexis
Open Mon-Fri 7:30-3:15

P LOWNDES COUNTY HISTORICAL SOCIETY & MUSEUM*, 305 W Central Ave, 31601-5404. (Mail add: PO Box 56, 31603-0056), SAN 370-520X. Tel: 229-247-4780. FAX: 229-247-2840. E-mail: research.LCHS@gmail.com. Web Site: valdostamuseum.com. *Dir,* Donald Davis
Founded 1967. Pop 55,000
Library Holdings: Bk Titles 1,200
Special Collections: Civil War (Colonel T A Faries Coll)
Subject Interests: Local hist
Function: Ref serv available
Open Mon-Fri 10-5, Sat 10-2

M SOUTH GEORGIA MEDICAL CENTER*, Medical Library, PO Box 1727, 31603-1727. SAN 325-0474. Tel: 229-259-4178. FAX: 229-245-6139. *Librn,* Susan T Leik
Library Holdings: Bk Titles 300; Per Subs 70
Restriction: Open to staff only, Restricted pub use

P SOUTH GEORGIA REGIONAL LIBRARY SYSTEM*, Valdosta-Lowndes County Public, 300 Woodrow Wilson Dr, 31602-2592. SAN 339-2643. Tel: 229-333-0086. Reference Tel: 229-333-0086, Ext 220. FAX: 229-333-7669. E-mail: sgrl@sgrl.org. Web Site: www.sgrl.org. *Dir,* Kelly Lenz; *Managing Librn,* David Peeples; *Librn for Blind & Physically Handicapped,* Diane Jernigan; *Adult Serv,* Eric Mathis; *Youth Serv,* Christie Paulk; Staff 35 (MLS 4, Non-MLS 31)
Founded 1876. Pop 100,000; Circ 500,000
Jul 2006-Jun 2007 Income (Main Library and Branch(s)) $1,043,700. Mats Exp $1,043,700. Sal $700,000
Library Holdings: AV Mats 18,000; Bk Vols 229,669; Per Subs 280
Special Collections: Birds
Automation Activity & Vendor Info: (Cataloging) Evergreen; (Circulation) Evergreen; (ILL) OCLC; (OPAC) Evergreen
Wireless access
Partic in PINES (Public Information Network for Electronic Services)
Special Services for the Blind - Talking bks
Open Mon-Thurs 9:30-8, Fri 9:30-5:30, Sat 11-5:30, Sun 2-6
Friends of the Library Group
Branches: 6
HAHIRA BRANCH, 220 E Main St, Hahira, 31632, SAN 339-2732. Tel: 229-794-3063. *Librn,* Janet Register
Library Holdings: Bk Vols 27,631
Open Mon-Thurs 11-7, Fri 11-5:30
EDITH G JOHNSTON LAKES BRANCH, 720 Lakes Blvd, Lake Park, 31636. (Mail add: PO Box 1350, Lake Park, 31636), SAN 372-0063. Tel: 229-559-8016.
Library Holdings: Bk Vols 27,681
Open Mon-Thurs 11-7, Fri 11-5:30
LAKELAND BRANCH, 18 S Valdosta Rd, Lakeland, 31635, SAN 339-2767. Tel: 229-482-2904. FAX: 229-482-1177. *Librn & Coordr, Echols & Lanier County Libr,* David Peeples; E-mail: dpeeples@sgrl.org; Staff 1.6 (MLS 1, Non-MLS 0.6)
Founded 1988. Pop 15,000; Circ 11,203
Library Holdings: Bk Vols 22,000
Function: Computer training, Computers for patron use, Copy machines, Electronic databases & coll, Family literacy, Free DVD rentals, Handicapped accessible, Music CDs, Online cat, Prog for adults, Prog for children & young adult, Spoken cassettes & CDs, VHS videos
Partic in OCLC Online Computer Library Center, Inc
Open Mon-Thurs 11-6, Fri 11-5:30
Friends of the Library Group
MAE WISENBAKER MCMULLEN MEMORIAL SOUTHSIDE LIBRARY, 527 Griffin Ave, 31601-6343, SAN 373-7128. Tel: 229-253-8313. *Mgr,* Beverly Sanders
Library Holdings: Bk Vols 23,000
Open Mon-Thurs 11-7, Fri 11-5:30
STATENVILLE BRANCH, US Hwy 129 & Jackson St, Statenville, 31648, SAN 339-2791. Tel: 229-559-8182. *Mgr,* Jackie Culpepper; E-mail: jculpepper@sgrl.org; Staff 1.2 (MLS 0.2, Non-MLS 1)
Library Holdings: Bk Vols 11,576
Special Collections: Echols County History
Function: Senior computer classes, Story hour, Summer reading prog, Teen prog, VHS videos
Partic in OCLC Online Computer Library Center, Inc
Open Mon-Fri 11-6
Friends of the Library Group
P TALKING BOOK CENTER, 300 Woodrow Wilson Dr, 31602, SAN 339-2678. Tel: 229-333-7658. Toll Free Tel: 800-246-6515. FAX: 229-333-0774. *In Charge,* Diane Jernigan
Founded 1974
Library Holdings: Bk Titles 20,000
Open Mon-Thurs 9:30-6, Fri 9:30-5:30
Bookmobiles: 1. Librn, Sara Elliott. Book Vols 15,000

C VALDOSTA STATE UNIVERSITY*, Odum Library, 1500 N Patterson St, 31698-0150. SAN 303-4313. Tel: 229-333-5860. Circulation Tel: 229-333-5869. Interlibrary Loan Service Tel: 229-333-5867. Reference Tel: 229-333-7149. FAX: 229-259-5055. Interlibrary Loan Service FAX: 229-333-5862. Web Site: www.valdosta.edu/library. *Univ Librn,* Alan Bernstein; E-mail: abernste@valdosta.edu; Staff 18 (MLS 18)
Founded 1913. Enrl 11,490; Fac 453; Highest Degree: Doctorate
Jul 2008-Jun 2009 Income $3,999,547. Mats Exp $1,241,744, Books $152,096, Per/Ser (Incl. Access Fees) $647,923, Micro $38,631, AV Mat $42,890, Electronic Ref Mat (Incl. Access Fees) $336,204, Presv $24,000. Sal $2,470,195 (Prof $1,259,809)
Library Holdings: Bk Titles 361,417; Bk Vols 539,557; Per Subs 2,732
Special Collections: Archives of Contemporary South Georgia History; Georgia History & Culture (Emily Hendree Park Memorial Coll). US Doc Dep, US Maps
Automation Activity & Vendor Info: (Acquisitions) Ex Libris Group; (Cataloging) Ex Libris Group; (Circulation) Ex Libris Group; (Course Reserve) Ex Libris Group; (Media Booking) Ex Libris Group; (OPAC) Ex Libris Group; (Serials) Ex Libris Group
Wireless access
Partic in Lyrasis; OCLC Online Computer Library Center, Inc; Peachnet

J WIREGRASS GEORGIA TECHNICAL COLLEGE LIBRARY, Valdosta Campus, 4089 Val Tech Rd, 31602. Tel: 229-259-5177. FAX: 229-259-5179. E-mail: library@wiregrass.edu. Web Site: www.wiregrass.edu/library. *Dir, Circ & Archives,* Kathryn S Tomlinson; Tel: 229-259-5178, E-mail: kathryn.tomlinson@wiregrass.edu; *Libr Asst,* Dorisanne Cardwell; E-mail: dorisanne.cardwell@wiregrass.edu; *Libr Asst,* Jennifer Whinnery; E-mail: jennifer.mcwilliams@wiregrass.edu; Staff 2 (MLS 1, Non-MLS 1)
Founded 1997. Enrl 2,500; Fac 180; Highest Degree: Associate
Jul 2013-Jun 2014. Mats Exp $27,700, Books $20,000, Per/Ser (Incl. Access Fees) $4,500, Electronic Ref Mat (Incl. Access Fees) $3,200
Library Holdings: AV Mats 75; Bks on Deafness & Sign Lang 16; Braille Volumes 1; CDs 723; DVDs 815; e-books 35,000; Electronic Media & Resources 650; High Interest/Low Vocabulary Bk Vols 9; Bk Vols 10,000; Per Subs 80; Videos 499
Automation Activity & Vendor Info: (Acquisitions) TLC (The Library Corporation); (Cataloging) TLC (The Library Corporation); (Circulation) TLC (The Library Corporation); (ILL) OCLC ILLiad; (OPAC) TLC (The Library Corporation); (Serials) EBSCO Online
Database Vendor: 3M Library Systems, CredoReference, EBSCO - WebFeat, EBSCOhost, LexisNexis, Medline, OCLC, ProQuest, TLC (The Library Corporation), WebMD
Wireless access
Function: CD-ROM, Computers for patron use, Copy machines, Electronic databases & coll, Fax serv, Free DVD rentals, ILL available, Notary serv, Online cat, Orientations, Photocopying/Printing, Ref serv in person, Scanner, VHS videos, Wheelchair accessible
Special Services for the Deaf - Bks on deafness & sign lang; Closed caption videos
Special Services for the Blind - Large screen computer & software; Low vision equip; Screen enlargement software for people with visual disabilities; ZoomText magnification & reading software

VIDALIA

P OHOOPEE REGIONAL LIBRARY SYSTEM, Vidalia-Toombs County Library Headquarters, 610 Jackson St, 30474-2835. SAN 339-2821. Tel: 912-537-9283. FAX: 912-537-3735. E-mail: vidalialib@ohoopeelibrary.org. Web Site: www.ohoopeelibrary.org. *Dir,* Martha Powers-Jones; E-mail:

powersm@ohoopeelibrary.org; *Asst Dir,* Tiffany Little; E-mail: littlet@ohoopeelibrary.org; Staff 9 (MLS 4, Non-MLS 5)
Founded 1938. Pop 52,000; Circ 150,000
Library Holdings: Bk Vols 130,000; Per Subs 110
Special Collections: Genealogy Coll; Local Newspaper (Vidalia Advance Coll, 1920 to date), micro
Automation Activity & Vendor Info: (Cataloging) Evergreen; (Circulation) Evergreen
Wireless access
Open Mon-9-7, Tues & Thurs 11-7, Wed, Fri & Sat 9-3
Branches: 6
NELLE BROWN MEMORIAL, 166 W Liberty St, Lyons, 30436-1432, SAN 339-2910. Tel: 912-526-6511. FAX: 912-526-6511. *Br Mgr,* Stephen Sisson; Staff 1 (Non-MLS 1)
Database Vendor: EBSCOhost, OCLC FirstSearch, ProQuest
Open Mon-Thurs 2-5:30, Fri 10-1
JEFF DAVIS PUBLIC LIBRARY, 189 E Jarman St, Hazlehurst, 31539, SAN 338-697X. Tel: 912-375-2386. Web Site: www.ohoopeelibrary.org/node/62. *Mgr,* Position Currently Open
Library Holdings: Bk Titles 12,500
Open Mon-Thurs 12-6, Sat 12-4
Friends of the Library Group
GLENNVILLE PUBLIC, 408 E Barnard St, Glennville, 30427, SAN 339-2856. Tel: 912-654-3812. FAX: 912-654-3812. *Br Mgr,* Patty R Wilson; Staff 2 (Non-MLS 2)
Database Vendor: EBSCOhost, OCLC FirstSearch, ProQuest
Open Mon & Thurs 10:30-8, Tues, Wed & Fri 10:30-6, Sat 10:30-2
LADSON GENEALOGICAL LIBRARY, 125 Church St, Ste 104, 30474. (Mail add: 610 Jackson St, 30474), SAN 339-2880. Tel: 912-537-8186. FAX: 912-537-8186. *Br Mgr,* Clint Moxley
Open Mon-Fri 10-1 & 2-6, Sat 10-2
Restriction: Non-circulating
MONTGOMERY COUNTY PUBLIC, 215 S Railroad St, Mount Vernon, 30445. (Mail add: PO Box 242, Mount Vernon, 30445-0242), SAN 339-2945. Tel: 912-583-2780. FAX: 912-583-2780.
Founded 1976
Open Mon & Wed 12-6, Tues & Thurs 12-7, Fri 10-2
TATTNALL COUNTY PUBLIC, 129 Tattnall St, Reidsville, 30453-0338, SAN 339-297X. Tel: 912-557-6247. FAX: 912-557-6247. *Br Mgr,* India K Sandford; Staff 1 (Non-MLS 1)
Open Mon & Tues 10:30-8, Wed-Fri 10:30-6, Sat 10:30-2
Bookmobiles: 1

J SOUTHEASTERN TECHNICAL COLLEGE, Vidalia Campus Library, 3001 E First St, 30474. Tel: 912-538-3132. FAX: 912-538-3156. Web Site: www.southeasterntech.edu/library/library.asp. *Dir, Libr Serv,* Jane L Summey; E-mail: jsummey@southeasterntech.edu; *Librn,* Leah Dasher; E-mail: ldasher@southeasterntech.edu; Staff 2 (MLS 2)
Founded 1990. Enrl 1,200; Highest Degree: Associate
Library Holdings: DVDs 40; e-books 29,000; Bk Vols 7,000; Per Subs 50; Talking Bks 10; Videos 350
Automation Activity & Vendor Info: (Cataloging) TLC (The Library Corporation); (Circulation) TLC (The Library Corporation); (OPAC) TLC (The Library Corporation)
Wireless access
Partic in GALILEO (Georgia Library Learning Online)
Open Mon & Tues 7:30am-9pm, Wed & Thurs 7:30-6

WACO

J WEST GEORGIA TECHNICAL COLLEGE*, Mary McClung Library-Murphy Campus, 176 Murphy Campus Blvd, 30182. Tel: 770-537-6066. FAX: 770-537-7997. E-mail: murphylibrary@westgatech.edu. Web Site: www.westgatech.edu. *Dir of Libr Serv,* Emanuel Sinclair Mitchell; E-mail: emanuel.mitchell@westgatech.edu; *Librn,* Farley Jenkins; E-mail: farley.jenkins@westgatech.edu; *Librn,* Matt Sunrich; E-mail: matthew.sunrich@westgatech.edu; *Libr Asst,* Cathy McWhorter; E-mail: cathy.mcwhorter@westgatech.edu; Staff 3 (MLS 2, Non-MLS 1)
Founded 2002. Highest Degree: Associate
Library Holdings: AV Mats 2,438; Bk Vols 24,000; Per Subs 215
Automation Activity & Vendor Info: (Cataloging) SirsiDynix; (Circulation) SirsiDynix; (OPAC) SirsiDynix
Wireless access
Partic in GALILEO (Georgia Library Learning Online)
Open Mon-Thurs 7:30am-9pm, Fri 8-Noon
Departmental Libraries:
DOUGLAS CAMPUS LIBRARY, 4600 Timber Ridge Dr, Douglasville, 30135. Tel: 770-947-7238. FAX: 770-947-7237. *Librn,* Mike Stephens; Tel: 770-947-7240, E-mail: michael.stephens@westgatech.edu; *Librn,* Chuck Davis; *Libr Asst,* Shawnta Patrick; E-mail: shawnta.patrick@westgatech.edu
Founded 1995. Highest Degree: Associate
Open Mon-Thurs 7:30am-9pm, Fri 7:30-Noon
LAGRANGE CAMPUS LIBRARY, One College Circle, LaGrange, 30240. Tel: 770-756-4557. FAX: 706-756-4631. Web Site: www.westgatech.edu/library. *Librn,* Linda Gavin; E-mail: linda.gavin@westgatech.edu; *Librn,* Linda Hamrick; Staff 2 (MLS 2)
Founded 1966. Enrl 1,950; Highest Degree: Associate
Library Holdings: AV Mats 70; e-books 15,000; Bk Vols 14,511; Per Subs 218; Videos 700
Automation Activity & Vendor Info: (Cataloging) TLC (The Library Corporation); (Circulation) TLC (The Library Corporation); (OPAC) TLC (The Library Corporation)
Partic in GALILEO (Georgia Library Learning Online)
Open Mon-Thurs 7:30am-9pm, Fri 7:30am-Noon
ROGER SCHOERNER TECHNICAL LIBRARY-CARROLL CAMPUS, 997 S Hwy 16, Carrollton, 30116. Tel: 770-836-4711. FAX: 770-836-6807. *Librn,* Chris Carroll; E-mail: chris.carroll@westgatech.edu; *Libr Asst,* Cathy Bost; Staff 1 (MLS 1)
Founded 1970. Highest Degree: Associate
Open Mon-Thurs 7:30am-9pm, Fri 7:30am-Noon

WALESKA

C REINHARDT UNIVERSITY, Hill Freeman Library & Spruill Learning Center, 7300 Reinhardt Circle, 30183. SAN 303-4321. Tel: 770-720-9120. Interlibrary Loan Service Tel: 770-720-5584. FAX: 770-720-5944. E-mail: library@reinhardt.edu. Web Site: library.reinhardt.edu. *Libr Dir,* Joel C Langford; Tel: 770-720-5985, E-mail: jcl@reinhardt.edu; Staff 6 (MLS 2, Non-MLS 4)
Founded 1883. Enrl 1,600; Fac 65; Highest Degree: Master
Library Holdings: e-books 100,000; e-journals 37,000; Bk Titles 68,375; Bk Vols 71,000; Per Subs 300
Automation Activity & Vendor Info: (Acquisitions) Ex Libris Group; (Cataloging) Ex Libris Group; (Circulation) Ex Libris Group; (OPAC) Ex Libris Group; (Serials) Ex Libris Group
Database Vendor: ABC-CLIO, Alexander Street Press, American Psychological Association (APA), ARTstor, BioOne, Brodart, Cinahl, CountryWatch, CQ Press, ebrary, EBSCOhost, Gale Cengage Learning, Greenwood Publishing Group, H W Wilson, Hoovers, infoUSA, JSTOR, Medline, Mergent Online, Modern Language Association, Newsbank, Newsbank-Readex, OCLC, OCLC ArticleFirst, OCLC FirstSearch, OCLC WorldShare Interlibrary Loan, OneSource, Oxford Online, ProQuest, ReferenceUSA, Springer-Verlag, Westlaw, Westlaw Business, Wilson - Wilson Web
Wireless access
Partic in Georgia Private Acad Librs Consortium (GPALS); Lyrasis
Open Mon-Thurs 8am-11pm, Fri 8-5, sat 1-5, Sun 2-11

WARM SPRINGS

M ROOSEVELT WARM SPRINGS INSTITUTE FOR REHABILITATION*, Professional Library, 6391 Roosevelt Hwy, 31830. (Mail add: PO Box 1000, 31830-1000), SAN 370-7180. Tel: 706-655-5616. FAX: 706-655-5630. *Librn,* Michael D Shadix; Staff 1 (MLS 1)
Founded 1940
Jul 2005-Jun 2006 Income $18,000. Mats Exp $12,000, Books $3,000, Per/Ser (Incl. Access Fees) $8,000, AV Mat $1,000
Library Holdings: Bk Titles 1,500; Per Subs 20
Special Collections: Polio Treatment Coll, photogs
Subject Interests: Vocational rehabilitation
Partic in Atlanta Health Science Libraries Consortium; Georgia Interactive Network for Medical Information

WARNER ROBINS

J CENTRAL GEORGIA TECHNICAL COLLEGE LIBRARY*, Warner Robins Campus, 80 Cohen Walker Dr, 31088. Tel: 478-988-6863. *Dir of Libr Serv,* Dr Dumont C Bunn; Tel: 478-218-3290, E-mail: dbunn@centralgatech.edu; Staff 4.45 (MLS 2, Non-MLS 2.45)
Founded 1998. Enrl 4,768; Highest Degree: Associate
Jul 2013-Jul 2014 Income $100,000. Mats Exp $72,807, Books $37,019, Per/Ser (Incl. Access Fees) $14,500, AV Equip $98, AV Mat $14,000, Electronic Ref Mat (Incl. Access Fees) $6,890, Presv $300
Library Holdings: AV Mats 2,079; CDs 686; DVDs 478; e-books 61,000; Bk Titles 24,993; Bk Vols 27,367; Per Subs 150; Videos 838
Automation Activity & Vendor Info: (Cataloging) TLC (The Library Corporation); (Circulation) TLC (The Library Corporation); (ILL) OCLC CatExpress; (OPAC) TLC (The Library Corporation)
Database Vendor: Cinahl, CredoReference, EBSCO Auto Repair Reference, EBSCOhost, LearningExpress, OCLC, OCLC WorldShare Interlibrary Loan, TLC (The Library Corporation), Westlaw
Partic in GALILEO
Open Mon-Thurs 7:30am-9pm, Fri 7:30-3:30

WASHINGTON

P BARTRAM TRAIL REGIONAL LIBRARY*, Mary Willis Library Headquarters, 204 E Liberty St, 30673. SAN 339-3003. Tel: 706-678-7736. FAX: 706-678-1615. Web Site: www.wilkes.public.lib.ga.us. *Dir,* Lillie Crowe; E-mail: lillie@btrl.net; *Tech Serv,* Jim Veatch; E-mail: jimv@btrl.net; Staff 4 (MLS 3, Non-MLS 1)
Founded 1888. Pop 33,615; Circ 10,410
Library Holdings: Bk Vols 101,000; Per Subs 75
Subject Interests: Ga, Local hist
Automation Activity & Vendor Info: (Cataloging) Evergreen; (Circulation) Evergreen; (ILL) OCLC; (OPAC) Evergreen
Wireless access
Partic in PINES (Public Information Network for Electronic Services)
Special Services for the Deaf - High interest/low vocabulary bks
Open Mon, Wed & Fri 8:30-5:30, Tues & Thurs 8:30-8, Sat 10-4
Friends of the Library Group
Branches: 2
TALIAFERRO COUNTY, 117 Askin St, Crawfordville, 30631. (Mail add: PO Box 129, Crawfordville, 30631-0129), SAN 339-3097. Tel: 706-456-2531. FAX: 706-456-2531. *Mgr,* Sharon DuBois; *Mgr,* Barbara Wolter
Open Mon, Tues, Thurs & Fri 10-5, Sat 10-1
Friends of the Library Group
THOMSON-MCDUFFIE COUNTY, 338 Main St, Thomson, 30824, SAN 339-3062. Tel: 706-595-1341. FAX: 706-597-9458. *Librn,* Suzan Harris
Open Mon, Wed & Fri 8:30-5:30, Tues & Thurs 8:30-8, Sat 10-4
Friends of the Library Group
Bookmobiles: 1

WAYCROSS

S GEORGIA DEPARTMENT OF CORRECTIONS, OFFICE OF LIBRARY SERVICES*, Ware State Prison, 3620 Harris Rd, 31503. Tel: 912-285-6400. FAX: 912-287-6520. Web Site: www.dcor.state.ga.us. *Librn, Media Spec,* Patti DeMarco
Library Holdings: Bk Vols 15,000; Per Subs 6
Special Collections: Law Coll
Open Mon-Wed 7:30-4:45, Thurs 7:30-4:45 & 6-8

P OKEFENOKEE REGIONAL LIBRARY*, 401 Lee Ave, 31501. SAN 339-3127. Tel: 912-287-4978. FAX: 912-284-2533. Web Site: www.okrls.org. *Dir,* Midge Galentine-Steis; *Circ,* Rosanne Moore; *Ref,* James Britton, III; *Tech Serv,* Linda K Lightfoot; Staff 5 (MLS 5)
Founded 1955. Pop 85,519; Circ 185,407
Library Holdings: Bk Titles 10,000; Bk Vols 230,000; Per Subs 123
Special Collections: Oral History
Subject Interests: Ga, Genealogy
Automation Activity & Vendor Info: (Cataloging) SirsiDynix; (Circulation) SirsiDynix; (ILL) OCLC WorldShare Interlibrary Loan; (OPAC) SirsiDynix
Open Mon & Thurs 10-9, Tues & Wed 10-6, Fri & Sat 10-4
Friends of the Library Group
Branches: 4
ALMA-BACON COUNTY PUBLIC, 201 N Pierce St, Alma, 31510, SAN 339-3216. Tel: 912-632-4710. FAX: 912-632-4512. *Mgr,* Theressa Anderson
Open Mon 9-12:30 & 1:30-8, Tues-Fri 9-12:30 & 1:30-5:30, Sat 9-12:30
APPLING COUNTY PUBLIC, 301 City Hall Dr, Baxley, 31513, SAN 339-3186. Tel: 912-367-8103. FAX: 912-367-8104. *Mgr,* Annette Osborne
Open Mon 10-8, Tues-Thurs 10-6, Fri 10-4, Sat 9-1
BLACKSHEAR MEMORIAL LIBRARY, 600 S Main St, Blackshear, 31516, SAN 339-3240. Tel: 912-449-7040. FAX: 912-449-2265. *Mgr,* Anita Bunkley
Open Mon, Tues, Thurs & Fri 9:30-1 & 2-6, Wed & Sat 9-1
Friends of the Library Group
CLINCH COUNTY PUBLIC, 478 W Dame St, Homerville, 31634, SAN 339-3275. Tel: 912-487-3200. FAX: 912-487-3304. *Mgr,* Jane Welch
Open Mon-Wed 10-1 & 2-6, Thurs 2-8, Fri 10-1, Sat 2-5
Friends of the Library Group
Bookmobiles: 1. In Charge, Katherine Smith

J OKEFENOKEE TECHNICAL COLLEGE*, Waycross Campus Library, 1701 Carswell Ave, 31503. Tel: 912-287-6655. FAX: 912-287-4865. E-mail: library@okefenokeetech.edu. Web Site: www.okefenokeetech.edu/library. *Dir, Libr Serv,* Cassie Clemons; Tel: 912-287-5834, E-mail: cclemons@okefenokeetech.edu; Staff 1.5 (MLS 1.5)
Enrl 1,100; Highest Degree: Associate
Library Holdings: DVDs 453; e-books 50,000; Bk Vols 7,000; Per Subs 120
Automation Activity & Vendor Info: (Cataloging) TLC (The Library Corporation); (Circulation) TLC (The Library Corporation); (ILL) OCLC FirstSearch; (OPAC) TLC (The Library Corporation)
Wireless access
Partic in GALILEO (Georgia Library Learning Online)
Open Mon-Thurs 7:45am-9pm

J SOUTH GEORGIA STATE COLLEGE, Waycross Campus Library, (Formerly Waycross College Library), 2001 S Georgia Pkwy, 31503. SAN 303-4356. Tel: 912-449-7515. FAX: 912-449-7611. Web Site: www.sgsc.edu. *Dir, Libr Serv,* Jacqueline Vickers; Tel: 912-260-4324, E-mail: jacqueline.vickers@sgsc.edu; *Coordr,* Janice Williams; Tel: 912-449-7519, E-mail: janice.williams@sgsc.edu; *Circ Serv Mgr,* Yolanda Crosby; Tel: 912-260-4335, E-mail: yolanda.crosby@sgsc.edu; *Tech Serv,* Sharon Williams; Tel: 912-449-7514, E-mail: sharon.william@sgsc.edu; Staff 4 (MLS 2, Non-MLS 2)
Founded 1976. Enrl 1,027; Fac 25; Highest Degree: Associate
Library Holdings: e-books 27,501; Bk Titles 27,500; Bk Vols 28,536; Per Subs 178
Special Collections: Okefenokee Swamp
Automation Activity & Vendor Info: (Cataloging) Ex Libris Group; (Circulation) Ex Libris Group; (OPAC) Ex Libris Group; (Serials) Ex Libris Group
Wireless access
Publications: Bay Leaf (Newsletter)
Partic in Georgia Libr Info Network
Open Mon-Thurs 8-8, Fri 8-Noon

WEST POINT

P HAWKES LIBRARY*, 100 W Eighth St, 31833. SAN 303-4364. Tel: 706-645-1549. FAX: 706-645-1549. *Dir, Children's Prog,* Nanci Hendrix; *Librn,* Rebecca Cotney; *Asst Librn,* Judy Crowder
Founded 1922. Pop 40,000
Library Holdings: Bk Vols 21,500; Per Subs 15
Special Collections: Confederate Memorabilia; Georgia Culture Coll
Subject Interests: Local hist
Wireless access
Open Mon, Tues, Thurs & Fri 12:30-5:30
Friends of the Library Group

WINDER

P PIEDMONT REGIONAL LIBRARY*, Regional Office, 189 Bellview St, 30680-1706. SAN 339-3399. Tel: 770-867-2762. FAX: 770-867-7483. Web Site: prlib.org. *Dir,* Beth McIntyre; E-mail: bmcintyre@prlib.org; *Asst Dir,* Anna R Hoover; *Cat Librn,* Nancy Holmes; *Computer Serv Librn,* George Tuttle; Staff 4 (MLS 4)
Founded 1954. Pop 148,247; Circ 582,027
Library Holdings: Bk Vols 582,027; Per Subs 262
Automation Activity & Vendor Info: (ILL) OCLC
Wireless access
Partic in PINES (Public Information Network for Electronic Services)
Open Mon-Fri 8:30-5
Friends of the Library Group
Branches: 10
AUBURN PUBLIC, 24 Fifth St, Auburn, 30011-3280. Tel: 770-513-2925. *Mgr,* Julia Simpson; E-mail: jsimpson@prlib.org
Open Mon 11–8, Tues–Thurs 11–7, Fri & Sat 1–5
BANKS COUNTY PUBLIC, 226 Hwy 51 S, Homer, 30547. (Mail add: PO Box 27, Homer, 30547-0027), SAN 339-3429. Tel: 706-677-3164. FAX: 706-677-3164. *Libr Mgr,* Stacy G Krumnow; E-mail: skrumnow@prlib.org; Staff 5 (Non-MLS 5)
Open Mon, Tues & Thurs 9-8, Wed 9-6, Sat 9-3
Friends of the Library Group
BRASELTON BRANCH, 132 W Broadway, Braselton, 30517. Tel: 706-654-1992. *Br Mgr,* Bev Adkins; E-mail: badkins@prlib.org
Open Mon, Wed & Fri 10-5, Tues & Thurs 10-7, Sat 10-2
COMMERCE PUBLIC, 1344 S Broad St, Commerce, 30529-2053, SAN 339-3453. Tel: 706-335-5946. FAX: 706-335-6879. *Libr Mgr,* Miguel J Vicente; E-mail: mvicente@prlib.org
Open Mon-Wed 10-6, Thurs 10-8, Fri 10-5, Sat 10-4
Friends of the Library Group
JEFFERSON PUBLIC, 379 Old Pendergrass Rd, Jefferson, 30549-2780, SAN 339-3488. Tel: 706-367-8012. *Libr Mgr,* Amy Carlan; E-mail: acarlan@prlib.org
Open Mon-Thurs 10-7, Fri 10-5, Sat 10-4
Friends of the Library Group
MAYSVILLE PUBLIC, 9247 Gillsville Rd, Maysville, 30558, SAN 374-6534. Tel: 706-652-2323. FAX: 706-652-2323. E-mail: maysville@prlib.org. *Libr Mgr,* Sherri Stephens
Open Mon & Fri 9-5, Tues & Thurs 9-7, Wed 9-1, Sat 10-2
STATHAM PUBLIC, 1928 Railroad St, Statham, 30666. Tel: 770-725-4785. *Libr Mgr,* Mary Spencer; E-mail: mspencer@prlib.org
Open Mon 10-6, Tues, Wed & Fri 10-5, Sat 10-1
HAROLD S SWINDLE PUBLIC LIBRARY, 5466 US Hwy 441 S, Nicholson, 30565, SAN 339-3607. Tel: 706-757-3577. FAX: 706-757-3246. *Libr Mgr,* Kelli McDaniel; E-mail: kmcdaniel@prlib.org; Staff 1 (Non-MLS 1)

Pop 2,000
Function: Bks on CD, Children's prog, Computers for patron use, Copy machines, Fax serv, Free DVD rentals, Handicapped accessible, Homework prog, Music CDs, Online cat, Prog for adults, Prog for children & young adult, Pub access computers, Story hour, Summer reading prog
Open Mon-Thurs 9-7, Fri 10-6, Sat 10-2
Friends of the Library Group

TALMO PUBLIC, 45 A J Irvin Rd, Talmo, 30575. Tel: 706-693-1905. E-mail: talmo@prlib.org. *Libr Mgr,* Jenna Wall
Open Mon-Fri 8:30-5:30

WINDER LIBRARY, 189 Bellview St, 30680-1706. *Libr Mgr,* Lisa Gannon; E-mail: lgannon@prlib.org
Library Holdings: Bk Vols 60,550

Bookmobiles: 1

WOODBINE

S BRYAN-LANG HISTORICAL LIBRARY*, Fourth St at Camden Ave, 31569. (Mail add: PO Box 715, 31569-0715), SAN 371-5337. Tel: 912-576-5841. FAX: 912-576-5841. *Librn,* John P Kennison
Founded 1984
Library Holdings: Bk Titles 4,265
Special Collections: Berrie Coll; Lang Coll
Open Mon-Fri 8-5

WRIGHTSVILLE

S GEORGIA DEPARTMENT OF CORRECTIONS, OFFICE OF LIBRARY SERVICES*, Johnson State Prison, PO Box 344, 31096-0344. Tel: 478-864-4100, Ext 4141. FAX: 478-864-4104. Web Site: www.dcor.state.ga.us.
Library Holdings: Bk Vols 2,500; Per Subs 10; Talking Bks 10
Special Collections: Law Coll
Database Vendor: LexisNexis
Open Mon & Wed 9-4, Tues & Thurs 9-8

YOUNG HARRIS

P MOUNTAIN REGIONAL LIBRARY SYSTEM*, Mountain Regional Library, 698 Miller St, 30582. (Mail add: PO Box 159, 30582-0159), SAN 339-3720. Tel: 706-379-3732. FAX: 706-379-2047. E-mail: mountain@mountainregionallibrary.org. Web Site: www.mountainregionallibrary.org. *Dir,* Donna W Howell; E-mail: howelld@mountainregionallibrary.org; *Tech Librn,* Curtis L Spiva; E-mail: spivac@mountainregionallibrary.org; *Br Mgr,* Sondra C Vaughn; E-mail: vaughns@mountainregionallibrary.org; *Training & Outreach Coordr,* Dyana Costello Banks; E-mail: costellobanksd@mountainregionallibrary.org; *Regional Asst,* Peggy Keys-Burrell; E-mail: keyspeggy@mountainregionallibrary.org; Staff 6.2 (MLS 2, Non-MLS 4.2)
Founded 1946. Pop 59,444; Circ 303,409
Special Collections: Appalachian Coll; Rare & Special Local Coll
Automation Activity & Vendor Info: (Acquisitions) Evergreen; (Cataloging) Evergreen; (Circulation) Evergreen; (ILL) OCLC; (OPAC) Evergreen
Database Vendor: LearningExpress, Overdrive, Inc
Wireless access
Function: Adult bk club, Audio & video playback equip for onsite use, Audiobks via web, AV serv, Bks on cassette, Bks on CD, Children's prog, Computer training, Computers for patron use, Copy machines, Digital talking bks, e-mail & chat, e-mail serv, Electronic databases & coll, Exhibits, Fax serv, Free DVD rentals, Handicapped accessible, ILL available, Instruction & testing, Magnifiers for reading, Mail & tel request accepted, Mus passes, Music CDs, Notary serv, Online cat, Outreach serv, Outside serv via phone, mail, e-mail & web, OverDrive digital audio bks, Preschool outreach, Preschool reading prog, Prog for adults, Prog for children & young adult, Pub access computers, Ref serv available, Senior computer classes, Senior outreach, Spoken cassettes & CDs, Story hour, Summer reading prog, Tax forms, Teen prog, Telephone ref, Web-catalog, Wheelchair accessible
Partic in GALILEO (Georgia Library Learning Online); Lyrasis; OCLC Online Computer Library Center, Inc; PINES (Public Information Network for Electronic Services)
Special Services for the Deaf - Assistive tech; Bks on deafness & sign lang
Special Services for the Blind - Accessible computers; Aids for in-house use; Assistive/Adapted tech devices, equip & products; Audio mat; Bks & mags in Braille, on rec, tape & cassette; Computer with voice synthesizer for visually impaired persons; Copier with enlargement capabilities; Digital talking bk; Digital talking bk machines; Extensive large print coll; Free checkout of audio mat; Home delivery serv; Internet workstation with adaptive software; Large print bks; Large screen computer & software; Lending of low vision aids; Magnifiers; Playaways (bks on MP3); Reader equip; Talking bk serv referral; Talking bks & player equip
Open Mon, Wed & Fri 9-5, Tues & Thurs 9-7, Sat 10-2
Friends of the Library Group

Branches: 3

FANNIN COUNTY PUBLIC LIBRARY, 400 W Main St, Ste 104, Blue Ridge, 30513, SAN 339-378X. Tel: 706-632-5263. FAX: 706-632-7719. *Librn,* Clare Barton; Staff 1 (MLS 1)
Pop 24,949; Circ 101,133
Automation Activity & Vendor Info: (Acquisitions) Evergreen; (Cataloging) Evergreen; (Circulation) Evergreen; (ILL) OCLC; (OPAC) Evergreen
Function: Audio & video playback equip for onsite use, Audiobks via web, AV serv, Bks on cassette, Bks on CD, Children's prog, Computers for patron use, Copy machines, Digital talking bks, e-mail serv, Exhibits, Free DVD rentals, Handicapped accessible, ILL available, Magnifiers for reading, Music CDs, Online cat, Outside serv via phone, mail, e-mail & web, OverDrive digital audio bks, Prog for adults, Prog for children & young adult, Story hour, Summer reading prog, Tax forms, Teen prog, Telephone ref
Special Services for the Deaf - Bks on deafness & sign lang
Special Services for the Blind - Accessible computers; Assistive/Adapted tech devices, equip & products; Audio mat; Bks & mags in Braille, on rec, tape & cassette; Bks on cassette; Bks on CD; Internet workstation with adaptive software; Large print & cassettes; Large print bks; Reader equip; Recorded bks; Talking bks & player equip
Open Mon & Fri 9-5, Tues 9-7, Thurs 11-7, Sat 9-1
Friends of the Library Group

TOWNS COUNTY PUBLIC LIBRARY, 99 S Berrong St, Hiawassee, 30546, SAN 328-8951. Tel: 706-896-6169. FAX: 706-896-2309. *Br Mgr,* Deborah Phillips; Staff 3 (Non-MLS 3)
Pop 11,469; Circ 41,747
Function: Audio & video playback equip for onsite use, Audiobks via web, AV serv, Bks on cassette, Bks on CD, Computers for patron use, Copy machines, Digital talking bks, e-mail serv, Electronic databases & coll, Fax serv, Free DVD rentals, Handicapped accessible, ILL available, Magnifiers for reading, Mail & tel request accepted, Notary serv, Online cat, OverDrive digital audio bks, Preschool outreach, Prog for adults, Prog for children & young adult, Pub access computers, Story hour, Summer reading prog, Tax forms, VHS videos, Wheelchair accessible
Special Services for the Deaf - Bks on deafness & sign lang
Special Services for the Blind - Bks on CD; Digital talking bk; Digital talking bk machines; Free checkout of audio mat; Large print bks; Local mags & bks recorded; Magnifiers; Playaways (bks on MP3); Screen enlargement software for people with visual disabilities; Talking bks & player equip
Open Mon-Wed & Fri 9-5, Thurs 10-6
Friends of the Library Group

UNION COUNTY PUBLIC LIBRARY, 303 Hunt Martin St, Blairsville, 30512, SAN 339-3755. Tel: 706-745-7491. FAX: 706-745-5652. E-mail: union@mountainregionallibrary.org. *Librn,* Susie Brendle; Staff 4.5 (MLS 1, Non-MLS 3.5)
Pop 22,269; Circ 175,657
Function: Adult bk club, Audiobks via web, Bks on CD, Children's prog, Computer training, Computers for patron use, Copy machines, Digital talking bks, e-mail & chat, Electronic databases & coll, Exhibits, Fax serv, Free DVD rentals, Handicapped accessible, ILL available, Instruction & testing, Magnifiers for reading, Mus passes, Music CDs, Notary serv, Online cat, Online ref, Outreach serv, OverDrive digital audio bks, Photocopying/Printing, Preschool outreach, Preschool reading prog, Prog for adults, Prog for children & young adult, Pub access computers, Ref serv available, Scanner, Senior computer classes, Story hour, Summer reading prog, Tax forms
Open Mon, Wed & Fri 9-5, Tues & Thurs 9-7, Sat 10-2
Friends of the Library Group

J YOUNG HARRIS COLLEGE*, Henry & J Lon Duckworth Memorial Library, One College St, 30582. (Mail add: PO Box 39, 30582-0039), SAN 303-4372. Tel: 706-379-4313. FAX: 706-379-4314. Web Site: www.yhc.edu. *Dir,* Dawn A Lamade; E-mail: dlamade@yhc.edu; *Cat,* Stephanie Short; E-mail: sshort@yhc.edu; *ILL, Pub Serv,* Joy Day; E-mail: joyday@yhc.edu; *Ref, Spec Coll Librn, Webmaster,* Debra March; E-mail: dbmarch@yhc.edu; Staff 4 (MLS 4)
Founded 1886. Enrl 600; Fac 40; Highest Degree: Associate
Jul 2005-Jun 2006. Mats Exp $73,190. Sal $202,197
Library Holdings: e-books 38,000; Bk Vols 40,000; Per Subs 130
Special Collections: Byron Herbert Reece & J A Sharp Coll; Merle Mann Indian Artifacts; Vietnam Veterans Oral History Project. Oral History
Subject Interests: Humanities, Music, Relig
Automation Activity & Vendor Info: (Cataloging) SirsiDynix; (Circulation) SirsiDynix; (ILL) OCLC; (OPAC) SirsiDynix
Database Vendor: EBSCOhost, LexisNexis, ProQuest, SirsiDynix, Wilson - Wilson Web
Wireless access
Partic in Georgia Online Database; Georgia Private Acad Librs Consortium (GPALS); Lyrasis
Open Mon-Thurs 7:45am-11pm, Fri 7:45-5, Sat Noon-5, Sun 2pm-11pm

ZEBULON

S GEORGIA DEPARTMENT OF CORRECTIONS, OFFICE OF LIBRARY SERVICES*, West Central Probation Detention Center Library, 335 County Farm Rd, 30295. Tel: 770-567-0531. FAX: 770-567-0257. *In Charge,* Lindolyn Green
Library Holdings: Bk Vols 530; Per Subs 20
Database Vendor: LexisNexis
Open Tues & Thurs 1-3

HAWAII

Date of Statistics: FY 2014
Population, 2010 U.S. Census: 1,360,301
Population, 2013: 1,404,054
Population Served by Public Libraries Statewide: 1,404,054
Total Volumes in Public Libraries (including State Library): 3,723,877
Volumes Per Capita: 2.65
Total Public Library Circulation (Includes Library for the Blind and Physically Handicapped): 6,519,688
Total Public Library Income: $33,963,167
Source of Income: State Legislative Appropriation (FY 2014), Federal LSTA Funds, and Special Funds
Expenditures Per Capita: $23.61
Number of County Libraries: 50 (all public libraries are in one integrated statewide system)
Number of Bookmobiles in State: 2
Grants-in-Aid to Public Libraries:
Library Services and Technology Act, FY 2014: $1,655,900
State Aid: State funded

FORT SHAFTER

A UNITED STATES ARMY*, Fort Shafter Library, APVG-GAF-RL (FS), Bldg 650, 96858-5009. SAN 339-5677. Tel: 808-438-9521. FAX: 808-438-3100. Web Site: www.mwrarmyhawaii.com. *Librn,* Donna Sviantek; Staff 3 (MLS 1, Non-MLS 2)
Founded 1943
Library Holdings: Bk Vols 18,000; Per Subs 86
Subject Interests: Hawaii
Wireless access
Open Mon-Thurs 10-7, Fri 10-3, Sun 11-3

HICKAM AFB

A JOINT BASE PEARL HARBOR-HICKAM LIBRARY*, Bldg 595, 990 Mills Blvd, 96853. SAN 339-3844. Tel: 808-449-8299. FAX: 808-449-8298. E-mail: hickamlibrary@gmail.com. *Dir,* Phyllis Frenzel; *Ref Serv,* Jeff Boling; Staff 7 (MLS 2, Non-MLS 5)
Founded 1957
Library Holdings: Bk Vols 36,000; Per Subs 75
Subject Interests: Hawaii
Automation Activity & Vendor Info: (Acquisitions) EOS International; (Cataloging) EOS International, (Circulation) EOS International
Database Vendor: EBSCOhost, Gale Cengage Learning, OCLC FirstSearch, ProQuest
Wireless access
Open Tues & Thurs 12-8, Wed, Fri & Sat 10-6
Friends of the Library Group

HILO

S HAWAII COMMUNITY CORRECTIONAL CENTER LIBRARY*, 60 Punahele St, 96720. Tel: 808-933-0428. FAX: 808-933-0425. *Librn,* Position Currently Open
Library Holdings: Bk Vols 6,000
Subject Interests: Law, Recreation
Restriction: Staff & inmates only

GL STATE SUPREME COURT*, Third Circuit Court-Law Library, Hale Kaulike Bldg, 777 Kilauea Ave, 96720-4212. SAN 303-4429. Tel: 808-961-7438. FAX: 808-961-7416. *Librn,* Debra Kaido
Library Holdings: Bk Vols 30,000
Open Mon-Fri 7:45-4:30

C UNIVERSITY OF HAWAII AT HILO LIBRARY, Edwin H Mookini Library, 200 W Kawili St, 96720. SAN 339-3933. Tel: 808-932-7286. Interlibrary Loan Service Tel: 808-932-7288. Administration Tel: 808-932-7280. Information Services Tel: 808-932-7296. Administration FAX: 808-932-7551. E-mail: mookini@hawaii.edu. Web Site: guides.library.uhh.hawaii.edu/home. *Univ Librn,* Helen Rogers; E-mail: hrogers@hawaii.edu; *Head, Coll Develop,* Brian Bays; E-mail: bbays@hawaii.edu; *Head, Coll Mgt,* Kathleen Stacey; E-mail: kstacey@hawaii.edu; *Head, Pub Serv,* Thora O Abarca; E-mail: tconnor@hawaii.edu; *Distance Learning Librn,* Amy Saxton; E-mail: saxton@hawaii.edu; Staff 22 (MLS 8, Non-MLS 14)
Founded 1947. Enrl 3,900; Fac 216; Highest Degree: Doctorate
Library Holdings: AV Mats 10,000; e-books 109,000; e-journals 35,000; Microforms 440,000; Bk Vols 232,000
Special Collections: Hawaiiana, bks & per. State Document Depository; US Document Depository
Subject Interests: E Asia
Automation Activity & Vendor Info: (Acquisitions) Ex Libris Group; (Cataloging) Ex Libris Group; (Circulation) Ex Libris Group; (Course Reserve) Ex Libris Group; (ILL) Ex Libris Group; (Media Booking) Ex Libris Group; (OPAC) Ex Libris Group; (Serials) Ex Libris Group
Database Vendor: EBSCOhost, JSTOR, LexisNexis
Wireless access
Function: ILL available, Ref serv available
Open Mon-Thurs 8am-10:30pm, Fri 8-6, Sat 11-6, Sun 2-10:30
Restriction: Open to fac, students & qualified researchers

HONOLULU

C ARGOSY UNIVERSITY*, Hawaii Library, 1001 Bishop St, Ste 400, 96813. Tel: 808-536-5555. Toll Free Tel: 888-323-2777. FAX: 808-536-5505. E-mail: auhnlibrary@argosy.edu. Web Site: www.auhawaii.net/library. *Dir of Libr Serv,* Jenny Foster; E-mail: jfoster@argosy.edu
Library Holdings: e-books 20,000; Bk Vols 4,600
Automation Activity & Vendor Info: (Acquisitions) Ex Libris Group; (Cataloging) Ex Libris Group; (Circulation) Ex Libris Group; (OPAC) Ex Libris Group; (Serials) Ex Libris Group
Database Vendor: EBSCOhost, Gale Cengage Learning, ProQuest
Partic in Georgia Online Database
Open Mon-Thurs 9-9, Fri 9-6:30, Sat 9-8, Sun 12-6

S BELT COLLINS HAWAII LLC, Information Center, 2153 N King St, Ste 200, 96819-4570. SAN 370-6850. Tel: 808-521-5361. FAX: 808-538-7819. E-mail: honolulu@bchdesign.com. *Info Res,* Lisa Minato; E-mail: lminato@bchdesign.com; Staff 1 (MLS 1)
Library Holdings: Bk Titles 4,500; Per Subs 100
Subject Interests: Eng, Environment, Landscape archit, Planning
Publications: Acquisition List; Departmental Catalogs of Holdings
Restriction: Circulates for staff only

S BERNICE P BISHOP MUSEUM LIBRARY & ARCHIVES*, 1525 Bernice St, 96817. SAN 303-447X. Tel: 808-848-4148. FAX: 808-847-8241. E-mail: archives@bishopmuseum.org, library@bishopmuseum.org. Web Site: www.bishopmuseum.org/research/library/libarch.html. *In Charge,* Position Currently Open
Founded 1889
Library Holdings: Bk Vols 115,000; Per Subs 1,100; Videos 90

Special Collections: Hawaii Maritime Center Coll; Hawaiian Language Newspapers; Hawaiiana (Carter Coll); Japanese Hawaii Imprints; Jerome Baker Coll; Pacific Island Languages; Pacificana (Fuller Coll); United States Geological Survey & South Pacific Commission
Subject Interests: Anthrop, Archaeology, Botany, Ethnology, Geog, Hawaii, Museology, Pacific, Photog, Zoology
Automation Activity & Vendor Info: (Cataloging) Ex Libris Group; (OPAC) Ex Libris Group
Database Vendor: OCLC FirstSearch
Publications: Catalog of B P Bishop Museum Library (Quarterly update)
Partic in OCLC Online Computer Library Center, Inc
Open Tues-Fri 12-4, Sat 9-12

L CADES SCHUTTE*, Law Library, 1000 Bishop St, Ste 1200, 96813-4212. (Mail add: PO Box 939, 96808-0939), SAN 303-4488. Tel: 808-521-9200. FAX: 808-521-9210. E-mail: cades@cades.com. Web Site: www.cades.com. *Librn,* Debra Anne Oandasan; E-mail: doandasan@cades.com; Staff 3 (Non-MLS 3)
Founded 1922
Library Holdings: Bk Titles 5,000; Bk Vols 15,000; Per Subs 215
Special Collections: Ecology (Hawaiian Water Rights); Hawaii Legislative Reports
Subject Interests: Corporate law, Med, Real estate, Securities
Function: Res libr
Restriction: Private libr

L CARLSMITH BALL LLP LIBRARY*, ASB Tower, Ste 2200, 1001 Bishop St, 96813. SAN 303-4496. Tel: 808-523-2500. FAX: 808-523-0842. Web Site: www.carlsmith.com. *Asst Librn,* Grace Yamada; E-mail: gyamada@carlsmith.com
Library Holdings: Bk Vols 20,000; Per Subs 150
Partic in Westlaw
Open Mon-Fri 8-4:30

C CHAMINADE UNIVERSITY OF HONOLULU*, Sullivan Family Library, 3140 Waialae Ave, 96816-1578. SAN 303-4518. Tel: 808-735-4725. Circulation Tel: 808-739-4665. Reference Tel: 808-739-4660. FAX: 808-735-4891. E-mail: library@chaminade.edu. Web Site: www.chaminade.edu/library. *Dir,* Sharon LePage; *Librn,* Puanani Akaka; *Librn,* Valerie Coleman; *Librn,* Eric Leong; Staff 3.75 (MLS 3.75)
Founded 1955. Enrl 2,400; Fac 80; Highest Degree: Master
Library Holdings: DVDs 1,200; e-books 36,000; e-journals 17,000; Bk Vols 75,000; Per Subs 230
Special Collections: Catholic Authors; Hawaiiana; Judaica
Automation Activity & Vendor Info: (Cataloging) SirsiDynix; (Circulation) SirsiDynix; (ILL) OCLC; (OPAC) SirsiDynix; (Serials) SirsiDynix
Database Vendor: EBSCOhost, ProQuest
Partic in Hawaii Library Consortium; OCLC Online Computer Library Center, Inc; Orbis Cascade Alliance
Open Mon-Thurs 7:45am-10pm, Fri 7:30-6, Sat 11-4, Sun 4-10

G CITY & COUNTY OF HONOLULU MUNICIPAL REFERENCE CENTER*, 558 S King St, 96813-3006. SAN 303-4895. Tel: 808-768-3765. E-mail: csdaccess@honolulu.gov. Web Site: www1.honolulu.gov/csd/mrc/index.htm. *Librn,* Position Currently Open
Founded 1929
Library Holdings: Bk Vols 32,200
Special Collections: Ordinances & Repository for Publications of the City & County of Honolulu
Subject Interests: Local govt
Restriction: Open by appt only

S LEO A DALY CO LIBRARY*, America Saving Bldg, Ste 1230, 1357 Kapiolani Blvd, 96814. SAN 303-5018. Tel: 808-521-8889. FAX: 808-521-3757. E-mail: ladhnl@pixi.com. *Librn,* Beverly Major
Founded 1960
Library Holdings: Bk Vols 1,500; Per Subs 40
Subject Interests: Art & archit, Structural eng
Restriction: Staff use only

S EAST-WEST CENTER*, Research Information Services, 1601 East-West Rd, 96848-1601. SAN 326-7520. Tel: 808-944-7345. FAX: 808-944-7600. E-mail: ris@eastwestcenter.org. Web Site: www.eastwestcenter.org. *Head Librn,* Phyllis Tabusa; Tel: 808-944-7450, E-mail: tabusap@eastwestcenter.org; *Head, Cat,* Jerilyn Sumida; Tel: 808-944-7379, E-mail: sumidaj@eastwestcenter.org; *Syst Librn,* Terese Leber; Tel: 808-944-7405, E-mail: lebert@eastwestcenter.org; *Tech Serv,* Audrey Minei; Tel: 808-944-7554, E-mail: mineia@eastwestcenter.org; Staff 4 (MLS 4)
Founded 1971
Library Holdings: Bk Titles 50,000; Bk Vols 66,000; Per Subs 40
Special Collections: Asian & Pacific Census; World Fertility Survey
Subject Interests: Econ, Energy, Environment, Intl relations
Automation Activity & Vendor Info: (Cataloging) EOS International; (Circulation) EOS International; (ILL) OCLC; (OPAC) EOS International; (Serials) EOS International
Database Vendor: ProQuest
Function: Doc delivery serv, ILL available, Ref serv available
Publications: Acquisitions Lists
Partic in OCLC Online Computer Library Center, Inc
Open Mon-Fri 8-4:30
Restriction: Restricted pub use

S HAWAII CENTER FOR THE DEAF & BLIND LIBRARY*, 3440 Leahi Ave, 96815. SAN 303-4690. Tel: 808-733-4831. FAX: 808-733-4824. Web Site: destiny.k12.hi.us. *Librn,* Laurianne Chun; *Curric Coordr,* Angela Nagata; Staff 2 (MLS 1, Non-MLS 1)
Founded 1976
Library Holdings: Bks on Deafness & Sign Lang 100; Braille Volumes 100; Large Print Bks 100; Bk Titles 6,000; Videos 5,000
Special Collections: Braille Textbooks; Captioned Media Program, VHS; Large Print Textbooks
Automation Activity & Vendor Info: (Acquisitions) Follett Software
Function: Accelerated reader prog, Online cat
Restriction: Open to students, fac & staff

S HAWAII CHINESE HISTORY CENTER LIBRARY*, 111 N King St, Ste 410, 96817-4703. SAN 303-4593. Tel: 808-521-5948. *In Charge,* Robert Tom
Founded 1970
Library Holdings: AV Mats 20; Bk Vols 850
Subject Interests: Chinese lang, Chinese-Am, Genealogy, Hawaii
Publications: Books & Papers (some with the cooperation of University Press of Hawaii); Hawaii Chinese History Center Newsletter
Open Mon, Wed & Fri 10-12

C HAWAII PACIFIC UNIVERSITY LIBRARIES, Meader Library, 1060 Bishop St, 96813-3192. SAN 303-4674. Tel: 808-544-0210. Reference Tel: 808-544-1133. Administration Tel: 808-544-0292. FAX: 808-521-7998. E-mail: reference@hpu.edu. Web Site: www.hpu.edu/Libraries_HPU/Webpages/index.html. *Dir of Libr,* Nori Leong; Fax: 808-544-0880, E-mail: nleong@hpu.edu; Staff 26 (MLS 14, Non-MLS 12)
Founded 1965. Highest Degree: Master
Library Holdings: e-books 50,000; e-journals 25,000; High Interest/Low Vocabulary Bk Vols 1,000; Bk Titles 90,000; Bk Vols 110,000; Per Subs 1,600; Videos 3,000
Special Collections: Atlas Coll; Closed Coll; Foreign Language Coll; Graduate Professional Paper Coll; Hawaiian-Pacific Coll; Index Center Coll; Topic Assistance Center Coll
Automation Activity & Vendor Info: (Circulation) TLC (The Library Corporation); (ILL) OCLC Online
Database Vendor: EBSCOhost
Wireless access
Function: AV serv, e-mail & chat, Photocopying/Printing, Ref serv available, VHS videos
Restriction: Open to students, fac & staff

Departmental Libraries:

ATHERTON LIBRARY, 45-045 Kamehameha Hwy, Kaneohe, 96744-5297, SAN 303-5050. Tel: 808-236-3505. Reference Tel: 808-236-5803. FAX: 808-236-5806. E-mail: atherton@hpu.edu. *Operations Mgr,* An Howell; E-mail: ahollowell@hpu.edu; Staff 6 (MLS 4, Non-MLS 2)
Founded 1967. Highest Degree: Master
Subject Interests: Hawaii, Nursing, Pacific, Sci
Database Vendor: ACM (Association for Computing Machinery), American Chemical Society, American Psychological Association (APA), BioOne, Cinahl, CQ Press, ebrary, JSTOR, ScienceDirect
Function: e-mail & chat, Electronic databases & coll, Photocopying/Printing

G HAWAII STATE ARCHIVES, Iolani Palace Grounds, 364 S King St, 96813. SAN 303-4704. Tel: 808-586-0329. FAX: 808-586-0330. E-mail: archives@hawaii.gov. Web Site: www.ags.hawaii.gov/archives. *Br Chief,* Luella H Kurkjian; E-mail: luella.ha.kurkjian@hawaii.gov; *Head, Coll Mgt,* Gina S Vergara-Bautista; E-mail: gina.s.vergara-bautista@hawaii.gov; *State Archivist,* Susan E Shaner; E-mail: susan.e.shaner@hawaii.gov; *Archivist,* Patricia Lai; E-mail: patricia.lai@hawaii.gov; *Archivist,* Alice Y Tran; E-mail: alice.y.tran@hawaii.gov; *Archivist,* Ju Sun Yi; E-mail: ju.sun.yi@hawaii.gov; *Libr Asst,* Melissa Shimonishi; E-mail: melissa.shimonishi@hawaii.gov; *Libr Tech,* Fredericka P Aikau; E-mail: fredericka.p.aikau@hawaii.gov; Staff 12 (MLS 6, Non-MLS 6)
Founded 1905
Library Holdings: Bk Vols 25,000
Special Collections: 19th Century Hawaiian Newspapers; Captain James Cook Memorial Coll; Hawaiian Government Publications Coll;

Immigration Records to 1900; National Territorial & State Archives, 1790 to date; Paul M Kahn Coll
Restriction: Closed stack

P HAWAII STATE PUBLIC LIBRARY SYSTEM, Office of the State Librarian, 44 Merchant St, 96813. SAN 339-3992. Tel: 808-586-3704. Circulation Tel: 808-586-3500. Interlibrary Loan Service Tel: 808-586-3551. Reference Tel: 808-586-3621. FAX: 808-586-3715. Web Site: www.librarieshawaii.org. *State Librn,* Richard Burns; *Head, Tech Serv,* Ann Fujioka; Tel: 808-831-6871, Fax: 808-831-7899; Staff 172 (MLS 171, Non-MLS 1)
Founded 1961. Pop 1,404,054; Circ 6,519,688
Jul 2013-Jun 2014 Income (Main Library and Branch(s)) $33,963,167, State $29,887,434, Federal $1,655,900, Other $2,419,833. Mats Exp $3,881,055, Books $1,975,964, Per/Ser (Incl. Access Fees) $142,634, Other Print Mats $38,182, Micro $38,549, AV Equip $518,497, Electronic Ref Mat (Incl. Access Fees) $1,167,229. Sal $22,147,533
Library Holdings: Audiobooks 114,902; AV Mats 177; Braille Volumes 17,971; CDs 117,273; DVDs 151,906; e-books 44,620; e-journals 159; Large Print Bks 28,663; Microforms 600; Bk Vols 3,295,163; Per Subs 2,703; Videos 4,043
Special Collections: Pacific Coll. State Document Depository; US Document Depository
Subject Interests: Chinese lang, Hawaii, Japanese (Lang), Korean (Lang)
Automation Activity & Vendor Info: (Acquisitions) SirsiDynix; (Cataloging) SirsiDynix; (Circulation) SirsiDynix; (OPAC) SirsiDynix
Database Vendor: Bowker, CQ Press, EBSCOhost, Gale Cengage Learning, JSTOR, LexisNexis, Marcive, Inc, Mergent Online, ProQuest, SerialsSolutions
Wireless access
Publications: Holo I Mua
Partic in Hawaii Library Consortium
Special Services for the Deaf - TTY equip
Special Services for the Blind - Braille bks; Braille servs; Descriptive video serv (DVS); Large print bks; Radio reading serv; Talking bks
Friends of the Library Group

Branches: 50

AIEA PUBLIC LIBRARY, 99-374 Pohai Place, Aiea, 96701, SAN 339-4654. Tel: 808-483-7333. FAX: 808-483-7336. *Br Mgr,* Baron Baroza; Staff 3 (MLS 3)
Founded 1964. Circ 125,013
Library Holdings: AV Mats 1; CDs 3,280; DVDs 4,381; Bk Vols 67,691; Per Subs 31; Videos 27
Special Services for the Deaf - TTY equip
Friends of the Library Group

AINA HAINA PUBLIC LIBRARY, 5246 Kalanianaole Hwy, 96821, SAN 339-4263. Tel: 808-377-2456. FAX: 808 377 2455. *Br Mgr,* Hueyduan Kwok; Staff 3 (MLS 3)
Founded 1962. Circ 140,491
Library Holdings: AV Mats 2; CDs 2,721; DVDs 2,385; Bk Vols 51,082; Per Subs 51; Videos 13
Friends of the Library Group

EWA BEACH PUBLIC & SCHOOL LIBRARY, 91-950 North Rd, Ewa Beach, 96706, SAN 339-4689. Tel: 808-689-1204. FAX: 808-689-1349. *Br Mgr,* Shari-Lynn Murphy; Staff 2 (MLS 2)
Founded 1971. Circ 89,143
Library Holdings: CDs 1,332; DVDs 1,854; Bk Vols 69,782; Per Subs 23; Videos 3
Special Collections: Oral History
Friends of the Library Group

HANA PUBLIC & SCHOOL LIBRARY, 4111 Hana Hwy, Hana, 96713. (Mail add: PO Box 490, Hana, 96713-0490), SAN 339-5480. Tel: 808-248-4848. FAX: 808-248-4849. *Br Mgr,* Frankie Pasion; Staff 1 (MLS 1)
Founded 1984. Circ 20,856
Library Holdings: AV Mats 11; CDs 1,162; DVDs 1,475; Bk Vols 31,128; Per Subs 55; Videos 150
Friends of the Library Group

HANAPEPE PUBLIC LIBRARY, 4490 Kona Rd, Hanapepe, 96716. (Mail add: PO Box B, Hanapepe, 96716), SAN 339-5316. Tel: 808-335-8418. FAX: 808-335-2120. *Br Mgr,* Karen Ikemoto; Staff 1 (MLS 1)
Founded 1950. Circ 55,954
Library Holdings: AV Mats 1; CDs 1,081; DVDs 2,128; Bk Vols 30,750; Per Subs 29; Videos 25
Friends of the Library Group

HAWAII KAI PUBLIC LIBRARY, 249 Lunalilo Home Rd, 96825, SAN 339-4298. Tel: 808-397-5833. FAX: 808-397-5832. *Br Mgr,* Colleen Lashway; Staff 4 (MLS 4)
Founded 1973. Circ 120,027
Library Holdings: AV Mats 1; CDs 1,954; DVDs 2,504; Bk Vols 73,602; Per Subs 52; Videos 12
Special Services for the Deaf - TTY equip
Friends of the Library Group

HAWAII STATE LIBRARY, 478 S King St, 96813, SAN 339-4050. Tel: 808-586-3500. Interlibrary Loan Service Tel: 808-586-3551. Reference Tel: 808-586-3621. FAX: 808-586-3943. TDD: 808-586-3471. *Managing Librn,* Diane Eddy; Staff 40 (MLS 40)
Founded 1913. Circ 345,237
Library Holdings: CDs 11,837; DVDs 7,153; Microforms 292; Bk Vols 558,191; Per Subs 267; Videos 1,169
Special Collections: Asian Language Materials; Federal Documents; Hawaii & Pacific Coll; Patent & Trademark Depository; Telephone References
Subject Interests: Art, Hist, Lit, Music, Philos, Recreation, Sci tech, Soc sci & issues, Tech
Special Services for the Deaf - TTY equip
Friends of the Library Group

HILO PUBLIC LIBRARY, 300 Waianuenue Ave, Hilo, 96720-2447, SAN 339-4891. Tel: 808-933-8888. FAX: 808-933-8895. TDD: 808-933-8890. *Ad,* Susan Collins; Staff 6 (MLS 6)
Founded 1880. Circ 437,318
Library Holdings: AV Mats 23; CDs 7,919; DVDs 8,136; Microforms 1; Bk Vols 235,690; Per Subs 174; Videos 415
Special Services for the Deaf - TTY equip
Friends of the Library Group

HONOKAA PUBLIC LIBRARY, Bldg 3, 45-3380 Mamane St, Honokaa, 96727, SAN 339-4980. Tel: 808-775-8881. FAX: 808-775-8882. *Br Mgr,* Tahirih Foster; Staff 1 (MLS 1)
Founded 1937. Circ 27,469
Library Holdings: AV Mats 4; CDs 828; DVDs 1,576; Bk Vols 19,489; Per Subs 13; Videos 12
Friends of the Library Group

KAHUKU PUBLIC & SCHOOL LIBRARY, 56-490 Kamehameha Hwy, Kahuku, 96731, SAN 339-4328. Tel: 808-293-8935. FAX: 808-293-8937. *Br Mgr,* Lea Domingo; Staff 2 (MLS 2)
Founded 1968. Circ 54,794
Library Holdings: CDs 1,228; DVDs 1,696; Bk Vols 45,847; Per Subs 53; Videos 49
Friends of the Library Group

KAHULUI PUBLIC LIBRARY, 90 School St, Kahului, 96732-1627, SAN 339-5499. Tel: 808-873-3097. FAX: 808-873-3094. *Br Mgr,* Sana Daliva; Staff 3 (MLS 3)
Founded 1963. Circ 167,027
Library Holdings: CDs 2,852; DVDs 3,350; e-journals 1; Microforms 1; Bk Vols 101,700; Per Subs 59; Videos 179
Friends of the Library Group

KAILUA-KONA PUBLIC LIBRARY, 75-138 Hualalai Rd, Kailua-Kona, 96740-1704, SAN 339-5014. Tel: 808-327-4327. FAX: 808-327-4326. *Br Mgr,* Irene Horvath; Staff 3 (MLS 3)
Founded 1972. Circ 149,727
Library Holdings: AV Mats 10; CDs 3,188; DVDs 3,121; Bk Vols 53,637; Per Subs 49; Videos 22
Friends of the Library Group

KAILUA PUBLIC LIBRARY, 239 Kuulei Rd, Kailua, 96734, SAN 339-4352. Tel: 808-266-9911. FAX: 808-266-9915. *Br Mgr,* Patti Mccrians; Staff 3.5 (MLS 3.5)
Founded 1960. Circ 263,935
Library Holdings: AV Mats 1; CDs 3,319; DVDs 2,344; Bk Vols 84,061; Per Subs 85; Videos 35
Friends of the Library Group

KAIMUKI PUBLIC LIBRARY, 1041 Koko Head Ave, 96816-3707, SAN 339-4387. Tel: 808-733-8422. FAX: 808-733-8426. *Br Mgr,* Maile Davis; Staff 5 (MLS 5)
Founded 1940. Circ 278,545
Library Holdings: AV Mats 1; CDs 3,419; DVDs 3,596; Bk Vols 82,029; Per Subs 83; Videos 57
Friends of the Library Group

KALIHI-PALAMA PUBLIC LIBRARY, 1325 Kalihi St, 96819, SAN 339-4417. Tel: 808-832-3466. FAX: 808-832-3469. *Br Mgr,* Marcia Nakama; Staff 3 (MLS 3)
Founded 1935. Circ 118,955
Library Holdings: AV Mats 1; CDs 2,928; DVDs 3,416; Bk Vols 53,853; Per Subs 41; Videos 29
Friends of the Library Group

KANEOHE PUBLIC LIBRARY, 45-829 Kamehameha Hwy, Kaneohe, 96744, SAN 339-4441. Tel: 808-233-5676. FAX: 808-233-5672. *Br Mgr,* Cynthia Chow; Staff 5 (MLS 5)
Founded 1961. Circ 253,405
Library Holdings: AV Mats 5; CDs 2,628; DVDs 2,233; Microforms 306; Bk Vols 112,447; Per Subs 84; Videos 1
Friends of the Library Group

KAPAA PUBLIC LIBRARY, 4-1464 Kuhio Hwy, Kapaa, 96746, SAN 339-5340. Tel: 808-821-4422. FAX: 808-821-4423. TDD: 808-821-4438. *Br Mgr,* Lani Kawahara; Staff 1 (MLS 1)
Founded 1955. Circ 94,493
Library Holdings: CDs 1,598; DVDs 3,271; Bk Vols 36,646; Per Subs 49; Videos 103

Special Services for the Deaf - TTY equip
Friends of the Library Group

KAPOLEI PUBLIC LIBRARY, 1020 Manawai St, Kapolei, 96707. Tel: 808-693-7050. FAX: 808-693-7062. *Br Mgr,* Elizabeth Stewart-Marshall; Staff 7 (MLS 7)
Founded 2004. Circ 396,610
Library Holdings: CDs 6,272; DVDs 7,251; Bk Vols 123,363; Per Subs 70; Videos 37
Friends of the Library Group

KEAAU PUBLIC & SCHOOL LIBRARY, 16-571 Keaau-Pahoa Rd, Keaau, 96749-8106, SAN 339-5049. Tel: 808-982-4281. FAX: 808-982-4242. *Br Mgr,* Maxine Aki; Staff 1 (MLS 1)
Founded 1974. Circ 60,387
Library Holdings: CDs 2,250; DVDs 2,209; Bk Vols 31,360; Per Subs 67; Videos 30

KEALAKEKUA PUBLIC LIBRARY, 81-6619 Mamalahoa Hwy, Kealakekua, 96750. (Mail add: PO Box 768, Kealakekua, 96750). Tel: 808-323-7585. FAX: 808-323-7586. *Actg Br Mgr,* Kipapa Kahelahela; Staff 1 (MLS 1)
Founded 1950. Circ 37,412
Library Holdings: CDs 1,174; DVDs 2,206; Bk Vols 18,688; Per Subs 24; Videos 4
Friends of the Library Group

KIHEI PUBLIC LIBRARY, 35 Waimahaihai St, Kihei, 96753-8015, SAN 326-8667. Tel: 808-875-6833. FAX: 808-875-6834. *Br Mgr,* Jessica Gleason; Staff 2 (MLS 2)
Founded 1988. Circ 143,759
Library Holdings: AV Mats 8; CDs 2,870; DVDs 3,527; Bk Vols 70,868; Per Subs 95; Videos 34
Friends of the Library Group

KOLOA PUBLIC & SCHOOL LIBRARY, 3451 Poipu Rd, Koloa, 96756. (Mail add: PO Box 9, Koloa, 96756-0009), SAN 339-5375. Tel: 808-742-8455. FAX: 808-742-8454. *Br Mgr,* David Thorp; Staff 1 (MLS 1)
Founded 1976. Circ 94,985
Library Holdings: CDs 337; DVDs 3,551; Bk Vols 31,538; Per Subs 51; Videos 28
Special Collections: Koloa, Kauai History Materials
Friends of the Library Group

LAHAINA PUBLIC LIBRARY, 680 Wharf St, Lahaina, 96761, SAN 339-5529. Tel: 808-662-3950. FAX: 808-662-3951. *Br Mgr,* Madeleine Buchanan; Staff 1 (Non-MLS 1)
Founded 1956. Circ 47,016
Library Holdings: AV Mats 25; CDs 1,633; DVDs 2,462; Bk Vols 27,857; Per Subs 130; Videos 136
Friends of the Library Group

LANAI PUBLIC & SCHOOL LIBRARY, 555 Fraser Ave, Lanai City, 96763. (Mail add: PO Box 630550, Lanai City, 96763-0550), SAN 339-5553. Tel: 808-565-7920. FAX: 808-565-7922. TDD: 808-565-6996. *Br Mgr,* Peggy Kim Hong Fink; Staff 1 (MLS 1)
Founded 1975. Circ 43,208
Library Holdings: AV Mats 13; CDs 1,113; DVDs 4,262; Bk Vols 30,260; Per Subs 61; Videos 2
Special Services for the Deaf - TTY equip
Friends of the Library Group

LAUPAHOEHOE PUBLIC & SCHOOL LIBRARY, 35-2065 Old Mamalahoa Hwy, Laupahoehoe, 96764. (Mail add: PO Box 249, Laupahoehoe, 96764-0249), SAN 339-5103. Tel: 808-962-2229. FAX: 808-962-2230. *Br Mgr,* Gabrielle Casart; Staff 1 (MLS 1)
Founded 1973. Circ 24,307
Library Holdings: AV Mats 1; CDs 1,553; DVDs 2,913; Bk Vols 24,369; Per Subs 21; Videos 13
Friends of the Library Group

LIBRARY FOR THE BLIND & PHYSICALLY HANDICAPPED
See Separate Entry

LIHUE PUBLIC LIBRARY, 4344 Hardy St, Lihue, 96766, SAN 339-5286. Tel: 808-241-3222. FAX: 808-241-3225. *Br Mgr,* Carolyn Larson; Staff 3 (MLS 3)
Founded 1969. Circ 92,148
Library Holdings: AV Mats 2; CDs 3,304; DVDs 3,805; Bk Vols 79,310; Per Subs 58; Videos 49
Special Services for the Deaf - TTY equip
Friends of the Library Group

LILIHA PUBLIC LIBRARY, 1515 Liliha St, 96817-3526, SAN 339-4476. Tel: 808-587-7577. FAX: 808-587-7579. *Br Mgr,* Sylvia Mitchell; Staff 3 (MLS 3)
Founded 1966. Circ 176,900
Library Holdings: CDs 2,606; DVDs 3,149; Bk Vols 85,401; Per Subs 40; Videos 106
Special Collections: Chinese Language Coll
Special Services for the Deaf - TTY equip
Friends of the Library Group

MAKAWAO PUBLIC LIBRARY, 1159 Makawao Ave, Makawao, 96768, SAN 339-5588. Tel: 808-573-8785. FAX: 808-573-8787. *Br Mgr,* Glenda Berry; Staff 2 (MLS 2)
Founded 1969. Circ 122,035
Library Holdings: AV Mats 2; CDs 2,437; DVDs 2,499; Bk Vols 43,242; Per Subs 90; Videos 36
Friends of the Library Group

MANOA PUBLIC LIBRARY, 2716 Woodlawn Dr, 96822-1841, SAN 339-4506. Tel: 808-988-0459. FAX: 808-988-0458. *Br Mgr,* Christel Collins; Staff 3 (MLS 3)
Founded 1966. Circ 196,586
Library Holdings: CDs 1,590; DVDs 4,489; Bk Vols 39,172; Per Subs 35; Videos 29
Friends of the Library Group

MCCULLY-MOILIILI PUBLIC LIBRARY, 2211 S King St, 96826, SAN 339-4530. Tel: 808-973-1099. FAX: 808-973-1095. *Br Mgr,* Hillary Chang; Staff 4 (MLS 4)
Founded 1969. Circ 269,428
Library Holdings: AV Mats 10; CDs 2,733; DVDs 4,969; Bk Vols 94,053; Per Subs 33; Videos 97
Special Collections: Korean Language Coll
Special Services for the Deaf - TTY equip
Friends of the Library Group

MILILANI PUBLIC LIBRARY, 95-450 Makaimoimo St, Mililani, 96789-3018, SAN 339-4700. Tel: 808-627-7470. FAX: 808-627-7309. *Br Mgr,* Wendi Woodstrup; Staff 4 (MLS 4)
Founded 1984. Circ 292,547
Library Holdings: CDs 3,274; DVDs 3,824; Bk Vols 73,277; Per Subs 43; Videos 3
Special Services for the Deaf - TTY equip
Friends of the Library Group

MOLOKAI PUBLIC LIBRARY, 15 Ala Malama St, Kaunakakai, 96748. (Mail add: PO Box 395, Kaunakakai, 96748-0395), SAN 339-5618. Tel: 808-553-1765. FAX: 808-553-1766. *Br Mgr,* Sri P TenCate; Staff 1 (MLS 1)
Founded 1937. Circ 39,053
Library Holdings: AV Mats 1; CDs 1,693; DVDs 2,312; Bk Vols 19,411; Per Subs 56; Videos 16
Special Services for the Deaf - TTY equip
Friends of the Library Group

MOUNTAIN VIEW PUBLIC & SCHOOL LIBRARY, 18-1235 Volcano Hwy, Mountain View, 96771. (Mail add: PO Box 380, Mountain View, 96771-0380), SAN 339-5138. Tel: 808-968-2322. FAX: 808-968-2323. *Br Mgr,* Carleen Corpuz; Staff 1 (MLS 1)
Founded 1977. Circ 35,288
Library Holdings: AV Mats 2; CDs 1,570; DVDs 2,205; Bk Vols 23,198; Per Subs 32; Videos 25
Friends of the Library Group

NAALEHU PUBLIC LIBRARY, 95-5669 Mamalahoa Hwy, Naalehu, 96772. (Mail add: PO Box 653, Naalehu, 96772-0653), SAN 339-5146. Tel: 808-939-2442. FAX: 808-939-2443. *Br Mgr,* Sara Kamibayashi; Staff 1 (MLS 1)
Founded 1994. Circ 31,142
Library Holdings: CDs 616; DVDs 1,287; Bk Vols 9,365; Per Subs 18; Videos 8
Friends of the Library Group

NORTH KOHALA PUBLIC LIBRARY, 54-3645 Akoni Pule Hwy, Kapaau, 96755. (Mail add: PO Box 248, Kapaau, 96755-0248). *Br Mgr, Librn IV,* Janet Lam; Tel: 808-889-6655, Fax: 808-889-6656; Staff 1 (MLS 1)
Founded 2010. Circ 71,880
Library Holdings: CDs 1,385; DVDs 2,491; Bk Vols 17,291; Per Subs 44; Videos 4
Friends of the Library Group

PAHALA PUBLIC & SCHOOL LIBRARY, 96-3150 Pikake St, Pahala, 96777. (Mail add: PO Box 400, Pahala, 96777-0400), SAN 339-5162. Tel: 808-928-2015. FAX: 808-928-2016. *Libr Tech VII,* Debra Wong Yuen
Founded 1963. Circ 9,168
Library Holdings: CDs 505; DVDs 967; Bk Vols 8,432; Per Subs 13; Videos 2
Friends of the Library Group

PAHOA PUBLIC & SCHOOL LIBRARY, 15-3070 Pahoa-Kalapana Rd, Pahoa, 96778, SAN 339-5197. Tel: 808-965-2171. FAX: 808-965-2199. *Br Mgr,* Gaila Vidunas; Staff 1 (MLS 1)
Founded 1967. Circ 108,612
Library Holdings: CDs 1,956; DVDs 2,514; Bk Vols 33,654; Per Subs 24; Videos 74
Friends of the Library Group

THELMA PARKER MEMORIAL PUBLIC & SCHOOL LIBRARY, 67-1209 Mamalahoa Hwy, Kamuela, 96743-8429. (Mail add: PO Box 698, Kamuela, 96743-0698), SAN 339-5227. Tel: 808-887-6067. FAX: 808-887-6066. *Br Mgr,* Pamela Akao; Staff 2 (MLS 2)
Founded 1978. Circ 99,445

Library Holdings: AV Mats 1; CDs 3,708; DVDs 3,475; Bk Vols 43,936; Per Subs 62; Videos 68
Friends of the Library Group

PEARL CITY PUBLIC LIBRARY, 1138 Waimano Home Rd, Pearl City, 96782, SAN 339-4719. Tel: 808-453-6566. FAX: 808-453-6570. *Br Mgr,* Vicky Bowie; Staff 5 (MLS 5)
Founded 1969. Circ 210,358
Library Holdings: AV Mats 1; CDs 3,197; DVDs 4,440; Bk Vols 150,428; Per Subs 30; Videos 65
Special Services for the Deaf - TTY equip
Friends of the Library Group

PRINCEVILLE PUBLIC LIBRARY, 4343 Emmalani Dr, Princeville, 96722. Tel: 808-826-4310. FAX: 808-826-4311. *Actg Br Mgr,* Eric Larsen; Staff 1 (MLS 1)
Founded 1999. Circ 84,387
Library Holdings: AV Mats 1; CDs 505; DVDs 2,872; Bk Vols 47,298; Per Subs 25; Videos 100
Friends of the Library Group

SALT LAKE-MOANALUA PUBLIC LIBRARY, 3225 Salt Lake Blvd, 96818, SAN 326-7393. Tel: 808-831-6831. FAX: 808-831-6834. *Br Mgr,* Duane Wenzel; Staff 3 (MLS 3)
Founded 1984. Circ 194,001
Library Holdings: AV Mats 1; CDs 2,794; DVDs 4,812; Bk Vols 67,383; Per Subs 45; Videos 26
Special Collections: Martial Art Coll
Friends of the Library Group

WAHIAWA PUBLIC LIBRARY, 820 California Ave, Wahiawa, 96786, SAN 339-4743. Tel: 808-622-6345. FAX: 808-622-6348. *Br Mgr,* Anthony Hooper; Staff 2 (MLS 2)
Founded 1940. Circ 57,748
Library Holdings: AV Mats 1; CDs 1,748; DVDs 2,153; Bk Vols 41,634; Per Subs 16; Videos 22
Friends of the Library Group

WAIALUA PUBLIC LIBRARY, 67-068 Kealohanui St, Waialua, 96791, SAN 339-4778. Tel: 808-637-8286. FAX: 808-637-8288. *Br Mgr,* Timothy Littlejohn; Staff 2 (MLS 2)
Founded 1952. Circ 55,576
Library Holdings: CDs 1,455; DVDs 1,974; Bk Vols 39,924; Per Subs 45; Videos 52
Friends of the Library Group

WAIANAE PUBLIC LIBRARY, 85-625 Farrington Hwy, Waianae, 96792, SAN 339-4808. Tel: 808-697-7868. FAX: 808-697-7870. *Br Mgr,* Laurie Barker-Perez; Staff 2 (MLS 2)
Founded 1966. Circ 56,422
Library Holdings: CDs 1,535; DVDs 2,541; Bk Vols 56,996; Per Subs 41; Videos 76
Friends of the Library Group

WAIKIKI-KAPAHULU PUBLIC LIBRARY, 400 Kapahulu Ave, 96815, SAN 339-4565. Tel: 808-733-8488. FAX: 808 733 8490. *Br Mgr,* Stephanie Strickland; Staff 3 (MLS 3)
Founded 1952. Circ 129,744
Library Holdings: CDs 2,059; DVDs 2,498; Bk Vols 37,244; Per Subs 42; Videos 12
Friends of the Library Group

WAILUKU PUBLIC LIBRARY, 251 High St, Wailuku, 96793, SAN 339-5464. Tel: 808-243-5766. FAX: 808-243-5768. *Br Mgr,* Susan Werner; Staff 2 (MLS 2)
Founded 1929. Circ 54,381
Library Holdings: AV Mats 6; CDs 2,548; DVDs 3,257; e-journals 1; Bk Vols 67,429; Per Subs 83; Videos 99
Friends of the Library Group

WAIMANALO PUBLIC & SCHOOL LIBRARY, 41-1320 Kalanianaole Hwy, Waimanalo, 96795, SAN 339-459X. Tel: 808-259-2610. FAX: 808-259-2612. *Br Mgr,* Cora Eggerman; Staff 1.5 (MLS 1.5)
Founded 1978. Circ 45,448
Library Holdings: CDs 1,170; DVDs 1,771; Bk Vols 41,363; Per Subs 18; Videos 25
Friends of the Library Group

WAIMEA PUBLIC LIBRARY, 9750 Kaumualii Hwy, Waimea, 96796. (Mail add: PO Box 397, Waimea, 96796-0397), SAN 339-5405. Tel: 808-338-6848. FAX: 808-338-6847. *Br Mgr,* Susan C Remoaldo
Founded 1950. Circ 8,447
Library Holdings: CDs 692; DVDs 1,252; Bk Vols 26,720; Per Subs 14; Videos 112
Friends of the Library Group

WAIPAHU PUBLIC LIBRARY, 94-275 Mokuola St, Waipahu, 96797, SAN 339-4832. Tel: 808-675-0358. FAX: 808-675-0360. *Br Mgr,* Christine Mogilewicz; Staff 3 (MLS 3)
Founded 1952. Circ 96,078
Library Holdings: CDs 1,658; DVDs 3,283; Bk Vols 65,685; Per Subs 32; Videos 120
Friends of the Library Group

Bookmobiles: 2

P HAWAII STATE PUBLIC LIBRARY SYSTEM, Library for the Blind & Physically Handicapped, 402 Kapahulu Ave, 96815. SAN 303-4712. Tel: 808-733-8444. FAX: 808-733-8449. *Actg Managing Librn,* Sue Sugimura; Staff 2 (MLS 2)
Founded 1931. Pop 150,659; Circ 48,026
Library Holdings: Audiobooks 114,902; AV Mats 41; Braille Volumes 17,971; CDs 2; DVDs 28; Large Print Bks 13,740; Bk Vols 14,779; Per Subs 47; Videos 232
Special Collections: Braille, Large Print, Cassettes & Books; Hawaiiana Titles, Described Videos & DVDs; Reference Material on Various Handicaps
Subject Interests: Braille
Wireless access
Publications: New Large Type Books (Quarterly); News is Getting Around the Pacific (Newsletter)
Special Services for the Deaf - Bks on deafness & sign lang; Deaf publ; Spec interest per; Staff with knowledge of sign lang; TTY equip
Special Services for the Blind - Accessible computers; Audio mat; Braille bks; Braille equip; Braille servs; Cassette playback machines; Closed circuit radio for broadcast serv; Computer with voice synthesizer for visually impaired persons; Ednalite Hi-Vision scope; Handicapped awareness prog; Large screen computer & software; Magnifiers; Mags & bk reproduction/duplication; Newsletter (in large print, Braille or on cassette); Photo duplicator for making large print; Production of talking bks; Recorded bks; Screen enlargement software for people with visual disabilities; Talking bk & rec for the blind cat; Talking bks & player equip; Talking calculator; Thermoform Brailon duplicator; Videos on blindness & phys handicaps; Volunteer serv
Friends of the Library Group

S HAWAIIAN HISTORICAL SOCIETY LIBRARY*, 560 Kawaiahao St, 96813. SAN 303-4763. Tel: 808-537-6271. FAX: 808-537-6271. Web Site: www.hawaiianhistory.org. *Dir,* Barbara E Dunn; E-mail: hhsbarb@lava.net; Staff 1 (MLS 1)
Founded 1892
Library Holdings: Bk Titles 16,000; Per Subs 20
Special Collections: History of Hawaii & Pacific Coll (Late 18th & 19th Centuries)
Automation Activity & Vendor Info: (OPAC) LibraryWorld, Inc
Wireless access
Publications: The Hawaiian Historical Society: A Guide to the Library Collections, 1991
Open Tues-Fri 10-4
Restriction: Open to pub for ref only
Friends of the Library Group

S HAWAIIAN MISSION CHILDREN'S SOCIETY LIBRARY*, Hawaiian Mission Houses Archives, 553 S King St, 96813. SAN 303-4771. Tel: 808-531-0481. FAX: 808-545-2280. E-mail: info@missionhouses.org. Web Site: www.missionhouses.org. *Archivist, Librn,* John Barker; E-mail: archives@missionhouses.org; Staff 1 (MLS 1)
Founded 1908
Library Holdings: AV Mats 50; Electronic Media & Resources 41; Bk Vols 13,000; Per Subs 10
Special Collections: American Board of Commissioners for Foreign Missions, including letters, ledgers, reports written by missionaries to the ABCFM in Boston; Hawaiian Evangelical Association Archives,including reports of native Hawaiian ministers; Hawaiian Language Imprints, 19th century; Lahainaluna Copperplate Engravings, 1830-1840; Marquesas Coll, including letters written by native Hawaiian missionaries to the Hawaiian Board of Missions in Hawaii; Micronesian Mission-HEA Papers, including letters from native Hawaiian ministers in Micronesia to the Hawaiian Board of Missions in Hawaii; Missionary Manuscripts, letters, reports, journals
Subject Interests: Hawaii
Wireless access
Function: Archival coll, Doc delivery serv, For res purposes, Handicapped accessible, Magnifiers for reading, Newsp ref libr, Photocopying/Printing, Prog for children & young adult, Ref serv available, Res libr, Telephone ref, Wheelchair accessible
Publications: A Guide to the Holdings of the Hawaiian Mission Children's Society Library; Engraved at Lahainaluna by David Forbes, 2012; Grapes of Canaan by Albertine Loomis; Hawaiian Language Imprints, 1822-1899; Ka Pai Palapala: Early Printing in Hawaii; Mission Houses Museum Guidebook, Na Hale Hoikeike o Na Mikanele, Honolulu, 2001; Missionary Album: Biographical Sketches & Portraits of the American Protestant Missionaries to Hawaii, HMCS, 1969; The Hawaii Journals of the New England Missionaries, 1813-1894; The Journals of Cochran Forbes; Voyages to Hawaii before 1860 by Bernice Judd, UH Press, 1974
Restriction: Closed stack, Non-circulating, Not a lending libr, Open to fac, students & qualified researchers, Open to pub for ref only, Private libr

J HEALD COLLEGE*, Learning Resource Center-Honolulu Campus, 1500 Kapiolani Blvd, 96814. Tel: 808-628-5525. FAX: 808-955-6964. Web Site: www.heald.edu. *Mgr,* Rachel Alsagoff; *Coordr,* Jason Harada; *Coordr,* Shaun Miyamoto; *Coordr,* Lionel Santos, II; *Coordr,* Shane Uehara

Library Holdings: AV Mats 200; Bk Vols 3,500; Per Subs 30
Database Vendor: EBSCOhost, Micromedex
Wireless access
Open Mon-Thurs 7:30am-10:30pm, Fri 8am-9:30pm, Sat 8:30-1

S HONOLULU ACADEMY OF ARTS, Robert C Allerton Library, 900 S Beretania St, 96814-1495. SAN 303-4798. Tel: 808-532-8754. FAX: 808-532-3683. Web Site: www.honoluluacademy.org. *Head Librn,* Kawaiaea F Sachiyo; E-mail: skawaiaea@honoluluacademy.org; Staff 1 (MLS 1)
Founded 1927
Library Holdings: Bk Titles 36,000; Bk Vols 45,000; Per Subs 45
Special Collections: Asian Islamic Art; Japanese Woodblock Prints
Wireless access
Open Wed & Thurs 10-3:30, Fri 10-3, Sat 10-2
Restriction: Non-circulating to the pub

J HONOLULU COMMUNITY COLLEGE LIBRARY, 874 Dillingham Blvd, 96817-4598. SAN 303-4801. Tel: 808-845-9199. Circulation Tel: 808-845-9221. Administration Tel: 808-845-9195. FAX: 808-845-3618. E-mail: honcclib@hawaii.edu. Web Site: www.honolulu.hawaii.edu/library. *Head Librn,* Irene Mesina; E-mail: imesina@hawaii.edu; *Libr Instruction, Ref Serv,* Carol Hasegawa; Tel: 808-845-9196; *Libr Instruction, Ref Serv,* Sarah Myhre; Tel: 808-845-9194; *Libr Instruction, Ref Serv,* Stefanie Sasaki; Tel: 808-845-9463; *Ref Serv, Tech Serv,* Nadine Leong-Kurio; Tel: 808-845-9198; Staff 10 (MLS 5, Non-MLS 5)
Founded 1965. Enrl 4,200; Fac 215; Highest Degree: Associate
Library Holdings: AV Mats 858; Bk Titles 45,000; Bk Vols 54,505; Per Subs 140
Special Collections: Automotive Technical Coll; Hawaii/Pacific Coll
Subject Interests: Liberal arts, Occupational
Automation Activity & Vendor Info: (Cataloging) Ex Libris Group; (Circulation) Ex Libris Group
Database Vendor: EBSCOhost, Gale Cengage Learning, ProQuest, ScienceDirect
Wireless access
Open Mon-Thurs 8-7, Fri 8-3, Sat 9-12

CM JOHN A BURNS SCHOOL OF MEDICINE*, Health Sciences Library, 651 Ilalo St, MEB, 96813. SAN 303-500X. Tel: 808-692-0810. FAX: 808-692-1244. E-mail: hslinfo@hawaii.edu. Web Site: hslib.jabsom.hawaii.edu. *Dir,* Virginia M Tanji; Tel: 808-692-0823, E-mail: tanji@hawaii.edu; *Info Serv & Instrul Librn,* Angela Lee; Tel: 808-692-0824; *Circ,* Hilda Baroza; Tel: 808-692-0816; Staff 8.5 (MLS 4.5, Non-MLS 4)
Founded 2005. Highest Degree: Doctorate
Library Holdings: Bk Titles 8,000; Bk Vols 11,000; Per Subs 150
Subject Interests: Med, Pub health
Automation Activity & Vendor Info: (Cataloging) OCLC; (Circulation) Ex Libris Group; (OPAC) Ex Libris Group; (Serials) SerialsSolutions
Database Vendor: EBSCOhost, ISI Web of Knowledge, McGraw-Hill, MD Consult, Medline, Natural Standard, OVID Technologies, ScienceDirect, STAT!Ref (Teton Data Systems), UpToDate, WebMD
Wireless access
Partic in OCLC Online Computer Library Center, Inc; Pacific Southwest Regional Medical Library (PSRML)
Open Mon-Thurs 8am-10pm, Fri 8-5, Sat 9-5, Sun Noon-5

J KAPI'OLANI COMMUNITY COLLEGE LIBRARY*, Lama Library, 4303 Diamond Head Rd, 96816. SAN 303-4852. Tel: 808-734-9268. Reference Tel: 808-734-9359. Administration Tel: 808-734-9259. FAX: 808-734-9453. E-mail: kapccref@hawaii.edu. Web Site: library.kcc.hawaii.edu. *Dir, Libr & Learning Res,* Susan Murata; Tel: 808-734-9267, E-mail: smurata@hawaii.edu; *Librn,* Joy Oehlers; Tel: 808-734-9352, E-mail: aichin@hawaii.edu; *Librn,* Kevin Roddy; Tel: 808-734-9354, E-mail: kroddy@hawaii.edu; *Digital Initiatives Librn,* Sunny Pai; Tel: 808-734-9755, E-mail: sunyeen@hawaii.edu; *Electronic Res Librn,* Stephanie Nelson; Tel: 808-734-9254, E-mail: stephnel@hawaii.edu; *Learning Res Librn,* Joyce Tokuda; Tel: 808-734-9357, E-mail: jtokuda@hawaii.edu; *Tech Serv Librn,* Michelle Sturges; Tel: 808-734-9163, E-mail: sturges@hawaii.edu; *Educ Spec,* Guy Inaba; Tel: 808-734-9206, E-mail: inaba@hawaii.edu; *Hawaiian Res Spec,* Anna Thomas; Tel: 808-734-9599, E-mail: athomas@hawaii.edu; *Res Support Spec,* Alva Kodama; Tel: 808-734-9217, E-mail: kodama@hawaii.edu. Subject Specialists: *Hawaii, Pacific,* Anna Thomas; Staff 22 (MLS 9, Non-MLS 13)
Founded 1992. Enrl 7,757; Fac 360; Highest Degree: Associate
Library Holdings: e-books 1,311; e-journals 17,000; Bk Titles 58,810; Bk Vols 73,114; Per Subs 300
Special Collections: Chinese History & Culture (Char Coll); Read (Developmental)
Subject Interests: Hawaii, Japan
Automation Activity & Vendor Info: (Cataloging) Ex Libris Group; (Circulation) Ex Libris Group; (OPAC) Ex Libris Group
Database Vendor: Gale Cengage Learning
Wireless access
Function: AV serv, Distance learning, Doc delivery serv, Handicapped accessible, ILL available, Magnifiers for reading, Photocopying/Printing, Ref serv available, Telephone ref, Wheelchair accessible

S LEGAL AID SOCIETY OF HAWAII LIBRARY*, 924 Bethel St, 96813. (Mail add: PO Box 37375, 96837-0375), SAN 323-4770. Tel: 808-527-8010, 808-536-4302. FAX: 808-527-8088. Web Site: www.legalaidhawaii.org. *In Charge,* Charles K Greenfield; E-mail: chgreen@lashaw.org
Library Holdings: Bk Vols 5,000; Per Subs 30
Open Mon-Fri 8-4:30

P MASONIC PUBLIC LIBRARY*, 1611 Kewalo St, 96822. Tel: 808-521-2070. FAX: 808-533-6493. *Mgr,* Jami Kaneshiro
Library Holdings: Bk Vols 6,000
Special Collections: Masonic Archival Coll
Subject Interests: Hawaii, Masonic heritage
Function: Photocopying/Printing
Open Mon-Fri 9-1

G NATIONAL MARINE FISHERIES SERVICE*, Honolulu Laboratory Library, 2570 Dole St, 96822-2396. SAN 303-4909. Tel: 808-983-5307. FAX: 808-983-2902. E-mail: ani.au@noaa.gov. Web Site: www.lib.noaa.gov.
Library Holdings: Bk Vols 11,000; Per Subs 60
Subject Interests: Marine biol, Oceanography
Function: Archival coll, ILL available, Photocopying/Printing, Ref serv available, Referrals accepted
Partic in OCLC Online Computer Library Center, Inc

S PACIFIC RESOURCES FOR EDUCATION & LEARNING*, Pacific Resource Center, 900 Fort Street Mall, Ste 1300, 96813. Tel: 808-441-1300. FAX: 808-441-1385. E-mail: askprel@prel.org. Web Site: www.prel.org. *Dir,* Jane Barnwell; Tel: 808-441-1320, E-mail: barnwellj@prel.org. Subject Specialists: *Pacific Islands,* Jane Barnwell; Staff 1 (MLS 1)
Library Holdings: AV Mats 150; Electronic Media & Resources 2; Bk Vols 3,000; Per Subs 40
Subject Interests: Educ, Educ tech, Health educ, Pacific Islands
Automation Activity & Vendor Info: (Cataloging) Follett Software; (Circulation) Follett Software; (OPAC) Follett Software
Database Vendor: EBSCOhost, STAT!Ref (Teton Data Systems)
Function: Ref serv available
Partic in Hawaii Library Consortium; Medical Libraries Consortium of Hawaii (MLCH); National Network of Libraries of Medicine
Restriction: Internal use only

C SCHOOL OF OCEAN & EARTH SCIENCE & TECHNOLOGY LIBRARY*, 2525 Correa Rd, HIG 133, 96822. SAN 303-464X. Tel: 808-956-7040. FAX: 808-956-2538. E-mail: pubslib@soest.hawaii.edu. *Mgr,* Diane J Henderson; Staff 2 (MLS 1, Non-MLS 1)
Founded 1963. Enrl 300; Fac 70; Highest Degree: Doctorate
Library Holdings: Bk Titles 3,800; Per Subs 83
Special Collections: Hawaii Earth Science Coll; HIG Reports
Subject Interests: Geol, Meteorology, Oceanography
Restriction: Open to students, fac & staff

M SHRINERS' HOSPITAL LIBRARY*, 1310 Punahou St, 96826-1099. SAN 303-4941. Tel: 808-941-4466, Ext 638. FAX: 808-942-8573. Web Site: www.shriners.com/shc/honolulu/index.html. *Coordr,* Ramona Fillman; Tel: 808-951-3693, E-mail: rfillman@shrinenet.org
Founded 1923
Library Holdings: Bk Vols 650; Per Subs 13

M STRAUB CLINIC & HOSPITAL*, Arnold Library, 888 S King St, 96813. SAN 303-495X. Tel: 808-522-4471. Web Site: www.straubhealth.com. *Med Librn,* David Coleman
Founded 1922
Library Holdings: Bk Vols 300; Per Subs 15
Special Collections: Physicians' Articles Coll
Subject Interests: Med
Function: Doc delivery serv, ILL available, Photocopying/Printing, Ref serv available, Res libr
Partic in Dialog Corp; National Network of Libraries of Medicine
Restriction: Staff use only

GL SUPREME COURT LAW LIBRARY*, 417 S King St, Rm 115, 96813. Tel: 808-539-4964. FAX: 808-539-4974. E-mail: lawlibrary@courts.hawaii.gov. Web Site: www.state.hi.us/jud/library/index.htm. *Pub Serv,* Marlene Cuenco; *Tech Serv,* Mark Skrimstad; Staff 8 (MLS 3, Non-MLS 5)
Founded 1851

Library Holdings: Bk Vols 85,000; Per Subs 206
Open Mon-Fri 7:45-4:15
Restriction: Open to pub for ref only

AM TRIPLER ARMY MEDICAL CENTER*, Medical Library, One Jarrett White Rd, 96859-5000. SAN 339-5790. Tel: 808-433-6391. FAX: 808-433-4892. *Librn,* Mabel Trafford; Tel: 808-433-4534; Staff 4 (MLS 2, Non-MLS 2)
Founded 1946
Library Holdings: Bk Vols 8,000; Per Subs 400
Partic in Docline; OCLC Online Computer Library Center, Inc

G UNESCO-INTERGOVERNMENTAL OCEANOGRAPHIC COMMISSION & NATIONAL WEATHER SERVICE*, International Tsunami Information Center Library, NOAA IRC-NWS/ITIC, 1845 Wasp Blvd, Bldg 176, 96818. SAN 326-3436. Tel: 808-725-6050. Administration Tel: 808-532-6423. FAX: 808-532-5576. Web Site: itic.ioc-unesco.org. *Tech Info Spec,* Nicolas P Arcos; E-mail: nicolas.arcos@noaa.org; Staff 2 (MLS 1, Non-MLS 1)
Founded 1965
Library Holdings: Bk Titles 2,000
Special Collections: Catalog of Tsunamis in Pacific, bks; Marigrams 2/65-1978, microfiche. UN Document Depository
Subject Interests: Earthquakes, Geophysics, Oceanography
Function: Ref serv available
Publications: Tsunami Newsletter; Tsunami Reports
Restriction: In-house use for visitors

GL UNITED STATES COURTS LIBRARY, 300 Ala Moana Blvd C-341, 96850. SAN 303-4992. Tel: 808-541-1797. FAX: 808-541-3667. *Librn,* Shannon L Lashbarok
Library Holdings: Bk Vols 30,000; Per Subs 25
Automation Activity & Vendor Info: (Acquisitions) SirsiDynix

CL UNIVERSITY OF HAWAII*, William S Richardson School of Law Library, 2525 Dole St, 96822-2328. SAN 326-5188. Tel: 808-956-5581, 808-956-7583. Reference Tel: 808-956-8991. FAX: 808-956-4615. TDD: 808-956-9577. Web Site: library.law.hawaii.edu. *Dir,* Leinaala Seeger; E-mail: seegerl@hawaii.edu; *Syst Librn,* Keiko Okuhara; *Info Tech, Ref,* Swee Lian Berkey; E-mail: berkey@hawaii.edu; *Pub Serv,* Diane F Frake; *Tech Serv,* Catherine Thomas; Staff 9 (MLS 5, Non-MLS 4)
Enrl 253; Fac 18; Highest Degree: Doctorate
Library Holdings: Bk Titles 304,000; Bk Vols 304,934; Per Subs 3,748
Special Collections: Pacific-Asian law. US Document Depository
Subject Interests: Environ law
Automation Activity & Vendor Info: (Acquisitions) Ex Libris Group; (Cataloging) Ex Libris Group; (Circulation) Ex Libris Group; (ILL) Ex Libris Group; (Media Booking) Ex Libris Group; (OPAC) Ex Libris Group; (Serials) Ex Libris Group
Partic in Hawaii Library Consortium; OCLC Online Computer Library Center, Inc
Open Mon-Thurs (Winter) 8am-11pm, Fri 8-7, Sat 9-7, Sun 10am-11pm; Mon-Fri (Summer) 8-5

C UNIVERSITY OF HAWAII AT MANOA LIBRARY, Thomas Hale Hamilton Library, 2550 McCarthy Mall, 96822. SAN 339-6096. Tel: 808-956-7203. Interlibrary Loan Service Tel: 808-956-8568. Reference Tel: 808-956-7214. Administration Tel: 808-956-7207. Automation Services Tel: 808-956-7853. FAX: 808-956-5968. TDD: 808-956-2534. E-mail: library@hawaii.edu. Web Site: library.manoa.hawaii.edu. *Univ Librn,* Irene Herold; E-mail: heroldi@hawaii.edu; Staff 133 (MLS 50, Non-MLS 83)
Founded 1907. Enrl 20,000; Highest Degree: Doctorate
Library Holdings: AV Mats 62,616; e-books 132,374; Music Scores 23,641; Bk Vols 3,206,032; Per Subs 44,000
Special Collections: Asia Coll; Book Arts; Congressional Papers Coll; Hawaiian Coll; Japanese American Veterans Coll; Jean Charlot Coll; Pacific Coll; Tsuzaki Reinecke Creole Coll; University Archives. State Document Depository; UN Document Depository; US Document Depository
Automation Activity & Vendor Info: (Acquisitions) Ex Libris Group; (Cataloging) Ex Libris Group; (Circulation) Ex Libris Group; (Course Reserve) Ex Libris Group; (ILL) OCLC ILLiad; (Media Booking) Ex Libris Group; (OPAC) Ex Libris Group; (Serials) Ex Libris Group
Wireless access
Publications: Acquisitions List of the Pacific Collection; Annual Report of the Univerity of Hawaii at Manoa Library; Current Hawaiiana; Ke Kukini (Newsletter); Selected Acquisitions of the Asia Collection
Partic in Association of Research Libraries (ARL); Greater Western Library Alliance; Hawaii Library Consortium; OCLC Online Computer Library Center, Inc
Open Mon-Thurs 8am-10pm, Fri 8-6, Sat 9-5, Sun 12-10

Departmental Libraries:
HAWAII RESEARCH CENTER FOR FUTURES STUDIES, Social Sciences Bldg, 2424 Maile Way, Rm 704 F, 96822, SAN 328-3607. Tel: 808-956-2888. FAX: 808-956-2889. *Dir,* Jim Dator; Tel: 808-956-6601
Library Holdings: Bk Titles 1,000
Special Collections: Futures Oriented Coll, bks, articles, periodicals
Subject Interests: Communication, Educ, Law, Media, Politics, Sci
GREGG M SINCLAIR LIBRARY, 2425 Campus Rd, 96822. (Mail add: 2550 McCarthy Mall, 96822), SAN 339-6126. Tel: 808-956-8308. FAX: 808-956-5952. E-mail: sinc@hawaii.edu. Web Site: www.sinclair.hawaii.edu. *Librn,* Kristen Anderson
Founded 1956
Open Mon-Thurs 7:30am-Midnight, Fri 7:30-7, Sat 9-5, Sun Noon-Midnight

S UNIVERSITY OF HAWAII-COLLEGE OF EDUCATION*, Western Curriculum Coordination Center, 1776 University Ave UA2-7, 96822. SAN 324-3451. Tel: 808-956-6496, 808-956-7834. FAX: 808-956-3374. E-mail: wccc@hawaii.edu. Web Site: www.hawaii.edu/wccc/. *Dir,* Lawrence Zane; Staff 1 (MLS 1)
Library Holdings: Bk Vols 20,000
Subject Interests: Vocational educ
Publications: Curriculum Materials (Subject bibliographies)

S USS BOWFIN SUBMARINE MUSEUM & PARK LIBRARY*, 11 Arizona Memorial Dr, 96818-3145. SAN 371-8395. Tel: 808-423-1341. FAX: 808-422-5201. E-mail: info@bowfin.org. Web Site: www.bowfin.org. *Dir of Educ,* Charles R Hinman. Subject Specialists: *Submarines, World War II,* Charles R Hinman; Staff 3 (Non-MLS 3)
Founded 1981
Library Holdings: Bk Titles 2,500; Bk Vols 5,000
Special Collections: Oral Histories of World War II Submariners; Submarine Photo Archives; US Navy Training Manuals for Submariners; USS Bowfin; War Patrol Reports of US Submarines in World War II; World War II Crew '35. Oral History
Subject Interests: Naval hist, Submarines, World War II
Function: Res libr
Publications: On Eternal Patrol
Restriction: Not a lending libr

KAHULUI

C UNIVERSITY OF HAWAII*, Maui Community College Library, 310 Kaahumanu Ave, 96732. SAN 303-5026. Tel: 808-984-3233. Reference Tel: 808-984-3298. Administration Tel: 808-984-3583. FAX: 808-244-9644. E-mail: mcclib@hawaii.edu. Web Site: www.hawaii.edu/maui/library. *Head Librn, Tech Serv, Webmaster,* Lisa Sepa; Tel: 808-984-3577, E-mail: sepa@hawaii.edu; *Ref Librn,* Dorothy Tolliver; E-mail: tolliver@hawaii.edu; *Distance Educ,* Lillian Mangum; Tel: 808-984-3584, E-mail: mangum@hawaii.edu; *Pub Serv,* Ellen Peterson; Tel: 808-984-3582, E-mail: epeterso@hawaii.edu; Staff 8 (MLS 4, Non-MLS 4)
Founded 1970. Enrl 2,794; Fac 92; Highest Degree: Bachelor
Jul 2005-Jun 2006 Income $415,395. Mats Exp $91,232. Sal $316,133 (Prof $223,901)
Library Holdings: AV Mats 3,703; Bks on Deafness & Sign Lang 17; CDs 1,719; DVDs 919; Bk Titles 49,258; Bk Vols 61,572; Per Subs 298; Videos 1,065
Subject Interests: Hawaii
Automation Activity & Vendor Info: (Cataloging) Ex Libris Group; (Circulation) Ex Libris Group; (Course Reserve) Ex Libris Group; (ILL) Ex Libris Group; (Media Booking) Ex Libris Group; (OPAC) Ex Libris Group
Database Vendor: ALLDATA Online, Baker & Taylor, Cinahl, Community of Science (COS), CountryWatch, CQ Press, Ebooks Corporation, ebrary, EBSCOhost, Ex Libris Group, Gale Cengage Learning, Gallup, H W Wilson, LexisNexis, OCLC WorldShare Interlibrary Loan, ScienceDirect, Wilson - Wilson Web
Wireless access
Partic in OCLC Online Computer Library Center, Inc
Open Mon-Thurs 8-8, Fri & Sat (Fall & Spring) 8-4:30

KALAHEO

S NATIONAL TROPICAL BOTANICAL GARDEN LIBRARY*, 3530 Papalina Rd, 96741. SAN 371-7852. Tel: 808-332-7324, Ext 214. FAX: 808-332-9765. Web Site: www.ntbg.org/resources/library.php. *In Charge,* David H Lorence; Staff 1 (MLS 1)
Founded 1971
Library Holdings: Bk Titles 15,500; Bk Vols 16,800; Per Subs 400
Special Collections: Tropical Botany, bks, journals. Oral History
Subject Interests: Botany, Hort
Open Mon-Fri 8-5
Friends of the Library Group

KANEOHE

M HAWAII STATE HOSPITAL*, Medical Library, 45-710 Keaahala Rd, 96744-3528. SAN 303-5069. Tel: 808-236-8201. FAX: 808-247-7335. *Librn,* Lisa Anne Matsumoto; E-mail: lisa.matsumoto@doh.hawaii.gov; Staff 1 (MLS 1)
Founded 1950
Library Holdings: Bk Titles 4,500; Per Subs 251
Subject Interests: Mental health, Neuropsychology, Psychiat, Psychol
Partic in Pacific Southwest Regional Medical Library (PSRML)
Restriction: Open by appt only

J WINDWARD COMMUNITY COLLEGE LIBRARY*, 45-720 Keaahala Rd, 96744. SAN 303-5077. Tel: 808-235-7436. Circulation Tel: 808-235-7441. Reference Tel: 808-235-7338. FAX: 808-235-7344. Web Site: library.wcc.hawaii.edu. *Dir,* Nancy Heu; Tel: 808-235-7435, E-mail: heu@hawaii.edu; *Pub Serv,* Tara Severns; Tel: 808-235-7440, E-mail: severns@hawaii.edu; Staff 3 (MLS 3)
Founded 1972. Enrl 1,800; Fac 77; Highest Degree: Associate
Library Holdings: AV Mats 4,648; Bk Titles 40,800; Bk Vols 48,552; Per Subs 147
Special Collections: Hawaiian Coll
Automation Activity & Vendor Info: (Cataloging) Ex Libris Group; (Circulation) Ex Libris Group; (Course Reserve) Ex Libris Group; (OPAC) Ex Libris Group
Database Vendor: EBSCOhost, LexisNexis
Publications: Audiovisual Materials in the WCC Library; Periodicals in the WCC Library
Open Mon & Tues (Winter) 8-8, Wed & Thurs 8-6, Fri 8-4; Mon-Fri (Summer) 8-4
Friends of the Library Group

KANEOHE BAY

A MARINE CORPS BASE HAWAII LIBRARIES, Marine Corps Base Hawaii, Bldg 219, 96863. (Mail add: PO Box 63073, 96863-3073), SAN 339-6037. Tel: 808-254-7624. FAX: 808-254-7623. Web Site: www.mccshawaii.com/library.htm. *Supvry Librn,* Meredith Healey; E-mail: meredith.healey@usmc-mccs.org; Staff 7 (MLS 1, Non-MLS 6)
Founded 1964
Oct 2006-Sept 2007 Income (Main Library and Branch(s)) $453,352. Mats Exp $75,751, Books $43,000, Per/Ser (Incl. Access Fees) $3,753, AV Equip $17,306, AV Mat $11,692. Sal $310,691 (Prof $80,741)
Library Holdings: Audiobooks 500; CDs 1,379; DVDs 385; Electronic Media & Resources 4; Microforms 1,199; Bk Titles 50,475; Bk Vols 58,368; Per Subs 239; Videos 8
Special Collections: Board Games; Children's Coll; Hawaiiana; Professional Military Education; Rosetta Stone Language Modules, 16 languages; US Marine (Professional) Reading List; US Marine Corps Coll
Subject Interests: Mil art & sci, Voluntary educ
Automation Activity & Vendor Info: (Acquisitions) SIRSI WorkFlows; (Cataloging) SIRSI WorkFlows; (Circulation) SIRSI WorkFlows; (ILL) SIRSI WorkFlows; (OPAC) SIRSI WorkFlows; (Serials) SIRSI WorkFlows
Database Vendor: Gale Cengage Learning
Wireless access
Partic in OCLC Online Computer Library Center, Inc
Restriction: Open to govt employees only
Branches:
CAMP SMITH BRANCH, Bldg 1, Rm 201, Camp H M Smith, 96861-4123. (Mail add: PO Box 64123, Camp H M Smith, 96861-4123), SAN 339-6061. Tel: 808-477-6348. *Librn,* Polly Chan; Staff 1 (MLS 1)
Library Holdings: Audiobooks 200; DVDs 46; Bk Titles 11,819; Bk Vols 13,513; Per Subs 72
Special Collections: Professional Military Education Coll; Rosetta Stone Language Modules; US Marine (Professional) Reading List
Subject Interests: Geopolitics, Mil art & sci, Voluntary educ
Restriction: Mil, family mem, retirees, Civil Serv personnel NAF only

KEALAKEKUA

C UNIVERSITY OF HAWAII CENTER, WEST HAWAII*, Library & Learning Center, 81-964 Halekii St, 96750. SAN 370-3800. Tel: 808-322-4858, 808-322-4862. FAX: 808-322-4859. *Dir,* Laurel Gregory; E-mail: lgregory@hawaii.edu; *Educ Spec,* Mike Hopson; E-mail: hopson@hawaii.edu; *ILL,* Karen Au; E-mail: karenau@hawaii.edu; Staff 2 (MLS 1, Non-MLS 1)
Founded 1989. Enrl 500; Highest Degree: Master
Library Holdings: Bk Vols 5,500
Subject Interests: Hawaii
Automation Activity & Vendor Info: (Acquisitions) TLC (The Library Corporation); (Cataloging) TLC (The Library Corporation); (Circulation) TLC (The Library Corporation); (Course Reserve) TLC (The Library Corporation); (ILL) TLC (The Library Corporation); (Media Booking) TLC (The Library Corporation); (OPAC) TLC (The Library Corporation); (Serials) TLC (The Library Corporation)
Database Vendor: EBSCOhost
Open Mon-Thurs 7:45-6:45, Fri 7:45-4:30, Sat 10-4:30

LAIE

C BRIGHAM YOUNG UNIVERSITY-HAWAII*, Joseph F Smith Library, 55-220 Kulanui St, BYU-Hawaii, No 1966, 96762-1294. SAN 303-5123. Tel: 808-675-3850. Circulation Tel: 808-675-3876. Reference Tel: 808-675-3878. FAX: 808-675-3877. Web Site: library.byuh.edu. *Univ Librn,* Michael Aldrich; Tel: 808-675-3851, E-mail: michael.aldrich@byuh.edu; *Head, Circ,* Yvonne Hernandez; E-mail: hernandy@byuh.edu; *Head, Ref,* Riley Moffat; Tel: 808-675-3884, E-mail: moffatr@byuh.edu; *Head, Tech Serv,* Marynelle Chew; Tel: 808-675-3863, E-mail: chewm@byuh.edu; *Outreach Serv Librn,* Rose Ram; Tel: 808-675-3882, E-mail: ramr@byuh.edu; *Ser Librn,* Kimball Boone; Tel: 808-675-3880, E-mail: kdb@byuh.edu; *Tech Librn,* Becky DeMartini; Tel: 808-675-3946, E-mail: becky.demartini@byuh.edu; *Archivist,* Matt Kester; Tel: 808-675-3869, E-mail: kesterm@byuh.edu; *ILL,* Andrea Clements; E-mail: andreakc@byuh.edu; Staff 10.5 (MLS 6, Non-MLS 4.5)
Founded 1955. Enrl 2,600; Fac 110; Highest Degree: Bachelor
Library Holdings: e-books 80,000; e-journals 50,000; Bk Vols 207,474; Per Subs 400
Special Collections: Mormonism Coll; Pacific Islands Coll. US Document Depository
Subject Interests: Pacific Islands
Automation Activity & Vendor Info: (Acquisitions) SirsiDynix; (Cataloging) SirsiDynix; (Circulation) SirsiDynix; (Course Reserve) SirsiDynix; (ILL) OCLC ILLiad; (Media Booking) SirsiDynix; (OPAC) SirsiDynix; (Serials) SirsiDynix
Database Vendor: Alexander Street Press, ARTstor, ebrary, EBSCOhost, ISI Web of Knowledge, JSTOR, LexisNexis, Newsbank, ProQuest, ScienceDirect, SirsiDynix, Wilson - Wilson Web
Wireless access
Partic in OCLC Online Computer Library Center, Inc
Open Mon-Thurs 7am-Midnight, Fri 7-6, Sat 9-9

LIHUE

C KAUAI COMMUNITY COLLEGE*, S W Wilcox II Learning Resource Center, 3-1901 Kaumualii Hwy, 96766. SAN 303-5131. Tel: 808-245-8233. Circulation Tel: 808-245-8322. Reference Tel: 808-245-8253. Administration Tel: 808-245-8236. FAX: 808-245-8294. Web Site: kauai.hawaii.edu/library/. *Head Librn,* Robert M Kajiwara; E-mail: kajiwara@hawaii.edu; *Distance Educ,* Anne McKenna; Tel: 808-245-8374, E-mail: mckenna@hawaii.edu; *Ref,* Michael Gmelin; E-mail: gmelin@hawaii.edu; *Tech Serv,* Diane M Johnson; Tel: 808-245-8240, E-mail: dianej@hawaii.edu. Subject Specialists: *Hist,* Robert M Kajiwara; *Bus, Health, Med,* Anne McKenna; *Fiction, Sports,* Diane M Johnson; Staff 7 (MLS 4, Non-MLS 3)
Founded 1967. Enrl 1,115; Fac 77; Highest Degree: Master
Library Holdings: CDs 169; Electronic Media & Resources 6,000; Bk Titles 42,023; Bk Vols 60,269; Per Subs 169; Videos 1,544
Special Collections: Hawaii & the Pacific, v-tapes
Subject Interests: Allied health, Nursing
Automation Activity & Vendor Info: (Cataloging) Ex Libris Group; (Circulation) Ex Libris Group; (Course Reserve) Ex Libris Group; (OPAC) Ex Libris Group
Database Vendor: EBSCOhost, OCLC FirstSearch
Function: Ref serv available
Publications: Circulation Policies; How to Locate Library Resources; Quick Reference
Open Mon & Tues (Winter) 7:30-7, Wed-Fri 7:30-4; Mon-Fri (Summer) 8-4

S KAUAI COMMUNITY CORRECTIONAL CENTER LIBRARY*, 3-5351 Kuhio Hwy, 96766. Tel: 808-241-3637. FAX: 808-241-3059. *Librn,* Position Currently Open
Library Holdings: Bk Titles 2,100; Per Subs 50
Database Vendor: LexisNexis
Friends of the Library Group

M WILCOX MEMORIAL HOSPITAL*, Robert J Emrick MD Medical Library, 3-3420 Kuhio Hwy, 96766-1099. SAN 303-5158. Tel: 808-245-1173. FAX: 808-246-2918. *Med Staff Spec,* Stephanie Ceron-Flores; E-mail: stephanie.ceron-flores@wilcoxhealth.org. Subject Specialists: *Med,* Stephanie Ceron-Flores
Founded 1939
Library Holdings: Per Subs 20
Partic in Pacific Southwest Regional Medical Library (PSRML)

PEARL CITY

J LEEWARD COMMUNITY COLLEGE LIBRARY*, 96-045 Ala Ike, 96782-3393. SAN 303-5182. Tel: 808-455-0379. Circulation Tel: 808-455-0210. FAX: 808-453-6729. Circulation E-mail: lcccirc@hawaii.edu. Reference E-mail: lccref@hawaii.edu. Web Site:

www.leeward.hawaii.edu/library. *Head Librn,* Chris Matz; Tel: 808-455-0673, E-mail: cmatz@hawaii.edu; *Instruction Librn,* Wayde Oshiro; Tel: 808-455-0378, E-mail: waydeo@hawaii.edu; *Pub Serv Librn,* Junie Hayashi; Tel: 808-455-0680, E-mail: junie@hawaii.edu; *Syst Librn,* Ralph Toyama; Tel: 808-455-0682, E-mail: rtoyama@hawaii.edu; *Tech Serv Librn,* Jue Wang; Tel: 808-455-0672, E-mail: juewang@hawaii.edu; *Circ Mgr,* Natalie Kahn; Tel: 808-455-0209, E-mail: nkahn@hawaii.edu; *Circ,* Carina Chernisky; Tel: 808-455-0301, E-mail: carinac@hawaii.edu; Staff 5 (MLS 5)
Founded 1968. Highest Degree: Associate
Library Holdings: Bk Titles 61,051; Bk Vols 76,169; Per Subs 249
Special Collections: Hawaiian/Pacific Coll, bks, pers. US Document Depository
Automation Activity & Vendor Info: (Cataloging) Ex Libris Group; (Circulation) Ex Libris Group; (Course Reserve) Ex Libris Group; (OPAC) Ex Libris Group
Database Vendor: Career Guidance Foundation, ebrary, EBSCOhost, LexisNexis, ScienceDirect
Wireless access
Publications: LCC Periodicals List
Open Mon-Thurs 8-8, Fri 8-3, Sat 9-1; Mon-Thurs (Summer) 7:30-4:30, Fri 7:30-2:30

C UNIVERSITY OF HAWAII - WEST OAHU LIBRARY*, 96-129 Ala Ike, 96782. SAN 303-4399. Tel: 808-455-0497, 808-455-0498. FAX: 808-456-7819. E-mail: uhwolib@hawaii.edu. Web Site: www2.hawaii.edu/~uhwolib. *Dir,* Position Currently Open
Founded 1976. Enrl 823; Fac 51; Highest Degree: Bachelor
Library Holdings: AV Mats 1,500; e-books 40,000; e-journals 25,000; Microforms 1,150; Bk Titles 28,000; Per Subs 40
Automation Activity & Vendor Info: (Cataloging) Ex Libris Group; (Circulation) Ex Libris Group; (Course Reserve) Ex Libris Group; (ILL) Ex Libris Group; (Media Booking) Ex Libris Group; (OPAC) Ex Libris Group; (Serials) Ex Libris Group
Database Vendor: American Psychological Association (APA), CQ Press, ebrary, EBSCOhost, Elsevier, H W Wilson, JSTOR, LexisNexis, Oxford Online, ProQuest, ScienceDirect, Springshare, LLC, Wilson - Wilson Web
Wireless access
Partic in Hawaii Library Consortium
Open Mon-Thurs 8-7, Fri 8-4

SCHOFIELD BARRACKS

A UNITED STATES ARMY*, SGT Yano Library, Bldg 560, 96857-5000. SAN 339 5707. Tel: 808 655 8002. Reference Tel: 808-655-8001. FAX: 808-655-6375. Web Site: mwrarmyhawaii.com. *Supvr,* Amy Nogami; E-mail: amy.nogami@us.army.mil; Staff 10 (MLS 4, Non-MLS 6)
Founded 1915
Library Holdings: AV Mats 1,000; Bk Vols 80,000; Per Subs 200
Special Collections: Hawaiian Islands (Hawaiiana)
Subject Interests: Mil hist
Partic in OCLC Online Computer Library Center, Inc
Open Mon & Tues 11-8, Wed-Sat 11-6

WAILUKU

GL HAWAII STATE CIRCUIT COURT-SECOND CIRCUIT*, Law Library, 2145 Main St, Rm 207, 96793. SAN 303-5212. Tel: 808-244-2959.
Library Holdings: Bk Vols 17,963
Automation Activity & Vendor Info: (Acquisitions) SirsiDynix
Restriction: By permission only

S MAUI CORRECTIONAL CENTER LIBRARY*, 600 Waiale Dr, 96753. Tel: 808-243-5855. FAX: 808-242-7867. *Librn,* Sandra Wada; Staff 1 (MLS 1)
Library Holdings: Bk Vols 52,000; Per Subs 25
Open Mon-Fri 8-3

S MAUI HISTORICAL SOCIETY*, Archival Resource Center, 2375 A Main St, 96793. SAN 326-3118. Tel: 808-244-3326. E-mail: info@mauimuseum.org. Web Site: www.mauimuseum.org. *Exec Dir,* Donald Craib
Founded 1957
Library Holdings: Bk Titles 7,650
Special Collections: Photographs
Publications: Index to the Maui News 1900-1973; Island of Maui Cemetery Directories
Open Tues-Fri 10-12 & 1-3

M MAUI MEMORIAL MEDICAL CENTER, Alyce L Haines Biomedical Library, 221 Mahalani St, 96793-2526. SAN 303-5204. Tel: 808-242-2337. FAX: 808-242-2340. *Dir,* Marilynn Mei Lin Wong; E-mail: mwong@hhsc.org; Staff 1 (MLS 1)
Founded 1967
Library Holdings: Bk Vols 7,000; Per Subs 150
Special Collections: Partial Federal Depository for Medical Government Documents for Maui County
Partic in Hawaii-Pacific Chapter of the Medical Library Association; Medical Library Association (MLA)
Restriction: Staff use only

S PACIFIC WHALE FOUNDATION LIBRARY*, 300 Maalaea Rd, Ste 211, 96793. SAN 373-4315. Tel: 808-249-8811 (Maui line), 808-879-8860. Toll Free Tel. 800-942-5311. FAX: 808-243-9021, 808-879-2615. E-mail: info@pacificwhale.org. Web Site: www.pacificwhale.org. *Pub Serv,* Anne Rillero
Library Holdings: Bk Vols 500; Per Subs 150
Wireless access
Restriction: Not open to pub, Staff use only

IDAHO

Date of Statistics: FY 2013
Population, 2010 U.S. Census: 1,567,582
Population, 2013 U.S. Census: 1,595,728
Population Served by Public Libraries: 1,407,299
Unserved: 204,837
Total Volumes in Public Libraries: 5,094,861
Volumes Per Capita: 3.13
Circulation Per Capita: 10.5
Total Public Library Income: $48,765,295
Local Taxes: $43,697,854
Local Taxes (ad valorem): 90%
Percent State Sales Tax: 1,176,951 (.024%)
Federal (LSTA): 60,880
Percent Other: 1,993,528 (.041%)
Total Expenditures: $45,024,764
Expenditures Per Capita: $31.99
Number of County or District Libraries: 54 (Includes 3 school/community)
Number of Public Libraries: 103 (including district/county libraries)
Number of Bookmobiles in State: 12

ABERDEEN

P ABERDEEN DISTRICT LIBRARY*, 76 E Central, 83210-1930. (Mail add: PO Box 207, 83210-0207), SAN 303-5247. Tel: 208-397-4427. FAX: 208-397-4427. E-mail: aberdeenlib@gmail.com. Web Site: aberdeen.lili.org. *Dir,* Stephanie Adamson
Circ 14,844
Library Holdings: Bk Vols 18,000; Per Subs 30
Automation Activity & Vendor Info: (Cataloging) SirsiDynix; (Circulation) SirsiDynix; (OPAC) SirsiDynix
Open Mon-Fri 10-6:30, Sat Noon-3

AMERICAN FALLS

P AMERICAN FALLS DISTRICT LIBRARY*, 308 Roosevelt St, 83211-1219. SAN 303-5255. Tel: 208-226-2335. FAX: 208-226-2303. E-mail: amlibrary@cableone.net. *Dir,* Harriet Newlin; Staff 5 (Non-MLS 5)
Pop 6,700; Circ 78,286
Library Holdings: Audiobooks 1,500; Bks on Deafness & Sign Lang 18; CDs 725; DVDs 1,600; Large Print Bks 3,612; Bk Titles 36,476; Bk Vols 36,700; Per Subs 100, Talking Bks 1,250; Videos 812
Special Collections: Idaho Coll; Large Print Coll; Music Coll; Spanish Lang Coll, bks on tape; Young Adult Coll
Automation Activity & Vendor Info: (Acquisitions) Winnebago Software Co; (Cataloging) OCLC; (Circulation) Follett Software; (ILL) OCLC
Wireless access
Open Mon-Thurs (Winter)10-8, Fri & Sat 10-6; Mon-Sat (Summer) 10-6
Restriction: Badge access after hrs
Friends of the Library Group

ARCO

P LOST RIVERS DISTRICT LIBRARY*, 126 S Front St, 83213. (Mail add: PO Box 170, 83213-0170), SAN 303-5263. Tel: 208-527-8511. *Dir,* Bettina Blattner; *Asst Librn,* Krickett Ray; *YA Serv,* Leslie Whitehead
Pop 2,907; Circ 15,716
Library Holdings: Bk Vols 13,000; Per Subs 50
Special Collections: American Classics; Antique Book Coll
Automation Activity & Vendor Info: (Acquisitions) Winnebago Software Co; (Cataloging) Winnebago Software Co; (Circulation) Winnebago Software Co; (Course Reserve) Winnebago Software Co; (ILL) Winnebago Software Co; (Media Booking) Winnebago Software Co; (OPAC) Winnebago Software Co; (Serials) Winnebago Software Co
Publications: Library Journal
Open Mon & Wed 10:30-6, Tues & Thurs 10:30-5:30, Fri 10:30-5
Branches: 1
HOWE BRANCH, 1523 Hwy 22, Howe, 83244. Tel: 208-767-3018. *Librn,* Janene Williams
Library Holdings: Bk Vols 2,500
Open Mon, Wed & Fri 1:30-6

ASHTON

P FREMONT COUNTY DISTRICT LIBRARY*, Ashton Branch, 925 Main, 83420. (Mail add: PO Box 854, 83420-0854), SAN 303-5271. Tel: 208-652-7280. E-mail: ashlib@ida.net. *Dir,* Kathy Henderson; *Ch Serv,* Barbara Moon
Pop 11,719; Circ 16,658
Library Holdings: Bk Vols 17,000; Per Subs 26
Subject Interests: Rare bks
Automation Activity & Vendor Info: (Cataloging) SirsiDynix; (Circulation) SirsiDynix; (OPAC) SirsiDynix
Open Mon-Thurs 10-6, Fri 10-5, Sat 10-1

BELLEVUE

P BELLEVUE PUBLIC LIBRARY*, 115 E Pine, 83313. (Mail add: PO Box 825, 83313-0268). Tel: 208-788-2128. FAX: 208-788-2128. E-mail: bellevuelibrary@bellevueidaho.us. *Librn,* Patty Gilman
Library Holdings: Bk Vols 8,000; Per Subs 10
Automation Activity & Vendor Info: (Cataloging) Follett Software; (Circulation) Follett Software; (OPAC) Follett Software
Open Mon & Wed 10-5, Tues 11-6:30, Thurs 11:30-6, Fri 12:30-5

BLACKFOOT

M BINGHAM MEMORIAL HOSPITAL*, Medical Library, 98 Poplar St, 83221. SAN 371-2052. Tel: 208-785-4100. FAX: 208-785-7606. Web Site: www.binghammemorial.org. *Librn,* Margaret Davis; Tel: 208-785-4100, Ext 3332, E-mail: mdavis@binghammemorial.org
Library Holdings: Bk Vols 500; Per Subs 50

P BLACKFOOT PUBLIC LIBRARY*, 129 N Broadway, 83221-2204. (Mail add: PO Box 610, 83221-0610), SAN 303-5298. Tel: 208-785-8628. FAX: 208-782-9688. E-mail: blackft@ida.net. *Dir,* Platte Lyman; *Librn,* Lisa Jensen Harral; *Librn,* Brenda K Wilcox; Staff 3 (MLS 1, Non-MLS 2)
Founded 1916. Pop 20,000; Circ 223,000
Library Holdings: CDs 1,906; Bk Vols 48,917; Per Subs 130; Videos 1,708
Special Collections: Local Newspaper Coll, 1880-, micro
Automation Activity & Vendor Info: (Cataloging) Follett Software; (Circulation) Follett Software; (OPAC) Follett Software
Database Vendor: ProQuest
Partic in Idaho Libr Asn
Open Mon-Thurs 10:30-8:30, Fri & Sat 10:30-5:30
Friends of the Library Group

P SNAKE RIVER SCHOOL COMMUNITY LIBRARY*, 924 W Hwy 39, 83221. SAN 303-5301. Tel: 208-684-3063. FAX: 208-684-3141. E-mail: snakeriverlibrary@gmail.com. Web Site: snakeriver.lili.org, snakeriverlibrary.com. *Dir,* Sherrilynn Bair
Founded 1951. Pop 7,700; Circ 90,473
Library Holdings: Bk Vols 34,000; Per Subs 52

Automation Activity & Vendor Info: (Cataloging) Follett Software; (Circulation) Follett Software; (ILL) OCLC; (OPAC) Follett Software
Open Mon-Thurs 7-8, Fri 7-6

BOISE

P ADA COMMUNITY LIBRARY*, Victory Branch, 10664 W Victory Rd, 83709. SAN 323-9756. Tel: 208-362-0181. FAX: 208-362-0303. Web Site: www.adalib.org. *Assoc Dir, Br Mgr,* Travis Porter; Tel: 208-362-0181, Ext 24, E-mail: tporter@adalib.org; *IT Coordr,* Dylan Baker; Tel: 208-362-0181, Ext 132, E-mail: dbaker@adalib.org
Founded 1984. Pop 50,000; Circ 900,000
Oct 2006-Sept 2007 Income (Main Library and Branch(s)) $2,982,989. Mats Exp $243,083
Library Holdings: CDs 3,164; DVDs 2,491; e-books 6,616; Bk Vols 138,000; Per Subs 200; Talking Bks 9,000; Videos 8,000
Automation Activity & Vendor Info: (Cataloging) Horizon; (Circulation) Horizon; (ILL) OCLC; (OPAC) Horizon; (Serials) Horizon
Database Vendor: EBSCOhost, Gale Cengage Learning
Partic in LYNX! Consortium; OCLC Online Computer Library Center, Inc
Open Mon-Thurs 9:30-9, Fri 9:30-6, Sat 9:30-5
Friends of the Library Group
Branches: 2
HIDDEN SPRINGS BRANCH, 5849 W Hidden Springs Dr, 83714. Tel: 208-229-2665. *Assoc Librn,* Mary Coles; E-mail: mcoles@adalib.org; Staff 2 (MLS 1, Non-MLS 1)
Founded 2001. Pop 1,800
Function: Audiobks via web, Bk reviews (Group), Bks on cassette, Bks on CD, Children's prog, Computer training, Computers for patron use, Copy machines, Digital talking bks, e-mail & chat, E-Reserves, Electronic databases & coll, Free DVD rentals, Handicapped accessible, Holiday prog, Homework prog, ILL available, Mail & tel request accepted, Music CDs, Online cat, Online ref, Online searches, Outreach serv, Outside serv via phone, mail, e-mail & web, Photocopying/Printing, Preschool outreach, Prog for adults, Prog for children & young adult, Pub access computers, Ref serv available, Ref serv in person, Spoken cassettes & CDs, Spoken cassettes & DVDs, Story hour, Summer reading prog, Tax forms, Teen prog, Telephone ref, VHS videos, Web-catalog
Open Mon-Fri 12-6
Friends of the Library Group
STAR BRANCH, 10706 W State St, Star, 83669. Tel: 208-286-9755. FAX: 208-286-9755. *Br Mgr,* Joy Lear
Library Holdings: Audiobooks 2,998; Bk Titles 30,254; Bk Vols 38,634; Per Subs 60; Videos 3,899
Open Mon-Thurs 10-7, Fri & Sat 10-5
Friends of the Library Group

S BOISE ART MUSEUM LIBRARY*, 670 Julia Davis Dr, 83702. SAN 320-149X. Tel: 208-345-8330, Ext 19. FAX: 208-345-2247. Web Site: www.boiseartmuseum.org. *Curator,* Sandy Harthorn; E-mail: sandy@boiseartmuseum.org
Library Holdings: Bk Titles 2,500; Per Subs 10
Subject Interests: Art hist
Function: Res libr
Open Tues, Wed, Fri & Sat 10-5, Thurs 10-8, Sun 12-5
Restriction: Non-circulating

CR BOISE BIBLE COLLEGE LIBRARY*, 8695 W Marigold St, 83714-1220. SAN 303-5328. Tel: 208-376-7731. FAX: 208-376-7743. E-mail: boisebible@boisebible.edu. Web Site: www.boisebible.edu. *Dir,* Glennis Thomas; Staff 1 (Non-MLS 1)
Founded 1945. Enrl 201; Fac 10; Highest Degree: Bachelor
Library Holdings: AV Mats 516; Bk Titles 29,731; Bk Vols 34,705; Per Subs 77; Videos 421
Special Collections: Restoration Movement materials
Subject Interests: Biblical studies, Church hist, Missions & missionaries
Automation Activity & Vendor Info: (Circulation) Follett Software; (OPAC) Follett Software
Database Vendor: ProQuest
Wireless access
Restriction: Borrowing privileges limited to fac & registered students, In-house use for visitors

P BOISE PUBLIC LIBRARY*, Main Library, 715 S Capitol Blvd, 83702. SAN 303-5344. Tel: 208-384-4076. Circulation Tel: 208-384-4340. Interlibrary Loan Service Tel: 208-384-4078. Administration Tel: 208-384-4238. Reference FAX: 208-384-4021. Administration FAX: 208-384-4025. TDD: 800-377-3529. Web Site: www.boisepubliclibrary.org. *Dir,* Kevin Wayne Booe; Tel: 208-384-4029, E-mail: kbooe@cityofboise.org; *Electronic Res Librn,* Lindsay Wyatt; Tel: 208-384-4442; *Main Libr & Pub Serv Mgr,* William Nation; Tel: 208-384-4210, E-mail: wnation@cityofboise.org; *Neighborhood Serv Mgr,* Laurel White; Tel: 208-384-4485, E-mail: lwhite@cityofboise.org; *Operations & Outreach Mgr,* Denise McNeley; Tel: 208-472-1958, E-mail: dmcneley@cityofboise.org; *Tech Serv Mgr,* Chrisanne Brown; Tel: 208-384-4464, E-mail: cbrown@cityofboise.org; *Govt Doc,* Julie Davis; Tel: 208-384-4441, E-mail: jdavis@cityofboise.org; *ILL,* Lisa McMillan; E-mail: lmcmillan@cityofboise.org; Staff 106.29 (MLS 19, Non-MLS 87.29)
Founded 1895. Pop 208,219; Circ 1,510,530
Library Holdings: AV Mats 28,588; Large Print Bks 5,043; Bk Titles 261,797; Bk Vols 356,772; Per Subs 299
Special Collections: Newspaper (Idaho Stateman), micro; Northwest & Idaho History. US Document Depository
Automation Activity & Vendor Info: (Acquisitions) SirsiDynix; (Cataloging) SirsiDynix; (Circulation) SirsiDynix; (ILL) OCLC Online; (OPAC) SirsiDynix; (Serials) SirsiDynix
Database Vendor: Dialog, EBSCOhost, Gale Cengage Learning, OCLC FirstSearch, SirsiDynix, Wilson - Wilson Web
Wireless access
Function: Handicapped accessible, Home delivery & serv to Sr ctr & nursing homes, Homebound delivery serv, ILL available, Magnifiers for reading, Outside serv via phone, mail, e-mail & web, Photocopying/Printing, Prog for children & young adult, Ref serv available, Summer reading prog
Partic in LYNX! Consortium
Special Services for the Deaf - TTY equip
Special Services for the Blind - Assistive/Adapted tech devices, equip & products
Open Mon-Thurs 10-9, Fri 10-6, Sat 10-5, Sun 12-5
Friends of the Library Group
Branches: 3
LIBRARY! AT COLE & USTICK, 7557 W Ustick Rd, 83704. (Mail add: 715 S Capitol Blvd, 83702), SAN 370-3649. Tel: 208-570-6900. Administration Tel: 208-384-4238. FAX: 208-376-1043. Administration FAX: 208-384-4025. *Dir,* Kevin Wayne Booe; Tel: 208-384-4029, E-mail: kbooe@cityofboise.org; *Br Supvr,* Kathy Stalder; E-mail: kstalder@cityofboise.org
Founded 2009
Open Tues-Thurs 10-9, Fri 10-6, Sat Noon-5, Sun 1-5
Friends of the Library Group
LIBRARY! AT COLLISTER, 4724 W State St, 83703. Tel: 208-562-4995. *Br Supvr,* Jim Jatkevicius
Founded 2008
Open Tues-Thurs 10-9, Fri 10-6, Sat Noon-5, Sun 1-5
Friends of the Library Group
LIBRARY! AT HILLCREST, 5246 W Overland Rd, 83705. Tel: 208-562-4996. Circulation Tel: 208-562-4927. Administration Tel: 208-384-4238. Administration FAX: 208-384-4025. TDD: 800-377-3529. *Br Supvr,* Diane Broom; Tel: 208-562-4931, E-mail: dbroom@cityofboise.org
Founded 2008
Open Tues-Thurs 10-9, Fri 10-6, Sat Noon-5, Sun 1-5
Friends of the Library Group
Bookmobiles: 1

C BOISE STATE UNIVERSITY*, Albertsons Library, 1865 Cesar Chavez Lane, 83725-1430. (Mail add: 1910 University Dr, 83725-1430), SAN 339-624X. Tel: 208-426-4321. Circulation Tel: 208-426-1204. Interlibrary Loan Service Tel: 208-426-3756. Reference Tel: 208-426-3301. Administration Tel: 208-426-1234. FAX: 208-334-2111. Web Site: library.boisestate.edu. *Dean,* Dr Tracy Bicknell-Holmes; E-mail: tracybicknell-holmes@boisestate.edu; *Assoc Dean,* Peggy Cooper; Tel: 208-426-2311, E-mail: pcooper@boisestate.edu; *Head, Acq,* Nancy Rosenheim; Tel: 208-426-1660, E-mail: nrosenhe@boisestate.edu; *Head, Spec Coll & Archives,* Cheryl Oestriecher; Tel: 208-426-3958, E-mail: cheryloestreicher@boisestate.edu; Staff 61.92 (MLS 22.92, Non-MLS 39)
Founded 1932. Enrl 18,936; Fac 611; Highest Degree: Doctorate
Special Collections: Cenarrusa Papers; Idaho Historical Manuscripts & Photos; Idaho Writers Archive, literary ms; Papers of Governor Cecil Andrus; Rare Books Coll; Senatorial Papers of Frank Church & Len B Jordan. US Document Depository
Automation Activity & Vendor Info: (Acquisitions) Ex Libris Group; (Cataloging) Ex Libris Group; (Circulation) Ex Libris Group; (Course Reserve) Docutek; (OPAC) Ex Libris Group; (Serials) Ex Libris Group
Wireless access
Open Mon-Thurs 7am-Midnight, Fri 7-7, Sat 10-7, Sun 10am-Midnight

GM DEPARTMENT OF VETERANS AFFAIRS*, Medical Center Library, 500 W Fort St, 531/142D, 83702-4598. SAN 303-545X. Tel: 208-422-1306. FAX: 208-422-1390. E-mail: vhaboilibrab@va.gov. *Libr Tech,* Gregg Whitmore; E-mail: gregory.whitmore@va.gov; Staff 1 (Non-MLS 1)
Founded 1930
Library Holdings: AV Mats 464; CDs 175; DVDs 183; e-books 3,000; e-journals 5,000; Microforms 1,440; Bk Titles 5,060; Per Subs 98; Videos 423
Special Collections: Clinical Medicine, bks, AV; Patient Education, bks, AV

Automation Activity & Vendor Info: (Acquisitions) Follett Software; (Cataloging) Follett Software; (Circulation) Follett Software; (Course Reserve) Follett Software; (Media Booking) Follett Software; (OPAC) Follett Software; (Serials) Follett Software
Function: For res purposes, Govt ref serv, Handicapped accessible, ILL available, Magnifiers for reading, Wheelchair accessible
Partic in National Network of Libraries of Medicine; Pacific NW Regional Health Sci Libr
Open Mon-Fri 8-4:30

SR DIOCESE OF BOISE*, Resource Center Library, 1501 S Federal Way, Ste 400, 83705. SAN 328-2074. Tel: 208-342-1311. FAX: 208-342-0224. E-mail: resourcecenter@rcdb.org. Web Site: www.catholicidaho.org. *Mgr,* Cathy Wheaton
Library Holdings: CDs 95; DVDs 110; Bk Titles 12,000; Videos 1,050
Special Services for the Blind - Audio mat
Open Mon-Fri 9-4

L HAWLEY TROXELL ENNIS & HAWLEY*, Law Library, 877 Main St, Ste 1000, 83702-1617. Tel: 208-344-6000. FAX: 208-342-3829. Web Site: www.hteh.com. *Librn,* Allison Terry
Library Holdings: Bk Vols 12,000; Per Subs 50
Restriction: Not open to pub

S HEALTHWISE INC*, Research Library, 2601 N Bogus Basin Rd, 83702. (Mail add: PO Box 1989, 83702-1989), SAN 377-2276. Tel: 208-331-6957. Interlibrary Loan Service Tel: 208-331-6958. FAX: 208-345-1897. E-mail: hwlibrary@healthwise.org. *Sr Res Libr Mgr,* Liisa Rogers; E-mail: lrogers@healthwise.org; Staff 2 (MLS 2)
Library Holdings: Bk Titles 675; Per Subs 65
Database Vendor: CyberTools for Libraries, Majors, ProQuest, PubMed, UpToDate
Function: ILL available, Res libr
Restriction: Co libr

G IDAHO COMMISSION FOR LIBRARIES, 325 W State St, 83702-6072. SAN 339-6363. Tel: 208-334-2150. FAX: 208-334-4016. Web Site: libraries.idaho.gov. *State Librn,* Ann Joslin; E-mail: ann.joslin@libraries.idaho.gov; *Assoc State Librn,* Marj Hooper; E-mail: marj.hooper@libraries.idaho.gov; *Admin Serv Mgr,* Roger Dubois; E-mail: roger.dubois@libraries.idaho.gov; *Prog Supvr,* Pamela Bradshaw; E-mail: pam.bradshaw@libraries.idaho.gov; Staff 19 (MLS 10, Non-MLS 9)
Founded 1901
Jul 2013-Jun 2014 Income $4,536,157, State $3,179,200, Federal $1,281,957, Other $75,000. Sal $2,203,735
Special Collections: NLS (Talking Book Service Coll); Shelf Project (Talking Book Service Coll); Stacks (Digital Repository of State Publications). State Document Depository
Automation Activity & Vendor Info: (Cataloging) OCLC; (OPAC) Keystone Systems, Inc (KLAS)
Database Vendor: EBSCO Auto Repair Reference, EBSCOhost, Gale Cengage Learning, LearningExpress
Wireless access
Function: Libr develop
Publications: Connections: TBS News (Quarterly newsletter); Envoy - Trustee News (Quarterly); Nexus - ICFL News (Bi-monthly); Public Library Statistics (Library statistics & report); The Scoop (Monthly newsletter)
Special Services for the Blind - Cassette playback machines; Cassettes; Digital talking bk; Digital talking bk machines; Machine repair; Newsletter (in large print, Braille or on cassette); Production of talking bks; Talking bks; Tel Pioneers equip repair group
Open Mon-Fri 8-5

P IDAHO COMMISSION FOR LIBRARIES*, Talking Book Service, 325 W State St, 83702-6072. SAN 303-5379. Tel: 208-334-2150. Toll Free Tel: 800-458-3271. E-mail: talkingbooks@libraries.idaho.gov. Web Site: libraries.idaho.org. *State Librn,* Ann Joslin; E-mail: ann.joslin@libraries.idaho.gov; Staff 1 (MLS 1)
Founded 1973. Pop 3,442; Circ 214,731
Special Collections: Braille & Audio Reading Download; Idaho & Pacific Northwest Recorded Books; Idaho Shelf Project
Automation Activity & Vendor Info: (OPAC) Keystone Systems, Inc (KLAS)
Wireless access
Publications: Connections: TBS News (Quarterly); Large Print Calendar
Open Mon-Fri 9-5

G IDAHO LEGISLATIVE REFERENCE LIBRARY*, Capitol Annex, 514 W Jefferson St, 83702. (Mail add: PO Box 83720, 83702), SAN 320-1759. Tel: 208-334-4822. FAX: 208-334-2125. Web Site: www.legislature.idaho.gov/. *Librn,* Kristin M Ford; Staff 2 (MLS 1, Non-MLS 1)
Founded 1978
Library Holdings: CDs 50; Bk Titles 2,500; Bk Vols 3,100; Per Subs 40
Subject Interests: Legislation
Automation Activity & Vendor Info: (Cataloging) Follett Software; (Circulation) Follett Software
Database Vendor: EBSCOhost, Gale Cengage Learning
Wireless access
Function: Photocopying/Printing, Telephone ref
Open Mon-Fri 8-5
Restriction: Circulates for staff only

S IDAHO POWER CO*, Corporate Library, 1221 W Idaho St, 83702. (Mail add: PO Box 70, 83707-0070), SAN 328-7890. Tel: 208-388-2696. FAX: 208-388-5505. *Librn,* Yvonne Thorusen; E-mail: ythorusen@idahopower.com
Library Holdings: Bks on Deafness & Sign Lang 2; Bk Titles 5,800; Per Subs 250
Wireless access
Open Mon-Fri 7:30-5

S IDAHO STATE HISTORICAL SOCIETY*, Public Archives & Research Library, Idaho History Ctr, 2205 Old Penitentiary Rd, 83712. SAN 339-6304. Tel: 208-334-3356. FAX: 208-334-3198. Web Site: www.idahohistory.net. *State Archivist,* Rod House; E-mail: rod.house@ishs.idaho.gov; *Archivist,* Steve Barrett; *Archivist,* Jim Riley; E-mail: jim.riley@ishs.idaho.gov; *Ref Archivist,* David Matte; E-mail: david.matte@ishs.idaho.gov; *Librn,* Carolyn Ruby; E-mail: carolyn.ruby@ishs.idaho.gov. Subject Specialists: *State archives,* Jim Riley; Staff 15 (MLS 2, Non-MLS 13)
Founded 1907
Library Holdings: Bk Titles 25,000
Special Collections: Idaho & Pacific Northwest History; Idaho Manuscripts including State & Local Governmental Records; Idaho Newspapers, microfilm, Idaho Photographs; Map Coll. Oral History
Subject Interests: Genealogy, Local hist
Function: For res purposes, ILL available, Newsp ref libr, Photocopying/Printing, Ref serv available, Res libr, Workshops
Publications: Idaho Landscapes (Periodical); Idaho Yesterdays (Periodical)
Open Wed-Sat 9-5
Restriction: Fee for pub use

L IDAHO STATE LAW LIBRARY*, 322 E Front St, Ste 560, 83702. SAN 303-5395. Tel: 208-364-4555. FAX: 208-334-2467. E-mail: lawlibrary@idcourts.net. Web Site: www.isll.idaho.gov. *Cataloger, Head, Tech Serv,* Kristin Quigley; Tel: 208-364-4557, E-mail: kquigley@idcourts.net; *Assoc Law Librn,* Michael Greenlee; Tel: 208-364-4554, E-mail: mjgreenl@uidaho.edu; *Libr Asst,* Nick Toennis; Tel: 208-364-4070, E-mail: ntoennis@uidaho.edu; Staff 4 (MLS 2, Non-MLS 2)
Founded 1869
Jul 2011-Jun 2012 Income $207,000, State $132,000, Other $75,000. Mats Exp $207,000, Books $107,000, Per/Ser (Incl. Access Fees) $50,000, Electronic Ref Mat (Incl. Access Fees) $50,000
Library Holdings: Bk Vols 31,000
Special Collections: US Document Depository
Subject Interests: Law, Legislation
Automation Activity & Vendor Info: (Acquisitions) Ex Libris Group; (Cataloging) Ex Libris Group; (Circulation) Ex Libris Group; (ILL) OCLC FirstSearch; (OPAC) Ex Libris Group; (Serials) Ex Libris Group
Database Vendor: OCLC FirstSearch, Westlaw
Wireless access
Function: Computers for patron use, Copy machines, e-mail serv, Electronic databases & coll, Fax serv, Handicapped accessible, ILL available, Mail & tel request accepted, Online cat, Online searches, Photocopying/Printing, Pub access computers, Ref & res, Ref serv available, Ref serv in person, Telephone ref, Web-catalog, Wheelchair accessible
Partic in WIN Library Network
Open Mon-Fri 8-5
Restriction: Borrowing requests are handled by ILL, Circ limited, Non-circulating coll, Non-circulating to the pub

S REAL ESTATE COMMISSION LIBRARY*, 633 N Fourth St, 83702-4510. (Mail add: PO Box 83720, 83720-0077), SAN 328-2236. Tel: 208-334-3285. Toll Free Tel: 866-447-5411 (Idaho only). FAX: 208-334-2050. Web Site: www.irec.idaho.gov. *Librn,* Jesama Rosensweig; Tel: 208-334-3285, Ext 106, E-mail: jesama.rosensweig@irec.idaho.gov
Library Holdings: Bk Vols 1,026
Open Mon-Fri 8-5
Restriction: Open to pub upon request

M SAINT ALPHONSUS HEALTH SYSTEM*, Kissler Library & Research Center, Central Tower, 1055 N Curtis Rd, 2nd Flr, 83706. SAN 303-5417. Tel: 208-367-3993. FAX: 208-367-2702. E-mail: bo-kisslerlibrary@sarmc.org. *Librn,* Sandra Hight
Founded 1970

Library Holdings: e-journals 10,000; Bk Titles 500; Per Subs 31
Database Vendor: EBSCOhost, MD Consult, OVID Technologies, UpToDate
Wireless access
Open Mon-Fri 7:30-3:30

M SAINT LUKE'S HEALTH SYSTEM LIBRARIES*, Dr Maurice M Burkholder Health Sciences Library, 190 E Bannock St, 83712-6297. SAN 303-5425. Tel: 208-381-2276. Automation Services Tel: 208-381-2277. FAX: 208-381-4317. E-mail: library@slrmc.org. *Dir,* Pamela Spickelmier; E-mail: spickelp@slrmc.org; *ILL, Libr Asst,* Jacque Gibson; *Applications Coordr,* Amy Claybaugh
Founded 1971
Library Holdings: Bk Titles 1,300; Bk Vols 1,500; Per Subs 1,100
Subject Interests: Cardiology, Internal med, Obstetrics & gynecology, Oncology, Pediatrics
Automation Activity & Vendor Info: (Cataloging) Softlink America; (Circulation) Softlink America; (OPAC) Softlink America
Wireless access
Open Mon-Fri 8-5

BONNERS FERRY

P BOUNDARY COUNTY DISTRICT LIBRARY*, 6370 Kootenai St, 83805. (Mail add: PO Box Y, 83805-1276), SAN 303-5468. Tel: 208-267-3750. FAX: 208-267-5231. E-mail: bcl@turbonet.com. Web Site: boundary.lili.org. *Dir,* Sandra Ashworth
Founded 1914. Pop 9,050; Circ 81,814
Library Holdings: Bk Vols 37,000; Per Subs 141
Subject Interests: Environ studies, Forestry
Automation Activity & Vendor Info: (Cataloging) OCLC WorldShare Interlibrary Loan; (Circulation) OCLC WorldShare Interlibrary Loan
Wireless access
Open Mon & Fri 9-8, Tues-Thurs 9-6, Sat 10-4

BRUNEAU

P BRUNEAU DISTRICT LIBRARY, 32073 Ruth St, 83604. (Mail add: PO Box 253, 83604). Tel: 208-845-2131. FAX: 208-845-2131. E-mail: bruneau_library@yahoo.com. *Dir,* Carol Copeland
Library Holdings: DVDs 50; Bk Titles 10,500; Videos 420
Wireless access
Open Tues & Thurs 10-6, Wed 10-4

BUHL

P BUHL PUBLIC LIBRARY*, 215 Broadway N, 83316-1624. SAN 303-5476. Tel: 208-543-6500. FAX: 208-543-2318. E-mail: libinbuhl@hotmail.com. *Dir,* C L Toppen; *Ch Serv,* Louise Nofziger
Pop 3,516; Circ 38,744
Library Holdings: Bk Vols 25,664; Per Subs 56; Talking Bks 1,688; Videos 1,191
Special Collections: Children's Art Coll; Idaho Coll; Quilting Coll
Automation Activity & Vendor Info: (Cataloging) Follett Software; (Circulation) Follett Software; (OPAC) Follett Software
Open Mon & Wed 10-9, Tues & Thurs 1-5 & 7-9, Sat 1-5

BURLEY

P BURLEY PUBLIC LIBRARY*, 1300 Miller Ave, 83318-1729. SAN 303-5492. Tel: 208-878-7708. FAX: 208-878-7018. E-mail: library@bplibrary.org. Web Site: www.bplibrary.org. *Dir,* Julie Woodford
Founded 1922. Pop 9,316; Circ 55,909
Library Holdings: Bk Vols 46,194; Per Subs 40
Special Collections: Idaho Coll
Automation Activity & Vendor Info: (Cataloging) Follett Software; (Circulation) Follett Software; (ILL) OCLC FirstSearch; (OPAC) Follett Software
Wireless access
Open Mon-Thurs 10-7, Fri 10-6, Sat 10-4
Friends of the Library Group

CALDWELL

P CALDWELL PUBLIC LIBRARY*, 1010 Dearborn, 83605-4195. SAN 303-5506. Tel: 208-459-3242. FAX: 208-459-7344. E-mail: caldwellweb@fiberpipe.net. Web Site: www.caldwell.lili.org. *Dir,* Elaine Leppert; *IT Dept Head,* Anne Adamson; *Ch,* Kimbre Chapman; *Ref,* Linda Hieb; Staff 4 (MLS 2, Non-MLS 2)
Founded 1887. Pop 46,237; Circ 183,944
Oct 2009-Sept 2010 Income $611,575, City $534,476, Locally Generated Income $77,099. Mats Exp $81,571, Books $64,851, AV Mat $5,411, Electronic Ref Mat (Incl. Access Fees) $11,309. Sal $351,024
Library Holdings: AV Mats 1,844; Bk Vols 95,092; Per Subs 153; Videos 1,821
Special Collections: Historical Photograph Coll. Oral History
Automation Activity & Vendor Info: (Acquisitions) SirsiDynix; (Cataloging) SirsiDynix; (Circulation) SirsiDynix; (OPAC) SirsiDynix
Wireless access
Partic in LYNX! Consortium; OCLC Online Computer Library Center, Inc
Open Mon-Thurs 10-9, Fri 10-6, Sat 10-5, Sun (Sept-May) 2-5
Friends of the Library Group

C THE COLLEGE OF IDAHO*, N L Terteling Library, 2112 Cleveland Blvd, 83605-4432. SAN 303-5514. Tel: 208-459-5506. Interlibrary Loan Service Tel: 208-459-5525. Reference Tel: 208-459-5524. FAX: 208-459-5299. E-mail: library@collegeofidaho.edu. Web Site: www.collegeofidaho.edu/academics/library/default.asp?ID=academics. *Dir,* Christine Schutz; E-mail: cschutz@collegeofidaho.edu; *Circ, ILL,* Kathryn Jepko; E-mail: kjepko@collegeofidaho.edu; Staff 4 (MLS 1, Non-MLS 3)
Founded 1891. Enrl 800; Highest Degree: Bachelor
Library Holdings: Bk Vols 190,000; Per Subs 340
Automation Activity & Vendor Info: (Cataloging) Innovative Interfaces, Inc; (Circulation) Innovative Interfaces, Inc; (Course Reserve) Innovative Interfaces, Inc; (ILL) OCLC; (OPAC) Innovative Interfaces, Inc
Function: ILL available
Open Mon-Thurs 8am-Midnight, Fri 8-5, Sat 1-5, Sun 1-Midnight
Restriction: Open to students, fac & staff
Friends of the Library Group

CAMBRIDGE

P CAMBRIDGE COMMUNITY LIBRARY*, Superior St, 83610. (Mail add: PO Box 10, 83610-0010), SAN 303-5522. Tel: 208-257-3434. E-mail: cambplib@ctcweb.net. *Dir,* Nina Hawkins; *Asst Librn,* Robin Stephens; *Ch Serv,* Janet Bunker
Founded 1973. Pop 1,725; Circ 9,000
Library Holdings: Bk Vols 15,000
Special Services for the Blind - Bks on cassette
Open Mon-Sat 2-6

CAREY

P LITTLE WOOD RIVER DISTRICT LIBRARY*, 16 Panther Ave, 83320-5063. (Mail add: PO Box 10, 83320-0218), SAN 303-5530. Tel: 208-823-4510. E-mail: lwrlibrary@yahoo.com. *Dir,* Mary Bowman
Founded 1976. Pop 1,000; Circ 15,000
Library Holdings: AV Mats 100; CDs 50; DVDs 360; Bk Titles 6,000; Videos 700
Wireless access
Open Mon 10-7:30, Wed & Thurs 3:30-7:30, Sat 10-1

CASCADE

P CASCADE PUBLIC LIBRARY*, 105 Front St, 83611. (Mail add: PO Box 10, 83611-0010), SAN 303-5549. Tel: 208-382-4757. FAX: 208-382-4757. E-mail: cplv@cableone.net. Web Site: cascade.lili.org. *Libr Dir,* Robin Mayfield; *Librn,* Valerie Rice Stewart; *Libr Tech,* Michele Keyes; Staff 2 (Non-MLS 2)
Founded 1914. Pop 1,001; Circ 12,250
Library Holdings: Audiobooks 305; CDs 96; DVDs 308; Large Print Bks 310; Bk Titles 15,200; Bk Vols 15,232; Per Subs 2; Videos 1,002
Special Collections: Genealogy Coll; Idaho Coll; National Geographic 1914-2010
Automation Activity & Vendor Info: (Cataloging) Biblionix; (Circulation) Biblionix; (ILL) OCLC FirstSearch
Wireless access
Function: Adult bk club, Bks on cassette, Bks on CD, CD-ROM, Children's prog, Computers for patron use, Copy machines, e-mail & chat, Electronic databases & coll, Fax serv, Free DVD rentals, Genealogy discussion group, Govt ref serv, Handicapped accessible, Homebound delivery serv, ILL available, Masonic res mat, Newsp ref libr, Photocopying/Printing, Preschool outreach, Prog for adults, Prog for children & young adult, Pub access computers, Ref serv in person, Spoken cassettes & CDs, Spoken cassettes & DVDs, Summer reading prog, Tax forms, Teen prog, Telephone ref, VHS videos, Wheelchair accessible
Special Services for the Blind - Bks on cassette; Cassette playback machines; Cassettes; Home delivery serv; Large print & cassettes; Talking bk serv referral; Talking bks; Talking bks & player equip
Open Mon-Fri 11-6, Sat 10-3:30
Friends of the Library Group

CHALLIS

P CHALLIS PUBLIC LIBRARY*, 501 Sixth St, 83226. (Mail add: PO Box 186, 83226-0186), SAN 303-5557. Tel: 208-879-4267. FAX: 208-879-4267. E-mail: cpl@custertel.net. *Librn,* Linda Hesse; *Asst Librn,* Kari Lind; Staff 1 (MLS 1)
Founded 1935. Pop 1,990; Circ 9,291
Library Holdings: Bk Titles 16,000; Per Subs 20
Automation Activity & Vendor Info: (Cataloging) New Generation Technologies Inc. (LiBRARYSOFT); (Circulation) New Generation

Technologies Inc. (LiBRARYSOFT); (OPAC) New Generation Technologies Inc. (LiBRARYSOFT)
Open Tues-Thurs 11-6, Fri & Sat 11-3

CHUBBUCK

P PORTNEUF DISTRICT LIBRARY, 5210 Stuart Ave, 83202-2214. SAN 303-6308. Tel: 208-237-2192. FAX: 208-237-2194. E-mail: notices@portneuflibrary.org. Web Site: portneuflibrary.org. *Dir,* Jezmynne Dene; E-mail: jezmynne.dene@portneuflibrary.org; *Asst Dir,* Josh Barnes; E-mail: josh.barnes@portneuflibrary.org; *Adult Serv/Young Adult Librarian,* Holly Jackson; *Ch,* Amanda Bowden; E-mail: amanda.bowden@portneuflibrary.org; Staff 3.03 (MLS 1, Non-MLS 2.03)
Founded 1958. Pop 22,000; Circ 117,717
Library Holdings: Audiobooks 4,633; Bks on Deafness & Sign Lang 10; CDs 500; DVDs 2,689; Large Print Bks 500; Bk Titles 43,190; Per Subs 29
Special Collections: Idaho Authors
Subject Interests: Idaho hist
Automation Activity & Vendor Info: (ILL) OCLC; (Serials) EBSCO Online
Database Vendor: Booklist Online, EBSCO Auto Repair Reference, EBSCOhost, LearningExpress, Medline, OCLC WorldShare Interlibrary Loan, ProQuest, TumbleBookLibrary
Wireless access
Function: 24/7 Electronic res, 24/7 Online cat, Accessibility serv available based on individual needs, Activity rm, After school storytime, Audiobks via web, Bilingual assistance for Spanish patrons, Bks on CD, Chess club, Children's prog, Citizenship assistance, Computer training, Computers for patron use, Copy machines, Digital talking bks, e-mail serv, Electronic databases & coll, Fax serv, Free DVD rentals, Handicapped accessible, Holiday prog, Homework prog, ILL available, Instruction & testing, Life-long learning prog for all ages, Literacy & newcomer serv, Magazines, Mango lang, Movies, Music CDs, Notary serv, Online ref, Online searches, Photocopying/Printing, Preschool outreach, Preschool reading prog, Prog for adults, Prog for children & young adult, Provide serv for the mentally ill, Pub access computers, Ref serv available, Ref serv in person, Senior computer classes, Senior outreach, Serves mentally handicapped consumers, Spanish lang bks, Spoken cassettes & CDs, Spoken cassettes & DVDs, Story hour, Study rm, Summer & winter reading prog, Summer reading prog, Teen prog, Web-catalog, Wheelchair accessible, Winter reading prog, Workshops
Partic in Library Consortium of Eastern Idaho
Open Mon-Thurs (Winter) 10-8, Fri & Sat 10-6; Mon-Sat (Summer) 10-6

CLARKIA

P CLARKIA DISTRICT LIBRARY*, 377 Poplar St, 83812. (Mail add: PO Box 1126, 83812-1126). Tel: 208-245-2908. FAX: 208-245-2908. E-mail: clarkialibrary@yahoo.com. *Dir,* Karen Anderson
Library Holdings: Bk Vols 7,000
Open Mon & Thurs 1-6:30, Tues & Wed 10-2

COEUR D'ALENE

P COEUR D'ALENE PUBLIC LIBRARY*, 702 E Front Ave, 83814-2373. SAN 303-5573. Tel: 208-769-2315. FAX: 208-769-2381. E-mail: info@cdalibrary.org. Web Site: www.cdalibrary.org. *Dir,* Bette Ammon; E-mail: bammon@cdalibrary.org; *Dep Dir, Ref/Tech Serv,* Sandy Pratt; *Circ Mgr,* Melissa Searle; E-mail: msearle@cdalibrary.org; *Info Serv,* Christopher Brannon; E-mail: christopher@cdalibrary.org; *ILL,* Sherry Bullard; E-mail: sbullard@cdalibrary.org; Staff 7 (MLS 2, Non-MLS 5)
Founded 1904. Pop 45,000; Circ 377,000
Special Collections: Human Rights Coll; Idaho Coll; Northwest Coll
Subject Interests: Local hist
Automation Activity & Vendor Info: (Cataloging) Ex Libris Group; (Circulation) ByWater Solutions; (OPAC) ByWater Solutions
Database Vendor: EBSCO Auto Repair Reference, Newsbank, OCLC FirstSearch, ProQuest, ReferenceUSA
Wireless access
Publications: Page Turner (Monthly newsletter)
Partic in Cooperative Information Network
Open Mon-Thurs 10-8, Fri 10-6, Sat & Sun 12-4
Friends of the Library Group

M KOOTENAI MEDICAL CENTER*, William T Wood Medical Library, 2003 Kootenai Health Way, 83814. SAN 328-0608. Tel: 208-666-2480. FAX: 208-666-2854. Web Site: www.kmcmedicallibrary.org, www.kootenaihealth.org/dearmondlibrary. *Libr Mgr,* Joan Wilson
Founded 1984
Library Holdings: Bk Titles 1,300; Per Subs 320
Special Collections: Alternative & Complementary Therapies
Subject Interests: Consumer health
Automation Activity & Vendor Info: (Acquisitions) Ex Libris Group
Wireless access
Publications: NIHIN (Newsletter)
Partic in Cooperative Information Network; IHIN; ILCN; National Network of Libraries of Medicine; NIHIN
Open Mon-Fri 8-4:30

S MUSEUM OF NORTH IDAHO INC ARCHIVES*, 115 Northwest Blvd, 83816. (Mail add: PO Box 812, 83816-0812), SAN 371-2966. Tel: 208-664-3448. E-mail: museum@museumni.org. Web Site: www.museumni.org. *Dir,* Dorothy Dahlgren
Library Holdings: Bk Vols 750
Subject Interests: Logging, Transportation
Publications: Newsletter (Quarterly)
Restriction: Open by appt only

J NORTH IDAHO COLLEGE LIBRARY*, Molstead Library, 1000 W Garden Ave, 83814-2199. SAN 303-5581. Tel: 208-769-3355. Interlibrary Loan Service Tel: 208-769-3269. Administration Tel: 208-769-3215. Information Services Tel: 208-769-3265. FAX: 208-769-3428. E-mail: librarian@nic.edu. Web Site: molstead.macminicolo.net. *Libr Dir,* George McAlister; E-mail: George_McAlister@nic.edu; *Coll Develop Librn, Pub Serv,* Siperly Brian; E-mail: Brian_Siperly@nic.edu; *Distance Educ Librn, Info Serv,* Jim DeMoss; Tel: 208-769-3253, E-mail: jim_demoss@nic.edu; *Tech Serv Librn,* Ann T Johnston; Tel: 208-769-3240, E-mail: ann_johnston@nic.edu; *Learning Res Coordr,* Andy Finney; Tel: 208-769-3266, E-mail: andy_finney@nic.edu; *Circ Supvr,* Cheryl Carroll; E-mail: cheryl-carroll@nic.edu; Staff 6.5 (MLS 4.5, Non-MLS 2)
Founded 1933. Enrl 3,405; Fac 175; Highest Degree: Associate
Library Holdings: Bk Vols 76,000
Special Collections: Pacific Northwest History & Indian Affairs (Special Coll & Veeder Coll). Oral History; State Document Depository
Automation Activity & Vendor Info: (Acquisitions) Ex Libris Group; (Cataloging) Ex Libris Group; (Circulation) Ex Libris Group; (OPAC) Ex Libris Group
Database Vendor: Baker & Taylor, BioOne, CQ Press, CredoReference, ebrary, EBSCO Auto Repair Reference, EBSCOhost, Ex Libris Group, Facts on File, Gale Cengage Learning, H W Wilson, OCLC WorldShare Interlibrary Loan, Oxford Online, ProQuest, Westlaw
Wireless access
Partic in Inland Northwest Library Automation Network (INLAN)
Open Mon-Thurs (Fall & Spring) 7:30am-9pm, Fri 7:30-2:30, Sun 1-8; Mon-Thurs (Summer) 8-5, Fri 8-2:30

COTTONWOOD

S NORTH IDAHO CORRECTIONAL INSTITUTION LIBRARY*, 236 Radar Rd, 83522. Tel: 208-962-3276, Ext 174. FAX: 208-962-5354. *Librn,* Emmett Wilson
Library Holdings: Bk Titles 7,800; Bk Vols 8,300; Per Subs 23

P PRAIRIE COMMUNITY LIBRARY*, 506 King St, 83522. (Mail add: PO Box 65, 83522-0065). Tel: 208-962-3714. E-mail: cottonwoodlib@gmail.com. *Librn,* Donna Watson
Pop 350, Circ 2,000
Library Holdings: DVDs 50; Large Print Bks 100; Bk Vols 13,000; Per Subs 1; Talking Bks 100; Videos 50
Wireless access
Open Tues & Thurs 10-5, Sat 10-1

COUNCIL

P COUNCIL DISTRICT LIBRARY*, Council Valley Free Library, 104 California Ave, 83612. (Mail add: PO Box E, 83612-0804), SAN 303-5611. Tel: 208-253-6004. FAX: 208-253-6004. E-mail: cvfl@ctcweb.net. Web Site: www.cvfl.ctc.net. *Dir,* Patty Gross
Circ 36,000
Oct 2011-Sept 2012 Income $48,816, County $47,460, Locally Generated Income $1,356. Mats Exp $8,187, Books $7,147, Other Print Mats $365, AV Mat $675. Sal $30,141
Library Holdings: AV Mats 670; Bk Vols 22,500; Per Subs 10
Database Vendor: LearningExpress, OCLC WorldShare Interlibrary Loan
Wireless access
Special Services for the Blind - Bks on cassette
Open Tues & Thurs 9:30-6, Sat 9:30-5:30
Friends of the Library Group

DOWNEY

P SOUTH BANNOCK LIBRARY DISTRICT*, 18 N Main St, 83234. (Mail add: PO Box D, 83234-0160), SAN 303-562X. Tel: 208-897-5270. FAX: 208-897-5270. E-mail: downylib@dcdi.net. Web Site: www.southbannocklibrary.org. *Dir,* Marcy Price
Pop 7,807; Circ 44,165
Library Holdings: AV Mats 594; Bk Titles 32,000; Per Subs 137
Automation Activity & Vendor Info: (Cataloging) Follett Software; (Circulation) Follett Software

Open Mon, Wed & Fri 1-5, Tues & Thurs 1-6, Sat 10-2
Friends of the Library Group
Branches: 1
LAVA HOT SPRINGS BRANCH, 33 E Main St, Lava Hot Springs, 83246-9999. (Mail add: PO Box 369, Lava Hot Springs, 83246-0369). Tel: 208-776-5301. FAX: 208-776-5301. E-mail: lavalib@dcdi.net. *Dir,* Marcy Price; *Asst Dir, Head Librn,* Debbie DePaola
Library Holdings: Bk Titles 17,000; Per Subs 69
Open Mon-Fri 1-5, Sat 10-2
Friends of the Library Group
Bookmobiles: 1

DUBOIS

P CLARK COUNTY DISTRICT LIBRARY*, 160 Main St, 83423. (Mail add: PO Box 67, 83423-0067), SAN 303-5638. Tel: 208-374-5267. *Dir,* DeAnn Taylor
Pop 1,022
Library Holdings: Bk Titles 7,500
Open Mon-Fri 3:30-6

EAGLE

P EAGLE PUBLIC LIBRARY*, 100 N Stierman Way, 83616-5162. SAN 303-5646. Tel: 208-939-6814. FAX: 208-939-1359. E-mail: eaglelibrary@cityofeagle.org. Web Site: www.eaglepubliclibrary.org. *Dir,* Steve Bumgarner; E-mail: sbumgarner@cityofeagle.org; *Asst Dir, Coll Develop, Youth Serv,* Janice Campbell; E-mail: jcampbell@cityofeagle.org; *Circ Mgr,* Carol Berry; E-mail: cberry@cityofeagle.org; *Tech Serv Mgr,* Megan Williamson; E-mail: mwilliamson@cityofeagle.org; Staff 13.5 (MLS 2, Non-MLS 11.5)
Founded 1963. Pop 20,000; Circ 288,501
Oct 2011-Sept 2012 Income $971,526, City $915,092, Locally Generated Income $56,434
Library Holdings: AV Mats 11,419; Bk Vols 86,964; Per Subs 151
Special Collections: Eagle Local History Coll
Automation Activity & Vendor Info: (Acquisitions) SirsiDynix; (Cataloging) SirsiDynix; (Circulation) SirsiDynix; (ILL) OCLC FirstSearch; (OPAC) SirsiDynix; (Serials) SirsiDynix
Database Vendor: 3M Library Systems, EBSCO Information Services, Ingram Library Services, LearningExpress, Newsbank, OCLC, OCLC FirstSearch, OCLC WorldShare Interlibrary Loan, Overdrive, Inc, ReferenceUSA, TumbleBookLibrary, WT Cox
Wireless access
Partic in LYNX! Consortium
Special Services for the Blind - Large print bks
Open Mon-Wed 9-8, Thurs 11-8, Fri 9-6, Sat 9-5
Friends of the Library Group

ELK CITY

P ELK CITY COMMUNITY LIBRARY*, 100 School Rd, 83525. (Mail add: PO Box 419, 83525-0419). Tel: 208-842-2218. FAX: 208-842-2225. *Librn,* Deborah Nevius
Library Holdings: Bk Vols 5,500
Open Wed 10-4

ELK RIVER

P ELK RIVER FREE LIBRARY DISTRICT*, 203 Main St, 83827. (Mail add: PO Box 187, 83827-0187), SAN 321-0294. Tel: 208-826-3539. E-mail: elkr.library@turbonet.com. Web Site: www.elkriveridaho.com. *In Charge,* Avis Trott
Pop 265; Circ 2,872
Library Holdings: Bk Vols 10,000; Per Subs 30
Open Mon, Wed & Fri 8:30-4:30, Tues & Thurs 8:30-4:30 & 6:30-8:30, Sat 2-4

EMMETT

P EMMETT PUBLIC LIBRARY*, 275 S Hayes St, 83617-2972. SAN 303-5654. Tel: 208-365-6057. FAX: 208-365-6060. E-mail: emmettpl@qwestoffice.net. Web Site: emmett.lili.org. *Dir,* Alyce Kelley; E-mail: alycek@qwestoffice.net
Founded 1924. Pop 6,000; Circ 53,178
Library Holdings: Bk Vols 61,000
Wireless access
Partic in LYNX! Consortium
Open Mon & Wed 12-7, Tues & Thurs 12-5, Fri 12-6
Friends of the Library Group

FAIRFIELD

P CAMAS COUNTY DISTRICT LIBRARY*, 607 Soldier Rd, 83327. (Mail add: PO Box 292, 83327-0292), SAN 303-5662. Tel: 208-764-2553. FAX: 208-764-2553. E-mail: camaslibrary@rtci.net. Web Site: camas.lili.org. *Librn,* Marilyn Ballard
Pop 1,000
Library Holdings: Bk Vols 12,000
Wireless access
Open Mon-Wed & Fri 12:30-5:30, Thurs 10-5:30

FERNWOOD

P BENEWAH COUNTY DISTRICT LIBRARY*, Tri Community Branch, 46 Isaacson St, 83830. (Mail add: PO Box 157, 83830-0157), SAN 377-4104. Tel: 208-245-4883. FAX: 208-245-0129. E-mail: readers@nidlink.com. *Librn,* Joanne O'Dwyer
Library Holdings: Bk Vols 18,500
Open Mon 1-8, Wed & Fri 10-5

FILER

P FILER PUBLIC LIBRARY*, 219 Main St, 83328-5349. (Mail add: PO Box 52, 83328-0052), SAN 303-5670. Tel: 208-326-4143. *Librn,* Margaret Holley
Founded 1923. Pop 1,850; Circ 13,567
Library Holdings: Bk Vols 15,000
Special Collections: Local History Archives
Subject Interests: Idaho
Automation Activity & Vendor Info: (Cataloging) Follett Software
Open Mon-Wed 3-6:30, Thurs 10:30-12 & 3-6:30, Sat 1:30-4:30

FORT HALL

P SHOSHONE-BANNOCK LIBRARY, Fort Hall Library, Pima & Bannock Dr, 83203. (Mail add: PO Box 306, 83203-0306), SAN 303-5689. Tel: 208-478-3882. *Dir,* Ardith Peyope; E-mail: rpeyope@shoshonebannocktribes.com
Circ 18,169
Library Holdings: Bk Titles 5,500
Special Collections: Oral History
Subject Interests: Indians
Open Mon-Fri 8-5

GARDEN CITY

P GARDEN CITY LIBRARY*, 6015 Glenwood St, 83714. SAN 303-5360. Tel: 208-472-2941. E-mail: gcpl@gardencitylibrary.org, reference@gardencitylibrary.org. Web Site: www.notaquietlibrary.org. *Dir,* Lisa Zeiter; Staff 5 (MLS 1, Non-MLS 4)
Founded 1962. Pop 12,000
Wireless access
Partic in LYNX! Consortium
Open Mon & Fri 9:30-5:30, Tues, Wed & Thurs 9:30-8, Sat 10-4
Friends of the Library Group
Bookmobiles: 1

GARDEN VALLEY

P GARDEN VALLEY DISTRICT LIBRARY*, 342 Village Circle, 83622-8040. SAN 303-5697. Tel: 208-462-3317. FAX: 208-462-3758. Web Site: www.lili.org/gardenvalley. *Dir,* Kathy Smith; E-mail: kathrynmsmith@yahoo.com; *Circ,* Carol Dansak; *Circ,* Carol Lynde; *Circ,* Diane Messick; Staff 5 (Non-MLS 5)
Pop 2,000; Circ 4,200
Library Holdings: AV Mats 3,000; Bks on Deafness & Sign Lang 20; Bk Titles 16,000; Per Subs 30
Special Collections: Idaho History
Automation Activity & Vendor Info: (Cataloging) Follett Software; (Circulation) Follett Software
Database Vendor: EBSCOhost, Gale Cengage Learning
Partic in Valley Mountain Library Consortium
Open Mon-Fri 10-6, Sat 10-4
Friends of the Library Group

GLENNS FERRY

P GLENNS FERRY PUBLIC LIBRARY*, 298 S Lincoln, 83623. (Mail add: PO Box 910, 83623-0910), SAN 303-5719. Tel: 208-366-2045. FAX: 208-366-2238. E-mail: glennsferrylib@yahoo.com. *Dir,* Lily Hampton; Staff 1 (Non-MLS 1)
Founded 1930. Pop 1,500; Circ 16,000
Library Holdings: Audiobooks 450; CDs 30; Large Print Bks 2,500; Bk Vols 14,500; Talking Bks 400; Videos 53
Special Collections: Christian Fiction
Function: ILL available
Open Mon 12-6, Tues-Sat 11-5
Restriction: Non-circulating

GOODING

P GOODING PUBLIC LIBRARY*, 306 Fifth Ave W, 83330-1205. SAN 303-5727. Tel: 208-934-4089. FAX: 208-934-4089. E-mail: sholib@shoshonecity.com. *Dir,* Pat A Hamilton; *Ch Serv,* Carolyn DeWitt
Founded 1910. Pop 3,230; Circ 24,100
Library Holdings: Bk Vols 22,000; Per Subs 52
Special Collections: Idaho Coll
Automation Activity & Vendor Info: (Cataloging) Follett Software; (Circulation) Follett Software
Open Mon, Fri & Sat 12-5, Tues & Thurs 1-8, Wed 10-5

P IDAHO SCHOOL FOR THE DEAF & BLIND LIBRARY*, 1450 Main St, 83330. Tel: 208-934-4457. FAX: 208-934-8352. Web Site: www.isdb.idaho.gov. *Librn,* Dorothy Ogden; Tel: 208-934-8751, E-mail: dorothy.ogden@iesdb.org
Library Holdings: Bks on Deafness & Sign Lang 2,000; Braille Volumes 500; Bk Vols 30,000; Talking Bks 75
Automation Activity & Vendor Info: (Acquisitions) Follett Software; (Cataloging) Follett Software; (Circulation) Follett Software
Wireless access
Open Mon-Thurs 7-4:30

GRACE

P GRACE DISTRICT LIBRARY*, 204 S Main, 83241. (Mail add: PO Box B, 83241-0200), SAN 303-5735. Tel: 208-425-3695. FAX: 208-425-3695. E-mail: gracedistlibra@dcdi.net. Web Site: grace.lili.org. *Dir, Libr & Info Serv,* Linda Rasmussen; *Asst Librn,* Margo May
Founded 1941. Pop 2,200; Circ 45,685
Library Holdings: Bk Titles 18,000; Per Subs 26
Partic in Library Consortium of Eastern Idaho
Open Mon 10-7, Tues-Fri 10-5

GRAND VIEW

P EAST OWYHEE COUNTY LIBRARY DISTRICT*, 520 Boise Ave, 83624. (Mail add: PO Box 100, 83624-0100), SAN 303-5743. Tel: 208-834-2785. *Dir,* Kathy Chick
Founded 1974. Pop 5,000
Library Holdings: Bk Vols 16,000; Per Subs 30
Database Vendor: EBSCOhost
Wireless access
Open Mon-Wed 10-5, Thurs 10-6, Fri 10-2

GRANGEVILLE

P GRANGEVILLE CENTENNIAL LIBRARY*, 215 W North St, 83530-1729. SAN 303-5751. Tel: 208-983-0951. FAX: 208-983-2336. E-mail: library@grangeville.us. Web Site: www.centennial library.org. *Dir,* Rebekah Hosman; E-mail: rhosman@grangeville.us; *Ch,* Andrea Solberg; *Asst Librn,* Debbie Urquhart; E-mail: durquhart@grangeville.us; Staff 2 (Non-MLS 2)
Founded 1899. Pop 3,228; Circ 26,275
Oct 2006-Sept 2007 Income $56,769. Mats Exp $11,420. Sal $20,539
Library Holdings: AV Mats 475; CDs 121; DVDs 82; Large Print Bks 133; Bk Vols 12,235; Per Subs 28; Talking Bks 241
Subject Interests: Genealogy
Automation Activity & Vendor Info: (Cataloging) Ex Libris Group; (Circulation) Ex Libris Group
Database Vendor: EBSCOhost, Gale Cengage Learning
Open Mon-Fri 10-6, Sat 10-2

HAILEY

P HAILEY PUBLIC LIBRARY*, Seven W Croy St, 83333. SAN 303-5778. Tel: 208-788-2036. FAX: 208-788-7646. Web Site: www.haileypubliclibrary.org. *Dir,* LeAnn Gelskey; E-mail: lgelskey@haileypubliclibrary.org; Staff 6 (Non-MLS 6)
Founded 1919. Pop 5,500; Circ 50,500
Library Holdings: Bk Titles 33,000; Bk Vols 34,000; Per Subs 85
Special Collections: Idaho Coll; Mallory Photo Coll - Historical Photographs of Wood River Valley
Automation Activity & Vendor Info: (Cataloging) Horizon; (Circulation) Horizon; (OPAC) Horizon
Database Vendor: EBSCOhost, Gale Cengage Learning, OCLC WorldShare Interlibrary Loan, SirsiDynix
Partic in LYNX! Consortium
Open Mon, Wed, Fri & Sat 10-6, Tues & Thurs 12-8
Friends of the Library Group

HANSEN

P HANSEN DISTRICT LIBRARY*, 120 Maple Ave W, 83334-4975. (Mail add: PO Box 150, 83334-0150), SAN 303-5794. Tel: 208-423-4122. E-mail: hanlib@cableone.net. *Dir,* Linda Oatman; *Librn,* Sarha Berry; Staff 0.55 (Non-MLS 0.55)
Founded 1975. Pop 2,811
Oct 2008-Sept 2009 Income $38,967, County $34,638, County $34,638, Locally Generated Income $4,329, Locally Generated Income $4,329. Mats Exp $8,691, Books $5,341, Books $5,341, AV Mat $350, AV Mat $350. Sal $17,247
Library Holdings: AV Mats 381; CDs 24; DVDs 1,181; Large Print Bks 83; Bk Vols 12,610; Per Subs 27; Talking Bks 75
Function: Accelerated reader prog, Adult literacy prog, Bks on cassette, Bks on CD, Children's prog, Computers for patron use, Free DVD rentals, ILL available, Music CDs, Photocopying/Printing, Prog for adults, Pub access computers, Ref serv available, Summer reading prog, VHS videos, Wheelchair accessible
Open Mon & Fri 1-6, Wed 1-7

HAYDEN

P COMMUNITY LIBRARY NETWORK, Hayden Branch, 8385 N Government Way, 83835-9280. SAN 303-5816. Tel: 208-772-5612. FAX: 208-215-2259. E-mail: hayden@communitylibrary.net. Web Site: www.communitylibrary.net. *Dir,* John W Hartung; *Mgr,* Clydene Blocker; Staff 50 (MLS 4, Non-MLS 46)
Founded 1976. Pop 66,750; Circ 467,000
Library Holdings: Bk Titles 103,500; Per Subs 103
Special Collections: North Idaho Genealogy Coll; North Idaho Land Surveyors Materials
Automation Activity & Vendor Info: (Cataloging) Ex Libris Group; (Circulation) Ex Libris Group; (ILL) Ex Libris Group; (OPAC) Ex Libris Group
Database Vendor: EBSCOhost, Gale Cengage Learning
Wireless access
Function: Adult bk club, Copy machines, Handicapped accessible, ILL available, Mail & tel request accepted, Music CDs, Photocopying/Printing, Preschool outreach, Prog for adults, Prog for children & young adult, Ref serv available, Spoken cassettes & CDs, Summer reading prog, Tax forms, Telephone ref, VHS videos, Video lending libr, Wheelchair accessible
Partic in Cooperative Information Network; WIN Library Network
Open Mon-Thurs 10-8, Fri & Sat 10-5, Sun 12-5
Friends of the Library Group
Branches: 5
ATHOL BRANCH, 30399 Third St, Athol, 83801. (Mail add: PO Box 70, Athol, 83801-0070), SAN 328-2228. Tel: 208-683-2979. FAX: 208-683-2979. *Mgr,* Barbara Broughton; E-mail: barbarab@communitylibrary.net; Staff 3 (Non-MLS 3)
Function: After school storytime, Copy machines, e-mail serv, Handicapped accessible, ILL available, Prog for adults, Prog for children & young adult
Open Mon-Fri 1-6, Sat 12-4
Friends of the Library Group
HARRISON PUBLIC, 111 Coeur d'Alene Ave, Harrison, 83833. (Mail add: PO Box 169, Harrison, 83833-0169), SAN 303-5808. Tel: 208-689-3976. FAX: 208-689-3976. *Mgr,* Dorothy Blackmore; Staff 2 (Non-MLS 2)
Pop 1,200; Circ 10,168
Function: Adult bk club, Copy machines, Handicapped accessible, ILL available, Music CDs, Prog for children & young adult
Open Mon 11-6, Wed 9-4, Sat 11-5, Fri (May-Sept) 1-5
Friends of the Library Group
PINEHURST-KINGSTON BRANCH, 107 Main St, Pinehurst, 83850. (Mail add: PO Box 634, Pinehurst, 83850-0634), SAN 303-6251. Tel: 208-682-3483. FAX: 208-682-3483. E-mail: pinehurst@communitylibrary.net. *Mgr,* Brenda Ludwick; Staff 3 (Non-MLS 3)
Pop 4,100; Circ 35,882
Function: Copy machines, Handicapped accessible, ILL available, Music CDs, Prog for children & young adult, Summer reading prog, Tax forms, VHS videos, Wheelchair accessible
Open Mon 11-8, Tues-Fri 11-5, Sat 11-2
Friends of the Library Group
RATHDRUM BRANCH, 16780 N Hwy 41, Rathdrum, 83858. (Mail add: PO Box 7, Rathdrum, 83858-0007), SAN 303-6359. Tel: 208-687-1029. FAX: 208-687-1029. E-mail: rathdrum@communitylibrary.net. *Mgr,* Sandy Burnett; Staff 4 (Non-MLS 4)
Pop 11,800; Circ 62,828
Function: Adult bk club, Copy machines, Electronic databases & coll, Handicapped accessible, ILL available, Mail & tel request accepted, Music CDs, Photocopying/Printing, Preschool outreach, Prog for adults, Prog for children & young adult, Spoken cassettes & CDs, Spoken cassettes & DVDs, Summer reading prog, Tax forms, Telephone ref, VHS videos, Video lending libr, Wheelchair accessible

Open Mon, Wed & Thurs 10-6, Tues 10-7, Fri 10-5, Sat 10-4
Friends of the Library Group
SPIRIT LAKE BRANCH, 32575 N Fifth Ave, Spirit Lake, 83869. (Mail add: PO Box 186, Spirit Lake, 83869-0186), SAN 328-2260. Tel: 208-623-5353. FAX: 208-623-5353. E-mail: spiritlake@communitylibrary.net. *Mgr,* Kathleen Werthman-Gizdich; Staff 2 (Non-MLS 2)
Pop 5,100; Circ 23,849
Function: Adult bk club, Copy machines, Handicapped accessible, ILL available, Music CDs, Photocopying/Printing, Preschool outreach, Prog for adults, Prog for children & young adult, Spoken cassettes & CDs, Spoken cassettes & DVDs, Summer reading prog, Tax forms, VHS videos, Wheelchair accessible
Open Mon 10-5, Tues-Thurs 1-6, Fri 12-5, Sat 12-4
Friends of the Library Group
Bookmobiles: 1. Mgr, Twylla Rehder

HOMEDALE

P HOMEDALE PUBLIC LIBRARY*, 125 W Owyhee, 83628. (Mail add: PO Box 1087, 83628-1087), SAN 303-5824. Tel: 208-337-4228. *Dir,* Position Currently Open
Founded 1921. Pop 2,619; Circ 8,759
Library Holdings: AV Mats 382; Bk Vols 8,790
Partic in Valley Mountain Library Consortium
Open Mon-Fri 1-5, Sat 1-4

HORSESHOE BEND

P HORSESHOE BEND DISTRICT LIBRARY*, 392 Hwy 55, 83629-9701. SAN 303-5832. Tel: 208-793-2460. FAX: 208-793-2871. E-mail: hsblib@hsb-idaho.com. *Librn,* June Brown; *Asst Librn,* Teresa Cooper
Founded 1917
Library Holdings: Bk Vols 14,000; Per Subs 37
Special Collections: Idaho History Coll
Automation Activity & Vendor Info: (Cataloging) Follett Software; (Circulation) Follett Software
Wireless access
Open Mon-Fri 10-5, Sat 10-12

IDAHO CITY

P BOISE BASIN LIBRARY DISTRICT*, 123 Montgomery St, 83631. SAN 303-5840. Tel: 208-392-4558. FAX: 208-392-4920. Web Site: boisebasin.lili.org. *Dir,* Marcy Rowe; Staff 5 (Non-MLS 5)
Founded 1962. Pop 3,700; Circ 21,009
Library Holdings: CDs 139; Large Print Bks 500; Bk Titles 11,000; Per Subs 24; Talking Bks 337; Videos 409
Special Collections: Boise Basin History Room; History of Idaho City Coll; The Idaho World Coll, photo
Automation Activity & Vendor Info: (Cataloging) Follett Software; (Circulation) Follett Software; (ILL) OCLC; (OPAC) Follett Software; (Serials) EBSCO Online
Database Vendor: EBSCOhost, ProQuest
Wireless access
Function: Homebound delivery serv, ILL available, Online searches, Photocopying/Printing, Prog for adults, Prog for children & young adult, Ref serv available, Summer reading prog, Telephone ref
Open Tues, Wed, Fri & Sat 11-6, Thurs 11-8
Friends of the Library Group
Bookmobiles: 1

IDAHO FALLS

M EASTERN IDAHO REGIONAL MEDICAL CENTER*, Medical Library, PO Box 2077, 83403-2077. SAN 320-636X. Tel: 208-529-6077. FAX: 208-529-7014. Web Site: www.eirmc.com. *Dir,* Kathy Fatkin
Founded 1950
Library Holdings: Bk Vols 500; Per Subs 140
Special Collections: History of Medicine
Subject Interests: Med
Publications: Library News
Open Mon-Fri 8-4:30

J EASTERN IDAHO TECHNICAL COLLEGE*, Richard & Lila J Jordon Library, Alexander Creek Bldg, Rm 551, 1600 S 25th E, 83404. SAN 371-8247. Tel: 208-524-3000, Ext 3312. Toll Free Tel: 800-662-0261. Web Site: www.eitc.edu/library.cfm. *Librn,* Suzanne Ricks; E-mail: suzanne.ricks@my.eitc.edu; Staff 2 (MLS 2)
Founded 1989. Enrl 2,500; Fac 43; Highest Degree: Associate
Jul 2006-Jun 2007 Income $170,810, Locally Generated Income $66,850, Parent Institution $103,960. Sal $91,510 (Prof $39,000)
Library Holdings: AV Mats 590; e-books 2,061; Bk Titles 18,500; Bk Vols 20,000; Per Subs 125; Spec Interest Per Sub 25; Videos 315
Automation Activity & Vendor Info: (Cataloging) SirsiDynix; (Circulation) SirsiDynix; (ILL) OCLC WorldShare Interlibrary Loan; (OPAC) SirsiDynix
Database Vendor: EBSCOhost, infoUSA, LexisNexis, Loislaw, OCLC FirstSearch, OCLC WorldShare Interlibrary Loan, ProQuest, SirsiDynix
Function: Mail loans to mem, Ref serv available, Wheelchair accessible
Partic in Library Consortium of Eastern Idaho
Open Mon-Thurs 7:30am-9pm, Fri 7:30-4:30, Sat 10-2
Restriction: Open to students, fac & staff

P IDAHO FALLS PUBLIC LIBRARY*, 457 W Broadway, 83402. SAN 303-5891. Tel: 208-612-8460. Interlibrary Loan Service Tel: 208-612-8334. Reference Tel: 208-612-8462. Administration Tel: 208-612-8155. Automation Services Tel: 208-612-8198. FAX: 208-612-8467. E-mail: rwright@ifpl.org. Web Site: www.ifpl.org. *Dir,* Robert Wright; E-mail: rwright@ifpl.org; *Adult Serv,* Jenniffer Hentzen; E-mail: jhentzen@ifpl.org; *Ch Serv,* Kim Bryant; E-mail: kimb@ifpl.org; *Tech Serv,* Tracie Chadwick; E-mail: tchadwick@ifpl.org; Staff 5 (MLS 4, Non-MLS 1)
Founded 1909. Pop 105,772; Circ 1,200,006
Library Holdings: Audiobooks 9,576; Braille Volumes 20; CDs 12; DVDs 20,762; e-books 300; Large Print Bks 24,809; Bk Vols 254,863; Per Subs 225; Talking Bks 3,669
Special Collections: Vardis Fisher Coll. State Document Depository
Automation Activity & Vendor Info: (Acquisitions) SirsiDynix; (Cataloging) SirsiDynix; (Circulation) SirsiDynix; (ILL) OCLC; (OPAC) SirsiDynix; (Serials) SirsiDynix
Database Vendor: EBSCOhost, Gale Cengage Learning, OCLC WorldShare Interlibrary Loan, SirsiDynix
Wireless access
Function: Adult bk club, After school storytime, Audiobks via web, Bk club(s), Bks on cassette, Bks on CD, Children's prog, Computers for patron use, Copy machines, Digital talking bks, Electronic databases & coll, Free DVD rentals, Handicapped accessible, Homebound delivery serv, ILL available, Microfiche/film & reading machines, Music CDs, Online cat, Orientations, Outreach serv, OverDrive digital audio bks, Photocopying/Printing, Preschool outreach, Printer for laptops & handheld devices, Prog for adults, Prog for children & young adult, Pub access computers, Ref serv available, Scanner, Story hour, Summer & winter reading prog, Summer reading prog, Teen prog, VHS videos, Web-catalog, Wheelchair accessible, Winter reading prog
Open Mon-Thurs 10-9, Fri & Sat 10-6
Friends of the Library Group

S IDAHO NATIONAL LABORATORY*, Technical Library, 1765 N Yellowstone Hwy, 83415-2300. (Mail add: PO Box 1625, 83415-2300), SAN 303-5859. Tel: 208-526-1185. FAX: 208-526-1697. Web Site: www.inl.gov. *Mgr,* Catherine Plowman; Tel: 208-526-4828; *Coll Develop Librn,* Marie Suhre; Tel: 208-526-1194; Staff 2 (MLS 1, Non-MLS 1)
Founded 1960
Library Holdings: AV Mats 128; e-books 1,604; e-journals 2,479; Bk Titles 33,900; Bk Vols 46,527; Per Subs 400
Subject Interests: Chem, Metallurgy, Nuclear eng, Nuclear sci, Physics
Publications: New Materials List
Partic in Dialog Corp; OCLC Online Computer Library Center, Inc
Open Mon-Fri 8-5

S IDAHO NATIONAL LABORATORY - RESEARCH LIBRARY, 2251 North Blvd, MS 2300, 83415-2300. (Mail add: PO Box 1625, 2525 Fremont Ave, 83415-2300), SAN 303-5875. Tel: 208-526-1185. Interlibrary Loan Service Tel: 208-526-1195. Administration Tel: 208-526-0841. Automation Services Tel: 208-526-1196. FAX: 208-526-0211. E-mail: lib@inl.gov. Web Site: www.inl.gov/library. *Mgr,* Carla Drake; E-mail: Carla.Drake@inl.gov; *Acq, Coll Develop & mgt,* Tam Ellingford; Tel: 208-526-6713, E-mail: Tamara.Ellingford@inl.gov; *ILL,* Tamera Waldron; E-mail: Tamera.Waldron@inl.gov; *Ref,* Jackie Loop; E-mail: Jackie.Loop@inl.gov; Staff 3 (MLS 1, Non-MLS 2)
Founded 1951
Library Holdings: e-books 3,000; e-journals 4,000; Bk Titles 20,000; Per Subs 250
Special Collections: AEC, ERDA & DOE Reports; DOE Public Reading Room: TMI-2 Research & Develop Program Files; Standards & Compliance Information
Subject Interests: Biochem, Chem, Chem eng, Computer sci, Earth sci, Energy, Eng, Environ sci, Geoscience, Mat sci, Math, Mgt, Nuclear eng, Nuclear physics, Nuclear safety, Nuclear sci, Occupational health, Occupational safety, Optics, Physics, Radioactive waste
Automation Activity & Vendor Info: (Cataloging) Ex Libris Group; (Circulation) Ex Libris Group; (OPAC) Ex Libris Group; (Serials) Ex Libris Group
Database Vendor: American Chemical Society, American Physical Society, CRC Press/Taylor & Francis Group, Dialog, Elsevier, HeinOnline, IEEE (Institute of Electrical & Electronics Engineers), IHS, IOP, Knovel, OCLC FirstSearch, Sage, Springer-Verlag, TDNet, Thomson - Web of Science, Wiley InterScience

Wireless access
Restriction: Secured area only open to authorized personnel

JEROME

P JEROME PUBLIC LIBRARY, 100 First Ave E, 83338-2302. SAN 303-5921. Tel: 208-324-5427. FAX: 208-324-6426. Web Site: www.jerome.lili.org. *Dir,* Linda Mecham; Staff 1 (MLS 1)
Founded 1921. Circ 72,300
Library Holdings: Bk Vols 38,000; Per Subs 14
Special Collections: Idaho History Coll; Large Print Coll
Automation Activity & Vendor Info: (Cataloging) SirsiDynix; (Circulation) SirsiDynix
Wireless access
Open Mon-Thurs 9-7, Fri 9-5, Sat 10-5
Friends of the Library Group

KELLOGG

P KELLOGG PUBLIC LIBRARY*, 16 W Market Ave, 83837-2499. SAN 303-593X. Tel: 208-786-7231. FAX: 208-784-1100. E-mail: kellogglibrary@usamedia.tv. *Dir,* Debra Gibler; *Asst Librn,* Jeannie Garnsey
Pop 2,491; Circ 14,533
Library Holdings: Bk Vols 11,500; Per Subs 30
Automation Activity & Vendor Info: (Cataloging) Ex Libris Group; (Circulation) Ex Libris Group; (OPAC) Ex Libris Group
Open Mon 12:30-8, Tues-Fri 12:30-5:30

KETCHUM

P COMMUNITY LIBRARY ASSOCIATION*, 415 Spruce Ave N, 83340. (Mail add: PO Box 2168, 83340-2168), SAN 303-5948. Tel: 208-726-3493. E-mail: info@thecommunitylibrary.org. *Exec Dir,* Cynthia Dillon; *Ch,* DeAnn Campbell; Tel: 208-726-3493, Ext 116; *Circ Coordr,* Pam Parker
Founded 1955. Pop 25,000; Circ 125,000
Library Holdings: AV Mats 12,853; Bk Titles 89,000; Per Subs 164; Talking Bks 5,380
Special Collections: John Lister Coll of Astrology & Occult Sciences; Sun Valley Ski Coll; Wood River Valley Coll, diaries, doc & letters. Oral History
Automation Activity & Vendor Info: (Cataloging) TLC (The Library Corporation); (Circulation) TLC (The Library Corporation); (ILL) TLC (The Library Corporation); (Media Booking) TLC (The Library Corporation)
Wireless access
Open Mon-Sat 10-6
Friends of the Library Group

KIMBERLY

P KIMBERLY PUBLIC LIBRARY, 120 Madison St W, 83341. (Mail add: PO Box 369, 83341-0369), SAN 303-5956. Tel: 208-423-4556. FAX: 208-423-4556. E-mail: kimblib@safelink.net. *Dir,* Helen McCord; Tel: 208-423-4262; *Children's & Youth Serv,* Kerri-Lynn Harris; Tel: 208-212-1565; Staff 1.325 (Non-MLS 1.325)
Founded 1978. Pop 3,216; Circ 31,317
Oct 2012-Sept 2013 Income $61,957, City $57,957, Locally Generated Income $3,000, Other $1,000. Mats Exp $7,715, Books $7,405, Other Print Mats $135, AV Mat $175. Sal $38,461
Library Holdings: Audiobooks 191; CDs 40; DVDs 275; Large Print Bks 66; Bk Titles 16,335; Bk Vols 16,350; Per Subs 25; Videos 200
Special Collections: Idaho Coll; Kipling's Works; Mark Twain Coll; O'Henry Coll; Writings of Abraham Lincoln
Database Vendor: OCLC FirstSearch, OCLC WebJunction, OCLC WorldShare Interlibrary Loan, ProQuest
Wireless access
Function: Accelerated reader prog, After school storytime, AV serv, Bks on cassette, Bks on CD, Children's prog, Computers for patron use, Copy machines, e-mail serv, Free DVD rentals, Handicapped accessible, ILL available, Music CDs, Preschool reading prog, Prog for adults, Prog for children & young adult, Pub access computers, Story hour, Summer & winter reading prog, VHS videos, Wheelchair accessible
Open Mon & Thurs 11-6, Tues 3-8, Wed & Fri 3-6, Sat 10-2

G UNITED STATES DEPARTMENT OF AGRICULTURE*, Agricultural Research Service, Northwest Irrigation & Soils Research Laboratory, 3793 N 3600 E, 83341-5776. SAN 321-771X. Tel: 208-423-5582. FAX: 208-423-6555. Web Site: sand.nwisrl.ars.usda.gov.
Library Holdings: Bk Titles 1,800
Subject Interests: Agr eng, Gen agr, Irrigation, Plants, Pollution, Soils, Water
Open Mon-Fri 8-4:30

KUNA

S IDAHO STATE CORRECTIONAL INSTITUTION LIBRARY*, 13500 S Pleasant Valley Rd, 83634. (Mail add: PO Box 14, Boise, 83707-0014). Tel: 208-424-3733. FAX: 208-424-3731.
Library Holdings: Bk Titles 34,349; Per Subs 32
Open Mon-Fri 8-11, 1-4 & 6-9
Branches:
IDAHO CORRECTIONAL INSTITUTION-OROFINO LIBRARY, 23 Hospital Dr N, Orofino, 83544. Tel: 208-476-3655. FAX: 208-476-4050.
Library Holdings: Bk Vols 2,000; Per Subs 30
Automation Activity & Vendor Info: (Cataloging) Follett Software; (Circulation) Follett Software
Open Mon-Fri 8-4
POCATELLO WOMEN'S CORRECTIONAL CENTER LIBRARY, 1451 Fore Rd, Pocatello, 83204. Tel: 208-236-6360. FAX: 208-236-6362.
Library Holdings: Bk Vols 13,075; Per Subs 19
Automation Activity & Vendor Info: (Cataloging) Follett Software; (Circulation) Follett Software
Open Mon-Fri 8-5
SOUTH BOISE WOMEN'S CORRECTIONAL CENTER LIBRARY, 13200 S Pleasant Valley Rd, 83634. (Mail add: PO Box 8509, Boise, 83707-8509). Tel: 208-424-3733.
Library Holdings: Bk Vols 5,000
Open Mon-Fri 8-11, 1-4 & 5-9
SOUTH IDAHO CORRECTIONAL INSTITUTION LIBRARY, 13900 S Pleasant Valley Rd, 83634. (Mail add: PO Box 8509, Boise, 83707-8509). Tel: 208-424-3733.
Library Holdings: Bk Vols 7,000
Open Mon-Fri 8-11, 1-4 & 5-9

P KUNA COMMUNITY LIBRARY*, 457 N Locust, 83634-1926. (Mail add: PO Box 129, 83634-0129), SAN 303-5964. Tel: 208-922-1025. FAX: 208-922-1026. Web Site: www.lili.org/kuna. *Dir,* Anne Hankins; E-mail: annh_1@yahoo.com
Founded 1964. Pop 12,000; Circ 101,960
Library Holdings: AV Mats 2,600; Bk Vols 68,000; Per Subs 65; Talking Bks 1,350
Subject Interests: Idaho
Automation Activity & Vendor Info: (Cataloging) Follett Software; (Circulation) Follett Software
Open Mon, Fri & Sat 10-5, Tues-Thurs 10-8
Friends of the Library Group

LAPWAI

P PRAIRIE-RIVER LIBRARY DISTRICT*, 103 N Main St, 83540. (Mail add: PO Box 1200, 83540-1200), SAN 339-6517. Tel: 208-843-7254. E-mail: email.riv@valnet.org. Web Site: www.prairieriver.lili.org.
Founded 1959. Pop 14,904; Circ 79,641
Library Holdings: Bk Vols 92,051; Per Subs 50; Talking Bks 1,287; Videos 2,029
Automation Activity & Vendor Info: (Cataloging) Ex Libris Group; (Circulation) Ex Libris Group; (OPAC) Ex Libris Group
Wireless access
Open Mon-Thurs 10-6
Branches: 7
CRAIGMONT COMMUNITY, 112 W Main St, Craigmont, 83523-9700. (Mail add: PO Box 144, Craigmont, 83523-0144), SAN 339-6533. Tel: 208-924-5510. FAX: 208-924-5510. E-mail: email.crg@valnet.org. *Br Mgr,* Gloria Reid
Open Tues-Thurs 10:30-3:30
Friends of the Library Group
CULDESAC COMMUNITY, 714 Main St, Culdesac, 83524-7806, SAN 339-6525. Tel: 208-843-5215. FAX: 208-843-5215. E-mail: email.cul@valnet.org. *Br Mgr, Librn,* Christie Wilson
Open Mon & Wed 12-5:30, Thurs 10-2
Friends of the Library Group
KAMIAH COMMUNITY, 505 Main St, Kamiah, 83536-9702. (Mail add: PO Box 846, Kamiah, 83536-0846), SAN 339-6541. Tel: 208-935-0428. FAX: 208-935-0428. E-mail: email.kam@valnet.org. Web Site: prairieriver.lili.org/node/70. *Br Mgr,* April Blankenship
Database Vendor: Ingram Library Services, Overdrive, Inc
Open Mon & Wed 10-5:30, Tues & Thurs 1-5, Fri 10-3:30
Friends of the Library Group
KOOSKIA COMMUNITY, 026 S Main St, Kooskia, 83539. (Mail add: PO Box 146, Kooskia, 83539-0146), SAN 377-8495. Tel: 208-926-4539. FAX: 208-926-4539. E-mail: email.koo@valnet.org. *Librn,* Dena Puderbaugh
Open Mon, Wed & Fri 12-5, Tues & Thurs 11-4
Friends of the Library Group
NEZPERCE COMMUNITY, 602 Fourth Ave, Nezperce, 83543. (Mail add: PO Box 124, Nezperce, 83543-0124), SAN 321-8902. Tel: 208-937-2458. FAX: 208-937-2458. E-mail: email.nzp@valnet.org. Web Site: nezperce.lili.org. *Br Mgr,* Sharon Harris

Open Mon, Wed & Fri 12-5
Friends of the Library Group
PECK COMMUNITY, 217 N Main St, Peck, 83545. (Mail add: PO Box 112, Peck, 83545-0112), SAN 339-655X. Tel: 208-486-6161. FAX: 208-486-6161. E-mail: email.pec@valnet.org. *Librn,* Doreen Schmidt
Open Mon 12-3, Tues-Thurs 12-3:30
Friends of the Library Group
WINCHESTER COMMUNITY, 314 Nezperce St, Winchester, 83555. (Mail add: PO Box 275, Winchester, 83555-0275). Tel: 208-924-5164. FAX: 208-924-5164. E-mail: email.wnc@valnet.org. *Br Mgr,* Carma Hammon
Open Tues-Thurs 1-6, Sat 9-12
Friends of the Library Group

LEADORE

P LEADORE COMMUNITY LIBRARY*, 202 S Railroad St, 83464-5022. (Mail add: PO Box 106, 83464-0106), SAN 303-5972. Tel: 208-768-2640. E-mail: leadorelibrary@centurytel.net. *Libr Dir,* Jeri Ann Beyeler
Founded 1961. Pop 114; Circ 200
Library Holdings: AV Mats 143; Bk Vols 5,175; Talking Bks 11
Database Vendor: EBSCO Auto Repair Reference, EBSCOhost, Gale Cengage Learning, LearningExpress, OCLC WorldShare Interlibrary Loan, SirsiDynix, World Book Online
Wireless access
Partic in Library Consortium of Eastern Idaho
Open Tues 10-5, Thurs 1-7 (12-6 Winter), Sat 10-2

LEWISTON

C LEWIS-CLARK STATE COLLEGE LIBRARY, 500 Eighth Ave, 83501. SAN 303-5980. Tel: 208-792-2236. Circulation Tel: 208-792-2396. Interlibrary Loan Service Tel: 208-792-2394. FAX: 208-792-2831. Web Site: www.lcsc.edu/library. *Dir,* Susan Niewenhous; Tel: 208-792-2395, E-mail: sniewenh@lcsc.edu; *Coll Mgt, Librn,* Samantha Thompson-Franklin; Tel: 208-792-2557, E-mail: sfranklin@lcsc.edu; *Electronic Res, Librn,* Lynne Bidwell; Tel: 208-792-2438, E-mail: lbidwell@lcsc.edu; *Instruction Librn,* Barbara Barnes; Tel: 208-792-2235, E-mail: blbarnes@lcsc.edu; *Instruction Librn,* Kate Flower; Tel: 208 792-2451, E-mail: klflower@lcsc.edu; *Circ, Pub Serv Librn,* Jennifer Cromer; Tel: 208-792-2829, E-mail: jjcromer@lcsc.edu; *Cat,* Shannon Casteel; Tel: 208-792-2229, E-mail: scasteel@lcsc.edu; *Circ,* Kaitlin Cushman; Tel: 208-792-2833, E-mail: kmcushman@lcsc.edu; *Circ,* Amanda Klone; Tel: 208-792-2830, E-mail: alklone@lcsc.edu; *ILL, Ser,* Becky Grinolds; E-mail: bgrinold@lcsc.edu; Staff 11 (MLS 6, Non-MLS 5)
Founded 1893. Fac 6; Highest Degree: Bachelor
Jul 2010-Jun 2011. Mats Exp $468,400. Sal $568,675
Special Collections: Audio-Visual Coll; Children's Literature; Curriculum Library; Pacific Northwest Coll. US Document Depository
Automation Activity & Vendor Info: (Acquisitions) Ex Libris Group; (Cataloging) Ex Libris Group; (Circulation) Ex Libris Group; (Course Reserve) Ex Libris Group; (ILL) OCLC; (OPAC) Ex Libris Group; (Serials) Ex Libris Group
Database Vendor: BioOne, CQ Press, EBSCOhost, Gale Cengage Learning, Modern Language Association, OCLC WorldShare Interlibrary Loan, Safari Books Online, Standard & Poor's, Westlaw, YBP Library Services
Wireless access
Function: Adult literacy prog
Partic in OCLC Online Computer Library Center, Inc; WIN Library Network
Open Mon-Thurs 8am-9:55pm, Fri 8-5:55, Sat Noon-5:55, Sun Noon-9:55

P LEWISTON CITY LIBRARY*, 428 Thain Rd, 83501-5399. SAN 339-6428. Tel: 208-743-6519. FAX: 208-798-4446. E-mail: library@cityoflewiston.org. Web Site: www.cityoflewiston.org/library. *Dir,* Dawn Wittman; *Cat, Ref, Tech Serv,* Randy Smith; *Ch Serv, YA Serv,* Heather Stout; Staff 8 (MLS 3, Non-MLS 5)
Founded 1901. Pop 30,906; Circ 211,904
Library Holdings: Bk Vols 75,000; Per Subs 128
Special Collections: Genealogy Coll; Idaho Coll
Automation Activity & Vendor Info: (Cataloging) Ex Libris Group; (Circulation) Ex Libris Group; (ILL) OCLC; (OPAC) Ex Libris Group; (Serials) Ex Libris Group
Database Vendor: EBSCO Auto Repair Reference, EBSCO Information Services, Gale Cengage Learning, H W Wilson, OCLC FirstSearch, OCLC WebJunction, OCLC WorldShare Interlibrary Loan, ProQuest
Wireless access
Function: After school storytime, Audiobks via web, Bk club(s), Bks on CD, Children's prog, Computers for patron use, Copy machines, Family literacy, Fax serv, Homebound delivery serv, Magnifiers for reading, Online cat, Preschool outreach, Prog for adults, Prog for children & young adult, Ref serv available, Story hour, Summer reading prog, Tax forms, Teen prog, Telephone ref
Partic in WIN Library Network
Special Services for the Blind - Audio mat; Bks available with recordings; Bks on cassette; Bks on CD; Cassettes; Digital talking bk; Extensive large print coll; Home delivery serv; Large print bks; Large type calculator; Lending of low vision aids; Magnifiers; Volunteer serv
Open Mon-Thurs 9-8, Fri 9-5, Sat 10-5
Friends of the Library Group

LEWISVILLE

P LEWISVILLE LEGACY LIBRARY, 3453 E 480 N, 83431. (Mail add: PO Box 158, 83431-0158). Tel: 208-754-8608. E-mail: lewisvillelibrary@live.com. Web Site: lewisville.lili.org. *Dir,* Merideth McElprang
Pop 467; Circ 1,064
Library Holdings: AV Mats 15; Bk Vols 7,000
Open Mon-Thurs (Winter) 4-6, Sat 10-Noon; Mon, Wed & Sat (Summer) 10-Noon, Tues & Thurs 4-6
Friends of the Library Group

MACKAY

P MACKAY DISTRICT LIBRARY*, 320 Capitol Ave, 83251. (Mail add: PO Box 355, 83251-0355). Tel: 208-588-3333. FAX: 208-588-3333. E-mail: library@atcnet.net. *Dir,* Shirley Olsen
Pop 1,500; Circ 9,000
Library Holdings: Large Print Bks 50; Bk Vols 9,000; Per Subs 12; Talking Bks 300
Automation Activity & Vendor Info: (Cataloging) Follett Software; (Circulation) Follett Software
Open Tues-Thurs 10-12 & 1-5, Fri & Sat 10-1:30

MACKS INN

P FREMONT COUNTY LIBRARY DISTRICT*, Island Park Public Library, 4388 Old Hwy 191, 83433. (Mail add: PO Box 74, 83433-0074). Tel: 208-558-0991. E-mail: Iplibrary1@gmail.com. Web Site: www.fretel.com/~iplibrary/. *Mgr,* Randa Dye
Library Holdings: Bk Vols 7,450
Automation Activity & Vendor Info: (Cataloging) SirsiDynix; (Circulation) SirsiDynix; (OPAC) SirsiDynix
Open Thurs & Fri (Sept-May) 12-5, Sat 11-4; Wed-Fri (June-Aug) 12-5, Sat 11-4
Friends of the Library Group

MALAD CITY

P ONEIDA COUNTY FREE LIBRARY*, 31 N 100 W, 83252-1234. (Mail add: PO Box 185, 83252-0185), SAN 303-6049. Tel: 208-766-2229. FAX: 208-766-2229. E-mail: oclib@atcnet.net. Web Site: www.maladidaho.org/library. *Dir,* Kathy Kent; Staff 3 (Non-MLS 3)
Founded 1954. Pop 3,246; Circ 42,407
Library Holdings: Bk Vols 20,000; Per Subs 50
Special Collections: Local History Coll
Automation Activity & Vendor Info: (Cataloging) Follett Software; (Circulation) Follett Software; (OPAC) Follett Software
Open Mon 11:30-6, Tues-Fri 11:30-5:30, Sat 10-1

MARSING

P LIZARD BUTTE PUBLIC LIBRARY*, 429 Main St, Ste 105, 83639. (Mail add: PO Box 60, 83639-0060), SAN 325-3058. Tel: 208-896-4690. FAX: 208-896-4472. E-mail: lizardbuttelibrary@yahoo.com. *Dir,* Janna Streibel; *YA Serv,* Andrea Pascoe; Staff 2 (Non-MLS 2)
Founded 1982. Pop 10,000
Oct 2005-Sept 2006 Income $41,951. Mats Exp $4,471. Sal $17,000
Library Holdings: Bk Titles 9,000
Database Vendor: EBSCOhost, OCLC FirstSearch
Function: ILL available
Open Mon-Fri 12-6

MCCALL

P MCCALL PUBLIC LIBRARY*, 218 E Park St, 83638. SAN 303-6030. Tel: 208-634-5522. E-mail: library@mccall.id.us. Web Site: www.mccall.lili.org. *Dir,* Anne Kantola; Staff 6 (MLS 2, Non-MLS 4)
Founded 1930. Pop 2,520
Library Holdings: Bk Titles 35,000; Per Subs 54
Special Collections: Building Trades; Idaho History Coll; Nature Studies Coll; Valley County Historical Coll
Subject Interests: Health promotion
Automation Activity & Vendor Info: (Cataloging) OCLC
Open Mon-Fri 10-6, Sat 11-3
Friends of the Library Group

MENAN

P JEFFERSON COUNTY DISTRICT LIBRARY*, Menan-Annis Public Library, 623A N 3500 E, 83434. SAN 377-4988. Tel: 208-754-0021. E-mail: menanlibrary@gmail.com. *Dir,* Laurie Willmore; Staff 3 (Non-MLS 3)
Founded 1972
Oct 2005-Sept 2006. Mats Exp $7,000
Library Holdings: Bk Titles 11,921; Per Subs 25
Automation Activity & Vendor Info: (Cataloging) Follett Software; (Circulation) Follett Software
Wireless access
Partic in Library Consortium of Eastern Idaho
Open Mon (Winter) 1-7, Tues, Thurs & Fri 1-5, Wed 10-5; Mon (Summer) 4-7, Tues-Fri 9-1
Friends of the Library Group
Branches: 2
HAMER BRANCH, 2450 E 2100 North, Hamer, 83425. (Mail add: PO Box 240, Hamer, 83425-0240), SAN 303-5786. Tel: 208-662-5275. FAX: 208-662-5213. E-mail: jldham@mudlake.net. Web Site: www.hamer.lili.org. *Dir,* Ethel Vadnais; *Asst Librn,* Rose Dixon
Founded 1972. Pop 800
Library Holdings: AV Mats 800; Bk Titles 15,000; Bk Vols 15,500; Per Subs 20; Talking Bks 500
Special Collections: Oral History
Automation Activity & Vendor Info: (Cataloging) SirsiDynix; (Circulation) SirsiDynix; (OPAC) SirsiDynix
Function: ILL available
Publications: Sands of Time - Desert in Bloom
Open Mon-Fri (Sept-May) 9-4; Tues & Wed (June-Aug) 9-4, Thurs 11-5
Friends of the Library Group
HEART OF THE VALLEY BRANCH, 1252 E 1500 N, Terreton, 83450. (Mail add: PO Box 45, Terreton, 83450-0045), SAN 377-5429. Tel: 208-663-4834. FAX: 208-663-4834. E-mail: hvpl@mudlake.net. Web Site: www.dcdi.net/~hvpl. *Dir,* Elaine Davies
Library Holdings: Bk Vols 21,000
Automation Activity & Vendor Info: (Cataloging) SirsiDynix; (Circulation) SirsiDynix; (OPAC) SirsiDynix
Open Mon, Tues, Thurs & Fri (Winter) 8-4, Wed 12:30-7; Tues & Thurs (Summer) 10-5, Wed 1-7
Friends of the Library Group

MERIDIAN

P MERIDIAN LIBRARY DISTRICT, 1326 W Cherry Lane, 83642. SAN 303-6057. Tel: 208-888-4451. FAX: 208-884-0745. Web Site: www.mld.org. *Libr Dir,* Gretchen Caserotti; E-mail: director@mld.org; *Mgr, Mat Serv,* Cheri Rendler; *Outreach Mgr,* Audra Green; *Pub Serv Mgr,* Natalie Nation; *Youth Serv Mgr,* Megan Egbert
Founded 1924. Pop 86,203; Circ 1,020,891
Automation Activity & Vendor Info: (Cataloging) Horizon; (Circulation) Horizon; (OPAC) Horizon
Database Vendor: EBSCOhost, Newsbank, OCLC WorldShare Interlibrary Loan, ProQuest, WebMD, World Book Online
Wireless access
Partic in LYNX! Consortium
Open Mon-Thurs 9-8, Fri 9-6, Sat 10-5
Friends of the Library Group
Branches: 1
SILVERSTONE BRANCH, 3531 E Overland Rd, 83642. Tel: 208-884-2616. *Br Mgr,* Travis Porter
Open Mon-Thurs 9-8, Fri 9-6, Sat 10-5, Sun 1-5
Bookmobiles: 1

MIDDLETON

P MIDDLETON PUBLIC LIBRARY*, 307 Cornell St, 83644. SAN 303-6065. Tel: 208-585-3931. *Dir,* Elaine Mathiasen; Staff 3 (Non-MLS 3)
Founded 1960. Pop 5,500
Library Holdings: Bk Vols 20,000; Per Subs 10
Automation Activity & Vendor Info: (ILL) Surpass
Wireless access
Mem of South Central Library System
Open Tues 10:30-8, Wed-Fri 10:30-5:30, Sat 10-4
Friends of the Library Group

MIDVALE

P MIDVALE DISTRICT LIBRARY*, 70 E Bridge St, 83645-2012. (Mail add: PO Box 127, 83645-0127), SAN 303-6073. Tel: 208-355-2213. E-mail: mcl@mtecom.net. *Dir,* Myrna Weikal
Founded 1976. Pop 800; Circ 10,606
Library Holdings: Bk Titles 12,038
Special Collections: Idaho Authors & History, bks & pamphlets. Oral History
Automation Activity & Vendor Info: (Cataloging) Follett Software
Open Mon-Thurs 1-5

MONTPELIER

P BEAR LAKE COUNTY FREE LIBRARY*, 138 N Sixth St, 83254-1556. SAN 303-609X. Tel: 208-847-1664. FAX: 208-847-1664. E-mail: blkcolib@dcdi.net. Web Site: bearlake.lili.org, www.lili.org/bearlake. *Dir,* Mary Nate
Founded 1959. Pop 7,250
Library Holdings: Bk Vols 60,000; Per Subs 120
Automation Activity & Vendor Info: (Cataloging) SirsiDynix; (Circulation) SirsiDynix; (OPAC) SirsiDynix
Open Mon-Thurs 11-7, Fri 9-5, Sat 9-2
Branches: 1
PARIS BRANCH, 62 S Main, Paris, 83261. (Mail add: PO Box 364, Paris, 83261-0364). Tel: 208-945-2253. FAX: 208-945-1327. *Librn,* David Matthews
Pop 7,250
Library Holdings: Bk Vols 5,000
Open Mon, Wed & Fri 1-5

MOSCOW

S APPALOOSA MUSEUM & HERITAGE CENTER*, Appaloosa Museum Library, 2720 W Pullman Rd, 83843. SAN 376-0820. Tel: 208-882-5578, Ext 279. FAX: 208-882-8150. E-mail: museum@appaloosa.com. Web Site: www.appaloosamuseum.org. *Dir,* Jennifer Hamilton; Tel: 208-882-5578, E-mail: museum@appaloosa.com
Library Holdings: AV Mats 40; Bk Titles 400
Open Mon-Thurs 12-5, Fri 10-5, Sat 10-4

S LATAH COUNTY HISTORICAL SOCIETY LIBRARY*, 327 E Second St, 83843. SAN 303-6103. Tel: 208-882-1004. FAX: 208-882-0759. E-mail: lchlibrary@moscow.com. Web Site: users.moscow.com/lchs. *Dir,* Daniel Crandall; *Curator,* Dulce Kersting
Founded 1968
Library Holdings: Bk Titles 450; Per Subs 500
Special Collections: Carol Ryrie Brink Coll (letters, interviews, photos, mss); Historic Preservation Coll; Psychiana Papers; Washington, Idaho & Montana Railroad Paper. Oral History
Publications: Guide to Historical & Genealogical Records in Latah County; Guide to the Latah County Oral History Collection; Guide to the Local History Library at the Latah County Historical Society; Latah Legacy (Quarterly); Newsletter (Quarterly)
Open Tues-Fri 9-5
Restriction: Not a lending libr

P LATAH COUNTY LIBRARY DISTRICT*, 110 S Jefferson, 83843-2833. SAN 339-6576. Tel: 208-882-3925. FAX: 208-882-5098. E-mail: moscow@latahlibrary.org. Web Site: www.latahlibrary.org. *Dir,* Anne Cheadle; E-mail: annec@latahlibrary.org; *Outreach Serv Librn,* Betsy Bybell; E-mail: betsyb@latahlibrary.org; *Mgr, Access Serv,* George Williams; *Bus & Human Res Mgr,* Carol Kampenhout; E-mail: carolk@latahlibrary.org; *Adult Serv,* Chris Sokol; E-mail: chriss@latahlibrary.org; *Ch Serv,* Cathy Ensley; E-mail: cathye@latahlibrary.org; *Tech Serv,* Jeannie Haag; E-mail: jeannieh@latahlibrary.org; Staff 7 (MLS 1, Non-MLS 6)
Founded 1901. Pop 35,000; Circ 235,000
Library Holdings: Bk Vols 98,518; Per Subs 237
Subject Interests: Local hist, Sci fict
Wireless access
Friends of the Library Group
Branches: 6
BOVILL BRANCH, 310 First Ave, Bovill, 83806. (Mail add: PO Box 210, Bovill, 83806-0210), SAN 371-3644. Tel: 208-826-3451. FAX: 208-826-3451. E-mail: bovill@latahlibrary.org. *Br Mgr,* Paula Winter
Library Holdings: Bk Vols 2,500
Friends of the Library Group
DEARY BRANCH, 304 Second Ave, Deary, 83823. (Mail add: PO Box 213, Deary, 83823-0213), SAN 339-6592. Tel: 208-877-1664. FAX: 208-877-1664. E-mail: deary@latahlibrary.org. *Br Mgr,* Debbie Fischer
Library Holdings: Bk Vols 5,000
Friends of the Library Group
GENESEE BRANCH, 140 E Walnut St, Genesee, 83832. (Mail add: PO Box 278, Genesee, 83832-0278), SAN 339-6606. Tel: 208-285-1398. FAX: 208-285-1398. E-mail: genesee@latahlibrary.org. *Br Mgr,* Sharon Steiger
Library Holdings: Bk Vols 5,000
Friends of the Library Group
JULIAETTA BRANCH, 205 Main St, Juliaetta, 83535. (Mail add: PO Box 471, Juliaetta, 83535-0470), SAN 339-6630. Tel: 208-276-7071. FAX: 208-276-7071. E-mail: juliaetta@latahlibrary.org. *Br Mgr,* Janice Welles
Library Holdings: Bk Vols 5,000
Friends of the Library Group

POTLATCH BRANCH, 1010 Onaway Rd, Potlatch, 83855. (Mail add: PO Box 335, Potlatch, 83855-0335), SAN 339-6665. Tel: 208-875-1036. FAX: 208-875-1036. E-mail: potlatch@latahlibrary.org. *Br Mgr,* Donna Quiring; E-mail: donnaq@latahlibrary.org
Library Holdings: Bk Vols 5,000
Friends of the Library Group

TROY BRANCH, 402 S Main St, Troy, 83871. (Mail add: PO Box 477, Troy, 83871-0477), SAN 339-669X. Tel: 208-835-4311. FAX: 208-835-4311. E-mail: troy@latahlibrary.org. *Br Supvr,* Margie Fitzmorris; E-mail: margief@latahlibrary.org
Library Holdings: Bk Vols 5,000
Friends of the Library Group

C UNIVERSITY OF IDAHO LIBRARY, Rayburn St, 83844. (Mail add: PO Box 442350, 83844-2350), SAN 339-672X. Tel: 208-885-6534. Circulation Tel: 208-885-6559. Interlibrary Loan Service Tel: 208-885-6843. Reference Tel: 208-885-6235, 208-885-6584. FAX: 208-885-6817. Web Site: www.lib.uidaho.edu. *Dean, Univ Libr,* Dr Lynn Baird; Fax: 208-885-7070, E-mail: lbaird@uidaho.edu; *Assoc Dean & Head, Tech Serv,* Benjamin Hunter; Tel: 208-885-5813, E-mail: bhunter@uidaho.edu; *Head, Govt Doc,* Ramirose Attebury; Tel: 208-885-2503, E-mail: rattebur@uidaho.edu; *Head, Spec Coll & Archives,* Dr Garth Reese; E-mail: garthr@uidaho.edu; *Head, User & Res Serv,* Rick Stoddart; Tel: 208-885-2504, E-mail: rstoddart@uidaho.edu; *Ref & Instrul Serv, Instr Coordr,* Diane Prorak; Tel: 208-885-2508, E-mail: prorak@uidaho.edu; *Ref Coordr,* Rochelle Smith; E-mail: rsmith@uidaho.edu; Staff 40 (MLS 17, Non-MLS 23)
Founded 1889. Enrl 10,764; Fac 871; Highest Degree: Doctorate
Jul 2011-Jun 2012 Income (Main Library Only) $5,639,326, State $5,437,175, Locally Generated Income $179,626, Other $22,525. Mats Exp $3,012,557. Sal $169,949 (Prof $790,634)
Library Holdings: AV Mats 10,728; e-books 30,039; e-journals 36,378; Microforms 2,549,720; Music Scores 13,613; Bk Titles 996,320; Bk Vols 1,283,419
Special Collections: Ezra Pound Coll; Idaho History (Day-Northwest Coll); Idaho State Publications; Imprints (Caxton Printers, Idaho); International Jazz Coll; Sir Walter Scott Coll. Oral History; State Document Depository; US Document Depository
Subject Interests: Mining, Natural res
Automation Activity & Vendor Info: (Acquisitions) Ex Libris Group; (Cataloging) OCLC; (Circulation) Ex Libris Group; (ILL) OCLC Online; (OPAC) OCLC WorldShare Interlibrary Loan; (Serials) Ex Libris Group
Database Vendor: Agricola, Alexander Street Press, American Chemical Society, American Psychological Association (APA), Annual Reviews, ARTstor, ASCE Research Library, BioOne, Blackwell, Cambridge Scientific Abstracts, EBSCOhost, Elsevier, Gale Cengage Learning, H W Wilson, HeinOnline, Ingram Library Services, IOP, ISI Web of Knowledge, JSTOR, Knovel, LexisNexis, Marcive, Inc, Marquis Who's Who, McGraw-Hill, Medline, Modern Language Association, Nature Publishing Group, Newsbank, OCLC ArticleFirst, OCLC FirstSearch, OCLC WorldShare Interlibrary Loan, Oxford Online, Project MUSE, ProQuest, PubMed, Sage, ScienceDirect, SerialsSolutions, Thomson - Web of Science, Westlaw, Wilson - Wilson Web
Wireless access
Function: Archival coll, Art exhibits, Audio & video playback equip for onsite use, Bus archives, CD-ROM, Computers for patron use, Copy machines, Distance learning, Doc delivery serv, e-mail & chat, e-mail serv, E-Reserves, Electronic databases & coll, Exhibits, For res purposes, Free DVD rentals, Govt ref serv, Handicapped accessible, Homework prog, ILL available, Jazz prog, Music CDs, Online cat, Online info literacy tutorials on the web & in blackboard, Online ref, Online searches, Orientations, Outreach serv, Outside serv via phone, mail, e-mail & web, Photocopying/Printing, Prog for adults, Ref & res, Ref serv available, Ref serv in person, Res libr, Tax forms, Telephone ref, VHS videos, Web-catalog, Wheelchair accessible
Publications: Towers
Partic in Orbis Cascade Alliance
Special Services for the Blind - Reader equip
Restriction: In-house use for visitors, Non-circulating of rare bks
Friends of the Library Group

Departmental Libraries:

CL COLLEGE OF LAW, 711 Rayburn St, 83844. (Mail add: 875 Perimeter Dr, PO Box 442324, 83844-2324). Tel: 208-885-6521. Interlibrary Loan Service Tel: 208-885-2159. Reference Tel: 208-885-5899. FAX: 208-885-2743. E-mail: lawlib@uidaho.edu. Web Site: www.uidaho.edu/law/library. *Dir,* John Hasko; E-mail: jhasko@uidaho.edu; *Head, Pub Serv,* Diana Gleason; Tel: 208-885-2161, E-mail: dgleason@uidaho.edu; *Head, Tech Serv,* Ruth Funabiki; E-mail: funabiki@uidaho.edu; *Ref & Coll Develop Librn,* Jean Mattimoe; Tel: 208-885-2162, E-mail: mattimoe@uidaho.edu; Staff 9 (MLS 4, Non-MLS 5)
Founded 1914. Enrl 360; Fac 33; Highest Degree: Doctorate
Jul 2010-Jun 2011 Income $1,714,934. Mats Exp $1,080,253. Sal $474,643 (Prof $287,906)
Library Holdings: Bk Titles 41,274; Bk Vols 250,747
Special Collections: Idaho Supreme Court Briefs. US Document Depository
Subject Interests: Native Am law, Natural res, Trial practice
Function: Ref serv available
Open Mon-Thurs 7:30am-10pm, Fri 7:30am-9pm, Sat 12-5, Sun 12-10
Restriction: Badge access after hrs

MOUNTAIN HOME

P MOUNTAIN HOME PUBLIC LIBRARY*, 790 N Tenth E, 83647-2830. SAN 303-6111. Tel: 208-587-4716. FAX: 208-587-6645. Web Site: www.mhlibrary.org. *Dir,* Luise House
Pop 8,533; Circ 39,518
Library Holdings: Bk Vols 32,480; Per Subs 70
Wireless access
Partic in LYNX! Consortium
Open Mon-Fri 10-7, Sat 9-5

MOUNTAIN HOME AFB

A UNITED STATES AIR FORCE, Mountain Home Air Force Base Library FL4897, 366 FSS/FSDL, 480 Fifth Ave, Ste 100, 83648. SAN 339-6789. Tel: 208-828-2326. FAX: 208-832-9840. E-mail: 366msg/baselibrary@us.af.mil. Web Site: www.mhafbfun.com. *Libr Dir,* Debbie Worthington; Staff 3.65 (MLS 1.25, Non-MLS 2.4)
Founded 1952
Library Holdings: Bk Vols 39,540
Subject Interests: Aeronaut, Idaho, Mil hist
Automation Activity & Vendor Info: (Cataloging) SirsiDynix; (Circulation) SirsiDynix; (ILL) OCLC WorldShare Interlibrary Loan; (OPAC) SirsiDynix; (Serials) SirsiDynix
Wireless access
Partic in OCLC Online Computer Library Center, Inc
Open Tues-Thurs 10-7, Fri 10-6, Sat 12-5

MULLAN

P MULLAN PUBLIC LIBRARY*, 117 Hunter Ave, 83846. (Mail add: PO Box 479, 83846-0479), SAN 303-612X. Tel: 208-744-1220. FAX: 208-744-1220. *Librn,* Barbara Baillie; *Asst Librn,* Linda Emerson; Staff 2 (Non-MLS 2)
Founded 1950. Pop 840; Circ 1,850
Library Holdings: AV Mats 600; Bk Vols 7,000
Open Mon 3-7, Wed & Fri 12-5:30
Friends of the Library Group

MURPHY

S OWYHEE COUNTY HISTORICAL SOCIETY*, Museum & Library Complex, 17085 Basey St, 83650. (Mail add: PO Box 67, 83650-0067), SAN 303-6138. Tel: 208-495-2319. FAX: 208-495-9824. E-mail: administration@owyheemuseum.org. Web Site: www.owyheemuseum.org. *Dir,* Thomas Couch
Founded 1960
Library Holdings: Bk Titles 1,000; Per Subs 13; Talking Bks 30
Special Collections: Newspaper (Owyhee Avalanche, Silver City), micro. Oral History; State Document Depository
Subject Interests: Archaeology, Genealogy, Geol, Hist, Mining
Publications: Owyhee Outpost (Annual historical book)
Open Tues-Sat 10-4
Restriction: Open to pub for ref only
Friends of the Library Group

NAMPA

M MERCY MEDICAL CENTER*, W B Ross Health Sciences Library, 1512 12th Avenue Rd, 83686. Tel: 208-463-5199. FAX: 208-463-5190. *Librn,* Adrianne Yoder
Library Holdings: Bk Vols 1,300; Per Subs 252
Open Mon-Fri 7:30-4

P NAMPA PUBLIC LIBRARY*, 101 11th Ave S, 83651. SAN 303-6146. Tel: 208-468-5800. FAX: 208-318-0530. E-mail: info@nampalibrary.org. Web Site: www.nampalibrary.org. *Dir,* Mark Rose; Tel: 208-468-5805, E-mail: mark@nampalibrary.org; *Pub Serv Dir,* Deborah Babbitt; Tel: 208-468-5814, E-mail: dbabbitt@nampalibrary.org; *Operations Mgr,* Claire Connley; Tel: 208-468-5806, E-mail: connleyc@nampalibrary.org; *Cat,* Beth Neunaber; Tel: 208-468-5807, E-mail: beth@nampalibrary.org; *Circ,* Vicki Oldham; Tel: 208-468-5812, E-mail: voldham@nampalibrary.org; Staff 23 (MLS 5, Non-MLS 18)
Founded 1904. Pop 83,000; Circ 749,000
Library Holdings: Audiobooks 10,161; AV Mats 8,142; e-books 500; Bk Vols 93,561; Per Subs 173
Special Collections: Local History Coll

Automation Activity & Vendor Info: (Acquisitions) SirsiDynix; (Cataloging) SirsiDynix; (Circulation) SirsiDynix; (ILL) OCLC Online; (OPAC) SirsiDynix; (Serials) SirsiDynix
Database Vendor: SirsiDynix
Wireless access
Function: Children's prog, Computer training
Partic in LYNX! Consortium
Open Mon-Thurs 10-7, Fri 10-6, Sat 10-5
Friends of the Library Group

C NORTHWEST NAZARENE UNIVERSITY*, John E Riley Library, 804 E Dewey St, 83686. (Mail add: 623 S University Blvd, 83686). Circulation Tel: 208-467-8607. Interlibrary Loan Service Tel: 208-467-8605. Reference Tel: 208-467-8611. FAX: 208-467-8610. E-mail: library@nnu.edu. Web Site: www.nnu.edu/library. *Dir, Libr & Archives,* Dr Sharon Bull; Tel: 208-467-8609, E-mail: sibull@nnu.edu; *Cat & Syst Librn,* Position Currently Open; *Instrul Serv Librn,* LaRita Schandorff; Tel: 208-467-8606, E-mail: llschandorff@nnu.edu; *Pub Serv Librn,* Position Currently Open; *Circ Supvr,* Deanna Wilde; Tel: 208-467-8614, E-mail: dwilde@nnu.edu; *Tech Serv Supvr,* Coral Mattei; E-mail: clmattei@nnu.edu; *Libr Tech,* Carol Poe; Tel: 208-467-8616, E-mail: cjpoe@nnu.edu; Staff 4 (MLS 4)
Founded 1913. Enrl 2,020; Highest Degree: Master
Library Holdings: Bk Titles 112,250; Bk Vols 174,533; Per Subs 855
Automation Activity & Vendor Info: (Cataloging) Innovative Interfaces, Inc; (Circulation) Innovative Interfaces, Inc; (ILL) Clio; (OPAC) Innovative Interfaces, Inc; (Serials) Innovative Interfaces, Inc
Database Vendor: Alexander Street Press, Children's Literature Comprehensive Database Company (CLCD), College Source, CQ Press, CredoReference, ebrary, EBSCOhost, Gale Cengage Learning, Innovative Interfaces, Inc, JSTOR, LexisNexis, Newsbank, OCLC FirstSearch, OCLC WorldShare Interlibrary Loan, ProQuest, RefWorks, SerialsSolutions, Springshare, LLC
Wireless access
Open Mon-Thurs 8am-11pm, Fri 8-5, Sat 11-5, Sun 8pm-11pm
Restriction: Open to pub for ref & circ; with some limitations

NEW MEADOWS

P MEADOWS VALLEY PUBLIC LIBRARY DISTRICT*, 400 Virginia St, 83654. (Mail add: PO Box 436, 83654-0436), SAN 303-6162. Tel: 208-347-3147. FAX: 208-347-4121. E-mail: mvpl@frontiernet.net. Web Site: www.lili.org/meadows. *Dir,* Audrey Crogh
Founded 1999. Pop 940
Library Holdings: Large Print Bks 35; Bk Vols 11,000; Talking Bks 500
Automation Activity & Vendor Info: (Cataloging) Follett Software; (Circulation) Follett Software
Partic in Valley Mountain Library Consortium
Special Services for the Blind - Braille bks; Descriptive video serv (DVS); Large print bks; Talking bks
Open Mon-Fri 11-6, Sat 11-2
Friends of the Library Group

NEW PLYMOUTH

P ARMORAL TUTTLE PUBLIC LIBRARY, 301 N Plymouth Ave, 83655. (Mail add: PO Box 158, 83655-0158), SAN 303-6170. Tel: 208-278-5338. FAX: 208-278-5330. E-mail: npl@cableone.net. *Librn,* Amy Gibbons
Founded 1916. Pop 1,186; Circ 11,810
Library Holdings: Large Print Bks 319; Bk Vols 9,361; Talking Bks 206
Automation Activity & Vendor Info: (Cataloging) Follett Software; (Circulation) Follett Software
Open Tues-Fri 10-6

OAKLEY

P OAKLEY LIBRARY DISTRICT*, 185 E Main, 83346. SAN 303-6197. Tel: 208-862-3434. E-mail: oaklib@pmt.org. *Libr Dir,* Pamelia Jenks; *Asst Librn,* Theresa Jenks
Founded 1973. Pop 1,500
Library Holdings: Bk Vols 9,884
Special Collections: Idaho History Coll
Automation Activity & Vendor Info: (Acquisitions) DEMCO; (Cataloging) OCLC Connexion; (Circulation) JayWil Software Development, Inc; (ILL) OCLC FirstSearch
Database Vendor: JayWil Software Development, Inc
Wireless access
Publications: Dusty Memories; History of the Latter Day Saints Community of Oakley; My Book & Me; The Twin Falls-Oakley Irrigation Project
Open Tues, Thurs & Sat 2-6

OROFINO

P CLEARWATER MEMORIAL PUBLIC LIBRARY*, 402 Michigan Ave, 83544. (Mail add: PO Box 471, 83544-0471), SAN 303-6200. Tel: 208-476-3411. FAX: 208-476-4527. E-mail: email.cmp@valnet.org. Web Site: www.orofinolibrary.org. *Dir,* Ellen Tomlinson; Staff 5 (MLS 1, Non-MLS 4)
Founded 1949. Pop 8,446; Circ 47,371
Library Holdings: AV Mats 646; Bks on Deafness & Sign Lang 12; Electronic Media & Resources 16; Bk Titles 33,630; Per Subs 75; Talking Bks 692
Special Collections: Lewis & Clark Coll; Pacific Northwest
Automation Activity & Vendor Info: (Cataloging) OCLC; (Circulation) LibLime
Wireless access
Special Services for the Blind - Talking bks
Open Mon-Fri 9-6, Sat 9-2
Friends of the Library Group
Bookmobiles: 1

OSBURN

P OSBURN PUBLIC LIBRARY*, 921 E Mullan, 83849. (Mail add: PO Box 809, 83849-0809), SAN 303-6219. Tel: 208-752-9711. FAX: 208-753-8585. E-mail: osburnpubliclibrary@usamedia.tv. Web Site: www.osburn.lili.org. *Dir,* Phyllis Keenan
Founded 1960. Pop 1,545; Circ 9,700
Oct 2009-Sept 2010 Income $33,511, State $8,662, City $22,036, Locally Generated Income $2,813. Mats Exp $3,353. Sal $22,950
Library Holdings: AV Mats 340; Bk Vols 9,400; Per Subs 20; Talking Bks 96
Automation Activity & Vendor Info: (Cataloging) Ex Libris Group; (Circulation) Ex Libris Group; (OPAC) Ex Libris Group
Open Mon & Wed (Winter) 12-8, Tues, Thurs & Fri 12-5; Mon & Wed (Summer) 11-8, Tues & Thurs 11-5
Friends of the Library Group

PARMA

P PATRICIA ROMANKO PUBLIC LIBRARY*, 121 N Third St, 83660. (Mail add: PO Box 309, 83660-0309), SAN 303-6227. Tel: 208-722-6605. E-mail: parmaromankolibrary@yahoo.com. *Librn,* Jack Jordan
Pop 3,138; Circ 9,614
Library Holdings: Bk Titles 18,900
Subject Interests: Idaho
Automation Activity & Vendor Info: (Cataloging) Follett Software; (Circulation) Follett Software
Partic in Idaho Libr Asn
Open Mon & Tues 12:30-8, Wed 11-6, Fri 12:30-5:30, Sat 9-1

PAYETTE

P PAYETTE PUBLIC LIBRARY*, 24 S Tenth St, 83661-2861. SAN 303-6235. Tel: 208-642-6029. FAX: 208-642-6046. E-mail: payettelib@cableone.net. *Dir,* Colleen Bonnell; Staff 3 (Non-MLS 3)
Founded 1920. Pop 6,170; Circ 36,755
Library Holdings: Bk Vols 40,800; Per Subs 88
Special Collections: Northwest Coll
Open Mon-Wed 10-7, Thurs & Fri 10-5:30, Sat 10-2
Friends of the Library Group

PIERCE

P PIERCE DISTRICT LIBRARY*, 208 S Main St, 83546. (Mail add: PO Box 386, 83546-0386), SAN 303-6243. Tel: 208-464-2823. FAX: 208-464-2823. Web Site: www.piercepubliclibrary.com/. *Dir,* Kim Ward; E-mail: kward@piercepubliclibrary.com
Founded 1919. Pop 1,000; Circ 13,899
Library Holdings: Bk Titles 14,945; Per Subs 51
Special Collections: Local History Artifacts
Automation Activity & Vendor Info: (Cataloging) Ex Libris Group; (Circulation) Ex Libris Group; (OPAC) Ex Libris Group
Open Mon-Thurs 10-6, Fri 11-5

PLUMMER

P PLUMMER PUBLIC LIBRARY, 800 D St, 83851. (Mail add: PO Box 309, 83851-0309). Tel: 208-686-1812. FAX: 208-686-1084. *Dir,* Paulina Freeburg
Library Holdings: Bk Vols 17,000; Per Subs 12
Automation Activity & Vendor Info: (Cataloging) Baker & Taylor; (Circulation) Baker & Taylor; (OPAC) Baker & Taylor
Wireless access
Open Mon-Wed 10-6, Thurs 2-6, Sat 10-2
Friends of the Library Group

POCATELLO

C IDAHO STATE UNIVERSITY*, Eli M Oboler Library, 850 S Ninth Ave, 83209-8089. (Mail add: 921 S Eighth Ave, Stop 8089, 83209-8089), SAN 303-6294. Tel: 208-282-2958. Circulation Tel: 208-282-3248. Interlibrary Loan Service Tel: 208-282-3127. Reference Tel: 208-282-3152.

Administration Tel: 208-282-2997. Toll Free Tel: 800-314-4781. FAX: 208-282-5847. Interlibrary Loan Service FAX: 208-282-4687. E-mail: refdesk@isu.edu. Web Site: www.isu.edu/library. *Dean & Univ Librn,* Sandra Shropshire; Tel: 208-282-2671, E-mail: shrosand@isu.edu; *Dir, Health Sci Libr,* Marcia Francis; Tel: 208-282-4182, Fax: 208-282-4295, E-mail: franmarc@isu.edu; *Interim Assoc Univ Librn, Pub Serv,* Jenny Semenza; Tel: 208-282-2581, E-mail: semmjenn@isu.edu; *Asst Univ Librn, Syst,* Janet Warnke; Tel: 208-282-2697, E-mail: higgjane@isu.edu; *Head, Spec Coll,* Karen Kearns; Tel: 208-282-3608, E-mail: kearkare@isu.edu; *Coordr, Instruction,* Spencer Jardine; Tel: 208-282-5609, E-mail: jardspen@isu.edu. Subject Specialists: *Archit, Art, English,* Sandra Shropshire; Staff 39 (MLS 15, Non-MLS 24)
Founded 1902. Enrl 14,664; Fac 621; Highest Degree: Doctorate
Jul 2009-Jun 2010 Income (Main and Other College/University Libraries) $4,997,306, State $4,791,602, Locally Generated Income $205,704. Mats Exp $4,763,044, Books $368,331, Per/Ser (Incl. Access Fees) $1,886,540, Other Print Mats $54,040, AV Mat $11,776, Electronic Ref Mat (Incl. Access Fees) $597,018, Presv $24,910. Sal $1,699,201 (Prof $857,898)
Library Holdings: Audiobooks 1,282; AV Mats 4,370; CDs 3,202; DVDs 653; e-books 741; e-journals 5,855; Microforms 2,004,535; Bk Titles 516,208; Bk Vols 541,668; Per Subs 8,185; Videos 2,435
Special Collections: Book Arts; Childrens' Readers; Early English Dictionaries; Elocution Coll; Samuel Johnson Coll. State Document Depository; US Document Depository
Subject Interests: Health sci, Law
Automation Activity & Vendor Info: (Acquisitions) Ex Libris Group; (Cataloging) Ex Libris Group; (Circulation) Ex Libris Group; (Course Reserve) Ex Libris Group; (ILL) Ex Libris Group; (Media Booking) Ex Libris Group; (OPAC) Ex Libris Group; (Serials) Ex Libris Group
Wireless access
Function: Archival coll, Distance learning, Doc delivery serv, For res purposes, Govt ref serv, Handicapped accessible, Health sci info serv, ILL available, Newsp ref libr, Online searches, Photocopying/Printing, Ref serv available, Telephone ref, Wheelchair accessible, Workshops
Publications: Between-the-Lines (Newsletter)
Partic in OCLC Online Computer Library Center, Inc
Special Services for the Deaf - Assistive tech
Special Services for the Blind - Assistive/Adapted tech devices, equip & products
Open Mon-Thurs 7:30am-Midnight, Fri 7:30-7, Sat 10-7, Sun Noon-Midnight
Friends of the Library Group

Departmental Libraries:

CM IDAHO HEALTH SCIENCES LIBRARY, 850 S Ninth Ave, 83201-5314. (Mail add: 921 S Eighth Ave, Stop 8089, 83209-8089). Tel: 208-282-4686. Toll Free Tel: 800-363-4781. FAX: 202-282-4295. E-mail: ihsl@isu.edu. Web Site: www.isu.edu/library/ihsl. *Dir,* Marcia Francis; Tel: 208-282-4182
Publications: Liaison (Newsletter)
Open Mon-Fri 8am-9pm, Sat 12-5

UNIVERSITY LIBRARY CENTER, 1776 Science Center Dr, Rm 250, Idaho Falls, 83402. Tel: 208-282-7906. Administration Tel: 208-282-7849. FAX: 208-282-7910. Web Site: www.isu.edu/idahofalls/library. *Librn,* Catherine Gray; E-mail: graycath@isu.edu; Staff 2 (MLS 1, Non-MLS 1)
Founded 1993. Enrl 2,180; Highest Degree: Doctorate
Library Holdings: Bk Vols 1,196
Function: Distance learning, Doc delivery serv, Ref serv available, Wheelchair accessible
Open Mon-Thurs 9-8, Fri & Sat 9-3
Restriction: Pub use on premises

P MARSHALL PUBLIC LIBRARY*, 113 S Garfield, 83204-5722. SAN 339-6819. Tel: 208-232-1263. FAX: 208-232-9266. Web Site: www.marshallpl.org. *Interim Dir,* Gardner Hanks; Tel: 208-232-1263, Ext 29; *Assoc Dir,* Position Currently Open; *Ref Librn,* Amy Campbell; *Readers' Advisor Librn,* Becky Hadley; *YA Librn,* Kath Ann Hendricks; Tel: 208-232-1263, Ext 28; Staff 10 (Non-MLS 10)
Founded 1905. Pop 50,600; Circ 463,159
Library Holdings: Bk Vols 151,903; Per Subs 198
Special Collections: Idaho Coll. State Document Depository
Automation Activity & Vendor Info: (Cataloging) SirsiDynix; (Circulation) SirsiDynix; (OPAC) SirsiDynix
Database Vendor: World Book Online
Open Mon-Thurs 9-9, Fri & Sat 9-6
Friends of the Library Group

POST FALLS

P POST FALLS PUBLIC LIBRARY*, 821 N Spokane St, 83854-9315. SAN 303-6316. Tel: 208-773-1506. FAX: 208-773-1507. *Dir,* Joe Reiss; Staff 10 (MLS 2, Non-MLS 8)
Founded 1915
Library Holdings: AV Mats 4,500; Large Print Bks 3,000; Bk Titles 50,000; Per Subs 110; Talking Bks 2,000
Automation Activity & Vendor Info: (Cataloging) Ex Libris Group; (Circulation) Ex Libris Group; (OPAC) Ex Libris Group
Database Vendor: OCLC FirstSearch
Partic in Cooperative Information Network; WIN Library Network
Open Mon-Thurs 10-8, Fri 10-6, Sat 10-5, Sun 12-5
Friends of the Library Group

PRESTON

P FRANKLIN COUNTY LIBRARY DISTRICT*, Larsen-Sant Public Library, 109 S First E, 83263. SAN 303-6324. Tel: 208-852-0175. FAX: 208-852-7148. E-mail: larsensantlib@dcdi.net. Web Site: larsen-sant.lil.org. *Dir,* Laura Wheatley; *Asst Dir,* Teresa Rasmussen
Pop 11,000; Circ 90,000
Library Holdings: Bk Vols 36,000; Per Subs 52
Wireless access
Partic in Library Consortium of Eastern Idaho
Open Mon-Thurs 10-7, Fri 10-6, Sat 11-4
Friends of the Library Group

PRIEST LAKE

P PRIEST LAKE PUBLIC LIBRARY*, 28769 N Hwy 57, 83856. SAN 303-6332. Tel: 208-443-2454. FAX: 208-443-2454. E-mail: plplibrary@hotmail.com. Web Site: www.priestlake.lili.org. *Dir,* Jody Pettit; *Asst Librn,* Jennifer Funk; *Asst Librn,* Anne Weitz
Founded 1974. Pop 1,786
Library Holdings: Bk Titles 8,500
Special Collections: History of Priest Lake
Function: Audio & video playback equip for onsite use, Handicapped accessible, Homebound delivery serv, ILL available, Music CDs, Online searches, Photocopying/Printing, Prog for children & young adult, Satellite serv, Spoken cassettes & CDs, Spoken cassettes & DVDs, Summer reading prog, Telephone ref, VCDs, VHS videos
Open Tues & Thurs (Winter) 11-4, Wed 11-6, Sat 10-2; Tues, Thurs & Fri (Summer) 11-4, Wed 11-6, Sat 10-2
Restriction: Pub use on premises
Friends of the Library Group

PRIEST RIVER

P WEST BONNER LIBRARY DISTRICT*, 118 Main St, 83856-5059. SAN 303-6340. Tel: 208-448-2207. E-mail: westbonnerlibrary@library.com. Web Site: westbonner.lili.org. *Dir,* Kathryn Crill; Staff 4 (Non-MLS 4)
Founded 1926. Pop 4,619; Circ 12,933
Library Holdings: Bk Vols 13,178
Function: Adult literacy prog, For res purposes, Handicapped accessible, ILL available, Photocopying/Printing, Prog for children & young adult, Summer reading prog, Telephone ref, Wheelchair accessible
Special Services for the Deaf - Bks on deafness & sign lang
Special Services for the Blind - Audio mat; Bks on cassette; Bks on CD; Large print bks; Talking bks
Open Mon, Wed & Fri 10-5, Tues & Thurs 10-7, Sat 10-2
Friends of the Library Group

REXBURG

C BRIGHAM YOUNG UNIVERSITY-IDAHO*, David O McKay Library, 525 S Center St, 83460-0405. SAN 303-6375. Tel: 208-496-9522. Interlibrary Loan Service Tel: 208-496-9524. FAX: 208-496-9503. Web Site: www.lib.byui.edu. *Dir of Libr Serv,* Ralph Kern; Tel: 208-496-9510, E-mail: kernr@byui.edu; *Head, Pub Serv,* Shane Cole; *Head, Tech Serv,* Debora Scholes; *Asst Univ Librn,* Brooks Haderlie; Staff 17 (MLS 10, Non-MLS 7)
Founded 1906. Enrl 13,368; Fac 603; Highest Degree: Bachelor
Library Holdings: Audiobooks 220; CDs 6,300; DVDs 1,600; e-books 432,000; e-journals 82,000; Electronic Media & Resources 336; Microforms 95,000; Music Scores 136,000; Bk Titles 157,000; Bk Vols 193,000; Per Subs 704; Videos 9,000
Special Collections: History of Writing (Scriptorium Coll); LDS Church Coll; Southeast Idaho Coll
Subject Interests: Genealogy
Automation Activity & Vendor Info: (Acquisitions) Horizon; (Cataloging) Horizon; (Circulation) Horizon; (Course Reserve) Horizon; (ILL) OCLC ILLiad; (OPAC) Horizon; (Serials) Horizon
Database Vendor: Alexander Street Press, ARTstor, Blackwell, Cambridge Scientific Abstracts, CQ Press, Dun & Bradstreet, ebrary, EBSCOhost, Elsevier MDL, Gale Cengage Learning, ISI Web of Knowledge, JSTOR, Knovel, LexisNexis, Newsbank, OCLC WorldShare Interlibrary Loan, Oxford Online, ProQuest, ScienceDirect, SirsiDynix, Wiley, Wilson - Wilson Web, World Book Online
Wireless access
Partic in Lyrasis; OCLC Online Computer Library Center, Inc
Open Mon-Thurs 7am-11:30pm, Fri 7am-9pm, Sat 9-9

P MADISON LIBRARY DISTRICT*, 73 N Center, 83440-1539. SAN 303-6367. Tel: 208-356-3461. Web Site: www.madisonlib.org. *Dir,* Judy Dewey; *Asst Dir, Cat,* Lorna Smith; *Prog Dir,* Amber Kent; *Cat Librn,* Robin Armstrong; *Adult Serv, Tech Serv,* Valerie Stohl; *Children's & YA Librn,* Vivian Milius; *ILL, Tech Serv,* Colleen Brewerton; Staff 7 (MLS 2, Non-MLS 5)
Founded 1920. Pop 32,000; Circ 393,379
Library Holdings: Bk Titles 65,000; Per Subs 105
Subject Interests: Idaho
Automation Activity & Vendor Info: (Cataloging) Horizon; (Circulation) Horizon; (ILL) OCLC FirstSearch; (OPAC) Horizon
Database Vendor: EBSCO Auto Repair Reference, EBSCOhost, ProQuest, ReferenceUSA
Wireless access
Partic in Library Consortium of Eastern Idaho
Open Mon-Thurs 9-8, Fri 9-6, Sat 10-4
Friends of the Library Group

RICHFIELD

P RICHFIELD DISTRICT LIBRARY*, 105 S Main, 83349. (Mail add: PO Box 146, 83349-0146), SAN 303-6383. Tel: 208-487-1242. E-mail: richdislib@gmail.com. *Dir,* Clay Ritter
Pop 1,050; Circ 3,373
Library Holdings: AV Mats 250; Bk Vols 10,000; Talking Bks 50
Function: Bks on cassette, Bks on CD, CD-ROM, Children's prog, Computers for patron use, Copy machines, Digital talking bks, Fax serv, Free DVD rentals, ILL available, Photocopying/Printing, Summer reading prog, VHS videos
Open Tues 2-6, Thurs 10-6
Friends of the Library Group

RIGBY

P RIGBY PUBLIC LIBRARY*, 110 N State St, 83442. (Mail add: PO Box 328, 83442), SAN 303-6391. Tel: 208-745-8231. FAX: 208-745-8231. E-mail: rcity1@ida.net. Web Site: www.rigby.lili.org. *Librn,* Marilynn Kamoe; *Asst Dir,* Bari Trost
Founded 1948. Pop 3,000; Circ 93,306
Library Holdings: Bk Vols 26,000; Per Subs 31
Automation Activity & Vendor Info: (Cataloging) SirsiDynix; (Circulation) SirsiDynix; (OPAC) SirsiDynix
Partic in Library Consortium of Eastern Idaho
Open Mon-Thurs 11-7, Fri 11-5, Sat 11-3
Friends of the Library Group

RIGGINS

P SALMON RIVER PUBLIC LIBRARY*, 126 N Main, 83549. (Mail add: PO Box 249, 83549-0249). Tel: 208-628-3394. FAX: 208-628-3792. E-mail: srplinfo@frontiernet.net. Web Site: rigginsidaho.org/library.html. *Dir,* Susan Long
Library Holdings: Bk Titles 10,000; Bk Vols 13,000
Automation Activity & Vendor Info: (Cataloging) Follett Software; (Circulation) Follett Software; (OPAC) Follett Software
Wireless access
Open Mon-Fri 10-5
Friends of the Library Group

RIRIE

P RIRIE CITY LIBRARY*, 464 Main St, 83443. (Mail add: PO Box 97, 83443-0097). Tel: 208-538-7974. FAX: 208-538-7974. E-mail: ririelibrary@yahoo.com. *Dir,* Janet Warren
Pop 545; Circ 6,315
Library Holdings: AV Mats 101; Bk Vols 11,000
Automation Activity & Vendor Info: (Cataloging) Follett Software; (Circulation) Follett Software; (OPAC) Follett Software
Open Mon, Tues, Thurs & Fri 1-5, Wed 1-7
Friends of the Library Group

ROBERTS

P ROBERTS PUBLIC LIBRARY*, 659 N 2870 East, 83444-5069. (Mail add: PO Box 305, 83444-0305). Tel: 208-228-2210. Web Site: www.roberts.lili.org. *Librn,* Lee Karlinsey
Library Holdings: CDs 50; DVDs 50; Bk Vols 10,000; Videos 100
Automation Activity & Vendor Info: (Cataloging) SirsiDynix; (Circulation) SirsiDynix; (OPAC) SirsiDynix
Wireless access
Open Mon & Wed 1-7, Tues & Thurs 3-5
Friends of the Library Group

ROCKLAND

P ROCKLAND SCHOOL COMMUNITY LIBRARY*, 321 E Center, 83271. (Mail add: PO Box 119, 83271-0119), SAN 303-6405. Tel: 208-548-2222. FAX: 208-548-2224. Web Site: rbulldogs.org/library.htm. *Dir,* Kindra Munk
Founded 1974. Pop 650; Circ 13,400
Library Holdings: Bk Vols 12,354; Per Subs 33
Automation Activity & Vendor Info: (Cataloging) Follett Software; (Circulation) Follett Software
Wireless access
Open Mon & Wed Fri (Winter) 8-3, Tues 8-3 & 5-7; Mon & Thurs (Summer) 12-4, Tues 12-7

RUPERT

P DEMARY MEMORIAL LIBRARY*, 417 Seventh St, 83350-1692. SAN 303-6413. Tel: 208-436-3874. FAX: 208-436-9719. E-mail: demary@pmt.org. Web Site: demary.lili.org. *Dir,* Sharon Kae Kimber; Staff 3.4 (Non-MLS 3.4)
Founded 1958. Pop 5,645; Circ 43,024
Library Holdings: Bk Vols 43,500; Per Subs 48
Special Collections: Idaho Coll; Local Archives
Database Vendor: EBSCOhost, Gale Cengage Learning, ProQuest
Wireless access
Open Mon-Fri 11-7, Sat 11-3
Friends of the Library Group

SAINT ANTHONY

P FREMONT COUNTY DISTRICT LIBRARY*, Saint Anthony Branch, 420 N Bridge, Ste E, 83445. SAN 303-6421. Tel: 208-624-3192. FAX: 208-624-3192. E-mail: ashlib@ida.net. *Dir,* Kathy Henderson
Founded 1920. Pop 3,182; Circ 47,924
Library Holdings: Bk Vols 16,000; Per Subs 30
Automation Activity & Vendor Info: (Cataloging) SirsiDynix; (Circulation) SirsiDynix; (OPAC) SirsiDynix
Open Mon-Wed 12-6, Thurs & Fri 12-5, Sat 10-1
Friends of the Library Group

S JUVENILE CORRECTION CENTER LIBRARY*, 2220 E 600 North, 83445. (Mail add: PO Box 40, 83445-0040). Tel: 208-624-3462. FAX: 208-624-0973. Web Site: www.idjc.idaho.gov. *Librn,* Lorene Hall; E-mail: lorene.hall@idjc.idaho.gov
Library Holdings: Bk Vols 5,000
Open Mon-Fri 8-2

SAINT MARIES

P SAINT MARIES PUBLIC LIBRARY*, 822 College Ave, 83861-1720. SAN 303 643X. Tel: 208-245-3732. FAX: 208-245-7102. E-mail: smlibrary@smgazette.com. *Librn,* Leslee Adams
Pop 2,872; Circ 23,811
Library Holdings: Bk Vols 15,500; Per Subs 36
Automation Activity & Vendor Info: (Cataloging) Ex Libris Group; (Circulation) Ex Libris Group; (OPAC) Ex Libris Group
Open Tues & Fri Noon-5, Sat 9-2
Friends of the Library Group

SALMON

G BUREAU OF LAND MANAGEMENT, Salmon District Office Library, 1206 S Challis St, 83467. SAN 303-6448. Tel: 208-756-5400. FAX: 208-756-5436. *Librn,* Position Currently Open
Library Holdings: Bk Vols 374; Per Subs 32
Open Mon-Fri 8-4:30

P SALMON PUBLIC LIBRARY*, 204 Main St, 83467-4111. SAN 303-6456. Tel: 208-756-2311. FAX: 208-756-2444. E-mail: salmonlibrary@centurytel.net. Web Site: www.salmonlibrary.org. *Librn,* Ramona Stauffer; Staff 1 (Non-MLS 1)
Founded 1916. Pop 7,806; Circ 51,922
Library Holdings: AV Mats 689; Large Print Bks 489; Bk Vols 22,722; Per Subs 60
Special Collections: Idaho Territorial & State Census Coll (1870-1930), microfilm; Lemhi Indian Agency Records, microfilm; Lewis & Clark Coll; Local Newspaper Coll (1882-2004), microfilm. Oral History
Automation Activity & Vendor Info: (Cataloging) SirsiDynix; (Circulation) SirsiDynix; (OPAC) SirsiDynix
Publications: History of Lemhi County
Partic in Library Consortium of Eastern Idaho
Open Mon-Wed 10-6, Thurs 10-7, Fri & Sat 10-5

SANDPOINT

S BONNER COUNTY HISTORICAL SOCIETY*, Research Library, 611 S Ella Ave, 83864. SAN 323-5378. Tel: 208-263-2344. E-mail: bcmuseum@frontier.com. Web Site: www.bonnercountyhistory.org.
Curator, Ann Ferguson
Founded 1972
Library Holdings: Bk Titles 1,000
Special Collections: Bonner County newspapers, 1891-present; Bonner County School Records, historic photos. Oral History
Subject Interests: Family hist, Idaho
Wireless access
Publications: "Beautiful Bonner History & Memories" Vol 2; "Beautiful Bonner," History of Bonner County, Idaho; "Morton Memories," History of Morton Community, Bonner County, Idaho

P EAST BONNER COUNTY FREE LIBRARY DISTRICT*, 1407 Cedar St, 83864-2052. SAN 303-6464. Tel: 208-263-6930. Circulation Tel: 208-263-6930, Ext 215. Interlibrary Loan Service Tel: 208-263-6930, Ext 203. Reference Tel: 208-263-6930, Ext 209. Administration Tel: 208-263-6930, Ext 208. Automation Services Tel: 208-263-6930, Ext 202. FAX: 208-263-8320. Web Site: www.ebcl.lib.id.us, www.ebonnerlibrary.org. *Dir,* Position Currently Open; *Dir, Human Res,* Craig Hofmeister; Tel: 208-263-6930, Ext 201, E-mail: craig@ebcl.lib.id.us; *Tech Coordr,* Gina Emory; E-mail: gina@ebcl.lib.id.us; *Cat,* Kate Walton; Tel: 208-263-6930, Ext 216, E-mail: kate@ebcl.lib.id.us; *Circ, Extn Serv,* Ann Nichols; Tel: 208-263-6930, Ext 257, E-mail: ann@ebcl.lib.id.us; *Coll Develop, Info Serv, Ref Serv,* Gloria Ray; Tel: 208-263-6930, Ext 204, E-mail: gloria@ebcl.lib.id.us; *ILL,* Sue Elsa; E-mail: suee@ebcl.lib.id.us; *Per,* Liz Duncan; *Youth Serv,* Suzanne Davis; Tel: 208-263-6930, Ext 211, E-mail: suzanne@ebcl.lib.id.us
Founded 1912. Pop 34,500; Circ 490,944
Library Holdings: AV Mats 25,464; Large Print Bks 4,719; Bk Vols 77,468; Per Subs 215
Special Collections: Pacific Northwest (Northwest Coll). State Document Depository
Automation Activity & Vendor Info: (Acquisitions) TLC (The Library Corporation); (Cataloging) TLC (The Library Corporation); (Circulation) TLC (The Library Corporation); (Course Reserve) TLC (The Library Corporation); (ILL) TLC (The Library Corporation); (OPAC) TLC (The Library Corporation)
Database Vendor: EBSCOhost, OCLC FirstSearch, OCLC WorldShare Interlibrary Loan, TLC (The Library Corporation)
Function: Homebound delivery serv, ILL available, Prog for children & young adult, Summer reading prog, Wheelchair accessible
Special Services for the Blind - Videos on blindness & phys handicaps
Open Mon-Thurs (Winter) 10-8, Fri & Sat 10-5; Mon-Thurs (Summer) 10-7, Fri & Sat 10-5
Friends of the Library Group
Branches: 1
CLARK FORK BRANCH, 601 Main St, Clark Fork, 83811. (Mail add: PO Box 219, Clark Fork, 83811-0219), SAN 328-6991. Tel: 208-266-1321. FAX: 208-266-1663.
Function: Adult bk club, Bks on CD, Children's prog, Citizenship assistance, Computer training, Computers for patron use, Copy machines, Digital talking bks, e-mail & chat, Electronic databases & coll, Exhibits, Fax serv, Free DVD rentals, Handicapped accessible, Home delivery & serv to Sr ctr & nursing homes, Homebound delivery serv, Homework prog, ILL available, Instruction & testing, Learning ctr, Magnifiers for reading, Mail & tel request accepted, Music CDs, Newsp ref libr, Notary serv, Online cat, Online info literacy tutorials on the web & in blackboard, Outreach serv, Outside serv via phone, mail, e-mail & web, OverDrive digital audio bks, Photocopying/Printing, Preschool outreach, Printer for laptops & handheld devices, Prog for adults, Prog for children & young adult, Pub access computers, Ref & res, Ref serv available, Ref serv in person, Res libr, Scanner, Senior computer classes, Senior outreach, Spoken cassettes & CDs, Spoken cassettes & DVDs, Story hour, Summer & winter reading prog, Summer reading prog, Tax forms, Teen prog, Telephone ref, Wheelchair accessible, Winter reading prog
Special Services for the Blind - Audio mat
Open Mon-Thurs 10-6, Fri & Sat 10-5
Friends of the Library Group
Bookmobiles: 1. Coordr, Robin Yeary

SHELLEY

P NORTH BINGHAM COUNTY DISTRICT LIBRARY*, 197 W Locust St, 83274-1139. SAN 303-6472. Tel: 208-357-7801. FAX: 208-357-2272. Web Site: www.ida.net/org/nbcdl. *Librn,* Heidi Riddoch; E-mail: hriddoch@cableone.net; Staff 1 (Non-MLS 1)
Pop 11,000; Circ 150,000
Library Holdings: AV Mats 1,000; Bk Vols 50,000; Talking Bks 600
Subject Interests: Local hist
Automation Activity & Vendor Info: (Cataloging) SirsiDynix
Open Mon, Tues, Thurs & Fri 10-6, Wed 10-8, Sat 10-2
Friends of the Library Group

SHOSHONE

P SHOSHONE PUBLIC LIBRARY*, 211 S Rail St, 83352-0236. SAN 303-6499. Tel: 208-886-2843. FAX: 208-886-2426. E-mail: sholib@shoshonecity.com. *Dir,* Pat Hamilton; Staff 3 (MLS 1, Non-MLS 2)
Pop 2,312; Circ 22,678
Library Holdings: Bks on Deafness & Sign Lang 10; Bk Titles 16,000; Per Subs 20
Special Collections: Idaho History
Subject Interests: Popular mat
Open Mon & Sat 12-5, Tues & Fri 10-5, Wed 12-8, Thurs 11-4

SODA SPRINGS

P SODA SPRINGS PUBLIC LIBRARY*, 149 S Main, 83276-1496. SAN 303-6502. Tel: 208-547-2606. FAX: 208-547-2606. E-mail: sspl@sodaspringsid.com. Web Site: soda.lili.org/. *Dir,* Cindy Erickson; *Ch,* Jennifer Balls; Staff 2 (Non-MLS 2)
Founded 1951. Pop 3,600; Circ 51,000
Library Holdings: Bks on Deafness & Sign Lang 12; High Interest/Low Vocabulary Bk Vols 100; Bk Vols 38,000; Per Subs 70
Special Collections: Idaho History (Southeast Idaho-especially Caribou County); Literature (Vardis Fisher Coll); Oregon Trail Newspapers (Caribou County Sun)
Subject Interests: Idaho
Automation Activity & Vendor Info: (Cataloging) SirsiDynix; (Circulation) SirsiDynix; (OPAC) SirsiDynix
Partic in Library Consortium of Eastern Idaho
Open Mon-Thurs 10-8, Fri 10-5
Friends of the Library Group

STANLEY

P STANLEY COMMUNITY PUBLIC LIBRARY*, 240 Niece Ave, 83278. (Mail add: PO Box 230, 83278-0230). Tel: 208-774-2470. FAX: 208-774-2470. E-mail: stanlib@ruralnetwork.net. Web Site: www.rualnetwork.net/~stanlib. *Dir,* Jane Somerville
Library Holdings: Audiobooks 150; Bk Vols 5,000; Per Subs 8
Automation Activity & Vendor Info: (Cataloging) Innovative Interfaces, Inc; (Circulation) Innovative Interfaces, Inc; (ILL) OCLC Online; (OPAC) Innovative Interfaces, Inc
Database Vendor: OCLC FirstSearch, OCLC WebJunction, OCLC WorldShare Interlibrary Loan
Wireless access
Partic in Library Consortium of Eastern Idaho
Open Mon & Thurs 12-6, Tues & Wed 12-4, Fri & Sat 10-6
Friends of the Library Group

SUGAR CITY

P SUGAR-SALEM SCHOOL COMMUNITY LIBRARY, One Digger Dr, 83448. SAN 303-6529. Tel: 208-356-0271. Web Site: www.sugarlib.org. *Libr Dir,* Chantelle Green; E-mail: cgreen@sugarsalem.com; Staff 1 (Non-MLS 1)
Pop 4,012
Library Holdings: Bk Vols 24,800; Per Subs 65; Videos 420
Automation Activity & Vendor Info: (Cataloging) Innovative Interfaces, Inc; (Circulation) Innovative Interfaces, Inc; (OPAC) Innovative Interfaces, Inc
Wireless access
Partic in Library Consortium of Eastern Idaho
Open Mon & Tues 7:30-6, Wed & Thurs 7:30-8, Fri 7:30-3:30, Sat 11-2; Mon, Wed & Fri (Summer) 9-2, Thurs 1-8

TWIN FALLS

J COLLEGE OF SOUTHERN IDAHO LIBRARY, 315 Falls Ave, 83301-3367. (Mail add: PO Box 1238, 83303-1238), SAN 303-6545. Tel: 208-732-6500. Interlibrary Loan Service Tel: 208-732-6503. Reference Tel: 208-732-6504. Administration Tel: 208-732-6501. FAX: 208-736-3087. Web Site: www.csi.edu/library. *Libr Dir,* Dr Teri Fattig; E-mail: tfattig@csi.edu; *Ref,* Stephen Poppino; E-mail: spoppino@csi.edu; Staff 3 (MLS 2, Non-MLS 1)
Founded 1965. Enrl 6,711; Fac 156; Highest Degree: Associate
Library Holdings: Bk Titles 61,000; Bk Vols 69,000; Per Subs 383
Automation Activity & Vendor Info: (Acquisitions) SirsiDynix; (Cataloging) SirsiDynix; (Circulation) SirsiDynix; (Course Reserve) SirsiDynix; (OPAC) SirsiDynix; (Serials) SirsiDynix
Database Vendor: Alexander Street Press, Cinahl, CQ Press, CredoReference, EBSCO Auto Repair Reference, EBSCOhost, Gale Cengage Learning, LearningExpress, LexisNexis, Micromedex, Newsbank,

OCLC FirstSearch, OCLC WorldShare Interlibrary Loan, Oxford Online, ProQuest, Sage, ScienceDirect, SirsiDynix, ValueLine, World Book Online
Wireless access
Function: 24/7 Electronic res, 24/7 Online cat, Audio & video playback equip for onsite use, Audiobks via web, Bks on CD, CD-ROM, Computers for patron use, Copy machines, Electronic databases & coll, Free DVD rentals, ILL available, Magazines, Magnifiers for reading, Music CDs, Online cat, Online info literacy tutorials on the web & in blackboard, Orientations, Pub access computers, Ref & res, Ref serv available, Ref serv in person, Study rm, Web-catalog
Open Mon-Thurs (Fall & Spring) 7:30am-10pm, Fri 7:30-6, Sat & Sun 10-5; Mon, Wed & Fri (Summer & Winter) 7:30-5, Tues & Thurs 7:30am-8pm, Sat 10-5

P TWIN FALLS PUBLIC LIBRARY, 201 Fourth Ave E, 83301-6397. SAN 303-6561. Tel: 208-733-2964. FAX: 208-733-2965. E-mail: tfpl@twinfallspubliclibrary.org. Web Site: www.twinfallspubliclibrary.org. *Dir,* Susan Ash; *Head, Adult Serv, ILL Supvr, Ref Librn,* Amy Mortensen; *Head, Circ Serv,* Craig Rasmusson; *Head, Youth Serv,* Erica Littlefield; *Admin/Personnel Mgr,* Barbara Ames; *Supvr, Acq,* Kate Morrison; *Cat, Tech Serv Supvr,* Kathleen Lambert; *Computer Support Spec,* Adam Day; Staff 10 (MLS 8, Non-MLS 2)
Founded 1909. Pop 44,564; Circ 464,343
Library Holdings: Bk Vols 171,507; Per Subs 358
Special Collections: Early Local Photography (Bisbee Coll); Idaho & Pacific Northwest History Coll; Large Print Coll; Pacific Northwest Americana Coll. State Document Depository
Subject Interests: Agr, Bus & mgt, Hist
Automation Activity & Vendor Info: (Acquisitions) SirsiDynix; (Cataloging) SirsiDynix; (Circulation) SirsiDynix; (OPAC) SirsiDynix; (Serials) SirsiDynix
Wireless access
Function: Adult bk club, Audiobks via web, Bks on CD, Children's prog, Computer training, Computers for patron use, Copy machines, Electronic databases & coll, Free DVD rentals, Handicapped accessible, ILL available, Microfiche/film & reading machines, Music CDs, Online cat, OverDrive digital audio bks, Photocopying/Printing, Prog for children & young adult, Pub access computers, Senior computer classes, Story hour, Summer reading prog
Partic in LYNX! Consortium
Open Mon-Thurs 9-9, Fri & Sat 9-6
Bookmobiles: 1. Outreach Librn, Beth Swenson

VICTOR

P VALLEY OF THE TETONS DISTRICT LIBRARY*, 56 N Main, 83455. (Mail add: PO Box 37, 83455-0037), SAN 303-657X. Tel: 208-787-2201. FAX: 208-787-2204. E-mail: library@silverstar.com. Web Site: www.tetons.lili.org. *Dir,* Carla Sherman; Staff 4 (Non-MLS 4)
Founded 1965. Pop 9,337; Circ 60,841
Oct 2009-Sept 2010 Income $212,055, State $14,318, County $182,515, Locally Generated Income $15,222. Mats Exp $36,929, Books $26,561, AV Mat $7,613, Electronic Ref Mat (Incl. Access Fees) $2,755. Sal $107,825
Library Holdings: Audiobooks 1,779; CDs 373; DVDs 912; Large Print Bks 598; Bk Titles 25,640; Per Subs 40; Videos 1,054
Automation Activity & Vendor Info: (Cataloging) Follett Software; (Circulation) Follett Software; (OPAC) Follett Software
Database Vendor: EBSCOhost, OCLC FirstSearch
Wireless access
Function: Audio & video playback equip for onsite use, Handicapped accessible, ILL available, Music CDs, Prog for children & young adult, Spoken cassettes & CDs, Summer reading prog, VHS videos, Wheelchair accessible
Special Services for the Blind - Talking bk serv referral
Open Mon, Tues & Thurs-Sat 11-5, Wed 11-7
Friends of the Library Group

WALLACE

P WALLACE PUBLIC LIBRARY*, 415 River St, 83873-2260. SAN 303-6596. Tel: 208-752-4571. FAX: 208-752-4571. E-mail: wallacelibrary@yahoo.com. *Librn,* Bernie Ludwick; *Asst Librn,* Betty Wise
Founded 1902. Pop 1,010; Circ 14,154
Library Holdings: Bk Titles 16,367; Per Subs 30
Special Collections: Idaho & Pacific Northwestern History, bks, microfiche, microfilm, slides; Large Print Coll; Scandinavian History & Literature
Automation Activity & Vendor Info: (Cataloging) Ex Libris Group; (Circulation) Ex Libris Group; (OPAC) Ex Libris Group
Publications: Booklist
Open Mon & Thurs 12-8, Tues, Wed & Fri 12-5:30

WEIPPE

P CLEARWATER COUNTY FREE LIBRARY DISTRICT*, Weippe Public Library, 204 Wood St, 83553. (Mail add: PO Box 435, 83553-0435). Tel: 208-435-4058. FAX: 208-435-4374. E-mail: weippelibrary@weippe.com. Web Site: www.weippelibrary.org. *Dir,* Terri Summerfield; E-mail: terris@weippe.com
Founded 1956
Library Holdings: Bk Vols 8,000; Per Subs 45
Automation Activity & Vendor Info: (Cataloging) Ex Libris Group; (Circulation) Ex Libris Group; (OPAC) Ex Libris Group
Function: ILL available, Photocopying/Printing
Open Mon, Thurs & Fri 10-5, Tues & Wed 10-7, Sat 10-1
Friends of the Library Group

WEISER

P WEISER PUBLIC LIBRARY*, 628 E First St, 83672-2241. SAN 303-660X. Tel: 208-549-1243. *Dir,* Pat Hamilton
Founded 1890. Pop 4,900; Circ 40,000
Library Holdings: Audiobooks 250; CDs 50; DVDs 300; Large Print Bks 200; Bk Titles 26,000; Per Subs 40
Automation Activity & Vendor Info: (Acquisitions) Follett Software; (Cataloging) Follett Software; (Circulation) Follett Software; (Course Reserve) Follett Software
Wireless access
Open Mon-Fri 9-6
Friends of the Library Group

WENDELL

P WENDELL PUBLIC LIBRARY*, 375 First Ave E, 83355. (Mail add: PO Box 208, 83355-0208), SAN 303-6618. Tel: 208-536-6195. E-mail: wendellpubliclibrary@yahoo.com. Web Site: wendelllibrary.org. *Librn,* Jennifer Hamilton
Pop 2,338; Circ 18,000
Library Holdings: Bk Vols 20,000
Open Tues 10-7, Wed 12-5, Thurs 12-7, Fri 12-6, Sat 10-3

WHITEBIRD

P WHITEBIRD COMMUNITY LIBRARY*, PO Box 33, 83554-0033. Tel: 208-839-2805. E-mail: wbclibrary@frontier.com. *Mgr,* Leah Harvey
Library Holdings: Bk Vols 5,500
Wireless access
Open Tues, Wed & Sat 10-1, Thurs 3-5

WILDER

P WILDER PUBLIC LIBRARY DISTRICT*, 207 A Ave, 83676-6099. (Mail add: PO Box 128, 83676-0128), SAN 303-6626. Tel: 208-482-7880. FAX: 208-482-7880. *Librn,* Susan Waldemer
Founded 1978. Pop 3,940; Circ 6,100
Library Holdings: Bk Vols 13,803
Wireless access
Open Mon-Fri 12-5:30, Sat 10-12:30
Friends of the Library Group

ILLINOIS

Date of Statistics: FY 2013
Population, 2010 U.S. Census: 12,830,632
Population Served by Tax-Supported Public Libraries: 11,792,327
Total Volumes in Public Libraries: 43,431,699 (books plus serials)
Volumes Per Capita: 3.39
Volumes Per Capita Served: 3.68
Total Non-book Resources Held: 6,012,336 (audio plus video)
Total Public Library Circulation Transactions: 117,975,337
Circulation Transactions Per Capita: 9.19
Circulation Transactions Per Capita Served: 10
Total Public Library Income (including some State & Federal Grants & Capital Income): $853,052,550
Source of Income: Primarily property tax
Total Operating Expenditures: $701,898,182
Expenditures Per Capita: $54.70
Expenditures Per Capita Served: $59.52
Number of System (Regional Libraries): 2 multitype; 1 public
Number of Central Public Libraries: 639
Counties Served: 102 whole or partial
Grants, awarded & monitored: 1,958 for $65,101,836

ABINGDON

P JOHN MOSSER PUBLIC LIBRARY DISTRICT*, 106 W Meek St, 61410-1451. SAN 303-6634. Tel: 309-462-3129. FAX: 309-462-3129. E-mail: j_mosser_pld@hotmail.com. *Dir,* Elizabeth Ann Kisler; *Asst Librn,* Jamie L Beil; *Asst Librn,* Mavis Meadows; *Ch Serv,* Linda Evelyn Crandall; Staff 4 (Non-MLS 4)
Founded 1895. Pop 3,600; Circ 20,131
Library Holdings: Bk Titles 22,618; Bk Vols 23,966; Per Subs 43
Special Collections: Abingdon Pottery Coll; County Histories; Cramer Coll, miniature vases; DAR Lineages from 1900; Hedding College Coll, memorabilia; Mosser Coll
Subject Interests: Genealogy
Wireless access
Special Services for the Blind - Bks on cassette
Open Tues & Fri 10-5, Wed 10-7, Thurs 3:30-6:30, Sat 10-3
Friends of the Library Group

ADDISON

P ADDISON PUBLIC LIBRARY, Four Friendship Plaza, 60101. SAN 303-6642. Tel: 630 543 3617. Reference Tel: 630-458-3318. FAX: 630-543-6645. E-mail: circ5@addisonlibrary.org, director@addisonlibrary.org. Web Site: www.addisonlibrary.org. *Dir,* Mary A Medjo-Me-Zengue; Tel: 630-458-3300, E-mail: medjo@addisonlibrary.org; *Head, Guest Serv,* Dianne Ludwig; Tel: 630-458-3322, E-mail: ludwig@addisonlibrary.org; *Head, Info Serv,* Uma Mirmira; Tel: 630-458-3314, E-mail: mirmira@addisonlibrary.org; *Head, Mat Mgt,* Brooke Sievers; Tel: 630-458-3329, E-mail: sievers@addisonlibrary.org; *Teen Librn,* Elizabeth Lynch; Tel: 630-458-3317, E-mail: lynch@addisonlibrary.org; *Digital Serv Coordr,* Jack Bower; Tel: 630-458-3354, E-mail: bower@addisonlibrary.org; *Pub Relations Coordr,* John Kokoris; Tel: 630-458-3303, E-mail: kokoris@addisonlibrary.org; *Ch Serv,* Mary Marshall; E-mail: marshall@addisonlibrary.org; *Info Tech,* Yabin Liu; Tel: 630-458-3350, E-mail: liu@addisonlibrary.org; *ILL,* Trish Schumacher; Tel: 630-458-3312, E-mail: schumacher@addisonlibrary.org; *Reader Serv,* Karen Dini; Tel: 630-458-3313, E-mail: dini@addisonlibrary.org; Staff 58 (MLS 14, Non-MLS 44)
Founded 1962. Pop 36,946
Automation Activity & Vendor Info: (Acquisitions) Innovative Interfaces, Inc; (Cataloging) Innovative Interfaces, Inc; (Circulation) Innovative Interfaces, Inc; (OPAC) Innovative Interfaces, Inc
Database Vendor: 3M Library Systems, Gale Cengage Learning, Innovative Interfaces, Inc, OCLC FirstSearch, ProQuest, ValueLine
Function: 24/7 Electronic res, 24/7 Online cat, Adult bk club, Adult literacy prog, Art exhibits, Audiobks via web, Bilingual assistance for Spanish patrons, Bk club(s), Bks on CD, Children's prog, Citizenship assistance, Computer training, Computers for patron use, Copy machines, Electronic databases & coll, Family literacy, Fax serv, Free DVD rentals, Handicapped accessible, ILL available, Life-long learning prog for all ages, Magazines, Movies, Music CDs, Notary serv, Online cat, Online ref, Online searches, Outreach serv, Photocopying/Printing, Preschool outreach, Preschool reading prog, Printer for laptops & handheld devices, Prog for adults, Prog for children & young adult, Pub access computers, Ref serv available, Ref serv in person, Referrals accepted, Scanner, Senior computer classes, Senior outreach, Spanish lang bks, Summer & winter reading prog, Tax forms, Teen prog, Telephone ref, Web-catalog, Workshops, Writing prog
Open Mon-Thurs 9-9, Fri & Sat 9-5, Sun 1-5
Friends of the Library Group

C DEVRY UNIVERSITY*, Addison Campus Library, 1221 Swift Rd, 60101. Tel: 630 652 8361. Administration Tel: 630-953-1300. FAX: 630-953-9665. Web Site: www.add.devry.edu/Library.html. *Dir,* Beverly Hughes; Tel: 630-652-8360, E-mail: BHughes@devry.edu; Staff 3 (MLS 1, Non-MLS 2)
Fac 50; Highest Degree: Master
Library Holdings: e-books 12,000; Bk Titles 17,000; Bk Vols 20,000; Per Subs 100
Automation Activity & Vendor Info: (Cataloging) Ex Libris Group; (Circulation) Ex Libris Group; (ILL) OCLC FirstSearch; (OPAC) Ex Libris Group
Database Vendor: EBSCOhost, ProQuest
Open Mon-Fri 7am-9pm, Sat 8-3

ALBANY

P ALBANY PUBLIC LIBRARY DISTRICT*, 302 S Main St, 61230. (Mail add: PO Box 516, 61230-0516), SAN 376-0952. Tel: 309-887-4193. *Librn,* Susie Boston
Library Holdings: Bk Titles 6,000; Per Subs 15
Open Mon, Tues & Thurs 6pm-7pm, Sat 9:30-10:30
Friends of the Library Group

ALBION

P ALBION PUBLIC LIBRARY*, Six N Fourth St, 62806. SAN 303-6669. Tel: 618-445-3314. *Head Librn,* Jane Gates; *Head Librn,* Rita Hortin; *Asst Librn,* Dixie Longbons
Founded 1818. Pop 7,000; Circ 19,044
Library Holdings: Bk Vols 14,798; Per Subs 50
Wireless access
Mem of Illinois Heartland Library System
Open Mon & Wed 1-5, Tues 1-7, Fri & Sat 9-12 & 1-5
Friends of the Library Group

ALEDO

P MERCER CARNEGIE LIBRARY*, 200 N College Ave, 61231. SAN 303-6677. Tel: 309-582-2032. FAX: 309-582-5155. E-mail: mercer.carnegie@mchsi.com. Web Site: mercercarnegielibrary.webs.com. *Dir,* Catherine Worlsey; Staff 1 (MLS 1)
Founded 1915. Pop 4,826
Library Holdings: Bk Titles 16,000; Per Subs 45

Subject Interests: Local hist
Mem of Reaching Across Illinois Library System (RAILS)
Open Mon, Wed & Fri 9-6, Tues & Thurs 9-7, Sat 9-2

ALGONQUIN

P ALGONQUIN AREA PUBLIC LIBRARY DISTRICT*, 2600 Harnish Dr, 60102-5900. SAN 303-6685. Tel: 847-458-6060, 847-658-4343. FAX: 847-458-9370. Interlibrary Loan Service FAX: 847-458-9359. TDD: 847-458-9573. Web Site: www.aapld.org. *Dir,* Lynn Elam; *Asst Dir,* Louise Nee; *Br Mgr,* Steven Slavick; *Circ,* Gary Christopherson; *Ref Serv,* Vicky Tobias; *Tech Serv,* Patrice Pearsall; *Youth Serv,* Alicia Parmele; Staff 78 (MLS 25, Non-MLS 53)
Founded 1921. Pop 40,809; Circ 1,313,887
Library Holdings: CDs 8,748; DVDs 21,723; e-books 21,452; Electronic Media & Resources 22; Large Print Bks 2,815; Bk Vols 195,176; Per Subs 404
Subject Interests: Local hist
Automation Activity & Vendor Info: (Acquisitions) SirsiDynix; (Cataloging) SirsiDynix; (Circulation) SirsiDynix; (OPAC) SirsiDynix
Database Vendor: EBSCO - WebFeat, Gale Cengage Learning, Newsbank, OCLC FirstSearch, Overdrive, Inc, ProQuest, ReferenceUSA, SirsiDynix
Wireless access
Function: Bk club(s), Bks on CD, Children's prog, e-mail serv, E-Reserves, Electronic databases & coll, Free DVD rentals, Handicapped accessible, Homebound delivery serv, ILL available, Music CDs, Online cat, Online ref, Online searches, Outside serv via phone, mail, e-mail & web, OverDrive digital audio bks, Photocopying/Printing, Prog for adults, Prog for children & young adult, Pub access computers, Summer reading prog, Teen prog
Publications: Library Leaves (Newsletter)
Partic in Cooperative Computer Services - CCS
Special Services for the Deaf - TDD equip
Open Mon-Thurs 9-9, Fri & Sat 9-5, Sun 1-5
Friends of the Library Group

ALSIP

P ALSIP-MERRIONETTE PARK PUBLIC LIBRARY DISTRICT*, 11960 S Pulaski Rd, 60803-1197. SAN 303-6693. Tel: 708-371-5666. FAX: 708-371-5672. E-mail: ampl@alsiplibrary.info. Web Site: www.alsiplibrary.info. *Dir,* Ruthann Swanson; E-mail: rswanson@alsiplibrary.info; *Adult Serv Mgr, Asst Dir,* Sue Pajor; E-mail: spajor@alsiplibrary.info; *Mgr, Circ & Tech Serv,* Doris Trela; E-mail: dtrela@alsiplibrary.info; *Mgr, Youth Serv,* Amy Malysa; E-mail: amalysa@alsiplibrary.info; Staff 29.6 (MLS 8.5, Non-MLS 21.1)
Founded 1973. Pop 22,280; Circ 165,948
Library Holdings: CDs 6,947; DVDs 9,332; Bk Vols 96,633; Per Subs 279
Automation Activity & Vendor Info: (Acquisitions) Innovative Interfaces, Inc; (Cataloging) Innovative Interfaces, Inc; (Circulation) Innovative Interfaces, Inc; (OPAC) Innovative Interfaces, Inc
Database Vendor: Baker & Taylor, EBSCO Auto Repair Reference, EBSCOhost, Innovative Interfaces, Inc, LearningExpress, Newsbank, OCLC FirstSearch, Overdrive, Inc, ProQuest, ReferenceUSA, World Book Online, WT Cox
Wireless access
Publications: NewsAmpler (Newsletter)
Mem of Reaching Across Illinois Library System (RAILS)
Open Mon-Thurs 9-9, Fri & Sat 9-5, Sun (Sept-May) 12-4

ALTAMONT

P ALTAMONT PUBLIC LIBRARY*, 121 W Washington St, 62411. SAN 303-6707. Tel: 618-483-5457. FAX: 618-483-5457. Web Site: www.altamontpubliclibrary.com. *Librn,* Beth Speers
Founded 1908. Pop 2,296; Circ 25,689
Library Holdings: Bk Vols 20,000; Per Subs 35
Mem of Illinois Heartland Library System
Open Mon-Wed 2-7, Thurs 5-8, Fri 2-6, Sat 9-1

ALTON

P HAYNER PUBLIC LIBRARY DISTRICT*, 326 Belle St, 62002. (Mail add: 401 State St, 62002-6137), SAN 303-6723. Tel: 618-462-0677. FAX: 618-462-0665. Administration FAX: 618-462-4919. E-mail: main.library@haynerlibrary.org. Web Site: www.haynerlibrary.org. *Exec Dir,* Jeffrey A Owen; E-mail: jeff.owen@haynerlibrary.org; *Asst Dir, Acq, Cat & Proc,* Lauren Erwin; *Asst Dir, Bus Operations & Human Res,* Sue Hardin; *Asst Dir, Libr Serv,* Catherine Schrimpf; *Asst Dir, Mkt & Pub Relations,* Bernadette Duvernoy; *Delivery Serv Mgr,* Esther Gillespie; *District Circ Mgr,* Mary Cordes; *Genealogy & Local Hist Mgr,* Cathie Lamere; *ILL Mgr,* Julie Belk; *Ref Serv Mgr,* Jean Shimunek; E-mail: jean.shimunek@haynerlibrary.org; *Vols Mgr,* Stephanie Munson; *Youth & Young Adult Mgr,* Sharon Windham; Staff 3 (MLS 3)
Founded 1891. Pop 58,155
Library Holdings: Bk Vols 208,267; Per Subs 374
Special Collections: Illinois History (Illinois Room), bks, microfilm, vf. Municipal Document Depository
Subject Interests: Hist
Automation Activity & Vendor Info: (Acquisitions) Innovative Interfaces, Inc; (Cataloging) Innovative Interfaces, Inc; (Circulation) Innovative Interfaces, Inc; (Course Reserve) Innovative Interfaces, Inc; (ILL) Innovative Interfaces, Inc; (Media Booking) Innovative Interfaces, Inc; (OPAC) Innovative Interfaces, Inc; (Serials) Innovative Interfaces, Inc
Database Vendor: SirsiDynix
Publications: The Hayner Public Library District (Newsletter)
Mem of Illinois Heartland Library System
Open Mon-Thurs 8-8, Fri 8-5, Sat 9-5, Sun 1-6
Friends of the Library Group
Branches: 2
ALTON SQUARE, 132 Alton Sq, 62002-6115. FAX: 618-463-1277. E-mail: branch.library@haynerlibrary.org. *In Charge,* Janet Schweppe
Open Mon-Sat 8:30am-9pm, Sun 12-6
GENEALOGY & LOCAL HISTORY, 401 State St, 62002-6113.
Open Mon-Thurs 8-8, Fri 8-5, Sat 9-5, Sun 1-4

ALTONA

P RANSOM MEMORIAL PUBLIC LIBRARY*, 110 E Main St, 61414-9998. SAN 303-6758. Tel: 309-484-6193. E-mail: ransompl@winco.net. *Dir,* Janice Larson; Staff 1 (Non-MLS 1)
Founded 1889. Pop 864; Circ 14,227
Library Holdings: Bk Vols 21,000; Per Subs 30
Function: ILL available
Open Mon & Thurs 3-8, Wed 10-5, Sat 9-12

AMBOY

P PANKHURST MEMORIAL LIBRARY*, Three S Jefferson Ave, 61310-1400. SAN 303-6766. Tel: 815-857-3925. FAX: 815-857-3065. E-mail: pmlamboy@essex1.com. *Librn,* Inez Vits; *Adult Serv,* Emily Goff; *Ch Serv,* Rebecca Gant; *Circ,* Staci Seier; Staff 3 (Non-MLS 3)
Founded 1928. Pop 2,561
Library Holdings: High Interest/Low Vocabulary Bk Vols 60; Bk Titles 19,280; Bk Vols 20,000; Per Subs 25
Database Vendor: Innovative Interfaces, Inc, OCLC FirstSearch, TLC (The Library Corporation), Wilson - Wilson Web
Mem of Reaching Across Illinois Library System (RAILS)
Partic in OWLSnet
Open Mon & Wed 1-7, Tues & Thurs 9-3, Fri & Sat 9-1
Friends of the Library Group

ANDALUSIA

P ANDALUSIA TOWNSHIP LIBRARY*, 503 W Second St, 61232. (Mail add: PO Box 268, 61232-0268), SAN 303-6774. Tel: 309-798-2542. FAX: 309-798-2310. Web Site: andalusialibrary.org. *Dir,* Leann Bredberg; *Circ,* Diane Gehn; Staff 2 (MLS 1, Non-MLS 1)
Pop 2,261; Circ 12,041
Library Holdings: Bk Vols 7,500; Per Subs 20
Wireless access
Mem of Reaching Across Illinois Library System (RAILS)
Open Mon-Thurs 1-8, Fri 2-6, Sat 9-1

ANNA

P STINSON MEMORIAL PUBLIC LIBRARY DISTRICT*, 409 S Main St, 62906. SAN 303-6790. Tel: 618-833-2521. FAX: 618-833-3560. Web Site: www.stinsonlibrary.org. *Dir,* Lisa Livesay; E-mail: llivesay@shawls.lib.il.us; *Head, Automation,* Thomas Sisler; Staff 11 (MLS 1, Non-MLS 10)
Founded 1914. Pop 15,408; Circ 28,631
Library Holdings: Bk Vols 32,658; Per Subs 44
Wireless access
Mem of Illinois Heartland Library System
Open Mon-Fri 10-6, Sat 10-3
Friends of the Library Group
Branches: 1
COBDEN BRANCH, 100 S Front St, Cobden, 62920. (Mail add: 409 S Main St, 62906). Tel: 618-893-4637. FAX: 618-893-4637. *Br Librn,* Doris Luther
Open Tues 2-6, Thurs 9-Noon

ANNAWAN

P ANNAWAN-ALBA TOWNSHIP LIBRARY*, 200 N Meadow Lane, Ste 2, 61234-7607. SAN 303-6804. Tel: 309-935-6483. FAX: 309-935-6483. Web Site: www.annawanillinois.org. *Dir,* Carole Stern; *Assoc Librn,* Michele Thurston
Founded 1930. Pop 1,332; Circ 25,989
Library Holdings: Bk Vols 13,320; Per Subs 27

Wireless access
Mem of Reaching Across Illinois Library System (RAILS)
Open Mon 1-5, Tues & Fri 9-12 & 1-5, Wed 1-7, Sat 9-4
Friends of the Library Group

ANTIOCH

P ANTIOCH PUBLIC LIBRARY DISTRICT, 757 Main St, 60002. SAN 303-6812. Tel: 847-395-0874. FAX: 847-395-5399. TDD: 847-395-0916. *Dir,* Kathy LaBuda; *Ch Serv,* Kim Zupkoff; Tel: 847-395-0874, Ext 232, E-mail: kzupkoff@apld.info; *Circ,* Lynn Floyd; Tel: 847-395-0874, Ext 228, E-mail: lfloyd@apld.info; *Ref,* Amy Blue; Tel: 847-395-0874, Ext 227, E-mail: ablue@apld.info; *Tech Serv,* Jennifer Norris; Tel: 847-395-0874, Ext 235, E-mail: jnorris@apld.info; Staff 5 (MLS 3, Non-MLS 2)
Founded 1921. Pop 26,111
Jul 2008-Jun 2009 Income $2,300,000, State $30,000, County $2,130,000, Locally Generated Income $117,000. Mats Exp $301,000, Books $200,000, Micro $3,000, AV Equip $10,000, AV Mat $38,000, Electronic Ref Mat (Incl. Access Fees) $45,000, Presv $5,000. Sal $774,000
Library Holdings: Audiobooks 9,557; CDs 12,951; DVDs 15,315; e-books 6,163; e-journals 65; Microforms 168; Bk Titles 122,716; Bk Vols 123,009; Per Subs 168; Videos 5,129
Subject Interests: City hist, Cooking, Craft, Games, Parenting
Automation Activity & Vendor Info: (Cataloging) TLC (The Library Corporation); (Circulation) TLC (The Library Corporation); (ILL) OCLC; (OPAC) TLC (The Library Corporation); (Serials) OCLC
Database Vendor: TLC (The Library Corporation)
Wireless access
Mem of Reaching Across Illinois Library System (RAILS)
Open Mon-Thurs 9-9, Fri & Sat 9-5, Sun 1-5
Friends of the Library Group

ARCOLA

P ARCOLA PUBLIC LIBRARY DISTRICT*, 407 E Main St, 61910-1513. SAN 303-6820. Tel: 217-268-4477. FAX: 217-268-4478. E-mail: arcolapl@consolidated.net. Web Site: www.arcola.lib.il.us. *Dir,* Cheryl Switzer; Staff 4 (Non-MLS 4)
Founded 1904. Pop 4,072; Circ 26,947
Library Holdings: Bk Titles 20,000; Per Subs 50
Database Vendor: OCLC FirstSearch, Wilson - Wilson Web
Wireless access
Mem of Illinois Heartland Library System
Open Mon 9:30-8, Tues-Fri 9:30-6, Sat 9-3

ARGENTA

P ARGENTA-OREANA PUBLIC LIBRARY DISTRICT*, Argenta Public Library, 100 E Water, 62501. (Mail add: PO Box 278, Oreana, 62554), SAN 303-6839. Tel: 217-795-2144. Automation Services Tel: 217-468-2340. FAX: 217-795-4763. Automation Services FAX: 217-468-2467. E-mail: director@aopld.lib.il.us. Web Site: www.aopld.lib.il.us. *Dir,* Julia Welzen; Staff 2 (Non-MLS 2)
Pop 5,507
Library Holdings: AV Mats 1,000; CDs 350; DVDs 1,000; High Interest/Low Vocabulary Bk Vols 1,000; Large Print Bks 3,000; Bk Titles 32,837; Per Subs 250; Talking Bks 1,000; Videos 1,755
Automation Activity & Vendor Info: (Acquisitions) SirsiDynix; (Cataloging) SirsiDynix; (Circulation) SirsiDynix; (ILL) SirsiDynix; (OPAC) SirsiDynix
Database Vendor: SirsiDynix
Wireless access
Mem of Illinois Heartland Library System
Open Mon & Wed 9-5, Tues & Thurs 12-7, Fri 9-1, Sat 9-Noon

ARGONNE

S ARGONNE NATIONAL LABORATORY*, Argonne Research Library, 9700 S Cass Ave, Bldg 240, 60439-4801. SAN 339-6878. Tel: 630-252-0007. Interlibrary Loan Service Tel: 630-252-4223. Administration Tel: 630-252-4275. FAX: 630-252-5024. Web Site: www.library.anl.gov. *Libr Mgr,* Yvette N Woell; *Sr Electronic Res Librn,* Carol Lepzelter Berry; Tel: 630-252-3876; *Sr Ref Librn,* Mary Straka; Tel: 630-252-7770; *Assoc Electronic Res Librn,* Sarah Leeman; Tel: 630-252-4224, E-mail: sleeman@anl.gov; *Cat/ILL Librn,* Mary Alice Buckley; *Coordr, Acq,* Virginia Razo; Tel: 630-252-4270. Subject Specialists: *Biol, Chem,* Carol Lepzelter Berry; *Eng, Mat sci, Physics,* Mary Straka; Staff 9 (MLS 5, Non-MLS 4)
Founded 1946
Oct 2011-Sept 2012 Income $3,800,000. Mats Exp $2,600,000
Library Holdings: e-books 2,400; e-journals 3,500; Bk Titles 85,000; Per Subs 500
Special Collections: DOE/ERDA/AEC Technical Report
Subject Interests: Chem, Chem eng, Computer sci, Environ sci, Mat sci, Math, Microbiology, Nuclear sci, Physics, Transportation
Automation Activity & Vendor Info: (Acquisitions) Livelink for Libraries; (Cataloging) Livelink for Libraries; (Circulation) Livelink for Libraries; (OPAC) Livelink for Libraries; (Serials) Livelink for Libraries
Wireless access
Function: Online cat, Online ref, Res libr
Restriction: Badge access after hrs, Employees only

ARLINGTON HEIGHTS

P ARLINGTON HEIGHTS MEMORIAL LIBRARY, 500 N Dunton Ave, 60004-5966. SAN 303-6863. Tel: 847-392-0100. Administration Tel: 847-506-2649. FAX: 847-506-2650. Interlibrary Loan Service FAX: 847-392-0136. TDD: 847-392-1119. Web Site: www.ahml.info. *Exec Dir,* Jason Kuhl; Tel: 847-506-2612, E-mail: jkuhl@ahml.info; *Dep Dir,* Jeremy Andrykowski; Tel: 847-502-2688, E-mail: jandryko@ahml.info; *Dir of Finance,* Mike Kelly; Tel: 847-506-2615, E-mail: MKelly@ahml.info; *Dir, Human Res,* Diane Schultz; Tel: 847-506-2648, E-mail: dschultz@ahml.info; *Dir, Mkt & Communications,* Debora Whisler; Tel: 847-506-2613, E-mail: dwhisler@ahml.info; *Mgr, Coll Serv,* Margaret Jasinski; Tel: 847-506-2643, E-mail: mjasinksi@ahml.info; *Customer Serv Mgr,* Jan Sissors; Tel: 847-506-2625, E-mail: jsissors@ahml.info; *Digital Serv Mgr,* Amy Pelman; Tel: 847-506-2674, E-mail: APelman@ahml.info; *Info Serv Mgr,* Nancy Kim Phillips; Tel: 847-506-2668, E-mail: nkimphillips@ahml.info; *IT Mgr,* Mike Driskell; Tel: 847-870-3695, E-mail: mdriskell@ahml.info; *Interim Spec Serv Mgr,* Shannon Distel; Tel: 847-870-3642, E-mail: SDistel@ahml.info; *Youth Serv Mgr,* Amber Creger; Tel: 847-506-2619, E-mail: acreger@ahml.info; *Prog Supvr,* Jennifer Czajka; Tel: 847-506-2348, E-mail: JCzajka@ahml.info; Staff 23.63 (MLS 23.63)
Founded 1926. Pop 76,031; Circ 2,300,000
Library Holdings: CDs 33,865; DVDs 47,667; Bk Titles 258,142; Per Subs 918
Subject Interests: Am lit, Educ, Fiction, Foreign lang, Genealogy, Ill, Law, Local hist
Automation Activity & Vendor Info: (Acquisitions) Innovative Interfaces, Inc - Millenium; (Cataloging) Innovative Interfaces, Inc - Millenium; (Circulation) Innovative Interfaces, Inc - Millenium; (ILL) Innovative Interfaces, Inc - Millenium; (OPAC) Innovative Interfaces, Inc - Millenium; (Serials) Innovative Interfaces, Inc - Millenium
Wireless access
Open Mon-Fri 9am-10pm, Sat 9-5:30, Sun 12-5:30
Friends of the Library Group
Bookmobiles: 1

S THE CENTER - RESOURCES FOR TEACHING & LEARNING LIBRARY*, 2626 S Clearbrook Dr, 6005-4626. SAN 324-3370. Tel: 224-366-8500. FAX: 224-366-8514. Web Site: www.thecenterweb.org. *Librn,* Kim Scannell; *Asst Librn,* Betty McMillan; Staff 3 (MLS 1, Non-MLS 2)
Founded 1974
Library Holdings: Bk Vols 24,000; Per Subs 60
Subject Interests: Adult basic educ, Bilingual educ, Early childhood educ, English as a second lang, GED programs, Literacy
Automation Activity & Vendor Info: (ILL) OCLC
Function: ILL available
Open Mon, Tues, Thurs & Fri 9-4:45, Wed 9-7

S INSTITUTE OF ENVIRONMENTAL SCIENCES & TECHNOLOGY LIBRARY*, 2340 S Arlington Heights Rd, Ste 100, 60005. SAN 373-4404. Tel: 847-981-0100. FAX: 847-981-4130. Web Site: www.iest.org.
Library Holdings: CDs 39; DVDs 42; Bk Vols 230

M NORTHWEST COMMUNITY HOSPITAL, Health Resource Library, 800 W Central Rd, 60005-2392. SAN 303-6871. Tel: 847-618-5180. Interlibrary Loan Service Tel: 847-618-5181. FAX: 847-618-5189. E-mail: library@nch.org. Web Site: www.nch.org. *Chief Librn, Coll Develop Librn,* Mary O'Connell; E-mail: maoconnell@nch.org
Founded 1963
Library Holdings: Bk Titles 6,189; Per Subs 281
Subject Interests: Consumer health, Med, Mgt, Nursing, Oncology
Automation Activity & Vendor Info: (Cataloging) Professional Software; (Circulation) Professional Software; (ILL) OCLC Connexion; (OPAC) Professional Software; (Serials) Professional Software
Database Vendor: EBSCOhost, Gale Cengage Learning, OCLC FirstSearch, OCLC WebJunction, OCLC WorldShare Interlibrary Loan, OVID Technologies, UpToDate
Wireless access
Partic in Metrop Consortium of Healthcare Librs
Open Mon-Fri 9-4

G OSHA-US DEPARTMENT OF LABOR*, H Lee Saltsgaver Library, 2020 S Arlington Heights Rd, 60005. SAN 375-9857. Tel: 847-759-7797. FAX: 847-759-7748. Web Site: www.osha.gov. *Librn,* Lewis Eberhardt; Staff 1 (MLS 1)
Library Holdings: Bk Titles 2,920; Per Subs 30

ARTHUR

P ARTHUR PUBLIC LIBRARY*, 225 S Walnut, 61911. SAN 303-6898. Tel: 217-543-2037. FAX: 217-543-4081. *Librn,* Alice Cisna; E-mail: alicecisna@rocketmail.com; Staff 3 (MLS 1, Non-MLS 2)
Founded 1901. Pop 5,097; Circ 71,000
Library Holdings: Bk Vols 20,000; Per Subs 53
Subject Interests: Amish
Automation Activity & Vendor Info: (Cataloging) SirsiDynix; (Circulation) SirsiDynix; (OPAC) SirsiDynix
Wireless access
Open Mon-Thurs 9-8, Fri & Sat 9-5

ASHLAND

P PRAIRIE SKIES PUBLIC LIBRARY DISTRICT, 125 W Editor St, 62612. (Mail add: PO Box 498, 62612-0498), SAN 303-6901. Tel: 217-476-3417. FAX: 217-476-8076. E-mail: pspld@yahoo.com. Web Site: www.pspld.com. *Dir,* Robin Krone; E-mail: robinkrone@gmail.com; *Cat,* Beth Harris; *ILL,* Suzi Mesojednik; *Ref Serv,* Patty Smith; *Youth Serv,* Liz Heady
Pop 1,351; Circ 6,355
Library Holdings: Bk Vols 22,000; Per Subs 80
Wireless access
Open Mon-Wed & Fri 9-5, Thurs 9-7, Sat 9-Noon
Branches: 1
PLEASANT PLAINS BRANCH, 555 Buckeye Rd, Pleasant Plains, 62677. (Mail add: PO Box 498, 62612-0498). Tel: 217-626-1553. FAX: 217-626-2433. *Dir,* Robin Krone; *Librn,* Beth Harris
Founded 2002
Library Holdings: Bk Titles 2,000; Per Subs 10
Automation Activity & Vendor Info: (Acquisitions) SirsiDynix
Database Vendor: ABC-CLIO, Baker & Taylor, OCLC ArticleFirst, OCLC FirstSearch, OCLC WebJunction, OCLC WorldShare Interlibrary Loan, SirsiDynix, Wilson - Wilson Web, World Book Online
Open Mon, Wed & Fri 9-5, Tues & Thurs 9-7, Sat 9-2
Friends of the Library Group

ASHLEY

P ASHLEY PUBLIC LIBRARY DISTRICT*, 70 N Second St, 62808. (Mail add: PO Box 246, 62808-0246), SAN 303-691X. Tel: 618-485-2295. FAX: 618-485-2295. E-mail: maindesk@ashleypubliclibrary.org. *Librn,* Margie Holtz
Pop 922; Circ 5,441
Library Holdings: Bk Vols 9,000; Per Subs 20
Mem of Illinois Heartland Library System
Open Mon 6pm-8pm, Tues & Fri 1-4:30, Sat 9-12
Friends of the Library Group

ASHTON

P MILLS & PETRIE MEMORIAL LIBRARY*, 704 N First St, 61006. (Mail add: PO Box 308, 61006), SAN 303-6928. Tel: 815-453-2213. FAX: 815-453-2723. *Dir, Librn,* Linda Dallam
Pop 1,142; Circ 9,090
Library Holdings: Bk Vols 12,200; Per Subs 60
Mem of Reaching Across Illinois Library System (RAILS)
Open Mon-Thurs 1-6:30, Sat 10-1

ASSUMPTION

P ASSUMPTION PUBLIC LIBRARY DISTRICT*, 205 N Oak St, 62510. SAN 303-6936. Tel: 217-226-3915. FAX: 217-226-3915. Web Site: assumptionpubliclibrary.com. *Dir,* Anna Adermann; E-mail: anna@assumptionpubliclibrary.com
Founded 1903. Pop 2,101; Circ 12,637
Library Holdings: Bk Titles 14,000; Per Subs 20
Automation Activity & Vendor Info: (Cataloging) SirsiDynix; (Circulation) SirsiDynix; (OPAC) SirsiDynix
Mem of Illinois Heartland Library System
Open Tues, Thurs & Fri 9-5, Wed 9-6, Sat 9-3

ASTORIA

P ASTORIA PUBLIC LIBRARY DISTRICT*, 220 W Broadway, 61501-9630. SAN 376-091X. Tel: 309-329-2423. FAX: 309-329-2842. E-mail: astorlib@astoriail.net. Web Site: astoria.lib.il.us. *Dir,* Whitney Parrillo; Staff 1 (Non-MLS 1)
Founded 1940. Pop 2,506
Function: For res purposes, Handicapped accessible, Home delivery & serv to Sr ctr & nursing homes, Large print keyboards, Magnifiers for reading, Mail loans to mem, Newsp ref libr, Online searches, Photocopying/Printing, Prog for adults, Prog for children & young adult, Ref serv available, Summer reading prog, Workshops
Special Services for the Blind - Audio mat; Cassette playback machines; Cassettes; Copier with enlargement capabilities; Home delivery serv; Large print & cassettes; Large print bks & talking machines; Large screen computer & software; Magnifiers; Screen enlargement software for people with visual disabilities; Talking bk & rec for the blind cat; Talking bks
Open Mon-Thurs 10-12 & 12:30-6, Fri 2-6
Restriction: Access at librarian's discretion
Friends of the Library Group

ATHENS

P ATHENS MUNICIPAL LIBRARY*, 410 E Hargrave St, 62613-9702. Tel: 217-636-8047. FAX: 217-636-8763. E-mail: athenslibrary@casscomm.com. Web Site: www.athenslibrary.weebly.com. *Dir,* Donna Cunningham
Library Holdings: Bk Titles 12,000
Automation Activity & Vendor Info: (Acquisitions) Horizon
Database Vendor: OCLC FirstSearch
Wireless access
Mem of Illinois Heartland Library System
Open Mon-Thurs 10-7, Sun 12-4
Friends of the Library Group

ATKINSON

P ATKINSON PUBLIC LIBRARY DISTRICT*, 109 S State, 61235. SAN 303-6944. Tel: 309-936-7606. FAX: 309-936-7606. E-mail: apld@geneseo.net. Web Site: www.atkinson-library.com. *Dir,* Ninette Carton; *Asst Dir,* Ruthann Carton
Founded 1920. Pop 1,498; Circ 15,516
Library Holdings: AV Mats 620; Large Print Bks 75; Bk Vols 16,974; Per Subs 69; Talking Bks 900
Special Collections: Bound local newspapers - 70 volumes (yearly)
Automation Activity & Vendor Info: (Cataloging) SirsiDynix; (Circulation) SirsiDynix; (ILL) OCLC; (OPAC) SirsiDynix
Function: Accelerated reader prog
Mem of Reaching Across Illinois Library System (RAILS)
Special Services for the Deaf - Closed caption videos
Special Services for the Blind - Talking bks
Open Mon & Thurs 2-6, Tues 9-12 & 2-6, Wed 2-8, Fri 2-5, Sat 9-12

ATLANTA

P ATLANTA PUBLIC LIBRARY DISTRICT*, 100 Race St, 61723. (Mail add: PO Box 568, 61723-0568), SAN 303-6952. Tel: 217-648-2112. FAX: 217-648-5269. E-mail: apldinformation@gmail.com. Web Site: www.apldinfo.org. *Dir,* Carol Begolka; *Libr Asst,* Ruth Ann Hieronymus; Staff 4 (Non-MLS 4)
Founded 1908. Pop 2,325; Circ 6,116
Library Holdings: Bk Vols 13,468
Special Collections: Local Newspaper Coll, micro. Oral History
Subject Interests: Abraham Lincoln
Database Vendor: OCLC FirstSearch, TLC (The Library Corporation)
Wireless access
Open Mon 10am-12:30pm, Tues & Thurs 10:30-8, Wed & Fri 10:30-4:30, Sat 9-3

ATWOOD

P ATWOOD-HAMMOND PUBLIC LIBRARY*, 123 N Main St, 61913. (Mail add: PO Box 440, 61913-0440), SAN 303-6960. Tel: 217-578-2727. FAX: 217-578-2727. E-mail: ahlibrary@hotmail.com. Web Site: www.ahlibrary.com. *Librn,* Marsha Burgener
Pop 2,996; Circ 23,000
Library Holdings: Bk Titles 18,000; Per Subs 42
Subject Interests: Local hist
Automation Activity & Vendor Info: (Cataloging) SirsiDynix; (Circulation) SirsiDynix; (OPAC) SirsiDynix
Mem of Illinois Heartland Library System
Open Mon & Fri 9-5, Tues-Thurs 12-8, Sat 9-1
Friends of the Library Group

AUBURN

P AUBURN PUBLIC LIBRARY*, 338 W Jefferson, 62615. SAN 303-6979. Tel: 217-438-6211. FAX: 217-438-9317. E-mail: library@royell.org. *Dir,* Laura Carter
Founded 1932. Pop 4,317; Circ 27,084
Library Holdings: AV Mats 1,500; Large Print Bks 1,700; Bk Vols 35,000; Per Subs 36; Talking Bks 870
Wireless access
Mem of Illinois Heartland Library System

Open Mon, Tues & Thurs 2-7, Wed 10-7, Fri 10-5, Sat 10-2
Friends of the Library Group

AUGUSTA

P GREATER WEST CENTRAL PUBLIC LIBRARY DISTRICT*, Augusta Branch, 202 Center St, 62311. (Mail add: PO Box 235, 62311-0235), SAN 303-6987. Tel: 217-392-2211. FAX: 217-392-2211. E-mail: gwclibraries@yahoo.com. Web Site: greaterwestcentral.com. *Dir,* Dodie Wessel; E-mail: gwclibraries@yahoo.com; *Librn,* Wanda Eddington. Subject Specialists: *Computer sci,* Wanda Eddington
Founded 1915. Pop 5,015; Circ 55,130
Library Holdings: Bk Titles 72,025; Per Subs 135
Subject Interests: Educ, Hist
Open Tues & Thurs 1-8, Wed 9-Noon, Sat 9-2
Branches: 4
BOWEN BRANCH, 116 Fifth St, Bowen, 62316. (Mail add: PO Box 235, 62311), SAN 303-7436. Tel: 217-842-5573. FAX: 217-842-5573. E-mail: gwcbowenlibrary@yahoo.com. *Librn,* Ginny Dorethy
Founded 1972. Pop 1,348; Circ 11,220
Library Holdings: Bk Vols 20,000; Per Subs 25
Open Tues 9-Noon, Thurs 2-5, Sat 9-11
GOLDEN BRANCH, 309 Quincy St, Golden, 62339. (Mail add: PO Box 87, Golden, 62339-0087), SAN 372-5235. Tel: 217-696-2428. FAX: 217-696-2428. E-mail: gwcgoldenlibrary@yahoo.com. *Librn,* Shelly Jones
Library Holdings: Bk Titles 10,000; Per Subs 30
Open Tues 9-12 & 2-5, Wed 2-5, Thurs 9-12 & 5-8, Sat 9-Noon
Friends of the Library Group
LITTLETON BRANCH, 210 S Center St, Littleton, 61452. (Mail add: PO Box 235, 62311), SAN 372-5243. Tel: 309-257-2202. FAX: 309-257-2202. E-mail: gwclittletonlibrary@yahoo.com. Web Site: greaterwestcentral.com/littleton. *Head Librn,* Waynette Caldwell
Library Holdings: Bk Titles 7,000; Per Subs 13
Open Wed 12-7, Fri 6pm-9pm, Sun 2-6
Friends of the Library Group
PLYMOUTH BRANCH, 103 W Side Sq, Plymouth, 62367. (Mail add: PO Box 251, Plymouth, 62367-0251), SAN 325-3929. Tel: 309-458-6616. FAX: 309-458-6616. E-mail: gwcplymouthlibrary@yahoo.com. *Librn,* Linda Switzer
Library Holdings: Bk Vols 10,000; Per Subs 10
Open Tues 10-1 & 3-6, Wed 3-6, Thurs 9-12 & 3-7, Sat 9-12

AURORA

P AURORA PUBLIC LIBRARY*, One E Benton St, 60505-4299. SAN 303-7002. Tel: 630-264-4100. Administration Tel: 630-264-4106. FAX: 630-896-3209. Administration FAX: 630-859-1909. Web Site: www.aurora.lib.il.us. *Exec Dir,* Daisy Porter-Reynolds; *Main Libr Coordr,* Elizabeth Bumgarner, Tel: 630-264-4120; *Coordr, Circ,* Surekha Pal; *Youth Serv Coordr,* Diane Christian; *Syst Adminr,* Linda Whitmill; Staff 100 (MLS 20, Non-MLS 80)
Founded 1881. Pop 164,681; Circ 1,360,833
Library Holdings: Bk Vols 397,133; Per Subs 8,891
Subject Interests: Local hist
Automation Activity & Vendor Info: (Acquisitions) TLC (The Library Corporation); (Cataloging) TLC (The Library Corporation); (Circulation) TLC (The Library Corporation); (ILL) OCLC; (OPAC) TLC (The Library Corporation)
Database Vendor: Gale Cengage Learning, OCLC FirstSearch, SirsiDynix, TLC (The Library Corporation), Wilson - Wilson Web
Wireless access
Function: ILL available
Mem of Reaching Across Illinois Library System (RAILS)
Partic in OCLC-LVIS
Open Mon-Thurs 9-9, Fri & Sat 9-5, Sun (Sept-May) 1-5
Friends of the Library Group
Branches: 2
EOLA, 555 S Eola Rd, 60504-8992. Tel: 630-264-3400. FAX: 630-898-5220. Reference FAX: 630-264-3409. *Br Coordr,* Shannon Halikias; *Ch Serv,* Carolyn Hewitt; Staff 11 (MLS 5, Non-MLS 6)
Founded 1993
Library Holdings: DVDs 2,993; Bk Vols 88,264; Per Subs 120
Open Mon-Thurs 9-9, Fri & Sat 9-5, Sun (Sept-May) 1-5
WEST BRANCH, 233 S Constitution Dr, 60506-0506. Tel: 630-264-3600. FAX: 630-844-8695. *Br Coordr,* Position Currently Open
Library Holdings: Bk Titles 75,000; Per Subs 150
Open Mon-Thurs 9-9, Fri & Sat 9-5, Sun (Sept-May) 1-5
Bookmobiles: 1

C AURORA UNIVERSITY*, Charles B Phillips Library, 315 S Gladstone, 60506-4877. (Mail add: 347 S Gladstone Ave, 60506-4877), SAN 303-6995. Tel: 630-844-5437, 630-892-6431. Circulation Tel: 630-844-7583. Interlibrary Loan Service Tel: 630-844-5439. Reference Tel: 630-844-7534. Toll Free Tel: 800-742-5281. FAX: 630-844-3848. Web Site: www.aurora.edu/academics/library/index.html. *Dir, Libr Serv,* John Law; *Info Serv Librn,* Kathy Clark; Tel: 630-844-5443, E-mail: kclark@aurora.edu; *Res & Electronic Resources Librn,* Dr Nancy Mactague; E-mail: nmactag@aurora.edu; *Tech Serv Librn,* Lauren Jackson-Beck; Tel: 630-844-5525, E-mail: lbeck@aurora.edu; *Acq Mgr,* Andi Seifrid; Tel: 630-844-5444, E-mail: aseifrid@aurora.edu; *Mgr, Access Serv,* Kay Culhane; E-mail: kculhane@aurora.edu; *Cataloger,* Anne McKearn; Tel: 630-844-5653, E-mail: amckearn@aurora.edu; Staff 10 (MLS 7, Non-MLS 3)
Founded 1893. Enrl 4,700; Highest Degree: Doctorate
Library Holdings: Bk Titles 78,893; Bk Vols 99,000; Per Subs 210
Special Collections: Adventism (Jenks Coll), bks, per
Subject Interests: Am Indians, Educ, English lit, Nursing, Soc serv (soc work)
Automation Activity & Vendor Info: (Cataloging) Ex Libris Group; (Circulation) Ex Libris Group; (OPAC) Ex Libris Group
Wireless access
Function: Ref serv available
Mem of Reaching Across Illinois Library System (RAILS)
Partic in Consortium of Academic & Research Libraries in Illinois; Fox Valley Health Science Library Consortium; LIBRAS, Inc; OCLC-LVIS

S ENGINEERING SYSTEMS INC LIBRARY*, 4215 Campus Dr, 60504-7900. SAN 375-3298. Tel: 630-851-4566, Ext 238. FAX: 630-851-4870. *Librn,* Cheryl A Hansen; E-mail: cahansen@esi-il.com; Staff 1 (MLS 1)
Founded 1990
Library Holdings: Bk Titles 2,000
Automation Activity & Vendor Info: (Cataloging) SydneyPlus; (OPAC) SydneyPlus
Database Vendor: Agricola, ASCE Research Library, Dialog, ebrary, Elsevier, IEEE (Institute of Electrical & Electronics Engineers), IHS, Infotrieve, PubMed, Sage, ScienceDirect, Wiley InterScience
Wireless access
Mem of Reaching Across Illinois Library System (RAILS)
Partic in Illinois Library & Information Network

S ILLINOIS MATHEMATICS & SCIENCE ACADEMY*, Leto M Furnas Information Resource Center, 1500 W Sullivan Rd, 60506-1000. SAN 375-9539. Tel: 630-907-5920. Interlibrary Loan Service Tel: 630 907-5075. Reference Tel: 630-907-5973. FAX: 630-907-5004. E-mail: irc@imsa.edu. Web Site: staff.imsa.edu/irc/. *Dir,* Paula Garrett; Tel: 630-907-5953; *Archives Librn, Coll Develop Librn, Ref & Instruction Librn,* Jean Evans; *Circ, ILL,* Angela Richardson; *Tech Serv,* Jean Bigger; Staff 5 (MLS 2, Non-MLS 3)
Founded 1986
Library Holdings: Bk Titles 42,000; Per Subs 120
Special Collections: IMSA Archives
Automation Activity & Vendor Info: (Cataloging) Ex Libris Group; (Circulation) Ex Libris Group; (OPAC) Ex Libris Group
Wireless access
Partic in Consortium of Academic & Research Libraries in Illinois; IOUG; LOEX; OCLC Online Computer Library Center, Inc
Restriction: Not open to pub

S MARMION ACADEMY LIBRARY*, 1000 Butterfield Rd, 60504-9742. SAN 375-9806. Tel: 630-897-6936. FAX: 630-897-7086. Web Site: www.marmion.org. *Librn,* Fr Mario Pedi
Library Holdings: Bk Titles 10,316
Open Mon-Fri 7:30-4

M PRESENCE MERCY MEDICAL CENTER*, Medical Library, 1325 N Highland Ave, 60506. SAN 303-7010. Tel: 630-859-2222. FAX: 630-801-2687. Web Site: www.provena.org/mercy. *Librn,* Janet Leach; Tel: 630-801-2686; Staff 1 (Non-MLS 1)
Founded 1965
Library Holdings: Bk Titles 3,000; Per Subs 70
Subject Interests: Hospital admin, Med, Nursing, Psychiat
Publications: Periodicals Directory, HSN Video Guide
Mem of Reaching Across Illinois Library System (RAILS)
Partic in Fox Valley Health Science Library Consortium; Illinois Library & Information Network; OCLC Online Computer Library Center, Inc
Open Mon-Thurs 8-1

C ROBERT MORRIS UNIVERSITY*, Dupage Library, 905 Meridian Lake Dr, 60504. Tel: 630-375-8209. FAX: 630-375-8193. Web Site: www.robertmorris.edu/library. *Br Librn,* Su Erickson; E-mail: serickson@robertmorris.edu; Staff 1 (MLS 1)
Highest Degree: Master
Library Holdings: CDs 905; DVDs 3,635; Bk Titles 6,500
Automation Activity & Vendor Info: (Acquisitions) Ex Libris Group; (Cataloging) Ex Libris Group; (Circulation) Ex Libris Group; (Course Reserve) Ex Libris Group; (OPAC) Ex Libris Group; (Serials) Ex Libris Group

Database Vendor: EBSCOhost, Ex Libris Group, Gale Cengage Learning, LexisNexis, OCLC FirstSearch, OCLC WorldShare Interlibrary Loan, ProQuest, Standard & Poor's, ValueLine, Westlaw
Wireless access
Mem of Reaching Across Illinois Library System (RAILS)
Open Mon-Thurs 8am-9:30pm, Fri & Sat 8-2

M RUSH-COPLEY MEDICAL CENTER*, Health Science Library, 2000 Ogden Ave, 60504. SAN 376-0065. Tel: 630-978-4917. FAX: 630-978-6854. Web Site: www.rushcopley.com. *Librn,* James Bohlen; E-mail: jbohlen@rushcopley.com
Library Holdings: Bk Vols 829
Special Collections: Management Coll; Nursing Coll
Automation Activity & Vendor Info: (Cataloging) OCLC; (ILL) OCLC; (OPAC) OCLC FirstSearch
Database Vendor: EBSCOhost, MD Consult, OCLC FirstSearch, OVID Technologies
Mem of Reaching Across Illinois Library System (RAILS)
Partic in Docline
Restriction: Not open to pub

AVON

P VILLAGE OF AVON PUBLIC LIBRARY*, 105 S Main St, 61415. (Mail add: PO Box 598, 61415-0598), SAN 303-7037. Tel: 309-465-3933. FAX: 309-465-3933. *Librn,* Linda Williams
Pop 1,019; Circ 6,631
Library Holdings: Bk Vols 11,000; Per Subs 42
Publications: Library Journal
Open Mon 9-11 & 2-6, Wed 2-6 & 6:30-8:30, Thurs & Fri 1:30-6, Sat 9-1

BARRINGTON

P BARRINGTON PUBLIC LIBRARY DISTRICT*, 505 N Northwest Hwy, 60010. SAN 303-7053. Tel: 847-382-1300. FAX: 847-382-1261. Web Site: www.barringtonarealibrary.org. *Exec Dir,* Detlev Pansch; E-mail: dpansch@barringtonarealibrary.org; *Head, Adult Serv,* Rose M Faber; E-mail: rfaber@barringtonarealibrary.org; *Head, Circ Serv,* Marie Thomas; E-mail: mthomas@barringtonarealibrary.org; *Head, Tech Serv,* Maripat Olson; E-mail: molson@barringtonarealibrary.org; *Head, Youth Serv,* Ryann Uden; E-mail: ruden@barringtonarealibrary.org; Staff 39 (MLS 23, Non-MLS 16)
Founded 1913. Pop 42,127; Circ 978,703
Library Holdings: CDs 18,681; DVDs 18,802; e-books 9,697; Bk Vols 243,847; Per Subs 439
Automation Activity & Vendor Info: (Acquisitions) SirsiDynix; (Cataloging) SirsiDynix; (Circulation) SirsiDynix; (ILL) OCLC ILLiad; (OPAC) SirsiDynix; (Serials) SirsiDynix
Database Vendor: Gale Cengage Learning, Newsbank, OCLC FirstSearch, OCLC WorldShare Interlibrary Loan, ProQuest, ReferenceUSA, Westlaw
Wireless access
Function: Computer training, Copy machines, E-Reserves, Electronic databases & coll, Handicapped accessible, Homebound delivery serv, Homework prog, ILL available, Magnifiers for reading, Mail & tel request accepted, Music CDs, Online ref, Online searches, Photocopying/Printing, Preschool outreach, Prog for adults, Prog for children & young adult, Ref serv available, Spoken cassettes & CDs, Spoken cassettes & DVDs, Summer reading prog, Tax forms, Telephone ref, VHS videos, Wheelchair accessible
Publications: Check It Out (Newsletter)
Open Mon-Fri 9-9, Sat 9-5, Sun 1-5
Friends of the Library Group

BARRY

P BARRY PUBLIC LIBRARY*, 880 Bainbridge St, 62312. SAN 303-7096. Tel: 217-335-2149. FAX: 217-335-2149. Web Site: www.barryil.org. *Librn,* Margaret L Rawlings
Founded 1856. Pop 1,391; Circ 17,492
Library Holdings: Bk Vols 12,000; Per Subs 100
Open Mon 2-6, Tues 10-9, Thurs 10-12 & 2-7, Fri 10-6, Sat 10-2

BARTLETT

P BARTLETT PUBLIC LIBRARY DISTRICT*, 800 S Bartlett Rd, 60103. SAN 303-710X. Tel: 630-837-2855. Interlibrary Loan Service Tel: 630-837-3560. FAX: 630-837-2669. TDD: 630-837-2922. E-mail: bpldref@bartlett.lib.il.us. Web Site: www.bartlett.lib.il.us. *Dir,* Karolyn Nance; E-mail: knance@bartlett.lib.il.us; *Asst Dir,* Susan Westgate; E-mail: swestgate@bartlett.lib.il.us; *Adult & Tech Serv Mgr,* Mary Jane O'Brien; *IT Mgr,* Al Ramirez; *Patron Serv Mgr,* Mary Bavido; *Youth Serv Mgr,* Ruth Anne Mielke; Staff 11 (MLS 11)
Founded 1972. Pop 35,942; Circ 510,000
Jul 2006-Jun 2007 Income $319,506, State $35,000, Locally Generated Income $284,506. Mats Exp $282,950, Books $144,400, Per/Ser (Incl. Access Fees) $18,200, AV Mat $55,350, Electronic Ref Mat (Incl. Access Fees) $65,000. Sal $1,233,000 (Prof $473,000)
Library Holdings: AV Mats 18,000; Bk Vols 107,000
Automation Activity & Vendor Info: (Cataloging) OCLC; (ILL) OCLC
Wireless access
Mem of Reaching Across Illinois Library System (RAILS)
Special Services for the Deaf - TDD equip
Open Mon-Thurs 9:30-9, Fri & Sat 9:30-5, Sun 12-5
Friends of the Library Group

BARTONVILLE

P ALPHA PARK PUBLIC LIBRARY DISTRICT*, 3527 S Airport Rd, 61607-1799. SAN 303-7118. Tel: 309-697-3822. Circulation Tel: 309-697-3822, Ext 10. Reference Tel: 309-697-3822, Ext 13. Administration Tel: 309-697-3822, Ext 12. FAX: 309-697-9681. TDD: 309-697-9470. E-mail: alpha@alphapark.org. Web Site: www.alphapark.org. *Dir,* John D Richmond; E-mail: jrichmond@alphapark.org; *Pub Serv,* Julia Niemeier; Tel: 309-697-3822, Ext 17, E-mail: jniemeier@alphapark.org; *Pub Serv,* Jason Zimmerman; Tel: 309-697-3822, Ext 25, E-mail: jzimmerman@alphapark.org; *Tech Serv,* Debbie Wenzel; Tel: 309-697-3822, Ext 16, E-mail: dwenzel@alphapark.org; *Youth Serv,* Katie McKeever; Tel: 309-697-3822, Ext 14, E-mail: kmckeever@alphapark.org; Staff 25 (MLS 1, Non-MLS 24)
Founded 1972. Pop 28,545; Circ 195,089
Library Holdings: Bk Vols 72,667; Per Subs 378
Special Collections: Peoria State Hospital Coll
Automation Activity & Vendor Info: (Circulation) TLC (The Library Corporation)
Database Vendor: OCLC FirstSearch, ProQuest, TLC (The Library Corporation)
Function: ILL available
Publications: Library Times (Bi-monthly)
Partic in Lyrasis; Resource Sharing Alliance
Special Services for the Deaf - TDD equip
Special Services for the Blind - Reader equip
Open Mon-Thurs 9-9, Fri 9-6, Sat 9-5

BATAVIA

P BATAVIA PUBLIC LIBRARY DISTRICT*, Ten S Batavia Ave, 60510-2793. SAN 303-7126. Tel: 630-879-1393. Reference Tel: 630-879-4777. FAX: 630-879-9118. TDD: 630-879-8335. E-mail: askus@bataviapubliclibrary.org. Web Site: www.bataviapubliclibrary.org. *Dir,* George H Scheetz; E-mail: gscheetz@bataviapubliclibrary.org; *Dep Dir, Head, Youth Serv,* Joanne C Zillman; E-mail: jzillman@bataviapubliclibrary.org; *Head, Adult Serv,* Stacey L Cisneros; E-mail: scisneros@bataviapubliclibrary.org; *Circ Serv Coordr,* Pamela W Weber; E-mail: pweber@bataviapubliclibrary.org; *Digital Serv & Info Tech Coordr,* James J Klyczek; E-mail: jklyczek@bataviapubliclibrary.org; *Promotional Serv Coordr,* Michele M Martzel; E-mail: mmartzel@bataviapubliclibrary.org; *Tech Serv Coordr,* Kerry K Halter; E-mail: khalter@bataviapubliclibrary.org; Staff 12.56 (MLS 9.75, Non-MLS 2.81)
Founded 1881. Pop 25,723; Circ 663,001
Jul 2008-Jun 2009 Income $3,099,738, State $68,078, Federal $2,719, Locally Generated Income $2,869,251, Other $159,690. Mats Exp $342,092. Sal $1,301,746
Library Holdings: AV Mats 24,831; Electronic Media & Resources 32; Bk Vols 185,139; Per Subs 249
Special Collections: American-Style Windmills Coll
Subject Interests: Batavia & Kane County hist
Automation Activity & Vendor Info: (Cataloging) SirsiDynix; (Circulation) SirsiDynix; (OPAC) SirsiDynix
Database Vendor: OCLC FirstSearch, OCLC WorldShare Interlibrary Loan, SirsiDynix
Wireless access
Publications: Neighbors of Batavia (Periodical); Wired (Monthly newsletter)
Mem of Reaching Across Illinois Library System (RAILS)
Special Services for the Deaf - Closed caption videos; TDD equip
Special Services for the Blind - BiFolkal kits; Descriptive video serv (DVS)
Open Mon-Thurs 9-9, Fri & Sat 9-5, Sun 12-5 (1-4 Summer)
Friends of the Library Group

S FERMI NATIONAL ACCELERATOR LABORATORY LIBRARY*, Information Resources Department, Kirk & Wilson Sts, 60510. (Mail add: PO Box 500, MS109, 60510-5011), SAN 303-7134. Tel: 630-840-3401. FAX: 630-840-4636. E-mail: library@fnal.gov. Web Site: library.fnal.gov. *Mgr,* Heath O'Connell; *Librn,* Sandra Lee; E-mail: slee@fnal.gov; *Libr Asst,* Kathy Saumell; Staff 3 (MLS 2, Non-MLS 1)
Founded 1967
Library Holdings: Bk Vols 20,000; Per Subs 160

Special Collections: High Energy Physics Preprints
Subject Interests: Computer sci, Energy, Eng
Wireless access
Function: Res libr
Open Mon-Fri 8-5:30

BEARDSTOWN

P BEARDSTOWN HOUSTON MEMORIAL LIBRARY*, 13 Boulevard Rd, 62618-8119. SAN 303-7142. Tel: 217-323-4204. FAX: 217-323-4217. E-mail: beardlib@casscomm.com. Web Site: www.beardstown.lib.il.us. *Dir,* Molly Rice; Staff 1 (Non MLS 1)
Founded 1904. Pop 6,000; Circ 21,000
Library Holdings: High Interest/Low Vocabulary Bk Vols 25; Bk Vols 25,000; Per Subs 60
Special Collections: Oral History
Automation Activity & Vendor Info: (Circulation) Follett Software
Partic in Resource Sharing Alliance
Open Mon 10-7, Tues-Thurs 12-6, Fri 12-4, Sat 10-12

BEDFORD PARK

P BEDFORD PARK PUBLIC LIBRARY DISTRICT*, 7816 W 65th Pl, 60501. SAN 303-6847. Tel: 708-458-6826. FAX: 708-458-9827. Web Site: www.bplib.net. *Dir,* Anne Murphy; E-mail: amurphy@bplib.net; *ILL,* Deborah Kalafut; *YA Serv,* Barbara Weber
Founded 1963. Pop 988; Circ 89,000
Library Holdings: Bk Vols 88,000; Per Subs 223
Automation Activity & Vendor Info: (Acquisitions) Innovative Interfaces, Inc; (Cataloging) Innovative Interfaces, Inc; (Circulation) Innovative Interfaces, Inc; (OPAC) Innovative Interfaces, Inc
Publications: Calendar & Booklist (Monthly); Newsletter (Quarterly)
Mem of Reaching Across Illinois Library System (RAILS)
Open Mon-Thurs 9-8, Fri & Sat 9-4

S ILLINOIS INSTITUTE OF TECHNOLOGY*, Institute for Food Safety & Health Library, Moffett Campus, 6502 S Archer Rd, 60501-1957. SAN 375-5363. Tel: 708-563-8160. FAX: 708-563-1873. Web Site: library.iit.edu/ifsh. *Br Librn,* David Griesemer; E-mail: dgriesem@iit.edu; Staff 2 (MLS 1, Non-MLS 1)
Founded 1993
Library Holdings: Bk Titles 5,000; Bk Vols 6,800; Per Subs 200
Automation Activity & Vendor Info: (Cataloging) EOS International; (Serials) EOS International
Wireless access
Partic in OCLC Online Computer Library Center, Inc
Open Mon-Fri 9-5:30

BEECHER

P BEECHER COMMUNITY LIBRARY*, 660 Penfield St, 60401. (Mail add: PO Box 818, 60401-0818). Tel: 708-946-9090. FAX: 708-946-2896. E-mail: director@beecherlibrary.com. Web Site: www.villageofbeecher.org. *Interim Dir,* Carol Harris
Founded 1994. Pop 4,302
Library Holdings: Bk Titles 20,000; Per Subs 35
Special Collections: Local history
Automation Activity & Vendor Info: (Cataloging) Innovative Interfaces, Inc; (Circulation) Innovative Interfaces, Inc; (OPAC) Innovative Interfaces, Inc
Mem of Reaching Across Illinois Library System (RAILS)
Open Mon & Wed 9-8, Tues, Thurs & Fri 1-6, Sat 9-12

BELLEVILLE

P BELLEVILLE PUBLIC LIBRARY*, 121 E Washington St, 62220. SAN 339-7203. Tel: 618-234-0441. FAX: 618-234-9474. TDD: 618-234-1496. E-mail: mainlibrary@bellevillepubliclibrary.org. Web Site: www.bellevillepubliclibrary.org. *Dir,* Leander Spearman; *Archivist,* Dana Prusacki; Tel: 618-234-0441, Ext 22; *Cat,* Karen Beiter; Tel: 618-234-0441, Ext 20, E-mail: karenb@lcls.org; *Ch Serv,* Terri Bassler; Tel: 618-234-0441, Ext 17, E-mail: terrib@lcls.org; *Circ,* Pat Miller; Tel: 618-234-0441, Ext 15, E-mail: patm@lcls.org; *Ref Serv,* Michelle Bruss; *Ref Serv,* Kent Willbanks; Tel: 618-234-0441, Ext 19; Staff 26 (MLS 1, Non-MLS 25)
Founded 1836. Pop 44,165; Circ 221,203
Library Holdings: Bk Vols 135,000; Per Subs 443
Special Collections: Geneology. State Document Depository
Subject Interests: Area hist, Local hist
Automation Activity & Vendor Info: (Acquisitions) SirsiDynix; (Cataloging) SirsiDynix; (Circulation) SirsiDynix; (OPAC) SirsiDynix
Database Vendor: EBSCOhost, OCLC FirstSearch, SirsiDynix
Function: ILL available
Publications: Anniversary booklet, Walking Tour Guide & Archives Bibliography
Open Mon-Thurs 9-8, Fri & Sat 9-5
Friends of the Library Group
Branches: 1
WEST BRANCH, 3414 W Main St, 62226, SAN 339-7238. Tel: 618-233-4366. FAX: 618-233-1482. E-mail: westbranch@bellevillepubliclibrary.org. *Br Mgr,* Pat Feldt; E-mail: pat.feldt@bellevillepubliclibrary.org
Open Mon, Wed & Sat 9-5, Tues & Thurs 12-8
Friends of the Library Group

M MEMORIAL HOSPITAL LIBRARY*, 4500 Memorial Dr, 62226-5360. SAN 321-6594. Tel: 618-257-5343. FAX: 618-257-6825. Web Site: www.memhosp.com. *Dir,* Barbara Grout; Staff 2 (MLS 1, Non-MLS 1)
Founded 1974
Library Holdings: Bk Titles 5,000; Per Subs 430
Publications: library infobooklet; Newsletter
Partic in Areawide Hospital Library Consortium of Southwestern Illinois; National Network of Libraries of Medicine; Regional Med Libr - Region 3
Open Mon-Fri 8-4:30
Friends of the Library Group

M SAINT ELIZABETH'S HOSPITAL*, Health Science Library, 211 S Third St, 62222. SAN 303-7169. Tel: 618-234-2120, Ext 2011. FAX: 618-222-4614. Web Site: www.steliz.org.
Founded 1956
Library Holdings: Bk Titles 2,500; Per Subs 323
Subject Interests: Med

J SOUTHWESTERN ILLINOIS COLLEGE LIBRARY*, SWIC Library, Belleville Campus, 2500 Carlyle Ave, 62221. SAN 303-7150. Tel: 618-235-2700, Ext 5204. Interlibrary Loan Service Tel: 618-222-5353. Reference Tel: 618-222-5236, 618-222-5597. Administration Tel: 618-235-2700, Ext 5220. Toll Free Tel: 866-942-7942. FAX: 618-222-8964. Web Site: www.swic.edu/library. *Dean,* Laurie Bingel; E-mail: laurie.bingel@swic.edu; Staff 2 (MLS 2)
Founded 1946. Enrl 8,000; Fac 165; Highest Degree: Associate
Library Holdings: AV Mats 251; Bk Titles 61,072; Bk Vols 62,917; Per Subs 200
Automation Activity & Vendor Info: (Cataloging) Ex Libris Group; (Circulation) Ex Libris Group; (OPAC) Ex Libris Group
Database Vendor: EBSCOhost, Gale Cengage Learning, LexisNexis, OCLC FirstSearch, OCLC WorldShare Interlibrary Loan
Mem of Illinois Heartland Library System
Partic in Consortium of Academic & Research Libraries in Illinois; Saint Louis Regional Library Network; Southern Ill Learning Resources Coop
Open Mon-Thurs (Winter) 7:30am-9:30pm, Fri 7:30-4, Sat 8-4; Mon-Thurs (Summer) 7:30am-9:30pm, Fri 7:30-4

BELLWOOD

P BELLWOOD PUBLIC LIBRARY*, 600 Bohland Ave, 60104-1896. SAN 303-7177. Tel: 708-547-7393. FAX: 708-547-9352. TDD: 708-547-7475. E-mail: bws@bellwoodlibrary.org. Web Site: www.bellwoodlibrary.org. *Dir,* Jimmi Wooten; E-mail: wootenj@bellwoodlibrary.org; *Bus Mgr,* Chris Randall; *Circ Mgr,* Jackie Spratt; E-mail: sprattj28@bellwoodlibrary.org; *Adult Serv,* Kristin Schultz; E-mail: schultzk@bellwoodlibrary.org; *Ch Serv,* Position Currently Open; *Info Tech,* Tony Brown; E-mail: brownt@bellwoodlibrary.org; *Ref Serv,* Natalie Cannestra; E-mail: cannestran@bellwoodlibrary.org; *Ref Serv, YA,* Karen Fredrickson; E-mail: fredrickson@bellwoodlibrary.org; Staff 5 (MLS 5)
Founded 1932. Pop 19,071; Circ 54,140
Library Holdings: CDs 1,008; DVDs 2,753; Large Print Bks 1,214; Bk Vols 77,699; Per Subs 96; Videos 549
Subject Interests: Ill
Publications: Bellwood, 1900-1975 (history)
Mem of Reaching Across Illinois Library System (RAILS)
Special Services for the Deaf - TDD equip
Open Mon-Thurs 9:30-9, Fri 9:30-6, Sat 9:30-4

BELVIDERE

P IDA PUBLIC LIBRARY*, 320 N State St, 61008-3299. SAN 303-7193. Tel: 815-544-3838. FAX: 815-544-8909. Web Site: www.idapubliclibrary.org. *Dir,* Debbie Bloom; E-mail: debbieb@idapubliclibrary.org; *AV,* Marjorie Hinrichs; *Ch Serv,* Pat Walter; *Tech Serv,* June Ottman; Staff 3 (MLS 3)
Founded 1885. Pop 23,532; Circ 165,000
Library Holdings: Bk Vols 77,000; Per Subs 250
Subject Interests: Local hist
Automation Activity & Vendor Info: (Cataloging) Innovative Interfaces, Inc; (Circulation) Innovative Interfaces, Inc; (ILL) Innovative Interfaces, Inc; (OPAC) Innovative Interfaces, Inc; (Serials) Innovative Interfaces, Inc
Publications: Ida-Lites (Newsletter)
Mem of Reaching Across Illinois Library System (RAILS)

Open Mon-Fri 10-8, Sat 9-5
Friends of the Library Group

BEMENT

P BEMENT PUBLIC LIBRARY DISTRICT*, 349 S Macon, 61813. SAN 303-7207. Tel: 217-678-7101. FAX: 217-678-7034. E-mail: bementlibrary@gmail.com. Web Site: www.bementpubliclibrary.org. *Dir,* Melinda Glover
Founded 1877. Pop 2,445; Circ 22,679
Library Holdings: Bk Vols 16,435; Per Subs 75
Subject Interests: Genealogy, Local hist, Ref bks
Wireless access
Function: ILL available, Photocopying/Printing
Mem of Illinois Heartland Library System
Open Mon & Wed 12-8, Tues, Thurs & Fri 12-5, Sat 9-2
Friends of the Library Group

BENLD

P FRANK BERTETTI BENLD PUBLIC LIBRARY*, 308 E Central Ave, 62009. Tel: 217-835-4045. FAX: 217-835-4045. E-mail: benldlibrary@gmail.com. Web Site: www.benldlibrary.org. *Librn,* Mary Newman
Founded 1997
Library Holdings: Bk Titles 9,000
Automation Activity & Vendor Info: (Circulation) Follett Software
Mem of Illinois Heartland Library System
Open Mon & Thurs 2-6, Tues 2-7, Wed & Fri 9-5, Sat 9-12

BENSENVILLE

P BENSENVILLE COMMUNITY PUBLIC LIBRARY*, 200 S Church Rd, 60106. SAN 303-7215. Tel: 630-766-4642. FAX: 630-766-0788. E-mail: bcplref@gmail.com. Web Site: www.benlib.org. *Dir,* Jill Rodriguez; Tel: 630-766-4642, Ext 426, E-mail: jrodriguez@benlib.org; *Asst Dir,* Bill Erbes; Tel: 630-766-4642, Ext 427, E-mail: berbes@benlib.org; *Circ Mgr,* Joan Baader; Tel: 630-766-4642, Ext 415, E-mail: jbaader@benlib.org; *Youth Serv Coordr,* Kelly Watson; E-mail: kwatson@benlib.org; Staff 37 (MLS 7, Non-MLS 30)
Founded 1960. Pop 21,640; Circ 130,000
Library Holdings: Bk Titles 80,000; Bk Vols 87,000; Per Subs 370
Special Collections: Large Print Books; Local History. Oral History
Automation Activity & Vendor Info: (Acquisitions) SirsiDynix; (Cataloging) SirsiDynix; (Circulation) SirsiDynix; (Course Reserve) SirsiDynix; (OPAC) SirsiDynix
Database Vendor: Grolier Online, Newsbank
Publications: Community News (Bi-monthly); Serendipity E News (Newsletter)
Mem of Reaching Across Illinois Library System (RAILS)
Open Mon-Thurs 9-9, Fri 9-5, Sun 1-5

C ROBERT MORRIS UNIVERSITY*, Bensenville Library, 1000 Tower Lane, 60106. Tel: 630-787-7879. Administration Tel: 630-787-7800. Toll Free Tel: 800-789-8735. FAX: 630-787-7802. Web Site: www.robertmorris.edu/library/branches. *Coordr,* E Pappas; E-mail: epappas@robertmorris.edu
Library Holdings: Bk Titles 1,500; Per Subs 21
Automation Activity & Vendor Info: (Acquisitions) Ex Libris Group
Open Mon & Wed 10-9:30, Tues & Thurs 8am-9:30pm, Fri 8:30-7:30, Sat 9-3

BENTON

P BENTON PUBLIC LIBRARY DISTRICT*, 502 S Main St, 62812. SAN 303-7223. Tel: 618-438-7511. FAX: 618-439-6139. Web Site: www.benton.lib.il.us. *Dir,* Erin Steinsultz; E-mail: erins@shawls.lib.il.us; Staff 3 (MLS 1, Non-MLS 2)
Founded 1916. Pop 10,452; Circ 60,000
Library Holdings: Bk Vols 42,000; Per Subs 60
Special Collections: Southern Illinois History
Subject Interests: Fiction, Genealogy, Local hist
Automation Activity & Vendor Info: (Cataloging) SirsiDynix; (Circulation) SirsiDynix; (OPAC) SirsiDynix
Mem of Illinois Heartland Library System
Partic in Illinois Library & Information Network
Open Mon-Thurs 9-8, Fri & Sat 9-5, Sun 1-5
Friends of the Library Group

BERKELEY

P BERKELEY PUBLIC LIBRARY, 1637 N Taft Ave, 60163-1499. SAN 303-7231. Tel: 708-544-6017. FAX: 708-544-7551. E-mail: mail@berkeleypl.org. Web Site: www.berkeleypl.org. *Dir,* Lenora Berendt; E-mail: lberendt@berkeleypl.org; Staff 2 (MLS 2)
Pop 5,409
Automation Activity & Vendor Info: (Acquisitions) Baker & Taylor; (Cataloging) Innovative Interfaces, Inc; (Circulation) Innovative Interfaces, Inc; (ILL) OCLC WorldShare Interlibrary Loan; (OPAC) Innovative Interfaces, Inc
Database Vendor: Baker & Taylor, EBSCOhost, Gale Cengage Learning, H W Wilson, Innovative Interfaces, Inc, OCLC, OCLC WorldShare Interlibrary Loan, Overdrive, Inc, ProQuest, ReferenceUSA, TumbleBookLibrary, World Book Online
Wireless access
Function: 24/7 Electronic res, 24/7 Online cat, Adult bk club, Audiobks via web, Bilingual assistance for Spanish patrons, Bk club(s), Bks on CD, Children's prog, Computer training, Computers for patron use, Copy machines, e-mail serv, Electronic databases & coll, Family literacy, Fax serv, Free DVD rentals, Govt ref serv, Handicapped accessible, Holiday prog, Homebound delivery serv, ILL available, Magazines, Mail & tel request accepted, Movies, Mus passes, Music CDs, Newsp ref libr, Online cat, Online info literacy tutorials on the web & in blackboard, Outreach serv, Outside serv via phone, mail, e-mail & web, OverDrive digital audio bks, Photocopying/Printing, Preschool outreach, Printer for laptops & handheld devices, Pub access computers, Ref & res, Ref serv available, Ref serv in person, Referrals accepted, Scanner, Senior outreach, Spanish lang bks, Story hour, Study rm, Summer & winter reading prog, Teen prog, Telephone ref, Video lending libr, Web-catalog, Wheelchair accessible, Workshops
Mem of Reaching Across Illinois Library System (RAILS)
Open Mon-Thurs 10-9, Fri 10-6, Sat 10-5
Restriction: ID required to use computers (Ltd hrs)
Friends of the Library Group

BERWYN

P BERWYN PUBLIC LIBRARY*, 2701 Harlem Ave, 60402. SAN 339-7262. Tel: 708-795-8000. Administration Tel: 708-795-8000, Ext 3029. FAX: 708-795-8101. TDD: 708-795-5998. Web Site: www.berwynlibrary.org. *Dir,* Bill Hensley; Staff 54 (MLS 7, Non-MLS 47)
Pop 54,016; Circ 367,210
Library Holdings: Bk Vols 200,000; Per Subs 388
Special Collections: Czechoslovakian Language Coll
Wireless access
Publications: Newsletter (Quarterly)
Mem of Reaching Across Illinois Library System (RAILS)
Open Mon-Thurs 9-9, Fri & Sat 9-5, Sun (Sept-May) 1-5
Friends of the Library Group

M MACNEAL HOSPITAL*, Health Sciences Resource Center, 3249 S Oak Park Ave, 60402. SAN 303-724X. Tel: 708-783-3089. FAX: 708-783-3369. *Med Librn,* Karly Vesely; Staff 1 (MLS 1)
Founded 1950
Subject Interests: Med, Nursing
Automation Activity & Vendor Info: (OPAC) CyberTools for Libraries; (Serials) SERHOLD
Database Vendor: EBSCOhost, Elsevier, OCLC FirstSearch, OVID Technologies, Sage, ScienceDirect, STAT!Ref (Teton Data Systems), Wilson - Wilson Web
Wireless access
Mem of Reaching Across Illinois Library System (RAILS)
Partic in National Network of Libraries of Medicine; OCLC Online Computer Library Center, Inc
Restriction: Hospital employees & physicians only

BETHALTO

P BETHALTO PUBLIC LIBRARY DISTRICT, 321 S Prairie St, 62010-1525. SAN 303-7266. Tel: 618-377-8141. FAX: 618-377-3520. E-mail: info@bethaltolibrary.org. Web Site: www.bethaltolibrary.org. *Dir,* Mary Brewster; Staff 8 (MLS 1, Non-MLS 7)
Founded 1947. Pop 15,828; Circ 144,229
Library Holdings: Audiobooks 641; DVDs 4,951; e-books 17,388; e-journals 168; Large Print Bks 1,000; Bk Vols 39,995; Per Subs 140
Automation Activity & Vendor Info: (Circulation) Innovative Interfaces, Inc
Database Vendor: 3M Library Systems, Gale Cengage Learning, Overdrive, Inc, TumbleBookLibrary
Wireless access
Function: 24/7 Online cat, Adult bk club, After school storytime, Audiobks via web, Bks on CD, Children's prog, Computers for patron use, Copy machines, Fax serv, Free DVD rentals, Handicapped accessible, Homebound delivery serv, ILL available, OverDrive digital audio bks, Scanner, Story hour, Summer reading prog, Tax forms, Wheelchair accessible
Mem of Illinois Heartland Library System
Open Mon-Thurs 9-8, Fri 9-7, Sat 10-5, Sun 1-5

BETHANY

P MARROWBONE PUBLIC LIBRARY DISTRICT*, 216 W Main St, 61914-8627. SAN 303-7274. Tel: 217-665-3014. FAX: 217-665-3246. Web Site: marrowbonepld.com. *Co-Dir,* Sally Ellen Ascenzo; E-mail: sea201@yahoo.com; *Co-Dir,* Lisa Marie Spracklen; E-mail: lms501@yahoo.com; *Ch,* Lesa Oathout; E-mail: leepod2003@yahoo.com; Staff 4 (Non-MLS 4)
Founded 1939. Pop 2,261; Circ 37,297
Library Holdings: Bks on Deafness & Sign Lang 10; High Interest/Low Vocabulary Bk Vols 100; Bk Titles 27,000; Per Subs 193
Automation Activity & Vendor Info: (Circulation) Innovative Interfaces, Inc
Database Vendor: SirsiDynix
Wireless access
Mem of Illinois Heartland Library System
Open Mon 9-8, Tues-Fri 9-6, Sat 10-4

BIGGSVILLE

P HENDERSON COUNTY PUBLIC LIBRARY DISTRICT*, 110 Hillcrest Dr, 61418-9736. SAN 303-7282. Tel: 309-627-2450. FAX: 309-627-2830. E-mail: hcpl61418@hotmail.com. Web Site: www.hendersoncolibrary.com. *Librn,* Anita Smith
Founded 1959. Pop 7,331; Circ 54,265
Library Holdings: Bk Vols 40,000; Per Subs 10
Subject Interests: Genealogy
Automation Activity & Vendor Info: (Cataloging) SirsiDynix; (Circulation) SirsiDynix; (OPAC) SirsiDynix
Database Vendor: Brodart, Gale Cengage Learning, Ingram Library Services, Overdrive, Inc
Wireless access
Function: Adult bk club, Bks on CD, Children's prog, Computers for patron use, Copy machines, Digital talking bks, e-mail serv, Fax serv, Free DVD rentals, Genealogy discussion group, Handicapped accessible, Microfiche/film & reading machines, Music CDs, Newsp ref libr, Online cat, OverDrive digital audio bks, Photocopying/Printing, Preschool outreach, Preschool reading prog, Prog for children & young adult, Scanner, Senior outreach, Story hour, Summer & winter reading prog, Tax forms, Web-catalog
Mem of Reaching Across Illinois Library System (RAILS)
Partic in RSA
Open Mon-Sat 9-5
Bookmobiles: 1. In Charge, Crystal Parsons

BLANDINSVILLE

P BLANDINSVILLE-HIRE DISTRICT LIBRARY*, 130 S Main St, 61420. (Mail add: PO Box 50, 61420-0050), SAN 303-7290. Tel: 309-652-3166. FAX: 309-652-3166. E-mail: blanhire@winco.net. *Librn,* Sherry Phillips; *Asst Librn,* Pat Hainline
Founded 1953. Pop 2,345; Circ 30,120
Library Holdings: AV Mats 1,550; Large Print Bks 580; Bk Titles 23,000; Bk Vols 23,200; Per Subs 91; Talking Bks 450
Subject Interests: Antiques, Genealogy, Hist, Local hist
Partic in RSA
Open Mon 12:30-8, Tues & Sat 8:30-5, Wed 8:30-8, Fri 12:30-5

BLOOMINGDALE

P BLOOMINGDALE PUBLIC LIBRARY*, 101 Fairfield Way, 60108-1579. SAN 303-7304. Tel: 630-529-3120. FAX: 630-529-3243. E-mail: bdref@mybpl.org. Web Site: www.mybpl.org. *Dir,* Timothy Jarzemsky; E-mail: tjarzemsky@mybpl.org; *Head, Adult Serv,* Julie Keating; E-mail: jkeating@mybpl.org; *Head, Circ & Tech Serv,* Kandice Krettler; E-mail: kkrettler@mybpl.org; *Head, Info Serv,* Sean Luster; E-mail: sluster@mybpl.org; *Head, Youth Serv,* Lisa Palmer; E-mail: lpalmer@mybpl.org; Staff 56 (MLS 12, Non-MLS 44)
Founded 1974. Pop 22,018; Circ 301,731
May 2010-Apr 2011 Income $2,751,689, State $3,555, City $2,657,999, Federal $3,177, Other $86,958. Mats Exp $338,450, Books $143,250, Manu Arch $3,000, Other Print Mats $8,500, AV Equip $5,000, AV Mat $66,700, Electronic Ref Mat (Incl. Access Fees) $110,500, Presv $1,500. Sal $1,504,207
Library Holdings: Audiobooks 31,317; DVDs 12,607; e-books 15,839; Electronic Media & Resources 68; Bk Titles 107,289; Per Subs 229
Automation Activity & Vendor Info: (Acquisitions) SirsiDynix; (Circulation) SirsiDynix; (OPAC) SIRSI-iBistro
Database Vendor: EBSCO Auto Repair Reference, Evanced Solutions, Inc, Gale Cengage Learning, infoUSA, Ingram Library Services, LearningExpress, Newsbank, OCLC FirstSearch, OCLC WorldShare Interlibrary Loan, Overdrive, Inc, ProQuest, ReferenceUSA, SerialsSolutions, SirsiDynix, TumbleBookLibrary, ValueLine, Wilson - Wilson Web, World Book Online, WT Cox
Wireless access
Publications: Off the Shelf (Newsletter)
Mem of Reaching Across Illinois Library System (RAILS)
Open Mon-Thurs 9-9, Fri & Sat 9-5, Sun 1-5
Friends of the Library Group

BLOOMINGTON

P BLOOMINGTON PUBLIC LIBRARY*, 205 E Olive St, 61701. (Mail add: PO Box 3308, 61702-3308), SAN 303-7312. Tel: 309-828-6091. FAX: 309-828-7312. Interlibrary Loan Service FAX: 309-821-9314. Web Site: www.bloomingtonlibrary.org. *Dir,* Georgia Bouda; E-mail: georgiab@bloomingtonlibrary.org; *Outreach Serv Librn,* Carol Torrens; E-mail: carolt@bloomingtonlibrary.org; *Bus Mgr,* Kathy Jeakins; E-mail: kathyj@bloomingtonlibrary.org; *Circ Mgr,* Lynne Rickard; E-mail: lynner@bloomingtonlibrary.org; *Human Res Mgr,* Gayle Tucker; E-mail: gaylet@bloomingtonlibrary.org; *Mgr, Info Tech,* Chuck Thacker; E-mail: chuckt@bloomingtonlibrary.org; *Tech Serv Mgr,* Linda Fitzgerald; E-mail: lindaf@bloomingtonlibrary.org; *Adult Serv,* Jane Chamberlain; E-mail: jchamber@bloomingtonlibrary.org; *Ch Serv,* Melissa Robinson; E-mail: melissar@bloomingtonlibrary.org; *Mkt,* Rhonda Massie; E-mail: rhondam@bloomingtonlibrary.org; Staff 47 (MLS 15, Non-MLS 32)
Founded 1867. Pop 74,975; Circ 705,332
Library Holdings: AV Mats 25,281; Bks on Deafness & Sign Lang 162; Bk Titles 178,864; Per Subs 500; Talking Bks 3,063
Special Collections: Illinois Coll
Subject Interests: Genealogy, Ill
Automation Activity & Vendor Info: (Cataloging) SirsiDynix; (Circulation) SirsiDynix; (OPAC) SirsiDynix
Database Vendor: SirsiDynix
Wireless access
Publications: Business Connection, News & Reviews (Newsletter)
Mem of Reaching Across Illinois Library System (RAILS)
Partic in Illinois Library & Information Network; OCLC Online Computer Library Center, Inc
Special Services for the Blind - Talking bks
Open Mon-Thurs 9-9, Fri & Sat 9-5, Sun 1-5
Friends of the Library Group
Bookmobiles: 1. Outreach Mgr, Carol Torrens. Bk titles 25,378

S ILLINOIS AGRICULTURAL ASSOCIATION*, Information Research Center, 1701 N Towanda Ave, 61701. (Mail add: PO Box 2901, 61701-2901), SAN 303-7339. Tel: 309-557-2552. FAX: 309-557-3185. E-mail: iaairc@ilfb.org. Web Site: www.ilfb.org. Staff 2 (Non-MLS 2)
Founded 1960
Sept 2008-Aug 2009. Mats Exp $120,000, Books $20,000, Per/Ser (Incl. Access Fees) $41,000, Electronic Ref Mat (Incl. Access Fees) $45,000, Presv $3,000
Library Holdings: Bk Titles 9,000; Per Subs 465
Automation Activity & Vendor Info: (Cataloging) Inmagic, Inc.; (Circulation) Inmagic, Inc.
Publications: Farm Facts
Mem of Reaching Across Illinois Library System (RAILS)
Partic in Illinois Library & Information Network; Libr User Info Syst
Open Mon-Fri 8-4:30

C ILLINOIS WESLEYAN UNIVERSITY*, The Ames Library, One Ames Plaza, 61701-7188. (Mail add: PO Box 2899, 61702-2899), SAN 339-7351. Tel: 309-556-3350. Interlibrary Loan Service Tel: 309-556-1040. FAX: 309-556-3706. Administration FAX: 309-556-3261. Web Site: www.iwu.edu/library. *Univ Librn,* Karen Schmidt; E-mail: kschmidt@iwu.edu; *Dir, Commun & Tech Serv,* Marcia Thomas; Tel: 309-556-3808, E-mail: mthomas@iwu.edu; *Libr Tech & Res Dir,* Suzanne Wilson; E-mail: swilson@iwu.edu; *Acad Outreach Librn,* Lynda Duke; Tel: 309-556-3220, E-mail: lduke@iwu.edu; *Fine Arts Librn,* Robert Delvin; Tel: 309-556-3003, E-mail: bdelvin@iwu.edu; *Info Literacy Librn,* Christopher Sweet; Tel: 309-556-3984, E-mail: csweet@iwu.edu; *Info Serv Librn,* Sue Anderson; *Scholarly Communications Librn,* Stephanie Davis-Kahl; Tel: 309-556-3010, E-mail: sdaviska@iwu.edu; *Spec Coll Librn, Univ Archivist,* Meg Miner; Tel: 556-309-1538, E-mail: mminer@iwu.edu; *Circ Mgr,* Tony Heaton; E-mail: theaton@iwu.edu; *Tech Serv Mgr,* Gloria Redinger; Tel: 309-556-3526, E-mail: gredinge@iwu.edu; *Coordr, Cat,* Julie Wood; E-mail: jwood@iwu.edu; *Coordr, Media Serv,* Michael Limacher; Tel: 309-556-3323, E-mail: limacher@iwu.edu; *Reserves & Digital Serv Coordr,* Amy Sutter; Tel: 309-556-3728, E-mail: asutter@iwu.edu; Staff 24 (MLS 9, Non-MLS 15)
Founded 1850. Enrl 2,100; Fac 175; Highest Degree: Bachelor
Library Holdings: Bk Vols 335,000; Per Subs 1,046
Special Collections: 20th Century Literature (Gernon Coll); Political Science & Government (Leslie Arends Coll), flm, memorabilia
Subject Interests: Music, Nursing
Automation Activity & Vendor Info: (Cataloging) Ex Libris Group; (Circulation) Ex Libris Group; (OPAC) Ex Libris Group; (Serials) Ex Libris Group
Wireless access
Mem of Reaching Across Illinois Library System (RAILS)

Partic in Consortium of Academic & Research Libraries in Illinois; Illinois Library & Information Network; OCLC Online Computer Library Center, Inc
Special Services for the Deaf - ADA equip
Special Services for the Blind - Accessible computers; Aids for in-house use; Bks available with recordings; Handicapped awareness prog; Large print bks & talking machines; Large screen computer & software; Mags & bk reproduction/duplication; Reader equip
Open Mon-Thurs 7:45am-1:30am, Fri 7:45am-10pm, Sat 10-10, Sun 11am-1:30am
Restriction: Authorized patrons, Authorized scholars by appt

S MCLEAN COUNTY MUSEUM OF HISTORY*, Stevenson-Ives Library, 200 N Main, 61701. SAN 303-7347. Tel: 309-827-0428. FAX: 309-827-0100. E-mail: library@mchistory.org. Web Site: www.mchistory.org. *Exec Dir,* Greg Koos; E-mail: gregkoos@mchistory.org; *Archivist/Librn,* Bill Kemp; Staff 2 (Non-MLS 2)
Founded 1892
Library Holdings: Bk Titles 12,000
Special Collections: Childrens Home Papers; Edward J Lewis Diaries & Civil War Correspondence; Ensenberger Furniture; Ezra M Prince Manuscripts & Correspondence; Hutton Family Coll; Illinois Soldiers & Sailors Coll; International Affairs (Adlai Stevenson Lectures), papers; McLean County Home Bureau Papers; McLean County Photographs, 1850-; McLean County, Civil War & Illinois History Coll; Milo Cluster Manuscripts; Minnie Salzman Stevens Papers; Moon Family Coll; Phoenix Nursery; Political & Social History of McLean County Archives; Sons of Union Veterans' Coll; William Brigham Papers; William Wantling Coll, correspondence, papers, poetry ms
Subject Interests: Genealogy, Local hist, Mat culture
Wireless access
Publications: Archive Index with Unpublished Calendar; Indexes
Mem of Reaching Across Illinois Library System (RAILS)
Partic in RSA
Open Mon-Sat 10-5, Tues 10-9
Restriction: Non-circulating to the pub

SR ST JOHN'S LUTHERAN CHURCH LIBRARY*, 1617 E Emerson St, 61701. SAN 371-9987. Tel: 309-827-6121. FAX: 309-829-3866. E-mail: info@stjohnsbloomington.org. Web Site: www.stjohnsbloomington.org.
Founded 1970
Library Holdings: AV Mats 50; Bk Titles 800
Subject Interests: Bible hist, Biblical, Christian educ, Family life

SR SECOND PRESBYTERIAN CHURCH, Capen Memorial Library, 313 N East St, 61701. SAN 303-7355. Tel: 309-828-6297. FAX: 309-828-7038. *In Charge,* Dorothy Kennett; Staff 3 (Non-MLS 3)
Library Holdings: Audiobooks 4; CDs 200; DVDs 100; Large Print Bks 17; Bk Vols 3,000; Spec Interest Per Sub 1; Talking Bks 30; Videos 400
Open Mon-Fri 8:30-4:30, Sun 8:30-11

BLUE ISLAND

P BLUE ISLAND PUBLIC LIBRARY*, 2433 York St, 60406-2011. SAN 303-738X. Tel: 708-388-1078. FAX: 708-388-1143. E-mail: info@blueislandlibrary.org. Web Site: blueislandlibrary.org. *Dir,* Colleen Waltman; Tel: 708-388-1078, Ext 14, E-mail: cwaltman@blueislandlibrary.org; *Head, Circ,* David Boras; Tel: 708-388-1078, Ext 15, E-mail: dboras@blueislandlibrary.org; *Mgr, Ref & Tech Serv,* Hope Standifer; Tel: 703-388-1078, Ext 21, E-mail: hstandifer@blueislandlibrary.org; *Events & Outreach,* Daniel Carroll; Tel: 708-388-1078, Ext 30, E-mail: dcarroll@blueislandlibrary.org; *Youth Serv,* Deborah Beasley; Tel: 708-388-1078, Ext 22, E-mail: dbeasley@blueislandlibrary.org; Staff 3 (MLS 3)
Founded 1897. Pop 23,463; Circ 112,000
Library Holdings: Bk Vols 79,000; Per Subs 315
Subject Interests: City hist
Database Vendor: EBSCOhost, Newsbank, ProQuest
Wireless access
Publications: The Bookworm (Newsletter)
Mem of Reaching Across Illinois Library System (RAILS)
Partic in System Wide Automated Network
Open Mon-Thurs 9-9, Fri & Sat 9-5, Sun (Sept-May) 1-5
Friends of the Library Group

M METROSOUTH MEDICAL CENTER*, Medical Library, 12935 S Gregory St, 60406. SAN 375-9431. Tel: 708-597-2000, Ext 5388. FAX: 708-824-4494. *Dir, Libr & Med Staff Serv,* Kathy Tobar; E-mail: kathy_tobar@metrosouthmedicalcenter.com
Founded 1938
Library Holdings: Bk Titles 800; Per Subs 75
Mem of Reaching Across Illinois Library System (RAILS)
Partic in Chicago & South Consortium
Restriction: Not open to pub

BLUE MOUND

P BLUE MOUND MEMORIAL LIBRARY DISTRICT*, 213 S St Marie St, 62513-9733. (Mail add: PO Box 317, 62513-0317), SAN 303-7401. Tel: 217-692-2774. FAX: 217-692-2191. E-mail: bluemoundlib@hotmail.com. Web Site: www.bluemoundlibrary.lib.il.us. *Head Librn,* Linda Perona; *Assoc Librn,* Alice Reed
Founded 1948. Pop 2,554; Circ 24,872
Library Holdings: Bk Titles 21,500; Per Subs 42
Mem of Illinois Heartland Library System
Partic in Heartland Consortia; Illinois Library & Information Network
Open Mon-Wed & Fri 10-6, Thurs 10-8, Sat 10-2

BLUFFS

P BLUFFS PUBLIC LIBRARY*, 110 N Bluffs St, 62621. (Mail add: PO Box 177, 62621-0177), SAN 303-741X. Tel: 217-754-3804. FAX: 217-754-3804. *Librn,* Ellen Graves
Pop 715; Circ 1,187
Library Holdings: Bk Vols 8,000; Per Subs 9
Wireless access
Mem of Reaching Across Illinois Library System (RAILS)
Open Tues & Thurs 1-5:30, Wed 9-12 & 1-7, Fri 1-5, Sat 9-12

BOLINGBROOK

P FOUNTAINDALE PUBLIC LIBRARY DISTRICT*, 300 W Briarcliff Rd, 60440. SAN 339-7475. Tel: 630-759-2102. FAX: 630-759-9519. Administration FAX: 630-759-6180. TDD: 630-754-4949, 815-886-4638. E-mail: info@fountaindale.org. Web Site: www.fountaindale.org. *Exec Dir,* Paul Mills; E-mail: pmills@fountaindale.org; *Dep Dir,* Catherine Yanikoski; E-mail: cyanikoski@fountaindale.org; *Head, Adult Serv, Head, Teen Serv,* Debra Dudek; E-mail: ddudek@fountaindale.org; *Ch Mgr,* Wendy Birkemeier; Tel: 630-685-4181, E-mail: wbirkemeier@fountaindale.org; *Circ Serv Mgr,* Theresa Hildebrand; Tel: 630-759-2102, Ext 4200, E-mail: thildebrand@fountaindale.org; *Mgr, Outreach Serv,* Marianne M Thompson; E-mail: mmthompson@fountaindale.org; Staff 75 (MLS 18, Non-MLS 57)
Founded 1970. Pop 71,474; Circ 826,075
Library Holdings: Bk Vols 285,727
Automation Activity & Vendor Info: (Circulation) SirsiDynix; (OPAC) SirsiDynix
Database Vendor: EBSCOhost, Gale Cengage Learning, Newsbank, OCLC FirstSearch, ProQuest
Mem of Reaching Across Illinois Library System (RAILS)
Partic in Pinnacle Library Cooperative
Special Services for the Deaf - TDD equip
Open Mon-Thurs 9-9, Fri & Sat 9-6, Sun 12-6
Friends of the Library Group
Bookmobiles: 1

BOURBONNAIS

P BOURBONNAIS PUBLIC LIBRARY DISTRICT*, 250 W John Casey Rd, 60914. SAN 324-5713. Tel: 815-933-1727. FAX: 815-933-1961. Web Site: www.bourbonnaislibrary.org. *Dir,* Diana Dillinger; *Adult & Teen Serv,* Fabiana Lopez; *Ch Serv,* Julie Ross; *Circ,* Stephen Bauman; *Tech Serv,* Chris Weybright
Founded 1982. Pop 23,223; Circ 138,162
Library Holdings: Bk Titles 44,796; Per Subs 103
Automation Activity & Vendor Info: (Circulation) SirsiDynix
Wireless access
Mem of Reaching Across Illinois Library System (RAILS)
Open Mon-Thurs 9-9, Fri 9-5, Sat 9-4
Friends of the Library Group

CR OLIVET NAZARENE UNIVERSITY*, Benner Library & Resource Center, One University Ave, 60914-2271. SAN 303-7428. Tel: 815-939-5354. Interlibrary Loan Service Tel: 815-928-5439. Reference Tel: 815-939-5355. Administration Tel: 815-939-5211. FAX: 815-939-5170. Web Site: library.olivet.edu. *Dir,* Kathryn R Boyens; E-mail: kboyens@olivet.edu; *Access Serv Librn,* Kyle Olney; Tel: 815-928-5490, E-mail: kolney1@olivet.edu; *Cat Librn,* Mary Ada Dillinger; Tel: 815-939-5144, E-mail: mdilling@olivet.edu; *Grad Sch Res Librn,* Pamela Greenlee; Tel: 815-939-5439, E-mail: pgreenle@olivet.edu; *Grad Sch Tech Librn,* Ann Johnston; Tel: 815-939-5061, E-mail: ajohnsto@olivet.edu; *Informatics Librn,* Craighton Hippenhammer; Tel: 815-939-5145, E-mail: chhammer@olivet.edu; *Instrul Serv Librn,* Jasmine Cieszynski; Tel: 815-928-5449, E-mail: jcieszyn@olivet.edu; *Ref Librn,* Judson Strain; Tel: 815-928-5438, E-mail: jlstrain@olivet.edu; *Evening Circ Supvr,* Sarah Kirkland. Subject Specialists: *Music,* Kathryn R Boyens; *Church hist,* Kyle Olney; *Educ,* Mary Ada Dillinger; *Nursing, Sci,* Pamela Greenlee; *Educ,* Ann Johnston; *Tech,* Craighton Hippenhammer; *Psychol,* Jasmine Cieszynski; *Law,* Judson Strain; Staff 8 (MLS 6, Non-MLS 2)
Founded 1909. Enrl 3,695; Fac 201; Highest Degree: Doctorate

Jul 2009-Jun 2010 Income $1,587,879. Mats Exp $444,720, Books $79,806, Per/Ser (Incl. Access Fees) $82,241, Other Print Mats $362, Micro $19,539, AV Mat $3,030, Electronic Ref Mat (Incl. Access Fees) $258,104, Presv $1,638. Sal $663,588 (Prof $276,531)
Library Holdings: CDs 831; DVDs 240; e-books 70,433; e-journals 38,767; Electronic Media & Resources 140; Music Scores 14,129; Bk Titles 146,352; Bk Vols 174,641; Per Subs 682; Videos 2,088
Special Collections: Jacob Arminus Coll, bks, microflm; John Wesley Coll; Olivet Nazarene Univ Archives. US Document Depository
Subject Interests: Educ, Nursing, Theol
Automation Activity & Vendor Info: (Acquisitions) Ex Libris Group; (Cataloging) Ex Libris Group; (Circulation) Ex Libris Group; (ILL) Ex Libris Group; (OPAC) Ex Libris Group; (Serials) Ex Libris Group
Database Vendor: Alexander Street Press, American Chemical Society, American Mathematical Society, American Psychological Association (APA), Annual Reviews, Baker & Taylor, Blackwell, Cambridge Scientific Abstracts, Cinahl, College Source, CQ Press, CredoReference, Dialog, Dun & Bradstreet, ebrary, EBSCO - WebFeat, EBSCOhost, Elsevier, Facts on File, Gale Cengage Learning, H W Wilson, Hoovers, JSTOR, LexisNexis, Medline, Mergent Online, Micromedex, Modern Language Association, OCLC ArticleFirst, OCLC CAMIO, OCLC FirstSearch, OCLC WorldShare Interlibrary Loan, OVID Technologies, Project MUSE, ProQuest, Sage, ScienceDirect, SerialsSolutions, STN International, Westlaw, Wiley InterScience, Wilson - Wilson Web
Wireless access
Function: Computers for patron use, Copy machines, Distance learning, Doc delivery serv, e-mail & chat, E-Reserves, Electronic databases & coll, Orientations
Mem of Reaching Across Illinois Library System (RAILS)
Partic in Consortium of Academic & Research Libraries in Illinois; Illinois Library & Information Network
Special Services for the Blind - Reader equip
Open Mon-Thurs & Sun 7:30am-Midnight, Fri 7:30-5, Sat 11-7
Restriction: In-house use for visitors

BRADFORD

P BRADFORD PUBLIC LIBRARY DISTRICT*, 111 S Peoria St, 61421. (Mail add: PO Box 249, 61421-0249), SAN 303-7444. Tel: 309-897-8400. FAX: 309-897-8314. Web Site: www.bpld.org. *Dir,* Sarah Boehm; *Ch Serv,* Cinda Scott
Founded 1924. Pop 1,699; Circ 14,123
Library Holdings: Bk Vols 7,079; Per Subs 20
Automation Activity & Vendor Info: (Cataloging) CARL.Solution (TLC); (Circulation) CARL.Solution (TLC)
Open Mon-Thurs 10-7, Fri 10-5, Sat 9-12

BRADLEY

P BRADLEY PUBLIC LIBRARY DISTRICT, 296 N Fulton Ave, 60915. SAN 303-7452. Tel: 815-932-6245. FAX: 815-932-6278. E-mail: info@bradleylibrary.org. Web Site: www.bradleylibrary.org. *Dir,* Jodie DePatis; Staff 4 (MLS 1, Non-MLS 3)
Founded 1944. Pop 13,295; Circ 99,846
Library Holdings: Audiobooks 1,378; DVDs 2,095; e-books 8,679; e-journals 22; Bk Vols 45,996; Per Subs 106
Automation Activity & Vendor Info: (Cataloging) Innovative Interfaces, Inc; (Circulation) Innovative Interfaces, Inc; (OPAC) Innovative Interfaces, Inc
Wireless access
Function: 24/7 Electronic res, Bk club(s), Bks on CD, Children's prog, Computer training, Computers for patron use, Copy machines, Electronic databases & coll, Fax serv, Free DVD rentals, Handicapped accessible, Homebound delivery serv, ILL available, Life-long learning prog for all ages, Magazines, Notary serv, Online cat, Outreach serv, OverDrive digital audio bks, Preschool reading prog, Prog for adults, Prog for children & young adult, Pub access computers, Scanner, Study rm, Summer reading prog, Tax forms, Wheelchair accessible
Mem of Reaching Across Illinois Library System (RAILS)
Open Mon-Thurs 9-8, Fri 9-6, Sat 9-5, Sun (Sept-May) 1-4
Friends of the Library Group

BRAIDWOOD

P FOSSIL RIDGE PUBLIC LIBRARY*, 386 W Kennedy Rd, 60408. SAN 303-7460. Tel: 815-458-2187. FAX: 815-458-2042. Web Site: www.fossilridge.org. *Libr Dir,* Richard Ashley; E-mail: rashley@fossilridge.org
Founded 1970. Pop 13,478; Circ 118,596
Library Holdings: Bk Vols 46,754; Per Subs 151
Wireless access
Mem of Reaching Across Illinois Library System (RAILS)
Open Mon-Thurs 9-8, Fri 9-5, Sat 9-3
Friends of the Library Group
Bookmobiles: 1

BREESE

P BREESE PUBLIC LIBRARY*, 530 N Third St, 62230. SAN 303-7479. Tel: 618-526-7361. FAX: 618-526-0143. E-mail: bra@breeselibrary.org. Web Site: www.breeselibrary.org. *Dir,* Jan Thomas; *Asst Librn,* Diane Holtgrave
Founded 1962. Pop 4,048; Circ 124,124
Library Holdings: Large Print Bks 200; Bk Titles 30,000; Bk Vols 32,000; Per Subs 75; Talking Bks 350
Automation Activity & Vendor Info: (Acquisitions) SirsiDynix; (Cataloging) SirsiDynix; (Circulation) SirsiDynix
Mem of Illinois Heartland Library System
Open Mon-Fri 10-8, Sat 10-3

BRIDGEVIEW

P BRIDGEVIEW PUBLIC LIBRARY*, 7840 W 79th St, 60455-1496. SAN 303-7487. Tel: 708-458-2880. FAX: 708-458-3553. E-mail: bridgeviewlibrary@hotmail.com. Web Site: www.bridgeviewlibrary.org. *Actg Dir, Head, Circ,* Lori Kinzel; Tel: 708-458-2880, Ext 101, E-mail: lkinzel@bridgeviewlibrary.org
Founded 1966. Pop 14,402; Circ 112,355
Library Holdings: AV Mats 2,859; Bk Vols 72,000; Per Subs 172
Automation Activity & Vendor Info: (Cataloging) TLC (The Library Corporation); (Circulation) TLC (The Library Corporation)
Database Vendor: EBSCOhost, Newsbank, OCLC FirstSearch
Mem of Reaching Across Illinois Library System (RAILS)
Open Mon, Wed & Fri 10-6, Tues & Thurs 12-8, Sat 9-5

BRIGHTON

P BRIGHTON MEMORIAL LIBRARY*, 110 N Main, 62012. (Mail add: PO Box 183, 62012-0183), SAN 375-9911. Tel: 618-372-8450. FAX: 618-372-7450. E-mail: books@brightonpubliclibrary.org. Web Site: www.brightonpubliclibrary.org. *Libr Dir,* Karen Sinks; E-mail: ksinks@brightonpubliclibrary.org; *Librn,* Sally Bland; E-mail: sbland@brightonpubliclibrary.org; *Librn,* Becky Huebener; E-mail: bhuebener@brightonpubliclibrary.org; *Librn,* Donna Watson; E-mail: dwatson@brightonpubliclibrary.org
Pop 2,500; Circ 26,000
Jul 2009-Jun 2010 Income $55,861, State $2,700, County $40,917, Locally Generated Income $9,588, Other $2,656. Mats Exp $5,875, Per/Ser (Incl. Access Fees) $500. Sal $33,722
Library Holdings: Audiobooks 517; Bks on Deafness & Sign Lang 5; CDs 120; DVDs 166; Electronic Media & Resources 5; Large Print Bks 505; Bk Titles 13,633; Per Subs 14; Videos 1,079
Automation Activity & Vendor Info: (Acquisitions) Innovative Interfaces, Inc - Millenium; (Cataloging) Innovative Interfaces, Inc - Millenium; (Circulation) Innovative Interfaces, Inc - Millenium; (ILL) Innovative Interfaces, Inc - Millenium; (Media Booking) Innovative Interfaces, Inc - Millenium; (OPAC) Innovative Interfaces, Inc - Millenium; (Serials) Innovative Interfaces, Inc - Millenium
Database Vendor: Gale Cengage Learning, OCLC FirstSearch, OCLC WebJunction, OCLC WorldShare Interlibrary Loan
Wireless access
Function: Audiobks via web, Bk club(s), Bks on cassette, Bks on CD, Children's prog, Computers for patron use, Copy machines, Electronic databases & coll, Exhibits, Fax serv, Free DVD rentals, Handicapped accessible, Home delivery & serv to Sr ctr & nursing homes, Homebound delivery serv, ILL available, Music CDs, Online cat, Online ref, Online searches, OverDrive digital audio bks, Photocopying/Printing, Preschool outreach, Prog for adults, Prog for children & young adult, Pub access computers, Ref serv available, Scanner, Spoken cassettes & CDs, Spoken cassettes & DVDs, Story hour, Summer & winter reading prog, Summer reading prog, VHS videos, Video lending libr, Wheelchair accessible
Mem of Illinois Heartland Library System
Special Services for the Deaf - Bks on deafness & sign lang; Closed caption videos
Special Services for the Blind - Audio mat; Bks on cassette; Bks on CD; Cassette playback machines; Cassettes; Large print & cassettes; Large print bks; Large type calculator; Photo duplicator for making large print; Recorded bks; Sound rec; Talking bk & rec for the blind cat
Open Mon, Wed & Thurs 10-6, Tues 10-7:30, Fri 10-5, Sat 10-3
Friends of the Library Group

BRIMFIELD

P BRIMFIELD PUBLIC LIBRARY*, 111 S Galena St, 61517. (Mail add: PO Box 207, 61517-0207), SAN 303-7495. Tel: 309-446-9575. FAX: 309-446-9357. Web Site: www.brimfieldlibrary.org. *Dir,* Patricia Smith; E-mail: psmith@brimfieldlibrary.org; *Asst Dir,* Glenda Wilson
Founded 1924. Circ 17,373
Library Holdings: Bk Vols 34,000; Per Subs 38
Automation Activity & Vendor Info: (Cataloging) SirsiDynix; (Circulation) SirsiDynix; (OPAC) SirsiDynix

Wireless access
Open Mon-Thurs (Winter) 10-7, Fri 10-6, Sat 10-2; Mon-Thurs (Summer) 10-7, Fri 10-6

BROADVIEW

P BROADVIEW PUBLIC LIBRARY DISTRICT, 2226 S 16th Ave, 60155-4000. SAN 303-7509. Tel: 708-345-1325. FAX: 708-345-5024. E-mail: brs@broadviewlibrary.org. Web Site: www.broadviewlibrary.org. *Dir,* Position Currently Open; *Pub Relations Coordr,* John Flanagan; *Pub Serv,* Joseph Bondi; *Tech Serv,* Robert Lafferty
Founded 1955. Pop 8,713; Circ 68,922
Library Holdings: Bk Vols 51,000; Per Subs 125
Automation Activity & Vendor Info: (Acquisitions) Innovative Interfaces, Inc - Millenium; (Cataloging) Innovative Interfaces, Inc - Millenium; (Circulation) Innovative Interfaces, Inc - Millenium
Wireless access
Mem of Reaching Across Illinois Library System (RAILS)
Open Mon-Thurs 10-9, Fri & Sat 10-5
Friends of the Library Group

BROOKFIELD

S AMERICAN SOKOL EDUCATIONAL & PHYSICAL CULTURE ORGANIZATION*, Library & Archives, 9126 Ogden Ave, 60513. SAN 326-7873. Tel: 708-255-5397. FAX: 708-255-5398. E-mail: aso@american-sokol.org. Web Site: www.american-sokol.org. *Curator,* Annette B Schabowski; Staff 1 (Non-MLS 1)
Founded 1976
Library Holdings: Bk Titles 3,166; Per Subs 3,836

P BROOKFIELD PUBLIC LIBRARY, 3609 Grand Blvd, 60513. SAN 303-7525. Tel: 708-485-6917. FAX: 708-485-5172. E-mail: director@brookfieldlibrary.info. Web Site: www.brookfieldlibrary.info. *Dir,* Kimberly Coughran
Founded 1913. Pop 18,978; Circ 296,000
Library Holdings: Bk Vols 73,366; Per Subs 164
Automation Activity & Vendor Info: (Acquisitions) Innovative Interfaces, Inc; (Cataloging) Innovative Interfaces, Inc; (Circulation) Innovative Interfaces, Inc; (OPAC) Innovative Interfaces, Inc; (Serials) Innovative Interfaces, Inc
Database Vendor: College Source, EBSCOhost, Newsbank, OCLC FirstSearch, ReferenceUSA
Wireless access
Mem of Reaching Across Illinois Library System (RAILS)
Partic in OCLC Online Computer Library Center, Inc; System Wide Automated Network
Open Mon-Thurs 10-9, Fri & Sat 10-6, Sun (Winter) 11-6
Friends of the Library Group

S CHICAGO ZOOLOGICAL SOCIETY*, Brookfield Zoo Library, 3300 Golf Rd, 60513. SAN 303-7533. Tel: 708-688-8583. FAX: 708-688-7583. *Mgr, Libr Serv,* Carla Owens; E-mail: carla.owens@czs.org; Staff 1 (MLS 1)
Founded 1964
Library Holdings: AV Mats 100; Bk Vols 8,000; Per Subs 100
Subject Interests: Animal behavior, Natural hist, Veterinary med, Zoology
Automation Activity & Vendor Info: (Cataloging) Innovative Interfaces, Inc
Database Vendor: BioOne, JSTOR
Wireless access
Publications: Gateways
Mem of Reaching Across Illinois Library System (RAILS)
Open Mon-Fri 9-3

BRUSSELS

P SOUTH COUNTY PUBLIC LIBRARY DISTRICT*, Main St, 62013. (Mail add: PO Box 93, 62013-0093), SAN 303-7541. Tel: 618-883-2522. *Librn,* Nancy Moennig
Founded 1974. Pop 1,298; Circ 3,046
Library Holdings: Bk Vols 8,571
Mem of Illinois Heartland Library System
Open Mon & Wed-Fri 9:30-4, Tues 9:30-8

BUDA

P MASON MEMORIAL PUBLIC LIBRARY*, 104 W Main St, 61314. (Mail add: PO Box 55, 61314-0055), SAN 303-755X. Tel: 309-895-7701. FAX: 309-895-7701. *Head Librn,* Jeannie Jarigese
Pop 597; Circ 5,357
Library Holdings: Bk Vols 13,770; Per Subs 44
Subject Interests: Genealogy, Local hist
Function: Homebound delivery serv, ILL available, Photocopying/Printing, Summer reading prog, Wheelchair accessible
Open Mon & Fri 1-5, Tues & Sat 11-5, Wed 1-8

BUNKER HILL

P BUNKER HILL PUBLIC LIBRARY DISTRICT*, 220 E Warren St, 62014. (Mail add: PO Box P, 62014-0664), SAN 303-7568. Tel: 618-585-4736. FAX: 618-585-6073. E-mail: bhlibrary1867@gmail.com. Web Site: www.bunkerhilllibrary.org. *Head Librn,* Susan Landreth; Staff 2 (Non-MLS 2)
Founded 1867. Pop 4,270
Mem of Illinois Heartland Library System
Open Mon, Wed & Fri 10-5, Tues & Thurs 1-7, Sat 8-1

BURBANK

P PRAIRIE TRAILS PUBLIC LIBRARY DISTRICT, 8449 S Moody, 60459-2525. SAN 303-7576. Tel: 708-430-3688. FAX: 708-430-5596. E-mail: pts@prairietrailslibrary.org. Web Site: www.prairietrailslibrary.org. *Dir,* Ruth E Faklis; E-mail: rfaklis@prairietrailslibrary.org; *Asst Librn,* Sheri Starr; E-mail: sstarr@prairietrailslibrary.org; *Adult Serv,* Mary Ann Lema; Staff 11 (MLS 5, Non-MLS 6)
Founded 1969. Pop 28,996; Circ 194,104
Library Holdings: Audiobooks 5,480; CDs 19,959; DVDs 40,529; Bk Titles 124,262; Per Subs 181
Special Collections: Arabic Language Coll; Polish Language Coll; Spanish Language Coll. Oral History
Subject Interests: Adult fiction
Automation Activity & Vendor Info: (Circulation) Innovative Interfaces, Inc; (OPAC) Innovative Interfaces, Inc; (Serials) EBSCO Online
Database Vendor: Innovative Interfaces, Inc
Wireless access
Function: Accelerated reader prog, Adult bk club, After school storytime, Art exhibits, Audio & video playback equip for onsite use, Audiobks via web, Bilingual assistance for Spanish patrons, Bk club(s), Bks on cassette, Bks on CD, CD-ROM, Children's prog, Computer training, Computers for patron use, Copy machines, Digital talking bks, E-Reserves, Electronic databases & coll, Exhibits, Free DVD rentals, Handicapped accessible, Holiday prog, ILL available, Magnifiers for reading, Mail & tel request accepted, Mus passes, Music CDs, Notary serv, Online cat, Orientations, Photocopying/Printing, Preschool outreach, Prog for adults, Prog for children & young adult, Pub access computers, Ref serv in person, Senior computer classes, Senior outreach, Serves mentally handicapped consumers, Spoken cassettes & CDs, Story hour, Summer reading prog, Tax forms, Teen prog, Telephone ref, Wheelchair accessible, Workshops
Publications: Newsletter (Monthly)
Mem of Reaching Across Illinois Library System (RAILS)
Partic in System Wide Automated Network
Open Mon-Thurs 9-9, Fri & Sat 9-5

BUREAU

P LEEPERTOWN TOWNSHIP PUBLIC LIBRARY, 201 E Nebraska, 61315. (Mail add: PO Box 80, 61315), SAN 303-7584. Tel: 815-659-3283. FAX: 815-659-3263. Web Site: leepertown.lib.il.us. *Interim Dir,* Rose Thompson; E-mail: rosemt@leepertown.lib.il.us
Founded 1976. Pop 518
Library Holdings: Bk Titles 4,500
Special Collections: Spanish language
Mem of Reaching Across Illinois Library System (RAILS)
Open Mon, Wed & Fri 2-6, Thurs 5-7, Sat 12-3

BURR RIDGE

P ILLINOIS TALKING BOOK OUTREACH CENTER*, 125 Tower Dr, 60527. SAN 340-6628. Tel: 630-734-5000. Toll Free Tel: 800-426-0709. FAX: 630-734-5055. E-mail: info@illinoistalkingbooks.org. Web Site: www.illinoistalkingbooks.org. *Dir,* Rose Chenoweth; Tel: 636-734-5210, E-mail: rose.chenoweth@railslibraries.info
Partic in National Network of Libraries of Medicine
Special Services for the Blind - Bks on cassette
Open Mon-Fri 8-5

BUSHNELL

P BUSHNELL PUBLIC LIBRARY*, 455 N Dean, 61422-1299. SAN 303-7592. Tel: 309-772-2060. FAX: 309-772-9038. E-mail: plibrary@frontier.com. *Dir,* Margaret Repp
Pop 4,706; Circ 25,639
Library Holdings: Bk Titles 25,000; Bk Vols 26,000; Per Subs 65
Special Collections: Peter Newell Coll
Automation Activity & Vendor Info: (Cataloging) Follett Software; (Circulation) Follett Software
Mem of Sumter County Library System
Open Mon-Wed 9-7, Thurs & Fri 10-5, Sat 10-2

BYRON

P BYRON PUBLIC LIBRARY DISTRICT*, 100 S Washington St, 61010-1460. (Mail add: PO Box 434, 61010-0434), SAN 303-7606. Tel: 815-234-5107. FAX: 815-234-5582. E-mail: library@byron.lib.il.us. Web Site: www.byron.lib.il.us. *Dir,* Penny O'Rourke; E-mail: pennyo@byron.lib.il.us; Staff 2 (MLS 2)
Founded 1916. Pop 7,989; Circ 138,289
Jul 2010-Jun 2011 Income $1,004,295. Mats Exp $125,868, Books $65,732, Per/Ser (Incl. Access Fees) $6,000, AV Equip $20,694, AV Mat $25,000, Electronic Ref Mat (Incl. Access Fees) $8,442. Sal $242,356
Library Holdings: Audiobooks 2,411; CDs 2,059; DVDs 4,067; e-books 170; Large Print Bks 3,284; Bk Vols 53,466; Per Subs 108
Special Collections: Commonwealth Edison
Automation Activity & Vendor Info: (Cataloging) SirsiDynix; (Circulation) SirsiDynix; (OPAC) SirsiDynix
Wireless access
Mem of Reaching Across Illinois Library System (RAILS)
Open Mon-Thurs 9-8, Fri & Sat 9-5

CAHOKIA

P CAHOKIA PUBLIC LIBRARY DISTRICT*, 140 Cahokia Park Dr, 62206-2129. SAN 303-7614. Tel: 618-332-1491. FAX: 618-332-1104. E-mail: info@cahokialibrary.org. Web Site: cahokialibrary.org. *Dir,* Kathleen Armstrong
Founded 1963. Pop 17,550; Circ 70,453
Library Holdings: Bk Vols 37,659; Per Subs 79
Automation Activity & Vendor Info: (Circulation) Innovative Interfaces, Inc
Mem of Illinois Heartland Library System
Open Mon-Thurs 9-7:30, Fri & Sat 9-5
Friends of the Library Group

CAIRO

P CAIRO PUBLIC LIBRARY*, 1609 Washington Ave, 62914. (Mail add: PO Box 151, 62914-0151), SAN 303-7630. Tel: 618-734-1840. FAX: 618-734-4799. E-mail: cplibrary@lazernetwireless.net. *Librn,* Monica L Smith
Founded 1884. Pop 2,846; Circ 32,800
Library Holdings: Bk Vols 52,000; Per Subs 60
Special Collections: Army & Navy Records; Census Microfilm for 16 Southern Illinois Counties; Civil War Coll; Jesuit Relations; Local Newspapers on Microfilm from 1848; WPA Art
Mem of Illinois Heartland Library System
Open Mon-Fri 10-5

CALUMET CITY

P CALUMET CITY PUBLIC LIBRARY*, 660 Manistee Ave, 60409. SAN 303-7649. Tel: 708-862-6220. Reference Tel: 708-862-6220, Ext 223. Administration Tel: 708-862-6220, Ext 241. FAX: 708 862 0872. E mail: info@calumetcitypl.org. Web Site: www.calumetcitypl.org. *Dir,* Jane Rowland; Tel: 708 862 6220, Ext 244, E mail: jrowland@calumetcitypl.org; *Head, Adult Serv,* Keisha Hester; Tel: 708-862-6220, Ext 2, E-mail: khester@calumetcity.org; *Head, Circ,* Lisa Ybarra; E-mail: lybarra@calumetcitypl.org; *Head, Tech Serv,* Margaret Wartak; E-mail: mwartak@calumetcitypl.org; *Head, Youth Serv,* Gale Krekovich; E-mail: gkrekovich@calumetcitypl.org; Staff 6 (MLS 5, Non-MLS 1)
Pop 39,071; Circ 174,726
Library Holdings: AV Mats 13,537; Large Print Bks 2,017; Bk Vols 126,932; Per Subs 33; Talking Bks 1,371
Automation Activity & Vendor Info: (Circulation) Innovative Interfaces, Inc; (OPAC) Innovative Interfaces, Inc; (Serials) Innovative Interfaces, Inc
Wireless access
Publications: Library Links (Quarterly newsletter)
Mem of Reaching Across Illinois Library System (RAILS)
Open Mon-Thurs 10-9, Fri & Sat 10-4, Sun (Sept-May) 12-4

CALUMET PARK

P CALUMET PARK PUBLIC LIBRARY, 1500 W 127th St, 60827. SAN 303-7657. Tel: 708-385-5768. FAX: 708-385-8816. *Dir,* Bernistine McCarter; E-mail: bernistinem@yahoo.com; *Youth Serv,* Debora Woods
Pop 8,788; Circ 15,770
Library Holdings: Bk Vols 25,000; Per Subs 80
Special Collections: Lupus
Automation Activity & Vendor Info: (Cataloging) Innovative Interfaces, Inc; (Circulation) Innovative Interfaces, Inc; (OPAC) Innovative Interfaces, Inc
Mem of Reaching Across Illinois Library System (RAILS)
Open Mon & Tues 11-8, Wed & Thurs 11-6, Fri & Sat 11-4

CAMBRIDGE

P CAMBRIDGE PUBLIC LIBRARY DISTRICT*, 212 W Center St, 61238-1239. SAN 303-7665. Tel: 309-937-2233. FAX: 309-937-2873. E-mail: camblib@geneseo.net. *Librn,* Eleanor Sponsel
Pop 3,394
Library Holdings: Bk Vols 28,000; Per Subs 65
Subject Interests: Local hist
Automation Activity & Vendor Info: (Cataloging) Follett Software; (Circulation) Follett Software
Open Mon-Thurs (Winter) 11-8, Fri 11-5, Sat 11-4; Mon-Thurs (Summer) 11-8, Fri & Sat 11-4

CAMP POINT

P CAMP POINT PUBLIC LIBRARY DISTICT, 206 E State St, 62320. (Mail add: PO Box 377, 62320-0377), SAN 303-7673. Tel: 217-593-7021. FAX: 217-593-6121. E-mail: cplibrary@adams.net. *Dir,* Debra Rossiter
Founded 1906. Pop 3,058; Circ 12,736
Jul 2013-Jun 2014 Income $60,897, State $3,835, County $56,462, Locally Generated Income $600. Mats Exp $8,879, Books $6,670, Per/Ser (Incl. Access Fees) $569, Electronic Ref Mat (Incl. Access Fees) $1,640. Sal $26,213
Library Holdings: Large Print Bks 750; Bk Titles 15,874; Per Subs 36
Automation Activity & Vendor Info: (Circulation) Follett Software
Database Vendor: Baker & Taylor, OCLC FirstSearch, OCLC WorldShare Interlibrary Loan
Wireless access
Function: Archival coll, Handicapped accessible, Home delivery & serv to Sr ctr & nursing homes, Homebound delivery serv, Homework prog, ILL available, Newsp ref libr, Online searches, Photocopying/Printing, Prog for adults, Prog for children & young adult, Ref serv available, Summer reading prog, Telephone ref, VHS videos, Video lending libr, Wheelchair accessible
Mem of Reaching Across Illinois Library System (RAILS)
Open Mon & Fri 2-6, Tues 10-7, Wed & Thurs 2-7, Sat 10-2
Restriction: Authorized patrons, In-house use for visitors, Non-circulating coll, Non-resident fee, Open to pub with supv only

CANTON

M GRAHAM HOSPITAL ASSOCIATION*, Medical Staff Library & School of Nursing Library, 210 W Walnut St, 61520. SAN 303-7681. Tel: 309-647-5240, Ext 2343. FAX: 309-649-5105. E-mail: library@grahamhospital.org. Web Site: www.grahamschoolofnursing.org. *Dir, Libr Serv,* Michelle Quinones; Tel: 309-647-5240, Ext 3388, E-mail: mquinones@grahamhospital.org; *Ref,* Lynette Murphy; Staff 1 (MLS 1)
Founded 1909
Library Holdings: AV Mats 600; Bk Vols 2,093; Per Subs 109
Special Collections: Oral History
Subject Interests: Med, Nursing
Automation Activity & Vendor Info: (Cataloging) OCLC Connexion; (Circulation) SIRSI WorkFlows; (ILL) OCLC; (OPAC) SIRSI WorkFlows; (Serials) EBSCO Online
Database Vendor: EBSCO Information Services, OCLC FirstSearch, OVID Technologies
Wireless access
Mem of Reaching Across Illinois Library System (RAILS)
Partic in Health Sci Librn of Ill (HSLI); Heart of Illinois Library Consortium
Open Mon-Fri 7-5
Restriction: Authorized patrons

S ILLINOIS DEPARTMENT OF CORRECTIONS*, Illinois River Correctional Center Library, 1300 W Locust St, 61520-8791. (Mail add: PO Box 999, 61520), SAN 371-6600. Tel: 309-647-7030, Ext 549, 309-647-7030, Ext 550. FAX: 309-647-0353. Web Site: www.idoc.state.il.us. *Librn,* Don Burkhart; Staff 1 (MLS 1)
Founded 1989
Library Holdings: High Interest/Low Vocabulary Bk Vols 50; Bk Titles 9,000; Bk Vols 19,000
Subject Interests: Law
Function: Ref serv available
Partic in Resource Sharing Alliance
Special Services for the Blind - Talking bks
Open Tues-Fri 7-5
Restriction: Circ limited

P PARLIN INGERSOLL PUBLIC LIBRARY, 205 W Chestnut St, 61520. SAN 303-769X. Tel: 309-647-0328. FAX: 309-647-8117. E-mail: parlin@parliningersoll.org. Web Site: www.parliningersoll.org. *Dir,* Kimberly Bunner; *Pub Serv,* Ben Smith; *Youth Serv,* Catherine Calvert; Staff 2 (MLS 1, Non-MLS 1)
Pop 14,704; Circ 147,000

Library Holdings: Audiobooks 4,600; CDs 4,800; DVDs 5,900; Large Print Bks 5,550; Bk Titles 73,450; Per Subs 125
Special Collections: Fulton County History Coll
Automation Activity & Vendor Info: (Cataloging) OCLC; (Circulation) Innovative Interfaces, Inc; (ILL) OCLC; (OPAC) Innovative Interfaces, Inc
Database Vendor: OCLC FirstSearch
Wireless access
Mem of Reaching Across Illinois Library System (RAILS)
Partic in OCLC Online Computer Library Center, Inc
Open Mon-Thurs 9-8, Fri 9-6, Sat 9-4 (9-1 Summer)

J SPOON RIVER COLLEGE LIBRARY, 23235 N County Rd 22, 61520. SAN 303-7703. Tel: 309-649-6222. Interlibrary Loan Service Tel: 309-649-6208. Information Services Tel: 309-649-6603. FAX: 309-649-6235. Web Site: www.src.edu. *Dir of Libr Serv,* Kathleen A Menanteaux; E-mail: kathleen.menanteaux@src.edu; *Cat & Circ Supvr,* Marla Turgeon; E-mail: marla.turgeon@src.edu; Staff 3 (MLS 1, Non-MLS 2)
Founded 1951. Enrl 2,400; Fac 60; Highest Degree: Associate
Jul 2014-Jun 2015 Income $187,718. Mats Exp $57,600
Library Holdings: AV Mats 2,500; CDs 48; DVDs 102; Electronic Media & Resources 21; Bk Titles 36,800; Bk Vols 47,000; Per Subs 30
Special Collections: College History Coll
Subject Interests: Career, Humanities, Sciences
Automation Activity & Vendor Info: (Acquisitions) CARL.Solution (TLC); (Cataloging) CARL.Solution (TLC); (Circulation) CARL.Solution (TLC); (Course Reserve) CARL.Solution (TLC); (ILL) OCLC Online; (OPAC) CARL.Solution (TLC)
Database Vendor: Baker & Taylor, Bowker, EBSCOhost, H W Wilson, LexisNexis, Newsbank, OCLC FirstSearch, OCLC WorldShare Interlibrary Loan, TLC (The Library Corporation), Wilson - Wilson Web, WT Cox, YBP Library Services
Publications: Faculty FYI (Acquisition list); Library Statistics Report (Monthly)
Partic in Consortium of Academic & Research Libraries in Illinois; Northern Ill Learning Resources Coop; OCLC Online Computer Library Center, Inc; Resource Sharing Alliance
Special Services for the Deaf - Assistive tech
Special Services for the Blind - Assistive/Adapted tech devices, equip & products; Reader equip; Scanner for conversion & translation of mats; ZoomText magnification & reading software
Open Mon-Fri 8-4:30
Restriction: 24-hr pass syst for students only

CARBONDALE

P CARBONDALE PUBLIC LIBRARY*, 405 W Main St, 62901-2995. SAN 303-7711. Tel: 618-457-0354. FAX: 618-457-0353. E-mail: cpllib@carbondale.lib.il.us. Web Site: www.carbondale.lib.il.us. *Dir,* Diana Brawley Sussman; Staff 4 (MLS 4)
Founded 1923. Pop 25,902; Circ 151,671
May 2011-Apr 2012 Income $1,019,312, State $114,221, City $844,859, Federal $10,845, Other $49,387. Mats Exp $146,472. Sal $446,362
Library Holdings: Audiobooks 4,168; e-books 36; Electronic Media & Resources 38; Bk Vols 95,423; Per Subs 213; Videos 4,825
Automation Activity & Vendor Info: (Cataloging) SirsiDynix; (Circulation) SirsiDynix; (OPAC) SirsiDynix
Wireless access
Function: Adult bk club, After school storytime, Art exhibits, Bks on cassette, Bks on CD, Children's prog, Computer training, Computers for patron use, Copy machines, Exhibits, Family literacy, Free DVD rentals, Handicapped accessible, Holiday prog, ILL available, Magnifiers for reading, Music CDs, Notary serv, Online ref, Orientations, OverDrive digital audio bks, Photocopying/Printing, Preschool outreach, Prog for adults, Prog for children & young adult, Pub access computers, Ref serv available, Spoken cassettes & CDs, Spoken cassettes & DVDs, Story hour, Summer & winter reading prog, Summer reading prog, Tax forms, Teen prog, Telephone ref, VHS videos, Wheelchair accessible, Writing prog
Mem of Illinois Heartland Library System
Open Mon-Thurs 9-8, Fri & Sat 9-6, Sun 1-6
Friends of the Library Group

C SOUTHERN ILLINOIS UNIVERSITY CARBONDALE*, Delyte W Morris Library, 605 Agriculture Dr, Mailcode 6632, 62901. SAN 339-7599. Tel: 618-453-2522. Circulation Tel: 618-453-1455. Interlibrary Loan Service Tel: 618-453-3374. Interlibrary Loan Service FAX: 618-453-8109. Administration FAX: 618-453-3440. Web Site: www.lib.siu.edu. *Dean, Libr Affairs,* Anne Cooper Moore; Staff 40 (MLS 30, Non-MLS 10)
Founded 1869. Highest Degree: Doctorate
Library Holdings: Bk Vols 2,800,000; Per Subs 36,000
Special Collections: American Philosophy Coll; Expatriates Coll; Irish Literary Renaissance Coll; John Dewey Coll; Lawrence Durrell Coll; Private Presses; Robert Graves, James Joyce, D H Lawrence & Henry Miller Colls, bks & mss; Ulysses S Grant Coll. Oral History; State Document Depository; UN Document Depository; US Document Depository
Automation Activity & Vendor Info: (Acquisitions) Ex Libris Group; (Cataloging) Ex Libris Group; (Circulation) Ex Libris Group; (Course Reserve) Ex Libris Group; (ILL) Ex Libris Group; (Media Booking) Ex Libris Group; (OPAC) Ex Libris Group; (Serials) Ex Libris Group
Database Vendor: EBSCOhost, LexisNexis, OCLC FirstSearch, OVID Technologies
Publications: Bibliographic Contributions (irregular)
Partic in Association of Research Libraries (ARL); Center for Research Libraries; Greater Western Library Alliance; Illinois Library & Information Network; OCLC Online Computer Library Center, Inc
Open Mon-Thurs 7:30am-11pm, Fri 7:30am-9pm, Sat 1-6, Sun 1-9
Friends of the Library Group

Departmental Libraries:

CL LAW LIBRARY, Lesar Law Bldg, 1150 Douglas Dr, 62901. (Mail add: Mailcode 6803, 1150 Douglas Dr, 62901), SAN 325-3295. Tel: 618-453-8796. FAX: 618-453-8728. E-mail: lawlib@siu.edu. Web Site: www.law.siu.edu/lawlib. *Dir, Law Libr,* Doug Lind; Tel: 618-453-8713, E-mail: dlind@siu.edu; *Head, Pub Serv,* Nancy L Strohmeyer; Tel: 618-453-8789, E-mail: nstrohmeyer@siu.edu; *Ref Librn,* Alicia Granby Jones; Tel: 618-453-8780, E-mail: agjones@siu.edu; *Ref Librn,* Nolan Wright; Tel: 618-453-8791, E-mail: nwright@siu.edu; *Acq & Cat,* Cornelius A Pereira; Tel: 618-453-8781, E-mail: cpereira@siu.edu; Staff 5 (MLS 5)
Founded 1973. Enrl 341; Fac 35; Highest Degree: Doctorate
Jul 2013-Jun 2014. Mats Exp $598,056, Books $424,556, Electronic Ref Mat (Incl. Access Fees) $169,000, Presv $2,000
Library Holdings: DVDs 1,093; Bk Vols 230,646; Per Subs 2,116
Special Collections: Dillard Coll; Lincoln as a Lawyer; Self-Help Legal Coll. State Document Depository; US Document Depository
Subject Interests: Law
Automation Activity & Vendor Info: (Acquisitions) Innovative Interfaces, Inc; (Cataloging) Innovative Interfaces, Inc; (Circulation) Innovative Interfaces, Inc; (Course Reserve) Innovative Interfaces, Inc; (ILL) OCLC WorldShare Interlibrary Loan; (OPAC) Innovative Interfaces, Inc; (Serials) Innovative Interfaces, Inc
Database Vendor: Bloomberg, EBSCOhost, Fastcase, Gale Cengage Learning, HeinOnline, Innovative Interfaces, Inc, LexisNexis, OCLC FirstSearch, OCLC WorldShare Interlibrary Loan, ProQuest, Westlaw
Function: ILL available, Ref serv available
Partic in Consortium of Academic & Research Libraries in Illinois
Open Mon-Thurs 8-9, Fri 8-6, Sat 9-5, Sun 1-9
Restriction: 24-hr pass syst for students only

CARLINVILLE

C BLACKBURN COLLEGE*, Lumpkin Library, 700 College Ave, 62626. SAN 303-772X. Tel: 217-854-3231, Ext 4220. Toll Free Tel: 800-233-3550. FAX: 217-854-3231, 217-854-8564. *Head Librn,* Carol Schaefer; E-mail: carol.schaefer@blackburn.edu; *Libr Mgr,* Andrew Ott; Staff 3 (MLS 2, Non-MLS 1)
Founded 1862. Enrl 550; Fac 40; Highest Degree: Bachelor
Library Holdings: Bk Titles 55,000; Bk Vols 80,000; Per Subs 100
Special Collections: US Document Depository
Mem of Illinois Heartland Library System
Partic in Consortium of Academic & Research Libraries in Illinois; OCLC-LVIS; Private Academic Libraries of Illinois; Sangamon Valley Academic Library Consortium
Open Mon-Thurs (Winter) 8am-11pm, Fri 8-4, Sun 4-11; Mon-Thurs (Summer) 8-5, Fri 8-4

P CARLINVILLE PUBLIC LIBRARY*, 510 N Broad St, 62626-1019. (Mail add: PO Box 17, 62626-0017), SAN 303-7738. Tel: 217-854-3505. FAX: 217-854-5349. E-mail: mail@carlinvillelibrary.org. Web Site: www.carlinvillelibrary.org. *Dir,* Janet Howard; Staff 1 (Non-MLS 1)
Founded 1927. Pop 5,416
Library Holdings: Bk Titles 24,000; Per Subs 120
Subject Interests: Genealogy
Automation Activity & Vendor Info: (Cataloging) SirsiDynix; (Circulation) SirsiDynix
Wireless access
Mem of Illinois Heartland Library System
Open Mon-Thurs 9-8, Fri 9-5, Sat 9-1, Sun 1-4

CARLOCK

P CARLOCK PUBLIC LIBRARY DISTRICT*, 202 E Washington, 61725. (Mail add: PO Box 39, 61725-0039), SAN 321-2718. Tel: 309-376-5651. FAX: 309-376-4027. E-mail: carlockpatron@hotmail.com. Web Site: www.carlocklibrary.org. *Dir,* Linda Spencer; Staff 3 (MLS 3)
Founded 1979. Pop 2,600; Circ 10,501
Library Holdings: Bk Vols 13,000; Per Subs 37
Automation Activity & Vendor Info: (Circulation) Follett Software

Open Mon 2-8:30, Tues & Thurs 9-11 & 2-8:30, Wed 9-11 & 2-6, Fri 2-6, Sat 9-1
Friends of the Library Group

CARMI

P CARMI PUBLIC LIBRARY*, 103 Slocumb St, 62821. SAN 303-7754. Tel: 618-382-5277. FAX: 618-384-3118. E-mail: carmilib@yahoo.com. *Librn,* Elaine Foster
Founded 1914. Pop 5,422; Circ 37,220
Library Holdings: Bk Vols 31,060; Per Subs 66; Talking Bks 602
Mem of Illinois Heartland Library System
Open Mon-Thurs 12-8, Fri 11-6, Sat 11-5
Friends of the Library Group

CAROL STREAM

P CAROL STREAM PUBLIC LIBRARY*, 616 Hiawatha Dr, 60188. SAN 303-7762. Tel: 630-653-0755. FAX: 630-653-6809. E-mail: cstream@cslibrary.org. Web Site: www.cslibrary.org. *Dir,* Ann L Kennedy; Tel: 630-344-6101, E-mail: akennedy@cslibrary.org; *Asst Dir,* Pam Leffler; Tel: 630-344-6107, E-mail: pleffler@cslibrary.org; *Dir, Tech Serv,* Ellen Marchessault; E-mail: emarchessault@cslibrary.org; *Circ,* Mary Clemens; E-mail: mclemens@cslibrary.org; *Ref Serv, Ad,* Laura Hays; E-mail: lhays@cslibrary.org; *Youth Serv,* Lynn Johnson; E-mail: ljohnson@cslibrary.org; Staff 38.2 (MLS 17.6, Non-MLS 20.6)
Founded 1962. Pop 39,711; Circ 497,465
May 2010-Apr 2011 Income $3,310,662, State $41,688, City $2,964, Locally Generated Income $3,261,897, Other $4,113. Mats Exp $467,715, Books $192,205, Per/Ser (Incl. Access Fees) $17,373, AV Mat $76,893, Electronic Ref Mat (Incl. Access Fees) $181,244. Sal $1,615,076 (Prof $941,885)
Library Holdings: Audiobooks 3,178; AV Mats 545; CDs 5,057; DVDs 7,545; Large Print Bks 4,161; Bk Vols 167,983; Per Subs 341; Videos 407
Automation Activity & Vendor Info: (Acquisitions) SirsiDynix; (Cataloging) SirsiDynix; (Circulation) SirsiDynix
Database Vendor: Baker & Taylor, EBSCOhost, Gale Cengage Learning, OCLC FirstSearch, SirsiDynix
Wireless access
Publications: Between the Lines (Periodical)
Mem of Reaching Across Illinois Library System (RAILS)
Open Mon-Thurs 9-9, Fri 9-6, Sat 9-5, Sun 1-5
Friends of the Library Group

CARRIER MILLS

P CARRIER MILLS-STONEFORT PUBLIC LIBRARY DISTRICT*, 109 W Oak St, 62917. (Mail add: PO Box 338, 62917-0338), SAN 303-7770. Tel: 618-994-2011. FAX: 618-994-2303. *Librn,* Beth Thomason; *Bus Mgr,* Louis Shaw; Staff 2 (Non-MLS 2)
Founded 1962. Pop 2,952; Circ 3,931
Jul 2007-Jun 2008 Income $51,959, State $7,390, Federal $6,112, County $35,856, Locally Generated Income $2,601. Mats Exp $4,121, Per/Ser (Incl. Access Fees) $4,010, AV Mat $111. Sal $30,525
Library Holdings: AV Mats 47; DVDs 100; Large Print Bks 400; Bk Vols 21,722; Per Subs 45; Videos 100
Special Collections: Genealogy Coll; Local History Coll
Mem of Illinois Heartland Library System
Open Mon, Tues & Thurs 9-12 & 1-7, Wed & Fri 9-12 & 1-5, Sat 9-12

CARROLLTON

P CARROLLTON PUBLIC LIBRARY*, 509 S Main St, 62016. SAN 303-7789. Tel: 217-942-6715. FAX: 217-942-6005. E-mail: carrolltonpl@gmail.com. *Dir,* Angie Custer
Founded 1901. Pop 2,605
Library Holdings: Bk Titles 22,000; Per Subs 50
Subject Interests: Genealogy, Ill
Wireless access
Mem of Illinois Heartland Library System
Partic in Amigos Library Services, Inc
Open Mon & Thurs 12-5, Tues & Wed 2-7, Fri 10-5, Sat 10-2
Friends of the Library Group

CARTERVILLE

J JOHN A LOGAN COLLEGE*, Learning Resources Center, 700 Logan College Rd, 62918. SAN 303-7800. Tel: 618-985-3741, Ext 8338. FAX: 618-985-3899. E-mail: library@jalc.edu. Web Site: www.jalc.edu/lrc/library. *Assoc Dean,* Judy Vineyard; Tel: 618-985-3741, Ext 8404, E-mail: judyvineyard@jalc.edu; *Ref Librn,* J Adam Rubin; Tel: 618-985-3741, Ext 8279, E-mail: adamrubin@jalc.edu; Staff 13 (MLS 4, Non-MLS 9)
Founded 1968. Enrl 6,000; Fac 92
Library Holdings: AV Mats 500; Bk Titles 57,338; Bk Vols 69,866; Per Subs 450
Special Collections: John A Logan Memorial Coll
Subject Interests: Genealogy, Ill, Nursing
Partic in Illinois Library & Information Network
Open Mon-Thurs (Winter) 7:30-7:30, Fri 7:30-4:30, Sat 10-Noon; Mon-Thurs (Summer) 7:30-7:30, Fri 8-4:30

P ANNE WEST LINDSEY DISTRICT LIBRARY*, 600 N Division St, 62918. SAN 303-7797. Tel: 618-985-3298. FAX: 618-985-9474. Web Site: www.awlindsey.lib.il.us. *Dir,* Jane Robertson
Founded 1965. Pop 11,309; Circ 31,983
Library Holdings: Bk Vols 35,000
Special Collections: Genealogy Coll; Local History Coll
Wireless access
Mem of Illinois Heartland Library System
Open Mon & Wed 10-7, Tues, Thurs & Fri 10-5, Sat 10-4
Friends of the Library Group

CARTHAGE

P CARTHAGE PUBLIC LIBRARY DISTRICT*, 500 Wabash Ave, 62321. SAN 303-7827. Tel: 217-357-3232. FAX: 217-357-2392. E-mail: cartlib@adams.net. Web Site: www.carthage.lib.il.us. *Dir,* Susan Hunt
Founded 1894. Pop 4,501; Circ 43,011
Library Holdings: AV Mats 1,300; High Interest/Low Vocabulary Bk Vols 40; Large Print Bks 1,200; Bk Vols 34,308; Per Subs 124
Special Collections: Local History & Genealogy
Automation Activity & Vendor Info: (Cataloging) SIRSI WorkFlows; (Circulation) SIRSI WorkFlows; (OPAC) SirsiDynix
Database Vendor: Wilson - Wilson Web
Wireless access
Mem of Reaching Across Illinois Library System (RAILS)
Partic in Resource Sharing Alliance
Open Mon-Thurs 11-8, Fri 11-5, Sat 9-5
Friends of the Library Group

CARY

P CARY AREA PUBLIC LIBRARY DISTRICT, 1606 Three Oaks Rd, 60013-1637. SAN 303-7843. Tel: 847-639-4210. Circulation Tel: 847-639-4210, Ext 221. Reference Tel: 847-693-4210, Ext 227. FAX: 847-639-8890. E-mail: librarybd@cary.lib.il.us. Web Site: www.cary.lib.il.us, www.caryarealibrary.info. *Dir,* Diane R McNulty; Tel: 847-639-4210, Ext 224, E-mail: dmcnulty@cary.lib.il.us; Staff 41 (MLS 2, Non-MLS 39)
Founded 1951. Pop 28,245; Circ 336,622
Jul 2013-Jun 2014 Income $1,918,669, State $50,776, Locally Generated Income $1,812,837, Other $55,056. Mats Exp $264,530, Books $135,608, Per/Ser (Incl. Access Fees) $9,214, AV Equip $14,370, AV Mat $42,145, Electronic Ref Mat (Incl. Access Fees) $63,193. Sal $840,121 (Prof $155,604)
Library Holdings: Audiobooks 1,392; CDs 2,814; DVDs 4,908; e-books 19,820; Bk Vols 66,639; Per Subs 212
Automation Activity & Vendor Info: (Cataloging) SirsiDynix; (Circulation) SirsiDynix, (ILL) SirsiDynix; (OPAC) SirsiDynix; (Serials) SirsiDynix
Database Vendor: 3M Library Systems, BiblioCommons, EBSCOhost, Evanced Solutions, Inc, Grolier Online, H W Wilson, LearningExpress, OCLC FirstSearch, OCLC WebJunction, OCLC WorldShare Interlibrary Loan, Overdrive, Inc, ProQuest, SirsiDynix, TumbleBookLibrary, ValueLine
Wireless access
Function: Handicapped accessible, Homebound delivery serv, ILL available, Magnifiers for reading, Prog for adults, Prog for children & young adult, Ref serv available, Summer reading prog, Telephone ref, Wheelchair accessible
Publications: Books & Bytes (Newsletter)
Partic in Cooperative Computer Services - CCS
Open Mon-Thurs 9-9, Fri & Sat 9-5, Sun (Sept-May) 1-5
Friends of the Library Group

CASEY

P CASEY TOWNSHIP LIBRARY*, 307 E Main St, 62420. SAN 303-7851. Tel: 217-932-2105. FAX: 217-932-2105. E-mail: kzlib@rr1.net. Web Site: www.caseytownship.lib.il.us. *Head Librn,* Sam Purcell; Staff 3 (Non-MLS 3)
Founded 1938. Pop 4,021; Circ 41,000
Library Holdings: Audiobooks 700; Bk Titles 22,000; Per Subs 51; Videos 1,000
Wireless access
Mem of Illinois Heartland Library System
Open Mon-Fri 11-5, Sat 10-3
Friends of the Library Group

CASEYVILLE

P CASEYVILLE PUBLIC LIBRARY DISTRICT, 419 S Second St, 62232. SAN 303-786X. Tel: 618-345-5848. FAX: 618-345-0081. Web Site: www.caseyvillelibrary.org. *Dir,* Christine Stewart; Staff 1 (Non-MLS 1)
Founded 1962. Pop 4,772
Library Holdings: Bk Titles 38,000; Per Subs 3
Automation Activity & Vendor Info: (Acquisitions) Innovative Interfaces, Inc - Millenium
Database Vendor: SirsiDynix
Wireless access
Mem of Illinois Heartland Library System
Open Mon, Wed & Fri 1-6, Tues & Thurs 10-12 & 1-8, Sat 9-2

CATLIN

P CATLIN PUBLIC LIBRARY DISTRICT*, 101 Mapleleaf Dr, 61817. (Mail add: PO Box 350, 61817-0350), SAN 303-7878. Tel: 217-427-2550. FAX: 217-427-9830. E-mail: catlinlibrary03@yahoo.com. *Librn,* Jeanette Nash
Founded 1972. Pop 3,402; Circ 20,422
Library Holdings: Bk Vols 15,115; Per Subs 43
Mem of Illinois Heartland Library System
Open Mon & Thurs 9-5, Tues & Wed 9-8, Fri 3-7, Sat 9-2

CENTRALIA

S CENTRALIA CORRECTIONAL CENTER LIBRARY*, 9330 Shattuc Rd, 62801. (Mail add: PO Box 1266, 62801-1266), SAN 371-5280. Tel: 618-533-4111, Ext 2710. *Libr Assoc,* J Wallace
Founded 1980
Library Holdings: Bk Vols 18,000; Per Subs 66
Open Tues-Fri 7-5

P CENTRALIA REGIONAL LIBRARY DISTRICT*, 515 E Broadway, 62801. SAN 303-7886. Tel: 618-532-5222. FAX: 618-532-8578. Web Site: www.centralialibrary.org. *Dir,* Joyce Jackson; E-mail: jjackson@shawls.lib.il.us; *Asst Dir,* Terri Rogers; *Circ Supvr,* Cindy Payne; *Ch Serv,* Rita Lewis; *Pub Relations,* Diana Donahoo
Founded 1874. Pop 31,204; Circ 127,170
Library Holdings: Audiobooks 3,409; DVDs 7,582; Bk Vols 92,934
Special Collections: Oral History
Automation Activity & Vendor Info: (Acquisitions) SirsiDynix; (Cataloging) SirsiDynix; (Circulation) SirsiDynix
Mem of Illinois Heartland Library System
Open Mon-Thurs 10-8, Fri 10-5, Sat 12-5, Sun 1:30-5
Friends of the Library Group
Branches: 4
IRVINGTON BRANCH, 208 S Fifth St, Irvington, 62848-0130. Tel: 618-249-8143. FAX: 618-249-8143. *Librn,* Carol Crenshaw
Open Tues & Wed 12-5, Thurs 12-7
ODIN COMMUNITY, 219 E Main St, Odin, 62870. Tel: 618-775-8309. FAX: 618-775-8309. *Librn,* Virgil Downen
Open Tues & Thurs 3-7, Wed & Fri 12-4, Sat 10-2
SANDOVAL BRANCH, 118 E Commercial, Sandoval, 62882. Tel: 618-247-3873. *Circ,* Mary O'Neill
Open Tues 12-7, Fri 10-5, Sat 10-4
RALPH W & BERNICE S SPREHE LIBRARY, 103 S Broadway, Hoffman, 62250. Tel: 618-495-9955. FAX: 618-495-9955. *Circ,* Lila Hoffman
Open Mon, Thurs & Fri 1-5, Sat 10-2

J KASKASKIA COLLEGE LIBRARY*, 27210 College Rd, 62801. SAN 303-7894. Tel: 618-545-3130. Toll Free Tel: 800-642-0859. FAX: 618-532-9241. E-mail: library@kaskaskia.edu. Web Site: www.kaskaskia.edu/library. *Dir,* Arlene Dueker; Tel: 618-545-3131, E-mail: adueker@kaskaskia.edu; *Librn,* Charles Rusiewski; E-mail: crusiewski@kaskaskia.edu; *Libr Serv Tech,* Linda Wimberly; Tel: 618-545-3135, E-mail: lkwimberly@kaskaskia.edu; Staff 4 (MLS 1, Non-MLS 3)
Founded 1940. Highest Degree: Associate
Jul 2006-Jun 2007. Mats Exp $62,281, Books $30,166, Per/Ser (Incl. Access Fees) $15,925, AV Mat $950, Electronic Ref Mat (Incl. Access Fees) $15,240
Library Holdings: CDs 10; DVDs 57; Bk Vols 23,357; Per Subs 169; Talking Bks 90; Videos 17
Automation Activity & Vendor Info: (Acquisitions) SirsiDynix; (Cataloging) SirsiDynix; (Circulation) SirsiDynix; (Serials) SirsiDynix
Database Vendor: EBSCOhost, Gale Cengage Learning, OCLC FirstSearch, ProQuest, SirsiDynix, Wilson - Wilson Web
Function: ILL available
Mem of Illinois Heartland Library System
Partic in Consortium of Academic & Research Libraries in Illinois; Northern Ill Learning Resources Coop; Southern Ill Learning Resources Coop
Open Mon-Thurs (Winter) 7:30-9, Fri 7:30-4, Sat 8-12; Mon-Thurs (Summer) 7:30-7, Fri 7:30-4

CENTREVILLE

P CENTREVILLE PUBLIC LIBRARY*, 701 S 47th St, 62207. (Mail add: PO Box 1260, Alorton, 62207-0260). Tel: 618-271-2040. FAX: 618-271-6893. E-mail: centreville@digitalesl.org. Web Site: centrevillelibrary.org. *Dir,* Jo Wanda Lindsey
Library Holdings: Bk Titles 6,000; Per Subs 15
Wireless access
Mem of Illinois Heartland Library System
Open Mon-Fri 2-6

CERRO GORDO

P HOPE WELTY PUBLIC LIBRARY DISTRICT*, 100 S Madison St, 61818. (Mail add: PO Box 260, 61818-0260), SAN 303-7908. Tel: 217-763-5001. FAX: 217-763-5391. Web Site: www.hopeweltylibrary.com. *Dir,* Position Currently Open; *Ch,* Shari Rawlings; *Circ Librn,* Jill Dodson
Pop 3,624; Circ 41,279
Library Holdings: Bk Vols 15,628; Per Subs 116
Automation Activity & Vendor Info: (Acquisitions) Horizon; (Cataloging) Horizon; (Circulation) Horizon; (ILL) Horizon
Database Vendor: OCLC FirstSearch
Wireless access
Mem of Illinois Heartland Library System
Partic in Illinois Library & Information Network
Open Mon 4-7, Tues, Wed & Fri 10-5, Thurs 10-7, Sat 10-1

CHADWICK

P CHADWICK PUBLIC LIBRARY DISTRICT*, 110 Main St, 61014. (Mail add: PO Box 416, 61014-0416), SAN 375-9946. Tel: 815-684-5215. FAX: 815-684-5215. Web Site: www.chadwicklibrary.org. *Dir,* Jo Nell Castellani; E-mail: jonell_castellani@yahoo.com
Founded 1988. Pop 1,221
Library Holdings: Bk Titles 10,000; Per Subs 20
Mem of Reaching Across Illinois Library System (RAILS)
Open Mon-Wed & Fri 1:30-6:30, Thurs 10:30-6:30, Sat 9-1

CHAMPAIGN

S CHAMPAIGN COUNTY HISTORICAL MUSEUM*, Barbara Peckham Research Library, 102 E University Ave, 61820-4111. SAN 373-4374. Tel: 217-356-1010. FAX: 217-356-1478. Web Site: www.champaignmuseum.org. *Dir,* Position Currently Open
Founded 1974
Library Holdings: Bk Vols 1,000
Special Collections: History of the Champaign County Area, incl Historic Preservation Issues, Memorabilia, Volumes Owned by Historic Figures, Local Histories & Studies of Local Buildings of Historic Value. Oral History
Subject Interests: Local hist
Function: Archival coll, For res purposes, Photocopying/Printing, Res libr
Publications: Champaign County Historical Museum Newsletter (Quarterly)
Open Sat & Sun Noon-5
Restriction: In-house use for visitors, Non-circulating

P CHAMPAIGN PUBLIC LIBRARY, 200 W Green St, 61820-5193. SAN 339-7831. Tel: 217-403-2050. Circulation Tel: 217-403-2000. Information Services Tel: 217-403-2070. FAX: 217-403-2053. Information Services FAX: 217-403-2073. TDD: 217-403-2055. Web Site: www.champaign.org. *Dir,* Marsha Grove; E-mail: mgrove@champaign.org; *Develop Dir,* Donna Pittman; E-mail: dpittman@champaign.org; *Asst Mgr, Adult Serv,* Nanette Donohue; E-mail: ndonohue@champaign.org; *Tech Mgr,* Amy Al-Shabibi; E-mail: aal-shabibi@champaign.org; *Adult Serv,* Kristina L Hoerner; E-mail: khoerner@champaign.org; *Ch Serv,* Stephanie Edwards; E-mail: sedwards@champaign.org; *Circ,* Laura Weis; E-mail: lweis@champaign.org; *Coll Develop,* Kelly S Strom; E-mail: kstrom@champaign.org
Founded 1876. Pop 81,055; Circ 2,500,000
Library Holdings: Audiobooks 8,000; CDs 29,000; DVDs 40,000; e-books 12,000; Bk Vols 270,000; Per Subs 506
Automation Activity & Vendor Info: (Acquisitions) Innovative Interfaces, Inc; (Cataloging) Innovative Interfaces, Inc; (Circulation) Innovative Interfaces, Inc; (ILL) Innovative Interfaces, Inc; (OPAC) Innovative Interfaces, Inc; (Serials) Innovative Interfaces, Inc
Database Vendor: Baker & Taylor, Ingram Library Services, OCLC FirstSearch, Overdrive, Inc, Tech Logic
Wireless access
Function: Online info literacy tutorials on the web & in blackboard
Publications: The Last Word (Monthly newsletter)
Mem of Illinois Heartland Library System
Partic in Illinois Library & Information Network
Special Services for the Deaf - TDD equip

Open Mon-Fri 9-9, Sat 9-6, Sun 1-6
Friends of the Library Group
Branches: 1
DOUGLASS BRANCH, 504 E Grove St, 61820-3239, SAN 339-7866. Tel: 217-403-2090, 217-403-4455. FAX: 217-356-9561. *Br Mgr,* Essie Harris
Open Mon-Thurs 10-8, Fri 10-6, Sat 10-4
Friends of the Library Group

S ILLINOIS EARLY INTERVENTION CLEARINGHOUSE*, Univ of Illinois-Urbana-Champaign, Children's Research Center, 51 Gerty Dr, 61820. SAN 371-523X. Tel: 217-333-1386. FAX: 217-244-7732. E-mail: Illinois eic@illinois.edu. Web Site: www.eiclearinghouse.org. *Dir,* Sarah Isaacs; Staff 2 (MLS 1, Non-MLS 1)
Founded 1986
Library Holdings: AV Mats 1,582; Bks on Deafness & Sign Lang 240; Bk Titles 8,864; Per Subs 25
Special Collections: Austism
Subject Interests: Disabilities, Early childhood, Parenting
Automation Activity & Vendor Info: (Cataloging) SirsiDynix; (Circulation) SirsiDynix; (ILL) OCLC; (OPAC) SirsiDynix; (Serials) EBSCO Online
Database Vendor: OCLC FirstSearch
Publications: Bibliography Series; Early Intervention (Newsletter)
Mem of Illinois Heartland Library System
Partic in Health Sci Libr Info Consortium; Illinois Library & Information Network
Special Services for the Deaf - Bks on deafness & sign lang; TDD equip; Videos & decoder
Open Mon-Fri 8-4:30

S NEWS-GAZETTE LIBRARY*, 15 Main St, 61820. (Mail add: PO Box 677, 61824-0677), SAN 324-4199. Tel: 217-351-5228. FAX: 217-351-5374. E-mail: library@news-gazette.com. *Head Librn,* Carolyn J Vance. Subject Specialists: *Local news,* Carolyn J Vance; Staff 2 (MLS 1, Non-MLS 1)
Founded 1946
Library Holdings: Bk Titles 521; Bk Vols 764; Per Subs 10
Special Collections: News-Gazette Microfilm (1953-present), Local Newspaper Clippings (mid 1946-July 1994) & Database of Local News Stories (July 27, 1994-present)
Subject Interests: Local hist, Local news
Restriction: Pub access by telephone only

A UNITED STATES ARMY CORPS OF ENGINEERS, Engineer Research & Development Center, 2902 Newmark Dr, 61822. (Mail add: PO Box 9005, 61826-9005), SAN 303-7959. Tel: 217-373-7217. FAX: 217-373-7258. E-mail: library-il@usace.army.mil. Web Site: www.erdc.usace.army.mil/library. *Libr Tech,* Pat Lacey; Staff 2 (Non-MLS 2)
Founded 1969
Library Holdings: Bk Titles 19,000
Subject Interests: Civil eng, Construction, Environ eng
Automation Activity & Vendor Info: (Acquisitions) SirsiDynix; (Cataloging) SirsiDynix; (Circulation) SirsiDynix; (OPAC) SirsiDynix
Function: Res libr
Mem of Illinois Heartland Library System
Partic in OCLC Online Computer Library Center, Inc
Restriction: Open to others by appt

CHANNAHON

P THREE RIVERS PUBLIC LIBRARY DISTRICT*, 25207 W Channon Dr, 60410-5028. (Mail add: PO Box 300, 60410-0300), SAN 321-0308. Tel: 815-467-6200. Circulation Tel: 815-467-6200, Ext 0. Administration Tel: 815-467-6200, Ext 208. FAX: 815-467-4012. Web Site: www.trpld.org. *Exec Dir,* Mary Soucie; E-mail: marys@trpld.org; *Asst Dir,* Lauren Offerman; E-mail: laureno@trpld.org; *Youth Serv Librn,* Lisa Berger; *Adult Serv Mgr,* Sarah Robertson; *Tech Serv Mgr,* Bev Markezich; Staff 4 (MLS 2, Non-MLS 2)
Founded 1976. Pop 17,189; Circ 191,764
Jul 2007-Jun 2008 Income $949,872, State $72,357, Locally Generated Income $714,896, Other $162,619. Mats Exp $174,475, Books $108,324, Per/Ser (Incl. Access Fees) $8,115, Other Print Mats $2,274, AV Mat $27,205, Electronic Ref Mat (Incl. Access Fees) $27,557, Presv $1,000. Sal $249,404 (Prof $177,298)
Library Holdings: Audiobooks 2,969; CDs 2,500; DVDs 2,118; High Interest/Low Vocabulary Bk Vols 50; Large Print Bks 1,200; Bk Vols 80,280; Per Subs 203; Talking Bks 744; Videos 60
Special Collections: Local History, Channahon & Minooka, IL
Automation Activity & Vendor Info: (Circulation) SirsiDynix; (ILL) OCLC; (OPAC) SirsiDynix
Database Vendor: Gale Cengage Learning, OCLC FirstSearch
Wireless access
Function: Adult bk club, Bks on CD, Children's prog, Copy machines, Fax serv, Handicapped accessible, Homebound delivery serv, Homework prog, ILL available, Notary serv, Online ref, Outside serv via phone, mail, e-mail & web, Photocopying/Printing, Prog for children & young adult, Ref serv available, Spoken cassettes & CDs, Story hour, Summer reading prog, Tax forms, Telephone ref, Wheelchair accessible
Publications: Newsletter (Quarterly)
Mem of Reaching Across Illinois Library System (RAILS)
Open Mon-Thurs 9-9, Fri 9-6, Sat 9-5, Sun 1-5; Mon-Thurs (Summer) 9-9, Fri 9-6, Sat 9-3

CHARLESTON

P CHARLESTON CARNEGIE PUBLIC LIBRARY*, 712 Sixth St, 61920. SAN 303-7967. Tel: 217-345-4913. FAX: 217-348-5616. E-mail: charlestonlibrary@yahoo.com. Web Site: www.charlestonlibrary.org. *Libr Dir,* Jeanne Hamilton; *Coll Develop Librn,* Judy Looby; *Circ Mgr,* Ruth Straith; *Adult & Teen Prog Coordr,* Kattie Livingston; *Adult Prog Coordr,* Beth Lugar; *Libr Assoc,* Tonya Morton
Founded 1896. Pop 20,398; Circ 163,143
Library Holdings: Bk Titles 48,000; Per Subs 175
Subject Interests: Educ, Med, Relig
Open Mon-Thurs 10-8, Fri & Sat 10-6, Sun 1-5

S COLES COUNTY HISTORICAL SOCIETY*, Research Library & Museum, 895 Seventh St, 61920. (Mail add: 1320 Lafayette Ave, Mattoon, 61938), SAN 370-8969. Tel: 217-235-6744. E-mail: coleshistory@consolidated.net. Web Site: www.coleshistory.net. *Spec Coll,* Norma Winkleblack; E-mail: nwink26@consolidated.net
Library Holdings: Bk Vols 2,000
Special Collections: Coles County Coll; Illinois History Coll
Restriction: Open by appt only

C EASTERN ILLINOIS UNIVERSITY*, Booth Library, 600 Lincoln Ave, 61920. SAN 303-7975. Circulation Tel: 217-581-6071. Interlibrary Loan Service Tel: 217-581-6074. Reference Tel: 217-581-6072. Administration Tel: 217-581-6061. Toll Free Tel: 866-862-6684. Interlibrary Loan Service FAX: 217-581-6066. Reference FAX: 217-581-6911. Administration FAX: 217-581-7534. Web Site: www.library.eiu.edu. *Dean, Libr Serv,* Dr Allen Lanham; E-mail: aklanham@eiu.edu; *Head, Acq,* Marlene Slough; Tel: 217-581-6021, Fax: 217-581-7379, E-mail: mmslough@eiu.edu; *Head Archivist,* Robert Hillman; Tel: 217-581-7552, Fax: 217-581-6409, E-mail: rvhillman@eiu.edu; *Head, Cat,* John Whisler; Tel: 217-581-7561, E-mail: jawhisler@eiu.edu; *Head, Circ,* Bradley Tolppanen; Tel: 217-581-6006, E-mail: bptolppanen@eiu.edu; *Electronic Res, Head, Coll Develop,* Karen Whisler; Tel: 217-581-7551, E-mail: klwhisler@eiu.edu; *Head, Media Serv,* John Looby; Tel: 217-581-7564, Fax: 217-581-6993, E-mail: jclooby@eiu.edu; *Head, Tech Serv,* Stacey Knight-Davis; Tel: 217-581-6091, E-mail: slknight@eiu.edu; *Head, Ref,* Position Currently Open; *Cat Librn,* Bill Schultz; Tel: 217-581-8457, E-mail: wnschultz@eiu.edu; *Cat/Digitization Libr,* Ellen Corrigan; Tel: 217-581-8456, E-mail: ekcorrigan@eiu.edu; *Institutional Repository Librn,* Todd Bruns; Tel: 217-581-8381, E-mail: tabruns@eiu.edu; *Circ, Night Supvr Librn,* Janice Derr; Tel: 217-549-1936, E-mail: jmderr@eiu.edu; *Ref Librn,* David Bell; Tel: 217-581-7547, E mail: dsbell@eiu.edu; *Ref Librn,* Ann Brownson; Tel: 217-581-6099, E-mail: aebrownson@eiu.edu; *Ref Librn,* Kirstin Duffin; Tel: 217-581-7550, E-mail: kduffin@eiu.edu; *Ref Librn,* Sarah Johnson; Tel: 217-581-7538, E-mail: sljohnson2@eiu.edu; *Ref Librn,* Pamela Ortega; Tel: 217-581-7548, E-mail: pfortega@eiu.edu; *Archivist,* Dr Robert Wiseman; Tel: 217-581-8454, E-mail: rcwiseman@eiu.edu. Subject Specialists: *Music,* Dr Allen Lanham; *Art, Family & consumer sci,* Marlene Slough; *Archives & Spec Coll,* Robert Hillman; *Hist, Mil sci,* Bradley Tolppanen; *English, Libr sci, Speech comm,* Karen Whisler; *Health, Nursing, Physics,* Stacey Knight-Davis; *Anthrop, Psychol, Sociol,* Bill Schultz; *Tech,* Todd Bruns; *Journalism, Leisure studies, Theatre arts,* David Bell; *Counseling, Educ, Secondary educ,* Ann Brownson; *Biological sci, Chem,* Kirstin Duffin; *Econ, Math,* Sarah Johnson; *Communication disorders, Foreign lang, Latin Am studies,* Pamela Ortega; *Photog,* Dr Robert Wiseman; Staff 56.66 (MLS 18, Non-MLS 38.66)
Founded 1896. Enrl 10,417; Fac 586; Highest Degree: Master
Jul 2011-Jun 2012 Income $5,150,411, State $3,357,853, Federal $20,458, Locally Generated Income $164,769, Other $19,409. Mats Exp $1,789,401, Books $433,944, Per/Ser (Incl. Access Fees) $778,370, Micro $26,498, AV Mat $44,051, Electronic Ref Mat (Incl. Access Fees) $441,750, Presv $64,788. Sal $3,087,060 (Prof $1,523,800)
Library Holdings: AV Mats 42,550; CDs 5,166; DVDs 11,497; e-books 44,320; e-journals 2,655; Microforms 481,753; Bk Vols 1,093,379; Per Subs 46,047; Videos 23,325
Special Collections: Art & Architecture in Illinois Libraries; Ballenger Teacher Center; Garner Sheet Music; Illinois Landscape Artists; Ned Brasel Coll of the Southwest; Remo Belli International Percussion Library. State Document Depository; US Document Depository
Subject Interests: Bus, Educ, Liberal arts
Automation Activity & Vendor Info: (Acquisitions) Ex Libris Group; (Cataloging) Ex Libris Group; (Circulation) Ex Libris Group; (Course

Reserve) Ex Libris Group; (ILL) Ex Libris Group; (OPAC) Ex Libris Group
Database Vendor: Alexander Street Press, American Chemical Society, American Mathematical Society, American Physical Society, Annual Reviews, ARTstor, Blackwell, Cinahl, EBSCO Information Services, EBSCOhost, Emerald, Ingenta, JSTOR, Lexi-Comp, LexisNexis, Medline, Mergent Online, Modern Language Association, OCLC FirstSearch, OCLC WorldShare Interlibrary Loan, OVID Technologies, Oxford Online, Plunkett Research, Ltd, Project MUSE, ProQuest, PubMed, Safari Books Online, Sage, SerialsSolutions, Springer-Verlag, Wiley InterScience, Wilson - Wilson Web, YBP Library Services
Wireless access
Function: Res libr
Mem of Illinois Heartland Library System
Partic in Consortium of Academic & Research Libraries in Illinois; OCLC Online Computer Library Center, Inc
Special Services for the Deaf - TTY equip
Special Services for the Blind - Accessible computers; Audio mat; Bks available with recordings; Cassette playback machines; Cassettes; HP Scan Jet with photo-finish software
Open Mon-Thurs (Winter) 8am-1am, Fri 8-5, Sat 9-5, Sun Noon-1am; Mon-Thurs (Summer) 8am-10pm, Fri 8-5, Sat 9-5, Sun 2-10
Restriction: Open to students, fac, staff & alumni, Pub use on premises

CHATHAM

P CHATHAM AREA PUBLIC LIBRARY DISTRICT*, 600 E Spruce St, 62629. SAN 376-0022. Tel: 217-483-2713. FAX: 217-483-2361. Web Site: www.chatham.lib.il.us. *Dir,* Amy Ihnen; Staff 4 (MLS 1, Non-MLS 3)
Pop 13,139; Circ 134,914
Library Holdings: Bk Vols 62,000; Per Subs 124
Automation Activity & Vendor Info: (Cataloging) SirsiDynix; (Circulation) SirsiDynix; (OPAC) SirsiDynix
Mem of Illinois Heartland Library System
Open Mon-Thurs 9-8, Fri 9-5, Sat 9-4
Friends of the Library Group

CHATSWORTH

P CHATSWORTH TOWNSHIP LIBRARY*, 432 E Locust St, 60921. (Mail add: PO Box 638, 60921-0638), SAN 303-7983. Tel: 815-635-3004. FAX: 815-635-3004. E-mail: chatslib@hotmail.com. *Dir,* Mary Fisher-Miller; E-mail: director.library@yahoo.com; *Asst Librn,* Norma Koerner
Pop 1,431; Circ 7,280
Library Holdings: Bk Vols 12,000; Per Subs 24
Open Tues-Fri 11-5, Sat (Fall & Spring) 9-12

CHENOA

P CHENOA PUBLIC LIBRARY DISTRICT*, 211 S Division St, 61726. SAN 303-7991. Tel: 815-945-4253. FAX: 815-945-4203. E-mail: chenoapl@frontier.com. Web Site: chenoalibrary.org. *Dir,* Sheryl Siebert
Pop 2,305; Circ 12,850
Library Holdings: AV Mats 150; Bks on Deafness & Sign Lang 10; DVDs 59; Large Print Bks 50; Bk Titles 14,083; Per Subs 70; Talking Bks 432; Videos 320
Database Vendor: Baker & Taylor, OCLC WorldShare Interlibrary Loan
Wireless access
Open Mon & Wed 2-7, Tues & Thurs 10-12 & 2-7, Fri 2-5, Sat 9-Noon

CHERRY VALLEY

P CHERRY VALLEY PUBLIC LIBRARY DISTRICT*, 755 E State St, 61016-9699. SAN 320-4731. Tel: 815-332-5161. FAX: 815-332-2441. Web Site: www.cherryvalley.lib.il.us. *Exec Dir,* Eve G Kirk; Tel: 815-332-5161, Ext 27, E-mail: evek@cherryvalley.lib.il.us; *Asst Dir,* Michele Arms; Tel: 815-332-5161, Ext 35; *Circ Mgr,* Jenny Hansen-Peterson; Tel: 815-332-5161, Ext 25; *Info Serv, ILL Mgr,* Blaine Cornelius; Tel: 815-332-5161, Ext 26; *Tech Serv Mgr,* Fran Schaible; Tel: 815-332-5161, Ext 32; *Youth Serv Mgr,* Stacey Chester; Tel: 815-332-5161, Ext 33; *Teen Serv,* Becky Yerk; Tel: 815-332-5161, Ext 34; Staff 22 (MLS 1, Non-MLS 21)
Founded 1977. Pop 17,000; Circ 172,510
Library Holdings: AV Mats 4,928; CDs 567; e-books 6,796; Electronic Media & Resources 11; Large Print Bks 1,248; Bk Titles 44,748; Bk Vols 46,855; Per Subs 160; Talking Bks 2,078; Videos 2,283
Subject Interests: Local hist
Automation Activity & Vendor Info: (Acquisitions) Innovative Interfaces, Inc; (Cataloging) Innovative Interfaces, Inc; (Circulation) Innovative Interfaces, Inc; (OPAC) Innovative Interfaces, Inc; (Serials) Innovative Interfaces, Inc
Database Vendor: Baker & Taylor, EBSCOhost, Innovative Interfaces, Inc, Newsbank, OCLC FirstSearch, OCLC WorldShare Interlibrary Loan, ProQuest
Function: Audio & video playback equip for onsite use, AV serv, ILL available, Magnifiers for reading, Photocopying/Printing, Prog for adults, Prog for children & young adult, Summer reading prog, Wheelchair accessible
Mem of Reaching Across Illinois Library System (RAILS)
Special Services for the Deaf - TDD equip
Special Services for the Blind - Assistive/Adapted tech devices, equip & products; Audio mat; Bks on cassette; Bks on CD; Large print bks; Reader equip; Talking bks
Open Mon-Thurs 9-8, Fri & Sat 9-5, Sun (Sept-May) 1-5
Friends of the Library Group

CHESTER

S CHESTER MENTAL HEALTH CENTER*, Patient Library, 1315 Lehmen Rd, 62233-2542. (Mail add: PO Box 31, 62233-0031), SAN 339-7955. Tel: 618-826-4571. FAX: 618-826-3581. *Supvr,* Lori Lrose; Tel: 618-826-4571, Ext 463; *Librn,* June Valentine; Tel: 618-826-4571, Ext 539
Founded 1968
Library Holdings: CDs 120; DVDs 50; Large Print Bks 200; Bk Titles 8,500; Per Subs 30; Videos 200
Special Collections: Large Print
Open Mon-Fri 8:30-4:30

P CHESTER PUBLIC LIBRARY*, 733 State St, 62233. SAN 303-8009. Tel: 618-826-3711. FAX: 618-826-2733. Web Site: www.chester.lib.il.us. *Admin Librn,* Tammy Grah; E-mail: graht@shawls.lib.il.us; *Librn II,* Lisa Whittenborne
Founded 1928. Pop 8,194; Circ 71,424
Library Holdings: Bk Vols 39,000; Per Subs 50
Special Collections: Rare Books (First Books Room)
Subject Interests: Environ studies, Ethnic studies, Genealogy, Local hist, Med, Relig, Sci tech
Automation Activity & Vendor Info: (Cataloging) SirsiDynix; (Circulation) SirsiDynix; (OPAC) SirsiDynix
Mem of Illinois Heartland Library System
Open Mon-Thurs 10-7, Fri 10-5, Sat 10-3
Friends of the Library Group

CHICAGO

S ADLER SCHOOL OF PROFESSIONAL PSYCHOLOGY*, Sol & Elaine Mosak Library, 17 N Dearborn St, 60602. SAN 303-8025. Tel: 312-261-4070. FAX: 312-201-8756. Web Site: www.adler.edu. *Dir of Libr Serv,* Kerry Cochrane; *Access Serv Librn,* Amanda Musacchio; *Tech Serv Librn,* Heather Cannon; Staff 3 (MLS 3)
Founded 1952. Enrl 300; Highest Degree: Doctorate
Library Holdings: AV Mats 500; Bk Titles 1,200; Per Subs 130; Videos 200
Special Collections: Adlerian Athenaeum Coll; Adlerian Psychology Coll; Individual Psychology Coll
Subject Interests: Art therapy, Cultural diversity, Family, Forensic psychol, Gender, Gerontology, Marriage, Psychiat, Psychol, Psychotherapy, Substance abuse
Automation Activity & Vendor Info: (Cataloging) SirsiDynix; (Circulation) SirsiDynix; (ILL) OCLC; (OPAC) SirsiDynix
Publications: Index to Individual Psychology
Partic in Asn Col & Res Librs; Consortium of Academic & Research Libraries in Illinois; Illinois Library & Information Network; OCLC Online Computer Library Center, Inc; OCLC-LVIS; Private Academic Libraries of Illinois; US National Library of Medicine
Restriction: Not open to pub

M ADVOCATE ILLINOIS MASONIC MEDICAL CENTER*, Medical Library, 836 W Wellington Ave, Rm 7501, 60657. SAN 320-4499. Tel: 773-296-5084. FAX: 773-296-7421. *Mgr,* Lisa Jacob; Staff 2 (MLS 1, Non-MLS 1)
Founded 1963
Library Holdings: Bk Vols 5,000; Per Subs 340
Subject Interests: Health sci
Automation Activity & Vendor Info: (Cataloging) Ex Libris Group; (Circulation) Ex Libris Group; (ILL) Clio; (OPAC) Ex Libris Group; (Serials) Ex Libris Group
Database Vendor: EBSCOhost, MD Consult, OCLC FirstSearch, OVID Technologies, SerialsSolutions, UpToDate
Wireless access
Publications: @ The Library (Intranet Newsletter)
Partic in National Network of Libraries of Medicine Greater Midwest Region

M ADVOCATE TRINITY HOSPITAL*, Department of Library Services, 2320 E 93rd St, 60617. SAN 377-5348. Tel: 773-967-5564. FAX: 773-967-5808. Web Site: www.advocatehealth.com/trin. *Mgr,* Candace Gwizdalski; Tel: 773-967-5564, Ext 5300
Library Holdings: Bk Vols 7,000; Per Subs 50
Subject Interests: Med, Nursing

Automation Activity & Vendor Info: (Cataloging) Ex Libris Group; (Circulation) Ex Libris Group; (OPAC) Ex Libris Group
Database Vendor: EBSCOhost, OVID Technologies
Mem of Reaching Across Illinois Library System (RAILS)
Restriction: Circulates for staff only

M ALZHEIMER'S ASSOCIATION, Benjamin B Green-Field National Alzheimer's Library & Resource Center, 225 N Michigan Ave, 17th Flr, 60601. SAN 371-9901. Tel: 312-335-9602. Toll Free Tel: 800-272-3900. E-mail: greenfield@alz.org. Web Site: www.alz.org/library. *Assoc Dir,* Mary Ann Urbashich; Tel: 312-335-5199, E-mail: maryann.urbashich@alz.org; Staff 1 (MLS 1)
Founded 1991
Jul 2014-Jun 2015. Mats Exp $111,556
Library Holdings: Audiobooks 5; AV Mats 200; CDs 60; DVDs 160; Electronic Media & Resources 50; Bk Titles 4,800; Bk Vols 6,400; Per Subs 160; Videos 1,200
Subject Interests: Aging, Care, Geriatrics, Gerontology, Nonprofit mgt
Automation Activity & Vendor Info: (Acquisitions) EOS International; (Cataloging) EOS International; (Circulation) EOS International; (ILL) OCLC; (OPAC) EOS International; (Serials) EOS International
Database Vendor: EBSCO Information Services, EBSCOhost, EOS International, Gale Cengage Learning, OCLC FirstSearch, OCLC WorldShare Interlibrary Loan, PubMed
Wireless access
Publications: Brochure; Resource Bibliographies
Mem of Reaching Across Illinois Library System (RAILS)
Partic in National Network of Libraries of Medicine Greater Midwest Region
Open Mon-Fri 8-5

M AMERICAN COLLEGE OF SURGEONS LIBRARY*, 633 N St Clair St, 60611. SAN 303-8084. Tel: 312-202-5239. FAX: 312-202-5011. Web Site: www.facs.org. *Mgr, Libr Serv,* Belinda Andry; E-mail: bandry@facs.org; Staff 1 (Non-MLS 1)
Founded 1913
Library Holdings: Bk Vols 500; Per Subs 100
Special Collections: History of Medicine; Surgical Artifacts Coll
Subject Interests: Surgery
Automation Activity & Vendor Info: (Cataloging) New Generation Technologies Inc. (LiBRARYSOFT)
Function: Res libr
Mem of Reaching Across Illinois Library System (RAILS)
Restriction: Non-circulating, Open by appt only

M AMERICAN DENTAL ASSOCIATION LIBRARY & ARCHIVES, 211 E Chicago Ave, 6th Flr, 60611-2678. SAN 303-8106. Tel: 312-440-2653. FAX: 312-440-2774. E-mail: library@ada.org. Web Site: www.ada.org. *Dir,* Jeff Gartman; Tel: 312-440-2642, E-mail: gartmanj@ada.org; *Cat & Ref Librn,* Penny Boyle; Tel: 312-440-2650, E-mail: boylec@ada.org; *Doc Delivery Mgr,* Diane Bartkowiak; Tel: 312-440-2652, E-mail: bartkowiakd@ada.org; *Archivist,* Andrea Matlak; Tel: 312-440-7722, E-mail: matlaka@ada.org; Staff 5 (MLS 4, Non-MLS 1)
Founded 1927
Library Holdings: e-books 54; e-journals 285; Bk Vols 15,000; Per Subs 505
Special Collections: Archives of American Dental Association; History of Dentistry
Subject Interests: Dentistry
Automation Activity & Vendor Info: (Acquisitions) EOS International; (Cataloging) EOS International; (ILL) OCLC ILLiad; (OPAC) EOS International; (Serials) EOS International
Database Vendor: Blackwell, DynaMed, EBSCOhost, Elsevier, EOS International, Haworth Pres Inc, Ingenta, Nature Publishing Group, OCLC FirstSearch, OVID Technologies, PubMed, Sage, ScienceDirect, Wiley
Wireless access
Function: 24/7 Electronic res, Archival coll, Doc delivery serv, Fax serv, ILL available, Online cat, Online searches, Photocopying/Printing, Ref serv in person, Res performed for a fee, Scanner, Telephone ref, Web-catalog
Mem of Reaching Across Illinois Library System (RAILS)
Restriction: Employee & client use only, Free to mem, Non-circulating, Not open to pub, Open by appt only, Private libr, Researchers by appt only, Staff & mem only

M AMERICAN HEALTH INFORMATION MANAGEMENT ASSOCIATION*, Fore Library, 233 N Michigan Ave, Ste 2150, 60601. SAN 303-8157. Tel: 312-233-1501. FAX: 312-233-1901. Web Site: www.ahima.org. *Dir, Libr Serv,* David A Sweet; E-mail: david.sweet@ahima.org; Staff 1 (MLS 1)
Founded 1965
Library Holdings: Bk Vols 3,000; Per Subs 175
Automation Activity & Vendor Info: (Cataloging) Inmagic, Inc.
Database Vendor: LexisNexis, OCLC FirstSearch
Function: Res libr
Mem of Reaching Across Illinois Library System (RAILS)
Partic in National Network of Libraries of Medicine South Central Region
Restriction: Mem only, Non-circulating, Open to others by appt

S AMERICAN HOSPITAL ASSOCIATION, Resource Center, 155 N Wacker Dr, 4th Flr, 60606. SAN 303-9455. Tel: 312-422-2050. FAX: 312-422-4700. E-mail: rc@aha.org. Web Site: www.aha.org/aha/resource-center/index.html. *Dir,* Sara Beazley. Subject Specialists: *Health policy, Hospital admin,* Sara Beazley; Staff 6 (MLS 3, Non-MLS 3)
Founded 1929
Library Holdings: Bk Vols 64,000; Per Subs 250
Special Collections: Center for Hospital & Healthcare Administration History; Ray E Brown Management Coll
Automation Activity & Vendor Info: (Cataloging) OCLC; (ILL) OCLC; (OPAC) TLC (The Library Corporation)
Database Vendor: Dialog, EBSCOhost, LexisNexis, OCLC WorldShare Interlibrary Loan, PubMed
Wireless access
Partic in National Network of Libraries of Medicine Greater Midwest Region; OCLC Online Computer Library Center, Inc
Open Mon-Fri 8:30-4:30

S AMERICAN LIBRARY ASSOCIATION LIBRARY, 50 E Huron St, 60611-2729. SAN 303-8122. Tel: 312-280-2153. Toll Free Tel: 800-545-2433, Ext 2153. FAX: 312-280-3255. E-mail: library@ala.org. Web Site: www.ala.org/library. *Dir,* Karen Muller; E-mail: kmuller@ala.org; Staff 3.5 (MLS 1.5, Non-MLS 2)
Founded 1924
Sept 2014-Aug 2015 Income $275,000. Mats Exp $27,800, Books $2,000, Per/Ser (Incl. Access Fees) $14,800, Electronic Ref Mat (Incl. Access Fees) $11,000. Sal $150,000
Library Holdings: DVDs 25; Microforms 1,500; Bk Vols 16,000; Per Subs 200
Special Collections: Library Annual Reports
Subject Interests: Ala hist, Issues & hist of librarianship, Libr & info sci
Automation Activity & Vendor Info: (Cataloging) SydneyPlus; (Circulation) SydneyPlus; (ILL) OCLC; (OPAC) SydneyPlus; (Serials) SydneyPlus
Database Vendor: EBSCOhost, LexisNexis, OCLC WorldShare Interlibrary Loan
Wireless access
Mem of Reaching Across Illinois Library System (RAILS)
Partic in Illinois Library & Information Network; OCLC Online Computer Library Center, Inc
Open Mon-Fri 8:30-4:30
Restriction: Circulates for staff only, External users must contact libr, Prof mat only

S AMERICAN PLANNING ASSOCIATION*, Merriam Library, 205 N Michigan Ave, Ste 1200, 60601. SAN 303-9714. Tel: 312-431-9100, Ext 6353. FAX: 312-431-9985. E-mail: library@planning.org. Web Site: www.planning.org, www.planning.org/library/index.htm. *Librn,* Rana Salzmann; E-mail: rsalzmann@planning.org
Founded 1932
Library Holdings: Bk Vols 5,800; Per Subs 100
Special Collections: Ira Bach Coll
Subject Interests: Urban planning
Function: Electronic databases & coll, Online cat, Online ref, Online searches, Ref serv available, Web-catalog
Restriction: Co libr, In-house use for visitors, Non-circulating coll, Open by appt only

S APPRAISAL INSTITUTE, Y T & Louise Lee Lum Library, 200 W Madison, Ste 1500, 60606. SAN 370-999X. Tel: 312-335-4467. FAX: 312-335-4486. Web Site: www.appraisalinstitute.org. *Sr Mgr,* Eric B Goodman; E-mail: egoodman@appraisalinstitute.org; Staff 1 (MLS 1)
Founded 1992
Library Holdings: e-books 71; Bk Titles 1,200; Per Subs 25
Subject Interests: Real estate
Automation Activity & Vendor Info: (Acquisitions) Softlink America; (Cataloging) Softlink America; (Circulation) Softlink America; (OPAC) Softlink America; (Serials) Softlink America
Database Vendor: EBSCOhost, Gale Cengage Learning
Wireless access
Mem of Reaching Across Illinois Library System (RAILS)
Open Mon-Fri 8:30-4

C ARGOSY UNIVERSITY*, Chicago Library, 225 N Michigan Ave, 60601. SAN 375-9601. Tel: 312-777-7653. Interlibrary Loan Service Tel: 312-777-7651. FAX: 312-777-7749. E-mail: auchilibrary@argosy.edu. Web Site: www.auchicagolib.org. *Dir, Libr Serv,* Fay Kallista; Tel: 312-777-7650, E-mail: fkallista@argosy.edu; Staff 3 (MLS 2, Non-MLS 1)
Founded 1979. Enrl 1,200; Fac 110; Highest Degree: Doctorate

Library Holdings: Bk Titles 11,000; Per Subs 120
Subject Interests: Bus, Educ, Psychol
Automation Activity & Vendor Info: (Acquisitions) Ex Libris Group; (Cataloging) Ex Libris Group; (Circulation) Ex Libris Group; (ILL) OCLC; (OPAC) Ex Libris Group
Database Vendor: EBSCOhost, LexisNexis, OCLC FirstSearch, ProQuest
Mem of Reaching Across Illinois Library System (RAILS)
Partic in OCLC
Open Mon-Thurs 8:30am-9pm, Fri 8:30-6:30, Sat 11-6

L ARNSTEIN & LEHR LLP LIBRARY*, 120 S Riverside Plaza, Ste 1200, 60606-3910. SAN 371-7623. Tel: 312-876-7170. FAX: 312-876-0288. Web Site: www.arnstein.com. *Dir, Libr Serv,* Frank Drake; E-mail: fldrake@arnstein.com; Staff 1 (MLS 1)
Library Holdings: AV Mats 30; Bk Titles 1,700; Bk Vols 12,000; Per Subs 100
Subject Interests: Law
Function: ILL available, Mail & tel request accepted, Online ref, Orientations, Ref serv available
Publications: Titles & Locations
Mem of Reaching Across Illinois Library System (RAILS)
Partic in Illinois Library & Information Network
Open Mon-Fri 9-5
Restriction: External users must contact libr, Open to pub by appt only

S ART INSTITUTE OF CHICAGO*, Ryerson & Burnham Libraries, 111 S Michigan Ave, 60603. SAN 339-8013. Tel: 312-443-3671. Reference Tel: 312-443-0964. FAX: 312-443-0849. Web Site: www.artic.edu. *Dir,* Jack Perry Brown; *Reader Serv Librn,* Melanie E Emerson; *Spec Coll & Archives Librn,* Mary Woolever; *Syst Librn,* Curtis Osmun; *Tech Serv Librn,* Anne Champagne; *Archivist,* Bart Ryckbosch; *Conservator,* Christine Fabian; Staff 23 (MLS 12, Non-MLS 11)
Founded 1879
Library Holdings: Bk Titles 508,000; Per Subs 1,500
Special Collections: Architecture, 18th & 19th Century (Percier & Fontaine Coll), bk, drawings; Catalan Art & Architectural (George R Collins Coll); Chicago & Midwestern Architecture, Archives, photog; Chicago Art & Artists Scrapbook, newsp 1890-to-date, micro: Russian Art (Ernest Hamill Coll); Surrealism (Mary Reynolds Coll); Whistler (Walter Brewster Coll). Oral History
Automation Activity & Vendor Info: (Acquisitions) Innovative Interfaces, Inc; (Cataloging) Innovative Interfaces, Inc; (Circulation) Innovative Interfaces, Inc; (Course Reserve) Innovative Interfaces, Inc; (OPAC) Innovative Interfaces, Inc; (Serials) Innovative Interfaces, Inc
Wireless access
Publications: Annual Exhibition Record of the Art Institute of Chicago 1888-1950 (1991); Architectural Records in Chicago (1981); Burnham Index to Architectural Literature (1990); Final Official Report of the Director of Works of the World's Columbian Exposition (1990); P B Wright (1980); Plan of Chicago (1909-1979); Ryerson Index to Art Periodicals; Surrealism & Its Affinities: The Mary Reynolds Coll; The Burnham Library of Architecture (1912-1987)
Partic in OCLC Online Computer Library Center, Inc
Restriction: Mem only, Open to students, fac & staff
Friends of the Library Group

SR ASSYRIAN UNIVERSAL ALLIANCE FOUNDATION*, Ashurbanipal Library, 7055 N Clark St, 60626. SAN 375-9903. Tel: 773-274-9262. FAX: 773-274-5866. E-mail: auaf@aol.com. Web Site: www.aua.net. *Librn,* Awayah Isho
Library Holdings: Bk Titles 7,000; Per Subs 30
Subject Interests: Hist, Linguistics, Lit
Function: Res libr
Open Mon-Fri 8:30-4:30
Restriction: Circ limited

S BALZEKAS MUSEUM OF LITHUANIAN CULTURE*, Reference & Research Library, 6500 S Pulaski Rd, 60629. SAN 303-822X. Tel: 773-582-6500. FAX: 773-582-5133. E-mail: info@balzekasmuseum.org. *Librn,* Irena Pumputiene
Founded 1966
Library Holdings: Bk Titles 65,000; Per Subs 1,700
Special Collections: Art Archives; History (Rare Books Coll); Lithuanian Genealogy, Personality & Photography Archives; Manuscripts, Pamphlets, Periodicals, Records
Subject Interests: Heraldry
Publications: Museum Review
Friends of the Library Group

L BANNER & WITCOFF, LTD LIBRARY*, Ten S Wacker Dr, Ste 3000, 60606. SAN 376-0944. Tel: 312-463-5455. FAX: 312-463-5001. Web Site: www.bannerwitcoff.com. *Libr Mgr,* Jan Whitis; E-mail: jwhitis@bannerwitcoff.com
Library Holdings: Bk Titles 6,290; Per Subs 10
Subject Interests: Law
Automation Activity & Vendor Info: (Cataloging) Inmagic, Inc.
Wireless access
Restriction: Staff use only

L BARACK, FERRAZZANO, KIRSHBAUM & NAGELBERG LIBRARY, 200 W Madison St, Ste 3900, 60606. SAN 376-1339. Tel: 312-984-3100. FAX: 312-984-3150. Web Site: www.bfkn.com. *Librn,* Carol Brosk
Library Holdings: Bk Titles 3,200; Per Subs 50
Automation Activity & Vendor Info: (Cataloging) EOS International; (OPAC) EOS International
Wireless access
Restriction: Staff use only

M THE NATALIE A & LOUIS D BOSHES LIBRARY FOR THE NEUROSCIENCES*, 912 S Wood St, 60612-7325. (Mail add: 912 S Wood St, MC 799, 60612). Tel: 312-996-4842. FAX: 312-996-9018. *Managing Librn,* James Stone; Staff 1 (MLS 1)
Founded 1998
Library Holdings: AV Mats 160; Bk Titles 3,000; Per Subs 120
Subject Interests: Neurology, Neurosurgery
Function: ILL available
Restriction: Non-circulating, Open to fac, students & qualified researchers, Open to others by appt

L BRINKS, HOFER, GILSON & LIONE*, Law Library, NBC Tower, 455 N Cityfront Plaza Dr, Ste 3600, 60611-5599. SAN 371-8506. Tel: 312-321-4200. FAX: 312-321-4299. Web Site: www.brinkshofer.com. *Law Librn,* Julia Jackson; E-mail: jjackson@brinkshofer.com; Staff 2 (MLS 1, Non-MLS 1)
Founded 1986
Library Holdings: Bk Titles 1,200; Per Subs 100
Special Collections: Patent Law
Automation Activity & Vendor Info: (Cataloging) Inmagic, Inc.
Wireless access
Mem of Reaching Across Illinois Library System (RAILS)
Restriction: Open to pub by appt only

M JESSE BROWN VA MEDICAL CENTER*, Library Services, 820 S Damen Ave, 60612. SAN 375-961X. Tel: 312-569-6116. Interlibrary Loan Service Tel: 312-569-6447. Reference Tel: 312-569-6445. Administration Tel: 312-569-6448. FAX: 312-569-6110. *Chief Librn,* Lydia Tkaczuk; E-mail: lydia.tkaczuk@va.gov; *Librn,* Position Currently Open; Staff 2 (MLS 2)
Library Holdings: AV Mats 500; Bk Titles 5,600; Per Subs 130
Automation Activity & Vendor Info: (Circulation) EOS International; (OPAC) EOS International; (Serials) EOS International
Partic in Docline; Metropolitan Consortium of Chicago

S BURRELL INFORMATION CENTER*, 233 N Michigan Ave, Ste 2900, 60601. SAN 375-992X. Tel: 312-297-9723. FAX: 312-297-9841. Web Site: www.burrell.com. *Dir,* Leslie Cole
Library Holdings: Bk Titles 1,000; Per Subs 200
Restriction: Staff use only

L BUTLER, RUBIN, SALTARELLI & BOYD LLP*, Law Library, Three First National Plaza, 70 W Madison St, Ste 1800, 60602. Tel: 312-444-9660. FAX: 312-444-9287. Web Site: www.butlerrubin.com. *Librn,* Robert Fabian
Library Holdings: Bk Titles 250; Bk Vols 375; Per Subs 25
Open Mon-Fri 9-5

GL WILLIAM J CAMPBELL LIBRARY OF THE US COURTS*, 219 S Dearborn St, Rm 1637, 60604-1769. SAN 304-0410. Tel: 312-435-5660. FAX: 312-408-5031. Web Site: www.lb7.uscourts.gov. *Circuit Librn,* Gretchen VanDam; E-mail: gretchen_van_dam@ca7.uscourts.gov; *Dep Circuit Librn,* Barry Herbert; *Acq Librn,* Jerry Lewis; *Cat Librn,* Kathleen Powers Goodridge; *Ref Librn,* John Klaus; *Ser Librn,* Sonja Nordstrom
Library Holdings: Bk Vols 30,000
Subject Interests: Govt publ
Partic in OCLC Online Computer Library Center, Inc
Open Mon-Fri 8:30-5

SR CATHOLIC THEOLOGICAL UNION*, Paul Bechtold Library, 5416 S Cornell Ave, 60615-5698. SAN 303-8335. Tel: 773-371-5464. FAX: 773-753-5340. Web Site: www.ctu.lib.il.us. *Libr Dir,* Melody Layton McMahon; Staff 6 (MLS 3, Non-MLS 3)
Founded 1968. Enrl 430; Fac 32; Highest Degree: Doctorate
Jul 2011-Jun 2012 Income $515,000. Mats Exp $120,200, Books $53,000, Per/Ser (Incl. Access Fees) $39,000, Manu Arch $200, Electronic Ref Mat (Incl. Access Fees) $28,000. Sal $348,000
Library Holdings: Bk Vols 127,000; Per Subs 450

Special Collections: Canon Law; Christian Art; Missiology; Religious Communities
Subject Interests: Franciscans, Roman Catholic theol
Automation Activity & Vendor Info: (Acquisitions) Ex Libris Group; (Cataloging) Ex Libris Group; (Circulation) Ex Libris Group; (Course Reserve) Ex Libris Group; (ILL) Ex Libris Group; (Media Booking) Ex Libris Group; (OPAC) Ex Libris Group; (Serials) Ex Libris Group
Wireless access
Publications: New Theology Review (Online only)
Mem of Reaching Across Illinois Library System (RAILS)
Partic in Association of Chicago Theological Schools; Consortium of Academic & Research Libraries in Illinois
Open Mon-Thurs 8am-10pm, Fri 8:30-4:30, Sat 11-4, Sun 4-9
Restriction: Circ privileges for students & alumni only

L CHAPMAN & CUTLER*, Law Library, 111 W Monroe, 60603-4096. SAN 303-8416. Tel: 312-845-3749. Interlibrary Loan Service Tel: 312-701-2372. FAX: 312-701-6620. *Librn,* Denis S Kowalewski; E-mail: kowalews@chapman.com; *Asst Librn,* David P Fanta; Tel: 312-845-3450, E-mail: fanta@chapman.com; *Asst Librn,* Robert Luberda; Tel: 312-845-3437, E-mail: luberda@chapman.com; *Asst Librn,* Jamie Stewart; Tel: 312-845-3435, E-mail: stewart@chapman.com; Staff 5 (MLS 4, Non-MLS 1)
Library Holdings: Bk Titles 3,000; Per Subs 50
Automation Activity & Vendor Info: (Acquisitions) ByWater Solutions; (Cataloging) ByWater Solutions; (Circulation) ByWater Solutions; (OPAC) ByWater Solutions; (Serials) ByWater Solutions
Partic in Illinois Library & Information Network
Restriction: Private libr

S CHICAGO ACADEMY OF SCIENCES*, Memorial Library, 2430 N Cannon Dr, 60614. SAN 303-8424. Tel: 773-755-5100. FAX: 773-755-5199. Web Site: www.naturemuseum.org. *Curator,* Steve Sullivan; Tel: 773-525-0166, E-mail: ssullivan@naturemuseum.org
Founded 1857
Library Holdings: Bk Vols 20,000
Subject Interests: Environ studies, Geol, Natural hist, Ornithology
Publications: Bulletin; Natural History Miscellania
Restriction: Not open to pub

S CHICAGO HISTORY MUSEUM*, Research Center, 1601 N Clark St, 60614-6099. SAN 303-8483. Tel: 312-642-4600. FAX: 312-266-2076. E-mail: research@chicagohistory.org. Web Site: libguides.chicagohistory.org/research. *Chief Librn, Dir of Res & Access,* Ellen Keith; Tel: 312-799-2030, E-mail: keith@chicagohistory.org; Staff 6 (MLS 4, Non-MLS 2)
Founded 1856
Library Holdings: Bk Vols 150,000; Per Subs 175
Subject Interests: Civil War, Ill, Metrop Chicago
Automation Activity & Vendor Info: (OPAC) Horizon
Database Vendor: OCLC FirstSearch, ProQuest, SirsiDynix
Wireless access
Function: Bus archives, e-mail serv, For res purposes, Online cat, Photocopying/Printing, Pub access computers, Ref serv available, Ref serv in person, Web catalog
Mem of Reaching Across Illinois Library System (RAILS)
Partic in Illinois Library & Information Network; OCLC Online Computer Library Center, Inc
Open Tues-Fri 1-4:30, Sat 10-4:30
Restriction: Fee for pub use, Internal circ only, Non-circulating to the pub, Not a lending libr, Off-site coll in storage - retrieval as requested, Open to pub for ref only, Photo ID required for access

S CHICAGO MERCANTILE EXCHANGE LIBRARY*, Information Resource Center, 20 S Wacker Dr, 60606. SAN 321-2726. Tel: 312-604-6552. Web Site: www.cmegroup.com. *Mgr,* Curt Zuckert; Staff 3 (MLS 1, Non-MLS 2)
Founded 1977
Library Holdings: Bk Titles 2,411; Per Subs 30
Subject Interests: Futures trading, Options trading
Mem of Reaching Across Illinois Library System (RAILS)
Partic in Dialog Corp; Illinois Library & Information Network
Open Mon-Fri 7-4
Restriction: Internal circ only

P CHICAGO PUBLIC LIBRARY*, 400 S State St, 60605. SAN 339-8102. Tel: 312-747-4300. Circulation Tel: 312-747-4396. Interlibrary Loan Service Tel: 312-747-4344. FAX: 312-747-4968. Interlibrary Loan Service FAX: 312-747-4918. Information Services FAX: 312-747-4329. Web Site: www.chicagopubliclibrary.org. *Commissioner,* Brian Bannon; Tel: 312-747-4090, E-mail: brian.bannon@chicagopubliclibrary.org; *Asst Commissioner, Admin & Finance,* Katie Ludwig; Tel: 312-747-4030, Fax: 312-747-4522, E-mail: kludwig@chicagopubliclibrary.org; *Asst Commissioner, Cent Libr Serv,* Greta M Bever; *Asst Commissioner, Coll,* Andrew Medlar; *Asst Commissioner, Neighborhood Serv,* Andrea Telli; Tel: 312-747-4212, Fax: 312-747-4076, E-mail: atelli@chicagopubliclibrary.org; *First Dep Commissioner,* Andrea Saenz; Tel: 312-747-4018, Fax: 312-745-1590, E-mail: asaenz@chicagopubliclibrary.org; *Dir, Adult Serv,* Craig Davis; Tel: 312-747-4252, E-mail: cdavis@chicagopubliclibrary.org; *Dir, Ch Serv, YA Serv,* Elizabeth McChesney; Tel: 312-747-4784, Fax: 312-747-4077, E-mail: emcchesn@chicagopubliclibrary.org; *Mgr, Acq Serv,* Diane Marshbank-Murphy; Tel: 312-747-4659, Fax: 312-747-4078, E-mail: marshban@chicagopubliclibrary.org
Founded 1872. Pop 2,695,598; Circ 9,556,918
Jan 2011-Dec 2011 Income (Main Library and Branch(s)) $110,629,437, State $6,702,370, Federal $1,044,145, Locally Generated Income $1,597,067. Mats Exp $7,000,000. Sal $52,611,171
Library Holdings: AV Mats 365,282; Bk Vols 5,790,289
Special Collections: US Document Depository
Automation Activity & Vendor Info: (Acquisitions) TLC (The Library Corporation); (Cataloging) TLC (The Library Corporation); (Circulation) TLC (The Library Corporation); (OPAC) TLC (The Library Corporation); (Serials) TLC (The Library Corporation)
Database Vendor: Booklist Online, Bowker, EBSCOhost, Facts on File, Gale Cengage Learning, infoUSA, JSTOR, Newsbank, OCLC FirstSearch, Oxford Online, ProQuest, Standard & Poor's, World Book Online
Wireless access
Partic in Illinois Library & Information Network; OCLC Online Computer Library Center, Inc
Special Services for the Deaf - Bks on deafness & sign lang; High interest/low vocabulary bks; Spec interest per; TDD equip; TTY equip; Videos & decoder
Special Services for the Blind - Assistive/Adapted tech devices, equip & products; Bks on cassette; Braille bks; Large print bks
Friends of the Library Group
Branches: 87
ALBANY PARK, 3401 W Foster Ave, 60625, SAN 339-8374. Tel: 773-539-5450. *Br Mgr,* John Glynn
Open Mon & Wed 10-6, Tues & Thurs 12-8, Fri & Sat 9-5
ALTGELD, 13281 S Corliss Ave, 60827. Tel: 312-747-3270. *Br Mgr,* Nicholas Saunders
Open Mon & Wed 12-8, Tues & Thurs 10-6, Fri & Sat 9-5
ARCHER HEIGHTS, 5055 S Archer Ave, 60632, SAN 339-8439. Tel: 312-747-9241. *Br Mgr,* Elzbieta Ptasik
Open Mon & Wed 12-8, Tues & Thurs 10-6, Fri & Sat 9-5
AUSTIN, 5615 W Race Ave, 60644, SAN 339-8498. Tel: 312-746-5038. *Br Mgr,* JoAnne Willis
Open Mon & Wed 12-8, Tues & Thurs 10-6, Fri & Sat 9-5
AUSTIN-IRVING, 6100 W Irving Park Rd, 60634, SAN 339-8528. Tel: 312-744-6222. *Br Mgr,* Anthony E Powers
Open Mon & Wed 12-8, Tues & Thurs 10-6, Fri & Sat 9-5
AVALON, 8148 S Stony Island, 60617, SAN 339-8552. Tel: 312-747-5234. *Br Mgr,* Mary Williams
Open Mon & Wed 12-8, Tues & Thurs 10-6, Fri & Sat 9-5
Friends of the Library Group
BACK OF THE YARDS, 2111 W 47th St, 60609. Tel: 312-747-9595. *Br Mgr,* Maggie Clemons
Open Mon & Wed 10-6, Tues & Thurs 12-8, Fri & Sat 9-5
BEVERLY, 1962 W 95th St, 60643, SAN 339-8617. Tel: 312-747-9673. *Br Mgr,* Joyce Colander
Open Mon & Wed 12-8, Tues & Thurs 10-6, Fri & Sat 9-5
BEZAZIAN, 1226 W Ainslie St, 60640, SAN 339-8641. Tel: 312-744-0019. *Br Mgr,* Mark Kaplan
Open Mon & Wed 12-8, Tues & Thurs 10-6, Fri & Sat 9-5
BLACKSTONE, 4904 S Lake Park Ave, 60615, SAN 339-8676. Tel: 312-747-0511. TDD: 312-747-3015. *Br Mgr,* Anne Keough
Special Services for the Deaf - TDD equip
Open Mon & Wed 12-8, Tues & Thurs 10-6, Fri & Sat 9-5
BRAINERD, 1350 W 89th St, 60620, SAN 339-8706. Tel: 312-747-6291. *Br Mgr,* Mary L Jones
Open Mon & Wed 10-6, Tues & Thurs 12-8, Fri & Sat 9-5
Friends of the Library Group
BRIGHTON PARK, 4314 S Archer Ave, 60632, SAN 339-8765. Tel: 312-747-0666. *Br Mgr,* Michael Conlon
Open Mon & Wed 10-6, Tues & Thurs 12-8, Fri & Sat 9-5
BUCKTOWN-WICKER PARK, 1701 N Milwaukee Ave, 60647. Tel: 312-744-6022. *Br Mgr,* Lisa Roe
Open Mon & Wed 12-8, Tues & Thurs 10-6, Fri & Sat 9-5
BUDLONG WOODS, 5630 N Lincoln Ave, 60659. Tel: 312-742-9590. *Br Mgr,* Thomas Stark
Open Mon & Wed 12-8, Tues & Thurs 10-6, Fri & Sat 9-5
BUSINESS-SCIENCE-TECHNOLOGY DIVISION, 400 S State St, 60605. Tel: 312-747-4400 (Bus), 312-747-4450 (Sci & Tech). *Div Chief,* Mark Andersen; Tel: 312-747-4470, E-mail: andersen@chicagopublibrary.org
Special Collections: Auto Repair Manuals & Price Guides; British Patents (1617- 1984); Complete US Patents (1790-date); Electrical Schematics; Industrial Standards & Specifications; Investment Services;

Jane's Defense Annuals; Product Directories; State & Foreign Industrial Directories
Subject Interests: Advertising, Bus & mgt, Careers, Computer sci, Culinary arts, Econ, Math, Med, Mil sci, Mkt, Real estate, Small bus
CANARYVILLE, 642 W 43rd St, 60609, SAN 374-6542. Tel: 312-747-0644. *Br Mgr,* Position Currently Open
Open Mon & Wed 12-8, Tues & Thurs 10-6, Fri & Sat 9-5
CHICAGO BEE, 3647 S State St, 60609, SAN 376-8902. Tel: 312-747-6872. *Br Mgr,* Marvin Bowen
Open Mon & Wed 12-8, Tues & Thurs 10-6, Fri & Sat 9-5
CHICAGO LAWN, 6120 S Kedzie Ave, 60629, SAN 339-882X. Tel: 312-747-0639. *Br Mgr,* Marvin Blackwell
Open Mon & Wed 10-6, Tues & Thurs 12-8, Fri & Sat 9-5
CHINATOWN, 2353 S Wentworth Ave, 60616, SAN 339-8854. Tel: 312-747-8013. *Br Mgr,* Si Chen
Open Mon & Wed 12-8, Tues & Thurs 10-6, Fri & Sat 9-5
CLEARING, 6423 W 63rd Pl, 60638, SAN 339-8889. Tel: 312-747-5657. *Br Mgr,* Robert Bitunjac
Open Mon & Wed 12-8, Tues & Thurs 10-6, Fri & Sat 9-5
BESSIE COLEMAN BRANCH, 731 E 63rd St, 60637, SAN 340-0689. Tel: 312-747-7760. *Br Mgr,* Veyshon Edmond
Open Mon & Wed 12-8, Tues & Thurs 10-6, Fri & Sat 9-5
RICHARD J DALEY LIBRARY, 3400 S Halsted St, 60608, SAN 339-8730. Tel: 312-747-8990. *Br Mgr,* Jeremy Kitchen
Open Mon & Wed 10-6, Tues & Thurs 12-8, Fri & Sat 9-5
RICHARD M DALEY, 733 N Kedzie Ave, 60612. Tel: 312-743-0555. *Br Mgr,* Jacob Cleary
Open Mon & Wed 10-6, Tues & Thurs Noon-8, Fri & Sat 9-5
DOUGLASS, 3353 W 13th St, 60623, SAN 339-8943. Tel: 312-747-3725. *Br Mgr,* Portia Latalladi
Open Mon & Wed 10-6, Tues & Thurs 12-8, Fri & Sat 9-5
DUNNING, 7455 W Cornelia Ave, 60634. Tel: 312-743-0480. *Br Mgr,* Melissa Kaszyski
Open Mon & Wed Noon-8, Tues & Thurs 10-6, Fri & Sat 9-5
EDGEBROOK, 5331 W Devon Ave, 60646, SAN 339-9036. Tel: 312-744-8313. *Br Mgr,* Jennifer Reynolds
Open Mon & Wed 12-8, Tues & Thurs 10-6, Fri & Sat 9-5
EDGEWATER, 6000 N Broadway, 60660. Tel: 312-742-1945. *Br Mgr,* Joanna Hazelden
Open Mon & Wed 10-6, Tues & Thurs 12-8, Fri & Sat 9-5
GAGE PARK, 2807 W 55th St, 60632, SAN 339-915X. Tel: 312-747-0032. *Br Mgr,* Kyleen Kenney
Open Mon & Wed 10-6, Tues & Thurs 12-8, Fri & Sat 9-5
GALEWOOD-MONT CLARE, 6871 W Belden Ave, 60707, SAN 339-9184. Tel: 312-746-0165. *Br Mgr,* Melissa Kaszyski
Open Mon & Wed 12-8, Tues & Thurs 10-6, Fri 9-5
GARFIELD RIDGE, 6348 S Archer Ave, 60638, SAN 339-9214. Tel: 312-747-6094. *Br Mgr,* Guillermina Duarte
Open Mon & Wed 10-6, Tues & Thurs 12-8, Fri & Sat 9-5
GENERAL INFORMATION SERVICES DIVISION, 400 S State St, 60605. Interlibrary Loan Service FAX: 312-747-4918. Information Services FAX: 312-747-4329. *Div Chief,* Carolyn Mulac; Tel: 312-747-4382, E-mail: cmulac@chicagopubliclibrary.org
Special Collections: Chicago Biography Index File; Chicago Curio Information; Early American Newspapers; National & International Telephone Directories & Newspapers; National, US, Foreign & Trade Bibliographies
Publications: CPL Serials List
GOVERNMENT PUBLICATIONS, 400 S State St, 60605. Tel: 312-747-4500. FAX: 312-747-4516. *Mgr,* Shah Tiwana; Tel: 312-747-4524, E-mail: stiwana@chicagopubliclibrary.org
Special Collections: American Statistics Index Microfiche Library (1974 retrospective-current); Chicago Municipal Reference Coll; CIS-Microfiche Library (1970-present); Congressional Committee Hearings (prior to 1953), microfiche; Congressional Committee Prints (prior to 1970), microfiche; Declassified Documents Reference System; Serial Set (1st-91st Congresses), microfiche. State Document Depository; US Document Depository
GREATER GRAND CROSSING, 1000 E 73rd St, 60619. Tel: 312-745-1608. *Br Mgr,* Kimberly Hagen
Open Mon & Wed 12-8, Tues & Thurs 10-6, Fri & Sat 9-5
HALL, 4801 S Michigan Ave, 60615, SAN 339-9249. Tel: 312-747-2541. *Br Mgr,* Donna Morris
Open Mon & Wed 10-6, Tues & Thurs 12-8, Fri & Sat 9-5
Friends of the Library Group
HEGEWISCH, 3048 E 130th St, 60633, SAN 339-9362. Tel: 312-747-0046. TDD: 773-646-8644. *Br Mgr,* Susan Puterko
Special Services for the Deaf - TDD equip
Open Mon & Wed 10-6, Tues & Thurs 12-8, Fri & Sat 9-5
THOMAS HUGHES CHILDREN'S LIBRARY, 400 S State St, 60605. Tel: 312-747-4200. FAX: 312-747-4223. *Unit Mgr,* Maria X Peterson; Tel: 312-747-4614, E-mail: mxpeters@chicagopubliclibrary.org
Special Collections: Dissertations on Children's Literature, microfiche; Mother Goose Coll; Opie Coll, microfiche; Retrospective Children's Literature (mostly 1900-1950); Walt Disney Coll
Subject Interests: Children's lit
HUMANITIES, 400 S State St, 60605. Tel: 312-747-4811. *Div Chief,* Michael Peters; E-mail: mpeters@chicagopubliclibrary.org
Special Collections: American Federation of Musicians (Chicago Chapter) Files; Ann Barzel Dance Film Archive; Arnold Jacobsen Recorded Sound Coll; Balaban & Katz Coll; Barrett Deems Coll; Charles Sengstock Coll; Chicago Artists' Archives; Chicago Blues Archive; Chicago Dance Coll; Chicago Public Library Programs Coll; Chicago Reader Motion Picture Stills Coll; Chicago Reader Touring Musicians Publicity Photos; Chicago Stagebills (1937-1978); Choral Sheet Music Coll; Clarence Hintze Jazz Drummer's Coll; Come For To Sing Archives; Crafts; Dick V Buckley's Archives of Jazz; Folk Dance Index; House Party International Coll; Illinois Entertainer Files; Jazz/Blues/Gospel Hall of Fame; Jewish Music Archives; Jubilee Showcase Coll; Jussi Bjorling Archives; Mail Order Catalogs (Sears, Wards, Aldens); Martin & Morris Coll; Mugsy Spanier Archives; Picture Coll; Stanley Paul Coll; University of Chicago Folk Festival Coll
Subject Interests: Archit, Communications, Criticism, Drama, Fiction, Fine arts, Journalism, Linguistics, Lit, Mass media, Music, Performing arts, Poetry
HUMBOLDT PARK, 1605 N Troy St, 60647, SAN 339-9427. Tel: 312-744-2244. *Br Mgr,* Sarah Tansley
Open Mon & Wed 12-8, Tues & Thurs 10-6, Fri & Sat 9-5
Friends of the Library Group
INDEPENDENCE, 3548 W Irving Park Rd, 60618, SAN 339-9540. Tel: 312-744-0900. *Br Mgr,* Kristy Kisler
Open Mon & Wed 10-6, Tues & Thurs 12-8, Fri & Sat 9-5
JEFFERSON PARK, 5363 W Lawrence Ave, 60630, SAN 339-9575. Tel: 312-744-1998. *Br Mgr,* Eileen Dohnalek
Open Mon & Wed 10-6, Tues & Thurs 12-8, Fri & Sat 9-5
JEFFERY MANOR, 2401 E 100th St, 60617, SAN 339-9605. Tel: 312-747-6479. *Br Mgr,* Lisa Burwell
Open Mon & Wed 10-6, Tues & Thurs 12-8, Fri & Sat 9-5
KELLY, 6151 S Normal Blvd, 60621, SAN 339-963X. Tel: 312-747-8418. *Br Mgr,* Gregory McClain
Open Mon & Wed 10-6, Tues & Thurs 12-8, Fri & Sat 9-5
MARTIN LUTHER KING JR BRANCH, 3436 S King Dr, 60616, SAN 339-9664. Tel: 312-747-7543. *Br Mgr,* Rosetta Coleman
Open Mon & Wed 10-6, Tues & Thurs 12-8, Fri & Sat 9-5
LEGLER, 115 S Pulaski Rd, 60624, SAN 339-9729. Tel: 312-746-7730. *Br Mgr,* Amber Proksa
Open Mon & Wed 12-8, Tues & Thurs 10-6, Fri & Sat 9-5
LINCOLN BELMONT, 1659 W Melrose St, 60657, SAN 339-9303. Tel: 312-744-0166. *Br Mgr,* Richard Dohnalek
Open Mon & Wed 10-6, Tues & Thurs 12-8, Fri & Sat 9-5
LINCOLN PARK, 1150 W Fullerton Ave, 60614, SAN 339-9753. Tel: 312-744-1926. *Br Mgr,* Mary Jo O'Toole
Open Mon & Wed 10-6, Tues & Thurs 12-8, Fri & Sat 9-5
LITTLE VILLAGE, 2311 S Kedzie Ave, 60623. Tel: 312-745-1862. *Br Mgr,* Teresa Madrigal
Open Mon & Wed 10-6, Tues & Thurs Noon-8, Fri & Sat 9-5
LOGAN SQUARE, 3030 W Fullerton Ave, 60647, SAN 339-9788. Tel: 312-744-5295. *Br Mgr,* Shirley Yee
Open Mon & Wed 10-6, Tues & Thurs 12-8, Fri & Sat 9-5
RUDY LOZANO LIBRARY, 1805 S Loomis St, 60608, SAN 340-014X. Tel: 312-746-4329. *Br Mgr,* Hector R Hernandez
Open Mon & Wed 10-6, Tues & Thurs 12-8, Fri & Sat 9-5
MABEL MANNING BRANCH, Six S Hoyne Ave, 60612, SAN 374-6550. Tel: 312-746-6800. *Br Mgr,* Rory Brown
Open Mon & Wed 12-8, Tues & Thurs 10-6, Fri & Sat 9-5
THURGOOD MARSHALL BRANCH, 7506 S Racine Ave, 60620, SAN 374-6569. Tel: 312-747-5927. *Br Mgr,* Jan Brooks
Open Mon & Wed 12-8, Tues & Thurs 10-6, Fri & Sat 9-5
MAYFAIR, 4400 W Lawrence Ave, 60630, SAN 339-9877. Tel: 312-744-1254. *Br Mgr,* Position Currently Open
Open Mon & Wed 12-8, Tues & Thurs 10-6, Fri & Sat 9-5
MCKINLEY PARK, 1915 W 35th St, 60609, SAN 339-9818. Tel: 312-747-6082. *Br Mgr,* Sheryll Adams
Open Mon & Wed 12-8, Tues & Thurs 10-6, Fri & Sat 9-5
JOHN MERLO BRANCH, 644 W Belmont Ave, 60657, SAN 339-9699. Tel: 312-744-1139. *Br Mgr,* Cynthia A Rodgers
Open Mon & Wed 12-8, Tues & Thurs 10-6, Fri & Sat 9-5
MOUNT GREENWOOD, 11010 S Kedzie Ave, 60655, SAN 339-9931. Tel: 312-747-2805. *Br Mgr,* Jessica Jeffers
Open Mon & Wed 10-6, Tues & Thurs 12-8, Fri & Sat 9-5
NEAR NORTH, 310 W Division, 60610, SAN 339-879X. Tel: 312-744-0991. *Br Mgr,* Scott Drawe
Open Mon & Wed 12-8, Tues & Thurs 10-6, Fri & Sat 9-5

NORTH AUSTIN, 5724 W North Ave, 60639, SAN 339-9990. Tel: 312-746-4233. *Br Mgr,* Shenita Mack
Open Mon & Wed 12-8, Tues & Thurs 10-6, Fri & Sat 9-5
NORTH PULASKI, 4300 W North Ave, 60639, SAN 340-0085. Tel: 312-744-9573. *Br Mgr,* Alex Fraser
Open Mon & Wed 10-6, Tues & Thurs 12-8, Fri & Sat 9-5
NORTHTOWN, 6435 N California Ave, 60645, SAN 340-0050. Tel: 312-744-2292. *Br Mgr,* Catharine Wilson
Open Mon & Wed 10-6, Tues & Thurs 12-8, Fri & Sat 9-5
ORIOLE PARK, 7454 W Balmoral Ave, 60656, SAN 340-0115. Tel: 312-744-1965. *Br Mgr,* Peter Iwanec
Open Mon & Wed 12-8, Tues & Thurs 10-6, Fri & Sat 9-5
Friends of the Library Group
POPULAR LIBRARY, 400 S State St, 60605. Tel: 312-747-4100. *Unit Mgr,* Katherine Linehan
Special Collections: Current Fiction & Non-Fiction, bks, music CDs; Educational & Entertainment Coll, audio bks, DVDs
PORTAGE-CRAGIN, 5108 W Belmont Ave, 60641, SAN 340-0174. Tel: 312-744-0152. *Br Mgr,* Susan Jorgensen
Open Mon & Wed 12-8, Tues & Thurs 10-6, Fri & Sat 9-5
PULLMAN, 11001 S Indiana Ave, 60628, SAN 340-0204. Tel: 312-747-2033. *Br Mgr,* Lolita Griffin
Open Mon & Wed 10-6, Tues & Thurs 12-8, Fri & Sat 9-5
RODEN, 6083 N Northwest Hwy, 60631, SAN 340-0263. Tel: 312-744-1478. *Br Mgr,* Bruce Fox
Open Mon & Wed 10-6, Tues & Thurs 12-8, Fri & Sat 9-5
Friends of the Library Group
ROGERS PARK, 6907 N Clark St, 60626, SAN 340-0298. Tel: 312-744-0156. *Br Mgr,* Shun-Ken Hui
Open Mon & Wed 12-8, Tues & Thurs 10-6, Fri & Sat 9-5
ROOSEVELT, 1101 W Taylor St, 60607, SAN 340-0328. Tel: 312-746-5656. *Br Mgr,* Layne Arens
Open Mon & Wed 12-8, Tues & Thurs 10-6, Fri & Sat 9-5
SCOTTSDALE, 4101 W 79th St, 60652, SAN 340-0352. Tel: 312-747-0193. *Br Mgr,* Bogdan Ptasik
Open Mon & Wed 10-6, Tues & Thurs 12-8, Fri & Sat 9-5
SHERMAN PARK, 5440 S Racine Ave, 60609, SAN 340-0387. Tel: 312-747-0477. *Br Mgr,* Lala Rogers
Open Mon & Wed 12-8, Tues & Thurs 10-6, Fri & Sat 9-5
SOCIAL SCIENCE & HISTORY DIVISION, 400 S State St, 60605. Tel: 312-747-4600. *Div Chief,* Margaret Kier; Tel: 312-747-4608, E-mail: mkier@chicagopubliclibrary.org
Special Collections: Abraham Lincoln Papers, 1809-1865 (Robert Todd Lincoln Coll), microfilm; Chicago Coll; Confederate Imprints, microfilm, Draper Manuscripts of American History, microfilm; Educational Resources Information Center, microfiche; Illinois County & Regional Histories & Atlases; Library & Information Science (Professional Library); Library of American Civilization, microfiche; Migne's Patrologia Cursus Completus, microfiche; Public & Private Papers of President John Adams, President John Quincy Adams & Charles Francis Adams, Papers of their Wives & Children, microfilm; Teacher Resource Center
Subject Interests: Anthrop, Educ, Hist, Law, Libr & info sci, Philos, Polit sci, Psychol, Relig, Sociol, Sports, Travel
SOUTH CHICAGO, 9055 S Houston Ave, 60617, SAN 340-0441. Tel: 312-747-8065. *Br Mgr,* Position Currently Open
Open Mon & Wed 12-8, Tues & Thurs 10-6, Fri & Sat 9-5
SOUTH SHORE, 2505 E 73rd St, 60649, SAN 340-0476. Tel: 312-747-5281. *Br Mgr,* Sandra Mohammad
Open Mon & Wed 10-6, Tues & Thurs 12-8, Fri & Sat 9-5
SPECIAL COLLECTIONS & PRESERVATION DIVISION, 400 S State St, 60605. Tel: 312-747-4875. E-mail: hwlcarch@chipublib.org. *Head, Spec Coll,* Glenn Humphreys; Tel: 312-747-1941, E-mail: ghumphre@chicagopubliclibrary.org; *Exhibits Curator, Spec Coll,* Elizabeth M Holland; Tel: 312-747-4883, E-mail: eholland@chicagopubliclibrary.org
Special Collections: Chicago History Coll; Chicago Public Library Achives; Chicago Public Library Art Coll; Chicago Theater Coll; Grand Army of the Republic & Civil War Coll; Harold Washinton Achives & Coll; Millennium Park Archives; World's Columbian Exposition Coll
CONRAD SULZER REGIONAL, 4455 N Lincoln Ave, 60625, SAN 339-9397. Tel: 312-744-7616. *Dir,* Position Currently Open
Special Collections: Northside Neighborhood History Coll, 1880s-present, artifacts, city directories, maps, memorabilia, newsclippings, sch year bks, transcribed interviews
Special Services for the Deaf - TDD equip
Open Mon-Thurs 9-9, Fri & Sat 9-5, Sun 1-5
TOMAN, 2708 S Pulaski Rd, 60623, SAN 340-059X. Tel: 312-745-1660. *Br Mgr,* Yvette Leigh
Open Mon & Wed 12-8, Tues & Thurs 10-6, Fri & Sat 9-5
UPTOWN, 929 W Buena Ave, 60613, SAN 374-6577. Tel: 312-744-8400. *Br Mgr,* Mary Clark
Open Mon & Wed 10-6, Tues & Thurs 12-8, Fri & Sat 9-5
VODAK-EAST SIDE, 3710 E 106th St, 60617, SAN 339-8978. Tel: 312-747-5500. *Br Mgr,* David Guilliams
Open Mon & Wed 12-8, Tues & Thurs 10-6, Fri & Sat 9-5
WALKER, 11071 S Hoyne Ave, 60643, SAN 340-0654. Tel: 312-747-1920. *Br Mgr,* Cristina Matera
Open Mon & Wed 10-6, Tues & Thurs 12-8, Fri & Sat 9-5
HAROLD WASHINGTON LIBRARY CENTER, 400 S State St, 60605. Tel: 312-747-4300. FAX: 312-747-4077. *Asst Commissioner, Cent Libr Serv,* Greta M Bever; Tel: 312-747-4070, E-mail: gbever@chicagopubliclibrary.org
Special Collections: US Document Depository
Partic in OCLC Online Computer Library Center, Inc
Special Services for the Deaf - Bks on deafness & sign lang; High interest/low vocabulary bks; Spec interest per; Videos & decoder
Open Mon-Thurs 9-9, Fri 9-5, Sun 1-5
WEST BELMONT, 3104 N Narragansett Ave, 60634, SAN 340-0743. Tel: 312-746-5142. *Br Mgr,* Robert Kostencki
Open Mon & Wed 10-6, Tues & Thurs 12-8, Fri & Sat 9-5
WEST CHICAGO AVENUE, 4856 W Chicago Ave, 60651. Tel: 312-743-0260. *Br Mgr,* Shirley Wallace
Open Mon & Wed 10-6, Tues & Thurs 12-8, Fri & Sat 9-5
WEST ENGLEWOOD, 1745 W 63rd St, 60636. Tel: 312-747-3481. *Br Mgr,* Keshia Gardner
Open Mon & Wed 12-8, Tues & Thurs 10-6, Fri & Sat 9-5
WEST LAWN, 4020 W 63rd St, 60629, SAN 340-0778. Tel: 312-747-7381. *Br Mgr,* Elizabeth Garcia
Open Mon & Wed 12-8, Tues & Thurs 10-6, Fri & Sat 9-5
WEST PULLMAN, 830 W 119th St, 60628. Tel: 312-747-1425. *Br Mgr,* Dewana Dorsey
Open Mon & Wed 12-8, Tues & Thurs 10-6, Fri & Sat 9-5
WEST TOWN, 1625 W Chicago Ave, 60622. Tel: 312-743-0450. *Br Mgr,* Stephanie Flinchbaugh
Open Mon & Wed 10-6, Tues & Thurs 12-8, Fri & Sat 9-5
CARTER G WOODSON REGIONAL, 9525 S Halsted St, 60628, SAN 340-0891. Tel: 312-747-6900. TDD: 312-747-0121. *Dir,* Position Currently Open
Special Collections: Afro-American History & Literature (Vivian G Harsh Coll), monographs; Afro-American Newspapers, 1927 to date, microfilm; Annual Reports of the National Association for the Advancement of Colored People, 1910-1970; Literary Manuscripts, such as Richard Wright & Langston Hughes; Papers of the American Missionary Association
Special Services for the Deaf - TDD equip
Open Mon-Thurs 9-9, Fri & Sat 9-5, Sun 1-5
WRIGHTWOOD-ASHBURN, 8530 S Kedzie Ave, 60652, SAN 340-0921. Tel: 312-747-2696. *Br Mgr,* Brent Lipinski
Open Mon & Wed 12-8, Tues & Thurs 10-6, Fri & Sat 9-5
WHITNEY M YOUNG JR BRANCH, 7901 S King Dr, 60619, SAN 340-0956. Tel: 312-747-0039. *Br Mgr,* Mitchell Smith
Open Mon & Wed 10-6, Tues & Thurs 12-8, Fri & Sat 9-5

S CHICAGO SCHOOL OF PROFESSIONAL PSYCHOLOGY LIBRARY*, 325 N Wells St, 6th Flr, 60610. SAN 329-7381. Tel: 312-329-6630. FAX: 312-644-6075. E-mail: library@thechicagoschool.edu. Web Site: www.thechicagoschool.edu/content.cfm/library. *Dir of Libr,* Indu Aggerwal; Tel: 312-329-6633; *Head, Instruction & Libr Access Serv,* Joanna Primus; Tel: 312-329-6632, E-mail: jprimus@thechicagoschool.edu; *Head, ILL,* Dan Patterson; Tel: 312-410-8956, E-mail: dpatterson@thechicagoschool.edu; Staff 9 (MLS 2, Non-MLS 7)
Library Holdings: Bk Titles 8,500; Bk Vols 10,000; Per Subs 220
Special Collections: Israel Goldiamond Special Coll
Subject Interests: Adolescent psychol, Assessment, Child psychology, Clinical psychol, Forensic psychol, Interpretation, Multicultural studies, Psychotherapy
Automation Activity & Vendor Info: (Cataloging) OCLC; (ILL) OCLC; (OPAC) OCLC; (Serials) OCLC
Mem of Reaching Across Illinois Library System (RAILS)
Partic in Health Science Libraries of Illinois (HSLI); Illinois Library & Information Network; OCLC Online Computer Library Center, Inc; OCLC-LVIS; Private Academic Libraries of Illinois
Open Mon-Thurs 8am-9pm, Fri & Sat 8-5

R CHICAGO SINAI CONGREGATION*, James & Leah Davis Memorial Library, 15 W Delaware Pl, 60610. SAN 303-8513. Tel: 312-867-7000. FAX: 312-867-7006. E-mail: library@chicagosinai.org. Web Site: www.chicagosinai.org. *Librn,* Lan Eng; E-mail: leng@chicagosinai.org; Staff 1 (MLS 1)
Founded 1950
Library Holdings: DVDs 100; Bk Titles 5,000; Per Subs 5
Subject Interests: Judaica (lit or hist of Jews)
Database Vendor: OCLC Amlib, OCLC FirstSearch
Wireless access
Function: Archival coll, Computers for patron use, ILL available, Online cat, Ref serv available, Video lending libr
Mem of Reaching Across Illinois Library System (RAILS)

Restriction: Circ to mem only
Friends of the Library Group

C CHICAGO STATE UNIVERSITY, University Library, 9501 S Martin Luther King Jr Dr, LIB 440, 60628-1598. SAN 303-8521. Tel: 773-995-2235. Circulation Tel: 773-995-2341. Interlibrary Loan Service Tel: 773-995-2222. Administration Tel: 773-995-2253. FAX: 773-995-3772. Interlibrary Loan Service FAX: 773-821-2581. E-mail: reference@csu.edu. Web Site: www.library.csu.edu. *Dean of Libr,* Dr Richard Darga; E-mail: rdarga@csu.edu; *Chair, Libr & Instruction Serv,* Gabrielle Toth; Tel: 773-995-2562, E-mail: gtoth@csu.edu; *Access Serv Librn,* Position Currently Open; *Electronic Res Librn,* Joanna Kolendo; Tel: 773-995-2542, E-mail: jkolendo@csu.edu; *Music & Performing Arts Librn,* Kathleen Haefliger; Tel: 773-995-2277, E-mail: khaeflig@csu.edu; *Ref & Instruction Librn, Educ,* Position Currently Open; *Ref & Instruction Librn, Sci,* Position Currently Open; *Ref Librn,* Rosalind Fielder; Tel: 773-821-2431, E-mail: rfielder@csu.edu; *Ref Librn,* Treadwell Merrill; Tel: 773-995-2550; *Tech Serv & Acq Librn/Coordr,* Azungwe Kwembe; Tel: 995-821-2848, E-mail: akwembe@csu.edu; *Pub Relations & Develop Coordr,* Tarshel Beards; Tel: 773-995-4414, E-mail: tbeards@csu.edu; *Ref & Instruction Coordr,* Charlene Snelling; Tel: 773-995-2557, E-mail: csnelling@csu.edu; *Syst Coordr,* Martin Kong; Tel: 773-995-3908, E-mail: mkong@csu.edu; *Spec Formats Cataloger,* Gayle Porter; Tel: 773-995-2551; *Univ Archivist,* Aaisha Haykal. Subject Specialists: *Foreign lang, Geog, Govt info,* Gabrielle Toth; *Humanities, Lit, Philos,* Joanna Kolendo; *Art, Design, Music,* Kathleen Haefliger; *Polit sci, Soc sci,* Rosalind Fielder; *African-Am studies, Hist,* Treadwell Merrill; *Mkt,* Azungwe Kwembe; *Humanities,* Tarshel Beards; *Health sci, Pharm,* Charlene Snelling; *Econ,* Martin Kong; *Sociol,* Gayle Porter; Staff 35 (MLS 15, Non-MLS 20)
Founded 1867. Enrl 5,701; Fac 420; Highest Degree: Doctorate
Jul 2012-Jun 2013. Mats Exp $938,747, Books $92,004. Sal $1,886,684 (Prof $1,285,166)
Library Holdings: AV Mats 8,688; e-books 33,371; e-journals 17,000; Bk Titles 467,544; Per Subs 1,005
Special Collections: Education (Learning Materials, Children's Books). State Document Depository; US Document Depository
Automation Activity & Vendor Info: (Acquisitions) Ex Libris Group; (Cataloging) Ex Libris Group; (Circulation) Ex Libris Group; (Course Reserve) Ex Libris Group; (ILL) Ex Libris Group; (OPAC) Ex Libris Group; (Serials) Ex Libris Group
Database Vendor: EBSCOhost, Gale Cengage Learning, LexisNexis, OCLC FirstSearch, OVID Technologies, ProQuest
Wireless access
Mem of Reaching Across Illinois Library System (RAILS)
Partic in Center for Research Libraries; Consortium of Academic & Research Libraries in Illinois; Illinois Library & Information Network
Open Mon-Thurs 8am-Midnight, Fri 8-7, Sat 9-5, Sun 2pm-Midnight

R CHICAGO THEOLOGICAL SEMINARY*, Learning Commons, 1407 E 60th St, 60637-2902. SAN 303-8556. Tel: 773-896-2450. FAX: 773-643-1334. E-mail: library@ctschicago.edu. Web Site: www.ctschicago.edu. *Assoc Prof, Dean of Libr,* Dr Neil Gerdes; Tel: 773-896-2451, E-mail: ngerdes@ctschicago.edu; *Asst Librn,* Evan Boyd; Tel: 773-896-2452, E-mail: eboyd@ctschicago.edu. Subject Specialists: *Relig,* Dr Neil Gerdes; Staff 3 (MLS 2, Non-MLS 1)
Founded 1855. Enrl 224; Fac 15; Highest Degree: Doctorate
Library Holdings: Bk Titles 116,000; Bk Vols 117,000; Per Subs 144
Subject Interests: Biblical studies, Counseling, Relig, Sexuality, Theol
Mem of Reaching Across Illinois Library System (RAILS)
Partic in Association of Chicago Theological Schools; Illinois Library & Information Network; OCLC Online Computer Library Center, Inc
Open Mon-Fri 9-5

S CHICAGO TRANSIT AUTHORITY-LAW LIBRARY*, 567 W Lake St, 60661-1498. (Mail add: PO Box 7564, 60680-7564), SAN 303-8572. Tel: 312-664-7200, Ext 12778, 312-681-2778. FAX: 312-681-2795. Web Site: www.transitchicago.com. *Coordr, Libr Serv,* Bart Lind Smith; Staff 1 (Non-MLS 1)
Founded 2000
Library Holdings: e-books 62; Bk Vols 8,950
Special Collections: Law (Legal)
Automation Activity & Vendor Info: (Acquisitions) New Generation Technologies Inc. (LiBRARYSOFT); (Cataloging) New Generation Technologies Inc. (LiBRARYSOFT); (Circulation) New Generation Technologies Inc. (LiBRARYSOFT); (Course Reserve) New Generation Technologies Inc. (LiBRARYSOFT); (OPAC) New Generation Technologies Inc. (LiBRARYSOFT); (Serials) New Generation Technologies Inc. (LiBRARYSOFT)
Database Vendor: LexisNexis, OCLC FirstSearch, Westlaw
Function: Archival coll, Doc delivery serv, For res purposes, Online searches, Photocopying/Printing, Ref serv available, Res libr, Workshops
Mem of Reaching Across Illinois Library System (RAILS)
Partic in American Association of Law Libraries (AALL); Call; OCLC Online Computer Library Center, Inc
Open Mon-Fri 8-4:30
Restriction: Circ limited, Co libr, In-house use for visitors, Internal circ only, Open to employees & special libr, Open to others by appt, Restricted borrowing privileges, Restricted pub use, Use of others with permission of librn

S CHICAGO URBAN LEAGUE*, Research & Planning Library, 4510 S Michigan Ave, 60653. SAN 320-6440. Tel: 773-285-5800. FAX: 773-285-7772. Web Site: www.cul-chicago.org. *Res,* Cynthia Jordan-Hubbard; Tel: 773-285-1500, E-mail: cjordan@thechicagourbanleague.org; Staff 1 (MLS 1)
Library Holdings: Bk Titles 1,900; Per Subs 50
Subject Interests: Race relations
Database Vendor: OCLC FirstSearch
Function: Res libr
Mem of Reaching Across Illinois Library System (RAILS)
Restriction: Circulates for staff only, Open to others by appt

CITY COLLEGES OF CHICAGO

J RICHARD J DALEY COLLEGE LIBRARY*, 7500 S Pulaski Rd, 60652-1200, SAN 376-2564. Tel: 773-838-7667. Circulation Tel: 773-838-7668. Interlibrary Loan Service Tel: 773-838-7676. Reference Tel: 773-838-7669. FAX: 773-838-7524. Web Site: daley.ccc.edu. *Chairperson,* Siew-Ben Chin; Tel: 773-838-7674, E-mail: schin@ccc.edu; Staff 11 (MLS 7, Non-MLS 4)
Founded 1965. Enrl 4,900; Fac 112; Highest Degree: Associate
Library Holdings: Bk Titles 65,000; Per Subs 200
Subject Interests: Local hist
Automation Activity & Vendor Info: (Acquisitions) Innovative Interfaces, Inc; (Cataloging) Innovative Interfaces, Inc; (Circulation) Innovative Interfaces, Inc; (Course Reserve) Innovative Interfaces, Inc; (ILL) OCLC FirstSearch; (OPAC) Innovative Interfaces, Inc; (Serials) Innovative Interfaces, Inc
Database Vendor: EBSCOhost, Gale Cengage Learning, OCLC FirstSearch, OCLC WorldShare Interlibrary Loan, ProQuest, Wilson - Wilson Web
Function: ILL available
Partic in Northern Illinois Learning Resources Cooperative (NILRC)
Mem of Reaching Across Illinois Library System (RAILS)
Open Mon-Thurs 7:45am-10pm, Fri 7:45-5, Sat 8-2
Restriction: Circ limited

J KENNEDY-KING COLLEGE LIBRARY, 6403 S Halsted, 60621. (Mail add: 747 W 63rd St, 60621), SAN 303-9390. Tel: 773-602-5449. Information Services Tel: 773-602-5491. FAX: 773-602-5450. E-mail: kkclibrarian@ccc.edu. Web Site: www.ccc.edu/colleges/kennedy/departments/Pages/Library-System.aspx. *Chairperson, Res Mgt Librn,* Ruth A Inman; *Ref & Instruction Librn,* Alecia Kerr. Subject Specialists: *Fine arts, Music,* Ruth A Inman; *Humanities,* Alecia Kerr; Staff 4 (MLS 4)
Founded 1934. Enrl 5,000; Fac 4; Highest Degree: Associate
Library Holdings: Bk Vols 51,000; Per Subs 40
Special Collections: Washburne Cookbook Coll
Automation Activity & Vendor Info: (Acquisitions) Ex Libris Group; (Cataloging) Ex Libris Group; (Circulation) Ex Libris Group; (Course Reserve) Ex Libris Group; (ILL) Ex Libris Group; (OPAC) Ex Libris Group; (Serials) Ex Libris Group
Database Vendor: 3M Library Systems, ABC-CLIO, Alexander Street Press, Baker & Taylor, CQ Press, CredoReference, EBSCOhost, Ex Libris Group, Gale Cengage Learning, Greenwood Publishing Group, JSTOR, LearningExpress, LexisNexis, OCLC, OCLC FirstSearch, OCLC WebJunction, OCLC WorldShare Interlibrary Loan, Oxford Online, PubMed, Sage, Springshare, LLC, Westlaw
Function: 24/7 Electronic res, 24/7 Online cat, Accessibility serv available based on individual needs, Archival coll, Art exhibits, CD-ROM, Computers for patron use, Copy machines, Distance learning, Electronic databases & coll, Handicapped accessible, ILL available, Large print keyboards, Magnifiers for reading, Online cat, Online info literacy tutorials on the web & in blackboard, Orientations, Photocopying/Printing, Ref serv available, Ref serv in person, Study rm, Telephone ref, Wheelchair accessible, Workshops
Partic in Consortium of Academic & Research Libraries in Illinois; Illinois Library & Information Network; Northern Illinois Learning Resources Cooperative (NILRC)
Mem of Reaching Across Illinois Library System (RAILS)
Open Mon-Thurs 8:30-8, Fri 8:30-4, Sat 9-1
Restriction: Open to pub for ref only

J OLIVE-HARVEY COLLEGE LIBRARY*, 10001 S Woodlawn Ave, Rm 2423, 60628, SAN 303-9978. Tel: 773-291-6354, 773-291-6477. FAX: 773-291-6463. Web Site: www.ccc.edu. *Librn,* Willa Lyn Fox; Tel: 773-291-6360, E-mail: wfox@ccc.edu; Staff 3 (MLS 1, Non-MLS 2)
Founded 1957. Enrl 7,000; Fac 123; Highest Degree: Doctorate
Library Holdings: Bk Titles 47,601; Bk Vols 57,095; Per Subs 260
Subject Interests: Spanish (Lang)
Automation Activity & Vendor Info: (OPAC) SirsiDynix
Partic in Illinois Library & Information Network

Special Services for the Blind - Braille Webster's dictionary
Open Mon-Thurs (Winter) 8am-9pm, Fri 8-3, Sat 8-1; Mon-Thurs (Summer) 8-8

J HARRY S TRUMAN - COSGROVE LIBRARY*, 1145 W Wilson Ave, 60640-5691, SAN 304-0380. Tel: 773-907-4865. FAX: 773-907-6803. *Chairperson,* Leone McDermot; Tel: 773-907-4877, E-mail: lmcdermott@ccc.edu; *Pub Serv,* Kwan-Yau Lam; Tel: 773-907-4869, E-mail: klam@ccc.edu; Staff 4 (MLS 4)
Founded 1956. Enrl 4,900; Fac 180; Highest Degree: Associate
Library Holdings: Bk Titles 63,000; Bk Vols 66,800; Per Subs 251
Partic in Illinois Library & Information Network; OCLC Online Computer Library Center, Inc
Open Mon-Thurs 8:30-8:30

J HAROLD WASHINGTON COLLEGE LIBRARY, 30 E Lake St, 60601-9996, SAN 303-9501. Tel: 312-553-5760. FAX: 312-553-5783. E-mail: hwc-library@ccc.edu. Web Site: hwclibrary.ccc.edu. *Instr,* Celia Perez; Tel: 312-553-5635, E-mail: cperez2@ccc.edu; Staff 10 (MLS 4, Non-MLS 6)
Founded 1962. Enrl 8,400; Fac 8; Highest Degree: Associate
Library Holdings: CDs 1,300; Bk Titles 69,802; Bk Vols 70,704; Per Subs 175; Videos 3,000
Subject Interests: Ethnic studies
Automation Activity & Vendor Info: (Acquisitions) Ex Libris Group; (Cataloging) Ex Libris Group; (Circulation) Ex Libris Group; (Course Reserve) Ex Libris Group; (ILL) Ex Libris Group; (Media Booking) Ex Libris Group; (OPAC) Ex Libris Group; (Serials) Ex Libris Group
Database Vendor: EBSCOhost, Gale Cengage Learning, OCLC FirstSearch, ProQuest, Wilson - Wilson Web
Partic in Consortium of Academic & Research Libraries in Illinois; Ill Regional Libr Coun; Illinois Library & Information Network; Northern Illinois Learning Resources Cooperative (NILRC)
Open Mon-Fri 8am-9pm, Sat 8:30-1:30

J WILBUR WRIGHT COLLEGE LIBRARY*, 4300 N Narragansett Ave, L-200, 60634-1500, SAN 304-0542. Tel: 773-481-8400. FAX: 773-481-8407. Web Site: www.ccc.edu/colleges/wright/departments/Pages/Library-System.aspx. ; Staff 3 (MLS 3)
Founded 1934. Enrl 6,250
Library Holdings: Bk Titles 48,000; Bk Vols 52,000; Per Subs 100
Automation Activity & Vendor Info: (Cataloging) Innovative Interfaces, Inc; (Circulation) Innovative Interfaces, Inc; (OPAC) Innovative Interfaces, Inc
Database Vendor: EBSCOhost, OCLC FirstSearch, ProQuest
Mem of Reaching Across Illinois Library System (RAILS)
Open Mon-Thurs 8am-9:30pm, Fri 8-4, Sat 8-2

GL CITY OF CHICAGO*, Department of Law Library, 30 N LaSalle, Ste 800, 60602. SAN 373-6172. Tel: 312-744-7632. FAX: 312-744-1974. Web Site: cityofchicago.org. *Librn,* Scott G Burgh; Staff 3 (MLS 2, Non-MLS 1)
Library Holdings: Bk Titles 700; Bk Vols 16,000
Mem of Reaching Across Illinois Library System (RAILS)
Restriction: Staff use only

L CLAUSEN MILLER RESEARCH SERVICES*, Ten S LaSalle St, 16th Flr, 60603-1098. SAN 371-635X. Tel: 312-606-7887. FAX: 312-606-7777. Web Site: www.clausen.com. *Dir, Res Serv,* Nancy L Tuohy; Tel: 312-606-7535, E-mail: ntuohy@clausen.com; *Mgr, Res,* Andrea Szabo; *Sr Res Spec,* Anton Kresich; *Res Spec,* Amanda Gruenwald; Staff 20 (MLS 2, Non-MLS 18)
Founded 1936
Library Holdings: Bk Vols 15,000; Per Subs 300
Mem of Reaching Across Illinois Library System (RAILS)
Partic in Illinois Library & Information Network; OCLC Online Computer Library Center, Inc
Open Mon-Fri 8:30-6

S COLLECTORS CLUB OF CHICAGO LIBRARY*, 1029 N Dearborn St, 60610. SAN 372-574X. Tel: 312-642-7981. *Pres,* George Fabian; Tel: 847-364-6868; *Acq,* James Duffy
Founded 1928
Library Holdings: Bk Titles 10,000; Per Subs 50
Special Collections: US Document Depository
Publications: Philatelic Hard Bound, bks

C COLUMBIA COLLEGE CHICAGO LIBRARY, 624 S Michigan Ave, 60605-1996. SAN 340-0980. Tel: 312-344-7900. Circulation Tel: 312-344-7152. Interlibrary Loan Service Tel: 312-344-7370. Reference Tel: 312-344-7153. FAX: 312-344-8062. Web Site: www.lib.colum.edu. *Dean of Libr,* Jan Chindlund; Tel: 312-369-7165, E-mail: jchindlund@colum.edu; *Head, Coll & Tech Serv,* Dennis McGuire; Tel: 312-369-7434, E-mail: dmcguire@colum.edu; *Head, Access Serv,* Roland Hansen; Tel: 312-369-7431, E-mail: rchansen@colum.edu; *Head, Archives & Spec Coll,* Heidi Marshall; *Head, Ref,* Arlie Sims; Tel: 312-369-7059, E-mail: asims@colum.edu; *Circ Mgr,* Jennifer Sauzer; Tel: 312-369-8540, E-mail: jsauzer@colum.edu; *Commun Engagement Mgr,* Kim Hale; Tel: 312-369-7355, E-mail: khale@colum.edu; Staff 19 (MLS 19)
Founded 1890. Enrl 11,500; Fac 1,100; Highest Degree: Master
Sept 2006-Aug 2007. Mats Exp $1,148,800, Books $632,500, Per/Ser (Incl. Access Fees) $197,000, AV Equip $11,200, AV Mat $83,200, Electronic Ref Mat (Incl. Access Fees) $210,500, Presv $14,400. Sal $2,032,078
Library Holdings: AV Mats 30,000; Bks on Deafness & Sign Lang 300; CDs 8,500; DVDs 3,300; e-books 4,379; Bk Titles 266,000; Bk Vols 283,000; Per Subs 1,300; Videos 14,000
Special Collections: Center for Black Music Research; Center for Book & Paper Arts; Fashion Columbia Study Coll
Subject Interests: Art, Dance, Films & filmmaking, Journalism, Photog, Radio, Television
Automation Activity & Vendor Info: (Acquisitions) Ex Libris Group; (Cataloging) Ex Libris Group; (Circulation) Ex Libris Group; (Course Reserve) Ex Libris Group; (ILL) Ex Libris Group; (OPAC) Ex Libris Group
Mem of Reaching Across Illinois Library System (RAILS)
Partic in Consortium of Academic & Research Libraries in Illinois; Illinois Library & Information Network; LIBRAS, Inc
Open Mon-Thurs 8am-9:30pm, Fri 8-6, Sat 9-5, Sun 12-5
Friends of the Library Group

S COMPASS LEXECON*, 332 S Michigan Ave, Ste 1300, 60604-4306. SAN 376-0111. Tel: 312-322-0200. FAX: 312-322-0218. Web Site: lexecon.com. *Librn,* Robert Blake
Library Holdings: Bk Titles 15,260; Per Subs 82

SR CONGREGATION RODFEI ZEDEK*, The Joseph J & Dora Abbell Library, 5200 S Hyde Park Blvd, 60615-4213. SAN 303-8653. Tel: 773-752-2770, Ext 106. FAX: 773-752-0330. Web Site: www.rodfei.org/Abbell_Library.aspx. *Adminr,* Sherry Gutman; E-mail: administrator@rodfei.org
Founded 1950
Library Holdings: Bk Vols 8,000; Per Subs 30
Subject Interests: Americana, Judaica (lit or hist of Jews)
Open Mon-Thurs 8:30-4:30, Fri & Sat 8:30-3, Sun 10-1

M COOK COUNTY HOSPITAL LIBRARIES*, 1900 W Polk St, 2nd fl, 60612. SAN 340-1073. Circulation Tel: 312-864-0506. E-mail: aclib2002@yahoo.com. *Dir,* Neera Kukreja; Tel: 312-864-0502
Library Holdings: Bk Titles 6,000; Bk Vols 8,000; Per Subs 500
Special Collections: Rare Medical Books by Notable Physicians
Subject Interests: Allied health, Med, Nursing
Database Vendor: SirsiDynix
Publications: Vanguard
Mem of Reaching Across Illinois Library System (RAILS)
Open Mon-Fri 8-6

GL COOK COUNTY LAW LIBRARY, 2900 Richard J Daley Ctr, 50 W Washington, 60602. SAN 303-8718. Tel: 312-603-5423. FAX: 312-603-4716. Web Site: cookcountyil.gov/law-library. *Exec Law Librn,* Montell Davenport; E-mail: montell.davenport@cookcountyil.gov; *Dep Law Librn,* Justin Piper; Tel: 312-603-2429, Fax: 312-603-9711, E-mail: justin.piper@cookcountyil.gov; *Head, Pub Serv,* Jean Wenger; Tel: 312-603-5131, E-mail: jean.wenger@cookcountyil.gov; *Head, Tech Serv,* Carolyn Hayes; Tel: 312-603-2433, E-mail: carolyn.hayes@cookcountyil.gov. Subject Specialists: *Foreign/Intl law, Govt doc,* Jean Wenger
Founded 1966
Library Holdings: e-journals 2,100; Bk Vols 375,000
Special Collections: Legal (All State, Federal, Foreign/International)
Automation Activity & Vendor Info: (Cataloging) Innovative Interfaces, Inc - Millenium; (OPAC) Innovative Interfaces, Inc - Millenium
Database Vendor: EBSCO Information Services, HeinOnline, LexisNexis, Westlaw
Wireless access
Function: Computers for patron use, Copy machines, Electronic databases & coll, Microfiche/film & reading machines, Online cat, Photocopying/Printing, Pub access computers, Ref & res, Ref serv available
Special Services for the Blind - Accessible computers; Computer with voice synthesizer for visually impaired persons; Copier with enlargement capabilities; Internet workstation with adaptive software; Low vision equip; Screen enlargement software for people with visual disabilities; Screen reader software
Open Mon-Fri 8:30am-9pm, Sat 9-4:30
Restriction: Circ limited
Branches:
BRIDGEVIEW BRANCH, 10220 S 76th Ave, Bridgeview, 60455, SAN 370-0313. Tel: 708-974-6201. FAX: 708-974-6053.
Database Vendor: EBSCOhost, HeinOnline, LexisNexis, Westlaw
Open Mon-Fri 8:30-4

CRIMINAL COURT, 2650 S California, 4th Flr, 60608, SAN 320-9903. Tel: 773-674-5039. FAX: 773-674-3413.
Automation Activity & Vendor Info: (OPAC) Innovative Interfaces, Inc - Millenium
Database Vendor: EBSCOhost, HeinOnline, LexisNexis, Westlaw
Open Mon-Fri 9-4:30

MARKHAM BRANCH, 16501 S Kedzie Pkwy, Markham, 60426, SAN 321-3900. Tel: 708-232-4125. FAX: 708-232-4374.
Automation Activity & Vendor Info: (OPAC) Innovative Interfaces, Inc - Millenium
Database Vendor: EBSCOhost, HeinOnline, LexisNexis, Westlaw
Open Mon-Fri 8:30-4

MAYWOOD BRANCH, 1500 Maybrook Dr, Maywood, 60153, SAN 321-3919. Tel: 708-865-6020. FAX: 708-865-5152.
Automation Activity & Vendor Info: (OPAC) Innovative Interfaces, Inc - Millenium
Database Vendor: EBSCOhost, HeinOnline, LexisNexis, Westlaw
Open Mon-Fri 8:30-4

SKOKIE BRANCH, 5600 W Old Orchard Rd, Skokie, 60077, SAN 321-8570. Tel: 847-470-7298. FAX: 847-470-7526.
Library Holdings: Bk Vols 2,500
Automation Activity & Vendor Info: (OPAC) Innovative Interfaces, Inc - Millenium
Database Vendor: EBSCOhost, HeinOnline, LexisNexis, Westlaw
Open Mon-Fri 8:30-4

S CRAIN COMMUNICATIONS INC*, Information Center, 360 N Michigan Ave, 6th Flr, 60601. SAN 303-8742. Tel: 312-649-5476. FAX: 312-649-5443. *Info Serv Mgr,* Debra Sims; E-mail: dsims@crain.com; Staff 3 (MLS 2, Non-MLS 1)
Founded 1930
Library Holdings: Bk Titles 1,000; Per Subs 50
Subject Interests: Advertising, Mkt
Publications: Newsletter
Restriction: Not open to pub

S DAWSON TECHNICAL INSTITUTE*, Learning Resource Center, 3901 S State St, 60609. SAN 325-6758. Tel: 773-451-2087. FAX: 773-451-2090. Web Site: www.ccc.edu. *In Charge,* Jacqueline Crosby
Library Holdings: Bk Titles 15,200; Bk Vols 16,250; Per Subs 90
Automation Activity & Vendor Info: (Cataloging) SirsiDynix; (Circulation) SirsiDynix
Database Vendor: OCLC FirstSearch, ProQuest, SirsiDynix
Function: Photocopying/Printing
Open Mon-Thurs 7:30-7, Fri 7:30-6

S DDB CHICAGO*, Information Center, 200 E Randolph, 60601. SAN 303-9889. Tel: 312-552-6000, Ext 6934. FAX: 312-552-2379. Web Site: www.ddb.com. *Dir,* Laura DeGraff; Staff 4 (MLS 2, Non-MLS 2)
Founded 1948
Library Holdings: Bk Titles 5,000; Per Subs 350
Subject Interests: Advertising
Publications: Bookends; Reference Shelf
Partic in Dialog Corp; Dow Jones News Retrieval; Illinois Library & Information Network
Restriction: Staff use only

C DEPAUL UNIVERSITY LIBRARIES*, John T Richardson Library, 2350 N Kenmore, 60614. SAN 340-1103. Tel: 773-325-3725, 773-325-7862. Interlibrary Loan Service Tel: 773-325-7818. Reference Tel: 773-325-7863. Administration Tel: 773-325-7849. FAX: 773-325-7870. Web Site: www.lib.depaul.edu. *Univ Librn,* Scott Walter; *Assoc Dir, Libr Info & Discovery Syst,* Megan Bernal; *Assoc Dir, Coll & Scholarly Res,* Position Currently Open; *Assoc Dir, Res & Info Serv,* Terry Taylor; E-mail: ttaylor@depaul.edu; *Assoc Dir, Admin Serv,* Christopher Hoeppner; E-mail: choeppner@depaul.edu; *VPres, Teaching & Learning Res,* Edward Udovic; E-mail: eudovic@depaul.edu; Staff 67 (MLS 31, Non-MLS 36)
Founded 1898. Enrl 21,363; Fac 1,500; Highest Degree: Doctorate
Library Holdings: Bk Vols 848,846; Per Subs 5,778
Special Collections: Art Books; Charles Dickens; Horace; Napoleon; Sports
Automation Activity & Vendor Info: (Acquisitions) Ex Libris Group; (Cataloging) Ex Libris Group; (Circulation) Ex Libris Group; (Course Reserve) Ex Libris Group; (ILL) Ex Libris Group; (Media Booking) Ex Libris Group; (OPAC) Ex Libris Group; (Serials) Ex Libris Group
Database Vendor: Gale Cengage Learning, LexisNexis, OCLC FirstSearch, OVID Technologies, ProQuest, Wilson - Wilson Web
Wireless access
Mem of Reaching Across Illinois Library System (RAILS)
Partic in Consortium of Academic & Research Libraries in Illinois; Illinois Library & Information Network
Open Mon-Thurs 7:30am-Midnight, Fri 7:30am-9pm, Sat 10-9, Sun 10am-Midnight
Friends of the Library Group

Departmental Libraries:

LOOP, One E Jackson Blvd, 10th Flr, 60604, SAN 340-1138. Tel: 312-362-5403. Circulation Tel: 312-362-8433. Reference Tel: 312-362-6186. *Instrul Serv Librn, Ref Serv,* Elisa Addlesperger; Tel: 312-362-5045, E-mail: eaddlesp@depaul.edu; *Instrul Serv Librn, Ref Serv,* Brian DeHart; *Access Serv, ILL,* Lorie Kolak; *Doc Delivery,* Paula Dempsey; E-mail: pdempsey@depaul.edu
Library Holdings: Bk Vols 250,000; Per Subs 200
Open Mon-Fri 8am-11pm, Sat 9-9
Friends of the Library Group

NAPERVILLE, 150 W Warrenville Rd, Naperville, 60563. Tel: 312-476-4500, 312-476-4554. *Instrul Serv Librn, Ref Serv,* Robert Acker; Tel: 312-476-4867, E-mail: racker@depaul.edu
Open Mon-Thurs 8am-10pm, Fri & Sat 8-5, Sun 12-5

OAK FOREST, 16333 S Kilbourn Ave, Ste 5350, Oak Forest, 60452, SAN 375-2895. Tel: 312-476-3000, 312-476-3049. FAX: 708-633-9095. *Ref Serv,* Pat McGreal; Tel: 630-636-3049, E-mail: pmcgreal@depaul.edu
Open Mon-Thurs 11-10, Fri 9-3, Sat 8:30-2
Friends of the Library Group

O'HARE, 3166 S River Rd, Des Plaines, 60018, SAN 329-000X. Tel: 312-476-3600, 312-476-3611. FAX: 847-296-4381. *Instrul Serv Librn, Ref Serv,* Elisa Addlesperger; Tel: 312-362-5045, E-mail: eaddlesp@depaul.edu; *Instrul Serv Librn, Ref Serv,* Celia Ross
Open Mon-Thurs 2-8, Fri 9-4, Sat 10-3
Friends of the Library Group

CL VINCENT G RINN LAW LIBRARY, 25 E Jackson Blvd, 5th Flr, 60604-2287, SAN 340-1197. Tel: 312-362-8121, 312-362-8701. FAX: 312-362-6908. Web Site: law.depaul.edu/library. *Dir,* Allen Moye; Tel: 312-362-6893; *Assoc Dir, Computing Serv,* Michael Schiffer; Tel: 312-362-6311, E-mail: mschiffe@depaul.edu; *Assoc Dir, Pub Serv,* Milta Hall; Tel: 312-362-5093; *Assoc Dir, Tech Serv,* Mary Lu Linnane; Tel: 312-362-6895; *Head, Cat,* Denise Glynn; *Acq Mgr,* Lenore Boehm; Tel: 312-362-5224; *Circ Mgr,* Heather Hummons; Tel: 312-362-8958, E-mail: hhummons@depaul.edu; *Mgr, Ser,* Candis Collins; Tel: 312-362-6155; *Cat, Doc,* Walter Baumann; Tel: 312-362-5225, E-mail: wbaumann@depaul.edu; *ILL,* Kimyatta Gainey; Tel: 312-362-5123, E-mail: kgainey@depaul.edu; Staff 18 (MLS 7, Non-MLS 11)
Founded 1920. Enrl 1,100; Fac 50; Highest Degree: Master
Library Holdings: Bk Titles 70,980; Bk Vols 402,000; Per Subs 5,348
Special Collections: Graduate Taxation Law; Health Law Coll; International Human Rights Law; Supreme Court Justices' Signatures (Nathan Schwartz Coll). US Document Depository
Subject Interests: Constitutional law, Environ law
Automation Activity & Vendor Info: (OPAC) Ex Libris Group
Database Vendor: H W Wilson, HeinOnline, Ingenta, JSTOR, Loislaw, PubMed, Thomson Carswell, Westlaw
Partic in Chicago Legal Acad Syst; OCLC Online Computer Library Center, Inc
Open Mon-Fri (Winter) 8am-11pm, Sat 9-6, Sun 12-10; Mon-Fri (Summer) 8am-10pm, Sat 9-6
Restriction: Photo ID required for access

C DEVRY UNIVERSITY*, Chicago Campus Library, 3300 N Campbell Ave, 60618. SAN 303-8807. Tel: 773-697-2214. FAX: 773-697-2714. Web Site: www.chi.devry.edu/library.html. *Dir,* Jason Rossi; Tel: 773-697-2215; Staff 1 (MLS 1)
Founded 1967. Highest Degree: Bachelor
Library Holdings: Bk Vols 20,000; Per Subs 30
Subject Interests: Bus & mgt, Computer sci, Electronics
Automation Activity & Vendor Info: (Cataloging) Ex Libris Group; (Circulation) Ex Libris Group; (Course Reserve) Ex Libris Group; (OPAC) Ex Libris Group
Database Vendor: EBSCOhost, OCLC FirstSearch, OCLC WorldShare Interlibrary Loan, ProQuest
Wireless access
Function: ILL available
Open Mon-Thurs 8am-10pm, Fri 8-8, Sat & Sun 8:30-4:30

L DLA PIPER US LLP, Law Library, 203 N LaSalle St, Ste 1900, 60601. SAN 372-1116. Tel: 312-849-3841. Interlibrary Loan Service Tel: 312-984-5855. FAX: 312-251-5845. *Sr Mgr, Libr Admin,* John M Klasey; Tel: 312-984-5222, E-mail: john.klasey@dlapiper.com; *Res Librn,* Sally Baker; Tel: 312-984-2615, E-mail: sally.baker@dlapiper.com; *Res Librn,* Megan C Butman; Tel: 312-849-8668, E-mail: megan.butman@dlapiper.com; *Res Librn,* Valerie Kropf; Tel: 312-984-5703, E-mail: valerie.kropf@dlapiper.com; *Res Serv Mgr,* Julie Pabarja; Tel: 312-849-8639, E-mail: julie.pabarja@dlapiper.com; Staff 6.2 (MLS 4.2, Non-MLS 2)
Database Vendor: Bloomberg, Dialog, Fastcase, HeinOnline, Hoovers, LexisNexis, OCLC FirstSearch, Westlaw
Wireless access
Mem of Reaching Across Illinois Library System (RAILS)
Partic in OCLC Online Computer Library Center, Inc

S DONORS FORUM LIBRARY*, 208 S La Salle St, Ste 1535, 60604-1006. SAN 303-884X. Tel: 312-578-0175. Toll Free Tel: 888-578-0090. FAX: 877-572-0160. E-mail: info@donorsforum.org. Web Site: www.donorsforum.org. *VPres of Libr & Nonprofit Serv,* Laura Zumdahl; E-mail: lzumdahl@donorsforum.org; Staff 2 (MLS 1, Non-MLS 1)
Founded 1974
Library Holdings: Bk Titles 2,500; Bk Vols 2,700; Per Subs 60
Special Collections: Foundation Center Regional Coll
Subject Interests: Philanthropy
Automation Activity & Vendor Info: (Cataloging) Inmagic, Inc.
Function: Homebound delivery serv, Orientations, Outside serv via phone, mail, e-mail & web, Photocopying/Printing, Ref & res, Wheelchair accessible, Workshops
Publications: A Guide to Funding Youth Development Programs; Chicago Area Grant Application; Chicago Area Grant Report; Duties & Responsibilities of Directors & Trustees of Illinois Private Foundations; Giving in Illinois; Principles for Community Health Care; The Directory of Illinois Foundations
Mem of Reaching Across Illinois Library System (RAILS)
Special Services for the Blind - Closed circuit TV
Open Mon-Fri Noon-5
Restriction: Circulates for staff only
Friends of the Library Group

L DRINKER, BIDDLE & REATH*, Library & Research Services, 191 N Wacker Dr, Ste 3700, 60606. SAN 376-1428. Tel: 312-569-1860. FAX: 312-569-3860. Web Site: www.drinkerbiddle.com. *Sr Res Librn,* Susane Yesnick
Library Holdings: Bk Titles 2,700
Automation Activity & Vendor Info: (Acquisitions) SydneyPlus; (Cataloging) SydneyPlus; (Circulation) SydneyPlus; (OPAC) SydneyPlus
Open Mon-Fri 9-5

S DUFF & PHELPS*, Research Library, 311 S Wacker Dr, Ste 4200, 60606. SAN 325-6367. Tel: 312-697-4600. FAX: 312-697-4609. Web Site: www.duffandphelps.com. *Mgr, Libr Serv,* Ramona Howerton; Tel: 312-697-4672; *Assoc Librn,* Michael Tebbe; Tel: 312-697-4535; Staff 3 (MLS 2, Non-MLS 1)
Library Holdings: Bk Titles 3,700; Bk Vols 4,500; Per Subs 200
Subject Interests: Finance
Automation Activity & Vendor Info: (Acquisitions) Inmagic, Inc.; (Cataloging) Inmagic, Inc.; (Circulation) Inmagic, Inc.; (Serials) Inmagic, Inc.
Mem of Reaching Across Illinois Library System (RAILS)

L DYKEMA GOSSETT PLLC*, Information Center, Ten S Wacker Dr, Ste 2300, 60606. SAN 304-0097. Tel: 312-876-1700. FAX: 312-876-1155. Web Site: www.dykema.com. *Ref Librn,* Sam Wertime; Staff 3 (MLS 1, Non-MLS 2)
Library Holdings: Bk Vols 16,000
Special Collections: Federal, Illinois & Indiana Law Coll
Database Vendor: OCLC FirstSearch, Westlaw
Restriction: Co libr

L EDWARDS WILDMAN PALMER, LLP*, 225 W Wacker Dr, Ste 3000, 60606. SAN 375-9199. Tel: 312-201-2000. FAX: 312-201-2555. E-mail: library@edwardswildman.com. *Libr & Info Res Coordr,* Camille S Jones; Tel: 312-201-2512, E-mail: csjones@edwardswildman.com; Staff 2 (Non-MLS 2)
Library Holdings: Bk Vols 30,000
Automation Activity & Vendor Info: (Cataloging) Inmagic, Inc.; (ILL) Inmagic, Inc.; (Serials) Inmagic, Inc.
Database Vendor: Dialog, LexisNexis, OCLC FirstSearch, Westlaw
Mem of Reaching Across Illinois Library System (RAILS)
Partic in Illinois Library & Information Network
Open Mon-Fri 8-5

SR EMANUEL CONGREGATION*, Joseph Taussig Memorial Library, 5959 N Sheridan Rd, 60660. SAN 371-6597. Tel: 773-561-5173. FAX: 773-561-5420. Web Site: www.emanuelcong.org.
Library Holdings: Bk Titles 5,012; Bk Vols 6,000; Per Subs 10
Subject Interests: Judaica
Restriction: Open by appt only, Open to pub for ref only

C ERIKSON INSTITUTE, Edward Neisser Library, 451 N LaSalle St, Ste 210, 60654. SAN 320-6459. Tel: 312-893-7210. FAX: 312-893-7213. E-mail: library@erikson.edu. Web Site: library.erikson.edu. *Libr Dir,* Karen Janke; E-mail: kjanke@erikson.edu; *Pub Serv Librn,* Alyssa Vincent; E-mail: avincent@erikson.edu; *Circ Supvr,* Deb Derylak; E-mail: dderylak@erikson.edu; Staff 3 (MLS 2, Non-MLS 1)
Founded 1966. Enrl 250; Fac 15; Highest Degree: Doctorate
Jul 2012-Jun 2013. Mats Exp $50,802, Books $12,219, Per/Ser (Incl. Access Fees) $19,940, AV Mat $2,000, Electronic Ref Mat (Incl. Access Fees) $16,643. Sal $168,020
Library Holdings: AV Mats 660; Braille Volumes 3; Bk Titles 25,321; Bk Vols 30,612; Per Subs 85; Spec Interest Per Sub 85
Subject Interests: Child develop, Early childhood educ, Soc work
Automation Activity & Vendor Info: (Acquisitions) Baker & Taylor; (Cataloging) OCLC; (Circulation) ByWater Solutions; (Course Reserve) Atlas Systems; (ILL) OCLC ILLiad; (OPAC) ByWater Solutions; (Serials) EBSCO Online
Database Vendor: Alexander Street Press, ByWater Solutions, EBSCOhost, Elsevier, JSTOR, MITINET, Inc, OCLC WorldShare Interlibrary Loan, Sage, SerialsSolutions, Wiley InterScience, YBP Library Services
Wireless access
Function: Archival coll, Audio & video playback equip for onsite use, Computer training, Computers for patron use, Copy machines, Distance learning, Doc delivery serv, Electronic databases & coll, ILL available, Online info literacy tutorials on the web & in blackboard, Online ref, Ref serv available, Telephone ref
Mem of Reaching Across Illinois Library System (RAILS)
Partic in Consortium of Academic & Research Libraries in Illinois
Open Mon-Thurs 8am-9pm, Fri 10-4
Restriction: Borrowing privileges limited to fac & registered students, Borrowing requests are handled by ILL, Circ privileges for students & alumni only, External users must contact libr, In-house use for visitors

S FEDERAL RESERVE BANK OF CHICAGO*, Knowledge Center, 230 S LaSalle St, 60604-1413. (Mail add: PO Box 834, 60690-0834), SAN 303-8912. Tel: 312-322-5824. Interlibrary Loan Service Tel: 312-322-4437. FAX: 312-322-5091. E-mail: library.chi@chi.frb.org. Web Site: www.chicagofed.org. *Mgr,* Susan Chenoweth. Subject Specialists: *Bus finance,* Susan Chenoweth; Staff 8 (MLS 6, Non-MLS 2)
Founded 1920
Library Holdings: Bk Titles 13,600; Per Subs 350
Subject Interests: Banks & banking, Econ, Finance, Monetary policy, Statistics
Automation Activity & Vendor Info: (Cataloging) SirsiDynix; (Circulation) SirsiDynix; (ILL) OCLC; (OPAC) SirsiDynix; (Serials) SirsiDynix
Mem of Reaching Across Illinois Library System (RAILS)
Partic in Illinois Library & Information Network

S FIELD MUSEUM OF NATURAL HISTORY LIBRARY, 1400 S Lake Shore Dr, 60605-2498. SAN 303-8955. Tel: 312-665-7894. FAX: 312-665-7893. E-mail: library@fieldmuseum.org. Web Site: fieldmuseum.org/explore/department/library. *Mus Librn,* Christine Giannoni; E-mail: cgiannoni@fieldmuseum.org; *Tech Serv Librn,* Diana Duncan; E-mail: dduncan@fieldmuseum.org; Staff 7 (MLS 2, Non-MLS 5)
Founded 1893
Library Holdings: Bk Vols 275,000; Per Subs 1,400
Special Collections: Berthold Laufer Coll of Far Eastern Studies; Edward E Ayer Ornithology Library Coll; Karl P Schmidt Herpetology Library Coll, bks & reprints
Subject Interests: Anthrop, Archaeology, Botany, Geol, Museology, Paleontology, Zoology
Database Vendor: OCLC Worldshare Management Services
Mem of Reaching Across Illinois Library System (RAILS)
Partic in Consortium of Academic & Research Libraries in Illinois; OCLC Online Computer Library Center, Inc
Restriction: Open by appt only

L FOLEY & LARDNER*, Law Library, 321 N Clark St, Ste 2800, 60610. SAN 373-8019. Tel: 312-832-4500. FAX: 312-832-4700. Web Site: www.foley.com. *Librn,* Christina Wagner
Founded 1988
Library Holdings: Bk Vols 10,000
Subject Interests: Commodities, Real estate, Securities

S FREEBORN & PETERS LIBRARY*, 311 S Wacker Dr, Ste 3000, 60606-6677. SAN 376-1711. Tel: 312-360-6000. FAX: 312-360-6575. E-mail: info@freebornpeters.com. Web Site: www.freebornpeters.com. *Librn, Mgr,* Maureen Newman
Library Holdings: Bk Titles 1,500; Per Subs 200
Subject Interests: Law
Automation Activity & Vendor Info: (Cataloging) Inmagic, Inc.; (Circulation) Inmagic, Inc.; (Serials) Inmagic, Inc.
Open Mon-Fri 9-5

S GREELEY & HANSEN ENGINEERING LIBRARY, 100 S Wacker Dr, Ste 1400, 60606-4004. SAN 303-9005. Tel: 312-578-2461. FAX: 312-558-1986. Web Site: www.greeley-hansen.com. *Librn,* Beth Spencer; E-mail: bspencer@greeley-hansen.com; Staff 1 (MLS 1)
Founded 1914
Library Holdings: Bk Titles 1,500; Per Subs 15
Subject Interests: Sewage, Water treatment

Automation Activity & Vendor Info: (Cataloging) Inmagic, Inc.; (Circulation) Inmagic, Inc.; (OPAC) Inmagic, Inc.
Database Vendor: IEEE (Institute of Electrical & Electronics Engineers), OCLC FirstSearch
Function: 24/7 Electronic res, 24/7 Online cat, Doc delivery serv, e-mail serv, Electronic databases & coll, Mail & tel request accepted, Online cat, Online searches, Ref serv available
Publications: Newsletter
Mem of Reaching Across Illinois Library System (RAILS)
Restriction: Employees & their associates

C HARRINGTON COLLEGE OF DESIGN LIBRARY, 200 W Madison St, Ste 336, 60606. SAN 320-1767. Tel: 312-697-3318. Circulation Tel: 312-939-4975, Ext 1118. FAX: 312-697-8115. E-mail: library@harrington.edu. Web Site: www.harrington.edu/StudentLife/Library. *Dir of Libr Serv,* Leigh Gates; E-mail: lgates@harrington.edu; Staff 2.6 (MLS 1.2, Non-MLS 1.4)
Founded 1975
Library Holdings: AV Mats 857; e-books 100,000; Bk Titles 31,000; Per Subs 83
Subject Interests: Archit, Art, Communication arts, Design, Furniture, Interior design, Photog, Web design, Web develop
Automation Activity & Vendor Info: (Acquisitions) Ex Libris Group; (Cataloging) Ex Libris Group; (Circulation) Ex Libris Group; (Course Reserve) Ex Libris Group; (ILL) OCLC; (OPAC) Ex Libris Group; (Serials) Ex Libris Group
Database Vendor: Alexander Street Press, Cambridge Scientific Abstracts, Cinahl, ebrary, EBSCO Information Services, EBSCOhost, Ex Libris Group, OCLC FirstSearch, OCLC WorldShare Interlibrary Loan, Oxford Online, ProQuest, Safari Books Online
Wireless access
Publications: Accessions Lists; Subject Bibliographies
Mem of Reaching Across Illinois Library System (RAILS)
Partic in Consortium of Academic & Research Libraries in Illinois; Illinois Library & Information Network; OCLC Online Computer Library Center, Inc
Open Mon-Thurs (Spring) 8am-9pm, Fri & Sat 8-3; Mon-Thurs (Summer) 8-4, Fri 8-2
Restriction: Open to students, fac & staff

S HEARTLAND INSTITUTE LIBRARY*, 19 S LaSalle No 903, 60603. SAN 377-5232. Tel: 312-377-4000. FAX: 312-377-5000. E-mail: think@heartland.org. Web Site: www.heartland.org. *Librn,* Cheryl Parker; Staff 1 (Non-MLS 1)
Founded 1984
Library Holdings: Bk Titles 1,500; Per Subs 25
Subject Interests: Agr, Econ, Educ, Environment, Global climate change, Politics, Regulation, Welfare
Function: Res libr
Open Mon-Fri 8-4

L HINSHAW & CULBERTSON LIBRARY*, 222 N LaSalle, Ste 300, 60601-1081. SAN 370-6052. Tel: 312-704-3000. FAX: 312-704-3951. Web Site: www.hinshawculbertson.com. *Mgr,* Jennifer Kiszka; *Acq, Tech Serv,* Nancy Hudson; *ILL, Ref Serv,* Virginia Brown; *ILL, Tech Serv,* Dan Sherman; Staff 4 (MLS 2, Non-MLS 2)
Library Holdings: Bk Titles 700; Bk Vols 15,000; Per Subs 75
Partic in American Association of Law Libraries (AALL); Chicago Association of Law Libraries (CALL); Illinois Library & Information Network

L HOLLAND & KNIGHT LLP*, Law Library, 131 S Dearborn, 30th Flr, 60603. SAN 325-6200. Tel: 312-578-6616. FAX: 312-578-6666. Web Site: www.hklaw.com. *Head Librn,* Carolyn Hosticka; E-mail: carolyn.hosticka@hklaw.com; Staff 3 (MLS 1, Non-MLS 2)
Library Holdings: Bk Vols 10,000; Per Subs 200
Automation Activity & Vendor Info: (Cataloging) Inmagic, Inc.; (Circulation) Inmagic, Inc.
Wireless access
Restriction: Staff use only

S J ALLEN HYNEK CENTER FOR UFO STUDIES, Information Center, PO Box 31335, 60631. SAN 370-615X. Tel: 773-271-3611. E-mail: infocenter@cufos.org. Web Site: www.cufos.org. *Librn,* George M Eberhart
Founded 1973
Library Holdings: Bk Titles 5,000; Per Subs 10
Special Collections: UFO Case Files, early 1900s-present
Wireless access
Restriction: Non-circulating to the pub, Open by appt only

CM ILLINOIS COLLEGE OF OPTOMETRY LIBRARY*, 3241 S Michigan Ave, Library, 60616-3878. Tel: 312-949-7160. Reference Tel: 312-949-7152. Administration Tel: 312-949-7153. Automation Services Tel: 312-949-7158. FAX: 312-949-6690. E-mail: cshepard@ico.edu. Web Site: library.ico.edu, www.visioncite.com. *Libr Dir,* Christine A Weber; E-mail: cweber@ico.edu; *Coll Mgt Librn,* Luke Sutton; Tel: 312-949-7163, E-mail: lsutton@ico.edu; *Electronic Serv Librn,* Amelia Prechel; E-mail: aprechel@ico.edu; *Pub Serv Librn,* Sandra Engram; E-mail: sengram@ico.edu; *Ser Librn,* Darlene Ward; Tel: 312-949-7151, E-mail: dward@ico.edu; *Circ Asst,* Irma Chavez; Tel: 312-949-7156, E-mail: ichavez@ico.edu. Subject Specialists: *Vision sci,* Christine A Weber; Staff 7 (MLS 5, Non-MLS 2)
Founded 1955. Enrl 680; Fac 75; Highest Degree: Doctorate
Library Holdings: AV Mats 929; Bks on Deafness & Sign Lang 46; CDs 135; e-journals 10,000; Microforms 1,522; Bk Titles 23,305; Bk Vols 41,793; Per Subs 114; Videos 700
Subject Interests: Aging, Allied health, Bus, Health sci, Med, Natural sci, Ophthalmology, Optics, Optometry
Automation Activity & Vendor Info: (Acquisitions) SirsiDynix; (Cataloging) SirsiDynix; (Circulation) SirsiDynix; (Course Reserve) SirsiDynix; (ILL) OCLC; (Media Booking) SirsiDynix; (OPAC) SirsiDynix; (Serials) SirsiDynix
Database Vendor: 3M Library Systems, Alexander Street Press, Baker & Taylor, Bowker, Brodart, Checkpoint Systems, Inc, Cinahl, CredoReference, EBSCO Information Services, EBSCOhost, Elsevier, Majors, Medline, OCLC, OCLC FirstSearch, OCLC WorldShare Interlibrary Loan, OVID Technologies, PubMed, RefWorks, Safari Books Online, Scopus, SirsiDynix, Springer-Verlag, Swets Information Services, WebMD, Wiley, Wiley InterScience, YBP Library Services
Wireless access
Function: Audio & video playback equip for onsite use, CD-ROM, Computers for patron use, Copy machines, Digital talking bks, e-mail & chat, E-Reserves, Electronic databases & coll, Fax serv, Handicapped accessible, Health sci info serv, ILL available, Magnifiers for reading, Microfiche/film & reading machines, Newsp ref libr, Notary serv, Online cat, Online ref, Online searches, Photocopying/Printing, Ref & res, Scanner, Tax forms, Telephone ref, Video lending libr, Web-catalog, Wheelchair accessible
Publications: ICO Library's proprietary citation index Database to Vision Science Journals; VisionCite
Mem of Reaching Across Illinois Library System (RAILS)
Partic in Association of Vision Science Librarians (AVSL); Medical Library Association (MLA); National Network of Libraries of Medicine Greater Midwest Region; OCLC Online Computer Library Center, Inc
Special Services for the Blind - Aids for in-house use; Assistive/Adapted tech devices, equip & products; Bks & mags in Braille, on rec, tape & cassette; Bks available with recordings; Closed circuit TV magnifier; Computer with voice synthesizer for visually impaired persons; Digital talking bk; Digital talking bk machines; Internet workstation with adaptive software; Large print bks; Large print bks & talking machines; Large screen computer & software; Magnifiers; Screen enlargement software for people with visual disabilities; Talking bks; Talking bks & player equip; Text reader; ZoomText magnification & reading software
Restriction: Access at librarian's discretion, Authorized patrons, Borrowing privileges limited to fac & registered students, Borrowing requests are handled by ILL, By permission only, Circ limited, Internal circ only, Non-circulating of rare bks, Non-circulating to the pub, Open to others by appt, Open to students, fac & staff, Photo ID required for access, Private libr, Pub by appt only, Researchers by appt only, Visitors must make appt to use bks in the libr

L ILLINOIS CRIMINAL JUSTICE INFORMATION AUTHORITY LIBRARY*, 300 W Adams, Ste 700, 60606-3997. SAN 329-5222. Tel: 312-793-8550. Interlibrary Loan Service Tel: 312-793-8901. FAX: 312-793-8422. Web Site: www.illinois.gov. *Librn,* Ideta Phillips
Library Holdings: Bk Vols 3,000; Per Subs 40
Mem of Illinois Heartland Library System
Open Mon-Fri 8:30-5

G ILLINOIS DEPARTMENT OF EMPLOYMENT SECURITY*, Law & Reference Library, 33 S State St, 60603. SAN 303-9110. Tel: 312-793-6202. FAX: 312-793-6292. Web Site: www.ides.state.il.us. *Head Librn,* Eunice Choi; E-mail: eunhee.milutinovic@illinois.gov; Staff 1 (MLS 1)
Founded 1976
Library Holdings: Bk Titles 3,000; Bk Vols 4,000; Per Subs 122
Subject Interests: Employment, Labor, Law, Mgt
Automation Activity & Vendor Info: (Cataloging) OCLC; (ILL) OCLC
Function: ILL available
Partic in Illinois Library & Information Network
Restriction: Not open to pub

C ILLINOIS INSTITUTE OF ART - CHICAGO LIBRARY*, 350 N Orleans St, 60654-1593. SAN 372-588X. Tel: 312-777-8728, 312-777-8730. Administration Tel: 312-777-8726. FAX: 312-777-8782. E-mail: iiaclibrary@aii.edu. *Librn,* Sean McCarthy; *Asst Librn,* Jennifer A Cox. Subject Specialists: *Applied arts,* Sean McCarthy; Staff 2 (MLS 2)
Founded 1995. Enrl 2,725; Fac 247; Highest Degree: Bachelor

Library Holdings: Electronic Media & Resources 28; Bk Vols 33,739; Per Subs 243
Special Collections: Fashion & Fashion History Coll (Vogue to 1938); Motion Clip Library; Online Digital Images; Sound Effects Library
Subject Interests: Advertising, Animation, Culinary, Fashion design, Gaming, Graphic design, Interior design, Web design
Automation Activity & Vendor Info: (Acquisitions) Ex Libris Group; (Cataloging) OCLC; (Circulation) Ex Libris Group; (Course Reserve) Ex Libris Group; (ILL) OCLC; (OPAC) Ex Libris Group; (Serials) Ex Libris Group
Database Vendor: CredoReference, ebrary, EBSCOhost, Electric Library, Ex Libris Group, Gale Cengage Learning, Greenwood Publishing Group, H W Wilson, Hoovers, Material ConneXion, Mergent Online, OCLC, OCLC ArticleFirst, OCLC CAMIO, OCLC FirstSearch, OCLC WorldShare Interlibrary Loan, Oxford Online, ProQuest, RefWorks, Safari Books Online, Wilson - Wilson Web, YBP Library Services
Wireless access
Function: CD-ROM, ILL available, Music CDs, Online searches, Orientations, Ref serv available, VHS videos, Wheelchair accessible
Mem of Reaching Across Illinois Library System (RAILS)
Partic in Consortium of Academic & Research Libraries in Illinois
Restriction: Borrowing requests are handled by ILL, Open to pub upon request, Open to students, fac & staff

C ILLINOIS INSTITUTE OF TECHNOLOGY, Paul V Galvin Library, 35 W 33rd St, 60616. SAN 340-1340. Tel: 312-567-3616. Circulation Tel: 312-567-6847. Interlibrary Loan Service Tel: 312-567-6846. FAX: 312-567-5318. E-mail: library@iit.edu. Web Site: library.iit.edu. *Dean of Libr,* Dr Sharon Bostick; Tel: 312-567-3293; Staff 29 (MLS 17, Non-MLS 12)
Founded 1891. Enrl 8,200; Highest Degree: Doctorate
Library Holdings: Bk Titles 294,066; Bk Vols 597,594; Per Subs 9,678
Special Collections: IIT Archives; Marvin Camras Coll, papers, inventions. Oral History; US Document Depository
Subject Interests: Art & archit, Computer sci, Econ, Eng, Environ studies, Math, Sci tech
Automation Activity & Vendor Info: (Acquisitions) Ex Libris Group
Database Vendor: ACM (Association for Computing Machinery), American Chemical Society, American Mathematical Society, Cambridge Scientific Abstracts, EBSCOhost, IEEE (Institute of Electrical & Electronics Engineers), JSTOR, OCLC WorldShare Interlibrary Loan, Project MUSE, ProQuest, Safari Books Online, Sage, ScienceDirect, Springer-Verlag, Thomson - Web of Science
Wireless access
Mem of Reaching Across Illinois Library System (RAILS)
Partic in Chicago Academic Libr Coun; Consortium of Academic & Research Libraries in Illinois; Illinois Library & Information Network; LCS; OCLC Online Computer Library Center, Inc
Special Services for the Deaf - TDD equip

Departmental Libraries:

LOUIS W BIEGLER LIBRARY, 201 East Loop Rd, Wheaton, 60187-8489. Tel: 630-682-6050. FAX: 630-682-6049. E-mail: biegler@iit.edu. Web Site: www.gl.iit.edu/biegler. *Br Librn,* Nichole Novak; Tel: 630 682 6047
Library Holdings: Bk Titles 4,500; Per Subs 15
Special Collections: Electrical Engineering (Alva C Todd Coll)
Automation Activity & Vendor Info: (Acquisitions) Ex Libris Group; (Cataloging) Ex Libris Group; (Circulation) Ex Libris Group; (ILL) OCLC; (OPAC) Ex Libris Group; (Serials) Ex Libris Group
Open Mon-Thurs 2-9:30, Sat 9-2

CENTER FOR THE STUDY OF ETHICS IN THE PROFESSIONS LIBRARY, Hermann Union Bldg/Mezzanine, Rm 205, 3241 S Federal St, 60616, SAN 326-6842. Tel: 312-567-6913. FAX: 312-567-3016. E-mail: cseplibrary@iit.edu. Web Site: ethics.iit.edu. *Librn,* Kelly Laas; Staff 1 (MLS 1)
Founded 1976. Enrl 7,000; Fac 200; Highest Degree: Doctorate
Library Holdings: AV Mats 90; e-journals 50; Bk Titles 2,500; Per Subs 34; Videos 60
Special Collections: Codes of Ethics Coll; Codes of Ethics Online Archive; Software Engineering Code of Ethics Archive
Function: Computers for patron use, Copy machines, e-mail & chat, Online cat, Online ref, Online searches, Orientations, Res libr, Res performed for a fee, Web-catalog
Publications: Perspectives on the Professions (Newsletter)
Open Mon-Fri 9-5
Restriction: Non-circulating to the pub

CL CHICAGO-KENT COLLEGE OF LAW LIBRARY, 565 W Adams St, 60661, SAN 340-1375. Tel: 312-906-5600. FAX: 312-906-5679. Web Site: library.kentlaw.edu. *Libr Dir,* Keith Ann Stiverson; Tel: 312-906-5610, E-mail: kstivers@kentlaw.iit.eduu; *Assoc Dir,* JoAnn Hounshell; Tel: 312-906-5675, E-mail: jhounshell@kentlaw.iit.edu; *Educ Tech Librn, Head, Fac Serv, Head, Res Serv,* Deborah Ginsberg; Tel: 312-906-5673, E-mail: dginsberg@kentlaw.iit.edu; *Access Serv Librn,* Eric Neagle; Tel: 312-906-5662, E-mail: eneagle@kentlaw.iit.edu; *Digital Res Librn,* Jona Whipple; E-mail: jwhipple@kentlaw.iit.edu; *Res/Fac Serv Librn,* Thomas Gaylord; Tel: 312-906-5643, E-mail: tgaylord@kentlaw.iit.edu; *Res/Fac Serv Librn,* Scott Vanderlin; E-mail: svanderlin@kentlaw.edu; *Res/Fac Serv Librn,* Clare Willis; E-mail: cwillis@kentlaw.iit.edu; *Res/Govt Doc Librn,* Kevin McClure; Tel: 312-906-5620, E-mail: kmcclure@kentlaw.iit.edu; *Web Technologist,* Emily Barney; E-mail: ebarney@kentlaw.iit.edu. Subject Specialists: *Law,* Keith Ann Stiverson; Staff 11 (MLS 11)
Enrl 1,100; Fac 95; Highest Degree: Doctorate
Library Holdings: Bk Titles 84,439; Bk Vols 574,899; Per Subs 9,158
Special Collections: Library of International Relations. UN Document Depository; US Document Depository
Subject Interests: Bus, Finance, Intl relations, Law
Automation Activity & Vendor Info: (Acquisitions) Ex Libris Group; (Cataloging) Ex Libris Group; (Circulation) Ex Libris Group; (Course Reserve) Ex Libris Group; (OPAC) Ex Libris Group; (Serials) Ex Libris Group
Open Mon-Thurs 8am-11pm, Fri 8-8, Sat 9-8, Sun 10am-11pm

S INSTITUTE FOR CLINICAL SOCIAL WORK LIBRARY*, Laura Kramer Fisher Library, 200 N Michigan Ave, Ste 407, 60601. SAN 375-2046. Tel: 312-726-8480. FAX: 312-726-7216. E-mail: librarian@icsw.edu. Web Site: icsw.edu. *Librn,* Steven Olderr; Staff 2 (MLS 1, Non-MLS 1)
Founded 1981. Enrl 100; Fac 75; Highest Degree: Doctorate
Library Holdings: Bk Vols 1,829; Per Subs 57
Special Collections: Faculty Publications; Student Dissertations
Subject Interests: Psychoanalysis, Psychol
Automation Activity & Vendor Info: (Cataloging) JayWil Software Development, Inc
Database Vendor: EBSCOhost, OCLC FirstSearch, ProQuest
Mem of Reaching Across Illinois Library System (RAILS)

S INSTITUTE FOR PSYCHOANALYSIS*, McLean Library, 122 S Michigan Ave, Ste 1300, 60603-6107. SAN 320-3719. Tel: 312-922-7474. FAX: 312-922-5656. Web Site: www.chicagoanalysis.org. *Dir, Libr Serv,* Scot Ausborn; Staff 1 (MLS 1)
Founded 1932
Library Holdings: Bk Titles 14,000; Per Subs 45
Special Collections: Gitelson Film Library Coll; Institute Archives; Kohut Archives
Subject Interests: Psychoanalysis
Wireless access
Restriction: Open to fac, students & qualified researchers

C INTERNATIONAL ACADEMY OF DESIGN & TECHNOLOGY*, Chicago Library, One N State St, Ste 526, 60602. SAN 375-5339. Tel: 312-980-9241. FAX: 312-960-1499. Web Site: www.iadtchicago.com. *Dir, Educ Res,* Alice McNeil; Staff 2 (MLS 1, Non-MLS 1)
Founded 1990. Enrl 900; Fac 40; Highest Degree: Bachelor
Library Holdings: Bk Titles 9,500; Per Subs 90
Subject Interests: Advertising, Archit, Art, Computer graphics, Design, Fashion, Interior design
Database Vendor: EBSCOhost, OCLC FirstSearch, ProQuest
Wireless access
Function: Ref serv available
Mem of Reaching Across Illinois Library System (RAILS)
Open Mon-Thurs 8:30am-9pm, Fri & Sat 9-5

M INTERNATIONAL MUSEUM OF SURGICAL SCIENCE LIBRARY*, 1524 N Lake Shore Dr, 60610. SAN 303-9269. Tel: 312-642-6502. FAX: 312-642-9516. E-mail: info@imss.org. *Curator,* Lindsey Thieman
Founded 1956
Library Holdings: Bk Vols 7,000
Subject Interests: Dentistry, Hist, Med, Surgery
Wireless access
Function: Archival coll, For res purposes
Restriction: Non-circulating to the pub, Open by appt only

L JENNER & BLOCK LIBRARY, 353 N Clark St, Ste 4300, 60654. SAN 303-9323. Tel: 312-222-9350. FAX: 312-527-0484. *Dir,* Mitchell Klaich; *Ref,* Mary Ruddy; *Res,* Jacqueline Norton; *Res,* Paul Ramonas; Staff 3 (MLS 3)
Founded 1914
Library Holdings: Bk Vols 35,000
Subject Interests: Law
Partic in Illinois Library & Information Network; Westlaw
Open Mon-Fri 8:45-5

L JONES DAY*, Law Library, 77 W Wacker Dr, Ste 3500, 60601-1692. SAN 371-8611. Tel: 312-782-3939. FAX: 312-782-8585. Web Site: www.jonesday.com. *Librn,* Sandy Jacobson; Tel: 312-269-4128, E-mail: sjacobson@jonesday.com; Staff 3 (MLS 2, Non-MLS 1)
Restriction: Private libr

L K&L GATES LLP*, 70 W Madison, Ste 3100, 60602-4207. SAN 376-1320. Tel: 312-372-1121. FAX: 312-827-8000. Web Site: www.klgates.com. *Libr Mgr,* James Wiederkehr; E-mail: james.wiederkehr@klgates.com
Library Holdings: Bk Titles 3,500; Bk Vols 30,000
Automation Activity & Vendor Info: (Cataloging) SirsiDynix
Restriction: Staff use only

L KATTEN, MUCHIN, ROSENMAN LLP LIBRARY*, 525 W Monroe St, Ste 1900, 60661-3693. SAN 321-3994. Tel: 312-902-5675. Interlibrary Loan Service Tel: 312-577-8170. Interlibrary Loan Service FAX: 312-902-1061. *Dir, Libr & Res Serv,* Deborah L Rusin; Staff 8 (MLS 5, Non-MLS 3)
Founded 1974
Library Holdings: Bk Vols 26,000; Per Subs 350
Automation Activity & Vendor Info: (Acquisitions) EOS International; (Cataloging) EOS International; (Circulation) EOS International; (OPAC) EOS International; (Serials) EOS International
Wireless access
Mem of Reaching Across Illinois Library System (RAILS)
Partic in OCLC Online Computer Library Center, Inc

C KENDALL COLLEGE LIBRARY*, 900 N North Branch St, 6th Flr, Rm 620, 60642. SAN 304-1778. Tel: 312-752-2530. FAX: 312-752-2541. Web Site: www.kendall.edu. *Dir,* Iva M Freeman; E-mail: ifreeman@kendall.edu; *Tech Serv Mgr,* Alexis Zanis; Tel: 312-752-2532, E-mail: azanis@kendall.edu; Staff 1.5 (MLS 1.5)
Founded 1934. Enrl 2,700; Fac 50; Highest Degree: Bachelor
Library Holdings: Bk Titles 32,800; Per Subs 210
Subject Interests: Bus, Culinary, Early childhood, Hospitality
Automation Activity & Vendor Info: (ILL) Ex Libris Group
Database Vendor: CQ Press, EBSCOhost, LexisNexis, OCLC FirstSearch, OCLC WorldShare Interlibrary Loan
Wireless access
Function: Computers for patron use, Copy machines, e-mail & chat, Electronic databases & coll, Fax serv, Free DVD rentals, Handicapped accessible, ILL available, Mail & tel request accepted, Online cat, Online ref, Online searches, Photocopying/Printing, Ref serv available, Ref serv in person, Scanner, Telephone ref, VHS videos, Web-catalog, Wheelchair accessible
Mem of Reaching Across Illinois Library System (RAILS)
Partic in Consortium of Academic & Research Libraries in Illinois; LIBRAS, Inc; OCLC Online Computer Library Center, Inc
Open Mon-Thurs 8-7, Fri 8-5, Sat 9-4
Restriction: External users must contact libr

L KIRKLAND & ELLIS LLP LIBRARY*, 300 N LaSalle St, 11th Flr, 60654. SAN 303-9412. Tel: 312-862-2358. Interlibrary Loan Service Tel: 312-862-3208. FAX: 312-862-2200. *Sr Dir for Libr Serv,* Joan Batchen; Tel: 312-862-2399; *Res,* Steve Abelson; Tel: 312-862-3246; *Res,* Brenda Burton; Tel: 312-862-3270; *Res,* Ken Desjardins; *Res,* Mary Eggert; Tel: 312-862-3851; *Res,* Mary Kamaraczewski; Tel: 312-862-6528; *Res,* Nancy McQueeny; *Res,* Renita Miller; *Res,* Clara Mosquera; Tel: 312-862-3189; *Res,* Carrie Pollack; Tel: 312-862-2305; *Res,* Anne Waldron; Tel: 312-862-2346; *Res,* Mindy Welch; Tel: 312-862-2492; Staff 14 (MLS 9, Non-MLS 5)
Founded 1918
Wireless access

S KORN FERRY INTERNATIONAL*, Research Library, 233 S Wacker Dr, Ste 3300, 60606. SAN 375-8117. Tel: 312-466-1834. FAX: 312-466-0451. *Dir, Res,* Janine Amilowski
Library Holdings: Bk Titles 300; Per Subs 64

S KPMG LLP LIBRARY*, 303 E Wacker Dr, 60601. SAN 372-4115. Tel: 312-665-5386. FAX: 312-665-6000. Web Site: www.kpmg.com. *Librn,* Pam Ragsdale; Staff 3 (MLS 2, Non-MLS 1)
Library Holdings: Bk Titles 75
Subject Interests: Tax law
Automation Activity & Vendor Info: (Cataloging) Sydney; (Serials) Sydney

L LATHAM & WATKINS*, Law Library, Sears Tower, 233 S Wacker Dr, Ste 5800, 60606. SAN 371-4071. Tel: 312-876-7700. Interlibrary Loan Service Tel: 312-993-2620. Reference Tel: 312-876-7710. FAX: 312-993-9767. Web Site: www.lw.com. *Ref Serv,* Deborah Rusin; Staff 4 (MLS 3, Non-MLS 1)
Library Holdings: Bk Vols 12,000; Per Subs 142
Open Mon-Fri 9-5

L LEGAL ASSISTANCE FOUNDATION OF METROPOLITAN CHICAGO LIBRARY*, 111 W Jackson, 3rd Flr, 60604. SAN 320-1775. Tel: 312-341-1070, Ext 8337. FAX: 312-341-1041. Web Site: www.lafchicago.org. *Librn,* Gail Tinney
Founded 1974
Library Holdings: Bk Titles 13,000; Bk Vols 18,000; Per Subs 160
Mem of Reaching Across Illinois Library System (RAILS)
Partic in Illinois Library & Information Network
Open Wed & Fri 9am-11am

C LEXINGTON COLLEGE LIBRARY*, 310 S Peoria, 60607. Tel: 312-226-6294. FAX: 312-226-6405. E-mail: library@lexingtoncollege.edu. Web Site: www.lexingtoncollege.edu.
Enrl 70; Fac 15; Highest Degree: Bachelor
Library Holdings: CDs 30; DVDs 25; Bk Titles 3,800; Per Subs 25; Videos 10
Subject Interests: Culinary, Events planning, Hospitality mgt
Database Vendor: EBSCOhost, OCLC FirstSearch, OCLC WorldShare Interlibrary Loan
Wireless access
Function: Online searches
Open Mon-Fri 8-4:30
Restriction: Open to students, fac & staff, Pub use on premises

CM LIBRARY OF RUSH UNIVERSITY MEDICAL CENTER*, Armour Academic Ctr, 600 S Paulina St, 5th Flr, 60612-3874. SAN 340-2304. Tel: 312-942-5950. Interlibrary Loan Service Tel: 312-942-5219. Reference Tel: 312-942-5220. FAX: 312-942-3143. E-mail: lib_ref@rush.edu. Web Site: www.lib.rush.edu/library. *Dir,* Christine D Frank; Tel: 312-942-8735, E-mail: christine_frank@rush.edu; *Asst Dir, Content Mgt,* Sandra Wenner; Tel: 312-942-2282, E-mail: sandra_wenner@rush.edu; *Asst Dir, Libr Tech,* Bill Fleming; Tel: 312-942-6832, Fax: 312-942-2234, E-mail: bill_fleming@rush.edu; *Asst Dir, Pub Serv,* Linda Ronan; Tel: 312-942-2280, E-mail: linda_ronan@rush.edu; *Archivist, Librn,* Heather Stecklein; Tel: 312-942-7214, Fax: 312-942-3342, E-mail: heather_j_stecklein@rush.edu; *Asst Archivist, Librn,* Nathalie Wheaton; Tel: 312-942-6358, Fax: 312-942-3342, E-mail: nathalie_wheaton@rush.edu; *Online Searching & Outreach Coordr, Ref Librn,* Jeanne Link; Tel: 312-942-6784, E-mail: jeanne_link@rush.edu; *Educ Coordr, Ref Librn,* Jonna Peterson; Tel: 312-942-2274, E-mail: jonna_peterson@rush.edu; *Cat/Archives Mgr,* Judith Dzierba; Tel: 312-942-2731, E-mail: judith_l_dzierba@rush.edu; *Circ Serv Mgr,* Toby Gibson; Tel: 312-942-2279, E-mail: toby_gibson@rush.edu; *Tech Serv Mgr,* Phillip Adrian; Tel: 312-942-2276, E-mail: phil_v_adrian@rush.edu; *Electronic Serv Coordr,* Ann Goliak; Tel: 312-942-8558, E-mail: ann_m_goliak@rush.edu; Staff 15 (MLS 12, Non-MLS 3)
Founded 1899. Enrl 1,800; Highest Degree: Doctorate
Special Collections: Imprints
Subject Interests: Health sci
Database Vendor: EBSCOhost, OCLC FirstSearch, OVID Technologies
Publications: InfoLINE
Partic in Docline; Greater Midwest Regional Medical Libr Network; OCLC Online Computer Library Center, Inc; Serials of Illinois Libraries Online (SILO)
Open Mon-Thurs 7am-Midnight, Fri 7am-8pm, Sat 9-6, Sun 1pm-Midnight

S LITHUANIAN RESEARCH & STUDIES CENTER, INC*, 5600 S Claremont Ave, 60636-1039. SAN 325-2728. Tel: 773-434-4545. FAX: 773-434-9363. E-mail: info@lithuanianresearch.org. Web Site: www.lithuanianresearch.org. *Pres,* Dr John A Rackauskas; *VPres,* Dr Robertas Vitas; *Dir, Archives,* Skirmante Miglinas; E-mail: miglinas@lithuanianresearch.org; *Head, Per,* Kristina Lapienyte-Bareikiene; Staff 10 (MLS 3, Non-MLS 7)
Founded 1982
Library Holdings: Bk Titles 146,000; Bk Vols 182,000; Per Subs 1,600
Special Collections: Cartography Dept; Dainauskas History Library; Krupavicius Coll; Lithuanian Historical Society; Lithuanian Institute of Education; Marian Fathers Coll; Pakstas Coll; Rare Book Coll; World Lithuanian Archives; World Lithuanian Community Coll; Zilevicius-Kreivenas Lithuanian Musicology Archive
Subject Interests: Costume, Culture, Customs, Dance, Economy, Educ, Folklore, Geog, Hist, Immigration, Lit, Lithuanian, Lithuanian-Am Art, Mil, Music, Politics, Sports, Traditions
Open Mon-Fri 11-5

L LOCKE LORD BISSELL & LIDDELL LLP*, Law Library, 111 S Wacker Dr, 60606. SAN 303-951X. Tel: 312-443-0646. FAX: 312-443-0336. *Dir,* Sandra Gold; Staff 8 (MLS 4, Non-MLS 4)
Library Holdings: Bk Vols 10,000
Partic in Illinois Library & Information Network

CR LOYOLA UNIVERSITY CHICAGO LIBRARIES, 1032 W Sheridan Rd, 60660. SAN 340-143X. Tel: 773-508-2641. Circulation Tel: 773-508-2632. Interlibrary Loan Service Tel: 773-508-6022. Reference Tel: 773-508-2654. E-mail: cud-ref@luc.edu. Web Site: libraries.luc.edu. *Dean of Libr,* Robert Seal; E-mail: rseal@luc.edu; *Asst Dean, Libr Serv & Coll,* Fred Barnhart; Tel: 773-508-2620, E-mail: fbarnha@luc.edu; *Asst Dean, Tech Serv &*

Planning, Anne Reuland; Tel: 773-508-2674, E-mail: areuland@luc.edu; Staff 63 (MLS 28, Non-MLS 35)
Founded 1870. Enrl 14,649; Fac 885; Highest Degree: Doctorate
Library Holdings: AV Mats 12,862; e-books 565,308; e-journals 52,963; Microforms 1,403,552; Bk Vols 1,854,100
Special Collections: Jesuitica; Paul Claudel Coll; Women & Leadership Archives. Oral History; State Document Depository; US Document Depository
Automation Activity & Vendor Info: (Acquisitions) Ex Libris Group; (Cataloging) Ex Libris Group; (Circulation) Ex Libris Group; (Course Reserve) Ex Libris Group; (Media Booking) Ex Libris Group; (OPAC) Ex Libris Group; (Serials) Ex Libris Group
Database Vendor: ABC-CLIO, ACM (Association for Computing Machinery), Agricola, Alexander Street Press, American Chemical Society, American Mathematical Society, American Psychological Association (APA), Annual Reviews, ARTstor, Atlas Systems, Bowker, Cinahl, CIOS (Communication Institute for Online Scholarship), CQ Press, CRC Press/Taylor & Francis Group, ebrary, EBSCOhost, Elsevier, Emerald, Ex Libris Group, Factiva.com, Foundation Center, Gale Cengage Learning, HeinOnline, IBISWorld, IEEE (Institute of Electrical & Electronics Engineers), ISI Web of Knowledge, JSTOR, LexisNexis, McGraw-Hill, Medline, Mergent Online, Modern Language Association, Nature Publishing Group, Newsbank, Newsbank-Readex, OCLC, OVID Technologies, Oxford Online, Project MUSE, ProQuest, PubMed, RefWorks, Safari Books Online, Sage, SBRnet (Sports Business Research Network), ScienceDirect, SerialsSolutions, Springer-Verlag, Springshare, LLC, Standard & Poor's, UpToDate, ValueLine, Wiley, Wiley InterScience, YBP Library Services
Wireless access
Partic in Association of Jesuit Colleges & Universities (AJCU); Chicago Area Theological Libr Asn; Chicago Collections Consortium; Illinois Library & Information Network
Restriction: Limited access for the pub
Friends of the Library Group

Departmental Libraries:

ELIZABETH M CUDAHY MEMORIAL LIBRARY, 6525 N Sheridan Rd, 60626, SAN 340-1464. Circulation Tel: 773-508-2632. Interlibrary Loan Service Tel: 773-508-6022. Reference Tel: 773-508-2654. Circulation FAX: 773-508-2993. Web Site: libraries.luc.edu/about/cudahy.htm. *Dean of Libr,* Robert Seal, Tel: 773-508-2641, E-mail: rseal@luc.edu; *Head, Access Serv,* Ursula Scholz; Tel: 773-508-2636, E-mail: uscholz@luc.edu
Library Holdings: Bk Titles 654,824; Bk Vols 912,292
Subject Interests: Arts, Humanities, Sciences, Soc sci
Special Services for the Deaf - Assistive tech
Special Services for the Blind - Assistive/Adapted tech devices, equip & products
Open Mon-Thurs 8am-10pm, Fri 8-5, Sat 12-5, Sun 12-8
Friends of the Library Group

CM HEALTH SCIENCES LIBRARY, Bldg 125, Rm 1526, 2160 S First Ave, Maywood, 60153-5585, SAN 340-1529. Tel: 708-216-9192. Interlibrary Loan Service Tel: 708-216-5308. Reference Tel: 708-216-9193. Administration Tel: 708-216-5301. FAX: 708-216-8115. Administration FAX: 708-216-6772. E-mail: hsl@luc.edu. Web Site: library.luhs.org/hslibrary/index.htm. *Libr Dir,* Gail Y Hendler; Tel: 708-216-5303, E-mail: ghendler@luc.edu; *Assoc Dir,* Jeanne Sadlik; Tel: 708-216-5304, E-mail: jsadlik@luc.edu; *Head, Coll Mgt,* Jean Gudenas; Tel: 708-216-4368, E-mail: jgudenas@luc.edu; *Info & Access Serv Librn,* Donald Nagolski; E-mail: dnagols@luc.edu; *Metadata & Discovery Librn,* Mackenzie Brooks; Tel: 708-216-3712, E-mail: mabrooks@luc.edu; Staff 25 (MLS 8, Non-MLS 17)
Enrl 627; Fac 1,642; Highest Degree: Doctorate
Library Holdings: AV Mats 6,789; e-books 172; e-journals 1,487; Electronic Media & Resources 7,432; Bk Titles 40,382; Bk Vols 198,189; Per Subs 4,943
Special Collections: History of Medicine
Subject Interests: Health sci, Med, Nursing
Automation Activity & Vendor Info: (Cataloging) Ex Libris Group; (Circulation) Ex Libris Group; (Course Reserve) Ex Libris Group; (ILL) Ex Libris Group; (OPAC) Ex Libris Group; (Serials) Ex Libris Group
Database Vendor: EBSCOhost, OVID Technologies
Partic in National Network of Libraries of Medicine
Publications: Circulation Manual; Collection Development Manual; Interlibrary Loan Manual
Open Mon-Thurs 8:30-7, Fri 8:30-5

CL LAW SCHOOL LIBRARY, 25 E Pearson St, 3rd Flr, 60611, SAN 340-1553. Tel: 312-915-7131, 312-915-7200, 312-915-7202. Circulation Tel: 312-915-6986. Interlibrary Loan Service Tel: 312-915-7198. Reference Tel: 312-915-7205. FAX: 312-915-6797. E-mail: law-library@luc.edu. Web Site: www.luc.edu/law_library. *Dir,* Julia Wentz; Tel: 312-915-7199, E-mail: jwentz@luc.edu; *Dir, Law Tech,* Mike Lonero; Tel: 315-915-7313, E-mail: mlonero@luc.edu; *Asst Dir, Access Serv,* Charles Fischer; E-mail: cfischer@luc.edu; *Asst Dir, Acq, Asst Dir, Cat, Asst Dir, Ser,* Carol Klink; E-mail: cklink@luc.edu; *Asst Dir, Res & Educ,* Patricia Scott; Tel: 312-915-8515, E-mail: pscott2@luc.edu; *Head, Coll Develop, Head, Fac Serv,* C Frederick LeBaron; Tel: 312-918-6842, E-mail: flebaro@luc.edu; *Electronic Serv/Ref Librn,* Joe Mitzenmacher; Tel: 312-915-6844, E-mail: jmitze1@luc.edu; *Foreign & Intl Law Librn,* Julienne Grant; Tel: 312-915-8520, E-mail: jgrant6@luc.edu; *Ref Librn,* Deborah Darin; *Ref Librn,* Nan Norton; Tel: 312-915-8517, E-mail: nnorton@luc.edu; *Cataloger,* Pam Cipkowski; Tel: 312-915-7191, E-mail: ccipkowski@luc.edu; Staff 16 (MLS 9, Non-MLS 7)
Founded 1909. Enrl 773; Fac 41; Highest Degree: Master
Library Holdings: Bk Titles 61,640; Bk Vols 180,732; Per Subs 1,313
Special Collections: GPO Depository; Medical Jurisprudence; Child Law. US Document Depository
Subject Interests: Antitrust law
Automation Activity & Vendor Info: (ILL) OCLC
Function: ILL available
Partic in Chicago Legal Acad Syst; Illinois Library & Information Network; Jesuit Law Libr Consortium
Mem of Reaching Across Illinois Library System (RAILS)
Open Mon-Thurs 8am-Midnight, Fri 8am-9pm, Sat 9-9, Sun Noon-Midnight
Restriction: Circ limited
Friends of the Library Group

LEWIS LIBRARY, 25 E Pearson St, 6th Flr, 60611, SAN 340-1499. Tel: 312-915-6625. Reference Tel: 312-915-6631. FAX: 312-915-6637. *Head of Libr,* Yolande Wersching; Tel: 312-915-6623, E-mail: ywersch@luc.edu
Subject Interests: Bus, Communication, Criminal justice, Econ, Educ, Soc work
Open Mon-Thurs 7:30am-Midnight, Fri 7:30am-9pm, Sat 9-9, Sun Noon-Midnight

M ANN & ROBERT H LURIE CHILDREN'S HOSPITAL OF CHICAGO*, Health Sciences Library, 225 E Chicago Ave, Box 12, 60611-2605. SAN 303-8599. Tel: 312-227-4707. Interlibrary Loan Service Tel: 312-227-4706. FAX: 312-227-9707. E-mail: healthsciencelibrary@luriechildrens.org. Web Site: www.luriechildrens.org. *Ref Librn,* Carol Ann Jeuell. Subject Specialists: *Pediatrics,* Carol Ann Jeuell; Staff 2 (MLS 1, Non-MLS 1)
Founded 1935
Library Holdings: e-journals 3,000; Bk Vols 600; Per Subs 50
Subject Interests: Adolescent psychol, Child psychology, Pediatrics
Automation Activity & Vendor Info: (Acquisitions) Ex Libris Group; (Cataloging) Ex Libris Group; (Circulation) Ex Libris Group; (OPAC) Ex Libris Group; (Serials) Ex Libris Group
Database Vendor: EBSCOhost, Ex Libris Group, ISI Web of Knowledge, JSTOR, MD Consult, Medline, Natural Standard, OCLC FirstSearch, OCLC WorldShare Interlibrary Loan, OVID Technologies, ProQuest, PubMed, ScienceDirect
Wireless access
Function: Computer training, Computers for patron use, Copy machines, e-mail serv, Health sci info serv, ILL available, Online cat, Online searches, Ref & res, Ref serv available, Ref serv in person, VHS videos, Web-catalog
Mem of Reaching Across Illinois Library System (RAILS)
Partic in Illinois Library & Information Network; Medical Library Association (MLA); National Network of Libraries of Medicine Greater Midwest Region; OCLC Online Computer Library Center, Inc
Restriction: Authorized personnel only

R LUTHERAN SCHOOL OF THEOLOGY AT CHICAGO & MCCORMICK THEOLOGICAL SEMINARY*, JKM Library, 1100 E 55th St, 60615-5199. SAN 303-9331. Tel: 773-256-0739. Reference Tel: 773-256-0703. FAX: 773-256-0737. E-mail: refdesk@jkmlibrary.org. Web Site: www.jkmlibrary.org. *Dir,* Dr Christine Wenderoth; Tel: 773-256-0735, E-mail: cwenderoth@jkmlibrary.org; *Spec Projects Librn,* Emilie Pulver; Tel: 773-256-0730, E-mail: epulver@jkmlibrary.org; *Assoc Librn, Pub Serv,* Barry C Hopkins; Tel: 773-256-0738, E-mail: bhopkins@jkmlibrary.org; *Mgr, Access Serv,* Elaine D Bonner; Tel: 773-256-0732, E-mail: ebonner@jkmlibrary.org; *Cataloger,* William Beermann; Tel: 773-256-0736, E-mail: wbeermann@jkmlibrary.org; Staff 6 (MLS 4, Non-MLS 2)
Founded 1975. Enrl 547; Fac 36; Highest Degree: Doctorate
Jul 2011-Jun 2012 Income $9,223,030. Mats Exp $917,002, Books $31,902, Per/Ser (Incl. Access Fees) $42,861, AV Mat $254, Electronic Ref Mat (Incl. Access Fees) $12,412, Presv $2,438. Sal $443,731 (Prof $406,345)
Library Holdings: CDs 643; DVDs 880; Electronic Media & Resources 25; Microforms 118,625; Bk Vols 307,640; Per Subs 454
Special Collections: Reformation Imprints (L Franklin Gruber Coll)
Subject Interests: Biblical studies, Lutheranism, Ministry, Reformation hist, Reformed theol, Theol
Automation Activity & Vendor Info: (Acquisitions) Horizon; (Cataloging) Horizon; (Circulation) Horizon; (OPAC) Horizon; (Serials) Horizon
Database Vendor: 3M Library Systems, EBSCOhost, JSTOR, OCLC FirstSearch, Oxford Online, SirsiDynix
Wireless access
Function: Res libr

Partic in Association of Chicago Theological Schools; Consortium of Academic & Research Libraries in Illinois; Illinois Library & Information Network; OCLC Online Computer Library Center, Inc
Open Mon-Thurs 8:30am-9pm, Fri 8:30-4:30, Sat 12-4:30, Sun 5-9
Restriction: Photo ID required for access

S JOHN D & CATHERINE T MACARTHUR FOUNDATION LIBRARY*, 140 S Dearborn St, Ste 1200, 60603-5285. SAN 375-8281. Tel: 312-726-8000. FAX: 312-920-6259. TDD: 312-920-6285. Web Site: www.macfound.org. *Sr Info Spec,* Elizabeth Quinlan
Library Holdings: Bk Titles 5,000; Per Subs 200
Restriction: Private libr

J MACCORMAC COLLEGE LIBRARY*, Borchardt Learning Center, 29 E Madison, 2nd Flr, 60602-4405. SAN 303-9552. Tel: 312-922-1884, Ext 215. FAX: 312-377-7572. Web Site: www.maccormac.edu/library. *Dir,* Greg Pekala; E-mail: gpekala@maccormac.edu; Staff 3 (Non-MLS 3)
Founded 1904. Enrl 400; Highest Degree: Associate
Library Holdings: AV Mats 105; High Interest/Low Vocabulary Bk Vols 30; Bk Vols 4,000; Per Subs 54
Subject Interests: Bus, Econ, Law
Database Vendor: EBSCOhost, OCLC FirstSearch
Mem of Reaching Across Illinois Library System (RAILS)
Partic in Illinois Library & Information Network
Open Mon-Thurs 9-7, Fri 9-6

J MALCOLM X COLLEGE LIBRARY*, Carter G Woodson Library, City Colleges of Chicago, 1900 W Van Buren St, 60612. SAN 303-9609. Tel: 312-850-7253. Reference Tel: 312-850-7244. FAX: 312-850-7249. E-mail: mxc-library@ccc.edu. Web Site: library.ccc.edu, malcolmx.ccc.edu/library. *Chairperson,* CM! Winters- Palacio; E-mail: cwinterspalacio@ccc.edu; Staff 3 (MLS 2, Non-MLS 1)
Founded 1934. Enrl 5,154; Highest Degree: Associate
Library Holdings: Bk Titles 50,134; Per Subs 450
Automation Activity & Vendor Info: (Acquisitions) Innovative Interfaces, Inc
Open Mon-Thurs 8-9, Fri 8-4
Restriction: Borrowing privileges limited to anthropology fac & libr staff

L THE JOHN MARSHALL LAW SCHOOL*, Louis L Biro Law Library, 315 S Plymouth Ct, 60604. SAN 303-9358. Tel: 312-427-2737. Circulation Tel: 312-427-2737, Ext 710. Reference Tel: 312-427-2737, Ext 729. FAX: 312-427-8307. Web Site: www.jmls.edu. *Dir,* June Liebert; *Asst Dir, Acad Tech,* Jessica Wittman; *Assoc Dir, Access & Organization,* Gwen Gregory; *Assoc Dir, Res & Instruction,* Claire Toomey Durkin; E-mail: 8durkin@jmls.edu; *Head, Access Serv,* Ramsey Donnell; *Head, Cat,* Liping Qin; *Evening Ref Librn,* Victor Salas; *Foreign & Intl Law Librn,* Anne Abramson; *Instrul Serv Librn,* Thomas Keefe; *Res Serv Librn,* Raizel Liebler; *Student Serv Librn,* Jamie Sommer; Staff 16 (MLS 8, Non-MLS 8)
Founded 1899. Enrl 1,600; Fac 60; Highest Degree: Doctorate
Library Holdings: Bk Titles 92,935; Bk Vols 392,150; Per Subs 6,047
Special Collections: CCH Tax Library Coll, ultrafiche; Chicago Bar Association Core Coll; IHS Legislative Histories; Illinois Appellate Court Unpublished Opinions; Illinois Supreme Court Briefs; National Reporter System Coll, First Series, ultrafiche; United States Circuit Court of Appeals 7th Circuit Briefs; United States Congressional Publications, 1970-date, micro; United States Supreme Court Records & Briefs, 1930-date. US Document Depository
Subject Interests: Anglo-Am law
Database Vendor: Checkpoint Systems, Inc, Gale Cengage Learning, HeinOnline, Innovative Interfaces, Inc, LexisNexis, OCLC FirstSearch, OCLC WorldShare Interlibrary Loan, Westlaw
Wireless access
Publications: The John Marshall Law School Publication Series
Partic in Chicago Legal Acad Syst; Illinois Library & Information Network; OCLC Online Computer Library Center, Inc
Open Mon-Thurs 8am-11pm, Fri 8-8, Sat 9-8, Sun 9am-10pm

L MAYER BROWN LLP*, Law Library, 71 S Wacker Dr, 60606. SAN 303-9668. Tel: 312-782-0600. FAX: 312-701-7711. Web Site: www.mayerbrown.com. *Libr Serv Mgr,* Bobby Towns
Mem of Reaching Across Illinois Library System (RAILS)
Partic in Dialog Corp; Westlaw

L MCDERMOTT, WILL & EMERY LAW LIBRARY*, 227 W Monroe St, 46th Flr, 60606-5096. SAN 303-9587. Tel: 312-984-7650. FAX: 312-984-2094. *Mgr,* Jerry Trenholm; Tel: 312-984-3289, E-mail: jtrenholm@mwe.com
Library Holdings: Bk Titles 60,000; Per Subs 500
Partic in Illinois Library & Information Network

CR MEADVILLE-LOMBARD THEOLOGICAL SCHOOL LIBRARY*, 610 S Michigan Ave, 60605. SAN 303-9684. Tel: 312-546-6483. Reference Tel: 312-546-0629. Web Site: www.meadville.edu. *Dean of Libr,* Dr Neil W Gerdes; E-mail: ngerdes@meadville.edu; *Asst Librn,* Eric Biddy; Tel: 312-546-6488, E-mail: ebiddy@meadville.edu; *Archivist,* John Leeker; E-mail: jleeker@meadville.edu; Staff 3 (MLS 2, Non-MLS 1)
Founded 1844. Enrl 122; Fac 7; Highest Degree: Doctorate
Jul 2005-Jun 2006 Income $157,602
Library Holdings: Bk Titles 112,000; Per Subs 130
Special Collections: English Philosophy; Ethics & Society; Unitarian-Universalist History & Liberal Religion; World Religion
Partic in Association of Chicago Theological Schools; Illinois Library & Information Network; OCLC Online Computer Library Center, Inc
Open Mon-Fri 9-5

M MERCY HOSPITAL & MEDICAL CENTER*, Medical Library, 2525 S Michigan Ave, 60616-2477. SAN 303-9706. Tel: 312-567-2363. FAX: 312-567-7086. *Librn,* Timothy Oh; *Asst Librn,* Marillyn Encarnado; Staff 1 (MLS 1)
Founded 1950
Library Holdings: e-journals 400; Bk Titles 4,000; Bk Vols 11,000
Special Collections: John B Murphy, MD Coll
Mem of Reaching Across Illinois Library System (RAILS)
Partic in Greater Midwest Regional Medical Libr Network; Medical Library Association (MLA); Midwest Health Sci Libr Network
Friends of the Library Group

G METROPOLITAN WATER RECLAMATION DISTRICT OF GREATER CHICAGO LIBRARY*, 100 E Erie St, 60611. SAN 303-9722. Tel: 312-751-6658, 312-751-6659. FAX: 312-751-6635. Web Site: www.mwrd.org. *Librn,* Gerald Austiff; E-mail: gerald.austiff@mwrd.org; Staff 2 (MLS 1, Non-MLS 1)
Founded 1966
Library Holdings: Bk Titles 3,000
Special Collections: Archives; Internal Reports & Proceedings of Metropolitan Sanitary District & Predecessors
Subject Interests: Environ studies
Partic in Ill Regional Libr Coun

S MONTGOMERY WATSON HARZA LIBRARY*, 175 W Jackson Blvd, 60604. SAN 329-8612. Tel: 312-831-3397. FAX: 312-831-3999. *Librn,* Lorraine Potrykus
Library Holdings: Bk Titles 10,000; Per Subs 100
Subject Interests: Eng
Open Mon-Fri 8-5

CR MOODY BIBLE INSTITUTE*, Crowell Library, 820 N La Salle Blvd, 60610-3284. SAN 340-1618. Tel: 312-329-4136. Interlibrary Loan Service Tel: 312-329-4078. Reference Tel: 312-329-4138. Administration Tel: 312-329-4140. Information Services Tel: 312-329-4175. Toll Free Tel: 800-356-6639. FAX: 312-329-8959. E-mail: library@moody.edu. Web Site: library.moody.edu. *Dir,* James Preston; E-mail: james.preston@moody.edu; *Head Librn, Pub Serv,* Christopher Ullman; *Cat Librn,* Susan Ruffolo. Subject Specialists: *Theol,* James Preston; Staff 7 (MLS 4, Non-MLS 3)
Founded 1889. Enrl 2,022; Fac 90; Highest Degree: Master
Library Holdings: Bks on Deafness & Sign Lang 27; Braille Volumes 128; CDs 11,428; DVDs 635; e-books 1,977; e-journals 16,025; Electronic Media & Resources 63; Large Print Bks 47; Music Scores 5,733; Bk Titles 121,450; Bk Vols 170,890; Per Subs 349; Videos 4,063
Special Collections: Curriculum Lab; Juvenile; D L Moody (Moodyana Coll), artifacts & bks; Moody Bible Institute Archives, docs, letters, newsp & photos
Subject Interests: Relig
Automation Activity & Vendor Info: (Acquisitions) OCLC; (Cataloging) SirsiDynix; (Circulation) SirsiDynix; (Course Reserve) SirsiDynix; (ILL) OCLC; (OPAC) SirsiDynix; (Serials) SirsiDynix
Database Vendor: ebrary, EBSCOhost, Electric Library, OCLC FirstSearch, OCLC WorldShare Interlibrary Loan, OVID Technologies, ProQuest, SirsiDynix, Wilson - Wilson Web
Wireless access
Function: Archival coll, Copy machines, ILL available, Online ref, Photocopying/Printing, Ref serv available
Mem of Reaching Across Illinois Library System (RAILS)
Partic in Asn of Christian Librs; Consortium of Academic & Research Libraries in Illinois; Illinois Library & Information Network; OCLC Online Computer Library Center, Inc
Special Services for the Blind - Braille bks
Open Mon-Sat 7:30am-Midnight
Restriction: Photo ID required for access, Restricted pub use

M MOUNT SINAI HOSPITAL MEDICAL CENTER*, Lewison Memorial Library, California Ave at 15th St, 60608. SAN 340-1677. Tel: 773-257-6240. FAX: 773-257-6135. *Librn,* Estella B Escudero; Tel: 773-257-6558, E-mail: esce@sinai.org; *ILL,* Merly M Arceo
Founded 1942
Library Holdings: Bk Vols 3,000; Per Subs 268
Subject Interests: Med, Nursing

S MURPHY-JAHN LIBRARY*, 35 E Wacker Dr, 60601. SAN 373-045X. Tel: 312-427-7300. FAX: 312-332-0274. *In Charge,* Joseph A Stypka
Library Holdings: CDs 430; DVDs 4; Bk Titles 20,000; Per Subs 210; Spec Interest Per Sub 210
Special Collections: Stone Samples
Subject Interests: Archit, Construction, Planning

S MUSEUM OF CONTEMPORARY ART LIBRARY*, 220 E Chicago Ave, 60611-2604. SAN 303-9773. Tel: 312-280-2660. FAX: 312-397-4099. Web Site: www.mcachicago.org. *In Charge,* Lynne Warren; *Librn,* Janice Dillard; Tel: 312-397-3894; Staff 1 (Non-MLS 1)
Founded 1981
Library Holdings: Bk Vols 13,500; Per Subs 40
Special Collections: Artist & Gallery Files; Artists' books; MCA Exhibition Catalogs
Subject Interests: Art
Automation Activity & Vendor Info: (ILL) OCLC FirstSearch
Database Vendor: Cambridge Scientific Abstracts, OCLC FirstSearch
Function: Res libr
Partic in Illinois Library & Information Network; OCLC Online Computer Library Center, Inc; RLIN (Research Libraries Information Network)
Restriction: Not open to pub, Open by appt only

G NATIONAL ARCHIVES & RECORDS ADMINISTRATION*, Great Lakes Region, 7358 S Pulaski Rd, 60629-5898. Tel: 773-948-9001. FAX: 773-948-9050. E-mail: chicago.archives@nara.gov. Web Site: www.archives.gov/great-lakes/contact/archives.html. *Archivist,* Douglas Bicknese; E-mail: douglas.bicknese@nara.gov; *Archivist,* Scott M Forsythe; *Archivist,* Glenn Longacre; Staff 4 (MLS 2, Non-MLS 2)
Special Collections: Archival Records of Federal Military, Civilian Agencies & Courts in Illinois, Indiana, Michigan, Minnesota, Ohio & Wisconsin from 1800 to 1990's; Indian Affairs Records, microfilm; Passenger Arrival & Naturalization Records, microfilm; Population Censuses for All States, 1790-1930, microfilm; Pre-Federal & Early Federal History Records, microfilm; Pre-World War I Military Service Records, microfilm; US Diplomatic Records, microfilm
Subject Interests: Fed govt rec
Function: Archival coll, Computers for patron use, Copy machines, Photocopying/Printing, Pub access computers, Workshops
Open Mon-Fri 7-3
Restriction: Closed stack, Internal use only, Non-circulating, Photo ID required for access

S NATIONAL ASSOCIATION OF REALTORS, Information Central, 430 N Michigan Ave, 60611-4087. SAN 303-982X. Tel: 312-329-8200. Toll Free Tel: 800-874-6500. FAX: 312-329-8835. E-mail: infocentral@realtors.org. Web Site: www.realtor.org/library. *Dir,* John Krukoff; Staff 15 (MLS 7, Non-MLS 8)
Founded 1923
Library Holdings: CDs 50; DVDs 50; e-books 4,000; e-journals 7,300; Bk Vols 15,000; Per Subs 150; Spec Interest Per Sub 600
Special Collections: NAR historical archives
Subject Interests: Real estate
Database Vendor: Factiva.com, Hoovers, LibLime, OCLC, OCLC WorldShare Interlibrary Loan, Overdrive, Inc, ProQuest, Springshare, LLC
Wireless access
Function: 24/7 Electronic res, 24/7 Online cat, Archival coll, Audiobks via web, Bks on CD, Bus archives, CD-ROM, Doc delivery serv, e-mail & chat, Electronic databases & coll, Literacy & newcomer serv, Magazines, Mail & tel request accepted, Online cat, Online ref, OverDrive digital audio bks, Prof lending libr, Ref & res, Ref serv available, Res libr, Spanish lang bks, Wheelchair accessible
Mem of Reaching Across Illinois Library System (RAILS)
Restriction: Authorized patrons, Authorized scholars by appt, Circ to mem only, Not open to pub, Open to researchers by request

C NATIONAL LOUIS UNIVERSITY LIBRARY & LEARNING SUPPORT, 122 S Michigan Ave, 60603. SAN 340-1820. Tel: 312-261-3376. Interlibrary Loan Service Tel: 847-947-5503. Toll Free Tel: 800-443-5522, Ext 3376. FAX: 312-261-3376. Interlibrary Loan Service FAX: 847-947-5503. E-mail: library@nl.edu. Web Site: www.nl.edu/library. *Dean, Libr & Learning Support,* Position Currently Open; *Interim Dean of Libr & Learning Support,* Rob Morrison; Tel: 312-261-3372, E-mail: rob.morrison@nl.edu; *Librn,* Amy Hall; Tel: 312-261-3565, E-mail: ahall17@nl.edu; *Librn,* Sarah Leeman; Tel: 312-261-3439, E-mail: sleeman@nl.edu; Staff 18 (MLS 9, Non-MLS 9)
Founded 1920. Enrl 4,426; Fac 863; Highest Degree: Doctorate
Library Holdings: Audiobooks 574; AV Mats 3,444; e-books 79,064; e-journals 17,978; Electronic Media & Resources 74; Bk Titles 56,242; Bk Vols 89,949; Videos 4,393
Special Collections: Adult Learning Materials (Maxwell Archive); American Coll at National Louis University (Children's & Young Adult Literature by Latin American Authors, Bilingual Spanish/English Materials, Literature with Latino Themes in English); Children's Literature (Weinstein Coll); Elizabeth Harrison Early Childhood Education Archives; OASIS Digital Commons
Automation Activity & Vendor Info: (Acquisitions) Ex Libris Group; (Cataloging) Ex Libris Group; (Circulation) Ex Libris Group; (Course Reserve) Ex Libris Group; (ILL) Ex Libris Group; (Media Booking) Ex Libris Group; (OPAC) Ex Libris Group; (Serials) Ex Libris Group
Database Vendor: Baker & Taylor, ebrary, EBSCOhost, Gale Cengage Learning, Hoovers, JSTOR, LexisNexis, OCLC, OVID Technologies, ProQuest, Sage, Springshare, LLC, TumbleBookLibrary, YBP Library Services
Wireless access
Partic in Consortium of Academic & Research Libraries in Illinois

Departmental Libraries:

LISLE, 850 Warrenville Rd, Lisle, 60532, SAN 321-5695. Tel: 630-874-4530. Toll Free Tel: 800-443-5522, Ext 4530. FAX: 630-960-4530. *Librn,* Position Currently Open

NORTH SHORE, 5202 Old Orchard Rd, Skokie, 60077, SAN 340-3866. Tel: 224-233-2288. Toll Free Tel: 800-443-5522, Ext 2288. FAX: 224-233-2288. *Librn,* Chris Diaz; Tel: 224-233-2277, Fax: 224-233-2277, E-mail: cdiaz10@nl.edu; *Librn,* Carol Moulden; Tel: 224-233-2235, E-mail: cmoulden@nl.edu; *Librn,* Toby Rajput; Tel: 224-233-2515, Fax: 224-233-2515, E-mail: toby.rajput@nl.edu

WHEELING, 1000 Capitol Dr, Wheeling, 60090-7201, SAN 378-0732. Tel: 847-947-5503. Toll Free Tel: 800-443-5522, Ext 5503. FAX: 847-947-5503. *Librn,* Amy LeFager; Tel: 847-947-5335, Fax: 847-947-5335, E-mail: amy.lefager@nl.edu

S NATIONAL OPINION RESEARCH CENTER LIBRARY*, Paul B Sheatsley Library, 1155 E 60th St, Rm 281, 60637-2667. SAN 303-9854. Tel: 773-256-6206. FAX: 773-753-7886. Web Site: www.norc.org. *Librn,* Ernest Tani; E-mail: tani-ernest@norc.uchicago.edu; Staff 3 (Non-MLS 3)
Founded 1941
Library Holdings: Bk Titles 9,000
Subject Interests: Demography, Survey res
Publications: NORC Bibliography of Publications, 1941-1991 (online)

L NEAL, GERBER & EISENBERG LLP, Law Library, Two N La Salle St, Ste 1700, 60602. SAN 323-8458. Tel: 312-269-5220. Administration Tel: 312-269-8087. FAX: 312-578-1793. E-mail: library@ngelaw.com. *Chief Knowledge Officer,* Monice M Kaczorowski; E-mail: mkaczorowski@ngelaw.com; *Competitive Intelligence Analyst Ref Librn,* Julie Swanson; Tel: 312-269-3096, E-mail: jswanson@ngelaw.com; *Ref Librn,* Carolyn A Hersch; Tel: 312-269-5275, E-mail: chersch@ngelaw.com; *Tech Serv Librn,* Sara M Castillo; Tel: 312-269-5294, E-mail: scastillo@ngelaw.com; *Mgr, Ref Serv,* Diana J Koppang; Tel: 312-269-5219, E-mail: dkoppang@ngelaw.com. Subject Specialists: *Healthcare, Labor,* Monice M Kaczorowski; *Intellectual property,* Diana J Koppang; Staff 7 (MLS 5, Non-MLS 2)
Founded 1986
Library Holdings: Bk Titles 3,000; Bk Vols 40,000; Per Subs 300
Subject Interests: Labor, Securities, Tax
Automation Activity & Vendor Info: (Acquisitions) Inmagic, Inc.; (Cataloging) Inmagic, Inc.; (Circulation) Inmagic, Inc., (ILL) Inmagic, Inc.; (OPAC) Inmagic, Inc.; (Serials) Inmagic, Inc.
Database Vendor: Bloomberg, Checkpoint Systems, Inc, Dialog, Dun & Bradstreet, Foundation Center, HeinOnline, Hoovers, LexisNexis, OCLC FirstSearch, OCLC WorldShare Interlibrary Loan, OneSource, Standard & Poor's
Wireless access
Function: 24/7 Electronic res, 24/7 Online cat
Partic in Illinois Library & Information Network
Restriction: Restricted access
Friends of the Library Group

S NEWBERRY LIBRARY, 60 W Walton St, 60610-3305. SAN 303-9900. Tel: 312-943-9090. Web Site: www.newberry.org. *Librn, Pres,* David Spadafora; Tel: 312-255-3600, Fax: 312-255-3712, E-mail: spadaforad@newberry.org; *VPres, Libr Serv,* Hjordis Halvorson; Tel: 312-255-3590, E-mail: halvorsonh@newberry.org; *Dir, Coll Serv,* Alan Leopold; Tel: 312-255-3629, E-mail: leopolda@newberry.org; *Dir, Conserv Serv,* Lesa Dowd; Tel: 312-255-3549, E-mail: dowdl@newberry.org; *Dir, Digital Initiatives & Serv,* Jennifer Thom; Tel: 312-255-3536, E-mail: thomj@newberry.org; *Dir, Reader Serv,* Will Hansen; Tel: 312-255-3527, E-mail: hansenw@newberry.org; *Maps & Modern Ms,* James Akerman; Tel: 312-255-3523, E-mail: akermanj@newberry.org; *Maps & Modern Ms,* Martha Briggs; Tel: 312-255-3554, E-mail: briggsm@newberry.org; Staff 61 (MLS 24, Non-MLS 37)
Founded 1887
Library Holdings: Bk Titles 868,810; Bk Vols 1,500,000; Per Subs 721
Special Collections: American & British History (Ruggles Coll); American Indian History & Americana (Ayer Coll); Arts, Business, Chicago, Civil War, Clubs & Organizations, Dance, Am Indians & Indigenous Studies, Newberry Library, Politics, Railroads, Social Action, Theater, Family papers, Journalism, Lit, Music, Printing Hist & Bk Arts (Amer Modern Manuscript Coll); Historical Linguistics (Bonaparte Coll); History of the

Book, Book Arts, Printing (Wing Coll); Maps, Atlases, & Travel (Baskes Coll); Portuguese & Brazilian History (Greenlee Coll); Western Americana (Graff Coll)
Subject Interests: Am hist & culture, British hist, British lit, Chicago & the Midwest, Dance, Genealogy & local hist, Hist of the bk, Maps, Maps, travel & exploration, Medieval, Renaissance & early modern studies, Music, Relig
Automation Activity & Vendor Info: (Acquisitions) Ex Libris Group; (Cataloging) Ex Libris Group; (OPAC) Ex Libris Group; (Serials) Ex Libris Group
Wireless access
Function: Res libr
Mem of Reaching Across Illinois Library System (RAILS)
Partic in Center for Research Libraries; Chicago Collections Consortium; Consortium of Academic & Research Libraries in Illinois; OCLC Online Computer Library Center, Inc; OCLC Research Library Partnership
Open Tues-Fri 9-5, Sat 9-1
Friends of the Library Group

NORTH PARK UNIVERSITY
C BRANDEL LIBRARY*, 5114 N Christiana Ave, 60625. (Mail add: 3225 W Foster Ave, 60625), SAN 340-1855. Tel: 773-244-5580, 773-244-6200. Interlibrary Loan Service Tel: 773-244-5588. Reference Tel: 773-244-5247. Administration Tel: 773-244-5583. FAX: 773-244-4891. Web Site: www.northpark.edu/library. *Dir,* Sarah Anderson; Tel: 773-244-5584, E-mail: saanderson@northpark.edu; *Archives Dir,* Anne Jenner; Tel: 773-244-6224, E-mail: ajenner@northpark.edu; *Dir, Media Serv,* Bill Hartley; Tel: 773-244-5579, E-mail: whartley@northpark.edu; *Head, Access Serv,* Richard Schwegel; E-mail: rschwegel@northpark.edu; *Bibliog Instr, Coll Mgt, Head, Ref,* Katie Maier-O'Shea; Tel: 773-244-5582, E-mail: kmaier@northpark.edu; *Bibliog Instr, Database Mgt, Ref Serv,* Laura Burt; Tel: 773-244-5587, E-mail: lburt@northpark.edu; *Ref Serv,* Norma Sutton; Tel: 773-244-6239, E-mail: nsutton@northpark.edu. Subject Specialists: *Music,* Richard Schwegel; *Seminary,* Norma Sutton; Staff 15 (MLS 8, Non-MLS 7)
Founded 1891. Enrl 2,972; Fac 127; Highest Degree: Master
Library Holdings: Bk Titles 203,563; Bk Vols 228,874; Per Subs 961
Special Collections: Bound Scores; China (Harold W Jacobson Coll); Evangelical Covenant Church Archives; G Anderson Coll; Jenny Lind, bks, coins, glass objects, letters, medals, music; Karl A Olsson Coll; Paul L Homer Coll; Scandinavian Coll; Scandinavian Literature (Nils William Olsson Coll); Swedish-American Historical Society Archives; Walter Johnson Coll
Subject Interests: Music, Nursing, Relig, Scandinavia, Theol
Automation Activity & Vendor Info: (Acquisitions) Ex Libris Group; (Cataloging) Ex Libris Group; (Circulation) Ex Libris Group; (ILL) OCLC; (OPAC) Ex Libris Group; (Serials) Ex Libris Group
Database Vendor: EBSCOhost, Gale Cengage Learning, JSTOR, LexisNexis, Newsbank, OCLC FirstSearch, OCLC WorldShare Interlibrary Loan, SerialsSolutions
Partic in Association of Chicago Theological Schools; LIBRAS, Inc
Publications: North Park Faculty Publications & Creative Works (1992 & 1997)
Special Services for the Blind - Magnifiers
Open Mon-Thurs 7:45am-Midnight, Fri 7:45am-10pm, Sat 10-6, Sun 1-Midnight
Restriction: Restricted access

C COVENANT ARCHIVES & HISTORICAL LIBRARY*, Brandel Library, F M Johnson Archives, 3225 W Foster Ave, Box 38, 60625-4823, SAN 325-6731. Tel: 773-244-6224. Toll Free Tel: 800-888-6728. FAX: 773-244-4891. E-mail: archives@northpark.edu. Web Site: www.northpark.edu/Brandel-Library/Archives. *Dir, Archives & Spec Coll,* Anna-Kajsa Anderson; E-mail: aanderson@northpark.edu; *Digitization Coordr, Tech Serv Coordr,* Joanna Wilkinson; Tel: 773-244-5244, E-mail: jwilkinson@northpark.edu; Staff 1 (Non-MLS 1)
Library Holdings: Bk Vols 3,000; Per Subs 15
Subject Interests: Evangelicalism
Restriction: Open by appt only

C SWEDISH-AMERICAN ARCHIVES OF GREATER CHICAGO*, 3225 W Foster Ave, 60625, SAN 304-0348. Tel: 773-244-6223. Toll Free FAX: 800-888-6728. E-mail: archives@northpark.edu. Web Site: www.campus.northpark.edu/library/archives. *Archivist,* Anne Jenner; Tel: 773-244-6224; Staff 1 (Non-MLS 1)
Founded 1968
Library Holdings: Bk Titles 3,000; Per Subs 20
Special Collections: Bengtsor Coll, doc; Chicago Swedes, doc; Chicago Swedes, newsp, orgn rec
Partic in Association of Chicago Theological Schools; Consortium of Academic & Research Libraries in Illinois; Illinois Library & Information Network; LIBRAS, Inc
Publications: Swedish American Historical Quarterly
Mem of Reaching Across Illinois Library System (RAILS)
Restriction: Open by appt only, Open to pub upon request
Friends of the Library Group

C NORTHEASTERN ILLINOIS UNIVERSITY*, Ronald Williams Library, 5500 N Saint Louis Ave, 60625-4699. SAN 340-191X. Tel: 773-442-4400. Circulation Tel: 773-442-4401. Interlibrary Loan Service Tel: 773-442-4509. Reference Tel: 773-442-4410. Administration Tel: 773-442-4470. FAX: 773-442-4531. Interlibrary Loan Service FAX: 773-442-4530. Web Site: library.neiu.edu. *Dean of Libr,* Carlos Melian; Tel: 773-442-4450, E-mail: c-melian@neiu.edu; *Assoc Dean of Libr,* Dave Green; Tel: 773-442-4414, E-mail: d-green3@neiu.edu; *Bus Librn,* Henry Owen, III; Tel: 773-442-4420, E-mail: h-owen3@neiu.edu; *Educ Librn,* James Rosenzweig; Tel: 773-442-4454, E-mail: J-Rosenzweig@neiu.edu; *Electronic Res & Ser Mgt Librn,* Susanna Bossenga; Tel: 773-442-4474, E-mail: s-bossenga@neiu.edu; *Humanities Librn,* Mary Thill; Tel: 773-442-4405, E-mail: m-thill@neiu.edu; *Ref Librn,* Michael Weinberg; Tel: 773-442-4455, E-mail: m-weinberg@neiu.edu; *Archivist, Ref Librn,* Dario Villa; Tel: 773-442-4416, E-mail: d-villa@neiu.edu; *Soc Sci Librn,* Michelle Guittar; Tel: 773-442-4445, E-mail: m-guittar@neiu.edu; *Web Serv Librn,* Lisa Wallis; Tel: 773-442-4571, E-mail: l-wallis@neiu.edu; *Tech Serv Coordr,* Joan Schuitema; Tel: 773-442-4446, E-mail: j-schuitema@neiu.edu. Subject Specialists: *Acctg, Bus law, Econ,* Henry Owen, III; *Reading, Spec educ, Teacher educ,* James Rosenzweig; *English, Linguistics, Philos,* Mary Thill; *Art, Psychol, Sci,* Michael Weinberg; *Environ studies, Geog, Polit sci,* Michelle Guittar; *Biol, Health, Phys educ,* Lisa Wallis; *Music,* Joan Schuitema; Staff 42 (MLS 17, Non-MLS 25)
Founded 1961. Enrl 11,000; Fac 715; Highest Degree: Master
Jul 2011-Jun 2012 Income (Main and Other College/University Libraries) $4,085,130, State $3,763,100, Federal $32,570, Locally Generated Income $288,926. Mats Exp $1,206,143, Books $138,186, Per/Ser (Incl. Access Fees) $613,986, Micro $5,022, AV Mat $20,570, Electronic Ref Mat (Incl. Access Fees) $416,390, Presv $11,989. Sal $2,555,430 (Prof $1,369,880)
Library Holdings: CDs 3,987; DVDs 4,652; e-books 50,562; e-journals 53,888; Bk Vols 705,949
Special Collections: Chicago & Cook County Archives (1831-1955). State Document Depository; US Document Depository
Subject Interests: Educ, Ethnic studies, Psychol
Automation Activity & Vendor Info: (Acquisitions) Ex Libris Group; (Cataloging) Ex Libris Group; (Circulation) Ex Libris Group; (Course Reserve) Ex Libris Group; (ILL) OCLC; (OPAC) Ex Libris Group; (Serials) Ex Libris Group
Database Vendor: Dialog, EBSCOhost, Gale Cengage Learning, LexisNexis, Newsbank, OCLC FirstSearch, OVID Technologies
Wireless access
Mem of Reaching Across Illinois Library System (RAILS)
Partic in Consortium of Academic & Research Libraries in Illinois; Illinois Library & Information Network

Departmental Libraries:

CARRUTHERS CENTER FOR INNER CITY STUDIES, 700 E Oakwood Blvd, 60653, SAN 340-1944. Tel: 773-256-2134, 773-268-7500, Ext 163. FAX: 773-442-4531. Web Site: www.neiu.edu/~neiulib. *Librn,* Sharon Scott
Subject Interests: African-Am
Open Mon-Thurs 1-9, Fri 10-5

J NORTHWESTERN COLLEGE, Edward G Schumacher Memorial Library, 4811 N Milwaukee Ave, 60630. SAN 375-4405. Tel: 773-777-4220. FAX: 773-205-2126. E-mail: library@nc.edu. Web Site: www.nc.edu/library. *Dir, Libr Serv,* Sarah Dulay; Tel: 708-237-5000, E-mail: sdulay@nc.edu; *Ref Librn,* Joseph Dane; E-mail: jdane@nc.edu; Staff 1 (MLS 1)
Founded 1991. Highest Degree: Associate
Library Holdings: Bk Titles 3,765; Bk Vols 12,160; Per Subs 88
Automation Activity & Vendor Info: (Cataloging) OCLC; (Circulation) Mandarin Library Automation; (ILL) OCLC; (OPAC) Mandarin Library Automation
Database Vendor: EBSCOhost, OCLC FirstSearch, OCLC WorldShare Interlibrary Loan, ProQuest, Westlaw
Wireless access
Function: Res libr
Mem of Reaching Across Illinois Library System (RAILS)
Partic in Illinois Library & Information Network; Metronet; Network of Illinois Learning Resources in Community Colleges; OCLC Online Computer Library Center, Inc
Open Mon-Thurs 8am-9pm, Fri 9-4, Sat 9-Noon

Departmental Libraries:

BRIDGEVIEW CAMPUS, 7725 S Harlem Ave, Bridgeview, 60455. Tel: 708-237-5000. FAX: 708-237-5005. *Dir of Libr Serv,* Sarah Dulay; E-mail: sdulay@nc.edu; *Ref & ILL Librn,* Joyce Tracy; E-mail: jtracy@nc.edu; Staff 2 (MLS 2)
Library Holdings: Bk Vols 7,095
Automation Activity & Vendor Info: (Cataloging) OCLC Connexion; (ILL) OCLC WorldShare Interlibrary Loan
Database Vendor: EBSCOhost, OCLC FirstSearch, OCLC WorldShare Interlibrary Loan, ProQuest, Westlaw
Partic in South Metrop Higher Education Consortium
Open Mon-Thurs 7:30am-9pm, Fri 7:30-4, Sat 8:30-Noon

M NORTHWESTERN MEMORIAL HOSPITAL*, Alberto Culver Health Learning Center, Galter Pavilion, Ste 3-304, 251 E Huron St, 60611. SAN 373-3556. Tel: 312-926-5465. FAX: 312-926-2125. E-mail: hlc@nmh.org. Web Site: www.nmh.org. *Mgr,* Nora St. Peter; *Health Educator,* Moira Workman; Staff 4 (MLS 2, Non-MLS 2)
Founded 1999
Library Holdings: Bk Vols 6,000
Special Collections: Women's Consumer Health
Subject Interests: Health
Wireless access
Function: Computer training, Computers for patron use, Copy machines, e-mail serv, Fax serv, Learning ctr, Mail & tel request accepted, Online cat, Online ref, Online searches, Outside serv via phone, mail, e-mail & web, Pub access computers, Ref serv available, Referrals accepted, Wheelchair accessible
Open Mon-Fri 9-5:30
Restriction: Hospital staff & commun, Med & nursing staff, patients & families, Med staff & students, Non-circulating

NORTHWESTERN UNIVERSITY, CHICAGO

CM GALTER HEALTH SCIENCES LIBRARY*, Montgomery Ward Bldg, 303 E Chicago Ave, 60611, SAN 340-2061. Tel: 312-503-8133. Circulation Tel: 312-503-8127. Interlibrary Loan Service Tel: 312-503-1908. Reference Tel: 312-503-8109. Information Services Tel: 312-503-8126. FAX: 312-503-1204. E-mail: ghsl-ref@northwestern.edu. Web Site: www.galter.northwestern.edu. *Dir,* James Shedlock; E-mail: j-shedlock@northwestern.edu; *Assoc Dir, Health Sci Libr,* Heidi Nickisch Duggan; Staff 30 (MLS 17, Non-MLS 13)
Founded 1927. Fac 15; Highest Degree: Doctorate
Sept 2006-Aug 2007. Mats Exp $1,887,017. Sal $1,368,995
Library Holdings: e-books 849; e-journals 7,966; Electronic Media & Resources 2,887; Bk Titles 125,940; Bk Vols 286,364
Special Collections: Dental History; Medical Classics; Medical History; Rare Books
Subject Interests: Basic med sci, Clinical med, Phys therapy
Automation Activity & Vendor Info: (Acquisitions) Ex Libris Group; (Cataloging) Ex Libris Group; (Circulation) Ex Libris Group; (OPAC) Ex Libris Group; (Serials) Ex Libris Group
Database Vendor: OVID Technologies, PubMed, ScienceDirect, UpToDate, Wiley
Publications: Guide Series; Library Guide; Library Notes
Restriction: Not open to pub
Friends of the Library Group

CL PRITZKER LEGAL RESEARCH CENTER*, 375 E Chicago Ave, 60611, SAN 340-2037. Tel: 312-503-8451. Reference Tel: 312-503-8450. Administration Tel: 312-503-4941. FAX: 312-503-9230. Web Site: www.law.northwestern.edu/lawlibrary/. *Interim Dir,* Eloise M Vondruska; Tel: 312-503-7369, E-mail: e-vondruska@law.northwestern.edu; *Acq Librn,* Eric C Parker; Tel: 312-503-7920, E-mail: ecp278@law.northwestern.edu; *Cat Librn,* Terence O'Connell; Tel: 312-503-7364, E-mail: t-oconnell@law.northwestern.edu; *Digital Serv & Emerging Tech Librn,* Kara Young; Tel: 312-503-0252, E-mail: k-young@law.northwestern.edu; *Doc Librn,* Pegeen Bassett; Tel: 312-503-7344, E-mail: p-bassett@law.northwestern.edu; *Fac Serv Librn,* Marcia Gold Lehr; Tel: 312-503-4356, E-mail: mglehr@law.northwestern.edu; *Foreign, Comparative & Intl Law Librn,* Heidi Frostestad Kuehl; Tel: 312-503-4725, E-mail: h-kuehl@law.northwestern.edu; *Instrul & Access Serv Librn,* Maribel Nash; Tel: 312-503-0300, E-mail: m-nash@law.northwestern.edu; *Res & Instrul Serv Librn,* Jamie Sommer; Tel: 312-503-0314, E-mail: j-sommer@law.northwestern.edu. Subject Specialists: *Foreign law, Intl law,* Heidi Frostestad Kuehl; Staff 23.5 (MLS 11, Non-MLS 12.5)
Founded 1859. Enrl 988; Fac 160; Highest Degree: Doctorate
Library Holdings: Bk Titles 244,052; Bk Vols 562,601; Per Subs 5,452
Special Collections: Foreign & International Law; Supreme Court Papers of Arthur J Goldberg
Automation Activity & Vendor Info: (Acquisitions) Ex Libris Group; (Cataloging) Ex Libris Group; (Circulation) Ex Libris Group; (Course Reserve) Ex Libris Group; (OPAC) Ex Libris Group; (Serials) Ex Libris Group
Partic in Chicago Legal Acad Syst; Committee on Institutional Cooperation; Illinois Library & Information Network; New England Law Library Consortium, Inc; OCLC Online Computer Library Center, Inc
Publications: Faculty Publications; Library Guide; New Books List
Mem of Reaching Across Illinois Library System (RAILS)
Open Mon-Thurs 7:30am-11pm, Fri 7:30am-8pm, Sat 9-6, Sun 9am-11pm

C JOSEPH SCHAFFNER LIBRARY*, Wieboldt Hall, 2nd Flr, 339 E Chicago Ave, 60611, SAN 340-2002. Tel: 312-503-8422. FAX: 312-503-8930. E-mail: schaffner-circulation@northwestern.edu, schaffner-reference@northwestern.edu. Web Site: www.library.northwestern.edu/schaffner. *Head of Libr,* Scott Garton; Tel: 312-503-0720, E-mail: s-garton@northwestern.edu
Library Holdings: Bk Vols 20,000
Subject Interests: Bus, Humanities
Open Mon-Thurs Noon-10, Fri Noon-9, Sat 9-5, Sun Noon-5

M NORWEGIAN AMERICAN HOSPITAL*, Seufert Memorial Library, 1044 N Francisco Ave, 60622. SAN 303-996X. Tel: 773-292-8200, Ext 4670. FAX: 773-292-5954. Web Site: www.n-ahs.org. *Educ Coordr, Librn,* Janethe Polo; E-mail: jpolo@nahospital.org
Founded 1922
Library Holdings: Bk Titles 800; Per Subs 45
Open Mon-Fri 8-4:30

SR ORDER OF SERVANTS OF MARY (SERVITES), USA PROVINCE*, Servite Provincial Library, 3121 W Jackson Blvd, 60612-2729. SAN 328-3461. Tel: 773-533-0360. FAX: 773-533-8307. Web Site: www.servite.org. *Archivist,* Conrad Borntrager; E-mail: conradbosm@yahoo.com
Library Holdings: Bk Vols 3,600; Per Subs 20; Videos 40
Restriction: Open by appt only

SR OUR LADY OF SORROWS BASILICA*, Archives Library, 3121 W Jackson Blvd, 60612-2729. SAN 323-4703. Tel: 773-638-5800, Ext 31. *Archivist,* Conrad Borntrager; E-mail: conradbosm@yahoo.com
Library Holdings: Bk Vols 300
Restriction: Open by appt only

M OUR LADY OF THE RESURRECTION MEDICAL CENTER LIBRARY*, 5645 W Addison, 60634-4455. SAN 303-9943. Tel: 773-282-7000, Ext 4332. Web Site: www.reshealth.org. *Mgr, Libr Serv,* Beth Robb
Founded 1972
Library Holdings: Bk Titles 900; Per Subs 100
Publications: Library Brochure
Mem of Reaching Across Illinois Library System (RAILS)
Partic in Metropolitan Consortium of Chicago; Regional Med Libr - Region 3
Restriction: Staff use only

SR PASSIONIST ACADEMIC INSTITUTE LIBRARY*, 5700 N Harlem Ave, 60631. SAN 373-0468. Tel: 773-631-1686, Ext 237. FAX: 773-631-1705, 773-631-8059. Web Site: www.passionistlibrary.org. *Librn,* Irene Horst; E-mail: irenebh@juno.com
Library Holdings: Bk Vols 20,000; Per Subs 35
Special Collections: John Henry (Cardinal) Newman Coll
Subject Interests: Philos, Theol

S PERKINS & WILL ARCHITECTS, INC*, Resource Center, 330 N Wabash Ave, Ste 3600, 60611-3608. SAN 373-3572. Tel: 312-755-0770. FAX: 312-755-0775. Web Site: www.perkinswill.com. *Librn,* Jenelle Dillman
Library Holdings: Bk Vols 1,000; Per Subs 100
Subject Interests: Manufacturers' catalogs

S PLAYBOY ENTERPRISES, INC*, Editorial Research Library, 680 N Lake Shore Dr, 60611. SAN 340-2096. Tel: 312-751-8000, Ext 2529. FAX: 312-751-2818. Web Site: www.playboyenterprises.com. *Res,* Mark Duran
Library Holdings: Bk Titles 10,000; Per Subs 75
Subject Interests: Civil rights, Films & filmmaking, Music, Sexuality, Sports
Restriction: Not open to pub
Branches:
PHOTO LIBRARY, 680 N Lake Shore Dr, 60611, SAN 340-2126. Tel: 312-751-8000, Ext 2730. FAX: 312-751-2818. *Librn,* Bonnie Jean Kenny
Restriction: Staff use only

S POLISH MUSEUM OF AMERICA LIBRARY*, 984 N Milwaukee Ave, 60642-4101. SAN 303-9994. Tel: 773-384-3352, Ext 101. FAX: 773-384-3799. E-mail: pma@polishmuseumofamerica.org. Web Site: www.polishmuseumofamerica.org. *Dir,* Jan Lorys; *Head Librn,* Malgorzata Kot; E-mail: malgorzata-kot@polishmuseumofamerica.org; *Librn,* Krystyna Grell; E-mail: krystyna-grell@polishmuseumofamerica.org; Staff 2 (MLS 1, Non-MLS 1)
Founded 1915
Library Holdings: Audiobooks 100; AV Mats 400; CDs 400; DVDs 100; Microforms 300; Music Scores 5,000; Bk Titles 100,000; Bk Vols 120,000; Per Subs 35; Videos 280
Special Collections: 19th Century Polish Emigre Coll; Old Manuscripts; Paderewski Coll; Polish Publishers in the US Coll; Polonica Americana Coll; Polonica in English Coll. Oral History
Subject Interests: Art, Genealogy, Heraldry, Hist, Poland, Polish lit
Function: Archival coll, Art exhibits, Copy machines, Exhibits, Genealogy discussion group, Holiday prog, Ref serv available, Ref serv in person, Wheelchair accessible, Workshops
Publications: Polish Past in America
Mem of Reaching Across Illinois Library System (RAILS)

Open Mon, Tues, Fri & Sat 10-4, Wed 1-7
Restriction: Access at librarian's discretion, Authorized patrons, Circ limited, Circ to mem only, Closed stack
Friends of the Library Group

S PRO-LIFE ACTION LEAGUE LIBRARY*, 6160 N Cicero Ave, Ste 600, 60646. SAN 373-3688. Tel: 773-777-2900. FAX: 773-777-3061. E-mail: info@prolifeaction.org. Web Site: www.prolifeaction.org. *Dir,* Ann Scheidler
Founded 1980
Library Holdings: Bk Vols 1,500; Per Subs 10
Special Collections: Articles on Pro Life
Subject Interests: Abortion, Euthanasia, Life
Publications: Action News (Quarterly)
Open Mon-Fri 9-5

M REHABILITATION INSTITUTE OF CHICAGO, LIFE Center, 345 E Superior St, 1st Flr, 60611. SAN 324-7317. Tel: 312-238-5433. FAX: 312-238-2860. E-mail: lifecenter@ric.org. Web Site: lifecenter.ric.org. *Mgr,* Lisa Rosen; *Med Librn,* Carol Stukey; Staff 1 (MLS 1)
Founded 2003
Library Holdings: Bk Titles 2,000; Per Subs 12; Videos 500
Subject Interests: Phys rehabilitation
Wireless access
Function: Health sci info serv
Restriction: Circulates for staff only, In-house use for visitors, Non-circulating to the pub

M RESURRECTION HEALTH CARE*, St Joseph Hospital Library, 2900 N Lake Shore Dr, 60657. SAN 304-016X. Tel: 773-665-3038. FAX: 773-665-3416. *Med Librn,* Eleanor Truex; E-mail: sjhlibrary@reshealthcare.org; Staff 1 (MLS 1)
Library Holdings: CDs 35; Bk Titles 3,465; Per Subs 110
Subject Interests: Med, Nursing
Database Vendor: EBSCOhost, Micromedex, OVID Technologies, UpToDate
Wireless access
Mem of Reaching Across Illinois Library System (RAILS)
Partic in Greater Midwest Regional Medical Libr Network; Illinois Library & Information Network; Metrop Consortium; Serials of Illinois Libraries Online (SILO)
Restriction: Borrowing requests are handled by ILL, Circ limited, Hospital employees & physicians only, Use of others with permission of librn

M RESURRECTION MEDICAL CENTER LIBRARY*, 7435 W Talcott Ave, 60631-3746. SAN 304-0062. Tel: 773-990-7638. Web Site: www.resurrectionmedicalcenter.org. *Mgr, Libr Serv,* Laura Wimmer; E-mail: lwimmer@reshealthcare.org
Founded 1953
Library Holdings: CDs 500; DVDs 30; e-books 20; e-journals 4,500; Bk Titles 900; Per Subs 80
Automation Activity & Vendor Info: (Cataloging) LibraryWorld, Inc; (Circulation) LibraryWorld, Inc; (OPAC) LibraryWorld, Inc; (Serials) LibraryWorld, Inc
Database Vendor: EBSCOhost, Elsevier, Marcive, Inc, MD Consult, Micromedex, OCLC FirstSearch, OVID Technologies, ProQuest, PubMed
Wireless access
Mem of Reaching Across Illinois Library System (RAILS)
Partic in Illinois Library & Information Network; Metro Consortium of Chicago; National Network of Libraries of Medicine
Open Mon-Fri 8-4

S THE RJA GROUP, INC*, 600 W Fulton St, Ste 500, 60661-1242. SAN 326-5293. Tel: 312-879-7220, Ext 30013. FAX: 312-879-7221. *Librn,* Krista Kountz; E-mail: kkountz@rjagroup.com; Staff 1 (MLS 1)
Library Holdings: AV Mats 100; CDs 150; Electronic Media & Resources 10; Bk Titles 25,000; Per Subs 50
Special Collections: Building Codes (National, City, State & Local); Fire Safety Engineering; NFPA Fire Codes
Restriction: Staff use only

C ROBERT MORRIS UNIVERSITY, Information Technology Library, 401 S State St, 60605. SAN 303-7835. Tel: 312-935-2202, 312-935-2203. Web Site: www.robertmorris.edu/library. *Libr Dir,* Sue Dutler; E-mail: sdutler@robertmorris.edu; Staff 5 (MLS 3, Non-MLS 2)
Founded 1913. Enrl 4,200; Highest Degree: Master
Library Holdings: Bk Titles 116,982; Per Subs 40
Automation Activity & Vendor Info: (Acquisitions) Ex Libris Group; (Cataloging) Ex Libris Group; (Circulation) Ex Libris Group; (Course Reserve) Ex Libris Group; (ILL) Ex Libris Group; (Media Booking) Ex Libris Group; (OPAC) Ex Libris Group
Wireless access
Partic in Consortium of Academic & Research Libraries in Illinois
Open Mon-Thurs 7:30am-10pm, Fri 7:30-4:30, Sat 9-4

C ROOSEVELT UNIVERSITY*, Murray-Green Library, 430 S Michigan Ave, 60605. SAN 340-224X. Circulation Tel: 312-341-3639, 312-341-3649. Interlibrary Loan Service Tel: 312-341-3638. Reference Tel: 312-341-3643, 312-341-3644. FAX: 312-341-2425. Web Site: www.roosevelt.edu/library. *Univ Librn,* Richard M Uttich; Tel: 312-341-3640, E-mail: ruttich@roosevelt.edu; *Dir, Performing Arts Libr,* Richard Schwegel; Tel: 312-341-3648, E-mail: rschwegel@roosevelt.edu; *Head, Access Serv,* Jacob Jeremiah; Tel: 312-341-6965, E-mail: jjeremiah@roosevelt.edu; *Head, Info Literacy & Instruction Serv,* Martinique Hallerduff; Tel: 312-341-2125, E-mail: mhaller@roosevelt.edu; *Head, Tech Serv,* David Pribyl; Tel: 312-341-3647, E-mail: dpribyl@roosevelt.edu; *Coll Develop Librn, Ref,* Geoff Greenburg; Tel: 312-341-2318, E-mail: ggreenberg@roosevelt.edu; *Distance Learning Librn,* Position Currently Open; *Electronic Res Mgt Librn, Ref & Instruction Librn, Webmaster,* Jefferson Micah; Tel: 312-341-2406, E-mail: mjefferson@roosevelt.edu; *Asst Archivist, Ref & Instruction Librn,* Michael Gabriel; Tel: 312-341-3645, E-mail: mgabriel@roosevelt.edu; *Scholarly Communications Librn,* Freeda Brook; Tel: 312-341-3652, E-mail: fbrook@roosevelt.edu; *Tech Serv Librn,* Erin Carlson; Tel: 312-341-3642, E-mail: ecarlson@roosevelt.edu; *Asst Music Librn,* Deborah Morris; Tel: 312-341-2328, E-mail: dmorris@roosevelt.edu; *Univ Archivist,* Laura Mills; Tel: 312-341-2280;312-341-2275, E-mail: lmills@roosevelt.edu; Staff 14 (MLS 14)
Founded 1945. Enrl 5,070; Fac 350; Highest Degree: Doctorate
Library Holdings: Bk Titles 174,907; Bk Vols 187,338; Per Subs 1,165
Special Collections: American Civilization & English Literature Coll; Music Coll, bks, recs, sheet music
Automation Activity & Vendor Info: (Acquisitions) Ex Libris Group; (Cataloging) Ex Libris Group; (Circulation) Ex Libris Group; (Course Reserve) SerialsSolutions; (ILL) OCLC ILLiad; (OPAC) Ex Libris Group; (Serials) EBSCO Online
Database Vendor: 3M Library Systems, ACM (Association for Computing Machinery), Alexander Street Press, American Chemical Society, American Mathematical Society, American Physical Society, American Psychological Association (APA), Annual Reviews, CQ Press, CredoReference, Dialog, Dun & Bradstreet, ebrary, EBSCOhost, Elsevier, Emerald, Ex Libris Group, Foundation Center, Gale Cengage Learning, Greenwood Publishing Group, H W Wilson, Ingenta, JSTOR, Knovel, LexisNexis, McGraw-Hill, Medline, Mergent Online, Nature Publishing Group, OCLC, OCLC WorldShare Interlibrary Loan, OneSource, Plunkett Research, Ltd, Project MUSE, ProQuest, PubMed, Sage, ScienceDirect, SerialsSolutions, Springer-Verlag, Springshare, LLC, Standard & Poor's, Wiley InterScience, Wilson - Wilson Web, YBP Library Services
Wireless access
Publications: Subject Research Guides
Partic in Black Metropolis Research Consortium (BMRC); Chicago Collections Consortium; Consortium of Academic & Research Libraries in Illinois

Departmental Libraries:

ROBERT R MCCORMICK TRIBUNE FOUNDATION LIBRARY, 1400 N Roosevelt Blvd, Schaumburg, 60173, SAN 376-9771. Tel: 847-619-7980. FAX: 847-619-7983. *Univ Librn,* Richard M Uttich; Tel: 312-341-3540, E-mail: ruttich@roosevelt.edu; *Dir, Head, Pub Serv,* Linda Wilkinson; Tel: 312-341-3659, E-mail: lpwilkinson@roosevelt.edu; *Asst Dir,* Position Currently Open; *Ref & Instruction Librn,* Joseph Davis; *Ref & Instruction Librn,* Laura McLoughlin; *Ref & Instruction Librn,* Renee Roth; Staff 9 (MLS 4, Non-MLS 5)
Library Holdings: Bk Titles 12,400; Per Subs 250
Mem of Reaching Across Illinois Library System (RAILS)
Open Mon-Thurs 9-8, Fri & Sat 9-4

PERFORMING ARTS LIBRARY, 430 S Michigan Ave, Rm 1111, 60605. Tel: 312-341-3651. FAX: 312-341-6394. Web Site: www.roosevelt.edu/library/locations/performingartslibrary.aspx. *Dir,* Richard C Schwegel; Tel: 312-341-3648, E-mail: rschwegel@roosevelt.edu; *Asst Dir,* Morris Deb; Tel: 312-341-2328, E-mail: dmorris@roosevelt.edu; *Tech Asst,* Anita Hwang; Tel: 312-341-2136, E-mail: ahwang@roosevelt.edu; Staff 3.5 (MLS 2, Non-MLS 1.5)
Enrl 500; Highest Degree: Master
Library Holdings: CDs 7,000; Music Scores 40,000; Bk Titles 39,678; Per Subs 90
Automation Activity & Vendor Info: (Course Reserve) Ex Libris Group
Database Vendor: OCLC WorldShare Interlibrary Loan
Restriction: Pub use on premises

M ROSELAND COMMUNITY HOSPITAL*, Health Science Library, 45 W 111th St, 60628. SAN 304-0100. Tel: 773-995-3191. FAX: 773-995-5863. Web Site: www.roselandhospital.org. *Dir,* Brenda Mitchell
Founded 1956
Library Holdings: Bk Vols 600; Per Subs 39
Subject Interests: Med, Nursing
Mem of Reaching Across Illinois Library System (RAILS)
Partic in Chicago & South Consortium; Illinois Library & Information Network; Regional Med Libr - Region 3
Restriction: Staff use only

S LURA LYNN RYAN PREVENTION RESEARCH LIBRARY*, 33 W Grand Ave, Ste 300, 60654. SAN 376-0367. Tel: 312-988-4646, Ext 252. Toll Free Tel: 800-572-5385, Ext 252 (Illinois only). FAX: 312-988-7096. E-mail: library@prevention.org. Web Site: www.prevention.org/library. *Libr Mgr,* Mary Simon; Staff 1 (MLS 1)
Library Holdings: Bk Titles 20,000; Per Subs 50
Database Vendor: OCLC FirstSearch
Open Mon-Fri 8:30-3

C SAINT AUGUSTINE COLLEGE LIBRARY*, 1345 W Argyle, 60640. SAN 375-9423. Tel: 773-878-3710. FAX: 773-878-0937. *Dir,* Elizabeth Murphy; E-mail: emurphy@staugustine.edu; Staff 4 (MLS 2, Non-MLS 2)
Founded 1980. Enrl 1,400; Highest Degree: Bachelor
Library Holdings: Bk Titles 15,000; Bk Vols 17,000; Per Subs 50
Automation Activity & Vendor Info: (Acquisitions) Brodart; (Cataloging) OCLC Online; (Circulation) Follett Software; (ILL) OCLC Online; (OPAC) Follett Software
Database Vendor: EBSCOhost, Newsbank, OCLC FirstSearch
Partic in Illinois Library & Information Network
Open Mon-Fri 8:30am-10pm, Sat 8:30-4
Restriction: By permission only

C SAINT XAVIER UNIVERSITY, Robert & Mary Rita Murphy Stump, 3700 W 103rd St, 60655-3105. SAN 304-0178. Tel: 773-298-3352. Interlibrary Loan Service Tel: 773-298-3353. Reference Tel: 773-298-3364. FAX: 773-779-5231. Web Site: www.sxu.edu/library. *Libr Dir,* David Stern; Tel: 773-298-3350, E-mail: stern@sxu.edu; *Assoc Librn,* Ursula Zyzik; Tel: 773-298-3354, E-mail: zyzik@sxu.edu; *Libr Tech,* Margaret Hoefferle; Tel: 773-298-3362; Staff 8 (MLS 8)
Founded 1916. Enrl 4,100; Fac 168; Highest Degree: Master
Library Holdings: Bk Vols 172,104; Per Subs 1,607
Subject Interests: Educ, Nursing, Relig
Automation Activity & Vendor Info: (Acquisitions) SirsiDynix; (Cataloging) OCLC WorldShare Interlibrary Loan; (Circulation) SirsiDynix; (Course Reserve) SirsiDynix; (ILL) SirsiDynix; (OPAC) SirsiDynix
Mem of Reaching Across Illinois Library System (RAILS)
Partic in CCMP; LIBRAS, Inc; OCLC Online Computer Library Center, Inc
Open Mon-Thurs 7:30am-Midnight, Fri 7:30-7, Sat 12-7, Sun Noon-Midnight

M SAINTS MARY & ELIZABETH MEDICAL CENTER*, Sister Stella Louise Health Science Library, 2233 W Division St, 60622. SAN 340-2363. Tel: 312-770-2219. FAX: 312-770-2221. E-mail: smmlib@yahoo.com. *Dir, Libr Serv,* Olivija Fistrovic; E-mail: ofistrovic@reshealthcare.org; *Asst Librn,* Mary LasQuety; Staff 2 (MLS 1, Non-MLS 1)
Founded 1949
Library Holdings: Bk Vols 2,250; Per Subs 100
Subject Interests: Internal med, Surgery
Publications: Acquisition List; Annual Report; Journal List
Partic in Illinois Library & Information Network; Metropolitan Consortium of Chicago

S SARGENT & LUNDY, LLC*, Resource Center, 55 E Monroe St, 24F60, 60603. SAN 340-2428. Tel: 312-269-3525. FAX: 312-269-3757. Web Site: www.sargentlundy.com. *Librn,* Gerard P Kenny; Staff 3 (MLS 2, Non-MLS 1)
Founded 1969
Library Holdings: Bk Titles 2,000; Per Subs 20
Subject Interests: Archit, Civil eng, Electrical eng, Energy, Mechanical eng
Automation Activity & Vendor Info: (Cataloging) Sydney
Mem of Reaching Across Illinois Library System (RAILS)
Partic in Illinois Library & Information Network
Open Mon-Fri 7:55-4:55
Restriction: Staff use only

L SCHIFF, HARDIN LLP LIBRARY*, 233 S Wacker Dr, Ste 6600, 60606. SAN 304-0186. Tel: 312-258-5500. FAX: 312-258-5600. Web Site: www.schiffhardin.com. *Dir,* Ruth Bridges; E-mail: rbridges@schiffhardin.com; Staff 5 (MLS 5)
Library Holdings: Bk Vols 40,000

C SCHOOL OF THE ART INSTITUTE OF CHICAGO, John M Flaxman Library, 37 S Wabash Ave, 60603-3103. SAN 339-8048. Tel: 312-899-5097. Reference Tel: 312-899-5096. FAX: 312-899-1851. E-mail: flaxman@saic.edu. Web Site: digital-libraries.saic.edu, libraryguides.saic.edu. *Dir,* Claire Eike; *Access & Res Serv Librn,* Holly Stec Dankert; *Cat & Acq,* Nathaniel Feis; *Coll Mgt Librn,* Sylvia Choi; *Digital Serv Librn,* Christopher Day; *Ref & Instruction Librn,* Nick Ferreira; *Ref & Instruction Librn,* Lindsay Harmon; *Ref & Instruction Librn,* Jenn Smith; *Spec Coll Librn,* Doro Boehme; *Access Serv Mgr,* Elizabeth Aubrey; *Mgr, Spec Coll,* Kayla Anderson; *Media Coll Mgr,* Carolyn Faber; *Acq Asst,* Keith Kostecki; *Cat & Metadata Asst,* Grace Gaynor; *Cat & Metadata Asst,* Joe Meads; *Cat & Metadata Asst,* Kathy Olsen; *Coll Mgt Asst,* Anna Di Cesare; *Digital Imaging Tech,* Elise Tanner; Staff 10.8 (MLS 8, Non-MLS 2.8)
Founded 1968. Enrl 3,290; Highest Degree: Master
Library Holdings: AV Mats 207,384; e-books 69,936; Microforms 150; Bk Vols 108,183; Per Subs 387
Special Collections: 16mm film; Film Study Coll; Joan Flasch Artists' Bks Coll; Mail Art; P-form Archives; Randolph Street Gallery Archives; SAIC Digital Libraries; Tony Zwicker Archives
Subject Interests: Animation, Archit, Art & tech, Art educ, Art therapy, Arts admin & policy, Contemporary art, Design, Film, Historic presv, New media, Video, Writing
Automation Activity & Vendor Info: (Cataloging) Ex Libris Group; (Circulation) Ex Libris Group; (ILL) OCLC; (OPAC) Ex Libris Group; (Serials) SerialsSolutions
Database Vendor: Alexander Street Press, American Psychological Association (APA), ARTstor, EBSCOhost, Ex Libris Group, Ingenta, JSTOR, LexisNexis, Material ConneXion, Modern Language Association, Nature Publishing Group, OCLC, OCLC FirstSearch, OCLC WebJunction, OCLC WorldShare Interlibrary Loan, Oxford Online, Project MUSE, ProQuest, Sage, SerialsSolutions, Springer-Verlag, YBP Library Services
Wireless access
Function: 24/7 Electronic res, 24/7 Online cat, Archival coll, Art exhibits, Audio & video playback equip for onsite use, Copy machines, e-mail serv, ILL available
Mem of Reaching Across Illinois Library System (RAILS)
Partic in Center for Research Libraries; Consortium of Academic & Research Libraries in Illinois; OCLC Online Computer Library Center, Inc
Special Services for the Deaf - Closed caption videos
Restriction: Open to students, fac & staff, Photo ID required for access

SR SEMINARY CONSORTIUM FOR URBAN PASTORAL EDUCATION, Resource Center, 205 W Monroe St, Ste 300, 60606. SAN 376-0340. Tel: 312-726-1200. FAX: 312-726-0425. E-mail: urbanmin@scupe.com. Web Site: www.scupe.com. *Pres,* Dr Shanta Premawardhana; E-mail: shanta@scupe.com
Founded 1976
Library Holdings: Bk Titles 3,500
Publications: Resource Review

S SEYFARTH SHAW*, 131 S Dearborn St, Ste 2400, 60603-5577. SAN 304-0224. Tel: 312-460-5000. FAX: 312-460-7000. Web Site: www.seyfarth.com. *Librn,* Gabrielle Lewis; E-mail: glewis@seyfarth.com; *Ref,* Nancy Faust; Staff 9 (MLS 3, Non-MLS 6)
Founded 1945
Library Holdings: Bk Vols 38,500; Per Subs 484
Special Collections: Arbitration Awards & Legal Memoranda (Seyfarth Shaw Coll), bd vols
Subject Interests: Employment law, Environ law, Labor law, Securities law
Function: ILL available
Mem of Reaching Across Illinois Library System (RAILS)
Partic in Illinois Library & Information Network; OCLC Online Computer Library Center, Inc
Restriction: Co libr

S JOHN G SHEDD AQUARIUM LIBRARY, 1200 S Lake Shore Dr, 60605. SAN 320-1791. Tel: 312-692-3217. Web Site: www.sheddaquarium.org. *Mgr, Libr Serv,* Alisun DeKock; E-mail: adekock@sheddaquarium.org; Staff 1 (MLS 1)
Founded 1975
Library Holdings: AV Mats 100; e-journals 20; Bk Titles 8,000; Per Subs 125
Special Collections: Aquatic Animals Coll, slide images
Subject Interests: Animals, behavior of, Aquarium mgt, Aquatic sci, Great Lakes
Automation Activity & Vendor Info: (Cataloging) SirsiDynix; (Circulation) SirsiDynix; (ILL) OCLC; (OPAC) SirsiDynix; (Serials) SirsiDynix
Database Vendor: EBSCO Discovery Service, EBSCO Information Services, EBSCOhost
Wireless access
Function: ILL available
Mem of Reaching Across Illinois Library System (RAILS)
Partic in International Environment Library Consortium (IELC); OCLC-LVIS; Serials of Illinois Libraries Online (SILO)
Restriction: Not open to pub, Staff use only

C SHIMER COLLEGE LIBRARY*, 3424 S State St, 60616-3893. SAN 304-4432. Tel: 312-235-3531. Web Site: www.shimer.edu. *Libr Dir,* Colleen McCarroll; Tel: 842-249-7898; Staff 3 (Non-MLS 3)
Founded 1904

Library Holdings: Bk Vols 20,000; Per Subs 25
Open Mon-Fri 9-5

S SHRINERS' HOSPITAL FOR CHILDREN*, Professional Library, 2211 N Oak Park Ave, 60707. SAN 323-7400. Tel: 773-385-5479. FAX: 773-385-5437. *Librn,* Laura Mueller; E-mail: lmueller@shrinenet.org; Staff 2 (MLS 1, Non-MLS 1)
Founded 1981
Jan 2010-Dec 2010. Mats Exp $25,600, Books $2,000, Per/Ser (Incl. Access Fees) $23,600
Library Holdings: AV Mats 300; CDs 40; Bk Titles 1,055; Per Subs 52; Videos 100
Subject Interests: Orthopedics, Pediatrics
Mem of Reaching Across Illinois Library System (RAILS)
Partic in Basic Health Sciences Library Network; Metropolitan Consortium of Chicago
Open Mon-Thurs 8:30-2

L SARGENT SHRIVER NATIONAL CENTER ON POVERTY LAW LIBRARY*, 50 E Washington, Ste 500, 60602. SAN 326-9574. Tel: 312-263-3830. FAX: 312-263-3846. Web Site: www.povertylaw.org.
Founded 1967
Library Holdings: Per Subs 150
Special Collections: Training Manuals & Poverty Law Analysis Coll
Open Mon-Fri 9-5

L SIDLEY AUSTIN LLP LIBRARY*, One S Dearborn St, 60603. SAN 304-0259. Tel: 312-853-7475. Interlibrary Loan Service Tel: 312-853-4600. FAX: 312-853-7036. Web Site: www.sidley.com. *Dir, Libr Serv,* Allyson D Withers
Library Holdings: Bk Vols 25,000
Subject Interests: Law
Partic in Illinois Library & Information Network; OCLC Online Computer Library Center, Inc

L SKADDEN, ARPS, SLATE, MEAGHER & FLOM LLP LIBRARY*, 155 N Wacker Dr, 60606. SAN 375-9652. Tel: 312-407-0941. Interlibrary Loan Service Tel: 312-407-0927. FAX: 312-407-0411. Web Site: www.skadden.com. *Head Law Librn,* Ann Morris; *Sr Librn, Ref,* Christine Morong; *Sr Librn, Ref,* Sandy Qiu; *Ref Librn,* Lauren Odom; Staff 5 (MLS 4, Non-MLS 1)
Automation Activity & Vendor Info: (Acquisitions) EOS International; (Cataloging) EOS International; (Circulation) EOS International; (OPAC) EOS International; (Serials) EOS International
Wireless access

S SKIDMORE, OWINGS & MERRILL LIBRARY*, 224 S Michigan Ave, Ste 1000, 60604. SAN 304-0267. Tel: 312-554-9090. FAX: 312-360-4545. Web Site: www.som.com. *Mgr,* Karen Widi
Founded 1972
Library Holdings: Bk Titles 7,000; Per Subs 50
Subject Interests: Art & archit, Eng
Mem of Reaching Across Illinois Library System (RAILS)
Partic in Illinois Library & Information Network
Restriction: Staff use only

L SONNENSCHEIN, NATH & ROSENTHAL*, Law Library, 8000 Sears Tower, 233 S Wacker Dr, Ste 7800, 60606-6404. SAN 304-0275. Tel: 312-876-8000. Interlibrary Loan Service Tel: 312-876-8001. Reference Tel: 312-876-7906. Toll Free Tel: 888-858-6429. FAX: 312-876-7934. Web Site: www.sonnenschein.com. *Head, Ref,* Nancy Henry; E-mail: nhenry@sonnenschein.com; *ILL,* Jeff Bent; *Ref,* Carol Dauler; *Tech Serv,* Susan Pateros
Library Holdings: Bk Titles 1,200; Bk Vols 15,000; Per Subs 200
Subject Interests: US law
Automation Activity & Vendor Info: (Acquisitions) EOS International; (Cataloging) EOS International; (Circulation) EOS International; (Course Reserve) EOS International; (ILL) EOS International; (Media Booking) EOS International; (OPAC) EOS International; (Serials) EOS International
Database Vendor: Dialog, LexisNexis, OCLC FirstSearch
Mem of Reaching Across Illinois Library System (RAILS)
Partic in CLS; OCLC Online Computer Library Center, Inc

S SPENCER STUART LIBRARY*, 401 N Michigan Ave, Ste 2600, 60611. SAN 304-0283. Tel: 312-822-0088. FAX: 312-822-0117. *Sr Mgr,* Laura Dear; E-mail: ldear@spencerstuart.com; Staff 5 (MLS 5)
Library Holdings: Per Subs 50
Subject Interests: Exec search
Mem of Reaching Across Illinois Library System (RAILS)

CR SPERTUS INSTITUTE OF JEWISH STUDIES*, Norman & Helen Asher Library, 610 S Michigan Ave, 60605. SAN 304-0291. Tel: 312-322-1712. Administration Tel: 312-322-1745. FAX: 312-922-0455. TDD: 312-922-4950. E-mail: resources@spertus.edu. Web Site: www.spertus.edu. *Coll Mgr,* Kathleen Bloch; E-mail: kbloch@spertus.edu; *Ser,* Camille Brown; Tel: 312-322-1751, E-mail: cbrown@spertus.edu; Staff 2 (MLS 1, Non-MLS 1)
Founded 1925. Enrl 900; Highest Degree: Doctorate
Library Holdings: Bk Titles 75,000; Bk Vols 100,000; Per Subs 550
Special Collections: Chicago Jewish Archives; Chicago Jewish History; Jewish Art (Badona Spertus Library of Art in Judaica); Jewish Music (Targ Center for Jewish Music); Non-Profit Management (Lewis Sulkin Human Services Coll)
Subject Interests: Jewish hist, Jewish holocaust, Judaica, Judaism (religion)
Automation Activity & Vendor Info: (Acquisitions) Ex Libris Group; (Cataloging) Ex Libris Group; (Circulation) Ex Libris Group; (OPAC) Ex Libris Group; (Serials) Ex Libris Group
Database Vendor: EBSCOhost, OCLC FirstSearch
Wireless access
Function: Bks on cassette, Bks on CD, Computers for patron use, Copy machines, Distance learning, Electronic databases & coll, Handicapped accessible, ILL available, Mail & tel request accepted, Mail loans to mem, Online cat, Online searches, Pub access computers, Ref serv in person, Spoken cassettes & CDs, Telephone ref, VHS videos, Video lending libr
Mem of Reaching Across Illinois Library System (RAILS)
Partic in Ill Regional Libr Coun
Special Services for the Deaf - TTY equip
Restriction: Open to students, fac, staff & alumni, Restricted borrowing privileges

M SWEDISH COVENANT HOSPITAL*, Joseph G Stromberg Library of the Health Sciences, 5145 N California Ave, 60625. SAN 304-033X. Tel: 773-878-8200, Ext 5312. FAX: 773-878-1624. Web Site: www.schosp.org. *Librn,* Liz Giese; Staff 1 (MLS 1)
Founded 1930
Library Holdings: Bk Titles 1,600; Per Subs 65
Subject Interests: Med
Mem of Reaching Across Illinois Library System (RAILS)
Partic in Metropolitan Consortium of Chicago
Restriction: Open to others by appt

S TECHNOMIC, INC*, Knowledge Center, 300 S Riverside Plaza, Ste 1200, 60606. SAN 326-3584. Tel: 312-876-3929. FAX: 312-876-1158. Web Site: www.technomic.com. *Dir,* Chris Urban; E-mail: curban@technomic.com; Staff 3 (MLS 2, Non-MLS 1)
Library Holdings: Bk Vols 2,000

S TETRA-TECH EM INC*, One S Wacker Dr 37th Flr, 60606. SAN 375-9717. Tel: 312-201-7718. FAX: 312-938-0118. *Info Spec,* Linda Zimnicki; Staff 1 (Non-MLS 1)
Library Holdings: Bk Titles 100; Per Subs 2
Mem of Reaching Across Illinois Library System (RAILS)
Open Mon-Fri 8-5

S GRANT THORNTON LLP*, Information Center, 175 W Jackson Blvd, 20th Flr, 60604. SAN 340-1227. Tel: 312-602-8828. FAX: 312-565-4719. *Librn,* Otis Joseph; E-mail: ojoseph@gt.com; Staff 2 (Non-MLS 2)
Founded 1972
Library Holdings: Bk Titles 93; Per Subs 50
Subject Interests: Acctg, Auditing
Automation Activity & Vendor Info: (Acquisitions) EOS International; (Cataloging) EOS International; (Circulation) EOS International; (ILL) OCLC; (Serials) EOS International
Function: ILL available
Mem of Reaching Across Illinois Library System (RAILS)
Restriction: Staff use only

M UKRAINIAN MEDICAL ASSOCIATION OF NORTH AMERICA*, Medical Archives & Library, 2247 W Chicago Ave, Ste 206, 60622. SAN 325-7185. Tel: 773-278-6262. Web Site: www.umana.org. *Archivist, Dir,* Dr M Hrycelak
Founded 1950
Library Holdings: Bk Vols 5,000
Subject Interests: Archives, Med, Ukraine
Function: Archival coll, Res libr
Restriction: Non-circulating, Staff use only

S UNGARETTI & HARRIS LIBRARY*, 3500 Three First National Plaza, 60602-4283. SAN 325-5131. Tel: 312-977-4378. FAX: 312-977-4405. *Libr Mgr,* Maria Chavez; E-mail: mchavez@uhlaw.com
Subject Interests: Corp law, Gen bus, Healthcare, Securities, Taxation
Automation Activity & Vendor Info: (Acquisitions) SydneyPlus
Database Vendor: OCLC FirstSearch, ProQuest, Westlaw
Partic in GSI Online; Illinois Library & Information Network; LivEdgar; Westlaw
Restriction: Private libr

S UNION LEAGUE CLUB OF CHICAGO LIBRARY, 65 W Jackson Blvd, 60604. SAN 304-0399. Tel: 312-435-4818. E-mail: librarian@ulcc.org. Web Site: www.ulcc.org. *Dir, Libr & Archives,* Anita Mechler; E-mail: amechler@ulcc.org; Staff 2 (MLS 2)
Library Holdings: Audiobooks 500; DVDs 1,700; Bk Vols 11,000; Per Subs 100; Spec Interest Per Sub 20
Special Collections: Chicago Metropolitan/Local Interest Fiction & Nonfiction Coll
Subject Interests: Am hist, Art & archit, Biol, Bus & mgt, Hist
Database Vendor: ComPanion Corp
Wireless access
Function: Adult bk club, Archival coll, Art exhibits, Audio & video playback equip for onsite use, Bi-weekly Writer's Group, Bks on CD, Bus archives, Chess club, Children's prog, Computer training, Computers for patron use, Copy machines, E-Reserves, Electronic databases & coll, Exhibits, Fax serv, Free DVD rentals, Handicapped accessible, Holiday prog, Magnifiers for reading, Mail & tel request accepted, Online cat, Orientations, Photocopying/Printing, Ref serv available, Scanner, Senior computer classes, Spoken cassettes & CDs, Summer & winter reading prog, Telephone ref, Writing prog
Publications: Check it Out (Quarterly); State of the Union (Bi-monthly)
Special Services for the Blind - Bks on CD; Large print bks
Open Mon-Sun 7am-9pm
Restriction: Private libr

G UNITED STATES DEPARTMENT OF JUSTICE*, Antitrust Division Library, 209 S LaSalle, Ste 600, 60604. SAN 304-0445. Tel: 312-353-7530. FAX: 312-353-1046. Web Site: www.usdoj.gov/atr. *In Charge,* Linda Irvin
Library Holdings: Bk Vols 3,800; Per Subs 20

G UNITED STATES ENVIRONMENTAL PROTECTION, Region 5 Library, 77 W Jackson Blvd (PL-16J), 60604. SAN 303-8882. Tel: 312-886-6822. FAX: 312-886-1492. E-mail: library.r05@epa.gov. Web Site: www.epa.gov/region5/library. *Fed Libr Mgr,* Jessica Wheatley; *Supvry Librn,* Karen Swanson; Staff 2 (MLS 1, Non-MLS 1)
Founded 1972
Special Collections: EPA Reports
Subject Interests: Air, Great Lakes, Waste, Water
Database Vendor: OCLC FirstSearch
Partic in EPA National Libr Network; Fedlink; OCLC Online Computer Library Center, Inc; OCLC-LVIS
Open Mon-Thurs 8:30-12 & 12:30-3

S UNITED STATES RAILROAD RETIREMENT BOARD LIBRARY*, 844 N Rush St, 60611-2031. SAN 304-0461. Tel: 312-751-4926. FAX: 312-751-4924. E-mail: library@rrb.gov. Web Site: usrrb.gov. *Head Librn,* Katherine Tsang; Staff 1 (MLS 1)
Founded 1940
Library Holdings: Bk Vols 45,000; Per Subs 162
Subject Interests: Law
Function: ILL available
Mem of Reaching Across Illinois Library System (RAILS)
Restriction: By permission only

C THE UNIVERSITY OF CHICAGO LIBRARY, Joseph Regenstein Library, 1100 E 57th St, 60637-1502. SAN 340-2630. Tel: 773-702-8740. Circulation Tel: 773-702-8701. Interlibrary Loan Service Tel: 773-702-7886, 773-702-8706. Reference Tel: 773-702-4685. FAX: 773-702-6623. Interlibrary Loan Service FAX: 773-834-2598. Web Site: www.lib.uchicago.edu. *Dir & Univ Librn,* Brenda L Johnson; E-mail: brendajohnson@uchicago.edu; *Assoc Univ Librn, Digital Serv,* Elisabeth Long; Tel: 773-702-3732, E-mail: elong@uchicago.edu; *Assoc Univ Librn, Coll & Serv,* James Mouw; Tel: 773-702-8732, E-mail: mouw@uchicago.edu; *Assoc Univ Librn, User Serv,* James Vaughan; Tel: 773-702-8351, E-mail: vau4@uchicago.edu; *Asst Univ Librn, Humanities, Soc Sci & Spec Coll,* Alice Schreyer; Tel: 773-702-0095, Fax: 773-702-3728, E-mail: schreyer@uchicago.edu; *Dir of Budget & Facilities,* David Borycz; Tel: 773-702-2494, E-mail: dnborycz@uchicago.edu; *Dir of Communications,* Rachel A Rosenberg; Tel: 773-834-1519, E-mail: rrosenb@uchicago.edu; *Dir of Develop,* Yasmin Omer; Tel: 773-834-3744, E-mail: yasminomer@uchicago.edu; *Dir, Human Res,* Jane Ciacci; Tel: 773-702-8755, E-mail: kjc2@uchicago.edu; *Dir, Admin Desktop Syst & Integrated Libr Syst,* Frances McNamara; Tel: 773-702-8465, E-mail: f-mcnamara@uchicago.edu; *Dir, Digital Libr Develop Ctr,* Charles Blair; Tel: 773-702-8459, E-mail: chas@uchicago.edu; *Co-Dir, Sci Libr, Head, Pub Serv,* Barbara Kern; Tel: 773-702-8717, Fax: 773-702-3317, E-mail: bkern@uchicago.edu; *Co-Dir, Sci Libr, Head, Coll Serv,* Andrea Twiss-Brooks; Tel: 773-702-8777, Fax: 773-702-3317, E-mail: atbrooks@uchicago.edu; *Asst Dir, Admin,* Position Currently Open. Subject Specialists: *Rare bks,* Alice Schreyer; *Astronomy, Tech,* Barbara Kern; *Chem, Physics, Sci,* Andrea Twiss-Brooks; Staff 247 (MLS 72, Non-MLS 175)
Founded 1891. Enrl 12,960; Fac 1,964; Highest Degree: Doctorate
Jul 2013-Jun 2014. Mats Exp $19,176,653, $19,176,653, Books $5,813,318, Per/Ser (Incl. Access Fees) $12,869,225. Sal $13,806,193 (Prof $5,809,150)
Library Holdings: Bk Titles 6,860,280; Bk Vols 11,560,575
Special Collections: American Drama (Atkinson & Morton Colls); Anatomical Illustration (Frank Coll); Balzac's Works (Croue Coll); Children's Books, Primarily 19th Century (Encyclopaedia Britannica Coll); Continental Literature (Hirsch-Bernays Coll); Cromwelliana (George Morris Eckels Coll); Dramatic Criticism (Briggs Coll); Early American School Books (Littlefield Coll); Early Theology & Biblical Criticism (American Bible Union & Hengstenberg Colls); English Bibles (Grant Coll); English Drama to 1800 (Celia & Delia Austrian Coll); Files of Poetry, a Magazine of Verse including The Personal Papers of Harriet Monroe; Fine Printing (Donnelley Coll); German Fiction, 1790-1850 (Lincke Coll); Goethe's Works (Heinemann Coll); History of Kentucky & Ohio River Valley (Durrett Coll); History of Science & Medicine (Crerar Coll); Judaica (Rosenberger Coll); Life Records of Geoffrey Chaucer & Canterbury Tales, in transcripts & photostat; Lincolniana (Barton Coll); Manuscripts of Manorial Records regarding Estates in Norfolk & Suffolk (Bacon Coll); Modern Poetry (Harriet Monroe Coll); New Testament Manuscripts (Edgar J Goodspeed Coll); Notarial Documents of Northern Italy (Rosenthal Coll); Personal Papers of William Beaumont, Stephen A Douglas, William H English (History of Indiana), Frank O Lowden, Ida B Wells; Photostats of German Folksongs (Wieboldt-Rosenwald Coll); Source Material Regarding First Contact of Whites & Indians in Mississippi Valley (Ethno-History Coll); Taschenbuecher; The John Crerar Library Rare Book Coll; University Archives (incl Papers of Edith & Grace Abbott, Thomas C Chamberlin, Enrico Fermi, James Franck, Samuel N Harper, William Rainey Harper, Robert Herrick, George Herbert Mead, William Vaughn Moody, Howard Taylor Ricketts, Marion Talbot, Herman Eduard von Holst). US Document Depository
Automation Activity & Vendor Info: (ILL) OCLC ILLiad; (OPAC) Horizon
Database Vendor: ABC-CLIO, ACM (Association for Computing Machinery), Agricola, Alexander Street Press, American Chemical Society, American Mathematical Society, American Physical Society, American Psychological Association (APA), Annual Reviews, ARTstor, Atlas Systems, Baker & Taylor, BioOne, Blackwell, Bowker, Cambridge Scientific Abstracts, CountryWatch, CQ Press, CRC Press/Taylor & Francis Group, CredoReference, Dialog, EBSCO Information Services, EBSCOhost, Elsevier, Emerald, Ex Libris Group, Factiva.com, Facts on File, Gallup, H W Wilson, Haworth Pres Inc, HeinOnline, IEEE (Institute of Electrical & Electronics Engineers), infoUSA, Ingenta, Innovative Interfaces, Inc, IOP, ISI Web of Knowledge, JSTOR, Knovel, LexisNexis, Marquis Who's Who, MD Consult, Medline, Mergent Online, Micromedex, Modern Language Association, Nature Publishing Group, OCLC ArticleFirst, OCLC FirstSearch, OCLC WorldShare Interlibrary Loan, OCLC-RLG, OneSource, OVID Technologies, Oxford Online, Project MUSE, ProQuest, PubMed, ReferenceUSA, RefWorks, Safari Books Online, Sage, ScienceDirect, SirsiDynix, Springer-Verlag, Standard & Poor's, Swets Information Services, Sybase, Thomson - Web of Science, TLC (The Library Corporation), UpToDate, WebMD, Westlaw, Wiley, Wiley InterScience, Wilson - Wilson Web, YBP Library Services
Wireless access
Function: Archival coll, Art exhibits, Audio & video playback equip for onsite use, AV serv, CD-ROM, Computers for patron use, Copy machines, Doc delivery serv, e-mail & chat, E-Reserves, Electronic databases & coll, Exhibits, For res purposes, Handicapped accessible, Health sci info serv, ILL available, Magnifiers for reading, Mail & tel request accepted, Music CDs, Online cat, Online ref, Online searches, Orientations, Outreach serv, Outside serv via phone, mail, e-mail & web, Photocopying/Printing, Pub access computers, Ref serv available, Ref serv in person, Res libr, Scanner, Telephone ref, VHS videos, Video lending libr, Web-catalog, Wheelchair accessible
Publications: Libra (Newsletter)
Partic in Association of Research Libraries (ARL); Center for Research Libraries; OCLC Online Computer Library Center, Inc
Special Services for the Deaf - ADA equip; Assisted listening device; Assistive tech
Special Services for the Blind - Accessible computers; Cassette playback machines; Cassettes; Computer access aids; Low vision equip; Magnifiers; Screen enlargement software for people with visual disabilities; Screen reader software; Sound rec
Restriction: Borrowing requests are handled by ILL, In-house use for visitors, Limited access for the pub, Non-circulating of rare bks, Open to pub upon request, Open to students, fac, staff & alumni, Res pass required for non-affiliated visitors, Restricted pub use
Friends of the Library Group

Departmental Libraries:

JOHN CRERAR LIBRARY, 5730 S Ellis Ave, 60637, SAN 303-8750. Tel: 773-702-7715. Circulation Tel: 773-702-7409. Interlibrary Loan Service Tel: 773-702-7031. Administration Tel: 773-702-7469. Administration FAX: 773-702-3317. Interlibrary Loan Service E-mail: crerar-circulation@lib.uchicago.edu. Reference E-mail: crerar-reference@lib.uchicago.edu. Web Site:

www.lib.uchicago.edu/e/crerar. *Co-Dir, Pub Serv, Head of Libr,* Barbara Kern; Tel: 773-702-8717, E-mail: bkern@uchicago.edu; *Co-Dir, Coll Develop, Head of Libr,* Andrea Twiss-Brooks; Tel: 773-702-8777, E-mail: atbrooks@uchicago.edu; *Ref & Instruction Librn,* Debra Werner; Tel: 773-702-8552, E-mail: dwerner@uchicago.edu; *Bibliographer,* Christa Modschiedler; Tel: 773-702-8759, E-mail: mods@uchicago.edu; *Bibliographer,* Brenda Rice; Tel: 773-702-8774, E-mail: bsr2@uchicago.edu. Subject Specialists: *Astronomy, Astrophysics, Tech,* Barbara Kern; *Chem, Geophysical sci, Physics,* Andrea Twiss-Brooks; *Biomed, Nursing,* Debra Werner; *Biomed sci,* Christa Modschiedler; *Computer sci, Math, Statistics,* Brenda Rice; Staff 18 (MLS 6, Non-MLS 12)
Founded 1891
Special Collections: Department of Special Collections; Incunabula; Joseph Regenstein Library
Subject Interests: Astrophysics, Botany, Clinical med, Hist of med, Hist of sci, Oceanography, Physics, Zoology
Partic in Comt for Institutional Coop; National Network of Libraries of Medicine; OCLC Online Computer Library Center, Inc
Publications: At Your Service (Newsletter)
Open Mon-Thurs 8:30am-10pm, Fri 8:30-6, Sat 9-5, Sun 12-10
Friends of the Library Group

CL D'ANGELO LAW LIBRARY, 1121 E 60th St, 60637-2786, SAN 340-2789. Tel: 773-702-9615. FAX: 773-702-2889. Web Site: www.lib.uchicago.edu/e/law. *Dir,* Sheri Lewis; Tel: 773-702-9614, E-mail: shl@uchicago.edu; *Head, Acq & Electronic Res,* Julie Stauffer; Tel: 773-702-0692; *Head, Cat & Ser,* Patricia Sayre McCoy; Tel: 773-702-9620; *Fac Serv Librn,* Margaret Schilt; Tel: 773-702-6716; *Foreign & Intl Law Librn,* Lyonette Louis-Jacques; Tel: 773-702-9612, E-mail: llou@uchicago.edu; *Ref Librn,* Todd Ito; Tel: 773-702-9617; *Assoc Librn, Tech Serv,* Lorna Tang; Tel: 773-702-9619, E-mail: L-tang@uchicago.edu; *Bibliographer,* William Schwesig; Tel: 773-702-3731, E-mail: w-schwesig@uchicago.edu; *Cataloger,* Michael D Brown; *Ref Serv,* Constance Fleischer; Tel: 773-702-0211, E-mail: mcf0@uchicago.edu. Subject Specialists: *US law,* Margaret Schilt; *Civil law, Intl law,* Lyonette Louis-Jacques; *US law,* Todd Ito; *Anglo-Am law,* William Schwesig; *Govt doc,* Constance Fleischer; Staff 26 (MLS 10, Non-MLS 16)
Founded 1902. Enrl 650; Fac 51; Highest Degree: Doctorate
Library Holdings: Bk Vols 672,917; Per Subs 8,450
Special Collections: Henry Simons Papers Coll; US Supreme Court Briefs & Records Depository. US Document Depository
Subject Interests: Anglo-Am law, Intl law
Automation Activity & Vendor Info: (Acquisitions) Innovative Interfaces, Inc; (Cataloging) Horizon; (Circulation) Horizon; (ILL) Relais International; (OPAC) Horizon; (Serials) Horizon
Database Vendor: Bloomberg, EBSCO Discovery Service, EBSCOhost, Factiva.com, Fastcase, Gale Cengage Learning, H W Wilson, HeinOnline, LexisNexis, Westlaw
Partic in Center for Research Libraries; Committee on Institutional Cooperation; Illinois Library & Information Network; OCLC Online Computer Library Center, Inc; OCLC Research Library Partnership
Mem of Reaching Across Illinois Library System (RAILS)
Restriction: Vols & interns use only

ECKHART LIBRARY, 1118 E 58th St, 60637, SAN 340-272X. Tel: 773-702-8778. FAX: 773-702-7535. E-mail: eckhart-library@lib.uchicago.edu. Web Site: www.lib.uchicago.edu/e/eck. *Librn,* Jennifer Hart; Tel: 773-702-8774; *Libr Asst,* Kiya Moody; Staff 1 (MLS 1)
Library Holdings: Bk Vols 55,000; Per Subs 520
Subject Interests: Computer sci, Math, Statistics
Open Mon, Wed & Thurs 8:30am-10pm, Tues 12-5, Fri 8:30-5, Sat 9-5

SOCIAL SERVICE ADMINISTRATION, 969 E 60th St, 60637-2627, SAN 340-2819. Tel: 773-702-1199. FAX: 773-702-0874. *Librn,* Eileen Libby; E-mail: lib3@midway.uchicago.edu; Staff 1 (MLS 1)
Library Holdings: Bk Vols 35,196; Per Subs 141
Subject Interests: Soc serv (soc work)
Open Mon-Thurs 8:30-8, Fri 8:30-5, Sat 10-5, Sun 12-5

C UNIVERSITY OF ILLINOIS AT CHICAGO*, Richard J Daley Library, MC 234, 801 S Morgan St, 60607. SAN 340-2932. Tel: 312-996-2716. Circulation Tel: 312-996-2724. Interlibrary Loan Service Tel: 312-996-4886. Reference Tel: 312-996-2726. FAX: 312-413-0424. Web Site: www.library.uic.edu. *Univ Librn,* Mary Case; E-mail: marycase@uic.edu; *Assoc Univ Librn,* Jay H Lambrecht; E-mail: jaylamb@uic.edu; *Asst Univ Librn, Health Sci,* Kathryn Carpenter; Tel: 312-996-2227, Fax: 312-996-9584, E-mail: khc@uic.edu; *Asst Univ Librn, Info Tech,* Robert Sandusky; E-mail: sandusky@uic.edu. Subject Specialists: *Health sci,* Kathryn Carpenter; *Info tech,* Robert Sandusky; Staff 65 (MLS 58, Non-MLS 7)
Founded 1946. Enrl 24,200; Fac 1,456; Highest Degree: Doctorate
Jul 2008-Jun 2009. Mats Exp $8,200,000. Sal $8,000,000
Library Holdings: Bk Vols 2,236,632
Special Collections: 17th Century French Political & Intellectual History; Architecture (Mies van der Rohe, Charles Genther, Burnham & Hammond Colls); Archives of the Chicago Rock Island & Pacific Railroad Company; Chicago Design Archive (contains business & organizational records & personal papers, including Institute of Design, Chicago Book Clinic, IDCA, 27 Chicago Designers, R Hunter Middleton, Robert Vogele, Bruce Beck, Gordon Monsen, Phillip Reed & William Stone Colls); Chicago Fairs & Expositions (A Century of Progress World's Fair archives); Chicago Literature & Literary Societies (Chicago literature to the present & Society of Midland Authors, Indiana Society, Boswell Club of Chicago Colls); Chicago Photographic Archive (Phillips, Italian-American Colls); Chicago Railroad Fair, archives; Chicagoana (Lawrence J Gutter Coll), contains pre-fire imprints, maps, lit, literary mss, hist, politics, transportation, archit, crime, prints; Corporate Archives of the Chicago Board of Trade; Franklin Roosevelt (Joseph M Jacob Coll); Jane Adams Memorial Coll (contains Hull-House Association records, papers of individuals & organizations associated with Hull-House such as: Immigrants Protective League, Travelers Aid Society, Juvenile Protective Association & Wallace Kirkland photographs); Midwest Women's Historical Coll (contains personal & organizational records, including Mary Hastings Bradley, Neva Leona Boyd, Haldeman-Julius Family, Adena-Miller Rich & Esther Saperstein); Papers of Lenox Riley Lohr & Helen Tieken Garaghty; Records of the Chicago Urban League; Sheet Music (American popular music, 1900-1945); Slavery & Anti-Slavery (Sierra Leone Coll); University Archives (contains the University's official records & papers of prominent members of the university's faculties). State Document Depository; US Document Depository
Automation Activity & Vendor Info: (Acquisitions) Ex Libris Group; (Cataloging) Ex Libris Group; (Circulation) Ex Libris Group; (OPAC) Ex Libris Group; (Serials) Ex Libris Group
Wireless access
Publications: ShelfLife
Partic in OCLC Online Computer Library Center, Inc
Open Mon-Thurs 7:30am-11pm, Fri 7:30-7, Sat 10-5, Sun 1-11

Departmental Libraries:

CM LIBRARY OF THE HEALTH SCIENCES, CHICAGO, 1750 W Polk St, 60612, SAN 340-3025. Tel: 312-996-8966. Circulation Tel: 312-996-8974. Interlibrary Loan Service Tel: 312-996-8991. Reference Tel: 312-996-9163. FAX: 312-996-9584. *Asst Univ Librn,* Kathryn Carpenter; E-mail: khc@uic.edu
Special Collections: Neurology & Psychiatry (Percival Bailey Coll); Pharmacopoeias, Herbals, Formularies, Dispensatories & History of the Health Sciences (Rare & Early Volumes); Urology & Anomalies (Joseph Kiefer Coll)
Subject Interests: Allied health, Dentistry, Environ studies, Med, Nursing
Open Mon-Thurs 8:30-6, Fri 8:30-5

CM LIBRARY OF THE HEALTH SCIENCES, PEORIA, One Illinois Dr, Peoria, 61605. (Mail add: PO Box 1649, Peoria, 61656-1649), SAN 304-5536. Tel: 309-671-8490. FAX: 309-671-8495. *Prof,* Josephine Dorsch; Tel: 309-671-8489, E-mail: jod@uic.edu
Open Mon-Thurs 7:30am-10pm, Fri 7:30-7, Sat 12-5, Sun 2-9

CM LIBRARY OF THE HEALTH SCIENCES, ROCKFORD, Crawford Library of the Health Sciences, 1601 Parkview Ave, Rockford, 61107, SAN 327-9987. Tel: 815-395-5650. Interlibrary Loan Service Tel: 815-395-5656. Information Services Tel: 815-395-5658. FAX: 815-395-5652. E-mail: lib-lhsr@uic.edu. Web Site: www.ulc.edu/depts/lib/lhsr. *Regional Head Librn,* Felicia A Barrett; Tel: 815-395-5660, E-mail: fbarrett@uic.edu; Staff 2 (MLS 2)
Founded 1972. Fac 2; Highest Degree: Doctorate
Partic in National Network of Libraries of Medicine Greater Midwest Region
Mem of Reaching Across Illinois Library System (RAILS)
Open Mon-Thurs 7:30am-9pm, Fri 7:30-5, Sat 1-5, Sun 1-9

CM LIBRARY OF THE HEALTH SCIENCES, URBANA, 102 Medical Sciences Bldg, MC-714, 506 S Mathews Ave, Urbana, 61801, SAN 340-8604. Tel: 217-333-4893. Reference Tel: 217-244-0607. FAX: 217-333-9559. E-mail: lib-lhsu@uic.edu. *Librn,* Mary Shultz; Tel: 217-244-2259, E-mail: shultz@uic.edu
Partic in Committee on Institutional Cooperation; Consortium of Academic & Research Libraries in Illinois
Open Mon-Thurs 8:30am-10pm, Fri 8:30-5, Sat 11-4, Sun 3-9

C VANDERCOOK COLLEGE OF MUSIC*, Harry Ruppel Memorial Library, 3140 S Federal St, 60616-3731. SAN 304-050X. Tel: 312-225-6288, Ext 301. FAX: 312-225-5211. Web Site: www.vandercook.edu/library/index.html. *Dir,* Rob DeLand; E-mail: rdeland@vandercook.edu. Subject Specialists: *Music,* Rob DeLand; Staff 1 (MLS 1)
Founded 1967. Enrl 150; Fac 25; Highest Degree: Master
Library Holdings: AV Mats 46; CDs 255; Music Scores 225; Bk Vols 332; Per Subs 186
Special Collections: H E Nutt Archives; Rare Book Coll; Ruth Artman Coll
Subject Interests: Educ, Music, Music educ, Psychol
Automation Activity & Vendor Info: (Acquisitions) SirsiDynix; (Cataloging) SirsiDynix; (Circulation) SirsiDynix; (Course Reserve)

SirsiDynix; (ILL) OCLC FirstSearch; (OPAC) SirsiDynix; (Serials) SirsiDynix
Database Vendor: Alexander Street Press, EBSCOhost, OCLC FirstSearch, OCLC WorldShare Interlibrary Loan, Oxford Online, ProQuest, SirsiDynix
Wireless access
Function: Res libr
Mem of Reaching Across Illinois Library System (RAILS)
Partic in Consortium of Academic & Research Libraries in Illinois
Open Mon-Thurs 8:30am-10pm, Fri 8:30-5, Sat 10-2, Sun 2-10
Restriction: Borrowing privileges limited to fac & registered students, Open to pub upon request, Photo ID required for access

L VEDDER, PRICE*, Law Library, 222 N LaSalle, 60601. SAN 304-0518. Tel: 312-609-7500. FAX: 312-609-5005. Web Site: www.vedderprice.com. *Librn,* Kenneth Halicki
Founded 1952
Library Holdings: Bk Vols 22,000
Subject Interests: Corporate law

M LOUIS A WEISS MEMORIAL HOSPITAL*, L Lewis Cohen Memorial Library, 4646 N Marine Dr, 60640. SAN 304-0526. Tel: 773-564-5820. FAX: 773-564-5829. Web Site: www.weisshospital.com. *Librn,* Connie Gibbon
Library Holdings: Bk Titles 2,000; Per Subs 175
Partic in Illinois Library & Information Network; Metrop Consortium; Regional Med Libr - Region 3
Open Mon-Fri 8-4:30

L WINSTON & STRAWN LLP LIBRARY*, 35 W Wacker Dr, 60601. SAN 304-0550. Tel: 312-558-5740. FAX: 312-558-5700. Web Site: www.winston.com. *Dir, Libr Serv,* Kathy Lefco; Staff 5 (MLS 4, Non-MLS 1)
Library Holdings: Bk Vols 30,000; Per Subs 750
Subject Interests: Law
Automation Activity & Vendor Info: (Acquisitions) SirsiDynix; (Cataloging) SirsiDynix; (Circulation) SirsiDynix; (ILL) SirsiDynix; (OPAC) SirsiDynix; (Serials) SirsiDynix
Database Vendor: CQ Press, Dialog, Dun & Bradstreet, HeinOnline, Hoovers, LexisNexis, Mergent Online, OCLC FirstSearch, OCLC WorldShare Interlibrary Loan, SirsiDynix, Westlaw, Westlaw Business
Wireless access
Partic in OCLC Online Computer Library Center, Inc
Restriction: By permission only, Private libr

S WORLD BOOK PUBLISHING*, Research Library, 233 N Michigan Ave, 20th Flr, 60601. SAN 304-0577. Tel: 312-729-5581. FAX: 312-729-5600. Web Site: www.worldbook.com. *Librn,* John Wills; E-mail: jwills@worldbook.com; Staff 2 (MLS 1, Non-MLS 1)
Founded 1920
Library Holdings: Bk Vols 16,000; Per Subs 100
Special Collections: Archives of Company Products
Automation Activity & Vendor Info: (Acquisitions) EOS International; (Cataloging) EOS International; (Circulation) EOS International; (OPAC) EOS International; (Serials) EOS International
Database Vendor: OCLC FirstSearch
Publications: Quartley Accessions List
Partic in Illinois Library & Information Network; OCLC Online Computer Library Center, Inc

CHICAGO HEIGHTS

P CHICAGO HEIGHTS PUBLIC LIBRARY*, 25 W 15th St, 60411-3488. SAN 304-0585. Tel: 708-754-0323. FAX: 708-754-0325. E-mail: chs@chicagoheightslibrary.org. Web Site: www.chicagoheightslibrary.org. *Admin Librn,* Michael Davis; *Asst Dir,* Carolyn Wagner; Staff 21 (MLS 5, Non-MLS 16)
Founded 1901. Pop 32,776; Circ 120,534
May 2007-Apr 2008 Income $1,053,255, State $40,101, City $981,261, Locally Generated Income $21,957, Other $9,936. Mats Exp $111,550, Books $97,138, Per/Ser (Incl. Access Fees) $10,912, Electronic Ref Mat (Incl. Access Fees) $3,500. Sal $533,944
Library Holdings: Bk Vols 132,681; Per Subs 294
Subject Interests: Local hist, Spanish (Lang)
Database Vendor: EBSCOhost, Innovative Interfaces, Inc, OCLC FirstSearch
Wireless access
Publications: Newsletter
Mem of Reaching Across Illinois Library System (RAILS)
Open Mon-Thurs 10-8, Fri 10-5, Sat 10-4, Sun (Sept-June) 1-5
Friends of the Library Group

J PRAIRIE STATE COLLEGE LIBRARY*, 202 S Halsted St, 60411-8200. SAN 304-0593. Tel: 708-709-3550. Circulation Tel: 708-709-3560. Interlibrary Loan Service Tel: 708-709-3559. Reference Tel: 708-709-2949, 708-709-3556. FAX: 708-709-3940. E-mail: library@prairiestate.edu. Web Site: library.prairiestate.edu. *Assoc Dean, Libr & Instrul Tech,* Anthony Molaro; Tel: 708-709-3551, E-mail: amolaro@prairiestate.edu; *Digital Serv & Coll Mgt Librn,* S Dubsky; *Lead Info Literacy Librn,* Kristina Marie Appelt; *Ref Librn,* T Tracy; E-mail: ttracy@prairiestate.edu; *Circ Tech,* A Madden; *Ser & ILL Tech,* A Altan; Staff 10 (MLS 3, Non-MLS 7)
Founded 1958. Enrl 9,000; Highest Degree: Associate
Jul 2006-Jun 2007 Income $579,000. Mats Exp $106,400, Books $32,000, Per/Ser (Incl. Access Fees) $30,000, AV Mat $4,000, Electronic Ref Mat (Incl. Access Fees) $40,000, Presv $400. Sal $400,000 (Prof $195,000)
Library Holdings: AV Mats 75; CDs 10; DVDs 25; Bk Titles 34,100; Bk Vols 40,000; Per Subs 490; Videos 2,010
Subject Interests: Communications, Dental, Nursing, Photog
Automation Activity & Vendor Info: (Acquisitions) Innovative Interfaces, Inc; (Cataloging) Innovative Interfaces, Inc; (Circulation) Innovative Interfaces, Inc; (ILL) OCLC Online; (OPAC) Innovative Interfaces, Inc; (Serials) Innovative Interfaces, Inc
Database Vendor: 3M Library Systems, ARTstor, Baker & Taylor, EBSCOhost, LexisNexis, Newsbank, OCLC FirstSearch, OCLC WorldShare Interlibrary Loan, SerialsSolutions
Wireless access
Function: ILL available, Ref serv available
Mem of Reaching Across Illinois Library System (RAILS)
Partic in Consortium of Academic & Research Libraries in Illinois; Northern Illinois Learning Resources Cooperative (NILRC)
Special Services for the Deaf - Assistive tech; Staff with knowledge of sign lang
Special Services for the Blind - Assistive/Adapted tech devices, equip & products
Open Mon-Thurs (Winter) 7:30am-9pm, Fri 7:30-4, Sat 8-3; Mon-Thurs (Summer) 7:30am-9pm
Restriction: Open to pub for ref & circ; with some limitations, Open to students, fac & staff

S SOUTH COOK ISC4 LIBRARY*, 253 W Joe Orr Rd, 60411. SAN 320-8559. Tel: 708-754-6600. FAX: 708-754-8687. Web Site: www.s-cook.org. *Exec Dir,* Dr Vanessa J Kinder; *Librn,* Danielle Washington
Special Collections: ERIC microfiche indexed by Council of Exceptional Children
Subject Interests: Educ
Automation Activity & Vendor Info: (Cataloging) Winnebago Software Co; (Circulation) Winnebago Software Co; (OPAC) Winnebago Software Co
Open Mon 8-8, Tues-Fri 8-4

CHICAGO RIDGE

P CHICAGO RIDGE PUBLIC LIBRARY, 10400 S Oxford Ave, 60415. SAN 304-0615. Tel: 708-423-7753. FAX: 708-423-2758. E-mail: refdesk@chicagoridgelibrary.org. Web Site: chicagoridgelibrary.org. *Dir,* Kathleen McSwain; *Adult Serv,* Angeline Powers; *Ch Serv,* Irene Ciciora; Staff 19 (MLS 5, Non-MLS 14)
Founded 1966. Pop 14,127; Circ 128,465
Library Holdings: Bk Titles 73,084; Per Subs 456
Automation Activity & Vendor Info: (Acquisitions) Innovative Interfaces, Inc; (Cataloging) Innovative Interfaces, Inc; (Circulation) Innovative Interfaces, Inc
Publications: CR Library Lines (Newsletter)
Mem of Reaching Across Illinois Library System (RAILS)
Open Mon-Thurs 9-9, Fri & Sat 9-5, Sun 1-5
Friends of the Library Group

CHILLICOTHE

P CHILLICOTHE PUBLIC LIBRARY DISTRICT*, 430 N Bradley Ave, 61523-1920. SAN 304-0623. Tel: 309-274-2719. FAX: 309-274-3000. E-mail: cpldstaff@yahoo.com. Web Site: www.chillicothepubliclibrary.org. *Libr Dir,* Susan K Drissi; E-mail: sdrissi@chillicothepubliclibrary.org; *Circ Coordr,* Teresa Storti; E-mail: teresa.storti@gmail.com; *Ch Serv,* Gail Hintz; E-mail: ghintze@chillicothepubliclibrary.org; *Illinois Libr Loan & Adult Acq,* Kathy D Sell; E-mail: ksell@chillicothepubliclibrary.org; *Tech & Ref,* Alex Jeffries; E-mail: ajeffries81@gmail.com; *Young Adult Serv & Family/Adult Serv,* Catharine Barnett; E-mail: cbarnett@chillicothepubliclibrary.org; Staff 6 (MLS 1, Non-MLS 5)
Founded 1916. Pop 13,250; Circ 86,000
Library Holdings: AV Mats 4,600; Bks on Deafness & Sign Lang 120; CDs 1,100; DVDs 250; Electronic Media & Resources 100; High Interest/Low Vocabulary Bk Vols 350; Large Print Bks 1,500; Music Scores 25; Bk Titles 33,500; Bk Vols 37,900; Per Subs 120; Spec Interest Per Sub 25; Talking Bks 10; Videos 600
Special Collections: Chillicothe Times-Bulletins, 1883-present; High School Yearbooks, 1918-present
Subject Interests: Local hist

Automation Activity & Vendor Info: (Cataloging) TLC (The Library Corporation); (Circulation) TLC (The Library Corporation); (OPAC) TLC (The Library Corporation)
Function: Adult bk club, Archival coll, Audiobks via web, Bi-weekly Writer's Group, Bk club(s), Bks on CD, Children's prog, Citizenship assistance, Computer training, Computers for patron use, Copy machines, Digital talking bks, e-mail & chat, e-mail serv, Exhibits, Fax serv, Free DVD rentals, Handicapped accessible, Holiday prog, Home delivery & serv to Sr ctr & nursing homes, Homebound delivery serv, ILL available, Magnifiers for reading, Mail & tel request accepted, Music CDs, Notary serv, Online searches, Outside serv via phone, mail, e-mail & web, OverDrive digital audio bks, Prog for adults, Prog for children & young adult, Pub access computers, Ref serv in person, Scanner, Senior computer classes, Story hour, Summer reading prog, Teen prog, Wheelchair accessible, Writing prog
Partic in Resource Sharing Alliance
Special Services for the Deaf - Staff with knowledge of sign lang
Special Services for the Blind - Accessible computers; Audio mat; Bks available with recordings; Bks on CD; Braille alphabet card; Cassette playback machines; Copier with enlargement capabilities; Extensive large print coll; Home delivery serv; Large print bks; Large screen computer & software; Lending of low vision aids; Magnifiers; Playaways (bks on MP3); Sound rec; Talking bks; Talking bks & player equip
Open Mon-Thurs 7:30am-8pm, Fri 7:30-5, Sat 9-1
Restriction: Open to pub for ref & circ; with some limitations, Pub ref by request, Pub use on premises

CHRISMAN

P CHRISMAN PUBLIC LIBRARY*, 108 N Illinois St, 61924. SAN 304-0631. Tel: 217-269-3011. FAX: 217-269-3011. E-mail: chrismanlib@midwestfirst.com. Web Site: www.ltls.org/cin.html. *Librn,* Mary E Galway; *Asst Librn,* Gwen Montgomery
Founded 1932. Pop 1,318
Library Holdings: Audiobooks 60; CDs 145; DVDs 51; Bk Vols 10,123; Per Subs 37; Videos 982
Automation Activity & Vendor Info: (Cataloging) SirsiDynix; (Circulation) SirsiDynix
Mem of Illinois Heartland Library System
Open Mon, Tues & Fri 1-5:30, Wed & Thurs 1-7, Sat 9-1

CHRISTOPHER

P CHRISTOPHER PUBLIC LIBRARY*, 204 E Market St, 62822-1759. (Mail add: PO Box 131, 62822-0131), SAN 304-064X. Tel: 618-724-7534. FAX: 618-724-7534. *Librn,* Patricia Brown; E-mail: pat1934@yahoo.com; *Asst Librn,* Linda Holland
Pop 2,836; Circ 18,117
Library Holdings: Bk Vols 19,200; Per Subs 10
Mem of Illinois Heartland Library System
Open Mon-Thurs 2-6, Fri 12-4, Sat 9-4

CICERO

P CICERO PUBLIC LIBRARY*, 5225 W Cermak Rd, 60804. SAN 304-0658. Tel: 708-652-8084. FAX: 708-652-8095. E-mail: ciceropublic@yahoo.com. Web Site: www.cicerolibrary.org. *Admin Dir,* Jane Schoen; E-mail: jschoen@cicerolibrary.org; *Asst Dir, Bus Mgr,* Victoria Totton; E-mail: vtotton@cicerolibrary.org; *Head, Ref,* Patricia Conroy; E-mail: pconroy@cicerolibrary.org; *Head, Youth Serv,* Colleen Gnat; E-mail: cgnat@cicerolibrary.org; Staff 33 (MLS 5, Non-MLS 28)
Founded 1921. Pop 85,616; Circ 219,688
Library Holdings: Bk Vols 111,770; Per Subs 465; Spec Interest Per Sub 12
Subject Interests: Polish (Lang), Spanish (Lang)
Database Vendor: Gale Cengage Learning, Innovative Interfaces, Inc, OCLC FirstSearch
Wireless access
Publications: Cicero Public Library News (Newsletter)
Mem of Reaching Across Illinois Library System (RAILS)
Special Services for the Blind - Radio reading serv
Open Mon-Fri 9-9, Sat 9-4, Sun 12-5

J MORTON COLLEGE LIBRARY*, 3801 S Central Ave, 60804. SAN 304-0666. Tel: 708-656-8000, Ext 321. Reference Tel: 708-656-8000, Ext 429. Administration Tel: 708-656-8000, Ext 320. FAX: 708-656-3297. Web Site: www.morton.edu/library. *Assoc Dean, Dir, Libr & Tech,* Jennifer Butler; Tel: 708-656-8000, Ext 322; Staff 9 (MLS 3, Non-MLS 6)
Founded 1924. Enrl 5,244; Fac 263; Highest Degree: Associate
Library Holdings: AV Mats 3,130; Bks on Deafness & Sign Lang 12; High Interest/Low Vocabulary Bk Vols 850; Per Subs 120
Special Collections: Adult New Readers
Subject Interests: Compact discs, Spanish (Lang)
Automation Activity & Vendor Info: (Circulation) Innovative Interfaces, Inc; (ILL) OCLC; (OPAC) Innovative Interfaces, Inc
Database Vendor: Baker & Taylor
Mem of Reaching Across Illinois Library System (RAILS)
Partic in Consortium of Academic & Research Libraries in Illinois; Dialog Corp; Innopac; System Wide Automated Network
Open Mon-Fri 7:45am-9:30pm, Sat 9-2, Sun 1-6

CISCO

P WILLOW BRANCH TOWNSHIP LIBRARY*, 330 N Eldon, 61830. (Mail add: PO Box 39, 61830), SAN 304-0674. Tel: 217-669-2312. FAX: 217-669-2312. Web Site: www.willowbranchtownshiplibrary.il.us. *Dir,* Joy Rathe; E-mail: joy.rathe@gmail.com; *Librn,* Charlene Brown; E-mail: cbrown@prairienet.net; *Cat Librn,* Linda Penney; E-mail: lindyp57@gmail.com; *Ch,* Heather Barrett; E-mail: hbarrett4@gmail.com
Pop 732; Circ 4,900
Library Holdings: Bk Vols 5,877; Per Subs 8
Special Collections: Biographies; Classics; Juvenile Fiction & Nonfiction; Westerns
Automation Activity & Vendor Info: (Acquisitions) SirsiDynix; (Cataloging) SirsiDynix; (Circulation) SirsiDynix; (Course Reserve) SirsiDynix; (ILL) SirsiDynix; (Media Booking) SirsiDynix; (OPAC) SirsiDynix; (Serials) SirsiDynix
Mem of Illinois Heartland Library System
Open Mon & Wed 1-8, Tues 9-12 & 1-5, Fri 1-5, Sat 9-1

CISSNA PARK

P CISSNA PARK COMMUNITY LIBRARY DISTRICT*, 511 N Second St, 60924. SAN 376-1304. Tel: 815-457-2452. FAX: 815-457-3033. *Librn,* Richard Dulaney
Founded 1991. Pop 1,806; Circ 32,100
Jul 2009-Jun 2010 Income $86,000. Mats Exp $17,000, Books $15,000, AV Mat $2,000. Sal $39,000 (Prof $3,000)
Library Holdings: Bk Titles 36,000; Per Subs 30
Subject Interests: Christian fiction
Mem of Illinois Heartland Library System
Open Mon, Wed & Fri 8-4, Tues & Thurs 8-8, Sat 8-2

CLARENDON HILLS

P CLARENDON HILLS PUBLIC LIBRARY*, Seven N Prospect Ave, 60514. SAN 304-0682. Tel: 630-323-8188. FAX: 630-323-8189. E-mail: cns@clarendonhillslibrary.org. *Dir,* Lori Craft; E-mail: craftl@clarendonhillslibrary.org; *Adult Serv,* Barbara Stepina; E-mail: stepinab@clarendonhillslibrary.org; *Ch Serv,* Krista Devlin; E-mail: devlink@clarendonhillslibrary.org; *ILL, Ref,* Kathleen Strange; E-mail: strange@clarendonhillslibrary.org; Staff 6 (MLS 3, Non-MLS 3)
Founded 1963. Pop 8,427; Circ 88,123
Library Holdings: AV Mats 1,439; Large Print Bks 253; Bk Titles 48,153; Bk Vols 51,176; Per Subs 146
Subject Interests: Local hist, Travel
Automation Activity & Vendor Info: (Circulation) Innovative Interfaces, Inc
Wireless access
Mem of Reaching Across Illinois Library System (RAILS)
Open Mon, Tues & Thurs 9:30-9, Wed & Fri 9:30-5, Sat 9:30-4
Friends of the Library Group

CLAYTON

P CLAYTON PUBLIC LIBRARY DISTRICT*, 211 E Maine St, 62324. (Mail add: PO Box 318, 62324-0318), SAN 304-0690. Tel: 217-894-6519. FAX: 217-894-6519. E-mail: claypld@adams.net. *Librn,* Sharol Busby
Pop 1,553
Library Holdings: Bk Vols 7,000; Per Subs 13
Wireless access
Open Tues & Wed 12:30-6, Thurs 1:30-7, Fri 2-5, Sat 9:30-3

CLIFTON

P CENTRAL CITIZENS' LIBRARY DISTRICT*, 1134 E 3100 North Rd, Ste C, 60927-7088. Tel: 815-694-2800. FAX: 815-694-3200. Web Site: www.ccld.org. *Dir,* Renee Wellborn; E-mail: rwellborn@cusd4.org; *Librn,* Connie Hitchens; Staff 2 (MLS 2)
Founded 1995. Pop 5,057; Circ 43,659
Library Holdings: Bk Vols 25,720; Per Subs 85
Automation Activity & Vendor Info: (Cataloging) SirsiDynix; (Circulation) SirsiDynix; (OPAC) SirsiDynix
Mem of Illinois Heartland Library System
Open Mon-Thurs 8-8, Fri 8-4, Sat 9-1
Friends of the Library Group

P CLIFTON PUBLIC LIBRARY, 150 E Fourth Ave, 60927. (Mail add: PO Box 452, 60927-0452). Tel: 815-694-2069. FAX: 815-694-2069. Web Site: www.cliftonlibrary.info. *Dir,* Carolyn Smith; Staff 1.25 (Non-MLS 1.25)
Founded 1903. Pop 1,317

Library Holdings: DVDs 400; Large Print Bks 60; Bk Titles 7,000; Per Subs 52
Wireless access
Function: Computers for patron use, Copy machines, Digital talking bks, Electronic databases & coll, Fax serv, Online ref, Online searches, Photocopying/Printing, Prog for adults, Prog for children & young adult, Ref & res, Scanner, VHS videos
Open Mon-Fri 2-7, Sat 9-Noon

CLINTON

P VESPASIAN WARNER PUBLIC LIBRARY DISTRICT*, 310 N Quincy, 61727. SAN 304-0704. Tel: 217-935-5174. FAX: 217-935-4425. Web Site: www.warner.lib.il.us. *Dir,* Joan Rhodes; *Asst Dir,* Bobbi Perryman; *Ch,* Paula Lopatic
Founded 1901. Pop 10,250; Circ 107,000
Library Holdings: Bk Vols 80,000; Per Subs 200
Special Collections: Early Illinois History & Geography (C H Moore Coll). US Document Depository
Automation Activity & Vendor Info: (Circulation) SirsiDynix
Wireless access
Mem of Illinois Heartland Library System
Open Mon-Thurs 9-9, Fri 9-5, Sat 9-4
Friends of the Library Group

COAL CITY

P COAL CITY PUBLIC LIBRARY DISTRICT*, 85 N Garfield St, 60416. SAN 304-0712. Tel: 815-634-4552. FAX: 815-634-2950. E-mail: ccpld@ccpld.org. Web Site: www.ccpld.org. *Dir,* Jolene Franciskovich; E-mail: jolene@ccpld.org; *Asst Dir,* Leah Bill; E-mail: leah@ccpld.org; *Head, Adult Serv,* Karla Welch; E-mail: karla@ccpld.org; *Head, Ch,* Rene Norris; E-mail: rene@ccpld.org; *Head, Circ,* Mary Jo Breneman; E-mail: maryjo@ccpld.org; *Head, Ref,* Irene Shepkowski; E-mail: irene@ccpld.org; *Head, Teen Serv,* Danielle Diamond; E-mail: danielle@ccpld.org; *Communications Coordr,* Dixie Wiley; E-mail: dixie@ccpld.org; Staff 12 (MLS 1, Non-MLS 11)
Founded 1886. Pop 11,257; Circ 232,502
Jul 2011-Jun 2012 Income $1,306,393, State $9,611, Locally Generated Income $1,294,771. Mats Exp $1,118,020, Books $67,291, Per/Ser (Incl. Access Fees) $8,509, AV Mat $18,729, Electronic Ref Mat (Incl. Access Fees) $34,870. Sal $651,289 (Prof $426,716)
Library Holdings: DVDs 3,794; e-books 6,163; Electronic Media & Resources 48; Bk Titles 65,992; Per Subs 282
Automation Activity & Vendor Info: (Cataloging) Innovative Interfaces, Inc; (Circulation) Innovative Interfaces, Inc; (OPAC) Innovative Interfaces, Inc
Database Vendor: CredoReference, EBSCOhost, Gale Cengage Learning, Grolier Online, OCLC FirstSearch, Overdrive, Inc, ProQuest
Wireless access
Function: Adult bk club, After school storytime, Audiobks via web, AV serv, Bk club(s), Bks on cassette, Bks on CD, CD-ROM, Children's prog, Computer training, Computers for patron use, Copy machines, e-mail & chat, e-mail serv, Electronic databases & coll, Fax serv, Free DVD rentals, Handicapped accessible, Holiday prog, Homebound delivery serv, Homework prog, ILL available, Music CDs, Notary serv, Online cat, Online ref, Online searches, Outreach serv, OverDrive digital audio bks, Photocopying/Printing, Preschool outreach, Prog for adults, Pub access computers, Ref & res, Ref serv available, Ref serv in person, Scanner, Senior computer classes, Senior outreach, Story hour, Summer & winter reading prog, Tax forms, Teen prog, Telephone ref, VHS videos, Wheelchair accessible
Mem of Reaching Across Illinois Library System (RAILS)
Open Mon-Thurs 9-8, Fri 9-6, Sat 9-4

COAL VALLEY

P ROBERT R JONES PUBLIC LIBRARY, 900 First St, 61240. (Mail add: PO Box 190, 61240-0190), SAN 304-0720. Tel: 309-799-3047. FAX: 309-799-5528. Web Site: robertrjoneslibrary.org. *Dir,* Jeffrey Stafford; E-mail: jstaf@coalval.lib.il.us
Founded 1967. Pop 4,955; Circ 34,699
Library Holdings: AV Mats 2,211; Bks on Deafness & Sign Lang 10; Large Print Bks 127; Bk Titles 34,194; Per Subs 150
Subject Interests: Coal mining, Coal Valley hist
Automation Activity & Vendor Info: (Circulation) Innovative Interfaces, Inc; (ILL) Innovative Interfaces, Inc; (OPAC) Innovative Interfaces, Inc
Database Vendor: EBSCO Information Services, Grolier Online, OCLC FirstSearch
Wireless access
Mem of Reaching Across Illinois Library System (RAILS)
Partic in Illinois Library & Information Network; Quad-Link Libr Consortium; RiverShare Libraries
Open Mon-Thurs 10-8, Fri 10-6, Sat 10-3
Friends of the Library Group

COLCHESTER

P COLCHESTER DISTRICT LIBRARY*, 203 Macomb St, 62326. (Mail add: PO Box 237, 62326-0237), SAN 304-0739. Tel: 309-776-4861. FAX: 309-776-4099. E-mail: colchesterlibrary@yahoo.com. Web Site: colchesterlibrary.com. *Dir,* Debbie Sullivan; *Circ Librn,* Waynette Caldwell
Pop 1,645; Circ 12,191
Library Holdings: AV Mats 150; Large Print Bks 200; Bk Vols 11,000; Per Subs 68; Talking Bks 20
Wireless access
Function: ILL available
Open Mon 1-6:45, Wed 9-6:45, Fri 1-5, Sat 9-1

COLFAX

P MARTIN TOWNSHIP PUBLIC LIBRARY*, 132 W Main St, 61728. (Mail add: PO Box 376, 61728-0376), SAN 304-0747. Tel: 309-723-2541. FAX: 309-723-5037. E-mail: mtpl_43@yahoo.com. Web Site: www.mtpl.lib.il.us/library. *Dir,* Joyce Carmack
Founded 1943. Pop 1,289; Circ 5,000
Library Holdings: Bk Vols 14,000; Per Subs 30
Special Collections: Colfax Press Coll (1896-1992), micro; Cooksville Interprise Coll (1879-1921), micro; Octavia Yearbooks; Ridgeview Review (1992-present)
Function: Computers for patron use, Copy machines, Fax serv, Free DVD rentals, Handicapped accessible, ILL available, Photocopying/Printing, Summer reading prog, Tax forms
Mem of Reaching Across Illinois Library System (RAILS)
Partic in Resource Sharing Alliance
Special Services for the Blind - Large print bks
Open Mon & Fri 1-5, Tues 9-5, Wed 1-8, Sat 9-12

COLLINSVILLE

P COLLINSVILLE MEMORIAL LIBRARY CENTER*, 408 W Main St, 62234. SAN 304-0755. Tel: 618-344-1112. FAX: 618-345-6401. E-mail: bxa@mvlibdist.org. Web Site: www.collinsvillelibrary.org. *Dir,* Barbara Rhodes; *Head, Circ,* Theresa Back; *Genealogy Librn, ILL Librn,* Leslee Hamilton; *Adult Serv,* Kyla Waltermire; *Cat,* Katie Heaton; *Youth Serv,* Alison Donnelly
Founded 1915. Pop 24,707; Circ 250,756
Library Holdings: AV Mats 4,500; e-books 7,100; Large Print Bks 500; Bk Vols 65,000; Per Subs 250
Subject Interests: Prog
Automation Activity & Vendor Info: (Acquisitions) Innovative Interfaces, Inc; (Cataloging) Innovative Interfaces, Inc; (Circulation) Innovative Interfaces, Inc
Database Vendor: SirsiDynix
Wireless access
Mem of Illinois Heartland Library System
Open Mon-Thurs 9-8, Fri & Sat 9-5, Sun 1-5
Friends of the Library Group

S ILLINOIS HISTORIC PRESERVATION AGENCY, Cahokia Mounds State Historic Site Library, 30 Ramey St, 62234. SAN 374-759X. Tel: 618-346-5160. FAX: 618-346-5162. E-mail: cahokia.mounds@sbcglobal.net. Web Site: www.cahokiamounds.org. *Mgr,* Mark Esarey
Library Holdings: Bk Vols 2,000
Subject Interests: Anthrop, Archaeology, Natural hist
Mem of Illinois Heartland Library System
Partic in Illinois Library & Information Network
Open Mon-Sun 9-5
Restriction: Internal circ only

S SOUTHWESTERN ILLINOIS METROPOLITAN & REGIONAL PLANNING COMMISSION*, Technical Library, 2511Vandalia St, 62234. SAN 326-9558. Tel: 618-344-4250. FAX: 618-344-4253. *Librn,* Stephenie Pratt; Tel: 618-344-4250, Ext 119
Publications: Grants & Miscellaneous Municality
Open Mon-Fri 9-5

COLONA

P COLONA DISTRICT PUBLIC LIBRARY*, 911 First St, 61241. SAN 304-2405. Tel: 309-792-0548. FAX: 309-792-2143. E-mail: contact@colonalibrary.com. Web Site: colonalibrary.com. *Dir,* Phyllis Von Arb; E-mail: pvonarb@colonalibrary.com; Staff 0.75 (MLS 0.75)
Pop 6,699; Circ 39,956
Library Holdings: Audiobooks 754; DVDs 1,600; e-books 5,766; Bk Vols 19,313; Per Subs 44
Subject Interests: Local hist
Database Vendor: OCLC FirstSearch, SirsiDynix
Wireless access
Function: After school storytime, Audiobks via web, Bks on cassette, Bks on CD, Children's prog, Computers for patron use, Copy machines, Digital

talking bks, e-mail & chat, Fax serv, Free DVD rentals, Handicapped accessible, ILL available, Online cat, OverDrive digital audio bks, Photocopying/Printing, Prog for adults, Prog for children & young adult, Pub access computers, Scanner, Story hour, Summer reading prog, Tax forms, VHS videos, Wheelchair accessible
Publications: Colona Library Link (Newsletter)
Mem of Reaching Across Illinois Library System (RAILS)
Special Services for the Blind - Talking bks
Open Mon-Fri 10-8, Sat 10-3
Friends of the Library Group

COLUMBIA

P COLUMBIA PUBLIC LIBRARY*, 106 N Metter Ave, 62236-2299. SAN 304-0771. Tel: 618-281-4237. FAX: 618-281-6977. Reference E-mail: reference@columbialibrary.org. Web Site: www.columbialibrary.org. *Dir & Head Librn,* Britta Krabill; E-mail: brittakrabill@columbialibrary.org; *Asst Dir,* Annette Bland; E-mail: annettebland@columbialibrary.org; *Cataloger,* Anna Hesterberg
Founded 1958. Pop 9,070; Circ 53,354
Library Holdings: CDs 65; Large Print Bks 1,316; Bk Vols 47,000; Per Subs 151; Talking Bks 1,247; Videos 1,691
Subject Interests: Genealogy, Local hist
Automation Activity & Vendor Info: (Acquisitions) Innovative Interfaces, Inc; (Cataloging) Innovative Interfaces, Inc; (Circulation) Innovative Interfaces, Inc; (OPAC) Innovative Interfaces, Inc
Database Vendor: OCLC FirstSearch, OCLC WorldShare Interlibrary Loan
Wireless access
Function: Audiobks via web, Bks on CD, Children's prog, Computers for patron use, Copy machines, Family literacy, Free DVD rentals, Handicapped accessible, Holiday prog, ILL available, Mail & tel request accepted, Music CDs, Online cat, Online ref, Online searches, Outside serv via phone, mail, e-mail & web, OverDrive digital audio bks, Photocopying/Printing, Preschool reading prog, Prog for adults, Prog for children & young adult, Pub access computers, Ref & res, Ref serv available, Ref serv in person, Summer reading prog, Teen prog, Telephone ref, Web-catalog, Wheelchair accessible
Mem of Illinois Heartland Library System
Special Services for the Blind - Extensive large print coll; Large print bks; Talking bk serv referral
Open Mon-Thurs 9-8:30, Fri 9-5, Sat 9-4
Friends of the Library Group

CORDOVA

P CORDOVA DISTRICT LIBRARY*, 402 Main Ave, 61242-9790. (Mail add: PO Box 247, 61242-0247), SAN 304-078X. Tel: 309-654-2330. FAX: 309-654-2290. Web Site: www.cordova.lib.il.us. *Dir,* Sue Hebel; E-mail: shebel@cordova.lib.il.us; *Head Librn,* Cheryl Lennox; E-mail: clennox@cordova.lib.il.us; *Head, ILL, Tech Serv Librn,* Traci Stratton; E-mail: tstratto@cordova.lib.il.us; Staff 2 (Non-MLS 2)
Founded 1876. Pop 1,031; Circ 31,625
Library Holdings: Bk Vols 15,000; Per Subs 35
Subject Interests: Miss river
Automation Activity & Vendor Info: (Cataloging) Infor Library & Information Solutions; (Circulation) Infor Library & Information Solutions; (OPAC) Infor Library & Information Solutions
Mem of Reaching Across Illinois Library System (RAILS)
Open Mon & Wed 9-8, Tues & Thurs 1-8, Fri 9-5, Sat 9-1

CORNELL

P AMITY TOWNSHIP PUBLIC LIBRARY*, 604 E Main St, 61319. (Mail add: PO Box 243, 61319-0243), SAN 376-1355. Tel: 815-358-2231. FAX: 815-358-2217. *Librn,* Judy Pharis; E-mail: jphar_22@yahoo.com
Library Holdings: Bk Titles 6,000; Per Subs 2
Open Mon & Wed 3-5, Tues 5-7, Thurs 2-4, Sat 10-12

CORTLAND

P CORTLAND COMMUNITY LIBRARY*, 63 S Somonauk Rd, 60112. (Mail add: PO Box 486, 60112-0486). Tel: 815-756-7274. FAX: 815-748-4491. E-mail: circ@cortlandlibrary.com. Web Site: www.cortlandlibrary.com. *Dir,* Barb Coward
Library Holdings: Bk Titles 23,500; Per Subs 65
Automation Activity & Vendor Info: (Acquisitions) SIRSI-iBistro; (Cataloging) SIRSI WorkFlows; (Circulation) SIRSI WorkFlows; (Course Reserve) SIRSI-iBistro; (ILL) SIRSI-iBistro; (Media Booking) SIRSI-iBistro; (OPAC) SIRSI-iBistro; (Serials) SIRSI WorkFlows
Database Vendor: SirsiDynix
Wireless access
Mem of Reaching Across Illinois Library System (RAILS)
Special Services for the Blind - Scanner for conversion & translation of mats
Open Mon & Thurs 9-9, Fri & Sat 9-5
Friends of the Library Group

COULTERVILLE

P COULTERVILLE PUBLIC LIBRARY*, 103 S Fourth St, 62237. (Mail add: PO Box 373, 62237-0373), SAN 304-0798. Tel: 618-758-3013. FAX: 618-758-3013. E-mail: coultervillepubliclibrary@gmail.com. Web Site: coultervillepubliclibrary.webs.com. *Librn,* Jennifer Grafton; *Librn,* Tammy Rieckenberg
Founded 1956. Pop 1,118; Circ 15,951
Library Holdings: Bk Vols 9,173
Special Collections: Education; Genealogy; History; Religion
Wireless access
Mem of Illinois Heartland Library System
Open Mon & Fri 10-3, Tues & Thurs 1-6, Sat 10-2

COWDEN

P DRY POINT TOWNSHIP LIBRARY*, S Rte 128, 62422. (Mail add: PO Box 275, 62422-0275), SAN 376-1479. Tel: 217-783-2616. *Librn,* Charlene Taylor
Founded 1972
Library Holdings: Bk Titles 15,000; Per Subs 25
Automation Activity & Vendor Info: (Cataloging) SirsiDynix; (Circulation) SirsiDynix
Mem of Illinois Heartland Library System
Open Mon & Thurs 8-8, Tues, Wed & Fri 8-4, Sat 8-12
Friends of the Library Group

CRESTON

P CRESTON-DEMENT LIBRARY DISTRICT*, 107 S Main St, 60113-0056. (Mail add: PO Box 193, 60113-0193). Tel: 815-384-3111. FAX: 815-384-3111. E-mail: staff@crestonlib.us. Web Site: crestonlib.us. *Dir,* Kristi Scherer
Founded 1986. Pop 731
Library Holdings: Audiobooks 257; CDs 3; DVDs 371; Large Print Bks 106; Bk Titles 15,000; Per Subs 27
Function: ILL available
Mem of Reaching Across Illinois Library System (RAILS)
Open Tues, Wed & Fri 9-5, Thurs 9-8, Sat 9-2
Friends of the Library Group

CRESTWOOD

P CRESTWOOD PUBLIC LIBRARY DISTRICT*, 4955 W 135th St, 60445. SAN 304-0801. Tel: 708-371-4090. FAX: 708-371-4127. E-mail: cws@crestwoodlibrary.org. Web Site: www.crestwoodlibrary.org. *Dir,* Suzanne Bleskin
Founded 1973. Circ 36,640
Library Holdings: Bk Vols 50,000; Per Subs 100
Automation Activity & Vendor Info: (Cataloging) Innovative Interfaces, Inc; (Circulation) Innovative Interfaces, Inc; (OPAC) Innovative Interfaces, Inc
Mem of Reaching Across Illinois Library System (RAILS)
Open Mon-Thurs 10-8, Fri & Sat 10-4

CRETE

P CRETE PUBLIC LIBRARY DISTRICT*, 1177 N Main St, 60417. SAN 304-081X. Tel: 708-672-8017. FAX: 708-672-3529. E-mail: cts@sslic.net. Web Site: www.cretelibrary.org. *Admin Dir,* Jane Schulten; *Adult Serv,* Tiffany Amschl; *Ch Serv,* Gail Scott; *Ref Serv, Ad,* Ellen Herrmann; Staff 21 (MLS 3, Non-MLS 18)
Founded 1985. Pop 19,500; Circ 124,000
Library Holdings: AV Mats 2,400; Bk Titles 61,000; Per Subs 197; Talking Bks 300
Special Collections: Caregiver Resource Center
Subject Interests: Antiques, Collectibles
Automation Activity & Vendor Info: (Acquisitions) Innovative Interfaces, Inc; (Cataloging) Innovative Interfaces, Inc; (Course Reserve) Innovative Interfaces, Inc
Database Vendor: EBSCOhost, OCLC FirstSearch
Mem of Reaching Across Illinois Library System (RAILS)
Open Mon-Thurs 10-9, Sat 10-3
Friends of the Library Group

CREVE COEUR

P CREVE COEUR PUBLIC LIBRARY DISTRICT*, 311 N Highland Ave, 61610. SAN 304-0828. Tel: 309-699-7921. FAX: 309-699-0949. E-mail: crcopld@hotmail.com. Web Site: www.crevecoeurpubliclibrary.com. *Dir,* Greg Wydert; Staff 4 (Non-MLS 4)
Founded 1945. Pop 5,448
Library Holdings: Bk Vols 23,279; Per Subs 48

Automation Activity & Vendor Info: (Cataloging) Follett Software; (Circulation) Follett Software
Open Mon 10-8, Tues-Fri 10-6

CRYSTAL LAKE

P CRYSTAL LAKE PUBLIC LIBRARY*, 126 Paddock St, 60014. SAN 304-0836. Tel: 815-459-1687. FAX: 815-459-9581. Web Site: www.crystallakelibrary.org. *Dir,* Kathryn I Martens; E-mail: kmartens@crystallakelibrary.org; *Asst Dir,* Karen Migaldi; E-mail: kmigaldi@crystallakelibrary.org; *Head, Adult Serv,* Cynthia Lopuszynski; E-mail: clopuszynski@crystallakelibrary.org; *Head, Circ,* Pamela Miller; E-mail: pmiller@crystallakelibrary.org; *Head, Youth Serv,* Jessie Exum; E-mail: jexum@crystallakelibrary.org; *Tech Serv & Automation,* Mary Van Sickle; E-mail: mvansickle@crystallakelibrary.org; Staff 86 (MLS 16, Non-MLS 70)
Founded 1913. Pop 39,788; Circ 1,001,075
Library Holdings: AV Mats 32,717; Bk Vols 176,627; Per Subs 360
Automation Activity & Vendor Info: (Acquisitions) SIRSI WorkFlows; (Cataloging) OCLC; (Circulation) SIRSI WorkFlows; (OPAC) SirsiDynix
Database Vendor: OCLC FirstSearch, ProQuest, SirsiDynix
Wireless access
Function: Adult bk club, Audiobks via web, AV serv, Bks on cassette, Bks on CD, CD-ROM, Chess club, Children's prog, Computer training, Computers for patron use, Copy machines, e-mail serv, E-Reserves, Electronic databases & coll, Fax serv, Free DVD rentals, Handicapped accessible, Holiday prog, Home delivery & serv to Sr ctr & nursing homes, Homebound delivery serv, ILL available, Mus passes, Music CDs, Notary serv, Online cat, Online ref, Online searches, Orientations, Outreach serv, Outside serv via phone, mail, e-mail & web, OverDrive digital audio bks, Photocopying/Printing, Preschool outreach, Prog for adults, Prog for children & young adult, Pub access computers, Ref serv available, Ref serv in person, Senior computer classes, Senior outreach, Story hour, Summer reading prog, Tax forms, Teen prog, Telephone ref, VHS videos, Wheelchair accessible
Publications: Beacon (Newsletter)
Partic in Cooperative Computer Services - CCS
Open Mon-Thurs 9-9, Fri & Sat 9-5, Sun 1-5
Restriction: Access at librarian's discretion
Friends of the Library Group

J MCHENRY COUNTY COLLEGE LIBRARY*, 8900 US Hwy 14, 60012-2738. SAN 304-0852. Tel: 815 455-8533. Reference Tel: 815-455-8762. FAX: 815-455-3999. Web Site: www.mchenry.edu/library/. *Dean,* Jonathan A Birnbaum; Tel: 815-479-7545; *Ref Serv,* Cynthia Letteri; E-mail: cletteri@mchenry.edu; *Ref Serv,* Janet Scott; E-mail: jscott@mchenry.edu; Staff 15 (MLS 7, Non-MLS 8)
Founded 1968. Enrl 1,850; Fac 84
Library Holdings: AV Mats 6,000; Bk Titles 35,000; Bk Vols 41,000; Per Subs 225
Subject Interests: Hort
Automation Activity & Vendor Info: (Cataloging) SirsiDynix; (Circulation) SirsiDynix; (Course Reserve) SirsiDynix; (OPAC) SirsiDynix; (Serials) SirsiDynix
Database Vendor: EBSCOhost, Gale Cengage Learning, LexisNexis, OCLC FirstSearch, ProQuest
Function: ILL available
Partic in Northern Illinois Learning Resources Cooperative (NILRC)
Open Mon-Thurs (Winter) 8am-9:30pm, Fri 8-4:30, Sat 8-2; Mon-Thurs (Summer) 8am-9pm, Fri 8-4:30

CUBA

P SPOON RIVER PUBLIC LIBRARY DISTRICT*, 201 S Third St, 61427. (Mail add: PO Box 140, 61427-0140), SAN 304-0860. Tel: 309-785-5496. FAX: 309-785-5439. E-mail: spoon_river_61427@yahoo.com. Web Site: www.cubaspoonriverlibrary.com/about-us. *Dir, Libr Serv,* Jean Twiss; Staff 6 (Non-MLS 6)
Founded 1912. Pop 3,402; Circ 27,164
Library Holdings: Bks on Deafness & Sign Lang 12; High Interest/Low Vocabulary Bk Vols 50; Bk Vols 20,000; Per Subs 47
Special Collections: Census on microfilm, Fulton County bks; Cuba High School Yearbook, microfilm; Cuba Journal, microfilm; Genealogy (family history files, obituaries, cemetery plot bks, etc)
Database Vendor: OCLC FirstSearch
Wireless access
Open Mon & Wed 9:30-4, Tues & Thurs 9:30-7, Fri & Sat 9:30-2

CUTLER

P CUTLER PUBLIC LIBRARY*, Civic Ctr, 409 S Main, 62238. SAN 376-1290. Tel: 618-497-2961. FAX: 618-497-8818. E-mail: cutlibcc@egyptian.net. *Librn,* Jackie Carrothers; *Asst Librn,* Judy Farris
Library Holdings: Bk Titles 2,700
Wireless access
Open Mon & Tues 4-7, Wed & Sat 9-12, Thurs & Fri 2-5

DAHLGREN

P DAHLGREN PUBLIC LIBRARY*, Third & Dale St, 62828. (Mail add: PO Box 237, 62828-0237). Tel: 618-736-2652. FAX: 618-736-2652. *Librn,* Judi Cockrum
Library Holdings: Bk Vols 5,000
Mem of Illinois Heartland Library System
Open Mon-Wed & Sun 2-4, Thurs 9am-11am

DANVERS

P DANVERS TOWNSHIP LIBRARY*, 117 E Exchange St, 61732-9347. (Mail add: PO Box 376, 61732-0376), SAN 304-0879. Tel: 309-963-4269. FAX: 309-963-4269. E-mail: danvers.tl.rsa@gmail.com. Web Site: www.danverstownshiplibrary.com. *Dir,* Lori Priebe; *Asst Librn,* Carol Bogue; *Asst Librn,* Cathy Frey; *Asst Librn,* Miriam Knoy; *Asst Librn,* Cindy Melick
Pop 1,925; Circ 21,000
Library Holdings: Audiobooks 307; CDs 50; DVDs 1,200; Bk Vols 20,000; Per Subs 88; Talking Bks 100; Videos 300
Database Vendor: OCLC FirstSearch, OCLC WorldShare Interlibrary Loan, Overdrive, Inc
Wireless access
Function: Computers for patron use, Copy machines, Fax serv, Free DVD rentals, Handicapped accessible, Holiday prog, ILL available, Online cat, OverDrive digital audio bks, Photocopying/Printing, Prog for adults, Scanner, Spoken cassettes & CDs, Story hour, Summer reading prog, Tax forms, VHS videos, Wheelchair accessible
Open Mon & Thurs 1-8, Tues 9-8, Wed & Fri 9-5, Sat 9-12

DANVILLE

J DANVILLE AREA COMMUNITY COLLEGE LIBRARY*, 2000 E Main St, 61832-5199. SAN 304-0887. Tel: 217-443-8734. Circulation Tel: 217-443-8883. Interlibrary Loan Service Tel: 217-443-8733. Reference Tel: 217-443-8739. FAX: 217-554-1623. E-mail: library@dacc.edu. Web Site: www.dacc.edu/library. *Dir,* Penny McConnell; *Head, Tech Serv & Cat,* Holly Nordheden; Tel: 217-443-8852; *Ref & Instrul Serv Librn,* Dr Ruth B Lindemann; Tel: 217-443-8735, E-mail: rlinde@dacc.edu; *Circ & ILL,* Kerry Bowden; *Tech Serv,* Glenda Hargan; Tel: 217-443-8737, E-mail: ghargan@dacc.edu; Staff 7 (MLS 4, Non-MLS 3)
Founded 1962. Enrl 2,100; Highest Degree: Associate
Library Holdings: CDs 200; DVDs 3,000; Bk Titles 30,000; Bk Vols 35,000; Per Subs 200
Automation Activity & Vendor Info: (Acquisitions) Ex Libris Group; (Cataloging) Ex Libris Group; (Circulation) Ex Libris Group; (ILL) Ex Libris Group; (OPAC) Ex Libris Group; (Serials) SerialsSolutions
Database Vendor: ABC-CLIO, Alexander Street Press, Baker & Taylor, Cinahl, CredoReference, ebrary, EBSCOhost, Elsevier, Facts on File, Gale Cengage Learning, LexisNexis, OCLC CAMIO, OCLC FirstSearch, OCLC WorldShare Interlibrary Loan, ProQuest, PubMed, Sage, Springer-Verlag, Springshare, LLC, Wilson - Wilson Web
Wireless access
Function: Audio & video playback equip for onsite use, Computers for patron use, Distance learning, Electronic databases & coll, ILL available, Magnifiers for reading, Ref serv available
Mem of Illinois Heartland Library System
Partic in Consortium of Academic & Research Libraries in Illinois; Illinois Library & Information Network; Network of Illinois Learning Resources in Community Colleges
Special Services for the Deaf - Closed caption videos; Described encaptioned media prog
Special Services for the Blind - Playaways (bks on MP3); Screen enlargement software for people with visual disabilities
Open Mon-Thurs (Fall & Spring) 7:30am-8pm, Fri 7:30-5
Restriction: Open to pub for ref & circ; with some limitations, Open to students, fac & staff

P DANVILLE PUBLIC LIBRARY*, 319 N Vermilion St, 61832. SAN 304-0895. Tel: 217-477-5220. Reference Tel: 217-477-5228. FAX: 217-477-5230. Web Site: www.danville.lib.il.us. *Dir,* Barbara J Nolan; Tel: 217-477-5223, Ext 113, E-mail: bnolan@danville.lib.il.us; *Asst Dir,* Phillip Cohee; Tel: 217-477-5223, Ext 118, E-mail: pcohee@danville.lib.il.us; *Outreach Serv Librn,* Mary Jane Starnes; Tel: 217-477-5227, E-mail: mstarnes@danville.lib.il.us; *Archivist, Ref,* Roberta Allen; E-mail: rallen@danville.lib.il.us; *AV,* Michael Boedicker; Tel: 217-477-5224, E-mail: mboedicker@hotmail.com; *Ch Serv,* Vonna Bley; Tel: 217-477-5225, E-mail: vbley@danville.lib.il.us; *Circ,* Patricia Lewis; Staff 7 (MLS 6, Non-MLS 1)
Founded 1883. Pop 33,828; Circ 313,669
Library Holdings: AV Mats 4,441; Bk Vols 161,415; Per Subs 353; Talking Bks 6,366
Special Collections: Gardening; Genealogy

Automation Activity & Vendor Info: (Cataloging) SirsiDynix; (Circulation) SirsiDynix; (OPAC) SirsiDynix
Database Vendor: OCLC FirstSearch
Publications: Danville Public Library News (Newsletter)
Mem of Illinois Heartland Library System
Open Mon-Thurs 9-8, Fri & Sat 9-5:30
Friends of the Library Group

DARIEN

P INDIAN PRAIRIE PUBLIC LIBRARY DISTRICT*, 401 Plainfield Rd, 60561-4207. SAN 324-1262. Tel: 630-887-8760. FAX: 630-887-8801. Administration FAX: 630-887-1018. E-mail: ippl@indianprairielibrary.org. Web Site: www.indianprairielibrary.org. *Dir,* Jamie Bukovac; E-mail: bukovacj@indianprairielibrary.org; *Asst Dir,* Laura Birmingham; E-mail: birminghaml@indianprairielibrary.org; *Adult Serv,* Debra Wordinger; E-mail: wordingerd@indianprairielibrary.org; *Circ,* Deborah Sheehan; E-mail: sheehand@indianprairielibrary.org; *Computer Serv, Tech Serv,* Ann Stovall; E-mail: stovalla@indianprairielibrary.org; *Youth Serv,* Monica Dzierzbicki; E-mail: dzierzbickim@indianprairielibrary.org; Staff 45 (MLS 12, Non-MLS 33)
Founded 1988. Pop 43,879; Circ 857,901
Jul 2008-Jun 2009 Income $343,728. Mats Exp $485,074, Books $282,504, Per/Ser (Incl. Access Fees) $33,078, AV Mat $98,603, Electronic Ref Mat (Incl. Access Fees) $70,889. Sal $1,715,714
Library Holdings: AV Mats 35,618; Bk Vols 151,256; Per Subs 457
Automation Activity & Vendor Info: (Acquisitions) Innovative Interfaces, Inc; (Cataloging) Innovative Interfaces, Inc; (Circulation) Innovative Interfaces, Inc; (ILL) Innovative Interfaces, Inc; (OPAC) Innovative Interfaces, Inc; (Serials) Innovative Interfaces, Inc
Database Vendor: Baker & Taylor, EBSCO Information Services, Gale Cengage Learning, infoUSA, OCLC FirstSearch, OCLC WorldShare Interlibrary Loan, ProQuest, ReferenceUSA
Wireless access
Function: Adult bk club, Adult literacy prog, Audio & video playback equip for onsite use, Audiobks via web, AV serv, BA reader (adult literacy), Bi-weekly Writer's Group, Bk club(s), Bks on CD, CD-ROM, Chess club, Children's prog, Computer training, Computers for patron use, Copy machines, E-Reserves, Electronic databases & coll, Fax serv, Free DVD rentals, Genealogy discussion group, Handicapped accessible, Home delivery & serv to Sr ctr & nursing homes, ILL available, Magnifiers for reading, Music CDs, Notary serv, Online cat, Online ref, Online searches, OverDrive digital audio bks, Photocopying/Printing, Preschool outreach, Prog for adults, Prog for children & young adult, Pub access computers, Ref serv available, Scanner, Senior computer classes, Senior outreach, Story hour, Summer reading prog, Tax forms, Teen prog, Telephone ref, VHS videos
Publications: Enewsletter (Newsletter); IPPL (Newsletter)
Mem of Reaching Across Illinois Library System (RAILS)
Special Services for the Deaf - Assisted listening device; Sign lang interpreter upon request for prog; Video relay serv
Special Services for the Blind - Ref serv; Screen enlargement software for people with visual disabilities
Open Mon-Fri 9-9, Sat 9-5, Sun 1-5
Friends of the Library Group

DE LAND

P GOOSE CREEK TOWNSHIP CARNEGIE LIBRARY*, 220 N Highway Ave, 61839. (Mail add: PO Box 237, 61839-0237), SAN 304-095X. Tel: 217-664-3572. FAX: 217-664-3624. E-mail: goosecreeklibrary@yahoo.com. *Dir,* Melinda DelMastro
Pop 852; Circ 6,383
Library Holdings: DVDs 300; Bk Titles 6,000; Per Subs 35
Wireless access
Mem of Illinois Heartland Library System
Open Mon, Tues, Thurs & Fri 1-5:30, Wed 3-7, Sat 9-12

DE PUE

P SELBY TOWNSHIP LIBRARY DISTRICT*, 101 Depot St, 61322. (Mail add: PO Box 49, 61322-0049), SAN 304-0968. Tel: 815-447-2660. FAX: 815-447-2598. *Dir,* Donna Dabler
Founded 1937. Pop 2,460; Circ 19,288
Library Holdings: Bk Vols 12,500; Per Subs 21
Special Collections: History of De Pue Coll, A-tapes. Oral History
Mem of Reaching Across Illinois Library System (RAILS)
Open Mon, Tues & Fri 12-5, Wed 10-8, Sat 8-12
Friends of the Library Group

DECATUR

S DECATUR GENEALOGICAL SOCIETY LIBRARY*, 1255 W South Side Dr, 62521-4024. (Mail add: PO Box 1548, 62525-1548), SAN 323-827X. Tel: 217-429-0135. E-mail: decaturgensoc@att.net. Web Site: www.rootsweb.com/~ildecgs/library.htm. *Pres,* Jan Camp; *Librn,* Cheri Hunter
Founded 1964
Library Holdings: Bk Titles 20,000; Bk Vols 30,000; Per Subs 16
Special Collections: County
Subject Interests: Bibles, Genealogy
Publications: Central Illinois Genealogical Quarterly
Open Mon 10-6, Wed & Sat 10-4

S DECATUR HERALD & REVIEW LIBRARY, 601 E William St, 62523-1142. SAN 304-0984. Tel: 217-421-6979. FAX: 217-421-7965. Web Site: www.herald-review.com. *Librn,* Position Currently Open
Founded 1890
Library Holdings: Bk Vols 500; Per Subs 10
Database Vendor: Newsbank
Open Mon-Fri 8-5

P DECATUR PUBLIC LIBRARY*, 130 N Franklin St, 62523-1327. SAN 340-3440. Tel: 217-424-2900. Circulation Tel: 217-421-9728, 217-424-2900, Ext 128. Interlibrary Loan Service Tel: 217-421-9747, 217-424-2900, Ext 147. Reference Tel: 217-421-9730. Administration Tel: 217-421-9712, 217-424-2900, Ext 112. Automation Services Tel: 217-421-9753, 217-424-2900, Ext 153. Information Services Tel: 217-421-9731, 217-424-2900, Ext 131. FAX: 217-233-4071. TDD: 217-421-9729. Web Site: www.decaturlibrary.org. *City Librn,* Rick Meyer; E-mail: rmeyer@decaturlibrary.org; *Asst City Librn,* Robert Edwards; Tel: 217-421-9702, E-mail: redwards@decaturlibrary.org; *Head, Adult Serv,* Alissa Henkel; Tel: 217-421-9771; *Head Bldg Serv,* Noah Tipton; Tel: 217-421-9738, E-mail: ntipton@decaturlibrary.org; *Head, Ch,* Catherine Gross; Tel: 217-421-9722, E-mail: kgross@decaturlibrary.org; *Head, Circ,* Robyn Hendricks; Tel: 217-421-9737, E-mail: rhendricks@decaturlibrary.org; *Head, Tech Serv,* Constance Strait; Tel: 217-421-9739, E-mail: cstrait@decaturlibrary.org; *ILL Librn,* John Wylder; E-mail: jwylder@decaturlibrary.org; *Archivist, Local Hist Librn,* Rebecca Damptz; Tel: 217-421-9711, E-mail: rdamptz@decaturlibrary.org; *Syst Adminr,* Matthew Wilkerson; E-mail: mwilkerson@decaturlibrary.org; Staff 61 (MLS 9, Non-MLS 52)
Founded 1876. Pop 76,122; Circ 593,111
May 2012-Apr 2013 Income $3,732,000, State $145,000, City $3,000,000, Other $587,000. Mats Exp $580,000, Books $373,000, Per/Ser (Incl. Access Fees) $24,000, AV Mat $43,000, Electronic Ref Mat (Incl. Access Fees) $140,000. Sal $2,635,201
Library Holdings: Audiobooks 8,540; CDs 9,223; DVDs 8,431; Microforms 3,910; Bk Vols 247,996; Per Subs 362; Videos 6,823
Special Collections: Abraham Lincoln Coll; Local History Coll, Decatur & Macon County. US Document Depository
Automation Activity & Vendor Info: (Acquisitions) SirsiDynix; (Cataloging) SirsiDynix; (Circulation) SirsiDynix; (OPAC) SirsiDynix
Wireless access
Function: Accelerated reader prog, Adult bk club, Adult literacy prog, Archival coll, Art exhibits, Bks on cassette, Bks on CD, Children's prog, Computer training, Computers for patron use, Copy machines, E-Reserves, Electronic databases & coll, Exhibits, Fax serv, Free DVD rentals, Handicapped accessible, Homebound delivery serv, ILL available, Microfiche/film & reading machines, Music CDs, Notary serv, Online cat, OverDrive digital audio bks, Prog for adults, Prog for children & young adult, Pub access computers, Ref & res, Ref serv available, Senior computer classes, Story hour, Summer reading prog, Tax forms, Teen prog, Telephone ref, VHS videos, Wheelchair accessible
Publications: Connections (Bi-monthly)
Mem of Illinois Heartland Library System
Open Mon-Thurs 9-9, Fri & Sat 9-5:30, Sun (Sept-May) 1-5
Friends of the Library Group

L MACON COUNTY LAW LIBRARY*, Macon County Courthouse, 253 E Wood St, Rm 303, 62523. SAN 326-9531. Tel: 217-424-1372. *Librn,* Victoria Burriss

C MILLIKIN UNIVERSITY*, Staley Library, 1184 W Main, 62522. SAN 304-1018. Tel: 217-424-6214. Interlibrary Loan Service Tel: 217-424-6215. FAX: 217-424-3992. Web Site: www.millikin.edu/staley. *Libr Dir,* Cindy Fuller; E-mail: cfuller@millikin.edu; *Archivist, Coordr, Access Serv,* Amanda Pippitt; *Coordr, Educ Tech,* Rachel Bicicchi; *Coordr, Instrul Serv,* Matthew Olsen; *Coordr, Tech Serv & Electronic Res,* Denise Green; Staff 11 (MLS 5, Non-MLS 6)
Founded 1902. Enrl 2,200; Fac 140; Highest Degree: Master
Library Holdings: Bk Vols 211,539; Per Subs 460; Videos 2,388
Subject Interests: Music
Automation Activity & Vendor Info: (Acquisitions) Ex Libris Group; (Cataloging) Ex Libris Group; (Circulation) Ex Libris Group; (Course Reserve) Ex Libris Group; (ILL) Ex Libris Group; (OPAC) Ex Libris Group; (Serials) Ex Libris Group
Database Vendor: Alexander Street Press, American Chemical Society, EBSCOhost, Gale Cengage Learning, H W Wilson, JSTOR, LexisNexis,

Marcive, Inc, OCLC FirstSearch, OVID Technologies, Standard & Poor's, ValueLine, Wiley InterScience
Mem of Illinois Heartland Library System
Partic in Consortium of Academic & Research Libraries in Illinois
Open Mon-Thurs 8am-Midnight, Fri 8-5, Sat 11-7, Sun 1-Midnight

J RICHLAND COMMUNITY COLLEGE*, Kitty Lindsay Learning Resources Center, One College Park, 62521. SAN 304-1026. Tel: 217-875-7200, Ext 296. FAX: 217-875-6961. Web Site: www.richland.cc.il.us. *Dir, Libr Serv,* Louise Greene; Tel: 217-875-7200, Ext 302, E-mail: lgreene@richland.edu; *Coordr, Access Serv,* Gavena Dahlman; Tel: 217-875-7200, Ext 301, E-mail: gdahlman@richland.edu; *Coordr, Instrul Serv,* Laura Mondt; Tel: 217-875-7200, Ext 294, E-mail: lmondt@richland.edu; *ILL,* Juanita Ball; Tel: 217-875-7200, Ext 328, E-mail: jball@richland.edu; *Ref Assoc,* Jill Stern; E-mail: jstern@richland.edu; Staff 5 (MLS 3, Non-MLS 2)
Founded 1972. Enrl 3,500; Fac 60; Highest Degree: Associate
Library Holdings: Bk Titles 23,000; Bk Vols 27,000; Per Subs 117
Automation Activity & Vendor Info: (Cataloging) Ex Libris Group; (Circulation) Ex Libris Group; (Course Reserve) Ex Libris Group; (OPAC) Ex Libris Group
Database Vendor: Alexander Street Press, Baker & Taylor, CQ Press, EBSCOhost, OCLC FirstSearch, ProQuest
Wireless access
Function: Archival coll, Art exhibits, AV serv, Bilingual assistance for Spanish patrons, Computers for patron use, Copy machines, Distance learning, Doc delivery serv, E-Reserves, Electronic databases & coll, Exhibits, Handicapped accessible, ILL available, Instruction & testing, Large print keyboards, Learning ctr, Magnifiers for reading, Newsp ref libr, Outside serv via phone, mail, e-mail & web, Photocopying/Printing, Printer for laptops & handheld devices, Prof lending libr, Pub access computers, Ref & res, Ref serv available, Ref serv in person, Scanner, Spanish lang bks, VHS videos, Wheelchair accessible
Publications: Media Index; Periodical Holdings List
Mem of Illinois Heartland Library System
Partic in Consortium of Academic & Research Libraries in Illinois
Open Mon-Thurs (Winter) 7:30am-9pm, Fri 7:30-5, Sat 9-2; Mon-Thurs (Summer) 7:30am-8pm, Fri 7:30-4
Restriction: By permission only, Open to pub for ref & circ; with some limitations, Open to students, fac, staff & alumni

M SAINT MARY'S HOSPITAL*, Health Science Library, 1800 E Lake Shore Dr, 62521-3883. SAN 304-1034. Tel: 217-464-2182. FAX: 217-464-1674. Web Site: www.stmarys-hospital.com. *Librn,* Laura Brosamer; E-mail: lbrosamer@smd.hshs.org; Staff 2 (MLS 1, Non-MLS 1)
Founded 1976
Library Holdings: Bk Titles 500
Subject Interests: Hospital admin, Med, Nursing
Automation Activity & Vendor Info: (Cataloging) SirsiDynix; (Circulation) SirsiDynix
Mem of Illinois Heartland Library System
Partic in Regional Med Libr - Region 3
Open Mon-Thurs 8-4:30, Fri 8-12

S TATE & LYLE*, Research Library, 2200 E Eldorado St, 62525-1801. SAN 304-1042. Tel: 217-421-2543. Administration Tel: 217-421-3283. FAX: 217-421-2519. *Dir, ILL,* Matt Harrington; Staff 1 (MLS 1)
Founded 1958
Library Holdings: Bk Titles 7,000; Per Subs 25; Videos 250
Special Collections: Company Internal Documents
Subject Interests: Food, Nutrition
Mem of Illinois Heartland Library System
Partic in OCLC Online Computer Library Center, Inc

DEER CREEK

P DEER CREEK DISTRICT LIBRARY*, 205 First St, 61733. (Mail add: PO Box 347, 61733-0347), SAN 304-1050. Tel: 309-447-6724. FAX: 309-447-6724. *Librn,* Carlene Mathis-Kull
Founded 1965. Pop 1,247; Circ 9,221
Library Holdings: Bk Vols 19,000; Per Subs 36
Wireless access
Partic in Resource Sharing Alliance
Open Mon 9-12 & 1-7, Tues, Thurs & Fri 9-12 & 1-6, Wed 1-8

DEERFIELD

P DEERFIELD PUBLIC LIBRARY*, 920 Waukegan Rd, 60015. SAN 304-1069. Tel: 847-945-3311. Circulation Tel: 847-945-3311, Ext 8822. FAX: 847-945-3402. TDD: 847-945-3372. Reference E-mail: reference@deerfieldlibrary.org. Web Site: www.deerfieldlibrary.org. *Dir,* Mary Pergander; E-mail: mpergander@deerfieldlibrary.org; Staff 13 (MLS 13)
Founded 1927. Pop 18,400; Circ 384,099
May 2008-Apr 2009 Income $2,864,322. Mats Exp $386,431, Books $233,519, AV Mat $77,538, Electronic Ref Mat (Incl. Access Fees) $75,374. Sal $1,429,816 (Prof $778,443)
Library Holdings: CDs 10,884; DVDs 8,080; Electronic Media & Resources 31; Bk Vols 152,351; Per Subs 338
Special Collections: Deerfield Local History
Automation Activity & Vendor Info: (Acquisitions) SirsiDynix; (Cataloging) SirsiDynix; (Circulation) SirsiDynix; (OPAC) SirsiDynix; (Serials) SirsiDynix
Database Vendor: Booksite, Children's Literature Comprehensive Database Company (CLCD), Elsevier, Gale Cengage Learning, Greenwood Publishing Group, Grolier Online, infoUSA, Newsbank, OCLC FirstSearch, OCLC WorldShare Interlibrary Loan, Oxford Online, ProQuest, ReferenceUSA, SirsiDynix
Wireless access
Function: Adult bk club, After school storytime, Audiobks via web, AV serv, Bk club(s), Bks on cassette, Bks on CD, Children's prog, Computer training, Computers for patron use, Copy machines, Electronic databases & coll, Free DVD rentals, Holiday prog, Home delivery & serv to Sr ctr & nursing homes, Homebound delivery serv, ILL available, Jazz prog, Mus passes, Music CDs, Notary serv, Online cat, Online searches, Outreach serv, Outside serv via phone, mail, e-mail & web, Photocopying/Printing, Preschool outreach, Prog for adults, Prog for children & young adult, Pub access computers, Ref serv available, Senior outreach, Story hour, Summer reading prog, Tax forms, Teen prog, Telephone ref, VHS videos, Wheelchair accessible, Writing prog
Publications: Browsing
Mem of South Central Library System
Open Mon-Thurs 9-9, Fri 9-6, Sat 9-5, Sun 1-5
Friends of the Library Group

G RYERSON NATURE LIBRARY*, 21950 N Riverwoods Rd, 60015. SAN 304-3495. Tel: 847-968-3320. FAX: 847-367-6649. E-mail: ryersonwoods@LCFPD.org. Web Site: lcfpd.org. *Mgr,* Jill Stites
Founded 1974
Library Holdings: Bk Titles 2,500
Special Collections: Botany (Wildflower Coll), pressed plants; Herbarium
Subject Interests: Biol, Botany, Ecology, Entomology, Environ studies, Forestry, Ill, Landscape archit, Zoology
Restriction: Not a lending libr

CR TRINITY INTERNATIONAL UNIVERSITY*, James E Rolfing Memorial Library, 2065 Half Day Rd, 60015-1241. SAN 320-1805. Tel: 847-317-4000. Circulation Tel: 847-317-4002. Interlibrary Loan Service Tel. 847-317-4008. Reference Tel: 847-317-4001. Administration Tel: 847-317-4004. Automation Services Tel: 847-317-4021. Information Services Tel: 847-317-4011. FAX: 847-317-4012. E-mail: libref@tiu.edu. Web Site: www.tiu.edu/library. *Libr Dir,* Dr Robert H Krapohl; E-mail: rkrapohl@tiu.edu; *Electronic Res, Head, Acq, Head, Ref,* Rebecca Miller; Tel: 847-317-4013, E-mail: rmiller@tiu.edu; *Head, ILL,* Jennine Goodart; E-mail: jgoodart@tiu.edu; *Head, Pub Serv,* Linda Fratt; Tel: 847-317-4003, E-mail: lfratt@tiu.edu; *Head, Ser,* Marie Hay; Tel: 847-317-4006, E-mail: mhay@tiu.edu; *Head, Syst, Head, Tech Serv,* Matt Ostercamp; Tel: 847-317-4005, E-mail: mosterca@tiu.edu; *Circ Supvr,* Hope Gibbs; E-mail: hgibbs@tiu.edu; *Acq,* Rebekah Hall, Tel. 847-317-4007, E-mail: rhall@tiu.edu; *Ref Serv,* Kevin Compton; Tel: 847-317-4010, E-mail: kcompton@tiu.edu; *Ref Serv,* Trisha Compton; Tel: 847-317-4009, E-mail: tcompton@tiu.edu. Subject Specialists: *Theol,* Kevin Compton; Staff 16 (MLS 7, Non-MLS 9)
Founded 1970. Enrl 4,132; Fac 168; Highest Degree: Doctorate
Library Holdings: AV Mats 5,195; Electronic Media & Resources 51; Bk Titles 172,314; Bk Vols 202,254; Per Subs 1,382
Special Collections: Evangelical Free Church of America Archives (partial); Papers of Wilbur Smith & Carl F H Henry; Trinity International University Archives
Subject Interests: Biblical studies, Bioethics, Church hist, Missions & missionaries, Theol
Automation Activity & Vendor Info: (Acquisitions) Ex Libris Group; (Cataloging) Ex Libris Group; (Circulation) Ex Libris Group; (Course Reserve) Ex Libris Group; (OPAC) Ex Libris Group; (Serials) Ex Libris Group
Database Vendor: EBSCOhost, JSTOR, LexisNexis, OCLC FirstSearch, ProQuest
Function: ILL available
Partic in Association of Chicago Theological Schools; OCLC Online Computer Library Center, Inc
Open Mon-Thurs 7:30am-Midnight, Fri 7:30am-10pm, Sat 9am-10pm, Sun 1-Midnight

DEKALB

P DEKALB PUBLIC LIBRARY*, Haish Memorial Library, 309 Oak St, 60115-3369. SAN 304-0941. Tel: 815-756-9568. FAX: 815-756-7837. TDD: 815-756-6553. E-mail: dkplref@dkpl.org. Web Site: www.dkpl.org. *Dir,* Dee Coover; E-mail: deec@dkpl.org; *Head, Info Serv/Readers*

Advisory, Teresa Iversen; E-mail: teresai@dkpl.org; *IT Mgr,* Patrick Smith; E-mail: patricks@dkpl.org; *Ch Serv,* Theresa Winterbauer; E-mail: theresaw@dkpl.org; *Circ,* Robert Aspatore; E-mail: roberta@dkpl.org; *Tech Serv,* Pat Adamkiewicz; E-mail: pata@dkpl.org; Staff 45 (MLS 8, Non-MLS 37)
Founded 1893. Pop 42,579; Circ 350,000
Jul 2009-Jun 2010 Income $1,838,355, State $78,964, City $1,574,213, Federal $20,000, Locally Generated Income $92,746, Other $72,432. Mats Exp $1,653,085, Books $156,878, Per/Ser (Incl. Access Fees) $8,240, Micro $796, AV Mat $18,508, Electronic Ref Mat (Incl. Access Fees) $48,142. Sal $723,085
Library Holdings: AV Mats 9,840; Bk Vols 141,238; Per Subs 238
Subject Interests: Local hist
Automation Activity & Vendor Info: (Cataloging) SirsiDynix; (Circulation) SirsiDynix; (ILL) SirsiDynix; (OPAC) SirsiDynix; (Serials) SirsiDynix
Database Vendor: EBSCOhost
Wireless access
Mem of Reaching Across Illinois Library System (RAILS)
Open Mon-Thurs 9-9, Fri 9-6, Sat 9-5, Sun 1-5
Friends of the Library Group

C NORTHERN ILLINOIS UNIVERSITY LIBRARIES*, Founders Memorial Library, 60115-2868. SAN 340-3297. Tel: 815-753-1094. Circulation Tel: 815-753-9844. Interlibrary Loan Service Tel: 815-753-9842. Reference Tel: 815-753-0152. Interlibrary Loan Service FAX: 815-753-2003. Administration FAX: 815-753-9803. TDD: 815-753-2000. E-mail: libadmin@niu.edu. Web Site: www.ulib.niu.edu. *Dean,* Patrick J Dawson; Tel: 815-753-9801, E-mail: pdawson@niu.edu; *Assoc Dean, Coll & Tech Serv,* Chalermsee Olson; Tel: 815-753-9805, E-mail: eteolson@niu.edu; *Assoc Dean, Pub Serv,* Rosanne M Cordell; Tel: 815-753-9804, E-mail: rcordell@niu.edu; *Asst Dean, Tech Initiatives & Support Serv,* T J Lusher; Tel: 815-753-0521, E-mail: tlusher@niu.edu; *Head, Ref & Res Serv,* Nestor Osorio; Tel: 815-753-9837, E-mail: nosorio@niu.edu; *Head, Tech Serv,* Jana Brubaker; Tel: 815-753-5914, E-mail: jbrubake@niu.edu; *Head, User Serv,* Sarah McHone-Chase; Tel: 815-753-9860, E-mail: mchonechase@niu.edu; *Unit Head, Govt Publ/Govt Doc,* Rachel Hradecky; Tel: 815-753-9841, E-mail: rhradecky@niu.edu; *Music Librn, Unit Head, Spec Coll,* Michael Duffy, IV; Tel: 815-753-9839, E-mail: mduffyiv@niu.edu; *Res & Ref Librn,* Meredith Ayers; Tel: 815-753-1872, E-mail: mayers@niu.edu; *Res & Ref Librn,* William Baker; Tel: 815-753-1857, E-mail: bbaker@niu.edu; *Res & Ref Librn,* Wayne Finley; Tel: 815-753-0991, E-mail: wfinley@niu.edu; *Res & Ref Librn,* Karen Hovde; Tel: 815-753-1770, E-mail: khovde@niu.edu; *Res & Ref Librn,* Wendell Johnson; Tel: 815-753-1634, E-mail: wjohnso1@niu.edu; *Res & Ref Librn,* Ladislava Khailova; Tel: 815-753-1351, E-mail: khailova@niu.edu; *Res & Ref Librn,* David Lonergan; Tel: 815-753-9866, E-mail: nemo@niu.edu; *Res & Ref Librn,* Beth McGowan; Tel: 815-753-1947, E-mail: bmcgowan@niu.edu; *Res & Ref Librn,* Junlin Pan; Tel: 815-753-0530, E-mail: jpan@niu.edu; *Res & Ref Librn,* Robert Ridinger; Tel: 815-753-1367, E-mail: rridinger@niu.edu; *Res & Ref Librn,* Leanne VandeCreek; Tel: 815-753-4025, E-mail: lvandecreek@niu.edu; *Tech Serv Librn,* Elizabeth Cribbs; Tel: 815-753-8392, E-mail: ecribbs@niu.edu; *Tech Serv Librn,* Matt Short; Tel: 815-753-9868, E-mail: mshort@niu.edu; *Acq Analysis & Relations,* James Millhorn; Tel: 815-753-1054, E-mail: millhorn@niu.edu; *Univ Archivist,* Cindy Ditzler; Tel: 815-753-9392, E-mail: cditzler@niu.edu; *Curator, Spec Coll, Rare Bks,* Lynne Thomas; Tel: 815-753-0255, E-mail: lmthomas@niu.edu. Subject Specialists: *Eng, Math, Sci,* Nestor Osorio; *English,* William Baker; Staff 94 (MLS 25, Non-MLS 69)
Founded 1899. Enrl 25,424; Fac 1,256; Highest Degree: Doctorate
Library Holdings: Bk Titles 1,469,412; Bk Vols 2,000,000; Per Subs 25,789
Special Collections: African-American Coll; American Popular Literature Coll; Angus Wilson Coll; Archives; Book Arts Coll; Burns Coll; Byron Coll; Chess Magazines; Chicago Lyric Opera Coll; Colorado-Henkle Coll; Comic Book Coll; Denson Coll; Dos Passos Coll; Drama Coll (includes University & Nisbett-Snydere Coll); Edward Ardizzone Coll; Fine Arts Coll; Gender Studies Coll; Graham Greene Coll; Hanley Manuscript Coll; Horatio Alger Coll; Imprint Society; James D Tobin Coll; Jeremy Taylor Coll; Johannsen Coll; Lovecraft Coll; Motley Coll; Music (Skinner Coll), ms; Private Press; Science Fiction Coll (includes Science Fiction Writers of America & the Science Fiction Magazine Coll); Southeast Asia Coll; Vincent Starrett Coll; Western Fiction Writers of America (WFMWA) Magazine Coll; Whitman Coll; Wordsworth Coll. State Document Depository; US Document Depository
Subject Interests: Bus & mgt, Econ, Educ, Hist, Natural sci, Sci tech
Automation Activity & Vendor Info: (Acquisitions) Ex Libris Group; (Cataloging) Ex Libris Group; (Circulation) Ex Libris Group; (OPAC) Ex Libris Group; (Serials) Ex Libris Group
Database Vendor: Dialog, EBSCOhost, Gale Cengage Learning, LexisNexis, OCLC FirstSearch, OVID Technologies, ProQuest, SirsiDynix, TLC (The Library Corporation)
Wireless access
Mem of Reaching Across Illinois Library System (RAILS)
Open Mon-Fri 8-4:30
Friends of the Library Group
Departmental Libraries:
FARADAY LIBRARY, Faraday Hall, Rm 212, 60115, SAN 340-3386. Tel: 815-753-1850. *In Charge,* Marcia Bradlee; Tel: 815-753-1257, E-mail: mbradlee@niu.edu; *Ref Serv,* Nestor Osorio; Tel: 815-753-9837, E-mail: nosorio@niu.edu
Subject Interests: Chem, Physics
Open Mon-Thurs 8am-10pm, Fri 8-5
MUSIC, School of Music, Rm 175, 60115. Tel: 815-753-1426. FAX: 815-753-9836. *Music Librn,* Michael Duffy, IV; Tel: 815-753-9839, E-mail: mduffyiv@niu.edu; Staff 2 (MLS 1, Non-MLS 1)
Highest Degree: Master
Library Holdings: AV Mats 17,000; CDs 3,000; Music Scores 25,000; Bk Vols 21,000; Per Subs 115
Special Collections: Jazz Recordings & Musical Scores Coll
Function: Audio & video playback equip for onsite use, CD-ROM, Doc delivery serv, ILL available, Music CDs, Orientations, Ref serv available
Open Mon-Thurs (Fall & Spring) 8am-10pm, Fri 8-5, Sat 1-5, Sun 1-10
REGIONAL HISTORY CENTER, Founders Library, 60115. Tel: 815-753-1779. *Dir,* Cindy Ditzler; Tel: 815-753-9392, E-mail: cditzler@niu.edu; *Curator of Ms,* Danielle Spalenka; Tel: 815-753-9394, E-mail: dspalenka@niu.edu
Special Collections: University Archives Coll
Open Mon-Fri 8-12 & 1-4:30

CL DAVID C SHAPIRO MEMORIAL LAW LIBRARY, Normal Rd, 60115-2890. (Mail add: 180 W Stadium Dr, 60115), SAN 304-2227. Tel: 815-753-0507. Reference Tel: 815-753-0519. FAX: 815-753-9499. Web Site: law.niu.edu/law/library/index.shtml. *Dir,* Heidi Kuehl; Tel: 815-753-9493, E-mail: hkuehl@niu.edu; *Assoc Dir, Admin & Pub Serv, Res Librn,* Therese Clarke Arado; Tel: 815-753-9497, E-mail: tclarke@niu.edu; *Assoc Dir, Tech Serv & Syst, Tech Serv Librn,* Sharon Nelson; Tel: 815-753-2021, E-mail: snelson@niu.edu; *Head, Ref & Res Serv, Res Librn,* Annie Mentkowski; Tel: 815-753-9492, E-mail: amentkowski@niu.edu; *Tech Serv Librn,* Karl Pettitt; Tel: 815-753-9495, E-mail: kpettitt@niu.edu; *Ref & Instrul Serv Librn,* Clanitra Stewart; Tel: 815-753-9487, E-mail: cstewart5@niu.edu; Staff 8 (MLS 6, Non-MLS 2)
Founded 1974. Enrl 292; Fac 21; Highest Degree: Doctorate
Jul 2013-Jun 2014. Mats Exp $706,142, Books $14,945, Per/Ser (Incl. Access Fees) $485,589, Micro $3,038, Electronic Ref Mat (Incl. Access Fees) $202,570
Library Holdings: Bk Titles 44,678; Bk Vols 267,214; Per Subs 1,810
Special Collections: US Document Depository
Subject Interests: Law
Automation Activity & Vendor Info: (ILL) Ex Libris Group
Database Vendor: Bloomberg, Ex Libris Group, Gale Cengage Learning, HeinOnline, LexisNexis, OCLC WorldShare Interlibrary Loan, Westlaw
Partic in Chicago Legal Acad Syst; Consortium of Academic & Research Libraries in Illinois; Mid-America Law Library Consortium; OCLC Online Computer Library Center, Inc
Open Mon-Thurs (Fall & Spring) 7:30am-11:30pm, Fri 7:30am-8pm, Sat 10-8, Sun Noon-11:30; Mon-Thurs (Summer) 8-8, Fri 8-5, Sun 1-5
Restriction: Badge access after hrs, Circ privileges for students & alumni only

DELAVAN

P AYER PUBLIC LIBRARY DISTRICT*, 208 Locust St, 61734. (Mail add: PO Box 500, 61734-0500), SAN 304-1107. Tel: 309-244-8236. FAX: 309-244-8237. E-mail: ayerpubliclibrary@yahoo.com. Web Site: www.ayerpubliclibrary.com. *Admin Librn,* Mary Ruth Lowry; Staff 5 (Non-MLS 5)
Founded 1907. Pop 2,807; Circ 27,668
Library Holdings: AV Mats 550; Bks on Deafness & Sign Lang 30; DVDs 1,100; Large Print Bks 1,000; Bk Vols 21,000; Per Subs 127; Videos 1,120
Special Collections: Delavan Times 1874-present, microfilm
Function: Bk club(s), Homebound delivery serv, ILL available, Music CDs, Online searches, Photocopying/Printing, Prog for adults, Prog for children & young adult, Ref serv available, Spoken cassettes & CDs, Spoken cassettes & DVDs, Summer reading prog, Telephone ref, VHS videos, Workshops
Open Mon & Thurs 1-8, Tues, Wed & Fri 10-5, Sat 10-3

DES PLAINES

S DES PLAINES HISTORICAL SOCIETY LIBRARY*, 781 Pearson St, 60016. SAN 304-1158. Tel: 847-391-5399. FAX: 847-297-4741. Web Site: www.desplaineshistory.org. *Exec Dir,* Shari Caine; E-mail: contact@desplaineshistory.org; Staff 6 (MLS 4, Non-MLS 2)
Founded 1969
Library Holdings: Bk Vols 500; Per Subs 10
Special Collections: Dr C A Earle Coll

P DES PLAINES PUBLIC LIBRARY*, 1501 Ellinwood St, 60016. SAN 304-1166. Tel: 847-827-5551. Reference Tel: 847-376-2841. FAX: 847-827-7974. TDD: 847-827-0515. E-mail: help@dppl.org. Web Site: dppl.org. *Dir,* Holly Richards Sorensen; E-mail: hsorensen@dppl.org; *Asst Dir,* Roberta Johnson; E-mail: rjohnson@dppl.org; *Head, Adult Serv,* Jo Bonell; E-mail: jbonell@dppl.org; *Head, Circ Serv,* Susan Farid; Tel: 847-376-2790, E-mail: sfarid@dppl.org; *Head, Pub Info,* Heather Imhoff; Tel: 847-376-2792, E-mail: himhoff@dppl.org; *Head, Youth Serv,* Stephanie Spetter; E-mail: sspetter@dppl.org; Staff 104 (MLS 22, Non-MLS 82)
Founded 1906. Pop 58,617; Circ 1,164,209
Library Holdings: Audiobooks 7,676; CDs 17,672, DVDs 32,688; e-books 11,945; e-journals 75; Large Print Bks 8,920; Bk Vols 254,339; Per Subs 706
Automation Activity & Vendor Info: (Cataloging) SirsiDynix; (Circulation) SirsiDynix; (ILL) SirsiDynix; (OPAC) SirsiDynix; (Serials) SirsiDynix
Database Vendor: EBSCOhost, Gale Cengage Learning, OCLC FirstSearch, ProQuest
Publications: eForeword (Newsletter)
Special Services for the Deaf - TDD equip; TTY equip
Special Services for the Blind - Accessible computers; Assistive/Adapted tech devices, equip & products; Copier with enlargement capabilities; Home delivery serv; Low vision equip; Magnifiers; Playaways (bks on MP3)
Open Mon-Fri 9-9, Sat 9-5, Sun 1-5
Friends of the Library Group

S GAS TECHNOLOGY INSTITUTE, Technical Information Center, 1700 S Mount Prospect Rd, 60018-1804. SAN 303-9226. Tel: 847-768-0664. FAX: 847-768-0669. E-mail: library@gastechnology.org. Web Site: www.gastechnology.org. *Supvr,* Carol Worster; Staff 1 (MLS 1)
Founded 1941
Library Holdings: Bk Vols 36,000; Per Subs 100
Special Collections: American Chemical Society Division of Fuel Chemistry, Preprints 1957 to present; Energy Reports (DOE, EPRI, GRI); Pipeline Simulation Interest Group, Proc
Subject Interests: Natural gas
Partic in Illinois Library & Information Network; OCLC Online Computer Library Center, Inc
Restriction: Access at librarian's discretion, Access for corporate affiliates, Circulates for staff only, External users must contact libr, Non-circulating coll, Open to pub by appt only

J OAKTON COMMUNITY COLLEGE LIBRARY*, 1600 E Golf Rd, Rm 1410, 60016. SAN 304-436X. Tel: 847-635-1642, 847-635-1644. Administration Tel: 847-635-1640. FAX: 847-635-1987. Administration FAX: 847-635-1887. Web Site: www.oakton.edu. *Dean, Libr & Media Serv,* Gary Newhouse, E-mail: garyn@oakton.edu; *Chair, Coll Develop Librn,* Jane Malik; Tel: 847-635-1715, E-mail: jmalik@oakton.edu; *Br Librn,* Rose Novil; Tel: 847-635-1474; *Cat Serv Librn,* Dr Sherrill Weaver; *Instrul Serv Librn & Coordr of Ref & Assessment,* Julia Fraas; Staff 5 (MLS 5)
Founded 1970. Enrl 5,400; Fac 154; Highest Degree: Associate
Library Holdings: AV Mats 690; DVDs 614; e-books 3,198; High Interest/Low Vocabulary Bk Vols 300; Microforms 4,237; Bk Titles 91,000; Bk Vols 107,578; Per Subs 27,700
Special Collections: US Document Depository
Automation Activity & Vendor Info: (Acquisitions) Ex Libris Group; (Cataloging) Ex Libris Group; (Circulation) Ex Libris Group; (Course Reserve) Ex Libris Group; (ILL) Ex Libris Group; (OPAC) Ex Libris Group; (Serials) Ex Libris Group
Database Vendor: Alexander Street Press, American Chemical Society, Baker & Taylor, Bowker, CQ Press, CredoReference, EBSCOhost, Facts on File, Gale Cengage Learning, LearningExpress, LexisNexis, Newsbank, OCLC FirstSearch, OCLC WorldShare Interlibrary Loan, Oxford Online, ProQuest, Sage, SerialsSolutions, Springshare, LLC, Westlaw
Function: Electronic databases & coll
Mem of Reaching Across Illinois Library System (RAILS)
Partic in Consortium of Academic & Research Libraries in Illinois; Network of Illinois Learning Resources in Community Colleges; OCLC Online Computer Library Center, Inc
Open Mon-Thurs (Winter) 7:30am-9pm, Fri 7:30-7:30, Sat 9-3; Mon-Thurs (Summer) 7:30am-9pm
Restriction: Open to pub for ref & circ; with some limitations

DIVERNON

P DIVERNON TOWNSHIP LIBRARY*, 221 S Second St, 62530. (Mail add: PO Box 140, 62530-0140), SAN 304-1204. Tel: 217-628-3813. FAX: 217-628-3813. *Librn,* Kathy Goleman; E-mail: kgoleman@hotmail.com; *Asst Librn,* Dorla Reavis; E-mail: dorlar@rpls.lib.il.us
Founded 1967. Pop 1,548
Library Holdings: Audiobooks 30; Bks on Deafness & Sign Lang 1; Large Print Bks 62; Bk Vols 2,500; Per Subs 14
Mem of Illinois Heartland Library System
Open Mon, Tues & Thurs 1-7, Wed & Fri 1-5, Sat 8:30-12:30

DIXON

M KATHERINE SHAW BETHEA HOSPITAL*, Medical Library, 403 E First St, 61021. SAN 377-225X. Tel: 815-285-5532. FAX: 815-285-5938. *Librn,* Judy Hallquist; E-mail: jhallquist@ksbhospital.com; Staff 1 (Non-MLS 1)
Founded 1970
Library Holdings: Bk Vols 158; Per Subs 14
Partic in Health Sci Librn of Ill (HSLI)
Open Mon-Fri 8-4:30

S DIXON CORRECTIONAL CENTER LIBRARY*, 2600 N Brinton Ave, 61021-9524. SAN 371-7208. Tel: 815-288-5561, Ext 3041. *In Charge,* Carole O'Neal
Library Holdings: Bk Titles 9,000; Bk Vols 10,000
Special Collections: Federal & Illinois Law
Mem of Reaching Across Illinois Library System (RAILS)
Open Mon-Thurs 8-4 & 6:30-8:30, Fri 8-4, Sat 8-3:30, Sun 8am-10:45am

P DIXON PUBLIC LIBRARY*, 221 S Hennepin Ave, 61021-3093. SAN 304-1212. Tel: 815-284-7261. FAX: 815-288-7323. TDD: 815-284-7261. E-mail: maillibrary@dixonpubliclibrary.org. Web Site: www.dixonpubliclibrary.org. *Dir,* Lynn A Roe; E-mail: dpdirector@dixonpubliclibrary.org; Staff 7 (MLS 1, Non-MLS 6)
Founded 1872. Pop 15,941; Circ 118,554
Library Holdings: Bks on Deafness & Sign Lang 15; Bk Vols 90,000; Per Subs 125
Special Collections: Dixon Evening Telegraph, 1851-present, micro; Lincoln Coll; Local History-Genealogy Coll
Automation Activity & Vendor Info: (Cataloging) TLC (The Library Corporation); (Circulation) TLC (The Library Corporation); (OPAC) TLC (The Library Corporation)
Function: ILL available
Publications: 1942-1945 (history book); Library Lines (Newsletter); Lincoln in Dixon (history book); Memories of the Green River Ordinance Plant
Mem of NorthNet Library System
Special Services for the Deaf - TTY equip
Special Services for the Blind - Closed circuit TV magnifier
Open Mon-Thurs 9-8, Fri 9-5, Sat 10-3
Friends of the Library Group

J SAUK VALLEY COMMUNITY COLLEGE*, Learning Resource Center, 173 IL Rte 2, 61021-9112. SAN 304-1239. Tel: 815-288-5511, Ext 247. FAX: 815-288-5651. Web Site: www.svcc.edu/departments/lrc/index.html. *Dir,* Melanie Armstrong; Tel: 815-288-5511, Ext 306, E-mail: melanie.s.armstrong@svcc.edu; *Coordr, Tech Serv,* Linda Dhaese; Tel: 815-288-5511, Ext 210, E-mail: linda.s.dhaese@svcc.edu
Founded 1966
Library Holdings: AV Mats 5,000; Bk Titles 56,000; Bk Vols 74,000, Per Subs 275
Special Collections: Illinois & Local History; Popular Culture (film, music & television)
Automation Activity & Vendor Info: (Acquisitions) Ex Libris Group; (Cataloging) Ex Libris Group; (Circulation) Ex Libris Group; (Course Reserve) Ex Libris Group; (ILL) Ex Libris Group; (OPAC) Ex Libris Group; (Serials) Ex Libris Group
Database Vendor: JSTOR, LexisNexis, Wilson - Wilson Web
Mem of Reaching Across Illinois Library System (RAILS)
Partic in Consortium of Academic & Research Libraries in Illinois; Northern Ill Learning Resources Coop
Open Mon-Thurs 8-8, Fri 8-3

DOLTON

P DOLTON PUBLIC LIBRARY DISTRICT*, 14037 Lincoln Ave, 60419-1091. SAN 304-1247. Tel: 708-849-2385. FAX: 708-841-6640. Web Site: www.doltonpubliclibrary.org. *Dir,* Jay Kalman; *Circ,* Frances Turner; *Tech Serv,* Laura Fazio; Staff 7 (MLS 4, Non-MLS 3)
Founded 1954. Pop 25,614; Circ 114,450
Library Holdings: AV Mats 8,300; Large Print Bks 2,256; Bk Vols 99,746; Per Subs 210; Talking Bks 1,282
Special Collections: Adult New Readers Coll
Subject Interests: African-Am hist, Local hist
Automation Activity & Vendor Info: (Cataloging) Innovative Interfaces, Inc; (Circulation) Innovative Interfaces, Inc; (ILL) Innovative Interfaces, Inc; (OPAC) Innovative Interfaces, Inc
Database Vendor: OCLC FirstSearch
Wireless access
Function: ILL available, Photocopying/Printing, Ref serv available
Mem of Reaching Across Illinois Library System (RAILS)
Open Mon-Thurs 9-9, Fri & Sat 9-5, Sun (Oct-April) Noon-4

DONGOLA

P DONGOLA PUBLIC LIBRARY DISTRICT*, 114 NE Front St, 62926. (Mail add: PO Box 113, 62926-0113), SAN 376-1487. Tel: 618-827-3622. FAX: 618-827-3622. E-mail: DongolaPLD@gmail.com. *Dir,* Alison Holderfield; Staff 1 (Non-MLS 1)
Founded 1983. Pop 1,907
Library Holdings: Bk Titles 15,000; Per Subs 15
Function: Children's prog, Computers for patron use, e-mail serv, Free DVD rentals, Handicapped accessible, Music CDs, Photocopying/Printing, Story hour, Summer reading prog
Mem of Illinois Heartland Library System
Open Tues & Wed 2-6, Thurs 10-12 & 1-7, Sat 9-1

DOWNERS GROVE

P DOWNERS GROVE PUBLIC LIBRARY*, 1050 Curtiss St, 60515. SAN 304-1255. Tel: 630-960-1200. FAX: 630-960-9374. Web Site: www.dglibrary.org. *Dir,* Rick Ashton; E-mail: libdirector@downersgrovelibrary.org; *Asst Dir, Pub Serv,* Bonnie Reid; E-mail: breid@dglibrary.org; *Asst Dir, Support Serv,* Sue O'Brien; E-mail: sobrien@dglibrary.org; *Adult & Teen Serv Mgr,* Nicole Wilhelms; E-mail: nwilhelms@dglibrary.org; *Mgr, Ch Serv,* Sara Pemberton; E-mail: spemberton@dglibrary.org; *Circ Mgr,* Melanie Mertz; E-mail: mmertz@dglibrary.org; *Tech Serv Mgr,* Jen Fredericks; E-mail: jfredericks@dglibrary.org; Staff 20 (MLS 20)
Founded 1891. Pop 47,833; Circ 969,191
Jan 2013-Dec 2013 Income $4,574,343, State $49,155, Locally Generated Income $4,352,324, Other $17,864. Mats Exp $545,604, Books $244,252, Other Print Mats $487, AV Mat $114,672, Electronic Ref Mat (Incl. Access Fees) $179,842. Sal $2,070,449
Library Holdings: CDs 21,173; DVDs 22,360; Bk Vols 238,669; Per Subs 400
Subject Interests: Art & archit, Educ, Humanities, Local hist
Automation Activity & Vendor Info: (Cataloging) Innovative Interfaces, Inc; (Circulation) Innovative Interfaces, Inc; (ILL) Innovative Interfaces, Inc; (OPAC) Innovative Interfaces, Inc
Database Vendor: Innovative Interfaces, Inc
Wireless access
Publications: Discoveries (Newsletter); E-ssentials (Newsletter)
Mem of Reaching Across Illinois Library System (RAILS)
Partic in System Wide Automated Network
Special Services for the Deaf - TDD equip
Special Services for the Blind - Closed circuit TV magnifier; Reader equip
Open Mon-Fri 9-9, Sat 9-5, Sun 1-5
Friends of the Library Group

CM MIDWESTERN UNIVERSITY, Downers Grove Campus Library, 555 31st St, 60515. SAN 339-8072. Tel: 630-515-6200. Reference Tel: 630-515-6197. FAX: 630-515-6195. E-mail: reference@midwestern.edu. Web Site: www.midwestern.edu. *Dir,* Natalie Reed; Tel: 630-515-6183, E-mail: nreedx@midwestern.edu; Staff 17.25 (MLS 7.5, Non-MLS 9.75)
Founded 1913. Fac 258; Highest Degree: Doctorate
Library Holdings: Bk Titles 9,486; Bk Vols 11,190; Per Subs 739
Subject Interests: Biomed sci, Dentistry, Occupational therapy, Osteopathic med, Pharm, Phys therapy, Speech-lang pathology
Database Vendor: Alexander Street Press, American Chemical Society, Annual Reviews, Atlas Systems, Backstage Library Works, Cinahl, CRC Press/Taylor & Francis Group, CredoReference, Dialog, DynaMed, ebrary, EBSCO Information Services, EBSCOhost, Elsevier, Foundation Center, Innovative Interfaces, Inc, Lexi-Comp, Majors, McGraw-Hill, MD Consult, Micromedex, Natural Standard, Nature Publishing Group, OCLC FirstSearch, OVID Technologies, ProQuest, Sage, ScienceDirect, SirsiDynix, Springer-Verlag, Springshare, LLC, STAT!Ref (Teton Data Systems), Thomson - Web of Science, UpToDate, Wiley, YBP Library Services
Wireless access
Publications: Newsletter (Quarterly)
Partic in Metropolitan Consortium of Chicago; National Network of Libraries of Medicine; Regional Med Libr - Region 3
Open Mon-Thurs 7:30am-Midnight, Fri 7:30am-10pm, Sat 9am-Midnight, Sun 10am-Midnight

DU QUOIN

P DU QUOIN PUBLIC LIBRARY*, 28 S Washington St, 62832. SAN 304-128X. Tel: 618-542-5045. FAX: 618-542-4735. Web Site: www.dpl.lib.il.us. *Libr Dir,* Pam Urban; *Asst Librn,* Linda Campenella
Founded 1934. Pop 6,400
Library Holdings: Bk Vols 22,000; Per Subs 65
Subject Interests: Genealogy
Automation Activity & Vendor Info: (Cataloging) SirsiDynix; (Circulation) SirsiDynix
Wireless access
Mem of Illinois Heartland Library System
Open Mon, Wed & Thurs 12-6, Tues 12-8, Fri 10-6, Sat 9-3
Friends of the Library Group

DUNDEE

P FOX RIVER VALLEY PUBLIC LIBRARY DISTRICT, Dundee Library, 555 Barrington Ave, 60118-1496. SAN 304-1298. Tel: 847-428-3661. FAX: 847-428-4021. Web Site: www.frvpld.info. *Dir,* Roxane Bennett; E-mail: rbennett@frvpld.info; *Asst Dir, Support Serv,* Lauren Rosenthal; E-mail: lrosenthal@frvpld.info; *Accounts Mgr,* Jeanne Etling; E-mail: jetling@frvpld.info; *Ch Mgr,* Elizabeth Novak; E-mail: enovak@frvpld.info; *Info Serv Mgr,* Carolyn Friedlund; E-mail: cfriedlund@frvpld.info; *IT Mgr, Tech Serv Mgr,* Karin Nelson; E-mail: knelson@frvpld.info; Staff 12 (MLS 12)
Founded 1876. Pop 69,338; Circ 522,766
Jul 2013-Jun 2014 Income (Main Library and Branch(s)) $3,180,637. Mats Exp $407,153. Sal $1,279,910
Library Holdings: Audiobooks 10,066; DVDs 14,523; e-books 7,825; Electronic Media & Resources 50; Bk Vols 124,638; Per Subs 130
Automation Activity & Vendor Info: (Acquisitions) SirsiDynix; (Cataloging) SirsiDynix; (Circulation) SirsiDynix; (OPAC) SirsiDynix
Wireless access
Publications: Newsletter
Partic in Cooperative Computer Services - CCS
Open Mon-Thurs 9-9, Fri & Sat 9-5:30, Sun (Sept-May) 1-4
Friends of the Library Group

DUNLAP

P DUNLAP PUBLIC LIBRARY DISTRICT*, 302 S First St, 61525. SAN 304-1301. Tel: 309-243-5716. FAX: 309-243-5874. E-mail: dunlaplibrary@mchsi.com. Web Site: dunlaplibrary.home.mchsi.com. *Automation Serv, Dir, Ref Serv,* Jane Sieck; *Head, Circ,* Debbie Gehrig; *Ch,* Chris Cobbs; *ILL,* Ana Shyu; Staff 8 (MLS 2, Non-MLS 6)
Founded 1954. Pop 5,184; Circ 59,115
Library Holdings: Bk Titles 30,698; Per Subs 88
Database Vendor: OCLC FirstSearch
Publications: The Library Connection (District newsletter)
Open Mon-Thurs 9-7, Fri 9-5, Sat 9-1

DUPO

P DAUGHERTY PUBLIC LIBRARY DISTRICT*, 220 S Fifth St, 62239. SAN 304-131X. Tel: 618-286-4444. FAX: 618-286-3636. Web Site: www.dupolibrary.org. *Dir,* Carol Brockmeyer; E-mail: carolb@dupolibrary.org
Founded 1971. Pop 7,700; Circ 40,529
Library Holdings: Bk Vols 28,000; Per Subs 53
Mem of Illinois Heartland Library System
Open Mon-Thurs 9-8, Fri & Sat 9-4
Friends of the Library Group

DWIGHT

S ILLINOIS DEPARTMENT OF CORRECTIONS*, Dwight Correctional Center Library, 23813 E 3200 N Rd, 60420. Tel: 815-584-2806, Ext 2228. FAX: 815-854-1432. Web Site: www.idoc.state.il.us. *Mgr,* Beatrice Stanley
Library Holdings: Bk Vols 15,000
Open Tues-Fri 8:30-10 & 12:30-3:30

P PRAIRIE CREEK PUBLIC LIBRARY*, 501 Carriage House Lane, 60420-1399. SAN 304-1328. Tel: 815-584-3061. FAX: 815-584-3120. Web Site: www.prairiecreeklibrary.org. *Dir,* Kristin Glatz; Staff 7 (MLS 1, Non-MLS 6)
Founded 1926. Pop 6,234; Circ 39,053
Library Holdings: Bks on Deafness & Sign Lang 20; High Interest/Low Vocabulary Bk Vols 100; Bk Titles 20,000; Bk Vols 31,500; Per Subs 70; Spec Interest Per Sub 10
Subject Interests: Am Civil War, Local hist
Automation Activity & Vendor Info: (Cataloging) Follett Software; (Circulation) Follett Software; (ILL) TLC (The Library Corporation); (OPAC) Follett Software
Database Vendor: OCLC FirstSearch
Publications: American Libraries (Annual report); Public Libraries (Annual report)
Open Mon-Thurs 10-8, Fri 10-5, Sat 10-3
Friends of the Library Group

EARLVILLE

P EARLVILLE LIBRARY DISTRICT*, 205 Winthrop St, 60518. (Mail add: PO Box 420, 60518-0420), SAN 304-1336. Tel: 815-246-9543. FAX: 815-246-6391. E-mail: inquiry@earlvillelibrary.org. Web Site: www.earlvillelibrary.org. *Tech Serv,* Paula Wold
Pop 2,653; Circ 21,350

Library Holdings: DVDs 234; Large Print Bks 148; Bk Vols 20,000; Per Subs 57; Talking Bks 364; Videos 642
Special Collections: Local Weekly Newspaper, 1914-present, micro. Oral History
Automation Activity & Vendor Info: (Acquisitions) SIRSI WorkFlows; (Cataloging) SIRSI WorkFlows; (Circulation) SIRSI WorkFlows
Wireless access
Mem of Reaching Across Illinois Library System (RAILS)
Open Mon & Wed 10-8, Tues & Fri 10-5, Sat 10-2
Friends of the Library Group

EAST ALTON

P EAST ALTON PUBLIC LIBRARY DISTRICT*, 250 Washington, 62024-1547. SAN 304-1344. Tel: 618-259-0787. FAX: 618-259-0788. E-mail: eastaltonlibrary@gmail.com. Web Site: www.eastaltonlibrary.org. *Dir,* Richard Chartrand; Staff 10 (MLS 1, Non-MLS 9)
Founded 1936. Pop 14,796; Circ 86,000
Library Holdings: Bk Vols 62,000; Per Subs 186
Automation Activity & Vendor Info: (Acquisitions) Innovative Interfaces, Inc
Mem of Illinois Heartland Library System
Open Mon-Thurs 9:30-7:30, Fri & Sat 9:30-5

EAST DUBUQUE

P EAST DUBUQUE DISTRICT LIBRARY*, 122 Wisconsin Ave, 61025-1325. SAN 304-1352. Tel: 815-747-3052. FAX: 815-747-6062. Web Site: www.eastdubuquelibrary.com. *Dir,* Michelle Wessels; E-mail: director@eastdubuquelibrary.com; *Asst Librn,* Rose Whisler; *Ch Serv,* Kathy Williams; Staff 3 (Non-MLS 3)
Founded 1937. Pop 4,459; Circ 18,011
Library Holdings: Bks on Deafness & Sign Lang 10; Bk Titles 14,997; Per Subs 33
Wireless access
Publications: Booklist; Illinois Libraries; Newsletter
Mem of Reaching Across Illinois Library System (RAILS)
Special Services for the Deaf - TTY equip
Special Services for the Blind - Bks on cassette; Talking bks
Open Mon-Thurs 10-8, Fri 10-5, Sat 10-2

EAST MOLINE

S EAST MOLINE CORRECTIONAL CENTER LIBRARY*, 100 Hillcrest Rd, 61244. SAN 376-088X. Tel: 309-755-4511, Ext 350. *Librn,* Patricia Hendrickson
Library Holdings: Bk Titles 7,141
Open Tues-Fri 10-8

P EAST MOLINE PUBLIC LIBRARY*, 740 16th Ave, 61244-2122. SAN 304-1379. Tel: 309-755-9614. FAX: 309-755-3901. E-mail: emp@empl.lib.il.us. Web Site: empl.lib.il.us. *Dir,* Cynthia K Coe; E-mail: coec@empl.lib.il.us; *Mgr,* Tami Cox; Staff 14 (MLS 1, Non-MLS 13)
Founded 1917. Pop 21,431; Circ 135,680
May 2005-Apr 2006 Income $773,817, State $130,712, City $450,210, Federal $33,406, Locally Generated Income $79,798. Mats Exp $112,292, Books $78,589, AV Mat $31,055, Electronic Ref Mat (Incl. Access Fees) $2,648. Sal $320,765
Library Holdings: DVDs 3,956; e-books 6,048; Electronic Media & Resources 15; Bk Vols 65,407; Per Subs 130; Talking Bks 6,236
Automation Activity & Vendor Info: (Circulation) SirsiDynix
Database Vendor: OCLC FirstSearch
Wireless access
Publications: EMPL Memo (Newsletter)
Mem of Reaching Across Illinois Library System (RAILS)
Partic in RiverShare Libraries
Friends of the Library Group

EAST PEORIA

P FONDULAC PUBLIC LIBRARY DISTRICT*, 140 E Washington St, 61611-2598. SAN 304-1395. Tel: 309-699-3917. FAX: 309-699-7851. E-mail: mail@fondulaclibrary.org. Web Site: www.fondulaclibrary.org.
Founded 1935. Pop 20,836; Circ 151,318
Library Holdings: AV Mats 4,613; e-books 325; Bk Vols 72,459; Per Subs 108
Special Collections: East Peoria & Tazewell County History
Subject Interests: Local hist
Automation Activity & Vendor Info: (Acquisitions) TLC (The Library Corporation); (Circulation) TLC (The Library Corporation); (OPAC) CARL.Solution (TLC)
Wireless access
Function: Handicapped accessible, ILL available, Photocopying/Printing, Prog for children & young adult, Ref serv available, Summer reading prog, Telephone ref, Wheelchair accessible
Open Mon-Thurs 9-9, Fri 9-6, Sat 9-5, Sun (Sept-May) 1-5
Friends of the Library Group

J ILLINOIS CENTRAL COLLEGE*, East Peoria Campus Library, Kenneth L Edward Library Administration Bldgs, L312, One College Dr, 61635-0001. SAN 304-1409. Tel: 309-694-5422. Reference Tel: 309-694-5355. FAX: 309-694-5473. E-mail: epref@icc.edu. Web Site: apps.icc.edu/library. *Libr Serv Dir,* Cate Kaufman; Tel: 309-694-8504, E-mail: cathryne.kaufman@icc.edu; *Electronic Res Librn,* Jessica Bastian; Tel: 309-694-5463, E-mail: jessica.bastian@icc.edu; *ILL Librn,* Gretchen Turvill; Tel: 309-694-5620, E-mail: gturvill@icc.edu; *Ref Librn,* Amy Glass; Tel: 309-694-5748, E-mail: amy.glass@icc.edu; *Ref Librn,* Michelle Nielsen Ott; Tel: 309-694-5617, E-mail: michelle.nielsenott@icc.edu; Staff 6 (MLS 6)
Founded 1967. Enrl 7,126; Fac 232; Highest Degree: Associate
Library Holdings: AV Mats 5,708; e-books 55,000; Bk Titles 95,000; Bk Vols 100,000; Per Subs 11,000
Automation Activity & Vendor Info: (Cataloging) Ex Libris Group; (Circulation) Ex Libris Group; (Course Reserve) Ex Libris Group; (OPAC) Ex Libris Group
Database Vendor: EBSCOhost, Gale Cengage Learning, LexisNexis, OCLC FirstSearch, ProQuest, Wilson - Wilson Web
Partic in Consortium of Academic & Research Libraries in Illinois; Northern Illinois Learning Resources Cooperative (NILRC); OCLC Online Computer Library Center, Inc; OCLC-LVIS
Open Mon-Thurs 7am-10pm, Fri 7-4, Sat 11-4, Sun 12-4

EAST SAINT LOUIS

J EAST SAINT LOUIS COMMUNITY COLLEGE CENTER*, Kenneth E Hall Learning Resource Center, 601 James R Thompson Blvd, 62201. SAN 304-1441. Tel: 618-874-8719. FAX: 618-874-6383. E-mail: eslccc.lrc@gmail.com. Web Site: eslccc.com/resource-center. *Dir,* Danielle O'Donnell; Tel: 618-874-8718, E-mail: dodonnell@eslccc.com; Staff 3 (MLS 1, Non-MLS 2)
Founded 1969. Enrl 1,000; Fac 100; Highest Degree: Associate
Library Holdings: CDs 3,000; DVDs 150; e-books 8,892; Bk Titles 15,000; Per Subs 200; Videos 700
Special Collections: African-American Coll (Authors, Personalities & Local History)
Subject Interests: African-Am
Automation Activity & Vendor Info: (Cataloging) Innovative Interfaces, Inc; (Circulation) Innovative Interfaces, Inc; (Course Reserve) Innovative Interfaces, Inc; (ILL) OCLC; (OPAC) Innovative Interfaces, Inc
Database Vendor: EBSCOhost, Gale Cengage Learning, Innovative Interfaces, Inc, OCLC ArticleFirst, OCLC FirstSearch, OCLC WorldShare Interlibrary Loan
Function: Audio & video playback equip for onsite use, Bks on CD, CD-ROM, Computers for patron use, Copy machines, Distance learning, Electronic databases & coll, For res purposes, Free DVD rentals, Handicapped accessible, ILL available, Music CDs, Online cat, Photocopying/Printing, Ref serv available, VHS videos
Mem of Illinois Heartland Library System
Partic in Illinois Library & Information Network
Restriction: Borrowing privileges limited to fac & registered students, Closed stack

P EAST SAINT LOUIS PUBLIC LIBRARY*, 5300 State St, 62203. SAN 304-1417. Tel: 618-397-0991. FAX: 618-397-1260. Web Site: www.esllibrary.org. *Head Librn,* Vera Beckwith; E-mail: beckwithd@sbcglobal.net; *Ch,* Lenora Cooper; *Ref Librn,* Regina Agnew
Founded 1872. Pop 46,000; Circ 175,000
Library Holdings: Bk Vols 53,000; Per Subs 40
Special Collections: Metro-East Journal since 1889, micro
Automation Activity & Vendor Info: (Acquisitions) SirsiDynix; (Cataloging) SirsiDynix; (Circulation) SirsiDynix
Mem of Illinois Heartland Library System
Open Mon-Thurs 9-8, Fri & Sat 9-5
Friends of the Library Group

S ILLINOIS DEPARTMENT OF CORRECTIONS*, Southwestern Illinois Correctional Center Library, 950 Kings Hwy, 62203. Tel: 618-394-2200, Ext 407. FAX: 618-394-2228. Web Site: www.idoc.state.il.us.
Library Holdings: Bk Vols 5,000; Per Subs 24
Open Mon-Wed 11-7, Thurs & Fri 7-3

GL UNITED STATES COURTS LIBRARY*, Southern District of Illinois, 750 Missouri Ave, 62202. Tel: 618-482-9477. FAX: 618-482-9234. Web Site: www.lb7.uscourts.gov. *Librn,* Chris Tighe
Library Holdings: Bk Vols 5,000
Wireless access
Restriction: Open by appt only

EDWARDSVILLE

P EDWARDSVILLE PUBLIC LIBRARY*, 112 S Kansas St, 62025. SAN 304-145X. Tel: 618-692-7556. FAX: 618-692-9566. E-mail: edereference@edwardsvillelibrary.org. Web Site: edwardsvillelibrary.org. *Dir,* Susan Carr; E-mail: scarr@edwardsvillelibrary.org; *Asst Dir,* Cary Harvangt; E-mail: caryh@edwardsvillelibrary.org; *Head, Tech Serv,* Gwen Bumpers; E-mail: gwenb@edwardsvillelibrary.org; *Ref Librn,* Judy Thompson; E-mail: judyt@edwardsvillelibrary.org; *Youth Serv Librn,* Anne Wolfe; E-mail: annwolfe@edwardsvillelibrary.org; Staff 32 (MLS 5, Non-MLS 27)
Founded 1818. Pop 25,073; Circ 281,357
Library Holdings: Bk Vols 112,171
Special Collections: Madison County Genealogical Society Coll
Wireless access
Function: Archival coll, Homebound delivery serv, ILL available, Magnifiers for reading, Online searches, Photocopying/Printing, Prog for adults, Prog for children & young adult, Ref serv available, Summer reading prog, Telephone ref, Wheelchair accessible
Mem of Illinois Heartland Library System
Partic in Coop Libr Agency for Syst & Servs
Open Mon-Thurs 9-9, Fri & Sat 9-5, Sun 1-5
Friends of the Library Group

S MADISON COUNTY HISTORICAL MUSEUM & ARCHIVAL LIBRARY*, 715 N Main St, 62025-1111. SAN 326-601X. Tel: 618-656-7562, 618-656-7569. FAX: 618-659-3457. E-mail: mtwesterhold@co.madison.il.us. Web Site: www.madisoncountymuseum.org. *Dir,* Suzanne Dietrich; E-mail: scdietrich@co.madison.il.us; *Operations Mgr,* Mary Westerhold; *Archivist,* LaVerne Bloemker; *Archivist,* Carol Frisse; *Archivist,* Marion Sperling; *Curator of Objects & Textiles,* Mary Louise Brown
Jan 2009-Dec 2009 Income $159,000, County $145,000, Parent Institution $14,000. Mats Exp $5,200, Books $100, Per/Ser (Incl. Access Fees) $100, Other Print Mats $500, Micro $500, AV Equip $1,500, Electronic Ref Mat (Incl. Access Fees) $1,000, Presv $1,500. Sal $90,000
Library Holdings: Bk Vols 3,000; Per Subs 12; Spec Interest Per Sub 10
Special Collections: Edwardsville Street Index & Housing Inventory (beginning 1894); Historic Photos; Index to First Sales of Land in Illinois; Madison County Poor Farm Records; N O Nelson-Village of Leclaire Papers; WPA Index to Alton Telegraph 1836-1940; WPA Index to Edwardsville Intelligencer 1862-1937
Subject Interests: Genealogy, Local hist
Publications: General Index for Brink's History of Madison County, Ill 1882; Madison County Poor Farm Index; Military Index for Brink's History of Madison County, Ill; Republication of Brink's History of Madison County Ill 1882
Open Wed-Fri 9-4, Sun 1-4
Restriction: Non-circulating to the pub
Friends of the Library Group

L MADISON COUNTY LAW LIBRARY*, 155 N Main St, 62025. Tel: 618-296-5921. FAX: 618-692-7475. Web Site: www.co.madison.il.us. *Law Librn,* Betsy Mahoney; E-mail: bemahoney@co.madison.il.us
Library Holdings: Bk Vols 5,000
Wireless access
Mem of Illinois Heartland Library System
Special Services for the Blind - Computer with voice synthesizer for visually impaired persons
Open Mon-Fri 8:30-4:30

C SOUTHERN ILLINOIS UNIVERSITY EDWARDSVILLE*, Elijah P Lovejoy Library, Campus Box 1063, 30 Hairpin Circle, 62026-1063. SAN 340-3777. Tel: 618-650-2615, 618-650-2711. Interlibrary Loan Service Tel: 618-650-2174. Toll Free Tel: 800-447-7483. FAX: 618-650-2717. Web Site: www.siue.edu/lovejoy/library. *Dean of Libr,* Regina McBride; Tel: 618-650-5198, E-mail: rmcbrid@siue.edu; *AV,* Gary Denue; Tel: 618-650-2632, E-mail: gdenue@siue.edu; *Circ,* Canduce Walter; Tel: 618-650-2277; *ILL,* Hope Myers; E-mail: hmyers@siue.edu
Founded 1957. Enrl 13,295; Fac 518; Highest Degree: Master
Library Holdings: AV Mats 29,495; e-books 1,629; Bk Titles 538,880; Bk Vols 788,003; Per Subs 14,371
Special Collections: Illinois Coll; Illinois, Missouri, & Regional Maps; Mormons in Illinois; Music Coll, sheet music, piano rolls, records, mss, cinema music, hymnals, song bks, instruments, photogs; Slavic-American Imprints Coll. State Document Depository; US Document Depository
Subject Interests: Bus, Educ, Eng, Ill, Nursing
Automation Activity & Vendor Info: (Acquisitions) Ex Libris Group; (Cataloging) Ex Libris Group; (Circulation) Ex Libris Group; (Course Reserve) Ex Libris Group; (ILL) Ex Libris Group; (OPAC) Ex Libris Group; (Serials) Ex Libris Group
Publications: Lovejoy Imprints (Newsletter)
Partic in Conference of Dirs of State Univ Librns of Ill; Consortium of Academic & Research Libraries in Illinois; Ill Coordinated Coll Mgt Prog; Illinois Library & Information Network; OCLC Online Computer Library Center, Inc; Saint Louis Regional Library Network
Open Mon-Thurs 7:30am-11pm, Fri 7:30-6, Sat 10-6, Sun 1-9
Friends of the Library Group

Departmental Libraries:

CM BIOMEDICAL LIBRARY, School of Dental Medicine, 2800 College Ave, Bldg 277, Alton, 62002, SAN 303-674X. Tel: 618-474-7277. FAX: 618-474-7270. Web Site: www.siue.edu/lovejoylibrary/biomed/contacts.shtml. *Dir,* Lydia Jackson; Tel: 618-650-2604, E-mail: ljackso@siue.edu; *Librn,* Jamie Conklin; Tel: 618-650-3129, E-mail: jconkli@siue.edu. Subject Specialists: *Health sci,* Jamie Conklin; Staff 2 (MLS 2)
Founded 1970
Library Holdings: Bk Vols 35,000; Per Subs 151
Automation Activity & Vendor Info: (Acquisitions) Ex Libris Group; (Cataloging) Ex Libris Group; (Circulation) Ex Libris Group; (Course Reserve) Ex Libris Group; (ILL) Ex Libris Group; (OPAC) Ex Libris Group; (Serials) Ex Libris Group
Database Vendor: Cambridge Scientific Abstracts, EBSCOhost, JSTOR, LexisNexis, OCLC FirstSearch, OCLC WorldShare Interlibrary Loan, OVID Technologies, ProQuest, Wilson - Wilson Web
Mem of Illinois Heartland Library System
Open Mon-Thurs 7:45am-11pm, Fri 7:45-5, Sat 1-7, Sun 1-10
Friends of the Library Group

EFFINGHAM

P HELEN MATTHES LIBRARY*, 100 E Market Ave, 62401-3499. SAN 304-1476. Tel: 217-342-2464. FAX: 217-342-2413. E-mail: hmlib@effinghamlibrary.org. Web Site: www.effinghamlibrary.org. *Dir,* Amanda D McKay; Tel: 217-342-2464, Ext 5, E-mail: amanda@effinghamlibrary.org; *Adult Serv Mgr,* Johnna Schultz; Tel: 217-342-2464, Ext 23, E-mail: johnna@effinghamlibrary.org; *Circ Mgr,* Margo Probst; Tel: 217-342-2464, Ext 2, E-mail: margo@effinghamlibrary.org; *Youth Serv Mgr,* Sara Smith; Tel: 217-342-2464, Ext 6, E-mail: sara@effinghamlibrary.org; Staff 21 (MLS 1, Non-MLS 20)
Founded 1883. Pop 12,300; Circ 165,000
Library Holdings: Bk Vols 56,000; Per Subs 50
Subject Interests: Genealogy, World War II
Automation Activity & Vendor Info: (Cataloging) Innovative Interfaces, Inc; (Circulation) Innovative Interfaces, Inc; (OPAC) Innovative Interfaces, Inc
Database Vendor: OCLC FirstSearch
Wireless access
Function: Ref serv available
Mem of Illinois Heartland Library System
Open Mon-Thurs 9-8, Fri 9-6, Sat 9-5

EL PASO

P EL PASO PUBLIC LIBRARY*, 149 W First St, 61738. SAN 304-1484. Tel: 309-527-4360. FAX: 309-527-7100. E-mail: eplibrary@fairpoint.net. Web Site: www.elpasopubliclibrary.net. *Ch,* Rene Griffith
Founded 1873. Pop 2,695; Circ 24,000
Library Holdings: Large Print Bks 1,000; Bk Vols 25,000; Per Subs 30
Special Collections: Local Newspaper, 1888-present
Automation Activity & Vendor Info: (Circulation) SirsiDynix
Open Mon, Wed & Fri 12-6, Tues 9-6, Thurs 9-7, Sat 10-3

ELBURN

P TOWN & COUNTRY PUBLIC LIBRARY DISTRICT, 320 E North St, 60119. SAN 304-1492. Tel: 630-365-2244. FAX: 630-365-2358. E-mail: library@elburn.lib.il.us. Web Site: www.elburn.lib.il.us. *Dir,* Mary Lynn Alms; E-mail: malms@elburn.lib.il.us; Staff 23 (MLS 3, Non-MLS 20)
Founded 1929. Pop 12,392; Circ 144,459
Jul 2013-Jun 2014 Income $1,438,608, Locally Generated Income $1,423,142, Other $15,466. Mats Exp $141,996, Books $60,422, Per/Ser (Incl. Access Fees) $3,442, Other Print Mats $2,571, AV Mat $30,624, Electronic Ref Mat (Incl. Access Fees) $36,937, Presv $8,000. Sal $483,248 (Prof $190,000)
Library Holdings: CDs 1,268; DVDs 3,939; e-books 7,280; Bk Vols 52,920; Per Subs 95
Special Collections: Local History Coll
Automation Activity & Vendor Info: (Acquisitions) SirsiDynix; (Cataloging) SirsiDynix; (Circulation) SirsiDynix; (OPAC) SirsiDynix
Database Vendor: Bowker, EBSCOhost, Gale Cengage Learning, Grolier Online, H W Wilson, LexisNexis, OCLC FirstSearch, OCLC WorldShare Interlibrary Loan, ProQuest, ReferenceUSA, ValueLine
Wireless access
Function: 24/7 Online cat, Adult bk club, Archival coll, Audiobks via web, Bks on CD, Chess club, Children's prog, Computer training, Computers for patron use, Copy machines, E-Reserves, Electronic databases & coll, eReaders, Family literacy, Fax serv, Free DVD rentals, Genealogy discussion group, Handicapped accessible, Holiday prog,

Homebound delivery serv, Homework prog, ILL available, Literacy & newcomer serv, Magnifiers for reading, Mus passes, Music CDs, Notary serv, Online cat, Online ref, Online searches, Outreach serv, OverDrive digital audio bks, Photocopying/Printing, Preschool outreach, Preschool reading prog, Prog for adults, Prog for children & young adult, Pub access computers, Ref serv available, Senior computer classes, Senior outreach, Story hour, Study rm, Summer & winter reading prog, Summer reading prog, Tax forms, Wheelchair accessible
Mem of Reaching Across Illinois Library System (RAILS)
Open Mon-Thurs 9-9, Fri & Sat 9-5, Sun 1-5
Friends of the Library Group

ELDORADO

P ELDORADO MEMORIAL PUBLIC LIBRARY DISTRICT, 1001 Grant St, 62930-1714. (Mail add: PO Box 426, 62930-0426), SAN 304-1506. Tel: 618-273-7922. FAX: 618-273-4402. E-mail: eldoradolibrary@yahoo.com. Web Site: eldoradomemoriallibrary.com, www.eldorado.lib.il.us. *Dir,* Felicia Murray; Staff 4 (MLS 1, Non-MLS 3)
Founded 1987. Pop 7,672; Circ 41,306
Library Holdings: Bk Vols 32,000; Per Subs 30
Automation Activity & Vendor Info: (Cataloging) OCLC Connexion
Database Vendor: 3M Library Systems, Gale Cengage Learning, OCLC WorldShare Interlibrary Loan, Overdrive, Inc
Wireless access
Mem of Illinois Heartland Library System
Open Mon-Thurs 9-7, Fri & Sat 9-5, Sun 1-5
Friends of the Library Group

ELGIN

P GAIL BORDEN PUBLIC LIBRARY DISTRICT*, 270 N Grove Ave, 60120-5596. SAN 304-1514. Tel: 847-742-2411. Circulation Tel: 847-695-6886. Interlibrary Loan Service Tel: 847-429-4682. Reference Tel: 847-429-4680. FAX: 847-742-0485. Circulation FAX: 847-608-5098. Interlibrary Loan Service FAX: 847-608-5221. Web Site: www.gailborden.info, www.gailborden.info/m/content/view/455/553. *Exec Dir,* Carole Medal; Tel: 847-429-4699, E-mail: cmedal@gailborden.info; *Dep Dir,* Karen E Maki; Tel: 847-429-5976, E-mail: kmaki@gailborden.info; *Dir, Access & Tech Serv,* Patricia K Noonan; Tel: 847-429-5983, Fax: 847-608 5201, E-mail: pnoonan@gailborden.info; *Dir, Br Serv,* Margaret Peebles; Tel: 847-931-2091, Fax: 847-531-7367, E-mail: mpeebles@gailborden.info; *Dir of Circ,* Laura Clark; Tel: 847-429-4681, E-mail: lclark@gailborden.info; *Dir, Info Tech,* Betsy O'Connell; Tel: 847-429-4689, Fax: 847-608-5029, E-mail: boconnell@gailborden.info; *Dir, Mkt, Develop & Communications,* Denise Raleigh; Tel: 847-429-5981, E-mail: draleigh@gailborden.info; *Dir, Pub Serv,* Patricia V Gebhardt; Tel: 847-429-5982, E-mail: pgebhardt@gailborden.info; *Dir, Staff & Organization Develop,* Sharon Wiseman; Tel: 847-289-5801, E-mail: swiseman@gailborden.info; *Dir, Youth Serv,* Position Currently Open; *Mgr, Info Serv,* Jennifer Ford; Tel: 847-695-4668, E-mail: jford@gailborden.info; Staff 27.4 (MLS 25.6, Non-MLS 1.8)
Founded 1873. Pop 133,959; Circ 2,076,271
Jul 2009-Jun 2010 Income $10,560,250, State $295,640, Federal $10,000, Locally Generated Income $9,858,738, Other $395,872. Mats Exp $1,114,986, Books $567,002, Per/Ser (Incl. Access Fees) $36,236, Micro $27,964, AV Equip $8,049, AV Mat $253,467, Electronic Ref Mat (Incl. Access Fees) $165,404. Sal $5,034,798 (Prof $2,476,891)
Library Holdings: Audiobooks 10,732; AV Mats 80,205; Bks on Deafness & Sign Lang 190; CDs 22,850; DVDs 20,612; e-books 3,101; High Interest/Low Vocabulary Bk Vols 1,170; Bk Titles 368,889; Bk Vols 394,167; Per Subs 404; Videos 6,354
Special Collections: Genealogy Coll; Local History Coll (Elgin & Kane County); Spanish Language Materials for Adults & Children
Automation Activity & Vendor Info: (Acquisitions) Innovative Interfaces, Inc; (Cataloging) Innovative Interfaces, Inc; (Circulation) Innovative Interfaces, Inc; (ILL) Innovative Interfaces, Inc; (OPAC) Innovative Interfaces, Inc; (Serials) Innovative Interfaces, Inc
Database Vendor: ABC-CLIO, Baker & Taylor, Booksite, BWI, Gale Cengage Learning, Grolier Online, infoUSA, Newsbank, OCLC FirstSearch, OCLC WorldShare Interlibrary Loan, ProQuest, TumbleBookLibrary
Wireless access
Function: Accelerated reader prog, Adult bk club, Adult literacy prog, After school storytime, Art exhibits, Audiobks via web, AV serv, Bilingual assistance for Spanish patrons, Bk club(s), Bks on cassette, Bks on CD, CD-ROM, Children's prog, Computer training, Computers for patron use, Copy machines, e-mail serv, Electronic databases & coll, Exhibits, Family literacy, Fax serv, Free DVD rentals, Genealogy discussion group, Handicapped accessible, Home delivery & serv to Sr ctr & nursing homes, Homebound delivery serv, ILL available, Magnifiers for reading, Mail & tel request accepted, Mus passes, Music CDs, Online cat, Outside serv via phone, mail, e-mail & web, OverDrive digital audio bks, Photocopying/Printing, Preschool outreach, Prog for adults, Prog for children & young adult, Pub access computers, Scanner, Senior computer classes, Senior outreach, Spoken cassettes & CDs, Spoken cassettes & DVDs, Story hour, Summer reading prog, Tax forms, Teen prog, Telephone ref, VHS videos, Wheelchair accessible, Workshops
Publications: Newsletter (Bi-monthly)
Special Services for the Deaf - Adult & family literacy prog; Assisted listening device; Assistive tech; Bks on deafness & sign lang; Closed caption videos; High interest/low vocabulary bks; Sign lang interpreter upon request for prog
Special Services for the Blind - Accessible computers; Assistive/Adapted tech devices, equip & products; BiFolkal kits; Bks available with recordings; Bks on CD; Extensive large print coll; Free checkout of audio mat, Handicapped awareness prog; Home delivery serv; Large print bks; Lending of low vision aids; Low vision equip; PC for handicapped; Playaways (bks on MP3); Recorded bks; Ref serv; VisualTek equip
Open Mon-Thurs 9-9, Fri & Sat 9-5:30, Sun 1-5:30
Friends of the Library Group

SR CHURCH OF THE BRETHREN*, Brethren Historical Library & Archives, 1451 Dundee Ave, 60120-1694. SAN 304-1522. Tel: 847-429-4368. FAX: 847-429-4378. Web Site: www.brethren.org/genbd/bhla/. *Dir,* Bill Kostlevy; E-mail: bkostlevy@brethren.org; Staff 1 (MLS 1)
Founded 1936
Jan 2011-Dec 2011 Income $125,270
Library Holdings: Bk Vols 10,291
Special Collections: Archives & Manuscripts Coll; Church of the Brethren History & Doctrines
Automation Activity & Vendor Info: (Cataloging) OCLC; (ILL) OCLC
Function: Archival coll, ILL available, Res libr
Publications: Guide for Local Church Historians; Guide to Research in Brethren Family History; Guide to Research in Brethren History; Guide to the Brethren in Europe
Partic in OCLC Online Computer Library Center, Inc
Restriction: Non-circulating to the pub, Open by appt only

J ELGIN COMMUNITY COLLEGE*, Renner Learning Resources Center, 1700 Spartan Dr, 60123. SAN 304-1530. Tel: 847-214-7337. Interlibrary Loan Service Tel: 847-214-7141. Reference Tel: 847-214-7354. Circulation FAX: 847-214-7995. Interlibrary Loan Service FAX: 847-622-3042. E-mail: libref@elgin.edu. Web Site: library.elgin.edu. *Assoc Dean,* Brian Beecher; Fax: 574-241-7595, E-mail: bbeecher@elgin.edu; *Cat/Ref Librn,* Mary Klemundt; *Distance Learning Librn,* Stacey Shah; *Archivist, ILL Librn,* Armando Trejo; *Pub Serv Librn,* Marge Schildknecht; Tel: 847-241-7174; *Ref Librn,* Tina Birkholz; *Ref Librn,* Lynn Ducar; *Ref Librn,* Connie James-Jenkin; *Ref Librn,* Jana Porter; *Ref Librn,* Himanshu Trivedi; *Tech Serv Librn,* Ellie Swanson; Staff 21 (MLS 11, Non-MLS 10)
Founded 1949. Enrl 7,010; Fac 470
Library Holdings: Audiobooks 323; CDs 1,782; DVDs 1,598; e-books 33,382; e-journals 43,656; Bk Vols 77,945; Per Subs 365; Videos 90
Automation Activity & Vendor Info: (Acquisitions) Innovative Interfaces, Inc; (Cataloging) Innovative Interfaces, Inc; (Circulation) Innovative Interfaces, Inc; (OPAC) Innovative Interfaces, Inc; (Serials) Innovative Interfaces, Inc
Database Vendor: EBSCOhost, Gale Cengage Learning, LexisNexis, OCLC FirstSearch, ProQuest
Wireless access
Partic in Illinois Library & Information Network; Northern Ill Learning Resources Coop; OCLC Online Computer Library Center, Inc
Open Mon-Thurs 7:45am-10pm, Fri 7:45-5, Sat 9-2

S ELGIN MENTAL HEALTH CENTER LIBRARY*, FTP Library, 750 S State St, 60123-7692. SAN 340-3807. Tel: 847-742-1040, Ext 3437. FAX: 847-429-4923. *Librn,* David Hagerman; E-mail: david.hagerman@illinois.gov; Staff 1 (MLS 1)
Founded 1995
Library Holdings: CDs 75; Bk Vols 10,000
Mem of Reaching Across Illinois Library System (RAILS)
Restriction: Authorized patrons

CR JUDSON UNIVERSITY*, Benjamin P Browne Library, 1151 N State St, 60123. SAN 304-1549. Tel: 847-628-2030. Interlibrary Loan Service Tel: 847-628-2032. Reference Tel: 847-628-2038. Administration Tel: 847-628-2036. FAX: 847-628-2045. Web Site: www.judsonu.edu/library. *Dir,* Larry C Wild; E-mail: lwild@judsonu.edu; *Per, Supvr, Access Serv,* Emily Tilsy; Tel: 847-628-2040, E-mail: etilsy@judsonu.edu; *ILL Supvr,* Ashley Fisher; E-mail: afisher@judsonu.edu; *Asst Supvr, Access Serv,* Karen McKeever; E-mail: kmckeever@judsonu.edu; *Asst Supvr, Access Serv,* Joshua Snyder; E-mail: jsnyder@judsonu.edu; *Ref & Instrul Serv, Instr Coordr,* Charlene Thompson; Tel: 847-628-2033, E-mail: cthompson@judsonu.edu; *Tech Serv,* Lynn Hammerlund; Tel: 847-628-2035, E-mail: lhammerlund@judsonu.edu. Subject Specialists: *Archit,* Ashley Fisher; Staff 5 (MLS 3, Non-MLS 2)
Founded 1963. Enrl 920; Highest Degree: Master
Library Holdings: Bk Titles 100,000; Bk Vols 104,693; Per Subs 350

Special Collections: Baptist History & Missions Coll; Edmundson Contemporary Christian Music Coll; Library of American Civilization Coll, micro, ultrafiche
Subject Interests: Archit, Music, Relig
Automation Activity & Vendor Info: (Acquisitions) Ex Libris Group; (Cataloging) Ex Libris Group; (Circulation) Ex Libris Group; (Course Reserve) Ex Libris Group; (ILL) OCLC Online; (OPAC) Ex Libris Group; (Serials) Ex Libris Group
Database Vendor: EBSCOhost, Gale Cengage Learning, LexisNexis, OCLC FirstSearch, Oxford Online, ValueLine
Wireless access
Partic in Consortium of Academic & Research Libraries in Illinois; LIBRAS, Inc; OCLC Online Computer Library Center, Inc

M PROVENA SAINT JOSEPH HOSPITAL*, Health Science Library, 77 N Airlite St, 60123. SAN 375-9458. Tel: 847-695-3200, Ext 5385. FAX: 847-888-3532. Web Site: www.provena.org/saintjoseph. *Librn,* Susan Anderson; E-mail: susan.anderson@provena.org
Library Holdings: Bk Titles 600; Per Subs 60
Mem of Reaching Across Illinois Library System (RAILS)
Open Mon-Thurs 8-1

ELIZABETH

P ELIZABETH TOWNSHIP LIBRARY, 210 E Myrtle St, 61028-9785. (Mail add: PO Box 243, 61028-0243), SAN 304-1565. Tel: 815-858-2212. FAX: 815-858-3475. Web Site: www.elizabethlibrary.org. *Adminr,* Deb Wunsch
Founded 1943. Pop 1,063; Circ 6,000
Library Holdings: Bk Vols 11,882; Per Subs 5
Automation Activity & Vendor Info: (Acquisitions) Follett Software; (Cataloging) Follett Software; (Circulation) Follett Software; (ILL) SIRSI WorkFlows; (OPAC) Follett Software
Wireless access
Function: Adult bk club, After school storytime, Audio & video playback equip for onsite use, Bk club(s), Bks on cassette, Bks on CD, Children's prog, Citizenship assistance, Computer training, Computers for patron use, Copy machines, Digital talking bks, Distance learning, e-mail & chat, Electronic databases & coll, Exhibits, Family literacy, Fax serv, Free DVD rentals, Games & aids for the handicapped, Handicapped accessible, Holiday prog, ILL available, Mail & tel request accepted, Music CDs, Online searches, Outreach serv, Photocopying/Printing, Prog for adults, Prog for children & young adult, Pub access computers, Ref serv available, Senior outreach, Spoken cassettes & CDs, Spoken cassettes & DVDs, Story hour, Summer reading prog, Tax forms, Teen prog, VHS videos, Video lending libr, Workshops
Mem of Reaching Across Illinois Library System (RAILS)
Open Mon & Wed 1-5:30, Thurs 1-7, Fri 9-12 & 1-5, Sat 9-1
Restriction: Non-resident fee

ELK GROVE VILLAGE

M ALEXIAN BROTHERS MEDICAL LIBRARY*, 800 Biesterfield Rd, 60007-3397. SAN 320-3751. Tel: 847-437-5500, Ext 4756. FAX: 847-981-5336. E-mail: alexianlibrary@alexian.net. *Med Librn,* Paul Deane; Tel: 847-437-5500, Ext 4750, E-mail: deanep@alexian.net; Staff 1 (MLS 1)
Founded 1967
Jan 2010-Dec 2010 Income $325,000. Mats Exp $325,000, Books $25,000, Electronic Ref Mat (Incl. Access Fees) $205,000. Sal $64,000
Library Holdings: CDs 250; DVDs 15; e-books 66; e-journals 4,000; Bk Titles 2,000; Per Subs 50
Subject Interests: Med, Nursing
Automation Activity & Vendor Info: (Cataloging) OCLC; (Circulation) CyberTools for Libraries; (OPAC) CyberTools for Libraries; (Serials) CyberTools for Libraries
Database Vendor: EBSCOhost, Majors, Medline, OCLC FirstSearch, OCLC WorldShare Interlibrary Loan, OVID Technologies, PubMed, UpToDate, WebMD
Partic in Docline; Fox Valley Consortium; Greater Midwest Regional Medical Libr Network; Illinois Library & Information Network; Metropolitan Consortium of Chicago; OCLC-LVIS
Open Mon-Fri 8-4:30

M AMERICAN ACADEMY OF PEDIATRICS*, Bakwin Library, 141 Northwest Point Blvd, 60007-1098. SAN 304-1689. Tel: 847-434-7635. FAX: 847-434-4993. Web Site: www.aap.org. *Dir,* Susan Bolda Marshall; Tel: 847-434-4722, E-mail: smarshall@aap.org; *Libr Mgr,* Chris Kwiat; E-mail: ckwiat@aap.org; *Archivist,* Rusty Heckaman; Tel: 847-434-7093, E-mail: rheckaman@aap.org; Staff 4 (MLS 3, Non-MLS 1)
Founded 1965
Library Holdings: Bk Titles 1,000; Per Subs 130
Special Collections: Pediatric History Center. Oral History
Automation Activity & Vendor Info: (Cataloging) EOS International; (Circulation) EOS International; (OPAC) EOS International
Database Vendor: Dialog, OVID Technologies
Partic in Illinois Library & Information Network; Metropolitan Consortium of Chicago; OCLC Online Computer Library Center, Inc
Open Mon-Fri 8-4:30

P ELK GROVE VILLAGE PUBLIC LIBRARY*, 1001 Wellington Ave, 60007-3391. SAN 304-1573. Tel: 847-439-0447. FAX: 847-439-0475. Information Services FAX: 847-439-1301. TDD: 847-439-0865. E-mail: contact@egvpl.org. Web Site: www.egvpl.org. *Dir,* Lee James Maternowski; E-mail: lee.maternowski@egvpl.org; *Adult Serv,* Lisa Malinowski; E-mail: lisa.malinowski@egvpl.org; *Circ,* Debra Nelson; E-mail: debra.nelson@egvpl.org; *Network Serv,* Judy Kennedy; E-mail: judy.kennedy@egvpl.org; *Pub Relations/Adult Prog,* Jill E Derkits; E-mail: jill.derkits@egvpl.org; *Ref,* Jeff Winterstein; E-mail: jeff.winterstein@egvpl.org; *Tech Serv,* Donna Page; E-mail: donna.page@egvpl.org; *YA Serv,* Adelaide Rowe; E-mail: arowe@egvpl.org; Staff 16.75 (MLS 6.75, Non-MLS 10)
Founded 1959. Pop 33,127; Circ 901,724
May 2010-Apr 2011 Income $4,651,538, State $23,371, City $4,476,052, Locally Generated Income $152,115. Mats Exp $828,324, Books $387,437, Per/Ser (Incl. Access Fees) $37,590, AV Mat $247,079, Electronic Ref Mat (Incl. Access Fees) $156,218. Sal $1,918,059 (Prof $494,117)
Library Holdings: Bks on Deafness & Sign Lang 50; Braille Volumes 21; CDs 35,108; DVDs 29,343; e-books 8,719; Electronic Media & Resources 64; Bk Vols 275,894; Per Subs 523
Subject Interests: Civil War, World War II
Automation Activity & Vendor Info: (Acquisitions) SirsiDynix; (Cataloging) OCLC; (Circulation) SirsiDynix; (OPAC) SirsiDynix; (Serials) SirsiDynix
Database Vendor: ALLDATA Online, EBSCO Information Services, EBSCOhost, Gale Cengage Learning, LearningExpress, Newsbank, OCLC FirstSearch, OCLC WorldShare Interlibrary Loan, ProQuest, ReferenceUSA, World Book Online
Wireless access
Publications: Elk Grove-The Peony Village (Local historical information); Highlights (Newsletter)
Special Services for the Deaf - Adult & family literacy prog; Closed caption videos; High interest/low vocabulary bks; Sign lang interpreter upon request for prog; TTY equip
Special Services for the Blind - Accessible computers; BiFolkal kits; Bks on cassette; Bks on CD; Braille bks; Children's Braille; Large print bks; Large screen computer & software; Talking bks from Braille Inst
Open Mon-Thurs 9am-10pm, Fri 9-7, Sat 9-5, Sun 1-5
Friends of the Library Group

ELKHART

P ELKHART PUBLIC LIBRARY DISTRICT*, 121 E Bohan St, 62634. (Mail add: PO Box 170, 62634-0170), SAN 376-1460. Tel: 217-947-2313. FAX: 217-947-2313. E-mail: elkhartlibrary@mchsi.com. *In Charge,* Vanda Liesman
Founded 1893. Pop 777
Library Holdings: Bk Titles 10,000
Automation Activity & Vendor Info: (Cataloging) Horizon; (Circulation) Horizon
Database Vendor: OCLC FirstSearch
Wireless access
Mem of Illinois Heartland Library System
Special Services for the Blind - Audio mat
Open Mon 4-8, Tues & Fri 9-4, Wed & Thurs 9-8, Sat 9-1

ELKVILLE

P RICK WARREN MEMORIAL PUBLIC LIBRARY DISTRICT, 114 S Fourth St, 62932-1097. SAN 376-1681. Tel: 618-568-1843. FAX: 618-568-1843. E-mail: rwlibrary@rickwarren.lib.il.us. Web Site: www.rickwarren.lib.il.us. *Librn,* Janet Eisenhauer; E-mail: jre_3@yahoo.com; *Asst Librn,* Johnnie Halstead
Founded 1970. Pop 3,301
Library Holdings: High Interest/Low Vocabulary Bk Vols 100; Bk Titles 15,000
Wireless access
Mem of Illinois Heartland Library System
Open Mon, Wed & Fri 12-5, Tues 9-8, Thurs 9-5, Sat 9-12

ELMHURST

C ELMHURST COLLEGE*, A C Buehler Library, 190 Prospect St, 60126. SAN 304-159X. Tel: 630-617-3160. Interlibrary Loan Service Tel: 630-617-3169. Reference Tel: 630-617-3173. FAX: 630-617-3332. E-mail: ref@elmhurst.edu. Web Site: www.elmhurst.edu/library. *Dir,* Susan Swords Steffen; Tel: 630-617-3172, E-mail: susanss@elmhurst.edu; *Head, Ref,* Donna Goodwyn; Tel: 630-617-3171; *Head, Tech Serv,* Elaine Fetyko Page; Tel: 630-617-3166; *Instrul Media Ctr Mgr,* Bonnie Torres; Tel: 630-617-3153; *Ref & Instruction Librn,* Jacob Hill; Tel: 630-617-3168; *Ref & Instruction Librn,* Jennifer Paliatka; Tel: 630-617-3158; *Ref Serv,* Ayanna Gaines; Staff 7 (MLS 6, Non-MLS 1)

Founded 1871. Enrl 2,775; Fac 119; Highest Degree: Master
Library Holdings: AV Mats 4,085; Bk Titles 219,915; Bk Vols 221,463; Per Subs 1,100
Subject Interests: Nursing
Automation Activity & Vendor Info: (Cataloging) Ex Libris Group; (Circulation) Ex Libris Group; (OPAC) Ex Libris Group
Partic in Consortium of Academic & Research Libraries in Illinois; LIBRAS, Inc; OCLC Online Computer Library Center, Inc
Open Mon-Thurs 7:30am-Midnight, Fri 7:30-7, Sat 8-5, Sun Noon-Midnight

S ELMHURST HISTORICAL MUSEUM LIBRARY*, 120 E Park Ave, 60126. SAN 326-0364. Tel: 630-833-1457. FAX: 630-833-1326. E-mail: ehm@elmhurst.org. Web Site: www.elmhurst.org/elmhurst/museum. *Dir,* Brian F Bergheger; *Curator of Coll,* Nancy Wilson
Founded 1975
Library Holdings: Bk Titles 577
Subject Interests: Local hist, Museology, Newsp on microfilm
Open Tues-Sun 1-5
Restriction: Non-circulating

M ELMHURST MEMORIAL HEALTHCARE*, Soukup Herter Library & Resource Center, 155 E Brush Hill Rd, 60126. SAN 304-1611. Tel: 331-221-1000, Ext 14130. FAX: 331-221-3788. *Libr Asst,* Diane Paulini; E-mail: libasst@emhc.org
Library Holdings: Bk Titles 8,000; Per Subs 240
Subject Interests: Med
Publications: Acquisition List (Monthly)
Mem of Reaching Across Illinois Library System (RAILS)
Partic in Fox Valley Health Science Library Consortium; Illinois Library & Information Network
Open Mon-Fri 8-4:30

P ELMHURST PUBLIC LIBRARY*, 125 S Prospect, 60126-3298. SAN 304-1603. Tel: 630-279-8696. FAX: 630-279-0636. TDD: 630-782-4310. E-mail: reference@elmhurst.org. Web Site: www.elmhurstpubliclibrary.org. *Dir,* Mary Beth Campe; Tel: 630-530-6300, Fax: 630-516-1364, E-mail: marybeth.campe@elmhurst.org; *Head, Adult Serv,* Catherine E Ingram; *Head, Circ,* Samantha Cresswell; *Head, Kids' Libr,* Sharon Karpiel; *Head, Tech Serv,* Kathleen Murphy; Staff 17.5 (MLS 17.5)
Founded 1916. Pop 44,121; Circ 1,482,430
May 2011-Apr 2012 Income $7,906,400, State $44,200, Locally Generated Income $6,731,000, Other $1,131,200. Mats Exp $877,600, Books $489,100, Per/Ser (Incl. Access Fees) $40,000, Other Print Mats $1,000, AV Mat $193,000, Electronic Ref Mat (Incl. Access Fees) $151,000, Presv $500. Sal $3,115,500
Library Holdings: Audiobooks 19,730; CDs 17,777; DVDs 18,799; e-books 7,062; Bk Vols 304,141; Per Subs 524; Videos 4,844
Automation Activity & Vendor Info: (Acquisitions) Innovative Interfaces, Inc; (Circulation) Innovative Interfaces, Inc; (ILL) Innovative Interfaces, Inc; (OPAC) Innovative Interfaces, Inc; (Serials) Innovative Interfaces, Inc
Wireless access
Publications: Newsletter-Fine Print
Mem of Reaching Across Illinois Library System (RAILS)
Partic in OCLC Online Computer Library Center, Inc
Special Services for the Blind - Assistive/Adapted tech devices, equip & products; Screen reader software
Open Mon-Fri 9-9, Sat 9-5, Sun 1-5
Friends of the Library Group

S LIZZADRO MUSEUM OF LAPIDARY ART LIBRARY, 220 Cottage Hill Ave, 60126. SAN 326-9493. Tel: 630-833-1616. FAX: 630-833-1225. E-mail: info@lizzadromuseum.org. Web Site: www.lizzadromuseum.org. *Dir,* Dorothy Asher
Library Holdings: Bk Titles 800
Subject Interests: Gemology, Geol, Mineral, Paleontology
Publications: Lizzadro Museum Publication
Restriction: Open by appt only

S THEATRE HISTORICAL SOCIETY OF AMERICA, Archive & Research Center, 152 N York Rd, 2nd Flr, 60126-2806. SAN 371-5256. Tel: 630-782-1800. Web Site: www.historictheatres.org. *Archives Dir,* Patrick Seymour; Tel: 630-936-4408, E-mail: archivedir@historictheatres.org
Founded 1969
Library Holdings: AV Mats 200; Bk Titles 1,100
Special Collections: Bill Clifford Coll, drawings & sketches; Bill Peterson Coll, photog; Blueprint Coll; Chicago Architectural Photographing Company Coll, theatre building negatives; Michael Miller Coll; Slide Coll; Terry Helgesen Coll
Subject Interests: Cinema, Theatre, Theatre archit
Wireless access
Function: Archival coll, Exhibits, Mail & tel request accepted, Res libr, Res performed for a fee
Publications: Marquee (Journal)
Restriction: Access at librarian's discretion, Authorized scholars by appt, Closed stack, Fee for pub use, Non-circulating, Not a lending libr, Open by appt only, Open to pub for ref only, Open to researchers by request, Private libr, Pub use on premises, Restricted access

ELMWOOD

P MORRISON & MARY WILEY LIBRARY DISTRICT*, 206 W Main St, 61529-9641. (Mail add: PO Box 467, 61529-0467), SAN 304-162X. Tel: 309-742-2431. FAX: 309-742-8298. E-mail: elmlib@elmnet.net. Web Site: elmwoodpubliclibrary.org. *Libr Dir,* Michelle Armbruster; *Asst Libr Dir,* Pat Keeter; *Libr Assoc,* April Estes; *Libr Assoc,* Carroll Inskeep; Staff 4 (Non-MLS 4)
Founded 1950. Pop 2,598; Circ 17,895
Library Holdings: Audiobooks 814; DVDs 3,305; e-books 2,568; Bk Titles 12,705; Bk Vols 19,000; Per Subs 35
Wireless access
Mem of Reaching Across Illinois Library System (RAILS)
Open Mon, Tues & Fri 1-5, Wed 9-6, Thurs 1-8, Sat 9-1

ELMWOOD PARK

P ELMWOOD PARK PUBLIC LIBRARY, One Conti Pkwy, 60707. SAN 304-1638. Tel: 708-453-7645. Reference Tel: 708-395-1219. FAX: 708-453-4671. E-mail: eps@elmwoodparklibrary.org. Web Site: www.elmwoodparklibrary.org. *Dir,* Tiffany Verzani; Tel: 708-395-1230, E-mail: tverzani@elmwoodparklibrary.org; *Head, Patron Serv,* Jason Stuhlmann; Tel: 708-395-1241, E-mail: jstuhlmann@elmwoodparklibrary.org; *Head, Adult Serv,* Mandy N McGee; Tel: 708-395-1240, E-mail: mmcgee@elmwoodparklibrary.org; *Head, Coll Serv,* Mary Moss; Tel: 708-395-1204, E-mail: mmoss@elmwoodparklibrary.org; *Head, Tech Serv,* Marcy Campagna; Tel: 708-395-1205, E-mail: mcampagna@elmwoodparklibrary.org; *Head, Youth Serv,* Kim Viita; Tel: 708-395-1242, E-mail: kviita@elmwoodparklibrary.org; Staff 24 (MLS 9, Non-MLS 15)
Founded 1936. Pop 24,883; Circ 243,658
Library Holdings: AV Mats 15,163; Bk Vols 120,198; Per Subs 218
Subject Interests: Italian (Lang), Lit, Local hist, Polish (Lang), Spanish (Lang)
Automation Activity & Vendor Info: (Acquisitions) Innovative Interfaces, Inc - Millenium; (Circulation) Innovative Interfaces, Inc; (OPAC) Innovative Interfaces, Inc - Millenium
Wireless access
Publications: What's Happening (Newsletter)
Mem of Reaching Across Illinois Library System (RAILS)
Partic in System Wide Automated Network
Open Mon-Thurs 9-9, Fri 9-6, Sat 9-5, Sun (Sept-May) 1-5
Friends of the Library Group

ELSAH

C PRINCIPIA COLLEGE*, Marshall Brooks Library, One Maybeck Pl, 62028-9703. SAN 304-1646. Tel: 618-374-5235. Reference Tel: 618-374-5070. FAX: 618-374-5107. Web Site: www.prin.edu/college/library. *Dir,* Lisa Roberts; E-mail: lisa.roberts@principia.edu; *Assoc Dir,* Edith List; Tel: 618-374-5076, E-mail: edith.list@principia.edu; *Librn,* Chelsea Sutton; *Acq Mgr,* Cathy Barlow; *Pub Serv Mgr,* Deb Wold; Staff 7 (MLS 5, Non-MLS 2)
Founded 1935. Enrl 550; Fac 62; Highest Degree: Bachelor
Library Holdings: Bk Titles 174,000; Bk Vols 205,000; Per Subs 800
Special Collections: Curriculum; US Govt Documents (Selective Depository)
Subject Interests: Art hist, Biblical studies, Christian scientists, Rare bks
Automation Activity & Vendor Info: (Acquisitions) SirsiDynix; (Cataloging) SirsiDynix; (Circulation) SirsiDynix; (Course Reserve) SirsiDynix; (OPAC) SirsiDynix; (Serials) SirsiDynix
Database Vendor: EBSCOhost, Gale Cengage Learning, LexisNexis, OCLC FirstSearch, ProQuest
Partic in IAC Expanded Acad, Inc; Illinois Library & Information Network; OCLC Online Computer Library Center, Inc; Saint Louis Regional Library Network
Open Mon-Thurs 8am-Midnight, Fri 8-6, Sat 9:30-8, Sun 1-Midnight

ERIE

P ERIE PUBLIC LIBRARY DISTRICT*, 802 Eighth Ave, 61250-7752. (Mail add: PO Box 436, 61250-0436), SAN 304-1654. Tel: 309-659-2707. FAX: 309-659-2707. E-mail: eriepubliclibrary@yahoo.com. *Dir,* Laurel M Reiss; E-mail: lreisspld@gmail.com; *Asst Librn, Ch,* Ellen Littrel
Founded 1964. Pop 3,345; Circ 18,690
Library Holdings: Audiobooks 954; CDs 702; Bk Titles 27,675; Per Subs 33
Mem of Reaching Across Illinois Library System (RAILS)
Open Mon, Wed & Thurs 9-11 & 2-8, Tues 2-8, Fri 2-5, Sat 9-2, Sun 2-4
Friends of the Library Group

EUREKA

C EUREKA COLLEGE*, Melick Library, 301 E College Ave, 61530-1563. SAN 304-1662. Tel: 309-467-6380. Reference Tel: 309-467-6892. Administration Tel: 309-467-6382. FAX: 309-467-6386. E-mail: library@eureka.edu. Web Site: www.eureka.edu/melick/melick.htm. *Libr Dir,* Anthony R Glass; E-mail: arglass@eureka.edu; *Pub Serv Librn,* Kelly A Fisher; *Tech Serv Librn,* Katrina Donaghy; *Coordr, Access Serv,* Nicolle Ebert; Staff 11 (MLS 3, Non-MLS 8)
Founded 1855. Enrl 500; Fac 43; Highest Degree: Bachelor
Library Holdings: Bk Titles 63,420; Bk Vols 77,695; Per Subs 250
Special Collections: Christian Church (Disciples of Christ Coll), archives; Eureka College Archives; History of Eureka Archives
Automation Activity & Vendor Info: (Cataloging) Ex Libris Group; (Circulation) Ex Libris Group; (ILL) Ex Libris Group; (OPAC) Ex Libris Group; (Serials) Ex Libris Group
Database Vendor: EBSCOhost, LexisNexis, OCLC FirstSearch
Partic in Consortium of Academic & Research Libraries in Illinois
Open Mon-Thurs 7:45am-11pm, Fri 7:45-4:30, Sat 1-5, Sun 6pm-11pm

P EUREKA PUBLIC LIBRARY DISTRICT*, 202 S Main St, 61530. SAN 304-1670. Tel: 309-467-2922. FAX: 309-467-3527. E-mail: info@eurekapl.org. Web Site: www.eurekapl.org. *Dir,* Nancy H Scott; E-mail: nscott@mtco.com; *Assoc Dir,* Ann Reeves; *Ch,* Robin Richey; Staff 7 (MLS 2, Non-MLS 5)
Founded 1930. Pop 6,618; Circ 106,608
Library Holdings: Bk Vols 40,725; Per Subs 251
Special Collections: Local History Coll
Automation Activity & Vendor Info: (Acquisitions) SirsiDynix; (Cataloging) OCLC Connexion; (Circulation) SIRSI WorkFlows; (OPAC) SirsiDynix
Database Vendor: Gale Cengage Learning, ProQuest
Wireless access
Function: Alaskana res, Archival coll, Art exhibits, BA reader (adult literacy), Bi-weekly Writer's Group, Bilingual assistance for Spanish patrons, Bk reviews (Group), Chess club, Citizenship assistance, e-mail & chat, Genealogy discussion group, Govt ref serv, Health sci info serv, Jail serv, Jazz prog, Large print keyboards, Learning ctr, Legal assistance to inmates, Mail loans to mem, Masonic res mat, Monthly prog for perceptually impaired adults, Mus passes, Newsp ref libr, Notary serv, Online info literacy tutorials on the web & in blackboard, Online ref, Passport agency, Prof lending libr, Provide serv for the mentally ill, Referrals accepted, Res libr, Res performed for a fee, Satellite serv, Serves mentally handicapped consumers, Specialized serv in classical studies, VCDs, Web-Braille, Words travel prog
Publications: Around the District (Newsletter)
Open Mon, Tues & Thurs 9-8, Wed & Fri 9-6, Sat (Sept-May) 9-2
Friends of the Library Group

EVANSTON

S EVANSTON HISTORY CENTER LIBRARY & ARCHIVES*, Frank B Foster Research Room, 225 Greenwood St, 60201. SAN 304-1719. Tel: 847-475-3410. FAX: 847-475-3599. Web Site: www.evanstonhistorycenter.org. *Exec Dir,* Eden Juron Pearlman; E-mail: ejpearlman@evanstonhistorycenter.org; *Archivist,* Lori Osborne; E-mail: losborne@evanstonhistorycenter.org; Staff 1 (Non-MLS 1)
Founded 1898
Library Holdings: Bk Titles 3,000
Special Collections: Charles Gates Dawes Coll
Function: Archival coll, Copy machines, Ref serv available
Publications: TimeLines (Newsletter)
Open Tues, Thurs & Sat 1-4, Wed 1-6
Restriction: Fee for pub use, Non-circulating

P EVANSTON PUBLIC LIBRARY*, 1703 Orrington, 60201. SAN 304-1735. Tel: 847-448-8600, 847-866-0300. Circulation Tel: 847-448-8605. Reference Tel: 847-448-8630. FAX: 847-866-0313. Web Site: www.epl.org. *Dir,* Mary Johns; *Bus Mgr,* Paul Gottschalk; *Adult Serv,* Lesley Williams; *AV,* Laura Hirshfield; Tel: 847-448-8620; *Ch Serv,* Jan Bojda; Tel: 847-448-8601; *Coll Develop,* Susan Robertson; Tel: 847-448-8619
Founded 1873. Pop 74,239; Circ 868,837
Library Holdings: AV Mats 26,234; Bk Vols 464,830; Per Subs 918
Special Collections: Antique Silver (Berg Coll); Music (Sadie Coe Coll)
Subject Interests: Art
Database Vendor: SirsiDynix
Partic in Dialog Corp; OCLC Online Computer Library Center, Inc
Open Mon-Thurs 9-9, Fri & Sat 9-6, Sun 12-6
Friends of the Library Group
Branches: 2
NORTH, 2026 Central St, 60201. Tel: 847-866-0330. FAX: 847-866-0331. *Br Mgr,* Constance Heneghan
Library Holdings: Bk Vols 30,000; Per Subs 39
Open Mon & Thurs 10-8, Tues & Wed 10-6, Sat 9-5
SOUTH, 949 Chicago Ave, 60202. Tel: 847-866-0333. FAX: 847-866-0332. *Br Mgr,* Jill Skwerski
Library Holdings: Bk Vols 25,000; Per Subs 25
Open Tues & Thurs 10-8, Wed & Fri 10-6, Sat 9-5

SR FIRST PRESBYTERIAN CHURCH*, Thomas E Boswell Memorial Library, 1427 Chicago Ave, 60201. SAN 304-1743. Tel: 847-864-1472. FAX: 847-864-1494. Web Site: www.firstpresevanston.org. *Dir,* Judith Akers; Staff 5 (MLS 3, Non-MLS 2)
Founded 1962
Library Holdings: Bk Titles 4,000; Per Subs 13
Subject Interests: Church hist, Fiction, Theol
Open Sun 8-2

S NATIONAL WOMAN'S CHRISTIAN TEMPERANCE UNION*, Frances E Willard Memorial Library, 1730 Chicago Ave, 60201-4585. SAN 304-1786. Tel: 847-864-1397. FAX: 847-864-9497. E-mail: archives@franceswillardhouse.org. Web Site: www.wctu.org. *Archivist/Librn,* Virginia L Beatty; Staff 2 (MLS 2)
Founded 1940
Library Holdings: Bk Titles 5,000
Special Collections: Frances E Willard Papers; WCTU Presidential Papers (eg, Anna Gordon, Lillian Stevens); WCTU Records
Subject Interests: Alcohol & drugs, Hist of Woman's Christian Temperance Union, Tobacco, Women's studies
Restriction: Open by appt only
Friends of the Library Group

C NORTHWESTERN UNIVERSITY LIBRARY, 1970 Campus Dr, 60208-2300. SAN 340-3920. Tel: 847-491-7658. Circulation Tel: 847-491-7633. Interlibrary Loan Service Tel: 847-491-7630, 847-491-7659. Reference Tel: 847-491-7656. Administration Tel: 847-491-7640. Interlibrary Loan Service FAX: 847-491-5685. Administration FAX: 847-491-8306. E-mail: refdept@northwestern.edu. Web Site: www.library.northwestern.edu. *Dean of Libr,* Sarah M Pritchard; E-mail: spritchard@northwestern.edu; *Head, Fac Operations & Stacks Mgt,* Suzette Radford; *Head, Res & Info Serv,* Harriet Lightman; *Actg Head, Access Serv, Head, User Experience,* Geoff Swindells; *Actg Head, Bibliog Serv,* Michael Babinec; *Assoc Univ Librn, Planning & Fac,* Elizabeth Hitchcock; *Assoc Univ Librn, Admin Serv,* Roxanne Sellberg; *Assoc Univ Librn, Pub Serv,* Marianne Ryan; *Actg Assoc Univ Librn, Spec Libr,* D.J. Hoek; *Art Librn,* Cara List; *Curator, Africana,* Esmeralda Kale; *Curator, Spec Coll,* Scott Krafft; *Pub Relations,* Clare Roccaforte; *Univ Archivist,* Kevin Leonard; Staff 226 (MLS 115, Non-MLS 111)
Founded 1851. Enrl 18,579; Fac 1,410; Highest Degree: Doctorate
Sept 2012-Aug 2013 Income (Main Library Only) $27,297,112. Mats Exp $12,173,767. Sal $12,107,221 (Prof $6,977,026)
Library Holdings: Bk Vols 5,295,648; Per Subs 54,604
Special Collections: Africana; Architecture (Frank Lloyd Wright Coll); Contemporary Music Scores; Dublin Gate Theatre; European Union, Orgn of Am States, World Trade Orgn; Manuscripts; Modern Movements in Art & Literature (German Expressionism, Italian Futurism, Dadaism, Surrealism, Concrete Poetry); Printing (Graphic Arts, Private Presses); Rare Books (Aldines, Deism, Elzeviers, Fichte, German Classics, Grundtvig, Ibsen, Kant, Kierkegaard, Little Magazines, Twain, Whitman); Women's Liberation Movement, 1960 to date. State Document Depository; UN Document Depository; US Document Depository
Automation Activity & Vendor Info: (Acquisitions) Ex Libris Group; (Cataloging) Ex Libris Group; (Circulation) Ex Libris Group; (Course Reserve) Atlas Systems; (ILL) OCLC ILLiad; (Media Booking) Ex Libris Group; (OPAC) Ex Libris Group; (Serials) Ex Libris Group
Database Vendor: ABC-CLIO, Alexander Street Press, American Chemical Society, American Geophysical Union, American Mathematical Society, American Physical Society, American Psychological Association (APA), Annual Reviews, ARTstor, Atlas Systems, Blackwell, Bowker, Cambridge Scientific Abstracts, Cinahl, CIOS (Communication Institute for Online Scholarship), CQ Press, CRC Press/Taylor & Francis Group, CredoReference, Dun & Bradstreet, Ebooks Corporation, ebrary, EBSCOhost, Elsevier, Elsevier MDL, Ex Libris Group, Factiva.com, Gale Cengage Learning, Greenwood Publishing Group, H W Wilson, Haworth Pres Inc, Hoovers, IBISWorld, IEEE (Institute of Electrical & Electronics Engineers), IHS, Ingenta, IOP, ISI Web of Knowledge, Jane's, JSTOR, Knovel, LexisNexis, Marcive, Inc, Marquis Who's Who, Mergent Online, Modern Language Association, Nature Publishing Group, Newsbank, Newsbank-Readex, OCLC FirstSearch, OCLC WorldShare Interlibrary Loan, OVID Technologies, Oxford Online, Paratext, Plunkett Research, Ltd, Project MUSE, ProQuest, PubMed, ReferenceUSA, Repere, Sage, SBRnet (Sports Business Research Network), ScienceDirect, Scopus, Springer-Verlag, Springshare, LLC, Standard & Poor's, Swets Information Services, Telus, Thomson - Web of Science, ValueLine, Wiley InterScience, YBP Library Services
Wireless access
Publications: Footnotes (Newsletter)
Partic in Association of Research Libraries (ARL); Center for Research Libraries; Committee on Institutional Cooperation; Consortium of

Academic & Research Libraries in Illinois; NISO Library Standards Alliance; OCLC Online Computer Library Center, Inc
Open Mon-Thurs 8:30am-3am, Fri & Sat 8:30am-11:45pm, Sun 10am-3am
Restriction: Restricted access

Departmental Libraries:

RALPH P BOAS MATHEMATICS LIBRARY, Lunt Bldg, Rm 130, 2033 Sheridan Rd, 60208, SAN 340-4013. Tel: 847-491-7627. E-mail: mathlib@northwestern.edu. Web Site: www.library.northwestern.edu/math. *Librn,* Cunera Buys; Staff 0.6 (MLS 0.1, Non-MLS 0.5)
Subject Interests: Math, Statistics
Open Mon-Fri 9:30-6

SEELEY G MUDD LIBRARY FOR SCIENCE & ENGINEERING, 2233 Tech Dr, 60208, SAN 340-4072. Tel: 847-491-3362. FAX: 847-491-4655. E-mail: sel@northwestern.edu. Web Site: www.library.northwestern.edu/sel. *Head, Br & Off-Campus Serv,* Scott Garton; Staff 7.3 (MLS 2.8, Non-MLS 4.5)
Subject Interests: Applied math, Astronomy, Chem, Computer sci, Eng, Life sci, Physics
Open Mon-Thurs 8:30am-3am, Fri & Sat 8:30am-Midnight, Sun 10am-3am

MUSIC, 1970 Campus Dr, 60208-2300. Tel: 847-491-3434. FAX: 847-467-7574. Web Site: www.library.northwestern.edu/music. *Head Music Libr,* D J Hoek; Tel: 847-491-2884, E-mail: djhoek@northwestern.edu; Staff 10 (MLS 4, Non-MLS 6)
Founded 1945
Library Holdings: CDs 30,000; Music Scores 175,000; Bk Vols 50,000; Per Subs 400
Special Collections: American Music Edition Archive; Ben Johnston Coll; Early Editions & Rare Publications of Treatises, Libretti & Scores; Foundation for Contemporary Performing Arts Coll, mss; Fritz Reiner Library; John Cage Archive; Moldenhauer Archives (Partial Coll); Music Manuscripts; Scores & Correspondence from the Ricordi Publishing House
Subject Interests: 20th Century music
Automation Activity & Vendor Info: (Acquisitions) Ex Libris Group
Publications: Music Library News (Current awareness service)

TRANSPORTATION LIBRARY, 1970 Campus Dr, 60208. Tel: 847-491-5273. Interlibrary Loan Service Tel: 847-491-8600. FAX: 847-491-8601. E-mail: trans@northwestern.edu. Web Site: www.library.northwestern.edu/transportation. *Head Librn,* Roberto A Sarmiento; Tel: 847-491-2913, E-mail: r-sarmiento@northwestern.edu; *Pub Serv Librn,* Mary K Geary; Tel: 847-467-5325, E-mail: m-geary@northwestern.edu; *Tech Serv Librn,* Paul R Burley; Tel: 847-491-5274, E-mail: p-burley@northwestern.edu; Staff 7 (MLS 3, Non-MLS 4)
Library Holdings: Electronic Media & Resources 3,818; Microforms 203,034; Bk Vols 320,748; Videos 44
Special Collections: Environmental Impact Statements; Transportation Companies Annual Reports
Subject Interests: Environ impact statements, Law enforcement, Transportation
Partic in Midwest Transportation Knowledge Network (MTKN)

M SAINT FRANCIS HOSPITAL*, Memorial Medical Library, 355 Ridge Ave, 60202. SAN 340-4137. Tel: 847-316-2460. Circulation Tel: 847-316-2456. FAX: 847-316-5816. *Mgr, Libr Serv,* Beth Carlin
Founded 1919
Library Holdings: Bk Vols 2,050
Wireless access
Publications: Newsletter
Partic in Metropolitan Consortium of Chicago
Open Mon-Fri 7:30-4

S SIGMA ALPHA EPSILON FRATERNITY & FOUNDATION*, Joseph W Walt Library, 1856 Sheridan Rd, 60201-3837. (Mail add: PO Box 1856, 60204-1856), SAN 304-1808. Tel: 847-475-1856. Toll Free Tel: 800-233-1856, Ext 204. FAX: 847-475-2250. Web Site: www.sae.net. *Exec Dir,* Steven K Priepke; Staff 1 (Non-MLS 1)
Founded 1930
Library Holdings: Bk Titles 2,000
Special Collections: Books By & About Members of Sigma Alpha Epsilon; Frances Willard Coll; History of SAE, 1856 to present, correspondence, mss, photogs; William C Levere Coll
Subject Interests: Stained glass
Open Mon-Fri 9-4
Restriction: Non-circulating

R THE UNITED LIBRARY*, 2121 Sheridan Rd, 60201. SAN 304-1751. Tel: 847-866-3909. Reference Tel: 847-866-3870. Administration Tel: 847-866-3877. Toll Free Tel: 877-600-8753. FAX: 847-866-3894. E-mail: united.library@garrett.edu. Web Site: library.garrett.edu. *Dir,* Dr Jaeyeon Lucy Chung; E-mail: jaeyeon.chung@garrett.edu; Staff 5 (MLS 3, Non-MLS 2)
Founded 1981. Highest Degree: Doctorate
Library Holdings: Bk Titles 220,000; Bk Vols 320,000; Per Subs 600
Special Collections: Egyptology (Hibbard Egyptian Coll); Keen Bible Coll
Subject Interests: Biblical studies, Church hist, Relig, Theol
Wireless access
Partic in Association of Chicago Theological Schools; Consortium of Academic & Research Libraries in Illinois; OCLC Online Computer Library Center, Inc
Open Mon & Wed 8:30am-10pm, Tues & Thurs 7:45am-10pm, Fri 8:30-6, Sat 11-5, Sun 2-8

EVANSVILLE

P EVANSVILLE PUBLIC LIBRARY*, 602 S Public St, 62242. (Mail add: PO Box 299, 62242-0299), SAN 304-1824. FAX: 618-853-2342. *Librn,* Sherri Herzog
Founded 1965. Pop 724
Library Holdings: Bk Vols 6,978; Per Subs 12
Subject Interests: Adult fiction, Hist
Mem of Illinois Heartland Library System
Open Tues & Thurs 12-6

EVERGREEN PARK

P EVERGREEN PARK PUBLIC LIBRARY*, 9400 S Troy Ave, 60805-2383. SAN 304-1832. Tel: 708-422-8522. FAX: 708-422-8665. Web Site: www.evergreenparklibrary.org. *Dir,* Nicolette Seidl; *Head, Circ,* Mary Lou Walsh; *Adult Serv, Ref,* Christine Raap; *Ch Serv,* Laura Meyer; Staff 13 (MLS 5, Non-MLS 8)
Founded 1944. Pop 20,860; Circ 125,000
Library Holdings: Bk Vols 70,000
Automation Activity & Vendor Info: (Acquisitions) Innovative Interfaces, Inc; (Cataloging) Innovative Interfaces, Inc; (Circulation) Innovative Interfaces, Inc
Wireless access
Mem of Reaching Across Illinois Library System (RAILS)
Open Mon-Thurs 9-9, Fri & Sat 9-5, Sun (Sept-May) 12-4

M LITTLE COMPANY OF MARY HOSPITAL*, Medical Library, 2800 W 95th St, 60805. SAN 304-1840. Tel: 708-229-5299. FAX: 708-229-5885. Web Site: www.lcmh.org. *Librn,* Teresa Luna; E-mail: tluna@lcmh.org
Library Holdings: Bk Vols 2,000; Per Subs 100
Wireless access
Open Mon-Thurs 7:30-1

FAIRBURY

P DOMINY MEMORIAL LIBRARY*, 201 S Third St, 61739. SAN 304-1859. Tel: 815-692-3231. FAX: 815-692-3503. E-mail: dominylibrary@yahoo.com. Web Site: www.dominymemoriallibrary.org. *Dir,* Debbie Oakland; *Asst Librn,* Marlene Walter; Staff 5 (Non-MLS 5)
Founded 1904. Pop 3,757; Circ 34,266
Library Holdings: High Interest/Low Vocabulary Bk Vols 20; Large Print Bks 382; Bk Vols 20,965; Per Subs 14
Automation Activity & Vendor Info: (Circulation) SIRSI WorkFlows
Database Vendor: OCLC FirstSearch, OCLC WebJunction, OCLC WorldShare Interlibrary Loan
Wireless access
Function: Home delivery & serv to Sr ctr & nursing homes, Homebound delivery serv, ILL available, Prog for children & young adult, Summer reading prog
Mem of Reaching Across Illinois Library System (RAILS)
Open Mon, Tues & Thurs 9-7, Wed & Fri 9-5, Sat 10-1
Friends of the Library Group

FAIRFIELD

P FAIRFIELD PUBLIC LIBRARY*, 300 SE Second St, 62837. SAN 304-1867. Tel: 618-842-4516. FAX: 618-842-6708. Web Site: www.fairfield.lib.il.us. *Head Librn,* Michelle Conard; Staff 2 (Non-MLS 2)
Founded 1923. Pop 5,428; Circ 60,119
Library Holdings: Bk Vols 40,000; Per Subs 84
Automation Activity & Vendor Info: (Cataloging) SirsiDynix; (Circulation) SirsiDynix; (OPAC) SirsiDynix
Mem of Illinois Heartland Library System
Open Mon-Thurs 10-7, Fri & Sat 10-5
Friends of the Library Group

J ILLINOIS EASTERN COMMUNITY COLLEGE*, Frontier Community College Library, Two Frontier Dr, 62837-9705. SAN 325-1810. Tel: 618-842-3711. Toll Free Tel: 877-464-3687. FAX: 618-842-4425. Web Site: www.iecc.edu/fcc/lrc. *Librn,* Merna Youngblood; E-mail: youngbloodm@iecc.edu; Staff 2 (MLS 1, Non-MLS 1)
Founded 1976. Enrl 650; Fac 500; Highest Degree: Associate

Jul 2009-Jun 2010 Income $106,468. Mats Exp $22,250, Books $9,000, Per/Ser (Incl. Access Fees) $4,500, AV Mat $4,000, Electronic Ref Mat (Incl. Access Fees) $4,750. Sal $80,418 (Prof $63,918)
Library Holdings: AV Mats 2,650; High Interest/Low Vocabulary Bk Vols 2,525; Bk Titles 20,250; Per Subs 100
Database Vendor: CredoReference, EBSCOhost, Facts on File, LexisNexis, McGraw-Hill, OCLC FirstSearch, OCLC WebJunction, OCLC WorldShare Interlibrary Loan
Wireless access
Function: Computers for patron use, Copy machines, e-mail & chat, Electronic databases & coll, Fax serv, Handicapped accessible, ILL available, Large print keyboards, Learning ctr, Magnifiers for reading, Online ref, Online searches, Orientations, Photocopying/Printing, Pub access computers, Scanner, Wheelchair accessible
Mem of Illinois Heartland Library System
Open Mon-Thurs 7:30am-8pm, Fri 7:30-4:30

FAIRMOUNT

P VANCE TOWNSHIP LIBRARY*, 107 S Main St, 61841. (Mail add: PO Box 230, 61841-0230), SAN 304-1875. Tel: 217-733-2164. FAX: 217-733-2164. E-mail: vantwplib@yahoo.com. *Dir,* Bonnie B Gilbert; Staff 2 (Non-MLS 2)
Founded 1940. Pop 1,027; Circ 4,674
Library Holdings: Bk Vols 10,263; Per Subs 32
Special Collections: History of Fairmount Coll; Jamaica Area; Senior Citizen Info; State of Illinois
Mem of Illinois Heartland Library System
Special Services for the Blind - Talking bk & rec for the blind cat
Open Tues-Fri 11-5, Sat 9-2

FAIRVIEW

P VALLEY DISTRICT PUBLIC LIBRARY*, Fairview Township Library, 515 Carter St, 61432. (Mail add: PO Box 200, 61432-0200), SAN 376-1215. Tel: 309-778-2240. FAX: 309-778-2240. E-mail: vdl61432@hotmail.com. *Librn,* Debbie Canevit
Library Holdings: Large Print Bks 75; Bk Titles 4,700
Open Mon, Wed & Fri 9-5

FAIRVIEW HEIGHTS

P FAIRVIEW HEIGHTS PUBLIC LIBRARY*, 10017 Bunkum Rd, 62208-1703. SAN 321-8961. Tel: 618-489-2070. Circulation Tel: 618-489-2073. Administration Tel: 618-489-2071. FAX: 618-489-2079. E-mail: fhpl@fhplibrary.org. Web Site: www.fairviewheightslibrary.org. *Dir,* Jill Pifer; Staff 11 (MLS 1, Non-MLS 10)
Founded 1972. Pop 15,034; Circ 135,000
May 2007-Apr 2008 Income $504,475, State $18,201, City $452,588, Locally Generated Income $33,686. Mats Exp $70,000, Books $40,000, AV Mat $20,000, Electronic Ref Mat (Incl. Access Fees) $10,000. Sal $283,417 (Prof $71,000)
Library Holdings: AV Mats 9,094; CDs 3,165; DVDs 2,300; Electronic Media & Resources 100; Large Print Bks 1,500; Bk Vols 40,000; Per Subs 135; Videos 200
Subject Interests: Music
Automation Activity & Vendor Info: (Cataloging) Innovative Interfaces, Inc; (Circulation) Innovative Interfaces, Inc; (ILL) Innovative Interfaces, Inc; (OPAC) Innovative Interfaces, Inc; (Serials) Innovative Interfaces, Inc
Database Vendor: Innovative Interfaces, Inc
Wireless access
Mem of Illinois Heartland Library System
Partic in Illinois Library & Information Network
Open Mon-Thurs 10-8, Fri & Sat 10-5
Friends of the Library Group

FARMER CITY

P FARMER CITY PUBLIC LIBRARY*, 105 E Green St, 61842-1508. (Mail add: PO Box 201, 61842-0201), SAN 304-1883. Tel: 309-928-9532. FAX: 309-928-2540. *Dir,* Catherine Hoffman
Pop 2,055; Circ 14,504
Library Holdings: Bk Vols 14,000; Per Subs 29
Subject Interests: Genealogy, Local hist
Wireless access
Open Mon & Wed 1-8, Tues & Thurs 3-6, Fri & Sat 9-1

FARMINGTON

P FARMINGTON AREA PUBLIC LIBRARY DISTRICT*, 266 E Fort St, 61531-1276. SAN 304-1891. Tel: 309-245-2175. FAX: 309-245-2294. E-mail: farmingtonpublic@yahoo.com. Web Site: www.farmingtonpublic.org. *Dir,* Barbara Love; Staff 5 (MLS 1, Non-MLS 4)
Founded 1901. Pop 7,267; Circ 22,664
Library Holdings: Bk Titles 27,000; Per Subs 50
Automation Activity & Vendor Info: (Cataloging) TLC (The Library Corporation)
Database Vendor: TLC (The Library Corporation)
Wireless access
Function: Adult bk club, After school storytime, CD-ROM, Copy machines, Digital talking bks, Fax serv, Home delivery & serv to Sr ctr & nursing homes, Homebound delivery serv, ILL available, Online ref, Photocopying/Printing, Prog for children & young adult, Spoken cassettes & CDs, Spoken cassettes & DVDs, Summer reading prog, Tax forms, VHS videos
Open Mon-Thurs 10-8, Fri 10-5, Sat 10-4

FLORA

P FLORA PUBLIC LIBRARY*, 216 N Main, 62839-1510. SAN 304-1905. Tel: 618-662-6553. FAX: 618-662-5007. E-mail: florapl@florapubliclibrary.org. Web Site: www.florapubliclibrary.org. *Dir,* Donna Corry; E-mail: dcorry@florapubliclibrary.org
Founded 1903. Pop 5,070; Circ 52,316
May 2011-Apr 2012 Income $221,757, State $5,205, Locally Generated Income $189,968, Other $26,584. Mats Exp $30,877. Sal $99,397
Library Holdings: Audiobooks 898; AV Mats 1,222; DVDs 1,142; Bk Vols 45,534; Per Subs 82; Videos 360
Wireless access
Mem of Illinois Heartland Library System
Open Mon-Thurs 1:30-8:30, Fri 10-6, Sat 10-5
Friends of the Library Group

FLOSSMOOR

P FLOSSMOOR PUBLIC LIBRARY*, 1000 Sterling Ave, 60422-1295. SAN 304-1913. Tel: 708-798-3600. FAX: 708-798-3603. E-mail: flossref@sslic.net. Web Site: www.flossmoorlibrary.org. *Adminr,* Megan Heligas; E-mail: heligasm@sslic.net; *Head, Tech Serv,* Deborah Majka; E-mail: majkad@sslic.net; *Adult Serv,* David Martin; E-mail: martind@sslic.net; *Youth Serv,* Margie Wegrzyn; E-mail: wegrzynm@sslic.net
Founded 1953. Pop 9,301; Circ 116,005
Library Holdings: Bk Vols 56,243; Per Subs 270
Special Collections: Helen Tenenbaum Women's Studies
Automation Activity & Vendor Info: (Circulation) Innovative Interfaces, Inc
Database Vendor: EBSCOhost, Innovative Interfaces, Inc
Mem of Reaching Across Illinois Library System (RAILS)
Partic in Illinois Library & Information Network
Open Mon-Thurs 9:30-9, Fri & Sat 9:30-5, Sun 1-5
Friends of the Library Group

FORD HEIGHTS

P FORD HEIGHTS PUBLIC LIBRARY DISTRICT*, 1537 Congress Lane, 60411. Tel: 708-757-0551. FAX: 708-757-0552. *Librn,* Kathy Parker
Library Holdings: Bk Titles 7,500; Per Subs 20
Open Mon, Wed & Fri 11-5, Tues & Thurs 1-7

FOREST PARK

P FOREST PARK PUBLIC LIBRARY*, 7555 Jackson Blvd, 60130. SAN 304-1921. Tel: 708-366-7171. FAX: 708-366-7293. Reference FAX: 708-366-7185. TDD: 708-366-9207. Web Site: www.forestparkpubliclibrary.org. *Dir,* Rodger Brayden; Tel: 708-366-7171, Ext 102; *Head, Tech Serv,* Erica Sanchez; *Mgr, Ad Serv,* Kate Niehoff; *Youth Serv Mgr,* Lindsey Kraft; *Circ,* Sandy Heitzman; Staff 20 (MLS 5, Non-MLS 15)
Founded 1916. Pop 15,688; Circ 95,000
Library Holdings: Bk Vols 80,000; Per Subs 180
Automation Activity & Vendor Info: (Circulation) Innovative Interfaces, Inc; (OPAC) Innovative Interfaces, Inc
Database Vendor: Gale Cengage Learning, Innovative Interfaces, Inc, OCLC FirstSearch, OVID Technologies, ProQuest
Wireless access
Mem of Reaching Across Illinois Library System (RAILS)
Special Services for the Blind - Bks on cassette; Bks on CD; Home delivery serv; Large print bks; Lending of low vision aids; Reader equip
Open Mon-Thurs 9-9, Fri 9-6, Sat 9-5, Sun (Sept-May) 1-5
Friends of the Library Group

FORREST

P FORREST PUBLIC LIBRARY DISTRICT*, 301 W James, 61741. (Mail add: PO Box 555, 61741-0555), SAN 304-193X. Tel: 815-657-8805. FAX: 815-657-8837. E-mail: forrestlibrary@sbcglobal.net. *Dir,* Elsie Evelsizer
Founded 1939. Pop 2,163; Circ 20,158
Library Holdings: Bk Vols 20,000; Per Subs 49
Special Collections: Louis L'Amour Westerns, large print bks
Subject Interests: Agr, Trains

Wireless access
Publications: Monthly Calendar
Open Mon & Wed 1-5, Tues & Thurs 10-7, Sat 9-12

FORRESTON

P FORRESTON PUBLIC LIBRARY*, 204 First Ave, 61030. (Mail add: PO Box 606, 61030-0606), SAN 304-1948. Tel: 815-938-2624. FAX: 815-938-2152. E-mail: forlib@frontier.com. Web Site: www.forrestonlibrary.org. *Dir,* Cindy Bahr; Staff 2 (Non-MLS 2)
Pop 1,469; Circ 17,000
Library Holdings: Bks on Deafness & Sign Lang 5; CDs 541; DVDs 440; Large Print Bks 500; Bk Vols 14,313; Per Subs 44; Videos 650
Special Collections: James Grisgby Arts Coll, art books, encyclopedias
Wireless access
Function: Adult bk club, Bks on CD, Children's prog, Computers for patron use, Copy machines, Fax serv, Free DVD rentals, Handicapped accessible, ILL available, Music CDs, Photocopying/Printing, Prog for adults, Prog for children & young adult, Pub access computers, Story hour, Tax forms
Mem of Reaching Across Illinois Library System (RAILS)
Open Mon 9-11:30 & 2:30-8, Tues-Thurs 9-11:30 & 2:30-6, Sat 9-1

FORSYTH

P FORSYTH PUBLIC LIBRARY*, 268 S Elwood, 62535. (Mail add: PO Box 20, 62535-0020), SAN 324-6124. Tel: 217-877-8174. FAX: 217-877-3533. Web Site: forsythlibrary.lib.il.us. *Dir,* Jean Campbell; Staff 8 (MLS 2, Non-MLS 6)
Founded 1981
Library Holdings: Bk Vols 40,000; Per Subs 153
Wireless access
Mem of Illinois Heartland Library System
Open Mon, Wed & Fri 9-5, Tues & Thurs 9-8, Sat 9-3

FOX LAKE

P FOX LAKE PUBLIC DISTRICT LIBRARY*, 255 E Grand Ave, 60020-1697. SAN 304-1956. Tel: 847-587-0198. FAX: 847-587-9493. TDD: 847-587-2448. Web Site: www.fllib.org. *Dir,* Harry J Bork; *Asst Librn,* Cynthia Lobaza; *Tech Serv Librn,* Carrie Jourdan; *Youth Serv,* Therese Johnson; Staff 2 (MLS 2)
Founded 1939. Pop 18,533; Circ 106,476
Library Holdings: Bk Titles 64,137; Per Subs 179
Wireless access
Publications: Footnotes; Newsletter (Bi-monthly)
Open Mon-Fri 9-9, Sat 9-5, Sun (Sept-May) 1-5
Friends of the Library Group

FOX RIVER GROVE

P FOX RIVER GROVE PUBLIC LIBRARY DISTRICT*, 407 Lincoln Ave, 60021-1406. SAN 304-1964. Tel: 847-639-2274. FAX: 847-639-0300. E-mail: frglibrary@frgml.lib.il.us. Web Site: www.frgml.lib.il.us. *Dir,* Linda Stoppenbach; E-mail: lstoppenbach@frgml.lib.il.us; Staff 9 (MLS 2, Non-MLS 7)
Founded 1954. Pop 4,235; Circ 50,402
Library Holdings: Bk Vols 32,000; Per Subs 120
Automation Activity & Vendor Info: (Circulation) Brodart; (OPAC) Brodart
Publications: Newsletter (Quarterly)
Open Mon-Fri 9-8:30, Sat 9-4
Friends of the Library Group

FRANKFORT

P FRANKFORT PUBLIC LIBRARY DISTRICT*, 21119 S Pfeiffer Rd, 60423-8699. SAN 304-1972. Tel: 815-469-2423. Circulation Tel: 815-534-6170. FAX: 815-469-9307. E-mail: fpl@frankfortlibrary.org. Web Site: www.frankfortlibrary.org. *Dir,* Pierre Gregoire; E-mail: pgregoire@frankfortlibrary.org; Staff 34 (MLS 9, Non-MLS 25)
Founded 1966. Pop 30,484; Circ 395,210
Jul 2011-Jun 2012 Income $2,001,362, State $36,184, Locally Generated Income $1,890,207, Other $74,971. Mats Exp $263,365, Books $160,374, AV Mat $43,776, Electronic Ref Mat (Incl. Access Fees) $59,215. Sal $1,065,261 (Prof $306,263)
Library Holdings: Audiobooks 3,686; AV Mats 7,167; CDs 6,909; DVDs 7,167; e-books 7,426; Electronic Media & Resources 2,350; Bk Titles 109,250; Per Subs 159
Automation Activity & Vendor Info: (Acquisitions) Innovative Interfaces, Inc - Millenium; (Cataloging) Innovative Interfaces, Inc; (Circulation) Innovative Interfaces, Inc; (ILL) OCLC FirstSearch; (OPAC) Innovative Interfaces, Inc; (Serials) Innovative Interfaces, Inc
Database Vendor: Baker & Taylor, EBSCOhost, Gale Cengage Learning, Newsbank, OCLC FirstSearch, OCLC WorldShare Interlibrary Loan
Wireless access
Publications: eNews (Online only)
Mem of Reaching Across Illinois Library System (RAILS)
Partic in System Wide Automated Network
Open Mon-Thurs 10-9, Fri & Sat 9-5, Sun (Sept-May) 1-5
Friends of the Library Group
Bookmobiles: 1. Bk titles 10,000

FRANKLIN GROVE

P FRANKLIN GROVE PUBLIC LIBRARY*, 112 S Elm St, 61031. (Mail add: PO Box 326, 61031-0326), SAN 304-1980. Tel: 815-456-2823. FAX: 815-456-2619. Web Site: www.franklingrovelibrary.org. *Dir,* Jeffrey Munson
Founded 1916. Pop 1,052
Mem of Reaching Across Illinois Library System (RAILS)
Open Mon-Thurs 10-8, Fri 10-5, Sat 10-2
Friends of the Library Group

FRANKLIN PARK

P FRANKLIN PARK PUBLIC LIBRARY DISTRICT*, 10311 Grand Ave, 60131. SAN 304-1999. Tel: 847-455-6016. FAX: 847-455-6416. Web Site: www.franklinparklibrary.org. *Dir,* Marie Saeli; E-mail: msaeli@franklinparklibrary.org; *Asst Dir,* Jean Erickson; E-mail: jerickson@franklinparklibrary.org; Staff 7 (MLS 6, Non-MLS 1)
Founded 1962
Library Holdings: CDs 5,000; DVDs 5,000; Bk Vols 170,000; Per Subs 246; Videos 5,000
Special Collections: Local History, artifacts, maps, print; Polish Language, av, print; Spanish Language, av, print
Automation Activity & Vendor Info: (Serials) SirsiDynix
Publications: Franklin Park Public Library Newsletter (Bi-monthly); The Franklin Park Library Electronic Newsletter (Monthly bulletin)
Mem of Reaching Across Illinois Library System (RAILS)
Partic in Libr Integrated Network Consortium
Open Mon-Thurs 9-9, Fri & Sat 9-5, Sun 1-5

FREEBURG

P FREEBURG AREA LIBRARY, 407 S Belleville, 62243. Tel: 618-539-5454. FAX: 618-539-5854. E-mail: frelib407@gmail.com. Web Site: www.freeburglibrary.com. *Dir,* Kristin Green
Founded 1996
Library Holdings: Bk Titles 37,000; Per Subs 60
Automation Activity & Vendor Info: (Acquisitions) Innovative Interfaces, Inc; (Cataloging) Innovative Interfaces, Inc; (Circulation) Innovative Interfaces, Inc
Wireless access
Mem of Illinois Heartland Library System
Open Mon, Tues & Thurs 11-7, Fri 11-6, Sat 11-2

FREEPORT

M FHN MEMORIAL HOSPITAL*, Health Science Library, 1045 W Stephenson St, 61032. SAN 371-6333. Tel: 815-599-6132. FAX: 815-599-6858. *Librn,* Mary Pat Gordon; E-mail: mgordon@fhn.org; Staff 1 (MLS 1)
Library Holdings: Bk Titles 750; Per Subs 70
Database Vendor: OCLC FirstSearch
Function: Health sci info serv, ILL available
Mem of Reaching Across Illinois Library System (RAILS)
Partic in Docline; Illinois Library & Information Network; OCLC-LVIS
Restriction: Authorized patrons, In-house use for visitors, Lending to staff only, Open by appt only

P FREEPORT PUBLIC LIBRARY*, 100 E Douglas St, 61032. SAN 304-2022. Tel: 815-233-3000. FAX: 815-233-1099. E-mail: information@freeportpubliclibrary.org. Web Site: www.freeportpubliclibrary.org. *Dir,* Carol Dickerson; E-mail: cdickerson@freeportpubliclibrary.org; *Head, Adult Serv,* Pat Vorwald; *Head, Tech Serv,* Margaret Morgan; *Head, Youth Serv,* Barbara Sowers; *Circ Supvr,* Lois Rees; *ILL,* Lou Ellen Shuey; Staff 32 (MLS 3, Non-MLS 29)
Founded 1874. Pop 25,840; Circ 310,324
Library Holdings: Bk Vols 119,688; Per Subs 396
Special Collections: Freeport & Stephenson County History, bks & pamphlet files; Local Newspapers, microfilm; Louis Sullivan Coll, pamphlet file. US Document Depository
Mem of Reaching Across Illinois Library System (RAILS)
Open Mon-Thurs (Winter) 9-9, Fri 9-6, Sat 9-5, Sun 1-4, Mon-Thurs (Summer) 9-8, Fri 9-6, Sat 9-5

J HIGHLAND COMMUNITY COLLEGE LIBRARY, Clarence Mitchell Library, 2998 W Pearl City Rd, 61032-9341. SAN 304-2030. Tel: 815-599-3539. Administration Tel: 815-599-3456. FAX: 815-599-3716. E-mail: library@highland.edu. Web Site: www.highland.edu/library. *Dir,*

Laura Watson; *User Serv Librn,* Michael Skwara; Tel: 815-599-3657; Staff 3 (MLS 2, Non-MLS 1)
Founded 1962. Enrl 1,100; Highest Degree: Associate
Library Holdings: AV Mats 300; Bk Vols 60,000; Per Subs 250
Special Collections: Local Authors Coll
Automation Activity & Vendor Info: (Acquisitions) Innovative Interfaces, Inc; (Cataloging) Innovative Interfaces, Inc; (Circulation) Innovative Interfaces, Inc; (Course Reserve) Innovative Interfaces, Inc; (ILL) Innovative Interfaces, Inc; (Media Booking) Innovative Interfaces, Inc; (OPAC) Innovative Interfaces, Inc; (Serials) Innovative Interfaces, Inc
Database Vendor: EBSCOhost, LexisNexis, OCLC FirstSearch, ProQuest
Wireless access
Mem of Reaching Across Illinois Library System (RAILS)
Partic in Consortium of Academic & Research Libraries in Illinois; Dubuque Area Library Information Consortium; Northern Illinois Learning Resources Cooperative (NILRC)
Special Services for the Blind - Assistive/Adapted tech devices, equip & products
Open Mon 8-7, Tues-Thurs 8-6, Fri 8-5

FULTON

P SCHMALING MEMORIAL PUBLIC LIBRARY DISTRICT, Fulton Public Library, 501 Tenth Ave, 61252. (Mail add: PO Box 125, 61252-0125), SAN 304-2057. Tel: 815-589-2045. FAX: 815-589-4483. E-mail: fulpublib@mchsi.com. Web Site: schmaling.lib.il.us. *Dir,* Britni Hartman; Staff 7 (MLS 3, Non-MLS 4)
Founded 1909. Pop 3,481; Circ 32,445
Library Holdings: Audiobooks 374; CDs 359; DVDs 865; Large Print Bks 742; Microforms 100; Bk Vols 18,367; Per Subs 35
Special Collections: Dutch Costumes & Books in Dutch Language; Local History Coll
Automation Activity & Vendor Info: (Acquisitions) JayWil Software Development, Inc; (Cataloging) JayWil Software Development, Inc; (Circulation) JayWil Software Development, Inc; (ILL) Innovative Interfaces, Inc; (OPAC) Innovative Interfaces, Inc; (Serials) JayWil Software Development, Inc
Wireless access
Function: Adult bk club, Bks on CD, Children's prog, Computers for patron use, Copy machines, e-mail serv, Electronic databases & coll, Free DVD rentals, Handicapped accessible, Homebound delivery serv, ILL available, Microfiche/film & reading machines, Music CDs, Online cat, Photocopying/Printing, Prog for adults, Prog for children & young adult, Pub access computers, Scanner, Story hour, Summer reading prog, Tax forms, Teen prog, Telephone ref, Video lending libr, Wheelchair accessible
Mem of Reaching Across Illinois Library System (RAILS)
Open Mon & Wed 2-7, Tues & Thurs 11-7, Fri 11-5, Sat 10-1
Restriction: Borrowing requests are handled by ILL, ID required to use computers (Ltd hrs), Non-circulating of rare bks, Non-resident fee
Friends of the Library Group

GALENA

P GALENA PUBLIC LIBRARY DISTRICT*, 601 S Bench St, 61036-2322. SAN 304-2065. Tel: 815-777-0200. FAX: 815-777-1542. E-mail: info@galenalibrary.org. Web Site: www.galenalibrary.org. *Libr Dir,* Susanna Ludwig-Ruppert; E-mail: ludwigs@galenalink.com
Founded 1894
Special Collections: Local History Coll, bks, micro, recs
Automation Activity & Vendor Info: (Acquisitions) SirsiDynix; (Cataloging) SirsiDynix; (Circulation) SirsiDynix; (ILL) OCLC WorldShare Interlibrary Loan; (OPAC) SIRSI-iBistro; (Serials) SirsiDynix
Database Vendor: EBSCOhost, OCLC WorldShare Interlibrary Loan, Overdrive, Inc, SirsiDynix
Wireless access
Mem of Reaching Across Illinois Library System (RAILS)
Partic in Dubuque Area Library Information Consortium
Special Services for the Blind - Braille bks
Open Mon-Thurs 11-8, Fri & Sat 11-5
Friends of the Library Group

S ILLINOIS HISTORIC PRESERVATION AGENCY*, Division of Historic Sites-US Grant's Home State Historic Site Library, 307 Decatur St, 61036. (Mail add: PO Box 333, 61036), SAN 325-6839. Tel: 815-777-3310. FAX: 815-777-3310. *Mgr,* Terry J Miller
Library Holdings: Bk Titles 1,500
Special Collections: E B Washburne Coll; Regional History, decorative arts, architecture, historic sites, local newspapers 1828-1930, historic photographs, 19th century artifacts; U S Grant Coll

GALESBURG

J CARL SANDBURG COLLEGE, Learning Resources Center, 2400 Tom L Wilson Blvd, 61401. SAN 340-4285. Tel: 309-341-5257. Interlibrary Loan Service Tel: 309-341-5206. FAX: 309-344-3526. E-mail: library@sandburg.edu. Web Site: www.sandburg.edu. *Dean of Libr,* Steven Noreln; *Coordr, Instrul Serv,* Jennie Archer; E-mail: jarcher@sandburg.edu; *Coordr, Libr Serv,* Amy Caulkins; E-mail: acaulkins@sandburg.edu; Staff 7 (MLS 3, Non-MLS 4)
Founded 1967. Enrl 3,614; Fac 69; Highest Degree: Associate
Jul 2006-Jun 2007 Income $393,469. Mats Exp $63,780, Books $41,080, Per/Ser (Incl. Access Fees) $21,470, Micro $1,130, Presv $100. Sal $314,031 (Prof $141,006)
Library Holdings: Bk Titles 31,644; Bk Vols 38,740; Per Subs 400
Special Collections: Bill Campbell Cartoon Art Coll, original graphic art; Carl Sandburg & Institutional Archives
Subject Interests: Vocational educ
Automation Activity & Vendor Info: (Circulation) TLC (The Library Corporation)
Wireless access
Function: Res libr
Partic in ALS Interlibr Servs; Consortium of Academic & Research Libraries in Illinois; Illinois Library & Information Network; OCLC Online Computer Library Center, Inc
Open Mon-Thurs 7:45am-8pm, Fri 8-4, Sat 9-Noon

Departmental Libraries:

CARTHAGE BRANCH CAMPUS, 305 Sandburg Dr, Carthage, 62321, SAN 340-4293. Tel: 217-357-3129. FAX: 217-357-3512. *Dean, Extn Serv,* Debra Miller; E-mail: dmiller@sandburg.edu; Staff 5 (MLS 2, Non-MLS 3)
Highest Degree: Associate
Library Holdings: AV Mats 250; Bk Vols 20,000; Per Subs 125
Function: Res libr
Open Mon-Thurs 7:45am-9pm, Fri 8-4, Sat 9-Noon

P GALESBURG PUBLIC LIBRARY, 40 E Simmons St, 61401-4591. SAN 340-4315. Tel: 309-343-6118. FAX: 309-343-4877. E-mail: reference@galesburglibrary.org. Web Site: www.galesburglibrary.org. *Dir,* Harriett Zipfel; E-mail: harriett.zipfel@galesburglibrary.org; *Asst Dir,* Jane Easterly; E-mail: jane.easterly@galesburglibrary.org; *Head, Ch,* Karen Marple; E-mail: karenm@galesburglibrary.org; *Head, Circ,* Sara Naslund; E-mail: sara.naslund@galesburglibrary.org; *Head, Tech Serv,* Nancy Terpening; E-mail: nancyt@galesburglibrary.org; *Ref Librn,* Faith Burdick; *Ref Librn,* Lucas Gorham; *Ref Librn, YA Librn,* Melinda Jones-Rhoades; *Ref Librn,* Lauren Pierce; *Archivist,* Patty Mosher; E-mail: pattym@galesburglibrary.org; Staff 20 (MLS 6, Non-MLS 14)
Founded 1874. Pop 32,195; Circ 279,690
Jan 2013-Dec 2013 Income $1,372,455. Mats Exp $250,000. Sal $776,525 (Prof $150,000)
Library Holdings: CDs 5,778; DVDs 5,931; Bk Titles 184,153; Per Subs 259
Special Collections: Local Newspapers, microfilm. Oral History
Subject Interests: Local hist
Automation Activity & Vendor Info: (Acquisitions) SIRSI WorkFlows; (Cataloging) SIRSI WorkFlows; (Circulation) SIRSI WorkFlows; (ILL) SIRSI WorkFlows; (OPAC) SIRSI WorkFlows; (Serials) SIRSI WorkFlows
Database Vendor: Baker & Taylor, OCLC ArticleFirst, OCLC FirstSearch, OCLC WebJunction, OCLC WorldShare Interlibrary Loan, SirsiDynix, Wilson - Wilson Web, World Book Online
Wireless access
Function: Accelerated reader prog, Adult bk club, Archival coll, Art exhibits, Audio & video playback equip for onsite use, Audiobks via web, AV serv, Bk club(s), Bks on cassette, Bks on CD, CD-ROM, Chess club, Children's prog, Computer training, Computers for patron use, Copy machines, e-mail serv, E-Reserves, Electronic databases & coll, Fax serv, Free DVD rentals, Handicapped accessible, Holiday prog, Home delivery & serv to Sr ctr & nursing homes, Homebound delivery serv, ILL available, Instruction & testing, Magnifiers for reading, Mail & tel request accepted, Music CDs, Newsp ref libr, Notary serv, Online cat, Online ref, Online searches, Orientations, Photocopying/Printing, Prof lending libr, Prog for adults, Prog for children & young adult, Pub access computers, Ref serv available, Scanner, Senior computer classes, Spoken cassettes & CDs, Story hour, Summer reading prog, Tax forms, Teen prog, Telephone ref, VHS videos, Video lending libr, Web-catalog, Wheelchair accessible, Workshops
Mem of Reaching Across Illinois Library System (RAILS)
Partic in Resource Sharing Alliance
Special Services for the Deaf - TTY equip
Open Mon-Thurs 9-8, Fri & Sat 9-5
Restriction: Non-circulating of rare bks
Friends of the Library Group

S HILL CORRECTIONAL CENTER LIBRARY*, 600 S Linwood Rd, 61401. (Mail add: PO Box 1327, 61401-1327), SAN 371-6449. Tel: 309-343-4212, Ext 360. FAX: 309-343-4212, Ext 123.
Founded 1986
Library Holdings: Bk Titles 12,000; Per Subs 22
Special Collections: Law Library Coll
Restriction: Staff & inmates only

C KNOX COLLEGE*, Henry W Seymour Library, Two E South St, 61401. SAN 340-4404. Tel: 309-341-7246. Interlibrary Loan Service Tel: 309-341-7244. Reference Tel: 309-341-7228. Administration Tel: 309-341-7248. FAX: 309-341-7799. Web Site: library.knox.edu. *Dir,* Jeffrey A Douglas; Tel: 309-341-7491, E-mail: jdouglas@knox.edu; *Assoc Librn,* Sharon Clayton; Tel: 309-341-7249, E-mail: sclayton@knox.edu; *Asst Librn, Pub Serv,* Anne Giffey; Tel: 309-341-7483, E-mail: agiffey@knox.edu; *IT Librn,* Laurie Sauer; Tel: 309-341-7788, E-mail: lsauer@knox.edu; Staff 7 (MLS 5, Non-MLS 2)
Founded 1837. Enrl 1,339; Fac 99; Highest Degree: Bachelor
Jul 2006-Jun 2007 Income $1,157,866. Mats Exp $336,320, Books $87,316, Per/Ser (Incl. Access Fees) $146,285, Micro $60, AV Mat $12,674, Electronic Ref Mat (Incl. Access Fees) $76,831, Presv $9,026. Sal $422,333
Library Holdings: AV Mats 7,924; Bk Titles 202,733; Bk Vols 316,918; Per Subs 519
Special Collections: American Civil War (Smith Coll), bks, mss, maps & photos; Ernest Hemingway & The Lost Generation (Hughes Coll), bks, mss; Lincoln Coll; Old Northwest Territory (Finley Coll), bks & maps; Upper Mississippi River Valley (Player Coll), bks, maps & prints
Automation Activity & Vendor Info: (Acquisitions) Ex Libris Group; (Cataloging) Ex Libris Group; (Circulation) Ex Libris Group; (Course Reserve) Ex Libris Group; (ILL) OCLC ILLiad; (OPAC) Ex Libris Group; (Serials) Ex Libris Group
Database Vendor: American Mathematical Society, American Psychological Association (APA), Annual Reviews, CredoReference, EBSCOhost, JSTOR, LexisNexis, OCLC FirstSearch
Wireless access
Partic in Consortium of Academic & Research Libraries in Illinois; OCLC Online Computer Library Center, Inc; OCLC-LVIS
Open Mon-Thurs 8am-1am, Fri 8am-9pm, Sat 10-9, Sun 11am-1am

GALVA

J BLACK HAWK COLLEGE*, Gust E Lundberg Learning Resources Center, 26230 Black Hawk Rd, 61434. SAN 304-3118. Tel: 309-852-5671, Ext 1731. FAX: 309-852-0038. Web Site: www.bhc.edu. *Coordr, Librn,* Jill Sodt; *AV,* Lavon Franklin; E-mail: franklinl@eastadmin.bhc.edu; Staff 3 (MLS 1, Non-MLS 2)
Founded 1967. Enrl 829; Fac 70; Highest Degree: Associate
Library Holdings: Bk Vols 18,000; Per Subs 128
Special Collections: Local Authors Coll
Subject Interests: Agr, Horses
Wireless access
Partic in Resource Sharing Alliance
Special Services for the Blind - Magnifiers
Open Mon-Thurs (Fall & Spring) 8-7:30, Fri 8-5; Mon-Fri (Summer) 8-5

P GALVA PUBLIC LIBRARY DISTRICT*, 120 NW Third Ave, 61434. SAN 304-2103. Tel: 309-932-2180. FAX: 309-932-2280. E-mail: galvalibrarystaff@yahoo.com. Web Site: www.galvalibrary.org. *Dir,* Melody Heck; *Asst Dir,* Linda Lipke; Staff 1 (Non-MLS 1)
Founded 1909. Pop 3,887; Circ 30,488
Library Holdings: AV Mats 209; Large Print Bks 689; Bk Titles 20,828; Bk Vols 21,243; Per Subs 75; Talking Bks 645; Videos 815
Special Collections: Galva News, 1879-present on microfilm; Swedish & Local History
Automation Activity & Vendor Info: (Circulation) TLC (The Library Corporation); (OPAC) TLC (The Library Corporation)
Partic in Resource Sharing Alliance
Open Mon-Wed (Sept-May) 9:30-8, Thurs 9:30-5, Fri 1-5, Sat 9-1; Mon & Wed (June-Aug) 9:30-11:30 & 1-6, Tues & Thurs 9:30-11:30 & 1-5, Fri 1-5, Sat 9-1

GENESEO

P GENESEO PUBLIC LIBRARY DISTRICT*, 805 North Chicago St, 61254. SAN 304-2111. Tel: 309-944-6452. FAX: 309-944-6721. E-mail: gpld@geneseo.lib.il.us. Web Site: geneseo.lib.il.us. *Dir,* Claire Crawford; E-mail: ccrawford@geneseo.lib.il.us; Staff 16 (MLS 1, Non-MLS 15)
Founded 1855. Pop 13,102; Circ 149,000
Library Holdings: Bk Titles 49,000; Per Subs 200
Special Collections: Early Geneseo Historical Material 1836-to-1920, including oral hist tapes. Oral History
Subject Interests: Compact discs
Wireless access
Publications: Library Events (Newsletter)
Mem of Reaching Across Illinois Library System (RAILS)
Special Services for the Blind - Talking bks
Open Mon-Thurs 9-8, Fri & Sat 9-5
Friends of the Library Group

GENEVA

M DELNOR COMMUNITY HOSPITAL*, Health Science Library, 300 Randall Rd, 60134. SAN 325-0776. Tel: 630-208-4299. FAX: 630-208-3497. E-mail: info@delnor.com. Web Site: www.delnor.com. *Librn,* Paula Olson; E-mail: paula.olson@delnor.com
Library Holdings: Bk Titles 900; Per Subs 110
Subject Interests: Med
Wireless access
Mem of Reaching Across Illinois Library System (RAILS)
Partic in Fox Valley Health Science Library Consortium; Illinois Library & Information Network
Open Mon-Fri 7:30-4

P GENEVA PUBLIC LIBRARY DISTRICT*, 127 James St, 60134. SAN 304-212X. Tel: 630-232-0780. Circulation Tel: 630-232-0780, Ext 222. Interlibrary Loan Service Tel: 630-232-0780, Ext 262. Reference Tel: 630-232-0780, Ext 251. FAX: 630-232-0881. Interlibrary Loan Service FAX: 630-232-2040. TDD: 630-845-3176. Web Site: www.geneva.lib.il.us. *Dir,* Matt Teske; Tel: 630-232-0780, Ext 224, E-mail: mteske@geneva.lib.il.us; *Head, Adult Serv,* Debbie Walsh; *Head, Tech & Automation Serv,* Dennis Winters; *Head, Youth Serv,* Kristi Miller-Pease; *Mgr, Automation Serv,* Lynnette Singh; *Circ Serv Supvr,* Margaret Johnston; Staff 66 (MLS 13, Non-MLS 53)
Founded 1894. Pop 28,500; Circ 479,000
Library Holdings: AV Mats 17,600; Bks on Deafness & Sign Lang 15; High Interest/Low Vocabulary Bk Vols 300; Large Print Bks 2,800; Bk Titles 127,800; Bk Vols 142,000; Per Subs 270; Talking Bks 9,616
Subject Interests: Art & archit, Folklore, Local hist
Automation Activity & Vendor Info: (Cataloging) SirsiDynix; (Circulation) SirsiDynix; (ILL) OCLC; (OPAC) SirsiDynix; (Serials) SirsiDynix
Database Vendor: EBSCOhost, Gale Cengage Learning, Newsbank, OCLC FirstSearch
Publications: Library Link (Newsletter)
Mem of Reaching Across Illinois Library System (RAILS)
Partic in LINC (Libraries IN Cooperation)
Special Services for the Deaf - TDD equip
Special Services for the Blind - Ednalite Hi-Vision scope; ZoomText magnification & reading software
Open Mon-Thurs 9-9, Fri & Sat 9-5, Sun (Sept-May) Noon-4
Friends of the Library Group

GENOA

P GENOA PUBLIC LIBRARY DISTRICT*, 232 W Main St, 60135. SAN 304-2138. Tel: 815-784-2627. FAX: 815-784-4829. E-mail: genoalibrary1@hotmail.com. Web Site: www.genoalibrary.org. *Dir,* Jennifer Barton
Pop 4,200; Circ 27,153
Library Holdings: Bk Vols 55,000; Per Subs 63
Wireless access
Mem of Reaching Across Illinois Library System (RAILS)
Open Mon 1-8, Tues-Thurs 10-8, Sat 10-2

GEORGETOWN

P GEORGETOWN PUBLIC LIBRARY*, 102 W West St, 61846. SAN 304-2146. Tel: 217-662-2164. FAX: 217-662-6790. *Librn,* Linda Davidson; E-mail: lddd97@advancenet.net
Founded 1936. Pop 3,628; Circ 19,000
Library Holdings: Bk Vols 16,000; Per Subs 30
Automation Activity & Vendor Info: (Acquisitions) SirsiDynix; (Cataloging) SirsiDynix; (Circulation) SirsiDynix; (ILL) SirsiDynix
Open Mon, Wed & Thurs 12:30-5:30, Tues & Fri 9-5:30, Sat 9-2
Friends of the Library Group

GERMANTOWN

P GERMANTOWN PUBLIC LIBRARY DISTRICT*, 403 Munster St, 62245. (Mail add: PO Box 244, 62245-0244). Tel: 618-523-4820. FAX: 618-523-4599. E-mail: gma@gtownlibrary.org. Web Site: www.gtownlibrary.org. *Dir,* Joan Young
Founded 1995. Pop 1,803; Circ 13,732
Library Holdings: AV Mats 379; Large Print Bks 300; Bk Titles 14,359; Per Subs 31
Wireless access
Mem of Illinois Heartland Library System
Open Mon & Wed 10-4, Tues & Thurs 1-8, Fri 1-6, Sat 9-Noon

GIBSON CITY

P MOYER DISTRICT LIBRARY*, 618 S Sangamon, 60936. SAN 304-2154. Tel: 217-784-5343. FAX: 217-784-5373. E-mail: moyerlibrary@yahoo.com. Web Site: www.moyer.lib.il.us. *Dir,* Sharon Heavilin; Staff 1 (Non-MLS 1)

Founded 1876. Pop 5,402
Library Holdings: Audiobooks 1,517; DVDs 2,655; Bk Titles 34,358; Per Subs 69
Automation Activity & Vendor Info: (Acquisitions) SirsiDynix; (Cataloging) SirsiDynix; (Circulation) SirsiDynix; (Course Reserve) SirsiDynix
Database Vendor: Baker & Taylor, OCLC FirstSearch
Wireless access
Function: After school storytime
Publications: Booklist; Illinois Libraries; Wilson Library Bulletin
Mem of Illinois Heartland Library System
Special Services for the Deaf - TTY equip
Open Mon-Thurs 10-8, Fri 10-5, Sat 10-3
Friends of the Library Group

GILLESPIE

P GILLESPIE PUBLIC LIBRARY, 201 W Chestnut, 62033. SAN 304-2162. Tel: 217-839-3614. FAX: 217-839-4854. E-mail: gillespiepubliclibrary@gmail.com. *Dir,* Steve Joyce; Staff 2 (MLS 1, Non-MLS 1)
Founded 1944. Pop 3,740; Circ 20,000
Library Holdings: Bk Vols 16,000; Per Subs 20
Mem of Illinois Heartland Library System
Open Mon 2-8, Tues & Thurs 2-6, Wed & Fri 9-5, Sat 9-1
Friends of the Library Group

GILMAN

P GILMAN-DANFORTH DISTRICT LIBRARY*, 715 N Maple St, 60938. SAN 304-2170. Tel: 815-265-7522. FAX: 815-265-4599. E-mail: gilmandanforthlib@live.com. *Dir,* Sally Newbury
Pop 3,049; Circ 19,000
Library Holdings: Bk Vols 20,000; Per Subs 25
Automation Activity & Vendor Info: (Cataloging) Horizon; (Circulation) Horizon
Wireless access
Mem of Illinois Heartland Library System
Open Mon, Tues & Thurs 10-6, Wed 10-7, Fri 10-5, Sat 10-2
Friends of the Library Group

GIRARD

P GIRARD TOWNSHIP LIBRARY*, 201 W Madison St, 62640-1551. SAN 304-2189. Tel: 217-627-2414. FAX: 217-627-2093. *Dir,* Sherry Hesterberg; Staff 2 (MLS 1, Non-MLS 1)
Founded 1947. Pop 2,000; Circ 16,933
Library Holdings: DVDs 25; Large Print Bks 200; Bk Titles 26,000; Per Subs 78; Talking Bks 100; Videos 250
Special Collections: City Ord/genealogy
Wireless access
Mem of Illinois Heartland Library System
Open Mon 9-12 & 1-5, Tues, Wed & Fri 1-5, Thurs 1-5 & 6-8, Sat 10-3
Friends of the Library Group

GLEN CARBON

P GLEN CARBON CENTENNIAL LIBRARY*, 198 S Main St, 62034. Tel: 618-288-1212. FAX: 618-288-1205. E-mail: gle@glencarbonlibrary.org. Web Site: www.glencarbonlibrary.org. *Dir,* Anne Hughes; E-mail: anneh@glencarbonlibrary.org; *Asst Dir,* Janet McAllister; *Cat,* Susan Kesler; *Youth Serv,* Magi Hendersen; Staff 16 (MLS 1, Non-MLS 15)
Founded 1992. Pop 12,400
Library Holdings: Bk Titles 35,000; Per Subs 45
Automation Activity & Vendor Info: (Circulation) Innovative Interfaces, Inc; (OPAC) Innovative Interfaces, Inc - Millenium
Database Vendor: BWI, EBSCOhost, Gale Cengage Learning, Ingram Library Services, OCLC WorldShare Interlibrary Loan, World Book Online
Wireless access
Function: ILL available
Mem of Illinois Heartland Library System
Special Services for the Deaf - TDD equip
Open Mon-Thurs 9-8, Fri & Sat 9-5, Sun 1-5
Friends of the Library Group

GLEN ELLYN

J COLLEGE OF DUPAGE LIBRARY*, 425 Fawell Blvd, 60137-6599. SAN 304-2197. Tel: 630-942-2350. Circulation Tel: 630-942-2106. Interlibrary Loan Service Tel: 630-942-2166. Reference Tel: 630-942-3364. FAX: 630-858-8757. Interlibrary Loan Service FAX: 630-942-4646. Web Site: www.cod.edu/library. *Dean, Learning Res,* Ellen Sutton; Tel: 630-942-2659, E-mail: suttone@cod.edu; *Ref Librn,* Christine Kickles; Tel: 630-942-2021, E-mail: kicklesc@cod.edu; *Ref Librn,* Debra Smith; *Tech Serv Mgr,* Mary S Konkel; Tel: 630-942-2662, E-mail: konkel@cod.edu; *Web Coordr,* Colin Koteles; Tel: 630-942-2923, E-mail: koteles@cod.edu; *Electronic Res, Ref,* Denise Cote; Tel: 630-942-2092, E-mail: cotede@cod.edu; *Ref,* Marianne Berger; Tel: 630-942-2338, E-mail: berger@cod.edu; *Ref,* Daniel Blewett; Tel: 630-942-2279, E-mail: blewett@cod.edu; *Ref,* Jason Ertz; Tel: 630-942-3317, E-mail: ertzja@cod.edu; *Ref,* Jennifer Kelley; Tel: 630-942-2383, E-mail: kelleyj@cod.edu; Staff 46 (MLS 14, Non-MLS 32)
Founded 1967. Enrl 34,000; Fac 308; Highest Degree: Associate
Library Holdings: AV Mats 24,000; Bk Vols 203,500; Per Subs 885
Special Collections: College & Career Information; College of DuPage Archives; Occupational & Technical Colls
Automation Activity & Vendor Info: (Acquisitions) Innovative Interfaces, Inc; (Cataloging) Innovative Interfaces, Inc; (Circulation) Innovative Interfaces, Inc; (Course Reserve) Innovative Interfaces, Inc; (OPAC) Innovative Interfaces, Inc; (Serials) Innovative Interfaces, Inc
Database Vendor: EBSCOhost, Gale Cengage Learning, OCLC FirstSearch, OCLC WorldShare Interlibrary Loan, ProQuest, SerialsSolutions
Mem of Reaching Across Illinois Library System (RAILS)
Partic in Illinois Library & Information Network; Northern Illinois Learning Resources Cooperative (NILRC); OCLC Online Computer Library Center, Inc
Special Services for the Deaf - Assistive tech
Special Services for the Blind - Assistive/Adapted tech devices, equip & products
Open Mon-Thurs 7:45am-10pm, Fri 7:45-4:30, Sat 9-4:30, Sun Noon-6

R FIRST UNITED METHODIST CHURCH LIBRARY*, 424 Forest Ave, 60137. SAN 304-2200. Tel: 630-469-3510. FAX: 630-469-2041. *Librn,* Kathryn E Collord
Founded 1954
Jan 2009-Dec 2009. Mats Exp $700, Books $600, AV Mat $100
Library Holdings: AV Mats 300; CDs 50; DVDs 75; Bk Vols 5,500; Videos 200
Special Collections: John Wesley & Church Coll
Special Services for the Blind - Cassettes
Open Sun 9-12:30

P GLEN ELLYN PUBLIC LIBRARY*, 400 Duane St, 60137-4508. SAN 304-2219. Tel: 630-469-0879. FAX: 630-469-1086. Web Site: www.gepl.org. *Dir,* Dawn A Bussey; E-mail: dbussey@gepl.org; *Dir, Adult Serv,* Rebecca Vnuk; *Dir of Circ,* Carrie Jeffries; *Dir, Tech Serv,* Jamie Simmons; *Dir, Youth Serv,* Kate Pierson; *Automated Serv Coordr,* Sharon Bannister; *ILL,* Teresa Olson; Staff 11 (MLS 11)
Founded 1907. Pop 26,093; Circ 519,423
Library Holdings: Bk Vols 201,138; Per Subs 800
Automation Activity & Vendor Info: (Circulation) SirsiDynix
Publications: Newsletter
Mem of Reaching Across Illinois Library System (RAILS)
Partic in Libr Integrated Network Consortium; OCLC Online Computer Library Center, Inc
Open Mon-Thurs 9-9, Fri & Sat 9-5, Sun (Sept-May) 1-5
Friends of the Library Group

GLENCOE

P GLENCOE PUBLIC LIBRARY*, 320 Park Ave, 60022-1597. SAN 304-2243. Tel: 847-835-5056. FAX: 847-835-5648. TDD: 847-835-7440. Web Site: www.glencoe.lib.il.us. *Exec Dir,* Margaret M Hamil; *Head, Circ,* Danny Burdett; *Adult Serv,* Teri Hennes; *Ch Serv,* Melissa Henderson; *Tech Serv,* Rebecca Halcli; Staff 31 (MLS 9, Non-MLS 22)
Founded 1909. Pop 8,762; Circ 228,519
Mar 2009-Feb 2010 Income $1,960,625, State $12,297, County $1,879,354, Locally Generated Income $68,974. Mats Exp $280,838, Books $138,380, Per/Ser (Incl. Access Fees) $19,889, AV Mat $43,662, Electronic Ref Mat (Incl. Access Fees) $73,284. Sal $933,730
Library Holdings: AV Mats 14,170; Bk Vols 82,223
Automation Activity & Vendor Info: (Cataloging) OCLC Connexion; (Circulation) SirsiDynix; (ILL) SirsiDynix; (OPAC) SirsiDynix
Database Vendor: Baker & Taylor, Electric Library, Gale Cengage Learning, Newsbank, OCLC FirstSearch, ProQuest, SirsiDynix
Wireless access
Function: AV serv, Homebound delivery serv, ILL available, Magnifiers for reading, Online searches, Outside serv via phone, mail, e-mail & web, Photocopying/Printing, Prog for children & young adult, Ref serv available, Summer reading prog, Telephone ref, Wheelchair accessible
Publications: Excerpts (Newsletter)
Partic in Cooperative Computer Services - CCS
Special Services for the Deaf - TTY equip
Special Services for the Blind - Talking bks
Open Mon-Thurs 9-9, Fri 9-5:30, Sat 9-5, Sun (Sept-May) 1-5
Friends of the Library Group

S LENHARDT LIBRARY OF THE CHICAGO BOTANIC GARDEN, 1000 Lake Cook Rd, 60022. SAN 304-2235. Tel: 847-835-8201. Reference Tel: 847-835-8200. FAX: 847-835-6885. E-mail: library@chicagobotanic.org.

Web Site: www.chicagobotanic.org/library. *Dir, Libr Serv,* Leora O Siegel; Tel: 847-835-8202, E-mail: lsiegel@chicagobotanic.org; *Sci Librn,* Donna Herendeen; Tel: 847-835-8273, E-mail: dherendeen@chicagobotanic.org; *Pub Serv Mgr,* Stacy Stoldt; E-mail: sstoldt@chicagobotanic.org; *Tech Serv Mgr,* Ann Anderson; Tel: 847-835-8381, E-mail: aanderson@chicagobotanic.org; *Curator, Rare Bks,* Edward J Valauskas; Tel: 847-835-8206, E-mail: ejv@chicagobotanic.org; Staff 4.75 (MLS 3.5, Non-MLS 1.25)
Founded 1951
Library Holdings: e-journals 50; Bk Titles 32,000; Bk Vols 125,000; Per Subs 400
Special Collections: Rare Book Coll
Subject Interests: Botany, Ecology, Garden design, Gardening, Hort, Hort therapy, Landscape archit
Automation Activity & Vendor Info: (Cataloging) EOS International; (Circulation) EOS International; (OPAC) EOS International; (Serials) EOS International
Database Vendor: Annual Reviews, BioOne, EBSCOhost, JSTOR, OCLC FirstSearch, OCLC WorldShare Interlibrary Loan
Wireless access
Publications: Current Books in Gardening & Botany (Bi-monthly)
Open Mon & Fri 10-4, Tues 10-6:30, Sat & Sun 12-4

SR NORTH SHORE CONGREGATION ISRAEL*, Romanek Library, 1185 Sheridan Rd, 60022. SAN 325-7010. Tel: 847-835-0724. FAX: 847-835-5613. Web Site: www.nsci.org. *Librn,* Janice B Footlik
Library Holdings: Bk Vols 20,000; Per Subs 24
Subject Interests: Archaeology
Partic in Nonpub Bk Asn
Open Mon-Thurs 9-5, Fri-9-3, Sun 8:45-1

GLENDALE HEIGHTS

P GLENSIDE PUBLIC LIBRARY DISTRICT*, 25 E Fullerton Ave, 60139-2697. SAN 304-2251. Tel: 630-260-1550. FAX: 630-260-1433. TDD: 630-260-1566. E-mail: ghdadmin@glensidepld.org. Web Site: glensidepld.org. *Dir,* Liz Fitzgerald; *Asst Admin,* Bill Forgette; *Commun Ambassador & Sch Spec,* Vincent Sovanski; *Automation & Tech Serv Mgr,* Ian Peery; *Adult Serv,* Karen Luster; *Ch Serv,* Tom Bartenfelder; *Circ,* Lucia Economos; Staff 18.5 (MLS 18.5)
Founded 1974. Pop 36,259; Circ 389,206
Jul 2010 Jun 2011 Income $3,078,152, Locally Generated Income $3,013,649, Other $57,643. Mats Exp $276,783, Books $128,564, AV Mat $107,310, Electronic Ref Mat (Incl. Access Fees) $40,909. Sal $1,454,447 (Prof $959,026)
Library Holdings: CDs 13,020; DVDs 5,631; e-books 11,093; Electronic Media & Resources 45; Bk Vols 116,773; Per Subs 271
Special Collections: ESL/Literacy; Learning Games; Signed English Children's Books
Automation Activity & Vendor Info: (Acquisitions) Baker & Taylor; (Cataloging) Innovative Interfaces, Inc; (Circulation) Innovative Interfaces, Inc; (OPAC) Innovative Interfaces, Inc
Database Vendor: EBSCOhost, Grolier Online, H W Wilson, Innovative Interfaces, Inc, Innovative Interfaces, Inc, LearningExpress, Medline, OCLC FirstSearch, Overdrive, Inc, Wilson - Wilson Web, World Book Online
Wireless access
Function: Bk club(s), Bks on CD, Chess club, Children's prog, Computer training, Computers for patron use, Copy machines, e-mail & chat, Electronic databases & coll, Fax serv, Free DVD rentals, Handicapped accessible, Homebound delivery serv, ILL available, Magnifiers for reading, Music CDs, Notary serv, Online cat, Online ref, Outreach serv, Outside serv via phone, mail, e-mail & web, OverDrive digital audio bks, Preschool outreach, Prog for adults, Prog for children & young adult, Pub access computers, Ref serv available, Scanner, Senior outreach, Spoken cassettes & CDs, Spoken cassettes & DVDs, Story hour, Summer & winter reading prog, Summer reading prog, Tax forms, Teen prog, Telephone ref, Web-catalog, Wheelchair accessible
Mem of Reaching Across Illinois Library System (RAILS)
Special Services for the Deaf - TDD equip
Special Services for the Blind - VisualTek equip
Open Mon-Thurs 9-9, Fri & Sat 9-5, Sun 1-5
Friends of the Library Group

GLENVIEW

S AON FIRE PROTECTION ENGINEERING CORP LIBRARY*, 1000 Milwaukee Ave, 5th Flr, 60025. SAN 375-1880. Tel: 847-953-7700. Web Site: www.schirmer.eng.com. *Librn,* Andrea Kiene; Staff 1 (MLS 1)
Library Holdings: Bk Vols 3,000; Per Subs 113
Automation Activity & Vendor Info: (Cataloging) Inmagic, Inc.
Function: Prof lending libr
Open Mon-Fri 8-5

P GLENVIEW PUBLIC LIBRARY*, 1930 Glenview Rd, 60025-2899. SAN 304-226X. Tel: 847-729-7500. FAX: 847-729-7558. TDD: 847-729-7529. E-mail: info@glenviewpl.org. Web Site: www.glenviewpl.org. *Libr Dir,* Vickie L Novak; E-mail: vnovak@glenviewpl.org; *Asst Dir,* Jane D Berry; E-mail: jberry@glenviewpl.org; *Communications Dir,* Jennifer S Black; E-mail: jblack@glenviewpl.org; *Head, Circ,* Maryann Bowler; E-mail: mbowler@glenviewpl.org; *Head, Reader Serv,* Linda Burns; E-mail: lburns@glenviewpl.org; *Head, Ref,* Diane Comen; E-mail: dcomen@glenviewpl.org; *Cat, Head, Tech Serv,* Muffet Schroer; E-mail: mschroer@glenviewpl.org; *Head, Youth Serv,* Barbara Littlefield; E-mail: blittlefield@glenviewpl.org; *Bus Off Mgr,* Christine Klimusko; E-mail: cklimusko@glenviewpl.org; *Fac Mgr,* Mark Depa; E-mail: mdepa@glenviewpl.org; *Acq,* Kim Faux Comerford; E-mail: kcomerford@glenviewpl.org; *ILL,* Gertrud Vepari; E-mail: gvepari@glenviewpl.org; *Tech Spec,* Allen Bettig; E-mail: abettig@glenviewpl.org; Staff 53.05 (MLS 21.98, Non-MLS 31.07)
Founded 1930. Pop 44,692; Circ 689,870
Library Holdings: Audiobooks 21,922; DVDs 15,197; e-books 42,172; Electronic Media & Resources 98; Bk Vols 262,532; Per Subs 548
Special Collections: Genealogy (Lundberg Coll)
Subject Interests: Med
Automation Activity & Vendor Info: (Acquisitions) SIRSI-iBistro; (Circulation) SIRSI WorkFlows
Wireless access
Publications: Events by Email (Online only); LINES (Quarterly)
Mem of Reaching Across Illinois Library System (RAILS)
Partic in Cooperative Computer Services - CCS
Special Services for the Deaf - ADA equip; Assisted listening device; Closed caption videos; Sign lang interpreter upon request for prog; TTY equip
Special Services for the Blind - Accessible computers; Assistive/Adapted tech devices, equip & products; BiFolkal kits; Bks available with recordings; Bks on cassette; Bks on CD; Cassette playback machines; Cassettes; Children's Braille; Computer access aids; Computer with voice synthesizer for visually impaired persons; Copier with enlargement capabilities; Dragon Naturally Speaking software; Extensive large print coll; Home delivery serv; Internet workstation with adaptive software; Large print bks; Large print bks & talking machines; Lending of low vision aids; Low vision equip; Magnifiers; Mags & bk reproduction/duplication; Open bk software on pub access PC; PC for handicapped; Recorded bks; Screen reader software; Sound rec; Talking bks; Talking bks & player equip; ZoomText magnification & reading software
Open Mon-Fri 9-9, Sat 9-5, Sun 1-5
Friends of the Library Group

M NORTH SHORE UNIVERSITY HEALTH SYSTEM-GLENBROOK HOSPITAL*, Medical Library, 2100 Pfingsten Rd, 60026-1301. SAN 374-8308. Tel: 847-657-5618. FAX: 847-657-5995. *Librn,* Hailan Wang; E-mail: hwang@northshore.org; Staff 1 (MLS 1)
Founded 1970
Library Holdings: Bk Titles 1,000; Bk Vols 1,100; Per Subs 115
Database Vendor: OCLC FirstSearch, OVID Technologies
Function: ILL available
Partic in Docline; Illinois Library & Information Network; Northeastern Ill Libr Consortia
Open Mon-Fri 8:30-2:30

S TRIODYNE INC, Beth Hamilton Safety Library, 3054 N Lake Terrace, 60026. SAN 320-5819. Tel: 847-677-4730. FAX: 847-647-2047. E-mail: infoserv@triodyne.com. Web Site: www.triodyne.com/library. *Mgr,* Jenny Warner; E-mail: jennyw@triodyne.com
Founded 1979
Library Holdings: Bk Vols 10,500; Per Subs 200
Special Collections: Expert Transcript Center, Bibcat 2500 (Bibliographies)
Subject Interests: Accident prevention, Automotive eng, Ergonomics, Forensic eng, Human factors, Safety
Database Vendor: Dialog, Factiva.com, OCLC FirstSearch, OCLC WorldShare Interlibrary Loan, Westlaw
Function: Doc delivery serv, ILL available, Res libr
Publications: BIBCAT 2500 (Bibliographies)
Restriction: Access at librarian's discretion

GLENWOOD

P GLENWOOD-LYNWOOD PUBLIC LIBRARY DISTRICT*, 19901 Stony Island Ave, 60411. SAN 304-2308. Tel: 708-758-0090. FAX: 708-758-0106. E-mail: gws@sslic.net. Web Site: www.glpld.org. *Dir,* Kathy Parker; E-mail: parkerk@sslic.net; *Circ Mgr,* Sheila Adams; E-mail: adamss@sslic.net; *Info Serv Mgr,* Rhonda Ruffin; E-mail: ruffinr@sslic.net; Staff 29 (MLS 3, Non-MLS 26)
Founded 1974. Pop 17,976; Circ 134,642
Library Holdings: Audiobooks 855; CDs 1,597; DVDs 2,674; Bk Vols 52,184; Per Subs 102

Automation Activity & Vendor Info: (Acquisitions) Innovative Interfaces, Inc; (Cataloging) Innovative Interfaces, Inc; (Circulation) Innovative Interfaces, Inc; (ILL) Innovative Interfaces, Inc; (OPAC) Innovative Interfaces, Inc; (Serials) Innovative Interfaces, Inc
Database Vendor: Innovative Interfaces, Inc
Wireless access
Publications: Newsletter
Mem of Reaching Across Illinois Library System (RAILS)
Open Mon-Thurs 9-9, Fri & Sat 9-5, Sun 1-5
Friends of the Library Group
Bookmobiles: 1

GODFREY

J LEWIS & CLARK COMMUNITY COLLEGE*, Reid Memorial Library, 5800 Godfrey Rd, 62035. SAN 304-2316. Tel: 618-468-4301. Reference Tel: 618-468-4304. FAX: 618-468-4301. Web Site: www.lc.edu. *Dir,* Dennis Krieb; Tel: 618-468-4330, E-mail: dkrieb@lc.edu; *Asst Dir,* Liz Burns; Tel: 618-468-4320, E-mail: lburns@lc.edu; *Asst Dir,* Greg Cash; Tel: 618-468-4340; *Cat,* Reva Van Hoose; Tel: 618-466-3411, Ext 4306, E-mail: rvanhoose@lc.cc.il.us; *Circ,* Debra Gipson; Tel: 618-466-3411, Ext 4301, E-mail: dgipson@lc.cc.il.us; *ILL,* Paula Seaman; Tel: 618-466-3411, Ext 4304, E-mail: pseaman@lc.cc.il.us; Staff 6 (MLS 3, Non-MLS 3)
Founded 1970. Enrl 4,500; Fac 100
Library Holdings: Bk Titles 45,000; Bk Vols 48,000; Per Subs 3,500
Special Collections: Lewis & Clark Coll; Monticello College History
Subject Interests: Local hist
Automation Activity & Vendor Info: (Cataloging) Ex Libris Group; (Circulation) Ex Libris Group; (Course Reserve) Ex Libris Group; (ILL) Ex Libris Group; (OPAC) Ex Libris Group
Database Vendor: EBSCOhost, OCLC FirstSearch, ProQuest
Wireless access
Partic in Consortium of Academic & Research Libraries in Illinois; Illinois Library & Information Network; SILRC
Open Mon-Thurs 8-8, Fri 8-4:30

GOLCONDA

P GOLCONDA PUBLIC LIBRARY*, 126 W Main St, 62938. (Mail add: PO Box 523, 62938-0523), SAN 304-2324. Tel: 618-683-6531. FAX: 618-683-6531. E-mail: golillib@shawneelink.com. *Chief Librn,* Maxine Houser; *Asst City Librn,* Peggy Conley
Founded 1915. Pop 823; Circ 12,450
Library Holdings: Bk Vols 18,267; Per Subs 20
Subject Interests: Genealogy, Local hist
Wireless access
Mem of Illinois Heartland Library System
Open Mon & Tues 9-5, Wed-Fri 1-5, Sat 9-12

GRAFTON

S IYC PERE MARQUETTE CORRECTIONAL INSTITUTION LIBRARY*, 17808 State Hwy 100 W, 62037-9799. Tel: 618-786-2371, Ext 133.
Library Holdings: Bk Vols 8,000

GRAND TOWER

P GRAND TOWER PUBLIC LIBRARY*, 111 Walnut St, 62942. (Mail add: PO Box 287, 62942-0287), SAN 376-141X. Tel: 618-565-2181. FAX: 618-565-2181. *Librn,* Art Burke
Library Holdings: Bk Titles 20,000; Per Subs 62
Open Mon & Wed-Fri 11:30-3:30, Sat 10-2

GRANITE CITY

P SIX MILE REGIONAL LIBRARY DISTRICT*, 2001 Delmar St, 62040-4590. SAN 304-2332. Tel: 618-452-6238. FAX: 618-876-6317. Web Site: sixmilerld.org. *Dir,* Tina Hubert; E-mail: tinahubert@sixmilerld.org; *Asst Dir,* Jeanette Kampen; *Head, Cat,* Lynda C Seegert; Staff 5 (MLS 5)
Founded 1912. Pop 46,088; Circ 331,637
Jul 2008-Jun 2009 Income $1,251,216. Mats Exp $164,000. Sal $1,060,829
Library Holdings: Bk Vols 176,583; Per Subs 250
Wireless access
Open Mon-Thurs 9-8, Fri & Sat 9-5
Friends of the Library Group
Branches: 1
DISTRICT BRANCH LIBRARY, 2145 Johnson Rd, 62040, SAN 376-2491. Tel: 618-452-6244. FAX: 618-452-6226. *Assoc Dir, Br Serv,* Gregg McGee; E-mail: greggmcgee@sixmilerld.org; Staff 1 (MLS 1)
Library Holdings: Bk Titles 20,000; Bk Vols 30,000; Per Subs 25
Open Mon & Thurs-Sat (Sept-May) 9-5, Tues & Wed 12-8; Mon & Wed-Sat (June-Aug) 9-5, Tues 12-8
Friends of the Library Group

J SOUTHWESTERN ILLINOIS COLLEGE*, Sam Wolf Granite City Campus Library, 4950 Maryville Rd, 62040. SAN 371-9111. Tel: 618-931-0600, Ext 7354. Reference Tel: 618-797-7354. Toll Free Tel: 800-222-5131, Ext 7354. E-mail: gcclibrary@swic.edu. Web Site: www.swic.edu/library. *Librn,* Jan Zuke, PhD; Tel: 618-797-7353, E-mail: jan.zuke@swic.edu; Staff 3 (MLS 3)
Founded 1983. Enrl 2,770; Fac 200; Highest Degree: Associate
Automation Activity & Vendor Info: (Course Reserve) Ex Libris Group
Database Vendor: EBSCOhost, LexisNexis, OCLC FirstSearch, SirsiDynix
Wireless access
Function: Pub access computers
Mem of Illinois Heartland Library System
Partic in Saint Louis Regional Library Network
Open Mon-Thurs (Winter) 8am-9:30pm, Fri 8-4, Sat 11-3; Mon-Thurs (Summer) 8am-9:30pm, Fri 8-4
Restriction: Open to pub for ref & circ; with some limitations, Open to students, fac & staff, Pub use on premises

GRANT PARK

P GRANT PARK PUBLIC LIBRARY*, 107 W Taylor St, 60940. (Mail add: PO Box 392, 60940-0302), SAN 304-2359. Tel: 815-465-6047. *Librn,* Mary Wilkening
Founded 1919. Pop 1,331; Circ 3,151
Library Holdings: Bk Vols 5,070
Special Collections: James Whitcomb Riley; Mark Twain; Zane Grey
Wireless access
Function: Accessibility serv available based on individual needs
Mem of Reaching Across Illinois Library System (RAILS)
Open Mon 1-6, Wed & Fri 12-6, Thurs 9-2, Sat 9-12

GRAYSLAKE

J COLLEGE OF LAKE COUNTY*, John C Murphy Memorial Library, 19351 W Washington St, 60030. SAN 304-2367. Tel: 847-543-2071. Administration Tel: 847-543-2463. FAX: 847-223-7690. Administration FAX: 847-543-3463. E-mail: library@clcillinois.edu. Web Site: library.clcillinois.edu. *Dean,* Brian Beecher; E-mail: bbeecher@clcillinois.edu; Erika Behling; Tel: 847-543-2892, E-mail: ebehling@clcillinois.edu; *Ref & Instruction Librn,* Uri Toch; Tel: 847-543-2466, E-mail: utoch@clcillinois.edu; *Tech Serv Librn,* Holly Ledvina; Tel: 847-543-2461, E-mail: hledvina@clcillinois.edu; *Tech Serv Supvr,* Kathleen VanVickle; Tel: 847-543-2893, E-mail: kvanvickle@clcillinois.edu; *ILL Spec,* Donna MacCartney; Tel: 847-543-2465, E-mail: dmaccartney@clcillinois.edu; *Libr Tech Spec,* Julie Ryan; Tel: 847-543-2734, E-mail: jryan@clcillinois.edu; *Circ,* Linda Burdette; Tel: 847-543-2438, E-mail: lburdette@clcillinois.edu; *Ref,* Michelle Carter; Tel: 847-543-2891, E-mail: mcarter@clcillinois.edu; *Ref,* Anne Chernaik; Tel: 847-543-2460, E-mail: achernaik@clcillinois.edu; *Ref,* Terry Sebastian; Tel: 847-543-2469, E-mail: tsebastian@clcillinois.edu. Subject Specialists: *Info literacy,* Kathleen Lovelace; *Automation,* Holly Ledvina; Staff 19 (MLS 7, Non-MLS 12)
Founded 1970. Enrl 15,000; Fac 215; Highest Degree: Associate
Jul 2011-Jun 2012. Mats Exp $614,088, Books $235,355, Per/Ser (Incl. Access Fees) $112,000, AV Mat $21,180, Electronic Ref Mat (Incl, Access Fees) $245,553. Sal $1,170,773 (Prof $860,277)
Library Holdings: DVDs 2,964; Bk Titles 109,570; Per Subs 575
Automation Activity & Vendor Info: (Acquisitions) Innovative Interfaces, Inc; (Cataloging) Innovative Interfaces, Inc; (Circulation) Innovative Interfaces, Inc; (Media Booking) Innovative Interfaces, Inc; (OPAC) Innovative Interfaces, Inc; (Serials) Innovative Interfaces, Inc
Database Vendor: OCLC FirstSearch
Function: Art exhibits, Audio & video playback equip for onsite use, Audiobks via web, Bks on CD, Computers for patron use, Copy machines, e-mail & chat, Electronic databases & coll
Partic in OCLC Online Computer Library Center, Inc
Open Mon-Thurs 8am-10pm, Fri 8-4:30, Sat 9-4:30, Sun 1-5

P GRAYSLAKE AREA PUBLIC LIBRARY DISTRICT*, 100 Library Lane, 60030-1684. SAN 304-2375. Tel: 847-223-5313. FAX: 847-223-6482. TDD: 847-223-5362. Web Site: www.grayslake.info. *Dir,* Roberta Thomas; E-mail: rthomas@grayslake.info; *Adult Serv,* Dawn Miller; *Tech Serv,* Jan Davis; Staff 55 (MLS 9, Non-MLS 46)
Founded 1931. Pop 25,399; Circ 419,838
Library Holdings: AV Mats 17,153; Bk Vols 128,447; Per Subs 374
Automation Activity & Vendor Info: (Acquisitions) TLC (The Library Corporation); (Cataloging) TLC (The Library Corporation); (Circulation) TLC (The Library Corporation); (ILL) TLC (The Library Corporation); (OPAC) TLC (The Library Corporation); (Serials) TLC (The Library Corporation)
Publications: Front Page (Newsletter)
Open Mon-Thurs 9:30-9, Fri 9:30-6, Sat 9:30-5, Sun (Winter) 1-5
Friends of the Library Group

GRAYVILLE

P GROFFE MEMORIAL LIBRARY*, 118 South Middle St, 62844. SAN 304-2383. Tel: 618-375-7121. FAX: 618-375-7121. *Dir,* Mickie Collard; E-mail: mcollard53@gmail.com; Staff 2 (Non-MLS 2)
Founded 1909. Pop 1,725; Circ 8,630
Library Holdings: Bk Titles 12,967; Per Subs 30
Special Collections: Rear Admiral James M Helm Coll, memorabilia
Mem of Illinois Heartland Library System
Open Mon-Thurs 10-7:30, Fri 10-6, Sat 10-2

GREAT LAKES

A UNITED STATES NAVY*, MWR Library, Bldg 160, 2601E Paul Jones St, 60088-2845. SAN 304-2391. Tel: 847-688-4617. FAX: 847-688-3602. Web Site: mwrgl.cnic.navy.mil/recreation/library/library.htm. *Dir,* Kevin R Jones; *Circ & Staff Develop Coordr,* Anny Swanson; Staff 4 (MLS 1, Non-MLS 3)
Founded 1912. Pop 32,000; Circ 35,000
Oct 2007-Sept 2008 Income $250,000. Mats Exp $60,000, Books $50,000, Per/Ser (Incl. Access Fees) $3,000, AV Equip $2,000, AV Mat $4,000. Sal $200,000 (Prof $70,000)
Library Holdings: AV Mats 600; Bk Vols 22,000; Per Subs 95; Talking Bks 450
Subject Interests: Naval hist, Naval sci
Automation Activity & Vendor Info: (Acquisitions) SIRSI Unicorn; (Cataloging) SIRSI Unicorn; (Circulation) SIRSI Unicorn; (OPAC) SIRSI-iBistro
Database Vendor: ProQuest
Wireless access
Open Mon-Thurs 10-8, Fri 10-2, Sat & Sun 1-5

GREENFIELD

P GREENFIELD PUBLIC LIBRARY*, 515 Chestnut, 62044-1304. (Mail add: PO Box 214, 62044-0214), SAN 304-2413. Tel: 217-368-2613. FAX: 217-368-2613. E-mail: gfe@greenfieldpl.org. *Dir,* Pat Theivagt; *Asst Librn,* Brenda Shipley
Founded 1914. Pop 1,192; Circ 6,000
Library Holdings: AV Mats 1,298; Bk Titles 10,498; Per Subs 18; Talking Bks 455
Open Mon & Tues (June-Aug) 3-6, Wed 1-7, Fri & Sat 9-12; Mon & Wed (Sept-May) 1-7, Tues 1-8, Fri & Sat 9-12
Friends of the Library Group

GREENUP

P GREENUP TOWNSHIP PUBLIC LIBRARY*, 101 N Franklin St, 62428. (Mail add: PO Box 275, 62428-0275), SAN 304-2421. Tel: 217-923-3616. FAX: 217-923-3616. *Dir,* Gayle Carr; *Asst Librn,* Elna Ochs
Pop 2,500; Circ 14,714
Library Holdings: Bk Vols 15,500; Per Subs 60
Special Collections: Genealogy Coll
Mem of Illinois Heartland Library System

GREENVILLE

C GREENVILLE COLLEGE*, Ruby E Dare Library, 301 N Elm, 62246. (Mail add: 315 E College Ave, 62246), SAN 304-243X. Tel: 618-664-6603. Reference Tel: 618-664-6599. FAX: 618-664-9578. E-mail: libgen@greenville.edu. Web Site: www.greenville.edu/library. *Dir,* Jane L Hopkins; E-mail: jane.hopkins@greenville.edu; *Head, Pub Serv,* Georgann Kurtz-Shaw; E-mail: georgann.kurtz-shaw@greenville.edu; Staff 5 (MLS 4, Non-MLS 1)
Founded 1892. Enrl 1,400; Fac 72; Highest Degree: Master
Library Holdings: Audiobooks 18; AV Mats 200; CDs 861; DVDs 300; e-books 7,000; e-journals 12,000; Electronic Media & Resources 200; Microforms 17,000; Bk Titles 112,283; Bk Vols 121,350; Per Subs 150; Videos 2,300
Special Collections: Free Methodist Church History Coll; Greenville College History Coll
Automation Activity & Vendor Info: (Acquisitions) Ex Libris Group; (Cataloging) Ex Libris Group; (Circulation) Ex Libris Group; (ILL) OCLC; (OPAC) Ex Libris Group
Database Vendor: Alexander Street Press, American Psychological Association (APA), CredoReference, EBSCOhost, LexisNexis, OCLC FirstSearch, OCLC WorldShare Interlibrary Loan, Sage, YBP Library Services
Wireless access
Publications: Annual report; Library Orientation Packet
Mem of Illinois Heartland Library System
Partic in Consortium of Academic & Research Libraries in Illinois; Illinois Library & Information Network; OCLC Online Computer Library Center, Inc
Special Services for the Deaf - Closed caption videos
Special Services for the Blind - Closed circuit TV; Computer with voice synthesizer for visually impaired persons; Copier with enlargement capabilities
Open Mon-Thurs 7:30am-11:45pm, Fri 7:30-5, Sat 12-5, Sun 6:30pm-10:30pm

P GREENVILLE PUBLIC LIBRARY*, 414 W Main St, 62246-1615. SAN 304-2448. Tel: 618-664-3115. FAX: 618-664-9442. Web Site: www.greenvillepubliclibrary.org. *Dir,* Hugh M Westbrook; *Librn,* Mary Hoiles
Founded 1856. Pop 6,955; Circ 40,000
Library Holdings: Bk Vols 25,219; Per Subs 75
Subject Interests: Genealogy
Mem of Illinois Heartland Library System
Open Mon & Tues 9-5, Wed & Thurs 12-8, Fri 8-5, Sat 8-3
Friends of the Library Group

GRIDLEY

P GRIDLEY PUBLIC LIBRARY DISTRICT*, 320 Center St, 61744. (Mail add: PO Box 370, 61744-0370), SAN 304-2456. Tel: 309-747-2284. FAX: 309-747-3195. E-mail: gpld@gridcom.net. *Dir,* Linda Zimmerman
Founded 1916. Pop 2,113
Library Holdings: Audiobooks 342; DVDs 1,061; e-books 2,967; Bk Titles 19,546; Per Subs 75
Special Collections: Library of America Coll
Automation Activity & Vendor Info: (Circulation) SIRSI WorkFlows
Wireless access
Open Mon 1:30-8:30, Tues & Thurs 9:30-6:30, Wed & Fri 1:30-6:30, Sat 9:30-2:30

GRIGGSVILLE

P NORTH PIKE DISTRICT LIBRARY*, 119 S Corey St, 62340. (Mail add: PO Box 419, 62340-0419), SAN 304-2464. Tel: 217-833-2633. FAX: 217-833-2283. E-mail: northpike@casscomm.com. *Dir,* Lee Jankowski
Founded 1887. Pop 3,500; Circ 27,960
Jul 2010-Jun 2011 Income $75,500, County $75,000, Locally Generated Income $500. Mats Exp $9,000, Books $5,000, Per/Ser (Incl. Access Fees) $500, Other Print Mats $500, AV Equip $2,000, AV Mat $1,000. Sal $25,000 (Prof $17,000)
Library Holdings: Audiobooks 540; AV Mats 700; Bks on Deafness & Sign Lang 5; Braille Volumes 1; DVDs 500; High Interest/Low Vocabulary Bk Vols 1,200; Large Print Bks 1,200; Microforms 24; Bk Titles 25,000; Bk Vols 19,788; Per Subs 32; Spec Interest Per Sub 12; Talking Bks 24; Videos 50
Special Collections: Municipal Document Depository; Oral History
Function: Home delivery & serv to Sr ctr & nursing homes, Homebound delivery serv, ILL available, Large print keyboards, Online searches, Photocopying/Printing, Preschool reading prog, Prog for children & young adult, Summer reading prog, Telephone ref
Mem of Reaching Across Illinois Library System (RAILS)
Partic in Illinois Library & Information Network; Resource Sharing Alliance
Open Mon-Fri 12-6, Sat 9-1

GURNEE

P WARREN-NEWPORT PUBLIC LIBRARY DISTRICT*, 224 N O'Plaine Rd, 60031. SAN 304-2472. Tel: 847-244-5150. FAX: 847-244-3499. TDD: 847-244-5195. E-mail: webcontact@wnpl.info. Web Site: www.wnpl.info. *Exec Dir,* Ryan Livergood; *Dep Dir,* Noreen Reese; Tel: 847-244-5150, Ext 3026, E-mail: nreese@wnpl.info; *Head, Communications,* Janice Marsh; Tel: 847-244-5150, Ext 3018, E-mail: jmarsh@wnpl.info; *Head, Circ,* Paula Pena; Tel: 847-244-5150, Ext 3024, E-mail: ppena@wnpl.info; *Head, Info Serv,* Kevin Getty; Tel: 847-244-5150, Ext 3015, E-mail: kgetty@wnpl.info; *Head, Outreach Serv,* Carol Brandon; E-mail: cbrandon@wnpl.info; *Head, Tech Serv,* Diane Stine; Tel: 847-244-5150, Ext 3048, E-mail: dstine@wnpl.info; *Head, Youth Serv,* Diana Sills; *Co-Mgr, Adult Serv,* Sandra Beda; Tel: 847-244-5150, Ext 3025, E-mail: sbeda@wnpl.info; *Co-Mgr, Adult Serv,* Kathie Fifer; Tel: 847-244-5150, Ext 3002, E-mail: kfifer@wnpl.info; Staff 82 (MLS 16, Non-MLS 66)
Founded 1973. Pop 66,690; Circ 1,339,836
Jul 2012-Jun 2013 Income $6,144,243, State $51,051, Federal $137,691, Locally Generated Income $5,738,312, Other $217,189. Mats Exp $500,344, Books $251,392, AV Mat $142,356, Electronic Ref Mat (Incl. Access Fees) $106,596. Sal $2,792,350
Library Holdings: AV Mats 11,341; Bks on Deafness & Sign Lang 140; CDs 24,019; High Interest/Low Vocabulary Bk Vols 87; Large Print Bks 2,458; Bk Titles 213,749; Per Subs 321; Talking Bks 13,553; Videos 26,930
Subject Interests: Ill
Automation Activity & Vendor Info: (Acquisitions) Innovative Interfaces, Inc - Millenium; (Cataloging) Innovative Interfaces, Inc - Millenium; (Circulation) Innovative Interfaces, Inc - Millenium; (OPAC) Innovative Interfaces, Inc - Millenium

Database Vendor: EBSCOhost, Gale Cengage Learning, OCLC FirstSearch, ReferenceUSA, SirsiDynix
Wireless access
Function: Adult bk club, Art exhibits, Bks on CD, Children's prog, Computer training, Computers for patron use, Copy machines, e-mail & chat, Electronic databases & coll, Handicapped accessible, Home delivery & serv to Sr ctr & nursing homes, Homebound delivery serv, ILL available, Magnifiers for reading, Mail & tel request accepted, Music CDs, Outreach serv, Outside serv via phone, mail, e-mail & web, OverDrive digital audio bks, Photocopying/Printing, Preschool outreach, Prog for adults, Prog for children & young adult, Pub access computers, Ref serv available, Senior outreach, Summer reading prog, Tax forms, Teen prog, Web-catalog
Publications: Inside Angle (Newsletter)
Partic in OCLC Online Computer Library Center, Inc
Special Services for the Deaf - TDD equip; TTY equip
Special Services for the Blind - Bks on CD; Children's Braille; Closed circuit TV; Screen enlargement software for people with visual disabilities; ZoomText magnification & reading software
Open Mon-Thurs 9-9, Fri 9-6, Sat 9-5, Sun (Oct-May) 1-5
Friends of the Library Group
Bookmobiles: 1. Head of Outreach, Carol Brandon

HAMILTON

P HAMILTON PUBLIC LIBRARY*, 861 Broadway St, 62341. SAN 304-2480. Tel: 217-847-2219. FAX: 217-847-3014. Web Site: www.hamiltonpubliclibrary.org. *Dir,* Nancy K Denton; *Tech Serv Librn,* Mary Patterson; Staff 4 (Non-MLS 4)
Founded 1902. Pop 3,029; Circ 17,610
Library Holdings: Bk Titles 21,595; Per Subs 50
Mem of Reaching Across Illinois Library System (RAILS)
Open Mon-Thurs 9-7, Fri 9-5, Sat 9-1
Friends of the Library Group

HAMPSHIRE

P ELLA JOHNSON MEMORIAL PUBLIC LIBRARY DISTRICT*, 109 S State St, 60140. (Mail add: PO Box 429, 60140-0429), SAN 304-2499. Tel: 847-683-4490. FAX: 847-683-4493. E-mail: library@ellajohnsonlibrary.org. Web Site: www.ellajohnsonlibrary.org. *Dir,* Carol Schrey; E-mail: cschrey@ellajohnsonlibrary.org; *Adult & Teen Serv Mgr,* Scott Grotto; E-mail: sgrotto@ellajohnsonlibrary.org; *Ch Mgr,* Dawn Cummings; E-mail: dcummings@ellajohnsonlibrary.org; *Circ Mgr,* Joy Kleiser; E-mail: jkleiser@ellajohnsonlibrary.org
Founded 1943. Pop 14,181; Circ 53,000
Library Holdings: Bk Titles 25,000; Bk Vols 28,000; Per Subs 108
Subject Interests: Local hist
Wireless access
Publications: Children Newsletter (Monthly)
Mem of Reaching Across Illinois Library System (RAILS)
Open Mon-Thurs 9:30-8, Fri 9:30-5, Sat 9:30-3, Sun Noon-4

HANOVER

P HANOVER TOWNSHIP LIBRARY, 204 Jefferson St, 61041. (Mail add: PO Box 475, 61041-0475), SAN 304-2510. Tel: 815-591-3517. FAX: 815-591-3517. E-mail: hanovertownshiplibrary@gmail.com. Web Site: www.hanover-lib.org. *Dir,* Denise Tollensdorf
Founded 1941. Pop 1,229; Circ 11,949
Library Holdings: Audiobooks 197; DVDs 935; Large Print Bks 247; Bk Titles 10,301; Per Subs 32; Videos 212
Subject Interests: Local hist
Wireless access
Mem of Reaching Across Illinois Library System (RAILS)
Open Mon & Thurs 2-7, Tues & Wed 12-5, Sat 9-2

HARRISBURG

P HARRISBURG PUBLIC LIBRARY DISTRICT*, Harrisburg District Library, Two W Walnut St, 62946-1261. SAN 304-2529. Tel: 618-253-7455. FAX: 618-252-1239. E-mail: hpld@harrisburglibrary.org. Web Site: www.harrisburglibrary.org. *Dir,* Ruth Miller; E-mail: rmiller@harrisburglibrary.org; Staff 1 (MLS 1)
Founded 1909. Pop 13,070; Circ 45,000
Library Holdings: Bk Vols 33,000; Per Subs 89
Subject Interests: Genealogy
Automation Activity & Vendor Info: (Cataloging) Innovative Interfaces, Inc; (Circulation) Innovative Interfaces, Inc
Wireless access
Function: Handicapped accessible, ILL available, Prog for children & young adult, Spoken cassettes & CDs, Summer reading prog, Wheelchair accessible
Mem of Illinois Heartland Library System
Open Mon-Fri 9-8, Sat 10-6, Sun 1-5
Friends of the Library Group

J SOUTHEASTERN ILLINOIS COLLEGE*, Melba Patton Library, 3575 College Rd, 62946. SAN 304-2537. Tel: 618-252-5400, Ext 2260, 618-252-5400, Ext 2261. Toll Free Tel: 866-338-2742. FAX: 618-252-2713. Web Site: www.sic.edu. *Librn,* Gary Jones; Staff 4 (MLS 1, Non-MLS 3)
Founded 1960. Enrl 2,300; Fac 85; Highest Degree: Associate
Library Holdings: Bk Vols 40,000; Per Subs 250
Automation Activity & Vendor Info: (Acquisitions) SirsiDynix; (Cataloging) SirsiDynix; (Circulation) SirsiDynix; (ILL) SirsiDynix; (Media Booking) SirsiDynix; (OPAC) SirsiDynix; (Serials) SirsiDynix
Partic in Northern Illinois Learning Resources Cooperative (NILRC); Southern Ill Learning Resources Coop
Open Mon-Thurs (Winter) 7:30am-9pm, Fri 7:30-4, Sun 2-8; Mon-Thurs (Summer) 7:30am-9pm, Sun 2-8

HARTFORD

P HARTFORD PUBLIC LIBRARY DISTRICT*, 143 W Hawthorne, 62048. SAN 304-2545. Tel: 618-254-9394. FAX: 618-254-6522. E-mail: libraryinfo@hartfordpld.org. *Dir,* Gloria Smith; *Cat,* Beverly Zagan
Founded 1965. Pop 1,545; Circ 13,743
Library Holdings: Bk Vols 27,791; Per Subs 50
Special Collections: Lewis & Clark Reference Center
Publications: Newsletter
Mem of Illinois Heartland Library System
Open Mon-Thurs 10-6, Fri & Sat 10-4

HARVARD

P HARVARD DIGGINS PUBLIC LIBRARY*, 900 E McKinley St, 60033. SAN 304-2553. Tel: 815-943-4671. FAX: 815-943-2312. E-mail: harpgeneral@harvard-diggins.org. Web Site: www.harvard-diggins.org. *Dir,* Harriet Roll
Founded 1908. Pop 9,000; Circ 54,000
Library Holdings: Bks on Deafness & Sign Lang 10; High Interest/Low Vocabulary Bk Vols 100; Bk Titles 24,000; Bk Vols 26,000; Per Subs 80
Special Collections: Butterfly Coll
Automation Activity & Vendor Info: (Cataloging) Innovative Interfaces, Inc; (Circulation) Innovative Interfaces, Inc; (ILL) Innovative Interfaces, Inc; (OPAC) Innovative Interfaces, Inc; (Serials) Innovative Interfaces, Inc
Database Vendor: Bowker, OCLC FirstSearch, OCLC WebJunction, ProQuest
Mem of Reaching Across Illinois Library System (RAILS)
Special Services for the Deaf - Am sign lang & deaf culture
Open Mon-Wed 9:30-8, Thurs 3-8, Fri & Sat 9:30-5:30

HARVEY

P HARVEY PUBLIC LIBRARY DISTRICT*, 15441 Turlington Ave, 60426-3683. SAN 304-257X. Tel: 708-331-0757. Circulation Tel: 708-331-0757, Ext 3200. Administration Tel: 708-331-0757, Ext 3201. FAX: 708-331-2835. TDD: 708-331-0767. E-mail: has@harvey.lib.il.us. Web Site: www.harvey.lib.il.us. *Admin Dir,* Sandra Flowers; Tel: 708-331-0757, Ext 3204, E-mail: sflowers@harvey.lib.il.us; Staff 10 (MLS 2, Non-MLS 8)
Founded 1903. Pop 25,300; Circ 65,098
Library Holdings: AV Mats 2,584; DVDs 5,674; e-books 680; Bk Vols 85,983; Per Subs 571
Subject Interests: Ethnic studies, Local hist
Automation Activity & Vendor Info: (Acquisitions) Innovative Interfaces, Inc; (Circulation) Innovative Interfaces, Inc
Database Vendor: Innovative Interfaces, Inc
Wireless access
Publications: Internal & Patron Newsletters
Mem of Reaching Across Illinois Library System (RAILS)
Special Services for the Deaf - TDD equip
Open Mon-Thurs 10-8, Fri & Sat 10-4

M INGALLS MEMORIAL HOSPITAL MEDICAL LIBRARY*, One Ingalls Dr, 60426. SAN 304-2588. Tel: 708-915-6881, 708-915-6882. FAX: 708-915-3109. Web Site: www.ingalls.org. *Dir, Health Sci Libr,* Clare Bonnema; Staff 1 (MLS 1)
Founded 1968
Library Holdings: Bk Titles 500; Bk Vols 700; Per Subs 50
Subject Interests: Clinical med, Nursing
Database Vendor: EBSCOhost, OVID Technologies
Function: Health sci info serv, ILL available, Online searches, Ref serv available
Partic in Chicago & South Consortium; Regional Med Libr - Region 3
Restriction: Staff & prof res

HARWOOD HEIGHTS

P EISENHOWER PUBLIC LIBRARY DISTRICT*, 4613 N Oketo Ave, 60706. SAN 304-2596. Tel: 708-867-7828. FAX: 708-867-1535. TDD: 708-867-6362. E-mail: essweb@eisenhowerpld.org. Web Site: www.eisenhowerlibrary.org. *Dir,* Stacy Wittmann; *Head, Ch,* Nancy Devlin; *Head, Circ,* Peggy Tomzik; *Head of Mkt,* Julianne Stam; *Head, Tech Serv,* Jessica Horvath; *Asst Head, Ref Serv,* Victoria Bitters; *Bus Mgr,* Linda Woyner; *Commun Serv, Mgr, YA Serv,* Penny Blubaugh; Staff 19 (MLS 17, Non-MLS 2)
Founded 1972. Pop 23,184; Circ 415,149
Library Holdings: Audiobooks 3,334; CDs 8,038; DVDs 8,861; e-books 11,770; Electronic Media & Resources 60; Large Print Bks 2,059; Bk Titles 134,771; Per Subs 250
Special Collections: Polish Language
Automation Activity & Vendor Info: (Circulation) Innovative Interfaces, Inc
Wireless access
Mem of Reaching Across Illinois Library System (RAILS)
Special Services for the Deaf - TTY equip
Open Mon-Thurs 9-9, Fri & Sat 9-5, Sun 1-5
Friends of the Library Group

HAVANA

P HAVANA PUBLIC LIBRARY DISTRICT*, 201 W Adams St, 62644-1321. SAN 304-260X. Tel: 309-543-4701. FAX: 309-543-2715. E-mail: library@casscomm.com. Web Site: www.havana.lib.il.us. *Dir,* Nancy I Glick; *Asst Dir, Youth Serv Librn,* Ellen R Mibbs; *Coll Develop,* Karen Elliott; Staff 11 (MLS 2, Non-MLS 9)
Founded 1896. Pop 8,313; Circ 30,000
Library Holdings: Bk Vols 45,000; Per Subs 122
Special Collections: Historic Photograph Coll; Mason County Genealogical & Historical Society Coll
Automation Activity & Vendor Info: (OPAC) SIRSI Unicorn
Database Vendor: OCLC FirstSearch, OCLC WorldShare Interlibrary Loan, SirsiDynix, Wilson - Wilson Web
Wireless access
Mem of Reaching Across Illinois Library System (RAILS)
Partic in RSA
Special Services for the Deaf - Interpreter on staff; Sign lang interpreter upon request for prog; Staff with knowledge of sign lang; TDD equip; TTY equip
Special Services for the Blind - Bks available with recordings; Bks on cassette; Bks on CD; Braille alphabet card; Cassette playback machines; Cassettes; Copier with enlargement capabilities; Home delivery serv; Large print & cassettes; Large print bks; Large print bks & talking machines; Micro-computer access & training; Radio reading serv; Recorded bks; Talking bk & rec for the blind cat; Talking bks; Talking bks & player equip; VisualTek equip
Open Mon-Wed 10-8, Thurs 10-7, Fri 10-5, Sat (Winter) 10-2
Friends of the Library Group

HAZEL CREST

P GRANDE PRAIRIE PUBLIC LIBRARY DISTRICT*, 3479 W 183rd St, 60429. SAN 304-2618. Tel: 708-798-5563. FAX: 708-798-5874. E-mail: gpsreference@yahoo.com. Web Site: grandeprairie.org. *Dir of Circ,* Donna Scholz; *Dir, Youth Serv,* Kim Peake; *Asst Dir, Adult Serv,* Linda S Ameling; Staff 18 (MLS 3, Non-MLS 15)
Founded 1960. Pop 30,985; Circ 124,071
Library Holdings: AV Mats 12,804; CDs 10,831; e-books 821; Bk Vols 78,426; Per Subs 210; Videos 3,759
Special Collections: Fiction Works by African American Writers
Automation Activity & Vendor Info: (Cataloging) Innovative Interfaces, Inc; (Circulation) Innovative Interfaces, Inc; (ILL) Innovative Interfaces, Inc; (OPAC) Innovative Interfaces, Inc
Database Vendor: ALLDATA Online, Baker & Taylor, Gale Cengage Learning, Grolier Online, Innovative Interfaces, Inc, LearningExpress, Newsbank, OCLC FirstSearch, OCLC WebJunction, OCLC WorldShare Interlibrary Loan, ProQuest, ReferenceUSA, World Book Online
Publications: Grande Prairie Public Library (Newsletter)
Mem of Reaching Across Illinois Library System (RAILS)
Open Mon-Thurs 9-9, Fri & Sat 9-5, Sun 1-5

S SOUTH SUBURBAN GENEALOGICAL & HISTORICAL SOCIETY LIBRARY, 3000 W 170th Pl, 60429-1174. SAN 304-6583. Tel: 708-335-3340. E-mail: info@ssghs.org. Web Site: www.ssghs.org. *Pres,* Patty Higgins; *Librn,* Laurie Coolidge
Founded 1972
Library Holdings: CDs 500; Microforms 2,000; Bk Titles 12,000; Spec Interest Per Sub 50
Special Collections: Federal Population Census 1790-1930, micro; Illinois - Cook & Will Counties; Naturalization Records for Calumet City; Obituary Files; Pullman Car Works, personnel rec; Roseland (Chicago) Church Hist; Township Records
Subject Interests: Genealogy, Local hist
Wireless access
Function: 24/7 Online cat
Publications: Cemetery Readings; Monthly Newsletter; Research Series; Where the Trails Cross (Quarterly)
Open Mon, Wed & Fri 10-4, Tues 1-5
Restriction: Non-circulating

HENNEPIN

P PUTNAM COUNTY PUBLIC LIBRARY DISTRICT*, 214 N Fourth St, 61327. (Mail add: PO Box 199, 61327-0199), SAN 340-4641. Tel: 815-925-7020. FAX: 815-925-7020. Web Site: www.putnamcountylibrary.org. *Dir,* Randie Dellatori; E-mail: rdellatori@putnamcountylibrary.org; Staff 4 (Non-MLS 4)
Founded 1938. Pop 6,087; Circ 38,000
Library Holdings: Bk Vols 33,000; Per Subs 40
Mem of Reaching Across Illinois Library System (RAILS)
Partic in Illinois Library & Information Network
Open Mon-Wed & Fri 9-5, Thurs 9-8, Sat 9-1
Branches: 5
GRANVILLE BRANCH, 212 S McCoy St, Granville, 61326. (Mail add: PO Box 495, Granville, 61326-0495), SAN 340-4676. Tel: 815-339-2038. FAX: 815-339-2038, 815-339-2480. *Librn,* Ann Wink
Open Tues & Sat 9-3, Wed 3-7
MAGNOLIA BRANCH, 114 N Chicago St, Magnolia, 61336. (Mail add: PO Box 167, Magnolia, 61336-0167), SAN 340-4765. Tel: 815-869-6038. FAX: 815-869-6038. *Librn,* Peggy Smith
Open Tues 3-8, Wed 4-8, Sat 9-11
MCNABB BRANCH, 322 W Main St, McNabb, 61335. (Mail add: PO Box 135, McNabb, 61336-0135). Tel: 815-882-2378. FAX: 815-882-2378. *Librn,* Marilyn Calbow
Open Mon & Sat 9-1, Wed 4-7
PUTNAM COUNTY - CONDIT BRANCH, 105 N Center St, Putnam, 60560. (Mail add: PO Box 4, Putnam, 61560-0004), SAN 340-479X. Tel: 815-437-2811. FAX: 815-437-2811. *Librn,* Sue Miller
Open Tues 9-1, Thurs 4-7, Sat 9-12
STANDARD BRANCH, 128 First St, Standard, 61363. (Mail add: PO Box 114, Standard, 61363-0217). Tel: 815-339-2471. FAX: 815-339-2471. *Librn,* Christie Biaja
Open Thurs 1-5

HENRY

P HENRY PUBLIC LIBRARY*, 702 Front St, 61537. (Mail add: PO Box 183, 61537-0183), SAN 304-2634. Tel: 309-364-2516. FAX: 309-364-2717. E-mail: henrypubliclibrary@mchsi.com. Web Site: www.henry.lib.il.us. *Dir,* Elizabeth Wild; E-mail: elizabeth@mchsi.com; *Asst Librn,* Mary Williams
Founded 1936. Pop 2,591; Circ 27,261
Library Holdings: Bk Vols 23,000; Per Subs 61
Subject Interests: Local hist
Open Mon & Fri 1-5, Tues 10-5, Wed 1-8, Thurs (Sept May) 1-5, Sat 10-3

HERRICK

P HERRICK TOWNSHIP PUBLIC LIBRARY*, 303 N Broadway, 62431. SAN 375-9482. Tel: 618-428-5223. FAX: 618-428-5222. Web Site: www.cowden-herrick.k12.il.us. *Librn,* Becky Wilson; E-mail: bewilson78@hotmail.com; Staff 1 (Non-MLS 1)
Founded 1979. Pop 687
Library Holdings: Bk Titles 10,000
Subject Interests: Genealogy
Database Vendor: OCLC FirstSearch, SirsiDynix
Mem of Illinois Heartland Library System
Open Mon & Tues 2-8, Thurs 9-5

HERRIN

P HERRIN CITY LIBRARY, 120 N 13th St, 62948-3233. SAN 304-2642. Tel: 618-942-6109. FAX: 618-942-4165. E-mail: herrincitylibrary@gmail.com. Web Site: search.herrin.lib.il.us, www.herrin.lib.il.us. *Dir/Acq Librn/Cat Mgr,* Michael Keepper; E-mail: keepperhcl@gmail.com; *Asst Dir, Asst Librn/Ch,* Irena Just; E-mail: ijusthcl@gmail.com; *Adult Serv, Circ Librn,* Kimberley Wild; E-mail: kwildhcl@gmail.com. Subject Specialists: *Am hist,* Michael Keepper; *Children's lit,* Irena Just; *Adult,* Kimberley Wild; Staff 4 (MLS 1, Non-MLS 3)
Founded 1917. Pop 12,501; Circ 75,000
May 2013-Apr 2014 Income $296,148, State $12,501, City $256,289, Locally Generated Income $27,358. Mats Exp $25,000, Books $16,000, Per/Ser (Incl. Access Fees) $5,000, AV Mat $1,000, Electronic Ref Mat (Incl. Access Fees) $2,000. Sal $128,131 (Prof $42,000)

Library Holdings: Audiobooks 211; CDs 211; DVDs 1,004; e-books 5,000; Large Print Bks 2,000; Bk Vols 50,000; Per Subs 50; Videos 1,672
Special Collections: Local History & Family Records (Herrin History Room)
Subject Interests: Local hist
Automation Activity & Vendor Info: (Acquisitions) Innovative Interfaces, Inc; (Cataloging) Innovative Interfaces, Inc; (ILL) Innovative Interfaces, Inc; (OPAC) Innovative Interfaces, Inc; (Serials) Innovative Interfaces, Inc
Database Vendor: EBSCOhost, H W Wilson, OCLC ArticleFirst, OCLC FirstSearch, OCLC WebJunction, OCLC WorldShare Interlibrary Loan
Wireless access
Function: Adult literacy prog, Archival coll, Audio & video playback equip for onsite use, Bks on cassette, Bks on CD, CD-ROM, Children's prog, Computers for patron use, Copy machines, Doc delivery serv, Electronic databases & coll, Family literacy, Fax serv, Free DVD rentals, Handicapped accessible, Homebound delivery serv, ILL available, Magnifiers for reading, Mail & tel request accepted, Music CDs, Newsp ref libr, Online cat, Online ref, Online searches, Outside serv via phone, mail, e-mail & web, OverDrive digital audio bks, Photocopying/Printing, Preschool outreach, Prog for adults, Prog for children & young adult, Pub access computers, Ref serv available, Scanner, Spoken cassettes & CDs, Spoken cassettes & DVDs, Story hour, Summer reading prog, Tax forms, Telephone ref, VCDs, VHS videos, Video lending libr, Web-catalog, Wheelchair accessible
Mem of Illinois Heartland Library System
Open Mon-Thurs 10-8, Fri 10-6, Sat 12-6
Restriction: In-house use for visitors, Non-resident fee
Friends of the Library Group

HEYWORTH

P HEYWORTH PUBLIC LIBRARY DISTRICT*, 119 E Main St, 61745. (Mail add: PO Box 469, 61745-0469), SAN 304-2650. Tel: 309-473-2313. FAX: 309-473-9253. E-mail: heylib@frontier.com. Web Site: heyworthlibrary.com. *Dir,* Beth Porter; E-mail: bethphpld@gmail.com; *Asst Librn,* Alice Gray; E-mail: aliceghpld@gmail.com; Staff 2 (Non-MLS 2)
Founded 1941. Pop 5,606; Circ 33,863
Library Holdings: Bk Titles 20,000; Bk Vols 22,329; Per Subs 102
Special Collections: Local History/Genealogy Coll. Oral History
Automation Activity & Vendor Info: (Cataloging) SirsiDynix; (Circulation) SirsiDynix; (ILL) OCLC FirstSearch
Database Vendor: OCLC FirstSearch, OCLC WebJunction, Overdrive, Inc, Wilson - Wilson Web
Wireless access
Function: Adult bk club, Audiobks via web, Bks on CD, Children's prog, Computers for patron use, Copy machines, e-mail serv, Exhibits, Fax serv, Genealogy discussion group, Handicapped accessible, ILL available, Mail & tel request accepted, Microfiche/film & reading machines, Music CDs, Online cat, Online searches, OverDrive digital audio bks, Photocopying/Printing, Preschool reading prog, Prog for adults, Prog for children & young adult, Summer reading prog, Tax forms, Wheelchair accessible
Mem of Reaching Across Illinois Library System (RAILS)
Open Mon & Thurs 10-8, Tues 1-8 (10-5 Summer), Wed & Fri 10-5, Sat 10-4

HIGHLAND

P LOUIS LATZER MEMORIAL PUBLIC LIBRARY*, 1001 Ninth St, 62249. SAN 304-2669. Tel: 618-654-5066. FAX: 618-654-1324. E-mail: hie@highlandillibrary.org. Web Site: www.highlandillibrary.org. *Dir,* Angela Kim; E-mail: angelak@highlandillibrary.org; *Ch,* Kay Schuette
Founded 1929. Pop 10,500; Circ 110,000
Library Holdings: Bk Vols 40,000; Per Subs 110
Wireless access
Mem of Illinois Heartland Library System
Partic in Health Sci Librn of Ill (HSLI); OCLC-LVIS
Special Services for the Blind - Rec of textbk mat
Open Mon & Wed 9-6, Tues & Thurs 9-8, Fri 9-5, Sat 9-3
Friends of the Library Group

HIGHLAND PARK

R CONGREGATION SOLEL LIBRARY*, 1301 Clavey Rd, 60035. SAN 304-2677. Tel: 847-433-3555. FAX: 847-433-3573. E-mail: soleloffice@solel.org. Web Site: www.solel.org/learning/library. *Exec Dir,* Sharon Diaz
Founded 1963
Library Holdings: Bk Titles 13,000; Bk Vols 15,000; Per Subs 40
Special Collections: Judaica (art, music)
Subject Interests: Biblical studies, Comparative relig, Holocaust, Israel, Jewish hist & lit
Automation Activity & Vendor Info: (Cataloging) Follett Software
Database Vendor: Surpass

P HIGHLAND PARK PUBLIC LIBRARY*, 494 Laurel Ave, 60035-2690. SAN 304-2685. Tel: 847-432-0216. Reference Tel: 847-681-7031. Administration Tel: 847-432-0216, Ext 119. FAX: 847-432-9139. Administration FAX: 847-681-7027. TDD: 847-432-7674. E-mail: hppla@hplibrary.org. Web Site: www.hplibrary.org. *Exec Dir,* Jane Conway; E-mail: jconway@hplibrary.org; *Circ Mgr,* Patricia Irvin; *Adult Serv,* Julia Johnas; E-mail: jjohnas@hplibrary.org; *AV,* Sylvana Osorio; E-mail: sosorio@hplibrary.org; *Ch Serv,* Linda Wicher; E-mail: lwicher@hplibrary.org; *Computer Serv,* Donna Beer; E-mail: dbeer@hplibrary.org; *Ref,* Gail Juris; E-mail: gjuris@nsls.info; *Tech Serv,* Bin Zhao; E-mail: bzhao@hplibrary.org; Staff 89 (MLS 20, Non-MLS 69)
Founded 1887. Pop 30,038; Circ 615,070
Library Holdings: AV Mats 27,049; CDs 15,070; Bk Vols 194,153; Per Subs 350
Subject Interests: Local hist
Automation Activity & Vendor Info: (Acquisitions) SirsiDynix; (Cataloging) SirsiDynix; (Circulation) SirsiDynix; (OPAC) SirsiDynix
Database Vendor: Baker & Taylor, EBSCOhost, Gale Cengage Learning, Grolier Online, OCLC FirstSearch, OCLC WorldShare Interlibrary Loan, ProQuest, ReferenceUSA, SirsiDynix
Wireless access
Publications: Laurels (Newsletter)
Special Services for the Deaf - TDD equip
Open Mon-Thurs 9-9, Fri 9-6, Sat 9-5, Sun 1-5
Friends of the Library Group

R NORTH SUBURBAN SYNAGOGUE BETH EL*, Maxwell Abbell Library, 1175 Sheridan Rd, 60035. SAN 304-2693. Tel: 847-432-8900. FAX: 847-432-9242. E-mail: nssbe@nssbethel.org. Web Site: www.nssbethel.org. *Librn,* Rachel Kamin; Staff 3 (MLS 1, Non-MLS 2)
Founded 1959
Library Holdings: Bk Titles 20,000; Per Subs 85
Special Collections: Judaica Video Coll
Subject Interests: Judaica (lit or hist of Jews)
Automation Activity & Vendor Info: (Cataloging) Follett Software
Open Mon-Thurs 8:30-5, Fri 8:30-3

HIGHWOOD

P HIGHWOOD PUBLIC LIBRARY*, 102 Highwood Ave, 60040-1597. SAN 304-2707. Tel: 847-432-5404. FAX: 847-432-5806. E-mail: info@highwoodlibrary.org. Web Site: www.highwoodlibrary.org. *Dir,* John Mitchell; E-mail: director@highwoodlibrary.org
Founded 1977
Wireless access
Open Mon-Thurs 12-8, Fri & Sat 12-5, Sun 1-5

HILLSBORO

S GRAHAM CORRECTIONAL CENTER LIBRARY*, PO Box 499, 62049. SAN 376-0871. Tel: 217-532-6961, Ext 2705. *In Charge,* Position Currently Open
Library Holdings: High Interest/Low Vocabulary Bk Vols 50; Large Print Bks 50; Bk Titles 15,000; Per Subs 25

P HILLSBORO PUBLIC LIBRARY*, 214 School St, 62049-1547. SAN 304-2715. Tel: 217-532-3055. FAX: 217-532-6813. E-mail: hillsboro2@consolidated.net. Web Site: www.hillsborolibrary.org. *Dir,* Cheryl J Sale; *Asst Dir,* Patty Paden; *Evening Mgr,* Harry Meyer
Pop 4,300; Circ 45,000
Library Holdings: Bk Titles 18,000; Bk Vols 20,000; Per Subs 55
Subject Interests: Genealogy
Automation Activity & Vendor Info: (Acquisitions) Follett Software; (Cataloging) Follett Software; (Circulation) Follett Software
Open Mon & Fri 9:30-5, Tues-Thurs 9:30-7:30, Sat 9:30-1

HILLSDALE

P MOORE MEMORIAL LIBRARY DISTRICT*, Hillsdale Library, 509 Main St, 61257-0325. (Mail add: PO Box 325, 61257-0325), SAN 304-2723. Tel: 309-658-2666. FAX: 309-658-2666. Web Site: hillsdale.lib.il.us. *Dir,* Lois Black; E-mail: mmemrl@mchsi.com
Founded 1942. Pop 864; Circ 3,900
Library Holdings: Large Print Bks 120; Bk Vols 6,100; Per Subs 20; Talking Bks 70
Mem of Reaching Across Illinois Library System (RAILS)
Open Mon 9-12 & 2-8, Tues 2-8, Wed 2-6, Thurs & Sat 9-Noon

HILLSIDE

P HILLSIDE PUBLIC LIBRARY*, 405 N Hillside Ave, 60162-1295. SAN 304-2731. Tel: 708-449-7510. FAX: 708-449-6119. Web Site: www.hillsidelibrary.org. *Dir,* Lori Anne Craft; *Circ,* Kathy Saleta; *Ref Serv,* Jane Chesham; E-mail: jchesham@hillsidelibrary.org; *Tech Serv,* Carmen Parker; *Youth Serv,* Maura McKee; E-mail: mmckee@hillsidelibrary.org; Staff 15 (MLS 4, Non-MLS 11)

Founded 1962. Pop 8,155; Circ 85,056
Library Holdings: AV Mats 4,953; Bk Vols 46,364; Per Subs 142
Automation Activity & Vendor Info: (Cataloging) Innovative Interfaces, Inc; (Circulation) Innovative Interfaces, Inc; (ILL) Innovative Interfaces, Inc; (OPAC) Innovative Interfaces, Inc
Database Vendor: EBSCOhost, Facts on File, Gale Cengage Learning, Greenwood Publishing Group, Grolier Online, infoUSA, Ingram Library Services, Innovative Interfaces, Inc, LearningExpress, OCLC ArticleFirst, OCLC FirstSearch, OCLC WorldShare Interlibrary Loan, ProQuest, World Book Online
Wireless access
Function: AV serv, Doc delivery serv, Handicapped accessible, ILL available, Photocopying/Printing, Prog for adults, Prog for children & young adult, Ref serv available, Summer reading prog, Telephone ref, Wheelchair accessible
Publications: Newsletter
Open Mon-Thurs 10-9, Fri & Sat 10-5, Sun (Winter) 12-4
Friends of the Library Group

HINCKLEY

P HINCKLEY PUBLIC LIBRARY DISTRICT*, 100 N Maple St, 60520. SAN 304-2758. Tel: 815-286-3220. FAX: 815-286-3664. Web Site: www.hinckley.lib.il.us. *Dir,* Shirley Wilhelmsen; E-mail: director@hinckley.lib.il.us; *Ch,* Lynne Stein; E-mail: lynnes@hinckley.lib.il.us; Staff 2 (Non-MLS 2)
Founded 1913. Pop 2,912; Circ 28,070
Jul 2007-Jun 2008 Income $168,366, State $3,711, Locally Generated Income $145,552, Other $19,103. Mats Exp $13,727, Books $11,687, AV Mat $2,040. Sal Prof $88,382
Library Holdings: Audiobooks 351; DVDs 962; e-books 839; Music Scores 240; Bk Vols 17,181; Per Subs 47
Automation Activity & Vendor Info: (Acquisitions) SIRSI WorkFlows; (Cataloging) SirsiDynix; (Circulation) SirsiDynix
Database Vendor: OCLC FirstSearch, OCLC WorldShare Interlibrary Loan
Wireless access
Function: Adult bk club, Bks on CD, Children's prog, Computers for patron use, Copy machines, Fax serv, Homebound delivery serv, ILL available, Music CDs, Online cat, Photocopying/Printing, Spoken cassettes & CDs, Story hour, Summer reading prog, Tax forms, VHS videos, Wheelchair accessible
Mem of Reaching Across Illinois Library System (RAILS)
Open Mon 2-8, Tues 10-6, Wed 10-8, Thurs & Fri 2-6, Sat 9-2
Friends of the Library Group

HINES

GM DEPARTMENT OF VETERANS AFFAIRS*, Library Service, PO Box 5000-142D, 60141-5142. SAN 304-2774. Tel: 708-202-2000. FAX: 708-202-2719. *Chief Librn,* John Cline; E-mail: john.cline@med.va.gov; *Librn,* Kathleen Kirk; *Libr Tech,* Charles Birchard; *Libr Tech,* Towanna Jelks; Staff 6 (MLS 2, Non-MLS 4)
Library Holdings: Bk Vols 9,500
Subject Interests: Allied health
Automation Activity & Vendor Info: (Cataloging) Follett Software; (Circulation) Follett Software
Database Vendor: OVID Technologies
Partic in Docline; OCLC Online Computer Library Center, Inc; Veterans Affairs Libr Network (VALNET)
Open Mon-Fri 8-4:30
Restriction: Non-circulating to the pub, Staff use only

HINSDALE

M ADVENTIST HINSDALE HOSPITAL*, Health Sciences Library, 120 N Oak St, 60521. SAN 304-2790. Tel: 630-856-7230. FAX: 630-856-7239. Web Site: www.keepingyouwell.com. *Mgr,* Bonnie Arnold; Staff 3 (MLS 1, Non-MLS 2)
Library Holdings: Bk Vols 4,000; Per Subs 230; Spec Interest Per Sub 10
Special Collections: E G White Coll
Subject Interests: Med, Nursing, Seventh Day Adventists
Automation Activity & Vendor Info: (Cataloging) EOS International; (Circulation) EOS International; (OPAC) EOS International
Database Vendor: OCLC FirstSearch, OCLC WorldShare Interlibrary Loan, OVID Technologies
Wireless access
Mem of Reaching Across Illinois Library System (RAILS)
Partic in Chicago & South Consortium; Illinois Library & Information Network; National Network of Libraries of Medicine Greater Midwest Region; OCLC-LVIS
Open Mon-Thurs 8-5, Fri 8-3

P HINSDALE PUBLIC LIBRARY, 20 E Maple St, 60521. SAN 304-2782. Tel: 630-986-1976. Reference Tel: 630-986-1982. FAX: 630-986-9654. E-mail: adultservices@hinsdalelibrary.info. Web Site: www.hinsdalelibrary.info. *Exec Dir,* Karen Kleckner Keefe; E-mail: kkeefe@hinsdalelibrary.info; *Adult Serv Mgr, Asst Dir,* Michaela Haberkern; E-mail: mhaberkern@hinsdalelibrary.info; *Circ Serv Mgr,* Pilar Shaker; E-mail: pshaker@hinsdalelibrary.info; *Mkt Mgr, Outreach Mgr,* Molly Castor; E-mail: mcastor@hinsdalelibrary.info; *Mat Mgt Mgr,* Ellen Smith; E-mail: esmith@hinsdalelibrary.info; Staff 46 (MLS 12, Non-MLS 34)
Founded 1893. Pop 16,594; Circ 339,180
Library Holdings: Bk Vols 125,934; Per Subs 295
Automation Activity & Vendor Info: (Circulation) Innovative Interfaces, Inc; (OPAC) Innovative Interfaces, Inc
Database Vendor: Gale Cengage Learning, OCLC FirstSearch, ProQuest
Wireless access
Publications: Beyond Books (Newsletter)
Special Services for the Deaf - TTY equip
Open Mon-Thurs 9-9, Fri 9-6, Sat 9-5, Sun 12-6
Friends of the Library Group

HODGKINS

P HODGKINS PUBLIC LIBRARY DISTRICT, 6500 Wenz Ave, 60525. SAN 321-4613. Tel: 708-579-1844. FAX: 708-579-1896. E-mail: contactus@hodgkinslibrary.org. Web Site: www.hodgkinslibrary.org. *Dir,* Samantha Millsap; *Ch Serv,* Carrie Cameron; Staff 1 (MLS 1)
Founded 1975. Pop 2,134
Library Holdings: Bk Vols 40,000; Per Subs 40
Wireless access
Mem of Reaching Across Illinois Library System (RAILS)
Open Mon-Fri 10-8, Sat 10-4

HOMER

P HOMER COMMUNITY LIBRARY*, 500 E Second St, 61849. SAN 304-2812. Tel: 217-896-2121. E-mail: homerlibrarian@gmail.com. Web Site: homervillage.com/HomerLibrary.htm. *Head Librn,* Christine Cunningham; Staff 0.7 (Non-MLS 0.7)
Founded 1971. Pop 1,200; Circ 18,000
Library Holdings: Audiobooks 200; AV Mats 990; CDs 300; DVDs 1,200; Large Print Bks 100; Bk Titles 18,000; Per Subs 27; Videos 75
Database Vendor: OCLC FirstSearch
Wireless access
Mem of Illinois Heartland Library System
Open Mon, Tues, Thurs & Fri 2-7, Wed 9-2, Sat 10-2

HOMER GLEN

P HOMER TOWNSHIP PUBLIC LIBRARY DISTRICT*, 14320 W 151st St, 60491. SAN 375-9490. Tel: 708-301-7908. FAX: 708-301-4535. Web Site: www.homerlibrary.org. *Exec Dir,* Sheree Kozel-La Ha; E-mail: sheree@homerlibrary.org; *Asst Dir,* Sara McCambridge; E-mail: sara@homerlibrary.org; *Dir, Adult Serv,* Alex Tyle-Annen; E-mail: alex@homerlibrary.org; *Youth Serv Dir,* Kathryn Mitchell; *Bus Mgr, Tech Serv,* Carol McSweeney; *Circ Supvr,* Jody Studer; E-mail: jody@homerlibrary.org; *Outreach Serv,* Jody Olivieri; E-mail: jolivieri@homerlibrary.org. Subject Specialists: *Admin, Grants,* Sheree Kozel-La Ha; Staff 30 (MLS 6, Non-MLS 24)
Founded 1982. Pop 40,000; Circ 267,340
Library Holdings: Audiobooks 5,000; DVDs 2,000; e-books 2,517; Electronic Media & Resources 50; Bk Titles 100,339; Per Subs 136; Talking Bks 5,000
Automation Activity & Vendor Info: (Acquisitions) SirsiDynix; (Cataloging) SirsiDynix; (Circulation) SirsiDynix; (Course Reserve) SirsiDynix; (ILL) SirsiDynix; (Media Booking) SirsiDynix; (OPAC) SirsiDynix; (Serials) SirsiDynix
Database Vendor: OCLC FirstSearch, ProQuest
Mem of Reaching Across Illinois Library System (RAILS)
Special Services for the Blind - Bks on cassette; Bks on CD; Large print bks; Magnifiers; Talking bks; ZoomText magnification & reading software
Open Mon-Thurs 8:30am-9pm, Fri 8:30-5, Sat 8:30-4, Sun 4-8
Friends of the Library Group
Bookmobiles: 1. Mgr, Jody Olivieri

HOMETOWN

P HOMETOWN PUBLIC LIBRARY, Jack R Ladwig Memorial Library, 4331 Southwest Hwy, 60456-1161. SAN 304-2820. Tel: 708-636-0997. FAX: 708-636-8127. E-mail: hometownlibrary@comcast.net. *Head Librn,* Annette Selmeister; *Asst Librn,* Eileen Greene
Founded 1956. Pop 4,349; Circ 25,814
Library Holdings: Bk Vols 25,186; Per Subs 480
Subject Interests: Hist, Local hist, Relig, Soc sci & issues
Mem of Reaching Across Illinois Library System (RAILS)
Open Mon, Wed & Thurs 1-7, Tues 9-9, Fri 1-5, Sat 10-2

HOMEWOOD

P HOMEWOOD PUBLIC LIBRARY*, 17917 Dixie Hwy, 60430-1703. SAN 304-2839. Tel: 708-798-0121. Reference Tel: 708-798-0121, Ext 216. FAX: 708-798-0662. E-mail: hws@notices.swanlibraries.net. Web Site: homewoodlibrary.org. *Adminr,* Amy Crump; Tel: 708-798-0121, Ext 214, E-mail: amyc@homewoodlibrary.net; *Dir, Tech Serv,* Claudia Miller; *Adult Serv, Mgr,* Judi Wolinsky; Staff 37 (MLS 7, Non-MLS 30)
Founded 1927. Pop 19,274; Circ 390,000
Library Holdings: Bk Vols 161,000; Per Subs 260
Automation Activity & Vendor Info: (Acquisitions) Innovative Interfaces, Inc; (Cataloging) Innovative Interfaces, Inc; (Circulation) Innovative Interfaces, Inc; (Course Reserve) Innovative Interfaces, Inc; (ILL) Innovative Interfaces, Inc; (Media Booking) Innovative Interfaces, Inc; (OPAC) Innovative Interfaces, Inc; (Serials) Innovative Interfaces, Inc
Database Vendor: Baker & Taylor, Checkpoint Systems, Inc, Gale Cengage Learning, Innovative Interfaces, Inc, Newsbank, OCLC FirstSearch, OCLC WorldShare Interlibrary Loan
Wireless access
Publications: Homewood Hi-Lites; Novel News
Mem of Metropolitan Library System
Open Mon-Thurs 9-9, Fri & Sat 9-5
Friends of the Library Group

HOOPESTON

P HOOPESTON PUBLIC LIBRARY*, 110 N Fourth St, 60942-1422. SAN 304-2847. Tel: 217-283-6711. FAX: 217-283-7077. TDD: 217-283-6999. E-mail: info@hooplib.org. Web Site: www.hooplib.org. *Dir,* Linda Mitchell
Founded 1898. Pop 10,838; Circ 55,412
Library Holdings: Bk Vols 38,000; Per Subs 100
Automation Activity & Vendor Info: (Acquisitions) Horizon; (Cataloging) Horizon; (Circulation) Horizon; (Course Reserve) Horizon; (ILL) Horizon; (Media Booking) Horizon; (OPAC) Horizon; (Serials) Horizon
Mem of Illinois Heartland Library System
Open Mon-Thurs 9:30-8, Fri 9:30-6, Sat 9:30-3
Friends of the Library Group

HUDSON

P HUDSON AREA PUBLIC LIBRARY DISTRICT*, 104 Pearl St, 61748. (Mail add: PO Box 461, 61748-0461), SAN 375-9504. Tel: 309-726-1103. FAX: 309-726-1646. E-mail: hudsonarealibrary@yahoo.com. Web Site: www.hudsonarealibrary.com. *Dir, Libr Serv,* Kari J Garman; Staff 8 (MLS 1, Non-MLS 7)
Founded 1992. Pop 2,985; Circ 39,006
Library Holdings: Audiobooks 965; AV Mats 566; CDs 200; DVDs 1,500; e-books 837; Bk Vols 18,512; Per Subs 49; Videos 33
Special Collections: Hudson History Room
Automation Activity & Vendor Info: (Circulation) SIRSI WorkFlows; (OPAC) SIRSI WorkFlows
Database Vendor: EBSCOhost, OCLC FirstSearch, TumbleBookLibrary, Wilson - Wilson Web
Wireless access
Function: Adult bk club, Archival coll, Audiobks via web, Bks on CD, Children's prog, Computers for patron use, Copy machines, Electronic databases & coll, Fax serv, Free DVD rentals, Handicapped accessible, Holiday prog, ILL available, Mail & tel request accepted, Music CDs, Notary serv, Online cat, Outside serv via phone, mail, e-mail & web, OverDrive digital audio bks, Prog for adults, Prog for children & young adult, Pub access computers, Ref serv in person, Scanner, Spoken cassettes & CDs, Story hour, Summer & winter reading prog, Summer reading prog, Teen prog, Telephone ref, VHS videos
Mem of Reaching Across Illinois Library System (RAILS)
Open Mon-Thurs 10-8, Fri 10-6, Sat 10-2

HUNTLEY

P HUNTLEY AREA PUBLIC LIBRARY DISTRICT*, 11000 Ruth Rd, 60142-7155. SAN 375-9512. Tel: 847-669-5386. Circulation Tel: 847-669-5386, Ext 10. Reference Tel: 847-669-5386, Ext 21. FAX: 847-669-5439. Web Site: www.huntleylibrary.org. *Dir,* Virginia Maravilla; E-mail: vmaravilla@huntleylibrary.org; *Head, Pub Serv,* Rosie Lukas; E-mail: rlukas@huntleylibrary.org; *Head, Tech Serv,* Jo Smolzer; E-mail: jsmolzer@huntleylibrary.org; Staff 31 (MLS 8, Non-MLS 23)
Founded 1989. Pop 50,000; Circ 468,908
Jul 2006-Jun 2007 Income $2,365,990, State $26,017, Locally Generated Income $2,339,973. Mats Exp $204,490, Books $120,730, Per/Ser (Incl. Access Fees) $19,914, AV Mat $57,523, Electronic Ref Mat (Incl. Access Fees) $6,323
Library Holdings: AV Mats 4,247; CDs 5,585; DVDs 3,869; Electronic Media & Resources 1,365; Large Print Bks 1,902; Bk Vols 70,921; Per Subs 188; Videos 3,372
Subject Interests: Ill, Local hist
Database Vendor: EBSCO Auto Repair Reference, Grolier Online, H W Wilson, OCLC ArticleFirst, OCLC FirstSearch, OCLC WorldShare Interlibrary Loan, Overdrive, Inc, ReferenceUSA, SirsiDynix
Function: Audiobks via web, AV serv, Bk club(s), Bks on cassette, Bks on CD, Children's prog, Computer training, Computers for patron use, Copy machines, Electronic databases & coll, ILL available, Music CDs, Online cat, Online ref, OverDrive digital audio bks, Photocopying/Printing, Preschool outreach, Prog for adults, Prog for children & young adult, Pub access computers, Ref serv available, Scanner, Summer reading prog, Tax forms, Teen prog, Telephone ref, VHS videos, Web-catalog, Wheelchair accessible
Publications: Library Links (Newsletter)
Partic in Cooperative Computer Services - CCS
Open Mon-Thurs 9-8, Fri 9-6, Sat 9-5, Sun (Sept-June) 12-4
Friends of the Library Group

ILLIOPOLIS

P ILLIOPOLIS-NIANTIC PUBLIC LIBRARY DISTRICT*, Sixth & Mary Sts, 62539. SAN 304-2863. Tel: 217-486-5561. FAX: 217-486-7811. Web Site: www.illiopolisniantic.lib.il.us. *Libr Dir,* Shelley Perry; *Ch Serv,* Mary Langloss; *Ch Serv,* Tari Parr
Founded 1935. Pop 2,198; Circ 19,739
Library Holdings: Bk Vols 16,977; Per Subs 50
Special Collections: War Plants Located at Illiopolis During WWII
Automation Activity & Vendor Info: (Acquisitions) Horizon; (Cataloging) Horizon; (Circulation) Horizon; (ILL) Horizon; (OPAC) Horizon; (Serials) Horizon
Wireless access
Mem of Illinois Heartland Library System
Open Mon & Fri 1-5, Tues & Thurs 1-8, Wed 10-5, Sat 10-4

INA

S ILLINOIS DEPARTMENT OF CORRECTIONS*, Big Muddy River Correctional Center Library, 251 N Illinois Hwy 37, 62846-2419. (Mail add: PO Box 1000, 62846-1000). Tel: 618-437-5300, Ext 467. FAX: 618-437-5627. Web Site: www.idoc.state.il.us. *Libr Mgr,* Jennifer Wilson
Library Holdings: Bk Vols 35,000
Open Tues-Fri 11-12, 1-2:30 & 5-7

J REND LAKE COLLEGE*, Learning Resource Center, 468 N Ken Gray Pkwy, 62846. SAN 304-2871. Tel: 618-437-5321. Circulation Tel: 618-437-5321, Ext 1308. Reference Tel: 618-437-5321, Ext 1276. Administration Tel: 618-437-5321, Ext 1277. Automation Services Tel: 618-437-5321, Ext 1249. FAX: 618-437-5677. Web Site: www.rlc.edu/electronic-library, www.rlc.edu/lrc-home. *Ref Librn,* Beth Mandrell; E-mail: mandrell@rlc.edu; *Coordr, Tech Serv,* Sandy West; E-mail: wests@rlc.edu; *Circ,* Kim Davis; E-mail: davis@rlc.edu. Subject Specialists: *Info literacy,* Beth Mandrell; Staff 3 (MLS 2, Non-MLS 1)
Founded 1956. Enrl 2,400; Fac 64; Highest Degree: Associate
Jul 2011-Jun 2012 Income $310,146. Mats Exp $103,310, Books $18,900, Per/Ser (Incl. Access Fees) $10,900, AV Mat $21,100, Electronic Ref Mat (Incl. Access Fees) $52,410. Sal $157,027 (Prof $84,279)
Library Holdings: Audiobooks 129; AV Mats 4,025; CDs 198; DVDs 774; e-books 2,074; Electronic Media & Resources 71; Large Print Bks 145; Bk Titles 21,252; Per Subs 123; Videos 741
Automation Activity & Vendor Info: (Cataloging) SirsiDynix; (Circulation) SirsiDynix; (ILL) OCLC Online; (OPAC) SirsiDynix; (Serials) SirsiDynix
Database Vendor: CQ Press, EBSCOhost, LexisNexis, OCLC FirstSearch, ProQuest
Wireless access
Function: Distance learning, Doc delivery serv, e-mail & chat
Mem of Illinois Heartland Library System
Partic in Consortium of Academic & Research Libraries in Illinois; Network of Illinois Learning Resources in Community Colleges; SILRC
Special Services for the Blind - Large print bks; Magnifiers
Open Mon-Thurs 7:30am-8pm, Fri 7:30-4

ITASCA

P ITASCA COMMUNITY LIBRARY*, 500 W Irving Park Rd, 60143. SAN 304-288X. Tel: 630-773-1699. FAX: 630-773-1707. E-mail: itascal@linc.lib.il.us. Web Site: www.itasca.lib.il.us. *Dir,* Tuki Sathaye; E-mail: tsathaye@linc.lib.il.us; *Head, Adult Serv,* Soon Har Tan; *Head, Circ,* Donna Reynertson; *Head, Youth Serv,* Jackie Stork; *Bus Mgr,* Izabela Wnuk; *Outreach Mgr,* Colleen Blanchard
Founded 1957. Pop 8,302; Circ 123,781
Library Holdings: Bk Vols 68,521; Per Subs 191
Special Collections: Learning Games Library; Parent Teacher Texts
Automation Activity & Vendor Info: (Cataloging) SirsiDynix; (Circulation) SirsiDynix; (OPAC) SirsiDynix
Database Vendor: EBSCOhost, OCLC FirstSearch
Mem of Reaching Across Illinois Library System (RAILS)
Partic in Libr Integrated Network Consortium

Open Mon-Thurs 9-9, Fri & Sat 9-5, Sun (Winter) 1-5
Friends of the Library Group

S NATIONAL SAFETY COUNCIL LIBRARY*, 1121 Spring Lake Dr, 60143. SAN 303-9870. Tel: 630-285-1121, Ext 2199. FAX: 630-285-0765. E-mail: library@nsc.org. Web Site: www.nsc.org. *Mgr, Libr Serv,* Position Currently Open; Staff 3 (MLS 3)
Founded 1915
Jul 2009-Jun 2010. Mats Exp $57,200, Books $13,000, Per/Ser (Incl. Access Fees) $28,000, Micro $1,000, Electronic Ref Mat (Incl. Access Fees) $15,000, Presv $200. Sal $170,000 (Prof $170,000)
Library Holdings: Bk Titles 171,000; Per Subs 90
Subject Interests: Accident prevention, Home & commun safety, Occupational health, Occupational safety, Traffic (safety)
Automation Activity & Vendor Info: (Cataloging) Inmagic, Inc.; (OPAC) Inmagic, Inc.
Database Vendor: Dialog, EBSCO Information Services, Elsevier, Gale Cengage Learning
Publications: Historical Index to the Occupational Safety & Health Data Sheets
Mem of Reaching Across Illinois Library System (RAILS)
Partic in Illinois Library & Information Network
Open Mon-Fri 8:30-4:45

JACKSONVILLE

C ILLINOIS COLLEGE*, Schewe Library, 245 Park St, 62650. (Mail add: 1101 W College Ave, 62650-2299), SAN 304-2898. Tel: 217-245-3020. Circulation Tel: 217-245-3021. Reference Tel: 217-245-3022. Automation Services Tel: 217-245-3023. FAX: 217-245-3082. E-mail: schewe@ic.edu. Web Site: www.ic.edu/library.htm. *Dir,* Martin H Gallas; E-mail: gallas@ic.edu; *Tech Serv Librn/Syst Adminr,* Beth Bala; E-mail: beth.bala@ic.edu; *Bibliog Instruction/Ref,* W Michael Westbrook; E-mail: mwestbro@ic.edu; Staff 6 (MLS 3, Non-MLS 3)
Founded 1829. Enrl 894; Fac 75; Highest Degree: Bachelor
Library Holdings: AV Mats 12,490; Bk Titles 147,000; Bk Vols 171,500; Per Subs 600
Special Collections: Civil War Coll; Lincoln Coll; Local History Coll
Automation Activity & Vendor Info: (Acquisitions) Ex Libris Group; (Cataloging) Ex Libris Group; (Circulation) Ex Libris Group; (Course Reserve) Ex Libris Group; (ILL) Ex Libris Group; (OPAC) Ex Libris Group; (Serials) Ex Libris Group
Database Vendor: ACM (Association for Computing Machinery), American Chemical Society, American Mathematical Society, American Psychological Association (APA), Annual Reviews, BioOne, EBSCO WebFeat, EBSCO Information Services, EBSCOhost, Ex Libris Group, Gale Cengage Learning, H W Wilson, JSTOR, LexisNexis, Modern Language Association, OCLC ArticleFirst, OCLC WorldShare Interlibrary Loan, ProQuest, Wilson - Wilson Web
Wireless access
Mem of Reaching Across Illinois Library System (RAILS)
Partic in Center for Research Libraries; OCLC Online Computer Library Center, Inc
Open Mon-Thurs 8am-Midnight, Fri 8-7, Sat 1-5, Sun 1-Midnight
Friends of the Library Group

S ILLINOIS DEPARTMENT OF CORRECTIONS*, Jacksonville Correctional Center Library, 2268 E Morton Ave, 62650-9347. SAN 375-5347. Tel: 217-245-1481, Ext 334. FAX: 217-245-1481, Ext 324. Web Site: www.idoc.state.il.us. *Librn I,* Susan Crowfoot; Staff 1 (MLS 1)
Founded 1984
Library Holdings: Bks on Deafness & Sign Lang 10; High Interest/Low Vocabulary Bk Vols 45; Large Print Bks 40; Bk Titles 5,621; Bk Vols 5,669; Per Subs 12
Special Collections: Federal/State Statutory & Case Law Coll; Self-Help Legal Books
Mem of Reaching Across Illinois Library System (RAILS)
Special Services for the Deaf - Bks on deafness & sign lang; TDD equip
Special Services for the Blind - Talking bks
Open Mon-Fri 7-3
Restriction: Inmate patrons, facility staff & vols direct access. All others through ILL only, Restricted access

S ILLINOIS SCHOOL FOR THE DEAF*, Library for the Deaf, 125 Webster, 62650. SAN 326-9477. Tel: 217-479-4240. FAX: 217-479-4244. Web Site: www.morgan.k12.il.us/isd. *Dir,* Nancy Kelly-Jones; E-mail: nancy.kelly-jones@illinois.gov; *Coordr,* Dave Cook, III; Tel: 217-479-4241, E-mail: dave.cook@illinois.gov; *Tech Serv,* Mike Aubry; E-mail: mike.aubry@illinois.gov; Staff 5 (Non-MLS 5)
Library Holdings: Bks on Deafness & Sign Lang 1,020; High Interest/Low Vocabulary Bk Vols 4,000; Bk Titles 15,050; Bk Vols 15,150; Per Subs 50
Subject Interests: Deaf educ, Deafness, Educ, Sign lang
Automation Activity & Vendor Info: (Cataloging) Follett Software; (Circulation) Follett Software; (OPAC) Follett Software
Database Vendor: OCLC FirstSearch, TLC (The Library Corporation)
Function: ILL available
Publications: Sights & Sounds
Special Services for the Deaf - Captioned film dep; Staff with knowledge of sign lang; TDD equip; TTY equip
Open Mon-Fri 8-3

S ILLINOIS SCHOOL FOR THE VISUALLY IMPAIRED LIBRARY*, 658 E State St, 62650-2184. SAN 326-9582. Tel: 217-479-4400, Ext 4471. FAX: 217-479-4479. Web Site: www.morgan.k12.il.us/isvi. *Libr Assoc,* Nancy Shive; Staff 1 (Non-MLS 1)
Library Holdings: Bk Titles 29,500; Per Subs 40; Talking Bks 1,500; Videos 450
Subject Interests: Blindness, Spec educ
Mem of Reaching Across Illinois Library System (RAILS)
Special Services for the Blind - Accessible computers; Aids for in-house use; Assistive/Adapted tech devices, equip & products; Audio mat; Audiovision-a radio reading serv; BiFolkal kits; Bks & mags in Braille, on rec, tape & cassette; Bks available with recordings
Open Mon-Fri 8-4:30

S JACKSONVILLE DEVELOPMENTAL CENTER LIBRARY*, 1201 S Main St, 62650-3396. SAN 304-2901. FAX: 217-479-2117. *Librn,* Jill Mayberry
Library Holdings: Bk Vols 225; Per Subs 25

P JACKSONVILLE PUBLIC LIBRARY, 201 W College Ave, 62650-2497. SAN 304-291X. Tel: 217-243-5435. FAX: 217-243-2182. TDD: 217-245-5022. Web Site: www.jaxpl.org. *Dir,* Chris Ashmore; E-mail: cashmore@jaxpl.org; *Asst Dir, Circ Supvr,* Kim Irvin; E-mail: kirvin@jaxpl.org; *Outreach Serv Librn,* Diane Hollendonner; E-mail: outreach201@hotmail.com; *Youth Serv Librn,* Cindy Boehlke; Staff 5 (MLS 3, Non-MLS 2)
Founded 1889. Pop 19,939; Circ 120,000
Library Holdings: AV Mats 7,842; Bk Vols 90,838; Per Subs 100; Talking Bks 4,112
Special Collections: Morgan County History
Automation Activity & Vendor Info: (Acquisitions) TLC (The Library Corporation); (Cataloging) TLC (The Library Corporation); (Circulation) TLC (The Library Corporation); (ILL) OCLC FirstSearch; (OPAC) TLC (The Library Corporation); (Serials) OCLC FirstSearch
Database Vendor: OCLC FirstSearch, TLC (The Library Corporation)
Wireless access
Function: Adult bk club, Chess club, Computer training, Copy machines, Doc delivery serv, e-mail serv, Handicapped accessible, Home delivery & serv to Sr ctr & nursing homes, Homebound delivery serv, ILL available, Mail & tel request accepted, Prog for children & young adult, Ref serv available, Senior computer classes, Serves mentally handicapped consumers, Spoken cassettes & CDs, Spoken cassettes & DVDs, Summer reading prog, VHS videos, Wheelchair accessible
Special Services for the Deaf - Bks on deafness & sign lang; Closed caption videos; TTY equip
Special Services for the Blind - Assistive/Adapted tech devices, equip & products; Audio mat; Bks on cassette; Bks on CD; Computer with voice synthesizer for visually impaired persons; Extensive large print coll; Home delivery serv; Large print bks; Talking bks
Open Mon-Thurs 9-9, Fri 9-6, Sat 9-5
Friends of the Library Group

C MACMURRAY COLLEGE*, Henry Pfeiffer Library, 447 E College Ave, 62650-2510. SAN 304-2928. Tel: 217-479-7110. FAX: 217-245-5214. Web Site: www.mac.edu/academ/lib.html. *Dir,* Susan Eilering; Tel: 217-479-7106, E-mail: susan.eilering@mac.edu; *Ref & Pub Serv Librn,* Jake Magnuson; Tel: 217-479-7105, E-mail: jake.magnuson@mac.edu; *Circ & ILL Mgr,* Dee Ann Roome; Tel: 217-479-7111, E-mail: deeann.roome@mac.edu; Staff 4 (MLS 3, Non-MLS 1)
Founded 1846. Enrl 875; Fac 55; Highest Degree: Bachelor
Library Holdings: Bks on Deafness & Sign Lang 350; Bk Vols 117,000; Per Subs 80
Special Collections: Lincoln Coll; McMurray College Archives. US Document Depository
Subject Interests: Deaf educ, Spec educ
Automation Activity & Vendor Info: (Cataloging) TLC (The Library Corporation); (Circulation) TLC (The Library Corporation); (OPAC) TLC (The Library Corporation)
Database Vendor: EBSCOhost, OCLC FirstSearch
Mem of Reaching Across Illinois Library System (RAILS)
Partic in Illinois Library & Information Network
Open Mon-Thurs 9am-9:30pm, Fri 9-4, Sun 3-9:30

M PASSAVANT AREA HOSPITAL, Sibert Library, 1600 W Walnut, 62650. SAN 304-2936. Tel: 217-245-9541, Ext 3424. FAX: 217-245-0230. E-mail: library@passavanthospital.com. Web Site: www.passavanthospital.com. *Librn,* Karen Douglas; Staff 1 (Non-MLS 1)

Founded 1902
Library Holdings: Bk Titles 925; Bk Vols 1,100; Per Subs 175
Special Collections: American Journal of Nursing, 1902 to present
Subject Interests: Allied health, Consumer health, Med, Nursing
Database Vendor: EBSCOhost, OCLC FirstSearch, OCLC WorldShare Interlibrary Loan, PubMed
Wireless access
Function: Prof lending libr
Mem of Reaching Across Illinois Library System (RAILS)
Partic in Illinois Library & Information Network; Nat Libr of Med/Docline; National Network of Libraries of Medicine; OCLC-LVIS
Open Mon-Thurs 8-1, Friday 8-12

JERSEYVILLE

P JERSEYVILLE PUBLIC LIBRARY*, 105 N Liberty St, 62052-1512. SAN 304-2944. Tel: 618-498-9514. FAX: 618-498-3036. E-mail: jpl@jerseyvillelibrary.org. Web Site: jerseyvillelibrary.org. *Dir,* Anita Driver; E-mail: anitad@jerseyvillelibrary.org; *Cataloger,* Chris Maness; *Circ Serv, ILL,* Beth Tittle; E-mail: betht@jerseyvillelibrary.org; *Youth Serv,* Laurie Ingram
Founded 1894. Pop 8,500; Circ 93,735
Library Holdings: CDs 5,771; DVDs 3,599; e-books 16,040; Bk Vols 51,017; Per Subs 145; Talking Bks 806
Automation Activity & Vendor Info: (Cataloging) Innovative Interfaces, Inc; (Circulation) Innovative Interfaces, Inc; (ILL) Innovative Interfaces, Inc; (OPAC) Innovative Interfaces, Inc; (Serials) Innovative Interfaces, Inc
Database Vendor: Gale Cengage Learning, OCLC FirstSearch, OCLC WorldShare Interlibrary Loan, Overdrive, Inc, ProQuest
Wireless access
Function: Bks on CD, Copy machines, Electronic databases & coll, Fax serv, Handicapped accessible, Homebound delivery serv, ILL available, Microfiche/film & reading machines, Music CDs, Online cat, OverDrive digital audio bks, Photocopying/Printing, Pub access computers, Scanner, Story hour, Summer reading prog, Tax forms, Video lending libr, Wheelchair accessible
Mem of Illinois Heartland Library System
Partic in Illinois Library & Information Network; OCLC Online Computer Library Center, Inc
Open Mon-Thurs 8:30am-9pm, Fri & Sat 8:30-5, Sun 1-4
Friends of the Library Group

JOHNSBURG

P JOHNSBURG PUBLIC LIBRARY DISTRICT*, 3000 N Johnsburg Rd, 60051. SAN 323-5491. Tel: 815-344-0077. FAX: 815-344-3524. Web Site: www.johnsburglibrary.org. *Dir,* Maria Zawacki; E-mail: mzawacki@johnsburglibrary.org; *Ch Serv,* Paulette Babchak; *Circ,* Melanie Ullrich; Staff 13 (MLS 1, Non-MLS 12)
Founded 1982. Pop 12,421; Circ 103,773
Library Holdings: Bk Vols 60,088; Per Subs 80
Special Collections: Homeschool Resource Center
Automation Activity & Vendor Info: (Cataloging) Follett Software; (Circulation) Follett Software; (OPAC) Follett Software
Database Vendor: OCLC FirstSearch
Wireless access
Publications: Newsletter (Quarterly)
Mem of Reaching Across Illinois Library System (RAILS)
Open Mon-Thurs 8:30am-9pm, Fri & Sat 8:30-5
Friends of the Library Group

JOHNSTON CITY

P JOHNSTON CITY PUBLIC LIBRARY*, 506 Washington Ave, 62951-1697. SAN 304-2952. Tel: 618-983-6359. FAX: 618-983-6359. E-mail: jcpublib@yahoo.com. Web Site: jcpublib.org. *Head Librn,* Cindy Pulsford; *Asst Librn,* Neloa Jent
Pop 3,557
Library Holdings: Bk Titles 15,177; Per Subs 40; Talking Bks 506; Videos 226
Wireless access
Mem of Illinois Heartland Library System
Open Mon-Thurs 1-7, Fri 11-5

JOLIET

S AMERICAN THEATRE ORGAN SOCIETY, INC*, Archives & Library, Five E Van Buren St, Ste 210, 60432-4223. SAN 325-5247. Tel: 708-562-8538. Web Site: www.atos.org. *Curator,* James Patak
Founded 1975
Library Holdings: CDs 200; Bk Titles 90
Special Collections: Glass Song Slides; Music Cassettes & LPs; Reel to Reel Radio Transcripts; Silent Motion Picture Cue Sheets & Scores; Wurlitzer Organ Rolls
Subject Interests: Exhibition of theatre pipe organs, Hist, Maintenance of theatre pipe organs, Presv, Restoration
Publications: Archives & Library catalogue; educator's guide
Restriction: Open by appt only

S ILLINOIS YOUTH CENTER*, Joliet Library, 2848 W McDonough St, 60436. SAN 375-9555. Tel: 815-725-1206. FAX: 815-725-9819. *Librn,* B McGregor
Library Holdings: Audiobooks 3; DVDs 35; Bk Titles 3,253; Bk Vols 3,478; Per Subs 30; Videos 257
Restriction: Staff & inmates only

J JOLIET JUNIOR COLLEGE*, Learning Resource Center, J-Bldg, 3rd Flr, 1215 Houbolt Rd, 60431-8938. SAN 304-2987. Tel: 815-729-9020, Ext 2350. Circulation Tel: 815-280-2665. Reference Tel: 815-280-2344. Administration Tel: 815-729-9020, Ext 2344. FAX: 815-744-2465. Web Site: www.jjc.edu/lrc. *Librn,* Gerald Anderson; E-mail: ganderso@jjc.edu; *Librn,* Susan Prokopeak; Tel: 815-729-9020, Ext 2215, E-mail: sprokope@jjc.edu; *Info Literacy Librn, Pub Serv,* Catherine Suchy; Tel: 815-729-9020, Ext 6604, E-mail: csuchy@jjc.edu; *Ref Librn,* Mark Arabadjief; E-mail: marabadj@jjc.edu; Staff 9 (MLS 3, Non-MLS 6)
Founded 1902. Enrl 5,000; Fac 150
Library Holdings: AV Mats 361; Bk Titles 53,000; Bk Vols 70,000; Per Subs 275
Special Collections: Children's books, soil surveys
Subject Interests: Agr, Criminal justice, Educ, English, Hist, Hort, Math, Nursing, Psychol, Veterinary tech
Automation Activity & Vendor Info: (Acquisitions) Ex Libris Group
Publications: Acquisitions report; film catalogue; video catalogue
Mem of Reaching Across Illinois Library System (RAILS)
Partic in Consortium of Academic & Research Libraries in Illinois; Ill Regional Libr Coun; Northern Ill Learning Resources Coop
Open Mon-Thurs (Fall & Spring) 7:30am-10pm, Fri 7:30-4:30, Sat 8-3:30; Mon-Thurs (Summer) 7:30am-10pm, Fri 7:30am-11:30am

P JOLIET PUBLIC LIBRARY*, 150 N Ottawa St, 60432-4192. SAN 340-4854. Tel: 815-740-2660. Reference Tel: 815-740-2666. FAX: 815-740-6161. Web Site: www.joliet.lib.il.us. *Dir,* James R Johnston; E-mail: jrjohnston@joliet.lib.il.us; *Assoc Dir,* Dianne Harmon; *Asst Dir,* John Mozga; *Ref,* Marcia Frowein; *Youth Serv,* Linda Ward-Callaghan; Staff 12 (MLS 10, Non-MLS 2)
Founded 1875. Pop 125,000
Library Holdings: Bk Titles 500,000; Per Subs 580
Special Collections: Granger Poetry; Herald News Microfilm Coll (1846-Present); Illinois History
Automation Activity & Vendor Info: (Circulation) SirsiDynix
Publications: Public & Staff Newsletters
Mem of Reaching Across Illinois Library System (RAILS)
Open Mon-Fri 9-9, Sat 9-4, Sun 1-5
Friends of the Library Group

M PROVENA SAINT JOSEPH MEDICAL CENTER*, Leon P Gardner Health Science Library, 333 N Madison St, 60435. SAN 304-2995. Tel: 815-725-7133, Ext 3530. FAX: 815-773-7755. Web Site: www.provena.orj/stjoes. *Librn,* Virginia Gale; *Media Serv Tech,* Darian Boyd; *Media Serv Tech,* Michael Schmuldt; Staff 3 (MLS 1, Non-MLS 2)
Founded 1975
Library Holdings: AV Mats 1,000; Bk Titles 1,500; Bk Vols 2,000; Per Subs 225
Subject Interests: Med, Nursing
Automation Activity & Vendor Info: (Cataloging) EOS International; (OPAC) EOS International
Database Vendor: OCLC FirstSearch, OVID Technologies
Mem of Reaching Across Illinois Library System (RAILS)
Partic in Chicago & South Consortium

M SILVER CROSS HOSPITAL MEDICAL LIBRARY*, Virtual Library, 1200 Maple Rd, 60432-9988. SAN 304-3002. Tel: 815-300-7477. FAX: 815-300-3567. *Med Librn,* Estelle Hu; E-mail: ehu@silvercross.org; Staff 1 (MLS 1)
Founded 1956
Oct 2011-Sept 2012 Income $51,000
Library Holdings: e-books 111; e-journals 360
Subject Interests: Health sci, Med
Database Vendor: Cinahl, MD Consult, Micromedex, OCLC FirstSearch, OCLC WorldShare Interlibrary Loan, OVID Technologies, PubMed
Wireless access
Function: Health sci info serv
Mem of Reaching Across Illinois Library System (RAILS)
Partic in Chicago & South Consortium
Restriction: Med staff only
Friends of the Library Group

S STATEVILLE CORRECTIONAL CENTER LIBRARIES*, PO Box 112, 60434-0112. Tel: 815-727-3607, Ext 5613. Web Site: www.idoc.state.il.us. *Librn,* Phyllis Baker; Staff 3 (MLS 3)
Founded 1936
Library Holdings: Bk Vols 39,000; Per Subs 140
Subject Interests: Criminal law & justice, Law, Recreation
Mem of Reaching Across Illinois Library System (RAILS)
Open Mon-Fri 8:30-2:30

CR UNIVERSITY OF ST FRANCIS*, 500 Wilcox St, 60435. SAN 304-2960. Tel: 815-740-5041. Circulation Tel: 815-740-3690. Interlibrary Loan Service Tel: 815-740-3446. Toll Free Tel: 800-726-6500. FAX: 815-740-3364. E-mail: circulation@stfrancis.edu. Web Site: www.stfrancis.edu/lib/libindex.htm. *Dir,* Terry Cottrell; Tel: 815-740-4292, E-mail: tcottrell@stfrancis.edu; *Head, Pub Serv,* Shannon Porte; Tel: 815-740-5061, E-mail: sporte@stfrancis.edu; *Head, Tech Serv,* Gail Gawlik; Tel: 815-740-3449, E-mail: ggawlik@stfrancis.edu; *Cat,* Judy Moroz; *Circ,* Marianne Kobe; E-mail: mkobe@stfrancis.edu
Founded 1930. Enrl 4,209; Highest Degree: Master
Library Holdings: Bk Vols 110,000; Per Subs 700
Special Collections: Contemporary Business Ethics
Subject Interests: Franciscans, Nursing
Automation Activity & Vendor Info: (Cataloging) Ex Libris Group; (Circulation) Ex Libris Group; (OPAC) Ex Libris Group; (Serials) Ex Libris Group
Database Vendor: EBSCOhost, Gale Cengage Learning, OCLC FirstSearch, ProQuest, SerialsSolutions
Mem of Reaching Across Illinois Library System (RAILS)
Partic in Library & Information Resources Network (LIRN); OCLC Online Computer Library Center, Inc; SMRHEC
Open Mon-Thurs 7:45am-10pm, Fri 7:45-4:30, Sat 9-2, Sun 3-10

L WILL COUNTY LAW LIBRARY*, 14 W Jefferson St, Ste 453, 60432-4300. SAN 373-0484. Tel: 815-727-8536. FAX: 815-727-8785. E-mail: lawlib@willcountyillinois.com. *Librn,* Karen Doyle; *Asst Librn,* Diane Brandolino
Database Vendor: Westlaw
Open Mon-Fri 8:30-4:30

JONESBORO

P JONESBORO PUBLIC LIBRARY*, 412 S Main, 62952. SAN 304-3010. Tel: 618-833-8121. FAX: 618-833-8121. E-mail: jonesborolibrary@frontier.com. *Librn,* Karen Hallam
Pop 1,853; Circ 4,269
Library Holdings: Bk Vols 8,000
Wireless access
Mem of Illinois Heartland Library System
Open Tues-Sat 1-5

JUSTICE

P JUSTICE PUBLIC LIBRARY DISTRICT, 7641 Oak Grove Ave, 60458-1358. SAN 320-474X. Tel: 708-496-1790. FAX: 708-496-1898. E-mail: jplonline@yahoo.com. Web Site: www.justicepubliclibrary.com. *Dir,* Juanita Durkin
Founded 1978. Pop 13,707; Circ 24,450
Library Holdings: Audiobooks 1,100; AV Mats 1,420; Bk Titles 47,123; Per Subs 81
Automation Activity & Vendor Info: (Cataloging) Innovative Interfaces, Inc - Millenium; (Circulation) Innovative Interfaces, Inc - Millenium; (ILL) Innovative Interfaces, Inc - Millenium; (OPAC) Innovative Interfaces, Inc
Database Vendor: EBSCOhost, OCLC WorldShare Interlibrary Loan, ProQuest
Wireless access
Function: 24/7 Electronic res, 24/7 Online cat, After school storytime, Audiobks via web, Bks on CD, Computers for patron use, Copy machines, Digital talking bks, Electronic databases & coll, Fax serv, ILL available, Life-long learning prog for all ages, Magazines, Movies, Mus passes, Music CDs, Notary serv, Online cat, Online ref, Online searches, OverDrive digital audio bks, Photocopying/Printing, Preschool reading prog, Printer for laptops & handheld devices, Prog for adults, Prog for children & young adult, Pub access computers, Summer & winter reading prog, Tax forms, Web-catalog
Publications: Cover to Cover (Newsletter)
Mem of Reaching Across Illinois Library System (RAILS)
Partic in System Wide Automated Network
Open Mon-Thurs 9:30-8, Fri & Sat 9:30-5

KAMPSVILLE

S CENTER FOR AMERICAN ARCHEOLOGY*, Research Library, PO Box 366, 62053-0366. SAN 371-165X. Tel: 618-653-4316. FAX: 618-653-4232. E-mail: caa@caa-archeology.org. Web Site: www.caa-archeology.org.
Library Holdings: Bk Vols 1,000
Restriction: Not open to pub

KANEVILLE

P KANEVILLE PUBLIC LIBRARY, Two S 101 Harter Rd, 60144. (Mail add: PO Box 29, 60144-0029), SAN 304-3029. Tel: 630-557-2441. FAX: 630-557-2553. E-mail: kanepublib@aol.com. Web Site: www.kanevillelibrary.org. *Dir,* Ray Christiansen; Staff 1 (Non-MLS 1)
Founded 1934. Pop 1,367; Circ 9,750
Library Holdings: Audiobooks 651; Bks on Deafness & Sign Lang 14; DVDs 753; e-books 55,000; Large Print Bks 1,100; Bk Titles 20,325; Bk Vols 25,412; Per Subs 41; Videos 753
Subject Interests: Fiction, Local hist
Automation Activity & Vendor Info: (Cataloging) SirsiDynix; (Circulation) SirsiDynix; (OPAC) SirsiDynix
Database Vendor: OCLC FirstSearch, OCLC WorldShare Interlibrary Loan, SirsiDynix
Wireless access
Function: 24/7 Online cat, Audio & video playback equip for onsite use, Bks on CD, CD-ROM, Computers for patron use, Copy machines, e-mail serv, Exhibits, Handicapped accessible, Holiday prog, ILL available, Magazines, Mail & tel request accepted, Mus passes, Photocopying/Printing, Preschool outreach, Prof lending libr, Prog for adults, Prog for children & young adult, Pub access computers, Ref serv available, Story hour, Tax forms, Telephone ref, Wheelchair accessible
Mem of Reaching Across Illinois Library System (RAILS)
Open Mon & Wed 10-6, Tues & Thurs 1-8, Sat 10-1
Friends of the Library Group

KANKAKEE

J KANKAKEE COMMUNITY COLLEGE*, Harold & Jean Miner Memorial Library, 100 College Dr, 60901-6505. SAN 304-3045. Tel: 815-802-8400. Reference Tel: 815-802-8403. Administration Tel: 815-802-8405. FAX: 815-802-8101. Web Site: www.kcc.edu/library. *Dir,* Position Currently Open; *Asst Dir,* Karen Becker; E-mail: kbecker@kcc.edu; *Librn,* Tracy Connor; E-mail: tconnor@kcc.edu; *Circ Serv,* Barbara Loudy; Tel: 815-802-8404, E-mail: bloudy@kcc.edu; Staff 6 (MLS 2, Non-MLS 4)
Founded 1966. Enrl 3,000; Highest Degree: Associate
Jul 2012-Jun 2013. Mats Exp $105,825, Books $37,000, Per/Ser (Incl. Access Fees) $17,000, AV Mat $7,325, Electronic Ref Mat (Incl. Access Fees) $44,500. Sal $134,602 (Prof $98,992)
Library Holdings: Bk Vols 34,000; Per Subs 100
Special Collections: Gordon Graves Environmental Coll; Reece L Ayers Soil & Water Conservation Coll
Automation Activity & Vendor Info: (Acquisitions) Baker & Taylor; (Cataloging) Ex Libris Group; (Circulation) Ex Libris Group; (Course Reserve) Ex Libris Group; (ILL) Ex Libris Group; (OPAC) Ex Libris Group; (Serials) Ex Libris Group
Wireless access
Mem of Reaching Across Illinois Library System (RAILS)
Partic in Consortium of Academic & Research Libraries in Illinois
Open Mon-Thurs (Fall-Spring) 7:45am-8pm, Fri 7:45-4, Sat 10am-1pm; Mon-Thurs (Summer) 7:45am-8pm

S KANKAKEE COUNTY HISTORICAL SOCIETY MUSEUM LIBRARY*, 801 S Eighth Ave, 60901-4744. SAN 304-3053. Tel: 815-932-5279. FAX: 815-932-5204. E-mail: kankakeecountymuseum@gmail.com. Web Site: www.kankakeecountymuseum.com. *Exec Dir,* Connie Licon
Founded 1906
Library Holdings: Bk Vols 3,500
Special Collections: Biographies; County History; Documents Coll; History of County Townships, bks, photog; Letters Coll; Manuscripts Coll
Subject Interests: Hist
Publications: Newsletter (Quarterly)
Restriction: In-house use for visitors, Open by appt only

P KANKAKEE PUBLIC LIBRARY*, 201 E Merchant St, 60901. SAN 304-3061. Tel: 815-939-4564. Circulation Tel: 815-937-6901. FAX: 815-939-9057. Web Site: www.lions-online.org. *Dir,* Stephen Bertrand; E-mail: sbertrand@lions-online.org; *Head, Tech Serv,* Melissa Landis-McFeeley; E-mail: mlandis@lions-online.org; *Head, Youth Serv,* Camille Rose; E-mail: ccrose@lions-online.org; *Adult Serv,* Allison Beasley; E-mail: abeasley@lions-online.org
Founded 1899. Pop 27,491; Circ 96,000
Library Holdings: Bk Vols 90,000; Per Subs 250
Subject Interests: Genealogy

Automation Activity & Vendor Info: (Acquisitions) SirsiDynix; (Cataloging) SirsiDynix; (Circulation) SirsiDynix; (ILL) SirsiDynix; (OPAC) SirsiDynix; (Serials) SirsiDynix
Publications: Between the Lions Newsletter (Bi-monthly)
Mem of Reaching Across Illinois Library System (RAILS)
Open Mon-Thurs 9-9, Fri 9-6, Sat 9-5, Sun (Sept-May) 1-5
Friends of the Library Group

P LIMESTONE TOWNSHIP LIBRARY, 2701 W Tower Rd, 60901. Tel: 815-939-1696. FAX: 815-939-1748. E-mail: info@limestonelibrary.org. Web Site: www.limestonelibrary.org. *Dir,* Lynne Noffke
Automation Activity & Vendor Info: (Acquisitions) Innovative Interfaces, Inc
Database Vendor: EBSCOhost, OCLC WorldShare Interlibrary Loan
Wireless access
Function: Bk club(s), Children's prog, Computer training, Computers for patron use, Copy machines, Fax serv, Free DVD rentals, ILL available, Notary serv, OverDrive digital audio bks, Prog for adults, Prog for children & young adult, Pub access computers, Scanner, Story hour, Summer & winter reading prog, Tax forms, Teen prog
Mem of Reaching Across Illinois Library System (RAILS)
Open Mon-Thurs 10-8, Fri 10-5, Sat 10-3
Friends of the Library Group

M PROVENA SAINT MARY'S HOSPITAL*, Medical Library, 500 W Court St, 60901. SAN 375-9466. Tel: 815-937-2477. FAX: 815-937-2466. Web Site: www.provena.org/stmarys. *Librn,* Sandy Kambic
Library Holdings: Bk Titles 200

S SHAPIRO DEVELOPMENTAL CENTER*, Resident Library, 100 E Jeffery St, 60901. SAN 326-9973. Tel: 815-939-8011, 815-939-8505. FAX: 815-939-8414. *Supvr,* Nina Williams
Library Holdings: Bk Titles 6,000; Per Subs 30
Open Mon, Wed & Fri 8-4:30

KANSAS

P KANSAS COMMUNITY MEMORIAL LIBRARY*, 107 N Front St, 61933. (Mail add: PO Box 319, 61933-0319), SAN 304-3096. Tel: 217-948-5484. FAX: 217-948-5484. *Librn,* Alison Phelps
Founded 1932. Pop 1,114; Circ 9,173
Library Holdings: Bk Vols 10,087; Per Subs 16
Mem of Illinois Heartland Library System
Open Mon & Wed-Fri 1-5, Tues 10-5, Sat 10-3

KENILWORTH

S KENILWORTH HISTORICAL SOCIETY*, Kilner Library, 415 Kenilworth Ave, 60043-1134. SAN 304-310X. Tel: 847-251-2565. FAX: 847-251-2565. E-mail: kenilworthhistory@sbcglobal.net. Web Site: www.kenilworthhistory.org. *Pres,* Carol Schulz; *Archivist, Curator,* Melinda Kwedar
Founded 1972
Library Holdings: Bk Titles 665; Bk Vols 674
Special Collections: Photograph Coll
Open Mon 9-4:30, Thurs 9-12
Restriction: Open to pub for ref only

KEWANEE

S ILLINOIS DEPARTMENT OF CORRECTIONS*, Kewanee Correctional Center Library, 2021 Kentville Rd, 61443. Tel: 309-852-4601, Ext 3331. FAX: 309-852-4617. Web Site: www.idoc.state.il.us. *Librn,* Linda Jaegers
Library Holdings: Bk Vols 5,561
Open Mon-Fri 8-4

S KEWANEE HISTORICAL SOCIETY MUSEUM & LIBRARY*, 211 N Chestnut St, 61443. SAN 374-9428. Tel: 309-854-9701. E-mail: kewaneehistory@kewanee.com. Web Site: www.kewaneehistory.com. *Pres,* Larry Lock
Library Holdings: Bk Vols 400
Special Collections: Cornhusking Hall of Fame
Subject Interests: Local hist
Open Thurs & Sat (April-Oct) 1:30-4

P KEWANEE PUBLIC LIBRARY DISTRICT*, 102 S Tremont St, 61443. SAN 304-3126. Tel: 309-852-4505. Information Services Tel: 309-852-0111. FAX: 309-852-4466. Administration FAX: 309-856-8445. TDD: 309-852-4505. E-mail: reference@kewaneelibrary.org. Web Site: www.kewaneelibrary.org. *Dir,* John E Sayers; *Head, Circ,* Heather Hollis; *Head, Info Serv,* Ann Turnbull; *Head, Tech Serv,* Amy Gould; *Head, Youth Serv,* Sara Darding; Staff 17 (MLS 2, Non-MLS 15)
Founded 1875. Pop 14,501; Circ 104,389
Library Holdings: AV Mats 7,553; High Interest/Low Vocabulary Bk Vols 451; Large Print Bks 1,463; Bk Vols 57,457; Per Subs 175; Talking Bks 2,218
Special Collections: Genealogy (Henry County Genealogical Coll); Local History
Automation Activity & Vendor Info: (Circulation) CARL.Solution (TLC); (OPAC) CARL.Solution (TLC)
Database Vendor: OCLC FirstSearch, TLC (The Library Corporation)
Publications: Between the Lines (Newsletter)
Open Mon & Thurs (Winter) 9-8, Tues, Wed & Fri 9-6, Sat 9-1; Mon-Fri (Summer) 9-6, Sat 9-1
Friends of the Library Group

KINMUNDY

P KINMUNDY PUBLIC LIBRARY*, 111 S Monroe St, 62854. (Mail add: PO Box 85, 62854-0085). Tel: 618-547-3250. FAX: 618-547-3258. *Librn,* Betty Eutsler
Pop 892
Apr 2009-Mar 2010 Income $12,253, State $1,079, City $8,344, Locally Generated Income $2,830. Mats Exp $5,996, Books $2,446, Other Print Mats $2,194, Electronic Ref Mat (Incl. Access Fees) $340
Library Holdings: Audiobooks 132; DVDs 171; Large Print Bks 200; Bk Titles 19,930; Per Subs 5; Spec Interest Per Sub 1; Videos 100
Wireless access
Mem of Illinois Heartland Library System
Open Mon 9-12 & 1-5, Tues-Fri 1-5, Sat 9-12

KIRKLAND

P KIRKLAND PUBLIC LIBRARY*, 513 W Main St, 60146. (Mail add: PO Box 89, 60146), SAN 304-3142. Tel: 815-522-6260. FAX: 815-522-6260. E-mail: kirklandlib@hotmail.com. Web Site: www.geocities.com/kirklandlib. *Dir,* Judy Nelson; *Asst Librn,* Britani Drexter; *Asst Librn,* Linda Felt; Staff 1 (Non-MLS 1)
Founded 1920. Pop 1,166; Circ 11,000
Library Holdings: High Interest/Low Vocabulary Bk Vols 56; Bk Vols 12,629; Per Subs 16
Automation Activity & Vendor Info: (Circulation) Follett Software
Database Vendor: OCLC FirstSearch
Function: ILL available
Mem of Reaching Across Illinois Library System (RAILS)
Special Services for the Deaf - TDD equip
Open Mon & Thurs 10-7, Tues & Wed 3-7, Sat 9-1
Friends of the Library Group

KNOXVILLE

P KNOXVILLE PUBLIC LIBRARY*, 200 E Main St, 61448-1351. SAN 304-3150. Tel: 309-289-2113. FAX: 309-289-8063. E-mail: kpl2@comcast.net. Web Site: www.kvillepub.lib.org. *Librn,* Patricia A Rose
Founded 1878. Pop 2,911; Circ 21,716
Library Holdings: Bk Vols 19,000; Per Subs 50
Open Mon-Thurs 2-8 (2-7 Summer), Fri & Sat 10-5

LA GRANGE

R GRACE LUTHERAN CHURCH LIBRARY*, 200 N Catherine Ave, 60525-1826. (Mail add: PO Box 207, 60525-0207), SAN 304-3185. Tel: 708-352-0730. FAX: 708-352-0737. *Librn,* Marilyn Burns; *Librn,* Grace Puls; E-mail: gracielib@aol.com; Staff 12 (MLS 1, Non-MLS 11)
Founded 1954
Library Holdings: Bk Vols 3,452
Subject Interests: Relig
Automation Activity & Vendor Info: (Cataloging) Follett Software
Open Thurs 10-1, Sun 8:30-12

M LA GRANGE MEMORIAL HOSPITAL*, Zitek Medical Library, 5101 Willow Springs Rd, 60525. SAN 304-3169. Tel: 708-245-7236. Interlibrary Loan Service Tel: 708-245-7230. FAX: 708-245-5613. *Mgr, Libr Serv,* Bonnie Arnold; E-mail: bonnie.arnold@ahss.org; Staff 2 (MLS 1, Non-MLS 1)
Founded 1956
Library Holdings: Bk Titles 600; Bk Vols 1,700; Per Subs 225
Subject Interests: Med, Nursing
Wireless access
Mem of Reaching Across Illinois Library System (RAILS)
Partic in Chicago & South Consortium; Greater Midwest Regional Medical Libr Network; Illinois Library & Information Network; Medical Library Association (MLA); OCLC-LVIS
Open Mon-Fri 8-4

P LA GRANGE PUBLIC LIBRARY*, Ten W Cossitt Ave, 60525. SAN 304-3193. Tel: 708-352-0576. Interlibrary Loan Service FAX: 708-352-1620. E-mail: lgref@lagrangelibrary.org. Web Site:

www.lagrangelibrary.org. *Dir,* Jeannie Dilger-Hill; Tel: 708-352-0576, Ext 11, E-mail: dilgerj@lagrangelibrary.org; *Head, Circ,* Pat Prohl; Tel: 708-352-0576, Ext 12, E-mail: prohlp@lagrangelibrary.org; *Head, Ref,* Debbie Darwine; Tel: 708-352-0576, Ext 24, E-mail: darwined@lagrangelibrary.org; *Head, Tech Serv,* Rebecca Bartlett; Tel: 708-352-0576, Ext 14, E-mail: bartlettr@lagrangelibrary.org; *Head, Youth Serv,* Caroline Schill; Tel: 708-352-0576, Ext 22, E-mail: schillc@lagrangelibrary.org; *ILL,* Pam Ferris; Tel: 708-352-0576, Ext 13, E-mail: ferrisp@lagrangelibrary.org; *Ref,* Nancy Bent; E-mail: bentn@lagrangelibrary.org; *Ref,* Gail Morrissey; E-mail: morrisse@lagrangelibrary.org; *Ref,* Victor Smith; E-mail: smithv@lagrangelibrary.org; *YA Serv,* Noel Zethmayr; Tel: 708-352-0576, Ext 35, E-mail: zethmayrn@lagrangelibrary.org; Staff 8 (MLS 8)
Founded 1905. Pop 15,550; Circ 289,035
May 2009-Apr 2010 Income $2,549,732, State $18,730, City $2,474,911, Locally Generated Income $56,091. Mats Exp $219,690, Books $161,529, Micro $800, AV Mat $28,505, Electronic Ref Mat (Incl. Access Fees) $28,856. Sal $960,334
Library Holdings: CDs 5,276; DVDs 3,085; Bk Vols 91,851; Per Subs 310
Special Collections: Business
Subject Interests: Genealogy, Local hist
Automation Activity & Vendor Info: (Acquisitions) Innovative Interfaces, Inc; (Cataloging) Innovative Interfaces, Inc; (Circulation) Innovative Interfaces, Inc; (ILL) Innovative Interfaces, Inc; (OPAC) Innovative Interfaces, Inc; (Serials) Innovative Interfaces, Inc
Database Vendor: EBSCOhost, Evanced Solutions, Inc, Gale Cengage Learning, Grolier Online, Innovative Interfaces, Inc, Newsbank, OCLC WorldShare Interlibrary Loan, Overdrive, Inc, ProQuest, ReferenceUSA, TumbleBookLibrary, Wilson - Wilson Web, World Book Online
Wireless access
Function: Bk club(s), Bks on CD, Children's prog, Computers for patron use, Copy machines, Electronic databases & coll, Exhibits, Fax serv, Free DVD rentals, Handicapped accessible, Holiday prog, ILL available, Mus passes, Music CDs, Online cat, Outside serv via phone, mail, e-mail & web, OverDrive digital audio bks, Photocopying/Printing, Preschool outreach, Prog for adults, Prog for children & young adult, Pub access computers, Ref serv available, Spoken cassettes & CDs, Story hour, Summer reading prog, Tax forms, Teen prog, Telephone ref, Web-catalog, Wheelchair accessible, Writing prog
Publications: BookNews (Online only); The Book Report (Newsletter)
Mem of Reaching Across Illinois Library System (RAILS)
Partic in System Wide Automated Network
Special Services for the Blind - Braille bks; Large print bks; Large screen computer & software; Low vision equip; Reader equip
Open Mon-Fri 9-9, Sat 9-5, Sun (Sept-May) 1-5
Friends of the Library Group

LA GRANGE PARK

P LA GRANGE PARK PUBLIC LIBRARY DISTRICT*, 555 N LaGrange Rd, 60526-5644. SAN 304-3215. Tel: 708-352-0100. FAX: 708-352-1606. TDD: 708-352-1970. E-mail: info@lplibrary.org. Web Site: www.lplibrary.org. *Dir,* Dixie M Conkis; *Adult Serv,* Kate Zdenek; *Ch Serv,* Meb Ingold; Staff 6 (MLS 5, Non-MLS 1)
Founded 1975. Pop 13,295; Circ 141,024
Library Holdings: Bk Vols 70,434; Per Subs 204; Videos 3,228
Automation Activity & Vendor Info: (Cataloging) Innovative Interfaces, Inc; (Circulation) Innovative Interfaces, Inc
Database Vendor: EBSCOhost, OCLC FirstSearch, ProQuest, ReferenceUSA
Wireless access
Publications: Newsletter (Quarterly)
Mem of Metropolitan Library System
Open Mon-Thurs 10-9, Fri & Sat 10-5, Sun 1-5
Friends of the Library Group

LA HARPE

P LA HARPE CARNEGIE PUBLIC LIBRARY DISTRICT*, 209 E Main St, 61450. (Mail add: PO Box 506, 61450-0506), SAN 304-3223. Tel: 217-659-7729. FAX: 217-659-7735. E-mail: lahalib@yahoo.com. Web Site: www.laharpe.lib.il.us/library/. *Head Librn,* Monica Carpenter; *Asst Librn,* Laurie Magee
Founded 1890. Pop 2,249; Circ 15,280
Library Holdings: Bk Vols 18,000; Per Subs 32
Special Collections: Hancock County Quill 1893-1982 (weekly newsp)
Automation Activity & Vendor Info: (Circulation) CARL.Solution (TLC)
Function: Homebound delivery serv, ILL available, Online searches, Photocopying/Printing, Prog for adults, Prog for children & young adult, Summer reading prog
Open Mon & Tues 9-5, Wed 2-7, Fri & Sat 9-12

LACON

P LACON PUBLIC LIBRARY DISTRICT, 205 Sixth St, 61540. SAN 304-3266. Tel: 309-246-2855. FAX: 309-246-4047. E-mail: laconlib@gmail.com. Web Site: www.Laconlibrary.org. *Dir,* Elizabeth Reed; Staff 0.6 (Non-MLS 0.6)
Founded 1839. Pop 1,979; Circ 25,796
Library Holdings: Audiobooks 670; CDs 115; DVDs 2,822; e-books 4,492; Large Print Bks 852; Bk Titles 10,997; Per Subs 54; Videos 35
Subject Interests: Local hist
Database Vendor: OCLC FirstSearch, OCLC WorldShare Interlibrary Loan
Wireless access
Function: Copy machines, Fax serv, ILL available, Summer reading prog, Tax forms
Mem of Reaching Across Illinois Library System (RAILS)
Partic in RSA
Open Mon-Wed 1-7, Fri 10-5, Sat 9-1

S MARSHALL COUNTY HISTORICAL SOCIETY LIBRARY*, 314 Fifth St, 61540. (Mail add: PO Box 123, 61540-0123), SAN 374-9371. Tel: 309-246-2349. E-mail: marshallcountyhistory@gmail.com. *Dir,* Jean Davis
Founded 1956
Library Holdings: Bk Vols 525
Special Collections: Doll Coll; Lincoln Coll
Subject Interests: Genealogy, Local hist
Publications: Reflections (Newsletter)
Open Tues & Wed 9-12
Restriction: Non-circulating, Ref only

LADD

P LADD PUBLIC LIBRARY DISTRICT*, 125 N Main St, 61329. (Mail add: PO Box 307, 61329-0307), SAN 304-3274. Tel: 815-894-3254. FAX: 815-894-3254. E-mail: ladd_library@frontier.com. Web Site: www.laddlibrary.com. *Dir,* Amy Galetti-Bosi; *Asst Librn,* Paula Corpus; *Asst Librn,* Ann King; Staff 3 (Non-MLS 3)
Founded 1930. Pop 1,684; Circ 8,088
Library Holdings: Bk Vols 7,000
Special Collections: Library of America Coll
Wireless access
Function: Adult bk club, After school storytime, Bk club(s), Bks on cassette, Bks on CD, Children's prog, Computers for patron use, Copy machines, Fax serv, ILL available, Magnifiers for reading, Music CDs, Prog for adults, Prog for children & young adult, Pub access computers, Story hour, Summer reading prog, Tax forms, VHS videos, Web-catalog, Wheelchair accessible
Mem of Reaching Across Illinois Library System (RAILS)
Open Mon & Tues 10-7, Wed 3-7, Fri 10-6, Sat 9-1

LAFAYETTE

P IRA C REED PUBLIC LIBRARY*, 302 Commercial St, 61449. (Mail add: PO Box 185, 61449-0185), SAN 304-3282. Tel: 309-995-3042. FAX: 309-995-3042. E-mail: irclibrary@winco.net. *Librn,* Marcine Rashid; Staff 3 (Non-MLS 3)
Founded 1909. Pop 227
Library Holdings: Large Print Bks 50; Bk Vols 8,355; Per Subs 12; Videos 250
Subject Interests: Local hist
Wireless access
Open Mon-Thurs 12-7, Fri 12-5:30

LAKE BLUFF

P LAKE BLUFF PUBLIC LIBRARY*, 123 E Scranton Ave, 60044. SAN 304-3290. Tel: 847-234-2540. FAX: 847-234-2649. Web Site: www.lakeblufflibrary.org. *Dir,* Eric Bailey; E-mail: ebailey@lakeblufflibrary.org; Staff 3 (MLS 3)
Founded 1926. Pop 6,056; Circ 71,752
May 2006-Apr 2007 Income $730,091. Mats Exp $92,869. Sal $332,767
Library Holdings: AV Mats 3,883; e-books 2,426; Bk Vols 47,101; Per Subs 130
Automation Activity & Vendor Info: (Cataloging) TLC (The Library Corporation); (Circulation) TLC (The Library Corporation); (OPAC) TLC (The Library Corporation)
Function: Adult bk club, Bk club(s), Bks on cassette, Bks on CD, Children's prog, Computers for patron use, Copy machines, Electronic databases & coll, Music CDs, Online cat, Online ref, Photocopying/Printing, Preschool outreach, Prog for adults, Prog for children & young adult, Pub access computers, Scanner, Summer reading prog, Tax forms, VHS videos, Wheelchair accessible, Workshops
Publications: Quarterly newsletter
Open Mon & Thurs 10-9, Tues, Wed & Fri 10-6, Sat 10-4, Sun (Sept-May) 1-5
Friends of the Library Group

LAKE FOREST

C LAKE FOREST COLLEGE*, Donnelley & Lee Library, 555 N Sheridan, 60045. SAN 340-4978. Tel: 847-735-5056. FAX: 847-735-6297. Web Site: www.library.lakeforest.edu. *Dir,* James Cubit; Tel: 847-735-5054, E-mail: cubit@lakeforest.edu; *Head, Circ,* Kristen Kinsella; E-mail: kkinsella@lakeforest.edu; *Head, Pub Serv,* Cory Stevens; Tel: 847-735-5072, E-mail: cstevens@lakeforest.edu; *Head, Tech Serv,* Eileen Karsten; Tel: 847-735-5066, E-mail: karsten@lakeforest.edu; *Govt Doc, Ref Librn, Ser,* Rita Koller; Tel: 847-735-5065, E-mail: koller@lakeforest.edu; *Archivist, Spec Coll Librn,* Arthur Miller, Jr; Tel: 847-735-5064, E-mail: amiller@lakeforest.edu; *Syst Librn, Tech Spec,* David Levinson; Tel: 847-735-5059, E-mail: levinson@lakeforest.edu; *ILL Coordr,* Susan Cloud; Tel: 847-735-5062, E-mail: cloud@lakeforest.edu; Staff 8 (MLS 8)
Founded 1857. Fac 91; Highest Degree: Master
Library Holdings: Bk Titles 240,000; Per Subs 1,000
Special Collections: Capt Joseph Medill Patterson Papers (NY Daily News Coll); Humanities, Rare Books (Hamill Coll); Printing History, Western Americana (O'Kieffe); Railroad (Elliott Donnelley, Munson Paddock & James Sloss Coll); Scotland (Stuart Coll); Theatre (Garrett Leverton Memorial. US Document Depository
Automation Activity & Vendor Info: (Acquisitions) Ex Libris Group; (Cataloging) Ex Libris Group; (Circulation) Ex Libris Group; (OPAC) Ex Libris Group
Partic in Center for Research Libraries; Illinois Library & Information Network
Open Mon-Thurs (Winter) 8am-Midnight, Fri 8-6, Sat 10-9, Sun 12-12; Mon-Fri (Summer) 8:30-4:30

P LAKE FOREST LIBRARY, 360 E Deerpath Ave, 60045-2252. SAN 304-3312. Tel: 847-234-0636. Circulation Tel: 847-810-4600. Interlibrary Loan Service Tel: 847-810-4629. Reference Tel: 847-810-4609. FAX: 847-234-1453. E-mail: reference@lfl.alibrary.com. Web Site: www.lakeforestlibrary.org. *Dir,* Kaye Grabbe; Tel: 847-810-4602, E-mail: kgrabbe@lfl.alibrary.com; *Head, Adult Serv,* Felicia Song; Tel: 847-810-4611; *Head, Ch,* Lorie Rohrer; Tel: 847-810-4632; *Head, Tech Serv,* Jian Tan; Tel: 847-810-4624; *Ad,* Jean Larson; Tel: 847-810-4613; *Ad/Virtual Serv,* Matt Neer; Tel: 847-810-4623; *Librn, Adult Serv,* Kate Buckardt; Tel: 847-810-4612; *Librn, Adult Serv,* Wendy Davis; Tel: 847-810-4615; *Ref Librn,* Judy Gummere; Tel: 847-810-4621; *Ch Serv,* Kate Parker; Tel: 847-810-4631; *Ch Serv,* Mary Webber; Tel: 847-810-4630; Staff 14 (MLS 14)
Founded 1898. Pop 19,375; Circ 450,876
May 2013-Apr 2014 Income $3,925,928, State $77,373, City $3,718,523, Locally Generated Income $130,032. Mats Exp $512,251, Books $222,147, Per/Ser (Incl. Access Fees) $19,000, AV Mat $104,336, Electronic Ref Mat (Incl. Access Fees) $166,768. Sal $2,362,252
Library Holdings: Audiobooks 6,391; AV Mats 25,138; CDs 6,527; DVDs 10,758; e-books 15,324; Electronic Media & Resources 58; Bk Vols 120,428; Per Subs 329
Subject Interests: Art & archit, Gardening, Local hist
Automation Activity & Vendor Info: (Cataloging) SirsiDynix; (Circulation) SirsiDynix; (ILL) OCLC; (OPAC) SirsiDynix
Database Vendor: 3M Library Systems, Baker & Taylor, CQ Press, EBSCO - WebFeat, EBSCOhost, Facts on File, Gale Cengage Learning, H W Wilson, infoUSA, Newsbank, OCLC ArticleFirst, OCLC FirstSearch, OCLC WebJunction, OCLC WorldShare Interlibrary Loan, Overdrive, Inc, ProQuest, ReferenceUSA, SirsiDynix, Standard & Poor's, ValueLine, Wilson - Wilson Web, World Book Online
Wireless access
Publications: Lake Forest Library (Newsletter)
Partic in OCLC Online Computer Library Center, Inc
Special Services for the Deaf - TDD equip
Special Services for the Blind - Assistive/Adapted tech devices, equip & products
Open Mon-Thurs 9-9, Fri & Sat 9-5, Sun 1-5
Friends of the Library Group

LAKE VILLA

P LAKE VILLA DISTRICT LIBRARY*, 1001 E Grand Ave, 60046. SAN 304-3320. Tel: 847-356-7711. FAX: 847-265-9595. Web Site: www.lvdl.org. *Dir,* Robert Watson; Tel: 847-356-7711, Ext 210; *Head, Admin Serv,* Andy Lentine; Tel: 847-356-7711, Ext 211; *Head, Adult Serv,* Paul Kaplan; Tel: 847-356-7711, Ext 230, E-mail: pkaplan@lvdl.org; *Head, Circ Serv,* Debbie Rosen; Tel: 847-356-7711, Ext 221, E-mail: debbie@lvdl.org; *Head, Commun Serv,* Liz Glazer; Tel: 847-356-7711, Ext 213, E-mail: lglazer@lvdl.org; *Head, Tech Serv,* Lois Wessale; Tel: 847-356-7711, Ext 233; *Head, Youth Serv,* Kerry Reed; Tel: 847-356-7711, Ext 246, E-mail: kreed@lvdl.org; *ILL,* Cindy McBrady; Tel: 847-356-7711, Ext 224; Staff 61 (MLS 7, Non-MLS 54)
Founded 1952. Pop 33,700; Circ 863,453
Library Holdings: AV Mats 27,445; e-books 11; Bk Vols 144,641; Per Subs 463
Automation Activity & Vendor Info: (Circulation) SirsiDynix; (OPAC) SirsiDynix
Database Vendor: Gale Cengage Learning, OCLC FirstSearch
Publications: Checking Out (Newsletter)
Partic in Cooperative Computer Services - CCS
Special Services for the Deaf - TTY equip
Special Services for the Blind - Closed circuit TV magnifier
Open Mon-Thurs 9-9, Fri 9-6, Sat 9-5, Sun (Sept-May) 1-5
Friends of the Library Group

LAKE ZURICH

P ELA AREA PUBLIC LIBRARY DISTRICT*, 275 Mohawk Trail, 60047. SAN 304-3347. Tel: 847-438-3433. FAX: 847-438-9290. TDD: 847-438-3799. E-mail: elaref1@eapl.org. Web Site: www.eapl.org. *Dir,* Matt Womack; *Asst Dir,* Brenda Duff; *Head, Circ,* Patti Paige; *Head, Ref,* Jennifer Plohr; *Head, Tech Serv,* Position Currently Open; *Head, Youth Serv,* Natalie Ziarnik; *Info Tech, Syst Adminr,* Warren Dawkins; *ILL,* Pam Braun; Staff 21 (MLS 20, Non-MLS 1)
Founded 1972. Pop 32,000; Circ 834,316
Library Holdings: AV Mats 38,336; Large Print Bks 6,824; Bk Vols 184,110; Per Subs 150
Automation Activity & Vendor Info: (Acquisitions) SirsiDynix; (Cataloging) SirsiDynix; (Circulation) SirsiDynix; (OPAC) SirsiDynix
Database Vendor: OCLC FirstSearch
Publications: Footnotes (Newsletter)
Partic in Cooperative Computer Services - CCS
Special Services for the Deaf - TDD equip
Open Mon-Thurs 9-9, Fri 9-6, Sat 9-5, Sun 12-5
Friends of the Library Group

LAMOILLE

P LAMOILLE-CLARION PUBLIC LIBRARY DISTRICT*, 81 Main St, 61330. (Mail add: PO Box 260, 61330-0260), SAN 304-3231. Tel: 815-638-2356. FAX: 815-638-2356. E-mail: llibrary@live.com. *Dir,* Joyce Sondgeroth; Staff 2 (Non-MLS 2)
Founded 1973. Pop 1,964; Circ 9,038
Jul 2006-Jun 2007 Income $50,867, State $2,403, County $42,900, Other $5,564. Mats Exp $5,863, Books $4,442, Per/Ser (Incl. Access Fees) $1,034, AV Mat $387. Sal $20,620
Library Holdings: DVDs 150; Large Print Bks 175; Bk Titles 16,393; Per Subs 52; Videos 621
Special Collections: Oral History
Database Vendor: Baker & Taylor
Wireless access
Mem of Reaching Across Illinois Library System (RAILS)
Open Mon & Wed 1-7, Tues & Fri 10-12 & 1-5, Thurs 1-5, Sat 10-3

LANARK

P LANARK PUBLIC LIBRARY*, 110 W Carroll St, 61046. SAN 304-3355. Tel: 815-493-2166. FAX: 815-493-8045. E-mail: lanarklibrary@yahoo.com. Web Site: www.lanarkil.com/lanarklibrary/. *Dir,* Janie A Dollinger
Founded 1957. Pop 1,583; Circ 16,000
Library Holdings: Large Print Bks 700; Bk Vols 25,000; Per Subs 40; Talking Bks 500
Subject Interests: Genealogy, Local hist
Automation Activity & Vendor Info: (Circulation) Follett Software
Mem of Reaching Across Illinois Library System (RAILS)
Special Services for the Deaf - TDD equip
Open Tues, Wed & Fri 12-5, Thurs 12-7:30, Sat 10-3
Friends of the Library Group

LANSING

P LANSING PUBLIC LIBRARY*, 2750 Indiana Ave, 60438. SAN 304-3363. Tel: 708-474-2447. Circulation Tel: 708-474-2447, Ext 102. Reference Tel: 708-474-2447, Ext 109. Information Services Tel: 708-474-2447, Ext 123. FAX: 708-474-9466. Web Site: www.lansing.lib.il.us. *Exec Dir,* Debbie Albrecht; Tel: 708-474-2447, Ext 100, E-mail: debbie@lansingpl.org; Staff 12 (MLS 3, Non-MLS 9)
Founded 1936. Pop 28,131; Circ 215,440
Library Holdings: Bk Titles 150,000; Per Subs 195
Automation Activity & Vendor Info: (Acquisitions) SirsiDynix; (Cataloging) SirsiDynix; (Circulation) SirsiDynix; (OPAC) SirsiDynix; (Serials) SirsiDynix
Mem of Reaching Across Illinois Library System (RAILS)
Partic in State of Iowa Libraries Online
Open Mon-Thurs 9-8, Fri & Sat 9-5
Friends of the Library Group

LASALLE

S CARUS CHEMICAL CO*, Research Library, 1500 Eighth St, 61301-3500. SAN 375-9938. Tel: 815-224-6886. Toll Free Tel: 800-435-6856. FAX: 815-224-6896. Web Site: www.caruscorporation.com. *Tech Info Spec,* Marsha Thorson; E-mail: marsha.thorson@caruschem.com
Library Holdings: Bk Titles 1,400; Per Subs 45
Mem of Reaching Across Illinois Library System (RAILS)
Restriction: Staff use only

P LASALLE PUBLIC LIBRARY*, 305 Marquette St, 61301. SAN 304-324X. Tel: 815-223-2341. FAX: 815-223-2353. Web Site: www.lasalle.lib.il.us. *Dir,* Cristy Stupegia; E-mail: estupegia@lasalle.lib.il.us; *Youth Serv,* Donna Blomquist; E-mail: dmblomquist@lasalle.lib.il.us; Staff 7 (MLS 2, Non-MLS 5)
Founded 1907. Pop 9,796
Library Holdings: Bk Vols 47,000; Per Subs 52
Special Collections: Local (LaSalle-Peru) History Materials & Original Documents Regarding History of Library; Spanish/Bilingual Coll
Automation Activity & Vendor Info: (Circulation) SirsiDynix
Wireless access
Mem of Reaching Across Illinois Library System (RAILS)
Open Mon & Wed 9-6, Tues & Thurs 9-8, Fri & Sat 9-5

LAWRENCEVILLE

P LAWRENCE PUBLIC LIBRARY DISTRICT*, 814 12th St, 62439. SAN 304-3371. Tel: 618-943-3016. FAX: 618-943-3215. E-mail: lawrencepubliclibrary@yahoo.com. Web Site: www.lawpubliclibrary.com. *Dir,* Theresa Marie Tucker
Founded 1921. Pop 15,452; Circ 66,702
Library Holdings: Bk Vols 40,000; Per Subs 60; Talking Bks 575
Mem of Illinois Heartland Library System
Open Mon, Wed & Fri 10-5, Tues & Thurs 10-6, Sat 10-3
Friends of the Library Group

LEAF RIVER

P BERTOLET MEMORIAL LIBRARY DISTRICT, 705 S Main St, 61047. (Mail add: PO Box 339, 61047-0339), SAN 321-5551. Tel: 815-738-2742. FAX: 815-738-2742. E-mail: bertolib@lrnet1.com. Web Site: www.bertoletmemoriallibrary.org. *Libr Dir,* Linda M Schreiber; *Asst Librn,* Julie Voss; Staff 1 (Non-MLS 1)
Founded 1981. Pop 2,145; Circ 9,180
Library Holdings: Bk Titles 8,624; Per Subs 25
Special Collections: Local History Coll, bks, diaries, ledgers
Wireless access
Mem of Reaching Across Illinois Library System (RAILS)
Open Mon-Thurs 10-7, Sat 8-12

LEBANON

P LEBANON PUBLIC LIBRARY*, 314 W Saint Louis St, 62254. SAN 304-3398. Tel: 618-537-4504. FAX: 618-537-4399. Web Site: lebanonpubliclibrary.org. *Librn,* Margaret Whaley
Founded 1946. Pop 3,523; Circ 13,655
Library Holdings: Bk Vols 15,000; Per Subs 35
Special Collections: Charles Dickens Coll
Mem of Illinois Heartland Library System
Partic in Midwest Collaborative for Library Services (MCLS)
Open Mon-Thurs 12-7, Fri 12-5, Sat 9-1

C MCKENDREE UNIVERSITY, Holman Library, 701 College Rd, 62254-1299. SAN 304-3401. Tel: 618-537-6950. Interlibrary Loan Service Tel: 618-537-6515. Reference Tel: 618-537-6952. Administration Tel: 618-537-6514. Toll Free Tel: 800-232-7228. FAX: 618-537-8411. E-mail: library_faculty@mckendree.edu. Web Site: www.mckendree.edu/library. *Libr Dir,* Rebecca Schreiner; E-mail: rlschreiner@mckendree.edu; *Govt Doc & Tech Serv Librn, Univ Archivist,* Deborah Houk; Tel: 618-537-6951, E-mail: djhouk@mckendree.edu; *Pub Serv Librn,* Jennifer Funk; E-mail: jafunk@mckendree.edu; *Ref/IT Librn,* Paula Martin; E-mail: phmartin@mckendree.edu. Subject Specialists: *Computer sci, Soc sci,* Deborah Houk; *Commun, Lang,* Jennifer Funk; *Educ, Nursing,* Paula Martin; Staff 5 (MLS 4, Non-MLS 1)
Founded 1828. Enrl 2,400; Fac 98; Highest Degree: Doctorate
Library Holdings: Audiobooks 20; AV Mats 10,000; DVDs 3,000; Bk Titles 74,000; Bk Vols 100,000; Per Subs 100
Special Collections: Abraham Lincoln (Warren Grauel Coll); Archives of the Southern Illinois Conference of the United Methodist Church; Journalism, Illinois History & Literature (Irving Dilliard Coll). US Document Depository
Subject Interests: Computer sci, Educ, Humanities, Nursing, Soc sci & issues
Automation Activity & Vendor Info: (Acquisitions) Ex Libris Group; (Cataloging) Ex Libris Group; (Circulation) Ex Libris Group; (Course Reserve) Ex Libris Group; (ILL) OCLC; (OPAC) Ex Libris Group; (Serials) Ex Libris Group
Database Vendor: Alexander Street Press, American Chemical Society, EBSCOhost, Gale Cengage Learning, LexisNexis, OCLC FirstSearch, OCLC WorldShare Interlibrary Loan, OVID Technologies, Oxford Online, ProQuest, Sage, ValueLine
Wireless access
Partic in Consortium of Academic & Research Libraries in Illinois; Ill Coordinated Coll Mgt Prog; Illinois Library & Information Network; Saint Louis Regional Library Network; SILRC
Open Mon-Thurs 7am Midnight, Fri 7 5, Sat 12 5, Sun 3pm Midnight

LEMONT

P LEMONT PUBLIC LIBRARY DISTRICT*, 50 E Wend St, 60439-6439. SAN 304-3428. Tel: 630-257-6541. FAX: 630-257-7737. E-mail: info@lemontlibrary.org. Web Site: www.lemontlibrary.org. *Dir,* Sandra Pointon; E-mail: spointon@lemontlibrary.org; Staff 5.5 (MLS 3.5, Non-MLS 2)
Founded 1943. Pop 22,017; Circ 158,876
Library Holdings: CDs 3,713; DVDs 4,707; Bk Vols 91,498; Per Subs 213
Automation Activity & Vendor Info: (Acquisitions) SirsiDynix
Wireless access
Function: Adult bk club, Bks on cassette, Bks on CD, CD-ROM, Children's prog, Computers for patron use, Copy machines, Handicapped accessible, Homework prog, ILL available, Music CDs, Notary serv, Online ref, Outreach serv, Photocopying/Printing, Prog for adults, Prog for children & young adult, Pub access computers, Ref serv available, Scanner, Senior outreach, Story hour, Summer reading prog, Tax forms, Teen prog, Telephone ref, VHS videos, Web-catalog, Wheelchair accessible
Publications: News For Kids (Newsletter); Read All About It (Newsletter)
Mem of Reaching Across Illinois Library System (RAILS)
Partic in Pinnacle Library Cooperative
Open Mon-Thurs 9-9, Fri 9-6, Sat 9-5, Sun 1-6
Restriction: Authorized patrons
Friends of the Library Group

LENA

P LENA COMMUNITY DISTRICT LIBRARY*, 300 W Mason St, 61048. (Mail add: PO Box 756, 61048-0756), SAN 304-3444. Tel: 815-369-3180. Administration Tel: 815-369-3182. FAX: 815-369-3181. E-mail: lenalibrary@le-win.net. *Dir,* Pennie V Miller; *Asst Librn,* Dixie Althoff; *Coordr, Ch Serv,* Kathy Andrews; Staff 3 (Non-MLS 3)
Founded 1912. Pop 5,184; Circ 43,000
Library Holdings: Bk Titles 20,000; Per Subs 82
Special Collections: Lena Stars since 1871 (local newspapers for genealogy research, microfilm)
Subject Interests: Child welfare, Health sci, Hist, Relig
Mem of Reaching Across Illinois Library System (RAILS)
Open Mon & Thurs 12-9, Tues 9-5 & 7-9, Wed 9-5, Fri & Sat 9-3

LEROY

P J T & E J CRUMBAUGH MEMORIAL PUBLIC LIBRARY*, 405 E Center St, 61752-1723. (Mail add: PO Box 129, 61752-0129), SAN 304-338X. Tel: 309-962-3911. E-mail: jtejcrumbaughlibrary@hotmail.com. *Head Librn,* Tracy Dotson; *Librn,* Denise Cox; *Librn,* Fae Morris; *Librn,* Kelly Stills
Founded 1927. Circ 39,797
Library Holdings: AV Mats 170; Bks on Deafness & Sign Lang 10; High Interest/Low Vocabulary Bk Vols 150; Large Print Bks 385; Bk Titles 14,000; Per Subs 30; Talking Bks 50
Special Collections: Local Cemetery Records; Spiritualist Section
Subject Interests: Fine arts, Genealogy, Hist, Local hist
Function: Archival coll, Res libr
Publications: J T & E J Crumbaugh Spiritualist Church & Memorial Library (history booklet); Tracing Your Roots (genealogy booklet)
Special Services for the Blind - Talking bks
Open Mon-Fri 10-5, Sat 10-3

LEWISTOWN

S DICKSON MOUNDS MUSEUM LIBRARY*, 10956 N Dickson Mounds Rd, 61542. SAN 375-1279. Tel: 309-547-3721. FAX: 309-547-3189. Web Site: www.museum.state.il.us/ismsites/dickson/. *Dir,* Dr Michael Wiant; E-mail: wiant@museum.state.il.us; *Librn,* Mary Hughes; E-mail: mhughes@museum.state.il.us
Library Holdings: Bk Titles 1,500; Per Subs 40
Wireless access
Function: Res libr
Publications: Illinois State Museum Scientific Reports; newsletter
Restriction: Non-circulating, Open by appt only

LEXINGTON

P LEXINGTON PUBLIC LIBRARY DISTRICT*, 207 S Cedar St, 61753. SAN 304-3460. Tel: 309-365-7801. FAX: 309-365-9028. E-mail: lexingtonl@yahoo.com. Web Site: www.lexington.lib.il.us. *Dir,* Evelyn Homan; E-mail: evelynhoman@yahoo.com
Founded 1896. Pop 3,000; Circ 33,500
Jul 2010-Jun 2011 Income $130,000, State $3,000, Locally Generated Income $95,000. Mats Exp $130,000, Books $18,000, Per/Ser (Incl. Access Fees) $2,000, AV Mat $2,000, Electronic Ref Mat (Incl. Access Fees) $600. Sal $82,000
Library Holdings: Audiobooks 600; CDs 468; DVDs 1,000; Large Print Bks 700; Bk Titles 25,000; Per Subs 80; Videos 500
Special Collections: Art prints, Library of America-Literacy Materials
Automation Activity & Vendor Info: (Acquisitions) SirsiDynix; (Cataloging) SIRSI WorkFlows; (Circulation) SIRSI WorkFlows; (ILL) OCLC FirstSearch; (OPAC) SIRSI WorkFlows
Database Vendor: OCLC ArticleFirst, OCLC FirstSearch, OCLC WorldShare Interlibrary Loan, Overdrive, Inc, SirsiDynix, TumbleBookLibrary
Function: Bks on CD, CD-ROM, Computers for patron use, Copy machines, e-mail & chat, Electronic databases & coll, Fax serv, Free DVD rentals, Home delivery & serv to Sr ctr & nursing homes, Homebound delivery serv, Music CDs, Online cat, Online ref, OverDrive digital audio bks, Prog for adults, Prog for children & young adult, Pub access computers, Ref serv available, Scanner, Story hour, Summer reading prog, Tax forms
Partic in Illinois Library & Information Network; OCLC Online Computer Library Center, Inc
Open Mon & Wed 9:30-11:30 & 1-8:30, Tues & Thurs 1-8:30, Fri 1-5, Sat 9-Noon

LIBERTYVILLE

M CONDELL MEDICAL CENTER*, Fohrman Library, 900 Garfield Ave, 60048. SAN 375-9385. Tel: 847-990-5265. FAX: 847-990-2806. Web Site: www.condell.org. *Dir,* Terri L Licari-DeMay; E-mail: tldemay@hotmail.com. Subject Specialists: *Med, Pharmaceuticals, Psychol,* Terri L Licari-DeMay; Staff 1 (MLS 1)
Library Holdings: Bk Titles 500; Per Subs 130; Spec Interest Per Sub 130
Database Vendor: OCLC FirstSearch
Function: Doc delivery serv, Health sci info serv, ILL available, Online searches, Ref serv available
Restriction: Med staff only

P COOK MEMORIAL PUBLIC LIBRARY DISTRICT*, 413 N Milwaukee Ave, 60048-2280. SAN 304-3479. Tel: 847-362-2330. FAX: 847-362-2354. Interlibrary Loan Service FAX: 847-362-0006. Reference FAX: 847-362-5105. Web Site: www.cooklib.org. *Dir,* Stephen Kershner; E-mail: skershner@cooklib.org; *Assoc Dir,* Mary Ellen Stembal; E-mail: mstembal@cooklib.org; *Asst Dir, Pub Serv,* David Archer; E-mail: darcher@cooklib.org; *Asst Dir, Support Serv,* Lauren Cerniglia; E-mail: lcerniglia@cooklib.org; *Adult Serv Mgr,* Jennifer Plohr; *Ch Mgr,* Melissa Henderson; Staff 94 (MLS 20, Non-MLS 74)
Founded 1921. Pop 60,069; Circ 1,589,191
Library Holdings: AV Mats 42,356; e-books 1,894; Bk Vols 203,457; Per Subs 624
Special Collections: Genealogy Coll; Lake County History Coll
Automation Activity & Vendor Info: (Cataloging) Infor Library & Information Solutions; (Circulation) Infor Library & Information Solutions; (OPAC) Infor Library & Information Solutions; (Serials) Infor Library & Information Solutions
Database Vendor: Gale Cengage Learning, OCLC FirstSearch, OCLC WorldShare Interlibrary Loan, ProQuest
Publications: INS & OUTS (Newsletter)
Special Services for the Deaf - TTY equip
Special Services for the Blind - Talking bks
Open Mon-Thurs 9-9, Fri 9-6, Sat 9-5, Sun (Sept-June) 1-5
Friends of the Library Group
Bookmobiles: 1

S HOLLISTER INCORPORATED*, Minnie Schneider Resource Center, 2000 Hollister Dr, 60048. SAN 326-9604. Tel: 847-680-1000. FAX: 847-918-3453. *Mgr, Libr Serv,* Elizabeth A LaGro; Tel: 847-918-3890, E-mail: elizabeth.lagro@hollister.com; *Librn,* Maureen Malinowski; Tel: 847-918-5805, E-mail: maureen.malinowski@hollister.com; *Info Res,* Marie Schultz; E-mail: marie.schultz@hollister.com; Staff 3 (MLS 3)
Founded 1983
Library Holdings: Bk Titles 4,500; Per Subs 200
Subject Interests: Med
Wireless access
Function: Archival coll, Audio & video playback equip for onsite use, Computers for patron use, Doc delivery serv, Electronic databases & coll, ILL available, Online cat, Online ref, Online searches, Orientations, Ref & res, Ref serv available, Scanner
Restriction: Co libr

S LAKE COUNTY PLANNING RESOURCE CENTER*, Research Library, Central Permit Facility, 500 W Winchester Rd, Unit 101, 60048-1331. SAN 329-952X. Reference Tel: 847-377-2600. FAX: 847-984-5743. Staff 1 (MLS 1)
Founded 1977
Library Holdings: Bk Vols 5,000; Per Subs 10
Special Collections: Lake County Aerial Maps, 1939-present
Subject Interests: Census data, Land use, Maps, Municipal info, Natural environ, Planning, Planning law
Automation Activity & Vendor Info: (OPAC) Inmagic, Inc.
Restriction: Open to pub for ref only

LINCOLN

CR LINCOLN CHRISTIAN UNIVERSITY, Jessie C Eury Library, 100 Campus View Dr, 62656. SAN 304-3509. Tel: 217-732-7788, Ext 2234. Toll Free Tel: 888-522-5228, Ext 2234. FAX: 217-732-3785. E-mail: library@lincolnchristian.edu. Web Site: lincolnchristian.edu/library. *Dir,* Nancy J Olson; Tel: 217-732-7788, Ext 2281, E-mail: nolson@lincolnchristian.edu; *Info Serv Librn,* Leslie Starasta; Tel: 217-732-7788, Ext 2203, E-mail: lstarasta@lincolnchristian.edu; *Asst Librn,* Mike Reid; Tel: 217-732-7788, Ext 2283, E-mail: mreid@lincolnchristian.edu; Staff 3 (MLS 3)
Founded 1944. Enrl 900; Fac 40; Highest Degree: Doctorate
Library Holdings: AV Mats 8,000; Bk Vols 90,000; Per Subs 350
Special Collections: Restoration Movement, sermons, hymnals, mission materials
Subject Interests: Biblical studies, Church hist, Educ, Theol
Automation Activity & Vendor Info: (Acquisitions) Ex Libris Group; (Cataloging) Ex Libris Group; (Circulation) Ex Libris Group; (Course Reserve) Ex Libris Group; (OPAC) Ex Libris Group; (Serials) Ex Libris Group
Wireless access
Mem of Illinois Heartland Library System
Partic in Christian Libr Network; Consortium of Academic & Research Libraries in Illinois
Open Mon-Thurs 7:30am-11pm, Fri 7:30-5, Sat 9:30-4, Sun 2-6

C LINCOLN COLLEGE*, McKinstry Library, 300 Keokuk, 62656. SAN 304-3517. Tel: 217-732-3155, Ext 290. Toll Free Tel: 800-569-0556. FAX: 217-732-4465. Web Site: www.lincolncollege.edu. *Dir,* Mike Starasta
Founded 1865. Enrl 642; Highest Degree: Doctorate
Library Holdings: Bk Vols 40,000; Per Subs 250
Special Collections: Lincoln
Mem of Illinois Heartland Library System
Partic in Sangamon Valley Academic Library Consortium
Open Mon-Thurs (Winter) 8:30-10, Fri 8:30-5, Sat 1-4, Sun 3:30-10; Mon-Fri (Summer) 8:30-4

S LINCOLN CORRECTIONAL CENTER LIBRARY*, 1098 1350th St, 62656-5094. (Mail add: RR 3, Box 549, 62656). Tel: 217-735-5411, Ext 368. FAX: 217-735-1361. *Librn,* Tracy Hill
Library Holdings: Bk Titles 6,000
Open Tues-Fri 7:30-4

P LINCOLN PUBLIC LIBRARY DISTRICT, 725 Pekin, 62656. SAN 304-3525. Tel: 217-732-5732, 217-732-8878. FAX: 217-732-6273. Web Site: www.lincolnpubliclibrary.org. *Dir,* Richard Sumrall; E-mail: directorlpld@gmail.com
Founded 1901. Pop 14,300
Jul 2014-Jun 2015 Income $661,000. Mats Exp $68,690. Sal $318,600
Library Holdings: CDs 1,877; DVDs 2,199; Bk Titles 55,400; Per Subs 150
Special Collections: Lincoln Coll; Logan County History & Genealogy
Automation Activity & Vendor Info: (Circulation) SirsiDynix; (OPAC) SirsiDynix
Wireless access
Publications: Human Services Directory
Mem of Illinois Heartland Library System
Open Mon, Wed & Fri 9-5, Tues & Thurs 9-7, Sat 9-1

S LOGAN CORRECTIONAL CENTER LIBRARY*, 1096 1350th St, Box 1000, 62656. SAN 376-0863. Tel: 217-735-5581, Ext 329. FAX: 217-735-4381. *Librn,* Kevin Brinton
Library Holdings: Bk Titles 6,160; Per Subs 12
Subject Interests: Easy bks, Spanish
Mem of Illinois Heartland Library System
Open Mon-Fri 7:30-3:30
Restriction: Staff use only

LINCOLNSHIRE

S AON HEWITT LIBRARY*, Four Overlook Point, 60069. SAN 304-3533. Tel: 847-295-5000. *Mgr, Client Res & Info Serv,* Patricia L Kuhl; E-mail: patti.kuhl@aonhewitt.com; Staff 7 (MLS 2, Non-MLS 5)
Founded 1946
Library Holdings: Bk Vols 300
Subject Interests: Benefits (Labor), Compensation (Labor), Human resources
Automation Activity & Vendor Info: (Circulation) EOS International
Database Vendor: EOS International

P VERNON AREA PUBLIC LIBRARY DISTRICT*, 300 Olde Half Day Rd, 60069-2901. SAN 304-5722. Tel: 847-634-3650. Interlibrary Loan Service Tel: 847-634-3650, Ext 160. FAX: 847-634-8449. Interlibrary Loan Service FAX: 847-634-8667. Web Site: www.vapld.info. *Dir,* Cynthia Fuerst; *Head, Adult Serv,* Keith Barlog; *Head, Circ Serv,* Stephen D Territo; *Head, Tech Serv,* Judy Nuernberger; *Head, Youth Serv,* Janice Kellman; *Mgr, Info Tech,* Reed Martin; Staff 130 (MLS 22, Non-MLS 108)
Founded 1974. Pop 43,000; Circ 76,846
Library Holdings: AV Mats 32,735; e-books 20,818; Bk Vols 227,957; Per Subs 924
Subject Interests: Local hist
Automation Activity & Vendor Info: (Acquisitions) Horizon; (Cataloging) Horizon; (Circulation) Horizon; (OPAC) Horizon; (Serials) Horizon
Database Vendor: Dialog, Gale Cengage Learning, LexisNexis, OCLC FirstSearch, ProQuest, Wilson - Wilson Web
Wireless access
Function: Adult bk club, After school storytime, Bk club(s), CD-ROM, Digital talking bks, Handicapped accessible, Home delivery & serv to Sr ctr & nursing homes, Homebound delivery serv, Homework prog, ILL available, Magnifiers for reading, Music CDs, Online searches, Photocopying/Printing, Prog for adults, Prog for children & young adult, Ref serv available, Spoken cassettes & CDs, Spoken cassettes & DVDs, Summer reading prog, Telephone ref, VHS videos, Wheelchair accessible
Publications: Columns (Newsletter)
Open Mon-Thurs 9-9, Fri & Sat 9-5, Sun 12-5
Friends of the Library Group

S ZENITH ELECTRONICS LLC*, Technical Library, 2000 Millbrook Dr, 60069. SAN 304-2294. Tel: 847 941 8000. FAX: 847-941-8555. *Dir,* Tim Laud; E-mail: tim.laud@zenith.com; Staff 1 (Non-MLS 1)
Founded 1956
Library Holdings: Bk Titles 2,014; Per Subs 46
Subject Interests: Bus, Eng, Math
Database Vendor: OCLC FirstSearch
Function: Res libr
Partic in Illinois Library & Information Network
Restriction: Not open to pub

LINCOLNWOOD

P LINCOLNWOOD PUBLIC LIBRARY DISTRICT*, 4000 W Pratt Ave, 60712. SAN 320-1813. Tel: 847-677-5277. FAX: 847-677-1937. Web Site: www.lincolnwoodlibrary.org. *Adult Serv, Coll Develop,* Gail Inman; *Ch Serv,* Sharon Levine; *Circ,* Vandana Sehgal; *Tech Serv,* Shao-Chen Lin; Staff 10 (MLS 7, Non-MLS 3)
Founded 1978. Pop 12,500; Circ 148,000
Library Holdings: AV Mats 10,000; Large Print Bks 5,000; Bk Vols 60,000; Per Subs 105; Talking Bks 5,000
Special Collections: David Zemsky Low Vision Center; Lincolnwood Historical Coll; Literacy Coll
Automation Activity & Vendor Info: (Cataloging) SirsiDynix; (Circulation) SirsiDynix; (ILL) SirsiDynix; (OPAC) SirsiDynix
Publications: Lincolnwood Library; The Acorn (quarterly newsletter)
Partic in Illinois Library & Information Network; OCLC Online Computer Library Center, Inc
Open Mon-Thurs 9-9, Fri 9-6, Sat 9-5, Sun 12:30-5
Friends of the Library Group

LISLE

C BENEDICTINE UNIVERSITY LIBRARY*, 5700 College Rd, 60532-0900. SAN 304-355X. Tel: 630-829-6050. Circulation Tel: 630-829-6058. Interlibrary Loan Service Tel: 630-829-6056. Reference Tel: 630-829-6057. Administration Tel: 630-829-6060. FAX: 630-960-9451. Web Site: www.ben.edu/library. *Univ Librn,* Jack Fritts; E-mail: jfritts@ben.edu; *Assoc Univ Librn,* Luann DeGreve; Tel: 630-829-6197, E-mail: ldegreve@ben.edu; *Archives & Spec Coll Librn,* Julie Wroblewski; *Bus Outreach Librn,* Kent Carrico; Tel: 630-829-6055, E-mail: kcarrico@ben.edu; *Digital Res Librn,* Amy Weidner; E-mail: aweidner@ben.edu; *Instruction Librn,* Joan Hopkins; E-mail: jhopkins@ben.edu; *Ref Librn,* Frances Gilles; E-mail: fgilles@ben.edu; *Ref Librn,* Mary Ocasek; E-mail: mocasek@ben.edu; *Sci Outreach Librn,* Joy McGehee; E-mail: jmcgehee@ben.edu; *ILL Coordr,* Diane Madrid; *Cataloger,* Mark A Kroll; E-mail: mkroll@ben.edu; Staff 14.5 (MLS 9.5, Non-MLS 5)
Founded 1887. Enrl 5,000; Fac 160; Highest Degree: Doctorate
Library Holdings: Bk Titles 85,000; Bk Vols 126,464; Per Subs 676
Special Collections: College Archives; John Erlenborn Papers; Rare Books & Manuscripts. State Document Depository
Subject Interests: Humanities, Theol
Automation Activity & Vendor Info: (Acquisitions) Ex Libris Group; (Cataloging) Ex Libris Group; (Circulation) Ex Libris Group; (Course Reserve) Ex Libris Group; (OPAC) Ex Libris Group; (Serials) Ex Libris Group
Database Vendor: EBSCOhost, Gale Cengage Learning, ProQuest
Wireless access
Mem of Reaching Across Illinois Library System (RAILS)
Partic in Consortium of Academic & Research Libraries in Illinois; LIBRAS, Inc; OCLC Online Computer Library Center, Inc

Departmental Libraries:

CHARLES E BECKER LIBRARY, 1500 N Fifth St, Springfield, 62702, SAN 304-6788. Tel: 217-525-1420, Ext 235. Toll Free Tel: 800-635-7289. FAX: 217-525-2651. *Br Dir, Libr Serv,* Brian Hickam; Tel: 217-525-1420, Ext 221, E-mail: bhickam@ben.edu; *Access Serv, Pub Serv Librn,* Pamm Collebrusco; E-mail: collebrusco@ben.edu; *Pub Serv Librn, Ref,* Eric Edwards; Staff 3 (MLS 3)
Founded 1929. Enrl 600; Fac 60; Highest Degree: Doctorate
Library Holdings: Bk Vols 20,000; Per Subs 200
Subject Interests: Humanities
Automation Activity & Vendor Info: (ILL) Ex Libris Group
Database Vendor: JSTOR, OCLC FirstSearch, Thomson - Web of Science
Function: ILL available, Photocopying/Printing
Mem of Illinois Heartland Library System
Open Mon-Thurs 8am-9pm, Fri 8-4, Sat & Sun 12-5
Restriction: Non-circulating to the pub, Open to students, fac & staff

P LISLE LIBRARY DISTRICT*, 777 Front St, 60532-3599. SAN 304-3568. Tel: 630-971-1675. FAX: 630-971-1701. Web Site: www.lislelibrary.org. *Dir, Libr Serv,* Katharine Seelig; E-mail: seeligk@lislelibrary.org; *Dir, Adult Serv,* Tatiana Weinstein; E-mail: tatiana@lislelibrary.org; *Circ Serv Dir,* Paul Hurt; E-mail: paulhurt@lislelibrary.org; *Dir, Tech Serv,* Beth McQuillan; E-mail: mcquil@lislelibrary.org; *Dir, Youth Serv,* Will Savage; E-mail: savagew@lislelibrary.org; *ILL Coordr,* Krista Kloepperk; E-mail: kloepperk@lislelibrary.org; *Literacy Coordr,* Jean Demas; E-mail: literacy@lislelibrary.org; Staff 15 (MLS 15)
Founded 1967. Pop 29,568; Circ 480,000
Library Holdings: Bk Vols 115,000; Per Subs 420
Subject Interests: Local hist, Oriental art
Automation Activity & Vendor Info: (Circulation) Innovative Interfaces, Inc; (Serials) EBSCO Online
Wireless access
Function: Adult literacy prog, AV serv, BA reader (adult literacy), Doc delivery serv, Homebound delivery serv, ILL available, Photocopying/Printing, Prog for children & young adult, Summer reading prog, Wheelchair accessible
Publications: Newsletter (Monthly)
Mem of Reaching Across Illinois Library System (RAILS)
Special Services for the Deaf - TTY equip; Videos & decoder
Open Mon-Fri 9:30-9, Sat 9:30-5, Sun 1-5
Friends of the Library Group

S MORTON ARBORETUM*, Sterling Morton Library, 4100 Illinois Rte 53, 60532-1293. SAN 304-3576. Tel: 630-719-2429. FAX: 630-719-7950. E-mail: library@mortonarb.org. Web Site: www.mortonarb.org, www.sterlingmortonlibrary.org. *Digital Assets Librn,* Maureen Murphy; *Coll Mgr,* Rita Hassert; E-mail: rhassert@mortonarb.org. Subject Specialists: *Archives, Digitization,* Maureen Murphy; *Botany, Hort, Rare bk cat,* Rita Hassert; Staff 4 (MLS 3, Non-MLS 1)
Founded 1922
Library Holdings: Bk Titles 28,000; Per Subs 200
Special Collections: Asia (E H Wilson Photo Coll); Botanical Art & Illustration; History & Topography Maps of Arboretum & Vicinity, 1922-present; Landscape Archives (Jens Jensen, Marshall Johnson & O C Simonds Coll) bks, letters, photos/slides, plans; May T Watts Coll, ms; Morton Arboretum Archives; Nursery Catalogs, pre-1920
Subject Interests: Birds, Botanical bibliography, Botanical hist, Botany, Environ studies, Forestry, Gardening, Hort, Landscape archit, Mammals, Natural hist, Plant sci
Automation Activity & Vendor Info: (Cataloging) OCLC; (Circulation) Innovative Interfaces, Inc - Millenium; (ILL) OCLC; (OPAC) Innovative Interfaces, Inc - Millenium; (Serials) Innovative Interfaces, Inc - Millenium
Database Vendor: EBSCOhost, OCLC FirstSearch
Wireless access
Function: Adult bk club, Archival coll, Art exhibits, e-mail serv, Exhibits, ILL available, Online cat, Photocopying/Printing, Ref serv available, Telephone ref, Wheelchair accessible

Mem of Reaching Across Illinois Library System (RAILS)
Partic in Illinois Library & Information Network; System Wide Automated Network
Open Tues-Fri 9-5, Sat 10-4
Restriction: Restricted borrowing privileges

LITCHFIELD

P LITCHFIELD CARNEGIE PUBLIC LIBRARY*, 400 N State St, 62056. SAN 304-3584. Tel: 217-324-3866. FAX: 217-324-3884. E-mail: library@litchfieldil.com. Web Site: www.litchfieldpubliclibrary.org. *Librn,* Sara Zumwalt; Staff 5 (Non-MLS 5)
Founded 1872. Pop 6,883; Circ 67,348
Library Holdings: Bk Vols 37,000; Per Subs 136
Special Collections: Genealogy & Local History
Subject Interests: Genealogy
Automation Activity & Vendor Info: (Cataloging) Follett Software; (Circulation) Follett Software
Mem of Illinois Heartland Library System
Open Mon, Wed & Fri 10-5, Tues & Thurs 1-8, Sat 10-2
Friends of the Library Group

LOCKPORT

P WHITE OAK LIBRARY DISTRICT*, Lockport Branch, 121 E Eighth St, 60441. SAN 340-5036. Tel: 815-838-0755. Web Site: www.whiteoaklibrary.org. *Dir,* Scott Pointon; E-mail: spointon@whiteoaklibrary.org; *Asst Dir,* Beverly Krakovec; E-mail: bkrakovec@dpvlib.org; *Br Mgr,* Patricia Jarog; E-mail: pjarog@dpvlib.org; Staff 8 (MLS 6, Non-MLS 2)
Founded 1921. Pop 77,893
Automation Activity & Vendor Info: (Cataloging) SirsiDynix; (Circulation) SirsiDynix
Wireless access
Publications: Check It Out (Newsletter)
Mem of Reaching Across Illinois Library System (RAILS)
Open Mon-Thurs 10-8:30, Fri & Sat 10-5, Sun 1-5
Friends of the Library Group
Branches: 2
CREST HILL BRANCH, 1298 Theodore St, Crest Hill, 60403, SAN 328-8692. Tel: 815-725-0234. *Br Mgr,* Amy Byrne-Henderson
Founded 1969
Open Mon-Thurs 10-8:30, Fri & Sat 10-5, Sun 1-5
Friends of the Library Group
ROMEOVILLE BRANCH, 201 W Normantown Rd, Romeoville, 60446. Tel: 815-886-2030. *Br Mgr,* Beverly Jean Krakovec; E-mail: bkrakovec@dpvlib.org; Staff 16 (MLS 9, Non-MLS 7)
Founded 1973
Open Mon-Thurs 10-8:30, Fri & Sat 10-5, Sun 1-5
Friends of the Library Group

LODA

P A HERR SMITH & E E SMITH LODA TOWNSHIP LIBRARY*, 105 E Adams St, 60948. (Mail add: PO Box 247, 60948-0247), SAN 304-3592. Tel: 217-386-2783. FAX: 217-386-2223. *Librn,* Nancy Seamands; E-mail: knabsea@prairieinet.net
Pop 1,306; Circ 5,010
Library Holdings: Bk Vols 5,100
Wireless access
Mem of Illinois Heartland Library System
Open Mon, Tues & Thurs 9-12 & 2-5, Wed 8-12, Sat 9-12

LOMBARD

S LOMBARD HISTORICAL SOCIETY LIBRARY, 23 W Maple St, 60148. SAN 374-9193. Tel: 630-629-1885. E-mail: lombardhistory@att.net. Web Site: www.lombardhistory.org. *Dir,* Natalie Troiani
Library Holdings: Bk Vols 350; Per Subs 20

CM NATIONAL UNIVERSITY OF HEALTH SCIENCES LEARNING RESOURCE CENTER*, Sordoni-Burich Library, 200 E Roosevelt Rd, Bldg C, 60148-4583. SAN 304-3614. Tel: 630-889-6612. Circulation Tel: 630-889-6612. Interlibrary Loan Service Tel: 630-889-6613. Reference Tel: 630-889-6617. Administration Tel: 630-889-6610. FAX: 630-495-6658. Web Site: www.nuhs.edu/lrc. *Dir,* Joyce Ellen Whitehead; E-mail: jwhitehead@nuhs.edu; *Asst Dir/Circ Mgr,* Patricia Genardo; Tel: 630-889-6597, E-mail: pgenardo@nuhs.edu; *Ref Librn,* Russell Iwami; E-mail: riwami@nuhs.edu; *Tech Serv Librn,* Anne Scott Hope; Tel: 630-889-6538, E-mail: ahope@nuhs.edu; Staff 8 (MLS 5, Non-MLS 3)
Founded 1920. Enrl 650; Fac 40; Highest Degree: Doctorate
Library Holdings: Bk Vols 16,000; Per Subs 375; Spec Interest Per Sub 300
Special Collections: Chiropractic Coll; History of National University of Health Sciences Coll
Subject Interests: Acupuncture, Alternative healing, Alternative med, Biomed sci, Chiropractic, Complementary med, Massage therapy, Naturopathic med, Neurology, Nutrition, Oriental med, Radiology, Sports med
Automation Activity & Vendor Info: (Cataloging) SirsiDynix; (Circulation) SirsiDynix; (OPAC) SirsiDynix; (Serials) SirsiDynix
Database Vendor: EBSCOhost, OCLC FirstSearch, OVID Technologies
Wireless access
Mem of Reaching Across Illinois Library System (RAILS)
Partic in Chiropractic Libr Consortium; Fox Valley Health Science Library Consortium; Illinois Library & Information Network
Open Mon-Thurs 7:30am-11pm, Fri 7:30-6, Sat & Sun 9-9

CR NORTHERN BAPTIST THEOLOGICAL SEMINARY*, Brimson Grow Library, 680 E Butterfield Rd, 60148. SAN 304-4904. Tel: 630-620-2104. Administration Tel: 630-620-2115. FAX: 630-620-2170. E-mail: library@seminary.edu. Web Site: www.seminary.edu/bgl. *Dir,* Blake Walter; E-mail: bwalter@seminary.edu; Staff 4 (MLS 2, Non-MLS 2)
Founded 1913. Enrl 220; Fac 16; Highest Degree: Master
Library Holdings: AV Mats 1,300; e-books 8,100; Bk Titles 45,320; Bk Vols 53,180; Per Subs 296; Videos 334
Special Collections: Library of John Peck & Hubbel Loomis
Subject Interests: Baptist hist, Bible, Christian hist, Christian theol, New Testament, Relig in Am, Theol, Women's studies in relig
Automation Activity & Vendor Info: (Acquisitions) Ex Libris Group; (Cataloging) Ex Libris Group; (Circulation) Ex Libris Group; (Course Reserve) Ex Libris Group; (ILL) OCLC; (OPAC) Ex Libris Group; (Serials) Ex Libris Group
Database Vendor: EBSCOhost, OCLC FirstSearch, OVID Technologies
Function: Res libr
Partic in Association of Chicago Theological Schools; Consortium of Academic & Research Libraries in Illinois; Illinois Library & Information Network
Open Mon-Thurs 9am-11pm, Fri 9am-10pm, Sat 9-5
Restriction: Non-circulating to the pub

P HELEN M PLUM MEMORIAL PUBLIC LIBRARY DISTRICT*, Lombard Public Library, 110 W Maple St, 60148-2594. SAN 304-3630. Tel: 630-627-0316. FAX: 630-627-0336. Web Site: www.helenplum.org. *Dir,* Robert A Harris; E-mail: bharris@helenplum.org; *Bus Mgr,* Denise Ragona; E-mail: dragona@helenplum.org; *Head, Adult Serv,* Linda Schehl; E-mail: lschehl@helenplum.org; *Head, Circ,* Karen Kee; E-mail: kkee@helenplum.org; *Head, Tech Proc,* Bronwen Culhane; E-mail: bculhane@helenplum.org; *Head, Youth Serv,* Claudia Krauspe; E-mail: ckrauspe@helenplum.org; *Mkt & Graphics Coordr,* Jennifer Amling; E-mail: jamling@helenplum.org; *Syst Support Spec,* Julie Adamski; E-mail: jadamski@helenplum.org; Staff 22 (MLS 15, Non-MLS 7)
Founded 1928. Pop 43,894; Circ 568,572
Library Holdings: Audiobooks 439; CDs 11,234; DVDs 3,184; Electronic Media & Resources 1,335; Bk Vols 196,688; Per Subs 432; Videos 759
Subject Interests: Art & archit, Local hist, Music
Automation Activity & Vendor Info: (Acquisitions) Innovative Interfaces, Inc - Millenium; (Cataloging) Innovative Interfaces, Inc - Millenium; (Circulation) Innovative Interfaces, Inc - Millenium; (ILL) Innovative Interfaces, Inc - Millenium; (OPAC) Innovative Interfaces, Inc - Millenium; (Serials) Innovative Interfaces, Inc - Millenium
Database Vendor: EBSCOhost, Gale Cengage Learning, OCLC FirstSearch, Overdrive, Inc, ProQuest, ReferenceUSA, Wilson - Wilson Web
Wireless access
Function: Adult bk club, AV serv, Bks on CD, CD-ROM, Children's prog, Computers for patron use, Copy machines, e-mail & chat, Electronic databases & coll, Exhibits, Fax serv, Free DVD rentals, Handicapped accessible, Homebound delivery serv, ILL available, Magnifiers for reading, Mail & tel request accepted, Music CDs, Online cat, Outreach serv, OverDrive digital audio bks, Photocopying/Printing, Preschool outreach, Prog for adults, Prog for children & young adult, Pub access computers, Ref serv in person, Spoken cassettes & CDs, Spoken cassettes & DVDs, Story hour, Summer & winter reading prog, Tax forms, Teen prog, Telephone ref, Wheelchair accessible
Publications: PLUM JAM (Monthly); PLUM TREE (Monthly)
Mem of Reaching Across Illinois Library System (RAILS)
Partic in Illinois Library & Information Network
Open Mon-Fri 9-9, Sat 9-5, Sun 1-5
Friends of the Library Group

LOSTANT

P LOSTANT COMMUNITY LIBRARY*, 102 W Third St, 61334. (Mail add: PO Box 189, 61334), SAN 304-3657. Tel: 815-368-3530. FAX: 815-368-8035. E-mail: lostantlibrary@yahoo.com. Web Site: lostant.lib.il.us. *Dir,* Christine Hubbard
Founded 1961. Pop 1,400; Circ 2,059
Library Holdings: Bk Vols 3,775
Subject Interests: Local hist

Wireless access
Mem of Reaching Across Illinois Library System (RAILS)
Open Tues 10-5, Wed 1-7, Thurs & Fri 1-5, Sat 9-1

LOVES PARK

P NORTH SUBURBAN LIBRARY DISTRICT*, 6340 N Second St, 61111. SAN 304-3665. Tel: 815-633-4247. Circulation Tel: 815-633-4247, Ext 16. Interlibrary Loan Service Tel: 815-633-4247, Ext 20. Reference Tel: 815-633-4247, Ext 12. FAX: 815-633-4249. Web Site: www.northsuburbanlibrary.org. *Dir,* Mary Petro; E-mail: maryp@northsld.org; *Head, Ref (Info Serv),* Nicole Johnson, *Ref Librn,* Linda Kapusta; *YA Librn,* Jessica Skaggs; *Acq, Coll Develop,* Denise Williams; *Cat,* Kathryn M Rasch; *Ch Serv,* Barb Jacobs; *Circ,* Peggy Miller; *ILL,* Mary Packer; Staff 7 (MLS 7)
Founded 1944. Pop 61,145; Circ 642,228
Library Holdings: Bk Vols 479,235; Per Subs 460
Subject Interests: Local hist
Automation Activity & Vendor Info: (Acquisitions) Innovative Interfaces, Inc; (Cataloging) Innovative Interfaces, Inc; (Circulation) Innovative Interfaces, Inc; (OPAC) Innovative Interfaces, Inc; (Serials) Innovative Interfaces, Inc
Wireless access
Publications: Elementary Education Newsletter; North Suburban District Library Newsletter; Secondary Education Newsletter; Staff Notes; Young Adult Committee Newsletter
Mem of Reaching Across Illinois Library System (RAILS)
Open Mon-Thurs 9-8:30, Fri & Sat 9-5:30
Friends of the Library Group
Branches: 1
ROSCOE BRANCH, 5562 Clayton Circle, Roscoe, 61073, SAN 329-2614. Tel: 815-623-6266. FAX: 815-623-8591. *Br Mgr, Ref Librn,* Linda Kapusta
Open Mon-Thurs 9-8, Fri & Sat 9-5

LOVINGTON

P LOVINGTON PUBLIC LIBRARY DISTRICT, 110 W State St, 61937. (Mail add: PO Box 199, 61937-0199), SAN 304-3673. Tel: 217-873-4468. FAX: 217-873-6068. E-mail: lovingtonpld@gmail.com. *Librn,* Darlene Barlow
Founded 1943. Pop 1,954; Circ 11,145
Jul 2009-Jun 2010 Income $70,000, State $1,116, County $65,173, Other $3,325. Mats Exp $4,100. Sal $37,135
Library Holdings: Bk Vols 20,722; Per Subs 38
Wireless access
Mem of Illinois Heartland Library System
Open Mon 10-8, Tues & Wed 1-6, Thurs & Sat 10-1, Fri 10-6
Friends of the Library Group

LYONS

P LYONS PUBLIC LIBRARY*, 4209 Joliet Ave, 60534-1597. SAN 304-3681. Tel: 708-447-3577. FAX: 708-447-3589. E-mail: lyons@lyonslibrary.org. Web Site: www.lyonslibrary.org. *Dir,* Sarah C Horn; *Circ & Tech Serv Mgr,* Bret Bieska; *Head, Adult Serv,* Linda Isaacson; *Head, Youth Serv,* Elisa Rodriguez; Staff 12 (MLS 3, Non-MLS 9)
Founded 1938. Pop 10,255
Library Holdings: Bk Vols 60,197; Per Subs 115
Special Collections: 17th, 18th, 19th Century Passenger Lists; Chicago Metropolitan History & Genealogy
Subject Interests: Genealogy, Ill
Automation Activity & Vendor Info: (Acquisitions) Innovative Interfaces, Inc; (Cataloging) Innovative Interfaces, Inc; (Circulation) Innovative Interfaces, Inc; (ILL) Innovative Interfaces, Inc; (OPAC) Innovative Interfaces, Inc; (Serials) Innovative Interfaces, Inc
Database Vendor: EBSCOhost, Grolier Online, H W Wilson, Innovative Interfaces, Inc, OCLC FirstSearch
Wireless access
Function: Accelerated reader prog, After school storytime, Art exhibits, Audio & video playback equip for onsite use, AV serv, Bk club(s), Bks on cassette, Bks on CD, CD-ROM, Children's prog, Computer training, Computers for patron use, Copy machines, e-mail serv, E-Reserves, Electronic databases & coll, Family literacy, Fax serv, Free DVD rentals, Games & aids for the handicapped, Handicapped accessible, Holiday prog, ILL available, Instruction & testing, Magnifiers for reading, Mail & tel request accepted, Mus passes, Music CDs, Notary serv, Online cat, Online searches, Outside serv via phone, mail, e-mail & web, Passport agency, Preschool outreach, Pub access computers, Ref serv available, Senior computer classes, Story hour, Summer reading prog, Tax forms, Telephone ref, Web-catalog, Wheelchair accessible, Workshops
Publications: Literally Lyons (Newsletter)
Mem of South Central Kansas Library System
Partic in System Wide Automated Network
Special Services for the Deaf - ADA equip; Bks on deafness & sign lang; Captioned film dep; Closed caption videos; Sign lang interpreter upon request for prog; Staff with knowledge of sign lang; TTY equip; Video & TTY relay via computer
Open Mon-Thurs 10-9, Fri 10-6, Sat 10-5

MACKINAW

P MACKINAW DISTRICT PUBLIC LIBRARY*, 117 S Main, 61755. (Mail add: PO Box 560, 61755-0560), SAN 304-372X. Tel: 309-359-8022. FAX: 309-359-6502. *Dir,* Vicky Dierker
Founded 1934. Pop 4,045; Circ 42,831
Jul 2008-Jun 2009 Income $145,700, State $4,894, County $133,431, Locally Generated Income $7,375. Mats Exp $36,824, Books $28,384, AV Mat $8,440. Sal $60,589
Library Holdings: CDs 2,090; DVDs 1,358; Bk Titles 28,544; Per Subs 59
Automation Activity & Vendor Info: (Circulation) SirsiDynix
Function: Homebound delivery serv
Partic in Illinois Library & Information Network; RSA
Open Mon 10-7, Tues & Thurs 12-6, Wed 12-7, Fri 12-5, Sat 9-12

MACOMB

P MACOMB PUBLIC LIBRARY DISTRICT*, 235 S Lafayette St, 61455-2231. SAN 304-3754. Tel: 309-833-2714. FAX: 309-833-2714. E-mail: library@macomb.com. Web Site: www.macomb.lib.il.us. *Dir,* Dennis Danowski; *Ch Serv,* Margaret Sowers; Staff 6 (MLS 1, Non-MLS 5)
Founded 1881. Pop 20,045; Circ 97,000
Jul 2011-Jun 2012 Income $365,000, State $25,000, Locally Generated Income $340,000. Mats Exp $55,500, Books $41,500, Per/Ser (Incl. Access Fees) $5,000, Micro $1,500, AV Mat $5,000, Presv $2,500. Sal $199,000
Library Holdings: Audiobooks 1,500; CDs 2,550; DVDs 329; Large Print Bks 600; Bk Vols 60,000; Per Subs 100; Videos 250
Special Collections: Illinois Local History Coll, bks & photog
Automation Activity & Vendor Info: (Circulation) SirsiDynix
Database Vendor: SirsiDynix
Wireless access
Open Mon, Tues, Thurs & Sat 9-6, Wed & Fri 9-9, Sun (Winter) 1-4
Friends of the Library Group

C WESTERN ILLINOIS UNIVERSITY, Leslie F Malpass Library, One University Circle, 61455. SAN 304-3762. Tel: 309-298-2762. Circulation Tel: 309-298-2705. Interlibrary Loan Service Tel: 309-298-2761. Reference Tel: 309-298-2700. FAX: 309-298-2791. Web Site: www.wiu.edu/library. *Dean of Libr,* Michael G Lorenzen; E-mail: MG-Lorenzen@wiu.edu; *Asst Dean, Libr,* Jeanne Stierman; Tel: 309-298-2739, E-mail: JD-Stierman@wiu.edu; Staff 15 (MLS 15)
Founded 1903. Enrl 13,000; Fac 650; Highest Degree: Doctorate
Library Holdings: Bk Titles 868,519; Bk Vols 998,041; Per Subs 3,200
Special Collections: Birds of Prey (Elton Fawks Coll); Center for Icarian Studies; Political Science (US Congressman Tom Railsback Coll); Theatre (Burl Ives Coll); West Central Illinois Local History Coll; Western Illinois University Theses; Wildlife Conservation (Virginia Eifert Coll). Oral History; State Document Depository; US Document Depository
Wireless access
Function: Archival coll
Partic in OCLC Online Computer Library Center, Inc
Open Mon, Wed & Fri 7:30-5, Tues 7:30-9, Sat 1-5

MACON

P SOUTH MACON PUBLIC LIBRARY DISTRICT*, 451 W Glenn St, 62544. SAN 304-3770. Tel: 217-764-3356. FAX: 217-764-5490. E-mail: southmaconlibrary@gmail.com. Web Site: southmacon.lib.il.us. *Dir,* Kay Burrous; *Asst Librn,* Carol Anne Smith; E-mail: casmith1@hotmail.com; *Webmaster,* Carol Robinett
Founded 1980. Pop 2,842; Circ 8,426
Library Holdings: AV Mats 1,029; Bk Titles 9,813; Per Subs 46
Automation Activity & Vendor Info: (Acquisitions) SirsiDynix; (Cataloging) SirsiDynix; (Circulation) SirsiDynix; (Course Reserve) SirsiDynix; (ILL) SirsiDynix; (Media Booking) SirsiDynix; (OPAC) SirsiDynix; (Serials) SirsiDynix
Wireless access
Mem of Illinois Heartland Library System
Open Mon, Tues, Fri & Sat 10-12 & 1:30-5:30, Wed 1:30-8, Thurs 1:30-5:30
Friends of the Library Group

MADISON

P MADISON PUBLIC LIBRARY*, 1700 Fifth St, 62060. SAN 304-3789. Tel: 618-876-8448. FAX: 618-876-8316. E-mail: madisonpublibrary@gmail.com. *Dir,* Judy Padgett; Staff 2 (MLS 2)
Pop 4,545; Circ 123,982

Library Holdings: Bk Vols 27,000
Mem of South Central Library System
Partic in Morris Automated Information Network
Open Tues & Fri 8-4:30, Sat 8-2

MAHOMET

P MAHOMET PUBLIC LIBRARY DISTRICT*, 1702 E Oak Street Mahomet, 61853-7427. SAN 304-3797. Tel: 217-586-2611. FAX: 217-586-5710. E-mail: staff@mahometpubliclibrary.org. Web Site: www.mahometpubliclibrary.org. *Dir,* Lynn Schmit; E-mail: lynn@mahometpubliclibrary.org; Staff 12 (MLS 2, Non-MLS 10)
Founded 1966. Pop 10,113; Circ 84,371
Library Holdings: Bk Vols 24,000; Per Subs 100
Automation Activity & Vendor Info: (Acquisitions) SirsiDynix; (Cataloging) SirsiDynix; (Circulation) SirsiDynix; (Media Booking) SirsiDynix; (OPAC) SirsiDynix; (Serials) SirsiDynix
Mem of Illinois Heartland Library System
Open Mon-Thurs 9-8, Fri 9-6, Sat 9-3, Sun 2-5
Friends of the Library Group

MALTA

J KISHWAUKEE COLLEGE LIBRARY*, 21193 Malta Rd, 60150-9699. SAN 304-3800. Tel: 815-825-2086, Ext 2250. Interlibrary Loan Service Tel: 815-825-2086, Ext 3030. Reference Tel: 815-825-2086, Ext 5700. FAX: 815-825-2072. Web Site: www.kish.cc.il.us/. *Dir, Libr Serv,* Anne-Marie Eggleston; Tel: 815-825-2086, Ext 3660, E-mail: egglestn@kishwaukeecollege.edu; *Ref Librn,* Tim Lockman; Tel: 815-825-2086, Ext 5660, E-mail: tlockman@kishwaukeecollege.edu; *Ref Librn,* Carol Wubbena; Tel: 815-825-2086, Ext 5670, E-mail: cwubbena@kishwaukeecollege.edu; Staff 10 (MLS 2, Non-MLS 8)
Founded 1968. Enrl 2,410; Fac 105; Highest Degree: Associate
Library Holdings: High Interest/Low Vocabulary Bk Vols 815; Bk Titles 38,966; Bk Vols 44,399; Per Subs 248
Special Collections: Oral History
Automation Activity & Vendor Info: (Acquisitions) Ex Libris Group; (Cataloging) Ex Libris Group; (Circulation) Ex Libris Group; (Course Reserve) Ex Libris Group; (Media Booking) Ex Libris Group; (OPAC) Ex Libris Group; (Serials) Ex Libris Group
Database Vendor: EBSCOhost, OCLC FirstSearch
Mem of Reaching Across Illinois Library System (RAILS)
Partic in Northern Illinois Learning Resources Cooperative (NILRC)
Special Services for the Blind - Computer with voice synthesizer for visually impaired persons
Open Mon-Thurs 7:30am-9:30pm, Fri 7:30-3:30, Sat 8:30-1:30
Friends of the Library Group

P MALTA TOWNSHIP PUBLIC LIBRARY, 203 E Adams, 60150. (Mail add: PO Box 54, 60150), SAN 304-3819. Tel: 815-825-2525. FAX: 815-825-1525. Web Site: www.maltalibrary.org. *Dir,* Peggy Wogen; E-mail: pjwogen@maltalibrary.org; Staff 2.6 (Non-MLS 2.6)
Founded 1921. Pop 1,608; Circ 13,823
Library Holdings: Audiobooks 717; CDs 446; DVDs 1,110; e-books 19,589; Large Print Bks 534; Bk Vols 12,084; Per Subs 37
Subject Interests: Am Indians, Civil War
Automation Activity & Vendor Info: (Cataloging) Innovative Interfaces, Inc; (Circulation) Innovative Interfaces, Inc; (ILL) Innovative Interfaces, Inc; (OPAC) Innovative Interfaces, Inc
Database Vendor: Baker & Taylor, Booklist Online, Facts on File, Ingram Library Services, OCLC FirstSearch, OCLC WebJunction, OCLC WorldShare Interlibrary Loan, Overdrive, Inc
Wireless access
Function: Adult bk club, Art exhibits, Audio & video playback equip for onsite use, Bks on cassette, Bks on CD, CD-ROM, Children's prog, Computers for patron use, Copy machines, Family literacy, Fax serv, Handicapped accessible, ILL available, Music CDs, Notary serv, Online cat, Online searches, Prog for adults, Prog for children & young adult, Pub access computers, Ref serv available, Scanner, Story hour, Summer reading prog, Teen prog, VHS videos, Wheelchair accessible
Mem of Reaching Across Illinois Library System (RAILS)
Open Mon & Wed-Fri 3:30-8, Tues 1-8, Sat 10-3

MANHATTAN

P MANHATTAN-ELWOOD PUBLIC LIBRARY DISTRICT*, 240 Whitson St, 60442. (Mail add: PO Box 53, 60442-0053), SAN 304-3827. Tel: 815-478-3987. FAX: 815-478-3988. Web Site: www.mpld.org. *Dir,* Judith Ann Pet; E-mail: jpet@mpld.org; *Asst Dir, Circ Mgr,* Barbara Hnetkovsky; E-mail: bhnetkovsky@mpld.org; *Ad,* Noreen Bormet; E-mail: nabormet@mpld.org; *Ch Mgr,* Amy Ingalls; E-mail: alingalls@mpld.org; *Tech Serv Mgr,* Mary Ellen Byford; E-mail: mebyford@mpld.org; *Teen Serv Mgr,* Mary Blatti; E-mail: mcblatti@mpld.org; Staff 21 (MLS 2, Non-MLS 19)
Founded 1909. Pop 13,166; Circ 162,047
Jul 2012-Jun 2013 Income $687,603, State $13,020, Locally Generated Income $646,833, Other $22,730. Mats Exp $59,637, Books $41,440, Per/Ser (Incl. Access Fees) $4,195, AV Mat $7,001, Electronic Ref Mat (Incl. Access Fees) $7,001. Sal $391,159
Library Holdings: CDs 2,146; DVDs 3,083; e-books 10,767; Electronic Media & Resources 1,625; Large Print Bks 2,227; Bk Vols 56,140; Per Subs 118
Subject Interests: Accelerated readers, Gardening, Local hist, Parenting
Automation Activity & Vendor Info: (Acquisitions) SirsiDynix; (Cataloging) Innovative Interfaces, Inc; (Circulation) SirsiDynix; (ILL) Innovative Interfaces, Inc; (OPAC) Innovative Interfaces, Inc; (Serials) Innovative Interfaces, Inc
Database Vendor: Baker & Taylor, Gale Cengage Learning, Medline, OCLC FirstSearch, Overdrive, Inc, SirsiDynix, TumbleBookLibrary, ValueLine, World Book Online
Wireless access
Function: Accelerated reader prog, Adult bk club, Audiobks via web, Bks on cassette, Bks on CD, Children's prog, Computers for patron use, Copy machines, Electronic databases & coll, Fax serv, Free DVD rentals, Handicapped accessible, Home delivery & serv to Sr ctr & nursing homes, Homebound delivery serv, ILL available, Magnifiers for reading, Mus passes, Music CDs, Notary serv, Online cat, Online ref, Online searches, Outreach serv, OverDrive digital audio bks, Photocopying/Printing, Prog for adults, Prog for children & young adult, Pub access computers, Ref serv available, Ref serv in person, Scanner, Senior computer classes, Senior outreach, Story hour, Summer & winter reading prog, Summer reading prog, Tax forms, Teen prog, Telephone ref, VHS videos, Video lending libr, Web-catalog, Wheelchair accessible
Mem of Reaching Across Illinois Library System (RAILS)
Partic in Prairienet
Special Services for the Blind - Assistive/Adapted tech devices, equip & products
Open Mon-Thurs 9-9, Fri 9-5, Sat 9-3
Friends of the Library Group

MANITO

P FORMAN VALLEY PUBLIC LIBRARY DISTRICT*, 404 1/2 S Harrison, 61546. (Mail add: PO Box 710, 61546-0710), SAN 320-8230. Tel: 309-968-6093. FAX: 309-968-7120. *Librn,* Debbie Horchem; *Ch Serv,* Michele Wyss
Pop 6,000
Library Holdings: Bk Vols 19,000; Per Subs 40
Automation Activity & Vendor Info: (Circulation) TLC (The Library Corporation)
Open Mon-Fri 8:30-6:30, Sat 9-1

MANSFIELD

P BLUE RIDGE TOWNSHIP PUBLIC LIBRARY*, Mansfield Public Library, 116 E Oliver St, 61854. (Mail add: PO Box 457, 61854-0457), SAN 304-3835. Tel: 217-489-9033. FAX: 217-489-9320. E-mail: mansfieldlibrary@yahoo.com. Web Site: www.mansfield.lib.il.us. *Libr Dir,* Brenda Edwards; *Asst Librn,* Sheila Roth
Founded 1923. Pop 1,418; Circ 12,970
Library Holdings: Bk Vols 10,000; Per Subs 55
Special Collections: Oral History
Mem of Illinois Heartland Library System
Open Mon, Wed & Fri 1-7, Tues & Thurs 4-7, Sat 8-12
Friends of the Library Group

MANTENO

S ILLINOIS VETERAN'S HOME LIBRARY*, One Veterans Dr, 60950-9466. Tel: 815-468-6581, Ext 272. FAX: 815-468-0570. *Dir,* Position Currently Open
Founded 1993. Pop 345; Circ 500
Library Holdings: CDs 1,250; DVDs 2,500; Music Scores 1,500; Bk Titles 2,300; Per Subs 140; Videos 1,000
Wireless access
Open Mon-Fri 8-4:30

MAPLE PARK

P MAPLE PARK PUBLIC LIBRARY DISTRICT*, 302 Willow St, 60151. (Mail add: PO Box 159, 60151), SAN 304-386X. Tel: 815-827-3362. FAX: 815-827-4072. E-mail: mppl@maplepark.lib.il.us. Web Site: maplepark.lib.il.us. *Dir,* Kimberly A Martin
Founded 1963. Pop 780; Circ 2,000
Library Holdings: Bk Vols 12,000
Wireless access
Function: Bks on cassette, Bks on CD, CD-ROM, Computers for patron use, Copy machines, Fax serv, Free DVD rentals, Homebound delivery serv, ILL available, Music CDs, Online cat, Photocopying/Printing, Pub access computers, Story hour, Summer reading prog, VHS videos
Mem of Reaching Across Illinois Library System (RAILS)

Open Mon & Wed (Winter) 9:30-12 & 3-8, Tues & Thurs 3-8, Fri 3-5, Sat 10-1; Mon & Wed (Summer) 9-4, Tues & Thurs 1-7, Sat 9-1
Friends of the Library Group

MAQUON

P MAQUON PUBLIC LIBRARY DISTRICT, 210 Main St, 61458-0230. SAN 304-3878. Tel: 309-875-3573. FAX: 309-875-3573. E-mail: maquon01@mymctc.net. *Dir,* Mary Payton
Founded 1943. Circ 10,215
Library Holdings: CDs 53; Large Print Bks 563; Bk Titles 14,920; Videos 395
Wireless access
Open Tues & Thurs 12-7, Wed & Fri 10-5, Sat 9-12

MARENGO

P MARENGO-UNION LIBRARY DISTRICT*, 200 S State St, 60152. SAN 304-3886. Tel: 815-568-8236. FAX: 815-568-5209. Web Site: www.muld.org. *Dir,* Kevin Drinka; *Head, Adult Serv,* Susan Parker; E-mail: susaneparker@muld.org; *Head, Youth Serv,* Sondra Terry; E-mail: sondrat@muld.org; *Circ Mgr/ILL,* Carol Clark
Founded 1878. Pop 12,110; Circ 70,223
Library Holdings: Bk Vols 52,657
Automation Activity & Vendor Info: (Cataloging) Follett Software; (Circulation) Follett Software; (OPAC) Follett Software
Database Vendor: OCLC FirstSearch
Function: ILL available
Mem of Reaching Across Illinois Library System (RAILS)
Open Mon-Thurs 9-8, Fri & Sat 9-5
Friends of the Library Group

MARION

P CRAB ORCHARD PUBLIC LIBRARY DISTRICT*, 20012 Crab Orchard Rd, 62959. SAN 376-0073. Tel: 618-982-2141. Toll Free Tel: 866-982-2141. FAX: 618-982-2141. Web Site: www.colibrary.org. *Dir,* Lola Morris; E-mail: lmorris@shawls.lib.il.us
Library Holdings: Bk Titles 20,000; Per Subs 55
Subject Interests: Genealogy
Mem of Illinois Heartland Library System
Open Tues-Thurs 11-7, Fri 9-5, Sat 1-5
Branches: 1
PITTSBURG BRANCH, 302 W Avery St, Pittsburg, 62974-1009. Tel: 618-997-8111. FAX: 618-997-8111. *Dir,* Lola Morris
Library Holdings: Bk Titles 2,000
Open Tues, Wed & Fri 2-6, Thurs 11-3

S GREATER EGYPT REGIONAL PLANNING & DEVELOPMENT COMMISSION*, Library Research Center, 3000 W DeYoung St, Ste 800B-3, 62959. SAN 326-9124. Tel: 618-997-9351. FAX: 618-997-9354. *Dir,* Cary Minnis; E-mail: caryminnis@greateregypt.org; *Prog Dir,* Margie Mitchell; E-mail: margiemitchell@greateregypt.org
Library Holdings: Bk Vols 400
Restriction: Staff & prof res

P MARION CARNEGIE LIBRARY*, 206 S Market St, 62959-2519. SAN 304-3894. Tel: 618-993-5935. FAX: 618-997-6485. Web Site: www.marioncarnegielibrary.org. *Dir,* David Patton; *Asst Dir,* Erica Hanke; *Admin Supvr,* Judy Wolf; Staff 17 (MLS 2, Non-MLS 15)
Founded 1916. Pop 17,193; Circ 105,652
Library Holdings: AV Mats 2,900; Bks on Deafness & Sign Lang 20; Large Print Bks 3,000; Bk Vols 62,217; Per Subs 80; Talking Bks 1,200; Videos 500
Special Collections: Williamson County Local History Coll
Subject Interests: Civil War, Genealogy, Local hist, Small bus
Automation Activity & Vendor Info: (Acquisitions) SirsiDynix; (Cataloging) SirsiDynix; (Circulation) SirsiDynix; (Course Reserve) SirsiDynix; (ILL) SirsiDynix; (Media Booking) SirsiDynix; (OPAC) SirsiDynix; (Serials) SirsiDynix
Database Vendor: Gale Cengage Learning, H W Wilson, OCLC FirstSearch, OCLC WebJunction, OCLC WorldShare Interlibrary Loan, SirsiDynix, World Book Online
Wireless access
Function: AV serv, Handicapped accessible, Home delivery & serv to Sr ctr & nursing homes, Homebound delivery serv, ILL available, Large print keyboards, Magnifiers for reading, Outside serv via phone, mail, e-mail & web, Photocopying/Printing, Prog for adults, Prog for children & young adult, Ref serv available, Summer reading prog, Telephone ref, Wheelchair accessible
Publications: The Container (Monthly newsletter)
Mem of Illinois Heartland Library System
Partic in Illinois Library & Information Network; OCLC Online Computer Library Center, Inc
Special Services for the Deaf - TTY equip
Special Services for the Blind - Computer with voice synthesizer for visually impaired persons
Open Mon-Thurs 9-8, Fri & Sat 9-5
Friends of the Library Group

MARISSA

P MARISSA PUBLIC LIBRARY*, 212 N Main, 62257. SAN 304-3916. Tel: 618-295-2825. FAX: 618-295-2435. E-mail: marissalibrary@hotmail.com. Web Site: www.marissa.lib.il.us. *Librn,* Linda Smith
Founded 1959. Pop 3,590; Circ 15,859
Jul 2006-Jun 2007 Income $63,815, State $4,450, Federal $2,035, County $54,600, Other $1,400. Mats Exp $5,650, Books $5,450, Per/Ser (Incl. Access Fees) $200. Sal $37,000
Library Holdings: Bk Titles 15,605; Per Subs 38
Mem of Illinois Heartland Library System
Open Tues & Thurs 10-7, Wed & Fri 10-5:30, Sat 9-12
Friends of the Library Group

MARKHAM

P MARKHAM PUBLIC LIBRARY*, 16640 S Kedzie Ave, 60428. SAN 304-3924. Tel: 708-331-0130. FAX: 708-331-0137. E-mail: markhampl@markhamlibrary.org. Web Site: www.markhamlibrary.org. *Dir,* Xavier Menzies; *Asst Dir,* Bridget Roland; Staff 1 (MLS 1)
Founded 1967. Pop 15,172; Circ 53,321
Library Holdings: Bk Titles 21,000; Bk Vols 27,000; Per Subs 35
Wireless access
Mem of Reaching Across Illinois Library System (RAILS)
Open Mon-Thurs 9-8, Fri & Sat 9-5
Friends of the Library Group

MAROA

P MAROA PUBLIC LIBRARY DISTRICT, 305 E Garfield St, 61756. SAN 304-3932. Tel: 217-794-5111. FAX: 217-794-3005. E-mail: maroalibrary@gmail.com. Web Site: maroa.lib.il.us. *Dir,* Amber Scott; *Asst Dir,* Penny Meece; E-mail: penigan@yahoo.com; Staff 3 (Non-MLS 3)
Founded 1945. Pop 2,902; Circ 61,661
Library Holdings: Bk Titles 23,160
Automation Activity & Vendor Info: (Cataloging) SirsiDynix; (Circulation) SirsiDynix
Database Vendor: OCLC FirstSearch
Wireless access
Mem of Illinois Heartland Library System
Open Tues-Fri 9-6, Sat 9-12
Friends of the Library Group

MARQUETTE HEIGHTS

P MARQUETTE HEIGHTS PUBLIC LIBRARY*, 715 Lincoln Rd, 61554-1313. SAN 304-3940. Tel: 309-382-3778. E-mail: mhplib@ntslink.net. Web Site: www.mhlibrary.com. *Librn,* Katie Sumner; E-mail: ksumner@ntslink.net
Founded 1959. Pop 2,824; Circ 4,456
Library Holdings: AV Mats 389; Electronic Media & Resources 31; Bk Vols 15,556; Per Subs 45
Wireless access
Mem of Reaching Across Illinois Library System (RAILS)
Open Mon & Wed 10-5, Tues & Thurs 12-8, Sat 10-3

MARSEILLES

P MARSEILLES PUBLIC LIBRARY, 155 E Bluff St, 61341-1499. SAN 304-3959. Tel: 815-795-4437. FAX: 815-795-5137. Web Site: www.marseilleslibrary.com. *Dir,* Jan Ambrose; Staff 5 (Non-MLS 5)
Founded 1904. Pop 5,090; Circ 19,880
Library Holdings: Bk Vols 20,463; Per Subs 50
Subject Interests: Local hist
Automation Activity & Vendor Info: (Circulation) Follett Software
Wireless access
Mem of Reaching Across Illinois Library System (RAILS)
Open Mon & Wed 10-8, Tues & Thurs 1-8, Fri 1-5, Sat 9-2
Friends of the Library Group

MARSHALL

P MARSHALL PUBLIC LIBRARY*, 612 Archer Ave, 62441. SAN 304-3967. Tel: 217-826-2535. FAX: 217-826-5529. Web Site: www.marshalllibrary.com. *Dir,* Nancy Claypool
Pop 3,392; Circ 26,000
Library Holdings: Bk Vols 25,289; Per Subs 70
Automation Activity & Vendor Info: (Acquisitions) SirsiDynix
Special Services for the Deaf - TDD equip
Open Mon-Wed 10-6, Thurs 10-8, Fri & Sat 10-5
Friends of the Library Group

MARTINSVILLE

P MARTINSVILLE PUBLIC LIBRARY DISTRICT*, 120 E Cumberland, 62442-1000. (Mail add: PO Box 190, 62442-0190), SAN 304-3975. Tel: 217-382-4113. FAX: 217-382-4113. E-mail: mvillelibrary@hotmail.com. *Librn,* Beth Hubbard; *Asst Librn,* Rusty Nave
Library Holdings: Bk Vols 14,000; Per Subs 55
Automation Activity & Vendor Info: (Cataloging) SirsiDynix; (Circulation) SirsiDynix
Mem of Illinois Heartland Library System
Open Mon-Wed & Fri 11-5, Thurs 11-7, Sat 9-1
Friends of the Library Group

MASCOUTAH

P MASCOUTAH PUBLIC LIBRARY*, Three W Church St, 62258. SAN 304-3983. Tel: 618-566-2562. FAX: 618-566-2563. Web Site: www.mascoutah.lib.il.us. *Dir,* Marian Albers; E-mail: malbers@shawls.lib.il.us; *Asst Librn,* Kerry Fangmeyer; Staff 6 (MLS 2, Non-MLS 4)
Founded 1929. Pop 6,737; Circ 43,571
Library Holdings: Bk Titles 42,000; Per Subs 105
Automation Activity & Vendor Info: (Acquisitions) SirsiDynix; (Cataloging) SirsiDynix; (Circulation) SirsiDynix; (Course Reserve) SirsiDynix; (ILL) SirsiDynix; (Media Booking) SirsiDynix; (OPAC) SirsiDynix; (Serials) SirsiDynix
Database Vendor: OVID Technologies, SirsiDynix
Open Mon-Thurs 10-8:30, Fri & Sat 10-5:30

MASON CITY

P MASON CITY PUBLIC LIBRARY DISTRICT*, 820 W Chestnut St, 62664-9768. SAN 304-3991. Tel: 217-482-3799. FAX: 217-482-3799. Web Site: www.masoncitylibrary.org. *Dir,* Diane Yeoman
Pop 3,431; Circ 14,523
Library Holdings: Bk Vols 20,000; Per Subs 20
Automation Activity & Vendor Info: (Acquisitions) SirsiDynix; (Cataloging) SirsiDynix; (Circulation) SirsiDynix; (Course Reserve) SirsiDynix; (ILL) SirsiDynix; (Media Booking) SirsiDynix; (OPAC) SirsiDynix; (Serials) SirsiDynix
Mem of Illinois Heartland Library System
Open Mon 10-7, Tues & Fri 12-5, Sat 10-12
Friends of the Library Group

MATTESON

P MATTESON PUBLIC LIBRARY, 801 S School St, 60443-1897. SAN 304-4009. Tel: 708-748-4431. FAX: 708-748-0510. Administration FAX: 708-748-0579. E-mail: mtslib@sslic.net. Web Site: www.mattesonpubliclibrary.org. *Dir,* Kathy Berggren; E-mail: berggren@sslic.net; *Asst Dir,* William W Madsen; *Head, Circ,* Renee Navarre; *Head, Computer Serv,* Andy Murgas; *Outreach Librn,* Colleen VanderHye; *Adult Serv, Ref,* Bill Downs; *Ch Serv,* Nikeda Webb; *Ref,* Marsha Lotz; Staff 11 (MLS 9, Non-MLS 2)
Founded 1964. Pop 19,009; Circ 232,437
May 2014-Apr 2015 Income $2,211,376. Mats Exp $274,115, Books $61,175, Per/Ser (Incl. Access Fees) $14,500, AV Mat $36,000, Electronic Ref Mat (Incl. Access Fees) $95,000. Sal $1,220,000 (Prof $540,000)
Library Holdings: Audiobooks 3,446; AV Mats 15,469; CDs 3,406; DVDs 7,200; e-books 13,145; Electronic Media & Resources 118; Bk Vols 85,265; Per Subs 207
Automation Activity & Vendor Info: (Acquisitions) Baker & Taylor; (Cataloging) Innovative Interfaces, Inc - Millenium; (Circulation) Innovative Interfaces, Inc - Millenium; (ILL) Innovative Interfaces, Inc - Millenium; (OPAC) Innovative Interfaces, Inc - Millenium
Database Vendor: Baker & Taylor, EBSCO Auto Repair Reference, EBSCOhost, Facts on File, Gale Cengage Learning, Grolier Online, Ingram Library Services, Innovative Interfaces, Inc, LearningExpress, Medline, Newsbank, OCLC ArticleFirst, OCLC FirstSearch, OCLC WorldShare Interlibrary Loan, Overdrive, Inc, ProQuest, World Book Online
Wireless access
Function: Workshops
Publications: Newsletter (Quarterly)
Mem of Reaching Across Illinois Library System (RAILS)
Partic in System Wide Automated Network
Special Services for the Blind - Aids for in-house use; Bks on CD; Descriptive video serv (DVS); Home delivery serv; Large print bks; Magnifiers
Open Mon-Thurs 9-9, Fri & Sat 9-5, Sun (Sept-May) 1-5
Friends of the Library Group

MATTOON

J LAKE LAND COLLEGE LIBRARY, 5001 Lake Land Blvd, 61938. SAN 304-4017. Tel: 217-234-5367. Interlibrary Loan Service Tel: 217-234-5235. Administration Tel: 217-234-5338. Information Services Tel: 217-234-5440. Toll Free Tel: 800-252-4121, Ext 5367 (Illinois only). FAX: 217-234-5533. Web Site: www.lakelandcollege.edu/library. *Dir, Libr Serv,* Scott Drone-Silvers; E-mail: sdronesi@lakelandcollege.edu; *Info Serv Librn,* Sarah B Hill; Tel: 217-234-5540, E-mail: shilll@lakelandcollege.edu; Staff 9 (MLS 2, Non-MLS 7)
Founded 1968. Enrl 3,800; Fac 120; Highest Degree: Associate
Jul 2014-Jun 2015 Income $562,851. Mats Exp $227,000, Books $37,000, Per/Ser (Incl. Access Fees) $14,000, AV Mat $3,000, Electronic Ref Mat (Incl. Access Fees) $173,000. Sal $268,578 (Prof $144,402)
Library Holdings: Audiobooks 336; CDs 365; DVDs 1,189; e-journals 27,500; Electronic Media & Resources 42; Bk Vols 35,800; Per Subs 114; Videos 204
Automation Activity & Vendor Info: (Cataloging) SirsiDynix; (Circulation) SirsiDynix; (ILL) OCLC; (OPAC) SirsiDynix
Database Vendor: ABC-CLIO, Alexander Street Press, American Psychological Association (APA), Baker & Taylor, CQ Press, CredoReference, ebrary, EBSCO Information Services, EBSCOhost, Elsevier, Facts on File, Gale Cengage Learning, JSTOR, LearningExpress, Medline, OCLC FirstSearch, OCLC WorldShare Interlibrary Loan, Oxford Online, ProQuest, PubMed, Sage, ScienceDirect, SerialsSolutions
Wireless access
Function: Art exhibits, AV serv, Copy machines, Electronic databases & coll, ILL available, Online info literacy tutorials on the web & in blackboard, Ref serv available
Mem of Illinois Heartland Library System
Partic in Consortium of Academic & Research Libraries in Illinois; Illinois Library & Information Network; Network of Illinois Learning Resources in Community Colleges
Special Services for the Deaf - Closed caption videos
Open Mon-Thurs (Fall & Spring) 7am-9pm, Fri 7-5, Sat 10-2, Sun 12-9; Mon-Thurs (Summer) 7am-9pm
Restriction: Open to pub for ref & circ; with some limitations

M SARAH BUSH LINCOLN HEALTH CENTER*, Medical Library, 1000 Health Center Dr, 61938. SAN 375-9474. Tel: 217-258-2262, 217-348-2263. FAX: 217-258-2288. E-mail: library@sblhs.org. Web Site: www.sarahbushlibrary.org. *Librn,* Nina Pals
Library Holdings: DVDs 100; e-books 60; e-journals 1,800; Bk Titles 1,300; Per Subs 150; Videos 40
Mem of Illinois Heartland Library System
Open Mon-Fri 8-4:30

P MATTOON PUBLIC LIBRARY*, 1600 Charleston Ave, 61938-3935. SAN 304-4025. Tel: 217-234-2621. FAX: 217-234-2660. E-mail: info@mattoonlibrary.org. Web Site: www.mattoonlibrary.org. *Dir,* Ryan A Franklin; E-mail: ryan@mattoonlibrary.org; Staff 6 (MLS 2, Non-MLS 4)
Founded 1893. Pop 18,291; Circ 82,665
Library Holdings: AV Mats 3,051; Bks on Deafness & Sign Lang 10; Bk Vols 55,000; Per Subs 170
Automation Activity & Vendor Info: (Cataloging) Innovative Interfaces, Inc; (Circulation) Innovative Interfaces, Inc
Database Vendor: OCLC FirstSearch, SirsiDynix
Wireless access
Function: ILL available
Mem of Illinois Heartland Library System
Open Mon-Fri 9-8, Sat 9-5
Friends of the Library Group

MAYWOOD

P MAYWOOD PUBLIC LIBRARY DISTRICT*, 121 S Fifth Ave, 60153. SAN 340-5095. Tel: 708-343-1847. FAX: 708-343-2115. TDD: 708-343-8452. Web Site: www.maywood.org. *Dir,* Stan Huntington; Tel: 703-343-1847, Ext 28, E-mail: shuntington@maywoodlibrary.org; *Dir, Info Serv,* Carol Clover; Tel: 708-343-1847, Ext 21, E-mail: cclover@maywoodlibrary.org; *Head, Computer Dept,* Marcia Burton; Tel: 708-343-1847, Ext 13, E-mail: mburton@maywoodlibrary.org; *Head, Lending Serv,* Felipe Altamirano; Tel: 708-343-1847, Ext 11, E-mail: faltamirano@maywoodlibrary.org; *Head, Tech Serv,* Kristin Flanders; Tel: 708-343-1847, Ext 15, E-mail: kflanders@maywoodlibrary.org; *Head, Youth Serv,* Sheila Ferrari; Tel: 708-343-1847, Ext 24, E-mail: sferrari@maywoodlibrary.org; *Bus Mgr,* Josephine Zaabel; Tel: 708-343-1847, Ext 29, E-mail: jzaabel@maywoodlibrary.org; *Ref Librn, Webmaster,* Victor Dixon; Tel: 708-343-1847, Ext 20, E-mail: vdixon@maywoodlibrary.org; *ILL Coordr,* Arthur Williams; Tel: 703-343-1847, Ext 19, E-mail: awilliams@maywoodlibrary.org; Staff 25 (MLS 5, Non-MLS 20)
Founded 1874. Pop 26,987
Library Holdings: AV Mats 7,489; Bks on Deafness & Sign Lang 50; CDs 1,351; DVDs 1,761; High Interest/Low Vocabulary Bk Vols 241; Large Print Bks 683; Bk Vols 77,870; Per Subs 97; Talking Bks 993; Videos 3,745
Subject Interests: African-Am, Local hist
Automation Activity & Vendor Info: (Circulation) Innovative Interfaces, Inc; (OPAC) Innovative Interfaces, Inc

Wireless access
Mem of Reaching Across Illinois Library System (RAILS)
Open Mon & Wed 9-9, Tues & Thurs-Sat 9-5:30

MCCOOK

P MCCOOK PUBLIC LIBRARY DISTRICT, 8419 W 50th St, 60525-3187. SAN 376-0146. Tel: 708-442-1242. FAX: 708-442-0148. E-mail: mccooklibrary@yahoo.com. Web Site: www.mccook.lib.il.us. *Dir,* Elisa Topper; Staff 3.8 (MLS 1, Non-MLS 2.8)
Founded 1984. Pop 254; Circ 33,997
Jul 2006-Jun 2007 Income $286,376, State $20,953, County $251,923, Locally Generated Income $13,500. Mats Exp $36,343, Books $22,542, Per/Ser (Incl. Access Fees) $3,773, AV Mat $10,028. Sal $103,273
Library Holdings: CDs 2,559; DVDs 3,827; Large Print Bks 150; Bk Vols 16,269; Per Subs 83
Automation Activity & Vendor Info: (Circulation) Innovative Interfaces, Inc; (ILL) Innovative Interfaces, Inc; (OPAC) Innovative Interfaces, Inc; (Serials) Innovative Interfaces, Inc
Database Vendor: OCLC FirstSearch
Wireless access
Function: Adult bk club, Bks on cassette, Bks on CD, Children's prog, Computers for patron use, Copy machines, e-mail serv, Electronic databases & coll, Fax serv, Handicapped accessible, ILL available, Music CDs, Online cat, Online searches, Photocopying/Printing, Prog for children & young adult, Pub access computers, Ref & res, Ref serv available, Summer reading prog, Tax forms, Teen prog, VHS videos, Web-catalog, Wheelchair accessible
Mem of Reaching Across Illinois Library System (RAILS)
Open Mon-Thurs 11-9, Fri 11-6, Sat 11-3
Restriction: Non-resident fee

MCHENRY

M CENTEGRA HEALTH SYSTEM*, Health Science Library, 4201 Medical Center Dr, 60050-8499. SAN 375-9814. Tel: 815-759-4076. FAX: 815-759-8088. Web Site: www.centegra.org. *Librn,* Mari-Clare Wendt; E-mail: mwendt@centegra.com
Library Holdings: Bk Titles 550; Per Subs 44
Mem of Reaching Across Illinois Library System (RAILS)
Open Mon-Fri 8-4:30

P MCHENRY PUBLIC LIBRARY DISTRICT, 809 N Front St, 60050. SAN 304-3711. Tel: 815-385-0036. FAX: 815-385-7085. Web Site: www.mchenrylibrary.org. *Exec Dir,* James C Scholtz; E-mail: jscholtz@mchenrylibrary.org; *Asst Dir,* R William Edminster; *Tech Coordr,* Terry Cashen; *Adult Serv,* Colette Myers; *Ch Serv,* Lesley Jakacki; *Circ,* Mary Amstadt; *ILL,* Bonnie Niepsuj; *Tech Serv,* Kevin Kimbrel; Staff 56 (MLS 11, Non-MLS 45)
Founded 1943. Pop 42,023; Circ 587,872
Jul 2013-Jun 2014 Income $3,382,967, State $52,529, Locally Generated Income $3,149,633, Other $180,805. Mats Exp $331,609, Books $143,410, AV Mat $98,459, Electronic Ref Mat (Incl. Access Fees) $89,740. Sal $1,574,762
Library Holdings: Audiobooks 9,482; AV Mats 2,118; Bks on Deafness & Sign Lang 38; CDs 8,699; DVDs 15,135; e-books 12,795; Electronic Media & Resources 49; Large Print Bks 4,379; Bk Vols 120,234; Per Subs 406; Videos 8
Special Collections: Large-Type Books Coll
Subject Interests: Genealogy
Automation Activity & Vendor Info: (Cataloging) SirsiDynix; (Circulation) SirsiDynix; (ILL) SirsiDynix; (OPAC) BiblioCommons; (Serials) SirsiDynix
Database Vendor: Baker & Taylor, Booksite, EBSCO Auto Repair Reference, Facts on File, Gale Cengage Learning, Grolier Online, H W Wilson, LearningExpress, Newsbank, OCLC FirstSearch, ProQuest, Thomson - Web of Science, TumbleBookLibrary
Wireless access
Publications: The Preface (Newsletter)
Partic in Cooperative Computer Services - CCS
Open Mon-Thurs 9-9, Fri & Sat 9-5, Sun 12-4
Friends of the Library Group

P RIVER EAST PUBLIC LIBRARY*, 813 W Rte 120, 60051. SAN 304-3703. Tel: 815-385-6303. FAX: 815-385-6337. Web Site: www.rivereastlibrary.org. *Dir,* Cherie Wright; E-mail: cherie@rivereastlibrary.org; Staff 5 (MLS 1, Non-MLS 4)
Founded 1960. Pop 4,266
Library Holdings: Bk Titles 13,987; Per Subs 41
Automation Activity & Vendor Info: (Circulation) Follett Software
Open Mon-Thurs 10-7, Fri & Sat 10-5
Friends of the Library Group

MCLEAN

P MOUNT HOPE-FUNKS GROVE TOWNSHIPS LIBRARY DISTRICT*, 111 S Hamilton St, 61754-7624. (Mail add: PO Box 320, 61754-0320), SAN 304-3738. Tel: 309-874-2291. FAX: 309-874-2291. E-mail: mhfglibrary1@hotmail.com. Web Site: geocities.com/mhfglibrary. *Dir,* Suzanne Kruger; *Libr Tech,* Sally Ann Carnahan; *Libr Tech,* Doris Yates
Founded 1917. Pop 1,348
Library Holdings: Bk Titles 13,431; Per Subs 35
Special Collections: McLean Lens Micro Film Coll
Wireless access
Mem of Reaching Across Illinois Library System (RAILS)
Open Mon & Sat 10-3, Tues, Wed & Thurs 2-8

MCLEANSBORO

P MCCOY MEMORIAL LIBRARY*, 118 S Washington St, 62859. SAN 304-3746. Tel: 618-643-2125. FAX: 618-643-2207. *Librn,* Brenda Ledford
Founded 1921. Pop 2,945; Circ 12,372
Library Holdings: Bk Titles 13,858; Per Subs 98
Subject Interests: Genealogy
Mem of Illinois Heartland Library System
Open Mon-Wed & Fri 11-5, Thurs 11-7, Sat 8-3

MELROSE PARK

S ALBERTO CULVER CO*, Research Library, 2525 Armitage Ave, 60160. SAN 304-4033. Tel: 708-450-3155. FAX: 708-450-2551. *Sr Librn,* Position Currently Open; Staff 1 (MLS 1)
Founded 1964
Library Holdings: Bk Titles 1,000; Per Subs 115
Subject Interests: Bus mgt, Cosmetics industry, Food indust
Database Vendor: KOSMET, OCLC FirstSearch, STN International

M GOTTLIEB MEMORIAL HOSPITAL*, Medical Library, 701 W North Ave, 60160. SAN 375-9393. Tel: 708-681-3200, Ext 1173. FAX: 708-681-3973. Web Site: www.gottliebhospital.org. *Librn,* Gloria Kroc; E-mail: gloria_kroc@ghr.org; Staff 1 (MLS 1)
Founded 1961
Library Holdings: Bk Titles 450; Per Subs 6
Restriction: Not open to pub

P MELROSE PARK PUBLIC LIBRARY, 801 N Broadway, 60160. SAN 304-405X. Tel: 708-343-3391. FAX: 708-531-5327. Web Site: mpplibrary.org. *Libr Dir,* Barbara Giordano; *Asst Dir, Circ & Tech Serv Mgr,* Cindy Gluecklich; Staff 9 (MLS 3, Non-MLS 6)
Founded 1898. Pop 23,171; Circ 54,234
Library Holdings: Bk Vols 87,000; Per Subs 183
Special Collections: Cinema
Automation Activity & Vendor Info: (Acquisitions) Innovative Interfaces, Inc
Database Vendor: EBSCOhost, Innovative Interfaces, Inc
Wireless access
Mem of Reaching Across Illinois Library System (RAILS)
Open Mon-Thurs 8-8, Fri 8-5, Sat 10-2

M WESTLAKE COMMUNITY HOSPITAL LIBRARY*, 1225 Lake St, 60160-4000. SAN 320-6572. Tel: 708-938-7215. FAX: 708-316-5816, 708-938-7496. *Librn,* Beth Carlin; Tel: 708-999-8406, E-mail: bcarlin@reshealthcare.org; Staff 2 (MLS 1, Non-MLS 1)
Library Holdings: Electronic Media & Resources 1,000; Bk Vols 200; Per Subs 12
Partic in BRS; Metrop Consortium
Restriction: Not open to pub, Staff use only

MELVIN

P MELVIN PUBLIC LIBRARY*, 102 S Center St, 60952. (Mail add: PO Box 129, 60952-0129), SAN 304-4084. Tel: 217-388-2421. FAX: 217-388-2421. *Librn,* Jacqueline Allen
Pop 614; Circ 6,900
Library Holdings: Bk Vols 8,500; Per Subs 40
Mem of Illinois Heartland Library System
Open Mon-Wed 12-6, Fri 12-5, Sat 10-3
Friends of the Library Group

MENDON

P FOUR STAR PUBLIC LIBRARY DISTRICT, 132 W South St, 62351. (Mail add: PO Box 169, 62351-0169), SAN 375-3271. Tel: 217-936-2131. FAX: 217-936-2132. E-mail: fourstar@adams.net. Web Site: www.fourstarlibrary.com. *Dir,* Jill Lucey
Founded 1990. Pop 4,314
Library Holdings: Bk Titles 14,000; Per Subs 36
Database Vendor: OCLC FirstSearch, SirsiDynix, TLC (The Library Corporation)

Wireless access
Partic in Resource Sharing Alliance
Open Mon-Thurs 2-8, Fri & Sat 10-2

MENDOTA

P GRAVES-HUME PUBLIC LIBRARY DISTRICT*, 1401 W Main, 61342. SAN 304-4092. Tel: 815-538-5142. FAX: 815-538-3816. *Dir,* Connie Beetz; E-mail: cmbeetz@graveshume.lib.il.us
Founded 1870. Pop 7,272; Circ 43,677
Jul 2010-Jun 2011 Income $213,117, State $20,355, Federal $602, County $186,427, Other $5,733. Mats Exp $24,450, Books $14,478, Per/Ser (Incl. Access Fees) $3,000, AV Mat $6,972. Sal $106,852 (Prof $47,545)
Library Holdings: Bk Vols 33,557; Per Subs 119
Mem of Reaching Across Illinois Library System (RAILS)
Friends of the Library Group

MEREDOSIA

P M-C RIVER VALLEY PUBLIC LIBRARY DISTRICT*, 304 Main St, 62665. (Mail add: PO Box 259, 62665-0259), SAN 304-4106. Tel: 217-584-1571. FAX: 217-584-1571. E-mail: vrevircm@adams.net. *Dir,* Janet Wells
Pop 1,904; Circ 16,032
Library Holdings: Bk Vols 17,000; Per Subs 50
Automation Activity & Vendor Info: (Cataloging) Follett Software; (Circulation) Follett Software; (OPAC) Follett Software
Open Mon & Thurs 6-9, Tues 9-5, Wed 9-9, Fri & Sat 1-5

METAMORA

P ILLINOIS PRAIRIE DISTRICT PUBLIC LIBRARY*, 208 E Partridge, 61548. (Mail add: PO Box 770, 61548-0770), SAN 340-515X. Tel: 309-367-4594. FAX: 309-367-2687. Web Site: www.ipdpl.org. *Dir,* Grant A Fredericksen; E-mail: grantf@mtco.com; Staff 1 (MLS 1)
Founded 1950. Pop 21,644; Circ 139,977
Library Holdings: Bk Vols 127,000; Per Subs 381
Special Collections: Local Newspaper (Metamora Herald 1887-present & Washburn Leader 1963-present), micro
Subject Interests: Agr, Antiques, Educ, Hist
Automation Activity & Vendor Info: (Cataloging) TLC (The Library Corporation); (Circulation) TLC (The Library Corporation); (ILL) OCLC; (OPAC) TLC (The Library Corporation)
Database Vendor: OCLC FirstSearch
Partic in OCLC Online Computer Library Center, Inc
Open Mon, Tues, Thurs & Fri 11-5, Wed 7pm-9pm, Sat 10-12
Branches: 6
BENSON BRANCH, 420 E Front, Benson, 61516. (Mail add: PO Box 17, Benson, 61516-0017), SAN 340-5184. Tel: 309-394-2542. FAX: 309-394-2542. *Librn,* Dawn Smith
Open Mon 3-7, Wed 2-5, Fri 2-6, Sat 10-12
GERMANTOWN-HILLS BRANCH, 101 Warrior Way, 61548, SAN 340-5214. Tel: 309-383-2263. FAX: 309-383-2263. *Librn,* Pat Staab
Open Mon & Thurs 2:30-7, Sat 10-12
METAMORA BRANCH, 208 E Partridge, 61548. (Mail add: PO Box 770, 61548-0770), SAN 340-5249. Tel: 309-367-4594. FAX: 309-367-2687. *Librn,* Sharon Thornton
Pop 19,179
Open Mon, Tues, Thurs & Fri 11-5, Wed 7pm-9pm, Sat 10-12
ROANOKE BRANCH, 123 Broad St, Roanoke, 61561. (Mail add: PO Box 657, Roanoke, 61561-0657), SAN 340-5273. Tel: 309-923-7686. FAX: 309-923-7601. *Librn,* Marge Braker
Open Mon 5pm-7pm, Tues & Thurs 1:30-5, Fri 9-Noon, Sat 9:30am-11:30am
SPRINGBAY BRANCH, 411 Illinois St, Springbay, 61611, SAN 340-5303. Tel: 309-822-0444. FAX: 309-822 0444. *Librn,* Lyn Wiegand
Library Holdings: Bk Titles 5,723
Open Mon 10-12 & 2-7, Thurs 2-7, Sat 10-12
WASHBURN BRANCH, 112 W Magnolia, Washburn, 61570. (Mail add: PO Box 128, Washburn, 61570-0128), SAN 340-5338. Tel: 309-248-7429. FAX: 309-248-7429. *Librn,* Donna Adami
Open Mon & Wed 2-5, Fri 4-7, Sat 10-12

METROPOLIS

P METROPOLIS PUBLIC LIBRARY*, 317 Metropolis St, 62960. SAN 304-4114. Tel: 618-524-4312. FAX: 618-524-3675. Web Site: www.metropolis.lib.il.us. *Dir,* Carrie L Stapleton
Pop 7,171; Circ 51,066
Library Holdings: e-books 3,000; Bk Vols 38,000; Per Subs 150
Special Collections: Genealogy Coll
Automation Activity & Vendor Info: (Cataloging) SirsiDynix; (Circulation) SirsiDynix; (Course Reserve) OCLC
Wireless access
Mem of Illinois Heartland Library System
Special Services for the Deaf - Assisted listening device; Bks on deafness & sign lang
Special Services for the Blind - Aids for in-house use; Assistive/Adapted tech devices, equip & products; Bks on CD; Copier with enlargement capabilities; Digital talking bk; Large print bks; Magnifiers; Playaways (bks on MP3); Recorded bks
Open Mon-Thurs 10-7, Fri & Sat 10-6

MIDLOTHIAN

P MIDLOTHIAN PUBLIC LIBRARY*, 14701 S Kenton Ave, 60445-4122. SAN 304-4122. Tel: 708-535-2027. FAX: 708-535-2053. E-mail: mds@midlothianlibrary.org. Web Site: www.midlothianlibrary.org. *Dir,* Mary Beth Sharples; *Head, Circ,* Susan Ross; E-mail: sross@midlothianlibrary.org; *Head, Ref,* Georgette Belisle; E-mail: gbelisle@midlothianlibrary.org; *Head, Youth Serv,* Zena Smith; Staff 23 (MLS 5, Non-MLS 18)
Founded 1931. Pop 14,315; Circ 106,182
May 2008-Apr 2009 Income $909,043, State $24,973, City $764,390, Federal $9,103, Locally Generated Income $110,577. Mats Exp $98,263, Books $67,740, Per/Ser (Incl. Access Fees) $4,000, AV Mat $11,925, Electronic Ref Mat (Incl. Access Fees) $14,598. Sal $370,677 (Prof $214,313)
Library Holdings: AV Mats 3,956; CDs 1,588; DVDs 2,368; Electronic Media & Resources 29; Bk Vols 61,560; Per Subs 261
Automation Activity & Vendor Info: (Cataloging) Innovative Interfaces, Inc; (Circulation) Innovative Interfaces, Inc; (ILL) Innovative Interfaces, Inc; (OPAC) Innovative Interfaces, Inc; (Serials) Innovative Interfaces, Inc
Database Vendor: EBSCOhost, Gale Cengage Learning, LearningExpress, OCLC FirstSearch
Wireless access
Function: Adult bk club, Bks on CD, Children's prog, Computers for patron use, Copy machines, Electronic databases & coll, Fax serv, Mus passes, Music CDs, Online cat, Prog for adults, Prog for children & young adult, Pub access computers, Spoken cassettes & CDs, Story hour, Summer reading prog, Tax forms, Teen prog
Mem of Reaching Across Illinois Library System (RAILS)
Partic in System Wide Automated Network
Open Mon-Thurs 9-8, Fri 9-5, Sat 9-4
Friends of the Library Group

MILFORD

P MILFORD DISTRICT LIBRARY*, Two S Grant Ave, 60953-1399. SAN 304-4130. Tel: 815-889-4722. FAX: 815-889-4722. *Librn,* Sue Crist
Founded 1896. Pop 3,415; Circ 23,284
Library Holdings: Bk Vols 23,000; Per Subs 32
Automation Activity & Vendor Info: (Acquisitions) SirsiDynix; (Cataloging) SirsiDynix; (Circulation) SirsiDynix; (Course Reserve) SirsiDynix; (ILL) SirsiDynix; (Media Booking) SirsiDynix; (OPAC) SirsiDynix; (Serials) SirsiDynix
Mem of Illinois Heartland Library System
Open Mon-Thurs 9-6, Fri 9-5, Sat 9-12

MILLEDGEVILLE

P WYSOX TOWNSHIP LIBRARY*, 18 W Fifth St, 61051-9416. SAN 304-4149. Tel: 815-225-7572. FAX: 815-225-7572. *Dir,* Jan McKean
Pop 1,865; Circ 8,968
Library Holdings: Bk Vols 12,193; Per Subs 24
Mem of Reaching Across Illinois Library System (RAILS)
Open Mon 1-8, Tues & Thurs 1-6, Wed 10-6, Sat 9-2

MILLSTADT

P MILLSTADT LIBRARY*, 115 W Laurel St, 62260. SAN 376-0901. Tel: 618-476-1887. FAX: 618-476-1887. Web Site: millstadt-library.org. *Dir,* Mary Eckert; *Librn,* Marilyn Gagliolo
Founded 1964
Library Holdings: Bk Titles 15,000; Per Subs 46
Automation Activity & Vendor Info: (Circulation) SirsiDynix
Mem of Illinois Heartland Library System
Open Mon-Thurs Noon-8, Fri & Sat 10-2

MINERAL

P MINERAL-GOLD PUBLIC LIBRARY DISTRICT*, 120 E Main St, 61344. (Mail add: PO Box 87, 61344-0087), SAN 304-4157. Tel: 309-288-3971. FAX: 309-288-3971. E-mail: minerallibrary@mchsi.com. *Librn,* Connie Baele
Pop 720; Circ 15,425
Library Holdings: Bk Vols 14,638; Per Subs 30
Subject Interests: Gardening, Local hist
Mem of Reaching Across Illinois Library System (RAILS)
Open Mon 1-6, Tues 9-12 & 1-5, Wed 1-8, Fri 9-12 & 1-4, Sat 9-12 & 1-3

MINIER

P H A PEINE MEMORIAL LIBRARY*, 202 N Main Ave, 61759. (Mail add: PO Box 19, 61759-0019), SAN 304-4165. Tel: 309-392-3220. FAX: 309-392-2697. E-mail: minierlibrary@yahoo.com. *Dir,* Denise Litwiller
Founded 1929. Pop 1,262; Circ 9,600
Library Holdings: Bk Vols 15,000; Per Subs 30
Open Mon-Thurs 12-8, Fri 12-6, Sat 9-1

MINONK

P FILGER PUBLIC LIBRARY*, 261 E Fifth St, 61760. SAN 304-4173. Tel: 309-432-2929. FAX: 309-432-2929. E-mail: filgerlibrary@frontier.com. Web Site: minonklibrary.wordpress.com. *Dir,* Karen Podzamsky; *Ch,* Debra Brunier
Founded 1915. Pop 1,984; Circ 25,412
Library Holdings: Bk Vols 28,000; Per Subs 65
Wireless access
Open Mon-Wed 9-5, Thurs 9-7, Fri & Sat 9-Noon

MOKENA

P MOKENA COMMUNITY PUBLIC LIBRARY DISTRICT*, 11327 W 195th St, 60448. SAN 304-4181. Tel: 708-479-9663. FAX: 708-479-9684. Web Site: www.mokena.lib.il.us. *Dir,* Phyllis A Jacobek; Fax: 708-479-1690, E-mail: pjacobek@sbcglobal.net; *Head, Circ,* Dawn Ellingham; E-mail: dellingham@mokena.lib.il.us; *Head, Tech Serv,* Nancy Baker; E-mail: nbaker@mokena.lib.il.us; *Head, YA,* Michaelene Cervantes-Squires; E-mail: mcervantes@mokena.lib.il.us; *Head, Youth Serv,* Pat Hoornaert; E-mail; phoornaert@mokena.lib.il.us; *Bus Librn,* Cathy Palmer; E-mail: cpalmer@mokena.lib.il.us; *Ref Serv,* Carol Tracy; E-mail: ctracy@mokena.lib.il.us; Staff 38 (Non-MLS 38)
Founded 1976. Pop 15,821; Circ 160,000
Library Holdings: Bk Vols 130,000; Per Subs 325
Subject Interests: Parenting
Automation Activity & Vendor Info: (Acquisitions) SirsiDynix; (Cataloging) SirsiDynix; (Circulation) SirsiDynix; (Course Reserve) SirsiDynix; (ILL) SirsiDynix; (Media Booking) SirsiDynix; (OPAC) SirsiDynix; (Serials) SirsiDynix
Database Vendor: EBSCOhost, Gale Cengage Learning, OCLC FirstSearch
Publications: Newsletter (in-house, monthly)
Mem of Reaching Across Illinois Library System (RAILS)
Open Mon-Thurs 9-9, Fri 9-6, Sat 9-5
Friends of the Library Group

MOLINE

J BLACK HAWK COLLEGE, 6600 34th Ave, 61265. SAN 340-5362. Tel: 309-796-5700. Reference Tel: 309-796-5147. FAX: 309-796-0393. E-mail: libraryref@bhc.edu. Web Site: www.bhc.edu/qclibrary. *Dir,* Ashtin Trimble; E-mail: trimblea@bhc.edu; *Ref & Instruction,* Position Currently Open; Staff 4.5 (MLS 2, Non-MLS 2.5)
Founded 1946. Enrl 4,887; Fac 312, Highest Degree: Associate
Automation Activity & Vendor Info: (Acquisitions) Innovative Interfaces, Inc; (Cataloging) Innovative Interfaces, Inc; (Circulation) Innovative Interfaces, Inc; (Course Reserve) Innovative Interfaces, Inc; (OPAC) Innovative Interfaces, Inc
Database Vendor: ABC-CLIO, American Psychological Association (APA), ARTstor, Cinahl, CQ Press, CredoReference, EBSCOhost, Facts on File, Gale Cengage Learning, JSTOR, LexisNexis, OCLC FirstSearch, OCLC WorldShare Interlibrary Loan, Oxford Online, ProQuest
Wireless access
Mem of Reaching Across Illinois Library System (RAILS)
Partic in Consortium of Academic & Research Libraries in Illinois; Network of Illinois Learning Resources in Community Colleges

S DEERE & CO LIBRARY, One John Deere Pl, 61265. SAN 340-5397. Tel: 309-765-3329. Interlibrary Loan Service Tel: 309-765-5200. FAX: 309-765-4088. E-mail: library@johndeere.com. Web Site: www.deere.com. *Mgr, Info, Knowledge & Internal Serv,* Sean O'Hanlon; E-mail: ohanlonsean@johndeere.com; *Mgr, Res,* Stacy Bell; *Info Mgt Team Leader,* Christine Walker; E-mail: walkerchristinea@johndeere.com; Staff 8 (MLS 2, Non-MLS 6)
Founded 1958
Library Holdings: Bk Titles 8,000; Bk Vols 10,000; Per Subs 500
Special Collections: Deere & Company History
Subject Interests: Agr, Bus & mgt, Construction, Econ, Eng, Finance, Forestry, Mkt
Automation Activity & Vendor Info: (Acquisitions) Softlink America; (Cataloging) Softlink America; (Circulation) Softlink America; (OPAC) Softlink America; (Serials) Softlink America
Partic in Illinois Library & Information Network; OCLC Online Computer Library Center, Inc

P MOLINE PUBLIC LIBRARY, 3210 41st St, 61265. SAN 340-5486. Tel: 309-524-2440. FAX: 309-524-2441. TDD: 309-762-0609. E-mail: reference@molinelibrary.org. Web Site: www.molinelibrary.com. *Libr Dir,* Lee Ann E Fisher; Tel: 309-736-2442, Fax: 309-797-3751, E-mail: lfisher@molinelibrary.org
Library Holdings: Bk Vols 203,417
Wireless access
Partic in RiverShare Libraries
Special Services for the Deaf - TDD equip
Open Mon-Thurs 9-8, Fri 9-5:30, Sat 9-5:30, Sun (Sept-May) 1-4

S ROCK ISLAND COUNTY ILLINOIS GENEALOGICAL SOCIETY LIBRARY*, 822 11th Ave, 61265. (Mail add: PO Box 3912, Rock Island, 61204-3912), SAN 370-8144. Tel: 309-234-5151, 309-786-3058. E-mail: ricigs@frontiernet.net. Web Site: www.rootsweb.com/~ilbgsrim. *Pres,* Position Currently Open
Library Holdings: Bk Vols 2,000; Spec Interest Per Sub 30
Special Collections: Cemetery Records; County Records; Newspaper Abstracts
Subject Interests: Genealogy
Restriction: Non-circulating to the pub
Friends of the Library Group

MOMENCE

P EDWARD CHIPMAN PUBLIC LIBRARY*, 126 N Locust St, 60954. SAN 304-4211. Tel: 815-472-2581. FAX: 815-472-2581. E-mail: edwardchipman@yahoo.com. *Dir, Head Librn,* Jean Stetson; *Librn,* Adrian Haut; *Librn,* Rebecca Wilson
Founded 1907. Pop 6,837; Circ 14,409
Library Holdings: Audiobooks 613; Large Print Bks 530; Microforms 74; Bk Vols 23,143; Per Subs 37; Videos 551
Mem of Reaching Across Illinois Library System (RAILS)
Open Mon-Wed 9:30-6, Fri 9:30-5, Sat 9:30-2

MONMOUTH

C MONMOUTH COLLEGE*, Hewes Library, 700 E Broadway, 61462-1963. SAN 304-422X. Tel: 309-457-2190. Interlibrary Loan Service Tel: 309-457-2188. Reference Tel: 309-457-2301, 309-457-2303. FAX: 309-457-2226. E-mail: library@monmouthcollege.edu. Web Site: library.monmouthcollege.edu. *Dir,* John Richard Sayre; Tel: 309-457-2192, E-mail: rsayre@monm.edu; *Pub Serv Librn,* Lauren Jensen; E-mail: ljensen@monmouthcollege.edu; *Ref & Ser Librn,* Pamela Kontowicz; Tel: 309-457-2278, E-mail: pkontowicz@monmouthcollege.edu; *Tech Serv Librn,* Lynn K Daw; Tel: 309-457-2187, E-mail: ldaw@monmouthcollege.edu; *Acq Mgr,* Marti Carwile; Tel: 309-457-2191, E-mail: mcarwile@monmouthcollege.edu; *AV, Coordr, Instrul Tech, Mgr,* Chris Buban; Tel: 309-457-2193, E-mail: cbuban@monmouthcollege.edu; *Mgr, Access Serv,* Bev McGuire; E-mail: bmcguire@monmouthcollege.edu; *Tech Proc Mgr,* Mindy Damewood; Tel: 309-457-2334, E-mail: damewood@monmouthcollege.edu; Staff 3.5 (MLS 3,5)
Founded 1853. Enrl 1,307; Fac 95; Highest Degree: Bachelor
Jul 2007-Jun 2008 Income $736,244. Mats Exp $275,213, Books $62,029, Per/Ser (Incl. Access Fees) $83,961, AV Mat $11,143, Electronic Ref Mat (Incl. Access Fees) $108,925, Presv $9,155. Sal $321,846 (Prof $164,297)
Library Holdings: AV Mats 12,304; DVDs 1,427; e-books 10,132; e-journals 1,059; Microforms 260,041; Bk Vols 191,866; Videos 2,103
Special Collections: Government Documents; James Christie Shields Coll of Ancient Art & Antiquities; Monmouth College Archives. US Document Depository
Automation Activity & Vendor Info: (Acquisitions) Ex Libris Group; (Cataloging) Ex Libris Group; (Circulation) Ex Libris Group; (Course Reserve) Ex Libris Group; (ILL) Clio; (OPAC) Ex Libris Group; (Serials) Ex Libris Group
Database Vendor: 3M Library Systems, ABC-CLIO, ACM (Association for Computing Machinery), Agricola, Alexander Street Press, American Chemical Society, American Physical Society, American Psychological Association (APA), Annual Reviews, ARTstor, Baker & Taylor, CQ Press, CredoReference, Dialog, EBSCO Information Services, EBSCOhost, Ex Libris Group, Facts on File, Gale Cengage Learning, H W Wilson, HeinOnline, JSTOR, LexisNexis, Modern Language Association, Nature Publishing Group, Newsbank-Readex, OCLC ArticleFirst, OCLC FirstSearch, OCLC WorldShare Interlibrary Loan, Oxford Online, ProQuest, PubMed, Sage, SerialsSolutions, SirsiDynix, Wilson - Wilson Web
Wireless access
Function: Archival coll, Art exhibits, Audio & video playback equip for onsite use, Computers for patron use, Copy machines, Doc delivery serv, Electronic databases & coll, Fax serv, ILL available, Online cat, Online searches, Orientations, Photocopying/Printing, Pub access computers, Telephone ref, Wheelchair accessible
Mem of Reaching Across Illinois Library System (RAILS)

Partic in Associated Colleges of the Midwest; Center for Research Libraries; Consortium of Academic & Research Libraries in Illinois; Illinois Library & Information Network
Open Mon-Thurs 8am-Midnight, Fri 8-5, Sat 9-5, Sun Noon-Midnight

P WARREN COUNTY PUBLIC LIBRARY DISTRICT*, 62 Public Sq, 61462. SAN 340-5516. Tel: 309-734-3166. FAX: 309-734-5955. E-mail: wcpl@wcplibrary.org. Web Site: www.wcplibrary.org. *Libr Dir,* Larisa Good; *Acq, Cat,* Donna Objartel; *Adult Serv,* Karen Vandeveer; *Ch Serv,* Genie Doty; Staff 2 (MLS 1, Non-MLS 1)
Founded 1868. Pop 18,735
Library Holdings: Bks on Deafness & Sign Lang 25; CDs 415; DVDs 1,234; Large Print Bks 3,706; Music Scores 3,000; Bk Titles 82,011; Bk Vols 96,029; Per Subs 161; Talking Bks 2,762; Videos 2,879
Special Collections: Lincoln Coll. Oral History
Subject Interests: Agr, Genealogy
Automation Activity & Vendor Info: (Acquisitions) Follett Software; (Cataloging) Follett Software; (Circulation) Follett Software; (Serials) EBSCO Online
Wireless access
Special Services for the Blind - Audio mat
Open Mon-Thurs 8-8 (8-5 Summer), Fri & Sat 8-5
Friends of the Library Group
Branches: 3
ALEXIS BRANCH, 102 W Broadway, Alexis, 61412, SAN 340-5540. Tel: 309-482-6109. *Librn,* Mary Richardson
Library Holdings: Bk Titles 3,013; Per Subs 15
Open Mon, Thurs & Fri 2-5, Wed 9-12 & 2-6, Sat 9-12
Friends of the Library Group
KIRKWOOD BRANCH, PO Box 249, Kirkwood, 61447-0249, SAN 340-5605. Tel: 309-768-2173. *Librn,* Linda Hollenberg
Library Holdings: Bk Titles 2,627; Per Subs 13
Open Mon-Wed & Fri 3:30-5:30, Thurs 5-7, Sat 9-12
ROSEVILLE BRANCH, 145 W Penn Ave, Roseville, 61473. (Mail add: PO Box 387, Roseville, 61473), SAN 340-5664. Tel: 309-426-2336. *Librn,* Ann McIntyre
Library Holdings: Bk Vols 4,348; Per Subs 15
Open Mon, Tues, Thurs & Fri 1-4, Sat 9-12
Friends of the Library Group

MONTICELLO

P ALLERTON PUBLIC LIBRARY DISTRICT, 201 N State St, 61856. SAN 304-4238. Tel: 217-762-4676. FAX: 217-762-2021. E-mail: librarian@monticellolibrary.org. Web Site: www.monticellolibrary.org. *Dir,* Lisa Winters; *Ch,* Cara Stoerger; E-mail: c.stoerger@monticellolibrary.org; *Circ Serv,* Kandace Heistand; E-mail: k.heistand@monticellolibrary.org; *Tech Serv,* Lorrie Taylor; E-mail: l.taylor@monticellolibrary.org; Staff 4 (MLS 1, Non-MLS 3)
Founded 1897. Pop 5,906; Circ 76,000
Library Holdings: Bk Vols 36,000; Per Subs 85
Special Collections: Census (Piatt County Coll), micro; Local History; Piatt County Newspaper Coll, micro. Oral History
Subject Interests: Genealogy
Automation Activity & Vendor Info: (Cataloging) SirsiDynix; (Circulation) SirsiDynix; (OPAC) SirsiDynix; (Serials) SirsiDynix
Database Vendor: Gale Cengage Learning, Grolier Online, ProQuest
Wireless access
Publications: Monticello 150 Years Later
Mem of Illinois Heartland Library System
Open Mon & Thurs 9-9, Tues, Wed & Fri 9-6, Sat 9-5, Sun 1-5

S PIATT COUNTY HISTORICAL & GENEALOGICAL SOCIETY LIBRARY*, Courthouse Annex, 301 S Charter, 61856-1856. SAN 372-5642. Tel: 217-762-9997. *Librn,* Lucia Wilkin; Tel: 217-649-1766
Founded 1980
Library Holdings: Bk Titles 500
Special Collections: Piatt County Illinois Local History (PGHGS Coll), bks & microflm
Publications: PCHGS (Quarterly newsletter)
Open Mon & Wed 1-4

MORRIS

P MORRIS AREA PUBLIC LIBRARY DISTRICT*, 604 Liberty St, 60450. SAN 304-4254. Tel: 815-942-6880. FAX: 815-942-6415. Web Site: www.morrislibrary.com. *Dir,* Lorene Kennard; E-mail: lkennard@morrislibrary.com; *Ch,* Carol Hutchings; E-mail: chutchings@morrislibrary.com; *Adult Serv Mgr,* Nancy Wilson; E-mail: nwilson@morrislibrary.com; *Circ Mgr,* Jenny Crisostomo; E-mail: jcrisostomo@morrislibrary.com; *Tech Serv Mgr,* Lois Feldman; E-mail: loisf@morrislibrary.com; Staff 7 (MLS 2, Non-MLS 5)
Founded 1913. Pop 18,501; Circ 189,000
Library Holdings: AV Mats 7,000; Bk Vols 53,816; Per Subs 130; Talking Bks 1,830
Special Collections: Local History (Morris-Grundy County Historical Coll), bks & photog. Oral History
Automation Activity & Vendor Info: (Acquisitions) Innovative Interfaces, Inc; (Cataloging) Innovative Interfaces, Inc; (Circulation) Innovative Interfaces, Inc; (ILL) Innovative Interfaces, Inc; (OPAC) Innovative Interfaces, Inc; (Serials) Innovative Interfaces, Inc
Wireless access
Mem of Reaching Across Illinois Library System (RAILS)
Open Mon-Thurs 9-8, Fri 9-6, Sat 9-4, Sun 1-4
Friends of the Library Group

MORRISON

P ODELL PUBLIC LIBRARY*, 307 S Madison St, 61270-2724. SAN 304-4270. Tel: 815-772-7323. FAX: 815-772-7323. E-mail: odell.library@gmail.com. Web Site: www.odellpubliclibrary.com. *Dir,* Connie Boonstra
Founded 1879. Pop 4,600; Circ 47,653
Library Holdings: Bk Vols 36,111; Per Subs 100
Subject Interests: Genealogy
Mem of Reaching Across Illinois Library System (RAILS)
Open Mon & Wed 10-8, Tues & Thurs 2-8, Fri 2-5, Sat 10-3

MORRISONVILLE

P KITCHELL MEMORIAL LIBRARY*, 300 SE Fifth St, 62546. (Mail add: PO Box 49, 62546), SAN 304-4289. Tel: 217-526-4553. FAX: 217-526-3695. E-mail: mvillelibrary@yahoo.com. Web Site: www.morrisonville.lib.il.us. *Librn,* Linda K Sheedy
Founded 1964. Pop 1,272; Circ 5,700
Library Holdings: CDs 70; DVDs 340; Large Print Bks 117; Bk Vols 8,620; Per Subs 25; Talking Bks 65; Videos 800
Special Collections: Historical Books of Christian Counties & Centennial Releases; Maps of Christian County, Morrisonville & Illinois; Morrisonville Public School Mohawk & Tomahawk Yearbooks; Morrisonville Times (1875 to present)
Function: Bks on cassette, Bks on CD, CD-ROM, Children's prog, Computer training, Computers for patron use, Copy machines, Free DVD rentals, Handicapped accessible, Magnifiers for reading, Music CDs, Notary serv, Photocopying/Printing, Prog for children & young adult, Senior computer classes, Spoken cassettes & CDs, Spoken cassettes & DVDs, Summer reading prog, Tax forms, VHS videos, Wheelchair accessible
Mem of Illinois Heartland Library System
Open Mon & Thurs 1-5, Tues 1-7, Fri 9-12 & 1-6, Sat 9-12

MORTON

P MORTON PUBLIC LIBRARY DISTRICT, 315 W Pershing St, 61550. SAN 304-4300. Tel: 309-263-2200. FAX: 309-266-9604. E-mail: mortonlibrary@hotmail.com, mortonlibraryref@gmail.com. Web Site: www.mortonlibrary.org. *Dir,* Janice Sherman; Staff 11 (MLS 2, Non-MLS 9)
Founded 1924. Pop 16,267; Circ 314,443
Jul 2012-Jun 2013 Income $877,000. Mats Exp $164,000. Sal $445,700
Library Holdings: Audiobooks 1,308; CDs 11,149; DVDs 8,350; e-books 5,329; Electronic Media & Resources 34; Bk Vols 95,854; Per Subs 138
Automation Activity & Vendor Info: (Acquisitions) SirsiDynix; (Cataloging) OCLC Connexion; (Circulation) SIRSI WorkFlows; (OPAC) SirsiDynix
Database Vendor: Baker & Taylor, Brodart, Electric Library, Facts on File, Gale Cengage Learning, Ingram Library Services, OCLC FirstSearch
Wireless access
Function: Adult literacy prog, Audiobks via web, Bk club(s), Bks on cassette, Bks on CD, Children's prog, Computer training, Computers for patron use, Copy machines, Digital talking bks, E-Reserves, Electronic databases & coll, Free DVD rentals, Handicapped accessible, Home delivery & serv to Sr ctr & nursing homes, ILL available, Magnifiers for reading, Music CDs, Notary serv, Online cat, OverDrive digital audio bks, Prog for adults, Prog for children & young adult, Pub access computers, Ref serv available, Tax forms, VHS videos, Wheelchair accessible
Mem of Reaching Across Illinois Library System (RAILS)
Open Mon-Thurs 9-9, Fri 9-6, Sat 9-5

MORTON GROVE

P MORTON GROVE PUBLIC LIBRARY*, 6140 Lincoln Ave, 60053-2989. SAN 304-4351. Tel: 847-965-4220. Circulation Tel: 847-929-5103. Interlibrary Loan Service Tel: 847-929-5101, Ext 156. Reference Tel: 847-929-5101. FAX: 847-965-7903. E-mail: info@webrary.org. Web Site: www.webrary.org. *Dir,* Debra Stombres; E-mail: dstombres@webrary.org; *Asst Dir,* Kevin Justie; Tel: 847-929-5110, E-mail: kjustie@webrary.org; *Head, Circ,* Caitlin Savage; Tel: 847-929-5125, E-mail: csavage@wwebrary.org; *Head, Ref,* Natalya Fishman; Tel: 847-929-5117, E-mail: nfishman@webrary.org; *Head, Tech Serv,* Helga Scherer; Tel: 847-929-5111, E-mail: hscherer@webrary.org; *Head, Youth Serv,* Theresa

Carey; Tel: 847-929-5113, E-mail: tcarey@webrary.org; *Commun Outreach Coordr/Librn,* Rosetta Metz; Tel: 847-929-5120, E-mail: rmetz@webrary.org; *YA Librn,* Jill Wehrheim; Tel: 847-929-5119, E-mail: jwehrheim@webrary.org; *Prog Coordr, Pub Relations Coordr,* Nancy Brothers; Tel: 847-929-5122, E-mail: nbrother@webrary.org; Staff 14 (MLS 14)
Founded 1938. Pop 22,451; Circ 337,000
Jan 2010-Dec 2010 Income $2,955,944
Library Holdings: Audiobooks 2,400; CDs 7,500; DVDs 5,800; Bk Vols 132,000; Per Subs 350; Videos 600
Automation Activity & Vendor Info: (Acquisitions) SirsiDynix; (Cataloging) SirsiDynix; (Circulation) SirsiDynix; (ILL) SirsiDynix; (OPAC) SirsiDynix; (Serials) SirsiDynix
Wireless access
Publications: Books & Beyond (Newsletter)
Partic in OCLC Online Computer Library Center, Inc
Special Services for the Deaf - TDD equip
Special Services for the Blind - Reader equip
Open Mon-Thurs 9-9, Fri 9-6, Sat 9-5, Sun 1-5
Friends of the Library Group

MOSSVILLE

S CATERPILLAR INC*, Technical Information Center, 14009 Old Galena Rd, 61552. (Mail add: PO Box 225, 61552-0225), SAN 340-6563. Tel: 309-578-6118. FAX: 309-578-6733. Web Site: www.cat.com. *Dir,* Dan Evans; Tel: 309-578-4473, E-mail: evans_dan_e@cat.com; Staff 5 (MLS 3, Non-MLS 2)
Founded 1939
Library Holdings: Bk Vols 9,200; Per Subs 532
Subject Interests: Mechanical eng
Wireless access
Mem of Reaching Across Illinois Library System (RAILS)
Partic in OCLC Online Computer Library Center, Inc
Open Mon-Fri 7-4

MOUND CITY

P MOUND CITY PUBLIC LIBRARY*, 224 High St, 62963. SAN 304-4386. Tel: 618-748-9427. *Librn,* Shirley Douglas
Founded 1935. Pop 692; Circ 2,966
Library Holdings: Bk Vols 5,000
Special Collections: Gun Boats; Naval Hospital
Open Mon-Fri 12-4
Friends of the Library Group

MOUNDS

P MOUNDS PUBLIC LIBRARY*, 418 First St, 62964. SAN 304-4394. Tel: 618-745-6610. *Dir, Librn,* Danielle Laird
Pop 1,700; Circ 4,277
Library Holdings: Bk Vols 7,362; Per Subs 30
Mem of Illinois Heartland Library System
Open Mon-Thurs 11-5

MOUNT CARMEL

P MOUNT CARMEL PUBLIC LIBRARY*, 727 Mulberry St, 62863-2047. SAN 304-4408. Tel: 618-263-3531. FAX: 618-262-4243. Web Site: www.mtcarmel.lib.il.us. *Dir,* Betty Louise Taylor
Founded 1911. Pop 8,000; Circ 85,025
Library Holdings: Bk Vols 50,000; Per Subs 128
Special Collections: Daily Republican-Register Local Newspaper (1844 to present), microfilm
Automation Activity & Vendor Info: (Acquisitions) SirsiDynix; (Cataloging) SirsiDynix; (Circulation) SirsiDynix
Mem of Illinois Heartland Library System
Open Mon-Thurs 11-7, Fri & Sat 11-5:30, Sun 1-5:30

J WABASH VALLEY COLLEGE*, Bauer Media Center, 2200 College Dr, 62863. SAN 304-4416. Tel: 618-262-8641, Ext 3400. FAX: 618-262-8962. Web Site: www.iecc.edu. *Dir,* Sandra Craig; Staff 1 (Non-MLS 1)
Founded 1961. Enrl 1,396
Library Holdings: Bk Titles 30,000; Bk Vols 32,000; Per Subs 85
Special Collections: Children's Book Coll
Subject Interests: Agr, Electronics, Environ studies, Mining, Nursing, Soc sci & issues
Wireless access
Open Mon-Thurs (Winter) 7:30am-8:30pm, Fri 7:30-4:30; Mon-Thurs (Summer) 7:30am-8pm, Fri 7:30-4

MOUNT CARROLL

P MOUNT CARROLL TOWNSHIP PUBLIC LIBRARY, 208 N Main St, 61053-1022. SAN 304-4424. Tel: 815-244-1751. FAX: 815-244-5203. Web Site: www.mountcarrollpubliclibrary.org. *Dir,* Pam Naples; Staff 3 (Non-MLS 3)
Founded 1908. Pop 2,473; Circ 10,609
Library Holdings: AV Mats 340; Large Print Bks 70; Bk Titles 17,136; Per Subs 21; Talking Bks 99
Special Collections: County Cemetary Directory Coll
Subject Interests: Genealogy, Local hist
Database Vendor: OCLC FirstSearch, ProQuest
Function: ILL available
Mem of Reaching Across Illinois Library System (RAILS)
Open Mon, Tues & Fri 1:30-5:30, Wed 9-5:30, Thurs 1:30-7, Sat 9-1
Friends of the Library Group

MOUNT MORRIS

P MOUNT MORRIS PUBLIC LIBRARY, 105 S McKendrie Ave, 61054. SAN 304-4440. Tel: 815-734-4927. FAX: 815-734-6035. E-mail: mmlib@mtmorris.il.org. Web Site: www.mtmorris-il.org. *Dir,* Rebecca McCanse; Staff 2 (MLS 1, Non-MLS 1)
Founded 1931. Pop 3,013; Circ 31,825
May 2013-Apr 2014 Income $100,626
Library Holdings: Audiobooks 600; CDs 535; DVDs 810; Electronic Media & Resources 300; High Interest/Low Vocabulary Bk Vols 80; Large Print Bks 1,022; Microforms 108; Bk Vols 23,335; Per Subs 58; Videos 634
Subject Interests: Local hist
Automation Activity & Vendor Info: (Circulation) Innovative Interfaces, Inc - Sierra
Database Vendor: Gale Cengage Learning, OCLC FirstSearch, OCLC WebJunction
Wireless access
Function: Adult bk club, Art exhibits, Audio & video playback equip for onsite use, AV serv, Bks on cassette, Bks on CD, Children's prog, Computers for patron use, Copy machines, Electronic databases & coll, Exhibits, Fax serv, Free DVD rentals, Handicapped accessible, Home delivery & serv to Sr ctr & nursing homes, Homebound delivery serv, ILL available, Magnifiers for reading, Mail & tel request accepted, Music CDs, Photocopying/Printing, Prog for adults, Prog for children & young adult, Pub access computers, Ref serv available, Spoken cassettes & CDs, Story hour, Summer reading prog, Tax forms, Teen prog, Telephone ref, VHS videos, Wheelchair accessible
Mem of Reaching Across Illinois Library System (RAILS)
Open Mon-Thurs 11-7, Fri 11-5, Sat 10-3

MOUNT OLIVE

P MOUNT OLIVE PUBLIC LIBRARY*, 100 N Plum St, 62069-1755. SAN 304-4459. Tel: 217-999-7311. FAX: 217-999-7360. E-mail: mtolivelibrary@yahoo.com. Web Site: mtolivepubliclibrary.org. *Librn,* Janice Thimsen; *Asst Librn,* Gina Schwartz
Founded 1973. Pop 2,150; Circ 21,578
Library Holdings: Bks on Deafness & Sign Lang 10; Bk Vols 30,000; Per Subs 30
Special Collections: Mount Olive Herald Newspaper, 1892-1998, micro
Mem of Illinois Heartland Library System
Special Services for the Deaf - TDD equip
Open Mon-Wed & Fri 10-6, Sat 10-2

MOUNT PROSPECT

P MOUNT PROSPECT PUBLIC LIBRARY, Ten S Emerson St, 60056. SAN 304-4475. Tel: 847-253-5675. FAX: 847-253-0642. TDD: 847-590-3797. Web Site: www.mppl.org. *Exec Dir,* Marilyn Genther; Fax: 847-253-5977, E-mail: mgenther@mppl.org; *IT Dir,* Timothy Loga; E-mail: tloga@mppl.org; *Mkt & Pub Relations Dir,* Carol Morency; E-mail: cmorency@mppl.org; *Dep Dir, Bus Operations,* Frank Corry; E-mail: fcorry@mppl.org; *Dep Dir, Pub Serv,* Catherine Deane; E-mail: cdeane@mppl.org; *Head, Circ,* Janine Sarto; E-mail: jsarto@mppl.org; *Head, Coll Mgt,* Nancy Prichard; E-mail: nancyp@mppl.org; *Head, Fiction/AV/Teen Serv,* Lawrence D'Urso; E-mail: ldurso@mppl.org; *Head, Registration Serv,* Martha Johnson; E-mail: mjohnson@mppl.org; *Head, Res Serv,* Dale Heath; E-mail: dheath@mppl.org; *Head, Tech Serv,* Rosemary Groenwald; E-mail: rosemary@mppl.org; *Head, Youth Serv,* Mary Smith; E-mail: msmith@mppl.org; *Asst Head, Circ Serv,* Sam Chiappone; E-mail: schiappone@mppl.org; *Asst Head, Fiction/AV/Teen,* John McInnes; E-mail: jmcinnes@mppl.org; *Asst Head, Res Serv,* Jo Robinson; E-mail: jor@mppl.org; *Asst Head, Youth Serv,* Mary Ann Sibrava; E-mail: msibrava@mppl.org; *Govt Doc Librn,* Julie Collins; E-mail: jcollins@mppl.org; *Librn, Virtual Serv,* Cynthia Dieden; E-mail: cdieden@mppl.org; *Teen Librn,* Barbara Fitzgerald; E-mail: bfitzgerald@mppl.org; *Teen Librn,* Colleen Seisser; E-mail: cseisser@mppl.org; *Mgr, Libr Develop,* Pamela Nelson; E-mail:

pnelson@mppl.org; *ILL Coordr,* Virginia Schlachter; E-mail: ginnys@mppl.org; *Human Res Officer,* Wendy Temko; E-mail: wtemko@mppl.org; Staff 48 (MLS 29, Non-MLS 19)
Founded 1943. Pop 54,167; Circ 1,084,724
Jan 2013-Dec 2013 Income (Main Library and Branch(s)) $8,678,119, State $59,356, City $8,437,202, Other $181,561. Mats Exp $719,876, Books $364,153, Per/Ser (Incl. Access Fees) $15,531, Micro $8,229, AV Mat $116,947, Electronic Ref Mat (Incl. Access Fees) $146,342. Sal $4,857,640
Library Holdings: AV Mats 61,773; Electronic Media & Resources 22,218; Bk Vols 371,939; Per Subs 494
Special Collections: Oral History; US Document Depository
Subject Interests: Genealogy, Local hist
Automation Activity & Vendor Info: (Acquisitions) Horizon; (Cataloging) Horizon; (Circulation) Horizon; (OPAC) EBSCO Online
Database Vendor: American Physical Society, Backstage Library Works, Baker & Taylor, Bowker, EBSCO Auto Repair Reference, EBSCOhost, Facts on File, Gale Cengage Learning, H W Wilson, infoUSA, LearningExpress, LexisNexis, Medline, OCLC ArticleFirst, OCLC CAMIO, OCLC FirstSearch, OCLC WorldShare Interlibrary Loan, Overdrive, Inc, Oxford Online, ProQuest, ReferenceUSA, SirsiDynix, Standard & Poor's, TumbleBookLibrary, ValueLine, Westlaw, Wilson - Wilson Web, World Book Online
Wireless access
Publications: Preview (Bi-monthly)
Mem of Reaching Across Illinois Library System (RAILS)
Special Services for the Deaf - Assisted listening device; Assistive tech; Bks on deafness & sign lang; TDD equip
Special Services for the Blind - Accessible computers; Bks on CD; Large print bks; Large screen computer & software; Magnifiers; Recorded bks; Talking bk serv referral; Text reader
Open Mon-Fri 9am-10pm, Sat 9-5, Sun 12-5
Friends of the Library Group
Branches: 1
SOUTH BRANCH, 1711 W Algonquin Rd, 60056. Tel: 847-590-4090. Web Site: www.mppl.org/southbranch. *Br Mgr,* Maria Garstecki; E-mail: mariag@mppl.org

MOUNT PULASKI

P MOUNT PULASKI PUBLIC LIBRARY DISTRICT*, 320 N Washington St, 62548. SAN 304-4483. Tel: 217-792-5919. FAX: 217-792-3449. *Libr Dir,* Marilyn Howe
Founded 1892. Pop 2,860; Circ 40,059
Library Holdings: Audiobooks 880; DVDs 1,330; Large Print Bks 1,144; Bk Titles 13,652; Per Subs 62
Subject Interests: Genealogy
Wireless access
Mem of Illinois Heartland Library System
Open Mon-Thurs 10-7, Fri 10-5, Sat 9-1

MOUNT STERLING

P BROWN COUNTY PUBLIC LIBRARY DISTRICT*, 143 W Main St, 62353. SAN 304-4491. Tel: 217-773-2013. FAX: 217-773-4723. E-mail: browncty@adams.net. *Librn,* Sharon Hillyer; Staff 7 (Non-MLS 7)
Founded 1915. Pop 5,812; Circ 23,396
Library Holdings: Bk Vols 25,000
Special Collections: Best Seller & Popular Fiction
Automation Activity & Vendor Info: (OPAC) SirsiDynix
Open Mon, Tues & Thurs 9-5 & 7-9, Wed 9-5, Fri 2-5, Sat 9am-Noon
Branches: 1
VERSAILLES BRANCH, 211 N Chestnut, Versailles, 62378. (Mail add: PO Box 294, Versailles, 62378-0294). Tel: 217-225-3102. FAX: 217-225-9082. *Br Librn,* Ruth Lucas
Library Holdings: Bk Titles 10,000; Per Subs 20
Open Mon & Thurs 1:30-6, Wed 1:30-5:30, Sat 9-12

S WESTERN ILLINOIS CORRECTIONAL CENTER LIBRARY*, 2500 Rt 99 S, 62353. SAN 376-1207. Tel: 217-773-4441, Ext 640. FAX: 217-773-3899. *Libr Assoc,* Michele Olsen
Library Holdings: Bk Vols 7,000; Per Subs 17
Special Collections: Illinois Legal Coll
Partic in Resource Sharing Alliance
Open Mon-Fri 8-4
Restriction: Staff & inmates only

MOUNT VERNON

P C E BREHM MEMORIAL PUBLIC LIBRARY DISTRICT, 101 S Seventh St, 62864. SAN 304-4521. Tel: 618-242-6322. FAX: 618-242-0810. Web Site: www.mtvbrehm.lib.il.us. *Libr Dir,* Bill Pixley; E-mail: bpixley@mtvbrehm.lib.il.us; *Asst Dir,* Esther Curry; *Ch,* Hannah Story; *Circ,* Jan Kreher; *Genealogy Serv,* Webb Marsha; E-mail: mwebb@mtvbrehm.lib.il.us; Staff 2 (MLS 2)
Founded 1899. Pop 37,918
Jul 2013-Jun 2014 Income $902,000, State $58,000, Federal $15,000, County $782,000, Locally Generated Income $45,000. Mats Exp $141,000. Sal $393,000 (Prof $110,000)
Special Collections: Genealogy Coll; Southern Illinois History Coll
Automation Activity & Vendor Info: (Acquisitions) Innovative Interfaces, Inc; (Cataloging) Innovative Interfaces, Inc; (Circulation) Innovative Interfaces, Inc; (ILL) Innovative Interfaces, Inc; (OPAC) Innovative Interfaces, Inc; (Serials) Innovative Interfaces, Inc
Database Vendor: 3M Library Systems, Baker & Taylor, EBSCO Auto Repair Reference, EBSCOhost, Overdrive, Inc, TumbleBookLibrary
Wireless access
Mem of Illinois Heartland Library System
Open Mon-Thurs 9-8, Fri 9-5, Sat 10-4, Sun 1-5

S CEDARHURST CENTER FOR THE ARTS*, Mitchell Museum Library, 2600 Richview Rd, 62864. (Mail add: PO Box 923, 62864-0019), SAN 304-4513. Tel: 618-242-1236. FAX: 618-242-9530. Web Site: www.cedarhurst.org. *Dir of Educ,* Jennifer Server; Staff 1 (Non-MLS 1)
Founded 1973
Library Holdings: AV Mats 117; Bk Vols 3,100; Per Subs 16; Spec Interest Per Sub 15
Subject Interests: Americana, Art, Paintings, Sculpture
Restriction: Circ limited, Open by appt only, Open to pub for ref only

M GOOD SAMARITAN REGIONAL HEALTH CENTER*, Health Science Library, 605 N 12th St, 62864. SAN 329-773X. Tel: 618-241-2062. FAX: 618-241-3817. *Librn,* Coleen Saxe; E-mail: coleen_saxe@ssmhc.com
Library Holdings: Bk Vols 1,000; Per Subs 45
Open Mon-Fri 8-12

GL ILLINOIS APPELLATE COURT*, Fifth District Law Library, 14th & Main Sts, 62864. (Mail add: PO Box 867, 62864-0018), SAN 304-4505. Tel: 618-242-6414. FAX: 618-242-9133. Web Site: www.state.il.us/court/appellatecourt. *Dir, Info Resources & Res,* Vito Mastrangelo; *Librn,* Janet Buchanan
Founded 1857
Library Holdings: Bk Vols 13,000; Per Subs 20
Subject Interests: Law
Open Mon-Fri 8:30-4:30

MOUNT ZION

P MOUNT ZION DISTRICT LIBRARY*, 115 W Main, 62549. SAN 304-453X. Tel: 217-864-3622. FAX: 217-864-5708. Web Site: www.mtzion.lib.il.us. *Dir,* Jennie Alexander; Staff 5 (MLS 1, Non-MLS 4)
Founded 1975. Pop 11,722; Circ 66,155
Library Holdings: Bk Vols 25,000; Per Subs 119
Automation Activity & Vendor Info: (Circulation) SirsiDynix
Publications: Newsletter (Monthly)
Mem of Illinois Heartland Library System
Special Services for the Deaf - TTY equip
Open Mon-Thurs 9-8, Fri 9-5, Sat 9-3

MOWEAQUA

P MOWEAQUA PUBLIC LIBRARY*, 600 N Putnam St, 62550. SAN 304-4548. Tel: 217-768-4700. FAX: 217-768-9070. Web Site: www.moweaqua.lib.il.us. *Libr Dir,* Barbara Collins
Founded 1893. Pop 2,850; Circ 25,211
Jul 2010-Jun 2011 Income $83,000, State $3,000, County $80,000. Mats Exp $7,000, Books $6,000, AV Mat $1,000
Library Holdings: Audiobooks 364; DVDs 751; Large Print Bks 724; Microforms 100; Bk Vols 13,000; Per Subs 6; Talking Bks 292; Videos 720
Subject Interests: Genealogy
Automation Activity & Vendor Info: (Circulation) SirsiDynix
Wireless access
Mem of Illinois Heartland Library System
Open Mon 9-12 & 1-7, Tues, Wed & Fri 9-12 & 1-5, Sat 9-12
Friends of the Library Group

MUNDELEIN

P FREMONT PUBLIC LIBRARY DISTRICT, 1170 N Midlothian Rd, 60060. SAN 304-4556. Tel: 847-566-8702. Circulation Tel: 847-918-3235. Reference Tel: 847-918-3206. FAX: 847-566-0204. TDD: 847-566-8722. E-mail: ref@fremontlibrary.org. Web Site: www.fremontlibrary.org. *Dir,* Scott Davis; *Asst Dir,* Rebecca Ingram; *Circ Mgr,* Karen Bolton; *Tech Serv Supvr,* Tracy Hucker; *Vols Serv Coordr,* Barbara Witte
Founded 1955. Pop 37,500; Circ 867,000
Library Holdings: Bk Vols 170,000; Per Subs 200
Special Collections: Local Newspapers, 1894-present, micro

Automation Activity & Vendor Info: (Cataloging) SIRSI WorkFlows; (Circulation) SIRSI-iBistro; (ILL) SIRSI WorkFlows; (OPAC) SIRSI-iBistro
Database Vendor: OCLC WebJunction, OCLC WorldShare Interlibrary Loan
Wireless access
Function: ILL available
Publications: Fremont (Newsletter)
Partic in Cooperative Computer Services - CCS
Special Services for the Blind - Bks on CD; Copier with enlargement capabilities; Home delivery serv; Large print bks; Low vision equip; Playaways (bks on MP3); Reader equip
Open Mon-Thurs 9-9, Fri 9-6, Sat 9-5, Sun 1-5
Friends of the Library Group

CR UNIVERSITY OF SAINT MARY OF THE LAKE - MUNDELEIN SEMINARY*, Feehan Memorial Library & McEssy Theological Resource Center, 1000 E Maple Ave, 60060. SAN 304-4572. Tel: 847-970-4820. Circulation Tel: 847-970-4821. FAX: 847-566-5229. Web Site: www.usml.edu/library. *Libr Dir,* Lorraine H Olley; E-mail: lolley@usml.edu; *Electronic Res Librn,* Christina Geuther; Tel: 847-970-8945, E-mail: cgeuther@usml.edu; *Circ & Stacks Coordr,* Anna Kielian; E-mail: akielian@usml.edu; *Tech Serv,* Lois Guebert; E-mail: lguebert@usml.edu; *Acq Asst,* Natalie Jordan; E-mail: njordan@usml.edu; Staff 4.5 (MLS 3, Non-MLS 1.5)
Founded 1929. Enrl 190; Fac 33; Highest Degree: Doctorate
Library Holdings: AV Mats 300; Bk Titles 102,000; Bk Vols 201,000; Per Subs 435
Special Collections: Incunabula Coll; Irish History & Literature (Carry Coll)
Subject Interests: Canon law, Catholicism, Roman Catholic relig, Scripture
Automation Activity & Vendor Info: (Acquisitions) Ex Libris Group; (Cataloging) Ex Libris Group; (Circulation) Ex Libris Group; (ILL) OCLC; (OPAC) Ex Libris Group; (Serials) EBSCO Online
Database Vendor: EBSCOhost
Wireless access
Partic in Association of Chicago Theological Schools; Consortium of Academic & Research Libraries in Illinois
Open Mon-Fri 8:30-4:30
Restriction: Borrowing requests are handled by ILL, In-house use for visitors, Non-circulating of rare bks, Non-circulating to the pub, Open to students, fac, staff & alumni, Use of others with permission of librn

MURPHYSBORO

P SALLIE LOGAN PUBLIC LIBRARY*, 1808 Walnut St, 62966. SAN 304-4580. Tel: 618-684-3271. FAX: 618-684-2392. Web Site: www.murphysboro.lib.il.us. *Dir,* Donella L Odum; E-mail: donella@shawls.lib.il.us; *Asst Librn,* Sherry Carlock; *Cat,* Barbara Corrington; *Circ,* Linda Kish
Founded 1936. Pop 8,950; Circ 89,335
Library Holdings: Large Print Bks 1,200; Bk Titles 56,000; Per Subs 38
Automation Activity & Vendor Info: (Acquisitions) SirsiDynix; (Cataloging) SirsiDynix; (Circulation) SirsiDynix; (ILL) SirsiDynix; (OPAC) SirsiDynix; (Serials) SirsiDynix
Database Vendor: SirsiDynix
Mem of Illinois Heartland Library System
Open Mon-Thurs 10-8, Fri & Sat 10-5
Friends of the Library Group

NAPERVILLE

SR COMMUNITY UNITED METHODIST CHURCH LIBRARY*, 20 N Center St, 60540-4611. SAN 372-641X. Tel: 630-355-1483. FAX: 630-778-2011. E-mail: info@communityunitedmethodist.org. Web Site: www.communityunitedmethodist.org. *Librn,* Forrest Rice; *Asst Librn,* Gertrude Brown; Staff 2 (MLS 1, Non-MLS 1)
Founded 1958
Library Holdings: Bk Titles 5,000; Per Subs 12
Special Collections: Illinois Evangelical Church 1850-1946, bks, papers, ledgers; Illinois Evangelical United Brethren Church 1946-1968, bks, papers, ledgers
Restriction: Open by appt only

M EDWARD HOSPITAL LIBRARY*, 801 S Washington St, 60540. SAN 371-7240. Tel: 630-527-3000. FAX: 630-355-9703. Web Site: www.edward.org.
Library Holdings: Bk Titles 2,500; Per Subs 253
Subject Interests: Consumer health, Med, Nursing
Mem of Reaching Across Illinois Library System (RAILS)
Partic in Fox Valley Health Science Library Consortium; Greater Midwest Regional Medical Libr Network; Health Sci Libr Network; Health Sci Librn of Ill (HSLI)
Open Mon-Fri 8-4:30

S GROUP TECHNOLOGY LIBRARY & INFORMATION SERVICES, BP Library, 150 W Warrenville Rd, MC F1, 60563. SAN 304-0313. Tel: 630-420-4850. Interlibrary Loan Service Tel: 630-961-7634. FAX: 630-420-3697. Web Site: www.bp.com. *Cont Mgt Team Lead,* Joyce Fedeczko; E-mail: joyce.fedeczko@bp.com; *Project Mgr,* Neal Rhutasel; Tel: 630-420-5784, E-mail: neal.rhutasel@bp.com; *Sr Res Spec,* Mona Suarez; Tel: 281-366-3387, E-mail: Mona.Suarez@bp.com; *Info Researcher,* Elizabeth Hatcher; E-mail: Elizabeth.Hatcher@bp.com; *Doc Delivery, Ref,* Debbie Buschman; E-mail: deborah.buschman@bp.com. Subject Specialists: *Knowledge mgt,* Joyce Fedeczko; *Bus,* Elizabeth Hatcher; Staff 11 (MLS 3, Non-MLS 8)
Founded 1972
Subject Interests: Chem, Eng, Environ studies, Geol, Petroleum
Automation Activity & Vendor Info: (Cataloging) Softlink America; (Circulation) Softlink America; (ILL) OCLC; (OPAC) Softlink America
Database Vendor: American Chemical Society, Dialog, Dun & Bradstreet, EBSCO Discovery Service, EBSCO Information Services, EBSCOhost, Elsevier, Factiva.com, IEEE (Institute of Electrical & Electronics Engineers), IHS, Knovel, LAC Group, LexisNexis, McGraw-Hill, Nature Publishing Group, OCLC, OCLC WebJunction, OCLC WorldShare Interlibrary Loan, OneSource, ScienceDirect, Springer-Verlag, STN International, Thomson - Web of Science, Wiley
Wireless access
Function: ILL available, Scanner
Mem of Reaching Across Illinois Library System (RAILS)
Open Mon-Fri 8-5
Restriction: Access for corporate affiliates

P NAPERVILLE PUBLIC LIBRARY*, Nichols Library, 200 W Jefferson Ave, 60540-5374. SAN 304-4602. Tel: 630-961-4100. FAX: 630-637-6389. Web Site: www.naperville-lib.info. *Exec Dir,* John Spears; Tel: 630-961-4100, Ext 6151; *Dep Dir,* Julie Rothenfluh; Tel: 630-961-4100, Ext 6144; *Bus Librn,* Kent Palmer; *Commun Serv Mgr,* Peggy Barry; Tel: 630-961-4100, Ext 2234; *IT Mgr,* Frances Tong; Tel: 630-961-4100, Ext 4980; *Libr Mgr,* Sue Prindiville; Tel: 630-961-4100, Ext 6307; *Tech Serv Mgr,* Rohini Bokka; *Adult Serv Supvr,* Amy Byrne; Tel: 630-961-4100, Ext 6312; *Cir/Check-In Supvr,* Helen Chow; Tel: 630-961-4100, Ext 6372; *Circ/Check-Out Supvr,* Carla Nolidis; Tel: 630-961-4100, Ext 6321; Staff 60 (MLS 39, Non-MLS 21)
Founded 1897. Pop 128,358; Circ 1,962,019
Library Holdings: Bk Vols 702,822
Automation Activity & Vendor Info: (Circulation) Innovative Interfaces, Inc - Millenium; (ILL) Innovative Interfaces, Inc - Millenium
Wireless access
Mem of Reaching Across Illinois Library System (RAILS)
Partic in Illinois Library & Information Network; OCLC Online Computer Library Center, Inc
Open Mon-Fri 9-9, Sat 9-5, Sun 1-5
Friends of the Library Group
Branches: 2
NAPER BOULEVARD, 2035 S Naper Blvd, 60565-3353, SAN 372-4999. Tel: 630-961-4100. FAX: 630-961-4119. TDD: 630-355-1585. *Mgr,* Karen Dunford; Tel: 630-961-4100, Ext 2210; *Adult Serv Supvr,* Yan Xu; Tel: 630-961-4100, Ext 2232; *Children's Serv Supvr,* Aynne Reist; Tel: 630-961-4100, Ext 2235; *Circ Supvr,* Marge Fay; Tel: 630-961-4100, Ext 2216
Pop 128,358; Circ 766,602
Library Holdings: Bk Vols 153,293
Special Services for the Deaf - TDD equip
Open Mon-Thurs 9-9, Fri & Sat 9-5, Sun 1-5
Friends of the Library Group
95TH STREET, 3015 Cedar Glade Dr, 60564. Tel: 630-961-4100. FAX: 630-637-4870. *Mgr,* Olya Tymciurak; Tel: 630-961-4100, Ext 4900; *Adult & Teen Serv Supvr,* Joe Filapek; Tel: 630-961-4100, Ext 4940; *Children's Serv Supvr,* Louise Brueggemann; Tel: 630-961-4100, Ext 4960; *Circ Serv Supvr,* Chris Murray; Tel: 630-961-4100, Ext 4920
Founded 2003. Circ 1,230,273
Library Holdings: Bk Vols 208,516
Open Mon-Fri 9-9, Sat 9-5, Sun 1-5

C NORTH CENTRAL COLLEGE*, Oesterle Library, 320 E School St, 60540. SAN 304-4610. Tel: 630-637-5700. Interlibrary Loan Service Tel: 630-637-5705. Reference Tel: 630-637-5715. FAX: 630-637-5716. Web Site: library.noctrl.edu. *Dir, Libr Serv,* Carolyn A Sheehy; Tel: 630-637-5701; *Archivist/Assoc Dir of Archives,* Kim Butler; Tel: 630-637-5714; *Info Serv Librn,* Ryan Williams; Tel: 630-637-5708; *Instrul Serv Librn,* Rosemary Henders; Tel: 630-637-5707; *Coordr, Access Serv,* Belinda Cheek; Tel: 630-637-5703; *Instrul Media Coordr,* Tom Gill; Tel: 630-637-5723; *Tech Serv Coordr,* Emily Prather; Tel: 630-637-5709; Staff 7 (MLS 5, Non-MLS 2)
Founded 1861. Enrl 2,267; Fac 151; Highest Degree: Master
Jul 2006-Jun 2007 Income $1,215,703. Mats Exp $415,964. Sal $655,601 (Prof $371,411)
Library Holdings: AV Mats 3,841; Bk Vols 146,179; Per Subs 3,427

Special Collections: History (Leffler Lincoln Coll); Literature (Sang Limited Edition Coll); Music (Sang Jazz Coll); Tholin Chicagoana Coll
Automation Activity & Vendor Info: (Acquisitions) Ex Libris Group; (Cataloging) Ex Libris Group; (Circulation) Ex Libris Group; (Course Reserve) Ex Libris Group; (ILL) Ex Libris Group; (OPAC) Ex Libris Group; (Serials) Ex Libris Group
Database Vendor: EBSCOhost, OCLC FirstSearch, OVID Technologies
Wireless access
Publications: EX LIBRIS (Newsletter)
Partic in Consortium of Academic & Research Libraries in Illinois; Illinois Library & Information Network; Illinois Library Computer Systems Organization (ILCSO); LIBRAS, Inc; OCLC Online Computer Library Center, Inc
Special Services for the Blind - Dragon Naturally Speaking software
Open Mon-Thurs 8am-Midnight, Fri 8-8, Sat 9-5:30, Sun Noon-Midnight
Restriction: Open to students, fac & staff, Restricted pub use

NASHVILLE

P NASHVILLE PUBLIC LIBRARY*, 219 E Elm St, 62263-1711. SAN 304-4629. Tel: 618-327-3827. FAX: 618-327-4820. Web Site: www.nashville.lib.il.us. *Libr Dir,* Linda Summers; *Asst Librn,* Dorothy Bahre; *Asst Librn,* Mary Schnake; *Asst Librn,* Sherrill Whitener
Founded 1943. Pop 3,147; Circ 26,585
Library Holdings: Bk Vols 17,000
Subject Interests: Genealogy, Local hist
Mem of Illinois Heartland Library System
Open Mon-Fri 10-7, Sat 10-2
Friends of the Library Group

NAUVOO

P NAUVOO PUBLIC LIBRARY*, 1270 Mulholland St, 62354. (Mail add: PO Box 276, 62354-0276), SAN 304-4637. Tel: 217-453-2707. FAX: 217-453-2707. E-mail: nauvoopl@mchsi.com. Web Site: www.nauvoo.lib.il.us. *Librn,* Jan Gerst
Founded 1913. Pop 1,063; Circ 10,125
Library Holdings: Large Print Bks 450; Bk Titles 10,000; Per Subs 20
Wireless access
Function: Photocopying/Printing, Prog for children & young adult, Summer reading prog
Open Mon 11-6:30, Tues & Thurs 11-6, Wed 9-4, Fri 10-5, Sat 10-2
Friends of the Library Group

NEOGA

P NEOGA PUBLIC LIBRARY DISTRICT*, 550 Chestnut St, 62447. (Mail add: PO Box 888, 62447-0888), SAN 376-0154. Tel: 217-895-3944. FAX: 217-895-3944. Web Site: www.neoga.lib.il.us. *Dir,* Patricia Andres
Library Holdings: AV Mats 913; Bk Titles 11,000; Bk Vols 15,749; Per Subs 31
Mem of Illinois Heartland Library System
Open Tues & Thurs 10-7, Wed & Fri 10-5:30, Sat 9-12

NEPONSET

P NEPONSET PUBLIC LIBRARY*, 201 W Commercial St, 61345. (Mail add: PO Box 110, 61345-0110), SAN 304-4645. Tel: 309-594-2204. FAX: 309-594-2204. E-mail: neponsetlibrary@yahoo.com. *Librn,* Carissa Faber; *Asst Librn, Ch Serv,* Nancy Hulslander
Founded 1875. Pop 819; Circ 13,758
Library Holdings: Bk Vols 16,817; Per Subs 23
Special Collections: Clippings File; Local History, bks, cassettes, flm, micro; School & Cemetary Records
Open Mon (Winter) 1-4, Tues 9-12 & 1-6, Wed & Fri 1-6, Sat 10-3; Tues (Summer) 9-12 & 1-6, Wed & Fri 1-4, Sat 10-3

NEW ATHENS

P NEW ATHENS DISTRICT LIBRARY, 201 N Van Buren St, 62264. SAN 304-4653. Tel: 618-475-3255. FAX: 618-475-9384. E-mail: newathenslibrary@gmail.com. *Dir,* Kathy Hagan
Founded 1963. Pop 4,032; Circ 14,365
Library Holdings: Bk Vols 40,000; Per Subs 40
Automation Activity & Vendor Info: (Acquisitions) Innovative Interfaces, Inc; (Cataloging) Innovative Interfaces, Inc; (Circulation) Innovative Interfaces, Inc; (Course Reserve) Innovative Interfaces, Inc; (ILL) Innovative Interfaces, Inc; (Media Booking) Innovative Interfaces, Inc; (OPAC) Innovative Interfaces, Inc; (Serials) Innovative Interfaces, Inc
Wireless access
Mem of Illinois Heartland Library System
Open Mon-Thurs 2-8, Fri 2-5, Sat 10-4

NEW BADEN

P NEW BADEN PUBLIC LIBRARY*, 210 N First St, 62265. SAN 376-2211. Tel: 618-588-4554. FAX: 618-588-4554. E-mail: newbadenlibrary@gmail.com. Web Site: www.newbaden.lib.il.us. *Dir,* Dennis Gregory; E-mail: dennisgregory6@gmail.com; *Librn,* Brenda Lehr
Library Holdings: Bk Titles 12,000; Bk Vols 15,000; Per Subs 22
Automation Activity & Vendor Info: (Acquisitions) SirsiDynix; (Cataloging) SirsiDynix; (Circulation) SirsiDynix; (Course Reserve) SirsiDynix; (ILL) SirsiDynix; (Media Booking) SirsiDynix; (OPAC) SirsiDynix; (Serials) SirsiDynix
Wireless access
Mem of Illinois Heartland Library System
Open Mon-Thurs 11-7, Fri 1-6, Sat 9-1

NEW BERLIN

P WEST SANGAMON PUBLIC LIBRARY DISTRICT*, 103 E Illinois St, 62670. (Mail add: PO Box 439, 62670-0439). Tel: 217-488-7733. Web Site: www.westsanglibrary.org. *Dir,* Jeanine Freeman Benanti
Founded 1999
Library Holdings: Bk Titles 19,000
Special Collections: Abraham Lincoln Coll
Automation Activity & Vendor Info: (Circulation) SirsiDynix
Wireless access
Function: ILL available
Mem of Illinois Heartland Library System
Open Tues & Thurs 12-7, Wed & Fri 10-5, Sat 9-1
Friends of the Library Group

NEW LENOX

P NEW LENOX PUBLIC LIBRARY DISTRICT*, 120 Veterans Pkwy, 60451. SAN 304-4661. Tel: 815-485-2605. FAX: 815-485-2548. TDD: 815-485-3963. E-mail: info@newlenoxlibrary.org. Web Site: www.newlenoxlibrary.org. *Interim Co-Dir,* Rose Gilman; *Head, Youth Serv, Interim Co-Dir,* Dana Russell; E-mail: drussell@newlenoxlibrary.org; *Head, Adult Serv,* Colleen Waltman; E-mail: cwaltman@newlenoxlibrary.org; *Circ Mgr,* Jennie Suttle; E-mail: jsuttle@newlenoxlibrary.org; Staff 3.26 (MLS 2.63, Non-MLS 0.63)
Founded 1946. Pop 35,000; Circ 283,969
Jul 2009-Jun 2010 Income $1,611,763, State $15,321, County $1,526,160, Locally Generated Income $70,282. Mats Exp $151,565, Books $76,188, Per/Ser (Incl. Access Fees) $9,843, AV Mat $21,450, Electronic Ref Mat (Incl. Access Fees) $44,084. Sal $879,930 (Prof $268,204)
Library Holdings: Audiobooks 2,623; CDs 3,629; DVDs 2,793; Electronic Media & Resources 27; Large Print Bks 2,290; Bk Titles 143,237; Per Subs 201; Videos 1,908
Subject Interests: Quilting
Automation Activity & Vendor Info: (Acquisitions) SIRSI WorkFlows; (Circulation) SirsiDynix; (ILL) OCLC FirstSearch
Database Vendor: Facts on File, Gale Cengage Learning, Grolier Online, infoUSA, Medline, Newsbank, OCLC FirstSearch, Overdrive, Inc, ProQuest, PubMed, ReferenceUSA, SirsiDynix
Wireless access
Function: Adult bk club, Audiobks via web, Bi-weekly Writer's Group, Bks on cassette, Bks on CD, Children's prog, Computers for patron use, Copy machines, e-mail & chat, E-Reserves, Electronic databases & coll, Fax serv, Handicapped accessible, ILL available, Magnifiers for reading, Mail & tel request accepted, Mus passes, Music CDs, Online cat, Online ref, Online searches, Photocopying/Printing, Prog for adults, Prog for children & young adult, Pub access computers, Ref serv available, Spoken cassettes & CDs, Story hour, Summer reading prog, Tax forms, Telephone ref, Wheelchair accessible
Mem of Reaching Across Illinois Library System (RAILS)
Special Services for the Deaf - Bks on deafness & sign lang; Sign lang interpreter upon request for prog; TDD equip
Special Services for the Blind - Aids for in-house use; Bks on cassette; Bks on CD; Cassettes; Large print bks; Magnifiers; Playaways (bks on MP3); Recorded bks; Screen enlargement software for people with visual disabilities; Talking bk serv referral
Open Mon-Thurs 10-8, Fri 10-6, Sat 10-4
Restriction: Non-resident fee
Friends of the Library Group

NEW WINDSOR

P NEW WINDSOR PUBLIC LIBRARY DISTRICT*, 412 Main St, 61465. SAN 304-467X. Tel: 309-667-2515. FAX: 309-667-2515. *Librn,* David Kruse; E-mail: dkruse@winco.net; Staff 3 (MLS 1, Non-MLS 2)
Founded 1959. Pop 1,268; Circ 14,772
Library Holdings: Bk Vols 10,700; Per Subs 22
Special Collections: Oral History
Subject Interests: Cooking, Gardening, Local hist

Open Mon & Thurs 3:30-8, Tues 9-11 & 5:30-8, Wed 1-8, Fri 9-11 & 1:30-5, Sat 9-1
Friends of the Library Group

NEWMAN

P NEWMAN REGIONAL LIBRARY DISTRICT*, 108 W Yates St, 61942. (Mail add: PO Box 118, 61942), SAN 304-4688. Tel: 217-837-2412. FAX: 217-837-2412. E-mail: librarian@newmanregionallibrary.org. Web Site: newmanregionallibrary.org. *Librn,* Renee Henry; Staff 1 (Non-MLS 1)
Pop 1,200; Circ 8,873
Jul 2007-Jun 2008 Income $52,473, State $4,640, Locally Generated Income $47,833. Mats Exp $8,308, Per/Ser (Incl. Access Fees) $433, Other Print Mats $5,709, AV Mat $1,817, Electronic Ref Mat (Incl. Access Fees) $349
Library Holdings: AV Mats 1,000; Large Print Bks 200; Bk Titles 10,841; Per Subs 40; Talking Bks 500
Automation Activity & Vendor Info: (Acquisitions) Horizon; (Cataloging) Horizon; (Circulation) Horizon; (ILL) Horizon; (OPAC) Horizon; (Serials) Horizon
Database Vendor: EBSCOhost, OCLC FirstSearch, OCLC WebJunction, OCLC WorldShare Interlibrary Loan
Wireless access
Function: ILL available, Magnifiers for reading, Online searches, Prog for adults, Prog for children & young adult, Summer reading prog, Wheelchair accessible
Mem of Illinois Heartland Library System
Partic in OCLC-LVIS
Open Mon & Wed 1-7, Tues, Thurs & Fri 1-6, Sat 9-Noon

NEWTON

P NEWTON PUBLIC LIBRARY & MUSEUM*, 100 S Van Buren St, 62448. SAN 304-4696. Tel: 618-783-8141. FAX: 618-783-8149. Web Site: www.newton.lib.il.us. *Dir,* Connie Davidson; *Librn,* Amanda Leonard; *Librn,* Roberta Menke
Founded 1927. Pop 3,186; Circ 20,677
Library Holdings: Bk Vols 17,000; Per Subs 45
Automation Activity & Vendor Info: (Acquisitions) SirsiDynix; (Cataloging) SirsiDynix; (Circulation) SirsiDynix; (Course Reserve) SirsiDynix; (ILL) SirsiDynix
Mem of Illinois Heartland Library System
Open Mon, Wed & Fri 10-5, Tues & Thurs 10-7, Sat 10-1
Friends of the Library Group

NILES

P NILES PUBLIC LIBRARY DISTRICT*, 6960 Oakton St, 60714. SAN 340-5907. Tel: 847-663-1234. FAX: 847-663-1350. Interlibrary Loan Service FAX: 847-663-6423. Administration FAX: 847-663-1360. TDD: 847-663-6500. E-mail: books@nileslibrary.org. Web Site: www.nileslibrary.org. *Dir,* Linda Weiss; *Bus Mgr,* Kevin Lockhart; *AV, Reader Serv,* Barbara Kruser; *Circ,* Kathy Pricone; *Ref,* Valerie Clark; *Tech Serv,* Ann Pasnick; *Youth Serv,* Susan Lempke; Staff 94 (MLS 26, Non-MLS 68)
Founded 1958. Pop 58,218; Circ 935,786
Library Holdings: AV Mats 29,672; Bk Vols 205,802; Per Subs 421
Database Vendor: SirsiDynix
Wireless access
Publications: Chapter One (Newsletter)
Partic in Cooperative Computer Services - CCS; OCLC Online Computer Library Center, Inc
Special Services for the Deaf - TTY equip
Open Mon-Thurs 9-9, Fri & Sat 9-5, Sun (Sept-May) 1-5
Friends of the Library Group

NOKOMIS

P NOKOMIS PUBLIC LIBRARY, 22 S Cedar St, Ste 2, 62075. SAN 304-4742. Tel: 217-563-2734. FAX: 217-563-2740. E-mail: admin@nokomispl.org. Web Site: www.nokomispl.org. *Dir,* Debra A Lehman; E-mail: dlehman@nokomispl.org
Pop 2,939; Circ 24,401
Apr 2013-Mar 2014 Income $61,564, State $5,278, Locally Generated Income $45,227, Other $11,059
Library Holdings: Audiobooks 680; AV Mats 4,920; CDs 914; DVDs 4,920; e-books 7,984; Large Print Bks 580; Bk Titles 18,767; Per Subs 18
Special Collections: Free Press-Progress, 1880 to present, micro
Subject Interests: Local hist
Wireless access
Function: Accelerated reader prog, Art exhibits, Audio & video playback equip for onsite use, Audiobks via web, AV serv, Bks on cassette, Bks on CD, CD-ROM, Children's prog, Computer training, Computers for patron use, Copy machines, Digital talking bks, e-mail serv, eReaders, Exhibits, Fax serv, Free DVD rentals, Handicapped accessible, Homebound delivery serv, ILL available, Life-long learning prog for all ages, Magazines, Magnifiers for reading, Mail & tel request accepted, Microfiche/film & reading machines, Music CDs, Online searches, Outside serv via phone, mail, e-mail & web, Photocopying/Printing, Preschool outreach, Printer for laptops & handheld devices, Prog for adults, Prog for children & young adult, Pub access computers, Ref serv available, Scanner, Senior computer classes, Spanish lang bks, Spoken cassettes & CDs, Spoken cassettes & DVDs, Story hour, Summer reading prog, Tax forms, Teen prog, Telephone ref, VHS videos, Video lending libr, Wheelchair accessible
Mem of Illinois Heartland Library System
Special Services for the Deaf - Bks on deafness & sign lang; Closed caption videos
Special Services for the Blind - Bks available with recordings; Bks on cassette; Bks on CD; Computer access aids; Copier with enlargement capabilities; Free checkout of audio mat; Large print bks; Large screen computer & software; Lending of low vision aids; Magnifiers; PC for handicapped; Playaways (bks on MP3); Screen enlargement software for people with visual disabilities
Open Mon 10-7, Tues, Thurs & Fri 9-5, Wed 10-6, Sat 9-2

NORMAL

M BROMENN HEALTHCARE*, A E Livingston Health Sciences Library, 1304 Franklin Ave, 61761. (Mail add: PO Box 2850, Bloomington, 61702-2850), SAN 339-7416. Tel: 309-827-4321, Ext 5281. Reference Tel: 309-827-4321, Ext 5207. FAX: 309-268-5953. Web Site: www.bromenn.org. *Dir,* Molly Horio; Staff 2 (MLS 2)
Founded 1973
Library Holdings: Bk Titles 4,500; Per Subs 300
Subject Interests: Med, Nursing
Automation Activity & Vendor Info: (Cataloging) CyberTools for Libraries; (OPAC) CyberTools for Libraries
Partic in Heart of Illinois Library Consortium
Open Mon-Fri 8-4:30

SR FIRST UNITED METHODIST CHURCH LIBRARY*, 211 N School St, 61761. SAN 325-6936. Tel: 309-452-2096. FAX: 309-452-1327. Web Site: www.normalfumc.org. *Librn,* Catherine Knight
Library Holdings: Bk Vols 1,000

J HEARTLAND COMMUNITY COLLEGE LIBRARY*, 1500 W Raab Rd, 61761. Tel: 309-268-8200. Reference Tel: 309-268-8293. Administration Tel: 309-268-8000. FAX: 309-268-7989. E-mail: library@heartland.edu. Web Site: www.heartland.edu/library. *Dir,* Rachelle Stivers; Tel: 309-268-8274, E-mail: rachelle.stivers@heartland.edu; *Librn,* Carol Reid; Tel: 309-268-8279, E-mail: carol.reid@heartland.edu; *Info & Instruction Librn,* Randi Sutter; Tel: 309-268-8275; *Info & Instruction Librn,* Chris Sweet; Tel: 309-268-8277, E-mail: chris.sweet@heartland.edu
Library Holdings: Bk Titles 13,000; Bk Vols 15,000; Per Subs 209
Automation Activity & Vendor Info: (Cataloging) TLC (The Library Corporation); (Circulation) TLC (The Library Corporation); (OPAC) TLC (The Library Corporation)
Open Mon-Thurs 7:30am-9:30pm, Fri 7:30-4, Sat 12-5, Sun 1-9:30

S ILLINOIS LODGE OF RESEARCH*, Louis L Williams Masonic Library, 614 E Lincoln Ave, 61761. Tel: 309-452-3109. E-mail: library@ilorlibrary.org. Web Site: www.ilorlibrary.org. *Librn,* John Dorner; E-mail: john@ilorlibrary.org; *Librn,* Jeff Fox; Tel: 309-219-1427, E-mail: jeff@ilorlibrary.org
Library Holdings: Bk Vols 10,000
Wireless access
Function: Photocopying/Printing, Pub access computers, Res libr
Open Thurs 6pm-10pm

C ILLINOIS STATE UNIVERSITY, Milner Library, 201 N School St, 61790-8900. (Mail add: Campus Box 8900, Milner Library, Illinois State University, 61790-8900), SAN 304-4777. Tel: 309-438-3481. Circulation Tel: 309-438-7321. Interlibrary Loan Service Tel: 309-438-3461. Reference Tel: 309-438-3451. FAX: 309-438-3676. Web Site: library.illinoisstate.edu. *Dean of Libr,* Dane Ward; E-mail: dmward@ilstu.edu; *Assoc Dean,* Chad Kahl; E-mail: cmkahl@ilstu.edu; *Assoc Dean,* Dallas Long; E-mail: dlong@ilstu.edu; Staff 94 (MLS 31, Non-MLS 63)
Founded 1890. Enrl 20,104; Fac 940; Highest Degree: Doctorate
Library Holdings: Bk Vols 1,632,215; Per Subs 4,873
Special Collections: 19th Century Elementary & Secondary School Textbooks; Children's Literature (Lenski, 19th Century); Circus & Allied Arts; Lincoln Coll. State Document Depository; US Document Depository
Subject Interests: Am hist, Educ, Math, Psychol
Automation Activity & Vendor Info: (Acquisitions) Ex Libris Group; (Cataloging) Ex Libris Group; (Circulation) Ex Libris Group; (ILL) Ex Libris Group; (OPAC) Ex Libris Group; (Serials) Ex Libris Group
Wireless access
Publications: Milner Memos
Partic in Consortium of Academic & Research Libraries in Illinois
Open Mon-Thurs 7am-2am, Fri 8-8, Sat 9-8, Sun Noon-2am
Friends of the Library Group

P NORMAL PUBLIC LIBRARY*, 206 W College Ave, 61761. (Mail add: PO Box 325, 61761-0325), SAN 304-4785. Tel: 309-452-1757. FAX: 309-452-5312. E-mail: normallibrary@normal.org. Web Site: normal-library.org. *Dir,* Brian Chase; *Adult Serv,* Ruth Reeves; *AV,* Jeanne Moonan; *Cat,* Kathy Packard; *Cat, Ch Serv,* Judy Poultney; *ILL,* Brenda Peden; *Pub Relations,* Mari McKeeth; *Ref Serv,* Lynn Freymann; *Youth Serv,* Linda Hutchins; Staff 3 (MLS 3)
Founded 1939. Pop 42,200; Circ 459,800
Library Holdings: Bk Vols 101,335; Per Subs 300
Automation Activity & Vendor Info: (Acquisitions) CARL.Solution (TLC)
Publications: Monthly Newsletter
Open Mon-Thurs 9-9, Fri & Sat 9-5, Sun 1-5
Friends of the Library Group

NORRIS CITY

P NORRIS CITY MEMORIAL PUBLIC LIBRARY DISTRICT*, 603 S Division St, 62869. SAN 304-4793. Tel: 618-378-3713. FAX: 618-378-3713. E-mail: libraryncil@yahoo.com. *Dir,* Judy Daubs; *Librn,* Denise Karns
Founded 1945. Pop 4,500; Circ 37,182
Library Holdings: Large Print Bks 1,200; Bk Titles 25,000; Per Subs 69; Talking Bks 945
Special Collections: Cookbooks
Subject Interests: Gardening, Genealogy, Hist, Ill, Nutrition
Wireless access
Publications: Periodical Guide
Mem of Illinois Heartland Library System
Open Mon-Thurs 12-7, Fri & Sat 10-5

NORTH AURORA

P MESSENGER PUBLIC LIBRARY OF NORTH AURORA, 113 Oak St, 60542. SAN 304-4807. Tel: 630-896-0240. Circulation Tel: 630-896-0240, Ext 4330. Administration Tel: 630-801-2345. Information Services Tel: 630-896-0240, Ext 4350. FAX: 630-896-4654. E-mail: director@northaurora.lib.il.us. Web Site: www.messengerpl.org. *Dir,* G Kevin Davis; Tel: 630-896-0240, Ext 2345, E-mail: gkdavis@northaurora.lib.il.us; Staff 10 (MLS 7, Non-MLS 3)
Founded 1937. Pop 16,760; Circ 234,413
Jun 2013-May 2014 Income $1,616,653, State $35,606, Locally Generated Income $1,534,929, Other $46,118. Mats Exp $198,185, Books $104,592, Per/Ser (Incl. Access Fees) $15,000, AV Mat $44,560, Electronic Ref Mat (Incl. Access Fees) $49,033. Sal $797,626
Library Holdings: Audiobooks 7,521; AV Mats 28,581; CDs 8,423; DVDs 12,503; e-books 9,489; e-journals 68; Electronic Media & Resources 43; Bk Vols 83,182; Per Subs 118
Subject Interests: N Aurora hist
Automation Activity & Vendor Info: (Cataloging) SirsiDynix; (Circulation) SirsiDynix
Wireless access
Function: 24/7 Electronic res, 24/7 Online cat, Activity rm, Adult bk club, Art exhibits, Audiobks via web, Bk club(s), Bks on CD, Children's prog, Computer training, Computers for patron use, Copy machines, Electronic databases & coll, eReaders, Genealogy discussion group, Holiday prog, Homebound delivery serv, ILL available, Magazines, Mango lang, Mus passes, Notary serv, Online cat, Outreach serv, OverDrive digital audio bks, Printer for laptops & handheld devices, Prog for adults, Pub access computers, Ref serv available, Ref serv in person, Scanner, Senior computer classes, Senior outreach, Spanish lang bks, Story hour, Study rm, Summer & winter reading prog, Summer reading prog, Tax forms, Teen prog, Telephone ref, Visual arts prog, Winter reading prog, Workshops, Writing prog
Mem of Reaching Across Illinois Library System (RAILS)
Partic in MAGIC (Multitype Automation Group in Cooperation)
Special Services for the Deaf - ADA equip; Assistive tech; Bks on deafness & sign lang; Closed caption videos; Sign lang interpreter upon request for prog
Open Mon-Thurs 9-9, Fri & Sat 9-5, Sun (Sept-May) 1-5
Restriction: Borrowing requests are handled by ILL

S NORTH EAST MULTI-REGIONAL TRAINING, Instructors' Library, 355 Smoke Tree Plaza Dr, 60542-1723. SAN 372-5782. Tel: 630-896-8860, Ext 108. FAX: 630-896-4422. Web Site: www.nemrt.com. *Librn,* Sarah Cole; E-mail: sarah@nemrt.com; Staff 1 (MLS 1)
Founded 1990
Jul 2014-Jun 2015 Income $8,000. Mats Exp $8,000, Books $1,500, Per/Ser (Incl. Access Fees) $2,000, AV Mat $2,000, Electronic Ref Mat (Incl. Access Fees) $2,500
Library Holdings: Audiobooks 40; Bk Titles 7,000; Per Subs 30; Videos 1,500
Special Collections: Law Enforcement
Function: Archival coll, For res purposes, ILL available
Mem of Reaching Across Illinois Library System (RAILS)
Open Mon-Fri 8:30-4:30
Restriction: Open to fac, students & qualified researchers, Photo ID required for access, Restricted borrowing privileges

NORTH CHICAGO

AM CAPTAIN JAMES A LOVELL FEDERAL HEALTH CARE CENTER*, Health Sciences Library, 3001 Green Bay Rd, 60064. SAN 324-0231. Tel: 224-610-3757. *Head, Med Libr,* Ann Baker
Founded 2010
Library Holdings: CDs 250; Bk Vols 3,000; Per Subs 240; Videos 200
Subject Interests: Clinical med, Health admin, Nursing
Open Mon-Fri 8-4

GM DEPARTMENT OF VETERANS AFFAIRS MEDICAL CENTER*, Learning Resource Center, 3001 Green Bay Rd, 60064. SAN 340-5966. Tel: 847-688-1900, Ext 83757. FAX: 847-578-3819. *Chief Librn,* William Nielson; E-mail: william.nielson@med.va.gov; *Librn,* Sylvia Ryan; Staff 2 (Non-MLS 2)
Library Holdings: Bk Titles 3,900; Bk Vols 20,000; Per Subs 80
Subject Interests: Med, Psychiat, Psychol, Soc serv (soc work)
Partic in Midwest Health Sci Libr Network; Northeastern Ill Libr Consortia
Restriction: Non-circulating to the pub, Staff use only

CM ROSALIND FRANKLIN UNIVERSITY OF MEDICINE & SCIENCE*, Boxer University Library, 3333 Green Bay Rd, 60064. SAN 340-2878. Tel: 847-578-3000. FAX: 847-578-3401. Web Site: www.rosalindfranklin.edu. *Electronic Res & Ref Librn,* Anne Baker; Tel: 847-578-8642, E-mail: anne.baker@rosalindfranklin.edu; *ILL Librn,* Kevin Robertson; Tel: 847-578-3243, E-mail: kevin.robertson@rosalindfranklin.edu
Founded 1912. Enrl 1,373; Fac 350; Highest Degree: Doctorate
Library Holdings: e-journals 1,829; Bk Vols 118,853; Per Subs 380
Subject Interests: Health sci, Med
Automation Activity & Vendor Info: (Cataloging) ComPanion Corp; (Circulation) ComPanion Corp; (ILL) OCLC FirstSearch; (OPAC) OCLC FirstSearch
Publications: Audiovisual catalog; Current Monographs & Serials, Resources; LRC Guide
Partic in Dialog Corp; National Network of Libraries of Medicine; OCLC Online Computer Library Center, Inc; Regional Med Libr - Region 3
Open Mon-Thurs 8am-Midnight, Fri 8am-10pm, Sat 9am-10pm, Sun Noon-Midnight

P NORTH CHICAGO PUBLIC LIBRARY*, 2100 Argonne Dr, 60064. SAN 304-4831. Tel: 847-689-0125. Circulation Tel: 847-689-0125, Ext 100. Reference Tel: 847-689-0125, Ext 113. FAX: 847-689-9117. E-mail: info@ncplibrary.org. Web Site: www.ncplibrary.org. *Dir,* Joan Battley; Tel: 847-689-0125, Ext 110, E-mail: joanb@ncplibrary.org; *Ch,* John Heideman; *Ref Librn,* Bob Palas; *Circ Mgr,* Rosetta Blount; E-mail: rosettab@ncplibrary.org; *Info Tech,* Barry Baker; *Tech Serv,* Maria Rapada San Ramon; Tel: 847-689-0125, Ext 105; Staff 10 (MLS 2, Non-MLS 8)
Founded 1916. Pop 34,978
Library Holdings: Bk Titles 66,000; Per Subs 140
Special Collections: African American Coll
Automation Activity & Vendor Info: (Cataloging) TLC (The Library Corporation); (Circulation) TLC (The Library Corporation); (ILL) OCLC; (OPAC) TLC (The Library Corporation)
Special Services for the Blind - Bks & mags in Braille, on rec, tape & cassette; Computer with voice synthesizer for visually impaired persons; Newsp on cassette; Talking bks
Open Mon-Thurs 9-7:45, Fri & Sat 9-4:45
Friends of the Library Group

NORTH RIVERSIDE

P NORTH RIVERSIDE PUBLIC LIBRARY DISTRICT*, 2400 S DesPlaines Ave, 60546. SAN 376-0197. Tel: 708-447-0869. FAX: 708-447-0526. Web Site: www.northriversidelibrary.org. *Dir,* Robert Lifka; Tel: 708-447-0869, Ext 225, E-mail: lifkar@northriversidelibrary.org; *Ref Librn,* Mary Cooper; E-mail: cooperm@northriversidelibrary.org; *Tech & Pub Serv Librn,* Kathleen Spale; Tel: 708-447-0869, Ext 245, E-mail: spalek@northriversidelibrary.org; *Ch Serv,* Susan Locander; Tel: 708-447-0869, Ext 224, E-mail: locanders@northriversidelibrary.org; *Circ Serv,* Mike Bradley; E-mail: bradleym@northriversidelibrary.org; *Ref,* John F Zmola; Tel: 708-447-0869, Ext 227, E-mail: zmola@northriversidelibrary.org; Staff 19.75 (MLS 4.75, Non-MLS 15)
Founded 1983. Pop 6,672
Library Holdings: Bk Titles 30,000; Per Subs 110
Automation Activity & Vendor Info: (Circulation) Innovative Interfaces, Inc; (ILL) Innovative Interfaces, Inc; (OPAC) Innovative Interfaces, Inc
Database Vendor: Innovative Interfaces, Inc, OCLC FirstSearch
Wireless access
Mem of Reaching Across Illinois Library System (RAILS)
Open Mon-Thurs 10-8, Fri 10-6, Sat 10-4
Friends of the Library Group

NORTHBROOK

SR CONGREGATION BETH SHALOM, Irving Rubenstein Memorial Library, 3433 Walters Ave, 60062-3298. SAN 371-7690. Tel: 847-498-4100. FAX: 847-498-9160. E-mail: library@bethshalomnb.org. Web Site: www.bethshalomnb.org/library-resource-center. *Librn,* Stephanie Gelb
Founded 1969
Library Holdings: Audiobooks 56; CDs 122; DVDs 393; Large Print Bks 100; Bk Titles 9,000; Bk Vols 11,125; Videos 312
Subject Interests: Holocaust
Automation Activity & Vendor Info: (Circulation) Follett Software
Open Tues 2-9, Sun 8-12:30

P NORTHBROOK PUBLIC LIBRARY*, 1201 Cedar Lane, 60062-4581. SAN 304-4866. Tel: 847-272-6224. FAX: 847-272-5362. Web Site: www.northbrook.info. *Dir,* Kate Hall; *Asst Dir,* Eric Robbins; E-mail: erobbins@northbrook.info; *Head, Ref,* Mary Munday; E-mail: mmunday@northbrook.info; *Head, Youth Serv,* Andrea Johnson; E-mail: ajohnson@northbrook.info; *Circ Mgr,* Ann Weston; E-mail: aweston@northbrook.info; *Multimedia,* Steve Gianni; E-mail: sgianni@northbrook.info; *Tech Serv,* Joyce Horvath; E-mail: jhorvath@northbrook.info; Staff 118 (MLS 34, Non-MLS 84)
Founded 1952. Pop 34,407; Circ 808,859
May 2008-Apr 2009 Income $6,295,802, State $175,000, County $5,632,802, Locally Generated Income $488,000. Mats Exp $761,000, Books $470,000, Per/Ser (Incl. Access Fees) $60,000, AV Mat $101,000, Electronic Ref Mat (Incl. Access Fees) $130,000. Sal $2,835,000
Library Holdings: Audiobooks 4,948; AV Mats 40,786; Bks on Deafness & Sign Lang 147; Braille Volumes 15; CDs 15,317; DVDs 8,914; High Interest/Low Vocabulary Bk Vols 74; Large Print Bks 8,902; Music Scores 1,650; Bk Titles 222,803; Bk Vols 272,660; Per Subs 613; Videos 6,506
Subject Interests: Archit, Art, Landscape archit, Sci tech
Automation Activity & Vendor Info: (Acquisitions) SirsiDynix
Database Vendor: Baker & Taylor, Children's Literature Comprehensive Database Company (CLCD), Dun & Bradstreet, EBSCO - WebFeat, EBSCO Auto Repair Reference, EBSCOhost, Electric Library, Gale Cengage Learning, Greenwood Publishing Group, Grolier Online, H W Wilson, LearningExpress, Marquis Who's Who, Newsbank, OCLC ArticleFirst, OCLC FirstSearch, OCLC WorldShare Interlibrary Loan, Overdrive, Inc, ProQuest, ReferenceUSA, SerialsSolutions, SirsiDynix, Standard & Poor's, ValueLine, World Book Online
Wireless access
Function: Adult literacy prog, After school storytime, Art exhibits, Digital talking bks, Govt ref serv, Home delivery & serv to Sr ctr & nursing homes, Homebound delivery serv, ILL available, Large print keyboards, Magnifiers for reading, Music CDs, Online searches, Photocopying/Printing, Prog for adults, Prog for children & young adult, Spoken cassettes & CDs, Summer reading prog, VCDs, VHS videos, Workshops
Publications: The Latest Edition (Newsletter)
Partic in Cooperative Computer Services - CCS
Special Services for the Deaf - Staff with knowledge of sign lang; TDD equip
Special Services for the Blind - Assistive/Adapted tech devices, equip & products; Audio mat; BiFolkal kits; Bks on cassette; Bks on CD, Computer with voice synthesizer for visually impaired persons; Home delivery serv; Large print bks; Large screen computer & software; Lending of low vision aids; PC for handicapped; Talking bks
Open Mon-Thurs 9-9, Fri 9-6, Sat 9-5, Sun 1-5
Friends of the Library Group

R SAINT GILES' EPISCOPAL CHURCH*, Saint Bede's Library, 3025 Walters Ave, 60062. SAN 304-4874. Tel: 847-272-6622. FAX: 847-272-7664. Web Site: saint-giles.org. *Librn,* Doug Downey
Founded 1952
Library Holdings: Bk Vols 1,100
Subject Interests: Relig
Restriction: Mem only, Open to others by appt

S WISS, JANNEY, ELSTNER ASSOCIATES, INC, 330 Pfingsten Rd, 60062. SAN 373-0492. Tel: 847-272-7400, Ext 4202, 847-753-7202. FAX: 847-498-0358. Web Site: www.wje.com. *Librn,* Penny Sympson; E-mail: psympson@wje.com; Staff 2 (MLS 2)
Library Holdings: Bk Vols 10,000; Per Subs 5
Subject Interests: Archit, Civil eng, Mat sci, Structural eng
Automation Activity & Vendor Info: (Cataloging) EOS International; (Circulation) EOS International
Database Vendor: OCLC FirstSearch
Function: ILL available, Photocopying/Printing
Partic in OCLC Online Computer Library Center, Inc
Restriction: Co libr, In-house use for visitors, Open by appt only

NORTHFIELD

S MCILVAINE CO*, Technical Library, 191 Waukegan Rd, Ste 208, 60093. SAN 373-4420. Tel: 847-784-0012. FAX: 847-784-0061. E-mail: editor@mcilvainecompany.com. Web Site: www.mcilvainecompany.com. *In Charge,* Robert Mcilvaine
Library Holdings: Per Subs 100
Subject Interests: Air pollution, Energy, Water pollution

S STEPAN CO*, Information Research Center, 22 W Frontage Rd, 60093. SAN 326-9647. Tel: 847-501-2389. FAX: 847-501-2466. Web Site: www.stepan.com. Staff 2 (MLS 1, Non-MLS 1)
Library Holdings: Bk Vols 3,899; Per Subs 155
Subject Interests: Chem
Database Vendor: OCLC FirstSearch
Restriction: Co libr

SR TEMPLE JEREMIAH*, Marshall B & Viola R Schwimmer Library, 937 Happ Rd, 60093. (Mail add: PO Box 8209, 60093-8209), SAN 374-5716. Tel: 847-441-5760. FAX: 847-441-5765. E-mail: info@templejeremiah.org. Web Site: www.templejeremiah.org. *In Charge,* Sue Kaufmann
Library Holdings: Bk Titles 4,500; Per Subs 32
Special Collections: Allan Tarshish Rabbinical Coll; Jewish Art
Restriction: Open by appt only

NORTHLAKE

P NORTHLAKE PUBLIC LIBRARY DISTRICT*, 231 N Wolf Rd, 60164. SAN 304-4890. Tel: 708-562-2301. FAX: 708-562-8120. E-mail: nls@northlakelibrary.org. Web Site: www.northlakelibrary.org. *Dir,* Jan Schmudde; E-mail: schmudde@northlakelibrary.org; *Adult Serv,* Mary Lopez; *Ch Serv,* Marianne Ryczek; *Tech Serv,* Mary Jane Garrett; Staff 20 (MLS 8, Non-MLS 12)
Founded 1957. Pop 26,653; Circ 192,676
Jul 2007-Jun 2008 Income $2,148,798, State $100,218, City $1,855,537, Locally Generated Income $32,394, Other $130,649. Mats Exp $193,124, Books $134,342, AV Mat $22,609, Electronic Ref Mat (Incl. Access Fees) $36,173. Sal $753,226 (Prof $413,572)
Library Holdings: AV Mats 5,776; CDs 3,198; DVDs 2,578; Electronic Media & Resources 36; High Interest/Low Vocabulary Bk Vols 60; Bk Titles 79,577; Per Subs 230
Subject Interests: Spanish
Automation Activity & Vendor Info: (Circulation) Innovative Interfaces, Inc; (ILL) Innovative Interfaces, Inc; (OPAC) Innovative Interfaces, Inc; (Serials) Innovative Interfaces, Inc
Database Vendor: Gale Cengage Learning, Innovative Interfaces, Inc
Wireless access
Function: Bilingual assistance for Spanish patrons, Bk club(s), Bks on cassette, Bks on CD, Computer training, Computers for patron use, Copy machines, E-Reserves, Electronic databases & coll, Free DVD rentals, Handicapped accessible, Home delivery & serv to Sr ctr & nursing homes, ILL available, Music CDs, Online cat, Photocopying/Printing, Prog for adults, Prog for children & young adult, Senior outreach, Spoken cassettes & CDs, Story hour, Summer reading prog, Tax forms, Teen prog, Telephone ref, Wheelchair accessible
Publications: Newsletter
Mem of Reaching Across Illinois Library System (RAILS)
Partic in Ill Regional Libr Coun

OAK BROOK

S CZECHOSLOVAK HERITAGE MUSEUM, LIBRARY & ARCHIVES*, 122 W 22nd St, 60523. SAN 326-5250. Tel: 630-472-0500. Toll Free Tel: 800-543-3272. FAX: 630-472-1100. Web Site: www.csafraternallife.org.
Founded 1974
Library Holdings: Bk Vols 1,000
Subject Interests: Czechoslovakia genealogy, Czechoslovakia hist, Czechoslovakia/Slovak Am
Open Tues & Fri 10-1

P OAK BROOK PUBLIC LIBRARY*, 600 Oak Brook Rd, 60523. SAN 304-4920. Tel: 630-368-7700. Circulation Tel: 630-368-7702. Reference Tel: 630-368-7725. FAX: 630-368-7704, 630-990-4509. Web Site: www.oak-brook.lib.il.us. *Dir,* Margaret G Klinkow Hartmann; Tel: 630-368-7706, Fax: 630-368-7707, E-mail: mklinkow@oak-brook.lib.il.us; *Head, Adult Serv,* Mary Williamson; Tel: 630-368-7722, E-mail: mwilliamson@oak-brook.lib.il.us; *Head, Circ,* Vernette R Richmond; Tel: 630-368-7712, E-mail: vrichmond@oak-brook.lib.il.us; *Head, Tech Serv,* Linda Fairbanks; Tel: 630-368-7716, E-mail: lfairbanks@oak-brook.lib.il.us; *Head, Youth Serv,* Sue Madorin; Tel: 630-368-7728, E-mail: smadorin@oak-brook.lib.il.us; Staff 20 (MLS 7, Non-MLS 13)
Founded 1960. Pop 8,702; Circ 96,414
Jan 2007-Dec 2007 Income $1,424,211, City $1,407,655, Locally Generated Income $16,556. Mats Exp $224,035. Sal $1,025,370

Library Holdings: AV Mats 11,574; Bk Titles 87,433; Bk Vols 94,471; Per Subs 10,080
Special Collections: Douglas Coll
Subject Interests: Gardening, Quilting
Automation Activity & Vendor Info: (Acquisitions) SirsiDynix; (Cataloging) SirsiDynix; (Circulation) SirsiDynix; (OPAC) SirsiDynix; (Serials) SirsiDynix
Function: Adult bk club, Art exhibits, Audiobks via web, AV serv, Bk club(s), Bks on cassette, Bks on CD, Computer training, Computers for patron use, Copy machines, Digital talking bks, E-Reserves, Electronic databases & coll, Handicapped accessible, Holiday prog, Homebound delivery serv, ILL available, Mail & tel request accepted, Music CDs, Online cat, Online searches, Photocopying/Printing, Prog for adults, Prog for children & young adult, Pub access computers, Ref & res, Senior outreach, Spoken cassettes & CDs, Spoken cassettes & DVDs, Summer reading prog, Tax forms, Teen prog, Telephone ref, VHS videos, Web-catalog, Wheelchair accessible
Mem of Reaching Across Illinois Library System (RAILS)
Partic in Dynix Consortium
Open Mon-Thurs 9:30-9, Fri & Sat 9:30-5, Sun 1-5
Friends of the Library Group

S RADIOLOGICAL SOCIETY OF NORTH AMERICA*, 820 Jorie Blvd, 60523-2251. SAN 371-4314. Tel: 630-571-2670. FAX: 630-571-7837. Web Site: www.rsna.org. *Asst Dir, Publications,* Roberta Arnold
Library Holdings: Bk Vols 400; Per Subs 40
Restriction: Mem only

OAK FOREST

P ACORN PUBLIC LIBRARY DISTRICT*, 15624 S Central Ave, 60452-3204. SAN 304-4955. Tel: 708-687-3700. FAX: 708-687-3712. E-mail: acorn@acornlibrary.org. Web Site: www.acornlibrary.org. *Dir,* Eric Werthmann; *Cat,* Patricia Kucher; *Ch Serv,* Jennifer Marquardt; E-mail: youthservices@acornlibrary.org; *Circ,* Donna Bos; E-mail: donnab@acornlibrary.org; *Ref,* Megan Marsch; E-mail: reference@acornlibrary.org; Staff 17 (MLS 3, Non-MLS 14)
Founded 1966. Pop 36,875; Circ 168,870
Library Holdings: Audiobooks 7,136; Bks on Deafness & Sign Lang 44; DVDs 3,358; High Interest/Low Vocabulary Bk Vols 125; Bk Vols 109,969; Per Subs 180
Automation Activity & Vendor Info: (Cataloging) Innovative Interfaces, Inc; (Circulation) Innovative Interfaces, Inc; (ILL) Innovative Interfaces, Inc; (OPAC) Innovative Interfaces, Inc; (Serials) Innovative Interfaces, Inc
Database Vendor: Baker & Taylor, EBSCO Auto Repair Reference, Gale Cengage Learning, Innovative Interfaces, Inc, LearningExpress, OCLC ArticleFirst, OCLC FirstSearch, OCLC WorldShare Interlibrary Loan, World Book Online
Wireless access
Publications: Community Awareness Brochures; Newsletter
Mem of Reaching Across Illinois Library System (RAILS)
Special Services for the Blind - Closed circuit TV
Open Mon-Thurs 9-9, Fri & Sat 9-5
Friends of the Library Group

SR MISSIONARY SISTERS OF SAINT BENEDICT LIBRARY*, 5900 W 147th St, 60452-1104. SAN 321-2289. Tel: 708-535-9623. *In Charge,* Sister Assumpta Wrobel
Library Holdings: Bk Titles 3,500; Per Subs 40
Special Collections: Oral History

OAK LAWN

P OAK LAWN PUBLIC LIBRARY*, 9427 S Raymond Ave, 60453-2434. SAN 304-498X. Tel: 708-422-4990. FAX: 708-422-5061. Web Site: www.olpl.org. *Dir,* Jim Deiters; *Ch Serv,* Jean Day; *Per,* Lana Magnavite; *Pub Serv,* Mary Pasek Williams; *Ref,* Mary Dunneback; *Tech Serv,* James Baker; Staff 90 (MLS 20, Non-MLS 70)
Founded 1943. Pop 56,000; Circ 500,000
Library Holdings: AV Mats 33,153; Bk Vols 281,342; Per Subs 735
Special Collections: Telephone Books on CD ROM & microfiche; US College Catalogs, microfiche. Oral History
Subject Interests: Careers, Law, Local hist
Automation Activity & Vendor Info: (Acquisitions) Brodart; (Circulation) Innovative Interfaces, Inc
Publications: Check It Out! (Newsletter)
Mem of Reaching Across Illinois Library System (RAILS)
Partic in BRS; Dialog Corp; Illinois Library & Information Network; OCLC Online Computer Library Center, Inc; System Wide Automated Network; Wilsonline
Special Services for the Deaf - Bks on deafness & sign lang; Captioned film dep
Special Services for the Blind - Talking bks
Open Mon-Thurs 9-9, Fri & Sat 9-5, Sun 1-5
Friends of the Library Group

OAK PARK

P OAK PARK PUBLIC LIBRARY, 834 Lake St, 60301. SAN 340-6148. Tel: 708-383-8200. Circulation Tel: 708-452-3409. FAX: 708-697-6900. Administration FAX: 708-697-6917. Web Site: www.oppl.org. *Exec Dir,* David J Seleb; Tel: 708-697-6911, E-mail: d.seleb@oppl.org; *Asst Dir, Admin Serv,* Jim Madigan; E-mail: jmadigan@oppl.org; *Asst Dir, Pub Serv,* Cynthia Landrum; E-mail: clandrum@oppl.org; Staff 26 (MLS 26)
Founded 1902. Pop 52,524; Circ 961,801
Library Holdings: Bk Vols 315,000; Per Subs 500
Special Collections: Frank Lloyd Wright & Ernest Hemingway (Local Authors), bks, pamphlets, papers; History, bks, photos, papers; Oak Park Local. US Document Depository
Subject Interests: Art & archit, Local hist
Automation Activity & Vendor Info: (Circulation) SirsiDynix
Wireless access
Open Mon-Thurs 9-9, Fri 9-6, Sat 9-5, Sun 1-6
Friends of the Library Group
Branches: 2
DOLE BRANCH, 255 Augusta St, 60302, SAN 340-6202. Tel: 708-386-9032. FAX: 708-445-2385. *Br Serv Mgr,* Lori Pulliam; E-mail: lpulliam@oppl.org
Open Tues-Thurs 10-9, Fri 10-6, Sat 10-5, Sun 1-6
Friends of the Library Group
MAZE BRANCH, 845 S Gunderson Ave, 60304, SAN 340-6172. Tel: 708-386-4751. FAX: 708-386-0023. *Mgr,* Lori Pulliam; E-mail: lpulliam@oppl.org
Library Holdings: Bk Vols 30,333
Open Mon-Fri 10-9, Sat 10-5, Sun 1-6
Friends of the Library Group

M RUSH OAK PARK HOSPITAL LIBRARY*, 520 S Maple, 60304. SAN 375-9830. Tel: 708-383-9300. FAX: 708-660-6480. Web Site: www.oakparkhospital.org. *Dir,* Wanda Mathews
Library Holdings: Bk Titles 200; Per Subs 42
Special Collections: Medical Reports; Survey Responses
Open Mon-Fri 7-3

S FRANK LLOYD WRIGHT PRESERVATION TRUST*, Research Center, 951 Chicago Ave, 60302. SAN 325-2949. Tel: 312-994-4035. Reference Tel: 708-848-1695. FAX: 708-848-1248. E-mail: info@gowright.org. Web Site: gowright.org/research/research-center.html. *Dir,* David Bagnall
Founded 1974
Library Holdings: Bk Titles 2,500; Per Subs 20
Special Collections: Artifacts; Frank Lloyd Wright Coll; John L Wright Toy Coll; Large Drawings; Maginal Wright Barney Archive; Prairie School of Architecture, mat; William Drummond Coll. Oral History
Subject Interests: Archit design, Arts & crafts
Publications: Frank Lloyd Wright (Newsletter)
Restriction: Open by appt only

OAKBROOK TERRACE

S THE JOINT COMMISSION*, Resource Center, One Renaissance Blvd, 60181. SAN 375-9784. Tel: 630-792-5474. FAX: 630-792-4474. *Dir,* Jan Aleccia; E-mail: jaleccia@jointcommission.org; Staff 2 (MLS 2)
Founded 1986
Jan 2012-Dec 2012 Income $250,000
Library Holdings: AV Mats 200; Bk Titles 2,500; Per Subs 100
Subject Interests: Health admin
Automation Activity & Vendor Info: (Cataloging) LibraryWorld, Inc
Database Vendor: Dialog, EBSCOhost, OCLC FirstSearch, PubMed, Thomson - Web of Science, Westlaw
Partic in Fox Valley Health Science Library Consortium; National Network of Libraries of Medicine

OAKWOOD

P OAKWOOD PUBLIC LIBRARY DISTRICT*, 110 E Finley, 61858. (Mail add: PO Box 99, 61858-0099), SAN 376-0162. Tel: 217-354-4777. FAX: 217-354-4782. Interlibrary Loan Service E-mail: OakwoodPublicLibrary@gmail.com. Web Site: www.oakwood.lib.li.us. *Dir,* Elizabeth Kent
Founded 1987. Pop 7,409
Library Holdings: Bk Titles 15,000; Per Subs 62
Special Collections: Audio Coll; Local History Room
Automation Activity & Vendor Info: (Cataloging) SirsiDynix; (Circulation) SirsiDynix
Mem of Illinois Heartland Library System
Open Mon, Wed & Fri 10-6, Tues & Thurs 12-8, Sat 9-2
Friends of the Library Group

ODELL

P ODELL PUBLIC LIBRARY DISTRICT, 301 E Richard St, 60460. (Mail add: PO Box 347, 60460-0347), SAN 304-5021. Tel: 815-998-2012. FAX: 815-998-2339. E-mail: odellpld@yahoo.com. Web Site: www.odelllibrary.com. *Chair,* Margaret Doran; *Libr Dir,* Cathy Grafton; Staff 1 (Non-MLS 1)
Founded 1905. Pop 2,341; Circ 6,984
Library Holdings: Audiobooks 308; CDs 312; DVDs 1,111; Large Print Bks 594; Bk Vols 14,171; Per Subs 12
Database Vendor: OCLC
Wireless access
Mem of Reaching Across Illinois Library System (RAILS)
Open Mon & Wed 1-8, Tues, Thurs & Fri 1-5, Sat 9-12
Restriction: Access for corporate affiliates
Friends of the Library Group

O'FALLON

P O'FALLON PUBLIC LIBRARY, 120 Civic Plaza, 62269-2692. SAN 304-503X. Tel: 618-632-3783. FAX: 618-632-3759. E-mail: reference@ofallonlibrary.org. Web Site: www.ofpl.info. *Dir,* Molly Scanlan; E-mail: molly@ofallonlibrary.org; *Adult Serv Mgr,* Ryan Johnson; E-mail: ryan@ofallonlibrary.org; *Circ,* Michael King; E-mail: michael@ofallonlibrary.org; *Youth Serv,* Teri Rankin; E-mail: teri@ofallonlibrary.org; Staff 3 (MLS 2, Non-MLS 1)
Founded 1943. Pop 28,396; Circ 348,532
Library Holdings: Audiobooks 4,694; CDs 4,500; DVDs 4,000; e-books 16,831; Electronic Media & Resources 55; Bk Vols 64,668; Per Subs 220
Special Collections: Learning Activities Resource Center (for teachers/homeschoolers)
Subject Interests: Popular mat
Automation Activity & Vendor Info: (Acquisitions) Innovative Interfaces, Inc; (Cataloging) Innovative Interfaces, Inc; (Circulation) Innovative Interfaces, Inc; (ILL) OCLC; (OPAC) Innovative Interfaces, Inc
Database Vendor: 3M Library Systems, EBSCO Discovery Service, EBSCOhost, Gale Cengage Learning, infoUSA, LearningExpress, Newsbank, OCLC FirstSearch, Overdrive, Inc, ProQuest
Wireless access
Mem of Illinois Heartland Library System
Open Mon-Thurs 9-8, Fri 9-5, Sat 9-4, Sun 1-5
Friends of the Library Group

OGDEN

P OGDEN ROSE PUBLIC LIBRARY*, 103 W Main, 61859. (Mail add: PO Box 297, 61859-0297), SAN 304-5048. Tel: 217-582-2411. FAX: 217-582-2411. E-mail: roselibrary@comcast.net. Web Site: home.comcast.net/~roselibrary. *Librn,* Sandra Wienke
Pop 800; Circ 1,800
Library Holdings: Bk Vols 17,000; Per Subs 20
Mem of Illinois Heartland Library System
Open Tues & Thurs 9-1 & 4-8, Wed 1-8, Sat 9-1
Friends of the Library Group

OGLESBY

J ILLINOIS VALLEY COMMUNITY COLLEGE*, Jacobs Memorial Library, 815 N Orlando Smith Ave, 61348-9692. SAN 304-5056. Tel: 815-224-0306. Interlibrary Loan Service Tel: 815-224-0305. FAX: 815-224-9147. E-mail: jacobs_library@ivcc.edu. Web Site: www.ivcc.edu/library. *Govt Doc, Head Librn,* Jane Norem; Tel: 815-224-0387, E-mail: jane_norem@ivcc.edu; *Coll Develop Librn,* Frances Whaley; Tel: 815-224-0263, E-mail: frances_whaley@ivcc.edu; *Circ, ILL,* Jan Vogelgesang; E-mail: jan_vogelgesang@ivcc.edu; *Electronic Res, Ser,* Joanne Jalley; Tel: 815-224-0237, E-mail: joanne_jalley@ivcc.edu; Staff 4 (MLS 2, Non-MLS 2)
Founded 1968. Enrl 4,500; Fac 91; Highest Degree: Associate
Library Holdings: AV Mats 1,214; e-books 10,738; Bk Vols 61,425
Special Collections: State Document Depository; US Document Depository
Automation Activity & Vendor Info: (Cataloging) Ex Libris Group; (Circulation) Ex Libris Group; (OPAC) Ex Libris Group
Database Vendor: EBSCOhost, Facts on File, JSTOR, LexisNexis, Newsbank, OCLC FirstSearch, ProQuest, SerialsSolutions
Wireless access
Mem of Reaching Across Illinois Library System (RAILS)
Partic in Consortium of Academic & Research Libraries in Illinois; Northern Ill Learning Resources Coop; OCLC Online Computer Library Center, Inc; OCLC-LVIS; State of Ill Librs Online
Open Mon-Thurs 7:30am-8pm, Fri 7:30-4:30
Restriction: Open to pub for ref & circ; with some limitations, Open to students, fac & staff

P OGLESBY PUBLIC LIBRARY*, 111 S Woodland St, 61348. SAN 304-5064. Tel: 815-883-3619. FAX: 815-883-3615. Web Site: www.oglesby.lib.il.us. *Librn,* Irene Claudnic
Founded 1925. Pop 3,979; Circ 12,819
Library Holdings: Bk Vols 23,000; Per Subs 75
Automation Activity & Vendor Info: (Circulation) SirsiDynix
Mem of Reaching Across Illinois Library System (RAILS)
Open Mon & Fri 10-5, Tues-Thurs 10-8, Sat 10-4
Friends of the Library Group

OHIO

P OHIO PUBLIC LIBRARY DISTRICT*, 112 N Main St, 61349. (Mail add: PO Box 187, 61349-0187), SAN 304-5072. Tel: 815-376-5422. FAX: 815-376-5422. E-mail: ohiolibrarybc@yahoo.com. *Dir,* Justin Mapes; E-mail: mapesjustin@hotmail.com
Founded 1949. Pop 1,043; Circ 6,075
Jul 2008-Jun 2009 Income $24,600, County $24,000, Other $600. Mats Exp $10,460, Books $3,000, Per/Ser (Incl. Access Fees) $500, AV Mat $100, Electronic Ref Mat (Incl. Access Fees) $300. Sal $14,140
Library Holdings: AV Mats 672; Bks on Deafness & Sign Lang 32; CDs 5; DVDs 120; Large Print Bks 418; Bk Vols 5,799; Per Subs 25; Spec Interest Per Sub 2; Talking Bks 5; Videos 571
Function: Adult bk club, Audio & video playback equip for onsite use, Computer training, Copy machines, e-mail serv, Fax serv, Handicapped accessible, Homebound delivery serv, Mail & tel request accepted, Music CDs, Newsp ref libr, Online ref, Online searches, Outside serv via phone, mail, e-mail & web, Photocopying/Printing, Prog for children & young adult, Ref serv available, Serves mentally handicapped consumers, Spoken cassettes & CDs, Summer reading prog, Tax forms, VHS videos, Video lending libr, Wheelchair accessible
Mem of Reaching Across Illinois Library System (RAILS)
Special Services for the Blind - Audio mat; Bks on cassette; Bks on CD; Cassette playback machines; Home delivery serv; Large print bks; Talking bk & rec for the blind cat; Talking bks; Talking bks & player equip
Open Mon & Fri 9-11:30 & 3:15-7, Wed 9-12 & 3:15-7, Sat 9-2
Restriction: In-house use for visitors, Non-circulating coll, Non-resident fee, Open to students, Pub ref by request, Pub use on premises, Registered patrons only, Residents only

OLIVE BRANCH

P DODGE MEMORIAL PUBLIC LIBRARY*, 22440 Railroad St, 62969. (Mail add: PO Box 65, 62969-0065), SAN 376-6764. Tel: 618-776-5115. FAX: 618-776-5115. E-mail; library1@lazernetwireless.net. *Librn,* Karen Schultz
Library Holdings: Bk Titles 4,500; Bk Vols 6,000
Mem of Illinois Heartland Library System
Open Tues 3-5, Wed-Fri 11-5

OLMSTED

P OLMSTED PUBLIC LIBRARY*, 160 N Front St, 62970. SAN 376-0170. Tel: 618-742-8296. FAX: 618-742-8296. *Librn,* Katherine Robertson; E-mail: krobolmpl@yahoo.com
Pop 299; Circ 1,161
Library Holdings: Bk Vols 5,000; Per Subs 25
Mem of Illinois Heartland Library System
Open Tues-Thurs 12:30-4:30

OLNEY

J OLNEY CENTRAL COLLEGE*, Anderson Learning Resource Center, 305 N West St, 62450. SAN 304-5080. Tel: 618-395-7777, Ext 2260. FAX: 618-392-3293. Web Site: www.iecc.edu/occ/lrc. *Dir,* Brittany Bass; E-mail: bassb@iecc.edu; *Libr Asst,* Rusty Foerster; E-mail: foersterr@iecc.edu; *Libr Asst,* Kyle Thomas; E-mail: thomask@iecc.edu
Founded 1963. Enrl 2,000; Fac 42; Highest Degree: Associate
Jul 2008-Jun 2009 Income $76,604, State $34,782, Federal $20,000, Locally Generated Income $20,992. Mats Exp $57,500, Books $20,000, Per/Ser (Incl. Access Fees) $4,500, AV Equip $20,000, AV Mat $1,000, Electronic Ref Mat (Incl. Access Fees) $12,000. Sal $112,436 (Prof $39,902)
Library Holdings: Audiobooks 70; AV Mats 742; Bks on Deafness & Sign Lang 27; CDs 139; DVDs 78; e-books 600; e-journals 1,600; Electronic Media & Resources 27; High Interest/Low Vocabulary Bk Vols 208; Large Print Bks 23; Music Scores 10; Bk Titles 20,953; Bk Vols 22,504; Per Subs 52; Spec Interest Per Sub 17; Talking Bks 50; Videos 664
Automation Activity & Vendor Info: (Acquisitions) Ex Libris Group; (Cataloging) Ex Libris Group; (Circulation) Ex Libris Group; (Course Reserve) Ex Libris Group; (ILL) Ex Libris Group; (OPAC) Ex Libris Group; (Serials) ADLiB
Database Vendor: Cinahl, CQ Press, CredoReference, EBSCOhost, Ex Libris Group, Facts on File, Ingenta, LexisNexis, Medline, Micromedex,

Newsbank, OCLC ArticleFirst, OCLC FirstSearch, OCLC WebJunction, OCLC WorldShare Interlibrary Loan, Oxford Online, PubMed, WebMD
Wireless access
Function: ILL available
Mem of Illinois Heartland Library System
Partic in Consortium of Academic & Research Libraries in Illinois
Special Services for the Deaf - Accessible learning ctr; ADA equip; Assistive tech; Closed caption videos
Special Services for the Blind - Accessible computers; Aids for in-house use; Assistive/Adapted tech devices, equip & products; Audio mat; Bks available with recordings
Open Mon-Thurs 7:30am-8pm, Fri 7:30-4:30
Friends of the Library Group

P OLNEY PUBLIC LIBRARY*, 400 W Main St, 62450. SAN 340-6237. Tel: 618-392-3711. FAX: 618-392-3139. Web Site: www.olney.lib.il.us. *Dir,* Judy Whitaker; *Asst Librn,* Roberta Eck; Staff 6 (Non-MLS 6)
Founded 1872. Pop 8,631; Circ 80,000
Library Holdings: Bk Titles 38,000; Per Subs 60
Special Collections: Antiques & Collectibles - Toys & Dolls; Civil War; Genealogy
Database Vendor: SirsiDynix
Mem of Illinois Heartland Library System
Open Mon-Thurs 11-7, Fri & Sat 10-5
Friends of the Library Group

OLYMPIA FIELDS

CM FRANCISCAN ST JAMES HEALTH, Olympia Fields Campus, (Formerly Midwestern University), 20201 S Crawford, 60461. SAN 304-5099. Tel: 708-747-4000. FAX: 708-747-0244.
Founded 1978
Library Holdings: Bk Titles 2,622; Per Subs 184
Wireless access
Partic in Illinois Library & Information Network; Midwest Health Sci Libr Network

ONARGA

P ONARGA COMMUNITY PUBLIC LIBRARY DISTRICT*, 209 W Seminary St, 60955-1131. SAN 304-5102. Tel: 815-268-7626. FAX: 815-268-4635. E-mail: onargalibrary@sbcglobal.net. Web Site: www.ltls.org/onn.html. *Dir,* Kim Heft
Pop 3,943; Circ 14,161
Automation Activity & Vendor Info: (Circulation) SirsiDynix
Wireless access
Mem of Illinois Heartland Library System
Open Mon-Wed & Fri 12-6, Thurs 10-6, Sat 9-12

ONEIDA

P GREIG MEMORIAL LIBRARY*, 110 S Joy St, 61467. (Mail add: PO Box 446, 61467-0446), SAN 304-5110. Tel: 309-483-3482. FAX: 309-483-3482. E-mail: greigmemlib@gmail.com. *Dir,* Dave Sheppard
Founded 1916. Pop 752; Circ 4,638
Library Holdings: Bk Vols 12,000
Wireless access
Mem of Reaching Across Illinois Library System (RAILS)
Open Tues 12-8, Wed 9-12 & 3-8, Fri & Sat 8-1
Friends of the Library Group

OREANA

P ARGENTA-OREANA PUBLIC LIBRARY DISTRICT*, Oreana Public Library, 100 S Rte 48, 62554-7901. (Mail add: PO Box 278, 62554-0261), SAN 304-5129. Tel: 217-468-2340. FAX: 217-468-2467. E-mail: director@aopld.lib.il.us. Web Site: www.aopld.lib.il.us. *Dir,* Julia Welzen
Pop 5,507
Library Holdings: CDs 200; DVDs 1,000; Bk Titles 32,837; Per Subs 25; Talking Bks 1,243; Videos 1,755
Automation Activity & Vendor Info: (Acquisitions) SirsiDynix; (Cataloging) SirsiDynix; (Circulation) SirsiDynix; (ILL) SirsiDynix; (OPAC) SirsiDynix
Database Vendor: SirsiDynix
Wireless access
Function: CD-ROM
Open Mon 9-7, Tues & Thurs 9-5, Wed 12-7, Fri 9-1, Sat 9-Noon

OREGON

P OREGON PUBLIC LIBRARY DISTRICT*, 300 Jefferson St, 61061. SAN 304-5137. Tel: 815-732-2724. FAX: 815-732-6643. E-mail: oregonlibrary@yahoo.com. Web Site: oregon.lib.il.us. *Dir,* Marsha Zaccone; *Adult Serv,* Kathe Wilson; *Ch Serv,* Deborah Herman
Pop 6,719; Circ 37,106
Library Holdings: Bk Vols 34,153; Per Subs 62
Special Collections: Laredo Taft Eagles Nest Art Coll
Subject Interests: Genealogy
Database Vendor: OCLC WorldShare Interlibrary Loan
Wireless access
Mem of Reaching Across Illinois Library System (RAILS)
Open Mon-Thurs 9-8, Fri & Sat 9-4
Friends of the Library Group

ORION

P WESTERN DISTRICT LIBRARY*, 1111 Fourth St, 61273. (Mail add: PO Box 70, 61273-0070), SAN 304-5145. Tel: 309-526-8375. FAX: 309-526-8375. Web Site: westerndistrictlibrary.org. *Dir,* Shirley Carney; *Ch,* Mary Ellison; Staff 1 (Non-MLS 1)
Founded 1905. Pop 4,913; Circ 40,161
Library Holdings: AV Mats 1,253; Bks on Deafness & Sign Lang 10; Bk Vols 26,057; Per Subs 89; Talking Bks 906
Automation Activity & Vendor Info: (Circulation) SirsiDynix; (ILL) SirsiDynix
Mem of Reaching Across Illinois Library System (RAILS)
Open Mon, Tues & Thurs 12-8, Wed 9-8, Fri 9-6, Sat 9-1

ORLAND HILLS

P ORLAND HILLS PUBLIC LIBRARY DISTRICT*, 16033 94th Ave, 60477-4623. SAN 376-1363. Tel: 708-349-6666. FAX: 708-349-1358. Web Site: www.orlandhills.org. *Chairperson,* Craig F Schmidt
Automation Activity & Vendor Info: (Circulation) Innovative Interfaces, Inc
Mem of Reaching Across Illinois Library System (RAILS)
Open Mon & Wed-Fri 8-4:30, Tues 8-7

ORLAND PARK

P ORLAND PARK PUBLIC LIBRARY*, 14921 Ravinia Ave, 60462. SAN 304-5153. Tel: 708-428-5100. FAX: 708-349-8322. E-mail: askoppl@orlandparklibrary.org. Web Site: www.orlandparklibrary.org. *Dir,* Mary Weimar; *Head, Adult Serv, ILL, Ref Serv,* Andrew Mosura; *Head, Ch,* Howard Griffin; *Head, Circ,* Peter Kuczynski; *Head, Tech Serv,* Kay Momsen; *Head, Youth Serv,* Mary Adamowski
Founded 1937. Pop 51,077
Library Holdings: Bk Vols 124,000; Per Subs 402
Automation Activity & Vendor Info: (Circulation) Innovative Interfaces, Inc
Publications: Newsletter (6 per year)
Mem of Reaching Across Illinois Library System (RAILS)
Open Mon-Fri 9-9, Sat 9-5, Sun (Sept-May) 1-5
Friends of the Library Group
Bookmobiles: 1

OSWEGO

P OSWEGO PUBLIC LIBRARY DISTRICT*, 32 W Jefferson St, 60543. SAN 304-5161. Tel: 630-554-3150. FAX: 630-978-1307. *Dir,* Sarah Skilton; E-mail: sskilton@oswego.lib.il.us; *Adult Serv,* Carolyn Leifheit; *Adult Serv,* Peggy Tegel; *Ch Serv,* Christy Kepler; *Tech Serv,* John Fallmaier; Staff 39 (MLS 9, Non-MLS 30)
Founded 1964. Pop 60,931
Library Holdings: Bk Vols 145,000
Special Collections: Fox Valley Genealogy Society; Illinois Census Coll (1820-1920), micro; Oswego Historical Records, micro
Subject Interests: Antiques, Collectibles
Automation Activity & Vendor Info: (Cataloging) Innovative Interfaces, Inc; (Circulation) SirsiDynix
Wireless access
Mem of Reaching Across Illinois Library System (RAILS)
Open Mon-Fri 9-9, Sat 9-5, Sun 12-4
Friends of the Library Group
Branches: 1
MONTGOMERY BRANCH, 1111 Reading Dr, Montgomery, 60538. *Dir,* Sarah Skilton; Tel: 630-554-3150, Fax: 630-978-1307, E-mail: sskilton@oswego.lib.il.us

OTTAWA

P REDDICK LIBRARY*, 1010 Canal St, 61350. SAN 304-517X. Tel: 815-434-0509. FAX: 815-434-2634. TDD: 815-434-0511. Web Site: www.reddicklibrary.org. *Dir,* Kathy Clair; E-mail: kclair@reddicklibrary.org; Staff 3 (MLS 1, Non-MLS 2)
Founded 1888. Pop 18,400; Circ 124,000
Library Holdings: High Interest/Low Vocabulary Bk Vols 200; Bk Vols 72,865; Per Subs 179
Special Collections: State & Local History (Illinois Coll)
Automation Activity & Vendor Info: (Circulation) SirsiDynix
Mem of Reaching Across Illinois Library System (RAILS)

Open Mon-Thurs (Winter) 9-9, Fri & Sat 9-5, Sun 1-5; Mon-Thurs (Summer) 9-7, Fri & Sat 9-5
Friends of the Library Group

GL THIRD DISTRICT APPELLATE COURT LIBRARY*, 1004 Columbus St, 61350. SAN 304-5188. Tel: 815-434-5050. FAX: 815-434-2442. *Librn,* Position Currently Open
Library Holdings: Bk Vols 15,000
Mem of Reaching Across Illinois Library System (RAILS)
Open Mon-Fri 8:30-4:30
Restriction: Open to pub for ref only

PALATINE

P PALATINE PUBLIC LIBRARY DISTRICT, 700 N North Ct, 60067-8159. SAN 304-5196. Tel: 847-358-5881. Administration FAX: 847-358-5998. E-mail: palatine@palatinelibrary.org. Web Site: www.palatinelibrary.org. *Dir,* Anthony Auston; *Asst Dir,* Position Currently Open; *Sr Mgr, Human Res,* Maureen Galvan; *Circ Mgr,* Rosalie Scarpelli; *Info Serv Mgr,* Kristine Kenney; *Mgr, Popular Mats,* Kathy Burns; *Tech Serv Mgr,* Shelby Ricci; *Tech Mgr,* Estevan Montano; Staff 129 (MLS 15, Non-MLS 114)
Founded 1923. Pop 88,983; Circ 1,578,994
Library Holdings: AV Mats 60,962; e-books 16,994; Bk Titles 255,115; Bk Vols 264,222; Per Subs 524
Automation Activity & Vendor Info: (Acquisitions) Innovative Interfaces, Inc; (Cataloging) Innovative Interfaces, Inc; (Circulation) Innovative Interfaces, Inc; (ILL) OCLC; (OPAC) Innovative Interfaces, Inc; (Serials) Innovative Interfaces, Inc
Database Vendor: 3M Library Systems, EBSCOhost, Gale Cengage Learning, Innovative Interfaces, Inc, OCLC FirstSearch, Overdrive, Inc, ProQuest, ReferenceUSA, Safari Books Online
Wireless access
Function: Accessibility serv available based on individual needs, Adult bk club, Art exhibits, Audio & video playback equip for onsite use, Bilingual assistance for Spanish patrons, Bk club(s), Bks on CD, Chess club, Children's prog, Computer training, Computers for patron use, Copy machines, Digital talking bks, e-mail & chat, Electronic databases & coll, Fax serv, Free DVD rentals, Handicapped accessible, Homebound delivery serv, ILL available, Magnifiers for reading, Mail & tel request accepted, Microfiche/film & reading machines, Mus passes, Music CDs, Online cat, Online ref, Outside serv via phone, mail, e mail & web, OverDrive digital audio bks, Photocopying/Printing, Printer for laptops & handheld devices, Prog for adults, Prog for children & young adult, Pub access computers, Ref serv available, Ref serv in person, Scanner, Senior computer classes, Spanish lang bks, Story hour, Summer & winter reading prog, Tax forms, Teen prog, Telephone ref, Web catalog, Wheelchair accessible
Publications: Pageturner (Newsletter)
Mem of Reaching Across Illinois Library System (RAILS)
Special Services for the Deaf - ADA equip; Assistive tech
Special Services for the Blind - Audio mat; Bks on CD; Braille bks; Braille equip; Children's Braille; Copier with enlargement capabilities; Digital talking bk; Dragon Naturally Speaking software; Home delivery serv; Large print bks; Magnifiers; Playaways (bks on MP3); Talking bks
Open Mon-Thurs 9-9, Fri 9-6, Sat 9-5, Sun 12-5
Friends of the Library Group
Branches: 2
NORTH HOFFMAN BRANCH, 3600 Lexington Dr, Hoffman Estates, 60192, SAN 370-3657. Tel: 847-934-0220. *Br Mgr,* Kathy Burns; *Supvr,* Karen Bollman; Staff 8 (MLS 1, Non-MLS 7)
Founded 1981. Pop 11,000; Circ 180,396
Library Holdings: Bk Vols 22,000; Per Subs 59
Function: ILL available, Photocopying/Printing, Prog for children & young adult, Ref serv available, Summer reading prog, Wheelchair accessible
Publications: Page Turner (Newsletter)
Open Mon-Fri 11-7, Sat 9-3
Friends of the Library Group
RAND ROAD, 1585 N Rand Rd, 60074. Tel: 847-202-1194. *Br Mgr,* Kathy Burns; *Br Supvr,* Karen Bollman; Staff 4 (Non-MLS 4)
Founded 2000. Pop 10,000; Circ 67,011
Library Holdings: Bk Titles 4,000; Bk Vols 6,800; Per Subs 16
Publications: Page Turner (Newsletter)
Open Mon & Thurs 11-7, Tues & Wed 10-6, Fri 10-4
Friends of the Library Group

J WILLIAM RAINEY HARPER COLLEGE LIBRARY*, Resources for Learning, 1200 W Algonguin Rd, 60067. SAN 304-520X. Tel: 847-925-6584. Interlibrary Loan Service Tel: 847-925-6768. Reference Tel: 847-925-6769. Automation Services Tel: 847-925-6550. Information Services Tel: 847-925-6184. FAX: 847-925-6164. Interlibrary Loan Service FAX: 847-925-6037. TDD: 847-925-6942. E-mail: library@harpercollege.edu. Web Site: harpercollege.edu/library. *Dean,* Njambi Kamoche; *Bibliog Instruction Coordr,* Amy Kammerman; Tel: 847-925-6555, E-mail: akammerm@harpercollege.edu; *Coordr, Coll Develop,* Kimberly Fournier; Tel: 847-925-6882, E-mail: kfournie@harpercollege.edu; *Ref Serv Coordr,* Tom Goetz; Tel: 847-925-6252, E-mail: tgoetz@harpercollege.edu; *Tech Serv Coordr,* Jim Edstrom; Tel: 847-925-6763, E-mail: jedstrom@harpercollege.edu; *Circ,* Patti Stricker; Tel: 847-925-6767, E-mail: pstricker@harpercollege.edu; *Electronic Res,* William Pankey; Tel: 847-925-6498, E-mail: wpankey@harpercollege.edu; *ILL,* Timothy Philbin; E-mail: tphilbin@harpercollege.edu. Subject Specialists: *Liberal arts,* Amy Kammerman; *Counseling, Wellness,* Tom Goetz; *Adult educ, Sign lang,* William Pankey; Staff 26 (MLS 9, Non-MLS 17)
Founded 1967. Enrl 39,124; Highest Degree: Associate
Library Holdings: AV Mats 21,000; e-books 1,900; Bk Titles 120,544; Bk Vols 127,573; Per Subs 279
Special Collections: Harper College Archives
Automation Activity & Vendor Info: (Acquisitions) Ex Libris Group; (Cataloging) Ex Libris Group; (Circulation) Ex Libris Group; (Course Reserve) Ex Libris Group; (OPAC) Ex Libris Group; (Serials) Ex Libris Group
Database Vendor: EBSCOhost, Gale Cengage Learning, OCLC FirstSearch
Function: Handicapped accessible, ILL available, Photocopying/Printing, Ref serv available
Publications: Library E-News (Newsletter)
Partic in Consortium of Academic & Research Libraries in Illinois; Ill State Libr Network; Northern Illinois Learning Resources Cooperative (NILRC)
Special Services for the Deaf - Assistive tech; Bks on deafness & sign lang; Closed caption videos
Special Services for the Blind - Assistive/Adapted tech devices, equip & products
Open Mon-Thurs (Winter) 7:30am-10pm; Mon-Fri (Summer) 7:30-4:30

PALESTINE

P PALESTINE PUBLIC LIBRARY DISTRICT*, 116 S Main St, 62451. SAN 320-4758. Tel: 618-586-5317. FAX: 618-586-9711. E-mail: palestinelibrary@hotmail.com. *Librn,* Susan Lockhart
Founded 1977. Pop 2,446
Library Holdings: Bk Vols 14,000; Per Subs 15
Mem of Illinois Heartland Library System
Friends of the Library Group

PALOS HEIGHTS

M PALOS COMMUNITY HOSPITAL*, Medical Library, 12251 S 80th Ave, 60463. SAN 340-6415. Tel: 708 923 4640. FAX: 708-923-4674. Web Site: www.paloshospital.org. *Librn,* Gail K Lahti
Founded 1972
Library Holdings: Bk Titles 2,000; Per Subs 68
Partic in Chicago & South Consortium
Restriction: Staff use only

P PALOS HEIGHTS PUBLIC LIBRARY*, 12501 S 71st Ave, 60463. SAN 301 5226. Tel: 708-448-1473. FAX: 708-448-8950. E-mail: phlibrary@palosheightslibrary.org. Web Site: www.palosheightslibrary.org. *Dir,* Elaine Savage, E-mail: savagee@palosheightslibrary.org
Founded 1944. Pop 12,188; Circ 155,380
Library Holdings: Bk Vols 70,245; Per Subs 223
Special Collections: Oral History
Subject Interests: Local hist
Automation Activity & Vendor Info: (Acquisitions) Innovative Interfaces, Inc; (Cataloging) Innovative Interfaces, Inc; (Circulation) Innovative Interfaces, Inc; (ILL) Innovative Interfaces, Inc; (OPAC) Innovative Interfaces, Inc; (Serials) Innovative Interfaces, Inc
Mem of Reaching Across Illinois Library System (RAILS)
Special Services for the Deaf - TTY equip
Open Mon-Thurs 9-9, Fri & Sat 9-5, Sun (Sept-May) 1-5
Friends of the Library Group

C TRINITY CHRISTIAN COLLEGE*, Jennie Huizenga Memorial Library, 6601 W College Dr, 60463. SAN 304-5234. Tel: 708-597-3000, Ext 4925. FAX: 708-385-5665. Web Site: www.trnty.edu/library. *Dir,* Marcille Frederick; Tel: 708-597-3000, Ext 4797, E-mail: marci.frederick@trnty.edu; *Access Serv Librn,* Tippi Price; Tel: 708-597-3000, Ext 4795; *Ref Outreach Librn,* Cynthia Bowen; Tel: 708-239-4841, E-mail: cynthia.bowen@trnty.edu; Staff 4.1 (MLS 3.1, Non-MLS 1)
Founded 1959. Enrl 1,533; Fac 128; Highest Degree: Master
Library Holdings: CDs 990; DVDs 839; e-books 5,412; e-journals 44,000; Music Scores 724; Bk Vols 73,590; Per Subs 100; Videos 60
Special Collections: DeKruyter Pastor's Library (Selection from the libr of Rev Arthur DeKruyter); Dutch Heritage Center
Subject Interests: Humanities, Music, Natural sci, Relig, Soc sci & issues
Automation Activity & Vendor Info: (Acquisitions) Ex Libris Group; (Cataloging) Ex Libris Group; (Circulation) Ex Libris Group; (ILL) OCLC; (OPAC) Ex Libris Group

Database Vendor: 3M Library Systems, Alexander Street Press, American Chemical Society, American Psychological Association (APA), Annual Reviews, ARTstor, BioOne, Bowker, Cinahl, CIOS (Communication Institute for Online Scholarship), EBSCOhost, Ex Libris Group, JSTOR, LexisNexis, Modern Language Association, OCLC WorldShare Interlibrary Loan, Oxford Online, Project MUSE, PubMed, Sage, Springer-Verlag, YBP Library Services
Wireless access
Function: Archival coll, Art exhibits, Audio & video playback equip for onsite use, CD-ROM, Computers for patron use, Copy machines, e-mail & chat, E-Reserves, Electronic databases & coll, Equip loans & repairs, Fax serv, Free DVD rentals, Handicapped accessible, ILL available, Mail & tel request accepted, Music CDs, Online cat, Online ref, Online searches, Orientations, Photocopying/Printing, Pub access computers, Ref serv available, Ref serv in person, Scanner, Spanish lang bks, Telephone ref, VHS videos, Web-catalog, Wheelchair accessible
Mem of Reaching Across Illinois Library System (RAILS)
Partic in Consortium of Academic & Research Libraries in Illinois; Council for Christian Colleges & Universities; LIBRAS, Inc
Open Mon-Thurs 8am-Midnight, Fri 8-6, Sat 10-5, Sun 7:30pm-Midnight
Restriction: Open to pub for ref only, Pub use on premises

PALOS HILLS

P GREEN HILLS PUBLIC LIBRARY DISTRICT*, 8611 W 103rd St, 60465. SAN 304-5242. Tel: 708-598-8446. Circulation Tel: 708-598-8446, Ext 110. Reference Tel: 708-598-8446, Ext 120. FAX: 708-598-0856. E-mail: ghs@greenhills.lib.il.us. Web Site: www.greenhills.lib.il.us. *Libr Dir,* Annette T Armstrong; Tel: 708-598-8446, Ext 111, E-mail: aarmstrong@greenhills.library.org; Staff 12 (MLS 2, Non-MLS 10)
Founded 1962. Pop 31,591; Circ 304,385
Jul 2013-Jun 2014 Income $2,721,688, County $2,589,640, Locally Generated Income $132,048. Mats Exp $221,760, Books $82,427, AV Mat $41,722, Electronic Ref Mat (Incl. Access Fees) $16,369. Sal $506,898 (Prof $252,844)
Library Holdings: Audiobooks 1,400; AV Mats 13,572; Bks on Deafness & Sign Lang 29; CDs 4,235; DVDs 7,649; e-books 1,332; Large Print Bks 125; Bk Titles 50,048; Bk Vols 65,938; Per Subs 49
Special Collections: Oral History
Subject Interests: Literary criticism, Local hist, Polish (Lang)
Automation Activity & Vendor Info: (Cataloging) SirsiDynix; (Circulation) SirsiDynix; (OPAC) SirsiDynix
Database Vendor: Gale Cengage Learning
Function: Adult bk club, Copy machines, Electronic databases & coll, ILL available, Music CDs, Prog for adults, Prog for children & young adult, Ref serv available, Spoken cassettes & CDs, Summer reading prog, VHS videos
Publications: Library Link (Newsletter)
Mem of Reaching Across Illinois Library System (RAILS)
Special Services for the Blind - Bks on CD
Open Mon-Fri 9-9, Sat 10-5, Sun 12-4
Friends of the Library Group

J MORAINE VALLEY COMMUNITY COLLEGE LIBRARY*, 9000 W College Pkwy, 60465. SAN 304-5250. Tel: 708-974-5709. Circulation Tel: 708-974-5235. Interlibrary Loan Service Tel: 708-974-5297. Reference Tel: 708-974-5234. Automation Services Tel: 708-974-5262. FAX: 708-974-1184. E-mail: library@morainevalley.edu. Web Site: lib.morainevalley.edu. *Dean,* Jane Long; E-mail: longJ53@morainevalley.edu; *Dept Chair, Pub Serv, Teaching & Learning Librn,* Troy Swanson; Tel: 708-974-5439, E-mail: swanson@morainevalley.edu; *Coll Mgt Librn, Pub Serv,* Joseph Mullarkey; Tel: 708-974-5293, E-mail: mullarkeyj@morainevalley.edu; *Info Literacy Librn, Pub Serv,* Position Currently Open; *Syst & Cat Librn,* Marie Martino; E-mail: martinom43@morainevalley.edu; *Mgr, Libr Serv,* Terra Jacobson; Tel: 708 974-5467, E-mail: jacobsont6@morainevalley.edu; *Distance Educ,* Lee Semmerling; Tel: 708-608-4009, E-mail: semmerling@morainevalley.edu; Staff 23 (MLS 6, Non-MLS 17)
Founded 1967. Enrl 19,249; Fac 991; Highest Degree: Associate
Library Holdings: AV Mats 9,805; Bk Titles 66,095; Bk Vols 77,731; Per Subs 553
Special Collections: Oral History; US Document Depository
Subject Interests: Allied health, Nursing
Automation Activity & Vendor Info: (Acquisitions) Innovative Interfaces, Inc; (Cataloging) Innovative Interfaces, Inc; (Circulation) Innovative Interfaces, Inc; (Course Reserve) Innovative Interfaces, Inc; (ILL) Innovative Interfaces, Inc; (OPAC) Innovative Interfaces, Inc; (Serials) Innovative Interfaces, Inc
Database Vendor: Career Guidance Foundation, EBSCOhost, Gale Cengage Learning, Newsbank, OCLC FirstSearch, OCLC WorldShare Interlibrary Loan, ProQuest, SerialsSolutions
Wireless access
Function: Handicapped accessible, ILL available, Photocopying/Printing, Ref serv available, Referrals accepted
Mem of Reaching Across Illinois Library System (RAILS)
Partic in Consortium of Academic & Research Libraries in Illinois; Illinois Library & Information Network; Northern Illinois Learning Resources Cooperative (NILRC)
Open Mon-Thurs 7:30am-10pm, Fri 7:30-5

PALOS PARK

P PALOS PARK PUBLIC LIBRARY*, 12330 S Forest Glen Blvd, 60464. SAN 304-5269. Tel: 708-448-1530. FAX: 708-448-3492. E-mail: info@palosparklibrary.org. Web Site: www.palosparklibrary.org. *Admin Librn,* Sheila M Sosnicki; Tel: 708-448-1534, E-mail: ssosnicki@palosparklibrary.org; *Acq,* Kathleen Strubin; E-mail: kstrubin@palosparklibrary.org; Staff 1 (MLS 1)
Founded 1936. Pop 4,847; Circ 42,460
Library Holdings: Large Print Bks 100; Bk Vols 37,182; Per Subs 130
Subject Interests: Local hist
Automation Activity & Vendor Info: (Circulation) Innovative Interfaces, Inc
Wireless access
Mem of Reaching Across Illinois Library System (RAILS)
Partic in System Wide Automated Network
Open Mon-Thurs 9:30-8, Fri & Sat 9:30-5

PANA

P CARNEGIE-SCHUYLER LIBRARY, Pana Public Library, 303 E Second St, 62557. SAN 304-5277. Tel: 217-562-2326. FAX: 217-562-2343. E-mail: panalibrary@consolidated.net. Web Site: panalibrary.com. *Dir,* Lisa Lynch; *Librn,* Janice Crowl; *Librn,* Lori Magnussen; *Librn,* Marla Miller; *Librn,* Donna Wagner
Founded 1903. Pop 5,873; Circ 82,728
Library Holdings: Bk Vols 28,000; Per Subs 25
Mem of Illinois Heartland Library System
Open Mon-Fri 11-6, Sat 9-1
Friends of the Library Group

PARIS

P PARIS CARNEGIE PUBLIC LIBRARY*, 207 S Main St, 61944. SAN 304-5285. Tel: 217-463-3950. FAX: 217-463-1155. E-mail: read@parispubliclibrary.org. Web Site: www.parispubliclibrary.org. *Dir,* Teresa Pennington; Staff 1.8 (MLS 0.9, Non-MLS 0.9)
Founded 1904. Pop 8,837; Circ 59,500
May 2010-Apr 2011 Income $177,506, State $22,440, City $115,729, Locally Generated Income $35,437, Other $3,900. Mats Exp $19,170, Books $9,100, Per/Ser (Incl. Access Fees) $3,590, Micro $1,500, AV Mat $2,007, Electronic Ref Mat (Incl. Access Fees) $2,973. Sal $97,209 (Prof $29,485)
Library Holdings: Audiobooks 359; AV Mats 1,331; DVDs 597; Large Print Bks 1,542; Microforms 64; Bk Vols 32,246; Per Subs 80; Videos 297
Automation Activity & Vendor Info: (Cataloging) Horizon; (Circulation) Horizon; (ILL) OCLC WorldShare Interlibrary Loan; (OPAC) Horizon
Database Vendor: Booksite, OCLC FirstSearch, Overdrive, Inc, ProQuest, TumbleBookLibrary, Wilson - Wilson Web
Wireless access
Function: Bk club(s), Bks on CD, Children's prog, Computers for patron use, Copy machines, Electronic databases & coll, Fax serv, Free DVD rentals, Handicapped accessible, ILL available, Online cat, OverDrive digital audio bks, Prog for adults, Pub access computers, Story hour, Summer reading prog, Tax forms, Telephone ref, Web-catalog
Mem of Illinois Heartland Library System
Open Mon-Thurs (Sept-May) 10-8, Fri 10-6, Sat 10-5; Mon (June-Aug) 10-8, Tues-Fri 10-6, Sat 10-4
Friends of the Library Group

PARK FOREST

P PARK FOREST PUBLIC LIBRARY, 400 Lakewood Blvd, 60466. SAN 304-5307. Tel: 708-748-3731. FAX: 708-748-8829. E-mail: pfpl@pfpl.org. Web Site: www.pfpl.org. *Dir,* Barbara Byrne Osuch; E-mail: barbara.osuch@pfpl.org; *Patron Serv Mgr,* Renee Wick-Brink; E-mail: renee.wickbrink@pfpl.org; *Admin Serv Coordr,* Mary VanSwol; E-mail: mary.vanswol@pfpl.org; Staff 4.25 (MLS 1.25, Non-MLS 3)
Founded 1955. Pop 26,963
Special Collections: Oral History
Automation Activity & Vendor Info: (Acquisitions) Innovative Interfaces, Inc; (Cataloging) Innovative Interfaces, Inc; (Circulation) Innovative Interfaces, Inc; (ILL) Innovative Interfaces, Inc; (OPAC) Innovative Interfaces, Inc; (Serials) Innovative Interfaces, Inc
Database Vendor: EBSCOhost, Gale Cengage Learning, Newsbank, OCLC ArticleFirst, OCLC FirstSearch, OCLC WorldShare Interlibrary Loan, World Book Online
Wireless access
Publications: Oh, Park Forest - Interpretation of Oral History Tapes
Mem of Reaching Across Illinois Library System (RAILS)
Partic in Illinois Library & Information Network

Open Mon-Thurs 10-9, Fri & Sat 10-5, Sun (Sept-May) 1-5
Friends of the Library Group

PARK RIDGE

M ADVOCATE LUTHERAN GENERAL HOSPITAL*, Advocate Health Sciences Library Network, 1775 Dempster St, 60068. SAN 304-5366. Tel: 847-723-5494. FAX: 847-692-9576. Web Site: www.advocatehealth.com. *Dir,* Marie T Burns; Staff 4 (MLS 4)
Founded 1966
Library Holdings: AV Mats 800; Bk Vols 16,500; Per Subs 250
Subject Interests: Med, Nursing
Automation Activity & Vendor Info: (Acquisitions) Ex Libris Group; (Cataloging) Ex Libris Group; (Circulation) Ex Libris Group; (OPAC) Ex Libris Group; (Serials) Ex Libris Group
Partic in Illinois Library & Information Network; OCLC Online Computer Library Center, Inc
Open Mon-Thurs 8-6, Fri 8-5
Restriction: Hospital staff & commun, In-house use for visitors, Prof mat only

S AMERICAN ASSOCIATION OF NURSE ANESTHETISTS*, Archives-Library, 222 S Prospect Ave, 60068-4001. SAN 374-6704. Tel: 847-655-1106. FAX: 847-692-6968. Web Site: www.aana.com/archives.aspx. *Archivist, Librn,* Kathy J Koch; E-mail: kkoch@aana.com; Staff 1 (MLS 1)
Library Holdings: Bk Titles 1,500; Bk Vols 2,000; Per Subs 70
Special Collections: AANA Archives; Nurse Anesthesia History. Oral History
Function: Archival coll, ILL available
Restriction: Access at librarian's discretion, Non-circulating, Open by appt only

P PARK RIDGE PUBLIC LIBRARY*, 20 S Prospect, 60068-4188. SAN 304-5374. Tel: 847-825-3123. Circulation Tel: 847-720-3271. Interlibrary Loan Service Tel: 847-720-3235. Reference Tel: 847-720-3230. Administration Tel: 847-825-7200. Information Services Tel: 847-720-3209. FAX: 847-825-0001. Web Site: www.parkridgelibrary.org. *Dir,* Janet Van De Carr; Tel: 847-720-3203, E-mail: librarydirector@prpl.org; *Asst Dir,* Linda Egebrecht; Tel: 847-720-3221, E-mail: legebrec@prpl.org; *Bus Mgr, Commun Network Mgr,* Angela Berger; Tel: 847-720-3202, E-mail: aberger@prpl.org; *Circ Serv Mgr,* John Doyle; E-mail: jdoyle@prpl.org; *Fac Mgr,* Jose Mestey; Tel: 847-720-3210, E-mail: jmestey@prpl.org; *IT Mgr,* Joe Basso; Tel: 847-720-3205, E-mail: jbasso@prpl.org; *Reader Serv Mgr,* Maggie Hommel; Tel: 847-720-3282, E-mail: mhommel@prpl.org; *Ref Serv Mgr,* Gretchen Kottkamp, Tel: 847-720-3245, E-mail: gkottkam@prpl.org; Staff 100 (MLS 23, Non-MLS 77)
Founded 1913. Pop 37,480; Circ 947,943
May 2011-Apr 2012 Income $4,332,357, State $89,725, City $4,044,332, Locally Generated Income $198,300. Mats Exp $574,600. Sal $2,470,815
Library Holdings: AV Mats 27,736; e-books 6,000; Bk Vols 215,881; Per Subs 400
Special Collections: Park Ridge History, newsp
Automation Activity & Vendor Info: (Acquisitions) Ex Libris Group, (Cataloging) SirsiDynix; (Circulation) SirsiDynix
Database Vendor: ALLDATA Online, Baker & Taylor, BiblioCommons, Booklist Online, CQ Press, Dun & Bradstreet, Gale Cengage Learning, infoUSA, Marquis Who's Who, OCLC FirstSearch, Overdrive, Inc, ReferenceUSA, Standard & Poor's, TumbleBookLibrary, World Book Online
Wireless access
Function: Adult bk club, After school storytime, Art exhibits, Audiobks via web, Bk club(s), Bks on CD, Children's prog, Computer training, Computers for patron use, Copy machines, Doc delivery serv, e-mail & chat, e-mail serv, E-Reserves, Electronic databases & coll, Exhibits, Free DVD rentals, Handicapped accessible, Holiday prog, Home delivery & serv to Sr ctr & nursing homes, Homebound delivery serv, ILL available, Large print keyboards, Magnifiers for reading, Mail & tel request accepted, Microfiche/film & reading machines, Mus passes, Music CDs, Newsp ref libr, Notary serv, Online cat, Online ref, Online searches, Outreach serv, Outside serv via phone, mail, e-mail & web, OverDrive digital audio bks, Photocopying/Printing, Preschool outreach, Preschool reading prog, Prog for adults, Prog for children & young adult, Pub access computers, Ref & res, Ref serv available, Ref serv in person, Scanner, Senior computer classes, Senior outreach, Story hour, Summer & winter reading prog, Tax forms, Teen prog, Telephone ref, Web-catalog, Wheelchair accessible, Workshops
Publications: Library Newsletter
Partic in Cooperative Computer Services - CCS
Special Services for the Deaf - Assisted listening device; Bks on deafness & sign lang; Closed caption videos; Sign lang interpreter upon request for prog; TDD equip
Special Services for the Blind - Accessible computers; Assistive/Adapted tech devices, equip & products; BiFolkal kits; Bks available with recordings; Bks on CD; Computer with voice synthesizer for visually impaired persons; Copier with enlargement capabilities; Home delivery serv; Info on spec aids & appliances; Internet workstation with adaptive software; Large print bks; Large screen computer & software; Lending of low vision aids; Magnifiers; Playaways (bks on MP3); Talking bk serv referral; ZoomText magnification & reading software
Open Mon-Thurs 9-9, Fri 9-6, Sat 9-5, Sun 12-5
Friends of the Library Group

M WOOD LIBRARY-MUSEUM OF ANESTHESIOLOGY*, 520 N Northwest Hwy, 60068-2573. SAN 304-5331. Tel: 847-825-5586. FAX: 847-825-2085. E mail: wlm@asahq.org. Web Site: www.woodlibrarymuseum.org. *Dir & Head Librn,* Karen Bieterman; Tel: 847-825-5586, Ext 158, E-mail: k.bieterman@asahq.org; *Librn,* Teresa Jimenez; E-mail: t.jimenez@asahq.org; *Archivist,* Felicia Reilly; E-mail: f.reilly@asahq.org; Staff 4 (MLS 4)
Founded 1933
Library Holdings: Bk Titles 13,000; Per Subs 65
Special Collections: Curare (R Gill Coll), mss; History of Anesthesia Coll; Mesmerism Coll. Oral History
Subject Interests: Anesthesiology
Automation Activity & Vendor Info: (Cataloging) Sydney
Publications: Historical Monographs; History of Anesthesia Reprint Series (annual)
Restriction: Open by appt only
Friends of the Library Group

PATOKA

P PATOKA PUBLIC LIBRARY*, 210 W Bond St, 62875. (Mail add: PO Box 58, 62875-0058), SAN 304-5382. Tel: 618-432-5019. FAX: 618-432-5019. E-mail: patokalibrary@yahoo.com. *Librn,* Nancy Snider
Founded 1934. Pop 633; Circ 1,815
Library Holdings: Bk Vols 5,023; Per Subs 10
Mem of Illinois Heartland Library System
Open Mon, Wed & Thurs 12-5

PAW PAW

P PAW PAW PUBLIC LIBRARY DISTRICT*, 362 Chicago Rd, 61353. (Mail add: PO Box 60, 61353-0060), SAN 304-5390. Tel: 815-627-9396. FAX: 815-627-3707. *Dir,* Nikki J Isakson
Founded 1925. Pop 852; Circ 6,733
Library Holdings: Bk Vols 18,417
Special Collections: Lee & DeKalb Counties Local History, includes written materials, census, newspaper slides, photos, scrapbooks & memorabilia
Open Tues-Fri 10-6, Sat 9-12

PAWNEE

P PAWNEE PUBLIC LIBRARY*, 613 Douglas St, 62558. (Mail add: PO Box 229, 62558-0229), SAN 304 5404. Tel: 217-625-7716. FAX: 217-625-7716. E-mail: pawpubl@family-net.net. Web Site: www.pawneepubliclibrary.org. *Librn,* Bennett A Bess
Founded 1951. Circ 10,135
Library Holdings: Bk Titles 14,500; Bk Vols 15,000
Subject Interests: Hist, Ill
Mem of Illinois Heartland Library System
Open Mon & Fri 11-5, Tues 11-8, Wed 10-5 & 7-9, Thurs 10-9, Sat 11-3

PAXTON

P PAXTON CARNEGIE LIBRARY*, 254 S Market St, 60957-1452. SAN 304-5412. Tel: 217-379-3431. E-mail: paxtonlibrary1@gmail.com. *Librn,* Anne Newman
Founded 1903. Pop 4,289; Circ 36,886
Library Holdings: Audiobooks 500; Bk Vols 24,000; Per Subs 60
Automation Activity & Vendor Info: (Circulation) SirsiDynix
Wireless access
Mem of Illinois Heartland Library System
Special Services for the Deaf - Bks on deafness & sign lang
Open Mon-Thurs 12-5 & 6:30-8:30, Fri 12-5, Sat 10-5

PEARL CITY

P PEARL CITY PUBLIC LIBRARY DISTRICT*, 221 S Main St, 61062. (Mail add: PO Box 158, 61062-0158), SAN 304-5420. Tel: 815-443-2832. FAX: 815-443-2832. Web Site: www.pearlcitylibrary.20m.com. *Chief Librn,* Mary E Vivian; E-mail: maryvpcpld@yahoo.com
Founded 1946. Pop 2,655; Circ 12,912
Library Holdings: Bk Titles 14,450; Per Subs 13
Mem of Reaching Across Illinois Library System (RAILS)
Open Mon & Thurs 3-7, Tues & Wed 3-9, Fri 11-7, Sat 10-2

PECATONICA

P PECATONICA PUBLIC LIBRARY DISTRICT, 400 W 11th St, 61063. SAN 304-5439. Tel: 815-239-2616. FAX: 815-239-2250. E-mail: director@pecatonicalibrary.com. Web Site: www.pecatonicalibrary.com/. *Dir,* Shari Hamilton; Staff 7 (Non-MLS 7)
Founded 1967. Pop 5,261; Circ 22,830
Library Holdings: AV Mats 1,286; Bks on Deafness & Sign Lang 10; Large Print Bks 220; Bk Titles 24,282; Per Subs 46
Special Collections: Local History (Pecatonica, Winnebago Co & Stephenson Co)
Automation Activity & Vendor Info: (Cataloging) PALS; (Circulation) SIRSI WorkFlows; (OPAC) SIRSI Unicorn
Database Vendor: OCLC, OCLC WebJunction, OCLC WorldShare Interlibrary Loan, SirsiDynix, World Book Online
Wireless access
Function: 24/7 Electronic res, 24/7 Online cat, Accelerated reader prog, Accessibility serv available based on individual needs, Activity rm, Adult bk club, Adult literacy prog, Art exhibits, Audiobks via web, AV serv, Bks on CD, CD-ROM, Children's prog, Computer training, Computers for patron use, Copy machines, Doc delivery serv, E-Reserves, Electronic databases & coll, Exhibits, Fax serv, Govt ref serv, Handicapped accessible, Homebound delivery serv, ILL available, Laminating, Magazines, Magnifiers for reading, Mango lang, Microfiche/film & reading machines, Music CDs, Notary serv, Online cat, Online searches, Outreach serv, OverDrive digital audio bks, Photocopying/Printing, Preschool reading prog, Prog for children & young adult, Pub access computers, Ref serv available, Scanner, Senior computer classes, Spanish lang bks, Story hour, Study rm, Summer reading prog, Tax forms, Wheelchair accessible, Workshops
Mem of Reaching Across Illinois Library System (RAILS)
Special Services for the Deaf - TTY equip
Open Mon-Thurs 10-4 & 6-8, Fri & Sat 9-1
Friends of the Library Group

PEKIN

P PEKIN PUBLIC LIBRARY*, 301 S Fourth St, 61554-4284. SAN 304-5455. Tel: 309-347-7111. FAX: 309-347-6587. E-mail: library@pekinpubliclibrary.org. Web Site: www.pekinpubliclibrary.org. *Dir,* Jeff Brooks; Tel: 309-347-7111, Ext 228, E-mail: jbrooks@pekinpubliclibrary.org; *Asst Dir,* Alissa Williams; Tel: 309-347-7111, Ext 226, E-mail: awilliams@pekinpubliclibrary.org; *Tech Serv,* Betty Wethington; E-mail: bwethington@pekin.net; *Youth Serv,* Julie Nutt; Tel: 309-347-7111, Ext 224, E-mail: jnutt@pekinpubliclibrary.org; Staff 4 (MLS 2, Non-MLS 2)
Founded 1896. Pop 33,857; Circ 277,993
Library Holdings: AV Mats 8,190; Bk Vols 129,314; Per Subs 196
Special Collections: History of Pekin; Tazewell Co
Automation Activity & Vendor Info: (Acquisitions) Baker & Taylor; (Cataloging) OCLC; (Circulation) SIRSI WorkFlows; (ILL) OCLC; (OPAC) SIRSI-iBistro
Database Vendor: Booksite, Gale Cengage Learning, OCLC FirstSearch
Wireless access
Function: Adult bk club, Bks on cassette, Bks on CD, Computers for patron use, Copy machines, e-mail & chat, Electronic databases & coll, Fax serv, Free DVD rentals, Homebound delivery serv, ILL available, Music CDs, Online cat, Scanner, Spoken cassettes & CDs, Spoken cassettes & DVDs, Story hour, Summer reading prog, Tax forms, Teen prog, Telephone ref, VHS videos
Publications: Newsletter
Partic in Illinois Library & Information Network; OCLC Online Computer Library Center, Inc
Open Mon-Thurs (Winter) 9-9, Fri 9-6, Sat 9-5; Mon-Thurs (Summer) 9-8, Fri 9-6, Sat 9-1
Friends of the Library Group

PEORIA

G AGRICULTURAL RESEARCH SERVICE*, National Agricultural Research Library, 1815 N University St, 61604. SAN 304-5528. Tel: 309-681-6526. FAX: 309-681-6681. *Libr Tech,* Michelle Archdale; Staff 1 (Non-MLS 1)
Founded 1941
Library Holdings: Bk Vols 7,380; Per Subs 48
Subject Interests: Biochem, Organic chem
Publications: Annual List of Publications & Patents
Partic in OCLC Online Computer Library Center, Inc
Open Mon-Fri 8:30-5
Restriction: In-house use for visitors, Staff use only

SR BAHAI REFERENCE LIBRARY OF PEORIA*, 5209 N University, 61614. SAN 304-5463. Tel: 309-691-9311. Administration Tel: 309-678-8153. FAX: 309-691-4407. *Asst Libm,* Pamela Jean Fox; E-mail: pamela.fox@att.net
Founded 1928
Library Holdings: High Interest/Low Vocabulary Bk Vols 426; Bk Titles 4,305; Bk Vols 4,808
Special Collections: Afro-American Coll, bks & videos; Baha'i (Star of the West, World Order Mag & Early United States Publications); Coll Letters of Early Believers; Meso-America & South American Cultures; Native American. Oral History
Subject Interests: Christianity, Educ, Human rights, Islam, Philos, Sociol
Function: Archival coll, For res purposes, Photocopying/Printing, Res libr
Restriction: Circ limited, Open by appt only

C BRADLEY UNIVERSITY*, Cullom-Davis Library, 1501 W Bradley Ave, 61625. SAN 340-6474. Tel: 309-677-2850. Interlibrary Loan Service Tel: 309-677-2837. FAX: 309-677-2558. Web Site: library.bradley.edu. *Exec Dir,* Barbara A Galik; Tel: 309-677-2830, E-mail: barbara@bradley.edu; *Coll Develop Librn,* Todd Spires; *Electronic Serv Librn,* Xiaotian Chen; *Info Literacy/Electronic Serv Librn,* Meg Frazier; *Ref Librn,* Dianne Happ; *Ref/Govt Doc Librn,* Denise Johnson; *Tech Serv Librn,* Deirdre Redington; *Circ & ILL Coordr,* Laura Corpuz; *Circ & ILL Coordr,* Marina Savoie; *Coordr, Access Serv,* Daniel Fuertges; *Coordr, Access Serv,* Michelle Viel; *Coordr, Acq,* Carol Rhoades; *Coordr, Ser,* Glynis Plym; *Electronic Serv Coordr,* Shawn Edwards; Staff 11 (MLS 11)
Founded 1897. Enrl 5,882; Fac 305; Highest Degree: Master
Library Holdings: Bk Titles 281,121; Bk Vols 435,394; Per Subs 1,488
Special Collections: Abraham Lincoln & Civil War (including Martin L Howser Coll); APCO (Public Safety Communications History Coll); Bradleyana; Industrial Arts History (Charles A Bennett Coll); Jubilee College (Philander Chase Coll & Citizens Committee to Preserve Jubilee College Coll); Peoria-Area History (Library of Peoria Historical Society). Oral History; State Document Depository; US Document Depository
Automation Activity & Vendor Info: (Acquisitions) Ex Libris Group; (Cataloging) Ex Libris Group; (Circulation) Ex Libris Group; (Course Reserve) Ex Libris Group; (OPAC) Ex Libris Group; (Serials) Ex Libris Group
Partic in Consortium of Academic & Research Libraries in Illinois; Heart of Ill Consortium; Illinois Library & Information Network
Open Mon-Thurs 8am-11pm, Fri 8-6, Sat 1-5, Sun 1pm-11pm
Friends of the Library Group

Departmental Libraries:
VIRGINIUS H CHASE SPECIAL COLLECTIONS CENTER, 1501 W Bradley Ave, 61625. Tel: 309-677-2822. *Spec Coll Librn,* Charles J Frey
Library Holdings: Bk Vols 17,000
Open Mon-Fri 9-12 & 1-4:30

J MIDSTATE COLLEGE*, Barbara Fields Memorial Library, 411 W Northmoor Rd, 61614. SAN 321-5032. Tel: 309-692-4092. FAX: 309-692-3918. E-mail: library@midstate.edu. Web Site: www.midstate.edu. *Librn,* Zack Brown; Tel: 800-251-4299, Ext 1200, E-mail: zbrown@midstate.edu; Staff 6 (MLS 1, Non-MLS 5)
Founded 1888. Enrl 625; Fac 40; Highest Degree: Bachelor
Library Holdings: Bk Titles 8,150; Per Subs 100
Automation Activity & Vendor Info: (Cataloging) SirsiDynix; (Circulation) SirsiDynix
Partic in RSA
Open Mon-Thurs 8am-9pm, Fri 8-4:30, Sat 8:30am-12:30pm

L PEORIA COUNTY LAW LIBRARY*, Peoria County Court House, Rm 211, 324 Main St, 61602. SAN 375-9865. Tel: 309-672-6084. FAX: 309-672-6957. Web Site: www.peoriacounty.org/courts/lawlibrary. *Librn,* Michele A Miller; E-mail: mmiller@peoriacounty.org
Library Holdings: Bk Vols 14,000
Database Vendor: Westlaw
Open Mon-Fri 8:30-5

P PEORIA PUBLIC LIBRARY*, 107 NE Monroe St, 61602-1070. SAN 340-6741. Tel: 309-497-2000. Circulation Tel: 309-497-2164. Interlibrary Loan Service Tel: 309-497-2153. FAX: 309-497-2007. Interlibrary Loan Service FAX: 309-674-0116. TDD: 309-497-2156. Web Site: www.peoriapubliclibrary.org. *Dir,* Leann Johnson; E-mail: leannjohnson@ppl.peoria.lib.il.us; *Assoc Dir,* Roberta Koscielski; E-mail: robertakoscielski@ppl.peoria.lib.il.us
Founded 1880. Pop 118,135; Circ 778,175
Library Holdings: Audiobooks 8,695; CDs 9,170; DVDs 6,488; Bk Vols 635,048; Videos 9,539
Special Collections: Genealogy, Local History, Government Documents. US Document Depository
Subject Interests: Census, Genealogy, Local hist
Automation Activity & Vendor Info: (Acquisitions) Baker & Taylor; (Cataloging) OCLC Connexion; (Circulation) SIRSI WorkFlows; (Serials) EBSCO Online
Database Vendor: OCLC FirstSearch
Publications: Passages (Newsletter)
Special Services for the Deaf - TDD equip
Open Mon-Sat 9-6
Friends of the Library Group

Branches: 4
LAKEVIEW, 1137 W Lake Ave, 61614-5935, SAN 340-6776. Tel: 309-497-2200. FAX: 309-497-2211. *Br Mgr,* Jennifer Sevier; Tel: 309-497-2204
Library Holdings: CDs 1,081; DVDs 553; Bk Vols 79,931; Talking Bks 1,343; Videos 2,490
Open Mon-Wed 10-8, Fri & Sat 10-6
Friends of the Library Group
LINCOLN, 1312 W Lincoln Ave, 61605-1976, SAN 340-6806. Tel: 309-497-2600. FAX: 309-497-2611. *Br Mgr,* Cynthia Smith; Tel: 309-497-2601, E-mail: cynthiasmith@ppl.peoria.lib.il.us
Open Mon-Tues & Thurs 10-8, Fri & Sat 10-6
MCCLURE, 315 W McClure Ave, 61604-3556, SAN 340-6830. Tel: 309-497-2700. FAX: 309-497-2711. *Br Mgr,* Patricia Pritchard; Tel: 309-497-2701, E-mail: patriciapritchard@ppl.peoria.lib.il.us; Staff 2 (MLS 1, Non-MLS 1)
Library Holdings: Audiobooks 500; CDs 191; DVDs 900; Bk Vols 25,838; Videos 300
Automation Activity & Vendor Info: (Circulation) SIRSI WorkFlows
Open Mon-Sat 9-6
Friends of the Library Group
NORTH BRANCH, 3001 W Grand Pkwy, 61615. Tel: 309-497-2100. *Br Mgr,* Anna Hudson
Open Mon, Wed & Thurs 10-8, Sun Noon-5
Bookmobiles: 1

CM SAINT FRANCIS MEDICAL CENTER COLLEGE OF NURSING*, The Sister Ludgera Library & Learning Resource Center, 511 NE Greenleaf St, 61603. SAN 340-692X. Tel: 309-655-2180. FAX: 309-655-3648. E-mail: CONLibrary@osfhealthcare.org. Web Site: www.sfmccon.edu/library. *Librn,* Leslie Menz; *Libr Tech,* Becky Rundall; Staff 3 (MLS 1, Non-MLS 2)
Founded 1936. Enrl 150; Fac 19; Highest Degree: Master
Library Holdings: Bk Titles 4,900; Bk Vols 5,300; Per Subs 130
Subject Interests: Educ
Database Vendor: Gale Cengage Learning, OCLC FirstSearch, OVID Technologies, TLC (The Library Corporation)
Partic in Consortium of Academic & Research Libraries in Illinois; Heart of Illinois Library Consortium; Illinois Library & Information Network
Open Mon-Thurs 7:30am-9pm, Fri 7:30-5, Sat 10-2, Sun 1-9

PEORIA HEIGHTS

P PEORIA HEIGHTS PUBLIC LIBRARY*, 816 E Glen Ave, 61616. SAN 304-5560. Tel: 309-682-5578. FAX: 309-682-4457. E-mail: phpl@peoriaheightslibrary.com. Web Site: www.peoriaheightslibrary.com. *Dir,* Marsha Westfall; *Ch Serv,* Lorri Ane Stotts; Staff 2 (MLS 2)
Founded 1935. Pop 6,930; Circ 42,186
Library Holdings: Bk Vols 32,800; Per Subs 126
Subject Interests: Art, Hist
Automation Activity & Vendor Info: (Circulation) TLC (The Library Corporation)
Publications: Newsletter: Check It Out
Partic in Illinois Library & Information Network
Open Mon & Tues 9-8, Wed & Thurs 9-6, Fri & Sat 9-5

PEOTONE

P PEOTONE PUBLIC LIBRARY DISTRICT*, 515 N First St, 60468. SAN 304-5579. Tel: 708-258-3436. FAX: 708-258-9796. E-mail: information@peotone.lib.il.us. Web Site: www.peotone.lib.il.us. *Dir,* Cynthia Cooper; *Asst Dir,* Sharon Garner; *Youth Serv,* Rosemary Wilson
Pop 15,513; Circ 75,000
Library Holdings: Bk Vols 65,000; Per Subs 100
Subject Interests: Genealogy
Wireless access
Mem of Reaching Across Illinois Library System (RAILS)
Open Mon-Thurs 10-8, Fri & Sat 10-5

PERU

M ILLINOIS VALLEY COMMUNITY HOSPITAL*, Medical Library, 925 West St, 61354. SAN 304-3258. Tel: 815-780-3485. FAX: 815-224-1747. Web Site: www.ivch.org. *Dir of Educ,* Maureen Rebholz
Library Holdings: Bk Vols 506
Restriction: Not open to pub

P PERU PUBLIC LIBRARY*, 1409 11th St, 61354. SAN 304-5587. Tel: 815-223-0229. FAX: 815-223-1559. Web Site: www.perulibrary.org. *Libr Dir,* Charm N Ruhnke; E-mail: cnruhnke@perulibrary.org; *Youth Serv Dir,* Laurie A Moss; E-mail: lamoss@perulibrary.org; Staff 4 (MLS 1, Non-MLS 3)
Founded 1911. Pop 9,835; Circ 90,000
Library Holdings: Bk Vols 50,000; Per Subs 140
Special Collections: Local newspaper 1906, micro. Oral History
Subject Interests: Local hist
Automation Activity & Vendor Info: (Acquisitions) SirsiDynix; (Cataloging) SirsiDynix; (Circulation) SirsiDynix; (OPAC) SirsiDynix; (Serials) SirsiDynix
Database Vendor: OCLC FirstSearch
Wireless access
Mem of Reaching Across Illinois Library System (RAILS)
Open Mon-Thurs 10-8, Fri & Sat 10-5
Friends of the Library Group

PETERSBURG

S ILLINOIS COLLEGE*, Starhill Forest Arboretum Library, 12000 Boy Scout Trail, 62675-9736. SAN 371-5477. Tel: 217-632-3685. Web Site: www.starhillforest.com. *Dir,* Guy Sternberg
Founded 1976
Library Holdings: Bk Titles 2,000; Bk Vols 2,200; Per Subs 10
Special Collections: Antiquarian Natural History; Modern Natural History, bks & slides
Subject Interests: Hort, Natural hist
Function: Ref serv available
Partic in Consortium of Academic & Research Libraries in Illinois; Illinois Library & Information Network
Restriction: Private libr, Staff use only

P PETERSBURG PUBLIC LIBRARY*, 220 S Sixth St, 62675. SAN 304-5595. Tel: 217-632-2807. FAX: 217-632-2833. Web Site: www.petersburgil.com/library. *Librn,* Mary Kleinschmidt; E-mail: mklib@yahoo.com
Founded 1906. Pop 2,419; Circ 29,000
Library Holdings: Bk Vols 12,900; Per Subs 86
Special Collections: Abraham Lincoln & Edgar Lee Masters
Automation Activity & Vendor Info: (Circulation) SirsiDynix
Open Tues & Thurs 10-8, Wed & Fri 10-5, Sat 9-1
Friends of the Library Group

PHILO

P PHILO PUBLIC LIBRARY DISTRICT*, 115 E Washington St, 61864. (Mail add: PO Box 199, 61864-0199), SAN 304-5609. Tel: 217-684-2896. FAX: 217-684-2719. E-mail: PhiloPubLib@gmail.com. Web Site: www.philolibrary.info. *Dir,* Don Thorsen; *Assoc Dir,* Susan Hale; Staff 5 (MLS 1, Non-MLS 4)
Founded 1961. Pop 1,954; Circ 21,483
Jul 2012-Jun 2013 Income $84,881, State $4,012, Locally Generated Income $75,973, Other $4,896. Mats Exp $9,947, Books $4,702, Per/Ser (Incl. Access Fees) $1,020, AV Mat $1,230, Electronic Ref Mat (Incl. Access Fees) $228. Sal $40,543
Library Holdings: Audiobooks 97; Braille Volumes 4; CDs 178; DVDs 852; Large Print Bks 220; Bk Titles 13,555; Bk Vols 13,575; Per Subs 60
Automation Activity & Vendor Info: (Circulation) Innovative Interfaces, Inc; (OPAC) Innovative Interfaces, Inc
Wireless access
Function: Accelerated reader prog, Adult bk club, Archival coll
Mem of Illinois Heartland Library System
Partic in Illinois Library & Information Network
Open Mon-Fri 9-12 & 3-7, Sat 9-1, Sun 2-5
Friends of the Library Group

PINCKNEYVILLE

P PINCKNEYVILLE PUBLIC LIBRARY*, 312 S Walnut St, 62274. SAN 304-5617. Tel: 618-357-2410. FAX: 618-357-2410. E-mail: library@pinckneyville.lib.il.us. Web Site: www.pinckneyville.lib.il.us. *Libr Dir,* Mark Urbanek
Founded 1917. Pop 5,648; Circ 16,405
Library Holdings: AV Mats 651; Bk Vols 17,375; Per Subs 50
Wireless access
Function: Bks on cassette, Bks on CD, Music CDs, Photocopying/Printing, Summer reading prog, VHS videos
Mem of Illinois Heartland Library System
Open Mon-Thurs 12-6, Fri & Sat 9-2

PIPER CITY

P PIPER CITY PUBLIC LIBRARY DISTRICT*, 39 W Main, 60959. (Mail add: PO Box 248, 60959-0248), SAN 304-5625. Tel: 815-686-9234. FAX: 815-686-9234. *Libr Dir,* Julie Kurtenbach
Founded 1927. Pop 1,149; Circ 6,966
Library Holdings: Bk Vols 7,997; Per Subs 37
Subject Interests: Local hist
Wireless access
Mem of Illinois Heartland Library System
Open Mon & Fri 9-12 & 1-5, Wed 9-12 & 1-7, Sat 9-12

PITTSFIELD

P PITTSFIELD PUBLIC LIBRARY, 205 N Memorial St, 62363-1406. SAN 304-5633. Tel: 217-285-2200. FAX: 217-285-9423. E-mail: pittsfieldlibrary@frontier.com. Web Site: www.pittsfieldpubliclibrary.com. *Dir,* Sara Bernard; *Asst Librn,* Clari Dees; *Ch Serv,* Lisa Feenstra
Founded 1906. Pop 4,600
Library Holdings: Bk Vols 35,000; Per Subs 95
Special Collections: Pike County History
Subject Interests: Hist, Miss river
Wireless access
Open Mon, Wed & Fri 10-5:30, Tues & Thurs 1-8, Sat 10-3

PLAINFIELD

P PLAINFIELD PUBLIC LIBRARY DISTRICT*, 15025 S Illinois St, 60544. SAN 304-565X. Tel: 815-436-6639. FAX: 815-439-2878. Web Site: www.plainfieldpubliclibrary.org. *Adminr,* Julie Milavec; Staff 50 (MLS 13, Non-MLS 37)
Founded 1925. Pop 75,337; Circ 668,332
Library Holdings: e-books 50,000; Bk Vols 140,000; Per Subs 195
Special Collections: Local History (state, county & city); Local Newspaper & Obituary Index (The Enterprise Coll), micro; Tornado (August 28, 1990), newsp clippings & pictures
Automation Activity & Vendor Info: (Acquisitions) Innovative Interfaces, Inc; (Cataloging) Innovative Interfaces, Inc; (Circulation) Innovative Interfaces, Inc; (ILL) OCLC WorldShare Interlibrary Loan; (OPAC) Innovative Interfaces, Inc; (Serials) Innovative Interfaces, Inc
Database Vendor: Baker & Taylor, Bowker, EBSCOhost, Facts on File, Gale Cengage Learning, Grolier Online, LearningExpress, Newsbank, OCLC FirstSearch, Overdrive, Inc, ProQuest, ReferenceUSA
Wireless access
Mem of Reaching Across Illinois Library System (RAILS)
Open Mon-Thurs 9-9, Fri & Sat 9-5, Sun (Sept-May) 1-5
Friends of the Library Group

PLANO

P PLANO COMMUNITY LIBRARY DISTRICT*, 15 W North St, 60545. SAN 304-5668. Tel: 630-552-2009. FAX: 630-552-1008. Web Site: www.plano.lib.il.us. *Dir,* Deanna Howard; E-mail: dhoward@plano.lib.il.us; *Mgr, Ad Serv,* Jeanne Valentine; *Mgr, Cat Dept,* Alesia Hacker; *Head, Circ,* Randy Struthers; Staff 17 (MLS 1, Non-MLS 16)
Founded 1905. Pop 10,995; Circ 143,034
Library Holdings: Bk Vols 33,127; Per Subs 112
Subject Interests: Local hist
Automation Activity & Vendor Info: (Acquisitions) SirsiDynix; (Cataloging) SirsiDynix; (Circulation) SirsiDynix; (ILL) SirsiDynix; (OPAC) SirsiDynix
Database Vendor: OCLC FirstSearch
Mem of Reaching Across Illinois Library System (RAILS)
Open Mon-Thurs 10-8, Fri 10-6, Sat 10-4
Friends of the Library Group

POLO

P POLO PUBLIC LIBRARY DISTRICT*, Polo Library, 302 W Mason St, 61064. SAN 304-5676. Tel: 815-946-2713. FAX: 815-946-4127. E-mail: library@polo.lib.il.us. Web Site: www.polo.lib.il.us. *Dir,* Ellen E Finfrock; Staff 2 (Non-MLS 2)
Founded 1871. Pop 2,813; Circ 34,124
Library Holdings: Audiobooks 420; DVDs 1,195; Bk Vols 15,558; Per Subs 65
Special Collections: Local hist
Automation Activity & Vendor Info: (Acquisitions) SirsiDynix; (Cataloging) SirsiDynix; (Circulation) SirsiDynix; (OPAC) SirsiDynix
Database Vendor: SirsiDynix
Wireless access
Function: Adult bk club, Audiobks via web, Children's prog, Computer training, Computers for patron use, Copy machines, Electronic databases & coll, Free DVD rentals, Handicapped accessible, Homebound delivery serv, ILL available, Magnifiers for reading, Music CDs, Online cat, Photocopying/Printing, Prog for adults, Scanner, Story hour, Summer & winter reading prog, Tax forms, VHS videos, Wheelchair accessible
Mem of Reaching Across Illinois Library System (RAILS)
Partic in OMNI
Special Services for the Deaf - TTY equip
Special Services for the Blind - Audio mat; Bks on CD; Digital talking bk; Digital talking bk machines; Large print bks; Low vision equip; Magnifiers; Talking bks & player equip
Open Mon-Thurs 10-7, Fri & Sat 10-3

PONTIAC

S PONTIAC CORRECTIONAL CENTER LIBRARY*, 700 W Lincoln St, 61764-2323. (Mail add: PO Box 99, 61764-0099), SAN 304-5684. Tel: 815-842-2816, Ext 2203. FAX: 815-842-3051. *Librn,* Kathy Donovan; Tel: 815-842-2816, Ext 672; Staff 4 (Non-MLS 4)
Library Holdings: Bk Vols 31,500; Per Subs 14
Subject Interests: Law
Partic in Corn Belt Libr Syst

P PONTIAC PUBLIC LIBRARY*, 211 E Madison St, 61764. SAN 304-5692. Tel: 815-844-7229. FAX: 815-844-3475. Web Site: www.pontiacpubliclibrary.com. *Interim Dir,* Michael Harms; E-mail: director@pontiacpubliclibrary.org; *Libr Dir,* Position Currently Open; *Cat,* Levada Lee; *Ch Serv,* Position Currently Open; *Circ,* Susan Strauch; *ILL,* Vicki Cunningham; Staff 8 (MLS 1, Non-MLS 7)
Founded 1858. Pop 11,500; Circ 70,000
Library Holdings: Bk Vols 60,000; Per Subs 50
Special Collections: Local History (Livingston County & Pontiac, Ill Coll)
Subject Interests: Agr
Automation Activity & Vendor Info: (Cataloging) OCLC Connexion; (Circulation) SIRSI WorkFlows; (OPAC) SIRSI WorkFlows
Database Vendor: OCLC FirstSearch
Wireless access
Open Mon-Thurs 9-7, Fri & Sat 9-5

PORT BYRON

P RIVER VALLEY DISTRICT LIBRARY*, 214 S Main St, 61275-9501. (Mail add: PO Box 10, 61275-0010), SAN 304-5706. Tel: 309-523-3440. FAX: 309-523-3516. E-mail: rivervalley5@mchsi.com. Web Site: rivervalleylibrary.org. *Dir,* Shelli R Fehr; E-mail: director@rivervalleylibrary.org; Staff 9 (MLS 1, Non-MLS 8)
Founded 1914. Pop 5,173; Circ 82,866
Special Collections: 1800's Local Newspaper Coll, microfilm; Rock Island County History
Automation Activity & Vendor Info: (Acquisitions) Innovative Interfaces, Inc; (Cataloging) Innovative Interfaces, Inc; (Circulation) Innovative Interfaces, Inc; (ILL) Innovative Interfaces, Inc; (OPAC) Innovative Interfaces, Inc; (Serials) Innovative Interfaces, Inc
Wireless access
Function: Audiobks via web, Bks on CD, Children's prog, Computer training, Computers for patron use, Copy machines, Electronic databases & coll, Fax serv, Handicapped accessible, ILL available, Microfiche/film & reading machines, Music CDs, Notary serv, Online cat, OverDrive digital audio bks, Photocopying/Printing, Preschool reading prog, Prog for adults, Prog for children & young adult, Pub access computers, Scanner, Senior computer classes, Story hour, Summer reading prog, Tax forms, Teen prog, Wheelchair accessible
Mem of Reaching Across Illinois Library System (RAILS)
Partic in RiverShare Libraries
Open Mon-Fri 9-8, Sat 9-1
Friends of the Library Group

POTOMAC

P POTOMAC PUBLIC LIBRARY*, 110 E State St, 61865. (Mail add: PO Box 171, 61865-0171), SAN 304-5714. Tel: 217-987-6457. FAX: 217-987-6457. *Librn,* Sara Kennel; E-mail: slkennel1@juno.com; *Asst Librn,* Karen Stevenson
Founded 1939. Pop 681; Circ 987
Library Holdings: Bk Vols 11,902
Special Collections: Large Print Coll
Mem of Illinois Heartland Library System
Open Tues & Thurs 9-2 & 4-8, Fri 4-8, Sat 9-12 (12-3 Summer)

PRINCETON

S BUREAU COUNTY HISTORICAL SOCIETY MUSEUM & LIBRARY*, 109 Park Ave W, 61356-1927. SAN 304-5730. Tel: 815-875-2184. E-mail: bchsmuseum@yahoo.com. Web Site: www.bureaucountymuseum.com. *Dir,* Pamela Lange
Founded 1948
Library Holdings: Bk Titles 1,000
Special Collections: Henry W Immke Photographic Coll
Subject Interests: Genealogy, Local hist
Open Wed-Sat 1-5

M PERRY MEMORIAL HOSPITAL*, Kenneth O Nelson Library of the Health Sciences, 530 Park Ave E, 61356. SAN 320-6602. Tel: 815-875-2811, Ext 4479. FAX: 815-872-1257. Web Site: www.perry-memorial.org. *Dir,* Linda Litherland
Founded 1954
Library Holdings: Bk Titles 421; Per Subs 15
Subject Interests: Nursing

Partic in Heart of Illinois Library Consortium
Open Mon-Fri 7-6

P PRINCETON PUBLIC LIBRARY*, 698 E Peru St, 61356. SAN 304-5749. Tel: 815-875-1331. FAX: 815-872-1376. E-mail: help@princetonpl.org. Web Site: www.princetonpl.org. *Dir,* Jane Wayland; *Head, Youth Serv,* Ron McCutchan; *Head, Youth Serv,* Paula Morrow; *Youth Serv Librn,* Mary Archer; *Youth Serv Librn,* Cheryl Bebej; *Curator,* Margaret Martinkus; E-mail: mmartinkus@princetonpl.org; Staff 1 (MLS 1)
Founded 1886. Pop 7,501; Circ 62,000
Library Holdings: Bk Titles 44,000; Per Subs 110
Special Collections: Bureau County (Illinois) Farm Architecture Exhibit, photog; Local History Coll, art, bks, blueprints, cassettes, Indian artifacts, micro, pamphlets, photog; World War II Coll, posters
Automation Activity & Vendor Info: (Circulation) SirsiDynix; (OPAC) SirsiDynix
Database Vendor: EBSCOhost, Gale Cengage Learning, OCLC FirstSearch
Open Mon-Thurs 10-9, Fri 10-6, Sat 9-2
Friends of the Library Group

PRINCEVILLE

P LILLIE M EVANS LIBRARY DISTRICT*, 207 N Walnut Ave, 61559. (Mail add: PO Box 349, 61559-0349), SAN 304-5757. Tel: 309-385-4540. FAX: 309-385-2661. E-mail: lill@lmelibrary.org. Web Site: www.lmelibrary.org. *Dir,* Beth Duttlinger; Staff 1 (MLS 1)
Founded 1956. Pop 3,834
Library Holdings: AV Mats 2,100; Bk Titles 22,000; Bk Vols 24,000; Per Subs 80; Talking Bks 1,250
Subject Interests: Local hist, Spanish (Lang)
Wireless access
Mem of Reaching Across Illinois Library System (RAILS)
Open Mon & Wed 9-8, Tues, Thurs & Fri 9-5, Sat 9-1
Friends of the Library Group

PROPHETSTOWN

P HENRY C ADAMS MEMORIAL LIBRARY*, 209 W Third St, 61277. SAN 304-5765. Tel: 815-537-5462. FAX: 815-537-5462. E-mail: hcadams1@yahoo.com. Web Site: prophetstownlibrary.com. *Dir,* Susan Miniel; Staff 3 (Non-MLS 3)
Founded 1929. Pop 2,023; Circ 15,648
Library Holdings: e-books 2,644; Large Print Bks 115, Bk Vols 12,484; Talking Bks 274; Videos 129
Special Collections: Civil War Records
Automation Activity & Vendor Info: (Acquisitions) SirsiDynix; (Cataloging) SirsiDynix; (Circulation) SirsiDynix; (Course Reserve) SirsiDynix; (ILL) SirsiDynix; (Media Booking) SirsiDynix; (OPAC) SirsiDynix, (Serials) SirsiDynix
Database Vendor: Baker & Taylor, EBSCOhost, OCLC FirstSearch, SirsiDynix
Function: Homebound delivery serv
Mem of Reaching Across Illinois Library System (RAILS)
Partic in RiverShare Libraries
Special Services for the Blind - Aids for in-house use; Computer with voice synthesizer for visually impaired persons; Talking bks
Open Mon, Tues & Thurs 2-8, Wed & Fri 2-5, Sat 9-1

PROSPECT HEIGHTS

P PROSPECT HEIGHTS PUBLIC LIBRARY DISTRICT*, 12 N Elm St, 60070-1450. SAN 304-5781. Tel: 847-259-3500. FAX: 847-259-4602. Web Site: www.phpl.info. *Exec Dir,* Alexander C Todd; *Head, Adult Serv,* Kim Murphy; *Head, Tech Serv,* Kimberly Last; E-mail: klast@phpl.info; *Head, Youth Serv,* Sue Seggeling; E-mail: sueann@phpl.info; *Circ,* Maureen Dunne; E-mail: mdunne@phpl.info; *Commun Serv,* Patricia Rustemeyer; E-mail: prusteme@phpl.info; Staff 31.5 (MLS 7.3, Non-MLS 24.2)
Founded 1955. Pop 14,073; Circ 214,769
Jul 2010-Jun 2011 Income $2,923,181, State $19,447, Locally Generated Income $2,870,487, Other $33,247. Mats Exp $227,547, Books $115,927, Per/Ser (Incl. Access Fees) $14,097, AV Mat $52,135, Electronic Ref Mat (Incl. Access Fees) $45,388. Sal $1,144,333
Library Holdings: Audiobooks 3,071; CDs 5,703; DVDs 6,200; e-books 3,866; Electronic Media & Resources 8,396; Bk Vols 89,209; Per Subs 220; Videos 42
Special Collections: Local History (Prospect Heights & Wheeling, IL)
Subject Interests: Antiques, Glass
Automation Activity & Vendor Info: (Cataloging) SirsiDynix; (Circulation) SirsiDynix; (ILL) SirsiDynix; (OPAC) SirsiDynix; (Serials) SirsiDynix
Database Vendor: 3M Library Systems, Baker & Taylor, Gale Cengage Learning, OCLC FirstSearch, SirsiDynix
Wireless access
Publications: Elm Leaf (Newsletter)
Partic in Cooperative Computer Services - CCS
Open Mon-Thurs 10-9, Fri 10-6, Sat 10-5, Sun 1-5
Friends of the Library Group

QUINCY

M BLESSING HEALTH PROFESSIONS LIBRARY*, Broadway at 11th St, 62305. (Mail add: PO Box 7005, 62305-7005), SAN 304-579X. Tel: 217-228-5520, Ext 6970. FAX: 217-223-6400. E-mail: librarian@brcn.edu. Web Site: www.library.brcn.edu. *Dir,* Arlis D Dittmer; Tel: 217-228-5520, Ext 6971, E-mail: adittmer@brcn.edu; *Pub Serv,* Julie Dietrich; E-mail: judietrich@brcn.edu; Staff 3 (MLS 1, Non-MLS 2)
Founded 1891
Library Holdings: Bk Titles 5,000; Per Subs 120
Subject Interests: Nursing
Automation Activity & Vendor Info: (Acquisitions) CARL.Solution (TLC); (Cataloging) CARL.Solution (TLC); (Course Reserve) CARL.Solution (TLC); (ILL) OCLC
Database Vendor: EBSCOhost, OCLC FirstSearch, OVID Technologies
Partic in Health Science Libraries of Illinois (HSLI); Illinois Library & Information Network; MCMLA; RSA

S HISTORICAL SOCIETY OF QUINCY & ADAMS COUNTY LIBRARY*, 425 S 12th St, 62301. SAN 326-145X. Tel: 217-222-1835. FAX: 217-222-8212. Web Site: adamscohistory.org. *Res Librn,* Jean Kay; E-mail: jeankay@adamscohistory.org
Founded 1896
Library Holdings: Bk Titles 1,060; Bk Vols 1,110
Special Collections: Civil War (Gen James D Morgan Coll), ms
Mem of Reaching Across Illinois Library System (RAILS)
Open Tues-Fri 10-2
Restriction: Non-circulating to the pub

J JOHN WOOD COMMUNITY COLLEGE LIBRARY*, 1301 S 48th St, 62305. SAN 320-1821. Tel: 217-641-4535, 217-641-4537. Interlibrary Loan Service Tel: 217-641-4565. Reference Tel: 217-641-4597. FAX: 217-641-4197. E-mail: circdesk@jwcc.edu, reference@jwcc.edu. Web Site: www.jwcc.edu/instruct/library. *Dir of Libr Serv,* Barb Lieber; *Mgr, Libr Serv,* Erin Ealy; Staff 2 (MLS 2)
Founded 1974. Enrl 2,640; Fac 50; Highest Degree: Associate
Library Holdings: Bk Titles 18,500; Per Subs 190
Subject Interests: Agr, Local hist, Nursing, Vocational educ
Automation Activity & Vendor Info: (Acquisitions) Ex Libris Group; (Cataloging) Ex Libris Group; (Circulation) Ex Libris Group; (Course Reserve) Ex Libris Group; (ILL) OCLC FirstSearch; (OPAC) Ex Libris Group; (Serials) Ex Libris Group
Database Vendor: CQ Press, CredoReference, Ebooks Corporation, EBSCOhost, Ex Libris Group, Gale Cengage Learning, OCLC FirstSearch, OCLC WorldShare Interlibrary Loan, Oxford Online, ProQuest, SerialsSolutions, Wilson - Wilson Web
Wireless access
Mem of Reaching Across Illinois Library System (RAILS)
Partic in Consortium of Academic & Research Libraries in Illinois; Northern Illinois Learning Resources Cooperative (NILRC)
Open Mon-Thurs 7:30am-8:30pm, Fri 7:30-5, Sat 12-4

P QUINCY PUBLIC LIBRARY, 526 Jersey St, 62301-3996. SAN 304-582X. Tel: 217-223-1309. Interlibrary Loan Service Tel: 217-223-1309, Ext 210. Reference Tel: 217-223-1309, Ext 502. Administration Tel: 217-223-1309, Ext 506. FAX: 217-222-5672. Reference FAX: 217-222-3052. E-mail: reference@quincylibrary.org. Web Site: www.quincylibrary.org. *Exec Dir,* Nancy J Dolan; Tel: 217-223-1309, Ext 204, E-mail: ndolan@quincylibrary.org; *AV Librn,* Mary B O'Brien; Tel: 217-223-1309, Ext 205, E-mail: mobrien@quincylibrary.org; *Ch Serv Librn,* Judy J Decker; Tel: 217-223-1309, Ext 219, E-mail: jdecker@quincylibrary.org; *Coll & Delivery Serv Mgr,* Pamela Clow; Tel: 217-223-1309, Ext 203, E-mail: pclow@quincylibrary.org; *Info Serv Mgr,* Katie Kraushaar; Tel: 217-223-1309, Ext 213, E-mail: kkraushaar@quincylibrary.org; *Sr Serv,* Patricia Woodworth; Tel: 217-223-1309, Ext 216, E-mail: pwoodworth@quincylibrary.org; Staff 9 (MLS 5, Non-MLS 4)
Founded 1888. Pop 53,000; Circ 701,716
Library Holdings: Audiobooks 9,700; DVDs 12,337; e-books 3,634; Bk Titles 145,844; Per Subs 304
Special Collections: State Document Depository
Subject Interests: Genealogy, Local hist
Automation Activity & Vendor Info: (Cataloging) SirsiDynix; (Circulation) SirsiDynix; (ILL) SirsiDynix
Database Vendor: Baker & Taylor, OCLC FirstSearch, Overdrive, Inc, ProQuest, SirsiDynix, TumbleBookLibrary, Wilson - Wilson Web
Wireless access
Function: After school storytime, Archival coll, Bk club(s), CD-ROM, Handicapped accessible, Home delivery & serv to Sr ctr & nursing homes, Homebound delivery serv, ILL available, Newsp ref libr, Online searches, Photocopying/Printing, Prog for adults, Prog for children & young adult, Summer reading prog

Mem of Reaching Across Illinois Library System (RAILS)
Special Services for the Deaf - TDD equip
Special Services for the Blind - Closed circuit TV; Large print bks; Reader equip; Talking bks
Open Mon-Thurs (Winter) 9-8, Fri & Sat 9-5, Sun 1-5; Mon (Summer) 9-8, Tues-Thurs 9-6, Fri & Sat 9-5
Friends of the Library Group

C QUINCY UNIVERSITY*, Brenner Library, 1800 College Ave, 62301-2699. SAN 304-5811. Tel: 217-228-5432, Ext 3801. Circulation Tel: 217-228-5432, Ext 3804. Reference Tel: 217-228-5432, Ext 3805. Administration Tel: 217-228-5432, Ext 3800. FAX: 217-228-5354. Web Site: www.quincy.edu/Library/index.php. *Dean of Libr,* Patricia Tomczak; E-mail: tomczpa@quincy.edu; *Assoc Librn, Head, Pub Serv,* Nancy Crow; E-mail: crowna@quincy.edu; *Access & Ser Librn,* Sharon Sample; *Ref/Archives Librn,* Brother Terry Santiapillai; Staff 6 (MLS 2, Non-MLS 4)
Founded 1860. Enrl 1,100; Fac 97; Highest Degree: Master
Library Holdings: AV Mats 5,850; Bks on Deafness & Sign Lang 25; CDs 845; DVDs 520; e-books 10; e-journals 15; Electronic Media & Resources 55; Music Scores 1,350; Bk Titles 155,355; Bk Vols 198,500; Per Subs 455; Spec Interest Per Sub 15; Talking Bks 15; Videos 2,350
Special Collections: Early Christian & Medieval (Bonaventure Library), Local History (Quincyana; East Asian Coll; Rare Book Library; Spanish-American History (Biblioteca Fraborese)
Subject Interests: Am lit, English lit, Theol
Automation Activity & Vendor Info: (Acquisitions) Ex Libris Group; (Cataloging) Ex Libris Group; (Circulation) Ex Libris Group; (Course Reserve) Ex Libris Group; (ILL) OCLC Connexion; (Media Booking) Ex Libris Group; (OPAC) Ex Libris Group; (Serials) EBSCO Online
Database Vendor: Baker & Taylor, Cambridge Scientific Abstracts, EBSCOhost, JSTOR, LexisNexis, OCLC FirstSearch, OCLC WorldShare Interlibrary Loan, OVID Technologies, ProQuest, SerialsSolutions
Publications: Bibliographies; Bibliography of the Spanish Borderlands in the Fraborese Coll; Catalog of the Incunabula in the Quincy University Library; Rare Book Collection
Partic in Consortium of Academic & Research Libraries in Illinois; Illinois Library & Information Network; OCLC Online Computer Library Center, Inc
Friends of the Library Group

S SOCIETY FOR ACADEMIC ACHIEVEMENT LIBRARY*, WCU Bldg, 510 Maine St, 62301. SAN 326-9779. Tel: 217-224-0570. *Pres,* Wayne Nelson; *Exec Dir, Librn,* Diane Weber
Library Holdings: Bk Vols 2,000
Subject Interests: Educ
Open Mon-Fri 9-4

RAMSEY

P RAMSEY PUBLIC LIBRARY*, 401 S Superior St, 62080. (Mail add: PO Box 128, 62080-0128), SAN 375-9733. Tel: 618-423-2019. FAX: 618-423-2120. E-mail: ramseylibrary@yahoo.com. *Dir,* Miriam Hargis-Poston; *Bus Mgr,* Carla Denton; Staff 1 (Non-MLS 1)
Pop 1,056; Circ 4,420
Library Holdings: Large Print Bks 200; Bk Vols 1,225; Per Subs 15
Subject Interests: Christian
Mem of Illinois Heartland Library System

RANTOUL

P RANTOUL PUBLIC LIBRARY*, 106 W Flessner, 61866. SAN 304-5838. Tel: 217-893-3955. FAX: 217-893-3961. TDD: 217-893-1439. E-mail: rantoullib@gmail.com. Web Site: www.rantoul.lib.il.us. *Dir,* Holly Thompson; E-mail: hollysrpl@gmail.com; *Youth Serv Librn,* Annette Davis; E-mail: andavster@gmail.com
Founded 1934. Pop 17,212; Circ 89,000
Library Holdings: Bk Vols 50,000; Per Subs 175
Special Collections: Aero-Space Coll
Automation Activity & Vendor Info: (Circulation) SirsiDynix
Mem of Illinois Heartland Library System
Special Services for the Deaf - TTY equip
Special Services for the Blind - Audio mat; Bks on cassette; Bks on CD; Braille bks; Talking bks
Open Mon-Thurs 9-9, Fri & Sat 9-5, Sun 1-5
Friends of the Library Group

RAYMOND

P DOYLE PUBLIC LIBRARY DISTRICT*, 109 S O'Bannon, 62560-5212. (Mail add: PO Box 544, 62560-0544). Tel: 217-229-4471. E-mail: doylepublic@gmail.com. *Dir,* Jane Whalen
Pop 1,888; Circ 7,605
Library Holdings: AV Mats 239; Bk Vols 7,800; Per Subs 16; Talking Bks 109
Special Collections: Raymond Independent & Raymond News Coll, newsp
Wireless access
Publications: Raymond Independent; Raymond News
Mem of Illinois Heartland Library System
Open Mon 11-6, Tues & Thurs 11-5, Wed 11-8, Fri 11-4, Sat 9-Noon

RED BUD

P RED BUD PUBLIC LIBRARY*, 925 S Main St, 62278. SAN 304-5846. Tel: 618-282-2255. FAX: 618-282-4055. *Dir,* Brenda Gilpatrick; E-mail: gilpatrickbrenda@hotmail.com; *Asst Librn,* Jancie Wall; Staff 2 (Non-MLS 2)
Founded 1945. Pop 3,334; Circ 8,000
Library Holdings: Bk Titles 14,000; Per Subs 60
Subject Interests: Ill
Wireless access
Mem of Illinois Heartland Library System
Open Mon-Thurs 12:30-8, Fri 12:30-4:30, Sat 10-2

RICHMOND

P NIPPERSINK DISTRICT LIBRARY*, 5418 Hill Rd, 60071. SAN 304-5854. Tel: 815-678-4014. FAX: 815-678-4484. E-mail: nippersink@nippersinklibrary.org. *Dir,* Cynthia Cole; Staff 12 (MLS 1, Non-MLS 11)
Founded 1972. Pop 11,169; Circ 82,500
Library Holdings: AV Mats 5,500; Bk Vols 46,000; Per Subs 68
Automation Activity & Vendor Info: (Circulation) Innovative Interfaces, Inc; (ILL) Innovative Interfaces, Inc; (OPAC) Innovative Interfaces, Inc
Publications: Library News (Quarterly)
Mem of Reaching Across Illinois Library System (RAILS)
Open Mon-Thurs 9-9, Fri & Sat 9-5, Sun 1-5
Friends of the Library Group

RICHTON PARK

P RICHTON PARK PUBLIC LIBRARY DISTRICT*, 4045 Sauk Trail, 60471. SAN 304-5862. Tel: 708-481-5333. FAX: 708-481-4343. E-mail: library@richtonparklibrary.org. Web Site: www.richtonparklibrary.org. *Libr Dir,* Kelley D Nichols-Brown; *Ad,* Donna Bailey; *Circ, ILL,* Doris Dougher; *Ref Librn,* Karissa Tatman; *Youth Serv,* Jennifer Fait; Staff 4 (MLS 3, Non-MLS 1)
Founded 1974. Pop 12,533; Circ 87,138
Jul 2007-Jun 2008 Income $714,028, State $68,022, County $565,414, Locally Generated Income $80,592. Mats Exp $74,260, Books $53,425, Per/Ser (Incl. Access Fees) $4,000, AV Mat $10,257, Electronic Ref Mat (Incl. Access Fees) $6,578. Sal $324,621 (Prof $189,000)
Library Holdings: AV Mats 1,500; Large Print Bks 200; Bk Titles 39,000; Bk Vols 41,000; Per Subs 175; Talking Bks 2,500
Automation Activity & Vendor Info: (Circulation) Innovative Interfaces, Inc; (ILL) Innovative Interfaces, Inc; (OPAC) Innovative Interfaces, Inc
Database Vendor: EBSCOhost, Innovative Interfaces, Inc, OCLC FirstSearch, OCLC WorldShare Interlibrary Loan
Wireless access
Function: Adult bk club, Bk club(s), Bks on CD, Children's prog, Computers for patron use, Copy machines, Free DVD rentals, Handicapped accessible, ILL available, Mail & tel request accepted, Music CDs, Notary serv, Online cat, Online searches, Photocopying/Printing, Prog for adults, Prog for children & young adult, Pub access computers, Ref serv available, Story hour, Summer reading prog, Tax forms, Telephone ref
Mem of Reaching Across Illinois Library System (RAILS)
Partic in System Wide Automated Network
Open Mon-Fri 10-9, Sat 10-5
Friends of the Library Group

RIDGE FARM

P ELWOOD TOWNSHIP CARNEGIE LIBRARY*, 104 N State St, 61870. (Mail add: PO Box 349, 61870-0349), SAN 304-5889. Tel: 217-247-2820. FAX: 217-247-2835. *Librn,* Lisa Davis; E-mail: booksld@yahoo.com
Founded 1909. Pop 1,672; Circ 6,213
Library Holdings: Bk Vols 10,751; Per Subs 20
Automation Activity & Vendor Info: (Cataloging) SirsiDynix; (Circulation) SirsiDynix
Mem of Illinois Heartland Library System
Open Tues-Thurs 2-7, Fri 12-5, Sat 9-2

RIVER FOREST

C CONCORDIA UNIVERSITY*, Klinck Memorial Library, 7400 Augusta St, 60305-1499. SAN 304-5897. Tel: 708-209-3050. Toll Free Tel: 866-733-8287. FAX: 708-209-3175. E-mail: crfilllib@cuchicago.edu, library@cuchicago.edu. Web Site: www.cuchicago.edu/library. *Dir,* Yana V Serdyuk; Tel: 708-209-3053, E-mail: yana.serdyuk@cuchicago.edu; *Access Serv Librn, ILL,* Dan Zamudio; Tel: 708-209-3057, E-mail: dan.zamudio@cuchicago.edu; *Ref Librn,* Marty J Breen; Tel:

708-209-3181, E-mail: marty.breen@cuchicago.edu; *Tech Serv Librn,* Lee Forrest; Tel: 708-209-3254, E-mail: lee.forrest@cuchicago.edu; *Ch Serv,* Maryanne Rusinak; Tel: 708-209-3587, E-mail: maryanne.rusinak@cuchicago.edu; Staff 5 (MLS 5)
Founded 1864. Enrl 2,781; Fac 88; Highest Degree: Master
Library Holdings: Bk Titles 170,000; Per Subs 534
Special Collections: Curriculum Library; Educational Resources Info Center, micro; Test file. Oral History
Subject Interests: Educ, Music, Relig
Automation Activity & Vendor Info: (Acquisitions) Ex Libris Group; (Cataloging) Ex Libris Group; (Circulation) Ex Libris Group; (Course Reserve) Ex Libris Group; (ILL) Ex Libris Group; (OPAC) Ex Libris Group; (Serials) Ex Libris Group
Database Vendor: Baker & Taylor, EBSCOhost, LexisNexis, OCLC FirstSearch, OCLC WorldShare Interlibrary Loan, ProQuest, SerialsSolutions
Partic in Consortium of Academic & Research Libraries in Illinois; Illinois Library & Information Network; LIBRAS, Inc; Minitex Library Information Network
Open Mon-Thurs 8-10, Fri 8-4:30, Sat 9:30-5:30

C DOMINICAN UNIVERSITY*, Rebecca Crown Library, 7900 W Division St, 60305-1066. SAN 304-5927. Tel: 708-524-6875. Circulation Tel: 708-524-6876. Interlibrary Loan Service Tel: 708-524-6877. FAX: 708-366-5360. Web Site: www.domweb.dom.edu/library/crown. *Univ Librn,* Bella Karr Gerlich, PhD; Tel: 708-524-6873, E-mail: bkarrgerlich@dom.edu; *Head, Tech Serv,* Position Currently Open; *Syst Librn,* Molly Beestrum; Staff 13.5 (MLS 7, Non-MLS 6.5)
Founded 1918. Enrl 3,100; Fac 150; Highest Degree: Master
Library Holdings: Bk Vols 300,000; Per Subs 16,000
Special Collections: US Document Depository
Subject Interests: Libr & info sci
Automation Activity & Vendor Info: (Acquisitions) Ex Libris Group; (Cataloging) Ex Libris Group; (Circulation) Ex Libris Group; (OPAC) Ex Libris Group
Wireless access
Publications: Bibliographies; Handbooks
Partic in Consortium of Academic & Research Libraries in Illinois; Illinois Library & Information Network; LIBRAS, Inc; OCLC Online Computer Library Center, Inc
Open Mon-Sun 8am-Midnight

P RIVER FOREST PUBLIC LIBRARY*, 735 Lathrop Ave, 60305-1883. SAN 304-5919. Tel: 708-366-5205. FAX: 708-366-8699, E-mail: reference@riverforestlibrary.org. Web Site: www.riverforestlibrary.org. *Dir,* Sophia Anastos; Tel: 708-366-5205, Ext 303, E-mail: sophia.anastos@riverforestlibrary.org; *Head, Strategic Planning,* Susan Quinn; Tel: 708-366-5205, Ext 319, E-mail: sue.quinn@riverforestlibrary.org; *Head, Circ,* Ted Bodewes; E-mail: ted.bodewes@riverforestlibrary.org; *Adult Serv,* Blaise Dierks; Tel: 708-366-5205, Ext 318, E-mail: blaise.dierks@riverforestlibrary.org; *Ch Serv,* Ashley Wescott; Tel: 708-366-5205, Ext 315, E-mail: ashley.wescott@riverforestlibrary.org; Staff 14 (MLS 9, Non-MLS 5)
Founded 1899. Pop 11,635; Circ 143,185
Automation Activity & Vendor Info: (Circulation) Innovative Interfaces, Inc
Database Vendor: Gale Cengage Learning
Wireless access
Publications: Newsletter (Bi-annually)
Mem of Reaching Across Illinois Library System (RAILS)
Open Mon-Thurs 9-9, Fri & Sat 9-5
Friends of the Library Group

RIVER GROVE

P RIVER GROVE PUBLIC LIBRARY DISTRICT, 8638 W Grand Ave, 60171. SAN 304-5935. Tel: 708-453-4484. FAX: 708-453-4517. E-mail: rgplreference@gmail.com. Web Site: rivergrovelibrary.org. *Dir,* Lisa Knasiak; *Ch Serv,* Dayna Tucker; *Circ,* Anastasia Daskalos; Staff 11 (MLS 1, Non-MLS 10)
Founded 1963. Pop 10,600; Circ 27,000
Library Holdings: Bk Vols 30,000; Per Subs 121
Special Collections: Local History
Automation Activity & Vendor Info: (OPAC) Innovative Interfaces, Inc
Database Vendor: Innovative Interfaces, Inc
Wireless access
Publications: Monthly Calender of Events; New Book List
Mem of Reaching Across Illinois Library System (RAILS)
Open Mon-Thurs 10-9, Fri & Sat 10-5

J TRITON COLLEGE LIBRARY*, 2000 N Fifth Ave, 60171. SAN 304-5943. Tel: 708-456-0300, Ext 3215. Reference Tel: 708-456-0300, Ext 3698. FAX: 708-583-3120. Interlibrary Loan Service FAX: 708-456-0300, Ext 3697. Web Site: www.triton.edu. *Chairperson,* Lucy Smith
Founded 1964. Highest Degree: Associate
Library Holdings: Bk Vols 84,000; Per Subs 410
Subject Interests: Nursing, Sci tech
Mem of Reaching Across Illinois Library System (RAILS)
Partic in Consortium of Academic & Research Libraries in Illinois; Network of Illinois Learning Resources in Community Colleges; OCLC Online Computer Library Center, Inc
Open Mon-Thurs 8am-10pm, Fri 8-5, Sat 8:30-4, Sun 12-4

RIVERDALE

P RIVERDALE PUBLIC LIBRARY DISTRICT*, 208 W 144th St, 60827-2788. SAN 304-5951. Tel: 708-841-3311. FAX: 708-841-1805. E-mail: rds@mls.lib.il.us. Web Site: www.riverdale.lib.il.us. *Adminr, Head of Libr,* Katrina Harris; *Asst Dir,* Brett Shelton; *Circ,* Sandy Schroeder; *Pub Serv,* Arlene Mallek; *Ref,* Dan O'Hara; *Tech Serv,* Barb Diehl; Staff 3 (MLS 1, Non-MLS 2)
Founded 1973. Pop 13,609; Circ 52,610
Library Holdings: Audiobooks 490; CDs 1,458; DVDs 1,790; Bk Titles 26,916; Bk Vols 35,447; Per Subs 65; Talking Bks 408
Automation Activity & Vendor Info: (Circulation) Innovative Interfaces, Inc
Database Vendor: EBSCOhost, Electric Library, Innovative Interfaces, Inc, Newsbank, OCLC FirstSearch
Wireless access
Mem of Reaching Across Illinois Library System (RAILS)
Open Mon-Thurs 10-6, Fri & Sat 12-4

RIVERSIDE

P RIVERSIDE PUBLIC LIBRARY*, One Burling Rd, 60546. SAN 304-596X. Tel: 708-442-6366. FAX: 708-442-9462. Circulation E-mail: circulation@riversidelibrary.org. Reference E-mail: reference@riversidelibrary.org. Web Site: www.riversidelibrary.org. *Dir,* Janice Fisher; E-mail: janicefisher@riversidelibrary.org; Staff 35 (MLS 5, Non-MLS 30)
Founded 1930. Pop 8,774; Circ 134,000
Library Holdings: Bk Titles 67,000; Per Subs 125
Special Collections: Frederick Law Olmsted
Subject Interests: Landscape archit, Local hist
Automation Activity & Vendor Info: (Circulation) Innovative Interfaces, Inc
Publications: Bibliography of Frederick Law Olmsted & Calvert Vaux; Local History Index; Local Newspaper Index 1912-39; Newsletter; Origins of Riverside Street Names
Mem of Reaching Across Illinois Library System (RAILS)
Open Mon-Thurs 9-9, Fri & Sat 9-5, Sun (Sept-May) 1-5
Friends of the Library Group

RIVERTON

P RIVERTON VILLAGE LIBRARY, 1200 E Riverton Rd, 62561-8200. Tel: 217-629-6353. FAX: 217-629-6353. E-mail: rvl1@casscomm.com. *Dir,* Nancy Blockyou
Founded 1996. Pop 3,455
Jan 2007-Dec 2007. Mats Exp $2,500
Automation Activity & Vendor Info: (Acquisitions) SirsiDynix; (Cataloging) SirsiDynix; (Circulation) SirsiDynix; (Course Reserve) SirsiDynix; (ILL) SirsiDynix; (Media Booking) SirsiDynix; (OPAC) SirsiDynix; (Serials) SirsiDynix
Database Vendor: OCLC FirstSearch
Wireless access
Mem of Illinois Heartland Library System
Open Mon-Thurs 9-2 & 4-8, Sat 10-3

ROBBINS

P WILLIAM LEONARD PUBLIC LIBRARY DISTRICT*, 13820 Central Park Ave, 60472-1999. SAN 304-5978. Tel: 708-597-2760. FAX: 708-597-2778. *Dir,* Coatney Priscilla
Founded 1973. Pop 8,853
Library Holdings: Bk Vols 21,000; Per Subs 88
Automation Activity & Vendor Info: (Circulation) Innovative Interfaces, Inc; (Course Reserve) Innovative Interfaces, Inc
Mem of Reaching Across Illinois Library System (RAILS)
Open Mon & Wed 12-8, Tues & Thurs 12-6, Fri 3-7, Sat 10-12
Friends of the Library Group

ROBINSON

J LINCOLN TRAIL COLLEGE*, Eagleton Learning Resources Center, 11220 State Hwy 1, 62454-5707. SAN 304-5986. Tel: 618-544-8657, Ext 1425. Toll Free Tel: 866-582-4322. FAX: 618-544-3957. Web Site: www.iecc.edu/ltc/lrc. *Dir,* Vicky Bonelli; Tel: 618-544-8657, Ext 1427, E-mail: bonelliv@iecc.edu
Founded 1970. Enrl 1,025

Library Holdings: Bk Vols 18,000; Per Subs 75
Automation Activity & Vendor Info: (Cataloging) Ex Libris Group; (Circulation) Ex Libris Group; (OPAC) Ex Libris Group
Open Mon-Thurs 7:45-7:30, Fri 7:30-4:30

P ROBINSON PUBLIC LIBRARY DISTRICT*, 606 N Jefferson St, 62454-2665. SAN 304-5994. Tel: 618-544-2917. FAX: 618-544-7172. E-mail: robinsonlibrarydistrict@hotmail.com. Web Site: www.robinson.lib.il.us. *Dir,* Breyanna Phipps; Staff 31 (Non-MLS 31)
Founded 1906. Pop 16,188; Circ 84,778
Library Holdings: DVDs 2,216; Electronic Media & Resources 18; Bk Vols 70,374; Per Subs 80; Talking Bks 710; Videos 5,320
Special Collections: Antiques & Collectibles; Crawford County History; Genealogy; Parenting
Subject Interests: Genealogy, Local hist
Automation Activity & Vendor Info: (Acquisitions) SirsiDynix; (Cataloging) SirsiDynix; (Circulation) SirsiDynix; (ILL) SirsiDynix; (OPAC) SirsiDynix; (Serials) SirsiDynix
Database Vendor: OCLC FirstSearch
Function: Homebound delivery serv, Ref serv available
Mem of Illinois Heartland Library System
Special Services for the Deaf - Bks on deafness & sign lang; Closed caption videos; TDD equip
Special Services for the Blind - Closed circuit TV magnifier; Reader equip; Talking bks
Open Mon-Thurs (Fall-Spring) 10-7, Fri & Sat 10-5:30; Mon (Summer) 10-7, Tues-Sat 10-5:30
Restriction: Non-circulating
Branches: 3
HUTSONVILLE BRANCH, 101 S Main St, Hutsonville, 62433. (Mail add: PO Box 08, Hutsonville, 62433-0008). Tel: 618-563-9603. FAX: 618-563-9603. E-mail: hutsonpubliclibrary@gmail.com. *Br Mgr,* Shannon Wells; Staff 2 (Non-MLS 2)
Founded 1994. Pop 1,151
Open Mon 3-5, Tues & Thurs 1-5, Sat 9-Noon
Friends of the Library Group
OBLONG BRANCH, 110 E Main St, Oblong, 62449. Tel: 618-592-3001. FAX: 618-592-3001. E-mail: doblibrary@yahoo.com. *Br Mgr,* Judy Plunkett; Staff 2 (Non-MLS 2)
Founded 1968. Pop 2,490
Open Tues-Fri 11-5, Sat 10-1
Friends of the Library Group
SUSIE WESLEY MEMORIAL, 105 S Main, Flat Rock, 62427. (Mail add: PO Box 185, Flat Rock, 62427-0185). Tel: 618-584-3636. FAX: 618-584-3636. E-mail: swlib@frtci.net. *Br Mgr,* Ellen Roberts; Staff 2 (Non-MLS 2)
Founded 1988. Pop 1,151
Open Tues & Thurs Noon-5, Sat 9-Noon
Friends of the Library Group

ROCHELLE

P FLAGG-ROCHELLE PUBLIC LIBRARY DISTRICT*, 619 Fourth Ave, 61068. SAN 304-6001. Tel: 815-562-3431. FAX: 815-562-3432. TDD: 815-562-3457. E-mail: library@rochelle.net. *Dir,* Barbara A Kopplin; *Ch Serv,* Connie Avery
Founded 1889. Pop 13,370; Circ 91,304
Library Holdings: Bk Vols 53,000; Per Subs 147
Subject Interests: Genealogy, Local hist
Wireless access
Mem of Reaching Across Illinois Library System (RAILS)
Open Mon-Thurs 10-8:30, Fri & Sat 10-5
Friends of the Library Group

ROCHESTER

P ROCHESTER PUBLIC LIBRARY DISTRICT*, One Community Dr, 62563. (Mail add: PO Box 617, 62563), SAN 376-1266. Tel: 217-498-8454. FAX: 217-498-8455. E-mail: info@rochesterlibrary.org. Web Site: www.rochesterlibrary.org. Staff 8 (MLS 1, Non-MLS 7)
Founded 1985. Pop 7,046
Library Holdings: Bk Titles 29,200; Per Subs 73
Automation Activity & Vendor Info: (Cataloging) SirsiDynix; (Circulation) SirsiDynix; (ILL) SirsiDynix; (OPAC) SirsiDynix
Function: Adult bk club, Audiobks via web, Bks on CD, Children's prog, Computer training, Computers for patron use, Copy machines, Electronic databases & coll, Equip loans & repairs, Exhibits, Fax serv, Free DVD rentals, Holiday prog, Home delivery & serv to Sr ctr & nursing homes, Homebound delivery serv, ILL available, Magnifiers for reading, Music CDs, Online cat, OverDrive digital audio bks, Photocopying/Printing, Preschool outreach, Prog for adults, Prog for children & young adult, Pub access computers, Ref serv available, Senior computer classes, Senior outreach, Story hour, Summer reading prog, Tax forms, Telephone ref, Web-catalog, Wheelchair accessible, Workshops, Writing prog
Publications: Bibliobits
Mem of Illinois Heartland Library System
Special Services for the Blind - Bks on cassette; Braille bks; Magnifiers
Open Mon-Thurs 10-8, Fri 10-5, Sat 10-4 (10-2 Summer)
Friends of the Library Group

ROCK FALLS

P ROCK FALLS PUBLIC LIBRARY DISTRICT*, 1007 Seventh Ave, 61071. SAN 304-601X. Tel: 815-626-3958. FAX: 815-626-8750. Web Site: www.rockfallslibrary.com. *Dir,* Amy Lego; *Librn,* Kendra Law; *Librn,* Peg Romanelli; *Ch,* Karen Borelli; Staff 7 (Non-MLS 7)
Founded 1939. Pop 11,000; Circ 48,000
Library Holdings: Bk Vols 36,000; Per Subs 131
Automation Activity & Vendor Info: (Cataloging) TLC (The Library Corporation); (Circulation) TLC (The Library Corporation); (OPAC) TLC (The Library Corporation)
Wireless access
Mem of Reaching Across Illinois Library System (RAILS)
Open Mon-Thurs 9-8, Fri 9-6, Sat 10-5

ROCK ISLAND

C AUGUSTANA COLLEGE LIBRARY*, Thomas Tredway Library, 3435 9 1/2 Ave, 61201-2296. (Mail add: 639 38th St, 61201-2296), SAN 304-6028. Tel: 309-794-7266. Interlibrary Loan Service Tel: 309-794-7585. FAX: 309-794-7640. Interlibrary Loan Service FAX: 309-794-7230. Web Site: www.augustana.edu/library. *Dir,* Carla Tracy; *Spec Coll Librn,* Sarah Horowitz; *Spec Coll Librn,* Jamie Nelson; *Ref,* Stefanie Bluemle; *Ref,* Anne Earel; *Ref,* Connie Ghinazzi; *Ref,* Amanda Makula; *Ref,* Margaret Rogal; *Tech Serv,* Mary Tatro; Staff 16 (MLS 10, Non-MLS 6)
Founded 1860. Enrl 2,441; Fac 223; Highest Degree: Bachelor
Jul 2009-Jun 2010 Income $1,461,512. Mats Exp $336,355, Books $106,798, Per/Ser (Incl. Access Fees) $203,866, Micro $1,781, AV Mat $12,507, Presv $11,403. Sal $627,295 (Prof $442,516)
Library Holdings: Bk Titles 173,734; Bk Vols 199,838; Per Subs 441
Special Collections: French Revolution (Charles XV Coll); John Hauberg Manuscript Coll; Upper Mississippi Valley Coll
Automation Activity & Vendor Info: (Acquisitions) Ex Libris Group; (Cataloging) Ex Libris Group; (Circulation) Ex Libris Group; (Course Reserve) Ex Libris Group; (ILL) OCLC ILLiad; (OPAC) Ex Libris Group
Database Vendor: EBSCOhost, LexisNexis, OCLC FirstSearch, ProQuest
Wireless access
Partic in Consortium of Academic & Research Libraries in Illinois; OCLC Online Computer Library Center, Inc
Open Mon-Thurs 7:30am-Midnight, Fri 7:30-7, Sat 10-6, Sun 10am-Midnight

L ROCK ISLAND COUNTY LAW LIBRARY*, Courthouse, 210 15th St, 61201. SAN 375-975X. Tel: 309-786-4451, Ext 3259. FAX: 309-558-3263. *Dir,* Victoria Bluedorn
Library Holdings: Bk Titles 10,000
Special Collections: Legal Item Coll
Mem of Reaching Across Illinois Library System (RAILS)
Open Mon-Fri 8-12 & 12:30-4:30

P ROCK ISLAND PUBLIC LIBRARY*, 401 19th St, 61201. SAN 340-7012. Tel: 309-732-7323. Reference Tel: 309-732-7341. FAX: 309-732-7342. Web Site: www.ripl.lib.il.us. *Dir,* Position Currently Open; *Asst Dir,* Amy M Penry; Tel: 309-732-7302, Fax: 309-732-7309, E-mail: apenry@libby.rbls.lib.il.us; *Dir, Br Serv,* Tricia L Kane; Tel: 309-732-7364, E-mail: tkane@libby.rbls.lib.il.us; *Dir, Ref,* Kristine Cawley; Tel: 309-732-7326; *Dir, Tech Serv,* Kimberly Brozovich; *Head, Circ,* Lisa M Davison; Tel: 309-732-7350, E-mail: ldaviso@libby.rbls.lib.il.us; *Ch Serv,* Susan A Foster; Tel: 309-732-7362, E-mail: sfoster@libby.rbls.lib.il.us; Staff 39 (MLS 6, Non-MLS 33)
Founded 1872. Pop 52,543; Circ 277,205
Library Holdings: Bk Titles 124,399; Bk Vols 190,313; Per Subs 382
Special Collections: Local History, Adults & Children's Large Print Bks
Subject Interests: Lit, Literary criticism
Database Vendor: OCLC FirstSearch, ProQuest
Wireless access
Publications: Rock Island Library Lines
Mem of Reaching Across Illinois Library System (RAILS)
Partic in RiverShare Libraries
Open Mon-Thurs 9-8, Fri 9-5:30, Sat 9-1
Friends of the Library Group
Branches: 2
SOUTHWEST, 9010 Ridgewood Rd, 61201, SAN 340-7071. Tel: 309-732-7338. FAX: 309-732-7337. *Br Mgr,* Tricia Kane; Tel: 309-732-7364
Library Holdings: Bk Titles 22,806; Bk Vols 23,991
Open Mon & Tues 10-8, Wed 9-8, Thurs-Sat 9-5:30

THIRTY-THIRTY-ONE BRANCH, 3059 30th St, 61201, SAN 340-7101. Tel: 309-732-7369. FAX: 309-732-7371. *Br Mgr,* Tricia Kane; Tel: 309-732-7364
Library Holdings: Bk Titles 17,649; Bk Vols 18,322
Open Mon-Thurs 9-8, Fri & Sat 9-5:30
Bookmobiles: 1

S SWENSON SWEDISH IMMIGRATION RESEARCH CENTER, Augustana College, 3520 Seventh Ave, 61201. (Mail add: Augustana College, 639 38th St, 61201-2296), SAN 326-9833. Tel: 309-794-7204. FAX: 309-794-7443. E-mail: sag@augustana.edu. Web Site: www.augustana.edu/swenson. *Dir,* Dr Dag Blanck, PhD; E-mail: dagblanck@augustana.edu; *Head, Genealogical Serv,* Jill Seaholm; E-mail: jillseaholm@augustana.edu; *Head, Libr Serv,* Susanne Titus; Tel: 309-794-7807, E-mail: susannetitus@augustana.edu; *Archivist, Librn,* Lisa Huntsha; Tel: 309-794-7496, E-mail: lisahuntsha@augustana.edu. Subject Specialists: *Family hist,* Jill Seaholm
Founded 1981
Library Holdings: Bk Titles 17,000; Per Subs 30
Special Collections: Chicago, Minneapolis & Saint Paul City Directories, microfilm; Name Indexes to Swedish Embarkation Ports, database; Swedish-American Churches, Societies, Organizations, Businesses & Personal Papers; Swedish-American Newspapers Coll, microfilm
Publications: Occasional Papers; Swedish American Genealogist (Quarterly); Swedish-American Newspapers: A Guide to Microfilms (1981); Swenson Center News
Partic in OCLC Online Computer Library Center, Inc
Restriction: Open by appt only

R TRI-CITY JEWISH CENTER LIBRARY, 2715 30th St, 61201. SAN 373-0514. Tel: 309-788-3426. E-mail: tcjc@mchsi.com. Web Site: tricityjewishcenter.org. *Librn,* Kristine Cawley; Tel: 309-787-2213, E-mail: kristinecawley@gmail.com
Library Holdings: Bk Vols 10,000
Special Collections: Coin Coll
Open Mon-Fri 9-5

M TRINITY IOWA HEALTH SYSTEM*, Health Sciences Library, 2701 17th St, 61201. SAN 304-419X. Tel: 309-779-2600. FAX: 309-779-2601. Web Site: www.trinityqc.com. Staff 1 (MLS 1)
Library Holdings: e-journals 5,000; Bk Vols 7,500; Per Subs 150
Subject Interests: Consumer health, Med, Nursing
Automation Activity & Vendor Info: (Cataloging) SirsiDynix; (Circulation) SirsiDynix; (OPAC) SirsiDynix; (Serials) SirsiDynix
Mem of Reaching Across Illinois Library System (RAILS)
Partic in Illinois Library & Information Network
Open Mon-Fri 8-4:30

A UNITED STATES ARMY*, Corps of Engineers Rock Island District Technical Library, Clock Tower Bldg, 61204. (Mail add: PO Box 2004, 61204-2004), SAN 340-7160. Tel: 309-794-5884. FAX: 309-794-5807. Web Site: www.mvr.usace.army.mil/library. *Librn,* Bob Romic
Founded 1975
Library Holdings: Bk Vols 11,500; Per Subs 75
Special Collections: Civil Engineering; Corps of Engineers History Coll; Environmental Resources; Hydraulics (Locks & Dams)
Subject Interests: Civil eng, Soil mechanics
Publications: Periodical Holding List
Mem of Reaching Across Illinois Library System (RAILS)
Partic in Dialog Corp; Lyrasis; OCLC Online Computer Library Center, Inc
Open Mon-Fri 8-4:30

S WESTERN ILLINOIS AREA AGENCY ON AGING*, Elderly Living & Learning Facility, 729 34th Ave, 61201. SAN 375-1775. Tel: 309-793-6800. FAX: 309-793-6807. Web Site: www.wiaaa.org.
Founded 1988
Library Holdings: Bk Titles 2,100; Per Subs 15
Subject Interests: Aging, Gerontology
Mem of Reaching Across Illinois Library System (RAILS)
Open Mon-Fri 8-12

ROCKFORD

M OSF SAINT ANTHONY MEDICAL CENTER*, Medical Library, 5666 E State St, 61108-2472. SAN 324-5969. Tel: 815-227-2558. FAX: 815-227-2904. E-mail: samc.library@osfhealthcare.org. Web Site: www.library.osfhealthcare.org. *Libr Dir,* Heather Klepitsch; E-mail: Heather.A.Klepitsch@osfhealthcare.org; *Med Librn,* Roberta Craig; E-mail: Roberta.J.Craig@osfhealthcare.org; *Libr Tech,* Mary (Mel) Finkbeiner; E-mail: Mary.E.Finkbeiner@osfhealthcare.org; Staff 3 (MLS 2, Non-MLS 1)
Oct 2013-Sept 2014 Income $159,870. Mats Exp $74,330, Books $17,960, Per/Ser (Incl. Access Fees) $55,520, Presv $850. Sal $70,940
Library Holdings: Bks on Deafness & Sign Lang 1; CDs 8; DVDs 10; e-books 225; e-journals 8,550; Electronic Media & Resources 25; Bk Titles 1,250; Bk Vols 1,295; Per Subs 83
Subject Interests: Clinical med, Healthcare admin, Nursing
Automation Activity & Vendor Info: (Acquisitions) Baker & Taylor; (Cataloging) EOS International; (Circulation) EOS International; (Course Reserve) EOS International; (ILL) OCLC; (OPAC) EOS International; (Serials) EOS International
Database Vendor: Blackwell, Cinahl, DynaMed, EBSCO Information Services, EBSCOhost, Elsevier, EOS International, Lexi-Comp, MD Consult, Medline, Micromedex, OCLC, OCLC ArticleFirst, OCLC FirstSearch, OCLC WebJunction, OCLC WorldShare Interlibrary Loan, OVID Technologies, PubMed, RefWorks, Sage, ScienceDirect, SerialsSolutions, STAT!Ref (Teton Data Systems), UpToDate, WebMD, Wiley
Wireless access
Publications: InTouch (Newsletter)
Mem of Reaching Across Illinois Library System (RAILS)
Partic in Health Sci Librn of Ill (HSLI); Illinois Library & Information Network; National Network of Libraries of Medicine Greater Midwest Region
Open Mon-Fri 8-4:30

C RASMUSSEN COLLEGE*, Rockford Campus Library, 6000 E State St, 4th Flr, 61108. Tel: 815-316-4800. FAX: 815-316-4801. *Librn,* Cynthia Reynolds; Tel: 815-316-4800, Ext 4841, E-mail: cynthia.reynolds@rasmussen.edu
Library Holdings: DVDs 100; Bk Vols 1,000; Per Subs 25
Open Mon-Thurs 9am-9:30pm, Fri 9-5, Sat 9-1

J ROCK VALLEY COLLEGE, Estelle M Black Library, 3301 N Mulford Rd, 61114. SAN 304-6052. Tel: 815-921-4615, 815-921-7821. Interlibrary Loan Service Tel: 815-921-4607. Reference Tel: 815-921-4619. Administration Tel: 815-921-4626. Toll Free Tel: 800-973-7821. FAX: 815-921-4629. E-mail: rvc-libref@rockvalleycollege.edu. Web Site: www.rockvalleycollege.edu/library. *Dir,* Dr Hsiao-Hung Lee; Tel: 815-921-4627, E-mail: H.Lee@rockvalleycollege.edu; *Archivist, Outreach Librn,* Steven Thompson; Tel: 815-921-4612, E-mail: S.Thompson@rockvalleycollege.edu; *Ref Librn,* Maria Figiel-Krueger; Tel: 815-921-4606, E-mail: M.Figiel-Krueger@rockvalleycollege.edu; *Syst Librn,* Yiluo Song; Tel: 815-921-4602, E-mail: Y.Song@rockvalleycollege.edu; *Tech Serv Librn,* Brent Eckert; Tel: 815-921-4604, E-mail: B.Eckert@rockvalleycollege.edu; *Access Serv Coordr,* Rebecca Whitlow; Tel: 815-921-4603, E-mail: R.Whitlow@rockvalleycollege.edu. Subject Specialists: *Archives,* Steven Thompson; Staff 6 (MLS 5, Non-MLS 1)
Founded 1965. Enrl 3,800; Fac 123; Highest Degree: Associate
Library Holdings: Audiobooks 1,828; AV Mats 10,903; CDs 5,102; DVDs 2,148; e-books 14,717; Bk Vols 91,326; Per Subs 459; Videos 2,208
Automation Activity & Vendor Info: (Acquisitions) Ex Libris Group; (Cataloging) Ex Libris Group; (Circulation) Ex Libris Group; (Course Reserve) Ex Libris Group; (ILL) OCLC; (OPAC) Ex Libris Group; (Serials) Ex Libris Group
Database Vendor: ABC-CLIO, Baker & Taylor, CredoReference, EBSCOhost, Gale Cengage Learning, JSTOR, LexisNexis, Micromedex, Newsbank, OCLC FirstSearch, OVID Technologies, Oxford Online, ProQuest, ScienceDirect, SerialsSolutions
Wireless access
Function: Accessibility serv available based on individual needs, Archival coll, Audio & video playback equip for onsite use, Bks on cassette, Bks on CD, CD-ROM, Computers for patron use, Copy machines, Electronic databases & coll, Handicapped accessible, ILL available, Music CDs, Online cat
Mem of Reaching Across Illinois Library System (RAILS)
Partic in Consortium of Academic & Research Libraries in Illinois; Illinois Library & Information Network; Network of Illinois Learning Resources in Community Colleges; OCLC Online Computer Library Center, Inc
Open Mon-Thurs 8am-9pm, Fri 8-5, Sat 8-1
Restriction: Open to pub for ref & circ; with some limitations, Open to students, fac & staff
Friends of the Library Group

S ROCKFORD INSTITUTE LIBRARY, 928 N Main St, 61103. SAN 377-4309. Tel: 815-964-5053. FAX: 815-964-9403. *Pres,* Thomas Piatak
Library Holdings: Bk Vols 400; Per Subs 30

M ROCKFORD MEMORIAL HOSPITAL*, Health Science Library, 2400 N Rockton Ave, 61103. SAN 321-9402. Tel: 815-971-6287. FAX: 815-968-7007. Web Site: www.insideweb/insideweb.htm. *Dir,* Amy Li; Tel: 815-971-6287, E-mail: ali@rhsnet.org; Staff 1 (MLS 1)
Founded 1974
Library Holdings: e-books 40; Bk Titles 3,000; Per Subs 150
Special Collections: Pediatrics (Hunter Memorial Coll)
Subject Interests: Med
Wireless access

Publications: Library Guide; New Acquisitions; Patient/Consumer Catalog
Mem of Reaching Across Illinois Library System (RAILS)
Open Mon-Fri 8-4:30

P ROCKFORD PUBLIC LIBRARY*, 215 N Wyman St, 61101-1023. SAN 340-7195. Tel: 815-965-7606. FAX: 815-965-0866. Web Site: www.rockfordpubliclibrary.org. *Exec Dir,* Lynn Stainbrook; *Asst Dir,* Fayrene Muhammad; E-mail: fmuhammad@rockfordpubliclibrary.org; *Chief Financial Officer,* Karen Mohr Powers; E-mail: kpowers@rockfordpubliclibrary.org; *Mgr, Ad Serv, Mgr, Youth Serv,* Jean Mangan; *Mgr, Circ Serv,* Erope Beckum; *Mgr Fac,* Donald Bergquist; *Mgr, Coll Mgt, Mgr, Info Tech,* Rose Peterson; *Asst Mgr, Adult Serv,* Amanda Gardner; *Asst Mgr, Circ,* Dunarene Hopson; *Develop Officer,* Renee Jensen; Staff 26 (MLS 18, Non-MLS 8)
Founded 1872. Pop 150,115; Circ 667,205
Library Holdings: Bk Titles 581,794; Bk Vols 437,929; Per Subs 20,553
Special Collections: Genealogy & Local History, bks, cemetery census, microtext
Subject Interests: Art & archit, Bus & mgt, Econ
Automation Activity & Vendor Info: (Circulation) SirsiDynix
Database Vendor: Innovative Interfaces, Inc
Wireless access
Publications: African Americans in Early Rockford; Confluence (Local historical information); That Men Know So Little of Men (Local Black History)
Mem of Reaching Across Illinois Library System (RAILS)
Special Services for the Deaf - Bks on deafness & sign lang; High interest/low vocabulary bks; TDD equip
Open Tues-Thurs Noon-8, Fri & Sat 10-6
Friends of the Library Group
Branches: 5
EAST, 6685 E State St, 61108, SAN 340-7268. Tel: 815-965-7606. FAX: 815-226-1538. *Br Mgr,* Sue Stevens
Founded 1986
Library Holdings: Bk Vols 27,773
Open Mon-Thurs Noon-8, Fri & Sat 10-6
LEWIS LEMON BRANCH, 1988 W Jefferson St, 61101-5671, SAN 375-6106. Tel: 815-965-7606, Ext 728. FAX: 815-962-4863. *Br Mgr,* Scharnae Walker; E-mail: swalker@rockfordpubliclibrary.org
Founded 1994
Open Mon-Fri 2-6
MONTAGUE, 1238 S Winnebago St, 61102-2944, SAN 340-7284. Tel: 815-965-7606, Ext 739. Administration Tel: 815-965-0866. FAX: 815-963-3264. Administration FAX: 815-987-6179. *Br Mgr,* Scharnae Black-Walker; Tel: 815-965-7606, E-mail: swalker@rockfordpubliclibrary.org
Founded 1923
Library Holdings: Bk Vols 17,560
Function: Homebound delivery serv
Open Tues-Thurs Noon-8, Fri 10-6
ROCK RIVER BRANCH, 3128 11th St, 61109-2202, SAN 340-7314. Tel: 815-965-7606, Ext 765. FAX: 815-398-1345. *Br Mgr,* Donna Hopson; E-mail: dhopson@rockfordpubliclibrary.org
Founded 1971
Library Holdings: Bk Vols 24,631
Open Tues-Thurs Noon-8, Fri 10-6
ROCKTON CENTRE, 3112 N Rockton Ave, 6110-2837, SAN 340-7349. Tel: 815-965-7606, Ext 778. FAX: 815-963-8855. *Br Mgr,* Donna Hopson; E-mail: dhopson@rockfordpubliclibrary.org
Founded 2000
Library Holdings: Bk Vols 26,554
Open Mon-Thurs 10-8, Fri & Sat 10-5

C ROCKFORD UNIVERSITY*, Howard Colman Library, 5050 E State St, 61108-2393. SAN 304-6079. Tel: 815-226-4000, 815-226-4035. Interlibrary Loan Service Tel: 815-394-5042. Reference Tel: 815-226-4165. FAX: 815-226-4084. Web Site: www.rockford.edu/library. *Actg Libr Dir,* Kelly James; E-mail: kjames@rockford.edu; *Circ Mgr,* Lori Erickson; *ILL Mgr,* Audrey Wilson; Staff 6 (MLS 2, Non-MLS 4)
Founded 1847. Enrl 1,200; Fac 62; Highest Degree: Master
Library Holdings: Bk Titles 122,277; Bk Vols 140,618; Per Subs 530
Special Collections: Jane Addams Coll
Automation Activity & Vendor Info: (Acquisitions) Innovative Interfaces, Inc; (Cataloging) Innovative Interfaces, Inc; (Circulation) Innovative Interfaces, Inc; (ILL) OCLC; (OPAC) Innovative Interfaces, Inc; (Serials) Innovative Interfaces, Inc
Database Vendor: EBSCOhost, Innovative Interfaces, Inc, LexisNexis, OCLC FirstSearch
Function: ILL available
Publications: Colman Lantern (Newsletter)
Mem of Reaching Across Illinois Library System (RAILS)
Partic in Consortium of Academic & Research Libraries in Illinois; Illinois Library & Information Network; OCLC Online Computer Library Center, Inc
Special Services for the Blind - Aids for in-house use
Open Mon-Fri 7:45am-11pm, Sat 1-5, Sun 1-11
Restriction: Borrowing privileges limited to fac & registered students
Friends of the Library Group

S SWEDISH HISTORICAL SOCIETY OF ROCKFORD*, Erlander Home Museum Library, 404 S Third St, 61104-2013. (Mail add: PO Box 5443, 61125-0443), SAN 375-0922. Tel: 815-963-5559. FAX: 815-963-5559. Web Site: www.swedishhistorical.org. *Pres,* Mike Lunde
Library Holdings: Bk Vols 2,000
Special Collections: Furniture Making in Rockford Coll; Swedish Immigration Coll. Oral History
Subject Interests: Immigration, Sweden
Publications: Swedish Heritage (Annual)
Restriction: Open by appt only

GL WINNEBAGO COUNTY LAW LIBRARY*, Courthouse Bldg, Ste 301, 61101-1221. SAN 304-6117. Tel: 815-319-4967. FAX: 815-319-4801. *Librn,* Brian L Buzard
Founded 1975
Library Holdings: Bk Vols 20,000; Per Subs 20
Special Collections: IICLE Handbooks; Illinois Law; Illinois Law School Law Reviews; ISBA Publications
Mem of Reaching Across Illinois Library System (RAILS)
Open Mon-Fri 8-5

ROCKTON

P TALCOTT FREE PUBLIC LIBRARY*, 101 E Main St, 61072. SAN 304-6125. Tel: 815-624-7511. FAX: 815-624-1176. Web Site: talcottfreelibrary.com. *Dir,* Bonnie Estrada
Founded 1888. Pop 13,534; Circ 115,000
Library Holdings: AV Mats 3,028; Large Print Bks 500; Bk Titles 46,500; Bk Vols 50,000; Per Subs 156; Talking Bks 2,568
Automation Activity & Vendor Info: (Cataloging) Innovative Interfaces, Inc; (Circulation) Innovative Interfaces, Inc; (OPAC) Innovative Interfaces, Inc
Database Vendor: Innovative Interfaces, Inc
Mem of Reaching Across Illinois Library System (RAILS)
Open Mon, Tues & Thurs 9-8, Wed & Fri 9-5:30, Sat 9-3
Friends of the Library Group

ROLLING MEADOWS

S NORTHROP GRUMMAN CORP*, Technical-Business Library, 600 Hicks Rd, MS M3300, 60008. SAN 376-0979. Tel: 224-625-4590. FAX: 224-625-5756. *Mgr,* Mary Crompton; Tel: 224-625-4592, E-mail: mary.crompton@ngc.com. Subject Specialists: *Aerospace, Defense, Eng,* Mary Crompton; Staff 1 (MLS 1)
Library Holdings: e-journals 12; Bk Titles 6,100; Bk Vols 7,000; Per Subs 212; Videos 15
Subject Interests: Aeronaut, Aviation, Electronics, Eng, Optics, Radar
Automation Activity & Vendor Info: (Cataloging) EOS International; (Circulation) EOS International; (OPAC) EOS International; (Serials) EOS International
Database Vendor: OCLC FirstSearch
Restriction: Co libr

P ROLLING MEADOWS LIBRARY*, 3110 Martin Lane, 60008. SAN 304-615X. Tel: 847-259-6050. FAX: 847-259-5319. Web Site: www.rmlib.org. *Exec Dir,* David C Ruff; E-mail: david.ruff@rmlib.org; *Asst Libr Dir, Dir, Youth Serv,* Lucia Khipple; E-mail: lucia.khipple@rmlib.org; *Dir of Circ,* Mary Sebela; E-mail: mary.sebela@rmlib.org; *Dir, Info Tech,* Patrick Graf; E-mail: patrick.graf@rmlib.org; *Dir, Reader Serv,* Mary Constance Back; E-mail: mary.back@rmlib.org; *Dir, Ref,* Jennifer Collette; E-mail: jennifer.collette@rmlib.org; *Spec Serv Dir,* Sharon Montague; E-mail: sharon.montague@rmlib.org; *Dir, Tech Serv,* Joyce Schweda; E-mail: joyce.schweda@rmlib.org; Staff 14.4 (MLS 9.9, Non-MLS 4.5)
Founded 1959. Pop 24,604; Circ 381,518
Jan 2008-Dec 2008 Income $3,625,785, State $104,668, City $3,418,959, Other $102,158. Mats Exp $435,471, Books $269,003, Other Print Mats $34,983, Micro $2,928, AV Mat $70,513, Electronic Ref Mat (Incl. Access Fees) $58,044. Sal $1,792,628
Library Holdings: Audiobooks 5,242; AV Mats 18,655; CDs 19,001; DVDs 11,864; Electronic Media & Resources 1; Bk Vols 166,812; Per Subs 581
Special Collections: Rolling Meadows History, photog
Automation Activity & Vendor Info: (Acquisitions) Baker & Taylor; (Cataloging) OCLC FirstSearch; (Circulation) Innovative Interfaces, Inc; (ILL) OCLC FirstSearch; (OPAC) Innovative Interfaces, Inc; (Serials) Innovative Interfaces, Inc
Function: Adult bk club, After school storytime, Art exhibits, Audiobks via web, Bi-weekly Writer's Group, Bilingual assistance for Spanish patrons, Bk club(s), Bk reviews (Group), Bks on cassette, Bks on CD, CD-ROM, Children's prog, Computer training, Computers for patron use,

Copy machines, e-mail serv, E-Reserves, Electronic databases & coll, Free DVD rentals, Games & aids for the handicapped, Handicapped accessible, Home delivery & serv to Sr ctr & nursing homes, Homebound delivery serv, ILL available, Jazz prog, Music CDs, Newsp ref libr, Online cat, Online ref, Online searches, Orientations, Outreach serv, Outside serv via phone, mail, e-mail & web, Photocopying/Printing, Preschool outreach, Prog for adults, Prog for children & young adult, Pub access computers, Senior computer classes, Spoken cassettes & CDs, Spoken cassettes & DVDs, Story hour, Summer reading prog, Tax forms, Telephone ref, Wheelchair accessible, Writing prog
Publications: They Took the Challenge: The Story of Rolling Meadows
Open Mon-Fri 9-9, Sat 9 5, Sun 1-5
Friends of the Library Group

ROMEOVILLE

CR LEWIS UNIVERSITY LIBRARY*, One University Pkwy, Unit 300, 60446-2200. SAN 340-7403. Tel: 815-836-5300. Interlibrary Loan Service Tel: 815-836-5678. Reference Tel: 815-836-5306. Administration Tel: 815-836-5015. Toll Free Tel: 800-897-9000. FAX: 815-838-9456. E-mail: reflib@lewisu.edu. Web Site: www.lewisu.edu/academics/library/index.htm. *Interim Co-Dir,* Mary Ann Atkins; E-mail: atkinsma@lewisu.edu; *Interim Co-Dir,* Jana Fast; *Head, Tech Serv,* Frederieke A Moskal; Tel: 815-836-5302, E-mail: moskalfr@lewisu.edu; *Ref/Govt Doc Librn,* Robert Pruter; Tel: 815-836-5664, E-mail: pruterro@lewisu.edu; *Circ Mgr,* Janet Dorencz; E-mail: dorencja@lewisu.edu; Staff 15 (MLS 10, Non-MLS 5)
Founded 1952. Enrl 5,000; Fac 169; Highest Degree: Doctorate
Library Holdings: Bk Vols 176,000; Per Subs 602
Special Collections: Contemporary Print Archives; I&M Canal Archives; Library of American Civilization, ultrafiche; Library of English Literatures, Part I & II, ultrafiche. US Document Depository
Subject Interests: Aviation, Bus & mgt, Nursing, Relig
Automation Activity & Vendor Info: (Acquisitions) Ex Libris Group; (Cataloging) Ex Libris Group; (Circulation) Ex Libris Group; (Course Reserve) Ex Libris Group; (ILL) Ex Libris Group; (OPAC) Ex Libris Group
Wireless access
Function: ILL available
Mem of Reaching Across Illinois Library System (RAILS)
Partic in Chicago & South Consortium; Consortium of Academic & Research Libraries in Illinois; Illinois Library & Information Network; LIBRAS, Inc; OCLC Online Computer Library Center, Inc

ROODHOUSE

P ROODHOUSE PUBLIC LIBRARY*, 220 W Franklin St, 62082-1412. SAN 304-6176. Tel: 217-589-5123. FAX: 217-589-5412. E-mail: rhe1926@gmail.com. Web Site: roodhouselibrary.org. *Dir & Librn,* Beth Huffines; *Asst Librn,* Carole Wells
Founded 1926. Pop 2,214; Circ 8,195
Library Holdings: Bk Vols 14,782; Per Subs 45
Mem of Illinois Heartland Library System
Open Mon-Fri 1-6, Sat 9-Noon

ROSELLE

P ROSELLE PUBLIC LIBRARY DISTRICT, 40 S Park St, 60172-2020. SAN 304-6184. Tel: 630-529-1641. Circulation Tel: 630-529-1641, Ext 222. Reference Tel: 630-529-1641, Ext 211. Administration Tel: 630-529-1641, Ext 311. FAX: 630-529-7579. TDD: 630-529-0394. Web Site: www.roselle.lib.il.us. *Exec Dir,* Amy Cawley; E-mail: acawley@roselle.lib.il.us; *Head, Circ,* Christy Snyders; Tel: 630-529-1641, Ext 221, E-mail: csnyders@roselle.lib.il.us; *Head, Ref & Adult Serv,* Marcia Bose; Tel: 630-529-1641, Ext 212; *Automation Coordr, Head, Tech Serv,* Lynn Dennis; Tel: 630-529-1641, Ext 241, E-mail: ldennis@roselle.lib.il.us; Staff 31 (MLS 4, Non-MLS 27)
Founded 1940. Pop 24,579
Library Holdings: CDs 498; DVDs 4,089; Electronic Media & Resources 12; Bk Vols 96,811; Per Subs 248; Talking Bks 4,753; Videos 4,089
Automation Activity & Vendor Info: (OPAC) TLC (The Library Corporation); (Serials) EBSCO Online
Database Vendor: EBSCOhost, Gale Cengage Learning, Grolier Online, OCLC FirstSearch, OCLC WorldShare Interlibrary Loan, ProQuest, TLC (The Library Corporation)
Wireless access
Publications: Library Lights (Newsletter)
Mem of Reaching Across Illinois Library System (RAILS)
Open Mon-Thurs 9:30-9, Fri & Sat 9:30-5, Sun 1-5
Friends of the Library Group

ROSICLARE

P ROSICLARE MEMORIAL PUBLIC LIBRARY*, Main St, 62982. (Mail add: PO Box 10, 62982). Tel: 618-285-6213. FAX: 618-285-6213. E-mail: rosilib@shawneelink.net. *Librn,* Judy Largent; Staff 2 (Non-MLS 2)
Founded 1936. Pop 1,213; Circ 4,335
Library Holdings: Bk Vols 12,497; Per Subs 27
Mem of Illinois Heartland Library System
Open Mon & Tues 12-6, Thurs & Fri 12-5, Sat 10-1

ROUND LAKE

P ROUND LAKE AREA PUBLIC LIBRARY DISTRICT*, 906 Hart Rd, 60073. SAN 304-6214. Tel: 847-546-7060. FAX: 847-546-7104. TDD: 847-546-7064. Web Site: www.rlalibrary.org. *Exec Dir,* James A DiDonato; Tel: 847-546-7060, Ext 127, E-mail: jdidonato@rlalibrary.org; *Head, Adult Serv,* Rich Erikson; Tel: 847-546-7060, Ext 123, E mail: rerikson@rlalibrary.org; *Head, Circ,* Margarita Rodriguez; Tel: 847-546-7060, Ext 115, E-mail: mrodriguez@rlalibrary.org; *Head, Outreach Serv,* Elena Lara; Tel: 847-546-7060, Ext 122, E-mail: elara@rlalibrary.org; *Head, Tech Serv,* Penny McMahon; Tel: 847-546-7060, Ext 116, E-mail: pmcmahon@rlalibrary.org; *Head, Tech,* John Haliotis; E-mail: jhaliotis@rlalibrary.org; *Head, Youth Serv,* Debbie Allen; Tel: 847-546-7060, Ext 129, E-mail: dallen@rlalibrary.org; *Admin Mgr,* Robbyn Allbee; Tel: 847-546-7060, Ext 105, E-mail: rallbee@rlalibrary.org; Staff 14 (MLS 8, Non-MLS 6)
Founded 1972. Pop 40,400; Circ 370,000
Library Holdings: AV Mats 18,000; Electronic Media & Resources 36; Bk Vols 52,000; Per Subs 200
Subject Interests: Spanish lang mat
Automation Activity & Vendor Info: (Acquisitions) SirsiDynix; (Cataloging) SirsiDynix; (Circulation) SirsiDynix; (ILL) OCLC; (OPAC) SirsiDynix; (Serials) SirsiDynix
Database Vendor: Baker & Taylor, BWI, Gale Cengage Learning, Grolier Online, Ingram Library Services, Medline, OCLC FirstSearch, OCLC WorldShare Interlibrary Loan, PubMed, ReferenceUSA, SirsiDynix
Wireless access
Publications: Paige Turner (Newsletter)
Partic in Cooperative Computer Services - CCS
Special Services for the Deaf - TDD equip; TTY equip
Special Services for the Blind - Assistive/Adapted tech devices, equip & products; Closed circuit TV; Home delivery serv; Magnifiers; PC for handicapped; Screen enlargement software for people with visual disabilities
Open Mon-Thurs 9-8, Fri & Sat 9-5, Sun 12-4
Friends of the Library Group

ROXANA

P ROXANA PUBLIC LIBRARY DISTRICT*, 200 N Central Ave, 62084-1102. SAN 304-6230. Tel. 618-254-6713. FAX: 618-254-6904. E-mail: library@roxanalibrary.org. Web Site: www.roxanalibrary.org. *Dir,* Jamie Morgan; Staff 8 (MLS 1, Non-MLS 7)
Founded 1941. Pop 1,562; Circ 31,306
Library Holdings: Bks on Deafness & Sign Lang 25; Bk Vols 26,779; Per Subs 71
Special Collections: Newbery & Caldicott Award Books; Reading Rainbow
Automation Activity & Vendor Info: (Cataloging) SirsiDynix; (Circulation) SirsiDynix; (OPAC) SirsiDynix
Database Vendor: Dialog, EBSCOhost, OCLC FirstSearch, SirsiDynix
Publications: Newsletter (Bi-annually)
Mem of Illinois Heartland Library System
Open Mon-Thurs 10-8, Fri & Sat 10-5

ROYALTON

P ROYALTON PUBLIC LIBRARY DISTRICT*, 305 South Dean St, 62983. (Mail add: PO Box 460, 62983-0460). Tel: 618-984-4463. FAX: 618-984-4463. Web Site: www.royaltonillinois.com/library.html. *Librn,* Bill McPhail; Staff 1 (Non-MLS 1)
Founded 1986. Pop 1,130; Circ 598
Jul 2006-Jun 2007 Income $19,500, State $1,500, County $13,000, Locally Generated Income $5,000. Mats Exp $2,100, Books $1,000, Per/Ser (Incl. Access Fees) $100, Electronic Ref Mat (Incl. Access Fees) $1,000. Sal $6,500
Library Holdings: AV Mats 50; CDs 110; Bk Titles 3,893; Per Subs 15; Videos 40
Wireless access
Mem of Illinois Heartland Library System
Open Mon, Wed & Fri 9-12 & 1-5

RUSHVILLE

P RUSHVILLE PUBLIC LIBRARY*, 104 N Monroe St, 62681-1364. SAN 304-6249. Tel: 217-322-3030. FAX: 217-322-3030. E-mail: library1@adams.net. Web Site: www.rushville.lib.il.us/library. *Dir,* Charlene Copeland; *Asst Librn,* Sandy Bullard; *Asst Librn,* Effie Snyder; Staff 3 (MLS 1, Non-MLS 2)
Founded 1878. Pop 3,212; Circ 30,646
Library Holdings: Bk Titles 20,000; Per Subs 74

Special Services for the Deaf - Bks on deafness & sign lang
Open Mon-Thurs 1-7, Fri 10-6, Sat 9-1

SAINT CHARLES

R BETHLEHEM LUTHERAN CHURCH LIBRARY*, 1145 N Fifth Ave, 60174-1230. (Mail add: PO Box 3850, 60174-9085), SAN 304-6265. Tel: 630-584-2199. FAX: 630-584-2674. E-mail: office@bethlehemluth.org. Web Site: www.bethlehemluth.org. *Dir,* Donna Blomquist; *Librn,* Theresa Meyer
Founded 1957
Library Holdings: Bk Titles 2,000; Per Subs 20
Open Mon-Fri 8-5

S ILLINOIS YOUTH CENTER*, Saint Charles Library, 3825 Campton Hills Rd, 60175. SAN 376-0448. Tel: 630-584-0506, Ext 284. FAX: 630-584-1126. *Librn,* Richard Fryer
Library Holdings: Bk Titles 12,000; Per Subs 14
Restriction: Staff & inmates only

P ST CHARLES PUBLIC LIBRARY DISTRICT, One S Sixth Ave, 60174-2105. SAN 304-6281. Tel: 630-584-0076. FAX: 630-584-3448. Administration FAX: 630-584-9262. E-mail: adultref@stcharleslibrary.org. Web Site: www.stcharleslibrary.org. *Dir,* Leffler M Pam; Tel: 630-584-0076, Ext 228, E-mail: pleffler@stcharleslibrary.org; *Asst Dir,* Bryan A Wood; Tel: 630-584-0076, Ext 227, E-mail: bwood@stcharleslibrary.org; *Coll Mgt Librn,* Sue Pfotenhauer; Tel: 630-584-0076, Ext 220, E-mail: spfotenhauer@stcharleslibrary.org; *Reader Serv Librn,* Marlise Schiltz; *YA Librn,* Marianne Weick; Tel: 630-584-0076, Ext 223; *Youth Serv Librn,* Michele Collette; Tel: 630-584-0076, Ext 235; *Youth Serv Librn,* Valerie Verscaj; Tel: 630-584-0076, Ext 207; *Circ Serv Mgr,* Bonni Ellis; Tel: 630-584-0076, Ext 257; *Outreach & Develop Mgr,* David Kelsey; Tel: 630-584-0076, Ext 219; *Ref Mgr,* Heidi Krueger; Tel: 630-584-0076, Ext 256; *Tech Serv Mgr,* Myung Sung; Tel: 630-584-0076, Ext 237, E-mail: msung@stcharleslibrary.org; *Youth Serv Mgr,* A Denise Farrugia; Tel: 630-584-0076, Ext 236; *Pub Info Officer,* Oam Salomone; Tel: 630-584-0076, Ext 246; Staff 25 (MLS 23, Non-MLS 2)
Founded 1906. Pop 47,855; Circ 1,491,873
Library Holdings: AV Mats 64,523; e-books 16,524; Bk Titles 276,362; Bk Vols 277,362; Per Subs 998
Special Collections: Adult New Reader Colls; Municipal
Subject Interests: Genealogy
Automation Activity & Vendor Info: (Acquisitions) SirsiDynix; (Cataloging) SirsiDynix; (Circulation) SirsiDynix; (ILL) SirsiDynix; (OPAC) SirsiDynix; (Serials) SirsiDynix
Wireless access
Publications: A Step Up: From Readers to Chapter Books; Action Rhymes
Mem of Reaching Across Illinois Library System (RAILS)
Partic in Libr Integrated Network Consortium; OCLC Online Computer Library Center, Inc
Special Services for the Deaf - TDD equip
Special Services for the Blind - Closed circuit TV
Open Mon-Thurs 9-9, Fri 9-8, Sat 9-5, Sun 12-5
Friends of the Library Group

SAINT ELMO

P SAINT ELMO PUBLIC LIBRARY DISTRICT*, 311 W Cumberland Rd, 62458. SAN 304-629X. Tel: 618-829-5544. FAX: 618-829-9104. Web Site: www.stelmolibrary.org. *Dir,* Terri Gillespie; *Librn,* Billie Enlow
Founded 1948. Pop 5,600; Circ 24,750
Library Holdings: Bk Vols 30,000; Per Subs 40
Wireless access
Function: Adult literacy prog
Mem of Illinois Heartland Library System
Open Mon 12-7, Tues, Wed & Fri 12-5, Thurs 4-7, Sat 10-2
Friends of the Library Group
Branches: 1
BEECHER CITY BRANCH, 108 N James St, Beecher City, 62414. Tel: 618-487-9400. *Dir,* Terri Gillespie; *Librn,* Jo An M Evans; *Librn,* Nola Larimore
Library Holdings: Bk Vols 8,000; Per Subs 15
Open Mon 12:30-7, Tues, Wed & Fri 12-5, Thurs 3:30-7, Sat 9:30-1:30

SAINT JOSEPH

P ST JOSEPH TOWNSHIP-SWEARINGEN MEMORIAL LIBRARY, 201 N Third, 61873. (Mail add: PO Box 259, 61873-0259), SAN 304-6303. Tel: 217-469-2159. FAX: 217-469-2159. E-mail: stjosephtownshiplibrary@gmail.com. Web Site: www.stjosephtownshiplibrary.info. *Librn,* Susan Dawn McKinney; E-mail: smckin@gmail.com; Staff 6 (MLS 1, Non-MLS 5)
Founded 1929. Pop 5,876; Circ 36,248
Apr 2013-Mar 2014 Income $138,739. Mats Exp $28,372, Books $16,000, Per/Ser (Incl. Access Fees) $1,000, AV Mat $9,239, Electronic Ref Mat (Incl. Access Fees) $2,133. Sal $85,748 (Prof $38,736)
Library Holdings: Audiobooks 1,480; CDs 430; DVDs 1,163; e-books 21,125; Large Print Bks 1,297; Bk Vols 24,872; Per Subs 62; Videos 101
Automation Activity & Vendor Info: (Acquisitions) Innovative Interfaces, Inc; (Cataloging) Innovative Interfaces, Inc; (Circulation) Innovative Interfaces, Inc; (ILL) Innovative Interfaces, Inc; (Serials) Innovative Interfaces, Inc
Database Vendor: 3M Library Systems, OCLC FirstSearch, Overdrive, Inc
Wireless access
Function: 24/7 Online cat, Activity rm, Adult bk club, Audiobks via web, AV serv, Bks on cassette, Bks on CD, Children's prog, Computers for patron use, Copy machines, e-mail serv, Electronic databases & coll, Fax serv, Free DVD rentals, Handicapped accessible, Homebound delivery serv, ILL available, Instruction & testing, Magazines, Mango lang, Movies, Music CDs, Online cat, Online searches, OverDrive digital audio bks, Photocopying/Printing, Prog for adults, Prog for children & young adult, Ref serv available, Ref serv in person, Scanner, Spoken cassettes & CDs, Spoken cassettes & DVDs, Story hour, Summer reading prog, Tax forms, Teen prog, Telephone ref, VHS videos, Wheelchair accessible
Mem of Illinois Heartland Library System
Special Services for the Deaf - Bks on deafness & sign lang; Sign lang interpreter upon request for prog
Special Services for the Blind - Bks on cassette; Bks on CD; Cassettes; Copier with enlargement capabilities; Extensive large print coll; Free checkout of audio mat; Home delivery serv; Large print bks
Open Mon & Wed 1-8, Tues & Thurs 9-6, Fri 9-7, Sat 9-3

SALEM

P BRYAN-BENNETT LIBRARY, 315 S Maple, 62881. (Mail add: PO Box 864, 62881), SAN 304-6311. Tel: 618-548-3006. FAX: 618-548-3096. Web Site: www.salembbl.lib.il.us. *Dir,* Kim Keller
Founded 1909. Pop 7,909; Circ 48,567
Library Holdings: Bk Vols 30,000; Per Subs 28
Automation Activity & Vendor Info: (Acquisitions) SirsiDynix; (Cataloging) SirsiDynix; (Circulation) SirsiDynix; (Serials) SirsiDynix
Wireless access
Mem of Illinois Heartland Library System
Open Mon-Thurs 12-8, Fri & Sat 9-2
Friends of the Library Group

SANDWICH

P SANDWICH PUBLIC LIBRARY DISTRICT, 925 S Main St, 60548-2304. SAN 304-632X. Tel: 815-786-8308. FAX: 815-786-9231. E-mail: contact@sandwichpld.org. Web Site: www.sandwichpld.org. *Dir,* Sarah Horn; E-mail: horns@sandwichpld.org; Staff 8 (MLS 1, Non-MLS 7)
Founded 1926. Pop 7,401; Circ 54,469
Library Holdings: AV Mats 1,250; CDs 624; DVDs 285; e-books 1,600; High Interest/Low Vocabulary Bk Vols 506; Large Print Bks 800; Bk Vols 29,377; Per Subs 88; Videos 953
Special Collections: Local Newspaper, 1878-present, microfilm
Automation Activity & Vendor Info: (Cataloging) SirsiDynix; (Circulation) SirsiDynix; (OPAC) SirsiDynix
Database Vendor: SirsiDynix
Wireless access
Function: Adult literacy prog, After school storytime, Copy machines, Fax serv, Home delivery & serv to Sr ctr & nursing homes, ILL available, Prog for children & young adult, Summer reading prog, Tax forms
Mem of Reaching Across Illinois Library System (RAILS)
Partic in Heritage Automated Libraries (HAL)
Open Mon-Thurs 10-8, Fri 10-6, Sat 10-4
Friends of the Library Group

SAUK VILLAGE

P NANCY L MCCONATHY PUBLIC LIBRARY*, 21737 Jeffery Ave, 60411. SAN 304-6338. Tel: 708-757-4771. Interlibrary Loan Service Tel: 708-757-4788. FAX: 708-757-3580. Web Site: www.at-the-library.org. *Dir,* Nanette Festa Wargo
Founded 1973. Pop 11,859; Circ 66,428
Library Holdings: Bk Vols 33,000; Per Subs 89
Special Collections: Cookbooks; Motion Picture Stars Biography
Mem of Reaching Across Illinois Library System (RAILS)
Open Mon-Thurs 9:30-6:50, Fri & Sat 9:30-3:50

SAVANNA

P SAVANNA PUBLIC LIBRARY DISTRICT*, 326 Third St, 61074. SAN 304-6346. Tel: 815-273-3714. FAX: 815-273-4634. E-mail: savpublib@mchsi.com. *Librn,* Mary Meyers; Staff 4 (Non-MLS 4)
Founded 1896. Pop 4,353; Circ 11,832
Library Holdings: Bk Vols 15,581; Per Subs 50
Special Collections: Savanna Times Journal, microfilm

Mem of Reaching Across Illinois Library System (RAILS)
Open Mon & Tues 1-7, Wed 10-5, Fri 1-5, Sat 9-1
Friends of the Library Group

SAYBROOK

P CHENEY'S GROVE TOWNSHIP LIBRARY*, 204 S State St, 61770. (Mail add: PO Box 58, 61770-0058), SAN 376-7817. Tel: 309-475-6131. FAX: 309-475-6131. Web Site: www.saybrook-il.com. *Librn,* Barb Lewis
Library Holdings: Audiobooks 140; Bks on Deafness & Sign Lang 3; Braille Volumes 1; CDs 98; Large Print Bks 450; Microforms 40; Bk Vols 15,000; Per Subs 10; Spec Interest Per Sub 7; Videos 430
Special Collections: Area Family History; Arrowsmith Newspapers 1920-1965, micro; Coins Coll; First Issue Stamps; Saybrook Newspapers 1890s-1985, micro; Township & Town History, photog; WWII Scrapbooks. Municipal Document Depository
Open Tues, Wed & Fri (Summer) 1-5, Thurs 6-8, Sat 9-12; Tues, Wed & Fri (Winter) 9:30-5:30, Thurs 6-8, Sat 9-12

SCHAUMBURG

M AMERICAN VETERINARY MEDICAL ASSOCIATION LIBRARY, 1931 N Meacham Rd, 90173-4360. Tel: 847-925-8070, Ext 6770. Toll Free Tel: 800-248-2862, Ext 6770. FAX: 847-925-9329. *Librn/Copyright & Permissions/Archives Electronic Access,* Diane A Fagen; E-mail: dfagen@avma.org. Subject Specialists: *Animal welfare, Food safety, Veterinary,* Diane A Fagen
Founded 1863
Library Holdings: AV Mats 634; DVDs 138; Bk Titles 8,524; Bk Vols 8,602; Per Subs 710; Spec Interest Per Sub 703; Videos 125
Special Collections: Veterinary History, 1877-present. Oral History
Subject Interests: Pub health, Veterinary
Wireless access
Function: Archival coll, e-mail serv, Health sci info serv, Outside serv via phone, mail, e-mail & web, Ref serv available, Res libr
Open Mon-Fri 8-4
Restriction: Authorized personnel only, Authorized scholars by appt, Borrowing requests are handled by ILL, By permission only, Circ limited, External users must contact libr, In-house use for visitors, Non-circulating of rare bks, Not a lending libr, Private libr, Pub ref by request

C ILLINOIS INSTITUTE OF ART*, Learning Resource Center, 1000 Plaza Dr, Ste 100, 60173-4990. SAN 372-5898. Tel: 847-619-3450. Toll Free Tel: 800-314-3450. FAX: 847-619-3064. Web Site: www.ilia.aii.edu. *Librn,* Rich Wilson; Staff 2 (MLS 2)
Founded 1986. Enrl 990; Fac 60; Highest Degree: Bachelor
Library Holdings: Bk Titles 6,020; Bk Vols 9,000; Per Subs 175
Subject Interests: Applied arts
Automation Activity & Vendor Info: (OPAC) Follett Software
Open Mon-Thurs 8am-10pm, Fri 8-5, Sat 8:30-3:30

S MOTOROLA, INC*, Research & Technical Library, 1301 E Algonquin Rd, Rm 1914, 60196-1078. SAN 304-6354. Tel: 847-576-8580. FAX: 847-576-4716. *Info Spec,* Nancy Snyder; Staff 3 (MLS 1, Non-MLS 2)
Founded 1978
Library Holdings: Bk Titles 9,800; Bk Vols 10,000; Per Subs 100
Special Collections: Communications Coll
Subject Interests: Electronics
Database Vendor: OCLC FirstSearch, ProQuest, SirsiDynix
Wireless access
Function: ILL available
Publications: Acquisitions; dissertations; journals; technical reports
Open Mon-Fri 9-4:30

P SCHAUMBURG TOWNSHIP DISTRICT LIBRARY*, 130 S Roselle Rd, 60193. SAN 340-7438. Tel: 847-985-4000. Circulation Tel: 847-923-3386. Interlibrary Loan Service Tel: 847-923-3349. Reference Tel: 847-923-3322. FAX: 847-923-3131. Web Site: www.schaumburglibrary.org. *Exec Dir,* Stephanie Sarnoff; Tel: 847-923-3200; *Dir, Popular Serv,* Judy Napier; Tel: 847-923-3180, Fax: 847-923-3188, E-mail: jnapier@stdl.org; *Dir, Ref,* Nelly Somerman; Tel: 847-923-3326, Fax: 847-923-3335, E-mail: nsomerman@stdl.org; *Dir, Youth Serv,* Melissa Jones; Tel: 847-923-3427, E-mail: mjones@stdl.org; *Head, Access Serv,* Victoria Akinde; Tel: 847-923-3227, E-mail: vakinde@stdl.org; *Adult Coll Develop Librn,* Suzanne Boudreau; Tel: 847-923-3336, E-mail: sboudreau@stdl.org; *ILL,* Linda Merkel; Tel: 847-923-3341, Fax: 847-923-3342, E-mail: lmerkel@stdl.org; *Online Serv,* Kristin Moo; Tel: 847-923-3328, E-mail: kmoo@stdl.org; Staff 174.42 (MLS 29.65, Non-MLS 144.77)
Founded 1963. Pop 126,849; Circ 2,342,000
Jul 2012-Jun 2013 Income (Main Library and Branch(s)) $15,534,211, State $129,598, Federal $19,023, Locally Generated Income $14,705,771, Other $679,819. Mats Exp $1,729,105, Books $954,155, AV Mat $287,600, Electronic Ref Mat (Incl. Access Fees) $487,350. Sal $9,266,321
Library Holdings: Audiobooks 68,171; DVDs 48,063; e-books 73,358; Bk Vols 448,002; Per Subs 939
Special Collections: Citizenship; English as a Second Language; Local History; World Languages
Automation Activity & Vendor Info: (Acquisitions) SIRSI WorkFlows; (Cataloging) SIRSI WorkFlows; (Circulation) SIRSI-iBistro; (OPAC) SirsiDynix
Wireless access
Special Services for the Deaf - Spec interest per
Special Services for the Blind - BiFolkal kits; Computer with voice synthesizer for visually impaired persons; Home delivery serv; Large print bks; Large screen computer & software; Lending of low vision aids; Low vision equip; Magnifiers; PC for handicapped; Playaways (bks on MP3)
Open Mon-Fri 9-10, Sat 10-5, Sun 12-9
Restriction: Access at librarian's discretion
Friends of the Library Group
Branches: 2
HANOVER PARK BRANCH, 1266 Irving Park Rd, Hanover Park, 60133, SAN 373-7136. Tel: 630-372-7800. FAX: 847-923-3488. *Br Coordr,* Gail Tobin; Tel: 847-923-3470; Staff 1 (MLS 1)
Library Holdings: AV Mats 4,406; Bk Titles 14,298
Open Mon-Thurs 10-9, Fri 10-5
HOFFMAN ESTATES BRANCH, 1550 Hassell Rd, Hoffman Estates, 60169, SAN 340-7462. Tel: 847-885-3511. FAX: 847-923-3466. *Br Coordr,* Jane Davey; Tel: 847-923-3456; Staff 1 (MLS 1)
Library Holdings: AV Mats 10,332; Bk Titles 29,276
Open Mon-Thurs 10-9, Fri & Sat 10-5
Friends of the Library Group

S SOCIETY OF ACTUARIES LIBRARY*, 475 N Martingale Rd, Ste 600, 60173-2226. SAN 329-2266. Tel: 847-706-3500. FAX: 847-706-3599. Web Site: www.soa.org. *Librn,* Ellen Bull; Staff 1 (MLS 1)
Founded 1949
Library Holdings: Bk Titles 1,650; Per Subs 60
Subject Interests: Actuarial sci, Employee benefits, Health ins, Life ins, Math
Partic in Chicago Association of Law Libraries (CALL); OCLC Online Computer Library Center, Inc; SLA

SCHILLER PARK

P SCHILLER PARK PUBLIC LIBRARY*, 4200 Old River Rd, 60176-1699. SAN 304-6362. Tel: 847-678-0433. FAX: 847-678-0567. Web Site: www.schillerparklibrary.org. *Dir,* Tina J Setzer; E-mail: tsetzer@ameritech.net
Founded 1962. Pop 11,189; Circ 59,594
Library Holdings: Bk Vols 80,000; Per Subs 150
Automation Activity & Vendor Info: (Circulation) Innovative Interfaces, Inc
Publications: Schiller Park Library PEN
Mem of Reaching Across Illinois Library System (RAILS)
Open Mon-Thurs 9-9, Fri-Sat 9-5, Sun (Sept-April) 1-5

SCOTT AFB

A UNITED STATES AIR FORCE, Scott Air Force Base Library FL4407, 375 FSS/FSDL, 510 Ward Dr, 62225-5360. SAN 340-7551. Tel: 618-256-5100. Interlibrary Loan Service Tel: 618-256-3028. FAX: 618-256-4558. E-mail: 375FSS.Library@us.af.mil. Web Site: www.375fss.com/scott_library.htm. *Libr Dir,* Tamela Smith; E-mail: tamela.smith.1@af.us.mil; Staff 2 (MLS 2)
Founded 1954
Library Holdings: Audiobooks 1,400; DVDs 3,300; Bk Vols 30,000; Per Subs 50
Special Collections: Professional Military Education Coll; Veteran Literacy Coll
Subject Interests: Mil hist
Wireless access
Function: Adult bk club, After school storytime, Art exhibits, Audio & video playback equip for onsite use, Bks on CD, CD-ROM, Children's prog, Computers for patron use, Copy machines, Doc delivery serv, Fax serv, Free DVD rentals, Govt ref serv, Handicapped accessible, ILL available, Music CDs, Online cat, Online ref, Online searches, Orientations, Outside serv via phone, mail, e-mail & web, OverDrive digital audio bks, Preschool outreach, Prof lending libr, Prog for adults, Prog for children & young adult, Pub access computers, Ref serv available, Scanner, Story hour, Summer reading prog, Tax forms, Teen prog, VHS videos, Wheelchair accessible
Open Mon-Thurs 10-8, Fri & Sat 9:30-5

SENECA

P SENECA PUBLIC LIBRARY DISTRICT*, 210 N Main St, 61360. SAN 304-6370. Tel: 815-357-6566. FAX: 815-357-6568. Web Site: www.senecalibrary.net. *Dir,* Margie Nolan; E-mail: mnolan@senecalibrary.net; *Adult Serv, Cat,* Jennifer Bilyeu; *Adult Serv, ILL,* Bonnie Anderson; *Cat, YA Serv,* Michelle Lawruk; *Children's Prog,*

Circ, Ruthanne Heaton; *Circ Serv,* Karen Einhaus; *Circ,* Ruth Ann Foehringer
Founded 1938. Pop 3,843; Circ 57,250
Library Holdings: CDs 1,473; DVDs 1,845; Large Print Bks 1,247; Bk Vols 51,330; Per Subs 120; Talking Bks 1,081; Videos 942
Special Collections: Seneca LST Shipyard Coll; WW II Coll
Automation Activity & Vendor Info: (Acquisitions) PALS; (Cataloging) SirsiDynix; (Circulation) SirsiDynix
Database Vendor: Baker & Taylor, OCLC FirstSearch, ProQuest, SirsiDynix
Wireless access
Function: Adult bk club, Audiobks via web, Bk club(s), Bks on cassette, Bks on CD, Children's prog, Computers for patron use, Copy machines, Digital talking bks, Fax serv, Free DVD rentals, Handicapped accessible, ILL available, Music CDs, Notary serv, Online cat, Online searches, Photocopying/Printing, Prog for adults, Prog for children & young adult, Pub access computers, Spoken cassettes & CDs, Story hour, Summer reading prog, Tax forms, Teen prog, Telephone ref, VHS videos, Wheelchair accessible
Publications: Seneca Library Newsletter (Bi-monthly)
Mem of Reaching Across Illinois Library System (RAILS)
Open Mon-Thurs 9-8, Fri 9-6, Sat 9-5

SESSER

P SESSER PUBLIC LIBRARY*, 303 W Franklin St, 62884. (Mail add: PO Box 538, 62884-0538), SAN 376-1274. Tel: 618-625-6566. FAX: 618-625-6566. E-mail: sesser@dtnspeed.net. Web Site: www.sesser.org/library.htm. *Librn,* Lowanda Johnston
Founded 1983
Library Holdings: AV Mats 45; Bk Titles 8,860; Videos 36
Mem of Illinois Heartland Library System
Open Mon-Fri (Winter) 1-5, Sat 9-12; Mon-Fri (Summer) 10-12 & 1-5, Sat 9-12

SHABBONA

P FLEWELLIN MEMORIAL LIBRARY*, 108 W Comanche Ave, 60550. (Mail add: PO Box 190, 60550-0190), SAN 304-6389. Tel: 815-824-2079. FAX: 815-824-2708. Web Site: www.shabbonalibrary.com. *Dir,* Vicki Bray
Pop 950; Circ 16,000
Library Holdings: Bk Vols 10,000; Per Subs 80
Special Collections: Chief Shabbona Coll
Automation Activity & Vendor Info: (Cataloging) Follett Software; (Circulation) Follett Software
Mem of Reaching Across Illinois Library System (RAILS)
Open Mon 4-8, Tues, Thurs & Fri 6-8:30, Wed 3-7:30, Sat 9-1

SHAWNEETOWN

P SHAWNEETOWN PUBLIC LIBRARY*, 320 N Lincoln Blvd E, 62984. (Mail add: PO Box 972, 62984-0972), SAN 304-6397. Tel: 618-269-3761. FAX: 618-269-3761. E-mail: shawls.lib.il.us@clearwave.com. *Dir,* Brenda Wood
Founded 1968. Pop 1,575; Circ 10,000
Library Holdings: Large Print Bks 560; Bk Vols 3,500; Per Subs 12
Subject Interests: Genealogy
Wireless access
Mem of Illinois Heartland Library System
Open Tues & Fri 10-12 & 1-5, Wed 1-5, Thurs 12-6, Sat 8-12

SHEFFIELD

P SHEFFIELD PUBLIC LIBRARY*, 136 E Cook St, 61361. SAN 304-6400. Tel: 815-454-2628. FAX: 815-454-2628. E-mail: sheffieldlib@yahoo.com. *Dir,* Tami Pettis
Founded 1896. Pop 946; Circ 3,120
Library Holdings: Bk Vols 10,300; Per Subs 29
Special Collections: Lincoln
Subject Interests: Hist
Function: Children's prog, Copy machines, Fax serv, Homebound delivery serv, ILL available, Magnifiers for reading, Mail & tel request accepted, Online searches, Photocopying/Printing, Spoken cassettes & CDs, Summer reading prog, Telephone ref, VHS videos, Video lending libr
Mem of Reaching Across Illinois Library System (RAILS)
Open Mon & Wed 1-7, Tues 9-5, Fri 1-5, Sat 9-12

SHELBYVILLE

P SHELBYVILLE FREE PUBLIC LIBRARY*, 154 N Broadway St, 62565-1698. SAN 304-6419. Tel: 217-774-4432. FAX: 217-774-2634. Web Site: shelbyville.lib.il.us. *Dir,* Shelley Koehler; *Asst Librn,* Nancy Pesch; *Asst Librn,* Pat Robertson
Founded 1902. Pop 5,259; Circ 68,219
Library Holdings: Bk Vols 28,000
Special Collections: 144 rolls of local & misc newspapers on microfilm dating 1812 to present
Subject Interests: Annual reports, Genealogy, Hist, Rare bks
Mem of Illinois Heartland Library System
Partic in Illinois Library & Information Network
Open Mon-Fri 9-7, Sat 9-1

SHELDON

P SHELDON PUBLIC LIBRARY DISTRICT*, 125 N Fifth, 60966. (Mail add: PO Box 370, 60966-0370), SAN 304-6427. Tel: 815-429-3521. FAX: 815-429-3804. *Dir,* Tammy Rice; E-mail: tamzr@hotmail.com
Founded 1917. Pop 2,082; Circ 5,339
Library Holdings: Bk Vols 12,151; Per Subs 30
Mem of Illinois Heartland Library System
Open Mon-Wed & Fri 10-6:30, Sat 10-3

SHERIDAN

S ILLINOIS DEPARTMENT OF CORRECTIONS*, Sheridan Correctional Center Library, 4017 E 2603 Rd, 60551. SAN 376-1010. Tel: 815-496-2181. *Libr Assoc,* Position Currently Open
Library Holdings: Bk Vols 5,000
Open Mon-Fri 8-4

P ROBERT W ROWE PUBLIC LIBRARY DISTRICT*, 120 E Si Johnson Ave, 60551. (Mail add: PO Box 358, 60551-0358), SAN 375-9741. Tel: 815-496-2031. FAX: 815-496-2067. Web Site: rwrlibrary.org. *Librn,* Debby Smith; E-mail: dsmith@robertrowe.lib.il.us; Staff 1 (Non-MLS 1)
Founded 1991. Pop 4,428; Circ 14,821
Jun 2008-Jul 2009 Income $195,253, State $5,357, Locally Generated Income $130,695, Other $59,201. Mats Exp $36,790, Books $13,610, Per/Ser (Incl. Access Fees) $1,358, Other Print Mats $1,951, Electronic Ref Mat (Incl. Access Fees) $2,311
Library Holdings: Bk Titles 17,000; Per Subs 40
Automation Activity & Vendor Info: (Cataloging) SirsiDynix; (Circulation) SirsiDynix; (OPAC) SirsiDynix
Wireless access
Mem of Reaching Across Illinois Library System (RAILS)
Open Mon, Thurs & Fri 10-5, Tues & Wed 1-8, Sat 10-2
Friends of the Library Group

SHERMAN

P SHERMAN PUBLIC LIBRARY DISTRICT*, 2100 E Andrew Rd, 62684-9676. (Mail add: PO Box 287, 62684-0287). Tel: 217-496-2496. FAX: 217-496-2357. E-mail: shermanlibrary@gcctv.com. Web Site: www.shermanlibrary.net. *Dir,* Anita Walters
Founded 1995. Pop 2,871
Library Holdings: Bk Vols 16,000; Per Subs 20
Automation Activity & Vendor Info: (Cataloging) Innovative Interfaces, Inc; (Circulation) Innovative Interfaces, Inc
Wireless access
Mem of Illinois Heartland Library System
Open Mon-Thurs 8-8, Fri 8-5, Sat 9-2

SHERRARD

P SHERRARD PUBLIC LIBRARY DISTRICT*, 200 Fifth Ave, 61281-8608. (Mail add: PO Box 345, 61281-0345), SAN 376-1223. Tel: 309-593-2178. FAX: 309-593-2179. E-mail: info@sherrardlibrary.org. Web Site: www.sherrardlibrary.org. *Dir,* Laura Evans; Staff 1 (MLS 1)
Founded 1976. Pop 7,288; Circ 15,000
Library Holdings: AV Mats 1,493; Large Print Bks 94; Bk Vols 18,910; Per Subs 86; Talking Bks 425
Subject Interests: Christian fiction
Partic in RiverShare Libraries
Open Mon-Fri 10-8, Sat 9-12
Friends of the Library Group

SHOREWOOD

P SHOREWOOD-TROY PUBLIC LIBRARY DISTRICT*, 650 Deerwood Dr, 60404. SAN 321-0278. Tel: 815-725-1715. FAX: 815-725-1722. TDD: 815-725-2173. E-mail: reference@shorewoodtroylibrary.org. Web Site: www.shorewood.lib.il.us. *Dir,* Jennie Cisna Mills; E-mail: jmills@shorewoodtroylibrary.org; *Asst Dir, Head, Tech Serv,* Leslie Lovato; E-mail: llovato@shorewoodtroylibrary.org; *Head, Adult Serv,* Sara Henry; E-mail: shenry@shorewoodtroylibrary.org; *Head, Circ,* Renee Daggers; E-mail: rdaggers@shorewoodtroylibrary.org; *Head, Youth Serv,* Will Savage; Tel: 815-725-4368, E-mail: wsavage@shorewoodtroylibrary.org; Staff 13 (MLS 6, Non-MLS 7)
Founded 1975. Pop 19,335; Circ 169,190
Library Holdings: Bk Titles 52,529
Special Collections: Township Records

Automation Activity & Vendor Info: (Circulation) Innovative Interfaces, Inc
Database Vendor: 3M Library Systems, OCLC FirstSearch, Overdrive, Inc
Wireless access
Mem of Reaching Across Illinois Library System (RAILS)
Partic in Pinnacle Library Cooperative
Open Mon-Thurs 9-9, Fri & Sat 9-5, Sun 1-5

SIDELL

P SIDELL DISTRICT LIBRARY*, 101 E Market St, 61876. (Mail add: PO Box 19, 61876-0019), SAN 304-6443. Tel: 217-288-9031. FAX: 217-288-9031. *Librn,* Mary Lue Tate; E-mail: mtate14780@aol.com
Founded 1947. Pop 2,445; Circ 16,000
Library Holdings: Bk Vols 9,389; Per Subs 57
Subject Interests: Fiction, Relig
Mem of Illinois Heartland Library System
Open Mon, Wed, Thurs & Sat 9-11:45 & 12:30-5

SIDNEY

P SIDNEY COMMUNITY LIBRARY*, 221 S David, 61877. (Mail add: PO Box 395, 61877), SAN 304-6451. Tel: 217-688-2332. E-mail: sidneylibrary@yahoo.com. *Librn,* Jeanne Daly; E-mail: dalyfam7@aol.com
Founded 1969. Pop 1,046; Circ 10,000
Library Holdings: Bk Vols 6,500; Per Subs 20
Automation Activity & Vendor Info: (Acquisitions) OCLC
Wireless access
Mem of Illinois Heartland Library System
Open Mon-Fri 9-12 & 4-7, Sat 9-12

SILVIS

M GENESIS MEDICAL CENTER, ILLINI CAMPUS*, Perlmutter Library of the Health Sciences, 855 Illini Dr, Ste 102, 61282. SAN 329-2231. Tel: 309-792-4360. FAX: 309-792-4362. *Coordr,* Barb Tharp; E-mail: tharpb@genesishealth.com; Staff 1 (Non-MLS 1)
Library Holdings: Bk Titles 1,600; Per Subs 300
Subject Interests: Consumer health, Nursing, Nutrition
Wireless access
Mem of Reaching Across Illinois Library System (RAILS)
Partic in Health Science Libraries of Illinois (HSLI); Illinois Library & Information Network; National Network of Libraries of Medicine
Open Mon-Fri 7:30-4

P ROCK RIVER LIBRARY DISTRICT*, Silvis Public Library, 105 Eighth St, 61282-1199. SAN 304-6478. Tel: 309-755-3393. FAX: 309-755-1816. Web Site: www.rbls.lib.il.us/svp. *Dir,* Imogene Jensen
Founded 1912. Pop 10,754; Circ 44,720
Library Holdings: Bk Vols 26,724; Per Subs 66; Talking Bks 1,919; Videos 733
Automation Activity & Vendor Info: (Circulation) SirsiDynix
Mem of Reaching Across Illinois Library System (RAILS)
Partic in RiverShare Libraries
Open Mon-Thurs 9-7, Fri & Sat 9-5
Friends of the Library Group

SKOKIE

CR HEBREW THEOLOGICAL COLLEGE*, Saul Silber Memorial Library, 7135 N Carpenter Rd, 60077-3263. SAN 340-7640. Tel: 847-982-2500. FAX: 847-674-6381. Web Site: www.htc.edu. *Head Librn,* Elie Ginsparg; E-mail: eginsparg@htc.edu; Staff 2 (MLS 1, Non-MLS 1)
Founded 1922
Library Holdings: Bk Vols 70,000; Per Subs 182
Special Collections: Bet Midrash Coll; Halakah (Rabbi Simon H Album Coll); Lazar Holocaust Coll; Rev M Newman Coll, per; Woman in Judaism (Moses Wolfe Coll)
Subject Interests: Biblical studies, Jewish hist & lit
Partic in Asn of Jewish Librs; Judaica Library Network Of Metropolitan Chicago
Open Mon-Thurs 9-3
Friends of the Library Group
Departmental Libraries:
BLITSTEIN INSTITUTE, 2606 W Touhy Ave, Chicago, 60645. Tel: 773-973-0241. FAX: 773-973-1627. E-mail: blitstein@htc.edu. *Actg Head Librn,* Eti Berland; Tel: 773-973-0241, Ext 123, E-mail: berland@htc.edu; Staff 2 (MLS 1, Non-MLS 1)
Library Holdings: Bk Vols 7,200
Special Collections: Dr Esther Levy Robinson Coll
Subject Interests: Judaica (lit or hist of Jews)
Friends of the Library Group

C KNOWLEDGE SYSTEMS INSTITUTE*, 3420 Main St, 60076. SAN 376-0103. Tel: 847-679-3135. FAX: 847-679-3166. E-mail: ksilibrary@ksi.edu. Web Site: www.ksi.edu. *Librn,* Maryann Mondrus; E-mail: mmondrus@ksi.edu; Staff 1 (MLS 1)
Founded 1975. Enrl 220; Fac 13; Highest Degree: Master
Library Holdings: Bk Vols 2,213; Per Subs 37
Subject Interests: Computer sci, Health informatics
Database Vendor: EBSCOhost
Wireless access
Restriction: Open to students, fac & staff

M NORTHSHORE UNIVERSITY HEALTHSYSTEM*, Carl Davis Jr, MD Medical Library, 9600 Gross Point Rd, 60076. SAN 373-1952. Tel: 847-933-6240. FAX: 847-933-3830. Web Site: www.northshore.org.
Founded 1970
Library Holdings: Bk Titles 1,450; Per Subs 77
Database Vendor: OCLC FirstSearch, OVID Technologies
Function: ILL available
Partic in Metro Consortium of Chicago
Restriction: Staff use only

J OAKTON COMMUNITY COLLEGE LIBRARY*, Ray Hartstein Campus, 7701 N Lincoln Ave, Rm A200, 60076-2895. Tel: 847-376-7632. Circulation Tel: 847-635-1432. FAX: 847-635-1449. Web Site: www.oakton.edu. *Head Librn,* Rose Novil; Staff 4 (MLS 1, Non-MLS 3)
Founded 1970. Highest Degree: Associate
Library Holdings: AV Mats 105; Bk Titles 15,000; Bk Vols 21,000; Per Subs 60
Automation Activity & Vendor Info: (Acquisitions) Ex Libris Group; (Cataloging) Ex Libris Group; (Circulation) Ex Libris Group; (Course Reserve) Ex Libris Group; (ILL) Ex Libris Group; (Media Booking) Ex Libris Group; (OPAC) Ex Libris Group; (Serials) Ex Libris Group
Open Mon-Thurs (Fall & Spring) 7:30am-10pm, Fri 7:30-6:30

S PORTLAND CEMENT ASSOCIATION*, Library Services, 5420 Old Orchard Rd, 60077-1083. SAN 340-7705. Tel: 847-966-6200. Interlibrary Loan Service Tel: 847-972-9178. Reference Tel: 847-972-9174. FAX: 847-966-6221. Reference FAX: 847-972-9175. Web Site: www.cement.org. *Mgr,* Connie N Field; E-mail: cfield@cement.org; Staff 3 (MLS 2, Non-MLS 1)
Founded 1950
Library Holdings: Bk Vols 105,000; Per Subs 200
Special Collections: ASTM Standards; Foreign Literature Studies; Limited Bibliographies; Occupational Health & Safety Coll; PCA Publications (out-of-print); Translations; TRB Coll
Subject Interests: Cement, Concrete, Construction
Automation Activity & Vendor Info: (Acquisitions) Sydney; (Cataloging) Sydney; (Circulation) Sydney; (OPAC) Sydney; (Serials) Sydney
Database Vendor: Dialog, OCLC FirstSearch, STN International
Publications: Library Update (bimonthly newsletter); Subject Bibliographies
Partic in Illinois Library & Information Network
Open Mon-Fri 8-4

R SAINT PAUL LUTHERAN CHURCH & SCHOOL LIBRARY*, 5201 Galitz St, 60077. SAN 304-6508. Tel: 847-673-5030. FAX: 847-673-9828. Web Site: www.stpaulskokie.org.
Library Holdings: Bk Vols 11,000; Per Subs 20
Open Mon-Fri 8:20-3
Friends of the Library Group

P SKOKIE PUBLIC LIBRARY, 5215 Oakton St, 60077-3680. SAN 304-6516. Tel: 847-673-7774. Reference Tel: 847-673-3733. FAX: 847-673-7797. TDD: 847-673-8926. E-mail: tellus@skokielibrary.info. Web Site: www.skokielibrary.info. *Dir,* Carolyn A Anthony; E-mail: canthony@skokielibrary.info; *Dep Dir,* Richard Kong; *Commun Engagement Mgr,* Susan Carlton; *Virtual Commun Engagement Mgr,* Brodie Austin; *Access Serv,* Laura McGrath; *Acq,* Pat Judge; *Adult Serv,* Lynnanne Pearson; *Ch Serv,* Jan Watkins; *Coll Develop,* Annabelle Mortensen; *Learning Experiences,* Mikael Jacobsen; *Learning Experiences,* Amita Lonial; *Ref,* Bruce Brigell; *YA Serv,* Jessi Schulte; Staff 36 (MLS 36)
Founded 1941. Pop 64,784; Circ 2,075,182
May 2013-Apr 2014 Income $11,896,838, State $473,100, City $11,157,670, Locally Generated Income $266,068. Mats Exp $1,330,670, Books $774,065, Per/Ser (Incl. Access Fees) $80,423, AV Mat $251,844, Electronic Ref Mat (Incl. Access Fees) $224,338. Sal $5,884,209
Library Holdings: CDs 45,516; DVDs 49,166; e-books 29,058; e-journals 23,301; Electronic Media & Resources 5,356; Bk Titles 299,954; Bk Vols 382,293; Per Subs 750
Special Collections: College Catalogs, micro; Local History (Cook County), bks & pamphlets; Organized File on Threat & Nazi March in Skokie, 1977

Subject Interests: Am lit, Art & archit, Bus & mgt, English lit, Foreign lang, Holocaust
Automation Activity & Vendor Info: (Acquisitions) Innovative Interfaces, Inc; (Cataloging) Innovative Interfaces, Inc; (Circulation) Innovative Interfaces, Inc; (ILL) Innovative Interfaces, Inc; (OPAC) Innovative Interfaces, Inc; (Serials) Innovative Interfaces, Inc
Database Vendor: EBSCO Auto Repair Reference, EBSCOhost, Gale Cengage Learning, OCLC FirstSearch, ProQuest
Wireless access
Publications: Skokie Public Library Newsletter (Quarterly)
Special Services for the Deaf - Assisted listening device; Bks on deafness & sign lang; High interest/low vocabulary bks; Sign lang interpreter upon request for prog; TDD equip
Special Services for the Blind - Assistive/Adapted tech devices, equip & products; Braille bks; Closed circuit TV; Large print bks; VisualTek equip
Open Mon-Fri 9-9, Sat 9-6, Sun 12-6
Bookmobiles: 1. Librn, Gail Dunlap

R TEMPLE JUDEA MIZPAH LIBRARY, 8610 Niles Center Rd, 60077. SAN 304-6532. Tel: 847-676-1566. FAX: 847-676-1579. E-mail: templejm@aol.com. Web Site: www.templejm.org. *Librn,* Judy Duesenberg
Library Holdings: Bk Vols 4,000
Special Collections: Jewish Authors, bks, publications

SMITHTON

P SMITHTON PUBLIC LIBRARY DISTRICT*, 109 S Main, 62285-1707. SAN 376-4958. Tel: 618-233-8057. FAX: 618-233-3670. E-mail: smithtonpl@smithtonpl.org. Web Site: www.smithtonpl.org. *Dir,* Jenna Nurnberger; Staff 3 (MLS 1, Non-MLS 2)
Founded 1988. Pop 4,807
Library Holdings: Bk Titles 14,000; Per Subs 18
Special Collections: Automotive Coll, Repairs & Collectables
Automation Activity & Vendor Info: (Cataloging) Innovative Interfaces, Inc; (Circulation) Innovative Interfaces, Inc; (OPAC) Innovative Interfaces, Inc
Database Vendor: OCLC FirstSearch
Wireless access
Mem of Illinois Heartland Library System
Open Mon-Thurs 9-8, Fri 9-6, Sat 9-5

SOMONAUK

P SOMONAUK PUBLIC LIBRARY DISTRICT*, 115 E Dekalb St, 60552-0307. (Mail add: PO Box 307, 60552-0307), SAN 304-6540. Tel: 815-498-2440. FAX: 815-498-2135. Web Site: somonauklibrary.org. *Dir,* Julie Harte Wasson; E-mail: jharte@somonauklibrary.org; Staff 1 (Non-MLS 1)
Founded 1921. Pop 8,401; Circ 36,500
Library Holdings: AV Mats 5,000; Bks on Deafness & Sign Lang 50; High Interest/Low Vocabulary Bk Vols 1,500; Large Print Bks 500; Bk Titles 32,000; Bk Vols 40,000; Per Subs 90,000; Spec Interest Per Sub 45; Talking Bks 450
Subject Interests: Am Indians
Automation Activity & Vendor Info: (Circulation) Infor Library & Information Solutions
Database Vendor: Gale Cengage Learning
Function: ILL available
Mem of Reaching Across Illinois Library System (RAILS)
Open Mon & Thurs 10-8, Tues, Wed & Fri 10-6, Sat 10-5
Friends of the Library Group

SOUTH BELOIT

P SOUTH BELOIT PUBLIC LIBRARY*, 630 Blackhawk Blvd, 61080-1919. SAN 304-6559. Tel: 815-389-2495. FAX: 815-389-0871. Web Site: www.southbeloit.lib.il.us. *Dir,* Ortus Dunbar; E-mail: odunbar@southbeloit.lib.il.us; Staff 2 (Non-MLS 2)
Founded 1952. Pop 7,892; Circ 16,257
Library Holdings: Bk Titles 21,727; Per Subs 78
Special Collections: Newbery Award & Coretta Scott King Award Books
Mem of Reaching Across Illinois Library System (RAILS)
Open Mon & Thurs 9-8, Tues & Wed 9-6, Fri 9-5, Sat 9-1

SOUTH HOLLAND

P SOUTH HOLLAND PUBLIC LIBRARY, 16250 Wausau Ave, 60473. SAN 304-6575. Tel: 708-331-5262. FAX: 708-331-6557. E-mail: library@southhollandlibrary.org. Web Site: www.southhollandlibrary.org. *Libr Dir,* Margaret Klinkow Hartmann; E-mail: meg@southhollandlibrary.org
Founded 1961. Pop 22,030; Circ 184,564
May 2014-Apr 2015 Income $1,849,832. Mats Exp $169,370. Sal $826,274
Library Holdings: AV Mats 10,052; DVDs 7,788; e-books 25,441; Bk Vols 94,202; Per Subs 353
Automation Activity & Vendor Info: (Cataloging) Innovative Interfaces, Inc; (Circulation) Innovative Interfaces, Inc; (ILL) Innovative Interfaces, Inc; (OPAC) Innovative Interfaces, Inc; (Serials) Innovative Interfaces, Inc
Database Vendor: EBSCOhost, Gale Cengage Learning, Newsbank, OCLC FirstSearch, ProQuest
Function: Bk club(s)
Mem of Reaching Across Illinois Library System (RAILS)
Partic in System Wide Automated Network
Special Services for the Deaf - Bks on deafness & sign lang; Closed caption videos
Special Services for the Blind - Audio mat; Bks on cassette; Bks on CD; Copier with enlargement capabilities; Large print bks; Talking bk & rec for the blind cat
Open Mon-Thurs 10-9, Fri 10-6, Sat 10-5

J SOUTH SUBURBAN COLLEGE LIBRARY*, Learning Resources Center, 15800 S State St, Rm 1249, 60473-1200. SAN 304-6591. Tel: 708-596-2000, Ext 2478. Circulation Tel: 708-596-2000, Ext 5751. Administration Tel: 708-596-2000, Ext 5807. Information Services Tel: 708-596-2000, Ext 5750. FAX: 708-210-5755. Web Site: www.southsuburbancollege.edu/en_US/Services/Library. *Librn,* Sangeeta Kumar; Tel: 708-596-2000, Ext 2574, E-mail: skumar@ssc.edu; *Librn,* Angeline D Nalepa; E-mail: analepa@ssc.edu; *Librn,* Marilyn Wells; Tel: 708-596-2000, Ext 2239, E-mail: mwells@ssc.edu. Subject Specialists: *Govt doc,* Angeline D Nalepa; Staff 7 (MLS 3, Non-MLS 4)
Founded 1927. Enrl 6,211; Fac 364; Highest Degree: Associate
Library Holdings: AV Mats 200; Bks on Deafness & Sign Lang 15; CDs 61; e-journals 1,500; Electronic Media & Resources 10; Music Scores 461; Bk Titles 24,000; Per Subs 55; Videos 800
Special Collections: US Document Depository
Subject Interests: Nursing
Automation Activity & Vendor Info: (Acquisitions) Baker & Taylor; (Serials) EBSCO Online
Database Vendor: CredoReference, EBSCOhost, ProQuest
Wireless access
Function: AV serv, Computers for patron use, Copy machines, e-mail & chat, Electronic databases & coll, Fax serv, Govt ref serv, Handicapped accessible, ILL available, Instruction & testing, Literacy & newcomer serv, Magnifiers for reading, Music CDs, Online cat, Orientations, Photocopying/Printing, Pub access computers, Ref serv available, Ref serv in person, Telephone ref, VHS videos, Wheelchair accessible
Mem of Reaching Across Illinois Library System (RAILS)
Partic in Consortium of Academic & Research Libraries in Illinois
Special Services for the Blind - Magnifiers
Open Mon-Thurs (Fall & Spring) 8am-9pm, Fri 8-4; Mon-Thurs (Summer) 8-8

SOUTH PEKIN

P SOUTH PEKIN PUBLIC LIBRARY*, 208 W Main St, 61564. (Mail add: PO Box 490, 61564-0490), SAN 304-6605. Tel: 309-348-2446. FAX: 309-348-2419. *Librn,* Sharon Thurman
Pop 1,243; Circ 3,195
Library Holdings: Bk Vols 2,771; Per Subs 11
Open Mon, Wed & Fri 3-5:30, Tues & Thurs 6-9

SPARTA

P SPARTA PUBLIC LIBRARY, 211 W Broadway, 62286. SAN 304-6613. Tel: 618-443-5014. FAX: 618-443-2952. E-mail: spartaillinoislibrary@gmail.com. Web Site: www.sparta.lib.il.us. *Admin Dir,* Susan Colbert; *Cat,* Lois Cunningham; E-mail: lpcun@hotmail.com; *Circ,* June Cohoon; *Circ,* Stacie Hicks; *Circ,* Jenny Hobeck; E-mail: jennyhobeck@hotmail.com; *Circ,* Jillian Mayer; *Circ,* Theresa Simpson; E-mail: tessimpson@earthlink.com. Subject Specialists: *Prog,* Stacie Hicks; *Prog,* Jillian Mayer; Staff 7 (Non-MLS 7)
Founded 1944. Pop 4,853; Circ 45,240
Library Holdings: Bks on Deafness & Sign Lang 10; Bk Vols 39,506; Per Subs 292
Subject Interests: Local hist
Automation Activity & Vendor Info: (Cataloging) Horizon; (Circulation) Horizon
Database Vendor: EBSCOhost, OVID Technologies
Wireless access
Function: Telephone ref
Mem of Illinois Heartland Library System
Special Services for the Deaf - Bks on deafness & sign lang
Open Mon, Tues & Thurs Noon-7, Wed & Fri 10-5, Sat 10-4
Friends of the Library Group

SPRING VALLEY

P RICHARD A MAUTINO MEMORIAL LIBRARY, 215 E Cleveland St, 61362. SAN 304-6621. Tel: 815-663-4741. FAX: 815-663-1040. E-mail: mautinolibrary@yahoo.com. Web Site: richardmautinolibrary.com. *Head*

Librn, Barbara White; *Ad,* Ruth Hedgespeth; *Ad,* Tari Sangston; *Ch Serv,* Jeri Loebach
Founded 1912. Pop 5,558; Circ 30,879
May 2014-Apr 2015. Mats Exp $43,000, Books $38,000, Per/Ser (Incl. Access Fees) $3,500, Electronic Ref Mat (Incl. Access Fees) $1,500. Sal $55,000
Library Holdings: CDs 1,505; DVDs 2,174; Bk Titles 37,442; Per Subs 59
Special Collections: Oral History
Automation Activity & Vendor Info: (Acquisitions) ResourceMATE; (Cataloging) JayWil Software Development, Inc
Database Vendor: JayWil Software Development, Inc
Wireless access
Mem of Reaching Across Illinois Library System (RAILS)
Special Services for the Deaf - TDD equip
Special Services for the Blind - Bks on CD
Open Mon-Wed 10-7, Thurs 2-7, Fri 10-5, Sat 9-2

SPRINGFIELD

S HANSON PROFESSIONAL SERVICES, INC*, Technical Library, 1525 S Sixth St, 62703-2886. SAN 304-663X. Tel: 217-747-9241. FAX: 217-747-9416. E-mail: library@hanson-inc.com. Web Site: www.hanson-inc.com. *Librn,* Cathy Popovitch; Staff 0.6 (MLS 0.6)
Founded 1975
Library Holdings: Bk Titles 16,002; Per Subs 278
Special Collections: Geology (Illinois Coll); Illinois Topo, maps; Walter E Hanson Coll
Subject Interests: Archit, Civil eng, Electrical eng, Mechanical eng
Automation Activity & Vendor Info: (Cataloging) Horizon; (Circulation) Horizon; (ILL) OCLC Online; (OPAC) Horizon; (Serials) Horizon
Database Vendor: OCLC FirstSearch, SirsiDynix
Mem of Illinois Heartland Library System
Partic in Capital Area Health Consortium; OCLC Online Computer Library Center, Inc
Restriction: Staff use only

G ILLINOIS AUDITOR GENERAL LIBRARY, 740 E Ash St, 62703. SAN 326-9914. Tel: 217-782-1055. FAX: 217-785-8222. E-mail: oag.auditor@illinois.gov. Web Site: www.auditor.illinois.gov. *Librn,* Renee O'Neil
Library Holdings: Bk Titles 2,600
Special Collections: Financial-Compliance & Performance Audits 1974-present
Partic in Illinois Library & Information Network
Open Mon-Fri 8-5

G ILLINOIS DEPARTMENT OF TRANSPORTATION*, Policy & Research Library, 320 Harry Hanley Bldg, 2300 S Dirksen Pkwy, 62764-0001. SAN 326-9957. Tel: 217-524-3834, 217-782-6680. E-mail: dot.policyresearchcenter@illinois.gov. *Dir,* Karen Perrin; Staff 1 (MLS 1)
Founded 1965
Library Holdings: Bk Vols 18,000; Per Subs 271
Subject Interests: Hwy eng, Transportation
Automation Activity & Vendor Info: (Cataloging) OCLC Connexion; (ILL) OCLC FirstSearch; (OPAC) Innovative Interfaces, Inc
Database Vendor: OCLC FirstSearch
Function: ILL available
Publications: Information Connection
Mem of Illinois Heartland Library System
Partic in Illinois Library & Information Network; Midwest Transportation Knowledge Network (MTKN); OCLC Online Computer Library Center, Inc
Restriction: Use of others with permission of librn

G ILLINOIS ENVIRONMENTAL PROTECTION AGENCY LIBRARY*, 1021 N Grand Ave E, 62702-4072. (Mail add: PO Box 19276, 62794-9276), SAN 321-897X. Tel: 217-782-9691. FAX: 217-524-4916. Web Site: www.epa.state.il.us. *Librn,* Tracy Pierceall; Staff 1 (Non-MLS 1)
Founded 1970
Library Holdings: Bk Titles 25,000; Per Subs 100
Subject Interests: Environ law, Environ protection
Mem of Illinois Heartland Library System
Partic in Capital Area Health Consortium; Illinois Library & Information Network; OCLC Online Computer Library Center, Inc
Open Mon-Fri 8:30-5

S ILLINOIS HISTORIC PRESERVATION AGENCY*, Abraham Lincoln Presidential Library, 112 N Sixth St, 62701. SAN 304-6656. Tel: 217-558-8844. FAX: 217-785-6250. Web Site: www.alplm.org. *Dir, Libr Serv,* Kathryn M Harris; Tel: 217-524-7219, E-mail: kathryn.harris@illinois.gov; *Head, Ref,* Jane Ehrenhart; Tel: 217-785-7945; *Newspaper Librn,* Jan Perone; Tel: 217-558-8856; *Ref Librn,* Gwen Podeschi; Staff 35 (MLS 9, Non-MLS 26)
Founded 1889
Library Holdings: AV Mats 400,000; Microforms 99,000; Bk Titles 199,000; Bk Vols 350,000; Per Subs 1,200
Special Collections: Illinois Newspapers; Lincolniana
Subject Interests: Civil War, Ill hist, Mormons
Automation Activity & Vendor Info: (Cataloging) Horizon; (ILL) OCLC; (OPAC) Horizon
Database Vendor: OCLC FirstSearch
Wireless access
Function: Res libr
Publications: Journal of Illinois History (Quarterly)
Mem of Reaching Across Illinois Library System (RAILS)
Partic in OCLC Online Computer Library Center, Inc
Open Mon-Fri 9-5
Restriction: Non-circulating to the pub

G ILLINOIS STATE DATA CENTER COOPERATIVE, Illinois Department of Commerce & Economic Opportunity, 607 E Adams St, IL-3, 62701. (Mail add: 500 E Monroe St, IL-3, 62701). Tel: 217-524-0187, 217-782-1381. FAX: 217-558-5146. Web Site: www.illinois.gov/dceo. *Coordr,* Sue Ebetsch; E-mail: sue.ebetsch@illinois.gov
Library Holdings: Bk Titles 5,000
Special Collections: US Bureau of the Census, Bureau of Economic Analysis, Bureau of Labor Statistics, print & electronic data
Publications: Illinois Population Trends - 2000-2030
Open Mon-Fri 9-4

P ILLINOIS STATE LIBRARY*, Gwendolyn Brooks Bldg, 300 S Second St, 62701-9713. SAN 304-6672. Tel: 217-782-2994. Circulation Tel: 217-782-7573. Interlibrary Loan Service Tel: 217-782-7523. Reference Tel: 217-782-7596. Toll Free Tel: 800-665-5576 (IL only). FAX: 217-785-4326. TDD: 800-965-0748. E-mail: islinformationline@ilsos.net. Web Site: www.cyberdriveillinois.com/departments/library/home.html. *Dir,* Anne Craig; E-mail: acraig@ilsos.net; *Assoc Dir, Grants & Prog,* Patricia Norris; Tel: 217-524-5867, E-mail: pnorris@ilsos.net; *Assoc Dir, Libr Automation & Tech,* Suzanne Schriar; Tel: 217-785-1533, E-mail: sschriar@ilsos.net; *Assoc Dir, Libr Operations,* Kathleen Bloomberg; Tel: 217-785-0052, Fax: 217-524-0041, E-mail: kbloomberg@ilsos.net; *Assoc Dir, Talking Bks & Braille Serv,* Sharon Ruda; Tel: 217-782-9435, E-mail: sruda@ilsos.net; *Chief Dep,* Lawren Tucker; Tel: 217-524-4200, E-mail: ltucker@ilsos.net; *Communications Mgr,* Pat McGuckin; Tel: 217-558-4029, E-mail: pmcguckin@ilsos.net; *Govt Doc Mgr,* Blaine Redemer; Tel: 217-782-5432, E-mail: bredemer@ilsos.net; *Mgr, Diversity Prog,* Vandella Brown; Tel: 217-785-9075, E-mail: vbrown@ilsos.net; *Fiscal Officer,* Greg McCormick; Tel: 217-782-3504, E-mail: gmccormick@ilsos.net; *Digital Imaging Prog Coordr,* Sandra Fritz; Tel: 217-558-2064, E-mail: sfritz@ilsos.net; *Ill Ctr for the Bk Coordr,* Bonnie Matheis; Tel: 217-558-2065, E-mail: bmatheis@ilsos.net; *Info Syst Coordr,* Jim Shepard; Tel: 217-782-5524, E-mail: jshepard@ilsos.net; *Literacy Coordr,* Cyndy Colletti; Tel: 217-524-3529, E-mail: ccolletti@ilsos.net; *LSTA Coordr,* Karen Egan; Tel: 217-782-7749, E-mail: kegan@ilsos.net; *Ref Outreach Coordr,* Debra Aggertt; Tel: 217-558-1945, E-mail: daggertt@ilsos.net; *State Data Coordr, YA Serv,* Robert Jones; Tel: 217-785-1168, E-mail: rjones1@ilsos.net; *Info Tech,* Andrew Bullen; Tel: 312-814-4386, E-mail: abullen@ilsos.net; *Network Serv,* Gwen Harrison; Tel: 217-785 5334, E-mail: gharrison@ilsos.net. Subject Specialists: *Govt,* Lawren Tucker
Founded 1839
Library Holdings: Bk Titles 1,694,500; Bk Vols 1,844,600; Per Subs 1,025
Special Collections: Illinois Authors Coll. State Document Depository; US Document Depository
Subject Interests: Govt, Polit sci
Automation Activity & Vendor Info: (Acquisitions) Ex Libris Group; (Cataloging) OCLC; (Cataloging) Ex Libris Group; (Circulation) Ex Libris Group; (ILL) OCLC; (OPAC) Ex Libris Group; (Serials) Ex Libris Group
Database Vendor: Dialog, EBSCOhost, Gale Cengage Learning, LexisNexis, OCLC FirstSearch
Wireless access
Function: Adult literacy prog, Doc delivery serv, For res purposes, Games & aids for the handicapped, Govt ref serv, Homebound delivery serv, ILL available, Libr develop, Newsp ref libr, Online searches, Photocopying/Printing, Ref serv available, Telephone ref, Wheelchair accessible, Workshops
Publications: E-news from the ISL (Newsletter); Insight (Newsletter)
Partic in OCLC Online Computer Library Center, Inc
Special Services for the Deaf - Assisted listening device; Assistive tech; Captioned film dep; Closed caption videos; Spec interest per
Special Services for the Blind - Assistive/Adapted tech devices, equip & products; Audio mat; Bks & mags in Braille, on rec, tape & cassette; Bks available with recordings; Braille Webster's dictionary; Cassette playback machines; Computer with voice synthesizer for visually impaired persons; GEAC Advance; Home delivery serv; Large print & cassettes; Large print bks & talking machines; Newsline for the Blind; Radio reading serv; Ref serv; Scanner for conversion & translation of mats; Talking bk & rec for

the blind cat; Talking bks & player equip; Tel Pioneers equip repair group; Videos on blindness & phys handicaps
Open Mon-Fri 8-4:30
Branches: 1

P TALKING BOOK & BRAILLE SERVICE, Gwendolyn Brooks Bldg, 300 S Second St, 62701-1796. Tel: 217-785-0022. Toll Free Tel: 800-665-5576. FAX: 217-558-4723. TDD: 888-261-2709. E-mail: isltbbs@ilsos.net. Web Site: www.ilbph.org. *Assoc Dir,* Sharon Ruda; Tel: 217-782-9435, E-mail: sruda@ilsos.net; Staff 14.5 (MLS 2, Non-MLS 12.5)
Founded 1931
Library Holdings: DVDs 535; Bk Titles 17,762; Talking Bks 166,754; Videos 2,045
Automation Activity & Vendor Info: (Cataloging) Keystone Systems, Inc (KLAS); (Circulation) Keystone Systems, Inc (KLAS); (OPAC) Keystone Systems, Inc (KLAS)
Function: 24/7 Electronic res, 24/7 Online cat, Audiobks via web, Bks on cassette, Computers for patron use, Digital talking bks, E-Reserves, Equip loans & repairs, eReaders, Free DVD rentals, Handicapped accessible, Home delivery & serv to Sr ctr & nursing homes, ILL available, Magazines, Mail & tel request accepted, Mail loans to mem, Online cat, Online searches, Pub access computers, Ref serv available, Ref serv in person, Spanish lang bks, Telephone ref, VHS videos, Video lending libr, Web-Braille, Web-catalog, Wheelchair accessible
Special Services for the Blind - Braille alphabet card; Braille bks; Descriptive video serv (DVS); Digital talking bk; Digital talking bk machines; Free checkout of audio mat; Machine repair; Magnifiers; Mags & bk reproduction/duplication; Music instrul cassettes; Musical scores in Braille & large print; Newsletter (in large print, Braille or on cassette); Newsline for the Blind; PC for handicapped; Recorded bks; Screen enlargement software for people with visual disabilities; Screen reader software; Spanish Braille mags & bks; Talking bks; Talking bks & player equip; Talking bks plus; Talking machines; Variable speed audiotape players; Web-Braille; ZoomText magnification & reading software
Open Mon-Fri 8-4:30
Restriction: Authorized patrons, Registered patrons only

S ILLINOIS STATE MUSEUM LIBRARY, 502 S Spring St, 62706-5000. SAN 304-6680. Tel: 217-524-0496, 217-782-6623. FAX: 217-782-1254, 217-785-2857. Web Site: www.museum.state.il.us. *Head Librn,* Patricia Burg; E-mail: pburg@museum.state.il.us; Staff 2 (MLS 1, Non-MLS 1)
Founded 1877
Library Holdings: Bk Vols 23,200; Per Subs 283
Special Collections: Anthropology (Thorne Deuel Coll); Art (Benjamin F Hunter Coll); Ornithology (R M Barnes Coll); Paleontology (Raymond E Janssen Coll); Zoology (Donald F Hoffmeister Coll)
Subject Interests: Anthrop, Art, Natural sci
Automation Activity & Vendor Info: (Cataloging) Horizon; (Circulation) Horizon; (ILL) OCLC; (OPAC) Horizon
Database Vendor: BioOne, JSTOR, OCLC FirstSearch, OCLC WorldShare Interlibrary Loan
Mem of Illinois Heartland Library System
Partic in Illinois Library & Information Network

L LEGISLATIVE REFERENCE BUREAU LAW LIBRARY*, State Capitol, Rm 112, 62706. SAN 304-6702. Tel: 217-782-6625. FAX: 217-785-4583. Web Site: www.ilga.gov. *Librn,* Mike Trudeau; E-mail: mtrudeau@ilga.gov
Founded 1913
Library Holdings: Bk Vols 20,000; Per Subs 29
Special Collections: Annotated Statutes for all Fifty States, Legislative Synopsis & Digests; Illinois Laws (since 1840)

J LINCOLN LAND COMMUNITY COLLEGE LIBRARY*, 5250 Shepherd Rd, 62794. (Mail add: PO Box 19256, 62794-9256), SAN 304-6710. Tel: 217-786-2354. Reference Tel: 217-786-2352. Administration Tel: 217-786-2353. Automation Services Tel: 217-786-9621. FAX: 217-786-2251. Web Site: www.llcc.edu/library. *Assoc Dean,* Tamara Schnell; E-mail: tammy.schnell@llcc.edu; *Dir, Tech Serv & e-Res,* Jared Wellman; E-mail: jared.wellman@llcc.edu; *Librn,* Jill Campbell; E-mail: jill.campbell@llcc.edu; *Librn,* Leslie Rios; E-mail: leslie.rios@llcc.edu; *Librn,* Ryan Roberts; Tel: 217-786-2771, E-mail: ryan.roberts@llcc.edu; *Libr Spec,* Dennis Suttles; E-mail: dennis.suttles@llcc.edu; Staff 10.5 (MLS 5.5, Non-MLS 5)
Founded 1968. Enrl 3,960; Fac 224; Highest Degree: Associate
Jul 2011-Jun 2012 Income $668,308. Mats Exp $195,300, Books $110,000, Per/Ser (Incl. Access Fees) $30,000, Micro $300, AV Mat $5,000, Electronic Ref Mat (Incl. Access Fees) $50,000. Sal $519,445 (Prof $299,913)
Library Holdings: AV Mats 1,290; CDs 375; DVDs 403; e-books 3,000; Bk Titles 53,458; Bk Vols 61,404; Per Subs 233; Videos 887
Subject Interests: Art, Hist, Lit
Automation Activity & Vendor Info: (Acquisitions) Ex Libris Group; (Cataloging) Ex Libris Group; (Circulation) Ex Libris Group; (Course Reserve) Ex Libris Group; (ILL) OCLC; (OPAC) Ex Libris Group; (Serials) Ex Libris Group
Database Vendor: ALLDATA Online, CQ Press, CredoReference, EBSCOhost, Facts on File, Gale Cengage Learning, H W Wilson, JSTOR, LexisNexis, OCLC FirstSearch, OCLC WorldShare Interlibrary Loan, Oxford Online, ProQuest, Springshare, LLC, Wilson - Wilson Web, YBP Library Services
Wireless access
Function: Audio & video playback equip for onsite use, Bks on CD, Computers for patron use, Copy machines, Doc delivery serv, Electronic databases & coll, Handicapped accessible, ILL available, Instruction & testing, Microfiche/film & reading machines, Music CDs, Online cat, Online info literacy tutorials on the web & in blackboard, Online ref, Orientations, Photocopying/Printing, Pub access computers, Ref & res, Ref serv available, Ref serv in person, Scanner, Telephone ref
Mem of Illinois Heartland Library System
Partic in Cap Area Libr Consortium; Consortium of Academic & Research Libraries in Illinois; Ill Coordinated Coll Mgt Prog; Northern Illinois Learning Resources Cooperative (NILRC); OCLC-LVIS
Open Mon-Thurs 7:30am-10pm, Fri 7:30-5, Sat 9-1, Sun 2-5; Mon-Thurs (Summer) 7am-8pm
Restriction: In-house use for visitors, Residents only

P LINCOLN LIBRARY*, The Public Library of Springfield, Illinois, 326 S Seventh St, 62701. SAN 340-7853. Tel: 217-753-4900. Circulation Tel: 217-763-4900, Ext 214. Reference Tel: 217-753-4900, Ext 230. FAX: 217-753-5329. TDD: 217-753-4947. Web Site: www.lincolnlibrary.info. *Dir,* Nancy Huntley; Tel: 217-753-4900, Ext 219, E-mail: nancy.huntley@lincolnlibrary.info; *Circ & ILL,* Lois Morse; E-mail: lois.morse@lincolnlibrary.info; *Ref,* Curtis Mann; Tel: 217-753-4900, Ext 232, E-mail: curtis.mann@lincolnlibrary.info; *Youth Serv,* Phyllis Barnard; Tel: 217-753-4900, Ext 215, E-mail: phyllis.barnard@lincolnlibrary.info; Staff 57 (MLS 18, Non-MLS 39)
Founded 1886. Pop 114,000; Circ 950,342
Library Holdings: Bk Vols 302,954; Per Subs 682
Special Collections: Local History; Newspaper Index; Vachel Lindsay (Sangamon Valley Coll)
Subject Interests: Hist, Music, Polit sci
Automation Activity & Vendor Info: (Cataloging) SirsiDynix; (Circulation) SirsiDynix; (OPAC) SirsiDynix
Wireless access
Publications: Lincoln Library Bulletin
Partic in OCLC Online Computer Library Center, Inc
Special Services for the Deaf - TTY equip
Open Mon-Wed 10-8, Thurs & Fri 10-6, Sat 10-5, Sun (Oct-April) 1-5
Friends of the Library Group

M ANDREW MCFARLAND MENTAL HEALTH CENTER*, 901 Southwind Rd, 62703. SAN 304-6729. Tel: 217-786-6983. FAX: 217-786-6803. *Coordr,* Melanie Bock
Library Holdings: Bk Vols 3,000; Per Subs 10
Subject Interests: Psychiat, Psychol
Restriction: Staff use only

M MEMORIAL MEDICAL CENTER*, Kenneth H Schnepp Professional Library, 701 N First St, 62781-0001. SAN 304-6737. Tel: 217-788-3331. FAX: 217-788-5540. Web Site: www.mhsil.com. *Coordr, Libr Serv,* Lynne Ferrell; E-mail: ferrell.lynne@mhsil.com
Founded 1943
Oct 2008-Sept 2009. Mats Exp $140,000
Library Holdings: e-books 50; e-journals 400; Bk Titles 1,975; Bk Vols 3,200; Per Subs 176
Subject Interests: Health sci
Automation Activity & Vendor Info: (Cataloging) OCLC Connexion; (Circulation) SirsiDynix; (ILL) OCLC
Database Vendor: OCLC FirstSearch, OVID Technologies, SirsiDynix
Function: ILL available, Photocopying/Printing, Prof lending libr, Res libr
Mem of Illinois Heartland Library System
Partic in Docline; Greater Regional Med Libr-Region 3; Illinois Library & Information Network; National Network of Libraries of Medicine; OCLC Online Computer Library Center, Inc; OCLC-LVIS
Restriction: Open to students, fac & staff

C ROBERT MORRIS UNIVERSITY*, Springfield Campus Library, 3101 Montvale Dr, 62704-4260. Tel: 217-726-1675, 217-726-1676. Web Site: www.robertmorris.edu/library/branches. *Librn,* Sarah Mueth; E-mail: smueth@robertmorris.edu; Staff 2 (Non-MLS 2)
Library Holdings: Bk Titles 4,000
Automation Activity & Vendor Info: (Acquisitions) Ex Libris Group; (Cataloging) Ex Libris Group; (Circulation) Ex Libris Group; (Course Reserve) Ex Libris Group; (ILL) Ex Libris Group; (Media Booking) Ex Libris Group; (OPAC) Ex Libris Group; (Serials) Ex Libris Group
Open Mon-Thurs 9-7

M ST JOHN'S HOSPITAL, Hospital Sisters Health System, Health Sciences Libraries, 800 E Carpenter, 62769. SAN 340-8000. Tel: 217-757-6700. Automation Services Tel: 217-544-6464, Ext 44567. Information Services Tel: 217-544-6464, Ext 44566. FAX: 217-525-2895. E-mail: library@hshs.org. Web Site: www.st-johns.org. *Dir,* Kathryn Wrigley; E-mail: kathryn.wrigley@hshs.org; *Librn,* Laura Brosamer; Tel: 217-464-2182, Fax: 217-464-1674, E-mail: Laura.Brosamer@hshs.org; *Asst Librn,* Sue Carter; E-mail: susan.carter@hshs.org; *Ref Librn,* Roger Swartzbaugh; Tel: 217-544-6464, Ext 44563, E-mail: roger.swartzbaugh@hshs.org; Staff 4 (MLS 3, Non-MLS 1)
Founded 1931
Library Holdings: AV Mats 604; e-books 25,255; e-journals 26,326; Bk Titles 4,644; Per Subs 79
Subject Interests: Cardiology, Nursing, Pediatrics, Surgery
Automation Activity & Vendor Info: (Acquisitions) SirsiDynix; (Cataloging) SirsiDynix; (Circulation) SirsiDynix; (Media Booking) SirsiDynix; (OPAC) SirsiDynix; (Serials) SirsiDynix
Database Vendor: OCLC FirstSearch, OVID Technologies
Wireless access
Mem of Illinois Heartland Library System
Partic in Illinois Library & Information Network; National Network of Libraries of Medicine; OCLC Online Computer Library Center, Inc
Open Mon-Fri 7:30-4:30

M SCHNEPP PROFESSIONAL LIBRARY*, Memorial Medical Ctr, 701 N First St, 62781. Tel: 217-788-3331. *Librn & Archivist,* Lynne Ferrell; E-mail: ferrell.lynne@mhsil.com

CM SOUTHERN ILLINOIS UNIVERSITY SCHOOL OF MEDICINE LIBRARY, 801 N Rutledge, 62702. (Mail add: PO Box 19625, 62794-9625), SAN 304-6761. Tel: 217-545-2658. Circulation Tel: 217-545-2122. Interlibrary Loan Service Tel: 217-545-2124. Reference Tel: 217-545-2113. FAX: 217-545-0988. Interlibrary Loan Service FAX: 217-545-7503. E-mail: reference@siumed.edu. Web Site: www.siumed.edu/lib. *Dir,* Connie Poole; E-mail: cpoole@siumed.edu; *Br Adminr,* Allison Sutphin; E-mail: asutphin@siumed.edu; *Head of Ref & Instrul Serv,* Rhona Kelley; E-mail: rkelley@siumed.edu; *Ref & Instrul Serv Librn,* Carol Gordon; E-mail: cgordon2@siumed.edu; Staff 20.11 (MLS 5.67, Non-MLS 14.44)
Founded 1970. Enrl 475; Highest Degree: Doctorate
Jul 2013-Jun 2014 Income $2,020,201, Locally Generated Income $13,857, Parent Institution $2,006,344. Mats Exp $906,008, Books $78,641, Per/Ser (Incl. Access Fees) $717,707, Electronic Ref Mat (Incl. Access Fees) $101,675, Presv $7,985. Sal $875,102
Library Holdings: AV Mats 3,316; e-books 8,200; e-journals 2,519; Bk Titles 56,635; Bk Vols 66,285; Per Subs 3,381
Special Collections: History of Medicine
Automation Activity & Vendor Info: (Acquisitions) Ex Libris Group; (Cataloging) Ex Libris Group; (Circulation) Ex Libris Group; (OPAC) Ex Libris Group; (Serials) Ex Libris Group
Database Vendor: Dialog, EBSCOhost, OCLC FirstSearch
Wireless access
Function: ILL available, Ref serv available
Publications: AV Titles; Serials Subjects; Serials Titles
Mem of Illinois Heartland Library System
Partic in Consortium of Academic & Research Libraries in Illinois; Illinois Library & Information Network; National Network of Libraries of Medicine
Open Mon-Thurs 8am-11pm, Fri 8-6, Sat 9-5, Sun 1-11

S SPRINGFIELD ART ASSOCIATION*, Michael Victor II Art Library, 700 N Fourth St, 62702-5232. SAN 304-677X. Tel: 217-523-2631. FAX: 217-523-3866. E-mail: mvlibrary@springfieldart.org. Web Site: www.springfieldart.org. *Libr Dir,* Jan Arnold
Founded 1964
Library Holdings: Bk Titles 4,000; Per Subs 8
Subject Interests: Art, Art hist, Arts & crafts, Paintings, Photog, Prints
Function: Art exhibits
Mem of Illinois Heartland Library System
Open Mon-Fri 9-5, Sat 10-3

GL SUPREME COURT OF ILLINOIS LIBRARY*, Supreme Court Bldg, 200 E Capital Ave, 62701-1791. SAN 304-6699. Tel: 217-782-2424. FAX: 217-782-5287. E-mail: sclibrary_questions@court.state.il.us. Web Site: www.state.il.us/court/supremecourt/library.asp. *Librn,* Geoff Pelzek; E-mail: gpelzek@illinoiscourts.gov; Staff 8 (MLS 4, Non-MLS 4)
Founded 1839
Library Holdings: Bk Titles 10,000; Bk Vols 100,000; Per Subs 500
Special Collections: SJI Depository. State Document Depository
Subject Interests: Ill, Law
Automation Activity & Vendor Info: (Cataloging) SirsiDynix
Database Vendor: SirsiDynix
Partic in OCLC Online Computer Library Center, Inc
Open Mon-Fri 8-4:30

L UNITED STATES COURTS LIBRARY*, 600 E Monroe St, Rm 305, 62701. SAN 372-1159. Tel: 217-492-4191. FAX: 217-492-4192. *Librn,* Martha Doyle
Library Holdings: Bk Vols 8,000; Per Subs 15
Partic in OCLC Online Computer Library Center, Inc
Restriction: Not open to pub

C UNIVERSITY OF ILLINOIS AT SPRINGFIELD*, Norris L Brookens Library, One University Plaza, MS BRK-140, 62703-5407. Tel: 217-206-6597. Circulation Tel: 217-206-6605. Interlibrary Loan Service Tel. 217-206-6601. Reference Tel: 217-206-6633. FAX: 217-206-6354. Reference FAX: 217-206-6208. Web Site: library.uis.edu. *Dean, Libr Instrul Serv,* Jane Treadwell; E-mail: jtrea1@uis.edu; *Dir, Info Syst & Tech Serv,* Jan Waterhouse; Tel: 217-206-7114, E-mail: jwate3@uis.e.du; *Instrul Serv Librn,* Pamela Salela; Tel: 217-206-6783, E-mail: psale2@uis.edu; *Archivist,* Thomas Wood; Tel: 217-206-6520, E-mail: wood.thomas@uis.edu; *Instrul Serv,* Amanda Binder; Tel: 217-206-8458, E-mail: binder2@uis.edu; *Instrul Serv,* Sarah Sagmoen; Tel: 217-206-6618, E-mail: ssagm2@uis.edu; *Instrul Serv,* Nancy Weichert; Tel: 217-206-6644, E-mail: nweic01s@uis.edu; Staff 26 (MLS 8, Non-MLS 18)
Founded 1970. Enrl 5,174; Fac 362; Highest Degree: Doctorate
Jul 2010-Jun 2011 Income $2,579,537. Mats Exp $1,072,269, Books $92,763, Per/Ser (Incl. Access Fees) $594,701, Other Print Mats $648, AV Mat $16,068, Electronic Ref Mat (Incl. Access Fees) $359,685, Presv $1,616. Sal $1,141,586 (Prof $545,038)
Library Holdings: Audiobooks 1,281; AV Mats 11,921; e-books 51,346; e-journals 57,341; Microforms 49,035; Music Scores 442; Bk Titles 476,774; Bk Vols 532,486; Per Subs 1,643; Videos 5,345
Special Collections: Central Illinois Oral Histories; Handy Colony Coll; Illinois Regional Archives Depository. Oral History; State Document Depository; US Document Depository
Subject Interests: Bus & mgt, Econ, Educ, Law
Automation Activity & Vendor Info: (Acquisitions) Ex Libris Group; (Cataloging) Ex Libris Group; (Circulation) Ex Libris Group; (Course Reserve) Ex Libris Group; (ILL) Ex Libris Group; (OPAC) Ex Libris Group; (Serials) Ex Libris Group
Database Vendor: EBSCOhost, JSTOR, LexisNexis, OCLC, ProQuest, Thomson - Web of Science
Wireless access
Publications: James Jones in Illinois: A Guide to the Handy Colony Collection, 1989
Mem of Illinois Heartland Library System
Partic in Consortium of Academic & Research Libraries in Illinois; Council of Directors of State University Libraries in Illinois; OCLC Online Computer Library Center, Inc
Special Services for the Blind - Aids for in-house use
Open Mon-Thurs 8:30am-Midnight, Fri 8:30-6, Sat 10-6, Sun 2-Midnight
Friends of the Library Group

STANFORD

P ALLIN TOWNSHIP LIBRARY*, 116 W Main St, 61774. (Mail add: PO Box 258, 61774-0258), SAN 376-0936. Tel: 309-379-4631. FAX: 309-379-4122. E-mail: allinlib@mchsi.com. *Librn,* Angie Gaddy
Library Holdings: Bk Vols 5,000
Open Mon & Wed 11:30-8, Fri 9-4:30, Sat 9-2:30
Friends of the Library Group

STAUNTON

P STAUNTON PUBLIC LIBRARY*, 306 W Main St, 62088. SAN 304-6796. Tel: 618-635-3852. FAX: 618-635-2246. E-mail: library@stauntonpl.org. *Dir,* Julie Jarman; E-mail: juliej@stauntonpl.org
Founded 1912. Pop 5,139; Circ 23,000
Library Holdings: Bk Vols 22,000; Per Subs 21
Special Collections: House the Macoupin Company Genealogical Coll
Wireless access
Mem of Illinois Heartland Library System
Open Mon-Thurs 10-7, Fri 10-5, Sat 10-3

STEELEVILLE

P STEELEVILLE AREA LIBRARY*, 625 S Florida St, 62288. SAN 376-494X. Tel: 618-965-9732. FAX: 618-965-3504. E-mail: svillelibrary@gmail.com. Web Site: www.steelevillelibrary.org. *Dir,* John Hostert; *Assoc Dir,* Sarah Duvall; *Cat Spec,* Betty Qualls; *Libr Spec,* Margo Block
Founded 1983
Jul 2012-Jun 2013. Mats Exp $1,700
Library Holdings: Bk Titles 25,000; Per Subs 35; Videos 1,300
Automation Activity & Vendor Info: (Acquisitions) SirsiDynix; (Cataloging) SirsiDynix; (Circulation) SirsiDynix; (Course Reserve) Follett Software; (ILL) Follett Software; (Media Booking) Follett Software; (OPAC) Follett Software; (Serials) Follett Software
Wireless access

Mem of Illinois Heartland Library System
Open Mon-Thurs 10-7, Fri 10-5, Sat 9-Noon
Friends of the Library Group

STEGER

P STEGER-SOUTH CHICAGO HEIGHTS PUBLIC LIBRARY DISTRICT*, 54 E 31st St, 60475. SAN 304-6567. Tel: 708-755-5040. FAX: 708-755-2504. E-mail: sts2@sslic.net. Web Site: www.ssch.lib.il.us. *Librn,* Lisa Korajczyk; *Adult Serv,* Janice Elmore; *Ch Serv,* Laura Oldenburg
Founded 1975. Pop 12,955
Library Holdings: Bk Vols 37,393; Per Subs 97
Publications: Newsletter (quarterly)
Mem of Reaching Across Illinois Library System (RAILS)
Open Mon-Thurs 10-8, Fri & Sat 10-5

STERLING

M CGH MEDICAL CENTER*, Health Sciences Library, 100 E LeFevre Rd, 61081-1278. SAN 375-2739. Tel: 815-625-0400, Ext 5794. *Librn,* Mellisa Cushman; Staff 1 (MLS 1)
Founded 1972
Library Holdings: Bk Vols 400; Per Subs 120
Database Vendor: OCLC FirstSearch
Mem of Reaching Across Illinois Library System (RAILS)
Restriction: Staff use only

P STERLING PUBLIC LIBRARY*, 102 W Third St, 61081-3504. SAN 304-680X. Tel: 815-625-1370. FAX: 815-625-7037. Web Site: www.sterlingpubliclibrary.org. *Dir,* Jennifer Slaney; E-mail: SPL-Director@comcast.net; Staff 13 (MLS 1, Non-MLS 12)
Pop 15,596; Circ 244,458
May 2013-Apr 2014 Income $535,469, State $19,479, City $500,990, Federal $15,000. Mats Exp $46,000, Books $30,000, AV Mat $8,000, Electronic Ref Mat (Incl. Access Fees) $8,000. Sal $302,745
Library Holdings: DVDs 1,235; Electronic Media & Resources 9; Bk Vols 110,128; Per Subs 100; Talking Bks 1,268; Videos 1,070
Subject Interests: Genealogy, Local hist, Polit sci
Automation Activity & Vendor Info: (Cataloging) TLC (The Library Corporation); (Circulation) TLC (The Library Corporation)
Database Vendor: Gale Cengage Learning, OCLC WorldShare Interlibrary Loan, TLC (The Library Corporation), World Book Online
Wireless access
Mem of Reaching Across Illinois Library System (RAILS)
Open Mon-Thurs 9-8, Fri 9-5, Sat 8-5

STICKNEY

P STICKNEY-FOREST VIEW PUBLIC LIBRARY DISTRICT*, 6800 W 43rd St, 60402. SAN 304-6818. Tel: 708-749-1050. FAX: 708-749-1054. Web Site: www.sfvpld.org. *Dir,* Heather Shlah; E-mail: shlahh@sfvpld.org; *Head, Adult Serv,* Oscar Arellano; E-mail: arellano@sfvpld.org; *Head, Circ Serv,* Jesse Blazek; E-mail: blazek@sfvpld.org; *Head, Tech Serv,* Marcos Arellano; *Head, Youth Serv,* Nancy Pajeau; E-mail: pajeaun@sfvpld.org; Staff 22 (MLS 7, Non-MLS 15)
Founded 1953. Pop 6,657; Circ 64,750
Library Holdings: Bk Vols 56,000; Per Subs 189
Automation Activity & Vendor Info: (Acquisitions) Baker & Taylor; (Cataloging) Innovative Interfaces, Inc; (Circulation) Innovative Interfaces, Inc; (Course Reserve) Innovative Interfaces, Inc
Wireless access
Mem of Reaching Across Illinois Library System (RAILS)
Open Mon-Thurs 9-8, Fri 9-5, Sat 9-3
Friends of the Library Group

STILLMAN VALLEY

P JULIA HULL DISTRICT LIBRARY*, 100 Library Lane, 61084. SAN 304-6826. Tel: 815-645-8611. FAX: 815-645-1341. Web Site: www.juliahull.org. *Dir,* Joanna Kluever; E-mail: jkluever@mail.meridian223.org; Staff 8 (MLS 1, Non-MLS 7)
Founded 1924. Pop 6,995; Circ 24,302
Library Holdings: AV Mats 180; CDs 339; DVDs 152; e-books 2,184; Electronic Media & Resources 56; Large Print Bks 341; Bk Vols 25,074; Per Subs 44; Videos 849
Subject Interests: Christian fiction
Wireless access
Mem of Reaching Across Illinois Library System (RAILS)
Open Mon-Thurs 9-8, Fri & Sat 9-5
Friends of the Library Group

STOCKTON

P STOCKTON TOWNSHIP PUBLIC LIBRARY, 140 W Benton Ave, 61085. SAN 304-6834. Tel: 815-947-2030. FAX: 815-947-2030. E-mail: stocktonlibrary@gmail.com. Web Site: www.stocktonlibrary.org. *Dir, Libr Serv,* Kim Scace
Founded 1926. Pop 2,555; Circ 16,915
Library Holdings: AV Mats 400; Large Print Bks 350; Bk Vols 18,000; Per Subs 54
Special Collections: Paintings (J Howard Smith Coll). Oral History
Subject Interests: Local hist
Wireless access
Mem of Reaching Across Illinois Library System (RAILS)
Open Mon & Wed 12:30-7, Tues & Thurs 12:30-6, Fri 12:30-3, Sat 9-1

STONINGTON

P STONINGTON TOWNSHIP PUBLIC LIBRARY*, 500 E North St, 62567. SAN 304-6842. Tel: 217-325-3512. FAX: 217-325-3750. Web Site: www.stonington.lib.il.us. *Librn,* Rita Stephens
Founded 1982. Pop 1,180
Library Holdings: CDs 43; Large Print Bks 48; Bk Titles 17,725; Bk Vols 22,417; Talking Bks 48; Videos 577
Mem of Illinois Heartland Library System
Open Mon & Thurs 1-6:30, Tues, Wed & Fri 10-12 & 1-5, Sat 9-11
Friends of the Library Group

STREAMWOOD

P POPLAR CREEK PUBLIC LIBRARY DISTRICT*, 1405 S Park Ave, 60107-2997. SAN 304-6850. Tel: 630-837-6800. FAX: 630-837-6823. Web Site: www.poplarcreek.lib.il.us. *Asst Dir,* Betty Cress; *Bus & Finance Mgr,* Darly Doyle; *Head, Circ,* Sue Melone; *Admin Librn,* Patricia Marie Hogan; Tel: 630-483-4917, E-mail: p-hogan@dupagels.lib.il.us; *Adult Serv,* Marjorie Kiefer Newman; *Ch Serv,* Elizabeth Drennan; *Doc,* Paulette Harding; *Reader Serv,* Jill Lauerman; *Tech Serv,* John Mitchell; *YA Serv,* Joyce Wagner; Staff 13 (MLS 10, Non-MLS 3)
Founded 1966. Pop 66,639
Library Holdings: CDs 11,676; Bk Vols 328,006; Per Subs 11,683; Videos 5,710
Special Collections: State Document Depository; US Document Depository
Automation Activity & Vendor Info: (Circulation) SirsiDynix
Database Vendor: OCLC FirstSearch, OCLC WorldShare Interlibrary Loan, SirsiDynix
Publications: Library Digest (Newsletter)
Mem of Reaching Across Illinois Library System (RAILS)
Open Mon-Thurs 9am-9:30pm, Fri & Sat 9-5, Sun 12-5
Branches: 1
SONYA CRAWSHAW BRANCH, 4300 Audrey Lane, Hanover Park, 60133, SAN 374-3578. Tel: 630-372-0052. FAX: 630-372-0024. *Mgr,* Vikki Hallack
Open Mon-Thurs 12-9, Fri-Sun 12-5

STREATOR

P STREATOR PUBLIC LIBRARY*, 130 S Park St, 61364. SAN 304-6869. Tel: 815-672-2729. FAX: 815-672-2729. E-mail: spl130spark@yahoo.com. *Dir,* Leslie Dianne Poldek; *Cat,* Rose Ann Negray; Staff 1 (Non-MLS 1)
Founded 1903. Pop 14,190; Circ 41,731
May 2007-Apr 2008 Income $328,632, State $56,713, City $232,369, Federal $342, Locally Generated Income $39,208. Mats Exp $118,390, Books $33,441, Per/Ser (Incl. Access Fees) $5,239, Micro $750, AV Mat $667, Electronic Ref Mat (Incl. Access Fees) $1,875. Sal $128,125
Library Holdings: Audiobooks 947; AV Mats 954; Bks on Deafness & Sign Lang 26; High Interest/Low Vocabulary Bk Vols 130; Large Print Bks 1,000; Bk Titles 42,800; Bk Vols 42,881; Per Subs 112; Talking Bks 947; Videos 954
Special Collections: History of Streator & La Salle County
Automation Activity & Vendor Info: (Acquisitions) SIRSI WorkFlows; (Cataloging) SIRSI WorkFlows; (Circulation) SIRSI WorkFlows; (Course Reserve) SIRSI WorkFlows; (ILL) SIRSI WorkFlows; (Media Booking) SIRSI WorkFlows; (OPAC) SIRSI WorkFlows; (Serials) SIRSI WorkFlows
Database Vendor: OCLC ArticleFirst, OCLC FirstSearch, OCLC WebJunction, OCLC WorldShare Interlibrary Loan
Wireless access
Mem of Reaching Across Illinois Library System (RAILS)
Open Mon-Thurs (Winter) 9-8, Fri & Sat 9-6; Mon-Fri (Summer) 9-6, Sat 9-1
Friends of the Library Group

SUGAR GROVE

P SUGAR GROVE PUBLIC LIBRARY DISTRICT*, 125 S Municipal Dr, 60554. SAN 304-6877. Tel: 630-466-4686. Interlibrary Loan Service Tel: 630-466-3956. Administration Tel: 630-466-1448. Information Services Tel:

630-466-3951. FAX: 630-466-4189. TDD: 800-526-0844 (relay). E-mail: library@sugargrove.lib.il.us. Web Site: www.sugargrove.lib.il.us. *Dir,* Shannon Halikias; E-mail: director@sugargrove.lib.il.us; Staff 11 (MLS 1, Non-MLS 10)
Founded 1962. Pop 15,476; Circ 83,582
Jul 2009-Jun 2010 Income $577,276, State $18,859, Locally Generated Income $558,417. Mats Exp $76,656. Sal $338,842
Library Holdings: Audiobooks 2,211; CDs 1,000; DVDs 300; Bk Vols 43,545; Per Subs 380; Videos 538
Automation Activity & Vendor Info: (Cataloging) SIRSI WorkFlows; (Circulation) SIRSI WorkFlows; (OPAC) SIRSI WorkFlows
Database Vendor: EBSCOhost, Gale Cengage Learning, Grolier Online, Newsbank
Wireless access
Mem of Reaching Across Illinois Library System (RAILS)
Open Tues-Thurs 9-9, Fri & Sat 9-1
Friends of the Library Group

J WAUBONSEE COMMUNITY COLLEGE*, Todd Library, State Rte 47 at Waubonsee Dr, 60554. SAN 304-6885. Tel: 630-466-2400. FAX: 630-466-7799. Web Site: library.waubonsee.edu. *Dean,* Mary Edith Butler; Tel: 630-466-2854, E-mail: mbutler@waubonsee.edu; *Librn,* Adam Burke; Tel: 630-466-2396, E-mail: aburke@waubonsee.edu; *Librn,* Stacia Happ; E-mail: shapp@waubonsee.edu; *Mgr, Libr Syst & Support Serv,* Laura A Michalek; Tel: 630-466-2405, E-mail: lmichalek@waubonsee.edu; *Tech Coordr,* John Wohlers; Tel: 630-466-2587, E-mail: jwohlers@waubonsee.edu; *Circ,* Rhea Hunter-Brodhead; Tel: 630-466-2401, E-mail: rhunter@waubonsee.edu; *Circ,* Rocio Limonez; Tel: 630-466-2943, E-mail: rlimonez@waubonsee.edu; *ILL,* Kendall Vance; Tel: 630-466-2333, E-mail: kvance@waubonsee.edu; Staff 16 (MLS 6, Non-MLS 10)
Founded 1967. Enrl 9,935; Fac 510; Highest Degree: Associate
Library Holdings: AV Mats 6,502; e-books 9,544; e-journals 14,717; Bk Vols 45,135; Per Subs 568
Automation Activity & Vendor Info: (Cataloging) SirsiDynix; (Circulation) SirsiDynix; (Course Reserve) SirsiDynix; (ILL) OCLC FirstSearch; (OPAC) SirsiDynix; (Serials) EOS International
Database Vendor: EBSCOhost, Gale Cengage Learning, LexisNexis, Newsbank, OCLC FirstSearch, OCLC WorldShare Interlibrary Loan, ProQuest, Wilson - Wilson Web
Partic in Consortium of Academic & Research Libraries in Illinois; Northern Illinois Learning Resources Cooperative (NILRC)
Special Services for the Blind - Closed circuit TV; Screen reader software
Open Mon-Thurs 7:30am-10pm, Fri 7:30-4:30, Sat 8-1, Sun 12-5:30

SULLIVAN

S MOULTRIE COUNTY HISTORICAL & GENEALOGICAL SOCIETY LIBRARY*, 117 E Harrison St, 61951. (Mail add: PO Box 588, 61951-0588), SAN 327-7917. Tel: 217-728-4085. E-mail: cardinal_61951@yahoo.com. *Librn,* Mary Storm
Special Collections: Family Histories, County Newspapers on Film; Illinois State Death Index (1916-1950)
Open Mon-Sat 1-5

P ELIZABETH TITUS MEMORIAL LIBRARY*, Two W Water St, 61951. SAN 304-6893. Tel: 217-728-7221. FAX: 217-728-2215. Web Site: www.sullivanil.us/library.html. *Dir,* Clem Uptmor; E-mail: knutesboys@yahoo.com; *Asst Dir,* Susan Wood; E-mail: susanew10@hotmail.com; *Ch,* Michelle Nolan; E-mail: mitchy13_69@yahoo.com; *Circ Librn,* Holly Aldendorf; *Circ Librn,* Jessica Bathe; *Tech Serv,* Christine Lane
Founded 1915. Pop 4,400; Circ 35,880
Library Holdings: AV Mats 4,546; Bk Vols 42,357; Per Subs 90
Automation Activity & Vendor Info: (Acquisitions) Innovative Interfaces, Inc; (Cataloging) Innovative Interfaces, Inc; (Circulation) Innovative Interfaces, Inc; (OPAC) Innovative Interfaces, Inc
Wireless access
Mem of Illinois Heartland Library System
Open Mon-Thurs 8:30-8, Fri 8:30-5, Sat 9-2

SUMMIT

P SUMMIT PUBLIC LIBRARY DISTRICT, 6233 S Archer Rd, 60501. SAN 304-6915. Tel: 708-458-1545. FAX: 708-458-1842. E-mail: summitlibrary@yahoo.com. Web Site: www.summitlibrary.info. *Dir,* Hadiya Drew; Staff 10 (MLS 1, Non-MLS 9)
Founded 1917. Pop 11,064
Subject Interests: Spanish (Lang)
Automation Activity & Vendor Info: (Circulation) Innovative Interfaces, Inc
Wireless access
Mem of Reaching Across Illinois Library System (RAILS)
Open Mon-Thurs 10-8, Fri 12-5, Sat 9-5
Friends of the Library Group

SUMNER

S ILLINOIS DEPARTMENT OF CORRECTIONS*, Lawrence Correctional Center Library, Rte 2, Box 36, 62466. Tel: 618-936-2064. FAX: 618-936-2842. Web Site: www.idoc.state.il.us. *Librn,* Sharon McCorkle
Library Holdings: Bk Vols 5,000
Open Tues-Fri 7-5

SYCAMORE

P SYCAMORE PUBLIC LIBRARY*, 103 E State St, 60178-1440. SAN 304-6923. Tel: 815-895-2500. FAX: 815-895-9816. E-mail: spl@sycamorelibrary.org. Web Site: www.sycamorelibrary.org. *Dir,* Sarah Tobias; Staff 22 (MLS 3, Non-MLS 19)
Founded 1891. Pop 14,866; Circ 206,717
Library Holdings: Audiobooks 3,000; CDs 2,000; DVDs 2,800; e-books 3,987; Bk Vols 56,730; Per Subs 121; Videos 300
Subject Interests: Local hist
Automation Activity & Vendor Info: (Acquisitions) SirsiDynix; (Cataloging) SirsiDynix; (Circulation) SirsiDynix; (Course Reserve) SirsiDynix; (ILL) SirsiDynix; (Media Booking) SirsiDynix; (OPAC) SirsiDynix; (Serials) SirsiDynix
Database Vendor: OCLC FirstSearch, SirsiDynix
Wireless access
Function: Bks on cassette, Bks on CD, Computer training, Computers for patron use, Copy machines, Home delivery & serv to Sr ctr & nursing homes, ILL available, Music CDs, Notary serv, Online cat, Online ref, Online searches, Photocopying/Printing, Preschool outreach, Prog for adults, Prog for children & young adult, Pub access computers, Ref serv available, Story hour, Summer reading prog, Tax forms, Teen prog, Web-catalog
Mem of Reaching Across Illinois Library System (RAILS)
Special Services for the Deaf - TDD equip
Open Mon-Thurs 9-9, Fri & Sat 9-5, Sun (Sept-May) 1-5
Restriction: Non-resident fee

TAYLORVILLE

S TAYLORVILLE CORRECTIONAL CENTER LIBRARY*, PO Box 1000, 62568. SAN 376-1185. Tel: 217-824-4004, Ext 5802. FAX: 217-824-4042. Web Site: www.idoc.state.il.us. *Librn,* Position Currently Open
Library Holdings: Bk Titles 4,000; Bk Vols 7,000

P TAYLORVILLE PUBLIC LIBRARY, 121 W Vine St, 62568. SAN 304-6931. Tel: 217-824-4736. FAX: 217-824-8921. E-mail: directortpl@yahoo.com. Web Site: www.taylorville.lib.il.us. *Dir,* Dorothy Siles; Staff 7 (MLS 1, Non-MLS 6)
Founded 1899. Pop 11,113; Circ 79,653
Library Holdings: CDs 1,000; High Interest/Low Vocabulary Bk Vols 200; Large Print Bks 2,000; Bk Vols 45,000; Per Subs 120
Subject Interests: Antiques
Automation Activity & Vendor Info: (Acquisitions) Innovative Interfaces, Inc; (Cataloging) Innovative Interfaces, Inc; (Circulation) Innovative Interfaces, Inc; (Course Reserve) Innovative Interfaces, Inc; (ILL) Innovative Interfaces, Inc; (Media Booking) Innovative Interfaces, Inc; (OPAC) Innovative Interfaces, Inc; (Serials) Innovative Interfaces, Inc
Database Vendor: OCLC FirstSearch
Wireless access
Mem of Illinois Heartland Library System
Open Mon-Thurs 10-8, Fri & Sat 10-5
Friends of the Library Group

THIRD LAKE

S JOE BULEY MEMORIAL LIBRARY*, 35240 N Grant St, 60030. (Mail add: PO Box 371, 60030). Tel: 847-223-5971. Administration Tel: 847-223-4300. *Dir,* Dr Nicholas T Groves; Staff 2 (MLS 1, Non-MLS 1)
Founded 2004
Library Holdings: Bk Titles 10,000; Bk Vols 15,000; Per Subs 50
Subject Interests: Orthodox theol & hist, Scriptural studies, Serbian archival mat, Serbian hist & culture
Function: Res libr
Restriction: Access at librarian's discretion

THOMSON

P YORK TOWNSHIP PUBLIC LIBRARY*, 1005 W Main St, 61285. SAN 304-694X. Tel: 815-259-2480. FAX: 815-259-2480. *Librn,* Deeann Kramer
Founded 1919. Pop 2,272; Circ 17,330
Library Holdings: Bk Vols 14,458; Per Subs 22
Subject Interests: Local hist
Mem of Reaching Across Illinois Library System (RAILS)
Open Mon & Wed 5:30-8, Tues & Thurs 9-4:30, Sat 9-2

THORNTON

P THORNTON PUBLIC LIBRARY*, 115 E Margaret St, 60476. SAN 304-6958. Tel: 708-877-2579. FAX: 708-877-2608. *Dir,* Kathy Vente; Staff 1 (Non-MLS 1)
Founded 1940. Pop 2,582; Circ 15,729
Library Holdings: Bk Vols 20,000; Per Subs 60
Special Collections: American Indians
Mem of Reaching Across Illinois Library System (RAILS)
Open Mon, Wed & Fri 12-5, Tues & Thurs 12-8, Sat 10-4

TINLEY PARK

C DEVRY UNIVERSITY*, Tinley Park Library, 18624 W Creek Dr, 60477. Tel: 708-342-3360, 708-342-3361. FAX: 708-342-3315. Web Site: www.tp.devry.edu/library.html. *Dir, Libr Serv,* Paul Burden; E-mail: pburden@devry.edu
Library Holdings: Bk Titles 12,000
Open Mon-Fri 7am-9pm, Sat 8-3

P TINLEY PARK PUBLIC LIBRARY*, 7851 Timber Dr, 60477-3398. SAN 304-6974. Tel: 708-532-0160. FAX: 708-532-2981. Reference FAX: 708-532-9813. E-mail: tp_library@tplibrary.org. Web Site: www.tplibrary.org. *Adminr,* Rich Wolff; Tel: 708-532-0160, Ext 8, E-mail: r_wolff@tplibrary.org; *Asst Admin,* Position Currently Open; *Mgr, Patron Serv,* Mary Ann Pyrzynski; Tel: 708-532-0160, Ext 3, E-mail: m_pyrzynski@tplibrary.org; *Adult Serv,* Robin Lauren; Tel: 708-532-0160, Ext 1, E-mail: r_lauren@tplibrary.org; *Ch Serv,* Sharon Dudeck; Tel: 708-532-0160, Ext 2, E-mail: s_dudeck@tplibrary.org; *Tech Serv,* Joy Anhalt; Tel: 708-532-0160, Ext 7, E-mail: j_anhalt@tplibrary.org
Founded 1959. Pop 65,031; Circ 556,106
Library Holdings: AV Mats 12,323; Bk Vols 141,957; Per Subs 813
Special Collections: Arabic Language Books; German Language Books; Hindi Language Books; Spanish Language Books
Automation Activity & Vendor Info: (Circulation) Innovative Interfaces, Inc
Database Vendor: EBSCOhost, LearningExpress, Newsbank, OCLC FirstSearch, ReferenceUSA
Wireless access
Mem of Reaching Across Illinois Library System (RAILS)
Open Mon-Fri 9-9, Sat 9-5, Sun 1-5
Friends of the Library Group
Bookmobiles: 1

TISKILWA

P TISKILWA PUBLIC LIBRARY*, 119 E Main, 61368. (Mail add: PO Box 150, 61368), SAN 304-6982. Tel: 815-646-4511. FAX: 815-646-4247. E-mail: tisklib@comcast.net. Web Site: www.tisklib.org. *Head Librn,* Karyn Stark; *Asst Librn,* Jean Cavada
Founded 1875. Pop 1,587; Circ 17,183
Library Holdings: Bk Vols 16,000; Per Subs 44
Special Collections: Oral History
Automation Activity & Vendor Info: (ILL) PALS
Wireless access
Mem of Reaching Across Illinois Library System (RAILS)
Open Mon & Thurs 1-7, Tues & Wed 9-12 & 1-7, Fri 9-12 & 1-5, Sat 9-12

TOLEDO

P SUMPTER TOWNSHIP LIBRARY*, 148 Courthouse Sq, 62468. (Mail add: PO Box 67, 62468-0067), SAN 304-6990. Tel: 217-849-2072. FAX: 217-849-2072. Web Site: www.r1.net. *Librn,* Cassandra Stewart
Pop 1,967; Circ 19,371
Library Holdings: Bk Vols 20,000; Per Subs 84
Mem of Illinois Heartland Library System
Open Tues & Thurs (Sept-May) 12-7, Wed 9-5, Fri 12-5, Sat 9-12; Tues (June-Aug) 11-6

TOLONO

P TOLONO PUBLIC LIBRARY DISTRICT*, 111 E Main St, 61880. (Mail add: PO Box 759, 61880-0759), SAN 304-7008. Tel: 217-485-5558. FAX: 217-485-3088. Web Site: www.tolonolibrary.org. *Dir,* Janet Cler; *Librn,* Dianne Bland
Founded 1968. Pop 8,130; Circ 104,000
Library Holdings: Bk Vols 25,000
Special Collections: Local Archives
Mem of Illinois Heartland Library System
Open Mon-Fri 10-8, Sat 10-4
Friends of the Library Group

TOLUCA

P TOLUCA PUBLIC LIBRARY*, 102 N Main St, 61369. (Mail add: PO Box 526, 61369), SAN 304-7016. Tel: 815-452-2211. FAX: 815-452-2211. *Librn,* Mary Cassidy
Founded 1974. Pop 1,339; Circ 5,030
Library Holdings: Bk Vols 8,079
Special Collections: National Geographic 1929-present
Wireless access
Mem of Reaching Across Illinois Library System (RAILS)
Open Mon & Wed 9-12, Tues & Fri 9-12 & 1-4:30, Thurs 9-12 & 1:30-4:30

TOULON

P TOULON PUBLIC LIBRARY DISTRICT*, 306 W Jefferson, 61483. SAN 304-7024. Tel: 309-286-5791. FAX: 309-286-4481. E-mail: toulonlibrary@gmail.com. Web Site: www.toulonpld.org. *Dir,* Laura Frisby; *Youth Serv,* Heather Hollis
Pop 2,886; Circ 22,254
Library Holdings: CDs 323; DVDs 838; e-books 825; Large Print Bks 865; Bk Vols 20,418; Per Subs 85; Talking Bks 379; Videos 1,542
Automation Activity & Vendor Info: (Circulation) TLC (The Library Corporation)
Database Vendor: TLC (The Library Corporation)
Wireless access
Publications: The Library Link (Newsletter)
Open Mon & Fri 10-5, Tues-Thurs 10-9, Sat 10-3

TOWANDA

P TOWANDA DISTRICT LIBRARY*, 301 S Taylor St, 61776. SAN 304-7032. Tel: 309-728-2176. FAX: 309-728-2139. E-mail: towandalib@yahoo.com. Web Site: towandalibrary.org. *Dir,* Karen Scott Bersche; Staff 1.75 (MLS 0.75, Non-MLS 1)
Founded 1939. Pop 1,989; Circ 16,600
Jul 2008-Jun 2009 Income $131,795, State $3,550, Federal $296, County $121,355, Locally Generated Income $6,594. Mats Exp $19,440, Books $13,945, Per/Ser (Incl. Access Fees) $1,600, AV Mat $3,895. Sal $64,167 (Prof $30,000)
Library Holdings: Audiobooks 419; CDs 1,221; DVDs 1,000; Large Print Bks 121; Bk Vols 16,650; Per Subs 53; Videos 362
Special Collections: History Coll; Illinois Coll; National Geographic Coll, 1916-present
Automation Activity & Vendor Info: (Cataloging) SirsiDynix; (Circulation) SirsiDynix; (ILL) SirsiDynix; (OPAC) SirsiDynix
Database Vendor: OCLC FirstSearch
Wireless access
Function: Adult bk club, Bks on cassette, Bks on CD, Children's prog, Computers for patron use, Copy machines, E-Reserves, Fax serv, Free DVD rentals, Handicapped accessible, Homebound delivery serv, ILL available, Music CDs, Prog for adults, Prog for children & young adult, Pub access computers, Ref serv in person, Spoken cassettes & CDs, Spoken cassettes & DVDs, Story hour, Summer reading prog, Tax forms, VHS videos, Web-catalog, Wheelchair accessible
Special Services for the Blind - Duplicating spec requests
Open Mon & Wed 10-6, Tues 1-7, Thurs & Fri 1-6, Sat 9-2
Restriction: Authorized patrons, Borrowing requests are handled by ILL
Friends of the Library Group

TREMONT

P TREMONT DISTRICT PUBLIC LIBRARY*, 215 S Sampson St, 61568. (Mail add: PO Box 123, 61568-0123), SAN 304-7040. Tel: 309-925-5432, 309-925-5597. FAX: 309-925-9953. E-mail: trdl@dpc.net. Web Site: www.tremont.lib.il.us/library. *Librn,* Judith Scheirer; *Ch Serv,* Adele Pollock; *Circ,* Jill Stout
Founded 1928. Pop 5,022; Circ 77,928
Jul 2007-Jun 2008 Income $236,019, State $8,013, Federal $2,559, Locally Generated Income $210,000, Other $15,447. Mats Exp $41,112, Books $27,598, Per/Ser (Incl. Access Fees) $5,177, AV Mat $5,177, Electronic Ref Mat (Incl. Access Fees) $3,160. Sal $103,000 (Prof $31,000)
Library Holdings: AV Mats 700; Bks on Deafness & Sign Lang 12; CDs 1,130; DVDs 787; High Interest/Low Vocabulary Bk Vols 110; Large Print Bks 400; Bk Titles 22,718; Bk Vols 24,532; Per Subs 83; Talking Bks 641
Subject Interests: Local hist
Automation Activity & Vendor Info: (Circulation) TLC (The Library Corporation); (ILL) OCLC FirstSearch; (OPAC) TLC (The Library Corporation)
Database Vendor: Baker & Taylor, OCLC FirstSearch, TLC (The Library Corporation)
Wireless access
Function: Adult bk club, Art exhibits, Computer training, Copy machines, Digital talking bks, Electronic databases & coll, Handicapped accessible, Home delivery & serv to Sr ctr & nursing homes, Homebound delivery serv, ILL available, Mail & tel request accepted, Music CDs, Online

searches, Photocopying/Printing, Prog for adults, Prog for children & young adult, Ref & res, Senior computer classes, Spoken cassettes & CDs, Summer reading prog, Tax forms, Telephone ref, Video lending libr, Wheelchair accessible
Mem of Reaching Across Illinois Library System (RAILS)
Partic in Resource Sharing Alliance
Open Mon, Tues & Thurs 10-12 & 2-8, Wed & Fri 10-5, Sat 9-1

TRENTON

P TRENTON PUBLIC LIBRARY*, 118 E Indiana, 62293. SAN 304-7059. Tel: 618-224-7662. FAX: 618-224-7671. Web Site: www.trenton.lib.il.us. *Libr Dir,* Linda L Richter; E-mail: lrich118@gmail.com; *Asst Librn,* Joe Billhartz; *Asst Librn,* Tracy Frey; Staff 2 (Non-MLS 2)
Founded 1974. Pop 2,715; Circ 11,236
Library Holdings: DVDs 350; Large Print Bks 954; Bk Vols 28,994; Per Subs 78; Talking Bks 290; Videos 921
Database Vendor: OCLC FirstSearch
Wireless access
Mem of Illinois Heartland Library System
Open Tues-Thurs 10-7, Fri 3-5, Sat 9-1

TROY

P TRI-TOWNSHIP PUBLIC LIBRARY DISTRICT*, 209 S Main St, 62294. SAN 375-9709. Tel: 618-667-2133. FAX: 618-667-9866. E-mail: info@troylibrary.org. Web Site: troylibrary.org. *Dir,* David Cassens, II; *Ch,* Robin Lovinggood; *Circ Supvr,* Jim Stuller; Staff 8 (MLS 1, Non-MLS 7)
Pop 13,215; Circ 70,000
Library Holdings: Bk Titles 30,000; Per Subs 195
Special Collections: Local Area Parenting Coll
Automation Activity & Vendor Info: (Circulation) SirsiDynix
Function: Doc delivery serv, ILL available, Online searches, Prog for children & young adult, Ref serv available, Summer reading prog, Telephone ref
Mem of Illinois Heartland Library System
Open Mon-Thurs 9-8, Fri 9-5, Sat 9-4
Friends of the Library Group

TUSCOLA

P TUSCOLA PUBLIC LIBRARY*, 112 E Sale St, 61953. SAN 304-7067. Tel: 217-253-3812. FAX: 217-253-4599. Web Site: www.tuscola.lib.il.us. *Ch Serv, Librn,* Bryan Penne; Staff 6 (MLS 1, Non-MLS 5)
Founded 1903. Pop 4,448
Library Holdings: Bk Vols 16,865; Per Subs 45
Function: Homebound delivery serv, ILL available, Magnifiers for reading, Photocopying/Printing, Prog for children & young adult, Summer reading prog, Telephone ref, Wheelchair accessible
Mem of Illinois Heartland Library System
Open Mon-Thurs 10-7, Fri & Sat 10-6
Friends of the Library Group

ULLIN

J SHAWNEE COMMUNITY COLLEGE LIBRARY*, 8364 Shawnee College Rd, 62992. SAN 304-7083. Tel: 618-634-3271. FAX: 618-634-3215. Web Site: www.shawnee.cc.il.us. *Librn,* Tracey Johnson; E-mail: traceyj@shawneecc.edu; Staff 1 (Non-MLS 1)
Founded 1969
Library Holdings: AV Mats 2,000; Bk Vols 38,300; Per Subs 175
Special Collections: Oral History
Automation Activity & Vendor Info: (Acquisitions) SirsiDynix; (Cataloging) SirsiDynix; (Circulation) SirsiDynix; (OPAC) SirsiDynix; (Serials) SirsiDynix
Wireless access
Mem of Illinois Heartland Library System
Partic in Illinois Library & Information Network; Southern Ill Learning Resources Coop
Open Mon-Thurs (Winter) 8-8, Fri 8-4; Mon-Fri (Summer) 8-4

UNION

S ILLINOIS RAILWAY MUSEUM*, Pullman Technical Library, 7000 Olson Rd, 60180. (Mail add: PO Box 427, 60180-0427), SAN 326-4009. Tel: 815-923-2020. FAX: 815-923-2006. E-mail: pullmanlibrary@irm.org. Web Site: www.irm.org. *Curator,* Ted Anderson; *Archivist,* Al Johanson; *Historian,* Bob Webber
Founded 1974
Special Collections: Pullman Company Linen Tracings & Blueprints Coll; T-Z Company Coll, blue prints
Function: Archival coll
Restriction: Open by appt only

UNIVERSITY PARK

C GOVERNORS STATE UNIVERSITY LIBRARY*, One University Pkwy, 60466-0975. SAN 304-5315. Tel: 708-534-4111. Circulation Tel: 708-534-4112. Interlibrary Loan Service Tel: 708-235-7508. Administration Tel: 708-534-4110. FAX: 708-534-4564. Web Site: www.govst.edu/library. *Dean,* Diane Dates Casey; Tel: 708-534-4110, E-mail: d-casey@govst.edu; *Acq, Ser,* Lydia Morrow-Ruetten; Tel: 708-534-4116, E-mail: l-morrow@govst.edu; *Libr Tech,* Michel Nguessan; Tel: 708-235-2143, E-mail: m-nguessan@govst.edu; *Ref,* Linda Geller; Tel: 708-534-4136, E-mail: l-geller@govst.edu; *Ref,* Paul Blobaum; Tel: 708-534-4139, E-mail: p-blobaum@govst.edu; *Ref,* Nancy Shlaes; Tel: 708-534-4137, E-mail: n-shlaes@govst.edu; Staff 29 (MLS 7, Non-MLS 22)
Founded 1969. Enrl 6,073; Fac 195; Highest Degree: Master
Library Holdings: AV Mats 26,720; CDs 356; DVDs 409; e-books 2,000; e-journals 20,165; Bk Titles 238,491; Bk Vols 263,953; Per Subs 1,917; Videos 9,008
Special Collections: Afro-American Literature (Schomberg Coll); ERIC Documents Coll, microfiche; Materials Center Coll. State Document Depository; US Document Depository
Subject Interests: Acctg, Biol, Bus & mgt, Chem, Computer sci, Counseling, Criminal law & justice, Educ, Finance, Humanities, Psychol
Automation Activity & Vendor Info: (Acquisitions) Ex Libris Group; (Cataloging) Ex Libris Group; (Circulation) Ex Libris Group; (Course Reserve) Ex Libris Group; (ILL) OCLC ILLiad; (OPAC) Ex Libris Group; (Serials) Ex Libris Group
Wireless access
Publications: Index to Non-print Materials; Information Please (Newsletter); Media Holdings List; Periodicals Holding List; Subject Guide to Indexes & Abstracts
Partic in Chicago & South Consortium; Chicago Academic Libr Coun; Consortium of Academic & Research Libraries in Illinois; OCLC Online Computer Library Center, Inc; SMRHEC
Special Services for the Deaf - Closed caption videos
Special Services for the Blind - Assistive/Adapted tech devices, equip & products
Open Mon-Thurs 8:30am-10:30pm, Fri & Sat 8:30-5, Sun 1-5
Friends of the Library Group

P UNIVERSITY PARK PUBLIC LIBRARY DISTRICT, 1100 Blackhawk Dr, 60466. SAN 304-5323. Tel: 708-534-2580. FAX: 708-534-2583. E-mail: universityparkpld@yahoo.com. Web Site: www.universityparklibrary.org. *Dir,* Tracy Ducksworth; *Head, Circ,* Position Currently Open; *Librn,* Shannon Perkins; *Pub Serv Coordr,* Sonje Lee
Founded 1974. Pop 6,245; Circ 16,314
Library Holdings: Bk Vols 23,000; Per Subs 95
Automation Activity & Vendor Info: (Circulation) SirsiDynix
Wireless access
Mem of Reaching Across Illinois Library System (RAILS)
Open Mon-Thurs 10-8, Fri & Sat 10-5
Friends of the Library Group

URBANA

S NATIONAL COUNCIL OF TEACHERS OF ENGLISH LIBRARY, 1111 W Kenyon Rd, 61801-1096. SAN 325-1535. Tel: 217-278-3619. FAX: 217-328-0977. Web Site: www.ncte.org. *Pub Div Dir,* Kurt Austin; E-mail: kaustin@ncte.org
Founded 1959
Library Holdings: Bk Titles 3,100; Bk Vols 4,800; Per Subs 35
Special Collections: NCTE Monographs - English Language Arts (NCTE Archives Coll), bks, microfiche, records, tapes
Subject Interests: Reading, Study, Teaching, Writing
Wireless access
Publications: Bibliographies; New Book List
Mem of Illinois Heartland Library System
Partic in Illinois Library & Information Network
Open Mon-Fri 8-4:30

M PROVENA COVENANT MEDICAL CENTER LIBRARY*, 1400 W Park St, 61801. SAN 304-7148. Tel: 217-337-2283. FAX: 217-337-2299. Web Site: www.provena.org/covenant. *Librn,* Elissa Cochran; E-mail: elissa.cochran@provena.org; Staff 1 (MLS 1)
Founded 1931
Library Holdings: Bk Titles 1,000; Per Subs 100
Subject Interests: Med, Nursing
Database Vendor: OCLC FirstSearch
Mem of Illinois Heartland Library System
Partic in Illinois Library & Information Network; Regional Med Libr - Region 3
Open Mon-Fri 8-4:30

C UNIVERSITY OF ILLINOIS LIBRARY AT URBANA-CHAMPAIGN*, 1408 W Gregory Drive, 61801. SAN 340-8124. Tel: 217-333-2290. Administration Tel: 217-333-0790. Administration FAX: 217-244-4358. E-mail: writeus@library.illinois.edu. Web Site: www.library.illinois.edu. *Dean, Libr & Univ Librn,* John P Wilkin; Staff 163 (MLS 110, Non-MLS 53)
Founded 1868. Enrl 42,000; Highest Degree: Doctorate
Library Holdings: Bk Vols 13,000,000
Special Collections: 16th & 17th Century Italian Drama; 17th Century Coll; 17th Century Newsletters; 17th Century Publishing (William Bentley & Grant Richards Coll); 18th Century English Literature (Nickell Coll); Abraham Lincoln Coll; American Humor & Folklore (Franklin J Meine Coll); Aquinas; Baskette Coll on Freedom of Expression; Carl Sandburg Coll; Cobbett (Muierhead Coll); Confederate Imprints (Richard B Harwell Coll); H G Wells Coll; Hollander Library of Economic History; Incunabula including St Thomas; John Milton Coll; Political & Religious Pamphlets; Shakespeare (Ernest Ingold Coll); Shana Alexander papers; T W Baldwin Elizabethan Library; W S Merwin papers; William Maxwell papers; William Shakespeare Coll. Oral History; US Document Depository
Database Vendor: Dialog, EBSCOhost, Gale Cengage Learning, Innovative Interfaces, Inc, OCLC FirstSearch, OVID Technologies, ProQuest, SirsiDynix
Wireless access
Publications: Friendscript
Mem of Illinois Heartland Library System
Partic in Association of Research Libraries (ARL); Consortium of Academic & Research Libraries in Illinois; Illinois Library & Information Network; Midwest Universities Consortium for Int Activities, Inc; OCLC Online Computer Library Center, Inc
Open Mon-Fri 8:30-5, Sat & Sun 1-5
Friends of the Library Group

Departmental Libraries:

APPLIED HEALTH SCIENCES LIBRARY, 146 Main Library, 1408 W Gregory Dr, 61801, SAN 340-8213. Tel: 217-333-3615. FAX: 217-333-8384. Web Site: www.library.illinois.edu/ahs. *Librn,* Mary Beth Allen; Tel: 217-244-1870, E-mail: mballen@illinois.edu; Staff 3 (MLS 1, Non-MLS 2)
Library Holdings: Bk Vols 25,000
Open Mon-Fri 8:30-5

ARCHITECTURE & ART LIBRARY, 208 Architecture, 608 E Lorado Taft Dr, 61801, SAN 340-8248. Tel: 217-333-0224. FAX: 217-244-5169. E-mail: rickerlibrary@library.uiuc.edu. Web Site: www.library.illinois.edu/arx. *Librn,* Jane Block; Tel: 217-333-7073, E-mail: block3@illinois.edu
Library Holdings: Bk Vols 58,274
Open Mon-Fri 8:30-5

ASIAN, 325 Main Library, 1408 W Gregory Dr, 61801, SAN 340-8264. Tel: 217-333-1501. FAX: 217-333-2214. Web Site: www.library.illinois.edu/asx. *Head Librn,* Karen Wei; Tel: 217-244-2046, E-mail: kwei@uiuc.edu
Founded 1965
Library Holdings: Bk Vols 420,000; Per Subs 1,250
Open Mon-Fri 8:30-5

BIOLOGY, Funk Library, 1101 S Goodwin, 61801, SAN 340-8272. Tel: 217-244-2249. FAX: 217-333-0558. E-mail: biolib@uiuc.edu. Web Site: www.library.illinois.edu/bix. *Librn,* Kelli Trei; Tel: 217-244-2503, E-mail: ktrei2@illinois.edu. Subject Specialists: *Biol,* Kelli Trei
Open Mon-Thurs 8:30am-3am, Fri 8:30am-10pm, Sat 10-10, Sun 10am-3am

BUSINESS & ECONOMICS, 101 Main Library, 1408 W Gregory, 61801, SAN 340-8396. Tel: 217-333-3619. FAX: 217-244-1931. Web Site: library.illinois.edu/bel. *Head Librn,* Rebecca Smith; Tel: 217-244-0388, E-mail: becky@illinois.edu; Staff 3 (MLS 3)
Library Holdings: Bk Vols 65,000; Per Subs 1,200
Open Mon-Fri 8:30-5

CHEMISTRY, 170 Noyes Lab, MC-712, 505 S Matthews, 61801, SAN 340-8302. Tel: 217-333-3737. Web Site: www.library.uiuc.edu/chx. *Librn,* Tina Chrazstowski
Library Holdings: Bk Vols 70,000
Open Mon-Thurs 8:30-7, Fri 8:30-5, Sat & Sun 1-5

CLASSICS, 1408 W Gregory Dr, 419A, 61801, SAN 340-8361. Tel: 217-333-1124. FAX: 217-333-2214. Web Site: www.library.illinois.edu/clx. *Librn,* Bruce W Swann; Tel: 217-244-1872, E-mail: bswann@uiuc.edu. Subject Specialists: *Classics,* Bruce W Swann
Library Holdings: Bk Titles 54,000
Open Mon-Fri 9-5

COMMUNICATIONS, 122 Gregory Hall, 61801, SAN 340-8426. Tel: 217-333-2216. Web Site: www.library.illinois.edu/cmx. *Librn,* Lisa Romero; Tel: 217-333-6348, E-mail: l-romero@uiuc.edu
Library Holdings: AV Mats 900; Bk Vols 16,600
Open Mon-Fri 9-5, Sat & Sun 1-5

FUNK LIBRARY, AGRICULTURAL, CONSUMER & ENVIRONMENTAL SCIENCES, 1101 S Goodwin, MC-633, 61801, SAN 340-8183. Tel: 217-333-2416. Reference Tel: 217-244-2249. FAX: 217-333-0558. Web Site: www.library.illinois.edu/funkaces. *Head Librn,* Robert Allen; Tel: 217-244-2245, E-mail: allen2@illinois.edu
Library Holdings: Bk Vols 119,815
Open Mon-Thurs 8:30am-3am, Fri 8:30am-10pm, Sat 10-10, Sun 10am-3am

GEOLOGY, 223 Natural History Bldg, 1301 W Green St, 61801, SAN 340-8574. Tel: 217-333-1266. FAX: 217-244-4319. Web Site: www.library.illinois.edu/gex. *Librn,* Lura Joseph; E-mail: luraj@uiuc.edu
Library Holdings: Bk Vols 100,359
Open Mon-Thurs 9-9, Fri 9-5
Friends of the Library Group

GOVERNMENT DOCUMENTS, 200-D Main Libr, 1408 W Gregory Dr, 61801, SAN 340-8434. Tel: 217-244-6445. FAX: 217-333-2214. E-mail: gdoclib@library.uiuc.edu. Web Site: www.library.illinois.edu/doc. *Librn,* Mary Mallory; Tel: 217-244-4621, E-mail: mmallory@illinois.edu; Staff 7 (MLS 4, Non-MLS 3)
Library Holdings: Bk Vols 230,000
Open Mon-Fri 9-5

GRAINGER ENGINEERING LIBRARY INFORMATION CENTER, 1301 W Springfield, 61801, SAN 340-8485. Tel: 217-333-3576. Reference Tel: 217-244-7826. FAX: 217-244-7764. E-mail: enginlib@uiuc.edu. Web Site: www.library.illinois.edu/grainger. *Librn,* William Mischo; E-mail: w-mischo@uiuc.edu
Library Holdings: Bk Vols 271,625
Open Mon-Sun 10-10

HISTORY, PHILOSOPHY & NEWSPAPER, 246 Main Library, 1408 W Gregory Dr, 61801, SAN 340-8639. Tel: 217-333-1509. Web Site: www.library.illinois.edu/hpnl. *Librn,* Mary Stuart; Tel: 217-244-0797, E-mail: m-stuart@illinois.edu; Staff 4 (MLS 1, Non-MLS 3)
Library Holdings: Bk Vols 40,944
Open Mon-Thurs 9-9, Fri 9-5, Sat 1-5, Sun 1-8

ILLINOIS HISTORY & LINCOLN COLLECTIONS, 322 Main Library, 1408 W Gregory Dr, 61801, SAN 340-8728. Tel: 217-333-1777. Web Site: www.library.illinois.edu/ihx. *Librn,* John Hoffmann; E-mail: jmhoffma@illinois.edu; Staff 1 (MLS 1)
Library Holdings: Bk Vols 25,000
Open Mon-Fri 8:30-5

LABOR & INDUSTRIAL RELATIONS, 147 ILIR, 504 E Armory Ave, Champaign, 61820, SAN 340-8752. Tel: 217-333-8021. FAX: 217-244-4091. Web Site: www.library.uiuc.edu/irx/location. *Librn,* Yoo-Seong Song; Tel: 217-333-7993, E-mail: yoosong@illinois.edu
Library Holdings: Per Subs 353

CL LAW, 142 Law Bldg, 504 E Pennsylvania Ave, Champaign, 61820, SAN 340-8787. Tel: 217-333-0931. Interlibrary Loan Service Tel: 217-333-1958. FAX: 217-244-8500. Web Site: www.law.uiuc.edu/library. *Dir,* Janis Johnston; Tel: 217-244-3046, E-mail: jljohnst@law.uiuc.edu; Staff 9.5 (MLS 9.5)
Founded 1897
Library Holdings: Bk Vols 761,652; Per Subs 8,800
Special Collections: European Economic Commun. State Document Depository; US Document Depository
Subject Interests: Foreign law
Publications: Law Library Aids; Law Library Collection Information
Open Mon-Fri 8:30-5

LIBRARY & INFORMATION SCIENCE VIRTUAL LIBRARY, 100 Main Library, 1408 W Gregory Dr, 61801, SAN 340-8817. Tel: 217-300-8439, 217-333-3804. E-mail: lislib@library.uiuc.edu. Web Site: www.library.illinois.edu/lis. *Librn,* Daniel G Tracy; E-mail: dtracy@illinois.edu. Subject Specialists: *Libr & info sci,* Daniel G Tracy; Staff 2 (MLS 2)
Function: Distance learning, e-mail & chat, e-mail serv, Electronic databases & coll, Online cat, Online info literacy tutorials on the web & in blackboard, Online ref, Orientations, Outside serv via phone, mail, e-mail & web, Ref & res, Ref serv in person, Workshops

LITERATURES & LANGUAGES, 225 Main Libr, 1408 W Gregory Dr, 61801, SAN 340-8515. Tel: 217-333-2220. FAX: 217-333-2214. Web Site: www.library.illinois.edu/llx. *Head, Lit & Lang Libr,* Paula Carns; Tel: 217-333-0076, E-mail: pcarns@illinois.edu; *English & Digital Humanities Librn,* Harriett Green; Tel: 217-333-4942, E-mail: green19@illinois.edu; *Cinema Studies & Media Serv Spec,* Dr Robert Cagle; Tel: 217-265-0737, E-mail: cagle@illinois.edu. Subject Specialists: *Western European,* Paula Carns; *Lit in English, Theatre,* Harriett Green; *Comparative lit, Film, Media,* Dr Robert Cagle; Staff 4 (MLS 2, Non-MLS 2)
Founded 2011
Library Holdings: Bk Vols 40,000
Subject Interests: Cinema, Eng lit, Fr lit, German lit, Italian, Latin Am lit, Linguistics, Medieval studies, Spanish
Open Mon-Thurs 9-7, Fri 9-5, Sat & Sun 1-5

MAP & GEOGRAPHY, 1408 W Gregory Dr, 418 Main Library, Mc-522, 61801, SAN 340-8841. Tel: 217-333-0827. FAX: 217-333-2214. Web Site: www.library.uiuc.edu/max. *Head Librn,* Jenny Marie Johnson; E-mail: jmj@illinois.edu; Staff 2 (MLS 1, Non-MLS 1)
Library Holdings: Bk Vols 590,641
Open Mon 8:30-8, Tues-Fri 8:30-5, Sat 1-5

MATHEMATICS, 1409 W Green St, 216 Altgeld Hall, 61801, SAN 340-8876. Tel: 217-333-0258. E-mail: math@library.uiuc.edu. Web Site: www.library.illinois.edu/mtx. *Librn,* Timothy Cole; Tel: 217-244-7837, E-mail: t-cole3@illinois.edu
Library Holdings: Bk Vols 100,000
Open Mon-Thurs 9-8, Fri 9-5, Sat & Sun 2-5

MODERN LANGUAGES & LINGUISTICS, 425 Main Library, MC-522, 1408 W Gregory Dr, 61801, SAN 340-8906. Tel: 217-333-0076. FAX: 217-333-2214. Web Site: www.library.illinois.edu/mdx. *Actg Head,* Bruce Swan; E-mail: bswann@illinois.edu; Staff 5 (MLS 3, Non-MLS 2)
Library Holdings: Bk Vols 17,000
Open Mon-Thurs 9-7, Fri 9-5, Sat & Sun 1-4

MUSIC & PERFORMING ARTS, 2146 Music Bldg, MC-056, 1114 W Nevada St, 61801-3859, SAN 340-8930. Tel: 217-333-1173. FAX: 217-244-9097. E-mail: musiclib@library.uiuc.edu. Web Site: library.illinois.edu/mux. *Head Librn,* John Wagstaff; Tel: 217-244-5070, E-mail: wagstaff@illinois.edu
Library Holdings: Microforms 19,000; Music Scores 520,000; Bk Vols 311,000
Open Mon-Fri 8:30-5

PHYSICS-ASTRONOMY, 204 Loomis Lab, 110 W Green St, 61801, SAN 340-9023. Tel: 217-244-8530. Web Site: www.library.illinois.edu/phx. *Librn,* Mary Schlembach; Tel: 217-333-3158, E-mail: schlemba@illinois.edu; Staff 17 (MLS 15, Non-MLS 2)
Library Holdings: Bk Vols 47,000
Automation Activity & Vendor Info: (Acquisitions) Ex Libris Group; (Cataloging) Ex Libris Group; (Circulation) Ex Libris Group; (Course Reserve) Ex Libris Group; (OPAC) Ex Libris Group
Open Mon, Wed & Fri 1-3 & by appt
Friends of the Library Group

PRAIRIE RESEARCH INSTITUTE LIBRARY, 1816 S Oak St, Champaign, 61820. Tel: 217-333-6892. FAX: 217-244-0802. E-mail: library@prairie.illinois.edu. Web Site: www.library.illinois.edu/prairie. *Head Inst Librn,* Susan M Braxton; Tel: 217-333-5856, E-mail: braxton@illinois.edu; *Inst Librn,* Beth Wohlgemuth; Tel: 217-244-4907, E-mail: wohlgemu@illinois.edu. Subject Specialists: *Natural res, Water res,* Susan M Braxton; *Ecology, Natural hist, Natural res,* Beth Wohlgemuth; Staff 4 (MLS 4)
Founded 2011
Jul 2010-Jun 2011 Income $342,855, Parent Institution $241,735, Other $101,120. Mats Exp $101,200, Books $12,700, Per/Ser (Incl. Access Fees) $88,500. Sal $216,035 (Prof $181,066)
Library Holdings: Microforms 185; Bk Titles 50,000; Per Subs 500; Videos 146
Special Collections: Aerial photographs; Field notes (ISGS); Images (INHS); Maps
Subject Interests: Atmospheric sci, Earth sci, Ecology, Environ educ, Environ sci, Environ sustainability, Natural hist, Natural res
Automation Activity & Vendor Info: (Acquisitions) Ex Libris Group; (Cataloging) Ex Libris Group; (Circulation) Ex Libris Group; (Course Reserve) Ex Libris Group; (ILL) OCLC ILLiad; (OPAC) Ex Libris Group
Function: Computers for patron use, e-mail serv, ILL available, Online cat, Ref serv available
The Prairie Research Institute Library is administered by the Prairie Research Institute, and formed from the merger of the Illinois Natural History Survey, Illinois State Geological Survey, Illinois State Water Survey, and Illinois Sustainable Technology Center libraries.
Open Mon-Fri 8-5

RARE BOOK & MANUSCRIPT LIBRARY, 346 Main Library, MC-522, 1408 W Gregory Dr, 61801, SAN 340-9058. Tel: 217-333-3777. FAX: 217-244-1755. Web Site: www.library.illinois.edu/rbx. *Librn,* Valerie Hotchkiss
Library Holdings: Bk Vols 172,983
Open Mon-Fri 8:30-5

SLAVIC & EAST EUROPEAN, 225 Main Library, 1408 W Gregory Dr, 61801, SAN 340-9066. Tel: 217-333-1349. FAX: 217-244-8976. E-mail: srscite@cliff.library.uiuc.edu. Web Site: gateway.library.uiuc.edu/spx. *Head of Libr,* Miranda Beaven Remnek; Tel: 217-333-1340, E-mail: mremnek@illinois.edu
Library Holdings: Bk Vols 17,140
Open Mon-Fri 8:30-5

SOCIAL SCIENCES, HEALTH & EDUCATION LIBRARY, 100 Main Library, MC-522, 1408 W Gregory Dr, 61801, SAN 340-8450. Tel: 217-333-2305. Reference Tel: 217-244-1864. FAX: 217-333-2214. E-mail: sshel@library.illinois.edu. Web Site: www.library.illinois.edu/sshel. *Head Librn,* Nancy O'Brien; Tel: 217-333-2408, E-mail: npobrien@illinois.edu; *Librn,* Peg Burnette; Tel: 217-300-5942, E-mail: phburn@illinois.edu; *Librn,* Cindy Ingold; Tel: 217-333-7998, E-mail: cingold@illinois.edu; *Librn,* Beth Sheehan; Tel: 217-244-1866, E-mail: edivince@illinois.edu; *Librn,* Yoo-Seong Song; Tel: 217-333-8021, E-mail: yoosong@illinois.edu; *Librn,* Dan Tracy; Tel: 217-300-8439, E-mail: dtracy@illinois.edu. Subject Specialists: *Children's lit, Curric, Educ,* Nancy O'Brien; *Biomed sci,* Peg Burnette; *Gender, Multicultural, Women's studies,* Cindy Ingold; *Anthrop, Geog, Sociol,* Beth Sheehan; *Econ, Labor relations,* Yoo-Seong Song; *Libr & info sci,* Dan Tracy; Staff 9.75 (MLS 8, Non-MLS 1.75)
Founded 2012
Library Holdings: Bk Vols 270,000; Per Subs 747
Special Collections: Arms Control, Disarmament & International Security Coll; Children's & Young Adult Literature (School Coll); Curriculum Coll of PreK-12 Classroom Teaching Materials; Human Relations Area Files; Instruments that Measure Intelligence (Test Coll); Occult Sciences (Mandeville Coll)
Subject Interests: Asian-Am studies, Gender studies, Polit sci, Recreation, Sports, Tourism

UNDERGRADUATE, 1402 W Gregory Dr, 61801. Tel: 217-333-3477. Reference Tel: 217-333-8589. FAX: 217-265-0936. TDD: 217-265-0967. E-mail: uglcirc@library.uiuc.edu. Web Site: www.library.illinois.edu/ugl. *Head of Libr,* Dr Lori Mestre; Tel: 217-244-4171, E-mail: lmestre@illinois.edu; Staff 16 (MLS 9, Non-MLS 7)
Library Holdings: Audiobooks 538; DVDs 30,000; Bk Vols 250,014; Per Subs 188
Special Collections: Gaming Resources; Graphic Novels; Loanable Technology; Popular Culture
Function: Audio & video playback equip for onsite use, Bks on CD, Computers for patron use, Copy machines, Doc delivery serv, e-mail & chat, E-Reserves, Electronic databases & coll, Equip loans & repairs, Exhibits, Free DVD rentals, ILL available, Magnifiers for reading, Online cat, Online info literacy tutorials on the web & in blackboard, Online ref, Online searches, Orientations, Printer for laptops & handheld devices, Ref & res, Ref serv available, Ref serv in person, Referrals accepted, Scanner, Video lending libr, Web-catalog, Workshops

UNIVERSITY ARCHIVES, 19 Main Library, 1408 W Gregory Dr, 61801, SAN 340-9082. Tel: 217-333-0798. FAX: 217-333-2868. E-mail: illiarch@illinois.edu. Web Site: www.library.uiuc.edu/archives. *Archivist,* William Maher; E-mail: w-maher@illinois.edu; Staff 6 (MLS 5, Non-MLS 1)
Founded 1963
Function: Archival coll
Open Mon, Tues, Thurs & Fri 8:30-12 & 1-5, Wed 10-12 & 1-5

UNIVERSITY LABORATORY HIGH SCHOOL, 1212 W Springfield Ave, Rm 201, 61801, SAN 340-9112. Tel: 217-333-1589. FAX: 217-333-4064. Web Site: www.uni.uiuc.edu/library. *Librn,* Frances Jacobsen Harris; E-mail: francey@illinois.edu
Library Holdings: Bk Vols 13,700
Open Mon-Fri 7:45-4:15

CM VETERINARY MEDICINE, 1257 Veterinary Med Basic Science Bldg, 2001 S Lincoln Ave, 61802, SAN 340-9147. Tel: 217-333-8778. FAX: 217-333-2286. Web Site: www.library.illinois.edu/vex. *Veterinary Med Librn,* Erin Kerby; Tel: 217-244-1295, E-mail: ekerb@illinois.edu; Staff 3 (MLS 1, Non-MLS 2)
Library Holdings: Bk Vols 52,000
Open Mon-Thurs 8am-10pm, Fri 8-5, Sat 1-5, Sun 1-10

P THE URBANA FREE LIBRARY, 210 W Green St, 61801. SAN 304-7164. Tel: 217-367-4057. Reference Tel: 217-367-4405. Administration Tel: 217-367-4058. FAX: 217-367-4061. Circulation FAX: 217-531-7089. E-mail: administration@tufl.info. Web Site: urbanafreelibrary.org. *Exec Dir,* Celeste Choate; E-mail: cchoate@tufl.info; *Assoc Dir,* Kathryn Wicks; E-mail: kwicks@tufl.info; *Dir, Ch Serv,* Lora Fegley; Tel: 217-367-4069, E-mail: lfegley@tufl.info; *Dir of Circ,* Dawn Cassady; E-mail: dcassady@tufl.info; *Dir, Spec Coll,* Anke Voss; Tel: 217-367-4025, E-mail: avoss@tufl.info; *Interm Dir, Adult Serv,* Mary Wilkes Towner; Tel: 217-367-4405, E-mail: mtowner@tufl.info; *Acq Mgr,* Keran Harrington; E-mail: kharrington@tufl.info; Staff 42 (MLS 17, Non-MLS 25)
Founded 1874. Pop 41,250; Circ 773,295
Jul 2013-Jun 2014 Income $3,527,475. Mats Exp $384,003. Sal $2,221,725
Library Holdings: Audiobooks 4,466; CDs 21,811; DVDs 21,858; Bk Vols 235,655
Special Collections: Champaign County Historical Archives (Champaign County records); City of Urbana Municipal Records. Municipal Document Depository; Oral History
Subject Interests: Genealogy, Local hist, Maps, Photog
Automation Activity & Vendor Info: (ILL) OCLC WorldShare Interlibrary Loan
Wireless access
Publications: This Month at the Urbana Free Library (Monthly)
Mem of Illinois Heartland Library System
Special Services for the Deaf - TTY equip
Special Services for the Blind - Low vision equip
Open Mon-Thurs 9-9, Fri & Sat 9-6, Sun 1-5
Friends of the Library Group

UTICA

P UTICA PUBLIC LIBRARY DISTRICT*, Mill & Grove Sts, 61373. (Mail add: PO Box 367, 61373-0367), SAN 304-7172. Tel: 815-667-4509. FAX: 815-667-4140. E-mail: uticalibrary@comcast.net. *Dir,* Marlene Ernat; *Asst Librn,* Gloria Alvarado; *Asst Librn,* Kathy Barbee

Founded 1952. Pop 2,589; Circ 115,644
Library Holdings: Large Print Bks 2,000; Bk Vols 50,000; Per Subs 20; Talking Bks 2,300
Special Collections: LaSalle County History Coll
Wireless access
Mem of Reaching Across Illinois Library System (RAILS)
Open Mon & Wed 2-8, Tues & Thurs 9-12 & 5-8, Fri 1-5, Sat 8:30-1:30
Friends of the Library Group

VANDALIA

P EVANS PUBLIC LIBRARY DISTRICT, 215 S Fifth St, 62471-2703. SAN 304-7180. Tel: 618-283-2824. FAX: 618-283-4705. E-mail: epldill@gmail.com. Web Site: evanspubliclibrary.org. *Libr Dir,* Jessica Blain; *Ch Serv,* Shawna Sprague; Staff 1 (Non-MLS 1)
Founded 1921. Pop 11,791; Circ 84,061
Jul 2013-Jun 2014 Income $329,366, State $16,167, County $273,075, Locally Generated Income $25,498. Mats Exp $44,701, Books $31,267, Per/Ser (Incl. Access Fees) $6,025, AV Mat $6,689, Electronic Ref Mat (Incl. Access Fees) $720. Sal $152,137 (Prof $59,339)
Library Holdings: Bk Vols 32,217; Per Subs 135; Videos 1,582
Special Collections: James Hall Coll; Lincoln (Rankin Coll); Local History & Genealogy; Vandalia Authors
Automation Activity & Vendor Info: (Cataloging) Innovative Interfaces, Inc; (Circulation) Innovative Interfaces, Inc; (OPAC) Innovative Interfaces, Inc; (Serials) Innovative Interfaces, Inc
Wireless access
Function: Bks on cassette, Bks on CD, CD-ROM, Children's prog, Computers for patron use, Copy machines, Electronic databases & coll, Handicapped accessible, Homebound delivery serv, ILL available, Magnifiers for reading, Music CDs, Online cat, Photocopying/Printing, Pub access computers, Ref serv available, Summer reading prog, Telephone ref, VHS videos, Wheelchair accessible
Mem of Illinois Heartland Library System
Partic in Illinois Library & Information Network
Special Services for the Deaf - TDD equip; TTY equip
Special Services for the Blind - Home delivery serv; Large print bks; Magnifiers; Talking bks
Open Mon-Thurs 9-7, Fri & Sat 9-5
Friends of the Library Group

S VANDALIA CORRECTIONAL CENTER LIBRARY, Rte 51 N, 62471. (Mail add: PO Box 500, 62471-0500), SAN 376-1193. Tel: 618-283-4170. *Interim Librn,* Position Currently Open

VENICE

P VENICE PUBLIC LIBRARY*, 325 Broadway, 62090. SAN 304-7199. Tel: 618-877-1330. FAX: 618-877-0633. E-mail: venicepubliclibrary@gmail.com. *Dir,* Diane West
Founded 1953. Pop 2,528; Circ 10,000
Library Holdings: Bk Vols 5,000; Per Subs 10
Wireless access
Mem of Illinois Heartland Library System
Special Services for the Deaf - TTY equip
Open Tues & Thurs 10-4, Wed & Fri 9-3, Sat 10-2

VERMONT

P VERMONT PUBLIC LIBRARY*, 101 N Main St, 61484. (Mail add: PO Box 199, 61484-0199), SAN 304-7202. Tel: 309-784-6291. FAX: 309-784-6291. *Head Librn,* Ann Patridge; *Librn,* Pat Nelson; Staff 2 (MLS 1, Non-MLS 1)
Founded 1947. Pop 806
Library Holdings: Bk Vols 5,676
Open Tues-Fri 12-5, Sat 12-3

VICTORIA

P VICTORIA PUBLIC LIBRARY DISTRICT*, 227 E Main St, 61485. (Mail add: PO Box 216, 61485-0216), SAN 375-9628. Tel: 309-879-2295. FAX: 309-879-2295. *Librn,* Carol Weedman
Pop 865; Circ 10,560
Library Holdings: Bk Vols 13,420; Per Subs 10
Open Mon-Sat 10-12 & 1-5

VIENNA

S ILLINOIS DEPARTMENT OF CORRECTIONS*, Shawnee Correctional Center Library, 6665 State Rte 146E, 62995. SAN 371-7429. Tel: 618-658-8331, Ext 2120. Web Site: www.idoc.state.il.us. *Librn,* Theresa Casteel; Staff 2 (Non-MLS 2)
Founded 1985
Jul 2010-Jun 2011 Income $30,000. Mats Exp $31,200, Per/Ser (Incl. Access Fees) $1,200, Other Print Mats $30,000. Sal $59,000
Library Holdings: Bk Titles 16,000; Per Subs 18
Special Collections: Federal & Illinois Law
Special Services for the Blind - Talking bks
Restriction: Staff & inmates only

P VIENNA CARNEGIE PUBLIC LIBRARY*, 401 Poplar St, 62995. (Mail add: PO Box 616, 62995-0616), SAN 304-7229. Tel: 618-658-5051. FAX: 618-658-5051. E-mail: viepub@yahoo.com. *Librn,* Margaret Mathis
Founded 1910. Pop 1,420; Circ 6,000
Library Holdings: Bk Vols 9,553
Special Collections: Old Books & Literature
Mem of Illinois Heartland Library System
Open Mon-Wed, Fri & Sat 1-5

S VIENNA CORRECTIONAL CENTER LIBRARY*, 6695 State Rte 146 E, 62995. (Mail add: PO Box 200, 62995- 0200), SAN 304-7210. Tel: 618-658-8371, Ext 270. *Librn,* J Karen Jones; Staff 2 (MLS 1, Non-MLS 1)
Founded 1972
Library Holdings: Bk Titles 17,000
Special Collections: Criminology Coll; Law Library; SW Reporter
Subject Interests: Law

VILLA GROVE

P CAMARGO TOWNSHIP DISTRICT LIBRARY*, 14 N Main St, 61956. SAN 304-7237. Tel: 217-832-5211. FAX: 217-832-7203. Web Site: www.camargotownship.lib.il.us. *Dir,* Jackie Jamison; E-mail: jackiejamison@hotmail.com
Founded 1919. Pop 4,034; Circ 38,459
Jul 2006-Jun 2007 Income $109,417, State $5,043, County $82,776, Locally Generated Income $21,598. Mats Exp $8,669, Books $7,385, AV Mat $1,284. Sal $53,474
Library Holdings: AV Mats 2,007; Large Print Bks 400; Bk Vols 22,085; Per Subs 126; Talking Bks 971
Automation Activity & Vendor Info: (Cataloging) Horizon; (Circulation) Horizon
Mem of Illinois Heartland Library System
Special Services for the Blind - Talking bks
Open Mon & Thurs 11-8, Tues, Wed & Fri 11-5, Sat 9-12 & 1-5
Friends of the Library Group

VILLA PARK

P VILLA PARK PUBLIC LIBRARY*, 305 S Ardmore Ave, 60181-2698. SAN 304-7245. Tel: 630-834-1164. FAX: 630-834-0489. TDD: 630-834-1165. E-mail: vpplinfo@vppl.info. Web Site: www.villapark.lib.il.us. *Libr Dir,* Sandra D Hill; Tel: 630-834-1164, Ext 111, E-mail: shill@linc.lib.il.us; *Head, Adult Serv,* Sean Birmingham; Tel: 630-834-1164, Ext 109, E-mail: sbirmingham@linc.lib.il.us; *Head, Automation & Tech Serv,* John Bradford; *Head, Circ,* Martha Bledsoe; *Head, Readers Advisory,* Candy Smith; *Head, Youth Serv,* Susan McKean; Tel: 630-834-1164, Ext 114, E-mail: smckeanmilcent@linc.lib.il.us; *Asst Head, Adult Serv,* Jan Wernette; *Asst Head, Youth Serv,* Jean Jansen; *Automation Serv Coordr,* Jeff Sand; Staff 45 (MLS 9, Non-MLS 36)
Founded 1928. Pop 22,517; Circ 316,516
Library Holdings: Bk Vols 109,850; Per Subs 286
Special Collections: Local History (Early History of Villa Park), bks, clippings, microfilm, slides, tapes
Automation Activity & Vendor Info: (Acquisitions) SirsiDynix; (Circulation) SirsiDynix
Database Vendor: Gale Cengage Learning, OCLC FirstSearch
Function: ILL available
Publications: The Resource (Newsletter)
Mem of Reaching Across Illinois Library System (RAILS)
Partic in Libr Integrated Network Consortium
Open Mon-Fri 9-9, Sat 9-5, Sun (Sept-May) 1-5

VIOLA

P VIOLA PUBLIC LIBRARY DISTRICT, 1705 14th St, 61486-9462. (Mail add: PO Box 479, 61486-0479), SAN 304-7253. Tel: 309-596-2620. FAX: 309-596-2822. E-mail: violapld@vhtmail.net. Web Site: violapubliclibrary.webs.com. *Dir,* Lill Batson; Staff 1 (Non-MLS 1)
Founded 1948. Pop 2,246; Circ 17,929
Library Holdings: Audiobooks 951; CDs 200; DVDs 951; e-books 2,917; Bk Titles 11,115; Per Subs 33; Videos 75
Wireless access
Function: Bks on cassette, Bks on CD, Children's prog, Computer training, Computers for patron use, Copy machines, e-mail serv, Fax serv, Free DVD rentals, Handicapped accessible, ILL available, Music CDs, Online cat, OverDrive digital audio bks, Photocopying/Printing, Prog for adults, Pub access computers, Summer reading prog, Tax forms, VHS videos
Mem of Reaching Across Illinois Library System (RAILS)
Open Mon-Thurs 9-12 & 2-6, Fri 9-12 & 2-5, Sat 9-12
Friends of the Library Group

VIRDEN

P GRAND PRAIRIE OF THE WEST PUBLIC LIBRARY DISTRICT*, 142 W Jackson St, 62690-1257. SAN 304-7261. Tel: 217-965-3015. FAX: 217-965-3801. *Dir,* Shirley Blankenship; *Ch Serv,* Margaret Hendricks
Pop 5,229; Circ 28,853
Library Holdings: Bk Vols 20,000; Per Subs 36
Mem of Illinois Heartland Library System
Open Mon-Wed & Fri 10-5, Thurs 10-8, Sat 10-1

VIRGINIA

P VIRGINIA MEMORIAL PUBLIC LIBRARY*, 100 N Main St, 62691-1364. SAN 304-727X. Tel: 217-452-3846. FAX: 217-452-3846. *Librn,* Karen Belmonte
Founded 1916. Pop 1,728; Circ 28,878
Library Holdings: AV Mats 264; Large Print Bks 838; Bk Vols 14,431; Per Subs 35; Talking Bks 70
Special Collections: Genealogy
Subject Interests: Local hist
Automation Activity & Vendor Info: (OPAC) TLC (The Library Corporation)
Publications: Illinois Libraries
Open Tues 12-5, Wed 1-6, Fri 9-4, Sat 9-Noon
Friends of the Library Group

WALNUT

P WALNUT PUBLIC LIBRARY DISTRICT, 101 Heaton, 61376. (Mail add: PO Box 728, 61376-0728), SAN 304-7288. Tel: 815-379-2159. FAX: 815-379-4098. E-mail: wpld2000@yahoo.com. *Dir,* Michele McAlvey; *Children's Coll Develop,* Kimberly Splitt; *ILL,* Rebecca Fritz
Founded 1939. Pop 1,894; Circ 29,700
Library Holdings: Bks on Deafness & Sign Lang 10; Bk Vols 24,218; Per Subs 40
Special Collections: Don Marquis Coll
Subject Interests: Local hist
Automation Activity & Vendor Info: (Acquisitions) Follett Software; (Cataloging) Follett Software; (Circulation) Follett Software; (ILL) SirsiDynix
Wireless access
Mem of Reaching Across Illinois Library System (RAILS)
Open Mon & Wed 9-7, Tues & Fri 12-5, Sat 9-2

WARREN

P WARREN TOWNSHIP PUBLIC LIBRARY*, 210 Burnett Ave, 61087. (Mail add: PO Box 427, 61087-0427), SAN 304-7296. Tel: 815-745-2076. FAX: 815-745-2076. E-mail: warp@aeroinc.net. *Dir,* Jennifer Lynne Carter; *Ch,* Summer Gurdak
Founded 1886. Pop 1,675
Library Holdings: Bk Vols 13,000; Per Subs 50
Subject Interests: Local hist
Mem of Reaching Across Illinois Library System (RAILS)
Open Tues & Wed 1-8, Thurs 9-12 & 1-5, Sat 9-1

WARRENSBURG

P BARCLAY PUBLIC LIBRARY DISTRICT*, 220 S Main St, 62573-9657. (Mail add: PO Box 349, 62573-0349), SAN 304-730X. Tel: 217-672-3621. FAX: 217-672-8404. E-mail: libriann@yahoo.com. Web Site: www.barclay.lib.il.us. *Dir,* Lacey Wright; Staff 1 (Non-MLS 1)
Founded 1942. Pop 7,600; Circ 48,000
Library Holdings: Bk Titles 28,145; Bk Vols 29,000; Per Subs 135
Automation Activity & Vendor Info: (Cataloging) SirsiDynix; (Circulation) SirsiDynix; (ILL) SirsiDynix; (OPAC) SirsiDynix
Database Vendor: OCLC FirstSearch
Mem of Illinois Heartland Library System
Open Mon, Wed & Fri 9-5, Tues & Thurs 9-8, Sat 9-1
Friends of the Library Group

WARRENVILLE

S ILLINOIS YOUTH CENTER*, Warrenville Library, 30 W 200 Ferry Rd, 60555. (Mail add: PO Box 828, 60555-0828), SAN 324-0045. Tel: 630-983-6231. Reference Tel: 630-983-6231, Ext 262. Administration Tel: 630-983-6231, Ext 260. FAX: 630-983-6213. *Librn,* Sheneta Graham; Tel: 630-983-6231, Ext 262; Staff 2 (MLS 1, Non-MLS 1)
Founded 1973
Library Holdings: AV Mats 300; Bk Titles 10,000; Bk Vols 11,000
Special Collections: Antique World Encyclopedia; Rare Album Recordings
Subject Interests: Romances, Young adult bks
Mem of Reaching Across Illinois Library System (RAILS)
Restriction: Not a lending libr, Not open to pub

P WARRENVILLE PUBLIC LIBRARY DISTRICT, 28 W 751 Stafford Pl, 60555. SAN 324-5144. Tel: 630-393-1171. FAX: 630-393-1688. Web Site: www.warrenville.com. *Dir,* Sandra Whitmer; E-mail: director@warrenville.com; *Head, Adult Serv,* Leila Heath; E-mail: leila@warrenville.com; *Head, Circ,* Patty Dybala; E-mail: patty@warrenville.com; *Head, Tech Serv,* Lou Carlile; E-mail: lou@warrenville.com; *Head, Youth Serv,* Sue Larson; E-mail: sue@warrenville.com; *Syst Adminr,* Cynthia Makowski; E-mail: cynthia@warrenville.com; Staff 16 (MLS 5, Non-MLS 11)
Founded 1979. Pop 13,551; Circ 233,411
Library Holdings: AV Mats 20,700; e-books 9,400; Bk Vols 99,500; Per Subs 200
Special Collections: Local Artist (Albright Coll), original art; Original Fine Arts Coll
Subject Interests: Local hist, Visual arts
Automation Activity & Vendor Info: (Cataloging) SirsiDynix; (Circulation) SirsiDynix; (OPAC) SirsiDynix
Database Vendor: Baker & Taylor, EBSCOhost, Gale Cengage Learning, Grolier Online, Newsbank, OCLC FirstSearch, ProQuest
Wireless access
Function: ILL available
Publications: Newsletter (Quarterly)
Mem of Reaching Across Illinois Library System (RAILS)
Open Mon-Thurs 9:30-9, Fri 9:30-7, Sat 9:30-5, Sun 1-5

WARSAW

P WARSAW PUBLIC LIBRARY*, 1025 Webster St, 62379-1454. SAN 304-7326. Tel: 217-256-3417. FAX: 217-256-3154. Web Site: www.warsawlib.org. *Librn,* Daniela Parish
Pop 1,793; Circ 23,658
Library Holdings: Bk Vols 18,000; Per Subs 68
Special Collections: Local History; Local Newspapers (on film from 1840-1973)
Open Mon-Thurs 10-12 & 2-8, Fri 10-12 & 2-5, Sat 10-2

WASHINGTON

P WASHINGTON DISTRICT LIBRARY*, 380 N Wilmor Rd, 61571. SAN 304-7334. Tel: 309-444-2241. FAX: 309-444-4711. E-mail: washlib@mtco.com. Web Site: washington.lib.il.us. *Exec Dir,* Randall Yelverton; *Ch Serv, Ref,* Veronica Walker; Staff 5 (MLS 2, Non-MLS 3)
Founded 1937. Pop 19,955; Circ 128,136
Library Holdings: Bk Titles 43,000; Bk Vols 65,000; Per Subs 165
Database Vendor: TLC (The Library Corporation)
Partic in OCLC Online Computer Library Center, Inc
Open Mon 9-6, Tues-Thurs 9-8, Fri 9-5, Sat (Sept-May) 9-5 & 9-1 (June-Aug)
Friends of the Library Group
Branches: 1
SUNNYLAND, Sunnyland Plaza, 61571. Tel: 309-745-3023. FAX: 309-745-3023. *Dir,* Pam Tomka
Pop 23,601
Library Holdings: Bk Titles 10,000; Per Subs 25
Mem of Reaching Across Illinois Library System (RAILS)
Open Mon & Wed 9-6, Tues 1-8, Thurs 1-6, Fri 9-5, Sat (Sept-May) 9-1
Friends of the Library Group

WASHINGTON PARK

P WASHINGTON PARK PUBLIC LIBRARY*, 5103 Bunkum Rd, No 2, 62204. Tel: 618-271-5103. FAX: 618-271-7511. *Dir,* Clifford Brown
Pop 5,345
Library Holdings: High Interest/Low Vocabulary Bk Vols 30; Bk Vols 5,100; Per Subs 10; Talking Bks 50
Mem of Illinois Heartland Library System
Open Mon-Fri 9-5, Sat 9-3

WATERLOO

P MORRISON-TALBOTT LIBRARY*, 215 Park St, 62298-1305. SAN 304-7342. Tel: 618-939-6232. Administration Tel: 618-939-2950. FAX: 618-939-4974. E-mail: mtl@waterloolibrary.org. Web Site: www.waterloolibrary.org. *Dir,* Elaine Steingrubey; E-mail: elaines@waterloolibrary.org; Staff 5.95 (Non-MLS 5.95)
Founded 1892. Pop 10,134; Circ 82,889
Library Holdings: Bk Vols 32,079; Per Subs 130
Special Collections: History & Genealogy of Monroe County, Ill
Automation Activity & Vendor Info: (Acquisitions) Innovative Interfaces, Inc; (Cataloging) Innovative Interfaces, Inc; (Circulation) Innovative Interfaces, Inc; (Course Reserve) Innovative Interfaces, Inc; (ILL) Innovative Interfaces, Inc; (OPAC) Innovative Interfaces, Inc; (Serials) Innovative Interfaces, Inc
Database Vendor: Gale Cengage Learning, Innovative Interfaces, Inc, OCLC ArticleFirst, OCLC FirstSearch, OCLC WebJunction, OCLC WorldShare Interlibrary Loan, Overdrive, Inc, ProQuest

Wireless access
Mem of Illinois Heartland Library System
Partic in GateNet; OCLC-LVIS
Open Mon-Thurs 10-8:30, Fri 10-5, Sat 10-4
Friends of the Library Group

WATERMAN

P CLINTON TOWNSHIP PUBLIC LIBRARY*, 110 S Elm St, 60556. (Mail add: PO Box 299, 60556-0299), SAN 304-7350. Tel: 815-264-3339. FAX: 815-264-3814. E-mail: ctplibrary@mchsi.com. *Librn,* Nancy Radtke; Staff 2 (Non-MLS 2)
Founded 1914. Pop 1,868
Library Holdings: Bk Vols 11,479; Per Subs 62
Subject Interests: Genealogy
Wireless access
Mem of Reaching Across Illinois Library System (RAILS)
Open Mon & Wed 1-9, Fri 1-6, Sat 9-1

WATSEKA

S IROQUOIS COUNTY GENEALOGICAL SOCIETY LIBRARY*, Old Courthouse Museum, 103 W Cherry St, 60970-1524. SAN 326-3916. Tel: 815-432-3730. FAX: 815-432-3730. E-mail: iroqgene@yahoo.com. Web Site: www.rootsweb.ancestry.com/~ilicgs. *Dir,* Mary Buhr; *Librn,* Debi LaFine Rhoads
Founded 1969
Library Holdings: Bk Vols 930; Per Subs 20
Special Collections: Iroquois County Census (1790-1920), micro; Iroquois County Newspapers (1850-1959), micro; Probates (1833-1913) & Civil Cases
Subject Interests: Cemeteries, Census, Marriage
Publications: Stalker (Quarterly)
Open Mon-Fri 10-4

P WATSEKA PUBLIC LIBRARY*, 201 S Fourth St, 60970. SAN 304-7369. Tel: 815-432-4544. FAX: 815-432-4545. E-mail: watsekalibrary@yahoo.com. Web Site: www.watsekalibrary.org. *Dir,* Kim Zumwalt
Founded 1898. Pop 5,543; Circ 54,442
Library Holdings: Audiobooks 1,130; DVDs 389; Large Print Bks 1,068; Bk Vols 35,250; Per Subs 100; Videos 227
Automation Activity & Vendor Info: (Acquisitions) Horizon; (Cataloging) Horizon; (Circulation) Horizon; (Course Reserve) Horizon; (ILL) Horizon; (Media Booking) Horizon; (OPAC) Horizon; (Serials) Horizon
Wireless access
Mem of Illinois Heartland Library System
Open Mon-Thurs (Sept-May) 10-8, Fri 10-5:30, Sat 10-3; Mon & Tues (June-Aug) 10-8, Wed-Fri 10-5:30, Sat 10-3
Friends of the Library Group

WAUCONDA

S LAKE COUNTY DISCOVERY MUSEUM*, Curt Teich Postcard Archives & Lake County History Archives, 27277 Forest Preserve Dr, 60084. SAN 376-1258. Tel: 847-968-3381. FAX: 847-526-1545. E-mail: teicharchives@lcfpd.org. Web Site: www.lakecountydiscoverymuseum.org, www.lcfpd.org. *Dir,* Katherine Hamilton-Smith; Tel: 847-968-3380, E-mail: khamilton-smith@LCFPD.org; *Res Ctr Mgr,* Andrew Osburne; Tel: 847-968-3383, E-mail: aosborne@LCFPD.org
Founded 1976
Library Holdings: Bk Titles 2,000; Per Subs 40
Special Collections: Curt Teich Postcard Archives; Lake County History Archives
Database Vendor: OCLC FirstSearch
Publications: Historian; Image File
Open Mon-Fri 10-4:30
Friends of the Library Group

P WAUCONDA AREA PUBLIC LIBRARY DISTRICT*, 801 N Main St, 60084. SAN 304-7377. Tel: 847-526-6225. FAX: 847-526-6244. E-mail: library@wauclib.org. Web Site: www.wauclib.org. *Dir,* Thomas D Kern; Tel: 847-526-6225, Ext 209, E-mail: tkern@wauclib.org; Staff 6 (MLS 6)
Founded 1939. Pop 25,150; Circ 652,000
Library Holdings: Audiobooks 4,000; AV Mats 27,000; CDs 7,000; DVDs 17,000; e-books 2,700; Large Print Bks 2,000; Bk Titles 97,000; Per Subs 300
Automation Activity & Vendor Info: (Cataloging) Innovative Interfaces, Inc; (ILL) OCLC FirstSearch; (OPAC) Innovative Interfaces, Inc; (Serials) EBSCO Online
Database Vendor: 3M Library Systems, Evanced Solutions, Inc, Gale Cengage Learning, Overdrive, Inc, ProQuest, ReferenceUSA, TumbleBookLibrary, Wilson - Wilson Web
Wireless access
Function: Adult bk club, Adult literacy prog, Art exhibits, Audio & video playback equip for onsite use, Audiobks via web, AV serv, Bilingual assistance for Spanish patrons, Bk club(s), Bk reviews (Group), Bks on cassette, Bks on CD, CD-ROM, Children's prog, Citizenship assistance, Computer training, Computers for patron use, Copy machines, Doc delivery serv, e-mail serv, Electronic databases & coll, Exhibits, Family literacy, Free DVD rentals, Handicapped accessible, Holiday prog, Home delivery & serv to Sr ctr & nursing homes, Homebound delivery serv, Homework prog, ILL available, Instruction & testing, Literacy & newcomer serv, Mus passes, Music CDs, Notary serv, Online cat, Online info literacy tutorials on the web & in blackboard, Online ref, Online searches, Orientations, Outreach serv, Outside serv via phone, mail, e-mail & web, OverDrive digital audio bks, Photocopying/Printing, Preschool outreach, Prof lending libr, Prog for adults, Prog for children & young adult, Pub access computers, Ref & res, Ref serv in person, Senior computer classes, Senior outreach, Story hour, Summer reading prog, Tax forms, Teen prog, Telephone ref, Video lending libr, Visual arts prog, Web-catalog, Workshops
Publications: Newsletter
Open Mon-Thurs 9-9, Fri 9-6, Sat 9-5, Sun 12-4
Friends of the Library Group

WAUKEGAN

GL WILLIAM D BLOCK MEMORIAL LAW LIBRARY, Lake County Law Library, 18 N County St, 60085-4359. SAN 304-7385. Tel: 847-377-2800. FAX: 847-984-5873. E-mail: lawlibrary@lakecountyil.gov. Web Site: 19thcircuitcourt.state.il.us/services/Pages/LawLibrary.aspx. *Librn,* Joanne N Vandestreek; Tel: 847-377-2267; Staff 3 (MLS 1, Non-MLS 2)
Founded 1845
Library Holdings: Bk Vols 20,000; Per Subs 20
Special Collections: 1964-present; Illinois Appellate Court Briefs of the Second Judicial District; Illinois Legal Practice Materials; Law Books on the State of Illinois
Automation Activity & Vendor Info: (Acquisitions) Inmagic, Inc.; (Cataloging) Inmagic, Inc.; (Circulation) Inmagic, Inc.; (OPAC) Inmagic, Inc.
Wireless access
Special Services for the Blind - Reader equip
Open Mon-Fri 8-5

M VISTA HEALTH SYSTEMS, EAST SITE*, 1324 N Sheridan Rd, 60085. SAN 304-7407. Tel: 847-360-3000, Ext 5144. FAX: 847-360-2402. Web Site: vistahealth.com. *Librn,* Nellie E Dorsey; E-mail: nellie_dorsey@chs.net
Founded 1969
Library Holdings: Bk Titles 1,000; Per Subs 64
Partic in Lake County Consortium
Open Mon-Fri 8-12
Restriction: Staff use only

P WAUKEGAN PUBLIC LIBRARY, 128 N County St, 60085. SAN 304-7415. Tel: 847-623-2041. FAX: 847-623-2092, 847-623-2094. Web Site: www.waukeganpl.org. *Exec Dir,* Richard Lee; E-mail: richardlee@waukeganpl.info; *Asst Dir, Commun Serv,* Elizabeth Stearns; E-mail: estearns@waukeganpl.info; *Asst Dir, Pub Serv,* Heidi Smith; E-mail: heidismith@waukeganpl.info
Founded 1898. Pop 91,962; Circ 650,000
Wireless access
Open Mon-Thurs 10-8, Fri 10-6, Sat & Sun 1-5
Friends of the Library Group
Bookmobiles: 1

WAVERLY

P WAVERLY PUBLIC LIBRARY*, 291 N Pearl St, 62692. SAN 304-7423. Tel: 217-435-2051. FAX: 217-435-2051. E-mail: wavpl@yahoo.com. Web Site: www.waverly.lib.il.us/library/. *Librn,* Julie Samaras
Founded 1880. Pop 1,402; Circ 11,000
Library Holdings: Bk Vols 11,000; Per Subs 29
Open Mon, Tues, Thurs & Fri 1-5:30, Wed 1-7, Sat 9-12
Friends of the Library Group

WAYNE CITY

P WAYNE CITY PUBLIC LIBRARY*, Wayne City Kissner Public Library, 102 S Main, 62895. (Mail add: PO Box 455, 62895-0455), SAN 304-7431. Tel: 618-895-2661. FAX: 618-895-2661. *Librn,* Sue Musgrave
Founded 1971. Pop 1,032; Circ 4,938
May 2010-Apr 2011 Income $17,436. Mats Exp $769, Books $626, Other Print Mats $143. Sal $12,878
Library Holdings: DVDs 243; Large Print Bks 223; Bk Vols 21,613; Per Subs 3; Videos 146
Subject Interests: Ill
Database Vendor: OCLC FirstSearch, OCLC WorldShare Interlibrary Loan, WebMD

Wireless access
Function: Archival coll, Bk reviews (Group), Computers for patron use, Copy machines, Free DVD rentals, Genealogy discussion group, Handicapped accessible, Homebound delivery serv, VCDs, VHS videos
Mem of Illinois Heartland Library System
Open Tues 1-7, Wed & Thurs 2-6, Fri 2-5, Sat 9-12
Restriction: Non-resident fee

WAYNESVILLE

P WAYNESVILLE TOWNSHIP LIBRARY*, 303 E Second St, 61778. (Mail add: PO Box 59, 61778-0059), SAN 304-744X. Tel: 217-949-5111. FAX: 217-949-5111. E-mail: waytlib@hotmail.com. Web Site: www.waynesvilletownshiplibrary.org. *Librn,* Margie Rich; *Asst Librn,* Margie Craig
Founded 1938. Pop 768; Circ 5,191
Library Holdings: Bk Vols 14,000
Open Tues & Sat 1-5:30, Wed 5-8:30, Thurs 9-12 & 1-5:30

WELDON

P WELDON PUBLIC LIBRARY DISTRICT*, 505 Maple St, 61882. (Mail add: PO Box 248, 61882-0248), SAN 304-7458. Tel: 217-736-2215. FAX: 217-736-2215. Web Site: www.weldon.lib.il.us. *Dir,* Lori Weaver; E-mail: lweaver@weldon.lib.il.us
Founded 1922. Pop 876; Circ 9,801
Library Holdings: Bk Vols 9,784; Per Subs 44
Automation Activity & Vendor Info: (Cataloging) SirsiDynix; (Circulation) SirsiDynix
Mem of Illinois Heartland Library System
Open Tues & Wed 1-7, Thurs 1-6, Fri 10-6, Sat 10-3

WENONA

P BOND PUBLIC LIBRARY*, 208 S Chestnut St, 61377. SAN 304-7466. Tel: 815-853-4665. FAX: 815-853-4665. *Head Librn,* Sharon Freise
Founded 1896. Pop 1,065; Circ 6,728
Library Holdings: Large Print Bks 175; Bk Titles 20,000; Per Subs 45
Special Collections: County History (Marshall, La Salle, Tazewell, Putnam, Livingston, McLean, Upper Ohio Valley, Logan); Local Newspapers, micro
Mem of Reaching Across Illinois Library System (RAILS)
Special Services for the Deaf - Bks on deafness & sign lang
Open Tues 10:30-7, Wed 1-6, Fri 10:30-6, Sat 9-1
Friends of the Library Group

WEST CHICAGO

P WEST CHICAGO PUBLIC LIBRARY DISTRICT*, 118 W Washington St, 60185. SAN 304-7474. Tel: 630-231-1552. FAX: 630-231-1709. Web Site: www.westchicago.lib.il.us. *Dir,* Benjamin R Weseloh; *Access Serv Mgr,* Ursula Salvesen; *Adult Serv Mgr,* Amanda Ghobrial; *Youth Serv Mgr,* Neena Nagpal; Staff 27 (MLS 7, Non-MLS 20)
Founded 1927. Pop 27,444; Circ 183,372
Library Holdings: Bk Vols 83,013; Per Subs 281
Special Collections: Book-plates Coll
Subject Interests: Railroads
Automation Activity & Vendor Info: (Acquisitions) SirsiDynix; (Cataloging) SirsiDynix; (Circulation) SirsiDynix; (Course Reserve) SirsiDynix; (ILL) SirsiDynix; (Media Booking) SirsiDynix; (OPAC) SirsiDynix; (Serials) SirsiDynix
Publications: Biblio News (Newsletter)
Mem of Reaching Across Illinois Library System (RAILS)
Open Mon-Thurs 9-9, Fri & Sat 9-5, Sun (Sept-May) 1-5
Friends of the Library Group

WEST FRANKFORT

P WEST FRANKFORT PUBLIC LIBRARY*, 402 E Poplar St, 62896. SAN 304-7482. Tel: 618-932-3313. FAX: 618-932-3313. Web Site: www.westfrankfort.lib.il.us. *Dir,* Pam Sevenski; Staff 4 (Non-MLS 4)
Founded 1927. Pop 8,182; Circ 50,000
Library Holdings: High Interest/Low Vocabulary Bk Vols 50; Bk Vols 40,000; Per Subs 45
Subject Interests: Antiques, Art, Fine arts, Furniture, Genealogy
Automation Activity & Vendor Info: (Acquisitions) Innovative Interfaces, Inc; (Cataloging) Innovative Interfaces, Inc; (Circulation) Innovative Interfaces, Inc; (ILL) Innovative Interfaces, Inc; (OPAC) Innovative Interfaces, Inc; (Serials) Innovative Interfaces, Inc
Database Vendor: OCLC FirstSearch
Wireless access
Mem of Illinois Heartland Library System
Special Services for the Blind - Bks on cassette; Talking bks
Open Mon-Fri 9-6, Sat 10-4
Friends of the Library Group

WEST SALEM

P WEST SALEM PUBLIC LIBRARY*, 112 W South St, 62476-1206. (Mail add: PO Box 128, 62476-0128), SAN 304-7490. Tel: 618-456-8970. FAX: 618-456-8970. E-mail: wslibrary@yahoo.com. *Dir,* Patricia Ann Fisher
Founded 1966. Pop 1,145
Library Holdings: Bk Vols 7,000; Per Subs 10
Mem of Illinois Heartland Library System
Open Mon, Tues & Thurs 1-7

WEST UNION

P WEST UNION DISTRICT LIBRARY*, 209 W Union St, 62477-0138. (Mail add: PO Box 138, 62477-0138), SAN 376-2769. Tel: 217-279-3556. FAX: 217-279-3556. *Head Librn,* Anita Dolson; Staff 1 (Non-MLS 1)
Founded 1986. Pop 914
Library Holdings: Bk Vols 23,000; Per Subs 40
Wireless access
Mem of Illinois Heartland Library System
Open Mon & Thurs 9-1, Tues 6-8, Wed 9-5, Fri 1-6, Sat 10-12
Friends of the Library Group

WESTCHESTER

P WESTCHESTER PUBLIC LIBRARY*, 10700 Canterbury St, 60154. SAN 304-7504. Tel: 708-562-3573. FAX: 708-562-1298. TDD: 708-562-9364. E-mail: wcs@westchesterpl.org. Web Site: www.westchesterpl.org. *Dir,* Fidencio Marbella; *Asst Dir,* Bonnie Schwanz; *Ref,* Ann Weaver; *Ref Serv, Ch,* Kristen Jacobson; Staff 9 (MLS 7, Non-MLS 2)
Founded 1956. Pop 16,824; Circ 149,005
May 2007-Apr 2008 Income $1,175,184, State $59,906, County $1,011,569, Locally Generated Income $103,709. Mats Exp $166,238, Books $58,277, Per/Ser (Incl. Access Fees) $28,650, AV Equip $15,000, AV Mat $25,035, Electronic Ref Mat (Incl. Access Fees) $39,276. Sal $529,144 (Prof $363,942)
Library Holdings: Audiobooks 1,504; AV Mats 10,005; CDs 3,144; DVDs 1,728; e-books 621; Electronic Media & Resources 42; Large Print Bks 1,588; Microforms 46; Bk Vols 81,498; Per Subs 267; Videos 3,204
Automation Activity & Vendor Info: (Acquisitions) Innovative Interfaces, Inc - Millenium; (Cataloging) Innovative Interfaces, Inc - Millenium; (Circulation) Innovative Interfaces, Inc - Millenium; (ILL) Innovative Interfaces, Inc; (OPAC) Innovative Interfaces, Inc - Millenium
Database Vendor: Comprise Technologies Inc, CQ Press, H W Wilson, Innovative Interfaces, Inc, LearningExpress, Medline, OCLC ArticleFirst, OCLC WorldShare Interlibrary Loan, ReferenceUSA, ValueLine, World Book Online
Wireless access
Mem of Reaching Across Illinois Library System (RAILS)
Partic in System Wide Automated Network
Open Mon-Thurs 9:30-9, Fri 9:30-6, Sat 9:30-5, Sun 1-5
Friends of the Library Group

WESTERN SPRINGS

P THOMAS FORD MEMORIAL LIBRARY*, Western Springs Library, 800 Chestnut Ave, 60558. SAN 304-7520. Tel: 708-246-0520. FAX: 708-246-0403. E-mail: info@fordlibrary.org. Web Site: www.fordlibrary.org. *Dir,* Anne Kozak; *Head, Adult Serv,* Richard Roche; *Head, Circ/ILL,* Sandy Frank; *Head, Youth Serv,* Uma Nori; *Ref Librn,* Rachiel Hoover; *Ref Librn,* Matthew Wenslauskis; *Youth Serv Librn,* Dana Folkerts; *Teen Serv,* Heather Booth; Staff 8 (MLS 8)
Founded 1932. Pop 12,876; Circ 157,203
Library Holdings: Bk Vols 75,000; Per Subs 250
Automation Activity & Vendor Info: (Cataloging) Innovative Interfaces, Inc; (Circulation) Innovative Interfaces, Inc; (OPAC) Innovative Interfaces, Inc
Wireless access
Publications: Quarterly Newsletter
Mem of Reaching Across Illinois Library System (RAILS)
Open Mon-Thurs 9:30-9, Fri & Sat 9:30-5, Sun 1-5
Friends of the Library Group

WESTMONT

P WESTMONT PUBLIC LIBRARY*, 428 N Cass, 60559-1502. SAN 304-7539. Tel: 630-969-5625. FAX: 630-969-6490. E-mail: wms@westmontlibrary.org. Web Site: westmontlibrary.org. *Dir,* Julia C Coen; E-mail: jcoen@westmontlibrary.org; *Dir, Support Serv,* Manisha Suri; E-mail: manisha.suri@westmontlibrary.org; *Adult Serv Coordr,* Anna Behm; E-mail: abehm@westmontlibrary.org; *Circ Coordr,* Brittany Hoornaert Smith; E-mail: bhoornaert@westmontlibrary.org; *Mkt Coordr,* Kate Buckson; E-mail: kbuckson@westmontlibrary.org; *Outreach Coordr,* Carmen Higgins; E-mail: carmenh@westmontlibrary.org; *Readers' Advisory Coordr,* Sheila Hope; E-mail: skhope@westmontlibrary.org; *Tech Coordr,* Scott Rosenberg; E-mail: scott@westmontlibrary.org; *Youth Serv Coordr,*

Lynn Thomas; E-mail: lthomas@westmontlibrary.org; Staff 6.57 (MLS 4.69, Non-MLS 1.88)
Founded 1943. Pop 24,685; Circ 277,108
May 2012-Apr 2013 Income $1,794,975. Mats Exp $226,051. Sal $806,860
Library Holdings: AV Mats 20,081; e-books 13,652; Bk Vols 103,737; Per Subs 178
Special Collections: Spanish Lang Coll; Westmont Town Crier & Westmont Progress Newspapers, 1943-present
Automation Activity & Vendor Info: (Cataloging) Innovative Interfaces, Inc; (Circulation) Innovative Interfaces, Inc; (ILL) Innovative Interfaces, Inc; (OPAC) Innovative Interfaces, Inc; (Serials) Innovative Interfaces, Inc
Database Vendor: Baker & Taylor, Booklist Online, Booksite, Brodart, EBSCOhost, Evanced Solutions, Inc, Gale Cengage Learning, infoUSA, Innovative Interfaces, Inc, LearningExpress, OCLC FirstSearch, OCLC WorldShare Interlibrary Loan, ProQuest, ReferenceUSA, TumbleBookLibrary, ValueLine, World Book Online
Wireless access
Function: Audiobks via web, Bilingual assistance for Spanish patrons, Bk club(s), Bks on CD, Children's prog, Computer training, Computers for patron use, Copy machines, Digital talking bks, Doc delivery serv, e-mail & chat, e-mail serv, Electronic databases & coll, Exhibits, Family literacy, Free DVD rentals, Handicapped accessible, Home delivery & serv to Sr ctr & nursing homes, ILL available, Mail & tel request accepted, Mus passes, Music CDs, Notary serv, Online cat, Outreach serv, Outside serv via phone, mail, e-mail & web, OverDrive digital audio bks, Photocopying/Printing, Preschool outreach, Prof lending libr, Prog for adults, Prog for children & young adult, Pub access computers, Ref serv in person, Scanner, Senior computer classes, Senior outreach, Spanish lang bks, Spoken cassettes & CDs, Spoken cassettes & DVDs, Story hour, Summer & winter reading prog, Tax forms, Teen prog, Telephone ref, VHS videos, Web-catalog, Writing prog
Mem of Reaching Across Illinois Library System (RAILS)
Partic in System Wide Automated Network
Special Services for the Deaf - Assistive tech; Bks on deafness & sign lang; Closed caption videos; High interest/low vocabulary bks; Sign lang interpreter upon request for prog; Staff with knowledge of sign lang
Special Services for the Blind - Audio mat; Bks on CD; Braille alphabet card; Copier with enlargement capabilities; Handicapped awareness prog; Home delivery serv; Large print bks; Newsletter (in large print, Braille or on cassette); Recorded bks; Ref serv; Sound rec
Open Mon-Thurs 10-9, Fri & Sat 10-5, Sun 1-5
Restriction: Non-resident fee
Friends of the Library Group

WESTVILLE

P WESTVILLE PUBLIC LIBRARY DISTRICT*, 233 S State St, 61883-1461. SAN 304-7547. Tel: 217-267-3170. FAX: 217-267-3468. Web Site: www.westvillepubliclibrarydistrict.org. *Dir,* Rick Balsamello; E-mail: rbalsa@lincolntrail.info
Founded 1937. Pop 12,499
Library Holdings: Audiobooks 1,046; CDs 266; e-books 30; Large Print Bks 430; Bk Titles 22,914; Per Subs 10; Videos 2,737
Special Collections: Antique & Collectibles Coll; History Coll
Wireless access
Mem of Illinois Heartland Library System
Open Mon, Tues, Thurs & Fri 9:30-6, Wed 9:30-7, Sat 9:30-1:30

WHEATON

SR COLLEGE CHURCH IN WHEATON LIBRARY*, 332 E Seminary Ave, 60187. SAN 304-7555. Tel: 630-668-0878. FAX: 630-668-0984. Web Site: www.college-church.org. *Librn,* Lisa Kern; Tel: 630-668-0878, Ext 138, E-mail: lkern@college-church.org
Library Holdings: Bk Vols 13,000; Per Subs 10
Subject Interests: Biblical studies, Missions & missionaries
Automation Activity & Vendor Info: (Cataloging) Follett Software; (Circulation) Follett Software
Publications: New in the Church Library (monthly)
Open Sun 9:15-12:30 & 5:45-6:15

S FIRST DIVISION MUSEUM AT CANTIGNY*, Colonel Robert R McCormick Research Center Library, One S 151 Winfield Rd, 60189-6097. SAN 375-1333. Tel: 630-260-8186. Interlibrary Loan Service Tel: 630-260-8211. Reference Tel: 630-260-8223. FAX: 630-260-9298. Web Site: www.firstdivisionmuseum.org. *Exec Dir,* Paul H Herbert; *Dir, Res,* Eric Gillespie; *Librn,* Tracy Cirar; *Ref Librn,* Mary Manning; *Archivist,* Kate Kleiderman; *Res,* Andrew Woods; Staff 5 (MLS 1, Non-MLS 4)
Library Holdings: Bk Vols 14,000; Per Subs 75
Special Collections: Oral History
Subject Interests: Mil hist
Database Vendor: OCLC FirstSearch
Function: Archival coll, Res libr
Mem of Reaching Across Illinois Library System (RAILS)
Open Tues-Fri 10-4 (10-5 Summer)
Restriction: Non-circulating to the pub, Open to pub with supv only

M MARIANJOY REHABILITATION HOSPITAL*, Medical Library, 26 W 171 Roosevelt Rd, 60187. SAN 324-4903. Tel: 630-909-7092. Interlibrary Loan Service Tel: 630-909-7090. FAX: 630-260-0143. E-mail: library@marianjoy.org. Web Site: www.marianjoylibrary.org. *Dir, Med Libr,* Nalini Mahajan; E-mail: nmahajan@marianjoy.org; Staff 2 (MLS 1, Non-MLS 1)
Founded 1974
Library Holdings: AV Mats 1,275; CDs 105; e-books 520; e-journals 6,253; Bk Titles 2,723; Per Subs 15; Spec Interest Per Sub 15; Videos 240
Special Collections: Rehabilitation Medicine
Subject Interests: Occupational therapy, Phys therapy, Rehabilitation, Speech therapy
Automation Activity & Vendor Info: (Acquisitions) Auto-Graphics, Inc; (Cataloging) Auto-Graphics, Inc; (Circulation) Auto-Graphics, Inc; (ILL) OCLC FirstSearch; (OPAC) Auto-Graphics, Inc; (Serials) Auto-Graphics, Inc
Database Vendor: DynaMed, EBSCOhost, MD Consult, Medline, Micromedex, Natural Standard, OCLC FirstSearch, OCLC WorldShare Interlibrary Loan, OVID Technologies, ProQuest, PubMed, ScienceDirect, SerialsSolutions, STAT!Ref (Teton Data Systems), UpToDate, Wiley InterScience
Function: Doc delivery serv, Handicapped accessible, Health sci info serv, ILL available, Mail loans to mem, Online searches, Photocopying/Printing, Ref serv available
Partic in Fox Valley Health Science Library Consortium; Illinois Library & Information Network
Restriction: Open to staff only

S THEOSOPHICAL SOCIETY IN AMERICA*, Henry S Olcott Memorial Library, 1926 N Main St, 60187. (Mail add: PO Box 270, 60187-0270), SAN 304-758X. Tel: 630-668-1571, Ext 304. FAX: 630-668-4976. E-mail: library@theosophical.org. Web Site: library.theosophical.org, www.theosophical.org. *Head Librn,* Marina Maestas; Staff 3 (MLS 3)
Founded 1926
Library Holdings: AV Mats 2,000; CDs 600; DVDs 400; Bk Titles 16,000; Bk Vols 20,000; Per Subs 85; Videos 1,200
Special Collections: Boris de Zirkoff Coll; Mary K Neff Coll; Rare Theosophical Journals Coll, microfilm
Subject Interests: Eastern philosophy, Mythology, Philos, Theosophy
Automation Activity & Vendor Info: (Cataloging) SirsiDynix; (Circulation) SirsiDynix; (ILL) OCLC Online; (OPAC) SirsiDynix
Database Vendor: OCLC WorldShare Interlibrary Loan
Wireless access
Mem of Reaching Across Illinois Library System (RAILS)
Partic in Illinois Library & Information Network; OCLC Online Computer Library Center, Inc
Open Tues-Sat (June-Aug) 10-12 & 1-5; Tues-Thurs (Sept-May) 5-7

C WHEATON COLLEGE*, Buswell Memorial Library, 510 Irving Ave, 60187-5593. (Mail add: 501 College Ave, 60187-5593), SAN 304-7598. Tel: 630-752-5102. Circulation Tel: 630-752-5354. Interlibrary Loan Service Tel: 630-752-5843. Reference Tel: 630-752-5169. Administration Tel: 630-752-5101. FAX: 630-752-5855. E-mail: reference@wheaton.edu. Web Site: library.wheaton.edu. *Dir,* Lisa Richmond; *Head, Ref,* Gregory Morrison; Tel: 630-752-5847, E-mail: gamori@wheaton.edu; *Archivist, Spec Coll Librn,* David Malone; Tel: 630-752-5707, E-mail: david.b.malone@wheaton.edu; *Syst Coordr,* Terry Huttenlock; Tel: 630-752-5352, E-mail: terry.huttenlock@wheaton.edu; *Coll Develop,* Stephen Spencer; Tel: 630-752-7104, E-mail: stephen.r.spencer@wheaton.edu; *Media Spec,* Keith Eiten; Tel: 630-752-5092, E-mail: keith.d.eiten@wheaton.edu; *Tech Serv,* Lynn Sue Gullickson; Tel: 630-752-5964, E-mail: lynn.h.gullickson@wheaton.edu. Subject Specialists: *Church hist, Theol,* Gregory Morrison; *Church hist, Instrul tech,* David Malone; *Hist, Theol,* Stephen Spencer; *Arts, Communication, Media, Music,* Keith Eiten; *Art, Art hist,* Lynn Sue Gullickson; Staff 14 (MLS 8, Non-MLS 6)
Founded 1860. Enrl 2,741; Fac 226; Highest Degree: Doctorate
Library Holdings: AV Mats 35,836; e-books 2,009; Bk Titles 259,664; Bk Vols 366,811; Per Subs 1,734
Special Collections: David Aikman, Frederick Buechner, John Bunyan, Anita & Peter Deyneka, Charles Dickens, Jaque Ellul, Samuel Johnson, Kenneth & Margaret Landon, Madeline L'Engle, Coleman Luck, Calvin Miller, Malcolm Muggeridge, Hans Rookmaaker, Luci Shaw, Norman Stone; Jonathan & Charles Blanchard Papers; Oswald Chambers, Senator Daniel R Coats. US Document Depository
Subject Interests: Am lit, Anthrop, English lit, Hist, Music, Philos, Polit sci, Relig
Automation Activity & Vendor Info: (Acquisitions) Ex Libris Group; (Cataloging) Ex Libris Group; (Circulation) Ex Libris Group; (Course Reserve) Ex Libris Group; (OPAC) Ex Libris Group; (Serials) Ex Libris Group
Mem of Reaching Across Illinois Library System (RAILS)

Partic in Association of Chicago Theological Schools; Lyrasis; OCLC Online Computer Library Center, Inc
Special Services for the Blind - Assistive/Adapted tech devices, equip & products; Computer with voice synthesizer for visually impaired persons
Open Mon-Thurs 7:30am-Midnight, Fri 7:30am-10pm, Sat 8:30am-10pm

Departmental Libraries:

MARION E WADE CENTER, 351 E Lincoln, 60187-4213. (Mail add: 501 College Ave, 60187-5501). Tel: 630-752-5908. FAX: 630-752-5459. E-mail: wade@wheaton.edu. Web Site: www.wheaton.edu/wadecenter. *Assoc Dir,* Marjorie L Mead; *Archivist,* Laura Schmidt; Staff 2 (MLS 1, Non-MLS 1)
Founded 1965
Library Holdings: Bk Vols 13,000; Per Subs 42
Special Collections: C S Lewis Coll, ms; Charles Williams Coll, ms; G K Chesterton Coll, ms; George MacDonald & Dorothy L Sayers Coll, ms; J R R Tolkien Coll, ms; Owen Barfield Coll, ms. Oral History
Subject Interests: Children's lit, Detective fiction, Fantasy, Sci fict, Theol
Function: Audio & video playback equip for onsite use, Bk club(s), Handicapped accessible
Publications: Seven: An Anglo-American Literary Review (Annual)
Open Mon-Fri 9-4, Sat 9-12
Restriction: Non-circulating

P WHEATON PUBLIC LIBRARY*, 225 N Cross St, 60187-5376. SAN 304-7601. Tel: 630-668-1374. Circulation Tel: 630-868-7510. Reference Tel: 630-868-7520. Administration Tel: 630-668-3097. Automation Services Tel: 630-868-7585. FAX: 630-668-8950. Administration FAX: 630-668-1465. TDD: 630-668-0256. E-mail: askref@wheatonlibrary.org. Web Site: www.wheatonlibrary.org. *Dir,* Betsy Adamowski; *Ch Serv,* Janet Dumas; Tel: 630-868-7543, E-mail: janet@wheatonlibrary.org; *Circ,* Ann Barnfield; Tel: 630-868-7512, E-mail: annb@wheatonlibrary.org; *Per,* Bev Jirsa; Tel: 630-868-7573, E-mail: beverly@wheatonlibrary.org; *Ref,* Carolyn Deare; Tel: 630-868-7592, E-mail: carolyn@wheatonlibrary.org; *Tech Serv,* Dawn Kovacs; E-mail: dawn@wheatonlibrary.org; Staff 13 (MLS 13)
Founded 1891. Pop 55,416; Circ 1,247,318
May 2008-Apr 2009 Income $4,105,214, State $67,801, City $3,700,000, Locally Generated Income $337,413. Mats Exp $658,430, Books $301,942, Per/Ser (Incl. Access Fees) $37,932, Micro $6,000, AV Mat $127,443, Electronic Ref Mat (Incl. Access Fees) $177,244, Presv $7,869. Sal $2,186,226 (Prof $797,992)
Library Holdings: Audiobooks 16,138; CDs 19,258; DVDs 8,524; Electronic Media & Resources 2,426; Large Print Bks 5,512; Microforms 4,768; Bk Vols 389,091; Per Subs 475; Videos 11,780
Special Collections: DuPage County History Coll
Subject Interests: Genealogy
Automation Activity & Vendor Info: (Acquisitions) Innovative Interfaces, Inc - Millenium; (Cataloging) Innovative Interfaces, Inc - Millenium; (Circulation) Innovative Interfaces, Inc - Millenium; (ILL) Innovative Interfaces, Inc; (OPAC) Innovative Interfaces, Inc - Millenium; (Serials) Innovative Interfaces, Inc - Millenium
Database Vendor: Baker & Taylor, Bowker, EBSCO - WebFeat, EBSCO Auto Repair Reference, Facts on File, Gale Cengage Learning, Greenwood Publishing Group, Grolier Online, Newsbank, OCLC FirstSearch, ProQuest, ReferenceUSA, ValueLine, Westlaw, World Book Online
Wireless access
Function: Audiobks via web, Bk club(s), Bks on cassette, Bks on CD, CD-ROM, Computer training, Computers for patron use, Copy machines, Electronic databases & coll, Free DVD rentals, Handicapped accessible, Homebound delivery serv, ILL available, Magnifiers for reading, Music CDs, Online cat, Online ref, Prog for adults, Prog for children & young adult, Scanner, Story hour, Summer reading prog, Tax forms, Telephone ref, VHS videos
Publications: Adult & Children's Newsletters; Bibliographies
Mem of Reaching Across Illinois Library System (RAILS)
Partic in OCLC Online Computer Library Center, Inc
Special Services for the Deaf - TDD equip
Special Services for the Blind - Bks on cassette; Bks on CD; Closed circuit TV magnifier; Home delivery serv; Large print bks; Text reader
Open Mon-Fri 9-9, Sat 9-5, Sun 1-5
Friends of the Library Group

WHEELING

P INDIAN TRAILS PUBLIC LIBRARY DISTRICT*, 355 S Schoenbeck Rd, 60090. SAN 304-761X. Tel: 847-459-4100. FAX: 847-459-4760. TDD: 847-459-5271. Web Site: www.indiantrailslibrary.org. *Dir,* Brian Shepard; *Head, Admin Serv,* Susan Beal; E-mail: sbeal@itpld.lib.il.us; *Head, Adult Serv,* Phil Spirito; *Head, Br & Outreach Serv,* Anna Yackle; *Head, Circ Serv,* Rosa Lloyd; *Head, Communication Serv,* Susan Dennison; *Head, Mat Serv,* Elizabeth Marszalik; *Head, Tech Serv,* Michael Jackiw; E-mail: mjackiw@itpld.lib.il.us; *Head, Youth Serv,* Michele Fenton; Staff 96 (MLS 15, Non-MLS 81)
Founded 1959. Pop 65,828; Circ 912,000
Library Holdings: AV Mats 33,939; e-books 500; Bk Titles 154,007; Bk Vols 213,170; Per Subs 410
Automation Activity & Vendor Info: (Acquisitions) SirsiDynix; (Cataloging) SirsiDynix; (Circulation) SirsiDynix; (OPAC) SirsiDynix; (Serials) SirsiDynix
Database Vendor: Baker & Taylor, BWI, OCLC FirstSearch, OCLC WorldShare Interlibrary Loan, SirsiDynix
Function: AV serv, Home delivery & serv to Sr ctr & nursing homes, Homebound delivery serv, ILL available, Magnifiers for reading, Outside serv via phone, mail, e-mail & web, Photocopying/Printing, Prog for children & young adult, Ref serv available, Summer reading prog, Wheelchair accessible
Publications: Children's Newsletter; General Library Newsletter; ITPLD News (Newsletter); Trails Tales (Newsletter)
Special Services for the Deaf - TDD equip; TTY equip
Special Services for the Blind - Computer with voice synthesizer for visually impaired persons; Large print bks; Large screen computer & software
Open Mon-Fri 9-9, Sat 9-5, Sun 12-5
Friends of the Library Group
Bookmobiles: 1. Head, Outreach Services, Chris Gibson. Bk titles 4000

WHITE HALL

P WHITE HALL TOWNSHIP LIBRARY*, 119 E Sherman St, 62092. SAN 304-7636. Tel: 217-374-6014. FAX: 217-374-6554. E-mail: whelib@gcctv.com. Web Site: whitehalltownshiplibrary.org. *Head Librn,* Alice Ford; *Asst Librn,* Janis Chapman; *Asst Librn,* Rene Seymoure; Staff 3 (Non-MLS 3)
Founded 1876. Pop 3,036; Circ 13,040
Apr 2011-Mar 2012 Income $41,676, State $3,823, Locally Generated Income $33,908, Other $3,945. Mats Exp $40,541. Sal $24,681
Library Holdings: Audiobooks 378; CDs 151; DVDs 151; Large Print Bks 100; Bk Vols 15,516; Per Subs 33; Videos 317
Special Collections: Green Prairie Press 1985-present, microfilm; Greene & Jersey History Coll; North Greene News June 7, 1979-April 1985, microfilm; White Hall Register 1869-July 1917, microfilm; White Hall Register-Republican August 1917-1979, microfilm
Wireless access
Mem of Illinois Heartland Library System
Special Services for the Deaf - Bks on deafness & sign lang
Special Services for the Blind - Bks on cassette
Open Mon-Thurs 2-8, Fri & Sat 9-5

WILLIAMSFIELD

P WILLIAMSFIELD PUBLIC LIBRARY DISTRICT*, 111 W Gale St, 61489. (Mail add: PO Box 268, 61489-0268), SAN 376-1398. Tel: 309-639-2630. FAX: 309-639-2611. E-mail: wpldgata@winco.net. Web Site: www.williamsfieldlibrary.org. *Dir,* Gayla Karrick
Founded 1991
Library Holdings: Bk Titles 6,200; Per Subs 29
Open Mon, Wed & Fri 9-4, Tues & Thurs 1-8, Sat 9-1
Friends of the Library Group

WILLIAMSVILLE

P WILLIAMSVILLE PUBLIC LIBRARY*, 102 S Elm St, 62693. (Mail add: 141 W Main St, 62693), SAN 304-7644. Tel: 217-566-3520. FAX: 217-566-3481. E-mail: billtownlib@yahoo.com. *Dir,* Jean Forness
Founded 1980. Pop 1,450; Circ 5,147
Library Holdings: Bk Titles 6,000
Automation Activity & Vendor Info: (Cataloging) Horizon; (Circulation) Horizon
Wireless access
Mem of Illinois Heartland Library System
Open Mon-Thurs 10-2 & 5-8, Sat 10-12

WILLOWBROOK

S VIBRATION INSTITUTE LIBRARY*, 6262 S Kingery Hwy, Ste 212, 60527. SAN 373-4447. Tel: 630-654-2254. FAX: 630-654-2271. E-mail: information@vi-institute.org. Web Site: www.vibinst.org. *Dir,* Karen E Bresson
Library Holdings: Bk Vols 200; Per Subs 50

WILMETTE

SR BETH HILLEL CONGREGATION LIBRARY*, 3220 Big Tree Lane, 60091. SAN 376-0057. Tel: 847-256-1213, Ext 29. FAX: 847-256-3225. E-mail: office@bhcbe.org. Web Site: www.bhcbe.org. *Librn,* Marcie Eskin; Staff 1 (MLS 1)
Library Holdings: Bk Titles 2,000
Restriction: Mem only

S WILMETTE HISTORICAL MUSEUM, Research Library, 609 Ridge Rd, 60091-2721. SAN 329-1154. Tel: 847-853-7666. E-mail: museum@wilmette.com. Web Site: www.wilmettehistory.org. *Dir,* K Hussey-Arntson; Staff 3 (Non-MLS 3)
Founded 1951
Library Holdings: Bk Titles 400; Bk Vols 500
Special Collections: Oral History
Subject Interests: Local hist
Publications: The Ouilmette Heritage (Newsletter)
Open Mon-Thurs & Sun 1-4:30
Restriction: Non-circulating to the pub
Friends of the Library Group

P WILMETTE PUBLIC LIBRARY DISTRICT*, 1242 Wilmette Ave, 60091-2558. SAN 304-7660. Tel: 847-256-5025. Circulation Tel: 847-256-6947. Interlibrary Loan Service Tel: 847-256-6955. Reference Tel: 847-256-6935. Administration Tel: 847-256-6912. FAX: 847-256-6933. TDD: 847-256-6931. E-mail: wilref@wilmettelibrary.info. Web Site: www.wilmettelibrary.info. *Dir,* Ellen Boates Clark; Tel: 847-256-6924, Fax: 847-256-6911, E-mail: ebclark@wilmettelibrary.info; *Head, Adult Serv,* Betty Giorgi; Tel: 847-256-6936, E-mail: blgiorgi@wilmettelibrary.info; *Bus Mgr,* Barbara Griffiths; Tel: 847-256-6910, Fax: 847-256-6911, E-mail: bgriffiths@wilmettelibrary.info; *Ch Serv,* Keren Joshi; Tel: 847-256-6940, Fax: 847-256-6943, E-mail: kjoshi@wilmettelibrary.info; *Circ Serv,* Luciano Ward; Tel: 847-256-6950, E-mail: lward@wilmettelibrary.info; *Commun Serv,* Bonnie Forkosh; Tel: 847-256-6925, E-mail: bforkosh@wilmettelibrary.info; *Tech Serv,* Gayle Rosenberg-Justman; Tel: 847-256-6920, Fax: 847-256-6944, E-mail: grjustman@wilmettelibrary.info; Staff 48 (MLS 15, Non-MLS 33)
Founded 1901. Pop 27,087; Circ 753,000
Jul 2011-Jun 2012 Income $6,155,917, State $75,391, County $5,557,633, Locally Generated Income $522,893. Mats Exp $770,248, Books $329,720, Per/Ser (Incl. Access Fees) $46,694, AV Mat $136,915, Electronic Ref Mat (Incl. Access Fees) $256,919. Sal $2,293,074 (Prof $1,036,754)
Library Holdings: AV Mats 45,739; e-books 34,877; Large Print Bks 7,138; Microforms 3,520; Bk Titles 200,491; Bk Vols 221,719; Per Subs 538
Special Collections: Oral History
Subject Interests: Art, Local hist, Travel
Automation Activity & Vendor Info: (Acquisitions) SirsiDynix; (Cataloging) SirsiDynix; (Circulation) SirsiDynix; (OPAC) SirsiDynix
Wireless access
Publications: Off the Shelf
Mem of Reaching Across Illinois Library System (RAILS)
Partic in Cooperative Computer Services - CCS
Open Mon-Fri & Sun (Sept-May) 9-9, Sat 9-5; Sun (June-Aug) 1-5
Friends of the Library Group

WILMINGTON

P WILMINGTON PUBLIC LIBRARY DISTRICT*, 201 S Kankakee St, 60481-1338. SAN 304-7679. Tel: 815-476-2834. FAX: 815-476-7805. Web Site: www.wilmingtonlibrary.org. *Dir,* Maria Meachum; E-mail: mfbmeachum@wilmingtonlibrary.org; *Asst Dir,* Nikeda F Webb; E-mail: nfwebb@wilmingtonlibrary.org; Staff 2 (MLS 1, Non-MLS 1)
Founded 1907. Pop 9,229; Circ 96,121
Jul 2007-Jun 2008 Income $532,126, State $30,282, County $468,283, Locally Generated Income $15,773, Other $17,788. Mats Exp $100,613, Books $61,848, Other Print Mats $21,680, Electronic Ref Mat (Incl. Access Fees) $17,085. Sal $253,433 (Prof $85,151)
Library Holdings: CDs 4,205; DVDs 3,788; e-books 4,645; Bk Titles 40,004; Per Subs 80
Subject Interests: Antiques, Genealogy, Local hist
Automation Activity & Vendor Info: (Cataloging) SirsiDynix; (Circulation) SirsiDynix; (ILL) SirsiDynix; (OPAC) SirsiDynix
Database Vendor: EBSCO Auto Repair Reference, EBSCOhost, Grolier Online, LearningExpress, Newsbank, ProQuest
Wireless access
Publications: Book Bytes (Newsletter)
Mem of Reaching Across Illinois Library System (RAILS)
Open Mon-Thurs 9-8, Fri-Sun 9-5
Friends of the Library Group

WINCHESTER

P WINCHESTER PUBLIC LIBRARY*, 215 N Main St, 62694. SAN 304-7687. Tel: 217-742-3150. FAX: 217-742-3150. E-mail: winplibrary@irtc.net. *Dir,* Darlene Smith; Staff 1 (Non-MLS 1)
Founded 1907. Pop 1,600; Circ 10,259
Library Holdings: Bk Vols 17,402; Per Subs 37
Subject Interests: Local hist
Automation Activity & Vendor Info: (Cataloging) SIRSI WorkFlows; (Circulation) SIRSI WorkFlows
Wireless access
Open Mon 1-6, Tues & Fri 1-5, Wed & Thurs 1-7, Sat 10-12

WINDSOR

P WINDSOR STORM MEMORIAL PUBLIC LIBRARY DISTRICT*, 102 S Maple, 61957. SAN 375-9342. Tel: 217-459-2498. FAX: 217-459-2499. Web Site: www.windsor.lib.il.us. *Libr Dir,* Stacey Stremming
Library Holdings: CDs 28,000; Bk Titles 14,000; Per Subs 59
Wireless access
Mem of Illinois Heartland Library System
Open Mon-Fri 10-5, Sat 10-1

WINFIELD

M CADENCE HEALTH-CENTRAL DUPAGE HOSPITAL, Knowledge Resource Library, 25 N Winfield Rd, 60190. SAN 304-7695. Tel: 630-933-4536. FAX: 630-933-4530. *Mgr, Libr of Cadence Health,* Julie Stielstra; E-mail: julie.stielstra@cadencehealth.org; Staff 1 (MLS 1)
Founded 1974
Library Holdings: Bk Titles 2,000; Per Subs 800
Subject Interests: Med, Nursing
Automation Activity & Vendor Info: (Cataloging) LibraryWorld, Inc; (Circulation) LibraryWorld, Inc; (OPAC) LibraryWorld, Inc
Database Vendor: DynaMed, EBSCOhost, Elsevier, LibraryWorld, Inc, OVID Technologies, STAT!Ref (Teton Data Systems)
Wireless access
Function: Health sci info serv
Mem of Reaching Across Illinois Library System (RAILS)
Partic in Fox Valley Health Science Library Consortium; Illinois Library & Information Network; OCLC Online Computer Library Center, Inc; Regional Med Libr - Region 3
Open Mon-Fri 7:30-3:30
Restriction: Circulates for staff only, In-house use for visitors

P WINFIELD PUBLIC LIBRARY, 0S291 Winfield Rd, 60190. SAN 304-7709. Tel: 630-653-7599. FAX: 630-653-7781. E-mail: wfdstaff@winfield.lib.il.us. Web Site: www.winfield.lib.il.us/winfield. *Dir,* Matthew Suddarth; E-mail: suddarth@winfield.lib.il.us; *Adult/YA Serv Librn,* Katie Clark; E-mail: kclark@winfield.lib.il.us; *Youth Serv,* Filomena Choate; Staff 5 (MLS 3, Non-MLS 2)
Founded 1968. Pop 9,080; Circ 104,646
May 2013-Apr 2014 Income $816,540. Sal $360,635 (Prof $224,134)
Library Holdings: AV Mats 5,451; Bk Vols 48,440; Per Subs 178
Subject Interests: Local hist
Automation Activity & Vendor Info: (Circulation) Auto-Graphics, Inc; (OPAC) Auto-Graphics, Inc
Database Vendor: Auto-Graphics, Inc, EBSCOhost, OCLC FirstSearch, OCLC WorldShare Interlibrary Loan, ProQuest, ReferenceUSA
Publications: The Inside Page (Newsletter)
Mem of Reaching Across Illinois Library System (RAILS)
Open Mon-Thurs 9-9, Fri & Sat 9-5
Friends of the Library Group

WINNEBAGO

P WINNEBAGO PUBLIC LIBRARY*, 210 N Elida St, 61088. (Mail add: PO Box 536, 61088-0536), SAN 324-5756. Tel: 815-335-7050. FAX: 815-335-7049. E-mail: director@winnebagopubliclibrary.org. Web Site: winnebagopubliclibrary.org. Staff 3 (Non-MLS 3)
Founded 1982. Pop 7,257
Library Holdings: AV Mats 3,013; Bks on Deafness & Sign Lang 30; CDs 216; DVDs 305; Large Print Bks 658; Bk Vols 31,848; Per Subs 102; Talking Bks 450; Videos 1,772
Subject Interests: Ill, Local hist
Automation Activity & Vendor Info: (Circulation) Follett Software
Mem of Reaching Across Illinois Library System (RAILS)
Open Mon-Thurs 10-8, Fri 10-6, Sat 10-4
Friends of the Library Group

WINNETKA

P WINNETKA-NORTHFIELD PUBLIC LIBRARY DISTRICT, 768 Oak St, 60093-2515. SAN 340-9171. Tel: 847-446-7220. FAX: 847-446-5085. Web Site: www.winnetkalibrary.org. *Dir,* Rebecca Wolf; E-mail: rwolf@winnetkalibrary.org; *Head, Adult Serv,* Shauna Porteus; *Head, Access Serv,* Kathy Roegge; *Head, Info Tech,* Mark Swenson; *Head, Youth Serv,* Sheila Cody; *Bus Mgr,* Alex Makstman; E-mail: alexmaks@winnetkalibrary.org; Staff 42 (MLS 12, Non-MLS 30)
Founded 1884. Pop 17,808; Circ 279,477
Library Holdings: AV Mats 7,244; e-books 2,622; Electronic Media & Resources 422; Bk Vols 127,028; Per Subs 146; Talking Bks 6,181; Videos 2,220
Subject Interests: Genealogy
Automation Activity & Vendor Info: (Cataloging) SirsiDynix; (Circulation) SirsiDynix; (ILL) SirsiDynix; (OPAC) SirsiDynix
Wireless access
Publications: Source (Newsletter)

Partic in Cooperative Computer Services - CCS
Open Mon-Thurs 9-9, Fri & Sat 9-5, Sun 1-5
Friends of the Library Group
Branches: 1
NORTHFIELD BRANCH, 1785 Orchard Ln, 60093, SAN 340-9201. Tel: 847-446-5990. FAX: 847-446-6586. *Br Mgr,* Kristin Carlson; E-mail: kristin@winnetkalibrary.org; Staff 3 (MLS 3)
Library Holdings: Bk Vols 16,000; Per Subs 50
Open Mon-Thurs 9-9, Fri & Sat 9-5, Sun 1-5
Friends of the Library Group

WITT

P WITT MEMORIAL PUBLIC LIBRARY*, 18 N Second St, 62094. (Mail add: PO Box 442, 62094-0442), SAN 304-7725. Tel: 217-594-7333. FAX: 217-594-7333. E-mail: witttownshippl@gmail.com. *Librn,* Sue VanOstran
Founded 1953. Pop 1,391; Circ 3,791
Library Holdings: Bk Vols 10,000
Wireless access
Open Tues-Thurs 9-12 & 2-5, Fri 2-5, Sat 9-12

WOOD DALE

P WOOD DALE PUBLIC LIBRARY DISTRICT*, 520 N Wood Dale Rd, 60191. SAN 304-7733. Tel: 630-766-6762. FAX: 630-766-5715. Web Site: www.wooddalelibrary.org. *Dir,* Yvonne Rae Beechler Bergendorf; *Mgr, Ch Serv,* Jenny Collier; E-mail: jcollier@wooddalelibrary.org; *Operations Mgr,* Joanna Klos; E-mail: jklos@wooddalelibrary.org; *Mgr, Pub Serv,* Karen Stier Pulver; E-mail: kspulver@wooddalelibrary.org; *Mgr, Tech Serv,* Jim Lindt; E-mail: jlindt@wooddalelibrary.org; Staff 21.55 (MLS 4.55, Non-MLS 17)
Founded 1962. Pop 11,868; Circ 188,757
Library Holdings: AV Mats 2,546; CDs 1,229; DVDs 3,715; Electronic Media & Resources 24; Large Print Bks 1,281; Bk Vols 86,165; Per Subs 193; Videos 1,749
Subject Interests: Local hist
Automation Activity & Vendor Info: (Cataloging) SirsiDynix; (Circulation) SirsiDynix; (ILL) OCLC Connexion; (OPAC) SirsiDynix
Database Vendor: Baker & Taylor, Gale Cengage Learning, OCLC ArticleFirst, OCLC FirstSearch, OCLC WebJunction, OCLC WorldShare Interlibrary Loan
Wireless access
Mem of Reaching Across Illinois Library System (RAILS)
Partic in MAGIC (Multitype Automation Group in Cooperation)
Special Services for the Deaf - Closed caption videos; High interest/low vocabulary bks; Sign lang interpreter upon request for prog
Special Services for the Blind - Accessible computers; Aids for in-house use; Audio mat; Bks available with recordings; Bks on CD; Extensive large print coll; Free checkout of audio mat; Large print bks; Large screen computer & software; Playaways (bks on MP3)
Open Mon-Thurs 10-9, Fri & Sat 10-5, Sun (Sept-May) 1-5

WOOD RIVER

P WOOD RIVER PUBLIC LIBRARY*, 326 E Ferguson Ave, 62095-2098. SAN 304-775X. Tel: 618-254-4832. FAX: 618-254-4836. E-mail: info@woodriverlibrary.org. Web Site: woodriverlibrary.org. *Dir,* Kate Kite; E-mail: kate@woodriverlibrary.org; *Asst Dir,* Jeremy Staicoff; *Tech Mgr,* Ernest Peters; *Youth Serv Mgr,* Ashley Bryant-Bennett; E-mail: ashleyb@woodriverlibrary.org
Founded 1920. Pop 10,493; Circ 129,980
Library Holdings: Bk Vols 65,316
Automation Activity & Vendor Info: (Circulation) Innovative Interfaces, Inc
Wireless access
Mem of Illinois Heartland Library System
Partic in Coop Libr Agency for Syst & Servs
Open Mon-Thurs 9:30-8, Fri & Sat 9:30-5, Sun 12:30-4
Friends of the Library Group

WOODHULL

P CLOVER PUBLIC LIBRARY DISTRICT*, 440 N Division St, 61490. (Mail add: PO Box 369, 61490-0369), SAN 304-7768. Tel: 309-334-2680. FAX: 309-334-2378. Web Site: www.woodhull.lib.il.us. *Dir,* Rene Bramlett
Founded 1965. Pop 2,398; Circ 21,000
Library Holdings: Bk Vols 22,000; Per Subs 54
Special Collections: Woodhull Hist Coll; World War II Coll
Automation Activity & Vendor Info: (Cataloging) SirsiDynix; (Circulation) SirsiDynix
Wireless access
Mem of Reaching Across Illinois Library System (RAILS)
Open Mon, Wed & Thurs 9-12 & 2-8, Tues 2-8, Fri 9-12 & 2-5, Sat 9-12

WOODRIDGE

P WOODRIDGE PUBLIC LIBRARY*, Three Plaza Dr, 60517-5014. SAN 304-7776. Tel: 630-964-7899. FAX: 630-964-0175. TDD: 630-964-7986. E-mail: wrs@woodridgelibrary.org. Web Site: www.woodridgelibrary.org. *Libr Adminr,* Susan McNeil-Marshall; E-mail: smmarshall@woodridgelibrary.org; *Head, Circ,* Julie Lombardo; E-mail: jlombardo@woodridgelibrary.org; *Head, Tech Serv,* Amy Weiss; E-mail: aweiss@woodridgelibrary.org; *Bus Mgr,* John Norton; E-mail: jnorton@woodridgelibrary.org; *Adult Serv, YA Serv,* George Kalinka; E-mail: gkalinka@woodridgelibrary.org; *Ch Serv,* Sheri Daun-Bedford; E-mail: sdbedford@woodridgelibrary.org; Staff 14 (MLS 10, Non-MLS 4)
Founded 1967. Pop 35,900; Circ 607,000
Library Holdings: Bk Vols 175,000; Per Subs 254
Automation Activity & Vendor Info: (Acquisitions) Innovative Interfaces, Inc; (Cataloging) Innovative Interfaces, Inc; (Circulation) Innovative Interfaces, Inc; (Course Reserve) Innovative Interfaces, Inc; (ILL) Innovative Interfaces, Inc; (OPAC) Innovative Interfaces, Inc
Database Vendor: OCLC FirstSearch, ProQuest
Wireless access
Function: Adult bk club, After school storytime, Art exhibits, Audiobks via web, AV serv, Bks on cassette, Bks on CD, CD-ROM, Children's prog, Computer training, Computers for patron use, Copy machines, e-mail serv, Electronic databases & coll, Fax serv, Free DVD rentals, Handicapped accessible, Holiday prog, Homebound delivery serv, ILL available, Magnifiers for reading, Mail & tel request accepted, Mus passes, Music CDs, Newsp ref libr, Notary serv, Online cat, Orientations, Outreach serv, OverDrive digital audio bks, Photocopying/Printing, Preschool outreach, Prog for adults, Prog for children & young adult, Pub access computers, Ref serv available, Ref serv in person, Spoken cassettes & DVDs, Story hour, Summer reading prog, Tax forms, Teen prog, Telephone ref, VHS videos, Video lending libr, Web-catalog, Wheelchair accessible
Mem of Reaching Across Illinois Library System (RAILS)
Special Services for the Deaf - TDD equip
Open Mon-Fri 9-9, Sat 9-5, Sun 1-5
Friends of the Library Group

WOODSTOCK

L MCHENRY COUNTY LAW LIBRARY*, McHenry County Government Ctr, 3rd Flr, 2200 N Seminary Ave, 60098. SAN 372-1140. Tel: 815-334-4166. FAX: 815-334-1005. Web Site: www.co.mchenry.il.us. *Librn,* Susana Huffman; E-mail: sxhuffman@co.mchenry.il.us
Library Holdings: Bk Vols 12,000
Database Vendor: LexisNexis, Westlaw
Wireless access
Open Mon-Fri 8-12 & 1-4:30

P WOODSTOCK PUBLIC LIBRARY*, 414 W Judd, 60098-3195. SAN 304-7792. Tel: 815-338-0542. FAX: 815-334-2296. E-mail: library@woodstockil.gov. Web Site: www.woodstockpubliclibrary.org. *Dir,* Position Currently Open; Staff 10 (MLS 8, Non-MLS 2)
Founded 1890. Pop 37,384, Circ 348,119
Library Holdings: Bk Titles 110,495
Special Collections: McHenry County History & Genealogy Coll
Automation Activity & Vendor Info: (Acquisitions) Innovative Interfaces, Inc; (Cataloging) Innovative Interfaces, Inc; (Circulation) Innovative Interfaces, Inc; (ILL) Innovative Interfaces, Inc; (OPAC) Innovative Interfaces, Inc; (Serials) Innovative Interfaces, Inc
Wireless access
Function: Adult bk club, Art exhibits, Audiobks via web, AV serv, Bilingual assistance for Spanish patrons, Bk club(s), Bks on cassette, Bks on CD, Children's prog, Computer training, Computers for patron use, Copy machines, e-mail serv, E-Reserves, Electronic databases & coll, Family literacy, Handicapped accessible, Home delivery & serv to Sr ctr & nursing homes, Homebound delivery serv, Homework prog, ILL available, Instruction & testing, Jail serv, Magnifiers for reading, Mail & tel request accepted, Music CDs, Online cat, Online ref, OverDrive digital audio bks, Photocopying/Printing, Prog for adults, Prog for children & young adult, Pub access computers, Ref serv available, Story hour, Summer reading prog, Tax forms, Teen prog, Telephone ref, VHS videos
Mem of Reaching Across Illinois Library System (RAILS)
Open Mon-Thurs 9-9, Fri 9-6, Sat 9-5, Sun 1-4
Friends of the Library Group

WORDEN

P WORDEN PUBLIC LIBRARY DISTRICT*, 111 E Wall St, 62097. (Mail add: PO Box 164, 62097-0164). Tel: 618-459-7171. E-mail: worden@outlook.com. *Dir,* Gary Naglich
Library Holdings: Bk Titles 7,084; Per Subs 7
Mem of Illinois Heartland Library System
Open Tues & Thurs 10-8, Wed 10-6, Fri 10-5, Sat 9-2

WYANET

P RAYMOND A SAPP MEMORIAL TOWNSHIP LIBRARY*, 103 E Main St, 61379. (Mail add: PO Box 23, 61379-0023), SAN 304-7814. Tel: 815-699-2342. FAX: 815-699-2342. *Dir,* Linda Kurth; *Asst Librn,* Sheila Johnsen; Staff 2 (Non-MLS 2)
Founded 1915. Pop 1,348; Circ 5,787
Library Holdings: AV Mats 564; Bk Vols 12,660; Per Subs 23; Talking Bks 100
Special Collections: Oral History
Wireless access
Mem of Reaching Across Illinois Library System (RAILS)
Partic in Illinois Library & Information Network
Open Mon, Tues, Wed & Fri 1-6, Thurs 3-8, Sat 8-1
Friends of the Library Group

WYOMING

P WYOMING PUBLIC LIBRARY DISTRICT*, 119 N Seventh St, 61491. SAN 304-7822. Tel: 309-695-2241. FAX: 309-695-2241. Web Site: www.wyomingpubliclibrary.com. *Dir,* Jane Scholl; E-mail: jscholl@wyomingpubliclibrary.com; *Librn,* Jane Jaggard
Pop 2,367; Circ 41,000
Library Holdings: Bk Vols 15,000; Per Subs 23
Open Mon & Tues 1-5:30, Wed 9-7:30, Thurs 1-7:30, Fri 1-5, Sat 8-12

YATES CITY

P SALEM TOWNSHIP PUBLIC LIBRARY DISTRICT*, 115 W Main St, 61572. (Mail add: PO Box 19, 61572-0019), SAN 304-7830. Tel: 309-358-1678. FAX: 309-358-1678. *Chief Librn,* Karen Siegel
Founded 1923. Pop 1,216; Circ 9,000
Library Holdings: Bk Titles 10,000; Per Subs 30
Open Mon, Wed & Fri 1:30-6:30, Tues & Thurs 10-7, Sat 9-1

YORKVILLE

P YORKVILLE PUBLIC MUNICIPAL LIBRARY*, 902 Game Farm Rd, 60560. SAN 304-7849. Tel: 630-553-4354. FAX: 630-553-0823. Web Site: www.yorkville.lib.il.us. *Dir,* Michelle Pfister
Founded 1915. Circ 35,900
Library Holdings: CDs 2,288; DVDs 1,183; Bk Vols 38,880; Per Subs 119
Special Collections: Irma Hardekopf Music Coll, bks, sheet music; Kendall County Record 1864-1978 Coll, microflm
Subject Interests: Art, Local hist, Music
Mem of Reaching Across Illinois Library System (RAILS)
Open Mon-Thurs 9-8:30, Fri 9-5, Sat 9-4, Sun 1-4
Friends of the Library Group

ZEIGLER

P ZEIGLER PUBLIC LIBRARY*, 102 E Maryland St, 62999. SAN 304-7857. Tel: 618-596-2041. FAX: 618-596-2041. *Librn,* Peggy Carpenter
Pop 1,748; Circ 7,500
Library Holdings: Bk Vols 9,000; Per Subs 30; Videos 72
Mem of Illinois Heartland Library System
Open Mon, Wed, Fri & Sat 12-5, Tues & Thurs 12-7

ZION

P ZION-BENTON PUBLIC LIBRARY DISTRICT*, 2400 Gabriel Ave, 60099. SAN 304-7873. Tel: 847-872-4680. FAX: 847-872-4942. TDD: 847-872-1163. E-mail: library@zblibrary.org. Web Site: www.zblibrary.org. *Asst Dir, Interim Dir,* Tara Caldara; Tel: 847-872-4680, Ext 109, E-mail: tcaldara@zblibrary.org; *Dir,* Position Currently Open; *Adult Serv Coordr,* Elsie Martinez; *Circ & Tech Serv Coordr,* Rosemary Kauth; Tel: 847-872-4680, Ext 124, E-mail: rkauth@zblibrary.org; *Youth Serv Coordr,* Sarah Washkoviak; Staff 29 (MLS 7, Non-MLS 22)
Founded 1937. Pop 40,526; Circ 276,000
Jul 2009-Jun 2010 Income $2,043,050. Mats Exp $229,000. Sal $926,000
Library Holdings: AV Mats 17,420; Bk Vols 123,350; Per Subs 152
Subject Interests: Genealogy, Local hist
Automation Activity & Vendor Info: (Acquisitions) SirsiDynix; (Cataloging) OCLC; (Circulation) SirsiDynix; (ILL) SirsiDynix; (OPAC) SirsiDynix; (Serials) SirsiDynix
Database Vendor: OCLC FirstSearch
Wireless access
Publications: ZB Reader (Newsletter)
Partic in Cooperative Computer Services - CCS; OCLC Online Computer Library Center, Inc
Special Services for the Deaf - TDD equip; TTY equip
Open Mon-Thurs 9-9, Sat 9-5
Friends of the Library Group

INDIANA

Date of Statistics: FY 2014
Population, 2010 U.S. Census: 6,483,802
Total Volumes in Public Libraries: 24,296,781
Volumes Per Capita: (Statewide) 3.75
Total Public Library Income: $333,034,531
Average Income: $1,405,209
Source of Income: Local property tax, optional local income tax, contractual revenue received for service, financial institution tax, license vehicle excise tax, commercial vehicle excise tax, private endorsements/grants, state grants-in-aid, license excise, county adjusted growth income tax, county option income tax, other state & federal income, LSTA
Number of County Libraries: 24
Counties Served: 92 (All receive complete or partial service)
Number of Bookmobiles in State: 26
Grants-in-Aid to Public Libraries:
Federal: $903,429
State: $824,500

AKRON

P AKRON CARNEGIE PUBLIC LIBRARY*, 205 E Rochester St, 46910. (Mail add: PO Box 428, 46910-0428), SAN 304-7881. Tel: 574-893-4113. FAX: 574-893-4113. E-mail: akronadm@akron.lib.in.us. Web Site: www.akron.lib.in.us. *Dir,* Velma Bright
Founded 1912. Pop 2,827; Circ 19,752
Library Holdings: Bk Vols 27,622; Per Subs 68
Special Collections: Local History, bks, microfilm. Oral History
Automation Activity & Vendor Info: (Cataloging) Follett Software; (Circulation) Follett Software
Partic in Midwest Collaborative for Library Services (MCLS)
Open Mon-Fri 9-6, Sat 9-5
Friends of the Library Group

ALBION

S CHAIN OF LAKES CORRECTIONAL FACILITY LIBRARY*, 3516 E 75th S, 46701. Tel: 206-636-3114. *Supvr,* Rod Kitchen
Library Holdings: Bk Vols 500

P NOBLE COUNTY PUBLIC LIBRARY*, 813 E Main St, 46701. SAN 340-9236. Tel: 260-636-7197. Toll Free Tel: 800-811-6861. FAX: 260-636-3321. Web Site: www.nobleco.lib.in.us. *Dir,* Sandy Petrie; Staff 13 (MLS 3, Non-MLS 10)
Founded 1914. Pop 23,102; Circ 236,073
Library Holdings: CDs 109; Large Print Bks 312; Bk Titles 86,305; Per Subs 376; Talking Bks 2,770; Videos 7,943
Special Collections: History & Genealogy (Noble County Coll); History (Albion Memories Coll)
Automation Activity & Vendor Info: (Acquisitions) Evergreen; (Cataloging) Evergreen; (Circulation) Evergreen; (ILL) Evergreen; (OPAC) Evergreen
Database Vendor: Baker & Taylor, Gale Cengage Learning, Inspire, OCLC WebJunction, ProQuest, Wilson - Wilson Web
Wireless access
Function: Adult bk club, After school storytime, CD-ROM, Computer training, Copy machines, Electronic databases & coll, Equip loans & repairs, Handicapped accessible, ILL available, Music CDs, Prog for adults, Prog for children & young adult, Ref serv available, Senior computer classes, Summer reading prog, Tax forms, VHS videos, Wheelchair accessible
Partic in Evergreen Indiana Consortium; Midwest Collaborative for Library Services (MCLS); Northeast Indiana Libraries Serving Communities Consortium; Northern Indiana Computer Consortium for Libraries (NICCL)
Open Mon, Tues & Thurs 9-7, Wed 9-8, Fri 9-6, Sat 10-2
Friends of the Library Group
Branches: 2
EAST, 104 Ley St, Avilla, 46710, SAN 340-9260. Tel: 260-897-3900. FAX: 260-897-3900. *Br Adminr,* Victoria Ferguson; Staff 3 (Non-MLS 3)
Open Mon, Wed & Fri 9-5, Tues & Thurs 9-7:30, Sat 9-2
Friends of the Library Group
WEST, 120 Jefferson St, Cromwell, 46732-0555, SAN 328-6592. Tel: 260-856-2119. FAX: 260-856-2119. *Br Admінr,* Janet Harper; Staff 3 (Non-MLS 3)
Open Mon, Tues, Thurs & Fri 9-5, Wed 9-7, Sat 9-2
Friends of the Library Group

ALEXANDRIA

P ALEXANDRIA-MONROE PUBLIC LIBRARY*, 117 E Church St, 46001-2005. SAN 304-789X. Tel: 765-724-2196. FAX: 765-724-2204. Web Site: www.alex.lib.in.us. *Dir,* Montie L Manning; E-mail: director@alex.lib.in.us; *Adult Serv, Outreach Librn,* Kathy Amos; E-mail: kamos@alex.lib.in.us; *Ch,* Elizabeth Spade; E-mail: bspade@alex.lib.in.us; Staff 2 (MLS 1, Non-MLS 1)
Founded 1903. Pop 10,233; Circ 77,985
Library Holdings: Bk Vols 43,116; Per Subs 136
Automation Activity & Vendor Info: (Acquisitions) TLC (The Library Corporation); (Cataloging) TLC (The Library Corporation); (Circulation) TLC (The Library Corporation); (OPAC) TLC (The Library Corporation); (Serials) TLC (The Library Corporation)
Partic in Evergreen Indiana Consortium; Midwest Collaborative for Library Services (MCLS)
Open Mon-Thurs 9-7, Fri & Sat 9-5

ANDERSON

P ANDERSON CITY, ANDERSON, STONY CREEK & UNION TOWNSHIPS PUBLIC LIBRARY, 111 E 12th St, 46016-2701. SAN 340-9295. Tel: 765-641-2456. Circulation Tel: 765-641-2441. FAX: 765-313-4759. E-mail: aplref@andersonlibrary.net. Web Site: www.andersonlibrary.net. *Dir,* Sarah Later; E-mail: slater@andersonlibrary.net; *Ind Rm Librn,* Beth Oljace; Tel: 765-641-2442, E-mail: boljace@andersonlibrary.net; *Bus Mgr,* Tonya Carman; Tel: 765-641-2197, E-mail: tcarman@andersonlibrary.net; *Mgr, Coll Serv,* Jackie Davis; Tel: 765-641-2455, E-mail: jdavis@andersonlibrary.net; *Ch Serv,* Staci Terrell; Tel: 765-241-2448, E-mail: sterrell@andersonlibrary.net; *Ref,* Jill Campbell; E-mail: jillcampbell@andersonlibrary.net; Staff 84 (MLS 16, Non-MLS 68)
Founded 1891. Pop 74,719; Circ 1,498,393
Library Holdings: Bk Titles 257,550; Bk Vols 436,612; Per Subs 673
Special Collections: Government Documents; Local History & Genealogy (Indiana Room), bks & microfilm; Music (Wendell Hall Coll), sheet music; Popular Records, CDs
Automation Activity & Vendor Info: (Acquisitions) SirsiDynix; (Cataloging) SirsiDynix; (Circulation) SirsiDynix
Database Vendor: EBSCOhost, Gale Cengage Learning, OCLC FirstSearch, SirsiDynix
Wireless access
Partic in Midwest Collaborative for Library Services (MCLS); OCLC Online Computer Library Center, Inc
Special Services for the Deaf - High interest/low vocabulary bks
Special Services for the Blind - Large print bks

Open Mon-Thurs 9:30-8, Fri & Sat 9:30-5:30, Sun 1-5
Friends of the Library Group
Branches: 1
LAPEL PUBLIC, 610 Main St, Lapel, 46051. (Mail add: PO Box 668, Lapel, 46051-0668), SAN 340-9325. Tel: 765-534-4654. FAX: 765-313-4759.
Founded 1972. Circ 937,700
Library Holdings: Large Print Bks 93; Bk Titles 38,091; Bk Vols 40,111; Per Subs 48
Function: Adult bk club, AV serv, Bk club(s), CD-ROM, Copy machines, Fax serv, ILL available, Music CDs, Online ref, Online searches, Photocopying/Printing, Preschool outreach, Prog for adults, Prog for children & young adult, Ref serv available, Spoken cassettes & CDs, Spoken cassettes & DVDs, Summer reading prog, Tax forms, Telephone ref
Open Mon & Tues 10-7, Wed & Thurs 11-7
Friends of the Library Group

ANDERSON UNIVERSITY
C ROBERT A NICHOLSON LIBRARY*, 1100 E Fifth St, 46012-3495, SAN 340-9384. Tel: 765-641-4280. Circulation Tel: 765-641-4286. Interlibrary Loan Service Tel: 765-641-4287. Administration Tel: 765-641-4272. FAX: 765-641-3850. Web Site: library.anderson.edu. *Dir,* Dr Janet L Brewer; E-mail: jlbrewer@anderson.edu; *Head, Ref,* Barbara Hoover; Tel: 765-641-4281, E-mail: heron@anderson.edu; *Ser Librn,* Jackie DeLong; Tel: 765-641-4277, E-mail: jsd@anderson.edu; *Spec Coll Librn,* Trish Janutolo; Tel: 765-641-4271, E-mail: tbj@anderson.edu; *Syst Librn,* Nathan Schwartz; Tel: 765-641-4275, E-mail: nrschwartz@anderson.edu; *Archivist,* Vivian Nieman; Tel: 765-641-4285, E-mail: vhnieman@anderson.edu; *Cataloger,* Becky Youngman; Tel: 765-641-4276, E-mail: rryoungman@anderson.edu; *Govt Doc, ILL, Ref,* Jill Branscum; E-mail: jeb@anderson.edu; Staff 10 (MLS 6.5, Non-MLS 3.5)
Founded 1917. Enrl 2,300; Fac 140; Highest Degree: Doctorate
Library Holdings: AV Mats 5,236; e-books 5,795; Bk Vols 279,045; Per Subs 457
Special Collections: Anderson University & Church of God Archives; Charles E Wilson Papers; Children's Literature & Modern Poetry (York Rare Books & Special Colls); Gaither Hymnal Coll. US Document Depository
Automation Activity & Vendor Info: (Acquisitions) SirsiDynix; (Cataloging) SirsiDynix; (Circulation) SirsiDynix; (Course Reserve) SirsiDynix; (ILL) SirsiDynix; (OPAC) SirsiDynix; (Serials) SirsiDynix
Database Vendor: Atlas Systems, CQ Press, EBSCOhost, Ex Libris Group, Gale Cengage Learning, Inspire, JSTOR, LexisNexis, OCLC FirstSearch, OCLC WorldShare Interlibrary Loan, Oxford Online, ProQuest, PubMed, Sage, SirsiDynix, YBP Library Services
Partic in Academic Libraries of Indiana; Private Academic Library Network of Indiana (PALNI)
Open Mon-Thurs 7:45am-Midnight, Fri 7:45-5, Sat 11-5, Sun 1:30-Midnight

J IVY TECH COMMUNITY COLLEGE*, Anderson Campus Library, 104 W 53rd St, 46013. SAN 372-493X. Tel: 765-643-7133, Ext 2313. Toll Free Tel: 800-644-4882. FAX: 765-643-3294. Web Site: wwwcc.ivytech.edu/eastcentral. *Dir,* Susan Clark; Tel: 765-289-2291, Ext 1321, E-mail: jsclark@ivytech.edu; Staff 2 (MLS 1, Non-MLS 1)
Enrl 392; Fac 9
Library Holdings: AV Mats 1,115; Bk Titles 1,170; Bk Vols 1,350; Per Subs 83
Partic in Midwest Collaborative for Library Services (MCLS)
Open Mon-Thurs 7:30am-9pm, Fri 7:30-4:30, Sat (Fall & Spring) 8-12

M SAINT JOHNS HEALTH SYSTEM*, Health Science Library, 2015 Jackson St, 46016-4339. SAN 304-792X. Tel: 765-646-8262. FAX: 765-646-8264. *Librn,* Scott Steven Loman; Staff 1 (Non-MLS 1)
Founded 1970
Library Holdings: Bk Titles 7,000; Bk Vols 7,300
Subject Interests: Med, Nursing
Wireless access
Partic in Midwest Health Sci Libr Network
Open Mon-Fri 7-3:30
Restriction: Staff use only

ANDREWS

P ANDREWS DALLAS TOWNSHIP PUBLIC LIBRARY*, 30 E Madison St, 46702. (Mail add: PO Box 367, 46702-0307), SAN 321-0502. Tel: 260-786-3574. FAX: 260-786-3574. E-mail: andrewsdirector@gmail.com. Web Site: andrews.lib.in.us. *Dir,* Nancy Disbro; Staff 1 (MLS 1)
Pop 2,243
Wireless access
Partic in Evergreen Indiana Consortium
Open Mon & Wed 10-5, Tues & Thurs 12-7, Sat 9-1
Friends of the Library Group

ANGOLA

P CARNEGIE PUBLIC LIBRARY OF STEUBEN COUNTY, 322 S Wayne St, 46703. SAN 304-7938. Tel: 260-665-3362. FAX: 260-665-8958. E-mail: info@steuben.lib.in.us. Web Site: www.steuben.lib.in.us. *Dir,* Sonya Dintaman; E-mail: sonyad@steuben.lib.in.us; Staff 16 (MLS 1, Non-MLS 15)
Founded 1915. Pop 14,000; Circ 120,000
Library Holdings: AV Mats 4,645; Bk Vols 64,000; Per Subs 145; Talking Bks 2,680
Subject Interests: Genealogy, Local hist
Automation Activity & Vendor Info: (Cataloging) Evergreen; (Circulation) Evergreen; (OPAC) Evergreen
Database Vendor: EBSCOhost, ProQuest
Partic in Evergreen Indiana Consortium; Midwest Collaborative for Library Services (MCLS)
Open Mon-Thurs 9-8, Fri 9-5, Sat 9-3
Friends of the Library Group

C TRINE UNIVERSITY, Sponsel Library & Information Services, 720 Thunder Dr, 46703. (Mail add: One University Ave, 46703). Tel: 260-665-4162. Administration Tel: 260-665-4161. FAX: 260-665-4283. E-mail: librarians@trine.edu. Web Site: trine.edu/academics/library. *Libr Dir,* Kristina Brewer; E-mail: brewerk@trine.edu; *Info Serv Librn,* Bob Freeman; Tel: 260-665-4287, E-mail: freemanr@trine.edu; *Info Serv Librn,* Sarah Wagner; Tel: 260-665-4179, E-mail: Wagnersarah@trine.edu; *Info Serv Assoc,* Renee Vanwagner; Tel: 260-665-4282, E-mail: vanwagnerr@trine.edu; Staff 3 (MLS 3)
Enrl 3,642; Fac 327; Highest Degree: Doctorate
Jun 2013-Apr 2014. Mats Exp $129,480, Books $20,205, Per/Ser (Incl. Access Fees) $13,692, Micro $482, AV Mat $7,550, Electronic Ref Mat (Incl. Access Fees) $87,551. Sal $186,543 (Prof $128,308)
Library Holdings: AV Mats 21,095; e-books 82,815; e-journals 27,212; Electronic Media & Resources 7,850; Music Scores 60; Bk Vols 32,395
Special Collections: Hershey Museum; Kostyshak Educational Media & Learning Resources Coll; University Archives
Subject Interests: Bus, Eng, Health sci, Humanities, Natural sci, Soc sci, Teacher educ
Automation Activity & Vendor Info: (Acquisitions) OCLC; (Cataloging) OCLC Connexion; (Circulation) OCLC; (Course Reserve) OCLC; (ILL) OCLC WorldShare Interlibrary Loan; (OPAC) OCLC; (Serials) OCLC
Database Vendor: American Chemical Society, American Psychological Association (APA), CQ Press, CredoReference, ebrary, EBSCOhost, Elsevier, Gale Cengage Learning, Hoovers, Inspire, LexisNexis, McGraw-Hill, OCLC, OCLC FirstSearch, OCLC WorldShare Interlibrary Loan, Overdrive, Inc, ProQuest, ScienceDirect
Wireless access
Publications: Triangle (School newspaper)
Partic in Academic Libraries of Indiana; Midwest Collaborative for Library Services (MCLS); Private Academic Library Network of Indiana (PALNI)
Special Services for the Deaf - Accessible learning ctr; Assistive tech
Special Services for the Blind - Assistive/Adapted tech devices, equip & products; Bks on CD; Dragon Naturally Speaking software; Screen reader software
Open Mon-Thurs 7:30am-11pm, Fri 7:30-5, Sat 1-5, Sun 1-9

ARGOS

P ARGOS PUBLIC LIBRARY*, 119 W Walnut St, 46501-1025. SAN 304-7954. Tel: 574-892-5818. FAX: 574-892-5818. Web Site: www.argos.lib.in.us. *Dir,* Jane Hall; E-mail: jehall@argos.lib.in.us; Staff 2 (MLS 1, Non-MLS 1)
Founded 1936. Pop 3,890; Circ 45,116
Library Holdings: CDs 219; Large Print Bks 323; Bk Vols 22,550; Per Subs 86; Talking Bks 191; Videos 1,148
Subject Interests: Art & archit
Automation Activity & Vendor Info: (Cataloging) Follett Software; (Circulation) Follett Software; (OPAC) Follett Software
Partic in Midwest Collaborative for Library Services (MCLS)
Open Mon, Wed & Fri 10-6, Tues & Thurs 12-8, Sat 10-2

ATTICA

P ATTICA PUBLIC LIBRARY*, 305 S Perry St, 47918. SAN 304-7962. Tel: 765-764-4194. FAX: 765-764-0906. Web Site: www.attica.lib.in.us. *Dir,* Norma Fink; E-mail: aplibnfink@netscape.net; *Asst Librn,* Lisa Mitton; E-mail: ljmitton@yahoo.com; Staff 3 (MLS 1, Non-MLS 2)
Founded 1902. Pop 4,429; Circ 35,920
Library Holdings: Bk Titles 28,911; Bk Vols 31,112; Per Subs 101; Talking Bks 218; Videos 317
Automation Activity & Vendor Info: (Acquisitions) Evergreen; (Cataloging) Evergreen; (OPAC) Evergreen
Wireless access
Partic in Wabash Valley Area Libr Servs Authority

Open Mon & Fri 10-6, Tues-Thurs 10-8, Sat 10-2
Friends of the Library Group

AUBURN

P ECKHART PUBLIC LIBRARY*, 603 S Jackson St, 46706-2298. SAN 304-7970. Tel: 260-925-2414. FAX: 260-925-9376. E-mail: reference@epl.lib.in.us. Web Site: www.epl.lib.in.us. *Dir,* Janelle Graber; *Mgr, Ch Serv,* Deborah Argast; *Genealogy Mgr,* Gregg Williamson; *Operations Mgr,* Christine Grogg; *Circ Serv Supvr,* Anni Bruns; *Tech Serv Supvr,* Paula Yoder; Staff 29 (MLS 2, Non-MLS 27)
Founded 1910. Pop 13,331; Circ 223,000
Jan 2008-Dec 2008 Income $865,148. Mats Exp $66,671, Books $28,558, Per/Ser (Incl. Access Fees) $3,941, AV Mat $22,317, Electronic Ref Mat (Incl. Access Fees) $11,855. Sal $606,522
Library Holdings: Audiobooks 4,010; CDs 2,587; DVDs 621; Large Print Bks 1,474; Bk Vols 69,323; Per Subs 188; Videos 2,637
Special Collections: Willennar Genealogy Center. Oral History
Automation Activity & Vendor Info: (Cataloging) TLC (The Library Corporation); (Circulation) TLC (The Library Corporation); (OPAC) TLC (The Library Corporation)
Database Vendor: Baker & Taylor, Booklist Online, Checkpoint Systems, Inc, Gale Cengage Learning, Inspire, ReferenceUSA, TLC (The Library Corporation)
Wireless access
Function: Adult bk club, After school storytime, Archival coll, Bi-weekly Writer's Group, Bk club(s), Bks on cassette, Bks on CD, CD-ROM, Children's prog, Computer training, Computers for patron use, Copy machines, Digital talking bks, Distance learning, e-mail serv, Electronic databases & coll, Equip loans & repairs, Fax serv, Free DVD rentals, Genealogy discussion group, Handicapped accessible, Holiday prog, Home delivery & serv to Sr ctr & nursing homes, Homebound delivery serv, Homework prog, ILL available, Instruction & testing, Learning ctr, Mail & tel request accepted, Mus passes, Music CDs, Online cat, Online ref, Online searches, Orientations, Outreach serv, Outside serv via phone, mail, e-mail & web, Photocopying/Printing, Preschool outreach, Prog for adults, Prog for children & young adult, Pub access computers, Ref serv available, Referrals accepted, Scanner, Senior computer classes, Senior outreach, Spoken cassettes & CDs, Spoken cassettes & DVDs, Story hour, Summer reading prog, Tax forms, Teen prog, Telephone ref, VHS videos, Web-catalog, Wheelchair accessible, Writing prog
Partic in Midwest Collaborative for Library Services (MCLS)
Open Mon-Thurs 9-8, Fri 9-7, Sat 9-5
Friends of the Library Group

AURORA

P AURORA PUBLIC LIBRARY DISTRICT, 414 Second St, 47001-1384. SAN 304-7989. Tel: 812-926-0646. FAX: 812-926-0665. Web Site: www.eapld.org. *Dir,* Mary Alice Horton; Staff 12 (MLS 2, Non-MLS 10)
Founded 1901. Pop 17,133; Circ 157,189
Library Holdings: Audiobooks 2,228; DVDs 2,000; Large Print Bks 1,000; Microforms 99; Bk Vols 53,857; Per Subs 181; Talking Bks 510; Videos 1,500
Automation Activity & Vendor Info: (Acquisitions) TLC (The Library Corporation); (Cataloging) TLC (The Library Corporation); (OPAC) TLC (The Library Corporation)
Wireless access
Partic in Midwest Collaborative for Library Services (MCLS)
Open Mon, Wed & Fri 10-6, Tues-Thurs 10-8, Sat 9-3
Branches: 1
DILLSBORO PUBLIC, 10151 Library Lane, Dillsboro, 47018. (Mail add: PO Box 547, Dillsboro, 47018-0547), SAN 377-7448. Tel: 812-432-5200. FAX: 812-432-5209. *Dir,* Mary Alice Horton; Staff 3 (MLS 1, Non-MLS 2)
Founded 1997
Library Holdings: Large Print Bks 260; Bk Titles 8,390; Bk Vols 9,800; Per Subs 43; Videos 280
Automation Activity & Vendor Info: (Circulation) TLC (The Library Corporation)
Database Vendor: EBSCOhost, Inspire, Overdrive, Inc, World Book Online
Open Mon-Fri 11-6, Sat 11-2

AVON

P AVON-WASHINGTON TOWNSHIP PUBLIC LIBRARY*, 498 N State Rd 267, 46123. SAN 376-5385. Tel: 317-272-4818. FAX: 317-272-7302. E-mail: reference@avonlibrary.net. Web Site: www.avon.lib.in.us. *Dir,* Laurel Setser; Staff 35 (MLS 8, Non-MLS 27)
Pop 26,319
Library Holdings: AV Mats 13,444; Large Print Bks 1,592; Bk Titles 75,766; Bk Vols 84,632; Per Subs 206
Special Collections: Washington Township Local History Coll
Automation Activity & Vendor Info: (Acquisitions) SirsiDynix; (Cataloging) SirsiDynix; (Circulation) SirsiDynix; (OPAC) SirsiDynix; (Serials) SirsiDynix
Database Vendor: EBSCOhost, Facts on File, Gale Cengage Learning, Grolier Online, LearningExpress, ProQuest, ReferenceUSA, Standard & Poor's, ValueLine
Wireless access
Publications: The Open Book (Newsletter)
Partic in Midwest Collaborative for Library Services (MCLS)
Open Mon-Thurs 9-8, Fri 9-6, Sat 9-5
Friends of the Library Group

BATESVILLE

P BATESVILLE MEMORIAL PUBLIC LIBRARY*, 131 N Walnut St, 47006. SAN 304-7997. Tel: 812-934-4706. FAX: 812-934-6288. E-mail: bmpl@cnz.com. Web Site: ebatesville.com/library. *Dir,* Michael J Kruse; Staff 9 (MLS 2, Non-MLS 7)
Founded 1937. Pop 10,852; Circ 192,991
Library Holdings: Audiobooks 1,217; AV Mats 135; Bks on Deafness & Sign Lang 40; CDs 1,408; DVDs 4,450; e-books 1,500; Electronic Media & Resources 130; Large Print Bks 700; Microforms 275; Bk Vols 45,219; Per Subs 120; Talking Bks 886; Videos 955
Special Collections: Hillenbrand Family Coll; James N Mahle Memorial Aviation Coll, bks, DVDs, mags, videos; Mary Stewart Center for Entrepreneurship Coll, audio, bks, DVDs, mags, periodicals, videos; Miriam Mason Coll, bks, drawings, original ms. Municipal Document Depository; Oral History
Subject Interests: Astronomy, Aviation, Entrepreneurship, Genealogy, Literacy, Local hist
Automation Activity & Vendor Info: (Cataloging) Evergreen; (Circulation) Evergreen; (ILL) Evergreen; (OPAC) Evergreen; (Serials) Evergreen
Database Vendor: Gale Cengage Learning, Inspire, OCLC WebJunction, OCLC WorldShare Interlibrary Loan, ProQuest, ReferenceUSA, World Book Online
Wireless access
Function: Art exhibits, Audio & video playback equip for onsite use, Audiobks via web, Bks on cassette, Bks on CD, Children's prog, Computer training, Computers for patron use, Copy machines, Distance learning, e-mail & chat, Electronic databases & coll, Exhibits, Free DVD rentals, Genealogy discussion group, Handicapped accessible, Holiday prog, Home delivery & serv to Sr ctr & nursing homes, ILL available, Jazz prog, Magnifiers for reading, Mail & tel request accepted, Microfiche/film & reading machines, Music CDs, Notary serv, Online cat, Online searches, OverDrive digital audio bks, Photocopying/Printing, Preschool outreach, Preschool reading prog, Prog for adults, Prog for children & young adult, Pub access computers, Ref serv available, Senior computer classes, Story hour, Summer reading prog, Tax forms, Teen prog, Telephone ref, VHS videos, Web catalog, Wheelchair accessible, Workshops
Partic in Midwest Collaborative for Library Services (MCLS)
Special Services for the Deaf - Bks on deafness & sign lang
Special Services for the Blind - Audio mat; Bks on cassette; Bks on CD; Digital talking bk machines; Info on spec aids & appliances; Large print bks; Low vision equip; Magnifiers; Playaways (bks on MP3)
Open Mon-Thurs 9-9, Fri 9-5, Sat 10-5, Sun 1-5
Restriction: In-house use for visitors, Non-circulating coll, Non-circulating of rare bks, Non-resident fee
Friends of the Library Group

BEDFORD

P BEDFORD PUBLIC LIBRARY*, 1323 K St, 47421. SAN 304-8004. Tel: 812-275-4471. FAX: 812-278-5244. E-mail: bpl@bedlib.com. Web Site: www.bedlib.org. *Dir,* Susan A Miller; E-mail: smiller@bedlib.com; *Adult Serv Mgr,* Mary Hall; E-mail: mhall@bedlib.com; *Mgr, Young Adult & Children's Serv,* Susan S Smith; E-mail: ssmith@bedlib.com; *Bus Mgr,* Shelly Fish; E-mail: sfish@bedlib.com; *Mgr, Outreach Serv,* Autumn Baughman; E-mail: abaughman@bedlib.com; *Tech Serv Mgr,* Susan Breidenbach; E-mail: sbreidenbach@bedlib.com; Staff 13 (MLS 5, Non-MLS 8)
Founded 1898. Pop 33,979; Circ 422,072
Jan 2010-Dec 2010 Income $1,283,163, County $1,228,163, Locally Generated Income $55,000. Mats Exp $123,257, Books $65,461, Other Print Mats $12,000, Micro $1,400, AV Equip $10,000, AV Mat $34,396
Library Holdings: Bk Vols 89,609; Per Subs 190
Special Collections: Genealogy Coll
Automation Activity & Vendor Info: (Acquisitions) SirsiDynix; (Cataloging) SirsiDynix; (Circulation) SirsiDynix
Database Vendor: OCLC FirstSearch
Open Mon-Thurs 9-8, Fri & Sat 9-5, Sun 1-5

S INDIANA LIMESTONE INSTITUTE OF AMERICA, INC*, Library & Information Center, Stone City Bank Bldg, Ste 400, 47421. SAN 371-1811. Tel: 812-275-4426. FAX: 812-279-8682. Web Site: www.iliai.com. *Exec Dir,* Jim Owens; Staff 1 (Non-MLS 1)
Library Holdings: Bk Titles 1,271; Bk Vols 1,419; Per Subs 16
Subject Interests: Gems
Open Mon-Fri 8:30-5
Restriction: Staff use only

BEECH GROVE

P BEECH GROVE PUBLIC LIBRARY*, 1102 Main St, 46107. SAN 304-8012. Tel: 317-788-4203. FAX: 317-788-0489. E-mail: bgplreference@bgpl.lib.in.us. Web Site: www.bgpl.lib.in.us. *Dir,* Diane Burns; *Ref,* Michele Patterson; Staff 16 (MLS 3, Non-MLS 13)
Founded 1949. Pop 14,880; Circ 129,961
Library Holdings: Bk Titles 73,891; Bk Vols 77,801; Per Subs 263; Talking Bks 391; Videos 1,123
Open Mon-Thurs 10-8, Fri 10-5, Sat 10-4
Friends of the Library Group

BERNE

P BERNE PUBLIC LIBRARY*, 166 N Sprunger St, 46711-1595. SAN 304-8039. Tel: 260-589-2809. FAX: 260-589-2940. E-mail: bpl@bernepl.lib.in.us. Web Site: www.bernepl.lib.in.us. *Libr Dir,* Kathryn Gerber; Staff 11 (MLS 1, Non-MLS 10)
Founded 1935. Pop 4,150
Library Holdings: Bk Titles 68,814; Bk Vols 69,814; Per Subs 128
Special Collections: Berne & Adams County Coll; Indiana History & Genealogy Coll; Mennonite History Coll
Database Vendor: Inspire
Wireless access
Open Mon-Wed & Fri 10-6, Thurs 12-8, Sat 10-2

BICKNELL

P BICKNELL-VIGO TOWNSHIP PUBLIC LIBRARY*, 201 W Second St, 47512. SAN 304-8047. Tel: 812-735-2317. FAX: 812-735-2018. Web Site: bicknell-vigo.lib.in.us. *Dir,* Debra Kean; E-mail: kean.debra@gmail.com; Staff 4 (MLS 2, Non-MLS 2)
Founded 1926. Pop 8,000; Circ 11,891
Library Holdings: AV Mats 433; Bk Titles 63,480; Bk Vols 65,111; Per Subs 65; Talking Bks 450; Videos 139
Automation Activity & Vendor Info: (Acquisitions) Brodart; (Cataloging) Brodart; (OPAC) Brodart
Partic in Ind Libr Asn
Open Mon-Thurs 10-8, Fri 10-5, Sat 10-3
Friends of the Library Group
Branches: 1
SANDBORN BRANCH, 112 Anderson St, Sandborn, 47578. Tel: 812-694-8403. *Supvr,* Colleen Bowman
Automation Activity & Vendor Info: (Circulation) Winnebago Software Co
Open Mon & Thurs 3-7, Tues, Wed & Fri 1-5, Sat 11-4

BLOOMFIELD

P BLOOMFIELD-EASTERN GREENE COUNTY PUBLIC LIBRARY*, 125 S Franklin St, 47424-1406. SAN 304-8055. Tel: 812-384-4125. FAX: 812-384-0820. E-mail: bloomfield@bloomfield.lib.in.us. Web Site: www.bloomfield.lib.in.us. *Dir,* Cassandra Thompson; Staff 10 (MLS 2, Non-MLS 8)
Founded 1905
Library Holdings: Bks on Deafness & Sign Lang 25; CDs 474; DVDs 450; High Interest/Low Vocabulary Bk Vols 42; Large Print Bks 1,063; Bk Vols 32,874; Per Subs 139; Talking Bks 2,117; Videos 1,445
Special Collections: Indiana Special Coll. Municipal Document Depository; State Document Depository
Automation Activity & Vendor Info: (Acquisitions) SirsiDynix; (Cataloging) SirsiDynix; (Circulation) SirsiDynix; (ILL) OCLC Online; (OPAC) SirsiDynix; (Serials) SirsiDynix
Database Vendor: ProQuest
Wireless access
Function: Adult bk club, Adult literacy prog, Computer training, Copy machines, Family literacy, Fax serv, Handicapped accessible, Homebound delivery serv, ILL available, Music CDs, Photocopying/Printing, Prog for adults, Prog for children & young adult, Ref & res, Spoken cassettes & CDs, Summer reading prog, Tax forms, Telephone ref, VHS videos, Wheelchair accessible, Workshops
Partic in Evergreen Indiana Consortium; Midwest Collaborative for Library Services (MCLS)
Open Mon-Thurs 10-8, Fri & Sat 10-5
Friends of the Library Group
Branches: 2
EASTERN, 11453 East St, Rd 54, 47424, SAN 373-8795. Tel: 812-825-2677. FAX: 812-825-2677. E-mail: easternlibrary@smithville.net. *Br Mgr,* Karen Holz; Staff 2 (MLS 1, Non-MLS 1)
Circ 10,042
Library Holdings: Bks on Deafness & Sign Lang 12; Large Print Bks 60; Bk Vols 6,159; Per Subs 32; Talking Bks 209; Videos 272
Database Vendor: OCLC WebJunction
Function: Computer training, Copy machines, E-Reserves, Fax serv, Handicapped accessible, ILL available, Music CDs, Prog for children & young adult, Tax forms, Telephone ref, VHS videos, Video lending libr, Wheelchair accessible
Open Mon, Wed & Fri 11-5, Tues & Thurs 2-8, Sat 9-12
Restriction: Non-resident fee
Friends of the Library Group
OWENSBURG, 11431 E Main St, Owensburg, 47453, SAN 373-8809. Tel: 812-863-2899. FAX: 812-863-2899. *Br Mgr,* Debra Hartsberg; Staff 0.5 (Non-MLS 0.5)
Circ 2,891
Library Holdings: CDs 90; Large Print Bks 23; Bk Titles 1,863; Per Subs 12; Talking Bks 45; Videos 31
Function: Senior computer classes, Spoken cassettes & CDs, Summer reading prog, Tax forms, Telephone ref, VHS videos
Open Mon & Thurs 3-7, Wed 9-1, Sat 9-12
Restriction: Non-resident fee
Friends of the Library Group

BLOOMINGTON

INDIANA UNIVERSITY
C INDIANA INSTITUTE ON DISABILITY & COMMUNITY*, 2853 E Tenth St, 47408-2601, SAN 371-6953. Tel: 812-855-9396. FAX: 812-855-9630. TDD: 812-855-9396. E-mail: cedir@indiana.edu. Web Site: www.iidc.indiana.edu/cedir. *Librn,* Christina Wray; Tel: 812-855-0077, E-mail: ccwray@indiana.edu; *Br Coordr,* Sharon Soto; Staff 2 (MLS 1, Non-MLS 1)
Library Holdings: Large Print Bks 280; Bk Titles 9,304; Bk Vols 9,670
Special Collections: Autism; Early Childhood Special Needs
Subject Interests: Aging, Disability awareness
Partic in Central Indiana Health Science Libraries Consortium
Publications: CeDIR Citings (Bi-annually)
Special Services for the Deaf - Accessible learning ctr; Bks on deafness & sign lang
Special Services for the Blind - Accessible computers
Open Mon-Fri 8-11:30 & 12:30-4

CL SCHOOL OF LAW LIBRARY*, Maurer School of Law, 211 S Indiana Ave, 47405, SAN 304-8071. Tel: 812-855-9666. Circulation Tel: 812-855-6404. Reference Tel: 812-855-2938. FAX: 812-855-7099. Web Site: www.law.indiana.edu/lawlibrary. *Dir,* Linda Fariss; E-mail: fariss@indiana.edu; *Head, Pub Serv,* Keith Buckley; Tel: 812-855-7216, E-mail: buckley@indiana.edu; *Head, Tech Serv,* Nona Watt; E-mail: wattn@indiana.edu; *Acq Librn,* Richard Vaughan; Tel: 812-855-4199, E-mail: rvaughan@indiana.edu; *Cat Librn,* Michael Maben; Tel: 812-855-1882, E-mail: mmaben@indiana.edu; *Doc Librn,* Jennifer Bryan Morgan; Tel: 812-855-4611, E-mail: jlbryan@indiana.edu; Staff 13 (MLS 9, Non-MLS 4)
Founded 1842. Enrl 645; Fac 34
Library Holdings: Bk Titles 250,000; Bk Vols 759,000
Special Collections: 7th Circuit Records & Briefs; Indiana Court of Appeals Briefs; Indiana Supreme Court Records & Briefs; Rare Books & Archives; US Government Publications; US Supreme Court Records & Briefs
Subject Interests: US law
Partic in Association of Research Libraries (ARL); GPO Access, Ind Coop Libr Servs Authority; OCLC Online Computer Library Center, Inc; Westlaw
Publications: Res Ipsa Loquitur (Newsletter)
Open Mon-Wed 7:30am-1am, Thurs & Fri 7:30am-Midnight, Sat 8am-10pm, Sun 9am-Midnight

C SINOR RESEARCH INSTITUTE FOR INNER ASIAN STUDIES, Indiana University, Goodbody Hall 144, 1011 E Third St, 47405-7005, SAN 324-3575. Tel: 812-855-1605, 812-855-9510. FAX: 812-855-7500. E-mail: SRIFIAS@indiana.edu. Web Site: www.indiana.edu/~rifias. *Dir,* Edward J Lazzerini; E-mail: elazzeri@indiana.edu; Staff 4 (MLS 2, Non-MLS 2)
Founded 1967
Library Holdings: Bk Titles 8,691; Bk Vols 8,950; Per Subs 26; Videos 34
Special Collections: Central Asian Archives/Tibetan Coll
Subject Interests: Cent Asia, Inner Asia, Mongol studies, Tibetan studies, Turkic studies, Uralic studies
Partic in Association of Research Libraries (ARL); Midwest Collaborative for Library Services (MCLS)
Restriction: Non-circulating, Open to pub for ref only

C INDIANA UNIVERSITY BLOOMINGTON*, Herman B Wells Library, 1320 E Tenth St, 47405-1801. SAN 340-9538. Tel: 812-855-0100. Circulation Tel: 812-855-4673. Reference Tel: 812-855-8028. FAX: 812-855-2576. E-mail: libref@indiana.edu. Web Site: www.libraries.iub.edu. *Dir, Libr Serv,* Brenda Johnson; *Exec Assoc Dean,* Carolyn Walters; E-mail: cwalters@indiana.edu; Staff 144 (MLS 92, Non-MLS 52)
Founded 1824. Enrl 37,821; Fac 1,823; Highest Degree: Doctorate
Library Holdings: Bk Vols 6,770,498; Per Subs 70,370
Special Collections: 19th Century British Plays; American Revolution; Aristotle Coll; Austrian History, 1790-1843; English History Coll; George Frederick Handel Coll; History of Science & Medicine (Archives of Herman Muller - Genetics & V Hlavety - Mathematics); Indiana History Coll; Lafayette Coll; Latin Americana through the Independence Period; Lilly Rare Book Library: English & American Literature, 1640- (Milton, Defoe, John Gray, Sterne, Wordsworth, Coleridge, Byron, Tennyson, Henty, Andrew Lang, Yeats, Joseph Conrad, Upton Sinclair, Sylvia Plath); Lincoln Coll; London Low Life, Early-Mid 19th Century (Sadleir Coll); Voyages & Explorations, especially Spanish, Portuguese & Dutch; War of 1812; Western Americana. State Document Depository; UN Document Depository; US Document Depository
Automation Activity & Vendor Info: (Acquisitions) SirsiDynix; (Cataloging) SirsiDynix; (Circulation) SirsiDynix; (OPAC) SirsiDynix; (Serials) SirsiDynix
Database Vendor: Dialog, EBSCOhost, Gale Cengage Learning, LexisNexis, OCLC FirstSearch, OVID Technologies, ProQuest, TLC (The Library Corporation), Wilson - Wilson Web
Function: Res libr
Publications: Indiana University Bookman (Newsletter); IUL News (Newsletter); The Source (Newsletter)
Partic in Area Libr Serv Authority; Digital Libr Fedn; OCLC Online Computer Library Center, Inc
Open Mon-Thurs 8am-Midnight, Fri 8am-9pm, Sat 10-9, Sun 11am-Midnight; Mon-Thurs 8am-10pm, Fri 8-5, Sat 10-5, Sun 1-10 (Summer)
Friends of the Library Group

Departmental Libraries:

BUSINESS/SPEA INFORMATION COMMONS, SPEA 150, 1315 E Tenth St, 47405, SAN 340-9627. Tel: 812-855-1957. FAX: 812-855-3398. E-mail: libbus@indiana.edu. Web Site: www.libraries.iub.edu/index.php?pageId=77. *Dept Head,* Christina Sheley; Staff 8 (MLS 3, Non-MLS 5)
Highest Degree: Doctorate
Library Holdings: Bk Vols 100,000
Automation Activity & Vendor Info: (Acquisitions) SIRSI WorkFlows; (Cataloging) SIRSI WorkFlows; (Circulation) SIRSI WorkFlows; (Course Reserve) SIRSI WorkFlows; (OPAC) SIRSI WorkFlows; (Serials) SIRSI WorkFlows

CHEMISTRY LIBRARY, Chemistry C003, 800 E Kirkwood Ave, 47405-7102, SAN 340-9651. Tel: 812-855-9452. E-mail: libchem@indiana.edu. Web Site: libraries.iub.edu/chem. *Head of Libr,* Jennifer Laherty; E-mail: jlaherty@indiana.edu; *Br Coordr,* Tiea Julian; E-mail: tmjulian@indiana.edu; Staff 1 (MLS 1)
Library Holdings: Bk Vols 47,839

WILLIAM & GAYLE COOK MUSIC LIBRARY, Simon Music Library & Recital Ctr M160, 200 S Jordan Ave, 47405, SAN 340-9953. Tel: 812-855-2970. FAX: 812-855-3843. E-mail: libmus@indiana.edu. *Dir,* Philip Ponella; E-mail: pponella@indiana.edu; *Assoc Dir,* Keith Cochran; E-mail: cochran6@indiana.edu
Library Holdings: AV Mats 138,622; Music Scores 106,769; Bk Vols 377,440
Subject Interests: Music
Open Mon-Thurs 8am-Midnight, Fri 8am-9pm, Sat 11-6, Sun 11-Midnight

EDUCATION LIBRARY, Wright Education 1160, 201 N Rose St, 47405-1006, SAN 340-9686. Tel: 812-856-8590. FAX: 812-856-8593. E-mail: libeduc@indiana.edu. *Head of Libr,* Gwendolyn Pershing; E-mail: pershing@indiana.edu
Library Holdings: Bk Vols 87,871
Special Collections: Childrens Coll; ERIC Documentation Coll; Indiana Textbook Repository
Open Mon-Thurs (Winter) 8am-10pm, Fri 8-5, Sat 9-5, Sun 1-10; Mon-Thurs (Summer) 8am-10pm, Fri 8-5, Sat 1-5, Sun 2-10

FINE ARTS LIBRARY, Fine Arts Museum 251, 1133 E Seventh St, 47405, SAN 340-9716. Tel: 812-855-3314. Reference Tel: 812-855-4597. FAX: 812-855-3443. E-mail: libart@indiana.edu. Web Site: www.libraries.iub.edu/index.php?pageId=80. *Interim Head of Libr,* Emilee Mathews; Tel: 812-855-5743; *Br Coordr,* Edwin Cheek; Tel: 812-855-4596; Staff 2 (MLS 2)
Founded 1939. Fac 2; Highest Degree: Doctorate
Library Holdings: AV Mats 350,000; CDs 236; DVDs 21; Electronic Media & Resources 50,000; Bk Vols 130,000; Per Subs 323; Videos 146
Special Collections: Artists Books
Function: Art exhibits, CD-ROM, Copy machines, E-Reserves, Electronic databases & coll, Handicapped accessible, ILL available, VHS videos, Wheelchair accessible
Open Mon-Thurs (Fall & Spring) 8am-9:30pm, Fri 8-5, Sat 10-5, Sun 1:30-9:30; Mon-Thurs (Summer) 8-7, Fri 8-5, Sat 10-3, Sun 12-5
Restriction: Restricted borrowing privileges

GEOLOGY LIBRARY, Geology 603, 1001 E Tenth St, 47405, SAN 340-9775. Tel: 812-855-1494. FAX: 812-855-6614. E-mail: libgeol@indiana.edu. Web Site: www.libraries.iub.edu/index.php?pageId=82. *Geology Librn,* Lou Malcomb; E-mail: malcomb@indiana.edu; Staff 1 (MLS 1)
Founded 1871. Enrl 86; Fac 31; Highest Degree: Doctorate
Library Holdings: Bk Vols 124,421
Friends of the Library Group

LIFE SCIENCES LIBRARY, Jordan Hall A304, 1001 E Third St, 47405-7005, SAN 340-9597. Tel: 812-855-8947. E-mail: liblife@indiana.edu. Web Site: libraries.iub.edu/life. *Head of Libr,* Jennifer Laherty; E-mail: jlaherty@indiana.edu; *Br Coordr,* Chris Phillips; E-mail: chphilli@indiana.edu; Staff 1 (MLS 1)
Library Holdings: Bk Vols 125,785

LILLY LIBRARY RARE BOOKS & MANUSCRIPTS, 1200 E Seventh St, 47405-5500, SAN 340-9899. Tel: 812-855-2452. FAX: 812-855-3143. E-mail: liblilly@indiana.edu. Web Site: www.indiana.edu/~liblilly. *Dir,* Joel Silver; E-mail: silverj@indiana.edu
Library Holdings: Bk Vols 413,781
Open Mon-Fri (Winter) 9-6, Sat 9-1; Mon-Thurs (Summer) 9-6, Fri 9-5, Sat 9-1
Friends of the Library Group

NEAL-MARSHALL BLACK CULTURE CENTER LIBRARY, Neal-Marshall Ctr, Rm A113, 275 N Jordan, 47405, SAN 373-5761. Tel: 812-855-3237. FAX: 812-856-4558. E-mail: bcclib@indiana.edu. *Head of Libr,* Deloice Holliday; E-mail: dehollid@indiana.edu; *Br Coordr,* Marianna Brough; E-mail: mabrough@indiana.edu
Founded 1972
Library Holdings: Bk Vols 8,403
Subject Interests: African-Am culture, African-Am hist
Open Mon-Thurs (Winter) 9-9, Fri 9-5, Sat 1-5, Sun 1-9; Mon-Fri (Summer) 9-5
Friends of the Library Group

CM OPTOMETRY LIBRARY, Optometry 202, 800 E Atwater Ave, 47405, SAN 340-9988. Tel: 812-855-8629. E-mail: libopt@indiana.edu. Web Site: www.libraries.iub.edu/index.php?pageId=91. *Head, Sci Libr,* Jian Liu; Tel: 812 855-4420, E-mail: jiliu@indiana.edu
Founded 1968
Library Holdings: Bk Vols 22,134
Database Vendor: ebrary, EBSCOhost, Elsevier, Ingenta, ISI Web of Knowledge, OVID Technologies, ProQuest, PubMed, RefWorks, Wiley
Partic in Association of Vision Science Librarians (AVSL); Center for Research Libraries; Midwest Collaborative for Library Services (MCLS)
Open Mon-Thurs 8am-10pm, Fri 8-5, Sat 10-4, Sun 1-10

PUBLIC HEALTH LIBRARY, 1025 E Seventh St, 47405, SAN 340-9562. Tel: 812-855-4420. FAX: 812-855 6778. E-mail: libhper@indiana.edu. *Head of Libr,* Jian Liu; E mail: jiliu@indiana.edu; Staff 1 (MLS 1)
Library Holdings: Bk Vols 22,873
Open Mon-Thurs (Winter) 8am-9pm, Fri 8-5, Sat 1-5, Sun 1-9; Mon-Thurs (Summer) 8-6, Fri 8-5, Sun 1-5

SWAIN HALL LIBRARY, Swain Hall West 208, 727 E Third St, 47405-7105, SAN 341-0048. Tel: 812-855-2758. FAX: 812-855-5533. E-mail: libswain@indiana.edu. *Head of Libr,* Robert Noel; E-mail: rnoel@indiana.edu; *Br Coordr,* Mohammad Rajaii; E-mail: mrajaii@indiana.edu
Library Holdings: Bk Vols 100,633
Subject Interests: Astronomy, Computer sci, Math, Physics
Open Mon-Thurs (Winter) 8am-10pm, Fri 8-6, Sat 1-5, Sun 1-10; Mon-Thurs (Summer) 8-7, Fri 8-5, Sun 1-5

WEIL JOURNALISM LIBRARY, Ernie Pyle Hall, 940 E Seventh St, 47405-7108, SAN 340-9864. Tel: 812-855-9247. FAX: 812-855-0901. E-mail: libjourn@indiana.edu. *Head of Libr,* Grace Jackson-Brown
Library Holdings: Bk Vols 26,523
Special Collections: Roy Howard Archives
Subject Interests: Communication, Culture, Journalism
Open Mon-Thurs 12-10, Fri & Sat 12-5, Sun 4-10

J IVY TECH COMMUNITY COLLEGE OF INDIANA*, Bloomington Campus Library, 200 Daniels Way, 47404. SAN 374-5317. Tel: 812-330-6080. Toll Free Tel: 866-447-0700. FAX: 812-330-6082. E-mail: bl-library@lists.ivytech.edu. Web Site: wwwcc.ivytech.edu/library/bloomington/index.html. *Dir,* Susan L Catt; Tel: 812-330-6079, E-mail: scatt@ivytech.edu; *Librn,* Carol Parkinson; Tel: 812-330-6236, E-mail: cparkinson@ivytech.edu; Staff 2 (MLS 2)
Enrl 6,000; Highest Degree: Associate
Library Holdings: AV Mats 1,200; DVDs 1,200; e-books 40,000; e-journals 25,000; Bk Titles 9,300; Per Subs 100
Subject Interests: Nursing

Automation Activity & Vendor Info: (Acquisitions) Ex Libris Group; (Cataloging) Ex Libris Group; (Circulation) Ex Libris Group; (Course Reserve) Ex Libris Group; (ILL) OCLC; (OPAC) Ex Libris Group
Database Vendor: Alexander Street Press, American Psychological Association (APA), ARTstor, Baker & Taylor, BioOne, Cinahl, CQ Press, CredoReference, ebrary, EBSCOhost, Facts on File, Gale Cengage Learning, Gallup, Inspire, IOP, JSTOR, LearningExpress, LexisNexis, McGraw-Hill, Natural Standard, Newsbank, OCLC FirstSearch, OCLC WorldShare Interlibrary Loan, Oxford Online, ProQuest, ScienceDirect, SerialsSolutions, World Book Online
Wireless access
Function: Computers for patron use, Copy machines, Doc delivery serv, e-mail & chat, Electronic databases & coll, Health sci info serv, ILL available, Online cat, Online info literacy tutorials on the web & in blackboard, Online ref, Orientations, Photocopying/Printing
Partic in Lyrasis; Midwest Collaborative for Library Services (MCLS)
Open Mon-Fri 8am-9:30pm, Sat 8-4

P MONROE COUNTY PUBLIC LIBRARY*, 303 E Kirkwood Ave, 47408. SAN 341-0072. Tel: 812-349-3050. Circulation Tel: 812-349-3090. Reference Tel: 812-349-3228. FAX: 812-349-3051. Web Site: www.mcpl.info. *Dir,* Marilyn Wood; *Mgr, Ad Serv,* Steve Backs; E-mail: sbacks@mcpl.info; *Mgr, Ch Serv,* Joshua Wolf; E-mail: jwolf@mcpl.info; *Mgr, Info Sys,* Ned Baugh; E-mail: nbaugh@mcpl.info; *Circ Mgr,* Bara Swinson; E-mail: bswinson@mcpl.info; *Commun Outreach Mgr,* Chris Jackson; E-mail: cjackson@mcpl.info; Staff 197 (MLS 36, Non-MLS 161)
Founded 1820. Pop 120,563; Circ 2,066,065
Library Holdings: AV Mats 74,910; Electronic Media & Resources 2,346; Bk Vols 380,098; Per Subs 1,078
Special Collections: CATS - Community Access Television; Indiana & Monroe County History (Indiana Coll), bks, mag, microfilm, newsp, pamphlets, hist tapes, maps, video & audio cassettes; VITAL - Volunteers in Tutoring Adult Learners. Oral History
Automation Activity & Vendor Info: (Acquisitions) Innovative Interfaces, Inc; (Cataloging) Innovative Interfaces, Inc; (Circulation) Innovative Interfaces, Inc; (OPAC) Innovative Interfaces, Inc; (Serials) Innovative Interfaces, Inc
Database Vendor: Baker & Taylor, BWI, EBSCOhost, Gale Cengage Learning, Inspire, Newsbank, OCLC FirstSearch, OCLC WorldShare Interlibrary Loan, ProQuest, Westlaw
Wireless access
Function: Adult bk club, Art exhibits, AV serv, Handicapped accessible, Home delivery & serv to Sr ctr & nursing homes, Homebound delivery serv, Homework prog, ILL available, Magnifiers for reading, Music CDs, Online searches, Photocopying/Printing, Prog for adults, Prog for children & young adult, Ref serv available, Spoken cassettes & CDs, Spoken cassettes & DVDs, Summer reading prog, VHS videos, Wheelchair accessible
Partic in OCLC Online Computer Library Center, Inc
Open Mon-Thurs 9-9, Fri 9-6, Sat 9-5, Sun 1-5
Friends of the Library Group
Branches: 1
ELLETTSVILLE BRANCH, 600 W Temperance St, Ellettsville, 47429, SAN 341-0102. Tel: 812-876-1272. FAX: 812-876-2515. *Br Mgr,* Mickey Needham; *Ch,* Stephanie Holman; E-mail: sholman@mcpl.info; Staff 9.25 (MLS 3, Non-MLS 6.25)
Circ 268,060
Open Mon-Thurs 10-9, Fri 10-6, Sat 9-5, Sun 1-5
Friends of the Library Group
Bookmobiles: 1

BLUFFTON

P WELLS COUNTY PUBLIC LIBRARY*, 200 W Washington St, 46714-1999. SAN 304-811X. Tel: 260-824-1612. FAX: 260-824-3129. E-mail: wcpl@wellscolibrary.org. Web Site: www.wellscolibrary.org. *Dir,* Stephanie Davis; E-mail: sdavis@wellscolibrary.org; *Br Coordr,* Susan M Dailey; Tel: 260-622-4691, Fax: 260-622-7030, E-mail: sdailey@wellscolibrary.org; *AV,* Jackie Dailey; E-mail: jdailey@wellscolibrary.org; *Ch Serv,* Amy G Greiner; E-mail: agreiner@wellscolibrary.org; *Circ,* Teresa Dustman; E-mail: tdustman@wellscolibrary.org; *Ref,* Vi Tester; E-mail: vtester@wellscolibary.org; *Ref Serv, YA,* Leah Baumgartner; E-mail: lbaumgartner@wellscolibrary.org; *Syst,* Christine Will; E-mail: cwill@wellscolibrary.org; *Tech Serv,* Judy Maxwell; E-mail: jmaxwell@wellscolibrary.org; *YA Serv,* Sarah MacNeill; E-mail: smacneill@wellscolibrary.org; Staff 28 (MLS 5, Non-MLS 23)
Founded 1902. Pop 27,176; Circ 391,233
Jan 2011-Dec 2011 Income (Main Library and Branch(s)) $1,863,397. Mats Exp $1,676,340, Books $133,421, Per/Ser (Incl. Access Fees) $11,871, Micro $2,369, AV Mat $413,884, Electronic Ref Mat (Incl. Access Fees) $64,010. Sal $872,504
Library Holdings: Audiobooks 4,341; CDs 3,079; DVDs 6,932; e-books 3,329; Bk Vols 103,159; Per Subs 275
Special Collections: Compton O Rider International Doll Coll; Harry Lindstand Art Coll; Large Print Books; Literacy Coll; Local Newspaper (Bluffton News-Banner & Ossian Journal, micro); Wells County History Coll
Automation Activity & Vendor Info: (Acquisitions) SirsiDynix; (Cataloging) SirsiDynix; (Circulation) SirsiDynix; (ILL) OCLC Online; (Media Booking) SirsiDynix; (OPAC) SirsiDynix; (Serials) SirsiDynix
Database Vendor: Baker & Taylor, EBSCO Auto Repair Reference, EBSCOhost, Facts on File, Gale Cengage Learning, Grolier Online, Inspire, LearningExpress, OCLC WebJunction, OCLC WorldShare Interlibrary Loan, Overdrive, Inc, Oxford Online, ProQuest, SirsiDynix, TumbleBookLibrary, World Book Online, WT Cox
Wireless access
Function: Adult bk club, After school storytime, Audio & video playback equip for onsite use, Audiobks via web, AV serv, Bk club(s), Bks on cassette, Bks on CD, CD-ROM, Children's prog, Computer training, Computers for patron use, Copy machines, Digital talking bks, Electronic databases & coll, Equip loans & repairs, Exhibits, Fax serv, Free DVD rentals, Handicapped accessible, Holiday prog, Home delivery & serv to Sr ctr & nursing homes, ILL available, Magnifiers for reading, Music CDs, Notary serv, Outreach serv, OverDrive digital audio bks, Photocopying/Printing, Preschool outreach, Prof lending libr, Prog for adults, Prog for children & young adult, Pub access computers, Ref serv available, Scanner, Senior computer classes, Spoken cassettes & CDs, Spoken cassettes & DVDs, Story hour, Summer & winter reading prog, Summer reading prog, Tax forms, Teen prog, Telephone ref, VHS videos, Web-catalog, Wheelchair accessible, Workshops
Publications: Librarian's Book Report (Newsletter)
Open Mon-Thurs 9-8, Fri 9-6, Sat 9-5
Friends of the Library Group
Branches: 1
OSSIAN BRANCH, 207 N Jefferson, Ossian, 46777, SAN 320-0892. Tel: 260-622-4691. FAX: 260-622-7030. E-mail: osslib@wellscolibrary.org. *Br Librn,* Susan Dailey; E-mail: sdailey@wellscolibrary.org; Staff 4 (MLS 1, Non-MLS 3)
Open Mon-Thurs 9-8, Fri 9-5, Sat 9-12
Friends of the Library Group

BOONVILLE

P BOONVILLE-WARRICK COUNTY PUBLIC LIBRARY*, 611 W Main St, 47601-1544. SAN 304-8136. Tel: 812-897-1500. FAX: 812-897-1508. *Librn,* Lois A Aigner; Staff 9 (MLS 4, Non-MLS 5)
Founded 1911. Pop 194,150; Circ 162,139
Library Holdings: CDs 88; Bk Titles 121,478; Bk Vols 123,391; Per Subs 221; Talking Bks 410; Videos 1,733
Special Collections: Indiana Coll; Lincoln Coll
Automation Activity & Vendor Info: (Acquisitions) SirsiDynix; (Cataloging) SirsiDynix; (OPAC) SirsiDynix
Publications: Between the Pages (Patrons newsletter); Book Ends (Staff newsletter)
Open Mon-Thurs 10-8, Fri 10-5, Sat 12-5
Friends of the Library Group
Branches: 3
ELBERFELD BRANCH, 175 Sycamore, Elberfeld, 47613, SAN 377-7596. Tel: 812-983-4029. *Librn,* Betty Grimes; Staff 2 (MLS 1, Non-MLS 1)
Library Holdings: Bk Titles 21,212; Bk Vols 22,911; Per Subs 33; Videos 112
Open Mon 2-5, Wed 10-12, Sat 9-12
Friends of the Library Group
LYNNVILLE BRANCH, 211 N Main, Lynnville, 47619, SAN 377-760X. Tel: 812-922-5409. *Librn,* Anice Howard; Staff 1 (MLS 1)
Library Holdings: DVDs 25; Bk Titles 15,111; Bk Vols 17,808; Per Subs 27; Videos 101
Open Tues 10-5, Thurs 3-8
Friends of the Library Group
TENNYSON BRANCH, 318 N Main St, Tennyson, 47637, SAN 377-7626. Tel: 812-567-8933. *Librn,* Jacqueline Franz; Staff 1 (MLS 1)
Library Holdings: Bk Titles 18,119; Bk Vols 19,640; Per Subs 37; Videos 112
Open Tues & Thurs 12-8, Sat 10-2
Friends of the Library Group
Bookmobiles: 2

BOSWELL

P BOSWELL & GRANT TOWNSHIP PUBLIC LIBRARY*, 101 E Main St, 47921. (Mail add: PO Box 315, 47921-0315), SAN 304-8144. Tel: 765-869-5428. FAX: 765-869-5428. E-mail: boswelllib@hotmail.com. *Dir,* Andrea Bowman; *Asst Librn,* Elizabeth Varner
Founded 1912. Pop 1,142; Circ 16,352
Library Holdings: AV Mats 1,450; Bk Vols 15,500; Per Subs 84; Talking Bks 250

Automation Activity & Vendor Info: (Acquisitions) SirsiDynix; (Cataloging) SirsiDynix; (Circulation) SirsiDynix; (ILL) SirsiDynix; (OPAC) SirsiDynix
Open Mon 12-7, Tues 10-5, Wed-Fri 12-5, Sat 9-12
Friends of the Library Group

BOURBON

P BOURBON PUBLIC LIBRARY*, 307 N Main St, 46504-1596. SAN 304-8152. Tel: 574-342-5655. FAX: 574-342-5001. Web Site: www.bourbon.lib.in.us/. *Dir,* Heather Barron; *Ch,* Dinah Thacker; *Tech Serv,* Denise Heckaman; Staff 4 (MLS 1, Non MLS 3)
Founded 1940. Pop 2,970; Circ 37,707
Library Holdings: AV Mats 1,615; CDs 27; Large Print Bks 100; Bk Titles 21,117; Bk Vols 28,580; Per Subs 103; Talking Bks 291; Videos 572
Automation Activity & Vendor Info: (Acquisitions) EOS International; (Cataloging) EOS International; (OPAC) EOS International
Open Mon-Wed 10-8, Thurs & Fri 10-5, Sat 10-3

BRANCHVILLE

S BRANCHVILLE CORRECTIONAL FACILITY LIBRARY*, 21390 Old State Rd 37, 47514. SAN 327-9006. Tel: 812-843-5921, Ext 4328. FAX: 812-843-4262. *Librn,* Gregg Roberts
Library Holdings: Bk Titles 15,000; Per Subs 70
Open Mon-Fri 10-6

BRAZIL

P BRAZIL PUBLIC LIBRARY*, 204 N Walnut St, 47834. SAN 304-8160. Tel: 812-448-1981. FAX: 812-446-3215. Web Site: www.brazil.lib.in.us. *Dir,* Jill Scarbrough; E-mail: jscarbrough@ticz.com; Staff 9 (MLS 1, Non-MLS 8)
Founded 1879. Pop 8,612; Circ 96,248
Library Holdings: CDs 59; Large Print Bks 161; Bk Titles 33,791; Bk Vols 35,815; Per Subs 89; Talking Bks 292; Videos 2,000
Automation Activity & Vendor Info: (Acquisitions) SirsiDynix; (Cataloging) SirsiDynix; (OPAC) SirsiDynix
Partic in Evergreen Indiana Consortium
Open Mon-Thurs 10-8, Fri & Sat 10-5
Friends of the Library Group

BREMEN

P BREMEN PUBLIC LIBRARY*, 304 N Jackson St, 46506. SAN 304-8179. Tel: 574-546-2849. FAX: 574-546-4938. E-mail: bremenpl@bremen.lib.in.us. Web Site: www.bremen.lib.in.us. *Dir,* Marsha L Patterson; *Head, Adult Serv,* Rose M Humphries; *Head, Ch,* Sandra J Krost; *Circ,* Lisa L Bixel; Staff 2 (Non-MLS 2)
Founded 1956. Pop 8,474; Circ 115,000
Library Holdings: Bk Titles 45,000; Bk Vols 45,325; Per Subs 220
Automation Activity & Vendor Info: (Acquisitions) Innovative Interfaces, Inc; (Cataloging) Innovative Interfaces, Inc - Millenium; (Circulation) Innovative Interfaces, Inc; (OPAC) Innovative Interfaces, Inc; (Serials) Innovative Interfaces, Inc
Database Vendor: Innovative Interfaces, Inc, Inspire, OCLC WorldShare Interlibrary Loan
Wireless access
Function: Accelerated reader prog, Adult bk club, Adult literacy prog, After school storytime, Bk club(s), Bks on cassette, Bks on CD, Children's prog, Computer training, Computers for patron use, Copy machines, E-Reserves, Electronic databases & coll, Exhibits, Fax serv, Handicapped accessible, Holiday prog, Home delivery & serv to Sr ctr & nursing homes, Homebound delivery serv, ILL available, Large print keyboards, Libr develop, Mail & tel request accepted, Music CDs, Online cat, Online searches, Photocopying/Printing, Preschool outreach, Prog for adults, Prog for children & young adult, Pub access computers, Ref & res, Ref serv available, Ref serv in person, Scanner, Senior computer classes, Serves mentally handicapped consumers, Spoken cassettes & CDs, Spoken cassettes & DVDs, Story hour, Summer reading prog, Tax forms, Telephone ref, VHS videos, Video lending libr, Web-catalog, Wheelchair accessible, Workshops
Publications: BLT, Bremen Libray Times (Newsletter)
Partic in Midwest Collaborative for Library Services (MCLS)
Open Mon-Thurs 9-8, Fri 9-5:30, Sat 9-5

BRISTOL

P BRISTOL-WASHINGTON TOWNSHIP PUBLIC LIBRARY*, 505 W Vistula St, 46507. (Mail add: PO Box 789, 46507-0789), SAN 304-8187. Tel: 574-848-7458. FAX: 574-848-4391. E-mail: bristolpublib@bristol.lib.in.us. Web Site: www.youseemore.com/bristolwash. *Dir,* Daryl Shrock; Staff 7 (MLS 1, Non-MLS 6)
Founded 1921. Pop 7,000
Library Holdings: AV Mats 8,000; Large Print Bks 450; Bk Titles 45,000; Per Subs 80; Talking Bks 500
Special Collections: Indiana History Coll
Automation Activity & Vendor Info: (Cataloging) TLC (The Library Corporation); (Circulation) TLC (The Library Corporation)
Function: ILL available
Partic in Midwest Collaborative for Library Services (MCLS)
Open Mon-Thurs 10-8, Fri 10-5, Sat 10-3

S ELKHART COUNTY HISTORICAL SOCIETY, INC*, Winifred Cosbey Library, 304 W Vistula, 46507. (Mail add: PO Box 434, 46507-0434), SAN 329-1286. Tel: 574-848-4322. FAX: 574-848-5703. E-mail: museum@elkhartcountyparks.org. Web Site: www.elkhartcountyparks.org. *Dir,* Nicholas James Hoffman; *Asst Dir,* Diana Zornow; *Educ Curator,* Rebecca Oestreich. Subject Specialists: *Ethnic studies, Labor hist,* Nicholas James Hoffman; Staff 3 (Non-MLS 3)
Founded 1968
Library Holdings: Bk Titles 2,200; Per Subs 10
Special Collections: Elkhart County from 1830, archives
Publications: Bibliographies
Restriction: Non-circulating

BROOK

P BROOK-IROQUOIS-WASHINGTON PUBLIC LIBRARY*, 100 W Main St, 47922. (Mail add: PO Box 155, 47922-0155), SAN 304-8195. Tel: 219-275-2471. FAX: 219-275-8471. E-mail: library@brooklib.in.us. Web Site: www.brook.lib.in.us/. *Dir,* Joyce K Whaley; E-mail: jwhaley@brook.lib.in.us; *Asst Librn,* Mandy Justice; *Libr Asst,* Maxine Dyer; Staff 2 (Non-MLS 2)
Founded 1910. Pop 1,389; Circ 14,123
Library Holdings: Bk Vols 28,000; Per Subs 35
Subject Interests: Indiana, Local hist
Automation Activity & Vendor Info: (Cataloging) Mandarin Library Automation; (Circulation) Mandarin Library Automation; (OPAC) Mandarin Library Automation
Wireless access
Open Mon & Wed 9-7, Tues & Fri 9-5, Sat 9-1

BROOKSTON

P BROOKSTON - PRAIRIE TOWNSHIP PUBLIC LIBRARY*, 111 W Second St, 47923. SAN 304-8209. Tel: 765-563-6511. FAX: 765-563-6833. E-mail: info@brookston.lib.in.us. Web Site: brookstonlibrary.org. *Libr Dir,* Marilyn Blessing; *Asst Librn,* Jennifer Norris; Staff 2 (Non-MLS 2)
Founded 1917. Pop 3,290; Circ 31,480
Library Holdings: DVDs 1,100; Bk Titles 32,890; Bk Vols 34,481; Per Subs 62; Talking Bks 1,011; Videos 445
Special Collections: Cookbooks; Crafts, Indiana History, bks, pamphlets. Oral History
Automation Activity & Vendor Info: (Acquisitions) Evergreen; (Cataloging) Evergreen; (OPAC) Evergreen
Wireless access
Partic in Midwest Collaborative for Library Services (MCLS)
Open Mon-Thurs 1-8, Fri 9-5, Sat 9-1
Friends of the Library Group

BROOKVILLE

P FRANKLIN COUNTY PUBLIC LIBRARY DISTRICT*, Brookville Public Library, 919 Main St, 47012-1498. SAN 304-8217. Tel: 765-647-4031. FAX: 765-647-0278. Web Site: www.fclibraries.org. *Dir,* Melody Gault; *Ch,* Amanda Van Winkle; *ILL,* Sara Dorrel; Staff 3 (Non-MLS 3)
Founded 1912. Pop 11,070; Circ 46,121
Library Holdings: Audiobooks 702; Electronic Media & Resources 3; Bk Titles 35,690; Bk Vols 39,972; Per Subs 132; Talking Bks 320; Videos 3,050
Special Collections: Family Histories; Genealogy Items; Heritage Art Coll; Local History Coll
Automation Activity & Vendor Info: (Cataloging) SirsiDynix; (Circulation) SirsiDynix; (OPAC) SirsiDynix
Database Vendor: Baker & Taylor, OCLC FirstSearch
Wireless access
Function: Adult literacy prog, Art exhibits, Audio & video playback equip for onsite use, CD-ROM, Handicapped accessible, Home delivery & serv to Sr ctr & nursing homes, Homebound delivery serv, ILL available, Music CDs, Online searches, Orientations, Photocopying/Printing, Prog for adults, Prog for children & young adult, Spoken cassettes & CDs, Summer reading prog, Telephone ref, VHS videos, Wheelchair accessible
Partic in Eastern Ind Area Libr Servs Authority; Evergreen Indiana Consortium; Midwest Collaborative for Library Services (MCLS)
Special Services for the Deaf - Adult & family literacy prog; Bks on deafness & sign lang; High interest/low vocabulary bks

Special Services for the Blind - Bks on cassette; Bks on CD; Home delivery serv; Large print bks; Large screen computer & software; Reader equip
Open Mon-Thurs 9-8, Fri 9-6, Sat 9-3
Restriction: In-house use for visitors, Non-resident fee
Friends of the Library Group
Branches: 1
LAUREL PUBLIC LIBRARY, 200 N Clay St, Laurel, 47024. Tel: 765-698-2582. FAX: 765-698-2626. *Dir,* Melody Gault; *Br Mgr,* Linda Bruns; *Cataloger,* Jodie Cregar; Staff 1 (Non-MLS 1)
Founded 1998. Pop 11,070
Automation Activity & Vendor Info: (ILL) LAC Group
Database Vendor: Inspire, ProQuest, SirsiDynix
Function: Adult literacy prog, Archival coll, Art exhibits, Handicapped accessible, Homebound delivery serv, ILL available, Online searches, Orientations, Photocopying/Printing, Prog for adults, Prog for children & young adult, Spoken cassettes & CDs, Summer reading prog, VHS videos, Workshops
Publications: Whitewater Valley Community Library (Newsletter)
Special Services for the Deaf - Adult & family literacy prog; Bks on deafness & sign lang; High interest/low vocabulary bks
Special Services for the Blind - Bks on cassette; Bks on CD; Copier with enlargement capabilities; Home delivery serv; Large print bks; Large screen computer & software; Videos on blindness & phys handicaps
Open Mon-Thurs 9-8, Fri 9-6, Sat 9-3
Restriction: Non-resident fee
Friends of the Library Group

BROWNSBURG

P BROWNSBURG PUBLIC LIBRARY*, 450 S Jefferson St, 46112-1310. SAN 304-8225. Tel: 317-852-3167. Circulation Tel: 317-852-3167, Ext 115. Interlibrary Loan Service Tel: 317-852-3167, Ext 109. Reference Tel: 317-852-3167, Ext 107. Administration Tel: 317-852-3167, Ext 100. FAX: 317-852-7734. TDD: 317-852-3168. E-mail: AccountInfo@brownsburg.lib.in.us, AskUs@brownsburg.lib.in.us. Web Site: www.brownsburg.lib.in.us. *Dir,* Wanda L Pearson; E-mail: wpearson@brownsburg.lib.in.us; *Asst Dir,* Denise Robinson; Tel: 317-852-3167, Ext 101, E-mail: drobinson@brownsburg.lib.in.us; *Pub Serv Adminr,* Amie Thomas; Tel: 317-852-3167, Ext 108, E-mail: athomas@brownsburg.lib.in.us; *Customer Serv Mgr,* Montoya Barker; Tel: 317-852-3167, Ext 118, E-mail: mbarker@brownsburg.lib.in.us; *Info Serv Mgr,* Emily Fleischer; Tel: 317-852-3167, Ext 127, E-mail: efleischer@brownsburg.lib.in.us; *Tech Serv Mgr,* Kelly Hale; Tel: 317-852-3167, Ext 103, E-mail: khale@brownsburg.lib.in.us; Staff 25 (MLS 11, Non-MLS 14)
Founded 1917. Pop 44,208; Circ 441,483
Jan 2012-Dec 2012 Income $1,303,572, State $76,427, Locally Generated Income $1,142,791, Other $84,354. Mats Exp $146,814, Books $78,908, Per/Ser (Incl. Access Fees) $7,422, AV Mat $27,520, Electronic Ref Mat (Incl. Access Fees) $32,964. Sal $761,294
Library Holdings: Audiobooks 4,462; CDs 1,239; DVDs 3,119; e-books 752; Large Print Bks 4,777; Bk Vols 108,352; Per Subs 293; Videos 1,040
Automation Activity & Vendor Info: (Acquisitions) Innovative Interfaces, Inc; (Cataloging) Innovative Interfaces, Inc; (Circulation) Innovative Interfaces, Inc; (ILL) Innovative Interfaces, Inc; (OPAC) Innovative Interfaces, Inc; (Serials) Innovative Interfaces, Inc
Database Vendor: Baker & Taylor, Evanced Solutions, Inc, Gale Cengage Learning, Ingram Library Services, Inspire, LearningExpress, Overdrive, Inc, ReferenceUSA, TumbleBookLibrary, ValueLine
Wireless access
Partic in Midwest Collaborative for Library Services (MCLS)
Special Services for the Deaf - TDD equip; TTY equip
Special Services for the Blind - Talking bks
Open Mon-Thurs 9-8, Fri 9-6, Sat 9-5, Sun 1-5
Friends of the Library Group

BROWNSTOWN

P BROWNSTOWN PUBLIC LIBRARY*, 120 E Spring St, 47220-1546. SAN 304-8233. Tel: 812-358-2853. FAX: 812-358-4116. Web Site: www.brownstown.lib.in.us. *Dir,* Sherri May; Staff 2 (Non-MLS 2)
Founded 1910. Pop 7,080; Circ 110,103
Jan 2011-Dec 2011 Income $321,224. Mats Exp $51,054, Books $27,949, Per/Ser (Incl. Access Fees) $2,029, AV Mat $21,076. Sal $227,636
Library Holdings: Audiobooks 575; CDs 244; DVDs 8,133; Large Print Bks 555; Bk Titles 33,112; Per Subs 70
Subject Interests: Indiana
Automation Activity & Vendor Info: (Acquisitions) Evergreen; (Cataloging) Evergreen; (Circulation) Evergreen; (OPAC) Evergreen
Wireless access
Partic in Evergreen Indiana Consortium
Open Mon-Thurs 9-7, Fri 9-6, Sat 9-4

BUNKER HILL

MIAMI CORRECTIONAL FACILITY
S PHASE I LIBRARY*, 3038 W 850 S, 46914. Tel: 765-689-8920. FAX: 765-689-5964. *Librn,* Robert Moore; Tel: 765-689-8920, Ext 5344
Founded 1999
Library Holdings: Large Print Bks 33; Bk Vols 10,500; Per Subs 8
Restriction: Inmate patrons, facility staff & vols direct access. All others through ILL only
S PHASE II LIBRARY*, 3038 W 850 S, 46914. Tel: 765-689-8920. FAX: 765-689-5964. *Librn,* Dr Barbara Kasper
Library Holdings: Bk Vols 3,000

BUTLER

P BUTLER PUBLIC LIBRARY*, 340 S Broadway, 46721. SAN 304-8241. Tel: 260-868-2351. FAX: 260-868-5491. Web Site: www.butlerpubliclibrary.net. *Dir,* Ellen Stuckey; E-mail: ellen@butlerpubliclibrary.net; *Cataloger, Ref Librn,* Bonnie Graham; E-mail: bonnie@butlerpubliclibrary.net; *Ch Serv,* Teri McKown; E-mail: teri@butlerpubliclibrary.net; Staff 3 (MLS 1, Non-MLS 2)
Founded 1906. Pop 3,905; Circ 54,718
Library Holdings: Bk Titles 44,343; Per Subs 110
Automation Activity & Vendor Info: (Cataloging) Evergreen; (Circulation) Evergreen; (OPAC) Evergreen
Wireless access
Partic in Evergreen Indiana Consortium
Open Mon-Thurs 10-7, Sat 9-1
Friends of the Library Group

CAMBRIDGE CITY

P CAMBRIDGE CITY PUBLIC LIBRARY*, 33 W Main St, 47327. SAN 304-825X. Tel: 765-478-3335. FAX: 765-478-6144. E-mail: ccitypl@yahoo.com. Web Site: www.cclib.lib.in.us. *Dir of Libr,* Melek Victoria; *Ch,* Denise Canady; Staff 2 (Non-MLS 2)
Founded 1936. Pop 5,508; Circ 65,000
Library Holdings: Bks on Deafness & Sign Lang 20; CDs 174; DVDs 622; Large Print Bks 604; Bk Titles 34,000; Per Subs 120; Talking Bks 649; Videos 1,158
Special Collections: History (Western Wayne County); Overbeck Pottery Coll
Automation Activity & Vendor Info: (Acquisitions) Surpass; (Cataloging) Surpass; (Circulation) Surpass; (Course Reserve) Surpass; (ILL) OCLC WorldShare Interlibrary Loan; (OPAC) Surpass; (Serials) Surpass
Database Vendor: Inspire
Function: After school storytime, Homebound delivery serv, ILL available, Music CDs, Online searches, Photocopying/Printing, Prog for adults, Prog for children & young adult, Ref serv available, Spoken cassettes & CDs, Summer reading prog, Telephone ref, VHS videos
Partic in Midwest Collaborative for Library Services (MCLS)
Open Mon & Wed 9-7:30, Tues, Thurs & Fri 9-5, Sat 10-5

CAMDEN

P CAMDEN-JACKSON TOWNSHIP PUBLIC LIBRARY*, 258 Main St, 46917. (Mail add: PO Box 24, 46917-0024), SAN 304-8268. Tel: 574-686-2120. FAX: 574-686-2120. E-mail: camlib@tds.net. *Dir,* Shirley L Schock; Staff 2 (MLS 1, Non-MLS 1)
Founded 1940. Pop 1,266; Circ 6,358
Library Holdings: Bk Titles 13,049; Bk Vols 15,691; Per Subs 27; Talking Bks 429; Videos 386
Partic in Wabash Valley Area Libr Servs Authority
Open Mon & Wed-Fri 1-5, Tues 7pm-9pm, Sat 9-12

CANNELTON

P CANNELTON PUBLIC LIBRARY*, 210 S Eighth, 47520. SAN 304-8276. Tel: 812-547-6028. E-mail: canneltonpl@yahoo.com. *Dir,* Sally Walker; Staff 2 (MLS 1, Non-MLS 1)
Founded 1893. Pop 1,209; Circ 7,890
Library Holdings: Large Print Bks 68; Bk Titles 21,068; Bk Vols 22,391; Per Subs 57; Talking Bks 99; Videos 219
Subject Interests: Indiana
Automation Activity & Vendor Info: (Acquisitions) Follett Software; (Cataloging) Follett Software; (OPAC) Follett Software
Partic in Midwest Collaborative for Library Services (MCLS)
Open Mon, Wed & Thurs 2-7, Tues 9-11, Fri & Sat 2-5

CARLISLE

WABASH VALLEY CORRECTIONAL FACILITY
S LEVEL FOUR LIBRARY*, 6908 S Old US Hwy 41, 47838. (Mail add: PO Box 500, 47838-0500). Tel: 812-398-5050, Ext 4573. FAX: 812-398-5032. Web Site: www.in.gov/idoc/2409.htm.
Library Holdings: Bk Titles 1,850; Bk Vols 2,060; Per Subs 42

Function: Adult literacy prog, Audio & video playback equip for onsite use, Distance learning, For res purposes, Homebound delivery serv, ILL available, Libr develop, Newsp ref libr, Photocopying/Printing, Prog for adults, Provide serv for the mentally ill, Ref serv available, Res libr, Serves mentally handicapped consumers, Spoken cassettes & CDs, Wheelchair accessible
Restriction: Circ limited

S LEVEL THREE LIBRARY*, 6908 S Old US Hwy 41, 47838. (Mail add: PO Box 500, 47838-0500). Tel: 812-398-5050, Ext 3271. FAX: 812-398-2125. Web Site: www.in.gov/idoc/2409.htm. *Librn,* Stephanie Sark; Staff 1 (Non-MLS 1)
Library Holdings: Bk Titles 5,160; Bk Vols 5,380; Per Subs 21

CARMEL

P CARMEL CLAY PUBLIC LIBRARY, 55 Fourth Ave SE, 46032-2278. SAN 304-8284. Tel: 317-814-3900. Circulation Tel: 317-844-3361. Reference Tel: 317-844-3362. Administration Tel: 317-844-6711. FAX: 317-571-4285. TDD: 317-571-4294. Web Site: www.carmel.lib.in.us. *Dir,* Wendy A Phillips; E-mail: wphillips@carmel.lib.in.us; Staff 46.95 (MLS 25, Non-MLS 21.95)
Founded 1904. Pop 86,293; Circ 2,025,415
Library Holdings: AV Mats 60,911; Bk Titles 226,336; Bk Vols 280,146; Per Subs 358
Automation Activity & Vendor Info: (Acquisitions) SirsiDynix; (Cataloging) SirsiDynix; (Circulation) SirsiDynix; (ILL) OCLC; (OPAC) SirsiDynix
Database Vendor: EBSCOhost, Gale Cengage Learning, OCLC FirstSearch, OCLC WorldShare Interlibrary Loan, ProQuest
Wireless access
Publications: Friends & Neighbors (Newsletter); Happenings (Newsletter)
Special Services for the Deaf - Assistive tech; Bks on deafness & sign lang; Closed caption videos; High interest/low vocabulary bks; TDD equip
Special Services for the Blind - Audio mat; Bks on cassette; Bks on CD; Large print bks; Screen enlargement software for people with visual disabilities
Open Mon-Thurs 9-9, Fri 9-7, Sat 9-5, Sun 1-5
Friends of the Library Group

CARTHAGE

P HENRY HENLEY PUBLIC LIBRARY*, Carthage Library, 102 N Main St, 46115. (Mail add: PO Box 35, 46115-0035), SAN 373-8671. Tel: 765-565-6631. *Librn,* Shelley Wilson
Founded 1890. Pop 1,100
Library Holdings: Bk Vols 10,500
Open Tues 1-7, Thurs 4-7, Sat 12-2
Friends of the Library Group

CENTERVILLE

P CENTERVILLE-CENTER TOWNSHIP PUBLIC LIBRARY*, 126 E Main St, 47330-1206. SAN 304-8292. Tel: 765-855-5223. FAX: 765-855-2009. E-mail: read@centervillelibrary.info. Web Site: www.centervillelibrary.info. *Dir,* Beth Treaster; E mail: btreaster@centervillelibrary.info; *Head, Youth Serv,* Celeste Badger; E-mail: cbadger@centervillelibrary.info; *Outreach Serv Librn,* Kristie Dickens, E-mail: kdickens@centervillelibrary.info; Staff 3 (MLS 2, Non-MLS 1)
Founded 1921. Pop 7,330; Circ 38,399
Library Holdings: Audiobooks 906; CDs 376; DVDs 643; Large Print Bks 2,000; Microforms 51; Bk Vols 39,247; Per Subs 86; Videos 1,050
Special Collections: Paintings by Local Artists
Subject Interests: Genealogy, Local hist
Automation Activity & Vendor Info: (Cataloging) Evergreen; (Circulation) Evergreen; (OPAC) Evergreen
Wireless access
Function: Art exhibits, Bk club(s), Computer training, Computers for patron use, Copy machines, Fax serv, Free DVD rentals, Genealogy discussion group, Handicapped accessible, Home delivery & serv to Sr ctr & nursing homes, ILL available, Online cat, OverDrive digital audio bks, Photocopying/Printing, Prog for adults, Prog for children & young adult, Pub access computers, Scanner, Senior computer classes, Story hour, Summer reading prog, Tax forms, Teen prog
Open Mon, Wed & Fri 10-5, Tues & Thurs 10-8, Sat 10-2

CHARLESTOWN

P CHARLESTOWN-CLARK COUNTY PUBLIC LIBRARY*, 51 Clark Rd, 47111. SAN 304-8306. Tel: 812-256-3337. FAX: 812-256-3890. Web Site: www.clarkco.lib.in.us. *Libr Dir,* Tamsie Meurer; *Ch Serv,* April Beckman; Staff 27 (MLS 9, Non-MLS 18)
Founded 1966. Pop 42,817; Circ 148,091
Library Holdings: Bk Titles 122,891; Per Subs 370; Talking Bks 762; Videos 1,934
Special Collections: Lexicography (J E Schmidt, MD Coll)
Subject Interests: Genealogy, Local hist
Automation Activity & Vendor Info: (Acquisitions) TLC (The Library Corporation); (Cataloging) TLC (The Library Corporation); (OPAC) TLC (The Library Corporation)
Publications: Monthly Calendar of Activities
Partic in Ind Area Libr Servs Authority; Midwest Collaborative for Library Services (MCLS)
Open Mon-Thurs 9-8, Fri & Sat 9-5
Branches: 4
BORDEN BRANCH, 117 W Main St, Borden, 47106. Tel: 812-967-3440. FAX: 812-967-3440. *Mgr,* Carla Akers
Library Holdings: AV Mats 1,221; DVDs 280; Bk Titles 15,906; Bk Vols 16,302; Per Subs 38; Videos 290
Open Mon 11-6, Tues & Thurs 11-7, Fri 9-6, Sat 10-2
HENRYVILLE BRANCH, 214 E Main St, Henryville, 47126. Tel: 812-294-4246. FAX: 812-294-1078. *Mgr,* June Kruer
Library Holdings: AV Mats 1,355; DVDs 280; Bk Titles 20,316; Bk Vols 20,943; Per Subs 34; Videos 214
Open Mon & Tues 9-6, Wed 12-6, Thurs 10-8, Fri 9-5, Sat 10-2
NEW WASHINGTON BRANCH, 210 S Poplar St, New Washington, 47162. Tel: 812-967-4577. FAX: 812-967-4577. *Mgr,* Nancy Bussy
Library Holdings: AV Mats 1,834; DVDs 728; Bk Titles 14,330; Bk Vols 14,772; Per Subs 33; Videos 177
Open Mon & Fri 9-5, Tues & Thurs 12-8, Sat 9-1
SELLERSBURG BRANCH, 430 N Indiana Ave, Sellersburg, 47172. Tel: 812-246-4493. FAX: 812-246-4382. *Mgr,* Cathy Hoover
Library Holdings: AV Mats 1,964; DVDs 313; Bk Titles 38,521; Bk Vols 39,845; Per Subs 64; Videos 792
Open Mon-Thurs 9-8, Fri & Sat 9-5

CHESTERTON

P WESTCHESTER PUBLIC LIBRARY, Thomas Library, 200 W Indiana Ave, 46304-3122. SAN 341-0137. Tel: 219-926-7696. FAX: 219-926-6424. Web Site: www.wpl.lib.in.us. *Dir,* Phil Baugher; E-mail: phil@wpl.lib.in.us; *Br Librn,* Leea Yelich; *Ch,* Heather Chaddock; *Acq Mgr,* Julie Bohannon; *AV Mgr,* Tracy McDonald; *Mgr, Automation & Ser,* Rhonda Mullin; *Circ Mgr,* Claire Williams; *IT Mgr,* Joseph Harry; *Tech Serv Mgr,* Rose Halpin; Tel: 219-921-0964; Staff 4 (MLS 4)
Founded 1972. Pop 18,341; Circ 340,000
Library Holdings: CDs 7,800; DVDs 4,200; Bk Vols 154,000; Per Subs 125; Talking Bks 950; Videos 10,900
Special Collections: Chesterton Tribune Photo Morgue; Prairie Club Archives
Subject Interests: Local hist
Automation Activity & Vendor Info: (Acquisitions) Innovative Interfaces, Inc; (Cataloging) Innovative Interfaces, Inc; (Circulation) Innovative Interfaces, Inc; (ILL) Innovative Interfaces, Inc; (OPAC) Innovative Interfaces, Inc
Wireless access
Function: Adult bk club, Adult literacy prog, After school storytime, Archival coll, AV serv, CD-ROM, Handicapped accessible, ILL available, Music CDs, Photocopying/Printing, Prog for adults, Prog for children & young adult, Ref serv available, Summer reading prog, VHS videos, Video lending libr
Open Mon Fri 9-9, Sat 9-5, Sun 1-5
Friends of the Library Group
Branches: 1
HAGEMAN, 100 Francis St, Porter, 46304, SAN 341-0161. Tel: 219-926-9080. *Br Mgr,* Susan Chomel
Open Mon-Fri 9-5, Sat 1-5
Friends of the Library Group

CHURUBUSCO

P CHURUBUSCO PUBLIC LIBRARY*, 116 N Mulberry St, 46723. SAN 304-8322. Tel: 260-693-6466. FAX: 260-693-6466. E-mail: buscolibrary@frontier.com. Web Site: buscolibrary.org. *Libr Dir,* Rachel Eyermann; Staff 2 (MLS 1, Non-MLS 1)
Founded 1914. Pop 5,050
Library Holdings: CDs 86; Bk Vols 23,383; Per Subs 55; Talking Bks 974
Open Mon-Fri 10-7, Sat 9-2
Friends of the Library Group

CICERO

P HAMILTON NORTH PUBLIC LIBRARY*, 209 W Brinton, 46034. SAN 340-9503. Tel: 317-984-5623. FAX: 317-984-7505. Web Site: www.hnpl.lib.in.us. *Libr Dir,* Samuel Mitchell; Staff 19 (MLS 1, Non-MLS 18)
Pop 9,968
Library Holdings: AV Mats 9,090; Bks on Deafness & Sign Lang 73; CDs 1,500; DVDs 1,000; High Interest/Low Vocabulary Bk Vols 74; Large Print Bks 1,063; Bk Vols 87,600; Per Subs 200; Talking Bks 2,000; Videos 4,590
Special Collections: Local History

Automation Activity & Vendor Info: (Acquisitions) Follett Software; (Cataloging) Follett Software; (OPAC) Follett Software
Function: Adult literacy prog, Archival coll, Art exhibits, AV serv, Handicapped accessible, Homebound delivery serv, ILL available, Music CDs, Photocopying/Printing, Prog for adults, Prog for children & young adult, Spoken cassettes & CDs, Summer reading prog, VHS videos, Wheelchair accessible
Partic in Evergreen Indiana Consortium; Midwest Collaborative for Library Services (MCLS)
Open Mon-Thurs 10-7, Fri 10-5, Sat 10-3
Friends of the Library Group
Branches: 1
ATLANTA BRANCH, 100 S Walnut St, Atlanta, 46031. (Mail add: PO Box 68, Atlanta, 46031-0068), SAN 340-9449. Tel: 765-292-2521. FAX: 765-292-2249. *Br Mgr,* Mary Palmiero; Staff 3 (MLS 1, Non-MLS 2)
Founded 1916. Circ 5,271
Library Holdings: Bk Vols 10,000
Function: Archival coll, Homebound delivery serv, ILL available, Music CDs, Photocopying/Printing, Prog for adults, Prog for children & young adult, Spoken cassettes & CDs, Summer reading prog, VHS videos
Open Mon-Thurs 2-7
Friends of the Library Group

CLAYTON

P CLAYTON-LIBERTY TOWNSHIP PUBLIC LIBRARY*, 5199 Iowa St, 46118-9174. (Mail add: PO Box E, 46118-4905), SAN 304-8330. Tel: 317-539-2991, 317-539-7052. FAX: 317-539-2050. E-mail: cltpl@tds.net. *Dir,* Jonnie Wallis-Halberstadt; Staff 5 (MLS 1, Non-MLS 4)
Founded 1929. Pop 5,072; Circ 12,308
Library Holdings: Bks on Deafness & Sign Lang 22; Large Print Bks 1,052; Bk Vols 27,000; Per Subs 78; Videos 230
Subject Interests: Local authors, Local hist
Automation Activity & Vendor Info: (Cataloging) Follett Software; (Circulation) Follett Software; (OPAC) Follett Software
Partic in Midwest Collaborative for Library Services (MCLS)
Special Services for the Deaf - Closed caption videos
Open Mon, Tues & Thurs 10-7, Fri 10-5, Sat 10-1

CLINTON

P CLINTON PUBLIC LIBRARY*, 313 S Fourth St, 47842-2398. SAN 304-8349. Tel: 765-832-8349. FAX: 765-832-3823. E-mail: cpl@clintonpl.lib.in.us. Web Site: www.clintonpl.lib.in.us. *Dir,* Becky Cuffle; E-mail: becky@clintonpl.lib.in.us; *Adult Serv,* Sue Vinyard; E-mail: sue@clintonpl.lib.in.us; *Ch Serv,* Stephanie Hoctor; E-mail: steph@clintonpl.lib.in.us; *YA Serv,* Judy Karanovich; E-mail: judy@clintonpl.lib.in.us; Staff 4.5 (MLS 1.5, Non-MLS 3)
Founded 1911. Pop 9,119; Circ 28,404
Jan 2011-Dec 2011 Income $331,874, State $43,062, County $278,561, Other $10,251. Mats Exp $20,568, Books $11,638, Per/Ser (Incl. Access Fees) $3,939, AV Mat $4,991. Sal $197,065 (Prof $30,898)
Library Holdings: AV Mats 2,690; Electronic Media & Resources 20; Bk Vols 45,088; Per Subs 78
Special Collections: Genealogy & Local History Coll, including Daily Clintonian on microfilm; Indiana Coll
Automation Activity & Vendor Info: (Cataloging) Evergreen; (Circulation) Evergreen; (ILL) Evergreen; (OPAC) Evergreen
Database Vendor: Inspire
Wireless access
Function: Accelerated reader prog, AV serv, Bk reviews (Group), Bks on cassette, Bks on CD, Children's prog, Computers for patron use, Copy machines, Fax serv, Free DVD rentals, ILL available, Instruction & testing, Mail & tel request accepted, Microfiche/film & reading machines, Music CDs, Online cat, OverDrive digital audio bks, Photocopying/Printing, Preschool reading prog, Prog for adults, Prog for children & young adult, Ref serv available, Scanner, Spoken cassettes & CDs, Summer reading prog, Teen prog, VHS videos, Web-catalog, Wheelchair accessible
Special Services for the Blind - Bks on cassette; Bks on CD; Large print bks; Talking bk serv referral
Open Mon-Thurs 9-8, Fri 9-5, Sat 9-2
Friends of the Library Group

COATESVILLE

P COATESVILLE-CLAY TOWNSHIP PUBLIC LIBRARY*, 4928 Milton St, 46121. (Mail add: PO Box 147, 46121-0147), SAN 304-8357. Tel: 765-386-2355. FAX: 765-386-6177. E-mail: cpl@ccrtc.com. *Librn,* Cheryl Steinborn; Staff 3 (MLS 1, Non-MLS 2)
Founded 1912. Pop 2,311; Circ 8,618
Library Holdings: Bk Titles 21,890; Bk Vols 23,450; Per Subs 72; Talking Bks 115; Videos 276
Special Collections: Coatesville Herald, 1910-1961, microfilm
Open Mon-Fri 1-7, Sat 10-5
Friends of the Library Group

COLFAX

P COLFAX-PERRY TOWNSHIP PUBLIC LIBRARY*, 207 S Clark St, 46035. (Mail add: PO Box 308, 46035-0308), SAN 304-8365. Tel: 765-324-2915. Circulation Tel: 765-324-2915, Ext 100. FAX: 765-324-2689. Web Site: www.colfaxptpl.org. *Ch, Interim Dir,* Brenda Kinslow; Tel: 765-324-2915, Ext 103, E-mail: bkinslow@colfaxptpl.org; *Asst Librn,* Janet Clawson; Tel: 765-324-2915, Ext 102; Staff 2 (MLS 1, Non-MLS 1)
Founded 1917. Pop 1,507; Circ 21,210
Library Holdings: Bk Titles 14,599; Bk Vols 15,981; Per Subs 82; Talking Bks 163; Videos 1,598
Subject Interests: Genealogy, Local hist
Automation Activity & Vendor Info: (Acquisitions) Follett Software; (Cataloging) Follett Software; (ILL) Follett Software; (OPAC) Follett Software
Wireless access
Publications: Periodic Newsletter
Partic in Evergreen Indiana Consortium
Open Mon & Wed 11-6, Tues & Thurs 1-7, Fri 11-5, Sat 10-3
Friends of the Library Group

COLUMBIA CITY

P PEABODY PUBLIC LIBRARY*, 1160 E Hwy Rd 205, 46725. (Mail add: PO Box 406, 46725-0406), SAN 304-8373. Tel: 260-244-5541. FAX: 260-244-5653. Web Site: ppl.lib.in.us. *Dir,* Mary Hartman; Staff 5 (MLS 4, Non-MLS 1)
Founded 1901. Pop 13,509; Circ 267,580
Library Holdings: AV Mats 9,986; Bk Vols 83,739; Per Subs 195
Special Collections: Oral History
Subject Interests: Local hist
Automation Activity & Vendor Info: (Cataloging) SirsiDynix; (Circulation) SirsiDynix; (OPAC) SirsiDynix; (Serials) SirsiDynix
Partic in Midwest Collaborative for Library Services (MCLS)
Open Mon & Fri 9-6, Tues-Thurs 9-8, Sat 9-5, Sun (Sept-May) 1-5
Friends of the Library Group

COLUMBUS

S BARTHOLOMEW COUNTY HISTORICAL SOCIETY*, Cline-Keller Library, 524 Third St, 47201. SAN 329-126X. Tel: 812-372-3541. FAX: 812-372-3113. Web Site: www.bartholomewhistory.org. *Exec Dir,* Julie Hughes
Founded 1921
Library Holdings: Bk Vols 1,310
Special Collections: Pence Coll. Oral History
Subject Interests: Genealogy, Hist, Local govt, Local hist
Publications: Quarterly Connection (Newsletter)
Restriction: Open by appt only

P BARTHOLOMEW COUNTY PUBLIC LIBRARY*, 536 Fifth St, 47201-6225. SAN 341-0196. Tel: 812-379-1255. Reference Tel: 812-379-1266. FAX: 812-379-1275. E-mail: library@barth.lib.in.us. Web Site: www.barth.lib.in.us. *Dir,* Elizabeth Booth-Poor; Tel: 812-379-1254; *Asst Dir,* Jason Hatton; E-mail: jhatton@barth.lib.in.us; *Teen Librn,* Christina Kelley; Tel: 812-379-1288, E-mail: children@barth.lib.in.us; *Syst Mgr,* Anna Smith; Tel: 812-379-1279, E-mail: aksmith@barth.lib.in.us; *Adult Serv, Circ,* Sonya Stretsberry; E-mail: circdesk@barth.lib.in.us; *Tech Serv,* Teresa Rhoades; E-mail: catalog1@barth.lib.in.us; *Youth Serv,* Jennifer Tchida; E-mail: jtchida@barth.lib.in.us. Subject Specialists: *Teen serv,* Christina Kelley; Staff 15 (MLS 11, Non-MLS 4)
Founded 1899. Pop 71,143; Circ 75,003
Jan 2012-Dec 2012 Income $3,343,941. Mats Exp $529,000, Books $310,000, Per/Ser (Incl. Access Fees) $16,000, Micro $5,000, AV Equip $10,000, AV Mat $108,000, Electronic Ref Mat (Incl. Access Fees) $80,000. Sal $1,547,815
Library Holdings: Audiobooks 11,519; Bks on Deafness & Sign Lang 362; CDs 6,201; DVDs 13,059; e-books 2,560; Electronic Media & Resources 1,090; Large Print Bks 6,688; Microforms 1,000; Bk Titles 160,888; Bk Vols 172,554; Per Subs 350; Talking Bks 25,000; Videos 918
Special Collections: Talking Books for Blind & Physically Handicapped, rec, cassettes, large print
Subject Interests: Am hist, Archit, Hist, Indiana
Automation Activity & Vendor Info: (Cataloging) SirsiDynix; (Circulation) SirsiDynix; (ILL) OCLC FirstSearch; (OPAC) SirsiDynix
Database Vendor: Baker & Taylor, Checkpoint Systems, Inc, EBSCOhost, Gale Cengage Learning, infoUSA, Inspire, OCLC, OCLC FirstSearch, OCLC WorldShare Interlibrary Loan, Overdrive, Inc, ProQuest, ReferenceUSA, SirsiDynix
Wireless access
Function: After school storytime, Archival coll, Audio & video playback equip for onsite use, Audiobks via web, AV serv, Bilingual assistance for Spanish patrons, Bks on cassette, Bks on CD, Bus archives, CD-ROM, Children's prog, Computer training, Computers for patron use, Digital talking bks, E-Reserves, Electronic databases & coll, Free DVD rentals,

Handicapped accessible, Holiday prog, ILL available, Mail & tel request accepted, Music CDs, Newsp ref libr, Online cat, Online info literacy tutorials on the web & in blackboard, Online ref, Online searches, Orientations, Outreach serv, OverDrive digital audio bks, Photocopying/Printing, Preschool outreach, Prof lending libr, Prog for adults, Prog for children & young adult, Pub access computers, Ref & res, Ref serv available, Scanner, Senior computer classes, Senior outreach, Serves mentally handicapped consumers, Spoken cassettes & CDs, Spoken cassettes & DVDs, Story hour, Summer reading prog, Tax forms, Teen prog, Telephone ref, VHS videos, Web-catalog, Wheelchair accessible, Workshops
Partic in Midwest Collaborative for Library Services (MCLS)
Special Services for the Deaf - ADA equip
Special Services for the Blind - Accessible computers; Assistive/Adapted tech devices, equip & products; Bks on cassette; Bks on CD; Bks on flash-memory cartridges; Braille alphabet card; Cassette playback machines; Cassettes; Closed circuit TV magnifier; Computer with voice synthesizer for visually impaired persons; Copier with enlargement capabilities; Daisy reader; Descriptive video serv (DVS); Digital talking bk; Digital talking bk machines; Dragon Naturally Speaking software; Extensive large print coll; Home delivery serv; HP Scan Jet with photo-finish software; Internet workstation with adaptive software; Large print & cassettes; Large print bks; Large print bks & talking machines; Large screen computer & software; Newsletter (in large print, Braille or on cassette); PC for handicapped; Recorded bks; Screen enlargement software for people with visual disabilities; Screen reader software; Talking bk & rec for the blind cat; Talking bks; Talking bks & player equip; ZoomText magnification & reading software
Open Mon-Thurs 8:30-9, Fri & Sat 8:30-6
Friends of the Library Group

Branches: 2

HOPE BRANCH, 635 Harrison St, Hope, 47246, SAN 341-0250. Tel: 812-546-5310. Web Site: www.barth.lib.in.us/hope.html. *Libr Mgr,* Dave Miller; E-mail: dmiller@barth.lib.in.us; Staff 1 (MLS 1)
Library Holdings: Audiobooks 200; CDs 200; DVDs 200; Large Print Bks 50; Bk Titles 12,000; Bk Vols 15,000; Per Subs 45; Videos 200
Database Vendor: OCLC Openly Informatics
Function: Audiobks via web, Bks on cassette, Bks on CD, CD-ROM, Children's prog, Computers for patron use, Copy machines, E-Reserves, Electronic databases & coll, Free DVD rentals, Handicapped accessible, Holiday prog, ILL available, Music CDs, Online cat, Orientations, OverDrive digital audio bks, Preschool outreach, Prog for children & young adult, Pub access computers, Ref serv available, Scanner, Spoken cassettes & CDs, Spoken cassettes & DVDs, Story hour, Summer reading prog, Tax forms, VHS videos, Wheelchair accessible
Special Services for the Blind - Bks on cassette; Bks on CD; Cassettes; Large print bks
Open Mon & Tues 9-8, Wed & Sat 9-4:30, Thurs & Fri 9-6
Friends of the Library Group

P SUBREGIONAL LIBRARY FOR THE BLIND & PHYSICALLY HANDICAPPED, 536 Fifth St, 47201. Tel: 812-379-1277. FAX: 812-379-1275. E-mail: talkingbooks@barth.lib.in.us. *Mgr,* Sharon Thompson
Founded 1969
Jan 2006 Dec 2006 Income $61,000. Mats Exp $8,100. Sal $46,675
Library Holdings: Bk Titles 21,117; Bk Vols 22,011; Per Subs 20
Publications: Newsletter for Talking Books Users
Open Mon-Fri 8:30-5:30

Bookmobiles: 1. Bk vols 25,000

C INDIANA UNIVERSITY-PURDUE UNIVERSITY*, University Library of Columbus, 4555 Central Ave, LC 1600, 47203. SAN 341-2830. Tel: 812-314-8703. Interlibrary Loan Service Tel: 812-314-8719. Administration Tel: 812-314-8712. FAX: 812-314-8722. E-mail: co-library@iupuc.edu. Web Site: www.iupuc.edu/library. *Exec Dir,* Emily A Dill; E-mail: eadill@iupuc.edu; *Asst Librn,* Madelyn Shackelford Washingtonc; E-mail: madwash@iupuc.edu; Staff 6 (MLS 4, Non-MLS 2)
Founded 1970. Enrl 6,000; Fac 400; Highest Degree: Master
Jul 2009-Jun 2010 Income $70,000. Mats Exp $70,000, Books $50,000, Per/Ser (Incl. Access Fees) $18,000. Sal $280,000 (Prof $200,000)
Library Holdings: Audiobooks 40; CDs 25; DVDs 200; e-books 30,000; e-journals 35,000; Bk Vols 45,000; Per Subs 200; Videos 600
Automation Activity & Vendor Info: (Acquisitions) SirsiDynix; (Cataloging) SirsiDynix; (Circulation) SirsiDynix; (ILL) OCLC ILLiad; (Media Booking) SirsiDynix; (OPAC) SirsiDynix; (Serials) SirsiDynix
Database Vendor: 3M Library Systems, ARTstor, Baker & Taylor, Blackwell, ebrary, EBSCOhost, H W Wilson, Infotrieve, Inspire, JSTOR, LexisNexis, Medline, Modern Language Association, Wilson - Wilson Web
Wireless access
Partic in Academic Libraries of Indiana; Midwest Collaborative for Library Services (MCLS)
Special Services for the Blind - Accessible computers; Assistive/Adapted tech devices, equip & products; Computer access aids; Computer with voice synthesizer for visually impaired persons; Premier adaptive tech software; Scanner for conversion & translation of mats; Screen reader software; Text reader
Open Mon-Thurs 8am-9pm, Fri 8-5, Sat 8-3

CONNERSVILLE

P FAYETTE COUNTY PUBLIC LIBRARY*, 828 N Grand Ave, 47331. SAN 304-839X. Tel: 765-827-0883. FAX: 765-825-4592. Web Site: www.fcplibrary.lib.in.us. *Interim Dir,* Marilyn Robinson; E-mail: marilyn@fcplibrary.lib.in.us; *Tech Coordr,* Melissa Scott; Staff 16 (MLS 2, Non-MLS 14)
Pop 25,855; Circ 165,873
Library Holdings: AV Mats 5,900; Bk Vols 90,192; Per Subs 240; Talking Bks 1,623
Automation Activity & Vendor Info: (Cataloging) SirsiDynix; (Circulation) SirsiDynix; (OPAC) SirsiDynix
Database Vendor: Baker & Taylor, EBSCOhost, ProQuest, SirsiDynix
Special Services for the Deaf - TDD equip
Special Services for the Blind - Bks on cassette; Bks on CD; Closed circuit TV; Computer with voice synthesizer for visually impaired persons; Home delivery serv; Internet workstation with adaptive software; Large print bks; ZoomText magnification & reading software
Open Mon-Fri 9-8, Sat 9-5
Friends of the Library Group
Bookmobiles: 1. Librn, Phyllis Dice. Bk titles 7600

CONVERSE

P CONVERSE JACKSON TOWNSHIP PUBLIC LIBRARY*, 108 S Jefferson St, 46919. (Mail add: PO Box 529, 46919-0529), SAN 304-8403. Tel: 765-395-3344. FAX: 765-395-3733. E-mail: lib@converselib.org. Web Site: www.converselib.org. *Dir,* Coleen Carlson; Staff 4 (MLS 1, Non-MLS 3)
Founded 1916. Pop 2,780; Circ 21,710
Library Holdings: Bk Titles 12,500; Per Subs 59; Talking Bks 292; Videos 1,228
Open Mon 10-6, Tues-Fri 10-5, Sat 10-12
Friends of the Library Group

CORYDON

P HARRISON COUNTY PUBLIC LIBRARY*, 105 N Capitol Ave, 47112. SAN 304-8411. Tel: 812 738 4110. Reference Tel: 812-738-5410. FAX: 812-738-5408. E-mail: hcpl@hcpl.lib.in.us. Web Site: www.hcpl.lib.in.us. *Libr Dir,* Vi Eckart; Tel: 812-738-5407; *Head, Ref,* Autumn Batman; *Syst Adminr,* Jessica Noorani; Staff 2 (MLS 2)
Founded 1904. Pop 34,325
Library Holdings: AV Mats 2,654; Bks on Deafness & Sign Lang 40; e-books 470; e-journals 150; Electronic Media & Resources 26; High Interest/Low Vocabulary Bk Vols 200; Large Print Bks 2,100; Bk Titles 62,644; Per Subs 137; Talking Bks 1,903
Special Collections: State Document Depository
Subject Interests: Genealogy, Indiana, Local hist, Spanish
Automation Activity & Vendor Info: (Acquisitions) Follett Software; (Cataloging) Follett Software; (Circulation) Follett Software; (OPAC) Follett Software; (Serials) Follett Software
Partic in Midwest Collaborative for Library Services (MCLS)
Open Mon-Thurs 9-8, Fri & Sat 9-5
Friends of the Library Group

COVINGTON

P COVINGTON-VEEDERSBURG PUBLIC LIBRARY, 622 Fifth St, 47932. SAN 341-034X. Tel: 765-793-2572. FAX: 765-793-2621. E-mail: cvpldirector@c-vpl.org. Web Site: www.c-vpl.org. *Libr Dir,* Regina George; *Circ Supvr,* Carolyn Story; E-mail: cstory@c-vpl.org; *Children's Prog Coordr,* Kim Kalweit; E-mail: kkalweit@c-vpl.org; Staff 6 (MLS 1, Non-MLS 5)
Founded 1914. Pop 6,922; Circ 95,000
Library Holdings: CDs 617; DVDs 1,031; Large Print Bks 2,029; Bk Titles 22,879; Per Subs 36; Talking Bks 1,523; Videos 1,960
Function: Adult bk club, Adult literacy prog, Bks on cassette, Bks on CD, Children's prog, Computers for patron use, Copy machines, Fax serv, Free DVD rentals, Handicapped accessible, Homebound delivery serv, Homework prog, ILL available, Music CDs, Photocopying/Printing, Preschool outreach, Prog for adults, Prog for children & young adult, Pub access computers, Referrals accepted, Scanner, Serves mentally handicapped consumers, Story hour, Summer reading prog, Tax forms, Teen prog, VHS videos, Wheelchair accessible
Publications: Newsletter
Partic in Midwest Collaborative for Library Services (MCLS)
Open Mon, Tues & Thurs 10-8, Wed & Fri 10-6, Sat 10-2
Friends of the Library Group

Branches: 1
VEEDERSBURG PUBLIC, 408 N Main St, Veedersburg, 47987, SAN 341-0374. Tel: 765-294-2808. FAX: 765-294-4648. E-mail: veedersburglibrary@sbcglobal.net. *Libr Dir,* Regina George; *Mgr,* Gale Nixon; *Children's Prog Coordr,* Paula Hering; *Children's Prog Coordr,* Darla Nine; Staff 2 (Non-MLS 2)
Circ 49,000
Library Holdings: CDs 347; DVDs 713; Large Print Bks 674; Bk Titles 16,243; Bk Vols 16,243; Per Subs 49; Talking Bks 468; Videos 923
Open Mon, Tues & Thurs 10-7, Wed & Fri 10-5, Sat 10-2
Friends of the Library Group

CRAWFORDSVILLE

P CRAWFORDSVILLE DISTRICT PUBLIC LIBRARY*, 205 S Washington St, 47933. SAN 304-842X. Tel: 765-362-2242. FAX: 765-362-7986. E-mail: web@cdpl.lib.in.us. Web Site: www.cdpl.lib.in.us. *Dir,* Laurence Hathaway; E-mail: dir@cdpl.lib.in.us; *Head, Ref Serv,* William Helling; *Electronic Res Librn,* Angela Clements; Staff 29 (MLS 6, Non-MLS 23)
Founded 1897. Pop 25,717; Circ 188,199
Library Holdings: Large Print Bks 391; Bk Titles 111,450; Bk Vols 114,122; Per Subs 311; Talking Bks 1,296; Videos 922
Special Collections: Crawfordsville History bks, microfilm, pamphlets
Subject Interests: Genealogy, Local hist
Automation Activity & Vendor Info: (Cataloging) Innovative Interfaces, Inc; (Circulation) Innovative Interfaces, Inc; (OPAC) Innovative Interfaces, Inc
Database Vendor: Inspire, OCLC FirstSearch
Function: ILL available
Partic in Midwest Collaborative for Library Services (MCLS)
Open Mon-Thurs 9-9, Fri & Sat 9-5, Sun 1-5
Friends of the Library Group

C WABASH COLLEGE*, Lilly Library, PO Box 352, 47933. SAN 304-8438. Tel: 765-361-6161. Circulation Tel: 765-361-6442. Interlibrary Loan Service Tel: 765-361-6376. Reference Tel: 765-361-6443. FAX: 765-361-6295. Web Site: www.wabash.edu/library. *Dir,* John Lamborn; Tel: 765-361-6081, E-mail: lambornj@wabash.edu; *Cat Librn,* Brian McCafferty; Tel: 765-361-6404, E-mail: mccaffeb@wabash.edu; *Ref Librn,* Jeff Beck; Tel: 765-361-6346, E-mail: beckj@wabash.edu; *Acq Mgr,* Susan Albrecht; Tel: 765-361-6216, E-mail: albrechs@wabash.edu; *Govt Doc Mgr,* Linda Petrie; Tel: 765-361-6361, E-mail: petriel@wabash.edu; *Mgr, ILL,* Deborah Polley; E-mail: polleyde@wabash.edu; *Mgr, Ser,* Laura Vogler; Tel: 765-361-6215, E-mail: voglerl@wabash.edu; *Archivist,* Elizabeth Swift; Tel: 765-361-6378, E-mail: swiftb@wabash.edu; Staff 9 (MLS 3, Non-MLS 6)
Founded 1832. Enrl 874; Fac 86; Highest Degree: Bachelor
Library Holdings: AV Mats 12,465; e-books 4,753; Electronic Media & Resources 5,735; Bk Titles 353,559; Bk Vols 438,204; Per Subs 1,010
Special Collections: College Archives. US Document Depository
Automation Activity & Vendor Info: (Acquisitions) Ex Libris Group; (Cataloging) Ex Libris Group; (Circulation) Ex Libris Group; (Course Reserve) Ex Libris Group; (ILL) Ex Libris Group; (Media Booking) Ex Libris Group; (OPAC) Ex Libris Group; (Serials) Ex Libris Group
Database Vendor: Dialog, EBSCOhost, JSTOR, LexisNexis, OCLC FirstSearch
Wireless access
Function: Archival coll, Bks on CD, CD-ROM, Computers for patron use, Copy machines, Distance learning, Doc delivery serv, e-mail serv, Electronic databases & coll, Fax serv, Govt ref serv, Handicapped accessible, Homework prog, ILL available, Libr develop, Music CDs, Orientations, Photocopying/Printing, Ref & res, Ref serv available, Res libr, Specialized serv in classical studies, Telephone ref, VHS videos, Wheelchair accessible
Partic in Academic Libraries of Indiana; Midwest Collaborative for Library Services (MCLS); OCLC Online Computer Library Center, Inc; Private Academic Library Network of Indiana (PALNI); The Oberlin Group
Open Mon-Fri 8am-Midnight, Sat 9am-Midnight, Sun Noon-Midnight

CROWN POINT

P CROWN POINT COMMUNITY LIBRARY*, 214 S Court St, 46307. SAN 304-8446. Tel: 219-663-0270, 219-663-0271. FAX: 219-663-0403. Web Site: cat.crownpoint.lib.in.us. *Dir,* Lynn M Frank; *Head, Circ,* Laurie Kingery; *Head, Ref Serv,* Mary Harrigan; *Head, Tech Serv,* Michael Sheets; *Head, Youth Serv,* Paula Newcom; *Spec Serv Librn,* Barb Houk; Staff 5 (MLS 5)
Founded 1906. Pop 33,069; Circ 344,522
Library Holdings: Bk Vols 93,755; Per Subs 212
Subject Interests: Indiana, Local hist, State hist
Automation Activity & Vendor Info: (Cataloging) Innovative Interfaces, Inc; (Circulation) Innovative Interfaces, Inc; (OPAC) Innovative Interfaces, Inc
Wireless access
Publications: Check It Out (Newsletter)
Partic in Midwest Collaborative for Library Services (MCLS)
Open Mon-Thurs 9-8, Fri & Sat 9-5, Sun 1-5
Friends of the Library Group
Branches: 1
WINFIELD, 10645 Randolph St, 46307. Tel: 219-662-4039. FAX: 219-662-4068. *Br Mgr,* Diane Keeney; Staff 1 (Non-MLS 1)
Pop 20,491; Circ 21,117
Library Holdings: Bk Titles 15,691; Bk Vols 17,801; Per Subs 46
Open Mon & Wed 10-6, Tues & Thurs 10-8, Fri 9-5, Sat 10-2

M SAINT ANTHONY MEDICAL CENTER*, Health Sciences Library, 1201 S Main St, 46307-8483. SAN 304-8462. Tel: 219-757-6345. FAX: 219-757-6161. *Mgr,* Monica A Nowesnick; E-mail: monica.nowesnick@ssfhs.org; Staff 1 (Non-MLS 1)
Library Holdings: Bk Titles 1,401; Bk Vols 1,680; Per Subs 99
Subject Interests: Med, Nursing
Open Mon-Fri 8:30-4:30

CULVER

P CULVER-UNION TOWNSHIP PUBLIC LIBRARY*, 107 N Main St, 46511-1595. SAN 304-8470. Tel: 574-842-2941. FAX: 574-842-3441. E-mail: staff@culver.lib.in.us. Web Site: www.culver.lib.in.us. *Dir,* Colleen McCarty; E-mail: director@culver.lib.in.us; Staff 7 (MLS 3, Non-MLS 4)
Founded 1915. Pop 3,088; Circ 56,315
Library Holdings: Audiobooks 1,306; Braille Volumes 20; CDs 2,238; DVDs 5,461; Large Print Bks 2,500; Bk Vols 39,057; Per Subs 120
Automation Activity & Vendor Info: (Acquisitions) Baker & Taylor; (Cataloging) Evergreen; (Circulation) Evergreen; (OPAC) Evergreen; (Serials) EBSCO Online
Database Vendor: Inspire
Wireless access
Partic in Evergreen Indiana Consortium
Special Services for the Deaf - Bks on deafness & sign lang; Closed caption videos
Special Services for the Blind - Bks on CD; Braille bks; Large print bks
Open Mon-Thurs 9-8, Fri 9-6, Sat 9-4
Friends of the Library Group

DALE

P LINCOLN HERITAGE PUBLIC LIBRARY*, 105 Wallace St, 47523-9267. (Mail add: PO Box 784, 47523-0784), SAN 376-6802. Tel: 812-937-7170. FAX: 812-937-7102. E-mail: director@lincolnheritage.lib.in.us. Web Site: www.lincolnheritage.lib.in.us. *Dir,* Lynn Mehringer; *Youth Serv Librn,* Rebecca Rau; *Bus Mgr,* Becky Hunter; Staff 11 (MLS 1, Non-MLS 10)
Founded 1989. Pop 11,347; Circ 27,901
Library Holdings: AV Mats 1,582; Large Print Bks 152; Bk Titles 52,119; Bk Vols 54,602; Per Subs 115; Videos 1,592
Subject Interests: Genealogy, Local hist
Automation Activity & Vendor Info: (Acquisitions) Evergreen; (Cataloging) Evergreen; (Circulation) Evergreen; (Serials) Evergreen
Database Vendor: Inspire
Wireless access
Function: Bk club(s), Bks on CD, Children's prog, Computers for patron use, Copy machines, e-mail serv, Electronic databases & coll, Exhibits, Fax serv, Free DVD rentals, Handicapped accessible, Holiday prog, Home delivery & serv to Sr ctr & nursing homes, ILL available, Instruction & testing, Microfiche/film & reading machines, Music CDs, Notary serv, Online cat, Outreach serv, Outside serv via phone, mail, e-mail & web, OverDrive digital audio bks, Photocopying/Printing, Preschool outreach, Prog for adults, Prog for children & young adult, Pub access computers, Ref serv in person, Scanner, Spanish lang bks, Spoken cassettes & CDs, Story hour, Summer reading prog, Tax forms, Teen prog, VHS videos, Web-catalog, Wheelchair accessible
Partic in Evergreen Indiana Consortium
Open Mon, Tues & Thurs 9-8, Wed & Fri 9-6, Sat 9-1
Friends of the Library Group

DANVILLE

P DANVILLE-CENTER TOWNSHIP PUBLIC LIBRARY*, 101 S Indiana St, 46122-1809. SAN 304-8489. Tel: 317-745-2604. FAX: 317-745-0756. Web Site: www.dpl.lib.in.us. *Dir,* Loren Malloy; *Adult Serv Mgr,* Janet Woodrum; Tel: 317-718-8008, Ext 12, E-mail: jwoodrum@dpl.lib.in.us; *Youth Serv,* Jodi Wingler; Tel: 317-718-8008, Ext 15, E-mail: jwingler@dpl.lib.in.us; Staff 15 (MLS 3, Non-MLS 12)
Founded 1903. Pop 9,744; Circ 99,602
Library Holdings: Bk Titles 55,617; Bk Vols 58,911; Per Subs 167; Talking Bks 1,206; Videos 1,371
Subject Interests: Genealogy
Automation Activity & Vendor Info: (Cataloging) Follett Software; (Circulation) Follett Software; (OPAC) Follett Software
Database Vendor: EBSCOhost, Gale Cengage Learning, Inspire, Newsbank, ReferenceUSA

Function: Archival coll, ILL available, Photocopying/Printing, Ref serv available, Telephone ref
Publications: "Spolight" Newsletter (6 times yr)
Partic in Midwest Collaborative for Library Services (MCLS)
Open Mon-Thurs 9-8, Fri & Sat 9-5, Sun 2-5
Friends of the Library Group

DARLINGTON

P DARLINGTON PUBLIC LIBRARY*, 203 W Main St, 47940. (Mail add: PO Box 248, 47940-0248), SAN 304-8497. Tel: 765-794-4813. FAX: 765-794-4813. *Dir,* John Dale; Staff 1 (Non-MLS 1)
Founded 1915. Pop 2,332; Circ 20,000
Library Holdings: Large Print Bks 83; Bk Titles 11,900; Bk Vols 12,000; Per Subs 45; Talking Bks 60; Videos 700
Special Collections: Oral History
Partic in Midwest Collaborative for Library Services (MCLS)
Open Mon & Wed 12-7, Tues & Thurs 12-6, Fri 12-5, Sat 9-12
Friends of the Library Group

DECATUR

P ADAMS PUBLIC LIBRARY SYSTEM*, 128 S Third St, 46733-1691. SAN 304-8500. Tel: 260-724-2605. FAX: 260-724-2877. Web Site: www.apls.lib.in.us. *Dir,* Kelly A Ehinger; *Adult Serv,* Louise A Wolpert; *Ch Serv,* Priscilla J Webber; Staff 4 (MLS 2, Non-MLS 2)
Founded 1905. Pop 10,698; Circ 167,442
Jan 2011-Dec 2011 Income (Main Library and Branch(s)) $694,603, State $36,213, County $86,066, Locally Generated Income $505,922, Other $66,402. Mats Exp $107,578, Books $80,672, Per/Ser (Incl. Access Fees) $6,779, AV Mat $13,224, Electronic Ref Mat (Incl. Access Fees) $6,903. Sal $499,646
Library Holdings: Audiobooks 3,827; Bk Vols 99,944; Per Subs 200; Videos 5,787
Special Collections: Adams County Genealogy Coll; Indiana Materials (Gene Stratton Porter Coll); Large Print Coll
Automation Activity & Vendor Info: (Cataloging) Evergreen; (Circulation) Evergreen; (OPAC) Evergreen
Database Vendor: EBSCOhost, infoUSA, Inspire
Wireless access
Function: Adult literacy prog, Audiobks via web, AV serv, Bk club(s), Bks on cassette, Bks on CD, Children's prog, Computer training, Computers for patron use, Copy machines, e-mail & chat, Family literacy, Fax serv, Free DVD rentals, Handicapped accessible, ILL available, Magnifiers for reading, Music CDs, Online ref, Online searches, Outreach serv, OverDrive digital audio bks, Photocopying/Printing, Preschool reading prog, Printer for laptops & handheld devices, Prog for adults, Prog for children & young adult, Pub access computers, Ref & res, Ref serv available, Story hour, Summer & winter reading prog, Summer reading prog, Tax forms, Teen prog, Telephone ref, Wheelchair accessible, Winter reading prog
Partic in Evergreen Indiana Consortium
Open Mon-Wed 9-8, Thurs & Fri 9-5, Sat 9-1; Sun (Sept-June) 1-5
Friends of the Library Group
Branches: 1
GENEVA BRANCH, 305 E Line St, Geneva, 46740-1026, SAN 304-9116. Tel: 260-368-7270. FAX: 260-368-9776. *Br Mgr,* Rose Bryan; E-mail: bryan@apls.lib.in.us; Staff 3 (MLS 1, Non-MLS 2)
Founded 1915. Pop 1,293
Library Holdings: AV Mats 1,668; Bk Titles 29,960; Bk Vols 31,415; Per Subs 62; Talking Bks 93; Videos 758
Function: Adult literacy prog, Archival coll, Distance learning, Doc delivery serv, Handicapped accessible, Homebound delivery serv, ILL available, Photocopying/Printing, Prog for children & young adult, Summer reading prog, Telephone ref, Wheelchair accessible
Partic in Ind Libr Asn
Special Services for the Deaf - Bks on deafness & sign lang; Closed caption videos
Special Services for the Blind - Audio mat; Bks on cassette; Bks on CD; Home delivery serv; Large print bks; Screen enlargement software for people with visual disabilities; Talking bk & rec for the blind cat; Talking bks
Open Mon, Wed & Fri 10-5, Tues 1-5, Thurs 1-5 & 6-8:30, Sat 9-12
Friends of the Library Group

DELPHI

P DELPHI PUBLIC LIBRARY, 222 E Main St, 46923. SAN 304-8519. Tel: 765-564-2929. FAX: 765-564-4746. E-mail: dplibrary@delphilibrary.org. Web Site: www.delphilibrary.org. *Dir,* Kelly D Currie; Tel: 765-564-2929, Ext 21, E-mail: kelly@delphilibrary.org; *Ad,* Sara Daly-Brosman; *Children's & YA Librn,* Lauren Brannon; *Ref Librn,* Jane Cruz; *Tech Serv,* Cathy Kesterson; Staff 15 (MLS 1, Non-MLS 14)
Founded 1905. Pop 7,724; Circ 113,364
Jan 2013-Dec 2013 Income (Main Library and Branch(s)) $805,413, State $50,203, Federal $2,831, Locally Generated Income $725,876, Other $26,503. Mats Exp $146,621, Books $85,783, Per/Ser (Incl. Access Fees) $8,173, AV Mat $21,879, Electronic Ref Mat (Incl. Access Fees) $30,786
Library Holdings: Audiobooks 5,275; DVDs 5,905; Bk Vols 61,087; Per Subs 194
Subject Interests: Indiana, Local hist
Automation Activity & Vendor Info: (Acquisitions) SirsiDynix; (Cataloging) SirsiDynix; (Circulation) SirsiDynix; (OPAC) SirsiDynix
Database Vendor: ABC-CLIO, Baker & Taylor, Bowker, EBSCO Auto Repair Reference, EBSCO Information Services, EBSCOhost, Gale Cengage Learning, Greenwood Publishing Group, Inspire, OCLC FirstSearch, OCLC WorldShare Interlibrary Loan, Overdrive, Inc, ProQuest, SirsiDynix, TumbleBookLibrary
Wireless access
Function: Adult bk club, Art exhibits, Audiobks via web, Bk club(s), Bks on cassette, Bks on CD, Children's prog, Computer training, Computers for patron use, Copy machines, Electronic databases & coll, Fax serv, Handicapped accessible, Holiday prog, Home delivery & serv to Sr ctr & nursing homes, Homebound delivery serv, ILL available, Magnifiers for reading, Music CDs, Notary serv, Online cat, OverDrive digital audio bks, Photocopying/Printing, Preschool outreach, Prog for adults, Prog for children & young adult, Pub access computers, Ref serv available, Scanner, Senior computer classes, Spoken cassettes & CDs, Story hour, Summer reading prog, Tax forms, Teen prog, Telephone ref, VHS videos, Web-catalog, Wheelchair accessible
Partic in Midwest Collaborative for Library Services (MCLS)
Open Mon-Thurs 9-8, Fri 10-6, Sat 10-5
Friends of the Library Group
Branches: 1
NORTHWEST CARROLL BRANCH, 164 W Forest St, Yeoman, 47997. Tel: 574-965-2382. *Br Librn,* Jane Cruz; Tel: 765-564-2929
Open Tues & Wed 10-7, Fri 10-6, Sat 10-4

DONALDSON

JR ANCILLA COLLEGE*, Gerald J Ball Library, 9601 S Union Rd, 46513. (Mail add: PO Box 1, 46513-0001), SAN 304-8527. Tel: 574-936-8898, Ext 323. FAX: 574-935-1773. Web Site: www.ancilla.edu/academics/library.html. *Dir,* Cassaundra Bash; E-mail: cassaundra.bash@ancilla.edu; *Ref Librn,* Karen Lopez; Staff 1.5 (MLS 1, Non-MLS 0.5)
Founded 1966. Enrl 578; Fac 53; Highest Degree: Associate
Library Holdings: Bk Titles 31,340; Bk Vols 32,941; Per Subs 201; Talking Bks 91; Videos 85
Special Collections: History of the Poor Handmaids of Jesus Christ, bks, photos, slides; Old & Rare Book Coll
Subject Interests: Art, Computer sci, Educ, Energy, Hist, Indiana, Libr & info sci, Relig
Wireless access
Partic in Private Academic Library Network of Indiana (PALNI)
Open Mon-Thurs 8am-9pm, Fri 8-4, Sat 8-12

DUBLIN

P DUBLIN PUBLIC LIBRARY*, 2249 E Cumberland, 47335. (Mail add: PO Box 188, 47335-0188), SAN 304-8535. Tel: 765-478-6206. FAX: 765-478 6206. E-mail: dublinpubliclibrary@yahoo.com. *Librn,* Kamala Narayanan; Staff 2 (MLS 1, Non-MLS 1)
Founded 1886. Pop 1,021; Circ 4,146
Library Holdings: Large Print Bks 15; Bk Titles 11,120; Bk Vols 11,800; Per Subs 25; Talking Bks 57
Special Collections: Dublin History Coll. Oral History; State Document Depository
Automation Activity & Vendor Info: (Acquisitions) TLC (The Library Corporation); (Cataloging) Surpass
Open Mon-Thurs 1:30-5:30, Sat 9-1

DUNKIRK

P DUNKIRK PUBLIC LIBRARY, 127 W Washington St, 47336-1218. SAN 376-5393. Tel: 765-768-6872. FAX: 765-768-6894. Web Site: www.dunkirk.lib.in.us. *Dir,* Beth Davidson; E-mail: bdavidson@dunkirk.lib.in.us; *Ch,* Mary Foor; Staff 4 (Non-MLS 4)
Founded 1917. Pop 2,693
Jan 2011-Dec 2011 Income $87,500, City $29,603, County $51,044, Locally Generated Income $5,545, Other $1,308. Mats Exp $33,000, Books $24,000, Per/Ser (Incl. Access Fees) $1,200, AV Equip $2,800, AV Mat $5,000. Sal $80,764 (Prof $33,496)
Library Holdings: Audiobooks 485; CDs 356; DVDs 1,969; Large Print Bks 1,340; Bk Vols 21,655; Per Subs 67; Videos 751
Automation Activity & Vendor Info: (Acquisitions) Evergreen; (Cataloging) Evergreen; (Circulation) Evergreen; (Course Reserve) Evergreen; (ILL) Evergreen; (Media Booking) Evergreen
Database Vendor: Baker & Taylor, Facts on File
Wireless access
Function: Bks on cassette, Bks on CD, Children's prog, Computers for patron use, Copy machines, Fax serv, Handicapped accessible, Holiday

prog, Homebound delivery serv, ILL available, Mail & tel request accepted, Music CDs, Prog for children & young adult, Scanner, Summer reading prog, Tax forms, Teen prog, VHS videos
Special Services for the Deaf - Closed caption videos; High interest/low vocabulary bks
Special Services for the Blind - Audio mat; Bks on cassette; Bks on CD; Cassette playback machines; Copier with enlargement capabilities; Home delivery serv; Large print bks; Talking bks
Open Mon & Thurs 10-7, Tues & Fri 10-5:30, Wed 10-4, Sat 10-2
Friends of the Library Group

DYER

R MID-AMERICA REFORMED SEMINARY LIBRARY*, 229 Seminary Dr, 46311. Tel: 219-864-2400. FAX: 219-864-2410. Web Site: www.midamerica.edu/resources/library. *Theological Librn,* Alan D Strange; *Assoc Librn,* Bart Voskuil; E-mail: bvoskuil@midamerica.edu; Staff 2 (MLS 1, Non-MLS 1)
Library Holdings: CDs 57; Bk Titles 38,828; Bk Vols 40,110; Per Subs 170
Automation Activity & Vendor Info: (Acquisitions) Follett Software; (Cataloging) TLC (The Library Corporation); (Circulation) TLC (The Library Corporation); (Serials) TLC (The Library Corporation)
Special Services for the Blind - Visunet prog (Canada)
Open Mon-Thurs 8am-10pm, Fri 8-4:30, Sat 10-4

M ST MARGARET MERCY HEALTHCARE CENTERS-SOUTH CAMPUS*, Health Sciences Library, 24 Joliet St, 46311-1799. SAN 304-8543. Tel: 219-865-2141, Ext 42133. FAX: 219-864-2146. Web Site: www.smmhc.com. *Coordr, Libr Serv,* Monica Nowesnick; E-mail: monica.nowesnick@ssfhs.org; Staff 1 (MLS 1)
Library Holdings: Bk Vols 1,000; Per Subs 27
Automation Activity & Vendor Info: (Cataloging) EOS International; (Circulation) EOS International; (OPAC) EOS International; (Serials) EOS International
Function: Doc delivery serv, Health sci info serv, ILL available
Open Mon-Fri 8:30-4:30
Restriction: Lending to staff only, Med staff only, Non-circulating to the pub

EARL PARK

P EARL PARK PUBLIC LIBRARY, 102 E Fifth St, 47942-8700. (Mail add: PO Box 97, 47942-0097), SAN 304-8551. Tel: 219-474-6932. FAX: 219-474-6932. E-mail: earlparklibrary@gmail.com. Web Site: www.earlpark.lib.in.us. *Dir,* Connie Sparenberg; Staff 3 (Non-MLS 3)
Founded 1914. Pop 900; Circ 7,721
Library Holdings: Audiobooks 200; DVDs 1,500; Large Print Bks 1,000; Bk Titles 20,530; Bk Vols 22,651; Per Subs 20
Automation Activity & Vendor Info: (Cataloging) Mandarin Library Automation; (Circulation) Mandarin Library Automation; (OPAC) Mandarin Library Automation
Database Vendor: Baker & Taylor
Wireless access
Partic in Wabash Valley Libr Network
Special Services for the Blind - Bks on CD
Open Mon & Tues 1-6, Wed 1-7, Fri 9-2, Sat 8-12
Friends of the Library Group

EAST CHICAGO

P EAST CHICAGO PUBLIC LIBRARY*, 2401 E Columbus Dr, 46312-2998. SAN 341-0439. Tel: 219-397-2453. FAX: 219-397-6715. Circulation FAX: 219-378-1951. TDD: 219-769-6506. Web Site: www.ecpl.org. *Dir,* Ophelia Georgiev Roop; E-mail: oroop@ecpl.org; *Adminr, Tech Serv,* Marla Spann; E-mail: mspann@ecpl.org; Staff 12 (MLS 3, Non-MLS 9)
Founded 1909. Pop 32,414; Circ 46,078
Jan 2009-Dec 2009 Income (Main Library and Branch(s)) $4,805,475, State $93,136, Locally Generated Income $4,640,891, Other $71,448. Mats Exp $151,877, Books $88,030, Per/Ser (Incl. Access Fees) $12,824, Micro $8,907, AV Equip $5,000, AV Mat $24,277, Electronic Ref Mat (Incl. Access Fees) $12,839. Sal $1,842,723 (Prof $552,265)
Library Holdings: AV Mats 2,520; Electronic Media & Resources 289; Large Print Bks 1,796; Bk Titles 187,031; Bk Vols 278,129; Per Subs 157; Talking Bks 6,301; Videos 7,071
Special Collections: History of East Chicago
Subject Interests: Ethnic studies
Automation Activity & Vendor Info: (ILL) Innovative Interfaces, Inc - Millenium
Database Vendor: Newsbank
Wireless access
Publications: Bibliographies; Historical Booklets
Partic in OCLC Online Computer Library Center, Inc
Special Services for the Blind - Bks available with recordings
Open Mon-Thurs 9-8, Fri & Sat 9-5:30
Branches: 1
ROBERT A PASTRICK BRANCH, 1008 W Chicago Ave, 46312, SAN 341-0463. Tel: 219-397-5505. FAX: 219-398-2827. *Dir,* Ophelia Georgiev Roop; Tel: 219-397-2453, Fax: 219-397-6715, E-mail: Oroop@ecpl.org; *Dep Dir, Finance,* Denise Carrasquillo; E-mail: dcarrasquillo@ecpl.org
Special Services for the Blind - Bks available with recordings
Bookmobiles: 1

M SAINT CATHERINE HOSPITAL*, McGuire Memorial Library, 4321 Fir St, 46312. SAN 304-8578. Tel: 219-392-7230. FAX: 219-392-7231. Web Site: www.comhs.org. *Librn,* Susan Miller
Founded 1946
Library Holdings: Bk Titles 1,600; Per Subs 60
Subject Interests: Allied health
Partic in Midwest Health Sci Libr Network
Open Mon-Fri 8-4:30

EDINBURGH

P EDINBURGH WRIGHT-HAGEMAN PUBLIC LIBRARY*, 119 W Main Cross, 46124-1499. SAN 304-8594. Tel: 812-526-5487. FAX: 812-526-7057. Web Site: www.edinburgh.lib.in.us. *Dir,* Cathy Hamm; E-mail: chamm@edinburgh.lib.in.us; Staff 3 (MLS 1, Non-MLS 2)
Founded 1921. Pop 4,800; Circ 51,860
Library Holdings: AV Mats 1,380; Large Print Bks 178; Bk Titles 29,801; Bk Vols 30,201; Per Subs 78; Talking Bks 700; Videos 520
Subject Interests: Genealogy
Open Mon-Thurs 9-8, Fri 9-6, Sat 9-1

ELKHART

R ASSOCIATED MENNONITE BIBLICAL SEMINARY LIBRARY*, 3003 Benham Ave, 46517. SAN 304-8608. Tel: 574-296-6253. FAX: 574-295-0092. Web Site: www.ambs.edu/library. *Dir,* Eileen K Saner; Tel: 574-296-6233, E-mail: esaner@ambs.edu; *Access Serv Librn,* Karl Stutzman; Tel: 574-296-6280, E-mail: kstutzman@ambs.edu; *Tech Serv Librn,* Brent Koehn; Tel: 574-296-6211, E-mail: bkoehn@ambs.edu; Staff 3 (MLS 3)
Founded 1945. Enrl 180; Highest Degree: Master
Library Holdings: Bk Vols 115,000; Per Subs 486
Special Collections: Studer Bible Coll
Subject Interests: Mennonites, Relig
Automation Activity & Vendor Info: (Acquisitions) Ex Libris Group
Database Vendor: EBSCOhost, Gale Cengage Learning, OCLC FirstSearch
Partic in Midwest Collaborative for Library Services (MCLS); OCLC Online Computer Library Center, Inc; Private Academic Library Network of Indiana (PALNI)

P ELKHART PUBLIC LIBRARY, 300 S Second St, 46516-3109. SAN 341-0587. Tel: 574-522-3333. Circulation Tel: 574-522-2665. Interlibrary Loan Service Tel: 574-522-5669. FAX: 574-293-9213, 574-522-2174. Web Site: www.myepl.org. *Dir,* Lisa Guedea Carreno; *Asst Dir, Pub Serv,* Marsha Eilers; E-mail: meilers@myepl.org; *Asst Dir, Support Serv,* Gwen Robison; E-mail: grobison@epl.org; Staff 80.5 (MLS 15, Non-MLS 65.5)
Founded 1903. Pop 90,792; Circ 1,004,652
Library Holdings: AV Mats 46,788; CDs 22,647; DVDs 23,861; Large Print Bks 9,709; Bk Vols 360,457; Per Subs 1,076
Subject Interests: Local hist
Automation Activity & Vendor Info: (Acquisitions) Innovative Interfaces, Inc; (Cataloging) Innovative Interfaces, Inc; (Circulation) Innovative Interfaces, Inc; (ILL) OCLC
Wireless access
Publications: Montage (Newsletter); Monthly Calendar of Programs
Partic in Ind Area Libr Servs Authority 2
Open Mon & Wed 9-8, Tues, Thurs & Fri 9-6, Sat 9-1
Branches: 3
DUNLAP, 58485 E County Rd 13, 46516, SAN 373-9066. Tel: 574-875-3100. FAX: 574-875-5512. E-mail: dunlap@elkhart.lib.in.us. *Assoc Dir,* Kevin Kilmer; E-mail: kkilmer@elkhart.lib.in.us; Staff 3 (MLS 1, Non-MLS 2)
Library Holdings: CDs 110; Bk Titles 34,891; Bk Vols 36,101; Per Subs 51; Talking Bks 88; Videos 391
Open Mon-Thurs 9-8, Fri & Sat 9-6, Sun 1-5
PIERRE MORAN BRANCH, 2400 Benham Ave, 46517, SAN 341-0641. Tel: 574-294-6418. FAX: 574-294-6419. E-mail: pmb@elkhart.lib.in.us, pmb@myepl.org. Web Site: www.myepl.org/epl/pierre-moran. *Br Mgr,* Antonio Martinez; Staff 3 (MLS 1, Non-MLS 2)
Library Holdings: CDs 36; Large Print Bks 114; Bk Titles 31,782; Bk Vols 33,199; Per Subs 51; Talking Bks 90; Videos 201
Open Mon, Wed & Fri 9-6, Tues & Thurs 9-8, Sat 9-1
Friends of the Library Group

OSOLO, 3429 E Bristol St, 46514, SAN 328-9133. Tel: 574-264-7234. FAX: 574-264-7343. E-mail: osolo@elkhart.lib.in.us. *Assoc Dir,* Charles Pieri; E-mail: cpieri@elkhart.lib.in.us; Staff 3 (MLS 1, Non-MLS 2)
Library Holdings: CDs 39; Large Print Bks 59; Bk Titles 26,781; Bk Vols 27,981; Per Subs 32; Videos 141
Open Mon-Thurs 9-8, Fri & Sat 9-6, Sun 1-5
Bookmobiles: 2

S RUTHMERE MUSEUM, Robert B Beardsley Arts Reference Library, 302 E Beardsley Ave, 46514. SAN 374-6275. Tel: 574-264-0330. Toll Free Tel: 888-287-7696. FAX: 574-266-0474. Web Site: www.ruthmere.org. *Curator, Librn & Archivist,* Jennifer Johns; Staff 1 (Non-MLS 1)
Founded 1980
Library Holdings: Bk Titles 1,917; Bk Vols 2,110; Per Subs 15
Subject Interests: Archit, Art, Decorative art
Publications: Ruthmere Record (Newsletter)
Partic in Midwest Collaborative for Library Services (MCLS)
Restriction: Open by appt only, Open to pub for ref only

ELWOOD

P NORTH MADISON COUNTY PUBLIC LIBRARY SYSTEM*, Elwood Public Library, 1600 Main St, 46036. SAN 304-8632. Tel: 765-552-5001. FAX: 765-552-0955. Web Site: www.elwood.lib.in.us. *Dir,* Jamie Scott; E-mail: jscott@elwood.lib.in.us; *Mgr, Ad Serv,* Katie Newby; E-mail: knewby@elwood.lib.in.us; *Mgr, Info Tech,* Clint Trice; E-mail: ctrice@elwood.lib.in.us; *Tech Serv Mgr,* Glenna Stewart; E-mail: gstewart@elwood.lib.in.us; *Mgr, Youth Serv,* Mary Hendrick; E-mail: mhendrick@elwood.lib.in.us; Staff 7 (MLS 1, Non-MLS 6)
Founded 1898. Pop 21,031; Circ 190,363
Library Holdings: Bk Vols 86,495; Per Subs 109
Special Collections: Local History (Indiana Coll); Wendell L Willkie Coll
Automation Activity & Vendor Info: (Acquisitions) TLC (The Library Corporation); (Cataloging) TLC (The Library Corporation); (Circulation) TLC (The Library Corporation)
Database Vendor: TLC (The Library Corporation)
Wireless access
Function: Adult literacy prog, After school storytime, Audio & video playback equip for onsite use, Bks on cassette, Bks on CD, Children's prog, Computer training, Computers for patron use, Copy machines, e-mail serv, E-Reserves, Exhibits, Fax serv, Free DVD rentals, Handicapped accessible, Holiday prog, ILL available, Music CDs, Newsp ref libr, Notary serv, Online cat, Photocopying/Printing, Preschool outreach, Prog for adults, Prog for children & young adult, Pub access computers, Ref serv in person, Scanner, Senior computer classes, Spoken cassettes & CDs, Story hour, Summer reading prog, Tax forms, Teen prog, Telephone ref, VHS videos, Video lending libr, Web-catalog, Wheelchair accessible
Partic in Midwest Collaborative for Library Services (MCLS); Northern Indiana Computer Consortium for Libraries (NICCL)
Open Mon-Thurs 10-7, Fri 10-6, Sat 10-4
Friends of the Library Group
Branches: 2
FRANKTON COMMUNITY LIBRARY, 102 S Church St, Frankton, 46044. (Mail add: PO Box 277, Frankton, 46044-0277), SAN 323-536X. Tel: 765 754-7116. FAX: 765-754-3312. *Br Mgr,* Barbara McAdams; E-mail: bmcadams@elwood.lib.in.us; Staff 1 (Non-MLS 1)
Function: Adult bk club, Adult literacy prog, Audio & video playback equip for onsite use, AV serv, Bks on cassette, Bks on CD, Children's prog, Computer training, Computers for patron use, Copy machines, e-mail & chat, e-mail serv, Fax serv, Free DVD rentals, Handicapped accessible, ILL available, Music CDs, Newsp ref libr, Online cat, Photocopying/Printing, Prog for adults, Prog for children & young adult, Pub access computers, Scanner, Senior computer classes, Spoken cassettes & CDs, Story hour, Summer reading prog, Tax forms, VHS videos, Wheelchair accessible
Open Mon, Tues & Thurs 10-7, Wed 12-7, Fri 12-5, Sat 10-1
Friends of the Library Group
RALPH E HAZELBAKER LIBRARY, 1013 W Church St, Summitville, 46070. (Mail add: PO Box 486, Summitville, 46070-0486), SAN 323-5386. Tel: 765-536-2335. FAX: 765-536-9050. *Br Mgr,* Jill Murray; E-mail: jmurray@elwood.lib.in.us; Staff 1 (Non-MLS 1)
Function: Accelerated reader prog, Adult literacy prog, After school storytime, Bks on cassette, Bks on CD, Children's prog, Computer training, Computers for patron use, Copy machines, e-mail & chat, e-mail serv, Exhibits, Fax serv, Free DVD rentals, Govt ref serv, Handicapped accessible, Holiday prog, Home delivery & serv to Sr ctr & nursing homes, ILL available, Music CDs, Newsp ref libr, Online cat, Outside serv via phone, mail, e-mail & web, Photocopying/Printing, Prog for adults, Prog for children & young adult, Pub access computers, Scanner, Senior computer classes, Spoken cassettes & CDs, Story hour, Summer reading prog, Tax forms, Teen prog, Telephone ref, VHS videos, Web-catalog, Wheelchair accessible
Open Mon-Thurs 10-7, Fri 10-5, Sat 10-1

ENGLISH

P CRAWFORD COUNTY PUBLIC LIBRARY, 203 Indiana Ave, 47118. (Mail add: PO Box 159, 47118-0159), SAN 304-8640. Tel: 812-338-2606. FAX: 812-338-3034. E-mail: ccpltech@gmail.com. Web Site: www.ccpl.lib.in.us. *Dir,* Tracy Underhill; E-mail: underhill.tracy@gmail.com
Founded 1954. Pop 10,000; Circ 69,556
Library Holdings: Bk Vols 35,000; Per Subs 120
Automation Activity & Vendor Info: (Acquisitions) ComPanion Corp; (Cataloging) ComPanion Corp; (Circulation) ComPanion Corp; (OPAC) ComPanion Corp
Wireless access
Special Services for the Blind - Computer with voice synthesizer for visually impaired persons
Open Tues-Thurs 10-7:30, Fri & Sat 10-4
Friends of the Library Group

EVANSVILLE

S ANGEL MOUNDS STATE HISTORIC SITE LIBRARY*, 8215 Pollack Ave, 47715. SAN 373-4471. Tel: 812-853-3956. FAX: 812-858-7686. Web Site: www.angelmounds.org. *Mgr,* Mike Linderman; Staff 1 (MLS 1)
Library Holdings: Bk Titles 410; Bk Vols 575; Per Subs 21
Subject Interests: Archaeology
Open Tues-Sat 9-5, Sun 1-5
Restriction: Staff use only

M DEACONESS HOSPITAL*, Grace O Hahn Health Science Library, 600 Mary St, 47747. SAN 304-8659. Tel: 812-450-3384, 812-450-3385. FAX: 812-450-7255. Web Site: www.deaconess.com/library. *Mgr, Libr Serv,* Julia Esparza; Staff 3 (MLS 1, Non-MLS 2)
Founded 1970
Oct 2005-Sept 2006. Mats Exp $142,000, Books $10,000, Per/Ser (Incl. Access Fees) $52,000, Electronic Ref Mat (Incl. Access Fees) $80,000
Library Holdings: Bk Titles 6,356; Bk Vols 7,400; Per Subs 140
Special Collections: Archive of Nursing; Hospital History
Subject Interests: Complementary med, Consumer health, Hospital admin, Med, Nursing
Automation Activity & Vendor Info: (Cataloging) Sydney; (Circulation) Sydney; (OPAC) Sydney; (Serials) Sydney
Function: Archival coll, Health sci info serv, ILL available, Ref serv available, Telephone ref
Partic in Evansville Area Library Consortium; Midwest Health Sci Libr Network; National Network of Libraries of Medicine
Open Mon & Wed-Fri 8-4:30, Tues 7-4:30
Restriction: Open to pub for ref & circ; with some limitations, Pub ref by request, Pub use on premises, Restricted access
Friends of the Library Group

S EVANSVILLE MUSEUM OF ARTS, HISTORY & SCIENCE LIBRARY*, 411 SE Riverside Dr, 47713. SAN 304-8675. Tel: 812-425-2406. FAX: 812-421-7509. Web Site: www.emuseum.org. *Curator of Coll,* Mary McNamee Bower; E-mail: mary@emuseum.org; *Curator of Hist,* Thomas R Lonnberg; E-mail: lonnberg@emuseum.org; Staff 2 (Non-MLS 2)
Founded 1904
Library Holdings: Bk Titles 6,210; Bk Vols 6,481; Per Subs 31
Special Collections: Henry B Walker Jr Memorial Art Books Coll; Vanderburgh County History Coll
Subject Interests: Anthrop, Antiques, Art & archit, Astronomy, Hist, Natural hist
Open Tues-Sat 10-5
Restriction: Non-circulating to the pub

M EVANSVILLE PSYCHIATRIC CHILDREN'S CENTER LIBRARY*, 3300 E Morgan Ave, 47715. SAN 304-8691. Tel: 812-477-6436, Ext 225. FAX: 812-474-4248. *Librn,* Brandy Fox; Staff 1 (Non-MLS 1)
Founded 1966
Library Holdings: Bk Titles 575; Bk Vols 610
Partic in Evansville Area Library Consortium
Open Mon-Fri 8-4:30

M EVANSVILLE STATE HOSPITAL*, Staff Library, 3400 Lincoln Ave, 47714. SAN 341-0919. Tel: 812-469-6800. FAX: 812-469-6801. *Training Dir,* Jeff Wedding; Staff 1 (MLS 1)
Founded 1944
Library Holdings: Bk Titles 2,610; Bk Vols 2,780; Per Subs 30
Subject Interests: Nursing, Psychiat, Psychol, Soc serv (soc work)
Partic in Evansville Area Library Consortium
Open Mon-Fri 9-4
Friends of the Library Group

Branches:
PATIENT LIBRARY, 3400 Lincoln Ave, 47714. Tel: 812-469-6800, Ext 4215. FAX: 812-469-6824. *Librn,* Kelly Kissel; E-mail: kelly.kissel@fssa.in.gov; Staff 1 (Non-MLS 1)
Founded 2003
Library Holdings: Bk Titles 781; Bk Vols 800; Per Subs 30
Open Mon-Fri 8-6, Sat 9-10
Friends of the Library Group

P EVANSVILLE VANDERBURGH PUBLIC LIBRARY, 200 SE Martin Luther King Jr Blvd, 47713-1604. SAN 341-0676. Tel: 812-428-8200. Circulation Tel: 812-428-8219. Interlibrary Loan Service Tel: 812-425-4721. Reference Tel: 812-428-8218. Administration Tel: 812-428-8204. Automation Services Tel: 812-428-8393. Administration FAX: 812-428-8397. Web Site: www.evpl.org. *Dir/Chief Exec Officer,* Marcia Learned Au; E-mail: mau@evpl.org; *Chief Operations Officer,* Larry Oathout; Tel: 812-428-8244, E-mail: larryo@evpl.org; *Communications & Develop Officer,* Amy Mangold; Tel: 812-428-8242, E-mail: amym@evpl.org; Staff 27 (MLS 22, Non-MLS 5)
Founded 1911. Pop 179,703; Circ 2,750,900
Jan 2013-Dec 2013 Income (Main Library and Branch(s)) $11,462,378, State $681,586, Federal $78,234, County $10,260,608, Locally Generated Income $441,950. Mats Exp $1,558,843, Books $681,688, Per/Ser (Incl. Access Fees) $81,027, AV Mat $349,275, Electronic Ref Mat (Incl. Access Fees) $404,682. Sal $6,693,077
Library Holdings: Audiobooks 7,206; AV Mats 48,971; Braille Volumes 35; CDs 75,463; DVDs 78,950; e-books 38,754; Large Print Bks 17,021; Bk Titles 538,135; Bk Vols 595,351; Per Subs 1,544; Talking Bks 26,156
Special Collections: Best Seller Express, bks, DVDs; Book Discussion; Business Central; Careers; Educational Materials Center; Foreign Language & ESL; Foundation Center; Local History; Online Audio Books; Online comic and graphic novels; Online eBooks; Online magazines; Science Projects; Streaming-downloadable music; Survivors of the Shoah Visual History Coll; Test Books. State Document Depository; US Document Depository
Subject Interests: Bus, Educ, Mgt, Relig
Automation Activity & Vendor Info: (Acquisitions) Innovative Interfaces, Inc; (Cataloging) Innovative Interfaces, Inc; (Circulation) Innovative Interfaces, Inc; (ILL) OCLC ILLiad; (Media Booking) EnvisionWare; (OPAC) Innovative Interfaces, Inc; (Serials) Innovative Interfaces, Inc
Database Vendor: Alexander Street Press, EBSCOhost, Gale Cengage Learning, Innovative Interfaces, Inc, Inspire, Newsbank, ProQuest, ValueLine
Wireless access
Partic in Lyrasis; Midwest Collaborative for Library Services (MCLS)
Special Services for the Blind - Talking bks
Open Mon-Thurs 9-9, Fri & Sat 9-6, Sun 1-5
Branches: 9
CENTRAL, 200 SE Martin Luther King Jr Blvd, 47713. Tel: 812-428-8200. Circulation Tel: 812-428-8219. Interlibrary Loan Service Tel: 812-425-4721. Reference Tel: 812-428-8218. Administration Tel: 812-428-8204. FAX: 812-428-8397. *Customer Serv Supvr,* Margaret Wilhite; E-mail: margiew@evpl.org
Library Holdings: CDs 28,874; DVDs 27,341; Large Print Bks 8,772; Bk Titles 236,334; Bk Vols 268,250; Per Subs 532
Special Collections: Municipal Document Depository; State Document Depository; US Document Depository
EAST BRANCH, 840 E Chandler, 47713, SAN 341-0706. Tel: 812-428-8231. FAX: 812-436-7320. E-mail: ea@evpl.org. *Customer Serv Supvr,* Beth Heil; E-mail: bethh@evpl.org
Library Holdings: CDs 2,953; DVDs 4,668; Large Print Bks 422; Bk Titles 14,825; Bk Vols 15,963; Per Subs 53
MCCOLLOUGH BRANCH, 5115 Washington Ave, 47715, SAN 341-0765. Tel: 812-428-8236. FAX: 812-473-0877. E-mail: mc@evpl.org. *Br Mgr,* Eleanor Nave; E-mail: eleanorn@evpl.org
Library Holdings: CDs 8,636; DVDs 7,601; Large Print Bks 2,076; Bk Titles 67,271; Bk Vols 74,272; Per Subs 175
NORTH PARK, 960 Koehler Dr, 47710, SAN 341-079X. Tel: 812-428-8237. FAX: 812-428-8243. E-mail: np@evpl.org. *Br Mgr,* Nancy Higgs; E-mail: nancyh@evpl.org
Library Holdings: CDs 10,392; DVDs 9,959; Large Print Bks 1,898; Bk Titles 59,934; Bk Vols 67,054; Per Subs 178
OAKLYN, 3001 Oaklyn Dr, 47711, SAN 341-0854. Tel: 812-428-8234. FAX: 812-428-8245. E-mail: oa@evpl.org. *Br Mgr,* Heather McNabb; E-mail: heatherm@evpl.org
Library Holdings: CDs 8,669; DVDs 10,731; Large Print Bks 1,682; Bk Titles 54,199; Bk Vols 61,406; Per Subs 167
RED BANK, 120 S Red Bank Rd, 47712, SAN 371-9774. Tel: 812-428-8205. FAX: 812-428-8240. E-mail: rb@evpl.org. *Br Mgr,* Kate Linderman; E-mail: katel@evpl.org
Library Holdings: CDs 9,119; DVDs 9,546; Large Print Bks 1,373; Bk Titles 54,638; Bk Vols 60,200; Per Subs 212
STRINGTOWN, 2100 Stringtown Rd, 47711, SAN 341-082X. Tel: 812-428-8233. FAX: 812-426-9792. E-mail: st@evpl.org. *Customer Serv Supvr,* Teresa Schneider; E-mail: teresas@evpl.org
Library Holdings: CDs 2,916; DVDs 4,250; Large Print Bks 323; Bk Titles 14,980; Bk Vols 15,786; Per Subs 58
P TALKING BOOKS SERVICE, 200 SE Martin Luther King Jr Blvd, 47713-1604. Tel: 812-428-8235. E-mail: tbs@evpl.org. *Talking Bks & Home Bound Supvr,* Grace Goins; E-mail: graceg@evpl.org
Founded 1977
Library Holdings: Bk Vols 26,156
WEST, 2000 W Franklin St, 47712, SAN 341-0889. Tel: 812-428-8232. FAX: 812-428-8230. E-mail: we@evpl.org. *Customer Serv Supvr,* Colt Hoskins; E-mail: colth@evpl.org
Library Holdings: CDs 3,619; DVDs 4,854; Large Print Bks 395; Bk Titles 23,195; Bk Vols 24,512; Per Subs 105
Bookmobiles: 1. Youth Serv Outreach Asst, Joann Burns. Bk titles 8,478

J IVY TECH COMMUNITY COLLEGE*, Carter Library, 3501 First Ave, 47710-3398. SAN 304-8713. Tel: 812-429-1412. FAX: 812-429-9802. Web Site: wwwcc.ivytech.edu/library/evansville. *Dir,* Maureen Barton; *Librn,* Lenore Bernard; E-mail: lbernard@ivytech.edu; *Librn,* Margaret Moutseous; E-mail: mmoutseous@ivytech.edu; *Librn,* Kate Sherrill; E-mail: ksherril@ivytech.edu; Staff 2 (MLS 2)
Founded 1969. Enrl 5,119; Fac 74; Highest Degree: Associate
Jul 2006-Jun 2007 Income $90,000. Mats Exp $74,500, Books $23,750, Per/Ser (Incl. Access Fees) $4,750, AV Mat $10,750, Electronic Ref Mat (Incl. Access Fees) $33,500
Library Holdings: AV Mats 2,400; e-books 48,000; Bk Vols 7,000; Per Subs 88
Subject Interests: Health, Sci tech
Automation Activity & Vendor Info: (Cataloging) Ex Libris Group; (Circulation) Ex Libris Group; (Course Reserve) Ex Libris Group; (ILL) OCLC; (OPAC) Ex Libris Group; (Serials) SerialsSolutions
Database Vendor: Alexander Street Press, ebrary, EBSCOhost, Gale Cengage Learning, Gallup, Inspire, LexisNexis, OVID Technologies, ProQuest, PubMed, Wilson - Wilson Web
Wireless access
Function: CD-ROM, Copy machines, Electronic databases & coll, ILL available
Partic in Evansville Area Library Consortium; Midwest Collaborative for Library Services (MCLS)
Open Mon-Fri 7:30am-9pm, Sat 10-2
Restriction: Open to pub for ref & circ; with some limitations

GL WILLIAM H MILLER LAW LIBRARY, 207 City-County Courts Bldg, 825 Sycamore, 47708-1849. SAN 304-8764. Tel: 812-435-5175. FAX: 812-435-5438. E-mail: evvlaw@evansville.net. Web Site: www.vanderburghgov.org/lawlibrary. *Librn,* Helen S Reed
Library Holdings: Microforms 4,900; Bk Vols 23,000
Wireless access
Open Mon-Fri 8-4
Restriction: Non-circulating

R SAINT PAUL'S UNITED CHURCH OF CHRIST LIBRARY*, 2227 W Michigan St, 47712. SAN 304-8756. Tel: 812-425-1522. FAX: 812-425-2145. Web Site: www.stpauls-evv.org.
Founded 1956
Library Holdings: Bk Titles 980; Bk Vols 1,170; Per Subs 18
Open Mon-Thurs 9-4

M SOUTHWESTERN BEHAVIORAL HEALTHCARE, INC*, Harold Zimmerman, M D Library, 415 Mulberry St, 47713-1298. SAN 341-0978. Tel: 812-436-4251. FAX: 812-422-7558. E-mail: library@southwestern.org. Staff 1 (MLS 1)
Founded 1975
Library Holdings: Bk Vols 2,200; Per Subs 70; Videos 675
Subject Interests: Mental disorders, Psychiat, Psychol, Psychotherapy, Substance abuse
Restriction: Open to staff only

C UNIVERSITY OF EVANSVILLE*, University Libraries, 1800 Lincoln Ave, 47722. SAN 341-1036. Tel: 812-488-2376. Interlibrary Loan Service Tel: 812-488-1062. FAX: 812-488-6996. E-mail: library@evansville.edu. Web Site: libraries.evansville.edu. *Univ Librn,* William F Louden; E-mail: bl9@evansville.edu; *Head Ref Librn,* Randy Abbott; Tel: 812-488-2727, E-mail: ra2@evansville.edu; *Cat Librn,* Steve Mussett; Tel: 812-488-2464, E-mail: sm37@evansville.edu; *Coll Mgt Librn,* Meg Atwater-Singer; Tel: 812-488-2487, E-mail: ma35@evansville.edu; *Per Librn,* Danielle Williams; Tel: 812-488-2732, E-mail: dw56@evansville.edu; Staff 13 (MLS 8, Non-MLS 5)
Founded 1872. Highest Degree: Master
Library Holdings: Bk Titles 278,690; Bk Vols 281,310; Per Subs 1,396
Special Collections: James L Clifford, 18th Century Materials; Knecht Cartoons Coll; Law (Kiltz Coll)

Partic in Evansville Area Library Consortium; Midwest Collaborative for Library Services (MCLS); OCLC Online Computer Library Center, Inc; State Univ Libr Automation Network
Open Mon-Thurs 7:45am-Midnight, Fri 7:45-6, Sat 10-6, Sun Noon-Midnight

C UNIVERSITY OF SOUTHERN INDIANA, David L Rice Library, 8600 University Blvd, 47712. SAN 304-8705. Tel: 812-464-1824, 812-464-8600. Circulation Tel: 812-464-1913. Interlibrary Loan Service Tel: 812-464-1683. Reference Tel: 812-464-1907. Toll Free Tel: 800-246-6173. FAX: 812-465-1693. E-mail: libweb@usi.edu. Web Site: www.usi.edu/library, *Libr Dir,* Marna Hostetler; E-mail: mmhostetle@usi.edu; *Assoc Dir, Coll Develop Librn,* Martha Niemeier; Tel: 812-464-1834, E-mail: mniemeie@usi.edu; *Asst Dir, Head, Ref Serv,* Joanne Artz; Tel: 812-465-1056, E-mail: jartz@usi.edu; *Distance Learning Librn,* Philip Orr; Tel: 812-461-5328, E-mail: porr@usi.edu; *Govt Doc & Tech Serv Librn,* Mona Meyer; Tel: 812-464-1920, E-mail: mmeyer@usi.edu; *Instrul Serv Librn,* Ashley Blinstrub; Tel: 812-465-1277, E-mail: aeclark3@usi.edu; *Monographs Tech Serv Librn,* Dianne Grayson; Tel: 812-464-1905, E-mail: dgrayson@usi.edu; *Ref/Archives Librn,* Jennifer Greene; Tel: 812-464-1832, E-mail: jagreene@usi.edu; *Ser Tech Serv Librn,* Peter Whiting; Tel: 812-465-1280, E-mail: pwhiting@usi.edu; *Circ Mgr,* Debbie Clark; Tel: 812-464-1922, E-mail: dclark@usi.edu; Staff 10 (MLS 9, Non-MLS 1)
Founded 1965. Enrl 7,821; Fac 682; Highest Degree: Doctorate
Jul 2013-Jun 2014 Income $2,828,389. Mats Exp $832,631. Sal $1,073,914 (Prof $613,567)
Library Holdings: Audiobooks 646; AV Mats 76; CDs 1,872; DVDs 2,657; e-books 208,825; e-journals 65,574; Microforms 102,387; Bk Titles 436,365; Per Subs 212
Special Collections: Communal Studies; Digital Colls; Regional Colls; University Archives. Oral History; US Document Depository
Automation Activity & Vendor Info: (Acquisitions) Ex Libris Group; (Cataloging) Ex Libris Group; (Circulation) Ex Libris Group; (Course Reserve) Ex Libris Group; (ILL) OCLC ILLiad; (OPAC) Ex Libris Group; (Serials) Ex Libris Group
Database Vendor: Alexander Street Press, American Chemical Society, American Psychological Association (APA), ARTstor, BioOne, Bowker, Checkpoint Systems, Inc, Cinahl, CQ Press, CredoReference, Dialog, ebrary, EBSCOhost, Elsevier, Ex Libris Group, Facts on File, Gale Cengage Learning, Hoovers, Inspire, JSTOR, LexisNexis, Marcive, Inc, McGraw-Hill, Medline, Modern Language Association, OCLC WorldShare Interlibrary Loan, OVID Technologies, Oxford Online, Project MUSE, ProQuest, PubMed, Safari Books Online, Sage, SerialsSolutions, Springer-Verlag, Springshare, LLC, STN International, UpToDate, ValueLine, Wiley, YBP Library Services
Wireless access
Partic in Academic Libraries of Indiana; Midwest Libr Consortium
Open Mon-Thurs (Winter) 7am-2am, Fri 7-7, Sat 9-9, Sun Noon-2am; Mon-Thurs (Summer) 8am-10pm, Fri 8-5, Sat 9-5, Sun 1-10

P WILLARD LIBRARY OF EVANSVILLE, 21 First Ave, 47710-1294. SAN 304-8772. Tel: 812-425-4309. FAX: 812-421-9742. E-mail: willard@willard.lib.in.us. Web Site. www.willard.lib.in.us. *Dir,* Gregory M Hager; E-mail: ghager@willard.lib.in.us; *Ad,* Eva Sanford; E-mail: esanford@willard.lib.in.us; *Ch,* Rhonda Mort; E-mail: rmort@willard.lib.in.us; *Spec Coll Librn,* Lyn Martin; Fax: 812 425-4303, E-mail: lmartin@willard.lib.in.us; *Tech Serv Librn,* John Scheer; E-mail: jscheer@willard.lib.in.us; *Bus Mgr,* Emily Phillips; E-mail: ephillips@willard.lib.in.us; *Archivist,* Patricia Sides; E-mail: psides@willard.lib.in.us; Staff 18 (MLS 5, Non-MLS 13)
Founded 1885. Pop 176,000; Circ 477,765
Library Holdings: AV Mats 2,687; Bk Vols 146,151; Per Subs 207
Special Collections: Architecture (Thrall Art Book Coll); Local History & Genealogy (Regional & Family History Center), bks, microfilm, ms; Nineteenth Century Periodical Lit, bd per
Subject Interests: Arts, Humanities, Popular fiction
Automation Activity & Vendor Info: (Cataloging) EOS International; (Circulation) EOS International; (OPAC) EOS International
Database Vendor: Baker & Taylor, EBSCOhost, EOS International, Gale Cengage Learning, Inspire, Newsbank, OCLC FirstSearch, OCLC WorldShare Interlibrary Loan, ProQuest
Wireless access
Partic in Midwest Collaborative for Library Services (MCLS)
Open Mon & Tues 9-8, Wed-Fri 9-5:30, Sat 9-5, Sun 1-5
Friends of the Library Group

FAIRMOUNT

P FAIRMOUNT PUBLIC LIBRARY*, 217 S Main St, 46928-1926. (Mail add: PO Box 27, 46928-0027), SAN 304-8780. Tel: 765-948-3177. FAX: 765-948-3194. Web Site: www.fairmountlibrary.com. *Dir,* Linda Magers; Staff 2 (MLS 1, Non-MLS 1)
Founded 1921. Pop 4,451; Circ 13,486
Jan 2008-Dec 2008 Income $75,800. Mats Exp $13,781. Sal $42,764
Library Holdings: Electronic Media & Resources 176; Bk Vols 12,433; Per Subs 75; Talking Bks 518; Videos 611
Special Collections: James Dean Coll, bks, mag & newsp articles
Subject Interests: Genealogy, Local hist
Automation Activity & Vendor Info: (Acquisitions) Follett Software; (Cataloging) Follett Software; (Circulation) Follett Software; (OPAC) Follett Software
Function: Bk reviews (Group), Bks on cassette, Bks on CD, Children's prog, Computer training, Computers for patron use, Copy machines, Fax serv, ILL available, Notary serv, Tax forms, VHS videos
Partic in Midwest Collaborative for Library Services (MCLS)
Special Services for the Blind - Bks on cassette
Open Mon, Wed & Fri 9:30-5:30, Tues 10-8, Sat 9:30-3:30
Friends of the Library Group

FARMLAND

P FARMLAND PUBLIC LIBRARY*, 116 S Main St, 47340. (Mail add: PO Box 189, 47340-0189), SAN 376-6772. Tel: 765-468-7292. FAX: 765-468-7292. E-mail: farmlandlibrary@frontier.com. Web Site: farmlandlibrary.org. *Dir,* Joseph Skeen; Staff 3 (MLS 1, Non-MLS 2)
Pop 1,780; Circ 9,291
Library Holdings: Bk Titles 11,415; Bk Vols 12,321; Per Subs 52; Talking Bks 215; Videos 152
Wireless access
Partic in Midwest Collaborative for Library Services (MCLS)
Open Mon & Sat 9-1, Tues & Thurs 11-7
Friends of the Library Group

FISHERS

R WESLEYAN CHURCH*, Archives & Historical Library, 13300 Olio Rd, 46037. (Mail add: PO Box 50434, Indianapolis, 46250-0434), SAN 305-0262. Tel: 317-774-7996. FAX: 317-774-7998. Web Site: www.wesleyan.org. *Archives Dir,* Greg Teegarden; E-mail: teegardeg@wesleyan.org; Staff 1 (MLS 1)
Founded 1968
Library Holdings: Bk Titles 6,180; Bk Vols 6,590; Per Subs 60
Open Mon-Fri 8-4:30

FLORA

P FLORA-MONROE TOWNSHIP PUBLIC LIBRARY*, 109 N Center St, 46929-1004. SAN 304-8799. Tel: 574 967-3912. FAX: 574-967-3671. E-mail: floralib@flora.lib.in.us. Web Site: www.flora.lib.in.us. *Dir,* Melissa Bishop; E-mail: mbishop@flora.lib.in.us; Staff 5 (MLS 1, Non-MLS 4)
Founded 1918. Pop 3,190; Circ 33,000
Jan 2011-Dec 2011 Income $131,998, County $125,761, Locally Generated Income $4,737, Other $1,500. Mats Exp $21,125, Books $13,835, Per/Ser (Incl. Access Fees) $3,096, AV Mat $4,194. Sal $87,557 (Prof $39,662)
Library Holdings: Bk Titles 30,884; Per Subs 62; Talking Bks 385; Videos 959
Automation Activity & Vendor Info: (Cataloging) Evergreen; (Circulation) Evergreen; (OPAC) Evergreen
Database Vendor: Inspire
Wireless access
Function: Adult bk club, Art exhibits, Audiobks via web, AV serv, Bks on CD, Chess club, Children's prog, Computer training, Computers for patron use, Copy machines, Exhibits, Fax serv, Free DVD rentals, Holiday prog, Homebound delivery serv, ILL available, Photocopying/Printing, Preschool outreach, Preschool reading prog, Printer for laptops & handheld devices, Prog for adults, Prog for children & young adult, Pub access computers, Ref serv available, Scanner, Senior computer classes, Story hour, Summer & winter reading prog, Tax forms, VHS videos, Wheelchair accessible
Partic in Midwest Collaborative for Library Services (MCLS); Northern Indiana Computer Consortium for Libraries (NICCL)
Open Mon & Fri 10-5:30, Tues & Thurs 10-7, Sat 10-2
Friends of the Library Group

FORT BRANCH

P FORT BRANCH-JOHNSON TOWNSHIP PUBLIC LIBRARY*, 107 E Locust St, 47648. SAN 304-8802. Tel: 812-753-4212. Web Site: www.fortbranchlibrary.com. *Dir,* Sabrina Frederick; E-mail: sabrina@fortbranchlibrary.com; Staff 2 (MLS 1, Non-MLS 1)
Founded 1916. Pop 7,416; Circ 72,641
Jan 2009-Dec 2009 Income $291,753. Mats Exp $65,474. Sal $156,760 (Prof $42,244)
Library Holdings: Audiobooks 1,235; AV Mats 4,148; Bk Titles 58,129; Per Subs 121
Automation Activity & Vendor Info: (Cataloging) Innovative Interfaces, Inc; (Circulation) Innovative Interfaces, Inc; (Serials) Innovative Interfaces, Inc
Open Mon, Wed & Thurs 9-5, Tues 12:30-8:30, Fri & Sat 12:30-5

FORT WAYNE

L ALLEN COUNTY LAW LIBRARY ASSOCIATION, INC*, Courthouse, Rm 105, 715 S Calhoun St, 46802. SAN 304-8829. Tel: 260-449-7638. E-mail: allencountylawlibrary@yahoo.com. *Librn*, Cynthia Ripley; Staff 1 (Non-MLS 1)
Founded 1910
Library Holdings: Bk Titles 19,111; Bk Vols 20,100; Per Subs 23
Special Collections: American Law Review; AmJur; Indiana Statutes; Regional Reporters; Supreme Court Reporter
Subject Interests: Law
Partic in Westlaw
Open Mon-Fri 8-4:30

P ALLEN COUNTY PUBLIC LIBRARY*, 900 Library Plaza, 46802. (Mail add: PO Box 2270, 46801-2270), SAN 341-1338. Tel: 260-421-1200. Circulation Tel: 260-421-2727, 260-421-2728, 260-421-2729. Reference Tel: 260-421-1235. Automation Services Tel: 260-421-1202. FAX: 260-421-1386. TDD: 260-424-2978. Web Site: www.acpl.lib.in.us. *Dir*, Greta Southard; Tel: 260-421-1201; *Mgr, Bibliog & Info Tech Serv*, Sean Robinson; Tel: 260-421-1288, E-mail: srobinson@acpl.lib.in.us; *Bus & Tech Mgr*, Mark Wendt; Tel: 260-421-1216, E-mail: mwendt@acpl.lib.in.us; *Mgr, Ch Serv*, Mary Voors; Tel: 260-421-1221, E-mail: mvoors@acpl.lib.in.us; *Mgr, Communications & Develop*, Cheryl Ferverda; Tel: 260-421-1265, E-mail: cferverda@acpl.lib.in.us; *Mgr, Digital Production Ctr*, Norm Compton; Tel: 260-421-1246, E-mail: ncompton@acpl.lib.in.us; *Financial Mgr*, Dave Sedestrom; Tel: 260-421-1270, Fax: 260-421-1388, E-mail: dsedestrom@acpl.lib.in.us; *Mgr, Genealogy Ctr*, Curt Witcher; Tel: 260-421-1226, E-mail: cwitcher@acpl.lib.in.us; *Mgr, Human Res*, Peter Ford; Tel: 260-421-1231, Fax: 260-421-1389, E-mail: pford@acpl.lib.in.us; *Properties Mgr*, Jim Gumbel; Tel: 260-421-1275, E-mail: jgumbel@acpl.lib.in.us; *Pub Serv Mgr*, Michael Clegg; Tel: 260-421-1301, E-mail: mclegg@acpl.lib.in.us; *Bibliographer*, Kathy Witwer; Tel: 260-421-1207, E-mail: kwitwer@acpl.lib.in.us; *Media Spec*, Stacy Pearson; Tel: 260-421-1211, E-mail: spearson@acpl.lib.in.us; *Reader Serv*, Carol Nahrwold; Tel: 260-421-1236, E-mail: cnahrwold@acpl.lib.in.us; *YA Serv*, Mari Hardacre; Tel: 260-421-1256, E-mail: mhardacre@acpl.lib.in.us; Staff 72 (MLS 72)
Founded 1895. Pop 353,888; Circ 7,831,650
Jan 2010-Dec 2010 Income (Main Library and Branch(s)) $28,663,076, State $24,762, City $443,022, County $32,750, Locally Generated Income $28,162,542. Mats Exp $3,426,587, Books $2,344,921, Per/Ser (Incl. Access Fees) $229,700, Micro $114,995, AV Mat $333,274, Electronic Ref Mat (Incl. Access Fees) $248,385, Presv $72,347. Sal $10,318,939 (Prof $4,075,981)
Library Holdings: AV Mats 353,932; e-books 10,351; Large Print Bks 82,789; Bk Vols 3,246,176; Per Subs 6,792
Special Collections: Fine Arts (Art & Music), bks & slides; Genealogy, Local History & Heraldry (Reynolds Historical Genealogy Coll), bks, film & micro. State Document Depository; US Document Depository
Automation Activity & Vendor Info: (Acquisitions) SirsiDynix; (Cataloging) SirsiDynix; (Circulation) SirsiDynix; (OPAC) SirsiDynix; (Serials) SirsiDynix
Database Vendor: OCLC FirstSearch
Wireless access
Function: Adult bk club, After school storytime, Art exhibits, Audiobks via web, Bks on cassette, Bks on CD, CD-ROM, Chess club, Children's prog, Computer training, Computers for patron use, Copy machines, Electronic databases & coll, Exhibits, Free DVD rentals, Genealogy discussion group, Handicapped accessible, Home delivery & serv to Sr ctr & nursing homes, Homework prog, ILL available, Music CDs, Online cat, Online ref, Outreach serv, OverDrive digital audio bks, Preschool outreach, Prog for adults, Prog for children & young adult, Pub access computers, Ref serv in person, Scanner, Spoken cassettes & CDs, Story hour, Summer reading prog, Tax forms, Teen prog, Telephone ref
Publications: Bookfriends; InSync; Legacy; What's Happening (Calendar)
Partic in Midwest Collaborative for Library Services (MCLS); OCLC Online Computer Library Center, Inc
Special Services for the Blind - Radio reading serv
Open Mon-Thurs 9-9, Fri & Sat 9-6, Sun 12-5
Friends of the Library Group
Branches: 13
ABOITE, 5630 Coventry Lane, 46804, SAN 370-0941. Tel: 260-421-1310. FAX: 260-432-2394. Web Site: www.acpl.lib.in.us/aboite. *Librn*, Susan Hunt; E-mail: shunt@acpl.lib.in.us; Staff 5 (MLS 3, Non-MLS 2)
Library Holdings: AV Mats 17,059; Large Print Bks 2,199; Bk Vols 88,580
Open Mon-Thurs 10-9, Fri & Sat 10-6
Friends of the Library Group
DUPONT, 536 E Dupont Rd, 46825, SAN 370-095X. Tel: 260-421-1315. FAX: 260-489-7756. Web Site: www.acpl.lib.in.us/dupont. *Librn*, Rebecca Wolfe; E-mail: rwolfe@acpl.lib.in.us; Staff 4 (MLS 3, Non-MLS 1)
Library Holdings: AV Mats 20,105; Large Print Bks 3,348; Bk Vols 120,351
Open Mon-Thurs 10-9, Fri & Sat 10-6
Friends of the Library Group
GEORGETOWN, 6600 E State Blvd, 46815, SAN 341-1397. Tel: 260-421-1320. FAX: 260-749-8513. Web Site: www.acpl.lib.in.us/georgetown. *Librn*, Lisa Armato; E-mail: larmato@acpl.lib.in.us; Staff 4 (MLS 3, Non-MLS 1)
Library Holdings: AV Mats 16,385; Large Print Bks 2,048; Bk Vols 110,731
Open Mon-Thurs 10-9, Fri & Sat 10-6
Friends of the Library Group
GRABILL BRANCH, 13521 State St, Grabill, 46741. (Mail add: PO Box 67, Grabill, 46741), SAN 341-1427. Tel: 260-421-1325. FAX: 260-627-7578. Web Site: www.acpl.lib.in.us/grabill. *Br Mgr*, Eric Fry; E-mail: efry@acpl.info; Staff 3 (MLS 2, Non-MLS 1)
Library Holdings: AV Mats 4,717; Large Print Bks 937; Bk Vols 32,427
Open Mon, Tues & Thurs 10-9, Wed, Fri & Sat 10-6
Friends of the Library Group
HESSEN CASSEL, 3030 E Paulding Rd, 46816, SAN 341-1451. Tel: 260-421-1330. FAX: 260-447-5978. Web Site: www.acpl.lib.in.us/hessencassel. *Librn*, Edith Helbert; E-mail: ehelbert@acpl.lib.in.us; Staff 4 (MLS 2, Non-MLS 2)
Library Holdings: AV Mats 7,082; Large Print Bks 1,036; Bk Vols 49,966
Open Mon, Tues & Thurs 10-9, Wed, Fri & Sat 10-6
Friends of the Library Group
LITTLE TURTLE, 2201 Sherman Blvd, 46808, SAN 341-1486. Tel: 260-421-1335. FAX: 260-424-5170. Web Site: www.acpl.lib.in.us/littleturtle. *Librn*, Rosie Stier; E-mail: rstier@acpl.lib.in.us; Staff 3 (MLS 2, Non-MLS 1)
Library Holdings: AV Mats 9,559; Large Print Bks 1,832; Bk Vols 59,483
Open Mon-Wed 10-9, Thurs-Sat 10-6
Friends of the Library Group
MONROEVILLE BRANCH, 115 Main St, Monroeville, 46773, SAN 341-1516. Tel: 260-421-1340. FAX: 260-623-6321. Web Site: www.acpl.lib.in.us/monroeville. *Librn*, Christopher Wiljer; E-mail: cwiljer@acpl.lib.in.us; Staff 2 (MLS 1, Non-MLS 1)
Library Holdings: AV Mats 3,664; Large Print Bks 1,086; Bk Vols 24,565
Open Mon & Wed 12-5 & 6-9, Tues, Thurs & Fri 10-12 & 1-6, Sat 10-2
Friends of the Library Group
NEW HAVEN BRANCH, 648 Green St, New Haven, 46774, SAN 341-1540. Tel: 260-421-1345. FAX: 260-493-0130. Web Site: www.acpl.lib.in.us/newhaven. *Librn*, Linda Jeffrey; E-mail: ljeffrey@acpl.lib.in.us; Staff 3 (MLS 2, Non-MLS 1)
Library Holdings: AV Mats 8,132; Large Print Bks 1,019; Bk Vols 50,749
Open Mon-Wed 10-9, Thurs & Fri 10-6, Sat (Sept-May) 10-6
Friends of the Library Group
PONTIAC, 2215 S Hanna St, 46803, SAN 341-1575. Tel: 260-421-1350. FAX: 260-744-5372. Web Site: www.acpl.lib.in.us/pontiac. *Librn*, Lisa Worrell; E-mail: lworrell@acpl.lib.in.us; Staff 3 (MLS 1, Non-MLS 2)
Library Holdings: AV Mats 5,502; Large Print Bks 276; Bk Vols 28,037
Open Mon, Tues & Thurs 10-9, Wed, Fri & Sat 10-6
Friends of the Library Group
SHAWNEE, 5600 Noll Ave, 46806, SAN 341-1605. Tel: 260-421-1355. FAX: 260-456-1871. Web Site: www.acpl.lib.in.us/shawnee. *Librn*, Pamela Martin-Diaz; E-mail: pmartin@acpl.lib.in.us; Staff 3 (MLS 2, Non-MLS 1)
Library Holdings: AV Mats 13,277; Large Print Bks 2,153; Bk Vols 76,736
Open Mon-Thurs 10-9, Fri & Sat 10-6
Friends of the Library Group
TECUMSEH, 1411 E State Blvd, 46805, SAN 341-163X. Tel: 260-421-1360. FAX: 260-482-5236. Web Site: www.acpl.lib.in.us/tecumseh. *Mgr*, Deborah L Noggle; Tel: 260-421-1361, E-mail: dnoggle@acpl.lib.in.us; Staff 3 (MLS 2, Non-MLS 1)
Library Holdings: AV Mats 7,731; Large Print Bks 907; Bk Vols 53,627
Open Mon-Wed 10-9, Thurs-Sat 10-6
Friends of the Library Group
WAYNEDALE, 2200 Lower Huntington Rd, 46819, SAN 341-1664. Tel: 260-421-1365. FAX: 260-747-4123. Web Site: www.acpl.lib.in.us/waynedale. *Librn*, Don Fisher; E-mail: dfisher@acpl.lib.in.us; Staff 3 (MLS 2, Non-MLS 1)
Library Holdings: AV Mats 15,252; Large Print Bks 2,987; Bk Vols 62,283
Open Mon, Tues & Thurs 10-9, Wed, Fri & Sat 10-6
Friends of the Library Group

WOODBURN BRANCH, 4701 State Rd 101 N, Woodburn, 46797, SAN 341-1699. Tel: 260-421-1370. FAX: 260-632-0101. Web Site: www.acpl.lib.in.us/woodburn. *Librn,* Genie Bishop; E-mail: gbishop@acpl.lib.in.us; Staff 3 (MLS 1, Non-MLS 2)
Library Holdings: AV Mats 3,756; Large Print Bks 408; Bk Vols 24,773
Open Mon, Wed & Fri 10-12 & 1-6, Tues & Thurs 12-5 & 6-9, Sat 10-2
Friends of the Library Group

R CONCORDIA THEOLOGICAL SEMINARY*, Walther Library, 6600 N Clinton St, 46825. SAN 304-8845. Tel: 260-452-2145. Circulation Tel: 260-452-2144. Interlibrary Loan Service Tel: 260-452 3145. Administration Tel: 260-452-2146. Automation Services Tel: 260-452-3148. Information Services Tel: 260-452-3149. FAX: 260-452-2126. E-mail: library@ctsfw.edu. Web Site: www.ctsfw.edu/library. *Dir, Libr Serv,* Robert V Roethemeyer; E-mail: robert.roethemeyer@ctsfw.edu; *Electronic Res Librn,* Robert E Smith; E-mail: robert.smith@ctsfw.edu; *Tech Serv Librn,* Timothy Faile; Tel: 260-452-3147, E-mail: timothy.faile@ctsfw.edu; *Tech Serv Librn,* Richard A Lammert; E-mail: richard.lammert@ctsfw.edu; Staff 7 (MLS 4, Non-MLS 3)
Founded 1846. Enrl 379; Fac 27; Highest Degree: Doctorate
Library Holdings: e-books 5,366; Bk Vols 169,541; Per Subs 719
Special Collections: 16th & 17th Century Lutheran Orthodoxy Coll; Hermann Sasse Coll; Missions Coll
Subject Interests: Theol
Automation Activity & Vendor Info: (Acquisitions) Ex Libris Group; (Cataloging) Ex Libris Group; (Circulation) Ex Libris Group; (Course Reserve) Ex Libris Group; (ILL) Ex Libris Group; (Media Booking) Ex Libris Group; (OPAC) Ex Libris Group; (Serials) Ex Libris Group
Database Vendor: EBSCOhost, H W Wilson, OCLC FirstSearch, OCLC WorldShare Interlibrary Loan, Oxford Online
Wireless access
Partic in Academic Libraries of Indiana; Midwest Collaborative for Library Services (MCLS); Private Academic Library Network of Indiana (PALNI)
Open Mon-Thurs 7:30am-9:30pm, Fri 7:30-5, Sat Noon-5, Sun 3-9:30
Restriction: Internal use only

S FORT WAYNE MUSEUM OF ART*, Auer Library, 311 E Main St, 46802. SAN 328-6312. Tel: 260-422-6467. FAX: 260-422-1374. Web Site: www.fwmoa.org. *Librn,* Anne Hall; E-mail: hall@fwmoa.org; Staff 0.75 (MLS 0.75)
Founded 1922
Library Holdings: Bk Titles 7,500; Per Subs 5
Automation Activity & Vendor Info: (Cataloging) LibLime; (Circulation) LibLime; (ILL) OCLC FirstSearch; (OPAC) LibLime
Open Tues-Fri 9:30 Noon
Friends of the Library Group

S FORT WAYNE NEWS-SENTINEL LIBRARY*, 600 W Main St, 46802. SAN 374-8367. Tel: 260-461-8468. FAX: 260-461-8817. Web Site: www.news-sentinel.com. *Mgr,* Laura Weston-Elchert; E-mail: lweston@news-sentinel.com; Staff 1 (Non-MLS 1)
Library Holdings: Bk Titles 2,198; Bk Vols 2,340
Special Collections: Fort Wayne Newspaper Coll
Open Mon-Fri 8:30-4:30

C INDIANA TECH*, McMillen Library, 1600 E Washington Blvd, 46803. SAN 304-8896. Tel: 260-422-5561, Ext 2215. FAX: 260-422-3189. Web Site: www.indianatech.edu. *Libr Dir,* Connie Scott; Tel: 260-422-5561, Ext 2224, E-mail: cescott@indianatech.edu; *Ref Librn,* Ben Moore; E-mail: bemoore@indianatech.edu; *Cataloger/Ref Librn,* Linda Paul; E-mail: lepaul@indianatech.edu; *Asst Librn,* Patricia Bone; E-mail: pibone@indianatech.edu; Staff 6 (MLS 4, Non-MLS 2)
Founded 1932. Highest Degree: Master
Library Holdings: Bk Titles 37,911; Bk Vols 39,808; Per Subs 262
Subject Interests: Bus, Eng, Sci tech
Automation Activity & Vendor Info: (Cataloging) Follett Software; (Circulation) Follett Software
Partic in Midwest Collaborative for Library Services (MCLS)
Open Mon-Thurs 8:30am-10pm, Fri 8:30-4, Sat 8-1, Sun 4-9

C INDIANA UNIVERSITY-PURDUE UNIVERSITY FORT WAYNE, Walter E Helmke Library, 2101 E Coliseum Blvd, 46805-1499. SAN 341-1214. Tel: 260-481-6512. Reference Tel: 260-481-6505. Administration Tel: 260-481-6514. FAX: 260-481-6509. Web Site: library.ipfw.edu. *Dean,* Cheryl Truesdell; E-mail: truesdel@ipfw.edu; *Head, Pub Serv,* Susan Anderson; Tel: 260-481-5404, E-mail: anderssm@ipfw.edu; *Coll Develop, Head, Tech Serv & Libr Technology Serv,* Marla Baden; Tel: 260-481-6086, E-mail: badenm@ipfw.edu; *Info Serv & Instrul Librn,* Tiff Adkins; Tel: 260-481-6708, E-mail: adkinst@ipfw.edu; *Info Serv & Instrul Librn,* Beth Boatright; Tel: 260-481-6499, E-mail: beth.boatright@ipfw.edu; *Info Serv & Instrul Librn,* Denise Buhr; Tel: 260-481-5759, E-mail: buhrd@ipfw.edu; *Info Serv & Instrul Librn,* David Dunham; Tel: 260-481-6513, E-mail: dunhamd@ipfw.edu; *Info Serv & Instrul Librn,* Shannon Johnson; Tel: 260-481-6502, E-mail: johnsons@ipfw.edu; *Info Serv & Instrul Librn,* Florence Mugambi; Tel: 260-481-6511, E-mail: mugambif@ipfw.edu; *Info Serv & Instrul Librn,* Susan Skekloff; Tel: 260-481-6011, E-mail: skekloff@ipfw.edu; *Mgr Serv Desk, Circ,* Joyce Saltsman; Tel: 260-481-4137. Subject Specialists: *Communication sci & disorder,* Susan Anderson; *Educ, Health, Phys educ, Recreation,* Tiff Adkins; *Bus, Emerging tech, Labor studies,* Beth Boatright; *Children's lit, Communication,* Denise Buhr; *Math, Sci,* David Dunham; *Consumer & family sci, Health sci, Human serv,* Shannon Johnson; *Computer sci, Eng, Tech,* Florence Mugambi; *Humanities, Linguistics, Soc sci,* Susan Skekloff; Staff 26 (MLS 10, Non-MLS 16)
Founded 1964. Enrl 8,996; Fac 819; Highest Degree: Doctorate
Jul 2013-Jun 2014. Mats Exp $835,005, Books $109,964, Per/Ser (Incl. Access Fees) $102,210, Micro $1,996, AV Mat $5,021, Electronic Ref Mat (Incl. Access Fees) $613,000, Presv $2,814. Sal $1,132,065 (Prof $769,438)
Library Holdings: AV Mats 7,745; e-books 223,907; e-journals 78,730; Microforms 280,198; Music Scores 1,492; Bk Vols 366,918
Special Collections: Faculty Publications; Sylvia Bowman Papers; University Archives. US Document Depository
Subject Interests: Bus & mgt, Sci tech
Automation Activity & Vendor Info: (Acquisitions) SirsiDynix; (Cataloging) SirsiDynix; (Circulation) SirsiDynix; (ILL) OCLC ILLiad; (OPAC) SirsiDynix; (Serials) SirsiDynix
Database Vendor: ABC-CLIO, ACM (Association for Computing Machinery), Alexander Street Press, American Chemical Society, American Mathematical Society, American Physical Society, American Psychological Association (APA), ARTstor, BioOne, Cambridge Scientific Abstracts, Cinahl, CQ Press, CredoReference, EBSCO Discovery Service, EBSCOhost, Elsevier, Emerald, Gale Cengage Learning, Greenwood Publishing Group, H W Wilson, Haworth Pres Inc, IEEE (Institute of Electrical & Electronics Engineers), Ingenta, Inspire, IOP, ISI Web of Knowledge, JSTOR, LexisNexis, Marcive, Inc, McGraw-Hill, Medline, Mergent Online, Modern Language Association, OCLC FirstSearch, OCLC WorldShare Interlibrary Loan, OVID Technologies, Oxford Online, Project MUSE, ProQuest, PubMed, Sage, ScienceDirect, Scopus, SerialsSolutions, SirsiDynix, Springer-Verlag, Springshare, LLC, Standard & Poor's, STN International, Thomson - Web of Science, ValueLine, Wiley
Wireless access
Function: 24/7 Online cat, Archival coll, Audio & video playback equip for onsite use, Bks on CD, CD-ROM, Computers for patron use, Copy machines, Doc delivery serv, e-mail & chat, Electronic databases & coll, Handicapped accessible, Microfiche/film & reading machines, Music CDs, Online cat, Online info literacy tutorials on the web & in blackboard, Photocopying/Printing, Pub access computers, Ref serv available, Ref serv in person, VHS videos, Wheelchair accessible
Publications: Helmke Highlights (Monthly newsletter); IPFW Faculty (Online only); Library Facts (Online only); Self-Guided Tour (Online only); Tutorials (Online only)
Partic in Academic Libraries of Indiana; Midwest Collaborative for Library Services (MCLS)
Special Services for the Deaf - ADA equip; Closed caption videos; Deaf publ; Sign lang interpreter upon request for prog
Special Services for the Blind - ABE/GED & braille classes for the visually impaired & print handicapped; Bks on CD; Closed circuit TV magnifier; Computer with voice synthesizer for visually impaired persons; Copier with enlargement capabilities; Dragon Naturally Speaking software; Duplicating spec requests; Free checkout of audio mat; Internet workstation with adaptive software; Networked computers with assistive software; PC for handicapped; Photo duplicator for making large print; Scanner for conversion & translation of mats; Screen enlargement software for people with visual disabilities; Screen reader software
Open Mon-Thurs 8-11, Fri 8-6, Sat 8:30-5:30, Sun 12-11

C INTERNATIONAL BUSINESS COLLEGE LIBRARY*, 5699 Coventry Ln, 46804-7145. SAN 375-4340. Tel: 260-459-4500. FAX: 260-436-1896. Web Site: www.intlbusinesscollege.edu. *Librn,* Cindy Rohlfing; E-mail: crohlfing@ibcfortwayne.edu; Staff 2 (Non-MLS 2)
Library Holdings: Bk Titles 2,191; Bk Vols 2,780; Per Subs 45
Database Vendor: Dialog, EBSCOhost, Hoovers, Inspire, LexisNexis, OCLC FirstSearch, OVID Technologies, ReferenceUSA, Westlaw
Open Mon-Thurs 8am-9pm, Fri 8-4:30

J ITT TECHNICAL INSTITUTE*, Learning Resource Center, 2810 Dupont Commerce Ct, 46825. Tel: 260-497-6260. Toll Free Tel: 800-866-4488. FAX: 260-484-0860. *Dean,* Elizabeth Beardmore; Staff 1 (MLS 1)
Library Holdings: Bk Titles 5,180; Bk Vols 5,390; Per Subs 48
Wireless access
Open Mon-Fri 8am-9:30pm

J IVY TECH COMMUNITY COLLEGE-NORTHEAST*, Fort Wayne Campus Library, 3800 N Anthony Blvd, 46805-1430. SAN 304-890X. Tel: 260-480-4172, 260-482-9171. Reference Tel: 260-480-2033. Administration Tel: 260-480-4280. Toll Free Tel: 888-489-5463. FAX: 260-480-4121. Web

Site: www.ivytech.edu/library/fortwayne. *Dir,* Sharon Shurtz Hultquist; E-mail: shultqui@ivytech.edu; *Circ,* Jonathan Puckett; Tel: 260-480-4246, E-mail: jpuckett@ivytech.edu; *Instr,* Jennifer Traore; Tel: 260-480-4176, E-mail: jheiding@ivytech.edu; *ILL,* Carol Gibbs; E-mail: cgibbs14@ivytech.edu; *Mat,* Ellie Lefand; Tel: 260-480-2032, E-mail: elefand@ivytech.edu; Staff 6 (MLS 2, Non-MLS 4)
Founded 1976. Enrl 7,527; Fac 281; Highest Degree: Associate
Library Holdings: AV Mats 3,950; CDs 445; DVDs 1,900; e-books 39,453; High Interest/Low Vocabulary Bk Vols 125; Large Print Bks 15; Bk Titles 21,419; Bk Vols 23,000; Per Subs 118; Spec Interest Per Sub 110
Special Collections: Family Reading Center, children's bks, per, parenting bks; Practical Nursing, bks, per; Respiratory Therapy, bks, per
Subject Interests: Child care, Children's fiction, Parenting, Puppets
Database Vendor: ABC-CLIO, Agricola, Alexander Street Press, American Psychological Association (APA), ARTstor, Baker & Taylor, Booklist Online, Bowker, BWI, CQ Press, CredoReference, ebrary, EBSCO - WebFeat, EBSCO Information Services, EBSCOhost, Facts on File, Gale Cengage Learning, Gallup, Greenwood Publishing Group, Grolier Online, Inspire, LexisNexis, Loislaw, Medline, OCLC FirstSearch, OCLC WorldShare Interlibrary Loan, Oxford Online, ProQuest, ScienceDirect, SerialsSolutions, Westlaw, Wilson - Wilson Web, YBP Library Services
Wireless access
Function: Computers for patron use, Copy machines, Distance learning, Doc delivery serv, e-mail serv, Electronic databases & coll, Family literacy, Handicapped accessible, ILL available, Magnifiers for reading, Music CDs, Online cat, Online info literacy tutorials on the web & in blackboard, Online ref, Online searches, Orientations, Outside serv via phone, mail, e-mail & web, Scanner, Spoken cassettes & CDs, Spoken cassettes & DVDs, Telephone ref
Publications: Bibliographies (Research guide); Guide to the Library; Newsletter (Monthly); OPAC Guide (Online only); Research Guides
Partic in Academic Libraries of Indiana; Midwest Collaborative for Library Services (MCLS)
Special Services for the Blind - Accessible computers; Assistive/Adapted tech devices, equip & products; Audio mat; Bks on cassette; Bks on CD; Copier with enlargement capabilities; HP Scan Jet with photo-finish software; Large print bks; Large screen computer & software; PC for handicapped; Screen enlargement software for people with visual disabilities; ZoomText magnification & reading software
Open Mon-Thurs 7:45am-8:45pm, Fri 7:45-6:45, Sat 8-2
Restriction: Open to students, fac, staff & alumni

S JOURNAL GAZETTE LIBRARY*, 600 W Main St, 46802. SAN 320-6661. Tel: 260-461-8377. FAX: 260-461-8648. E-mail: jgnews@jg.net. Web Site: www.journalgazette.net. *Mgr, News Tech,* Tom Pellegrene; E-mail: tpellegrene@jg.net; *Asst Librn,* Juanita Smith; Tel: 260-461-8456, E-mail: juanitasmith@jg.net; *Asst Librn,* Lyn Winchell; Tel: 260-461-8258, E-mail: lwinchel@jg.net; *Webmaster,* Mitchell Surface; Tel: 260-461-8196, E-mail: msurface@jg.net. Subject Specialists: *Texts,* Lyn Winchell; Staff 3.5 (MLS 0.5, Non-MLS 3)
Founded 1977
Library Holdings: Bk Titles 1,279; Bk Vols 1,410; Per Subs 27
Special Collections: Journal-Gazette-1885 to Present, micro
Subject Interests: News
Function: Archival coll, Res libr
Open Mon-Fri 6am-10pm
Restriction: Private libr

M PARK CENTER PROFESSIONAL LIBRARY*, Corporate Services, 909 E State Blvd, 46805. SAN 320-183X. Tel: 260-481-2700, Ext 2188. FAX: 260-481-2885. *Mgr,* Virginia Moore; Staff 1 (Non-MLS 1)
Founded 1983
Library Holdings: CDs 10; DVDs 25; Bk Titles 1,041; Bk Vols 15; Per Subs 1; Videos 40
Subject Interests: Mental health, Psychiat, Psychol, Soc serv (soc work)
Partic in Area Libr Serv Authority; Region 3
Restriction: Staff use only

M PARKVIEW HOSPITAL*, Ridderheim Health Science Library, 2200 Randallia Dr, 46805. SAN 304-8934. Tel: 260-373-3690. FAX: 260-373-3692. E-mail: library@parkview.com. *Mgr,* Julie Hughbanks; Staff 2 (MLS 1, Non-MLS 1)
Library Holdings: Bk Vols 2,500; Per Subs 200
Special Collections: Patient Information
Subject Interests: Allied health, Med, Nursing
Automation Activity & Vendor Info: (Cataloging) LibraryWorld, Inc
Database Vendor: EBSCOhost, Elsevier
Wireless access
Function: Doc delivery serv, Electronic databases & coll, Online searches, Prof lending libr
Partic in Midwest Collaborative for Library Services (MCLS); Midwest Health Sci Libr Network
Restriction: Med staff only

C UNIVERSITY OF SAINT FRANCIS, Lee & Jim Vann Library, 201 Pope John Paul II Ctr, 2701 Spring St, 46808. SAN 304-8942. Tel: 260-399-8060. Information Services Tel: 260-479-5001. FAX: 260-399-8166. E-mail: library@sf.edu. Web Site: library.sf.edu. *Exec Dir, Info & Instrul Serv,* Karla Alexander; Tel: 260-399-7700, Ext 6060, E-mail: kalexander@sf.edu; *Assoc Dir, Tech Serv,* Maureen McMahan; Tel: 260-399-7700, Ext 6059, E-mail: mmcmahan@sf.edu; *Health Sci, Ref & Instrul Librn,* Cort Eyer; Tel: 260-399-7700, Ext 6057, E-mail: ceyer@sf.edu; *Pub Serv, Ref Librn,* Cindy Kump; Tel: 260-399-7700, Ext 6056, E-mail: ckump@sf.edu; *Syst Librn,* Celia Price; Tel: 260-399-7700, Ext 6066, E-mail: cprice@sf.edu; *Supvr, User Serv,* Michael Ashby; Tel: 260-399-7700, Ext 6058, E-mail: mashby@sf.edu; *Doc Delivery Spec, ILL,* Barbara Chen; Tel: 260-399-7700, Ext 6061, E-mail: bchen@sf.edu; *Instrul Designer,* Melissa Rasmussen; Tel: 260-399-7700, Ext 6046, E-mail: mrasmussen@sf.edu; *Ser Spec,* Elizabeth Wages; Tel: 260-399-7700, Ext 6068, E-mail: ewages@sf.edu; Staff 8 (MLS 7, Non-MLS 1)
Founded 1890. Enrl 2,350; Fac 193; Highest Degree: Master
Special Collections: ERIC Document Coll
Subject Interests: Art, Counseling, Educ, Nursing, Psychol, Spec educ
Automation Activity & Vendor Info: (Acquisitions) OCLC; (Cataloging) OCLC Connexion; (Circulation) OCLC; (Course Reserve) OCLC; (ILL) OCLC ILLiad; (OPAC) OCLC; (Serials) OCLC
Database Vendor: Alexander Street Press, American Chemical Society, Annual Reviews, ARTstor, Blackwell, Cinahl, CredoReference, EBSCOhost, Elsevier, H W Wilson, Haworth Pres Inc, Hoovers, Inspire, JSTOR, LexisNexis, MD Consult, Medline, Newsbank, OCLC, OCLC ArticleFirst, OCLC WorldShare Interlibrary Loan, OVID Technologies, ProQuest, PubMed, ScienceDirect, Springshare, LLC
Wireless access
Function: Audio & video playback equip for onsite use, Copy machines, Electronic databases & coll, Handicapped accessible, Online searches, Orientations, Ref serv available, Scanner, VHS videos, Wheelchair accessible
Partic in Private Academic Library Network of Indiana (PALNI)
Open Mon-Thurs 7:30am-10pm, Fri 7:30-6, Sat 10-8, Sun 12-10
Restriction: Limited access for the pub, Open to students, fac, staff & alumni, Restricted loan policy

GM VA-NORTHERN INDIANA HEALTH CARE SYSTEM*, Medical Center Library, 2121 Lake Ave, 142D, 46805. SAN 304-8969. Tel: 260-426-5431, Ext 71330. FAX: 260-460-1490. Web Site: www.northernindiana.va.gov. *Librn,* Laveta Diem; Staff 1 (Non-MLS 1)
Founded 1950
Library Holdings: Bk Titles 1,250; Bk Vols 1,500; Per Subs 55
Subject Interests: Allied health, Nursing
Open Mon-Fri 8:30-4:30
Friends of the Library Group

FORTVILLE

P FORTVILLE-VERNON TOWNSHIP PUBLIC LIBRARY*, 625 E Broadway, 46040-1549. SAN 304-8977. Tel: 317-485-6402. FAX: 317-485-4084. Web Site: www.fortville.lib.in.us. *Dir,* Richard Bell; Staff 3 (MLS 2, Non-MLS 1)
Founded 1918. Pop 6,894; Circ 131,673
Library Holdings: Bk Titles 36,999; Talking Bks 2,427; Videos 7,129
Wireless access
Open Mon-Thurs 10-8, Fri & Sat 10-5

FOWLER

P BENTON COUNTY PUBLIC LIBRARY*, 102 N Van Buren Ave, 47944-1299. SAN 304-8985. Tel: 765-884-1720. FAX: 765-884-1720. E-mail: bcpl64@yahoo.com. Web Site: www.benton.lib.in.us. *Dir,* Sandra Furr; Staff 2 (Non-MLS 2)
Founded 1906. Pop 5,059; Circ 42,960
Library Holdings: Bk Titles 30,000; Per Subs 80
Special Collections: Burton Berry Coll; Louis L'Amour Westerns
Subject Interests: Agr, Art & archit, Cookbks, Environ studies, Genealogy
Automation Activity & Vendor Info: (Acquisitions) Evergreen; (Cataloging) Evergreen; (Circulation) Evergreen; (OPAC) Evergreen
Wireless access
Function: Children's prog, Computers for patron use, Copy machines, Fax serv, Free DVD rentals, Home delivery & serv to Sr ctr & nursing homes, ILL available, Microfiche/film & reading machines, Music CDs, Online cat, Online searches, Outreach serv, OverDrive digital audio bks, Photocopying/Printing, Preschool reading prog, Pub access computers, Ref serv available, Scanner, Spoken cassettes & CDs, Story hour, Tax forms, Web-catalog
Partic in Evergreen Indiana Consortium
Open Mon & Wed 9-5, Tues & Thurs 9-8, Sat 9-1
Restriction: Authorized patrons, Non-resident fee
Friends of the Library Group

FRANCESVILLE

P FRANCESVILLE-SALEM TOWNSHIP PUBLIC LIBRARY*, 201 W Montgomery, 47946. (Mail add: PO Box 577, 47946-0577), SAN 304-8993. Tel: 219-567-9433. FAX: 219-567-9433. E-mail: francesvillelibrary@yahoo.com. Web Site: www.pulaski-libraries.lib.in.us/francesville. *Librn,* Helen Vollmer; Staff 1 (Non-MLS 1)
Founded 1916. Pop 1,500; Circ 31,744
Library Holdings: CDs 150; DVDs 800; Large Print Bks 122; Bk Titles 26,000; Per Subs 75; Talking Bks 220; Videos 1,000
Automation Activity & Vendor Info: (Cataloging) AmLib Library Management System; (Circulation) AmLib Library Management System
Wireless access
Open Mon, Wed & Fri 11-5, Tues & Thurs 11-5 & 6:15-8:30, Sat 10-2

FRANKFORT

P FRANKFORT COMMUNITY PUBLIC LIBRARY, 208 W Clinton St, 46041. SAN 304-9000. Tel: 765-654-8746. FAX: 765-654-8747. TDD: 765-659-3047. E-mail: fcpl@accs.net. Web Site: www.accs.net/fcpl. *Dir,* Position Currently Open; *Asst Dir, Head Ref Librn,* Tom Smith; E-mail: tsmith@accs.net; *Head, Ch,* Peggy Williams; E-mail: pwilliams@accs.net; *Head, Tech/Teen Serv,* Jessica Barnes; E-mail: jbarnes@accs.net; *Head, Circ,* Carol Scott; E-mail: cscott@accs.net; *Head, Genealogical Serv,* Grace Gouveia; E-mail: ggouveia@accs.net; Staff 16 (MLS 5, Non-MLS 11)
Founded 1880. Pop 33,000; Circ 266,913
Library Holdings: AV Mats 8,397; CDs 3,508; DVDs 3,339; Large Print Bks 3,377; Bk Vols 141,506; Per Subs 200; Talking Bks 3,473
Special Collections: Genealogy (Fugate & Culver Coll)
Automation Activity & Vendor Info: (Acquisitions) Innovative Interfaces, Inc; (Cataloging) Innovative Interfaces, Inc; (Circulation) Innovative Interfaces, Inc; (OPAC) Innovative Interfaces, Inc
Database Vendor: EBSCOhost, ProQuest
Wireless access
Publications: Library Lines (Newsletter)
Partic in Midwest Collaborative for Library Services (MCLS)
Special Services for the Deaf - TDD equip
Special Services for the Blind - Assistive/Adapted tech devices, equip & products
Open Mon-Thurs 9-8, Fri & Sat 9-5, Sun (Winter) 1-5
Friends of the Library Group
Branches: 3
MICHIGAN ROAD COMMUNITY LIBRARY, 2489 N St, Rd 29, Michigantown, 46057-9566. (Mail add: PO Box 300, Michigantown, 46057-0300), SAN 376-8384. Tel: 765-249-2303. FAX: 765-249-2303. Web Site: www.accs.net/fcpl/mich.htm. *Br Librn,* Rosie McKinney; E-mail: rmckinney@accs.net; Staff 2 (Non-MLS 2)
Founded 1984
Library Holdings: AV Mats 51; CDs 209; DVDs 184; Large Print Bks 121; Bk Vols 20,630; Per Subs 25; Talking Bks 197; Videos 868
Open Mon & Tues 12:30-7, Thurs 9-5:30, Sat 10-2
Friends of the Library Group
MULBERRY COMMUNITY LIBRARY, 615 E Jackson St, Mulberry, 46058-9539. (Mail add: PO Box 489, Mulberry, 46058-0489), SAN 376-8392. Tel: 765-296-2604. FAX: 765-296-2604. Web Site: www.accs.net/fcpl/mulb.htm. *Br Mgr,* Michelle Ogden; E-mail: mogden@accs.net; Staff 2 (MLS 1, Non-MLS 1)
Founded 1984
Library Holdings: AV Mats 40; CDs 341; DVDs 490; Large Print Bks 207; Bk Vols 18,931; Per Subs 37; Talking Bks 489; Videos 881
Open Mon & Wed 1-7, Thurs 1-6, Fri 9-5, Sat 10-2
Friends of the Library Group
ROSSVILLE COMMUNITY LIBRARY, 400 W Main St, Rossville, 46065-9446, SAN 376-8406. Tel: 765-379-2246. FAX: 765-379-2246. Web Site: www.accs.net/fcpl/ross.htm. *Br Librn,* Kathy Scircle; E-mail: kscircle@accs.net; Staff 3 (MLS 1, Non-MLS 2)
Founded 1984
Library Holdings: AV Mats 1,075; CDs 394; DVDs 1,000; Large Print Bks 306; Bk Vols 26,769; Per Subs 50; Talking Bks 374
Open Mon, Wed & Fri 9-5, Tues & Thurs 1-7, Sat 10-2
Friends of the Library Group
Bookmobiles: 1

FRANKLIN

C FRANKLIN COLLEGE*, B F Hamilton Library, 101 Branigin Blvd, 46131-2623. SAN 304-9019. Tel: 317-738-8164. Circulation Tel: 317-738-8162. FAX: 317-738-8787. E-mail: library@franklincollege.edu. Web Site: library.franklincollege.edu. *Dir,* Ronald L Schuetz; E-mail: rschuetz@franklincollege.edu; *Instruction & Ref Librn,* Jessica Mahoney; E-mail: jmahoney@franklincollege.edu; *Tech & Technical Serv Librn,* Susan Leach-Murray; E-mail: sleach-murray@franklincollege.edu; *Circ Mgr,* Heather Myers; E-mail: hmyers@franklincollege.edu; *Acq,* Rebecca Wallace; E-mail: rwallace@franklincollege.edu; *Archivist,* Ruth Ellen Dorrel; E-mail: rdorrel@franklincollege.edu; *Tech Serv & ILL Asst,* Erin Cataldi; E-mail: ecataldi@franklincollege.edu; Staff 6.38 (MLS 3, Non-MLS 3.38)
Founded 1834. Enrl 1,012; Fac 79; Highest Degree: Bachelor
Library Holdings: Audiobooks 768; AV Mats 72; CDs 790; DVDs 1,631; e-books 141,668; e-journals 4,494; Microforms 301,815; Music Scores 611; Bk Titles 104,363; Bk Vols 127,247; Per Subs 226; Videos 6,354
Special Collections: David Demaree Banta Coll; Indiana Baptist Coll; Roger D Branigin Papers
Automation Activity & Vendor Info: (Acquisitions) Ex Libris Group; (Cataloging) Ex Libris Group; (Circulation) Ex Libris Group, (ILL) OCLC; (OPAC) Ex Libris Group; (Serials) Ex Libris Group
Database Vendor: Agricola, American Chemical Society, BioOne, College Source, CQ Press, ebrary, EBSCOhost, Ex Libris Group, Facts on File, Gale Cengage Learning, Hoovers, JSTOR, LexisNexis, Marquis Who's Who, Medline, OCLC FirstSearch, OCLC WebJunction, OCLC WorldShare Interlibrary Loan, Oxford Online, Project MUSE, ProQuest, PubMed
Wireless access
Publications: Catalog of the David Demaree Banta Collection
Partic in Academic Libraries of Indiana; Midwest Collaborative for Library Services (MCLS); OCLC Online Computer Library Center, Inc; Private Academic Library Network of Indiana (PALNI)

P JOHNSON COUNTY PUBLIC LIBRARY, 401 State St, 46131-2545. SAN 304-9027. Tel: 317-738-2833. Interlibrary Loan Service Tel: 317-738-3133. Administration Tel: 317-738-9835. FAX: 317-738-9635. Administration FAX: 317-738-9354. Web Site: www.jcplin.org. *Dir,* Beverly A Martin; E-mail: bmartin@jcplin.org; *Br Mgr, Mgr, Ch Serv,* Sarah Taylor; E-mail: staylor@jcplin.org; *Mgr, Ad Serv,* David Allen; E-mail: dallen@jcplin.org; *Mgr, Coll Serv,* Melanie Johnson; E-mail: mjohnson@jcplin.org; *Mgr, Human Res,* Amber Turner; E-mail: aturner@jcplin.org; *Mgr, Info Tech,* Georgia Vaught; E-mail: gvaught@jcplin.org; *Circ Supvr,* Lori Roberts; E-mail: lroberts@jcplin.org; *Commun Relations Coordr,* Amy Kitchen; Tel: 317-738-2957, E-mail: akitchen@jcplin.org; *Adult Learning Ctr Spec,* Wendy Preilis; Tel: 317-738-4677, E-mail: wpreilis@jcplin.org; Staff 100 (MLS 33, Non-MLS 67)
Founded 1911. Pop 95,000; Circ 1,089,000
Library Holdings: AV Mats 41,091; e-books 16; Large Print Bks 8,198; Bk Titles 296,412; Bk Vols 362,351; Per Subs 556
Special Collections: Johnson County History
Subject Interests: Careers, Consumer, Spanish, Travel
Automation Activity & Vendor Info: (Acquisitions) SirsiDynix; (Cataloging) SirsiDynix; (Circulation) SirsiDynix; (ILL) SirsiDynix; (Media Booking) SirsiDynix; (OPAC) SIRSI-iBistro; (Serials) SirsiDynix
Wireless access
Publications: Connections (Bi-monthly)
Partic in Johnson County Commun Network; OCLC Online Computer Library Center, Inc
Open Mon-Thurs 9-9, Fri 9-6, Sat 9-5, Sun (Sept-May) 1-5
Friends of the Library Group
Branches: 3
CLARK PLEASANT LIBRARY, 530 Tracy Rd, Ste 250, New Whiteland, 46184-9699, SAN 376-9445. Tel: 317-535-6206. FAX: 317-535-6018. E-mail: cpl_ref@jcplin.org. *Br Mgr,* Tiffany Wilson; E-mail: twilson@jcplin.org; *Ch Serv Librn,* Sue Salamone; E-mail: ssalamone@jcplin.org; *Circ Mgr,* Holly Kubancsek; E-mail: hkubancsek@jcplin.org; Staff 7 (MLS 4, Non-MLS 3)
Function: Adult literacy prog, Audio & video playback equip for onsite use, AV serv, Bk club(s), CD-ROM, Computer training, Copy machines, e-mail serv, E-Reserves, Electronic databases & coll, Handicapped accessible, Home delivery & serv to Sr ctr & nursing homes, Homebound delivery serv, ILL available, Magnifiers for reading, Music CDs, Photocopying/Printing, Preschool outreach, Prog for adults, Prog for children & young adult, Ref serv available, Senior computer classes, Serves mentally handicapped consumers, Summer reading prog, Tax forms, Telephone ref, VHS videos, Video lending libr, Wheelchair accessible, Workshops
Open Mon-Thurs 9-8, Fri 9-6, Sat 9-5
Friends of the Library Group
TRAFALGAR BRANCH, 424 Tower St, Trafalgar, 46181. Tel: 317-878-9560. FAX: 317-878-4093. E-mail: tra-ref@jcplin.org. *Br Mgr,* Todd Jones; E-mail: tjones@jcplin.org; *Ch Serv Librn,* Annemarie Wallace; E-mail: awallace@jcplin.org; *Circ Supvr,* Jen Sinclair; E-mail: jsinclair@jcplin.org; *Ch Serv,* Laura Harris; E-mail: lharris@jcplin.org; Staff 8 (MLS 4, Non-MLS 4)
Open Mon-Thurs 9-8, Fri 9-6, Sat 9-5
WHITE RIVER LIBRARY, 1664 Library Blvd, Greenwood, 46142, SAN 320-9539. Tel: 317-885-1330. FAX: 317-882-4117. E-mail: wrl_ref@jcplin.org. *Br Mgr,* Linda Kilbert; E-mail: lkilbert@jcplin.org; *Ad,* Erin Kirchhoff; E-mail: ekirchhoff@jcplin.org; *Ch Serv Librn,* Laura Carr; E-mail: lcarr@jcplin.org; *Digital Serv Librn,* Davin Kolderup; E-mail: dkolderup@jcplin.org; *Spec Pop Librn,* Beth Hayes; E-mail: bhayes@jcplin.org; *Mgr, Ch Serv,* Beth Martin; E-mail: emartin@jcplin.org; Staff 18 (MLS 8, Non-MLS 10)

Open Mon-Thurs 9-9, Fri 9-6, Sat 9-5, Sun (Sept-May) 1-5
Friends of the Library Group

FREMONT

P FREMONT PUBLIC LIBRARY, 1004 W Toledo St, 46737. (Mail add: PO Box 7, 46737-0007), SAN 376-2653. Tel: 260-495-7157. Administration Tel: 260-495-9227. FAX: 260-495-7127. E-mail: library@fremont.lib.in.us. Web Site: www.fremont.lib.in.us. *Dir,* Hope Wilson; E-mail: hwilson@fremont.lib.in.us; Staff 9 (MLS 3, Non-MLS 6)
Founded 1919. Pop 7,041; Circ 78,282
Library Holdings: Audiobooks 2,998; DVDs 6,322; e-books 3,322; Large Print Bks 2,740; Bk Titles 51,145; Per Subs 147
Automation Activity & Vendor Info: (Cataloging) TLC (The Library Corporation); (Circulation) TLC (The Library Corporation); (OPAC) TLC (The Library Corporation)
Database Vendor: Inspire, ProQuest
Wireless access
Function: Adult bk club, Audio & video playback equip for onsite use, Audiobks via web, Bk club(s), Bks on cassette, Bks on CD, Children's prog, Computer training, Computers for patron use, Copy machines, Doc delivery serv, e-mail & chat, Electronic databases & coll, Exhibits, Free DVD rentals, Holiday prog, Homebound delivery serv, Homework prog, ILL available, Photocopying/Printing, Printer for laptops & handheld devices, Prog for adults, Prog for children & young adult, Pub access computers, Scanner, Senior computer classes, Story hour, Summer & winter reading prog, Summer reading prog, Tax forms, Teen prog, VHS videos, Wheelchair accessible, Winter reading prog
Open Mon-Thurs 9-8, Fri 10-6, Sat 10-4
Restriction: Non-circulating coll, Non-resident fee
Friends of the Library Group

FRENCH LICK

P MELTON PUBLIC LIBRARY*, 8496 W College St, 47432-1026. SAN 304-9035. Tel: 812-936-2177. FAX: 812-936-7524. Web Site: www.melton.lib.in.us. *Dir,* Suzie Owen; Staff 3 (MLS 2, Non-MLS 1)
Pop 4,767; Circ 36,400
Library Holdings: Bk Titles 31,610; Bk Vols 33,190; Per Subs 61; Talking Bks 374; Videos 1,269
Database Vendor: SirsiDynix
Wireless access
Partic in Evergreen Indiana Consortium
Open Mon & Fri 10-5, Tues & Thurs 10-7, Sat 10-3
Friends of the Library Group

GARRETT

P GARRETT PUBLIC LIBRARY*, 107 W Houston St, 46738. SAN 304-9043. Tel: 260-357-5485. FAX: 260-357-5170. Web Site: www.gpl.lib.in.us. *Dir,* Catherine Birdseye; E-mail: cbirdseye@gpl.lib.in.us; *Adult Serv,* Andrea Basinger; E-mail: abasinger@gpl.lib.in.is; *Ch Serv,* Deborah Buechner; E-mail: dbuechner@gpl.lib.in.us; *Tech Serv,* Tammy Savage; E-mail: tsavage@gpl.lib.in.us; Staff 13 (MLS 1, Non-MLS 12)
Founded 1914. Pop 8,065; Circ 80,000
Library Holdings: AV Mats 3,000; Large Print Bks 650; Bk Titles 30,000; Bk Vols 33,000; Per Subs 109
Special Collections: Cameron Park Indian Relics Coll
Automation Activity & Vendor Info: (Cataloging) TLC (The Library Corporation); (Circulation) TLC (The Library Corporation); (OPAC) TLC (The Library Corporation)
Wireless access
Function: Handicapped accessible, Homebound delivery serv, ILL available, Large print keyboards, Prog for children & young adult, Ref serv available, Summer reading prog, Wheelchair accessible
Special Services for the Deaf - TTY equip
Open Mon-Thurs 9-8, Fri 9-6, Sat 9-4
Friends of the Library Group

GARY

P GARY PUBLIC LIBRARY*, Administrative Office, 220 W Fifth Ave, 46402-1215. SAN 341-1729. Tel: 219-886-2484. FAX: 219-886-6829.
Founded 1908
Wireless access
Branches: 4
BRUNSWICK BRANCH, 4030 W Fifth Ave, 46406. Tel: 219-944-9402. FAX: 219-944-9644. *Librn,* Kenneth Green
Open Mon-Thurs 12-8, Fri & Sat 10-5
W E B DU BOIS BRANCH, 1835 Broadway, 46407-2298, SAN 341-1753. Tel: 219-886-9120. FAX: 219-886-9319. *Head Librn,* Diana Morrow; Staff 2 (MLS 1, Non-MLS 1)
Founded 1979
Library Holdings: AV Mats 1,012; Large Print Bks 115; Bk Titles 71,410; Bk Vols 73,911; Per Subs 68; Videos 290
Special Collections: Afro-American Rare Book Coll, micro-fiche
Open Mon-Thurs 12-8, Fri & Sat 10-5
Friends of the Library Group
JOHN F KENNEDY BRANCH, 3953 Broadway, 46408-1799, SAN 341-1818. Tel: 219-887-8112. FAX: 219-887-5967. *Head Librn,* Brenda Moore; Staff 2 (Non-MLS 2)
Library Holdings: AV Mats 815; Large Print Bks 91; Bk Titles 74,911; Bk Vols 75,612; Per Subs 56; Videos 211
Open Mon-Thurs 12-8, Fri & Sat 10-5
Friends of the Library Group
CARTER G WOODSON BRANCH, 501 S Lake St, 46403-2408, SAN 341-1907. Tel: 219-938-3941. FAX: 219-938-8759. *Br Mgr,* Patience A Ojomo; E-mail: ojompa@garypubliclibrary.org; Staff 2 (MLS 1, Non-MLS 1)
Library Holdings: AV Mats 791; Bk Titles 58,911; Bk Vols 59,612; Per Subs 52; Videos 231
Open Mon-Thurs 12-8, Fri & Sat 10-5
Friends of the Library Group

C INDIANA UNIVERSITY NORTHWEST, John W Anderson Library, 3400 Broadway, 46408. SAN 304-9051. Tel: 219-980-6580. Circulation Tel: 219-980-6585. Interlibrary Loan Service Tel: 219-980-6933. Reference Tel: 219-980-6582. FAX: 219-980-6558. E-mail: iunlib@iun.edu. Web Site: www.iun.edu/~lib. *Dir of Libr Serv,* Timothy Sutherland; Tel: 219-980-6946; *Head, Tech Serv,* Cynthia Szymanski; Tel: 219-980-6521, E-mail: cszymans@iun.edu; *Archivist/Librn,* Stephen McShane; Tel: 219-980-6628, E-mail: smshane@iun.edu; *GIS/Adaptive Technologies Librn,* Scott Sandberg; Tel: 219-980-6928, E-mail: smsandbe@iun.edu; *Coordr of Ref Serv, Libr Instruction,* Arena Stevens; Tel: 219-980-6625, E-mail: astevens@iun.edu; *Coordr, Libr Instruction, Ref Serv,* Latrice Booker; Tel: 219-980-6547, E-mail: lbooker@iun.edu; *Syst Coordr, Web Coordr,* Nicholas Rosselli; Tel: 219-980-6929, E-mail: rosselli@iun.edu; Staff 14 (MLS 7, Non-MLS 7)
Founded 1940. Enrl 4,200; Fac 175; Highest Degree: Master
Library Holdings: Bk Vols 264,000
Special Collections: Calumet Regional Archives; Northwest Center for Data & Analysis. US Document Depository
Automation Activity & Vendor Info: (Acquisitions) SirsiDynix; (Cataloging) SirsiDynix; (Circulation) SirsiDynix; (ILL) SirsiDynix; (OPAC) SirsiDynix; (Serials) SirsiDynix
Database Vendor: American Chemical Society, Annual Reviews, BioOne, Blackwell, Cambridge Scientific Abstracts, Checkpoint Systems, Inc, College Source, Community of Science (COS), CountryWatch, CQ Press, Dialog, EBSCOhost, Gale Cengage Learning, Inspire, JSTOR, LexisNexis, Mergent Online, OCLC WorldShare Interlibrary Loan, OVID Technologies, ProQuest, SirsiDynix
Wireless access
Partic in Academic Libraries of Indiana; Midwest Collaborative for Library Services (MCLS); OCLC Online Computer Library Center, Inc
Open Mon-Thurs 8am-8:30pm, Fri 8-3, Sat 10-5, Sun 1-5

CM INDIANA UNIVERSITY SCHOOL OF MEDICINE-NORTHWEST CENTER FOR MEDICAL EDUCATION*, Steven C Beering Medical Library, 3400 Broadway, 46408-1197. SAN 320-1848. Tel: 219-980-6709, 219-980-6852. Toll Free Tel: 800-437-5409, Ext 6852. FAX: 219-980-6524. Web Site: www.medicine.iu.edu/body.cfm?id=4973. *Coordr,* Corona Wiley; E-mail: cwiley@iun.edu; Staff 2 (MLS 1, Non-MLS 1)
Library Holdings: Bk Titles 1,800; Per Subs 15
Wireless access
Open Mon-Thurs 8-5, Fri 8-4

J IVY TECH COMMUNITY COLLEGE-NORTHWEST*, Gary Campus Library, 1440 E 35th Ave, 46409-1499. SAN 304-906X. Tel: 219-981-4410. FAX: 219-981-4415. Web Site: wwwcc.ivytech.edu/library/northwest. *Regional Dir,* Barbara K Weaver; E-mail: bweaver@ivytech.edu; *Asst Mgr, Tech Serv,* Nick Vasil; E-mail: nvasil@ivytech.edu; *Computer Lab Tech,* Linda Holcomb; E-mail: lholcomb@ivytech.edu; Staff 4 (MLS 1, Non-MLS 3)
Founded 1972. Enrl 5,000
Library Holdings: AV Mats 4,295; e-books 28,029; e-journals 14,235; Electronic Media & Resources 42; Bk Titles 13,805; Per Subs 160
Automation Activity & Vendor Info: (Cataloging) Ex Libris Group; (OPAC) Ex Libris Group
Partic in Duplicate Exchange Union; Midwest Collaborative for Library Services (MCLS)
Open Mon-Thurs 8am-9:30pm, Fri 8-6, Sat 9-2

M METHODIST HOSPITAL*, North Lake Campus-Health Science Libraries, 600 Grant St, 46402. SAN 304-9086. Tel: 219-886-4554. FAX: 219-886-4271. Web Site: www.methodisthospitals.org. *Librn,* Fannie Ilievski; Staff 2 (MLS 1, Non-MLS 1)
Founded 1950
Library Holdings: Bk Titles 3,000; Bk Vols 3,500; Per Subs 150
Subject Interests: Cardiology, Internal med, Oncology
Function: AV serv, ILL available, Photocopying/Printing

Open Mon-Fri 8-4
Restriction: Staff use only
Friends of the Library Group

GAS CITY

P GAS CITY-MILL TOWNSHIP PUBLIC LIBRARY*, 135 E Main St, 46933-1496. SAN 304-9108. Tel: 765-674-4718. FAX: 765-674-5176. E-mail: gascitypl@yahoo.com. Web Site: www.gcmtpl.lib.in.us. *Libr Dir,* Nancy Lynn Bryant; E-mail: nlb723@yahoo.com; Staff 10 (Non-MLS 10)
Founded 1913. Pop 9,449; Circ 77,959
Library Holdings: AV Mats 4,841; Bk Vols 35,926; Per Subs 136
Automation Activity & Vendor Info: (Acquisitions) Innovative Interfaces, Inc; (Cataloging) Innovative Interfaces, Inc; (Circulation) Innovative Interfaces, Inc; (OPAC) Innovative Interfaces, Inc
Partic in Midwest Collaborative for Library Services (MCLS)
Open Mon-Thurs 10-8, Fri & Sat 10-5

GOODLAND

P GOODLAND & GRANT TOWNSHIP PUBLIC LIBRARY, 111 S Newton St, 47948. (Mail add: PO Box 405, 47948-0405), SAN 304-9124. Tel: 219-297-4431. FAX: 219-297-4431. *Dir,* Joyce Crane; E-mail: jcrane@goodland.lib.in.us; Staff 2 (Non-MLS 2)
Founded 1907. Pop 1,100; Circ 9,829
Jan 2014-Dec 2014 Income $165,000
Library Holdings: Bk Titles 16,791; Bk Vols 18,919; Per Subs 50; Talking Bks 175; Videos 1,000
Subject Interests: Indiana
Automation Activity & Vendor Info: (Acquisitions) Koha; (Cataloging) Koha; (OPAC) Koha
Wireless access
Open Mon-Wed & Fri 12-5, Thurs 12-8, Sat 9-1

GOSHEN

GOSHEN COLLEGE

C HAROLD & WILMA GOOD LIBRARY, 1700 S Main, 46526-4794, SAN 341-1931. Tel: 574-535-7427. Interlibrary Loan Service Tel: 574-535-7430. Reference Tel: 574-535-7431. FAX: 574-535-7438. E-mail: library@goshen.edu. Web Site: www.goshen.edu/library. *Dir,* Fritz Hartman; Tel: 574-535-7423, E-mail: fritzdh@goshen.edu; *Head, Ref & Instruction,* Eric Bradley; Tel: 574-535-7424, E-mail: ebradley@goshen.edu; *Head, Tech Serv, Ser & Syst,* Position Currently Open; *Ref & Instruction Librn,* Position Currently Open; *Day Circ Mgr,* Ruth Hochstetler; E-mail: rutheh2@goshen.edu; *Evening Circ Supvr,* Esther Guedea; E-mail: esthergg@goshen.edu; *Libr Asst,* Yoder Tillie; Tel: 574-535-7637, E-mail: matildaky@goshen.edu. Subject Specialists: *Bus, Communications, English,* Fritz Hartman; *Educ, Hist, Psychol,* Eric Bradley; Staff 3.5 (MLS 3.5)
Founded 1894. Enrl 889; Highest Degree: Master
Jul 2014-Jun 2015 Income (Main Library and Branch(s)) $522,915. Mats Exp $233,507, Books $28,400, Per/Ser (Incl. Access Fees) $112,000, Micro $2,500, Electronic Ref Mat (Incl. Access Fees) $3,145. Sal $209,764 (Prof $156,464)
Library Holdings: AV Mats 3,176; e-books 8,996; Bk Vols 134,453; Per Subs 416
Special Collections: Early American Hymnody (Jesse Hartzler Coll)
Subject Interests: Peace, Relig
Automation Activity & Vendor Info: (Acquisitions) OCLC; (Cataloging) OCLC; (Circulation) OCLC; (Course Reserve) OCLC; (ILL) OCLC; (OPAC) OCLC; (Serials) OCLC
Database Vendor: American Chemical Society, American Psychological Association (APA), BioOne, Bowker, Cinahl, College Source, CQ Press, CredoReference, EBSCOhost, Ex Libris Group, Gale Cengage Learning, H W Wilson, IBISWorld, Inspire, JSTOR, LexisNexis, McGraw-Hill, Medline, Modern Language Association, OCLC FirstSearch, OCLC WorldShare Interlibrary Loan, Oxford Online, Project MUSE, ProQuest, PubMed, Sage, Springshare, LLC
Function: Art exhibits, Copy machines, Electronic databases & coll, Exhibits, Handicapped accessible, ILL available, Online cat, Online ref, Pub access computers
Partic in Academic Libraries of Indiana; Midwest Collaborative for Library Services (MCLS); OCLC Online Computer Library Center, Inc; Private Academic Library Network of Indiana (PALNI)
Open Mon-Thurs 7:30am-11pm, Fri 7:30-5, Sat 1-5, Sun 3-11
Restriction: In-house use for visitors, Pub use on premises

C MENNONITE HISTORICAL LIBRARY*, 1700 S Main, 46526, SAN 341-1966. Tel: 574-535-7418. FAX: 574-535-7438. E-mail: mhl@goshen.edu. Web Site: www.goshen.edu/mhl. *Dir,* Dr John D Roth; *Assoc Librn,* Victoria M Waters; *Curator,* Joe A Springer; Staff 2 (MLS 2)
Founded 1906. Enrl 1,000; Highest Degree: Master
Library Holdings: Bk Vols 77,000; Per Subs 400
Subject Interests: Amish, Anabaptists, Genealogy, Mennonite
Automation Activity & Vendor Info: (Acquisitions) Ex Libris Group; (Cataloging) Ex Libris Group; (Circulation) Ex Libris Group; (OPAC) Ex Libris Group; (Serials) Ex Libris Group
Database Vendor: EBSCOhost, JSTOR, OCLC WorldShare Interlibrary Loan
Partic in OCLC Online Computer Library Center, Inc; Private Academic Library Network of Indiana (PALNI)
Publications: Mennonite Quarterly Review
Open Mon-Fri 8-5
Restriction: Circ limited

P GOSHEN PUBLIC LIBRARY*, 601 S Fifth St, 46526-3994. SAN 304-9132. Tel: 574-533-9531. FAX: 574-533-5211. E-mail: gpl@goshenpl.lib.in.us. Web Site: www.goshenpl.lib.in.us. *Dir,* Andrew Waters; *Head, Adult/Teen Serv, Head, Circ,* Ann-Margaret Rice; *Head, Ch,* Margaret Kownover; *Coll Develop Coordr, Head, Ref Serv,* Ann Kauffman; *Head, Tech Serv,* Elizabeth Rinehart; *Automation Mgr,* Ross Riker; *Bus Mgr,* Gregory Laughlin; *AV Coordr,* Janet Showalter; *Sr Cataloger,* Susanne Friesen; Staff 14 (MLS 11, Non-MLS 3)
Founded 1901. Pop 37,608; Circ 481,931
Jan 2011-Dec 2011 Income $1,681,467. Mats Exp $224,270. Sal $953,112
Library Holdings: AV Mats 26,686; Bk Titles 137,306; Per Subs 299
Special Collections: Indiana History & Local Genealogy Coll; Large Print Coll; Spanish Language Coll
Automation Activity & Vendor Info: (Acquisitions) SirsiDynix; (Cataloging) SirsiDynix; (Circulation) SirsiDynix; (OPAC) SirsiDynix; (Serials) SirsiDynix
Wireless access
Partic in Midwest Collaborative for Library Services (MCLS)
Special Services for the Blind - Computer with voice synthesizer for visually impaired persons
Open Mon, Wed & Thurs 10-8, Tues 1-8, Fri 10-6, Sat 10-4, Sun (Winter) 1-5
Friends of the Library Group

GREENCASTLE

C DEPAUW UNIVERSITY*, Roy O West Library, 11 E Larrabee St, 46135. SAN 341-1990. Tel: 765-658-4420. FAX: 765-658-4017. Web Site: www.depauw.edu/library. *Dir,* Rick Provinc; E-mail: provine@depauw.edu; *Archivist, Spec Coll Librn,* Wesley Wilson; *Cat,* Bruce Sanders; *Coll Develop,* Joyce Dixon-Fyle; Staff 22 (MLS 12, Non-MLS 10)
Founded 1837. Enrl 2,400; Fac 220; Highest Degree: Bachelor
Library Holdings: AV Mats 25,000; Bk Titles 400,000
Special Collections: Archives of DePauw University & Indiana United Methodism, doc, flm, ms; Bret Harte Library of First Editions; German (Bence Coll); Latin (Simison Coll); Pre-Law (Williams Coll), bks, per. Oral History; State Document Depository; US Document Depository
Subject Interests: Bus & mgt, Econ, Music
Automation Activity & Vendor Info: (OPAC) Ex Libris Group
Wireless access
Partic in Midwest Collaborative for Library Services (MCLS)

Departmental Libraries:

PREVO LIBRARY, Julian Science & Math Ctr, 46135, SAN 341-2059. Tel: 765-658-4515. *Sci Librn,* Caroline Gilson; E-mail: cgilson@depauw.edu; Staff 3 (Non-MLS 3)
Automation Activity & Vendor Info: (OPAC) Ex Libris Group

P PUTNAM COUNTY PUBLIC LIBRARY*, 103 E Poplar St, 46135-1655. (Mail add: PO Box 116, 46135-0116), SAN 304-9159. Tel: 765-653-2755. FAX: 765-653-2756. E-mail: library@putnam.lib.in.us. Web Site: www.putnam.lib.in.us. *Dir,* Alice Greenburg; E-mail: alice@putnam.lib.in.us; *Dir, Commun Relations,* Margot Payne; *Ch Serv,* Cortina Zuichkovski; *Ref,* Lynne Tweedie; Staff 7.6 (MLS 4.6, Non-MLS 3)
Founded 1902. Pop 36,323; Circ 248,610
Jan 2010-Dec 2010 Income $963,478. Mats Exp $826,927
Library Holdings: AV Mats 11,292; Large Print Bks 1,625; Bk Titles 63,244; Bk Vols 71,961; Per Subs 244
Special Collections: Oral History
Subject Interests: Genealogy, Local hist
Automation Activity & Vendor Info: (Acquisitions) Innovative Interfaces, Inc; (Cataloging) Innovative Interfaces, Inc; (Circulation) Innovative Interfaces, Inc; (OPAC) Innovative Interfaces, Inc
Database Vendor: Baker & Taylor, Booksite, ReferenceUSA
Wireless access
Function: Archival coll, Bk club(s), Bks on CD, Children's prog, Computers for patron use, Copy machines, e-mail & chat, Exhibits, Fax serv, Free DVD rentals, Handicapped accessible, Home delivery & serv to Sr ctr & nursing homes, Jail serv, Music CDs, Online cat, Outreach serv, Photocopying/Printing, Preschool outreach, Prog for adults, Prog for children & young adult, Pub access computers, Ref serv in person, Scanner, Spoken cassettes & CDs, Spoken cassettes & DVDs, Story hour, Summer & winter reading prog, Tax forms, Telephone ref, Web-catalog, Wheelchair accessible

Open Mon & Fri 9-5:30, Tues-Thurs 9-8, Sat 9-5
Friends of the Library Group
Bookmobiles: 1. Librn, Jane Glier. Bk titles 4,000

S PUTNAMVILLE CORRECTIONAL FACILITY*, Learning Resource Center, 1946 W US 40, 46135-9275. SAN 304-9140. Tel: 765-653-8441. FAX: 765-653-4157. *Dir,* Jimmie Bowman; *Media Spec,* Brent Roark; Staff 1 (Non-MLS 1)
Founded 1954
Library Holdings: Bk Titles 10,191; Bk Vols 11,216; Per Subs 80
Open Mon-Fri 7:30-3:30

GREENFIELD

P HANCOCK COUNTY PUBLIC LIBRARY*, 900 W McKenzie Rd, 46140-1741. SAN 304-9167. Tel: 317-462-5141. Reference Tel: 317-467-6672. FAX: 317-462-5711. E-mail: hcpl@hcplibrary.org. Web Site: www.hcplibrary.org. *Libr Dir,* Dianne Osborne; Tel: 317-467-6663; *Asst Dir,* Barbara Roark; *Pub Serv Mgr,* Golam Kibreah; Staff 53 (MLS 7, Non-MLS 46)
Founded 1898. Pop 48,497; Circ 634,072
Library Holdings: Bk Titles 140,000; Bk Vols 188,000; Per Subs 275
Special Collections: James Whitcomb Riley Coll, digitized
Subject Interests: Genealogy, Indiana
Automation Activity & Vendor Info: (Acquisitions) SirsiDynix; (Cataloging) SirsiDynix; (Circulation) SirsiDynix; (OPAC) SirsiDynix; (Serials) SirsiDynix
Database Vendor: AVC Technology Corp, Baker & Taylor, EBSCOhost, Gale Cengage Learning, Inspire, OCLC FirstSearch, OCLC WebJunction, OCLC WorldShare Interlibrary Loan, ProQuest, ReferenceUSA, SirsiDynix
Wireless access
Function: Adult literacy prog, AV serv, Distance learning, Health sci info serv, Home delivery & serv to Sr ctr & nursing homes, Homebound delivery serv, ILL available, Magnifiers for reading, Monthly prog for perceptually impaired adults, Online searches, Photocopying/Printing, Prog for children & young adult, Ref serv available, Satellite serv, Serves mentally handicapped consumers, Summer reading prog, Telephone ref, Wheelchair accessible, Workshops
Publications: Newsletter (Monthly)
Partic in Midwest Collaborative for Library Services (MCLS)
Special Services for the Deaf - Bks on deafness & sign lang; High interest/low vocabulary bks
Special Services for the Blind - Audio mat; Bks on CD; Home delivery serv; Large print bks; Magnifiers; Talking bks; Volunteer serv
Open Mon-Thurs 9-9, Fri 9-6, Sat 9-5, Sun 1-4
Friends of the Library Group
Branches: 1
SUGAR CREEK BRANCH, 5087 W US 52, New Palestine, 46163. (Mail add: PO Box 262, New Palestine, 46163-8728). Tel: 317-861-6618. FAX: 317-861-2061. *Br Mgr,* Jeanette Sherfield; Tel: 317-861-6618, Ext 20
Library Holdings: Bk Vols 35,000
Open Mon-Thurs 9-8, Fri 9-6, Sat 9-5, Sun 1-4
Bookmobiles: 1

GREENSBURG

P GREENSBURG-DECATUR COUNTY PUBLIC LIBRARY*, 1110 E Main St, 47240. SAN 304-9183. Tel: 812-663-2826. FAX: 812-663-5617. E-mail: grefdesk@greensburglibrary.org. Web Site: www.greensburglibrary.org. *Libr Dir,* Andrea Ingmire; E-mail: aingmire@greensburglibrary.org; *Ch,* Jill Pratt; E-mail: jpratt@greensburglibrary.org; *Ref Librn,* Vanessa Martin; E-mail: vmartin@greensburglibrary.org; *Ref Librn,* Lori Osting; E-mail: losting@greensburglibrary.org; *Ref Librn,* Rebecca Perkins; E-mail: rperkins@greensburglibrary.org. Subject Specialists: *Genealogy, Local hist,* Lori Osting; Staff 8 (MLS 4, Non-MLS 4)
Founded 1905. Pop 24,555; Circ 250,594
Jan 2011-Dec 2011 Income (Main Library and Branch(s)) $788,532, State $45,606, Locally Generated Income $693,894, Other $49,032. Mats Exp $95,172, Books $46,051, Per/Ser (Incl. Access Fees) $8,120, AV Mat $23,157, Electronic Ref Mat (Incl. Access Fees) $17,844. Sal $59,933 (Prof $467,573)
Library Holdings: Audiobooks 5,430; AV Mats 8,699; Electronic Media & Resources 436; Bk Vols 109,701; Per Subs 206
Special Collections: Oral History
Subject Interests: Local hist
Automation Activity & Vendor Info: (Cataloging) Evergreen; (Circulation) Evergreen; (OPAC) Evergreen
Database Vendor: Evanced Solutions, Inc, Gale Cengage Learning, ProQuest, TumbleBookLibrary, Wilson - Wilson Web
Wireless access
Function: Audiobks via web, Bk club(s), Bks on cassette, Bks on CD, Children's prog, Computer training, Computers for patron use, Copy machines, Digital talking bks, Electronic databases & coll, Fax serv, Free DVD rentals, Holiday prog, Home delivery & serv to Sr ctr & nursing homes, ILL available, Music CDs, Notary serv, Online cat, Online searches, OverDrive digital audio bks, Photocopying/Printing, Preschool outreach, Preschool reading prog, Printer for laptops & handheld devices, Prog for adults, Prog for children & young adult, Pub access computers, Ref serv available, Scanner, Senior computer classes, Spanish lang bks, Story hour, Summer & winter reading prog, Summer reading prog, Tax forms, Teen prog, Web-catalog
Open Mon-Thurs 8:30-8:30, Fri 8:30-5, Sat 9-4, Sun 12-4
Friends of the Library Group
Branches: 1
WESTPORT BRANCH, 205 W Main St, Westport, 47283-9601, SAN 371-3830. Tel: 812-591-2330. FAX: 812-591-2330. *Librn,* Deb Smith; E-mail: dsmith@greensburglibrary.org
Founded 1989. Circ 17,407
Open Mon-Thurs 2-8, Sat 9-1
Friends of the Library Group
Bookmobiles: 1

GREENTOWN

P GREENTOWN PUBLIC LIBRARY*, 421 S Harrison St, 46936-1496. SAN 304-9191. Tel: 765-628-3534. FAX: 765-628-3759. Web Site: www.greentownlib.org. *Dir,* Margi Bontrager; Staff 9 (MLS 1, Non-MLS 8)
Founded 1919. Pop 6,000; Circ 123,249
Library Holdings: Bks on Deafness & Sign Lang 12; Large Print Bks 869; Bk Vols 47,440; Per Subs 181
Special Collections: Civil War Coll; Large Print Books Coll
Automation Activity & Vendor Info: (Circulation) Follett Software; (OPAC) Follett Software
Database Vendor: EBSCOhost
Open Mon, Wed & Fri 8-4, Tues & Thurs 8-8, Sat 9-1

GREENWOOD

P GREENWOOD PUBLIC LIBRARY*, 310 S Meridian St, 46143-3135. SAN 304-9205. Tel: 317-881-1953. Reference Tel: 317-883-4224. FAX: 317-881-1963. Reference FAX: 317-883-4227. TDD: 317-883-4226. E-mail: questions@greenwoodlibrary.us. Web Site: www.greenwoodlibrary.us. *Dir,* Cheryl Dobbs; E-mail: cdobbs@greenwoodlibrary.us; *Head, Ref,* Emily Ellis; *Head, Tech Serv,* Janet Buckley; Tel: 317-883-4246, E-mail: jbuckley@mail.greenwood.lib.in.us; *Ch Serv,* Linda Oldham Messick; Tel: 317-883-4248; Staff 45 (MLS 14, Non-MLS 31)
Founded 1917. Pop 26,849; Circ 224,321
Library Holdings: AV Mats 6,000; Bk Vols 100,000; Per Subs 360
Automation Activity & Vendor Info: (Acquisitions) SirsiDynix; (Cataloging) SirsiDynix; (Circulation) SirsiDynix; (OPAC) SirsiDynix; (Serials) SirsiDynix
Database Vendor: SirsiDynix
Wireless access
Function: Distance learning, Handicapped accessible, Homebound delivery serv, ILL available, Libr develop, Magnifiers for reading, Prog for children & young adult, Ref serv available, Summer reading prog, Telephone ref, Wheelchair accessible
Partic in Ind Libr Asn; Midwest Collaborative for Library Services (MCLS)
Open Mon-Thurs 9-8, Fri & Sat 1-5
Friends of the Library Group

CR INDIANA BAPTIST COLLEGE LIBRARY*, Leon F Maurer Library, 1301 W County Line Rd, 46142. SAN 304-9612. Tel: 317-882-2327, 317-882-2345. FAX: 317-885-2960. E-mail: info@indianabaptistcollege.com. Web Site: www.indianabaptistcollege.com. *Libr Serv Mgr,* Edna Kehrt; Staff 1 (Non-MLS 1)
Founded 1955. Enrl 130; Fac 23; Highest Degree: Doctorate
Library Holdings: Bk Titles 21,116; Bk Vols 23,410; Per Subs 33
Special Collections: Carl Byrd Antiquarian Coll
Subject Interests: Relig
Open Mon-Fri 8:30-5

HAGERSTOWN

P HAGERSTOWN JEFFERSON TOWNSHIP PUBLIC LIBRARY*, Ten W College St, 47346. SAN 304-9213. Tel: 765-489-5632. FAX: 765-489-5808. E-mail: info@hagerstownlibrary.org. Web Site: www.hagerstown.lib.in.us. *Dir,* Ruth Fraur; E-mail: director@hagerstownlibrary.org; Staff 1 (MLS 1)
Founded 1928. Pop 3,427; Circ 73,706
Jan 2007-Dec 2007 Income $249,767. Mats Exp $49,500, Books $35,000, Per/Ser (Incl. Access Fees) $4,000, AV Mat $9,000, Electronic Ref Mat (Incl. Access Fees) $1,500. Sal $97,912 (Prof $36,858)
Library Holdings: Audiobooks 72; Bks on Deafness & Sign Lang 13; CDs 126; DVDs 1,024; Large Print Bks 502; Bk Titles 33,410; Per Subs 81; Videos 1,200
Special Collections: Indiana Coll, bks, microfilm, newspaper

Automation Activity & Vendor Info: (Cataloging) Evergreen; (Circulation) Evergreen; (OPAC) Evergreen
Wireless access
Function: Adult bk club, Bks on cassette, Bks on CD, CD-ROM, Children's prog, Computers for patron use, Copy machines, Fax serv, Free DVD rentals, Handicapped accessible, Holiday prog, ILL available, Music CDs, Online cat, Outside serv via phone, mail, e-mail & web, Prof lending libr, Prog for adults, Prog for children & young adult, Ref serv available, Story hour, Summer reading prog, Tax forms, Telephone ref, VHS videos
Partic in Evergreen Indiana Consortium; Midwest Collaborative for Library Services (MCLS)
Special Services for the Deaf - Bks on deafness & sign lang; Closed caption videos
Special Services for the Blind - Bks on cassette; Bks on CD; Large print bks
Open Mon, Tues, Thurs & Fri 10:30-7, Wed 3-7, Sat 10:30-2:30
Restriction: Non-resident fee
Friends of the Library Group

HAMMOND

C AMERICAN CONSERVATORY OF MUSIC*, Robert R McCormick Memorial Library, 252 Wildwood Rd, 46324. SAN 303-8092. Tel: 219-931-6000. FAX: 219-931-6089. *Dir,* Theodora Schulze; E-mail: president@americanconservatory.edu
Founded 1962. Highest Degree: Doctorate
Library Holdings: DVDs 100; Music Scores 2,000; Bk Vols 1,600
Special Collections: Bach, Neue Ausgabe; Bach-Gesellshaft; Beethoven, Werke; Choral Music, Mini Scores, Orch Scor/pts; Haydn, Werke; International Library Piano Music; Mozart, Neue Ausgabe; Musik in Geschichte und Gegenwart; New Grove Dict Music & Musicians; New Oxford HM; NG Dict American Music
Subject Interests: Music
Restriction: Not open to pub

P HAMMOND PUBLIC LIBRARY*, 564 State St, 46320-1532. SAN 341-2113. Tel: 219-931-5100. FAX: 219-931-3474. E-mail: hpl@hammond.lib.in.us. Web Site: www.hammond.lib.in.us. *Dir,* Rene L Greenleaf; *Head, Circ,* Zora Ludwig; Tel: 219-931-5100, Ext 331; *Head, Info Serv,* Rosalie Ruff; Tel: 219-931-5100, Ext 327; *Head, Tech Serv,* Jennifer Wells Bull; Tel: 219-931-5100, Ext 320; *Head, Youth Serv,* Melody Scott; Tel: 219-931-5100, Ext 330; Staff 17 (MLS 10, Non-MLS 7)
Founded 1902. Pop 83,048; Circ 363,749
Library Holdings: Bk Vols 206,810; Per Subs 466
Special Collections: Hammond Area History (Susan G Long, Local History Room), a-tapes, bks, maps, monographs, pictures, photog, videos. Oral History; US Document Depository
Automation Activity & Vendor Info: (Acquisitions) Innovative Interfaces, Inc; (Cataloging) Innovative Interfaces, Inc; (Circulation) Innovative Interfaces, Inc; (OPAC) Innovative Interfaces, Inc
Publications: Bookends
Partic in Midwest Collaborative for Library Services (MCLS)
Open Mon-Thurs 9-9, Fri & Sat 9-5
Friends of the Library Group

C PURDUE UNIVERSITY*, Calumet Library, 2200 169th St, 46323-2094. SAN 304-9272. Tel: 219-989-2224. Interlibrary Loan Service Tel: 219-989-2720. FAX: 219-989-2070. Circulation FAX: 219-989-2553. Web Site: purduecal.edu/library. *Dir, Learning & Res Serv,* Tammy S Guerrero; Tel: 219-989-2675, E-mail: guerrero@purduecal.edu; *Asst Dir, Learning & Res Serv,* LaShawn M Jones; Tel: 219-989-2138, E-mail: joneslm@purduecal.edu; *Educ Librn,* Sheila A Rezak; Tel: 219-989-2677, E-mail: rezak@purduecal.edu; *Humanities Librn,* Lan Shen; Tel: 219-989-2678, E-mail: shenlan@purduecal.edu; *Sci & Bus Librn,* Sammy Chapman, Jr; Tel: 219-989-2903, E-mail: Sammy.Chapman@purduecal.edu; Staff 19 (MLS 6, Non-MLS 13)
Founded 1947. Enrl 9,325; Fac 531; Highest Degree: Master
Jul 2008-Jun 2009 Income $1,418,813. Mats Exp $485,032, Books $154,267, Per/Ser (Incl. Access Fees) $267,693, AV Mat $1,357, Electronic Ref Mat (Incl. Access Fees) $55,672. Sal $718,557 (Prof $682,652)
Library Holdings: Bks on Deafness & Sign Lang 126; CDs 5; DVDs 412; e-books 2,993; e-journals 9,039; Electronic Media & Resources 1,058; Large Print Bks 54; Microforms 792,765; Music Scores 7; Bk Titles 256,194; Bk Vols 269,280; Per Subs 603; Videos 850
Special Collections: Archives (Non-Current University Records); Calumet Region Materials. US Document Depository
Automation Activity & Vendor Info: (Acquisitions) Ex Libris Group; (Cataloging) OCLC; (Circulation) Ex Libris Group; (Course Reserve) Ex Libris Group; (ILL) OCLC; (OPAC) Ex Libris Group; (Serials) Ex Libris Group
Database Vendor: Cambridge Scientific Abstracts, EBSCOhost, LexisNexis, OCLC FirstSearch, OCLC WorldShare Interlibrary Loan, OVID Technologies, Oxford Online, ProQuest, Wilson - Wilson Web
Wireless access
Partic in Academic Libraries of Indiana; Committee on Institutional Cooperation (CIC); Lyrasis; Midwest Collaborative for Library Services (MCLS); OCLC Online Computer Library Center, Inc
Special Services for the Deaf - Assistive tech
Special Services for the Blind - Braille equip; Dragon Naturally Speaking software; Internet workstation with adaptive software

M SAINT MARGARET MERCY-NORTH CAMPUS*, Sallie M Tyrrell MD Memorial Library, 5454 Hohman Ave, 46320. SAN 304-9280. Tel: 219-932-2300, Ext 34633, 219-933-2133. FAX: 219-933-2146. *Coordr,* Monica Nowesnick; Tel: 219-933-2133, Ext 32133
Founded 1937
Library Holdings: Bk Titles 950; Bk Vols 1,200; Per Subs 60
Subject Interests: Med, Nursing
Publications: Newsletter
Partic in Docline
Open Mon-Fri 9-12

HANOVER

C HANOVER COLLEGE*, Duggan Library, 121 Scenic Dr, 47243. (Mail add: PO Box 287, 47243-0287), SAN 304-9302. Tel: 812-866-7165. Reference Tel: 812-866-7171. FAX: 812-866-7172. Web Site: www.hanover.edu/Library. *Coll Develop, Dir,* Ken Gibson; Tel: 812-866-7160, E-mail: gibson@hanover.edu; *Head, Cat,* Alynza Henderson; E-mail: henderson@hanover.edu; *Head, ILL, Head, Ser,* Kelly Joyce; Tel: 812-866-7166, E-mail: joyce@hanover.edu; *Acq,* Mary Royalty; Tel: 812-866-7161, E-mail: royalty@hanover.edu; *Archivist & Curator of Rare Bks,* Doug Denne; Tel: 812-866-7182, E-mail: denne@hanover.edu; *Circ, ILL & Ser,* Victoria Bramwell; Tel: 812-866-7169, E-mail: bramwell@hanover.edu; *Circ Asst,* Patricia Lawrence; Tel: 812-866-7176, E-mail: lawrence@hanover.edu; *Govt Doc,* Position Currently Open; *Info Serv,* Heather Loehr; Tel: 812-866-7170, E-mail: loehr@hanover.edu; Staff 9 (MLS 5, Non-MLS 4)
Founded 1827. Enrl 920; Fac 100; Highest Degree: Bachelor
Special Collections: Church History (Archives of the Presbyterian Church of Indiana) bks, micro; Civil War (Daugherty Coll); Hanover College Archives; Indiana History (I M Bridgman Coll); Judith Moffett Papers; Pacifica & Northwest Exploration (Dr Ronald Kleopfer Coll); Senator William E Jenner Papers. US Document Depository
Automation Activity & Vendor Info: (Acquisitions) Ex Libris Group; (Cataloging) Ex Libris Group; (Circulation) Ex Libris Group; (Course Reserve) Ex Libris Group; (OPAC) Ex Libris Group; (Serials) Ex Libris Group
Database Vendor: Baker & Taylor, Cambridge Scientific Abstracts, EBSCOhost, JSTOR, LexisNexis, OCLC FirstSearch, OCLC WorldShare Interlibrary Loan, Project MUSE, Springshare, LLC
Wireless access
Publications: INFORMER (Newsletter)
Partic in Academic Libraries of Indiana; Lyrasis; Midwest Collaborative for Library Services (MCLS); OCLC Online Computer Library Center, Inc; OCLC-LVIS; Private Academic Library Network of Indiana (PALNI)
Restriction: 24-hr pass syst for students only

HARTFORD CITY

P HARTFORD CITY PUBLIC LIBRARY*, 314 N High St, 47348-2143. SAN 304-9310. Tel: 765-348-1720. FAX: 765-348-5090. E-mail: hartfordcitylibrary@yahoo.com. Web Site: www.hcpubliclibrary.com. *Dir,* Vicki Cecil; E-mail: vickicecil@earthlink.net; *Ch Serv,* Andrea Landis; E-mail: allandis99@hotmail.com; Staff 11 (MLS 1, Non-MLS 10)
Founded 1903. Pop 7,122; Circ 166,660
Library Holdings: AV Mats 3,100; Large Print Bks 98; Bk Titles 61,914; Bk Vols 63,411; Per Subs 321; Talking Bks 71; Videos 1,040
Special Collections: Indiana Genealogy Coll; Music (George Leonard Fulton Memorial Record Library)
Subject Interests: Genealogy, Indiana
Automation Activity & Vendor Info: (ILL) Follett Software
Database Vendor: OCLC FirstSearch
Function: ILL available
Open Mon-Thurs (Winter) 10-8, Fri 10-5:30, Sat 10-5; Mon-Thurs (Summer) 10-7, Fri 10-5:30, Sat 10-2
Friends of the Library Group

HENRYVILLE

S HENRYVILLE CORRECTIONAL FACILITY LIBRARY*, PO Box 148, 47126. Tel: 812-294-4372. *Librn,* Steve Bonsett; Staff 1 (Non-MLS 1)
Library Holdings: Bk Titles 1,080; Bk Vols 1,200; Per Subs 21
Open Mon-Fri 8-4

HOBART

S HOBART HISTORICAL SOCIETY, INC*, Mariam Pleak Library, 706 E Fourth St, 46342-4411. (Mail add: PO Box 24, 46342-0024), SAN 304-9337. Tel: 219-942-0970. *Archivist, Curator,* Elin Christianson
Founded 1973
Library Holdings: Bk Titles 500; Per Subs 10
Special Collections: Genealogy; Local Newspapers; Photographs
Subject Interests: Hist, Indiana, Local hist
Open Sat 10-12

M SAINT MARY MEDICAL CENTER*, Reference Library, 1500 S Lake Park Ave, 46342. SAN 304-9094. Tel: 219-947-6230. FAX: 219-947-6331. *Med Librn,* Lucinda Macko; Staff 1 (MLS 1)
Library Holdings: Bk Titles 268; Per Subs 25
Subject Interests: Hospital admin, Med, Nursing
Partic in National Network of Libraries of Medicine Greater Midwest Region
Open Mon-Fri 8:30-5

HUNTINGBURG

P HUNTINGBURG PUBLIC LIBRARY*, 419 N Jackson St, 47542. SAN 304-9345. Tel: 812-683-2052. FAX: 812-683-2056. Web Site: www.huntingburg.lib.in.us. *Dir,* Kathleen M Lett; E-mail: klett@huntingburg.lib.in.us; Staff 6 (Non-MLS 6)
Founded 1922. Pop 7,178; Circ 71,402
Library Holdings: Bk Vols 34,394; Per Subs 87
Automation Activity & Vendor Info: (Cataloging) SirsiDynix; (Circulation) SirsiDynix; (OPAC) SirsiDynix
Database Vendor: SirsiDynix
Wireless access
Partic in Evergreen Indiana Consortium; Midwest Collaborative for Library Services (MCLS)
Open Mon-Thurs 9-8, Fri & Sat 9-5

HUNTINGTON

P HUNTINGTON CITY-TOWNSHIP PUBLIC LIBRARY*, 200 W Market St, 46750-2655. SAN 304-9353. Tel: 260-356-0824. FAX: 260-356-3073. Web Site: huntingtonpub.lib.in.us. *Exec Dir,* Rebecca Lemons; *Tech Serv,* Nancy Ross
Founded 1903. Pop 23,000; Circ 167,347
Library Holdings: Bk Titles 110,640; Bk Vols 148,000; Per Subs 186; Talking Bks 3,000
Special Collections: Genealogy; Local & State History; Trains Coll
Automation Activity & Vendor Info: (Acquisitions) SirsiDynix; (Cataloging) SirsiDynix; (Circulation) SirsiDynix
Database Vendor: EBSCOhost
Partic in Midwest Collaborative for Library Services (MCLS)
Open Mon-Thurs 9-8, Fri & Sat 9-5
Friends of the Library Group
Branches: 1
MARKLE PUBLIC LIBRARY, 197 E Morse St, Markle, 46770. (Mail add: PO Box 578, Markle, 46770-0578), SAN 376-5342. Tel: 260-758-3332. FAX: 260-758-3332. *Dir,* Kathryn Holst; Staff 5 (MLS 1, Non-MLS 4)
Founded 1937. Pop 1,259; Circ 5,689
Library Holdings: AV Mats 750; Bk Titles 8,914; Bk Vols 11,610; Per Subs 56; Talking Bks 59; Videos 359
Open Mon, Tues, Thurs & Fri 1-7, Wed 10-12 & 1-7, Sat 9-12

CR HUNTINGTON UNIVERSITY*, RichLyn Library, 2303 College Ave, 46750. SAN 304-9361. Tel: 260-359-4063. Circulation Tel: 260-359-4054. Interlibrary Loan Service Tel: 260-359-4061. FAX: 260-358-3698. Web Site: huntington.edu. *Dir of Libr Serv,* Anita L Gray; E-mail: agray@huntington.edu; *Assoc Dir, Libr Serv,* Randy Neuman; E-mail: rneuman@huntington.edu
Founded 1897. Enrl 950; Fac 55; Highest Degree: Master
Library Holdings: Bk Vols 180,000
Special Collections: Archives of Huntington College; Curriculum Materials Center; United Brethren in Christ Church. US Document Depository
Automation Activity & Vendor Info: (Acquisitions) Ex Libris Group; (Cataloging) Ex Libris Group; (Circulation) Ex Libris Group; (Course Reserve) Ex Libris Group; (OPAC) Ex Libris Group; (Serials) Ex Libris Group
Wireless access
Partic in Midwest Collaborative for Library Services (MCLS); OCLC Online Computer Library Center, Inc; Private Academic Library Network of Indiana (PALNI)
Special Services for the Blind - ZoomText magnification & reading software
Open Mon, Tues & Thurs (Winter) 7:30am-11pm, Wed 7:30am-Midnight, Fri 7:30-5, Sat 12-6, Sun 2-11; Mon-Thurs (Summer) 7:30-7, Fri 7:30-5, Sat 12-5

INDIANAPOLIS

SR ALL SOULS UNITARIAN CHURCH*, E Burdette Backus Memorial Library, 5805 E 56th St, 46226-1526. SAN 304-937X. Tel: 317-545-6005. FAX: 317-545-4662. Web Site: www.allsoulsuuindy.org. *Dir of Educ,* Nancy Renner Clear
Library Holdings: Bk Titles 1,290; Bk Vols 1,398; Per Subs 11
Subject Interests: Comparative relig, Philos, Relig, Soc sci & issues, Unitarianism
Restriction: Not open to pub

S AMERICAN LEGION NATIONAL HEADQUARTERS LIBRARY*, 700 N Pennsylvania St, 4th Flr, 46204-1172. (Mail add: PO Box 1055, 46206-1055), SAN 304-9388. Tel: 317-630-1366. FAX: 317-630-1241. E-mail: library@legion.org. Web Site: www.legion.org. *Dir, Libr & Mus Serv,* Howard Trace; Staff 6 (MLS 2, Non-MLS 4)
Founded 1923
Library Holdings: Microforms 1,200; Bk Vols 12,000
Special Collections: Archives of The American Legion National Organization; National Defense; Patriotism (1919-date); Veterans' Affairs; World War I & II Posters
Subject Interests: Mil hist
Automation Activity & Vendor Info: (Cataloging) Inmagic, Inc.; (Circulation) Inmagic, Inc.; (Serials) Inmagic, Inc.
Restriction: Access at librarian's discretion, Authorized scholars by appt, Circulates for staff only, Non-circulating, Restricted access

C ART INSTITUTE OF INDIANAPOLIS LIBRARY*, 3500 Depauw Blvd, Ste 1010, 46268. Tel: 317-613-4800, 317-613-4803. Administration Tel: 317-613-4957. FAX: 317-613-4808. E-mail: AIIndyLibrary@aii.edu. *Dir of Libr Serv,* Michael Piper; E-mail: mpiper@aii.edu; Staff 1 (MLS 1)
Founded 2006. Enrl 1,100; Fac 120; Highest Degree: Bachelor
Jul 2013-Jun 2014. Mats Exp $5,408, Books $5,000, Per/Ser (Incl. Access Fees) $90, AV Equip $18, AV Mat $250, Electronic Ref Mat (Incl. Access Fees) $50
Library Holdings: AV Mats 200; Bks on Deafness & Sign Lang 10; DVDs 180; Bk Titles 5,000; Per Subs 90; Videos 20
Special Collections: Indiana
Subject Interests: Culinary arts, Digital photog, Fashion design, Fashion retail mgt, Graphic design, Interior design, Media arts & multimedia design
Automation Activity & Vendor Info: (Acquisitions) Ex Libris Group; (Cataloging) Ex Libris Group; (Circulation) Ex Libris Group; (OPAC) Ex Libris Group; (Serials) EBSCO Online
Database Vendor: CQ Press, CredoReference, ebrary, EBSCOhost, Inspire, LearningExpress, Material Connexion, Mergent Online, OCLC FirstSearch, OCLC WebJunction, OCLC WorldShare Interlibrary Loan, ReferenceUSA, RefWorks, Wilson - Wilson Web, WT Cox
Wireless access
Function: Art exhibits, Audio & video playback equip for onsite use, CD-ROM, Computers for patron use, Copy machines, Distance learning, e-mail serv, E-Reserves, Electronic databases & coll, Free DVD rentals, Handicapped accessible, Online ref, Online searches, Orientations, Outside serv via phone, mail, e-mail & web, Photocopying/Printing, Ref serv available, Scanner, Telephone ref, Web-catalog, Writing prog
Partic in Lyrasis; Midwest Collaborative for Library Services (MCLS); OCLC Online Computer Library Center, Inc
Open Mon-Fri 7:30am-8pm
Restriction: Authorized patrons, Borrowing privileges limited to fac & registered students, Circ privileges for students & alumni only, ID required to use computers (Ltd hrs), Not open to pub, Open to students, fac & staff, Photo ID required for access

S EDWARD A BLOCK FAMILY LIBRARY*, Riley Hospital, 702 Barnhill Dr, Rm 1719, 46202-5128. SAN 304-9809. Tel: 317-274-1149, 317-278-1645. FAX: 317-278-1631. *Librn,* Tom Lund; E-mail: tlund@clarian.org; *Librn,* Dena Vincent; E-mail: dvincent@clarian.org; Staff 2 (MLS 1, Non-MLS 1)
Founded 1922
Library Holdings: Bks on Deafness & Sign Lang 11; CDs 147; DVDs 1,000; Bk Vols 7,900; Per Subs 30; Videos 750
Special Collections: Lay Medical Information
Wireless access
Publications: Consumer Medical Bibliography
Partic in Midwest Collaborative for Library Services (MCLS)

L BOSE MCKINNEY & EVANS LLP*, Law Library, 111 Monument Circle, Ste 2700, 46204. SAN 372-1213. Tel: 317-684-5166. Interlibrary Loan Service Tel: 317-684-5275. FAX: 317-223-0166. E-mail: bmelibrary@boselaw.com. Web Site: www.boselaw.com. *Dir, Libr & Info Serv,* Cheryl Lynn Niemeier; E-mail: cniemeier@boselaw.com; Staff 2 (MLS 1, Non-MLS 1)
Library Holdings: Bk Vols 27,000; Per Subs 150

Subject Interests: Bus operations, Civil rights, Intellectual property, Labor, Litigation, Securities, Tax
Automation Activity & Vendor Info: (Acquisitions) LibraryWorld, Inc; (Cataloging) OCLC Online; (Circulation) LibraryWorld, Inc; (ILL) OCLC Online; (OPAC) LibraryWorld, Inc; (Serials) LibraryWorld, Inc
Database Vendor: Dialog, LexisNexis, Westlaw
Function: For res purposes, ILL available
Restriction: Co libr, Not open to pub, Private libr, Prof mat only, Staff use only

C BUTLER UNIVERSITY LIBRARIES*, Irwin Library, 4600 Sunset Ave, 46208. SAN 341-2474. Tel: 317-940-9227. Interlibrary Loan Service Tel: 317-940-9677. Reference Tel: 317-940-9235. Administration Tel: 317-940-9714. FAX: 317-940-9711. Web Site: www.butler.edu. *Dean of Libr,* Lewis R Miller; E-mail: lmiller@butler.edu; *Asst Dean, Pub Serv,* Sally Neal; Tel: 317-940-9949, E-mail: sneal@butler.edu; *Asst Dean, Tech Serv,* Dan Roose; Tel: 317-940-9236, E-mail: droose@butler.edu; *Music Librn,* Sheridan Stormes; Tel: 317-940-9218, E-mail: sstormes@butler.edu; *Access Serv,* Brad Matthies; Tel: 317-940-9549, E-mail: bmatthies@butler.edu; *ILL,* Susan Berger; E-mail: sberger@butler.edu; *Ser,* Virginia Rumph; Tel: 317-940-6491, E-mail: vrumph@butler.edu; *Spec Coll & Archives Librn,* Sally Childs-Helton; Tel: 317-940-9265, E-mail: schildsh@butler.edu. Subject Specialists: *Fine arts, Music,* Sheridan Stormes; Staff 24 (MLS 12, Non-MLS 12)
Founded 1855. Enrl 4,246; Fac 305; Highest Degree: Master
Jun 2008-May 2009 Income (Main and Other College/University Libraries) $2,883,362. Mats Exp $1,092,668, Books $142,294, Per/Ser (Incl. Access Fees) $284,405, Micro $4,741, AV Mat $21,102, Electronic Ref Mat (Incl. Access Fees) $604,095, Presv $36,031. Sal $1,130,150 (Prof $668,810)
Library Holdings: AV Mats 17,536; e-books 14,455; e-journals 32,423; Music Scores 18,196; Bk Titles 237,058; Bk Vols 359,470; Per Subs 538
Special Collections: 19th Century American Sheet Music; 20th Century American Poetry, bks, mss; Abraham Lincoln, bks, mss, pamphlets, prints; Botanical & Zoological Prints 16th-19th Century; Jean Sibelius, publ & unpubl scores, recordings & secondary sources; Kin Hubbard-Gaar Williams Coll of Original Cartoons, bks, mss, memorabilia; Mme de Stael Research Coll; National Track & Field Historical Research Library; Pacific Islands 16th-20th Century; Rare Books Coll, bks, mss, prints; USABA Archives. US Document Depository
Automation Activity & Vendor Info: (Acquisitions) Ex Libris Group; (Cataloging) Ex Libris Group; (Circulation) Ex Libris Group; (Course Reserve) Ex Libris Group; (OPAC) Ex Libris Group; (Serials) Ex Libris Group
Database Vendor: EBSCOhost, Gale Cengage Learning, JSTOR, Medline, OCLC FirstSearch
Wireless access
Publications: Catalogues of Special Collections; New Acquisitions List
Partic in Academic Libraries of Indiana; Lyrasis; Private Academic Library Network of Indiana (PALNI)
Open Mon-Thurs 7:30am-1am, Fri 7:30-6, Sat 10-6, Sun 10am-1am

Departmental Libraries:

RUTH LILLY SCIENCE LIBRARY, 740 W 46th St, 46208-3485. Tel: 317-940-9401. FAX: 317-940-9519. Web Site: www.butler.edu/libraries. *Dean of Libr,* Lewis R Miller; Tel: 317-940-9714, Fax: 317-940-9711, E-mail: lmiller@butler.edu; *Librn,* Barbara Howes; E-mail: bhowes@butler.edu; Staff 1 (MLS 1)
Subject Interests: Chem, Math
Open Mon-Thurs 8am-12am, Fri 8-7, Sat 1-7, Sun 10am-12am

M LARUE D CARTER MEMORIAL HOSPITAL*, Professional Library, 2601 Cold Spring Rd, 46222-2202. SAN 341-2563. Tel: 317-941-4154. FAX: 317-941-4385. *Librn,* Judith K Smith; Staff 1 (Non-MLS 1)
Founded 1952
Library Holdings: Bk Titles 5,000; Per Subs 28; Videos 500
Special Collections: Murray Coll; Psychiatry & Mental Health (Hahn Coll, McMahan Coll, Barrows Coll, Reed Coll)
Subject Interests: Mental health, Psychiat, Psychol
Open Mon-Fri 8:45-4:45
Restriction: Circ limited

R CHRIST CHURCH CATHEDRAL*, Margaret Ridgely Memorial Library, 125 Monument Circle, 46204-2993. (Mail add: 55 Monument Circle, Ste 600, 46204-2917), SAN 304-9485. Tel: 317-636-4577. FAX: 317-635-1040. Web Site: www.ccindy.org. *Librn,* Cornell Lumpkin
Founded 1928
Library Holdings: Bk Titles 3,370; Bk Vols 3,510; Per Subs 39
Subject Interests: Relig
Publications: Acquisitions List (Quarterly)
Open Mon-Fri 9-3
Friends of the Library Group

R CHRISTIAN THEOLOGICAL SEMINARY LIBRARY, 1000 W 42nd St, 46208. SAN 304-9507. Tel: 317-924-1331. Circulation Tel: 317-931-2361. Reference Tel: 317-931-2367. Toll Free Tel: 800-585-0108. FAX: 317-931-2363. E-mail: research@cts.edu. Web Site: cts.libguides.com/home. *Dir,* Anthony Elia; E-mail: aelia@cts.edu; *Actg Ser Librn, Head, Pub Serv,* Cheryl Miller Maddox; E-mail: cmaddox@cts.edu; *Sysy & Acad Tech Librn,* Dr Alan R Rhoda; Tel: 317-931-2362, E-mail: arhoda@cts.edu; *Acq Mgr, Admin Serv,* Rebecca Furnish; Tel: 317-931-2370, E-mail: rfurnish@cts.edu; *Archives, Spec Coll,* Dr Scott Seay; Tel: 317-931-2347, E-mail: sseay@cts.edu; Staff 4 (MLS 3, Non-MLS 1)
Founded 1942. Enrl 200; Fac 10; Highest Degree: Doctorate
Library Holdings: Bk Vols 220,000; Per Subs 700
Special Collections: Disciples of Christ History (Literature of the Restoration Movement), bks, ms, per
Subject Interests: Culture, Hist, Music, Relig, Soc sci & issues, Theol
Database Vendor: EBSCOhost
Wireless access
Publications: Encounter (Quarterly)
Partic in Academic Libraries of Indiana; Midwest Collaborative for Library Services (MCLS); OCLC Online Computer Library Center, Inc; Private Academic Library Network of Indiana (PALNI)
Special Services for the Blind - Audio mat

M CLARIAN HEALTH PARTNERS*, IU Health Medical Library, 1701 N Senate Blvd, Rm D1422, 46206-1367. SAN 304-9760. Tel: 317-962-8021. Interlibrary Loan Service Tel: 317-962-2979. FAX: 317-962-8397. Web Site: www.clarian.org. Staff 6 (MLS 1, Non-MLS 5)
Founded 1947
Library Holdings: AV Mats 500; Bk Titles 2,700; Bk Vols 4,680; Per Subs 680
Special Collections: Audiovisuals; Health Education
Subject Interests: Med, Nursing
Automation Activity & Vendor Info: (Acquisitions) EBSCO Online; (Cataloging) EOS International; (OPAC) EBSCO Online
Database Vendor: OVID Technologies
Partic in BRS; Central Indiana Health Science Libraries Consortium; Dialog Corp; Midwest Collaborative for Library Services (MCLS); Midwest Health Sci Libr Network
Open Mon-Thurs 7-5:30, Fri 7-4:30

M COMMUNITY HEALTH NETWORK LIBRARY*, 1500 N Ritter Ave, 46219. SAN 304-9515. Tel: 317-355-3600. Interlibrary Loan Service Tel: 317-355-5504. FAX: 317-351-7816. E-mail: library@ecommunity.com. Web Site: www.ecommunity.com/library. *Mgr,* Position Currently Open; *Circuit Librn,* Amy Hughes; Tel: 317-621-5811, E-mail: ahughes2@ecommunity.com; *Circuit Librn,* Liz Orban; Tel: 765-298-2100, E-mail: eorban@ecommunity.com; Staff 4 (MLS 3, Non-MLS 1)
Founded 1960
Library Holdings: e-books 100; e-journals 2,000; Bk Titles 2,781; Bk Vols 3,190; Per Subs 349
Subject Interests: Bus & mgt, Med, Nursing
Automation Activity & Vendor Info: (Acquisitions) LibraryWorld, Inc; (Cataloging) LibraryWorld, Inc; (Circulation) LibraryWorld, Inc; (Course Reserve) ADLiB; (OPAC) LibraryWorld, Inc; (Serials) EBSCO Online
Database Vendor: American Psychological Association (APA), Blackwell, Cinahl, EBSCO Information Services, EBSCOhost, Elsevier, Inspire, Medlib, Medline, Micromedex, OVID Technologies, STAT!Ref (Teton Data Systems), UpToDate, Wiley InterScience
Wireless access
Function: ILL available, Newsp ref libr, Online info literacy tutorials on the web & in blackboard, Online ref, Online searches, Ref serv available, Ref serv in person
Partic in Central Indiana Health Science Libraries Consortium; Health Sci Libr Network; Midwest Collaborative for Library Services (MCLS)
Open Mon-Fri 8:30-5
Restriction: 24-hr pass syst for students only, Access for corporate affiliates, Authorized patrons, Authorized personnel only, Authorized scholars by appt, Badge access after hrs, Circ limited, External users must contact libr, Hospital employees & physicians only, Hospital staff & commun, ID required to use computers (Ltd hrs), Med & nursing staff, patients & families, Med staff & students, Med staff only

R CONGREGATION BETH-EL ZEDECK*, Religious School Library, 600 W 70th St, 46260. SAN 329-2762. Tel: 317-253-3441. FAX: 317-259-6849. Web Site: www.bez613.org. *Librn,* Jane Gabovitch Morrison; E-mail: librarian@bez613.org; Staff 1 (Non-MLS 1)
Founded 1964
Library Holdings: Bk Titles 6,200; Bk Vols 6,400; Per Subs 15
Subject Interests: Judaica
Wireless access

CR CROSSROADS BIBLE COLLEGE*, Kathryn Ulmer Library, 601 N Shortridge Rd, 46219. SAN 327-974X. Tel: 317-352-8736. Toll Free Tel: 800-822-3119. FAX: 317-352-9145. E-mail: librarian@crossroads.edu. Web Site: www.crossroads.edu. *Actg Librn,* Nicholas Piotrowski; Staff 2 (MLS 2)

Founded 1980. Enrl 256; Fac 8; Highest Degree: Bachelor
Library Holdings: Bk Titles 30,156; Bk Vols 35,799
Special Collections: Afro-American History & the Black Church Coll
Subject Interests: Theol
Automation Activity & Vendor Info: (Cataloging) Follett Software; (Circulation) Follett Software; (OPAC) Follett Software
Partic in Midwest Collaborative for Library Services (MCLS)
Open Mon-Thurs 10-7

GM DEPARTMENT OF VETERANS AFFAIRS*, Health Science Library, 1481 W Tenth St, 46202. SAN 304-985X. Tel: 317-554-0000. FAX: 317-988-4846. *Chief Librn,* Linda Bennett; E-mail: linda.bennett@med.va.gov
Founded 1952
Library Holdings: AV Mats 1,500; Bk Vols 6,050; Per Subs 500
Subject Interests: Allied health, Med, Nursing
Automation Activity & Vendor Info: (Acquisitions) EOS International; (Cataloging) EOS International; (Circulation) EOS International; (OPAC) EOS International; (Serials) EOS International
Database Vendor: EBSCOhost
Partic in National Network of Libraries of Medicine
Open Mon-Fri 8-4:30

L KRIEG DEVAULT LLP LIBRARY*, One Indiana Sq, Ste 2800, 46204-2017. SAN 323-5920. Tel: 317-636-4341. Reference Tel: 317-238-6396. FAX: 317-636-1507. Web Site: www.kriegdevault.com. *Librn,* Ann Levy; Staff 2 (MLS 1, Non-MLS 1)
Library Holdings: Bk Titles 20,108; Bk Vols 22,707; Per Subs 36
Partic in Midwest Collaborative for Library Services (MCLS)
Restriction: Staff use only

S DOW AGROSCIENCES*, Information Management Center, 9330 Zionsville Rd, 46268. SAN 375-3972. Tel: 317-337-3517. FAX: 317-337-3245. *Mgr,* Margaret B Hentz; E-mail: mhentz@dow.com; Staff 5 (MLS 3, Non-MLS 2)
Library Holdings: Bk Titles 7,890; Bk Vols 8,140; Per Subs 150
Subject Interests: Agr, Organic chem
Partic in Midwest Collaborative for Library Services (MCLS)
Open Mon-Fri 7:30-4:30

R DOWNEY AVENUE CHRISTIAN CHURCH LIBRARY*, 111 S Downey Ave, 46219. SAN 328-2015. Tel: 317-359-5304. *Librn,* Lois Leamon; Staff 2 (MLS 1, Non-MLS 1)
Library Holdings: Bk Titles 1,025; Bk Vols 1,300; Per Subs 22
Open Mon-Fri 9-3

S EITELJORG MUSEUM OF AMERICAN INDIANS & WESTERN ART*, Watanabe Family Library, 500 W Washington St, 46204-2707. SAN 325-6820. Tel: 317-636-9378, Ext 1346. FAX: 317-264-1446. E-mail: library@eiteljorg.com. *In Charge,* Kitty Jansen; Staff 1 (MLS 1)
Library Holdings: CDs 55; DVDs 40; Bk Vols 6,000; Per Subs 13; Videos 540
Special Collections: The Sidney & Rosalyn Wiener Coll, bks, illustrations, pers
Subject Interests: Am Western art, hist & culture, Native Am art, hist & culture
Partic in Midwest Collaborative for Library Services (MCLS); OCLC Online Computer Library Center, Inc
Open Tues-Sun 12-5

S ELI LILLY & CO*, LINK (Lilly Information & Knowledge), Lilly Corporate Ctr, Drop Code 0737, 46285. SAN 341-3551. Tel: 317-433-0936. FAX: 317-276-4418. Web Site: www.lilly.com. *Mgr,* Nancy F Michael; Tel: 317-651 2259; Staff 21 (MLS 14, Non-MLS 7)
Founded 1890
Library Holdings: e-journals 7,000; Bk Titles 1,000
Special Collections: Domestic & Foreign Drug Encyclopedias Coll; Drug Product Information, cards; Foreign Pharmacopeias Coll
Subject Interests: Biol, Chem, Econ, Law, Med, Toxicology
Automation Activity & Vendor Info: (Cataloging) SirsiDynix; (Circulation) SirsiDynix; (OPAC) SirsiDynix
Wireless access
Partic in Midwest Collaborative for Library Services (MCLS); Midwest Health Sci Libr Network; OCLC Online Computer Library Center, Inc
Open Mon-Fri 9-3
Restriction: Co libr

R ENGLEWOOD CHRISTIAN CHURCH LIBRARY*, 57 N Rural St, 46201. SAN 304-9566. Tel: 317-639-1541. FAX: 317-639-3447. Web Site: www.englewoodcc.com. *Librn,* Norene Martin; Staff 1 (MLS 1)
Founded 1961
Library Holdings: Bk Titles 8,100; Bk Vols 8,310
Special Collections: Children's Library (980 vols)
Subject Interests: Biblical studies, Christianity, Missions & missionaries, Philos, Relig
Open Sun 8-9 & 11:30-12:15

L FAEGRE BAKER DANIELS LIBRARY*, Information Resources, 300 N Meridian St, Ste 2700, 46204. SAN 304-9418. Tel: 317-237-0300. Interlibrary Loan Service Tel: 317-237-1353. FAX: 317-237-1000. *Dir, Res Serv,* Constance Matts; Tel: 317-237-0300, Ext 1353; Staff 6 (MLS 3, Non-MLS 3)
Founded 1952
Automation Activity & Vendor Info: (Cataloging) SydneyPlus; (Serials) SydneyPlus
Wireless access
Partic in Midwest Collaborative for Library Services (MCLS); OCLC Online Computer Library Center, Inc
Restriction: Staff use only

S FEDERAL HOME LOAN BANK OF INDIANAPOLIS LIBRARY*, 8250 Woodfield Crossing Blvd, 46240-7324. SAN 375-0493. Tel: 317-465-0438. FAX: 317-465-0397. Web Site: www.fhlbi.com. *Librn,* Miriam Lemen; Staff 2 (Non-MLS 2)
Library Holdings: Bk Titles 2,375; Bk Vols 2,500; Per Subs 35
Special Collections: Thrift Industry, bks, per, printouts
Publications: Current Library Selections
Partic in Midwest Collaborative for Library Services (MCLS)
Open Mon-Fri 8-5

M FRANCISCAN ST FRANCIS HEALTH, Medical Library, (Formerly Saint Francis Hospital & Health Centers), 8111 S Emerson Ave, 46237. SAN 304-8020. Tel: 317-528-7136. FAX: 317-782-6934. E-mail: asflibrary@franciscanalliance.org. Web Site: www.franciscanalliance.org. *Mgr, Libr Serv,* Ryan M Ayers; Staff 1 (Non-MLS 1)
Founded 1972
Library Holdings: Bk Vols 500; Per Subs 180
Subject Interests: Nursing
Automation Activity & Vendor Info: (Serials) LibraryWorld, Inc
Database Vendor: EBSCOhost, Elsevier, OCLC FirstSearch, OVID Technologies
Wireless access
Partic in BRS; Cent Ind Health Sci Libr Asn; Ind Health Libr Asn; Ind State Libr Asn; Medical Library Association (MLA)
Open Mon-Fri 8-4:30

SR FREE METHODIST CHURCH OF NORTH AMERICA*, Marston Memorial Historical Center & Archives, 770 N High School Rd, 46214. (Mail add: PO Box 535002, 46253-5002), SAN 326-5552. Tel: 317-244-3660. Toll Free Tel: 800-342-5531. FAX: 317-244-1247. E-mail: history@fmcna.org. Web Site: marston.freemethodistchurch.org. *Dir,* Cathy Fortner; E-mail: cathyf@fmcna.org; *Digital Librn,* Kyle Moran; *Archivist,* Kate McGinn; E-mail: katem@fmcna.org; Staff 3 (MLS 2, Non-MLS 1)
Founded 1969
Jan 2011-Dec 2011 Income $62,202, Locally Generated Income $10,044, Parent Institution $40,158, Other $12,000. Mats Exp $3,075, Books $275, Per/Ser (Incl. Access Fees) $120, Manu Arch $500, Micro $680, Presv $1,500. Sal $42,249
Library Holdings: CDs 1; DVDs 10; Bk Titles 11,191; Bk Vols 12,470; Per Subs 10; Videos 170
Special Collections: Methodism (John Wesley Coll), Wesleyana Material, Free Methodist Memoribilia. Oral History
Wireless access
Function: Res libr
Publications: Free Methodist Historical Society (Newsletter)
Restriction: Open by appt only

C HARRISON COLLEGE*, Learning Resources Center, 550 E Washington St, 46204. Tel: 317-447-6216. E-mail: harrison.librarian@harrison.edu. *Librn,* Laura Menard; Staff 6 (MLS 2, Non-MLS 4)
Founded 2006. Enrl 2,000; Fac 125; Highest Degree: Bachelor
Jul 2007-Jun 2008. Mats Exp $22,000, Books $20,000, Per/Ser (Incl. Access Fees) $2,000, Electronic Ref Mat (Incl. Access Fees) $5,000
Library Holdings: AV Mats 15; CDs 10; DVDs 25; Bk Titles 2,500; Bk Vols 3,000; Per Subs 100; Videos 100
Automation Activity & Vendor Info: (Cataloging) Innovative Interfaces, Inc; (Circulation) Innovative Interfaces, Inc; (OPAC) Innovative Interfaces, Inc
Database Vendor: Inspire, OCLC WorldShare Interlibrary Loan, ProQuest, YBP Library Services
Function: Computer training, Copy machines, Distance learning, e-mail serv, Electronic databases & coll, Equip loans & repairs, ILL available, Instruction & testing, Mail & tel request accepted, Online cat, Orientations, Ref serv available, Wheelchair accessible
Open Mon-Thurs 8-9, Fri 10-4
Restriction: Borrowing privileges limited to fac & registered students

L ICE MILLER LLP*, Law Library, One American Sq, Ste 2900, 46282-0020. SAN 321-7698. Tel: 317-236-2414. FAX: 317-592-4207. Web Site: www.icemiller.com. *Dir of Libr Serv,* Melanie A Kelley; E-mail: melanie.kelley@icemiller.com; Staff 5 (MLS 2, Non-MLS 3)
Founded 1910
Library Holdings: Bk Titles 27,891; Bk Vols 30,000; Per Subs 71
Subject Interests: Law, State law
Automation Activity & Vendor Info: (Acquisitions) SIMA, Inc; (Cataloging) SIMA, Inc; (OPAC) SIMA, Inc; (Serials) SIMA, Inc
Wireless access
Partic in Midwest Collaborative for Library Services (MCLS); OCLC Online Computer Library Center, Inc
Open Mon-Fri 8:30-5
Restriction: Clients only

S INDIANA ACADEMY OF SCIENCE*, John Shepard Wright Memorial Library, Indiana State Library, 140 N Senate Ave, 46204-2296. SAN 373-0530. Tel: 317-232-3686. FAX: 317-232-3728. Web Site: www.indianaacademyofscience.org. *Interim Librn,* Doug Conrads; E-mail: dconrads@library.in.gov
Founded 1885
Library Holdings: Bk Vols 13,000
Subject Interests: Natural hist

S INDIANA CHAMBER OF COMMERCE*, Business Research & Information Center, 115 W Washington St S, Ste 850, 46204-3497. SAN 329-1162. Tel: 317-264-3110. FAX: 317-264-6855. Web Site: www.indianachamber.com. Staff 2 (MLS 1, Non-MLS 1)
Library Holdings: Bk Titles 200; Bk Vols 300; Per Subs 100
Special Collections: Indiana Companies & Unions
Subject Interests: Econ, Employee benefits, Employee relations, Mkt, Unions
Publications: Top 200 Indiana Employers
Open Mon-Fri 7-3
Restriction: Mem only, Staff use only

S INDIANA DEPARTMENT OF ENVIRONMENTAL MANAGEMENT*, Office of Legal Counsel Library, 100 N Senate Ave, IGCN 1307, MC 60-01, 46204-2215. SAN 329-4897. Tel: 317-233-3706. FAX: 317-233-5517. *Librn,* Sally Palin
Library Holdings: Bk Titles 1,451; Bk Vols 1,690; Per Subs 88
Subject Interests: Environment, Pollution
Open Mon-Fri 8:30-5

M INDIANA HAND TO SHOULDER CENTER LIBRARY, Ruth Lilly Hand Surgery Library, 8501 Harcourt Rd, 46260-2046. SAN 372-6436. Tel: 317-471-4340. Web Site: www.indianahandtoshoulder.com. *Librn,* Bernie English; E-mail: benglish@ihtsc.com; Staff 1 (MLS 1)
Founded 1980
Library Holdings: DVDs 100; Bk Vols 1,400; Per Subs 16; Videos 200
Special Collections: Hand Rehabilitation; Surgery of Upper Extremity
Subject Interests: Orthopaedic surgery
Automation Activity & Vendor Info: (Cataloging) LibraryWorld, Inc; (OPAC) LibraryWorld, Inc
Database Vendor: EBSCOhost, Inspire, LibraryWorld, Inc, OCLC WorldShare Interlibrary Loan, OVID Technologies, PubMed
Wireless access
Function: Doc delivery serv, For res purposes, Online cat, Online ref, Online searches
Partic in National Network of Libraries of Medicine
Restriction: Staff use only

S INDIANA HISTORICAL SOCIETY LIBRARY, William Henry Smith Memorial Library, 450 W Ohio St, 46202-3269. SAN 304-9639. Tel: 317-232-0321. Toll Free Tel: 800-447-1830. FAX: 317-234-0168. TDD: 317-233-6615. Web Site: www.indianahistory.org. *VPres, Archives & Libr,* Suzanne Hahn; Tel: 317-234-0039, E-mail: shahn@indianahistory.org; Staff 13 (MLS 10, Non-MLS 3)
Founded 1934
Library Holdings: Music Scores 14,000; Bk Titles 45,000
Special Collections: African American History, images, papers; Agricultural History, bks, images, papers; Architectural History, papers; Business History, bks, images, papers; Ethnic History, images, papers; Indiana Mills, images, papers; Indiana Politics, images, paper; Local History, bks, images, papers; Medical History, bks, papers; Military History, images, papers; Northwest Territory & Indiana Territory, papers; Notable Hoosiers, images, papers; Social Services, papers; Transportation, images, papers (Midwestern railroads, interurbans, covered bridges)
Subject Interests: Civil War, Indiana
Database Vendor: Inspire, OCLC Worldshare Management Services, ProQuest
Wireless access
Publications: Black History News & Notes; Indiana Historical Society (Annual report)
Partic in OCLC Online Computer Library Center, Inc
Open Tues-Sat 10-5
Restriction: Closed stack, Non-circulating coll

S INDIANA LANDMARKS, Information Center, (Formerly Historic Landmarks Foundation of Indiana), 1201 Central Ave, 46202-2660. SAN 326-8896. Tel: 317-639-4534. Toll Free Tel: 800-450-4534. FAX: 317-639-6734. E-mail: info@indianalandmarks.org. Web Site: www.indianalandmarks.org. *Dir of Educ,* Suzanne Stanis; E-mail: sstanis@indianalandmarks.org; Staff 1 (MLS 1)
Library Holdings: Bk Titles 3,000; Per Subs 90
Subject Interests: Archit
Automation Activity & Vendor Info: (Acquisitions) LibraryWorld, Inc; (Cataloging) LibraryWorld, Inc; (Circulation) LibraryWorld, Inc
Publications: The Indiana Preservationist
Partic in Midwest Collaborative for Library Services (MCLS)

P INDIANA STATE LIBRARY*, 315 W Ohio St, 46202. (Mail add: 140 N Senate, 46204), SAN 341-2628. Tel: 317-232-3675. Reference Tel: 317-232-3678. Administration Tel: 317-232-3692. Information Services Tel: 317-232-3697. Toll Free Tel: 866-683-0008. FAX: 317-232-0002. Administration FAX: 317-232-3682. TDD: 317-232-7763. E-mail: ldo@library.in.gov. Web Site: www.in.gov/library. *State Librn,* Jacob Speer; *Assoc Dir,* Connie Bruder; Tel: 317-232-3693, E-mail: cbruder@library.in.gov; *Assoc Dir, Statewide Serv,* Wendy Knapp; Tel: 317-232-3691, E-mail: wknapp@library.in.gov; *Head, Syst,* Adam Bowling; Tel: 317-232-3290, E-mail: adbowling@library.in.gov; *Digital Initiatives Librn,* Connie Rendfeld; Tel: 317-232-3694, E-mail: crendfeld@library.in.gov; *Librn for Blind & Physically Handicapped,* Maggie Ansty; Tel: 317-232-3738, E-mail: mansty@library.in.gov; *Supvr, Libr Develop,* Steven J Schmidt; Tel: 317-232-3715, E-mail: steschmidt@library.in.gov; *LSTA Coordr,* Jennifer Clifton; Tel: 317-234-6550, E-mail: jclifton@library.in.gov; *Acq,* Mary Kelley; Tel: 317-232-1939; *Sr Info Spec,* Position Currently Open; Staff 75 (MLS 37, Non-MLS 38)
Founded 1825
Special Collections: Americana (Holliday Coll); Genealogy (Darrach Coll of Indianapolis Pub Libr); Hymn Books (Levering Sunday School); Indiana Academy of Science; Indiana Newspapers; Manuscripts; Shorthand & Typewriting (Strachan Coll). State Document Depository; US Document Depository
Subject Interests: Am hist, Genealogy, Indiana, Libr & info sci, State hist
Automation Activity & Vendor Info: (Cataloging) Evergreen; (Circulation) Evergreen; (ILL) OCLC ILLiad; (OPAC) Evergreen
Database Vendor: EBSCOhost, Gale Cengage Learning
Wireless access
Function: Archival coll, Govt ref serv, Handicapped accessible, ILL available, Libr develop, Newsp ref libr, Prog for adults, Ref serv available, Res libr, Wheelchair accessible, Workshops
Publications: Indiana Insights (Newsletter); Wednesday Word (Current awareness service)
Partic in Evergreen Indiana Consortium; Lyrasis; OCLC Online Computer Library Center, Inc
Special Services for the Deaf - Bks on deafness & sign lang
Special Services for the Blind - Bks & mags in Braille, on rec, tape & cassette; Braille bks; Children's Braille; Screen reader software; Talking bks & player equip; Tel Pioneers equip repair group
Open Mon-Wed & Fri 8-4:30, Thurs 8-7, Sat 8-4

P INDIANA STATE LIBRARY*, Indiana Talking Book & Braille Library, 140 N Senate Ave, 46204-2207. SAN 304-9655. Tel: 317-232-3684. Toll Free Tel: 800-622-4970. FAX: 317-232-3728. TDD: 317-233-5025. E-mail: lbph@library.IN.gov. Web Site: www.in.gov/library/tbbl.html. *Regional Librn,* Margaret Ansty; Tel: 317-232-3738; Staff 5 (MLS 2, Non-MLS 3)
Founded 1934
Library Holdings: Braille Volumes 42,187; Large Print Bks 24,022; Per Subs 19; Talking Bks 305,230; Videos 130
Special Collections: Indiana History & Literature Coll, cassettes, digital talking bk cartridge
Automation Activity & Vendor Info: (Circulation) Keystone Systems, Inc (KLAS)
Wireless access
Publications: In Touch (Newsletter); Indiana Insights (Newsletter)
Special Services for the Blind - Braille equip; Reader equip
Open Mon-Fri 8-4:30, Sat 8-4

GL INDIANA SUPREME COURT LAW LIBRARY*, 316 State House, 200 W Washington St, 46204-2788. SAN 304-968X. Tel: 317-232-2557. FAX: 317-233-8693. Web Site: www.in.gov/judiciary/library. *Librn,* Terri Ross; Staff 3 (MLS 2, Non-MLS 1)
Founded 1867
Library Holdings: Bk Titles 81,290; Bk Vols 83,460; Per Subs 198
Special Collections: US Document Depository
Subject Interests: State law

Automation Activity & Vendor Info: (Cataloging) LibLime; (ILL) OCLC FirstSearch; (OPAC) LibLime
Database Vendor: HeinOnline, LexisNexis, Westlaw
Wireless access
Partic in Midwest Collaborative for Library Services (MCLS); OCLC Online Computer Library Center, Inc
Open Mon-Fri 8:30-4:30

INDIANA UNIVERSITY
CM RUTH LILLY MEDICAL LIBRARY, 975 W Walnut St, IB 100, 46202, SAN 341-2741. Tel: 317-274-7182. Interlibrary Loan Service Tel: 317-274-7184. Administration Tel: 317-274-1404. FAX: 317-278-2385. E-mail: medlref@iupui.edu. Web Site: library.medicine.iu.edu. *Dean,* Dr Jay L Hess; *Dir,* Gabe Rios; Tel: 317-274-1408, E-mail: grrios@iu.edu; *Asst Dir, Libr Operations,* Rick Ralston; Tel: 317-274-1409, E-mail: rralston@iu.edu; *Biomedical Librn,* Kellie Kaneshiro; Tel: 317-274-1612, E-mail: kkaneshi@iu.edu; *Knowledge Mgr, Outreach Coordr,* Elaine Skopelja; Tel: 317-274-8358, E-mail: eskopelj@iu.edu; Staff 16 (MLS 12, Non-MLS 4)
Founded 1908. Enrl 3,591; Fac 1,002; Highest Degree: Doctorate
Library Holdings: Bk Vols 191,853; Per Subs 310; Videos 115
Special Collections: History of Medicine
Subject Interests: Allied health, Med, Nursing
Automation Activity & Vendor Info: (Cataloging) NOTIS
Partic in Association of Research Libraries (ARL); Dialog Corp; National Network of Libraries of Medicine; OCLC Online Computer Library Center, Inc

CM SCHOOL OF DENTISTRY LIBRARY*, 1121 W Michigan St, Rm 128, 46202-5186, SAN 341-2687. Tel: 317-274-7204. Interlibrary Loan Service Tel: 317-274-5203. FAX: 317-278-1256. E-mail: ds-libry@iupui.edu. Web Site: www.iusd.iupui.edu/depts/lib/default.aspx. *Head Librn,* Jan Cox; Tel: 317-274-5207, E-mail: jcox2@iupui.edu; Staff 5 (MLS 2, Non-MLS 3)
Founded 1927. Enrl 619; Fac 129; Highest Degree: Doctorate
Library Holdings: AV Mats 5,940; e-books 40; Bk Vols 26,903; Per Subs 463
Special Collections: Archives Coll
Subject Interests: Dentistry, Med
Automation Activity & Vendor Info: (Acquisitions) SirsiDynix; (Cataloging) SirsiDynix; (Circulation) SirsiDynix; (Course Reserve) SirsiDynix; (ILL) OCLC ILLiad; (OPAC) SirsiDynix; (Serials) SirsiDynix
Database Vendor: OCLC WorldShare Interlibrary Loan, OVID Technologies, PubMed, ScienceDirect, STAT!Ref (Teton Data Systems), Wiley
Function: ILL available, Ref serv available
Partic in National Network of Libraries of Medicine; OCLC Online Computer Library Center, Inc
Open Mon-Thurs 7:30am-10pm, Fri 7:30-5, Sat 9-4:30, Sun 1-5

CL RUTH LILLY LAW LIBRARY*, 530 W New York St, 46202-3225, SAN 341-2717. Tel: 317-274-3884, 317-274-4028. Reference Tel: 317-274-4026. FAX: 317-274-8825. E-mail: circlawl@iupui.edu. Web Site: www.indylaw.indiana.edu/library. *Dir,* Judith Ford Anspach; E-mail: juanspac@iupui.edu; *Assoc Dir,* Miriam A Murphy; E-mail: mimurphy@iupui.edu; *Head, Info Serv,* Catherine Lemmer; E-mail: calemmer@iupui.edu; *Cat Librn,* Chris Evan Long; E-mail: clong@iupui.edu; *Cat & Govt Doc Librn,* Wendell Johnting; E-mail: wjohntin@iupui.edu; *Ref Librn,* Richard E Humphrey; E-mail: rhumphre@iupui.edu; *Res & Instrul Serv Librn,* Susan deMaine; E-mail: sdemaine@iupui.edu; *Res & Instrul Serv Librn,* Benjamin Keele; E-mail: bkeele@iupui.edu; Staff 11 (MLS 3, Non-MLS 8)
Founded 1944. Highest Degree: Doctorate
Library Holdings: Bk Titles 240,391; Bk Vols 584,622; Per Subs 6,300
Special Collections: Commonwealth Coll; Council of Europe; European Communities, law & law-related publications; International & Comparative Materials; OAS Official Records; Rare Book Coll (especially in legal history). UN Document Depository; US Document Depository
Subject Interests: State law, US law
Partic in Academic Libraries of Indiana; Association of Research Libraries (ARL)
Publications: Bibliography of Indiana Legal Materials; Recent Monthly Acquisitions Lists
Open Mon-Fri 7:30am-Midnight, Sat 9-9, Sun 10am-Midnight

C INDIANA UNIVERSITY-PURDUE UNIVERSITY INDIANAPOLIS, University Libraries, 755 W Michigan St, 46202-5195. SAN 341-2776. Tel: 317-274-8278. Circulation Tel: 317-274-0472. Interlibrary Loan Service Tel: 317-274-0500. Reference Tel: 317-274-0483. Administration Tel: 317-274-9833. Information Services Tel: 317-274-0469. FAX: 317-278-0368. Administration FAX: 317-278-2300. Information Services FAX: 317-274-0469. Web Site: www.ulib.iupui.edu. *Dean,* David Lewis; Tel: 317-274-0493, E-mail: dlewis@iupui.edu; *Assoc Dean, Admin & Spec Coll,* Todd Daniels-Howell; Tel: 317-274-0466, E-mail: tjdaniel@iupui.edu; *Assoc Dean, Coll & Info Access,* Position Currently Open; *Assoc Dean, Teaching, Learning & Res,* William Orme; Tel: 317-274-0485, E-mail: orme@iupui.edu; *Assoc Dean, Digital Scholarship,* Kristi Palmer; Tel: 317-278-2327, E-mail: klpalmer@iupui.edu. Subject Specialists: *Archives,* Todd Daniels-Howell; *Film, Liberal arts, Polit sci,* William Orme; Staff 49 (MLS 29, Non-MLS 20)
Founded 1939. Enrl 28,756; Fac 3,178; Highest Degree: Doctorate
Jul 2013-Jun 2014 Income (Main and Other College/University Libraries) $9,795,253, Locally Generated Income $103,000, Parent Institution $9,692,253. Mats Exp $3,739,004, Books $573,666, Per/Ser (Incl. Access Fees) $3,165,338. Sal $3,539,446 (Prof $2,706,626)
Library Holdings: AV Mats 15,838; Bks on Deafness & Sign Lang 724; CDs 2,188; DVDs 3,405; e-books 457,716; e-journals 101,899; Large Print Bks 92; Microforms 96,783; Music Scores 418; Bk Titles 997,269; Bk Vols 1,385,645; Per Subs 2,475; Talking Bks 26; Videos 4,225
Special Collections: Archives Coll; Artists' & Fine Press Book; Digital Colls; German Americana; Philanthropy Coll. Oral History; US Document Depository
Subject Interests: Bus & mgt, Educ, Eng, Humanities, Sci tech, Soc sci & issues
Automation Activity & Vendor Info: (Cataloging) SirsiDynix
Database Vendor: ABC-CLIO, ACM (Association for Computing Machinery), Alexander Street Press, American Chemical Society, American Geophysical Union, American Mathematical Society, American Physical Society, American Psychological Association (APA), Annual Reviews, ARTstor, ASCE Research Library, BioOne, Bloomberg, Booklist Online, Bowker, Brodart, Cambridge Scientific Abstracts, Cinahl, CIOS (Communication Institute for Online Scholarship), College Source, Corbis, CQ Press, CRC Press/Taylor & Francis Group, CredoReference, Dun & Bradstreet, ebrary, EBSCOhost, Elsevier, Emerald, Factiva.com, Foundation Center, Gale Cengage Learning, Greenwood Publishing Group, HeinOnline, IBISWorld, IEEE (Institute of Electrical & Electronics Engineers), infoUSA, Ingenta, Inspire, Integrated Technology Group, IOP, ISI Web of Knowledge, JSTOR, LexisNexis, Marquis Who's Who, McGraw-Hill, Medline, Mergent Online, Modern Language Association, Nature Publishing Group, Newsbank, Newsbank-Readex, OCLC, OCLC FirstSearch, OCLC WorldShare Interlibrary Loan, OVID Technologies, Oxford Online, Plunkett Research, Ltd, Project MUSE, ProQuest, ReferenceUSA, Sage, ScienceDirect, SerialsSolutions, SirsiDynix, Springer-Verlag, Standard & Poor's, STAT!Ref (Teton Data Systems), ValueLine, Wiley, Wiley InterScience, YBP Library Services
Wireless access
Function: Archival coll, Art exhibits, Audio & video playback equip for onsite use, AV serv, Bk club(s), Bks on cassette, Bks on CD, Bus archives, CD-ROM, Computers for patron use, Copy machines, Distance learning, Doc delivery serv, e-mail & chat, E-Reserves, Electronic databases & coll, Exhibits, Fax serv, Free DVD rentals, Games & aids for the handicapped, Govt ref serv, Handicapped accessible, ILL available, Instruction & testing, Large print keyboards, Libr develop, Literacy & newcomer serv, Magazines, Magnifiers for reading, Microfiche/film & reading machines, Movies, Music CDs, Newsp ref libr, Online cat, Online info literacy tutorials on the web & in blackboard, Online ref, Online searches, Orientations, Outreach serv, Outside serv via phone, mail, e-mail & web, Photocopying/Printing, Pub access computers, Ref serv available, Ref serv in person, Scanner, Spanish lang bks, Spoken cassettes & CDs, Spoken cassettes & DVDs, Study rm, Telephone ref, VCDs, VHS videos, Video lending libr, Web-catalog, Wheelchair accessible, Workshops
Partic in Academic Libraries of Indiana; Lyrasis; Midwest Collaborative for Library Services (MCLS); OCLC Online Computer Library Center, Inc
Special Services for the Deaf - Sorenson video relay syst; TTY equip
Special Services for the Blind - Assistive/Adapted tech devices, equip & products; Bks available with recordings; Bks on cassette; Bks on CD; Blind students ctr; Cassettes; Closed caption display syst; Closed circuit TV; Large print bks; Magnifiers; Premier adaptive tech software; Soundproof reading booth; Talking bks; Text reader; Textbks on audio-cassettes; ZoomText magnification & reading software
JAWS; Kurzweil 3000 book reader software
Open Mon-Thurs 7:30am-Midnight, Fri 7:30am-9pm, Sat 8-6, Sun 10am-Midnight
Restriction: Authorized patrons, Borrowing requests are handled by ILL, Circ limited, External users must contact libr, ID required to use computers (Ltd hrs), In-house use for visitors, Limited access based on advanced application, Limited access for the pub, Non-circulating coll, Non-circulating of rare bks, Open to pub for ref & circ; with some limitations, Open to students, fac, staff & alumni, Photo ID required for access, Restricted borrowing privileges, Restricted loan policy, Secured area only open to authorized personnel

Departmental Libraries:

HERRON ART LIBRARY, Herron School of Art & Design, 735 W New York St, 46202, SAN 341-2806. Tel: 317-278-9484. Reference Tel: 317-278-9461. FAX: 317-278-9497. E-mail: herron@iupui.edu. Web Site: www.ulib.iupui.edu/herron. *Dir,* Sonja Staum-Kuniej; Tel: 317-278-9417, E-mail: sstaumku@iupui.edu; *Circ Supvr,* Seth Kong; Tel: 317-278-9434, E-mail: pkong@iupui.edu; *Visual Res Spec,* Danita Davis; Tel: 317-278-9439, E-mail: dldavis@iupui.edu; Staff 4 (MLS 2, Non-MLS 2)
Founded 1970. Enrl 900; Fac 70; Highest Degree: Master

Library Holdings: Bk Vols 24,000; Per Subs 181; Videos 210
Open Mon-Thurs 8-6, Fri 8-5

S INDIANA WOMEN'S PRISON LIBRARY*, 401 N Randolph St, 46201. SAN 304-9701. Tel: 317-639-2671, Ext 248. FAX: 317-684-9643. *In Charge,* Judith Richey; Staff 6 (MLS 1, Non-MLS 5)
Founded 1932
Library Holdings: Bk Titles 12,600; Bk Vols 13,900; Per Subs 44
Open Mon-Thurs 1-9, Fri 9-5

S THE INDIANA YOUTH INSTITUTE*, Virgina Beall Ball Library, 603 E Washington St, Ste 800, 46204-2692. Tel: 317-396-2700. Toll Free Tel: 800-343-7060. FAX: 317-396-2701. E-mail: library@iyi.org. Web Site: www.iyi.org. *Dir of Libr Serv,* Lisa Habegger
Library Holdings: Bk Titles 7,000
Open Mon-Fri 8-5

P INDIANAPOLIS-MARION COUNTY PUBLIC LIBRARY, 2450 N Meridian St, 46208. (Mail add: PO Box 211, 46206-0211), SAN 341-289X. Tel: 317-275-4100. Circulation Tel: 317-275-4105. Interlibrary Loan Service Tel: 317-275-4242. Automation Services Tel: 317-275-4910. FAX: 317-269-5300. Interlibrary Loan Service FAX: 317-229-4510. Administration FAX: 317-269-5220. Automation Services FAX: 317-269-5319. Information Services FAX: 317-229-4507. TDD: 317-269-1833. Web Site: www.imcpl.org. *Chief Exec Officer,* Jackie Nytes; Tel: 317-275-4001, E-mail: jnytes@indypl.org; *Chief Financial Officer,* Rebecca Dixon; Tel: 317-275-4850, E-mail: rdixon@indypl.org; *Dir, Human Res,* Katherine Lerg; Tel: 317-275-4806, Fax: 317-269-5248, E-mail: klerg@indypl.org; *Dir, Coll Mgt,* Deborah Lambert; Tel: 317-275-4721, E-mail: dlambert@indypl.org; *Dir, Prog Develop,* Christine Cairo; Tel: 317-275-4080, E-mail: ccairo@indypl.org; *IT Dir,* Debra Champ; E-mail: dchamp@indypl.org; *Dep Dir, Pub Serv,* Laura Johnson; Tel: 317-275-4012, E-mail: ljohnson@indypl.org; *Area Res Mgr, Cent Libr,* Michael Williams; Tel: 317-275-4302, E-mail: mwilliams@indypl.org; *Area Res Mgr, E Region,* Betsy Crawford; Tel: 317-275-4465, E-mail: bcrawford@indypl.org; *Area Res Mgr, Mid-Region,* Sharon Bernhardt; Tel: 317-275-4475, E-mail: sbernhardt@indypl.org; *Area Res Mgr, W Region,* Carol Schlake; Tel: 317-275-4485, E-mail: cschlake@indypl.org; *Mgr Fac,* Sharon Smith; Tel: 317-275-4301, E-mail: ssmith@indypl.org; *Mgr, Organizational Learning & Development,* Cheryl Wright; Tel: 317-275-4808, E-mail: cwright@indypl.org; *Mgr, Support Serv & Vols Res,* Nancy Stephenson; E-mail: nstephenson@indypl.org; Staff 134 (MLS 134)
Founded 1873. Pop 877,389; Circ 15,977,141
Jan 2013-Dec 2013 Income (Main Library and Branch(s)) $37,725,413, State $2,801,287, Federal $317,508, County $32,367,128, Other $2,239,490. Mats Exp $6,601,615, Books $3,272,688, Per/Ser (Incl. Access Fees) $144,600, AV Mat $1,173,346, Electronic Ref Mat (Incl. Access Fees) $1,249,785. Sal $15,602,466
Library Holdings: AV Mats 169,409; e-books 106,823; Bk Vols 1,635,945; Per Subs 1,999; Videos 121,899
Special Collections: Arthur H Rumpf Menu Coll; Fine Printing Coll; Foundation Coll; Illustrated Children's Books; Indianapolis Authors; James Whitcomb Riley Coll; Julia Connor Thompson Coll; Local Indianapolis History; Storytelling; Wright Marble Cookbook Coll. US Document Depository
Subject Interests: Arts, Bus, Local hist, Music, Patents
Automation Activity & Vendor Info: (Acquisitions) Horizon; (Cataloging) Horizon; (Circulation) Horizon; (ILL) OCLC; (Serials) Horizon
Database Vendor: ABC-CLIO, ALLDATA Online, CQ Press, Dun & Bradstreet, EBSCOhost, Gale Cengage Learning, infoUSA, Inspire, LearningExpress, Mergent Online, Newsbank, ProQuest, Standard & Poor's Wireless access
Function: Adult bk club, After school storytime, Archival coll, Art exhibits, Audio & video playback equip for onsite use, Audiobks via web, Bilingual assistance for Spanish patrons, Bk club(s), Bks on cassette, Bks on CD, Bus archives, CD-ROM, Children's prog, Computer training, Computers for patron use, Copy machines, Digital talking bks, e-mail & chat, E-Reserves, Electronic databases & coll, Exhibits, Free DVD rentals, Govt ref serv, Handicapped accessible, Holiday prog, Home delivery & serv to Sr ctr & nursing homes, Homebound delivery serv, Homework prog, ILL available, Jazz prog, Large print keyboards, Life-long learning prog for all ages, Magazines, Magnifiers for reading, Microfiche/film & reading machines, Music CDs, Online cat, Online searches, Orientations, Outreach serv, OverDrive digital audio bks, Photocopying/Printing, Preschool outreach, Printer for laptops & handheld devices, Prog for adults, Prog for children & young adult, Pub access computers, Ref serv available, Scanner, Senior computer classes, Spanish lang bks, Spoken cassettes & CDs, Spoken cassettes & DVDs, Story hour, Study rm, Summer reading prog, Tax forms, Teen prog, Telephone ref, VHS videos, Video lending libr, Web-catalog, Wheelchair accessible, Workshops
Publications: A Live Thing in the Whole Town (Local historical information); Indianapolis in the World of Books (Local historical information); Stacks: A History of the Indianapolis-Marion County Public Library (Local historical information)
Partic in Midwest Collaborative for Library Services (MCLS); OCLC Online Computer Library Center, Inc
Special Services for the Deaf - Assisted listening device; Assistive tech; Closed caption videos; Sign lang interpreter upon request for prog; Sorenson video relay syst; Video relay serv
Special Services for the Blind - Accessible computers; Assistive/Adapted tech devices, equip & products; Bks on cassette; Bks on CD; Cassettes; Closed circuit TV magnifier; Digital talking bk; Dragon Naturally Speaking software; Home delivery serv; Internet workstation with adaptive software; Large print & cassettes; Large print bks; Lending of low vision aids; Magnifiers; PC for handicapped; Screen enlargement software for people with visual disabilities; Screen reader software; Text reader; ZoomText magnification & reading software
Open Mon-Wed 10-8, Thurs & Fri 10-6, Sat 10-5, Sun 12-5
Friends of the Library Group
Branches: 22
BRIGHTWOOD, 2435 N Sherman Dr, 46218-3852, SAN 341-292X. Tel: 317-275-4310. *Br Mgr,* Rhonda Oliver; Tel: 317-275-4315, E-mail: roliver@indypl.org
Founded 1901
Library Holdings: Bk Vols 15,435
Open Mon-Wed 10-8, Thurs & Fri 10-6, Sat 10-5
COLLEGE AVENUE, 4180 N College Ave, 46205, SAN 341-2989. Tel: 317-275-4320. *Br Mgr,* Rodney Freeman; Tel: 317-275-4325, E-mail: rfreeman@indypl.org
Founded 2000
Library Holdings: Bk Vols 55,216
Open Mon-Thurs 10-8, Fri 10-6, Sat 10-5
Friends of the Library Group
DECATUR, 5301 Kentucky Ave, 46221-6540, SAN 341-3195. Tel: 317-275-4330. *Br Mgr,* Gregory Hill; Tel: 317-275-4335, E-mail: ghill@indypl.org
Founded 1990
Library Holdings: Bk Vols 51,820
Open Mon-Wed 10-8, Thurs & Fri 10-6, Sat 10-5
EAGLE, 3325 Lowry Rd, 46222-1240, SAN 341-3047. Tel: 317-275-4340. *Br Mgr,* Mary Agnes Hylton; Tel: 317-275-4345, E-mail: mhylton@indypl.org
Founded 1970
Library Holdings: Bk Vols 37,927
Open Mon-Wed 10-8, Thurs & Fri 10-6, Sat 10-5
EAST THIRTY-EIGHTH STREET, 5420 E 38th St, 46218-1873, SAN 341-3101. Tel: 317-275-4350. *Br Mgr,* Shanika Heyward; Tel: 317-275-4355, E-mail: sheyward@indypl.org
Founded 1957
Library Holdings: Bk Vols 31,193
Open Mon-Wed 10-8, Thurs & Fri 10-6, Sat 10-5
EAST WASHINGTON, 2822 E Washington St, 46201-4215, SAN 341-3071. Tel: 317-275-4360. *Br Mgr,* Doriene Smither; Tel: 317-275-4365, E-mail: dsmither@indypl.org
Founded 1911
Library Holdings: Bk Vols 12,168
Open Mon-Wed 10-8, Thurs & Fri 10-6, Sat 10-5
FLANNER HOUSE, 2424 Dr Martin Luther King Jr St, 46208-5598, SAN 341-311X. Tel: 317-275-4370. *Br Mgr,* Denyce Malone; Tel: 317-275-4375, E-mail: dmalone@indypl.org
Founded 1979
Library Holdings: Bk Vols 13,384
Open Mon & Tues 10-8, Wed-Fri 10-6
FOUNTAIN SQUARE, 1066 Virginia Ave, 46203, SAN 341-3284. Tel: 317-275-4390. *Br Mgr,* Peggy Wehr; Tel: 317-275-4395, E-mail: pwehr@indypl.org
Library Holdings: Bk Vols 15,623
Open Mon-Wed 10-8, Thurs & Fri 10-6, Sat 10-5
FRANKLIN ROAD, 5550 S Franklin Rd, 46239, SAN 341-3403. Tel: 317-275-4380. *Br Mgr,* Jill Wetnight; Tel: 317-275-4385, E-mail: jwetnight@indypl.org
Founded 2000
Library Holdings: Bk Vols 83,379
Open Mon-Wed 10-8, Thurs & Fri 10-6, Sat 10-5
GARFIELD PARK, 2502 Shelby St, 46203-4236, SAN 341-3314. Tel: 317-275-4490. *Br Mgr,* Judy Clem; Tel: 317-275-4495, E-mail: jclem@indypl.org
Founded 1965
Library Holdings: Bk Vols 32,076
Open Mon-Wed 10-8, Thurs & Fri 10-6, Sat 10-5
GLENDALE, Glendale Town Ctr, 6101 N Keystone Ave, 46220, SAN 341-2954. Tel: 317-275-4410. *Br Mgr,* Melissa Wooton; Tel: 317-275-4415, E-mail: mwooton@indypl.org
Founded 2000
Library Holdings: Bk Vols 105,746
Open Mon-Wed 10-8, Thurs & Fri 10-6, Sat 10-5, Sun 12-5

HAUGHVILLE, 2121 W Michigan St, 46222-3862, SAN 341-3136. Tel: 317-275-4420. *Br Mgr,* Nancy Mobley; Tel: 317-275-4425, E-mail: nmobley@indypl.org
Founded 1897
Library Holdings: Bk Vols 27,583
Open Mon-Wed 10-8, Thurs & Fri 10-6, Sat 10-5

INFOZONE, The Children's Museum, 3000 N Meridian St, 46208. Tel: 317-275-4430. *Br Mgr,* Joan Emmert; Tel: 317-275-4435, E-mail: jemmert@indypl.org
Founded 2000
Library Holdings: Bk Vols 10,122
Open Tues-Thurs (Sept-Feb) 10-8, Fri-Sun 10-5; Mon-Thurs (March-Aug) 10-8, Fri-Sun 10-5

IRVINGTON, 5625 E Washington St, 46219-6411, SAN 341-3012. Tel: 317-275-4450. *Br Mgr,* Sue Kennedy; Tel: 317-275-4455, E-mail: skennedy@indypl.org
Founded 1903
Library Holdings: Bk Vols 68,216
Open Mon-Wed 10-8, Thurs & Fri 10-6, Sat 10-5

LAWRENCE, 7898 N Hague Rd, 46256-1754, SAN 341-3160. Tel: 317-275-4460. *Br Mgr,* Ann Grilliot; Tel: 317-275-4463, E-mail: agrilliot@indypl.org
Founded 1983
Library Holdings: Bk Vols 92,722
Open Mon-Wed 10-8, Thurs & Fri 10-6, Sat 10-5, Sun 12-5

NORA, 8625 Guilford Ave, 46240-1835, SAN 341-3225. Tel: 317-275-4470. *Br Mgr,* Delia Blanchard; Tel: 317-275-4473, E-mail: dblanchard@indypl.org
Library Holdings: Bk Vols 93,963
Open Mon-Wed 10-8, Thurs & Fri 10-6, Sat 10-5, Sun 12-5

PIKE, 6525 Zionsville Rd, 46268-2352, SAN 341-3527. Tel: 317-275-4480. *Br Mgr,* Tia Jah Wynne Ayers; Tel: 317-275-4487, E-mail: twayers@indypl.org
Library Holdings: Bk Vols 84,230
Open Mon-Wed 10-8, Thurs & Fri 10-6, Sat 10-5, Sun 12-5

SOUTHPORT, 2630 E Stop 11 Rd, 46227-8899, SAN 341-3349. Tel: 317-275-4510. *Br Mgr,* Cathy Gage; Tel: 317-275-4517, E-mail: cgage@indypl.org
Founded 1974
Library Holdings: Bk Vols 99,133
Open Mon-Wed 10-8, Thurs & Fri 10-6, Sat 10-5, Sun 12-5

SPADES PARK, 1801 Nowland Ave, 46201-1158, SAN 341-3373. Tel: 317-275-4520. *Br Mgr,* Adam Todd; Tel: 317-275-4522, E-mail: atodd@indypl.org
Founded 1912
Library Holdings: Bk Vols 17,436
Open Mon-Wed 10-8, Thurs & Fri 10-6, Sat 10-5

WARREN, 9701 E 21st St, 46229-1707, SAN 341-3438. Tel: 317-275-4550. *Br Mgr,* Ruth Hans; Tel: 317-275-4555, E-mail: rhans@indypl.org
Founded 1980
Library Holdings: Bk Vols 78,399
Open Mon-Wed 10-8, Thurs & Fri 10-6, Sat 10-5, Sun 12-5

WAYNE, 198 S Girls School Rd, 46231-1120, SAN 341-3462. Tel: 317-275-4530. *Br Mgr,* Melinda Mullican; Tel: 317-275-4537, E-mail: mmullican@indypl.org
Founded 1969
Library Holdings: Bk Vols 73,803
Open Mon-Wed 10-8, Thurs & Fri 10-6, Sat 10-5, Sun 12-5

WEST INDIANAPOLIS, 1216 S Kappes St, 46221-1540, SAN 341-3497. Tel: 317-275-4540. *Br Mgr,* Kimberly Andersen; Tel: 317-275-4545, E-mail: kandersen@indypl.org
Library Holdings: Bk Vols 17,002
Open Mon-Wed 10-8, Thurs & Fri 10-6, Sat 10-5

Bookmobiles: 2. Margaret Wagoner, Manager, Outreach Services

S INDIANAPOLIS MUSEUM OF ART*, Stout Reference Library, 4000 Michigan Rd, 46208-3326. SAN 304-9728. Tel: 317-920-2647. FAX: 317-926-8931. E-mail: library@imamuseum.org. Web Site: www.imamuseum.org. *Head, Libr & Archives,* Alba Fernandez-Keys; E-mail: afernandez-keys@imamuseum.org; *Cat/Ref Librn,* Deborah Evans-Cantrell; E-mail: devans-cantrell@imamuseum.org; *Archivist,* Jennifer Whitlock; E-mail: jwhitlock@imamuseum.org; *Libr Asst,* Megan Bettag; E-mail: mbettag@imamuseum.org; Staff 3.5 (MLS 3, Non-MLS 0.5)
Founded 1908
Library Holdings: Bk Vols 100,000; Per Subs 160
Special Collections: Contemporary Design Manufacturer's Catalogs; Indiana Artists Files; Miller House & Garden Coll; Sales & Auction Catalogs
Automation Activity & Vendor Info: (Cataloging) OCLC Connexion; (Circulation) Horizon; (ILL) OCLC ILLiad; (Serials) EBSCO Online
Database Vendor: EBSCOhost, JSTOR, OCLC, Oxford Online, YBP Library Services
Wireless access
Function: Ref serv available, Res libr
Open Tues, Wed & Fri 2-5, Thurs 2-8
Restriction: Non-circulating

J INTERNATIONAL BUSINESS COLLEGE LIBRARY*, 7205 Shadeland Sta, 46256. SAN 375-4456. Tel: 317-841-6400, Ext 194. Administration Tel: 317-813-2311. FAX: 317-841-6419. Web Site: www.intlbusinesscollege.com. *Librn,* Nikki Johnson; Staff 1 (MLS 1)
Founded 2000. Enrl 301; Fac 25; Highest Degree: Associate
Library Holdings: Bk Titles 1,297; Bk Vols 1,462; Per Subs 63
Automation Activity & Vendor Info: (Cataloging) Book Systems; (Circulation) Book Systems; (OPAC) Book Systems
Open Mon-Fri 8-3
Restriction: Non-circulating to the pub

J IVY TECH COMMUNITY COLLEGE*, North Meridian Campus Library, 50 W Fall Creek Pkwy N Dr, 46208-5752. SAN 304-9698. Tel: 317-921-4782. FAX: 317-917-5719. Web Site: wwwcc.ivytech.edu/library/central-indiana. *Dir,* Jan Woodall; Tel: 317-917-5742, E-mail: jwoodall1@ivytech.edu; *Asst Dir,* Erica McFarland; Tel: 317-917-7178, E-mail: emcfarland8@ivytech.edu; *Instrul Librn, Tech Serv Librn,* Donna Funk; Tel: 317-917-7143, E-mail: dfunk@ivytech.edu; *Ref & Instruction Librn,* Meridith Hayden; Tel: 317-916-7993, E-mail: mhayden17@ivytech.edu; *Ref & Instruction Librn,* Kim Hurson; Tel: 317-917-7149, E-mail: khurson@ivytech.edu; Staff 7 (MLS 2, Non-MLS 5)
Founded 1969. Enrl 3,341; Fac 394
Library Holdings: AV Mats 1,216; Bk Titles 23,416; Bk Vols 24,911; Per Subs 100
Subject Interests: Allied health, Bus & mgt, Educ, Sci tech, Vocational educ
Wireless access
Publications: Annual Serials List; Bibliographies; LRC (Newsletter); Periodical Holdings (Annual); reading lists
Partic in Midwest Collaborative for Library Services (MCLS); OCLC Online Computer Library Center, Inc
Open Mon-Thurs 8am-10pm, Fri 8-5, Sat 8-3, Sun 3-10

S LILLY ENDOWMENT LIBRARY*, 2801 N Meridian St, 46208. SAN 304-9744. Tel: 317-924-5471. FAX: 317-926-4431. *Librn,* Elizabeth Hansen; Tel: 317-916-7316, E-mail: hansenb@lei.org; Staff 1 (MLS 1)
Founded 1974
Library Holdings: Bk Titles 4,000; Bk Vols 4,050; Per Subs 100
Subject Interests: Higher educ, Philanthropy, Relig
Automation Activity & Vendor Info: (Acquisitions) Book Systems; (Cataloging) Book Systems; (Circulation) Book Systems; (OPAC) Book Systems; (Serials) Book Systems
Database Vendor: Factiva.com
Partic in Consortium of Foundation Libraries
Restriction: Staff use only

L LOCKE REYNOLDS LLP*, Locke Reynolds Library, 1000 Capital Center S, 201 N Illinois St, Ste 1000, 46204-4210. SAN 323-7397. Tel: 317-237-3800, 317-237-3831. FAX: 317-237-3900. Web Site: www.locke.com. *Librn,* Kimberly Cage; E-mail: kcage@locke.com; Staff 1 (MLS 1)
Founded 1913
Wireless access
Open Mon-Fri 8-4:30

C MARIAN COLLEGE*, Mother Theresa Hackelmeier Memorial Library, 3200 Cold Spring Rd, 46222. SAN 304-9752. Tel: 317-955-6090. Interlibrary Loan Service Tel: 317-955-6008. FAX: 317-955-6418. E-mail: librarystaff@marian.edu. Web Site: www.marian.edu/library. *Dir,* Nancy Kirpatrick; Tel: 317-955-6224, E-mail: nkirkpatrick@marian.edu; *Asst Dir,* Elizabeth Pearson; Tel: 317-955-6223, E-mail: epearson@marian.edu; *Asst Librn,* Sister Patricia Connor; E-mail: gladys@marian.edu; Staff 5 (MLS 3, Non-MLS 2)
Founded 1937. Enrl 1,325; Fac 96; Highest Degree: Bachelor
Library Holdings: Bk Titles 142,690; Bk Vols 145,911; Per Subs 402
Special Collections: Am far west; Archbishop Paul C Schulte, bks, papers; Monsignor Doyle Coll
Subject Interests: Educ, Nursing, Roman Catholic Church
Database Vendor: SirsiDynix
Publications: Annual Report; Marian College Library Guide
Partic in Midwest Collaborative for Library Services (MCLS); OCLC Online Computer Library Center, Inc; Private Academic Library Network of Indiana (PALNI)

S PRESIDENT BENJAMIN HARRISON RESEARCH LIBRARY*, 1230 N Delaware St, 46202. SAN 326-5064. Tel: 317-631-1888. FAX: 317-632-5488. E-mail: harrison@bhpsite.org. Web Site: www.presidentbenjaminharrison.org. *Curator,* Jennifer Capps
Library Holdings: Bk Titles 2,700

Special Collections: Benjamin Harrison Coll
Restriction: Open by appt only

S ROLLS-ROYCE*, Library Information Services, Mail Code S5, 2001 S Tibbs Ave, 46241. (Mail add: Mail Code S5, PO Box 420, 46206-0420), SAN 304-9590. Tel: 317-230-4751. FAX: 317-230-8901. *Librn,* Gabriel Hysong; Staff 3 (MLS 3)
Founded 1941
Library Holdings: Bk Titles 11,210; Bk Vols 12,350; Per Subs 350
Special Collections: Aeronautical Research Council Reports; Allison Archives; Partial Federal Depository for medical government documents for Maui County
Subject Interests: Aerospace, Gas turbines, Metallurgy
Partic in Midwest Collaborative for Library Services (MCLS)
Open Mon-Fri 7:30-5

M ST VINCENT HOSPITAL & HEALTH SERVICES*, Garceau Library, 2001 W 86th St, 46260. SAN 304-9825. Tel: 317-338-2095. FAX: 317-338-6516. Web Site: www.stvincent.org. *Mgr, Libr Serv,* Denise H Rumschlag; Tel: 317-338-3757; Staff 2 (MLS 2)
Founded 1935
Library Holdings: Bk Titles 3,530; Bk Vols 5,000; Per Subs 225
Special Collections: Consumer Senior Health; Hospital Archives Coll
Subject Interests: Hospital admin, Med, Nursing, Spirituality
Automation Activity & Vendor Info: (OPAC) Inmagic, Inc.
Database Vendor: OVID Technologies
Function: Ref serv available
Partic in Central Indiana Health Science Libraries Consortium; Midwest Collaborative for Library Services (MCLS)
Open Mon-Fri 8-4
Restriction: Circulates for staff only

R UNITED PRESBYTERIAN CHURCH*, First Meridian Heights Library, 4701 N Central Ave, 46205. SAN 304-9841. Tel: 317-283-1305. FAX: 317-921-2266. E-mail: fmhpc@live.com. Web Site: www.fmhpc.org. *Adminr,* Rachel Stutsman; Staff 1 (Non-MLS 1)
Founded 1964
Library Holdings: Bk Titles 1,260; Bk Vols 1,550
Subject Interests: Relig
Open Mon-Wed & Fri 10-2

GL UNITED STATES COURTS LIBRARY*, Southern District of Indiana, 46 E Ohio St, Rm 445, 46204. Tel: 317-229-3925. FAX: 317-229-3927. Web Site: www.lb7.uscourts.gov. *Librn,* Sonja Simpson
Library Holdings: Bk Vols 10,000; Per Subs 55
Automation Activity & Vendor Info: (Cataloging) SirsiDynix; (OPAC) SirsiDynix
Database Vendor: LexisNexis, Westlaw
Wireless access
Restriction: Staff use only

C UNIVERSITY OF INDIANAPOLIS*, Krannert Memorial Library, 1400 E Hanna Ave, 46227-3697. SAN 304-9620. Tel: 317-788-3268. Interlibrary Loan Service Tel: 317-788-3398, 317-788-3402. Reference Tel: 317-788-2100, 317-788-6124. Administration Tel: 317-788-3399. Automation Services Tel: 317-788-6106. FAX: 317-788-3275. Web Site: www.kml.uindy.edu. *Dir,* Francesca Busch; E-mail: fbusch@uindy.edu; *Archivist,* Christine Guyonneau; Tel: 317-788-3431, E-mail: guyonneau@uindy.edu; *Cat/Metadata Librn,* Lucy Fields; E-mail: lfields@uindy.edu; *Computer Serv,* Noah Brubaker; E-mail: nbrubaker@uindy.edu; *ILL,* Kim Wenning; E-mail: kwenning@uindy.edu; *Ref & Libr Instruction,* Tedra Richter; E-mail: trichter@uindy.edu; Staff 7 (MLS 7)
Founded 1902. Enrl 5,000; Fac 225; Highest Degree: Doctorate
Jul 2007-Jun 2008 Income $1,240,244. Mats Exp $491,893, Books $83,545, Per/Ser (Incl. Access Fees) $165,748, Other Print Mats $24,211, AV Mat $21,592, Electronic Ref Mat (Incl. Access Fees) $196,451, Presv $346. Sal $471,293 (Prof $317,690)
Library Holdings: AV Mats 4,404; e-books 30,000; e-journals 15; Bk Titles 135,031; Bk Vols 154,257; Per Subs 650
Special Collections: Evangelical United Brethren Memorial Coll; Krannert Coll (specially bd limited editions)
Subject Interests: Educ, Hist, Nursing, Phys therapy, Psychol, Relig
Automation Activity & Vendor Info: (Acquisitions) Ex Libris Group; (Cataloging) Ex Libris Group; (Circulation) Ex Libris Group; (Course Reserve) Ex Libris Group; (ILL) Ex Libris Group; (OPAC) Ex Libris Group; (Serials) Ex Libris Group
Database Vendor: ABC-CLIO, American Psychological Association (APA), ARTstor, BioOne, Cinahl, CredoReference, EBSCOhost, Gale Cengage Learning, LexisNexis, Newsbank, OCLC FirstSearch, OCLC WorldShare Interlibrary Loan, ProQuest, Westlaw
Wireless access
Function: Archival coll, For res purposes, Handicapped accessible, ILL available, Magnifiers for reading, Res libr, Telephone ref, Wheelchair accessible
Partic in Academic Libraries of Indiana; Midwest Collaborative for Library Services (MCLS); Private Academic Library Network of Indiana (PALNI)
Open Mon-Thurs 7:30am-11pm, Fri 7:30am-9pm, Sat 10am-11pm, Sun 1-11pm
Restriction: Open to students, fac & staff, Pub use on premises

JAMESTOWN

P TRI-AREA LIBRARY*, Two W Main St, 46147. (Mail add: PO Box 315, 46147-0315). Tel: 765-676-6190. Web Site: www.bccn.boone.in.us/tri. *Head Librn,* Suzy Rich
Founded 1981
Library Holdings: Bk Titles 10,000
Open Mon 3-6, Tues & Thurs 1-8, Wed 9-6, Fri 1-5, Sat 10-12

JASONVILLE

P JASONVILLE PUBLIC LIBRARY*, 611 W Main St, 47438-0105. SAN 304-9884. Tel: 812-665-2025. E-mail: jvillepl@att.net. *Librn,* Judy Stone; Staff 2 (MLS 1, Non-MLS 1)
Founded 1924. Pop 2,560; Circ 16,890
Library Holdings: CDs 191; Bk Titles 23,411; Bk Vols 25,121; Per Subs 31; Videos 1,041
Special Collections: Indiana History Holdings
Subject Interests: Genealogy
Open Mon 12-7, Wed 12-5, Sat 9-5

JASPER

P JASPER-DUBOIS COUNTY CONTRACTUAL PUBLIC LIBRARY, 1116 Main St, 47546-2899. SAN 304-9892. Tel: 812-482-2712. FAX: 812-482-7123. Web Site: www.jdcpl.us. *Actg Dir,* Christine Golden; E-mail: cgolden@jdcpl.us; *Ch Serv,* Christine Howard; E-mail: choward@jdcpl.us; Staff 23 (MLS 3, Non-MLS 20)
Founded 1934. Pop 32,000; Circ 390,000
Library Holdings: CDs 600; Bk Vols 95,000; Per Subs 220; Talking Bks 3,800; Videos 3,500
Subject Interests: Genealogy, Hist, Indiana
Automation Activity & Vendor Info: (Acquisitions) TLC (The Library Corporation); (Cataloging) TLC (The Library Corporation); (Circulation) TLC (The Library Corporation); (OPAC) TLC (The Library Corporation)
Database Vendor: Baker & Taylor, EBSCOhost, infoUSA, Ingram Library Services, Inspire, LearningExpress, ProQuest, ReferenceUSA, TLC (The Library Corporation), World Book Online
Wireless access
Partic in Midwest Collaborative for Library Services (MCLS)
Open Mon-Thurs 9-8, Fri & Sat 9-5, Sun 12-5
Restriction: Open to pub for ref & circ; with some limitations
Branches: 2
DUBOIS BRANCH LIBRARY, 5506 E Main St, Dubois, 47527. Tel: 812-678-2548. FAX: 812-678-2549. *Mgr,* Anita Murphy; E-mail: amurphy@jdcpl.lib.in.us
Library Holdings: Bk Titles 10,000
Open Mon & Wed 10-8, Tues & Thurs 10-6, Fri & Sat 10-5
FERDINAND BRANCH, 112 E 16th St, Ferdinand, 47542, SAN 371-3717. Tel: 812-367-1671. FAX: 812-367-1063. *Br Mgr,* Trina James; E-mail: tjames@jdcpl.us; Staff 3 (Non-MLS 3)
Founded 1960. Pop 12,000
Library Holdings: Bk Vols 21,000
Automation Activity & Vendor Info: (Serials) TLC (The Library Corporation)
Function: ILL available, Prog for adults, Prog for children & young adult, Ref serv available, Summer reading prog, Telephone ref
Open Mon-Wed 10-8, Thurs-Sat 10-5

JEFFERSONVILLE

P JEFFERSONVILLE TOWNSHIP PUBLIC LIBRARY*, 211 E Court Ave, 47130. (Mail add: PO Box 1548, 47131-1548), SAN 304-9906. Tel: 812-285-5630. Circulation Tel: 812-285-5631. Reference Tel: 812-285-5634. Administration Tel: 812-285-5632. Automation Services Tel: 812-285-5644. FAX: 812-285-5639. Web Site: jefflibrary.org. *Dir,* Libby Pollard; Tel: 812-285-5633, E-mail: lpollard@jefflibrary.org; *Pub Serv Librn,* Harriet Goldberg; E-mail: hgoldberg@jefflibrary.org; *Pub Serv Librn,* Jennifer Wyatt; Tel: 812-285-5640, Fax: 812-285-5642, E-mail: jwyatt@jefflibrary.org; *Adult Serv,* Becky Kelien; E-mail: bkelien@jefflibrary.org; *Youth Serv,* Lori Morgan; Tel: 812-285-5636, E-mail: lmorgan@jefflibrary.org; Staff 11 (MLS 8, Non-MLS 3)
Founded 1900. Pop 56,695; Circ 335,851
Jan 2008-Dec 2008 Income (Main Library and Branch(s)) $1,796,379, State $138,801, Locally Generated Income $1,594,367, Other $63,211. Mats Exp $217,286, Books $157,584, Per/Ser (Incl. Access Fees) $12,230,

AV Mat $44,414, Electronic Ref Mat (Incl. Access Fees) $3,058. Sal $791,071 (Prof $299,844)
Library Holdings: AV Mats 6,184; CDs 4,320; DVDs 1,587; Bk Titles 146,149; Bk Vols 177,767; Per Subs 287; Talking Bks 3,656; Videos 8,427
Special Collections: Local & Indiana History (Indiana Coll), bk, microfilm, photographs
Automation Activity & Vendor Info: (Cataloging) Infor Library & Information Solutions; (Circulation) Infor Library & Information Solutions; (OPAC) Infor Library & Information Solutions
Database Vendor: Baker & Taylor, Booklist Online, EBSCOhost, Infor Library & Information Solutions, Inspire, LearningExpress, OCLC WebJunction, OCLC WorldShare Interlibrary Loan, ProQuest, ValueLine, World Book Online
Wireless access
Function: Adult bk club, AV serv, Bk club(s), Bks on cassette, Bks on CD, Children's prog, Computer training, Computers for patron use, Copy machines, e-mail serv, Electronic databases & coll, Exhibits, Fax serv, Free DVD rentals, Handicapped accessible, Holiday prog, ILL available, Mail & tel request accepted, Music CDs, Notary serv, Online cat, Online ref, Online searches, Orientations, Outreach serv, Outside serv via phone, mail, e-mail & web, Photocopying/Printing, Preschool outreach, Prog for adults, Prog for children & young adult, Pub access computers, Ref serv available, Ref serv in person, Story hour, Summer reading prog, Teen prog, Telephone ref, VHS videos, Web-catalog, Wheelchair accessible, Workshops
Partic in Midwest Collaborative for Library Services (MCLS)
Open Mon-Thurs 10-8, Fri & Sat 9-5
Friends of the Library Group
Branches: 1
CLARKSVILLE BRANCH, 1312 Eastern Blvd, Clarksville, 47129-1704. Tel: 812-285-5640. FAX: 812-285-5642. *Pub Serv Librn,* Jennifer Wyatt; E-mail: jwyatt@jefflibrary.org
Library Holdings: Bk Titles 45,880; Bk Vols 50,461; Per Subs 82
Automation Activity & Vendor Info: (Acquisitions) Baker & Taylor; (Serials) Infor Library & Information Solutions
Database Vendor: Baker & Taylor, Checkpoint Systems, Inc, OCLC FirstSearch, OCLC WorldShare Interlibrary Loan
Open Mon-Thurs 9-9, Fri 9-5:30, Sat 9-5
Friends of the Library Group

C MID-AMERICA COLLEGE OF FUNERAL SERVICE LIBRARY*, 3111 Hamburg Pike, 47130. Tel: 812-288-8878. Toll Free Tel: 800-221-6158. FAX: 812-288-5942. Web Site: www.mid-america.edu. *Librn,* Sonja Pierce
Enrl 125; Fac 9
Library Holdings: AV Mats 110; Bk Titles 1,019; Bk Vols 1,150; Per Subs 19; Spec Interest Per Sub 25
Automation Activity & Vendor Info: (Cataloging) Follett Software
Function: Res libr
Restriction: Not open to pub

JONESBORO

P JONESBORO PUBLIC LIBRARY*, 124 E Fourth St, 46938-1105. SAN 304-9914. Tel: 765-677-9080. E-mail: jonesborolibrary56@yahoo.com. *Dir,* Carol Jones; *Asst Librn,* Terry Jones; Staff 3 (MLS 1, Non-MLS 2)
Founded 1941. Pop 2,073; Circ 10,464
Library Holdings: AV Mats 1,194; Bk Titles 12,668; Bk Vols 14,071; Per Subs 76; Videos 668
Wireless access
Open Mon-Fri 12-7

KENDALLVILLE

P KENDALLVILLE PUBLIC LIBRARY*, 221 S Park Ave, 46755-2248. SAN 341-3675. Tel: 260-343-2010. FAX: 260-343-2011. E-mail: info@kendallvillelibrary.org. Web Site: www.kendallvillelibrary.org. *Dir,* Jenny Draper; E-mail: jdraper@kendallvillelibrary.org; *Head, Tech Serv,* Barb Huth; E-mail: bhuth@kendallvillelibrary.org; *Head, Tech, Syst Adminr,* Reagan Smith; E-mail: rsmith@kendallvillelibrary.org; *Ch,* Beth Munk; E-mail: bmunk@kendallvillelibrary.org; *YA Librn,* Katie Mullins; E-mail: kmullins@kendallvillelibrary.org; *Circ Mgr,* Lynette Barnett; E-mail: lbarnett@kendallvillelibrary.org; *Adult Serv,* Mary Hartman; E-mail: mhartman@kendallvillelibrary.org; Staff 5 (MLS 3, Non-MLS 2)
Founded 1913. Pop 17,241; Circ 207,619
Library Holdings: AV Mats 10,175; Bk Titles 66,782; Bk Vols 68,452; Per Subs 226; Videos 943
Special Collections: Gene Stratton-Porter Coll; M F Owen Scrapbook
Subject Interests: Local hist
Automation Activity & Vendor Info: (Cataloging) TLC (The Library Corporation); (Circulation) TLC (The Library Corporation); (OPAC) TLC (The Library Corporation)
Database Vendor: EBSCOhost
Publications: Annual Report; Newsletter (Monthly); Topic Supplement (Quarterly)
Partic in Evergreen Indiana Consortium; Midwest Collaborative for Library Services (MCLS)
Open Mon-Thurs 9-8, Fri 9-6, Sat 9-3
Friends of the Library Group
Branches: 1
LIMBERLOST PUBLIC LIBRARY, 164 Kelly St, Rome City, 46784. (Mail add: PO Box 447, Rome City, 46784-0447), SAN 341-3705. Tel: 260-854-2775. FAX: 260-854-3382. *Br Mgr,* Bridgett Coe; E-mail: bcoe@kendallvillelibrary.org; *Asst Br Mgr,* Annie Fleck; E-mail: afleck@kendallvillelibrary.org; *Ch Serv,* Joan Miller; E-mail: jmiller2@kendallvillelibrary.org; Staff 2 (MLS 1, Non-MLS 1)
Library Holdings: AV Mats 561; Bk Titles 12,612; Bk Vols 13,141; Per Subs 60; Videos 217
Open Mon 9-8, Tues-Fri 9-5:30, Sat 9-3
Friends of the Library Group

KENTLAND

P KENTLAND-JEFFERSON TOWNSHIP PUBLIC LIBRARY*, 201 E Graham St, 47951-1233. SAN 304-9922. Tel: 219-474-5044. FAX: 219-474-5351. E-mail: kentlandpubliclibrary@gmail.com. Web Site: www.kentland.lib.in.us. *Dir,* Roberta Dewing; Staff 1 (Non-MLS 1)
Founded 1912. Pop 2,000; Circ 22,802
Jan 2012-Dec 2012. Mats Exp $41,000, Books $26,000, Per/Ser (Incl. Access Fees) $3,000, AV Mat $12,000. Sal $38,000
Library Holdings: Audiobooks 612; DVDs 590; Large Print Bks 1,495; Microforms 198; Bk Titles 29,956; Per Subs 65
Automation Activity & Vendor Info: (Acquisitions) Mandarin Library Automation; (Cataloging) Mandarin Library Automation; (Circulation) Mandarin Library Automation; (OPAC) Mandarin Library Automation
Wireless access
Function: Audiobks via web, Bks on CD, Children's prog, Computers for patron use, Copy machines, Fax serv, Free DVD rentals, Handicapped accessible, Holiday prog, ILL available, Microfiche/film & reading machines, Online cat, OverDrive digital audio bks, Photocopying/Printing, Preschool reading prog, Prog for adults, Prog for children & young adult, Pub access computers, Scanner, Story hour, Summer reading prog, Tax forms, Wheelchair accessible
Open Mon 9-8, Tues & Thurs 11-6, Wed 1-8, Fri 9-5, Sat 8-Noon
Friends of the Library Group

KEWANNA

P KEWANNA PUBLIC LIBRARY*, 210 E Main St, 46939-9529. (Mail add: PO Box 365, 46939-0365), SAN 304-9930. Tel: 574-653-2011. FAX: 574-653-2130. E-mail: kewannapublib@yahoo.com. *Dir,* Linda Hawkey; Staff 4 (MLS 2, Non-MLS 2)
Founded 1914. Pop 1,657; Circ 13,100
Jan 2007-Dec 2007 Income $122,350. Mats Exp $28,000. Sal $34,000 (Prof $25,000)
Library Holdings: AV Mats 1,650; Large Print Bks 160; Bk Titles 30,000; Bk Vols 30,000; Per Subs 311; Talking Bks 311; Videos 875
Special Collections: Fulton County; Indiana
Subject Interests: Antiques, Arts & crafts
Open Mon-Fri 10-6, Sat 9-3

KINGMAN

P KINGMAN PUBLIC LIBRARY, 123 W State St, 47952. (Mail add: PO Box 116, 47952-0116), SAN 304-9949. Tel: 765-397-3138. FAX: 765-397-3566. E-mail: kingmanlib@sbcglobal.net. Web Site: www.kingmanlibrary.com. *Dir,* Shannon Hart; Staff 3 (Non-MLS 3)
Founded 1916. Pop 1,610; Circ 3,849
Library Holdings: Audiobooks 100; Bks on Deafness & Sign Lang 4; DVDs 600; Large Print Bks 300; Bk Titles 13,900; Bk Vols 14,000; Per Subs 30; Videos 1,600
Subject Interests: Local hist
Automation Activity & Vendor Info: (Cataloging) Follett Software; (Circulation) Follett Software; (OPAC) Follett Software
Wireless access
Partic in Midwest Collaborative for Library Services (MCLS)
Special Services for the Blind - Talking bks
Open Mon & Tues 2-8, Wed & Thurs 1-5, Fri & Sat 9-3

KIRKLIN

P KIRKLIN PUBLIC LIBRARY*, 115 N Main, 46050. (Mail add: PO Box 8, 46050-0008), SAN 304-9957. Tel: 765-279-8308. FAX: 765-279-8258. Web Site: www.kirklinlibrary.com. *Librn,* Heidi Turner; E-mail: hturner@kirklinlibrary.com; *Ch,* Julie Lafferty; Staff 3 (Non-MLS 3)
Founded 1913. Pop 1,476; Circ 14,764
Library Holdings: Bk Vols 18,000; Per Subs 50
Special Collections: Kirklin History Archives
Automation Activity & Vendor Info: (Acquisitions) Follett Software; (Cataloging) Follett Software; (Serials) Follett Software
Partic in Midwest Collaborative for Library Services (MCLS)

Open Mon & Wed 12-7, Tues & Thurs 10-5, Fri 12-5, Sat 10-3
Friends of the Library Group

KNIGHTSTOWN

P KNIGHTSTOWN PUBLIC LIBRARY*, Five E Main St, 46148-1248. SAN 304-9965. Tel: 765-345-5095. FAX: 765-345-5377. E-mail: ktown_library@hrtc.net. *Dir,* Vanda Carnes; Staff 3 (MLS 1, Non-MLS 2)
Founded 1912. Pop 2,270; Circ 15,911
Library Holdings: AV Mats 1,159; Large Print Bks 151; Bk Titles 18,711; Bk Vols 20,094; Per Subs 67; Talking Bks 65; Videos 615
Special Collections: Knightstown, Henry County & Indiana History; Local Newspaper Coll, 1908-present
Automation Activity & Vendor Info: (Acquisitions) LibraryWorld, Inc; (Cataloging) LibraryWorld, Inc; (Circulation) LibraryWorld, Inc; (OPAC) LibraryWorld, Inc; (Serials) LibraryWorld, Inc
Database Vendor: LibraryWorld, Inc
Wireless access
Function: Bks on cassette, Bks on CD, CD-ROM, Children's prog, Computer training, Computers for patron use, Copy machines, Distance learning, e-mail & chat, e-mail serv, E-Reserves, Electronic databases & coll, Fax serv, Free DVD rentals, Govt ref serv, Holiday prog, Home delivery & serv to Sr ctr & nursing homes, Homebound delivery serv, ILL available, Mail & tel request accepted, Microfiche/film & reading machines, Music CDs, Newsp ref libr, Notary serv, Online cat, Online ref, Online searches, Orientations, Outreach serv, Outside serv via phone, mail, e-mail & web, Photocopying/Printing, Preschool outreach, Preschool reading prog, Printer for laptops & handheld devices, Prog for adults, Prog for children & young adult, Pub access computers, Ref serv available, Ref serv in person, Res libr, Scanner, Senior computer classes, Senior outreach, Serves mentally handicapped consumers, Spoken cassettes & CDs, Story hour, Summer & winter reading prog, Summer reading prog, Tax forms, Teen prog, Telephone ref, VHS videos, Video lending libr, Web-catalog
Partic in Midwest Collaborative for Library Services (MCLS)
Open Mon & Fri 10-5, Tues & Thurs 10-8, Sat 10-3
Friends of the Library Group

KNOX

P STARKE COUNTY PUBLIC LIBRARY SYSTEM*, Henry F Schricker (Main Library), 152 W Culver Rd, 46534-2220. SAN 304-9973. Tel: 574-772-7323. Web Site: www.starkecountylibrary.org. *Dir,* Sheila R Urwiler; E-mail: surwiler@starkecountylibrary.org; *Syst Adminr,* Rob Pitts; *Ch Serv,* Janine Tuttle-Gassere; *Circ,* Mary Wharton; *Patron Serv,* Nancy Barton, *Ref Serv,* Ellen Pitcher; *Tech Serv,* Lisa Hamand; Staff 12 (MLS 3, Non-MLS 9)
Founded 1919. Pop 18,569; Circ 169,497
Jan 2011-Dec 2011 Income (Main Library and Branch(s)) $918,373. Mats Exp $183,665. Sal $533,801
Library Holdings: AV Mats 9,544; Electronic Media & Resources 31; Large Print Bks 2,000; Bk Vols 102,468; Per Subs 287
Subject Interests: Genealogy, Local hist
Automation Activity & Vendor Info: (Acquisitions) Innovative Interfaces, Inc; (Cataloging) Innovative Interfaces, Inc; (Circulation) Innovative Interfaces, Inc; (OPAC) Innovative Interfaces, Inc
Database Vendor: Baker & Taylor, EBSCO Information Services, H W Wilson, Inspire, LearningExpress, ProQuest, ReferenceUSA, TumbleBookLibrary
Wireless access
Function: Art exhibits, AV serv, Bk club(s), Bks on CD, Children's prog, Citizenship assistance, Computer training, Computers for patron use, Copy machines, e-mail & chat, Electronic databases & coll, Exhibits, Fax serv, Free DVD rentals, Genealogy discussion group, Handicapped accessible, ILL available, Music CDs, Notary serv, Online cat, Photocopying/Printing, Prog for adults, Prog for children & young adult, Pub access computers, Ref serv available, Scanner, Spoken cassettes & CDs, Story hour, Summer & winter reading prog, Tax forms, Teen prog, Telephone ref, Wheelchair accessible, Writing prog
Partic in Midwest Collaborative for Library Services (MCLS); Northern Indiana Computer Consortium for Libraries (NICCL)
Special Services for the Deaf - Bks on deafness & sign lang; Closed caption videos
Special Services for the Blind - Audio mat; Bks on cassette; Bks on CD; Copier with enlargement capabilities; Large print bks; Magnifiers; Sound rec
Open Mon-Thurs 9-7, Fri & Sat 9-5
Branches: 3
HAMLET BRANCH, Six N Starke St, Hamlet, 46532. (Mail add: PO Box 8, Hamlet, 46532-0008), SAN 324-2498. Tel: 574-867-6033. *Br Mgr,* Barbara Pilger
Open Mon, Wed & Fri 9-5, Sat 9-12
KOONTZ LAKE BRANCH, 7954 N State Rd 23, Walkerton, 46574, SAN 321-415X. Tel: 574-586-3353. *Br Mgr,* Bonita Davis
Open Mon, Wed & Fri 9-5, Sat 8-11
SAN PIERRE BRANCH, 103 Broadway, San Pierre, 46374. (Mail add: PO Box 218, San Pierre, 46374-0218), SAN 321-4168. Tel: 219-828-4352. *Br Mgr,* Lisa Jakich
Open Mon, Wed & Fri 9-5, Sat 9-12

KOKOMO

C INDIANA UNIVERSITY KOKOMO LIBRARY, 2300 S Washington St, 46904. (Mail add: PO Box 9003, 46904-9003), SAN 305-0009. Tel: 765-455-9265. Circulation Tel: 765-455-9513. Reference Tel: 765-455-9521. E-mail: iuklib@iuk.edu. Web Site: www.iuk.edu/library. *Dean,* Polly Boruff-Jones; Tel: 765-455-9343, E-mail: pboruffj@iuk.edu; *Digital User Experience Librn,* Angie Thorpe; E-mail: atthorpe@iuk.edu; *Info Literacy Librn,* Yan He; E-mail: yh4@iuk.edu; *Ref/Info Serv Librn,* Diane J Bever; E-mail: dbever@iuk.edu; *Tech Serv Librn,* Ria Lukes; E-mail: rlukes@iuk.edu; Staff 8 (MLS 5, Non-MLS 3)
Founded 1945. Enrl 3,648; Fac 120; Highest Degree: Master
Jul 2013-Jun 2014 Income $1,046,151. Mats Exp $418,000, Books $80,000, Per/Ser (Incl. Access Fees) $3,462,323. Sal $352,151 (Prof $257,822)
Library Holdings: CDs 1,005; DVDs 1,664; e-books 500,735; e-journals 89,208; Electronic Media & Resources 567; Microforms 297,087; Bk Vols 158,457; Per Subs 17; Videos 127
Special Collections: State Document Depository; US Document Depository
Automation Activity & Vendor Info: (Acquisitions) SirsiDynix; (Cataloging) SirsiDynix; (Circulation) SirsiDynix; (Course Reserve) SirsiDynix; (ILL) OCLC ILLiad; (Media Booking) SirsiDynix; (OPAC) SirsiDynix; (Serials) SirsiDynix
Wireless access
Publications: Check It Out (Newsletter)
Partic in Academic Libraries of Indiana; Lyrasis; Midwest Collaborative for Library Services (MCLS)
Open Mon-Thurs (Winter) 8am-9pm, Fri 8-5, Sat 12-5, Sun 1-5; Mon-Thurs (Summer) 8-8, Fri 8-5, Sat 12-5

P KOKOMO-HOWARD COUNTY PUBLIC LIBRARY*, 220 N Union St, 46901-4614. SAN 305-0017. Tel: 765-457-3242. Reference Tel: 765-454-4710. FAX: 765-457-3683. E-mail: info@khcpl.org. Web Site: www.khcpl.org. *Dir,* Faith Brautigam; E-mail: fbrautigam@khcpl.org; *Asst Dir,* Peg Harmon; E-mail: pharmon@khcpl.org; *Head, Coll Mgt,* Tammy Keith; E-mail: tkeith@khcpl.org; *Head, Genealogy & Local Hist,* Amy Russell; E-mail: arussell@khcpl.org; *Adult Coll Develop Librn,* Dawn VanBibber; E-mail: dvanbibber@khcpl.org; *Juv Coll Develop Librn,* Debra Andrews; E-mail: dandrews@khcpl.org; *Young Adult Coll Develop Librn,* Melissa Wheelock; E-mail: mwheelock@khcpl.org; *Syst Coordr,* Jennifer Budenz; E-mail: jbudenz@khcpl.org; *Adult Serv,* Trisha Shively; E-mail: tshively@khcpl.org; *AV,* Tonya McClain; E-mail: tmcclain@khcpl.org; *Ch Serv,* Nicole Porter; E-mail: nporter@khcpl.org; *Circ,* Aaron Smith; E-mail: asmith@khcpl.org; *Outreach Serv,* Doug Workinger; E-mail: dworkinger@khcpl.org; *Principal Cataloger,* Eddie Clem; E-mail: eclem@khcpl.org; Staff 102 (MLS 23, Non-MLS 79)
Founded 1885. Pop 76,265; Circ 1,031,349
Jan 2012-Dec 2012 Income $5,087,732, County $5,060,609, Locally Generated Income $27,123. Mats Exp $684,867, Books $397,095, Per/Ser (Incl. Access Fees) $26,579, AV Mat $144,629, Electronic Ref Mat (Incl. Access Fees) $100,122. Sal $2,319,892
Library Holdings: Audiobooks 13,569; Braille Volumes 144; CDs 14,583; DVDs 20,225; e-books 14,297; Electronic Media & Resources 590; Large Print Bks 10,668; Microforms 431; Bk Titles 153,672; Bk Vols 291,799; Per Subs 650; Videos 3,912
Special Collections: Hoosier Art Coll; Howard County Indiana Genealogy & History
Automation Activity & Vendor Info: (Acquisitions) Innovative Interfaces, Inc; (Cataloging) Innovative Interfaces, Inc; (Circulation) Innovative Interfaces, Inc; (ILL) Atlas Systems; (OPAC) Innovative Interfaces, Inc
Database Vendor: ABC-CLIO, EBSCOhost, Foundation Center, Gale Cengage Learning, Grolier Online, Innovative Interfaces, Inc, Inspire, Library Ideas, LLC, OCLC, OCLC FirstSearch, OCLC WorldShare Interlibrary Loan, Overdrive, Inc, ProQuest, ReferenceUSA, TumbleBookLibrary, ValueLine, World Book Online
Wireless access
Function: Telephone ref
Publications: More Than Just Books (Newsletter)
Open Mon-Thurs 9-8, Fri & Sat 9-5:30, Sun 2-5:30
Friends of the Library Group
Branches: 2
RUSSIAVILLE BRANCH, 315 Mesa Dr, Russiaville, 46979, SAN 370-0054. Tel: 765-883-5112. FAX: 765-883-5974. *Br Mgr,* Meredith Wagner; E-mail: mwagner@khcpl.org; Staff 4 (MLS 1, Non-MLS 3)
Founded 1989
Library Holdings: Audiobooks 603; CDs 851; DVDs 2,043; Electronic Media & Resources 95; Large Print Bks 561; Bk Titles 21,145; Bk Vols 21,754; Per Subs 78

Open Mon-Thurs 9-8, Fri & Sat 9-5:30, Sun 2-5:30
Friends of the Library Group
SOUTH BRANCH, 1755 E Center Rd, 46902-5322, SAN 321-8589. Tel: 765-453-4150. FAX: 765-453-6677. *Br Mgr,* Lori Hugley; E-mail: lhugley@khcpl.org; Staff 16 (MLS 3, Non-MLS 13)
Founded 1978
Library Holdings: Audiobooks 3,273; CDs 3,053; DVDs 4,665; Electronic Media & Resources 504; Large Print Bks 1,173; Bk Titles 37,027; Bk Vols 35,987; Per Subs 123; Videos 2,110
Special Collections: Chinese Language Coll, bks, DVDs, mags
Open Mon-Thurs 9-8, Fri & Sat 9-5:30, Sun 2-5:30
Friends of the Library Group
Bookmobiles: 2

M ST VINCENT HEALTH*, St Joseph Hospital Health Science Library, 1907 W Sycamore St, 46901-4113. (Mail add: PO Box 9004, 46904-9004), SAN 305-0025. Tel: 765-456-5499. FAX: 765-456-5823. Web Site: www.stvincent.org. *Librn,* Marie Becker
Founded 1970
Library Holdings: Bk Vols 250; Per Subs 55
Subject Interests: Allied health, Nursing
Wireless access
Partic in Docline
Open Mon-Thurs 9-3

LA CROSSE

P LA CROSSE PUBLIC LIBRARY*, 307 E Main St, 46348. (Mail add: PO Box 300, 46348-0300), SAN 376-5369. Tel: 219-754-2606. FAX: 219-754-2606. E-mail: librarylacrossepublic@gmail.com. Web Site: www.lacrosselibraryonline.org. *Dir,* Patricia Spiess; Staff 5 (Non-MLS 5)
Pop 1,128; Circ 25,000
Library Holdings: Audiobooks 450; AV Mats 1,509; DVDs 2,200; Large Print Bks 450; Bk Titles 19,600; Bk Vols 20,250; Per Subs 50
Automation Activity & Vendor Info: (Acquisitions) Follett Software; (Cataloging) Follett Software; (Circulation) Follett Software
Wireless access
Open Mon 3-8:30, Tues 9-6, Wed 9-8:30, Thurs 3-7, Fri 9-5:30, Sat 9-1

LA PORTE

P LA PORTE COUNTY PUBLIC LIBRARY*, 904 Indiana Ave, 46350-3435. SAN 305-0033. Tel: 219-362-6156. FAX: 219-362-6158. Web Site: www.laportelibrary.org. *Dir,* Fonda Owens; E-mail: fowens@lapcat.org; *Head, Circ,* Keith Kuric; *Ad, AV,* Monicah Fratena; *Ch Mgr,* Susan Bannwart; *Extn Serv Mgr,* Elizabeth Johnson; *IT Mgr,* Rebecca Tomerlin; *Tech Serv,* Kym Ogden; Staff 62 (MLS 13, Non-MLS 49)
Founded 1897. Pop 64,696; Circ 903,285
Jan 2008-Dec 2008 Income (Main Library and Branch(s)) $3,330,000, State $350,000, County $2,800,000, Locally Generated Income $180,000. Mats Exp $611,000, Books $300,000, Per/Ser (Incl. Access Fees) $30,000, Micro $1,000, AV Equip $2,500, AV Mat $210,000, Electronic Ref Mat (Incl. Access Fees) $65,000, Presv $2,500. Sal $1,865,000 (Prof $940,000)
Library Holdings: Audiobooks 12,500; Bks on Deafness & Sign Lang 50; CDs 15,000; DVDs 19,125; e-books 702; Electronic Media & Resources 250; High Interest/Low Vocabulary Bk Vols 2,000; Large Print Bks 30,000; Microforms 11,276; Bk Titles 225,000; Bk Vols 316,000; Per Subs 255; Videos 14,855
Special Collections: History of La Porte County, City of La Porte & State of Indiana
Automation Activity & Vendor Info: (Acquisitions) Innovative Interfaces, Inc; (Cataloging) Innovative Interfaces, Inc; (Circulation) Innovative Interfaces, Inc; (OPAC) Innovative Interfaces, Inc
Database Vendor: Baker & Taylor, Brodart, BWI, EBSCOhost, Innovative Interfaces, Inc, Inspire, Newsbank, OCLC WorldShare Interlibrary Loan, Overdrive, Inc, ReferenceUSA
Wireless access
Partic in Midwest Collaborative for Library Services (MCLS); OCLC Online Computer Library Center, Inc
Open Mon-Thurs 9-8, Fri 9-6, Sat 9-5
Friends of the Library Group
Branches: 6
COOLSPRING, 7089 W 400 N, Michigan City, 46360, SAN 322-5798. Tel: 219-879-3272. FAX: 219-879-3333. *Br Mgr,* Alice Mathews; E-mail: amathews@lapcat.org; Staff 5 (MLS 1, Non-MLS 4)
Function: Adult bk club, Bks on CD, Children's prog, Computers for patron use, Copy machines, Fax serv, Free DVD rentals, Handicapped accessible, Homework prog, ILL available, Magnifiers for reading, Music CDs, Notary serv, Online cat, Photocopying/Printing, Preschool outreach, Prog for adults, Prog for children & young adult, Pub access computers, Ref serv available, Serves mentally handicapped consumers, Spoken cassettes & CDs, Summer reading prog, Tax forms, Teen prog
Restriction: Restricted pub use
Friends of the Library Group
FISH LAKE, 7981 E State Rd 4, Walkerton, 46574. (Mail add: PO Box 125, Walkerton, 46574-0125), SAN 341-3764. Tel: 219-369-1337. FAX: 219-369-1337. *Br Mgr,* Laurie Dittmar; Staff 0.625 (Non-MLS 0.625)
Library Holdings: CDs 250; DVDs 250; Large Print Bks 100; Bk Titles 8,761; Bk Vols 9,414; Per Subs 40
Open Tues 11-7, Wed & Fri 2-6, Thurs 2-7, Sat 10-2
HANNA BRANCH, 202 N Thompson, Hanna, 46340. (Mail add: PO Box 78, Hanna, 46340-0078), SAN 341-3799. Tel: 219-797-4735. FAX: 219-797-4735. *Br Mgr,* Jennifer Zimmerman; Staff 0.75 (Non-MLS 0.75)
Library Holdings: CDs 350; DVDs 800; Bk Titles 8,156; Bk Vols 8,391; Per Subs 32
Open Mon 12-6, Wed 1-7, Thurs & Fri 1-6, Sat 9-1
KINGSFORD HEIGHTS BRANCH, 436 Evanston, Kingsford Heights, 46346. (Mail add: PO Box 219, Kingsford Heights, 46346-0219), SAN 341-3829. Tel: 219-393-3280. FAX: 219-393-3280. *Br Mgr,* Maria Posey; Staff 0.725 (Non-MLS 0.725)
Library Holdings: CDs 350; DVDs 800; Bk Titles 10,158; Bk Vols 11,900; Per Subs 40
Open Mon, Wed & Thurs 1-7, Fri 1-6, Sat 9-2
ROLLING PRAIRIE BRANCH, One E Michigan Ave, Rolling Prairie, 46371. (Mail add: PO Box 157, Rolling Prairie, 46371-0157), SAN 341-3853. Tel: 219-778-2390. FAX: 219-778-2390. *Br Mgr,* Jennifer Monhaut; Staff 0.725 (Non-MLS 0.725)
Library Holdings: CDs 350; DVDs 800; Bk Titles 19,199; Bk Vols 21,140; Per Subs 47
Open Tues 11-6, Wed & Fri 1-6, Thurs 1-7, Sat 9-1
UNION MILLS BRANCH, 3727 W 800 South, Union Mills, 46382-9672. (Mail add: PO Box 189, Union Mills, 46382-0189), SAN 341-3888. Tel: 219-767-2604. FAX: 219-767-2604. *Br Mgr,* Anna Arnett; Staff 0.75 (Non-MLS 0.75)
Library Holdings: CDs 350; DVDs 800; Bk Titles 9,649; Bk Vols 10,112; Per Subs 32
Open Mon 12-7, Tues & Fri 1-6, Wed 1-7, Sat 9-2
Bookmobiles: 1

LADOGA

P LADOGA-CLARK TOWNSHIP PUBLIC LIBRARY*, 128 E Main St, 47954. (Mail add: PO Box 248, 47954-0248), SAN 373-8965. Tel: 765-942-2456. FAX: 765-942-2457. E-mail: ladoga@ladoga.lib.in.us. Web Site: www.ladoga.lib.in.us. *Dir,* Wanda Bennett; Staff 1 (Non-MLS 1)
Founded 1919. Pop 3,372; Circ 11,125
Jan 2011-Dec 2011 Income $74,000. Mats Exp $15,050, Books $10,050, Per/Ser (Incl. Access Fees) $1,000, AV Mat $3,000, Electronic Ref Mat (Incl. Access Fees) $1,000. Sal $35,525 (Prof $25,455)
Library Holdings: AV Mats 100; CDs 65; DVDs 10; Large Print Bks 44; Bk Titles 16,500; Bk Vols 17,000; Per Subs 41; Videos 5
Special Collections: Local History & Genealogy (Maude Long Neff Coll), bks, newsps on microfilm
Automation Activity & Vendor Info: (Acquisitions) Evergreen; (Cataloging) Evergreen; (Circulation) Evergreen; (ILL) Evergreen; (OPAC) Evergreen; (Serials) Evergreen
Database Vendor: Inspire
Wireless access
Publications: Newsletter (Quarterly)
Partic in Evergreen Indiana Consortium
Special Services for the Deaf - Bks on deafness & sign lang
Special Services for the Blind - Audio mat
Open Mon 12-5, Tues & Thurs 1-7, Wed & Fri 10-5, Sat 9-1
Friends of the Library Group

LAFAYETTE

M FRANCISCAN ST ELIZABETH HEALTH*, Bannon Health Sciences Library, 1701 S Creasy Lane, 47905. SAN 341-3918. Tel: 765-502-4010. FAX: 765-502-4011. Web Site: www.ste.org. *Librn,* Patricia A Lunsford; E-mail: patty.lunsford@franciscanalliance.org; *Libr Asst,* Ana Ramirez; Tel: 765-423-6125, Fax: 765-423-6385, E-mail: ana.ramirez@franciscanalliance.org; Staff 2 (MLS 1, Non-MLS 1)
Founded 1919
Library Holdings: Bk Titles 7,680; Bk Vols 8,000; Per Subs 350
Special Collections: Bioethics Coll
Subject Interests: Clinical med, Hospital admin
Automation Activity & Vendor Info: (Cataloging) OCLC Connexion; (Circulation) Mandarin Library Automation; (ILL) SERHOLD; (OPAC) Mandarin Library Automation; (Serials) Basch Subscriptions, Inc
Database Vendor: EBSCOhost, Inspire, Medline, OCLC FirstSearch, OCLC WorldShare Interlibrary Loan, OVID Technologies, PubMed, Sage, ScienceDirect, UpToDate, WebMD
Wireless access
Partic in Docline; Greater Midwest Regional Medical Libr Network; Indiana Health Sciences Librarians Association (IHSLA); Midwest Collaborative for Library Services (MCLS)
Open Mon-Fri 6am-8pm

S TIPPECANOE COUNTY HISTORICAL ASSOCIATION*, Alameda McCollough Research Library, 1001 South St, 47901. SAN 305-0068. Tel: 765-476-8411. FAX: 765-476-8414. E-mail: library@tippecanoehistory.org. Web Site: www.tippecanoehistory.org.
Founded 1925
Library Holdings: Bk Titles 7,684; Bk Vols 8,391; Per Subs 53; Videos 28
Special Collections: Archives Coll, diaries, letters, photos; Local History Coll; Marriage & Local Court Records. Oral History
Subject Interests: Genealogy, Local hist
Wireless access
Function: Res libr
Publications: 100 Years of the TC Courthouse; Grist Mills of Tippecanoe County, Indiana; Indians & A Changing Frontier, The Art of George Winter; Lafayette Newspapers, 150 years; Old Lafayette 1811-1853; Old Lafayette 1854-1875; Recollections of the Early Settlement of the Wabash Valley; Sandford Cox, Tippecanoe Tales (pamphlets on various local subjects); The House That Moses Fowler Built
Partic in Midwest Collaborative for Library Services (MCLS)
Open Thurs & Fri 1-5
Restriction: Non-circulating to the pub
Friends of the Library Group

J TIPPECANOE COUNTY-IVY TECH LIBRARY*, Campus Library, 3101 S Creasy Lane, 47903. (Mail add: PO Box 6299, 47903-6299), SAN 305-0041. Tel: 765-269-5380. Reference Tel: 765-269-5389. Toll Free Tel: 800-669-4882. FAX: 765-269-5383. Web Site: www.ivytech.edu/library/lafayette, www.tcpl.lib.in.us/branch/index.htm. *Managing Librn,* Leanne York; Tel: 765-269-5400, E-mail: lyork@tcpl.lib.in.us; *Col Librn,* Cindy Mitchell; Tel: 765-269-5381, E-mail: cmitchell42@ivytech.edu; *Librn,* Evelyn Samad; Tel: 765-269-5382, E-mail: esamad@ivytech.edu; *Youth Serv Librn,* Kelley Lethgo; Tel: 765-269-5392, E-mail: klethgo@tcpl.lib.in.us; *Circ Supvr,* Joan Strother; E-mail: jstrother@tcpl.lib.in.us; Staff 13 (MLS 5, Non-MLS 8)
Founded 1973. Enrl 6,500; Fac 135; Highest Degree: Associate
Library Holdings: AV Mats 2,000; e-books 34,000; e-journals 7,000; Bk Titles 50,618; Bk Vols 51,000; Per Subs 250
Subject Interests: Bus & mgt, Med, Sci tech
Automation Activity & Vendor Info: (Cataloging) SirsiDynix; (Circulation) SirsiDynix; (Course Reserve) SirsiDynix; (ILL) SirsiDynix; (OPAC) SirsiDynix
Database Vendor: Baker & Taylor, ebrary, EBSCOhost, Gale Cengage Learning, Inspire, LexisNexis, Newsbank, OCLC FirstSearch, OCLC WorldShare Interlibrary Loan, ProQuest, ReferenceUSA, SerialsSolutions, SirsiDynix
Partic in Midwest Collaborative for Library Services (MCLS)
Open Mon-Thurs 8-8, Fri 8-5, Sat 9:30-5, Sun 1-5

P TIPPECANOE COUNTY PUBLIC LIBRARY*, 627 South St, 47901-1470. SAN 305-0076. Tel: 765-429-0100. FAX: 765-429-0150. Web Site: www.tcpl.lib.in.us. *County Librn,* Jos N Holman; *Asst County Librn,* Amy Paget; E-mail: amypaget@tcpl.lib.in.us; *Head, Ref,* Alison Moss; E-mail: amoss@tcpl.lib.in.us; *Head, Youth Serv,* Carol Stults; E-mail: cstults@tcpl.lib.in.us; *Managing Librn,* Leanne York; E-mail: lyork@tcpl.lib.in.us; *Tech Serv,* Terry Travis; E-mail: tmtravis@tcpl.lib.in.us; Staff 24 (MLS 20, Non-MLS 4)
Founded 1882. Pop 121,891; Circ 1,143,198
Library Holdings: AV Mats 11,945; CDs 180; Large Print Bks 495; Bk Titles 301,117; Bk Vols 302,011; Per Subs 1,947; Videos 1,865
Special Collections: Indiana Coll; Large Print Books; Local Newspaper Coll, 1831-date, micro; New Reader's Coll
Subject Interests: Mental health
Automation Activity & Vendor Info: (Acquisitions) SirsiDynix; (Circulation) SirsiDynix
Publications: Notes & Quotes (Newsletter); The Pocket Edition (Newsletter)
Special Services for the Blind - Computer with voice synthesizer for visually impaired persons
Open Mon-Thurs 9-9, Fri & Sat 9-6, Sun 1-6
Friends of the Library Group
Branches: 1
KLONDIKE BRANCH, 3062 Lindberg Rd, West Lafayette, 47906. Tel: 765-463-5893. FAX: 765-463-5894. *Br Mgr,* Neal Starkey
Library Holdings: Bk Vols 35,000
Open Mon, Wed, Fri & Sat 10-6, Tues & Thurs 12-9, Sun 1-5
Bookmobiles: 1

LAGRANGE

P LAGRANGE COUNTY PUBLIC LIBRARY*, 203 W Spring St, 46761-1845. SAN 341-3977. Tel: 260-463-2841. FAX: 260-463-2843. E-mail: info@lagrange.lib.in.us. Web Site: www.lagrange.lib.in.us. *Dir,* Mary Hooley; Staff 20 (MLS 1, Non-MLS 19)
Founded 1919. Pop 37,032; Circ 250,000
Library Holdings: AV Mats 5,700; CDs 2,200; DVDs 1,700; Large Print Bks 3,800; Bk Titles 65,000; Bk Vols 100,000; Per Subs 150; Videos 1,000
Special Collections: Census Records (LaGrange County: 1830-1940), microfilm; Genealogy Department (Local Hist bks, Ohio & Pennsylvania Histories); Local Newspaper (LaGrange Standard: 1863 to present), microfilm; Local Newspaper (Topeka Journal: 1905-1957), microfilm
Automation Activity & Vendor Info: (Cataloging) Evergreen; (Circulation) Evergreen; (ILL) OCLC FirstSearch; (OPAC) Evergreen
Database Vendor: TLC (The Library Corporation)
Wireless access
Function: Bk club(s), Bks on CD, Children's prog, Computers for patron use, Copy machines, E-Reserves, Fax serv, Free DVD rentals, Handicapped accessible, ILL available, Microfiche/film & reading machines, Music CDs, Online cat, Online searches, Prog for adults, Prog for children & young adult, Pub access computers, Ref serv available, Scanner, Story hour, Summer reading prog, Tax forms, Teen prog, Wheelchair accessible, Writing prog
Special Services for the Deaf - Bks on deafness & sign lang
Special Services for the Blind - Bks on CD; Copier with enlargement capabilities; Extensive large print coll; Large print bks; Recorded bks
Open Mon-Thurs 9-8, Fri & Sat 9-5
Friends of the Library Group
Branches: 2
SHIPSHEWANA BRANCH, 350 Depot St, Shipshewana, 46565. (Mail add: PO Box 636, Shipshewana, 46565-0636). Tel: 260-768-7444. FAX: 260-768-7290. E-mail: shipshe@lagrange.lib.in.us. *Br Mgr,* Vickie Short
Founded 1989
Library Holdings: Bk Titles 8,000; Per Subs 20
Function: Computers for patron use, Copy machines, Fax serv, Free DVD rentals, ILL available, Music CDs, Online cat
Open Mon, Tues, Thurs & Fri 11:30-6, Wed & Sat 8:30-3
TOPEKA BRANCH, 133 N Main St, Topeka, 46571. (Mail add: PO Box 236, Topeka, 46571), SAN 341-406X. Tel: 260-593-3030. FAX: 260-593-3032. E-mail: topeka@lagrange.lib.in.us. *Br Mgr,* Heidi Trivett
Founded 1939
Library Holdings: Bk Titles 7,000; Bk Vols 10,000; Per Subs 73
Function: Computers for patron use, Copy machines, Fax serv, Free DVD rentals, ILL available, Music CDs, Online cat, Teen prog
Open Mon, Tues, Thurs & Fri 11:30-6, Wed & Sat 8:30-3
Bookmobiles: 1

LAKE VILLAGE

P NEWTON COUNTY PUBLIC LIBRARY*, Lake Village Memorial Township Library, 9444 N 315 W, 46349. (Mail add: PO Box 206, 46349-0206), SAN 305-0084. Tel: 219-992-3490. FAX: 219-992-9198. E-mail: lakevil@netnitco.net. Web Site: www.newton.lib.in.us. *Br Mgr,* Sandra J Canaday; Staff 5 (MLS 1, Non-MLS 4)
Founded 1947. Pop 9,235; Circ 106,184
Jan 2012-Dec 2012 Income (Main Library and Branch(s)) $707,032, State $28,558, Locally Generated Income $657,123, Other $21,351. Mats Exp $88,517, Books $50,267, Per/Ser (Incl. Access Fees) $5,141, AV Mat $24,391, Electronic Ref Mat (Incl. Access Fees) $8,718. Sal $361,355 (Prof $48,000)
Library Holdings: Audiobooks 968; Bks on Deafness & Sign Lang 37; DVDs 7,902; e-books 11,368; Electronic Media & Resources 14; Large Print Bks 1,347; Bk Titles 66,350; Bk Vols 80,681; Per Subs 151
Special Collections: Jennie Milk Conrad Coll; Kankakee River, Bogus Island & Beaver Lake Information
Subject Interests: Local hist
Automation Activity & Vendor Info: (Acquisitions) Evergreen; (Cataloging) Evergreen; (Circulation) Evergreen; (OPAC) Evergreen
Database Vendor: Gale Cengage Learning, Inspire, Library Ideas, LLC, Overdrive, Inc, TumbleBookLibrary
Wireless access
Function: Bks on CD, Computers for patron use, Copy machines, e-mail & chat, Exhibits, Fax serv, Free DVD rentals, Handicapped accessible, Homebound delivery serv, ILL available, Notary serv, Online cat, Photocopying/Printing, Prog for adults, Prog for children & young adult, Pub access computers, Scanner, Story hour, Summer reading prog, Tax forms, Telephone ref, Wheelchair accessible
Publications: Literary Speaking (Monthly newsletter)
Partic in Evergreen Indiana Consortium; Midwest Collaborative for Library Services (MCLS)
Special Services for the Deaf - Bks on deafness & sign lang; Closed caption videos; High interest/low vocabulary bks
Special Services for the Blind - Aids for in-house use; Bks on CD; Home delivery serv; Large print bks; Recorded bks; Talking bk serv referral
Open Mon & Thurs 9:30-7:30, Tues, Wed & Fri 9:30-5:30, Sat 9:30-2:30
Branches: 2
MOROCCO COMMUNITY LIBRARY, 205 S West St, Morocco, 47963. (Mail add: PO Box 87, Morocco, 47963-0087), SAN 375-9008. Tel: 219-285-2664. FAX: 219-285-0009. E-mail: morocco@netnitco.net. *Br Mgr,* T Jane Gulley; Staff 6 (MLS 1, Non-MLS 5)
Founded 1963

Special Collections: Carlson Family Arrowhead Coll; Glenwood Perkins Arrowhead Coll
Function: AV serv, Bks on cassette, Bks on CD, Children's prog, Computers for patron use, Copy machines, e-mail & chat, Exhibits, Fax serv, Free DVD rentals, Handicapped accessible, Homebound delivery serv, ILL available, Notary serv, Outreach serv, Photocopying/Printing, Prog for children & young adult, Ref serv available, Story hour, Summer reading prog, Tax forms, Telephone ref, VHS videos, Wheelchair accessible
Special Services for the Deaf - Bks on deafness & sign lang; Closed caption videos; High interest/low vocabulary bks
Special Services for the Blind - Bks on CD; Copier with enlargement capabilities; Extensive large print coll; Home delivery serv; Large print bks
Open Mon, Tues, Thurs & Fri 9:30-5:30, Wed 9:30-7:30, Sat 9:30-1:30
ROSELAWN LIBRARY, 4421 East State Rd 10, Roselawn, 46372. (Mail add: PO Box 57, Roselawn, 46372-0057), SAN 375-9016. Tel: 219-345-2010. FAX: 219-345-2117. E-mail: rosln@netnitco.net. *Br Mgr,* Leposava Tepavcevich; Staff 6 (MLS 1, Non-MLS 5)
Founded 1962
Special Collections: Beaver Lake History Coll; Bogus Island History Coll; Kankakee River History Coll
Function: Bks on CD, Children's prog, Computers for patron use, Copy machines, e-mail & chat, Fax serv, Free DVD rentals, Handicapped accessible, Homebound delivery serv, ILL available, Magnifiers for reading, Prog for children & young adult, Pub access computers, Ref serv available, Story hour, Summer reading prog, Tax forms, Telephone ref, Wheelchair accessible
Special Services for the Deaf - Bks on deafness & sign lang; Closed caption videos; High interest/low vocabulary bks
Special Services for the Blind - Bks on CD; Large print bks; Magnifiers; Talking bk serv referral
Open Mon & Wed-Fri 9:30-5:30, Tues 9:30-7:30, Sat 9:30-2:30

LAWRENCEBURG

M DEARBORN COUNTY HOSPITAL*, Medical Library, 600 Wilson Creek, 47025. SAN 375-1058. Tel: 812-537-1010. FAX: 812-537-2833. *Librn,* Carol Gillespie; Staff 2 (MLS 1, Non-MLS 1)
Library Holdings: Bk Titles 680; Bk Vols 790; Per Subs 41
Subject Interests: Med, Nursing
Restriction: Not open to pub

P LAWRENCEBURG PUBLIC LIBRARY DISTRICT*, 150 Mary St, 47025-1995. SAN 305-0092. Tel: 812-537-2775. Interlibrary Loan Service Tel: 812-537-2775, Ext 29. Administration Tel: 812-537-2775, Ext 21. Automation Services Tel: 812-537-2775, Ext 25. FAX: 812-537-2810. E-mail: lawplib@lpld.lib.in.us. Web Site: www.lpld.lib.in.us. *Dir,* Barbara Bonney; E-mail: bbonney@lpld.lib.in.us; *ILS Syst Mgr,* Debra Beckett; E-mail: dbeckett@lpld.lib.in.us; *Operations & Bus Mgr,* Margie Kleier; E-mail: mkleier@lpld.lib.in.us; *Youth Serv Mgr,* Jody Maples; Tel: 812-537-2775, Ext 23, E-mail: jlmaples@lpld.lib.in.us; Staff 8 (MLS 3, Non-MLS 5)
Founded 1910. Pop 29,000; Circ 176,000
Library Holdings: Bk Titles 75,000; Bk Vols 126,000; Per Subs 310
Special Collections: Dearborn County Indiana Cemetery Records
Subject Interests: Genealogy, Local hist
Automation Activity & Vendor Info: (Cataloging) Innovative Interfaces, Inc; (Circulation) Innovative Interfaces, Inc; (OPAC) Innovative Interfaces, Inc; (Serials) Innovative Interfaces, Inc
Database Vendor: Baker & Taylor, Inspire, OCLC FirstSearch, OCLC WorldShare Interlibrary Loan, ProQuest
Wireless access
Function: Archival coll, Art exhibits, Audio & video playback equip for onsite use, AV serv, Distance learning, Handicapped accessible, Home delivery & serv to Sr ctr & nursing homes, Homebound delivery serv, ILL available, Magnifiers for reading, Music CDs, Online searches, Outside serv via phone, mail, e-mail & web, Photocopying/Printing, Prog for adults, Prog for children & young adult, Ref serv available, Satellite serv, Spoken cassettes & CDs, Summer reading prog, Telephone ref, VHS videos, Wheelchair accessible
Partic in Midwest Collaborative for Library Services (MCLS)
Special Services for the Deaf - Bks on deafness & sign lang; Closed caption videos
Special Services for the Blind - Audio mat; BiFolkal kits; Bks on cassette; Bks on CD; Cassette playback machines; Extensive large print coll; Home delivery serv; Large print bks; Magnifiers; Talking bks
Open Mon-Thurs 9-8, Fri 9-5, Sat 10-5
Friends of the Library Group
Branches: 1
NORTH DEARBORN BRANCH, 25969 Dole Rd, West Harrison, 47060. Tel: 812-637-0777. FAX: 812-637-0797. *Br Mgr,* Phil Kuhn; E-mail: pkuhn@lpld.lib.in.us; Staff 6 (MLS 1, Non-MLS 5)
Pop 29,111; Circ 116,291
Library Holdings: Audiobooks 2,274; AV Mats 6,516; Bks on Deafness & Sign Lang 14; CDs 876; DVDs 860; e-books 208; Bk Titles 96,036; Bk Vols 149,088; Per Subs 482; Talking Bks 323; Videos 5,013
Automation Activity & Vendor Info: (Acquisitions) Innovative Interfaces, Inc; (Cataloging) Innovative Interfaces, Inc; (Circulation) Innovative Interfaces, Inc; (ILL) OCLC WorldShare Interlibrary Loan; (OPAC) Innovative Interfaces, Inc; (Serials) Innovative Interfaces, Inc
Open Mon-Thurs 10-8, Sat 10-5
Friends of the Library Group
Bookmobiles: 1. Outreach Coordr, Jim Farris. Bk titles 5,000

LEAVENWORTH

P BREEDEN MEMORIAL LIBRARY & LITERACY CENTER*, 529 West Old State Rd 62, 47137. Tel: 812-739-4092. FAX: 812-739-2143. E-mail: breedenlibrary@yahoo.com. *Librn,* Sharon A Harvey; E-mail: sharvey58@yahoo.com; Staff 1 (Non-MLS 1)
Founded 1997
Wireless access
Function: Bks on cassette, Bks on CD, Children's prog, Computers for patron use, Copy machines, Free DVD rentals, Handicapped accessible, ILL available, Music CDs, Pub access computers, Scanner, Story hour, Summer reading prog, Tax forms, VHS videos, Wheelchair accessible
Open Mon, Wed, Fri & Sat 10-6
Restriction: Private libr
Friends of the Library Group

LEBANON

P LEBANON PUBLIC LIBRARY*, 104 E Washington St, 46052. SAN 305-1684. Tel: 765-482-3460. FAX: 317-873-5059. Web Site: www.bccn.boone.in.us/LPL. *Dir,* Kay K Martin; E-mail: kay@leblib.org; *Asst Dir, Head Audio/Visual,* Connie Bruder; E-mail: lplav@bccn.boone.in.us; *Head, Children's Dept,* Christina Johnson; Tel: 765-483-2570, E-mail: lplchild@bccn.boone.in.us; *Head, Circ,* Chase Martin; *Head, Genealogical Serv,* Jamey Hickson; E-mail: lplgen@bccn.boone.in.us; *Head, Outreach Serv,* Tammy Culley; E-mail: lplkids@bccn.boone.in.us; *Head, Ref Serv, Webmaster,* Anna Goben; E-mail: lplref@bccn.boone.in.us; *Head, Tech Serv,* Jocelyn Lewis; E-mail: lpltech@bccn.boone.in.us; *Head, YA,* Sarah Bourg; E-mail: lplya@bccn.boone.in.us; *Bus Mgr,* Glenna Lenox; E-mail: lplmgr@bccn.boone.in.us; *IT Coordr,* James Brown; E-mail: lpltech1@bccn.boone.in.us; Staff 12 (MLS 4, Non-MLS 8)
Founded 1905. Pop 17,102; Circ 170,749
Library Holdings: Bks on Deafness & Sign Lang 100; CDs 1,550; DVDs 1,400; Electronic Media & Resources 11; High Interest/Low Vocabulary Bk Vols 200; Large Print Bks 2,400; Music Scores 1,500; Bk Titles 67,015; Per Subs 234; Talking Bks 2,400; Videos 3,000
Special Collections: Abraham Lincoln; Indiana Coll
Subject Interests: Local genealogy
Database Vendor: EBSCOhost, Gale Cengage Learning, LearningExpress, ProQuest, ReferenceUSA, Westlaw
Wireless access
Function: Adult bk club, Archival coll, AV serv, Bi-weekly Writer's Group, Bilingual assistance for Spanish patrons, Bk club(s), Bks on cassette, Bks on CD, Children's prog, Computers for patron use, Copy machines, Electronic databases & coll, Equip loans & repairs, Handicapped accessible, Holiday prog, Home delivery & serv to Sr ctr & nursing homes, Homebound delivery serv, Homework prog, ILL available, Instruction & testing, Music CDs, Online cat, Online ref, Prog for adults, Prog for children & young adult, Ref & res, Summer reading prog, Tax forms, Teen prog, Telephone ref, VHS videos, Video lending libr, Wheelchair accessible, Workshops
Open Mon-Thurs 9-8, Fri 9-6, Sat 9-5 (9-2 Summer)
Friends of the Library Group

LIBERTY

P UNION COUNTY PUBLIC LIBRARY*, Two E Seminary St, 47353-1398. SAN 305-0114. Tel: 765-458-5355, 765-458-6227. FAX: 765-458-9375. E-mail: ucplibrary@gmail.com. Web Site: ucplibrary.org. *Dir,* Karen Kahl; E-mail: karenkahl@hotmail.com; Staff 8 (MLS 1, Non-MLS 7)
Founded 1913. Pop 7,598; Circ 67,840
Library Holdings: CDs 90; Bk Titles 27,867; Bk Vols 29,011; Per Subs 112; Talking Bks 590; Videos 2,644
Subject Interests: Genealogy, Indiana
Automation Activity & Vendor Info: (Cataloging) SirsiDynix; (Circulation) SirsiDynix
Partic in Eastern Ind Area Libr Servs Authority
Open Mon-Fri 9-7, Sat 9-2
Friends of the Library Group

LIGONIER

P LIGONIER PUBLIC LIBRARY*, 300 S Main St, 46767-1812. SAN 305-0122. Tel: 260-894-4511. FAX: 260-894-4509. Web Site: www.ligonier.lib.in.us. *Dir,* Jerry L Nesbitt; E-mail: jnesbitt@ligonier.lib.in.us; Staff 4 (MLS 1, Non-MLS 3)
Founded 1907. Pop 4,410; Circ 26,870
Library Holdings: Bk Titles 24,210; Bk Vols 25,681; Per Subs 102; Talking Bks 159
Special Collections: Jewish Culture (Jewish Historical)
Automation Activity & Vendor Info: (Acquisitions) Mandarin Library Automation; (Cataloging) Mandarin Library Automation; (OPAC) Mandarin Library Automation
Open Mon-Fri 10-7, Sat 8-1

LINCOLN CITY

S US NATIONAL PARK SERVICE*, Lincoln Boyhood National Memorial Library, 2916 E South St, 47552. (Mail add: PO Box 1816, 47552-1816), SAN 323-8652. Tel: 812-937-4541. FAX: 812-937-9929. Web Site: www.nps.gov/libo. *Supvr,* Randy Wester; Staff 2 (Non-MLS 2)
Library Holdings: Bk Titles 1,210; Bk Vols 1,340; Per Subs 22
Special Collections: Abraham Lincoln
Open Mon-Fri (Dec-Feb) 8-4:30; Mon-Fri (March-Nov) 8-5
Restriction: Open to pub for ref only

LINTON

P LINTON PUBLIC LIBRARY, 95 SE First St, 47441. SAN 305-0149. Tel: 812-847-7802. FAX: 812-847-4695. E-mail: lintonpl@lintonpl.lib.in.us. Web Site: www.lintonpl.lib.in.us. Staff 6 (MLS 1, Non-MLS 5)
Founded 1907. Pop 8,447; Circ 60,000
Library Holdings: Bk Vols 33,000; Per Subs 60
Automation Activity & Vendor Info: (Acquisitions) Evergreen; (Cataloging) Evergreen; (Circulation) Evergreen; (OPAC) Evergreen
Database Vendor: Inspire
Wireless access
Open Mon-Thurs (Winter) 10-8, Fri 10-5, Sat 10-3; Mon-Thurs (Summer) 9:30-6, Fri 9:30-5, Sat 9:30-3
Friends of the Library Group

LOGANSPORT

J IVY TECH COMMUNITY COLLEGE OF INDIANA*, One Ivy Way, 46947. SAN 372-722X. Tel. 574-753-5101. FAX: 574-753-5103. Web Site: wwwcc.ivytech.edu/library/kokomo. *Mgr,* Karen Davis; E-mail: kdavis@ivytech.edu; Staff 1 (Non-MLS 1)
Founded 1992. Enrl 500; Fac 7
Library Holdings: AV Mats 720; Bk Titles 1,110; Bk Vols 1,282; Per Subs 47
Open Mon & Thurs 8-8, Tues & Wed 8-6, Fri 8-4:30, Sat 8-12
Friends of the Library Group

P LOGANSPORT-CASS COUNTY PUBLIC LIBRARY*, 616 E Broadway, 46947-3187. SAN 341-4124. Tel: 574-753-6383. FAX: 574-722-5889. E-mail: library@logan.lib.in.us. Web Site: www.logan.lib.in.us. *Dir,* David Ivey; *Asst Dir,* Scott Pletka; *Mgr, Ch Serv,* Patricia Moore; *Tech Serv Mgr,* Sara Borden; Staff 24 (MLS 4, Non-MLS 20)
Founded 1894. Pop 34,992; Circ 625,899
Jan 2012-Dec 2012 Income $1,402,860
Library Holdings: AV Mats 8,688; DVDs 27,458; e-books 3,725; Bk Vols 198,856; Per Subs 290
Automation Activity & Vendor Info: (Cataloging) Innovative Interfaces, Inc; (Circulation) Innovative Interfaces, Inc; (OPAC) Innovative Interfaces, Inc
Database Vendor: Baker & Taylor, EBSCOhost, Gale Cengage Learning, Overdrive, Inc, TumbleBookLibrary
Wireless access
Function: Audio & video playback equip for onsite use, Bks on CD, Children's prog, Copy machines, Electronic databases & coll, Free DVD rentals, Handicapped accessible, Holiday prog, ILL available, Microfiche/film & reading machines, Music CDs, Online cat, Photocopying/Printing, Prog for adults, Prog for children & young adult, Pub access computers, Ref serv available, Spanish lang bks, Story hour, Summer & winter reading prog, Telephone ref, Web-catalog, Wheelchair accessible, Workshops
Open Mon-Fri 9-9, Sat 9-6, Sun Noon-6
Restriction: Non-resident fee
Branches: 1
GALVESTON BRANCH, 304 E Jackson, Galveston, 46932, SAN 341-4159. Tel: 574-699-6170. FAX: 574-699-6171. *Librn,* Patricia Hamilton; Staff 1 (Non-MLS 1)
Library Holdings: DVDs 3,780; Bk Vols 8,250
Open Mon & Wed 10-6, Tues, Thurs & Fri 1-6, Sat 10-3

M LOGANSPORT STATE HOSPITAL*, Staff Library, 1098 S State Rd 25, 46947-9699. Tel: 574-737-3712. FAX: 574-737-3909. TDD: 574-732-0069. *Librn,* Brian Newell
Founded 1938
Library Holdings: Bk Titles 2,000; Per Subs 5
Subject Interests: Forensic psychiat, Nursing, Psychiat, Psychol
Partic in Midwest Collaborative for Library Services (MCLS)

LOOGOOTEE

P LOOGOOTEE PUBLIC LIBRARY*, Frances L Folks Memorial Library, 106 N Line St, 47553. SAN 305-0165. Tel: 812-295-3713. FAX: 812-295-4579. Web Site: www.loogootee.lib.in.us. *Dir,* Darla Wagler; E-mail: dwagler@loogootee.lib.in.us; *Asst Librn,* Terri Trotter; E-mail: ttrotter@loogootee.lib.in.us; Staff 3 (MLS 2, Non-MLS 1)
Founded 1939. Pop 2,958; Circ 15,318
Library Holdings: AV Mats 1,215; Bk Vols 16,000; Per Subs 76; Videos 29
Subject Interests: Bus & mgt, Econ, Hist, Sci tech
Automation Activity & Vendor Info: (Acquisitions) Follett Software; (Cataloging) Follett Software; (Serials) Follett Software
Partic in Evergreen Indiana Consortium; Four Rivers Area Libr Serv Authority
Open Mon 12-7, Tues 10-7, Thurs 10-5, Fri 12-5, Sat 9-1

LOWELL

P LOWELL PUBLIC LIBRARY*, 1505 E Commercial Ave, 46356-1899. SAN 305-0173. Tel: 219-696-7704. FAX: 219-696-5280. Web Site: www.lowellpl.lib.in.us. *Dir,* Eugene Pidzarko; *Asst Dir,* Bethany Gray; *Head, Ref,* Darlene Rigg; *Ad,* Beverly Schoon; Staff 5 (MLS 3, Non-MLS 2)
Pop 17,325; Circ 250,000
Library Holdings: AV Mats 3,259; Large Print Bks 207; Bk Titles 85,065; Bk Vols 87,050; Per Subs 169; Videos 2,701
Subject Interests: Genealogy, Indiana, Local hist
Automation Activity & Vendor Info: (Cataloging) Horizon; (Circulation) Horizon
Wireless access
Publications: Newsletters
Open Mon-Thurs 9-8, Fri & Sat 9-5
Friends of the Library Group
Branches: 2
SCHNEIDER BRANCH, 24002 Parrish Ave, Schneider, 46376. (Mail add: PO Box 19, Schneider, 46376-0019). Tel: 219-552-1000. FAX: 219-552-0137. *Br Head,* Christine Stavros
Library Holdings: Bk Vols 2,000
Open Mon (Winter) 2-7, Tues & Wed 3-6, Thurs 3-7, Sat 10-12; Mon (Summer) 10-1 & 5-7, Tues-Thurs & Sat 10-1
SHELBY BRANCH, 23323 Shelby Rd, Shelby, 46377. (Mail add: PO Box 237, Shelby, 46377-0237). Tel: 219-552-0809. *Br Head,* Ashlee Criner
Library Holdings: Bk Vols 4,000
Open Mon (Winter) 9-12 & 3-7, Tues-Thurs 3-7, Sat 9-2, Mon (Summer) 9-12 & 3-7, Tues-Thurs 9-1, Sat 9-2

LYNN

P LYNN-WASHINGTON TOWNSHIP PUBLIC LIBRARY*, 107 N Main St, 47355. (Mail add: PO Box 127, 47355-0127), SAN 305-0181. Tel: 765-874-1488. FAX: 765-874-1427. E-mail: washtwplib@hotmail.com. Web Site: lynnlibrary.lib.in.us. *Dir,* Suzanne Robinson; Staff 3 (MLS 1, Non-MLS 2)
Founded 1942. Pop 4,108; Circ 93,710
Jan 2013-Dec 2013 Income $72,000. Mats Exp $9,000
Library Holdings: AV Mats 1,096; Bk Titles 20,000; Bk Vols 25,000; Per Subs 67; Talking Bks 32; Videos 112
Automation Activity & Vendor Info: (Acquisitions) Evergreen; (Cataloging) Evergreen; (OPAC) Evergreen

MADISON

J IVY TECH COMMUNITY COLLEGE*, Madison Campus Library, 590 Ivy Tech Dr, 47250. SAN 372-4077. Tel: 812-265-2580, Ext 4102. Toll Free Tel: 800-403-2190. FAX: 812-265-4028. Web Site: wwwcc.ivytech.edu/library/southeast. *Dir,* Tim Renners; Tel: 800-403-2190, Ext 4106, E-mail: trenners@ivytech.edu; Staff 3 (MLS 1, Non-MLS 2)
Founded 1972. Enrl 1,200; Fac 30; Highest Degree: Associate
Library Holdings: e-books 10,000; Large Print Bks 25; Bk Titles 8,000; Bk Vols 8,500; Per Subs 95
Subject Interests: Bus, Computer, Early childhood, Electronics, Nursing, Paralegal, Psychol
Database Vendor: EBSCOhost, Gale Cengage Learning, LexisNexis, ProQuest
Function: Audio & video playback equip for onsite use, AV serv, CD-ROM, Digital talking bks, Distance learning, For res purposes, Handicapped accessible, Health sci info serv, ILL available, Large print

keyboards, Magnifiers for reading, Mail loans to mem, Online searches, Orientations, Outside serv via phone, mail, e-mail & web, Photocopying/Printing, Res libr, Satellite serv, Telephone ref, VHS videos, Wheelchair accessible
Partic in Jefferson County Libr Coop; Midwest Collaborative for Library Services (MCLS); SE Ind Area Libr Servs Authority
Special Services for the Deaf - High interest/low vocabulary bks
Special Services for the Blind - Assistive/Adapted tech devices, equip & products; Braille equip; Cassette playback machines; Computer with voice synthesizer for visually impaired persons; Copier with enlargement capabilities; Dragon Naturally Speaking software; Large print bks; Reader equip; Talking bks
Open Mon-Thurs 9-9, Fri 9-4

P MADISON-JEFFERSON COUNTY PUBLIC LIBRARY*, 420 W Main St, 47250-3796. SAN 305-019X. Tel: 812-265-2744. FAX: 812-265-2217. E-mail: director@mjcpl.org. Web Site: www.mjcpl.org. *Dir,* Position Currently Open; *Asst Dir,* Virgie Dowell; E-mail: asstdir@mjcpl.org; *Ch,* Kara Pettey; Staff 5 (MLS 5)
Founded 1818. Pop 31,700; Circ 188,934
Jan 2008-Dec 2008 Income $1,020,970, County $923,093, Locally Generated Income $94,672, Other $3,205. Mats Exp $154,000, Books $106,000, Per/Ser (Incl. Access Fees) $12,000, AV Mat $30,000, Electronic Ref Mat (Incl. Access Fees) $6,000. Sal $442,175 (Prof $193,210)
Library Holdings: AV Mats 2,551; High Interest/Low Vocabulary Bk Vols 336; Large Print Bks 6,714; Bk Titles 105,905; Per Subs 200; Talking Bks 2,211
Special Collections: Lemen Photog Coll; Local Newspapers 1840-date (Courier Coll), micro
Subject Interests: Genealogy, Local hist
Automation Activity & Vendor Info: (Cataloging) OCLC; (OPAC) LibLime
Database Vendor: Baker & Taylor, Inspire, LearningExpress, OCLC WorldShare Interlibrary Loan, ProQuest
Wireless access
Publications: @ Your Library (Bi-monthly)
Partic in Evergreen Indiana Consortium; Midwest Collaborative for Library Services (MCLS)
Open Mon-Thurs 9-9, Fri 9-6, Sat 9-5, Sun (Sept-May) 1-5
Friends of the Library Group

MARION

C INDIANA WESLEYAN UNIVERSITY*, Lewis A Jackson Library, 4201 S Washington St, 46953. SAN 305-022X. Tel: 765-677-2184. Interlibrary Loan Service Tel: 765-677-2981. Reference Tel: 765-677-2603. FAX: 765-677-2676. Web Site: www2.indwes.edu/library. *Dir,* Sheila O Carlblom; Tel: 765-677-2191, E-mail: sheila.carlblom@indwes.edu; *Off-Campus Libr Serv Dir,* Jule Kind; Tel: 765-672-2980, E-mail: jule.kind@indwes.edu; *Asst Libr Dir,* Alison Johnson; Tel: 765-677-2383, E-mail: alison.johnson@indwes.edu; *Ref & Instruction Librn,* Laura Kelsey; Tel: 765-677-2403, E-mail: laura.kelsey@indwes.edu; *Ref Librn,* Bruce Brinkley; Tel: 765-677-2179, E-mail: bruce.brinkley@indwes.edu; *Ref Librn,* Sarah Crume; Tel: 765-677-2334, E-mail: sarah.crume@indwes.edu; *Ref Librn,* David Dial; Tel: 216-525-6171, E-mail: david.dial@indwes.edu; *Ref Librn,* Lisa Hayes; Tel: 513-881-3611, E-mail: lisa.hayes@indwes.edu; *Ref Librn,* Amy Lorson; Tel: 502-261-5019, E-mail: amy.lorson@indwes.edu; *Ref Librn,* Jaime Painter; Tel: 765-677-2445, E-mail: jaime.painter@indwes.edu; *Ref Librn,* Curt Rice; Tel: 219-769-5173, E-mail: curt.rice@indwes.edu; *Ref Librn,* Jay Wise; Tel: 614-529-7563, E-mail: jay.wise@indwes.edu; *Tech Serv Librn,* Stephen Brown; Tel: 765-677-2197, E-mail: steve.brown@indwes.edu; *Coordr, Acq,* Cheri Colter; Tel: 765-677-2193, E-mail: cheri.colter@indwes.edu; *Cat Tech,* Sharon Cecil; Tel: 765-677-2982, E-mail: sharon.cecil@indwes.edu; *ILL Tech,* Lynn Crawford; E-mail: lynn.crawford@indwes.edu; Staff 20 (MLS 13, Non-MLS 7)
Founded 1920. Enrl 14,901; Fac 1,010; Highest Degree: Doctorate
Jul 2010-Jun 2011. Mats Exp $714,005, Books $272,248, Per/Ser (Incl. Access Fees) $205,130, AV Mat $20,967, Electronic Ref Mat (Incl. Access Fees) $198,090, Presv $17,570. Sal $898,558 (Prof $681,042)
Library Holdings: AV Mats 13,183; CDs 1,120; DVDs 1,538; e-books 80,704; Microforms 315,156; Bk Titles 137,086; Bk Vols 168,115; Per Subs 742
Special Collections: Holiness; Wesleyan Church History
Subject Interests: Counseling, Educ, Nursing, Relig
Automation Activity & Vendor Info: (Acquisitions) Innovative Interfaces, Inc; (Cataloging) Innovative Interfaces, Inc; (Circulation) Innovative Interfaces, Inc; (Course Reserve) Innovative Interfaces, Inc; (OPAC) Innovative Interfaces, Inc; (Serials) Innovative Interfaces, Inc
Database Vendor: ACM (Association for Computing Machinery), Alexander Street Press, American Chemical Society, BCR: Christian Periodical Index, ebrary, EBSCOhost, Emerald, Facts on File, Gale Cengage Learning, infoUSA, Inspire, JSTOR, LexisNexis, OCLC FirstSearch, OVID Technologies, Project MUSE, ProQuest, ValueLine
Wireless access
Function: Audio & video playback equip for onsite use, Handicapped accessible, ILL available, Online searches, Photocopying/Printing, Ref serv available
Partic in Academic Libraries of Indiana; Midwest Collaborative for Library Services (MCLS); OCLC Online Computer Library Center, Inc
Open Mon-Thurs 7:30am-Midnight, Fri 7:30-6, Sat 11-8

M MARION GENERAL HOSPITAL*, Medical Library, 441 N Wabash Ave, 46952. SAN 328-381X. Tel: 765-662-4760. FAX: 765-662-4523. Web Site: www.mgh.net. *Educ Serv Supvr,* Nancy Pyle; Staff 1 (MLS 1)
Library Holdings: Bk Vols 1,301; Per Subs 50; Talking Bks 16
Wireless access
Partic in National Network of Libraries of Medicine
Restriction: Not open to pub

P MARION PUBLIC LIBRARY*, 600 S Washington St, 46953-1992. SAN 305-0238. Tel: 765-668-2900. FAX: 765-668-2911. TDD: 765-668-2907. E-mail: mpl@marion.lib.in.us. Web Site: www.marion.lib.in.us. *Dir,* Mary Theresa Eckerle; E-mail: meckerle@marion.lib.in.us; *Head, Ch,* Clare Jozwiak; *Head, Circ,* Michelle Morgan; *Head, Genealogical Serv,* Rhonda Stoffer; *Mgr, Ref Serv,* Mary Leffler; *Tech Serv,* Karen E Blinn. Subject Specialists: *Genealogy, Hist, Indiana,* Rhonda Stoffer; Staff 49 (MLS 3, Non-MLS 46)
Founded 1884. Pop 31,320; Circ 370,649
Library Holdings: AV Mats 13,179; Bk Vols 136,774; Per Subs 436
Subject Interests: Genealogy, Local hist
Automation Activity & Vendor Info: (Acquisitions) SirsiDynix; (Cataloging) SirsiDynix; (Circulation) SirsiDynix; (OPAC) SirsiDynix
Database Vendor: SirsiDynix
Publications: Special Edition (Newsletter)
Open Mon-Fri 9-8, Sat 9-5, Sun (Winter) 1-4
Friends of the Library Group

GM VA NORTHERN INDIANA HEALTHCARE SYSTEMS*, Hospital Medical Library, 1700 E 38th St, 46953. SAN 305-0254. Tel: 765-677-3110. FAX: 765-677-3111. Web Site: www.northernindiana.va.gov. *Librn,* Karen A Davis; E-mail: karen.davis@va.gov; Staff 2 (Non-MLS 2)
Library Holdings: Bk Titles 5,380; Bk Vols 5,600; Per Subs 50
Subject Interests: Geriatrics & gerontology, Med, Nursing, Psychiat, Psychol
Automation Activity & Vendor Info: (Cataloging) EOS International; (Circulation) EOS International; (OPAC) EOS International
Database Vendor: EBSCOhost
Publications: AV Catalog; Newsletter
Partic in Eastern Ind Area Libr Servs Authority; Greater Midwest Regional Medical Libr Network; Midwest Collaborative for Library Services (MCLS)
Open Mon-Thurs 7:30-4

MARTINSVILLE

P MORGAN COUNTY PUBLIC LIBRARY*, 110 S Jefferson St, 46151. SAN 305-0270. Tel: 765-342-3451. FAX: 765-342-9992. Web Site: morg.lib.in.us. *Dir,* Krista Ledbetter; *Asst Dir,* Jennifer McKinley; *Ch,* Alyssa Morgan; *Ref Librn/Genealogy,* Janice Kistler; *YA Librn,* Cassie Jones; Staff 11 (MLS 5, Non-MLS 6)
Founded 1906. Pop 53,198; Circ 191,669
Library Holdings: AV Mats 2,524; Large Print Bks 480; Bk Titles 119,311; Bk Vols 166,369; Per Subs 225; Videos 416
Subject Interests: Genealogy
Automation Activity & Vendor Info: (Acquisitions) Evergreen; (Cataloging) Evergreen; (OPAC) Evergreen
Database Vendor: EBSCOhost, Evanced Solutions, Inc, Gale Cengage Learning, ProQuest, ReferenceUSA
Wireless access
Function: Accelerated reader prog, After school storytime, Art exhibits, Bk club(s), Bks on cassette, Bks on CD, CD-ROM, Children's prog, Computers for patron use, Copy machines, e-mail & chat, E-Reserves, Electronic databases & coll, Exhibits, Free DVD rentals, Genealogy discussion group, Handicapped accessible, Holiday prog, Home delivery & serv to Sr ctr & nursing homes, ILL available, Instruction & testing, Mail & tel request accepted, Newsp ref libr, Online cat, Outreach serv, Outside serv via phone, mail, e-mail & web, Photocopying/Printing, Prog for adults, Prog for children & young adult, Pub access computers, Ref & res, Ref serv available, Ref serv in person, Story hour, Summer reading prog, Tax forms, Teen prog, Telephone ref, VHS videos, Web-catalog, Wheelchair accessible
Publications: Audio Cassettes List; Children's Calendar (Monthly); Guide to Services; Irregular Bookmark & Handouts for Special Programs; New Book List (Monthly); Newspaper Column (Weekly); Video List
Partic in Ind Libr Film Serv; Midwest Collaborative for Library Services (MCLS)
Open Mon-Thurs 9-8:30, Fri & Sat 9-5:30, Sun 1-5

Branches: 5

BROOKLYN BRANCH, Six E Mill St, Brooklyn, 46111. Tel: 317-834-2003. *Br Mgr,* Pam Shelburne
Library Holdings: Bk Vols 7,777
Database Vendor: EBSCOhost, Gale Cengage Learning, ProQuest, ReferenceUSA
Open Tues & Thurs 12-7, Fri & Sat 9-4:30

EMINENCE BRANCH, Eminence Lion's Club, Walters Rd, Eminence, 46125. (Mail add: 110 S Jefferson St, 46151). Tel: 765-528-2117. *Br Mgr,* Stephanie Wigal
Library Holdings: Bk Vols 4,139
Open Mon & Wed 3-7

MONROVIA BRANCH, 145 S Chestnut St, Monrovia, 46157. (Mail add: PO Box 218, Monrovia, 46157). Tel: 317-996-4307. FAX: 317-996-3439. E-mail: monrovia@mail.morg.lib.in.us. *Br Mgr,* Lorie Long
Library Holdings: Bk Vols 17,444
Open Mon-Thurs 9-8:30, Fri & Sat 9-5:30, Sun 1-5
Friends of the Library Group

MORGANTOWN BRANCH, 79 W Washington St, Morgantown, 46160. Tel: 812-597-0889. E-mail: morgantownlibrary@hotmail.com. *Br Mgr,* Sandy Ball
Library Holdings: Bk Vols 8,300
Database Vendor: EBSCOhost, Gale Cengage Learning, ProQuest, ReferenceUSA
Open Mon & Thurs Noon-7, Wed & Sat 9-4

WAVERLY BRANCH, 9410 State Rd 144, 46151. Tel: 317-422-9915. FAX: 317-422-9415. E-mail: nebranch@hotmail.com. *Br Mgr,* Charles Thrawley
Library Holdings: Bk Vols 30,365
Database Vendor: EBSCOhost, Gale Cengage Learning, ProQuest, ReferenceUSA
Open Mon-Thurs 9-8:30, Fri & Sat 9-5:30, Sun 1-5

MENTONE

P BELL MEMORIAL PUBLIC LIBRARY*, 101 W Main St, 46539. (Mail add: PO Box 368, 46539-0368), SAN 305-0289. Tel: 574-353-7234. FAX: 574-353-1307. Web Site: www.bell.lib.in.us. *Dir,* Krystal Smith; E-mail: ksmith@bell.lib.in.us; Staff 8 (MLS 1, Non-MLS 7)
Founded 1916. Pop 4,281; Circ 59,803
Library Holdings: Bk Titles 36,391; Bk Vols 37,142; Per Subs 490; Talking Bks 1,000, Videos 798
Subject Interests: Agr, Arts & crafts, Genealogy, Hist, Indiana, Local hist, Med, Natural sci, Relig, Sci tech
Partic in Midwest Collaborative for Library Services (MCLS)
Open Mon, Wed, Fri & Sat 9-5, Thurs 9-8, Sun 1-5
Friends of the Library Group

MERRILLVILLE

P LAKE COUNTY PUBLIC LIBRARY*, 1919 W 81st Ave, 46410-5488. SAN 341-4337. Tel: 219-769-3541. FAX: 219-769-0690. Web Site: www.lcplin.org. *Dir,* Ingrid Norris; *Asst Dir, Br Operations,* Carolyn Strickland; E-mail: cstrickland@lakeco.lib.in.us; Staff 153.55 (MLS 32.81, Non-MLS 120.74)
Founded 1959. Pop 217,349; Circ 2,494,480
Jan 2008-Dec 2008 Income (Main Library and Branch(s)) $14,463,409. Mats Exp $1,489,331
Library Holdings: Bk Vols 1,044,948; Per Subs 803; Talking Bks 2,985; Videos 93,682
Special Collections: Indiana Coll, bks, pamphlets
Automation Activity & Vendor Info: (Acquisitions) SirsiDynix; (Circulation) SirsiDynix
Database Vendor: SirsiDynix
Publications: Happenings (Newsletter)
Partic in OCLC Online Computer Library Center, Inc
Special Services for the Deaf - Bks on deafness & sign lang; Captioned film dep; High interest/low vocabulary bks; Spec interest per; Videos & decoder
Open Mon-Thurs 9-9, Fri 9-6, Sat 9-5, Sun 12-4
Friends of the Library Group

Branches: 11

BLACK OAK, 5921 W 25th Ave, Gary, 46406-3024, SAN 341-4396. Tel: 219-844-8809. FAX: 219-844-5824. *Librn,* Chris Rettig; Staff 2 (MLS 1, Non-MLS 1)
Library Holdings: Large Print Bks 38; Bk Titles 38,911; Bk Vols 40,111; Per Subs 56; Talking Bks 191; Videos 210
Open Mon, Wed & Fri 10-6
Friends of the Library Group

CEDAR LAKE BRANCH, 10010 W 133rd Ave, Cedar Lake, 46303, SAN 341-4426. Tel: 219-374-7121. FAX: 219-374-6333. *Br Mgr,* Linda Johnsen; Staff 2 (MLS 2)
Library Holdings: Large Print Bks 83; Bk Titles 52,340; Bk Vols 55,680; Per Subs 49; Talking Bks 81; Videos 310
Open Mon & Wed 12:30-8:30, Tues, Thurs & Fri 10-6, Sat 9-5
Friends of the Library Group

DYER-SCHERERVILLE BRANCH, 1001 W Lincoln Hwy, Schererville, 46375-1552, SAN 341-4450. Tel: 219-322-4731. FAX: 219-865-5478. *Mgr,* Pam Maud; Staff 2 (MLS 1, Non-MLS 1)
Library Holdings: Large Print Bks 103; Bk Titles 101,670; Bk Vols 102,700; Per Subs 88; Talking Bks 139; Videos 410
Open Mon-Thurs 10-8:30, Fri 10-6, Sat 9-5
Friends of the Library Group

FORTY-FIRST AVENUE, 3491 W 41st Ave, Gary, 46408-3007, SAN 341-4485. Tel: 219-980-5180. FAX: 219-985-8057. *Mgr,* Mark Furukawa; Staff 2 (MLS 1, Non-MLS 1)
Library Holdings: Large Print Bks 101; Bk Titles 42,610; Bk Vols 44,912; Per Subs 52; Talking Bks 78; Videos 310
Open Mon & Wed 12:30-8:30, Tues, Thurs & Fri 10-6, Sat 9-5
Friends of the Library Group

GRIFFITH BRANCH, 940 N Broad St, Griffith, 46319-1528, SAN 341-4515. Tel: 219-838-2825. Web Site: www.lcplin.org/gr.htm. *Br Mgr,* Chris Rettig; Staff 2 (MLS 1, Non-MLS 1)
Library Holdings: Audiobooks 1,450; AV Mats 10,000; CDs 2,200; DVDs 3,900; High Interest/Low Vocabulary Bk Vols 30; Large Print Bks 1,400; Bk Titles 60,000; Bk Vols 60,300; Per Subs 75; Videos 820
Function: Adult bk club, After school storytime, Audio & video playback equip for onsite use, Bks on cassette, Bks on CD, CD-ROM, Children's prog, Computer training, Computers for patron use, Copy machines, Electronic databases & coll, Free DVD rentals, Handicapped accessible, Holiday prog, ILL available, Music CDs, Online cat, Outreach serv, Preschool outreach, Prog for adults, Prog for children & young adult, Pub access computers, Ref serv available, Spoken cassettes & CDs, Story hour, Summer reading prog, Tax forms, VHS videos, Video lending libr, Web-catalog, Wheelchair accessible
Open Mon-Thurs 10-8:30, Fri 10-6, Sat 9-5
Friends of the Library Group

HIGHLAND BRANCH, 2841 Jewett St, Highland, 46322-1617, SAN 341-454X. Tel: 219-838-2394. *Br Mgr,* Bob Mele; E-mail: bmele@lcplin.org; Staff 3 (MLS 2, Non-MLS 1)
Library Holdings: Bk Titles 81,200; Bk Vols 83,556; Per Subs 75
Open Mon-Thurs 10-8:30, Fri 10-6, Sat 9-5
Friends of the Library Group

HOBART BRANCH, 100 Main St, Hobart, 46342-4391, SAN 341-4574. Tel: 219-942-2243. FAX: 219-947-1823. ; Staff 2 (MLS 1, Non-MLS 1)
Pop 25,000
Library Holdings: AV Mats 1,641; Bk Titles 82,819; Bk Vols 84,202; Per Subs 107; Talking Bks 83; Videos 261
Subject Interests: Investing
Open Mon-Thurs 10-8:30, Fri 10-6, Sat 9-5
Friends of the Library Group

LAKE STATION-NEW CHICAGO BRANCH, 2007 Central Ave, Lake Station, 46405-2061, SAN 341-4698. Tel: 219-962-2409. FAX: 219-962-8460. *Mgr,* Carol Daumer-Gutjahr; Staff 2 (MLS 1, Non-MLS 1)
Library Holdings: Large Print Bks 62; Bk Titles 33,491; Bk Vols 35,814; Per Subs 53; Talking Bks 119; Videos 281
Open Mon & Wed 12:30-8:30, Tues, Thurs & Fri 10-6, Sat 9-5
Friends of the Library Group

MUNSTER BRANCH, 8701 Calumet Ave, Munster, 46321-2526, SAN 341-4663. Tel: 219-836-8450. FAX: 219-836-5694. *Br Mgr,* Linda Dunn; *Librn,* Chris Retseck; Staff 3 (MLS 2, Non-MLS 1)
Library Holdings: AV Mats 1,121; Large Print Bks 84; Bk Titles 75,615; Bk Vols 78,065; Per Subs 71; Videos 219
Open Mon-Thurs 10-8:30, Fri 10-6, Sat 9-5
Friends of the Library Group

SAINT JOHN BRANCH, 9450 Wicker Dr, Saint John, 46373-9646, SAN 341-4728. Tel: 219-365-5379. FAX: 219-365-5963. *Mgr,* Pam Maud; Staff 1 (MLS 1)
Library Holdings: AV Mats 780; Bk Titles 33,610; Bk Vols 35,118; Per Subs 43; Talking Bks 170; Videos 281
Open Mon & Wed 12:30-8:30, Tues, Thurs & Fri 10-6, Sat 9-5
Friends of the Library Group

P TALKING BOOK SERVICE, 1919 W 81st Ave, 46410-5382. Tel: 219-769-3541, Ext 323. *Librn,* Dawn Mogle; Staff 2 (MLS 1, Non-MLS 1)
Founded 1970
Library Holdings: AV Mats 1,140; Large Print Bks 80; Bk Titles 26,450; Bk Vols 28,112; Per Subs 53; Talking Bks 78; Videos 219
Special Collections: Descriptive Videos
Open Mon-Thurs 9-9, Fri 9-6, Sat 9-5
Friends of the Library Group

S SUN-TIMES NEWS GROUP*, Post Tribune Library, 1433 E 83rd Ave, 46410. SAN 329-0190. Tel: 219-648-3135. FAX: 219-648-3026. Web Site: www.post-trib.com. *Librn,* Carol Chisholm; Staff 3 (MLS 1, Non-MLS 2)
Founded 1935
Library Holdings: Bk Titles 850; Bk Vols 1,000

Special Collections: Golden Jubilee Edition, films & bound; Newspapers, Post Tribune from 1935-Present
Restriction: Staff use only

MICHIGAN CITY

S INDIANA STATE PRISON*, Michael S Thomas Learning Resource Center, One Park Row St, 46360-6597. SAN 341-4787. Tel: 219-874-7256, Ext 6100. FAX: 219-874-0335. *Media Spec,* Kenneth J Boyle; Staff 11 (MLS 1, Non-MLS 10)
Founded 1969
Library Holdings: AV Mats 649; Bk Titles 14,468; Bk Vols 15,212; Per Subs 27
Subject Interests: Careers, Current events, Fiction
Function: Doc delivery serv, For res purposes, Newsp ref libr, Photocopying/Printing, Res libr
Restriction: Internal circ only, Non-circulating to the pub, Not open to pub, Open to students, Private libr

P MICHIGAN CITY PUBLIC LIBRARY*, 100 E Fourth St, 46360-3302. SAN 341-4906. Tel: 219-873-3044. Circulation Tel: 219-873-3042. Information Services Tel: 219-879-4561. FAX: 219-873-3067. Administration FAX: 219-873-3475. E-mail: refdesk@mclib.org. Web Site: www.mclib.org. *Dir,* Don Glossinger; Tel: 219-873-3050, E-mail: dgloss@mclib.org; *Asst Dir,* Andrew W Smith; Tel: 219-873-3056, E-mail: awsmith@mclib.org; Staff 19 (MLS 7, Non-MLS 12)
Founded 1897. Pop 40,350; Circ 478,484
Library Holdings: Bk Titles 108,527; Bk Vols 137,151; Per Subs 420
Special Collections: Genealogy Coll; Indiana Coll. Oral History
Automation Activity & Vendor Info: (Cataloging) SirsiDynix; (Circulation) SirsiDynix; (OPAC) SirsiDynix
Wireless access
Function: Homebound delivery serv, ILL available, Ref serv available
Open Mon-Thurs 9-8, Fri & Sat 9-6, Sun (Sept-May) 1-5
Friends of the Library Group

MIDDLEBURY

P MIDDLEBURY COMMUNITY PUBLIC LIBRARY, 101 E Winslow St, 46540. (Mail add: PO Box 192, 46540-0192), SAN 375-2860. Tel: 574-825-5601. FAX: 574-825-5150. E-mail: mclib@mdy.lib.in.us. Web Site: www.mdy.lib.in.us. *Libr Dir,* Teresa Rheinheimer; E-mail: terry@mdy.lib.in.us; Staff 16 (MLS 3, Non-MLS 13)
Founded 1978. Pop 17,099; Circ 288,279
Library Holdings: AV Mats 17,222; Large Print Bks 5,375; Bk Titles 72,222; Bk Vols 83,050; Per Subs 126
Subject Interests: Amish, Mennonite
Automation Activity & Vendor Info: (Acquisitions) TLC (The Library Corporation); (Cataloging) TLC (The Library Corporation); (Circulation) TLC (The Library Corporation); (Course Reserve) TLC (The Library Corporation); (OPAC) TLC (The Library Corporation)
Database Vendor: ABC-CLIO, Baker & Taylor, Booklist Online, Booksite, EBSCOhost, Gale Cengage Learning, Inspire, TumbleBookLibrary, Wilson - Wilson Web
Wireless access
Function: 24/7 Online cat, Adult bk club, Archival coll, Audiobks via web, Bilingual assistance for Spanish patrons, Bk club(s), Bks on CD, Children's prog, Computers for patron use, Copy machines, Digital talking bks, Electronic databases & coll, Fax serv, Free DVD rentals, Handicapped accessible, Home delivery & serv to Sr ctr & nursing homes, Homebound delivery serv, ILL available, Laminating, Magazines, Mail & tel request accepted, Microfiche/film & reading machines, Movies, Music CDs, Notary serv, Online cat, Online ref, Outside serv via phone, mail, e-mail & web, Photocopying/Printing, Preschool outreach, Preschool reading prog, Printer for laptops & handheld devices, Prog for adults, Prog for children & young adult, Pub access computers, Ref serv in person, Scanner, Story hour, Study rm, Summer & winter reading prog, Tax forms, Teen prog, Telephone ref, Wheelchair accessible
Partic in Midwest Collaborative for Library Services (MCLS); Northern Indiana Computer Consortium for Libraries (NICCL)
Special Services for the Deaf - Bks on deafness & sign lang
Special Services for the Blind - Bks on cassette; Bks on CD; Copier with enlargement capabilities; Large print bks; Playaways (bks on MP3)
Open Mon-Thurs 9-8, Fri 9-6, Sat 9-2
Friends of the Library Group

MIDDLETOWN

P MIDDLETOWN FALLCREEK TOWNSHIP PUBLIC LIBRARY*, 780 High St, 47356-1399. SAN 305-0351. Tel: 765-354-4071. FAX: 765-354-9578. Web Site: www.mfc.lib.in.us. *Dir,* Teresa Holden; Staff 1 (Non-MLS 1)
Founded 1929. Pop 4,811; Circ 122,354
Library Holdings: AV Mats 1,000; Large Print Bks 300; Bk Titles 100,000; Per Subs 104
Special Collections: Local Genealogy Coll
Automation Activity & Vendor Info: (Circulation) Winnebago Software Co; (Serials) EBSCO Online
Partic in Evergreen Indiana Consortium
Open Mon & Wed 9-8, Tues & Thurs 12-8, Fri 9-5, Sat 10-3
Friends of the Library Group

MILFORD

P MILFORD PUBLIC LIBRARY, 101 N Main St, 46542. SAN 305-036X. Tel: 574-658-4312. FAX: 574-658-9454. Web Site: www.milford.lib.in.us. *Dir,* Julie Frew; E-mail: jfrew@milford.lib.in.us; Staff 3 (MLS 2, Non-MLS 1)
Founded 1907. Pop 4,597; Circ 35,690
Library Holdings: AV Mats 3,000; Bk Vols 35,000; Per Subs 80; Videos 3,500
Special Collections: PBS Video Coll; Town of Milford & Van Buren & East Jefferson Townships History
Wireless access
Open Mon & Thurs 10-8, Tues, Wed & Fri 10-6, Sat 10-2

MISHAWAKA

C BETHEL COLLEGE*, Otis & Elizabeth Bowen Library, 1001 Bethel Circle, 46545. SAN 305-0386. Tel: 574-807-7180. Interlibrary Loan Service Tel: 574-807-3389. Reference Tel: 574-807-7170. FAX: 574-807-7964. Web Site: www.bethelcollege.edu/library. *Dir of Libr,* Dr Clyde R Root; E-mail: rootc@bethelcollege.edu; *Head, Ref,* Mark Root; E-mail: rootm1@bethelcollege.edu; *Head, Tech Serv,* Kevin Blowers; Tel: 574-807-7720, E-mail: blowersk@bethelcollege.edu; *Archivist,* Tim Erdel; Tel: 574-807-7153, E-mail: erdelt@bethelcollege.edu; *Circ,* Tim Amstutz. Subject Specialists: *Nursing,* Dr Clyde R Root; *Educ, Hist,* Mark Root; *Lit,* Kevin Blowers; *Philos, Relig,* Tim Erdel; Staff 4 (MLS 4)
Founded 1947. Enrl 1,701; Fac 116; Highest Degree: Master
Library Holdings: AV Mats 8,368; Bks on Deafness & Sign Lang 325; CDs 252; Bk Titles 125,000; Bk Vols 133,241; Per Subs 457; Videos 707
Special Collections: Bethel College Archives; Dr Otis Bowen Museum & Archives; Missionary Church Archives & Historical Coll. Oral History
Subject Interests: Educ, Nursing, Relig
Automation Activity & Vendor Info: (Cataloging) Ex Libris Group; (Circulation) Ex Libris Group; (ILL) OCLC; (OPAC) Follett Software
Database Vendor: Cambridge Scientific Abstracts, EBSCOhost, Gale Cengage Learning, JSTOR, OCLC FirstSearch, OCLC WorldShare Interlibrary Loan, OVID Technologies
Wireless access
Partic in Dialog Corp; Michiana Acad Libr Consortium; OCLC Online Computer Library Center, Inc
Open Mon-Thurs 8am-Midnight, Fri 8-6, Sat 10-6, Sun 7pm-11pm

P MISHAWAKA-PENN-HARRIS PUBLIC LIBRARY, 209 Lincoln Way E, 46544-2084. SAN 341-4965. Tel: 574-259-5277. Circulation Tel: 574-259-5277, Ext 213. Interlibrary Loan Service Tel: 574-259-5277, Ext 222. Reference Tel: 574-259-5277, Ext 218. Administration Tel: 574-259-5277, Ext 288. Automation Services Tel: 574-259-5277, Ext 209. FAX: 574-254-5585, 574-255-8489. Web Site: www.mphpl.org. *Dir,* David J Eisen; Tel: 574-259-5277, Ext 300, E-mail: d.eisen@mphpl.org; *Br Mgr,* Donna Meeks; Tel: 574-259-5277, Ext 228, E-mail: d.meeks@mphpl.org; *Coordr, Media Serv,* Eric Mims; Tel: 574-259-5277, Ext 200, E-mail: e.mims@mphpl.org; *Tech Serv Coordr,* Sheila Makala; Tel: 574-259-5277, Ext 278, E-mail: s.makala@mphpl.org; *Circ Serv,* Bruce Friedline; E-mail: b.friedline@mphpl.org; Staff 23 (MLS 23)
Founded 1907. Pop 89,652; Circ 715,889
Jan 2013-Dec 2013 Income (Main Library and Branch(s)) $4,470,383, State $306,087, Federal $41,774, County $3,917,723, Locally Generated Income $204,799. Mats Exp $676,392, Books $348,663, Per/Ser (Incl. Access Fees) $47,812, Micro $8,275, AV Equip $15,878, AV Mat $194,115, Electronic Ref Mat (Incl. Access Fees) $61,649. Sal $2,540,580
Library Holdings: Audiobooks 15,411; AV Mats 70,069; CDs 21,516; DVDs 23,925; e-books 3,429; Electronic Media & Resources 3,095; Microforms 13,360; Bk Vols 289,298; Per Subs 355; Videos 1,023
Special Collections: Heritage Center Coll
Subject Interests: Auto repair, Local hist
Automation Activity & Vendor Info: (Acquisitions) Innovative Interfaces, Inc; (Cataloging) Innovative Interfaces, Inc; (Circulation) Innovative Interfaces, Inc; (ILL) Innovative Interfaces, Inc; (Media Booking) Innovative Interfaces, Inc; (OPAC) Innovative Interfaces, Inc; (Serials) Innovative Interfaces, Inc
Database Vendor: Innovative Interfaces, Inc
Wireless access
Publications: Hi-Lites (Newsletter of Friends of Library)
Partic in Midwest Collaborative for Library Services (MCLS); OCLC Online Computer Library Center, Inc
Open Mon-Thurs 9-9, Fri 9-6, Sat 9-5
Friends of the Library Group

Branches: 2
BITTERSWEET, 602 Bittersweet Rd, 46544-4155, SAN 322-5887. Tel: 574-259-0392. FAX: 574-259-0399. *Br Mgr,* Chris Granatino; Tel: 574-259-0392, Ext 223, E-mail: c.granatino@mphpl.org; *Children's Serv Supvr,* Sue Reber; Tel: 574-259-0392, Ext 225, E-mail: s.reber@mphpl.org; *Circ Serv Supvr,* Mitzi Miller; Tel: 574-259-0392, Ext 230, E-mail: m.miller@mphpl.org; Staff 17 (MLS 5, Non-MLS 12)
Open Mon-Thurs 9-9, Fri 9-6, Sat 9-5
Friends of the Library Group
HARRIS, 51446 Elm Rd, Granger, 46530-7171. Tel: 574-271-3179. FAX: 574-271-3183. *Br Mgr,* Susie Cleaver; Tel: 574-271-3179, Ext 311; *Children's Serv Supvr,* Kathy Winkel; Tel: 574-271-3179, Ext 310, E-mail: k.winkel@mphpl.org; Staff 14 (MLS 5.5, Non-MLS 8.5)
Open Mon-Thurs 9-9, Fri 9-6, Sat 9-5
Friends of the Library Group

MITCHELL

P MITCHELL COMMUNITY PUBLIC LIBRARY*, 804 Main St, 47446. SAN 305-0394. Tel: 812-849-2412. FAX: 812-849-2665. E-mail: info@mitchell.lib.in.us. Web Site: www.mitchell.lib.in.us. *Dir,* Alexis Caudell
Founded 1917. Pop 12,007; Circ 78,851
Library Holdings: AV Mats 1,796; Large Print Bks 310; Bk Titles 50,000; Bk Vols 60,000; Per Subs 80; Videos 511
Special Collections: Local History; Virgil "Gus" Grissom
Automation Activity & Vendor Info: (Acquisitions) Evergreen; (Cataloging) Evergreen; (Circulation) Evergreen; (OPAC) Evergreen
Wireless access
Publications: Newsletter (Bi-monthly)
Partic in Evergreen Indiana Consortium; Midwest Collaborative for Library Services (MCLS)
Open Mon, Tues & Thurs 9-8, Fri & Sat 9-5:30
Friends of the Library Group

MONON

P MONON TOWN & TOWNSHIP PUBLIC LIBRARY*, 427 N Market, 47959. (Mail add: PO Box 305, 47959-0305), SAN 305-0408. Tel: 219-253-6517. FAX: 219-253-8373. E-mail: mononplstaff@yahoo.com. Web Site: www.monon.lib.in.us. *Dir,* Jo Minnick; *Youth Serv Librn,* Peggy Horton
Founded 1914. Pop 3,272; Circ 26,388
Library Holdings: AV Mats 2,148; Bk Vols 28,296; Per Subs 120; Talking Bks 885
Automation Activity & Vendor Info: (Cataloging) SirsiDynix; (Circulation) SirsiDynix; (OPAC) SirsiDynix; (Serials) SirsiDynix
Partic in Midwest Collaborative for Library Services (MCLS)
Open Mon & Wed 10-8, Tues, Thurs & Fri 10-6, Sat 10-3

MONTEREY

P MONTEREY-TIPPECANOE TOWNSHIP PUBLIC LIBRARY*, 6260 E Main St, 46960. (Mail add: PO Box 38, 46960-0038), SAN 305-0416. Tel: 574-542-2171. FAX: 574-542-2171. Web Site: www.pulaski-libraries.lib.in.us. *Dir,* Renita Potthoff; E-mail: renita@monterey-tipp.lib.in.us; *Asst Librn,* Toni Mersch; *Circ,* Sharon Weldon; Staff 3 (Non-MLS 3)
Founded 1918. Pop 1,031; Circ 24,218
Library Holdings: AV Mats 1,335; CDs 121; DVDs 933; Large Print Bks 125; Bk Titles 12,730; Bk Vols 13,250; Per Subs 31; Videos 788
Special Collections: Indiana Coll
Automation Activity & Vendor Info: (Cataloging) Brodart; (Circulation) Brodart; (OPAC) Brodart
Function: Handicapped accessible, ILL available, Photocopying/Printing, Prog for children & young adult, Summer reading prog, VHS videos, Wheelchair accessible
Partic in Midwest Collaborative for Library Services (MCLS)
Open Mon & Wed 11-7, Tues, Thurs & Fri 11-5, Sat 10-2

MONTEZUMA

P MONTEZUMA PUBLIC LIBRARY*, 270 Crawford St, 47862. (Mail add: PO Box 70, 47862-0070), SAN 305-0424. Tel: 765-245-2772. FAX: 765-245-0677. E-mail: library@montezuma.lib.in.us. Web Site: www.montezuma.lib.in.us. *Dir,* Barbara Rumple
Founded 1932. Pop 1,597; Circ 12,370
Jan 2007-Dec 2007. Mats Exp $12,500, Books $8,000, Per/Ser (Incl. Access Fees) $1,500, AV Mat $3,000. Sal $26,000
Library Holdings: AV Mats 2,000; Bk Vols 14,580; Per Subs 55
Automation Activity & Vendor Info: (Cataloging) Book Systems; (Circulation) Book Systems
Wireless access
Partic in Midwest Collaborative for Library Services (MCLS)
Open Tues & Wed Noon-5, Thurs 2-8, Sat 9-1

MONTICELLO

P MONTICELLO-UNION TOWNSHIP PUBLIC LIBRARY*, 321 W Broadway, 47960-2047. SAN 305-0432. Tel: 574-583-2665. FAX: 574-583-2782. Circulation E-mail: circulationclerk@monticello.lib.in.us. Web Site: www.monticello.lib.in.us. *Libr Dir,* Monica Casanova; E-mail: director@monticello.lib.in.us; *Adult Serv,* Portia Kapraun; E-mail: adult@monticello.lib.in.us; *Ch Serv,* Sandy Wagner; E-mail: childrens@monticello.lib.in.us; *Circ Serv Librn,* Scott Miller; E-mail: smiller@monticello.lib.in.us; Staff 11 (MLS 3, Non-MLS 8)
Founded 1903. Pop 11,238; Circ 127,339
Library Holdings: AV Mats 2,400; Bks on Deafness & Sign Lang 60; Large Print Bks 219; Bk Titles 61,980; Bk Vols 63,410; Per Subs 131; Videos 1,016
Automation Activity & Vendor Info: (Cataloging) Follett Software; (Circulation) Follett Software; (OPAC) Follett Software
Wireless access
Partic in Midwest Collaborative for Library Services (MCLS)
Open Mon-Thurs 9-8, Fri & Sat 9-5
Friends of the Library Group

MONTPELIER

P MONTPELIER PUBLIC LIBRARY*, 301 S Main St, 47359. SAN 305-0440. Tel: 765-728-5969. FAX: 765-728-5969. E-mail: mhtpl@hotmail.com. *Librn,* Laura Lee; Staff 2 (MLS 1, Non-MLS 1)
Pop 3,042; Circ 44,118
Library Holdings: AV Mats 1,038; Large Print Bks 108; Bk Titles 26,819; Bk Vols 28,100; Per Subs 79; Videos 248
Automation Activity & Vendor Info: (Acquisitions) Follett Software; (Cataloging) Follett Software; (Serials) Follett Software
Open Mon-Thurs 10-7, Fri 10-5, Sat 10-2

MOORESVILLE

P MOORESVILLE PUBLIC LIBRARY*, 220 W Harrison St, 46158-1633. SAN 305-0459. Tel: 317-831-7323. FAX: 317-831-7383. E-mail: wecare@mooresville.lib.in.us. Web Site: www.mooresvillelib.org. *Dir,* Diane Huerkamp; E-mail: dianeh@mooresville.lib.in.us; *Youth Serv Librn,* Suzanne Walker; E-mail: suzannew@mooresville.lib.in.us; *Circ Coordr,* Rosemary Mayo; E-mail: corkym@mooresville.lib.in.us; *ILL Coordr,* Shirley Martin; E-mail: shirleym@mooresville.lib.in.us; *Tech Serv Coordr,* Judy Morehouse; E-mail: judym@mooresville.lib.in.us; Staff 15 (MLS 4, Non-MLS 11)
Founded 1912. Pop 18,110; Circ 119,412
Library Holdings: AV Mats 2,080; Large Print Bks 180; Bk Titles 61,411; Bk Vols 63,108; Per Subs 245; Videos 411
Special Collections: Local History Coll (Clifford C Furnas, John Dillinger & Paul Hadley); Mooresville Area Obituary Database
Subject Interests: Local hist
Automation Activity & Vendor Info: (Cataloging) SirsiDynix; (Circulation) SirsiDynix; (OPAC) SirsiDynix
Function: ILL available
Publications: Bookmark (Newsletter)
Partic in Evergreen Indiana Consortium; Midwest Collaborative for Library Services (MCLS)
Open Mon-Thurs 9-8, Fri 9-5, Sat 9-4
Friends of the Library Group

MOUNT VERNON

P ALEXANDRIAN PUBLIC LIBRARY*, 115 W Fifth St, 47620. SAN 305-0467. Tel: 812-838-3286. FAX: 812-838-9639. E-mail: alexpl@evansville.net. Web Site: www.apl.lib.in.us. *Dir,* Marissa Priddis; *Head, Adult Serv,* Patty Vahey; *Head, Coll Serv,* Charles Kendall; *Head, Commun Relations,* Stan Campbell; *Head, Outreach Serv,* Jeanne Burns; *Head, Syst Admin,* Carrie Robb; *Head, Youth Serv,* Anne Cottrell; *YA Librn,* Trisha Seidensticker; Staff 20 (MLS 4, Non-MLS 16)
Founded 1895. Pop 23,000; Circ 125,000
Library Holdings: Bk Vols 85,000; Per Subs 114
Special Collections: Curriculum Enrichment
Subject Interests: Genealogy, Indiana, Local hist
Automation Activity & Vendor Info: (Acquisitions) SirsiDynix; (Cataloging) SirsiDynix; (Circulation) SirsiDynix; (OPAC) SirsiDynix; (Serials) SirsiDynix
Database Vendor: EBSCOhost
Function: AV serv, Handicapped accessible, Homebound delivery serv, ILL available, Photocopying/Printing, Prog for adults, Prog for children & young adult, Ref serv available, Summer reading prog
Publications: APL Core (Newsletter)
Partic in Midwest Collaborative for Library Services (MCLS); OCLC Online Computer Library Center, Inc
Open Mon-Thurs 9-8, Fri & Sat 9-5, Sun 1-5
Friends of the Library Group
Bookmobiles: 1. Outreach Servs, Jeanne Burns. Bk titles 22,000

MUNCIE

M BALL MEMORIAL HOSPITAL*, Library & Information Center, 2401 W University Ave, 47303-3499. SAN 305-0491. Tel: 765-747-3204. FAX: 765-747-0137. E-mail: bmhmedlib@iuhealth.org. Web Site: www.iuhealth.org/library. *Dir, Libr Serv,* Lorna Springston; Tel: 765-747-4229, E-mail: lspringston@iuhealth.org; *Coordr,* Janelle Cunningham; E-mail: jcunningham@iuhealth.org; *Acq & Cat,* Dana Nunn; Tel: 765-747-4470, E-mail: dnunn@iuhealth.org; *Doc Delivery,* Paula McCown; Tel: 765-741-1959, E-mail: pmccown@iuhealth.org; *Digital Serv, Ref Serv,* Barbara Hendrixson; E-mail: bhendrixson@iuhealth.org; Staff 5 (MLS 1, Non-MLS 4)
Founded 1931
Library Holdings: Bk Vols 2,700; Per Subs 430
Special Collections: Clinical, Medical & Nursing Journals & Textbooks; Consumer Health Information
Subject Interests: Allied health, Commun health, Med, Nursing
Function: ILL available, Photocopying/Printing, Ref serv available
Open Mon-Fri 7-4:30

C BALL STATE UNIVERSITY LIBRARIES*, Alexander M Bracken Library, 2000 W University Ave, 47306-1099. SAN 341-5023. Tel: 765-285-5277. Circulation Tel: 765-285-5143. Interlibrary Loan Service Tel: 765-285-1324. Reference Tel: 765-285-1101. FAX: 765-285-2008. E-mail: library@bsu.edu. Web Site: www.bsu.edu/library. *Dean, Univ Libr,* Dr Arthur W Hafner, PhD; E-mail: ahafner@bsu.edu; *Asst Dean, Coll Res Mgt,* Sharon A Roberts; Tel: 765-285-1305, E-mail: sroberts@bsu.edu; *Asst Dean, Libr Info Tech,* Bradley D Faust; E-mail: bfaust@bsu.edu; *Asst Dean, Digital Initiatives & Spec Coll,* John B Straw; E-mail: jstraw@bsu.edu; *Asst Dean, Pub Serv,* Suzanne S Rice; Tel: 765-285-1307, Fax: 765-285-2644, E-mail: srice@bsu.edu; *Head of Acq Serv,* Rebecca Susanne Sheffield; Tel: 765-285-8031, E-mail: rsheffie@bsu.edu; *Head, Coll Develop,* Hilde M Calvert; Tel: 765-285-8033, E-mail: hcalvert@bsu.edu; *Head, Info Serv,* Diane L Calvin; Tel: 765-285-3327, E-mail: dcalvin@bsu.edu; *Financial & Bus Serv Mgr,* Dixie D DeWitt; E-mail: ddewitt@bsu.edu; *Mgr, Univ Copyright Ctr,* Dr Fritz Dolak; Tel: 765-285-5330, E-mail: fdolak@bsu.edu. Subject Specialists: *Archit,* Dr Fritz Dolak; Staff 117 (MLS 47, Non-MLS 70)
Founded 1918. Enrl 19,655; Highest Degree: Doctorate
Library Holdings: AV Mats 487,825; e-books 1,986; e-journals 10,272; Bk Titles 798,187; Bk Vols 1,201,500; Per Subs 3,408
Special Collections: Althea L Stoeckel Delaware County Archives & Local History Coll; Elisabeth Ball World War I Coll, posters; Frederic W Goudy Coll; Glass Industry (Richard Roller Coll); John Steinbeck Coll; Middletown Studies Coll; Modern American Poetry Coll; Nazi Coll; Sir Norman Angell Coll; University Archives. US Document Depository
Automation Activity & Vendor Info: (Acquisitions) SirsiDynix; (Cataloging) SirsiDynix; (Circulation) SirsiDynix; (Course Reserve) SirsiDynix; (ILL) OCLC ILLiad; (Media Booking) SirsiDynix; (OPAC) SirsiDynix; (Serials) SirsiDynix
Wireless access
Function: Doc delivery serv, ILL available, Photocopying/Printing
Publications: The Library Insider (Monthly newsletter)
Partic in Academic Libraries of Indiana; Midwest Collaborative for Library Services (MCLS); OCLC Online Computer Library Center, Inc
Open Mon-Thurs 7:30am-3am, Fri 7:30am-9pm, Sat 9-7:30, Sun 10am-3am
Friends of the Library Group

Departmental Libraries:

ARCHITECTURE, Architecture Bldg, Rm 116, 47306, SAN 341-5058. Tel: 765-285-5857. FAX: 765-285-2644. Web Site: cms.bsu.edu/academics/libraries/collectionsanddept/architecture.aspx. *Archit Librn,* Amy E Trendler; Tel: 765-285-5858, E-mail: aetrendler@bsu.edu. Subject Specialists: *Archit, Art,* Amy E Trendler; Staff 3 (MLS 1, Non-MLS 2)
Founded 1966
Subject Interests: Archit, Landscape archit, Urban planning
Automation Activity & Vendor Info: (Acquisitions) SirsiDynix
Open Mon-Thurs 7:30am-10pm, Fri 7:30-6, Sat 9-5, Sun 1pm-10pm
Friends of the Library Group

ARCHIVES & SPECIAL COLLECTIONS, Bracken Library, Rm 210, 47306-0161, SAN 373-532X. Tel: 765-285-5078. FAX: 765-285-8149. E-mail: libarchives@bsu.edu. Web Site: www.bsu.edu/libraries/archives. *Asst Dean, Spec Coll,* John B Straw, Jr; Staff 5 (MLS 3, Non-MLS 2)
Open Mon & Tues 8-8, Wed-Fri 8-6
Friends of the Library Group

MUSIC COLLECTIONS, Bracken Library BL-106, 47306, SAN 341-5112. Tel: 765-285-5065. FAX: 765-285-2644. Web Site: www.bsu.edu/library/collections/musiccoll. *Music Librn,* Amy L Edmonds; E-mail: aledmonds@bsu.edu. Subject Specialists: *Music,* Amy L Edmonds; Staff 2 (MLS 1, Non-MLS 1)
Founded 1975
Special Collections: Tubists Universal Brotherhood Association Resources, scores
Friends of the Library Group

SCIENCE-HEALTH SCIENCE, Cooper Science Bldg, CN16, 47306, SAN 341-5147. Tel: 765-285-5079. FAX: 765-285-2644. Web Site: www.bsu.edu/library/collections/shsl. *Sci Librn,* Kevin E Brooks; E-mail: kbrooks2@bsu.edu. Subject Specialists: *Nursing,* Kevin E Brooks; Staff 1 (Non-MLS 1)
Library Holdings: Bk Titles 57,881; Bk Vols 62,921; Per Subs 281
Database Vendor: EBSCOhost
Open Mon-Thurs 7:30am-9pm, Fri 7:30-6, Sat 9-5, Sun 1-9
Friends of the Library Group

P MUNCIE PUBLIC LIBRARY*, Maring-Hunt Library, 2005 S High St, 47302. Tel: 765-747-8200. Administration Tel: 765-747-8228. FAX: 765-747-8221. Web Site: www.munpl.org. *Dir,* Virginia Nilles; Tel: 765-747-8201, E-mail: gnilles@munpl.org
Pop 67,500; Circ 1,016,000
Library Holdings: AV Mats 45,607; CDs 16,193; DVDs 13,423; e-books 76; Electronic Media & Resources 1,146; Large Print Bks 6,575; Bk Vols 204,320; Per Subs 494; Talking Bks 4,930; Videos 21,017
Automation Activity & Vendor Info: (Acquisitions) Horizon; (Cataloging) Horizon; (Circulation) Horizon; (Course Reserve) Horizon; (OPAC) Horizon; (Serials) Brodart
Database Vendor: Baker & Taylor, EBSCOhost, Gale Cengage Learning, OCLC FirstSearch, Wilson - Wilson Web
Wireless access
Function: Archival coll, AV serv, CD-ROM, Digital talking bks, ILL available, Magnifiers for reading, Meeting rooms, Outside serv via phone, mail, e-mail & web, Photocopying/Printing, Prog for adults, Prog for children & young adult, Ref serv available, Spoken cassettes & CDs, Story hour, Summer reading prog, Telephone ref, VHS videos, Wheelchair accessible, Workshops
Publications: MPL Now (Newsletter)
Special Services for the Blind - Assistive/Adapted tech devices, equip & products; Audio mat; Bks on cassette; Bks on CD; Computer with voice synthesizer for visually impaired persons; Low vision equip; Magnifiers; Talking bks; Videos on blindness & phys handicaps
Open Mon-Thurs 9-8, Fri & Sat 9-6
Friends of the Library Group

Branches: 2

CARNEGIE LIBRARY, 301 E Jackson St, 47305, SAN 341-5171. Tel: 765-747-8208. Administration Tel: 765-747-8201. *Br Mgr,* Lorraine Sinclair; Tel: 765-741-5157
Founded 1875. Pop 72,465
Special Collections: Genealogy Coll; Local History Coll
Function: Meeting rooms
Open Mon, Tues & Thurs 9-6
Friends of the Library Group

JOHN F KENNEDY BRANCH, 1700 W McGalliard Rd, 47304, SAN 341-5325. Tel: 765-741-9727. Information Services Tel: 765-747-8225. FAX: 765-747-8213. *Adult Serv,* Donna Catron; Tel: 765-747-8215, E-mail: dcatron@munpl.org; *Ch Serv,* Annetta Terrell; Tel: 765-741-7333, E-mail: aterrell@munpl.org
Founded 1964
Function: Meeting rooms, Story hour
Open Mon-Thurs 10-8, Fri & Sat 9-6, Sun 1-5

NAPPANEE

P NAPPANEE PUBLIC LIBRARY*, 157 N Main St, 46550. SAN 305-0513. Tel: 574-773-7919. FAX: 574-773-7910. E-mail: readmore@nappaneelibrary.org. Web Site: www.nappaneelibrary.org. *Dir,* Lissa Krull; Staff 5 (MLS 1, Non-MLS 4)
Founded 1921. Pop 10,082; Circ 183,370
Library Holdings: Bk Titles 63,880; Bk Vols 65,960; Per Subs 195
Special Collections: Heritage Center
Automation Activity & Vendor Info: (Acquisitions) Innovative Interfaces, Inc; (Cataloging) Innovative Interfaces, Inc; (Circulation) Innovative Interfaces, Inc; (OPAC) Innovative Interfaces, Inc; (Serials) Innovative Interfaces, Inc
Database Vendor: Inspire, Overdrive, Inc
Wireless access
Partic in Ind Libr Asn; Midwest Collaborative for Library Services (MCLS)
Open Mon-Thurs 9-9, Fri 9-5:30, Sat 9-5, Sun 1-5
Friends of the Library Group

NASHVILLE

P BROWN COUNTY PUBLIC LIBRARY, 205 Locust Lane, 47448. (Mail add: PO Box 8, 47448-0008), SAN 305-0521. Tel: 812-988-2850. FAX: 812-988-8119. Web Site: www.browncounty.lib.in.us. *Dir,* Stori Snyder; Tel: 812-988-1230, E-mail: ssnyder@browncounty.lib.in.us; Staff 4 (MLS 4)
Founded 1919. Pop 14,080; Circ 150,870
Library Holdings: Bk Vols 60,000; Per Subs 100
Special Collections: Brown County Artists & Authors

Automation Activity & Vendor Info: (Acquisitions) Follett Software; (Cataloging) Follett Software; (OPAC) Follett Software
Wireless access
Function: Homebound delivery serv, ILL available
Publications: Annual Report
Special Services for the Deaf - TDD equip
Special Services for the Blind - Aids for in-house use; Audio mat; Bks on cassette; Bks on CD; Closed circuit TV; Large print bks; Talking bks
Open Mon-Thurs 9-8, Fri & Sat 9-5, Sun 1-5
Friends of the Library Group
Branches: 1
CORDRY SWEETWATER, 8451 Nineveh Rd, Nineveh, 46164. Tel: 317-933-9229. *Dir,* Yvonne Oligea; Tel: 812-988-2850
Library Holdings: Bk Vols 4,743
Open Tues 2-5, Wed & Thurs 4-7

NEW ALBANY

C INDIANA UNIVERSITY SOUTHEAST LIBRARY*, 4201 Grant Line Rd, 47150. SAN 305-053X. Tel: 812-941-2262. Circulation Tel: 812-941-2485. FAX: 812-941-2656. Administration FAX: 812-941-2493. Web Site: www.ius.edu/library. *Dir, Libr Serv,* Claude Martin Rosen; Tel: 812-941-2631, E-mail: crosen@ius.edu; *Coordr, Access Serv,* Gabrielle Carr; E-mail: gcarr@ius.edu; *Coordr, Automation & Tech Serv,* Melanie Hughes; E-mail: mehughes@ius.edu; *Head, Coll Develop & Spec Coll,* Jacqueline Fessard Johnson; E-mail: jfessard@ius.edu; *Coordr, Electronic Res,* Benita Mason; E-mail: bkmason@ius.edu; *Coordr, Libr Instruction,* Maria Accardi; Tel: 812-941-2551, E-mail: maccardi@ius.edu; *Coordr, Pub Serv,* Nancy T Totten; E-mail: ntotten@ius.edu; *Acq Asst,* Phyllis Nachand; E-mail: pnachand@ius.edu; *Cat Asst,* Elizabeth McMahan; E-mail: emcmahan@ius.edu; *Govt Doc Asst,* Robin King; E-mail: raking@isu.edu; *ILL Asst,* Janice Bush; Tel: 812-941-2487, E-mail: jfbush@isu.edu; Staff 16 (MLS 6, Non-MLS 10)
Founded 1941. Enrl 6,400; Fac 241; Highest Degree: Master
Library Holdings: Bk Titles 250,000; Per Subs 1,040
Special Collections: Ars Femina Musical Scores; Center for Cultural Resources; IUS Archives; William L Simon Sheet Music. US Document Depository
Automation Activity & Vendor Info: (Acquisitions) SirsiDynix; (Cataloging) SirsiDynix; (Circulation) SirsiDynix; (Course Reserve) SirsiDynix; (ILL) SirsiDynix; (OPAC) SirsiDynix; (Serials) SirsiDynix
Database Vendor: EBSCOhost, Gale Cengage Learning, LexisNexis, OCLC FirstSearch, OVID Technologies, ProQuest, TLC (The Library Corporation)
Partic in Kentuckiana Metroversity, Inc; Midwest Collaborative for Library Services (MCLS)
Special Services for the Blind - Assistive/Adapted tech devices, equip & products
Open Mon-Thurs 8am-10pm, Fri 8-5, Sat 9-5, Sun 12-6

P NEW ALBANY-FLOYD COUNTY PUBLIC LIBRARY*, 180 W Spring St, 47150-3692. SAN 305-0548. Tel: 812-944-8464. Administration Tel: 812-949-3734. FAX: 812-949-3532. Web Site; www.nafclibrary.org. *Dir,* Rose Frost; *Teen Librn,* Renata Sancken; *Archivist,* Matt Eidem; *Ch Serv,* Abby Johnson; *Circ, Media Serv,* Marilyn Powell; *ILL,* Paula Zellers; *Ref,* Paulette Gibbs; *Tech Serv,* Cyndi Kepley; *Hispanic Outreach,* Lori Eskridge; Staff 41 (MLS 9, Non-MLS 32)
Founded 1884. Pop 74,578; Circ 413,069
Library Holdings: Bk Vols 225,759; Per Subs 405
Special Collections: Oral History; State Document Depository
Subject Interests: Genealogy, Local hist
Automation Activity & Vendor Info: (Cataloging) SirsiDynix; (Circulation) SirsiDynix; (Media Booking) SirsiDynix; (OPAC) SirsiDynix
Wireless access
Function: Adult bk club, Archival coll, Art exhibits, Audiobks via web, Bk reviews (Group), Bks on cassette, Bks on CD, Children's prog, Computer training, Computers for patron use, Copy machines, Electronic databases & coll, Fax serv, Free DVD rentals, Homebound delivery serv, ILL available, Microfiche/film & reading machines, Music CDs, Online cat, Outreach serv, OverDrive digital audio bks, Photocopying/Printing, Prog for adults, Prog for children & young adult, Pub access computers, Scanner, Spanish lang bks, Story hour, Summer reading prog, Teen prog, Telephone ref, Web-catalog
Partic in Midwest Collaborative for Library Services (MCLS)
Open Mon-Thurs 9-8:30, Fri & Sat 9-5:30, Sun (Sept-May) 1-5
Restriction: Residents only
Friends of the Library Group

NEW CARLISLE

P NEW CARLISLE & OLIVE TOWNSHIP PUBLIC LIBRARY*, 408 S Bray St, 46552. (Mail add: PO Box Q, 46552-0837), SAN 305-0556. Tel: 574-654-3046. FAX: 574-654-8260. Web Site: www.ncpl.lib.in.us. *Dir,* Stephen J Boggs; E-mail: sboggs@ncpl.lib.in.us; *Asst Dir,* Amy Schrock; *Ch Serv,* Sara Smigielski; Staff 1 (MLS 1)
Founded 1894. Pop 5,019; Circ 140,504
Library Holdings: AV Mats 7,697; Bk Titles 40,853; Bk Vols 49,905; Per Subs 105; Talking Bks 3,868
Subject Interests: Arts & crafts, Fiction, Local hist
Automation Activity & Vendor Info: (Cataloging) TLC (The Library Corporation); (Circulation) Follett Software; (OPAC) Follett Software
Partic in Midwest Collaborative for Library Services (MCLS)
Open Mon-Thurs 9-8, Fri & Sat 9-5, Sun 1-5
Friends of the Library Group

NEW CASTLE

P NEW CASTLE-HENRY COUNTY PUBLIC LIBRARY*, 376 S 15th St, 47362-3205. (Mail add: PO Box J, 47362-1050), SAN 305-0572. Tel: 765-529-0362, 765-529-0362, Ext 300. Reference Tel: 765-529-0362, Ext 309. FAX: 765-521-3581. Web Site: www.nchcpl.lib.in.us. *Dir,* Jan Preusz; Tel: 765-529-0362, Ext 301, E-mail: janp@nchcpl.lib.in.us; *Asst Dir,* Winnifred Price; Tel: 765-529-0362, Ext 302, E-mail: winniep@nchcpl.lib.in.us; *Ch & Youth Librn,* Jan Gillispie; Tel: 765-529-0362, Ext 366, E-mail: jang@nchcpl.lib.in.us; Staff 28 (MLS 4, Non-MLS 24)
Founded 1913. Pop 39,349; Circ 324,841
Library Holdings: AV Mats 19,688; High Interest/Low Vocabulary Bk Vols 300; Bk Titles 180,291; Per Subs 384
Special Collections: Indiana History Coll; New Castle & Henry County Coll
Automation Activity & Vendor Info: (Acquisitions) SirsiDynix; (Cataloging) SirsiDynix; (Circulation) SirsiDynix; (ILL) SirsiDynix; (OPAC) SirsiDynix
Database Vendor: EBSCOhost
Wireless access
Partic in Midwest Collaborative for Library Services (MCLS)
Open Mon-Thurs 9-9, Fri 9-6, Sat 9-5, Sun 1-5
Friends of the Library Group
Bookmobiles: 1

NEW HARMONY

S WORKING MEN'S INSTITUTE LIBRARY*, 407 W Tavern St, 47631. (Mail add: PO Box 368, 47631-0368), SAN 305-0599. Tel: 812-682-4806. FAX: 812-682-4806. Web Site: www.workingmensinstitute.org. *Dir,* Ryan Rokicki; E-mail: director@workingmensinstitute.org; Staff 1 (MLS 1)
Founded 1838
Library Holdings: AV Mats 100; Bk Vols 32,000; Per Subs 50; Talking Bks 50
Special Collections: New Harmony History Manuscript Coll; Rare Books Coll, from 1538
Automation Activity & Vendor Info: (Cataloging) Follett Software; (Circulation) Follett Software; (OPAC) Follett Software
Wireless access
Open Tues-Thurs 10-7, Fri & Sat 10-4:30, Sun 12-4
Friends of the Library Group

NEWBURGH

J ITT TECHNICAL INSTITUTE*, Learning Resource Center, 10999 Stahl Rd, 47630. Tel: 812-858-1600. Toll Free Tel: 800-832-4488. Web Site: www.itttech.edu. *In Charge,* Joseph Wilbur; Staff 2 (MLS 1, Non-MLS 1)
Highest Degree: Bachelor
Library Holdings: Bk Titles 3,000; Bk Vols 3,260; Per Subs 58
Wireless access
Open Mon-Fri 9-9

P OHIO TOWNSHIP PUBLIC LIBRARY SYSTEM*, 4111 Lakeshore Dr, 47630-2274. (Mail add: PO Box 850, 47629-0850), SAN 305-0602. Tel: 812-853-5468. FAX: 812-853-0509. Web Site: www.ohio.lib.in.us. *Dir,* Stephen Thomas; E-mail: sthomas@ohio.lib.in.us; *Br Mgr,* Renee Beard; *Head, Computer Serv,* Allen Tate; E-mail: atate@ohio.lib.in.us; *Ch Serv,* Linda Spillman Bruns; *Ref Serv, Ad,* Diane Sprick; *Ref Serv, YA,* Jacalyn Lincoln; *Tech Serv,* Joan Elliott Parker; Staff 43 (MLS 5, Non-MLS 38)
Founded 1897. Pop 31,002; Circ 465,074
Jan 2008-Dec 2008 Income (Main Library and Branch(s)) $1,394,766, County $1,305,946, Locally Generated Income $88,820. Mats Exp $184,347, Books $101,871, Per/Ser (Incl. Access Fees) $13,268, AV Mat $65,033, Electronic Ref Mat (Incl. Access Fees) $4,175. Sal $801,970 (Prof $295,516)
Library Holdings: Bk Vols 104,939; Per Subs 308
Special Collections: Warrick County Families Genealogy; Warrick County History. State Document Depository; US Document Depository
Subject Interests: Local hist
Automation Activity & Vendor Info: (Acquisitions) Innovative Interfaces, Inc; (Cataloging) Innovative Interfaces, Inc; (Circulation) Innovative Interfaces, Inc; (OPAC) Innovative Interfaces, Inc
Database Vendor: 3M Library Systems, ALLDATA Online, Baker & Taylor, Checkpoint Systems, Inc, Inspire, OCLC WorldShare Interlibrary Loan

Wireless access
Function: ILL available, Prog for children & young adult, Summer reading prog
Partic in Midwest Collaborative for Library Services (MCLS)
Open Mon-Thurs 9-9, Fri & Sat 9-5, Sun 1-5
Friends of the Library Group
Branches: 2
CHANDLER LIBRARY, 402 S Jaycee St, Chandler, 47610, SAN 324-3079. Tel: 812-925-7179. FAX: 812-925-7192. *Br Mgr,* Position Currently Open; Staff 7.5 (Non-MLS 7.5)
Library Holdings: Bk Titles 22,840; Bk Vols 25,290; Per Subs 59; Videos 310
Open Mon & Thurs 10-6, Tues & Wed 10-8, Fri 10-5, Sat 1-5
Friends of the Library Group
NEWBURGH LIBRARY, 30 W Water St, 47630, SAN 370-1069. Tel: 812-858-1437. FAX: 812-858-9390. *Br Mgr,* Caryl Hulgus; E-mail: chulgus@ohio.lib.in.us; Staff 3 (Non-MLS 3)
Library Holdings: Bk Titles 53,640; Bk Vols 56,910; Per Subs 72; Videos 314
Open Mon 11-7, Tues-Thurs 10-6, Fri & Sat 1-5
Friends of the Library Group

NEWPORT

P VERMILLION COUNTY PUBLIC LIBRARY*, 385 E Market St, 47966. (Mail add: PO Box 100, 47966-0100), SAN 341-5384. Tel: 765-492-3555. FAX: 765-492-9558. E-mail: newport_library@hotmail.com. Web Site: www.newportlibrary.info. *Dir,* Brigit Steinbrenner; Staff 5 (Non-MLS 5)
Founded 1929. Pop 7,670; Circ 45,928
Jan 2008-Dec 2008 Income $230,600. Mats Exp $12,000. Sal $89,000
Library Holdings: Audiobooks 212; Bks on Deafness & Sign Lang 11; DVDs 200; Large Print Bks 370; Bk Titles 52,331; Bk Vols 62,428; Per Subs 50; Talking Bks 400; Videos 350
Subject Interests: Cooking, Genealogy
Wireless access
Partic in Midwest Collaborative for Library Services (MCLS)
Open Mon, Wed & Fri 9-5, Tues & Thurs 10-6, Sat 10-2

NOBLESVILLE

P HAMILTON EAST PUBLIC LIBRARY*, Noblesville Library, One Library Plaza, Cumberland Rd, 46060-5639. SAN 305-0610. Tel: 317-773-1384. FAX: 317-776-6936. Web Site: www.hepl.lib.in.us. *Dir,* Edra Waterman; E-mail: ewaterman@hepl.lib.in.us; *Head of Outreach Serv,* Melissa A Stewart; Tel: 317-770-3235, E-mail: stewartm@hepl.lib.in.us; *Head, Circ,* Mary Kay Patterson; Tel: 317-770-3226, E-mail: pattersonm@hepl.lib.in.us; *Head, Ref,* Linda Shaw; Tel: 317-770-3207, E-mail: shawl@hepl.lib.in.us; *Head, Tech Serv,* Theresa Tyner; Tel: 317-770-3220, E-mail: tynert@hepl.lib.in.us
Founded 1909. Pop 148,721; Circ 2,019,986
Jan 2011-Dec 2011 Income (Main Library and Branch(s)) $6,381,133, State $213,959, County $5,585,747, Other $581,427. Mats Exp $535,134, Books $268,199, Per/Ser (Incl. Access Fees) $88,218, AV Mat $178,717. Sal $3,912,443
Library Holdings: Bk Titles 394,564; Bk Vols 524,957; Per Subs 799
Special Collections: Hamilton County History & Genealogy, bk & microfilm
Automation Activity & Vendor Info: (Acquisitions) SirsiDynix; (Cataloging) SirsiDynix; (Circulation) SirsiDynix; (OPAC) SirsiDynix
Database Vendor: Gale Cengage Learning, infoUSA, Inspire, ReferenceUSA
Wireless access
Publications: Abstracts of the Will Records of Hamilton County, Indiana 1824-1901
Partic in Midwest Collaborative for Library Services (MCLS)
Special Services for the Deaf - Bks on deafness & sign lang; TDD equip; Videos & decoder
Open Mon-Thurs 9-9, Fri & Sat 9-5:30, Sun 1:30-5:30
Friends of the Library Group
Branches: 1
FISHERS BRANCH, Five Municipal Dr, Fishers, 46038-1574. Tel: 317-579-0300. FAX: 317-579-0309. *Dir,* David L Cooper
Library Holdings: Bk Vols 252,830
Database Vendor: ProQuest
Open Mon-Thurs 9-9, Fri & Sat 9-5:30, Sun 1:30-5:30

C INDIANA CHRISTIAN UNIVERSITY LIBRARY*, 10511 Greenfield Ave, 46060. Tel: 317-773-3909. FAX: 317-773-1403. Web Site: www.icu.icuniversityonline.com. *Exec Dir,* Lucy Sheets
Enrl 100; Fac 3; Highest Degree: Doctorate
Library Holdings: Bk Vols 10,000; Per Subs 10
Open Mon, Tues, Thurs & Fri 9-12, 1-3 & 7-9
Restriction: Open to students, fac, staff & alumni

NORTH JUDSON

P NORTH JUDSON-WAYNE TOWNSHIP PUBLIC LIBRARY*, 208 Keller Ave, 46366. SAN 305-0629. Tel: 574-896-2841. FAX: 574-896-2892. Web Site: www.njwt.lib.in.us. *Dir,* Jane Ellen Felchuk; Staff 2 (MLS 1, Non-MLS 1)
Founded 1921. Pop 4,987; Circ 20,970
Jan 2007-Dec 2007 Income $184,529, State $18,539, Locally Generated Income $153,370, Other $12,620. Mats Exp $17,490, Books $14,887, Per/Ser (Incl. Access Fees) $2,171, AV Mat $432. Sal $96,439 (Prof $27,400)
Library Holdings: Audiobooks 179; AV Mats 399; CDs 196; DVDs 95; Large Print Bks 220; Microforms 255; Bk Titles 33,267; Bk Vols 35,171; Per Subs 82; Videos 1,318
Special Collections: Excalibur Coll; Mint Growing. Oral History
Automation Activity & Vendor Info: (Cataloging) Follett Software; (Circulation) Follett Software; (OPAC) Follett Software
Wireless access
Function: Adult bk club, AV serv, Bk club(s), Computer training, Copy machines, Electronic databases & coll, Handicapped accessible, Homebound delivery serv, ILL available, Learning ctr, Mail & tel request accepted, Online searches, Photocopying/Printing, Prog for adults, Prog for children & young adult, Ref & res, Spoken cassettes & CDs, Spoken cassettes & DVDs, Summer reading prog, Tax forms, Telephone ref, VCDs, VHS videos, Video lending libr, Wheelchair accessible, Workshops
Partic in Midwest Collaborative for Library Services (MCLS); Northern Indiana Computer Consortium for Libraries (NICCL)
Open Mon-Thurs 11-8, Fri 11-6, Sat 10-3
Friends of the Library Group

NORTH MANCHESTER

C MANCHESTER UNIVERSITY*, Funderburg Library, 604 E College Ave, 46962. SAN 305-0637. Tel: 260-982-5364. FAX: 260-982-5362. Web Site: www.manchester.edu/oaa/library. *Libr Dir,* Jill Lichtsinn; Tel: 260-982-5015, E-mail: jslichtsinn@manchester.edu; *Subj Librn, Tech Serv,* Darla Vornberger Haines; Tel: 260-982-5949, E-mail: dvhaines@manchester.edu; *Tech & Sci Librn,* Doris Stephenson; Tel: 260-982-5028, E-mail: dfstephenson@manchester.edu; *Archivist,* Jeanine Wine; Tel: 260-982-5361, E-mail: jmwine@manchester.edu; Staff 4.25 (MLS 3.75, Non-MLS 0.5)
Founded 1889. Enrl 1,300; Highest Degree: Master
Library Holdings: Bk Vols 176,052
Special Collections: Church of the Brethren Coll; College Archives; Peace Studies
Automation Activity & Vendor Info: (Acquisitions) Ex Libris Group; (Cataloging) Ex Libris Group; (Circulation) Ex Libris Group; (OPAC) Ex Libris Group; (Serials) Ex Libris Group
Wireless access
Function: Archival coll, Audio & video playback equip for onsite use, Computers for patron use, Copy machines, Doc delivery serv, e-mail serv, Electronic databases & coll, Exhibits, Free DVD rentals, Handicapped accessible, ILL available, Music CDs, Online cat, Online ref, Photocopying/Printing, Ref & res, Ref serv available, Ref serv in person, Scanner, Tax forms, Telephone ref, VHS videos, Video lending libr, Wheelchair accessible
Partic in Academic Libraries of Indiana; Midwest Collaborative for Library Services (MCLS); OCLC Online Computer Library Center, Inc; Private Academic Library Network of Indiana (PALNI)
Open Mon-Thurs (Winter) 8am-11pm, Fri 8-5, Sat 10-5, Sun 12:30-11; Mon-Fri (Summer) 8-5
Restriction: Circ limited, In-house use for visitors

P NORTH MANCHESTER PUBLIC LIBRARY*, 405 N Market St, 46962. SAN 305-0645. Tel: 260-982-4773. FAX: 260-982-6342. E-mail: nmpl@nman.lib.in.us. Web Site: www.nman.lib.in.us. *Dir,* Theresa Tyner; *Ch Serv,* Nancy Lance; Staff 4 (MLS 1, Non-MLS 3)
Founded 1912. Pop 6,020; Circ 128,754
Library Holdings: Bk Titles 64,225; Bk Vols 67,377; Per Subs 121
Special Collections: North Manchester News-Journal, 1882-present
Subject Interests: Genealogy, Local hist
Automation Activity & Vendor Info: (Cataloging) Follett Software; (Circulation) Follett Software; (OPAC) Follett Software
Wireless access
Partic in Midwest Collaborative for Library Services (MCLS); Northern Indiana Computer Consortium for Libraries (NICCL)
Special Services for the Deaf - Closed caption videos
Special Services for the Blind - Audio mat; Bks on cassette; Bks on CD; Copier with enlargement capabilities; Home delivery serv; Large print bks; Playaways (bks on MP3)
Open Mon-Thurs 9-8, Fri & Sat 9-5
Friends of the Library Group

NORTH VERNON

P JENNINGS COUNTY PUBLIC LIBRARY*, 2375 N State Hwy 3, 47265-1596. SAN 305-0653. Tel: 812-346-2091. FAX: 812-346-2127. E-mail: jlibrary@seidata.com. Web Site: www.jenningscounty.lib.in.us. *Dir,* Mary Hougland; E-mail: Mary.Hougland@jenningslib.org; *Asst Dir,* Ed Kellar; *Head, Youth Serv,* Misti Harris; *Ad,* Bette Eggleston; Staff 10 (MLS 3, Non-MLS 7)
Founded 1813. Pop 28,510; Circ 100,000
Library Holdings: CDs 900; Large Print Bks 1,200; Bk Titles 72,000; Bk Vols 90,000; Per Subs 236; Talking Bks 1,500; Videos 5,000
Subject Interests: Genealogy, Local hist
Automation Activity & Vendor Info: (Cataloging) Auto-Graphics, Inc; (Circulation) Auto-Graphics, Inc; (OPAC) Auto-Graphics, Inc
Partic in Evergreen Indiana Consortium; Midwest Collaborative for Library Services (MCLS)
Open Mon-Thurs 9-9, Fri 9-6, Sat 9-4
Friends of the Library Group

NORTH WEBSTER

P NORTH WEBSTER COMMUNITY PUBLIC LIBRARY*, 301 N Main St, 46555. (Mail add: PO Box 825, 46555-0008). Tel: 574-834-7122. FAX: 574-834-7122. E-mail: info@nweb.lib.in.us. Web Site: www.nweb.lib.in.us. *Dir,* Helen Leinbach; E-mail: hleinbach@nweb.lib.in.us; Staff 6 (MLS 2, Non-MLS 4)
Founded 2004. Pop 6,700; Circ 91,372
Jan 2011-Dec 2011 Income $505,622, City $359,757, County $126,289, Locally Generated Income $19,576. Mats Exp $61,678, Books $31,360, Per/Ser (Incl. Access Fees) $4,000, AV Equip $1,000, AV Mat $16,318, Electronic Ref Mat (Incl. Access Fees) $9,000. Sal $223,823 (Prof $78,785)
Library Holdings: Audiobooks 2,162; Bks on Deafness & Sign Lang 30; Braille Volumes 4; CDs 504; DVDs 3,595; Electronic Media & Resources 43; High Interest/Low Vocabulary Bk Vols 100; Large Print Bks 2,062; Bk Titles 53,021; Per Subs 165; Videos 1,425
Automation Activity & Vendor Info: (Acquisitions) Baker & Taylor; (Cataloging) Evergreen; (Circulation) Evergreen; (Course Reserve) Evergreen; (ILL) Evergreen; (OPAC) Evergreen
Database Vendor: Gale Cengage Learning, Inspire, Overdrive, Inc, ProQuest, ReferenceUSA
Wireless access
Function: Accelerated reader prog, Adult bk club, Art exhibits, Audiobks via web, AV serv, Bi-weekly Writer's Group, Bk club(s), Bks on cassette, Bks on CD, Children's prog, Computer training, Computers for patron use, Copy machines, Digital talking bks, e-mail serv, E-Reserves, Electronic databases & coll, Exhibits, Fax serv, Free DVD rentals, Genealogy discussion group, Handicapped accessible, Holiday prog, Homebound delivery serv, ILL available, Mail & tel request accepted, Music CDs, Online cat, Online ref, Online searches, Outreach serv, Outside serv via phone, mail, e-mail & web, OverDrive digital audio bks, Photocopying/Printing, Preschool outreach, Preschool reading prog, Printer for laptops & handheld devices, Prog for adults, Prog for children & young adult, Pub access computers, Ref serv available, Ref serv in person, Scanner, Spoken cassettes & CDs, Spoken cassettes & DVDs, Story hour, Summer reading prog, Tax forms, Teen prog, VHS videos, Video lending libr, Wheelchair accessible
Publications: Lily Pad Press (Monthly newsletter); Local History & Genealogy Center: From the Library (Local historical information)
Partic in Evergreen Indiana Consortium; Midwest Collaborative for Library Services (MCLS); Northeast Indiana Libraries Serving Communities Consortium
Special Services for the Deaf - Accessible learning ctr; Bks on deafness & sign lang; Closed caption videos; High interest/low vocabulary bks; Interpreter on staff; Staff with knowledge of sign lang
Special Services for the Blind - Bks on cassette; Bks on CD; Braille bks; Home delivery serv; Large print & cassettes; Large print bks; Low vision equip; Magnifiers
Open Mon-Thurs 10-7, Fri 10-6, Sat 10-3
Friends of the Library Group

NOTRE DAME

C HESBURGH LIBRARIES*, 221 Hesburgh Library, University of Notre Dame, 46556. SAN 341-5414. Tel: 574-631-5252. FAX: 574-631-6772. Web Site: www.library.nd.edu. *Edward H Arnold Univ Librn,* Diane Parr Walker; E-mail: Diane.Parr.Walker@nd.edu; *Assoc Librn,* Zheng Wang; E-mail: zheng.wang@nd.edu; *Assoc Librn,* Louis Jordan; E-mail: ljordan@nd.edu; Staff 174 (MLS 62, Non-MLS 112)
Founded 1873. Enrl 11,793; Fac 1,051; Highest Degree: Doctorate
Jul 2011-Jun 2012. Mats Exp $11,919,149. Sal $8,920,429
Library Holdings: Bk Titles 3,110,579; Bk Titles 3,110,579; Bk Vols 3,865,693
Special Collections: 1798 Irish Rebellion Coll; 17th-Early 19th Century Books from Religious Libraries Near Olmutz (Olmutz Coll); Anastos Byzantine Coll; Armed Services Editions Coll; Autographed Books (Theodore M Hesburgh Coll); Catholic Americana; Chesterton (John Bennett Shaw Coll); Dante (John A Zahm Coll); Descartes (Denisoff Coll); Early American Newspapers (Thackenbruch Coll); Early Editions of the Works of Edmund Burke (William Todd Coll); Early Printed Books (Astrik L Gabriel Coll); Early Printed Maps of Ireland Coll; Edward Gorey Coll; Eric Gill Coll; Fundamentalist/Evangelical Magazines (Adam L Lutzweiler Coll); Garcilaso de la Vega & the History of Peru (Durand Coll); George Berkeley (A A Luce Coll); Historical Botany (Edward Greene Coll); Irish Music (Captain Francis O'Neill Coll); Jacques Maritain Coll; Jorge Luis Borges Coll; McDevitt Inquisition Coll; Medieval & Renaissance Manuscripts; Modern Manuscript Coll; Notre Dame Coll; Penguin Paperbacks, 1935-1965; R H Gore, Sr Orchid Coll; Robert H Gore Numismatic Coll; Sports (Edmund Joyce Coll); Vatican II Documents Coll; Wolf Irish Stamp Coll. US Document Depository
Automation Activity & Vendor Info: (Acquisitions) Ex Libris Group; (Cataloging) Ex Libris Group
Database Vendor: EBSCOhost, Elsevier, Ex Libris Group, OCLC, YBP Library Services
Wireless access
Publications: Access (Quarterly)
Partic in Association of Research Libraries (ARL); Center for Research Libraries; Midwest Collaborative for Library Services (MCLS); Northeast Research Libraries Consortium (NERL); OCLC Online Computer Library Center, Inc; RLIN (Research Libraries Information Network)
Restriction: In-house use for visitors

Departmental Libraries:

ARCHITECTURE, 117 Bond Hall, 46556-5652, SAN 341-5449. Tel: 574-631-6654. FAX: 574-631-9662. E-mail: library.archlib.1@nd.edu. Web Site: architecture.library.nd.edu. *Br Mgr,* Deborah Webb; *Archit Librn,* Jennifer Parker; Tel: 574-631-9401; Staff 4 (MLS 1, Non-MLS 3)
Founded 1931. Enrl 250; Fac 20; Highest Degree: Master
Library Holdings: DVDs 174; e-journals 45; Bk Vols 34,444; Per Subs 95; Videos 130
Subject Interests: Archit, Interior design, Landscape archit, Rare bks, Urban planning
Publications: New Acquisitions
Open Mon-Thurs 8am-11pm, Fri 8-6, Sat 1-5, Sun 1-11
Restriction: Circ limited

CHEMISTRY-PHYSICS, 231 Nieuwland Science Hall, 46556, SAN 341-5473. Tel: 574-631-7203. FAX: 574-631-9661. Web Site: chemistry.library.nd.edu. *Br Librn,* Thurston D Miller; *Br Supvr,* Diane M Gram; Staff 4 (MLS 1, Non-MLS 3)
Library Holdings: e-journals 580; Bk Vols 34,253; Per Subs 96
Subject Interests: Astronomy, Chem, Physics
Publications: New Acquisitions
Open Mon-Thurs 8am-10pm, Fri 8-5, Sun 1-10

ENGINEERING, 149 Fitzpatrick Hall, 46556, SAN 341-5503. Tel: 574-631-6665. FAX: 574-631-9208. E-mail: library.engrlib.1@nd.edu. Web Site: engineering.library.nd.edu. *Br Librn,* Carol A Brach. Subject Specialists: *Eng,* Carol A Brach; Staff 1 (MLS 1)
Library Holdings: e-journals 1,430; Bk Vols 56,426; Per Subs 134
Publications: New Book List (Accession list)
Open Mon-Thurs 8am 11pm, Fri 8-5, Sat 1-5, Sun 1-11

KELLOGG-KROC INFORMATION CENTER, 318 Hesburgh Ctr International Studies, 46556-5677, SAN 378-0430. Tel: 574-631-8534. FAX: 574-631-6717. E-mail: library.kic.1@nd.edu. Web Site: www.kkic.library.nd.edu.
Library Holdings: Per Subs 21
Special Collections: Newletters & Journals covering Latin American & European Affairs
Open Mon-Fri 1-5

THOMAS J MAHAFFEY JR BUSINESS INFORMATION CENTER, L001 Mendoza College of Business, 46556, SAN 378-0414. Tel: 574-631-9098. FAX: 574-631-6367. E-mail: library.bic.1@nd.edu. Web Site: bic.library.nd.edu. *Bus Librn,* Stephen M Hayes; Tel: 574-631-5268, E-mail: shayes1@nd.edu; *Asst Bus Librn,* Barbara Pietraszewski; Tel: 574-631-9099, E-mail: bpietras@nd.edu; Staff 4 (MLS 2, Non-MLS 2)
Founded 1995. Highest Degree: Master
Library Holdings: AV Mats 10; Electronic Media & Resources 51; Bk Vols 417
Subject Interests: Bus
Function: Res libr
Open Mon-Wed 8am-9pm, Thurs 8-8, Fri 8-5, Sat 12-4, Sun 1-9

MEDIEVAL INSTITUTE LIBRARY, 715 Hesburgh Library, 46556-5629, SAN 341-5651. Tel: 574-631-5724, 574-631-6603. FAX: 574-631-8644. Web Site: www.nd.edu/~medvllib. *Head, Spec Coll,* Louis Jordan; Tel: 574-631-3778; Staff 1 (MLS 1)
Founded 1948
Library Holdings: Bk Vols 90,000; Per Subs 470
Special Collections: Ambrosiana (Frank M Folsom Microfilm & Photographic Coll); History of Medieval Universities
Subject Interests: Byzantine studies, Medieval studies
Open Mon-Fri 8-5

O'MEARA MATHEMATICS LIBRARY, 001 Hayes-Healy Ctr, 46556-5641, SAN 341-5627. Tel: 574-631-7278. FAX: 574-631-9660. E-mail: library.mathlib.1@nd.edu. Web Site: mathematics.library.nd.edu. *Math & Life Sci Librn,* Parker Ladwig; E-mail: ladwig.1@nd.edu; *Br Supvr,* Karen Lanser; Staff 3 (MLS 1, Non-MLS 2)
Library Holdings: e-journals 440; Bk Vols 53,100; Per Subs 71; Videos 10
Special Collections: Marston Morse
Subject Interests: Computer sci, Math
Publications: Acquisitions List
Open Mon-Thurs 9-9, Fri 9-5, Sat 1-5, Sun 1-9
Friends of the Library Group

RADIATION CHEMISTRY READING ROOM, 105 Radiation Research Bldg, 46556. Tel: 574-631-6163. E-mail: chemlib.1@nd.edu. Web Site: library.nd.edu/radlab. *Br Librn,* Thurston D Miller; Tel: 574-631-4549, E-mail: tmiller5@nd.edu. Subject Specialists: *Chem, Physics,* Thurston D Miller; Staff 1 (MLS 1)
Library Holdings: e-journals 24; Bk Vols 5,006; Per Subs 6
Open Mon-Fri 8-5

C HOLY CROSS COLLEGE*, McKenna Library, 54515 State Rd 933 N, 46556-0308. SAN 305-0661. Tel: 574-239-8391. FAX: 574-239-8324. Web Site: www.hcc-nd.edu. *Dir of Libr Serv,* Mary Ellen Hegedus; Tel: 574-239-8360, E-mail: mhegedus@hcc-nd.edu; *Assoc Dir, Libr Serv,* Sarah Kolda; E-mail: skolda@hcc-nd.edu; *Cat Librn,* Sean Walton; E-mail: swalton@hcc-nd.edu; *Libr Tech,* Paula Morrow; E-mail: pmorrow@hcc-nd.edu; Staff 4 (MLS 3, Non-MLS 1)
Founded 1966. Fac 45; Highest Degree: Bachelor
Automation Activity & Vendor Info: (Circulation) Ex Libris Group
Wireless access
Partic in Academic Libraries of Indiana; Michiana Acad Libr Consortium; Midwest Collaborative for Library Services (MCLS)
Open Mon-Thurs 8:30am-Midnight, Fri 8:30-4:30, Sat 1-5, Sun 1-Midnight

C SAINT MARY'S COLLEGE*, Cushwa-Leighton Library, 46556-5001. SAN 305-067X. Tel: 574-284-5280. Circulation Tel: 574-284-5278. Reference Tel: 574-284-5288. FAX: 574-284-4791. Web Site: www.saintmarys.edu/~library. *Dir,* Janet Fore; Tel: 219-284-5281, E-mail: jfore@saintmarys.edu; *Cat Librn,* Katherine Marschall; Tel: 574-284-4438, E-mail: marschal@saintmarys.edu; *Per Librn,* Sue Wiegand; Tel: 574-284-4789, E-mail: swiegand@saintmarys.edu; *ILL, Ref Librn,* Jill Hobgood; Tel: 574-284-4804, E-mail: jhobgood@saintmarys.edu; *Bibliog Instruction Coordr, Ref Librn,* Catherine Pellegrino; Tel: 574-284-5286, E-mail: cpellegr@saintmarys.edu; *Ref & Instruction Librn,* Robert Hohl; Tel: 219-284-5287, E-mail: rhohl@saintmarys.edu; *Col Archivist,* John Kovach; Tel: 574-284-5282, E-mail: jkovach@saintmarys.edu; *Circ,* Lisa Karle; Tel: 574-284-5396, E-mail: lkarle@saintmarys.edu; *Coll Develop,* Julie Long; Tel: 574-284-5289, E-mail: jlong@saintmarys.edu; Staff 13 (MLS 7, Non-MLS 6)
Founded 1855. Enrl 1,602; Fac 150; Highest Degree: Bachelor
Library Holdings: AV Mats 2,657; Bk Titles 166,301; Bk Vols 229,484; Per Subs 584; Videos 210
Special Collections: Dante
Automation Activity & Vendor Info: (Acquisitions) Ex Libris Group; (Cataloging) Ex Libris Group; (Circulation) Ex Libris Group; (ILL) OCLC; (OPAC) Ex Libris Group; (Serials) Ex Libris Group
Database Vendor: Dialog, EBSCOhost, Gale Cengage Learning, OCLC FirstSearch, Wilson - Wilson Web
Function: Audio & video playback equip for onsite use, ILL available
Partic in Michiana Acad Libr Consortium; Midwest Collaborative for Library Services (MCLS); OCLC Online Computer Library Center, Inc
Open Mon-Thurs 7:45am-Midnight, Fri 7:45am-10pm, Sat 9-5, Sun 1-Midnight
Restriction: Open to pub for ref & circ; with some limitations

CL UNIVERSITY OF NOTRE DAME*, Kresge Law Library, Notre Dame Law School, 2345 Biolchini Hall of Law, 46556-4640. SAN 341-5562. Tel: 574-631-7024. Reference Tel: 574-631-5993. FAX: 574-631-6371. E-mail: lawlib@nd.edu. Circulation E-mail: lawcirc@nd.edu. Web Site: law.nd.edu/library-and-technology. *Assoc Dean, Dir,* Ed Edmonds; Tel: 574-631-5916, E-mail: edmonds.7@nd.edu; *Head, Access Serv,* Carmela Kinslow; Tel: 574-631-5990, E-mail: ckinslow@nd.edu; *Head, Tech Serv,* Joseph Thomas; Tel: 574-631-5992, E-mail: jthomas@nd.edu; *Head, Res Serv,* Dwight King; E-mail: dwight.b.king.1@nd.edu; *Head, Tech Serv,* Daniel Manier; Tel: 574-631-3939, E-mail: manier@nd.edu; *Acq/Coll Develop Librn,* Sandra Klein; Tel: 574-631-8447, E-mail: klein.26@nd.edu; *Bibliog Control Librn,* Laurel Cochrane; Tel: 574-631-0983, E-mail: lcochran@nd.edu; *Res Librn,* Christopher O'Byrne; Tel: 574-631-5664; *Res Librn,* Patti Ogden; Tel: 574-631-5996, E-mail: pogden@nd.edu; *Res Librn,* Warren Rees; Tel: 574-631-4436, E-mail: warren.d.rees.2@nd.edu; Staff 21.5 (MLS 9, Non-MLS 12.5)
Founded 1869. Enrl 540; Fac 9; Highest Degree: Doctorate
Library Holdings: AV Mats 1,785; CDs 687; DVDs 1,175; e-books 7,500; e-journals 35,000; Microforms 1,807,829; Bk Titles 222,433; Bk Vols 690,000; Per Subs 4,250
Automation Activity & Vendor Info: (Acquisitions) Innovative Interfaces, Inc - Millenium; (Cataloging) Innovative Interfaces, Inc - Millenium; (Circulation) Innovative Interfaces, Inc - Millenium; (ILL) OCLC ILLiad; (OPAC) Innovative Interfaces, Inc - Millenium; (Serials) Innovative Interfaces, Inc - Millenium
Wireless access
Open Mon-Fri (Winter) 8am-10pm, Sat 9am-10pm, Sun 10-10; Mon-Fri (Summer) 8-5
Restriction: 24-hr pass syst for students only

OAKLAND CITY

P OAKLAND CITY-COLUMBIA TOWNSHIP PUBLIC LIBRARY*, 210 S Main, 47660. SAN 305-0696. Tel: 812-749-3559. FAX: 812-749-3558. E-mail: occtpl@gmail.com. Web Site: www.occtpl.lib.in.us. *Dir,* Julie Elmore; Staff 3 (Non-MLS 3)
Founded 1917. Pop 4,149; Circ 24,211
Library Holdings: CDs 279; DVDs 122; Bk Titles 29,110; Bk Vols 31,470; Per Subs 87; Talking Bks 1,038; Videos 920
Special Collections: History of Pike & Gibson Counties
Database Vendor: Inspire
Partic in Midwest Collaborative for Library Services (MCLS)
Open Mon-Wed & Fri 9-6, Thurs 9-8, Sat 9-1
Friends of the Library Group

C OAKLAND CITY UNIVERSITY*, Barger-Richardson LRC, 605 W Columbia St, 47660. SAN 305-0688. Tel: 812-749-1269. FAX: 812-749-1414. Web Site: oak.oak.edu. *Dir,* Denise J Pinnick; Tel: 812-749-1267, E-mail: dpinnick@oak.edu; *Asst Dir,* Emily Eberhardt; Tel: 812-749-1268, E-mail: eeberhard@oak.edu; Staff 3 (MLS 1, Non-MLS 2)
Founded 1890. Enrl 1,668; Fac 37; Highest Degree: Doctorate
Library Holdings: Bk Titles 110,115; Bk Vols 115,340; Per Subs 301
Special Collections: General Baptist Denomination Materials
Automation Activity & Vendor Info: (Acquisitions) Ex Libris Group; (Cataloging) Ex Libris Group; (Circulation) Ex Libris Group; (Course Reserve) Ex Libris Group; (OPAC) Ex Libris Group; (Serials) Ex Libris Group
Database Vendor: EBSCOhost, Gale Cengage Learning, Inspire, JSTOR, LexisNexis, OCLC FirstSearch, OCLC WorldShare Interlibrary Loan, OVID Technologies, ProQuest
Function: Res libr
Partic in Academic Libraries of Indiana; Midwest Collaborative for Library Services (MCLS); Private Academic Library Network of Indiana (PALNI)
Open Mon-Thurs 8am-10pm, Fri 8-4:30, Sat 10-2, Sun 6pm-10pm

ODON

P ODON WINKELPLECK PUBLIC LIBRARY, 202 W Main St, 47562. SAN 305-070X. Tel: 812-636-4949. FAX: 812-636-4949. E-mail: owpl@mail.odon.lib.in.us. Web Site: www.odon.lib.in.us. *Dir,* Marsha Lynn; *Asst Librn,* Sandra Armstrong; *Asst Librn,* Lynn Brown; Staff 3 (Non-MLS 3)
Founded 1906. Pop 2,793; Circ 19,400
Library Holdings: Audiobooks 220; AV Mats 310; CDs 95; Large Print Bks 300; Bk Titles 15,000; Bk Vols 16,250; Per Subs 40; Videos 1,750
Automation Activity & Vendor Info: (Cataloging) Evergreen; (Circulation) Evergreen; (OPAC) Evergreen
Database Vendor: Inspire
Wireless access
Function: Bks on cassette, Computers for patron use, Copy machines, Fax serv, Online cat, Photocopying/Printing, Scanner, Summer reading prog, Tax forms, VHS videos, Video lending libr
Partic in Evergreen Indiana Consortium
Open Tues 1-8, Wed & Sat 9-1, Thurs 4-8, Fri 1-5
Restriction: Non-resident fee
Friends of the Library Group

ORLAND

P JOYCE PUBLIC LIBRARY*, 9490 W State Rd 120, 46776-6329. (Mail add: PO Box 240, 46776-0240), SAN 376-5350. Tel: 260-829-6329. *Librn,* Wava Albright; Staff 1 (Non-MLS 1)
Founded 1903. Pop 1,841; Circ 4,868
Jan 2010-Dec 2010 Income $16,000. Mats Exp $4,500
Library Holdings: CDs 15; DVDs 200; Bk Titles 13,491; Bk Vols 14,122; Per Subs 16; Talking Bks 284; Videos 157
Wireless access
Open Tues 4-8, Wed 1-5, Sat 8-12

ORLEANS

P ORLEANS TOWN & TOWNSHIP PUBLIC LIBRARY*, 174 N Maple St, 47452-1424. (Mail add: PO Box 142, 47452-0142), SAN 305-0718. Tel: 812-865-3270. FAX: 812-865-3270. E-mail: orleanslibrary@hotmail.com.

Web Site: www.orleans.lib.in.us. *Dir,* Deborah M Stone; Staff 2 (Non-MLS 1, Non-MLS 1)
Founded 1913. Pop 2,273; Circ 15,583
Library Holdings: CDs 222; DVDs 25; Large Print Bks 122; Bk Vols 19,287; Per Subs 26; Talking Bks 285; Videos 601
Automation Activity & Vendor Info: (Acquisitions) Book Systems
Database Vendor: Inspire, OCLC FirstSearch
Wireless access
Open Mon 10-7, Tues & Thurs 10-6:30, Fri 9-5, Sat 10-2

OSGOOD

P OSGOOD PUBLIC LIBRARY*, 136 W Ripley St, 47037-1229. SAN 305-0726. Tel: 812-689-4011. FAX: 812-689-5062. E-mail: opl@osgoodlibrary.org. Web Site: www.osgoodlibrary.org. *Dir,* Vicki Butz; E-mail: vbutz@osgoodlibrary.org; Staff 4 (MLS 1, Non-MLS 3)
Founded 1912. Pop 9,533; Circ 26,910
Library Holdings: AV Mats 1,590; Bk Titles 29,840; Bk Vols 32,708; Per Subs 50; Talking Bks 270; Videos 940
Special Collections: Peoples History of Ripley County; Township Geneological Papers
Automation Activity & Vendor Info: (Cataloging) Book Systems
Partic in SE Ind Area Libr Servs Authority
Open Mon & Thurs 10-6, Tues & Wed 10-7, Fri 10-5, Sat 10-2
Friends of the Library Group

OTTERBEIN

P OTTERBEIN PUBLIC LIBRARY*, 23 E First St, 47970. (Mail add: PO Box 550, 47970-0550), SAN 305-0734. Tel: 765-583-2107. FAX: 765-583-2337. E-mail: otterbeinlibrary@hotmail.com. Web Site: www.otterbeinpubliclibrary.org. *Dir,* Sarah Rainey; E-mail: sarah@otterbeinpubliclibrary.org; *Adult Serv,* Chris McCallister; E-mail: cmccalli@otterbeinpubliclibrary.org; *Ch Serv,* Cindy Jackson; E-mail: cindyj@otterbeinpubliclibrary.org; Staff 5 (MLS 1, Non-MLS 4)
Founded 1919. Pop 1,666; Circ 32,898
Library Holdings: Audiobooks 403; CDs 208; DVDs 2,536; Large Print Bks 190; Bk Titles 14,576; Per Subs 38; Videos 1,300
Special Collections: Adam Kennedy Coll; Gene Stratton Porter Coll
Subject Interests: Local hist
Automation Activity & Vendor Info: (Acquisitions) Evergreen; (Cataloging) Evergreen; (Circulation) Evergreen; (ILL) Evergreen; (OPAC) Evergreen; (Serials) Evergreen
Wireless access
Function: After school storytime, Bks on cassette, Bks on CD, CD-ROM, Children's prog, Computer training, Computers for patron use, Copy machines, e-mail serv, Fax serv, Free DVD rentals, Handicapped accessible, Holiday prog, Homebound delivery serv, ILL available, Instruction & testing, Libr develop, Music CDs, Online cat, Outreach serv, Photocopying/Printing, Prog for adults, Prog for children & young adult, Pub access computers, Ref serv available, Ref serv in person, Senior computer classes, Story hour, Summer reading prog, Teen prog, VHS videos, Wheelchair accessible
Partic in Evergreen Indiana Consortium
Open Mon 3-8, Tues & Thurs 10-7, Wed & Fri 11-7, Sat 10-2

OWENSVILLE

P OWENSVILLE CARNEGIE PUBLIC LIBRARY*, 110 S Main St, 47665. (Mail add: PO Box 219, 47665-0219), SAN 305-0742. Tel: 812-724-3335. FAX: 812-724-3336. E-mail: owensvillelibrary@gmail.com. Web Site: www.owensvillelibrary.org. *Dir,* Peggy Callis; *Ch,* April Yockey; *Asst Librn,* Donna Keller
Founded 1917. Pop 3,742
Jan 2007-Dec 2007 Income $243,685, County $218,014, Locally Generated Income $10,297, Other $15,374. Mats Exp $91,317, Books $49,267, Per/Ser (Incl. Access Fees) $9,376, AV Mat $16,866. Sal $82,267
Library Holdings: CDs 1,009; DVDs 3,148; Large Print Bks 9,000; Bk Vols 27,008; Per Subs 145; Talking Bks 400
Subject Interests: Local hist
Partic in Midwest Collaborative for Library Services (MCLS)
Open Mon & Wed 10-6, Tues 10-8, Thurs & Fri 10-5, Sat 10-3

OXFORD

P OXFORD PUBLIC LIBRARY*, 201 E Smith, 47971. (Mail add: PO Box 6, 47971-0006), SAN 305-0750. Tel: 765-385-2177. FAX: 765-385-2313. E-mail: oxfordlibrary@sbcglobal.net. *Dir,* Danielle A Payne; Staff 3 (Non-MLS 3)
Founded 1917. Pop 1,694; Circ 33,880
Library Holdings: AV Mats 2,200; DVDs 400; Large Print Bks 300; Bk Titles 23,450; Bk Vols 26,100; Per Subs 70; Talking Bks 100; Videos 1,642
Automation Activity & Vendor Info: (Acquisitions) SirsiDynix; (Cataloging) SirsiDynix; (OPAC) SirsiDynix
Open Mon, Wed & Fri 10-6, Tues & Thurs 12-7, Sat 10-2
Friends of the Library Group

PAOLI

P PAOLI PUBLIC LIBRARY*, Ten E Court, 47454. SAN 305-0769. Tel: 812-723-3841. FAX: 812-723-3841. E-mail: paolilibrary@hotmail.com. *Dir,* Carole Vance; *Ch Serv,* Glenda Hess
Founded 1918. Pop 5,780; Circ 32,907
Library Holdings: AV Mats 1,103; Bks on Deafness & Sign Lang 10; Large Print Bks 100; Bk Vols 24,117; Per Subs 50; Talking Bks 382
Subject Interests: Genealogy, Local hist
Open Mon, Thurs & Fri 12:30-5:30, Tues 11-7, Sat 9-1

PENDLETON

P PENDLETON COMMUNITY LIBRARY*, 595 E Water St, 46064-1070. SAN 305-0777. Tel: 765-778-7527. Toll Free Tel: 800-242-2935. FAX: 765-778-7529. Web Site: www.pendleton.lib.in.us. *Dir,* Lynn Hobbs; Tel: 765-778-7527, Ext 107, E-mail: lhobbs@pendleton.lib.in.us; *Asst Dir, Ch,* Alicia Pitman; Tel: 765-778-7527, Ext 105, E-mail: apitman@pendleton.lib.in.us; *Adult Ref Librn,* Barb Donnell; Tel: 765-778-7527, Ext 109, E-mail: bdonnell@pendleton.lib.in.us; *Bus Mgr,* Jo Ann Fryback; Tel: 765-778-7527, Ext 108, E-mail: jfryback@pendleton.lib.in.us; Staff 3 (MLS 3)
Founded 1912. Pop 20,704; Circ 137,530
Library Holdings: AV Mats 7,000; Bk Vols 53,426; Per Subs 175
Special Collections: Quaker Manuscripts
Subject Interests: Genealogy, Local hist
Automation Activity & Vendor Info: (Acquisitions) Innovative Interfaces, Inc; (Cataloging) Innovative Interfaces, Inc; (Circulation) Innovative Interfaces, Inc; (OPAC) Innovative Interfaces, Inc; (Serials) Innovative Interfaces, Inc
Database Vendor: Baker & Taylor, ProQuest
Wireless access
Partic in Midwest Collaborative for Library Services (MCLS)
Open Mon-Thurs 9-8, Fri 9-6, Sat 9-5, Sun 1-5
Friends of the Library Group

S PENDLETON CORRECTIONAL FACILITY*, Offender Library, 4490 W Reformatory Rd, 46064. SAN 341-5716. Tel: 765-778-2107, Ext 1221. FAX: 765-778-1431. *In Charge,* Larry Fowler; Staff 1 (Non-MLS 1)
Founded 1897
Library Holdings: Bk Titles 15,810; Bk Vols 16,900; Per Subs 48
Subject Interests: Sci fict
Wireless access
Open Mon-Fri 6:15-5
Branches:
LAW, 4490 W Reformatory Rd, 46064, SAN 341-5724. Tel: 765-778-2107. FAX: 765-778-3395. *In Charge,* Larry Fowler; Staff 1 (Non-MLS 1)
Library Holdings: Bk Titles 11,290; Bk Vols 12,300; Per Subs 41
Open Mon-Fri 6:15am-8pm

PENNVILLE

P PENNVILLE TOWNSHIP PUBLIC LIBRARY*, 195 N Union, 47369. (Mail add: PO Box 206, 47369-0206), SAN 305-0785. Tel: 260-731-3333. FAX: 260-731-3333. *Dir,* Brenda L Cash
Pop 1,236; Circ 7,045
Library Holdings: Bk Vols 12,000; Per Subs 35
Open Tues-Thurs 3-8, Fri 4-6, Sat (May-Oct) 9-12

PERU

P PERU PUBLIC LIBRARY*, 102 E Main St, 46970-2338. SAN 305-0793. Tel: 765-473-3069. FAX: 765-473-3060. E-mail: perupubliclibrary@yahoo.com. Web Site: www.peru.lib.in.us. *Dir,* Charles A Wagner; *Asst Dir,* Maryanne Farnham; *Adult Serv,* Michael Rasor; *Ch Serv,* Carla Murtha; *Ref,* Laura Marshall; *Tech Serv,* Terri Hall; Staff 7 (MLS 2, Non-MLS 5)
Founded 1902. Pop 34,165; Circ 162,810
Library Holdings: DVDs 500; Large Print Bks 108; Bk Titles 37,910; Bk Vols 55,000; Per Subs 185; Talking Bks 1,500; Videos 1,200
Subject Interests: Genealogy, Indiana
Publications: Miami County (encyclopedia 12 vols, genealogies 9 vols); Miami County Obituaries
Open Mon-Thurs (Winter) 9-9, Fri & Sat 9-5:30; Mon-Sat (Summer) 9-6
Restriction: Residents only
Friends of the Library Group

PETERSBURG

P PIKE COUNTY PUBLIC LIBRARY, Petersburg Branch, 1008 E Maple St, 47567-1736. SAN 305-0807. Tel: 812-354-6257. FAX: 812-354-6259. E-mail: petersburg@pikeco.lib.in.us. Web Site: www.pikeco.lib.in.us.

Interim Dir, Thomas Behme; E-mail: director@pikeco.lib.in.us; *Adult & Teen Prog Coordr,* Dana Hughes; *Tech Serv,* Pat Weathers; E-mail: pweathers@pikeco.lib.in.us; Staff 1 (MLS 1)
Founded 1953. Pop 12,837; Circ 86,838
Library Holdings: AV Mats 5,022; Bk Titles 100,000; Per Subs 142
Subject Interests: Genealogy, Indiana, Local hist
Automation Activity & Vendor Info: (Cataloging) Evergreen; (Circulation) Evergreen; (OPAC) Evergreen
Wireless access
Function: Holiday prog, Home delivery & serv to Sr ctr & nursing homes, Homebound delivery serv, ILL available, Instruction & testing, Mail loans to mem, Music CDs, Newsp ref libr, Online cat, Photocopying/Printing, Preschool outreach, Prog for adults, Prog for children & young adult, Scanner, Senior computer classes, Senior outreach, Spoken cassettes & CDs, Spoken cassettes & DVDs, Summer reading prog, Tax forms, Teen prog, Telephone ref, VHS videos, Wheelchair accessible
Open Mon & Thurs 9-8, Tues, Wed, Fri & Sat 9-5
Restriction: Lending limited to county residents, Non-circulating coll, Non-resident fee, Off-site coll in storage - retrieval as requested, Use of others with permission of librn
Friends of the Library Group
Branches: 2
OTWELL BRANCH, 2301 N Spring St, Otwell, 47564. Tel: 812-380-0066. FAX: 812-380-0037. *Actg Dir,* Dana Hughes
Open Tues, Wed & Fri 9-5, Thurs Noon-8, Sat 9-2
Friends of the Library Group
WINSLOW BRANCH, 105 E Center St, Winslow, 47598, SAN 376-818X. Tel: 812-789-5423. FAX: 812-789-9496. *Actg Dir,* Dana Hughes; Staff 3 (Non-MLS 3)
Library Holdings: Bk Titles 10,800; Bk Vols 12,000; Per Subs 23; Videos 210
Open Tues, Wed & Fri 9-5, Thurs Noon-8, Sat 9-2
Friends of the Library Group

PIERCETON

P PIERCETON & WASHINGTON TOWNSHIP LIBRARY*, 101 Catholic St, 46562. (Mail add: PO Box 328, 46562-0328), SAN 305-0815. Tel: 574-594-5474. E-mail: pierceton.library@mchsi.com. *Dir,* Pamela Myers; Staff 3 (MLS 1, Non-MLS 2)
Founded 1915. Pop 4,815; Circ 6,891
Library Holdings: AV Mats 590; Bk Titles 25,930; Bk Vols 28,861; Per Subs 41; Talking Bks 120
Wireless access
Open Tues & Thurs 11:30-5, Wed & Fri 1-5, Sat 9-1

PLAINFIELD

G INDIANA LAW ENFORCEMENT ACADEMY*, Learning Resources Center, 5402 Sugar Grove Rd, 46168. (Mail add: PO Box 313, 46168-0313), SAN 305-0823. Tel: 317-837-3236. Reference Tel: 317-837-3290. FAX: 317-839-9741. Web Site: www.state.in.us/ilea. *Librn,* Connie Beck; E-mail: cbeck@ilea.in.gov; Staff 2 (MLS 1, Non-MLS 1)
Founded 1975
Library Holdings: Bk Titles 6,290; Bk Vols 7,100; Per Subs 121; Videos 72
Subject Interests: Law, Law enforcement, Photog
Database Vendor: LexisNexis, ProQuest
Function: Ref serv available
Partic in Midwest Collaborative for Library Services (MCLS); Nat Criminal Justice Ref Serv
Restriction: Open to others by appt

P PLAINFIELD-GUILFORD TOWNSHIP PUBLIC LIBRARY*, 1120 Stafford Rd, 46168. SAN 305-0831. Tel: 317-839-6602. Circulation Tel: 317-838-3800. Administration Tel: 317-838-3803. FAX: 317-838-3805. Web Site: www.plainfieldlibrary.net. *Dir,* Rachel Ziegler; Tel: 317-839-6602, Ext 2111; *Asst Dir, IT Mgr,* Kerry Green; Tel: 317-839-6602, Ext 2121; *Coll Develop Librn, Libr Mgr,* Mary Glaser; Tel: 317-839-6602, Ext 2147, E-mail: mglaser@plainfieldlibrary.net; *ILL Librn, Ref Supvr,* Debra Shaw; Tel: 317-839-6602, Ext 2113; *Youth Serv Mgr,* Joyce Welkie; Tel: 317-839-6602, Ext 2127; *Circ Supvr,* Paula Hilton; Tel: 317-839-6602, Ext 2122; Staff 12 (MLS 8, Non-MLS 4)
Founded 1901. Pop 22,961; Circ 274,061
Library Holdings: Bk Titles 179,443; Per Subs 282
Special Collections: Guilford Township Historical Coll
Subject Interests: Indiana, Local hist
Automation Activity & Vendor Info: (Acquisitions) Evergreen; (Cataloging) Evergreen; (Circulation) Evergreen; (OPAC) Evergreen; (Serials) Evergreen
Database Vendor: EBSCOhost
Wireless access
Publications: Novel News (Newsletter)
Partic in Evergreen Indiana Consortium; Midwest Collaborative for Library Services (MCLS)
Open Mon-Thurs 9-9, Fri 9-6, Sat 9-5, Sun 1-5
Friends of the Library Group

PLYMOUTH

S MARSHALL COUNTY HISTORICAL SOCIETY LIBRARY*, Research Library, 123 N Michigan St, 46563. SAN 305-0858. Tel: 574-936-2306. FAX: 574-936-9306. E-mail: lindarippy@mchistoricalsociety.org. Web Site: www.mchistoricalsociety.org. *Exec Dir,* Linda Rippy; *Archives Mgr,* Judy McCullough; *Photo Archivist, Res Spec,* Karin Rettinger
Founded 1957
Library Holdings: Bk Titles 550
Special Collections: Marshall County History Coll
Subject Interests: Genealogy
Wireless access
Open Tues-Sat 10-4

P PLYMOUTH PUBLIC LIBRARY*, 201 N Center St, 46563. SAN 305-0866. Tel: 574-936-2324. FAX: 574-936-7423. E-mail: info@plymouth.lib.in.us. Interlibrary Loan Service E-mail: ill@plymouth.lib.in.us. Web Site: www.plymouth.lib.in.us. *Dir,* Susie Reinholt; E-mail: reinholt@plymouth.lib.in.us; *AV,* Susan Mitchell; E-mail: mitchell@plymouth.lib.in.us; *Ch Serv,* Marie Dylag; E-mail: dylag@plymouth.lib.in.us; *Circ,* Marilee Douglass; Staff 30 (MLS 1, Non-MLS 29)
Founded 1910. Pop 18,609; Circ 355,000
Jan 2007-Dec 2007 Income $2,717,095. Mats Exp $1,243,512. Sal $671,999
Library Holdings: DVDs 7,000; Large Print Bks 30,000; Bk Vols 220,000; Per Subs 215; Talking Bks 3,100
Special Collections: Indiana History; Marshall County Authors
Automation Activity & Vendor Info: (Circulation) Innovative Interfaces, Inc
Open Mon-Thurs 9-8, Fri & Sat 9-5:30, Sun 1-5
Friends of the Library Group

PORTLAND

P JAY COUNTY PUBLIC LIBRARY*, 315 N Ship St, 47371. SAN 305-0874. Tel: 260-726-7890. FAX: 260-726-7317. Web Site: www.jaycpl.lib.in.us. *Dir,* Eric Hinderliter; E-mail: ehinderliter@jaycpl.lib.in.us; Staff 22 (MLS 2, Non-MLS 20)
Founded 1898. Pop 17,998; Circ 372,000
Library Holdings: CDs 1,572; DVDs 709; Large Print Bks 4,548; Bk Vols 80,949; Per Subs 210; Talking Bks 3,171; Videos 10,000
Wireless access
Function: Adult bk club, After school storytime, Art exhibits, AV serv, Bks on cassette, Bks on CD, Children's prog, Computers for patron use, Copy machines, Fax serv, Free DVD rentals, Handicapped accessible, Holiday prog, Home delivery & serv to Sr ctr & nursing homes, ILL available, Music CDs, Online cat, Online searches, Outreach serv, Preschool outreach, Prog for adults, Prog for children & young adult, Pub access computers, Ref serv in person, Scanner, Spoken cassettes & CDs, Spoken cassettes & DVDs, Story hour, Summer reading prog, Tax forms, VHS videos, Wheelchair accessible
Publications: Library Newsnotes (Newsletter)
Partic in Evergreen Indiana Consortium
Open Mon-Fri 8-8, Sat 8-5
Friends of the Library Group
Bookmobiles: 1

POSEYVILLE

P POSEYVILLE CARNEGIE PUBLIC LIBRARY*, 55 S Cale St, 47633. (Mail add: PO Box 220, 47633-0220), SAN 305-0882. Tel: 812-874-3418. FAX: 812-874-2026. E-mail: circulation@pcpl.lib.in.us. Web Site: www.pcpl.lib.in.us. *Dir,* Heather McNabb; Staff 1 (MLS 1)
Founded 1905. Pop 4,727; Circ 33,044
Library Holdings: Audiobooks 320; CDs 524; DVDs 695; Bk Titles 12,391; Per Subs 58
Automation Activity & Vendor Info: (Acquisitions) Evergreen; (Cataloging) Evergreen; (Circulation) Evergreen; (ILL) Evergreen; (OPAC) Evergreen; (Serials) Evergreen
Database Vendor: Inspire, WebClarity Software Inc
Wireless access
Function: Adult bk club, After school storytime, Archival coll, Art exhibits, Audiobks via web, Bk club(s), Bks on CD, Chess club, Children's prog, Computers for patron use, Copy machines, Electronic databases & coll, Family literacy, Fax serv, Free DVD rentals, Handicapped accessible, Holiday prog, ILL available, Magnifiers for reading, Music CDs, Newsp ref libr, Online cat, Outreach serv, OverDrive digital audio bks, Photocopying/Printing, Preschool outreach, Prog for adults, Prog for children & young adult, Pub access computers, Ref serv available, Ref serv in person, Scanner, Serves mentally handicapped consumers, Spoken cassettes & CDs, Spoken cassettes & DVDs, Story hour, Summer & winter

reading prog, Tax forms, Teen prog, Telephone ref, Wheelchair accessible, Workshops, Writing prog
Partic in Evergreen Indiana Consortium
Open Mon, Fri & Sat 9-4, Tues & Thurs 9-8, Wed 1-8

PRINCETON

P PRINCETON PUBLIC LIBRARY*, 124 S Hart St, 47670. SAN 305-0890. Tel: 812-385-4464. FAX: 812-386-1662. E-mail: director@princetonpl.lib.in.us. Web Site: www.princetonpl.lib.in.us. *Dir,* Brenda Williams; Staff 4 (MLS 1, Non-MLS 3)
Founded 1883. Pop 12,290; Circ 88,063
Library Holdings: Audiobooks 2,041; DVDs 2,976; Microforms 371; Bk Titles 50,564; Per Subs 66; Videos 875
Special Collections: History of Gibson County, North Gibson area
Subject Interests: Genealogy, Local hist
Automation Activity & Vendor Info: (Cataloging) Evergreen; (Circulation) Evergreen; (OPAC) Evergreen
Wireless access
Open Mon-Fri 9-8, Sat 9-5, Sun 1-5
Friends of the Library Group

REMINGTON

P REMINGTON-CARPENTER TOWNSHIP PUBLIC LIBRARY*, 105 N Ohio St, 47977. (Mail add: PO Box 65, 47977-0065), SAN 305-0904. Tel: 219-261-2543. FAX: 219-261-3800. E-mail: director@rctpl.com. Web Site: www.rctpl.com. *Dir,* Sue Waibel; *Asst Librn,* Agnes J Dombrowski; Staff 1 (Non-MLS 1)
Founded 1913. Pop 2,096; Circ 13,963
Jan 2008-Dec 2008 Income $153,000. Mats Exp $14,322
Library Holdings: AV Mats 2,162; Bk Titles 31,459; Per Subs 34
Special Collections: Geneology
Automation Activity & Vendor Info: (Cataloging) Follett Software; (Circulation) Follett Software
Function: Children's prog, Computer training, Computers for patron use, Copy machines, ILL available, Music CDs, Online cat, Online searches, Preschool outreach, Prog for adults, Prog for children & young adult, Senior computer classes, Summer reading prog, Tax forms, VHS videos
Partic in Northwest Ind Area Libr Servs Authority
Open Mon & Wed 10-7, Tues & Fri 10-5, Sat 9-12
Friends of the Library Group

RENSSELAER

P JASPER COUNTY PUBLIC LIBRARY*, Rensselaer Public, 208 W Susan St, 47978. SAN 341-5805. Tel: 219-866-5881. FAX: 219-866-7378. Web Site: www.myjcpl.org. *Dir,* Patty Stringfellow; E-mail: pstringfellow@myjcpl.org; *Managing Librn,* Linda Poortenga; *Tech Serv Librn,* Rebecca Amalong; E-mail: ramalong@myjcpl.org; *Syst Adminr,* Sheila Maxwell; E-mail: sheila@jasperco.lib.in.us; *Webmaster,* Melissa Widner; E-mail: mwidner@myjcpl.org; Staff 19 (MLS 4, Non-MLS 15)
Founded 1904. Pop 31,525; Circ 301,174
Library Holdings: AV Mats 24,457; Electronic Media & Resources 3,409; Bk Vols 150,732; Per Subs 577
Special Collections: Mementos of Civil War (Major General Robert H Milroy Coll)
Subject Interests: Humanities, Natural sci
Automation Activity & Vendor Info: (Acquisitions) TLC (The Library Corporation); (Cataloging) TLC (The Library Corporation); (Circulation) TLC (The Library Corporation); (OPAC) TLC (The Library Corporation); (Serials) TLC (The Library Corporation)
Database Vendor: Baker & Taylor, EBSCOhost, Gale Cengage Learning
Publications: Community Connections (Newsletter)
Partic in Midwest Collaborative for Library Services (MCLS)
Open Mon-Thurs 9-8, Fri & Sat 9-5
Friends of the Library Group
Branches: 2
DEMOTTE BRANCH, 901 Birch St SW, DeMotte, 46310. (Mail add: PO Box 16, DeMotte, 46310-0016), SAN 341-583X. Tel: 219-987-2221. FAX: 219-987-2220. *Br Mgr,* Brenda Thompson; Staff 9 (Non-MLS 9)
Open Mon, Tues & Thurs 9-8, Wed 9-6, Fri & Sat 9-5
Friends of the Library Group
WHEATFIELD BRANCH, 350 S Bierma St, Wheatfield, 46392, SAN 341-5864. Tel: 219-956-3774. FAX: 219-956-4808. *Librn,* Diana Kooy; E-mail: dkooy@jasperco.lib.in.us; Staff 5 (Non-MLS 5)
Open Mon, Wed & Thurs 9:30-5:30, Tues 9:30-8, Fri & Sat 9-5
Friends of the Library Group

C SAINT JOSEPH'S COLLEGE*, Keith & Kate Robinson Memorial Library, Hwy 231 S, 47978. (Mail add: PO Box 990, 47978-0990), SAN 305-0912. Tel: 219-866-6209. Interlibrary Loan Service Tel: 219-866-6213. Administration Tel: 219-866-6187. FAX: 219-866-6135. Web Site: www.saintjoe.edu/library. *Dir,* Catherine Salyers; Tel: 219-866-6212, E-mail: cathys@saintjoe.edu; *Archives Mgr, Circ,* Pamela Brown-Seeley; E-mail: pseely@saintjoe.edu; *Per, Tech Serv Librn,* Nancy Leibee; Tel: 219-866-6390, E-mail: nancyel@saintjoe.edu; *Asst Librn, Ref,* Jody Taylor-Watkins; Tel: 219-866-6210, E-mail: jodyt@saintjoe.edu; *Coordr, Doc,* Cheryl Witty; E-mail: cwitty@saintjoe.edu; *Acq, ILL,* Carla Luzadder; E-mail: carlal@saintjoe.edu; *Multimedia,* Sandra Greene; Tel: 219-866-6190, E-mail: srgreene@saintjoe.edu; Staff 10 (MLS 3, Non-MLS 7)
Founded 1892. Enrl 938; Fac 63; Highest Degree: Master
Library Holdings: AV Mats 23,000; Bk Vols 132,000; Per Subs 425
Special Collections: US Document Depository
Subject Interests: Latin Am, Music, Relig, Women's studies
Partic in BRS; OCLC Online Computer Library Center, Inc
Open Mon-Thurs (Winter) 7:30am-11pm, Fri 7:30-5, Sat 12-5, Sun 1-11; Mon-Fri (Summer) 8-4:30

RICHMOND

C EARLHAM COLLEGE, Lilly Library, 801 National Rd W, 47374-4095. SAN 341-5899. Tel: 765-983-1360. Circulation Tel: 765-983-1287. Interlibrary Loan Service Tel: 765-983-1307. Information Services Tel: 765-973-2106. FAX: 765-983-1304. Web Site: library.earlham.edu. *Libr Dir,* Neal Baker; Tel: 765-983-1355, E-mail: bakerne@earlham.edu; *Assoc Libr Dir, Head, Ref,* Amy Bryant; Tel: 765-983-1302, E-mail: bryanam@earlham.edu; *Curator, Friends Coll, Dir, Spec Coll, Prof of Hist,* Dr Thomas D Hamm; Tel: 765-983-1511, E-mail: tomh@earlham.edu; *Head, Wildman Sci Libr, Sci Tech Learning Spec,* Jose Ignacio Pareja; Tel: 765-983-1612, E-mail: parejjo@earlham.edu; *Acad Outreach Librn,* Kate Blinn; Tel: 765-983-1408, E-mail: blinnka@earlham.edu; *Acad Outreach/Sem Librn,* Jane Pinzino; Tel: 765-983-1290, E-mail: pinzija@earlham.edu; *Tech Serv Librn,* Mary A Bogue; Tel: 765-983-1363, E-mail: boguema@earlham.edu; *Asst Archivist,* Jenny Freed; Tel: 765-983-1743, E-mail: freedje@earlham.edu. Subject Specialists: *Film studies, Japanese studies, Lang,* Neal Baker; *Mus studies, Visual arts, Women's studies,* Amy Bryant; *Global studies, Peace, Soc sci,* Kate Blinn; *Humanities, Jewish studies, Relig,* Jane Pinzino; Staff 13 (MLS 8, Non-MLS 5)
Founded 1847. Enrl 992; Fac 109; Highest Degree: Master
Jul 2013-Jun 2014. Mats Exp $438,103, Books $58,299, Per/Ser (Incl. Access Fees) $26,279, AV Mat $7,578, Electronic Ref Mat (Incl. Access Fees) $339,635, Presv $6,312. Sal $625,903 (Prof $385,844)
Library Holdings: AV Mats 30,268; CDs 3,437; DVDs 6,510; Microforms 159,946; Bk Vols 381,766; Per Subs 33,200
Special Collections: East Asian Materials, bks, micro, ms; Society of Friends, bks, micro, ms
Automation Activity & Vendor Info: (Acquisitions) OCLC, (Cataloging) OCLC; (Circulation) OCLC; (Course Reserve) OCLC; (ILL) OCLC ILLiad; (Media Booking) OCLC; (OPAC) OCLC; (Serials) OCLC
Database Vendor: ABC-CLIO, ACM (Association for Computing Machinery), Alexander Street Press, American Chemical Society, American Mathematical Society, American Psychological Association (APA), Annual Reviews, Backstage Library Works, BioOne, Blackwell, CQ Press, CredoReference, ebrary, EBSCOhost, Elsevier, Emerald, Foundation Center, Gale Cengage Learning, Greenwood Publishing Group, IEEE (Institute of Electrical & Electronics Engineers), Ingenta, Ingram Library Services, Inspire, ISI Web of Knowledge, JSTOR, LexisNexis, Medline, Modern Language Association, Nature Publishing Group, Newsbank, Newsbank-Readex, OCLC, OCLC FirstSearch, OCLC WorldShare Interlibrary Loan, OCLC Worldshare Management Services, Oxford Online, Paratext, Project MUSE, ProQuest, PubMed, RefWorks, ScienceDirect, Springshare, LLC, Standard & Poor's, Thomson - Web of Science, WebMD, Wiley, YBP Library Services
Wireless access
Partic in Academic Libraries of Indiana; OCLC Online Computer Library Center, Inc; Private Academic Library Network of Indiana (PALNI)
Open Mon-Thurs 8am-Midnight, Fri 8am-10pm, Sat 10-10, Sun Noon-Midnight

S THE S W HAYES RESEARCH FOUNDATION*, Hayes Arboretum Library, 801 Elks Rd, 47374. SAN 326-0925. Tel: 765-962-3745. FAX: 765-966-1931. Web Site: www.hayesarboretum.org. *Dir,* Rodney Waltz; E-mail: rjwaltz@aol.com; Staff 2 (MLS 1, Non-MLS 1)
Library Holdings: Bk Titles 750; Bk Vols 890; Per Subs 12
Subject Interests: Flowers, Trees
Open Mon-Sat 9-5

C INDIANA UNIVERSITY EAST CAMPUS LIBRARY*, Library Services, 2325 Chester Blvd, 47374. SAN 320-9113. Tel: 765-973-8311. Interlibrary Loan Service Tel: 765-973-8309. Reference Tel: 765-973-8279. Web Site: www.iue.edu/library. *Assoc Librn, Electronic Res,* Sue A McFadden; Tel: 765-973-8325, E-mail: smcfadde@indiana.edu; *Assoc Librn, Info Tech Serv,* Lora K Baldwin; Tel: 765-973-8326, E-mail: mcclell@indiana.edu; *Coordr, Instrul Serv,* Lajmar Anderson; Tel: 765-973-8434, E-mail: ldanders@iue.edu; *Ref Serv Coordr,* Matthew Dilworth; Tel: 765-973-8279, E-mail: mdilwort@indiana.edu; *Archivist, Coordr, User Serv,* Elizabeth Brockman; Tel: 765-973-8204, E-mail: eabrockm@iue.edu; *ILL,* Marcia

Sloan; E-mail: masloan@indiana.edu. Subject Specialists: *English, Fine arts,* Lajmar Anderson; Staff 6 (MLS 3, Non-MLS 3)
Founded 1975
Library Holdings: AV Mats 1,080; Bk Titles 68,911; Bk Vols 71,022; Per Subs 488; Videos 319
Automation Activity & Vendor Info: (OPAC) SIRSI Unicorn
Database Vendor: Alexander Street Press, American Chemical Society, BioOne, CredoReference, ebrary, EBSCOhost, Facts on File, Gale Cengage Learning, Greenwood Publishing Group, JSTOR, LexisNexis, OCLC WorldShare Interlibrary Loan, OVID Technologies, ProQuest, RefWorks, Thomson - Web of Science, Wiley InterScience, Wilson - Wilson Web, YBP Library Services
Wireless access
Partic in OCLC Online Computer Library Center, Inc
Open Mon-Thurs 8-7, Fri 8-5
Friends of the Library Group

S RICHMOND ART MUSEUM LIBRARY*, 350 Hub Etchison Pkwy, 47374-0816. SAN 305-0920. Tel: 765-966-0256. FAX: 765-973-3738. Web Site: www.richmondartmuseum.org. *Curator,* Glenn Markoe; Staff 3 (MLS 3)
Founded 1898
Library Holdings: Bk Vols 800
Subject Interests: Art
Open Tues-Fri 10-4, Sun 1-4

M RICHMOND STATE HOSPITAL*, Professional Library, 498 NW 18th St, 47374. SAN 305-0939. Tel: 765-966-0511. Reference Tel: 765-966-0511, Ext 4307. FAX: 765-966-6993. Web Site: www.richmondstatehospital.org. *Dir, Libr & Info Serv, Info Spec,* Ron Richmond
Founded 1968
Library Holdings: Bk Titles 500; Per Subs 15
Partic in Ind Libr Film Serv; Ind State Libr Asn; Midwest Collaborative for Library Services (MCLS); Midwest Health Sci Libr Network
Restriction: Staff use only

S WAYNE COUNTY, INDIANA, HISTORICAL MUSEUM LIBRARY*, 1150 North A St, 47374. SAN 305-0947. Tel: 765-962-5756. FAX: 765-939-0909. Web Site: www.waynecountyhistoricalmuseum.com. *Dir,* Jim Harlan; E-mail: harlanjd@aol.com; Staff 3 (MLS 1, Non-MLS 2)
Founded 1929
Library Holdings: Bk Titles 1,000; Bk Vols 1,200
Special Collections: Cartoons (Gaar Williams Coll); Early Agricultural Tools & Implements Coll; Early Transportation Coll (autos & carriages); Motion Pictures & Early Television (C Francis Jenkins Coll), doc; Textile Coll
Subject Interests: Genealogy, Local authors, Local hist, State hist
Publications: Newsletter (Quarterly)
Open Mon-Fri 9-4, Sat & Sun 1-4

P WAYNE TOWNSHIP LIBRARY*, Morrisson-Reeves Library, 80 N Sixth St, 47374-3079. SAN 341-5988. Tel: 765-966-8291. FAX: 765-962-1318. E-mail: library@mrlinfo.org. Web Site: www.mrlinfo.org. *Dir,* Paris Pegg; *Adult Serv Mgr,* Sue King; *AV Mgr,* Alex Sarkissian; *Bus Mgr,* Barbara Judy; *Ch Mgr,* Lou Spicer; *Human Res Mgr,* Laura Kehlenbrink; *IT Support, Tech Serv Mgr,* Sarah Morey; *Pub Relations/Mkt/Web Site,* Jenie Lahmann; Staff 27.5 (MLS 8, Non-MLS 19.5)
Founded 1864. Pop 51,398; Circ 456,119
Jan 2013-Dec 2013 Income (Main Library and Branch(s)) $1,803,136. Mats Exp $150,000, Books $112,000, Per/Ser (Incl. Access Fees) $12,000, AV Mat $26,000. Sal $820,135 (Prof $82,615)
Library Holdings: AV Mats 11,546; Bk Titles 157,687; Bk Vols 263,000; Per Subs 313
Special Collections: Cookbooks; Large Print; Local Newspapers (1831 to date), indexed, microfilm; Popular & Semi-Popular Music (Singin' Sam), sheet music. US Document Depository
Automation Activity & Vendor Info: (Acquisitions) SirsiDynix; (Cataloging) SirsiDynix; (Circulation) SirsiDynix; (ILL) SirsiDynix; (Media Booking) SirsiDynix; (OPAC) SirsiDynix; (Serials) SirsiDynix
Database Vendor: SirsiDynix
Wireless access
Function: Accelerated reader prog, Accessibility serv available based on individual needs, Adult literacy prog, After school storytime, Archival coll, Audio & video playback equip for onsite use, Audiobks via web, AV serv, BA reader (adult literacy), Bks on CD, Bus archives, CD-ROM, Children's prog, Computer training, Computers for patron use, Copy machines, Digital talking bks, e-mail serv, Electronic databases & coll, Exhibits, Free DVD rentals, Govt ref serv, Handicapped accessible, Holiday prog, ILL available, Magnifiers for reading, Mail & tel request accepted, Microfiche/film & reading machines, Music CDs, Newsp ref libr, Online cat, Online ref, Online searches, Outside serv via phone, mail, e-mail & web, OverDrive digital audio bks, Photocopying/Printing, Preschool outreach, Preschool reading prog, Prog for adults, Prog for children & young adult, Pub access computers, Ref & res, Ref serv available, Ref serv in person, Scanner, Spanish lang bks, Spoken cassettes & DVDs, Story hour, Summer reading prog, Tax forms, Teen prog, Telephone ref, Web-catalog, Wheelchair accessible, Workshops, Writing prog
Partic in Midwest Collaborative for Library Services (MCLS)
Open Mon-Thurs 9-7:30, Fri & Sat 9-5
Friends of the Library Group
Branches: 1
WAYNE COUNTY CONTRACTUAL LIBRARY, 80 N Sixth St, 47374, SAN 341-6070. Tel: 765-966-8291. FAX: 765-962-1318. *Dir,* Paris Pegg

RIDGEVILLE

P RIDGEVILLE PUBLIC LIBRARY*, 308 N Walnut St, 47380. (Mail add: PO Box 63, 47380-0063), SAN 305-0955. Tel: 765-857-2025. FAX: 765-857-2025. E-mail: rplibrary@jayco.net. *Dir,* Marcella McCormick; Staff 2 (MLS 1, Non-MLS 1)
Founded 1912. Pop 1,539; Circ 5,000
Jan 2008-Dec 2008 Income $18,011. Mats Exp $4,450, Books $3,355, Per/Ser (Incl. Access Fees) $630, Micro $65, AV Equip $400. Sal $8,536 (Prof $6,734)
Library Holdings: AV Mats 30; Bk Vols 15,998; Per Subs 50
Partic in Midwest Collaborative for Library Services (MCLS)
Open Tues 12:30-8, Wed 1-5, Thurs 12:30-7
Friends of the Library Group

RISING SUN

P OHIO COUNTY PUBLIC LIBRARY*, 100 N High St, 47040-1022. SAN 305-0963. Tel: 812-438-2257. FAX: 812-438-2257. Web Site: ocpl.lib.in.us/. *Dir,* Cynthia Schmid-Perry; Staff 4 (MLS 1, Non-MLS 3)
Founded 1916. Pop 5,623; Circ 33,119
Library Holdings: AV Mats 1,281; Large Print Bks 88; Bk Titles 26,780; Bk Vols 28,818; Per Subs 51; Talking Bks 410; Videos 759
Special Collections: Local News & History (Ohio County Newspapers, 1834-1970), microfilm (1970-present), loose files
Automation Activity & Vendor Info: (Cataloging) Follett Software; (Circulation) Follett Software
Open Mon, Wed & Fri 9-5, Tues & Thurs 9-7:30, Sat 9-1

ROACHDALE

P ROACHDALE-FRANKLIN TOWNSHIP PUBLIC LIBRARY, 100 E Washington, 46172. (Mail add: PO Box 399, 46172-0399), SAN 305-0971. Tel: 765-522-1491. FAX: 765-522-4149. E-mail: roachdalepl@tds.net. *Interim Dir,* Jennifer Stranger; *Librn,* Debbie Keffer; Staff 3 (MLS 1, Non-MLS 2)
Founded 1913. Pop 2,117; Circ 14,400
Library Holdings: Bk Titles 19,840; Bk Vols 21,680; Per Subs 30; Talking Bks 350; Videos 666
Partic in Midwest Collaborative for Library Services (MCLS)
Open Mon & Fri 12-5, Tues & Wed 10-5, Thurs 12-8, Sat 9-1

ROANN

P ROANN PAW PAW TOWNSHIP PUBLIC LIBRARY*, 240 S Chippewa Rd, 46974. (Mail add: PO Box 248, 46974-0248), SAN 305-098X. Tel: 765-833-5231. FAX: 765-833-5231. E-mail: roannlibrary@yahoo.com. Web Site: www.geocities.com/roannlibrary. *Dir,* Joy Harber; *Asst Librn,* Eleanore Draper; *Asst Librn,* Krys Eckelbarger; Staff 3 (Non-MLS 3)
Founded 1914. Pop 1,616; Circ 7,983
Jan 2008-Dec 2008 Income $65,321. Mats Exp $6,000, Books $2,000, Per/Ser (Incl. Access Fees) $2,000, AV Equip $1,300, AV Mat $400, Electronic Ref Mat (Incl. Access Fees) $300. Sal $30,000 (Prof $22,000)
Library Holdings: AV Mats 450; CDs 310; Large Print Bks 45; Bk Vols 17,151; Per Subs 25; Videos 1,600
Subject Interests: Local genealogy
Special Services for the Blind - Bks on cassette; Talking bks
Open Mon-Wed 1-6, Thurs & Fri 9-12 & 1-6, Sat 9-12
Friends of the Library Group

ROANOKE

P ROANOKE PUBLIC LIBRARY*, 314 N Main St, Ste 120, 46783-1073. (Mail add: PO Box 249, 46783-0249), SAN 305-0998. Tel: 260-672-2989. FAX: 260-676-2239. E-mail: director@roanoke.lib.in.us. Web Site: www.roanoke.lib.in.us. *Dir,* Celia Bandelier; Staff 1.5 (MLS 1, Non-MLS 0.5)
Founded 1910. Pop 1,720; Circ 10,111
Library Holdings: Bk Titles 14,760; Bk Vols 16,340; Per Subs 27; Talking Bks 190; Videos 633
Special Collections: Roanoke Review, 1919 to 1981, CD-ROM
Automation Activity & Vendor Info: (Cataloging) Evergreen; (Circulation) Evergreen; (ILL) Evergreen; (OPAC) Evergreen; (Serials) Evergreen
Database Vendor: Inspire, OCLC WebJunction, Overdrive, Inc
Wireless access

Function: Bks on CD, Children's prog, Computer training, Computers for patron use, Copy machines, Family literacy, Fax serv, Free DVD rentals, Govt ref serv, Handicapped accessible, ILL available, Mail & tel request accepted, Music CDs, Notary serv, Online cat, Online searches, Outside serv via phone, mail, e-mail & web, OverDrive digital audio bks, Photocopying/Printing, Preschool reading prog, Prog for adults, Prog for children & young adult, Pub access computers, Ref & res, Ref serv available, Scanner, Senior computer classes, Spanish lang bks, Story hour, Summer reading prog, Tax forms, Teen prog, Telephone ref, VHS videos, Web-catalog, Workshops
Open Mon-Thurs 9-7, Sat 9-1
Friends of the Library Group

ROCHESTER

S FULTON COUNTY HISTORICAL SOCIETY, INC*, Museum & Library, 37 E 375 N, 46975-8384. SAN 371-9103. Tel: 574-223-4436. FAX: 574-224-4436. E-mail: fchs@rtcol.com. Web Site: www.fultoncountyhistory.org. *Pres,* Fred A Oden; *Dir,* Melinda Clinger; Staff 3 (Non-MLS 3)
Founded 1963
Library Holdings: Bk Titles 15,000; Per Subs 100
Special Collections: Fulton County, Indiana Coll; Potawatomi Indians Trail of Death Coll; Round Barns Coll. Oral History
Publications: Fulton County Folk Finder; Fulton County Historical Power Association (Newsletter); Fulton County Images; Potawatomi Trail of Death Association (Newsletter)
Open Mon-Sat 9-5
Restriction: In-house use for visitors, Not a lending libr

P FULTON COUNTY PUBLIC LIBRARY*, Rochester Library, 320 W Seventh St, 46975-1332. SAN 341-6100. Tel: 574-223-2713. Circulation Tel: 574-223-1006. Interlibrary Loan Service Tel: 574-223-1004. Reference Tel: 574-223-1003. FAX: 574-223-5102. E-mail: rochester@fulco.lib.in.us. Web Site: www.fulco.lib.in.us. *Dir,* Rebecca J Williams; E-mail: director@fulco.lib.in.us; *Head, Circ,* Rose Krull; E-mail: circ@fulco.lib.in.us; *Head, Ref,* Position Currently Open; *Syst Coordr,* April Gross; E-mail: sysadmin@fulco.lib.in.us; *AV,* Tami Holloway; E-mail: av@fulco.lib.in.us; *Ch Serv,* Becky Williams; E-mail: kids@fulco.lib.in.us; *ILL,* Tami Holloway; E-mail: ill@fulco.lib.in.us; Staff 34 (MLS 1, Non-MLS 33)
Founded 1906. Pop 16,227; Circ 372,403
Jan 2011-Dec 2011 Income (Main Library and Branch(s)) $1,432,610. Mats Exp $192,500, Books $105,000, Per/Ser (Incl. Access Fees) $12,500, AV Mat $75,000. Sal $856,975 (Prof $50,000)
Library Holdings: CDs 9,062; DVDs 20,335; Bk Vols 135,286; Per Subs 187
Special Collections: Indiana Local & State History Coll
Subject Interests: Agr, Bus & mgt, Hist, Indiana
Automation Activity & Vendor Info: (Acquisitions) Evergreen; (Cataloging) Evergreen; (Circulation) Evergreen; (OPAC) Evergreen
Database Vendor: Inspire
Wireless access
Function: Adult literacy prog
Publications: American Libraries (Monthly); Booklist; Focus; Library Administration Digest; Mosaic
Partic in Midwest Collaborative for Library Services (MCLS)
Open Mon-Thurs 10-8, Fri 10-6, Sat 9-5
Friends of the Library Group
Branches: 2
AUBBEE, 7432 Olson Rd, Leiters Ford, 46945. (Mail add: PO Box 566, Leiters Ford, 46945-0566), SAN 341-6135. Tel: 574-542-4859. FAX: 574-542-4859. E-mail: aubbee@fulco.lib.in.us. *Br Librn,* Carol Chileen; Staff 2 (MLS 1, Non-MLS 1)
Library Holdings: AV Mats 981; Large Print Bks 190; Bk Titles 21,110; Bk Vols 22,690; Per Subs 41; Videos 210
Open Mon 10-7, Tues-Fri 10-6, Sat 9-3
Friends of the Library Group
FULTON BRANCH, 514 State Rd 25, Fulton, 46931. (Mail add: PO Box 307, Fulton, 46931-0307), SAN 341-616X. Tel: 574-857-3895. FAX: 574-857-2215. E-mail: fulton@fulco.lib.in.us. *Br Librn,* Selena Rouch; Staff 2 (MLS 1, Non-MLS 1)
Library Holdings: AV Mats 871; Large Print Bks 88; Bk Titles 22,112; Bk Vols 23,490; Per Subs 46; Videos 226
Open Mon & Thurs 9-6, Tues, Wed & Fri 9-5, Sat 9-12
Friends of the Library Group

ROCKPORT

P SPENCER COUNTY PUBLIC LIBRARY*, 210 Walnut St, 47635-1398. SAN 305-1005. Tel: 812-649-4866. FAX: 812-649-4018. E-mail: reference@rockport-spco.lib.in.us. Web Site: www.rockport-spco.lib.in.us. *Dir,* Beverly Jo Symon; E-mail: symonb@rockport-spco.lib.in.us; *Ch,* Carol Evrard; E-mail: evrardc@rockport-spco.lib.in.us; Staff 2 (MLS 1, Non-MLS 1)
Founded 1917. Pop 9,393; Circ 177,736
Jan 2009-Dec 2009 Income (Main Library and Branch(s)) $992,896, State $61,371, County $909,579, Locally Generated Income $21,946. Mats Exp $61,125, Books $50,179, Per/Ser (Incl. Access Fees) $6,622, Micro $432, AV Mat $3,892. Sal $566,061
Library Holdings: Bks on Deafness & Sign Lang 84; High Interest/Low Vocabulary Bk Vols 140; Large Print Bks 1,798; Bk Titles 106,025; Per Subs 153; Talking Bks 2,282; Videos 5,101
Special Collections: Lincoln Coll, bks, pamphlets, pictures, vf
Subject Interests: Genealogy, Hist, Local hist, Relig
Automation Activity & Vendor Info: (Cataloging) Evergreen; (Circulation) Evergreen
Database Vendor: Inspire
Wireless access
Open Mon & Fri 8-5, Tues-Thurs 8am-9pm, Sat 9-3
Branches: 3
GRANDVIEW BRANCH, 403 Main St, Grandview, 47615-0717. Tel: 812-649-9732. E-mail: grandview@rockport-spco.lib.in.us. *Br Mgr,* Jennie Weatherholt
Open Mon 8am-9pm, Tues-Fri 8-5, Sat 9-3
PARKER BRANCH, 925 N County Rd 900W, Hatfield, 47617. Tel: 812-359-4030. FAX: 812-359-4048. E-mail: hatfield@rockport-spco.lib.in.us. *Br Mgr,* Pat Lashley
Library Holdings: Bk Vols 5,000
Open Mon-Fri 9-5, Sat 9-12
MARYLEE VOGEL BRANCH, 6014 W Division St, Richland, 47634. Tel: 812-359-4146. FAX: 812-359-4223. E-mail: richland@rockport-spco.lib.in.us. *Br Mgr,* Charlynn Bruggenschmidt
Library Holdings: Bk Vols 17,000
Open Mon-Fri 9-5, Sat 9-Noon

ROCKVILLE

S ROCKVILLE CORRECTIONAL FACILITY LIBRARY*, 811 W 50 N, 47872. Tel: 765-569-3178. FAX: 765-569-0149. *Librn,* April Bonomo
Library Holdings: Bk Vols 9,000
Database Vendor: LexisNexis
Open Mon-Fri 8-4

P ROCKVILLE PUBLIC LIBRARY*, 106 N Market St, 47872. SAN 305-1013. Tel: 765-569-5544. FAX: 765-569-5546. E-mail: rockvillelib@gmail.com. Web Site: rockvillepl.lib.in.us. *Dir,* Cindy Hein; *Asst Librn,* Lynn Lee; Staff 3 (Non-MLS 3)
Founded 1915. Pop 5,399; Circ 28,000
Jan 2005-Dec 2005 Income $350,267. Mats Exp $57,931. Sal $126,800
Library Holdings: Bk Vols 26,000; Per Subs 81; Talking Bks 76; Videos 572
Special Collections: Census Records, including Illinois, Ohio & New York 1820-1900; County Newspapers 1871-1974, microfilm; Genealogy Coll; Indiana Coll
Automation Activity & Vendor Info: (Acquisitions) Follett Software; (Cataloging) Follett Software; (OPAC) Follett Software
Wireless access
Open Mon-Fri 9-6, Sat 9-2

ROYAL CENTER

P ROYAL CENTER-BOONE TOWNSHIP PUBLIC LIBRARY*, 203 N Chicago, 46978. (Mail add: PO Box 459, 46978-0459), SAN 305-1021. Tel: 574-643-3185. FAX: 574-643-5003. E-mail: royalcenterlib@frontier.com. *Dir,* Phyllis J Gray; Staff 3 (MLS 1, Non-MLS 2)
Founded 1915. Pop 1,581; Circ 16,439
Library Holdings: Audiobooks 341; DVDs 700; Bk Titles 32,680; Bk Vols 35,160; Per Subs 20
Subject Interests: Ethnic studies, Relig, Soc sci & issues
Wireless access
Partic in Wabash Valley Area Libr Servs Authority
Open Mon, Wed & Fri 12:30-5, Thurs 12:30-6, Sat 8:30-3

RUSHVILLE

P RUSHVILLE PUBLIC LIBRARY*, 130 W Third St, 46173-1899. SAN 305-103X. Tel: 765-932-3496. FAX: 765-932-4528. E-mail: rpl@rpl.lib.in.us. Web Site: www.rushvillelibrary.com. *Dir,* Sue Prifogle Otte; E-mail: sueotte@rpl.lib.in.us; *Adult/YA Serv Librn,* Jan Marlene Garrison; E-mail: janmg@rpl.lib.in.us; *Ch Serv Librn,* Pamela Jean Vogel; E-mail: pamvogel@rpl.lib.in.us; *Tech Serv/Ref Librn,* Mary Patricia Coons; E-mail: mpcoons@rpl.lib.in.us; *Bus Mgr,* Rhonda Kay Albrecht; E-mail: ralbrecht@rpl.lib.in.us; *Circ,* Virginia May Holdman; E-mail: ginny@rpl.lib.in.us; Staff 7 (MLS 1, Non-MLS 6)
Founded 1910. Pop 5,995; Circ 34,000
Jan 2011-Dec 2011 Income $293,800, City $267,300, Locally Generated Income $26,500. Mats Exp $22,940, Books $16,940, Per/Ser (Incl. Access Fees) $3,800, AV Mat $1,700, Electronic Ref Mat (Incl. Access Fees) $500. Sal $183,414 (Prof $46,177)

Library Holdings: AV Mats 2,260; Bk Titles 32,130; Per Subs 85
Special Collections: Indiana History Coll; Rush County History Coll; Wendell Wilkie File Coll
Automation Activity & Vendor Info: (Cataloging) Innovative Interfaces, Inc; (Circulation) Innovative Interfaces, Inc; (OPAC) Innovative Interfaces, Inc
Wireless access
Open Mon-Thurs 8:30-6:30, Fri 8:30-5, Sat 9-3

SAINT MARY-OF-THE-WOODS

C SAINT MARY-OF-THE-WOODS COLLEGE LIBRARY*, The Mary & Andrew Rooney Library, 3301 Saint Mary's Rd, 47876. SAN 305-1048. Tel: 812-535-5223. FAX: 812-535-5127. E-mail: library@smwc.edu. Web Site: library.smwc.edu. *Dir,* Judith Tribble; Tel: 812-535-5255, E-mail: jtribble@smwc.edu; Staff 2 (MLS 2)
Founded 1840. Enrl 1,687; Fac 57; Highest Degree: Master
Jul 2006-Jun 2007. Mats Exp $64,922, Books $25,800, Per/Ser (Incl. Access Fees) $39,122. Sal $107,409 (Prof $83,409)
Library Holdings: Bk Titles 90,668; Bk Vols 132,673; Per Subs 150
Special Collections: Catholic Americana; Fore-edge Painting Coll; Seventeenth & Eighteenth Century French Religious Books
Partic in Academic Libraries of Indiana; Midwest Collaborative for Library Services (MCLS); OCLC Online Computer Library Center, Inc
Open Mon-Thurs 8am-10pm, Fri 8-4:30, Sat 10-4:30, Sun 6pm-10pm

SAINT MEINRAD

R SAINT MEINRAD ARCHABBEY & SCHOOL OF THEOLOGY*, Archabbey Library, 200 Hill Dr, 47577. SAN 305-1056. Tel: 812-357-6401. Interlibrary Loan Service Tel: 812-357-6717. Toll Free Tel: 800-987-7311. FAX: 812-357-6398. E-mail: library@saintmeinrad.edu. Web Site: www.saintmeinrad.edu. *Dir,* Dan Kolb; *Acq, ILL,* Mary Ellen Seifrig; *Cat,* Ruth Denning; *Per,* Fr Joseph Cox; Staff 5 (MLS 3, Non-MLS 2)
Founded 1854. Enrl 127; Fac 24; Highest Degree: Master
Jul 2006-Jun 2007. Mats Exp $86,970, Books $49,514, Per/Ser (Incl. Access Fees) $33,554, Presv $3,902
Library Holdings: Bk Titles 140,449; Bk Vols 174,531; Per Subs 333
Subject Interests: Humanities, Relig, Theol
Automation Activity & Vendor Info: (Acquisitions) Ex Libris Group; (Cataloging) OCLC; (Circulation) Ex Libris Group; (ILL) Ex Libris Group; (OPAC) Ex Libris Group; (Serials) Ex Libris Group
Database Vendor: EBSCOhost, Gale Cengage Learning, OCLC WorldShare Interlibrary Loan
Partic in Midwest Collaborative for Library Services (MCLS); Private Academic Library Network of Indiana (PALNI); Theological Education Association of Mid America
Open Mon-Thurs 8-12, 1-5 & 7-10, Fri 8-12 & 1-5, Sat 9-11, 1-5 & 7-10, Sun 1-5 & 7-10
Restriction: Borrowing privileges limited to fac & registered students, In-house use for visitors

SALEM

P SALEM PUBLIC LIBRARY*, 212 N Main St, 47167. SAN 305-1064. Tel: 812-883-5600. FAX: 812-883-1609. E-mail: salemindianalibrary@hotmail.com. Web Site: www.salemlib.lib.in.us. *Dir,* Jill DuChemin; Staff 3 (MLS 2, Non-MLS 1)
Founded 1903. Pop 9,129; Circ 36,000
Library Holdings: AV Mats 780; Bk Titles 36,080; Bk Vols 37,110; Per Subs 151; Videos 1,000
Subject Interests: Local hist
Automation Activity & Vendor Info: (Cataloging) Follett Software; (Circulation) Follett Software; (OPAC) Follett Software
Open Mon-Thurs 10-7, Fri & Sat 10-5, Sun 1-5
Friends of the Library Group

S WASHINGTON COUNTY HISTORICAL SOCIETY LIBRARY*, Stevens Museum - The John Hay Center, 307 E Market St, 47167. SAN 305-1072. Tel: 812-883-6495. Web Site: www.stevensmuseum.com. *Librn,* Kathy Wade; *Asst Librn,* Dawn Camp
Library Holdings: Bk Titles 5,000
Subject Interests: Genealogy
Open Tues-Sat 9-5

SCOTTSBURG

P SCOTT COUNTY PUBLIC LIBRARY*, 108 S Main St, 47170. SAN 305-1080. Tel: 812-752-2751. FAX: 812-752-2878. Web Site: www.scott.lib.in.us. *Dir,* Darlene Hall; E-mail: darlene@scott.lib.in.us; *Br Mgr,* Dona Lacey; E-mail: dona@scott.lib.in.us; *Asst Librn,* Joyce Hickman; E-mail: joyce@scott.lib.in.us; Staff 12 (MLS 2, Non-MLS 10)
Founded 1921. Pop 22,718; Circ 88,111
Jan 2008-Dec 2008 Income $500,000. Mats Exp $50,000, Books $30,000, Per/Ser (Incl. Access Fees) $7,500, Micro $10,000, Presv $800. Sal $350,000 (Prof $45,000)
Library Holdings: Braille Volumes 10; CDs 350; DVDs 350; Large Print Bks 150; Bk Titles 76,539; Bk Vols 79,110; Per Subs 209; Spec Interest Per Sub 20; Talking Bks 300; Videos 350
Special Collections: Carl R Bogardus Sr, MD Coll
Subject Interests: Genealogy, Local hist, State hist
Automation Activity & Vendor Info: (Cataloging) Innovative Interfaces, Inc; (Circulation) Innovative Interfaces, Inc; (OPAC) Innovative Interfaces, Inc
Wireless access
Function: After school storytime, Archival coll, Audio & video playback equip for onsite use, AV serv, Bi-weekly Writer's Group, Handicapped accessible, Homebound delivery serv, ILL available, Orientations, Photocopying/Printing, Prog for adults, Prog for children & young adult, Ref serv available, Spoken cassettes & CDs, Summer reading prog, VHS videos, Wheelchair accessible, Workshops
Partic in Midwest Collaborative for Library Services (MCLS)
Special Services for the Deaf - Staff with knowledge of sign lang
Special Services for the Blind - Audio mat; Bks & mags in Braille, on rec, tape & cassette; Bks available with recordings; Bks on cassette; Bks on CD; Talking bks
Open Mon & Thurs 9-8, Tues, Wed & Fri 9-6, Sat 9-5
Friends of the Library Group
Branches: 2
AUSTIN BRANCH, 26 Union Ave, Austin, 47102-1344. Tel: 812-794-2721. FAX: 812-794-4550. *Br Mgr,* Donna Lacey
Library Holdings: Bk Vols 15,000
Open Mon, Thurs & Fri 9-5, Tues 9-8, Wed & Sat 9-3
LEXINGTON BRANCH, 2781 Cherry St, Lexington, 47138-8620. Tel: 812-889-3831. FAX: 812-889-3846. *Br Mgr,* Kathy Napier
Library Holdings: Bk Titles 5,000
Open Mon-Thurs 9-6, Fri 1-6, Sat 9-1

SELLERSBURG

J IVY TECH COMMUNITY COLLEGE*, Ogle Virtual Library, 8204 Hwy 311, 47172-1897. SAN 320-6718. Tel: 812-246-3301, Ext 4225. FAX: 812-246-9905. Web Site: www.ivytech.edu/library/sellersburg. *Dir,* Marie White; *Commun Outreach Librn,* Gool Randelia; Staff 3 (MLS 1, Non-MLS 2)
Founded 1974. Highest Degree: Master
Library Holdings: AV Mats 838; Bk Titles 3,911; Bk Vols 4,180; Per Subs 162
Subject Interests: Med
Open Mon-Thurs 8:30am-9pm, Fri 8-5, Sat 9-1

SEYMOUR

P JACKSON COUNTY PUBLIC LIBRARY*, Seymour Library, 303 W Second St, 47274-2147. SAN 341-6194. Tel: 812-522-3412. Circulation Tel: 812-522-3412, Ext 243. Interlibrary Loan Service Tel: 812-522-3412, Ext 240. Administration Tel: 812-522-3412, Ext 253. FAX: 812-522-5456. E-mail: admin@myjclibrary.org. Web Site: www.myjclibrary.org. *Dir,* Julia Aker; Tel: 812-522-3412, Ext 223, E-mail: jaker@myjclibrary.org; *IT Dir,* Jason Boyer; Tel: 812-522-3412, Ext 227, E-mail: jasonb@myjclibrary.org; *Adminr,* Mary Reed; Tel: 812-522-3412, Ext 233, E-mail: mreed@myjclibrary.org; *Head, Info Serv,* Becky Brewer; Tel: 812-522-3412, Ext 239, E-mail: bbb@myjclibrary.org; *Head, Youth Serv,* Melessa Wiesehan; Tel: 812-522-3412, Ext 231, E-mail: melessa@myjclibrary.org; *Circ Mgr,* Christina Hime; Tel: 812-522-3412, Ext 238, E-mail: chime@myjclibrary.org; *Mgr, Outreach Serv,* Fay Gardner; Tel: 812-522-3412, Ext 234, E-mail: fgardner@myjclibrary.org; *Tech Serv Mgr,* Terri Wichman; Tel: 812-522-3412, Ext 226, E-mail: terriw@myjclibrary.org; *Info Serv,* Charlotte Sellers; Tel: 812-522-3412, Ext 224, E-mail: csellers@myjclibrary.org. Subject Specialists: *Family hist, Local hist,* Charlotte Sellers; Staff 3 (MLS 3)
Founded 1905. Pop 34,423; Circ 384,807
Jan 2010-Dec 2010 Income (Main Library and Branch(s)) $2,912,611, County $1,758,161, Other $1,154,450. Mats Exp $162,394, Books $105,402, Per/Ser (Incl. Access Fees) $9,309, AV Mat $47,683. Sal $916,451
Library Holdings: AV Mats 13,658; Bk Vols 73,208; Per Subs 193
Special Collections: Digital Archive Coll. Oral History
Subject Interests: Local hist
Automation Activity & Vendor Info: (Circulation) Evergreen; (ILL) OCLC; (OPAC) Evergreen
Database Vendor: Baker & Taylor
Wireless access
Function: Adult bk club, Archival coll, Art exhibits, Audio & video playback equip for onsite use, Bk club(s), CD-ROM, Distance learning, Handicapped accessible, Home delivery & serv to Sr ctr & nursing homes, Homebound delivery serv, ILL available, Magnifiers for reading, Online searches, Outside serv via phone, mail, e-mail & web,

Photocopying/Printing, Prog for adults, Prog for children & young adult, Ref serv available, Satellite serv, Spoken cassettes & CDs, Spoken cassettes & DVDs, Summer reading prog, Telephone ref, VHS videos, Wheelchair accessible
Publications: Browse (Bi-monthly)
Partic in Midwest Collaborative for Library Services (MCLS)
Special Services for the Deaf - Assistive tech; Bks on deafness & sign lang; Closed caption videos
Special Services for the Blind - BiFolkal kits; Bks on cassette; Bks on CD; Computer with voice synthesizer for visually impaired persons; Descriptive video serv (DVS); Large print bks; Magnifiers
Open Mon Thurs 8:30-8:30, Fri 8.30-6, Sat 9-5, Sun 1-5
Restriction: Non-circulating coll
Friends of the Library Group
Branches: 2
CROTHERSVILLE BRANCH, 120 E Main St, Crothersville, 47229, SAN 341-6224. Tel: 812-793-2927. FAX: 812-793-3721. *Br Mgr,* Georgiana Boss; E-mail: gboss@myjclibrary.org; Staff 4 (Non-MLS 4)
Pop 1,570
Automation Activity & Vendor Info: (Serials) Evergreen
Function: Accelerated reader prog, Adult bk club, Bk club(s), Bks on CD, CD-ROM, Children's prog, Computers for patron use, Copy machines, E-Reserves, Electronic databases & coll, Free DVD rentals, Handicapped accessible, Holiday prog, ILL available, Music CDs, Online cat, Photocopying/Printing, Preschool outreach, Prog for adults, Prog for children & young adult, Pub access computers, Senior outreach, Summer reading prog, Tax forms, VHS videos
Open Mon-Thurs 10-8, Fri & Sat 12-5
Friends of the Library Group
MEDORA BRANCH, 27 Main St, Medora, 47260. (Mail add: PO Box 400, Medora, 47260-0400), SAN 371-3458. Tel: 812-966-2278. FAX: 812-966-2229. *Br Mgr,* Georgiana Boss; E-mail: gboss@myjclibrary.org; Staff 2 (Non-MLS 2)
Founded 1992. Pop 915
Automation Activity & Vendor Info: (ILL) Evergreen
Function: Adult bk club, After school storytime, Bk club(s), Bks on CD, CD-ROM, Computers for patron use, Copy machines, Free DVD rentals, Handicapped accessible, Holiday prog, ILL available, Music CDs, Online cat, Photocopying/Printing, Prog for adults, Prog for children & young adult, Spoken cassettes & CDs, Spoken cassettes & DVDs, Summer reading prog, Tax forms, Telephone ref, VHS videos, Web-catalog, Wheelchair accessible
Open Mon-Fri 2-6, Sat 12-5
Friends of the Library Group
Bookmobiles: 1. Mgr, Fay Gardner

SHELBYVILLE

P SHELBY COUNTY PUBLIC LIBRARY*, 57 W Broadway, 46176. SAN 305-1099. Tel: 317-398-7121, 317-835-2653. FAX: 317-398-4430. Web Site: www.myshelbylibrary.org. *Dir,* Janet Wallace; E-mail: jwallace@sscpl.lib.in.us. *Youth Serv Dir,* Brandy Graves; *Head, Tech Serv,* Beverly Compton; *Hist Coll Librn,* Judy Cheatham; *Adult Serv,* Diane Anderson; *Ref,* Carol Antle; E-mail: cantle@sscpl.lib.in.us; Staff 36 (MLS 3, Non-MLS 33)
Founded 1898. Pop 44,310; Circ 132,610
Library Holdings: High Interest/Low Vocabulary Bk Vols 50; Bk Titles 91,840; Bk Vols 93,210; Per Subs 267; Talking Bks 1,402; Videos 1,520
Special Collections: Oral History
Subject Interests: Local hist
Automation Activity & Vendor Info: (Cataloging) Evergreen; (Circulation) Evergreen
Wireless access
Partic in Midwest Collaborative for Library Services (MCLS)
Open Mon-Thurs 9-9, Fri 9-7, Sat 9-5
Friends of the Library Group
Bookmobiles: 1. Outreach Mgr, Pam Weakley

SHERIDAN

P SHERIDAN PUBLIC LIBRARY*, 103 W First St, 46069. SAN 305-1102. Tel: 317-758-5201. FAX: 317-758-0045. Web Site: www.sheridan.lib.in.us. *Dir,* Stephen H Martin; E-mail: steve@sheridan.lib.in.us; *Asst Dir,* Kim Riley; E-mail: kim@sheldon.lib.in.us; *Librn,* Patty Barker; *Librn,* Dorothy Bishop; *Ch Serv,* Nancy Urban; Staff 4 (MLS 1, Non-MLS 3)
Founded 1912. Pop 4,892; Circ 37,812
Library Holdings: AV Mats 1,290; Large Print Bks 110; Bk Titles 36,727; Bk Vols 38,910; Per Subs 54; Videos 410
Partic in Cent Ind Libr Asn
Open Mon-Thurs 10-7, Fri 10-5:30, Sat 9-12
Friends of the Library Group

SHOALS

P SHOALS PUBLIC LIBRARY*, 404 N High St, 47581. (Mail add: PO Box 909, 47581-0909), SAN 305-1110. Tel: 812-247-3838. FAX: 812-247-3838. E-mail: shoalspubliclibrary@gmail.com. Web Site: www.spl.lib.in.us. *Dir,* Linda Jones; Staff 2 (MLS 1, Non-MLS 1)
Pop 809; Circ 15,650
Jan 2008-Dec 2008 Income $41,610. Mats Exp $5,000
Library Holdings: Bk Titles 10,214; Bk Vols 11,810; Per Subs 6; Talking Bks 50; Videos 375
Wireless access
Partic in Evergreen Indiana Consortium
Open Mon-Wed, Fri & Sat 9-12, Thurs 12-7

SOUTH BEND

C INDIANA UNIVERSITY SOUTH BEND, Franklin D Schurz Library, 1700 Mishawaka Ave, 46615. (Mail add: PO Box 7111, 46634-7111), SAN 305-1145. Tel: 574-520-4449. Circulation Tel: 574-520-4440. Interlibrary Loan Service Tel: 574-520-4433. Reference Tel: 574-520-4441. FAX: 574-520-4472. Web Site: iusb.edu/library. *Dean, Libr Serv,* Vicki Bloom; Tel: 574-520-4448, E-mail: vdbloom@iusb.edu; *Dir, Access Support,* Scott Opasik; Tel: 574-520-4446, E-mail: sopasik@iusb.edu; *Dir, Coll Serv,* Susan Thomas; Tel: 574-520-5500, E-mail: suethoma@iusb.edu; *Dir, Res, Instruction & Outreach,* Linda Fisher; Tel: 574-520-4442, E-mail: lfisher@iusb.edu; *Head, Electronic Res,* Feng Shan; Tel: 574-520-4189, E-mail: fshan@iusb.edu; *Head, Info Literacy,* Nancy Colborn; Tel: 574-520-4321, E-mail: ncolborn@iusb.edu; *Head, Info Tech,* Kirby Cheng; Tel: 574-520-4421, E-mail: xicheng@iusb.edu; *Head, Pub Relations & Outreach,* Julie Elliott; Tel: 574-520-4410, E-mail: jmfelli@iusb.edu; *Head, Web Serv,* Vincci Kwong; Tel: 574-520-4444, E-mail: vkwong@iusb.edu; *Scholarly Communications Librn,* Stephen Craig Finlay; Tel: 574-520-4209, E-mail: scfinlay@iusb.edu; *Bus Operations Mgr,* Angela Huff; Tel: 574-520-4404, E-mail: adhuff@iusb.edu; *Circ Supvr,* Katherin Plodowski; Tel: 574-520-4380, E-mail: kplodows@iusb.edu; *Dorothy J Wiekamp Educ Res Commons Supvr,* Kimberly Parker; Tel: 574-520-5548, E-mail: kparker@iusb.edu; *ILL Supvr,* Maureen Kennedy; E-mail: maurkenn@iusb.edu; *Archivist,* Alison Stankrauff; Tel: 574-520-4392, E-mail: astankra@iusb.edu. Subject Specialists: *New media, Visual arts,* Vicki Bloom; *Astronomy, Chem, Math,* Scott Opasik; *Allied health, Polit sci, Pub affairs,* Susan Thomas; *Biol, Criminal justice, Psychol,* Linda Fisher; *Communication arts, East Asian studies,* Feng Shan; *Anthrop, Educ, Sociol,* Nancy Colborn; *Computer sci, Informatics, World lang,* Kirby Cheng; *Dance, English, Theatre,* Julie Elliott; *Bus, Econ,* Vincci Kwong; *Latin Am studies, Music, Philos,* Stephen Craig Finlay; *African-Am studies, Gender studies, Hist,* Alison Stankrauff; Staff 21 (MLS 11, Non-MLS 10)
Founded 1940. Enrl 8,075; Fac 300; Highest Degree: Master
Jul 2013-Jun 2014 Income $2,223,560. Mats Exp $750,138. Sal $983,172 (Prof $781,321)
Library Holdings: CDs 1,702; DVDs 2,215; e-books 251,233; e-journals 70,254; Music Scores 6,285; Bk Vols 253,872; Per Subs 303; Videos 4,670
Special Collections: Annie Belle Boss Papers; James Lewis Casaday Theatre Coll; Lincoln Coll; Torrington Company Coll. US Document Depository
Automation Activity & Vendor Info: (Acquisitions) SirsiDynix; (Cataloging) SirsiDynix; (Circulation) SirsiDynix; (ILL) OCLC; (OPAC) SirsiDynix; (Serials) SirsiDynix
Database Vendor: ACM (Association for Computing Machinery), Alexander Street Press, American Chemical Society, American Geophysical Union, American Physical Society, Annual Reviews, ARTstor, Blackwell, Bowker, Cambridge Scientific Abstracts, Checkpoint Systems, Inc, CQ Press, CredoReference, ebrary, EBSCO Discovery Service, EBSCO Information Services, EBSCOhost, Elsevier, Emerald, Gale Cengage Learning, Greenwood Publishing Group, Ingenta, ISI Web of Knowledge, JSTOR, LexisNexis, Marcive, Inc, Nature Publishing Group, OCLC FirstSearch, OCLC WorldShare Interlibrary Loan, OVID Technologies, Oxford Online, Paratext, Project MUSE, ProQuest, PubMed, ScienceDirect, SerialsSolutions, SirsiDynix, Springer-Verlag, Springshare, LLC, Standard & Poor's, Thomson - Web of Science, ValueLine, Wiley InterScience, YBP Library Services
Wireless access
Function: Archival coll, Audio & video playback equip for onsite use, AV serv, Computers for patron use, Copy machines, Distance learning, Doc delivery serv, e-mail & chat, e-mail serv, Electronic databases & coll, Govt ref serv, Handicapped accessible, ILL available, Learning ctr, Magnifiers for reading, Microfiche/film & reading machines, Music CDs, Online cat, Online info literacy tutorials on the web & in blackboard, Online ref, Printer for laptops & handheld devices, Pub access computers, Ref & res, Ref serv available, Ref serv in person, Res libr, Scanner, Telephone ref, Wheelchair accessible
Publications: News from IU South Bend Libraries (Bi-annually)
Partic in Academic Libraries of Indiana; Lyrasis; Midwest Collaborative for Library Services (MCLS); OCLC Online Computer Library Center, Inc
Open Mon-Thurs 8am-Midnight, Fri 8-5, Sat 10-5, Sun Noon-Midnight

Restriction: Open to pub for ref & circ; with some limitations, Open to students, fac & staff
Friends of the Library Group

J IVY TECH COMMUNITY COLLEGE*, South Bend Campus Library, 220 Dean Johnson Blvd, 46601. SAN 305-1153. Tel: 574-289-7001, Ext 5343. FAX: 574-236-7165. Web Site: wwwcc.ivytech.edu/library/northcentral. *Libr Dir,* John Fribley; Tel: 574-289-7001, Ext 5341, E-mail: jfribley@ivytech.edu; *Librn,* Daniel Sanford; Tel: 574-289-7001, Ext 1125, E-mail: dsanford1@ivytech.edu; Staff 3 (MLS 1, Non-MLS 2)
Founded 1968. Enrl 2,500; Highest Degree: Associate
Library Holdings: AV Mats 941; Bk Titles 5,280; Bk Vols 5,690; Per Subs 70
Subject Interests: Art & archit, Bus & mgt, Med, Photog, Sci tech
Automation Activity & Vendor Info: (Acquisitions) Ex Libris Group; (Cataloging) Ex Libris Group; (Circulation) Ex Libris Group; (OPAC) Ex Libris Group
Database Vendor: Gale Cengage Learning, OVID Technologies, SirsiDynix, Wilson - Wilson Web
Open Mon-Thurs (Winter) 7:45am-8pm, Fri 7:45-5, Sat (Fall & Spring) 8-Noon

GL LIBRARY OF THE US COURTS*, Robert A Grant Courthouse, 204 S Main St, Rm 316, 46601. SAN 372-1183. Tel: 574-246-8050. FAX: 574-246-8002. Web Site: www.lb7.uscourts.gov. *Asst Satellite Librn,* John Fox; E-mail: john_fox@ca7.uscourts.gov; *Libr Tech,* Karen M Shandor; E-mail: karen_shandor@lb7.uscourts.gov. Subject Specialists: *Law,* John Fox; Staff 1 (Non-MLS 1)
Founded 1986
Automation Activity & Vendor Info: (Acquisitions) SirsiDynix; (Cataloging) SirsiDynix; (ILL) OCLC Connexion; (OPAC) SirsiDynix; (Serials) SirsiDynix
Database Vendor: Dialog, HeinOnline, LexisNexis, OCLC FirstSearch, Oxford Online, SirsiDynix, Westlaw
Partic in Law Library Microform Consortium (LLMC)
Restriction: Not open to pub

M MEMORIAL HOSPITAL OF SOUTH BEND*, Library Services, 615 N Michigan, 46601. SAN 329-1316. Tel: 574-647-7389, 574-647-7491. FAX: 574-647-3319. Web Site: www.qualityoflife.org. *Coordr, Libr & Educ Serv,* Charles A LeGuern; E-mail: cleguern@memorialsb.org; Staff 1 (MLS 1)
Founded 1978
Jan 2011-Dec 2011 Income $200,000. Mats Exp $110,000, Books $5,000, Per/Ser (Incl. Access Fees) $30,000, Electronic Ref Mat (Incl. Access Fees) $75,000
Library Holdings: e-books 100; e-journals 6,000; Per Subs 60
Subject Interests: Family practice, Gen med, Healthcare, Nursing, Rehabilitation
Automation Activity & Vendor Info: (Cataloging) OCLC Connexion; (ILL) OCLC FirstSearch
Database Vendor: Dialog, EBSCOhost, Inspire, MD Consult, Micromedex, OCLC FirstSearch, OCLC WorldShare Interlibrary Loan, UpToDate
Wireless access
Function: Computers for patron use, Doc delivery serv, e-mail serv, Electronic databases & coll, Fax serv, For res purposes, Online ref, Online searches, Photocopying/Printing, Ref & res, Scanner
Partic in Midwest Collaborative for Library Services (MCLS); National Network of Libraries of Medicine Greater Midwest Region; OCLC Online Computer Library Center, Inc
Open Mon-Fri 8-5
Restriction: Hospital employees & physicians only

GL SAINT JOSEPH COUNTY LAW LIBRARY*, Court House, 101 S Main St, 46601. SAN 305-117X. Tel: 574-235-9657. FAX: 574-235-9905. E-mail: stjoebar@gmail.com. Web Site: www.sjcba.org. *Librn,* Amy McGuire
Library Holdings: Bk Vols 15,000
Special Collections: Law Books Coll; Reporters Coll; Statutes Coll
Open Mon-Fri 9-3

P SAINT JOSEPH COUNTY PUBLIC LIBRARY, 304 S Main, 46601-2125. SAN 341-6259. Tel: 574-282-4646. Circulation Tel: 574-282-4617. Interlibrary Loan Service Tel: 574-282-4671. Reference Tel: 574-282-4630. FAX: 574-280-2763. TDD: 574-235-4194. Web Site: www.libraryforlife.org. *Dir,* Donald J Napoli; E-mail: donald.napoli@sjcpl.org; *Asst Dir,* Debra Futa; E-mail: debra.futa@sjcpl.org; *Human Res Adminr,* Consuelo Nicely; E-mail: c.nicely@sjcpl.org; *Mgr, AV Serv,* Marianne Kruppa; E-mail: m.kruppa@sjcpl.org; *Cat Mgr,* Pamela Armstrong; E-mail: p.armstrong@sjcpl.org; *Ch Mgr,* Theresa Horn; E-mail: t.horn@sjcpl.org; *Circ Serv Mgr,* Lisa O'Brien; E-mail: l.obrien@sjcpl.org; *Coll Develop Mgr,* Rona Plummer; E-mail: r.plummer@sjcpl.org; *IT Mgr,* David Haslett; E-mail: d.haslett@sjcpl.org; *Local & Family Hist Mgr,* Joseph Sipocz; E-mail: j.sipocz@sjcpl.org; *Ref, Fiction & Teen Serv Mgr,* David Heidt; E-mail: d.heidt@sjcpl.org; *Br Coordr,* Patricia Coleman; E-mail: t.coleman@sjcpl.org; *Coordr, Develop & Communication,* Nicholas Schafer; E-mail: n.schafer@sjcpl.org; *Coordr, Pub Serv,* Linda Conyers; Tel: 574-282-4659, E-mail: l.conyers@sjcpl.org; *Chief Financial Officer,* Nancy Korpal; E-mail: nancy.korpal@sjcpl.org; Staff 35 (MLS 35)
Founded 1888. Pop 167,606; Circ 2,330,262
Jan 2013-Dec 2013 Income (Main Library and Branch(s)) $12,392,566, State $799,167, Federal $128,678, Locally Generated Income $10,433,967, Other $1,030,754. Mats Exp $2,363,587, Books $1,439,712, Per/Ser (Incl. Access Fees) $143,850, AV Mat $566,827, Electronic Ref Mat (Incl. Access Fees) $213,198. Sal $5,094,019
Library Holdings: DVDs 60,760; Electronic Media & Resources 10,172; Bk Vols 513,806; Per Subs 3,440
Special Collections: Local History & Genealogy Coll (necrology & clippings file)
Automation Activity & Vendor Info: (Acquisitions) Innovative Interfaces, Inc; (Cataloging) Innovative Interfaces, Inc; (Circulation) Innovative Interfaces, Inc; (ILL) OCLC FirstSearch; (OPAC) Innovative Interfaces, Inc; (Serials) Innovative Interfaces, Inc
Database Vendor: Innovative Interfaces, Inc, OCLC FirstSearch
Wireless access
Function: Computers for patron use, Fax serv, Homebound delivery serv, ILL available, Mus passes, Music CDs, Online cat, Online ref, Photocopying/Printing, Prog for children & young adult, Pub access computers, Scanner, Story hour, Summer reading prog, Tax forms, Teen prog, Telephone ref
Special Services for the Deaf - TTY equip
Special Services for the Blind - Large print bks
Open Mon-Thurs 10-8, Fri & Sat 10-6, Sun 1-5
Friends of the Library Group
Branches: 9
CENTRE TOWNSHIP BRANCH, 1150 E Kern Rd, 46614. Tel: 574-251-3700. *Br Mgr,* Dawn Matthews; E-mail: d.matthews@sjcpl.org
ROGER B FRANCIS BRANCH, 52655 N Ironwood Rd, 46635, SAN 341-6283. Tel: 574-282-4641. *Br Mgr,* Dana Labrum; E-mail: d.labrum@sjcpl.org
GERMAN TOWNSHIP BRANCH LIBRARY, 52807 Lynnewood Ave, 46628. Tel: 574-271-5144. *Br Mgr,* Kristine Springer; E-mail: k.springer@sjcpl.org
LAKEVILLE BRANCH, 120 N Michigan, Lakeville, 46536, SAN 370-9248. Tel: 574-784-3446.
LASALLE BRANCH, 3232 W Ardmore, 46628-3232, SAN 341-6313. Tel: 574-282-4633. *Br Mgr,* Michael Moriconi; E-mail: m.moriconi@sjcpl.org
NORTH LIBERTY BRANCH, 105 E Market, North Liberty, 46554, SAN 329-6822. Tel: 574-656-3664. *Br Mgr,* Debra Palguta; E-mail: d.palguta@sjcpl.org
RIVER PARK BRANCH, 2022 Mishawaka Ave, 46615, SAN 341-6348. Tel: 574-282-4635. *Br Mgr,* Scott Sinnett; E-mail: s.sinnett@sjcpl.org
VIRGINIA M TUTT BRANCH, 2223 S Miami St, 46613, SAN 341-6372. Tel: 574-282-4637. *Br Mgr,* Judith Falzon; E-mail: j.falzon@sjcpl.org
WESTERN BRANCH, 611 S Lombardy Dr, 46619, SAN 341-6402. Tel: 574-282-4639. *Br Mgr,* Jesus Moya; E-mail: j.moya@sjcpl.org

M SAINT JOSEPH'S REGIONAL MEDICAL CENTER*, Medical Library, 801 E LaSalle, 46617. SAN 325-7231. Tel: 574-237-7228. FAX: 574-472-6307. *Librn,* Jennifer Helmen; E-mail: helmenj@sjrmc.com; Staff 1 (Non-MLS 1)
Library Holdings: Bk Titles 1,100; Bk Vols 1,225; Per Subs 150
Subject Interests: Med, Nursing
Open Mon-Fri 9-5

S SOUTH BEND MUSEUM OF ART LIBRARY*, 120 S St Joseph St, 46601. SAN 305-1129. Tel: 574-235-9102. FAX: 574-235-5782. E-mail: info@southbendart.org. Web Site: www.sbrma.org. *Dir,* Susan Visser
Founded 1947
Library Holdings: Bk Titles 1,578; Bk Vols 1,690; Per Subs 45
Special Collections: Art Books; Art Coll, flm, slides; Art Exhibition Catalogues; Carlotta Murray Banta Coll
Open Wed-Sun 12-5
Restriction: Non-circulating to the pub

S STUDEBAKER NATIONAL MUSEUM ARCHIVES*, 201 S Chapin St, 46601. SAN 325-4526. Tel: 574-235-9714, 574-235-9983. FAX: 574-235-5522. E-mail: archives@studebakermuseum.org. Web Site: www.studebakermuseum.org. *Archivist,* Andrew Beckman
Library Holdings: Bk Titles 400; Per Subs 20
Special Collections: Industrial History Transcriptions; Labor History Coll; South Bend Area Business, Labor & Industry, photogs, vf; South Bend Labor Oral History Project; Transportation History (Studebaker Coll), flms, mss, photogs, trade lit. Oral History
Subject Interests: General indust hist, Local indust hist
Restriction: Non-circulating to the pub

SOUTH WHITLEY

P SOUTH WHITLEY-CLEVELAND TOWNSHIP PUBLIC LIBRARY*, 201 E Front St, 46787-1315. SAN 305-1196. Tel: 260-723-5321. FAX: 260-723-5326. Web Site: www.swhitley.lib.in.us. *Dir,* Darci Kessie; E-mail: dkessie@swhitley.lib.in.us
Founded 1913. Pop 5,195
Library Holdings: Bk Vols 40,057; Per Subs 140
Special Collections: Oral History
Subject Interests: Local hist
Wireless access
Open Mon 10-6, Tues-Thurs 10-8, Fri & Sat 10-4

SPEEDWAY

P SPEEDWAY PUBLIC LIBRARY*, 5633 W 25th St, 46224-3899. SAN 305-120X. Tel: 317-243-8959. FAX: 317-243-9373. Web Site: www.speedway.lib.in.us. *Dir,* Darsi Bohr; *Adult Serv,* Toni Sekula; *Ch Serv,* Wendy Zishka; Staff 3 (MLS 3)
Founded 1965. Pop 11,812; Circ 122,156
Library Holdings: AV Mats 8,060; Bk Vols 87,362; Per Subs 116; Talking Bks 5,676
Special Collections: Auto Racing (Indianapolis 500). Municipal Document Depository
Subject Interests: Genealogy
Automation Activity & Vendor Info: (Acquisitions) SirsiDynix; (Cataloging) SirsiDynix; (ILL) OCLC; (OPAC) SirsiDynix
Wireless access
Publications: Speedreader (Newsletter)
Partic in Midwest Collaborative for Library Services (MCLS)
Open Mon-Thurs (Winter) 9-9, Fri & Sat 9-5; Mon-Thurs (Summer) 9-8, Fri & Sat 9-5
Friends of the Library Group

SPENCER

P OWEN COUNTY PUBLIC LIBRARY, Ten S Montgomery St, 47460-1738. SAN 305-1218. Tel: 812-829-3392. FAX: 812-829-6165. *Dir,* Ginger Rogers; E-mail: grogers@owenlib.org; *Dir, Tech Serv,* Debbie Campbell; Staff 22 (MLS 2, Non-MLS 20)
Founded 1912. Pop 21,575; Circ 140,620
Library Holdings: Bk Titles 67,391; Per Subs 122
Subject Interests: Genealogy
Automation Activity & Vendor Info: (Acquisitions) SirsiDynix; (Cataloging) SirsiDynix; (Circulation) SirsiDynix; (OPAC) SirsiDynix; (Serials) SirsiDynix
Database Vendor: EBSCOhost, Gale Cengage Learning, ProQuest, SirsiDynix
Function: AV serv, ILL available, Photocopying/Printing, Prog for children & young adult, Ref serv available, Summer reading prog, Wheelchair accessible
Open Mon-Thurs 9-8, Fri 9-5, Sat 9-3
Friends of the Library Group

SPICELAND

P SPICELAND TOWN-TOWNSHIP PUBLIC LIBRARY*, 106 W Main St, 47385. (Mail add: PO Box 445, 47385-0445), SAN 305-1226. Tel: 765-987-7472. *Dir,* Brenda Baldauf; Staff 2 (MLS 1, Non-MLS 1)
Pop 2,200; Circ 7,891
Library Holdings: DVDs 75; Bk Titles 25,621; Bk Vols 27,890; Per Subs 45; Talking Bks 286; Videos 737
Automation Activity & Vendor Info: (Cataloging) TLC (The Library Corporation); (Circulation) TLC (The Library Corporation)
Open Mon & Tues 3-7, Wed & Thurs 10-3

SULLIVAN

P SULLIVAN COUNTY PUBLIC LIBRARY*, 100 S Crowder St, 47882. SAN 341-6437. Tel: 812-268-4957. FAX: 812-268-5370. Web Site: sullivan.lib.in.us. *Dir,* Rebecca C Cole; E-mail: rcole@sullivan.lib.in.us; *Ch Serv,* Carol Swisher; *Circ,* Cindy Goodman; *Ref Serv,* Pat Osburn; Staff 13 (Non-MLS 13)
Founded 1904. Pop 21,751; Circ 125,595
Library Holdings: AV Mats 4,335; Bks on Deafness & Sign Lang 33; CDs 1,140; DVDs 144; High Interest/Low Vocabulary Bk Vols 42; Large Print Bks 2,587; Bk Titles 49,427; Bk Vols 99,211; Per Subs 346; Talking Bks 1,243; Videos 2,968
Special Collections: Indiana Coll
Subject Interests: Genealogy, Local hist
Automation Activity & Vendor Info: (Cataloging) SydneyPlus; (Circulation) SirsiDynix; (OPAC) SirsiDynix; (Serials) SirsiDynix
Database Vendor: SirsiDynix
Wireless access
Function: AV serv, Copy machines, Digital talking bks, Distance learning, Fax serv, Home delivery & serv to Sr ctr & nursing homes, Homebound delivery serv, ILL available, Music CDs, Online ref, Photocopying/Printing, Prog for adults, Prog for children & young adult, Provide serv for the mentally ill, Spoken cassettes & CDs, Summer reading prog, Tax forms, VHS videos, Wheelchair accessible, Workshops
Partic in Midwest Collaborative for Library Services (MCLS)
Open Mon-Thurs (Winter) 9-8, Fri 9-6, Sat 9-5; Mon-Fri (Summer) 9-6, Sat 9-5
Friends of the Library Group
Branches: 5
CARLISLE PUBLIC, 201 N Ledgerwood St, Carlisle, 47838. (Mail add: PO Box 297, Carlisle, 47838-0297). Tel: 812 398-4480. E-mail: carlisle1@cebridge.net. *Librn,* Agnes Cox
Founded 1965
Automation Activity & Vendor Info: (Cataloging) Innovative Interfaces, Inc; (Circulation) Innovative Interfaces, Inc; (OPAC) Innovative Interfaces, Inc
Open Mon-Fri 11-5, Sat 1-4
DUGGER PUBLIC, 8007 E Main St, Dugger, 47848. (Mail add: PO Box 277, Dugger, 47848-0277). Tel: 812-648-2822. E-mail: duggerpl@gmail.com. *Librn,* Deborah Loveless
Founded 1928
Automation Activity & Vendor Info: (Cataloging) LibLime; (Circulation) LibLime
Database Vendor: LearningExpress, ProQuest
Open Tues-Fri Noon-5, Sat 9-2
FARMERSBURG PUBLIC, 116 W Main St, Farmersburg, 47850. (Mail add: PO Box 530, Farmersburg, 47850-0530). Tel: 812-696-2194. E-mail: fpl47850@frontier.com. *Librn,* Rose Ann Gaskins
Automation Activity & Vendor Info: (Cataloging) LibLime; (Circulation) LibLime
Database Vendor: LearningExpress, ProQuest
Open Tues-Fri 12-5, Sat 9-2
MEROM PUBLIC, 8554 W Market St, Merom, 47861. (Mail add: PO Box 146, Merom, 47861-0146). Tel: 812-356-4612. E-mail: merompubliclibrary@frontier.com. *Librn,* Kim Cox
Open Tues-Fri Noon-5, Sat 9-2
SHELBURN PUBLIC, 17 W Griffith, Shelburn, 47879. (Mail add: PO Box 10, Shelburn, 47879-0010). Tel: 812-397-2210. E-mail: shelburnpubliclibrary@frontier.com. *Librn,* Nondus Murray
Automation Activity & Vendor Info: (Cataloging) LibLime; (Circulation) LibLime
Database Vendor: LearningExpress, ProQuest
Open Mon-Wed & Fri 12-5, Sat 9-2

SWAYZEE

P SWAYZEE PUBLIC LIBRARY*, 301 S Washington, 46986. (Mail add: PO Box 307, 46986-0307). Tel: 765-922-7526. FAX: 765-922-4538. E-mail: swaypub@swayzee.com. *Dir,* Dianna King; Staff 1 (Non-MLS 1)
Founded 1919
Library Holdings: Bk Vols 19,000; Per Subs 28; Talking Bks 22; Videos 700
Open Mon & Wed 12-6, Tues & Fri 11-5, Sat 9-11

SYRACUSE

P SYRACUSE TURKEY CREEK TOWNSHIP PUBLIC LIBRARY*, 115 E Main St, 46567. SAN 305-1242. Tel: 574-457-3022. FAX: 574-457-8971. Web Site: www.syracuse.lib.in.us. *Dir,* John Castleman; E-mail: jcastleman@syracuse.lib.in.us; Staff 7 (MLS 3, Non-MLS 4)
Founded 1909. Pop 9,680; Circ 41,120
Library Holdings: AV Mats 4,192; Large Print Bks 188; Bk Titles 54,691; Bk Vols 57,381; Per Subs 83; Talking Bks 323; Videos 2,122
Special Collections: Local Newspaper Coll, micro; Old historical photographs & slides. Oral History
Automation Activity & Vendor Info: (Acquisitions) SirsiDynix; (Cataloging) SirsiDynix; (OPAC) SirsiDynix
Partic in Area Libr Serv Authority
Open Mon-Wed 10-8, Thurs 12-7, Fri 10-6, Sat 10-5
Friends of the Library Group

TELL CITY

P TELL CITY-PERRY COUNTY PUBLIC LIBRARY*, 2328 Tell St, 47586. SAN 305-1250. Tel: 812-547-2661. FAX: 812-547-3038. Web Site: www.tcpclibrary.org. *Dir,* John Mundy; E-mail: jmundy@tcpclibrary.org; *Dir, Children & YA,* Lisa Hammack; E-mail: lhammack@tcpclibrary.org; Staff 4 (MLS 1, Non-MLS 3)
Founded 1905. Pop 17,984; Circ 156,000
Library Holdings: Bk Titles 62,000; Bk Vols 80,000; Per Subs 215
Subject Interests: Genealogy, Local hist
Automation Activity & Vendor Info: (Cataloging) Mandarin Library Automation; (Circulation) Mandarin Library Automation; (OPAC) Mandarin Library Automation
Wireless access
Partic in Midwest Collaborative for Library Services (MCLS)

Special Services for the Blind - Computer with voice synthesizer for visually impaired persons
Open Mon-Wed 9-8, Thurs & Fri 9-5:30, Sat 9-4:30
Friends of the Library Group
Bookmobiles: 1

TERRE HAUTE

R CENTRAL PRESBYTERIAN CHURCH LIBRARY*, 125 N Seventh St, 47807-3195. SAN 305-1269. Tel: 812-232-5049. E-mail: CPCOffice@thcpc.org. *Librn,* Marsha Harder; *Librn,* Eunice Pate
Founded 1960
Library Holdings: Bk Vols 2,492
Special Collections: Archives on Central Presbyterian Church & Presbyterian Church in the U S
Subject Interests: Church hist, Relig
Publications: CP Annual Report; Herald & Sunday Bulletin

R IMMANUEL EVANGELICAL LUTHERAN CHURCH LIBRARY*, 645 Poplar St, 47807. SAN 305-1331. Tel: 812-232-4972. FAX: 812-234-3935. Web Site: www.immanuelevluth.org. *In Charge,* Kathy Tschudny; E-mail: kathy@ImmanuelTH.org; Staff 1 (Non-MLS 1)
Founded 1973
Library Holdings: Bk Titles 3,100; Videos 10
Subject Interests: Relig
Restriction: Mem only, Not open to pub

C INDIANA STATE UNIVERSITY, Cunningham Memorial Library, 510 North 6 1/2 St, 47809. SAN 341-6496. Tel: 812-237-3700. Circulation Tel: 812-237-2541. Interlibrary Loan Service Tel: 812-237-2566. Reference Tel: 812-237-2580. Toll Free Tel: 800-851-4279. FAX: 812-237-3376. Interlibrary Loan Service FAX: 812-237-2567. Web Site: library.indstate.edu. *Dean of Libr Serv,* Robin A Crumrin; E-mail: Robin.Crumrin@indstate.edu; *Assoc Dean, Libr Serv,* Gregory Youngen; E-mail: Gregory.Youngen@indstate.edu; *Chair, Systems,* Stephen Patton; E-mail: Stephen.Patton@IndState.edu; *Chair, Spec Coll Project Dir,* Cinda May; E-mail: Cinda.May@indstate.edu; *Chair, Tech Serv,* Valentine Muyumba; E-mail: Valentine.Muyumba@indstate.edu; *Dir, Pub Serv,* Brian Bunnett; E-mail: Brian.Bunnett@indstate.edu; *Data Curation Librn,* Kayla Siddell; E-mail: Kayla.Siddell@indstate.edu; *Emerging Tech Librn,* Heather Rayl; *Metadata Librn,* Natalie Bulick; E-mail: Natalie.Bulick@indstate.edu; *Ref & Instruction Librn,* Shelley Arvin; E-mail: Shelley.Arvin@indstate.edu; *Ref & Instruction Librn,* Cheryl Blevens; *Ref & Instruction Librn,* Edith Campbell; *Ref & Instruction Librn,* Karen Evans; *Ref & Instruction Librn,* Steve Hardin; *Ref & Instruction Librn,* Rolland McGiverin; Tel: 812-237-2615, E-mail: rolland.mcgiverin@indstate.edu; *Ref & Instruction Librn,* Marsha Miller; *Tech Serv Librn,* Susan Frey; Tel: 812-237-2545, E-mail: susan.frey@indstate.edu; *Univ Archivist,* Katie Sutrina-Haney; E-mail: Katie.Sutrina-Haney@indstate.edu; Staff 21 (MLS 19, Non-MLS 2)
Founded 1870. Enrl 8,832; Fac 603; Highest Degree: Doctorate
Jul 2008-Jun 2009 Income $5,516,579, State $5,429,124, Locally Generated Income $18,442, Other $69,013. Mats Exp $2,005,503, Books $324,993, Per/Ser (Incl. Access Fees) $1,580,713, Micro $9,450, AV Mat $83,660, Presv $6,687. Sal $2,739,340 (Prof $1,486,691)
Library Holdings: Audiobooks 1,184; AV Mats 91,628; CDs 5,119; DVDs 8,481; e-books 52,522; e-journals 46,997; Microforms 51,118; Bk Vols 1,069,443
Special Collections: American Education, Classics (Cunningham Coll) & Textbooks (Walker Coll); American Labor Movement (Debs Coll); History, Culture, Travel & Literature (Rare Books Coll); Human Memory (Hermann Coll); Indiana Education (Floyd Family Coll); Indiana Federal Writers Project/Program Coll; Indiana History & Culture (Indiana Coll); Local Publishing History & Culture (Faculty Coll); Pre-1901 Dictionaries & Word Books (Cordell Coll); Sheet & Orchestra Music (Kirk Coll); US Civil War (Neff-Guttridge Coll); Wabash Valley Visions & Voices Digital Memory Project. State Document Depository; UN Document Depository; US Document Depository
Automation Activity & Vendor Info: (Acquisitions) Ex Libris Group; (Cataloging) Ex Libris Group; (Circulation) Ex Libris Group; (Course Reserve) Docutek; (ILL) OCLC ILLiad; (OPAC) Ex Libris Group; (Serials) Concepts Logiques 4DI Inc
Database Vendor: 3M Library Systems, ABC-CLIO, ACM (Association for Computing Machinery), Alexander Street Press, American Chemical Society, American Mathematical Society, American Psychological Association (APA), Annual Reviews, ARTstor, ASCE Research Library, Baker & Taylor, Blackwell, Cambridge Scientific Abstracts, College Source, CQ Press, CRC Press/Taylor & Francis Group, EBSCO - WebFeat, EBSCOhost, Elsevier, Emerald, Ex Libris Group, Facts on File, Faulkner Information Services, Greenwood Publishing Group, H W Wilson, Haworth Pres Inc, Ingenta, Inspire, ISI Web of Knowledge, JSTOR, LearningExpress, LexisNexis, McGraw-Hill, Medline, Modern Language Association, Nature Publishing Group, OCLC FirstSearch, OCLC WorldShare Interlibrary Loan, OVID Technologies, Oxford Online, Project MUSE, ProQuest, PubMed, Safari Books Online, Sage, ScienceDirect, Springer-Verlag, Swets Information Services, Westlaw, Wiley, Wiley InterScience, YBP Library Services
Wireless access
Function: Archival coll, Art exhibits, Bks on CD, Computers for patron use, Copy machines, Distance learning, Doc delivery serv, e-mail & chat, E-Reserves, Electronic databases & coll, Equip loans & repairs, Exhibits, Free DVD rentals, Handicapped accessible, ILL available, Music CDs, Online cat, Online ref, Orientations, Photocopying/Printing, Pub access computers, Ref serv in person, Res libr, Scanner, Senior computer classes, Senior outreach, Wheelchair accessible, Workshops
Publications: Floyd Family Collection: Catalog of Textbooks & Related Materials; Sycamore.net; Walker Collection: Catalog of Textbooks
Partic in Academic Libraries of Indiana; Lyrasis; Midwest Collaborative for Library Services (MCLS); MLC; OCLC Online Computer Library Center, Inc
Special Services for the Deaf - Closed caption videos
Special Services for the Blind - Accessible computers; Aids for in-house use; Audio mat; Bks & mags in Braille, on rec, tape & cassette; Bks available with recordings; Bks on CD; Closed caption display syst; Handicapped awareness prog; Large print bks; Large screen computer & software; Scanner for conversion & translation of mats; Sound rec; ZoomText magnification & reading software
Friends of the Library Group

J IVY TECH COMMUNITY COLLEGE*, 8000 S Education Dr, 47802. SAN 341-6550. Tel: 812-298-2307. Toll Free Tel: 800-377-4882, Ext 2307. FAX: 812-299-5723. Web Site: wwwcc.ivytech.edu/library/wabashvalley. *Libr Dir,* David Barton; E-mail: dbarton@ivytech.edu
Founded 1967. Enrl 1,600; Fac 45
Library Holdings: AV Mats 730; Bk Titles 4,680; Bk Vols 4,870; Per Subs 71
Subject Interests: Bus & mgt, Health sci, Vocational educ
Open Mon-Thurs 7:30am-10pm, Fri 7:30-4:30

C ROSE-HULMAN INSTITUTE OF TECHNOLOGY*, John A Logan Library, 5500 Wabash Ave, 47803. SAN 305-1374. Tel: 812-877-8200. FAX: 812-877-8579. Web Site: www.rose-hulman.edu/Library. *Dir,* Rachel Crowley; E-mail: rachel.crowley@rose-hulman.edu; Staff 2 (MLS 2)
Founded 1874. Enrl 1,300; Fac 101; Highest Degree: Master
Library Holdings: Bk Titles 76,911; Bk Vols 78,110; Per Subs 480
Special Collections: Institute Archives
Subject Interests: Sci tech
Database Vendor: EBSCOhost, OCLC FirstSearch
Partic in OCLC Online Computer Library Center, Inc
Open Mon-Thurs 8am-11pm, Fri 8-5, Sat 1-6, Sun 2-11

S SHELDON SWOPE ART MUSEUM LIBRARY*, 25 S Seventh St, 47807. SAN 305-1382. Tel: 812-238-1676. FAX: 812-238-1677. Web Site: www.swope.org. *Exec Dir,* Marianne Richter; E-mail: richter@swope.org
Library Holdings: Bk Titles 1,250; Bk Vols 1,575; Per Subs 23
Special Collections: Rare Books
Subject Interests: Am archit, Arts & crafts (Am)
Partic in Midwest Collaborative for Library Services (MCLS)
Restriction: Not a lending libr, Open by appt only

M UNION HOSPITAL*, Medical Library, 1606 N Seventh St, 47804. SAN 305-1412. Tel: 812-238-7641. FAX: 812-238-7595. E-mail: mehelp@uhhg.org. Web Site: www.uhhg.org. *Asst Librn,* Lorraine Brett; *Asst Librn,* RosaLee Weir; *Coordr,* Cheryl Stearley; E-mail: cstearley@uhhg.org; Staff 3 (MLS 2, Non-MLS 1)
Founded 1976
Library Holdings: CDs 44; Bk Titles 335; Bk Vols 1,119; Per Subs 60; Videos 27
Restriction: Staff use only

S VIGO COUNTY HISTORICAL MUSEUM LIBRARY*, 1411 S Sixth St, 47802. SAN 323-4398. Tel: 812-235-9717. FAX: 812-235-4998. E-mail: vchs@joink.com. Web Site: www.vchs.co. *Exec Dir,* Marylee Hagan; *Asst Dir,* Barbara Carney
Library Holdings: Bk Titles 1,500
Open Tues-Sun 1-4
Friends of the Library Group

P VIGO COUNTY PUBLIC LIBRARY*, One Library Sq, 47807. SAN 341-6615. Tel: 812-232-1113. Circulation Tel: 812-232-1113, Ext 2250. Interlibrary Loan Service Tel: 812-232-1113, Ext 2243. Reference Tel: 812-232-1113, Ext 2241, 812-232-1113, Ext 2242. Administration Tel: 812-232-1113, Ext 2201, 812-232-1113, Ext 2202. Automation Services Tel: 812-232-1113, Ext 2272. FAX: 812-232-3208. Administration FAX: 812-235-1439. TDD: 812-232-2055. E-mail: questions@vigo.lib.in.us. Web Site: www.vigo.lib.in.us. *Dir,* Kristi Howe; E-mail: khowe@vigo.lib.in.us; *Admin Coordr,* Libby Walker; Tel: 812-232-1113, Ext 2203, E-mail: lwalker@vigo.lib.in.us; *Commun Serv & Mkt Coordr,* Chris Schellenberg; Tel: 812-232-1113, Ext 2281, E-mail: cschellenberg@vigo.lib.in.us; *Pub &*

Info Serv Coordr, Jeff Trinkle; Tel: 812-232-1113, Ext 2214, E-mail: jtrinkle@vigo.lib.in.us; *Coordr, Youth Serv,* June Dunbar; Tel: 812-232-1113, Ext 2222, E-mail: jdunbar@vigo.lib.in.us; Staff 20 (MLS 15, Non-MLS 5)
Founded 1882. Pop 105,848; Circ 877,129
Jan 2009-Dec 2009 Income (Main Library and Branch(s)) $5,713,945, State $448,308, Federal $24,894, County $5,174,159, Other $66,584. Mats Exp $513,947, Books $212,932, Per/Ser (Incl. Access Fees) $50,957, AV Mat $96,849, Electronic Ref Mat (Incl. Access Fees) $153,209. Sal $2,536,167
Library Holdings: AV Mats 32,837; e-books 1,780; Electronic Media & Resources 661; Bk Vols 171,999; Per Subs 865
Special Collections: Adult & Family Literacy; ESL (LifeLong Learning Center Literacy Materials); Community Archives Coll; Eugene V Debs Coll; Max Ehrmann Coll; Vigo County Marriage & Obituary Databases. Oral History
Automation Activity & Vendor Info: (Acquisitions) Innovative Interfaces, Inc - Millenium; (Cataloging) Innovative Interfaces, Inc - Millenium; (Circulation) Innovative Interfaces, Inc - Millenium; (Course Reserve) Innovative Interfaces, Inc - Millenium; (ILL) Innovative Interfaces, Inc - Millenium; (OPAC) Innovative Interfaces, Inc - Millenium; (Serials) Innovative Interfaces, Inc - Millenium
Database Vendor: Baker & Taylor, EBSCO - WebFeat, EBSCO Auto Repair Reference, EBSCO Information Services, EBSCOhost, Gale Cengage Learning, Grolier Online, infoUSA, Innovative Interfaces, Inc, Inspire, LearningExpress, LexisNexis, Newsbank, OCLC WorldShare Interlibrary Loan, ProQuest, ReferenceUSA, Westlaw, World Book Online
Wireless access
Function: Adult bk club, Adult literacy prog, After school storytime, Archival coll, Art exhibits, Bilingual assistance for Spanish patrons, Bk club(s), Bks on cassette, Bks on CD, Bus archives, Children's prog, Citizenship assistance, Computer training, Computers for patron use, Copy machines, Distance learning, Electronic databases & coll, Exhibits, Family literacy, Free DVD rentals, Handicapped accessible, Health sci info serv, Holiday prog, Home delivery & serv to Sr ctr & nursing homes, Homebound delivery serv, Homework prog, ILL available, Instruction & testing, Large print keyboards, Learning ctr, Literacy & newcomer serv, Magnifiers for reading, Mail & tel request accepted, Music CDs, Newsp ref libr, Online cat, Online info literacy tutorials on the web & in blackboard, Online ref, Online searches, Outreach serv, Outside serv via phone, mail, e-mail & web, Photocopying/Printing, Preschool outreach, Prog for adults, Prog for children & young adult, Provide serv for the mentally ill, Pub access computers, Ref serv available, Ref serv in person, Senior computer classes, Senior outreach, Serves mentally handicapped consumers, Spoken cassettes & CDs, Spoken cassettes & DVDs, Story hour, Summer reading prog, Tax forms, Teen prog, Telephone ref, VCDs, VHS videos, Wheelchair accessible, Workshops, Writing prog
Publications: History of the Public Library in Vigo County, 1816-1975 (Local historical information); Preview (Monthly); Tutortalk (Newsletter)
Partic in Econ Develop Info Network; Indiana Public Library Internet Consortium; Library Consortium of Vigo County (LCVC); Midwest Collaborative for Library Services (MCLS)
Special Services for the Deaf - Bks on deafness & sign lang; Closed caption videos; TDD equip
Special Services for the Blind - Audio mat, BiFolkal kits; Bks on cassette; Bks on CD; Computer with voice synthesizer for visually impaired persons; Descriptive video serv (DVS); Extensive large print coll; Handicapped awareness prog; Home delivery serv; Videos on blindness & phys handicaps
Open Mon-Thurs 9-9, Fri 9-6, Sat 9-5, Sun 1-5
Restriction: Non-resident fee
Friends of the Library Group
Branches: 1
WEST TERRE HAUTE BRANCH, 626 National Ave, West Terre Haute, 47885. SAN 341-6763. Tel: 812-232-1113, Ext 2211. FAX: 812-478-9602. *In Charge,* Raina Konazeski; Tel: 812-232-1113, Ext 287, E-mail: rkonazeski@vigo.lib.in.us; Staff 1 (MLS 1)
Library Holdings: AV Mats 1,790; Bk Titles 11,464; Bk Vols 12,523; Talking Bks 330
Function: Adult bk club, Electronic databases & coll, Family literacy, Homebound delivery serv, ILL available, Online ref, Online searches, Photocopying/Printing, Preschool outreach, Prog for adults, Prog for children & young adult, Ref serv available, Spoken cassettes & CDs, Spoken cassettes & DVDs, Summer reading prog, Tax forms, VHS videos
Open Mon-Fri 10-6
Friends of the Library Group

THORNTOWN

P THORNTOWN PUBLIC LIBRARY*, 124 N Market St, 46071-1144. SAN 305-1455. Tel: 765-436-7348. FAX: 765-436-7011. Web Site: www.bccn.boone.in.us/tpl. *Dir,* Christine Sterle; E-mail: csterle@thorntown.lib.in.us; *Local Hist & Genealogy Librn, Syst Adminr,* Linda White; *Head, Youth Serv,* Kathy Bowen; E-mail: kbowen@thorntown.lib.in.us; *Ad,* Karen Niemeyer; E-mail: kniemeyer@thorntown.lib.in.us; *Cataloger, YA Librn,* Britta Dorsey; E-mail: bdorsey@thorntown.lib.in.us; *Circ,* Myrtle Cox; E-mail: mcox@thorntown.lib.in.us; *Circ,* Bonnie Deakins; E-mail: bdeakins@thorntown.lib.in.us; *Circ,* Becki Osborne; E-mail: bosborne@thorntown.lib.in.us; *Tech Serv,* Linda Porter; E-mail: lporter@thorntown.lib.in.us; *Treas,* Barbara Darnell; E-mail: bdarnell@thorntown.lib.in.us; Staff 12 (MLS 3, Non-MLS 9)
Pop 5,010; Circ 53,818
Library Holdings: AV Mats 5,293; Bk Titles 38,000; Per Subs 105; Videos 560
Special Collections: Local Indian Coll
Subject Interests: Local hist
Automation Activity & Vendor Info: (Cataloging) Evergreen; (Circulation) Evergreen; (ILL) Evergreen; (OPAC) Evergreen
Database Vendor: Evanced Solutions, Inc, Overdrive, Inc
Wireless access
Partic in Evergreen Indiana Consortium
Open Mon & Fri 9-6, Tues-Thurs 9-8, Sat 10-4
Friends of the Library Group

TIPTON

P TIPTON COUNTY PUBLIC LIBRARY, 127 E Madison St, 46072-1993. SAN 341-6798. Tel: 765-675-8761. FAX: 765-675-4475. E-mail: tipton@tiptonpl.lib.in.us. Web Site: www.tiptonpl.lib.in.us. *Dir,* Cherie Spencer; E-mail: cspencer@tiptonpl.org; *Asst Dir,* Beau Cunnyngham; E-mail: bcunnyngham@tiptonpl.org; Staff 16 (MLS 4, Non-MLS 12)
Founded 1902. Pop 16,532
Library Holdings: Bk Titles 89,000; Per Subs 318
Special Collections: Tipton & Indiana, bks, clippings & newspapers
Subject Interests: Indians
Automation Activity & Vendor Info: (Acquisitions) SirsiDynix; (Cataloging) SirsiDynix; (Circulation) SirsiDynix; (OPAC) SirsiDynix
Wireless access
Partic in Midwest Collaborative for Library Services (MCLS)
Open Mon-Thurs 9:30-8, Fri & Sat 9:30-5
Friends of the Library Group
Branches: 1
WINDFALL BRANCH, 109 McClellen St, Windfall, 46076. (Mail add: PO Box 458, Windfall, 46076), SAN 341-6828. Tel: 765-945-7655. FAX: 765-945-7655. E-mail: windfall@tiptonpl.lib.in.us. *Dir,* Cherie Spencer
Library Holdings: Bk Vols 3,000
Open Mon, Tues & Thurs 2-7, Wed 9-5, Fri 12-5

UNION CITY

P UNION CITY PUBLIC LIBRARY*, 408 N Columbia St, 47390-1404. SAN 305-1463. Tel: 765-964-4748. FAX: 765-964-0017. Web Site: www.unioncity.lib.in.us. *Dir,* Virginia M Hiatt; E-mail: vhiatt@unioncity.lib.in.us; Staff 1 (MLS 1)
Founded 1904. Pop 3,622; Circ 9,315
Jan 2012-Dec 2012 Income $143,720, State $6,555, County $130,164, Other $7,001. Mats Exp $17,974, Books $14,948, Per/Ser (Incl. Access Fees) $1,556, Micro $210, Electronic Ref Mat (Incl. Access Fees) $1,260. Sal $69,207 (Prof $46,249)
Library Holdings: Microforms 570; Bk Titles 19,449; Per Subs 51; Talking Bks 140; Videos 882
Special Collections: Local Newspapers, micro
Subject Interests: Genealogy, Local hist
Partic in Midwest Collaborative for Library Services (MCLS)
Special Services for the Blind - Bks on cassette; Bks on CD

UPLAND

P BARTON REES POGUE MEMORIAL LIBRARY, 29 W Washington St, 46989. (Mail add: PO Box 488, 46989-0488), SAN 305-1471. Tel: 765-998-2971. FAX: 765-998-2961. E-mail: bdlibrarydirector@yahoo.com. Web Site: www.upland.lib.in.us. *Dir,* Barbara Dixon; *Asst Librn,* Martha Wenger; Staff 1 (Non-MLS 1)
Founded 1934. Pop 3,800; Circ 16,800
Library Holdings: Bk Vols 15,327; Per Subs 41; Videos 112
Automation Activity & Vendor Info: (Acquisitions) Evergreen; (Cataloging) Evergreen; (Circulation) Evergreen; (ILL) Evergreen; (OPAC) Evergreen
Database Vendor: Overdrive, Inc
Wireless access
Function: 24/7 Electronic res, 24/7 Online cat, Bks on cassette, Bks on CD, Children's prog, Computers for patron use, Copy machines, Electronic databases & coll, eReaders, Exhibits, Fax serv, Free DVD rentals, Homebound delivery serv, ILL available, Instruction & testing, Magazines, Music CDs, Online cat, OverDrive digital audio bks, Photocopying/Printing, Prog for adults, Prog for children & young adult, Pub access computers, Scanner, Spoken cassettes & CDs, Story hour, Summer reading prog, Tax forms, Web-catalog
Open Tues & Thurs 2-8, Wed 2-6, Fri 2-5, Sat 9-1

C TAYLOR UNIVERSITY, Zondervan Library, 236 W Reade Ave, 46989-1001. SAN 305-148X. Tel: 765-998-5522. Reference Tel: 765-998-4357. FAX: 765-998-5569. E-mail: zonlib@taylor.edu. Web Site: www.taylor.edu/academics/library. *Univ Librn/Libr Dir,* Daniel J Bowell; Tel: 765-998-5241, E-mail: dnbowell@taylor.edu; *Asst Dir/Res Librn,* Lana J Wilson; Tel: 765-998-5267, E-mail: lnwilson@taylor.edu; *Assessment & Mkt Librn, Univ Archivist,* Ashley N Chu; Tel: 765-998-5242, E-mail: aschu@taylor.edu; *Info Serv Librn,* Shawn D Denny; Tel: 765-998-5243, E-mail: shdenny@taylor.edu; *Instrul Serv Librn,* Linda J Lambert; Tel: 765-998-5270, E-mail: ldlambert@taylor.edu; *Acq,* Shari Michael; Tel: 765-998-5264, E-mail: shmichael@taylor.edu; *Circ/Ser,* Marsha Becker; Tel: 765-998-5266, E-mail: mrbecker@taylor.edu; *ILL,* Jo Ann Cosgrove; Tel: 765-998-5530, E-mail: jncosgrov@taylor.edu; *Tech Serv,* Sharon Eib; Tel: 765-998-5265, E-mail: sheib@taylor.edu; Staff 10 (MLS 5, Non-MLS 5)

Founded 1846. Enrl 1,925; Fac 140; Highest Degree: Master

Jun 2014-May 2015 Income $1,004,581. Mats Exp $228,000, Books $27,000, Per/Ser (Incl. Access Fees) $35,000, Other Print Mats $15,000, AV Mat $3,000, Electronic Ref Mat (Incl. Access Fees) $145,000, Presv $3,000. Sal $372,817 (Prof $278,393)

Library Holdings: AV Mats 15,841; Bk Titles 125,715; Bk Vols 202,766; Per Subs 370

Automation Activity & Vendor Info: (Acquisitions) OCLC; (Cataloging) OCLC; (Circulation) OCLC; (ILL) OCLC; (Media Booking) OCLC; (OPAC) OCLC

Database Vendor: CountryWatch, CQ Press, CredoReference, Dialog, ebrary, EBSCO Information Services, EBSCOhost, Gale Cengage Learning, JSTOR, LexisNexis, OCLC WorldShare Interlibrary Loan, OCLC Worldshare Management Services, PubMed, STN International

Wireless access

Function: 24/7 Electronic res, 24/7 Online cat, Electronic databases & coll, ILL available, Online ref

Partic in Midwest Collaborative for Library Services (MCLS); OCLC Online Computer Library Center, Inc; Private Academic Library Network of Indiana (PALNI)

Open Mon-Thurs 7:45am-Midnight, Fri 7:45am-10pm, Sat 9am-10pm, Sun 7pm-Midnight

VALPARAISO

P PORTER COUNTY PUBLIC LIBRARY SYSTEM*, 103 Jefferson St, 46383-4820. SAN 341-6852. Tel: 219-462-0524. FAX: 219-477-4866. TDD: 219-462-4948. Web Site: www.pcpls.lib.in.us. *Dir,* James D Cline; Tel: 219-462-0524, Ext 126; *Asst Dir,* Phyllis A Nelson; Tel: 219-462-0524, Ext 103; *Genealogy Librn,* Larry Clark; Staff 82 (MLS 10, Non-MLS 72)

Founded 1905. Pop 128,665; Circ 1,322,429

Library Holdings: AV Mats 163,358; Bks on Deafness & Sign Lang 300; High Interest/Low Vocabulary Bk Vols 1,500; Bk Vols 434,315; Per Subs 1,199

Special Collections: Oral History

Subject Interests: Genealogy, Indiana

Automation Activity & Vendor Info: (Acquisitions) SirsiDynix; (Circulation) SirsiDynix; (OPAC) SirsiDynix

Publications: Between-the-Stacks; Calendar of Events (Bi-monthly); Summer Reading Booklet, Baby Talk Bibliography

Special Services for the Deaf - High interest/low vocabulary bks; TDD equip

Special Services for the Blind - Closed circuit TV magnifier; Computer with voice synthesizer for visually impaired persons; Reader equip

Open Mon-Thurs 9-9, Fri 9-6, Sat 9-5

Friends of the Library Group

Branches: 5

HEBRON PUBLIC, 201 W Sigler St, Hebron, 46341. (Mail add: PO Box 97, Hebron, 46341-0097), SAN 371-9561. Tel: 219-996-3684. FAX: 219-996-3680. Reference E-mail: hebref@pcpls.lib.in.us. *Br Mgr,* Pamela Gibbs Ferber; E-mail: pferber@pcpls.lib.in.us; Staff 9 (MLS 2, Non-MLS 7)

Founded 1917

Library Holdings: CDs 2,802; DVDs 4,312; Bk Vols 48,051

Automation Activity & Vendor Info: (OPAC) Innovative Interfaces, Inc

Function: 24/7 Online cat, Bk club(s), Bks on CD, Children's prog, Computers for patron use, Copy machines, Electronic databases & coll, Fax serv, Free DVD rentals, Handicapped accessible, ILL available, Magazines, Magnifiers for reading, Mango lang, Music CDs, Online cat, Photocopying/Printing, Preschool outreach, Prog for adults, Prog for children & young adult, Pub access computers, Scanner, Story hour, Study rm, Summer reading prog, Tax forms, Teen prog, Telephone ref, Web-catalog, Wheelchair accessible

Open Mon & Wed 10-9, Tues, Thurs & Fri 10-6, Sat 9-5

Friends of the Library Group

KOUTS PUBLIC, 101 E Daumer Rd, Kouts, 46347, SAN 341-6917. Tel: 219-766-2271. FAX: 219-766-2273. Reference E-mail: koref@pcpls.lib.in.us. *Br Mgr,* Hayley Dwyer; Staff 7 (MLS 1, Non-MLS 6)

Founded 1969

Library Holdings: Bk Vols 33,007

Open Mon, Wed & Fri 10-6, Tues & Thurs 10-9, Sat 9-5

Friends of the Library Group

PORTAGE PUBLIC, 2665 Irving St, Portage, 46368-3504, SAN 341-6941. Tel: 219-763-1508. FAX: 219-762-0101. Reference E-mail: porref@pcpls.lib.in.us. *Br Mgr,* Anne M Wood; E-mail: amgwood@pcpls.lib.in.us; Staff 16 (MLS 3, Non-MLS 13)

Founded 1970

Library Holdings: Bk Vols 109,858

Special Collections: Local History Coll (Portage, Portage Township & Ogden Dunes)

Subject Interests: Careers

Database Vendor: SirsiDynix

Open Mon-Thurs 9-9, Fri 9-6, Sat 9-5

Friends of the Library Group

SOUTH HAVEN, 403 West, 700 North, 46385-8407, SAN 341-6976. Tel: 219-759-4474. FAX: 219-759-4454. Reference E-mail: shref@pcpls.lib.in.us. *Br Mgr,* Linda Cronk; Staff 6 (MLS 1, Non-MLS 5)

Founded 1974

Library Holdings: Bk Vols 47,048

Open Mon & Wed 10-9, Tues, Thurs & Fri 10-6, Sat 9-5

Friends of the Library Group

VALPARAISO PUBLIC (CENTRAL), 103 Jefferson St, 46383-4820, SAN 341-6887. Tel: 219-462-0524. FAX: 219-477-4867. TDD: 800-743-3333. *Br Mgr,* Connie Sullivan

Founded 1905

Library Holdings: Bk Vols 178,247

Subject Interests: Genealogy, Local hist

Open Mon-Thurs 9-9, Fri 9-6, Sat 9-5

Friends of the Library Group

C VALPARAISO UNIVERSITY, Christopher Center for Library & Information Resources, 1410 Chapel Dr, 46383-6493. SAN 341-700X. Tel: 219-464-5500. Circulation Tel: 219-464-5366. Interlibrary Loan Service Tel: 219-464-5363. Administration Tel: 219-464-5364. Web Site: library.valpo.edu. *Dean of Libr Serv,* Bradford Lee Eden, PhD; E-mail: brad.eden@valpo.edu; *Assoc Dean, Libr Serv,* Donna R Resetar; Tel: 219-464-6183, E-mail: donna.resetar@valpo.edu; *Dir, Res Serv,* Trisha Mileham; Tel: 219-464-5693, E-mail: trisha.mileham@valpo.edu; *Asst Prof, Res Serv Librn,* Mark Robison; Tel: 219-464-6286, E-mail: mark.robison@valpo.du; *Electronic Serv Librn,* Ruth Connell; Tel: 219-464-5360, E-mail: ruth.connell@valpo.edu; *Media Cat Serv Librn,* Pat Hogan-Vidal; Tel: 219-464-6128, E-mail: pat.hoganvidal@valpo.edu; *Res Serv Librn,* Rachael Muszkiewicz; Tel: 219-464-5464, E-mail: rachael.muszkiewicz@valpo.edu; *Res Serv Librn,* Kimberly Whalen; Tel: 219-464-5754, E-mail: kimberly.whalen@valpo.edu; *Res Serv, Sci/Eng Librn,* Nora Belzowski; Tel: 219-464-5023, E-mail: nora.belzowski@valpo.edu; *Scholarly Communication Serv Librn,* Jonathan Bull; Tel: 219-464-5771, E-mail: jon.bull@valpo.edu; *Spec Coll Librn,* Judith Miller; Tel: 219-464-5808, E-mail: judith.miller@valpo.edu; *Circ Mgr,* Shannon Howe; Tel: 219-464-5168, E-mail: Shannon.Howe@valpo.edu; *Circ Mgr,* Sam Simpson; E-mail: Sam.Simpson@valpo.edu; *Evening Circ Mgr,* Colette Mancini; Tel: 219-464-5129, E-mail: Colette.Mancini@valpo.edu; *ILL Mgr,* Stephanie Frederick; E-mail: stephanie.frederick@valpo.edu; *Weekend Cir Mgr,* Timothy Blewett; Tel: 219-464-5125, E-mail: Timothy.Blewett@valpo.edu; *Acq Spec,* Rachel Volk; E-mail: rachel.volk@valpo.edu; *Cat Spec,* Stacy Fellers; Tel: 219-464-5160, E-mail: Stacy.Fellers@valpo.edu; *Govt Doc/Per Spec,* Kathy Rhynard; Tel: 219-464-6121, E-mail: kathy.rhynard@valpo.edu. Subject Specialists: *Govt info,* Mark Robison; *Health sci,* Kimberly Whalen; Staff 13 (MLS 12, Non-MLS 1)

Founded 1859. Enrl 4,293; Fac 376; Highest Degree: Master

Library Holdings: AV Mats 16,604; e-books 125,179; e-journals 51,971; Microforms 847,858; Bk Vols 341,508

Special Collections: University Archives. US Document Depository

Subject Interests: Lutheran studies, Theol

Automation Activity & Vendor Info: (Acquisitions) Innovative Interfaces, Inc - Millenium; (Cataloging) Innovative Interfaces, Inc; (Circulation) Innovative Interfaces, Inc - Millenium; (Course Reserve) Innovative Interfaces, Inc - Millenium; (ILL) OCLC ILLiad; (OPAC) Innovative Interfaces, Inc; (Serials) SerialsSolutions

Database Vendor: ABC-CLIO, Agricola, American Chemical Society, American Mathematical Society, American Physical Society, American Psychological Association (APA), Annual Reviews, ARTstor, ASCE Research Library, Bowker, Career Guidance Foundation, Cinahl, CQ Press, CRC Press/Taylor & Francis Group, CredoReference, ebrary, EBSCOhost, Elsevier, Foundation Center, Gale Cengage Learning, Ingenta, Inspire, JSTOR, LexisNexis, Marcive, Inc, Medline, Modern Language Association, Newsbank, OCLC, OCLC FirstSearch, OCLC WorldShare Interlibrary Loan, OVID Technologies, Oxford Online, Project MUSE, ProQuest, PubMed, ScienceDirect, SerialsSolutions, Springshare, LLC, Standard & Poor's, Thomson - Web of Science, ValueLine, Wiley, Wiley InterScience, YBP Library Services

Wireless access
Partic in Academic Libraries of Indiana; Lyrasis; Midwest Collaborative for Library Services (MCLS); OCLC Online Computer Library Center, Inc; Private Academic Library Network of Indiana (PALNI)
Special Services for the Deaf - Closed caption videos
Special Services for the Blind - Bks on CD; ZoomText magnification & reading software
Open Mon-Thurs (Winter) 7:30am-2am, Fri 7:30am-9pm, Sat 9-6, Sun 10am-2am; Mon-Thurs (Summer) 8am-10pm, Fri 8-5

Departmental Libraries:

CL SCHOOL OF LAW LIBRARY, 656 S Greenwich St, 46383, SAN 341-7034. Tel: 219-465-7827. FAX: 219-465-7917. Web Site: www.valpo.edu/law. *Assoc Dean,* Emily M Janoski-Haehlen; E-mail: emily.janoskihaehlen@valpo.edu; *Assoc Law Librn,* Michael Bushbaum; E-mail: michael.bushbaum@valpo.edu; *Cat & Acq,* Larissa Sullivant; Tel: 219-465-7878, E-mail: larissa.sullivant@valpo.edu; *Digital Serv Librn, Outreach Librn,* Jesse Bowman; Tel: 219-465-7911, E-mail: jesse.bowman@valpo.edu; *Educ Serv Librn,* Steven Probst; E-mail: steven.probst@valpo.edu; *Fac Serv Librn,* Debra Denslaw; Tel: 219-465-7876, E-mail: debra.denslaw@valpo.edu; *Govt Info/Ref Librn,* Sally Holterhoff; E-mail: sally.holterhoff@valpo.edu; Staff 12 (MLS 7, Non-MLS 5)
Founded 1879. Enrl 560; Fac 37; Highest Degree: Doctorate
Library Holdings: AV Mats 2,332; Microforms 983,622; Bk Titles 185,131; Bk Vols 349,068; Per Subs 2,458
Special Collections: Supreme Court Records & Briefs Coll. State Document Depository; US Document Depository
Automation Activity & Vendor Info: (Acquisitions) Innovative Interfaces, Inc; (Cataloging) Innovative Interfaces, Inc; (Circulation) Innovative Interfaces, Inc; (Course Reserve) Innovative Interfaces, Inc; (ILL) OCLC ILLiad; (OPAC) Innovative Interfaces, Inc; (Serials) Innovative Interfaces, Inc
Database Vendor: ebrary, Gale Cengage Learning, H W Wilson, HeinOnline, Innovative Interfaces, Inc, LexisNexis, Marcive, Inc, ProQuest, Westlaw, Wilson - Wilson Web
Partic in Academic Libraries of Indiana
Publications: Valparaiso University Law Review
Open Mon-Thurs 7:30am-Midnight, Fri 7:30am-10pm, Sat 9am-10pm, Sun 9-Midnight

VAN BUREN

P VAN BUREN PUBLIC LIBRARY*, 115 S First St, 46991. (Mail add: PO Box 405, 46991-0405), SAN 305-151X. Tel: 765-934-2171. FAX: 765-934-4926. E-mail: vbpl2003@yahoo.com. Web Site: www.shideler.net/vbpl.html. *Dir,* Stephanie Beck; Staff 1 (Non-MLS 1)
Founded 1917. Pop 2,046; Circ 23,000
Library Holdings: Bk Titles 23,911; Bk Vols 24,688; Per Subs 57; Talking Bks 48; Videos 1,511
Automation Activity & Vendor Info: (Cataloging) Follett Software; (Circulation) Follett Software
Function: After school storytime, Computer training, Copy machines, e-mail serv, Fax serv, Homebound delivery serv, ILL available, Photocopying/Printing, Prog for adults, Prog for children & young adult, Summer reading prog, Tax forms, VHS videos
Open Mon 10-6, Tues-Fri 10-5, Sat 10-12:30

VERSAILLES

P TYSON LIBRARY*, 325 W Tyson St, 47042. (Mail add: PO Box 769, 47042-0769), SAN 376-5326. Tel: 812-689-5894. FAX: 812-689-7401. E-mail: info@tysonlibrary.org. Web Site: www.tysonlibrary.org. *Dir,* Andy Rowden; Staff 5 (MLS 1, Non-MLS 4)
Founded 1942. Pop 3,000
Library Holdings: Audiobooks 500; CDs 300; DVDs 1,000; Bk Titles 8,000; Bk Vols 10,000; Per Subs 50; Videos 1,000
Special Collections: Indiana Coll; James Tyson Coll; Ripley Coll; Versailles Coll
Subject Interests: Fiction, Hist, Lit, Relig
Automation Activity & Vendor Info: (Cataloging) Innovative Interfaces, Inc; (Circulation) Innovative Interfaces, Inc; (OPAC) Innovative Interfaces, Inc
Open Mon-Thurs 10-8, Fri 10-6, Sat 10-3

VEVAY

P SWITZERLAND COUNTY PUBLIC LIBRARY*, 205 Ferry St, 47043. SAN 305-1528. Tel: 812-427-3363. FAX: 812-427-3654. *Dir,* Kristi Harms; *Adult Serv, Distance Educ,* Shannon Phipps; E-mail: sphipps@scpl.us; *Ch Serv,* Greta Griffin; E-mail: ggriffin@scpl.us; Staff 3 (MLS 1, Non-MLS 2)
Founded 1915. Pop 9,162; Circ 34,561
Library Holdings: Bk Titles 37,390; Bk Vols 39,684; Per Subs 78; Talking Bks 210; Videos 376
Special Collections: Switzerland County History, bks, VF, microfilm, a-tapes. Oral History
Automation Activity & Vendor Info: (Acquisitions) Innovative Interfaces, Inc; (Cataloging) Innovative Interfaces, Inc; (OPAC) Innovative Interfaces, Inc
Partic in Evergreen Indiana Consortium; Midwest Collaborative for Library Services (MCLS)
Open Mon-Thurs 9-8, Fri 9-6, Sat 9-5

VINCENNES

M GOOD SAMARITAN HOSPITAL LIBRARY*, 520 S Seventh St, 47591. SAN 305-1536. Tel: 812-882-5220, 812-885-3228. FAX: 812-885-3089. Web Site: www.gshvin.org. *Librn,* Carmon Graves-Onken; E-mail: cgraves@gshvin.org; Staff 1 (Non-MLS 1)
Library Holdings: Bk Titles 500; Bk Vols 615; Per Subs 39
Partic in Evansville Area Library Consortium
Open Mon-Fri 8-4

P KNOX COUNTY PUBLIC LIBRARY*, 502 N Seventh St, 47591-2119. SAN 305-1544. Tel: 812-886-4380. FAX: 812-886-0342. E-mail: publib@kcpl.lib.in.us. Web Site: www.kcpl.lib.in.us. *Dir,* Emily Cooper Bunyan; E-mail: ebunyan@kcpl.lib.in.us; *Asst Dir,* Steven Smith; E-mail: ssmith@kcpl.lib.in.us; *Supvr, Youth Serv,* Amy Blake; E-mail: ablake@kcpl.lib.in.us; *Tech Coordr,* Harold Lambertson; E-mail: hlambertson@kcpl.lib.in.us; *Circ,* Mary Studley; E-mail: mstudley@kcpl.lib.in.us; *Tech Serv,* Bernice Doades; E-mail: ebdoades@kcpl.lib.in.us; Staff 6 (MLS 4, Non-MLS 2)
Founded 1889. Pop 33,978; Circ 240,000
Jan 2007-Dec 2007 Income $1,233,305. Mats Exp $115,758. Sal $500,000
Library Holdings: Audiobooks 8,867; AV Mats 8,424; CDs 1,259; DVDs 1,452; High Interest/Low Vocabulary Bk Vols 250; Large Print Bks 3,000; Bk Titles 92,431; Bk Vols 123,895; Per Subs 253; Talking Bks 3,392; Videos 3,318
Special Collections: Daughters of the American Revolution, Francis Vigo Chapter; Early Vincennes Court Records 1532-1805; Knox County Records; Northwest Territory History; Vincennes History; Vincennes University-Lewis Library Genealogy Coll
Subject Interests: Genealogy, Hist
Automation Activity & Vendor Info: (Cataloging) Innovative Interfaces, Inc; (Circulation) Innovative Interfaces, Inc; (OPAC) Innovative Interfaces, Inc
Wireless access
Function: Archival coll, ILL available, Newsp ref libr, Ref serv available, Telephone ref
Publications: Friends (Newsletter)
Partic in OCLC Online Computer Library Center, Inc
Special Services for the Deaf - TDD equip
Special Services for the Blind - Bks on cassette; Computer with voice synthesizer for visually impaired persons; Home delivery serv
Open Mon-Wed 8:30am-9pm, Thurs-Sat 8:30-5:30, Sun 1-5
Friends of the Library Group

SR OLD CATHEDRAL LIBRARY*, 205 Church St, 47591-1133. Tel: 812-882-5638. FAX: 812-882-4042. *Mgr,* John Schipp, Staff 1 (Non-MLS 1)
Founded 1794
Library Holdings: Bk Titles 11,000; Bk Vols 12,100
Special Collections: Brute Coll
Subject Interests: Hist, Theol
Function: Res libr
Restriction: Open by appt only

C VINCENNES UNIVERSITY*, Shake Library, Shake Learning Resources Center, 1002 N First St, 47591. SAN 341-7069. Tel: 812-888-5130. Circulation Tel: 812-888-4165. Reference Tel: 812-888-5810. FAX: 812-888-5471. E-mail: libref@vinu.edu. Web Site: www.vinu.edu. *Dean,* David M Peter; Tel: 812-888-5815, E-mail: dpeter@vinu.edu; *Info Serv Librn,* Anita Slack; Tel: 812-888-5377, E-mail: aslack@vinu.edu; *Pub Serv Librn,* Marissa Ellermann; Tel: 812-888-4427, E-mail: mellermann@vinu.edu; *Tech Serv & Syst Librn,* Abigail Creitz; Tel: 812-888-5807, E-mail: acreitz@vinu.edu; *Media Serv,* Jay Wolf; Tel: 812-888-4172, E-mail: jwolf@vinu.edu; *Ref,* Richard King; Tel: 812-888-5411, E-mail: rking@vinu.edu; Staff 18 (MLS 4, Non-MLS 14)
Founded 1959. Enrl 6,368; Fac 250; Highest Degree: Bachelor
Library Holdings: CDs 2,264; DVDs 378; e-books 12,568; Bk Titles 76,467; Bk Vols 98,508; Per Subs 508; Videos 2,261
Special Collections: Lewis Historical Coll Library. Oral History
Subject Interests: Archives, Indiana, Local hist
Automation Activity & Vendor Info: (Acquisitions) Ex Libris Group; (Cataloging) Ex Libris Group; (Circulation) Ex Libris Group; (Course Reserve) Ex Libris Group; (ILL) Ex Libris Group; (OPAC) Ex Libris Group; (Serials) EBSCO Online
Database Vendor: ABC-CLIO, ARTstor, Baker & Taylor, CredoReference, EBSCO - WebFeat, EBSCOhost, Ex Libris Group, Facts on File, Gale Cengage Learning, Inspire, LexisNexis, Loislaw, Newsbank, OCLC WorldShare Interlibrary Loan, Oxford Online, ProQuest, SerialsSolutions

Wireless access
Function: Archival coll, Audio & video playback equip for onsite use, AV serv, Computer training, Computers for patron use, Copy machines, Distance learning, Doc delivery serv, e-mail & chat, E-Reserves, Electronic databases & coll, Equip loans & repairs, Exhibits, Handicapped accessible, ILL available, Instruction & testing, Mail & tel request accepted, Masonic res mat, Music CDs, Newsp ref libr, Online cat, Online ref, Online searches, Orientations, Photocopying/Printing, Prof lending libr, Pub access computers, Ref & res, Ref serv available, Ref serv in person, Referrals accepted, Res libr, Scanner, Telephone ref, VHS videos, Wheelchair accessible, Workshops
Partic in Academic Libraries of Indiana; Lyrasis; Midwest Collaborative for Library Services (MCLS)
Open Mon-Thurs 7:30am-Midnight, Fri 7:30am-9pm, Sat 11-9, Sun 2-Midnight
Restriction: Residents only

WABASH

P WABASH CARNEGIE PUBLIC LIBRARY*, 188 W Hill St, 46992-3048. SAN 305-1560. Tel: 260-563-2972. FAX: 260-563-0222. E-mail: general@wabash.lib.in.us. Web Site: www.wabash.lib.in.us. *Dir,* Ware W Wimberly, III; *Ch Serv,* Nancy Snyder; *Ref,* Polly Howell; *Tech Serv,* Ruth Lord; Staff 10 (MLS 3, Non-MLS 7)
Founded 1903. Pop 11,743; Circ 145,000
Library Holdings: AV Mats 6,755; Bk Vols 67,466; Per Subs 168
Special Collections: Gene Stratton-Porter Coll. Oral History
Subject Interests: Gardening, Genealogy, Local hist, Travel
Automation Activity & Vendor Info: (Cataloging) Innovative Interfaces, Inc; (Circulation) Innovative Interfaces, Inc; (OPAC) Innovative Interfaces, Inc
Wireless access
Open Mon-Thurs 9-8, Fri & Sat 9-5

WAKARUSA

P WAKARUSA PUBLIC LIBRARY*, Wakarusa-Olive & Harrison Township Public Library, 124 N Elkhart St, 46573. (Mail add: PO Box 485, 46573-0485), SAN 305-1579. Tel: 574-862-2465. FAX: 574-862-4156. E-mail: info@wakarusa.lib.in.us. Web Site: www.wakarusa.lib.in.us. *Dir,* Jo Geleske; E-mail: jgeleske@wakarusa.lib.in.us; *Archivist,* Linda Hartman; *Ch Serv,* Matt Bowers; E-mail: mbowers@wakarusa.lib.in.us; Staff 9 (Non-MLS 9)
Founded 1945. Pop 7,500; Circ 110,000
Library Holdings: Audiobooks 1,300; CDs 1,000; DVDs 2,500; Large Print Bks 1,200; Bk Titles 54,000; Per Subs 110
Special Collections: Local History (Wakarusa, Indiana), pictures, clippings, oral, pamphlets
Automation Activity & Vendor Info: (Acquisitions) SirsiDynix; (Cataloging) SirsiDynix; (Circulation) SirsiDynix; (OPAC) SirsiDynix
Wireless access
Partic in Midwest Collaborative for Library Services (MCLS)
Open Mon, Tues & Thurs 9-8, Wed & Fri 9-5:30, Sat 9-2
Friends of the Library Group

WALKERTON

P WALKERTON-LINCOLN TOWNSHIP PUBLIC LIBRARY*, 300 Michigan St, 46574. SAN 305-1587. Tel: 574-586-2933. FAX: 574-586-2933. *Dir,* Connie Jo Swanson
Founded 1913. Pop 3,053; Circ 14,866
Library Holdings: Large Print Bks 500; Bk Vols 17,268; Per Subs 22; Talking Bks 681; Videos 300
Subject Interests: Local hist
Automation Activity & Vendor Info: (Cataloging) Surpass; (Circulation) Surpass
Partic in Midwest Collaborative for Library Services (MCLS)
Open Mon, Wed & Thurs 9:30-5:30, Tues 9:30-7, Fri 12-5:30, Sat 9:30-1:30

WALTON

P WALTON & TIPTON TOWNSHIP PUBLIC LIBRARY*, Walton Public, 110 N Main St, 46994-0406. (Mail add: PO Box 406, 46994-0406), SAN 305-1595. Tel: 574-626-2234. FAX: 574-626-2234. E-mail: waltonlibrary@walton.lib.in.us. Web Site: www.walton.lib.in.us. *Dir, Ref Librn,* Gordon T Southern; E-mail: gsouthern@walton.lib.in.us; Staff 3 (Non-MLS 3)
Founded 1914. Pop 2,490; Circ 43,000
Jan 2013-Dec 2013 Income $146,273. Mats Exp $17,394, Books $7,693, Per/Ser (Incl. Access Fees) $1,200, AV Mat $7,155. Sal $80,119 (Prof $25,000)
Library Holdings: Audiobooks 172; AV Mats 732; CDs 147; DVDs 603; e-books 93; Large Print Bks 685; Bk Titles 23,884; Bk Vols 24,120; Per Subs 68; Talking Bks 62; Videos 1,908
Subject Interests: Indiana
Database Vendor: AVC Technology Corp
Wireless access
Function: Accelerated reader prog, Adult bk club, Adult literacy prog, After school storytime, Art exhibits, Audio & video playback equip for onsite use, AV serv, Bilingual assistance for Spanish patrons, Children's prog, Citizenship assistance, Computer training, Computers for patron use, Copy machines, Fax serv, Handicapped accessible, Home delivery & serv to Sr ctr & nursing homes, ILL available
Publications: Newsletter (Monthly)
Open Tues-Fri 9-6:30, Sat 10-2
Restriction: Lending limited to county residents
Friends of the Library Group

WANATAH

P WANATAH PUBLIC LIBRARY, 114 S Main St, 46390. (Mail add: PO Box 299, 46390-0299), SAN 305-1609. Tel: 219-733-9303. FAX: 219-733-2763. E-mail: wanatahl@hotmail.com. Web Site: www.wanatahlibrary.com. *Dir,* Don Parker; Staff 3 (Non-MLS 3)
Founded 1935. Pop 1,677; Circ 14,586
Library Holdings: Audiobooks 200; AV Mats 1,000; Bks on Deafness & Sign Lang 10; CDs 50; DVDs 800; e-books 1; Large Print Bks 500; Microforms 1; Bk Vols 20,000; Per Subs 30; Videos 500
Special Collections: Wanatah Mirror Newspaper Complete Coll 1896-1969
Subject Interests: Hist
Automation Activity & Vendor Info: (Acquisitions) Follett Software; (Cataloging) Follett Software; (Circulation) Follett Software; (OPAC) Follett Software; (Serials) Follett Software
Wireless access
Special Services for the Blind - Talking bk serv referral
Open Mon & Wed 11-7, Tues & Thurs 11-6, Fri 11-5, Sat 9-1

WARREN

P WARREN PUBLIC LIBRARY*, 123 E Third St, 46792. (Mail add: PO Box 327, 46792-0327), SAN 305-1617. Tel: 260-375-3450. FAX: 260-375-3450. E-mail: warrenpl@warren.lib.in.us. Web Site: www.warren.lib.in.us. *Dir,* Robert Neuenschwander; *Asst Dir,* Susan Mills; Staff 2 (MLS 1, Non-MLS 1)
Founded 1916. Pop 2,629; Circ 15,078
Library Holdings: Bk Titles 19,911; Bk Vols 21,112; Per Subs 89; Talking Bks 162; Videos 574
Special Collections: Local Newspaper, micro
Automation Activity & Vendor Info: (Cataloging) Evergreen; (Circulation) Evergreen; (OPAC) Evergreen; (Serials) Evergreen
Database Vendor: Inspire, World Book Online
Wireless access
Partic in Northern Indiana Computer Consortium for Libraries (NICCL)
Open Mon, Tues & Thurs 1-6, Wed 3-8, Fri 10-6, Sat 10-2
Friends of the Library Group

WARSAW

S KOSCIUSKO COUNTY HISTORICAL SOCIETY, Research Library & Archives, 121 N Indiana St, 46581. (Mail add: PO Box 1071, 46581-1071), SAN 373-4501. Tel: 574-269-1078. E-mail: librarian@kosciuskohistory.com. Web Site: www.kosciuskohistory.com. *Librn,* Sharon Sucec
Library Holdings: Bk Titles 32,911; Bk Vols 34,100; Per Subs 120
Special Collections: County Newspapers (except Warsaw); County Records, 1830-present
Subject Interests: Genealogy, Local hist
Wireless access
Open Wed-Sat 10-4
Friends of the Library Group

P WARSAW COMMUNITY PUBLIC LIBRARY, 310 E Main St, 46580-2882. SAN 305-1625. Tel: 574-267-6011. FAX: 574-269-7739. E-mail: info@warsawlibrary.org. Web Site: www.warsawlibrary.org. *Dir,* Ann M Zydek; E-mail: azydek@warsawlibrary.org; *Asst Dir, Cat,* Joni L Brookins; *Ch Serv,* Duane Herendeen; *Info Serv,* Dana L Owen; Staff 36 (MLS 5, Non-MLS 31)
Founded 1915. Pop 27,780; Circ 552,919
Library Holdings: Audiobooks 5,472; CDs 16,802; DVDs 6,436; e-books 5,937; e-journals 10; Large Print Bks 4,544; Bk Vols 157,306; Per Subs 268
Special Collections: Old & Current Local Papers, microfilms
Subject Interests: Genealogy, Local hist
Automation Activity & Vendor Info: (Acquisitions) SirsiDynix; (Cataloging) SirsiDynix; (Circulation) SirsiDynix; (ILL) OCLC; (OPAC) SirsiDynix; (Serials) SirsiDynix
Wireless access
Function: Activity rm, Art exhibits, Audiobks via web, Bk club(s), Bks on CD, Chess club, Computers for patron use, Copy machines, Digital talking bks, Electronic databases & coll, Fax serv, Genealogy discussion group, Handicapped accessible, Holiday prog, Homebound delivery serv, ILL

available, Magazines, Mango lang, Microfiche/film & reading machines, Movies, Music CDs, Online cat, OverDrive digital audio bks, Photocopying/Printing, Prog for adults, Prog for children & young adult, Pub access computers, Ref serv available, Scanner, Senior outreach, Spanish lang bks, Story hour, Study rm, Summer & winter reading prog, Tax forms, Telephone ref, Web-catalog, Wheelchair accessible, Writing prog
Publications: Check It Out (Newsletter)
Partic in Midwest Collaborative for Library Services (MCLS)
Open Mon & Tues 9-8, Wed-Fri 9-6, Sat 10-2

WASHINGTON

P WASHINGTON CARNEGIE PUBLIC LIBRARY*, 300 W Main St, 47501-2698. SAN 305-1633. Tel: 812-254-4586. FAX: 812-254-4585. E-mail: info@washingtonpubliclibrary.org. Web Site: www.washingtonpubliclibrary.org. *Dir,* Teresa Heidenreich; Tel: 812-254-4586, Ext 222, E-mail: teresah@washingtonpubliclibrary.org; *Ref Librn,* Elizabeth Dowling; E-mail: libbyd@washingtonpubliclibrary.org; *Youth Serv Librn,* Lori Osmon; E-mail: lorio@washingtonpubliclibrary.org; *Mgr, Prog & Outreach,* Rick Chambon. Subject Specialists: *Acctg, Admin, Human resource mgt,* Teresa Heidenreich; *Genealogy, Local hist,* Elizabeth Dowling; *Prog,* Lori Osmon; *Prog,* Rick Chambon; Staff 5 (MLS 3, Non-MLS 2)
Founded 1902. Pop 11,509; Circ 137,000
Jan 2013-Dec 2013 Income (Main Library and Branch(s)) $413,604, State $24,494, Locally Generated Income $337,408, Other $51,702. Mats Exp $55,000, Books $29,000, Per/Ser (Incl. Access Fees) $6,500, AV Mat $11,000, Electronic Ref Mat (Incl. Access Fees) $8,500. Sal $216,500 (Prof $154,220)
Library Holdings: Audiobooks 1,267; Bks on Deafness & Sign Lang 16; Braille Volumes 2; CDs 543; DVDs 658; e-books 10,816; Large Print Bks 647; Bk Titles 44,105; Per Subs 75; Videos 820
Special Collections: Daviess County Indiana History
Subject Interests: Local hist
Automation Activity & Vendor Info: (Acquisitions) Follett Software; (Cataloging) Follett Software; (Circulation) Follett Software; (OPAC) Follett Software
Database Vendor: Gale Cengage Learning, Inspire, Overdrive, Inc, ProQuest
Wireless access
Function: Ref & res
Partic in Midwest Collaborative for Library Services (MCLS)
Open Mon & Tues 10-8, Wed & Thurs 10-6, Fri 10-5, Sat 10-2
Restriction: Circ to mem only
Friends of the Library Group
Branches: 1
PLAINVILLE BRANCH, 858 Second St, Plainville, 47568. (Mail add: PO Box 8, Plainville, 47568-0008). Tel: 812-687-7271. FAX: 812-687-7271. *In Charge,* Rita Tribby
Library Holdings: Bk Vols 4,000
Open Mon-Wed 9-5, Thurs 2-6, Sat 9-1

WATERLOO

P WATERLOO-GRANT TOWNSHIP PUBLIC LIBRARY*, 300 S Wayne St, 46793-0707. SAN 305-1641. Tel: 260-837-4491. FAX: 260-837-9148. E-mail: waterloo@waterloo.lib.in.us. Web Site: www.waterloo.lib.in.us. *Dir,* Linda Dunn; *Ch,* Sallie Pease; Staff 2 (Non-MLS 2)
Founded 1913. Pop 3,100; Circ 51,000
Library Holdings: Audiobooks 1,510; AV Mats 2,030; Bk Vols 28,000; Per Subs 100
Automation Activity & Vendor Info: (Acquisitions) Evergreen; (Cataloging) Evergreen; (Circulation) Evergreen; (OPAC) Evergreen
Wireless access
Partic in Evergreen Indiana Consortium
Open Mon-Thurs 9-8, Fri 9-5, Sat 9-3 (9-12 Summer)
Friends of the Library Group

WAVELAND

P WAVELAND-BROWN TOWNSHIP PUBLIC LIBRARY*, 115 E Green, 47989. (Mail add: PO Box 158, 47989-0158), SAN 305-165X. Tel: 765-435-2700. FAX: 765-435-2434. *Dir,* Suzie Baldwin; E-mail: suzie_baldwin@sbcglobal.net; *Asst Librn,* Sandra L Greene; Staff 2 (Non-MLS 2)
Founded 1916. Pop 1,750; Circ 18,000
Library Holdings: AV Mats 1,000; Large Print Bks 300; Bk Vols 13,000; Per Subs 50; Talking Bks 150
Open Mon 9-5, Tues & Thurs 1-5 & 6:30-8, Wed & Fri 1-5, Sat 9:30-12:30

WEST LAFAYETTE

S INDIANA VETERAN'S HOME*, Lawrie Library, 3851 North River Rd, 47906. SAN 371-6384. Tel: 765-463-1502, Ext 8654. *Librn,* Sonya Hill; Tel: 765-463-1502, Ext 8200; Staff 2 (MLS 1, Non-MLS 1)
Library Holdings: Bk Titles 11,740; Bk Vols 12,390; Per Subs 47
Open Mon-Fri 8:30-4

C PURDUE UNIVERSITY LIBRARIES*, 504 W State St, 47907-2058. SAN 341-7158. Tel: 765-494-2900. Interlibrary Loan Service Tel: 765-494-2800. FAX: 765-494-0156. Web Site: www.lib.purdue.edu. *Dean of Libr,* Dr James L Mullins; E-mail: jmullins@purdue.edu; *Assoc Dean, Acad Affairs,* Beth McNeil; Tel: 765-496-2261, E-mail: memcneil@purdue.edu; *Assoc Dean, Digital Prog & Info Access,* Paul J Bracke; Tel: 765-496-3606, E-mail: pbracke@purdue.edu; *Assoc Dean, Planning & Admin,* Nancy S Hewison; E-mail: nhewison@purdue.edu; *Assoc Dean, Res,* D Scott Brandt; Tel: 765-494-2889, E-mail: techman@purdue.edu; *ILL,* Amy Winks; E-mail: ill@purdue.edu; Staff 194 (MLS 84, Non-MLS 110)
Founded 1874. Enrl 40,090; Fac 2,743; Highest Degree: Doctorate
Jul 2007-Jun 2008. Mats Exp $10,580,220, Books $1,447,270, Per/Ser (Incl. Access Fees) $7,022,039. Sal $11,043,835 (Prof $5,891,096)
Library Holdings: Bk Vols 2,509,158; Per Subs 40,094
Special Collections: Aviation, Women Pilots, History of Flight (The George Palmer Putnam Coll of Amelia Earhart Papers); Design of The Golden Gate Bridge (Charles A Ellis Papers); Economic History (Krannert Special Coll); English & American Literature (George Ade Manuscripts, Charles Major Manuscripts); History of Engineering (Goss Coll, Andrey A Potter Papers); Industrial Management, Home Economics, Time & Motion Studies (Frank & Lillian Gilbreth Papers); Political Cartoons (John T McCutcheon Coll); Psychedelics (Psychoactive Substances Research Coll); Space Exploration (Neil Armstrong Papers, Janice Voss Papers, Roy Bridges Papers); Typography & Book Design (Bruce Rogers Coll-Anna Embree Baker Rogers Coll). State Document Depository; UN Document Depository; US Document Depository
Database Vendor: American Chemical Society, Cambridge Scientific Abstracts, EBSCOhost, Elsevier MDL, Factiva.com, Gale Cengage Learning, IEEE (Institute of Electrical & Electronics Engineers), IHS, ISI Web of Knowledge, JSTOR, Lexi-Comp, LexisNexis, Newsbank, OCLC FirstSearch, OVID Technologies, ProQuest, Springer-Verlag, Wiley, Wilson - Wilson Web
Wireless access
Partic in Academic Libraries of Indiana; Association of Research Libraries (ARL); Midwest Collaborative for Library Services (MCLS); OCLC Online Computer Library Center, Inc
Departmental Libraries:
AVIATION TECHNOLOGY, Terminal Bldg 163, 47907-2058, SAN 341-7182. Tel: 765-494-7640. FAX: 765-494-0156. E-mail: avtlib@purdue.edu. Web Site: www.lib.purdue.edu/avte/index.html. *Librn,* Dania Remaly; E-mail: dremaly@purdue.edu
Open Mon-Thurs 8-7, Fri 8-6, Sat & Sun 1-5
EARTH & ATMOSPHERIC SCIENCES, Civil Engineering Bldg, Rm 2215, 550 Stadium Mall Dr, 47907-2058, SAN 341-7360. Tel: 765-494-3264. FAX: 765-496-1210. E-mail: easlib@purdue.edu. Web Site: www.lib.purdue.edu/eas/index.html. *Librn,* Michael Fosmire; Tel: 765-494-2858, E-mail: fosmire@purdue.edu
Open Mon-Thurs (Winter) 8am-10pm, Fri 8-6, Sat 1-10; Mon-Fri (Summer) 8-5
JOHN W HICKS UNDERGRADUATE LIBRARY, Hicks Undergraduate Library, Ground Flr, 504 W State St, 47907-2058, SAN 341-7166. Tel: 765-494-9153. Reference Tel: 765-494-6733. FAX: 765-494-6744. E-mail: ugrl@purdue.edu. Web Site: www.lib.purdue.edu/ugrl. *Head of Libr,* Doan Tomalee; Tel: 765-494-6728, E-mail: tdoan@purdue.edu
Open Mon-Thurs 7am-2am, Fri 7-6, Sun 11am-2am
HUMANITIES, SOCIAL SCIENCE & EDUCATION LIBRARY, Stewart Ctr 135, 504 W State St, 47907-2058, SAN 341-7336. Tel: 765-494-2831. FAX: 765-494-9007. E-mail: hsselib@purdue.edu. Web Site: www.lib.purdue.edu/hsse/index.html. *Head of Libr,* Tomalee Doan; E-mail: tdoan@purdue.edu
Open Mon-Thurs 8am-Midnight, Fri 8-6, Sat 11-5, Sun 11-Midnight
LIFE SCIENCES, Lilly Hall of Life Sciences, Rm 2400, 915 W State St, 47907-2058. (Mail add: Purdue University Libraries - LIFE, 504 W State St, 47907-2058), SAN 341-7425. Tel: 765-494-2910. E-mail: lifelib@purdue.edu. Web Site: www.lib.purdue.edu/life. *Head of Libr,* Vicki Killion; Tel: 765-494-1417, E-mail: vkillion@purdue.edu; Staff 8 (MLS 4, Non-MLS 4)
Enrl 40,000; Highest Degree: Doctorate
Open Mon-Thurs 8am-10pm, Fri 8-5, Sat 1-5, Sun 1-10
MANAGEMENT & ECONOMICS, Krannert Bldg, 2nd Flr, 403 W State St, 47907-2058, SAN 341-7395. Tel: 765-494-2920. Circulation Tel: 765-494-2919. FAX: 765-494-2923. E-mail: kranlib@purdue.edu. Web Site: www.lib.purdue.edu/mel. *Head, Mgt & Econ Libr,* Tomalee Doan; Tel: 765-494-2928, E-mail: tdoan@purdue.edu

MATHEMATICAL SCIENCES, Mathematical Sciences Bldg 311, 105 N University St, 47907-2058, SAN 341-745X. Tel: 765-494-2855. FAX: 765-494-0548. E-mail: mathlib@purdue.edu. Web Site: www.lib.purdue.edu/math. *Librn,* Stewart Saunders; E-mail: ssaunder@purdue.edu
Open Mon-Thurs 8am-10pm, Fri 8-6, Sat 1-5, Sun 1-10

M G MELLON LIBRARY OF CHEMISTRY, Wetherill Lab of Chemistry Bldg, Rm 301, 47907-1333, SAN 341-7484. Tel: 765-494-2862. *Librn,* Jeremy Garritano

CM PHARMACY, NURSING & HEALTH SCIENCES, Heine Pharmacy Bldg 272, 575 Stadium Mall Dr, 47907-2058, SAN 341-7514. Tel: 765-494-1416. E-mail: pharlib@purdue.edu. Web Site: www.lib.purdue.edu/pnhs. *Head of Libr,* Vicki Killion; Tel: 765-494-1417, E-mail: vkillion@purdue.edu

PHYSICS, Physics Bldg, Rm 290, 47907-1321, SAN 341-7549. Tel: 765-494-2858. FAX: 765-494-0706. E-mail: physlib@purdue.edu. Web Site: www.lib.purdue.edu/phys. *Librn,* Michael Fosmire; Tel: 765-494-2859, E-mail: fosmire@purdue.edu
Open Mon-Thurs (Winter) 8am-10pm, Fri 8-6, Sat 1-5, Sun 1-10; Mon-Fri (Summer) 8-5

SIEGESMUND ENGINEERING LIBRARY, Potter Ctr 160, 500 Central Dr, 47907-2058, SAN 341-7301. Tel: 765-494-2869. Reference Tel: 765-494-2873. FAX: 765-496-3572. E-mail: enginlib@purdue.edu. Web Site: www.lib.purdue.edu/engr. *Head of Libr,* Michael Fosmire; Tel: 765-494-2859, E-mail: fosmire@purdue.edu
Open Mon-Thurs 8am-Midnight, Fri 8-6, Sat 11-5, Sun 11am-Midnight

CM VETERINARY MEDICAL, Lynn Hall of Veterinary Medicine 1133, 625 Harrison St, 47907-2058, SAN 341-7603. Tel: 765-494-2853. E-mail: vetmlib@purdue.edu. *Librn,* Gretchen Stephens; Tel: 765-494-2852, E-mail: gms@purdue.edu
Partic in Center for Research Libraries
Open Mon-Thurs (Winter) 8am-Midnight, Fri 8-6, Sat 11-5, Sun 11am-Midnight; Mon, Tues & Thurs (Summer) 8-8, Wed 8am-10pm, Fri 8-5, Sat & Sun 1-5

P WEST LAFAYETTE PUBLIC LIBRARY*, 208 W Columbia St, 47906. SAN 305-1676. Tel: 765-743-2261. FAX: 765-743-0540. E-mail: refdesk@wlaf.lib.in.us. Web Site: www.westlafayettepubliclibrary.org. *Dir,* Nick Schenkel; E-mail: nick@wlaf.lib.in.us; *Cat,* Jane Dolan; *Ch Serv,* Pam Koehler; *Circ,* Ruth Cushman; *Circ,* Phyllis Heath; *Ref & Info Serv, Web Coordr,* Nancy Hartman; Staff 12 (MLS 3, Non-MLS 9)
Founded 1922. Pop 28,787; Circ 308,613
Library Holdings: AV Mats 4,834; Bk Titles 116,421; Bk Vols 118,111; Per Subs 484; Videos 598
Special Collections: Cancer Coll; Children's Literature Award Winners (Dickey Coll); Cookbooks (Reisner Coll); ESL/English as a Second Language Coll; Foreign Language Coll (Chinese, Korean, Hindi & Other Languages); Large Print Books Coll; Young Adult & Adult Graphic Novels
Automation Activity & Vendor Info: (Acquisitions) TLC (The Library Corporation); (Cataloging) TLC (The Library Corporation); (OPAC) TLC (The Library Corporation)
Wireless access
Publications: Friend's (Newsletter)
Partic in Midwest Collaborative for Library Services (MCLS); Wabash Valley Area Libr Servs Authority
Special Services for the Deaf - Staff with knowledge of sign lang; TDD equip
Open Mon & Tues 10-9, Wed & Thurs 10-8, Fri 10-6, Sat 10-5, Sun 1-5
Friends of the Library Group

WEST LEBANON

P WEST LEBANON-PIKE TOWNSHIP PUBLIC LIBRARY*, 200 N High St, 47991. (Mail add: PO Box 277, 47991-0277), SAN 376-5377. Tel: 765-893-4605. FAX: 765-893-4605. E-mail: westleblibrary@hotmail.com. Web Site: www.westlebanon.lib.in.us. *Dir,* Terri Wargo; Staff 1 (Non-MLS 1)
Founded 1916. Pop 1,185; Circ 9,624
Jan 2010-Dec 2010. Mats Exp $14,305, Books $11,937, Per/Ser (Incl. Access Fees) $1,057, AV Mat $1,311. Sal $43,500 (Prof $33,000)
Library Holdings: CDs 163; DVDs 767; Microforms 6; Bk Titles 13,303; Per Subs 38
Database Vendor: Inspire
Wireless access
Function: Magnifiers for reading, Notary serv, Photocopying/Printing, Pub access computers, Summer reading prog, VHS videos
Open Mon & Wed 11-7, Tues, Thurs & Fri 11-5, Sat 9-2

WEST TERRE HAUTE

R FIRST BAPTIST CHURCH OF WEST TERRE HAUTE LIBRARY*, 205 S Fifth, 47885. (Mail add: PO Box 126, 47885), SAN 305-1293. Tel: 812-533-2016. E-mail: libraryfbcwth@gmail.com. *Librn,* Ruth Ridener; *Librn,* Stardust Watson; *Circ,* Dale Marshall; *Libr Tech,* Paul Watson; Staff 5 (Non-MLS 5)
Founded 1966
Library Holdings: Audiobooks 5; AV Mats 20; Bks on Deafness & Sign Lang 2; Braille Volumes 1; CDs 7; DVDs 7; Bk Titles 6,500; Bk Vols 6,605; Videos 40
Subject Interests: Christianity, Fiction, Missions & missionaries, Music, Relig
Automation Activity & Vendor Info: (Cataloging) JayWil Software Development, Inc; (Circulation) JayWil Software Development, Inc
Database Vendor: JayWil Software Development, Inc
Function: AV serv
Open Wed 6:30pm-9pm, Sun 9-12 & 5:30-7:30

WESTFIELD

P WESTFIELD WASHINGTON PUBLIC LIBRARY*, 333 W Hoover St, 46074-9283. SAN 305-1692. Tel: 317-896-9391. FAX: 317-896-3702. Web Site: www.wwpl.lib.in.us. *Dir,* Sheryl A Sollars; E-mail: ssollars@wwpl.lib.in.us; *Asst Dir,* Sandra M Rowland; E-mail: srowland@wwpl.lib.in.us; *Ch Mgr,* Vicki J M Parker; E-mail: vparker@wwpl.lib.in.us; *Info/Ref Serv Mgr,* Nancy Lee; E-mail: nlee@wwpl.lib.in.us; Staff 42 (MLS 9, Non-MLS 33)
Founded 1901. Pop 18,500; Circ 486,803
Library Holdings: Audiobooks 5,777; CDs 5,541; DVDs 7,068; Bk Vols 121,315; Per Subs 266; Videos 5,076
Special Collections: American Quaker Genealogy Coll
Automation Activity & Vendor Info: (Cataloging) Evergreen; (Circulation) Evergreen; (OPAC) Evergreen
Database Vendor: Newsbank
Wireless access
Publications: Friends (Newsletter)
Partic in Midwest Collaborative for Library Services (MCLS)
Open Mon-Thurs 9:30-8, Fri 9:30-6, Sat 9:30-5
Friends of the Library Group

WESTVILLE

C PURDUE UNIVERSITY NORTH CENTRAL LIBRARY*, Library-Student-Faculty Bldg, 2nd Flr, 1401 S US Hwy 421, 46391. SAN 305-1706. Tel: 219-785-5248. Administration Tel: 219-785-5249. FAX: 219-785-5501. Web Site: www.pnc.edu/ls. *Libr Dir,* KR Johnson; E-mail: kjohnson@pnc.edu; *Tech Serv Librn,* Tricia Jauquet; Tel: 219-785-5234, E-mail: tjauquet@pnc.edu; Staff 6 (MLS 3, Non MLS 3)
Founded 1967. Enrl 3,500; Fac 95; Highest Degree: Master
Library Holdings: Bk Vols 84,900; Per Subs 390
Open Mon-Thurs 7:30am-8:30pm, Fri 7:30-5, Sat 9:30-2:30
Friends of the Library Group

S WESTVILLE CORRECTIONAL FACILITY*, Resident Library, 5501 S 1100 W, 46391. SAN 341-7662. Tel: 219-785-2511, Ext 4672. FAX: 219-785-4864. Web Site: www.in.gov/idoc/2401.htm. *Dir, Libr Serv,* Brad Stigler; Staff 1 (MLS 1)
Founded 1951
Library Holdings: Bk Titles 28,918; Bk Vols 29,100; Per Subs 90
Automation Activity & Vendor Info: (Cataloging) Follett Software; (Circulation) Follett Software
Partic in Midwest Collaborative for Library Services (MCLS)

P WESTVILLE-NEW DURHAM TOWNSHIP PUBLIC LIBRARY*, 153 Main St, 46391. (Mail add: PO Box 789, 46391-0789), SAN 305-1714. Tel: 219-785-2015. FAX: 219-785-2015. E-mail: wvpubliclibrary@yahoo.com. Web Site: westville.lib.in.us. *Dir,* Courtney Cassler; E-mail: director@westville.lib.in.us; Staff 3 (Non-MLS 3)
Founded 1915. Pop 4,095; Circ 23,498
Library Holdings: Large Print Bks 110; Bk Vols 18,140; Per Subs 52; Talking Bks 680; Videos 1,450
Subject Interests: Cemetery, Veterans
Wireless access
Open Mon 2-8, Tues-Thurs 1-6, Sat 10-2

WHITING

CR CALUMET COLLEGE OF SAINT JOSEPH*, Specker Memorial Library, 2400 New York Ave, 46394. SAN 304-9248. Tel: 219-473-4373. FAX: 219-473-4259. E-mail: library@ccsj.edu, reference@ccsj.edu. Web Site: www.ccsj.edu/library. *Interim Dir,* Marcia Keith; Tel: 219-473-4375, E-mail: mkeith@ccsj.edu; *Electronic Res Librn,* Richard O'Boyle; Tel: 219-473-4282, E-mail: roboyle@ccsj.edu; *Circ Supvr,* Robert Bussie; Tel: 219-473-4332, E-mail: rbussie@ccsj.edu; *Ref Coordr,* Joe Coates; Tel: 219-473-4376, E-mail: jcoates@ccsj.edu; Staff 6 (MLS 3, Non-MLS 3)
Enrl 1,300; Fac 60; Highest Degree: Master
Library Holdings: AV Mats 6,580; Bk Vols 110,000; Per Subs 74
Automation Activity & Vendor Info: (Acquisitions) Ex Libris Group; (Cataloging) Ex Libris Group; (Circulation) Ex Libris Group; (ILL) Ex Libris Group; (OPAC) Ex Libris Group; (Serials) Ex Libris Group
Database Vendor: EBSCOhost, OCLC FirstSearch, ProQuest, Westlaw

Function: Adult bk club, Art exhibits, Handicapped accessible, ILL available, Music CDs, Online searches, Orientations, Photocopying/Printing, Prog for adults, Ref serv available, Referrals accepted, Spoken cassettes & CDs, Spoken cassettes & DVDs, VCDs, VHS videos, Workshops
Open Mon, Wed & Thurs 9-7, Tues 9-9, Fri 9-5, Sat 9-1
Restriction: Open to pub by appt only, Open to students, fac & staff

P WHITING PUBLIC LIBRARY*, 1735 Oliver St, 46394-1794. SAN 305-1722. Tel: 219-473-4700, 219-659-0269. Circulation Tel: 219-473-4700, Ext 10. Interlibrary Loan Service Tel: 219-473-4700, Ext 20. Reference Tel: 219-473-4700, Ext 14. Administration Tel: 219-473-4700, Ext 11. FAX: 219-659-5833. E-mail: wpl@whiting.lib.in.us. Web Site: www.whiting.lib.in.us. *Dir,* Rachael DeLuna; *Asst Dir,* Mary Kershner; *Head, Tech Serv,* Deanna Valentine; Tel: 219-473-4700, Ext 15; *Ch Serv, YA Librn,* Inglada Montserrat; Tel: 219-473-4700, Ext 13; Staff 3 (MLS 3)
Founded 1906. Pop 17,000; Circ 140,000
Library Holdings: AV Mats 4,070; CDs 1,825; DVDs 336; Bk Vols 90,687; Per Subs 245; Talking Bks 1,120; Videos 3,047
Special Collections: Books on Early Settlement of Lake County, Indiana (prehistoric period to 1800's); Local City Directory 1900's; Local History Room; Whiting, Indiana (early 1900's)
Subject Interests: Consumer, Finance
Automation Activity & Vendor Info: (Acquisitions) SirsiDynix; (Cataloging) SirsiDynix; (Circulation) SirsiDynix; (ILL) OCLC; (OPAC) SirsiDynix; (Serials) SirsiDynix
Database Vendor: OCLC FirstSearch
Function: Homebound delivery serv, ILL available
Publications: The WPL Newsletter (Quarterly)
Partic in Midwest Collaborative for Library Services (MCLS)
Open Mon-Thurs 9-8, Fri & Sat 9-5
Friends of the Library Group

S WHITING-ROBERTSDALE HISTORICAL SOCIETY MUSEUM*, 1610 119th St, 46394. SAN 371-6570. Tel: 219-659-1432. *Curator,* Mary Skvara; Staff 1 (Non-MLS 1)
Library Holdings: Bk Titles 1,180; Bk Vols 1,310; Per Subs 21
Subject Interests: Local hist
Open Tues & Sat 1-4

WILLIAMSPORT

P WILLIAMSPORT-WASHINGTON TOWNSHIP PUBLIC LIBRARY*, 28 E Second St, 47993-1299. SAN 305-1730. Tel: 765-762-6555. FAX: 765-762-6588. Web Site: www.wwtpl.lib.in.us. *Dir,* Christopher Brown; E-mail: cbrown@wwtpl.lib.in.us; Staff 7 (MLS 2, Non-MLS 5)
Founded 1915. Pop 2,384; Circ 45,690
Jan 2010-Dec 2010 Income $186,950. Mats Exp $30,000, Books $14,000, Per/Ser (Incl. Access Fees) $3,000, AV Equip $1,000, AV Mat $12,000. Sal $113,225 (Prof $34,000)
Library Holdings: Audiobooks 1,728; AV Mats 7; Bks on Deafness & Sign Lang 23; CDs 828; DVDs 2,269; Large Print Bks 734; Bk Vols 28,353; Per Subs 83; Videos 518
Automation Activity & Vendor Info: (Acquisitions) Follett Software; (Cataloging) Follett Software; (Circulation) Follett Software; (Course Reserve) Follett Software; (OPAC) Follett Software; (Serials) Follett Software
Database Vendor: Baker & Taylor
Wireless access
Function: Bks on CD, CD-ROM, Children's prog, Computer training, Computers for patron use, Copy machines, Digital talking bks, Distance learning, Doc delivery serv, e-mail & chat, E-Reserves, Electronic databases & coll, Equip loans & repairs, Exhibits, Fax serv, Free DVD rentals, Genealogy discussion group, Handicapped accessible, Holiday prog, Home delivery & serv to Sr ctr & nursing homes, Homebound delivery serv, ILL available, Instruction & testing, Jail serv, Large print keyboards, Learning ctr, Magnifiers for reading, Mail & tel request accepted, Music CDs, Newsp ref libr, Online cat, Online ref, Online searches, Outreach serv, Photocopying/Printing, Preschool outreach, Prog for adults, Prog for children & young adult, Pub access computers, Ref & res, Ref serv available, Ref serv in person, Referrals accepted, Scanner, Senior computer classes, Senior outreach, Spoken cassettes & CDs, Spoken cassettes & DVDs, Story hour, Summer reading prog, Tax forms, Web-catalog, Wheelchair accessible, Writing prog
Partic in Midwest Collaborative for Library Services (MCLS)
Special Services for the Deaf - Accessible learning ctr; Closed caption videos
Special Services for the Blind - Accessible computers; Audio mat; Bks available with recordings; Bks on CD; Digital talking bk; Home delivery serv; Large print bks; Low vision equip; Playaways (bks on MP3); Recorded bks; Sound rec; Talking bks
Open Mon & Fri 10-5, Tues & Thurs 10-7, Wed 10-8, Sat 9-2
Friends of the Library Group

WINAMAC

P PULASKI COUNTY PUBLIC LIBRARY*, 121 S Riverside Dr, 46996-1596. SAN 341-7697. Tel: 574-946-3432. FAX: 574-946-6598. TDD: 574-946-6981. Web Site: www.pulaski-libraries.lib.in.us. *Exec Dir,* MacKenzie Inez Ledley; Staff 4 (MLS 1, Non-MLS 3)
Founded 1905. Pop 10,646; Circ 113,937
Jul 2009-Jun 2010 Income (Main Library and Branch(s)) $440,190, County $87,718, Other $352,472. Mats Exp $51,011, Books $34,529, Per/Ser (Incl. Access Fees) $4,582, AV Mat $11,900. Sal $238,005
Library Holdings: Audiobooks 2,508; AV Mats 2,343; CDs 1,065; DVDs 2,706; Large Print Bks 935; Bk Titles 57,534; Bk Vols 47,832; Per Subs 154
Special Collections: Local Newspapers 1869-, micro. Oral History
Subject Interests: Genealogy, Indiana, Local hist
Automation Activity & Vendor Info: (Acquisitions) AmLib Library Management System
Wireless access
Function: Adult bk club, After school storytime, Bk reviews (Group), Bks on cassette, Bks on CD, CD-ROM, Children's prog, Computer training, Computers for patron use, Copy machines, e-mail & chat, e-mail serv, E-Reserves, Electronic databases & coll, Exhibits, Free DVD rentals, Genealogy discussion group, Handicapped accessible, Holiday prog, Home delivery & serv to Sr ctr & nursing homes, Homebound delivery serv, ILL available, Jail serv, Magnifiers for reading, Masonic res mat, Music CDs, Newsp ref libr, Notary serv, Outreach serv, Photocopying/Printing, Preschool outreach, Prog for adults, Prog for children & young adult, Provide serv for the mentally ill, Pub access computers, Ref serv in person, Senior outreach, Serves mentally handicapped consumers, Spoken cassettes & CDs, Spoken cassettes & DVDs, Story hour, Summer & winter reading prog, Tax forms, Teen prog, Telephone ref, VHS videos
Partic in Midwest Collaborative for Library Services (MCLS)
Special Services for the Deaf - TDD equip
Open Mon-Thurs 9-7, Fri 9-6, Sat 9-4
Branches: 1
MEDARYVILLE BRANCH, 510 E Main, Medaryville, 47957, SAN 341-7727. Tel: 219-843-3021. FAX: 219-843-3024.
Founded 1965
Library Holdings: Audiobooks 330; CDs 362; DVDs 973; Large Print Bks 241; Bk Titles 4,726; Per Subs 33
Open Mon, Wed & Fri 12-6, Tues & Thurs 2-7, Sat 12-3

WINCHESTER

GL RANDOLPH CIRCUIT COURT*, Law Library, 100 S Main, 47394. SAN 305-1749. Tel: 765-584-0465, Ext 230. FAX: 765-584-7186. *Librn,* Mike O'Neal; Tel: 765-584-4128; Staff 1 (MLS 1)
Library Holdings: Bk Titles 750; Bk Vols 1,000
Subject Interests: State law
Open Mon-Fri 8-4

P WINCHESTER COMMUNITY LIBRARY*, 125 N East St, 47394-1698. SAN 305-1757. Tel: 765-584-4824. FAX: 765-584-3624. E-mail: wincomlib@yahoo.com. *Dir,* Jana Barnes; *Dir, Ch Serv,* Cheryl Study; Staff 2 (Non-MLS 2)
Founded 1912. Pop 8,622; Circ 99,000
Jan 2011-Dec 2011 Income $336,367. Mats Exp $25,000. Sal $222,000
Library Holdings: AV Mats 464; DVDs 1,761; Large Print Bks 1,838; Bk Vols 53,025; Per Subs 69; Videos 2,924
Subject Interests: Abraham Lincoln
Automation Activity & Vendor Info: (Acquisitions) Baker & Taylor; (Cataloging) Evergreen; (Circulation) Evergreen; (OPAC) Evergreen
Wireless access
Function: Adult bk club, AV serv, Bks on cassette, Bks on CD, Children's prog, Computer training, Computers for patron use, Copy machines, Fax serv, Free DVD rentals, Handicapped accessible, Home delivery & serv to Sr ctr & nursing homes, Homebound delivery serv, ILL available, Magnifiers for reading, Online cat, Photocopying/Printing, Prog for adults, Prog for children & young adult, Pub access computers, Ref & res, Ref serv in person, Story hour, Summer reading prog, Tax forms, Teen prog, Telephone ref, VHS videos, Wheelchair accessible
Partic in Midwest Collaborative for Library Services (MCLS)
Open Mon-Thurs 9-8, Fri & Sat 9-5
Friends of the Library Group

WINONA LAKE

CR GRACE COLLEGE & GRACE THEOLOGICAL SEMINARY*, Morgan Library, 200 Seminary Dr, 46590. SAN 305-1765. Tel: 574-372-5100, Ext 6294. Reference Tel: 574-372-5100, Ext 6297. FAX: 574-372-5176. Web Site: www.grace.edu/resources/library. *Dir of Libr Serv,* Tonya Fawcett; Tel: 574-372-5100, Ext 6291, E-mail: fawcettl@grace.edu; *Assoc Dir, Pub & Electronic Serv,* Rhoda Palmer; E-mail: rfpalmer@grace.edu; *Assoc Dir, Tech Serv,* Steve Robbins; Tel: 574-372-5100, Ext 6292, E-mail: robbinsl@grace.edu; Staff 4 (MLS 3, Non-MLS 1)
Founded 1939. Enrl 1,401; Fac 59; Highest Degree: Doctorate

Library Holdings: AV Mats 4,626; CDs 1,426; e-books 85,502; e-journals 59,546; Microforms 24,760; Bk Titles 195,340; Bk Vols 212,194; Per Subs 204; Videos 328
Special Collections: Billy Sunday Papers Coll; Winona Lake Historical Coll; Winona Railroad Special Coll
Subject Interests: Biblical studies
Automation Activity & Vendor Info: (Acquisitions) Ex Libris Group; (Cataloging) Ex Libris Group; (Circulation) Ex Libris Group; (Course Reserve) Ex Libris Group; (ILL) Ex Libris Group; (Media Booking) Ex Libris Group; (OPAC) Ex Libris Group; (Serials) Ex Libris Group
Wireless access
Partic in Christian Library Consortium; Midwest Collaborative for Library Services (MCLS); OCLC Online Computer Library Center, Inc; Private Academic Library Network of Indiana (PALNI)
Open Mon-Thurs 8:30am-10pm, Fri 8:30-5, Sat 10-7

WOLCOTT

P WOLCOTT COMMUNITY PUBLIC LIBRARY*, 101 E North St, 47995. (Mail add: PO Box 376, 47995-0376), SAN 305-1773. Tel: 219-279-2695. FAX: 219-279-2692. E-mail: wolcottlibrary@mywcpl.com. Web Site: www.mywcpl.com. *Dir,* Deanna Dreblow; Staff 33 (Non-MLS 33)
Founded 1923. Pop 2,193; Circ 10,766
Library Holdings: Audiobooks 786; CDs 32; DVDs 575; e-books 11,368; Large Print Bks 300; Bk Titles 24,522; Per Subs 18; Videos 645
Automation Activity & Vendor Info: (Acquisitions) Evergreen; (Cataloging) Evergreen; (Circulation) Evergreen; (Course Reserve) Evergreen; (OPAC) Evergreen; (Serials) DEMCO
Database Vendor: Overdrive, Inc
Wireless access
Function: Bks on cassette, Bks on CD, Children's prog, Computers for patron use, Copy machines, Homebound delivery serv, ILL available, Music CDs, Online cat, OverDrive digital audio bks, Photocopying/Printing, Preschool outreach, Preschool reading prog, Prog for adults, Prog for children & young adult, Pub access computers, Ref serv available, Senior outreach, Spoken cassettes & CDs, Spoken cassettes & DVDs, Story hour, Summer & winter reading prog, Summer reading prog, Tax forms, Teen prog, VHS videos, Winter reading prog
Open Mon 1-7, Tues 10-7, Thurs & Fri 10-5, Sat 9-1
Restriction: Access for corporate affiliates

WORTHINGTON

P WORTHINGTON-JEFFERSON TOWNSHIP PUBLIC LIBRARY*, 26 N Commercial St, 47471-1415. SAN 305-1781. Tel: 812-875-3815. FAX: 812-875-3815. E-mail: wjtpl@yahoo.com. *Dir,* Andrea Fuller; Staff 4 (MLS 2, Non-MLS 2)
Founded 1918. Pop 2,409; Circ 21,610
Jan 2008-Dec 2008. Mats Exp $8,126, Books $7,626, Per/Ser (Incl. Access Fees) $500
Library Holdings: AV Mats 1,200; Bk Vols 18,467; Per Subs 30; Videos 1,100
Automation Activity & Vendor Info: (Acquisitions) SirsiDynix; (Cataloging) SirsiDynix; (OPAC) SirsiDynix
Partic in Stone Hills Area Libr Servs Authority
Open Mon & Wed Noon-5, Tues & Thurs Noon-8, Fri 9-5, Sat 9-1

YORKTOWN

P YORKTOWN-MOUNT PLEASANT TOWNSHIP PUBLIC LIBRARY*, 8920 W Adaline St, 47396. Tel: 765-759-9723. FAX: 765-759-7260. Web Site: yorktownlib.org. *Dir,* Liz Rozelle; Staff 5 (MLS 1, Non-MLS 4)
Founded 2001. Pop 12,600; Circ 141,700
Library Holdings: Audiobooks 1,528; Bks on Deafness & Sign Lang 42; CDs 1,065; DVDs 4,753; Electronic Media & Resources 6; Large Print Bks 1,266; Bk Titles 39,132; Bk Vols 40,755; Per Subs 130; Talking Bks 1,528
Special Collections: Yorktown, Mount Pleasant Township & Delaware County Local History Coll
Automation Activity & Vendor Info: (Acquisitions) Follett Software; (Cataloging) Follett Software; (Circulation) Follett Software; (OPAC) Follett Software; (Serials) EBSCO Online
Database Vendor: Grolier Online, Inspire
Wireless access
Function: Bks on CD, Children's prog, Computer training, Computers for patron use, Copy machines, Digital talking bks, Electronic databases & coll, Exhibits, Free DVD rentals, Handicapped accessible, Holiday prog, Home delivery & serv to Sr ctr & nursing homes, Homebound delivery serv, ILL available, Mus passes, Music CDs, Notary serv, Online cat, Outreach serv, Photocopying/Printing, Prog for adults, Prog for children & young adult, Pub access computers, Ref serv available, Scanner, Senior computer classes, Story hour, Summer reading prog, Tax forms, Teen prog, VHS videos, Web-catalog, Wheelchair accessible
Publications: The Yorktown Quarterly (Newsletter)
Partic in Midwest Collaborative for Library Services (MCLS)
Special Services for the Deaf - Bks on deafness & sign lang
Special Services for the Blind - Bks on cassette; Bks on CD; Home delivery serv; Large print bks
Open Mon & Wed 10-5:30, Tues & Thurs 10-8, Fri 10-6, Sat 10-4
Restriction: Non-resident fee, Residents only
Friends of the Library Group

ZIONSVILLE

P HUSSEY-MAYFIELD MEMORIAL PUBLIC LIBRARY, 250 N Fifth St, 46077-1324. (Mail add: PO Box 840, 46077-0840), SAN 305-179X. Tel: 317-873-3149. Circulation Tel: 317-873-3149, Ext 11810. Interlibrary Loan Service Tel: 317-873-3149, Ext 12454. Reference Tel: 317-873-3149, Ext 12400. Administration Tel: 317-873-3149, Ext 13001. Automation Services Tel: 317-873-3149, Ext 13003. Information Services Tel: 317-873-3149, Ext 11900. FAX: 317-873-8339. Web Site: www.zionsville.lib.in.us. *Dir,* Karry Green; E-mail: karryg@zionsvillelibrary.org; *Dir, Info & Fac,* Steve Olson; E-mail: steveo@zionsvillelibrary.org; *Dir, Pub & Tech Serv,* Mary Rueff; Tel: 317-873-3149, Ext 13002, E-mail: maryr@zionsvillelibrary.org; *Circ Serv Dept Head,* Virginia Hilbert; Tel: 317-873-3149, Ext 11280, E-mail: virginiah@zionsvillelibrary.org; *Cat Librn, Dept Head, Tech Serv,* Sarah Childs; Tel: 317-873-3149, Ext 13330, E-mail: sarahc@zionsvillelibrary.org; *Teen/Adult Serv Dept Head,* Jane Ferger; Tel: 317-873-3149, Ext 12450, E-mail: janef@zionsvillelibrary.org; *Youth Serv Dept Head,* Jamie Schlenk; Tel: 317-873-3149, Ext 11650, E-mail: jamies@zionsvillelibrary.org; Staff 46 (MLS 3, Non-MLS 43)
Founded 1989. Pop 15,924; Circ 464,508
Jan 2007-Dec 2007 Income $1,708,358. Mats Exp $223,174, Books $109,136, Per/Ser (Incl. Access Fees) $10,476, AV Equip $40,637, AV Mat $59,418, Electronic Ref Mat (Incl. Access Fees) $3,507. Sal $951,839
Library Holdings: AV Mats 18,919; Bk Vols 101,480; Per Subs 260
Special Collections: Business & Investing Room
Subject Interests: Arts & crafts, Bus, Civil War, Gardening, Investment
Automation Activity & Vendor Info: (Acquisitions) OCLC Connexion; (Cataloging) Evergreen; (Circulation) Evergreen; (OPAC) Evergreen
Database Vendor: EBSCOhost, Gale Cengage Learning, Ingram Library Services, Inspire, ReferenceUSA
Wireless access
Publications: Seasons (Newsletter)
Partic in Evergreen Indiana Consortium; Lyrasis; Midwest Collaborative for Library Services (MCLS)
Open Mon-Thurs 9:30-8:30, Fri & Sat 9:30-5, Sun 1-5
Friends of the Library Group

S SULLIVANMUNCE CULTURAL CENTER*, Local History Museum & Genealogy Library, 225 W Hawthorne St, 46077. SAN 373-4528. Tel: 317-873-4900. *Exec Dir,* Cynthia Young; *Mus Dir,* Melissa Fanning; Staff 1 (MLS 1)
Library Holdings: Electronic Media & Resources 2; Bk Vols 7,000
Special Collections: Early Photographs of Zionsville & Boone County (Part of Archival Coll); Indiana Paintings including Portrait of William Zion (Part of Museum Coll); Local Newspapers on microfilm, locally compiled surname & family files (Part of Genealogy Library Coll)
Subject Interests: Genealogy, Local hist
Function: Archival coll, Computers for patron use, Electronic databases & coll, Online cat
Open Tues-Sat 10-4
Restriction: Non-circulating, Not a lending libr

Date of Statistics: FY 2012-2013
Population, 2010 U.S. Census: 3,046,355
Total Titles in Public Libraries: 13,642,394
Titles Per Capita: 4.4
Total Public Library Circulation: 28,318,507
Circulation Per Capita: 9.3
Total Public Library Income (including Grants-in-Aid): $117,451,937
Average Income: $224,145
Source of Income: Mainly public funds
Expenditures Per Capita: $48.04
Number of County & Regional Libraries: 3 county
State Aid: $2,174,229
Federal (LSTA): $1,844,037

ACKLEY

P ACKLEY PUBLIC LIBRARY*, 401 State St, 50601. SAN 305-1803. Tel: 641-847-2233. FAX: 641-847-2233. E-mail: ackleypl@mchsi.com. Web Site: www.ackley.lib.ia.us. *Ch, Dir,* Janice Miller; *Asst Librn,* Dianne Nolte
Founded 1902. Pop 1,809; Circ 19,643
Library Holdings: Bk Vols 13,468; Per Subs 51
Open Mon 10:30-5, Tues & Thurs 11-7, Wed & Fri 9-5, Sat 9-2

ADAIR

P ADAIR PUBLIC LIBRARY*, 310 Audubon, 50002. (Mail add: PO Box 276, 50002-0276), SAN 305-1811. Tel: 641-742-3323. FAX: 641-742-3323. *Dir,* Bertha Fagan; *Ch,* Joan Maas
Founded 1936. Pop 839; Circ 6,231
Library Holdings: Bk Titles 9,300; Per Subs 25
Mem of Southwest Iowa Library Services District
Open Tues & Thurs 1-5, Sat 9-1

ADEL

P ADEL PUBLIC LIBRARY*, 303 S Tenth St, 50003-1797. SAN 305-182X. Tel: 515-993-3512. FAX: 515-993-3191. Web Site: www.adelpl.org. *Dir,* Paula James; E-mail: paula@adelpl.org; *Asst Dir,* Lynne Schlaht; E-mail: lynne@adelpl.org; *Youth Serv Dir,* Laura Guth; E-mail: laura@adelpl.org
Pop 3,435; Circ 46,000
Library Holdings: Bk Titles 28,022; Per Subs 64
Mem of Central Iowa Library Services
Open Mon-Thurs 10:30-8, Fri 10:30-5:30, Sat 10:30-1:30
Friends of the Library Group

AGENCY

P AGENCY PUBLIC LIBRARY*, 104 E Main St, 52530. (Mail add: PO Box 346, 52530-0346), SAN 305-1838. Tel: 641-937-6002. FAX: 641-937-5241. E-mail: agencypubliclibrary@gmail.com. *Dir,* Kim Schwartz
Founded 1955. Pop 524; Circ 4,260
Library Holdings: Bk Vols 7,000; Per Subs 20
Special Collections: Iowa History
Open Mon 1-8, Tues & Thurs 4-8, Wed 9:30-11:30 & 4-9, Fri 4-6, Sat 8:30-11:30, Sun 2-5

AKRON

P AKRON PUBLIC LIBRARY*, 350 Reed St, 51001. (Mail add: PO Box 348, 51001-0348), SAN 305-1846. Tel: 712-568-2601. FAX: 712-568-2601. E-mail: akronlib@hickorytech.net. Web Site: www.akron.lib.ia.us. *Dir,* Jeannie Frerichs; *Asst Dir,* Roxanne Michael; *Ch, Teen Librn,* Mary Campbell
Pop 1,489; Circ 33,000
Jul 2007-Jun 2008 Income $76,667, State $650, City $60,721, County $12,496, Locally Generated Income $2,800. Mats Exp $8,672, Books $6,620, Per/Ser (Incl. Access Fees) $1,240, Micro $62, AV Mat $750. Sal $56,417
Library Holdings: CDs 60; DVDs 346; Large Print Bks 531; Bk Titles 13,000; Per Subs 62; Videos 277
Automation Activity & Vendor Info: (Acquisitions) Follett Software; (Circulation) Follett Software; (ILL) Brodart
Database Vendor: EBSCOhost, Medline
Wireless access
Function: Adult bk club, Art exhibits, Bk club(s), Bks on cassette, Bks on CD, Children's prog, Computer training, Computers for patron use, Copy machines, Fax serv, Handicapped accessible, Holiday prog, Homebound delivery serv, ILL available, Photocopying/Printing, Preschool outreach, Prog for adults, Prog for children & young adult, Pub access computers, Ref serv in person, Senior computer classes, Story hour, Summer reading prog, Tax forms, Telephone ref, VHS videos, Workshops
Mem of Northwest Iowa Library Services
Open Mon 9-6, Tues, Thurs & Fri 9:30-5:30, Wed 9:30-5:30 & 6:45-8:45, Sat 9-3

ALBERT CITY

P ALBERT CITY PUBLIC LIBRARY*, 215 Main, 50510. (Mail add: PO Box 368, 50510-0368), SAN 305-1854. Tel: 712-843-2012. FAX: 712-843-2058. Web Site: www.albertcity.lib.ia.us. *Dir,* Mary Johnson; E-mail: mjohnson@albertcity.lib.ia.us; *Asst Librn,* Kathy Landgraf; E-mail: klandgraf@albertcity.lib.ia.us
Pop 709; Circ 15,542
Library Holdings: AV Mats 683; Electronic Media & Resources 31; Bk Titles 10,429; Per Subs 36; Talking Bks 144
Automation Activity & Vendor Info: (Acquisitions) Follett Software
Mem of Northwest Iowa Library Services
Open Mon & Wed 10-12:30 & 1-6:30, Tues, Thurs & Fri 10-12:30 & 1-5:30, Sat (Winter) 8:30-11:30
Friends of the Library Group

ALBIA

P CARNEGIE-EVANS PUBLIC LIBRARY*, 203 Benton Ave E, 52531-2036. SAN 305-1862. Tel: 641-932-2469. FAX: 641-932-2469. E-mail: albialibrary@netscape.net. *Dir,* Marilyn Woods; *Asst Librn,* Betty Reeves; *Ch Serv,* Ruth Raskie; E-mail: ruthraskie631@hotmail.com
Founded 1906. Pop 3,706; Circ 173,000
Library Holdings: Bk Titles 40,000; Per Subs 25
Open Mon-Fri Noon-6, Sat 10-3

ALBION

P ALBION MUNICIPAL LIBRARY*, 400 N Main St, 50005. (Mail add: PO Box 118, 50005-0118), SAN 321-8295. Tel: 641-488-2226. FAX: 641-488-2272. E-mail: albionlib@heartofiowa.net. *Librn,* Julia E Ohrt
Founded 1982. Pop 505; Circ 29,829
Library Holdings: Bk Titles 7,458; Per Subs 10
Automation Activity & Vendor Info: (Acquisitions) Biblionix

Database Vendor: EBSCOhost, LearningExpress
Wireless access
Function: Bk club(s), Bks on cassette, Bks on CD, Children's prog, Computers for patron use, Copy machines, Exhibits, Free DVD rentals, Games & aids for the handicapped, Genealogy discussion group, Handicapped accessible, Holiday prog, Homebound delivery serv, Homework prog, Literacy & newcomer serv, Magnifiers for reading, Mail & tel request accepted, Online info literacy tutorials on the web & in blackboard, Online ref, Online searches, Preschool outreach, Pub access computers, Ref & res, Summer reading prog, VHS videos, Wheelchair accessible
Open Mon & Tues 10-6, Wed & Thurs Noon-6, Sat 10-Noon
Friends of the Library Group

ALDEN

P DR GRACE O DOANE ALDEN PUBLIC LIBRARY*, 1012 Water St, 50006. SAN 305-1870. Tel: 515-859-3820. FAX: 515-859-3919. E-mail: aldenlibrary@wmtel.net. Web Site: aldenlibrary.org. *Dir,* Janeice Murra; *Ch,* Sarah Day
Pop 905; Circ 18,023
Library Holdings: Bk Titles 12,000; Per Subs 72
Automation Activity & Vendor Info: (Cataloging) Follett Software
Wireless access
Partic in Hardin County Libr Asn
Open Mon 1:30-6:30, Tues & Fri 9-11:30 & 1:30-5:30, Sat 11-5:30
Friends of the Library Group

ALEXANDER

P ALEXANDER PUBLIC LIBRARY*, 409 Harriman St, 50420. (Mail add: PO Box 27, 50420-0027), SAN 305-1889. Tel: 641-692-3238. FAX: 641-692-3238. E-mail: alexlib@frontiernet.net. Web Site: mayors-office.town.alexander.ia.us. *Dir,* Kaye Vanness
Founded 1962. Pop 165; Circ 8,077
Library Holdings: Bk Titles 6,500; Per Subs 30
Automation Activity & Vendor Info: (Cataloging) Follett Software
Open Mon 8:30-12 & 1-5, Tues-Thurs 2:30-5, Fri 2:30-6, Sat 8:30-12

ALGONA

P ALGONA PUBLIC LIBRARY*, 210 N Phillips St, 50511. SAN 305-1897. Tel: 515-295-5476. FAX: 515-295-3307. Web Site: www.youseemore.com/NILC/AlgonaPL. *Dir,* Kyle Neugebauer; E-mail: kneugebauer@algona.lib.ia.us; *Asst Dir,* Sheila Foxhoven; E-mail: sfoxhoven@algona.lib.ia.us; Staff 3 (MLS 2, Non-MLS 1)
Founded 1904. Pop 5,741; Circ 97,900
Subject Interests: Hist, Iowa, Local hist
Automation Activity & Vendor Info: (Cataloging) TLC (The Library Corporation); (Circulation) TLC (The Library Corporation); (OPAC) TLC (The Library Corporation)
Wireless access
Open Mon-Thurs 9:30-8, Fri 9:30-5, Sat 9:30-4
Friends of the Library Group

ALLERTON

P ALLERTON PUBLIC LIBRARY*, 103 South Central Ave, 50008. (Mail add: PO Box 216, 50008-9760), SAN 305-1900. Tel: 641-873-4575. E-mail: alrtnlib@grm.net. *Librn,* Sharon Sinclair; *Ch,* Sheryl Hefner
Pop 559
Library Holdings: Bk Titles 8,500; Per Subs 10
Open Mon-Fri 2-5, Sat 9-Noon

ALLISON

P ALLISON PUBLIC LIBRARY*, 412 Third St, 50602. (Mail add: PO Box 605, 50602-0605), SAN 305-1919. Tel: 319-267-2562. FAX: 319-267-2562. Web Site: www.allison.lib.ia.us. *Dir,* Patty Hummel; E-mail: phummel@allison.lib.ia.us
Founded 1929. Pop 1,006; Circ 30,027
Library Holdings: Bk Titles 13,643; Per Subs 76
Open Mon 10-12 & 2-6, Tues & Thurs 2-7, Wed & Fri 2-6, Sat 9-3

ALTA

P ALTA COMMUNITY LIBRARY*, 1009 S Main St, 51002. SAN 305-1927. Tel: 712-200-1250. E-mail: admin@alta.lib.ia.us. Web Site: www.alta.lib.ia.us. *Dir,* Andrea Hogrefe; *Ch,* Laura Turnquist; E-mail: laura.turnquist@alta.lib.ia.us
Founded 1911. Pop 1,865
Library Holdings: Bk Titles 20,553; Per Subs 39
Automation Activity & Vendor Info: (Acquisitions) Follett Software; (Cataloging) Follett Software
Wireless access
Open Mon-Fri (Winter) 8:30-7, Sat 9-1; Mon, Wed, Fri & Sat (Summer) 9-1, Tues & Thurs 3-7

ALTA VISTA

P ALTA VISTA PUBLIC LIBRARY*, 203 S White Ave, 50603. (Mail add: PO Box 167, 50603-0167), SAN 376-6551. Tel: 641-364-6009. FAX: 641-364-6009. E-mail: llibrary@iowatelecom.net. *Dir,* Jackie Andrea
Pop 286
Library Holdings: Bk Vols 7,700; Per Subs 30
Open Mon & Wed 3-8, Tues & Thurs 9-1 & 4-7, Fri 4-7, Sat 9-Noon

ALTON

P ALTON PUBLIC LIBRARY*, 605 Tenth St, 51003. SAN 305-1943. Tel: 712-756-4516. FAX: 712-756-4140. Web Site: www.alton.lib.ia.us. *Dir,* Cheryl Hoekstra; E-mail: cherylhoekstra@alton.lib.ia.us; *Ch,* Dawn Streff; E-mail: dawnstreff@alton.lib.ia.us
Founded 1923. Pop 1,095; Circ 15,000
Library Holdings: Bk Vols 10,000; Per Subs 77
Special Collections: Local Newspaper (Alton Democrat, 1883-present), micro
Automation Activity & Vendor Info: (Circulation) Follett Software
Wireless access
Mem of Northwest Iowa Library Services
Open Mon-Wed 10-7, Thurs 10-8:30, Fri 10-5, Sat 10-4

ALTOONA

P ALTOONA PUBLIC LIBRARY, 700 Eighth St SW, 50009. SAN 305-1951. Tel: 515-967-3881. FAX: 515-967-6934. *Dir,* Kim Kietzman; E-mail: kkietzman@altoona.lib.ia.us; *Asst Dir,* Amy Turgasen; *Ch,* Jerry Goulden
Founded 1971. Pop 15,000; Circ 120,000
Library Holdings: Bk Titles 50,000; Per Subs 75
Automation Activity & Vendor Info: (Cataloging) Innovative Interfaces, Inc
Wireless access
Open Mon-Thurs 9-9, Fri & Sat 9-5:30, Sun 2-5:30
Friends of the Library Group

AMES

P AMES PUBLIC LIBRARY*, 515 Douglas Ave, 50010. SAN 305-1978. Tel: 515-239-5656. Circulation Tel: 515-239-5646. Interlibrary Loan Service Tel: 515-239-5659. Administration Tel: 515-239-5630. FAX: 515-233-9001. Administration FAX: 515-232-4571. Web Site: www.amespubliclibrary.org. *Dir,* Lynne Carey; Tel: 515-239-5640, E-mail: lcarey@amespubliclibrary.org; *Adult Serv,* Mary Logsdon; E-mail: mlogsdon@amespubliclibrary.org; *Youth Serv,* Jerri Heid; Tel: 515-239-5643, E-mail: jheid@amespubliclibrary.org; Staff 12 (MLS 8, Non-MLS 4)
Founded 1903. Pop 64,126; Circ 1,388,273
Jul 2010-Jun 2011 Income $3,368,167, State $69,299, City $2,911,494, County $133,307, Locally Generated Income $116,980, Other $137,087. Mats Exp $402,424, Books $234,539, Per/Ser (Incl. Access Fees) $14,739, AV Mat $112,223, Electronic Ref Mat (Incl. Access Fees) $40,923. Sal $1,957,555 (Prof $791,116)
Library Holdings: Audiobooks 6,726; AV Mats 49,183; Bks on Deafness & Sign Lang 44; Braille Volumes 56; CDs 20,746; DVDs 19,747; e-books 1,964; Electronic Media & Resources 43; High Interest/Low Vocabulary Bk Vols 577; Large Print Bks 6,344; Bk Vols 176,140; Per Subs 323
Special Collections: Local History (Farwell T Brown Photographic Archives)
Subject Interests: Photog
Automation Activity & Vendor Info: (Acquisitions) Horizon; (Cataloging) OCLC; (Circulation) Horizon; (ILL) OCLC; (OPAC) Horizon; (Serials) Horizon
Database Vendor: Booksite, EBSCO Auto Repair Reference, EBSCOhost, infoUSA, Newsbank, OCLC FirstSearch, Overdrive, Inc, ProQuest, ReferenceUSA, TumbleBookLibrary, ValueLine, World Book Online
Wireless access
Function: Adult bk club, Adult literacy prog, After school storytime, Audio & video playback equip for onsite use, Audiobks via web, Bk club(s), Bk reviews (Group), Bks on CD, Children's prog, Computers for patron use, Copy machines, e-mail serv, E-Reserves, Electronic databases & coll, Fax serv, Free DVD rentals, Genealogy discussion group, Handicapped accessible, Home delivery & serv to Sr ctr & nursing homes, Homebound delivery serv, ILL available, Mail & tel request accepted, Music CDs, Notary serv, Online cat, Online ref, Online searches, Outreach serv, OverDrive digital audio bks, Photocopying/Printing, Preschool outreach, Prog for adults, Prog for children & young adult, Pub access computers, Ref serv in person, Scanner, Senior outreach, Spoken cassettes & CDs, Spoken cassettes & DVDs, Story hour, Summer & winter reading

prog, Summer reading prog, Tax forms, Teen prog, Telephone ref, Web-catalog, Wheelchair accessible, Winter reading prog, Writing prog
Publications: Page One (Monthly newsletter)
Mem of Central Iowa Library Services
Special Services for the Deaf - Bks on deafness & sign lang; High interest/low vocabulary bks
Special Services for the Blind - Audio mat; Bks available with recordings; Bks on CD; Children's Braille; Home delivery serv; Large print bks; PC for handicapped; Recorded bks; Ref serv; Sound rec
Open Mon-Thurs 9-9, Fri & Sat 9-6, Sun 1-5
Friends of the Library Group
Bookmobiles: 1. Outreach Supvr, Valerie Donnell. Bk titles 3,000

M MARY GREELEY MEDICAL CENTER LIBRARY*, 1111 Duff Ave, 50010. SAN 377-5623. Tel: 515-239-2154. FAX: 515-239-2020. *Librn,* Emily H Erickson; E-mail: erickson@mgmc.com
Library Holdings: Bk Vols 3,000; Per Subs 80
Wireless access
Partic in Polk County Biomedical Consortium

G IOWA DEPARTMENT OF TRANSPORTATION LIBRARY*, 800 Lincoln Way, 50010-6915. SAN 305-1994. Tel: 515-239-1200. *Librn,* Leighton Christiansen; E-mail: leighton.christiansen@dot.iowa.gov
Founded 1970
Library Holdings: Bk Vols 20,000; Per Subs 20
Special Collections: Iowa Historic Road Files 1914-1930, photogs; Iowa State Parks 1920-1945, photogs; Rock Island Railroad, newsp & mag clippings 1958-, 5 vol Iowa coverage
Subject Interests: Air transportation, Bus & mgt, Environ studies, Iowa, Manuscripts, Railroads, Transportation
Automation Activity & Vendor Info: (Cataloging) LibLime Koha; (Circulation) LibLime Koha; (OPAC) LibLime Koha
Publications: Library Bulletin (Monthly)
Partic in Dialog Corp; Midwest Transportation Knowledge Network (MTKN); OCLC Online Computer Library Center, Inc

C IOWA STATE UNIVERSITY LIBRARY, 302 Parks Library, 50011-2140. SAN 341-7751. Tel: 515-294-1442, 515-294-1443. Interlibrary Loan Service Tel: 515-294-8073. Reference Tel: 515-294-3642. FAX: 515-294-5525. Interlibrary Loan Service FAX: 515-294-1885. Web Site: www.lib.iastate.edu. *Interim Dean of Libr,* Joyce Garnett; E-mail: garnettj@iastate.edu; *Assoc Dean, Coll & Tech Serv,* Karen Lawson; Tel: 515-294-2485, E-mail: klawson@iastate.edu; *Assoc Dean, Ref & Instruction,* Christine King; Tel: 515-294-0904, E-mail: cking1@iastate.edu; *Asst Dir, Info Tech,* Gregory Davis; Tel: 515-294-2445, E-mail: davisg1@iastate.edu; *Head, Access Serv,* Kathy A Parsons; Tel: 515-294-9630, E-mail: kap@iastate.edu; *Bus Mgr, Head, Bus Serv,* Shelley Hawkins; Tel: 515-294-4954, E-mail: shawkins@iastate.edu; *Head, Humanities & Soc Sci,* Rebecca Jackson; Tel: 515-294-9030, E-mail: rjackson@iastate.edu; *Head, Libr Human Res,* Hilary Deike; Tel: 515-294-0443, E-mail: hdeike@iastate.edu; *Head, Libr Instruction,* Susan Vega Garcia; Tel: 515-294-4052, E-mail: savega@iastate.edu; *Head, Metadata & Cat,* Lori O Kappmeyer; Tel: 515-294-4281, E-mail: losmus@iastate.edu; *Head, Presv & Spec Coll,* Hilary Seo; Tel: 515-294-3540, E-mail: hseo@iastate.edu; *Head, Sci & Tech,* Lorraine Pellack; Tel: 515-294-5569, E-mail: pellack@iastate.edu; *Circ Coordr/Access Serv,* Angie Brown; Tel: 515-294-0448, E-mail: ambrown@iastate.edu. Subject Specialists: *Kinesiology,* Christine King; *Psychol,* Rebecca Jackson; *African-Am studies, Educ, Latino studies,* Susan Vega Garcia; *Agr educ, Food & nutrition,* Lorraine Pellack; Staff 120 (MLS 39, Non-MLS 81)
Founded 1869. Enrl 29,410; Fac 1,445; Highest Degree: Doctorate
Jul 2013-Jun 2014 Income (Main and Other College/University Libraries) $23,901,855, State $22,647,496, Locally Generated Income $632,645, Other $621,714. Mats Exp $13,756,647, Books $1,074,069, Per/Ser (Incl. Access Fees) $233,147, Other Print Mats $227,722. Sal $6,942,790 (Prof $2,595,348)
Library Holdings: AV Mats 1,199,194; e-books 384,019; Microforms 3,534,371; Bk Vols 2,858,602
Special Collections: Archives of Women in Science & Engineering. Oral History; State Document Depository; US Document Depository
Subject Interests: Agr, Hist of sci, Soil conservation, Veterinary med
Automation Activity & Vendor Info: (Acquisitions) Ex Libris Group; (Cataloging) Ex Libris Group; (Circulation) Ex Libris Group; (Course Reserve) Ex Libris Group; (ILL) Ex Libris Group; (Media Booking) Ex Libris Group; (OPAC) Ex Libris Group; (Serials) Ex Libris Group
Database Vendor: ACM (Association for Computing Machinery), Agricola, Alexander Street Press, American Chemical Society, American Mathematical Society, American Psychological Association (APA), Annual Reviews, BioOne, Blackwell, Bowker, Cambridge Scientific Abstracts, CQ Press, ebrary, EBSCOhost, Elsevier, Emerald, Ex Libris Group, Facts on File, Gale Cengage Learning, Greenwood Publishing Group, H W Wilson, Haworth Pres Inc, IEEE (Institute of Electrical & Electronics Engineers), IOP, ISI Web of Knowledge, Jane's, JSTOR, Knovel, LexisNexis, Mergent Online, Modern Language Association, Nature Publishing Group, Newsbank, OCLC FirstSearch, OCLC WorldShare Interlibrary Loan, OCLC-RLG, OVID Technologies, ProQuest, PubMed, ScienceDirect, SerialsSolutions, SirsiDynix, Springer-Verlag, Swets Information Services, Thomson - Web of Science, ValueLine, Westlaw, Wiley, YBP Library Services
Wireless access
Partic in Association of Research Libraries (ARL); Center for Research Libraries; Coalition for Networked Information (CNI); Greater Western Library Alliance; National Initiative for a Networked Cultural Heritage; OCLC Online Computer Library Center, Inc
Special Services for the Blind - Braille equip; Reader equip

Departmental Libraries:

CM VETERINARY MEDICAL LIBRARY, 2280 College of Veterinary Med, 50011. Tel: 515-294-2225. FAX: 515-294-5525. *Librn,* Jeff Alger; E-mail: jalger@iastate.edu; Staff 4 (MLS 1, Non-MLS 3)
Enrl 706; Fac 171; Highest Degree: Doctorate
Function: Res libr
Partic in National Network of Libraries of Medicine

SR SAINT THOMAS AQUINAS CHURCH*, Barr Memorial Library, 2210 Lincoln Way, 50014. SAN 327-9081. Tel: 515-292-3810. FAX: 515-292-3841. Web Site: www.staparish.net. *Librn,* Anne Recker
Library Holdings: Bk Vols 5,500

G UNITED STATES DEPARTMENT OF AGRICULTURE*, National Centers for Animal Health Library, 1920 Dayton Ave, 50010. (Mail add: PO Box 70, 50010), SAN 305-2001. Tel: 515-337-7271. *Librn,* Janice K Eifling; E-mail: janice.k.eifling@aphis.usda.gov; Staff 1 (MLS 1)
Founded 1961
Library Holdings: Bk Vols 3,000; Per Subs 75
Subject Interests: Immunology, Microbiology, Veterinary med
Open Mon-Fri 8-4:30

ANAMOSA

P ANAMOSA PUBLIC LIBRARY & LEARNING CENTER*, 600 E First St, 52205. SAN 305-201X. Tel: 319-462-2183. FAX: 319-462-5349. Web Site: anamosa.lib.ia.us. *Dir,* Marg Folkerts; E-mail: mfolkerts@anamosa.lib.ia.us; *Ch,* Loretta Brickley
Founded 1902. Pop 5,494; Circ 39,120
Jul 2006-Jun 2007 Income $157,629, State $5,416, City $121,657, County $14,936, Locally Generated Income $15,620. Mats Exp $18,907, Books $13,707, Per/Ser (Incl. Access Fees) $4,215, AV Mat $985. Sal $94,839
Library Holdings: CDs 713; DVDs 176; Large Print Bks 538; Bk Vols 24,864; Per Subs 94; Talking Bks 724; Videos 1,043
Automation Activity & Vendor Info: (Acquisitions) Baker & Taylor; (Cataloging) MITINET, Inc; (Circulation) Winnebago Software Co
Database Vendor: EBSCOhost
Wireless access
Open Mon-Thurs 10-8, Fri 10-5, Sat 10-3
Friends of the Library Group

S ANAMOSA STATE PENITENTIARY*, Men's Reformatory Library, 406 N High St, 52205. SAN 305-2028. Tel: 319-462-3504, Ext 2237. FAX: 319-462-3013. *Librn,* Joe Beadle; *Librn,* Mary Wilfer
Library Holdings: Bk Titles 10,684; Per Subs 102
Special Collections: Science Fiction Coll
Open Mon-Fri 7:50-8:45, 9:30-12 & 1-4:45, Sat & Sun 10-Noon

ANITA

P ANITA PUBLIC LIBRARY, 812 Third St, 50020. (Mail add: PO Box 366, 50020), SAN 305-2036. Tel: 712-762-3639. FAX: 712-762-3178. E-mail: anitapl@midlands.net. Web Site: www.anitalibrary.org. *Dir,* Vicki Lynn Christensen; *Asst Librn,* Carolyn Modrell; Staff 2 (Non-MLS 2)
Pop 997; Circ 13,713
Automation Activity & Vendor Info: (Cataloging) Follett Software; (Circulation) Follett Software; (OPAC) Follett Software
Database Vendor: EBSCOhost, OCLC FirstSearch
Wireless access
Mem of Southwest Iowa Library Services District
Open Mon 2-8, Tues, Thurs & Fri 2-6:30, Wed 10-6:30, Sat 9-1
Friends of the Library Group

ANKENY

J DES MOINES AREA COMMUNITY COLLEGE LIBRARY*, Ankeny Campus, 2006 S Ankeny Blvd, 50023. SAN 305-2044. Tel: 515-964-6317. FAX: 515-965-7126. Web Site: www.library.dmacc.edu. *Dir,* Rebecca Funke; Tel: 515-964-6328, E-mail: rsfunke@dmacc.edu; *ILL, Pub Serv, Ref,* Diana Messersmith; Tel: 515-964-6573, E-mail: djmessersmith@dmacc.edu; *Tech Serv,* Shirley Petersen; Tel: 515-964-6634, E-mail: gspetersen@dmacc.edu
Library Holdings: Bk Vols 40,000; Per Subs 200

Partic in OCLC Online Computer Library Center, Inc
Open Mon-Thurs 7:30am-9pm, Fri 7:30-4, Sat 8-1

CR FAITH BAPTIST BIBLE COLLEGE & THEOLOGICAL SEMINARY*, John L Patten Library, 1900 NW Fourth St, 50023. SAN 305-2052. Tel: 515-964-0601. FAX: 515-964-1638. Web Site: www.faith.edu. *Libr Dir,* John Hartog, II; E-mail: hartogj2@faith.edu; Staff 4 (MLS 1, Non-MLS 3)
Enrl 347; Fac 33; Highest Degree: Master
Jul 2010-Jun 2011 Income $117,695. Mats Exp $117,575. Sal $60,845
Library Holdings: Bk Vols 69,621; Per Subs 358
Special Collections: Bible Coll; Theology Coll
Automation Activity & Vendor Info: (Cataloging) Follett Software; (Circulation) Follett Software; (OPAC) Follett Software
Database Vendor: OCLC FirstSearch
Wireless access
Partic in OCLC Online Computer Library Center, Inc; State of Iowa Libraries Online
Open Mon, Tues & Thurs 7am-10:30pm, Wed & Fri 7-5:30, Sat 10-5

P KIRKENDALL PUBLIC LIBRARY*, 1210 NW Prairie Ridge Dr, 50021. SAN 305-2060. Tel: 515-965-6460. Administration Tel: 515-965-6463. FAX: 515-965-6474. Web Site: www.ci.ankeny.ia.us/library. *Dir,* Sarah Willeford; E-mail: swilleford@ankenyiowa.gov; *Asst Dir,* Eric Melton; *Ch, Teen Librn,* Sherry Schlundt; E-mail: children@ankeny.k12.ia.us; Staff 39 (MLS 2, Non-MLS 37)
Founded 1960. Pop 27,711
Library Holdings: AV Mats 7,641; Large Print Bks 3,291; Bk Vols 64,967; Per Subs 275; Talking Bks 1,849
Automation Activity & Vendor Info: (Acquisitions) SirsiDynix; (Cataloging) SirsiDynix; (Circulation) SirsiDynix; (OPAC) SirsiDynix
Database Vendor: OCLC FirstSearch, SirsiDynix
Mem of Central Iowa Library Services
Open Mon-Thurs 9-9, Fri & Sat 9-5:30, Sun 2-5

ANTHON

P HAMANN MEMORIAL LIBRARY*, 311 E Main, 51004. (Mail add: PO Box 293, 51004-0293), SAN 305-2079. Tel: 712-373-5275. FAX: 712-373-5275. Web Site: www.anthon.lib.ia.us. *Asst Dir,* Kathleen Sauser; Staff 2 (MLS 2)
Founded 1903. Pop 649; Circ 900
Library Holdings: Bk Titles 5,697; Per Subs 29
Automation Activity & Vendor Info: (Acquisitions) Book Systems; (OPAC) Book Systems
Wireless access
Mem of Northwest Iowa Library Services
Partic in Woodbury County Libr Syst
Open Mon-Tues 3-7:30, Wed & Fri 1-5, Sat 10-1:30

APLINGTON

P APLINGTON LEGION MEMORIAL LIBRARY*, 929 Parrot St, 50604. (Mail add: PO Box 38, 50604-0038), SAN 305-2087. Tel: 319-347-2432. FAX: 319-347-2432. *Dir,* Nancy Huisman; E-mail: huisman@aplington.lib.ia.us
Pop 1,054; Circ 24,000
Library Holdings: Bk Vols 16,000; Per Subs 60
Automation Activity & Vendor Info: (Cataloging) Follett Software
Open Mon, Tues & Fri 1-5:30, Wed 9-5:30, Thurs 1-7, Sat 9-12
Friends of the Library Group

ARCHER

P ARCHER PUBLIC LIBRARY*, 203 Sanford St, 51231. (Mail add: PO Box 165, 51231-0165), SAN 376-5024. Tel: 712-723-5629. E-mail: archerp1@netins.net. Web Site: www.archer.lib.ia.us. *Dir,* Marla Erick
Founded 1989. Pop 126; Circ 3,698
Library Holdings: Bk Vols 5,500; Per Subs 18
Wireless access
Mem of Northwest Iowa Library Services
Open Tues & Thurs 4-8, Sat 9-12
Friends of the Library Group

ARLINGTON

P ARLINGTON PUBLIC LIBRARY*, 711 Main St, 50606. (Mail add: PO Box 176, 50606-0176), SAN 305-2095. Tel: 563-633-3475. FAX: 563-633-3475. E-mail: director@arlington.lib.ia.us. Web Site: www.arlington.lib.ia.us. *Dir,* Linda K Adams; *Asst Librn,* Roberta Smith
Founded 1875. Pop 490; Circ 7,000
Library Holdings: Bk Vols 6,120; Per Subs 20
Wireless access
Open Mon & Fri 2-6, Tues & Sat 9-12, Wed 9-12 & 6-8, Thurs 6-8

ARMSTRONG

P ARMSTRONG PUBLIC LIBRARY*, 308 Sixth St, 50514. (Mail add: PO Box 169, 50514-0169), SAN 305-2109. Tel: 712-868-3353. FAX: 712-868-3779. E-mail: apl@iowatelecom.net. Web Site: www.armstrongiowa.net/libmus.php. *Dir,* Gertrude Jensen
Founded 1945. Pop 979; Circ 15,254
Library Holdings: AV Mats 442; Bk Titles 9,657; Bk Vols 14,000; Per Subs 38; Talking Bks 150
Special Collections: Spiritual Books
Subject Interests: Art & archit, Med, Natural sci, Relig, Sci tech
Automation Activity & Vendor Info: (Cataloging) Winnebago Software Co; (Circulation) Winnebago Software Co
Special Services for the Blind - Bks on cassette; Large print bks
Open Mon & Fri 1-5, Wed 10:30-3:30, Sat 9-1

ARNOLDS PARK

P ARNOLDS PARK PUBLIC LIBRARY*, Hwy 71, 51331. (Mail add: PO Box 556, 51331-0556), SAN 305-2117. Tel: 712-332-2033. Web Site: www.arnoldsparklib.ia.us. *Librn,* Susan Sup; E-mail: sue@arnoldspark.lib.ia.us; *Asst Librn,* Grace Cummins
Pop 1,162; Circ 25,043
Library Holdings: Bk Titles 10,000; Per Subs 50
Automation Activity & Vendor Info: (Cataloging) Book Systems; (Circulation) Book Systems; (OPAC) Book Systems; (Serials) Book Systems
Wireless access
Mem of Northwest Iowa Library Services
Open Mon & Tues 9-6, Wed-Fri 9-5, Sat 10-12
Friends of the Library Group

ARTHUR

P ARTHUR PUBLIC LIBRARY*, 224 S Main St, 51431-8054. (Mail add: PO Box 77, 51431-0077), SAN 305-2125. Tel: 712-367-2240. FAX: 712-367-2240. Web Site: www.arthur.lib.ia.us. *Dir,* Pat Bell; E-mail: pat@arthur.lib.ia.us
Founded 1925. Pop 245; Circ 8,346
Library Holdings: Bk Titles 8,500; Per Subs 15
Mem of Northwest Iowa Library Services
Open Mon 2-6:30, Thurs 2-8:30, Sat 9-2:30

ASBURY

P DUBUQUE COUNTY LIBRARY*, Asbury Branch, 5900 Saratoga Plaza, Ste 5, 52002. SAN 305-3628. Tel: 563-582-0008. FAX: 563-582-0022. E-mail: library@dubcolib.lib.ia.us. Web Site: www.dubcolib.lib.ia.us. *Dir,* Rebecca S Heil
Jul 2008-Jun 2009 Income (Main Library and Branch(s)) $535,000. Mats Exp $60,000, Books $45,000, Per/Ser (Incl. Access Fees) $5,000, AV Mat $6,000, Electronic Ref Mat (Incl. Access Fees) $4,000
Library Holdings: Audiobooks 2,000; DVDs 2,000; Bk Vols 46,000; Per Subs 100; Videos 2,000
Subject Interests: Local hist
Automation Activity & Vendor Info: (Acquisitions) TLC (The Library Corporation); (Cataloging) TLC (The Library Corporation); (Circulation) TLC (The Library Corporation); (OPAC) TLC (The Library Corporation)
Database Vendor: Baker & Taylor, BWI, EBSCOhost, OCLC FirstSearch, OCLC WebJunction, OCLC WorldShare Interlibrary Loan, TLC (The Library Corporation)
Wireless access
Open Mon-Thurs 9-8, Sat 9-3, Sun 1-5
Branches: 3
EPWORTH BRANCH, 110 Bierman Rd, Epworth, 52045. (Mail add: PO Box 50, Epworth, 52045-0050). Tel: 563-876-3388. FAX: 563-876-3388. *Librn,* Becky Heil
Library Holdings: Bk Titles 6,000; Per Subs 32
Automation Activity & Vendor Info: (Circulation) TLC (The Library Corporation)
Database Vendor: Baker & Taylor, BWI, EBSCOhost, OCLC FirstSearch, OCLC WebJunction, OCLC WorldShare Interlibrary Loan, TLC (The Library Corporation)
Open Mon, Tues & Thurs 3-7, Wed 9-12 & 1-7, Sat 9-1
FARLEY BRANCH, 205 First St, NE, Farley, 52046. (Mail add: PO Box 10, Farley, 52046). Tel: 563-744-3577. FAX: 563-744-3577.
Library Holdings: Bk Vols 6,000; Per Subs 32
HOLY CROSS BRANCH, 938 Church St, Holy Cross, 52053. (Mail add: PO Box 307, Holy Cross, 52053), SAN 376-6543. Tel: 563-870-2082. *Librn,* Becky Heil
Pop 339
Library Holdings: Bk Vols 3,500; Per Subs 32
Automation Activity & Vendor Info: (Serials) TLC (The Library Corporation)
Open Mon & Thurs 4-7, Wed 1-6, Sat 9-1
Bookmobiles: 1

ASHTON

P ASHTON PUBLIC LIBRARY*, 3029 Third St, 51232. (Mail add: PO Box 277, 51232-0277), SAN 305-2133. Tel: 712-724-6426. FAX: 712-724-6426. E-mail: ashtlib@nethtc.net. Web Site: www.ashton.lib.ia.us. *Dir,* Heather Grotluschen
Pop 461; Circ 15,870
Library Holdings: DVDs 850; Large Print Bks 85; Bk Titles 12,260; Per Subs 53; Talking Bks 298; Videos 40
Automation Activity & Vendor Info: (Cataloging) Book Systems; (Circulation) Book Systems
Database Vendor: EBSCOhost, OCLC FirstSearch
Wireless access
Mem of Northwest Iowa Library Services
Open Tues & Thurs 4-7, Wed 9-12 & 2-8, Sat 9-2

ATKINS

P ATKINS PUBLIC LIBRARY*, 84 Main Ave, 52206. (Mail add: PO Box 217, 52206), SAN 305-2141. Tel: 319-446-7676. FAX: 319-446-7676. E-mail: director@atkins.lib.ia.us. *Dir,* Cathy Becker
Pop 1,297; Circ 14,244
Library Holdings: Bk Titles 8,800; Per Subs 43
Automation Activity & Vendor Info: (Cataloging) Follett Software
Open Mon, Tues & Thurs 9-12 & 2-6, Wed 2-8, Fri 2-6, Sat 9-12

ATLANTIC

P ATLANTIC PUBLIC LIBRARY, 507 Poplar St, 50022. SAN 305-215X. Tel: 712-243-5466. FAX: 712-243-5011. E-mail: atlanticpubliclibrary@gmail.com. Web Site: www.atlantic.lib.ia.us. *Dir,* Michelle Johnson; *Adult Coll Coordr,* Jody Allumbaugh; E-mail: jallumbaugh@atlantic.lib.ia.us; *Ch Serv,* Julie Tjepkes; E-mail: jtjpekes@atlantic.lib.ia.us; *ILL,* Diane McFadden; E-mail: dmcfad@atlantic.lib.ia.us; Staff 8 (MLS 1, Non-MLS 7)
Founded 1903. Pop 7,112; Circ 90,280
Jul 2011-Jun 2012 Income $261,798, State $5,201, City $198,558, County $13,000, Locally Generated Income $5,819, Other $39,220. Mats Exp $261,798, Books $30,530, Per/Ser (Incl. Access Fees) $3,000, Micro $1,500, Electronic Ref Mat (Incl. Access Fees) $5,982. Sal $147,900 (Prof $45,100)
Library Holdings: CDs 2,441; DVDs 26,811; e-books 8,100; Large Print Bks 1,688; Bk Vols 35,600; Per Subs 84
Subject Interests: Genealogy, Local hist
Automation Activity & Vendor Info: (Cataloging) Biblionix; (Circulation) Biblionix; (OPAC) Biblionix
Database Vendor: EBSCO Information Services, EBSCOhost, Newsbank, OCLC FirstSearch, Overdrive, Inc, ProQuest, TumbleBookLibrary
Wireless access
Function: Audiobks via web, Bks on CD, Computers for patron use, Copy machines, Distance learning, e-mail & chat, E-Reserves, Electronic databases & coll, Exhibits, Fax serv, Free DVD rentals, Genealogy discussion group, Handicapped accessible, Holiday prog, Home delivery & serv to Sr ctr & nursing homes, Homebound delivery serv, ILL available, Music CDs, Online cat, OverDrive digital audio bks, Prog for adults, Prog for children & young adult, Provide serv for the mentally ill, Serves mentally handicapped consumers, Story hour, Summer reading prog, Tax forms, Teen prog, Telephone ref
Partic in State of Iowa Libraries Online
Special Services for the Deaf - Interpreter on staff
Open Mon, Tues, Thurs & Fri 9:30-6, Wed 9:30-8, Sat 9:30-2:30
Friends of the Library Group

AUBURN

P AUBURN PUBLIC LIBRARY*, 209 Pine St, 51433. (Mail add: PO Box 40, 51433), SAN 373-7586. Tel: 712-688-2264. FAX: 712-688-2264. E-mail: auburnpl@iowatelecom.net. *Dir,* Donetta Stewart
Pop 322
Library Holdings: Bk Titles 11,000; Per Subs 25
Function: Children's prog, Computers for patron use, Copy machines, Free DVD rentals, ILL available, Music CDs, Photocopying/Printing, Prog for children & young adult, Pub access computers, Summer reading prog
Open Mon 2-7, Tues-Thurs 3-7, Sat 9-12

AUDUBON

P AUDUBON PUBLIC LIBRARY*, 401 N Park Pl, 50025-1258. SAN 305-2168. Tel: 712-563-3301. FAX: 712-563-2580. Web Site: www.audubon.swilsa.lib.ia.us. *Dir,* Gail P Richardson; E-mail: gailr@metc.net; *Ch,* Robin Killeen
Founded 1893. Pop 2,382; Circ 31,000
Library Holdings: Bk Vols 27,000; Per Subs 128
Special Collections: Local History & Geneaology
Mem of Southwest Iowa Library Services District
Open Mon 12-5 & 7-8:30, Tues, Wed & Thurs 10-5 & 7-8:30, Fri 10-5, Sat 10-2
Friends of the Library Group

AURELIA

P AURELIA PUBLIC LIBRARY*, 232 Main St, 51005. (Mail add: PO Box 188, 51005-0188), SAN 305-2176. Tel: 712-434-5330. FAX: 712-434-5330. E-mail: aurelia.library@aurelia.lib.ia.us. Web Site: www.aurelia.lib.ia.us. *Dir,* Sherri Stevenson; *Librn,* Janet Laursen; Staff 2 (Non-MLS 2)
Founded 1917. Pop 1,062; Circ 15,000
Library Holdings: Bk Titles 15,000; Per Subs 34
Special Collections: Iowa Coll
Subject Interests: Hist, Natural sci, Relig
Automation Activity & Vendor Info: (Circulation) Book Systems
Wireless access
Function: Prof lending libr
Mem of Northwest Iowa Library Services
Open Mon-Fri 10-6, Sat 9-1
Friends of the Library Group

AURORA

P AURORA PUBLIC LIBRARY*, 401 Woodruff St, 50607. (Mail add: PO Box 7, 50607-0007), SAN 376-7396. Tel: 319-634-3660. FAX: 319-634-3960. E-mail: director@aurora.lib.ia.us. Web Site: www.aurora.lib.ia.us. *Librn,* Elaine Rosburg
Pop 194
Library Holdings: Bk Vols 3,000; Per Subs 12
Open Mon 4-8, Tues 2-5, Wed 2-6, Thurs 9-12 & 4-8, Fri 9-11

AVOCA

P AVOCA PUBLIC LIBRARY*, Edwin M Davis Memorial Library, 213 N Elm St, 51521. (Mail add: PO Box 219, 51521-0219), SAN 305-2184. Tel: 712-343-6358. FAX: 712-343-6358. E-mail: avocapl@walnutel.net. Web Site: www.avoca.swilsa.lib.ia.us. *Dir,* Serena Riesgaard; *Ch,* Joy Krohn; E-mail: joyapl@walnutel.net
Pop 1,610; Circ 30,000
Library Holdings: DVDs 1,000; Bk Vols 20,063; Per Subs 66; Talking Bks 650
Wireless access
Open Mon, Tues, Thurs & Fri 10-5, Wed 10-8, Sat 9-12

BADGER

P BADGER PUBLIC LIBRARY*, 211 First Ave SE, 50516. (Mail add: PO Box 255, 50516-0255), SAN 376-5229. Tel: 515-545-4793. FAX: 515-545-4440. E-mail: badger@wccta.net. *Dir,* Eric Jones
Pop 610
Library Holdings: Bk Vols 8,000; Per Subs 25
Automation Activity & Vendor Info: (Cataloging) Follett Software
Partic in Small Libr Asn
Open Mon 4-6, Tues, Wed & Thurs 4-8, Sat 10-2
Friends of the Library Group

BAGLEY

P BAGLEY PUBLIC LIBRARY, 117 Main, 50026. (Mail add: PO Box 206, 50026-0206), SAN 305-2192. Tel: 641-427-5214. FAX: 641-427-5214. E-mail: bagleypl@iowatelecom.net. *Dir,* Carole Honold; Tel: 712-999-5621, E-mail: honoldc@crmu.net; Staff 1 (Non-MLS 1)
Founded 1976. Pop 354; Circ 3,433
Library Holdings: Audiobooks 255; DVDs 430; Large Print Bks 230; Bk Titles 5,100; Per Subs 24; Talking Bks 250; Videos 100
Special Collections: Town Depository
Subject Interests: Christian fiction
Database Vendor: EBSCOhost, OCLC FirstSearch
Wireless access
Function: Bks on cassette, Bks on CD, Children's prog, Computers for patron use, Copy machines, e-mail & chat, Fax serv, Free DVD rentals, Handicapped accessible, Homebound delivery serv, ILL available, Instruction & testing, Photocopying/Printing, Pub access computers, Story hour, Summer reading prog, Tax forms, VHS videos
Mem of Southwest Iowa Library Services District
Open Tues, Thurs & Fri 2-6, Wed 11-6, Sat 11-2
Restriction: Restricted access
Friends of the Library Group

BANCROFT

P BANCROFT PUBLIC LIBRARY*, 208 E Ramsey St, 50517. (Mail add: PO Box 347, 50517-0347), SAN 305-2206. Tel: 515-885-2753. FAX: 515-885-2753. Web Site: www.bancroft.lib.ia.us. *Dir,* Mary Richter;

E-mail: m.richter@bancroft.lib.ia.us; *Asst Librn,* Maureen Ingalls; *Asst Librn,* Diane Hellman
Founded 1961. Pop 808; Circ 27,064
Library Holdings: Bk Titles 15,260; Per Subs 94
Automation Activity & Vendor Info: (Cataloging) Follett Software; (Circulation) Follett Software
Open Mon, Thurs & Fri 1-5:30, Tues 9-11 & 1-5:30, Wed 1-8, Sat 9-12

BATAVIA

P BATAVIA PUBLIC LIBRARY*, 902 Third St, 52533. SAN 305-2214. Tel: 641-662-2317. *Librn,* Judy Dovico
Pop 500; Circ 2,761
Library Holdings: Bk Titles 5,112; Bk Vols 5,400; Per Subs 20
Open Tues & Thurs 2-5

BATTLE CREEK

P BATTLE CREEK PUBLIC LIBRARY*, 115 Main St, 51006. SAN 305-2222. Tel: 712-365-4912. FAX: 712-365-4912. E-mail: bcpublib@frontier.com. *Dir,* Sheila Petersen
Pop 743; Circ 9,676
Library Holdings: Bk Titles 11,989; Per Subs 29
Open Mon & Thurs 2-7, Tues & Wed 2-6, Fri 2-5, Sat 11-3

BAXTER

P BAXTER PUBLIC LIBRARY*, 202 E State St, 50028. (Mail add: PO Box 586, 50028-0586), SAN 376-5059. Tel: 641-227-3934. FAX: 641-227-3217. *Dir,* Elaine Montgomery; E-mail: elaine@partnercom.net
Pop 1,055
Library Holdings: Bk Vols 25,000; Per Subs 30
Mem of Central Iowa Library Services
Open Mon-Thurs 9-12 & 3:30-7, Fri 9-12, Sat 10-12
Friends of the Library Group

BAYARD

P BAYARD PUBLIC LIBRARY*, 315 Main St, 50029. (Mail add: PO Box 338, 50029-0338), SAN 305-2230. Tel: 712-651-2238. FAX: 712-651-2238. *Dir,* Jeannie Stone; Staff 1.5 (Non-MLS 1.5)
Founded 1936. Pop 471; Circ 17,176
Jul 2010-Jun 2011 Income $72,705, State $1,621, City $52,200, County $11,644, Locally Generated Income $5,619, Other $1,621. Mats Exp $13,414, Books $10,537, Other Print Mats $380, AV Mat $1,780, Electronic Ref Mat (Incl. Access Fees) $717. Sal $40,665
Library Holdings: Audiobooks 370; AV Mats 366; Bks on Deafness & Sign Lang 2; CDs 370; DVDs 656; e-books 5,607; Bk Titles 14,096; Per Subs 52
Subject Interests: Antiques, Quilting, Sports
Automation Activity & Vendor Info: (Acquisitions) Follett Software; (Cataloging) Follett Software; (Circulation) Follett Software; (Course Reserve) Follett Software; (ILL) Follett Software; (Media Booking) Follett Software; (OPAC) Follett Software; (Serials) Follett Software
Wireless access
Partic in State of Iowa Libraries Online; WILBOR Consortium (West/Central Iowa Libraries Building Online Resources)
Open Mon, Tues, Thurs & Fri 1-5, Wed 10-8, Sat 9-Noon
Friends of the Library Group

BEAMAN

P BEAMAN COMMUNITY MEMORIAL LIBRARY*, 223 Main St, 50609. (Mail add: PO Box 135, 50609-0135), SAN 305-2249. Tel: 641-366-2912. FAX: 641-366-2912. E-mail: library@beaman.lib.ia.us. Web Site: library.beaman.lib.ia.us. *Dir,* LaVonne Sternhagen; *Asst Dir,* Darla Whitmire; Staff 2 (Non-MLS 2)
Founded 1955. Pop 210; Circ 6,978
Library Holdings: AV Mats 29; DVDs 76; Bk Titles 6,361; Per Subs 51; Videos 329
Subject Interests: Local hist
Automation Activity & Vendor Info: (Cataloging) Follett Software; (Circulation) Follett Software
Mem of Northeast Iowa Library Services
Open Mon, Wed & Fri 2-6, Tues & Thurs 3-6, Sat 10-12

BEDFORD

P BEDFORD PUBLIC LIBRARY*, 507 Jefferson, 50833-1314. SAN 305-2257. Tel: 712-523-2828. E-mail: bedfordlibrary@mchsi.com. Web Site: www.bedford.lib.ia.us. *Dir,* Sandy Kennedy; *Asst Dir,* Belinda Spencer
Founded 1915. Pop 1,620; Circ 14,326
Library Holdings: Bk Titles 22,078; Per Subs 41
Special Collections: Genealogical Coll, bks, prints; Local Newspapers; Taylor County Census, microfilm
Mem of Southwest Iowa Library Services District
Partic in GMILCS, Inc; Midwest Collaborative for Library Services (MCLS)

BELLE PLAINE

P BELLE PLAINE COMMUNITY LIBRARY*, 904 12th St, 52208-1711. SAN 305-2265. Tel: 319-444-2902. FAX: 319-444-2902. E-mail: director@belleplaine.lib.ia.us. Web Site: www.belleplaine.lib.ia.us. *Dir,* Kristi Sorensen; E-mail: kristi@belleplaine.lib.ia.us; *Asst Librn,* Sonya Johnson; *Asst Librn,* Jackie Rupp; *Asst Librn,* Sonya Thiessen; *Asst Librn,* Nadine Thomasson; *Libr Asst,* Reda Prichard
Founded 1907. Pop 2,950; Circ 20,000
Library Holdings: Bk Vols 19,000; Per Subs 80
Subject Interests: Iowa
Open Mon-Thurs 12-8, Fri & Sat 10-4

BELLEVUE

P BELLEVUE PUBLIC LIBRARY*, 106 N Third St, 52031. SAN 305-2273. Tel: 563-872-4991. FAX: 563-872-4094. Web Site: www.bellevue.lib.ia.us. *Dir,* Marian L Meyer; E-mail: MarianMeyer4@aol.com; *Asst Dir,* Sheila Bragg; *Ch,* Tish Jackson
Pop 2,350; Circ 51,766
Library Holdings: Bk Vols 19,000; Per Subs 55
Open Mon, Tues, Thurs & Fri 10-5:30, Wed 10-7, Sat 10-3
Friends of the Library Group

BELMOND

P TALBOT BELMOND PUBLIC LIBRARY*, 440 E Main St, 50421-1224. SAN 305-2281. Tel: 641-444-4160. FAX: 641-444-3457. *Dir,* Chris Adcock; E-mail: cadcock@belmond.lib.ia.us; *Ch,* Amy Bates
Founded 1917. Pop 2,560; Circ 38,000
Library Holdings: Bk Vols 20,000; Per Subs 80
Automation Activity & Vendor Info: (Cataloging) Follett Software; (Circulation) Follett Software; (OPAC) Follett Software
Open Mon-Thurs 10-6, Fri 10-3, Sat 10-2
Friends of the Library Group

BENNETT

P BENNETT PUBLIC LIBRARY*, 203 Main St, 52721. (Mail add: PO Box 299, 52721-0299), SAN 305-229X. Tel: 563-890-2238. FAX: 563-890-2711. E-mail: benetlib@fbcom.net. Web Site: www.fbcom.net/web. *Dir,* Lisa Studer
Founded 1942. Pop 395; Circ 800
Library Holdings: Bk Titles 5,543
Open Tues, Fri & Sat (Fall & Winter) 9-12, Wed 2-6, Thurs 1-6; Tues & Thurs (Spring & Summer) 9-1, Wed 2-6, Fri & Sat 9-12

BETTENDORF

P BETTENDORF PUBLIC LIBRARY INFORMATION CENTER*, 2950 Learning Campus Dr, 52722. (Mail add: PO Box 1330, 52722-1330), SAN 305-2311. Tel: 563-344-4175. Circulation Tel: 563-344-4195. Reference Tel: 563-344-4179. Administration Tel: 563-344-4183. FAX: 563-344-4185. E-mail: info@bettendorflibrary.com. Web Site: www.bettendorflibrary.com. *Dir,* Sue Mannix; E-mail: smannix@bettendorf.org; *Adult Serv Mgr,* Maria Levetzow; Tel: 563-344-4191, E-mail: mlevetzow@bettendorf.org; *Circ Mgr,* Carol Anne Chouteau; E-mail: cachouteau@bettendorf.org; *Tech Serv Mgr,* Susan Green; Tel: 593-344-4193, E-mail: sgreen@bettendorf.org; *Youth Serv Mgr,* Paul Odell; Tel: 563-344-4189, E-mail: podell@bettendorf.org; Staff 23 (MLS 10, Non-MLS 13)
Founded 1957. Pop 31,258; Circ 620,206
Library Holdings: AV Mats 19,400; e-books 7,956; Bk Vols 150,206; Per Subs 348
Special Collections: Iowa Hist Coll
Automation Activity & Vendor Info: (Acquisitions) Innovative Interfaces, Inc; (Cataloging) Innovative Interfaces, Inc; (Circulation) Innovative Interfaces, Inc; (OPAC) Innovative Interfaces, Inc; (Serials) Innovative Interfaces, Inc
Wireless access
Publications: Pages (Newsletter)
Partic in RiverShare Libraries
Open Mon-Thurs 9-9, Fri & Sat 9-5:30, Sun 1-5
Friends of the Library Group

J SCOTT COMMUNITY COLLEGE LIBRARY*, 500 Belmont Rd, 52722. SAN 305-3253. Tel: 563-441-4150. Interlibrary Loan Service Tel: 563-441-4153. Administration Tel: 563-441-4152. FAX: 563-441-4154. E-mail: scclibrary@eicc.edu. Web Site: www.eicc.edu/library. *Dir,* Jane Campagna; *ILL,* Carol Brade; E-mail: cbrade@eicc.edu; *Ref,* Linda Nelson; Tel: 563-441-4151, E-mail: lnelson@eicc.edu; *Web Coordr,* Joyce Haack; Tel: 563-441-4156, E-mail: jhaack@eicc.edu; Staff 6 (MLS 1, Non-MLS 5)
Founded 1968. Enrl 4,506; Fac 120; Highest Degree: Associate

Library Holdings: Bk Titles 39,851; Per Subs 176
Automation Activity & Vendor Info: (Cataloging) Infor Library & Information Solutions; (Circulation) Infor Library & Information Solutions; (OPAC) Infor Library & Information Solutions
Database Vendor: EBSCOhost, OVID Technologies
Function: Distance learning, ILL available
Publications: Infotrac
Mem of Reaching Across Illinois Library System (RAILS)
Partic in Quad-Link Libr Consortium
Open Mon-Thurs 7:30-8:30, Fri 7:30-4:30, Sat 9-1

BIRMINGHAM

P BIRMINGHAM PUBLIC LIBRARY*, 310 Main St, 52535. (Mail add: PO Box 167, 52535-0167), SAN 305-232X. Tel: 319-498-4423. *Dir,* Michele Mitchell
Pop 488; Circ 1,075
Jul 2011-Jun 2012 Income $2,443, City $500, County $1,943
Library Holdings: AV Mats 15; Bk Titles 6,976; Per Subs 20; Videos 332
Function: Summer reading prog
Open Mon (April-Oct) 7pm-8:30pm, Wed 1-5, Sat 11-4
Restriction: Pub use on premises

BLAIRSTOWN

P BLAIRSTOWN PUBLIC LIBRARY*, 305 Locust St, Ste 2, 52209. (Mail add: PO Box 187, 52209-0187), SAN 305-2338. Tel: 319-454-6497. FAX: 319-454-6495. E-mail: btown@netins.net. Web Site: www.blairstown.lib.ia.us. *Dir,* Beth Crow
Founded 1930. Pop 682
Library Holdings: Bk Titles 11,500; Per Subs 20
Wireless access
Open Mon 10-7, Tues-Thurs 1-7, Fri 1-6, Sat 10-1

BLAKESBURG

P BLAKESBURG PUBLIC LIBRARY, 407 S Wilson St, 52536. (Mail add: PO Box 87, 52536-0087), SAN 373-6954. Tel: 641-938-2834. FAX: 641-938-2834. E-mail: library@blakesburg.lib.ia.us. Web Site: www.blakesburg.lib.ia.us. *Dir,* Cheryl Talbert; *Asst Librn,* Chris Johnson
Pop 374
Library Holdings: DVDs 200; e-books 10,000; Large Print Bks 500; Bk Titles 5,398; Per Subs 14
Database Vendor: EBSCOhost, LearningExpress
Wireless access
Special Services for the Blind - Large print bks
Open Mon 5:30-8:30, Tues & Thurs 3:30-6, Fri 8:30-4:30, Sat 8:30-12:30
Friends of the Library Group

BLOOMFIELD

P BLOOMFIELD PUBLIC LIBRARY*, 107 N Columbia St, 52537-1431. SAN 305-2354. Tel: 641-664-2209. FAX: 641-664-2506. E-mail: bpl@netins.net. Web Site: www.bloomfield.lib.ia.us. *Dir,* Beth Sullivan, E-mail: beth.sullivan@bloomfield.lib.ia.us
Founded 1913. Pop 2,601; Circ 41,230
Library Holdings: DVDs 113; Large Print Bks 1,194; Bk Titles 20,711; Per Subs 51; Talking Bks 871; Videos 383
Special Collections: Davis County Genealogy Society
Subject Interests: Iowa, Local hist
Open Mon & Wed-Fri 10-5:30, Tues 10-6, Sat 10-2
Friends of the Library Group

BODE

P BODE PUBLIC LIBRARY*, 114 Humboldt Ave, 50519. (Mail add: PO Box 122, 50519-0122), SAN 305-2362. Tel: 515-379-1258. FAX: 515-379-1486. *Librn,* Orlys Maassen
Pop 327; Circ 5,149
Library Holdings: Bk Vols 4,682; Per Subs 32
Wireless access
Open Mon 1-8, Tues & Thurs 1-5, Fri 9-5

BONAPARTE

P BONAPARTE PUBLIC LIBRARY*, 602 Second St, 52620. (Mail add: PO Box 158, 52620-1058), SAN 305-2370. Tel: 319-592-3677. FAX: 319-592-3677. E-mail: blibrary@netins.net. *Adminr,* Kathy Meyer; Fax: 319-592-3577
Pop 458; Circ 5,026
Library Holdings: Bk Titles 8,000
Open Mon 9-12:30, Tues-Thurs 1:30-6, Sat 9-12

BONDURANT

P BONDURANT COMMUNITY LIBRARY*, 104 Second St NE, 50035. (Mail add: PO Box 160, 50035-0160), SAN 320-4766. Tel: 515-967-4790. FAX: 515-967-2668. E-mail: library@cityofbondurant.com. *Dir,* Karen Burkett-Pederson
Founded 1977. Pop 5,318; Circ 40,543
Automation Activity & Vendor Info: (Acquisitions) Follett Software; (Cataloging) Follett Software; (Circulation) Follett Software; (Course Reserve) Follett Software; (ILL) OCLC FirstSearch; (Media Booking) OCLC FirstSearch; (OPAC) Follett Software; (Serials) Follett Software
Wireless access
Open Mon-Thurs 10:30-7, Fri 10:30-5, Sat 9-4
Friends of the Library Group

BOONE

J DES MOINES AREA COMMUNITY COLLEGE*, Boone Campus Library, 1125 Hancock Dr, 50036-5326. SAN 305-2389. Tel: 515-433-5043. FAX: 515-433-5044. Web Site: www.library.dmacc.edu. *Dir,* Rebecca Funke; Tel: 515-433-5040, E-mail: rsfunke@dmacc.edu; *Asst Librn,* Karen Messler; Tel: 515-433-5041; Staff 3 (MLS 1, Non-MLS 2)
Founded 1966
Library Holdings: Bk Vols 19,000; Per Subs 115
Special Collections: Iowa Fiction; Railroads
Database Vendor: EBSCOhost, OCLC FirstSearch
Partic in OCLC Online Computer Library Center, Inc
Open Mon-Thurs 7:30am-9pm, Fri 7:30-4

P ERICSON PUBLIC LIBRARY*, 702 Greene St, 50036. SAN 341-7816. Tel: 515-432-3727. FAX: 515-432-1103. E-mail: ericson@boone.lib.ia.us. Web Site: www.boone.lib.ia.us. *Dir,* Jamie Williams; E-mail: jwilliams@boone.lib.ia.us; *Ch,* Zach Stier; E-mail: zstier@boone.lib.ia.us; Staff 3 (Non-MLS 3)
Founded 1901. Pop 12,803; Circ 205,411
Jul 2012-Jun 2013 Income $639,000. Mats Exp $48,953, Books $38,166, Per/Ser (Incl. Access Fees) $2,287, AV Mat $7,342. Sal $268,277 (Prof $56,220)
Library Holdings: AV Mats 14,105; Large Print Bks 6,769; Bk Vols 62,412; Per Subs 94
Subject Interests: Antiques, Genealogy, Iowa, Railroads
Automation Activity & Vendor Info: (Cataloging) Innovative Interfaces, Inc; (Circulation) Innovative Interfaces, Inc; (OPAC) Innovative Interfaces, Inc
Wireless access
Mem of Central Iowa Library Services
Partic in OCLC Online Computer Library Center, Inc
Open Mon & Tues 9-8, Wed-Fri 9-6, Sat 9-3
Friends of the Library Group

BOYDEN

P BOYDEN PUBLIC LIBRARY*, 609 Webb St, 51234. (Mail add: PO Box 249, 51234-0249), SAN 305-2397. Tel: 712-725-2281. FAX: 712-725-2224. Web Site: www.boyden.lib.ia.us. *Dir,* Shari Fedders; E-mail: sfedders@boyden.lib.ia.us
Pop 672
Library Holdings: AV Mats 2,919; Bk Vols 23,478; Per Subs 62
Mem of Northwest Iowa Library Services
Open Tues, Thurs & Fri 1-5:30, Wed 1-6, Sat 9-12

BRITT

P BRITT PUBLIC LIBRARY*, 132 Main Ave S, 50423-1628. SAN 305-2400. Tel: 641-843-4245. FAX: 641-843-4245. E-mail: brittpubliclibrary@mchsi.com. *Dir,* Linda Friedow; *Ch,* Corinne Ball; Staff 3 (Non-MLS 3)
Founded 1917. Pop 2,052; Circ 14,500
Library Holdings: AV Mats 1,766; Large Print Bks 400; Bk Vols 17,366; Per Subs 54
Subject Interests: Hospice
Automation Activity & Vendor Info: (Cataloging) Follett Software; (Circulation) Follett Software
Database Vendor: EBSCOhost
Open Mon 10-6, Tues-Thurs 10-8, Fri 10-5, Sat 9-12
Friends of the Library Group

BROOKLYN

P BROOKLYN PUBLIC LIBRARY*, 306 Jackson St, 52211. (Mail add: PO Box 515, 52211-0515), SAN 305-2419. Tel: 641-522-9272. FAX: 641-522-9272. E-mail: brooklyn@netins.net. *Dir,* LuAnn Jahlas
Pop 1,367
Library Holdings: Bk Titles 8,000; Per Subs 50
Database Vendor: OCLC FirstSearch

Open Mon-Fri 11-6, Sat 9-1
Friends of the Library Group

BUFFALO CENTER

P BUFFALO CENTER PUBLIC LIBRARY*, 221 N Main St, 50424. (Mail add: PO Box 350, 50424-1037), SAN 305-2427. Tel: 641-562-2546. FAX: 641-562-2546. E-mail: bclib@wctatel.net. Web Site: www.buffalocenter.lib.ia.us. *Dir,* Sharon Hippen; *Asst Librn,* Betty Delgado; *Asst Librn,* Cindy Steffensen
Pop 963; Circ 8,063
Library Holdings: Bk Titles 8,000; Per Subs 20
Automation Activity & Vendor Info: (Circulation) Follett Software
Open Mon, Wed & Fri 2-5:30, Tues 9:30-11:30 & 2-5:30, Thurs 2-7, Sat 9:30-11:30

BURLINGTON

P BURLINGTON PUBLIC LIBRARY*, 210 Court St, 52601. SAN 305-2443. Tel: 319-753-1647. FAX: 319-753-0789. Web Site: www.burlington.lib.ia.us. *Dir,* Rhonda J Frevert; E-mail: rfrevert@burlington.lib.ia.us; *Pub Serv Mgr,* Dawn Hayslett; E-mail: dhayslett@burlington.lib.ia.us; *Tech Serv Mgr,* Paula J Buhrow; E-mail: pbuhrow@burlington.lib.ia.us; *Youth Serv Mgr,* Angie Pilkington; E-mail: apilkington@burlington.lib.ia.us; *IT Supvr,* Lois J Blythe; E-mail: lblythe@burlington.lib.ia.us; Staff 5 (MLS 5)
Founded 1868. Pop 26,839; Circ 518,417
Library Holdings: CDs 3,439; DVDs 7,119; Large Print Bks 3,700; Music Scores 10,066; Bk Titles 117,874; Bk Vols 111,212; Per Subs 457; Talking Bks 3,740; Videos 3,577
Subject Interests: County hist, Genealogy, Local hist
Automation Activity & Vendor Info: (Acquisitions) SirsiDynix; (Cataloging) SirsiDynix; (Circulation) SirsiDynix; (OPAC) SirsiDynix; (Serials) SirsiDynix
Database Vendor: OCLC FirstSearch, OCLC WorldShare Interlibrary Loan
Wireless access
Open Mon-Thurs 9-9, Fri & Sat 9-5
Friends of the Library Group

BURT

P BURT PUBLIC LIBRARY*, 119 Walnut St, 50522. (Mail add: PO Box 128, 50522-0128), SAN 305-2451. Tel: 515-924-3680. FAX: 515-924-3681. E-mail: burtpl@netins.net. Web Site: www.burtiowa.com/burtlibrary.htm. *Dir,* Trisha Hicks
Pop 556; Circ 4,474
Library Holdings: Bk Vols 6,500; Per Subs 25
Open Mon 9-12 & 1-8, Wed & Fri 1-5:30, Sat 9-12

BUSSEY

P BUSSEY COMMUNITY PUBLIC LIBRARY, (Formerly Bussey Community Public Library), 401 Merrill St, 50044. (Mail add: PO Box 29, 50044-0039), SAN 376-5423. Tel: 641-944-5994. E-mail: bclib@iowatelecom.net. *Dir,* Betty Schmaltz
Pop 450
Library Holdings: Bk Vols 11,000
Mem of Central Iowa Library Services
Open Mon 1-4, Tues 12-6, Wed 10-4, Thurs 11-5, Sat 10-12

CALLENDER

P CALLENDER HERITAGE LIBRARY*, 505 Thomas St, 50523. (Mail add: PO Box 69, 50523-0069), SAN 305-2478. Tel: 515-548-3803. FAX: 515-548-3801. *Dir,* Tina Twito
Founded 1903. Pop 424; Circ 9,230
Library Holdings: Bk Titles 10,000; Per Subs 40
Open Mon & Thurs 5-8, Tues, Wed & Fri 1:30-5, Sat 9-12

CALMAR

P CALMAR PUBLIC LIBRARY*, 101 S Washington St, 52132. (Mail add: PO Box 806, 52132-0806), SAN 305-2486. Tel: 563-562-3010. FAX: 563-562-3010. E-mail: calmarlib@mchsi.com. Web Site: www.calmarlibrary.com. *Librn,* Linda Crossland
Pop 1,058; Circ 8,314
Library Holdings: Audiobooks 921; DVDs 189; Large Print Bks 626; Bk Titles 16,500; Per Subs 29; Videos 800
Automation Activity & Vendor Info: (Acquisitions) Follett Software; (Cataloging) Follett Software; (Circulation) Follett Software; (Course Reserve) Follett Software; (ILL) Follett Software; (Media Booking) Follett Software
Database Vendor: Booklist Online, EBSCO Information Services, Facts on File, Ingram Library Services, Natural Standard, OCLC FirstSearch, WebMD
Wireless access
Mem of Yellowhead Regional Library
Partic in North Eastern Iowa Bridge to Online Resource Sharing (NEIBORS)
Open Mon-Fri 12-6, Sat 10-1

J NORTHEAST IOWA COMMUNITY COLLEGE*, Wilder Library, 1625 Hwy 150, 52132. (Mail add: PO Box 400, 52132-0400), SAN 305-2494. Tel: 563-562-3263. Toll Free Tel: 800-728-2256. FAX: 563-562-4361. Web Site: www.nicc.edu. *Coordr,* Karen Davidson; Tel: 563-562-3263, Ext 257, E-mail: davidsok@nicc.edu; *ILL,* Heather Busta; E-mail: bustah@portal.nicc.edu; Staff 4 (MLS 1, Non-MLS 3)
Founded 1966. Enrl 1,500; Fac 140; Highest Degree: Associate
Library Holdings: Bk Vols 19,200; Per Subs 305
Special Collections: Holocaust Coll
Subject Interests: Agr, Bus & mgt, Nursing, Sci tech
Automation Activity & Vendor Info: (Acquisitions) SirsiDynix; (Cataloging) SirsiDynix; (Circulation) SirsiDynix
Database Vendor: EBSCOhost, OCLC FirstSearch
Open Mon-Thurs 7am-8pm, Fri 7-6, Sat 10-2

CAMANCHE

P CAMANCHE PUBLIC LIBRARY*, 102 12th Ave, 52730. SAN 305-2508. Tel: 563-259-1106. FAX: 563-259-1106. Web Site: www.camanche.lib.ia.us. *Dir,* Beth Thilmany; E-mail: bthilmany@camanche.lib.ia.us; *Ch,* Sondra Taylor; E-mail: staylor@camanche.lib.ia.us; *Libr Asst,* Mary Hehlke; *Libr Asst,* Maureen Vogel
Founded 1965. Pop 4,215; Circ 35,780
Library Holdings: Bk Titles 24,000; Per Subs 150
Special Collections: Iowa Coll; Mississippi River Coll
Open Mon & Tues 2-8:30, Wed & Thurs 11-8:30, Fri 1-5, Sat 11-5
Friends of the Library Group

CAMBRIDGE

P CAMBRIDGE MEMORIAL LIBRARY, 224 Water St, 50046. Tel: 515-220-4542. FAX: 515-220-4542. E-mail: cambridgejmt@yahoo.com. *Librn,* Janet Thorson
Pop 819
Library Holdings: Bk Vols 15,000
Wireless access
Mem of Central Iowa Library Services
Open Mon 9-2 & 4-5:30, Wed 1-6, Fri 4-8, Sat 10-2:30

CANTRIL

P CANTRIL PUBLIC LIBRARY*, 104 W Third, 52542. (Mail add: PO Box 158, 52542-0158), SAN 376-5482. Tel: 319-397-2366. FAX: 319-397-2366. E-mail: cantril@netins.net. *Actg Exec Dir,* Yvonne Pauline Klett
Pop 257
Library Holdings: Bk Vols 7,000
Special Services for the Blind - Large print bks; Talking bks
Open Mon 9-11 & 3:30-5:30, Tues & Thurs 9-11, Wed & Fri 9-11 & 3:30-5

CARLISLE

P CARLISLE PUBLIC LIBRARY*, 135 School St, 50047-8702. (Mail add: PO Box S, 50047-0718), SAN 305-2532. Tel: 515-989-0909. FAX: 515-989-4328. E-mail: carlpl1@mchsi.com. Web Site: www.carlisle.lib.ia.us. *Dir,* Robert Berning; *Ch,* Cathy Spratt
Pop 3,497; Circ 29,097
Jul 2007-Jun 2008 Income $108,023, State $2,340, City $87,860, County $6,656, Locally Generated Income $1,000, Other $730
Library Holdings: Bk Vols 26,466; Per Subs 28
Special Collections: Carlisle/Hartford Scrapbook Coll; Iowa Coll
Automation Activity & Vendor Info: (Cataloging) Follett Software; (Circulation) Follett Software
Mem of Central Iowa Library Services
Open Mon & Thurs 10-9, Tues, Wed, Fri & Sat 10-5
Friends of the Library Group

CARROLL

P CARROLL PUBLIC LIBRARY*, 118 E Fifth St, 51401. SAN 305-2540. Tel: 712-792-3432. FAX: 712-792-0141. E-mail: carrollpublic@yahoo.com. Web Site: www.carroll-library.org. *Dir,* Kelly Fischbach; E-mail: kfischbach@carroll-library.org; *Ch,* Nancy Pudenz; Staff 1 (MLS 1)
Founded 1893. Pop 10,098; Circ 111,846
Library Holdings: Bk Vols 79,000; Per Subs 181
Subject Interests: Genealogy, Sci fict
Automation Activity & Vendor Info: (Cataloging) ComPanion Corp; (Circulation) ComPanion Corp

Database Vendor: EBSCO Auto Repair Reference, EBSCOhost
Wireless access
Mem of Northwest Iowa Library Services
Open Mon-Thurs 9-8, Fri 10-6, Sat 10-5
Friends of the Library Group

J DES MOINES AREA COMMUNITY COLLEGE LIBRARY*, Carroll Campus Library, 906 N Grant Rd, 51401. Tel: 712-792-1755, 712-792-8316. Circulation Tel: 712-792-8317. FAX: 712-792-8500. Web Site: go.dmacc.edu/library/pages/welcome.aspx. *Librn,* Lisa Dreesman; E-mail: ladreesman@dmacc.edu; *Libr Asst,* Jane Riley, E-mail: jcriley@dmacc.edu; Staff 2 (MLS 1, Non-MLS 1)
Enrl 800; Fac 26; Highest Degree: Bachelor
Library Holdings: Bk Vols 6,000; Per Subs 125
Subject Interests: Bus, Educ, Nursing, Psychol
Automation Activity & Vendor Info: (Acquisitions) Innovative Interfaces, Inc; (Cataloging) Innovative Interfaces, Inc; (Circulation) Innovative Interfaces, Inc; (Course Reserve) Innovative Interfaces, Inc; (OPAC) Innovative Interfaces, Inc; (Serials) Innovative Interfaces, Inc
Database Vendor: ABC-CLIO, CQ Press, EBSCOhost, Gale Cengage Learning, JSTOR, Medline, OCLC FirstSearch, Westlaw
Wireless access
Function: Audio & video playback equip for onsite use, Audiobks via web, Bks on CD, Computers for patron use, Copy machines, Electronic databases & coll, ILL available, Online cat, Online searches

CARTER LAKE

P EDWARD F OWEN MEMORIAL LIBRARY*, 1120 Willow Dr, 51510-1332. SAN 305-2559. Tel: 712-347-5492. FAX: 712-347-5013. E-mail: owenlibrary@cox.net. Web Site: www.carterlake.swilsa.lib.ia.us. *Dir,* Theresa Hawkins; *Ch Serv,* Mary Schomer
Founded 1977. Pop 3,248; Circ 13,292
Library Holdings: Bk Titles 14,900; Per Subs 75
Automation Activity & Vendor Info: (Cataloging) Follett Software
Open Mon-Thurs 9-7, Sat 9-2

CASCADE

P CASCADE PUBLIC LIBRARY, 310 First Ave W, 52033. (Mail add: PO Box 117, 52033-0117), SAN 305-2567. Tel: 563-852-3201. FAX: 563-852-6011. E-mail: cpl@netins.net. Web Site: www.cascade.lib.ia.us. *Dir,* Melissa A Kane; *Libr Asst,* Carol Cigrand; *Libr Asst,* Rebecca Johnson; *Libr Asst,* Joyce Kremer; *Libr Asst,* Jane Strang
Founded 1968. Pop 1,958; Circ 26,055
Library Holdings: Bk Vols 16,000; Per Subs 28
Automation Activity & Vendor Info: (Acquisitions) Biblionix/Apollo; (Cataloging) Biblionix/Apollo; (Circulation) Biblionix/Apollo
Database Vendor: EBSCOhost, Overdrive, Inc
Wireless access
Partic in Dubuque Area Library Information Consortium
Open Mon & Tues 1-7, Wed 9:30-8:30, Thurs & Fri 1-5, Sat 9-12
Friends of the Library Group

CASEY

P CASEY PUBLIC LIBRARY*, 604 Antique Country Dr, 50048. (Mail add: PO Box 178, 50048-0178), SAN 305-2575. Tel: 641-746-2670. FAX: 641-746-2670. E-mail: caseylib@netins.net. Web Site: www.casey.swilsa.lib.ia.us. *Dir,* Kim Westphal
Founded 1941. Pop 478; Circ 3,263
Library Holdings: AV Mats 282; High Interest/Low Vocabulary Bk Vols 150; Large Print Bks 30; Bk Titles 10,000; Bk Vols 12,023; Per Subs 10; Talking Bks 155
Special Collections: A-C Yearbooks; Adair News 1951-present; Casey Obituaries; Casey School Alumni Class Pictures; Casey Vindicator on microfilm 1878-1950
Automation Activity & Vendor Info: (ILL) OCLC
Mem of Southwest Iowa Library Services District
Special Services for the Deaf - Closed caption videos
Special Services for the Blind - Bks on cassette; Bks on CD; Large print bks
Open Mon 1-5:30, Wed 1-6, Fri 9-12, Sat 2-5
Friends of the Library Group

CEDAR FALLS

S CEDAR FALLS HISTORICAL SOCIETY ARCHIVES*, 308 W Third St, 50613. SAN 325-7282. Tel: 319-266-5149. FAX: 319-268-1812. E-mail: cfhistory@cfu.net. *Exec Dir,* Jeffery Kurtz; Staff 2 (Non-MLS 2)
Founded 1962
Special Collections: Local Authors
Subject Interests: Local hist
Open Mon-Fri 8-4

P CEDAR FALLS PUBLIC LIBRARY*, 524 Main St, 50613-2830. SAN 305-2583. Tel: 319-273-8643. FAX: 319-273-8648. E-mail: cedarfallslibrary@gmail.com. Web Site: www.cedar-falls.lib.ia.us/. *Dir,* Sheryl Groskurth; Tel: 319-268-5541, E-mail: sheryl.groskurth@gmail.com; Staff 18 (MLS 4, Non-MLS 14)
Founded 1865. Pop 36,145; Circ 269,786
Library Holdings: Bk Vols 115,757; Per Subs 253; Talking Bks 2,176; Videos 5,468
Automation Activity & Vendor Info: (Acquisitions) Innovative Interfaces, Inc; (Cataloging) Innovative Interfaces, Inc; (Circulation) Innovative Interfaces, Inc; (OPAC) Innovative Interfaces, Inc
Wireless access
Function: Bk club(s), Handicapped accessible, Home delivery & serv to Sr ctr & nursing homes, Homebound delivery serv, ILL available, Magnifiers for reading, Prog for children & young adult, Ref serv available, Spoken cassettes & CDs, Spoken cassettes & DVDs, Summer reading prog, VHS videos, Wheelchair accessible
Partic in Cedar Valley Libr Consortium
Special Services for the Blind - Low vision equip
Open Mon-Thurs 9-9, Fri & Sat 9-5, Sun 1-5
Friends of the Library Group

C KAPLAN UNIVERSITY*, Cedar Falls Campus Library, 7009 Nordic Dr, 50613. Tel: 319-277-0220. FAX: 319-268-0978. *Librn,* Kim Masheck; Staff 1 (MLS 1)
Library Holdings: Bk Vols 9,000; Per Subs 20
Subject Interests: Acctg, Bus, Law, Tourism, Travel
Open Mon-Thurs 8-8, Fri 8-5

C UNIVERSITY OF NORTHERN IOWA LIBRARY*, Rod Library, 1227 W 27th St, 50613-3675. SAN 305-2605. Tel: 319-273-2737. Circulation Tel: 319-273-2462. Interlibrary Loan Service Tel: 319-273-2912. Reference Tel: 319-273-2838. FAX: 319-273-2913. E-mail: libill@uni.edu. Web Site: www.library.uni.edu. *Dean of Libr Serv,* Christopher Cox; E-mail: chris.cox@uni.edu; *Head, Access Serv,* Linda L McLaury; Tel: 319-273-3610, E-mail: linda.mclaury@uni.edu; *Head, Coll Mgt & Spec Serv,* Katherine F Martin; Tel: 319-273-7255, E-mail: katherine.martin@uni.edu; *Head, Info Tech,* Jerry Caswell; Tel: 319-273-7059, E-mail: jerry.caswell@uni.edu; *Head, Ref, Instrul Serv Librn,* Jerilyn Marshall; Tel: 319-273-3721, E-mail: jerilyn.marshall@uni.edu; *Head, Tech Serv,* Cynthia M Coulter; Tel: 319-273-2801, E-mail: cynthia.coulter@uni.edu; *Fine & Performing Arts Librn,* Angela Pratesi; Tel: 319-273-6257, E-mail: Angela.Pratesi@uni.edu; *Bibliographer, Instrul Serv Librn, Ref Serv,* Chris Neuhaus; Tel: 319-273-3718, E-mail: chris.neuhaus@uni.edu; *Bibliographer, Maps Librn, Ref Librn,* Gretchen Gould; Tel: 319-273-6327, E-mail: gretchen.gould@uni.edu; *Outreach Serv Librn,* Leila Rod-Welch; Tel: 319-273-3730, E-mail: Leila.Rod-Welch@uni.edu; *Archivist, Bibliographer, Spec Coll Librn,* Gerry L Peterson; Tel: 319-273-6307, E-mail: gerald.peterson@uni.edu; *Acq, Bibliographer,* Thomas Kessler; E-mail: thomas.kessler@uni.edu; *Bibliographer, Ref Serv,* Barbara Allen; Tel: 319-273-3715, E-mail: barbara.allen@uni.edu; *Bibliographer, Ref Serv,* Stanley Lyle; Tel: 319-273-2843, E-mail: stanley.lyle@uni.edu; *Bibliographer, Cat,* Clint Wrede; Tel: 319-273-3654, E-mail: clint.wrede@uni.edu; *Bibliographer, Cat,* Susan Moore; Tel: 319-273-3661, E-mail: susan.moore@uni.edu; *Bibliographer, Distance Educ, Ref Serv,* Ellen Neuhaus; Tel: 319-273-3739, E-mail: ellen.neuhaus@uni.edu; *Bibliographer, Ref Serv,* Barbara Weeg; Tel: 319-273-3705, E-mail: barbara.weeg@uni.edu; *Curator, Mus & Coll,* Position Currently Open; *Info Tech,* John Wynstra; Tel: 319-273-3619, E-mail: john.wynstra@uni.edu; *YA Serv,* Position Currently Open; Staff 29 (MLS 19, Non-MLS 10)
Founded 1876. Enrl 12,159; Fac 788; Highest Degree: Doctorate
Jul 2012-Jun 2013 Income $6,918,850, State $6,172, Locally Generated Income $40,138, Parent Institution $6,872,540. Mats Exp $2,575,750, Books $248,916, Per/Ser (Incl. Access Fees) $450,260, Other Print Mats $248,916, Micro $25,152, Electronic Ref Mat (Incl. Access Fees) $1,584,755, Presv $17,751. Sal $3,317,869 (Prof $2,116,183)
Library Holdings: AV Mats 30,668; CDs 10,346; DVDs 5,267; e-books 8,659; e-journals 59,434; Music Scores 16,630; Bk Titles 674,281; Bk Vols 784,462; Per Subs 1,126; Videos 9,203
Special Collections: American Fiction; Center for the History of Rural Iowa Education & Culture; Grassley Papers; Iowa History; University Archives. State Document Depository; US Document Depository
Subject Interests: Art, Children's lit, Educ, Music
Automation Activity & Vendor Info: (Acquisitions) Innovative Interfaces, Inc; (Cataloging) Innovative Interfaces, Inc; (Circulation) Innovative Interfaces, Inc; (Course Reserve) Innovative Interfaces, Inc; (ILL) OCLC ILLiad; (Media Booking) Innovative Interfaces, Inc; (OPAC) Innovative Interfaces, Inc; (Serials) Innovative Interfaces, Inc
Database Vendor: ABC-CLIO, ACM (Association for Computing Machinery), Agricola, Alexander Street Press, American Chemical Society, American Mathematical Society, American Physical Society, American Psychological Association (APA), Annual Reviews, ARTstor, Baker & Taylor, Blackwell, Bowker, Cambridge Scientific Abstracts, Career

Guidance Foundation, Children's Literature Comprehensive Database Company (CLCD), CIOS (Communication Institute for Online Scholarship), College Source, CQ Press, CRC Press/Taylor & Francis Group, Dialog, Dun & Bradstreet, EBSCO Information Services, EBSCOhost, Elsevier, Emerald, Facts on File, Foundation Center, Gale Cengage Learning, Greenwood Publishing Group, H W Wilson, Haworth Pres Inc, Hoovers, IBISWorld, IEEE (Institute of Electrical & Electronics Engineers), infoUSA, Ingenta, Innovative Interfaces, Inc, IOP, JSTOR, LexisNexis, Marcive, Inc, Marquis Who's Who, McGraw-Hill, Mergent Online, Modern Language Association, Nature Publishing Group, Newsbank, OCLC FirstSearch, OCLC WorldShare Interlibrary Loan, OVID Technologies, Oxford Online, Paratext, Project MUSE, ProQuest, PubMed, ReferenceUSA, Sage, ScienceDirect, Springer-Verlag, Standard & Poor's, STN International, Swets Information Services, ValueLine, Westlaw, Wiley, Wiley InterScience, Wilson - Wilson Web, YBP Library Services
Wireless access
Publications: Guide to the Library; Library User's Guide Series
Partic in Cedar Valley Libr Consortium; Lyrasis; OCLC Online Computer Library Center, Inc
Special Services for the Deaf - ADA equip; Assistive tech; Bks on deafness & sign lang; Closed caption videos; Coll on deaf educ; Sign lang interpreter upon request for prog; Videos & decoder
Special Services for the Blind - Accessible computers; Aids for in-house use; Assistive/Adapted tech devices, equip & products; Audio mat; Braille alphabet card; Braille equip; Cassette playback machines; Children's Braille; Closed caption display syst; Closed circuit TV magnifier; Computer access aids; Computer with voice synthesizer for visually impaired persons; Copier with enlargement capabilities; Free checkout of audio mat; HP Scan Jet with photo-finish software; IBM screen reader; Info on spec aids & appliances; Internet workstation with adaptive software; Large screen computer & software; Low vision equip; Magnifiers; Micro-computer access & training; Networked computers with assistive software; Open bk software on pub access PC; PC for handicapped; Photo duplicator for making large print; Playaways (bks on MP3); Rec; Ref serv; Rental typewriters & computers; Scanner for conversion & translation of mats; Screen enlargement software for people with visual disabilities; Screen reader software; Sound rec; Talking calculator; Text reader; Videos on blindness & phys handicaps; VisualTek equip; ZoomText magnification & reading software
Open Mon-Thurs 7am-Midnight, Fri 7-7, Sat 10-5, Sun Noon-Midnight

CEDAR RAPIDS

S AFRICAN AMERICAN MUSEUM OF IOWA LIBRARY*, 55 12th Ave SE, 52401. Tel: 319-862-2101, Ext 227. FAX: 319-862-2105. Web Site: www.blackiowa.org. *Curator,* Brianna Wright; E-mail: bwright@blackiowa.org; Staff 1 (Non-MLS 1)
Founded 1993
Jan 2012-Dec 2012 Income $415,000, State $15,000, City $40,000, Federal $20,000, County $6,000, Locally Generated Income $40,000, Other $294,000. Mats Exp $10,000. Sal $32,000 (Prof $32,000)
Library Holdings: Bk Vols 4,500
Special Collections: African American History; African American History in Iowa. Oral History
Subject Interests: African hist, African-Am hist
Wireless access
Open Mon-Sat 10-4

S CEDAR RAPIDS MUSEUM OF ART*, Herbert S Stamats Library, 410 Third Ave SE, 52401. SAN 325-1438. Tel: 319-366-7503. FAX: 319-366-4111. E-mail: info@crma.org. Web Site: www.crma.org. *Exec Dir,* Terence Pitts
Founded 1905
Special Collections: Grant Wood Art Coll; Marvin Cone Art Coll
Subject Interests: Art
Restriction: Non-circulating to the pub

P CEDAR RAPIDS PUBLIC LIBRARY WEST*, 2600 Edgewood Rd SW, Ste 330, 52404. SAN 341-7875. Tel: 319-398-5123. FAX: 319-398-0476. E-mail: ill@crlibrary.org, info@crlibrary.org. Web Site: www.crlibrary.org. *Libr Dir,* Position Currently Open; *Children's & Prog Serv Mgr,* Carol Hoke; E-mail: hokec@crlibrary.org; *Coll Mgr,* Karen Johnson; E-mail: johnsonk@crlibrary.org; *IT Mgr,* Roy Johnston; E-mail: johnstonr@crlibrary.org; Staff 44.6 (MLS 12.5, Non-MLS 32.1)
Founded 1896. Pop 126,326; Circ 810,115
Library Holdings: Bk Vols 103,182; Per Subs 233
Automation Activity & Vendor Info: (Acquisitions) SirsiDynix; (Cataloging) SirsiDynix; (Circulation) SirsiDynix; (OPAC) SirsiDynix; (Serials) SirsiDynix
Database Vendor: EBSCOhost, Gale Cengage Learning, Innovative Interfaces, Inc
Wireless access
Function: Bks on CD, Children's prog, Computer training, Computers for patron use, Copy machines, e-mail serv, Free DVD rentals, Homebound delivery serv, ILL available, Music CDs, Notary serv, OverDrive digital audio bks, Photocopying/Printing, Preschool outreach, Prog for adults, Prog for children & young adult, Pub access computers, Ref serv in person, Story hour, Summer & winter reading prog, Tax forms, Teen prog, Telephone ref, Visual arts prog, Wheelchair accessible
Publications: News from the Cedar Rapids Public Library (Newsletter)
Partic in Metro Library Network
Open Mon-Fri 9-9, Sat 10-5, Sun 1-5
Friends of the Library Group

C COE COLLEGE*, Stewart Memorial Library, 1220 First Ave NE, 52402-5092. SAN 305-2621. Tel: 319-399-8023. Circulation Tel: 319-399-8585. Interlibrary Loan Service Tel: 319-399-8018. Reference Tel: 319-399-8586. Administration Tel: 319-399-8024. FAX: 319-399-8019. Web Site: www.library.coe.edu. *Dir,* Jill Jack; E-mail: Jjack@coe.edu; *Head, Ref & Info Serv,* Katelyn Handler; Tel: 319-399-8017, E-mail: Khandler@coe.edu; *Archives,* Rob DeSpain; Tel: 319-399-8787, E-mail: Rdespain@coe.edu; *AV,* Laura Riskedahl; Tel: 319-399-8211, E-mail: lriskedahl@coe.edu; *Cat, Tech Serv,* Hongbo Xie; Tel: 319-399-8026, E-mail: hxie@coe.edu; *Circ,* Sandy Blanchard; Tel: 319-399-8595, E-mail: sblancha@coe.edu; *ILL,* Harlene Hansen; Tel: 319-399-8016, E-mail: hhansen@coe.edu; Staff 4 (MLS 4)
Founded 1900. Enrl 1,303; Fac 123; Highest Degree: Master
Jul 2013-Jun 2014 Income $1,100,000. Mats Exp $400,000. Sal $470,000 (Prof $250,000)
Library Holdings: AV Mats 15,000; CDs 4,001; DVDs 4,787; e-books 193,392; e-journals 2,924; Microforms 5,979; Music Scores 385; Bk Titles 379,276; Per Subs 6,000; Videos 2,231
Special Collections: Paul Engle Papers; William Shirer Papers
Subject Interests: Art & archit, Hist, Relig, Soc sci & issues
Automation Activity & Vendor Info: (Acquisitions) SirsiDynix; (Cataloging) SirsiDynix; (Circulation) SirsiDynix; (Course Reserve) SirsiDynix; (ILL) OCLC ILLiad; (OPAC) SirsiDynix; (Serials) SirsiDynix
Database Vendor: American Chemical Society, American Psychological Association (APA), ARTstor, BioOne, Cinahl, CQ Press, CredoReference, ebrary, EBSCO Information Services, EBSCOhost, Elsevier, H W Wilson, Ingenta, JSTOR, LexisNexis, Modern Language Association, OCLC ArticleFirst, OCLC CAMIO, OCLC FirstSearch, OCLC WorldShare Interlibrary Loan, Project MUSE, ProQuest, RefWorks, ScienceDirect, SerialsSolutions, SirsiDynix
Wireless access
Publications: Coe College Library Association (Newsletter)
Partic in OCLC Online Computer Library Center, Inc
Open Mon-Thurs 7:45am-1am, Fri 7:45-6, Sat 9-6, Sun 11am-1am
Friends of the Library Group

S GENEALOGICAL SOCIETY OF LINN COUNTY IOWA, 813 First Ave SE, 52402. (Mail add: PO Box 175, 52406-0175), SAN 370-1697. Tel: 319-369-0022. *Pres,* Jeanette Bea Haars
Founded 1965
Library Holdings: CDs 300; Bk Titles 12,000
Special Collections: Linn County Cemetery & Court House Records
Function: Res libr
Publications: Linn County Heritage Hunter (Newsletter)
Open Tues-Sat 10-4

S GRAND LODGE OF IOWA, AF & AM, Iowa Masonic Library, 813 First Ave SE, 52406. (Mail add: PO Box 279, 52406-0279), SAN 305-2613. Tel: 319-365-1438. FAX: 319-365-1439. E-mail: librarian@gl-iowa.org. Web Site: www.gl-iowa.org. *Librn,* Craig Davis; E-mail: gliowa@qwest.net; *Asst Librn,* William Kreuger; Staff 2 (MLS 1, Non-MLS 1)
Founded 1845
Library Holdings: Bk Titles 100,000
Special Collections: Abraham Lincoln Coll; Arthur Edward Waite Coll; Cedar Rapids Gazette, micro; Dr Erskine Medical Coll; Early Cedar Rapids, micro, paper; Prince Hall Masonic Coll; Robert Burns Coll
Subject Interests: Hist, Iowa, Poetry, Relig
Open Mon-Fri 8-12 & 1-5

C KAPLAN UNIVERSITY*, Cedar Rapids Campus Library, 3165 Edgewood Pkwy SW, 52404. Tel: 319-363-0481, Ext 123. FAX: 319-363-3812. *Adminr,* Madelyn Wagner
Library Holdings: Bk Vols 5,000; Per Subs 60
Subject Interests: Acctg, Bus, Computers, Travel
Automation Activity & Vendor Info: (Acquisitions) Follett Software; (Cataloging) Follett Software; (Circulation) Follett Software; (Course Reserve) Follett Software; (OPAC) Follett Software
Database Vendor: EBSCOhost, OCLC FirstSearch, OVID Technologies
Partic in Iowa Libr Asn
Open Mon-Thurs 8am-9pm, Fri 8-4, Sat 9-1

J KIRKWOOD COMMUNITY COLLEGE LIBRARY, Benton Hall, 6301 Kirkwood Blvd SW, 52404-5260. (Mail add: PO Box 2068, 52406-2068), SAN 305-2664. Tel: 319-398-5553. Circulation Tel: 319-398-5696. Interlibrary Loan Service Tel: 319-398-1254. Reference Tel: 319-398-5697.

FAX: 319-398-4908. E-mail: library@kirkwood.edu. Web Site: www.kirkwood.edu/library. *Dean, Learning & Libr Serv,* Arron Wings; E-mail: awings@kirkwood.edu; *Access Serv Librn,* Sue Miller; Tel: 319-398-5887, E-mail: sue.miller@kirkwood.edu; *Coll Librn,* Steve Sickels; *Digital Serv Librn,* Nicole Forsythe; *Circ Coordr,* Cindy Wiese; *Electronic Res Coordr,* Ryan Strempke-Durgin; E-mail: ryan.strempke-durgin@kirkwood.edu; *Tech Spec,* Shelley Schultz; Staff 15 (MLS 9, Non-MLS 6)
Founded 1967. Enrl 15,466; Fac 929; Highest Degree: Associate
Library Holdings: AV Mats 3,944; Bks on Deafness & Sign Lang 138; Bk Vols 66,153; Per Subs 594
Automation Activity & Vendor Info: (Acquisitions) OCLC; (Cataloging) OCLC; (Circulation) OCLC; (Course Reserve) OCLC; (ILL) OCLC; (OPAC) OCLC; (Serials) OCLC
Database Vendor: ACM (Association for Computing Machinery), American Psychological Association (APA), CQ Press, EBSCOhost, Gale Cengage Learning, OCLC, OCLC FirstSearch, OVID Technologies, Oxford Online, ProQuest
Wireless access
Publications: Faculty Handbook; Student Handbook
Open Mon-Thurs 7:30am-11pm, Fri 7:30-5, Sat 8:30-4, Sun 3-8
Departmental Libraries:
IOWA CITY CAMPUS LIBRARY, 1816 Lower Muscatine Rd, Iowa City, 52240. Tel: 319-887-3612. FAX: 319-887-3606. E-mail: refdesk@kirkwood.edu. Web Site: www.kirkwood.edu/iclibrary. *Ref Librn,* Glenda Davis-Driggs; *Ref Librn,* David Strass; *Coordr,* Kate Hess; E-mail: khess@kirkwood.edu; *Libr Spec,* Missy Molleston; Staff 6 (MLS 3, Non-MLS 3)
Highest Degree: Associate
Open Mon-Thurs 8-8, Fri 8-5, Sat 11-4

GL LINN COUNTY LAW LIBRARY*, Linn County Courthouse, 52401. SAN 305-2672. Tel: 319-398-3920, Ext 1322.
Founded 1925
Library Holdings: Electronic Media & Resources 10,000; Bk Titles 5,000
Database Vendor: Westlaw
Open Mon-Fri 8-4:30

C MOUNT MERCY UNIVERSITY*, Busse Library, 1330 Elmhurst Dr NE, 52402-4797. SAN 305-2699. Tel: 319-368-6465. FAX: 319-363-9060. E-mail: library@mtmercy.edu. Web Site: www.mtmercy.edu/busselibrary.html. *Dir,* Marilyn Murphy; E-mail: mmurphy@mtmercy.edu; *Acad Tech Librn,* Vicky Maloy; E-mail: vmaloy@mtmercy.edu; *Access Serv Librn,* Boyd Broughton; E-mail: bbroughton@mtmercy.edu; *Archives, Ref Serv,* Kristy Raine; E-mail: kraine@mtmercy.edu; *Cat, Tech Serv,* Janis Dickes; Staff 8 (MLS 6, Non-MLS 2)
Founded 1958. Enrl 1,305; Fac 84; Highest Degree: Master
Library Holdings: AV Mats 5,188; e-books 11,490; e-journals 2,250; Bk Vols 130,573; Per Subs 500
Automation Activity & Vendor Info: (Acquisitions) SirsiDynix; (Cataloging) SirsiDynix; (Circulation) SirsiDynix; (OPAC) SirsiDynix; (Serials) SirsiDynix
Database Vendor: Annual Reviews, College Source, CQ Press, CredoReference, EBSCOhost, LexisNexis, Newsbank, OCLC FirstSearch, OCLC WorldShare Interlibrary Loan, Oxford Online, ProQuest
Wireless access
Partic in OCLC Online Computer Library Center, Inc

M SAINT LUKE'S HOSPITAL*, Health Science Library, 1026 A Ave NE, 52406-3026. SAN 305-2710. Tel: 319-369-7864. FAX: 319-369-8036. Web Site: www.stlukescr.org. *Librn,* Elizabeth Hoover de Galvez; Staff 1 (MLS 1)
Founded 1969
Library Holdings: Bk Titles 4,000; Bk Vols 4,500; Per Subs 350
Subject Interests: Admin law, Allied health, Child welfare
Automation Activity & Vendor Info: (Cataloging) EOS International; (Circulation) EOS International; (Serials) EOS International
Open Mon-Fri 7:30-4

R TEMPLE JUDAH LIBRARY*, 3221 Lindsay Lane SE, 52403. SAN 305-2729. Tel: 319-362-1261. FAX: 319-365-6276. E-mail: office@templejudah.org.
Founded 1950
Library Holdings: Bk Titles 1,850
Subject Interests: Judaica (lit or hist of Jews)
Open Fri 7:30-9:30

CENTER POINT

P CENTER POINT PUBLIC LIBRARY*, 720 Main St, 52213. (Mail add: PO Box 279, 52213-0279), SAN 305-2737. Tel: 319-849-1509. FAX: 319-849-1509. E-mail: cpulib@centerpoint.lib.ia.us. Web Site: www.centerpoint.lib.ia.us. *Tech Librn,* Janine Walters; E-mail: jwalters@centerpoint.lib.ia.us
Pop 2,007; Circ 32,000
Library Holdings: Bk Titles 15,000; Per Subs 52
Open Mon & Thurs 1-8, Tues 8:30-1, Wed 1-5:30, Fri 8:30-5:30, Sat 9-3:30

CENTERVILLE

P DRAKE PUBLIC LIBRARY*, 115 Drake Ave, 52544. SAN 305-2745. Tel: 641-856-6676. FAX: 641-856-6135. E-mail: drake@centerville.lib.ia.us. Web Site: www.centerville.lib.ia.us. *Dir,* Jami Livingston; *Circ Librn,* Julie Buban; Staff 8 (Non-MLS 8)
Founded 1903. Pop 5,924; Circ 108,138
Library Holdings: Bk Titles 30,478; Per Subs 105
Automation Activity & Vendor Info: (Circulation) Follett Software
Function: ILL available
Open Mon, Wed & Thurs 12-8, Fri & Sat 10-6, Sun 1-4
Friends of the Library Group

J INDIAN HILLS COMMUNITY COLLEGE*, Centerville Library, 721 N First St, Bldg CV06, 52544. SAN 305-2753. Tel: 641-856-2143, Ext 2237. Toll Free Tel: 800-670-3641, Ext 2237. FAX: 641-856-5527. Web Site: www.ihcc.cc.ia.us/libraries. *Libr Asst,* Becky Morrow; *Pub Serv Asst,* Debra Yeomans; E-mail: dyeomans@indianhills.edu
Library Holdings: Bk Vols 24,000; Per Subs 98
Open Mon-Thurs 7:15am-9pm

CENTRAL CITY

P JOHN C CLEGG PUBLIC LIBRARY*, 137 Fourth St N, 52214. SAN 305-2761. Tel: 319-438-6685. FAX: 319-438-6685. Web Site: www.centralcity.lib.ia.us. *Dir,* Denise Levenhagen; E-mail: dlevenhagen@centralcity.lib.ia.us; Staff 1 (MLS 1)
Founded 1895. Pop 1,157; Circ 6,793
Library Holdings: Bk Titles 8,435; Per Subs 33
Automation Activity & Vendor Info: (Circulation) Follett Software; (OPAC) Follett Software
Database Vendor: EBSCOhost, OCLC FirstSearch
Open Mon-Wed 8:30-5, Thurs 8:30-7:00, Fri 12-4:30
Friends of the Library Group

CHARITON

P CHARITON FREE PUBLIC LIBRARY*, 803 Braden Ave, 50049. SAN 305-277X. Tel: 641-774-5514. FAX: 641-774-8695. E-mail: charitonlibrary@iowatelecom.net. Web Site: www.chariton.lib.ia.us. *Dir,* Kris Murphy
Founded 1898. Pop 4,573; Circ 40,517
Library Holdings: Bk Titles 35,000; Per Subs 100
Special Collections: Iowa Census Coll; Lucas County, Federal Census, micro; Newspapers (Chariton Coll)
Automation Activity & Vendor Info: (Cataloging) Follett Software
Mem of Southwest Iowa Library Services District
Open Mon-Wed 1-7, Thurs & Fri 10-6, Sat 10-3
Friends of the Library Group

CHARLES CITY

P CHARLES CITY PUBLIC LIBRARY*, 106 Milwaukee Mall, 50616-2281. SAN 305-2788. Tel: 641-257-6319. FAX: 641-257-6325. *Dir,* Jill Gray; *Ch,* Dana Schwickerath; E-mail: dschwickerath@charles-city.lib.ia.us; Staff 2 (MLS 2)
Founded 1904. Pop 7,812; Circ 125,000
Library Holdings: Audiobooks 666; Bk Titles 52,000; Per Subs 156; Videos 1,000
Special Collections: Iowa History; Mooney Art Coll
Subject Interests: Art, Genealogy
Automation Activity & Vendor Info: (Acquisitions) Follett Software
Open Mon-Thurs 10-8, Fri 10-5, Sat & Sun 1-5
Friends of the Library Group

S FLOYD COUNTY HISTORICAL SOCIETY MUSEUM LIBRARY*, 500 Gilbert St, 50616-2738. SAN 373-4536. Tel: 641-228-1099. FAX: 641-228-1157. E-mail: fchs@fiai.net. Web Site: www.floydcountymuseum.org. *Dir,* Mary Ann Townsend
Library Holdings: Bk Vols 1,000
Special Collections: Oliver Hart Parr Coll
Subject Interests: Genealogy
Publications: Floyd County Heritage (Newsletter)

CHARTER OAK

P CHARTER OAK PUBLIC LIBRARY*, 461 Railroad, 51439. (Mail add: PO Box 58, 51439), SAN 320-8249. Tel: 712-678-3425. E-mail: colibry@frontiernet.net. *Librn,* Connie Wiegel
Pop 530
Library Holdings: Bk Vols 5,000
Wireless access
Mem of Northwest Iowa Library Services
Open Wed 1-6, Sat 8:30-1:30
Friends of the Library Group

CHELSEA

P CHELSEA PUBLIC LIBRARY*, 600 Station St, 52215. (Mail add: PO Box 187, 52215-0187), SAN 305-280X. Tel: 641-489-2525. FAX: 641-489-2525. *Dir,* Dianna Dunning; E-mail: diannadunning@hotmail.com
Founded 1974. Pop 287; Circ 4,767
Library Holdings: Bk Vols 7,000; Per Subs 25
Mem of Harrison Regional Library System
Open Mon 11:30-4:30, Tues & Wed 1:30-5:30, Thurs 2-7, Sat 9-12

CHEROKEE

M CHEROKEE MENTAL HEALTH INSTITUTE*, Health Science Library, 1251 W Cedar Loop, 51012. SAN 375-2747. Tel: 712-225-2594, Ext 2239. FAX: 712-225-6974. *In Charge,* Diane Knaack; Tel: 712-225-6919
Library Holdings: Bk Vols 500; Per Subs 5
Restriction: Open to staff only

P CHEROKEE PUBLIC LIBRARY*, 215 S Second St, 51012. SAN 305-2818. Tel: 712-225-3498. FAX: 712-225-4964. Web Site: www.cherokee.lib.ia.us. *Dir,* Mary Jo Ruppert
Founded 1886. Pop 5,369; Circ 65,000
Library Holdings: AV Mats 125; CDs 400; DVDs 300; Large Print Bks 900; Bk Titles 32,000; Per Subs 90; Talking Bks 1,500; Videos 1,400
Automation Activity & Vendor Info: (Cataloging) Follett Software; (Circulation) Follett Software
Database Vendor: Baker & Taylor, MITINET, Inc
Wireless access
Open Mon, Wed & Thurs 10-8, Tues & Fri 10-5, Sat 10-2
Friends of the Library Group

S SANFORD MUSEUM & PLANETARIUM*, Reference Library, 117 E Willow, 51012. SAN 305-2826. Tel: 712-225-3922. FAX: 712-225-0446. E-mail: sanfordmuseum@iowatelecom.net. *Dir,* Linda Burkhart
Founded 1951
Library Holdings: Bk Vols 5,000
Subject Interests: Anthrop, Archaeology, Astronomy, Hist, Museology, Paleontology

CHURDAN

P CHURDAN CITY LIBRARY*, 414 Sand St, 50050. (Mail add: PO Box 185, 50050-0185), SAN 305-2834. Tel: 515-389-3423. FAX: 515-389-3401. Web Site: www.churdan.lib.ia.us. *Dir,* Shari Minnehan; E-mail: shari@churdan.lib.ia.us; *Youth Serv Dir,* Marilyn Tilley; E-mail: marilyn@churdan.lib.ia.us
Pop 418; Circ 25,016
Library Holdings: AV Mats 1,115; DVDs 165; Bk Titles 10,040; Per Subs 32; Talking Bks 400
Automation Activity & Vendor Info: (Acquisitions) Book Systems; (Cataloging) Book Systems; (Circulation) Book Systems
Mem of Central Iowa Library Services
Open Mon, Tues, Thurs & Fri Noon-5:30, Wed 9:30-6, Sat 8:30-Noon

CLARE

P CLARE PUBLIC LIBRARY*, 119 E Front St, 50524. (Mail add: PO Box 5, 50524-0005), SAN 376-5164. Tel: 515-546-6222. Administration Tel: 515-546-6173. FAX: 515-546-6222. E-mail: clarepl@wccta.net. *Librn,* Kathy Allen
Founded 1980. Pop 190
Jul 2007-Jun 2008 Income $15,215, City $4,500, County $10,715. Mats Exp $4,414, Books $3,500, Per/Ser (Incl. Access Fees) $304, AV Mat $610. Sal $6,847
Library Holdings: AV Mats 25; Large Print Bks 50; Bk Titles 8,680; Per Subs 11; Talking Bks 74; Videos 919
Special Services for the Blind - Large print bks
Open Mon 5-8, Wed & Fri 1:30-5:30, Sat 9-1

CLARENCE

P EDNA ZYBELL MEMORIAL LIBRARY, 309 Sixth Ave, 52216-4400. SAN 305-2842. Tel: 563-452-3734. FAX: 563-452-3520. Web Site: www.clarence.lib.ia.us. *Librn,* Tami Finley; E-mail: t.finley@clarence.lib.ia.us; *Asst Librn,* Karolyn Rouse
Pop 989; Circ 7,590
Library Holdings: Bk Vols 7,842; Per Subs 13
Wireless access
Open Tues 1-5, Wed 9-12 & 1-6, Thurs 1-6, Fri 9-12 & 1-5, Sat 9-Noon
Friends of the Library Group

CLARINDA

J IOWA WESTERN COMMUNITY COLLEGE-CLARINDA CAMPUS*, Edith Lisle Library, 923 E Washington, 51632. SAN 305-2869. Tel: 712-542-5117, Ext 234. FAX: 712-542-3604. Web Site: www.iwcc.edu. *Coordr,* Shelly Anderson; E-mail: sanderson@iwcc.edu; Staff 1 (MLS 1)
Founded 1963. Enrl 350
Automation Activity & Vendor Info: (Cataloging) SirsiDynix; (Circulation) SirsiDynix; (Serials) SirsiDynix
Open Mon-Thurs 8am-9pm, Fri 8-4

P LIED PUBLIC LIBRARY*, 100 E Garfield St, 51632. SAN 305-2850. Tel: 712-542-2416. FAX: 712-542-3590. Web Site: www.clarindapubliclibrary.org. *Dir,* Andrew Hoppman; *Youth Serv Librn,* Marissa Gruber
Pop 7,500; Circ 60,000
Library Holdings: AV Mats 609; CDs 6,600; Bk Titles 36,000; Per Subs 96
Automation Activity & Vendor Info: (Acquisitions) Book Systems
Wireless access
Mem of Southwest Iowa Library Services District
Open Mon 12-8, Tues-Thurs 9:30-6, Fri 9:30-5, Sat 9:30-1
Friends of the Library Group

CLARION

P CLARION PUBLIC LIBRARY*, 302 N Main St, 50525. SAN 305-2877. Tel: 515-532-3673. FAX: 515-532-6322. Web Site: www.clarion.lib.ia.us. *Librn,* Nola Waddingham; E-mail: nola@clarion.lib.ia.us; *Ch,* Nancy Nail
Pop 2,968; Circ 36,000
Library Holdings: Bk Titles 23,000; Per Subs 45
Automation Activity & Vendor Info: (Acquisitions) Follett Software; (Cataloging) Follett Software; (Circulation) Follett Software; (ILL) Follett Software; (Media Booking) Follett Software; (OPAC) Follett Software; (Serials) Follett Software
Open Mon-Wed 12-8, Thurs-Sat 10-5

CLARKSVILLE

P CLARKSVILLE PUBLIC LIBRARY*, 103 W Greene St, 50619-0039. SAN 305-2885. Tel: 319-278-1168. FAX: 319-278-1168. E-mail: clarksville@butler-bremer.com. Web Site: www.clarksville.lib.ia.us. *Dir,* Kristen Clark; *Asst Librn,* Patricia Calease
Founded 1929. Pop 1,441; Circ 28,000
Library Holdings: Bk Titles 17,000; Bk Vols 17,119; Per Subs 80
Open Mon & Wed 10-6, Tues & Thurs 10-5, Fri 10-4, Sat 10-2

CLEAR LAKE

P CLEAR LAKE PUBLIC LIBRARY*, 200 N Fourth St, 50428-1698. SAN 305-2893. Tel: 641-357-6133, 641-357-6134. FAX: 641-357-4645. E-mail: clplib@netins.net. Web Site: www.cityofclearlake.com/html/library.html. *Dir,* Jean Casey; *Ch,* Martha Boyes; E-mail: librarylady831@yahoo.com; Staff 16 (MLS 1, Non-MLS 15)
Founded 1889. Pop 8,161; Circ 153,585
Library Holdings: Audiobooks 1,390; CDs 395; DVDs 2,372; Large Print Bks 2,150; Bk Titles 45,182; Bk Vols 46,453; Per Subs 164
Automation Activity & Vendor Info: (Cataloging) TLC (The Library Corporation); (Circulation) TLC (The Library Corporation); (OPAC) TLC (The Library Corporation)
Database Vendor: EBSCOhost
Wireless access
Open Mon-Thurs 10-8, Fri & Sat 10-5
Friends of the Library Group

CLEARFIELD

P CLEARFIELD PUBLIC LIBRARY*, 401 Broadway, Ste 200, 50840-0028. SAN 305-2907. Tel: 641-336-2944. E-mail: clfdlib@iowatelecom.net. *Librn,* Suzanne Brown; Tel: 641-336-2939
Founded 1916. Pop 371; Circ 4,127
Library Holdings: Bk Vols 7,007; Talking Bks 48
Mem of Southwest Iowa Library Services District

Special Services for the Blind - Bks available with recordings; Large print bks
Open Wed & Fri 12-5
Bookmobiles: 1

CLEGHORN

P M-C COMMUNITY LIBRARY*, 200 W Grace St, 51014. (Mail add: PO Box 124, 51014-0124), SAN 305-2915. Tel: 712-436-2521. FAX: 712-436-2695. E-mail: mclib@netins.net. *Dir,* Vangie Cowen
Pop 250; Circ 6,000
Library Holdings: Bk Vols 14,699; Per Subs 18
Automation Activity & Vendor Info: (Cataloging) Follett Software
Mem of Northwest Iowa Library Services
Open Mon 8-7, Tues-Fri 8-6, Sat 9-12

CLERMONT

P CLERMONT PUBLIC LIBRARY*, 503 Larabee St, 52135. (Mail add: PO Box 49, 52135-0049), SAN 305-2923. Tel: 563-423-7286. FAX: 563-423-7286. Web Site: www.clermont.lib.ia.us. *Dir,* Helena Zweibohmer; E-mail: helenaz@clermont.lib.ia.us
Pop 716; Circ 10,230
Library Holdings: AV Mats 420; Bk Titles 6,231; Per Subs 36
Open Mon-Wed 1-6, Fri 9:30-11:30 & 1-5, Sat 9-12

CLINTON

C ASHFORD UNIVERSITY LIBRARY*, 400 N Bluff Blvd, 52732. SAN 305-294X. Tel: 563-242-4023, Ext 3211. FAX: 563-242-2003. Web Site: www.ashford.edu. *Dir,* Flora S Lowe; Tel: 563-242-4023, Ext 7844; *ILL,* Sabrina Aude; Staff 3 (MLS 2, Non-MLS 1)
Founded 1918. Highest Degree: Bachelor
Library Holdings: Bk Vols 105,000; Per Subs 500
Special Collections: St Francis, St Clare & the Medieval Woman Autograph Coll
Automation Activity & Vendor Info: (Cataloging) SirsiDynix; (Circulation) SirsiDynix; (OPAC) SirsiDynix
Database Vendor: EBSCOhost, LexisNexis, OCLC FirstSearch, ProQuest
Partic in Iowa Private Academic Library Consortium (IPAL); Quad-Link Libr Consortium; RiverShare Libraries
Open Mon-Thurs 7:30am-11pm, Fri 7:30-5, Sat 1-5, Sun 1-11

S BICKELHAUPT ARBORETUM LIBRARY*, 340 S 14th St, 52732-5432. SAN 324-7813. Tel: 563-242-4771. FAX: 563-242-7373. Web Site: www.bickarb.org. *Dir,* David Horst; Staff 3 (MLS 3)
Founded 1970
Library Holdings: Bk Titles 800; Bk Vols 845; Per Subs 10
Subject Interests: Hort
Open Mon-Fri 8-5

J CLINTON COMMUNITY COLLEGE LIBRARY*, 1000 Lincoln Blvd, 52732. SAN 305-2931. Tel: 563-244-7046. Reference Tel: 563-244-7106. FAX: 563-244-7107. E-mail: ccclibrary@eicc.edu. Web Site: www.eicc.edu/library/. *Librn,* Jane Campagna, *Libr Spec,* Charlotte Darsidan; Staff 3 (MLS 1, Non-MLS 2)
Founded 1966. Enrl 1,300
Library Holdings: Bk Titles 17,422; Bk Vols 18,439; Per Subs 65
Automation Activity & Vendor Info: (Cataloging) SIRSI WorkFlows; (Circulation) SIRSI WorkFlows; (Course Reserve) SIRSI-iBistro; (OPAC) SIRSI-iBistro; (Serials) SIRSI WorkFlows
Database Vendor: CountryWatch, CQ Press, EBSCO - WebFeat, EBSCOhost, Gale Cengage Learning, Micromedex, OCLC FirstSearch, OCLC WorldShare Interlibrary Loan, Oxford Online, SirsiDynix, STAT!Ref (Teton Data Systems)
Wireless access
Function: ILL available
Partic in Regional Med Libr - Region 3; RiverShare Libraries
Open Mon-Thurs (Winter) 7:30am-9pm, Fri 7:30-4, Sat 8-1; Mon, Tues & Thurs (Summer) 7:30-7, Wed & Fri 7:30-4

P CLINTON PUBLIC LIBRARY*, 306 Eighth Ave S, 52732. SAN 341-8022. Tel: 563-242-8441. FAX: 563-242-8162. E-mail: clintonlib@clinton.lib.ia.us, reference@clinton.lib.ia.us. Web Site: www.clinton.lib.ia.us. *Dir,* Amy Birtell; E-mail: abirtell@clinton.lib.ia.us; *Ch,* Kay Spittler; *Ref Librn,* Kim Limond; *Cataloger,* Beth Mosher; *Tech Spec,* Sharon Hess; Staff 27 (MLS 3, Non-MLS 24)
Founded 1904. Pop 27,772; Circ 183,130
Library Holdings: AV Mats 1,038; Bks on Deafness & Sign Lang 68; CDs 2,432; High Interest/Low Vocabulary Bk Vols 186; Large Print Bks 10,050; Bk Titles 148,725; Per Subs 266; Talking Bks 5,656; Videos 2,572
Special Collections: Clinton & Lyons Newspapers on Microfilm 1854 to date; Clinton Authors. State Document Depository
Subject Interests: Genealogy
Automation Activity & Vendor Info: (Cataloging) SirsiDynix; (Circulation) SirsiDynix; (OPAC) SirsiDynix
Database Vendor: EBSCOhost, OCLC FirstSearch, SirsiDynix, TLC (The Library Corporation)
Function: ILL available
Partic in RiverShare Libraries
Special Services for the Deaf - TDD equip
Open Mon-Thurs 9-8, Fri & Sat 9-5
Friends of the Library Group
Branches: 1
LYONS, 105 Main St, 52732. (Mail add: 306 Eighth Ave S, 52732), SAN 341-8057. Tel: 563-242-5355. FAX: 563-243-6553. E-mail: lyons@clinton.lib.ia.us. *Circ Asst,* Mary Bertrand; E-mail: mbertrand@clinton.lib.ia.us; Staff 5 (Non-MLS 5)
Library Holdings: AV Mats 585; Bk Vols 17,486; Per Subs 51
Automation Activity & Vendor Info: (Circulation) SirsiDynix
Database Vendor: ProQuest, SirsiDynix
Function: ILL available
Open Mon-Thurs 1-8, Fri & Sat 9-5
Friends of the Library Group

M MERCY MEDICAL CENTER LIBRARY*, 1410 N Fourth St, 52732. SAN 377-5445. Tel: 563-244-5555. FAX: 563-244-5592. *Dir,* Diane Grantz; *Coordr,* Donna Herkelman; E-mail: herkelmd@mercyhealth.com
Library Holdings: Bk Vols 200; Per Subs 50
Wireless access
Open Mon-Fri 7:30-4

CLIVE

P CLIVE PUBLIC LIBRARY*, 1900 NW 114th St, 50325. SAN 920-6965. Tel: 515-453-2221. FAX: 515-453-2246. Web Site: www.cityofclive.com/departments/library. *Dir,* Todd Seaman; E-mail: tseaman@cityofclive.com; *Libr Mgr,* Nicole Morgan; E-mail: nmorgan@cityofclive.com; *Ch,* Suzanne Piel; Staff 9 (MLS 3, Non-MLS 6)
Founded 2000. Pop 14,125; Circ 223,623
Jul 2007-Jun 2008 Income $707,772, City $706,772, County $1,000. Mats Exp $110,000
Library Holdings: Bk Titles 66,000; Per Subs 190
Automation Activity & Vendor Info: (Acquisitions) Innovative Interfaces, Inc; (Cataloging) Innovative Interfaces, Inc; (Circulation) Innovative Interfaces, Inc; (OPAC) Innovative Interfaces, Inc; (Serials) Innovative Interfaces, Inc
Database Vendor: 3M Library Systems, Baker & Taylor, BCR: Christian Periodical Index, Bowker, EBSCO Information Services, EBSCOhost, Facts on File, Innovative Interfaces, Inc, OCLC FirstSearch, OCLC WebJunction, OCLC WorldShare Interlibrary Loan, Overdrive, Inc, ProQuest
Wireless access
Mem of Central Iowa Library Services
Open Mon-Thurs 9-8, Fri 9-6, Sat 9-5, Sun 1-5
Friends of the Library Group

CLUTIER

P CLUTIER PUBLIC LIBRARY*, 404 Main St, 52217. (Mail add: PO Box 182, 52217-0182), SAN 376-7450. Tel: 319-479-2171. FAX: 319-479-2903. *Dir,* Michelle Parizek
Pop 229
Library Holdings: AV Mats 382; Bk Vols 5,000; Per Subs 18
Open Mon 9-12 & 2:30-6, Tues-Thurs 2:30-6, Fri 9:15-12, Sat 9-12
Friends of the Library Group

COGGON

P COGGON PUBLIC LIBRARY*, 216 E Main St, 52218-0182. (Mail add: PO Box 79, 52218-0079), SAN 376-5407. Tel: 319-435-2542. FAX: 319-435-2542. E-mail: coggonpl@qwestoffice.net. *Dir,* Diane Knott
Founded 1938. Pop 745
Library Holdings: Large Print Bks 150; Bk Vols 15,000; Per Subs 35
Open Tues 9-6, Wed & Fri 9-5, Sat 9-Noon
Friends of the Library Group

COIN

P COIN PUBLIC LIBRARY*, 115 Main St, 51636. SAN 376-5202. Tel: 712-583-3684. *Pres,* Bonnie Jackson
Founded 1981. Pop 252
Library Holdings: e-journals 14,190; Large Print Bks 33; Bk Vols 13,437; Talking Bks 53; Videos 86
Mem of Southwest Iowa Library Services District
Open Mon 9-10:30 & 2:30-4:30, Tues, Thurs & Fri 9am-10:30am, Wed 2:30-4:30, Sat 8:30am-10am

COLESBURG

P COLESBURG PUBLIC LIBRARY*, 220 Main St, 52035. (Mail add: PO Box 159, 52035-0159), SAN 376-5237. Tel: 563-856-5800. FAX: 563-856-5800. E-mail: colepl@windstream.net. Web Site: www.colesburg.lib.ia.us/. *Libr Dir,* Carol Walthart; E-mail: cwalthart@colesburg.lib.ia.us
Founded 1983. Pop 412; Circ 5,150
Library Holdings: Bks on Deafness & Sign Lang 20; Bk Vols 13,570; Per Subs 33
Automation Activity & Vendor Info: (Circulation) Follett Software
Open Mon 1-6, Tues 10-8, Wed 4-8, Thurs 9-2, Fri 1-5, Sat 9-Noon
Friends of the Library Group

COLFAX

P COLFAX PUBLIC LIBRARY, 25 W Division St, 50054. SAN 305-2966. Tel: 515-674-3625. E-mail: colfaxlib@mediacombb.net. *Dir,* Jill Miller
Pop 2,223; Circ 9,000
Library Holdings: Bk Vols 7,110; Per Subs 25
Wireless access
Open Mon 2-8, Tues-Fri 2-6, Sat 9-12

COLLINS

P COLLINS PUBLIC LIBRARY*, 212 Main St, 50055. (Mail add: PO Box 79, 50055), SAN 305-2974. Tel: 641-385-2464. FAX: 641-385-2205. E-mail: collinspubliclibrary@gmail.com. Web Site: www.collinspubliclibrary.org. *Dir,* Deanne Marie Jolly; *Children's Prog Coordr,* Darlene Marie Newton; *Storyhour Coordr,* Kesha Christie
Founded 1936. Pop 499; Circ 20,033
Library Holdings: AV Mats 650; CDs 152; DVDs 889; Large Print Bks 270; Music Scores 150; Bk Titles 10,380; Per Subs 16; Talking Bks 45; Videos 378
Special Collections: Samual Clemems (Complete Authorized); Set of 24 (Rare book set)
Function: Adult bk club, Audio & video playback equip for onsite use, Bks on cassette, Bks on CD, CD-ROM, Children's prog, Computer training, Computers for patron use, Copy machines, e-mail & chat, e-mail serv, Electronic databases & coll, Equip loans & repairs, Family literacy, Free DVD rentals, Govt ref serv, Handicapped accessible, Holiday prog, Homebound delivery serv, Homework prog, ILL available, Magnifiers for reading, Mail & tel request accepted, Mail loans to mem, Music CDs, Newsp ref libr, Outreach serv, Outside serv via phone, mail, e-mail & web, Photocopying/Printing, Preschool outreach, Prog for children & young adult, Pub access computers, Ref serv in person, Referrals accepted, Scanner, Senior computer classes, Senior outreach, Story hour, Summer reading prog, Tax forms, Teen prog, VHS videos, Wheelchair accessible
Special Services for the Deaf - Bks on deafness & sign lang; High interest/low vocabulary bks
Special Services for the Blind - Audio mat; Bks on cassette; Bks on CD; Braille alphabet card; Cassette playback machines; Cassettes; Home delivery serv; Large print & cassettes; Large print bks; Magnifiers
Open Tues 8-10 & 4-7, Wed 9-11 & 3-6, Thurs 4-7, Fri 2-6, Sat 9-Noon
Friends of the Library Group

COLO

P COLO PUBLIC LIBRARY*, 309 Main St, 50056. (Mail add: PO Box 324, 50056-0324), SAN 305-2982. Tel: 641-377-2900. FAX: 641-377-2468. E-mail: cololibrary@netins.net. Web Site: www.colo.lib.ia.us. *Dir,* Joanie Jamison; *Ch,* Carla Smith
Pop 868; Circ 21,786
Library Holdings: Bk Vols 15,000; Per Subs 40; Videos 1,100
Mem of Central Iowa Library Services
Open Mon, Wed, Thurs & Fri 11-6, Sat 8-6

COLUMBUS JUNCTION

P COLUMBUS JUNCTION PUBLIC LIBRARY*, 232 Second St, 52738-1028. (Mail add: PO Box 109, 52738-0109), SAN 305-2990. Tel: 319-728-7972. FAX: 319-728-2303. Web Site: www.columbusjct.lib.ia.us. *Dir,* Cathy Crawford; E-mail: cathy.crawford@columbusjct.lib.ia.us
Founded 1948. Pop 1,900; Circ 16,579
Library Holdings: AV Mats 566; Bk Titles 14,000; Per Subs 50
Special Collections: Videos, Large Print & Audiotapes
Open Mon-Fri 10-12, Sat 9-12
Friends of the Library Group

CONRAD

P CONRAD PUBLIC LIBRARY*, 114 N Main Ave, 50621. (Mail add: PO Box 189, 50621-0189), SAN 305-3008. Tel: 641-366-2583. FAX: 641-366-3105. E-mail: conradlibrary@conrad.lib.ia.us. Web Site: www.conrad.lib.ia.us. *Dir,* Susan Blythe; E-mail: susan@conrad.lib.ia.us; *Ch,* Sarah German; Staff 3 (Non-MLS 3)
Founded 1936. Pop 1,055
Library Holdings: Bk Vols 16,051; Per Subs 113
Subject Interests: Genealogy
Automation Activity & Vendor Info: (Cataloging) Follett Software; (Circulation) Follett Software; (OPAC) Follett Software
Open Mon, Tues & Thurs 2-8, Wed 9-8, Fri 2-6, Sat 9-12

COON RAPIDS

P COON RAPIDS PUBLIC LIBRARY*, 123 Third Ave, 50058-1601. SAN 305-3016. Tel: 712-999-5410. FAX: 712-999-5410. *Dir,* Faye Seidl; E-mail: faye.seidl@coonrapids.lib.ia.us
Pop 1,305; Circ 19,097
Library Holdings: AV Mats 802; Bk Titles 15,074; Per Subs 60; Videos 539
Automation Activity & Vendor Info: (Acquisitions) Baker & Taylor; (Circulation) Book Systems; (OPAC) Book Systems
Wireless access
Mem of Northwest Iowa Library Services
Open Mon, Tues, Thurs & Fri 11-6, Wed 11-8, Sat 11-3
Friends of the Library Group

CORALVILLE

P CORALVILLE PUBLIC LIBRARY*, 1401 Fifth St, 52241. SAN 305-3024. Tel: 319-248-1850. FAX: 319-248-1890. E-mail: corallib@coralville.lib.ia.us. Web Site: www.coralvillepubliclibrary.org. *Dir,* Alison Ames Galstad; E-mail: agalstad@coralville.lib.ia.us; *Asst Dir,* Ellen L Hampe; E-mail: ehampe@coralville.lib.ia.us; *Ch,* Sara Glenn; E-mail: sglenn@coralville.lib.ia.us; *Youth Serv Coordr,* Linda Parker; Staff 12.5 (MLS 5.5, Non-MLS 7)
Founded 1965. Pop 17,269; Circ 254,932
Jul 2007-Jun 2008 Income $724,783. Mats Exp $107,000. Sal $350,000
Library Holdings: Bk Titles 90,186; Per Subs 200
Automation Activity & Vendor Info: (Acquisitions) SirsiDynix; (Cataloging) SirsiDynix; (Circulation) SirsiDynix; (OPAC) Horizon; (Serials) SirsiDynix
Database Vendor: Baker & Taylor, BWI, EBSCOhost, Facts on File, infoUSA, LearningExpress, Marquis Who's Who, Newsbank, OCLC ArticleFirst, OCLC FirstSearch, OCLC WorldShare Interlibrary Loan, Oxford Online, ReferenceUSA, SirsiDynix, Standard & Poor's, ValueLine
Open Mon-Thurs 10-8:30, Fri 10-6, Sat 9-4:30
Friends of the Library Group

CORNING

P CORNING PUBLIC LIBRARY*, 603 Ninth St, 50841-1304. SAN 305-3032. Tel: 641-322-3866. FAX: 641-322-3491. E-mail: cornpl@mchsi.com. Web Site: www.corning.swilsa.lib.ia.us. *Dir,* Becky Rike; *Asst Dir, Ch,* Roxann Moore; *Ad,* Gayle Anstey
Founded 1916. Pop 1,783; Circ 44,618
Library Holdings: AV Mats 1,800; Bk Vols 29,000; Per Subs 45
Special Collections: American Indian Literature
Partic in Iowa Libr Asn
Open Mon, Tues, Thurs & Fri 9:30-5:30, Wed 9:30-8, Sat 9:30-1

CORRECTIONVILLE

P CORRECTIONVILLE PUBLIC LIBRARY*, 532 Driftwood, 51016. (Mail add: PO Box 308, 51016), SAN 305-3040. Tel: 712-342-4203. FAX: 712-342-4203. Web Site: www.correctionville.lib.ia.us. *Dir,* Kristen Wilen; E-mail: kristen.wilen@correctionville.lib.ia.us
Founded 1899. Pop 851; Circ 8,047
Library Holdings: Audiobooks 58; Bks on Deafness & Sign Lang 2; DVDs 158; Large Print Bks 96; Bk Vols 11,945; Per Subs 4; Videos 324
Database Vendor: EBSCOhost
Wireless access
Mem of Northwest Iowa Library Services
Open Mon & Thurs 1-5, Wed 3-7, Sat 9-2
Friends of the Library Group

CORWITH

P CORWITH PUBLIC LIBRARY*, 110 NW Elm, 50430. (Mail add: PO Box 308, 50430-0308), SAN 305-3059. Tel: 515-583-2536. FAX: 515-583-2536. E-mail: corlib@comm1net.net. *Dir,* Kathy Olthoff
Pop 309; Circ 9,072
Library Holdings: Bk Vols 7,651; Per Subs 15
Automation Activity & Vendor Info: (Acquisitions) TLC (The Library Corporation)
Wireless access
Partic in N Iowa Libr Exten
Open Mon & Fri 1-6, Wed 1-8, Thurs 6-8, Sat 9-Noon

CORYDON

P KARL MILES LECOMPTE MEMORIAL LIBRARY*, 110 S Franklin, 50060-1518. SAN 305-3067. Tel: 641-872-1621. FAX: 641-872-1621. E-mail: lecompte@grm.net. *Dir,* Kay Milner
Pop 1,591; Circ 30,192
Library Holdings: Bk Titles 16,000; Per Subs 30
Mem of Southwest Iowa Library Services District
Open Mon-Wed & Fri 12-5, Thurs 12-6, Sat 10-2

S WAYNE COUNTY HISTORICAL SOCIETY, Prairie Trails Museum of Wayne County Iowa Library, Hwy 2, 515 E Jefferson St, 50060. (Mail add: PO Box 104, 50060), SAN 375-1783. Tel: 641-872-2211. E-mail: ptmuseum@grm.net. Web Site: www.prairietrailsmuseum.org. *Head Librn,* Jan Donaldson; Staff 8 (Non-MLS 8)
Founded 1975
Library Holdings: Microforms 50; Bk Vols 750
Special Collections: County Census Records 1850-1920; Doctor's Records; Early Wills & Birth Certificates; Obituaries; Old Newspapers & Newspaper Clippings
Subject Interests: Obituary info
Wireless access

COULTER

P COULTER PUBLIC LIBRARY*, 111 Main St, 50431. (Mail add: PO Box 87, 50431-0087), SAN 305-3075. Tel: 641-866-6798. FAX: 641-866-6798. *Librn,* Barb Gardner
Founded 1971. Pop 262; Circ 4,391
Library Holdings: Bk Titles 7,081; Per Subs 12
Automation Activity & Vendor Info: (Acquisitions) Follett Software; (Cataloging) Follett Software; (Circulation) Follett Software; (ILL) Follett Software; (Media Booking) Follett Software; (OPAC) Follett Software; (Serials) Follett Software
Wireless access
Open Tues-Thurs 1-5, Fri 1-6, Sat 9-12

COUNCIL BLUFFS

P COUNCIL BLUFFS PUBLIC LIBRARY*, 400 Willow Ave, 51503-4269. SAN 305-3091. Tel: 712-323-7553. Circulation Tel: 712-323-7553, Ext 110. Interlibrary Loan Service Tel: 712-323-7553, Ext 117. Reference Tel: 712-323-7553, Ext 132. Administration Tel: 712-323-7553, Ext 120. Automation Services Tel: 712-323-7553, Ext 111. FAX: 712-323-1269. TDD: 712-322-6338. Web Site: www.cbpl.lib.ia.us. *Dir,* Kathy Rieger; Tel: 712-323-7553, Ext 123, E-mail: krieger@cbpl.lib.ia.us; *Automation & Networking Mgr,* Tom Ryan; E-mail: tryan@cbpl.lib.ia.us; *Circ & Adult Serv Mgr,* Marlys Lien; Tel: 712-323-7553, Ext 118, E-mail: mlien@cbpl.lib.ia.us; *Support Serv Mgr,* Mary Carpenter; Tel: 712-323-7553, Ext 127, E-mail: mcarp@cbpl.lib.ia.us; *Youth Serv Mgr,* Dianne Herzog; Tel: 712-323-7553, Ext 113, E-mail: dherzog@cbpl.lib.ia.us; *Teen Librn,* Anna Hartmann; Tel: 712-323-7553, Ext 105, E-mail: ahartmann@cbpl.lib.ia.us; Staff 8 (MLS 7, Non-MLS 1)
Founded 1866. Pop 61,324; Circ 600,372
Jul 2012-Jun 2013 Income $2,205,560. Mats Exp $300,000
Library Holdings: Audiobooks 12,017; DVDs 8,745; e-books 400; Electronic Media & Resources 4,012; Bk Vols 169,278; Per Subs 314
Special Collections: Lewis Carroll Coll; Railroads (Grenville Mellen Dodge Coll); Woman Suffrage (Amelia Bloomer Coll)
Automation Activity & Vendor Info: (Acquisitions) Innovative Interfaces, Inc; (Cataloging) Innovative Interfaces, Inc; (Circulation) Innovative Interfaces, Inc; (ILL) Innovative Interfaces, Inc; (Media Booking) Innovative Interfaces, Inc - Millenium; (OPAC) Innovative Interfaces, Inc; (Serials) Innovative Interfaces, Inc
Database Vendor: Baker & Taylor, Booklist Online, Booksite, EBSCO Auto Repair Reference, EBSCOhost, Foundation Center, infoUSA, Innovative Interfaces, Inc, Newsbank, OCLC FirstSearch, OCLC WorldShare Interlibrary Loan, WT Cox
Wireless access
Function: Accelerated reader prog, Adult bk club, Archival coll, Art exhibits, Audiobks via web, AV serv, Bk club(s), Bks on CD, Chess club, Children's prog, Computer training, Computers for patron use, Copy machines, Digital talking bks, e-mail & chat, e-mail serv, E-Reserves, Electronic databases & coll, Exhibits, Fax serv, Free DVD rentals, Handicapped accessible, Holiday prog, Homebound delivery serv, ILL available, Magnifiers for reading, Mail & tel request accepted, Music CDs, Newsp ref libr, Online cat, Online ref, Online searches, Outside serv via phone, mail, e-mail & web, Photocopying/Printing, Preschool outreach, Prog for adults, Prog for children & young adult, Provide serv for the mentally ill, Pub access computers, Ref serv available, Ref serv in person, Senior computer classes, Senior outreach, Story hour, Summer reading prog, Tax forms, Teen prog, Telephone ref, Web-catalog, Wheelchair accessible
Publications: Friends FLYLEAF (Newsletter)
Mem of Southwest Iowa Library Services District
Special Services for the Deaf - TTY equip
Open Mon-Thurs 9-9, Fri & Sat 9-5, Sun 1-5
Friends of the Library Group

J IOWA WESTERN COMMUNITY COLLEGE*, Herbert Hoover Library, 2700 College Rd, 51503-7057. (Mail add: PO Box 4C, 51502-3004), SAN 341-8081. Tel: 712-325-3247. Toll Free Tel: 800-432-5852. FAX: 712-325-3244. Web Site: www.iwcc.cc.ia.us. *Dir,* Ellen VanWaart; E-mail: evanwaart@iwcc.edu; *Librn,* Cindy Nelson; Staff 4 (MLS 2, Non-MLS 2)
Founded 1966. Enrl 3,000; Fac 150
Library Holdings: Bk Titles 52,237; Per Subs 150
Special Collections: State Document Depository
Subject Interests: Deaf, Nursing, Vocational educ
Automation Activity & Vendor Info: (Acquisitions) Winnebago Software Co; (Cataloging) Winnebago Software Co; (Circulation) Winnebago Software Co; (OPAC) Winnebago Software Co
Database Vendor: EBSCOhost, OCLC FirstSearch, ProQuest
Mem of Southwest Iowa Library Services District
Open Mon-Thurs (Fall & Spring) 8-9, Fri 8-4, Sat 10-2; Mon-Thurs (Summer) 8-4:30, Fri 8-4

C KAPLAN UNIVERSITY*, Council Bluffs Campus Library, 1751 Madison Ave, Ste 750, 51503. Tel: 712-328-4212. FAX: 712-328-4061. *Dir of Libr Serv,* Elzbieta Ciborowski; E-mail: eciborowski@kaplan.edu
Library Holdings: Bk Vols 4,000
Automation Activity & Vendor Info: (Cataloging) Follett Software; (Circulation) Follett Software
Wireless access
Open Mon-Thurs 9-9, Fri 9-2

L SMITH PETERSON LAW LIBRARY*, 35 Main Pl, Ste 300, 51503-0702. (Mail add: PO Box 249, 51502-0249), SAN 326-050X. Tel: 712-328-1833. FAX: 712-328-8320. E-mail: email@smithpeterson.com. Web Site: smithpeterson.com. *Mgr,* William Melvin
Library Holdings: Bk Titles 7,392
Restriction: Staff use only

CRESCO

P CRESCO PUBLIC LIBRARY*, 320 N Elm St, 52136-1452. SAN 305-3105. Tel: 563-547-2540. FAX: 563-547-1769. Web Site: www.cresco.lib.ia.us. *Dir,* Carmen Buss; E-mail: cbuss@cresco.lib.ia.us
Founded 1915. Pop 3,905; Circ 139,956
Library Holdings: Bk Titles 30,780; Per Subs 106
Wireless access
Open Mon-Thurs 9-8, Fri 9-5, Sat 9-1
Friends of the Library Group

CRESTON

P GIBSON MEMORIAL LIBRARY*, 200 W Howard, 50801-2339. SAN 305-3113. Tel: 641-782-2277. FAX: 641-782-4604. E-mail: clibrary@iowatelecom.net. Web Site: www.creston.lib.ia.us. *Dir,* Marilyn Ralls; *Ch Serv,* Sue Teutsch; Staff 6 (MLS 1, Non-MLS 5)
Founded 1932
Library Holdings: Bk Titles 30,000; Per Subs 100
Subject Interests: Genealogy
Automation Activity & Vendor Info: (Cataloging) Follett Software; (Circulation) Follett Software; (OPAC) Follett Software
Mem of Southwest Iowa Library Services District
Open Mon & Wed 10-8, Tues, Thurs & Fri 10-6, Sat 10-3
Friends of the Library Group

J SOUTHWESTERN COMMUNITY COLLEGE*, Learning Resource Center, 1501 W Townline, 50801. SAN 305-3121. Tel: 641-782-1462. FAX: 641-782-1301. Web Site: www.swcciowa.edu. *Dir, Libr Serv,* Ann Coulter; Tel: 641-782-1340, E-mail: coulter@swcciowa.edu; *ILL,* Helen Waigand; E-mail: waigand@swcc.cc.ia.us; Staff 4 (MLS 1, Non-MLS 3)
Founded 1965. Enrl 1,200
Library Holdings: Bk Titles 14,320; Bk Vols 15,194; Per Subs 170
Automation Activity & Vendor Info: (Circulation) Innovative Interfaces, Inc; (OPAC) Innovative Interfaces, Inc
Database Vendor: OCLC FirstSearch
Open Mon-Fri (Fall & Spring) 7am-9pm, Sun 4-8; Mon-Fri (Summer) 7-4:30

CRYSTAL LAKE

P JUANITA EARP MEDIA CENTER LIBRARY*, 120 E Fifth & Summit St, 50432. (Mail add: PO Box 130, 50432-0130), SAN 377-547X. Tel: 641-565-3325. FAX: 641-565-3325. *Dir,* Lisa Swingen; E-mail: lswingen@woden-crystallake.k12.ia.us
Pop 285
Library Holdings: AV Mats 100; Bk Titles 5,300; Per Subs 48

Automation Activity & Vendor Info: (Acquisitions) Follett Software; (Cataloging) Follett Software; (Circulation) Follett Software; (ILL) Follett Software; (OPAC) Follett Software
Open Mon, Wed & Fri 8-3:30, Tues & Thurs 8-7, Sat 9-11

CUMBERLAND

P CUMBERLAND PUBLIC LIBRARY*, 119 Main St, 50843-9900. (Mail add: PO Box 150, 50843-0150), SAN 305-313X. Tel: 712-774-5334. FAX: 712-774-5334. E-mail: cmblibry@netins.net. Web Site: www.cumberland.swilsa.lib.ia.us. *Dir,* Caroline Hartman; E-mail: harty@netins.net
Pop 281; Circ 6,400
Library Holdings: AV Mats 400; Bk Vols 6,500; Per Subs 25
Mem of Indianhead Federated Library System
Open Mon 9-6, Wed 8-5, Sat 9-10

CUSHING

P CUSHING COMMUNITY LIBRARY*, 202 Main St, 51018. (Mail add: PO Box 13, 51018-0013). Tel: 712-384-2501. E-mail: cushinglibrary2@schallertel.net. Web Site: www.cushing.lib.ia.us. *Dir,* Elaine Droegmiller
Pop 246
Library Holdings: AV Mats 385; CDs 19; Bk Vols 4,588; Videos 255
Open Mon 2-7, Thurs 5-7, Sat 10-12
Friends of the Library Group

DALLAS CENTER

P ROY R ESTLE MEMORIAL LIBRARY*, 1308 Walnut St, 50063. (Mail add: PO Box 521, 50063-0521), SAN 305-3148. Tel: 515-992-3185. FAX: 515-992-4929. Web Site: dallascenter.lib.ia.us. *Dir,* Shelly Cory; E-mail: scory@dallascenter.lib.ia.us; Staff 4 (Non-MLS 4)
Founded 1945. Pop 1,595; Circ 38,524
Jul 2009-Jun 2010 Income $149,963, State $2,991, City $96,920, County $17,319, Locally Generated Income $3,048, Other $29,685. Mats Exp $20,141, Books $15,095, Per/Ser (Incl. Access Fees) $2,363, AV Mat $2,610, Electronic Ref Mat (Incl. Access Fees) $73. Sal $78,618
Library Holdings: Audiobooks 4,676; DVDs 605; Large Print Bks 1,093; Bk Titles 18,940; Per Subs 63; Talking Bks 3,178; Videos 231
Special Collections: County Newspapers, 1890 to present, micro; Dallas County Cemetery Records; Dallas County Genealogical Coll
Subject Interests: Local hist
Automation Activity & Vendor Info: (Acquisitions) Follett Software; (Circulation) Follett Software; (OPAC) Follett Software
Database Vendor: EBSCOhost, OCLC FirstSearch
Wireless access
Function: Adult bk club, After school storytime, Archival coll, Bk club(s), Bks on cassette, Bks on CD, Children's prog, Computers for patron use, Copy machines, Free DVD rentals, Handicapped accessible, Home delivery & serv to Sr ctr & nursing homes, Homebound delivery serv, ILL available, Prog for children & young adult, Pub access computers, Ref serv available, Scanner, Spoken cassettes & CDs, Story hour, Summer reading prog, Tax forms, Telephone ref, VHS videos, Web-catalog, Wheelchair accessible
Mem of Central Iowa Library Services
Open Mon & Fri 9-5, Tues-Thurs 9-7, Sat 9-12
Friends of the Library Group

DAVENPORT

P DAVENPORT PUBLIC LIBRARY*, 321 Main St, 52801-1490. SAN 305-3172. Tel: 563-326-7832. Reference Tel: 563-326-7844. FAX: 563-326-7809. TDD: 563-326-7843. Web Site: www.davenportlibrary.com. *Dir,* Kenneth Wayne Thompson; E-mail: kwthompson@davenportlibrary.com; *Assoc Dir, Customer Serv,* Stephanie Schulte; Tel: 563-328-6838, E-mail: sschulte@davenportlibrary.com; *Assoc Dir, Res,* Amy Groskopf; Tel: 563-328-6850, E-mail: agroskopf@davenportlibrary.com. Subject Specialists: *Customer serv,* Stephanie Schulte; *Spec coll,* Amy Groskopf; Staff 18 (MLS 18)
Founded 1877. Pop 100,802; Circ 946,114
Library Holdings: Audiobooks 36,353; AV Mats 18,971; e-books 5,047; Bk Vols 313,042; Per Subs 889
Special Collections: Iowa Authors Coll; Patent & Trademark Resource Center. State Document Depository; US Document Depository
Subject Interests: Bus & mgt, Econ, Genealogy
Automation Activity & Vendor Info: (Acquisitions) Innovative Interfaces, Inc; (Cataloging) Innovative Interfaces, Inc; (Circulation) Innovative Interfaces, Inc; (ILL) OCLC FirstSearch
Wireless access
Function: Bks on cassette
Publications: Main Entries (Newsletter)
Partic in OCLC Online Computer Library Center, Inc; RiverShare Libraries
Special Services for the Deaf - TDD equip
Open Mon-Thurs 9:30-8, Fri & Sat 9:30-5:30, Sun (Fall-Spring) 1-4
Friends of the Library Group
Branches: 2
FAIRMOUNT STREET, 3000 N Fairmount St, 52804-1160, SAN 324-2552. Tel: 563-326-7893. FAX: 563-326-7806. *Br Supvr,* Valerie Farrar; Tel: 563-328-6830; *Br Supvr,* Sue Ring; Tel: 563-888-3390
Open Mon & Thurs-Sat 9:30-5:30, Tues & Wed 12-8
RICHARDSON-SLOANE SPECIAL COLLECTIONS CENTER, 321 Main St, 52801-1409. (Mail add: PO Box 3132, 52808-3132), SAN 371-8646. Tel: 563-326-7902. FAX: 563-326-7901. *Dir,* Kenneth Wayne Thompson; E-mail: kwthompson@davenportlibrary.com; *Assoc Dir, Res Serv,* Amy Groskopf; E-mail: agroskopf@davenportlibrary.com
Library Holdings: Bk Titles 1,600; Per Subs 20
Open Mon 12-8, Tues-Sat 9-5:30
Friends of the Library Group

M GENESIS HEALTH SYSTEM, Clinical Library, 1227 E Rusholme St, 52803. SAN 375-9369. Tel: 563-421-2287. FAX: 563-421-2288. E-mail: library@genesishealth.com. *Med Librn,* Erin Moore; E-mail: mooreerin@genesishealth.com; Staff 2 (MLS 2)
Library Holdings: Bk Titles 1,500; Per Subs 100
Database Vendor: EBSCOhost, OCLC FirstSearch, OVID Technologies
Wireless access
Partic in Quad City Area Biomedical Consortium
Open Mon-Fri 7-4

C KAPLAN UNIVERSITY, Gail Katherine Barrigar Library, 1801 E Kimberly Rd, Ste 1, 52807. SAN 371-7062. Tel: 563-441-2467. Circulation Tel: 563-441-2449. Toll Free Tel: 800-747-1035. FAX: 563-355-1320. Web Site: library.kaplan.edu/dav. *Dir,* Marlene Metzgar; E-mail: mmetzgar@kaplan.edu; Staff 2 (MLS 1, Non-MLS 1)
Founded 1938. Enrl 760; Fac 45; Highest Degree: Master
Library Holdings: AV Mats 300; Bk Titles 9,000; Bk Vols 10,000; Per Subs 40
Subject Interests: Bus admin, Criminal justice, Info tech
Automation Activity & Vendor Info: (Circulation) SirsiDynix; (ILL) OCLC; (OPAC) SirsiDynix
Database Vendor: EBSCOhost, LexisNexis, OCLC FirstSearch, Wilson - Wilson Web
Wireless access
Function: Res libr
Partic in RiverShare Libraries
Open Mon-Thurs 8-8, Fri 9-5

CM PALMER COLLEGE OF CHIROPRACTIC-DAVENPORT CAMPUS*, David D Palmer Health Sciences Library, 1000 Brady St, 52803-5287. SAN 305-3202. Tel: 563-884-5641. Reference Tel: 563-884-5896. Administration Tel: 563-884-5441. FAX: 563-884-5897. Web Site: www.palmer.edu. *Sr Dir for Libr Serv,* Chabha Tepe; Tel: 563-884-5442, E-mail: chabha.tepe@palmer.edu; Staff 6 (MLS 6)
Founded 1897. Enrl 1,433; Fac 101; Highest Degree: Doctorate
Jul 2007-Jun 2008 Income $1,289,625. Mats Exp $287,489, Books $58,137, Per/Ser (Incl. Access Fees) $74,664, AV Mat $15,088, Electronic Ref Mat (Incl. Access Fees) $65,463, Presv $5,273. Sal $767,812 (Prof $307,695)
Library Holdings: AV Mats 24,190; e-books 10,600; e-journals 15,805; Bk Titles 30,643; Bk Vols 59,774; Per Subs 151
Special Collections: BJ Palmer Papers Coll; Gustave Dubbs Papers; Kenneth Cronk Papers; Lyndon Lee Papers Coll; Palmer College Archives Coll; Russel Gibbons Papers; Ted Shrader Papers; Walter Wardwell Papers
Subject Interests: Alternative & complimentary health care, Basic sci, Chiropractic health care, Diagnosis, Imaging
Automation Activity & Vendor Info: (Acquisitions) Horizon; (Cataloging) Horizon; (Circulation) Horizon; (Course Reserve) Horizon; (ILL) Horizon; (Media Booking) Horizon; (OPAC) Horizon; (Serials) Horizon
Database Vendor: Cinahl, Dialog, EBSCOhost, Elsevier, MD Consult, Natural Standard, OCLC FirstSearch, OCLC WorldShare Interlibrary Loan, OVID Technologies, PubMed, RefWorks, ScienceDirect, Wiley, Wiley InterScience
Wireless access
Function: Audio & video playback equip for onsite use, Computers for patron use, Doc delivery serv, Electronic databases & coll, Fax serv, Health sci info serv, ILL available, Online cat, Online searches, Photocopying/Printing, Pub access computers, Ref serv available, VHS videos
Publications: The Nexus (Current awareness service)
Partic in Greater Midwest Regional Medical Libr Network; Iowa Private Academic Library Consortium (IPAL); Quad City Area Biomedical Consortium
Open Mon-Thurs 7:15am-11pm, Fri 7:15-5, Sat 9-5, Sun 3-11
Restriction: Open to pub for ref & circ; with some limitations

S PUTNAM MUSEUM OF HISTORY & NATURAL SCIENCE*, 1717 W 12th St, 52804. SAN 305-3229. Tel: 563-324-1933, Ext 216. FAX: 563-324-6638. E-mail: museum@putnam.org. Web Site: www.putnam.org. *Dir,* Christopher J Reich; *Curator,* Eunice Schlichting
Founded 1867
Library Holdings: Bk Titles 30,000
Special Collections: Manuscripts (A LeClaire, I Hall, L Summers, I Wetherby, R Cram, Black Store, Putnam Family, James Grant); Steamboats, files, photog
Subject Interests: Art, Hist, Local hist, Sci tech
Restriction: Open by appt only

CR SAINT AMBROSE UNIVERSITY LIBRARY, 518 W Locust St, 52803. SAN 305-3237. Tel: 563-333-6246. Reference Tel: 563-333-6245. FAX: 563-333-6248. *Exec Dir, Info Res, Libr Dir,* Mary B Heinzman; Tel: 563-333-6241, E-mail: heinzmanmaryb@sau.edu; *Asst Libr Dir,* Julia B Dickinson; Tel: 563-333-6244, E-mail: dickinsonjuliab@sau.edu; *Ref Librn,* James R O'Gorman; Tel: 563-333-6035, E-mail: ogormanjamesr@sau.edu; *Circ Mgr,* Yvonne Conlon; Tel: 563-333-6474, E-mail: conlonyvonne@sau.edu; *Evening Circ Supvr,* Bryan Hinds; Tel: 563-333-6475, E-mail: hindsbryant@sau.edu; *Archivist,* Onnica F Marquez; Tel: 563-333-6444, E-mail: marquezonnicaf@sau.edu; *Cat,* Beth Shoemaker; Tel: 563-333-6469, E-mail: shoemakerelizabetha@sau.edu; *Evening Ref (Info Serv),* Conrad w Bendixon; Tel: 563-333-6473, E-mail: bendixenconradw@sau.edu; *Ref,* Stella Herzig; Tel: 563-333-6056, E-mail: herzigstellaj@sau.edu; *Ref,* Anita J Niemczyk; Tel: 563-333-5813, E-mail: niemczykanitaj@sau.edu; *Ref,* Leslie Ross; Tel: 563-333-6472, E-mail: rosslesliem@sau.edu. Subject Specialists: *Acctg, Bus, Gen ref,* Mary B Heinzman; *Commun, Hist, Polit sci,* James R O'Gorman; *Archives, Art,* Onnica F Marquez; *Music,* Beth Shoemaker; *Nursing, Occupational therapy, Phys therapy,* Conrad w Bendixon; *Philos, Theol, Women's studies,* Stella Herzig; *Eng, Environ, Sci,* Anita J Niemczyk; *Art, English, Modern lang,* Leslie Ross; Staff 16.5 (MLS 8, Non-MLS 8.5)
Founded 1882. Enrl 3,306; Fac 337; Highest Degree: Doctorate
Jul 2012-Jun 2013 Income $1,471,239, Federal $61,470, Locally Generated Income $1,409,769. Mats Exp $635,550, Books $150,000, Per/Ser (Incl. Access Fees) $335,000, Micro $1,800, AV Equip $6,000, AV Mat $14,000, Electronic Ref Mat (Incl. Access Fees) $120,000, Presv $8,750. Sal $837,253
Library Holdings: Audiobooks 150; AV Mats 4,200; CDs 325; DVDs 506; e-books 75,000; e-journals 33,189; Bk Titles 145,638; Bk Vols 172,091; Per Subs 502
Subject Interests: Bus & mgt, Econ, Liberal arts, Occupational therapy, Phys therapy, Relig
Automation Activity & Vendor Info: (Acquisitions) Innovative Interfaces, Inc; (Cataloging) Innovative Interfaces, Inc; (Circulation) Innovative Interfaces, Inc; (ILL) Clio; (OPAC) Innovative Interfaces, Inc; (Serials) Innovative Interfaces, Inc
Database Vendor: ABC-CLIO, Alexander Street Press, American Chemical Society, American Psychological Association (APA), ARTstor, Atlas Systems, Cinahl, CRC Press/Taylor & Francis Group, CredoReference, EBSCO Information Services, EBSCOhost, Elsevier, JSTOR, LearningExpress, LexisNexis, Modern Language Association, Newsbank, OCLC ArticleFirst, OCLC FirstSearch, OCLC WorldShare Interlibrary Loan, Overdrive, Inc, Plunkett Research, Ltd, ProQuest, PubMed, ScienceDirect, Springshare, LLC, ValueLine, Wiley InterScience, YBP Library Services
Wireless access
Function: Archival coll
Partic in Lyrasis; RiverShare Libraries
Special Services for the Deaf - Accessible learning ctr

DAYTON

P DAYTON PUBLIC LIBRARY, 22 First St NW, 50530. (Mail add: PO Box 378, 50530-0378), SAN 305-3288. Tel: 515-547-2700. FAX: 515-547-2700. E-mail: dpl@lvcta.com. Web Site: www.youseemore.com/nilc/Dayton. *Dir,* Tanya E Campbell; Staff 0.6 (Non-MLS 0.6)
Founded 1900. Pop 830; Circ 14,674
Jul 2012-Jun 2013 Income $44,567, State $1,492, City $18,100, Federal $840, County $15,659, Locally Generated Income $9,316
Library Holdings: Audiobooks 237; Bks-By-Mail 99,999; DVDs 1,021; e-books 9,139; e-journals 13; Large Print Bks 564; Bk Titles 12,564; Bk Vols 12,564; Per Subs 39; Talking Bks 237; Videos 1,036
Subject Interests: Christian fiction
Automation Activity & Vendor Info: (Cataloging) TLC (The Library Corporation); (Circulation) TLC (The Library Corporation); (Serials) EBSCO Online
Database Vendor: EBSCOhost, Overdrive, Inc
Wireless access
Function: 24/7 Electronic res, 24/7 Online cat, Audio & video playback equip for onsite use, Audiobks via web, Bks on CD, Children's prog, Computers for patron use, Copy machines, Digital talking bks, e-mail serv, Electronic databases & coll, Fax serv, Handicapped accessible, Homebound delivery serv, ILL available, Magazines, Movies, Online cat, Online ref, Online searches, Outside serv via phone, mail, e-mail & web, OverDrive digital audio bks, Photocopying/Printing, Prog for adults, Prog for children & young adult, Pub access computers, Ref serv available, Ref serv in person, Scanner, Summer reading prog, Tax forms, VHS videos, Web-catalog, Wheelchair accessible
Partic in North Eastern Iowa Bridge to Online Resource Sharing (NEIBORS)
Open Mon, Wed & Fri 11-6, Sat 9-Noon
Friends of the Library Group

DE SOTO

P DE SOTO PUBLIC LIBRARY*, 405 Walnut St, 50069. (Mail add: PO Box 585, 50069-0585), SAN 305-3296. Tel: 515-834-2690. FAX: 515-834-2131. E-mail: desotolibrary@mchsi.com. Web Site: www.desoto.lib.ia.us. *Dir,* Mary Murphy; *Ch,* Sara Tessmer; Staff 3 (MLS 3)
Pop 1,035
Library Holdings: Bk Vols 9,000; Per Subs 28
Function: Adult literacy prog, For res purposes, Home delivery & serv to Sr ctr & nursing homes, Homebound delivery serv, ILL available, Photocopying/Printing, Prog for children & young adult, Summer reading prog, Telephone ref, Wheelchair accessible
Mem of Central Iowa Library Services
Open Mon-Wed 10-6,Thurs 10-8, Fri 1-6, Sat 10-1

DECORAH

P DECORAH PUBLIC LIBRARY*, 202 Winnebago St, 52101. SAN 305-3318. Tel: 563-382-3717. FAX: 563-382-4524. E-mail: dpllib@decorah.lib.ia.us. Web Site: www.decorah.lib.ia.us. *Dir,* Lorraine Borowski; E-mail: lborowsk@decorah.lib.ia.us; *Ch,* Sally Stromseth; *Youth Serv Coordr,* Heidi Swets; Staff 4 (Non-MLS 4)
Founded 1893. Pop 8,200; Circ 13,682
Jul 2005-Jun 2006 Income $754,226, State $38,000, City $279,148, County $49,000, Locally Generated Income $320,000, Other $68,078. Mats Exp $40,000. Sal $274,429
Library Holdings: Large Print Bks 9,942; Bk Vols 73,905; Per Subs 200; Talking Bks 3,548
Special Collections: County Historical Archives; Vera Harris Large Print Book Coll
Automation Activity & Vendor Info: (Cataloging) Follett Software; (Circulation) Follett Software
Database Vendor: Baker & Taylor, Gale Cengage Learning
Publications: Annual Report
Special Services for the Blind - Large print bks; Talking bks
Open Mon-Thurs 10-8, Fri & Sat 10-5, Sun (Oct-April) 1-4
Friends of the Library Group

C LUTHER COLLEGE, Preus Library, 700 College Dr, 52101. SAN 305-3326. Tel: 563-387-1166. Reference Tel: 563-387-1163. FAX: 563-387-1657. E-mail: library@luther.edu. Web Site: www.luther.edu/library. *Exec Dir, Libr & Info Serv,* Paul Mattson; Tel: 563-387-1717, E-mail: paul.mattson@luther.edu; *Dept Head, Res & Instruction Librn,* Dr Andrea Beckendorf; Tel: 563-387-1227, E-mail: beckenan@luther.edu; *Digital Initiatives Librn, Head, Libr Operations,* Ryan Gjerde; Tel: 563-387-1288, E-mail: gjerdery@luther.edu; *First Year Experience Librn,* Germano Streese; Tel: 563-387-2223, E-mail: strege01@luther.edu; *Innovative Serv Librn,* Jennifer Rian; Tel: 563-387-1790, E-mail: rianje01@luther.edu; *Instrul Design Librn,* Christine Vivian; Tel: 563-387-1297, E-mail: vivich01@luther.edu; *Ref Librn,* Lindy Moeller; Tel: 563-387-1498, E-mail: moellind@luther.edu; *Tech Serv Librn,* John Goodin; Tel: 563-387-2124, E-mail: goodinjo@luther.edu; *Col Archivist,* Position Currently Open; Staff 9.75 (MLS 8.75, Non-MLS 1)
Founded 1861. Enrl 2,423; Fac 225; Highest Degree: Bachelor
Library Holdings: CDs 3,608; DVDs 2,512; e-books 13,065; e-journals 31,893; Music Scores 5,377; Bk Vols 333,314; Per Subs 823
Special Collections: Luther College Archives; Norwegian-American Newspapers
Subject Interests: Fine arts, Norwegian hist, Rare bks
Automation Activity & Vendor Info: (Acquisitions) OCLC; (Cataloging) OCLC; (Circulation) OCLC; (Course Reserve) OCLC; (ILL) OCLC ILLiad; (Media Booking) OCLC; (OPAC) OCLC WorldShare Interlibrary Loan; (Serials) OCLC
Database Vendor: American Chemical Society, American Physical Society, Annual Reviews, ARTstor, BioOne, Cambridge Scientific Abstracts, CQ Press, CredoReference, EBSCOhost, Gale Cengage Learning, ISI Web of Knowledge, JSTOR, LearningExpress, Micromedex, Nature Publishing Group, OCLC WorldShare Interlibrary Loan, Oxford Online, Project MUSE, ProQuest, PubMed, ScienceDirect, Springshare, LLC
Wireless access
Partic in Iowa Private Academic Library Consortium (IPAL); OCLC Online Computer Library Center, Inc

S VESTERHEIM NORWEGIAN-AMERICAN MUSEUM*, Special Library, 502 W Water St, 52101. (Mail add: PO Box 379, 52101), SAN 325-5727. Tel: 563-382-9681. FAX: 563-382-8828. E-mail: info@vesterheim.org. Web Site: vesterheim.org. *Registrar,* Jennifer Kovarik; E-mail: jkovarik@vesterheim.org
Library Holdings: Bk Titles 10,000; Bk Vols 11,000; Per Subs 20
Special Collections: Norwegian Lang Works Published in America
Subject Interests: Norwegian & Norwegian-Am folk art, Norwegian-Am fine art, Norwegian-Am hist
Publications: Vesterheim (Magazine); Vesterheim Current (Online only)
Open Mon-Fri 9-12 & 1-4

DELHI

P DELHI PUBLIC LIBRARY*, 316A Franklin St, 52223-9602. (Mail add: PO Box 233, 52223-0233), SAN 305-3342. Tel: 563-922-2037. FAX: 563-922-2037. E-mail: delhilibrary@iowatelecom.net. *Dir,* Mary Lahr; E-mail: maryl@delhi.lib.ia.us; Staff 1 (Non-MLS 1)
Founded 1940. Pop 452; Circ 6,041
Library Holdings: Bk Titles 8,388; Per Subs 20
Automation Activity & Vendor Info: (Cataloging) Follett Software
Open Mon 1-6, Wed 10-6, Thurs 4-8 & Sat 9-12
Friends of the Library Group

DENISON

P NORELIUS COMMUNITY LIBRARY*, 1403 First Ave S, 51442-2014. SAN 305-3350. Tel: 712-263-9355. FAX: 712-263-8578. E-mail: denlib@frontiernet.net. Web Site: www.denison.lib.ia.us. *Dir,* Deb McKeown; E-mail: norlib@frontiernet.net; *Asst Dir, Teen Librn,* Sandra Haynes; *Ch,* Mary Siegner; Staff 8 (MLS 1, Non-MLS 7)
Founded 1904. Pop 7,339; Circ 111,376
Library Holdings: CDs 228; DVDs 107; Large Print Bks 785; Bk Vols 46,750; Per Subs 191; Talking Bks 1,854; Videos 1,512
Automation Activity & Vendor Info: (Cataloging) Book Systems; (Circulation) Book Systems
Database Vendor: EBSCOhost
Mem of Northwest Iowa Library Services
Open Mon-Thurs 9-8, Fri & Sat 9-5
Friends of the Library Group

DENVER

P DENVER PUBLIC LIBRARY*, 100 Washington St, 50622. (Mail add: PO Box 692, 50622-0692), SAN 305-3369. Tel: 319-984-5140. FAX: 319-984-5140. Web Site: www.denver.lib.ia.us. *Dir,* Kelly Platte; E-mail: kplatte@denver.lib.ia.us
Pop 3,654; Circ 50,187
Library Holdings: Bk Titles 35,000; Per Subs 50
Wireless access
Open Mon 10-7, Tues & Wed 10-6, Thurs 10-8, Fri 10-5, Sat 9-12
Friends of the Library Group

DES MOINES

C AIB COLLEGE OF BUSINESS LIBRARY*, 2500 Fleur Dr, 50321-1749. SAN 371-0955. Tel: 515-244-4221. Circulation Tel: 515-246-5330. Interlibrary Loan Service Tel: 515-246-5331. FAX: 515-288-4366. *Dir,* Leslie Bintner; E-mail: bintnerl@aib.edu; Staff 2 (MLS 2)
Enrl 900; Fac 40; Highest Degree: Bachelor
Library Holdings: Bk Titles 5,100; Bk Vols 5,400; Per Subs 160
Special Collections: Court & Realtime Reporting (Speedbuilding Tape Library Coll), audio & video tapes
Automation Activity & Vendor Info: (Cataloging) Follett Software; (Circulation) Follett Software; (OPAC) Follett Software
Database Vendor: EBSCO Information Services, EBSCOhost, Newsbank, OCLC FirstSearch, OCLC WorldShare Interlibrary Loan, ProQuest
Wireless access
Function: ILL available
Partic in Iowa Private Academic Library Consortium (IPAL); State of Iowa Libraries Online
Special Services for the Deaf - Bks on deafness & sign lang
Open Mon-Thurs 7am-9:30pm, Fri 7-4:30, Sun 5-8
Restriction: Open to students, fac & staff

M BROADLAWNS MEDICAL CENTER*, Health Sciences Library, 1801 Hickman Rd, 50314. SAN 305-3385. Tel: 515-282-2394. FAX: 515-282-5634. *Librn,* Elaine Hughes
Library Holdings: Bk Vols 1,400; Per Subs 160
Subject Interests: Clinical med, Nursing, Psychiat
Partic in Greater Midwest Regional Medical Libr Network; Polk County Biomedical Consortium
Open Mon-Fri 8-4:30

L DAVIS BROWN LAW FIRM*, 215 Tenth St, Ste 1300, 50309. SAN 305-3504. Tel: 515-288-2500. FAX: 515-243-0654. E-mail: info@lawiowa.com. Web Site: www.lawiowa.com. *In Charge,* Susan Prunty; E-mail: susanprunty@davisbrownlaw.com
Library Holdings: Bk Vols 11,000
Restriction: Staff use only

G DEAF SERVICES COMMISSION OF IOWA*, Library on Deafness, Iowa Dept Human Rights, Lucas State Office Bldg, 2nd Flr, 50319. Tel: 515-281-3164. FAX: 515-242-6119. E-mail: dhr.dsci@iowa.gov. Web Site: www.deafservices.iowa.gov.
Library Holdings: Bk Vols 1,000; Per Subs 10

J DES MOINES AREA COMMUNITY COLLEGE LIBRARY, Urban Campus, 1100 Seventh St, 50314. Tel: 515-248-7210. FAX: 515-248-7534. Web Site: www.library.dmacc.edu. *Librn,* Polly Mumma; Tel: 515-697-7739, E-mail: psmumma@dmacc.edu; *Libr Spec,* Brooke Vance; Tel: 515-278-7238, E-mail: bavance2@dmacc.edu
Library Holdings: Bk Vols 13,000; Per Subs 50
Subject Interests: Law
Automation Activity & Vendor Info: (Acquisitions) Innovative Interfaces, Inc - Millenium; (Cataloging) Innovative Interfaces, Inc - Millenium; (Circulation) Innovative Interfaces, Inc - Millenium; (Course Reserve) Innovative Interfaces, Inc - Millenium; (OPAC) Innovative Interfaces, Inc - Millenium; (Serials) Innovative Interfaces, Inc - Millenium
Wireless access
Open Mon-Thurs 7:30am-8:30pm, Fri 7:30-4:30, Sat 9-Noon

S DES MOINES ART CENTER LIBRARY*, 4700 Grand Ave, 50312-2099. SAN 305-3415. Tel: 515-277-4405. FAX: 515-271-0357. Web Site: desmoinesartcenter.org.
Founded 1950
Library Holdings: AV Mats 120; Bk Titles 16,500; Per Subs 20
Subject Interests: 21st Century art, Art (19th Century), Art (20th Century)
Wireless access
Restriction: Open by appt only

P DES MOINES PUBLIC LIBRARY*, 1000 Grand Ave, 50309. SAN 341-8294. Tel: 515-283-4152. Interlibrary Loan Service Tel: 515-283-4292. FAX: 515-237-1654. E-mail: reference@dmpl.org. Web Site: www.dmpl.org. *Dir,* Greg Heid; Tel: 515-283-4288, E-mail: ggheid@dmpl.org; *Dep Dir,* Linda L Roe; Tel: 515-283-4102, E-mail: llroe@dmpl.org; *Supv Librn, Tech Serv,* Dawn E Work-Makinne; Tel: 515-283-4155, E-mail: deworkmakinne@dmpl.org; *Cent Libr Mgr,* Nyla L Wobig; Tel: 515-283-4265, E-mail: nlwobig@dmpl.org; *Mkt Mgr,* Jan D Kaiser; Tel: 515-283-4103, E-mail: jdkaiser@dmpl.org; Staff 89.43 (MLS 36.75, Non-MLS 52.68)
Founded 1866. Pop 198,682; Circ 1,421,567
Jul 2011-Jun 2012 Income (Main Library and Branch(s)) $8,675,871, State $70,456, City $7,666,379, County $49,748, Other $889,288. Mats Exp $766,957, Books $488,995, AV Mat $177,199, Electronic Ref Mat (Incl. Access Fees) $100,763. Sal $5,583,850
Library Holdings: Audiobooks 60,479; CDs 7,847; DVDs 26,764; e-books 3,401; Bk Vols 494,233; Per Subs 843
Special Collections: Foundation Center. Oral History; US Document Depository
Subject Interests: Iowa, Sheet music
Automation Activity & Vendor Info: (Acquisitions) Horizon; (Cataloging) Horizon; (Circulation) Horizon; (OPAC) Horizon
Database Vendor: EBSCOhost, OCLC FirstSearch, ProQuest
Wireless access
Publications: Annual Report; Insight (Newsletter); What's Happening Calendar (Online events calendar)
Special Services for the Blind - Bks on cassette; Bks on CD; Large print bks; Magnifiers
Open Mon-Thurs 9-8, Fri 9-6, Sat 10-5, Sun 1-5
Friends of the Library Group
Branches: 5
EAST SIDE, 2559 Hubbell Ave, 50317, SAN 341-8324. Tel: 515-283-4152. FAX: 515-248-6256. *Br Mgr,* Carolyn Greufe; E-mail: cegreufe@dmpl.org
Library Holdings: Bk Vols 58,393
Open Mon & Tues 10-8, Thurs & Fri 10-6, Sat 10-5
Friends of the Library Group
FOREST AVENUE, 1326 Forest Ave, 50314, SAN 341-8383. Tel: 515-283-4152. FAX: 515-242-2853. E-mail: forelib@netins.net. *Br Mgr,* Sue Woody
Library Holdings: Bk Vols 43,092
Open Mon & Thurs 10-8, Tues & Wed 10-6, Sat 10-5
Friends of the Library Group
FRANKLIN AVENUE, 5000 Franklin Ave, 50310, SAN 341-8359. Tel: 515-283-4152. FAX: 515-271-8734. *Br Mgr,* Pam Deitrick; E-mail: psdeitrick@dmpl.org
Library Holdings: Bk Vols 116,106

Open Mon & Tues 10-8, Wed & Fri 10-6, Sat 10-5
Friends of the Library Group
NORTH SIDE, 3516 Fifth Ave, 50313, SAN 341-8413. Tel: 515-283-4152. FAX: 515-242-2684. *Br Mgr,* Carolyn E Greufe
Library Holdings: Bk Vols 50,369
Open Tues & Wed 10-8, Thurs & Fri 10-6, Sat 10-5
Friends of the Library Group
SOUTH SIDE, 1111 Porter Ave, 50315, SAN 341-8448. Tel: 515-283-4152. FAX: 515-256-2567. E-mail: southlib@netins.net. *Br Mgr,* Sue Woody
Library Holdings: Bk Vols 71,057
Open Mon & Wed 10-8, Thurs & Fri 10-6, Sat 10-5
Friends of the Library Group

S DES MOINES REGISTER, Newsroom Library, 400 Locust St, Ste 500, 50309-3703. SAN 305-3423. Tel: 515-284-8077. FAX: 515-286-2511. *Coordr,* Joann J Donaldson; Staff 1 (Non-MLS 1)
Special Collections: Des Moines Register & Tribune Coll 1920 to present, clippings, photog
Wireless access
Restriction: Not open to pub

C DRAKE UNIVERSITY*, Cowles Library, 2725 University Ave, 50311. (Mail add: 2507 University Ave, 50311-4505), SAN 341-8111. Tel: 515-271-3993. Circulation Tel: 515-271-2111. Interlibrary Loan Service Tel: 515-271-4819. Reference Tel: 515-271-2113. Toll Free Tel: 800-443-7253. FAX: 515-271-3933. E-mail: cowles-ill@drake.edu. Web Site: library.drake.edu. *Dean of Libr,* Rod Neal Henshaw; E-mail: rod.henshaw@drake.edu; *Dir, Digital Libr & Instruction,* Bruce Gilbert; Tel: 515-271-4821, E-mail: bruce.gilbert@drake.edu; *Digital Projects Librn,* Bart Schimdt; Tel: 515-271-2940, E-mail: bart.schmidt@drake.edu; *ILS LIbrn,* Andrew Welch; Tel: 515-271-2862, E-mail: andrew.welch@drake.edu; *Instrul Serv Librn,* Marcia Keyser; Tel: 515-271-3989, E-mail: marcia.keyser@drake.edu; *Librn, Digital Literacy & Gen Educ,* Carrie Dunham-LaGree; Tel: 515-271-2175, E-mail: carrie.dunham-lagree@drake.edu; *Pharm & Health Sci Librn,* Priya Shenoy; Tel: 515-271-2879, E-mail: priya.shenoy@drake.edu; *Ref Librn,* Mark Stumme; Tel: 515-271-3192, E-mail: mark.stumme@drake.edu; *Admin Mgr,* Jordan Flynn; Tel: 515-272-1936, E-mail: jordan.flynn@drake.edu; *Mgr, Electronic Res,* Kay Kelly; Tel: 515-271-2119, E-mail: kay.kelly@drake.edu; *Coordr, Digital Initiatives,* Claudia Frazer; Tel: 515-271-3776, E-mail: claudia.frazer@drake.edu; *Coordr, Access Serv, ILL Supvr,* Liga L Briedis; Tel: 515-271-3908, E-mail: liga.briedis@drake.edu; *Coordr, Acq, Coordr, Electronic Res, Coordr, Ser,* Teri Koch; Tel: 515-271-2941, E-mail: teri.koch@drake.edu; *Ref & Instrul Serv, Instr Coordr,* Karl Schaefer; Tel: 515-271-2924, E-mail: karl.schaefer@drake.edu; *Serv Quality & Training Coordr,* Karen A Jurasek; Tel: 515-271-2903, E-mail: karen.jurasek@drake.edu; *ILL,* Kris Mogle; E-mail: kristine.mogle@drake.edu; *Libr Project/Cat Spec,* Laura Krossner; Tel: 515-271-2475, E-mail: laura.krossner@drake.edu; *Prog, Planning & Projects Spec,* Marc Davis; Tel: 515-271-1934, E-mail: marc.davis@drake.edu; *Web Developer,* Daniel Taylor; Tel: 515-271-2975, E-mail: daniel.taylor@drake.edu; Staff 22 (MLS 12, Non-MLS 10)
Founded 1881. Enrl 5,139; Fac 289; Highest Degree: Doctorate
Jun 2012-Jun 2013 Income $3,604,501. Mats Exp $1,034,624, Books $174,137, Per/Ser (Incl. Access Fees) $816,457, Micro $5,064, AV Mat $10,805, Electronic Ref Mat (Incl. Access Fees) $17,514, Presv $10,647. Sal $1,211,181 (Prof $1,059,592)
Library Holdings: AV Mats 2,969; CDs 1,342; DVDs 1,683; e-books 337,967; e-journals 32,000; Microforms 936,702; Music Scores 9,718; Bk Titles 1,177,547; Bk Vols 551,472; Per Subs 1,887; Videos 940
Special Collections: Digital Colls; Ding Darling Coll; Drake Related Materials; ERIC Documents to 2004, microfiche; eScholarShare; Gardner Cowles Papers; Heritage Coll. State Document Depository; US Document Depository
Subject Interests: Health sci, Mus, Relig
Automation Activity & Vendor Info: (Acquisitions) SirsiDynix; (Cataloging) SirsiDynix; (Circulation) SirsiDynix; (Course Reserve) SirsiDynix; (ILL) OCLC ILLiad; (OPAC) SirsiDynix; (Serials) SirsiDynix
Database Vendor: SirsiDynix
Wireless access
Partic in OCLC Online Computer Library Center, Inc; OCLC-LVIS; Scholarly Publ & Acad Resources Coalition
Open Mon-Thurs 7:30am-1am, Fri 7:30am-8pm, Sat 10-8, Sun 10am-1am
Restriction: Badge access after hrs

Departmental Libraries:

CL DRAKE LAW LIBRARY, Opperman Hall, 2615 Carpenter Ave, 50311-4505. (Mail add: 2507 University Ave, 50311-4516), SAN 341-8146. Tel: 515-271-2141. Circulation Tel: 515-271-3189. Interlibrary Loan Service Tel: 515-271-3759. Reference Tel: 515-271-2053. FAX: 515-271-2530. Web Site: www.law.drake.edu. *Assoc Dean,* John D Edwards; E-mail: john.edwards@drake.edu; *Acq,* Deborah E Sulzbach; Tel: 515-271-3784, E-mail: deborah.sulzbach@drake.edu; *Circ,* Karen Wallace; Tel: 515-271-2989, E-mail: karen.wallace@drake.edu; *Electronic Res,* David B Hanson; Tel: 515-271-2077, E-mail: david.hanson@drake.edu; *Ref Serv,* Rebecca Lutkenhaus; E-mail: rebecca.lutkenhaus@drake.edu; *Tech Serv,* Julie A Thomas; Tel: 515-271-2052, E-mail: julie.thomas@drake.edu; Staff 10.2 (MLS 6, Non-MLS 4.2)
Founded 1865. Enrl 374; Fac 25; Highest Degree: Doctorate
Jul 2013-Jun 2014. Mats Exp $752,679, Books $64,553, Per/Ser (Incl. Access Fees) $477,303, Electronic Ref Mat (Incl. Access Fees) $204,207, Presv $6,616
Library Holdings: AV Mats 498; Electronic Media & Resources 25; Microforms 125,662; Bk Titles 86,277; Bk Vols 356,990; Per Subs 3,349
Special Collections: Iowa Legal History. State Document Depository; US Document Depository
Automation Activity & Vendor Info: (Acquisitions) SIRSI WorkFlows; (Cataloging) SIRSI WorkFlows; (Circulation) SIRSI WorkFlows; (OPAC) SIRSI-iLink; (Serials) SIRSI WorkFlows
Partic in Iowa Private Academic Library Consortium (IPAL); Law Library Microform Consortium (LLMC); Mid-America Law Library Consortium
Publications: Acquisitions Lists; Newsletter
Special Services for the Blind - Computer with voice synthesizer for visually impaired persons
Open Mon-Thurs 7am-11pm, Fri 7-7, Sat 10-7, Sun 11-11
Friends of the Library Group

C GRAND VIEW UNIVERSITY LIBRARY*, 1350 Morton Ave, 50316-1494. SAN 305-3431. Tel: 515-263-2877. Reference Tel: 515-263-2949. Administration Tel: 515-263-2878. FAX: 515-263-2998. E-mail: library@grandview.edu. Web Site: library.gvc.edu. *Dir,* Pam Rees; E-mail: prees@grandview.edu; *Fac Develop & Instruction Librn,* Cara Stone; E-mail: cstone@grandview.edu; *Res Serv Librn,* Sheri Muller; Tel: 515-263-6199; *User Serv & Instruction Design Librn,* Daniel Chibnal; Tel: 515-263-2879, E-mail: dchibnall@grandview.edu; Staff 7 (MLS 4, Non-MLS 3)
Founded 1896. Enrl 1,660; Fac 100; Highest Degree: Master
Library Holdings: Bk Vols 120,000; Per Subs 400
Special Collections: Iowa Danish Immigrant Archives. State Document Depository
Subject Interests: Bus, Communication, Educ, Graphic design, Liberal arts, Nursing
Automation Activity & Vendor Info: (Acquisitions) Ex Libris Group; (Cataloging) Ex Libris Group; (Circulation) Ex Libris Group; (Course Reserve) Ex Libris Group; (ILL) OCLC; (OPAC) Ex Libris Group; (Serials) Ex Libris Group
Database Vendor: EBSCOhost, Gale Cengage Learning, LexisNexis, Newsbank, OCLC FirstSearch, OCLC WorldShare Interlibrary Loan, PubMed, SerialsSolutions
Partic in Docline; Iowa Private Academic Library Consortium (IPAL); OCLC Online Computer Library Center, Inc; State of Iowa Libraries Online
Special Services for the Blind - Reader equip
Open Mon-Thurs 8am-Midnight, Fri 8 4:30, Sat 12-4, Sun 3-Midnight
Restriction: Open to students, fac & staff, Pub use on premises
Friends of the Library Group

S IOWA GENEALOGICAL SOCIETY LIBRARY*, 628 E Grand Ave, 50309-1924. SAN 321-5741. Tel: 515-276-0287. Administration Tel: 515-276-0287, Ext 101. FAX: 515-727-1824. E-mail: igs@iowagenealogy.org. Web Site: www.iowagenealogy.org. *Librn,* Judy McClain
Founded 1965
Library Holdings: Microforms 11,730; Bk Vols 12,000; Per Subs 70
Special Collections: Iowa Cemetery, Census & Court House Records; Iowa Pioneers; US Federal Census Microfilm; World War I Draft Records
Subject Interests: Genealogy, Hist
Wireless access
Function: Res libr
Publications: Hawkeye Heritage (Quarterly); IGS Newsletter (Bi-monthly)
Open Mon, Wed, Fri & Sat 10-4, Tues & Thurs 10-9
Restriction: Non-circulating

G IOWA LEAGUE OF CITIES LIBRARY*, 317 Sixth Ave, Ste 800, 50309-4111. SAN 320-1872. Tel: 515-244-7282. FAX: 515-244-0740. *Asst Dir,* Mickey Shields
Founded 1961
Library Holdings: Bk Vols 450; Per Subs 12
Special Collections: Iowa Municipal Codes Coll; League Monthly Magazine-Iowa Coll (1899-present); Local Government Subjects Coll
Subject Interests: Law, Local govt
Restriction: Pub use on premises

M IOWA METHODIST MEDICAL CENTER, Health Sciences Library, 1200 Pleasant St, 50309. SAN 341-8235. Tel: 515-241-6490. FAX: 515-241-3383. E-mail: mlb.library@unitypoint.org. Web Site:

www.unitypoint.org/desmoines/health-sciences-library.aspx. *Dir,* Nancy O'Brien; Staff 5 (MLS 2, Non-MLS 3)
Founded 1940
Library Holdings: Bk Titles 5,000; Per Subs 300
Subject Interests: Allied health, Consumer health, Health sci, Med, Nursing, Nutrition
Partic in Greater Midwest Regional Medical Libr Network; Polk County Biomedical Consortium
Open Mon-Fri 7:30-4

P IOWA REGIONAL LIBRARY FOR THE BLIND & PHYSICALLY HANDICAPPED*, 524 Fourth St, 50309-2364. SAN 305-344X. Tel: 515-281-1333. Toll Free Tel: 800-362-2587. FAX: 515-281-1378. TDD: 515-281-1355. E-mail: library@blind.state.ia.us. Web Site: www.blind.state.ia.us. *Dir,* Randall E Landgrebe; Tel: 515-281-1291, E-mail: randy.landgrebe@blind.state.ia.us; Staff 24 (MLS 4, Non-MLS 20)
Founded 1960
Library Holdings: Large Print Bks 6,445; Bk Titles 94,168; Bk Vols 310,630; Per Subs 75; Talking Bks 49,897
Special Collections: Print Coll of Books about Blindness
Special Services for the Deaf - TDD equip
Special Services for the Blind - Assistive/Adapted tech devices, equip & products; Braille bks; Computer with voice synthesizer for visually impaired persons; Talking bks
Open Mon-Fri 8-4:30
Friends of the Library Group

C KAPLAN UNIVERSITY*, Urbandale Des Moines Campus Library, 4655 NW 121st St, 50323. Tel: 515-727-2100, Ext 208. FAX: 515-727-2115. *Dir, Libr Serv,* Andrew M Gress; E-mail: agress@hamiltonia.edu
Library Holdings: Bk Vols 5,200; Per Subs 50
Special Collections: Kaplan Training Library
Subject Interests: Bus, Criminal justice, Info tech
Open Mon-Thurs 7:30am-10pm, Fri 8-5, Sat 9-1

S LEGISLATIVE SERVICES AGENCY LIBRARY*, State Capitol Bldg, Ground Flr, 50319. SAN 320-6750. Tel: 515-281-3566. FAX: 515-281-8027. Web Site: www.legis.state.ia.us. *Sr Librn,* Jonetta Douglas; Tel: 515-281-3312, E-mail: jonetta.douglas@legis.state.ia.us; *Asst Librn,* Judy Neff; Tel: 515-281-3569, E-mail: judy.neff@legis.state.ia.us; Staff 2 (Non-MLS 2)
Founded 1960
Library Holdings: Bk Vols 5,790; Per Subs 37
Special Collections: Bill Drafts; Bills introduced in the General Assembly with amendments filed since 1953; Interim Committee Reports & Minutes
Publications: Interim Study Reports to the General Assembly (Intermittent); Legislative Guides
Open Mon-Fri 9-5
Restriction: Circ limited

CM MERCY COLLEGE OF HEALTH SCIENCES LIBRARY*, 928 Sixth Ave, 50309-1239. SAN 377-0990. Tel: 515-643-6613. FAX: 515-643-6695. Web Site: www.mchs.edu. *Dir,* Roy Meador, III; Tel: 515-643-6612, E-mail: rmeador@mercydesmoines.org; *Asst Dir,* Jennifer Thompson; E-mail: jthompson@mercydesmoines.org
Library Holdings: Bk Titles 9,261; Bk Vols 10,497; Per Subs 111
Wireless access
Partic in Docline; OCLC Online Computer Library Center, Inc
Open Mon-Thurs (Fall & Spring) 7:30am-10pm, Fri 7:30-5, Sat 9-2, Sun 5-10; Mon-Fri (Summer) 7:30am-9:30pm, Fri 7:30-4, Sat 9-2, Sun 5-10

M MERCY MEDICAL CENTER, Levitt Library, 1111 Sixth Ave, 50314-2611. SAN 305-3482. Tel: 515-247-4189. FAX: 515-643-8809. E-mail: library@mercydesmoines.org. Web Site: www.mercydesmoines.org. *Mgr,* Jeanette Stonebraker; E-mail: jstonebraker@mercydesmoines.org
Founded 1961
Library Holdings: Bk Vols 4,384; Per Subs 139
Automation Activity & Vendor Info: (Cataloging) TLC (The Library Corporation); (Circulation) TLC (The Library Corporation); (OPAC) OCLC
Partic in Docline
Open Mon-Fri 8-4:30

L PRINCIPAL FINANCIAL GROUP*, Law Library, 711 High St, S006 W80, 50392. SAN 375-3352. Tel: 515-247-5893. FAX: 515-248-3011. *Mgr, Libr Serv,* Brent Chesson; E-mail: chesson.brent@principal.com
Founded 1939
Library Holdings: Bk Titles 800; Bk Vols 5,000; Per Subs 20
Subject Interests: Ins, Pensions, State law
Open Mon-Fri 9-6

S STATE HISTORICAL SOCIETY OF IOWA-DES MOINES LIBRARY*, 600 E Locust, 50319-0290. SAN 305-3466. Tel: 515-281-6200. Interlibrary Loan Service Tel: 515-281-5070. FAX: 515-282-0502. Web Site: www.iowahistory.org. *Head Librn,* Carol Kirsch; *ILL, Ref Librn,* Shari Stelling; *Ref Librn,* Susan Jellinger; *Archives Supvr,* Jeffrey Dawson; *Archivist,* Sharon Avery; *Archivist,* Meaghan McCarthy; *Archives Assoc,* Bruce Krueger; *Microfilm Presv Spec,* Delpha Musgrave; *Ref Serv,* Rosie Springer; *Spec Coll & Archives Librn,* Becki Plunkett; Staff 10 (MLS 3, Non-MLS 7)
Founded 1892
Jul 2007-Jun 2008 Income $1,352,449. Mats Exp $101,529, Books $17,681, Per/Ser (Incl. Access Fees) $6,204, Micro $77,644. Sal $1,156,604
Special Collections: Manuscripts; Photo Archives; State Archives
Subject Interests: Agr, Genealogy, Iowa hist, Maps
Automation Activity & Vendor Info: (Cataloging) Ex Libris Group
Wireless access
Open Tues-Sat 9-4:30

GL STATE LIBRARY OF IOWA*, Iowa State Law Library, State Capitol Bldg, 1007 E Grand Ave, 50319. SAN 372-1248. Tel: 515-281-5124. FAX: 515-281-6515. E-mail: law@lib.state.ia.us. Web Site: www.silo.lib.ia.us/lawlib.html. *Librn,* Mandy Easter; E-mail: mandy.easter@lib.state.ia.us; *Librn,* Cory Quist; E-mail: cory.quist@lib.state.ia.us; Staff 3 (MLS 2, Non-MLS 1)
Founded 1835
Library Holdings: Bk Vols 160,000
Special Collections: English law; Iowa law. State Document Depository; US Document Depository
Database Vendor: LexisNexis, Westlaw
Open Mon-Fri 8-4:30
Restriction: Open to pub for ref only

P STATE LIBRARY OF IOWA*, 1112 E Grand Ave, 50319. SAN 341-8472. Tel: 515-281-4105. FAX: 515-281-6191. Web Site: www.statelibraryofiowa.org. *Interim State Librn,* Barbara Corson; *Librn,* Helen Dagley; *Librn,* Nancy Lee; *Info Spec,* Annette Wetteland; E-mail: annette.wetteland@lib.state.ia.us; Staff 26 (MLS 16, Non-MLS 10)
Founded 1838. Pop 2,776,755
Library Holdings: Bk Titles 259,449; Bk Vols 363,539; Per Subs 1,228
Special Collections: Attorney General Opinions; Bar Association Proceedings; Iowa State Publications; Medical Coll, bks & journals; Patent. State Document Depository; US Document Depository
Automation Activity & Vendor Info: (Cataloging) Horizon
Database Vendor: EBSCOhost, LexisNexis, OCLC FirstSearch, OCLC WebJunction, ProQuest, Westlaw
Wireless access
Function: Art exhibits, Audio & video playback equip for onsite use, Computer training, Computers for patron use, Copy machines, Distance learning, Doc delivery serv, e-mail & chat, e-mail serv, Electronic databases & coll, Fax serv, Govt ref serv, Handicapped accessible, ILL available, Legal assistance to inmates, Libr develop, Mail & tel request accepted, Mail loans to mem, Newsp ref libr, Online cat, Online ref, Online searches, Outside serv via phone, mail, e-mail & web, Photocopying/Printing, Prof lending libr, Pub access computers, Ref serv available, Ref serv in person, Referrals accepted, Summer reading prog, Telephone ref, Web-catalog, Wheelchair accessible, Workshops
Publications: CE Calendar; Documents Catalog & Index; Footnotes; Inservice to Iowa (Public Libraries Measures of Quality); Iowa Certification Manual for Public Libraries; Library Directory; Long Range Plan; Public Library Statistics; Summer Reading Program
Partic in Iowa Resource & Info Sharing; OCLC Online Computer Library Center, Inc
Open Mon-Fri 8-4:30

GL UNITED STATES COURT OF APPEALS*, Branch Library, 110 E Court Ave, Ste 358, 50309. SAN 325-4305. Tel: 515-284-6228. FAX: 515-284-6296. E-mail: library8th@ca8.uscourts.gov. *Librn,* Melissa Miller
Library Holdings: Bk Vols 17,000; Per Subs 50
Partic in Westlaw
Open Mon-Fri 8-4:30

DEWITT

P THE FRANCES BANTA WAGGONER COMMUNITY LIBRARY, 505 Tenth St, 52742-1335. SAN 305-330X. Tel: 563-659-5523. FAX: 563-659-2901. E-mail: fbwclib@dewitt.lib.ia.us. Web Site: www.dewitt.lib.ia.us. *Dir,* Jane Kedley; E-mail: janekedley@dewitt.lib.ia.us; *Asst Dir,* Ruth Fatchett; *Ch,* Pamela Danley; *Tech Librn,* Erin McDonnell; *Circ/Customer Serv Mgr,* Joellyn McDonnell; Staff 5 (Non-MLS 5)
Founded 1897. Pop 5,049; Circ 111,644
Library Holdings: AV Mats 3,080; DVDs 2,832; Large Print Bks 60; Bk Vols 35,761; Per Subs 91
Subject Interests: Newsp on microfilm
Automation Activity & Vendor Info: (Acquisitions) Book Systems; (Cataloging) Book Systems; (Circulation) Book Systems; (OPAC) Book Systems

Database Vendor: EBSCOhost, LearningExpress, ProQuest, TumbleBookLibrary
Wireless access
Function: Writing prog
Partic in Iowa Libr Asn
Open Mon, Tues & Thurs 10-8, Wed & Fri 10-5, Sat 10-4, Sun 1-4
Friends of the Library Group

DEXTER

P DEXTER PUBLIC LIBRARY*, 724 Marshall St, 50070. (Mail add: PO Box 37, 50070-0037), SAN 305-3520. Tel: 515-789-4490. FAX: 515-789-4490. E-mail: dexterpl@mchsi.com. *Librn,* Mary McColloch; *Asst Librn,* Rachel Findlay
Founded 1930. Pop 669; Circ 10,065
Library Holdings: AV Mats 628; Bk Vols 8,147; Per Subs 17
Open Mon-Wed 1-6, Thurs 6pm-9pm, Fri 1-5, Sat 9-12
Friends of the Library Group

DICKENS

P DICKENS PUBLIC LIBRARY, 210 Main, 51333. (Mail add: PO Box 38, 51333-0038), SAN 376-530X. Tel: 712-836-2217. *Dir,* Bonnie Hagedorn
Library Holdings: Bk Vols 4,900
Mem of Northwest Iowa Library Services
Open Mon-Thurs 4-8

DIKE

P DIKE PUBLIC LIBRARY*, 133 E Elder, 50624-9612. SAN 305-3547. Tel: 319-989-2608. FAX: 319-989-2984. E-mail: dikepubliclibrary@dike.lib.ia.us. Web Site: www.dike.lib.ia.us. *Dir,* Patricia Renee Boe; *Asst City Librn,* Margaret Nielsen; Staff 2 (Non-MLS 2)
Pop 1,025; Circ 52,146
Jul 2007-Jun 2008 Income $86,000, City $64,246, County $19,054. Mats Exp $25,551. Sal $22,574 (Prof $19,802)
Library Holdings: Large Print Bks 200; Bk Vols 18,000; Per Subs 100; Talking Bks 1,100
Automation Activity & Vendor Info: (Cataloging) Follett Software; (Circulation) Follett Software
Database Vendor: EBSCOhost, OCLC FirstSearch
Wireless access
Function: Homebound delivery serv, ILL available
Open Mon & Wed 9-12 & 1-7, Tues, Thurs & Fri 9-12 & 1-5, Sat 9-12

DONNELLSON

P DONNELLSON PUBLIC LIBRARY*, 500 Park St, 52625. (Mail add: PO Box 290, 52625-0290), SAN 305-3555. Tel: 319-835-5545. FAX: 319-835-5545. Web Site: www.donnellson.lib.ia.us. *Dir,* Brenda Christine Knox; E-mail: bknox@donnellson.lib.ia.us; *Asst Dir,* Carolyn Sue Lind; Staff 3 (Non-MLS 3)
Founded 1937. Pop 940; Circ 43,149
Jul 2007-Jun 2008 Income $66,482, City $25,925, County $7,826, Locally Generated Income $13,052, Other $19,446. Mats Exp $28,380, Books $8,570, Per/Ser (Incl. Access Fees) $914, Other Print Mats $14,190, AV Equip $3,205, AV Mat $1,195, Electronic Ref Mat (Incl. Access Fees) $306. Sal $37,137
Library Holdings: AV Mats 1,020; DVDs 340; Bk Titles 15,740; Bk Vols 15,749; Per Subs 63; Talking Bks 1,600; Videos 900
Special Collections: Genealogy Coll; Local History Coll
Automation Activity & Vendor Info: (Circulation) Follett Software; (OPAC) Follett Software
Database Vendor: EBSCOhost, OCLC FirstSearch
Wireless access
Function: ILL available
Partic in State of Iowa Libraries Online
Open Mon-Fri 11:30-7:30, Sat 10-3:30

DOON

P DOON PUBLIC LIBRARY*, 207 Barton Ave, 51235. (Mail add: PO Box 218, 51235-0218), SAN 305-3563. Tel: 712-726-3526. FAX: 712-726-3526. E-mail: doonlib@speednet.com. *Dir,* Amy Zevenbergen
Pop 537; Circ 6,407
Library Holdings: Bk Titles 12,000; Per Subs 22
Wireless access
Mem of Northwest Iowa Library Services
Open Mon 2-5:30, Tues & Wed 11-3, Thurs 4-8, Fri 2-5, Sat 10-12

DOWS

P DOWS COMMUNITY LIBRARY*, 114 Ellsworth, 50071. (Mail add: PO Box 427, 50071-0427), SAN 305-358X. Tel: 515-852-4326. FAX: 515-852-4326. E-mail: dowslib@wmtel.net. Web Site: dows.lib.ia.us. *Dir,* Deb Olson
Founded 1925. Pop 538; Circ 8,852
Library Holdings: Bk Titles 9,000; Bk Vols 9,400; Per Subs 15
Special Collections: Newspapers 1896-present, microfilm. Oral History
Wireless access
Partic in OCLC Online Computer Library Center, Inc
Open Mon 1-6, Tues & Fri 1-5, Wed 10-12 & 1-5:30, Sat 9-2
Friends of the Library Group

DUBUQUE

P CARNEGIE-STOUT PUBLIC LIBRARY*, 360 W 11th St, 52001. SAN 305-3601. Tel: 563-589-4225. Administration Tel: 563-589-4313. FAX: 563-589-4217. Web Site: www.dubuque.lib.ia.us. *Dir,* Susan Henricks; Tel: 563-589-4126, E-mail: shenricks@dubuque.lib.ia.us; *Youth Serv Librn,* Danielle Day; Tel: 563-589-4138, E-mail: dday@dubuque.lib.ia.us; *IT Supvr,* Jason Burds; Tel: 563-589-4225, Ext 2229, E-mail: jburds@dubuque.lib.ia.us; *Adult Serv,* Michelle Hellmer; Tel: 563-589-4137, E-mail: mhellmer@dubuque.lib.ia.us; *Circ,* Deb Stephenson; Tel: 563-589-4139, E-mail: dstephen@dubuque.lib.ia.us; *Tech Serv,* Deborah Fliegel; Tel: 563-589-4243, E-mail: dfliegel@dubuque.lib.ia.us; Staff 28 (MLS 11, Non-MLS 17)
Founded 1902. Pop 58,646; Circ 705,000
Jul 2010-Jun 2011 Income $2,925,435, State $44,220, City $2,784,302, Locally Generated Income $74,570, Other $22,343. Mats Exp $334,261, Books $179,353, Per/Ser (Incl. Access Fees) $32,589, AV Mat $76,450, Electronic Ref Mat (Incl. Access Fees) $45,869. Sal $1,261,841
Library Holdings: Audiobooks 10,442; DVDs 15,121; e-books 1,333; Bk Vols 149,598; Per Subs 496
Special Collections: Municipal Document Depository; State Document Depository
Subject Interests: Iowa, Local hist
Automation Activity & Vendor Info: (Acquisitions) Horizon; (Cataloging) Horizon; (Circulation) Horizon; (OPAC) SirsiDynix
Database Vendor: Baker & Taylor, Booksite, Brodart, EBSCO Auto Repair Reference, EBSCOhost, Ingram Library Services, LearningExpress, Newsbank, OCLC, OCLC FirstSearch, OCLC WorldShare Interlibrary Loan, Overdrive, Inc, ProQuest, ReferenceUSA, SirsiDynix
Wireless access
Function: ILL available
Publications: Brochures; Magazine & Newspaper Holdings (Annual)
Partic in Dubuque Area Library Information Consortium; State of Iowa Libraries Online
Open Mon-Wed 9-9, Thurs 1-9, Fri 9-5, Sat 10-5, Sun 1-5
Friends of the Library Group

CR CLARKE UNIVERSITY*, Nicholas J Schrup Library, 1550 Clarke Dr, 52001. SAN 305-361X. Tel: 563-588-6320. Reference Tel: 563-588-6421. Administration Tel: 563-588-6580. FAX: 563-588-8160. E-mail: library@clarke.edu. Web Site: www.clarke.edu/page.aspx?id=23174. *Libr Dir,* Sue Leibold; E-mail: susanne.leibold@clarke.edu; *Ref Librn,* Becky Alford; E-mail: becky.alford@clarke.edu; *Circ Desk Mgr,* Brian Gomoll; E-mail: brian.gomoll@clarke.edu; *Acq,* Vicki Larson; Tel: 563-588-6424, E-mail: vicki.larson@clarke.edu; *Archives,* Sara McAlpin; Tel: 563-588-6556, E-mail: sara.mcalpin@clarke.edu; Staff 5 (MLS 3, Non-MLS 2)
Founded 1843. Enrl 1,200; Fac 105; Highest Degree: Doctorate
Jun 2011-May 2012 Income $324,325. Mats Exp $179,000, Books $15,000, Per/Ser (Incl. Access Fees) $50,000, Micro $3,000, AV Mat $500, Electronic Ref Mat (Incl. Access Fees) $110,000, Presv $500. Sal $200,000 (Prof $135,000)
Library Holdings: DVDs 400; e-books 90,000; e-journals 100; Microforms 5,000; Bk Titles 100,000; Bk Vols 125,000; Videos 50
Special Collections: BVM Heritage Coll; Rare Books
Automation Activity & Vendor Info: (Cataloging) ComPanion Corp; (Circulation) ComPanion Corp; (Course Reserve) ComPanion Corp; (ILL) OCLC ILLiad; (OPAC) ComPanion Corp; (Serials) ComPanion Corp
Database Vendor: 3M Library Systems, American Chemical Society, Annual Reviews, ARTstor, Checkpoint Systems, Inc, ComPanion Corp, CredoReference, EBSCOhost, Elsevier, Gale Cengage Learning, JSTOR, LexisNexis, Mergent Online, Newsbank-Readex, OCLC FirstSearch, OCLC WorldShare Interlibrary Loan, OVID Technologies, Oxford Online, Project MUSE, ProQuest, ScienceDirect
Wireless access
Function: Adult bk club, Archival coll, Art exhibits, Audio & video playback equip for onsite use, AV serv, Copy machines, Distance learning, Electronic databases & coll, Equip loans & repairs, Free DVD rentals, Handicapped accessible, ILL available, Instruction & testing, Learning ctr, Music CDs, Online cat, Online info literacy tutorials on the web & in blackboard, Online searches, Orientations, Ref serv available, Ref serv in person, Scanner, VHS videos, Wheelchair accessible
Partic in Dubuque Area Library Information Consortium

CR EMMAUS BIBLE COLLEGE LIBRARY, 2570 Asbury Rd, 52001-3096. SAN 304-4998. Tel: 563-588-8000, Ext 1003. FAX: 563-588-1216. *Dir,* John Rush; E-mail: jrush@elearn.emmaus.edu; *Librn,* Beth Young; Tel:

563-588-8000, Ext 1002, E-mail: byoung@elearn.emmaus.edu; Staff 2 (MLS 2)
Founded 1941. Enrl 210; Highest Degree: Bachelor
Library Holdings: Bk Titles 99,000; Bk Vols 120,000; Per Subs 240
Special Collections: Plymouth Brethren Writings, bibliog & flm
Subject Interests: Biblical studies
Automation Activity & Vendor Info: (OPAC) Winnebago Software Co
Database Vendor: EBSCOhost
Wireless access
Partic in Chicago Area Theological Libr Asn; Dubuque Area Library Information Consortium

M FINLEY HOSPITAL*, Resource Center, 350 N Grandview Ave, 52001. Tel: 563-589-2496. FAX: 563-557-2813. Web Site: www.finleyhospital.org. *In Charge,* Julie Harris
Library Holdings: Bk Vols 2,500; Per Subs 105
Subject Interests: Consumer health, Nursing
Open Mon-Fri 8-4:30

C LORAS COLLEGE LIBRARY, 1450 Alta Vista St, 52004-4327. (Mail add: PO Box 164, 52004-0164), SAN 305-3644. Tel: 563-588-7189. Interlibrary Loan Service Tel: 563-588-4969. Reference Tel: 563-588-7042. Administration Tel: 563-588-7164. Toll Free Tel: 800-245-6727. FAX: 563-588-7147. Web Site: www.loras.edu/library. *Dir,* Joyce A Meldrem; E-mail: joyce.meldrem@loras.edu; *E-Res & Research Serv Librn,* Kristen Smith; E-mail: kristen.smith@loras.edu; *Instrul Serv Librn,* Julie Arensdorf; Tel: 563-588-7917, E-mail: julie.arensdorf@loras.edu; *Spec Coll & Tech Serv Librn,* Heidi Pettitt; Tel: 563-588-7873, E-mail: heidi.pettitt@loras.edu; *Circ Supvr,* Position Currently Open; *Night Supvr,* Position Currently Open; *Coordr, Acq,* Position Currently Open; *ILL & Reserves Coordr,* Suzanne Ward; E-mail: suzanne.ward@loras.edu; *Coordr, Ser,* Donna Welter; Tel: 563-588-7654, E-mail: donna.welter@loras.edu; Staff 7.74 (MLS 4, Non-MLS 3.74)
Founded 1839. Enrl 1,516; Fac 136; Highest Degree: Master
Library Holdings: Audiobooks 257; DVDs 2,296; Bk Vols 334,675; Per Subs 198; Videos 472
Special Collections: Center for Dubuque History Coll; Dubuque County Document Depository; Horace Coll; Loras College Archives; T S Eliot Coll; Torch Press Imprints Coll; William Boyd Allison Government Document Coll. State Document Depository; US Document Depository
Subject Interests: Educ, Hist
Automation Activity & Vendor Info: (Acquisitions) SirsiDynix; (Cataloging) SirsiDynix; (Circulation) SirsiDynix; (Course Reserve) SirsiDynix; (OPAC) SirsiDynix; (Serials) SirsiDynix
Database Vendor: American Chemical Society, ARTstor, EBSCOhost, Gale Cengage Learning, JSTOR, Newsbank, OCLC FirstSearch, SirsiDynix
Wireless access
Partic in Dubuque Area Library Information Consortium; OCLC Online Computer Library Center, Inc

M MERCY MEDICAL CENTER*, Anthony C Pfohl Health Sciences Library, 250 Mercy Dr, 52001-7398. SAN 305-3652. Tel: 563-589-9620. FAX: 563-589-8185. Web Site: www.mercydubuque.com/educat/index.htm/library. *Librn,* Pam Kress-Dunn; E-mail: kressp@mercyhealth.com; Staff 1 (MLS 1)
Founded 1973
Library Holdings: Bk Titles 1,144; Bk Vols 1,155; Per Subs 74
Subject Interests: Health sci
Automation Activity & Vendor Info: (Acquisitions) EOS International; (Cataloging) EOS International; (OPAC) EOS International; (Serials) EBSCO Online
Database Vendor: Cinahl, EBSCOhost, Elsevier, EOS International, MD Consult, PubMed, STAT!Ref (Teton Data Systems)
Wireless access
Function: Computers for patron use, Copy machines, ILL available
Partic in Dubuque Area Library Information Consortium; National Network of Libraries of Medicine
Open Mon-Fri 8-4:30
Restriction: Authorized patrons, Badge access after hrs, Circ limited, Hospital employees & physicians only, In-house use for visitors, Non-circulating to the pub

S TELEGRAPH HERALD LIBRARY*, 801 Bluff St, 52001. (Mail add: PO Box 688, 52001-0688), SAN 305-3695. Tel: 563-588-5770. FAX: 563-588-5745. E-mail: thonline@wcinet.com. Web Site: www.thonline.com. *Librn,* Steve McAuliff
Founded 1970
Library Holdings: Bk Vols 800
Special Collections: City Directories (from 1856, incomplete); History-Dubuque & area; Necrology Card File (from 1974)
Open Mon-Fri 8-5

C UNIVERSITY OF DUBUQUE LIBRARY*, Charles C Myers Library, 2000 University Ave, 52001. SAN 305-3687. Tel: 563-589-3100. FAX: 563-589-3722. E-mail: libcirc@dbq.edu. Web Site: www.dbq.edu/library. *Univ Librn,* Mary Anne Knefel; E-mail: mknefel@dbq.edu; *Dir, Curric Libr, Ref Librn,* Carolyne Lathrop; *Asst Dir, Libr Instruction & Pub Serv,* Anne Marie Gruber; *Asst Dir, Libr Syst & Tech Serv,* Jonathan Helmke; *Ref & Instruction Librn,* Becky Canovan; *Circ Supvr,* Jaimie Shaffer; *Cat, ILL,* Sue Reiter; Staff 8 (MLS 4, Non-MLS 4)
Founded 1852. Enrl 1,268; Fac 71; Highest Degree: Doctorate
Library Holdings: e-journals 17,026; Bk Vols 172,670; Per Subs 484
Special Collections: German Presbyterian Coll; Walter F Peterson Coll; William J Petersen Coll
Subject Interests: Native Am, Relig
Automation Activity & Vendor Info: (Acquisitions) SirsiDynix; (Cataloging) SirsiDynix; (Circulation) SirsiDynix; (OPAC) SirsiDynix; (Serials) SirsiDynix
Partic in Dubuque Area Library Information Consortium; OCLC Online Computer Library Center, Inc
Open Mon-Thurs 7am-Midnight, Fri 7am-9pm, Sat 10-9, Sun 12-Midnight

SR WARTBURG THEOLOGICAL SEMINARY*, Reu Memorial Library, 333 Wartburg Pl, 52004. (Mail add: PO Box 5004, 52004-5004), SAN 325-5808. Tel: 563-589-0267. Interlibrary Loan Service Tel: 563-589-0266. FAX: 563-589-0333. E-mail: library@wartburgseminary.edu. Web Site: www.wartburgseminary.edu. *Dir,* Susan J Ebertz; E-mail: sebertz@wartburgseminary.edu; *Coordr, Libr Serv,* Loretta Haskell; *Libr Asst,* Sarah Nessan; Staff 4 (Non-MLS 4)
Founded 1853. Enrl 162
Library Holdings: Bk Vols 85,148; Per Subs 246
Partic in Dubuque Area Library Information Consortium
Open Mon-Thurs 8-10, Fri 8-4:30, Sat 9-4:30, Sun 3-10

DUMONT

P DUMONT COMMUNITY LIBRARY*, 602 Second St, 50625. (Mail add: PO Box 159, 50625-0159), SAN 305-3725. Tel: 641-857-3304. FAX: 641-857-3304. Web Site: www.dumont.lib.ia.us. *Dir,* Deb Eisentrager; E-mail: deb@dumont.lib.ia.us; *Asst Librn,* Jodi Angstman
Founded 1927. Pop 650; Circ 14,233
Jul 2005-Jun 2006 Income $28,600. Mats Exp $7,700, Books $6,000, Per/Ser (Incl. Access Fees) $700, AV Mat $1,000
Library Holdings: Bk Titles 11,000; Per Subs 52
Open Mon & Tues 1-5, Wed & Fri 9-12 & 1-5, Thurs Noon-7, Sat 9-12
Friends of the Library Group

DUNCOMBE

P DUNCOMBE PUBLIC LIBRARY*, 621 Prince St, 50532. (Mail add: PO Box 178, 50532-0178), SAN 376-5210. Tel: 515-543-4646. FAX: 515-543-8186. *Dir,* Arrin Balsley; Staff 2 (Non-MLS 2)
Founded 1978. Pop 410
Library Holdings: Audiobooks 99; DVDs 566; Large Print Bks 160; Bk Vols 6,084; Per Subs 44; Videos 280
Automation Activity & Vendor Info: (Acquisitions) TLC (The Library Corporation); (Cataloging) TLC (The Library Corporation); (Circulation) TLC (The Library Corporation); (Course Reserve) TLC (The Library Corporation); (ILL) TLC (The Library Corporation)
Database Vendor: EBSCOhost, Ingram Library Services, WebMD
Wireless access
Open Mon 10-12 & 1-6, Tues-Thurs 1-5, Fri 1-6, Sat 9-12

DUNKERTON

P DUNKERTON PUBLIC LIBRARY*, 203 E Tower St, 50626. (Mail add: PO Box 249, 50626-0249), SAN 305-3733. Tel: 319-822-4610. FAX: 319-822-4664. E-mail: dunkpublib@dunkerton.net. Web Site: www.dunkerton.lib.ia.us. *Dir,* Michelle Wheeler
Pop 1,100; Circ 5,800
Library Holdings: Bk Titles 8,200
Automation Activity & Vendor Info: (Cataloging) Biblionix; (Circulation) Biblionix
Wireless access
Open Mon, Tues & Thurs 2-7, Wed, Fri & Sat 10-2
Friends of the Library Group

DUNLAP

P DUNLAP PUBLIC LIBRARY*, 102 S Tenth St, 51529. SAN 305-3741. Tel: 712-643-5311. FAX: 712-643-5311. *Librn,* Paula Hess; E-mail: pjhess@hotmail.com
Pop 1,217; Circ 16,483
Jul 2005-Jun 2006 Income $31,000. Mats Exp $11,000
Library Holdings: Bk Titles 11,000; Bk Vols 13,175; Per Subs 38
Mem of Southwest Iowa Library Services District
Open Mon-Thurs 8:30-6, Fri 8:30-5, Sat 11-2
Friends of the Library Group

DYERSVILLE

P JAMES KENNEDY PUBLIC LIBRARY*, 320 First Ave E, 52040. SAN 305-375X. Tel: 563-875-8912. FAX: 563-875-6162. Web Site: www.dyersville.lib.ia.us. *Dir,* Shirley J Vonderhaar; E-mail: svonderhaar@dyersville.lib.ia.us; *Ad,* Diana Schmitt; E-mail: dschmitt@dyersville.lib.ia.us; *Sr Serv,* Lisa Gaylor; E-mail: lgaylor@dyersville.lib.ia.us; *Youth Serv,* Kimshiro Benton; E-mail: kbenton@dyersville.lib.ia.us; Staff 2.5 (MLS 1, Non-MLS 1.5)
Founded 1956. Pop 4,035; Circ 130,000
Library Holdings: Bk Titles 44,000; Per Subs 125
Automation Activity & Vendor Info: (Acquisitions) Follett Software
Wireless access
Partic in Dubuque Area Library Information Consortium
Open Mon-Thurs 9-8, Fri & Sat 9-5, Sun 1-4
Friends of the Library Group

DYSART

P NORMA ANDERS PUBLIC LIBRARY*, 320 Main St, 52224. (Mail add: PO Box 519, 52224-0519), SAN 305-3768. Tel: 319-476-5210. FAX: 319-476-2671. *Dir,* Deborah Reed; *Ch,* Rachelle Frost
Founded 1882. Pop 1,379; Circ 26,238
Library Holdings: Bk Vols 29,000; Per Subs 82
Automation Activity & Vendor Info: (Acquisitions) Biblionix; (Cataloging) Biblionix; (Circulation) Biblionix; (Course Reserve) Biblionix; (ILL) Biblionix; (Media Booking) Biblionix; (OPAC) Biblionix; (Serials) Biblionix
Wireless access
Open Mon 9-12 & 1-6, Tues & Fri 1-6, Wed 12-6, Thurs 9-12 & 2-7, Sat 9-12

EAGLE GROVE

P EAGLE GROVE MEMORIAL LIBRARY*, 101 S Cadwell, 50533. SAN 305-3776. Tel: 515-448-4115. FAX: 515-448-5279. Web Site: www.eaglegrove.lib.ia.us. *Dir,* Jan Grandgeorge; E-mail: jgrandgeorge@eaglegrove.lib.ia.us; *Ch,* Renee Simons; E-mail: rsimons@eaglegrove.lib.ia.us; *Circ,* Marilyn Schnell; Staff 1 (Non-MLS 1)
Founded 1903. Pop 6,231; Circ 63,430
Library Holdings: AV Mats 557; Large Print Bks 1,289; Bk Vols 30,000; Per Subs 99; Talking Bks 1,725
Automation Activity & Vendor Info: (Circulation) Follett Software; (OPAC) Follett Software
Database Vendor: EBSCO Information Services, EBSCOhost, MITINET, Inc, OCLC FirstSearch
Wireless access
Special Services for the Blind - Bks on cassette; Bks on CD; Large print bks
Open Mon-Thurs 10-7, Fri & Sat 10-4:30

EARLHAM

P EARLHAM PUBLIC LIBRARY, 120 S Chestnut Ave, 50072. (Mail add: PO Box 310, 50072-0310), SAN 305-3792. Tel: 515 758-2121. FAX: 515-758-2121. E-mail: library@earlham.lib.ia.us. Web Site: www.earlham.lib.ia.us. *Dir,* Michelle Sandquist; *Asst Librn,* Lorraine Bailey; *Asst Librn,* Ellyn Reel; *Asst Librn,* Phyllis Sheely; Staff 1.18 (Non-MLS 1.18)
Pop 1,450; Circ 14,800
Library Holdings: Audiobooks 232; DVDs 817; e-books 10,042; Bk Titles 17,900; Per Subs 38
Automation Activity & Vendor Info: (Cataloging) Biblionix
Wireless access
Function: Adult bk club, Archival coll, Audiobks via web, Bk club(s), Bks on CD, Children's prog, Computers for patron use, Copy machines, Electronic databases & coll, Fax serv, Free DVD rentals, ILL available, Online cat, Online info literacy tutorials on the web & in blackboard, OverDrive digital audio bks, Photocopying/Printing, Prog for adults, Prog for children & young adult, Pub access computers, Scanner, Story hour, Summer reading prog, Web-catalog
Partic in WILBOR Consortium (West/Central Iowa Libraries Building Online Resources)
Open Mon, Tues & Thurs 10-7, Wed 9-7, Fri 10-5, Sat 9-12
Friends of the Library Group

EARLVILLE

P RUTH SUCKOW MEMORIAL LIBRARY*, 122 Northern Ave, 52041. (Mail add: PO Box 189, 52041-0189), SAN 305-3806. Tel: 563-923-5235. FAX: 563-923-5235. E-mail: librarian@earlville.lib.ia.us. *Dir,* Laurie Ellen Boies
Founded 1937. Pop 900; Circ 11,293
Library Holdings: AV Mats 321; Bk Titles 10,232; Per Subs 32; Talking Bks 50
Special Collections: Ruth Suckow Coll
Open Mon & Fri 1-5, Wed 9-12, 1-5 & 6-8, Sat 9-12

EARLY

P EARLY PUBLIC LIBRARY*, 107 Main St, 50535-5010. (Mail add: PO Box 399, 50535-0399), SAN 305-3814. Tel: 712-273-5334. FAX: 712-273-5251. E-mail: earlylib@ruralwaves.us. *Librn,* Christine Drey
Founded 1926. Pop 800; Circ 15,228
Library Holdings: Bk Vols 24,000; Per Subs 69
Mem of Northwest Iowa Library Services
Open Mon & Wed 9-12 & 1-5:30, Tues 1-6, Sat 9-3
Friends of the Library Group

EDDYVILLE

P EDDYVILLE PUBLIC LIBRARY*, Akers Memorial Bldg, 202 S Second St, 52553. (Mail add: PO Box 399, 52553-0399), SAN 305-3822. Tel: 641-969-4815. FAX: 641-969-4040. Web Site: www.eddyville.lib.ia.us. *Dir,* Vicki Vroegh
Founded 1897. Pop 1,064; Circ 10,181
Library Holdings: AV Mats 470; Large Print Bks 66; Bk Vols 10,000; Per Subs 37
Automation Activity & Vendor Info: (Cataloging) Follett Software; (Circulation) Follett Software
Open Mon-Thurs 9:30-1 & 1:30-6:30, Fri 9:30-2, Sat 9-12

EDGEWOOD

P EDGEWOOD PUBLIC LIBRARY*, 203 W Union St, 52042. (Mail add: PO Box 339, 52042-0339), SAN 305-3830. Tel: 563-928-6242. FAX: 563-928-6242. Web Site: www.edgewood.lib.ia.us. *Dir,* Cathy Shaw; E-mail: cshaw@edgewood.lib.ia.us; *Asst Librn,* Rayma Fisher
Founded 1933. Pop 925; Circ 23,677
Library Holdings: Bk Titles 12,000; Per Subs 52
Automation Activity & Vendor Info: (Circulation) Follett Software
Function: Adult bk club, Handicapped accessible, Home delivery & serv to Sr ctr & nursing homes, Homebound delivery serv, Homework prog, ILL available, Online searches, Prog for adults, Prog for children & young adult, Spoken cassettes & CDs, Summer reading prog, VHS videos, Wheelchair accessible
Open Mon 12-7, Tues 10-5, Wed 1-8, Thurs 12-6, Fri 12-4, Sat 9-1

ELBERON

P ELBERON PUBLIC LIBRARY*, 106 Main St, 52225. SAN 377-581X. Tel: 319-439-5476. FAX: 319-439-5476. E-mail: elbronpl@netins.net. Web Site: www.elberon.lib.ia.us. *Dir,* Kim Banes
Founded 1990
Library Holdings: Bk Vols 10,593; Per Subs 24
Open Tues 11-6, Wed & Fri 11-5, Sat 8:30-10:30

ELDON

P ELDON CARNEGIE PUBLIC LIBRARY*, 608 W Elm St, 52554. (Mail add: PO Box 430, 52225-0430), SAN 305-389X. Tel: 641-652-7517. FAX: 641-652-7517. Web Site: www.eldon.lib.ia.us. *Dir,* Suzanne Streeby; E-mail: sstreeby@eldon.lib.ia.us; *Asst Librn,* Christina Albert; *Asst Librn,* Sharon Glasgow
Founded 1913. Pop 1,070; Circ 7,000
Library Holdings: AV Mats 510; Bk Vols 10,200; Per Subs 35
Subject Interests: Genealogy
Wireless access
Open Mon & Fri 1-5, Tues & Wed 11-5:30, Thurs 11:30-6, Sat 9-Noon
Friends of the Library Group

ELDORA

P ELDORA PUBLIC LIBRARY*, 1202 Tenth St, 50627. SAN 305-3857. Tel: 641-939-2173. FAX: 641-939-7563. Web Site: www.eldora.lib.ia.us. *Dir,* Dan Gehring; E-mail: dgehring@eldora.lib.ia.us; *Ch,* Karen Feht; Staff 2 (MLS 1, Non-MLS 1)
Pop 3,035; Circ 45,000
Library Holdings: Bk Vols 25,000; Per Subs 95
Open Mon & Wed 9-8, Tues, Thurs & Fri 9-6, Sat 9-3
Friends of the Library Group

ELDRIDGE

P SCOTT COUNTY LIBRARY SYSTEM*, 200 N Sixth Ave, 52748. SAN 341-8561. Tel: 563-285-4794. FAX: 563-285-4743. Web Site: www.scottcountylibrary.org. *Dir,* Paul H Seelau; E-mail: pseelau@scottcountylibrary.org; *Ref Serv Librn, YA Librn,* Sarah Carlin; E-mail: scarlin@scottcountylibrary.org; *Youth Serv Librn,* Crystal Kehoe; E-mail: ckehoe@scottcountylibrary.org; *Tech Serv,* Connie Owings; E-mail: cowings@scottcountylibrary.org; *Circ,* Joan Hennigan; E-mail:

jhennigan@scottcountylibrary.org; *ILL,* Lorna Lillis; Staff 55 (MLS 3, Non-MLS 52)
Founded 1950. Pop 27,756; Circ 310,463
Library Holdings: Bk Vols 136,491; Per Subs 645
Special Collections: Scott County History
Automation Activity & Vendor Info: (Acquisitions) SirsiDynix; (Cataloging) SirsiDynix; (Circulation) SirsiDynix; (ILL) OCLC; (OPAC) SirsiDynix; (Serials) SirsiDynix
Database Vendor: EBSCO Auto Repair Reference, EBSCOhost, Grolier Online, infoUSA, OCLC FirstSearch, ProQuest, ReferenceUSA
Wireless access
Partic in Quad-Link Libr Consortium; RiverShare Libraries
Open Mon-Thurs 8-8, Fri 8-4:30, Sat 9:30-4:30
Friends of the Library Group
Branches: 5
BLUE GRASS BRANCH, 114 N Mississippi St, Blue Grass, 52726, SAN 341-8596. Tel: 563-381-2868. FAX: 563-381-2868. *Ch,* Gina Chesling
Pop 1,169
Library Holdings: Bk Vols 5,000
Database Vendor: EBSCO Information Services, SirsiDynix
Open Tues, Thurs & Fri 3-7, Wed & Sat 9-1,
Friends of the Library Group
BUFFALO BRANCH, 329 Dodge St, Buffalo, 52728, SAN 341-8626. Tel: 563-381-1797. FAX: 563-381-1797. *Assoc Librn,* Cindy Mosier; Staff 0.5 (Non-MLS 0.5)
Pop 1,321
Library Holdings: Bk Vols 5,000
Database Vendor: EBSCO Information Services
Open Mon, Tues & Thurs 2-7, Wed 9-1 & 2-7, Sat 8-12
DURANT BRANCH, 402 Sixth St, Durant, 52747, SAN 341-8650. Tel: 563-785-4725. FAX: 563-785-4725. *Assoc Librn,* Kim Olson; Staff 0.5 (Non-MLS 0.5)
Library Holdings: Bk Vols 10,000
Database Vendor: EBSCO Information Services, SirsiDynix
Open Mon, Wed & Fri 2-7, Thurs & Sat 9-12
PRINCETON BRANCH, 328 River Dr, Princeton, 52768, SAN 341-8804. Tel: 563-289-4282. FAX: 563-289-4282. *Librn,* Dawn McMeen; *Librn,* Penne Miller; Staff 0.75 (Non-MLS 0.75)
Library Holdings: Bk Vols 6,000
Database Vendor: EBSCO Information Services, SirsiDynix
Open Mon & Sat 9-12, Tues & Fri 3-7, Thurs 4-8
Friends of the Library Group
WALCOTT BRANCH, 207 S Main St, Walcott, 52773. (Mail add: PO Box 698, Walcott, 52773-0698), SAN 341-8839. Tel: 563-284-6612. FAX: 563-284-6612. *Librn,* Sheri Roberts; E-mail: sroberts@scottcountylibrary.org; Staff 0.5 (Non-MLS 0.5)
Pop 1,528
Library Holdings: Bk Vols 6,000
Database Vendor: EBSCO Information Services, SirsiDynix
Open Mon & Wed 2-7, Tues 1-5, Fri 9-1, Sat 9-12
Friends of the Library Group
Bookmobiles: 1. In Charge, Cathy Zimmerman

ELGIN

P ELGIN PUBLIC LIBRARY*, 214 Main St, 52141. (Mail add: PO Box 36, 52141-0036), SAN 305-3865. Tel: 563-426-5313. FAX: 563-426-5999. Web Site: www.elgin.lib.ia.us. *Dir,* Lisa Leuck; E-mail: librarylisa@elgin.lib.ia.us; *Asst Librn,* Jolene Bennett; *Ch,* Kris Stark
Founded 1927. Pop 702; Circ 24,603
Library Holdings: Bk Vols 15,000; Per Subs 51
Publications: Annual Report
Partic in OCLC Online Computer Library Center, Inc
Open Mon, Tues & Fri 1:30-5:30, Wed 11:30-5:30, Thurs 1:30-7:30, Sat 9:30-12:30
Friends of the Library Group

ELK HORN

P ELK HORN PUBLIC LIBRARY, 2027 Washington St, 51531. (Mail add: PO Box 119, 51531-0119), SAN 305-3873. Tel: 712-764-2013. FAX: 712-764-5515. E-mail: ehlib@metc.net. *Dir,* Alissa LaCanne
Pop 875
Library Holdings: Bk Titles 3,000; Bk Vols 4,000; Per Subs 24
Wireless access
Open Mon, Tues, Thurs & Fri 12:30-4:30, Wed 12:30-6:30, Sat 9-11

ELKADER

P ELKADER PUBLIC LIBRARY, 130 N Main St, 52043. (Mail add: PO Box 310, 52043-0310), SAN 305-3881. Tel: 563-245-1446. FAX: 563-245-1446. Web Site: www.elkader.lib.ia.us. *Dir,* Lisa Pope; E-mail: director@elkader.lib.ia.us; *Asst Librn,* Hila Garms; *Asst Librn,* Carol Hauge; Staff 2 (MLS 1, Non-MLS 1)
Founded 1926
Library Holdings: Audiobooks 600; CDs 300; DVDs 1,100; Large Print Bks 900; Bk Vols 21,500; Per Subs 45
Wireless access
Open Mon 9:30-6, Tues, Wed & Fri 9:30-5, Thurs 9:30-8, Sat 9:30-1

ELLIOTT

P ELLIOTT PUBLIC LIBRARY*, 401 Main St, 51532. (Mail add: PO Box 306, 51532-0306), SAN 376-5156. Tel: 712-767-2355. FAX: 712-767-2355. E-mail: elliotlib@netins.net. *Dir,* Laura Weston; Staff 2 (Non-MLS 2)
Founded 1917. Pop 670; Circ 5,654
Library Holdings: DVDs 26; Large Print Bks 502; Bk Titles 10,000; Per Subs 23; Talking Bks 107; Videos 612
Database Vendor: OCLC FirstSearch
Wireless access
Function: ILL available
Mem of Southwest Iowa Library Services District
Open Mon & Fri 1-5, Tues 12-5, Wed 1-6, Sat 8-10
Friends of the Library Group

ELLSWORTH

P ELLSWORTH PUBLIC LIBRARY*, 1549 Dewitt St, 50075. (Mail add: PO Box 338, 50075-0338), SAN 305-3903. Tel: 515-836-4852. FAX: 515-836-2162. Web Site: www.ellsworth.lib.ia.us. *Dir,* Debra Caudle
Pop 480; Circ 6,977
Library Holdings: Bk Titles 6,000; Bk Vols 6,571; Per Subs 23
Automation Activity & Vendor Info: (Cataloging) Follett Software
Mem of Indianhead Federated Library System
Open Mon, Tues, Thurs & Fri 1-5, Wed 1-6, Sat 9-12

ELMA

P ELMA PUBLIC LIBRARY*, 710 Busti Ave, 50628. (Mail add: PO Box 287, 50628-0287), SAN 305-3911. Tel: 641-393-8100. FAX: 641-393-8100. *Dir,* Barbara Schroeder; *Asst Librn,* Marileen Nibaur
Founded 1915. Pop 1,828; Circ 13,000
Library Holdings: AV Mats 583; Bk Titles 9,085; Per Subs 45
Special Collections: Local Newspaper on microflim
Wireless access
Mem of Buffalo & Erie County Public Library System
Open Mon & Thurs 10-8, Tues & Wed 2-8, Sat 9-3

ELY

P ELY PUBLIC LIBRARY*, 1595 Dows St, 52227. (Mail add: PO Box 249, 52227-0249), SAN 305-392X. Tel: 319-848-7616. FAX: 319-848-4056. Web Site: www.ely.lib.ia.us. *Dir,* Sarah L Sellon; E-mail: ssellon@ely.lib.ia.us; *Tech Serv Librn,* Paula Bradway; E-mail: pbradway@ely.lib.ia.us; *Youth Serv Librn,* Liz Pearson; E-mail: lpearson@ely.lib.ia.us; *Asst Librn,* Becky Cheesman; E-mail: bcheesman@ely.lib.ia.us; *Asst Librn,* Carolyn Wilson; E-mail: cwilson@ely.lib.ia.us
Founded 1974. Pop 1,526; Circ 47,350
Library Holdings: Audiobooks 387; Bk Vols 19,658; Per Subs 33; Videos 2,305
Subject Interests: Czechoslovakia, Hist, Iowa
Wireless access
Open Mon & Thurs 9-8, Tues & Wed 1-8, Fri 1-5, Sat 9-4
Friends of the Library Group

EMERSON

P EMERSON PUBLIC LIBRARY*, 701 Morton Ave, 51533. (Mail add: PO Box 282, 51533-0282), SAN 328-0756. Tel: 712-824-7867. FAX: 712-824-7867. E-mail: emlib@pointenet.com. *Librn,* Karen Gage; Staff 1 (MLS 1)
Founded 1982. Pop 2,350; Circ 10,945
Library Holdings: AV Mats 577; Large Print Bks 85; Bk Titles 12,450; Per Subs 21; Talking Bks 164
Subject Interests: Local hist
Wireless access
Function: Prog for children & young adult
Open Mon 8:30-12:30 & 1-4, Tues, Thurs & Fri 9-12, Wed 8:30-12:30 & 3-7, Sat 9-1
Bookmobiles: 1

EMMETSBURG

P EMMETSBURG PUBLIC LIBRARY*, 707 N Superior St, 50536. SAN 305-3938. Tel: 712-852-4009. FAX: 712-852-3785. E-mail: info@emmetsburg.lib.ia.us. Web Site: www.emmetsburg.lib.ia.us. *Dir,* Nathan R E Clark; E-mail: nclark@emmetsburg.lib.ia.us; *Asst Dir,* Donna Mason; *Youth Serv Dir,* Kari Gramowski; E-mail: kgramowski@iowalakes.edu; Staff 5 (Non-MLS 5)
Founded 1908. Pop 4,900; Circ 50,525

Library Holdings: Bk Titles 39,270; Per Subs 115; Talking Bks 1,252
Automation Activity & Vendor Info: (Acquisitions) Follett Software; (Cataloging) Follett Software; (Circulation) Follett Software; (OPAC) Follett Software
Mem of Northwest Iowa Library Services
Open Mon-Thurs 11-8, Fri & Sat 11-4
Friends of the Library Group

J IOWA LAKES COMMUNITY COLLEGE LIBRARY*, 3200 College Dr, 50536. Tel: 712-852-5317. Toll Free Tel: 800-242-5108. FAX: 712-852-3094. Web Site: www.iowalakes.edu/library/index.htm. *Dir, Libr Serv,* Brenda Colegrove; E-mail: bcolegrove@iowalakes.edu; *ILL,* Judy Johnson
Automation Activity & Vendor Info: (Cataloging) Follett Software; (Circulation) Follett Software
Open Mon-Thurs 7:30am-8:30pm, Fri 7:30-4

EPWORTH

CR DIVINE WORD COLLEGE, Matthew Jacoby Memorial Library, 102 Jacoby Dr SW, 52045-0380. SAN 305-3946. Tel: 563-876-3353, Ext 207. Interlibrary Loan Service Tel: 563-876-3353, Ext 262. Administration FAX: 563-876-3407. Web Site: intranet.dwci.edu/library/home.asp. *Dir,* Daniel Boice; E-mail: dboice@dwci.edu; *Asst Librn, ILL,* Brother Anthony Kreinus; E-mail: akreinus@dwci.edu; Staff 3 (MLS 2, Non-MLS 1)
Founded 1915. Enrl 112; Fac 33; Highest Degree: Bachelor
Jul 2013-Jun 2014. Mats Exp $46,424, Books $21,560, Per/Ser (Incl. Access Fees) $15,649, Micro $137, AV Mat $5,169, Electronic Ref Mat (Incl. Access Fees) $1,861, Presv $1,585. Sal $126,415 (Prof $100,318)
Library Holdings: AV Mats 13,081; Bks on Deafness & Sign Lang 11; CDs 971; DVDs 1,486; Bk Titles 68,197; Bk Vols 89,892; Per Subs 264; Talking Bks 151; Videos 580
Special Collections: Vietnamese Literature
Subject Interests: Cross-cultural studies, Philos, Relig
Automation Activity & Vendor Info: (Cataloging) Follett Software; (Circulation) Follett Software; (OPAC) Follett Software
Database Vendor: EBSCOhost, OCLC
Wireless access
Partic in Dubuque Area Library Information Consortium; Iowa Private Academic Library Consortium (IPAL)
Restriction: Open to others by appt

ESSEX

P LIED PUBLIC LIBRARY*, 508 Iowa St, 51638. (Mail add: PO Box 298, 51638-0298), SAN 305-3954. Tel: 712-379-3355. FAX: 712-379-3355. E-mail: elibrar@heartland.net. Web Site: www.essexiowalibrary.com. *Dir,* Brenda Franks; *Ch,* Linda Hesson
Founded 1939. Pop 1,001; Circ 13,259
Library Holdings: AV Mats 694; Bk Titles 9,321; Bk Vols 11,740; Per Subs 25
Wireless access
Mem of Southwest Iowa Library Services District
Open Mon & Fri 3-6, Tues & Thurs 9:30-12 & 3-6, Wed 3-8, Sat 10-Noon

ESTHERVILLE

P ESTHERVILLE PUBLIC LIBRARY*, 613 Central Ave, 51334-2294. SAN 305-3962. Tel: 712-362-7731. FAX: 712-362-3509. E-mail: info@estherville.lib.ia.us. Web Site: www.estherville.lib.ia.us. *Dir,* Tena Hanson; *Asst Dir,* Beth Reineke; Staff 5.75 (Non-MLS 5.75)
Founded 1882. Pop 6,250; Circ 64,730
Jul 2012-Jun 2013 Income $413,168, State $2,588, City $390,875, County $19,500, Other $205. Mats Exp $25,327. Sal $173,203
Library Holdings: AV Mats 232; CDs 1,101; Bk Titles 44,290; Per Subs 80; Talking Bks 1,533; Videos 576
Subject Interests: Genealogy, Iowa
Automation Activity & Vendor Info: (Acquisitions) Biblionix; (Cataloging) Biblionix; (Circulation) Biblionix; (ILL) Biblionix; (Serials) EBSCO Online
Database Vendor: Baker & Taylor, EBSCOhost
Wireless access
Publications: Friends of Library Newsletter (Quarterly)
Mem of Northwest Iowa Library Services
Partic in State of Iowa Libraries Online
Special Services for the Deaf - Bks on deafness & sign lang; High interest/low vocabulary bks
Open Mon & Thurs 10-8, Tues & Wed 10-6, Fri 10-5, Sat 10-1
Friends of the Library Group

J IOWA LAKES COMMUNITY COLLEGE LIBRARY*, 300 S 18th St, 51334. SAN 305-3970. Tel: 712-362-7936. Interlibrary Loan Service Tel: 712-362-7991. FAX: 712-362-5970. Web Site: www.iowalakes.edu/library/index.htm. *Dir,* Brenda Colegrove; E-mail: bcolegrove@iowalakes.edu; *ILL,* Janet Kirchner; E-mail: jkirchner@iowalakes.edu; Staff 2 (MLS 2)
Founded 1964. Enrl 3,100
Library Holdings: Bk Vols 30,812; Per Subs 195; Videos 1,480
Automation Activity & Vendor Info: (Cataloging) Follett Software; (Circulation) Follett Software
Database Vendor: EBSCOhost, LexisNexis, OCLC FirstSearch
Function: Doc delivery serv, ILL available, Photocopying/Printing
Open Mon-Thurs 7:30am-8:30pm, Fri 7:30-4

EVANSDALE

P EVANSDALE PUBLIC LIBRARY*, 123 N Evans Rd, 50707. SAN 305-3989. Tel: 319-232-5367. FAX: 319-232-5367. E-mail: eplib@mchsi.com. Web Site: www.evansdale.lib.ia.us. *Dir,* Shannon Jensen; *Ch, Libr Asst,* Anne Johnson
Founded 1968. Pop 5,003; Circ 9,655
Library Holdings: Bk Vols 12,000; Per Subs 35
Automation Activity & Vendor Info: (Acquisitions) Book Systems; (Cataloging) Book Systems; (Circulation) Book Systems; (Course Reserve) Book Systems; (ILL) Book Systems; (Media Booking) Book Systems; (OPAC) Book Systems; (Serials) Book Systems
Open Mon & Thurs 11-7, Tues, Wed, Fri & Sat 11-5
Friends of the Library Group

EVERLY

P EVERLY PUBLIC LIBRARY*, 308 N Main St, 51338-0265. (Mail add: PO Box 265, 51338-0265), SAN 305-3997. Tel: 712-834-2390. FAX: 712-834-2390. E-mail: library1@evertek.net. *Dir,* Sue Biederman
Founded 1917. Pop 850; Circ 4,387
Library Holdings: AV Mats 205; Bk Titles 4,866; Bk Vols 6,121; Per Subs 16
Mem of Northwest Iowa Library Services
Open Tues, Thurs & Fri 9:30-12 & 1-5:30, Wed 9:30-12 & 1-6, Sat 10-12
Friends of the Library Group

EXIRA

P EXIRA PUBLIC LIBRARY, 114 W Washington St, 50076. (Mail add: PO Box 368, 50076-0368), SAN 320-8257. Tel: 712-268-5489. FAX: 712-268-5489. E-mail: exiralib@metc.net. Web Site: www.exira.lib.ia.us. *Dir,* Sandra Bauer; *Ch,* Katie Wheeler
Pop 810; Circ 10,506
Library Holdings: Bk Vols 17,500; Per Subs 60
Wireless access
Mem of Southwest Iowa Library Services District
Open Mon & Thurs 9-6, Tues, Wed & Fri 2-5, Sat 9-Noon

FAIRBANK

P FAIRBANK PUBLIC LIBRARY*, 212 Main St, 50629. (Mail add: PO Box 426, 50629-0426), SAN 305-4004. Tel: 319-635-2487. FAX: 319-635-2487. E-mail: f.library@mchsi.com. Web Site: www.fairbank-iowa.org. *Dir,* Karen Tiedt
Pop 980; Circ 12,832
Library Holdings: Bk Titles 11,000; Per Subs 36
Open Mon 2:30-6:30, Tues, Thurs & Fri 1-5, Wed 9-11 & 2:30-6:30, Sat 10-1

FAIRFAX

P FAIRFAX PUBLIC LIBRARY*, 313 Vanderbilt St, 52228. (Mail add: PO Box 187, 52228-0187), SAN 305-4012. Tel: 319-846-2994. FAX: 319-846-2889. Web Site: www.fairfax.lib.ia.us. *Dir,* Cathy Bayne; E-mail: cathy.bayne@fairfax.lib.ia.us
Pop 980; Circ 20,000
Library Holdings: Bk Vols 9,000; Per Subs 21
Open Mon-Thurs 12-7, Fri 12-6, Sat 9-12

FAIRFIELD

P FAIRFIELD PUBLIC LIBRARY*, 104 W Adams, 52556. SAN 305-4020. Tel: 641-472-6551. FAX: 641-472-3249. E-mail: fplib@fairfield.lib.ia.us. Web Site: www.fairfield.lib.ia.us. *Dir,* Rebecca Huggins; E-mail: bhuggins@fairfield.lib.ia.us; *Youth Serv Librn,* Simon Soderberg; Staff 5 (MLS 2, Non-MLS 3)
Founded 1853. Pop 10,000; Circ 212,000
Library Holdings: Bk Titles 67,000; Per Subs 231
Automation Activity & Vendor Info: (Circulation) SirsiDynix; (OPAC) SirsiDynix
Database Vendor: EBSCOhost
Open Mon-Wed 9:30-8, Thurs & Fri 9:30-6, Sat & Sun 1-5
Friends of the Library Group

C MAHARISHI UNIVERSITY OF MANAGEMENT LIBRARY, 1000 N Fourth St, 52557. SAN 305-4039. Tel: 641-472-1148. Circulation Tel: 641-472-1154. Interlibrary Loan Service Tel: 641-472-7000, Ext 3334. Reference Tel: 641-472-7000, Ext 3733. FAX: 641-472-1137. E-mail: library@mum.edu. Web Site: www.mum.edu/library. *Dir,* Rouzanna Vardanyan; E-mail: rvardanyan@mum.edu; *Ref Librn,* Martin Schmidt; E-mail: mschmidt@mum.edu; *Tape Librn,* Peter Freund; *ILL Officer,* Lyle Nelson; Tel: 641-472-1121, E-mail: ill@mum.edu; *Acq Mgr,* Elizabeth Pommier; Staff 4 (MLS 3, Non-MLS 1)
Founded 1971. Enrl 1,054; Fac 165; Highest Degree: Doctorate
Jul 2012-Jun 2013. Mats Exp $107,000, Books $46,000, Per/Ser (Incl. Access Fees) $60,000
Library Holdings: Bk Vols 140,000; Per Subs 115,000
Special Collections: Maharishi Vedic Science (Maharishi Mahesh Yogi & MUM Faculty), a-tapes, bks, flm, v-tapes; Vedic Literature
Subject Interests: Am lit, Art, Computer sci, Educ, English lit, Med, Mgt, Organic gardening, Physics, Physiology
Automation Activity & Vendor Info: (Acquisitions) Mandarin Library Automation; (Cataloging) Mandarin Library Automation; (Circulation) Mandarin Library Automation; (Course Reserve) Mandarin Library Automation; (ILL) OCLC; (OPAC) Mandarin Library Automation; (Serials) Mandarin Library Automation
Database Vendor: EBSCOhost, OCLC FirstSearch
Wireless access
Publications: Bibliography of General Reference Works; Bibliography on WWW Sites for Business Management; Index to Modern Science & Vedic Science; Serials Holdings Lists
Partic in Iowa Librs Ariel Network; Iowa Private Academic Library Consortium (IPAL); Iowa Res & Educ Network; National Network of Libraries of Medicine; OCLC Online Computer Library Center, Inc
Friends of the Library Group

FARMERSBURG

P FARMERSBURG PUBLIC LIBRARY*, 208 S Main St, 52047. (Mail add: PO Box 167, 52047-0167), SAN 305-4047. Tel: 563-536-2229. FAX: 563-536-2229. Web Site: www.farmersburg.lib.ia.us. *Dir,* Kim Scherf; E-mail: kims@farmersburg.lib.ia.us; *Libr Asst,* Jen Johanningmeier
Founded 1920. Pop 291; Circ 1,519
Library Holdings: Bk Titles 6,900
Subject Interests: Local hist
Open Mon-Thurs 4-7, Fri 9-2, Sat 9-12

FARMINGTON

P FARMINGTON PUBLIC LIBRARY*, 205 Elm St, 52626. (Mail add: PO Box 472, 52626-0472), SAN 305-4055. Tel: 319-878-3702. FAX: 319-878-3727. E-mail: farmingtonlib52626@gmail.com. *Dir,* Jill Dennis
Pop 750; Circ 10,975
Library Holdings: AV Mats 550; High Interest/Low Vocabulary Bk Vols 68; Bk Titles 18,442; Bk Vols 26,500; Per Subs 77
Database Vendor: EBSCOhost
Open Tues 1-6, Wed & Fri 1-5:30, Sat 9-11:30 & 1-5

FARNHAMVILLE

P FARNHAMVILLE PUBLIC LIBRARY*, 240 Hardin St, 50538. (Mail add: PO Box 216, 50538-0216), SAN 376-5261. Tel: 515-544-3660. FAX: 515-544-3703. E-mail: farnlib@wccta.net. Web Site: www.farnhamville.lib.ia.us. *Librn,* Kristin Fields
Founded 1927. Pop 430
Library Holdings: Bk Vols 5,200; Per Subs 28
Database Vendor: EBSCOhost
Wireless access
Mem of Northwest Iowa Library Services
Special Services for the Blind - Bks on CD; Large print bks
Open Mon, Wed & Fri 1-6, Sat 9-12

FAYETTE

P FAYETTE COMMUNITY LIBRARY*, 104 W State St, 52142. (Mail add: PO Box 107, 52142-0107), SAN 305-4071. Tel: 563-425-3344. FAX: 563-425-3344. E-mail: director@fayettelibrary.lib.ia.us. Web Site: www.fayettelibrary.lib.ia.us. *Dir,* Linda K Adams; *Asst Librn,* Melanie Morell
Founded 1934. Pop 1,380; Circ 15,000
Library Holdings: Bk Vols 15,000; Per Subs 35
Automation Activity & Vendor Info: (Acquisitions) Follett Software; (Cataloging) Follett Software; (Circulation) Follett Software; (ILL) Follett Software; (Media Booking) Follett Software; (OPAC) Follett Software; (Serials) Follett Software
Open Mon & Fri 10-5, Tues & Wed 1-8, Thurs & Sat 1-5

C UPPER IOWA UNIVERSITY*, Henderson-Wilder Library, 605 Washington St, 52142. (Mail add: PO Box 1858, 52142-1858), SAN 305-408X. Tel: 563-425-5270. Interlibrary Loan Service Tel: 563-425-5217. Reference Tel: 563-425-5261. FAX: 563-425-5271. E-mail: library@uiu.edu. Web Site: www.uiu.edu/library. *Dir,* Becky Wadian; E-mail: wadianb@uiu.edu; *Asst Dir, Libr Serv,* Jodi Hilleshiem; E-mail: hilleshiemj@uiu.edu; *Asst Dir, Libr Serv,* Mary White; E-mail: whitem@uiu.edu; *Assoc Dir, Libr Serv,* Carol Orr; E-mail: orrc@uiu.edu; Staff 4 (MLS 1, Non-MLS 3)
Founded 1901. Enrl 3,276; Fac 125; Highest Degree: Master
Library Holdings: Bk Titles 60,516; Bk Vols 69,023; Per Subs 290
Special Collections: NASA Coll, slides, pictures & clippings. US Document Depository
Automation Activity & Vendor Info: (Acquisitions) Ex Libris Group; (Cataloging) Ex Libris Group; (Circulation) Ex Libris Group; (ILL) Ex Libris Group; (OPAC) Ex Libris Group; (Serials) Ex Libris Group
Database Vendor: Dialog, EBSCOhost, Gale Cengage Learning, OCLC FirstSearch
Partic in OCLC Online Computer Library Center, Inc
Open Mon-Thurs (Winter) 7:30-11, Fri 7:30-5, Sat 2-5, Sun 2-11; Mon-Thurs (Summer) 7:30am-8pm, Fri 7:30-3

FENTON

P FENTON PUBLIC LIBRARY*, 605 Maple, 50539-0217. (Mail add: PO Box 217, 50539-0217). Tel: 515-889-2333. FAX: 515-889-2333. E-mail: flibrary@netins.net. *Dir,* Vickie Gochenour
Library Holdings: Bk Vols 7,766; Per Subs 24
Automation Activity & Vendor Info: (Cataloging) Follett Software; (Circulation) Follett Software; (OPAC) Follett Software
Open Mon & Fri 1:30-6, Tues 12-4:30, Wed 9-12, Sat 8:30-12

FERTILE

P FERTILE PUBLIC LIBRARY, 204 W Main St, 50434-1020. (Mail add: PO Box 198, 50434-0198), SAN 305-4101. Tel: 641-797-2787. FAX: 641-797-2787. E-mail: ferlib@wctatel.net. Web Site: www.youseemore.com/NILC/FertilePL. *Dir,* Nancy Suby; *Asst Dir,* Ramona Kinseth; Staff 2 (Non-MLS 2)
Founded 1968. Pop 360
Library Holdings: Bk Vols 10,003; Per Subs 42
Database Vendor: EBSCOhost
Special Services for the Blind - Bks on cassette; Copier with enlargement capabilities; Large print bks
Open Mon & Wed 1-6, Thurs 3-6, Fri 9-12 & 2-6, Sat 9-Noon
Friends of the Library Group

FONDA

P FONDA PUBLIC LIBRARY, 104 W Second & Main, 50540. (Mail add: PO Box 360, 50540-0360), SAN 305-411X. Tel: 712-288-4467. FAX: 712-288-6633. Web Site: www.fonda.lib.ia.us. *Dir,* Linda Mercer; E-mail: linda.mercer@fonda.lib.ia.us
Founded 1942. Pop 1,500; Circ 7,449
Library Holdings: AV Mats 1,000; Bk Titles 6,970; Per Subs 18
Wireless access
Mem of Northwest Iowa Library Services
Open Mon, Thurs & Fri 1-5, Wed 10-8, Sat 9-12

FONTANELLE

P FONTANELLE PUBLIC LIBRARY*, 303 Washington St, 50846. (Mail add: PO Box 387, 50846-0387), SAN 305-4128. Tel: 641-745-4981. FAX: 641-745-3017. E-mail: fplibrary@iowatelecom.net. Web Site: www.fontanelle.swilsa.lib.ia.us. *Dir,* Kay Marckmann; *Asst Librn,* Phyllis Jacobson
Pop 805; Circ 2,833
Library Holdings: Bk Titles 9,500; Per Subs 18
Mem of Southwest Iowa Library Services District
Open Mon, Tues, Thurs & Fri 1:30-6, Sat 9:30-11:30

FOREST CITY

P FOREST CITY PUBLIC LIBRARY*, 115 East L St, 50436. SAN 305-4136. Tel: 641-585-4542. FAX: 641-585-2939. E-mail: fcpublib@wctatel.net. Web Site: www1.youseemore.com/nilc/forestcitypl. *Dir,* Christa Cosgriff
Founded 1897. Pop 4,151; Circ 40,760
Subject Interests: Scandinavia
Automation Activity & Vendor Info: (Cataloging) TLC (The Library Corporation); (Circulation) TLC (The Library Corporation); (OPAC) TLC (The Library Corporation)
Wireless access
Open Mon-Thurs 10-7, Fri 10-5, Sat 10-2

CR WALDORF COLLEGE*, Luise V Hanson Library, 106 S Sixth St, 50436. SAN 305-4144. Tel: 641-585-8110. FAX: 641-585-8111. E-mail: library@waldorf.edu. Web Site: www.waldorf.edu. *Interim Dir,* Scott

Searcy; *Dir,* Position Currently Open; *Ref & Instruction Librn,* Rebekal Vrabel; E-mail: rebekah.vrabel@waldorf.edu; Staff 2 (MLS 2)
Founded 1903. Enrl 513; Fac 45; Highest Degree: Bachelor
Library Holdings: Bk Vols 65,000; Per Subs 125
Special Collections: Bible Coll
Automation Activity & Vendor Info: (Cataloging) EOS International; (Circulation) EOS International; (OPAC) EOS International
Wireless access
Function: ILL available, Online searches, Photocopying/Printing, Ref serv available
Open Mon-Thurs 7:30am-10:45pm, Fri 7:30-4, Sat 2-5, Sun 3-10:45

FORT ATKINSON

P FORT ATKINSON PUBLIC LIBRARY*, 302 Third St NW, 52144. (Mail add: PO Box 277, 52144-0277), SAN 305-4152. Tel: 563-534-2222. FAX: 563-534-2222. Web Site: www.fortatkinson.lib.ia.us. *Dir,* Chris Bodensteiner; *Ch,* Cindy Luzum; E-mail: cluzum@fortatkinson.lib.ia.us
Founded 1964. Pop 389; Circ 4,248
Library Holdings: Bk Titles 6,335; Per Subs 31
Automation Activity & Vendor Info: (Acquisitions) Biblionix; (Cataloging) Biblionix; (Circulation) Biblionix; (ILL) Biblionix; (Media Booking) Biblionix; (OPAC) Biblionix; (Serials) Biblionix
Open Mon-Thurs 2:30-6:30, Fri 10-5, Sat 9-11

FORT DODGE

S FORT DODGE CORRECTIONAL FACILITY LIBRARY*, 1550 L St, 50501. Tel: 515-574-4700. FAX: 515-574-4718. *Librn,* Ruth Collins
Library Holdings: Bk Vols 7,803; Per Subs 45
Open Mon-Fri 8-4

P FORT DODGE PUBLIC LIBRARY*, 424 Central Ave, 50501. SAN 341-8863. Tel: 515-573-8167. FAX: 515-573-5422. Web Site: www.fortdodgeiowa.org/library. *Dir,* Barbara J Shultz; Tel: 515-573-8167, Ext 231, E-mail: barb@fortdodge.lib.ia.us; *Asst Dir,* Rita Schmidt; Tel: 515-573-8167, Ext 229, E-mail: rschmidt@fortdodge.lib.ia.us; *Youth Serv Dir,* Laurie Hotz; Tel: 515-573-8167, Ext 244, E-mail: lhotz@fortdodge.lib.ia.us; Staff 10 (MLS 2, Non-MLS 8)
Founded 1890. Pop 25,206; Circ 230,101
Library Holdings: Bk Vols 80,728; Per Subs 200
Special Collections: Iowa Coll; Webster County Coll
Subject Interests: Local hist
Automation Activity & Vendor Info: (Cataloging) OCLC CatExpress; (Circulation) TLC (The Library Corporation); (OPAC) TLC (The Library Corporation)
Database Vendor: 3M Library Systems, Comprise Technologies Inc, EBSCO Auto Repair Reference, EBSCOhost, MITINET, Inc, OCLC FirstSearch, OCLC WorldShare Interlibrary Loan, ProQuest, TLC (The Library Corporation)
Wireless access
Publications: Newsletter (Quarterly)
Open Mon & Tues 8:30-8, Wed-Fri 8:30-5:30, Sat 9-5:30
Friends of the Library Group

J IOWA CENTRAL COMMUNITY COLLEGE*, Fort Dodge Center Library, 330 Ave M, 50501. SAN 370-3177. Tel: 515-576-7201, Ext 2618. FAX: 515-576-0099, Ext 2631. Web Site: www.iccc.cc.ia.us. *Dir,* Dan Schiefelbein; E-mail: schiefelbein@iowacentral.edu; Staff 12 (MLS 2, Non-MLS 10)
Founded 1967. Enrl 2,836
Library Holdings: Bk Vols 55,000; Per Subs 350
Subject Interests: Educ, Iowa, Local hist
Automation Activity & Vendor Info: (Cataloging) Innovative Interfaces, Inc; (Circulation) Innovative Interfaces, Inc; (Serials) Innovative Interfaces, Inc
Open Mon-Thurs 7:30am-9pm, Fri 7:30-4:30, Sun 12:30-8:30
Departmental Libraries:
EAGLE GROVE, 316 NW Third St, Eagle Grove, 50533, SAN 377-7367. Tel: 515-448-4723. FAX: 515-448-2800. *Dir,* Sherry Hohensee; *ILL,* Dan Schiefelbein; E-mail: schiefelbein@iowacentral.edu
Open Mon-Thurs 8-5, Fri 8-4:30
WEBSTER CITY CENTER, 1725 Beach St, Webster City, 50595, SAN 305-7747. Tel: 515-832-1632, Ext 2821. FAX: 515-576-0099, Ext 2820. *Dir,* Dan Schiefelbein; E-mail: schiefelbein@iowacentral.edu; *Adminr,* Cindy Hafs; Staff 3 (MLS 1, Non-MLS 2)
Enrl 200; Fac 20
Library Holdings: Bk Titles 18,000; Per Subs 115
Open Mon-Thurs 8-8, Fri 8-4:30

FORT MADISON

P FORT MADISON PUBLIC LIBRARY*, Cattermole Memorial Library, 1920 Avenue E, 52627. SAN 305-4187. Tel: 319-372-5721. FAX: 319-372-5726. E-mail: fmpl@ft-madison.lib.ia.us. Web Site: www.fortmadisonlibrary.org. *Dir,* Sarah Clendineng; E-mail: SarahClen@fortmadison.lib.ia.us; *Circ Supvr,* Deborah Albee
Founded 1894. Pop 10,717; Circ 63,000
Library Holdings: Bk Titles 70,000; Bk Vols 85,000; Per Subs 150
Special Collections: Black History (Dr Harry D Harper Sr Coll); Genealogy & Local History; Railroad (Chester S Gross Memorial Coll)
Open Mon, Wed & Fri 9-5, Tues & Thurs 10-7, Sat 9-4:30
Friends of the Library Group

S IOWA STATE PENITENTIARY*, John Bennett Correctional Center Library, Three John Bennett Dr, 52627. Tel: 319-372-5432, Ext 439.
Library Holdings: Bk Vols 12,000; Per Subs 19
Open Mon, Thurs & Fri 8-10 & 12-2, Tues & Wed 12-2 & 3:30-5

FREDERICKSBURG

P UPHAM MEMORIAL LIBRARY*, 138 W Main St, 50630. (Mail add: PO Box 281, 50630-0281), SAN 305-4217. Tel: 563-237-6498. FAX: 563-237-6218. E-mail: director@fredericksburg.lib.ia.us. Web Site: www.fredericksburg.lib.ia.us. *Dir,* Joan Schultz; *Ch,* Mary Stabe; Staff 3 (Non-MLS 3)
Founded 1935. Pop 986
Library Holdings: Bk Titles 11,555; Per Subs 50; Talking Bks 370
Automation Activity & Vendor Info: (Acquisitions) Follett Software; (Cataloging) Follett Software; (Circulation) Follett Software
Partic in State of Iowa Libraries Online
Open Tues 9-12 & 1-5:30, Wed 1-7, Thurs & Fri 1-5:30, Sat 9-1
Friends of the Library Group

GALVA

P GALVA PUBLIC LIBRARY*, 203 S Main St, 51020. (Mail add: PO Box 203, 51020-0203), SAN 305-4225. Tel: 712-282-4400. FAX: 712-282-4400. E-mail: bookwrm203@yahoo.com. Web Site: www.galvaiowa.bluffsonline.net. *Dir,* Judy Lynn Whitmer
Pop 398; Circ 6,700
Library Holdings: AV Mats 340; Bk Vols 5,800; Per Subs 31
Mem of Northwest Iowa Library Services
Open Mon 1-6, Tues, Thurs & Fri 1-5, Sat 9-12
Friends of the Library Group

GARDEN GROVE

P GARDEN GROVE PUBLIC LIBRARY*, 103 Main St, 50103. (Mail add: PO Box 29, 50103-0029), SAN 376-6829. Tel: 641-443-2172. E-mail: gglibry@grm.net. *Librn,* Diane Fenton
Pop 165; Circ 4,673
Jan 2011-Dec 2011 Income $960, County $760, Other $200. Sal $1,200
Library Holdings: Audiobooks 162; DVDs 20; Large Print Bks 280; Bk Vols 3,300; Per Subs 10; Videos 510
Wireless access
Mem of Southwest Iowa Library Services District
Open Mon & Wed 12-3
Friends of the Library Group

GARNAVILLO

P GARNAVILLO PUBLIC LIBRARY*, 122 Main St, 52049. SAN 305-4241. Tel: 563-964-2119. FAX: 563-964-2119. Web Site: www.garnavillo.lib.ia.us. *Dir,* Mary Fran Nikolai; E-mail: mfnikolai@garnavillo.lib.ia.us; *Ch,* Karolyn Balk; *Asst Librn,* June Wolter
Founded 1939. Pop 757; Circ 36,641
Library Holdings: Bk Vols 21,000; Per Subs 38
Special Collections: Garnavillo History & Genealogy Coll
Automation Activity & Vendor Info: (Acquisitions) Biblionix; (Cataloging) Biblionix; (Circulation) Biblionix
Database Vendor: EBSCOhost, Electric Library, OCLC WebJunction, OCLC WorldShare Interlibrary Loan
Wireless access
Special Services for the Blind - Large print bks; Talking bks
Open Tues 10-4, Wed 10-8, Thurs 3-8, Sat 10-2

GARNER

P GARNER PUBLIC LIBRARY*, 416 State St, 50438. (Mail add: PO Box 406, 50438-0406), SAN 305-425X. Tel: 641-923-2850. FAX: 641-923-2339. E-mail: garner.library@mchsi.com. Web Site: www.youseemore.com/nilc/garner. *Dir,* Ellen Petty; Staff 1 (MLS 1)
Founded 1873. Pop 3,129; Circ 33,700
Jul 2012-Jun 2013 Income $154,698, State $2,252, City $111,987, County $28,834, Locally Generated Income $11,625. Mats Exp $28,049, Books $16,500, Per/Ser (Incl. Access Fees) $2,635, AV Mat $6,870, Electronic Ref Mat (Incl. Access Fees) $472. Sal $71,574 (Prof $38,030)
Library Holdings: Audiobooks 4,061; CDs 35; DVDs 996; e-books 5,834; Large Print Bks 623; Bk Titles 15,471; Bk Vols 15,896; Per Subs 78

Automation Activity & Vendor Info: (Acquisitions) TLC (The Library Corporation); (Cataloging) TLC (The Library Corporation); (Circulation) TLC (The Library Corporation); (OPAC) TLC (The Library Corporation)
Database Vendor: Booklist Online, EBSCOhost, LearningExpress, Library Ideas, LLC, Overdrive, Inc, TLC (The Library Corporation)
Wireless access
Partic in North Eastern Iowa Bridge to Online Resource Sharing (NEIBORS)
Open Mon 10-8, Tues & Wed 10-5:30, Thurs 12-8, Fri 12-5:30, Sat 10-2
Friends of the Library Group

GARRISON

P GARRISON PUBLIC LIBRARY*, 100 N Birch Ave, 52229. (Mail add: PO Box 26, 52229-0026), SAN 320-8265. Tel: 319-477-5531. FAX: 319-477-5531. E-mail: garrison@netins.net. *Dir,* Betty Hendryx
Founded 1975. Pop 413
Library Holdings: Bk Titles 5,428; Per Subs 18
Open Mon 3-7, Tues-Fri 2:30-5, Sat 9-11

GARWIN

P GARWIN PUBLIC LIBRARY*, 208 Main St, 50632. (Mail add: PO Box 216, 50632-0216), SAN 305-4268. Tel: 641-499-2024. FAX: 641-499-2024. E-mail: glibrary@iowatelecom.net. *Librn,* Shirley Delfs
Pop 565; Circ 6,208
Library Holdings: DVDs 51; Bk Titles 8,475; Per Subs 20; Talking Bks 76; Videos 828
Open Mon 1-5:30, Tues 8-12, Wed 2-7, Fri 2-5:30, Sat 8-12:30

GEORGE

P GEORGE PUBLIC LIBRARY*, 119 S Main St, 51237. (Mail add: PO Box 738, 51237-0738), SAN 305-4276. Tel: 712-475-3897. E-mail: geolibry@mtcnet.net. Web Site: www.george.lib.ia.us. *Dir,* Nadine Dykstra; Staff 1 (Non-MLS 1)
Founded 1937. Pop 1,051; Circ 28,356
Jul 2009-Jun 2010 Income $56,600, State $1,359, City $29,029, County $13,303, Locally Generated Income $8,014. Mats Exp $14,350, Books $7,142, Per/Ser (Incl. Access Fees) $643, Other Print Mats $3,254, AV Mat $3,254, Electronic Ref Mat (Incl. Access Fees) $57. Sal $28,120 (Prof $24,755)
Library Holdings: Audiobooks 287; DVDs 917; Large Print Bks 564; Bk Vols 10,782; Per Subs 44; Videos 69
Wireless access
Mem of Northwest Iowa Library Services
Open Mon, Tues & Thurs 1-5, Wed 1-8, Fri 10-5, Sat 8:30-10:30

GILMAN

P GILMAN PUBLIC LIBRARY*, 106 N Main St, 50106. (Mail add: PO Box 383, 50106-0383), SAN 305-4284. Tel: 641-498-2120. E-mail: gillib@partnercom.net. *Dir,* Wilma Smith
Pop 642; Circ 4,706
Library Holdings: Bk Vols 5,000
Mem of Central Iowa Library Services
Open Mon & Wed 8:30-11, Tues & Thurs 1-6, Sat 8:30-12
Friends of the Library Group

GILMORE CITY

P GILMORE CITY PUBLIC LIBRARY*, 308 S Gilmore St, 50541-0283. Tel: 515-373-6562. E-mail: Gilcplib@qwestoffice.net. *Dir,* Marilyn Dunn
Pop 556
Library Holdings: AV Mats 633; Bk Titles 3,000; Bk Vols 9,569; Per Subs 56; Videos 547
Open Mon & Fri 3-7, Wed 12-7, Thurs 1-5, Sat 9:30-3:30

GLADBROOK

P GLADBROOK PUBLIC LIBRARY, 301 Second St, 50635. (Mail add: PO Box 399, 50635-0399), SAN 305-4306. Tel: 641-473-3236. FAX: 641-473-3236. E-mail: gladlib@iowatelecom.net. *Asst Librn,* Pat Sievers
Pop 1,015; Circ 10,394
Library Holdings: Bk Titles 11,221; Bk Vols 12,300; Per Subs 37
Automation Activity & Vendor Info: (Circulation) Biblionix/Apollo
Wireless access
Open Mon 2-6, Tues-Fri 12-6, Sat 10-12

GLENWOOD

P GLENWOOD PUBLIC LIBRARY*, 109 N Vine St, 51534-1516. SAN 305-4314. Tel: 712-527-5252. FAX: 712-527-3619. E-mail: library@glenwood.lib.ia.us. Web Site: www.glenwood.lib.ia.us. *Dir,* Angela Campbell; *Ad,* Teresa R Buckingham; E-mail: tbuckingham@glenwood.lib.ia.us; *Ch,* Debbie Schmidt; E-mail: dschmidt@glenwood.lib.ia.us; Staff 6 (Non-MLS 6)
Founded 1896. Pop 5,358; Circ 54,912
Jul 2009-Jun 2010 Income $213,333, State $3,873, City $141,438, County $23,820, Locally Generated Income $44,202. Mats Exp $29,287, Books $17,904, Per/Ser (Incl. Access Fees) $2,500, Micro $200, AV Mat $1,677, Electronic Ref Mat (Incl. Access Fees) $7,006. Sal $137,935
Library Holdings: CDs 800; DVDs 2,313; Bk Vols 36,770; Per Subs 100; Videos 1,100
Subject Interests: Genealogy, Local hist
Automation Activity & Vendor Info: (Cataloging) Follett Software; (Circulation) Follett Software
Database Vendor: EBSCOhost, OCLC FirstSearch
Wireless access
Function: Adult bk club, Art exhibits, Bks on cassette, Bks on CD, Children's prog, Computers for patron use, Copy machines, Fax serv, Free DVD rentals, Handicapped accessible, Home delivery & serv to Sr ctr & nursing homes, Homebound delivery serv, ILL available, Music CDs, Prog for adults, Prog for children & young adult, Ref serv available, Spoken cassettes & CDs, Spoken cassettes & DVDs, Summer reading prog, Tax forms, Telephone ref, VHS videos, Wheelchair accessible
Open Mon, Tues, Thurs & Fri 10-6, Wed 12-8, Sat 9-12
Friends of the Library Group

S GLENWOOD RESOURCE CENTER*, Staff Library, 711 S Vine St, 51534. SAN 305-4322. Tel: 712-527-2438. FAX: 712-527-2280. *Dir,* Connie Brown
Founded 1960
Library Holdings: Bk Vols 5,000; Per Subs 20
Open Mon-Fri 8-4:30

GLIDDEN

P GLIDDEN PUBLIC LIBRARY*, 110 Idaho St, 51443. (Mail add: PO Box 345, 51443-0345), SAN 305-4330. Tel: 712-659-3781. FAX: 712-659-3805. E-mail: glibrary@mchsi.com. *Dir,* Erin Wolf
Pop 1,076; Circ 21,572
Library Holdings: AV Mats 437; Bk Titles 11,000; Bk Vols 12,000; Per Subs 41
Mem of Northwest Iowa Library Services
Open Mon-Fri 1-6, Sat 9-1

GOWRIE

P GOWRIE PUBLIC LIBRARY*, 1204 Market St, 50543. (Mail add: PO Box 137, 50543-0137), SAN 305-4349. Tel: 515-352-3315. FAX: 515-352-3713. E-mail: gowriepl@wccta.net. *Dir,* Shelly Nelson
Founded 1930. Pop 1,038; Circ 15,282
Library Holdings: Bk Vols 9,500; Per Subs 31
Automation Activity & Vendor Info: (Acquisitions) Follett Software; (Cataloging) Follett Software; (Circulation) Follett Software; (ILL) Follett Software; (Media Booking) Follett Software; (OPAC) Follett Software; (Serials) Follett Software
Open Mon, Tues, Thurs & Fri 1-5, Wed 1-5 & 7-9, Sat 9-12

GRAETTINGER

P GRAETTINGER PUBLIC LIBRARY*, 115 W Robins St, 51342. (Mail add: PO Box 368, 51342-0368), SAN 305-4357. Tel: 712-859-3592. FAX: 712-859-3197. Web Site: www.graettinger.lib.ia.us. *Dir,* Nicole Harris; E-mail: nharris@graettinger.lib.ia.us
Founded 1939. Pop 820; Circ 13,136
Library Holdings: AV Mats 418; Bk Titles 12,000; Per Subs 30
Automation Activity & Vendor Info: (Acquisitions) Follett Software
Mem of Northwest Iowa Library Services
Special Services for the Blind - Bks on cassette; Bks on CD
Open Mon 11-7, Tues-Fri 9-5

GRAFTON

P GRAFTON PUBLIC LIBRARY*, 203 Fourth Ave, 50440-0025. (Mail add: PO Box 25, 50440-0025), SAN 305-4365. Tel: 641-748-2735. FAX: 641-748-2739. E-mail: graftonlib@wctatel.net. Web Site: www.wctatel.net/web/graftonlib. *Librn,* Loraine Kalvig
Pop 300; Circ 8,425
Library Holdings: Audiobooks 112; Bks on Deafness & Sign Lang 3; CDs 5; DVDs 1,060; Large Print Bks 216; Bk Vols 11,033; Per Subs 65; Talking Bks 211; Videos 1,867
Automation Activity & Vendor Info: (Acquisitions) Winnebago Software Co; (Cataloging) Follett Software; (Circulation) Winnebago Software Co; (ILL) Winnebago Software Co
Database Vendor: Baker & Taylor
Wireless access
Open Mon-Fri 2-6:30, Sat 9-3

GRAND JUNCTION

P GRAND JUNCTION PUBLIC LIBRARY*, 106 E Main St, 50107. (Mail add: PO Box 79, 50107-0079), SAN 305-4373. Tel: 515-738-2506. FAX: 515-738-2506. Web Site: www.grandjunction.lib.ia.us. *Dir,* Jenon Cody; E-mail: jenon.cody@grandjunction.lib.ia.us; Staff 2 (Non-MLS 2)
Founded 1929. Pop 970; Circ 16,850
Library Holdings: Audiobooks 130; Bks on Deafness & Sign Lang 10; DVDs 410; Large Print Bks 480; Bk Titles 8,954; Per Subs 40
Automation Activity & Vendor Info: (Acquisitions) Book Systems; (Cataloging) Book Systems; (Circulation) Book Systems; (Course Reserve) Book Systems; (ILL) Book Systems; (Media Booking) Book Systems; (OPAC) Book Systems; (Serials) Book Systems
Database Vendor: EBSCOhost
Wireless access
Mem of Central Iowa Library Services
Open Mon, Tues & Thurs 2-6, Wed 1-7, Fri 2-5, Sat 9-12

GRANGER

P GRANGER PUBLIC LIBRARY, 2216 Broadway, 50109. SAN 305-4381. Tel: 515-999-2088. FAX: 515-999-9156. Web Site: www.grangeriowa.org/library. *Dir,* Janette Friesen; E-mail: janette.friesen@granger.lib.ia.us
Pop 619
Library Holdings: Bk Titles 6,062; Per Subs 30
Wireless access
Mem of Central Iowa Library Services
Open Mon & Thurs 2-7, Tues & Wed 9-12 & 1-7, Sat 9:30-1:30
Friends of the Library Group

GREENE

P GREENE PUBLIC LIBRARY*, 231 W Traer St, 50636-9406. (Mail add: PO Box 280, 50636-0280), SAN 305-439X. Tel: 641-816-5642. FAX: 641-816-4838. E-mail: gpl@myomnitel.com. Web Site: www.greene.lib.ia.us. *Dir,* Cynthia Siemons; E-mail: cynthias@greene.lib.ia.us; *Ch,* Dorothy Leavens
Founded 1872. Pop 2,600; Circ 27,707
Library Holdings: AV Mats 1,227; Bk Titles 17,046; Per Subs 89
Special Collections: The Greene Recorder (1876-1996), microfilm
Automation Activity & Vendor Info: (Acquisitions) Follett Software; (Cataloging) Follett Software; (Circulation) Follett Software
Open Mon & Wed 9-9, Tues & Thurs Noon-5, Fri 9-5, Sat 9-3

GREENFIELD

P GREENFIELD PUBLIC LIBRARY*, 202 S First St, 50849. (Mail add: PO Box 328, 50849), SAN 305-4403. Tel: 641-743-6120. E-mail: greenpl@iowatelecom.net. Web Site: www.greenpl@iowatelecom.net. *Co-Dir,* Lynn Heinbuch; *Co-Dir,* Lorraine Schneider
Founded 1916. Pop 2,129; Circ 27,531
Library Holdings: Bk Vols 23,000; Per Subs 100
Subject Interests: Genealogy
Automation Activity & Vendor Info: (Acquisitions) Book Systems; (Cataloging) Book Systems; (Circulation) Book Systems; (ILL) Book Systems; (Media Booking) Book Systems; (OPAC) Book Systems; (Serials) Book Systems
Mem of Southwest Iowa Library Services District
Open Mon-Wed & Fri 10-5:30, Thurs 10-7, Sat 10-Noon
Friends of the Library Group

GRIMES

P GRIMES PUBLIC LIBRARY*, 200 N James, 50111. (Mail add: PO Box 290, 50111-0290), SAN 305-4411. Tel: 515-986-3551. FAX: 515-986-9553. E-mail: library@grimes.lib.ia.us. Web Site: www.grimes.lib.ia.us. *Dir,* Karla D Pfaff; E-mail: karla@grimes.lib.ia.us; *Asst Dir,* Karalee Kerr; *Head, Circ,* Katelyn Wazny; *Youth Serv Librn,* Janet Rice; Staff 9 (Non-MLS 9)
Founded 1972. Pop 5,098
Library Holdings: Bk Titles 30,804; Bk Vols 33,260; Per Subs 40
Automation Activity & Vendor Info: (Cataloging) Follett Software; (Circulation) Follett Software; (OPAC) Follett Software
Database Vendor: OCLC FirstSearch
Mem of Central Iowa Library Services
Open Mon-Thurs 9-9, Fri 9-6, Sat 9-3, Sun 1-4

GRINNELL

P DRAKE COMMUNITY LIBRARY*, 930 Park St, 50112-2016. SAN 305-4438. Tel: 641-236-2661. FAX: 641-236-2667. E-mail: grinlib@iowatelecom.net. Web Site: www.grinnell.lib.ia.us. *Dir,* Marilyn Kennett; E-mail: marilyn@grinnelliowa.gov; *Asst Dir,* Stephanie Sueppel; E-mail: stephanie@grinnelliowa.gov; *Youth Serv Librn,* Karen Neal; E-mail: karen@grinnelliowa.gov; *Syst Adminr,* Monique Shore; E-mail: monique@grinnelliowa.gov; Staff 9 (MLS 3, Non-MLS 6)
Founded 1901. Pop 9,218; Circ 106,885
Jul 2012-Jun 2013 Income $498,285, State $5,135, City $468,144, County $13,006, Locally Generated Income $12,000. Mats Exp $62,300, Books $35,500, Per/Ser (Incl. Access Fees) $7,600, Micro $1,000, AV Mat $6,200, Electronic Ref Mat (Incl. Access Fees) $12,000. Sal $169,507 (Prof $134,271)
Library Holdings: Audiobooks 2,459; AV Mats 3,550; Bks on Deafness & Sign Lang 48; CDs 333; DVDs 1,692; e-books 13,090; Electronic Media & Resources 294, Large Print Bks 2,337; Bk Vols 62,040; Per Subs 175
Special Collections: State Document Depository
Subject Interests: Local hist
Automation Activity & Vendor Info: (Acquisitions) Baker & Taylor; (Cataloging) SirsiDynix; (Circulation) SirsiDynix; (OPAC) SirsiDynix; (Serials) EBSCO Online
Database Vendor: EBSCOhost, Gale Cengage Learning, LearningExpress, OCLC FirstSearch, Wilson - Wilson Web
Wireless access
Function: After school storytime, Audio & video playback equip for onsite use, Audiobks via web, Bks on cassette, Bks on CD, Children's prog, Computers for patron use, Copy machines, e-mail serv, E-Reserves, Electronic databases & coll, Equip loans & repairs, Exhibits, Fax serv, Free DVD rentals, Handicapped accessible, Holiday prog, Homebound delivery serv, Homework prog, ILL available, Microfiche/film & reading machines, Music CDs, Notary serv, Online cat, Online ref, Online searches, Outreach serv, Outside serv via phone, mail, e-mail & web, OverDrive digital audio bks, Photocopying/Printing, Preschool outreach, Preschool reading prog, Prog for adults, Prog for children & young adult, Pub access computers, Ref serv available, Ref serv in person, Scanner, Senior outreach, Serves mentally handicapped consumers, Spanish lang bks, Spoken cassettes & CDs, Spoken cassettes & DVDs, Story hour, Summer & winter reading prog, Summer reading prog, Tax forms, Teen prog, Telephone ref, VHS videos, Video lending libr, Wheelchair accessible, Winter reading prog
Open Mon-Thurs 10-8, Fri 10-6, Sat 10-5, Sun 1:30-4
Friends of the Library Group

C GRINNELL COLLEGE LIBRARIES, Burling Library, 1111 Sixth Ave, 50112-1770. SAN 305-442X. Tel: 641-269-3350. Interlibrary Loan Service Tel: 641-269-3005. Reference Tel: 641-269-3353. Administration Tel: 641-269-3351. FAX: 641-269-4283. E-mail: query@grinnell.edu. Web Site: www.grinnell.edu/library. *Librn,* Richard Fyffe; Fax: 641-269-3488, E-mail: fyffe@grinnell.edu; *Assoc Librn, Soc Studies & Data Serv Librn,* Julia Bauder; Tel: 641-269-4431, E-mail: bauderj@grinnel.edu; *Acq & Discovery Librn,* R Cecilia Knight; Tel: 641-269-3368, E-mail: knight@grinnell.edu; *Discovery & Integrated Syst Librn,* Becky Yoose; Tel: 641-269-4775, E-mail: yoosebec@grinnell.edu; *Coordr of Res Serv, Humanities Librn,* Phillip Jones; Tel: 641-269-3355, E-mail: jonesphi@grinnell.edu; *Humanities Librn,* Jieun Kang; Tel: 641-269-3362, E-mail: kangjieu@grinnell.du; *Sci Librn,* Kevin Engel; Tel: 641-269-4234, E-mail: engelk@grinnell.edu; *Col Archivist & Spec Coll Librn,* Chris Jones; Tel: 641-269-3364, E-mail: joneschr@grinnell.edu. Subject Specialists: *Philos,* Richard Fyffe; *Econ, Global studies,* Julia Bauder; *Art, Gender, Women's & sexuality studies,* R Cecilia Knight; *Computer sci,* Becky Yoose; *English, Relig studies, Spanish,* Phillip Jones; *Am studies, Classics, East Asian studies,* Jieun Kang; *Sciences,* Kevin Engel; *Hist, Prairie studies,* Chris Jones; Staff 22.5 (MLS 8, Non-MLS 14.5)
Enrl 1,635; Fac 165; Highest Degree: Bachelor
Jul 2012-Jun 2013. Mats Exp $4,169,400, Books $297,566, Per/Ser (Incl. Access Fees) $1,184,985, AV Mat $30,233, Presv $25,671. Sal $1,244,001 (Prof $786,163)
Library Holdings: AV Mats 35,440; e-books 288,547; Microforms 27,067; Per Subs 1,839
Special Collections: East Asian Coll; Iowa, Local History & College Archives, bks & ms; James Norman Hall Coll, paper & ms; Pinne Coll, bks & ms. State Document Depository; US Document Depository
Automation Activity & Vendor Info: (Acquisitions) Innovative Interfaces, Inc; (Cataloging) Innovative Interfaces, Inc; (Circulation) Innovative Interfaces, Inc; (Course Reserve) Innovative Interfaces, Inc; (ILL) OCLC ILLiad; (OPAC) Innovative Interfaces, Inc; (Serials) Innovative Interfaces, Inc
Wireless access
Function: 24/7 Electronic res, 24/7 Online cat, Accessibility serv available based on individual needs, Archival coll, Art exhibits, Computers for patron use, Copy machines, Doc delivery serv, e-mail & chat, E-Reserves, Electronic databases & coll, Equip loans & repairs, eReaders, Exhibits, Handicapped accessible, ILL available, Large print keyboards, Magazines, Magnifiers for reading, Mail & tel request accepted, Microfiche/film & reading machines, Movies, Music CDs, Newsp ref libr, Online cat, Online ref, Online searches, Orientations, Outreach serv, Photocopying/Printing, Printer for laptops & handheld devices, Prof lending libr, Pub access computers, Ref & res, Ref serv available, Ref serv in person, Scanner, Study rm, VHS videos, Video lending libr, Web-catalog, Wheelchair accessible

Special Services for the Blind - Assistive/Adapted tech devices, equip & products; Computer with voice synthesizer for visually impaired persons
Open Mon-Thurs 7:45am-1am, Fri 7:45am-10pm, Sat 10-10, Sun 10am-1am
Restriction: Borrowing requests are handled by ILL

GRISWOLD

P GRISWOLD PUBLIC LIBRARY, 505 Main, 51535. (Mail add: PO Box 190, 51535-0190), SAN 305-4446. Tel: 712-778-4130. FAX: 712-778-4140. E-mail: grislib@netins.net. Web Site: www.griswold.lib.ia.us. *Libr Dir,* Lisa Metheny; *Asst Librn,* Susan Peterson; Staff 1 (Non-MLS 1)
Founded 1977. Pop 1,039; Circ 18,482
Library Holdings: Bk Vols 10,134; Per Subs 33
Automation Activity & Vendor Info: (Acquisitions) Follett Software; (Cataloging) Follett Software; (Circulation) Follett Software; (ILL) Follett Software; (Media Booking) Follett Software; (OPAC) Follett Software; (Serials) Follett Software
Database Vendor: EBSCOhost
Wireless access
Function: Bks on CD, Children's prog, Computers for patron use, Copy machines, e-mail serv, E-Reserves, Electronic databases & coll, Fax serv, Free DVD rentals, Handicapped accessible, Homebound delivery serv, ILL available, Online cat, Outreach serv, Preschool outreach, Prog for adults, Prog for children & young adult, Scanner, Story hour, Summer reading prog, Tax forms, VHS videos, Wheelchair accessible
Mem of Southwest Iowa Library Services District
Open Tues & Thurs 10-12 & 1-6:30, Wed & Fri 10-12 & 1-5, Sat 10-12
Restriction: In-house use for visitors
Friends of the Library Group

GRUNDY CENTER

P KLING MEMORIAL LIBRARY*, 708 Seventh St, 50638-1430. SAN 305-4454. Tel: 319-825-3607. FAX: 319-825-5863. E-mail: library@grundycenter.lib.ia.us. Web Site: www.grundycenter.lib.ia.us. *Dir,* Molly Mauer; Tel: 319-825-3607, E-mail: molly@grundycenter.lib.ia.us; *Asst Dir,* Brenda Brown
Pop 2,596; Circ 57,306
Library Holdings: AV Mats 1,222; Large Print Bks 1,378; Bk Vols 25,679; Per Subs 127; Talking Bks 532
Special Collections: Herbert Quick Coll
Subject Interests: Iowa
Wireless access
Open Mon, Wed & Fri 10-5, Tues & Thurs 10-7, Sat 10-12
Friends of the Library Group

GUTHRIE CENTER

P MARY BARNETT MEMORIAL LIBRARY*, 400 Grand St, 50115-1439. SAN 305-4462. Tel: 641-747-8110. FAX: 641-747-8110. E-mail: mjblib@netins.net. Web Site: www.guthriecenter.lib.ia.us. *Dir,* Patricia Sleister; E-mail: mjbdirector@guthriecenter.lib.ia.us; *Asst Librn,* Sandy Vaughan; Staff 1 (MLS 1)
Founded 1902. Pop 2,000; Circ 40,000
Library Holdings: Bk Titles 30,000; Per Subs 85
Mem of Southwest Iowa Library Services District
Open Mon & Wed 1-7, Tues & Thurs 1-6, Fri 9-1, Sat 9-12
Friends of the Library Group

GUTTENBERG

P GUTTENBERG PUBLIC LIBRARY*, 603 S Second St, 52052. (Mail add: PO Box 130, 52052-0130), SAN 305-4470. Tel: 563-252-3108. E-mail: guttlib@alpinecom.net, librarian@guttenberg.lib.ia.us. Web Site: www.guttenberg.lib.ia.us. *Dir,* Sandra Barron; *Ch,* Caroline Rosacker
Pop 2,000; Circ 27,000
Automation Activity & Vendor Info: (Acquisitions) Follett Software; (Cataloging) Follett Software; (Circulation) Follett Software; (ILL) Follett Software; (Media Booking) Follett Software; (OPAC) Follett Software; (Serials) Follett Software
Wireless access
Open Mon 10-7:30, Tues, Thurs & Fri 10-5, Wed 1-7:30, Sat 9-3

HAMBURG

P HAMBURG PUBLIC LIBRARY, 1301 Main St, 51640. SAN 305-4489. Tel: 712-382-1395. FAX: 712-382-1405. E-mail: libraryhamburg@gmail.com. Web Site: www.hamburglibrary.com. *Dir,* Ruth Lauman; Staff 1 (Non-MLS 1)
Founded 1919. Pop 1,684; Circ 7,000
Library Holdings: Bk Titles 11,000
Wireless access
Open Mon 12-5 & 7-8:30, Tues, Wed & Thurs 12-5, Fri 11-5, Sat 9-Noon
Friends of the Library Group

HAMPTON

P HAMPTON PUBLIC LIBRARY*, Four Federal St S, 50441-1934. SAN 305-4497. Tel: 641-456-4451. FAX: 641-456-2377. E-mail: hplibrary@mchsi.com. *Dir,* Kim Bell; Staff 2 (MLS 2)
Founded 1889. Pop 4,133
Library Holdings: Bk Titles 35,000; Per Subs 103
Subject Interests: Genealogy, Iowa
Automation Activity & Vendor Info: (Acquisitions) Follett Software; (Cataloging) Follett Software; (Circulation) Follett Software; (ILL) Follett Software; (OPAC) Follett Software; (Serials) Follett Software
Open Mon & Thurs 10-5:30, Tues & Wed 10-8, Fri & Sat 10-3
Friends of the Library Group

HANLONTOWN

P KINNEY MEMORIAL LIBRARY*, 214 Main St, 50444. (Mail add: PO Box 58, 50444-0058), SAN 305-4500. Tel: 641-896-2888. FAX: 641-896-2890. E-mail: redhawks@wctatel.net. Web Site: www.hanlontown.lib.ia.us. *Dir,* Ramona Kinseth; E-mail: director@hanlontown.lib.ia.us; *Asst Dir,* Cindy Sorenson
Pop 193; Circ 2,975
Library Holdings: Bk Titles 5,114; Per Subs 21
Open Mon, Tues & Thurs 3-7, Wed & Sat 9-1

HARCOURT

P HARCOURT COMMUNITY LIBRARY*, 106 W Second St, 50544. (Mail add: PO Box 358, 50544-0358), SAN 305-4519. Tel: 515-354-5391. FAX: 515-354-5391. E-mail: harcourt@lvcta.com. *Librn,* Kathy Hay
Founded 1950. Pop 700; Circ 5,200
Library Holdings: Bk Vols 6,000; Per Subs 45
Open Tues 2:30-8, Wed 4-8, Thurs 2:30-8:30, Sat 8:30-1

HARLAN

P HARLAN COMMUNITY LIBRARY*, 718 Court St, 51537. SAN 305-4527. Tel: 712-755-5934. FAX: 712-755-3952. E-mail: harlanpl@harlannet.com. Web Site: www.harlan.lib.ia.us. *Dir,* Michael Burris; *Asst Dir,* Elaine Sprague; *Ch,* Patricia Engemann; *Circ,* Jan Phifer; *ILL,* Linda Burger; Staff 6 (MLS 1, Non-MLS 5)
Pop 5,282; Circ 102,447
Library Holdings: Bk Titles 50,000; Bk Vols 50,250; Per Subs 126
Special Collections: Iowa History Coll
Automation Activity & Vendor Info: (Cataloging) Follett Software; (Circulation) Follett Software; (OPAC) Follett Software
Database Vendor: EBSCOhost, OCLC FirstSearch
Mem of Southwest Iowa Library Services District
Open Mon-Wed & Fri 9:30-5:30, Thurs 9:30-8:30, Sat 9:30-12:30

HARPERS FERRY

P DOLORES TILLINGHAST MEMORIAL LIBRARY*, 234 N Fourth St, 52146. (Mail add: PO Box 57, 52146-0057), SAN 376-5040. Tel: 563-586-2524. FAX: 563-586-2524. E-mail: harplib@acegroup.cc. Web Site: harpersferryiowa.com/library.htm. *Dir,* Jody Delaney
Founded 1990. Pop 330
Jul 2005-Jun 2006 Income $10,477, City $4,700, County $5,777
Library Holdings: Bk Vols 9,641; Per Subs 70
Open Mon, Tues & Sat 9-12, Wed 4-7, Thurs 5-7, Fri 2-5

S US NATIONAL PARK SERVICE*, Effigy Mounds National Monument Library, 151 Hwy 76, 52146-7519. SAN 370-3185. Tel: 563-873-3491. FAX: 563-873-3743. *In Charge,* Florenceia M Wiles
Library Holdings: Bk Vols 10,000
Special Collections: Ellison Orr Coll, mss
Subject Interests: Natural hist
Restriction: Non-circulating, Open to others by appt, Pub ref by request

HARTLEY

P HARTLEY PUBLIC LIBRARY*, 91 First St SE, 51346. SAN 305-4535. Tel: 712-928-2080. FAX: 712-928-2823. E-mail: libdirector@hartley.lib.ia.us. Web Site: www.hartley.lib.ia.us. *Dir,* Cynthia Ann Gelderman; *Adult Coordr,* Ellen Treimer; E-mail: ellen@hartley.lib.ia.us; *Children's & Teen Serv Coordr,* Tarisa Smith; E-mail: tarisa@hartley.lib.ia.us
Founded 1942. Pop 1,733
Library Holdings: AV Mats 905; Large Print Bks 82; Bk Vols 21,665; Per Subs 104; Talking Bks 574
Automation Activity & Vendor Info: (Cataloging) Follett Software; (Circulation) Follett Software
Wireless access
Function: Handicapped accessible, Home delivery & serv to Sr ctr & nursing homes, Homebound delivery serv, ILL available,

Photocopying/Printing, Prog for children & young adult, Summer reading prog
Open Mon & Wed 1-8, Tues & Thurs 10-5:30, Fri 1-5:30, Sat 8:30-12:30
Friends of the Library Group

HAWARDEN

P HAWARDEN PUBLIC LIBRARY*, 803 Tenth St, 51023. SAN 305-456X. Tel: 712-551-2244. FAX: 712-551-1720. E-mail: haw_library@acsnet.com. Web Site: www.hawarden.lib.ia.us. *Dir,* Valerie Haverhals; E-mail: valerie.haverhals@hawarden.lib.ia.us
Founded 1901. Pop 2,480; Circ 49,582
Library Holdings: Bk Titles 26,730; Bk Vols 27,112; Per Subs 121
Special Collections: Hawarden Historical Slides; Hawarden History; Howard Olsen Map Coll; Iowa Coll
Automation Activity & Vendor Info: (Cataloging) Book Systems; (Circulation) Book Systems; (OPAC) Book Systems
Database Vendor: OCLC FirstSearch
Mem of Northwest Iowa Library Services
Partic in State of Iowa Libraries Online
Open Mon, Wed & Thurs 10-8, Tues 10-6, Fri 10-5, Sat 10-2

HAWKEYE

P HAWKEYE PUBLIC LIBRARY*, 104 S Second St, 52147-0216. (Mail add: PO Box 216, 52147-0216), SAN 305-4586. Tel: 563-427-5536. FAX: 563-427-5536. E-mail: director@hawkeye.lib.ia.us. Web Site: www.hawkeye.lib.ia.us. *Dir,* Annie Lee
Pop 480; Circ 6,300
Library Holdings: Bk Titles 7,829; Per Subs 30
Subject Interests: Civil War
Automation Activity & Vendor Info: (Acquisitions) Follett Software; (Cataloging) Follett Software; (Circulation) Follett Software; (Serials) Follett Software
Database Vendor: EBSCOhost, OCLC FirstSearch
Open Mon, Wed & Fri 12-5:30, Tues 4-7:30

HEDRICK

P HEDRICK PUBLIC LIBRARY*, 109 N Main St, 52563. (Mail add: PO Box 427, 52563-0427), SAN 305-4594. Tel: 641-653-2211. FAX: 641-653-2487. *Dir,* Jan Brink
Pop 837
Library Holdings: AV Mats 185; Bk Titles 7,765; Per Subs 16; Videos 120
Open Mon, Tues & Fri 2-5, Wed 12:30-4:30, Thurs 2-6, Sat 8:30-11:30

HIAWATHA

P HIAWATHA PUBLIC LIBRARY*, 150 W Willman St, 52233. SAN 305-4608. Tel: 319-393-1414. FAX: 319-393-6005. Web Site: www.hiawathalibrary.com. *Dir,* Jeaneal C Weeks; *Asst Dir,* Patricia Struttmann; E-mail: struttmanp@crlibrary.org; *Youth Serv Librn,* Alicia Mangin. Staff 7 (Non-MLS 7)
Founded 1960. Pop 7,024; Circ 181,401
Library Holdings: Bk Titles 38,351; Per Subs 94
Automation Activity & Vendor Info: (Cataloging) SirsiDynix; (Circulation) SirsiDynix
Database Vendor: SirsiDynix
Wireless access
Open Mon-Thurs 10-8, Fri & Sat 10-5, Sun 1-4
Friends of the Library Group

HILLSBORO

P HILLSBORO PUBLIC LIBRARY*, 100 W Commercial St, 52630. (Mail add: PO Box 117, 52630-0117), SAN 305-4616. Tel: 319-253-4000. FAX: 319-253-4000. E-mail: hillsborobooks@iowatelecom.net. *Dir,* Kelly Heitmeier
Founded 1937. Pop 208; Circ 3,120
Library Holdings: Bk Titles 8,000
Wireless access
Open Mon, Wed & Fri 3:30-5:30

HOLSTEIN

P STUBBS MEMORIAL LIBRARY*, 207 E Second St, 51025. (Mail add: PO Box 290, 51025-0290), SAN 305-4624. Tel: 712-368-4563. FAX: 712-368-4483. E-mail: stubbslibrary@holstein.lib.ia.us. Web Site: www.holstein.lib.ia.us. *Dir,* Bonnie Barkema; E-mail: bonnie@holstein.lib.ia.us; *Ch,* Roxanne Stevenson
Pop 1,477; Circ 33,312
Library Holdings: Bk Titles 24,000; Per Subs 75
Mem of Northwest Iowa Library Services
Open Mon 2-8, Tues, Thurs & Fri 2-6, Wed 10-12 & 2-6, Sat 9-1

HOPKINTON

P HOPKINTON PUBLIC LIBRARY*, 110 First St SE, 52237. (Mail add: PO Box 220, 52237-0220), SAN 305-4632. Tel: 563-926-2514. FAX: 563-926-2065. *Librn,* Kim Ungs
Founded 1944. Pop 685; Circ 12,000
Library Holdings: Bks-By-Mail 36; CDs 110; Large Print Bks 200; Bk Titles 13,000; Per Subs 28; Talking Bks 25; Videos 890
Special Collections: Iowa Coll
Special Services for the Blind - Audio mat; Large print bks
Open Tues & Thurs 10-5, Wed 10-6, Fri & Sat 9-Noon

HOSPERS

P HOSPERS PUBLIC LIBRARY*, 213 Main St, 51238. (Mail add: PO Box 6, 51238-0248). Tel: 712-752-8400. FAX: 712-752-8601. E-mail: hosperslibrary@hospers.lib.ia.us. Web Site: www.hospers.lib.ia.us. *Dir,* Hope Hofland
Library Holdings: AV Mats 250; Bk Vols 8,000; Per Subs 20; Talking Bks 150
Special Collections: Local Artists Paintings Coll
Automation Activity & Vendor Info: (Cataloging) Book Systems; (Circulation) Book Systems; (OPAC) Book Systems
Open Mon 11:30-8, Tues 11-7:30, Wed 9-1, Thurs 11:30-7, Fri 11:30-5, Sat 10-2

HUBBARD

P HUBBARD PUBLIC LIBRARY*, 218 E Maple St, 50122. (Mail add: PO Box 339, 50122-0339), SAN 305-4640. Tel: 641-864-2771. FAX: 641-864-2712. E-mail: hubbardlibrary@gmail.com. Web Site: hubbard.lib.ia.us. *Dir,* Susan Winter
Founded 1930. Pop 850; Circ 20,000
Jul 2013-Jun 2014 Income $63,000, City $38,000, County $15,000, Other $10,000. Mats Exp $12,960, Books $10,000, Per/Ser (Incl. Access Fees) $1,500, AV Mat $1,000, Electronic Ref Mat (Incl. Access Fees) $460. Sal $42,000 (Prof $14,000)
Automation Activity & Vendor Info: (Acquisitions) TLC (The Library Corporation); (Cataloging) TLC (The Library Corporation); (Circulation) TLC (The Library Corporation)
Database Vendor: EBSCOhost
Wireless access
Function: Adult bk club, After school storytime, Audiobks via web, Bk club(s), Bks on CD, Children's prog, Computer training, Computers for patron use, Copy machines, e-mail & chat, e-mail serv, Electronic databases & coll, Equip loans & repairs, Exhibits, Fax serv, Free DVD rentals, Genealogy discussion group, Handicapped accessible, Holiday prog, Home delivery & serv to Sr ctr & nursing homes, Homebound delivery serv, ILL available, Instruction & testing, Large print keyboards, Magnifiers for reading, Mail & tel request accepted, Mail loans to mem, Newsp ref libr, Online cat, Online info literacy tutorials on the web & in blackboard, Online searches, Preschool outreach, Preschool reading prog, Printer for laptops & handheld devices, Prof lending libr, Prog for adults, Prog for children & young adult, Pub access computers, Scanner, Senior computer classes, Story hour, Summer reading prog, Teen prog, Telephone ref, VHS videos, Video lending libr, Web-catalog, Wheelchair accessible, Workshops
Open Mon, Wed & Fri 9-6, Tues & Thurs 1-6, Sat 9-Noon

HUDSON

P HUDSON PUBLIC LIBRARY*, 401 Fifth St, 50643. (Mail add: PO Box 480, 50643-0480), SAN 305-4659. Tel: 319-988-4217. E-mail: staff@hudson.lib.ia.us. Web Site: www.hudson.lib.ia.us. *Dir,* Mary L Bucy; *Asst Dir,* Kathy Holst; E-mail: kholst@hudson.lib.ia.us; Staff 3.09 (Non-MLS 3.09)
Pop 3,621; Circ 29,587
Jul 2006-Jun 2007 Income $160,724. Mats Exp $25,169. Sal $76,318
Library Holdings: Bk Titles 26,648; Per Subs 73
Automation Activity & Vendor Info: (Circulation) Follett Software; (OPAC) Follett Software
Database Vendor: EBSCOhost
Function: Archival coll, AV serv, Distance learning, Homebound delivery serv, ILL available, Photocopying/Printing, Prog for adults, Prog for children & young adult, Ref serv available, Summer reading prog, Telephone ref, Wheelchair accessible
Special Services for the Blind - Large print bks; Talking bks
Open Mon, Wed & Thurs 10-8, Tues 8-8, Fri 8-6, Sat 10-5

HULL

P HULL PUBLIC LIBRARY*, 1408 Main St, 51239. SAN 305-4667. Tel: 712-439-1321. FAX: 712-439-1534. E-mail: hulllib@hickorytech.net. *Dir,* Matt Hoehamer; *Ch,* Marge Vander Esch; Staff 6 (Non-MLS 6)
Pop 1,960; Circ 65,000

Jul 2005-Jun 2006 Income $102,120, State $2,320, City $80,913, County $18,887. Mats Exp $17,105, Books $12,513, Per/Ser (Incl. Access Fees) $1,741, Other Print Mats $1,406, Micro $62, Electronic Ref Mat (Incl. Access Fees) $1,383. Sal $41,971
Special Collections: Local Newspaper, 1892-, micro
Automation Activity & Vendor Info: (Acquisitions) Follett Software; (Cataloging) Follett Software; (Circulation) Follett Software
Database Vendor: EBSCOhost
Wireless access
Mem of Northwest Iowa Library Services
Open Mon & Wed 12:30-9, Tues & Thurs 9:30-5:30, Fri 12:30-5:30, Sat 9-12:30
Friends of the Library Group

HUMBOLDT

P HUMBOLDT PUBLIC LIBRARY*, 30 Sixth St N, 50548. SAN 305-4675. Tel: 515-332-1925. FAX: 515-332-1926. E-mail: director@humboldtpubliclibrary.com. Web Site: www.humboldtpubliclibrary.com. *Dir,* Nikki Ehlers; *Ch,* Jean Holste; *Teen Librn,* Demi Johnson; Staff 3 (MLS 1, Non-MLS 2)
Founded 1908. Pop 4,452; Circ 82,395
Library Holdings: AV Mats 1,967; Bk Titles 26,547; Per Subs 80
Automation Activity & Vendor Info: (Acquisitions) Follett Software; (Cataloging) Follett Software; (Circulation) Follett Software; (ILL) Follett Software; (Media Booking) Follett Software; (OPAC) Follett Software; (Serials) Follett Software
Open Mon & Tues 10-8, Wed-Fri 10-5:30, Sat 9-3
Friends of the Library Group

HUMESTON

P HUMESTON PUBLIC LIBRARY, 302 Broad St, 50123. (Mail add: PO Box 97, 50123-0097), SAN 305-4683. Tel: 641-877-4811. E-mail: humlib@iowatelecom.net. Web Site: www.humeston.lib.ia.us. *Libr Dir,* Jackie Gunzenhauser; *Asst Libr Dir,* Leona Darrah
Founded 1925. Pop 494; Circ 7,690
Library Holdings: Audiobooks 150; DVDs 345; Large Print Bks 200; Bk Titles 9,500; Per Subs 10
Automation Activity & Vendor Info: (Cataloging) Biblionix/Apollo; (Circulation) Biblionix/Apollo
Database Vendor: EBSCOhost, OCLC FirstSearch
Wireless access
Function: Bk club(s), Computers for patron use, ILL available, Preschool outreach, Story hour, Summer reading prog, Wheelchair accessible
Mem of Southwest Iowa Library Services District
Special Services for the Blind - Bks on CD; Large print bks
Open Mon & Fri 1-5, Tues 2-5, Wed 1-6, Sat 9-Noon

HUXLEY

P HUXLEY PUBLIC LIBRARY*, 515 N Main Ave, 50124. (Mail add: PO Box 5, 50124-0005), SAN 305-4691. Tel: 515-597-2552. FAX: 515-597-2554. E-mail: huxlib@gmail.com. Web Site: www.huxleyiowa.org. *Dir of Libr Serv,* Mike Hanks; Staff 5 (Non-MLS 5)
Founded 1972. Pop 2,800; Circ 74,565
Library Holdings: AV Mats 1,253; Bk Vols 36,000; Per Subs 50; Talking Bks 581
Special Collections: Iowa History; Norwegian Language Books
Automation Activity & Vendor Info: (Cataloging) Follett Software; (Circulation) Follett Software
Mem of Central Iowa Library Services
Open Mon-Thurs 7:30am-8pm, Fri 7:30-5, Sat 10-3
Friends of the Library Group

IDA GROVE

P IDA GROVE PUBLIC LIBRARY*, 100 E Second St, 51445. SAN 305-4705. Tel: 712-364-2306. FAX: 712-364-3228. Web Site: www.idagrove.lib.ia.us. *Dir,* Angela Scales; E-mail: angela.scales@idagrove.lib.ia.us
Pop 2,268
Library Holdings: Bk Titles 15,000; Per Subs 65
Mem of Northwest Iowa Library Services
Open Mon 10-6, Tues 11-5, Wed Noon-5, Thurs Noon-7, Fri 10-7, Sat 9-2
Friends of the Library Group

INDEPENDENCE

P INDEPENDENCE PUBLIC LIBRARY*, 805 First St E, 50644. SAN 305-4713. Tel: 319-334-2470. FAX: 319-332-0306. E-mail: indylib@indytel.com. Web Site: www.indylibrary.org. *Dir,* Laura Blaker; *Asst Dir,* Amy McGraw; Staff 7 (MLS 1, Non-MLS 6)
Founded 1857. Pop 6,000; Circ 89,611
Jul 2010-Jun 2011 Income $286,866. Mats Exp $36,915. Sal $192,555
Library Holdings: Audiobooks 1,584; DVDs 1,064; Bk Vols 32,160; Per Subs 84
Automation Activity & Vendor Info: (Cataloging) Follett Software; (Circulation) Follett Software; (OPAC) Follett Software
Database Vendor: EBSCOhost, World Book Online
Wireless access
Function: Art exhibits, Audiobks via web, Bks on CD, Children's prog, Computer training, Computers for patron use, Copy machines, e-mail & chat, Electronic databases & coll, Fax serv, Free DVD rentals, Handicapped accessible, Online cat, Online ref, Online searches, OverDrive digital audio bks, Photocopying/Printing, Preschool outreach, Prog for adults, Prog for children & young adult, Pub access computers, Ref serv available, Story hour, Summer reading prog, Tax forms, Teen prog, Telephone ref, Wheelchair accessible
Mem of Northeast Iowa Library Services
Open Mon-Thurs 9:30-8, Fri 9:30-5, Sat 9:30-4, Sun 1-4
Restriction: Authorized patrons
Friends of the Library Group

INDIANOLA

P INDIANOLA PUBLIC LIBRARY*, 207 North B St, 50125. SAN 305-473X. Tel: 515-961-9418. FAX: 515-961-9419. E-mail: info@indianola.lib.ia.us. Web Site: www.indianola.lib.ia.us. *Dir,* Joyce Godwin; E-mail: jgodwin@indianola.lib.ia.us; *Asst Dir,* Alice Gaumer; E-mail: agaumer@indianola.lib.ia.us; *Youth Serv Librn,* Jane Carlson; E-mail: jcarlson@indianola.lib.ia.us; Staff 10 (MLS 2, Non-MLS 8)
Founded 1884. Pop 14,132; Circ 151,631
Jul 2005-Jun 2006 Income $445,329, City $369,200, County $42,000, Locally Generated Income $19,300, Other $14,829. Mats Exp $68,350, Books $45,000, Per/Ser (Incl. Access Fees) $7,000, AV Mat $10,500, Electronic Ref Mat (Incl. Access Fees) $5,850. Sal $201,376 (Prof $55,000)
Library Holdings: Bk Vols 45,000; Per Subs 123
Subject Interests: Genealogy, Local hist
Automation Activity & Vendor Info: (Acquisitions) Innovative Interfaces, Inc; (Cataloging) Innovative Interfaces, Inc; (Circulation) Innovative Interfaces, Inc; (Serials) Innovative Interfaces, Inc
Function: Bk club(s), Homebound delivery serv, ILL available, Prog for children & young adult, Ref serv available, Summer reading prog, Telephone ref
Mem of Central Iowa Library Services
Partic in OCLC Online Computer Library Center, Inc
Open Mon-Thurs 10-8:30, Fri 10-6, Sat 10-5, Sun 1-4
Friends of the Library Group

CR SIMPSON COLLEGE*, Dunn Library, 508 North C St, 50125-1216. SAN 305-4748. Tel: 515-961-1663. Circulation Tel: 515-961-1518. Interlibrary Loan Service Tel: 515-961-1815. Reference Tel: 515-961-1520. Administration Tel: 515-961-1519. Automation Services Tel: 515-961-1748. FAX: 515-961-1363. E-mail: dunnlib@simpson.edu. Web Site: www.simpson.edu/library. *Col Librn/Archivist,* Cyd Dyer; E-mail: cyd.dyer@simpson.edu; *Res Librn,* Steve Duffy; E-mail: steve.duffy@simpson.edu; *Res Librn,* Liz Grimsbo; Tel: 515-961-1485, E-mail: liz.grimsbo@simpson.edu; *Res Librn,* Mary Peterson; E-mail: mary.peterson@simpson.edu; Staff 7 (MLS 4, Non-MLS 3)
Founded 1860. Enrl 1,767; Fac 138; Highest Degree: Master
Jun 2012-May 2013 Income $830,723, State $845, Parent Institution $829,878. Mats Exp $276,761, Books $49,599, Per/Ser (Incl. Access Fees) $145,206, AV Equip $20,550, AV Mat $2,796, Electronic Ref Mat (Incl. Access Fees) $58,610. Sal $371,021 (Prof $192,814)
Library Holdings: CDs 1,299; DVDs 1,523; e-books 7,462; e-journals 24,971; Microforms 9,898; Music Scores 3,144; Bk Titles 109,343; Bk Vols 133,346; Per Subs 267; Videos 1,485
Special Collections: Avery O Craven Coll
Automation Activity & Vendor Info: (Acquisitions) Innovative Interfaces, Inc; (Cataloging) OCLC; (Circulation) Innovative Interfaces, Inc; (Course Reserve) Innovative Interfaces, Inc; (ILL) OCLC; (OPAC) Innovative Interfaces, Inc; (Serials) Innovative Interfaces, Inc
Database Vendor: 3M Library Systems, Alexander Street Press, American Chemical Society, ARTstor, Baker & Taylor, BioOne, Cambridge Scientific Abstracts, CredoReference, EBSCOhost, Gale Cengage Learning, Innovative Interfaces, Inc, JSTOR, LearningExpress, LexisNexis, Mergent Online, OCLC FirstSearch, OCLC WorldShare Interlibrary Loan, Oxford Online, Project MUSE, ProQuest, ScienceDirect, ValueLine, Wiley
Wireless access
Publications: Annual Report; Archives & Subject Guides (Online only); Bookmark (Brochure)
Partic in Iowa Private Academic Library Consortium (IPAL); OCLC Online Computer Library Center, Inc

INWOOD

P INWOOD PUBLIC LIBRARY*, 103 S Main, 51240. (Mail add: PO Box 69, 51240-0069), SAN 305-4756. Tel: 712-753-4814. E-mail: admin@inwood.lib.ia.us. Web Site: www.inwood.lib.ia.us. *Dir,* Donna Bos; E-mail: donnab@inwood.lib.ia.us; *Asst Dir,* Clarene Burgers
Founded 1924. Pop 1,200; Circ 34,250
Library Holdings: CDs 150; DVDs 700; Large Print Bks 100; Bk Titles 16,470; Per Subs 48; Talking Bks 626; Videos 1,000
Subject Interests: Best sellers
Automation Activity & Vendor Info: (Acquisitions) Follett Software; (Cataloging) Follett Software; (Circulation) Follett Software
Mem of Northwest Iowa Library Services
Open Mon & Wed 2-5:30, Tues 9-11 & 2-5:30, Thurs 2-5:30 & 7-9, Sat 9-1

IONIA

P IONIA COMMUNITY LIBRARY*, 101 W Iowa St, 50645-0130. (Mail add: PO Box 130, 50645-0130), SAN 305-4764. Tel: 641-394-4803. FAX: 641-394-4803. E-mail: director@ionia.lib.ia.us. Web Site: www.ionia.lib.ia.us. *Dir,* Jane McGrane; Staff 1 (MLS 1)
Founded 1974. Pop 350
Library Holdings: Bk Titles 6,000; Per Subs 24
Automation Activity & Vendor Info: (Acquisitions) Follett Software; (Cataloging) Follett Software; (Circulation) Follett Software; (ILL) Follett Software; (Media Booking) Follett Software; (OPAC) Follett Software; (Serials) Follett Software
Partic in Lakeland Library Cooperative
Open Mon 3-8, Tues 9-11:30 & 1-5, Wed & Thurs 1-5, Sat 9-11:30

IOWA CITY

S ACT INFORMATION RESOURCE CENTER*, 200 ACT Dr, 52243. (Mail add: PO Box 168, 52243-0168), SAN 305-4772. Tel: 319-337-1166. FAX: 319-337-1538. *Mgr,* Jacqueline Snider; Staff 3 (MLS 1, Non-MLS 2)
Founded 1968
Library Holdings: Bk Titles 30,000; Per Subs 600
Special Collections: ERIC Coll
Subject Interests: Educ
Function: ILL available, Ref serv available
Partic in OCLC Online Computer Library Center, Inc
Restriction: Co libr, Not open to pub

P IOWA CITY PUBLIC LIBRARY*, 123 S Linn St, 52240. SAN 305-4780. Tel: 319-356-5200. FAX: 319-356-5494. Web Site: www.icpl.org. *Dir,* Susan Craig; Tel: 319-356-5241, E-mail: scraig@icpl.org; *Dir of Develop,* Patty McCarthy; Tel: 319-356-5249, E-mail: pmccarthy@icpl.org; *Admin Coordr,* Elyse Miller; Tel: 319-887-6003, E-mail: emiller@icpl.org; *Adult Serv Coordr,* Maeve Clark; Tel: 319-887-6004, E-mail: maeve-clark@icpl.org; *Children's Serv Coordr,* Vicki Pasicznyuk; Tel: 319-887-6019, E-mail: vickie-pasicznyuk@icpl.org; *Coordr, Coll Serv,* Anne Mangano; Tel: 319-887-6006, E-mail: anne-mangano@icpl.org; *Commun & Access Serv Coordr,* Kara Logsden; Tel: 319-887-6007, E-mail: kara-logsden@icpl.org; *IT Coordr,* Brent Palmer, Tel: 319-887-6035, E-mail: brent palmer@icpl.org; Staff 42 (MLS 15, Non MLS 27)
Founded 1896. Pop 67,862; Circ 1,512,852
Library Holdings: AV Mats 40,887; Electronic Media & Resources 53; Bk Vols 195,036; Per Subs 546
Automation Activity & Vendor Info: (Acquisitions) Innovative Interfaces, Inc; (Cataloging) Innovative Interfaces, Inc; (Circulation) Innovative Interfaces, Inc; (ILL) Innovative Interfaces, Inc; (OPAC) Innovative Interfaces, Inc; (Serials) Innovative Interfaces, Inc
Database Vendor: Innovative Interfaces, Inc
Wireless access
Function: Audio & video playback equip for onsite use, Audiobks via web, AV serv, Bks on cassette, Bks on CD, CD-ROM, Children's prog, Computer training, Computers for patron use, Copy machines, e-mail serv, Electronic databases & coll, Free DVD rentals, Handicapped accessible, Holiday prog, Home delivery & serv to Sr ctr & nursing homes, Homebound delivery serv, Homework prog, ILL available, Jail serv, Mail & tel request accepted, Mail loans to mem, Music CDs, Online cat, Online ref, Online searches, OverDrive digital audio bks, Photocopying/Printing, Preschool outreach, Prog for adults, Prog for children & young adult, Ref serv available, Senior outreach, Spoken cassettes & CDs, Spoken cassettes & DVDs, Summer reading prog, Tax forms, Teen prog, Telephone ref, VHS videos, Video lending libr, Web-catalog, Wheelchair accessible, Workshops, Writing prog
Publications: Window (Newsletter)
Open Mon-Thurs 10-9, Fri 10-8, Sat 10-6, Sun 12-5

S STATE HISTORICAL SOCIETY OF IOWA, Iowa City Library, 402 Iowa Ave, 52240-1806. SAN 305-4802. Tel: 319-335-3916. FAX: 319-335-3935. Web Site: www.iowahistory.org. *Spec Coll Librn,* Mary Bennett; Staff 7 (MLS 4, Non-MLS 3)
Founded 1857
Jul 2007-Jun 2008 Income $1,352,449. Mats Exp $101,529, Books $17,681, Per/Ser (Incl. Access Fees) $6,204, Micro $77,644. Sal $1,156,604
Special Collections: Manuscripts; Photo Archives
Subject Interests: Agr, Civil law, Genealogy, Hist, Iowa, Labor law, Maps, Women's hist
Automation Activity & Vendor Info: (Cataloging) Ex Libris Group
Wireless access
Function: Res libr
Partic in OCLC Online Computer Library Center, Inc
Open Thurs-Sat 9-4:30
Restriction: Non-circulating to the pub, Not a lending libr

UNIVERSITY OF IOWA

C BLOMMERS MEASUREMENT RESOURCES LIBRARY*, 304 Lindquist Ctr, 52242-1587, SAN 322-6840. Tel: 319-335-5416. FAX: 319-335-6038. Web Site: www.education.uiowa.edu/itp/blommers. *Librn,* Anna Marie Guengerich; E-mail: anna-guengerich@uiowa.edu; Staff 2 (MLS 1, Non-MLS 1)
Founded 1973
Library Holdings: Bk Titles 4,000; Per Subs 40
Special Collections: Current Tests; Historical Tests
Subject Interests: Educ testing, Measurements, Statistics
Automation Activity & Vendor Info: (Cataloging) Follett Software; (Circulation) Follett Software; (OPAC) Follett Software; (Serials) Follett Software
Open Mon-Fri 8-12 & 1-5

C SOJOURNER TRUTH LIBRARY*, 130 N Madison, 52242, SAN 325-7304. Tel: 319-335-1486. FAX: 319-353-1985. E-mail: wrac@uiowa.edu. Web Site: www.uiowa.edu/~wrac/library. *Dir,* Linda Kroon; E-mail: linda-kroon@uiowa.edu
Library Holdings: Bk Vols 500
Subject Interests: Eating disorders, Family, Gender, Health, Money, Safety
Open Mon-Fri 9-5

CM UNIVERSITY OF IOWA HOSPITALS & CLINICS*, Patients Library, 8016 JCP, 200 Hawkins Dr, 52242-1046. SAN 305-4829. Tel: 319-356-2468. FAX: 319-353-8793. Web Site: www.uihealthcare.com/patlib. *Dir,* Mindwell S Egeland; Tel: 319-384-8908, E-mail: mindwell-egeland@uiowa.edu; Staff 2 (MLS 1, Non-MLS 1)
Founded 1932
Library Holdings: Bk Titles 11,000
Special Collections: Consumer Health Information; Popular recreational materials
Subject Interests: Consumer health
Automation Activity & Vendor Info: (OPAC) Follett Software
Database Vendor: Gale Cengage Learning
Function: Telephone ref
Open Mon-Fri 9-4, Sat & Sun 1-4

C UNIVERSITY OF IOWA LIBRARIES*, 100 Main Library, 125 W Washington St, 52242-1420. SAN 341-8928. Circulation Tel: 319-335-5912. Interlibrary Loan Service Tel: 319-335-5917. Reference Tel: 319-335-5429. Administration Tel: 319-335-5867. Automation Services Tel: 319-384-4778. Information Services Tel: 319-335-5299. Interlibrary Loan Service FAX: 319-335-5830. Administration FAX: 319-335-5900. E-mail: lib-ref@uiowa.edu. Web Site: www.lib.uiowa.edu. *Univ Librn,* John P Culshaw; E-mail: john-culshaw@uiowa.edu; *Assoc Univ Librn & Dir, Libr Info Tech,* Paul Soderdahl; E-mail: paul-soderdahl@uiowa.edu; *Interim Assoc Univ Librn & Dir, Coll & Scholarly Communication,* Michael Wright; E-mail: michael-wright@uiowa.edu; *Interim Assoc Univ Librn & Dir, Serv,* David Martin; Staff 173 (MLS 60, Non-MLS 113)
Founded 1855. Enrl 29,642; Fac 1,690; Highest Degree: Doctorate
Special Collections: State Document Depository; UN Document Depository; US Document Depository
Automation Activity & Vendor Info: (Acquisitions) Ex Libris Group
Wireless access
Partic in Association of Research Libraries (ARL); OCLC Online Computer Library Center, Inc
Friends of the Library Group

Departmental Libraries:

ART, 235 Art Bldg W, 141 N Riverside Dr, 52242, SAN 341-8952. Tel: 319-335-3089. FAX: 319-335-5900. E-mail: lib-art@uiowa.edu. Web Site: www.lib.uiowa.edu/art. *Head Librn,* Rijn Templeton; E-mail: rijn-templeton@uiowa.edu
Library Holdings: Bk Vols 132,000
Friends of the Library Group

RITA BENTON MUSIC LIBRARY, 2006 Main Library, 52242, SAN 341-9258. Tel: 319-335-3086. E-mail: lib-mus@uiowa.edu. Web Site: www.lib.uiowa.edu/music/. *Librn,* Position Currently Open
Enrl 30,000; Highest Degree: Doctorate

Library Holdings: Bk Vols 99,484
Friends of the Library Group

CL COLLEGE OF LAW LIBRARY, 200 Boyd Law Bldg, 52242-1166, SAN 341-9169. Tel: 319-335-9002. Reference Tel: 319-335-9005. FAX: 319-335-9039. Reference E-mail: lawlib-ref@uiowa.edu. Web Site: www.law.uiowa.edu/library. *Assoc Dean, Res,* Arthur E Bonfield; Tel: 319-335-9020, E-mail: arthur-bonfield@uiowa.edu; *Head, Continuing Coll,* Sherri Bethke; Tel: 319-335-9041, E-mail: sherri-bethke@uiowa.edu; *Head, Pub Serv,* Ted Potter; Tel: 319-335-9017, E-mail: ted-potter@uiowa.edu; *Circ Librn, ILL Librn,* John Bergstrom; Tel: 319-335-9015, E-mail: john-bergstrom@uiowa.edu; *Conbtiuning Coll Librn,* Virginia Melroy; Tel: 319-335-9077, E-mail: virginia-melroy@uiowa.edu; *Intl Law Librn,* Don Ford; Tel: 319-335-9068, E-mail: donald-ford@uiowa.edu; *Bibliographer, Ref Librn,* Druet Cameron-Klugh; Tel: 319-335-9038, E-mail: druet-klugh@uiowa.edu; *Ref Librn,* Ellen Jones; Tel: 319-335-6829, E-mail: ellen-jones@uiowa.edu; *Collection Access Mgt,* Karen Nobbs; Tel: 319-335-9029, E-mail: karen-nobbs@uiowa.edu; Staff 14 (MLS 14)
Founded 1868. Enrl 680; Fac 44; Highest Degree: Doctorate
Library Holdings: Bk Vols 1,200,000; Per Subs 9,500
Special Collections: UN Doc (Readex Coll). US Document Depository
Subject Interests: Environ studies, Law
Partic in Committee on Institutional Cooperation; National Network of Libraries of Medicine South Central Region; OCLC Online Computer Library Center, Inc; RLIN (Research Libraries Information Network)
Publications: Law Library User's Guide; News Briefs
Open Mon-Thurs 7:30am-Midnight, Fri 7:30am-10pm, Sat 9am-10pm, Sun Noon-Midnight

ENGINEERING, 2001 Seamans Center, 52242-1420. Tel: 319-335-6047. FAX: 319-335-5900. E-mail: lib-engineering@uiowa.edu. Web Site: www.lib.uiowa.edu/eng/. *Librn,* John W Forys, Jr; E-mail: john-forys@uiowa.edu
Library Holdings: Bk Vols 109,563
Friends of the Library Group

CM HARDIN LIBRARY FOR THE HEALTH SCIENCES, 600 Newton Rd, 52242, SAN 341-9134. Tel: 319-335-9871. Interlibrary Loan Service Tel: 319-335-9874. Information Services Tel: 319-335-9151. FAX: 319-353-3752. E-mail: lib-hardin@uiowa.edu. Web Site: www.lib.uiowa.edu/hardin. *Assoc Univ Librn, Dir,* Linda Walton; E-mail: linda-walton@uiowa.edu; *Asst Dir,* Janna Lawrence; E-mail: janna-lawrence@uiowa.edu
Founded 1882
Library Holdings: Bk Vols 285,241
Subject Interests: Hist of med
Partic in National Network of Libraries of Medicine South Central Region
Publications: Heirs of Hippocrates
Friends of the Library Group

MARVIN A POMERANTZ BUSINESS LIBRARY, 10 E Jefferson St, 52242, SAN 341-8987. Tel: 319-335-3077. FAX: 319-335-3752. E-mail: lib-bus@uiowa.edu. Web Site: www.lib.uiowa.edu/biz/. *Head Librn,* J David Martin; E-mail: j-martin@uiowa.edu
Library Holdings: Bk Vols 32,989
Friends of the Library Group

SCIENCES, 120 Iowa Ave, 52242-1325, SAN 341-9312. Tel: 319-335-3083. FAX: 319-335-2698. E-mail: lib-sciences@uiowa.edu. Web Site: www.lib.uiowa.edu/sciences/. *Head Librn,* Leo Clougherty; E-mail: leo-clougherty@uiowa.edu
Library Holdings: Bk Vols 46,541
Friends of the Library Group

IOWA FALLS

P ROBERT W BARLOW MEMORIAL LIBRARY*, 921 Washington Ave, 50126. SAN 305-4845. Tel: 641-648-2872. FAX: 641-648-2872. Web Site: www.iowafalls.lib.ia.us. *Dir,* Terry Tikovitsch; E-mail: terryt@iowafalls.lib.ia.us; *Asst Dir,* Nancy Hoffman; *Ch,* Judy Afdahl
Founded 1896. Pop 6,100; Circ 76,000
Library Holdings: Bk Titles 52,000; Per Subs 170
Special Collections: Travel Guides
Automation Activity & Vendor Info: (Cataloging) TLC (The Library Corporation); (Circulation) TLC (The Library Corporation); (OPAC) TLC (The Library Corporation)
Open Mon-Thurs 9-8, Fri & Sat 10-5, Sun 1-5
Friends of the Library Group

J ELLSWORTH COMMUNITY COLLEGE*, Osgood Library, 1100 College Ave, 50126-1199. SAN 305-4853. Tel: 641-648-4611, Ext 233. FAX: 641-648-3128. E-mail: ecclib@iavalley.edu. *Mgr,* Sandra Greufe
Founded 1890. Enrl 950
Library Holdings: Bk Titles 24,689; Bk Vols 25,664; Per Subs 240
Partic in Iowa Higher Educ Instrul Resource Consortia
Open Mon-Thurs 7:30-9:30, Fri 7:30-3:30, Sun 5-9

IRWIN

P LIED IRWIN PUBLIC LIBRARY*, 509 Ann St, 51446. (Mail add: PO Box 255, 51446-0255). Tel: 712-782-3335. FAX: 712-782-3335. E-mail: irwinlibrarian@yahoo.com. Web Site: www.irwinlibrary.com. *Dir,* Karen Plagman
Pop 372
Library Holdings: Bk Vols 2,506
Open Wed & Sat 11-2, Thurs & Fri 2-5

JAMAICA

P JAMAICA PUBLIC LIBRARY*, 316 Main St, 50128. (Mail add: PO Box 122, 50128-0122), SAN 305-4861. Tel: 641-429-3362. FAX: 641-429-3362. *Librn,* Dana Lowry
Founded 1948. Pop 237; Circ 3,994
Library Holdings: Bk Titles 6,500; Per Subs 12; Talking Bks 100
Subject Interests: Genealogy, Local hist
Open Mon-Wed 1-6, Thurs 9am-11am
Friends of the Library Group

JANESVILLE

P JANESVILLE PUBLIC LIBRARY*, 227 Main St, 50647. (Mail add: PO Box 328, 50647-0328), SAN 305-487X. Tel: 319-987-2925. FAX: 319-987-2925. E-mail: janesvillelibrary@mchsi.com. Web Site: www.janesville.lib.ia.us. *Dir,* Beth Ann Scott
Pop 825; Circ 15,783
Library Holdings: Audiobooks 27; DVDs 829; Bk Vols 9,898; Per Subs 53; Videos 321
Automation Activity & Vendor Info: (Acquisitions) Follett Software; (Cataloging) Follett Software; (Circulation) Follett Software; (ILL) Follett Software; (Media Booking) Follett Software; (OPAC) Follett Software; (Serials) Follett Software
Wireless access
Open Mon, Tues & Thurs 12-6, Wed 10-6, Fri 1-5, Sat 9-12

JEFFERSON

P JEFFERSON PUBLIC LIBRARY, 200 W Lincoln Way, 50129-2185. SAN 305-4888. Tel: 515-386-2835. FAX: 515-386-8163. E-mail: jeflib@netins.net. Web Site: www.jefferson.lib.ia.us. *Dir,* Jane Millard; *Ch,* Terry Clark
Founded 1903. Pop 4,600; Circ 80,000
Library Holdings: Bk Titles 45,000; Per Subs 60
Special Collections: Greene County. Oral History
Subject Interests: Genealogy
Automation Activity & Vendor Info: (Cataloging) Innovative Interfaces, Inc; (Circulation) Innovative Interfaces, Inc; (OPAC) Innovative Interfaces, Inc
Database Vendor: OCLC FirstSearch
Wireless access
Open Mon & Wed 1-8, Tues & Thurs 11-8, Fri 1-5:30 Sat 9-1
Friends of the Library Group

JESUP

P JESUP PUBLIC LIBRARY*, 721 Sixth St, 50648-0585. (Mail add: PO Box 585, 50648-0585), SAN 305-4896. Tel: 319-827-1533. FAX: 319-827-1580. Web Site: www.jesup.lib.ia.us. *Dir,* Cynthia A Lellig; E-mail: clellig@jesup.lib.ia.us; *Asst Librn,* Julia Darby; *Ch,* Candy Lompe; Staff 3 (Non-MLS 3)
Pop 2,299; Circ 33,453
Jul 2009-Jun 2010 Income $111,152, State $5,288, City $84,230, County $17,962, Locally Generated Income $1,742, Other $1,930. Mats Exp $20,004, Books $11,798, Per/Ser (Incl. Access Fees) $1,625, AV Equip $2,343, AV Mat $4,238. Sal $72,027 (Prof $72,027)
Library Holdings: Audiobooks 561; CDs 288; DVDs 150; Large Print Bks 368; Bk Titles 18,526; Per Subs 56; Videos 376
Automation Activity & Vendor Info: (Cataloging) Follett Software; (Circulation) Follett Software
Wireless access
Open Mon, Wed & Fri 11-6, Tues & Thurs 11-8, Sat 10-2
Friends of the Library Group

JEWELL

P MONTGOMERY MEMORIAL LIBRARY*, 711 Main St, 50130. (Mail add: PO Box 207, 50130-0207), SAN 305-490X. Tel: 515-827-5112. FAX: 515-827-5112. E-mail: jewell-library@globalccs.net. Web Site: www.jewell.lib.ia.us. *Dir,* Kris Koehnk; *Asst Librn,* Marcia Wheeler; E-mail: mwheeler@jewell.lib.ia.us; *Ch,* Roseann Amundson; E-mail: ramundson@jewell.lib.ia.us
Founded 1947. Pop 1,200
Special Collections: History of Hamilton County, Jewell Township

Automation Activity & Vendor Info: (Cataloging) Follett Software; (Circulation) Follett Software
Open Mon-Wed 1-7, Thurs & Fri 10-5, Sat 10-1

JOHNSTON

P JOHNSTON PUBLIC LIBRARY*, 6700 Merle Hay Rd, 50131-0327. (Mail add: PO Box 327, 50131-0327), SAN 376-5458. Tel: 515-278-5233. FAX: 515-278-4975. E-mail: info@johnstonlibrary.com. Web Site: www.johnstonlibrary.com. *Dir,* Willona Goers; E-mail: goers@johnstonlibrary.com; *Asst Dir,* Maurine Myers; E-mail: myers@johnstonlibrary.com; *Ch,* Kinney Carnahan; E-mail: carnahan@johnstonlibrary.com; *Teen Librn,* Jessica Young; *Pub Serv,* Cheryl Heid; E-mail: heid@johnstonlibrary.com; Staff 13.5 (MLS 2, Non-MLS 11.5)
Founded 1988. Pop 17,285; Circ 309,405
Jul 2009-Jun 2010 Income $1,048,850, State $28,372, City $931,974, County $61,892, Locally Generated Income $24,648, Other $1,964. Mats Exp $103,428, Books $60,494, Per/Ser (Incl. Access Fees) $4,148, AV Mat $31,469, Electronic Ref Mat (Incl. Access Fees) $7,317. Sal $562,760 (Prof $168,000)
Library Holdings: Audiobooks 11,000; CDs 5,000; DVDs 4,818; Electronic Media & Resources 4,200; Bk Vols 62,609; Per Subs 198; Videos 100
Automation Activity & Vendor Info: (Cataloging) SirsiDynix; (Circulation) SirsiDynix
Database Vendor: EBSCOhost, Facts on File, Ingram Library Services, LearningExpress, OCLC FirstSearch, SirsiDynix, ValueLine, World Book Online
Wireless access
Mem of Central Iowa Library Services
Open Mon-Thurs 10-8, Fri & Sat 10-5:30, Sun 1-5
Friends of the Library Group

S PIONEER HI-BRED INTERNATIONAL, INC*, Research Library, 7300 NW 62nd Ave, 50131. (Mail add: PO Box 1004, 50131-9412), SAN 324-7120. Tel: 515-535-4199. FAX: 515-535-2184. Web Site: www.pioneer.com. *Librn,* Ken Braun; Tel: 515-535-4818, E-mail: ken.braun@pioneer.com; *Mgr,* Dana Smith; E-mail: dana.smith@pioneer.com; Staff 4 (MLS 2, Non-MLS 2)
Founded 1983
Library Holdings: Bk Titles 1,700; Per Subs 220
Subject Interests: Agr, Law, Plant genetics
Automation Activity & Vendor Info: (Acquisitions) EOS International; (Cataloging) EOS International; (Circulation) EOS International; (OPAC) EOS International; (Serials) EOS International
Wireless access
Function: ILL available
Restriction: Co libr

JOICE

P JOICE PUBLIC LIBRARY*, 201 Main St, 50446. (Mail add: PO Box 183, 50446-0183), SAN 305-4918. Tel: 641-588-3330. FAX: 641-588-3330. E-mail: jhawks@wctatel.net. *Dir,* Mary Hrubetz
Pop 3,500; Circ 6,000
Library Holdings: Bk Titles 5,000; Bk Vols 7,000; Per Subs 17; Videos 645
Automation Activity & Vendor Info: (Acquisitions) Follett Software; (Cataloging) Follett Software; (Circulation) Follett Software; (ILL) Follett Software; (Media Booking) Follett Software; (OPAC) Follett Software; (Serials) Follett Software
Wireless access
Open Tues 9-12 & 1-6, Wed & Thurs 1-6, Fri 2-5, Sat 9-11

KALONA

P KALONA PUBLIC LIBRARY*, 510 C Ave, 52247. (Mail add: PO Box 1212, 52247-1212), SAN 305-4926. Tel: 319-656-3501. FAX: 319-656-3503. Web Site: www.kalona.lib.ia.us. *Dir,* Anne Skaden; E-mail: askaden@kalona.lib.ia.us
Pop 2,200; Circ 26,729
Library Holdings: Bk Titles 16,000; Per Subs 50
Subject Interests: Amish
Automation Activity & Vendor Info: (Cataloging) ComPanion Corp; (Circulation) ComPanion Corp
Wireless access
Open Mon-Thurs 9:30-8, Fri 9:30-5, Sat 9:30-3
Friends of the Library Group

KANAWHA

P KANAWHA PUBLIC LIBRARY, 120 N Main, 50447. (Mail add: PO Box 148, 50447-0148), SAN 305-4934. Tel: 641-762-3595. FAX: 641-762-3966. E-mail: norby@comm1net.net. Web Site: www.youseemore.com/nilc/Kanawha. *Dir,* Christine Guthmiller
Pop 652; Circ 8,321
Library Holdings: Audiobooks 155; DVDs 785; e-books 8,200; Electronic Media & Resources 7; Bk Titles 8,337; Per Subs 38; Talking Bks 4,080
Automation Activity & Vendor Info: (Cataloging) TLC (The Library Corporation); (Circulation) TLC (The Library Corporation); (ILL) TLC (The Library Corporation); (OPAC) TLC (The Library Corporation)
Database Vendor: EBSCOhost
Wireless access
Open Mon & Fri 11-5:30, Wed 11-6, Sat 9-Noon

KENSETT

P KENSETT PUBLIC LIBRARY*, 214 Fifth St, 50448. (Mail add: PO Box 55, 50448-0055), SAN 305-4942. Tel: 641-845-2222. FAX: 641-845-2222. E-mail: kensettlibrary@mchsi.com. *Librn,* Barbara Luckason
Pop 280; Circ 7,200
Library Holdings: Bk Titles 6,400; Per Subs 27
Open Mon-Thurs 2:30-6:30, Sat 9-1

KEOKUK

M KEOKUK AREA HOSPITAL*, Health Science Library, 1600 Morgan St, 52632. Tel: 319-524-7150. FAX: 319-524-5317. Web Site: www.keokuthealthsystems.org. *Dir, Libr Serv,* Dixie Fink
Library Holdings: Bk Vols 1,500; Per Subs 45
Open Mon-Fri 8-4:30
Restriction: Staff use only

P KEOKUK PUBLIC LIBRARY*, 210 N Fifth St, 52632. SAN 305-4950. Tel: 319-524-1483. FAX: 319-524-2320. E-mail: keokukpl@keokuk.lib.ia.us. Web Site: www.keokuk.lib.ia.us. *Dir,* Emily Rohlfs; E-mail: erohlfs@keokuk.lib.ia.us; Staff 1 (MLS 1)
Founded 1893. Pop 10,511; Circ 90,398
Library Holdings: Bk Titles 70,000; Per Subs 200
Subject Interests: Local hist
Open Mon-Thurs 9-8 (9-7 Summer), Fri 9-5, Sat 9-3

KEOSAUQUA

P KEOSAUQUA PUBLIC LIBRARY*, 608 First St, 52565. (Mail add: PO Box 160, 52565-0160), SAN 305-4977. Tel: 319-293-3766. FAX: 319-293-3766. E-mail: keolib@netins.net. Web Site: www.keosauqua.ia.lib.us *Libr Dir,* Nicole Annis; *Ch,* Darlea Westercamp; *Ref Librn,* Michael Miller. Subject Specialists: *Cataloging,* Darlea Westercamp; *Genealogy,* Michael Miller
Founded 1910. Pop 1,020; Circ 18,450
Library Holdings: Audiobooks 300; DVDs 375; Large Print Bks 200; Bk Titles 17,000
Subject Interests: Genealogy, Iowa, Natural hist
Automation Activity & Vendor Info: (Acquisitions) Baker & Taylor; (Cataloging) Follett Software; (Circulation) Follett Software; (ILL) Follett Software
Database Vendor: Baker & Taylor, Booklist Online, EBSCOhost, OCLC FirstSearch, OCLC WebJunction, OCLC WorldShare Interlibrary Loan
Wireless access
Special Services for the Deaf - Closed caption videos
Open Mon, Tues & Fri 1-5, Wed 1-8, Thurs 10-5, Sat 10-1

KEOTA

P WILSON MEMORIAL LIBRARY*, 109 E Washington Ave, 52248. SAN 305-4985. Tel: 641-636-3850. FAX: 641-636-3050. E-mail: wilsonlib@keota.lib.ia.us. Web Site: www.keota.lib.ia.us. *Dir,* Juli Hisel; E-mail: jhisel@keota.lib.ia.us
Founded 1877. Pop 1,100; Circ 15,000
Library Holdings: Bk Titles 11,617; Bk Vols 11,741; Per Subs 16
Automation Activity & Vendor Info: (Cataloging) Follett Software; (Circulation) Follett Software; (OPAC) Follett Software; (Serials) Follett Software
Wireless access
Open Mon-Wed 11-6, Thurs & Fri 10-5, Sat 10-3

KEYSTONE

P SCHROEDER PUBLIC LIBRARY*, 93 Main St, 52249. (Mail add: PO Box 305, 52249-0305), SAN 305-4993. Tel: 319-442-3329. FAX: 319-442-3327. E-mail: keystnpl@netins.net. Web Site: www.keystone.lib.ia.us. *Dir,* Pat Jans; *Librn,* Laura Hopper; Staff 1 (Non-MLS 1)
Pop 622; Circ 12,630
Library Holdings: Audiobooks 322; CDs 115; DVDs 726; Large Print Bks 150; Bk Titles 6,773; Per Subs 64; Videos 100
Automation Activity & Vendor Info: (Acquisitions) Book Systems; (Cataloging) Book Systems; (Circulation) Book Systems; (OPAC) Book Systems
Wireless access

Mem of Northeast Iowa Library Services
Open Mon-Thurs 9-12 & 2-5, Fri 9-12 & 2-6, Sat 9-12

KIMBALLTON

P KIMBALLTON PUBLIC LIBRARY*, 118 Main St, 51543. (Mail add: PO Box 67, 51543-0067), SAN 305-5000. Tel: 712-773-3002. *Dir,* Rose Anne Poldberg
Pop 1,000
Library Holdings: Bk Vols 7,000; Per Subs 36
Mem of Southwest Iowa Library Services District
Open Mon-Fri 1-5

KINGSLEY

P KINGSLEY PUBLIC LIBRARY, 220 Main St, 51028. (Mail add: PO Box 400, 51028-0400), SAN 305-5019. Tel: 712-378-2410. FAX: 712-378-2410. E-mail: library@wiatel.net. Web Site: kingsleylibrary.com. *Dir,* Marilyn Lindgren
Founded 1966. Pop 1,500; Circ 30,804
Library Holdings: Bk Titles 17,595; Per Subs 41
Wireless access
Mem of Northwest Iowa Library Services
Open Mon 9:30-11:30, 1-5 & 7-9, Tues-Fri 9:30-11:30 & 1-5, Sat 8:30-12

KLEMME

P KLEMME PUBLIC LIBRARY, 204 E Main St, 50449. (Mail add: PO Box 275, 50449-0275), SAN 305-5027. Tel: 641-587-2369. FAX: 866-380-3876. E-mail: klemlibr@comm1net.net. Web Site: www1.youseemore.com/nilc/klemme. *Dir,* Kathy Olthoff
Founded 1967. Pop 509; Circ 4,865
Library Holdings: Bk Vols 8,000; Per Subs 60
Automation Activity & Vendor Info: (Acquisitions) Follett Software; (Cataloging) Follett Software; (Circulation) Follett Software; (ILL) Follett Software; (Media Booking) Follett Software; (OPAC) Follett Software; (Serials) Follett Software
Wireless access
Open Mon-Wed & Fri 10-12 & 1-5, Thurs 10-12 & 1-6, Sat 9am-11pm

KNOXVILLE

P KNOXVILLE PUBLIC LIBRARY*, 213 E Montgomery St, 50138-2296. SAN 305-5035. Tel: 641-828-0585. FAX: 641-828-0513. E-mail: knoxlib@mediacombb.net. Web Site: www.knoxville.lib.ia.us. *Dir,* Roslin I Thompson; *Asst Dir,* Staci Stanton; E-mail: stantons@iowatelecom.net; *Youth Serv Librn,* Holly A Shelford. Subject Specialists: *Lit,* Roslin I Thompson; *Elem educ,* Holly A Shelford; Staff 9 (MLS 1, Non-MLS 8)
Founded 1912. Pop 7,731; Circ 119,146
Jul 2006-Jun 2007 Income $248,502, State $5,170, City $199,943, County $26,871, Locally Generated Income $11,084, Other $5,434. Mats Exp $32,506, Books $21,903, Per/Ser (Incl. Access Fees) $4,507, AV Mat $6,096. Sal $110,617 (Prof $46,146)
Library Holdings: AV Mats 4,404; CDs 521; DVDs 489; Large Print Bks 1,795; Bk Vols 26,544; Per Subs 123; Talking Bks 1,719; Videos 2,067
Automation Activity & Vendor Info: (Cataloging) TLC (The Library Corporation); (Circulation) TLC (The Library Corporation); (OPAC) TLC (The Library Corporation)
Database Vendor: EBSCOhost, Newsbank, OCLC FirstSearch
Wireless access
Function: Handicapped accessible, Home delivery & serv to Sr ctr & nursing homes, ILL available, Photocopying/Printing, Prog for children & young adult, Summer reading prog, Wheelchair accessible
Open Mon-Thurs 10-8, Fri 10-5, Sat 10-3, Sun (Sept-May) 2-4
Friends of the Library Group

GM VETERANS AFFAIRS CENTRAL IOWA HEALTH CARE SYSTEMS*, Medical Center Library - 142D, 1515 W Pleasant St, 50138-3399. SAN 305-5043. Tel: 641-828-5127. FAX: 641-828-5084. *Librn,* Judith L Gottshall; E-mail: judith.gottshall@med.va.gov; Staff 1 (MLS 1)
Founded 1924
Library Holdings: Bk Titles 7,000
Subject Interests: Allied health, Psychiat, Psychol
Database Vendor: EBSCOhost, OCLC FirstSearch
Open Mon-Fri 7:45-4:30

LA PORTE CITY

P HAWKINS MEMORIAL LIBRARY*, 308 Main St, 50651. SAN 305-5051. Tel: 319-342-3025. FAX: 319-342-3025. *Dir,* Laura Hammersley; E-mail: lhammersley@laportecity.lib.ia.us; *Ch,* Elaine Gross
Founded 1945. Pop 2,200; Circ 21,712
Library Holdings: Bk Vols 19,280; Per Subs 65
Open Mon 8-4, Tues, Thurs & Fri 1-6, Sat 9-1

LACONA

P LACONA PUBLIC LIBRARY*, 107 E Main, 50139. (Mail add: PO Box 75, 50139-1014), SAN 376-5466. Tel: 641-534-4400. FAX: 641-534-4430. E-mail: laconalibrary@iowatelecom.net. Web Site: www.lacona.lib.ia.us. *Dir,* Kate Cloudsparks
Library Holdings: Audiobooks 60; DVDs 300; Bk Vols 7,400; Per Subs 24
Special Collections: Lacona History/Genealogy; Warren/Marion/Lucas Cty, births. marriages, obits
Database Vendor: EBSCOhost
Wireless access
Mem of Central Iowa Library Services
Open Mon 3-6, Tues 11-5, Wed Noon-3, Thurs 3-8, Sat 9-Noon
Friends of the Library Group

LAKE CITY

P LAKE CITY PUBLIC LIBRARY*, 110 E Washington St, 51449-1718. SAN 305-506X. Tel: 712-464-3413. FAX: 712-464-3413. Web Site: www.lakecity.lib.ia.us. *Dir,* Michele Deluhery; E-mail: director@lakecity.lib.ia.us; *Asst Dir,* Kim Olson; *Asst Librn,* Justina Wuebker; *Ch,* Vicki Tasler
Founded 1901. Pop 3,200; Circ 25,819
Library Holdings: Bk Vols 17,000; Per Subs 60
Wireless access
Function: Adult bk club, Art exhibits, Audiobks via web, Bks on CD, CD-ROM, Children's prog, Computer training, Computers for patron use, Copy machines, Free DVD rentals, Handicapped accessible, Home delivery & serv to Sr ctr & nursing homes, ILL available, Magnifiers for reading, Music CDs, Online cat, Photocopying/Printing, Preschool reading prog, Prog for adults, Prog for children & young adult, Pub access computers, Scanner, Senior computer classes, Senior outreach, Spoken cassettes & CDs, Summer reading prog, Tax forms, Teen prog, Video lending libr, Web-catalog, Wheelchair accessible
Mem of Northwest Iowa Library Services
Open Mon & Fri 12:30-5:30, Tues, Wed & Thurs 9-8, Sat 9-12
Friends of the Library Group

LAKE MILLS

P LAKE MILLS PUBLIC LIBRARY*, 102 S Lake St, 50450. SAN 305-5078. Tel: 641-592-0092. FAX: 641-592-0093. Web Site: www.lakemills.lib.ia.us. *Dir,* Toni Johnson; E-mail: director@lakemills.lib.ia.us; *Asst Dir,* Melissa Johanson
Pop 2,281; Circ 31,000
Library Holdings: Bk Titles 26,000; Per Subs 64
Automation Activity & Vendor Info: (Acquisitions) TLC (The Library Corporation); (Cataloging) TLC (The Library Corporation); (Circulation) TLC (The Library Corporation)
Database Vendor: TLC (The Library Corporation)
Wireless access
Open Mon-Thurs 10-12 & 1-7, Fri 10-12 & 1-6, Sat 9-1

LAKE PARK

P LAKE PARK PUBLIC LIBRARY*, 905 S Market St, 51347. (Mail add: PO Box 344, 51347-0344), SAN 305-5086. Tel: 712-832-9505. FAX: 712-832-9507. E-mail: lpplibrary@mchsi.com. Web Site: www.lakepark.lib.ia.us. *Libr Dir,* Diane Duitsman; *Libr Asst,* Pam Kruger
Founded 1922. Pop 1,023; Circ 6,066
Library Holdings: AV Mats 270; Large Print Bks 50; Bk Titles 7,700; Per Subs 35; Talking Bks 15
Automation Activity & Vendor Info: (Acquisitions) Follett Software; (OPAC) Follett Software
Wireless access
Partic in Northeast Iowa Library Services Erate Consortia
Open Tues 9:30-12 & 12:30-6, Wed-Fri 9:30-12 & 12:30-5:30, Sat 9-Noon
Friends of the Library Group

LAKE VIEW

P LAKE VIEW PUBLIC LIBRARY*, 202 Main St, 51450. (Mail add: PO Box 20, 51450-0020), SAN 305-5094. Tel: 712-657-2310. FAX: 712-657-2310. E-mail: lvl@netins.net. *Dir,* Kay Montano; *Asst Librn,* Paula Wilson
Founded 1920. Pop 1,301; Circ 25,398
Library Holdings: Audiobooks 828; Bk Titles 20,334; Per Subs 85; Videos 1,294
Special Collections: Civil War (Goffrey C Ward Coll), bk, v-tapes; Des Moines Register; Lake View Resort 1941-to-date (weekly paper); Library of America; Wall Street Journal
Mem of Northwest Iowa Library Services
Partic in OCLC Online Computer Library Center, Inc
Special Services for the Blind - Talking bks

Open Mon 10-12 & 2-8, Tues, Thurs & Fri 2-8, Wed 8:30-11:30 & 2-8, Sat 10-3
Friends of the Library Group

LAKOTA

P LAKOTA PUBLIC LIBRARY*, 204 Third St, 50451-7084. (Mail add: PO Box 178, 50451-0178), SAN 305-5108. Tel: 515-886-2312. FAX: 515-886-2312. Web Site: www.youseemore.com/NILC/Lakota. *Dir,* Susan Kearney; E-mail: susank@lakota.lib.ia.us
Pop 281; Circ 4,400
Jul 2010-Jun 2011 Income $19,653, State $1,550, City $4,509, County $12,444, Other $1,150. Mats Exp $19,653
Library Holdings: Audiobooks 45; CDs 109; DVDs 650; Bk Vols 5,090; Per Subs 29
Automation Activity & Vendor Info: (Acquisitions) TLC (The Library Corporation); (Cataloging) TLC (The Library Corporation); (Circulation) TLC (The Library Corporation); (ILL) TLC (The Library Corporation); (Media Booking) TLC (The Library Corporation); (OPAC) TLC (The Library Corporation); (Serials) TLC (The Library Corporation)
Database Vendor: EBSCOhost, OCLC FirstSearch, OCLC WorldShare Interlibrary Loan
Wireless access
Open Tues & Thurs 1-5 & 6pm-8pm, Wed 9-2, Sat 9-12

LAMONI

C GRACELAND UNIVERSITY*, Frederick Madison Smith Library, One University Pl, 50140. SAN 305-5116. Tel: 641-784-5301. Circulation Tel: 641-784-5361. Interlibrary Loan Service Tel: 641-784-5306. Administration Tel: 641-784-5302. Information Services Tel: 641-784-5303. FAX: 641-784-5497. E-mail: library@graceland.edu. Web Site: www.graceland.edu/academics/library. *Dir, Libr Serv,* Alisha Linam; E-mail: amlinam1@graceland.edu; *Coll Mgt, Govt Doc,* Marsha Jackel; E-mail: jackel@graceland.edu; *ILL, Per,* Betsy Folkins; Tel: 641-784-5483, E-mail: folkins@graceland.edu; Staff 8.5 (MLS 3, Non-MLS 5.5)
Founded 1895. Enrl 2,103; Fac 81; Highest Degree: Master
Jun 2008-May 2009 Income $536,539, Locally Generated Income $2,532, Parent Institution $534,007. Mats Exp $218,474, Books $37,284, Per/Ser (Incl. Access Fees) $160,654, Micro $5,334, AV Mat $1,660, Electronic Ref Mat (Incl. Access Fees) $11,548, Presv $1,994. Sal $231,543 (Prof $93,420)
Library Holdings: AV Mats 3,681; CDs 329; e-books 6,592; e-journals 479; Electronic Media & Resources 8,607; Microforms 131,737; Bk Titles 150,938; Bk Vols 194,765; Per Subs 558; Videos 1,352
Special Collections: Mormon History Manuscripts, bks & micro. State Document Depository; US Document Depository
Subject Interests: Allied health, Mormons, Nursing
Automation Activity & Vendor Info: (Acquisitions) Innovative Interfaces, Inc; (Cataloging) Innovative Interfaces, Inc; (Circulation) Innovative Interfaces, Inc; (Course Reserve) Innovative Interfaces, Inc; (ILL) OCLC; (OPAC) Innovative Interfaces, Inc; (Serials) Innovative Interfaces, Inc
Database Vendor: American Psychological Association (APA), Career Guidance Foundation, CredoReference, EBSCOhost, Elsevier, LexisNexis, Medline, Mergent Online, OCLC FirstSearch, OCLC WorldShare Interlibrary Loan, World Book Online
Wireless access
Function: Archival coll, Audio & video playback equip for onsite use, AV serv, Copy machines, Distance learning, Doc delivery serv, E-Reserves, Electronic databases & coll, ILL available, Online searches, Outside serv via phone, mail, e-mail & web, Photocopying/Printing, Ref serv available, Telephone ref, Video lending libr
Partic in OCLC Online Computer Library Center, Inc
Open Mon-Thurs (Winter) 8am-1:45am, Fri 8am-4:45pm, Sat 1pm-4:45pm, Sun 1pm-1:45am; Mon-Fri (Summer) 8-4:45

P LAMONI PUBLIC LIBRARY, 301 W Main St, 50140. SAN 305-5124. Tel: 641-784-6686. FAX: 641-784-6693. E-mail: lamonipl@grm.net. Web Site: www.lamoni.lib.ia.us. *Dir,* Rebecca Ramsey
Founded 1922. Pop 2,444; Circ 46,577
Library Holdings: AV Mats 1,513; Large Print Bks 881; Bk Titles 23,764; Bk Vols 25,000; Per Subs 36; Talking Bks 1,700
Automation Activity & Vendor Info: (Circulation) Follett Software
Mem of Southwest Iowa Library Services District
Open Mon, Wed & Fri 1-5:30, Tues 10:30-9, Thurs 10-5:30, Sat 10-1

LAMONT

P LAMONT PUBLIC LIBRARY*, 616 Bush St, 50650. (Mail add: PO Box 116, 50650-0116), SAN 305-5132. Tel: 563-924-3203. FAX: 563-924-3203. Web Site: www.lamont.lib.ia.us. *Librn,* Jane A Seedorff; E-mail: jseedorff@lamont.lib.ia.us
Pop 1,147; Circ 7,927
Library Holdings: Bk Titles 4,000; Per Subs 12
Open Tues, Thurs & Fri 1:30-5:30, Wed 2-7, Sat 8-12

LANSING

P MEEHAN MEMORIAL LANSING PUBLIC LIBRARY, 515 Main St, 52151. SAN 305-5140. Tel: 563-538-4693. FAX: 563-538-4693. E-mail: library@lansing.lib.ia.us. Web Site: www.lansing.lib.ia.us. *Dir,* Derva Burke
Pop 1,207; Circ 12,211
Library Holdings: Bk Vols 10,137; Per Subs 35; Talking Bks 266
Automation Activity & Vendor Info: (Acquisitions) ComPanion Corp; (Cataloging) ComPanion Corp; (Circulation) ComPanion Corp
Database Vendor: ComPanion Corp
Wireless access
Special Services for the Blind - Large print bks; Talking bks
Open Mon & Sat 9-Noon, Tues, Thurs & Fri 11-7
Friends of the Library Group

LARCHWOOD

P LARCHWOOD PUBLIC LIBRARY, 1020 Broadway, 51241. (Mail add: PO Box 97, 51241-0097), SAN 305-5159. Tel: 712-477-2583. FAX: 712-477-2572. E-mail: lpblib@alliancecom.net. *Dir,* Gayle L Bruns; *Asst Dir, Admin,* Kathy Sorlie; *Children's & Teen Serv Coordr,* Esther Knutson
Founded 1927. Pop 866
Jul 2013-Jun 2014 Income $63,911, State $2,279, City $43,099, County $15,283, Locally Generated Income $2,935, Other $315. Mats Exp $63,485, Books $6,436, Per/Ser (Incl. Access Fees) $573, AV Mat $3,500, Electronic Ref Mat (Incl. Access Fees) $371. Sal $30,698
Library Holdings: Audiobooks 1,161; DVDs 1,629; e-books 6,620; Bk Titles 14,172; Per Subs 31
Automation Activity & Vendor Info: (Acquisitions) Book Systems; (Cataloging) Book Systems; (Circulation) Book Systems; (OPAC) Book Systems
Database Vendor: Baker & Taylor
Wireless access
Function: Bks on CD, Children's prog, Computers for patron use, Homebound delivery serv, Magazines, Story hour, Summer reading prog
Open Mon & Tues 9-11 & 1-6, Thurs 2-6, Sat 9-1
Restriction: Authorized personnel only
Friends of the Library Group

LAURENS

P LAURENS PUBLIC LIBRARY, 273 N Third St, 50554. SAN 305-5167. Tel: 712-841-4612. FAX: 712-841-4612. Web Site: www.laurenspubliclibrary.com. *Dir,* Glenda Mulder; E-mail: director@laurenspubliclibrary.com; *Asst Dir,* Deb Hertz; E-mail: assistantdir@laurenspubliclibrary.com; *Ch,* Kayla Graff; E-mail: childrens@laurenspubliclibrary.com; Staff 4 (Non-MLS 4)
Founded 1910. Pop 1,476; Circ 30,612
Library Holdings: Bk Vols 25,000; Per Subs 75
Mem of Northwest Iowa Library Services
Open Mon-Wed 11-8, Thurs & Fri 11-5, Sat 9-1
Friends of the Library Group

LAWLER

P LAWLER PUBLIC LIBRARY*, 412 E Grove, 52154. (Mail add: PO Box 235, 52154-0235), SAN 305-5175. Tel: 563-238-2191. FAX: 563-238-2191. E-mail: lawlerlibrary@iowatelecom.net. *Dir,* Cathy Humpal
Founded 1964. Pop 461; Circ 5,468
Library Holdings: AV Mats 396; CDs 95; DVDs 21; Large Print Bks 12; Bk Titles 6,833; Per Subs 40; Talking Bks 238; Videos 375
Open Mon, Tues & Thurs 1-5, Wed 1-6, Sat 8:30-12

LE GRAND

P LE GRAND PIONEER HERITAGE LIBRARY*, 206 N Vine St, 50142. (Mail add: PO Box 188, 50142-0188), SAN 373-918X. Tel: 641-479-2122. FAX: 641-479-2122. Web Site: www.legrand.lib.ia.us. *Dir,* Shelley Barron; E-mail: sbarron@legrand.lib.ia.us
Pop 854; Circ 14,809
Library Holdings: Bk Titles 9,516; Bk Vols 9,581; Per Subs 42
Special Collections: Native American Legends
Automation Activity & Vendor Info: (Cataloging) Follett Software; (Circulation) Follett Software
Mem of Central Iowa Library Services
Open Tues 10-8, Wed 9-12 & 5-8, Thurs 10-5, Sun 3-6
Friends of the Library Group

LE MARS

P LE MARS PUBLIC LIBRARY*, 46 First St SW, 51031-3696. SAN 305-5183. Tel: 712-546-5004. FAX: 712-546-5797. Web Site: www.lemars.lib.ia.us. *Dir,* Sue Kroesche; E-mail: kroesche@lemars.lib.ia.us; *Asst Dir,* Cathy Hovden; E-mail: cathy.hovden@lemars.lib.ia.us; *Ch,* Lisa Vander Sluis; E-mail: lisa.vandersluis@lemars.lib.ia.us

Founded 1894. Pop 9,500
Library Holdings: Bk Vols 40,000; Per Subs 149
Subject Interests: Local hist
Wireless access
Publications: Library Movers (Quarterly newsletter)
Mem of Northwest Iowa Library Services
Open Mon-Thurs 10-8, Fri & Sat 10-5
Friends of the Library Group

LECLAIRE

P LECLAIRE COMMUNITY LIBRARY, 323 Wisconsin St, 52753. SAN 341-8685. Tel: 563-289-4242, Ext 4. Administration Tel: 563-289-6002. E-mail: library@leclaireiowa.gov. Web Site: www.leclairelibrary.org. *Dir,* Jillian Aschliman; E-mail: jaschliman@leclaireiowa.gov
Library Holdings: AV Mats 5,000; Bk Vols 23,000; Per Subs 60
Partic in RiverShare Libraries
Open Mon-Thurs 10-8, Fri 10-5, Sat 10-2
Friends of the Library Group

LEDYARD

P LEDYARD PUBLIC LIBRARY*, 220 Edmunds St, 50556. (Mail add: PO Box 8, 50556-0008), SAN 305-5205. Tel: 515-646-3111. FAX: 515-646-3111. E-mail: llibrary@iowatelecom.net. *Dir Gen, Published Heritage,* Erna R Lunn; *Ch,* Position Currently Open
Founded 1971. Pop 616; Circ 3,951
Library Holdings: Audiobooks 446; Bks on Deafness & Sign Lang 2; CDs 98; DVDs 104; Large Print Bks 94; Bk Titles 5,702; Per Subs 12; Videos 206
Special Collections: Ledyard Yearbooks; Ledyard, Connecticut Informational Books. Municipal Document Depository
Database Vendor: MITINET, Inc
Wireless access
Open Mon 2:30-6:30, Wed 1-5, Sat 8-12

LEHIGH

P LEHIGH PUBLIC LIBRARY, 241 Elm St, 50557. (Mail add: PO Box 138, 50557-0138), SAN 305-5213. Tel: 515-359-2967. FAX: 515-359-2973. E-mail: director@lehigh.lib.ia.us. *Dir,* Melanie Murray
Founded 1927. Pop 497; Circ 12,605
Library Holdings: AV Mats 910; Bk Titles 7,000; Per Subs 44
Automation Activity & Vendor Info: (Circulation) Follett Software
Open Mon 11-6, Tues, Wed & Fri 12:30-5:30, Sat 10-12

LENOX

P LENOX PUBLIC LIBRARY, 101 N Main St, 50851. SAN 305-5221. Tel: 641-333-4411. FAX: 641-333-4411. E-mail: library@lenoxia.com. Web Site: www.lenox.lib.ia.us. *Dir,* Shari Burger; Staff 0.86 (Non-MLS 0.86)
Founded 1941. Pop 1,500; Circ 10,000
Library Holdings: DVDs 290; Bk Titles 4,800; Per Subs 113
Automation Activity & Vendor Info: (Cataloging) Biblionix; (Circulation) Biblionix
Database Vendor: Biblionix/Apollo, EBSCOhost
Wireless access
Function: 24/7 Online cat, Adult bk club, Archival coll, Bks on cassette, Bks on CD, Children's prog, Computer training, Computers for patron use, Copy machines, Fax serv, Free DVD rentals, Handicapped accessible, ILL available, Magazines, Microfiche/film & reading machines, Movies, Online cat, Photocopying/Printing, Prog for children & young adult, Pub access computers, Scanner, Senior computer classes, Spanish lang bks, Summer reading prog, VHS videos, Wheelchair accessible
Mem of Southwest Iowa Library Services District
Open Mon 10-12 & 1-6, Tues-Fri 10-12 & 1-5:30, Sat 9-12

LEON

P LEON PUBLIC LIBRARY*, 200 W First St, 50144. SAN 305-523X. Tel: 641-446-3746, 641-446-6332. FAX: 641-446-3746. E-mail: leonpl@grm.net. Web Site: www.leon.lib.ia.us. *Dir,* Darlene Richardson
Pop 1,983; Circ 21,199
Library Holdings: Bk Vols 16,594; Per Subs 39
Wireless access
Mem of Southwest Iowa Library Services District
Open Mon 12:30-7:30, Tues & Thurs 10:30-5:30, Wed & Fri 12:30-5:30, Sat 10:30-1:30

LETTS

P LETTS PUBLIC LIBRARY*, 135 S Cherry St, 52754. (Mail add: PO Box B, 52754-0410), SAN 305-5248. Tel: 319-726-5121. FAX: 319-726-5121. Web Site: www.letts.lib.ia.us. *Dir,* Karen Koppe; E-mail: karenk@letts.lib.ia.us
Founded 1910. Pop 473; Circ 2,094
Library Holdings: Bk Titles 7,500; Per Subs 25
Automation Activity & Vendor Info: (Cataloging) Follett Software
Publications: Newsletter (Quarterly)
Open Tues & Fri 1-6, Wed 9-1, Thurs 1-7, Sat 8:30-10:30

LEWIS

P LEWIS PUBLIC LIBRARY*, 412 W Main, 51544. (Mail add: PO Box 202, 51544-0202), SAN 376-5172. Tel: 712-769-2228. FAX: 712-769-2228. E-mail: lewislibrary@netins.net. Web Site: www.lewis.swilsa.lib.ia.us. *Dir & Librn,* Susie Campbell
Pop 430
Library Holdings: DVDs 30; Large Print Bks 50; Bk Titles 3,999; Bk Vols 5,050; Per Subs 3; Videos 125
Database Vendor: Baker & Taylor, EBSCOhost
Wireless access
Mem of Southwest Iowa Library Services District
Open Mon 1:30-6, Wed 1:30-5:30, Sat 10-12

LIME SPRINGS

P LIME SPRINGS PUBLIC LIBRARY*, 112 W Main St, 52155. (Mail add: PO Box 68, 52155-0068), SAN 305-5264. Tel: 563-566-2207. FAX: 563-566-2207. E-mail: lspublib@mchsi.com. *Dir,* Janet DeVries
Library Holdings: Audiobooks 211; CDs 155; DVDs 220; Bk Titles 6,406; Per Subs 58; Videos 301
Open Mon, Tues & Thurs 2-8, Wed & Sat 10-5, Fri 2-5

LINDEN

P LINDEN PUBLIC LIBRARY*, 131 S Main, 50146. (Mail add: PO Box 18, 50146-0018), SAN 305-5272. Tel: 641-744-2124. *Dir,* Maribe Burnham; E-mail: robbee@iowatelecom.net; *Ch,* Dorothy Lamb
Pop 264; Circ 2,334
Library Holdings: Bk Titles 4,696; Per Subs 10
Open Mon-Wed & Fri 2-5, Thurs 9-12 & 4-6, Sat 9-12

LINN GROVE

P LINN GROVE PUBLIC LIBRARY, 110 Weaver St, 51033. SAN 305-5280. Tel: 712-296-3919. FAX: 712-296-3919. *Dir,* Emily Brown; E-mail: director@linngrove.lib.ia.us
Founded 1934. Pop 145; Circ 1,200
Library Holdings: AV Mats 578; Large Print Bks 15; Bk Vols 7,389; Talking Bks 65; Videos 534
Subject Interests: Christian fiction, Iowa, Relig
Function: Accelerated reader prog, Copy machines, Fax serv, ILL available
Mem of Northwest Iowa Library Services
Open Tues & Fri 2:30-5, Wed 11-6, Sat 1-3

LISBON

P LISBON PUBLIC LIBRARY, 101 E Main St, 52253. (Mail add: PO Box 217, 52253-0217), SAN 305-5299. Tel: 319-455-2800. FAX: 319-455-2800. *Dir,* Amy White; E-mail: amy@lisbon.lib.ia.us
Founded 1936. Pop 2,000; Circ 14,000
Library Holdings: Bk Titles 10,000; Per Subs 18
Special Collections: Local History
Wireless access
Open Mon 9-1 & 2-5, Tues 2-5, Wed 2-8:30, Thurs 10-5, Fri 12-5, Sat 9-1
Friends of the Library Group

LITTLE ROCK

P LITTLE ROCK PUBLIC LIBRARY*, 402 Main St, 51243. (Mail add: PO Box 308, 51243-0308), SAN 376-5288. Tel: 712-479-2298. FAX: 712-479-2298. E-mail: lrbooks@mtcnet.net. *Dir,* LeAnn Gerken
Library Holdings: Bk Vols 6,300; Per Subs 32
Wireless access
Open Tues & Thurs 1-5, Wed 2-8, Fri & Sat 9-12

LIVERMORE

P LIVERMORE PUBLIC LIBRARY*, 402 Fifth St, 50558. (Mail add: PO Box 18, 50558-0018), SAN 305-5329. Tel: 515-379-2078. FAX: 515-379-2078. *Dir,* Pansy Streit; E-mail: pansy@livermore.lib.ia.us
Founded 1935. Pop 515; Circ 4,056
Library Holdings: Bk Vols 7,666; Per Subs 22; Talking Bks 232; Videos 536
Function: Prog for children & young adult
Open Mon 1-6, Wed & Thurs 9-12 & 1-5, Fri 1-5, Sat 9-12

LOGAN

P LOGAN PUBLIC LIBRARY*, 121 E Sixth St, 51546. SAN 305-5337. Tel: 712-644-2551. FAX: 712-644-2551. Web Site: www.logan.lib.ia.us. *Dir,* Connie Johnson; E-mail: cjohnson@logan.lib.ia.us; *Ch Serv,* Jody Powell
Founded 1920. Pop 1,900; Circ 23,400
Library Holdings: Bk Vols 16,700; Per Subs 69
Automation Activity & Vendor Info: (Acquisitions) Follett Software
Mem of Central Kansas Library System
Open Mon & Wed 11-8, Tues, Thurs & Fri 11-5, Sat 11-3
Friends of the Library Group
Bookmobiles: 1

LOHRVILLE

P J J HANDS LIBRARY*, 609 Second St, 51453. (Mail add: PO Box 277, 51453-0277), SAN 305-5345. Tel: 712-465-4115. FAX: 712-465-4115. E-mail: jjhand@iowatelecom.net. Web Site: www.lohrville.org. *Dir,* Jane Beschorner; *Teen Librn,* Pam Haberl
Founded 1935. Pop 771; Circ 11,000
Library Holdings: AV Mats 512; Bk Vols 16,500; Per Subs 58
Automation Activity & Vendor Info: (Acquisitions) Book Systems; (Cataloging) Book Systems; (Circulation) Book Systems
Mem of Northwest Iowa Library Services
Open Mon, Tues & Fri 1-6, Wed 9-6, Thurs & Sat 9-12
Friends of the Library Group

LOST NATION

P LOST NATION PUBLIC LIBRARY*, 410 Main St, 52254. (Mail add: PO Box 397, 52254-0397), SAN 376-4974. Tel: 563-678-2114. FAX: 563-678-2368. E-mail: lnchlib@netins.net. *Dir,* Janene Shannon
Pop 467; Circ 2,346
Library Holdings: Bk Titles 9,000
Wireless access
Open Mon, Wed & Thurs 9-11 & 3:30-5:30, Tues 9-1 & 3:30-5:30, Fri & Sat 9-11

LOWDEN

P LOWDEN PUBLIC LIBRARY*, 605 Main St, 52255. (Mail add: PO Box 307, 52255-0307), SAN 320-8273. Tel: 563-941-7629. Web Site: www.lowden.lib.ia.us. *Dir,* Vicki Mohr; E-mail: vjmohr@lowden.lib.ia.us
Pop 790; Circ 9,439
Library Holdings: Bk Titles 9,400; Per Subs 10
Open Mon & Wed 10-12 & 1-7, Tues & Fri 8-12 & 1-5, Sat 9-12
Friends of the Library Group

LUVERNE

P LUVERNE PUBLIC LIBRARY*, 117 DeWitt St, 50560. (Mail add: PO Box 37, 50560-0037), SAN 305-5361. Tel: 515-882-3436. FAX: 515-882-3436. E-mail: director@luverne.lib.ia.us. Web Site: www.luverne.lib.ia.us. *Dir,* Marilyn Johnson
Pop 418; Circ 10,200
Library Holdings: Bk Vols 10,606; Per Subs 45
Open Mon & Wed 1:30-8, Fri 1:30-5:30, Sat 10-4

LYNNVILLE

P LYNNVILLE PUBLIC LIBRARY*, 301 South St, 50153. (Mail add: PO Box 96, 50153-9600), SAN 376-4982. Tel: 641-527-2590. FAX: 641-527-2592. E-mail: lynnlibrary@netins.net. Web Site: www.lynnville.lib.ia.us. *Dir,* Linda James
Library Holdings: AV Mats 1,958; Bk Titles 9,300; Bk Vols 11,700; Per Subs 49
Mem of Central Iowa Library Services
Open Mon 3-6, Wed 2-6, Thurs 4-7, Sat 10-12

LYTTON

P LYTTON PUBLIC LIBRARY*, 118 Main St, 50561. (Mail add: PO Box 136, 50561-0136), SAN 376-5318. Tel: 712-466-2522. FAX: 712-466-2522. E-mail: lyttnlib@iowatelecom.net. *Dir,* Myra Jones; E-mail: mjones@iowatelecom.net; *Ch,* Susan Miltner
Pop 350
Library Holdings: Bk Vols 5,000
Mem of Northwest Iowa Library Services
Open Mon & Wed 10-5, Tues & Thurs 10-7, Fri 10-4, Sat 9-1
Friends of the Library Group

MADRID

P MADRID PUBLIC LIBRARY, 100 W Third St, 50156. SAN 305-5388. Tel: 515-795-3846. FAX: 515-795-3697. E-mail: circdesk@madrid.lib.ia.us. Web Site: www.madrid.lib.ia.us. *Dir,* Angie Strong; E-mail: angie@madrid.lib.ia.us; *Children & Teen Librn,* Stephanie Fogarty; E-mail: stephanie@madrid.lib.ia.us
Founded 1934. Pop 2,395; Circ 23,687
Library Holdings: Bk Vols 15,000; Per Subs 80; Talking Bks 979; Videos 868
Automation Activity & Vendor Info: (Circulation) Book Systems; (OPAC) Book Systems
Wireless access
Mem of Central Iowa Library Services
Open Mon-Thurs 9-12 & 1-7, Fri 9-12 & 1-5:30, Sat 9-12
Friends of the Library Group

MALLARD

P MALLARD PUBLIC LIBRARY*, 605 Inman St, 50562. SAN 320-8281. Tel: 712-425-3330. FAX: 712-425-3236. E-mail: mallardl@ncn.net. Web Site: www.mallard.lib.ia.us. *Dir,* Anna McDevitt
Founded 1943. Pop 420; Circ 8,007
Library Holdings: Bk Vols 8,000; Per Subs 20
Mem of Northwest Iowa Library Services
Open Mon 1-6, Wed 9-12 & 1-5:30, Fri 1-5:30, Sat 9-12

MALVERN

P MALVERN PUBLIC LIBRARY*, 502 Main St, 51551. (Mail add: PO Box 180, 51551-0180), SAN 305-5396. Tel: 712-624-8554. FAX: 712-624-8245. E-mail: malvernlibrary@qwestoffice.net. Web Site: www.malvernlibrary.org. *Dir,* Stacey Buick
Founded 1914. Pop 1,200; Circ 16,424
Library Holdings: Bk Vols 13,000; Per Subs 50
Special Collections: Malvern Leader Coll
Automation Activity & Vendor Info: (Cataloging) Follett Software
Mem of Southwest Iowa Library Services District
Open Mon, Tues, Thurs & Fri 9:30-6, Wed 2-7, Sat 9:30-3
Friends of the Library Group

MANCHESTER

P MANCHESTER PUBLIC LIBRARY*, 304 N Franklin St, 52057. SAN 305-540X. Tel: 563-927-3719. FAX: 563-927-3058. E-mail: manchpl@manchester.lib.ia.us. Web Site: www.manchester.lib.ia.us. *Dir,* Kristy Folsom; *Asst Dir,* Kathy Heyer; *Ch,* Angie Shere; Staff 1 (MLS 1)
Founded 1903. Pop 5,179; Circ 108,020
Special Collections: Manchester Newspapers, 1871-2011
Subject Interests: Genealogy, Hist, Local hist
Automation Activity & Vendor Info: (Circulation) Biblionix
Database Vendor: EBSCOhost, Grolier Online
Wireless access
Function: Bks on cassette, Bks on CD, Children's prog, Computers for patron use, Copy machines, Electronic databases & coll, Fax serv, Free DVD rentals, Handicapped accessible, ILL available, Microfiche/film & reading machines, Music CDs, Online cat, OverDrive digital audio bks, Photocopying/Printing, Preschool reading prog, Prog for adults, Prog for children & young adult, Pub access computers, Ref serv available, Senior outreach, Story hour, Summer reading prog, Teen prog, Telephone ref, VHS videos, Wheelchair accessible
Open Mon-Thurs 9:30-8, Fri 9:30-5, Sat 9-3
Friends of the Library Group

MANILLA

P MANILLA PUBLIC LIBRARY*, 447 Main St, 51454. (Mail add: PO Box 459, 51454-0459), SAN 305-5418. Tel: 712-654-5192. *Dir,* Ann Macumber
Founded 1932. Pop 839; Circ 5,795
Library Holdings: Bk Titles 5,241; Bk Vols 6,200
Mem of Southwest Iowa Library Services District
Open Wed 2-5, Sat 9-11 & 2-5

MANLY

P MANLY PUBLIC LIBRARY*, 127 S Grant, 50456. (Mail add: PO Box 720, 50456-0720), SAN 305-5426. Tel: 641-454-2982. FAX: 641-454-2252. E-mail: director@manly.lib.ia.us. Web Site: www.manly.lib.ia.us. *Dir,* Marilyn Pinta
Pop 1,342; Circ 25,613
Jul 2007-Jun 2008 Income $48,794, State $2,251, City $26,700, Federal $692, County $12,500, Locally Generated Income $3,351, Other $3,300. Mats Exp $15,465, Books $6,665, Per/Ser (Incl. Access Fees) $1,038, Other Print Mats $4,197, AV Mat $3,565. Sal $32,517
Library Holdings: Audiobooks 392; CDs 10; Large Print Bks 358; Bk Titles 15,202; Bk Vols 14,148; Per Subs 47; Talking Bks 392; Videos 788
Automation Activity & Vendor Info: (Acquisitions) Follett Software; (Circulation) Winnebago Software Co; (Course Reserve) Winnebago Software Co
Database Vendor: EBSCOhost

Wireless access
Open Mon 2-8, Tues & Wed 2-6, Thurs 10-12 & 2-8, Fri 2-5, Sat 10-4

MANNING

P MANNING PUBLIC LIBRARY*, 310 Main St, 51455. SAN 305-5434. Tel: 712-655-2260. FAX: 712-655-2260. E-mail: mannplib@mmctsu.com. *Dir,* Renee Pfannkuch; *Ch,* Judi Stribe
Pop 1,490; Circ 10,536
Library Holdings: AV Mats 100; Bk Titles 13,900; Per Subs 25
Mem of Northwest Iowa Library Services
Open Mon, Tues, Thurs & Fri 10:30-5, Wed 11-7, Sat 10-12

MANSON

P MANSON PUBLIC LIBRARY, 1312 10th Ave, 50563. (Mail add: PO Box 309, 50563-0309), SAN 305-5442. Tel: 712-469-3986. FAX: 712-469-3076. Web Site: www.manson.lib.ia.us. *Dir,* Laura Koons; E-mail: lkoons@manson.lib.ia.us
Founded 1922. Pop 1,848
Library Holdings: Bk Vols 17,266; Per Subs 36
Automation Activity & Vendor Info: (Circulation) Book Systems
Wireless access
Mem of Northwest Iowa Library Services
Open Mon & Fri 1-5, Tues & Wed 10-5, Thurs 1-8, Sat 9-Noon

MAPLETON

P FISHER-WHITING MEMORIAL LIBRARY*, 609 Courtright St, 51034. SAN 305-5450. Tel: 712-881-1312. FAX: 712-881-1312. *Librn,* Position Currently Open; *Librn,* Linda Miller; *Asst Librn,* Jean Wessling
Pop 1,495; Circ 24,617
Library Holdings: Bk Titles 17,676; Per Subs 45
Publications: Library Journal
Mem of Northwest Iowa Library Services
Open Mon & Fri 12-8, Tues & Thurs 12-5, Wed 10-8, Sat 10-4
Friends of the Library Group

MAQUOKETA

P MAQUOKETA PUBLIC LIBRARY*, 126 S Second St, 52060. SAN 305-5469. Tel: 563-652-3874. Web Site: www.maquoketa.lib.ia.us. *Dir,* Elena Lanz; E-mail: director@maquoketa.lib.ia.us
Founded 1878. Pop 6,101; Circ 72,644
Library Holdings: Bk Vols 35,000; Per Subs 92
Subject Interests: Iowa, Lit, Local hist
Automation Activity & Vendor Info: (Acquisitions) Follett Software
Wireless access
Partic in Dubuque Area Library Information Consortium
Special Services for the Deaf - Closed caption videos
Special Services for the Blind - Audio mat; Bks available with recordings; Bks on cassette; Bks on CD; Cassette playback machines; Cassettes; Home delivery serv; Large print bks; Recorded bks; Screen enlargement software for people with visual disabilities; Sound rec
Open Mon, Tues & Thurs 10-8, Wed & Fri 10-6, Sat 9-3
Friends of the Library Group

MARATHON

P MARATHON PUBLIC LIBRARY, 306 W Attica St, 50565. SAN 305-5477. Tel: 712-289-2200. *Dir,* Jeanne Cox; E-mail: jeannec@marathon.lib.ia.us
Pop 280
Library Holdings: Bk Titles 9,000; Per Subs 37
Wireless access
Open Tues 10-4, Wed 10-6, Thurs 1-5, Sat 9-Noon

MARBLE ROCK

P MARBLE ROCK PUBLIC LIBRARY*, 105 S Main St, 50653. (Mail add: PO Box 236, 50653-0236), SAN 305-5485. Tel: 641-315-4480. FAX: 641-315-4480. E-mail: mrlib@myomnitel.com. *Dir,* Elaine Ott
Founded 1946. Pop 334; Circ 6,000
Library Holdings: Bk Vols 4,500; Per Subs 40
Open Mon, Tues, Thurs & Fri 1:30-5, Wed 9-11 & 1:30-6, Sat 9-12

MARCUS

P MARCUS PUBLIC LIBRARY, 106 N Locust St, 51035. (Mail add: PO Box 528, 51035-0528), SAN 305-5493. Tel: 712-376-2328. FAX: 712-376-4628. E-mail: marcuspl@midlands.net. Web Site: www.marcus.lib.ia.us. *Dir,* Beth Kingdon; Staff 1.12 (Non-MLS 1.12)
Founded 1908. Pop 1,200; Circ 21,300
Jul 2013-Jun 2014 Income $65,677, State $1,113, City $54,714, County $8,700, Locally Generated Income $1,150. Mats Exp $11,731, Books $7,833, Per/Ser (Incl. Access Fees) $1,724, AV Mat $2,103, Electronic Ref Mat (Incl. Access Fees) $71. Sal $19,344
Library Holdings: Audiobooks 307; CDs 95; DVDs 890; Large Print Bks 678; Bk Titles 16,262; Per Subs 60; Videos 389
Subject Interests: Local hist, Sci tech
Automation Activity & Vendor Info: (Cataloging) Follett Software; (Circulation) Follett Software
Database Vendor: EBSCOhost, OCLC FirstSearch
Wireless access
Mem of Northwest Iowa Library Services
Open Mon, Tues & Fri 12:30-5:30, Wed & Thurs 12:30-8, Sat 10-4
Friends of the Library Group

MARENGO

P MARENGO PUBLIC LIBRARY*, 235 E Hilton St, 52301. SAN 305-5507. Tel: 319-741-3825. FAX: 319-741-3825. Web Site: www.marengo.lib.ia.us. *Dir,* Tina Hootman-Vick; E-mail: director@marengo.lib.ia.us; Staff 3 (Non-MLS 3)
Founded 1904. Pop 2,535; Circ 35,648
Jul 2007-Jun 2008 Income $110,619, State $1,859, City $90,120, County $18,640. Mats Exp $17,845, Books $11,765, Per/Ser (Incl. Access Fees) $1,300, AV Equip $1,465, AV Mat $3,315. Sal $63,000
Library Holdings: Audiobooks 350; AV Mats 1,016; CDs 200; DVDs 450; Large Print Bks 300; Bk Titles 20,225; Bk Vols 20,245; Per Subs 92; Videos 1,200
Special Collections: Iowa County History, bd vols, micro
Automation Activity & Vendor Info: (Acquisitions) Follett Software; (Cataloging) Follett Software; (Circulation) Follett Software; (OPAC) Follett Software
Database Vendor: EBSCOhost, Medline, OCLC FirstSearch, OCLC WebJunction
Wireless access
Open Mon-Thurs 10-7:30, Fri 10-6, Sat 10-3
Friends of the Library Group

MARION

P MARION PUBLIC LIBRARY*, 1095 Sixth Ave, 52302. SAN 305-5515. Tel: 319-377-3412. FAX: 319-377-0113. E-mail: mplinfo@cityofmarion.org. Web Site: marionpubliclibrary.org. *Dir,* Doug Raber; E-mail: draber@cityofmarion.org; *Asst Dir,* Jo Pearson; E-mail: jpearson@cityofmarion.org; *Ch,* Olivia Stoner; E-mail: ostoner@cityofmarion.org; *Circ Librn,* Jill Law; E-mail: jlaw@cityofmarion.org; *Ref Librn,* Judy Winistorfer; E-mail: jwinistorfer@cityofmarion.org; *YA Librn,* Cressant Swarts; E-mail: cswarts@cityofmarion.org; Staff 28 (MLS 3, Non-MLS 25)
Pop 25,000; Circ 365,312
Library Holdings: CDs 2,868; DVDs 16,421; Bk Vols 171,718; Per Subs 302; Talking Bks 5,292
Automation Activity & Vendor Info: (Acquisitions) SirsiDynix; (Cataloging) SirsiDynix; (Circulation) SirsiDynix
Database Vendor: EBSCOhost, LearningExpress, Newsbank, OCLC WorldShare Interlibrary Loan, Overdrive, Inc
Wireless access
Open Mon-Thurs 9:30-9, Fri-Sat 9:30-5, Sun (Sept-May) 2-5
Friends of the Library Group

MARSHALLTOWN

S EMERSON PROCESS MANAGEMENT*, Fisher Control International Information Center, RA Engel Technical Ctr, 1700 12th Ave, 50158. SAN 329-0557. Tel: 641-754-2161. FAX: 641-754-3159. *Mgr, Knowledge Network & Info Serv,* Mark Heindselman; E-mail: mark.heindselman@emerson.com; *Info Ctr Analyst,* Brian Herman; E-mail: brian.herman@emerson.com; *Webmaster,* Herb Rickert, Jr; E-mail: herb.rickert@emerson.com
Library Holdings: AV Mats 3,000; Bk Titles 3,500; Per Subs 175
Subject Interests: Chem, Electronics, Mat sci, Petrochemicals, Software eng
Partic in BRS; Dialog Corp; Vutext
Open Mon-Fri 7:30-4:30

S IOWA VETERAN'S HOME LIBRARY*, 1301 Summit St, 50158-5484. SAN 305-5531. Tel: 641-753-4412. FAX: 641-753-4373. *Librn,* Sonia Hayek
Library Holdings: Bk Vols 5,000; Per Subs 50
Subject Interests: Geriatrics & gerontology
Open Mon-Fri 9-4

J MARSHALLTOWN COMMUNITY COLLEGE*, B J Harrison Library, 3700 S Center St, 50158. SAN 320-6777. Tel: 641-844-5690. FAX: 641-754-1442. E-mail: library@iavalley.edu. Web Site: www.iavalley.edu/district/library. *Libr Supvr,* Linda Moore; E-mail: linda.moore@iavalley.edu; Staff 2 (MLS 1, Non-MLS 1)
Founded 1927. Highest Degree: Associate
Library Holdings: Bk Vols 58,000; Per Subs 1,224

Automation Activity & Vendor Info: (Cataloging) SIRSI WorkFlows; (Circulation) SIRSI WorkFlows; (OPAC) SirsiDynix; (Serials) SIRSI WorkFlows
Database Vendor: EBSCOhost, Facts on File, ProQuest, SerialsSolutions
Wireless access
Function: Electronic databases & coll, Fax serv, Handicapped accessible, ILL available, Music CDs, Online cat, Online ref, Orientations, Photocopying/Printing, Prof lending libr, Scanner, Wheelchair accessible
Open Mon-Thurs 7:30am-9pm, Fri 7:30-3, Sun 5pm-9pm
Restriction: Fee for pub use

P MARSHALLTOWN PUBLIC LIBRARY*, 105 W Boone St, 50158-4911. SAN 341-9347. Tel: 641-754-5738. FAX: 641-754-5708. Web Site: www.marshalltownlibrary.org. *Dir,* Sarah Rosenblum; E-mail: srosenblum@ci.marshalltown.ia.us; Staff 8 (MLS 2, Non-MLS 6)
Founded 1898. Pop 33,518; Circ 315,070
Jul 2010-Jun 2011 Income $850,964, State $16,395, City $738,057, County $36,231, Locally Generated Income $59,431, Other $850. Mats Exp $105,378, Books $64,553, AV Mat $12,497. Sal $590,609 (Prof $67,308)
Library Holdings: Audiobooks 6,374; DVDs 8,482; Bk Vols 104,736; Per Subs 225; Talking Bks 3,676
Subject Interests: Genealogy, Local hist
Automation Activity & Vendor Info: (Cataloging) SirsiDynix; (Circulation) SirsiDynix; (OPAC) SirsiDynix
Database Vendor: OCLC FirstSearch, ProQuest, SirsiDynix
Wireless access
Mem of Central Iowa Library Services
Open Mon-Thurs 9-8, Fri 9-6, Sat 9-5
Friends of the Library Group

MARTELLE

P MARTELLE PUBLIC LIBRARY*, 202 South St, 52305. (Mail add: PO Box 86, 52305-0086), SAN 305-5558. Tel: 319-482-4121. FAX: 319-482-4121. Web Site: www.martelle.lib.ia.us. *Dir,* Theresa Pennington; E-mail: tpennington@martelle.lib.ia.us
Founded 1950. Pop 316; Circ 3,831
Library Holdings: Bk Titles 4,600; Per Subs 18
Open Tues & Thurs 2-6, Wed 9-5, Sat 9-12

MASON CITY

C KAPLAN UNIVERSITY*, Mason City Campus Library, 2570 Fourth St SW - Plaza West, 50401. SAN 375-3255. Tel: 641-423-2530. Reference Tel: 641-421-8267. Toll Free Tel: 800 274-2530. FAX: 641-423-7512. E-mail: mclibrary@kaplan.edu. *Dir, Libr Serv,* Kim Mashek; Staff 2 (MLS 1, Non-MLS 1)
Founded 1900. Enrl 250; Fac 10; Highest Degree: Master
Library Holdings: Bk Vols 5,000; Per Subs 10
Automation Activity & Vendor Info: (Acquisitions) TLC (The Library Corporation); (Cataloging) TLC (The Library Corporation); (Circulation) TLC (The Library Corporation); (OPAC) TLC (The Library Corporation)
Wireless access
Function: For res purposes, ILL available, Mail loans to mem, Photocopying/Printing, Ref serv available, Telephone ref
Publications: Inside Hamilton (Newsletter)
Special Services for the Deaf - High interest/low vocabulary bks
Restriction: Open to students

S CHARLES H MACNIDER MUSEUM LIBRARY*, 303 Second St SE, 50401-3925. SAN 305-5566. Tel: 641-421-3666. FAX: 641-422-9612. E-mail: macniderinformation@masoncity.net. Web Site: www.macnider.art.org. *Dir,* Edith Blanchard; E-mail: eblanchard@masoncity.net; *Assoc Curator,* Mara Linskey-Deegan
Founded 1966
Library Holdings: Bk Vols 1,500; Per Subs 10
Subject Interests: Art, Art hist
Open Tues, Wed, Fri & Sat 9-5, Thurs 9-9
Restriction: In-house use for visitors, Not a lending libr

P MASON CITY PUBLIC LIBRARY*, 225 Second St SE, 50401. SAN 305-5574. Tel: 641-421-3668. Reference Tel: 641-421-3670. Administration Tel: 641-421-3669. FAX: 641-423-2615. E-mail: librarian@mcpl.org. Web Site: www.mcpl.org. *Dir,* Mary Markwalter; *Asst Dir,* Penny V Weitzel; *Head, Youth Serv,* Kellie Jensen; *Archivist,* Terrence Harrison; Staff 15 (MLS 1, Non-MLS 14)
Founded 1876. Pop 29,172; Circ 55,000
Jul 2013-Jun 2014 Income $1,001,200, State $7,200, City $881,000, Federal $1,000, County $82,000, Locally Generated Income $30,000. Mats Exp $95,000, Books $30,000, Per/Ser (Incl. Access Fees) $8,000, AV Mat $18,000, Electronic Ref Mat (Incl. Access Fees) $39,000. Sal $875,870 (Prof $76,640)
Library Holdings: Bk Titles 107,000; Bk Vols 109,000; Per Subs 325
Special Collections: Lee P Loomis Archive of Mason City History; Prairie School Architecture Coll. State Document Depository
Subject Interests: Art & archit, Civil War, Local hist
Automation Activity & Vendor Info: (Acquisitions) Innovative Interfaces, Inc; (Cataloging) Innovative Interfaces, Inc; (Circulation) Innovative Interfaces, Inc; (OPAC) Innovative Interfaces, Inc; (Serials) Innovative Interfaces, Inc
Database Vendor: AudioBookCloud, Baker & Taylor, EBSCO Auto Repair Reference, EBSCOhost, Gale Cengage Learning, Library Ideas, LLC, OCLC WorldShare Interlibrary Loan, ProQuest, Wilson - Wilson Web
Wireless access
Publications: Annual Report
Special Services for the Blind - World Bk Encyclopedia on cassette
Open Mon-Thurs 9-8, Fri & Sat 9-5
Friends of the Library Group

M MERCY MEDICAL CENTER - NORTH IOWA*, Medical Library, 1000 Fourth St SW, 50401. SAN 305-5604. Tel: 641-428-7699. FAX: 641-422-7698. Web Site: www.mercynorthiowa.com/library-services. *Librn,* Position Currently Open; Staff 1 (MLS 1)
Library Holdings: Bk Titles 1,900; Per Subs 250; Videos 46
Subject Interests: Med, Nursing
Automation Activity & Vendor Info: (Acquisitions) EOS International; (Cataloging) EOS International; (OPAC) EOS International; (Serials) EOS International
Database Vendor: EBSCOhost
Partic in Greater Midwest Regional Medical Libr Network; National Network of Libraries of Medicine
Open Mon-Fri 8-4:30

J NORTH IOWA AREA COMMUNITY COLLEGE LIBRARY*, 500 College Dr, 50401. SAN 305-5590. Tel: 641-422-4232. Interlibrary Loan Service Tel: 641-422-4407. Reference Tel: 641-422-4327. FAX: 641-422-4131. Web Site: www.niacc.edu/library. *Dir,* Karen F Dole; E-mail: dolekare@niacc.edu; *ILL,* Cindy Eyeberg; E-mail: eybercin@niacc.edu; Staff 4 (MLS 1, Non-MLS 3)
Founded 1918. Enrl 3,181; Fac 84; Highest Degree: Associate
Library Holdings: Audiobooks 325; AV Mats 2,134; CDs 29; DVDs 274; e-books 13,631; e-journals 65; Electronic Media & Resources 71; Microforms 433; Bk Titles 19,885; Bk Vols 27,129; Per Subs 279; Videos 826
Automation Activity & Vendor Info: (Cataloging) Innovative Interfaces, Inc; (Circulation) Innovative Interfaces, Inc; (ILL) OCLC; (OPAC) Innovative Interfaces, Inc
Database Vendor: ABC-CLIO, Alexander Street Press, CredoReference, EBSCOhost, Gale Cengage Learning, LexisNexis, McGraw-Hill, Micromedex, Newsbank, OCLC FirstSearch, OCLC WorldShare Interlibrary Loan, OVID Technologies, ProQuest, SerialsSolutions
Wireless access
Publications: NIACC Library Handbook
Partic in Lyrasis; OCLC Online Computer Library Center, Inc
Open Mon-Thurs 7:30am-8pm, Fri 7:30-4

MASSENA

P MASSENA PUBLIC LIBRARY*, 122 Main, 50853. (Mail add: PO Box 86, 50853-0086), SAN 305-5612. Tel: 712-779-3726. *Interim Dir,* Paul L Schaffer
Founded 1918. Pop 414; Circ 5,281
Library Holdings: DVDs 50; Bk Titles 3,806; Per Subs 17; Videos 60
Wireless access
Open Mon & Thurs 9-12, Tues & Wed 1-4:30, Fri 1-6, Sat 9am-11am
Friends of the Library Group

MAXWELL

P MAXWELL PUBLIC LIBRARY*, 111 Main St, 50161. (Mail add: PO Box 128, 50161-0128), SAN 305-5620. Tel: 515-387-8780. FAX: 515-387-8780. E-mail: maxwell_public_library2011@hotmail.com. *Dir,* Meggan Lawrence; *Libr Asst,* Carol Newton
Pop 800; Circ 6,977
Library Holdings: Bk Vols 5,586
Subject Interests: Iowa
Mem of Central Iowa Library Services
Open Mon 8-10 & 2-6, Tues & Wed 3-7, Thurs 2-6, Sat 10-2

MAYNARD

P MAYNARD COMMUNITY LIBRARY*, 225 Main St W, 50655. (Mail add: PO Box 225, 50655-0255), SAN 376-5253. Tel: 563-637-2330. FAX: 563-637-2330. E-mail: maynardlibrary@mchsi.com. Web Site: www.maynard.lib.ia.us. *Dir,* Lezlie Barry
Library Holdings: Bk Vols 6,200; Per Subs 37
Automation Activity & Vendor Info: (Cataloging) Follett Software
Open Tues & Wed 1-5, Thurs 1-7:30, Fri & Sat 9-12

MCGREGOR

P MCGREGOR PUBLIC LIBRARY*, 334 Main St, 52157. (Mail add: PO Box 398, 52157-0398), SAN 305-537X. Tel: 563-873-3318. FAX: 563-873-3318. E-mail: mplib@mchsi.com. Web Site: www.mcgregor.lib.ia.us/. *Dir,* Michele Pettit; *Teen Librn,* Jane Lundquist
Pop 797; Circ 23,462
Library Holdings: Bk Titles 14,500; Per Subs 31
Subject Interests: Local hist
Mem of East Central Regional Library
Open Mon & Wed 2:30-8:30, Tues & Thurs 10:30-5:30, Fri 2:30-5:30, Sat 9:30-3:30

MECHANICSVILLE

P MECHANICSVILLE PUBLIC LIBRARY*, 218 E First St, 52306. (Mail add: PO Box 370, 52306-0370), SAN 305-5647. Tel: 563-432-7135. FAX: 563-432-7135. E-mail: jkhartman@mechanicsville.lib.ia.us. Web Site: www.mechanicsville.lib.ia.u. *Dir,* Judy Hartman; E-mail: jkhartman@mechanicsville.lib.ia.us; *Asst Dir,* Shannon Walshire; E-mail: swalshire@mechanicsville.lib.ia.us; *Asst Librn,* Carrie Albaugh
Pop 1,012; Circ 7,497
Library Holdings: Bk Vols 11,000; Per Subs 45
Open Mon 1-7:30, Tues & Thurs 1-5, Wed 1-8:30, Fri 10-11:30 & 1-5, Sat 9-1

MEDIAPOLIS

P MEDIAPOLIS PUBLIC LIBRARY*, 128 N Orchard St, 52637. (Mail add: PO Box 39, 52637-0039), SAN 305-5655. Tel: 319-394-3895. FAX: 319-394-3916. E-mail: director@mediapolis.lib.ia.us. Web Site: www.mediapolis.lib.ia.us. *Dir,* Kim Earnest; E-mail: kearnest@mediapolis.lib.ia.us; Staff 4 (Non-MLS 4)
Founded 1915. Pop 1,650; Circ 3,500
Library Holdings: AV Mats 500; Bks on Deafness & Sign Lang 10; High Interest/Low Vocabulary Bk Vols 1,000; Large Print Bks 550; Bk Vols 17,571; Per Subs 73; Talking Bks 200
Automation Activity & Vendor Info: (Cataloging) Follett Software; (Circulation) Follett Software; (OPAC) Follett Software
Database Vendor: EBSCOhost, OCLC FirstSearch
Function: AV serv, Handicapped accessible, ILL available, Photocopying/Printing, Prog for children & young adult, Summer reading prog, Wheelchair accessible
Open Mon, Wed & Fri 10-6, Tues & Thurs 10-7, Sat 10-2
Friends of the Library Group

MELBOURNE

P MELBOURNE PUBLIC LIBRARY, 603 Main St, 50162. SAN 376-5431. Tel: 641-482-3115. Web Site: www.melbourne.lib.ia.us. *Dir,* Amy Hill; Staff 2 (Non-MLS 2)
Founded 1975
Library Holdings: Large Print Bks 300; Bk Titles 14,000; Per Subs 24; Talking Bks 428
Automation Activity & Vendor Info: (Cataloging) Follett Software; (Circulation) Follett Software
Wireless access
Mem of Central Iowa Library Services
Open Mon & Wed 11-5, Tues 9-11 & 3-7, Thurs 3-7, Fri 1-5, Sat 9-12
Friends of the Library Group

MELCHER-DALLAS

P MELCHER-DALLAS PUBLIC LIBRARY*, 101 E Center St, 50163. (Mail add: PO Box 684, 50163). Tel: 641-947-6700. FAX: 641-947-6700. Web Site: www.melcher-dallaspubliclibrary.com. *Dir,* Lori Davis; E-mail: m-dpl-1@hotmail.com
Pop 1,298; Circ 7,580
Library Holdings: AV Mats 215; Bk Vols 8,267
Mem of Central Iowa Library Services
Open Mon-Tues & Thurs-Fri 11-5, Wed 12-6, Sat 8-Noon
Friends of the Library Group

MELVIN

P MELVIN PUBLIC LIBRARY*, 232 Main St, 51350. SAN 376-5148. Tel: 712-736-2107. *Librn,* Helen Wimmer; *Libr Asst,* Norma Griese
Pop 985; Circ 8,522
Library Holdings: Audiobooks 366; Bk Vols 3,522; Per Subs 34
Wireless access
Open Mon 2-6, Wed 1-5, Sat 9-12

MENLO

P MENLO PUBLIC LIBRARY*, Menlo Community Bldg, 504 Fifth St, 50164. (Mail add: PO Box 39, 50164-0039), SAN 305-568X. Tel: 641-524-4201. FAX: 641-524-2682. Web Site: www.menlo.lib.ia.us. *Dir,* Annette Murphy; E-mail: annette@menlo.lib.ia.us; *Asst Librn,* Patty Jacobson; E-mail: patty@menlo.lib.ia.us
Founded 1942. Pop 365; Circ 9,996
Library Holdings: Audiobooks 15; Bks on Deafness & Sign Lang 5; Braille Volumes 1; CDs 35; DVDs 250; Electronic Media & Resources 5; High Interest/Low Vocabulary Bk Vols 50; Large Print Bks 100; Bk Vols 9,580; Per Subs 23; Videos 15
Wireless access
Mem of Southwest Iowa Library Services District
Special Services for the Deaf - Am sign lang & deaf culture; Bks on deafness & sign lang
Special Services for the Blind - Accessible computers; Audio mat
Open Mon 1-6, Tues & Thurs 4-7, Wed & Sat 9-12, Fri 2-5
Friends of the Library Group

MERRILL

P MERRILL PUBLIC LIBRARY*, 608 Main St, 51038. SAN 305-5698. Tel: 712-938-2503. FAX: 712-938-2402. E-mail: merrilllibrary@mtcnet.net. *Dir,* Norma Philips; *Ch,* Julie Schultz
Pop 752; Circ 7,950
Library Holdings: Bk Vols 6,400; Per Subs 71
Wireless access
Mem of Northwest Iowa Library Services
Open Mon & Wed 6-8, Tues & Thurs 1:30-5, Fri & Sat 9-12

MESERVEY

P MESERVEY PUBLIC LIBRARY*, 719 First St, 50457. (Mail add: PO BOx 68, 50457), SAN 305-5701. Tel: 641-358-6274. FAX: 641-358-6274. Web Site: www.meservey.lib.ia.us. *Dir,* Tonya Uhde; E-mail: tonya.uhde@meservey.lib.ia.us
Founded 1965. Pop 580; Circ 5,296
Library Holdings: AV Mats 271; Bk Titles 7,844; Per Subs 22
Open Mon 6:30-9, Tues & Wed 1-5, Thurs 1-5 & 6:30-9, Sat 9-12

MILFORD

P MILFORD MEMORIAL LIBRARY*, 1009 Ninth St, Ste 5, 51351. SAN 305-571X. Tel: 712-338-4643. FAX: 712-338-4859. E-mail: info@milfordlibrary.net. Web Site: www.milford.lib.ia.us. *Dir,* Beth K Sorenson
Founded 1923. Pop 2,474; Circ 86,000
Library Holdings: Audiobooks 12,639; CDs 631; DVDs 728; e-books 10,042; e-journals 73; Large Print Bks 1,479; Bk Vols 23,804; Per Subs 175
Automation Activity & Vendor Info: (Cataloging) OCLC CatExpress; (Circulation) Biblionix; (OPAC) Biblionix
Database Vendor: EBSCOhost, LearningExpress, OCLC FirstSearch, Overdrive, Inc
Wireless access
Function: Photocopying/Printing
Mem of Northwest Iowa Library Services
Open Mon, Tues, Thurs & Fri 9:30-5:30, Wed 9:30-8, Sat 10-1:30
Friends of the Library Group

MILO

P MILO PUBLIC LIBRARY*, 123 Main St, 50166. SAN 305-5728. Tel: 641-942-6557. FAX: 641-942-6557. E-mail: milolibrary@iowatelecom.net. *Librn,* Paula J Griggs; *Ch,* Renee Minton
Founded 1955. Pop 839; Circ 13,657
Jul 2005-Jun 2006 Income $31,712, State $1,088, City $22,257, County $5,598, Locally Generated Income $2,769. Mats Exp $5,768, Books $4,102, Per/Ser (Incl. Access Fees) $1,371, AV Mat $280, Electronic Ref Mat (Incl. Access Fees) $15. Sal Prof $18,158
Library Holdings: AV Mats 438; Large Print Bks 236; Bk Titles 12,474; Per Subs 78
Special Collections: Local History Coll, bks, newsp, obituaries, photogs
Mem of Central Iowa Library Services
Open Mon 2-7:30, Tues 6-8, Wed & Thurs 2-5:30, Fri 9-11 & 2-5:30, Sat 9-12

MILTON

P MILTON PUBLIC LIBRARY*, 422 N Main St, 52570. SAN 305-5736. Tel: 641-656-4611. FAX: 641-656-4611. E-mail: mlp@iowatelecom.net. *Vols Librn,* Jane Hargrove
Pop 443; Circ 1,218
Library Holdings: Bk Vols 7,416
Open Wed-Fri 1:30-4:30

MINBURN

P MINBURN PUBLIC LIBRARY, 315 Baker St, 50167. (Mail add: PO Box 23, 50167-0023), SAN 305-5744. Tel: 515-677-2712. FAX: 515-677-2245. E-mail: minburnlib@minburncomm.net. Web Site: www.minburn.lib.ia.us. *Dir,* Anne Pepper
Pop 390; Circ 1,532
Library Holdings: Bk Vols 6,000; Per Subs 28
Wireless access
Mem of Central Iowa Library Services
Open Mon, Tues & Thurs 12-5:30, Fri 11-7, Sat 9-1

MISSOURI VALLEY

P MISSOURI VALLEY PUBLIC LIBRARY*, 420 E Huron St, 51555. SAN 305-5752. Tel: 712-642-4111. Web Site: www.missourivalley.lib.ia.us. *Dir,* Frankie Hannan; E-mail: fhannan@missourivalley.lib.ia.us; *Ch,* DeAnn Kruempel; E-mail: dkruempel@missourivalley.lib.ia.us
Founded 1881. Pop 2,800; Circ 33,000
Library Holdings: Bk Titles 30,900; Per Subs 50
Wireless access
Mem of Southwest Iowa Library Services District
Open Mon-Wed & Fri 10-5:30, Thurs 1-8, Sat 10-2
Friends of the Library Group

MITCHELLVILLE

S IOWA CORRECTIONAL INSTITUTION FOR WOMEN*, 300 Elm Ave SW, 50169. SAN 305-6740. Tel: 515-967-4236, Ext 1221. FAX: 515-967-5347. *Librn,* Nancy Ellingson; Staff 1 (Non-MLS 1)
Library Holdings: Bk Vols 20,000; Per Subs 20
Subject Interests: Ethnic studies, Feminism
Restriction: Staff & inmates only

P MITCHELLVILLE PUBLIC LIBRARY*, 204 Center Ave N, 50169. (Mail add: PO Box 727, 50169-0727), SAN 305-5779. Tel: 515-967-3339. FAX: 515-967-1868. E-mail: mplibr@mitchellville.lib.ia.us. Web Site: www.mitchellvillelibrary.org. *Dir,* Gisela Veatch; *Asst Dir,* Dorothy Johnson
Pop 2,017; Circ 20,747
Library Holdings: Bk Titles 13,096; Per Subs 45
Automation Activity & Vendor Info: (Circulation) Follett Software
Database Vendor: EBSCOhost
Mem of Central Iowa Library Services
Open Mon 1-8,Tues, Wed & Thurs 1-7, Fri 1-5, Sat 9-12, Sun 1-4
Friends of the Library Group

MODALE

P MODALE PUBLIC LIBRARY*, 511 N Main St, 51556. (Mail add: PO Box 28, 51556-0028), SAN 305-5787. Tel: 712-645-2826. FAX: 712-645-2826. Web Site: www.modale.swilsa.lib.ia.us. *Librn,* Margaret Vittitoe; *Asst Librn,* Jennifer Skinner
Circ 5,080
Library Holdings: Bk Vols 8,371; Per Subs 20; Talking Bks 100
Mem of Southwest Iowa Library Services District
Open Wed 1:30-6:30, Sat 9-2
Friends of the Library Group

MONDAMIN

P MONDAMIN PUBLIC LIBRARY, 201 Maple St, 51557. (Mail add: PO Box 190, 51557-0190), SAN 305-5795. Tel: 712-646-2888. E-mail: mpl@iowatelecom.net. Web Site: www.mondamin.swilsa.lib.ia.us. *Dir,* Susan Hardy
Founded 1934. Pop 1,743; Circ 3,664
Library Holdings: AV Mats 50; Bk Titles 6,895; Per Subs 15; Videos 202
Automation Activity & Vendor Info: (Cataloging) Follett Software
Mem of Southwest Iowa Library Services District
Open Tues & Thurs 1-6, Wed 3-8, Sat 9-2

MONONA

P MURPHY MEMORIAL LIBRARY*, 111 N Page, 52159-0430. (Mail add: PO Box 942, 52159-0942), SAN 305-5809. Tel: 563-539-2356. FAX: 563-539-2306. E-mail: murphy@monona.lib.ia.us. Web Site: www.monona.lib.ia.us. *Dir,* Christine Bee; *Ch,* Heidi Feuerhelm
Founded 1934. Pop 1,550; Circ 15,572
Library Holdings: Bk Titles 13,500; Per Subs 65
Wireless access
Open Mon & Wed 1-8, Tues & Thurs 9:30-5:30, Fri 1-5, Sat 10-2

MONROE

P MONROE PUBLIC LIBRARY*, 416 S Buchanan St, 50170. (Mail add: PO Box 780, 50170-0780), SAN 376-5474. Tel: 641-259-3065. FAX: 641-259-3065. *Dir,* Randy Bellinger; Staff 2 (MLS 1, Non-MLS 1)
Pop 1,808
Jul 2010-Jun 2011. Mats Exp $52,850
Library Holdings: Bk Vols 21,250; Per Subs 22
Subject Interests: Local hist
Automation Activity & Vendor Info: (Cataloging) Follett Software; (Circulation) Follett Software
Database Vendor: EBSCOhost, OCLC FirstSearch
Wireless access
Function: Adult bk club, Bks on cassette, Bks on CD, Computers for patron use, Copy machines, Fax serv, Free DVD rentals, Handicapped accessible, Holiday prog, ILL available, Music CDs, Photocopying/Printing, Story hour, Summer reading prog, Tax forms, VHS videos, Wheelchair accessible
Mem of South Central Library System
Open Mon-Thurs 12-7, Fri 12-5, Sat 9-12
Friends of the Library Group

MONTEZUMA

P MONTEZUMA PUBLIC LIBRARY*, 500 E Main St, 50171. (Mail add: PO Box 158, 50171-0158), SAN 305-5817. Tel: 641-623-3417. FAX: 641-623-3339. E-mail: montepl@zumatel.net. *Dir,* Diane M Kitzmann; *Asst Librn,* Hazel Shultz
Founded 1916. Circ 20,500
Library Holdings: Bk Vols 15,407; Per Subs 55
Wireless access
Open Mon-Thurs 11:30-5:30, Fri 10-4, Sat 9:30-12

MONTICELLO

P ROSS & ELIZABETH BATY MONTICELLO PUBLIC LIBRARY*, 205 E Grand St, 52310-1617. SAN 376-7493. Tel: 319-465-3354. FAX: 319-465-4587. Web Site: www.monticello.lib.ia.us. *Dir,* Michelle Turnis; E-mail: michelleturnis@monticello.lib.ia.us
Library Holdings: Bk Vols 15,485; Per Subs 85
Open Mon-Thurs 9-8, Fri 9-6, Sat 9-3
Friends of the Library Group

MONTROSE

P MONTROSE PUBLIC LIBRARY*, 200 Main St, 52639-0100. (Mail add: PO Box 100, 52639-0100), SAN 305-5833. Tel: 319-463-5532. FAX: 319-463-5532. E-mail: montroselibrary12@yahoo.com. Web Site: www.leeco.lib.ia.us/montrose. *Dir,* Lana Clark; *Ch,* Joann Fenn
Founded 1928. Pop 957; Circ 14,334
Library Holdings: Bk Titles 10,034; Per Subs 28
Subject Interests: Local hist
Wireless access
Open Mon & Wed-Fri 3-7, Sat 9-1

MOORHEAD

P MOORHEAD PUBLIC LIBRARY*, PO Box 33, 51558-0033. Tel: 712-886-5211. *Dir,* Carolyn Archer; *Ch,* LaBerta Hinrichsen
Library Holdings: Bk Vols 3,500; Per Subs 11
Mem of Northwest Iowa Library Services
Open Sat 1-4
Friends of the Library Group

MORAVIA

P MORAVIA PUBLIC LIBRARY*, 100 E Chariton, 52571-9530. SAN 305-5841. Tel: 641-724-3440. FAX: 641-724-3440. Web Site: www.moravia.lib.ia.us. *Dir,* Deena Hoffman
Founded 1941. Pop 688
Library Holdings: CDs 220; DVDs 862; Large Print Bks 315; Bk Titles 12,015; Per Subs 12; Spec Interest Per Sub 3; Talking Bks 28
Subject Interests: Genealogy, Local hist
Automation Activity & Vendor Info: (Cataloging) Follett Software; (Circulation) Follett Software
Wireless access
Open Mon & Thurs 10-6, Wed 9-2:30, Sat 9-1:30
Friends of the Library Group

MORLEY

P MORLEY PUBLIC LIBRARY*, 507 Vine St, 52312. SAN 305-585X. Tel: 319-489-9271. FAX: 319-489-9271. E-mail: morlib@netins.net. *Librn,* Sue VonBehren
Pop 95; Circ 1,600
Library Holdings: Bk Titles 7,000; Per Subs 10

Wireless access
Open Mon & Wed 4-6, Sat 9-11

MORNING SUN

P MELLINGER MEMORIAL LIBRARY*, 11 Division St, 52640. (Mail add: PO Box 8, 52640-0008), SAN 305-5868. Tel: 319-868-7505. FAX: 319-868-7505. E-mail: mslib@louisacomm.net. Web Site: www.morningsun.lib.ia.us. *Dir,* Alethea LaMar; *Asst Dir,* Amanda Herrick
Founded 1915. Pop 956; Circ 9,538
Library Holdings: Bk Titles 8,664; Per Subs 41
Wireless access
Open Mon 10:30-6, Tues-Fri 10:30-5:30, Sat 10-2
Friends of the Library Group

MOULTON

P GARRETT MEMORIAL LIBRARY*, 123 S Main, 52572-1327. SAN 305-5876. Tel: 641-642-3664. FAX: 641-642-3664. Web Site: www.moulton.lib.ia.us. *Libr Dir,* Sandy Gooden; *Asst Libr Dir,* Wilma Stephenson
Founded 1968. Pop 658; Circ 6,831
Library Holdings: Bk Vols 10,000; Per Subs 35
Subject Interests: Genealogy
Automation Activity & Vendor Info: (Circulation) Follett Software
Wireless access
Open Mon 1-6, Tues-Thurs 1-5, Fri & Sat 10-1

MOUNT AYR

P MOUNT AYR PUBLIC LIBRARY*, 121 W Monroe St, 50854. SAN 305-5884. Tel: 641-464-2159. FAX: 641-464-2159. E-mail: mlibrary@mchsi.com. Web Site: www.mtayr.lib.ia.us. *Librn,* Mary Kathryn Gepner; *Assoc Librn,* Bobbie Bainum; *Asst Librn,* Dorothy Main
Founded 1916. Pop 1,938; Circ 33,124
Library Holdings: Bk Vols 14,000; Per Subs 65
Subject Interests: Genealogy, Local hist
Automation Activity & Vendor Info: (Cataloging) Follett Software; (Circulation) Follett Software
Mem of Southwest Iowa Library Services District
Open Mon-Wed & Fri 1:30-5, Thurs 10-:30-6, Sat 9:30-12

MOUNT PLEASANT

GM IOWA DEPARTMENT OF HUMAN SERVICES*, Mental Health Institute Library, 1200 E Washington, 52641. SAN 305-5892. Tel: 319-385-9511, Ext 2263. FAX: 319-385-8465. *Librn,* Position Currently Open; Staff 1 (MLS 1)
Founded 1861
Library Holdings: AV Mats 600; Bk Titles 5,000; Per Subs 50; Talking Bks 75
Subject Interests: Alcohol & drugs, Drug abuse, Med, Nursing, Psychiat, Soc sci & issues
Automation Activity & Vendor Info: (Cataloging) Follett Software; (Circulation) Follett Software
Partic in Lyrasis; Regional Med Libr - Region 3

C IOWA WESLEYAN COLLEGE*, J Raymond Chadwick Library, 107 W Broad St, 52641. SAN 305-5906. Tel: 319-385-6316. Circulation Tel: 319-385-6317. Interlibrary Loan Service Tel: 319-385-6318. FAX: 319-385-6324. E-mail: reference@iwc.edu. Web Site: chadwick.iwc.edu. *Dir,* Paula Kinney; E-mail: pkinney@iwc.edu; *E-Res/Instrul Librn,* Kate Adams; *Circ Assoc,* Joy Conwell; E-mail: jconwell@iwc.edu; Staff 3 (MLS 3)
Founded 1857. Enrl 605; Fac 48; Highest Degree: Bachelor
Library Holdings: Bk Titles 74,509; Bk Vols 109,567; Per Subs 441
Special Collections: German-Americanism; Iowa Conference of the United Methodist Church Archives; Iowa History. State Document Depository
Automation Activity & Vendor Info: (Circulation) Mandarin Library Automation; (Media Booking) Mandarin Library Automation; (OPAC) Mandarin Library Automation
Database Vendor: EBSCOhost, Gale Cengage Learning, Newsbank, OCLC FirstSearch
Publications: Library Guides
Partic in Iowa Private Academic Library Consortium (IPAL); OCLC Online Computer Library Center, Inc
Open Mon-Thurs 8am-Midnight, Fri 8-5, Sat 1-5, Sun 6pm-10pm

S MOUNT PLEASANT CORRECTIONAL FACILITY LIBRARY*, 1200 E Washington, 52641. SAN 371-5876. Tel: 319-385-9511, Ext 2263. FAX: 319-385-8465. *Librn,* Position Currently Open; Staff 2 (Non-MLS 2)
Founded 1984
Library Holdings: Bk Vols 8,000; Per Subs 40; Talking Bks 50; Videos 200
Automation Activity & Vendor Info: (Cataloging) Follett Software; (Circulation) Follett Software; (OPAC) Follett Software

P MOUNT PLEASANT PUBLIC LIBRARY*, 307 E Monroe, Ste 101, 52641. SAN 305-5914. Tel: 319-385-1490. FAX: 319-385-1491. E-mail: directormppl@iowatelecom.net. Web Site: www.mountpleasantiowalibrary.com. *Dir,* Gayle Trede; *Ch,* Susan Mast; Staff 10 (MLS 2, Non-MLS 8)
Founded 1901. Pop 8,027
Jul 2009-Jun 2010 Income $316,119, State $6,606, City $255,840, County $25,460, Locally Generated Income $28,213. Mats Exp $97,231, Books $45,309, Per/Ser (Incl. Access Fees) $7,900, Other Print Mats $38,378, AV Mat $4,455, Electronic Ref Mat (Incl. Access Fees) $1,189. Sal $210,821 (Prof $168,838)
Library Holdings: Audiobooks 1,807; AV Mats 2,007; Bks on Deafness & Sign Lang 22; Braille Volumes 1; CDs 343; DVDs 2,007; Electronic Media & Resources 4; Large Print Bks 4,434; Microforms 5; Bk Vols 46,005; Per Subs 121; Videos 868
Special Collections: Henry County & Mt Pleasant History
Automation Activity & Vendor Info: (Acquisitions) Biblionix; (Cataloging) Biblionix; (Circulation) Biblionix; (OPAC) Biblionix
Database Vendor: EBSCOhost
Wireless access
Special Services for the Deaf - TDD equip
Open Mon-Thurs 10-8, Fri 10-5:30, Sat 10-5
Friends of the Library Group

MOUNT VERNON

C CORNELL COLLEGE*, Russell D Cole Library, 620 Third St SW, 52314-1012. SAN 305-5922. Tel: 319-895-4271. Reference Tel: 319-895-4122. E-mail: library@cornellcollege.edu. Web Site: www.cornellcollege.edu/library. *Dir,* Paul Waelchli; Tel: 319-895-4260, E-mail: pwaelchli@cornellcollege.edu; *Ref/Tech Serv Librn,* Glenda Davis-Driggs; Tel: 319-895-4256, E-mail: gdavisdriggs@cornellcollege.edu; *Syst Librn,* Gregory Cotton; Tel: 319-895-4454, E-mail: gcotton@cornellcollege.edu; *Libr Asst,* Kristin Reimann; Tel: 319-895-4201, E-mail: kreimann@cornellcollege.edu; Staff 6 (MLS 6)
Founded 1853. Enrl 1,150; Fac 70; Highest Degree: Bachelor
Library Holdings: AV Mats 7,599; Bk Vols 139,670; Per Subs 600; Talking Bks 1,871
Automation Activity & Vendor Info: (Acquisitions) Ex Libris Group; (Cataloging) Ex Libris Group; (Circulation) Ex Libris Group; (Course Reserve) Ex Libris Group; (Serials) Ex Libris Group
Partic in OCLC Online Computer Library Center, Inc

MOVILLE

P WOODBURY COUNTY LIBRARY*, 825 Main St, 51039. (Mail add: Box 625, 51039-0606), SAN 341-9401. Tel: 712-873-3322. FAX: 712-873-3744. E-mail: wcolib@wiatel.net. Web Site: www.moville.lib.ia.us. *Dir,* Donna Chapman; Staff 1 (MLS 1)
Founded 1949. Pop 12,000
Library Holdings: Bk Titles 53,000; Per Subs 40
Subject Interests: Local hist
Mem of Northwest Iowa Library Services
Open Mon & Wed 8-6, Tues, Thurs & Fri 8-5, Sat 8-1
Friends of the Library Group
Branches: 3
CORD MEMORIAL LIBRARY, 215 Main St, Danbury, 51019, SAN 341-9436. Tel: 712-883-2207. *Librn,* JoLynn Wright
Pop 384
Library Holdings: Bk Vols 3,500
Open Tues & Thurs 1-4:30 & 7-9, Sat 9:30-4:30
Friends of the Library Group
HORNICK BRANCH, 510 Main St, Hornick, 51026. (Mail add: Box 153, Hornick, 51026), SAN 341-9460. Tel: 712-874-3616.
Library Holdings: Bk Vols 3,500
Open Wed 9-11 & 2-6, Sat 9-12
Friends of the Library Group
PIERSON BRANCH, 321 Fourth St, Pierson, 51048, SAN 341-9495. Tel: 712-375-5022. E-mail: piersonlibrary@evertek.com. *Librn,* Dian Bush
Library Holdings: Bk Vols 3,500
Open Mon-Fri 9-4, Sat 9-12
Friends of the Library Group
Bookmobiles: 1

MURRAY

P MURRAY PUBLIC LIBRARY*, 416 Maple St, 50174. (Mail add: PO Box 21, 50174-0021), SAN 305-5930. Tel: 641-447-2711. E-mail: mplibrary@hotmail.com. *Dir,* Joan Callison
Pop 750; Circ 2,400
Library Holdings: Bk Titles 7,500; Per Subs 87
Mem of Southwest Iowa Library Services District
Open Mon 12-5, Wed 12-6, Fri 1-5, Sat 9-12

MUSCATINE

S MUSCATINE ART CENTER*, Art Reference Library, 1314 Mulberry Ave, 52761. SAN 373-4544. Tel: 563-263-8282. FAX: 563-263-4702. E-mail: art@muscatineiowa.gov. Web Site: www.muscatineartcenter.org. *Coordr,* Lynn Bartenhagen; E-mail: lbartenhagen@muscatineiowa.gov
Library Holdings: Bk Vols 1,000; Per Subs 24
Subject Interests: Am fine art, Decorative art
Open Tues, Wed & Fri 10-5, Thurs 10-7, Sat & Sun 1-5

P MUSSER PUBLIC LIBRARY*, 304 Iowa Ave, 52761-3875. SAN 305-5965. Tel: 563-263-3065. Reference Tel: 563-263-3472. FAX: 563-264-1033. E-mail: refmus@muscatineiowa.gov. Web Site: www.musserpubliclibrary.org. *Dir,* Pam Collins; E-mail: pcollins@muscatineiowa.gov; *Asst Dir,* Robert Fiedler; E-mail: rfiedler@muscatineiowa.gov; *Acq, Head, Tech Serv,* Marianna Haas; E-mail: mhaas@muscatineiowa.gov; *Outreach Serv Librn,* Jenny Howell; E-mail: jhowell@muscatinelibrary.us; *ILL,* Dan Chapman; E-mail: dchapman@muscatineiowa.gov; Staff 20 (MLS 4, Non-MLS 16)
Founded 1901. Pop 33,592; Circ 268,295
Library Holdings: Bk Titles 130,673; Bk Vols 135,997; Per Subs 225
Special Collections: Area Servicemen; The Little House Books by Laura Ingalls Wilder. Oral History
Subject Interests: Local hist, WWII
Automation Activity & Vendor Info: (Circulation) SirsiDynix
Database Vendor: EBSCOhost, OCLC FirstSearch
Wireless access
Partic in RiverShare Libraries
Friends of the Library Group

NEVADA

P NEVADA PUBLIC LIBRARY, 631 K Ave, 50201. SAN 305-5981. Tel: 515-382-2628. FAX: 515-382-3552. E-mail: npl@nevada.lib.ia.us. Web Site: nevada.lib.ia.us. *Dir,* Beth Williams; E-mail: beth@nevada.lib.ia.us; *Ch,* Lucinda Anderson; E-mail: cindy@nevada.lib.ia.us; Staff 5 (MLS 3, Non-MLS 2)
Founded 1876. Pop 7,000; Circ 120,000
Jul 2013-Jun 2014 Income $490,006, State $6,705, City $413,005, County $43,960, Locally Generated Income $26,336. Mats Exp $47,428, Books $33,289, Per/Ser (Incl. Access Fees) $4,000, AV Mat $9,926, Electronic Ref Mat (Incl. Access Fees) $213. Sal $292,292
Library Holdings: Audiobooks 4,393; DVDs 1,200, Large Print Bks 3,540; Bk Vols 58,383; Per Subs 137; Videos 2,808
Special Collections: Geneology (Obits)
Automation Activity & Vendor Info: (Cataloging) Baker & Taylor; (Circulation) Follett Software; (OPAC) Follett Software
Database Vendor: EBSCOhost, OCLC FirstSearch, OCLC WebJunction, OCLC WorldShare Interlibrary Loan
Wireless access
Function: Adult bk club, After school storytime, Audio & video playback equip for onsite use, Audiobks via web, Bk club(s), Bks on cassette, Bks on CD, CD ROM, Children's prog, Computer training, Computers for patron use, Copy machines, Digital talking bks, e-mail serv, E-Reserves, Electronic databases & coll, Exhibits, Fax serv, Free DVD rentals, Handicapped accessible, Holiday prog, Home delivery & serv to Sr ctr & nursing homes, Homebound delivery serv, ILL available, Instruction & testing, Mail & tel request accepted, Music CDs, Online cat, Online ref, Outreach serv, Outside serv via phone, mail, e-mail & web, OverDrive digital audio bks, Photocopying/Printing, Preschool outreach, Prog for adults, Prog for children & young adult, Pub access computers, Ref & res, Ref serv in person, Referrals accepted, Scanner, Senior computer classes, Senior outreach, Serves mentally handicapped consumers, Spoken cassettes & CDs, Spoken cassettes & DVDs, Story hour, Summer & winter reading prog, Summer reading prog, Tax forms, Teen prog, Telephone ref, VHS videos, Wheelchair accessible, Workshops
Mem of Central Iowa Library Services
Partic in WILBOR Consortium (West/Central Iowa Libraries Building Online Resources)
Open Mon-Thurs 10-8, Fri 10-6, Sat 10-4
Friends of the Library Group

NEW ALBIN

P NEW ALBIN PUBLIC LIBRARY, 176 Elm St, 52160. (Mail add: PO Box 12, 52160-0012), SAN 305-599X. Tel: 563-544-4747. FAX: 563-544-4757. E-mail: library@acegroup.cc. *Dir,* Krislyn Curry
Pop 534; Circ 3,821
Library Holdings: Bk Titles 5,500; Per Subs 45
Wireless access
Open Mon, Wed & Fri 4-7, Tues & Thurs 9-11 & 4-7, Sat 9-11

NEW HAMPTON

P NEW HAMPTON PUBLIC LIBRARY*, 20 W Spring St, 50659. SAN 305-6007. Tel: 641-394-2184. FAX: 641-394-5482. Web Site: www.newhampton.lib.ia.us. *Dir,* Patricia Ipsen; E-mail: pipsen@newhampton.lib.ia.us; Staff 3 (MLS 1, Non-MLS 2)
Pop 3,660; Circ 57,100
Library Holdings: CDs 128; Bk Vols 25,000; Per Subs 75; Talking Bks 1,506; Videos 650
Automation Activity & Vendor Info: (Cataloging) Follett Software; (Circulation) Follett Software
Open Mon-Thurs 10-8:30, Fri 10-6, Sat 10-4
Friends of the Library Group

NEW HARTFORD

P ELIZABETH RASMUSSEN MARTIN MEMORIAL LIBRARY*, 406 Packwaukee, 50660. (Mail add: PO Box 292, 50660-0292), SAN 305-6015. Tel: 319-983-2533. FAX: 319-983-2533. Web Site: www.newhartford.lib.ia.us. *Dir,* Sue Meyer; E-mail: sue@newhartford.lib.ia.us; *Asst Dir,* Chris Thompson; E-mail: christhompson@newhartford.lib.ia.us
Pop 764; Circ 5,672
Library Holdings: Bk Titles 10,733; Per Subs 18
Open Tues-Fri 11-6, Sat 9-11

NEW LONDON

P H J NUGEN PUBLIC LIBRARY*, 103 E Main St, 52645. SAN 305-6023. Tel: 319-367-7704. FAX: 319-367-7710. Web Site: www.newlondon.lib.ia.us. *Dir,* Rhonda Mixon; E-mail: rmixon@newlondon.lib.ia.us; *Asst Dir,* Linda Geer; *Libr Asst,* Dorothy Jacobs
Founded 1937. Pop 1,922
Library Holdings: Bk Titles 15,000; Per Subs 60
Open Mon 10-8, Tues, Thurs & Fri 10-6, Wed 1-6, Sat 9-1

NEW MARKET

P NEW MARKET PUBLIC LIBRARY*, 407 Main St, 51646. (Mail add: PO Box 68, 51646-0116), SAN 305-6031. Tel: 712-585-3467. *Librn,* Tonya Kennedy
Pop 584; Circ 1,841
Library Holdings: Bk Titles 3,474; Per Subs 20
Wireless access
Mem of Southwest Iowa Library Services District
Open Tues 2-4:30, Thurs 2-6, Sat 9-11

NEW PROVIDENCE

S HONEY CREEK CHURCH PRESERVATION LIBRARY*, 31031 PP Ave, 50206-8008. (Mail add: 31083 PP Ave, 50206), SAN 372-638X. Tel: 641-497-5499. *In Charge,* Dee Reece
Founded 1973
Special Collections: Community & School Records, minutes, alumni; Local legal papers, personal memorabilia; Quaker History, bks, flms, tapes, pictures
Subject Interests: Artifacts
Publications: Annual Newsletter; Diaries; Local Authors
Restriction: Open by appt only
Friends of the Library Group

NEW SHARON

P NEW SHARON PUBLIC LIBRARY*, 107 W Maple, 50207. (Mail add: PO Box 92, 50207-0092), SAN 305-604X. Tel: 641-637-4049. E-mail: newslib19@hotmail.com. *Dir,* Arlene Stilwell; Tel: 641-637-2689
Pop 1,225; Circ 50,013
Library Holdings: Bk Titles 10,000; Bk Vols 15,000
Open Mon-Fri 2-5, Sat 10-3

NEW VIRGINIA

P NEW VIRGINIA PUBLIC LIBRARY*, 504 Book Alley, 50210. (Mail add: PO Box 304, 50210-0304), SAN 305-6058. Tel: 641-449-3614. E-mail: nvlibr@windstream.net. Web Site: newvirginialibrary.org. *Dir,* Joan Stuart; *Libr Asst,* Beth Coles
Founded 1972. Circ 4,129
Library Holdings: Bks on Deafness & Sign Lang 25; Bk Vols 8,000; Per Subs 20
Database Vendor: EBSCOhost
Wireless access
Mem of Central Iowa Library Services
Open Tues & Thurs 4-8, Wed 9-11 & 1-8, Sat 9-12
Friends of the Library Group

NEWELL

P NEWELL PUBLIC LIBRARY*, 205 E Second, 50568. (Mail add: PO Box 667, 50568-0667), SAN 305-6066. Tel: 712-272-4334. FAX: 712-272-4334. Web Site: www.newell.lib.ia.us. *Libr Dir,* Sherrie Peterson
Founded 1883. Pop 889; Circ 7,492
Library Holdings: AV Mats 667; Bk Vols 16,113; Per Subs 47; Talking Bks 112
Automation Activity & Vendor Info: (Cataloging) Book Systems; (Circulation) Book Systems
Wireless access
Mem of Northwest Iowa Library Services
Open Mon 10-8, Tues-Fri 2-5, Sat 9-11
Friends of the Library Group

NEWHALL

P NEWHALL PUBLIC LIBRARY*, 14 Main St, 52315. (Mail add: PO Box 348, Newell, 52315-0348), SAN 376-5415. Tel: 319-223-5510. FAX: 319-223-5510. Web Site: www.newhall.lib.ia.us. *Dir,* Karen McClain; E-mail: kmcclain@newhall.lib.ia.us
Library Holdings: Bk Vols 7,200; Per Subs 21
Automation Activity & Vendor Info: (Cataloging) Follett Software; (Circulation) Follett Software
Open Mon 3-8, Tues & Thurs 1-6, Wed & Fri 9-12 & 1-6, Sat 9-11
Friends of the Library Group

NEWTON

NEWTON CORRECTIONAL FACILITY

S CORRECTIONAL RELEASE CENTER LIBRARY*, 307 S 60th Ave W, 50208. (Mail add: PO Box 218, 50208-0218). Tel: 641-792-7552, Ext 357. FAX: 641-792-9288.
Library Holdings: Bk Vols 5,000; Per Subs 40
Open Mon-Fri 7:30-4

S NCF LIBRARY*, 307 S 60th Ave W, 50208. (Mail add: PO Box 218, 50208-0218). Tel: 641-792-7552, Ext 568. FAX: 641-791-1680. *In Charge,* Brian Pfeifer
Library Holdings: Bk Vols 5,000; Per Subs 25
Open Mon-Fri 8-10:30 & 12:30-4

P NEWTON PUBLIC LIBRARY*, 100 N Third Ave W, 50208. (Mail add: PO Box 746, 50208-0746), SAN 305-6082. Tel: 641-792-4108. FAX: 641-791-0729. E-mail: newtonpl@newton.lib.ia.us. Web Site: www.newton.lib.ia.us. *Dir,* Sue Padilla; E-mail: spadilla@newton.lib.ia.us; *Asst Dir,* Susan Beise; *Circ,* Christine Nida; *Pub Serv Librn,* Nicole Lindstrom; *Youth Serv Librn,* Phylis Peter
Founded 1896. Pop 17,000; Circ 161,468
Library Holdings: Bk Vols 80,014; Per Subs 141
Automation Activity & Vendor Info: (Acquisitions) SirsiDynix; (Cataloging) SirsiDynix; (Circulation) SirsiDynix; (OPAC) SirsiDynix; (Serials) SirsiDynix
Database Vendor: EBSCO Auto Repair Reference, EBSCOhost, Facts on File, LearningExpress, Newsbank, ProQuest, World Book Online
Wireless access
Partic in OCLC Online Computer Library Center, Inc
Open Mon-Thurs 10-8, Fri 10-6, Sat 10-2
Friends of the Library Group

NORA SPRINGS

P NORA SPRINGS PUBLIC LIBRARY*, 45 N Hawkeye, 50458. (Mail add: PO Box 337, 50458-0337), SAN 305-6090. Tel: 641-749-5569. E-mail: nslib1@myomnitel.com. Web Site: www.norasprings.lib.ia.us. *Dir,* Marlene Stirling
Pop 1,532; Circ 10,706
Library Holdings: Bk Vols 8,000; Per Subs 46
Automation Activity & Vendor Info: (Cataloging) Follett Software; (Circulation) Follett Software
Open Mon & Fri 9-12 & 1:30-5:30, Tues & Thurs 1:30-5:30, Wed 1:30-6, Sat 9-12

NORTH ENGLISH

P NORTH ENGLISH PUBLIC LIBRARY*, 123 S Main, 52316. (Mail add: PO Box 427, 52316-0427), SAN 305-6104. Tel: 319-664-3725. FAX: 319-664-3725. Web Site: www.northenglish.lib.ia.us. *Dir,* Jane McCartney; E-mail: janem@northenglish.lib.ia.us
Founded 1934. Pop 991; Circ 16,905
Library Holdings: Bk Titles 9,800; Bk Vols 10,000; Per Subs 35
Special Collections: North English Record (paper) 1902-1999
Automation Activity & Vendor Info: (Acquisitions) Follett Software
Partic in Iowa Libr Asn
Open Mon, Tues & Thurs 1-5:30, Wed 1-6, Fri 9-5, Sat 9-12:30

NORTH LIBERTY

P NORTH LIBERTY COMMUNITY LIBRARY, 520 W Cherry St, 52317-9797. (Mail add: PO Box 320, 52317-0320), SAN 323-5998. Tel: 319-626-5701. Administration Tel: 319-626-5778. E-mail: nlcl@northlibertyiowa.org. Web Site: www.northlibertylibrary.org. *Libr Dir,* Jennie Garner; E-mail: jgarner@northlibertyiowa.org; *Asst Dir,* Jennifer Jordebrek; Staff 9 (MLS 4, Non-MLS 5)
Founded 1986. Pop 13,775; Circ 206,000
Library Holdings: CDs 1,800; DVDs 3,458; Large Print Bks 540; Bk Vols 38,207; Per Subs 112
Special Collections: Christian Fiction
Subject Interests: Early childhood
Automation Activity & Vendor Info: (Acquisitions) Insignia Software; (Cataloging) Insignia Software; (Circulation) Insignia Software; (OPAC) Insignia Software; (Serials) Insignia Software
Database Vendor: EBSCOhost, OCLC, Overdrive, Inc, TumbleBookLibrary, World Book Online
Wireless access
Publications: Brochure
Partic in Iowa Libr Asn; State of Iowa Libraries Online
Open Mon & Wed 9-8, Tues & Thurs 8-8, Fri 9-5, Sat 10-5, Sun (Sept-May) 1-4
Friends of the Library Group

NORTHWOOD

P NORTHWOOD PUBLIC LIBRARY*, 906 First Ave S, 50459. (Mail add: PO Box 137, 50459-0137), SAN 305-6112. Tel: 641-324-1340. Web Site: www.northwood.lib.ia.us. *Dir,* Connie Kenison
Pop 2,193; Circ 26,149
Library Holdings: Bk Titles 19,000; Bk Vols 22,000; Per Subs 56
Wireless access
Open Mon 7pm-9pm, Tues & Thurs 1-8, Fri 1-5:30, Sat 9-4
Friends of the Library Group

NORWALK

P NORWALK EASTER PUBLIC LIBRARY*, 1051 North Ave, 50211. SAN 305-6120. Tel: 515-981-0217. FAX: 515-981-4346. Web Site: www.norwalk.iowa.gov/Departments/Library. *Libr Dir,* Holly Sealine; E-mail: hsealine@norwalk.iowa.gov; *Youth Serv Mgr,* Annette Clark; Staff 13 (MLS 2, Non-MLS 11)
Founded 1962. Pop 8,500; Circ 71,943
Automation Activity & Vendor Info: (Acquisitions) ComPanion Corp; (Cataloging) ComPanion Corp; (Circulation) ComPanion Corp; (OPAC) ComPanion Corp
Database Vendor: EBSCOhost, OCLC FirstSearch
Wireless access
Function: Handicapped accessible, ILL available, Online cat, OverDrive digital audio bks, Photocopying/Printing, Preschool outreach, Prog for adults, Prog for children & young adult, Pub access computers, Ref serv available, Senior outreach, Story hour, Summer reading prog, Tax forms, Wheelchair accessible
Special Services for the Deaf - Closed caption videos
Special Services for the Blind - Bks on CD
Open Mon-Thurs 10-8, Fri & Sat 10-5
Friends of the Library Group

NORWAY

P NORWAY PUBLIC LIBRARY*, 108 Railroad St, 52318. (Mail add: PO Box 7, 52318-0007), SAN 320-829X. Tel: 319-227-7487. FAX: 319-227-7487. E-mail: norwaypl@southslope.net. *Dir,* Wendy Chesnes
Founded 1976. Pop 633; Circ 5,348
Library Holdings: Bk Titles 7,000; Per Subs 23
Open Tues & Thurs 2-7, Wed 9-12 & 1-3, Fri 3-5, Sat 9-12
Friends of the Library Group

OAKLAND

P ECKELS MEMORIAL LIBRARY*, 207 S Hwy, 51560. (Mail add: PO Box 519, 51560-0519), SAN 305-6147. Tel: 712-482-6668. FAX: 712-482-6668. E-mail: eckelslibrary@yahoo.com. Web Site: www.oakland.swilsa.lib.ia.us. *Dir,* Patrice Vance
Pop 1,700; Circ 13,027
Library Holdings: Bk Titles 26,000; Per Subs 38
Mem of Southwest Iowa Library Services District
Open Tues & Wed 12-5, Thurs 12-7, Fri 7-9, Sat 10-2

OCHEYEDAN

P OCHEYEDAN PUBLIC LIBRARY*, 874 Main St, 51354. (Mail add: PO Box 427, 51354-0427), SAN 305-6155. Tel: 712-758-3352. FAX: 712-758-3352. E-mail: director@ocheyedan.lib.ia.us. Web Site:

www.ocheyedan.lib.ia.us. *Co-Dir,* Connie Schuster; *Co-Dir,* Diane Truckenmiller; *Asst Librn,* Ruth Hoekstra
Founded 1912. Pop 536; Circ 13,000
Library Holdings: DVDs 170; Bk Vols 11,180; Per Subs 45; Talking Bks 100; Videos 1,083
Mem of Northwest Iowa Library Services
Open Tues, Wed & Fri 1-5:30, Thurs 1:30-6, Sat 10-12

ODEBOLT

P FIELD-CARNEGIE LIBRARY*, 200 Walnut St, 51458. SAN 305-6163. Tel: 712-668-2718. FAX: 712-668-4380. E-mail: fieldcar@netins.net. Web Site: www.odebolt.lib.ia.u. *Dir,* Julie Childers
Pop 1,256; Circ 17,150
Library Holdings: Bk Vols 13,922; Per Subs 53
Wireless access
Mem of Northwest Iowa Library Services
Open Mon & Fri 2-6, Tues & Thurs 2-5, Wed 10-12 & 2-7:30, Sat 9-12
Friends of the Library Group

OELWEIN

P OELWEIN PUBLIC LIBRARY*, 201 E Charles St, 50662-1939. SAN 305-6171. Tel: 319-283-1515. FAX: 319-283-6646. E-mail: oelwein@oelwein.lib.ia.us. Web Site: www.oelwein.lib.ia.us. *Dir,* Susan Macken; E-mail: smacken@oelwein.lib.ia.us; *Asst Dir,* Edith Biddinger; E-mail: ebiddinger@oelwein.lib.ia.us
Founded 1909. Pop 7,564; Circ 70,842
Library Holdings: Bk Vols 44,000; Per Subs 120
Special Collections: Oral History
Automation Activity & Vendor Info: (Cataloging) Follett Software; (Circulation) Follett Software
Wireless access
Open Mon-Thurs 9:30-8, Fri 9:30-5:30, Sat 11-5:30, Sun 2-5:30
Friends of the Library Group

OGDEN

P LEONARD A GOOD COMMUNITY LIBRARY*, 208 W Mulberry St, 50212. (Mail add: PO Box 696, 50212-0696), SAN 305-618X. Tel: 515-275-4550. Web Site: www.ogden.lib.ia.us. *Dir,* Debi Carlson; E-mail: debi.carlson@ogden.lib.ia.us
Founded 1948. Pop 2,000; Circ 38,911
Library Holdings: Bk Titles 12,000; Per Subs 31
Wireless access
Mem of Central Iowa Library Services
Open Mon 10-7, Tues & Fri 1-5, Wed & Thurs 9-5, Sat 9-Noon

OLIN

P OLIN PUBLIC LIBRARY*, 301 Parkway St, 52320. (Mail add: PO Box 318, 52320-0318), SAN 305-6198. Tel: 319-484-2944. FAX: 319-484-2944. Web Site: www.olin.lib.ia.us. *Dir,* Dolores Wood; E-mail: dwood@olin.lib.ia.us
Pop 735; Circ 3,376
Library Holdings: Bk Titles 6,365; Per Subs 29
Open Mon, Wed & Fri 1-5, Thurs 1-7, Sat 9-1

ONAWA

P ONAWA PUBLIC LIBRARY*, 707 Iowa Ave, 51040. SAN 305-6201. Tel: 712-423-1733. FAX: 712-433-4622. E-mail: onawalib@onawave.net. Web Site: www.onawa.lib.ia.us. *Dir,* Lori Beck; *Asst Dir,* Chris Zink; Staff 2 (Non-MLS 2)
Founded 1907. Pop 6,401; Circ 53,028
Library Holdings: Bk Titles 22,650; Bk Vols 26,421; Per Subs 80
Subject Interests: Astronomy, Local hist
Automation Activity & Vendor Info: (Cataloging) Book Systems; (Circulation) Book Systems
Mem of Northwest Iowa Library Services
Open Mon-Thurs 11-8, Fri & Sat 11-5
Friends of the Library Group

ORANGE CITY

C NORTHWESTERN COLLEGE*, Ramaker Library & Learning Resource Center, 101 Seventh St SW, 51041. SAN 305-621X. Tel: 712-707-7234. Interlibrary Loan Service Tel: 712-707-7311. FAX: 712-707-7247. E-mail: library@nwciowa.edu. Web Site: library.nwciowa.edu. *Dir,* Tim Schlak; Tel: 712-707-7238, E-mail: tim.schlak@nwciowa.edu; *Info Literacy Librn, Sr Ref Librn,* Anita Vogel; Tel: 712-707-7249, E-mail: avogel@nwciowa.edu; *Electronic Res & Ref Librn,* Anne Mead; Tel: 712-707-7237, E-mail: amead@nwciowa.edu; *Ref/Syst Librn,* Greta Grond; Tel: 712-707-7248, E-mail: ggrond@nwciowa.edu; *Access Serv Coordr,* Ben Karnish; E-mail: bkarnish@nwciowa.edu; *Acq & Ser Coordr,* Heather Sas; Tel: 712-707-7235, E-mail: heather.sas@nwciowa.edu; *Cataloger, Libr Syst Spec,* Sherri Langton; Tel: 712-707-7236, E-mail: slangton@nwciowa.edu; Staff 7 (MLS 4, Non-MLS 3)
Founded 1882. Enrl 1,280; Fac 65; Highest Degree: Bachelor
Library Holdings: Bk Titles 98,000; Bk Vols 108,000; Per Subs 530
Special Collections: Dutch Related-Reformed Church, bks, newsp, micro. US Document Depository
Subject Interests: Hist, Lit, Relig
Automation Activity & Vendor Info: (Acquisitions) EOS International; (Cataloging) EOS International; (Circulation) EOS International; (OPAC) EOS International
Database Vendor: EBSCOhost, OCLC FirstSearch
Partic in Christian Library Consortium; Cooperating Libraries in Consortium; Illinois Library & Information Network; Iowa Private Academic Library Consortium (IPAL); Minitex Library Information Network; OCLC Online Computer Library Center, Inc
Open Mon-Thurs (Fall & Spring) 7:30am-Midnight, Fri 7:30am-10pm, Sat 8-5, Sun 1:30-Midnight; Mon-Thurs (Summer) 8am-8:30pm, Fri 8-4

P ORANGE CITY PUBLIC LIBRARY*, 112 Albany Ave SE, 51041-1730. (Mail add: PO Box 436, 51041-0436), SAN 305-6228. Tel: 712-707-4302. FAX: 712-707-4431. E-mail: oclibrar@orangecitycomm.net. Web Site: www.orangecity.lib.ia.us. *Dir,* Karla Chase; Staff 5.35 (Non-MLS 5.35)
Founded 1915. Pop 6,004; Circ 212,292
Library Holdings: AV Mats 13,529; Bk Vols 63,771; Per Subs 170
Special Collections: Dutch Costume Patterns for Dutch Festival in May
Automation Activity & Vendor Info: (Cataloging) Follett Software; (Circulation) Follett Software; (OPAC) Follett Software
Database Vendor: EBSCOhost, OCLC FirstSearch
Wireless access
Mem of Northwest Iowa Library Services
Open Mon-Thurs 8am-9pm, Fri 8-5, Sat 9-5

OSAGE

P OSAGE PUBLIC LIBRARY*, 406 Main St, 50461-1125. SAN 305-6236. Tel: 641-732-3323. FAX: 641-732-4419. E-mail: osagepl@osage.net. Web Site: www.osage.net/~osagepl. *Dir,* Audrey Hancock; Staff 1 (MLS 1)
Founded 1876. Circ 98,089
Library Holdings: Bk Vols 39,741; Per Subs 47
Special Collections: Hamlin Garland Coll; Iowa Coll
Automation Activity & Vendor Info: (Circulation) Follett Software; (OPAC) Follett Software
Wireless access
Open Mon-Thurs (Winter) 10-9, Fri 10-5:30, Sat 10-4; Mon-Thurs (Summer) 10-8, Fri 10-5:30, Sat 10-4

OSCEOLA

P OSCEOLA PUBLIC LIBRARY*, 300 S Fillmore St, 50213-2237. SAN 305-6244. Tel: 641-342-2237. FAX: 641-342-6057. E-mail: osceolalib@osceola.lib.ia.us. Web Site: www.osceola.lib.ia.us. *Dir,* Judy Coe; E-mail: jcoe@osceola.lib.ia.us
Founded 1909. Pop 4,150; Circ 84,880
Library Holdings: Bk Vols 22,000; Per Subs 102
Automation Activity & Vendor Info: (Cataloging) Follett Software; (Circulation) Follett Software
Wireless access
Mem of Southwest Iowa Library Services District
Open Mon & Wed 9-7, Tues, Thurs & Fri 12-5, Sat 9-12:30

OSKALOOSA

P OSKALOOSA PUBLIC LIBRARY, 301 S Market St, 52577. SAN 305-6252. Tel: 641-673-0441. FAX: 641-673-6237. E-mail: opl@oskaloosalibrary.org. Web Site: www.oskaloosalibrary.org. *Dir,* William Ottens; *Ch,* Kilie Steel; *Teen Librn,* Susan Hasso; *Cat,* Marion Gaughan; *Libr Tech,* Paulette Groet; E-mail: pgroet@oskaloosalibrary.org; Staff 10 (MLS 2, Non-MLS 8)
Founded 1903. Pop 22,507; Circ 198,518
Library Holdings: Bk Titles 54,316; Bk Vols 55,000; Per Subs 198
Subject Interests: Hist
Automation Activity & Vendor Info: (Circulation) SirsiDynix; (OPAC) SirsiDynix
Database Vendor: OCLC FirstSearch, SirsiDynix
Function: Telephone ref
Mem of Southeast Iowa Library Services
Open Mon, Tues & Thurs 10-8, Wed, Fri & Sat 10-5
Friends of the Library Group

C WILLIAM PENN UNIVERSITY*, Wilcox Library, 201 Trueblood Ave, 52577. SAN 305-6260. Tel: 641-673-1096. FAX: 641-673-1098. E-mail: cwalibrarian@wmpenn.edu. Web Site: www.wmpenn.edu/library/library.html. *Librn,* Julie E Hansen; Tel: 641-673-1197, E-mail: hansenj@wmpenn.edu; *Instrul Serv Librn,* Jennifer Sterling; E-mail: sterlingj@wmpenn.edu; Staff 2 (MLS 2)
Founded 1873. Highest Degree: Bachelor

Library Holdings: Bk Vols 68,291; Per Subs 349
Special Collections: Quakerism (Quaker Coll)
Subject Interests: Educ, Indust arts, Soc sci & issues
Automation Activity & Vendor Info: (Cataloging) SirsiDynix; (Circulation) SirsiDynix; (OPAC) SirsiDynix
Partic in OCLC Online Computer Library Center, Inc
Open Mon-Thurs 8am-12am, Fri 8-8, Sat 1-5, Sun Noon-Midnight

OSSIAN

P OSSIAN PUBLIC LIBRARY, 123 W Main, 52161. (Mail add: PO Box 120, 52161-0120), SAN 305-6279. Tel: 563-532-9461. FAX: 563-532-9461. E-mail: director@ossian.lib.ia.us. Web Site: www.ossian.lib.ia.us. *Dir,* Jude Zweibohmer; Staff 1 (Non-MLS 1)
Founded 1956. Pop 842; Circ 10,502
Library Holdings: CDs 115; DVDs 15; Bk Vols 8,910; Per Subs 30; Talking Bks 150; Videos 290
Automation Activity & Vendor Info: (Cataloging) Follett Software; (Circulation) Follett Software
Open Mon, Tues & Thurs 2-5:30, Wed & Fri 2-7, Sat 9-12

OTTUMWA

J INDIAN HILLS COMMUNITY COLLEGE LIBRARY, 525 Grandview Ave, 52501-1398. SAN 305-6287. Tel: 641-683-5199. Administration Tel: 641-683-5174. Automation Services Tel: 641-683-5178. Toll Free Tel: 800-726-2585, Ext 5199. FAX: 641-683-5184. E-mail: library@indianhills.edu. Web Site: www.indianhills.edu. *Exec Dean,* Darlas Shockley; E-mail: Darlas.Shockley@indianhills.edu; *Librn,* Cheryl Talbert; E-mail: Cheryl.Talbert@indianhills.edu
Founded 1960. Enrl 3,500; Fac 250; Highest Degree: Associate
Library Holdings: Bk Vols 30,000; Per Subs 270
Automation Activity & Vendor Info: (Cataloging) TLC (The Library Corporation); (Circulation) TLC (The Library Corporation); (Course Reserve) TLC (The Library Corporation)
Publications: Monthly Acquisitions List
Open Mon-Thurs 7:15am-9pm, Sun 4:30-9

P OTTUMWA PUBLIC LIBRARY*, 102 W Fourth St, 52501. SAN 305-6295. Tel: 641-682-7563. FAX: 641-682-4970. Web Site: www.ottumwapubliclibrary.org. *Dir,* Sonja Ferrell; Tel: 641-682-7563, Ext 202, E-mail: sferrell@ottumwapubliclibrary.org; *Asst Dir,* Ron Houk; Tel: 641-682-7563, Ext 203, E-mail: rhouk@ottumwapubliclibrary.org; *Ch,* Jenna Bates; Tel: 641-682-7563, Ext 210, E-mail: jbates@ottumwapubliclibrary.org; *Ref Librn/Genealogy,* Patricia Essick; Tel: 641-682-7563, Ext 205, E-mail: ref@ottumwapubliclibrary.org; Staff 11 (MLS 1, Non-MLS 10)
Founded 1872. Pop 24,000
Library Holdings: AV Mats 1,500; Bk Vols 70,000; Per Subs 120; Talking Bks 400
Special Collections: Ottumwa & Wapello County History (Iowa Coll), bks, clippings, pictures
Automation Activity & Vendor Info: (Cataloging) SirsiDynix; (Circulation) SirsiDynix; (OPAC) SirsiDynix
Database Vendor: SirsiDynix
Wireless access
Function: ILL available
Open Mon-Thurs 9-7, Fri & Sat 9-5
Friends of the Library Group

M OTTUMWA REGIONAL HEALTH CENTER MEDICAL LIBRARY*, 1003 Pennsylvania Ave, 52501. SAN 377-4856. Tel: 641-684-2450. FAX: 641-684-2455. *Librn,* Jason Young
Library Holdings: Bk Vols 1,300
Open Mon-Fri 8-4

OXFORD

P OXFORD PUBLIC LIBRARY*, 112 Augusta Ave, 52322. (Mail add: PO Box 160, 52322-0160), SAN 376-6799. Tel: 319-828-4087. FAX: 319-828-4087. E-mail: oxfordlibrary@southslope.net. *Dir,* Sarah Uthoff
Library Holdings: Bk Vols 8,047; Per Subs 18
Mem of Chester County Library System; South Central Kansas Library System
Partic in Bibliomation Inc
Open Thurs 2-5, Fri 2-6, Sat 9-11:30 & 1-4
Friends of the Library Group

OXFORD JUNCTION

P WREGIE MEMORIAL LIBRARY*, 105 W Broadway, 52323. (Mail add: PO Box 345, 52323-0345), SAN 305-6325. Tel: 563-826-2450. FAX: 563-826-2450. E-mail: wregieml@netins.net. Web Site: www.netins.net/showcase/wregiememlib. *Dir,* Angela Shirley
Founded 1940
Library Holdings: Bk Titles 5,891; Per Subs 24
Special Collections: Oxford Mirror 1879-1952, micro
Open Tues & Sat 9-12, Wed 2-6, Thurs & Fri 12-5

PALMER

P PALMER PUBLIC LIBRARY*, 520 Hanson Ave, 50571. (Mail add: PO Box 114, 50571-0114), SAN 320-8222. Tel: 712-359-2296. E-mail: palib@ncn.net. *Dir,* Ramona Miller
Pop 230; Circ 6,457
Library Holdings: Bk Titles 11,187; Per Subs 21
Partic in Iowa Libr Asn
Open Mon 1-5, Wed 1:30-6, Sat 9-12

PANORA

P PANORA PUBLIC LIBRARY*, 102 N First St, 50216. SAN 305-6341. Tel: 641-755-2529. FAX: 641-755-3009. E-mail: pnralib@netins.net. Web Site: www.panora.org/library. *Dir,* Kimberly Finnegan; *Asst Librn,* Camille Kemble
Founded 1902. Pop 1,211; Circ 16,787
Library Holdings: Bk Titles 15,000; Per Subs 78
Database Vendor: EBSCOhost
Wireless access
Function: Bks on cassette, ILL available, Prog for children & young adult, Tax forms
Mem of Southwest Iowa Library Services District
Open Mon 1-7, Tues & Thurs 12-5, Wed 1-8, Fri 9:30-5, Sat 9:30-12
Friends of the Library Group

PARKERSBURG

P KOTHE MEMORIAL LIBRARY*, 309 Third St, 50665-1030. (Mail add: PO Box 160, 50665-0160), SAN 305-635X. Tel: 319-346-2442. FAX: 319-346-2442. Web Site: www.parkersburg.lib.ia.us. *Dir,* Marty Stahl; E-mail: marty@parkersburg.lib.ia.us; *Asst Librn,* Phyllis Arends
Pop 1,968; Circ 35,283
Library Holdings: AV Mats 1,300; Bk Vols 13,000; Per Subs 51
Automation Activity & Vendor Info: (Circulation) Follett Software
Open Mon & Wed 10-8, Tues, Thurs & Fri 10-5:30, Sat 10-1

PATON

P WILLIAM PATON PUBLIC LIBRARY*, 105 Main St, 50217. (Mail add: PO Box 70, 50217-0070), SAN 305-6368. Tel: 515-968-4559. E-mail: patonlib@wccta.net. *Dir,* Virginia Wilson
Pop 255; Circ 7,270
Library Holdings: Bk Titles 13,888; Per Subs 15
Mem of Central Iowa Library Services
Open Mon 2-7, Wed-Fri 2-6, Sat 9-12

PAULLINA

P PAULLINA PUBLIC LIBRARY*, 113 S Mickley St, 51046. (Mail add: PO Box 60, 51046-0060), SAN 305-6376. Tel: 712-949-3941. FAX: 712-949-3866. E-mail: director@paullina.lib.ia.us. Web Site: www.paullina.lib.ia.us. *Dir,* Terri L Tesch; E-mail: territesch@paullina.lib.ia.us; *Asst Librn,* Jean Gnade; E-mail: jeang@paullina.lib.ia.us
Founded 1908. Circ 17,436
Library Holdings: Bk Vols 20,623; Per Subs 46; Talking Bks 774; Videos 760
Automation Activity & Vendor Info: (Acquisitions) Winnebago Software Co; (Cataloging) Winnebago Software Co; (Circulation) Winnebago Software Co
Database Vendor: EBSCOhost
Wireless access
Mem of Northwest Iowa Library Services
Special Services for the Blind - Bks on cassette; Bks on CD; Large print bks
Open Mon 2-6, Tues & Wed 10-6, Thurs 2-8, Fri 1-5, Sat 10-2

PELLA

C CENTRAL COLLEGE, Geisler Library, Campus Box 6500, 812 University St, 50219-1999. SAN 341-955X. Tel: 641-628-5219. Interlibrary Loan Service Tel: 641-628-5193. FAX: 641-628-5327. Web Site: www.central.edu/library. *Dir,* Elizabeth McMahon; Tel: 641-628-5345, E-mail: mcmahone@central.edu; *Tech Serv Librn,* Kyle Winward; Tel: 641-628-5158, E-mail: winwardk@central.edu; *Libr Office Mgr,* Sue Van Vark; E-mail: vanvarks@central.edu; *Media Ctr Mgr,* Debra Phipps; E-mail: phippsd@central.edu; *Circ Supvr,* Lana Goodrich; E-mail: goodrichl@central.edu; *ILL Coordr,* Kelly Taylor; E-mail: taylork@central.edu; Staff 6.39 (MLS 3, Non-MLS 3.39)
Founded 1853. Enrl 1,500; Fac 120; Highest Degree: Bachelor

Library Holdings: AV Mats 7,796; CDs 1,659; DVDs 2,788; e-books 11,682; e-journals 115; Electronic Media & Resources 12,000; Music Scores 4,848; Bk Vols 165,053; Per Subs 379; Videos 5,057
Special Collections: Dutch in America & Iowa (Scholte Coll), bks & letters; George Enescu Coll of Romanian Music; Helen Van Dyke Miniature Book Coll; Pella History, newsp & docs. Oral History
Automation Activity & Vendor Info: (Acquisitions) Innovative Interfaces, Inc; (Cataloging) Innovative Interfaces, Inc; (Circulation) Innovative Interfaces, Inc; (Course Reserve) Innovative Interfaces, Inc; (ILL) OCLC; (OPAC) Innovative Interfaces, Inc; (Serials) Innovative Interfaces, Inc
Database Vendor: ACM (Association for Computing Machinery), American Chemical Society, CQ Press, CredoReference, EBSCOhost, Gale Cengage Learning, JSTOR, OCLC FirstSearch, OCLC WorldShare Interlibrary Loan, ProQuest
Wireless access
Publications: Annual Report; Collection Guides (Online only)
Partic in Greater Western Library Alliance; Iowa Private Academic Library Consortium (IPAL); OCLC Online Computer Library Center, Inc
Special Services for the Deaf - Am sign lang & deaf culture
Open Mon-Thurs 8am-Midnight, Fri 8-5, Sat 1-5, Sun 2-Midnight

P PELLA PUBLIC LIBRARY, 603 Main St, 50219-1592. SAN 305-6384. Tel: 641-628-4268. FAX: 641-628-1735. Web Site: www.cityofpella.com/library. *Dir,* Wendy Street; E-mail: wstreet@cityofpella.com; *Asst Dir,* Christopher Brown; *Youth Serv Librn,* Katie Dreyer; Staff 3 (MLS 2, Non-MLS 1)
Founded 1903. Pop 11,000; Circ 282,865
Automation Activity & Vendor Info: (Acquisitions) Innovative Interfaces, Inc; (Cataloging) Innovative Interfaces, Inc; (Circulation) Innovative Interfaces, Inc; (OPAC) Innovative Interfaces, Inc; (Serials) Innovative Interfaces, Inc
Database Vendor: EBSCOhost, Overdrive, Inc, ProQuest
Wireless access
Partic in OCLC Online Computer Library Center, Inc
Open Mon-Thurs 10-9, Fri 10-6, Sat 10-5
Friends of the Library Group

PEOSTA

R NEW MELLERAY LIBRARY*, 6632 Melleray Circle, 52068. SAN 375-4332. Tel: 563-588-2319, Ext 426. FAX: 563-588-4117. *Librn,* David Bock
Founded 1849
Library Holdings: Bk Titles 32,000; Per Subs 40
Subject Interests: Comparative relig, Hist, Psychol
Wireless access
Restriction: Mem only, Residents only, Restricted access

J NORTHEAST IOWA COMMUNITY COLLEGE*, Peosta Library, 8342 NICC Dr, 52068. SAN 305-3598. Tel: 563-556-5110, Ext 224. FAX: 563-557-0340. Web Site: www.nicc.edu. *Dir,* Deborah Seiffert; E-mail: seiffertd@nicc.edu; *Acq,* Phyllis Mausser; *ILL,* Julie Conolly
Founded 1971. Enrl 2,402
Library Holdings: Bk Vols 17,000; Per Subs 150
Subject Interests: Bus, Health
Automation Activity & Vendor Info: (Cataloging) SirsiDynix; (Circulation) Horizon; (OPAC) SirsiDynix; (Serials) Surpass
Wireless access
Partic in Dubuque Area Library Information Consortium
Open Mon-Thurs 7am-8pm, Fri 7-5

PERRY

P PERRY PUBLIC LIBRARY*, 1101 Willis Ave, 50220-1649. SAN 305-6392. Tel: 515-465-3569. FAX: 515-465-9881. Web Site: www.perry.lib.ia.us. *Dir,* Mary Murphy
Founded 1904. Pop 10,000; Circ 108,000
Library Holdings: Bk Titles 45,000; Per Subs 110
Automation Activity & Vendor Info: (Cataloging) OCLC; (Circulation) Innovative Interfaces, Inc; (ILL) OCLC; (OPAC) Innovative Interfaces, Inc; (Serials) Innovative Interfaces, Inc
Mem of Pioneer Library System
Open Mon-Thurs 10-8, Fri & Sat 10-5, Sun 1-4
Friends of the Library Group

PETERSON

P KIRCHNER-FRENCH MEMORIAL LIBRARY*, 101 Main St, 51047. (Mail add: PO Box 203, 51047-0203), SAN 305-6406. Tel: 712-295-6705. FAX: 712-295-6705. E-mail: kirchner@iowatelecom.net. *Dir,* Linda Eaton; E-mail: leaton@peterson.lib.ia.us; *Youth Serv,* Ruth Paff; Staff 1 (Non-MLS 1)
Founded 1926. Pop 362; Circ 4,787
Library Holdings: Bk Titles 6,505; Per Subs 24; Talking Bks 94; Videos 567
Special Collections: Peterson Patriot (1869-1983)
Function: Bk club(s), Homebound delivery serv, ILL available, Prog for adults, Prog for children & young adult, Ref serv available, Summer reading prog, Telephone ref, VHS videos
Mem of Northwest Iowa Library Services
Open Mon & Sat 9:30-12:30 & 1:30-5:30, Tues, Thurs & Fri 1:30-5:30, Wed 1:30-6

PLAINFIELD

P PLAINFIELD PUBLIC LIBRARY*, 723 Main St, 50666. (Mail add: PO Box 327, 50666-0327), SAN 305-6414. Tel: 319-276-4461. FAX: 319-276-4461. E-mail: bookit@butler-bremer.com. *Dir,* Debra Caudle
Circ 9,000
Library Holdings: Bk Vols 8,000; Per Subs 33
Automation Activity & Vendor Info: (Cataloging) Follett Software; (Circulation) Follett Software
Partic in Libraries of Middlesex Automation Consortium
Open Mon & Fri 1-5, Tues 9-4:30, Wed 12-6, Sat 10-12

PLEASANT HILL

P PLEASANT HILL PUBLIC LIBRARY*, 5151 Maple Dr, 50327-8456. SAN 376-5032. Tel: 515-266-7815. FAX: 515-266-7793. E-mail: phlib@pleasanthill.lib.ia.us. Web Site: www.ci.pleasant-hill.ia.us/library. *Dir,* John Lerdal; E-mail: jlerdal@pleasanthill.lib.ia.us; Staff 5 (MLS 1, Non-MLS 4)
Founded 1982. Pop 6,961; Circ 87,472
Library Holdings: Bks on Deafness & Sign Lang 9; CDs 380; DVDs 481; High Interest/Low Vocabulary Bk Vols 15; Large Print Bks 365; Bk Titles 35,871; Bk Vols 37,427; Per Subs 124; Talking Bks 1,604; Videos 998
Automation Activity & Vendor Info: (Cataloging) Follett Software; (Circulation) Follett Software; (OPAC) Follett Software
Database Vendor: EBSCO Auto Repair Reference, EBSCOhost
Wireless access
Open Mon-Thurs 10-8, Fri 10-6, Sat 10-5, Sun 1-4
Friends of the Library Group

PLEASANTVILLE

P WEBB SHADLE MEMORIAL LIBRARY*, 301 W Dallas, 50225. (Mail add: PO Box 338, Plesantville, 50225-0338), SAN 305-6422. Tel: 515-848-5617. FAX: 515-848-3272. *Dir,* Larry A Conn; E-mail: lconn27769@aol.com
Founded 1955. Pop 2,000; Circ 26,000
Library Holdings: Bk Vols 15,000; Per Subs 65
Special Collections: Americana Coll
Mem of Central Iowa Library Services
Open Mon, Tues & Fri 10-12 & 1-5, Wed 10-12, 1-5, & 6-8, Sat 9-12

PLOVER

P PLOVER PUBLIC LIBRARY, 301 Main St, 50573. (Mail add: PO Box 112, 50573-0112), SAN 305-6430. Tel: 712-857-3532. E-mail: plover@ncn.net. *Dir,* Jerry Depew
Pop 380; Circ 2,463
Library Holdings: AV Mats 312; DVDs 75; Bk Titles 2,500; Per Subs 23; Talking Bks 50; Videos 310
Subject Interests: Local hist
Automation Activity & Vendor Info: (Cataloging) ResourceMATE; (Circulation) ResourceMATE
Wireless access
Mem of Northwest Iowa Library Services
Open Mon & Thurs 3-6, Sat 9-Noon

POCAHONTAS

P POCAHONTAS PUBLIC LIBRARY, 14 Second Ave NW, 50574. SAN 305-6457. Tel: 712-335-4471. FAX: 712-335-4471. E-mail: pocahontaspl@pocahontas.lib.ia.us. Web Site: www.pocahontas.lib.ia.us. *Dir,* Lola DeWall; *Ch & Youth Librn,* Marge Spear; *Librn,* Linda Ferguson; *Librn,* Gabrielle Mackinnon; *Librn,* Jane Schott; *Adult Serv,* Mona Zhorne; Staff 5 (Non-MLS 5)
Founded 1922. Pop 1,970; Circ 22,993
Jul 2006-Jun 2007 Income $83,024, State $2,310, City $62,500, County $7,875, Locally Generated Income $2,500, Other $7,839. Mats Exp $11,400, Books $9,600, Per/Ser (Incl. Access Fees) $1,800. Sal $49,068
Library Holdings: Bk Vols 19,684; Per Subs 65
Subject Interests: Genealogy, Local hist, Railroads
Automation Activity & Vendor Info: (Cataloging) Book Systems; (Circulation) Book Systems; (OPAC) Book Systems
Database Vendor: EBSCOhost, LearningExpress, OCLC FirstSearch
Wireless access
Mem of Northwest Iowa Library Services
Open Mon, Tues & Fri 11-5, Wed & Thurs 11-8, Sat 9-2

POLK CITY

P POLK CITY COMMUNITY LIBRARY*, 1500 W Broadway St, 50226-2001. (Mail add: PO Box 259, 50226-0259), SAN 305-6465. Tel: 515-984-6119. FAX: 515-984-9273. E-mail: library@polkcitylibrary.org. Web Site: www.polkcitylibrary.org. *Dir,* Kim Kellogg
Founded 1974. Pop 1,908; Circ 14,730
Library Holdings: Bk Titles 12,000
Automation Activity & Vendor Info: (Cataloging) Follett Software; (Circulation) Follett Software
Wireless access
Publications: Booklist
Mem of Central Iowa Library Services
Open Mon-Thurs 10-8, Fri 10-6, Sat 10-4
Friends of the Library Group

POMEROY

P POMEROY PUBLIC LIBRARY*, 114 S Ontario St, 50575-7702. (Mail add: Box 187, 50575-0187), SAN 305-6473. Tel: 712-468-2311. FAX: 712-468-2311. *Dir,* Marcia Ehr; E-mail: director@pomeroy.lib.ia.us
Pop 895; Circ 10,462
Library Holdings: DVDs 45; Large Print Bks 60; Bk Vols 9,000; Per Subs 35; Talking Bks 85; Videos 150
Wireless access
Mem of Northwest Iowa Library Services
Open Mon 10-12 & 1-5, Wed & Fri 1-5, Thurs 1-6, Sat 9-12

POSTVILLE

P POSTVILLE PUBLIC LIBRARY*, 235 W Tilden, 52162. SAN 305-6481. Tel: 563-864-7600. FAX: 563-864-7600. E-mail: library@postville.lib.ia.us. Web Site: www.postville.lib.ia.us. *Dir,* Cindy Berns
Pop 2,200; Circ 19,594
Library Holdings: Bk Titles 18,000; Per Subs 52
Automation Activity & Vendor Info: (Cataloging) ComPanion Corp; (Circulation) ComPanion Corp
Wireless access
Open Mon & Fri 9:30-5:30, Tues & Thurs 2-5:30, Wed 9:30-7:30, Sat 9-12

PRAIRIE CITY

P PRAIRIE CITY PUBLIC LIBRARY*, 100 E Fifth, 50228. (Mail add: PO Box 113, 50228-0113), SAN 376-7507. Tel: 515-994-2308. E-mail: pclibrar@mchsi.com. Web Site: www.prairiecity.lib.ia.us. *Dir,* Sue Ponder
Library Holdings: Bk Vols 8,524; Per Subs 34
Mem of Central Iowa Library Services
Open Mon & Fri 1-5, Tues & Thurs 4-8, Wed 9-11 & 1-5, Sat 9-12

PRESCOTT

P PRESCOTT PUBLIC LIBRARY*, 607 Second St, 50859-0177. SAN 376-5199. Tel: 641-335-2238. FAX: 641-335-2238. *Dir,* Veda McCarty
Pop 611; Circ 1,346
Library Holdings: Bk Vols 3,517; Per Subs 10
Open Mon & Thurs 9-5, Wed 1-5

PRESTON

P PRESTON PUBLIC LIBRARY*, One W Gillet, 52069. (Mail add: PO Box 605, 52069-0605), SAN 305-649X. Tel: 563-689-3581. FAX: 563-689-3581. E-mail: director@preston.lib.ia.us. Web Site: www.preston.lib.ia.us. *Co-Dir,* Carolyn Bradekamp; *Co-Dir,* Mary Snopek
Founded 1974. Circ 14,297
Library Holdings: Bk Vols 13,000; Per Subs 75
Automation Activity & Vendor Info: (Cataloging) Follett Software; (Circulation) Follett Software
Partic in Southeastern Libraries Cooperating
Open Mon & Wed 1-8, Tues 9:30-11:30 & 1-5, Thurs 1-5, Fri 10-5, Sat (Sept-May) 10-3

PRIMGHAR

P PRIMGHAR PUBLIC LIBRARY*, 320 First St NE, 51245. (Mail add: PO Box 9, 51245-0009), SAN 305-6503. Tel: 712-957-8981. FAX: 712-957-8981. E-mail: primlib@tcaexpress.net. Web Site: www.primghar.com. *Dir,* Leann Langfitt
Pop 1,050; Circ 22,640
Library Holdings: Bk Titles 14,000; Per Subs 31
Mem of Northwest Iowa Library Services
Open Tues & Wed 1-5, Thurs 1-6, Fri 9-12 & 1-5, Sat 8-12

QUIMBY

P QUIMBY PUBLIC LIBRARY*, 201 N Main, 51049. (Mail add: PO Box 186, 51049-0186), SAN 305-6511. Tel: 712-445-2413. FAX: 712-445-2688. E-mail: qpl@midlands.net. Web Site: www.quimby.lib.ia.us. *Dir,* Linda Sones
Pop 334; Circ 2,736
Library Holdings: Bk Titles 6,433; Per Subs 30
Mem of Northwest Iowa Library Services
Open Mon-Wed & Fri 1-5, Thurs 4-6, Sat 10-12

RADCLIFFE

P RADCLIFFE PUBLIC LIBRARY*, 210 Isabella, 50230. (Mail add: PO Box 348, 50230-0348), SAN 305-652X. Tel: 515-899-7914. FAX: 515-899-7914. E-mail: rad_lib@netins.net. *Dir,* Marilyn Raska-engelson
Pop 593; Circ 11,193
Library Holdings: Bk Titles 15,756; Per Subs 50
Open Mon 2-5 & 7-9, Tues 10-5, Wed 10-5 & 7-9, Thurs & Fri 2-5, Sat 10-3

RAKE

P RAKE PUBLIC LIBRARY, 123 N Main St, 50465. (Mail add: PO Box 166, 50465), SAN 305-6538. Tel: 641-566-3388. FAX: 641-566-3388. E-mail: rakelibrary@wctatel.net. *Dir,* Virginia Cooper
Founded 1962. Pop 230; Circ 5,000
Library Holdings: Bk Titles 5,400
Automation Activity & Vendor Info: (Cataloging) Follett Software
Wireless access
Open Tues, Wed & Fri 9-11:30 & 1:30-5, Thurs 9-11:30 & 1:30-6, Sat 9am-10:30am

RANDOLPH

P RANDOLPH PUBLIC LIBRARY*, 106 S Main St, 51649. (Mail add: PO Box 112, 51649-0112), SAN 305-6546. Tel: 712-625-3561. FAX: 712-625-3561. *Dir,* Debbie Lesher
Founded 1960. Pop 820; Circ 5,000
Library Holdings: AV Mats 413; Bks on Deafness & Sign Lang 25; DVDs 450; Bk Titles 10,000; Per Subs 12
Special Collections: Randolph Enterprise Newspapers, 1895-1970
Wireless access
Mem of Southwest Iowa Library Services District
Open Mon 4-7, Tues-Thurs 4-6, Sat 8:30-11:30

READLYN

P READLYN COMMUNITY LIBRARY*, 309 Main St, 50668. (Mail add: PO Box 249, 50668-0249), SAN 305-6554. Tel: 319-279-3432. FAX: 319-279-3432. E-mail: readlynlib@gmail.com. Web Site: www.readlyn.lib.ia.us. *Dir,* Barb Sowers
Founded 1965. Pop 858; Circ 17,185
Library Holdings: Bk Titles 14,000; Per Subs 73
Wireless access
Open Mon & Thurs 10-7, Tues, Wed & Fri 10-5, Sat 9-12

RED OAK

P RED OAK PUBLIC LIBRARY*, 400 N Second St, 51566-2251. SAN 305-6562. Tel: 712-623-6516. FAX: 712-623-6518. Web Site: www.redoak.lib.ia.us. *Dir,* Kathi Wagner; Staff 1 (Non-MLS 1)
Founded 1908. Pop 6,264; Circ 65,000
Special Collections: State & Local History
Wireless access
Mem of Southwest Iowa Library Services District
Open Mon & Wed 10-8, Tues, Thurs, Fri & Sat 10-5

REDFIELD

P REDFIELD PUBLIC LIBRARY*, 1112 Thomas St, 50233. (Mail add: PO Box L, 50233-0911), SAN 305-6570. Tel: 515-833-2200. E-mail: r.library@mchsi.com. *Librn,* Lori Stonehocker
Pop 959; Circ 11,000
Library Holdings: Bk Titles 10,500; Per Subs 36
Mem of Central Iowa Library Services
Open Mon & Wed-Fri 1-6, Tues & Sat 9-12 & 1-6

REINBECK

P REINBECK PUBLIC LIBRARY*, 501 Clark St, 50669. SAN 305-6589. Tel: 319-788-2652. FAX: 319-788-2826. E-mail: reinlibr@reinbeck.net. Web Site: www.reinbeck.lib.ia.us. *Dir,* Janet Slessor; E-mail: janets@reinbeck.lib.ia.us; *Asst Librn,* Ann Rae Billerbeck; *Asst Librn,* Cherie Eckhoff
Pop 1,664; Circ 25,899

Jul 2011-Jun 2012 Income $94,620, State $1,662, City $67,103, Federal $253, County $22,291, Locally Generated Income $3,311. Mats Exp $17,113, Books $13,652, Per/Ser (Incl. Access Fees) $1,500, AV Mat $1,412, Electronic Ref Mat (Incl. Access Fees) $549. Sal $49,340 (Prof $33,000)
Library Holdings: Audiobooks 653; AV Mats 1,211; CDs 500; DVDs 350; Bk Titles 20,000; Bk Vols 21,000; Per Subs 77; Videos 108
Automation Activity & Vendor Info: (Acquisitions) Follett Software; (Circulation) Follett Software

REMBRANDT

P REMBRANDT PUBLIC LIBRARY*, Main St & Broadway, 50576. (Mail add: PO Box 169, 50576-0186), SAN 373-8906. Tel: 712-286-6801. FAX: 712-286-6801. Web Site: www.rembrandt.lib.ia.us. *Dir,* Joleen Anderson; E-mail: joleenj@rembrandt.lib.ia.us; Staff 1 (MLS 1)
Founded 1930. Pop 229; Circ 3,237
Library Holdings: Bk Titles 6,000; Per Subs 11
Open Tues 10-5, Wed 4-6, Thurs 10-6, Sat 9-12

REMSEN

P REMSEN PUBLIC LIBRARY*, 211 Fulton, 51050. SAN 305-6600. Tel: 712-786-2911. FAX: 712-786-3255. E-mail: rploff@midlands.net. *Co-Dir,* Valerie Loutsch; *Co-Dir,* Rita Nuebel
Founded 1939
Library Holdings: DVDs 50; Large Print Bks 500; Bk Titles 16,000; Per Subs 60; Talking Bks 200; Videos 200
Automation Activity & Vendor Info: (Cataloging) Follett Software; (Circulation) Follett Software
Mem of Northwest Iowa Library Services
Open Mon & Fri 1-5, Tues & Thurs 9-5, Wed 9-8, Sat 9-1

RENWICK

P RENWICK PUBLIC LIBRARY*, 204 Stoddard St, 50577-0038. (Mail add: PO Box 38, 50577-0038), SAN 305-6619. Tel: 515-824-3209. FAX: 515-824-3209. E-mail: renwickl@wmtel.net. *Librn,* Jan Thompson
Pop 280; Circ 6,814
Library Holdings: Bk Titles 4,000; Bk Vols 4,500; Per Subs 15
Open Mon 10-6, Tues 1-5, Wed 10-5, Fri & Sat 9-12

RICEVILLE

P RICEVILLE PUBLIC LIBRARY*, 307 Woodland Ave, 50466. SAN 305-6627. Tel: 641-985-2273. FAX: 641-985-4002. E-mail: director@riceville.lib.ia.us. Web Site: www.riceville.lib.ia.us. *Dir,* Jim Cross; *Asst Librn,* Diane Brownell
Founded 1928. Pop 1,300; Circ 30,535
Library Holdings: AV Mats 943; Large Print Bks 789; Bk Titles 12,000; Bk Vols 13,050; Per Subs 36; Talking Bks 560
Automation Activity & Vendor Info: (Cataloging) Follett Software; (Circulation) Follett Software; (OPAC) Follett Software
Wireless access
Open Mon 10-7, Tues-Fri 10-6, Sat 10-1
Friends of the Library Group

RICHLAND

P RICHLAND PUBLIC LIBRARY*, 100 E Main St, 52585. SAN 305-6635. Tel: 319-456-6541. FAX: 319-456-6541. E-mail: richlib@iowatelecom.net. Web Site: www.richland.lib.ia.us. *Dir,* Cindy McCan
Pop 1,221; Circ 9,565
Library Holdings: AV Mats 406; Bk Titles 9,000; Per Subs 15
Automation Activity & Vendor Info: (Acquisitions) Follett Software
Wireless access
Open Tues-Thurs 2:30-6:30, Fri 12-5, Sat 9-12

RINGSTED

P RINGSTED PUBLIC LIBRARY*, Eight W Maple St, 50578. SAN 305-6651. Tel: 712-866-0878. FAX: 712-866-0879. E-mail: rlibrary@ringtelco.com. *Dir,* Lola Meyer; *Ch,* Chris Struecker
Pop 440; Circ 3,584
Library Holdings: Bk Titles 9,674; Per Subs 16
Mem of Northwest Iowa Library Services
Open Mon, Tues & Fri 9-11:30, Wed & Thurs 1:30-6, Sat 8:30-12

RIPPEY

P RIPPEY PUBLIC LIBRARY, 224 Main St, 50235. (Mail add: PO Box 184, 50235-0184), SAN 305-666X. Tel: 515-436-7714. E-mail: rippeyli@windstream.net. Web Site: www.rippey.lib.ia.us.
Wireless access
Mem of Central Iowa Library Services
Special Services for the Blind - Large print bks
Open Mon 1-6, Tues 1:30-5:30, Wed 3-8, Thurs 10-2

ROCK RAPIDS

P ROCK RAPIDS PUBLIC LIBRARY*, 102 S Greene St, 51246. SAN 305-6678. Tel: 712-472-3541. FAX: 712-472-3541. E-mail: rrlib@hickorytech.net. Web Site: www.rockrapids.lib.ia.us. *Dir,* Linda McCormack
Founded 1893. Pop 2,549; Circ 62,135
Jul 2010-Jun 2011 Income $155,643, State $1,663, City $125,406, County $16,828, Locally Generated Income $1,697, Other $10,049. Mats Exp $16,206, Books $12,202, Per/Ser (Incl. Access Fees) $2,201, AV Mat $1,803. Sal $90,584
Library Holdings: Bk Vols 38,965; Per Subs 51
Automation Activity & Vendor Info: (Cataloging) Book Systems; (Circulation) Book Systems; (OPAC) Book Systems
Database Vendor: EBSCOhost
Wireless access
Mem of Northwest Iowa Library Services
Open Mon & Wed 12-5:30 & 7-9, Tues & Thurs 10-5:30 & 7-9, Fri 12-5:30, Sat 10-3:30
Friends of the Library Group

ROCK VALLEY

P ROCK VALLEY PUBLIC LIBRARY*, 1531 Main St, 51247-1127. SAN 305-6686. Tel: 712-476-5651. FAX: 712-476-5261. E-mail: rvplorna@hickorytech.net. Web Site: www.rockvalley.lib.ia.us. *Dir,* Lorna Van Maanen; E-mail: lornavm@rockvalley.lib.ia.us; *Ch,* Beth Vandenberg; *Asst Librn,* Linda Wissink
Founded 1916. Pop 3,700; Circ 115,980
Library Holdings: Bk Vols 46,000; Per Subs 50
Special Collections: Oral History
Mem of Northwest Iowa Library Services
Open Mon & Wed 10-9, Tues & Thurs-Sat 10-5

ROCKFORD

P ROCKFORD PUBLIC LIBRARY, 202 W Main Ave, 50468-1212. (Mail add: PO Box 496, 50468-0496), SAN 305-6694. Tel: 641-756-3725. FAX: 641-756-3725. E-mail: rkfdlib@myomnitel.com. *Dir,* Jill Gray; *Ch,* Stacy Tynan; Staff 2 (MLS 1, Non-MLS 1)
Founded 1917. Pop 860; Circ 17,403
Jan 2005-Dec 2005 Income $35,379, City $15,406, County $12,608, Other $7,365. Mats Exp $4,998, Books $3,436, Per/Ser (Incl. Access Fees) $719, AV Mat $843. Sal $15,789
Library Holdings: AV Mats 710; Bk Titles 7,189; Per Subs 42; Talking Bks 572
Automation Activity & Vendor Info: (Acquisitions) Biblionix/Apollo; (Cataloging) Biblionix/Apollo; (Circulation) Biblionix/Apollo; (ILL) Biblionix/Apollo; (OPAC) Biblionix/Apollo; (Serials) Biblionix/Apollo
Wireless access
Open Mon, Tues, Thurs & Fri 1-5:30, Wed 1-7:30, Sat 9-12

ROCKWELL

P ROCKWELL PUBLIC LIBRARY*, 307 Main St, 50469. (Mail add: PO Box 419, 50469-0419), SAN 305-6708. Tel: 641-822-3268. FAX: 641-822-3168. E-mail: rkwlpl@netins.net. Web Site: www.rockwell.lib.ia.us. *Dir,* Linda Dunning
Founded 1900. Pop 989; Circ 20,654
Library Holdings: Large Print Bks 183; Bk Titles 11,316; Bk Vols 12,961; Per Subs 60; Talking Bks 242
Automation Activity & Vendor Info: (Cataloging) Follett Software; (Circulation) Follett Software
Open Mon, Wed & Thurs 9-12 & 2-8, Tues 9-12, Fri 9-12 & 2-6, Sat 9-3

ROCKWELL CITY

S NORTH CENTRAL CORRECTIONAL FACILITY*, Inmate Library, 313 Lanedale, 50579. SAN 375-3263. Tel: 712-297-7521, Ext 229. FAX: 712-297-9316. *Librn,* Joe Bush; Staff 9 (MLS 1, Non-MLS 8)
Library Holdings: Bk Titles 6,000; Per Subs 20
Subject Interests: Law
Open Mon-Fri 8:30-4

P ROCKWELL CITY PUBLIC LIBRARY*, 424 Main St, 50579-1415. SAN 305-6732. Tel: 712-297-8422. FAX: 712-297-8422. E-mail: director@rockwellcity.lib.ia.us. Web Site: www.rockwellcity.lib.ia.us. *Dir,* Denise Pohl; *Ch Serv,* Sarah Weiss
Founded 1897. Pop 1,919; Circ 21,176
Library Holdings: High Interest/Low Vocabulary Bk Vols 80; Bk Titles 17,762; Bk Vols 18,178; Per Subs 72
Special Collections: Calhoun County Genealogical Society Library
Publications: Column Inches (Newsletter)
Mem of Northwest Iowa Library Services

Open Mon & Tues 11-7, Wed- Fri 10-5, Sat 9-12
Friends of the Library Group

ROLAND

P ROLAND PUBLIC LIBRARY*, 218 N Main, 50236. (Mail add: PO Box 409, 50236-0409), SAN 376-544X. Tel: 515-388-4086. E-mail: rolandlib@globalccs.net. Web Site: www.roland.lib.ia.us. *Dir,* Laura Urbanek
Library Holdings: Bk Vols 12,000; Per Subs 75
Mem of Central Iowa Library Services
Open Mon-Fri 10-7, Sat 10-4, Sun 12-4
Friends of the Library Group

ROLFE

P ROLFE PUBLIC LIBRARY, 319 Garfield St, 50581-1118. SAN 305-6759. Tel: 712-848-3143. FAX: 712-848-3143. E-mail: rplib@ncn.net. *Librn,* Penny Tilden
Founded 1926. Pop 575; Circ 4,270
Library Holdings: Bk Vols 10,791; Per Subs 17
Special Collections: Local Hist Coll, pictures, papers. Oral History
Wireless access
Mem of Northwest Iowa Library Services
Open Mon 1-6, Tues-Fri 2-5, Sat 9:30-12:30
Friends of the Library Group

ROWAN

P ROWAN PUBLIC LIBRARY*, 101 Main St, 50470-5005. (Mail add: PO Box 182, 50470-0182), SAN 305-6767. Tel: 641-853-2327. FAX: 641-853-2327. Web Site: www.rowan.lib.ia.us. *Dir,* Joyce Erikson; E-mail: joyceeriksen@rowan.lib.ia.us
Founded 1964. Pop 259; Circ 11,214
Library Holdings: Bk Vols 6,300
Open Mon & Wed 10-6, Fri 10-5, Sat 9-Noon

ROYAL

P ROYAL PUBLIC LIBRARY*, 302 Main St, 51357. (Mail add: PO Box 199, 51357-0199), SAN 305-6775. Tel: 712-933-5500. E-mail: rlibrary@royaltelco.net. *Librn,* Barbara Fletcher
Pop 479; Circ 4,379
Library Holdings: Bk Vols 6,558; Per Subs 86
Open Mon, Wed & Fri 2-4:30, Tues & Sat 9:30-11:30, Thurs 4:30-6:30
Friends of the Library Group

RUDD

P RUDD PUBLIC LIBRARY*, 308 Chickasaw St, 50471. (Mail add: PO Box 305, 50471-0305), SAN 305-6783. Tel: 641-395-2385. FAX: 641-395-2385. E-mail: ruddlib@myomnitel.com. Web Site: www.rudd.lib.ia.us. *Librn,* Susan Pifer
Founded 1956. Pop 430; Circ 16,875
Library Holdings: Bk Vols 7,000; Per Subs 48
Open Mon & Wed 1-7, Fri 12-6, Sat 9-12

RUNNELLS

P RUNNELLS COMMUNITY LIBRARY*, 6575 SE 116th St, 50237-1193. Tel: 515-966-2068. Web Site: www.cityofrunnells.com/communitylibrary. *Dir,* Carole Adams
Pop 352
Library Holdings: Bk Titles 4,500
Automation Activity & Vendor Info: (Cataloging) Book Systems; (Circulation) Book Systems
Wireless access
Open Tues & Thurs 5:30-8, Sat 9-12

RUTHVEN

P RUTHVEN PUBLIC LIBRARY*, 1301 Gowrie St, 51358. (Mail add: PO Box 280, 51358-0280), SAN 305-6791. Tel: 712-837-4820. FAX: 712-837-4820. Web Site: www.ruthven.lib.ia.us. *Dir,* Nathan R E Clark; E-mail: nclark@ruthven.lib.ia.us; *Asst Dir,* Donna Johnson; E-mail: djohnson@ruthven.lib.ia.us; Staff 2 (Non-MLS 2)
Pop 711; Circ 7,000
Library Holdings: Bk Vols 6,000; Per Subs 30
Function: ILL available
Open Mon & Fri 1-5:30, Tues & Thurs 6-8, Wed 9:30-11:30 & 3-8, Sat 9-12
Friends of the Library Group

SABULA

P KRABBENHOFT PUBLIC LIBRARY*, 512 Elk St, 52070. (Mail add: PO Box 340, 52070-0340), SAN 305-6805. Tel: 563-687-2950. FAX: 563-687-2950. E-mail: sabulapubliclibrary@mchsi.com. Web Site: www.sabula.lib.ia.us. *Dir,* Ronda Taplin
Founded 1961. Pop 670; Circ 12,724
Library Holdings: AV Mats 700; Bk Vols 15,000; Per Subs 40
Open Tues, Thurs & Fri 1-5, Wed 7-9, Sat 9-4

SAC CITY

P SAC CITY PUBLIC LIBRARY*, 1001 W Main St, 50583. SAN 305-6813. Tel: 712-662-7276. FAX: 712-662-7802. Web Site: www.saccity.lib.ia.us. *Dir,* Brandie Ledford; E-mail: bledford@saccity.lib.ia.us; *Asst Librn,* Joyce O'Tool; *Ch,* Cathie Hass
Founded 1912. Pop 2,460; Circ 11,000
Library Holdings: AV Mats 500; Large Print Bks 300; Bk Titles 32,000; Per Subs 78; Talking Bks 600
Special Collections: Oral History
Subject Interests: Local hist
Mem of Northwest Iowa Library Services
Open Mon, Tues, Wed & Fri 10-6, Thurs 10-7, Sat 10-1
Friends of the Library Group

SAINT ANSGAR

P NISSEN PUBLIC LIBRARY*, Saint Ansgar Public Library, 217 W Fifth, 50472-0040. (Mail add: PO Box 40, 50472-0040), SAN 305-6821. Tel: 641-713-2218. FAX: 641-713-4716. Web Site: www.saintansgar.lib.ia.us. *Dir,* Marsha Kuntz; *Asst Dir,* S Stohr; *Asst Librn,* J Kuntz; Staff 5 (Non-MLS 5)
Founded 1927. Pop 1,030
Library Holdings: Bk Titles 10,569; Per Subs 60; Talking Bks 541
Automation Activity & Vendor Info: (Cataloging) Follett Software; (Circulation) Follett Software; (ILL) Follett Software
Open Mon & Wed 1-5:30 & 7-9, Tues, Thurs & Sat 1-5:30, Fri 9-12 & 1-5:30

SAINT CHARLES

P SAINT CHARLES PUBLIC LIBRARY*, 210 N Cross St, 50240. (Mail add: PO Box 2, 50240-0118). Tel: 641-396-2945. E-mail: scplibrary@netins.net. Web Site: www.stcharles.lib.ia.us. *Dir,* Joan Naylor
Pop 619; Circ 2,804
Library Holdings: Bk Vols 7,199; Per Subs 17
Database Vendor: EBSCOhost
Open Tues & Thurs 10:30-7, Wed 3-6, Sat 9-12

SALEM

P CREW PUBLIC LIBRARY*, 107 E Cherry St, 52649. (Mail add: PO Box 117, 52649-0117), SAN 305-683X. Tel: 319-258-9007. FAX: 319-258-9007. E-mail: crew2009@iowatelecom.net. *Dir,* Kelly Patterson
Founded 1940. Pop 500; Circ 13,500
Library Holdings: Bk Titles 10,000; Per Subs 20
Open Mon 11:30-3, Wed 1-6, Sat 9:30-11:30

SANBORN

P SANBORN PUBLIC LIBRARY*, 407 Main St, 51248. (Mail add: PO Box 430, 51248-0430), SAN 305-6848. Tel: 712-930-3215. FAX: 712-930-3170. E-mail: spl@tcaexpress.net. Web Site: www.sanborn.lib.ia.us. *Dir,* Alvina Reitsma
Founded 1911. Pop 1,353
Library Holdings: DVDs 378; Large Print Bks 47; Bk Vols 20,000; Per Subs 76; Talking Bks 591; Videos 425
Automation Activity & Vendor Info: (Cataloging) Follett Software; (Circulation) Follett Software
Database Vendor: Baker & Taylor
Wireless access
Function: ILL available, Prog for children & young adult, Spoken cassettes & CDs, Spoken cassettes & DVDs, Summer reading prog, VHS videos
Mem of Northwest Iowa Library Services
Open Mon & Wed 11:30-7, Thurs 11:30-5:30, Fri & Sat 8:30-12
Restriction: Restricted loan policy
Friends of the Library Group

SCHALLER

P SCHALLER PUBLIC LIBRARY*, 103 S Main St, 51053. (Mail add: PO Box 427, 51053-0427), SAN 305-6856. Tel: 712-275-4741. *Dir,* Barb Jorgensen
Pop 779
Library Holdings: Bk Titles 9,000; Bk Vols 11,476; Per Subs 20; Talking Bks 191

Database Vendor: OCLC FirstSearch
Wireless access
Mem of Northwest Iowa Library Services
Partic in State of Iowa Libraries Online
Open Mon & Fri 2:30-5:30, Tues & Thurs 9:30-10:30 & 2:30-5:30, Wed 2-6, Sat 10-Noon

SCHLESWIG

P SCHLESWIG PUBLIC LIBRARY*, 202 Cedar St, 51461-0306. SAN 305-6864. Tel: 712-676-3470. E-mail: burdan@windstream.net. *Dir,* Dee Lyon
Founded 1940. Pop 2,000; Circ 4,810
Library Holdings: Bk Titles 11,017
Special Collections: Schleswig Leader Coll (1909 to 1981), 75th Anniversary, microflim, sound flm
Mem of Northwest Iowa Library Services
Open Mon 3-8, Wed 3-5, Sat 9-2
Friends of the Library Group

SCRANTON

P SCRANTON PUBLIC LIBRARY*, 1102 Main St, 51462. (Mail add: PO Box 68, 51462-0068), SAN 305-6872. Tel: 712-652-3453. E-mail: admin@scranton.lib.ia.us, scrpblib@netins.net. *Dir,* Sarah Stephens
Pop 602; Circ 15,350
Library Holdings: Bk Vols 10,000; Per Subs 44
Automation Activity & Vendor Info: (Cataloging) Book Systems; (Circulation) Book Systems
Mem of Central Iowa Library Services
Open Mon-Wed & Fri 2-6, Thurs 2-7, Sat 8-11
Friends of the Library Group

SEYMOUR

P SEYMOUR COMMUNITY LIBRARY*, 123 N Fifth, 52590. SAN 305-6880. Tel: 641-898-2966. FAX: 641-898-2305. E-mail: seycomlib@lisco.net. *Librn,* Lisa Perkins
Founded 1940. Pop 1,036; Circ 7,662
Library Holdings: Bk Titles 10,000
Mem of Southwest Iowa Library Services District
Open Mon-Fri 1-5, Sat 10-12

SHEFFIELD

P SHEFFIELD PUBLIC LIBRARY*, 123 S Third St, 50475. (Mail add: PO Box 616, 50475-0616), SAN 305-6899. Tel: 641-892-4717. FAX: 641-892-4248. Web Site: www.sheffield.lib.ia.us. *Dir,* Jill Peterson; E-mail: jpeterson@sheffield.lib.ia.us
Pop 930; Circ 22,793
Library Holdings: Bk Titles 17,381; Per Subs 64
Automation Activity & Vendor Info: (Cataloging) Follett Software; (Circulation) Follett Software; (OPAC) Follett Software
Database Vendor: EBSCOhost, OCLC FirstSearch
Open Mon 10-7, Tues-Fri 1:30-6:30, Sat 9-3

SHELDON

J NORTHWEST IOWA COMMUNITY COLLEGE LIBRARY*, 603 W Park St, 51201. SAN 305-6902. Tel: 712-324-5061. FAX: 712-324-4157. Web Site: www.nwicc.edu. *Dir,* Molly Galm; E-mail: mgalm@nwicc.edu; *ILL,* Rhonda Huisman
Founded 1974. Enrl 850; Fac 50
Library Holdings: Bk Titles 13,000; Bk Vols 15,000; Per Subs 250
Subject Interests: Bus & mgt, Electronics, Mechanical eng, Sci tech
Automation Activity & Vendor Info: (Cataloging) Innovative Interfaces, Inc; (Circulation) Innovative Interfaces, Inc; (OPAC) Innovative Interfaces, Inc
Partic in OCLC Online Computer Library Center, Inc; State of Iowa Libraries Online
Open Mon-Thurs 7:30-7, Fri 7:30-4:30

P SHELDON PUBLIC LIBRARY, 925 Fourth Ave, 51201-1517. SAN 305-6910. Tel: 712-324-2442. FAX: 712-324-5609. E-mail: sheldonpubliclibrary@gmail.com. Web Site: www.sheldon.lib.ia.us. *Dir,* Ruth A Rodvik; *Asst Dir,* Brenda Klaahssen
Founded 1904. Pop 5,003; Circ 94,680
Library Holdings: AV Mats 746; Bk Titles 29,802; Per Subs 100; Talking Bks 801
Special Collections: Local Newspaper 1874-1997, micro
Automation Activity & Vendor Info: (Serials) EBSCO Online
Database Vendor: Book Systems
Wireless access
Open Mon & Tues 9:30-8, Wed-Fri 9:30-5, Sat 9:30-3
Friends of the Library Group

SHELL ROCK

P BENNY GAMBAIANI PUBLIC LIBRARY*, 104 S Cherry St, 50670. (Mail add: PO Box 320, 50670-0811), SAN 305-6929. Tel: 319-885-4345. FAX: 319-885-6209. E-mail: gambaian@butler-bremer.com. Web Site: www.shellrocklibrary.org. *Dir,* Diane L Harms; *Asst Librn,* Debra Heidemann; Staff 2 (Non-MLS 2)
Pop 1,298; Circ 25,000
Library Holdings: Large Print Bks 79; Bk Titles 14,000; Per Subs 69; Talking Bks 359
Special Collections: Shell Rock Newspapers, microfilm
Automation Activity & Vendor Info: (Circulation) Follett Software
Function: Handicapped accessible, Home delivery & serv to Sr ctr & nursing homes, Homebound delivery serv, ILL available, Libr develop, Mail loans to mem, Online searches, Outside serv via phone, mail, e-mail & web, Photocopying/Printing, Prog for children & young adult, Summer reading prog, Workshops
Open Mon & Fri 12-5, Tues & Thurs 12-8, Wed 9-5, Sat 9am-11am

SHELLSBURG

P SHELLSBURG PUBLIC LIBRARY*, 110 Main St, 52332. (Mail add: PO Box 248, 52332-0248), SAN 305-6937. Tel: 319-436-2112. FAX: 319-436-2112. E-mail: director@shellsburg.lib.ia.us. Web Site: www.shellsburg.lib.ia.us. *Dir,* Edward Kraft; *Asst Librn,* Phyllis Judas; Staff 1 (Non-MLS 1)
Founded 1970. Pop 998; Circ 21,179
Jul 2011-Jun 2012 Income $43,464, State $1,377, City $34,842, County $7,245
Library Holdings: CDs 42; DVDs 175; Large Print Bks 72; Bk Titles 12,725; Per Subs 12; Videos 64
Automation Activity & Vendor Info: (Acquisitions) Follett Software
Database Vendor: EBSCOhost
Wireless access
Function: Bk club(s), Bks on cassette, Bks on CD, Children's prog, Computers for patron use, Copy machines, e-mail & chat, Fax serv, Free DVD rentals, Handicapped accessible, ILL available, Magnifiers for reading, Online cat, OverDrive digital audio bks, Photocopying/Printing, Pub access computers, Summer reading prog, Tax forms, VHS videos, Video lending libr, Wheelchair accessible
Open Mon & Wed 10-12 & 2-6, Tues, Thurs & Fri 2-6, Sat 10-12
Restriction: Authorized patrons, Borrowing requests are handled by ILL, Circ limited
Friends of the Library Group

SHENANDOAH

P SHENANDOAH PUBLIC LIBRARY*, 201 S Elm St, 51601. SAN 305-6945. Tel: 712-246-2315. FAX: 712-246-5847. E-mail: libraryq@qwestoffice.net. Web Site: www.shenandoah.lib.ia.us. *Dir,* Jan Frank-de Ois; *Circ,* Janet Hensen; *Ch Serv,* Elizabeth Trippler; *Tech Coordr,* Carrie Falk; Staff 4 (MLS 2, Non-MLS 2)
Founded 1904. Pop 5,546; Circ 65,564
Library Holdings: Bk Vols 55,000
Automation Activity & Vendor Info: (Cataloging) Follett Software; (Circulation) Follett Software; (OPAC) Follett Software
Database Vendor: OCLC FirstSearch
Mem of Southwest Iowa Library Services District
Open Mon-Wed & Fri-Sat 10-6, Thurs 10-9
Friends of the Library Group

SIBLEY

P SIBLEY PUBLIC LIBRARY*, 406 Ninth St, 51249. SAN 305-6953. Tel: 712-754-2888. FAX: 712-754-2590. Web Site: www.sibley.lib.ia.us. *Dir,* Constance Diane Mataloni; E-mail: connie.mataloni@sibley.lib.ia.us; *Ch Serv,* Sonia Ernst; E-mail: sonia.ernst@sibley.lib.ia.us; Staff 4 (Non-MLS 4)
Founded 1917. Pop 2,796; Circ 48,594
Jul 2006-Jun 2007 Income $135,575, State $2,537, City $94,624, County $10,000, Locally Generated Income $9,652, Other $18,762. Mats Exp $24,505, Books $16,470, Per/Ser (Incl. Access Fees) $2,968, AV Mat $4,263, Electronic Ref Mat (Incl. Access Fees) $804. Sal $66,278
Library Holdings: Audiobooks 111; DVDs 656; Large Print Bks 48; Bk Titles 21,151; Per Subs 56
Automation Activity & Vendor Info: (Cataloging) Follett Software; (Circulation) Follett Software
Database Vendor: OVID Technologies
Mem of Northwest Iowa Library Services
Open Mon, Tues & Thurs 10-8, Wed & Fri 10-5, Sat 10-2

SIDNEY

P SIDNEY PUBLIC LIBRARY, 1002 Illinois St, 51652. (Mail add: PO Box 479, 51652-0479), SAN 305-6961. Tel: 712-374-6203. FAX: 712-374-6303. E-mail: spl@sidney.lib.ia.us. Web Site: www.sidney.lib.ia.us. *Dir,* Chris Moyer
Pop 1,499; Circ 8,715
Library Holdings: DVDs 175; Large Print Bks 250; Bk Vols 10,750; Per Subs 33; Talking Bks 216; Videos 845
Automation Activity & Vendor Info: (Cataloging) Follett Software
Mem of Southwest Iowa Library Services District
Open Mon & Wed Noon-7:30, Tues & Sat 9-1, Fri 10-5

SIGOURNEY

P SIGOURNEY PUBLIC LIBRARY*, 720 E Jackson, 52591-1505. SAN 305-697X. Tel: 641-622-2890. FAX: 641-622-3391. E-mail: sigopl@lisco.com. Web Site: www.sigourney.lib.ia.us. *Dir,* Andi Wallerich
Pop 2,220; Circ 32,989
Library Holdings: Bk Vols 12,500; Per Subs 40
Automation Activity & Vendor Info: (Cataloging) Follett Software; (Circulation) Follett Software
Open Mon-Wed 11-7, Thurs & Fri 11-6, Sat 11-3
Friends of the Library Group

SILVER CITY

P SILVER CITY PUBLIC LIBRARY*, 408 Main St, 51571. Tel: 712-525-9053. FAX: 712-525-9053. Web Site: www.silvercity.lib.ia.us. *Dir,* Dee Ferguson; E-mail: dee.f@silvercity.lib.ia.us; *Ch,* Donna Schoening
Library Holdings: AV Mats 608; DVDs 70; Large Print Bks 40; Bk Titles 6,030; Per Subs 21; Videos 512
Open Mon 2-7, Wed 8:30-2:30, Thurs 4-8

SIOUX CENTER

CR DORDT COLLEGE*, John & Louise Hulst Library, 498 Fourth Ave NE, 51250. SAN 305-6996. Tel: 712-722-6040. Interlibrary Loan Service Tel: 712-722-6041. Reference Tel: 712-722-6042, 712-722-6043. FAX: 712-722-1198. E-mail: library@dordt.edu. Web Site: www.dordt.edu/academics/library. *Dir, Libr Serv,* Sheryl Sheeres Taylor; Tel: 712-722-6047, E-mail: staylor@dordt.edu; *Ch Serv, YA Serv,* Gerlene Meyer; Tel: 712-722-6045; *ILL,* Dawn Van Den Hul; E-mail: ill@dordt.edu; *Pub Serv,* Darlene Reichert; *Ref,* Jennifer Breems; *Ref Serv,* Jan Versluis; *Ser,* Ingrid Mulder; Tel: 712-722-6048; *Tech Serv,* Elaine Wassink; Tel: 712-722-6046; Staff 7 (MLS 2, Non-MLS 5)
Founded 1955. Enrl 1,300; Fac 88; Highest Degree: Master
Library Holdings: Bk Titles 124,000; Bk Vols 303,000; Per Subs 650
Special Collections: Dutch History Coll
Subject Interests: Educ, Hist, Relig
Automation Activity & Vendor Info: (Acquisitions) SirsiDynix; (Cataloging) SirsiDynix; (Circulation) SirsiDynix; (Course Reserve) SirsiDynix; (OPAC) SirsiDynix; (Serials) SirsiDynix
Database Vendor: EBSCOhost, LexisNexis, OCLC FirstSearch, OVID Technologies, ProQuest
Partic in OCLC Online Computer Library Center, Inc

P SIOUX CENTER PUBLIC LIBRARY*, 102 S Main Ave, 51250-1801. SAN 305-7003. Tel: 712-722-2138. FAX: 712-722-1235. Web Site: www.siouxcenter.lib.ia.us. *Dir,* Becky Bilby; E-mail: bbilby@siouxcenter.lib.ia.us; *Ch, Vols Coordr,* Judy Dirkse; *Circ,* Laurey Zwart; *Cat/Circ,* Jamie Lyman; Staff 7 (MLS 1, Non-MLS 6)
Founded 1927. Pop 16,000; Circ 153,249
Library Holdings: Large Print Bks 3,300; Bk Titles 62,179; Per Subs 143
Special Collections: Genealogy of Sioux County. Oral History
Subject Interests: Genealogy, Hist, Iowa, Spanish lang mat
Automation Activity & Vendor Info: (Cataloging) Book Systems; (OPAC) Book Systems
Mem of Northwest Iowa Library Services
Partic in State of Iowa Libraries Online
Special Services for the Deaf - Bks on deafness & sign lang; High interest/low vocabulary bks
Special Services for the Blind - Bks on cassette; Home delivery serv
Open Mon-Thurs 9-9, Fri & Sat 9-5

SIOUX CITY

C BRIAR CLIFF UNIVERSITY*, The Bishop Mueller Library, 3303 Rebecca St, 51104-2324. SAN 305-7011. Tel: 712-279-5449. FAX: 712-279-1723. E-mail: library@briarcliff.edu. Web Site: library.briarcliff.edu/. *Instrul Serv Librn, Interim Dir,* Julius Fleschner; Tel: 712-279-5451, E-mail: julius.fleschner@briarcliff.edu; *Circ Supvr, Reserves,* Kathy Weber; *ILL, Tech Serv,* Sister Mary Jane Koenigs; Tel: 712-279-5535, E-mail: koenigs@briarcliff.edu; Staff 3 (MLS 1, Non-MLS 2)
Founded 1930. Enrl 928; Fac 64; Highest Degree: Master
Subject Interests: Nursing, Soc serv (soc work), Sociol, Theol
Automation Activity & Vendor Info: (Cataloging) SirsiDynix; (Circulation) SirsiDynix; (OPAC) SirsiDynix
Database Vendor: EBSCOhost, ProQuest, SirsiDynix, Wilson - Wilson Web
Function: ILL available
Partic in Iowa Private Academic Library Consortium (IPAL); Sioux City Library Cooperative
Open Mon-Thurs 7:45am-Midnight, Fri 7:45-6, Sat 11-6, Sun 1-Midnight
Friends of the Library Group

M MERCY MEDICAL CENTER*, Health Science Library, 801 Fifth St, 51101. SAN 305-7038. Tel: 712-279-2310. E-mail: library@mercyhealth.com. *Head Librn,* Donna Phillips; E-mail: phillidm@mercyhealth.com; *Librn,* Barbara Groom
Founded 1976
Library Holdings: Bk Titles 1,000; Per Subs 250
Subject Interests: Clinical med, Hospital admin, Med, Nursing, Soc sci & issues
Partic in Basic Health Sciences Library Network; Greater Midwest Regional Medical Libr Network; Massachusetts Health Sciences Libraries Network; Polk County Biomedical Consortium; Sioux City Library Cooperative
Open Mon-Fri 8-4:30

C MORNINGSIDE COLLEGE*, Hickman-Johnson-Furrow Learning Center, 1501 Morningside Ave, 51106. SAN 305-7046. Tel: 712-274-5195. Reference Tel: 712-274-5193. FAX: 712-274-5224. Web Site: library.morningside.edu. *Assoc Dean,* Karmen Ten Napel; Tel: 712-274-5191, E-mail: tennapel@morningside.edu; *Digital & Archival Serv Librn,* Adam Fullerton; E-mail: fullertona@morningside.edu; *Ref & Instruction Librn,* Holly Petersen; Tel: 712-274-5246, E-mail: petersenh@morningside.edu; *Circ Mgr,* Karen Johnson; Tel: 712-274-5245, E-mail: johnsonka@morningside.edu; Staff 6 (MLS 3, Non-MLS 3)
Founded 1894. Enrl 1,369; Fac 70; Highest Degree: Master
Library Holdings: AV Mats 2,763; Bk Titles 86,228; Bk Vols 99,121; Per Subs 443
Automation Activity & Vendor Info: (Cataloging) SirsiDynix; (Circulation) SirsiDynix; (Course Reserve) SirsiDynix; (ILL) SirsiDynix; (OPAC) SirsiDynix; (Serials) SirsiDynix
Database Vendor: American Chemical Society, EBSCO Information Services, EBSCOhost, JSTOR, Micromedex, OCLC ArticleFirst, OCLC FirstSearch, OCLC WorldShare Interlibrary Loan, PubMed
Wireless access
Function: Web-catalog
Publications: Newsletter
Partic in Council of Independent Colleges (CIC); Iowa Private Academic Library Consortium (IPAL); Iowa Resource & Info Sharing; LibraryLinkNJ, The New Jersey Library Cooperative; OCLC Online Computer Library Center, Inc
Open Mon-Thurs 7:30am-Midnight, Fri 7:30-5, Sat 10-3, Sun 1-Midnight
Restriction: Open to pub for ref & circ; with some limitations

CM ST LUKE'S COLLEGE LIBRARY*, 2620 Pierce St, 51104. (Mail add: 2720 Stone Park Blvd, 51104). Tel: 712-279-3156. Toll Free Tel: 800-352-4660, Ext 3156. Web Site: www.stlukescollege.edu/body.cfm?id=122. *Dept Chair,* Nancy Zubrod; Tel: 712-279-4961, E-mail: zubrodnj@stlukescollege.edu
Library Holdings: Bk Titles 2,260; Bk Vols 2,900; Per Subs 70
Subject Interests: Family practice, Med, Nursing
Automation Activity & Vendor Info: (Cataloging) CyberTools for Libraries; (Circulation) CyberTools for Libraries; (OPAC) CyberTools for Libraries
Database Vendor: EBSCOhost
Wireless access
Open Mon-Thurs 7:30-5, Fri 7:30-4, Sun 12-5

S SIOUX CITY ART CENTER*, Margaret Avery Heffernan Reference Library, 225 Nebraska St, 51101. SAN 305-7062. Tel: 712-279-6272. Reference Tel: 712-279-6272, Ext 208. FAX: 712-255-2921. *Admin Serv,* Kjersten Welch
Library Holdings: CDs 12; Bk Vols 1,500; Videos 63
Subject Interests: Art (20th Century)
Function: Res libr
Restriction: Non-circulating to the pub, Open by appt only

P SIOUX CITY PUBLIC LIBRARY*, Wilbur Aalfs Main Library, 529 Pierce St, 51101-1203. SAN 341-9673. Tel: 712-255-2933. E-mail: questions@siouxcitylibrary.org. Web Site: www.siouxcitylibrary.org. *Dir,* Betsy J Thompson; E-mail: bthompson@siouxcitylibrary.org; *Ch Serv,* Jeanette E Bobeen; *Circ,* Marla Kerr; *Coll Develop, Ref Serv, Ad,* Sara A Doyle; *Tech Serv,* Troy S Jennings; Staff 18 (MLS 7, Non-MLS 11)
Founded 1877. Pop 82,678; Circ 564,516

Jul 2011-Jun 2012 Income (Main Library and Branch(s)) $2,830,326, State $31,326, City $2,600,000, Locally Generated Income $77,000, Other $122,000. Mats Exp $295,000, Books $203,000, Per/Ser (Incl. Access Fees) $18,000, AV Mat $38,000, Electronic Ref Mat (Incl. Access Fees) $36,000. Sal $2,057,000
Library Holdings: AV Mats 9,921; Large Print Bks 2,331; Bk Vols 127,268; Per Subs 144
Special Collections: US Document Depository
Automation Activity & Vendor Info: (Acquisitions) SirsiDynix; (Cataloging) SirsiDynix; (Circulation) SirsiDynix; (OPAC) SirsiDynix
Wireless access
Publications: Book Remarks (Newsletter)
Open Mon-Wed 9-8, Thurs-Sat 9-5, Sun 1-5
Friends of the Library Group
Branches: 2
PERRY CREEK BRANCH LIBRARY, 2912 Hamilton Blvd, 51104-2410, SAN 341-9797. Tel: 712-255-2926. *Circ Mgr,* Marla Kerr
Library Holdings: AV Mats 716; Large Print Bks 414; Bk Vols 10,369; Per Subs 25
Friends of the Library Group
SCHROEDER-MORNINGSIDE BRANCH LIBRARY, 4005 Morningside Ave, 51106-2448, SAN 341-9738. Tel: 712-255-2924. *Br Supvr,* Jennifer Delperdang
Library Holdings: AV Mats 5,007; Large Print Bks 3,075; Bk Vols 40,580; Per Subs 59
Friends of the Library Group

J WESTERN IOWA TECHNICAL COMMUNITY COLLEGE, Library Services, 4647 Stone Ave, 51106. (Mail add: PO Box 5199, 51102-5199), SAN 305-7089. Tel: 712-274-8733, Ext 1239. Administration Tel: 712-274-8733, Ext 1324. FAX: 712-274-6423. E-mail: library@witcc.edu. Web Site: www.witcc.edu/library. *Libr Serv Dir,* Sharon Kay Dykshoorn; E-mail: Sharon.Dykshoorn@witcc.edu; *Pub Serv,* Position Currently Open; Staff 2 (MLS 1, Non-MLS 1)
Founded 1966. Enrl 6,399; Highest Degree: Associate
Jul 2013-Jun 2014 Income $95,624. Mats Exp $93,126, Books $14,030, Per/Ser (Incl. Access Fees) $65,494, AV Mat $8,602, Electronic Ref Mat (Incl. Access Fees) $5,000. Sal $116,620 (Prof $98,817)
Automation Activity & Vendor Info: (Cataloging) SirsiDynix; (Circulation) SirsiDynix; (Course Reserve) SirsiDynix; (OPAC) SirsiDynix
Database Vendor: EBSCOhost, Gale Cengage Learning, OCLC FirstSearch, Westlaw
Wireless access
Partic in Sioux City Library Cooperative
Open Mon-Thurs 7:30-7, Fri 7:30-5, Sat 8-Noon
Friends of the Library Group

SIOUX RAPIDS

P SIOUX RAPIDS MEMORIAL LIBRARY*, 215 Second St, 50585. SAN 305-7100. Tel: 712-283-2064. FAX: 712-283-2064. Web Site: www.siouxrapids.lib.ia.us. *Librn,* Martha Landsness; E-mail: mlandsness@siouxrapids.lib.ia.us
Pop 817; Circ 18,432
Library Holdings: Bk Vols 21,500; Per Subs 35
Special Collections: Sioux Rapids Bulletin Press (1800's-current), micro
Mem of Northwest Iowa Library Services
Open Mon, Wed & Thurs 12-6, Tues & Sat 9-3, Fri 9-12

SLATER

P SLATER PUBLIC LIBRARY*, 105 N Tama St, 50244. (Mail add: PO Box 598, 50244-0598), SAN 305-7119. Tel: 515-228-3558. FAX: 515-228-3558. Web Site: slaterlibrary.org. *Dir,* Ben Miller; E-mail: director@slaterlibrary.org; Staff 4 (MLS 1, Non-MLS 3)
Founded 1970. Pop 2,000; Circ 22,074
Library Holdings: Bk Vols 15,000; Per Subs 40; Videos 1,000
Special Collections: Slater News & Tri County Times, 1890-present, microfilm
Automation Activity & Vendor Info: (Cataloging) Follett Software; (Serials) EBSCO Online
Database Vendor: EBSCOhost
Open Mon & Fri 10-5, Tues, Wed & Thurs 10-8, Sat 10-12
Friends of the Library Group

SLOAN

P SLOAN PUBLIC LIBRARY*, 311 Fourth St, 51055. (Mail add: PO Box 8, 51055-0008), SAN 305-7127. Tel: 712-428-4200. E-mail: slolib@longlines.com. *Co-Dir,* Tami Coil; *Librn,* Mary Parker
Founded 1935. Pop 1,032; Circ 14,856
Jul 2010-Jun 2011 Income $33,502, State $911, City $22,100, County $6,428, Locally Generated Income $4,063. Mats Exp $8,358, Books $5,386, Per/Ser (Incl. Access Fees) $1,486, AV Mat $1,486. Sal $18,175
Library Holdings: Audiobooks 105; DVDs 801; Large Print Bks 75; Bk Titles 9,135; Per Subs 32
Subject Interests: Hist, Iowa
Automation Activity & Vendor Info: (Cataloging) Book Systems
Function: Bks on cassette, Bks on CD, Children's prog, Computers for patron use, Copy machines, Fax serv, Free DVD rentals, Home delivery & serv to Sr ctr & nursing homes, Homebound delivery serv, ILL available, Outreach serv, Outside serv via phone, mail, e-mail & web, Photocopying/Printing, Preschool outreach, Pub access computers, Ref serv in person, Scanner, Senior outreach, Story hour, Summer reading prog, Tax forms, VHS videos
Mem of Northwest Iowa Library Services
Special Services for the Deaf - Bks on deafness & sign lang; Captioned film dep
Open Mon 1:30-6:30, Wed 9-12 & 1:30-6:30, Thurs 1:30-6:30, Fri & Sat 9-12

SOLDIER

P SOLDIER PUBLIC LIBRARY*, 108 Oak St, 51572-6237. (Mail add: PO Box 45, 51572-0045), SAN 376-5296. Tel: 712-884-2266. FAX: 712-884-2264. *Librn,* Barb Jensen; E-mail: bjensen@longlines.com
Library Holdings: Bk Vols 2,000
Mem of Northwest Iowa Library Services
Open Mon-Fri 9-4

SOLON

P SOLON PUBLIC LIBRARY*, 320 W Main St, 52333-9504. SAN 305-7135. Tel: 319-624-2678. FAX: 319-624-5034. E-mail: admin@solon.lib.ia.us. Web Site: www.solon.lib.ia.us. *Dir,* Kris Brown; *Youth Serv Librn,* Carey Major; E-mail: cmajor@solon.lib.ia.us
Founded 1965. Pop 2,000; Circ 97,498
Library Holdings: Audiobooks 2,358; DVDs 2,556; Bk Titles 29,296; Per Subs 59
Automation Activity & Vendor Info: (Acquisitions) Auto-Graphics, Inc
Database Vendor: EBSCOhost, TumbleBookLibrary
Wireless access
Function: Adult bk club, Bks on CD, Children's prog, Computers for patron use, Copy machines, Electronic databases & coll, Fax serv, Free DVD rentals, Handicapped accessible, Holiday prog, ILL available, Music CDs, Online searches, Outreach serv, OverDrive digital audio bks, Preschool outreach, Preschool reading prog, Prog for adults, Prog for children & young adult, Pub access computers, Scanner, Summer reading prog, Tax forms, Teen prog, Web-catalog
Partic in North Eastern Iowa Bridge to Online Resource Sharing (NEIBORS)
Open Mon-Thurs 12-8, Fri & Sat 10-5
Restriction: Access at librarian's discretion
Friends of the Library Group

SOMERS

P SOMERS PUBLIC LIBRARY*, 502 Sixth St, 50586. (Mail add: PO Box 114, 50586-0114), SAN 305-7143. Tel: 515-467-5522. FAX: 515-467-5603. E-mail: somlib@yahoo.com. *Librn,* Linda Welter
Founded 1973. Pop 167; Circ 3,768
Library Holdings: Bk Titles 5,475
Open Mon & Tues 2-5, Wed 6-9, Sat 8:30-11:30

SOUTH ENGLISH

P SOUTH ENGLISH PUBLIC LIBRARY*, 407 Ives St, 52335. (Mail add: PO Box 162, 52335-0162), SAN 305-7151. Tel: 319-667-2715. FAX: 319-667-4507. E-mail: slibrary@netins.net. Web Site: www.southenglish.lib.ia.us. *Dir,* Pauline Smith; E-mail: psmith@southenglish.lib.ia.us
Founded 1936. Pop 213; Circ 5,015
Library Holdings: Bk Titles 3,804
Open Tues 3-4:30, Wed 4-7, Thurs 2-6, Sat 8-11:30

SPENCER

P SPENCER PUBLIC LIBRARY*, 21 E Third St, 51301-4188. SAN 305-716X. Tel: 712-580-7290. FAX: 712-580-7468. E-mail: info@spencerlibrary.com. Web Site: www.spencerlibrary.com. *Dir,* Malinda Roberts; E-mail: mroberts@spencerlibrary.com; *Asst Dir,* Paula Brown; E-mail: pbrown@spencerlibrary.com; *Ch,* Sarah Beth Beaver; *YA Librn,* Kayla Williams; Staff 12 (MLS 1, Non-MLS 11)
Founded 1904. Pop 11,317
Jul 2005-Jun 2006 Income $466,301, State $8,405, City $420,234, County $14,861, Locally Generated Income $16,729, Other $6,072. Mats Exp $52,277, Books $33,161, Per/Ser (Incl. Access Fees) $6,412, Other Print Mats $6,211, Micro $650, AV Equip $1,900, AV Mat $1,830, Electronic Ref Mat (Incl. Access Fees) $2,113. Sal $309,968

Library Holdings: CDs 2,384; DVDs 691; Large Print Bks 2,843; Bk Vols 49,735; Per Subs 217; Talking Bks 1,122; Videos 447
Special Collections: Career-Related Materials; Charlotte Brett Genealogy Coll
Subject Interests: Local hist
Automation Activity & Vendor Info: (Cataloging) TLC (The Library Corporation); (Circulation) TLC (The Library Corporation); (OPAC) TLC (The Library Corporation)
Database Vendor: Checkpoint Systems, Inc, EBSCOhost, OCLC FirstSearch, TLC (The Library Corporation), WebMD
Wireless access
Publications: SPLASH (Newsletter)
Mem of Northwest Iowa Library Services
Special Services for the Blind - Computer with voice synthesizer for visually impaired persons
Open Mon-Thurs 9-9, Fri & Sat 9-5
Friends of the Library Group

SPILLVILLE

P SPILLVILLE PUBLIC LIBRARY*, 201 Oak St, 52168. (Mail add: PO Box 197, 52168-0197), SAN 325-2558. Tel: 563-562-4373. FAX: 563-562-4373. E-mail: spillville.library@mchsi.com. Web Site: www.spillvillelibrary.com. *Dir,* Renae Franzen; *Asst Librn,* Romana Ryant
Founded 1980
Library Holdings: Bks on Deafness & Sign Lang 10; CDs 109; DVDs 41; Bk Titles 5,500; Bk Vols 6,052; Per Subs 25; Talking Bks 168; Videos 428
Automation Activity & Vendor Info: (Cataloging) Follett Software; (Circulation) Follett Software
Open Mon-Fri 2-6, Sat 9-12

SPIRIT LAKE

J IOWA LAKES COMMUNITY COLLEGE*, Spirit Lake Campus, 800 21st St, 51360. Tel: 712-336-3439, 712-336-6564. FAX: 712-336-1357. Web Site: www.iowalakes.edu/library/index.htm. *Supvr,* Kendra Hough
Wireless access
Open Mon-Thurs 9-5, Fri 9-1

P SPIRIT LAKE PUBLIC LIBRARY*, 702 16th St, 51360. SAN 305-7178. Tel: 712-336-2667. FAX: 712-336-0511. E-mail: slpublib@ncn.net. Web Site: www.spiritlakepubliclibrary.org. *Dir,* Linda Bolluyt; Staff 4 (Non-MLS 4)
Founded 1912. Pop 4,840; Circ 111,297
Jul 2010-Jun 2011 Income $201,033, City $166,123, County $18,877, Locally Generated Income $16,033. Mats Exp $37,730, Books $23,982, Per/Ser (Incl. Access Fees) $3,200, AV Mat $10,548
Library Holdings: Audiobooks 2,333; DVDs 1,062; Bk Vols 26,242; Per Subs 231
Special Collections: Northwest Iowa History Coll. Oral History
Automation Activity & Vendor Info: (Cataloging) OCLC CatExpress; (Circulation) Book Systems; (OPAC) Book Systems
Wireless access
Mem of Northwest Iowa Library Services
Open Mon-Thurs 10-7, Fri 10-5, Sat 10-3
Friends of the Library Group

SPRINGVILLE

P SPRINGVILLE MEMORIAL LIBRARY*, 264 Broadway St, 52336. (Mail add: PO Box 78, 52336-0078), SAN 305-7186. Tel: 319-854-6444. FAX: 319-854-6443. E-mail: sprlibry@netins.net. *Dir,* Mary LaGrange; Staff 2 (Non-MLS 2)
Founded 1949. Pop 1,091; Circ 13,487
Library Holdings: Bk Vols 14,500; Per Subs 25
Open Mon-Wed 10-6, Thurs 10-8, Fri 10-5, Sat 10-3
Friends of the Library Group

STACYVILLE

P STACYVILLE PUBLIC LIBRARY*, 106 N Broad St, 50476. (Mail add: PO Box 219, 50476-0219), SAN 305-7194. Tel: 641-710-2531. FAX: 641-710-2531. E-mail: stacylib@myomnitel.com. Web Site: www.youseemore.com/nilc/stacyville. *Dir,* Barb Klapperich
Founded 1967. Pop 494; Circ 38,000
Library Holdings: Bk Titles 16,000
Special Collections: Oral History
Automation Activity & Vendor Info: (Cataloging) TLC (The Library Corporation); (Circulation) TLC (The Library Corporation)
Wireless access
Open Mon, Tues & Fri 10-12 & 2-6:30, Wed & Thurs 2-6:30, Sat 10-2:30

STANHOPE

P STANHOPE PUBLIC LIBRARY*, 665 Iowa St, 50246. (Mail add: PO Box 67, 50246-0067), SAN 305-7208. Tel: 515-826-3211. FAX: 515-826-3211. E-mail: stanpl@netins.net. *Dir,* Dee Weir
Founded 1950. Pop 488; Circ 4,000
Library Holdings: Bk Vols 7,000; Per Subs 22
Open Tues, Wed & Thurs 1-6:30, Fri & Sat 9-12

STANTON

§P STANTON PUBLIC LIBRARY, 501 Elliott St, Ste A, 51573. (Mail add: PO Box 130, 51573). Tel: 712-829-2290. FAX: 712-829-2570. E-mail: stanlib@myfmtc.com. Web Site: www.stanton.lib.ia.us. *Dir,* Jerry S Gilliland

STANWOOD

P STANWOOD PUBLIC LIBRARY*, 202 E Broadway, 52337-0234. (Mail add: PO Box 234, 52337-0234), SAN 305-7224. Tel: 563-942-3531. FAX: 563-942-3531. Web Site: www.stanwood.lib.ia.us. *Dir,* Michelle Potter; E-mail: mlpotter@stanwood.lib.ia.us
Founded 1949. Pop 705; Circ 3,366
Library Holdings: Bk Titles 9,000
Open Mon 2-5, Tues & Thurs 2-7, Fri 8-12 & 2-5, Sat 8-11
Friends of the Library Group

STATE CENTER

P GUTEKUNST PUBLIC LIBRARY*, 309 Second St SE, 50247-0550. (Mail add: PO Box 603, 50247-0550), SAN 305-7232. Tel: 641-483-2741. FAX: 641-483-2131. Web Site: www.statecenter.lib.ia.us. *Dir,* Catherine Noble; E-mail: cnoble.lib@gmail.com; *Librn,* Katey Lively; *Ch,* Andria Cosolotto
Circ 55,000
Library Holdings: Bk Titles 19,536; Bk Vols 23,283; Per Subs 90
Automation Activity & Vendor Info: (Cataloging) Follett Software; (Circulation) Follett Software
Mem of Central Iowa Library Services
Open Mon-Thurs 9-12 & 2-7, Fri 9-5, Sat 10-3
Friends of the Library Group

STEAMBOAT ROCK

P STEAMBOAT ROCK PUBLIC LIBRARY*, 511 Market St, 50672. (Mail add: PO Box 416, 50672-0416), SAN 305-7240. Tel: 641-868-2300. FAX: 641-868-2300. *Dir,* Lois Luiken; E-mail: ljluiken@steamboatrock.lib.ia.us
Founded 1959. Pop 336; Circ 11,586
Library Holdings: Bk Titles 2,390; Bk Vols 8,000; Per Subs 33
Open Mon 1:30-6:30, Tues, Thurs & Sat 9-11 & 1:30-5:30, Wed & Fri 1:30-5:30

STOCKPORT

P STOCKPORT PUBLIC LIBRARY*, 113 E Beswick St, 52651. (Mail add: PO Box 62, 52651-0062), SAN 305-7259. Tel: 319-796-4681. FAX: 319-796-4681. E-mail: stocklib@netins.net. *Dir,* Bev Runyon
Pop 847; Circ 1,553
Library Holdings: Bk Vols 7,800; Per Subs 10
Open Mon & Wed 3-6, Thurs 9-12, Sat 8-10:30

STORM LAKE

C BUENA VISTA UNIVERSITY LIBRARY*, 610 W Fourth St, 50588. SAN 305-7267. Tel: 712-749-2127, 712-749-2203. Interlibrary Loan Service Tel: 712-749-2096. Toll Free Tel: 877-288-2240. FAX: 712-749-2059. E-mail: library@bvu.edu. Web Site: www.bvu.edu/library. *Actg Dir, Ref Librn,* Jodie Morin; Tel: 712-749-2097, E-mail: morinj@bvu.edu; *Dir,* Position Currently Open; *Ref Librn,* Jackie AlSaffar; Tel: 712-749-2089, E-mail: alsaffarj@bvu.edu; *Tech Serv & Syst Librn,* Margaret Stangohr; Tel: 712-749-2092, E-mail: stangohrm@bvu.edu; *Coordr, Access Serv,* Florene Cork; E-mail: corkf@bvu.edu; *Access Serv,* Kelly Olson; Tel: 712-749-2098, E-mail: olsonk@bvu.edu; *Acq,* Juliann Berg; Tel: 712-749-2091; *Cataloger,* Joan Curbow; Tel: 712-749-2094, E-mail: curbowj@bvu.edu; Staff 8 (MLS 4, Non-MLS 4)
Founded 1891. Enrl 2,526; Fac 81; Highest Degree: Master
Jul 2009-Jun 2010 Income $933,263. Mats Exp $364,735, Books $54,159, Per/Ser (Incl. Access Fees) $302,933, Micro $2,058, AV Mat $5,585. Sal $352,956 (Prof $240,246)
Library Holdings: AV Mats 6,726; CDs 1,492; DVDs 899; e-books 11,534; e-journals 49; Bk Vols 126,204; Per Subs 465; Videos 3,649
Subject Interests: Hist, Iowa
Automation Activity & Vendor Info: (Acquisitions) Horizon; (Cataloging) Horizon; (Circulation) Horizon; (Course Reserve) Horizon; (ILL) OCLC ILLiad; (OPAC) Horizon; (Serials) Horizon
Database Vendor: ABC-CLIO, ACM (Association for Computing Machinery), American Chemical Society, CQ Press, CredoReference,

EBSCOhost, Elsevier, JSTOR, LexisNexis, OCLC WorldShare Interlibrary Loan, Project MUSE, Sage, SerialsSolutions, SirsiDynix, ValueLine, Westlaw
Wireless access
Function: Photocopying/Printing, Ref serv available
Partic in Iowa Private Academic Library Consortium (IPAL); OCLC-LVIS
Open Mon-Thurs 8am-Midnight, Fri 8-6, Sat 9-6, Sun 1-Midnight; Mon-Fri (Summer) 8-5
Restriction: Open to pub for ref & circ; with some limitations

P STORM LAKE PUBLIC LIBRARY*, 609 Cayuga St, 50588. SAN 305-7275. Tel: 712-732-8026. FAX: 712-732-7609. E-mail: admin@stormlake.lib.ia.us. Web Site: www.stormlake.lib.ia.us. *Dir,* Misty Gray; E-mail: misty.gray@stormlake.lib.ia.us; *Asst Dir,* Elizabeth Huff; Staff 7 (MLS 1, Non-MLS 6)
Founded 1905. Pop 10,600; Circ 88,287
Library Holdings: Bk Titles 42,176; Bk Vols 42,502; Per Subs 86
Special Collections: Spanish Coll
Automation Activity & Vendor Info: (Cataloging) Follett Software; (Circulation) Follett Software; (OPAC) Follett Software
Database Vendor: OCLC FirstSearch
Publications: Annual Report; Newsletter (Quarterly)
Mem of Northwest Iowa Library Services
Partic in WILBOR Consortium (West/Central Iowa Libraries Building Online Resources)
Open Mon & Fri (Winter) 9-6, Tues & Wed 9-7, Thurs 9-8, Sat 9-2; Mon-Fri (Summer) 9-6, Sat 9-2
Friends of the Library Group

STORY CITY

P BERTHA BARTLETT PUBLIC LIBRARY*, 503 Broad St, 50248-1133. SAN 305-7283. Tel: 515-733-2685. FAX: 515-733-2843. E-mail: scbbpl@windstream.net. Web Site: www.storycity.lib.ia.us. *Dir,* Kolleen Taylor-Breven; E-mail: scbbpl@iowatelecom.net; *Asst Dir,* Denise Froehlich; *Ch,* Julia Humphrey; Staff 4 (Non-MLS 4)
Founded 1922. Pop 3,228
Jul 2006-Jun 2007 Income $104,007, State $4,752, City $86,853, County $8,560, Locally Generated Income $3,842. Mats Exp $16,704, Books $12,937, Per/Ser (Incl. Access Fees) $1,698, AV Mat $1,247, Electronic Ref Mat (Incl. Access Fees) $122. Sal $75,576
Library Holdings: AV Mats 1,053; Bks on Deafness & Sign Lang 14; CDs 283; DVDs 315; Large Print Bks 1,280; Bk Vols 37,019; Per Subs 53; Talking Bks 1,121; Videos 654
Automation Activity & Vendor Info: (Cataloging) ComPanion Corp; (Circulation) ComPanion Corp, (OPAC) ComPanion Corp; (Serials) EBSCO Online
Database Vendor: EBSCOhost, Facts on File
Wireless access
Function: Adult bk club, After school storytime, Audiobks via web, Bilingual assistance for Spanish patrons, Bk club(s), Bks on CD, CD-ROM, Children's prog, Computer training, Computers for patron use, Copy machines, e-mail & chat, Fax serv, Free DVD rentals, Handicapped accessible, Home delivery & serv to Sr ctr & nursing homes, ILL available, Music CDs, Photocopying/Printing, Preschool outreach, Prog for adults, Prog for children & young adult, Ref serv available, Scanner, Spanish lang bks, Spoken cassettes & CDs, Summer reading prog, Tax forms, Teen prog, VHS videos, Web-catalog
Open Mon, Tues & Thurs 10-8, Wed, Fri & Sat 10-5, Sun (Winter) 1-5
Friends of the Library Group
Branches: 1
GILBERT BRANCH, 207 Broad St, Gilbert, 50105.
Open Tues & Thurs 3:30-7:30, Sat 10-Noon

STRATFORD

P STRATFORD PUBLIC LIBRARY*, 816 Shakespeare, 50249. (Mail add: PO Box 320, 50249-0320), SAN 305-7291. Tel: 515-838-2131. FAX: 515-838-2131. E-mail: stratlib@globalccs.net. *Dir,* Marna Navara
Founded 1926. Pop 720; Circ 9,500
Library Holdings: AV Mats 370; Bk Vols 6,454; Per Subs 41; Talking Bks 165
Special Collections: Stratford Courier Newspaper 1892-1959, micro 1978-present, paper
Open Mon-Fri 1-6, Sat 9-12

STRAWBERRY POINT

P STRAWBERRY POINT PUBLIC LIBRARY, 401 Commercial St, 52076. (Mail add: PO Box 340, 52076-0340), SAN 305-7305. Tel: 563-933-4340. FAX: 563-933-4340. Web Site: www.strawberrypt.com/Library/library.htm. *Dir,* Patty Lincoln; E-mail: plincoln@strawberrypoint.lib.ia.us
Pop 1,115; Circ 32,872
Library Holdings: e-books 4,449; Bk Titles 25,883; Per Subs 63
Automation Activity & Vendor Info: (Media Booking) Biblionix/Apollo; (OPAC) Biblionix/Apollo
Database Vendor: EBSCOhost
Wireless access
Open Mon & Fri 2-6:30, Tues & Thurs 9-12 & 2-6:30, Wed 11-6:30, Sat 9-12

STUART

P STUART PUBLIC LIBRARY*, 111 NE Front St, 50250. (Mail add: PO Box 220, 50250 0220), SAN 305-7313. Tel: 515-523-2152. FAX: 515-523-2152. Web Site: www.stuart.lib.ia.us. *Dir,* Sandy Pollard; E-mail: sandy.pollard@stuart.lib.ia.us
Founded 1901. Pop 1,650; Circ 28,961
Library Holdings: Bk Vols 18,751; Per Subs 70
Subject Interests: Iowa
Mem of Southwest Iowa Library Services District
Open Mon, Tues & Fri 1-5, Wed 10-5, Thurs 1-7, Sat 9-12
Friends of the Library Group

SULLY

P SULLY COMMUNITY LIBRARY*, 318 Sixth Ave, 50251. (Mail add: PO Box 227, 50251-0227), SAN 371-5434. Tel: 641-594-4148. FAX: 641-594-2978. E-mail: sullylib@netins.net. Web Site: www.sullylibrary.com. *Dir,* Kathy Zylstra
Library Holdings: Bk Vols 10,000
Automation Activity & Vendor Info: (Acquisitions) OCLC CatExpress; (Cataloging) Follett Software; (Circulation) Follett Software
Wireless access
Mem of Central Iowa Library Services
Open Mon 12-7:30, Wed 10-7:30, Thurs 3-7:30, Sat 9-12
Friends of the Library Group

SUMNER

P SUMNER PUBLIC LIBRARY*, 206 N Railroad St, 50674. SAN 305-7321. Tel: 563-578-3324. FAX: 563-578-3324. E-mail: library@sumner.lib.ia.us. Web Site: www.sumner.lib.ia.us. *Dir,* Denise Hoins
Pop 2,100; Circ 35,000
Library Holdings: Bk Titles 25,000; Per Subs 70
Automation Activity & Vendor Info: (Cataloging) Follett Software; (Circulation) Follett Software
Open Mon, Wed & Thurs 9-8, Tues & Fri 1-5, Sat 9-4

SUTHERLAND

P GENERAL N B BAKER PUBLIC LIBRARY*, 315 Ash St, 51058. (Mail add: PO Box 370, 51058-0280), SAN 305-733X. Tel: 712-446-3839. FAX: 712-446-3839. *Dir,* Mary Draper; Staff 2 (Non-MLS 2)
Founded 1875. Pop 714; Circ 9,835
Library Holdings: Bk Vols 8,142; Per Subs 54
Special Collections: Iowa Coll
Subject Interests: Hist
Mem of Northwest Iowa Library Services
Open Mon & Wed 2-7, Tues & Fri 2-5, Sat 10-2

SWALEDALE

P SWALEDALE PUBLIC LIBRARY*, 504 Main St, 50477. (Mail add: PO Box 114, 50477-0114), SAN 305-7348. Tel: 641-995-2352. FAX: 641-995-2352. E-mail: swdl@frontiernet.net. *Dir,* Heather M Jones; *Asst Librn,* Lori Rasmuson
Founded 1972. Pop 185; Circ 1,778
Library Holdings: Bk Vols 5,818; Per Subs 38; Videos 542
Function: After school storytime, Children's prog, Computers for patron use, Copy machines, Digital talking bks, Fax serv, Free DVD rentals, Handicapped accessible, Holiday prog, ILL available, Instruction & testing, Mail & tel request accepted, Music CDs, Photocopying/Printing, Prog for children & young adult, Pub access computers, Scanner, Summer reading prog, Teen prog, VHS videos, Wheelchair accessible, Workshops
Special Services for the Blind - Large print bks
Open Mon 9-1 & 3:30-6, Wed 1-8, Thurs 6-8, Fri 3:30-6, Sat 10-Noon

SWEA CITY

P SWEA CITY PUBLIC LIBRARY*, 208 Third St N, 50590. (Mail add: PO Box 368, 50590-1013), SAN 305-7356. Tel: 515-272-4216. FAX: 515-272-4216. E-mail: swcpl@mchsi.com. *Librn,* Angie Kintzle
Founded 1900. Pop 642; Circ 19,000
Library Holdings: Bk Titles 15,988; Per Subs 35; Talking Bks 131
Open Mon 12-6, Wed 12-5, Fri 9-5, Sat 9-12
Friends of the Library Group

TABOR

P TABOR PUBLIC LIBRARY*, 805 Main St, 51653. (Mail add: PO Box 27, 51653-0027), SAN 305-7364. Tel: 712-629-2735. FAX: 712-629-6004. Web Site: www.tabor.lib.ia.us. *Dir,* Dawn Miller; E-mail: dawn.miller@tabor.lib.ia.us
Pop 993; Circ 3,954
Library Holdings: Bk Vols 8,286; Per Subs 13
Mem of Southwest Iowa Library Services District
Open Tues, Thurs & Fri 1-5:30, Wed 1:30-8, Sat 9-1

TAMA

P THE LOUISE & LUCILLE HINK-TAMA PUBLIC LIBRARY*, 401 Siegel St, 52339. SAN 305-7372. Tel: 641-484-4484. FAX: 641-484-4484. E-mail: tamalibrary@tama.lib.ia.us. Web Site: www.tama.lib.ia.us. *Dir,* Julie D Shook; Tel: 641-484-2194, E-mail: julies@tama.lib.ia.us
Founded 1907. Pop 2,731
Jul 2009-Jun 2010 Income $142,617, State $4,770, City $112,859, County $8,539, Locally Generated Income $12,349, Other $4,100. Mats Exp $18,837, Books $14,265, Other Print Mats $2,179, AV Mat $2,286, Electronic Ref Mat (Incl. Access Fees) $107. Sal $64,158
Library Holdings: Audiobooks 174; CDs 37; DVDs 326; Electronic Media & Resources 8; Large Print Bks 521; Bk Titles 28,249; Per Subs 56; Videos 1,130
Special Collections: Mesquakie Indian Coll
Automation Activity & Vendor Info: (Acquisitions) Book Systems; (Cataloging) Book Systems; (Circulation) Book Systems; (Course Reserve) Book Systems; (ILL) Book Systems; (Media Booking) Book Systems; (OPAC) Book Systems; (Serials) Book Systems
Database Vendor: EBSCOhost, OCLC FirstSearch
Open Mon & Wed (Oct-April) 12-5, Tues & Thurs 12-8, Fri 9-5, Sat 9-12, Sun 1-4; Mon & Wed (May-Sept) 12-5, Tues & Thurs 12-8, Fri 9-5

TERRIL

P TERRIL COMMUNITY LIBRARY*, 115 N State St, 51364. (Mail add: PO Box 38, 51364-0038), SAN 305-7380. Tel: 712-853-6224. FAX: 712-853-6599. E-mail: library@terril.net. Web Site: www.terril.lib.ia.us. *Dir,* Rebekah Schnelle; E-mail: rschnelle@terril.lib.ia.us
Founded 1933. Pop 400; Circ 8,001
Library Holdings: Bk Vols 8,000
Special Collections: Terril Record Coll, 1929-52; Terril Tribune Coll, 1900-03
Mem of Northwest Iowa Library Services
Open Mon 12-5, Wed 9-6, Fri 9-12, Sat 9-2

THOMPSON

P THOMPSON PUBLIC LIBRARY*, 142 Jackson St N, 50478. (Mail add: PO Box 81, 50478-0081), SAN 305-7399. Tel: 641-584-2829. Web Site: www.thompson.lib.ia.us. *Dir,* Susan Shaw; E-mail: sshaw@thompson.lib.ia.us
Founded 1937. Pop 668
Library Holdings: Bk Titles 4,000; Bk Vols 5,300; Per Subs 20
Open Tues 9-11 & 2-6, Wed 2-7, Thurs 2-6, Fri 2-5, Sat 9-11

THORNTON

P THORNTON PUBLIC LIBRARY*, 412 Main St, 50479. SAN 305-7402. Tel: 641-998-2416. FAX: 641-998-2470. E-mail: maplest@frontiernet.net. Web Site: www.thornton-iowa.com. *Dir,* Trevett Gloria
Pop 442; Circ 19,400
Library Holdings: Bk Titles 9,000; Per Subs 20
Open Mon 1-3:30, Tues 1:30-4:30, Wed 2-6, Thurs 9-4:30, Fri 8-11 & 2-4:30, Sat 9-11:30

TIFFIN

P SPRINGMIER COMMUNITY LIBRARY*, 311 W Marengo Rd, 52340-9308. Tel: 319-545-2960. FAX: 319-545-2863. E-mail: springlb@southslope.net. *Dir,* Kris Petersen
Pop 1,032
Library Holdings: Bk Titles 10,400
Automation Activity & Vendor Info: (Cataloging) ComPanion Corp; (Circulation) ComPanion Corp
Open Mon-Thurs 10-6, Fri & Sat 9-Noon

TIPTON

P TIPTON PUBLIC LIBRARY*, 206 Cedar St, 52772-1753. SAN 305-7410. Tel: 563-886-6266. FAX: 563-886-6257. E-mail: staff@tipton.lib.ia.us. Web Site: www.tipton.lib.ia.us. *Dir,* Denise Smith; E-mail: denises@tipton.lib.ia.us
Founded 1901. Circ 40,619
Library Holdings: Bks-By-Mail 15; Large Print Bks 861; Bk Titles 21,000; Per Subs 59; Talking Bks 150
Special Collections: Cedar County Genealogical Society; Cedar County History Coll; Grant Wood Lithographs; Marvin Cone & Polly Kemp Works
Automation Activity & Vendor Info: (Cataloging) Follett Software; (Circulation) Follett Software
Open Mon-Thurs 10-8, Fri 10-5, Sat 10-1
Friends of the Library Group

TITONKA

P TITONKA PUBLIC LIBRARY*, 136 Main St N, 50480. (Mail add: PO Box 323, 50480-0323), SAN 305-7429. Tel: 515-928-2509. FAX: 515-928-2519. E-mail: tykeplib@netins.net. Web Site: www.youseemore.com/nilc/Titonka. *Co-Dir,* Laurie Lee; *Co-Dir,* Avon Rurup; E-mail: tykeplib1@netins.net
Founded 1913
Library Holdings: Bk Titles 6,800; Bk Vols 7,270; Per Subs 50
Special Collections: Wood carving
Automation Activity & Vendor Info: (Cataloging) Follett Software; (Circulation) Follett Software; (OPAC) Follett Software
Database Vendor: Gale Cengage Learning, OCLC FirstSearch
Function: ILL available
Special Services for the Blind - Large print bks
Open Mon 10-1 & 2-7, Tues-Thurs 10-1 & 2-6, Sat 10-Noon
Friends of the Library Group

TOLEDO

S TAMA COUNTY HISTORICAL SOCIETY*, Museum Library, 200 N Broadway, 52342. SAN 371-9200. Tel: 641-484-6767. Circulation Tel: 641-484-6563. FAX: 641-484-7677. E-mail: tracers@pcpartner.net. *Pres,* Joyce Wiese; Staff 6 (MLS 6)
Founded 1974
Library Holdings: Bk Titles 5,500; Per Subs 22
Open Tues-Sat 1-4:30

P TOLEDO PUBLIC LIBRARY*, 206 E High St, 52342-1617. SAN 305-7437. Tel: 641-484-3362. FAX: 641-484-2058. E-mail: tpl@toledo.lib.ia.us. Web Site: www.toledo.lib.ia.us. *Dir,* Jenny Bledsoe; E-mail: jennyb@toledo.lib.ia.us
Pop 2,539; Circ 23,000
Library Holdings: Bk Titles 21,000; Per Subs 74
Special Collections: Iowa Coll
Automation Activity & Vendor Info: (Cataloging) Follett Software; (Circulation) Follett Software
Open Mon-Thurs 11-7, Fri 11-5, Sat 9-12

TRAER

P TRAER PUBLIC LIBRARY*, 531 Second St, 50675. SAN 305-7445. Tel: 319-478-2180. FAX: 319-478-2180. Web Site: www.traer.lib.ia.us. *Dir,* Rosanne Foster; E-mail: rfoster@traer.lib.ia.us; Staff 2 (Non-MLS 2)
Founded 1916. Pop 1,794; Circ 41,880
Library Holdings: Audiobooks 689; DVDs 2,535; Large Print Bks 1,279; Bk Vols 14,409; Per Subs 126; Videos 135
Automation Activity & Vendor Info: (Acquisitions) Biblionix; (Cataloging) Biblionix; (Circulation) Biblionix
Database Vendor: Baker & Taylor, Brodart, EBSCO Auto Repair Reference, EBSCOhost, Ingram Library Services, OCLC FirstSearch, OCLC WorldShare Interlibrary Loan, TumbleBookLibrary
Wireless access
Function: Accelerated reader prog, Adult bk club, Audiobks via web, Bks on cassette, Bks on CD, Children's prog, Computer training, Computers for patron use, Copy machines, e-mail serv, Fax serv, Free DVD rentals, Handicapped accessible, Home delivery & serv to Sr ctr & nursing homes, Homebound delivery serv, ILL available, Mail & tel request accepted, Photocopying/Printing, Prog for adults, Prog for children & young adult, Pub access computers, Senior computer classes, Spoken cassettes & CDs, Spoken cassettes & DVDs, Story hour, Summer reading prog, Tax forms, VHS videos, Wheelchair accessible
Open Mon 1-7, Tues & Fri 1-5, Wed 10-5, Thurs 10-7, Sat 10-12
Friends of the Library Group

TRIPOLI

P TRIPOLI PUBLIC LIBRARY, 101 Fourth Ave SW, 50676. (Mail add: PO Box 430, 50676-0430), SAN 305-7453. Tel: 319-882-4807. FAX: 319-882-3580. E-mail: director@tripoli.lib.ia.us. Web Site: www.tripoli.lib.ia.us. *Librn,* Annette Martin; E-mail: Ann@tripoli.lib.ia.us; Staff 3 (MLS 1, Non-MLS 2)
Founded 1951. Pop 1,280; Circ 31,855
Library Holdings: Bk Titles 13,200; Per Subs 48
Subject Interests: Hist, Iowa
Open Mon 9-7, Tues 1:30-5:30, Wed 10-5, Thurs 9-4:30, Fri 2-6:30, Sat 9-12
Friends of the Library Group

TRURO

P TRURO PUBLIC LIBRARY*, 114 E Center St, 50257. (Mail add: PO Box 49, 50257-0049), SAN 305-7461. Tel: 641-765-4220. FAX: 641-765-4220. E-mail: trurolib@netins.net. *Dir,* Betty Green; E-mail: betty@truro.lib.ia.us
Founded 1929. Pop 407; Circ 8,134
Library Holdings: Bk Vols 13,965; Per Subs 83
Mem of Central Iowa Library Services
Partic in Cape Libraries Automated Materials Sharing Network
Open Mon 9-11 & 1:30-8, Tues 1:30-5, Wed & Thurs 1:30-8, Fri 1:30-6:30, Sat 9-3

UNION

P UNION PUBLIC LIBRARY*, 406 Commercial St, 50258. (Mail add: PO Box 146, 50258), SAN 305-747X. Tel: 641-486-5561. FAX: 641-486-2284. Web Site: www.union.lib.ia.us. *Dir,* Laura Newby; E-mail: director@union.lib.ia.us
Founded 1968. Pop 1,875; Circ 25,000
Library Holdings: Bk Vols 23,000; Per Subs 86
Database Vendor: EBSCO Information Services, EBSCOhost, OCLC FirstSearch
Wireless access
Open Mon & Wed 1-7, Tues, Thurs & Fri 10-5, Sat 10-2

URBANDALE

P URBANDALE PUBLIC LIBRARY*, 3520 86th St, 50322-4056. SAN 305-7496. Tel: 515-278-3945. Reference Tel: 515-331-4488. FAX: 515-278-3918. Reference FAX: 515-331-6737. E-mail: reference@urbandale.org. Web Site: www.urbandalelibrary.org. *Dir,* Julie Wells; *Asst Dir,* Trish Dimond; *Ref Serv Librn,* Jeanette Andrews; *Youth Serv Librn,* Carmen Epstein; Staff 19 (MLS 6, Non-MLS 13)
Founded 1961. Pop 35,904; Circ 644,028
Jul 2007-Jun 2008 Income $2,096,714, State $105,606, City $1,638,489, County $12,458, Locally Generated Income $85,335, Other $254,826. Mats Exp $2,080,037, Books $169,634, Per/Ser (Incl. Access Fees) $15,360, AV Mat $58,025, Electronic Ref Mat (Incl. Access Fees) $12,535. Sal $1,367,059
Library Holdings: AV Mats 15,118; DVDs 10,869; Bk Vols 130,897; Per Subs 362
Automation Activity & Vendor Info: (Cataloging) SirsiDynix; (Circulation) SirsiDynix; (ILL) OCLC; (OPAC) SirsiDynix; (Serials) SirsiDynix
Wireless access
Mem of Central Iowa Library Services
Partic in OCLC Online Computer Library Center, Inc
Open Mon-Thurs 9-9, Fri & Sat 9-6, Sun 1-5

UTE

P UTE PUBLIC LIBRARY, 130 Main St, 51060. (Mail add: PO Box 255, 51060-0255), SAN 376-7485. Tel: 712-885-2237. FAX: 712-885-2237. *Librn,* Position Currently Open
Library Holdings: High Interest/Low Vocabulary Bk Vols 300; Bk Vols 2,500
Mem of Northwest Iowa Library Services
Friends of the Library Group

VAN HORNE

P VAN HORNE PUBLIC LIBRARY*, 114 Main St, 52346. (Mail add: PO Box 280, 52346-0280), SAN 305-750X. Tel: 319-228-8744. FAX: 319-228-8744. E-mail: director@vanhorne.lib.ia.us. Web Site: www.vanhorne.lib.ia.us. *Dir,* Nancy Pickering; *Asst Librn,* Judy Wallace
Pop 1,400; Circ 9,760
Library Holdings: Bk Vols 9,835
Open Mon-Thurs 9-11 & 3:30-7, Fri & Sat 9-11

VAN METER

P VAN METER PUBLIC LIBRARY*, 505 Grant St, 50261. (Mail add: PO Box 94, 50261-0094), SAN 305-7518. Tel: 515-996-2435. FAX: 515-996-2207. E-mail: vanmeterpl@mchsi.com. *Dir,* Jolena Welker; E-mail: jwelker@vanmeteria.gov
Pop 866; Circ 9,743
Library Holdings: Bk Vols 8,000; Per Subs 21
Mem of Central Iowa Library Services
Open Mon & Fri 9-5, Tues 3-8, Wed & Thurs 9-8, Sat 9-Noon

VENTURA

P VENTURA PUBLIC LIBRARY*, Seven W Ventura St, 50482. (Mail add: PO Box 200, 50482-0200), SAN 305-7534. Tel: 641-829-4410. FAX: 641-829-4410. E-mail: ventpl@netins.net. Web Site: showcase.netins.net/web/venturalibrary. *Dir,* Carol Clemens
Founded 1968. Pop 614; Circ 11,000
Library Holdings: Bks on Deafness & Sign Lang 20; Bk Titles 10,500; Per Subs 50
Wireless access
Function: Homebound delivery serv
Open Mon-Thurs 11-5, Fri 1-6, Sat 9-12

VICTOR

P VICTOR PUBLIC LIBRARY*, 710 Second St, 52347. (Mail add: PO Box 686, 52347-0686), SAN 305-7542. Tel: 319-647-3646. FAX: 319-647-3646. E-mail: vpl4@netins.net. *Librn,* Elaine Roberts
Library Holdings: Bk Vols 11,480; Per Subs 51
Open Mon, Wed & Fri 9-6, Sat 9-12

VILLISCA

P VILLISCA PUBLIC LIBRARY*, 204 S Third Ave, 50864. SAN 305-7550. Tel: 712-826-2452. FAX: 712-826-2686. Web Site: www.villisca.swilsa.lib.ia.us. *Dir,* Pat Means; *Ch,* Janet Scholey
Founded 1903. Pop 2,500; Circ 13,232
Jul 2010-Jun 2011. Mats Exp $48,280
Library Holdings: Bk Vols 14,000; Per Subs 55
Special Collections: Chinese Coll, Native American Arrowhead Coll, Pitcher Coll
Automation Activity & Vendor Info: (Acquisitions) Follett Software; (Cataloging) Follett Software; (Circulation) Follett Software; (Course Reserve) Follett Software; (ILL) Follett Software; (Media Booking) Follett Software; (OPAC) Follett Software; (Serials) Follett Software
Database Vendor: EBSCOhost
Wireless access
Mem of Southwest Iowa Library Services District
Open Mon & Wed 10-6, Tues, Thurs & Fri 1-5, Sat 9-1

VINTON

P VINTON PUBLIC LIBRARY*, 510 Second Ave, 52349. SAN 305-7569. Tel: 319-472-4208. FAX: 319-472-2548. E-mail: vintonpl@mchsi.com. Web Site: www.vintonlibrary.com. *Dir,* Virginia Holsten; *Ch,* Amy Noe
Founded 1902. Pop 5,102; Circ 78,727
Jul 2011-Jun 2012 Income $229,305, State $3,334, City $181,173, County $12,970, Locally Generated Income $1,855. Mats Exp $22,261, Books $13,823, Electronic Ref Mat (Incl. Access Fees) $3,823. Sal $114,244
Library Holdings: Audiobooks 1,141; Bks on Deafness & Sign Lang 5; DVDs 372; e-books 4,026; Large Print Bks 1,829; Bk Titles 26,828; Bk Vols 26,928; Per Subs 67; Talking Bks 868; Videos 301
Automation Activity & Vendor Info: (Cataloging) Book Systems; (Circulation) Book Systems; (OPAC) Book Systems
Database Vendor: EBSCOhost, Ingram Library Services, OCLC FirstSearch, OCLC WorldShare Interlibrary Loan
Wireless access
Function: Handicapped accessible, Homebound delivery serv, ILL available, Photocopying/Printing, Prog for children & young adult, Ref serv available, Summer reading prog, Telephone ref, Wheelchair accessible
Open Mon & Thurs 9-8, Tues & Wed 9-5:30, Fri 9-5, Sat 9-12

VOLGA

P VOLGA PUBLIC LIBRARY, 505 Washington St, 52077. (Mail add: PO Box 131, 52077-0131), SAN 305-7577. Tel: 563-767-3511. FAX: 563-767-3511. E-mail: volgalib@iowatelecom.net. *Dir,* Heather L Thomas
Founded 1923. Circ 4,537
Library Holdings: CDs 110; DVDs 70; Bk Titles 5,836; Per Subs 27; Talking Bks 138; Videos 454
Automation Activity & Vendor Info: (Acquisitions) Winnebago Software Co; (Cataloging) Winnebago Software Co; (Circulation) Winnebago Software Co
Database Vendor: EBSCOhost, MITINET, Inc
Wireless access
Special Services for the Blind - Large print bks; Talking bks
Open Mon 1-6, Wed 1-8, Thurs 12-5, Sat 9-12

WADENA

P WADENA PUBLIC LIBRARY*, 136 S Mill St, 52169. (Mail add: PO Box 19, 52169-0019), SAN 305-7585. Tel: 563-774-2039. FAX: 563-774-2039. E-mail: wadenapl@windstream.net. Web Site: www.wadena.lib.ia.us. *Dir,* Dawn Thompson
Founded 1950. Pop 242; Circ 5,677
Library Holdings: Bk Titles 8,164; Per Subs 15
Subject Interests: Educ, Hist
Open Mon 1:30-6, Wed & Sat 9-2

WALL LAKE

P WALL LAKE PUBLIC LIBRARY*, 116 Main St, 51466. (Mail add: PO Box 68, 51466-0068), SAN 305-7593. Tel: 712-664-2983. FAX: 712-664-2577. Web Site: www.walllake.lib.ia.us. *Dir,* Jody Fischer; E-mail: jody.fischer@walllake.lib.ia.us
Founded 1909. Pop 950; Circ 7,200
Library Holdings: Bk Vols 10,000; Per Subs 28
Mem of Northwest Iowa Library Services
Open Mon 2-6, Tues, Thurs & Fri 2-5:30, Wed 11-5, Sat 10-12

WALNUT

P WALNUT PUBLIC LIBRARY*, 224 Antique City Dr, 51577-0347. (Mail add: PO Box 347, 51577-0347), SAN 305-7607. Tel: 712-784-3533. E-mail: wlntlib@walnutel.net. Web Site: www.walnutiowa.org. *Librn,* Margo Matthies
Pop 897; Circ 8,981
Library Holdings: Bk Vols 10,000; Per Subs 46
Mem of Southwest Iowa Library Services District
Open Mon, Tues, Thurs & Fri 1-5, Wed 1-6, Sat 9-12

WAPELLO

P KECK MEMORIAL LIBRARY*, 119 N Second St, 52653-1501. SAN 305-7615. Tel: 319-523-5261. FAX: 319-523-5261. Web Site: www.wapello.lib.ia.us. *Dir,* Llewann Bryant; E-mail: lbryant@wapello.lib.ia.us
Pop 2,124; Circ 39,291
Library Holdings: Bk Vols 29,144; Per Subs 50
Open Mon & Wed 9-8, Tues, Thurs & Fri 9-5, Sat 9-12
Friends of the Library Group

WASHINGTON

P WASHINGTON PUBLIC LIBRARY*, 115 W Washington St, 52353. SAN 305-7623. Tel: 319-653-2726. FAX: 319-653-3095. Web Site: www.washington.lib.ia.us. *Dir,* Debbie Stanton; *Ch,* Jolisa Weidner; Staff 6.5 (MLS 1, Non-MLS 5.5)
Founded 1877. Pop 13,750; Circ 82,838
Jul 2011-Jun 2012 Income $421,048, State $3,542, City $336,634, County $66,649, Locally Generated Income $6,851, Other $7,372. Mats Exp $38,734, Books $24,384, AV Mat $9,277, Electronic Ref Mat (Incl. Access Fees) $5,073. Sal $179,461 (Prof $45,000)
Library Holdings: Audiobooks 2,385; AV Mats 8,362; DVDs 986; e-books 7,956; Bk Titles 39,473; Per Subs 136
Special Collections: Art Coll (Circulating Art Coll); Board Games (Circulating Board Game Coll)
Subject Interests: Genealogy
Automation Activity & Vendor Info: (Acquisitions) Baker & Taylor; (ILL) OCLC WorldShare Interlibrary Loan; (Serials) EBSCO Online
Database Vendor: ComPanion Corp
Wireless access
Function: Art exhibits, Audiobks via web, Bilingual assistance for Spanish patrons, Bks on CD, CD-ROM, Children's prog, Computers for patron use, Copy machines, Electronic databases & coll, Exhibits, Fax serv, Free DVD rentals, Handicapped accessible, Holiday prog, Home delivery & serv to Sr ctr & nursing homes, ILL available, Magnifiers for reading, Mail & tel request accepted, Microfiche/film & reading machines, Music CDs, Notary serv, Online cat, Outreach serv, Outside serv via phone, mail, e-mail & web, OverDrive digital audio bks, Photocopying/Printing, Preschool outreach, Preschool reading prog, Prog for adults, Prog for children & young adult, Pub access computers, Ref serv available, Spanish lang bks, Story hour, Summer reading prog, Tax forms, Teen prog, Telephone ref, Wheelchair accessible, Winter reading prog
Partic in WILBOR Consortium (West/Central Iowa Libraries Building Online Resources)
Special Services for the Deaf - Bks on deafness & sign lang
Special Services for the Blind - Bks available with recordings; Bks on CD; Extensive large print coll; Free checkout of audio mat; Home delivery serv; Large print bks; Magnifiers; Ref serv
Open Mon-Thurs 9-8, Fri & Sat 9-5

WASHTA

P WASHTA PUBLIC LIBRARY*, 100 S Fifth Ave, 51061. (Mail add: PO Box 121, 51061-0121), SAN 305-7631. Tel: 712-447-6546. FAX: 712-447-6158. *Dir,* Ruby Wych
Pop 284
Library Holdings: Per Subs 16
Mem of Northwest Iowa Library Services
Open Mon-Wed 10-12 & 3-6, Thurs 3-6, Fri 10-12 & 3-4:30, Sat 1-Midnight
Friends of the Library Group

WATERLOO

CM ALLEN COLLEGE*, Barrett Library, 1825 Logan Ave, 50703. SAN 325-5905. Tel: 319-226-2005. FAX: 319-226-2020, 319-226-2053. Web Site: www.allencollege.edu. *Librn,* Dr Ruth Yan; Tel: 319-226-2080, E-mail: yanl2@ihs.org; *Instrul Tech,* David R Wu; Tel: 319-226-2054, E-mail: wudr@ihs.org; Staff 2 (MLS 1, Non-MLS 1)
Founded 1995. Enrl 350; Fac 50; Highest Degree: Master
Library Holdings: AV Mats 40; Bk Titles 400; Per Subs 90
Automation Activity & Vendor Info: (Acquisitions) Innovative Interfaces, Inc; (Cataloging) Innovative Interfaces, Inc; (Circulation) Innovative Interfaces, Inc; (Course Reserve) Innovative Interfaces, Inc; (ILL) Innovative Interfaces, Inc; (Media Booking) Innovative Interfaces, Inc; (OPAC) Innovative Interfaces, Inc; (Serials) Innovative Interfaces, Inc
Database Vendor: EBSCOhost
Function: Doc delivery serv, For res purposes, Health sci info serv, ILL available, Online searches, Ref serv available, Res libr, Telephone ref
Open Mon-Fri 8-4
Restriction: Open to students, fac & staff

M COVENANT MEDICAL CENTER*, Health Sciences Library, 3421 W Ninth St, 50702. Tel: 319-272-7385. FAX: 319-272-7313. *Librn,* Mary Ann Upchurch; Staff 1 (MLS 1)
Jul 2005-Jun 2006 Income $19,000
Library Holdings: Bk Vols 1,000; Per Subs 51
Partic in Docline
Open Tues-Thurs 7:30-4

S GROUT MUSEUM OF HISTORY & SCIENCE*, Hans J Chryst Archival Library, 503 South St, 50701. SAN 305-7666. Tel: 319-234-6357. FAX: 319-236-0500. E-mail: info@gmdistrict.org. Web Site: www.groutmuseumdistrict.org. *Archivist,* Catreva Manning; E-mail: clmkell@hotmail.com
Founded 1956
Library Holdings: Bk Titles 1,520
Special Collections: Iowa Authors Coll, clippings & memoirs; Photogs; Rare Books Coll (Indian & Iowa History)
Subject Interests: Genealogy, Local hist
Open Tues-Sat 9-5

J HAWKEYE COMMUNITY COLLEGE LIBRARY*, 1501 E Orange Rd, 50701-9014. (Mail add: PO Box 8015, 50704-8015), SAN 305-7674. Tel: 319-296-4006. FAX: 319-296-9140. E-mail: hcclibrary@hawkeyecollege.edu. Web Site: www.hawkeyecollege.edu/library/index.aspx. *Dir,* Candace Havely; *Ref Librn,* Judy Mitchell; Staff 5 (MLS 2, Non-MLS 3)
Founded 1970. Enrl 5,765; Fac 274; Highest Degree: Associate
Automation Activity & Vendor Info: (Cataloging) Innovative Interfaces, Inc; (Circulation) Innovative Interfaces, Inc; (ILL) OCLC; (OPAC) Innovative Interfaces, Inc; (Serials) Innovative Interfaces, Inc
Database Vendor: CQ Press, ebrary, EBSCOhost, Gale Cengage Learning, LexisNexis, Micromedex, Newsbank, OCLC FirstSearch, OCLC WorldShare Interlibrary Loan, Oxford Online, ReferenceUSA, SerialsSolutions
Wireless access
Partic in Cedar Valley Libr Consortium
Open Mon-Thurs 7am-8pm, Fri 7-4:30, Sun 12-8

M NORTHEAST IOWA MEDICAL EDUCATION FOUNDATION LIBRARY*, 2055 Kimball Ave, 50702. Tel: 319-272-2525. FAX: 319-272-2527. *Librn,* Jean Camarata
Library Holdings: Bk Vols 500; Per Subs 22
Wireless access
Open Mon-Fri 8-5

P WATERLOO PUBLIC LIBRARY*, 415 Commercial St, 50701-1385. SAN 341-9851. Tel: 319-291-4521. Circulation Tel: 319-291-4480. Reference Tel: 319-291-4476. Administration Tel: 319-291-4496. Automation Services Tel: 319-291-4497. FAX: 319-291-6736. Administration FAX: 319-291-9013. TDD: 319-291-3823. E-mail: infowiz.wpl@gmail.com. Web Site: www.waterloo.lib.ia.us. *Dir,* Sheryl McGovern; E-mail: mcgovern.sheryl@gmail.com; *Tech Serv Adminr,* Lori Petersen; *Youth Serv Librn,* Kelly Stern; *Ref,* Michael Dargan; Staff 49 (MLS 9, Non-MLS 40)
Founded 1896. Pop 68,747; Circ 466,903
Library Holdings: AV Mats 16,740; Bk Vols 205,960; Per Subs 376
Special Collections: AIDS Lending Library
Automation Activity & Vendor Info: (Acquisitions) Innovative Interfaces, Inc; (Cataloging) Innovative Interfaces, Inc; (Circulation) Innovative Interfaces, Inc
Partic in Cedar Valley Libr Consortium
Special Services for the Deaf - TDD equip
Special Services for the Blind - Computer with voice synthesizer for visually impaired persons
Open Mon-Thurs 9-9, Fri & Sat 9-5, Sun 1-5
Friends of the Library Group

WATERVILLE

P WATERVILLE PUBLIC LIBRARY*, 82 Main St, 52170. (Mail add: PO Box 68, 52170-0068), SAN 376-5245. Tel: 563-535-7295. FAX: 563-535-7030. E-mail: director@waterville.lib.ia.us. Web Site: www.waterville.lib.ia.us. *Dir,* Heather Bente; Staff 1 (Non-MLS 1)
Founded 1995. Pop 250
Library Holdings: DVDs 30; Large Print Bks 35; Bk Titles 4,200; Bk Vols 4,400; Per Subs 12; Talking Bks 50; Videos 100
Function: Home delivery & serv to Sr ctr & nursing homes, Photocopying/Printing, Prog for children & young adult, VHS videos
Open Tues 3-7, Thurs 10-1 & 2-6, Sat 9-12

WAUCOMA

P WAUCOMA PUBLIC LIBRARY*, 103 First Ave, 52171. (Mail add: PO Box 131, 52171), SAN 321-5180. Tel: 563-776-4042. FAX: 563-776-4042. E-mail: director@waucoma.lib.ia.us. Web Site: www.waucoma.lib.ia.us. *Dir,* Lois Ann Langreck; Tel: 563-776-9971, E-mail: flois@iowatelecom.net
Founded 1978. Pop 699; Circ 5,000
Library Holdings: Bk Titles 6,000; Per Subs 10
Wireless access
Open Mon & Thurs 4-8, Tues 9-11 & 1-5, Fri 2-6, Sat 9-11

WAUKEE

P WAUKEE PUBLIC LIBRARY*, 950 Warrior Lane, 50263. (Mail add: PO Box 68, 50263-0068), SAN 305-7690. Tel: 515-987-1280. FAX: 515-987-5262. Web Site: www.waukee.lib.ia.us. *Interim Libr Dir, Youth Serv Librn,* Keri Weston-Stoll; E-mail: kweston-stoll@waukee.org; *Dir,* Position Currently Open; *Asst Dir,* Devon Murphy-Petersen; E-mail: dmurphy-petersen@waukee.org; Staff 9 (MLS 2, Non-MLS 7)
Founded 1929. Pop 15,000; Circ 162,000
Jul 2012-Jun 2013 Income $466,097, State $16,392, City $426,000, County $7,850, Locally Generated Income $15,855. Mats Exp $49,000, Books $30,000, Per/Ser (Incl. Access Fees) $2,000, AV Mat $15,000, Electronic Ref Mat (Incl. Access Fees) $2,000. Sal $198,785
Library Holdings: Audiobooks 4,198; AV Mats 4,439; CDs 720; DVDs 3,593; e-books 1,002; Electronic Media & Resources 2,379; Large Print Bks 800; Bk Vols 37,785; Per Subs 122; Videos 272
Automation Activity & Vendor Info: (Acquisitions) TLC (The Library Corporation); (Cataloging) TLC (The Library Corporation); (Circulation) TLC (The Library Corporation); (OPAC) TLC (The Library Corporation)
Database Vendor: EBSCOhost, MITINET, Inc, OCLC FirstSearch, OCLC WorldShare Interlibrary Loan, Overdrive, Inc, TLC (The Library Corporation)
Wireless access
Function: Adult bk club, After school storytime, Archival coll, Bi-weekly Writer's Group, Bilingual assistance for Spanish patrons, Bk club(s), Bks on CD, Children's prog, Computers for patron use, Copy machines, Digital talking bks, e-mail & chat, Electronic databases & coll, Equip loans & repairs, Exhibits, Family literacy, Fax serv, Free DVD rentals, Genealogy discussion group, Govt ref serv, Handicapped accessible, Holiday prog, Home delivery & serv to Sr ctr & nursing homes, Homebound delivery serv, ILL available, Music CDs, Online cat, OverDrive digital audio bks, Preschool outreach, Prog for adults, Prog for children & young adult, Scanner, Story hour, Summer reading prog, Tax forms, Teen prog, Telephone ref, Web-catalog, Writing prog
Publications: City Newsletter (Monthly)
Mem of Central Iowa Library Services
Open Mon-Thurs 9:30-8:30, Fri 9:30-5:30, Sat 9:30-3:30, Sun 1-4
Friends of the Library Group

WAUKON

P ROBEY MEMORIAL LIBRARY*, 401 First Ave NW, 52172-1803. SAN 305-7704. Tel: 563-568-4424. FAX: 563-568-5026. E-mail: robeymemorial@waukon.lib.ia.us. Web Site: www.waukon.lib.ia.us. *Dir,* Position Currently Open
Founded 1920. Pop 4,863; Circ 50,948
Library Holdings: Bk Vols 25,457; Per Subs 101
Special Collections: Iowa Coll; Large Print Coll
Automation Activity & Vendor Info: (Cataloging) Follett Software; (Circulation) Follett Software
Database Vendor: EBSCOhost
Wireless access
Open Mon-Thurs 10-8, Fri 10-6, Sat 10-4

WAVERLY

C WARTBURG COLLEGE LIBRARY*, Vogel Library, 100 Wartburg Blvd, 50677-0903. SAN 305-7712. Tel: 319-352-8500. Interlibrary Loan Service Tel: 319-352-8258. Reference Tel: 319-352-8506. Administration Tel: 319-352-8462. FAX: 319-352-8312. Web Site: library.wartburg.edu. *Col Librn, Libr Dir,* Curtis Brundy; E-mail: curtis.brundy@wartburg.edu; *Archivist, Cat Librn,* Pamela Madden; Tel: 319-352-8461, E-mail: pamela.madden@wartburg.edu; *Info Literacy Librn,* Christine Elliott; *Info Literacy Librn,* Karen Lehmann; Tel: 319-352-8460, E-mail: karen.lehmann@wartburg.edu; *Info Literacy Librn,* Eric Leong; *Info Literacy Librn,* Jill Westen; *Circ & Reserves Supvr,* Linda Hennings; Tel: 319-352-8524, E-mail: linda.hennings@wartburg.edu; *ILL Supvr,* Paula Hemingson; E-mail: paula.hemingson@wartburg.edu; *Supvr, Access Serv,* Eileen Myers; Tel: 319-352-8464, E-mail: eileen.myers@wartburg.edu; *Tech Serv Assoc,* Margaret Hubbard; E-mail: margaret.hubbard@wartburg.edu; Staff 10.5 (MLS 6.5, Non-MLS 4)
Founded 1852. Enrl 1,764; Fac 107; Highest Degree: Bachelor
Library Holdings: AV Mats 5,051; e-books 11,131; e-journals 19,338; Electronic Media & Resources 932; Microforms 8,480; Bk Titles 145,810; Bk Vols 184,335; Per Subs 801
Special Collections: Archives of Iowa Broadcasting History; College Archives
Automation Activity & Vendor Info: (Acquisitions) Innovative Interfaces, Inc - Millenium; (Cataloging) Innovative Interfaces, Inc - Millenium; (Circulation) Innovative Interfaces, Inc - Millenium; (Course Reserve) Innovative Interfaces, Inc - Millenium; (ILL) OCLC; (OPAC) Innovative Interfaces, Inc - Millenium; (Serials) Innovative Interfaces, Inc - Millenium
Database Vendor: ABC-CLIO, Alexander Street Press, American Chemical Society, American Psychological Association (APA), Annual Reviews, ARTstor, BioOne, Cambridge Scientific Abstracts, CQ Press, CredoReference, ebrary, EBSCOhost, Facts on File, Gale Cengage Learning, Gallup, Ingenta, JSTOR, LexisNexis, McGraw-Hill, Newsbank, OCLC FirstSearch, OCLC WorldShare Interlibrary Loan, Oxford Online, Project MUSE, ProQuest, Wiley InterScience
Wireless access
Partic in Iowa Private Academic Library Consortium (IPAL)
Open Mon-Thurs 7:30am-12am, Fri 7:30-5, Sat 10-5, Sun 1pm-12am

P WAVERLY PUBLIC LIBRARY*, 1500 W Bremer Ave, 50677-2836. SAN 305-7720. Tel: 319-352-1223. FAX: 319-352-0872. E-mail: waverly@waverly.lib.ia.us. *Dir,* Sarah Meyer-Ryerson; E-mail: smeyer@waverly.lib.ia.us
Founded 1857. Pop 8,968; Circ 148,000
Library Holdings: High Interest/Low Vocabulary Bk Vols 100; Bk Titles 60,000; Bk Vols 68,000; Per Subs 162
Subject Interests: Local hist
Automation Activity & Vendor Info: (Cataloging) SirsiDynix; (Circulation) SirsiDynix; (OPAC) SirsiDynix
Open Mon-Thurs 10-8, Fri & Sat 10-5, Sun 2-5
Friends of the Library Group

WEBB

P WEBB PUBLIC LIBRARY*, 124 Main St, 51366. (Mail add: PO Box 97, 51366-0097), SAN 305-7739. Tel: 712-838-7719. E-mail: webblibrary@webbwireless.net. *Dir,* Linda Adams; Staff 1 (Non-MLS 1)
Pop 222; Circ 3,487
Library Holdings: Bk Titles 8,000; Per Subs 35
Subject Interests: Local hist
Mem of Northwest Iowa Library Services
Open Tues & Thurs (Winter) 12-6, Fri 9-2, Sat 9-12; Tues & Thurs (Summer) 12-6, Wed 9-12, Fri 9-2

WEBSTER CITY

P KENDALL YOUNG LIBRARY*, 1201 Willson Ave, 50595-2294. SAN 305-7755. Tel: 515-832-9100. FAX: 515-832-9102. E-mail: info@kendall-young.lib.ia.us. Web Site: www.kendall-young.lib.ia.us. *Dir,* Paul Elliott Dahl; *Asst Dir/Ch,* Linda Brown; Tel: 515-832-9101; Staff 17 (MLS 3, Non-MLS 14)
Founded 1898. Pop 8,176; Circ 73,640
Jan 2008-Dec 2008 Income $586,670, State $6,789, City $20,260, County $19,309, Locally Generated Income $540,312. Mats Exp $73,068, Books $56,275, Per/Ser (Incl. Access Fees) $6,773, Micro $81, AV Mat $7,997, Electronic Ref Mat (Incl. Access Fees) $1,942. Sal $297,281
Library Holdings: Audiobooks 1,860; Bks on Deafness & Sign Lang 35; CDs 495; DVDs 673; Large Print Bks 1,250; Bk Vols 59,391; Per Subs 144; Videos 833
Special Collections: Clark R Mollenhoff Coll; MacKinlay Kantor Coll
Subject Interests: Genealogy, Local hist
Automation Activity & Vendor Info: (Cataloging) TLC (The Library Corporation); (Circulation) TLC (The Library Corporation)
Database Vendor: EBSCOhost, OCLC FirstSearch, ProQuest
Wireless access
Function: Adult bk club, After school storytime, Archival coll, Art exhibits, Audiobks via web, AV serv, Bks on cassette, Bks on CD, CD-ROM, Children's prog, Computer training, Computers for patron use, Copy machines, Digital talking bks, e-mail & chat, E-Reserves, Electronic databases & coll, Exhibits, Fax serv, Free DVD rentals, Genealogy discussion group, Handicapped accessible, Holiday prog, Home delivery & serv to Sr ctr & nursing homes, Homebound delivery serv, ILL available,

Magnifiers for reading, Mail & tel request accepted, Music CDs, Online cat, Online searches, Outside serv via phone, mail, e-mail & web, OverDrive digital audio bks, Photocopying/Printing, Preschool outreach, Prog for adults, Prog for children & young adult, Pub access computers, Ref & res, Ref serv available, Ref serv in person, Scanner, Senior computer classes, Spoken cassettes & CDs, Spoken cassettes & DVDs, Story hour, Summer reading prog, Tax forms, Teen prog, Telephone ref, VHS videos, Video lending libr, Wheelchair accessible, Workshops
Partic in North Eastern Iowa Bridge to Online Resource Sharing (NEIBORS)
Special Services for the Deaf - Closed caption videos
Special Services for the Blind - Audio mat; Bks on cassette; Bks on CD; Copier with enlargement capabilities; Extensive large print coll; Home delivery serv; Low vision equip
Open Mon-Thurs 10-8, Fri 10-6, Sat 10-5
Friends of the Library Group

WELLMAN

P WELLMAN SCOFIELD PUBLIC LIBRARY*, 711 Fourth St, 52356. (Mail add: PO Box 420, 52356), SAN 305-7763. Tel: 319-646-6858. FAX: 319-646-6561. Web Site: www.wellman.lib.ia.us. *Dir,* Steve Miller; E-mail: steve@wellman.lib.ia.us; *Asst Dir,* Kathy Carlson; Staff 2.5 (Non-MLS 2.5)
Founded 1909. Pop 1,393; Circ 24,000
Library Holdings: Bk Titles 17,756; Per Subs 25
Automation Activity & Vendor Info: (Cataloging) Follett Software; (Circulation) Follett Software; (OPAC) Follett Software
Database Vendor: EBSCOhost, OCLC FirstSearch
Wireless access
Function: ILL available
Open Mon & Thurs 10-6, Tues & Wed 1-6, Fri 1-5, Sat 10-4
Friends of the Library Group

WELLSBURG

P WELLSBURG PUBLIC LIBRARY*, 411 N Adams, 50680. (Mail add: PO Box 489, 50680-0489), SAN 305-7771. Tel: 641-869-5234. FAX: 641-869-5234. Web Site: www.wellsburg.lib.ia.us. *Dir,* Karen Mennenga; E-mail: Karen@wellsburg.lib.ia.us; *Librn,* Joyce Meyeraan; *Asst Librn,* Janice Schafer; Staff 2 (Non-MLS 2)
Pop 709
Library Holdings: Bk Titles 9,000; Per Subs 40
Special Collections: Ortssippen Books (German genealogy)
Database Vendor: Baker & Taylor, EBSCOhost, Gale Cengage Learning, Ingram Library Services, LearningExpress, OCLC FirstSearch
Wireless access
Open Tues, Wed & Fri 10-5, Thurs 10-7, Sat 10-12

WESLEY

P WESLEY PUBLIC LIBRARY*, 206 W Main St, 50483. (Mail add: PO Box 37, 50483-0037), SAN 305-778X. Tel: 515-679-4214. FAX: 515-679-4214. E-mail: wplbooks@yahoo.com. *Dir,* Lany Mitchell
Founded 1950. Pop 467; Circ 9,849
Library Holdings: Bk Titles 6,877; Bk Vols 7,091; Per Subs 44
Open Mon & Wed 1-7, Thurs & Fri 9-Noon

WEST BEND

P WEST BEND PUBLIC LIBRARY*, 316 S Broadway, 50597. (Mail add: PO Box 46, 50597-0046), SAN 305-7798. Tel: 515-887-6411. FAX: 515-887-6412. E-mail: wbplib@ncn.net. *Dir, Operations,* Jennifer Gambell; *Ch,* Lisa Riesenberg
Founded 1939. Pop 902; Circ 54,000
Library Holdings: AV Mats 800; Large Print Bks 300; Bk Titles 13,100; Bk Vols 13,380; Per Subs 70; Talking Bks 130
Automation Activity & Vendor Info: (Cataloging) Follett Software; (Circulation) Follett Software; (OPAC) Follett Software; (Serials) EBSCO Online
Open Mon 10:30-7:30, Tues-Fri 10:30-5:30, Sat 9-3
Friends of the Library Group

WEST BRANCH

S NATIONAL ARCHIVES & RECORDS ADMINISTRATION, Herbert Hoover Presidential Library-Museum, 210 Parkside Dr, 52358-9685. (Mail add: PO Box 488, 52358-0488), SAN 305-781X. Tel: 319-643-5301. FAX: 319-643-6045. E-mail: hoover.library@nara.gov. Web Site: www.hoover.archives.gov. *Dir,* Dr Thomas Schwartz
Founded 1962
Library Holdings: AV Mats 40,000; Microforms 3,000; Bk Vols 20,000; Per Subs 7
Special Collections: Bourke Hickenlooper Coll; Clark R Mollenhoff Coll; Gerald P Nye Coll; H R Gross Coll; Hanford MacNider Coll; Herbert Hoover Coll; Hugh R Wilson Coll; James P Goodrich Coll; James Westbrook Pegler Coll; Lewis L Strauss Coll; Lou Henry Hoover Coll; Nathan W MacChesney Coll; Robert E Wood Coll; Rose Wilder Lane Coll; Verne Marshall Coll; Walter Trohan Coll; William C Mullendore Coll; William P MacCracken Coll; William R Castle Coll
Subject Interests: Econ, Hist, Polit sci
Wireless access
Partic in RLIN (Research Libraries Information Network)
Open Mon-Fri 8:45-4:45
Friends of the Library Group

P WEST BRANCH PUBLIC LIBRARY*, 300 N Downey, 52358. (Mail add: PO Box 460, 52358-0460), SAN 305-7801. Tel: 319-643-2633. FAX: 319-643-2845. Web Site: www.westbranch.lib.ia.us. *Dir,* Nick Shimmin; E-mail: nshimmin@westbranch.lib.ia.us; *Asst Dir/Ch,* Becky Knoche; E-mail: bknoche@westbranch.lib.ia.us
Pop 2,108; Circ 2,500
Library Holdings: Bk Titles 40,000; Per Subs 55
Open Mon-Thurs 12-8, Fri 10-5, Sat 10-2
Friends of the Library Group

WEST BURLINGTON

M GREAT RIVER MEDICAL CENTER LIBRARY*, 1221 S Gear Ave, 52655-1679. SAN 305-2435. Tel: 319-768-4075. FAX: 319-768-4080. Web Site: www.greatrivermedical.org/library. *Librn,* Sarah Goff; E-mail: sgoff@grhs.net; Staff 1 (MLS 1)
Library Holdings: Bk Vols 2,000; Per Subs 283
Wireless access
Open Mon 9-1, Tues-Fri 7:30-4

J SOUTHEASTERN COMMUNITY COLLEGE LIBRARY*, Yohe Memorial Library, 1500 W Agency Rd, 52655. (Mail add: PO Box 180, 52655-0180), SAN 341-9916. Tel: 319-752-2731, Ext 8143. FAX: 319-753-0322. Web Site: www.scciowa.edu. *Dir,* Brian P McAtee; Tel: 319-752-2731, Ext 5091, E-mail: bmcatee@scciowa.edu; Staff 7 (MLS 3, Non-MLS 4)
Founded 1920. Enrl 2,000; Fac 80
Library Holdings: Bk Vols 30,000; Per Subs 300
Subject Interests: Anthrop, Art & archit, Environ studies
Automation Activity & Vendor Info: (Cataloging) Innovative Interfaces, Inc; (Circulation) Innovative Interfaces, Inc; (OPAC) Innovative Interfaces, Inc
Database Vendor: EBSCOhost, OCLC FirstSearch
Open Mon-Thurs (Winter) 7am-9pm, Fri 7-4:30; Mon-Fri (Summer) 7-4:30
Departmental Libraries:
FRED KARRE MEMORIAL LIBRARY-KEOKUK CAMPUS, 335 Messenger Rd, Keokuk, 52632. (Mail add: PO Box 6007, Keokuk, 52632-6007), SAN 328-9141. Tel: 319-524-3221, Ext 8456. FAX: 319-524-6433. E-mail: sclib1@secc.cc.ia.us. *Librn,* Brian P McAtee; Staff 1 (MLS 1)
Library Holdings: Bk Vols 9,500; Per Subs 75
Subject Interests: Art
Partic in SE Regional Libr Servs
Open Mon-Thurs (Winter) 7:30am-9pm, Fri 7:30-4; Mon-Thurs (Summer) 7:30-5, Fri 7:30am-11:30am

WEST DES MOINES

P WEST DES MOINES PUBLIC LIBRARY*, 4000 Mills Civic Pkwy, 50265-2049. SAN 305-7836. Tel: 515-222-3400. Circulation Tel: 515-222-3404. Reference Tel: 515-222-3403. FAX: 515-222-3401. Web Site: www.wdmlibrary.org. *Dir,* Darryl Eschete; *Head, Circ,* Heather Hildreth; *Head, Pub Serv,* Shirley Houghtaling; Staff 7 (MLS 6, Non-MLS 1)
Founded 1940. Pop 51,744; Circ 812,092
Jul 2007-Jun 2008. Mats Exp $316,038. Sal $1,284,101
Library Holdings: AV Mats 24,342; Bk Vols 150,536; Per Subs 309
Database Vendor: EBSCOhost
Wireless access
Publications: WDM (Magazine)
Mem of Central Iowa Library Services
Open Mon-Thurs (Oct-Apr) 9-9, Fri 9-6, Sat 9-5, Sun 2-5; Mon-Thurs (May-Sept) 9-9, Fri 9-6, Sat 10-4
Friends of the Library Group

WEST LIBERTY

P WEST LIBERTY FREE PUBLIC LIBRARY*, 400 N Spencer St, 52776. SAN 305-7844. Tel: 319-627-2084. FAX: 319-627-2135. E-mail: wllibrary@wlpl.org. Web Site: www.wlpl.org. *Dir,* Janette E McMahon; E-mail: jmcmahon@wlpl.org; Staff 5 (Non-MLS 5)
Founded 1904. Pop 3,300; Circ 28,000
Library Holdings: Bk Titles 18,000; Per Subs 52
Special Collections: Spanish & Laosian materials
Automation Activity & Vendor Info: (Cataloging) Follett Software; (Circulation) Follett Software
Database Vendor: EBSCOhost

Open Mon 2-7, Tues-Thurs 10-7, Fri & Sun 2-5, Sat 10-1
Friends of the Library Group

WEST POINT

P WEST POINT PUBLIC LIBRARY*, 317 Fifth St, 52656. (Mail add: PO Box 236, 52656-0236), SAN 305-7852. Tel: 319-837-6315. FAX: 319-837-6250. *Dir,* Cathy Schwartz; E-mail: cschwartz@westpoint.lib.ia.us
Founded 1946. Pop 1,000; Circ 25,139
Library Holdings: Bk Titles 10,000; Per Subs 60
Open Mon-Thurs 12-7, Fri 12-6, Sat 9-3

WEST UNION

S FAYETTE COUNTY HISTORICAL SOCIETY LIBRARY*, 100 N Walnut St, 52175-1347. SAN 371-7763. Tel: 563-422-5797. *Librn,* Steve Story; *Asst Librn,* Mary Richmond
Founded 1975
Library Holdings: Bk Titles 250
Special Collections: Oral History
Open Mon-Fri 10-3

P WEST UNION COMMUNITY LIBRARY*, 210 N Vine St, 52175. SAN 305-7860. Tel: 563-422-3103. FAX: 563-422-3103. Web Site: www.westunionlibrary.org. *Dir,* Tara Johnson; Staff 5 (Non-MLS 5)
Founded 1928. Pop 2,594; Circ 49,182
Library Holdings: Bk Vols 25,638; Per Subs 73; Talking Bks 800
Special Collections: Lincoln Coll
Automation Activity & Vendor Info: (Cataloging) Follett Software; (Circulation) Follett Software; (OPAC) Follett Software
Database Vendor: EBSCOhost, OCLC FirstSearch
Open Mon, Wed & Fri 11-5:30, Tues & Thurs 1:30-7:30, Sat 11-3

WESTGATE

P WESTGATE PUBLIC LIBRARY*, Three Main St, 50681. (Mail add: PO Box 10, 50681-0010). Tel: 563-578-5151. FAX: 563-578-5151. E-mail: westgatelibrary@iowatelecom.net. Web Site: www.westgate.lib.ia.us. *Dir,* Rhonda Harn
Pop 263; Circ 6,510
Library Holdings: Bk Titles 6,110; Per Subs 30
Open Mon & Thurs 1:30-7, Tues, Wed & Sat 9-12

WHAT CHEER

P WHAT CHEER PUBLIC LIBRARY*, 308 S Barnes St, 50268-0008. (Mail add: PO Box 324, 50268), SAN 321-1770. Tel: 641-634-2859. FAX: 641-634-2007. E-mail: admin@whatcheer.lib.ia.us, wc.library@mchsi.com. Web Site: www.whatcheer.lib.ia.us. *Dir,* William Miller; Staff 1 (Non-MLS 1)
Founded 1897. Pop 803
Library Holdings: Bk Titles 5,000
Wireless access
Open Mon 11-6, Wed 8:30-3:30, Thurs 1:30-5:30, Sat 9-11

WHEATLAND

P CURTIS MEMORIAL LIBRARY*, 116 S Main, 52777. (Mail add: PO Box 429, 52777), SAN 320-8303. Tel: 563-374-1534. FAX: 563-374-1534. E-mail: wheatlib@fbcom.net. *Librn,* Jill Bachus
Pop 840; Circ 5,665
Special Collections: Old Local Newspaper Coll (1860-1962), microfilm
Subject Interests: Local hist
Database Vendor: EBSCOhost
Wireless access
Open Mon 10-1 & 2-7, Tues-Thurs 10-1 & 2-6, Fri 10-1 & 2-5, Sat 10-1

WHITING

P WHITING PUBLIC LIBRARY*, 407 Whittier St, 51063. (Mail add: PO Box 288, 51063-0288), SAN 305-7917. Tel: 712-455-2612. FAX: 712-455-2612. Web Site: www.whiting.lib.ia.us. *Dir,* Margaret A Polly; E-mail: meg.polly@whiting.lib.ia.us; *Asst Dir,* Pamela Rasmussen; E-mail: pamela.rasmussen@whiting.lib.ia.us
Founded 1912. Pop 702; Circ 22,072
Jul 2010-Jun 2011 Income $63,067, State $2,134, City $48,469, County $4,001, Locally Generated Income $6,981, Other $1,482. Mats Exp $13,807, Books $9,113, Per/Ser (Incl. Access Fees) $1,519, AV Mat $3,126, Electronic Ref Mat (Incl. Access Fees) $49. Sal $30,897
Library Holdings: Audiobooks 639; Bks on Deafness & Sign Lang 7; DVDs 1,485; Large Print Bks 841; Bk Titles 13,856; Bk Vols 13,900; Per Subs 95; Videos 142
Database Vendor: EBSCOhost, Ingram Library Services, Overdrive, Inc
Wireless access
Function: Audiobks via web
Partic in WILBOR Consortium (West/Central Iowa Libraries Building Online Resources)
Open Mon-Wed 1-7, Thurs 9-7, Fri 9-12, Sat 1-5

WHITTEMORE

P WHITTEMORE PUBLIC LIBRARY*, 405 Fourth St, 50598. (Mail add: PO Box 356, 50598-0356), SAN 305-7925. Tel: 515-884-2680. FAX: 515-884-2323. Web Site: www.whittemore.lib.ia.us. *Dir,* Sandy Long; E-mail: sandyl@whittemore.lib.ia.us; *Asst Dir,* Joy Metzger; E-mail: joym@whittemore.lib.ia.us
Founded 1940. Pop 504; Circ 15,352
Jul 2011-Jun 2012 Income $76,218, State $1,465, City $45,400, County $12,516, Locally Generated Income $16,337, Other $500. Mats Exp $13,278, Books $10,266, Per/Ser (Incl. Access Fees) $917, AV Mat $2,054, Electronic Ref Mat (Incl. Access Fees) $41. Sal $40,991
Library Holdings: CDs 883; DVDs 1,548; Large Print Bks 475; Bk Vols 18,657; Per Subs 55; Videos 300
Automation Activity & Vendor Info: (Acquisitions) TLC (The Library Corporation); (Cataloging) TLC (The Library Corporation); (Circulation) TLC (The Library Corporation); (OPAC) TLC (The Library Corporation)
Database Vendor: EBSCO Information Services, TLC (The Library Corporation)
Wireless access
Open Mon 2-6, Tues & Thurs 9-11 & 2-7:30, Wed & Fri 2-5:30, Sat 9-1
Friends of the Library Group

WILLIAMS

P WILLIAMS PUBLIC LIBRARY*, 216 Main St, 50271. (Mail add: PO Box 36, 50271-0036), SAN 305-7933. Tel: 515-854-2643. FAX: 515-854-2643. E-mail: willpl@wmtel.net. Web Site: www.williams.lib.ia.us. *Dir,* Diane Sinclair; Staff 1 (Non-MLS 1)
Founded 1948. Pop 512; Circ 5,907
Library Holdings: Audiobooks 3,305; AV Mats 715; CDs 183; DVDs 785; e-books 6,044; Electronic Media & Resources 3; High Interest/Low Vocabulary Bk Vols 58; Large Print Bks 178; Bk Titles 20,225; Per Subs 35; Videos 35
Wireless access
Function: Adult bk club, Art exhibits, Audio & video playback equip for onsite use, Bk club(s), Bks on cassette, Bks on CD, Children's prog, Computer training, Computers for patron use, Copy machines, e-mail & chat, Fax serv, Free DVD rentals, Handicapped accessible, Health sci info serv, Holiday prog, ILL available, Online cat, Online ref, Online searches, Photocopying/Printing, Prog for adults, Prog for children & young adult, Scanner, Senior computer classes, Serves mentally handicapped consumers, Spoken cassettes & CDs, Spoken cassettes & DVDs, Story hour, Summer reading prog, VHS videos, Wheelchair accessible, Workshops
Open Mon 2-7:30, Tues-Fri 2-6, Sat 8:30-12:30

WILLIAMSBURG

P WILLIAMSBURG PUBLIC LIBRARY*, 300 W State St, 52361. (Mail add: PO Box 48, 52361-0048), SAN 305-7941. Tel: 319-668-1195. FAX: 319-668-9621. E-mail: wpl.lkli@mchsi.com. Web Site: www.williamsburg.lib.ia.us. *Dir,* Loretta Hanson; *Asst Dir,* Patrick Lienemann; *Ch,* Kristin Carlson; *Libr Asst,* Perla Josue; Staff 2.5 (Non-MLS 2.5)
Founded 1934. Pop 3,000; Circ 42,468
Jul 2012-Jun 2013 Income $197,153, State $381, City $177,334, County $18,640, Locally Generated Income $798. Mats Exp $29,014, Books $27,164, AV Mat $600, Electronic Ref Mat (Incl. Access Fees) $1,250. Sal $118,701 (Prof $31,000)
Library Holdings: Audiobooks 1,693; DVDs 2,212; e-books 3,305; Bk Titles 19,951; Per Subs 73
Partic in North Eastern Iowa Bridge to Online Resource Sharing (NEIBORS)
Open Mon & Wed 10-7, Tues & Thurs 10-5, Fri 10-6, Sat 10-1
Friends of the Library Group

WILTON

P WILTON PUBLIC LIBRARY*, 106 E Fourth St, 52778. (Mail add: PO Box 447, 52778-0114), SAN 305-795X. Tel: 563-732-2583. FAX: 563-732-2593. E-mail: wplstaff@netwtc.net. Web Site: www.wilton.lib.ia.us. *Dir,* Sharon Bowers; E-mail: s_bowers@wilton.lib.ia.us; *Asst Dir,* Sue Hoskins; E-mail: s_hoskins@wilton.lib.ia.us
Founded 1935. Pop 2,829; Circ 28,753
Library Holdings: AV Mats 1,000; Large Print Bks 500; Bk Vols 20,000; Per Subs 85
Special Collections: Wilton Advocate (high school yearbook)
Subject Interests: Local hist
Automation Activity & Vendor Info: (Cataloging) Winnebago Software Co; (Circulation) Winnebago Software Co

Open Mon & Wed 12-8, Tues & Thurs 12-6, Fri 10-5, Sat 10-3, Sun 2-5
Friends of the Library Group

WINFIELD

P WINFIELD PUBLIC LIBRARY*, 112 W Ash, 52659-9511. (Mail add: PO Box 47, 52469), SAN 305-7968. Tel: 319-257-3247. FAX: 319-257-3247. E-mail: director47@winfield.lib.ia.us. Web Site: www.winfield.lib.ia.us. *Dir,* Claire Matthews; Staff 2 (MLS 1, Non-MLS 1)
Founded 1916. Pop 2,200; Circ 8,171
Jul 2012-Jun 2013 Income $55,000, State $900, City $41,800, County $9,955, Locally Generated Income $2,300, Other $50. Mats Exp $11,600. Sal $15,000
Library Holdings: Audiobooks 75; DVDs 485; e-books 10,040; Large Print Bks 375; Bk Titles 13,940; Per Subs 76
Subject Interests: Agr, Educ, Relig
Wireless access
Function: Adult bk club, Audiobks via web, Bks on CD, Children's prog, Computers for patron use, Copy machines, E-Reserves, Electronic databases & coll, Free DVD rentals, ILL available, Magnifiers for reading, Mail & tel request accepted, Microfiche/film & reading machines, Online cat, Online searches, OverDrive digital audio bks, Preschool outreach, Pub access computers, Scanner, Senior outreach, Story hour, Summer reading prog, Web-catalog
Open Mon, Wed & Fri 10-6, Tues & Thurs 2-6, Sat 9-12

WINTERSET

P WINTERSET PUBLIC LIBRARY*, 123 N Second St, 50273-1508. SAN 305-7976. Tel: 515-462-1731. FAX: 515-462-4196. E-mail: library@winterset.lib.ia.us. Web Site: www.winterset.lib.ia.us. *Dir,* Nancy Trask; E-mail: nancy.trask@winterset.lib.ia.us; *Ch,* Ann Newbury; Staff 5 (MLS 1, Non-MLS 4)
Founded 1891. Pop 5,130; Circ 97,508
Jul 2012-Jun 2013 Income $511,725, State $3,565, City $396,428, County $48,580, Locally Generated Income $12,999, Other $50,153. Mats Exp $495,381, Books $34,845, Per/Ser (Incl. Access Fees) $4,000, AV Mat $5,188, Electronic Ref Mat (Incl. Access Fees) $5,904. Sal $232,321 (Prof $54,432)
Library Holdings: Audiobooks 9,119; DVDs 3,590; e-books 6,989; Electronic Media & Resources 5,241; Large Print Bks 600; Microforms 300; Bk Titles 43,715; Per Subs 130
Special Collections: Antiques & Collectibles; Audio Books; Genealogy Coll; Iowa History Coll; John Wayne Videos; Large Print Coll; Madison County Court Records; Madison County Land & Probate Records; Madison County Newspaper, microfilm
Automation Activity & Vendor Info: (Cataloging) OCLC; (Circulation) Innovative Interfaces, Inc; (ILL) OCLC; (OPAC) Innovative Interfaces, Inc
Database Vendor: EBSCO Auto Repair Reference, EBSCOhost, Ingram Library Services, LearningExpress, OCLC FirstSearch, OCLC WorldShare Interlibrary Loan, Overdrive, Inc, ProQuest, TumbleBookLibrary
Wireless access
Function: Adult bk club, Audio & video playback equip for onsite use, Audiobks via web, AV serv, Bi-weekly Writer's Group, Bk club(s), Bks on CD, Children's prog, Computer training, Computers for patron use, Copy machines, Digital talking bks, Doc delivery serv, Electronic databases & coll, Exhibits, Fax serv, Free DVD rentals, Genealogy discussion group, Handicapped accessible, Health sci info serv, Holiday prog, Homebound delivery serv, ILL available, Instruction & testing, Mail & tel request accepted, Microfiche/film & reading machines, Music CDs, Online cat, Outside serv via phone, mail, e-mail & web, OverDrive digital audio bks, Photocopying/Printing, Preschool outreach, Prog for adults, Prog for children & young adult, Pub access computers, Ref & res, Scanner, Senior computer classes, Serves mentally handicapped consumers, Story hour, Summer reading prog, Tax forms, Teen prog, Telephone ref, VHS videos, Web-catalog, Wheelchair accessible
Mem of Central Iowa Library Services
Partic in OCLC Online Computer Library Center, Inc
Open Mon-Thurs 10-8, Fri & Sat 10-5
Friends of the Library Group

WINTHROP

P WINTHROP PUBLIC LIBRARY, 354 W Madison, 50682. (Mail add: PO Box 159, 50682-0159), SAN 305-7984. Tel: 319-935-3374. FAX: 319-935-3574. E-mail: winlib@netins.net. Web Site: www.east-buc.k12.ia.us/Winthrop/Lib/lib.htm. *Dir,* Mary Kenyon; Staff 3 (Non-MLS 3)
Pop 871; Circ 12,402
Library Holdings: Bk Titles 9,250; Per Subs 30
Automation Activity & Vendor Info: (Circulation) Follett Software
Mem of Traverse Des Sioux Library Cooperative
Partic in Minitex Library Information Network
Open Mon 1-8, Tues-Fri 1-5, Sat 9-12

WODEN

P WODEN PUBLIC LIBRARY*, 304 Main St, 50484. (Mail add: PO Box 156, 50484-0156), SAN 305-7992. Tel: 641-926-5716. FAX: 641-926-5716. *Dir,* Jeanne Tollagsen
Founded 1960. Pop 240; Circ 6,895
Library Holdings: Bk Titles 5,000; Per Subs 40
Open Mon, Tues, Thurs & Fri 9-10:30 & 3-5, Wed 9-10:30 & 3:30-6, Sat 9:30-11:30 & 3-5

WOODBINE

P WOODBINE PUBLIC LIBRARY*, 58 Fifth St, 51579. SAN 305-800X. Tel: 712-647-2750. FAX: 712-647-2750. Web Site: www.woodbine.lib.ia.us. *Dir,* Rita Bantam; E-mail: Rita@woodbine.lib.ia.us; *Youth Serv Librn,* Wendy Doyel; E-mail: Wendy@woodbine.lib.ia.us
Pop 1,500; Circ 23,000
Library Holdings: Bk Titles 24,000; Per Subs 67
Wireless access
Mem of Southwest Iowa Library Services District
Open Tues, Thurs & Fri 10-5, Wed 10-7, Sat 9-12

WOODWARD

P WOODWARD PUBLIC LIBRARY, 118 S Main St, 50276. (Mail add: PO Box 510, 50276-0510), SAN 305-8018. Tel: 515-438-2636. FAX: 515-438-2166. E-mail: wpublib@minburncomm.net. Web Site: www.woodwardlibrary.org. *Dir,* Leah White; E-mail: wpldirector@minburncomm.net; *Libr Asst,* Susan Lemon; Staff 1.3 (Non-MLS 1.3)
Founded 1946. Pop 1,500; Circ 18,748
Library Holdings: AV Mats 750; Bk Vols 19,000; Per Subs 68
Automation Activity & Vendor Info: (Circulation) Follett Software
Wireless access
Function: Accessibility serv available based on individual needs, Adult bk club, Art exhibits, Audiobks via web, AV serv, Bk club(s), Bks on CD, Children's prog, Computer training, Computers for patron use, Copy machines, Free DVD rentals, Handicapped accessible, Holiday prog, Homebound delivery serv, ILL available, Instruction & testing, Magnifiers for reading, Music CDs, Notary serv, OverDrive digital audio bks, Photocopying/Printing, Preschool outreach, Prog for adults, Prog for children & young adult, Pub access computers, Scanner, Story hour, Summer & winter reading prog, Teen prog, Wheelchair accessible
Mem of Central Iowa Library Services
Open Mon & Wed-Fri 9-12 & 1-5, Tues 4-7, Sat 9-12
Friends of the Library Group

WYOMING

P WYOMING PUBLIC LIBRARY*, 109 Main St, 52362. (Mail add: PO Box 139, 52362-0139), SAN 305-8026. Tel: 563-488-3975. FAX: 563-488-3975. E-mail: admin@wyoming.lib.ia.us. Web Site: www.wyoming.lib.ia.us. *Librn,* Nicole Rushford; E-mail: nrushford@wyoming.lib.ia.us
Founded 1947. Pop 878; Circ 16,135
Library Holdings: Bk Titles 7,000; Per Subs 24
Open Tues 2-6, Wed & Fri 12-5, Thurs & Sat 9-12

ZEARING

P ZEARING PUBLIC LIBRARY, 101 E Main, 50278. (Mail add: PO Box 197, 50278-0197), SAN 305-8034. Tel: 641-487-7888. FAX: 641-487-7886. E-mail: zearing@zearing.lib.ia.us, zearinglibrary@netins.net. Web Site: www.zearing.lib.ia.us. *Dir,* P J McBride
Founded 1975. Pop 630; Circ 7,270
Library Holdings: Large Print Bks 95; Bk Titles 10,636; Per Subs 20; Talking Bks 538
Subject Interests: Iowa, World War II
Automation Activity & Vendor Info: (Circulation) Follett Software
Database Vendor: Baker & Taylor
Wireless access
Mem of Central Iowa Library Services
Open Mon, Tues, Thurs & Fri 3-7, Wed 10-7, Sat 10-3

KANSAS

Date of Statistics: FY 2013
Population, 2010 U.S. Census: 2,853,118
Population Served by Public Libraries: 2,487,027
Total Volumes in Public Libraries: 9,238,057
Volumes Per Capita: 3.71
Total Public Library Circulation: 26,206,200
Circulation Per Capita: 10.54
Total Public Library Income: $115,146,655
Source of Income: Public funds, donations, federal & state aid
Expenditures Per Capita: $44.66
Number of County & Multi-County (Regional) Libraries: 32
Number of Bookmobiles in State: 4
Grants-in-Aid to Public Libraries: **$888,392**
State Aid: $1,332,588

ABILENE

P ABILENE PUBLIC LIBRARY*, 209 NW Fourth, 67410-2690. SAN 305-8042. Tel: 785-263-3082. FAX: 785-263-2274. E-mail: apl@abilenelibrary.org. Web Site: abilene.mykansaslibrary.org. *Dir,* Wendy Moulton; E-mail: wmoulton@abilenelibrary.org; *Assoc Dir,* Kara Cromwell; *Ch,* Sheryl Davidson; Tel: 785-263-1303
Founded 1908. Pop 7,378; Circ 93,420
Library Holdings: CDs 704; Bk Vols 61,157; Per Subs 106; Videos 1,718
Automation Activity & Vendor Info: (Acquisitions) Follett Software; (Cataloging) Follett Software; (Circulation) Follett Software; (OPAC) Follett Software
Wireless access
Partic in OCLC Online Computer Library Center, Inc
Special Services for the Deaf - TTY equip
Open Mon-Wed 9-6, Thurs 9-7, Fri 9-5, Sat 9-4
Friends of the Library Group

S MUSEUM OF INDEPENDENT TELEPHONY LIBRARY, 412 S Campbell, 67410. SAN 326-0984. Tel: 785-263-2681. FAX: 785-263-0380. E-mail: heritagecenterdk@sbcglobal.net. Web Site: www.heritagecenterdk.com. *Dir,* Jeff Sheets
Founded 1973
Library Holdings: Bk Vols 600; Per Subs 10
Special Collections: Oral History
Restriction: Open by appt only, Open to pub for ref only

S NATIONAL ARCHIVES & RECORDS ADMINISTRATION*, Dwight D Eisenhower Library, 200 SE Fourth St, 67410-2900. (Mail add: PO Box 339, 67410), SAN 305-8050. Tel: 785-263-6700. Toll Free Tel: 877-746-4453. FAX: 785-263-6715, 785-263-6718. E-mail: eisenhower.library@nara.gov. Web Site: eisenhower.archives.gov. *Dir,* Karl Weissenbach; Staff 11 (MLS 1, Non-MLS 10)
Founded 1962
Library Holdings: Bk Vols 27,000; Per Subs 75
Special Collections: World War II & Eisenhower Administration Manuscript Coll
Subject Interests: Presidents (US), World War II
Function: Archival coll
Publications: Overview (Newsletter)
Open Mon-Fri 9-4:45 (8-5:45 Summer)
Friends of the Library Group

ALLEN

P LYON COUNTY, LIBRARY DISTRICT ONE*, 421 Main St, 66833. (Mail add: PO Box 447, 66833-0447), SAN 320-4774. Tel: 620-528-3451. FAX: 620-528-3451. E-mail: library@satelephone.com. *Librn,* Shirley Williams
Founded 1976. Pop 1,104; Circ 5,774
Library Holdings: Bk Titles 9,000
Special Collections: Microfilms of Old Local Newspapers
Mem of North Central Kansas Libraries System
Open Mon 10-12 & 5-8, Tues, Thurs & Fri 9-12, Wed 4-6, Sat 9-2

ALMENA

P ALMENA CITY LIBRARY*, 415 Main, 67622. (Mail add: PO Box 153, 67622-0153), SAN 320-1880. Tel: 785-669-2336. E-mail: almenlib@ruraltel.net. *In Charge,* Clara Irene Oman; Staff 1 (Non-MLS 1)
Founded 1903. Pop 373; Circ 4,313
Library Holdings: Bk Vols 4,500; Per Subs 10
Function: ILL available
Mem of Northwest Kansas Library System
Open Tues & Thurs 2-5, Sat 9-12

ALTAMONT

P ALTAMONT PUBLIC LIBRARY*, 407 Houston St, 67330. (Mail add: PO Box 219, 67330-0219), SAN 305-8077. Tel: 620-784-5530. E-mail: library@altamontks.com. *Dir,* Freda Edwards; Staff 1 (Non-MLS 1)
Founded 1928
Library Holdings: Bk Vols 14,372; Per Subs 50
Open Mon, Tues & Fri 1-5, Wed & Thurs 1-5 & 6-8

ALTOONA

P ALTOONA PUBLIC LIBRARY*, 713 Main St, 66710. (Mail add: PO Box 68, 66710-0068), SAN 305-8085. Tel: 620-568-6645. E-mail: altoonakansas@yahoo.com. *Librn,* Veda Roets; Tel: 620-568-6681
Pop 564; Circ 2,970
Library Holdings: Bk Vols 5,000; Per Subs 20
Open Mon, Wed & Fri 1-6

AMERICUS

P AMERICUS TOWNSHIP LIBRARY*, 710 Main St, 66835. (Mail add: PO Box 404, 66835-0404), SAN 305-8093. Tel: 620-443-5503. FAX: 620-443-5218. E-mail: americuslibrary@fairpoint.net. *Dir,* Anita Westcott
Pop 1,591; Circ 33,124
Library Holdings: Bk Vols 18,000; Per Subs 28
Automation Activity & Vendor Info: (Cataloging) SirsiDynix
Mem of North Central Kansas Libraries System
Open Mon-Wed & Fri 1-5:30, Thurs 9-12 & 1-7, Sat 9-12 & 1-5

ANDALE

P ANDALE DISTRICT LIBRARY*, 328 Main St, 67001. (Mail add: PO Box 58, 67001-0071). Tel: 316-444-2363. FAX: 316-444-2363. *Librn,* Sonya Horsch; *Librn,* Lori Lane
Library Holdings: Audiobooks 29; AV Mats 291; Bk Titles 15,529; Per Subs 10
Automation Activity & Vendor Info: (Cataloging) Follett Software; (Circulation) Follett Software; (OPAC) Follett Software
Wireless access

Mem of South Central Kansas Library System
Open Mon 3-7, Thurs 9-11 & 3-7, Sat 9-Noon
Friends of the Library Group

ANDOVER

P ANDOVER PUBLIC LIBRARY, 1511 E Central Ave, 67002. SAN 305-8107. Tel: 316-558-3500. FAX: 316-558-3503. Web Site: www.andoverlibrary.org. *Dir,* Tom Taylor; E-mail: tomtaylor@andoverlibrary.org; *Asst Dir,* Cheri Nienke; E-mail: cnienke@andoverlibrary.org; *Admin Dir,* Karyn Schemm; E-mail: kmschemm@andoverlibrary.org; *Ch,* Cathy Catt; E-mail: ccatt@andoverlibrary.org; *YA Librn,* Tori Hamilton; E-mail: thamilton@andoverlibrary.org; *ILL,* Kathy Pyles; E-mail: kpyles@andoverlibrary.org; Staff 4 (MLS 1, Non-MLS 3)
Pop 17,532; Circ 196,309
Library Holdings: AV Mats 2,779; DVDs 4,328; Large Print Bks 1,010; Bk Vols 44,517; Per Subs 57
Automation Activity & Vendor Info: (Acquisitions) Innovative Interfaces, Inc; (Cataloging) Innovative Interfaces, Inc; (Circulation) Innovative Interfaces, Inc; (ILL) Auto-Graphics, Inc; (OPAC) Innovative Interfaces, Inc; (Serials) EBSCO Online
Wireless access
Function: Handicapped accessible, Home delivery & serv to Sr ctr & nursing homes, Homebound delivery serv, ILL available, Photocopying/Printing, Prog for children & young adult, Summer reading prog
Open Mon-Thurs 9-8, Fri 9-5, Sat 9-3
Friends of the Library Group

ANTHONY

P ANTHONY PUBLIC LIBRARY*, 624 E Main, 67003-2738. SAN 305-8115. Tel: 620-842-5344. Administration Tel: 620-842-5344, Ext 2. FAX: 620-842-5684. E-mail: anthonylib@gmail.com. *Dir,* Eldon Younce
Founded 1897. Pop 9,640; Circ 21,216
Library Holdings: Bk Vols 49,661; Per Subs 45
Special Collections: County Cemetery Records; County Newspaper Coll, micro; Dawes Indian Rolls (Enrollment cards for the five civilized tribes 1898-1914)
Automation Activity & Vendor Info: (Cataloging) Follett Software; (Circulation) Follett Software
Wireless access
Function: Accelerated reader prog, AV serv, Bks on cassette, Bks on CD, CD-ROM, Children's prog, Computers for patron use, Copy machines, e-mail & chat, Fax serv, Free DVD rentals, ILL available, Music CDs, Online searches, Photocopying/Printing, Prog for children & young adult, Pub access computers, Scanner, Spoken cassettes & CDs, Spoken cassettes & DVDs, Story hour, Summer reading prog, Tax forms, Telephone ref, VHS videos, Wheelchair accessible
Mem of South Central Kansas Library System
Open Mon-Thurs 10-7, Fri 10-5, Sat 1-5

ARGONIA

P DIXON TOWNSHIP LIBRARY*, 120 W Walnut, 67004. (Mail add: PO Box 95, 67004-0095), SAN 305-8123. Tel: 620-435-6979. E-mail: dixtwplib@havilandtelco.com. *Dir,* Gaylene Larson
Pop 783; Circ 7,366
Library Holdings: Bk Vols 5,500; Per Subs 15
Mem of South Central Kansas Library System
Open Mon & Wed 2-7, Sat 9-2

ARKANSAS CITY

P ARKANSAS CITY PUBLIC LIBRARY, 120 E Fifth Ave, 67005-2695. SAN 305-8131. Tel: 620-442-1280. FAX: 620-442-4277. E-mail: arkcitypl@acpl.org. Web Site: www.acpl.org. *Dir,* Mendy Pfannenstiel; Staff 8.6 (Non-MLS 8.6)
Founded 1908. Pop 12,000; Circ 97,699
Automation Activity & Vendor Info: (Cataloging) Innovative Interfaces, Inc; (Circulation) Innovative Interfaces, Inc; (ILL) Auto-Graphics, Inc; (OPAC) Innovative Interfaces, Inc
Wireless access
Mem of South Central Kansas Library System
Open Mon & Thurs 9-8, Fri & Sat 10-6

J COWLEY COUNTY COMMUNITY COLLEGE*, Renn Memorial Library, 131 S Third St, 67005. SAN 305-814X. Tel: 620-441-5257. Circulation Tel: 620-441-5334. Automation Services Tel: 620-442-0430. FAX: 620-441-5356. Web Site: www.cowley.edu/library/. *Dir, Libr Serv,* Rhoda M MacLaughlin; Tel: 620-441-5280, E-mail: maclaughlinr@cowley.edu; Staff 3 (MLS 1, Non-MLS 2)
Founded 1922. Enrl 3,098; Fac 47
Library Holdings: AV Mats 200; e-books 1,200; Bk Titles 26,000; Per Subs 80
Special Collections: Kansas Room, bks & per
Automation Activity & Vendor Info: (Cataloging) Follett Software; (Circulation) Follett Software; (ILL) Auto-Graphics, Inc; (OPAC) Follett Software
Database Vendor: Baker & Taylor, EBSCOhost, Gale Cengage Learning, OCLC FirstSearch, Wilson - Wilson Web
Function: ILL available
Mem of South Central Kansas Library System
Open Mon-Thurs (Winter) 7:45am-10pm, Fri 7:45-4, Sun 2-10; Mon & Thurs (Summer) 7-5, Tues & Wed 7am-8pm
Restriction: Open to pub with supv only, Open to students, fac & staff

ARLINGTON

P ARLINGTON CITY LIBRARY*, 900 W Main St, 67514. (Mail add: PO Box 396, 67514-0396), SAN 305-8158. Tel: 620-538-2471. E-mail: arllib@yahoo.com. *Librn,* Ginger Stiggins
Founded 1933. Pop 442; Circ 4,550
Library Holdings: Bk Titles 5,500; Bk Vols 6,671
Wireless access
Mem of South Central Kansas Library System
Open Mon, Wed & Thurs 2-7, Tues 9-Noon
Friends of the Library Group

ARMA

P ARMA CITY LIBRARY*, 508 E Washington, 66712. (Mail add: PO Box 822, 66712-0822), SAN 376-7671. Tel: 620-347-4811. FAX: 620-347-4977. E-mail: armalibrary@hotmail.com. *Dir,* Christie Wilson; Staff 1 (Non-MLS 1)
Founded 1993. Circ 6,500
Library Holdings: Bk Vols 6,500; Per Subs 20
Special Collections: Local Newspaper, 1915-1974 microfilm
Automation Activity & Vendor Info: (Circulation) Follett Software
Mem of Southeast Kansas Library System
Open Mon-Wed & Fri 11-5, Thurs 12-6

ASHLAND

P ASHLAND CITY LIBRARY*, 604 Main St, 67831. (Mail add: PO Box 397, 67831-0397), SAN 305-8166. Tel: 620-635-2589. FAX: 620-635-2931. E-mail: ashlib@ucom.net. *Dir,* Cara Vanderree; *Asst Librn,* Khristi Branson
Founded 1920. Pop 1,000; Circ 10,987
Library Holdings: Bk Titles 18,778; Per Subs 45; Talking Bks 266
Special Collections: Local newspaper 1884-1989 micro
Automation Activity & Vendor Info: (Cataloging) OCLC; (Circulation) Follett Software; (ILL) Auto-Graphics, Inc
Database Vendor: Gale Cengage Learning, OCLC FirstSearch
Mem of Southwest Kansas Library System
Open Mon, Fri & Sat 1:30-5:30, Tues & Thurs 11-5:30, Wed 1:30-7:30

ATCHISON

P ATCHISON PUBLIC LIBRARY*, 401 Kansas Ave, 66002-2495. SAN 305-8174. Tel: 913-367-1902. FAX: 913-367-2717. Web Site: www.atchisonlibrary.org. *Dir,* Gary Landeck; Tel: 913-367-1902, Ext 208, E-mail: glandeck@atchisonlibrary.org; *Youth Serv Librn,* Holly Hutchinson; *Circ Supvr,* Mary Domann; Tel: 913-367-1902, Ext 203; *Adult Serv,* Jennifer George; *ILL,* Cindy Kloepper; Staff 2 (MLS 1, Non-MLS 1)
Pop 11,000; Circ 100,000
Library Holdings: Bk Vols 63,000; Per Subs 80
Special Collections: Local History Coll, microfilm, newsp & prints
Subject Interests: Hist, Music
Automation Activity & Vendor Info: (Acquisitions) SirsiDynix; (Cataloging) SirsiDynix; (Circulation) SirsiDynix; (ILL) SirsiDynix; (OPAC) SirsiDynix
Mem of Northeast Kansas Library System
Open Mon-Thurs 9-8, Fri & Sat 9-5
Friends of the Library Group

C BENEDICTINE COLLEGE LIBRARY*, 1020 N Second St, 66002-1499. SAN 342-0000. Tel: 913-360-7608. FAX: 913-360-7622. Web Site: www.benedictine.edu/library. *Dir, Libr Serv,* Steven Gromatzky; Tel: 913-360-7511; *Asst Dir,* Darla Meyer; Tel: 913-360-7516; *Circ,* Angie Gomez; *Govt Doc,* Miriam O'Hare; Tel: 913-360-7513; *ILL,* Jane Schuele; Tel: 913-360-7609; *Ser,* Wilma Dague; Tel: 913-360-7610; Staff 2 (MLS 2)
Founded 1858. Enrl 1,352; Fac 70; Highest Degree: Doctorate
Library Holdings: Bk Vols 368,558; Per Subs 300
Special Collections: Belloc; Chesterton; Church Fathers (Abbey Coll); Gerontology (Jay Gatson Coll); Monasticism; Philosophy (Ture Snowden Coll)
Subject Interests: Agr, Educ, Hist, Relig
Automation Activity & Vendor Info: (Acquisitions) SirsiDynix; (Cataloging) SirsiDynix; (Circulation) SirsiDynix; (Course Reserve) SirsiDynix; (ILL) SirsiDynix; (OPAC) SirsiDynix; (Serials) SirsiDynix

Database Vendor: EBSCOhost, Gale Cengage Learning, OCLC FirstSearch
Mem of Northeast Kansas Library System
Partic in Health Sciences Library Network of Kansas City, Inc; OCLC Online Computer Library Center, Inc
Open Mon-Thurs (Winter) 7:45am-11pm, Fri 7:45-5, Sat Noon-5, Sun 1-11; Mon-Fri (Summer) 8-5

ATTICA

P ATTICA CITY LIBRARY*, 125 N Main St, 67009. (Mail add: PO Box 137, 67009-0137), SAN 305-8190. Tel: 620 254-7767. E-mail: acl@attica.net. *Librn,* Lillian Tubb; Tel: 620-254-7683
Founded 1900. Pop 630; Circ 5,184
Library Holdings: AV Mats 356; Bk Vols 11,779; Per Subs 45; Talking Bks 136
Mem of South Central Kansas Library System
Open Tues-Fri 1-5, Sat 9-12

ATWOOD

P ATWOOD PUBLIC LIBRARY*, 102 S Sixth St, 67730-1998. SAN 305-8204. Tel: 785-626-3805. FAX: 785-626-3805. E-mail: atwoodli@ruraltel.net. *Librn,* Pamela A Luedke
Pop 2,250; Circ 11,500
Library Holdings: Bk Titles 22,372; Per Subs 48
Automation Activity & Vendor Info: (Circulation) Follett Software; (OPAC) Follett Software
Wireless access

AUGUSTA

P AUGUSTA PUBLIC LIBRARY*, 1609 State St, 67010-2098. SAN 305-8212. Tel: 316-775-2681. FAX: 316-775-7692. *Dir,* Lynne Thorn Holloway; Staff 5 (MLS 1, Non-MLS 4)
Founded 1919. Pop 8,500; Circ 78,000
Jan 2005-Dec 2005 Income $260,000
Library Holdings: Bk Vols 30,000; Per Subs 100
Automation Activity & Vendor Info: (Cataloging) Follett Software; (Circulation) Follett Software; (OPAC) Follett Software
Function: Chess club
Mem of South Central Kansas Library System
Open Mon-Thurs 9:30-8, Fri 9:30-5, Sat 9:30-3
Friends of the Library Group

AXTELL

P AXTELL PUBLIC LIBRARY*, 401 Maple, 66403. SAN 305-8220. Tel: 785-736-2858. E-mail: axtellpl@bluevalley.net. *Actg Librn,* Diane Tate
Founded 1937. Pop 435; Circ 2,075
Library Holdings: Large Print Bks 243; Bk Vols 5,046; Per Subs 21; Talking Bks 146
Open Tues, Wed & Fri 2-5, Sat 9-12

BALDWIN CITY

C BAKER UNIVERSITY, Collins Library, 518 Eighth St, 66006. (Mail add: PO Box 65, 66006-0065), SAN 305-8239. Tel: 785-594-8414. Interlibrary Loan Service Tel: 785-594-8585. Reference Tel: 785-594-8442. FAX: 785-594-6721. E-mail: reference@bakeru.edu. Web Site: www.bakeru.edu/library. *Dir, Libr Serv, Librn, Quayle Rare Bible Coll,* Kay Bradt; Tel: 785-594-8390, E-mail: kay.bradt@bakeru.edu; *Instruction Librn,* Carolyn Craycraft Clark; Tel: 785-594-4543, E-mail: carolyn.clark@bakeru.edu; *Archivist,* Jen McCollough; Tel: 785-594-8380, E-mail: jmccollough@bakeru.edu; *Electronic Serv, Govt Doc,* Ray Walling; Tel: 785-594-8389, E-mail: ray.walling@bakeru.edu; *Ref Serv,* Irene Weiner; Tel: 785-594-8445, E-mail: irene.weiner@bakeru.edu; *Tech Serv,* Nate Poell; Tel: 785-594-4582, E-mail: nathan.poell@bakeru.edu; Staff 6 (MLS 5, Non-MLS 1)
Founded 1858. Enrl 2,299; Fac 197; Highest Degree: Doctorate
Jul 2013-Jun 2014 Income $500,000. Mats Exp $152,000, Books $27,000, Per/Ser (Incl. Access Fees) $19,000, Manu Arch $3,000, Electronic Ref Mat (Incl. Access Fees) $103,000. Sal $230,000
Library Holdings: CDs 1,457; DVDs 560; e-books 108,000; Electronic Media & Resources 28; Microforms 18,000; Music Scores 1,270; Bk Vols 56,000; Per Subs 32; Videos 356
Special Collections: Baker University Archives; Kansas Area Archives of the United Methodist Church; Quayle Rare Bible Coll. US Document Depository
Subject Interests: Biol, Western US hist
Automation Activity & Vendor Info: (Cataloging) OCLC; (Circulation) OCLC; (Course Reserve) OCLC; (ILL) OCLC WorldShare Interlibrary Loan; (OPAC) OCLC; (Serials) OCLC
Database Vendor: Alexander Street Press, CQ Press, CredoReference, ebrary, EBSCOhost, Gale Cengage Learning, JSTOR, LexisNexis, Nature Publishing Group, Oxford Online, ProQuest, PubMed
Function: Archival coll, Computers for patron use, Copy machines, e-mail & chat, Electronic databases & coll, Exhibits, Govt ref serv, ILL available, Microfiche/film & reading machines, Online cat, Online info literacy tutorials on the web & in blackboard, Ref serv available, Study rm, Wheelchair accessible
Open Mon-Thurs 8am-11pm, Fri 8-4:30, Sun 3-11

P BALDWIN CITY LIBRARY*, 800 Seventh St, 66006. SAN 305-8247. Tel: 785-594-3411. FAX: 785-594-3411. E-mail: baldwinpl@baldwin.lib.ks.us. Web Site: www.baldwincitylibrary.org. *Dir,* Kathy Johnston; *Asst Librn,* Phyllis Braun
Founded 1916. Pop 4,145; Circ 47,336
Library Holdings: Audiobooks 1,278; AV Mats 1,031; CDs 277; DVDs 680; Large Print Bks 288; Bk Titles 22,649; Per Subs 78; Videos 1,031
Special Collections: The Kansas Shelf Coll
Automation Activity & Vendor Info: (Cataloging) Follett Software; (Circulation) Follett Software; (ILL) Follett Software; (OPAC) Follett Software
Wireless access
Mem of Northeast Kansas Library System
Partic in Kansas Info Circuit
Open Mon & Wed 9-9, Tues, Thurs & Fri 9-5, Sat 9-12
Friends of the Library Group

BASEHOR

P BASEHOR COMMUNITY LIBRARY DISTRICT 2*, 1400 158th St, 66007. SAN 326-3967. Tel: 913-724-2828. FAX: 913-724-2898. Web Site: www.basehorlibrary.org. *Dir,* Diana Weaver; E-mail: dweaver@basehorlibrary.org; *Asst Dir,* Jenne Laytham; E-mail: jlaytham@basehorlibrary.org; Staff 11 (Non-MLS 11)
Founded 1985. Pop 8,730; Circ 138,746
Library Holdings: Audiobooks 1,565; DVDs 4,500; Bk Vols 40,000; Per Subs 136
Wireless access
Mem of Northeast Kansas Library System
Partic in NExpress Consortium
Open Mon-Thurs 9-8, Fri & Sat 9-5, Sun 1-5
Friends of the Library Group

BAXTER SPRINGS

P JOHNSTON PUBLIC LIBRARY*, 210 W Tenth St, 66713-1611. SAN 305-8255. Tel: 620-856-5591. *Dir,* Muriel E Burrows; Staff 1 (MLS 1)
Founded 1905. Pop 4,348; Circ 44,573
Library Holdings: Bk Vols 40,329; Per Subs 77
Subject Interests: Am Indians, Civil War, Kansas
Open Mon & Thurs 9:30-12 & 1-7, Tues & Wed 9:30-12 & 1-6, Fri 9:30-12 & 1-5

BEATTIE

§P BEATTIE PUBLIC LIBRARY, 715 Main St, 66406. Tel: 785-353-2348. Web Site: beattie.mykansaslibrary.org. *Dir,* Jan Studer; E-mail: jwstuder@bluevalley.net
Open Tues, Thurs & Sat 10-1

BELLE PLAINE

P BELLE PLAINE CITY LIBRARY*, 222 W Fifth Ave, 67013. (Mail add: PO Box 700, 67013-0700), SAN 305-8263. Tel: 620-488-3431. E-mail: bplib@sktc.net. Web Site: belleplainelibrary.com. *Dir,* Vicki Bohannon; *Asst Librn,* Sharlene Slaughter
Founded 1915. Pop 1,800; Circ 9,411
Library Holdings: Bk Vols 11,500; Per Subs 25
Open Mon 6-8, Tues 2-5, Wed-Fri 9-12 & 1-5, Sat 9-12

BELLEVILLE

P BELLEVILLE PUBLIC LIBRARY*, 1327 19th St, 66935-2296. SAN 305-8271. Tel: 785-527-5305. FAX: 785-527-5305. Web Site: www.bellevillelibrary.org. *Dir,* Leah Krotz; E-mail: leahkrotz@nckcn.com
Founded 1927. Pop 2,517; Circ 33,841
Library Holdings: Bk Vols 23,000; Per Subs 67
Special Collections: Republic County History Coll; Republic County New papers, 1870-1995, micro; World War II Veterans. Oral History
Automation Activity & Vendor Info: (Cataloging) Follett Software; (Circulation) Follett Software; (OPAC) Follett Software
Open Mon-Thurs 10-7, Fri 10-5, Sat 10-3
Friends of the Library Group

BELOIT

S KANSAS DEPARTMENT OF CORRECTIONS*, Beloit Juvenile Correctional Facility Library, 1720 N Hersey, 67420. (Mail add: PO Box 427, 67420-0427). Tel: 785-738-5735, Ext 245. FAX: 785-738-6483. *Librn,* Delycia Zimmer; E-mail: delycia.zimmer@greenbush.org
Library Holdings: Bk Vols 5,000; Per Subs 25
Automation Activity & Vendor Info: (Acquisitions) Follett Software; (Cataloging) Follett Software; (Circulation) Follett Software; (OPAC) Follett Software; (Serials) Follett Software
Open Mon-Fri 8-12 & 1-2:30

P PORT LIBRARY*, Beloit City Library, 1718 N Hersey, 67420. (Mail add: PO Box 427, 67420), SAN 305-828X. Tel: 785-738-3936. E-mail: portlib@nckcn.com. Web Site: portlibrary.weebly.com. *Dir,* Rachel Malay; E-mail: portlibdir@nckcn.com; Staff 5 (MLS 1, Non-MLS 4)
Founded 1931. Pop 3,500; Circ 38,378
Library Holdings: AV Mats 600; CDs 200; Large Print Bks 450; Bk Vols 28,000; Per Subs 83; Talking Bks 1,000
Special Collections: Kindles & Nooks; Local Cookbooks; Local History Coll; Quilts & Quilting Coll
Automation Activity & Vendor Info: (Cataloging) Book Systems; (Circulation) Book Systems; (ILL) Auto-Graphics, Inc
Wireless access
Function: Adult bk club, After school storytime, Audio & video playback equip for onsite use, Audiobks via web, Bilingual assistance for Spanish patrons, Bk club(s), Bk reviews (Group), Bks on cassette, Bks on CD, Children's prog, Computers for patron use, Copy machines, e-mail serv, E-Reserves, Free DVD rentals, Handicapped accessible, Holiday prog, Home delivery & serv to Sr ctr & nursing homes, ILL available, Large print keyboards, Mail & tel request accepted, Microfiche/film & reading machines, Music CDs, Online cat, OverDrive digital audio bks, Photocopying/Printing, Preschool outreach, Preschool reading prog, Prog for adults, Prog for children & young adult, Pub access computers, Ref & res, Ref serv in person, Res performed for a fee, Serves mentally handicapped consumers, Spoken cassettes & CDs, Story hour, Summer & winter reading prog, Summer reading prog, Tax forms, Teen prog, Telephone ref, VHS videos, Web-catalog, Wheelchair accessible
Mem of Central Kansas Library System
Open Mon-Wed & Fri 10-6, Thurs 10-8, Sat 10-2
Restriction: Non-circulating of rare bks
Friends of the Library Group

BELPRE

P HENRY LAIRD LIBRARY*, PO Box 128, 67519-0128. SAN 305-8298. Tel: 620-995-3322. *Librn,* Joyce Gales
Circ 3,552
Library Holdings: Bk Vols 4,000; Per Subs 30
Special Collections: Oil Painting (L Winters Coll)
Mem of Southwest Kansas Library System
Open Tues, Thurs & Sat 1-5

BERN

P BERN COMMUNITY LIBRARY*, 401 Main St, 66408. SAN 376-5598. Tel: 785-336-3000. FAX: 785-336-3000. E-mail: librarian@bernlibrary.org. Web Site: bern.mykansaslibrary.org. *Coll Develop, Dir,* Kathie Platt; *Asst Librn,* Sheila Huls; Staff 3 (Non-MLS 3)
Founded 1995. Pop 455; Circ 4,768
Jan 2005-Dec 2005 Income $36,595. Mats Exp $4,470. Sal $18,556
Library Holdings: Bk Vols 8,625; Per Subs 12
Automation Activity & Vendor Info: (Cataloging) Follett Software; (Circulation) Follett Software
Mem of Northeast Kansas Library System
Open Mon, Thurs & Fri 2-5, Wed 2-8, Sat 9-Noon

BIRD CITY

P BIRD CITY PUBLIC LIBRARY*, 110 E Fourth St, 67731. (Mail add: PO Box 175, 67731-0175), SAN 305-8301. Tel: 785-734-2203. E-mail: bcpl@bcks.net. *Librn,* Darla Deeds
Pop 620; Circ 3,491
Library Holdings: Bk Vols 7,323; Per Subs 30
Database Vendor: Gale Cengage Learning, OCLC FirstSearch
Mem of Northwest Kansas Library System
Open Mon, Tues & Thurs 2-5:30, Fri 2-7, Sat 9:30-1

BISON

P BISON COMMUNITY LIBRARY*, 202 Main St, 67520. (Mail add: PO Box 406, 67520-0406), SAN 305-831X. Tel: 785-356-4803. FAX: 785-356-2403. E-mail: bisonlib@gbta.net. *Librn,* Lila Vondracek
Pop 313; Circ 2,246
Library Holdings: Bk Vols 5,293; Per Subs 20
Wireless access
Mem of Central Kansas Library System
Open Mon, Tues & Fri 2-5, Wed 5-8, Thurs 9-12

BLUE MOUND

P LINN COUNTY LIBRARY DISTRICT NO 3*, 316 Main St, 66010. (Mail add: PO Box 13, 66010-0013), SAN 305-8328. Tel: 913-756-2628. FAX: 913-756-2628. *Dir, Librn,* Brenda Curtis
Founded 1964. Pop 584; Circ 6,815
Library Holdings: Bk Vols 6,000
Special Collections: Oral History
Automation Activity & Vendor Info: (Cataloging) Winnebago Software Co; (Circulation) Winnebago Software Co
Mem of Southeast Kansas Library System
Open Tues-Fri 11-5, Sat 9-3

BLUE RAPIDS

P BLUE RAPIDS PUBLIC LIBRARY*, 14 Public Sq, 66411. (Mail add: PO Box 246, 66411-0246), SAN 305-8336. Tel: 785-363-7709. *Librn,* Lynne Turner
Founded 1874. Pop 1,047; Circ 4,251
Library Holdings: AV Mats 89; Bk Vols 5,577; Per Subs 24; Videos 64
Mem of North Central Kansas Libraries System
Open Mon & Fri 1-5, Wed 11-7:30, Sat 9-12
Friends of the Library Group

BONNER SPRINGS

P BONNER SPRINGS CITY LIBRARY*, 201 N Nettleton Ave, 66012-1047. SAN 305-8344. Tel: 913-441-2665. FAX: 913-441-2660. Web Site: www.bonnerlibrary.org. *Libr Dir,* Kimberly Beets; E-mail: kbeets@bonnerlibrary.org; *Asst Dir,* Kathleen Schram; E-mail: kschram@bonnerlibrary.org; *Teen/YA Librn,* Lesley Lard; *Children's Coordr,* Jeanne Dunbar; *Circ Coordr,* Katy Konovalske; *ILL Coordr,* Cheryl Morisse; E-mail: cmorisse@bonnerlibrary.org; Staff 6.23 (MLS 1, Non-MLS 5.23)
Founded 1946. Pop 10,000; Circ 100,000
Library Holdings: Bk Vols 50,000; Per Subs 65
Automation Activity & Vendor Info: (Cataloging) SirsiDynix; (Circulation) SirsiDynix; (OPAC) SirsiDynix; (Serials) SirsiDynix
Mem of Northeast Kansas Library System
Open Mon-Thurs 9-8, Fri & Sat 9-5, Sun 1-5
Friends of the Library Group

S WYANDOTTE COUNTY MUSEUM*, Trowbridge Research Library, 631 N 126th St, 66012. SAN 305-8352. Tel: 913-721-1078. FAX: 913-721-1394. *Dir,* Trish Schurkamp; *Archivist,* Joel Thornton; *Curator,* Jennifer Laughlin
Founded 1956
Library Holdings: Bk Vols 2,000
Special Collections: Census Records; Early Family Records; Photographic File; Wyandotte County Genealogical Materials
Open Mon-Sat 10-4

BREWSTER

S NORTHWEST KANSAS HERITAGE CENTER*, Library & Museum, 401 Kansas Ave, 67732. (Mail add: PO Box 284, 67732-0284), SAN 376-768X. Tel: 785-694-2891. *Librn,* Betty Wolfe
Library Holdings: Bk Vols 6,000
Mem of Northwest Kansas Library System
Open Mon & Wed 1-4, Sat 9-11

BRONSON

P BRONSON PUBLIC LIBRARY*, 509 Clay St, 66716. SAN 305-8360. Tel: 620-939-4910. FAX: 620-939-4569. E-mail: bronson_library@yahoo.com. *Dir,* Diana Huff
Pop 419; Circ 5,656
Library Holdings: Bk Vols 4,600; Per Subs 19
Mem of Southeast Kansas Library System
Open Tues & Thurs 9-12 & 2-5, Wed 1-8, Sat 9-12

BROWNELL

P BROWNELL PUBLIC LIBRARY*, PO Box 135, 67521-0135. SAN 305-8379. Tel: 785-481-2300. *Dir,* June Ruff; Tel: 785-481-2345
Founded 1941. Pop 85; Circ 3,000
Library Holdings: AV Mats 84; Bk Vols 4,200
Mem of Southwest Kansas Library System
Open Tues 8-4

BUCKLIN

P BUCKLIN PUBLIC LIBRARY*, 201 N Main, 67834. (Mail add: PO Box 596, 67834-0596), SAN 305-8387. Tel: 620-826-3223. FAX: 620-826-3794. E-mail: bplibrary2@unitedwireless.com. Web Site: www.bucklinpubliclibrary.org/. *Dir,* Kathy Leon; *Asst Librn,* Eva Meredith; *Asst Librn,* Edna M Ringwald; Staff 2 (Non-MLS 2)
Founded 1964. Pop 719; Circ 4,300
Library Holdings: AV Mats 602; CDs 97; DVDs 35; Large Print Bks 629; Music Scores 35; Bk Titles 18,162; Per Subs 35; Talking Bks 368; Videos 439
Special Collections: Art Coll; Kansas History Coll; Oprah's Book Club
Subject Interests: Best sellers, Inspirational reading, Mystery, Sci fict, Western
Automation Activity & Vendor Info: (Cataloging) Follett Software; (Circulation) Follett Software; (OPAC) Follett Software
Mem of Southwest Kansas Library System
Open Mon & Wed 9-7, Fri 9-6, Sat 10-1

BUHLER

P BUHLER PUBLIC LIBRARY*, 121 N Main St, 67522-0664. SAN 305-8395. Tel: 620-543-2241. FAX: 620-543-2241. E-mail: library@buhlerks.net. *Dir,* Pam Fast
Pop 1,200; Circ 8,398
Library Holdings: Bk Vols 11,000; Per Subs 30
Wireless access
Mem of South Central Kansas Library System
Open Mon, Wed & Fri 12-5, Tues & Thurs 10-5:30

BURDETT

P BURDETT COMMUNITY LIBRARY*, 207 Elm St, 67523. SAN 305-8409. Tel: 620-525-6588. *Librn,* Beverly Steffen
Library Holdings: Bk Vols 2,000
Mem of Central Kansas Library System
Open Sat 9-11

BURLINGAME

P BURLINGAME COMMUNITY LIBRARY, 122 W Sante Fe Ave, 66413. SAN 305-8417. Tel: 785-654-3400. FAX: 785-654-3411. E-mail: director@burlingame.lib.ks.us. Web Site: burlingame.mykansaslibrary.org. *Dir,* Sara Worcester
Founded 1970. Pop 913; Circ 6,493
Library Holdings: Bk Vols 12,000
Automation Activity & Vendor Info: (Cataloging) Follett Software; (Circulation) Follett Software; (Serials) Follett Software
Wireless access
Mem of Northeast Kansas Library System
Open Mon, Tues & Fri 1-5, Wed 10-8, Thurs 10-5, Sat 9-Noon
Friends of the Library Group

BURLINGTON

P COFFEY COUNTY LIBRARY*, 410 Juniatta St, 66839. SAN 305-8425. Tel: 620-364-2010. FAX: 620-364-2603. Web Site: www.cclibraryks.org. *Dir,* Valerie Williams; Staff 36 (MLS 2, Non-MLS 34)
Founded 1987. Pop 8,743; Circ 166,264
Library Holdings: Bk Vols 86,939; Per Subs 288
Subject Interests: Genealogy
Automation Activity & Vendor Info: (Cataloging) SirsiDynix; (Circulation) SirsiDynix; (OPAC) SirsiDynix
Database Vendor: SirsiDynix
Mem of Southeast Kansas Library System
Open Mon-Fri 8-5
Branches: 6
BURLINGTON BRANCH, 410 Juniatta, 66839. Tel: 620-364-5333. FAX: 620-364-2603. E-mail: burlington@mail.cclibks.org. *Dir,* Valerie Williams; E-mail: vpwilliams7@yahoo.com; Staff 6 (MLS 1, Non-MLS 5)
Open Mon-Thurs 9:30-8:30, Fri 9:30-5, Sat 9:30-3
GRIDLEY BRANCH, 512 Main St, Gridley, 66852, SAN 305-9316. Tel: 620-836-3905. FAX: 620-836-3401. E-mail: gridley@mail.cclibks.org. *Dir,* Janet Birk; E-mail: janetbirk23@yahoo.com; Staff 4 (Non-MLS 4)
Open Mon, Wed & Fri 9-5, Tues 9-7, Thurs 10-7, Sat 9-12
LEBO BRANCH, 327 S Ogden St, Lebo, 66856-9306, SAN 306-0012. Tel: 620-256-6452. FAX: 620-256-6301. E-mail: lebo@mail.cclibks.org. *Dir,* Mary Barker; E-mail: maryebarker@yahoo.com; Staff 4 (Non-MLS 4)
Open Mon, Wed & Fri 9-5, Tues & Thurs 9-7, Sat 9-12
LEROY BRANCH, 725 Main St, LeRoy, 66857, SAN 306-0063. Tel: 620-964-2321. FAX: 620-964-2394. E-mail: leroy@mail.cclibks.org. *Dir,* Cindy Stohs; E-mail: cjstohs1619@yahoo.com; Staff 3 (Non-MLS 3)
Library Holdings: Bk Vols 16,000
Open Mon, Tues, Thurs & Fri 8:30-5, Wed 8:30-7:30, Sat 9-12
Friends of the Library Group
NEW STRAWN BRANCH, 365 N Main St, New Strawn, 66839, SAN 373-5729. Tel: 620-364-8910. FAX: 620-364-5354. E-mail: newstrawn@mail.cclibks.org.
Open Mon & Wed-Fri 9-5, Tues 9-6, Sat 9-12
WAVERLY BRANCH, 608 Pearson, Waverly, 66871-9688, SAN 306-1760. Tel: 785-733-2400. FAX: 785-733-2474. E-mail: waverly@mail.cclibks.org. *Dir,* Marcella Chapman; E-mail: mechapman@yahoo.com; Staff 4 (Non-MLS 4)
Publications: Waverly City History Book
Open Mon 9-7, Tues-Thurs 9-5:30, Fri 9-5, Sat 9-12

BURNS

P BURNS PUBLIC LIBRARY*, 104 N Washington, 66840. (Mail add: PO Box 233, 66840-0233), SAN 305-8433. Tel: 620-726-5717. *Librn,* Anne Welch
Pop 363; Circ 1,319
Library Holdings: Bk Vols 4,500
Wireless access
Mem of North Central Kansas Libraries System
Open Tues & Fri 10-12 & 3:45-7, Sat 10-Noon

BURR OAK

P BURR OAK CITY LIBRARY*, 221 A Main St, 66936. Tel: 785-647-5597. FAX: 785-647-5597. *Librn,* Tammy Finnell
Pop 366; Circ 1,696
Library Holdings: AV Mats 232; Bk Vols 10,000; Per Subs 17
Mem of Central Kansas Library System
Open Mon, Wed & Fri 2-5, Tues 7-9

BURRTON

P RUTH DOLE MEMORIAL LIBRARY*, 121 N Burrton Ave, 67020. SAN 305-845X. Tel: 620-463-7902. *Librn,* Rhonda Corwin
Pop 1,000; Circ 7,834
Library Holdings: Bk Vols 9,712; Per Subs 12
Open Mon & Fri 1-5, Wed 9-5, Sat 9-12

CALDWELL

P CALDWELL PUBLIC LIBRARY*, 120 S Main St, 67022. SAN 305-8476. Tel: 620-845-6879. *Dir,* Lisa Moreland
Founded 1912. Pop 1,275
Library Holdings: Bk Vols 8,000; Per Subs 20
Wireless access
Mem of South Central Kansas Library System
Open Mon 10-6, Wed-Sat 10-2
Friends of the Library Group

CANEY

P CANEY CITY LIBRARY*, 100 N Ridgeway, 67333. (Mail add: PO Box 38, 67333-2035), SAN 305-8484. Tel: 316-879-5341. FAX: 620-879-5829. E-mail: caneylibrary@yahoo.com. *Dir,* Sandra Freidline
Pop 2,284; Circ 13,104
Library Holdings: AV Mats 200; Bk Vols 15,000; Per Subs 35
Mem of Southeast Kansas Library System
Open Mon 12-6, Tues 2-7, Wed & Fri 1-6, Thurs 8-1, Sat 8-2

CANTON

P CANTON TOWNSHIP CARNEGIE LIBRARY*, 203 N Main St, 67428. (Mail add: PO Box 336, 67428-0336), SAN 305-8492. Tel: 620-628-4349. *Dir,* Doris Evans
Founded 1909. Pop 1,187; Circ 6,012
Library Holdings: Bk Vols 4,200; Per Subs 15
Mem of South Central Kansas Library System
Open Tues & Thurs 1-5, Wed 4-6

CARBONDALE

P CARBONDALE CITY LIBRARY*, 234 Main St, 66414-9635. (Mail add: PO Box 330, 66414-0330), SAN 305-8506. Tel: 785-836-7638. FAX: 785-836-7789. *Dir,* Alice Smith; *Asst Librn,* Margie Kleier
Founded 1971. Pop 1,500
Library Holdings: Bk Vols 8,000; Per Subs 10
Mem of Northeast Kansas Library System
Open Mon 1-5, Tues & Fri 9-12 & 1-5, Wed 9-1, Thurs 10-12 & 1-6, Sat 9-12
Friends of the Library Group

CAWKER CITY

P CAWKER CITY PUBLIC LIBRARY, 802 Locust, 67430. (Mail add: PO Box 136, 67430-0136), SAN 305-8514. Tel: 785-781-4925. E-mail: cawkerlib@nckcn.com. *Dir,* Kathy Bowles
Founded 1884. Pop 500; Circ 3,500
Library Holdings: Audiobooks 40; CDs 34; DVDs 216; e-books 2; Large Print Bks 129; Microforms 106; Bk Titles 9,600; Per Subs 18; Talking Bks 120
Wireless access
Function: Bk reviews (Group), Bks on cassette, Bks on CD, CD-ROM, Children's prog, Computers for patron use, Copy machines, e-mail & chat, e-mail serv, Exhibits, Free DVD rentals, Genealogy discussion group, Handicapped accessible, Holiday prog, Home delivery & serv to Sr ctr & nursing homes, ILL available, Prog for adults, Prog for children & young adult, Pub access computers, Scanner, Story hour, Summer reading prog, Tax forms, VHS videos, Workshops
Mem of Central Kansas Library System
Open Tues 10-1, Wed 1-7, Thurs & Fri 1-5, Sat 9-12

CEDAR VALE

P CEDAR VALE MEMORIAL LIBRARY, 608 Cedar St, 67024. (Mail add: PO Box 369, 67024-0369), SAN 376-5555. Tel: 620-758-2598. FAX: 620-758-2598. E-mail: cvmemlib@sktc.net. *Dir,* Katie Boyle; *Head Librn,* MaKailah Marin McKinley
Pop 600
Library Holdings: Bk Vols 4,100
Wireless access
Mem of Southeast Kansas Library System
Open Mon-Wed 2-6, Thurs-Sat 9-Noon

CENTRALIA

P CENTRALIA COMMUNITY LIBRARY*, 520 Fourth St, 66415. SAN 305-8522. Tel: 785-857-3331. E-mail: centlb@bluevalley.net. Web Site: centralia.mykansaslibrary.org. *Librn,* Sonny Gore; Staff 2 (Non-MLS 2)
Founded 1880. Pop 504; Circ 10,324
Library Holdings: DVDs 287; Bk Vols 9,020; Per Subs 50; Videos 986
Automation Activity & Vendor Info: (Acquisitions) LibLime; (Cataloging) LibLime; (Circulation) LibLime; (Course Reserve) LibLime; (ILL) LibLime; (Media Booking) LibLime; (OPAC) LibLime; (Serials) LibLime
Wireless access
Mem of Northeast Kansas Library System
Open Mon & Fri 9-12 & 4-6, Wed 1-6, Sat 9-12

CHANUTE

P CHANUTE PUBLIC LIBRARY*, 111 N Lincoln, 66720-1819. SAN 305-8530. Tel: 620-431-3820. FAX: 620-431-3848. *Dir,* Susan Willis; Staff 4 (MLS 1, Non-MLS 3)
Founded 1905. Pop 16,500; Circ 120,617
Library Holdings: AV Mats 6,170; Large Print Bks 1,500; Bk Vols 59,960; Per Subs 130
Special Collections: Esther Clark Hill Coll; Nora B Cunningham Coll, letters
Subject Interests: Local hist
Automation Activity & Vendor Info: (Circulation) Follett Software; (OPAC) Follett Software
Mem of Southeast Kansas Library System
Open Mon-Thurs 9:30-8, Fri & Sat 9-5, Sun 1-5
Friends of the Library Group

S MARTIN & OSA JOHNSON SAFARI MUSEUM*, Stott Explorers Library, 111 N Lincoln Ave, 66720. SAN 325-7320. Tel: 620-431-2730. FAX: 620-431-2730. E-mail: osajohns@safarimuseum.com. Web Site: www.safarimuseum.com. *Dir,* Conrad G Froehlich
Founded 1980
Library Holdings: Bk Vols 10,000
Subject Interests: Africa, Natural hist, Pacific
Publications: Wait-A-Bit News
Open Mon-Sat 10-5, Sun 1-5
Restriction: Not a lending libr

J NEOSHO COUNTY COMMUNITY COLLEGE*, Chapman Library, 800 W 14th St, 66720-2699. SAN 305-8549. Tel: 620-431-2820, Ext 244. Interlibrary Loan Service Tel: 620-431-2820, Ext 296. Interlibrary Loan Service Toll Free Tel: 800-729-6222, Ext 296. FAX: 620-432-9841. E-mail: library@neosho.edu. Web Site: www.neosho.edu/library/index.asp. *Dir,* Susan Weisenberger; Tel: 620-431-2820, Ext 246, E-mail: sweisenberger@neosho.edu; *Circ, ILL,* Joan Gill; E-mail: jgill@neosho.edu; Staff 4 (MLS 1, Non-MLS 3)
Founded 1936. Highest Degree: Associate
Library Holdings: Bk Vols 31,000; Per Subs 80
Special Collections: Genealogy
Automation Activity & Vendor Info: (Circulation) Follett Software; (OPAC) Follett Software
Database Vendor: EBSCOhost, Gale Cengage Learning, OCLC FirstSearch, OCLC WorldShare Interlibrary Loan
Wireless access
Open Mon-Thurs 8-8, Fri 8-5

CHAPMAN

P CHAPMAN PUBLIC LIBRARY*, 402 N Marshall, 67431. (Mail add: PO Box F, 67431-2644), SAN 305-8557. Tel: 785-922-6548. FAX: 785-922-6548. E-mail: chaplib@cityofchapman.org. Web Site: skyways.lib.ks.us/library/chapman. *Dir,* Carol Frasure; Staff 0.05 (Non-MLS 0.05)
Pop 1,428; Circ 7,798
Library Holdings: Bk Vols 14,516; Per Subs 50
Special Collections: KS History (Chapman Coll)
Automation Activity & Vendor Info: (Cataloging) Follett Software; (Circulation) Follett Software
Mem of North Central Kansas Libraries System
Open Tues & Thurs (Winter) 9-12 & 1-6, Wed 3-7, Sat 9-12; Mon (Summer) 1-6, Tues & Thurs 9-12 & 1-6, Wed 1-7, Sat 9-12

CHENEY

P CHENEY PUBLIC LIBRARY*, 203 N Main St, 67025. (Mail add: PO Box 700, 67025-0700), SAN 305-8565. Tel: 316-542-3331. E-mail: cheneypubliclibrary@cheneyks.org. Web Site: www.cheneypubliclibrary.org. *Dir,* Susan Woodard
Founded 1940. Pop 1,800; Circ 25,363
Library Holdings: Bk Vols 13,000; Per Subs 17
Automation Activity & Vendor Info: (Cataloging) Innovative Interfaces, Inc; (Circulation) Innovative Interfaces, Inc
Database Vendor: Gale Cengage Learning, OCLC FirstSearch
Mem of South Central Kansas Library System
Open Mon-Wed & Fri 9-1 & 2-5, Thurs 3-7, Sat 9-1
Friends of the Library Group

CHERRYVALE

P CHERRYVALE PUBLIC LIBRARY*, 329 E Main St, 67335-1413. SAN 305-8573. Tel: 620-336-3460. FAX: 620-336-3460. E-mail: librarian@cherryvalelibrary.org. Web Site: cherryvalelibrary.org. *Librn,* April Read
Founded 1913. Pop 2,770; Circ 20,526
Library Holdings: Large Print Bks 93; Bk Vols 16,400; Per Subs 26; Talking Bks 80
Wireless access
Mem of Southeast Kansas Library System
Open Mon-Fri 11-6:30, Sat 9-2
Friends of the Library Group

CHETOPA

P CHETOPA CITY LIBRARY*, 312 Maple, 67336-0206. (Mail add: PO Box 206, 67336-0206), SAN 305-8581. Tel: 620-236-7194. E-mail: chetopacitylibrary@yahoo.com. *Dir,* Tiffany LaPee
Founded 1875. Pop 1,850; Circ 16,236
Library Holdings: Audiobooks 50; DVDs 400; Large Print Bks 1,200; Bk Vols 25,000; Per Subs 25
Wireless access
Function: Adult bk club, Adult literacy prog, Alaskana res, Art exhibits
Mem of Southeast Kansas Library System
Open Mon, Tues & Fri 1-5, Wed 2-6, Thurs 9-1
Restriction: 24-hr pass syst for students only, Access at librarian's discretion, Authorized personnel only
Friends of the Library Group
Bookmobiles: 2. Dir, Tiffany LaPee

CIMARRON

P CIMARRON CITY LIBRARY*, 120 N Main, 67835. (Mail add: PO Box 645, 67835-0645), SAN 305-859X. Tel: 620-855-3808. FAX: 620-855-3884. E-mail: cimar1lb@ucom.net. Web Site: www.cimarroncitylibrary.org. *Dir,* Candi Cook; *Asst Librn,* Sandy Unruh; E-mail: cimlib@hotmail.com; Staff 3 (Non-MLS 3)
Founded 1934. Pop 1,934; Circ 35,286
Jan 2005-Dec 2005 Income $109,441, State $3,522, City $61,557, County $26,138, Other $18,224. Mats Exp $15,787, Books $10,497, Per/Ser (Incl. Access Fees) $1,389, AV Mat $3,651, Electronic Ref Mat (Incl. Access Fees) $250. Sal $57,424
Library Holdings: AV Mats 1,127; Electronic Media & Resources 100; Bk Vols 36,303; Per Subs 73; Talking Bks 1,448
Automation Activity & Vendor Info: (Circulation) Follett Software; (OPAC) Follett Software

Wireless access
Mem of Southwest Kansas Library System
Open Mon-Wed & Fri 9-6, Thurs 9-8, Sat 10-12 & 1-4
Friends of the Library Group
Branches: 2
ENSIGN BRANCH, 108 Aubrey, Ensign, 67841. (Mail add: PO Box 25, Ensign, 67841-0025). Tel: 620-865-2199. E-mail: ensignlib@yahoo.com. *Librn,* Pam Renfro
Pop 200
Library Holdings: Bk Vols 1,000
Automation Activity & Vendor Info: (Circulation) Auto-Graphics, Inc
Open Mon-Fri 3:30-5:30
INGALLS BRANCH, 220 S Main St, Ingalls, 67853. Tel: 620-335-5580. E-mail: ingallslibrary@yahoo.com. *Librn,* Debbie Milne
Library Holdings: Bk Titles 4,000
Automation Activity & Vendor Info: (Cataloging) Auto-Graphics, Inc; (Circulation) Auto-Graphics, Inc
Open Mon-Thurs 4-6, Fri 9am-11am

CLAFLIN

P INDEPENDENT TOWNSHIP LIBRARY*, 108 Main St, 67525. (Mail add: PO Box 163, 67525-0163), SAN 305-8603. Tel: 316-587-3488. FAX: 620-587-3488. *Dir,* Judy Wondra; E-mail: jwondra@hbcomm.net
Founded 1962. Pop 887; Circ 8,358
Library Holdings: AV Mats 148; DVDs 10; Large Print Bks 100; Bk Titles 9,205; Per Subs 20; Talking Bks 65; Videos 300
Special Collections: Arts & Crafts Coll; Kansas Book Title Coll; Original Claflin Clarion Newspaper Coll, dated back to 1800's
Mem of Central Kansas Library System
Open Mon 3:30-8, Tues & Fri 9-12:30, Thurs 1-5:30, Sat 9-12

CLAY CENTER

P CLAY CENTER CARNEGIE LIBRARY, 706 Sixth St, 67432-2997. SAN 305-8611. Tel: 785-632-3889. E-mail: director@cckslibrary.org. Web Site: claycenter.mykansaslibrary.org. *Dir,* Crystal Applegarth; *Ch,* Pixie Knepper
Founded 1901. Pop 4,640; Circ 44,349
Library Holdings: Bk Titles 40,264; Per Subs 97
Wireless access
Mem of North Central Kansas Libraries System
Open Mon & Wed 2-8, Tues & Thurs 10-8, Fri 2-6, Sat 10-2
Friends of the Library Group

CLAYTON

P CLAYTON CITY LIBRARY*, HC 1, Box 76, 67629. SAN 305-862X, *Librn,* Mary Vanover
Pop 117; Circ 600
Library Holdings: Bk Vols 1,877
Mem of Northwest Kansas Library System
Open Wed 5:30-7

CLEARWATER

P CLEARWATER PUBLIC LIBRARY, 109 E Ross St, 67026-7824. SAN 305-8638. Tel: 620-584-6474. FAX: 620-584-2995. Web Site: www.clearwaterkslibrary.org. *Dir,* Sue Koenig; Staff 4 (MLS 1, Non-MLS 3)
Pop 2,481; Circ 22,273
Library Holdings: Bk Vols 15,757; Per Subs 32
Automation Activity & Vendor Info: (Cataloging) Innovative Interfaces, Inc; (Circulation) Innovative Interfaces, Inc; (ILL) Auto-Graphics, Inc; (OPAC) Innovative Interfaces, Inc
Wireless access
Open Tues & Thurs 10-7, Wed & Fri 10-5, Sat 10-2
Friends of the Library Group

CLIFTON

P CLIFTON PUBLIC LIBRARY*, 104 E Parallel, 66937. (Mail add: PO Box J, 66937-0310), SAN 305-8646. Tel: 785-455-2222. E-mail: clifpblib@hotmail.com. Web Site: clifton.mykansaslibrary.org. *Librn,* Pat Bloomfield
Founded 1954. Pop 600; Circ 400
Library Holdings: Bk Vols 3,000
Open Mon & Fri 1-5, Tues 2-5, Wed 9-12 & 2-5, Sat 9-Noon

CLYDE

P CLYDE PUBLIC LIBRARY*, Randolph-Decker Library, 101 S Green St, 66938. (Mail add: PO Box 85, 66938-0085), SAN 305-8654. Tel: 785-446-3563. Web Site: skyways.lib.ks.us. *Librn,* Virginia Racette; *Ch,* Lee Ann Brady
Founded 1920. Pop 722; Circ 12,305
Library Holdings: Bk Vols 15,000
Wireless access
Open Mon 2-8, Tues-Thurs 2-6, Fri & Sat 1-5

COFFEYVILLE

J COFFEYVILLE COMMUNITY COLLEGE*, Graham Library, 400 W 11th, 67337-5064. SAN 305-8662. Tel: 620-252-7220. FAX: 620-252-7366. Web Site: coffeyville.edu/academics/library/index.htm. *Dir,* Marty Evensvold; E-mail: martye@coffeyville.edu; Staff 1 (MLS 1)
Founded 1923. Enrl 1,170; Fac 45; Highest Degree: Associate
Library Holdings: Bks on Deafness & Sign Lang 12; Bk Titles 25,108; Bk Vols 27,626; Per Subs 308
Automation Activity & Vendor Info: (Acquisitions) Follett Software; (Cataloging) Follett Software; (Circulation) Follett Software; (OPAC) Follett Software; (Serials) Follett Software
Mem of Southeast Kansas Library System
Special Services for the Blind - ZoomText magnification & reading software
Open Mon-Thurs (Winter) 7:45am-9pm, Fri 7:45-3:30, Sun 2-7; Mon-Fri (Summer) 8-4

P COFFEYVILLE PUBLIC LIBRARY*, 311 W Tenth St, 67337. SAN 305-8670. Tel: 620-251-1370. FAX: 620-251-1512. E-mail: cvillepl@coffeyvillepl.org. Web Site: www.cvillepublib.org. *Dir,* Jennifer Dalton; E-mail: jd@coffeyvillepl.org; *Ch,* Cindy Powell; E-mail: coffeygal2000@yahoo.com; *ILL, Ref,* Joy Duvall; E-mail: joy@coffeyvillepl.org; Staff 6 (MLS 2, Non-MLS 4)
Founded 1906. Pop 10,517; Circ 76,287
Library Holdings: Bks on Deafness & Sign Lang 52; CDs 505; DVDs 400; Large Print Bks 1,800; Bk Titles 74,239; Per Subs 101; Talking Bks 400; Videos 1,121
Subject Interests: Genealogy
Automation Activity & Vendor Info: (Cataloging) Auto-Graphics, Inc; (Circulation) Follett Software; (ILL) Auto-Graphics, Inc; (OPAC) Follett Software
Wireless access
Mem of Southeast Kansas Library System
Special Services for the Deaf - Bks on deafness & sign lang; High interest/low vocabulary bks
Special Services for the Blind - BiFolkal kits; Bks on CD; Copier with enlargement capabilities; Extensive large print coll; Home delivery serv; Lending of low vision aids; Magnifiers; Talking bks
Open Mon-Thurs 9-8, Fri & Sat 9-5
Restriction: Non-resident fee

COLBY

J COLBY COMMUNITY COLLEGE*, H F Davis Memorial Library, 1255 S Range Ave, 67701. SAN 305-8689. Tel: 785-460-4689. FAX: 785-460-4600. Web Site: www.colbycc.edu. *Coordr,* Tara Schroer; Tel: 785-462-3984, Ext 5487; *Acq,* Amy Torrance; E-mail: amy.torrance@colbycc.edu; *Govt Doc,* Sena Bailey; Tel: 785-462-3984, Ext 5494, E-mail: sena.bailey@colbycc.edu; Staff 3 (MLS 1, Non-MLS 2)
Founded 1964. Enrl 2,402; Fac 150; Highest Degree: Associate
Library Holdings: AV Mats 2,222; CDs 69; DVDs 2,937; e-books 44; Bk Titles 28,347; Per Subs 200
Special Collections: Cookbook Coll
Subject Interests: Kansas
Automation Activity & Vendor Info: (Acquisitions) EOS International; (Cataloging) EOS International; (Circulation) EOS International; (OPAC) EOS International
Database Vendor: Gale Cengage Learning, LexisNexis, OCLC FirstSearch, OCLC WorldShare Interlibrary Loan, ProQuest
Wireless access
Mem of Northwest Kansas Library System
Partic in State Library of Kansas
Open Mon-Thurs 8-8, Fri 8-5, Sun 4-8
Restriction: Circ privileges for students & alumni only

P PIONEER MEMORIAL LIBRARY*, 375 W Fourth St, 67701-2197. SAN 305-8697. Tel: 785-460-4470. FAX: 785-460-4472. E-mail: colbykslibrary@yahoo.com. Web Site: www.colbylibrary.com. *Dir,* Melany A Wilks; E-mail: director@colbylibrary.com; *Asst Dir,* Debbie Tittle; E-mail: assistantdirector@colbylibrary.com; *Circ Supvr,* Carol Bohme; *Adult Serv, ILL,* Nancy Saddler; E-mail: adult@colbylibrary.com; *Ch Serv,* Judy Kleinsorge; E-mail: child-youth@colbylibrary.com; Staff 5 (MLS 1, Non-MLS 4)
Founded 1926. Pop 8,219; Circ 153,460
Jan 2012-Dec 2012 Income $288,724, State $2,300, City $240,824, Locally Generated Income $20,000, Other $25,600. Mats Exp $283,203. Sal $174,886
Library Holdings: Audiobooks 1,674; AV Mats 276; Bks on Deafness & Sign Lang 3; Braille Volumes 4; CDs 936; DVDs 816; Large Print Bks 2,145; Bk Titles 40,156; Bk Vols 44,641; Per Subs 135; Videos 2,292
Special Collections: Kansas Coll

Automation Activity & Vendor Info: (Acquisitions) Auto-Graphics, Inc; (Cataloging) Auto-Graphics, Inc; (Circulation) Auto-Graphics, Inc; (ILL) Auto-Graphics, Inc; (OPAC) Auto-Graphics, Inc; (Serials) Auto-Graphics, Inc
Database Vendor: Ingram Library Services
Wireless access
Function: Photocopying/Printing
Publications: Annual Report (Library statistics & report); The Library Link
Special Services for the Deaf - Am sign lang & deaf culture; Bks on deafness & sign lang; Closed caption videos
Special Services for the Blind - Audio mat; Bks available with recordings; Bks on cassette; Bks on CD; Cassette playback machines; Cassettes; Large print & cassettes; Large print bks; Large print bks & talking machines; Talking bks; Talking bks & player equip
Open Mon-Thurs (Winter) 9-8, Fri 9-5, Sat 9-4, Sun 1-4; Mon-Wed (Summer) 9-6, Thurs 9-8, Fri 9-5, Sat 9-4, Sun 1-4
Friends of the Library Group

COLDWATER

P COLDWATER-WILMORE REGIONAL LIBRARY*, 221 E Main, 67029. (Mail add: PO Box 606, 67029-0606), SAN 342-006X. Tel: 620-582-2333. FAX: 620-582-2333. E-mail: coldlibrary@unitedwireless.com. Web Site: www.coldwaterkansas.com/library.html. *Dir,* Ellen Selzer; Staff 1 (MLS 1)
Founded 1912. Pop 800
Library Holdings: Bk Vols 14,000; Per Subs 15
Wireless access
Mem of Southwest Kansas Library System
Open Mon 3:30-7:30, Tues-Sat 9-12 & 1:30-5:30
Branches: 1
WILMORE BRANCH, 100 Taft St, Wilmore, 67155, SAN 342-0094. Tel: 620-738-4464. *Librn,* Pat White
Library Holdings: Bk Titles 335
Open Tues & Fri 1-6

COLONY

P COLONY CITY LIBRARY*, 339 Cherry St, 66015. (Mail add: PO Box 85, 66015-0085), SAN 305-8719. Tel: 620-852-3530. FAX: 620-852-3107. E-mail: colonylibrary@yahoo.com. *Librn,* LaNell Knoll; E-mail: colonylibrary@yahoo.com
Pop 397; Circ 1,517
Library Holdings: Bks on Deafness & Sign Lang 10; DVDs 70; Large Print Bks 100; Music Scores 39; Bk Titles 4,500; Per Subs 20; Talking Bks 16; Videos 352
Wireless access
Mem of Southeast Kansas Library System
Partic in SE Kans Libr Asn
Open Mon-Fri 8-11:30 & 12:30-5

COLUMBUS

P COLUMBUS PUBLIC LIBRARY*, 205 N Kansas, 66725-1221. SAN 305-8727. Tel: 620-429-2086. FAX: 620-429-1950. Web Site: skyways.lib.ks.us/library/columbus/. *Dir,* Danielle Dougherty
Founded 1905. Pop 3,597; Circ 30,418
Library Holdings: Bk Vols 15,000; Per Subs 70
Automation Activity & Vendor Info: (Acquisitions) Follett Software
Open Mon & Thurs 12-6, Tues & Wed 12-8, Fri & Sat 10-3

COLWICH

P COLWICH COMMUNITY LIBRARY, 432 W Colwich, 67030. (Mail add: PO Box 8, 67030-0008), SAN 305-8735. Tel: 316-796-1521. E-mail: library@colwich.kscoxmail.com. *Dir,* Joanna Kraus; *Asst Librn,* Jenny Hemmen; Staff 2 (Non-MLS 2)
Founded 1961. Pop 2,257; Circ 16,821
Library Holdings: Bk Vols 14,100; Per Subs 62
Automation Activity & Vendor Info: (Circulation) Innovative Interfaces, Inc
Database Vendor: Booklist Online
Wireless access
Publications: Website
Mem of South Central Kansas Library System
Open Mon-Thurs 8-11 & 3-8, Fri 8-11 & 3-6, Sat 10-2

CONCORDIA

P FRANK CARLSON LIBRARY*, 702 Broadway, 66901. SAN 305-8743. Tel: 785-243-2250. Web Site: www.fcarlsonlib.org. *Librn,* Denise De Rochefort-Reynolds; Staff 4 (MLS 1, Non-MLS 3)
Founded 1892. Pop 5,300; Circ 75,000
Jan 2009-Dec 2009 Income $150,000
Library Holdings: Bk Vols 38,000; Per Subs 131
Special Collections: Business Resources; Frank Carlson Coll; Kansas Coll; US Constitution
Automation Activity & Vendor Info: (Cataloging) LibLime; (Circulation) LibLime; (OPAC) LibLime
Wireless access
Mem of Central Kansas Library System
Open Mon-Thurs 9-8, Fri & Sat 9-5

J CLOUD COUNTY COMMUNITY COLLEGE LIBRARY*, 2221 Campus Dr, 66901-5305. (Mail add: PO Box 1002, 66901-1002), SAN 305-8751. Tel: 785-243-1435, Ext 224. Interlibrary Loan Service Tel: 785-243-1435, Ext 225. Administration Tel: 785-243-1435, Ext 226. Toll Free Tel: 800-729-5101. FAX: 785-243-1043. E-mail: library@cloud.edu. Web Site: www.cloud.edu/Academics/Library/index. *Libr Dir,* Jennifer Schroeder; Staff 2 (MLS 1, Non-MLS 1)
Founded 1968. Enrl 1,680; Fac 139; Highest Degree: Associate
Library Holdings: AV Mats 1,666; e-books 9,151; Bk Titles 18,308; Bk Vols 21,067; Per Subs 30
Special Collections: Child Care Coll
Automation Activity & Vendor Info: (Cataloging) Auto-Graphics, Inc; (Circulation) Auto-Graphics, Inc; (ILL) Auto-Graphics, Inc; (OPAC) Auto-Graphics, Inc
Database Vendor: EBSCOhost, Gale Cengage Learning, OCLC FirstSearch, OCLC WorldShare Interlibrary Loan, ProQuest
Wireless access
Function: Bi-weekly Writer's Group
Open Mon-Thurs 7:45am-9pm, Fri 7:45-5, Sun 6pm-8pm

S CLOUD COUNTY HISTORICAL SOCIETY MUSEUM LIBRARY*, 635 Broadway, 66901. SAN 325-7347. Tel: 785-243-2866. E-mail: museum@cloudcountyks.org. Web Site: www.cloudcountyks.org. *Curator, Dir,* Cindy Reimann
Founded 1959
Library Holdings: Bk Vols 550
Special Collections: Municipal Document Depository
Open Tues-Sat 1-5

CONWAY SPRINGS

P CONWAY SPRINGS CITY LIBRARY*, 210 W Spring St, 67031. (Mail add: PO Box 183, 67031-0183), SAN 376-5563. Tel: 620-456-2859. FAX: 620-456-3294. E-mail: cwslibrary@havilandtelco.com. *Dir,* Danna Fulkerson
Library Holdings: Bk Vols 11,000; Per Subs 20
Mem of South Central Kansas Library System
Open Mon-Fri 8-11 & 12:30-6

COPELAND

P COPELAND PUBLIC LIBRARY*, 109 Santa Fe St, 67837. (Mail add: PO Box 121, 67837-0121), SAN 305-8778. Tel: 620-668-5559. E-mail: copelandlibrary@hotmail.com. *Librn,* Melissa Dahlke
Pop 310; Circ 1,033
Library Holdings: Bk Vols 6,000
Automation Activity & Vendor Info: (Cataloging) Brodart; (Circulation) Brodart
Wireless access
Open Mon-Thurs 10-12 & 2-5

CORNING

P CORNING CITY LIBRARY*, 6221 Fifth St, 66417-8485. SAN 305-8786. Tel: 785-868-2755. FAX: 785-868-2755. Web Site: www.corningcitylibrary.org. *Libr Dir,* Mandy Deters; E-mail: mdeters@corningcitylibrary.org
Founded 1920. Pop 167; Circ 2,072
Library Holdings: DVDs 22; Large Print Bks 164; Bk Vols 7,000; Per Subs 12; Videos 462
Mem of Northeast Kansas Library System
Open Mon 12:30-5:30, Wed 3:30-8:30, Sat 9-1

COTTONWOOD FALLS

P BURNLEY MEMORIAL LIBRARY*, 401 Oak, 66845. (Mail add: PO Box 509, 66845-0509), SAN 376-558X. Tel: 620-273-8588. FAX: 620-273-8588. E-mail: burnleylibrary@sbcglobal.net. *Librn,* Susan Davis
Library Holdings: Bk Vols 10,000; Per Subs 22
Automation Activity & Vendor Info: (Acquisitions) ComPanion Corp; (Cataloging) ComPanion Corp; (Circulation) ComPanion Corp; (OPAC) ComPanion Corp
Mem of North Central Kansas Libraries System
Open Mon, Tues, Thurs & Sat 2-5, Wed 2-5 & 7-9, Fri 12-5

COUNCIL GROVE

P COUNCIL GROVE PUBLIC LIBRARY*, 829 W Main St, 66846. SAN 305-8794. Tel: 620-767-5716. FAX: 620-767-7312. E-mail: cglib@tctelco.net. Web Site: cgpl.mykansaslibrary.org. *Dir,* Lee Dobratz; *Ch,* Erica Smith; *Asst Librn,* Kathy Avers; Staff 5 (Non-MLS 5)
Founded 1876. Pop 2,280; Circ 23,190
Library Holdings: Audiobooks 1,300; AV Mats 1,235; DVDs 500; Large Print Bks 834; Bk Titles 20,422; Per Subs 36
Automation Activity & Vendor Info: (Cataloging) Follett Software; (Circulation) Follett Software; (ILL) Auto-Graphics, Inc; (OPAC) Follett Software; (Serials) Follett Software
Database Vendor: Gale Cengage Learning, OCLC FirstSearch
Wireless access
Function: Audio & video playback equip for onsite use, Bk club(s), Bks on cassette, Bks on CD, Children's prog, Computers for patron use, Copy machines, Electronic databases & coll, Fax serv, Free DVD rentals, Handicapped accessible, ILL available, Music CDs, Online cat, OverDrive digital audio bks, Prog for adults, Prog for children & young adult, Pub access computers, Scanner, Story hour, Summer reading prog, Tax forms, VHS videos, Wheelchair accessible
Mem of North Central Kansas Libraries System
Open Mon-Fri 9-6, Sat 10-2
Friends of the Library Group

COURTLAND

P COURTLAND COMMUNITY LIBRARY*, 403 Main St, 66939. (Mail add: PO Box 85, 66939-0085), SAN 305-8808. Tel: 785-374-4260. E-mail: library@courtland.net. Web Site: www.courtland.net. *Dir,* Dolores Erickson
Founded 1922. Pop 377
Library Holdings: Bk Vols 5,000; Per Subs 21
Mem of Central Kansas Library System
Open Mon & Fri 2:30-6, Wed 5-8

CUBA

P HILLCREST PUBLIC LIBRARY*, 804 Bristol, 66940-3024. (Mail add: PO Box 167, 66940-0167). Tel: 785-729-3333, 785-729-3355. FAX: 785-729-3692. *Dir,* Lori Swiercinsky; E-mail: lori6263@yahoo.com
Founded 2000. Pop 920
Library Holdings: Bk Vols 12,000; Per Subs 50; Talking Bks 125; Videos 200
Automation Activity & Vendor Info: (Cataloging) Follett Software; (Circulation) Follett Software
Mem of Central Kansas Library System
Open Mon & Wed 8-7, Tues, Thurs & Fri 8-4

DELPHOS

P DELPHOS PUBLIC LIBRARY*, 114 W Second, 67436. (Mail add: PO Box 284, 67436-0284), SAN 376-5679. Tel: 785-523-4668. E-mail: delphoslib@nckcn.com. Web Site: skyways.lib.ks.us/towns/delphos/our_town/the_library.html. *Dir,* Sharon Snively
Library Holdings: Bk Vols 6,000; Per Subs 10
Mem of Central Kansas Library System
Open Mon & Fri 1-5, Tues 10-2, Thurs 1-7, Sat 10-Noon

DERBY

P DERBY PUBLIC LIBRARY*, 1600 E Walnut Grove, 67037. SAN 305-8816. Tel: 316-788-0760. FAX: 316-788-7313. Web Site: www.derbylibrary.com. *Dir,* Eric Gustafson; E-mail: eric@derbylibrary.com; *Asst Dir,* Debbie Thomas; E-mail: debbie@derbylibrary.com; *ILL & Cat Coordr,* Joanne Condon; E-mail: joanne@derbylibrary.com; *Pub Support Serv Coordr,* Kristy Norman; E-mail: kristy@derbylibrary.com; *Tech Coordr,* Justin Ball; E-mail: justin@derbylibrary.com; *Youth Serv Coordr,* Carri Fry; E-mail: carri@derbylibrary.com; Staff 18.6 (MLS 1, Non-MLS 17.6)
Founded 1958. Pop 22,000; Circ 323,908
Jan 2013-Dec 2013 Income $866,652, State $13,000, City $784,652, Locally Generated Income $40,000, Other $29,000. Mats Exp $166,493, Books $79,493, Per/Ser (Incl. Access Fees) $7,000, AV Mat $45,000, Electronic Ref Mat (Incl. Access Fees) $35,000. Sal $494,000 (Prof $69,120)
Library Holdings: AV Mats 4,540; Braille Volumes 32; CDs 2,459; DVDs 4,357; Electronic Media & Resources 38; High Interest/Low Vocabulary Bk Vols 208; Large Print Bks 4,788; Bk Titles 60,000; Bk Vols 80,000; Per Subs 100
Automation Activity & Vendor Info: (Acquisitions) LibLime; (Cataloging) LibLime; (Circulation) LibLime; (ILL) Auto-Graphics, Inc; (OPAC) LibLime
Database Vendor: Baker & Taylor, EBSCO Auto Repair Reference, EBSCO Information Services, EBSCOhost, Gale Cengage Learning, LearningExpress, LibLime, Newsbank, OCLC FirstSearch, OCLC WebJunction, OCLC WorldShare Interlibrary Loan, Overdrive, Inc, ProQuest, TLC (The Library Corporation), World Book Online
Wireless access
Function: Adult bk club, After school storytime, Art exhibits, Audiobks via web, Bk club(s), Bks on CD, Children's prog, Computers for patron use, Copy machines, Electronic databases & coll, Free DVD rentals, Handicapped accessible, Holiday prog, Home delivery & serv to Sr ctr & nursing homes, ILL available, Music CDs, Online cat, Online searches, OverDrive digital audio bks, Prog for adults, Prog for children & young adult, Pub access computers, Story hour, Summer reading prog, Tax forms, Teen prog, Web-catalog, Wheelchair accessible
Mem of South Central Kansas Library System
Special Services for the Deaf - Closed caption videos; High interest/low vocabulary bks; Sign lang interpreter upon request for prog
Special Services for the Blind - Large print bks; PC for handicapped
Open Mon-Thurs 9-8:30, Fri 9-6, Sat 9-5, Sun (Sept-May) 1-5

DIGHTON

P LANE COUNTY LIBRARY*, 144 South Lane, 67839. (Mail add: PO Box 997, 67839-0997), SAN 305-8824. Tel: 620-397-2808. FAX: 620-397-5937. E-mail: lanelib@st-tel.net. Web Site: lanecolibrary.info. *Dir,* Ruby Martin; *Asst Librn,* Mona Peck
Founded 1934. Pop 2,211; Circ 33,323
Jan 2005-Dec 2005 Income (Main Library and Branch(s)) $58,881, Federal $1,356, County $48,535, Other $8,990. Mats Exp $8,639, Books $6,434, Per/Ser (Incl. Access Fees) $2,000, Other Print Mats $160, Electronic Ref Mat (Incl. Access Fees) $45. Sal $35,472
Library Holdings: Bks on Deafness & Sign Lang 18; CDs 111; DVDs 270; Large Print Bks 54; Bk Vols 20,400; Per Subs 76; Talking Bks 563; Videos 1,451
Special Collections: Our Kansas Room-Kansas Books
Subject Interests: Genealogy
Automation Activity & Vendor Info: (Acquisitions) Auto-Graphics, Inc; (Cataloging) Follett Software; (Circulation) Follett Software; (Course Reserve) Relais International; (ILL) Follett Software
Wireless access
Function: Adult bk club, Audio & video playback equip for onsite use, CD-ROM, Copy machines, e-mail serv, Genealogy discussion group, Home delivery & serv to Sr ctr & nursing homes, Homebound delivery serv, Homework prog, ILL available, Online ref, Online searches, Outside serv via phone, mail, e-mail & web, Photocopying/Printing, Preschool outreach, Prog for children & young adult, Spoken cassettes & CDs, Spoken cassettes & DVDs, Summer reading prog, Tax forms, VHS videos, Video lending libr
Mem of Southwest Kansas Library System
Open Mon & Thurs 9-8, Tues, Wed & Fri 9-5
Friends of the Library Group
Branches: 1
HEALY EXTENSION, 2009 W Hwy 4, Healy, 67850-5088. (Mail add: PO Box 144, Healy, 67850-0144). Tel: 620-398-2267. E-mail: healylib@st-tel.net. *Dir,* Roberta Barnett
Library Holdings: Bk Vols 3,500
Open Mon 9-1, Wed 1:30-5:30
Friends of the Library Group

DODGE CITY

S BOOT HILL MUSEUM*, Special Library & Archives, Front St, 67801. SAN 373-4552. Tel: 620-227-8188. FAX: 620-227-7673. Web Site: www.boothill.org. *Asst Curator,* Kathie Bell
Library Holdings: Bk Vols 1,450; Per Subs 20
Special Collections: Historic Photographs Coll
Partic in Dodge City Library Consortium
Restriction: Open by appt only

J DODGE CITY COMMUNITY COLLEGE*, Learning Resources Center-Library Services, 2501 N 14th, 67801. SAN 305-8840. Tel: 620-225-1321, Ext 287, 620-227-9287. Administration Tel: 620-227-9285. E-mail: library@dc3.edu. Web Site: www.dc3.edu/lrc. *Dir,* Shelly Huelsman; E-mail: shuelsman@dc3.edu; *Circ, ILL,* Rachel Turner; *Govt Doc,* Jolene Durler; Staff 1 (MLS 1)
Founded 1935. Enrl 2,414; Fac 85; Highest Degree: Associate
Jul 2013-Jun 2014 Income $52,950. Mats Exp $30,681, Books $12,000, Per/Ser (Incl. Access Fees) $8,500, AV Mat $181, Electronic Ref Mat (Incl. Access Fees) $10,000. Sal $89,000 (Prof $52,000)
Library Holdings: CDs 171; DVDs 632; Bk Titles 33,112; Per Subs 210
Special Collections: US Document Depository
Automation Activity & Vendor Info: (Acquisitions) Auto-Graphics, Inc; (Cataloging) Auto-Graphics, Inc; (Circulation) Auto-Graphics, Inc; (Course Reserve) Auto-Graphics, Inc; (ILL) Auto-Graphics, Inc; (OPAC) Auto-Graphics, Inc; (Serials) Auto-Graphics, Inc
Database Vendor: Auto-Graphics, Inc, CredoReference, EBSCO Auto Repair Reference, EBSCOhost, Gale Cengage Learning, Medline, OCLC

FirstSearch, OCLC WorldShare Interlibrary Loan, ProQuest, PubMed, WebMD
Wireless access
Function: Archival coll, Computers for patron use, Copy machines, Distance learning, e-mail serv, Electronic databases & coll, Free DVD rentals, Govt ref serv, Handicapped accessible, ILL available, Instruction & testing, Mail & tel request accepted, Microfiche/film & reading machines, Orientations, Photocopying/Printing, Pub access computers, Scanner, Video lending libr
Mem of Southwest Kansas Library System
Partic in Dodge City Library Consortium
Open Mon-Thurs 8am-9pm, Fri 8-4, Sun 6pm-9pm

P DODGE CITY PUBLIC LIBRARY*, 1001 N Second Ave, 67801-4484. SAN 305-8859. Tel: 620-225-0248. FAX: 620-225-2761. Interlibrary Loan Service FAX: 620-225-0868. Administration FAX: 620-225-1931. E-mail: library@dcpl.info. Web Site: www.dcpl.info. *Dir,* Cathy Reeves; E-mail: cathyr@dcpl.info; *Dir, Pub Serv,* Michael Biltz; E-mail: michaelb@trails.net; *ILL,* Cindy Shipley; *Ref,* Sam Shipley; Staff 19 (MLS 3, Non-MLS 16)
Founded 1905. Pop 26,101; Circ 125,962
Jan 2008-Dec 2008 Income $1,024,760, State $17,912, City $928,903, Locally Generated Income $59,605, Other $18,340. Mats Exp $214,670, Books $96,310, Per/Ser (Incl. Access Fees) $8,800, Other Print Mats $105,110, Electronic Ref Mat (Incl. Access Fees) $4,450. Sal $672,634
Library Holdings: AV Mats 3,949; DVDs 7,935; Electronic Media & Resources 44; Bk Vols 126,671; Per Subs 202
Special Collections: Kansas Coll. State Document Depository
Subject Interests: Gardening, Hist, Kansas, Spanish (Lang)
Automation Activity & Vendor Info: (Acquisitions) SirsiDynix; (Cataloging) SirsiDynix; (Circulation) SirsiDynix; (Media Booking) SirsiDynix; (OPAC) SirsiDynix; (Serials) SirsiDynix
Database Vendor: EBSCO Auto Repair Reference, EBSCOhost, Gale Cengage Learning, Ingram Library Services, OCLC WebJunction, OCLC WorldShare Interlibrary Loan, Overdrive, Inc, ProQuest, SirsiDynix, World Book Online
Wireless access
Mem of Southwest Kansas Library System
Partic in OCLC Online Computer Library Center, Inc
Open Mon-Wed & Fri 9-6, Thurs 9-8, Sat 9-5
Friends of the Library Group

S KANSAS HERITAGE CENTER LIBRARY, 1000 N Second Ave, 67801-4415. (Mail add: PO Box 1207, 67801-1207), SAN 305-8832. Tel: 620-227-1616. FAX: 620-227-1701. E-mail: library@ksheritage.org. Web Site: ksheritagestore.org/research. *Librn,* Janice Scott; Staff 4 (MLS 1, Non-MLS 3)
Founded 1966
Library Holdings: Bk Titles 6,400; Bk Vols 9,000; Per Subs 45; Videos 500
Special Collections: Dodge City & Kansas Research Files; Dodge City Newspaper, 1876-present, micro
Subject Interests: Kansas
Wireless access
Publications: 399 Kansas Characters; Color Kansas Characters Poster/Coloring Book; Color Oklahoma Characters Poster/Coloring Book; Dodge City, Cowboy Capital; Kansas Symbols Coloring Book; Oklahoma Symbols Coloring Book; Santa Fe Trail Adventures; Sentinel to the Cimarron: The Frontier Experience of Fort Dodge, Kansas; West by Southwest
Open Mon-Fri 8-5

P SOUTHWEST KANSAS LIBRARY SYSTEM, 100 Military Ave, Ste 210, 67801-4484. SAN 342-0124. Tel: 620-225-1231. Toll Free Tel: 800-657-2533. FAX: 620-225-0252. E-mail: swkls@swkls.org. Web Site: www.swkls.org. *Dir,* Emily Sitz; E-mail: esitz@swkls.org; *Tech Coordr,* Charlene McGuire; E-mail: cmcguire@swkls.org; *ILL,* Patti Cummins; E-mail: pcummins@swkls.org; Staff 10 (MLS 2, Non-MLS 8)
Founded 1968. Pop 151,689
Library Holdings: Bk Vols 14,709; Per Subs 12
Special Collections: Spanish (Popular Reading)
Automation Activity & Vendor Info: (Acquisitions) Auto-Graphics, Inc; (Cataloging) Auto-Graphics, Inc; (Circulation) Auto-Graphics, Inc
Publications: Southwest Kansas Library System Newsletter; System Scene
Member Libraries: Ashland City Library; Brownell Public Library; Bucklin Public Library; Cimarron City Library; Coldwater-Wilmore Regional Library; Dodge City Community College; Dodge City Public Library; Dudley Township Public Library; Finney County Public Library; Ford City Library; Grant County Library; Greeley County Library; Hamilton County Library; Hanston City Library; Haskell Township Library; Henry Laird Library; Jetmore Public Library; Kearny County Library; Kinsley Public Library; Kismet Public Library; Lane County Library; Liberal Memorial Library; Meade Public Library; Meadowlark Public Library; Minneola City Library; Montezuma Township Library; Morton County Library; Ness City Public Library; Plains Community Library; Protection Township Library; Ransom Public Library; Scott County Library; Seward County Community College Library; Spearville Township Library; Stanton County Library; Stevens County Library; Utica Library Association
Partic in Telecommunications Libr Info Network
Open Mon-Fri 8-5
Branches: 1
P TALKING BOOKS, 100 Military Ave, Ste 210, 67801-4484. Tel: 620-225-1231. Toll Free Tel: 800-657-2533. FAX: 620-225-0252. ; Staff 1 (Non-MLS 1)
Library Holdings: Bk Vols 500
Open Mon-Fri 8-5
Bookmobiles: 1

DOUGLASS

P DOUGLASS PUBLIC LIBRARY*, 319 S Forrest St, 67039. (Mail add: PO Box 190, 67039-0190), SAN 305-8875. Tel: 316-746-2600. FAX: 316-746-3936. Web Site: www.douglasslibrary.com. *Dir,* Polly Bloom
Founded 1941. Pop 2,626
Library Holdings: Bk Vols 20,000; Per Subs 51
Automation Activity & Vendor Info: (Cataloging) Follett Software; (Circulation) Follett Software
Mem of South Central Kansas Library System
Open Mon, Wed & Fri 10-5, Tues & Thurs 11-6, Sat 9-2
Friends of the Library Group

DOWNS

P DOWNS CARNEGIE LIBRARY*, 504 S Morgan, 67437-2019. SAN 305-8883. Tel: 785-454-3821. FAX: 785-454-3821. E-mail: downslibrary@ruraltel.net. *Librn,* Jody Marihugh
Founded 1905. Pop 1,170; Circ 15,000
Library Holdings: Bk Vols 12,500; Per Subs 40
Subject Interests: Hist, Kansas
Automation Activity & Vendor Info: (Cataloging) Follett Software; (Circulation) Follett Software
Mem of Central Kansas Library System
Open Mon & Wed 1-7, Tues & Thurs 1-5, Fri & Sat 11-5

DWIGHT

P DWIGHT LIBRARY*, 637 Main, 66849. (Mail add: PO Box 278, 68849-0278), SAN 305-8891. Tel: 785-482-3804. E-mail: dwlibrary@tctelco.net. *In Charge,* Karen Byrd
Pop 392; Circ 2,847
Library Holdings: Bk Vols 3,300; Per Subs 16
Wireless access
Mem of North Central Kansas Libraries System
Open Mon 9-10, Wed 10-12 & 1:30-4:30, Sat 10-12 & 1-3

EDNA

P EDNA PUBLIC LIBRARY*, 105 N Delaware, 67342. (Mail add: PO Box 218, 67342-0218), SAN 305-8905. Tel: 620-922-3470. E-mail: ednalibrary@yahoo.com. *Librn,* Eva Rexwinkle
Founded 1950. Pop 537
Library Holdings: Large Print Bks 292; Bk Vols 6,249; Per Subs 10; Talking Bks 18
Wireless access
Mem of Southeast Kansas Library System
Special Services for the Blind - Talking bks
Open Mon & Wed 9-11 & 1-6, Thurs 2:30-5:30

EFFINGHAM

P EFFINGHAM COMMUNITY LIBRARY*, 414 Main St, 66023. (Mail add: PO Box 189, 66023-0189), SAN 305-8913. Tel: 913-833-5881. FAX: 913-833-5881. E-mail: efflibrary@yahoo.com. *Librn,* Rosie Falk
Founded 1927. Pop 548; Circ 600
Library Holdings: CDs 90; Electronic Media & Resources 20; Large Print Bks 120; Bk Vols 7,461; Per Subs 20; Talking Bks 36; Videos 200
Database Vendor: OCLC FirstSearch
Mem of Northeast Kansas Library System
Open Mon & Thurs 1-5, Wed 9-12 & 1-5, Sat 9-12

EL DORADO

P BRADFORD MEMORIAL LIBRARY*, 611 S Washington St, 67042. SAN 305-8921. Tel: 316-321-3363. FAX: 316-321-5546. E-mail: bmlibadm@eldoks.com. Web Site: skyways.lib.ks.us/library/bradford. *Dir,* Hollis Helmeci; E-mail: bmlibdir@eldoks.com; Staff 14 (MLS 2, Non-MLS 12)
Founded 1897. Pop 12,686; Circ 156,705

Jan 2007-Dec 2007 Income $392,183, City $352,761, Federal $11,922, County $15,000, Locally Generated Income $12,500. Mats Exp $59,000, Books $41,000, Per/Ser (Incl. Access Fees) $4,000, AV Mat $14,000. Sal $224,159 (Prof $39,600)
Library Holdings: AV Mats 8,425; Bks on Deafness & Sign Lang 64; Large Print Bks 7,971; Bk Titles 67,337; Bk Vols 65,542; Per Subs 108
Special Collections: Mental Health Coll; Ornithology Coll
Automation Activity & Vendor Info: (Acquisitions) Follett Software; (Cataloging) Follett Software; (Circulation) Follett Software
Database Vendor: Gale Cengage Learning, OCLC FirstSearch
Wireless access
Function: Adult bk club, Bks on cassette, Bks on CD, Computers for patron use, Copy machines, Digital talking bks, Electronic databases & coll, Equip loans & repairs, Fax serv, Free DVD rentals, Games & aids for the handicapped, Handicapped accessible, Home delivery & serv to Sr ctr & nursing homes, Homebound delivery serv, ILL available, Mail & tel request accepted, Music CDs, Online cat, Online searches, Outreach serv, OverDrive digital audio bks, Photocopying/Printing, Prog for adults, Prog for children & young adult, Pub access computers, Ref serv available, Spoken cassettes & CDs, Story hour, Summer reading prog, Tax forms, Teen prog, Telephone ref, VHS videos, Web-catalog, Wheelchair accessible
Open Mon-Thurs 9-8, Fri & Sat 9-5, Sun 1-5
Friends of the Library Group

J BUTLER COMMUNITY COLLEGE LIBRARY, L W Nixon Library, 901 S Haverhill Rd, 67042-3280. SAN 305-893X. Tel: 316-322-3234. Interlibrary Loan Service Tel: 316-322-3351. Reference Tel: 316-323-6843. Automation Services Tel: 316-323-6810. FAX: 316-322-3315. E-mail: lwnixon@butlercc.edu. Web Site: www.butlercc.edu/nixon_library. *Dir,* Micaela Ayers; Tel: 316-322-3235, E-mail: mayers@butlercc.edu; *IT Librn,* Ronda Holt; Tel: 316-323-6410, E-mail: rholt@butlercc.edu; *Ref & Instruction Librn,* Judy Bastin; E-mail: jbastin@butlercc.edu; *Tech/Pub Serv Librn,* Martha Gregg; Tel: 316-323-6842, E-mail: mgregg@butlercc.edu; Staff 7 (MLS 4, Non-MLS 3)
Founded 1927. Enrl 6,353; Fac 511; Highest Degree: Associate
Jul 2012-Jun 2013 Income $474,474. Mats Exp $101,737, Books $34,080, Per/Ser (Incl. Access Fees) $4,700, Electronic Ref Mat (Incl. Access Fees) $40,361. Sal $372,737 (Prof $153,351)
Library Holdings: Audiobooks 361; Bks on Deafness & Sign Lang 37; CDs 435; DVDs 2,411; e-books 2,160; Electronic Media & Resources 13; Bk Titles 32,496; Bk Vols 30,000; Per Subs 100; Videos 296
Special Collections: Koke Memorial Folk Arts Coll,; McCormick Pioneer Women Coll,; McCormick Science & Technology Coll
Subject Interests: Folk art, Pioneer women
Automation Activity & Vendor Info: (Cataloging) Auto-Graphics, Inc; (Circulation) Auto-Graphics, Inc; (ILL) Auto-Graphics, Inc; (OPAC) Auto-Graphics, Inc
Database Vendor: Alexander Street Press, CredoReference, EBSCOhost, Facts on File, Gale Cengage Learning, Ingram Library Services, LexisNexis, Micromedex, Newsbank, ProQuest, Springshare, LLC, WT Cox
Wireless access
Function: Audio & video playback equip for onsite use, Audiobks via web, Bks on cassette, Bks on CD, Computer training, Computers for patron use, Copy machines, Distance learning, Electronic databases & coll, Free DVD rentals, Handicapped accessible, Holiday prog, Homework prog, ILL available, Music CDs, Online cat, Online info literacy tutorials on the web & in blackboard, Online ref, Online searches, Orientations, OverDrive digital audio bks, Photocopying/Printing, Pub access computers, Ref & res, Scanner
Mem of South Central Kansas Library System
Partic in Southeast Kansas Academic Librarians Council (SEKALC)
Special Services for the Deaf - Bks on deafness & sign lang
Special Services for the Blind - Accessible computers; Bks on cassette; Bks on CD; Closed caption display syst; Computer access aids; Copier with enlargement capabilities; Free checkout of audio mat; IBM screen reader; Internet workstation with adaptive software; Screen enlargement software for people with visual disabilities; Screen reader software; ZoomText magnification & reading software
Open Mon-Thurs (Winter) 8am-9pm, Fri 8-5, Sat 9-1, Sun 5-9; Mon-Fri (Summer) 8-5

S ROLLA A CLYMER RESEARCH LIBRARY, Olive Clifford Stone Library, 383 E Central, 67042. SAN 326-4629. Tel: 316-321-9333. FAX: 316-321-3619. E-mail: education@kansasoilmuseum.org. *Res Librn & Mus Educator,* Ardath Lawson; Staff 1 (MLS 1)
Founded 1977
Library Holdings: Bk Titles 3,902; Bk Vols 4,008
Special Collections: Walnut Valley Times, El Dorado Republican & El Dorado Times Local Newspaper Coll, 1870-present, micro; William Allen White Coll. Oral History
Subject Interests: Kansas, Local hist, Petroleum indust
Wireless access
Function: Res libr
Open Mon-Sat (June-Sept) 9-5; Tues-Fri (Oct-May) 10-4, Sat 12-5
Restriction: Not a lending libr

S KANSAS DEPARTMENT OF CORRECTIONS*, El Dorado Correctional Facility Library, 1737 SE Hwy 54, 67042. (Mail add: PO Box 311, 67042). Tel: 316-321-7284. FAX: 316-322-2018. *Librn,* Margaret Adamson
Library Holdings: Bk Vols 10,000; Per Subs 20
Automation Activity & Vendor Info: (Cataloging) Follett Software; (Circulation) Follett Software; (OPAC) Follett Software
Database Vendor: LexisNexis

ELKHART

P MORTON COUNTY LIBRARY*, 410 Kansas, 67950. (Mail add: PO Box 938, 67950), SAN 305-8948. Tel: 620-697-2025. FAX: 620-697-4205. Web Site: mclib.elkhart.com. *Dir,* Virginia Johnson; E-mail: director@mocolib.info
Founded 1922. Pop 3,408; Circ 144,007
Library Holdings: Bk Vols 35,000; Per Subs 110
Special Collections: Doll Coll; Quilt & Cookbook Coll
Automation Activity & Vendor Info: (Cataloging) Auto-Graphics, Inc; (Circulation) Auto-Graphics, Inc; (ILL) Auto-Graphics, Inc; (Serials) EBSCO Online
Wireless access
Mem of Southwest Kansas Library System; Southwest Kansas Library System
Open Mon-Fri 9-5:30
Branches: 2
RICHFIELD BRANCH, HC 1, Box 99, Richfield, 67953.
Library Holdings: Bk Vols 4,000
Open Wed 2-4:30
ROLLA BRANCH, 202 Third St, Rolla, 67954. (Mail add: PO Box 412, Rolla, 67954-0412). Tel: 620-593-4328. FAX: 620-593-4276. E-mail: library@usd217.org. *Br Dir,* Cindy Hittle; E-mail: chittle@usd217.org; Staff 3 (Non-MLS 3)
Founded 1970. Pop 500
Library Holdings: Audiobooks 401; CDs 75; DVDs 583; Large Print Bks 154; Bk Vols 17,896; Per Subs 36; Videos 907
Automation Activity & Vendor Info: (Acquisitions) Auto-Graphics, Inc; (OPAC) Auto-Graphics, Inc
Open Mon-Fri 8-5
Bookmobiles: 1

ELLINWOOD

P ELLINWOOD SCHOOL & COMMUNITY LIBRARY*, 210 N Schiller Ave, 67526-1651. SAN 305-8956. Tel: 620-564-2306. FAX: 620-564-2848. *Librn,* Sharon Sturgis; E-mail: ssturgis@usd355.org; *ILL,* Julie Blakeslee; *Tech Serv,* Mary Lowenthal; Staff 3 (MLS 1, Non-MLS 2)
Pop 2,300; Circ 21,334
Library Holdings: Bk Vols 30,000; Per Subs 85
Automation Activity & Vendor Info: (Cataloging) Follett Software; (Circulation) Follett Software; (ILL) Follett Software
Mem of Central Kansas Library System
Open Mon-Thurs 8-7, Fri 8-4, Sat 10-2

SR SAINT JOHN'S LUTHERAN CHURCH LIBRARY*, 512 N Wilhelm, 67526. SAN 325-5921. Tel: 620-564-2044. *Librn,* Paula Knop
Library Holdings: Audiobooks 40; CDs 200; DVDs 706; Electronic Media & Resources 1; Large Print Bks 135; Bk Titles 5,275; Per Subs 5; Videos 1,103

ELLIS

P ELLIS PUBLIC LIBRARY*, 907 Washington St, 67637. (Mail add: PO Box 107, 67637-0107), SAN 305-8964. Tel: 785-726-3464. FAX: 785-726-3900. E-mail: ellispl@eaglecom.net. *Librn,* Steve Arthur; Staff 1 (Non-MLS 1)
Founded 1876. Pop 1,873
Library Holdings: CDs 30; DVDs 200; Bk Vols 1,440; Per Subs 40
Special Collections: EPL Archives, docs, oral hist; Kansas Coll. Oral History
Subject Interests: Eastern European immigration, Local hist, Railroad hist, Transportation, Westward US expansion
Automation Activity & Vendor Info: (Cataloging) Follett Software; (Circulation) Follett Software
Database Vendor: OCLC FirstSearch
Wireless access
Function: e-mail serv
Mem of Central Kansas Library System
Open Mon-Thurs 12-8, Fri 12-6, Sat 10-2

ELLSWORTH

S KANSAS DEPARTMENT OF CORRECTIONS*, Ellsworth Correctional Facility Inmate Library, 1607 State St, 67439. (Mail add: PO Box 107, 67439-0107). Tel: 785-472-5501, Ext 250; 785-472-6250. FAX: 785-472-4032. *Librn,* Francis J Devadason; E-mail: francisd@doc.ks.gov; *Libr Asst III,* Ellen R Rose; Staff 2 (MLS 2)
Library Holdings: Bks on Deafness & Sign Lang 12; Electronic Media & Resources 1; Bk Titles 11,346; Bk Vols 12,467; Per Subs 28
Automation Activity & Vendor Info: (Cataloging) Follett Software; (Circulation) Follett Software; (OPAC) Follett Software
Function: Copy machines, Electronic databases & coll, ILL available, Jail serv, Legal assistance to inmates, Photocopying/Printing, Ref serv available, Spanish lang bks, Wheelchair accessible
Restriction: Staff & inmates only

P J H ROBBINS MEMORIAL LIBRARY*, City Library, 219 N Lincoln, 67439-3313. SAN 305-8972. Tel: 785-472-3969. FAX: 785-472-4191. E-mail: libirobbins@yahoo.com. Web Site: skyways.lib.ics.us. *Dir,* Linda Homolka
Founded 1913. Pop 3,500; Circ 48,000
Library Holdings: Bk Vols 21,941; Per Subs 69
Special Collections: Cemetery Records of Ellsworth County. Oral History
Automation Activity & Vendor Info: (Cataloging) Follett Software; (Circulation) Follett Software
Mem of Central Kansas Library System
Open Mon & Wed 10-7, Tues, Thurs & Fri 10-6, Sat 10-2

EMPORIA

P EMPORIA PUBLIC LIBRARY*, 110 E Sixth Ave, 66801-3960. SAN 305-8980. Tel: 620-340-6462. Reference Tel: 620-340-6450. Administration Tel: 620-340-6464. FAX: 620-340-6444. Web Site: www.emporialibrary.org, www.skyways.lib.ks.us/library/emporia. *Dir,* Sue Blechl; E-mail: blechls@emporialibrary.org; *Adult Serv,* Lynette Olson; Tel: 620-340-6451, E-mail: olsonlyn@emporialibrary.org; *Ch Serv,* Lori Heller; Tel: 620-340-6467, E-mail: hellerl@emporialibrary.org; *ILL,* Sarah Pound; Staff 3 (MLS 3)
Founded 1869. Pop 35,100; Circ 200,000
Jan 2011-Dec 2011 Income $706,000
Library Holdings: Bk Vols 95,724; Per Subs 203
Subject Interests: Art & archit, Bus & mgt, Genealogy, Local hist, Music, Philos, Theol
Automation Activity & Vendor Info: (Cataloging) SirsiDynix; (Circulation) SirsiDynix; (Serials) SirsiDynix
Database Vendor: Gale Cengage Learning, OCLC FirstSearch
Wireless access
Function: Homebound delivery serv
Mem of North Central Kansas Libraries System
Partic in OCLC Online Computer Library Center, Inc
Open Mon-Thurs 9-8, Fri 9-6, Sat 11-5, Sun 2-5
Friends of the Library Group

C EMPORIA STATE UNIVERSITY*, William Allen White Library, 1200 Commercial St, Box 4051, 66801. SAN 342-0183. Tel: 620-341-5207. Circulation Tel: 620-341-5205. Interlibrary Loan Service Tel: 620-341-5050. Administration Tel: 620-341-5208. Automation Services Tel: 620-341-5058. Toll Free Tel: 877-613-7323. FAX: 620-341-5997. Administration FAX: 620-341-6208. Web Site: library.emporia.edu. *Dean,* Joyce Davis; E-mail: jdavis@emporia.edu; *Head, Instrul Serv,* Cynthia Akers; Tel: 620-341-5480, E-mail: cakers@emporia.edu; *Access Serv,* Terri Summey; E-mail: tsummey@emporia.edu; *Acq,* Betty Norton; Tel: 620-341-5084, E-mail: bnorton@emporia.edu; *Cat,* Beth Hanschu; Tel: 620-341-5055, E-mail: bhanschu@emporia.edu; *Circ,* Kathy Redeker; E-mail: kredeker@emporia.edu; *Info Serv,* Mary E Bogan; Tel: 620-341-5037, E-mail: mbogan@emporia.edu; *ILL,* Candy Johnson; E-mail: cjohnso1@emporia.edu; Staff 19 (MLS 7, Non-MLS 12)
Founded 1863. Enrl 6,000; Fac 347; Highest Degree: Doctorate
Library Holdings: AV Mats 8,012; e-books 8,090; Bk Titles 566,924; Bk Vols 649,621; Per Subs 1,438
Special Collections: Children's Books (May Massee Coll), bk, orig illust; Children's Literature (Mary White Coll); Elizabeth Yates Coll; Emporia State University Materials (Normaliana); Lois Lenski Coll, mss, illust; William Allen White Coll, bks, mss, letters. State Document Depository; US Document Depository
Automation Activity & Vendor Info: (Acquisitions) Innovative Interfaces, Inc; (Cataloging) Innovative Interfaces, Inc; (Circulation) Innovative Interfaces, Inc; (Course Reserve) Innovative Interfaces, Inc; (ILL) Innovative Interfaces, Inc; (Media Booking) Innovative Interfaces, Inc; (OPAC) Innovative Interfaces, Inc; (Serials) Innovative Interfaces, Inc
Database Vendor: Dialog, OVID Technologies, ProQuest
Open Mon-Thurs 7:30am-11pm, Fri 7:30-6, Sat 9-6, Sun Noon-11

C FLINT HILLS TECHNICAL COLLEGE LIBRARY*, 3301 W 18th Ave, 66801. Tel: 620-341-1323. Toll Free Tel: 800-711-6947. FAX: 620-343-4610. Web Site: fhtc.edu/fhtc/library. *Dir,* Janet Anderson-Story; E-mail: janderson@fhtc.edu; Staff 1 (MLS 1)
Founded 1963. Enrl 700; Fac 75; Highest Degree: Associate
Library Holdings: AV Mats 200; Bk Vols 2,500; Per Subs 40
Automation Activity & Vendor Info: (Acquisitions) Auto-Graphics, Inc; (Cataloging) Auto-Graphics, Inc; (Circulation) Auto-Graphics, Inc; (Course Reserve) Auto-Graphics, Inc; (ILL) Auto-Graphics, Inc; (OPAC) Auto-Graphics, Inc
Database Vendor: EBSCOhost, Gale Cengage Learning, OCLC FirstSearch, ProQuest
Wireless access
Function: Computer training, Copy machines, e-mail serv, Electronic databases & coll, Handicapped accessible, Health sci info serv, Homework prog, ILL available, Online searches, Orientations, Outside serv via phone, mail, e-mail & web, Photocopying/Printing, Ref serv available, Telephone ref, VHS videos, Wheelchair accessible, Workshops
Mem of North Central Kansas Libraries System
Open Mon-Fri 7:30am-4pm

P KANSAS STATE LIBRARY*, Kansas Talking Books Service, ESU Memorial Union, 1200 Commercial, Box 4055, 66801-5087. SAN 306-1515. Tel: 620-341-6280. Toll Free Tel: 800-362-0699. E-mail: kslib_talking_books@library.ks.gov. Web Site: kslib.info/talking. *Dir,* Toni Harrell; E-mail: toni.harrell@library.ks.gov; Staff 9 (MLS 5, Non-MLS 4)
Founded 1970. Circ 260,000
Function: Digital talking bks, Handicapped accessible, Mail & tel request accepted, Online cat, Outreach serv, Outside serv via phone, mail, e-mail & web, Summer reading prog, Web-Braille, Web-catalog
Publications: Newsletter
Special Services for the Blind - Braille bks; Descriptive video serv (DVS)
Open Mon-Fri 8-5
Friends of the Library Group

ENTERPRISE

P ENTERPRISE PUBLIC LIBRARY, 202 S Factory, 67441. (Mail add: PO Box 307, 67441-0307), SAN 305-9006. Tel: 785-263-8351. E-mail: eprisepublib@gmail.com. Web Site: enterprise.mykansaslibrary.org. *Librn,* Stephanie Widler
Pop 995; Circ 12,723
Library Holdings: Bk Vols 17,500; Per Subs 48
Wireless access
Publications: Readers Guide
Open Tues & Fri 12-5, Wed & Thurs 1-6

ERIE

P ERIE CITY PUBLIC LIBRARY*, 204 S Butler, 66733-1349. SAN 305-9014. Tel: 620-244-5119. FAX: 620-244-5119. *Librn,* Kindra Holland; E-mail: kindra@erielibrary.kscoxmail.com
Pop 1,400; Circ 14,508
Library Holdings: Bk Vols 13,500; Per Subs 25
Special Collections: Kansas Coll
Automation Activity & Vendor Info: (Cataloging) Follett Software; (Circulation) Follett Software
Mem of Southeast Kansas Library System
Open Mon & Thurs 10-7, Tues, Wed & Fri 10-5, Sat 9-1

ESBON

P ESBON LIBRARY*, 168 Sunflower St, 66941. (Mail add: PO Box 145, 66941-0145). Tel: 785-725-3991. *Librn,* Shirley Marihugh; E-mail: buddym1@hotmail.com
Library Holdings: Bk Vols 2,000
Open Wed 1-5

EUDORA

P EUDORA PUBLIC LIBRARY, 14 E Ninth St, 66025-9478. (Mail add: PO Box 370, 66025-0370), SAN 305-9022. Tel: 785-542-2496. FAX: 785-542-2496. E-mail: eudorapl@sunflower.com. *Dir,* Carol Wohlford
Founded 1967. Pop 4,000; Circ 25,000
Library Holdings: Bk Vols 10,000; Per Subs 40
Automation Activity & Vendor Info: (Cataloging) Follett Software; (Circulation) Follett Software
Wireless access
Mem of Northeast Kansas Library System
Open Mon & Wed 10-8, Tues, Thurs & Fri 10-5, Sat 10-1
Friends of the Library Group

EUREKA

P EUREKA PUBLIC LIBRARY, 606 N Main St, 67045. SAN 305-9030. Tel: 620-583-6222. FAX: 620-583-6222. E-mail: carnegie@fox-net.net. *Dir,* Constance Mitchell; Staff 3 (MLS 1, Non-MLS 2)
Founded 1892. Pop 2,663; Circ 35,000
Jan 2013-Dec 2013 Income $114,932, State $1,052, City $74,887, Locally Generated Income $10,035, Other $28,958. Mats Exp $11,783, Books $8,937, Per/Ser (Incl. Access Fees) $1,656, AV Mat $1,190. Sal $56,912 (Prof $39,937)
Library Holdings: Audiobooks 417; DVDs 747; Large Print Bks 613; Bk Titles 17,500; Bk Vols 18,338; Per Subs 54; Talking Bks 203; Videos 978
Automation Activity & Vendor Info: (Cataloging) SirsiDynix; (Circulation) SirsiDynix; (ILL) Auto-Graphics, Inc; (OPAC) SirsiDynix
Database Vendor: OCLC FirstSearch, Overdrive, Inc, ProQuest, World Book Online
Wireless access
Mem of Southeast Kansas Library System
Open Mon-Sat 10-5:30
Friends of the Library Group

S GREENWOOD COUNTY HISTORICAL SOCIETY LIBRARY*, 120 W Fourth, 67045-1445. SAN 371-7941. Tel: 316-583-6682. E-mail: gwhistory@sbcglobal.net. *Pres,* Barbara Robison
Library Holdings: Bk Titles 500
Special Collections: Oral History
Subject Interests: Genealogy

EVEREST

P BARNES READING ROOM*, 640 Main St, 66424. (Mail add: PO Box 204, 66424-0204), SAN 305-9049. Tel: 785-548-7733 (www.everest.mykanaslibrary.org). FAX: 785-548-7733. E-mail: barnesreadingroom@rainbowtel.net. *Dir,* Nancy Linck
Pop 433; Circ 3,134
Library Holdings: Bk Vols 7,413; Per Subs 10
Mem of Northeast Kansas Library System
Open Tues 3:30-7:30, Wed & Fri 3:30-6:30, Thurs 3:30-5, Sat 8-11:30

FALL RIVER

P FALL RIVER PUBLIC LIBRARY*, 314 Merchant Ave, 67047. SAN 376-804X. Tel: 620-658-4973. E-mail: fallriverlibrary@yahoo.com. *Librn,* Carol Palsmeier
Library Holdings: Bk Vols 6,000
Open Mon 1-5, Thurs 2-6

FLORENCE

P FLORENCE PUBLIC LIBRARY*, 324 Main St, 66851. SAN 305-9057. Tel: 620-878-4649. E-mail: library.florence@gmail.com. *Dir,* Alice Johnson
Pop 672; Circ 7,000
Library Holdings: Bk Vols 8,200; Per Subs 21
Open Tues, Thurs & Fri 2-5, Wed 2 7, Sat 9-Noon

FORD

P FORD CITY LIBRARY*, E Eighth St, 67842-0108. (Mail add: PO Box 68, 67842), SAN 376-7221. Tel: 620-369-2820. FAX: 620-369-2216. E-mail: fordlib@ucom.net. Web Site: www.trails.net/wkls/fordlibrary.htm. *Librn,* Kay Johnson-Craig
Library Holdings: Bk Vols 5,200; Per Subs 23
Mem of Southwest Kansas Library System
Open Mon 9-2, Tues 9-1, Thurs 1-7

FORMOSO

P FORMOSO PUBLIC LIBRARY*, 204 Main St, 66942-9802. (Mail add: PO Box 10, 66942-0010), SAN 305-9065. Tel: 785-794-2424. E-mail: libfor@nckcn.com. *Librn,* Barbara Langston
Pop 124; Circ 1,800
Library Holdings: Bk Vols 4,202
Mem of Central Kansas Library System

FORT LEAVENWORTH

UNITED STATES ARMY

A COMBINED ARMS RESEARCH LIBRARY*, US Army Command & General Staff College, Eisenhower Hall, 250 Gibbon Ave, 66027-2314, SAN 342-0302. Tel: 913-758-3001. Circulation Tel: 913-758-3002. Interlibrary Loan Service Tel: 913-758-3017. Reference Tel: 913-758-3053. Administration Tel: 913-758-3033. FAX: 913-758-3014. Web Site: carl.army.mil. *Dir,* Edwin B Burgess; E-mail: edwin.b.burgess.civ@mail.mil; *Dep Dir, Pub Serv Librn,* Pamela S Bennett; Tel: 913-758-3058, E-mail: pamela.bennett@us.army.mil; *Acq Librn,* Tiffany L Konczey; Tel: 913-758-3013, E-mail: tiffany.konczey@us.army.mil; *Chief Doc Librn,* Rusty P Rafferty; Tel: 913-758-3128, E-mail: russ.rafferty@us.army.mil; *Sr Ref Librn,* Joanne E Knight; E-mail: joanne.knight@us.army.mil; *Archives Chief,* Kathleen M Buker; Tel: 913-758-3161, E-mail: kathleen.buker@us.army.mil; *Circ Supvr,* Kelsey Reed; Tel: 913-758-3005, E-mail: kelsey.e.reed.civ@mail.mil; *Syst Adminr,* Patricia E Knuth; Tel: 913-758-3019, E-mail: pat.knuth@us.army.mil; Staff 29 (MLS 19, Non-MLS 10)
Founded 1882
Library Holdings: Bk Vols 320,000; Per Subs 642
Special Collections: Combined Arms & Fort Leavenworth Archives
Subject Interests: Land warfare, Leadership, Mil hist, Nat security
Automation Activity & Vendor Info: (Acquisitions) Horizon; (Cataloging) Horizon; (Circulation) Horizon; (ILL) OCLC; (OPAC) Horizon; (Serials) Horizon
Database Vendor: ABC-CLIO, Baker & Taylor, Blackwell, CountryWatch, EBSCOhost, Gale Cengage Learning, LexisNexis, Newsbank, OCLC FirstSearch, OCLC WorldShare Interlibrary Loan, Overdrive, Inc, ProQuest, SirsiDynix
Function: Bks on cassette, Bks on CD, Children's prog, Digital talking bks, e-mail serv, Electronic databases & coll, Free DVD rentals, ILL available, Online ref, Online searches, Orientations, Outreach serv, Outside serv via phone, mail, e-mail & web, OverDrive digital audio bks, Prog for children & young adult, Pub access computers, Ref & res, Ref serv available, Ref serv in person, Res libr, Scanner, Spoken cassettes & CDs, Spoken cassettes & DVDs, Story hour, Summer reading prog, Telephone ref, VHS videos, Workshops
Partic in Fedlink; MECC/LWG
Open Mon-Thurs 7-7, Fri 7-4:30, Sat & Sun 10-5
Restriction: Open to fac, students & qualified researchers, Open to pub for ref & circ; with some limitations

A UNITED STATES DISCIPLINARY BARRACKS LIBRARY*, 1301 N Warehouse Rd, 66027-2304. Tel: 913-758-3864. FAX: 913-758-3927. *Librn,* Angela Perry; E-mail: angela.e.perry@us.army.mil; Staff 2 (MLS 1, Non-MLS 1)
Library Holdings: Bk Vols 11,300; Per Subs 13
Function: Adult literacy prog, Jail serv
Restriction: Clients only, Govt use only, Inmate patrons, facility staff & vols direct access. All others through ILL only, Not a lending libr, Not open to pub

FORT RILEY

UNITED STATES ARMY

A FORT RILEY POST LIBRARY*, Bldg 5306, Hood Dr, 66442-6416, SAN 342-0337. Tel: 785-239-5305. FAX: 785-239-4422. *Librn, Project Mgr,* Terri Seaman; E-mail: terri.seaman@us.army.mil; *Cataloger/Ref Librn,* John Triplett; Tel: 785-239-9582, E-mail: john.triplett@us.army.mil; Staff 4 (MLS 1, Non-MLS 3)
Library Holdings: AV Mats 3,000; DVDs 700; Large Print Bks 45; Bk Titles 21,000; Bk Vols 22,000; Per Subs 60; Talking Bks 320; Videos 1,800
Subject Interests: Mil hist
Automation Activity & Vendor Info: (Cataloging) OCLC Connexion; (Circulation) Horizon; (OPAC) Horizon; (Serials) Horizon
Function: Electronic databases & coll, Family literacy, Handicapped accessible, Prog for children & young adult, Spoken cassettes & CDs, Summer reading prog
Special Services for the Blind - Bks on CD; Home delivery serv; Talking bks & player equip
Open Tues-Sat 11-6, Sun 12-5

AM IRWIN ARMY COMMUNITY HOSPITAL MEDICAL LIBRARY, CDR USAMEDDAC-Med Libr, 600 Caisson Hill Rd, 66442-7037, SAN 320-9288. Tel: 785-239-7874. FAX: 785-239-7626. *Med Librn,* Phyllis Whiteside; E-mail: phyllis.j.whiteside.civ@mail.mil
Partic in Midcontinental Regional Med Libr Program
Open Mon-Fri 7:30-11 & 12-4:30

S UNITED STATES CAVALRY ASSOCIATION*, United States Cavalry Memorial Research Library, Bldg 247, Cameron Ave, 66442. (Mail add: PO Box 2325, 66442-0325). Tel: 785-784-5797. FAX: 785-784-5797. E-mail: cavalry@flinthills.com. Web Site: www.uscavalry.org. *Exec Dir,* Patricia Spurrier-Bright; *Curator,* Robert Smith
Founded 1999
Library Holdings: Bk Vols 4,000; Per Subs 20
Special Collections: Cavalry Biography, biographical data files, Hiram Tuttle Papers (US Army Officer, Member of US Olympic Equestrian Team 1932 & 1936)
Subject Interests: Archives, Equine/equestrian, Manuscripts
Open Mon-Fri 8-4

S US CAVALRY MUSEUM*, Museum Division Library & Archives, Bldg 263, Cameron Ave, 66442. (Mail add: Bldg 500, Huebner Rd, 66442), SAN 329-3025. Tel: 785-239-8234. FAX: 785-239-6243. Web Site: www.rileymwr.com. *Dir,* Bill McKale

Library Holdings: Bk Titles 8,000; Per Subs 34
Subject Interests: First infantry div hist, Mil hist, US cavalry hist
Open Mon-Fri 8-12 & 12:30-4:30
Restriction: Open to pub upon request

FORT SCOTT

J FORT SCOTT COMMUNITY COLLEGE LIBRARY, 2108 S Horton, 66701. SAN 305-9073. Tel: 620-223-2700, Ext 3441. FAX: 620-223-6530. Web Site: www.fortscott.edu/academics/library.asp. *Dir,* Stacy Dzbenski; E-mail: stacyd@fortscott.edu; Staff 4 (MLS 2, Non-MLS 2)
Founded 1919. Enrl 2,660; Fac 48
Library Holdings: Bk Vols 10,000; Per Subs 10
Subject Interests: Kansas
Automation Activity & Vendor Info: (Cataloging) SirsiDynix; (Circulation) SirsiDynix
Database Vendor: EBSCOhost, Gale Cengage Learning
Wireless access
Open Mon-Fri 8-5

P FORT SCOTT PUBLIC LIBRARY*, 201 S National, 66701. SAN 305-9081. Tel: 620-223-2882. *Dir,* Lisa Walter; *Ch Serv,* Julie Townsend
Pop 8,893
Library Holdings: Bk Vols 38,000; Per Subs 50
Subject Interests: Kansas, Local hist
Automation Activity & Vendor Info: (Cataloging) Follett Software; (Circulation) Follett Software
Mem of Southeast Kansas Library System
Open Mon-Fri 9-6, Sat 9-2

FOWLER

P FOWLER PUBLIC LIBRARY*, 510 Main St, 67844-0135. SAN 305-909X. Tel: 620-646-5550. FAX: 620-646-5439. E-mail: director@fowlerlibrary.info. Web Site: www.fowlerlibrary.info. *Dir,* Becky Heinz
Founded 1963. Pop 650
Library Holdings: Bk Titles 11,180; Per Subs 30
Open Mon Noon-7, Tues & Sat 10-3, Wed 10-5

FRANKFORT

P FRANKFORT CITY LIBRARY*, 104 E Second St, 66427-1403. SAN 305-9103. Tel: 785-292-4320. E-mail: franklib@bluevalley.net. *Dir,* Alice Jones
Founded 1888
Library Holdings: Bk Vols 10,000; Per Subs 25
Special Collections: Kansas History
Wireless access
Mem of North Central Kansas Libraries System
Open Mon 1-5, Tues, Thurs & Fri 9-12 & 1-5, Wed 1-8

FREDONIA

P FREDONIA PUBLIC LIBRARY*, 807 Jefferson, 66736. SAN 305-9111. Tel: 620-378-2863. FAX: 620-378-2645. E-mail: fredodir@twinmounds.com. Web Site: www.skyways.lib.ks.us/town/fredonia/index.html. *Dir,* Michelle Hulse; *Asst Dir,* Pamela Medkey
Founded 1914. Circ 27,865
Jan 2006-Dec 2006 Income $72,000
Library Holdings: Bk Vols 35,000; Per Subs 25
Automation Activity & Vendor Info: (Cataloging) Follett Software; (Circulation) Follett Software
Open Mon-Thurs 10-8, Fri 10-6, Sat 10-12
Friends of the Library Group

S WILSON COUNTY HISTORICAL SOCIETY*, Museum Library, 420 N Seventh St, 66736-1315. SAN 325-5948. Tel: 620-378-3965. E-mail: wilcohisoc@twinmounds.com. *Pres,* Emma Crites; *Curator,* Nadine Dishman
Founded 1968
Jul 2005-Jun 2006 Income $12,000, County $5,500. Sal $5,700
Library Holdings: Bk Vols 1,000
Special Collections: Family Histories; History & Genealogy Coll. Oral History
Subject Interests: Local hist
Publications: Our Yesteryear II (Newsletter)
Open Mon-Fri 1-4:30

GALENA

P GALENA PUBLIC LIBRARY*, 315 W Seventh St, 66739-1293. SAN 305-912X. Tel: 620-783-5132. FAX: 620-783-5030. E-mail: galenapubliclibrary@yahoo.com. *Librn,* Nellie Hoskins
Pop 3,731; Circ 22,483
Library Holdings: Bk Vols 35,000; Per Subs 52
Special Collections: Cemetary records for Cherokee County; Genealogy Coll; Local Newspapers, 1877
Mem of Southeast Kansas Library System
Open Mon, Wed & Fri 9-1, Tues & Thurs 1-5
Friends of the Library Group

GARDEN CITY

P FINNEY COUNTY PUBLIC LIBRARY*, 605 E Walnut St, 67846. SAN 305-9146. Tel: 620-272-3680. FAX: 620-272-3682. Web Site: www.fcpl.homestead.com. *Dir,* Erin Francoeur; *Dep Dir,* Elaine Scheuerman; *Youth Serv,* Judy Cole; E-mail: judyc_fcpl@hotmail.com; Staff 16 (Non-MLS 16)
Founded 1897. Pop 40,000; Circ 240,000
Library Holdings: AV Mats 4,216; Bk Vols 100,000; Per Subs 300
Special Collections: Kansas Coll; Powell Coll; Spanish & Vietnamese Literature
Subject Interests: Genealogy, Kansas
Automation Activity & Vendor Info: (Cataloging) SirsiDynix; (Circulation) SirsiDynix
Database Vendor: OCLC FirstSearch
Wireless access
Mem of Southwest Kansas Library System
Special Services for the Blind - Internet workstation with adaptive software; Reader equip
Open Mon-Thurs 9-9, Fri & Sat 9-6, Sun 1-6
Friends of the Library Group

J GARDEN CITY COMMUNITY COLLEGE*, Thomas F Saffell Library, 801 Campus Dr, 67846. SAN 305-9138. Tel: 620-276-9511. FAX: 620-276-9630. E-mail: library@gcccks.edu. Web Site: www.gcccks.edu/library/saffell/index.htm. *ILL,* Kathy Winter; Tel: 620-276-9656, E-mail: kathy.winter@gcccks.edu; Staff 4 (MLS 1, Non-MLS 3)
Founded 1919. Enrl 2,233; Fac 110; Highest Degree: Associate
Library Holdings: Bk Titles 33,000; Bk Vols 47,000; Per Subs 100
Automation Activity & Vendor Info: (Cataloging) Follett Software; (Circulation) Follett Software; (OPAC) Follett Software
Database Vendor: Gale Cengage Learning, LexisNexis, OCLC FirstSearch
Function: ILL available
Open Mon-Thurs 8am-10pm, Fri 8-4:30, Sun 6pm-10pm

GARDEN PLAIN

P GARDEN PLAIN COMMUNITY LIBRARY*, 502 N Main, 67050. Tel: 316-535-2990. FAX: 316-535-2990. E-mail: gpcomlib@yahoo.com. *Head Librn,* Joyce Loehr; *Asst Librn,* Michelle Mannebach
Library Holdings: Bk Vols 7,747
Mem of South Central Kansas Library System
Open Mon & Tues 3-5, Wed 3-5 & 6-8, Sat 10-12

GARNETT

P GARNETT PUBLIC LIBRARY*, 125 W Fourth St, 66032-1350. (Mail add: PO Box 385, 66032-0385), SAN 305-9154. Tel: 785-448-3388. FAX: 785-448-3936. E-mail: garnettlibrary@yahoo.com. *Dir,* Andrea Sobba; *Actg Head Librn,* Rose Scarlet
Founded 1912. Pop 3,179; Circ 54,000
Library Holdings: Bk Vols 30,000; Per Subs 35
Special Collections: Mary Bridget McAuliffe Walker Art Coll
Automation Activity & Vendor Info: (Acquisitions) Follett Software; (Cataloging) Follett Software; (OPAC) Follett Software
Mem of Southeast Kansas Library System
Open Mon, Tues & Thurs 10-8, Wed & Fri 10-5:30, Sat 10-4
Friends of the Library Group

GAYLORD

P GAYLORD CITY LIBRARY*, 505 Main, 67638-3884. SAN 376-5121. Tel: 785-697-2650. *Librn,* Donna Muck
Library Holdings: Bk Vols 3,000
Mem of Central Kansas Library System
Open Tues, Thurs & Sat 9-11

GENESEO

P GENESEO PUBLIC LIBRARY, 725 Main St, 67444-9702. (Mail add: PO Box 166, 67444-0166), SAN 305-9162. Tel: 620-824-6140. E-mail: gplib@hometelco.net. *Librn,* Veronica Bauer
Pop 521; Circ 5,350
Library Holdings: Bk Vols 5,000; Per Subs 70
Special Collections: Kansas History Coll
Mem of South Central Kansas Library System
Open Mon 9-12 & 1-5, Wed & Fri 1-5

GIRARD

P GIRARD PUBLIC LIBRARY*, 128 W Prairie Ave, 66743-1498. SAN 305-9170. Tel: 620-724-4317. FAX: 620-724-8374. E-mail: girardpl@ckt.net. Web Site: girardpubliclibrary.net. *Dir,* Terri Harley; Staff 6 (Non-MLS 6)
Founded 1899. Pop 3,160; Circ 38,859
Library Holdings: Audiobooks 2,579; AV Mats 3,508; Bks on Deafness & Sign Lang 22; e-books 99; Large Print Bks 523; Bk Titles 33,048; Per Subs 79
Special Collections: Crawford County History Coll; Halderman-Julius (Little Blue Books), Kansas Authors; The Girard Press (1869-1999), micro
Automation Activity & Vendor Info: (Circulation) ComPanion Corp; (Serials) EBSCO Online
Wireless access
Mem of Southeast Kansas Library System
Special Services for the Blind - Accessible computers; Audio mat; Bks on cassette; Bks on CD; Cassettes; Copier with enlargement capabilities; Large print bks; Playaways (bks on MP3); Radio reading serv; Recorded bks; Talking bk & rec for the blind cat
Open Mon 9:30-7, Tues-Thurs 9:30-6, Fri 9:30-5, Sat 9:30-3

GLASCO

P GLASCO CITY LIBRARY*, 206 E Main St, 67445. (Mail add: PO Box 595, 67445-0595), SAN 305-9189. Tel: 785-568-2313. *Librn,* Patricia Horn
Founded 1916. Pop 600; Circ 5,700
Library Holdings: Bk Vols 10,250; Per Subs 40
Mem of Central Kansas Library System
Open Tues & Fri 2-6, Wed 2-5, Thurs 10-Noon, Sat 9-Noon

GLEN ELDER

P GLEN ELDER LIBRARY*, 105 S Mill, 67446. (Mail add: PO Box 188, 67446-0188). Tel: 785-545-3632. *Librn,* Rachel Jones
Pop 475; Circ 1,716
Library Holdings: Large Print Bks 100; Bk Titles 3,966; Per Subs 12; Talking Bks 10
Special Collections: Glen Elder History Coll; School History of Glen Elder Coll
Wireless access
Mem of Central Kansas Library System
Open Tues 10-12 & 1:30-5:30, Thurs 1:30-5:30
Friends of the Library Group

GODDARD

P GODDARD PUBLIC LIBRARY*, 315 S Main St, 67052. (Mail add: PO Box 443, 67052-0443), SAN 305-9200. Tel: 316-794-8771. E-mail: goddardlib@yahoo.com. *Librn,* Kendra Mork
Founded 1969. Pop 1,900; Circ 20,120
Library Holdings: Bk Vols 15,049; Per Subs 50
Mem of South Central Kansas Library System
Open Mon, Wed & Fri 1-5, Tues & Thurs 10-7, Sat 9-Noon

GOESSEL

P GOESSEL PUBLIC LIBRARY*, 101 S Cedar, 67053. (Mail add: PO Box 36, 67053-0036), SAN 305-9219. Tel: 620-367-8440. FAX: 620-367-2774. E-mail: goeslib@mtelco.net. Web Site: skyways.lib.ks.us/library/goessel. *Dir,* Laura Dailey; Staff 2 (Non-MLS 2)
Founded 1968. Pop 565; Circ 3,000
Library Holdings: Large Print Bks 100; Bk Vols 700; Per Subs 20; Spec Interest Per Sub 10; Talking Bks 200; Videos 400
Automation Activity & Vendor Info: (Cataloging) Book Systems; (Circulation) Book Systems
Function: Computers for patron use, Copy machines, Free DVD rentals, ILL available, Online cat, Preschool reading prog, Scanner, Story hour, Summer reading prog
Mem of North Central Kansas Libraries System
Open Mon 4-8, Tues 5-7, Fri 9-2, Sat 9-12

GOODLAND

P GOODLAND PUBLIC LIBRARY*, 812 Broadway, 67735. SAN 305-9227. Tel: 785-899-5461. FAX: 785-899-5461. Web Site: www.goodlandlibrary.org. *Dir,* Karen Gillihan; E-mail: karen@gplibrary.org; *Adult Serv,* Laura McClung; E-mail: lauraj@eaglecom.net; *Ch Serv,* Marcy Melia; E-mail: marcy@eaglecom.net; Staff 5 (Non-MLS 5)
Founded 1912. Pop 5,000; Circ 51,000
Jan 2006-Dec 2006 Income $167,000, State $3,200, City $122,000, County $15,000, Locally Generated Income $7,800. Mats Exp $167,000, Books $18,000, Per/Ser (Incl. Access Fees) $4,500, AV Equip $4,300, Electronic Ref Mat (Incl. Access Fees) $1,000. Sal $86,000
Library Holdings: CDs 800; DVDs 345; Large Print Bks 1,717; Bk Vols 46,000; Per Subs 150; Talking Bks 1,800; Videos 1,031
Automation Activity & Vendor Info: (Cataloging) Follett Software; (Circulation) Follett Software; (OPAC) Follett Software
Database Vendor: Gale Cengage Learning, OCLC FirstSearch
Wireless access
Mem of Northwest Kansas Library System
Open Mon-Thurs (Winter) 10-8, Fri & Sat 10-5; Mon-Thurs (Summer) 10-7, Fri & Sat 10-5

GOVE

P GOVE CITY LIBRARY*, 519 Broad St, 67736. (Mail add: PO Box 66, 67736-0066), SAN 305-9235. Tel: 785-938-2242. E-mail: govelib@ruraltel.net. *Librn,* Rayna Kopriva
Founded 1937. Pop 148; Circ 1,964
Library Holdings: Bk Vols 3,623
Mem of Northwest Kansas Library System
Open Tues & Thurs 2:30-5:30, Wed 4-7

GRAINFIELD

P GRAINFIELD CITY LIBRARY*, 242 Main, 67737. (Mail add: PO Box 154, 67737-0154), SAN 305-9243. Tel: 785-673-4770. E-mail: grain1lb@ruraltel.net. *Librn,* Anna Whiteman
Pop 417; Circ 2,410
Library Holdings: Bk Vols 4,086
Wireless access
Mem of Northwest Kansas Library System
Open Tues & Wed 3-6, Thurs 9:30-11:30

GREAT BEND

J BARTON COUNTY COMMUNITY COLLEGE LIBRARY*, 245 NE 30 Rd, 67530. SAN 305-9251. Tel: 620-792-9362. FAX: 620-792-3238. Web Site: www.bartonccc.edu/library. *Dir, Learning Res,* ReGina Reynolds-Casper; E-mail: casperr@bartonccc.edu
Founded 1969
Library Holdings: Bk Vols 30,000; Per Subs 130
Special Collections: Rural Gerontology Grant Coll
Subject Interests: Nursing
Automation Activity & Vendor Info: (Cataloging) Book Systems; (Circulation) Book Systems
Database Vendor: Gale Cengage Learning
Mem of Central Kansas Library System
Open Mon-Thurs 7:30am-9:30pm, Fri 7:30-4:30, Sun 3:30-9:30

P CENTRAL KANSAS LIBRARY SYSTEM*, 1409 Williams St, 67530-4020. SAN 305-926X. Tel: 620-792-4865. Toll Free Tel: 800-362-2642 (Kansas only). FAX: 620-792-5495. Administration FAX: 620-793-7270. Web Site: www.ckls.org. *Dir,* Harry Willems; *Admin Mgr,* Vickie Herl; E-mail: vherl@ckls.org; *Supvr, Automation Serv,* Steve Thomas; E-mail: sthomas@ckls.org; *Supvr, Ref & Outreach Serv,* Gail Santy; E-mail: gsanty@ckls.org; *Supvr, Tech Serv & ILL,* Kathleen Rippel; E-mail: kdr@ckls.org; *Supvr, Youth Serv,* Patty Collins; Staff 8 (MLS 4, Non-MLS 4)
Founded 1968. Pop 202,000
Library Holdings: Bk Vols 30,000; Per Subs 50
Wireless access
Publications: Post (Newsletter); Trustee Handbook
Member Libraries: Barnard Library; Barton County Community College Library; Bison Community Library; Burdett Community Library; Burr Oak City Library; Cawker City Public Library; Clyde Public Library; Courtland Community Library; Delphos Public Library; Downs Carnegie Library; Ellinwood School & Community Library; Ellis Public Library; Formoso Public Library; Fort Hays State University; Frank Carlson Library; Gaylord City Library; Glasco City Library; Glen Elder Library; Great Bend Public Library; Gypsum Community Library; Hays Public Library; Hillcrest Public Library; Hoisington Public Library; Independent Township Library; J H Robbins Memorial Library; Jamestown City Library; Jewell Public Library; Jordaan Memorial Library; Kanopolis Public Library; Kansas Department of Corrections; Kansas State University at Salina; Kensington Community-School Library; Kirwin City Library; Lang Memorial Library; Larned State Hospital; Lebanon-Community Library; Lincoln Carnegie Library; Logan Public Library; Mankato City Library; McCracken Public Library; Minneapolis Public Library; Osborne Public Library; Otis Community Library; Palco Public Library; Phillipsburg City Library; Plainville Memorial Library; Port Library; Rae Hobson Memorial Library; Randall Public Library; Russell Public Library; Salina Public Library; Scandia City Library; Smith Center Public Library; Stockton Public Library; Sunshine City Library; Sylvan Grove Public Library
Special Services for the Blind - Low vision equip
Open Mon-Fri 9-5

Branches: 1

P SUBREGIONAL LIBRARY FOR THE BLIND & PHYSICALLY HANDICAPPED, 1409 Williams St, 67530-4020. Tel: 620-792-4865. Toll Free Tel: 800-362-2642 (Kansas only). FAX: 620-792-5495. *Supvr,* Cathy Rhan
Founded 1973. Circ 34,000
Library Holdings: Large Print Bks 3,198; Talking Bks 20,088
Open Mon-Fri 9-5

Bookmobiles: 1. Gail Santy, Supervisor

P GREAT BEND PUBLIC LIBRARY*, 1409 Williams St, 67530-4090. SAN 305-9286. Tel: 620-792-2409. FAX: 620-792-5495, 620-793-7270. *Dir,* Harry A Willems; *AV, Dir, Pub Relations, Pub Serv,* Terri Hurley; E-mail: thurley@ckls.org; *Head, Ch,* Sandy Dayton; E-mail: sdayton@ckls.org; *Head, Circ,* Marilyn Malbrough; E-mail: mmalbro@ckls.org; *Coll Develop, Head, Ref,* Cara Negaard; E-mail: cnegaard@ckls.org; *Automation Serv, Head, Tech Serv,* Romona Newsome; E-mail: romona@ckls.org; Staff 2 (MLS 2)
Founded 1908. Pop 15,000; Circ 200,000
Jan 2006-Dec 2006 Income $720,481
Library Holdings: Bk Vols 100,000; Per Subs 300
Special Collections: Petroleum Geology (American Petroleum Institute Coll). Oral History
Automation Activity & Vendor Info: (Acquisitions) Follett Software; (Cataloging) Follett Software; (Circulation) Follett Software; (OPAC) Follett Software
Mem of Central Kansas Library System
Partic in OCLC Online Computer Library Center, Inc
Open Mon 12-9, Tues-Thurs 10-9, Fri & Sat 10-5, Sun 1-5

GREENSBURG

P KIOWA COUNTY LIBRARY*, 320 S Main, Ste 120, 67054. SAN 305-9294. Tel: 620-723-1118. *Head Librn,* Debby Allison; *Asst Librn,* Cassie Blackburn; Staff 2 (Non-MLS 2)
Founded 1936
Library Holdings: Bk Vols 12,000; Per Subs 18
Automation Activity & Vendor Info: (Cataloging) Biblionix; (Circulation) Biblionix
Wireless access
Open Mon-Fri 9:30-5:30, Sat 9:30-Noon

Branches: 2

HAVILAND BRANCH, 112 N Main, Haviland, 67059. (Mail add: PO Box 295, Haviland, 67059). Tel: 620-862-5350. E-mail: kwcolib@hotmail.com. *Br Librn,* Charles Townsend
Founded 1936
Library Holdings: Bk Vols 44,825; Per Subs 52
Open Mon-Fri 1-5

MULLINVILLE BRANCH, 115 N Main, Mullinville, 67109. (Mail add: PO Box 137, Mullinville, 67109-0137). Tel: 620-548-2630. *Br Librn,* Jodi Behee; Staff 0.5 (Non-MLS 0.5)
Pop 200; Circ 2,353
Open Mon-Fri 2-5

GRENOLA

P GRENOLA PUBLIC LIBRARY*, 205 S Main St, 67346. (Mail add: PO Box 131, 67346-0131), SAN 305-9308. Tel: 620-358-3707. FAX: 620-358-3820. E-mail: grenlib@sktc.net. *Librn,* Dixie A Conklin; Staff 1 (Non-MLS 1)
Founded 1950. Pop 347; Circ 2,082
Library Holdings: Bk Vols 5,500; Per Subs 15
Mem of Southeast Kansas Library System
Open Mon 4-7, Wed 2-6, Fri 9-12, Sat 9-4

GRINNELL

P MOORE FAMILY LIBRARY*, 95 S Adams, 67738. (Mail add: PO Box 159, 67738-0159), SAN 376-5512. Tel: 785-824-3885. E-mail: moorefamilylibrary@yahoo.com. *Dir,* Pat Baalman
Founded 1985
Library Holdings: Bk Vols 5,000
Wireless access
Function: ILL available, Ref serv available, Summer reading prog
Mem of Northwest Kansas Library System
Open Mon & Wed 4:30-6:30, Sat 9:30-11:30

GYPSUM

P GYPSUM COMMUNITY LIBRARY*, 521 Maple, 67448-9783. (Mail add: PO Box 19, 67448-0019), SAN 305-9324. Tel: 785-536-4319. FAX: 785-536-4296. *Librn,* Peggy Woods
Founded 1910. Pop 423; Circ 2,827
Library Holdings: Bk Vols 9,500; Per Subs 20
Mem of Central Kansas Library System
Open Mon (Winter) 4-8, Wed 1-6, Sat 10-3; Mon (Summer) 4-8, Wed 1-6, Fri 10-3

HALSTEAD

P HALSTEAD PUBLIC LIBRARY*, 264 Main St, 67056-0285. SAN 305-9332. Tel: 316-835-2170. FAX: 316-835-2170. E-mail: halpublib@hotmail.com. *Pres,* Joan Parnell; *Dir,* Elizabeth Cain
Founded 1905. Pop 2,000; Circ 14,000
Jan 2009-Dec 2009 Income $81,000
Library Holdings: Bk Vols 18,000; Per Subs 33
Special Collections: Halstead City History Coll; Kansas Coll
Mem of South Central Kansas Library System
Open Mon, Wed & Fri 10-5, Tues & Thurs 10-8, Sat 10-2

HAMILTON

P HAMILTON CITY LIBRARY*, 21 E Main St, 66853-9768. (Mail add: PO Box 128, 66853-0128), SAN 305-9359. Tel: 620-678-3646. FAX: 620-678-3646. E-mail: hclibrary66853@yahoo.com. *Librn,* Leta Harrell
Founded 1970. Pop 380; Circ 2,213
Library Holdings: Bk Titles 7,400; Per Subs 14
Mem of Southeast Kansas Library System
Open Tues & Wed 3-7, Thurs 3-6, Fri 10-6

HANOVER

P HANOVER PUBLIC LIBRARY*, 205 Jackson St, 66945-8874. (Mail add: PO Box 97, 66945-0097), SAN 305-9367. Tel: 785-337-2424. E-mail: hanlib@bluevalley.net. *Librn,* Judy Springer
Founded 1954. Pop 839
Library Holdings: Bk Vols 18,000; Per Subs 50
Open Tues, Thurs & Sat 12-5, Wed 8-1

HANSTON

P HANSTON CITY LIBRARY*, 105 N Logan, 67849-9409. SAN 373-8981. Tel: 620-623-2798. *Dir,* Karen S Salmans; E-mail: salmans@ucom.net; *Asst City Librn,* Barb Ewy; Tel: 620-623-4987; Staff 2 (Non-MLS 2)
Founded 1963. Pop 287; Circ 2,469
Library Holdings: AV Mats 379; Bk Vols 5,138; Per Subs 23; Talking Bks 106
Function: Homebound delivery serv, ILL available, Online searches, Photocopying/Printing, Prog for children & young adult, Summer reading prog
Mem of Southwest Kansas Library System
Open Mon 1-6, Wed 1-5, Sat 9-12

HARDTNER

P HARDTNER PUBLIC LIBRARY*, 102 E Central, 67057. (Mail add: PO Box 36, 67057-0036), SAN 305-9375. Tel: 620-296-4586. E-mail: hardtlb@kanokla.net. Web Site: skyways.lib.ks.us/towns/Hardtner/. *Librn,* Joy Helmer
Founded 1913. Pop 336; Circ 1,638
Library Holdings: Bk Vols 10,000; Per Subs 20
Mem of South Central Kansas Library System
Open Tues 2-8, Sat 1-5
Friends of the Library Group

HARPER

P HARPER PUBLIC LIBRARY, 708 W 14th, 67058-1233. SAN 305-9383. Tel: 620-896-2959. FAX: 620-896-2778. E-mail: harperlib@cyberlodge.com. *Dir,* Tina Welch; *Asst Librn,* Michelle Harder; Staff 2 (Non-MLS 2)
Founded 1876. Pop 1,700; Circ 16,354
Library Holdings: Bk Vols 16,800; Per Subs 62
Mem of South Central Kansas Library System
Open Mon 1:30-8, Tues, Thurs & Fri 1:30-5:30, Wed 9-12 & 1:30-8, Sat 9-1

HARTFORD

P ELMENDARO TOWNSHIP LIBRARY*, 224 Commercial St, 66854. (Mail add: PO Box 38, 66854-0038), SAN 305-9391. Tel: 620-392-5518. E-mail: elmlibhartford@gmail.com. *Dir,* Catherine Schmidt
Founded 1966. Pop 1,700
Library Holdings: Bk Vols 10,000; Per Subs 40
Subject Interests: Econ, Health, Soc sci & issues, Spec needs
Wireless access
Mem of North Central Kansas Libraries System
Special Services for the Blind - Talking bks
Open Mon & Thurs 2-6, Tues 9:30-2, Wed 3-7, Fri 9:30-1

HAVEN

P HAVEN PUBLIC LIBRARY*, 121 N Kansas Ave, 67543. (Mail add: PO Box 340, 67543-0340), SAN 373-8973. Tel: 620-465-3524. FAX: 620-465-3524. E-mail: havenlibrarian@gmail.com. *Admin Librn,* Trudy Littlestar; *Ch,* Stephanie Confer; Staff 2 (Non-MLS 2)
Founded 1902. Pop 1,175; Circ 12,391
Library Holdings: Bk Vols 11,325; Per Subs 52
Wireless access
Mem of South Central Kansas Library System
Open Tues & Thurs 12-7, Wed 12-5, Fri & Sat 9-2
Friends of the Library Group

HAVILAND

C BARCLAY COLLEGE*, Worden Memorial Library, 100 E Cherry St, 67059. SAN 305-9413. Tel: 620-862-5274. FAX: 620-862-5403. E-mail: interlibraryloan@barclaycollege.edu, library@barclaycollege.edu. Web Site: www.barclaycollege.edu/academics/library.asp. *Libr Dir,* Pat Hall; Staff 1 (MLS 1)
Founded 1892. Enrl 197; Fac 18; Highest Degree: Master
Library Holdings: Bk Vols 50,000; Per Subs 75
Special Collections: Quaker Rare Books
Subject Interests: Relig
Automation Activity & Vendor Info: (Cataloging) Follett Software; (Circulation) Follett Software; (Serials) Follett Software
Database Vendor: EBSCOhost, Gale Cengage Learning, OCLC FirstSearch, ProQuest
Function: CD-ROM, For res purposes, ILL available, Music CDs, VHS videos
Open Mon & Wed 7:50-5:30 & 7-11, Tues & Thurs 7:50-10:45, 12:30-5:30 & 7-11, Fri 7:50-4, Sat 1-5, Sun 2-10

HAYS

S ELLIS COUNTY HISTORICAL SOCIETY ARCHIVES*, 100 W Seventh St, 67601. SAN 329-7489. Tel: 785-628-2624. FAX: 785-628-0386. E-mail: archive@elliscountyhistoricalsociety.org. Web Site: www.elliscountyhistoricalmuseum.org. Staff 5 (MLS 2, Non-MLS 3)
Founded 1972
Special Collections: County; Local History, docs, photog; Volga German History, docs, photog
Function: Archival coll, Res libr
Open Tues-Fri 10-12 & 1-5

C FORT HAYS STATE UNIVERSITY*, Forsyth Library, 600 Park St, 67601-4099. SAN 305-9421. Tel: 785-628-4431. Interlibrary Loan Service Tel: 785-628-4351. Reference Tel: 785-628-5283. FAX: 785-628-4096. Web Site: www.fhsu.edu/forsyth_lib/. *Dir,* John Ross; E-mail: jross@fhsu.edu; *Supvr, Acq,* Jean Wesselowski; Tel: 785-628-4343, E-mail: jwesselo@fhsu.edu; *Cat,* Jerry Wilson; Tel: 785-628-5282, E-mail: jwilson@fhsu.edu; *Circ,* Lacey Wegner; Tel: 785-628-5837, E-mail: llwegner@fhsu.edu; *Govt Doc,* Sharolyn Legleiter; E-mail: slegleit@fhsu.edu; *ILL,* Sheran Powers; E-mail: spowers@fhsu.edu; *Per,* Angela Barger; Tel: 785-628-4529, E-mail: abarger@fhsu.edu; *Pub Serv,* Lynn Haggard; Tel: 785-628-5566, E-mail: jhaggard@fhsu.edu; *Ref Serv,* Judy Salm; Tel: 785-628-4537, E-mail: jasalm@fhsu.edu; *Ser,* Nona Barton; Tel: 785-628-5262, E-mail: nbarton@fhsu.edu; Staff 18 (MLS 9, Non-MLS 9)
Founded 1902. Enrl 5,600; Fac 300
Library Holdings: Bk Vols 350,000; Per Subs 1,800
Special Collections: Children's Literature; History (Ethnic Coll, Volga Germans) bks, tapes; History (Western Coll, Western Kansas). Oral History; State Document Depository; US Document Depository
Automation Activity & Vendor Info: (Acquisitions) Ex Libris Group; (Cataloging) Ex Libris Group; (Circulation) Ex Libris Group; (Course Reserve) Ex Libris Group; (ILL) OCLC; (OPAC) Ex Libris Group; (Serials) Ex Libris Group
Mem of Central Kansas Library System
Partic in OCLC Online Computer Library Center, Inc
Open Mon-Thurs (Winter) 7:30am-Midnight, Fri 7:30-7, Sat 10-5, Sun 1-Midnight; Mon-Fri (Summer) 8-5

P HAYS PUBLIC LIBRARY*, 1205 Main, 67601-3693. SAN 305-943X. Tel: 785-625-9014. FAX: 785-625-8683. Web Site: www.hayspublib.org. *Dir,* Eric Norris; E-mail: enorris@hayspublib.org; *Spec Coll Librn,* Mary Ann Thompson; *Adult Serv,* Marleah Augustine; *Ch Serv,* Norleen Knoll; Tel: 785-625-5916; *YA Serv,* Brandon Hines; E-mail: bhines@hayspublib.org; Staff 40 (MLS 2, Non-MLS 38)
Founded 1899. Pop 19,827
Jan 2006-Dec 2006 Income $1,219,542, State $21,500, Provincial $25,000, City $1,119,042, Locally Generated Income $54,000. Mats Exp $234,000, Books $130,000, Per/Ser (Incl. Access Fees) $11,000, Micro $700, AV Equip $15,000, AV Mat $62,000, Electronic Ref Mat (Incl. Access Fees) $15,000, Presv $300. Sal $611,000 (Prof $103,500)
Library Holdings: AV Mats 26,000; Bks on Deafness & Sign Lang 158; High Interest/Low Vocabulary Bk Vols 105; Large Print Bks 5,700; Bk Vols 146,000; Per Subs 200
Subject Interests: Kansas, Local hist
Automation Activity & Vendor Info: (Cataloging) SirsiDynix; (Circulation) SirsiDynix; (OPAC) SirsiDynix
Publications: The Bookmark (Newsletter)
Mem of Central Kansas Library System
Special Services for the Deaf - TTY equip
Special Services for the Blind - Braille bks
Open Mon-Thurs 9-8, Fri 9-6, Sat 9-5, Sun 1-5
Friends of the Library Group

HAYSVILLE

P HAYSVILLE COMMUNITY LIBRARY*, 210 S Hays, 67060. (Mail add: PO Box 285, 67060-0285), SAN 320-4782. Tel: 316-524-5242. FAX: 316-524-0142. E-mail: hcl@haysvillecommunitylibrary.org. Web Site: www.haysvillecommunitylibrary.org. *Dir,* Betty Cattrell; Staff 12 (MLS 2, Non-MLS 10)
Founded 1977. Pop 9,627; Circ 75,970
Library Holdings: Bk Vols 45,000; Per Subs 132
Special Collections: Genealogy Coll; Kansas (Kansas & Local History), bks, newspapers; Quilting bks; Sports bks
Automation Activity & Vendor Info: (Cataloging) Innovative Interfaces, Inc; (Circulation) Innovative Interfaces, Inc; (OPAC) Innovative Interfaces, Inc
Database Vendor: OCLC FirstSearch
Wireless access
Function: Adult bk club, Art exhibits, Bks on cassette, Bks on CD, Children's prog, Computer training, Computers for patron use, Copy machines, Electronic databases & coll, Free DVD rentals, Handicapped accessible, ILL available, Notary serv, Photocopying/Printing, Pub access computers, Scanner, Senior computer classes, Story hour, Summer reading prog, Tax forms, Telephone ref, VHS videos, Web-catalog, Wheelchair accessible
Mem of South Central Kansas Library System
Open Mon-Thurs 9-9, Fri & Sat 10-5, Sun 1-4
Friends of the Library Group

HEPLER

P HEPLER CITY LIBRARY*, 105 S Prairie, 66746. (Mail add: PO Box 148, 66746-0148), SAN 305-9448. Tel: 620-368-4379. FAX: 620-368-4379. E-mail: heplerlibrary@yahoo.com. *Librn,* Samantha Kennedy
Pop 187; Circ 2,155
Library Holdings: Bk Vols 4,126
Mem of Southeast Kansas Library System
Open Mon-Fri 6:30pm-8:30pm

HERINGTON

P HERINGTON PUBLIC LIBRARY*, 102 S Broadway, 67449-2634. SAN 305-9456. Tel: 785 258-2011. FAX: 785-258-2011. E-mail: director@heringtonlib.info. *Librn,* Shelly Wirtz
Founded 1897. Pop 3,000; Circ 31,250
Library Holdings: Bk Vols 15,000; Per Subs 20
Automation Activity & Vendor Info: (Cataloging) Auto-Graphics, Inc
Wireless access
Mem of North Central Kansas Libraries System
Open Mon-Thurs 11-6, Fri & Sat 9-3

HESSTON

C HESSTON COLLEGE, Mary Miller Library, 325 S Main St, 67062-8901. (Mail add: PO Box 3000, 67062-2093), SAN 342-0361. Tel: 620-327-8245. FAX: 620-327-8300. Web Site: www.hesston.edu/academic/lrc/mml.html. *Dir,* Margaret Wiebe; E-mail: margaret@hesston.edu; Staff 1 (MLS 1)
Founded 1908. Enrl 435; Fac 50; Highest Degree: Associate
Library Holdings: AV Mats 3,000; Bk Titles 30,000; Per Subs 225
Automation Activity & Vendor Info: (Acquisitions) Auto-Graphics, Inc; (Cataloging) Auto-Graphics, Inc; (Circulation) Auto-Graphics, Inc; (ILL) Auto-Graphics, Inc; (OPAC) Auto-Graphics, Inc
Database Vendor: Amigos Library Services, Auto-Graphics, Inc, College Source, CQ Press, ebrary, EBSCOhost, Gale Cengage Learning, LearningExpress, LexisNexis, OCLC FirstSearch, ProQuest
Wireless access
Mem of South Central Kansas Library System
Open Mon-Thurs 8am-Midnight, Fri 8-5, Sat 1-5, Sun 2-Midnight

P HESSTON PUBLIC LIBRARY, 300 N Main St, 67062. (Mail add: PO Box 640, 67062-0640), SAN 305-9472. Tel: 620-327-4666. FAX: 620-327-4459. E-mail: hesstonpubliclibrary@gmail.com. Web Site: www.hesstonpubliclibrary.com. *Dir,* Libby Albers; Staff 6 (MLS 1, Non-MLS 5)

Founded 1937. Pop 3,618; Circ 49,020
Jan 2013-Dec 2013 Income $204,920, State $1,499, City $178,511, County $13,003, Locally Generated Income $10,408, Other $1,499. Mats Exp $23,698, Books $17,464, Per/Ser (Incl. Access Fees) $4,019, AV Mat $1,143, Electronic Ref Mat (Incl. Access Fees) $1,072. Sal $110,450 (Prof $50,000)
Library Holdings: AV Mats 2,172; Bk Vols 36,650; Per Subs 75
Special Collections: Children's Videos; Educational Toys; Family Diversity; Sewing Patterns
Subject Interests: Aging, Amish, Ecology, Landscape archit, Lifelong wellness, Mennonites, Quilts, Spirituality, Transportation
Automation Activity & Vendor Info: (Cataloging) Follett Software; (Circulation) Follett Software; (OPAC) Follett Software
Function: ILL available, Photocopying/Printing, Telephone ref
Mem of South Central Kansas Library System
Open Mon-Wed & Fri 9-6, Thurs 9-8, Sat 9-2

HIAWATHA

P MORRILL PUBLIC LIBRARY*, 431 Oregon, 66434-2290. SAN 305-9480. Tel: 785-742-3831. FAX: 785-742-2054. E-mail: morrill@hiawathalibrary.org. Web Site: www.hiawathalibrary.org. *Dir,* Jenny Marr
Founded 1882. Pop 3,410; Circ 92,676
Library Holdings: Bk Vols 38,727; Per Subs 100
Wireless access
Mem of Northeast Kansas Library System
Friends of the Library Group

HIGHLAND

J HIGHLAND COMMUNITY COLLEGE LIBRARY*, 606 W Main, 66035. SAN 305-9499. Tel: 785-442-6053. FAX: 785-442-6101. Web Site: www.highlandcc.edu. *Dir, Libr Serv,* Penny Donaldson; Tel: 785-442-6054, E-mail: pdonaldson@highlandcc.edu; Staff 3 (MLS 1, Non-MLS 2)
Founded 1858. Enrl 3,500; Fac 79; Highest Degree: Associate
Library Holdings: DVDs 125; Bk Titles 22,500; Bk Vols 23,000; Per Subs 125; Videos 1,750
Special Collections: Local History, videocassettes
Subject Interests: Soc sci & issues
Automation Activity & Vendor Info: (Circulation) TLC (The Library Corporation)
Database Vendor: Gale Cengage Learning, OCLC FirstSearch
Open Mon-Thurs (Winter) 7:30am-10pm, Fri 7:30-4, Sun 3:30-10; Mon-Fri (Summer) 7:30-4

HILL CITY

P GRAHAM COUNTY PUBLIC LIBRARY*, 414 N West St, 67642-1646. SAN 305-9502. Tel: 785-421-2722. FAX: 785-421-5583. E-mail: gract1lb@ruraltel.net. Web Site: www.ghcopublib.org. *Librn,* Mary Allen; *Libr Asst,* Carol Nickelson; Staff 4 (Non-MLS 4)
Founded 1972. Pop 3,219
Library Holdings: Bk Vols 31,219; Per Subs 60
Special Collections: Graham County Newspapers 1879-present; Wildflowers of Graham County
Wireless access
Open Mon-Wed & Fri 9:30-5:30, Thurs 9:30-8:30, Sat 9:30-2:30
Friends of the Library Group

HILLSBORO

P HILLSBORO PUBLIC LIBRARY, 120 E Grand, 67063-1598. SAN 305-9510. Tel: 620-947-3827. FAX: 620-947-3810. E-mail: hillsboropubliclib@gmail.com. Web Site: hillsboro.mykansaslibrary.org. *Dir,* Cathleen J Fish; *Ch,* Delora Kaufman; Staff 3 (Non-MLS 3)
Founded 1926. Pop 2,833; Circ 38,430
Jan 2005-Dec 2005 Income $65,839. Mats Exp $13,388. Sal $33,000
Library Holdings: AV Mats 968; Bks on Deafness & Sign Lang 13; Large Print Bks 74; Bk Titles 20,489; Per Subs 65; Talking Bks 209
Automation Activity & Vendor Info: (Cataloging) Auto-Graphics, Inc; (Circulation) Auto-Graphics, Inc
Database Vendor: Auto-Graphics, Inc
Wireless access
Function: ILL available, Online searches, Photocopying/Printing, Prog for adults, Prog for children & young adult, Summer reading prog, Telephone ref, Wheelchair accessible
Member Libraries: North Central Kansas Libraries System
Mem of North Central Kansas Libraries System
Open Mon 9:30-7, Tues-Fri 9:30-5

C TABOR COLLEGE LIBRARY, 400 S Jefferson St, 67063. SAN 305-9529. Tel: 620-947-3121, Ext 1201. FAX: 620-947-2607. E-mail: library@tabor.edu. Web Site: www.tabor.edu/library. *Dir of Libr Serv,* Janet L Williams; Tel: 620-947-3121, Ext 1202, E-mail: janetw@tabor.edu; Staff 2.5 (MLS 1, Non-MLS 1.5)
Founded 1908. Enrl 535; Fac 53
Jul 2013-Jun 2014. Mats Exp $75,945, Books $27,366, Per/Ser (Incl. Access Fees) $18,796, AV Equip $918, AV Mat $865, Electronic Ref Mat (Incl. Access Fees) $28,000. Sal $45,000
Library Holdings: Bk Titles 60,016; Bk Vols 82,536; Per Subs 156
Special Collections: Center for Mennonite Brethren Studies, bks, mss, per
Subject Interests: Germans from Russia, Hymnals, Kansas, Relig
Automation Activity & Vendor Info: (Acquisitions) OCLC Online; (Cataloging) OCLC Online; (Circulation) OCLC Online; (Course Reserve) OCLC Online; (ILL) OCLC WorldShare Interlibrary Loan; (OPAC) OCLC Online; (Serials) OCLC Online
Database Vendor: OCLC
Wireless access
Function: Art exhibits, AV serv, CD-ROM, Distance learning, Doc delivery serv, ILL available, Music CDs, Online searches, Orientations, Outside serv via phone, mail, e-mail & web, Prof lending libr, Ref serv available, VHS videos, Wheelchair accessible, Workshops
Open Mon-Thurs 7:30am-11pm, Fri 7:30-5:30, Sat 1-5, Sun (Sept-May) 1-11

HOISINGTON

P HOISINGTON PUBLIC LIBRARY, 169 S Walnut, 67544. SAN 305-9537. Tel: 620-653-4128. FAX: 620-653-4128. E-mail: hoisington_library@hotmail.com. *Dir,* Melissa Nech
Founded 1928. Pop 3,820
Library Holdings: AV Mats 620; Large Print Bks 178; Bk Vols 22,480; Per Subs 93
Automation Activity & Vendor Info: (Cataloging) Book Systems; (Circulation) Book Systems
Mem of Central Kansas Library System
Open Mon & Wed 10-6, Tues, Thurs & Fri 12-6, Sat 12-4

HOLTON

P BECK BOOKMAN LIBRARY*, 420 W Fourth St, 66436-1572. SAN 305-9545. Tel: 785-364-3532. FAX: 785-364-5402. E-mail: holtoncitylib@gmail.com. Web Site: www.holtonks.net/library/index.html. *Dir,* Candee Jacobs; *Circ,* Dylan Calhoon; *Circ,* Gail Schmitz; *Tech Serv & Automation,* Helen Plankinton-Murphy
Founded 1897. Pop 15,000; Circ 59,319
Library Holdings: Bk Vols 28,370; Per Subs 52
Special Collections: Campbell College Coll; Kansas Coll
Automation Activity & Vendor Info: (Cataloging) ByWater Solutions; (Circulation) ByWater Solutions
Wireless access
Mem of Northeast Kansas Library System
Open Mon-Thurs 10-7:30, Fri 10-6:30, Sat 10-2:30

HOPE

P HOPE COMMUNITY LIBRARY*, 216 N Main St, 67451. SAN 376-7663. Tel: 785-366-7219. E-mail: hopelibrary@tctelco.net. Web Site: hope.mykansaslibrary.org. *Dir,* Denise Hull
Wireless access
Mem of North Central Kansas Libraries System
Open Tues, Wed & Fri 3-6, Thurs 9-1, Sat 9-12
Friends of the Library Group

HORTON

P HORTON FREE PUBLIC LIBRARY*, 809 First Ave E, 66439-1898. SAN 305-9553. Tel: 785-486-3326. FAX: 785-486-2116. E-mail: hortonlibrary@hortonlibrary.org. Web Site: www.hortonkansas.net/community/horton-free-public-library-1. *Dir,* Rita L Higley; E-mail: rhigley@hortonlibrary.org; *Librn,* Carolyn Olsen
Founded 1925. Pop 2,000; Circ 18,000
Library Holdings: Bk Vols 16,000; Per Subs 41
Special Collections: Kansas Coll
Automation Activity & Vendor Info: (Cataloging) Follett Software; (Circulation) Follett Software; (OPAC) Follett Software
Database Vendor: OCLC FirstSearch
Mem of Northeast Kansas Library System
Open Mon & Thurs 1-8, Tues 9-1, Wed & Fri 1-6, Sat 10-2
Friends of the Library Group

HOWARD

P HOWARD CITY LIBRARY*, 126 S Wabash, 67349. (Mail add: PO Box 785, 67349-0785), SAN 305-9561. Tel: 620-374-2890. *Librn,* Judith Harsh
Founded 1921. Pop 976; Circ 6,057
Library Holdings: Bk Vols 17,600; Per Subs 15
Special Collections: Kansas Coll
Mem of Southeast Kansas Library System
Special Services for the Blind - Large print bks
Open Mon, Wed & Fri 2-5

HOXIE

P SHERIDAN COUNTY LIBRARY*, 801 Royal Ave, 67740. (Mail add: PO Box 607, 67740-0607), SAN 305-957X. Tel: 785-675-3102. *Dir,* Cindy Eller; *Asst Librn,* Kristine Moss
Pop 3,500; Circ 34,473
Library Holdings: Bk Vols 18,400; Per Subs 61
Subject Interests: Kansas
Automation Activity & Vendor Info: (Cataloging) Follett Software; (Circulation) Follett Software
Database Vendor: Gale Cengage Learning, OCLC FirstSearch
Mem of Northwest Kansas Library System
Open Mon-Fri 9:30-4:30
Friends of the Library Group

HUGOTON

P STEVENS COUNTY LIBRARY*, 500 Monroe, 67951-2639. SAN 305-9588. Tel: 620-544-2301. FAX: 620-544-2322. E-mail: library@stevenscountylibrary.com. Web Site: www.stevenscountylibrary.com. *Dir,* Eunice M Schroeder; *Asst Dir, Youth Serv,* Stacey L Strickland; *Tech Serv,* Marikate Harvey; Staff 10 (MLS 2, Non-MLS 8)
Founded 1914. Pop 5,056; Circ 79,002
Jan 2010-Dec 2010 Income $484,877, State $3,849, County $458,062, Other $12,000. Mats Exp $84,591, Books $32,938, Per/Ser (Incl. Access Fees) $4,386, AV Mat $42,035, Electronic Ref Mat (Incl. Access Fees) $5,232. Sal $110,046 (Prof $85,000)
Library Holdings: CDs 3,219; DVDs 3,044; Electronic Media & Resources 48; Bk Vols 41,159; Per Subs 125
Special Collections: Art Print Coll; Kansas Room Coll; Stevens County Genealogical Society Coll
Automation Activity & Vendor Info: (Cataloging) Auto-Graphics, Inc; (Circulation) Auto-Graphics, Inc; (ILL) Auto-Graphics, Inc; (OPAC) Auto-Graphics, Inc
Database Vendor: EBSCO Information Services, Gale Cengage Learning, Ingram Library Services, OCLC FirstSearch, OCLC WorldShare Interlibrary Loan, ProQuest, World Book Online
Wireless access
Function: Art exhibits, Audiobks via web, AV serv, Bilingual assistance for Spanish patrons, Bks on CD, CD-ROM, Children's prog, Computer training, Computers for patron use, Copy machines, Digital talking bks, Distance learning, e-mail & chat, e-mail serv, E-Reserves, Electronic databases & coll, Exhibits, Family literacy, Fax serv, For res purposes, Free DVD rentals, Genealogy discussion group, Govt ref serv, Handicapped accessible, Health sci info serv, Holiday prog, Home delivery & serv to Sr ctr & nursing homes, Homebound delivery serv, Homework prog, ILL available, Instruction & testing, Jail serv, Libr develop, Literacy & newcomer serv, Magnifiers for reading, Mail & tel request accepted, Masonic res mat, Music CDs, Newsp ref libr, Notary serv, Online cat, Online info literacy tutorials on the web & in blackboard, Online ref, Online searches, Orientations, Outreach serv, Outside serv via phone, mail, e-mail & web, OverDrive digital audio bks, Photocopying/Printing, Preschool outreach, Printer for laptops & handheld devices, Prog for adults, Prog for children & young adult, Pub access computers, Ref & res, Ref serv available, Ref serv in person, Referrals accepted, Satellite serv, Scanner, Senior computer classes, Senior outreach, Spoken cassettes & CDs, Spoken cassettes & DVDs, Story hour, Summer & winter reading prog, Summer reading prog, Tax forms, Teen prog, Telephone ref, Video lending libr, Wheelchair accessible, Winter reading prog, Workshops
Mem of Southwest Kansas Library System
Partic in Tri-State Libr Consortium
Open Mon-Fri 8-7, Sat 9-5

HUMBOLDT

P HUMBOLDT PUBLIC LIBRARY*, 916 Bridge St, 66748-1834. SAN 305-9596. Tel: 620-473-2243. *Dir,* Melinda Herder
Founded 1939. Pop 3,500; Circ 19,000
Library Holdings: Bk Vols 19,500; Per Subs 52
Special Collections: City History; high school year bks
Subject Interests: Parenting, Photog, Relig, Sci fict
Automation Activity & Vendor Info: (Cataloging) Follett Software; (Circulation) Follett Software
Partic in OCLC Online Computer Library Center, Inc
Open Tues-Thurs 9:30-8:30, Fri & Sat 9:30-5:30

HUTCHINSON

J HUTCHINSON COMMUNITY COLLEGE*, John F Kennedy Library, 1300 N Plum St, 67501. SAN 305-9618. Tel: 620-665-3547. Toll Free Tel: 800-289-3501, Ext 3547. FAX: 620-665-3392. E-mail: jfk@hutchcc.edu. Web Site: www.hutchcc.edu/library. *Coordr, Libr Serv,* Robert Kelly; Tel: 620-665-3548, E-mail: kellyr@hutchcc.edu; *Access & Tech Serv Librn,* Cheryl Warkentin; Tel: 620-665-3489, E-mail: warkentinc@hutchcc.edu; *Hist Instr/Pub Serv Librn,* Brad Fenwick; Tel: 620-665-3338, E-mail: fenwickb@hutchcc.edu; *ILL,* Sylvia Call; Tel: 620-665-3418, E-mail: calls@hutchcc.edu; Staff 4 (MLS 2.5, Non-MLS 1.5)
Founded 1928. Enrl 5,000; Fac 400; Highest Degree: Associate
Jul 2011-Jun 2012 Income $7,000. Mats Exp $55,280, Books $9,200, Per/Ser (Incl. Access Fees) $16,080, AV Mat $3,500, Electronic Ref Mat (Incl. Access Fees) $26,500. Sal $136,000 (Prof $103,750)
Library Holdings: AV Mats 2,799; e-books 13,000; Bk Vols 42,883; Per Subs 161
Special Collections: FAA Resource Center
Automation Activity & Vendor Info: (Cataloging) Spydus; (Circulation) Spydus; (OPAC) Spydus; (Serials) Spydus
Database Vendor: ARTstor, CredoReference, EBSCOhost, JSTOR, LexisNexis, Oxford Online
Function: Audio & video playback equip for onsite use, Computers for patron use, Copy machines, Electronic databases & coll, ILL available, Online cat, Video lending libr
Mem of South Central Kansas Library System
Open Mon-Thurs (Winter) 7:30am-9pm, Fri 7:30-5, Sun 4-8; Mon-Thurs (Summer) 8-7, Fri 8-4
Restriction: ID required to use computers (Ltd hrs)

P HUTCHINSON PUBLIC LIBRARY*, 901 N Main, 67501-4492. SAN 305-9626. Tel: 620-663-5441. FAX: 620-663-9506. Interlibrary Loan Service FAX: 620-663-1215. Reference FAX: 620-663-1583. Web Site: www.hutchpl.org. *Dir,* Gregg Wamsley; E-mail: gwamsley@hutchpl.org; *Asst Dir, Pub Serv,* Position Currently Open; *Head, Circ,* Dianna Brown; E-mail: dbrown@hutchpl.org; *Head, ILL, Head, Ref,* Cheryl Canfield; E-mail: cherylc@hutchpl.org; *Tech Serv Team Leader,* Ruth Heidebrecht; E-mail: rheidebrecht@hutchpl.org; *Ch Serv,* Terry Christner; E-mail: tchristn@hutchpl.org; Staff 44 (MLS 5, Non-MLS 39)
Founded 1901. Pop 62,155; Circ 456,985
Library Holdings: Bk Titles 32,631; Bk Vols 289,081; Per Subs 396
Special Collections: State Document Depository; US Document Depository
Automation Activity & Vendor Info: (Acquisitions) Innovative Interfaces, Inc; (Cataloging) Innovative Interfaces, Inc; (Circulation) Innovative Interfaces, Inc; (OPAC) Innovative Interfaces, Inc; (Serials) Innovative Interfaces, Inc
Database Vendor: LexisNexis, Overdrive, Inc, Standard & Poor's
Wireless access
Function: Adult bk club, Archival coll, Art exhibits, Audiobks via web, Bk club(s), Bks on CD, Children's prog, Computer training, Computers for patron use, Copy machines, e-mail serv, Electronic databases & coll, Exhibits, Free DVD rentals, Handicapped accessible, Home delivery & serv to Sr ctr & nursing homes, Homebound delivery serv, ILL available, Magnifiers for reading, Mail & tel request accepted, Music CDs, Online cat, Online ref, Online searches, Outreach serv, OverDrive digital audio bks, Photocopying/Printing, Preschool outreach, Prog for adults, Prog for children & young adult, Pub access computers, Scanner, Senior computer classes, Senior outreach, Story hour, Summer reading prog, Teen prog, Workshops
Open Mon-Thurs 9-9, Fri & Sat 9-6, Sun 1-5
Friends of the Library Group

S KANSAS DEPARTMENT OF CORRECTIONS*, Hutchinson Correctional Facility Central Library, 500 S Reformatory Rd, 67501. (Mail add: PO Box 1568, 67504-1568). Tel: 620-662-2321, Ext 4365. FAX: 620-662-5986. *Dir,* Kate Field
Library Holdings: Bk Vols 5,000; Per Subs 21
Automation Activity & Vendor Info: (Cataloging) Follett Software; (Circulation) Follett Software; (OPAC) Follett Software
Mem of Central Kansas Library System

INDEPENDENCE

J INDEPENDENCE COMMUNITY COLLEGE LIBRARY, 1057 W College Ave, 67301. Tel: 620-331-4100. FAX: 620-331-6821. Web Site: www.indycc.edu/library. *Dir,* Lily Morgan; E-mail: Lmorgan@indycc.edu; Staff 4 (MLS 2, Non-MLS 2)
Founded 1925. Enrl 1,190; Highest Degree: Associate
Jul 2006-Jun 2007. Mats Exp $30,454, Books $15,000, Per/Ser (Incl. Access Fees) $6,700, AV Mat $2,700, Electronic Ref Mat (Incl. Access Fees) $2,525
Library Holdings: AV Mats 778; Bk Vols 30,098; Per Subs 54
Special Collections: William Inge Coll
Automation Activity & Vendor Info: (Acquisitions) Follett Software; (Cataloging) Follett Software; (Circulation) Follett Software; (ILL) Auto-Graphics, Inc; (Serials) Follett Software
Database Vendor: Gale Cengage Learning, OCLC FirstSearch

P INDEPENDENCE PUBLIC LIBRARY*, 220 E Maple, 67301-3899. SAN 305-9642. Tel: 620-331-3030. FAX: 620-331-4093. Web Site: www.iplks.org. *Dir,* Pete Daniels; E-mail: pete.daniels@iplks.org; *Asst Dir,* Julie Hildebrand; E-mail: julie.hildebrand@iplks.org; *Mgr, Tech Serv,*

Rebecca Passaur; E-mail: becky.passauer@iplks.org; *Ch,* Blinn Sheffield; Staff 11 (MLS 2, Non-MLS 9)
Founded 1882. Pop 13,500; Circ 121,613
Jan 2007-Dec 2007 Income $422,829, State $9,291, City $230,362, County $120,695, Locally Generated Income $18,732, Other $43,749. Mats Exp $62,660, Books $38,866, Per/Ser (Incl. Access Fees) $5,087, Other Print Mats $4,546, AV Mat $13,444, Electronic Ref Mat (Incl. Access Fees) $717. Sal $209,777
Library Holdings: Audiobooks 1,604; AV Mats 195; DVDs 1,625; High Interest/Low Vocabulary Bk Vols 50; Large Print Bks 899; Microforms 62; Bk Titles 37,964; Per Subs 128
Special Collections: Business Coll; Genealogy Coll; Local Newspapers, micro
Automation Activity & Vendor Info: (Acquisitions) Follett Software; (Cataloging) Follett Software; (Circulation) Follett Software; (Course Reserve) Follett Software; (ILL) Follett Software; (Media Booking) Follett Software; (OPAC) Follett Software; (Serials) Follett Software
Wireless access
Function: ILL available
Mem of Southeast Kansas Library System; Winding Rivers Library System
Open Mon 10-8, Tues-Fri 10-6, Sat 10-4
Friends of the Library Group

INMAN

P INMAN PUBLIC LIBRARY*, 100 N Main, 67546. (Mail add: PO Box 416, 67546-0416), SAN 305-9650. Tel: 620-585-2474. E-mail: library@inmanks.net. Web Site: inmanlibrary.com. *Librn,* Donna Sallee
Founded 1943. Pop 1,000; Circ 10,000
Library Holdings: AV Mats 250; Bk Vols 18,000; Per Subs 30
Automation Activity & Vendor Info: (Circulation) Auto-Graphics, Inc
Wireless access
Mem of South Central Kansas Library System
Open Mon-Fri 1-7, Sat 9-12

IOLA

J ALLEN COMMUNITY COLLEGE LIBRARY*, 1801 N Cottonwood, 66749-1648. SAN 305-9669. Tel: 620-365-5116, Ext 208. Interlibrary Loan Service Tel: 620-365-5116, Ext 207. FAX: 620-365-3284. E-mail: accclib@allencc.edu. Web Site: www.allencc.edu/accc/library/library.html. *Dir,* Steven W Anderson; Tel: 620-365-5116, Ext 235, E-mail: anderson@allencc.edu; *Libr Tech,* Jill Hoffman; E-mail: hoffman@allencc.edu; *Libr Tech,* Alice Williamson; E-mail: williamson@allencc.edu; Staff 3 (MLS 1, Non-MLS 2)
Founded 1970. Enrl 3,128; Fac 65; Highest Degree: Associate
Jul 2006-Jun 2007. Mats Exp $56,357, Books $16,660, Per/Ser (Incl. Access Fees) $18,980, Electronic Ref Mat (Incl. Access Fees) $11,054. Sal $92,425 (Prof $55,248)
Library Holdings: Audiobooks 22; AV Mats 521; Bks on Deafness & Sign Lang 16; CDs 415; e-books 12,874; e-journals 8,953; Electronic Media & Resources 353; High Interest/Low Vocabulary Bk Vols 108; Large Print Bks 48; Music Scores 63; Bk Titles 38,326; Bk Vols 39,261; Per Subs 104; Videos 521
Subject Interests: Local genealogy
Automation Activity & Vendor Info: (Cataloging) Follett Software; (Circulation) Follett Software; (Course Reserve) Follett Software; (OPAC) Follett Software
Database Vendor: Alexander Street Press, Checkpoint Systems, Inc, EBSCO Information Services, EBSCOhost, Facts on File, Gale Cengage Learning, Ingram Library Services, MITINET, Inc, OCLC WorldShare Interlibrary Loan, Oxford Online, ProQuest, World Book Online
Wireless access
Function: Ref serv available
Publications: Policies & Procedures Manual
Mem of Southeast Kansas Library System
Special Services for the Deaf - Assistive tech; Closed caption videos; High interest/low vocabulary bks
Special Services for the Blind - Assistive/Adapted tech devices, equip & products; Bks available with recordings; Bks on cassette; Bks on CD; Computer with voice synthesizer for visually impaired persons; Dragon Naturally Speaking software; Large print bks; Magnifiers; Music instrul cassettes; PC for handicapped; Reader equip; Rec of textbk mat; Screen enlargement software for people with visual disabilities; Screen reader software; ZoomText magnification & reading software
Open Mon-Thurs (Winter) 8am-9pm, Fri 8-4, Sun 6-9; Mon-Fri (Summer) 8-4

P IOLA PUBLIC LIBRARY*, 218 E Madison Ave, 66749. SAN 305-9677. Tel: 620-365-3262. FAX: 620-365-5137. E-mail: iolaref@sekls.org. Web Site: iola.mykansaslibrary.org. *Dir,* Roger L Carswell; E-mail: rcarswell@sekls.org; *Ch Serv,* Leah Oswald; E-mail: loswald@sekls.org; *Pub Serv,* Lesa Cole; E-mail: lcole@sekls.org; Staff 3 (MLS 1, Non-MLS 2)
Founded 1884. Pop 5,704; Circ 77,275
Jan 2013-Dec 2013 Income $267,328, State $2,288, City $208,000, Locally Generated Income $28,830, Other $28,210. Mats Exp $24,500, Books $9,825, Per/Ser (Incl. Access Fees) $5,400, Micro $575, AV Mat $7,800. Sal $146,989
Library Holdings: Audiobooks 1,010; CDs 956; DVDs 1,742; Microforms 1,120; Bk Vols 35,211; Per Subs 75; Videos 612
Special Collections: Kansas History Coll
Subject Interests: Genealogy, State hist
Automation Activity & Vendor Info: (Cataloging) ByWater Solutions; (Circulation) ByWater Solutions; (OPAC) ByWater Solutions
Wireless access
Mem of Southeast Kansas Library System
Open Mon-Thurs 9:30-8, Fri & Sat 9-5
Friends of the Library Group

P SOUTHEAST KANSAS LIBRARY SYSTEM*, 218 E Madison Ave, 66749. SAN 305-9685. Tel: 620-365-5136. Toll Free Tel: 800-279-3219. FAX: 620-365-5137. Web Site: www.sekls.org. *Dir,* Roger L Carswell; E-mail: rcarswell@sekls.org; *Tech Coordr,* Melissa Geist; E-mail: mgeist@sekls.org; *ILL,* Brenda Cash; E-mail: bcash@sekls.org; *Talking Bks,* Beckye Parker; Fax: bparker@sekls.org; *Tech Serv,* Kim Burns; E-mail: kburns@sekls.org; *Youth Serv Consult,* Sandy Wilkerson; E-mail: swilkerson@sekls.org; Staff 15 (MLS 3, Non-MLS 12)
Founded 1966
Jan 2013-Dec 2013 Income $1,563,483, State $97,133, Locally Generated Income $350, Other $1,466,000. Mats Exp $67,300, Books $49,000, Per/Ser (Incl. Access Fees) $1,650, AV Mat $6,500. Sal $563,625
Library Holdings: Audiobooks 416; DVDs 995; Microforms 11,483; Bk Vols 58,512; Per Subs 24
Special Collections: Kansas Census
Subject Interests: Genealogy
Automation Activity & Vendor Info: (Cataloging) ByWater Solutions; (Circulation) ByWater Solutions; (OPAC) ByWater Solutions
Wireless access
Publications: SEKLS Stacks of News (Newsletter)
Member Libraries: Allen Community College Library; Arma City Library; Bronson Public Library; Caney City Library; Cedar Vale Memorial Library; Chanute Public Library; Cherryvale Public Library; Chetopa City Library; Coffey County Library; Coffeyville Community College; Coffeyville Public Library; Colony City Library; Edna Public Library; Erie City Public Library; Eureka Public Library; Fort Scott Public Library; Fredonia Public Library; Galena Public Library; Garnett Public Library; Girard Public Library; Graves Memorial Public Library; Grenola Public Library; Hamilton City Library; Hepler City Library; Howard City Library; Independence Public Library; Iola Public Library; Labette Community College Library; Linn County Library District No 2; Linn County Library District No 3; Linn County Library District No 5; Linn County Library District Number 1; Longton Library; Mary Sommerville Free Library; McCune Osage Township Library; Moline Public Library; Moran Public Library; Mound Valley Public Library; Oswego Public Library; Pittsburg Public Library; Prescott City Public Library; Savonburg Public Library; Sedan Public Library; Thayer Friday Reading Club City Library; W A Rankin Memorial Library; Weir Public Library; Yates Center Public Library

JAMESTOWN

P JAMESTOWN CITY LIBRARY*, 311 D Walnut St, 66948. (Mail add: PO Box 287, 66948-0287), SAN 305-9693. Tel: 785-439-6258. E-mail: jameslib@nckcn.com. *Actg Libr Dir,* Debbie Kearn; Staff 1 (MLS 1)
Founded 1898. Pop 325; Circ 6,928
Library Holdings: Bk Vols 8,100; Per Subs 22; Spec Interest Per Sub 10
Special Collections: Children Around the World Coll
Mem of Central Kansas Library System
Open Tues & Thurs 3-5, Sat 9-12 & 1-4

JENNINGS

P JENNINGS CITY LIBRARY*, Kansas Ave, 67643. (Mail add: PO Box 84, 67643-0084), SAN 305-9707. Tel: 785-678-2666. FAX: 785-678-2666. E-mail: jenlibsg@ruraltel.net. *Librn,* Helen Rhodes
Pop 194; Circ 3,804
Library Holdings: Bk Vols 4,711; Per Subs 10
Subject Interests: Local hist
Wireless access
Mem of Northwest Kansas Library System
Open Mon 3-6, Wed & Sat 9-11

JETMORE

P JETMORE PUBLIC LIBRARY*, 310 Main St, 67854. (Mail add: PO Box 608, 67854), SAN 305-9715. Tel: 620-357-8336. E-mail: jetpl@jetpl.info. Web Site: www.jetpl.info. *Dir,* Jacque Sherrill; Staff 1 (MLS 1)
Library Holdings: Bk Titles 15,386; Per Subs 18

Special Collections: Hodgemon County Census & Newspapers, micro; Hodgemon County Genealogy Coll
Automation Activity & Vendor Info: (Acquisitions) Auto-Graphics, Inc; (Cataloging) Auto-Graphics, Inc; (Circulation) Auto-Graphics, Inc; (ILL) Auto-Graphics, Inc
Database Vendor: Auto-Graphics, Inc
Wireless access
Mem of Southwest Kansas Library System
Open Mon 10-1 & 2-7, Tues & Thurs 10-1, & 2-5:30, Wed & Fri 2-5:30
Friends of the Library Group

JEWELL

P JEWELL PUBLIC LIBRARY*, 216 Delaware, 66949. (Mail add: PO Box 283, 66949-0283), SAN 305-9723. Tel: 785-428-3630. FAX: 785-428-3630. E-mail: jewellpl@nckcn.com. *Dir,* Carla Feigal; *Asst Librn,* Janice Schmacher
Founded 1926. Pop 478; Circ 5,049
Library Holdings: AV Mats 80; Bks-By-Mail 5,000; Large Print Bks 40; Bk Vols 5,060; Per Subs 15
Special Collections: Quilting Coll
Mem of Central Kansas Library System
Open Mon 2-5:30, Tues, Wed & Sat 2-5, Thurs 2:30-7:30, Fri 9-11 & 2-5

JOHNSON

P STANTON COUNTY LIBRARY*, 103 E Sherman, 67855. (Mail add: PO Box 480, 67855-0480), SAN 305-9731. Tel: 620-492-2302. FAX: 620-492-2203. E-mail: stcpl@stantoncountylib.info. Web Site: www.stantoncountylib.info. *Dir,* Denise Smith; *Ch,* Michelle Perez; *Circ,* Peggy Stiles
Pop 2,339; Circ 36,568
Library Holdings: AV Mats 2,000; Large Print Bks 35; Bk Vols 3,900; Per Subs 70; Talking Bks 1,700
Automation Activity & Vendor Info: (Cataloging) Follett Software; (Circulation) Follett Software
Database Vendor: Gale Cengage Learning, OCLC FirstSearch
Wireless access
Publications: Library Journal (Weekly)
Mem of Southwest Kansas Library System
Open Mon-Fri 8:30-5:30, Sat 10-2

JUNCTION CITY

P DOROTHY BRAMLAGE PUBLIC LIBRARY*, 230 W Seventh, 66441-3097. SAN 305-974X. Tel: 785-238-4311. FAX: 785-238-7873. E-mail: jclibrary@jclib.org. Web Site: www.jclib.org. *Dir,* Susan Moyer; E-mail: susanm@jclib.org; *Asst Dir,* Cheryl Jorgensen; E-mail: cherylj@jclib.org; *Ch Serv,* Patty Collins; E-mail: pattyc@jclib.org
Founded 1907. Pop 31,099; Circ 139,000
Library Holdings: Bk Vols 75,000
Automation Activity & Vendor Info: (Acquisitions) Baker & Taylor; (Cataloging) Auto-Graphics, Inc; (Circulation) Auto-Graphics, Inc
Database Vendor: Gale Cengage Learning, OCLC FirstSearch
Wireless access
Publications: Community Information Directory (Annual); LIFE Directory (Periodical)
Mem of North Central Kansas Libraries System
Open Mon-Thurs 9-9, Fri 9-6, Sat 9-5, Sun 1-5
Friends of the Library Group

KANOPOLIS

P KANOPOLIS PUBLIC LIBRARY*, 221 N Kansas, 67454. (Mail add: PO Box 205, 67454), SAN 376-5652. Tel: 785-472-3053. E-mail: kanopolis@eaglecom.net. Web Site: kanopoliskansas.com/library. *Librn,* Gloria Ploutz
Pop 525
Library Holdings: Bk Vols 6,100; Per Subs 25
Wireless access
Mem of Central Kansas Library System
Open Tues-Fri 3:30-6:30, Sat 9-Noon

KANSAS CITY

C DONNELLY COLLEGE, Trant Memorial Library, 608 N 18th St, 66102. SAN 305-9774. Tel: 913-621-8735. FAX: 913-621-8719. Web Site: www.donnelly.edu/library. *Libr Dir,* Jane Ballagh De Tovar; E-mail: jane@donnelly.edu; *Asst Libr Dir,* Michael Washburn; E-mail: mwashburn@donnelly.edu; Staff 6 (MLS 1, Non-MLS 5)
Founded 1949. Enrl 500; Fac 80; Highest Degree: Bachelor
Library Holdings: Bk Vols 38,000; Per Subs 75
Special Collections: African-American Heritage (Roe Coll)
Subject Interests: Biblical studies, Women's studies
Automation Activity & Vendor Info: (OPAC) SirsiDynix
Database Vendor: ProQuest, SirsiDynix
Wireless access
Function: Ref serv available
Mem of Northeast Kansas Library System
Partic in Mid-America Library Alliance/Kansas City Metropolitan Library & Information Network
Open Mon-Wed 8-7, Thurs 8-7:30, Fri 8-4:30

J KANSAS CITY KANSAS COMMUNITY COLLEGE LIBRARY*, 7250 State Ave, 66112-3098. SAN 305-9782. Tel: 913-288-7650. Interlibrary Loan Service Tel: 913-288-7698. FAX: 913-288-7606. Web Site: www.kckcc.edu/services/library. *Dir,* Cheryl Postlewait; Tel: 913-288-7230, E-mail: cpostlewait@kckcc.edu; *Pub Serv Librn,* Joseph Grasela, Jr; E-mail: jgrasela@kckcc.edu; *Ref Librn,* Barbara Stransky; E-mail: bstransky@kckcc.edu; *Ref/Media Serv Librn,* Penny Mahon; E-mail: pennymah@kckcc.edu; Staff 11 (MLS 5, Non-MLS 6)
Founded 1923. Enrl 7,000; Fac 3; Highest Degree: Associate
Jul 2012-Jun 2013. Mats Exp $208,000, Books $30,000, Per/Ser (Incl. Access Fees) $25,000, Micro $1,000, AV Mat $12,000, Electronic Ref Mat (Incl. Access Fees) $140,000
Library Holdings: AV Mats 12,000; CDs 2,500; DVDs 2,500; e-books 49,000; Bk Titles 60,000; Bk Vols 75,000; Per Subs 100; Videos 2,500
Special Collections: US Document Depository
Subject Interests: Educ, Mortuary sci, Nursing
Automation Activity & Vendor Info: (Acquisitions) EOS International; (Cataloging) EOS International; (Circulation) EOS International; (Course Reserve) EOS International; (ILL) EOS International; (Media Booking) EOS International; (OPAC) EOS International; (Serials) EOS International
Database Vendor: 3M Library Systems, Alexander Street Press, ALLDATA Online, CredoReference, ebrary, EBSCO Auto Repair Reference, EBSCOhost, EOS International, Facts on File, Gale Cengage Learning, LearningExpress, LexisNexis, Newsbank, OCLC FirstSearch, OCLC WorldShare Interlibrary Loan, Oxford Online, ProQuest, PubMed, Safari Books Online, Sage, WT Cox
Wireless access
Partic in Kansas City Library Service Program; Mid-America Library Alliance/Kansas City Metropolitan Library & Information Network; OCLC Online Computer Library Center, Inc
Special Services for the Deaf - Assistive tech; Closed caption videos
Special Services for the Blind - Assistive/Adapted tech devices, equip & products
Open Mon-Thurs (Winter) 7:30am-9pm, Fri 7:30-4:30, Sat 9-3:30; Mon-Thurs (Summer) 7:30am-9pm
Restriction: Open to pub for ref & circ; with some limitations

P KANSAS CITY, KANSAS PUBLIC LIBRARY*, 625 Minnesota Ave, 66101. SAN 342-0515. Tel: 913-551-3280. Circulation Tel: 913-279-2206. Interlibrary Loan Service Tel: 913-279-2239. Reference Tel: 913-279-2212. Administration Tel: 913-279-2219. FAX: 913-279-2033. Administration FAX: 913-551-3243. Web Site: www.kckpl.org. *Dir,* Carol Levers; Tel: 913-279-2219; *Asst Dir,* Chris Barnickel; Tel: 913-279-2223, E-mail: cbarnickel@kckpl.org; *Head, Cat,* John Byrd; Tel: 913-279-2108, E-mail: jbyrd@kckpl.org; *Computer Serv Mgr,* Nancy Haag; Tel: 913-279-2670, E-mail: nhaag@kckpl.org; *Extn Serv Mgr,* Patti Myers; E-mail: pmyers@kckpl.org; *Human Res Mgr,* Tammie Sharp; Tel: 913-279-2256, E-mail: tsharp@kckpl.org; *Supvr, Computer Serv,* Mike Fairley; Tel: 913-279-2361; *Network Serv Coordr,* Brig McCoy; Tel: 913-279-2349, E-mail: bmccoy@kckpl.org; *Pub Relations Coordr,* Sarah Lehman; Tel: 913-279-2106. Subject Specialists: *Computer,* Nancy Haag; *Pub relations,* Sarah Lehman; Staff 130 (MLS 32, Non-MLS 98)
Founded 1892. Pop 150,314; Circ 959,256
Library Holdings: AV Mats 56,955; Electronic Media & Resources 2,198; Bk Vols 487,863; Per Subs 980
Special Collections: Fine Arts; Spanish Language; Wyandot Indians (Connelley Coll), bks & ms. State Document Depository
Subject Interests: Kansas
Automation Activity & Vendor Info: (Acquisitions) SirsiDynix
Database Vendor: Baker & Taylor, EBSCOhost, Gale Cengage Learning, Newsbank, OCLC FirstSearch, ProQuest, SirsiDynix, Wilson - Wilson Web
Function: Fax serv, Photocopying/Printing, Ref serv available
Publications: Advice from the Experts; Divulgacion; Happy Kids; Health Notes; New Ideas for Non Profits; Real Money; Taking Stock; The Fiction Connection
Mem of Northeast Kansas Library System
Partic in Mid-America Library Alliance/Kansas City Metropolitan Library & Information Network; OCLC Online Computer Library Center, Inc
Open Mon-Thurs 8:30-8:30, Fri & Sat 8:30-5, Sun 1-5
Friends of the Library Group
Branches: 4
MAIN BRANCH, 625 Minnesota Ave, 66101. Tel: 913-279-2206. FAX: 913-279-2032. *Br Mgr,* Linda Wolford; Tel: 913-279-2202, E-mail: lwolford@kckpl.org
MR & MRS F L SCHLAGLE, 4051 West Dr, 66109. Tel: 913-299-2384. FAX: 913-299-9967. *Br Mgr,* Craig Hensley; E-mail: chensley@kckpl.org

SOUTH BRANCH, 3401 Strong Ave, 66106, SAN 342-054X. Tel: 913-722-7400. FAX: 913-722-7402. *Br Mgr,* Jack Granath; E-mail: jgranath@kckpl.org; Staff 13 (MLS 2, Non-MLS 11)
Library Holdings: AV Mats 9,468; Bk Vols 66,671; Per Subs 87
Special Collections: Spanish Language Coll
Open Mon-Thurs 8:30-8:30, Fri & Sat 8:30-5, Sun 1-5
Friends of the Library Group

WEST WYANDOTTE, 1737 N 82nd St, 66112. Tel: 913-596-5800. FAX: 913-596-5806. *Br Mgr,* Laura Loveless; Tel: 913-596-5800, Ext 1001, E-mail: llove@kckpl.org
Bookmobiles: 1

S KANSAS UNIVERSITY MEDICAL CENTER*, Clendening History of Medicine Library, 1020-1030 Robinson Bldg, 3901 Rainbow Blvd, 66160-7311. (Mail add: University of Kansas Medical Center, MS 1024, 3901 Rainbow Blvd, 66160), SAN 375-4375. Tel: 913-588-7244. FAX: 913-588-7060. E-mail: clendening@kumc.edu. Web Site: clendening.kumc.edu. *Dir,* Dr Christopher Crenner; Tel: 913-588-7040, E-mail: crenner@kumc.edu; *Archivist,* Nancy Hulston; Tel: 913-588-7243, E-mail: nhulston@kumc.edu; *Rare Bks,* Dawn McInnis; E-mail: dmcinnis@kumc.edu; Staff 1 (Non-MLS 1)
Founded 1945
Library Holdings: Bk Vols 26,000; Per Subs 40
Special Collections: Anesthesia, Roentgenology, Hemotology & Microscopy Colls; Florence Nightingale & Joseph Lister Letters; Rudolf Virchow Manuscripts; Samuel Crumbine Papers
Subject Interests: Bioethics, Hist of med
Automation Activity & Vendor Info: (Acquisitions) Ex Libris Group; (Cataloging) Ex Libris Group; (Circulation) Ex Libris Group
Wireless access
Open Mon & Wed 9-1, Tues & Thurs 12-4
Restriction: Circ limited, Closed stack
Friends of the Library Group

M PROVIDENCE MEDICAL CENTER LIBRARY, 8929 Parallel Pkwy, 66112-0430. SAN 342-0604. Tel: 913-596-3990. FAX: 913-596-3436. *Librn,* Marin Goodier; Staff 1 (Non-MLS 1)
Founded 1964
Library Holdings: Bk Titles 500; Per Subs 50
Subject Interests: Consumer health, Health sci
Open Mon-Fri 8-4:30

GL UNITED STATES COURTS*, Kansas City, Kansas Branch Library, 624 US Courthouse, 500 State Ave, 66101-2448. Tel: 913-735-2200. *Br Librn,* Position Currently Open; *Libr Tech,* Linda A Wassberg; Tel: 913-551-6546, E-mail: linda_wassberg@ca10.uscourts.gov; Staff 2 (MLS 1, Non-MLS 1)
Founded 1994
Library Holdings: Bk Vols 8,000; Per Subs 12
Automation Activity & Vendor Info: (Acquisitions) SirsiDynix; (Cataloging) SirsiDynix; (OPAC) SirsiDynix
Restriction: Not open to pub, Secured area only open to authorized personnel

CM UNIVERSITY OF KANSAS MEDICAL CENTER, Archie R Dykes Library of Health Sciences, 2100 W 39th Ave, 66160-7180. (Mail add: 3901 Rainbow Blvd, Mail Stop 1050, 66160), SAN 305-9812. Tel: 913-588-7166. Interlibrary Loan Service Tel: 913-588-5073. Administration Tel: 913-588-7300. Toll Free Tel: 800-332-4193. E-mail: dykesref@kumc.edu. Web Site: www.library.kumc.edu. *Dir,* Jameson Watkins; E-mail: jwatkins@kumc.edu; *Asst Dir, Content Mgt,* Crystal Cameron-Vedros; E-mail: cvedros@kumc.edu; *Res & Ref Librn,* Deborah Carman; Tel: 913-588-7118; Staff 17 (MLS 9, Non-MLS 8)
Founded 1906. Enrl 2,560; Highest Degree: Doctorate
Library Holdings: e-journals 12,000; Bk Titles 54,000; Bk Vols 62,476; Per Subs 1,000
Special Collections: History & Philosophy of Medicine (Clendening Coll)
Subject Interests: Health sci
Automation Activity & Vendor Info: (Acquisitions) Ex Libris Group; (Cataloging) Ex Libris Group; (Circulation) Ex Libris Group; (Course Reserve) Blackboard Inc
Database Vendor: 3M Library Systems, Blackwell, EBSCOhost, Gale Cengage Learning, JSTOR, OCLC FirstSearch, OVID Technologies, ProQuest, PubMed, ScienceDirect, SerialsSolutions, UpToDate, Wiley
Wireless access
Function: Computer training, Copy machines, Doc delivery serv, E-Reserves, Electronic databases & coll, Health sci info serv, ILL available, Online searches, Photocopying/Printing
Partic in BRS; Health Sciences Library Network of Kansas City, Inc; Midcontinental Regional Med Libr Program; OCLC Online Computer Library Center, Inc

GL WYANDOTTE COUNTY LAW LIBRARY*, Court House, 710 N Seventh St, Ste 500, 66101-3999. SAN 305-9820. Tel: 913-573-2899. FAX: 913-573-2892. *Librn,* Brenda Eaton
Founded 1925
Library Holdings: Bk Vols 50,000
Open Mon-Fri 8:30-5

KENSINGTON

P KENSINGTON COMMUNITY-SCHOOL LIBRARY, 203 S Jackson, 66951. (Mail add: PO Box 188, 66951-0188), SAN 376-5660. Tel: 785-476-2219. FAX: 785-476-2215. E-mail: kensingtonlibrary@hotmail.com. *Dir,* Erica L Barnes; E-mail: ebarnes@usd110.net; Staff 2 (Non-MLS 2)
Library Holdings: Bk Vols 12,000; Per Subs 70
Automation Activity & Vendor Info: (Serials) ByWater Solutions
Database Vendor: ByWater Solutions
Wireless access
Mem of Central Kansas Library System
Open Mon 8-8, Tues-Fri 8-4, Sat 9-2; Mon-Sat (Summer) 9-2

KINGMAN

P KINGMAN CARNEGIE PUBLIC LIBRARY*, 455 N Main St, 67068-1395. SAN 305-9839. Tel: 620-532-3061. FAX: 620-532-2528. Web Site: www.kingmanlibrary.org. *Librn,* Grace G Helm; E-mail: graceg@kingmanlibrary.org; *Asst Librn,* Joy Stroot; *Youth Serv Librn,* Aaron Rohrer
Founded 1913. Pop 3,200; Circ 56,827
Library Holdings: AV Mats 636; High Interest/Low Vocabulary Bk Vols 162; Large Print Bks 718; Bk Vols 30,235; Per Subs 68; Talking Bks 332
Subject Interests: Local newsp
Automation Activity & Vendor Info: (Acquisitions) Follett Software; (Circulation) Follett Software
Wireless access
Open Mon, Tues & Thurs 10-8, Wed & Fri 10-6, Sat 10-2
Friends of the Library Group

KINSLEY

P KINSLEY PUBLIC LIBRARY*, 208 E Eighth St, 67547-1422. SAN 305-9855. Tel: 620-659-3341. E-mail: director@kinsleylibrary.info. Web Site: www.kinsleylibrary.info. *Dir,* Joan Weaver; *Librn,* Rosetta Graff; Staff 2.1 (Non-MLS 2.1)
Founded 1904. Pop 1,200; Circ 19,100
Library Holdings: AV Mats 1,000; Large Print Bks 285; Bk Titles 23,000; Per Subs 70; Talking Bks 300
Special Collections: DAR Magazines 1914-1963; Kinsley Historical Downtown Digital Map on line; Kinsley Newspapers 1878-present, micro; Local Oral Histories. Oral History
Subject Interests: Carnivals, Genealogy, Local hist
Automation Activity & Vendor Info: (Circulation) Auto-Graphics, Inc
Wireless access
Mem of Southwest Kansas Library System
Open Mon & Wed 9-8, Tues, Thurs & Fri 9-11 & 1-5, Sat 1-5
Friends of the Library Group

KIOWA

P KIOWA PUBLIC LIBRARY*, 123 N Seventh St, 67070. SAN 305-9863. Tel: 620-825-4630. FAX: 620-825-4630. E-mail: kiowalb@sctelcom.net. Web Site: skyways.lib.ks.us/towns/kiowa/library. *Dir,* Gayle Bowdes
Founded 1950. Pop 1,160; Circ 9,000
Library Holdings: DVDs 60; Large Print Bks 1,300; Bk Vols 15,000; Per Subs 30; Videos 500
Automation Activity & Vendor Info: (Cataloging) Follett Software; (Circulation) Follett Software
Wireless access
Function: Accelerated reader prog, Audio & video playback equip for onsite use, Bks on cassette, Bks on CD, Computers for patron use, Copy machines, e-mail serv, Fax serv, Free DVD rentals, Handicapped accessible, Home delivery & serv to Sr ctr & nursing homes, Homebound delivery serv, ILL available, Newsp ref libr, Pub access computers, Summer reading prog, Tax forms, VCDs, Video lending libr, Wheelchair accessible
Mem of South Central Kansas Library System
Special Services for the Blind - Accessible computers; Bks on cassette; Bks on CD; Cassette playback machines; Copier with enlargement capabilities; Large print bks
Open Mon 7pm-9pm, Tues 12-5, Thurs 2-5 & 7-9, Sat 10-1
Friends of the Library Group

KIRWIN

P KIRWIN CITY LIBRARY*, First & Main, 67644. (Mail add: PO Box 445, 67644-0445), SAN 305-9871. Tel: 785-543-6652. FAX: 785-543-6168. *Librn,* Wanda Jameson
Pop 267; Circ 5,000
Library Holdings: Bk Vols 7,900; Per Subs 15; Talking Bks 58

Special Collections: Papers Published in Kirwin, 1889-1942
Publications: History of Kirwin, Kansas 1869-1969; The Saga of Fort Kirwin
Mem of Central Kansas Library System
Open Mon-Thurs 9-12 & 1-4:30

KISMET

P KISMET PUBLIC LIBRARY*, 503 Main St, 67859-9615. (Mail add: PO Box 66, 67859-0066), SAN 326-5536. Tel: 620-563-7357. FAX: 620-563-7143. E-mail: director@kismetlibrary.info. Web Site: www.kismetlibrary.info. *Dir,* Pam Orth
Library Holdings: Bk Vols 3,500; Per Subs 16
Function: AV serv, ILL available
Mem of Southwest Kansas Library System
Open Mon 1-7, Tues & Thurs 1-6, Wed 8-12 & 1-5, Sat 9-1

LA CROSSE

P BARNARD LIBRARY*, 521 Elm, 67548. (Mail add: PO Box 727, 67548-0727), SAN 305-988X. Tel: 785-222-2826. FAX: 785-222-2826. E-mail: blibrary@gbta.net. *Dir,* Linda Seymour
Founded 1926. Pop 1,800
Library Holdings: Bk Titles 17,000; Per Subs 41
Special Collections: Kansas Coll
Automation Activity & Vendor Info: (Cataloging) Follett Software; (Circulation) Follett Software
Mem of Central Kansas Library System
Open Mon, Tues & Fri 11-4:30, Wed 1-6, Thurs 11-7, Sat 10-3

LA CYGNE

P LINN COUNTY LIBRARY DISTRICT NO 2, 209 N Broadway, 66040. (Mail add: PO Box 127, 66040-0127), SAN 305-9898. Tel: 913-757-2151. FAX: 913-757-2405. E-mail: lacyg1lb@peoplestelecom.net. Web Site: www.lacygnelibrary.org. *Dir,* Christine Waddell; *Asst Librn, Ch Serv, Tech Serv,* Janet Reynolds; *Ch Serv,* LaVeda Riggs; Staff 3 (Non-MLS 3)
Founded 1908. Pop 2,500; Circ 23,266
Jan 2007-Dec 2007 Income $248,100, State $1,100, County $247,000. Mats Exp $22,100, Books $19,000, Per/Ser (Incl. Access Fees) $3,100. Sal $61,400
Library Holdings: Audiobooks 534; Bks on Deafness & Sign Lang 15; CDs 135; DVDs 1,737; High Interest/Low Vocabulary Bk Vols 600; Large Print Bks 3,588; Bk Titles 35,088; Bk Vols 35,250; Per Subs 95; Talking Bks 322; Videos 150
Special Collections: Genealogy; Kansas Books & Authors; LaCygne Journal (1870-2000 on microfilm)
Automation Activity & Vendor Info: (Cataloging) Follett Software; (Circulation) Follett Software; (ILL) Auto-Graphics, Inc; (OPAC) Follett Software
Database Vendor: Evanced Solutions, Inc, OCLC FirstSearch
Wireless access
Function: 24/7 Online cat, After school storytime, Audiobks via web, Bk club(s), Bks on CD, Children's prog, Computer training, Computers for patron use, Copy machines, e-mail & chat, Electronic databases & coll, Fax serv, Free DVD rentals, Genealogy discussion group, Handicapped accessible, Holiday prog, Laminating, Life-long learning prog for all ages, Magazines, Mail & tel request accepted, Mango lang, Microfiche/film & reading machines, Movies, Music CDs, Notary serv, Online cat, Photocopying/Printing, Preschool outreach, Preschool reading prog, Printer for laptops & handheld devices, Prog for adults, Prog for children & young adult, Pub access computers, Scanner, Senior computer classes, Spanish lang bks, Story hour, Summer reading prog, Tax forms, Teen prog, VHS videos, Web-catalog, Wheelchair accessible
Mem of Southeast Kansas Library System
Open Mon, Tues & Thurs 9-6, Wed 9-4, Fri 9-5, Sat 9-Noon
Friends of the Library Group

LAKIN

P KEARNY COUNTY LIBRARY*, 101 E Prairie, 67860. (Mail add: PO Box 773, 67860-0773), SAN 305-9901. Tel: 620-355-6674. FAX: 620-355-6801. *Dir,* Richard Brookman; *Asst Dir,* Tammy Dickey; *ILL,* Dora Lynch; Staff 4 (MLS 1, Non-MLS 3)
Founded 1956. Pop 4,177; Circ 30,794
Library Holdings: Bk Titles 27,697; Per Subs 69
Special Collections: Foundation Center for Grant Writing; Graphic Novels; Native American Coll
Subject Interests: Kansas
Function: Photocopying/Printing
Publications: Weekly Newspaper
Mem of Southwest Kansas Library System
Open Mon, Wed & Fri 9-5, Tues & Thurs 9-9, Sat 10-1
Friends of the Library Group

LANSING

S KANSAS DEPARTMENT OF CORRECTIONS*, Lansing Correctional Facility Library, 801 E Kansas Hwy, 66043. (Mail add: PO Box 2, 66043-0002). Tel: 913-727-3235. FAX: 913-727-2997. *Librn,* Mark York
Library Holdings: Bk Vols 20,000; Per Subs 18
Database Vendor: LexisNexis
Open Mon-Fri 8-10:30, 12:30-2:30 & 5:30-8:30, Sat 1-2:30

P LANSING COMMUNITY LIBRARY*, 108 S Second St, 66043. Tel. 913-727-2929. FAX: 913-727-1538. Web Site: www.lansing.ks.us. *Librn,* Darlene Dean
Library Holdings: Bk Titles 32,000
Automation Activity & Vendor Info: (Cataloging) Follett Software; (Circulation) Follett Software
Mem of Northeast Kansas Library System
Open Mon-Thurs 10-7, Fri 10-5, Sat 9-1

LARNED

S FORT LARNED HISTORICAL SOCIETY, INC*, Santa Fe Trail Center Library, 1349 K-156 Hwy, 67550. SAN 305-9928. Tel: 620-285-2054. FAX: 620-285-7491. E-mail: curator@santafetrailcenter.org. Web Site: www.santafetrailcenter.org.
Founded 1974
Library Holdings: Bk Titles 3,450; Per Subs 10
Special Collections: Grand Army of the Republic Records (B F Larned Post); Official Records & Correspondence; Pawnee County, Kansas School Records; R R Smith Glass Magic Lantern Slide Coll; War of the Rebellion Coll
Subject Interests: Kansas

P JORDAAN MEMORIAL LIBRARY*, 724 Broadway, 67550-3051. SAN 305-991X. Tel: 620-285-2876. FAX: 620-285-7275. Web Site: www.jordaanlibrary.com. *Dir,* Margaret Larson; E-mail: mlarson@jordaanlibrary.com; Staff 4.5 (Non-MLS 4.5)
Founded 1915. Pop 5,000; Circ 30,000
Library Holdings: Large Print Bks 3,000; Bk Vols 36,180; Per Subs 107; Talking Bks 465
Subject Interests: Hist, Kansas
Automation Activity & Vendor Info: (Cataloging) Follett Software
Mem of Central Kansas Library System
Open Mon-Thurs (Winter) 11-8, Fri 10-6, Sat 10-4; Mon-Fri (Summer) 9-6, Sat 10-4

S KANSAS DEPARTMENT OF CORRECTIONS*, Larned Correctional Mental Health Facility Library, 1318 KS Hwy 264, 67550. Tel: 620-285-6249. FAX: 620-285-8070.
Library Holdings: Bk Vols 2,000; Per Subs 52; Talking Bks 30
Open Mon & Sun 1-8, Tues & Thurs 8-4, Wed & Fri 8-5

LARNED STATE HOSPITAL

M J T NARAMORE MEMORIAL LIBRARY*, 1301 KS Hwy 264, 67550-9365, SAN 342-0728. Tel: 620-285-4303. FAX: 620-285-4325.
Founded 1953
Library Holdings: Bk Vols 1,500; Per Subs 30
Special Collections: Dr Homer Davis Coll; J T Naramore Coll
Open Mon-Fri 8-5

M PATIENTS' LIBRARY*, 1301 KS Hwy 264, 67550-9365, SAN 342-0752. Tel: 620-285-4303. FAX: 620-285-4325.
Founded 1948
Library Holdings: Bk Vols 3,000; Per Subs 15
Subject Interests: Local hist
Mem of Central Kansas Library System; Central Kansas Library System
Special Services for the Deaf - Videos & decoder
Special Services for the Blind - Braille bks; Large print bks & talking machines
Open Mon-Fri 8-5

S US NATIONAL PARK SERVICE*, Fort Larned National Historic Site Library, 1767 Hwy 156, 67550-9803. SAN 370-3150. Tel: 620-285-6911. FAX: 620-285-3571. Web Site: www.nps.gov/fols. *Librn,* Celeste Dixon
Library Holdings: Bk Vols 1,600; Per Subs 10
Special Collections: Fort Larned Documents 1859-1878; Microfilm Coll
Function: Res libr
Open Mon-Sun 8:30-4:30

LAWRENCE

C HASKELL INDIAN NATIONS UNIVERSITY*, Tommaney Library, 155 Indian Ave, 66046. SAN 305-9936. Tel: 785-832-6661. FAX: 785-749-8473. Web Site: www.haskell.edu. *Libr Dir,* Dr Marilyn L Russell; E-mail: mrussell@haskell.edu; Staff 5 (MLS 1, Non-MLS 4)
Founded 1884. Enrl 900; Fac 34; Highest Degree: Bachelor
Library Holdings: DVDs 250; Bk Vols 75,000; Per Subs 250
Special Collections: Indians of North America Coll

Subject Interests: Indians
Automation Activity & Vendor Info: (Acquisitions) SirsiDynix; (Cataloging) OCLC CatExpress; (Circulation) SirsiDynix; (ILL) SirsiDynix; (OPAC) SirsiDynix
Database Vendor: EBSCOhost, HeinOnline, JSTOR, Project MUSE, ProQuest
Wireless access
Function: ILL available
Publications: American Indian Periodicals & Tribal Newspapers
Partic in Kans City Pub Libr Consortium
Open Mon-Thurs 8am-10pm, Fri 8-5, Sun 1-10
Restriction: Staff & prof res, Students only, Teacher & adminr only

G KANSAS GEOLOGICAL SURVEY LIBRARY*, Core Library, 1930 Constant Ave, 66047-3726. SAN 324-0096. Tel: 785-864-4909. FAX: 785-864-5317. Web Site: www.kgs.ku.edu. *Librn,* Janice Sorensen
Founded 1973
Library Holdings: Bk Titles 17,000; Per Subs 55
Subject Interests: Energy, Geol, Kansas, Natural res, Water res
Publications: Bibliography of Kansas Geology; Kansas State Geological Survey Open-file Reports
Open Mon-Fri 8-5

P LAWRENCE PUBLIC LIBRARY, 707 Vermont St, 66044-2371. SAN 305-9952. Tel: 785-843-3833. FAX: 785-843-3368. E-mail: custserv@lawrence.lib.ks.us. Web Site: www.lawrencepubliclibrary.org. *Exec Dir,* Brad Allen; Tel: 785-843-3833, Ext 102, E-mail: ballen@lawrence.lib.ks.us; *Dir, Develop & Strategic Partnerships,* Kathleen Morgan; Tel: 785-843-3833, Ext 131, E-mail: kmorgan@lawrence.lib.ks.us; *Dir of Libr Operations,* Sherri Turner; Tel: 785-843-3833, Ext 126, E-mail: sturner@lawrence.lib.ks.us; *Tech Librn,* Kim Fletcher; Tel: 785-843-3833, Ext 116, E-mail: kfletcher@lawrence.lib.ks.us; *Coll Serv Mgr,* Tricia Karlin; Tel: 785-843-3833, Ext 109, E-mail: tkarlin@lawrence.lib.ks.us; *Fac & Tech Mgr,* Tom Davin; Tel: 785-843-3833, Ext 135, E-mail: tdavin@lawrence.lib.ks.us; *Pub Serv Mgr,* Amanda McConnell; Tel: 785-843-3833, Ext 120, E-mail: amcconnell@lawrence.lib.ks.us; *Coll Develop Coordr,* Charlee Glinka; Tel: 785-843-3833, Ext 104, E-mail: cglinka@lawrence.lib.ks.us; *Info Serv Coordr,* Ransom Jabara; Tel: 785-843-3833, Ext 113, E-mail: rjabara@lawrence.lib.ks.us; *Mkt Coordr,* Jeni Daley; Tel: 785-843-3833, Ext 123, E-mail: jdaley@lawrence.lib.ks.us; *Prog & Events Coordr,* Kristin Soper; Tel: 785-843-3833, Ext 122, E-mail: ksoper@lawrence.lib.ks.us; *Reader's Serv Coordr,* Polli Kenn; Tel: 785-843-3833, Ext 132, E-mail: pkenn@lawrence.lib.ks.us; *Tech Coordr,* Aaron Brumley; Tel: 785-843-3833, Ext 106, E-mail: abrumley@lawrence.lib.ks.us; *Youth Serv Coordr,* Karen Allen; Tel: 785-843-3833, Ext 121, E-mail: kallen@lawrence.lib.ks.us; Staff 54 (MLS 17, Non-MLS 37)
Founded 1904. Pop 90,000; Circ 1,300,000
Jan 2014-Dec 2014 Income $3,660,800, State $32,000, City $3,383,260, Other $245,540. Mats Exp $520,000. Sal $1,960,000
Library Holdings: AV Mats 40,000; Bk Vols 140,000; Per Subs 200
Special Collections: Osma Local History Coll
Automation Activity & Vendor Info: (Acquisitions) Innovative Interfaces, Inc; (Cataloging) Innovative Interfaces, Inc; (Circulation) Innovative Interfaces, Inc; (ILL) Innovative Interfaces, Inc; (OPAC) BiblioCommons; (Serials) Innovative Interfaces, Inc
Database Vendor: Baker & Taylor, BiblioCommons, EBSCOhost, Evanced Solutions, Inc, Gale Cengage Learning, Innovative Interfaces, Inc, OCLC FirstSearch, Overdrive, Inc, Tech Logic
Wireless access
Function: 24/7 Electronic res, 24/7 Online cat, Activity rm, Adult bk club, Art exhibits, Audiobks via web, Bk club(s), Bks on CD, Computers for patron use, Copy machines, e-mail & chat, Electronic databases & coll, eReaders, Fax serv, Free DVD rentals, Handicapped accessible, Home delivery & serv to Sr ctr & nursing homes, Homebound delivery serv, ILL available, Magazines, Movies, Music CDs, Online cat, Outreach serv, OverDrive digital audio bks, Photocopying/Printing, Prog for adults, Prog for children & young adult, Pub access computers, Ref serv available, Senior outreach, Story hour, Study rm, Summer & winter reading prog, Summer reading prog, Tax forms, Teen prog, Telephone ref, Web-catalog
Mem of Northeast Kansas Library System
Special Services for the Blind - Computer with voice synthesizer for visually impaired persons
Open Mon-Thurs 9-9, Fri 9-7, Sat 9-6, Sun 12-6
Restriction: Authorized patrons
Friends of the Library Group

P NORTHEAST KANSAS LIBRARY SYSTEM*, 4317 W Sixth St, 66049. SAN 306-1302. Tel: 785-838-4090. Toll Free Tel: 888-296-6963 (KS only). FAX: 785-838-3989. Web Site: www.nekls.org. *Dir,* Jim Minges; E-mail: jminges@nekls.org; *Bus Mgr/Consult,* Laura A DeBaun; E-mail: ldebaun@nekls.org; *Libr Develop Consult,* Mickey Coalwell; E-mail: mcoalwell@nekls.org; *Tech Consult,* Sharon Moreland; E-mail: smoreland@nekls.or; Staff 7 (MLS 6, Non-MLS 1)
Founded 1966. Pop 834,867
Jan 2009-Dec 2009 Income $2,164,542, State $119,645, Federal $225,678, County $1,503,362, Other $315,857. Mats Exp $14,500
Subject Interests: Libr sci, Tech
Automation Activity & Vendor Info: (Cataloging) LibLime; (Circulation) LibLime; (ILL) LibLime; (OPAC) LibLime
Wireless access
Publications: Directory; Librarians Report; Loose Change (Newsletter)
Member Libraries: Atchison Public Library; Baldwin City Library; Barnes Reading Room; Basehor Community Library District 2; Beck Bookman Library; Benedictine College Library; Bern Community Library; Bonner Springs City Library; Burlingame Community Library; Carbondale City Library; Centralia Community Library; Corning City Library; Delaware Township Library; Donnelly College; Effingham Community Library; Eudora Public Library; Horton Free Public Library; Johnson County Library; Kansas City, Kansas Public Library; Lansing Community Library; Lawrence Public Library; Leavenworth Public Library; Library District Number One, Doniphan County; Linwood Community Library; Louisburg Public Library; Lyndon Carnegie Library; Mary Cotton Public Library; McLouth Public Library; Meriden Community Library; MidAmerica Nazarene University; Morrill Public Library; Nortonville Public Library; Olathe Public Library; Osage City Public Library; Osawatomie Public Library; Osawatomie State Hospital; Ottawa Library; Ottawa University; Overbrook Public Library; Paola Free Library; Rossville Community Library; Seneca Free Library; Silver Lake Library; Tonganoxie Public Library; Topeka & Shawnee County Public Library; Wellsville City Library; Wetmore Public Library; Williamsburg Community Library

CR UNIVERSITY OF KANSAS, DEPARTMENT OF RELIGIOUS STUDIES*, William J Moore Reading Room, Smith Hall, Rm 109, 1300 Oread Ave, 66045-7615. SAN 305-9944. Tel: 785-864-4663. FAX: 785-864-5205. E-mail: wjmoore@mail.ku.edu. *In Charge,* Melissa Fisher Isaacs
Library Holdings: Bk Titles 12,000; Bk Vols 14,000; Per Subs 46
Subject Interests: Bible studies, Buddhism, Christianity, Hinduism, Islam, Judaism
Restriction: Private libr

C UNIVERSITY OF KANSAS LIBRARIES*, Watson Library, 1425 Jayhawk Blvd, 66045-7544. SAN 342-0787. Tel: 785-864-3956. FAX: 785-864-5311. Web Site: www.lib.ku.edu. *Dean of Libr,* Lorraine Haricombe; *Asst Dean,* Kent Miller; *Asst Dean,* Mary Roach; *ILL,* Lars Leon; Staff 87 (MLS 54, Non-MLS 33)
Founded 1866. Enrl 29,260; Fac 2,328; Highest Degree: Doctorate
Library Holdings: Bk Vols 4,194,283; Per Subs 48,037
Special Collections: 18th Century English History & Literature; 19th Century Spanish Plays; Anglo-Saxon Types; Botany; Children's Books; Chinese Classics; Colombia; Continental Renaissance; Economics; Edmund Curll Coll; English Poetical Miscellanies; French Revolution; Historical Cartography; Irish History & Literature; Joyce Coll; Kansas History; Linnaeus Coll; Modern American Poetry; Modern Extremist Politics; Opera; Ornithology; Rilke Coll; Sir Robert Walpole Coll; Travel; Women; Yeats Coll. Oral History; State Document Depository; UN Document Depository; US Document Depository
Automation Activity & Vendor Info: (Acquisitions) Ex Libris Group; (Cataloging) Ex Libris Group; (Circulation) Ex Libris Group; (Course Reserve) Docutek; (OPAC) Ex Libris Group; (Serials) Ex Libris Group
Publications: Bibliographical Contributions, Books & Libraries
Partic in Association of Research Libraries (ARL); Center for Research Libraries; Greater Western Library Alliance; OCLC Online Computer Library Center, Inc
Open Mon-Thurs 8am-Midnight, Fri 8-8, Sat 10-5, Sun 10am-Midnight

Departmental Libraries:

ANSCHUTZ LIBRARY, 1301 Hoch Auditoria Dr, 66045-7537. Tel: 785-864-4928. FAX: 785-864-5705. *Dean,* Lorraine Haricombe
Open Mon-Thurs (Sept-May) 8am-Midnight, Fri 8-8, Sat 10-8; Mon-Thurs (June-July) 8am-9pm, Fri 8-5, Sat 12-5, Sun 10-5; Mon-Fri (Aug) 8-5, Sat 1-5

GORTON MUSIC & DANCE LIBRARY, 1530 Naismith Dr, 66045-3102, SAN 342-1058. Tel: 785-864-3496. FAX: 785-864-5310. *Head of Libr,* George Gibbs; Tel: 785-864-3282, E-mail: ggibbs@ku.edu
Subject Interests: Applied music, Composition, Music educ, Music theory, Music therapy
Open Mon-Thurs 8am-10pm, Fri 8-5, Sat 12-5, Sun 1-10

MURPHY ART & ARCHITECTURE LIBRARY, 1301 Mississippi St, 66045-7500, SAN 342-0817. Tel: 785-864-3020. FAX: 785-864-4608. *Librn,* Susan Craig
Subject Interests: Archit, Art, Art hist, Design, Photog hist
Open Mon-Thurs 8am-10pm, Fri 8-6, Sat Noon-5, Sun 1-10

SPAHR ENGINEERING LIBRARY, 1532 W 15th St, 66045-7611, SAN 342-099X. Tel: 785-864-3866. FAX: 785-864-5755. *Librn,* Channette Alexander; E-mail: calexander@ku.edu

SPENCER RESEARCH LIBRARY, 1450 Poplar Lane, 66045-7616, SAN 342-1112. Tel: 785-864-4334. FAX: 785-864-5803. *Librn,* Sheryl Williams
Open Mon-Fri 8-5, Sat 12-4

CL WHEAT LAW LIBRARY, Green Hall, Rm 200, 1535 W 15th St, 66045-7608, SAN 342-0930. Tel: 785-864-3025. FAX: 785-864-3680. Web Site: www.law.ku.edu/library. *Dir,* Joyce Pearson; E-mail: jpearson@ku.edu; *Assoc Dir, Head, Tech Serv,* Joseph A Custer; E-mail: jcuster@ku.edu; *Head, Pub Serv,* Pamela Tull; E-mail: ptull@ku.edu; *Cat Librn,* Lauren VanWaardhuizen; E-mail: ldwaard@ku.edu; *Digital Librn, Info Tech,* Tammy Steinle-McLain; E-mail: tsteinle@ku.edu; *Instrul Serv Librn,* W Blake Wilson; E-mail: wilsonwb@ku.edu; *Fac Serv, Res Librn,* Chris Steadham; E-mail: csteadham@ku.edu; *Automation Serv,* Katherine Greene; E-mail: kgreene@ku.edu; Staff 13 (MLS 8, Non-MLS 5)
Founded 1878. Highest Degree: Doctorate
Library Holdings: Bk Vols 360,139; Per Subs 3,702
Special Collections: State Document Depository; US Document Depository
Automation Activity & Vendor Info: (Course Reserve) Blackboard Inc; (ILL) OCLC
Database Vendor: 3M Library Systems, Gale Cengage Learning, HeinOnline, LexisNexis, OCLC WorldShare Interlibrary Loan, Westlaw
Open Mon-Thurs (Winter) 7:30am-11pm, Fri 7:30-7, Sat 9-5, Sun 10am-11pm; Mon-Thurs (Summer) 7:30am-10pm, Fri 7:30-5, Sat 9-5, Sun 10-10
Friends of the Library Group

S UNIVERSITY OF KANSAS LIFE SPAN INSTITUTE*, Research & Training Center on Independent Living Library, 1000 Sunnyside Dr, Rm 4089, 66045-7555. SAN 375-1899. Tel: 785-864-4095. FAX: 785-864-5063. TDD: 785-864-0706. E-mail: rtcil@ku.edu. Web Site: www.rtcil.org. *In Charge,* Pam Willits
Library Holdings: Bk Vols 300; Per Subs 15
Open Mon-Fri 8-5

LEAVENWORTH

P LEAVENWORTH PUBLIC LIBRARY*, 417 Spruce St, 66048. SAN 305-9960. Tel: 913-682-5666. FAX: 913-682-1248. Web Site: www.leavenworthpubliclibrary.org. *Dir,* Matthew Nojonen; E-mail: mnojonen@lvplks.org; *Asst Dir, Ref Serv,* Marguerite Spencer; E-mail: mspencer@leavenworth.lib.ks.us; *Tech Coordr,* Fred Postlewait; E-mail: fpostlewait@leavenworth.lib.ks.us; Staff 28 (MLS 7, Non-MLS 21)
Founded 1895. Pop 35,000
Jan 2011-Dec 2011 Income $1,105,648, State $46,415, City $1,022,603, Locally Generated Income $36,630. Mats Exp $146,862, Books $87,018, Per/Ser (Incl. Access Fees) $11,835, Micro $2,000, AV Mat $25,277, Electronic Ref Mat (Incl. Access Fees) $20,732. Sal $740,429
Library Holdings: Audiobooks 2,113; CDs 2,384; DVDs 2,990; e-books 384; Large Print Bks 2,918; Bk Vols 85,846; Per Subs 120
Special Collections: Oral History; State Document Depository
Subject Interests: Kansas, Local hist
Automation Activity & Vendor Info: (Acquisitions) ByWater Solutions; (Cataloging) ByWater Solutions; (Circulation) ByWater Solutions; (ILL) Auto-Graphics, Inc; (OPAC) ByWater Solutions
Database Vendor: Gale Cengage Learning
Wireless access
Publications: Leavenworth Legacy
Mem of Northeast Kansas Library System
Open Mon-Thurs 9-9, Fri & Sat 9-5, Sun 1-5
Friends of the Library Group

C UNIVERSITY OF SAINT MARY*, De Paul Library, 4100 S Fourth St Trafficway, 66048-5082. SAN 305-9979. Tel: 913-758-6306. Administration Tel: 913-758-6111. FAX: 913-758-6200. Web Site: www.stmary.edu/library. *Acq, Coll Develop, Dir,* Penelope Lonergan; E-mail: lonergan@stmary.edu; *Access Serv, ILL,* Ashley Creek; E-mail: creek91@stmary.edu; *Cat,* James Bass; E-mail: bassj@stmary.edu; *Ref,* Sister Madonna Fink; E-mail: finksm@stmary.edu; Staff 3 (MLS 3)
Founded 1923. Enrl 1,044; Fac 52; Highest Degree: Doctorate
Library Holdings: AV Mats 1,970; e-books 5,000; Bk Titles 94,280; Bk Vols 118,566; Per Subs 205; Talking Bks 15
Special Collections: Abraham Lincoln, bks, clippings, music, pamphlets; Americana (including Ethnic Minorities), bks, doc, letters, micro; Bible, bks, incunabula, ms; Music, orchestral scores; Shakespeare, bks, microfilm
Automation Activity & Vendor Info: (Acquisitions) EOS International; (Cataloging) EOS International; (Circulation) EOS International; (OPAC) EOS International; (Serials) EOS International
Database Vendor: EBSCOhost
Partic in State Library of Kansas
Open Mon-Thurs 8am-9:30pm, Fri 8-4:30, Sun 5:30-9:30

LEBANON

P LEBANON-COMMUNITY LIBRARY*, 404 N Main St, 66952-9721. (Mail add: PO Box 67, 66952-0067), SAN 306-0004. Tel: 785-389-5711. FAX: 785-389-5711. E-mail: leblibrary@ruraltel.net. *Librn,* Esther Delimont; Staff 1 (Non-MLS 1)
Founded 1901. Pop 440; Circ 2,798
Jan 2011-Dec 2011 Income $13,277, State $124, City $5,653, Other $7,500. Mats Exp $2,067, Books $1,656, Per/Ser (Incl. Access Fees) $363, Electronic Ref Mat (Incl. Access Fees) $48. Sal $7,346
Library Holdings: Large Print Bks 600; Bk Titles 9,000; Per Subs 19
Special Collections: Kansas; Lebanon
Subject Interests: Environ studies, Hist, Med, Music, Natural sci, Relig
Wireless access
Mem of Central Kansas Library System
Open Tues, Wed & Fri 1-5, Sat 1-4

LENEXA

G US ENVIRONMENTAL PROTECTION AGENCY*, Region 7 Library, 11201 Renner Blvd, 66219. SAN 309-0302. Tel: 913-551-7979. FAX: 913-551-8762. E-mail: r7-library@epa.gov. Web Site: www.epa.gov/region7/citizens/irc/index.htm. *Fed Libr Mgr,* Vincent Shawver; Staff 1 (MLS 1)
Founded 1970
Subject Interests: Ecology, Environ educ, Environment, Pollution control, Toxicology
Function: e-mail serv, Mail & tel request accepted, Pub access computers, Ref serv in person, Telephone ref
Restriction: Borrowing requests are handled by ILL, Open to others by appt

LENORA

P LENORA PUBLIC LIBRARY*, 125 1/2 E Washington St, 67645. (Mail add: PO Box 247, 67645-0247), SAN 306-0020. Tel: 785-567-4432. E-mail: lenoralib@ruraltel.net. *Librn,* Gloria Heikes
Founded 1930. Pop 444; Circ 4,041
Library Holdings: Bk Vols 6,500
Automation Activity & Vendor Info: (Cataloging) Gateway; (Circulation) Gateway
Mem of Northwest Kansas Library System
Open Tues & Thurs 2-5:30, Sat 10-1
Friends of the Library Group

LEON

P LEON PUBLIC LIBRARY*, 113 S Main St, 67074-9785. (Mail add: PO Box 57, 67074-0057), SAN 306-0039. Tel: 316-742-3438. *In Charge,* Barbara Templin
Pop 667; Circ 5,409
Library Holdings: Bk Vols 4,450
Open Sat 9-1

LEONARDVILLE

P LEONARDVILLE CITY LIBRARY*, 117 N Erpelding Ave, 66449. (Mail add: PO Box 141, 66449-0141), SAN 306-0047. Tel: 785-293-5606. E-mail: llibrary@twinvalley.net. Web Site: leonardville.mykansaslibrary.org. *Librn,* Barbara Lee
Founded 1963. Pop 348; Circ 6,144
Library Holdings: Bk Vols 5,000
Database Vendor: Auto-Graphics, Inc
Wireless access
Mem of North Central Kansas Libraries System
Open Tues 12:45-5:30, Wed 2-3:30, Thurs 2-5:30, Sat 9-Noon

LEOTI

P WICHITA COUNTY LIBRARY*, 208 S Fourth St, 67861. (Mail add: PO Box 490, 67861-0490), SAN 306-0055. Tel: 620-375-4322. E-mail: wicolib@wbsnet.org. *Dir,* Deandra Gittlein
Founded 1928. Pop 2,900; Circ 18,103
Library Holdings: Bk Titles 19,605; Per Subs 81
Special Collections: Kansas Historical Library; Kansas International Portrait Gallery
Automation Activity & Vendor Info: (Acquisitions) Follett Software; (Cataloging) Follett Software; (Circulation) Follett Software; (OPAC) Follett Software
Open Mon 10-8, Tues-Fri 10-5:30, Sat 9-12

LEWIS

P MEADOWLARK PUBLIC LIBRARY*, 208 Main St, 67552. (Mail add: PO Box 331, 67552-0331), SAN 306-0071. Tel: 620-324-5743. E-mail: meadowlk@gmail.com. Web Site: skyways.lib.ks.us/library/meadowlark. *Librn,* Mary Cross

Founded 1925. Pop 500; Circ 4,289
Library Holdings: Bk Vols 16,000; Per Subs 23
Wireless access
Mem of Southwest Kansas Library System
Open Tues & Thurs 9-12:30 & 1-5, Sat 9-2

LIBERAL

P LIBERAL MEMORIAL LIBRARY*, 519 N Kansas, 67901-3345. SAN 306-008X. Tel: 620-626-0180. FAX: 620-626-0182. Web Site: www.lmlibrary.org. *Dir,* Jill Pannkuk; E-mail: director@lmlibrary.org; *Asst Dir, ILL,* Paulina Poplawska; E-mail: asstdirector@lmlibrary.org; *Tech Supvr,* Doreen Wright; E-mail: tech@lmlibrary.org; *Circ,* Kim Potter; E-mail: circdesk@lmlibrary.org; *Pub Serv,* Connie Yoxall; E-mail: connie@lmlibrary.org; *Youth Serv,* Carol Rittscher; E-mail: childrens@lmlibrary.org; Staff 17 (MLS 2, Non-MLS 15)
Founded 1904. Pop 25,000; Circ 150,000
Library Holdings: Audiobooks 3,307; CDs 1,250; DVDs 2,510; e-books 295; Bk Titles 68,075; Per Subs 170; Videos 2,451
Special Collections: Map Coll of Southwest Kansas & Oklahoma Panhandle; Seward County Newspapers, 1886-1999 (microfiche)
Subject Interests: Local genealogy
Automation Activity & Vendor Info: (Cataloging) Auto-Graphics, Inc; (Circulation) Auto-Graphics, Inc; (ILL) Auto-Graphics, Inc
Wireless access
Publications: Novel Ideas Newsletter; Weekly Newspaper Articles
Mem of Southwest Kansas Library System
Special Services for the Deaf - Videos & decoder
Special Services for the Blind - Bks on cassette
Open Mon-Thurs 9-8, Fri 9-5, Sat 9-1

J SEWARD COUNTY COMMUNITY COLLEGE LIBRARY*, 1801 N Kansas, 67901. (Mail add: PO Box 1137, 67905-1137), SAN 306-0098. Tel: 620-417-1160. FAX: 620-629-2725. E-mail: library@sccc.edu. Web Site: www.sccc.edu/academics/library/index.html. *Dir,* Matthew Pannkuk; Tel: 620-417-1161, E-mail: matthew.pannkuk@sccc.edu
Founded 1967
Library Holdings: Bk Titles 40,000; Per Subs 250
Automation Activity & Vendor Info: (Cataloging) EOS International; (Circulation) EOS International; (OPAC) EOS International
Mem of Southwest Kansas Library System
Open Mon-Thurs 7:45am-10pm, Fri 7:45am-4:45pm, Sat 9-3, Sun 1-9

LINCOLN

P LINCOLN CARNEGIE LIBRARY*, 203 S Third, 67455. SAN 306-0101. Tel: 785-524-4034. E-mail: lincolnlibrary@hotmail.com. Web Site: www.lincolncl.blogspot.com. *Dir,* Nancy Jensen
Founded 1913. Pop 1,200; Circ 12,000
Library Holdings: AV Mats 500; Large Print Bks 75; Bk Vols 17,000; Per Subs 25
Special Collections: Lincoln County Papers, 1873-present
Wireless access
Function: Bk club(s), Bks on CD, Children's prog, Computers for patron use, Copy machines, ILL available, Mail & tel request accepted, Online cat, Photocopying/Printing, Prog for children & young adult, Pub access computers, Summer reading prog, Tax forms, VHS videos
Mem of Central Kansas Library System
Open Mon, Tues, Thurs & Fri 10-1 & 2-6, Wed 10-1 & 2-7, Sat 9-12
Friends of the Library Group

LINDSBORG

C BETHANY COLLEGE*, Wallerstedt Library, 235 E Swensson Ave, 67456-1896. SAN 306-011X. Tel: 785-227-3380, Ext 8165. Web Site: www.bethanylb.edu. *Dir,* Denise Carson; Tel: 785-227-3380, Ext 8342; Staff 1 (MLS 1)
Founded 1907. Enrl 600; Fac 40
Library Holdings: Bk Vols 121,000; Per Subs 60
Automation Activity & Vendor Info: (Cataloging) Innovative Interfaces, Inc; (Circulation) Innovative Interfaces, Inc; (OPAC) Innovative Interfaces, Inc
Database Vendor: EBSCOhost, LexisNexis, OCLC FirstSearch
Mem of South Central Kansas Library System
Partic in Associated Colleges of Central Kansas; Lyrasis
Open Mon-Thurs 7:30am-10:30pm, Fri 7:30-5, Sat 1-5, Sun 3-10:30

P LINDSBORG COMMUNITY LIBRARY*, 111 S Main St, 67456-2417. SAN 306-0128. Tel: 785-227-2710. E-mail: lindsborglibrary@sbcglobal.net. Web Site: www.lindsborglibrary.org. *Dir,* Holly Lofton; Staff 3 (Non-MLS 3)
Circ 26,000
Library Holdings: Bk Vols 24,000; Per Subs 35
Special Collections: Civil War Coll; Swedish Heritage Coll
Subject Interests: Kansas, Scandinavia
Automation Activity & Vendor Info: (Acquisitions) Innovative Interfaces, Inc; (Cataloging) Innovative Interfaces, Inc; (Circulation) Innovative Interfaces, Inc; (OPAC) Innovative Interfaces, Inc; (Serials) Innovative Interfaces, Inc
Wireless access
Function: Bks on cassette, Bks on CD, Children's prog, Computers for patron use, Copy machines, Free DVD rentals, ILL available, Photocopying/Printing, Scanner, Serves mentally handicapped consumers, Story hour, Summer reading prog, Tax forms, VHS videos, Web-catalog, Wheelchair accessible
Mem of South Central Kansas Library System
Open Mon-Wed & Fri 10-6, Thurs 10-8, Sat 10-2
Friends of the Library Group

LINWOOD

P LINWOOD COMMUNITY LIBRARY*, 19649 Linwood Rd, 66052. (Mail add: PO Box 80, 66052-0080), SAN 320-9997. Tel: 913-301-3686. FAX: 913-301-3686. E-mail: linwoodlib@linwoodlibrary.org. Web Site: www.linwoodcommunitylibrary.org. *Dir,* Chris Bohling; Staff 2 (Non-MLS 2)
Founded 1977. Pop 2,768; Circ 44,648
Library Holdings: CDs 284; DVDs 664; Bk Titles 15,791; Per Subs 59; Videos 674
Special Collections: Indian Coll; Kansas Coll; Reference Coll
Automation Activity & Vendor Info: (Acquisitions) Follett Software; (Cataloging) Follett Software; (Circulation) Follett Software; (OPAC) Follett Software
Wireless access
Function: Bk club(s), Computer training, Copy machines, Fax serv, Genealogy discussion group, Homework prog, ILL available, Mail & tel request accepted, Photocopying/Printing, Preschool outreach, Prog for adults, Prog for children & young adult, Ref serv available, Summer reading prog, VHS videos, Video lending libr, Workshops
Mem of Northeast Kansas Library System
Open Mon-Wed 10-7:30,Thurs 10-9, Fri 10-6, Sat 10-3
Friends of the Library Group

LITTLE RIVER

P LITTLE RIVER COMMUNITY LIBRARY*, 125 Main St, 67457. (Mail add: PO Box 98, 67457-0098), SAN 306-0136. Tel: 620-897-6610. E-mail: lrcomlib@lrmutual.com. Web Site: skyways.lib.ks.us/towns/LittleRiver/library.html. *Librn,* Marilyn Kay Carlson
Founded 1932. Pop 734; Circ 12,171
Library Holdings: Bk Titles 12,381; Per Subs 30
Subject Interests: Kansas
Database Vendor: Gale Cengage Learning
Wireless access
Function: ILL available, Prog for children & young adult, Ref serv available, Summer reading prog
Mem of South Central Kansas Library System
Open Mon 2-6:30, Tues-Fri 9:30-12 & 1-5
Friends of the Library Group

LOGAN

P LOGAN PUBLIC LIBRARY*, 109 W Main St, 67646. (Mail add: PO Box 356, 67646-0356), SAN 306-0144. Tel: 785-689-4333. E-mail: loganlib@ruraltel.net. *Librn,* Norma Mullen
Founded 1900. Pop 538; Circ 3,700
Library Holdings: Bk Vols 5,065; Per Subs 25
Subject Interests: Local hist
Automation Activity & Vendor Info: (Acquisitions) ByWater Solutions; (Cataloging) ByWater Solutions
Database Vendor: LibLime
Wireless access
Mem of Central Kansas Library System
Special Services for the Blind - Bks on cassette; Bks on CD; Home delivery serv; Large print & cassettes; Talking bks & player equip
Open Mon 6-8, Tues-Thurs 1:30-5:30, Sat 10-Noon

LONG ISLAND

P LONG ISLAND COMMUNITY LIBRARY*, Main St, 67647-0195. (Mail add: PO Box 68, 67647-0068), SAN 306-0152. Tel: 785-854-7474. E-mail: longipat@ruraltel.net. *Librn,* Beth Ponstein
Founded 1921. Pop 187; Circ 1,510
Library Holdings: Bk Titles 3,416; Per Subs 12
Wireless access
Open Mon 9-Noon, Tues & Thurs 3-5, Sat 8:30-11:30

LONGTON

P LONGTON LIBRARY*, 512A Kansas Ave, 67352. (Mail add: PO Box 163, 67352-0163). Tel: 620-642-6012. FAX: 620-642-6012. E-mail: longtonbooks@yahoo.com. Web Site: longton.mykansaslibrary.org. *Libr Dir,* Jolie Gerding; *Librn,* Ammie Rankin
Library Holdings: Audiobooks 75; Bks-By-Mail 1,000; DVDs 50; Large Print Bks 500; Bk Titles 3,000; Per Subs 5; Talking Bks 600; Videos 100
Wireless access
Mem of Southeast Kansas Library System
Special Services for the Blind - Bks available with recordings; Bks on cassette; Bks on CD; Copier with enlargement capabilities; Talking bks; Talking bks & player equip
Open Mon-Fri 10-12 & 1-5
Friends of the Library Group

LOUISBURG

P LOUISBURG PUBLIC LIBRARY*, 206 S Broadway, 66053. SAN 306-0179. Tel: 913-837-2217. FAX: 913-837-2218. Web Site: www.louisburglibrary.org. *Dir,* Kiersten Allen; E-mail: kallen@louisburglibrary.org; *Coll Develop,* Dawn Eggers; *ILL,* Kathy Baker; *Adult Serv Coordr,* Holly Gillogly; *Youth Serv Coordr,* Elizabeth Ellis; Staff 2 (MLS 1, Non-MLS 1)
Founded 1968. Pop 8,500; Circ 52,000
Library Holdings: Bk Titles 41,614; Per Subs 85
Automation Activity & Vendor Info: (Cataloging) Follett Software; (Circulation) Follett Software; (ILL) Follett Software; (OPAC) Follett Software
Database Vendor: Gale Cengage Learning, OCLC FirstSearch
Function: ILL available
Mem of Northeast Kansas Library System
Open Mon-Thurs 9-7, Fri 9-5, Sat 9-3, Sun 1-5
Restriction: Pub use on premises
Friends of the Library Group

LYNDON

P LYNDON CARNEGIE LIBRARY*, 127 E Sixth, 66451. (Mail add: PO Box 563, 66451-0563), SAN 306-0195. Tel: 785-828-4520. FAX: 785-828-4565. E-mail: lyndonlibrary@lyndonlibrary.org. Web Site: www.lyndonlibrary.org. *Dir,* Sarah Walker-Hitt; *Asst Librn,* Sharon Culley
Pop 1,536; Circ 2,968
Library Holdings: Bk Vols 17,000; Per Subs 10
Automation Activity & Vendor Info: (Cataloging) SirsiDynix; (Circulation) SirsiDynix
Mem of Northeast Kansas Library System
Open Mon 9-12:30 & 2-7, Tues-Thurs 9-12:30 & 2-6, Fri 9-12:30, Sat 9-12
Friends of the Library Group

LYONS

P LYONS PUBLIC LIBRARY*, 217 East Ave S, 67554-2721. SAN 306-0209. Tel: 620-257-2961. E-mail: lyonslibr@hotmail.com. *Dir,* Becky McBeth; Staff 1 (MLS 1)
Founded 1908. Pop 4,395; Circ 47,575
Library Holdings: Bk Vols 28,140; Per Subs 90
Special Collections: Kansas Coll, bks by Kansas authors & bks about Kansas; Local Newspaper Coll; Lyons Daily News on Microfilm; Santa Fe Trail, Coronado & Quivira
Automation Activity & Vendor Info: (Cataloging) Follett Software; (Circulation) Follett Software
Database Vendor: OCLC FirstSearch
Open Mon-Thurs (Winter) 10-8, Fri & Sat 10-6; Mon-Sat (Summer) 10-6

MACKSVILLE

P MACKSVILLE CITY LIBRARY*, 333 N Main St, 67557. (Mail add: PO Box 398, 67557-0398), SAN 306-0241. Tel: 620-348-3555. FAX: 620-348-3555. E-mail: macksvillecitylibrary@hotmail.com. Web Site: macksville.scklf.info. *Dir,* Jody Suiter
Founded 1935. Pop 488
Library Holdings: AV Mats 247; Bk Vols 11,601; Per Subs 15
Wireless access
Mem of South Central Kansas Library System
Open Mon & Wed 1-6, Sat 9-12

MADISON

P MADISON PUBLIC LIBRARY*, 110 S First St, 66860. SAN 306-0284. Tel: 620-437-2634. FAX: 620-437-2631. E-mail: madison.library@madtel.net. *Dir,* Virginia Pedroja
Pop 826
Library Holdings: Bk Vols 8,234; Per Subs 47
Subject Interests: Kansas
Open Tues-Sat 1-5

MANHATTAN

C KANSAS STATE UNIVERSITY LIBRARIES*, 137 Hale Library, 1100 Mid-Campus Dr, 66506. SAN 342-1201. Tel: 785-532-3014. Circulation Tel: 785-532-7425. Interlibrary Loan Service Tel: 785-532-7441. Reference Tel: 785-532-7421. Administration Tel: 784 432-7400. FAX: 785-532-7415. E-mail: library@k-state.edu. Web Site: www.lib.k-state.edu. *Dean of Libr,* Lori A Goetsch; Tel: 785-532-7402, E-mail: lgoetsch@k-state.edu; Staff 123.65 (MLS 80.15, Non-MLS 43.5)
Founded 1863. Enrl 24,581; Fac 968; Highest Degree: Doctorate
Jul 2012-Jun 2013 Income (Main and Other College/University Libraries) $15,200,459. Mats Exp $6,258,943, Books $448,288, Per/Ser (Incl. Access Fees) $5,461,223, Micro $22,814, AV Mat $29,762, Presv $29,089. Sal $7,125,562 (Prof $5,037,919)
Library Holdings: AV Mats 148,382; e-books 1,033,462; e-journals 86,115; Bk Titles 1,343,343; Bk Vols 1,367,976; Per Subs 21,429
Special Collections: Agriculture & Rural Life Coll; Clementine Paddleford Papers; Consumer Movement Coll; Cookery Coll; Dan D Casement Papers; Donald V R Drenner Papers; Gail Kubik Papers; Grain Science & Milling Coll; Historic Costume & Textiles; History of Higher Education & Land Grant Universities Coll; Kansas & Kansas State University History Coll; Kenneth S Davis Papers; L Frank Baum & The Wizard of Oz Coll; Linnaeana; Louis Zukofsky Papers; Manuscript Cookbooks, Miniature Books & Photographs; McDill "Huck" Boyd Papers; Military History Coll; Repository for Permanent Records of Kansas State University; Richard L D Morse Papers; Robert Graves Coll; Science Fiction Coll; Society for Military History Coll. State Document Depository; US Document Depository
Automation Activity & Vendor Info: (Acquisitions) Ex Libris Group; (Cataloging) Ex Libris Group; (Circulation) Ex Libris Group; (ILL) OCLC; (OPAC) Ex Libris Group; (Serials) Ex Libris Group
Wireless access
Partic in Center for Research Libraries; Greater Western Library Alliance; Lyrasis; OCLC Online Computer Library Center, Inc
Special Services for the Deaf - Assistive tech
Special Services for the Blind - Assistive/Adapted tech devices, equip & products
Friends of the Library Group

Departmental Libraries:

MATHEMATICS & PHYSICS LIBRARY, 105 Cardwell Hall, 66506, SAN 342-1295. Tel: 785-532-6827. FAX: 785-532-6806. Web Site: www.lib.k-state.edu/branches/physics. *Librn,* Barbara Steward; E-mail: drawets@k-state.edu
Subject Interests: Math, Physics
Open Mon-Thurs 8-5 & 7-9, Fri 8-5

CM VETERINARY MEDICAL LIBRARY, Veterinary Medical Complex, 408 Trotter Hall, 66506-5614, SAN 342-1325. Tel: 785-532-6006. FAX: 785-532 2838. E-mail: vetlib@vet.k-state.edu. Web Site: www.vet.ksu.edu/depts/library. *Dir,* Gayle Willard; E-mail: gwillard@vet.k state.edu
Special Collections: Animal Nutrition; Human-Animal Relationships; Veterinary History
Subject Interests: Animals, behavior of, Health sci, Human relations, Nutrition, Veterinary med
Open Mon-Wed 8am-10pm, Thurs 8am-11pm, Fri 8-5, Sun 1-10

PAUL WEIGEL LIBRARY OF ARCHITECTURE, PLANNING & DESIGN, 323 Seaton Hall, 66506, SAN 342-1236. Tel: 785-532-5968. FAX: 785-532-6722. Web Site: www.lib.k-state.edu/branches/arch. *Libr Asst III,* Maxine Ganske; Tel: 785-532-5978, E-mail: mlganske@k-state.edu
Subject Interests: Archit, Construction, Eng, Landscape archit, Planning, Regional studies
Open Mon-Fri 8-12 & 1-5

C MANHATTAN CHRISTIAN COLLEGE LIBRARY, 1415 Anderson Ave, 66502-4081. SAN 306-0314. Tel: 785-539-3571, Ext 110. Interlibrary Loan Service Tel: 785-539-3571, Ext 113. Administration Tel: 785-539-3571, Ext 111. FAX: 785-539-0832. E-mail: mcclib@mccks.edu. Web Site: www.mccks.edu/academics/library. *Dir of Libr Serv,* Mary Ann Buhler; E-mail: mabuhler@mccks.edu; *Ref Librn,* Ron Ratliff; E-mail: rratliff@mccks.edu; Staff 2 (MLS 2)
Founded 1927. Enrl 345; Fac 10; Highest Degree: Bachelor
Library Holdings: CDs 142; DVDs 243; e-books 3,899; e-journals 11,467; Bk Titles 37,227; Bk Vols 43,123; Per Subs 80; Videos 450
Special Collections: Restoration Movement, commentaries
Subject Interests: Biblical studies, Counseling, Missions & missionaries, Music, Relig educ, Theol studies
Automation Activity & Vendor Info: (Cataloging) OCLC Connexion; (Circulation) EOS International; (Course Reserve) EOS International; (ILL) OCLC WorldShare Interlibrary Loan; (OPAC) EOS International

Database Vendor: Amigos Library Services, CredoReference, EBSCOhost, EOS International, Gale Cengage Learning, OCLC, OCLC FirstSearch, OCLC WorldShare Interlibrary Loan, SirsiDynix, WT Cox
Wireless access
Function: Telephone ref, VCDs, VHS videos, Video lending libr, Web-catalog, Wheelchair accessible
Partic in OCLC Online Computer Library Center, Inc; OCLC-LVIS; Private Academic Libraries Section, Kansas Library Association; State Library of Kansas
Open Mon 7:30am-10pm, Tues-Thurs 7:30-11, Fri 7:30-5, Sun 4-11
Restriction: Authorized patrons, Fee for pub use, In-house use for visitors, Open to pub for ref & circ; with some limitations, Open to students, fac, staff & alumni, Photo ID required for access

P MANHATTAN PUBLIC LIBRARY*, 629 Poyntz Ave, 66502-6086. SAN 306-0322. Tel: 785-776-4741. Toll Free Tel: 800-432-2796. FAX: 785-776-1545. Web Site: www.manhattan.lib.ks.us. *Dir,* Linda Knupp; E-mail: lknupp@manhattan.lib.ks.us; *Asst Dir,* John Pecoraro; *Adult Serv Mgr,* Susan Withee; E-mail: swithee@manhattan.lib.ks.us; *Mgr, Ch Serv,* Jennifer Adams; E-mail: jadams@manhattan.lib.ks.us; *Circ Mgr,* Marilyn Fulkerson; E-mail: marilynf@manhattan.lib.ks.us; *YA Librn,* Janene Hill; E-mail: jhill@manhattan.lib.ks.us; *Coll Develop,* Marcy Allen; E-mail: mallen@manhattan.lib.ks.us; Staff 22 (MLS 5, Non-MLS 17)
Founded 1904. Pop 44,831; Circ 547,571
Library Holdings: Bk Vols 173,954; Per Subs 325; Talking Bks 5,065
Special Collections: State Document Depository
Automation Activity & Vendor Info: (Acquisitions) SirsiDynix; (Cataloging) SirsiDynix; (Circulation) SirsiDynix; (OPAC) SirsiDynix
Database Vendor: CQ Press, LearningExpress, Oxford Online, ReferenceUSA, SirsiDynix, World Book Online
Publications: Friends Newsletter
Mem of North Central Kansas Libraries System
Partic in OCLC Online Computer Library Center, Inc
Special Services for the Blind - Assistive/Adapted tech devices, equip & products
Open Mon-Thurs 9-9, Fri 9-8, Sat 9-6, Sun 1-6
Friends of the Library Group

P NORTH CENTRAL KANSAS LIBRARIES SYSTEM*, 629 Poyntz Ave, 66502-6086. SAN 306-0330. Tel: 785-776-4741. Toll Free Tel: 800-432-2796. FAX: 785-776-1545. Web Site: www.nckl.info. *Dir,* Linda Knupp; Tel: 785-776-4741, Ext 129, E-mail: lknupp@manhattan.lib.ks.us; *Asst Dir,* Carol R Barta; Tel: 785-776-4741, Ext 140; *Coll Develop,* Marcia Allen; E-mail: mallen@manhattan.lib.ks.us; Staff 11.8 (MLS 1.3, Non-MLS 10.5)
Founded 1968. Pop 221,265
Jan 2011-Dec 2011 Income (Main Library Only) $850,463, State $83,241, Federal $36,800, Locally Generated Income $693,923, Other $34,098. Mats Exp $38,500. Sal $510,670
Library Holdings: Bk Vols 58,140
Automation Activity & Vendor Info: (Acquisitions) Auto-Graphics, Inc; (Cataloging) OCLC Connexion; (Circulation) Auto-Graphics, Inc; (ILL) Auto-Graphics, Inc; (OPAC) Auto-Graphics, Inc
Database Vendor: Auto-Graphics, Inc, OCLC FirstSearch, SirsiDynix
Function: Home delivery & serv to Sr ctr & nursing homes, ILL available, Prof lending libr, Ref & res, Summer reading prog, Workshops
Publications: North Central Kansas Libraries (Newsletter)
Member Libraries: Americus Township Library; Axtell Public Library; Blue Rapids Public Library; Burnley Memorial Library; Burns Public Library; Chapman Public Library; Clay Center Carnegie Library; Council Grove Public Library; Dorothy Bramlage Public Library; Dwight Library; Elm Creek Township Library; Elmendaro Township Library; Emporia Public Library; Enterprise Public Library; Flint Hills Technical College Library; Frankfort City Library; Goessel Public Library; Herington Public Library; Hillsboro Public Library; Hope Community Library; Leonardville City Library; Lyon County, Library District One; Manhattan Public Library; Marion City Library; Marysville Public Library; Peabody Township Library; Pottawatomie Wabaunsee Regional Library; Riley City Library; Solomon Public Library; Vermillion Public Library; Wamego Public Library; Washington Public Library; White City Public Library
Partic in OCLC Online Computer Library Center, Inc
Special Services for the Blind - Assistive/Adapted tech devices, equip & products
Open Mon-Fri 8-5

S RILEY COUNTY HISTORICAL MUSEUM*, Seaton Memorial Library, 2309 Claflin Rd, 66502-3421. SAN 306-0349. Tel: 785-565-6490. FAX: 785-565-6491. Web Site: www.rileycountyks.gov. *Dir,* D Cheryl Collins; *Archivist, Librn,* Linda Glasgow; Staff 1 (Non-MLS 1)
Founded 1916
Library Holdings: Bk Titles 4,500
Special Collections: Local History Coll, photog
Subject Interests: County hist, Frontier & pioneer life, Hist, Kansas
Publications: Historic Homes, Manhattan; Indices to Riley County Marriage Records 1887-1918; Land Grant Ladies: KSU Presidential Wives; Memory Lane Map 1976; Parades & Pastimes, Play & Picnics (photographs); Riley County Officials & Their Families 1855-1900 (monograph); The Churches of Manhattan & Vicinity; This Land is Our Land: The Public Domain in the Vicinity of Riley County & Manhattan, Kansas; Tracing Traditions (juvenile coloring book)
Restriction: Non-circulating to the pub, Open by appt only

S RILEY COUNTY KANSAS GENEALOGICAL SOCIETY LIBRARY*, 2005 Claflin, 66502-3415. SAN 326-2421. Tel: 785-565-6495. E-mail: rcgs03@cox.net. Web Site: www.rileycgs.com. *Pres,* Fred DeLano; *Coordr, Libr Serv,* Glee Eggers; *Acq,* Rebecca Rose; *Cat,* Muriel Wilson; *Computer Serv,* Patricia Wadick; *Res,* Libby Wolffing; Staff 32 (Non-MLS 32)
Founded 1962
Jan 2006-Dec 2006 Income $14,000. Mats Exp $5,100, Books $900, Per/Ser (Incl. Access Fees) $100, Other Print Mats $4,000, Presv $100
Library Holdings: CDs 50; Bk Titles 4,500; Per Subs 450
Special Collections: Genealogy Coll; Local Family History Coll; Pioneers of Riley County, Kansas Family Histories, 1853-1860
Subject Interests: Genealogy
Publications: Kansas Kin Newsletter (Quarterly)
Open Tues, Thurs & Sat 10-4, Wed 1-4 & 7-9, Sun 2-5
Restriction: Non-circulating

MANKATO

P MANKATO CITY LIBRARY*, 210 N Commercial St, 66956-2006. SAN 306-0357. Tel: 785-378-3885. E-mail: manpl@nckcn.com. *Librn,* Linda Eaton
Founded 1902. Pop 1,205; Circ 15,383
Library Holdings: Bk Vols 13,265; Per Subs 44
Mem of Central Kansas Library System
Open Mon & Wed 12:30-4:30 & 7-8:30, Tues, Thurs & Fri 12:30-4:30, Sat 10-12

MARION

P MARION CITY LIBRARY*, 101 Library St, 66861. SAN 306-0365. Tel: 620-382-2442. E-mail: mlibrary@eaglecom.net. Web Site: www.cityofmarion.kansasgov.com. *Dir,* Janet Marler
Pop 1,951; Circ 19,276
Library Holdings: Bk Vols 24,000; Per Subs 60
Special Collections: Kansas Coll
Subject Interests: Genealogy
Automation Activity & Vendor Info: (Cataloging) Follett Software; (Circulation) Follett Software; (OPAC) Follett Software
Mem of North Central Kansas Libraries System
Open Mon & Thurs 10-8, Tues, Wed & Fri 10-5, Sat 9-1

MARQUETTE

P MARQUETTE COMMUNITY LIBRARY*, 121 N Washington, 67464-0389. (Mail add: PO Box 389, 67464), SAN 306-0373. Tel: 785-546-2561. E-mail: marqlib@ks-usa.net. *Librn,* Donna Elvin
Founded 1964. Pop 655; Circ 7,190
Library Holdings: Audiobooks 100; CDs 15; DVDs 150; Large Print Bks 100; Bk Vols 7,730; Per Subs 22; Videos 305
Wireless access
Mem of South Central Kansas Library System
Open Tues, Wed & Sat 10-12 & 2-5

MARYSVILLE

P MARYSVILLE PUBLIC LIBRARY*, 1009 Broadway, 66508-1814. SAN 306-0381. Tel: 785-562-2491. FAX: 785-562-4086. *Dir,* Jamie D Kelley; E-mail: jkelley@bluevalley.net; *ILL, Youth Serv,* Janice Lyhane; E-mail: jlyhane@bluevalley.net; Staff 3 (MLS 1, Non-MLS 2)
Founded 1935. Pop 3,140; Circ 31,525
Jan 2006-Dec 2006 Income $180,600, State $2,000, City $139,600, Locally Generated Income $6,500, Other $8,500. Mats Exp $29,300, Books $20,750, Per/Ser (Incl. Access Fees) $2,700, AV Mat $5,850. Sal $92,700 (Prof $34,500)
Library Holdings: AV Mats 1,929; Bks on Deafness & Sign Lang 33; Large Print Bks 793; Bk Vols 37,138; Per Subs 156
Special Collections: Marshall County Coll
Subject Interests: Kansas
Automation Activity & Vendor Info: (Cataloging) Auto-Graphics, Inc; (Circulation) Auto-Graphics, Inc; (ILL) Auto-Graphics, Inc; (OPAC) Auto-Graphics, Inc
Wireless access
Function: Homebound delivery serv
Mem of North Central Kansas Libraries System
Special Services for the Blind - Magnifiers; Talking bks
Open Mon-Wed & Fri 10-6, Thurs 10-7:30, Sat 10-2

MCCRACKEN

P MCCRACKEN PUBLIC LIBRARY*, 303 Main St, 67556. (Mail add: PO Box 125, 67556-0125), SAN 306-0217. Tel: 785-394-2444. FAX: 785-394-2444. E-mail: mccrpul@gbta.net. *Dir,* Ruth Crawshaw; *Asst Librn,* Mamie Crawshaw
Founded 1936. Pop 292; Circ 1,964
Library Holdings: Bk Vols 8,500; Per Subs 25
Special Collections: McCracken Newspapers, 1887-1945 & 1951-1997, micro
Mem of Central Kansas Library System
Open Mon, Tues, Thurs & Fri 2-5, Wed 2-5 & 7-9, Sat 10-12

MCCUNE

P MCCUNE OSAGE TOWNSHIP LIBRARY*, 509 Sixth St, 66753. (Mail add: PO Box 73, 66753-0073), SAN 306-0225. Tel: 620-632-4112. E-mail: books@ckt.net. *Libr Dir,* Doni S Gray
Pop 423; Circ 2,300
Library Holdings: DVDs 40; Large Print Bks 400; Bk Vols 3,900; Per Subs 12; Talking Bks 40; Videos 600
Special Collections: History/Genealogy Coll
Wireless access
Mem of Southeast Kansas Library System
Open Tues & Thurs 10-12 & 3-6:30, Sat 9-12

MCDONALD

P MCDONALD PUBLIC LIBRARY*, PO Box 89, 67745-0089. SAN 306-0233. Tel: 785-538-2441. *Librn,* Karlyne Atchison
Pop 238; Circ 3,100
Library Holdings: Bk Vols 4,500; Per Subs 10; Talking Bks 58
Open Tues 12-3, Sat 10-12

MCLOUTH

P MCLOUTH PUBLIC LIBRARY*, 215 S Union, 66054. (Mail add: PO Box 69, 66054-0069). Tel: 913-796-2225. FAX: 913-796-2230. Web Site: mclouth.mykansaslibrary.org. *Dir,* Katherin Jones; E-mail: director@mclouth.lib.ks.us
Library Holdings: Bk Vols 5,000; Per Subs 10
Wireless access
Mem of Northeast Kansas Library System
Open Mon, Thurs & Fri 11-5, Tues & Wed 11-6, Sat 9-12
Friends of the Library Group

MCPHERSON

CR CENTRAL CHRISTIAN COLLEGE OF KANSAS*, Briner Library, 1200 S Main, 67460. (Mail add: PO Box 1403, 67460), SAN 306-025X. Tel: 620-241-0723, Ext 359. Administration Tel: 620-241-0723, Ext 360. FAX: 620-241-6032. Web Site: www.centralchristian.edu/library.html. *Dir, Libr Serv,* Beverly Kelley; E-mail: bev.kelley@centralchristian.edu; *Asst Dir,* Hatsue Aizawa; E-mail: hatsue.aizawa@centralchristian.edu; Staff 2 (MLS 1, Non-MLS 1)
Founded 1894. Enrl 315; Fac 19; Highest Degree: Bachelor
Jul 2012-Jun 2013 Income $73,300, Locally Generated Income $300. Mats Exp $28,100. Books $2,700, Per/Ser (Incl. Access Fees) $4,500, Other Print Mats $2,000, AV Mat $1,800, Electronic Ref Mat (Incl. Access Fees) $16,100, Presv $1,000. Sal $47,000 (Prof $31,000)
Library Holdings: AV Mats 177; CDs 265; e-books 6,873; Bk Titles 25,716; Bk Vols 28,156; Per Subs 136; Videos 629
Special Collections: Free Methodist Coll (By or about Free Methodist persons); Japanese Coll (Books written in Japanese)
Subject Interests: Bus, Liberal studies, Psychol, Relig, Sports sci
Automation Activity & Vendor Info: (Acquisitions) Follett Software; (Circulation) Auto-Graphics, Inc; (Course Reserve) Auto-Graphics, Inc; (ILL) Auto-Graphics, Inc; (OPAC) Auto-Graphics, Inc; (Serials) EBSCO Online
Database Vendor: American Chemical Society, Auto-Graphics, Inc, EBSCOhost, LexisNexis, OCLC WorldShare Interlibrary Loan, Oxford Online
Wireless access
Function: ILL available, Music CDs, Online searches, Orientations, Photocopying/Printing, Ref serv available, VHS videos, Wheelchair accessible
Mem of South Central Kansas Library System
Partic in Kans Libr Asn
Open Mon-Thurs 8am-11pm, Fri 8-5, Sat 12:30-2, Sun 2-4 & 6-11

C MCPHERSON COLLEGE*, Miller Library, 1600 E Euclid, 67460-3899. (Mail add: PO Box 1402, 67460-1402), SAN 306-0268. Tel: 620-242-0487, 620-242-0490. Interlibrary Loan Service Tel: 620-242-0488. FAX: 620-241-8443. E-mail: library@mcpherson.edu. Web Site: www.mcpherson.edu. *Dir, Libr Res,* Mary Hester; E-mail: hesterm@mcpherson.edu; Staff 1 (MLS 1)
Founded 1887. Enrl 656; Fac 40; Highest Degree: Bachelor
Library Holdings: Bk Vols 95,000; Per Subs 300
Special Collections: Automobile Restoration Special Coll; Church of the Brethren Archives; McPherson College Archives
Automation Activity & Vendor Info: (Cataloging) Book Systems; (Circulation) Book Systems; (Course Reserve) Book Systems; (ILL) OCLC; (OPAC) Book Systems; (Serials) Book Systems
Database Vendor: CredoReference, EBSCOhost, Gale Cengage Learning, LexisNexis, McGraw-Hill, OCLC WorldShare Interlibrary Loan, WT Cox
Wireless access
Function: Archival coll, Audio & video playback equip for onsite use, AV serv, Bks on cassette, Bks on CD, Copy machines, Electronic databases & coll, Exhibits, Free DVD rentals, Handicapped accessible, ILL available, Literacy & newcomer serv, Music CDs, Online cat, Online ref, Online searches, Orientations, Outside serv via phone, mail, e-mail & web, OverDrive digital audio bks, Photocopying/Printing, Ref & res, Ref serv available, Scanner, Spoken cassettes & CDs, Spoken cassettes & DVDs, Telephone ref, VHS videos
Mem of South Central Kansas Library System
Partic in Associated Colleges of Central Kansas
Open Mon-Thurs 7:30am-11pm, Fri 7:30-5, Sun 2-11
Restriction: Open to pub for ref & circ; with some limitations

P MCPHERSON PUBLIC LIBRARY, 214 W Marlin, 67460-4299. SAN 306-0276. Tel: 620-245-2570. FAX: 620-245-2567. E-mail: library@macpl.org. Web Site: www.macpl.org. *Dir,* Steven D Read; *Adult Serv,* Jennie Hall; *Ch Serv,* Mandy Martin; *Tech Serv,* Rachel Brandt; Staff 13 (MLS 1, Non-MLS 12)
Founded 1902. Pop 13,672; Circ 190,162
Jan 2013-Dec 2013 Income $866,739, State $5,303, City $792,093, Locally Generated Income $35,745, Other $33,598. Mats Exp $75,787, Books $54,403, Per/Ser (Incl. Access Fees) $10,209, AV Mat $6,171, Electronic Ref Mat (Incl. Access Fees) $5,004. Sal $431,440
Library Holdings: Audiobooks 1,628; AV Mats 3,309; CDs 1,195; DVDs 2,904; Large Print Bks 2,522; Bk Vols 92,005; Per Subs 166
Special Collections: Kansas Coll; Local History. Oral History
Subject Interests: Genealogy
Automation Activity & Vendor Info: (Acquisitions) Innovative Interfaces, Inc; (Cataloging) Innovative Interfaces, Inc; (Circulation) Innovative Interfaces, Inc; (OPAC) Innovative Interfaces, Inc; (Serials) Innovative Interfaces, Inc
Wireless access
Function: Adult bk club, After school storytime, Archival coll, Art exhibits, Bks on CD, Children's prog, Computers for patron use, Copy machines, Electronic databases & coll, Exhibits, Free DVD rentals, Handicapped accessible, ILL available, Magnifiers for reading, Mail & tel request accepted, Microfiche/film & reading machines, Music CDs, Newsp ref libr, Online cat, Online ref, Online searches, Photocopying/Printing, Preschool outreach, Preschool reading prog, Printer for laptops & handheld devices, Prog for adults, Prog for children & young adult, Pub access computers, Ref serv available, Spoken cassettes & CDs, Story hour, Summer & winter reading prog, Summer reading prog, Tax forms, Teen prog, Telephone ref, Winter reading prog
Mem of South Central Kansas Library System
Special Services for the Blind - Bks on cassette; Bks on CD; Closed circuit TV magnifier; Large print bks; Large screen computer & software; Talking bk serv referral
Open Mon-Fri 9-8, Sat 9-5, Sun 2-5

MEADE

P MEADE PUBLIC LIBRARY*, 104 E West Plains, 67864. (Mail add: PO Box 609, 67864-0609), SAN 306-039X. Tel: 620-873-2522. FAX: 620-873-2522. Web Site: www.meadelibrary.info. *Dir,* May Caleb; E-mail: director@meadelibrary.info
Founded 1895. Pop 1,600; Circ 30,000
Library Holdings: Bk Vols 24,000; Per Subs 60
Subject Interests: Antiques, Collectibles, Landscaping, Parenting
Automation Activity & Vendor Info: (Cataloging) Follett Software; (Circulation) Follett Software
Wireless access
Mem of Southwest Kansas Library System
Partic in OCLC Online Computer Library Center, Inc
Open Mon & Thurs 9:30-7, Tues, Wed & Fri 9:30-5, Sat 9:30-1
Friends of the Library Group

MEDICINE LODGE

P LINCOLN LIBRARY, 201 N Main St, 67104. SAN 306-0403. Tel: 620-886-5746. FAX: 620-886-9985. Web Site: www.cyberlodg.com/lincoln/index.html. *Librn,* Rosalee Armstrong
Founded 1898. Pop 3,000; Circ 40,804
Library Holdings: Bk Vols 21,412; Per Subs 52
Special Collections: Indians; Kansas History

Wireless access
Open Mon & Thurs 10-7, Tues, Wed & Fri 10-5:30, Sat 10-4

MERIDEN

P MERIDEN COMMUNITY LIBRARY*, 100 Main St, 66512. (Mail add: PO Box 221, 66512-0221), SAN 306-0411. Tel: 785-484-3393. FAX: 785-484-3393. E-mail: meridenlib@hotmail.com. *Dir,* Jerie Tichenor
Founded 1968. Circ 15,250
Library Holdings: Bk Vols 14,000; Per Subs 12
Automation Activity & Vendor Info: (Cataloging) Follett Software
Mem of Northeast Kansas Library System
Open Mon & Thurs 10-12 & 1-6, Fri 10-12 & 1-4, Sat 9-11

MINNEAPOLIS

P MINNEAPOLIS PUBLIC LIBRARY*, 519 Delia Ave, 67467. SAN 306-0438. Tel: 785-392-3205. FAX: 785-392-2934. E-mail: mplibrary@nckcn.com. *Librn,* Ronald D Brubaker
Founded 1892. Circ 20,382
Library Holdings: Bk Vols 20,000; Per Subs 50
Automation Activity & Vendor Info: (Cataloging) Follett Software; (Circulation) Follett Software
Wireless access
Mem of Central Kansas Library System
Partic in Metronet; Metropolitan Library Service Agency; Minitex Library Information Network
Open Mon, Tues & Thurs 12-8, Wed 12-6, Fri 10-5, Sat 10-3

MINNEOLA

P MINNEOLA CITY LIBRARY*, 112 Main St, 67865-8544. (Mail add: PO Box 95, 67865-0095), SAN 306-0446. Tel: 620-885-4749. FAX: 620-885-4278. *Dir,* Barbara Wilson; *Librn,* Stephanie Swonger
Founded 1930. Pop 700; Circ 10,000
Library Holdings: Bk Vols 14,000; Per Subs 25
Automation Activity & Vendor Info: (Acquisitions) Auto-Graphics, Inc; (Cataloging) Auto-Graphics, Inc; (ILL) Auto-Graphics, Inc; (OPAC) Auto-Graphics, Inc
Wireless access
Mem of Southwest Kansas Library System
Open Mon & Wed 1-6, Thurs 9-12, Sat 9-2

MOLINE

P MOLINE PUBLIC LIBRARY*, 107 N Main, 67353. (Mail add: PO Box 235, 67353-0235), SAN 306-0462. Tel: 620-647-3310. FAX: 620-647-3310. *Librn,* Cindy Jordan
Pop 553; Circ 8,128
Library Holdings: Bk Vols 5,000; Per Subs 16
Mem of Southeast Kansas Library System
Open Tues & Sat 9-12, Wed 9-5

MONTEZUMA

P MONTEZUMA TOWNSHIP LIBRARY, 309 N Aztec, 67867. (Mail add: PO Box 416, 67867-0416), SAN 306-0470. Tel: 620-846-7032. FAX: 620-846-7032. E-mail: library@montelib.info. Web Site: montezuma.mykansaslibrary.org. *Dir,* Angie Zehr
Founded 1923. Pop 1,587; Circ 5,835
Library Holdings: Bk Vols 15,587
Automation Activity & Vendor Info: (Cataloging) Auto-Graphics, Inc; (Circulation) Auto-Graphics, Inc
Wireless access
Function: After school storytime, Audio & video playback equip for onsite use, Audiobks via web, Bks on cassette, Bks on CD, CD-ROM, Children's prog, Computer training, Computers for patron use, Copy machines, Distance learning, e-mail serv, E-Reserves, Electronic databases & coll, Handicapped accessible, Home delivery & serv to Sr ctr & nursing homes, Homebound delivery serv, Homework prog, ILL available, Instruction & testing, Online cat, Online ref, Online searches, Outside serv via phone, mail, e-mail & web, OverDrive digital audio bks, Photocopying/Printing, Prog for children & young adult, Pub access computers, Ref & res, Ref serv in person, Scanner, Story hour, Summer reading prog, VHS videos, Web-catalog
Mem of Southwest Kansas Library System
Open Mon-Wed & Fri 1-5:30, Thurs 9-11 & 1-5:30

MORAN

P MORAN PUBLIC LIBRARY*, 335 N Cedar, 66755. (Mail add: PO Box 186, 66755-0186), SAN 306-0489. Tel: 620-237-4334. E-mail: moranlibrary@yahoo.com. *Librn,* Audrey Maley
Founded 1957. Pop 674; Circ 5,000
Library Holdings: AV Mats 500; Large Print Bks 350; Bk Titles 9,000; Per Subs 15; Talking Bks 75
Mem of Southeast Kansas Library System
Open Mon-Wed & Fri 2-5, Sat 9-Noon

MOUND CITY

P MARY SOMMERVILLE FREE LIBRARY*, 509 Main St, 66056. (Mail add: PO Box 325, 66056-0325), SAN 306-0497. Tel: 913-795-2788. FAX: 913-795-2801. E-mail: marysommervillelibrary@yahoo.com. *Dir,* Lena Dick
Pop 874; Circ 10,491
Library Holdings: Bk Vols 12,000; Per Subs 30
Automation Activity & Vendor Info: (Cataloging) Follett Software; (Circulation) Follett Software
Mem of Southeast Kansas Library System
Open Mon-Fri 9-4:30, Sat 9-1

MOUND VALLEY

P MOUND VALLEY PUBLIC LIBRARY*, 411 Hickory, 67354. (Mail add: PO Box 179, 67354-0179), SAN 306-0500. Tel: 620-328-3341. FAX: 620-328-3341. E-mail: mound_valley_library@hotmail.com. *Librn,* Melinda Thrash
Founded 1973. Pop 496; Circ 5,293
Library Holdings: Bk Vols 5,000; Per Subs 15
Mem of Southeast Kansas Library System
Open Mon & Tues 3:30-8, Thurs & Sat 10-Noon

MOUNDRIDGE

P MOUNDRIDGE PUBLIC LIBRARY*, 220 S Christian, 67107. SAN 306-0519. Tel: 620-345-6355. E-mail: moundlib@mtelco.net. *Dir,* Connie Olson; Staff 2 (MLS 1, Non-MLS 1)
Founded 1967. Pop 1,575; Circ 32,900
Jan 2012-Dec 2012 Income $68,150, State $1,150, City $61,000, Locally Generated Income $1,000, Other $5,000. Mats Exp $18,500, Books $13,000, Per/Ser (Incl. Access Fees) $2,500, AV Mat $3,000. Sal $35,000
Library Holdings: Audiobooks 50; DVDs 500; Large Print Bks 50; Bk Vols 20,000; Per Subs 110
Automation Activity & Vendor Info: (Cataloging) Innovative Interfaces, Inc; (Circulation) Innovative Interfaces, Inc; (ILL) Innovative Interfaces, Inc
Wireless access
Mem of South Central Kansas Library System
Open Mon 9-1 & 3:30-8, Tues-Fri 9-1 & 3:30-6, Sat 9-12

MOUNT HOPE

P MOUNT HOPE PUBLIC LIBRARY*, 109 S Ohio St, 67108. (Mail add: PO Box 309, 67108-0309), SAN 306-0527. Tel: 316-667-2665. Web Site: mthope.polarislibrary.com. *Dir,* Sandra West
Pop 1,096; Circ 12,668
Library Holdings: Bk Vols 9,000; Per Subs 36
Wireless access
Mem of South Central Kansas Library System
Open Mon-Wed & Fri 1-7, Sat 10-2

MULVANE

P MULVANE PUBLIC LIBRARY*, 101 E Main St, 67110. SAN 306-0535. Tel: 316-777-1211. FAX: 316-777-1755. E-mail: mulvanelib@yahoo.com. *Librn,* Kristi McEachern; Staff 5 (MLS 1, Non-MLS 4)
Pop 5,488; Circ 41,463
Library Holdings: Bk Vols 24,458; Per Subs 71
Automation Activity & Vendor Info: (Acquisitions) Follett Software; (Cataloging) Follett Software; (Circulation) Follett Software; (OPAC) Follett Software
Database Vendor: OCLC FirstSearch
Mem of South Central Kansas Library System
Open Mon & Thurs 10-7, Tues & Wed 10-5:30, Fri 10-5, Sat 10-1

NEODESHA

P W A RANKIN MEMORIAL LIBRARY*, 502 Indiana St, 66757-1532. SAN 306-0543. Tel: 620-325-3275. FAX: 620-325-3275. E-mail: rankin.library@neodesha.com. *Dir,* Mary Meckley; *Asst Dir,* Rita Banta; *Ch Serv,* Alicia Newland
Founded 1912. Pop 2,837; Circ 37,000
Library Holdings: AV Mats 1,455; Large Print Bks 2,000; Bk Titles 19,046; Per Subs 88; Talking Bks 950
Special Collections: Altoona Advocate (Aug 27, 1886-1977); Neodesha Daily Sun (Mar 1891-Oct 27, 1983), micro; Neodesha Derrick (Aug 18, 1994-2004); Neodesha Register (Nov 1883-Dec 29, 1983); Neodesha Sun Register (Jan 1990-Aug 11, 1994)
Mem of Southeast Kansas Library System
Open Mon-Wed 9:30-6:30, Thurs & Fri 9:30-5:30, Sat 9-12
Friends of the Library Group

NESS CITY

P NESS CITY PUBLIC LIBRARY*, 113 S Iowa Ave, 67560-1992. SAN 306-0551. Tel: 785-798-3415. FAX: 785-798-2313. E-mail: director@nesscitylibrary.org. Web Site: nesscitylibrary.org. *Dir,* Jean Schlegel; *Asst Librn, ILL,* Laurie Dinges; Staff 2 (Non-MLS 2)
Founded 1887. Pop 1,476; Circ 20,268
Library Holdings: Audiobooks 786; AV Mats 1,303; Bk Titles 17,727; Per Subs 43
Subject Interests: Genealogy
Automation Activity & Vendor Info: (Circulation) Auto-Graphics, Inc; (OPAC) Auto-Graphics, Inc
Wireless access
Mem of Southwest Kansas Library System
Special Services for the Blind - Reading & writing aids; Talking bks
Open Tues 10-9, Wed-Fri 10-5:30, Sat 9-12

NEWTON

P NEWTON PUBLIC LIBRARY*, 720 N Oak, 67114. SAN 306-056X. Tel: 316-283-2890. FAX: 316-283-2916. E-mail: library@newtonplks.org. Web Site: www.newtonplks.org. *Libr Dir,* Marianne Eichelberger; E-mail: meichelb@newtonplks.org; *Adult Serv,* Anne Ethen; E-mail: aethen@newtonplks.org; *Coll Develop,* Betsy Davis; E-mail: bdavis@newtonplks.org; *Info Tech,* Carr Nathan; *Spec Serv,* Susan Bartel; E-mail: sbartel@newtonplks.org; *Youth Serv,* Amy Bayes; E-mail: abayes@newtonplks.org; *Youth Serv Asst Supvr,* Jannell Johannes; E-mail: jjohanne@newtonplks.org; Staff 20 (MLS 3, Non-MLS 17)
Founded 1886. Pop 19,200; Circ 161,774
Jan 2012-Dec 2012 Income $808,432, State $11,648, City $693,976, County $15,532, Locally Generated Income $25,031, Other $62,245. Mats Exp $131,187, Books $72,293, Per/Ser (Incl. Access Fees) $13,045, AV Mat $39,604, Electronic Ref Mat (Incl. Access Fees) $6,245. Sal $345,690
Library Holdings: Audiobooks 2,119; AV Mats 6,136; CDs 1,324; DVDs 1,315; e-books 119; Large Print Bks 10,845; Microforms 421; Bk Titles 92,278; Bk Vols 85,833; Per Subs 273; Videos 1,718
Special Collections: Oral History
Subject Interests: Genealogy, Kansas, Spanish
Automation Activity & Vendor Info: (Acquisitions) Innovative Interfaces, Inc; (Cataloging) Innovative Interfaces, Inc; (Circulation) Innovative Interfaces, Inc; (ILL) Auto-Graphics, Inc; (OPAC) Innovative Interfaces, Inc; (Serials) Innovative Interfaces, Inc
Database Vendor: 3M Library Systems, Auto-Graphics, Inc, Baker & Taylor, Booksite, EBSCO Auto Repair Reference, EBSCO Information Services, EBSCOhost, Gale Cengage Learning, LearningExpress, MITINET, Inc, OCLC FirstSearch, OCLC WorldShare Interlibrary Loan, Overdrive, Inc, ProQuest, ValueLine
Wireless access
Function: Audiobks via web, Bks on CD, CD-ROM, Children's prog, Computer training, Computers for patron use, Copy machines, Digital talking bks, e-mail serv, Electronic databases & coll, Equip loans & repairs, Exhibits, Fax serv, Free DVD rentals, Genealogy discussion group, Holiday prog, Home delivery & serv to Sr ctr & nursing homes, ILL available, Microfiche/film & reading machines, Music CDs, Newsp ref libr, Online searches, OverDrive digital audio bks, Photocopying/Printing, Preschool reading prog, Prog for adults, Prog for children & young adult, Pub access computers, Ref serv available, Ref serv in person, Scanner, Spanish lang bks, Spoken cassettes & CDs, Spoken cassettes & DVDs, Story hour, Summer & winter reading prog, Tax forms, Teen prog, Telephone ref, VCDs, VHS videos, Visual arts prog, Wheelchair accessible, Workshops
Mem of South Central Kansas Library System
Special Services for the Blind - BiFolkal kits; Bks on CD; Large print bks; Recorded bks; Sound rec; Talking bks
Open Mon-Thurs 9-9, Fri & Sat 9-6
Friends of the Library Group

NICKERSON

P NICKERSON PUBLIC LIBRARY*, 23 N Nickerson, 67561. (Mail add: PO Box 368, 67561-0368), SAN 306-0578. Tel: 620-422-3361. Toll Free Tel: 800-234-0529. FAX: 620-422-3361. E-mail: nickpublib@yahoo.com. *Dir,* Gay Sykes
Founded 1916
Library Holdings: Bk Vols 11,500; Per Subs 25
Mem of South Central Kansas Library System
Open Mon 10-12:30 & 1:30-7, Tues-Fri 1:30-7
Friends of the Library Group

NORTH NEWTON

C BETHEL COLLEGE LIBRARY*, 300 E 27th St, 67117-0531. SAN 342-135X. Tel: 316-284-5361. FAX: 316-284-5843. E-mail: library@bethelks.edu. Web Site: www.bethelks.edu/services/library. *Co-Dir, Libr & Dir Pub Serv,* Gail Stucky; *Co-Dir, Libr & Dir Tech Serv,* Barbara Thiesen; *ILL,* Greta Hiebert; Staff 3 (MLS 2, Non-MLS 1)
Founded 1891. Enrl 514; Fac 45; Highest Degree: Bachelor
Library Holdings: AV Mats 3,042; CDs 828; DVDs 39; e-books 1,000; Music Scores 1,366; Bk Titles 79,463; Bk Vols 102,219; Per Subs 291; Videos 428
Subject Interests: Music, Relig
Automation Activity & Vendor Info: (Acquisitions) Ex Libris Group; (Cataloging) Ex Libris Group; (Circulation) Ex Libris Group; (Course Reserve) Ex Libris Group; (ILL) Ex Libris Group; (Media Booking) Ex Libris Group; (OPAC) Ex Libris Group; (Serials) Ex Libris Group
Database Vendor: EBSCOhost, Gale Cengage Learning, OCLC FirstSearch, OVID Technologies
Mem of South Central Kansas Library System
Partic in Associated Colleges of Central Kansas; OCLC Online Computer Library Center, Inc
Open Mon-Thurs (Winter) 8am-Midnight, Fri 8-5, Sat 1-5, Sun 1pm-Midnight; Mon-Fri (Summer) 8-12 & 1-5

Departmental Libraries:

MENNONITE LIBRARY & ARCHIVES, 300 E 27th St, 67117-0531. Tel: 316-284-5304. FAX: 316-284-5843. E-mail: mla@bethelks.edu. Web Site: www.bethelks.edu/mla. *Archivist, Dir,* John Thiesen; *Archivist,* James Lynch; *Cat,* Barbara Thiesen
Founded 1936
Library Holdings: AV Mats 161,534; CDs 224; Bk Titles 27,054; Bk Vols 32,928; Per Subs 280; Videos 171
Special Collections: 17th Century Dutch Art Coll; Cheyenne Indian (Rodolphe Petter Coll), bk, mss & photog; Hopi Indian (H R Voth Coll), bk, mss & photog; Peace (H P Krehbiel Coll), bk & mss; Showalter Oral History Coll (numerous topics, especially World War I conscientious objectors & World War II Civilian Public Service)
Subject Interests: Biblical studies, Dutch (Lang), Genealogy, German (Lang), Hist, Mennonites, Reformation
Database Vendor: LexisNexis, OCLC FirstSearch, OCLC WorldShare Interlibrary Loan
Publications: Mennonite Life (Quarterly)
Open Mon-Thurs 10-12 & 1-5
Friends of the Library Group

NORTON

P NORTHWEST KANSAS LIBRARY SYSTEM, Two Washington Sq, 67654-1615. SAN 306-0608. Tel: 785-877-5148. Toll Free Tel: 800-432-2858 (Kansas only). FAX: 785-877-5697. E-mail: nwklsbus@ruraltel.net, nwklscon@ruraltel.net. Web Site: www.nwkls.org. *Dir,* George Seamon, Jr; E-mail: nwklsdir@ruraltel.net; *Bus Mgr,* Alice Evans; *Acq, ILL,* Kama Mandl; E-mail: illoan@ruraltel.net; *Cataloger,* Aurelia Jackson; E-mail: nwklscat@ruraltel.net; *Libr Develop Consult,* Meagan Zampieri; *Tech Consult,* Dave Fisher; E-mail: nwklstec@sbcglobal.net; Staff 8 (MLS 3, Non-MLS 5)
Founded 1966. Pop 38,364
Library Holdings: AV Mats 847; CDs 400; DVDs 420; Large Print Bks 5,746; Bk Vols 10,028
Special Collections: 6 by 6: Ready to Read Kits; KHC TALK Books Series. State Document Depository
Automation Activity & Vendor Info: (Cataloging) Auto-Graphics, Inc; (Circulation) Auto-Graphics, Inc; (ILL) Auto-Graphics, Inc; (OPAC) Auto-Graphics, Inc
Database Vendor: Gale Cengage Learning, OCLC FirstSearch, OCLC WorldShare Interlibrary Loan, Overdrive, Inc
Wireless access
Function: ILL available
Publications: NWKLS Vertical Files (Newsletter)
Member Libraries: Almena City Library; Bird City Public Library; Clayton City Library; Colby Community College; Goodland Public Library; Gove City Library; Grainfield City Library; Jay Johnson Public Library; Jennings City Library; Lenora Public Library; Moore Family Library; Northwest Kansas Heritage Center; Norton Correctional Facility; Norton Public Library; Oakley Public Library; Oberlin City Library; Pioneer Memorial Library; Selden Public Library; Sharon Springs Public Library; Sheridan County Library; St Francis Public Library; WaKeeney Public Library
Partic in Lyrasis
Special Services for the Blind - Talking bks
Open Mon-Fri 8-5

G NORTON CORRECTIONAL FACILITY*, Inmate Library, PO Box 546, 67654. SAN 325-6006. Tel: 785-877-3389, Ext 333. FAX: 785-877-3972. *In Charge,* Lori Van Eaton
Library Holdings: Bk Titles 1,500; Per Subs 17
Automation Activity & Vendor Info: (Cataloging) Follett Software; (Circulation) Follett Software
Mem of Northwest Kansas Library System
Open Mon-Fri 1-9:30

P NORTON PUBLIC LIBRARY*, One Washington Sq, 67654-1615. SAN 306-0616. Tel: 785-877-2481. Circulation FAX: 785-874-4404. E-mail: nortonpl2@ruraltel.net. *Dir,* Mary Luehrs; *Ch,* Amy Husted; *Librn,* Candia Colby; *Librn,* Rosalie McMullen; *Librn,* Bette Townsend; Staff 3.75 (Non-MLS 3.75)
Founded 1909. Pop 5,500; Circ 64,800
Library Holdings: Bk Vols 78,000; Per Subs 46
Special Collections: Masonic Coll
Function: Chess club, Children's prog, Computer training, Computers for patron use, Copy machines, Digital talking bks, e-mail serv, E-Reserves, Exhibits, Fax serv, Free DVD rentals, Handicapped accessible, Home delivery & serv to Sr ctr & nursing homes, Homebound delivery serv, ILL available, Music CDs, Online cat, Online ref, Online searches, OverDrive digital audio bks, Photocopying/Printing, Preschool outreach, Prog for children & young adult, Ref serv available, Ref serv in person, Story hour, Summer reading prog, Tax forms, Telephone ref, VHS videos, Wheelchair accessible
Mem of Northwest Kansas Library System
Partic in SAILS Library Network
Open Mon-Thurs 10-8, Fri 10-6, Sat 1-5
Friends of the Library Group

NORTONVILLE

P NORTONVILLE PUBLIC LIBRARY*, 407 Main, 66060-4001. (Mail add: PO Box 179, 66060-0179), SAN 306-0624. Tel: 913-886-2060. Interlibrary Loan Service Tel: 913-843-3654. FAX: 913-886-3070. E-mail: nortlib@hotmail.com. *Dir,* Diane Trinkle; Staff 1 (Non-MLS 1)
Founded 1897. Pop 1,110; Circ 12,127
Library Holdings: AV Mats 894; Electronic Media & Resources 61; Large Print Bks 248; Bk Vols 8,384; Per Subs 38; Talking Bks 709
Mem of Northeast Kansas Library System
Open Tues & Sat 9-Noon, Wed 10-6, Thurs & Fri 9-6

OAKLEY

P OAKLEY PUBLIC LIBRARY*, 700 W Third St, 67748-1256. SAN 306-0640. Tel: 785-671-4776. FAX: 785-671-3868. E-mail: oaklib@st-tel.net. Web Site: oakley.mykansaslibrary.org. *Dir,* Victoria Halbleib; *ILL,* Patricia Keyes; Staff 1 (Non-MLS 1)
Founded 1923. Pop 2,029; Circ 38,019
Library Holdings: Bk Vols 17,550; Per Subs 20
Automation Activity & Vendor Info: (Acquisitions) Auto-Graphics, Inc; (Cataloging) Auto-Graphics, Inc; (Circulation) Auto-Graphics, Inc; (ILL) Auto-Graphics, Inc; (Serials) Auto-Graphics, Inc
Database Vendor: Auto-Graphics, Inc
Wireless access
Mem of Northwest Kansas Library System
Special Services for the Blind - Assistive/Adapted tech devices, equip & products; Audio mat; BiFolkal kits; Bks available with recordings; Bks on cassette; Bks on CD; Cassette playback machines; Cassettes; Copier with enlargement capabilities; Digital talking bk; Extensive large print coll; Home delivery serv; Large print & cassettes; Large print bks & talking machines; Reader equip; Rec & flexible discs; Talking bks & player equip; Videos on blindness & phys handicaps
Open Mon-Thurs 9-6, Fri 9-5, Sat 9-3
Friends of the Library Group

OBERLIN

P OBERLIN CITY LIBRARY*, 104 E Oak, 67749-1997. SAN 306-0659. Tel: 785-475-2412. *Librn,* Carol Smith
Founded 1903. Pop 2,300; Circ 31,000
Library Holdings: Bk Vols 24,000; Per Subs 40
Automation Activity & Vendor Info: (Cataloging) Follett Software; (Circulation) Follett Software
Mem of Northwest Kansas Library System
Open Mon-Thurs 9:30-8, Fri 9:30-5, Sat 10-3

OGDEN

P OGDEN LIBRARY*, 220 Willow St, 66517. (Mail add: PO Box 266, 66517-0266). Tel: 785-537-0351. E-mail: ogdenlibrary@hotmail.com. *Dir,* Virginia Shepard
Library Holdings: AV Mats 150; Bk Vols 5,000
Open Mon-Fri 9-5:30

OLATHE

GL JOHNSON COUNTY LAW LIBRARY*, Courthouse, Rm 101, 100 N Kansas Ave, 66061. SAN 306-0667. Tel: 913-715-4154. FAX: 913-715-4152. Web Site: lawlibrary.jocogov.org. *Dir,* John Pickett; E-mail: john.pickett@jocogov.org; Staff 4 (MLS 1, Non-MLS 3)
Founded 1952
Jan 2009-Dec 2009 Income $610,000. Mats Exp $274,000, Books $270,000, Per/Ser (Incl. Access Fees) $4,000. Sal $268,000
Library Holdings: AV Mats 100; Bk Titles 2,200; Bk Vols 23,000; Per Subs 50
Automation Activity & Vendor Info: (Cataloging) EOS International; (Circulation) EOS International; (OPAC) EOS International; (Serials) EOS International
Database Vendor: Westlaw
Wireless access
Function: Computers for patron use, Copy machines, Doc delivery serv, Fax serv, Notary serv, Online cat, Photocopying/Printing, Pub access computers, Ref serv available, Telephone ref, Web-catalog
Open Mon-Fri 8-5
Restriction: Circ limited, Non-circulating to the pub, Pub use on premises

C MIDAMERICA NAZARENE UNIVERSITY*, Mabee Library & Learning Resource Center, 2030 E College Way, 66062-1899. SAN 306-0683. Tel: 913-971-3485. Interlibrary Loan Service Tel: 913-971-3562. Reference Tel: 913-971-3569. FAX: 913-971-3285. E-mail: library@mnu.edu. Web Site: www.mnu.edu/mabee-library.html. *Libr Dir,* Bruce Flanders; Tel: 913-971-3568, E-mail: blflanders@mnu.edu; *Computer Serv Librn, Univ Archivist,* Lon E Dagley; Tel: 913-971-3566, E-mail: ledagley@mnu.edu; *Instrul & Res Librn,* Lauren Hays; Tel: 913-971-3561, E-mail: ldhays@mnu.edu; Staff 5 (MLS 3, Non-MLS 2)
Founded 1968. Enrl 1,700; Fac 90; Highest Degree: Master
Jul 2005-Jun 2006 Income $478,251. Mats Exp $113,000, Books $37,000, Per/Ser (Incl. Access Fees) $76,000. Sal $300,676 (Prof $100,000)
Library Holdings: AV Mats 360,000; CDs 1,145; DVDs 71; Bk Titles 95,110; Per Subs 225
Special Collections: Americana; Church of the Nazarene Publications; Teacher Education Resource Center
Automation Activity & Vendor Info: (Acquisitions) Innovative Interfaces, Inc; (Cataloging) Innovative Interfaces, Inc; (Circulation) Innovative Interfaces, Inc; (Course Reserve) Innovative Interfaces, Inc; (ILL) Innovative Interfaces, Inc; (Media Booking) Innovative Interfaces, Inc; (OPAC) Innovative Interfaces, Inc; (Serials) Innovative Interfaces, Inc
Database Vendor: EBSCOhost, Westlaw
Wireless access
Mem of Northeast Kansas Library System
Open Mon-Thurs 7am-11pm, Fri 7-6, Sat 12-5, Sun 8pm-11pm
Restriction: Fee for pub use

P OLATHE PUBLIC LIBRARY*, 201 E Park St, 66061. SAN 306-0691. Tel: 913-971-6850. Reference Tel: 913-971-6888. FAX: 913-971-6839. TDD: 913-971-6855. Web Site: www.olathelibrary.org. *Dir,* Emily F Baker; Tel: 913-971-6880, E-mail: ebaker@olatheks.org; *Head, Info Tech Serv,* Steve Nielsen; Tel: 913-971-6863, E-mail: snielsen@olatheks.org; *Head, Customer Serv,* Leslie K Ellsworth; Tel: 913-971-6856, E-mail: lellsworth@olatheks.org; *Head, Adult Serv,* Maggie Baker; Tel: 913-971-6849, E-mail: mbaker@olatheks.org; *Commun Relations Librn,* Rita Patterson; Tel: 913-971-6879, E-mail: rpatterson@olatheks.org; *Ch Serv,* Jennifer Adamson; Tel: 913-971-6869, E-mail: jadamson@olatheks.org; *ILL,* Susan Smith; Tel: 913-971-6854, E-mail: sssmith@olatheks.org; Staff 65 (MLS 12, Non-MLS 53)
Founded 1909. Pop 128,000; Circ 1,533,000
Special Collections: Business & Automotive Reference Coll; Kansas Room; Microfilm Coll; Music & Books on CD's Coll
Automation Activity & Vendor Info: (Acquisitions) SirsiDynix; (Cataloging) SirsiDynix; (Circulation) SIRSI WorkFlows; (OPAC) SirsiDynix
Database Vendor: SirsiDynix
Wireless access
Mem of Northeast Kansas Library System
Partic in Mid-America Library Alliance/Kansas City Metropolitan Library & Information Network
Special Services for the Deaf - TDD equip
Special Services for the Blind - Computer with voice synthesizer for visually impaired persons; Sec-Tec enlarger; ZoomText magnification & reading software
Open Mon-Thurs 10-8:30, Fri 10-6, Sat Noon-5, Sun 1-5
Friends of the Library Group
Branches: 1
INDIAN CREEK, 12990 S Black Bob Rd, 66062. Tel: 913-971-5235. FAX: 913-971-5239. *Br Mgr,* Kathleen O'Leary; Tel: 913-971-5240, E-mail: koleary@olatheks.org; Staff 35 (MLS 4, Non-MLS 31)
Library Holdings: AV Mats 19,702; Bk Vols 91,608
Function: ILL available
Special Services for the Deaf - TDD equip
Special Services for the Blind - Computer with voice synthesizer for visually impaired persons; ZoomText magnification & reading software
Open Mon-Thurs 10-8:30, Fri 10-6, Sat Noon-5, Sun 1-5
Friends of the Library Group

OSAGE CITY

P OSAGE CITY PUBLIC LIBRARY*, 515 Main St, 66523. SAN 306-0705. Tel: 785-528-2620, 785-528-3727. FAX: 785-528-4502. Web Site: www.osagecitylibrary.org. *Dir,* Jeanette Stromgren; E-mail: jstromgren@osagecitylibrary.org; *ILL,* Mavet Cooper; E-mail: mcooper@osagecitylibrary.org; Staff 1 (MLS 1)
Founded 1922. Pop 2,667; Circ 55,359
Library Holdings: Bk Vols 22,691; Per Subs 60
Special Collections: Cake Pan Coll
Automation Activity & Vendor Info: (Cataloging) Follett Software; (Circulation) Follett Software; (OPAC) Follett Software
Wireless access
Function: Adult bk club, Bk club(s), Children's prog, Computer training, Computers for patron use, Copy machines, e-mail serv, Family literacy, Fax serv, Free DVD rentals, Handicapped accessible, Holiday prog, Home delivery & serv to Sr ctr & nursing homes, Homebound delivery serv, Homework prog, ILL available, Instruction & testing, Music CDs, Newsp ref libr, Photocopying/Printing, Preschool outreach, Prog for adults, Prog for children & young adult, Ref serv available, Spoken cassettes & CDs, Story hour, Summer reading prog, Tax forms, Teen prog, Telephone ref, VHS videos, Web-catalog, Wheelchair accessible, Writing prog
Mem of Northeast Kansas Library System
Open Mon-Thurs 10-8, Fri 10-5, Sat 10-2
Friends of the Library Group

OSAWATOMIE

P OSAWATOMIE PUBLIC LIBRARY*, 527 Brown Ave, 66064-1367. SAN 306-0713. Tel: 913-755-2136. FAX: 913-755-2335. E-mail: osawlibrary@yahoo.com. Web Site: www.osawatomie.org. *Dir,* Elizabeth Trigg
Pop 4,413; Circ 28,292
Library Holdings: Bk Titles 20,221; Per Subs 60
Special Collections: Kansas Coll
Automation Activity & Vendor Info: (Cataloging) Follett Software; (Circulation) Follett Software; (ILL) Follett Software
Mem of Northeast Kansas Library System
Open Mon, Wed & Fri 9-5:30, Tues & Thurs 9-8:30, Sat 10-4
Friends of the Library Group

M OSAWATOMIE STATE HOSPITAL*, Rapaport Professional Library, 500 State Hospital Dr, 66064-1813. SAN 306-0721. Tel: 913-755-7212. FAX: 913 755-7089. *Librn,* Rhonda Magee; E-mail: rhonda.magee@osh.ks.gov; Staff 1 (MLS 1)
Founded 1949
Library Holdings: Bk Vols 3,000
Subject Interests: Med, Nursing, Psychiat, Psychol, Soc sci & issues
Database Vendor: EBSCOhost, Medline, OCLC FirstSearch, OCLC WorldShare Interlibrary Loan, PubMed
Function: Ref serv available
Mem of Northeast Kansas Library System
Partic in Medical Library Association (MLA); Midcontinental Regional Med Libr Program
Open Mon-Fri 12-4

OSBORNE

P OSBORNE PUBLIC LIBRARY*, 325 W Main St, 67473-2425. SAN 306-073X. Tel: 785-346-5486. FAX: 785-346-2888. E-mail: osbor1lb@ruraltel.net. *Dir,* Karen Wallace
Founded 1913. Pop 2,120; Circ 34,226
Library Holdings: Bk Titles 22,000; Per Subs 28
Subject Interests: Genealogy, Local hist
Automation Activity & Vendor Info: (ILL) Auto-Graphics, Inc
Wireless access
Function: AV serv, Handicapped accessible, Homebound delivery serv, ILL available, Prog for children & young adult, Summer reading prog, Telephone ref
Mem of Central Kansas Library System
Partic in Kans Libr Asn
Open Mon & Thurs 1-8, Tues 1-5, Wed & Fri 10-5, Sat 10-2

OSKALOOSA

P OSKALOOSA PUBLIC LIBRARY*, 315 Jefferson St, 66066. (Mail add: PO Box 347, 66066-0347), SAN 306-0748. Tel: 785-863-2475. FAX: 785-863-2088. Web Site: www.oskielibrary.org. *Libr Dir,* Paula J Ware; E-mail: pware@oskielibrary.org
Pop 1,900; Circ 18,000
Jan 2007-Dec 2007 Income $61,243, State $1,512, City $31,000, Locally Generated Income $12,281, Other $16,450. Mats Exp $12,621, Books $7,973, Per/Ser (Incl. Access Fees) $1,075, AV Mat $3,573. Sal $29,771
Library Holdings: CDs 133; DVDs 151; Bk Vols 10,900; Per Subs 36; Talking Bks 333; Videos 641
Subject Interests: Kansas
Automation Activity & Vendor Info: (Cataloging) Follett Software; (Circulation) Follett Software
Wireless access
Open Mon 10-6, Tues-Fri 10-5, Sat 10-1 (9-1 Summer)
Friends of the Library Group

OSWEGO

P OSWEGO PUBLIC LIBRARY*, 704 Fourth St, 67356. SAN 306-0756. Tel: 620-795-4921. FAX: 620-795-4921. Web Site: www.oswegolibrary.org. *Librn,* Liz Turner
Pop 2,218; Circ 26,500
Library Holdings: Audiobooks 150; CDs 250; DVDs 735; Bk Titles 14,000; Per Subs 68; Videos 325
Automation Activity & Vendor Info: (Cataloging) LibLime; (Circulation) LibLime; (ILL) LibLime; (OPAC) LibLime
Database Vendor: LibLime
Mem of Southeast Kansas Library System
Open Tues 1-8, Wed 10-5:30, Thurs & Fri 1-5:30, Sat 9-1

OTIS

P OTIS COMMUNITY LIBRARY*, 121 S Main, 67565. (Mail add: PO Box 9, 67565-0009), SAN 306-0764. Tel: 785-387-2287. *Librn,* L J Krestine
Pop 410; Circ 5,181
Library Holdings: Bk Vols 6,000; Per Subs 33
Special Collections: Children's Video Coll; Kansas Shelf
Mem of Central Kansas Library System
Open Mon 7pm-9pm, Tues 9-12, Thurs 1:30-5, Fri 9-12 & 1:30-5, Sat 9-12:30

OTTAWA

P OTTAWA LIBRARY*, 105 S Hickory St, 66067-2306. SAN 306-0772. Tel: 785-242-3080. FAX: 785-242-8789. E-mail: ottawalibraryreference@yahoo.com. Web Site: www.ottawa.lib.ks.us. *Dir,* Robin Flory; *Acq, Ref Serv,* Heidi Van der Heuvel; *Ch Serv,* Leanna Heth; *Ch Serv,* Shannon Leonard; *Circ, Webmaster,* Rosemary Honn; *ILL,* Martie Livingston; *Network Adminr,* Hal Bundy; *Ref Serv,* Linda Knight; *Tech Serv,* Pam Miller; Staff 12 (MLS 2, Non-MLS 10)
Founded 1872. Pop 12,000; Circ 119,957
Library Holdings: AV Mats 4,403; Bk Vols 58,000; Per Subs 124
Subject Interests: Genealogy, Local hist
Automation Activity & Vendor Info: (Cataloging) SirsiDynix; (Circulation) SirsiDynix; (OPAC) SirsiDynix
Database Vendor: Gale Cengage Learning, OCLC FirstSearch
Mem of Northeast Kansas Library System
Partic in Kansas Info Circuit
Open Mon-Thurs 9-8, Fri & Sat 9-5, Sun (Fall & Spring) 1:30-5
Friends of the Library Group

CR OTTAWA UNIVERSITY*, Myers Library, 1001 S Cedar, 66067-3399. SAN 306-0780. Tel: 785-248-2538. Interlibrary Loan Service Tel: 785-248-2535. Administration Tel: 785-248-2536. Toll Free Tel: 800-755-5200. FAX: 785-229 1012. Web Site: myottawa.ottawa.edu/ics/Resources/Myers_Library_Online. *Dir, Libr Serv,* Gloria Creed-Dikeogu; Tel: 785-248-2537, E-mail: gloria.creeddikeogu@ottawa.edu; *Assoc Dir, Libr Serv,* Janice Lee; E-mail: jan.lee@ottawa.edu; *Tech Serv,* Celia Davis; E-mail: celia.davis@ottawa.edu; Staff 3 (MLS 2, Non-MLS 1)
Founded 1865. Enrl 533; Fac 44; Highest Degree: Master
Library Holdings: Audiobooks 50; AV Mats 385; CDs 1,000; DVDs 4,000; e-books 120,000; Microforms 1,123; Music Scores 300; Bk Titles 70,000; Bk Vols 71,193; Per Subs 30; Videos 300
Special Collections: Baptist Church History Coll; Chinese Art & Related Asiatic Studies; J H Kilbuck Coll; Native American Indian Artifact Coll
Automation Activity & Vendor Info: (Cataloging) EOS International; (Circulation) EOS International; (Course Reserve) EOS International; (ILL) OCLC; (OPAC) EOS International; (Serials) EOS International
Database Vendor: 3M Library Systems, Alexander Street Press, American Psychological Association (APA), CQ Press, CredoReference, EBSCOhost, LexisNexis, McGraw-Hill, OCLC FirstSearch, OCLC WorldShare Interlibrary Loan, PubMed
Wireless access
Function: Archival coll, Art exhibits, Audiobks via web, Bks on cassette, Bks on CD, Computers for patron use, Copy machines, Distance learning, e-mail serv, Electronic databases & coll, Exhibits, ILL available, Music CDs, Online info literacy tutorials on the web & in blackboard, Online searches, OverDrive digital audio bks, Photocopying/Printing, Pub access computers, Ref & res, Scanner, Spoken cassettes & DVDs, VHS videos, Video lending libr
Mem of Northeast Kansas Library System
Partic in Mid-America Library Alliance/Kansas City Metropolitan Library & Information Network
Open Mon-Thurs (Fall & Spring) 7:45am-Midnight, Fri 7:45-5, Sun 4-Midnight; Mon-Fri (Summer) 9-5

OVERBROOK

P OVERBROOK PUBLIC LIBRARY*, 317 Maple St, 66524. (Mail add: PO Box 389, 66524), SAN 306-0799. Tel: 785-665-7266. FAX: 785-665-7973. Web Site: overbrook.mykansaslibrary.org/. *Librn,* Peggy Waldman; E-mail: pwaldman@overbrook.lib.ks.us
Founded 1928. Pop 973; Circ 14,557
Jan 2005-Dec 2005 Income $46,163, State $669, City $33,319, Other $12,175. Mats Exp $7,919, Books $6,152, Per/Ser (Incl. Access Fees) $412, Manu Arch $15, Other Print Mats $1,340. Sal $27,738
Library Holdings: Large Print Bks 910; Bk Titles 18,751; Per Subs 14
Special Collections: Kansas Coll
Wireless access
Function: Adult bk club, Bks on cassette, Bks on CD, CD-ROM, Computer training, Computers for patron use, Copy machines, Fax serv, Home delivery & serv to Sr ctr & nursing homes, ILL available, Music CDs, Online ref, Online searches, Photocopying/Printing, Prog for children & young adult, Summer reading prog, Tax forms, VHS videos
Mem of Northeast Kansas Library System
Open Mon, Wed & Fri 9-1 & 2-6, Tues & Thurs 2-7:30, Sat 9-1
Friends of the Library Group

OVERLAND PARK

R BETH SHALOM CONGREGATION*, Blanche & Ira Rosenblum Memorial Library, 14200 Lamar Ave, 66223. SAN 309-0221. Tel: 913-647-7279. FAX: 913-647-7277. *Exec Dir,* Elaine Levine; Staff 1 (Non-MLS 1)
Library Holdings: Bk Titles 10,102; Bk Vols 10,408; Per Subs 20; Videos 42
Open Sun 9-Noon

S BLACK & VEATCH*, Central Library, 11401 Lamar, 66211. SAN 309-023X. Tel: 913-458-7884. FAX: 913-458-2934. *Coll Develop, Dir,* Kevin Nelson; E-mail: nelsonk@bv.com; *Web Serv Mgr,* Charlette Weber; *Acq,* Marva Jefferson; *Ref,* Tom Jongeling; *Ref,* Jennifer Langlois; Staff 6 (MLS 2, Non-MLS 4)
Founded 1915
Library Holdings: Bk Titles 40,160; Bk Vols 45,000; Per Subs 50
Subject Interests: Eng
Automation Activity & Vendor Info: (Acquisitions) EOS International; (Cataloging) EOS International; (Circulation) EOS International; (Media Booking) EOS International; (OPAC) EOS International; (Serials) EOS International
Partic in Info Mgt & Eng Ltd

CM CLEVELAND CHIROPRACTIC COLLEGE*, Ruth R Cleveland Memorial Library, 10850 Lowell Ave, 66210. SAN 324-7147. Tel: 913-234-0814. FAX: 913-234-0901. *Dir,* Marcia M Thomas; Tel: 913-234-0809, E-mail: marcia.thomas@cleveland.edu; *Asst Dir,* Simone Briand; Tel: 913-234-0810, E-mail: simone.briand@cleveland.edu; Staff 3 (MLS 1, Non-MLS 2)
Founded 1976. Enrl 486; Fac 53
Library Holdings: Bk Titles 13,900; Bk Vols 15,000; Per Subs 301
Special Collections: Chiropractic texts, journals
Subject Interests: Acupuncture, Chiropractic, Nutrition, Orthopedics, Radiology
Automation Activity & Vendor Info: (Cataloging) EOS International; (Circulation) EOS International
Publications: Library News (monthly); quarterly list of new books; Subject bibliographies
Partic in Health Sciences Library Network of Kansas City, Inc
Open Mon-Fri 8-5
Friends of the Library Group

J JOHNSON COUNTY COMMUNITY COLLEGE*, Billington Library, 12345 College Blvd, Box 21, 66210. SAN 306-0802. Tel: 913-469-3871. Circulation Tel: 913-469-4484. Reference Tel: 913-469-8500. FAX: 913-469-3816. Web Site: library.jccc.edu. *Dir,* Mark Daganaar; Tel: 913-469-3882, E-mail: mdaganaar@jccc.edu; *Ref/Copyright Librn,* Mark Swails; Tel: 913-469-8500, Ext 3773, E-mail: mswails@jccc.edu; *Ref/Digital Librn,* Barry Bailey; Tel: 913-469-8500, Ext 4841, E-mail: bbaile14@jccc.edu; *Evening/Weekend Ref Librn,* Jessica Tipton; Tel: 913-469-8500, Ext 3286, E-mail: jtipton4@jccc.edu; *Tech Serv Librn,* Judith Guzzy; Tel: 913-469-8500, Ext 4151, E-mail: jguzzy@jccc.edu; *Ref/Archives (Info Serv),* John Russell; Tel: 913-469-8500, Ext 3284, E-mail: jrussell@jccc.edu; *Ref,* Marsha Cousino; Tel: 913-469-8500, Ext 3987, E-mail: mcousino@jccc.edu; *Ref,* Judith Vaughn; E-mail: jvaughn@jccc.edu; Staff 12 (MLS 7, Non-MLS 5)
Founded 1969. Enrl 30,000; Fac 800; Highest Degree: Associate
Library Holdings: Bk Titles 89,000; Bk Vols 100,000; Per Subs 600
Automation Activity & Vendor Info: (Acquisitions) Ex Libris Group; (Cataloging) Ex Libris Group; (Circulation) Ex Libris Group; (Course Reserve) Ex Libris Group; (OPAC) Ex Libris Group; (Serials) Ex Libris Group
Partic in Mid-America Library Alliance/Kansas City Metropolitan Library & Information Network
Special Services for the Deaf - Bks on deafness & sign lang; Spec interest per; Staff with knowledge of sign lang
Open Mon-Thurs (Fall & Spring) 7:30am-10pm, Fri 7:30-5, Sat 8-5, Sun 1-5; Mon-Thurs (Summer) 7:30am-10pm, Fri 7:30-5, Sat 8-5

P JOHNSON COUNTY LIBRARY*, 9875 W 87th St, 66212. (Mail add: PO Box 2933, Shawnee Mission, 66201-1333), SAN 342-1627. Tel: 913-495-2400. Reference Tel: 913-495-9100. FAX: 913-495-2460. TDD: 913-495-2433. Web Site: www.jocolibrary.org. *County Librn,* Sean Casserley; *Dep County Librn,* Tricia Suellentrop; *Assoc Dir, Br Serv,* Tensae Roger; Tel: 913-495-2549; *Assoc Dir, Cent Libr Serv,* Carolyn Weeks; Tel: 913-495-2467; *Coll Mgr,* Mary Anne Hile; Tel: 913-495-2434; *Communications Mgr,* Kasey Riley; Tel: 913-495-2345; *Info & Reader Serv Mgr,* Whitney Davison-Turley; Tel: 913-495-2473; *YA Serv,* Kate Pickett; Tel: 913-261-2332; Staff 280 (MLS 61, Non-MLS 219)
Founded 1952. Pop 400,600
Jan 2007-Dec 2007 Income (Main Library and Branch(s)) $19,578,528, State $494,057, County $17,972,489, Locally Generated Income $1,111,758. Mats Exp $3,240,407, Books $1,447,367, Per/Ser (Incl. Access Fees) $711,265, Other Print Mats $14,066, AV Mat $516,528, Electronic Ref Mat (Incl. Access Fees) $551,181. Sal $12,788,821
Library Holdings: AV Mats 210,992; e-books 1,400; Bk Vols 1,196,429; Per Subs 2,851
Special Collections: State Document Depository; US Document Depository
Subject Interests: Bus, Genealogy, Local hist
Automation Activity & Vendor Info: (Acquisitions) SirsiDynix; (Cataloging) SirsiDynix; (Circulation) SirsiDynix; (OPAC) SirsiDynix; (Serials) SirsiDynix
Database Vendor: EBSCOhost, Gale Cengage Learning, Newsbank, OCLC FirstSearch, ProQuest
Mem of Northeast Kansas Library System
Partic in Mid-America Library Alliance/Kansas City Metropolitan Library & Information Network; OCLC Online Computer Library Center, Inc
Open Mon-Thurs 9-9, Fri 9-6, Sat 9-5, Sun 1-5
Friends of the Library Group
Branches: 13
ANTIOCH, 8700 Shawnee Mission Pkwy, Merriam, 66202. (Mail add: PO Box 2933, Shawnee Mission, 55201-1333), SAN 376-883X. Tel: 913-261-2300. FAX: 913-261-2320. TDD: 913-261-2337. *Mgr,* Ken Werne; Tel: 913-261-2328; Staff 4 (MLS 4)
Founded 1955. Pop 38,426; Circ 557,000
Library Holdings: AV Mats 19,000; Bk Vols 111,000; Per Subs 131
Open Mon-Thurs 10-9, Fri 10-6, Sat 9-5, Sun 1-5
Friends of the Library Group
BLUE VALLEY, 9000 W 151st, 66221, SAN 342-1678. Tel: 913-495-3850. FAX: 913-495-3821. TDD: 913-495-3855. *Mgr,* Cyndi Chappell; Tel: 913-495-3826; Staff 3 (MLS 3)
Founded 1982. Pop 75,712; Circ 871,815
Library Holdings: AV Mats 24,872; Bk Vols 109,687; Per Subs 123
Open Mon-Fri 10-9, Sat 9-5, Sun 1-5
Friends of the Library Group
CEDAR ROE, 5120 Cedar, Roeland Park, 66205, SAN 342-1686. Tel: 913-384-8590. FAX: 913-384-8597. *Mgr,* Meredith Roberson; Tel: 913-384-8595; Staff 1 (MLS 1)
Founded 1969. Pop 16,138; Circ 331,013
Library Holdings: AV Mats 12,379; Bk Vols 77,478
Open Mon-Thurs 10-9, Fri 10-6, Sat 9-5
Friends of the Library Group
CENTRAL RESOURCE, 9875 W 87th St, 66212. (Mail add: PO Box 2933, Shawnee Mission, 66201-1333). Tel: 913-826-4600. FAX: 913-495-2480. *Assoc Dir, Cent Libr Serv,* Carolyn Weeks; Staff 87 (MLS 20, Non-MLS 67)
Founded 1995. Circ 1,042,841
Library Holdings: AV Mats 40,697; Bk Vols 288,644; Per Subs 874
Subject Interests: Genealogy, Regional
Open Mon-Thurs 9-9, Fri 9-6, Sat 9-5, Sun 1-5
Friends of the Library Group
CORINTH, 8100 Mission Rd, Prairie Village, 66208, SAN 342-1716. Tel: 913-967-8650. FAX: 913-967-8663. TDD: 913-967-8665. *Mgr,* Stuart Hinds; Tel: 913-967-8653; Staff 3 (MLS 3)
Founded 1963. Pop 43,102; Circ 779,534
Library Holdings: AV Mats 23,677; Large Print Bks 3,599; Bk Vols 160,635; Per Subs 170
Open Mon-Thurs 10-9, Fri 10-6, Sat 9-5, Sun 1-5
Friends of the Library Group
DE SOTO BRANCH, 33145 W 83rd St, De Soto, 66018, SAN 342-1740. Tel: 913-583-3106. FAX: 913-583-1702. *Mgr,* Leslie Nord; Tel: 913-495-7542; Staff 1 (MLS 1)
Founded 1967. Pop 6,062; Circ 86,843
Library Holdings: AV Mats 5,036; Bk Vols 20,347; Per Subs 47
Open Tues, Wed & Fri 10-6, Thurs 10-8, Sat 10-2
Friends of the Library Group

EDGERTON BRANCH, 319 E Nelson, Edgerton, 66021. Tel: 913-893-6720. FAX: 913-893-6723. *Mgr,* Terry Velasquez; Tel: 913-495-3888
Founded 2000. Pop 2,062; Circ 45,337
Library Holdings: AV Mats 2,876; Bk Vols 9,998; Per Subs 23
Open Tues 10-6, Wed 1-8, Thurs-Sat 10-2
Friends of the Library Group

GARDNER BRANCH, 137 E Shawnee, Gardner, 66030, SAN 342-1775. Tel: 913-856-7223. FAX: 913-495-3881. TDD: 913-495-3880. *Mgr,* Terry Velasquez; Tel: 913-495-3888; Staff 2 (MLS 2)
Founded 1960. Pop 17,869; Circ 252,509
Library Holdings: AV Mats 10,108; Bk Vols 42,096; Per Subs 89
Open Mon-Thurs 10-9, Fri 10-6, Sat 9-5
Friends of the Library Group

LACKMAN, 15345 W 87th St Pkwy, Lenexa, 66219, SAN 328-6630. Tel: 913-495-7540. FAX: 913-495-7556. TDD: 913-888-8483. *Mgr,* Leslie Nord; Tel: 913-495-7542; Staff 3 (MLS 3)
Founded 1986. Pop 38,771; Circ 561,511
Library Holdings: AV Mats 18,185; Bk Vols 95,921; Per Subs 165
Open Mon-Thurs 10-9, Fri 10-6, Sat 9-5, Sun 1-5
Friends of the Library Group

LEAWOOD PIONEER BRANCH, 4700 Town Center Dr, Leawood, 66211, SAN 375-6300. Tel: 913-344-0250. FAX: 913-344-0253. TDD: 913-344-0260. *Mgr,* Sandra Sutter; Tel: 913-344-0255; Staff 2 (MLS 2)
Founded 1994. Pop 34,202; Circ 536,621
Library Holdings: AV Mats 15,190; Bk Vols 77,207; Per Subs 117
Open Mon-Thurs 10-9, Fri 10-6, Sat 9-5
Friends of the Library Group

OAK PARK, 9500 Bluejacket, 66214, SAN 342-1805. Tel: 913-752-8700. FAX: 913-752-8709. TDD: 913-752-8711. *Mgr,* Magaly Vallazza; Tel: 913-752-8705; Staff 2 (MLS 2)
Founded 1969. Pop 34,732; Circ 615,485
Library Holdings: AV Mats 21,278; Bk Vols 121,042; Per Subs 165
Open Mon-Fri 10-9, Sat 9-5, Sun 1-5
Friends of the Library Group

SHAWNEE BRANCH, 13811 Johnson Dr, Shawnee, 66216, SAN 371-9839. Tel: 913-962-3800. FAX: 913-962-3809. *Mgr,* Roxanne Belcher; Tel: 913-962-3806; Staff 10 (MLS 1, Non-MLS 9)
Founded 1992. Pop 28,304; Circ 424,170
Library Holdings: AV Mats 11,792; Bk Vols 69,047; Per Subs 122
Open Mon-Thurs 10-9, Fri 10-6, Sat 9-5
Friends of the Library Group

SPRING HILL BRANCH, 109 S Webster, Spring Hill, 66083, SAN 342-183X. Tel: 913-592-3232. FAX: 913-686-2004. *Mgr,* Terry Velasquez; Tel: 913-495-3888; Staff 2 (Non-MLS 2)
Founded 1971. Pop 4,816; Circ 110,552
Jan 2005-Dec 2005. Mats Exp $130,414
Library Holdings: AV Mats 4,281; Bk Vols 16,617; Per Subs 35
Open Mon, Wed & Thurs 10-6, Tues 10-8, Sat 10-2
Friends of the Library Group

M MENORAH MEDICAL CENTER*, Robert Uhlmann Medical Library, 5721 W 119th St, 66209. SAN 309-0450. Tel: 913-498-6625. FAX: 913-498-6642. E-mail: library-mmc@hcamidwest.com. Web Site: www.hcamidwest.com. *Coordr,* Dick Kammer; Staff 3 (MLS 2, Non-MLS 1)
Founded 1931
Library Holdings: Bk Titles 800; Per Subs 150
Special Collections: Jewish Medical Ethics
Subject Interests: Allied health, Med, Nursing
Partic in Health Sciences Library Network of Kansas City, Inc
Open Mon-Fri 7-3:30

C NATIONAL AMERICAN UNIVERSITY*, Learning Resource Center, 10310 Mastin, 66212-5451. Tel: 913-981-8700. Toll Free Tel: 800-770-2959. Web Site: national.edu. *Campus Librn,* Anna Wong; E-mail: awong@national.edu; Staff 1 (MLS 1)
Founded 2000. Fac 25; Highest Degree: Master
Database Vendor: EBSCOhost, LexisNexis, ProQuest
Wireless access
Function: Computers for patron use, Copy machines, Distance learning, e-mail serv, Electronic databases & coll, Learning ctr, Online cat, Online ref, Online searches, Orientations, Outside serv via phone, mail, e-mail & web, Photocopying/Printing, Ref serv in person, Web-catalog
Restriction: Internal circ only, Open to students, fac & staff

OXFORD

P OXFORD PUBLIC LIBRARY*, 115 S Sumner St, 67119. (Mail add: PO Box 266, 67119-0266), SAN 306-0829. Tel: 620-455-2221. FAX: 620-455-2221. E-mail: oxfordkslib@gmail.com. Web Site: oxfordkslib.org. *Dir & Librn,* Claudia Hopkins; Staff 1.5 (Non-MLS 1.5)
Pop 1,172; Circ 6,490
Library Holdings: Audiobooks 50; Bk Vols 8,000
Subject Interests: Hist, Kansas
Automation Activity & Vendor Info: (Cataloging) Innovative Interfaces, Inc; (Circulation) Innovative Interfaces, Inc
Wireless access
Open Mon-Fri 9-12 & 1-5

PALCO

P PALCO PUBLIC LIBRARY*, 311 Main St, 67657. (Mail add: PO Box 218, 67657-0218), SAN 306-0837. Tel: 785-737-4286. *Librn,* Pat Kern
Pop 550; Circ 5,637
Library Holdings: Bk Vols 7,500; Per Subs 15
Mem of Central Kansas Library System
Open Tues, Fri & Sat 9-12, Thurs 9-12 & 2-5

PAOLA

P PAOLA FREE LIBRARY*, 101 E Peoria, 66071-1798. SAN 306-0845. Tel: 913-259-3655. FAX: 913-259-3656. Web Site: skyways.lib.ks.us/library/paola. *Dir,* Rosemary King; E-mail: rking@cityofpaola.com; *Cat,* Beverly Looney; *Circ,* Linda Prothe; E-mail: lprothe@cityofpaola.com; *ILL,* Helen Roberts; E-mail: hroberts@cityofpaola.com; *Per,* Peg Turney; *Youth Serv,* Elizabeth Trigg; E-mail: youthservices@cityofpaola.com; Staff 9 (MLS 1, Non-MLS 8)
Founded 1876. Pop 5,000; Circ 50,000
Library Holdings: Bks on Deafness & Sign Lang 25; Large Print Bks 480; Bk Vols 37,874; Per Subs 75; Spec Interest Per Sub 27; Talking Bks 1,355
Automation Activity & Vendor Info: (Circulation) Follett Software; (ILL) Auto-Graphics, Inc; (OPAC) Follett Software
Mem of Northeast Kansas Library System
Special Services for the Blind - Talking bks
Open Mon-Thurs 10-8:30, Fri 10-5, Sat 10-4
Friends of the Library Group

PARK CITY

P PARK CITY COMMUNITY PUBLIC LIBRARY*, 2107 E 61st St N, 67219. Tel: 316-744-6318. FAX: 316-744-6319. Web Site: www.parkcitypubliclibrary.com. *Librn,* Kelly Blurton; E-mail: kblurton@parkcitypubliclibrary.com; *Asst Librn,* Linda Halley; Staff 4.5 (MLS 1.5, Non-MLS 3)
Founded 2000. Pop 7,500
Library Holdings: Audiobooks 500; DVDs 1,500; Large Print Bks 500; Bk Vols 22,500; Per Subs 22
Automation Activity & Vendor Info: (Cataloging) ComPanion Corp; (Circulation) ComPanion Corp; (OPAC) ComPanion Corp
Wireless access
Mem of South Central Kansas Library System
Open Mon & Tues 9-7, Wed-Fri 9-6, Sat 9-1
Friends of the Library Group

PARKER

P LINN COUNTY LIBRARY DISTRICT NUMBER 1, 234 W Main St, 66072. (Mail add: PO Box 315, 66072-0315), SAN 376-771X. Tel: 913-898-4650. FAX: 913-898-4650. E-mail: parkerlibrary@yahoo.com. Web Site: parker.mykansaslibrary.org. *Dir & Librn,* Kay Bowman
Library Holdings: Bk Vols 10,000; Per Subs 37
Wireless access
Mem of Southeast Kansas Library System
Open Mon-Fri 10-6
Friends of the Library Group

PARSONS

J LABETTE COMMUNITY COLLEGE LIBRARY*, 200 S 14th St, 67357. SAN 306-0853. Tel: 620-820-1167. Interlibrary Loan Service Tel: 620-820-1154. Administration Tel: 620-820-1168. Toll Free Tel: 888-522-3883. FAX: 620-421-1469. Web Site: www.labette.edu/library. *Dir,* Scotty M Zollars; E-mail: scottz@labette.edu; *Cat, ILL,* Phylis A Coomes; E-mail: phylisc@labette.edu; *Patron Serv,* Erlene Cares; E-mail: erlenec@labette.edu; *Pub Relations, User Serv,* Lee Ann M Eggers; E-mail: leeanne@labette.edu; Staff 4 (MLS 1, Non-MLS 3)
Founded 1923. Enrl 1,084; Fac 69; Highest Degree: Associate
Jul 2012-Jun 2013 Income $199,316. Mats Exp $84,094, Books $11,710, Per/Ser (Incl. Access Fees) $13,838, Micro $3,500, Electronic Ref Mat (Incl. Access Fees) $47,349. Sal $115,222 (Prof $50,459)
Library Holdings: Bk Titles 23,925; Bk Vols 25,942; Per Subs 262
Special Collections: Carnegie Art Book Coll; Labette County & Kansas History
Subject Interests: Acad, Children's lit
Automation Activity & Vendor Info: (Cataloging) LibLime; (Circulation) LibLime; (ILL) LibLime; (OPAC) LibLime; (Serials) LibLime
Database Vendor: Baker & Taylor, CredoReference, Facts on File, Gale Cengage Learning, JSTOR, Newsbank, OCLC FirstSearch, ProQuest, Wilson - Wilson Web

Wireless access
Function: Archival coll, Distance learning, ILL available, Online searches, Orientations, Photocopying/Printing, Ref serv available, Telephone ref
Mem of Southeast Kansas Library System
Open Mon-Thurs (Winter) 8am-9pm, Fri 8-Noon; Mon & Tues (Summer) 7-7, Wed & Thurs 7-4:30
Restriction: Non-circulating coll, Photo ID required for access

P PARSONS PUBLIC LIBRARY, 311 S 17th St, 67357. SAN 306-0861. Tel: 620-421-5920. FAX: 620-421-3951. E-mail: staff@parsonslibrary.org. Web Site: www.parsonslibrary.org. *Dir,* Jean Strader; Staff 10 (MLS 1, Non-MLS 9)
Founded 1908. Pop 11,177; Circ 92,696
Library Holdings: Bk Vols 69,934; Per Subs 110
Subject Interests: Kansas
Automation Activity & Vendor Info: (Cataloging) Follett Software; (Circulation) Follett Software; (OPAC) Follett Software
Wireless access
Open Mon-Thurs (Winter) 9-7:30, Fri 9-5, Sat 10-4; Mon & Thurs (Summer) 9-7:30, Tues & Wed 9-5:30, Fri 9-5, Sat 10-4

M PARSONS STATE HOSPITAL & TRAINING CENTER*, The Learning Center, 2601 Gabriel, 67357-2399. (Mail add: PO Box 738, 67357-0738), SAN 342-1473. Tel: 620-421-6550, Ext 1781. *Librn,* Nancy Holding
Founded 1956
Library Holdings: Bk Vols 6,600; Per Subs 10
Open Mon-Fri 8-5

PARTRIDGE

P PARTRIDGE PUBLIC LIBRARY*, 23 S Main St, 67566. (Mail add: PO Box 96, 67566-0096), SAN 306-087X. Tel: 620-567-2467. FAX: 620-567-2467. E-mail: ppl@twotrees.net. *Dir,* Margo A Garton
Pop 338; Circ 6,496
Library Holdings: Bk Vols 16,798; Per Subs 23
Special Collections: Kansas Author's Coll; Kansas Coll
Mem of South Central Kansas Library System
Open Mon, Tues & Thurs 1-6, Fri 9-2

PEABODY

P PEABODY TOWNSHIP LIBRARY*, 214 Walnut St, 66866. SAN 306-0896. Tel: 620-983-2502. E-mail: peabodytownshiplibrary@gmail.com. Web Site: www.peabody.mykansaslibrary.org. *Libr Dir,* Rodger L Charles
Founded 1914. Pop 1,705; Circ 10,909
Library Holdings: Bk Vols 10,000; Per Subs 26
Automation Activity & Vendor Info: (Cataloging) Follett Software; (Circulation) Follett Software
Mem of North Central Kansas Libraries System
Open Tues 9-Noon & 3-8, Wed-Fri 2-5, Sat 9-Noon

PHILLIPSBURG

P PHILLIPSBURG CITY LIBRARY*, 888 Fourth St, 67661. SAN 306-090X. Tel: 785-543-5325. FAX: 785-543-5374. E-mail: pblib1@ruraltel.net. Web Site: www.phillipsburgks.us/index.aspx?NID=136. *Dir,* Kayla Kreller; *Ch Serv,* Position Currently Open
Founded 1926. Pop 2,500; Circ 53,441
Library Holdings: Bk Titles 35,137; Per Subs 75
Subject Interests: Genealogy, Kansas
Automation Activity & Vendor Info: (Acquisitions) ByWater Solutions; (Cataloging) ByWater Solutions; (Circulation) ByWater Solutions; (OPAC) ByWater Solutions
Database Vendor: LibLime
Wireless access
Function: Bks on cassette, Bks on CD, Children's prog, Computer training, Computers for patron use, Copy machines, Exhibits, Fax serv, Genealogy discussion group, Handicapped accessible, Home delivery & serv to Sr ctr & nursing homes, ILL available, Magnifiers for reading, Photocopying/Printing, Prog for adults, Prog for children & young adult, Pub access computers, Scanner, Story hour, Summer reading prog, Tax forms, Telephone ref, VHS videos
Mem of Central Kansas Library System
Open Mon-Fri 10-6, Sat 9-3

PITTSBURG

P PITTSBURG PUBLIC LIBRARY*, 308 N Walnut, 66762-4732. SAN 306-0918. Tel: 620-231-8110. FAX: 620-232-2258. Web Site: pplonline.org. *Dir,* Pat Clement; E-mail: pclement@pplonline.org; *Asst Dir,* Bev Clarkson; E-mail: bclarkson@pplonline.org; *Head, Adult Serv,* Carol Ann Robb; E-mail: carobb@pplonline.org; *Head, Circ,* Cindy Gier; E-mail: cgier@pittsburgpubliclibrary.org; *Head, Info Tech,* James Swafford; E-mail: jswafford@pittsburgpubliclibrary.org; *Head, Tech Serv,* Becky Galindo; E-mail: bgalindo@pittsburgpubliclibrary.org; *Head, Youth Serv,* Gail Sheppard; E-mail: gsheppard@pittsburgpubliclibrary.org; Staff 19 (MLS 2, Non-MLS 17)
Founded 1902. Pop 19,646; Circ 239,419
Jan 2011-Dec 2011 Income $823,578, State $29,072, City $713,054, Federal $9,651, Locally Generated Income $71,801. Mats Exp $69,156, Books $47,662, Per/Ser (Incl. Access Fees) $6,606, AV Mat $14,888. Sal $637,962
Library Holdings: CDs 8,641; DVDs 3,370; Bk Vols 55,777; Per Subs 142
Special Collections: Crawford County Genealogical Society Coll
Subject Interests: Local hist, Med, Relig
Automation Activity & Vendor Info: (Cataloging) SirsiDynix; (Circulation) SirsiDynix; (OPAC) SirsiDynix
Database Vendor: EBSCOhost, Gale Cengage Learning, ProQuest
Wireless access
Function: Audiobks via web, Bks on CD, Children's prog, Computer training, Computers for patron use, Copy machines, Electronic databases & coll, Fax serv, Free DVD rentals, Handicapped accessible, Holiday prog, Homebound delivery serv, Homework prog, ILL available, Magnifiers for reading, Mail & tel request accepted, Music CDs, Online cat, OverDrive digital audio bks, Photocopying/Printing, Prog for adults, Prog for children & young adult, Pub access computers, Ref serv available, Scanner, Senior computer classes, Story hour, Summer reading prog, Tax forms, Teen prog, Telephone ref, VHS videos, Wheelchair accessible
Mem of Southeast Kansas Library System
Open Mon-Thurs 9-8, Fri & Sat 9-5, Sun 1-5
Friends of the Library Group

C PITTSBURG STATE UNIVERSITY*, Leonard H Axe Library, 1605 S Joplin St, 66762-5889. (Mail add: 1701 S Broadway, 66762-5876), SAN 306-0926. Tel: 620-235-4878. Circulation Tel: 620-235-4882. Interlibrary Loan Service Tel: 620-235-4890. Reference Tel: 620-235-4894. Administration Tel: 620-235-4879. Automation Services Tel: 620-235-4087. Information Services Tel: 620-235-4888. FAX: 620-235-4090. E-mail: libr@pittstate.edu. Web Site: library.pittstate.edu. *Dean of Libr Serv,* Randy Roberts; E-mail: reroberts@pittstate.edu; *Cat Librn,* Morgan McCune; Tel: 620-235-4895, E-mail: mmccune@pittsstate.edu; *Per/Ref Librn,* Barbara Pope; Tel: 620-235-4884, E-mail: bpope@pittstate.edu; *Ref Librn,* Robert Lindsey; Tel: 620-235-4887, E-mail: rlindsey@pittstate.edu; *Libr Syst Mgr,* David Nance; E-mail: dnance@pittstate.edu; *Syst Coordr,* Susan Johns-Smith; Tel: 620-235-4115, E-mail: sjohnssmith@pittstate.edu; *Tech Serv Coordr,* Earl W Lee; Tel: 620-235-4885, E-mail: elee@pittstate.edu; *Spec Coll,* Janette Mauk; Tel: 620-235-4883, E-mail: jmauk@pittstate.edu; Staff 21 (MLS 9, Non-MLS 12)
Founded 1903. Enrl 7,200; Fac 298; Highest Degree: Master
Jul 2012-Jun 2013 Income $1,905,143. Mats Exp $752,000, Books $175,500, Per/Ser (Incl. Access Fees) $355,239, AV Mat $500, Electronic Ref Mat (Incl. Access Fees) $118,000, Presv $10,000. Sal $1,568,000
Library Holdings: Bks on Deafness & Sign Lang 145; Bk Titles 328,745; Bk Vols 497,639; Per Subs 3,425
Special Collections: Historic Map Coll; Southeast Kansas Coll, bks, per, ms, tapes, photog; University Archives, bks, per, ms, tapes, photog. State Document Depository; US Document Depository
Automation Activity & Vendor Info: (Acquisitions) SirsiDynix; (Cataloging) SirsiDynix; (Circulation) SirsiDynix; (Course Reserve) SirsiDynix; (OPAC) SirsiDynix; (Serials) SirsiDynix
Database Vendor: Gale Cengage Learning, LexisNexis, OCLC FirstSearch, OVID Technologies, Wilson - Wilson Web
Wireless access
Special Services for the Blind - Large screen computer & software
Open Mon-Thurs (Winter) 7:30am-Midnight, Fri 7:30-5, Sat 9-5, Sun Noon-Midnight; Mon-Thurs (Summer) 7:30am-10pm, Fri 7:30-5, Sun 4-10
Friends of the Library Group

PLAINS

P PLAINS COMMUNITY LIBRARY, 500 Grand Ave, 67869. (Mail add: PO Box 7, 67869-0007), SAN 376-5571. Tel: 620-563-7326. FAX: 620-563-6114. E-mail: plainslibrary@plainslibrary.info. Web Site: www.plainslibrary.info. *Dir,* Carolyn Chase; Staff 1 (Non-MLS 1)
Founded 1969. Pop 1,485; Circ 16,000
Library Holdings: Audiobooks 420; Bk Titles 19,000; Per Subs 62; Videos 725
Automation Activity & Vendor Info: (Cataloging) Auto-Graphics, Inc; (Circulation) Auto-Graphics, Inc; (Serials) EBSCO Online
Database Vendor: Gale Cengage Learning, OCLC FirstSearch
Wireless access
Mem of Southwest Kansas Library System
Open Mon & Thurs 10-6:30, Tues & Fri 10-5, Sat 9-1
Friends of the Library Group

PLAINVILLE

P PLAINVILLE MEMORIAL LIBRARY*, 200 SW First St, 67663. SAN 306-0942. Tel: 785-434-2786. FAX: 785-434-2786. E-mail: pville2@ruraltel.net. *Librn,* Margaret Wilson; *Asst Librn,* Brenda Frederking
Pop 2,458; Circ 12,000
Library Holdings: Bk Vols 13,000; Per Subs 30
Automation Activity & Vendor Info: (Cataloging) Book Systems; (Circulation) Book Systems; (OPAC) Book Systems
Wireless access
Mem of Central Kansas Library System
Open Mon-Fri 9-5:30, Sat 9-12 & 1-4

PLEASANTON

P LINN COUNTY LIBRARY DISTRICT NO 5*, Pleasanton Lincoln Library, 752 Main St, 66075. (Mail add: PO Box 101, 66075-0101), SAN 306-0950. Tel: 913-352-8554. FAX: 913-352-8556. E-mail: pleaslinlib@ckt.net. Web Site: pleasanton.mykansaslibrary.org. *Dir,* Wendy Morlan; *Circ,* Frances Marshall; *Circ,* Brenda Mitchell
Founded 1881. Pop 1,832; Circ 15,945
Library Holdings: Audiobooks 155; DVDs 1,385; Bk Titles 9,013; Per Subs 44
Automation Activity & Vendor Info: (Acquisitions) LibLime; (Cataloging) LibLime; (Circulation) LibLime; (OPAC) LibLime
Wireless access
Mem of Southeast Kansas Library System
Open Mon, Wed & Fri 10-5, Tues & Thurs 10-6, Sat 10-1:30
Friends of the Library Group

S LINN COUNTY MUSEUM & GENEALOGY LIBRARY*, Dunlap Park, 307 E Park St, 66075. (Mail add: PO Box 137, 66075-0137), SAN 325-6022. Tel: 913-352-8739. FAX: 913-352 8739. E-mail: linncohist-gen@ckt.net. *Pres,* Ola May Earnest
Library Holdings: Bk Titles 500; Per Subs 135
Subject Interests: Civil War, Genealogy, Kansas, State hist
Open Tues & Thurs (Oct-May) 9-4, Sat & Sun 1-5; Mon-Sun (June-Sept) 1-5

POTWIN

P POTWIN PUBLIC LIBRARY*, 126 N Randall, 67123. SAN 306-0969. Tel: 620-752-3421. FAX: 620-752-3421. E-mail: whesta40@wheatstate.com. *Librn,* Amber Howell
Founded 1932
Library Holdings: Bk Vols 4,000
Function: Homebound delivery serv, ILL available, Prog for children & young adult, Summer reading prog
Mem of South Central Kansas Library System
Open Mon 4-7, Wed 11-1 & 4-8, Fri 10-1

PRAIRIE VIEW

P SUNSHINE CITY LIBRARY*, Prairie View City Library, 207 Kansas St, 67664. (Mail add: PO Box 424, 67664), SAN 306-0977. Tel: 785-973-2265. E-mail: read@ruraltel.net. Web Site: skyways.lib.ks.us. *Librn,* Gloria DeWitt
Founded 1966. Pop 131; Circ 1,552
Jan 2006-Dec 2006 Income $5,157, State $92, City $1,655, Locally Generated Income $2,030, Other $1,380. Mats Exp $658, Books $606, Per/Ser (Incl. Access Fees) $52. Sal $470
Library Holdings: Bk Vols 3,485; Per Subs 15; Talking Bks 80; Videos 125
Mem of Central Kansas Library System
Open Mon 4-8, Wed, Thurs & Sat 9-11

PRAIRIE VILLAGE

R VILLAGE CHURCH LIBRARY*, 6641 Mission Rd, 66208-1799. (Mail add: PO Box 8050, 66208-8050), SAN 306-0985. Tel: 913-262-4200. FAX: 913-262-0304. Web Site: villagepres.org. *Librn,* Karen Lundgrin; E-mail: karen.lundgrin@villagepres.org
Library Holdings: Large Print Bks 22; Bk Vols 3,974; Per Subs 3
Open Mon-Fri 8:30-5, Sun 8:30-1

PRATT

J PRATT COMMUNITY COLLEGE*, Linda Hunt Memorial Library, 348 NE State Rd 61, 67124. SAN 306-0993. Tel: 620-450-2253. Circulation Tel: 620-672-5641, Ext 172. FAX: 620-672-2519. Web Site: www.prattcc.edu. *Dir, Librn,* Carol Matulka; E-mail: carolma@prattcc.edu. Subject Specialists: *Computer sci, Elem educ,* Carol Matulka; Staff 2.5 (MLS 1, Non-MLS 1.5)
Founded 1938. Enrl 1,000; Fac 45; Highest Degree: Associate
Jul 2008-Jun 2009 Income $152,000. Mats Exp $52,000, Books $8,000, Per/Ser (Incl. Access Fees) $18,000, AV Equip $5,000, AV Mat $2,000, Electronic Ref Mat (Incl. Access Fees) $1,000, Presv $250. Sal $58,000 (Prof $35,000)
Library Holdings: Audiobooks 98; AV Mats 2,490; e-books 1,000; Bk Titles 27,938; Bk Vols 32,351; Per Subs 250; Videos 2,000
Automation Activity & Vendor Info: (Acquisitions) Follett Software; (Cataloging) Follett Software; (Circulation) Follett Software; (Serials) EBSCO Online
Database Vendor: OCLC FirstSearch
Wireless access
Function: Audiobks via web, AV serv, Bks on cassette, Bks on CD, CD-ROM, Computers for patron use, Copy machines, Digital talking bks, Electronic databases & coll, Equip loans & repairs, ILL available, Learning ctr, Libr develop, Mail & tel request accepted, Online searches, Outside serv via phone, mail, e-mail & web, Photocopying/Printing, Pub access computers, Ref & res, Ref serv available, Referrals accepted, Scanner, Spoken cassettes & CDs, Spoken cassettes & DVDs, VHS videos, Web-catalog, Wheelchair accessible
Open Mon-Thurs 8am-10pm, Fri 8-4, Sun 4-8

P PRATT PUBLIC LIBRARY, 401 S Jackson St, 67124. SAN 306-1000. Tel: 620-672-3041, 620-672-5842. FAX: 620-672-5151. E-mail: staff@prattpubliclibrary.org. Web Site: www.prattpubliclibrary.org. *Libr Dir,* Rochelle A Westerhaus; E-mail: rochelle@prattpubliclibrary.org; Staff 4 (Non-MLS 4)
Founded 1910. Pop 9,544; Circ 73,328
Library Holdings: Audiobooks 552; Bks on Deafness & Sign Lang 94; DVDs 1,000; Large Print Bks 670; Bk Titles 45,785; Bk Vols 51,012; Per Subs 45
Special Collections: Genealogy; Kansas History
Automation Activity & Vendor Info: (Cataloging) Biblionix; (Circulation) Biblionix
Wireless access
Special Services for the Deaf - Bks on deafness & sign lang
Special Services for the Blind - Recorded bks; Screen enlargement software for people with visual disabilities; Screen reader software; Sec-Tec enlarger; ZoomText magnification & reading software
Open Mon-Thurs 10-7, Fri & Sat 10-6

PRESCOTT

P PRESCOTT CITY PUBLIC LIBRARY*, 174 W Third, 66767. SAN 306-1019. Tel: 913-471-4593. E-mail: prescottkansaslibrary@yahoo.com. *Librn,* Jean Mayhugh
Founded 1975. Pop 600; Circ 3,915
Library Holdings: Bk Vols 5,000; Per Subs 15
Special Collections: Kansas History
Wireless access
Mem of Southeast Kansas Library System
Open Mon-Thurs 3-6, Fri & Sat 9-Noon

PRETTY PRAIRIE

P PRETTY PRAIRIE PUBLIC LIBRARY*, 119 W Main St, 67570. (Mail add: PO Box 68, 67570), SAN 306-1027. Tel: 620-459-6392. FAX: 620-459-7354. E-mail: pprairie@btsskynet.net. Web Site: www.skyways.org/towns/PrettyPrairie. *Coll Develop, Dir,* Patti Brace; *Asst City Librn,* Carol Atkins Ray; Staff 3 (MLS 2, Non-MLS 1)
Founded 1945. Pop 657; Circ 7,533
Library Holdings: Bk Titles 11,000; Per Subs 40
Automation Activity & Vendor Info: (Cataloging) Auto-Graphics, Inc; (Circulation) Auto-Graphics, Inc; (OPAC) Auto-Graphics, Inc
Mem of South Central Kansas Library System
Open Mon-Fri 9-12 & 1-5, Sat 9-12

PROTECTION

P PROTECTION TOWNSHIP LIBRARY*, 404 N Broadway, 67127. (Mail add: PO Box 265, 67127-0265). Tel: 620-622-4886. FAX: 620-622-4492. E-mail: pclibrary@protectionlibrary.com. Web Site: www.protectionlibrary.com. *Libr Dir,* Mary Ehret Holler
Founded 1934. Pop 700
Library Holdings: Bk Vols 5,000
Special Collections: Stan Herd Art Gallery
Wireless access
Function: Fax serv, Handicapped accessible, Home delivery & serv to Sr ctr & nursing homes, Homebound delivery serv, Homework prog, Large print keyboards, Wheelchair accessible
Mem of Southwest Kansas Library System
Open Mon-Fri 12-6

QUINTER

P JAY JOHNSON PUBLIC LIBRARY*, 411 Main St, 67752. (Mail add: PO Box 369, 67752-0369), SAN 306-1035. Tel: 785-754-2171. E-mail: jjpl@ruraltel.net. Web Site: www.quinterlibrary.org. *Dir,* Sara Linden
Founded 1932. Pop 952; Circ 24,084
Library Holdings: Bk Vols 17,000; Per Subs 35
Special Collections: Geneaology & Community History (Heritage Room)
Automation Activity & Vendor Info: (Cataloging) Auto-Graphics, Inc
Wireless access
Mem of Northwest Kansas Library System
Open Mon, Wed & Fri 10-5, Tues & Thurs 10-8, Sat 10-1
Friends of the Library Group

RANDALL

P RANDALL PUBLIC LIBRARY*, 107 Main St, 66963. (Mail add: PO Box 101, 66963-0101), SAN 306-1043. Tel: 785-739-2380. FAX: 785-739-2331. E-mail: ranlib@nckcn.com. *Dir,* Amy Topliff
Pop 154; Circ 999
Library Holdings: Bk Vols 3,764; Per Subs 10
Mem of Central Kansas Library System
Open Mon 3-5, Tues 3-6, Wed & Thurs 8:30am-11am

RANSOM

P RANSOM PUBLIC LIBRARY*, 411 S Vermont, 67572. (Mail add: PO Box 263, 67572-0263), SAN 306-1051. Tel: 785-731-2855. FAX: 785-731-2518. E-mail: director@ransomlibrary.info. Web Site: www.ransomlibrary.info. *Librn,* Debbie Erb
Pop 468; Circ 9,860
Library Holdings: Bk Vols 5,400; Per Subs 30
Automation Activity & Vendor Info: (Cataloging) Follett Software; (Circulation) Follett Software
Database Vendor: Gale Cengage Learning, OCLC FirstSearch
Mem of Southwest Kansas Library System
Open Mon, Wed & Fri 12-6, Sat 9-12

REPUBLIC

P RAE HOBSON MEMORIAL LIBRARY*, PO Box 3, 66964-0003. SAN 306-106X. Tel: 785-361-2481. *Librn,* Vera Burge
Pop 300; Circ 2,301
Library Holdings: Bk Vols 4,000; Per Subs 10
Subject Interests: Fiction
Mem of Central Kansas Library System
Open Tues & Sat 1-6
Friends of the Library Group

RICHMOND

P RICHMOND PUBLIC LIBRARY*, 107 E Central, 66080-4035. (Mail add: PO Box 237, 66080-0237), SAN 306-1078. Tel: 785-835-6163. FAX: 785-835-6163. Web Site: richmond.mykansaslibrary.org. *Dir,* Connie A Weber; E-mail: cweber@richmond.lib.ks.us; Staff 2 (Non-MLS 2)
Founded 1938. Pop 500; Circ 7,707
Library Holdings: Audiobooks 40; CDs 50; DVDs 400; Large Print Bks 290; Bk Titles 4,000; Per Subs 20; Videos 150
Wireless access
Function: Children's prog, Computers for patron use, Copy machines, Fax serv, Free DVD rentals, ILL available, Music CDs, Photocopying/Printing, Prog for adults, Prog for children & young adult, Scanner, Spoken cassettes & DVDs, Summer reading prog, VHS videos
Partic in Public Library InterLINK
Open Mon & Fri 3-6, Wed & Thurs 10-6, Sat 12-2
Friends of the Library Group

RILEY

P RILEY CITY LIBRARY*, 206 S Broadway, 66531. (Mail add: PO Box 204, 66531-0204). Tel: 785-485-2978. E-mail: rc3lib@kansas.net. *Dir,* Kathleen J Caster; *Circ Librn,* Laura Gayle Coon
Library Holdings: Bk Vols 4,000
Automation Activity & Vendor Info: (ILL) Auto-Graphics, Inc
Wireless access
Mem of North Central Kansas Libraries System
Open Mon 5-7, Tues 1-5, Wed & Fri 1:30-5:30, Sat 10-12

ROSE HILL

P ROSE HILL PUBLIC LIBRARY*, 306 N Rose Hill Rd, 67133. (Mail add: PO Box 157, 67133-0157). Tel: 316-776-3013. *Librn,* Cindy Maxey; E-mail: cmaxey@cityofrosehill.com
Library Holdings: Bk Vols 2,000; Per Subs 11; Talking Bks 400
Automation Activity & Vendor Info: (Cataloging) Chancery SMS; (Circulation) Chancery SMS; (OPAC) Chancery SMS
Mem of South Central Kansas Library System
Open Mon, Wed & Sat 9-1, Tues & Thurs 1-7

ROSSVILLE

P ROSSVILLE COMMUNITY LIBRARY*, 407 Main St, 66533. (Mail add: PO Box 618, 66533-0618), SAN 306-1086. Tel: 785-584-6454. FAX: 785-584-6454. *Dir,* Sean Bird; E-mail: seancbird@gmail.com; Staff 1 (MLS 1)
Pop 1,635; Circ 19,023
Library Holdings: Bk Vols 11,720; Per Subs 43
Mem of Northeast Kansas Library System
Open Mon, Tues, Thurs & Fri 1-6, Wed 9:30-7, Sat 8-12

RUSSELL

P RUSSELL PUBLIC LIBRARY, 126 E Sixth St, 67665-2041. SAN 306-1108. Tel: 785-483-2742. FAX: 785-483-6254. E-mail: ruspublib@gmail.com. Web Site: www.russellpubliclibrary.com. *Dir,* Jessica McGuire; Staff 8 (Non-MLS 8)
Founded 1906. Pop 4,696; Circ 2,249
Library Holdings: Audiobooks 800; DVDs 347; e-books 20; Large Print Bks 2,600; Bk Titles 21,163; Per Subs 45
Automation Activity & Vendor Info: (Cataloging) ByWater Solutions; (Circulation) ByWater Solutions; (OPAC) ByWater Solutions
Wireless access
Function: 24/7 Online cat, Activity rm, Adult bk club, After school storytime, Audiobks via web, Bk club(s), Bks on CD, Children's prog, Computers for patron use, Copy machines, e-mail serv, Electronic databases & coll, eReaders, Fax serv, Free DVD rentals, Handicapped accessible, Holiday prog, Laminating, Magazines, Magnifiers for reading, Microfiche/film & reading machines, Movies, Music CDs, Newsp ref libr, Online cat, OverDrive digital audio bks, Photocopying/Printing, Preschool outreach, Preschool reading prog, Prog for children & young adult, Pub access computers, Res performed for a fee, Scanner, Spoken cassettes & CDs, Spoken cassettes & DVDs, Story hour, Study rm, Summer reading prog, Teen prog, Wheelchair accessible, Workshops
Mem of Central Kansas Library System
Open Mon-Thurs 10-6, Fri 10-5, Sat 10-3

SABETHA

P MARY COTTON PUBLIC LIBRARY*, 915 Virginia, 66534-1950. (Mail add: PO Box 70, 66534-0070), SAN 306-1124. Tel: 785-284-3160. FAX: 785-284-3605. Web Site: www.sabethalibrary.org. *Dir,* Kim Priest; E-mail: kimpriest@sabethalibrary.org; Staff 3 (Non-MLS 3)
Founded 1912. Pop 2,500; Circ 56,000
Library Holdings: Bks on Deafness & Sign Lang 20; DVDs 1,000; High Interest/Low Vocabulary Bk Vols 12,000; Large Print Bks 500; Bk Titles 29,000; Bk Vols 30,000; Per Subs 30; Talking Bks 1,200; Videos 1,062
Special Collections: Albany School/Town Pictures; Sabetha Herald Newspaper Coll, 1880
Subject Interests: Genealogy, Local hist
Automation Activity & Vendor Info: (Cataloging) LibLime Koha; (Circulation) LibLime Koha; (ILL) LibLime Koha
Database Vendor: EBSCOhost, Gale Cengage Learning, ProQuest
Function: Home delivery & serv to Sr ctr & nursing homes, ILL available, Magnifiers for reading, Photocopying/Printing, Prog for children & young adult, Serves mentally handicapped consumers, Summer reading prog, Wheelchair accessible
Mem of Northeast Kansas Library System
Open Mon & Wed 10-8, Tues, Thurs & Fri 10-5:30, Sat 10-4
Friends of the Library Group

SAINT FRANCIS

P ST FRANCIS PUBLIC LIBRARY*, 121 N Scott St, 67756. (Mail add: PO Box 688, 67756-0688), SAN 306-1132. Tel: 785-332-3292. E-mail: library@cityofstfrancis.net. *Librn,* Pat Leibbrandt
Circ 21,202
Library Holdings: Bk Vols 15,000; Per Subs 48
Wireless access
Open Mon-Fri 10:30-5:30, Sat 10:30-1

SAINT JOHN

P IDA LONG GOODMAN MEMORIAL LIBRARY, 406 N Monroe, 67576-1836. SAN 306-1140. Tel: 620-549-3227. FAX: 620-549-6589. E-mail: ilgml@usd350.com. *Dir,* Christie Snyder; E-mail: snyder@usd350.com; Staff 1 (Non-MLS 1)
Founded 1969. Pop 1,173; Circ 20,466
Library Holdings: Audiobooks 212; Bk Titles 29,171
Special Collections: Sheet Music; St John News (1880-)
Subject Interests: Educ, Genealogy, Hist, Kansas, Local hist
Automation Activity & Vendor Info: (Acquisitions) Baker & Taylor; (Circulation) ComPanion Corp; (ILL) Auto-Graphics, Inc

Database Vendor: OCLC FirstSearch
Wireless access
Function: Accelerated reader prog, Accessibility serv available based on individual needs, Adult bk club, After school storytime, Audiobks via web, Bilingual assistance for Spanish patrons, Bks on cassette, Bks on CD, Children's prog, Computer training, Computers for patron use, Copy machines, Digital talking bks, Family literacy, Fax serv, Free DVD rentals, Handicapped accessible, Holiday prog, Homework prog, Microfiche/film & reading machines, Online searches, Orientations, Outreach serv, Outside serv via phone, mail, e-mail & web, Photocopying/Printing, Preschool outreach, Preschool reading prog, Prog for adults, Prog for children & young adult, Scanner, Senior outreach, Spanish lang bks, Spoken cassettes & CDs, Story hour, Summer reading prog, Tax forms, VCDs, VHS videos, Wheelchair accessible
Mem of South Central Kansas Library System
Open Mon-Thurs 7:30-7, Fri 8-5, Sun 2-5
Friends of the Library Group

SAINT MARYS

P POTTAWATOMIE WABAUNSEE REGIONAL LIBRARY*, St Marys Headquarters Library, 306 N Fifth St, 66536-1404. SAN 342-1503. Tel: 785-437-2778. FAX: 785-437-2778. E-mail: illpowab@oct.net. Web Site: skyways.lib.ks.us/library/pottwablib, www.pottwab.org. *Dir,* Judith Cremer; E-mail: cremerj@oct.net; Staff 13.53 (MLS 2, Non-MLS 11.53)
Founded 1962. Pop 24,362; Circ 79,522
Jan 2011-Dec 2012 Income (Main Library and Branch(s)) $536,031, State $10,280, County $478,847, Locally Generated Income $2,710, Other $44,194. Mats Exp $65,253, Books $55,206, Per/Ser (Incl. Access Fees) $3,946, Micro $279, AV Mat $5,601, Electronic Ref Mat (Incl. Access Fees) $221. Sal $311,656
Library Holdings: Audiobooks 3,738; Bks-By-Mail 5,851; e-books 10,000; e-journals 5,000; Electronic Media & Resources 50; Large Print Bks 8,822; Microforms 490; Bk Vols 82,752; Per Subs 107; Videos 325
Automation Activity & Vendor Info: (Cataloging) Auto-Graphics, Inc; (Circulation) Auto-Graphics, Inc; (ILL) Auto-Graphics, Inc; (OPAC) Auto-Graphics, Inc
Database Vendor: Auto-Graphics, Inc
Wireless access
Function: Audiobks via web, Bks on cassette, Bks on CD, Children's prog, Computers for patron use, Copy machines, Digital talking bks, e mail & chat, e-mail serv, E-Reserves, Electronic databases & coll, Fax serv, Free DVD rentals, Handicapped accessible, Homework prog, ILL available, Mail & tel request accepted, Microfiche/film & reading machines, Music CDs, Newsp ref libr, Online cat, Outside serv via phone, mail, e-mail & web, OverDrive digital audio bks, Photocopying/Printing, Preschool reading prog, Prog for children & young adult, Pub access computers, Ref serv available, Spoken cassettes & CDs, Story hour, Summer reading prog, Tax forms, Telephone ref, VHS videos, Web-catalog, Wheelchair accessible
Mem of North Central Kansas Libraries System
Special Services for the Blind - Audio mat; Bks on cassette; Cassettes; Large print & cassettes; Large print bks
Open Mon, Tues & Fri 8:30 5, Wed 8:30-6, Thurs 8:30-7, Sat 9-1
Branches: 3
ALMA BRANCH, 115 W Third St, Alma, 66401. (Mail add: PO Box 420, Alma, 66401-0420), SAN 342-1538. Tel: 785-765-3647. FAX: 785-765-3647. E-mail: powabalm@gmail.com. *Br Librn,* Joyce Mathies; *Asst Br Librn,* Paula Moege; Staff 1 (Non-MLS 1)
Function: Audiobks via web, Bks on cassette, Bks on CD, Children's prog, Computers for patron use, Copy machines, Digital talking bks, e-mail & chat, E-Reserves, Electronic databases & coll, Fax serv, Free DVD rentals, Handicapped accessible, ILL available, Mail & tel request accepted, Microfiche/film & reading machines, Music CDs, Newsp ref libr, Online cat, OverDrive digital audio bks, Photocopying/Printing, Preschool reading prog, Prog for children & young adult, Pub access computers, Ref serv available, Story hour, Summer reading prog, Tax forms, Telephone ref, Web-catalog, Wheelchair accessible
Special Services for the Blind - Audio mat; Bks on cassette; Cassettes; Large print & cassettes; Large print bks
Open Mon, Tues & Fri 9-12:15 & 12:45-5, Wed 9-12:15 & 12:45-7
ESKRIDGE BRANCH, 115 S Main St, Eskridge, 66423. (Mail add: PO Box 87, Eskridge, 66423-0087), SAN 342-1562. Tel: 785-449-2296. FAX: 785-449-2296. E-mail: powabesk@gmail.com. *Br Librn,* Jan Brown; *Asst Br Librn,* Judy Morton; Staff 1 (Non-MLS 1)
Function: Audiobks via web, Bks on cassette, Bks on CD, Children's prog, Computers for patron use, Copy machines, e-mail & chat, e-mail serv, E-Reserves, Electronic databases & coll, Fax serv, Free DVD rentals, Handicapped accessible, Homework prog, ILL available, Mail & tel request accepted, Microfiche/film & reading machines, Newsp ref libr, Outside serv via phone, mail, e-mail & web, OverDrive digital audio bks, Photocopying/Printing, Prog for children & young adult, Pub access computers, Ref serv available, Story hour, Summer reading prog, Tax forms, Telephone ref, Web-catalog, Wheelchair accessible
Special Services for the Blind - Audio mat; Bks on cassette; Cassettes; Large print & cassettes; Large print bks; Talking bk serv referral
Open Mon-Wed 8:30-12:30 & 1-5, Fri 9-12:30 & 1-4, Sat 10-12
ONAGA BRANCH, 313 Leonard St, Onaga, 66521. (Mail add: PO Box 310, Onaga, 66521-0310), SAN 342-1597. Tel: 785-889-4531. FAX: 785-889-4531. E-mail: powabona@gmail.com. *Br Librn,* Ivy Rash; *Asst Br Librn,* Emma Schreiber; Staff 1 (Non-MLS 1)
Function: Audiobks via web, Bks on cassette, Bks on CD, Children's prog, Computers for patron use, Copy machines, e-mail & chat, e-mail serv, E-Reserves, Electronic databases & coll, Fax serv, Free DVD rentals, Homework prog, ILL available, Mail & tel request accepted, Microfiche/film & reading machines, Music CDs, Newsp ref libr, Online cat, Outside serv via phone, mail, e-mail & web, OverDrive digital audio bks, Photocopying/Printing, Preschool reading prog, Prog for children & young adult, Pub access computers, Ref serv available, Story hour, Summer reading prog, Tax forms, Telephone ref, Web-catalog
Special Services for the Blind - Audio mat; Bks on cassette; Cassettes; Large print & cassettes; Large print bks; Talking bk serv referral
Open Mon 9-12:30 & 1-7, Tues & Fri 9-12:30 & 1-5, Wed 9-12:30 & 1-6:30

SAINT PAUL

P GRAVES MEMORIAL PUBLIC LIBRARY*, 717 Central Ave, 66771. (Mail add: PO Box 354, 66771-0354), SAN 306-1159. Tel: 620-449-2001. FAX: 620-449-2001. E-mail: gmpldirector@hotmail.com. Web Site: stpaul.mykansaslibrary.org. *Dir,* C Wesley Filkel; E-mail: gmpldirector@hotmail.com
Founded 1955. Pop 927; Circ 6,292
Library Holdings: Bk Vols 5,537; Per Subs 18
Special Collections: Local Newspaper 1901-1961; W W Graves, writings & bks
Wireless access
Mem of Southeast Kansas Library System
Open Mon-Fri 9-12 & 2-6, Sat 9-2
Restriction: Authorized patrons

SALINA

C KANSAS STATE UNIVERSITY AT SALINA*, College of Technology & Aviation Library, Technology Center Bldg, 2310 Centennial Rd, Rm 111, 67401. SAN 306-1175. Tel: 785-826-2637. FAX: 785-826-2937. Web Site: www.sal.ksu.edu/library/. *Dir,* Alysia Starkey; Tel: 785-826-2616, E-mail: astarkey@ksu.edu; Staff 4 (MLS 2, Non-MLS 2)
Founded 1965. Enrl 1,000; Fac 100; Highest Degree: Doctorate
Jul 2005-Jun 2006 Income $78,630. Mats Exp $23,000
Library Holdings: Bk Vols 30,000; Per Subs 100
Subject Interests: Aeronaut, Aviation, Bus & mgt, Computer info, Computer sci, Construction eng tech, Electronic tech, Math, Mechanical tech
Automation Activity & Vendor Info: (Acquisitions) Ex Libris Group; (Cataloging) Ex Libris Group; (Circulation) Ex Libris Group; (OPAC) Ex Libris Group; (Serials) Ex Libris Group
Mem of Central Kansas Library System
Open Mon-Thurs (Winter) 8am-11:30pm, Fri 8-5, Sat 1-4, Sun 6pm-9pm; Mon-Thurs (Summer) 8am-9pm, Fri 8-5
Friends of the Library Group

C KANSAS WESLEYAN UNIVERSITY*, Memorial Library, 100 E Claflin Ave, 67401-6100. SAN 306-1183. Tel: 785-827-5541, Ext 4120. Interlibrary Loan Service Tel: 785-827-5541, Ext 4150. Toll Free Tel: 800-874-1154. FAX: 785-827-0927. E-mail: library@kwu.edu. Web Site: www.kwu.edu/library. *Dir, Libr & Info Serv,* Angela A Allen; E-mail: angelaa@kwu.edu; *Assoc Librn,* Lynda Linder; E-mail: lyndal@kwu.edu; Staff 2 (MLS 2)
Founded 1886. Enrl 900; Fac 50; Highest Degree: Master
Library Holdings: e-books 7,500; Bk Titles 78,500; Per Subs 117
Automation Activity & Vendor Info: (Circulation) Follett Software; (OPAC) Follett Software
Database Vendor: EBSCOhost, Gale Cengage Learning, LexisNexis, OCLC FirstSearch, ProQuest, SerialsSolutions
Function: ILL available
Partic in Associated Colleges of Central Kansas; OCLC Online Computer Library Center, Inc
Open Mon-Thurs (Winter) 8am-11pm, Fri 8-5, Sat 1-5, Sun 2-11; Mon-Fri (Summer) 8-5
Restriction: Open to pub for ref & circ; with some limitations

P SALINA PUBLIC LIBRARY, 301 W Elm St, 67401. SAN 306-1205. Tel: 785-825-4624. FAX: 785-823-0706. Web Site: www.salinapubliclibrary.org. *Dir,* Joe McKenzie; E-mail: joemcken@salpublib.org; *Head of Acq/Cataloging,* Nick Berezovsky; E-mail: nickbere@salpublib.org; *Coll Develop, Head, Info Serv,* Angela Allen; E-mail: aallen@salpublib.org; *Head, Outreach Serv,* Lori Berezovsky; E-mail: loribere@salpublib.org; *Head, Youth Serv,* Kristi Hansen; E-mail: khansen@salpublib.org; *Bus &*

Human Res Mgr, Sandy Wilcox; E-mail: swilcox@salpublib.org; *Tech Ctr Mgr,* Melanie Hedgespeth; E-mail: melanie@salpublib.org; *Circ,* Dianna Waite; E-mail: diawaite@salpublib.org; *ILL,* Connie Hocking; E-mail: chocking@salpublib.org; Staff 38 (MLS 7, Non-MLS 31)
Founded 1897. Pop 48,045; Circ 574,651
Jan 2013-Dec 2013 Income $2,866,254. Mats Exp $301,341, Books $126,828, Per/Ser (Incl. Access Fees) $21,802, AV Mat $97,888, Electronic Ref Mat (Incl. Access Fees) $54,823. Sal $1,389,379
Special Collections: Campbell Room of Kansas History
Subject Interests: Art, Educ, Hist
Automation Activity & Vendor Info: (Cataloging) LibLime Koha; (Circulation) LibLime Koha; (OPAC) LibLime Koha
Wireless access
Function: Adult bk club, After school storytime, Archival coll, Art exhibits, Audiobks via web, AV serv, Bk club(s), Bks on CD, Children's prog, Computer training, Computers for patron use, Copy machines, e-mail & chat, eReaders, Exhibits, Free DVD rentals, Genealogy discussion group, Handicapped accessible, Holiday prog, Home delivery & serv to Sr ctr & nursing homes, Homebound delivery serv, ILL available, Learning ctr, Life-long learning prog for all ages, Magazines, Mango lang, Microfiche/film & reading machines, Movies, Music CDs, Online cat, Online ref, Online searches, Orientations, Outreach serv, Outside serv via phone, mail, e-mail & web, OverDrive digital audio bks, Photocopying/Printing, Preschool outreach, Preschool reading prog, Printer for laptops & handheld devices, Prog for adults, Prog for children & young adult, Pub access computers, Ref serv in person, Scanner, Senior computer classes, Senior outreach, Spanish lang bks, Story hour, Study rm, Summer & winter reading prog, Summer reading prog, Tax forms, Telephone ref, Web-catalog, Winter reading prog, Workshops
Publications: Class Catalog; Cover to Cover (Newsletter)
Mem of Central Kansas Library System
Open Mon-Thurs 9-9, Fri & Sat 9-6, Sun 1-6
Friends of the Library Group

SATANTA

P DUDLEY TOWNSHIP PUBLIC LIBRARY*, 105 N Sequoyah St, 67870. (Mail add: PO Box 189, 67870-0189). Tel: 620-649-2213. FAX: 620-649-2213. E-mail: satantalibrary@gmail.com. Web Site: satanta.mykansaslibrary.org. *Dir,* Lennet Froelich
Founded 1932
Library Holdings: Bk Vols 29,000; Per Subs 24
Special Collections: Kansas Coll
Wireless access
Mem of Southwest Kansas Library System
Open Mon-Wed & Fri 10:30-5:30, Thurs 10:30-8, Sat 10-2

SAVONBURG

P SAVONBURG PUBLIC LIBRARY*, 101A S Walnut, 66772. SAN 306-123X. Tel: 620-754-3835. E-mail: lib@savonburg.net. *Dir,* Kathy Hale
Founded 1963. Pop 113; Circ 4,017
Library Holdings: Bk Vols 5,000; Per Subs 20
Automation Activity & Vendor Info: (Acquisitions) LibLime; (Cataloging) LibLime; (Circulation) LibLime
Wireless access
Mem of Southeast Kansas Library System
Open Tues & Thurs 2-6, Sat 1-5

SCANDIA

P SCANDIA CITY LIBRARY*, 409 Fourth St, 66966. (Mail add: PO Box 20, 66966-0020), SAN 306-1248. Tel: 785-335-2271. FAX: 785-335-2271. *Librn,* Kathryn Gile; E-mail: kgile@nckcn.com
Pop 650
Library Holdings: Bk Titles 9,000; Per Subs 40
Subject Interests: Swedish (Lang)
Mem of Central Kansas Library System
Open Mon, Wed, Fri & Sat 2-6

SCOTT CITY

P SCOTT COUNTY LIBRARY*, 110 W Eighth, 67871-1599. SAN 306-1256. Tel: 620-872-5341. FAX: 620-872-0248. E-mail: sclib@wbsnet.org. *Dir,* Julie O'Brien
Founded 1923. Pop 5,582
Library Holdings: Bk Titles 45,000; Per Subs 100
Automation Activity & Vendor Info: (Cataloging) Follett Software; (Circulation) Follett Software
Database Vendor: OCLC FirstSearch
Mem of Southwest Kansas Library System
Open Mon & Thurs 10-8, Tues & Wed 10-6, Fri & Sat 10-5

SEDAN

P SEDAN PUBLIC LIBRARY*, 115 N Chautauqua St, 67361-1301. SAN 306-1264. Tel: 620-725-3405. FAX: 620-725-3405. *Librn,* Ellen Rushing; *Asst Librn,* Annmarie Cunningham; Staff 2 (Non-MLS 2)
Pop 1,450
Library Holdings: Bk Vols 9,400; Per Subs 29
Mem of Southeast Kansas Library System
Open Mon-Thurs 12:30-5:30, Fri 9-5:30, Sat 9-Noon

SEDGWICK

P LILLIAN TEAR LIBRARY*, 501 N Commercial, 67135. (Mail add: PO Box 28, 67135-0028), SAN 306-1272. Tel: 316-772-5727. E-mail: sedgwicktearlib@cityofsedgwick.org. *Libr Dir,* Cathy Lynn Medlin
Founded 1929. Pop 1,450; Circ 10,000
Library Holdings: Bk Vols 6,000; Per Subs 20
Special Collections: Sheet Music Coll
Wireless access
Open Mon-Fri 10-6

SELDEN

P SELDEN PUBLIC LIBRARY*, 109 S Kansas Ave, 67757. (Mail add: PO Box 244, 67757-0244), SAN 376-513X. Tel: 785-386-4321. E-mail: seldenpl@ruraltel.net. *Librn,* Marsha Rogers
Library Holdings: Audiobooks 50; AV Mats 50; CDs 10; DVDs 15; Large Print Bks 2,500; Bk Titles 5,000; Bk Vols 7,000; Videos 40
Wireless access
Mem of Northwest Kansas Library System
Open Mon & Sat 9am-11am, Wed 6:30pm-8:30pm

SENECA

P SENECA FREE LIBRARY*, 606 Main St, 66538. SAN 306-1280. Tel: 785-336-2377. FAX: 785-336-3699. E-mail: librarian@senecafreelibrary.org. Web Site: senecafreelibrary.org. *Libr Dir,* Kate Haynie; E-mail: khaynie@senecafreelibrary.org; Staff 1 (Non-MLS 1)
Founded 1917. Pop 2,000; Circ 60,000
Jan 2008-Dec 2009 Income $130,715, State $1,415, City $113,000, Locally Generated Income $3,000, Other $16,000. Mats Exp $29,800, Books $19,000, Per/Ser (Incl. Access Fees) $700, AV Equip $300, AV Mat $9,500, Electronic Ref Mat (Incl. Access Fees) $200, Presv $100. Sal $50,000 (Prof $26,500)
Library Holdings: Audiobooks 900; CDs 700; DVDs 1,300; Large Print Bks 500; Bk Vols 26,000; Per Subs 54; Videos 400
Automation Activity & Vendor Info: (Acquisitions) LibLime; (Cataloging) LibLime; (Circulation) LibLime; (ILL) Auto-Graphics, Inc
Database Vendor: LibLime
Wireless access
Function: Adult bk club, Archival coll, Bk club(s), Bks on cassette, Children's prog, Computer training, Computers for patron use, Copy machines, e-mail & chat, Exhibits, Family literacy, Fax serv, For res purposes, Free DVD rentals, Handicapped accessible, Home delivery & serv to Sr ctr & nursing homes, Homebound delivery serv, ILL available, Instruction & testing, Libr develop, Mail & tel request accepted, Mail loans to mem, Online ref, Online searches, Orientations, Outreach serv, Outside serv via phone, mail, e-mail & web, OverDrive digital audio bks, Photocopying/Printing, Prof lending libr, Prog for children & young adult, Pub access computers, Ref & res, Ref serv in person, Res performed for a fee, Spoken cassettes & CDs, Story hour, Summer reading prog, Tax forms, Teen prog, VHS videos, Video lending libr, Web-catalog, Wheelchair accessible
Mem of Northeast Kansas Library System
Open Mon-Thurs 10-8, Fri 10-5, Sat 10-2

SHARON SPRINGS

P SHARON SPRINGS PUBLIC LIBRARY*, 113 W Second St, 67758. (Mail add: PO Box 640, 67758-0640), SAN 306-1299. Tel: 785-852-4685. FAX: 785-852-4687. E-mail: sspl@wbsnet.org. *Head Librn,* Cathy Van Allen
Founded 1930. Pop 1,064; Circ 8,093
Library Holdings: AV Mats 13; Bk Vols 8,200; Per Subs 14
Subject Interests: Local hist
Automation Activity & Vendor Info: (Cataloging) Winnebago Software Co; (Circulation) Winnebago Software Co
Mem of Northwest Kansas Library System
Open Mon-Thurs 2-6, Fri & Sat 9-12 & 2-6

SHAWNEE

R CENTRAL BAPTIST THEOLOGICAL SEMINARY LIBRARY*, 6601 Monticello Rd, 66226-3513. SAN 305-9766. Tel: 913-667-5700, 913-667-5725. Administration Tel: 913-667-5729. FAX: 913-371-8110. Web Site: libguides.cbts.edu/home. *Libr Dir,* Vance M Thomas; Fax:

913-667-5789, E-mail: vmthomas@cbts.edu; *Libr Asst,* Linda Kiesling; Tel: 913-667-5733, E-mail: lkiesling@cbts.eud; Staff 2 (MLS 1, Non-MLS 1)
Founded 1901. Highest Degree: Master
Library Holdings: Bk Vols 105,000; Per Subs 75
Subject Interests: Baptists, Relig
Automation Activity & Vendor Info: (Cataloging) SirsiDynix; (Circulation) SirsiDynix
Database Vendor: SirsiDynix
Wireless access
Partic in ECUNET/ABNET; Kansas City Library Service Program
Open Mon, Tues & Thurs (Fall & Spring) 10-10, Wed & Fri 10-4:30; Mon-Fri (Summer) 10-4:30

SHAWNEE MISSION

M SHAWNEE MISSION MEDICAL CENTER MEDICAL LIBRARY*, 9100 W 74th St, 66204. SAN 320-1899. Tel: 913-676-2101. Interlibrary Loan Service Tel: 913-676-2103. FAX: 913-676-2106. *Mgr, Med Librn,* Clifford L Nestell; *Med Librn,* Melody J Senecal; E-mail: melody.senecal@shawneemission.org; Staff 1.7 (MLS 1.5, Non-MLS 0.2)
Founded 1963
Library Holdings: CDs 1,820; DVDs 100; e-books 1,000; e-journals 3,400; Bk Vols 9,325; Per Subs 175
Automation Activity & Vendor Info: (Acquisitions) EOS International; (Cataloging) EOS International; (Circulation) EOS International; (ILL) OCLC; (OPAC) EOS International; (Serials) EOS International
Wireless access
Partic in OCLC Online Computer Library Center, Inc
Open Mon-Thurs 8-5:30, Fri 8-4:30

SILVER LAKE

P SILVER LAKE LIBRARY*, 203 Railroad St, 66539. (Mail add: PO Box 248, 66539-0248), SAN 306-1310. Tel: 785-582-5141. FAX: 785-582-4282. Web Site: skyways.lib.ks.us/library/silverlake. *Dir,* Cathy Newland; *Asst Dir,* Alphie Dick; *Youth Serv Librn,* Tracey DeShazo; *Circ Librn,* Karla Bahret; *Circ Librn,* Amber Hamilton; *Circ Librn,* Nancy Huske; *Circ Librn,* Danielle Larson; *Circ Librn,* Matt McClain; Staff 2 (Non-MLS 2)
Founded 1975
Library Holdings: Bks on Deafness & Sign Lang 20; Bk Titles 8,000; Bk Vols 9,000; Per Subs 50
Special Collections: Children with Disabilities
Subject Interests: Inspirational
Automation Activity & Vendor Info: (Cataloging) SirsiDynix; (Circulation) SirsiDynix; (ILL) SirsiDynix
Function: Fax serv, Photocopying/Printing, Prog for children & young adult
Publications: Silver Lake Library Times
Mem of Northeast Kansas Library System
Special Services for the Blind - Audio mat
Open Mon, Wed & Fri 9-5, Tues & Thurs 9-6, Sat 10-2
Friends of the Library Group

SMITH CENTER

P SMITH CENTER PUBLIC LIBRARY*, 117 W Court St, 66967-2601. SAN 306-1329. Tel: 785-282-3361. FAX: 785-282-6740. E-mail: smcntpl@ruraltel.net. *Libr Dir,* Joanna Runyon; *Asst Librn,* Diane Depperschmidt
Pop 2,100; Circ 30,603
Library Holdings: Bk Vols 17,000; Per Subs 59
Wireless access
Mem of Central Kansas Library System
Open Mon-Wed & Fri 10-5, Thurs 10-8, Sat 10-12 & 1-5

SOLOMON

P SOLOMON PUBLIC LIBRARY*, 108 N Walnut, 67480. (Mail add: PO Box 246, 67480-0246), SAN 306-1337. Tel: 785-655-3521. E-mail: slibrary@eaglecom.net. *Librn,* Connie Avery
Founded 1934. Pop 1,192; Circ 9,492
Library Holdings: Bk Vols 12,500; Per Subs 35
Automation Activity & Vendor Info: (Acquisitions) Auto-Graphics, Inc; (Circulation) Auto-Graphics, Inc; (ILL) Auto-Graphics, Inc
Wireless access
Mem of North Central Kansas Libraries System
Open Mon & Wed 12-6, Tues, Thurs & Fri 3:30-6, Sat 10-4

SOUTH HAVEN

P SOUTH HAVEN TOWNSHIP LIBRARY*, 104 W Baird, 67140. (Mail add: PO Box 227, 67140-0027), SAN 306-1345. Tel: 620-892-5268. E-mail: libraryboard@hotmail.com. *Librn,* Wynetta Schaffer
Founded 1937. Pop 733; Circ 3,545
Library Holdings: Bk Vols 7,870
Mem of South Central Kansas Library System
Open Thurs, Fri & Sat 1-4:30

SOUTH HUTCHINSON

P SOUTH CENTRAL KANSAS LIBRARY SYSTEM*, 321 N Main St, 67505-1146. SAN 342-0426. Tel: 620-663-3211. Toll Free Tel: 800-234-0529. FAX: 620-663-9797. Web Site: www.sckls.info. *Dir,* Paul Hawkins; E-mail: paul@sckls.info; *IT Dir,* Larry Papenfuss; E-mail: larry@sckls.info; *Mem Serv Coordr,* Tom Taylor; E-mail: tom@sckls.info; *Tech Serv Coordr,* Tram Nguyen; E-mail: tram@sckls.info; *Admin Serv,* Mia Wilson; E-mail: mia@sckls.info; *Libr Support Spec,* Katherine Goodenberger; E-mail: katherine@sckls.info; *Outreach Serv Spec,* Nicole Penley; E-mail: nicole@sckls.info; *Tech Consult,* Sharon Barnes; E-mail: sharon@sckls.info; *Tech Consult,* Lee Scott; E-mail: lee@sckls.info; *Tech Consult,* Lisa Sharbaugh; E-mail: lisa@sckls.info; *Youth Serv Consult,* Julie Tomlianovich; E-mail: julie@sckls.info; Staff 11 (MLS 8, Non-MLS 3)
Founded 1967. Pop 762,000
Jan 2011-Dec 2011 Income $2,340,762, State $94,333, Locally Generated Income $2,246,429. Mats Exp $83,000. Sal $496,585
Library Holdings: Bk Vols 50,000; Per Subs 20
Special Collections: Book Discussion Sets Coll; Children's Puppet Play Resource Coll; Professional Coll
Automation Activity & Vendor Info: (OPAC) Auto-Graphics, Inc
Wireless access
Function: Computer training, Distance learning, e-mail serv, Handicapped accessible, Libr develop, Online cat, Orientations, Prof lending libr, Summer reading prog, Web-catalog, Workshops
Member Libraries: Andale District Library; Andover Public Library; Anthony Public Library; Arkansas City Public Library; Arlington City Library; Attica City Library; Augusta Public Library; Bethany College; Bethel College Library; Buhler Public Library; Butler Community College Library; Caldwell Public Library; Canton Township Carnegie Library; Central Christian College of Kansas; Cheney Public Library; Colwich Community Library; Conway Springs City Library; Cowley County Community College; Derby Public Library; Dixon Township Library; Douglass Public Library; Garden Plain Community Library; Geneseo Public Library; Goddard Public Library, Halstead Public Library; Hardtner Public Library; Harper Public Library; Haven Public Library; Haysville Community Library; Hesston College; Hesston Public Library; Hutchinson Community College; Hutchinson Public Library; Ida Long Goodman Memorial Library; Inman Public Library; Kiowa Public Library; Lindsborg Community Library; Little River Community Library; Lyons Public Library; Macksville City Library; Marquette Community Library; McPherson College; McPherson Public Library; Moundridge Public Library; Mount Hope Public Library; Mulvane Public Library; Newton Public Library; Nickerson Public Library; Norwich Public Library; Oxford Public Library; Park City Community Public Library; Partridge Public Library; Potwin Public Library; Pretty Prairie Public Library; Rose Hill Public Library; South Haven Township Library; Sterling College; Sterling Public Library; Sylvia Public Library; Towanda Public Library; Turon Community Library; Udall Public Library; Valley Center Public Library; Walton Community Library; Wellington Public Library; Whitewater Memorial Library; Wichita Public Library; Zenda Public Library
Partic in South Central Kansas Automation Network (SCKAN)

SPEARVILLE

P SPEARVILLE TOWNSHIP LIBRARY, 414 N Main St, 67876. (Mail add: PO Box 464, 67876-0464), SAN 306-1353. Tel: 620-385-2501. E-mail: slibrary@ucom.net. Web Site: www.spearvillelibrary.org. *Dir,* Leesa Shafer; Staff 1 (Non-MLS 1)
Founded 1929. Pop 1,232; Circ 14,780
Library Holdings: Bk Vols 25,000; Per Subs 70
Automation Activity & Vendor Info: (Cataloging) Auto-Graphics, Inc; (Circulation) Auto-Graphics, Inc; (ILL) Auto-Graphics, Inc; (OPAC) Auto-Graphics, Inc
Database Vendor: Gale Cengage Learning, OCLC FirstSearch
Wireless access
Mem of Southwest Kansas Library System
Open Mon 1-8, Tues 10-6, Wed 9-3, Thurs 9-3 & 5-8

STAFFORD

P NORA E LARABEE MEMORIAL LIBRARY, 108 N Union St, 67578-1339. SAN 306-1361. Tel: 620-234-5762. E-mail: dako@southwind.net. *Dir,* Dixie A Osborn; E-mail: dako@southwind.net
Founded 1906. Pop 1,027; Circ 35,000
Library Holdings: Bk Vols 25,000; Per Subs 50
Wireless access
Open Mon, Fri & Sat 2-6, Tues & Thurs 2-6 & 7-9, Wed 10-12, 2-6 & 7-9

STERLING

C STERLING COLLEGE*, Mabee Library, 125 W Cooper, 67579-1533. SAN 306-137X. Tel: 620-278-4234. Administration Tel: 620-278-4209. Toll Free Tel: 800-346-1017. FAX: 620-278-4414. E-mail: library@sterling.edu. Web Site: www.sterling.edu/academics/mabee-library. *Dir,* Jeremy Labosier; *Asst Librn,* Brooke Sutton; E-mail: bsutton@sterling.edu; *Asst Librn,* Laurel Watney; E-mail: lwatney@sterling.edu; Staff 4 (MLS 1, Non-MLS 3)
Founded 1887. Enrl 600; Fac 40; Highest Degree: Bachelor
Library Holdings: Bk Titles 52,000; Per Subs 173
Automation Activity & Vendor Info: (Cataloging) LibLime Koha; (Circulation) LibLime Koha; (Course Reserve) LibLime Koha; (OPAC) LibLime Koha; (Serials) LibLime Koha
Database Vendor: EBSCOhost, LexisNexis, ProQuest
Wireless access
Function: Ref serv available
Partic in OCLC Online Computer Library Center, Inc; Private Academic Libraries Section, Kansas Library Association
Open Mon-Thurs 8am-Midnight, Fri 8-5, Sun 3-6 & 9-Midnight

P STERLING FREE PUBLIC LIBRARY*, 138 N Broadway, 67579-2131. SAN 306-1388. Tel: 620-278-3191. FAX: 620-278-3891. Web Site: skyways.lib.ks.us/towns/Sterling/library.html.
Founded 1917. Pop 2,600; Circ 36,000
Library Holdings: AV Mats 1,200; Large Print Bks 100; Bk Titles 15,802; Bk Vols 18,716; Per Subs 100; Talking Bks 300
Automation Activity & Vendor Info: (Cataloging) Follett Software; (Circulation) Follett Software; (OPAC) Follett Software
Database Vendor: Gale Cengage Learning, OCLC FirstSearch
Open Mon-Thurs (Winter) 1-8, Fri & Sat 1-6; Mon-Fri (Summer) 1-8

STOCKTON

P STOCKTON PUBLIC LIBRARY*, 124 N Cedar, 67669-1636. SAN 306-1396. Tel: 785-425-6372. FAX: 785-425-6372. E-mail: stocklib@ruraltel.net. Web Site: www.skyways.org/library/stockton. *Dir,* Christine D Sander; *Librn,* Brook J Dix
Pop 1,500; Circ 20,000
Library Holdings: Audiobooks 458; Bks on Deafness & Sign Lang 8; CDs 77; DVDs 111; Large Print Bks 484; Microforms 116; Music Scores 24; Bk Vols 15,944; Per Subs 32; Spec Interest Per Sub 18; Videos 824
Special Collections: Genealogy (Rooks County Record, 1878-1983)
Automation Activity & Vendor Info: (Circulation) LibLime; (ILL) Auto-Graphics, Inc; (Serials) EBSCO Online
Database Vendor: OCLC FirstSearch
Wireless access
Mem of Central Kansas Library System
Partic in OCLC Online Computer Library Center, Inc
Open Mon, Tues & Thurs 10-7, Wed & Fri 10-5, Sat 10-1

SUBLETTE

P HASKELL TOWNSHIP LIBRARY*, 700 Choteau St, 67877. (Mail add: PO Box 937, 67877-0937), SAN 306-140X. Tel: 620-675-2771. FAX: 620-675-2771. E-mail: haskelllib@gmail.com. Web Site: www.swkls.org/haskell/. *Dir,* Jamie Wright
Founded 1922. Pop 1,900; Circ 9,000
Library Holdings: Bk Vols 24,000; Per Subs 80
Automation Activity & Vendor Info: (Cataloging) Follett Software
Mem of Southwest Kansas Library System
Open Mon, Wed & Fri 10-5:30, Tues & Thurs 10-8, Sat 10-12

SUMMERFIELD

P SUMMERFIELD PUBLIC LIBRARY*, 300 Main, 66541. (Mail add: PO Box 146, 66541-0146), SAN 306-1418. Tel: 785-244-6531. *Librn,* ViAnne Routon
Founded 1939. Pop 225; Circ 1,542
Library Holdings: Large Print Bks 50; Bk Titles 2,850
Subject Interests: Kansas
Wireless access
Open Mon & Wed 3-5, Sat 1-4

SYLVAN GROVE

P SYLVAN GROVE PUBLIC LIBRARY*, 122 S Main St, 67481. (Mail add: PO Box 96, 67481-0096), SAN 306-1426. Tel: 785-526-7188. FAX: 785-526-7189. E-mail: sylvanpl@wtciweb.com. Web Site: skyways.lib.ks.us/towns/SylvanGrove/library.html. *Librn,* Ramie Schulteis
Founded 1931. Pop 376; Circ 3,245
Library Holdings: Bk Vols 4,236; Per Subs 25
Mem of Central Kansas Library System
Open Tues 9:30-4:30, Wed 3-7, Fri 1-5

SYLVIA

P SYLVIA PUBLIC LIBRARY*, 121 S Main St, 67581-9700. (Mail add: PO Box 68, 67581-0068), SAN 306-1434. Tel: 620-486-2472. FAX: 620-486-2070. E-mail: sylvialibrary@hotmail.com. *Librn,* Thelma Ward
Pop 310; Circ 550
Library Holdings: Bk Titles 4,731; Per Subs 13
Mem of South Central Kansas Library System
Open Tues & Fri 1-6

SYRACUSE

P HAMILTON COUNTY LIBRARY*, 102 W Ave C, 67878. (Mail add: PO Box 1307, 67878-1307), SAN 306-1442. Tel: 620-384-5622. FAX: 620-384-5623. E-mail: hamcolib@yahoo.com. Web Site: syracuselibrary.info. *Dir,* Joyce Armstrong; E-mail: director@syracuselibrary.info; Staff 3 (Non-MLS 3)
Founded 1931. Pop 2,650; Circ 29,000
Library Holdings: Bk Vols 26,500; Per Subs 70
Subject Interests: Genealogy
Automation Activity & Vendor Info: (Cataloging) OCLC CatExpress; (Circulation) Auto-Graphics, Inc
Database Vendor: Gale Cengage Learning, OCLC FirstSearch, OCLC WorldShare Interlibrary Loan
Wireless access
Function: CD-ROM, Copy machines, Digital talking bks, Distance learning, Family literacy, Fax serv, Genealogy discussion group, Home delivery & serv to Sr ctr & nursing homes, Homebound delivery serv, Homework prog, ILL available, Online searches, Prog for adults, Prog for children & young adult, Summer reading prog, Tax forms, VHS videos
Mem of Southwest Kansas Library System
Open Mon, Wed & Fri 9-5, Tues & Thurs 9-6

TESCOTT

P TESCOTT PUBLIC LIBRARY*, PO Box 53, 67484-0053. Tel: 785-283-4437. FAX: 785-283-4435. E-mail: tescottcity@twinvalley.net. *Librn,* Joanne Schwindt
Library Holdings: Bk Vols 2,000
Open Mon & Thurs 8-5

THAYER

P THAYER FRIDAY READING CLUB CITY LIBRARY*, 200 W Neosho Ave, 66776. (Mail add: PO Box 37, 66776-0037), SAN 306-1450. Tel: 620-839-5646. FAX: 620-839-5646. E-mail: thayerfrc@terraworld.net. *Librn,* Janet Stafford; Staff 1 (Non-MLS 1)
Pop 500
Library Holdings: Bk Vols 8,615; Per Subs 13
Mem of Southeast Kansas Library System
Open Mon & Thurs 10-12 & 2-5, Tues & Wed 2-5, Sat 10-12
Friends of the Library Group
Bookmobiles: 1

TIPTON

P TIPTON LIBRARY*, Main St, 67485. (Mail add: 313 Grasshopper, 67485-9616). Tel: 785-373-6975. *In Charge,* Pat Allen
Library Holdings: Bk Vols 3,000
Open Thurs 9-4:30

TONGANOXIE

P TONGANOXIE PUBLIC LIBRARY*, 303 S Bury St, 66086-5504. SAN 306-1469. Tel: 913-845-3281. FAX: 913-845-2962. Web Site: www.tonganoxielibrary.org. *Dir,* Kelly Fann; E-mail: director@tonganoxielibrary.org; Staff 9 (MLS 1, Non-MLS 8)
Founded 1899. Pop 5,000; Circ 70,000
Library Holdings: Audiobooks 1,090; CDs 1,603; DVDs 2,777; Electronic Media & Resources 573; High Interest/Low Vocabulary Bk Vols 30; Large Print Bks 1,500; Bk Vols 26,023; Per Subs 40; Spec Interest Per Sub 12; Talking Bks 110
Special Collections: Kansas Coll
Automation Activity & Vendor Info: (ILL) Auto-Graphics, Inc
Database Vendor: LibLime
Wireless access
Function: Bks on CD, Children's prog, Computer training, Computers for patron use, Copy machines, Fax serv, Free DVD rentals, ILL available, Magnifiers for reading, Microfiche/film & reading machines, Music CDs, Online cat, OverDrive digital audio bks, Photocopying/Printing, Prog for adults, Prog for children & young adult, Pub access computers, Scanner, Senior computer classes, Senior outreach, Spanish lang bks, Story hour, Summer reading prog, Tax forms, Teen prog, Web-catalog, Wheelchair accessible, Winter reading prog
Mem of Northeast Kansas Library System

Special Services for the Blind - Talking bks
Open Mon-Thurs 9-8, Fri 9-5, Sat 10-5, Sun 1-5

TOPEKA

GM DEPARTMENT OF VETERANS AFFAIRS*, Karl A Menninger Medical Library, Colmery O'Neil VA Medical Ctr, 2200 SW Gage Blvd, 66622. SAN 306-1582. Tel: 785-350-3111, Ext 2779. Circulation Tel: 785-350-3111, Ext 2777. FAX: 785-350-4421. *Librn,* Rosemarie Adkins; E-mail: rosemarie.adkins@med.va.gov
Founded 1946
Library Holdings: Bk Titles 6,565; Bk Vols 7,000; Per Subs 142
Subject Interests: Med, Psychiat, Soc sci & issues
Database Vendor: EBSCOhost
Open Mon-Fri 8-4:30

S GRAND LODGE OF KANSAS LIBRARY*, 320 S W Eight Ave, 66601. (Mail add: PO Box 1217, 66601-1217). Tel: 785-234-5518. FAX: 785-357-4036. Web Site: www.kansasmason.org. *Librn,* Robert Tomlinson; E-mail: rltomlinsonjr@aol.com
Library Holdings: Bk Vols 13,000
Open Mon-Fri 9-4

S KANSAS DEPARTMENT OF CORRECTIONS*, Topeka Juvenile Correctional Facility Library, PO Box 8098, 66608-0098. Tel: 785-354-9800. FAX: 785-354-9798. *Librn,* Greg Hopkins
Library Holdings: Bk Vols 9,000; Per Subs 12
Automation Activity & Vendor Info: (Acquisitions) Follett Software; (Cataloging) Follett Software; (Circulation) Follett Software; (OPAC) Follett Software; (Serials) Follett Software
Open Mon-Fri 7:45-3:30

G KANSAS DEPARTMENT OF TRANSPORTATION LIBRARY*, Eisenhower Bldg, 700 SW Harrison St, 66603-3754. SAN 306-1493. Tel: 785-291-3854. FAX: 785-291-3717.
Founded 1962
Library Holdings: Bk Vols 10,200; Per Subs 10
Subject Interests: Eng
Open Mon-Fri 8-4:30

S KANSAS STATE HISTORICAL SOCIETY*, Library & Archives Division, 6425 SW Sixth Ave, 66615-1099. SAN 306-1507. Tel: 785-272-8681. Reference Tel: 785-272-8681, Ext 117. FAX: 785-272-8682. TDD: 785-272-8683. E-mail: reference@kshs.org. Web Site: www.kshs.org. *Div Head,* Dr Patricia Michaelis; *Head Librn,* Margaret Knecht; *Librn,* Susan Forbes; *Head, Ref,* Lin Fredricksen; *Curator,* Bob Knecht; Staff 17 (MLS 6, Non-MLS 11)
Founded 1875
Library Holdings: Bk Vols 180,814; Per Subs 475
Special Collections: Kansas State Archives, AV, maps, ms, newsp & photos. Oral History; State Document Depository; US Document Depository
Subject Interests: Am Indians, Civil War, Genealogy, Kansas
Automation Activity & Vendor Info: (Cataloging) OCLC Connexion; (OPAC) Innovative Interfaces, Inc; (Serials) Innovative Interfaces, Inc
Function: Archival coll, ILL available
Open Tues-Sat 9-4:30
Restriction: Non-circulating

GL KANSAS SUPREME COURT*, Law Library, Kansas Judicial Ctr, 301 SW Tenth St, 66612-1502. SAN 306-1523. Tel: 785-296-3257. FAX: 785-296-1863. E-mail: lawlibrary@kscourts.org. Web Site: www.kscourts.org/kansas-courts/law-library. *Asst Law Librn, Ref,* Claire King; E-mail: kingc@kscourts.org; *Automation Librn, Ref,* Laura Schafer; Tel: 785-296-3258, E-mail: schaferl@kscourts.org; *Coll Develop, Ref,* Jan Cook; Tel: 785-368-7369, E-mail: cookj@kscourts.org; Staff 4 (MLS 1, Non-MLS 3)
Founded 1855
Jul 2010-Jun 2011 Income $574,829, State $569,250, Locally Generated Income $5,579. Mats Exp $515,260, Books $26,852, Per/Ser (Incl. Access Fees) $396,491, Electronic Ref Mat (Incl. Access Fees) $85,690, Presv $6,227. Sal $450,376
Library Holdings: Bk Vols 205,162; Per Subs 400
Special Collections: Judicial Administration. US Document Depository
Automation Activity & Vendor Info: (Cataloging) Innovative Interfaces, Inc; (OPAC) Innovative Interfaces, Inc
Database Vendor: Innovative Interfaces, Inc, Westlaw
Wireless access
Open Mon-Fri 8-5

P STATE LIBRARY OF KANSAS, State Capitol Bldg, 300 SW Eight Ave, 66612. (Mail add: 300 SW Tenth Ave, Rm 312-W, 66612), SAN 342-1864. Tel: 785-296-3296. Toll Free Tel: 800-432-3919 (KS Only). FAX: 785-368-7291. E-mail: infodesk@library.ks.gov. Web Site: www.kslib.info. *State Librn,* Joanne Budler; E-mail: jo.budler@library.ks.gov; *Dir, Ref,* Cindy Roupe; *Dir, Statewide Libr Serv,* Jeff Hixon; *Dir, Talking Bks,* Toni Harrell; *State Data Coordr,* Megan Schulz; *ILL,* Tom Roth; *Res Sharing Spec,* Rhonda Machlan; *State Doc Cataloger,* Bill Sowers; Staff 27 (MLS 16, Non-MLS 11)
Founded 1855
Special Collections: Kansas Legislative Materials. State Document Depository; US Document Depository
Subject Interests: Demographics, Govt, Pub policy issues
Automation Activity & Vendor Info: (Cataloging) Evergreen; (Circulation) Evergreen; (ILL) Auto-Graphics, Inc; (OPAC) Evergreen; (Serials) Evergreen
Database Vendor: LearningExpress, Newsbank, OCLC, OCLC FirstSearch
Wireless access
Partic in OCLC Online Computer Library Center, Inc
Special Services for the Blind - Descriptive video serv (DVS)
Open Mon-Fri 8-5
Branches: 2
KANSAS TALKING BOOKS SERVICE
See Separate Entry in Emporia
SPECIAL PROJECTS, 300 SW Tenth Ave, 66612, SAN 377-6883. Tel: 785-296-3296. Administration Tel: 785-296-3296. Toll Free Tel: 800-432-3919.
Open Mon-Fri 8-5

M STORMONT-VAIL HEALTHCARE*, Stauffer Health Science Library, 1500 SW Tenth St, 66604-1353. SAN 327-7933. Tel: 785-354-5800. FAX: 785-354-5059. E-mail: hslibemail@stormontvail.org. *Dir,* Lenora Kinzie; Staff 3 (MLS 1, Non-MLS 2)
Library Holdings: Bk Titles 8,000; Per Subs 200
Subject Interests: Med, Nursing
Open Mon-Thurs 7-5

P TOPEKA & SHAWNEE COUNTY PUBLIC LIBRARY*, 1515 SW Tenth Ave, 66604-1374. SAN 342-1929. Tel: 785-580-4400. Interlibrary Loan Service Tel: 785-580-4425. Reference Tel: 785-580-4555. FAX: 785-580-4496. TDD: 785-580-4544. Web Site: www.tscpl.org. *Exec Dir,* Gina Millsap; E-mail: gmillsap@tscpl.org; *Dep Dir, Finance,* Nancy Watkins; E-mail: nwatkins@tscpl.org; *Dep Dir, Operations,* Robert Banks; E-mail: rbanks@tscpl.org; *Circ Mgr,* Ruth Rodden; E-mail: rrodden@tscpl.org; *Digital Br & Serv Mgr,* David Lee King; E-mail: dking@tscpl.org; *Pub Relations Mgr,* Diana Friend; E-mail: dfriend@tscpl.org; *Pub Serv Mgr,* Marie Pyko; E-mail: mpyko@mail.tscpl.org, *Mgr, Spec Coll,* Susan Marchant; E-mail: smarchant@mail.tscpl.org; *Mgr, Youth Serv,* Jeffery Dawson; E-mail: jdawson@tscpl.org; *Supvr, Tech Serv,* Scarlett Fisher-Herreman; *Cat,* Renee Patzer; E-mail: rpatzer@tscpl.org; Staff 176 (MLS 27, Non MLS 149)
Founded 1870. Pop 167,747; Circ 2,141,520
Jan 2005-Dec 2005 Income $16,679,883. Mats Exp $1,857,000. Sal $6,505,141 (Prof $1,365,978)
Library Holdings: AV Mats 98,784; Large Print Bks 27,070; Bk Vols 386,435; Per Subs 1,301; Talking Bks 28,340
Special Collections: Federal Census Depository Coll; Miniature Books; Topeka, bks, photos & film
Subject Interests: Art & archit, Illustrated bks, Music
Automation Activity & Vendor Info: (Acquisitions) SirsiDynix; (Cataloging) SirsiDynix; (Circulation) SirsiDynix; (ILL) SirsiDynix; (OPAC) SirsiDynix; (Serials) SirsiDynix
Database Vendor: SirsiDynix
Wireless access
Function: Archival coll, AV serv, Games & aids for the handicapped, Handicapped accessible, Home delivery & serv to Sr ctr & nursing homes, Homebound delivery serv, ILL available, Large print keyboards, Libr develop, Magnifiers for reading, Online searches, Outside serv via phone, mail, e-mail & web, Photocopying/Printing, Prog for adults, Prog for children & young adult, Ref serv available, Serves mentally handicapped consumers, Summer reading prog, Wheelchair accessible, Workshops
Publications: Library Edition
Special Services for the Deaf - Bks on deafness & sign lang; Closed caption videos; Spec interest per; Staff with knowledge of sign lang; TDD equip; TTY equip
Special Services for the Blind - Reader equip
Open Mon-Fri 9-9, Sat 9-6, Sun Noon-9
Friends of the Library Group
Bookmobiles: 3. In Charge, Ann Newel. Bk vols 56,100

P TOPEKA GENEALOGICAL SOCIETY LIBRARY*, 2717 SE Indiana Ave, 66605-1440. (Mail add: PO Box 4048, 66604-0048), SAN 370-7334. Tel: 785-233-5762. E-mail: library@tgstopeka.org. Web Site: www.tgstopeka.org. *Librn,* Lynn Hutchinson
Founded 1968
Library Holdings: Bk Titles 5,800; Bk Vols 6,000; Per Subs 612
Special Collections: Original Shawnee County Kansas Probate Books 1856-1920; Shawnee County Cemetery Files; Shawnee County Kansas Naturalization Records; Surname Card File

Subject Interests: Genealogy, Hist
Publications: Topeka Genealogical Society Quarterly; Topeka Society Newsletter
Open Mon, Wed, Thurs & Sat 1-4
Restriction: Circ limited

S TOPEKA ZOOLOGICAL PARK LIBRARY*, 635 SW Gage Blvd, 66606-2079. SAN 371-540X. Tel: 785-368-9180. FAX: 785-368-9152. Web Site: www.topeka.org. *Dir,* Brendan Wiley; E-mail: bwiley@topeka.org
Founded 1963
Library Holdings: Bk Titles 832; Per Subs 10
Open Mon-Fri 10-4:30

C WASHBURN UNIVERSITY*, Mabee Library, 1700 SW College Ave, 66621. SAN 342-1988. Tel: 785-670-1179. Circulation Tel: 785-670-1485. Interlibrary Loan Service Tel: 785-670-1489. Reference Tel: 785-670-1483. Toll Free Tel: 800-736-9060. FAX: 785-670-3223. Web Site: www.washburn.edu/mabee. *Dean of Libr,* Dr Alan Bearman; E-mail: alan.bearman@washburn.edu; *Asst Dean, Univ Libr,* Sean Bird; Tel: 785-670-1550, E-mail: sean.bird@washburn.edu; *Head, Circ/ILL,* Andrea Leon; E-mail: andrea.leon@washburn.edu; *First Year Experience Librn,* Keith Rocci; Tel: 785-670-1490, E-mail: keith.rocci@washburn.edu; *Health Sci Librn,* Gwen Wilson; Tel: 785-670-2609, E-mail: gwen.wilson@washburn.edu; *Info Literacy Librn,* Elise Blas; Tel: 785-670-2507, E-mail: elise.blas@washburn.edu; *Pub Serv Librn,* Position Currently Open; *Ser Librn,* David Winchester; Tel: 785-670-1193, E-mail: david.winchester@washburn.edu; *Spec Coll Librn,* Martha Imparato; Tel: 785-670-1981, E-mail: martha.imparato@washburn.edu; *Educ Librn,* Royce Kitts; Tel: 785-670-1956, E-mail: royce.kitts@washburn.edu; *Tech Librn,* Lori Fenton; Tel: 785-670-1984, E-mail: lori.fenton@washburn.edu; *Sch of Bus Librn,* Kelley Weber; Tel: 785-670-1503, E-mail: kelley.weber@washburn.edu; Staff 20 (MLS 10, Non-MLS 10)
Founded 1865. Enrl 6,000; Fac 342; Highest Degree: Master
Jul 2005-Jun 2006 Income $1,715,365. Mats Exp $788,710, Books $192,973, Per/Ser (Incl. Access Fees) $342,858, Micro $14,178, AV Mat $10,432, Electronic Ref Mat (Incl. Access Fees) $215,783, Presv $12,486. Sal $953,260 (Prof $592,554)
Library Holdings: AV Mats 14,531; CDs 1,049; e-books 10,496; e-journals 21,255; Bk Vols 345,642; Per Subs 1,672; Videos 2,092
Special Collections: Bradbury Thompson Materials; College & University History (Washburn Archives); Curriculum Resources Center; William I Koch Art History Coll. State Document Depository; US Document Depository
Automation Activity & Vendor Info: (Acquisitions) Innovative Interfaces, Inc; (Cataloging) Innovative Interfaces, Inc; (Circulation) Innovative Interfaces, Inc; (Course Reserve) Innovative Interfaces, Inc; (ILL) Innovative Interfaces, Inc; (OPAC) Innovative Interfaces, Inc; (Serials) Innovative Interfaces, Inc
Database Vendor: Cambridge Scientific Abstracts, EBSCOhost, Gale Cengage Learning, Haworth Pres Inc, JSTOR, LexisNexis, OCLC FirstSearch, OCLC WorldShare Interlibrary Loan, OVID Technologies, ProQuest, ReferenceUSA, ScienceDirect, SerialsSolutions, Wiley, Wilson - Wilson Web
Wireless access
Publications: Among Friends (Newsletter)
Partic in OCLC Online Computer Library Center, Inc
Special Services for the Deaf - Assistive tech
Special Services for the Blind - Assistive/Adapted tech devices, equip & products
Open Mon-Thurs 7:45am-11pm, Fri 7:45-6, Sat 10-5, Sun 1-11
Friends of the Library Group
Departmental Libraries:
CARNEGIE EDUCATION LIBRARY, 1700 SW College Ave, 66621, SAN 342-2011. Tel: 785-670-1436. Web Site: www.washburn.edu/mabee/crc. *Libr Asst II,* Paula Inman; E-mail: paula.inman@washburn.edu; Staff 2 (MLS 1, Non-MLS 1)
Founded 1984
Jul 2011-Jun 2012. Mats Exp $9,054
Open Mon-Thurs 8-6, Fri 8-5; Mon-Fri (Spring) 8:30-5:30
CL SCHOOL OF LAW LIBRARY, 1700 SW College Ave, 66621, SAN 342-2046. Tel: 785-670-1088. FAX: 785-670-3194. E-mail: lawlibrary@washburnlaw.edu. Web Site: www.washburnlaw.edu/library. *Dir,* John E Christensen; *Asst Dir, Head, Tech Serv,* Martin Wisneski; Tel: 785-670-1788; *Head Ref/Govt Doc Librn,* Andrew Evans; Tel: 785-670-1787; *Cat,* Rebecca Alexander; *Circ,* Nancy Gray; Tel: 785-670-1783; *Digital Projects,* Janet Todwong; Tel: 785-670-3191; *Electronic Serv,* Barbara Ginzburg; Tel: 785-670-1087; *Instrul Media,* Glen McBeth; Tel: 785-670-1778; *Res & Bibliog Instruction,* Creighton Miller; Tel: 785-670-1041
Founded 1903. Enrl 454; Fac 36; Highest Degree: Doctorate
Library Holdings: Bk Vols 395,673
Special Collections: Brown vs Board of Education Historic Document Coll; Kansas Supreme Court Briefs. State Document Depository; US Document Depository
Automation Activity & Vendor Info: (Acquisitions) Innovative Interfaces, Inc; (Cataloging) Innovative Interfaces, Inc; (Circulation) Innovative Interfaces, Inc; (Course Reserve) Innovative Interfaces, Inc; (OPAC) Innovative Interfaces, Inc; (Serials) Innovative Interfaces, Inc
Database Vendor: Gale Cengage Learning, HeinOnline, LexisNexis, OCLC WorldShare Interlibrary Loan, Westlaw
Partic in Mid-America Law Library Consortium; New England Law Library Consortium, Inc; OCLC Online Computer Library Center, Inc
Open Mon-Thurs 7am-11pm, Fri 7am-9pm, Sat 8-8, Sun Noon-11

TORONTO

P TORONTO PUBLIC LIBRARY*, 107 W Main, 66777. (Mail add: PO Box 244, 66777-0244), SAN 376-7213. Tel: 620-637-2661. FAX: 620-637-2661. E-mail: torlib@embarqmail.com. *Dir,* Deb McLean
Library Holdings: Bk Titles 8,000; Per Subs 30
Open Tues-Fri 2-6:30

TOWANDA

P TOWANDA PUBLIC LIBRARY*, 620 Highland, 67144-9042. (Mail add: PO Box 580, 67144-0580), SAN 306-1604. Tel: 316-536-2464. FAX: 316-536-2847. E-mail: towandalibrary@gmail.com. Web Site: towandalibrary.info/. *Libr Dir,* Rachel Ayers; *Storytime Dir,* Shawna Mosier; *Asst Librn,* Joy Barron; Staff 2 (Non-MLS 2)
Founded 1936. Pop 1,426; Circ 5,357
Library Holdings: High Interest/Low Vocabulary Bk Vols 50; Large Print Bks 50; Bk Titles 13,048; Bk Vols 15,048; Per Subs 35; Talking Bks 150
Subject Interests: Local hist, Reading
Automation Activity & Vendor Info: (ILL) OCLC
Wireless access
Function: Adult literacy prog, Homebound delivery serv, ILL available, Prog for children & young adult
Special Services for the Blind - Bks on CD
Open Mon, Wed & Fri 10-6, Sat 10-12
Friends of the Library Group

TRIBUNE

P GREELEY COUNTY LIBRARY, 517 Broadway, 67879. (Mail add: PO Box 300, 67879-0300). Tel: 620-376-4801. FAX: 620-376-4077. E-mail: director@greeleycolibrary.info. Web Site: www.greeleycolibrary.info. *Libr Dir,* Ronna Schmidt
Library Holdings: Bk Vols 15,000; Per Subs 20
Automation Activity & Vendor Info: (Cataloging) Auto-Graphics, Inc; (Circulation) Auto-Graphics, Inc; (ILL) Auto-Graphics, Inc; (OPAC) Auto-Graphics, Inc; (Serials) Auto-Graphics, Inc
Wireless access
Function: Computers for patron use
Mem of Southwest Kansas Library System
Open Mon, Tues, Thurs & Fri 9:30-5, Wed 1-7

TROY

P LIBRARY DISTRICT NUMBER ONE, DONIPHAN COUNTY*, 105 N Main, 66087. (Mail add: PO Box 220, 66087-0220), SAN 306-1612. Tel: 785-985-2597. FAX: 785-985-2602. E-mail: librarydist1@carsoncomm.com. *Dir,* Judy Fuemmeler; Staff 12 (Non-MLS 12)
Founded 1974
Special Collections: Doniphan County Hist. Oral History
Subject Interests: Genealogy, Kansas
Wireless access
Mem of Northeast Kansas Library System
Special Services for the Deaf - Closed caption videos
Special Services for the Blind - Playaways (bks on MP3)
Open Mon & Fri 8-5:30, Tues-Thurs 8-7, Sat 8-1
Friends of the Library Group
Branches: 3
ELWOOD BRANCH, 410 N Ninth, Elwood, 66024. (Mail add: PO Box 208, Elwood, 66024). Tel: 913-365-2409. *Librn,* Carla Watkins
Special Services for the Deaf - Closed caption videos
Special Services for the Blind - Large print bks
Open Mon, Wed & Thurs 9-1 & 2-6, Fri 1-6
Friends of the Library Group
HIGHLAND BRANCH, 306 W Main, Highland, 66035. (Mail add: PO Box 257, Highland, 66035). Tel: 785-442-3078. *Librn,* Mary Lou Glynn; *Librn,* Betty Snyder
Library Holdings: Audiobooks 150; CDs 40; DVDs 100; Large Print Bks 20; Bk Vols 6,000; Videos 40
Open Mon-Thurs 10-6
WATHENA BRANCH, 206 St Joseph, Wathena, 66090. Tel: 785-989-4711. *Br Librn,* Shelley Anderson
Library Holdings: Bk Vols 2,000
Open Tues 1-5, Wed 3-7, Fri 8-12 & 1-5
Friends of the Library Group

TURON

P TURON COMMUNITY LIBRARY*, 501 E Price, 67583-9464. (Mail add: PO Box 357, 67583-0357), SAN 306-1620. Tel: 620-497-6409. E-mail: turonlib@sctelcom.net. *Librn,* Sharon Nitzsche
Pop 430
Library Holdings: Bk Vols 5,386; Per Subs 12
Mem of South Central Kansas Library System
Open Tues, Wed & Thurs 1-5, Sat 9-Noon

UDALL

P UDALL PUBLIC LIBRARY*, 109 E First St, 67146. (Mail add: PO Box 135, 67146-0135), SAN 306-1639. Tel: 620-782-3435. Web Site: www.cityofudall.com/library.html. *Librn,* Bertha Rhoads
Pop 910; Circ 3,000
Library Holdings: Bk Vols 3,600
Mem of South Central Kansas Library System
Open Mon-Fri 3-6

ULYSSES

P GRANT COUNTY LIBRARY*, 215 E Grant Ave, 67880-2958. SAN 306-1647. Tel: 620-356-1433. FAX: 620-356-1344. E-mail: frances@pld.com. Web Site: www.grantcolib.info. *Dir,* Frances Roberts; *Asst Librn,* Norma Strickland; *Spec Coll Librn,* Nidia Gallegos; *Ch Serv,* Holly Mathes; *YA Serv,* Position Currently Open
Founded 1915. Pop 10,000; Circ 95,000
Jan 2006-Dec 2006 Income $944,766, State $5,500, County $472,633, Locally Generated Income $464,133, Other $2,500. Mats Exp $73,925, Books $38,913, Per/Ser (Incl. Access Fees) $7,000, AV Equip $4,000, AV Mat $20,000, Electronic Ref Mat (Incl. Access Fees) $1,000. Sal $298,751 (Prof $41,400)
Library Holdings: Bk Vols 50,000; Per Subs 140
Special Collections: Large Print Books; Local Newspapers (to 1989), cassettes, micro; Spanish Coll, bks, micro, per & rec. Oral History
Subject Interests: Art & archit, Frontier & pioneer life, Genealogy, Kansas, Relig, Soc sci & issues
Automation Activity & Vendor Info: (Acquisitions) Follett Software; (Cataloging) Follett Software; (Circulation) Follett Software
Database Vendor: Gale Cengage Learning, LexisNexis, OCLC FirstSearch
Open Mon-Fri 9-6
Friends of the Library Group

UTICA

P UTICA LIBRARY ASSOCIATION*, 249 N Ohio, 67584-0146. SAN 306-1655. Tel: 785-391-2419. E-mail: uticalibrary1@gmail.com. *Librn,* Nevada Linck
Pop 288; Circ 3,000
Library Holdings: Bk Vols 2,100; Per Subs 12
Mem of Southwest Kansas Library System
Open Mon & Wed 3-7, Tues Noon-3

VALLEY CENTER

P VALLEY CENTER PUBLIC LIBRARY*, Edna Buschow Memorial Library, 321 W First St, 67147-2516. SAN 306-1663. Tel: 316-755-7350. FAX: 316-755-7351. E-mail: valleycenterlibrary@yahoo.com. Web Site: www.valleycenterlibrary.org. *Dir,* Janice Sharp; E-mail: director@valleycenterlibrary.org
Founded 1923. Pop 6,861; Circ 49,573
Library Holdings: Bk Vols 49,000; Per Subs 48
Special Collections: Ark Valley News Coll, 1975-1998, micro; Kansas Writers Coll; Valley Center Index Coll, 1897-1975, micro; Valley Center News Coll, 1882-1890, micro
Automation Activity & Vendor Info: (Acquisitions) Innovative Interfaces, Inc; (Cataloging) Innovative Interfaces, Inc; (Circulation) Innovative Interfaces, Inc; (ILL) Auto-Graphics, Inc
Database Vendor: Overdrive, Inc
Wireless access
Function: Bks on CD, Children's prog, Computers for patron use, Copy machines, Free DVD rentals, Homebound delivery serv, ILL available, Instruction & testing, Microfiche/film & reading machines, Notary serv, Online cat, OverDrive digital audio bks, Photocopying/Printing, Preschool reading prog, Prog for adults, Prog for children & young adult, Pub access computers, Story hour, Summer reading prog, Tax forms, Teen prog
Mem of South Central Kansas Library System
Partic in South Central Kansas Automation Network (SCKAN)
Open Mon-Wed & Fri 10-6, Thurs 10-8, Sat 10-4
Friends of the Library Group

VALLEY FALLS

P DELAWARE TOWNSHIP LIBRARY*, 421 Mary St, No A, 66088. SAN 306-1671. Tel: 785-945-3990. FAX: 785-945-3341. Web Site: valleyfalls.mykansaslibrary.org. *Dir,* Kay Lassiter
Founded 1945. Pop 1,200; Circ 7,024
Library Holdings: Bk Vols 12,800; Per Subs 24
Automation Activity & Vendor Info: (Acquisitions) Follett Software; (Circulation) Follett Software; (ILL) Follett Software; (Serials) Follett Software
Mem of Northeast Kansas Library System
Open Mon 9-5, Tues 9-12 & 1-6, Wed 9-8, Thurs 9-12 & 1-5, Fri 9-Noon, Sat 9-12 & 1-5

VERMILLION

P VERMILLION PUBLIC LIBRARY*, 102 Main St, 66544. (Mail add: PO Box 95, 66544-0095), SAN 376-5504. Tel: 785-382-6227. *Librn,* Audrey Broxterman; E-mail: abbrox@bluevalley.net
Circ 1,430
Library Holdings: AV Mats 400; Bk Vols 4,500
Mem of North Central Kansas Libraries System
Open Mon & Tues 1:30-5:30, Wed & Sat 9-11:30

VIOLA

P VIOLA TOWNSHIP LIBRARY*, 100 N Grice, 67149. (Mail add: PO Box 547, 67149-0547), SAN 306-168X. Tel: 620-584-6679. *Dir,* Claire Charlebois
Pop 200; Circ 604
Library Holdings: Bk Vols 5,000; Per Subs 32
Automation Activity & Vendor Info: (Cataloging) Autolib Library & Information Management Systems; (Circulation) Autolib Library & Information Management Systems; (OPAC) Autolib Library & Information Management Systems
Open Mon & Thurs 9-12 & 3-6

WAKEENEY

P WAKEENEY PUBLIC LIBRARY*, 610 Russell Ave, 67672-2135. SAN 306-1698. Tel: 785-743-2960. FAX: 785-743-5802. E-mail: waklib@ruraltel.net. Web Site: skyways.lib.ks.us/kansas/nwkls/trego/wakeeney.htm. *Dir,* Louella Kaiser
Founded 1906. Pop 1,924; Circ 23,945
Library Holdings: AV Mats 851; Bk Titles 23,268; Per Subs 61
Subject Interests: Kansas
Function: ILL available, Photocopying/Printing, Ref serv available, Telephone ref
Mem of Northwest Kansas Library System
Special Services for the Blind - Talking bks
Open Mon & Fri 1-5, Tues 9-6, Thurs 1-6, Sat 9:30-1:30

WAKEFIELD

P WAKEFIELD PUBLIC LIBRARY*, 205 Third St, 67487. (Mail add: PO Box 348, 67487-0348), SAN 306-1701. Tel: 785-461-5510. FAX: 785-461-5510. E-mail: wplibrary@eaglecom.net. Web Site: www.wakefieldks.com. *Dir,* Rita Braden
Founded 1914. Pop 900; Circ 3,800
Library Holdings: Bk Vols 8,500; Per Subs 30
Subject Interests: Local hist
Open Mon & Wed 1-7, Fri & Sat 10-4:30

WALNUT

P WALNUT PUBLIC LIBRARY*, 511 W Robbins, 66780. SAN 306-171X. Tel: 620-354-6794. FAX: 620-354-6795. E-mail: walnutlibrary@ckt.net. Web Site: walnut.mykansaslibrary.org. *Librn,* Sierra Kirkpatrick
Library Holdings: Bk Vols 3,000; Per Subs 16
Open Mon-Thurs 5-7:30

WALTON

P WALTON COMMUNITY LIBRARY*, 122 Main St, 67151. (Mail add: PO Box 200, 67151-0200), SAN 306-1728. Tel: 620-837-3252. FAX: 620-837-3252. E-mail: waltoncommunitylibrary@pixius.net. *Librn,* Carmen South
Pop 260; Circ 3,600
Library Holdings: Bk Vols 3,000; Per Subs 25
Mem of South Central Kansas Library System
Open Mon-Fri 8-12 & 1-4

WAMEGO

P WAMEGO PUBLIC LIBRARY*, 431 Lincoln, 66547-1620. SAN 306-1736. Tel: 785-456-9181. FAX: 785-456-8986. E-mail: info@wamegopubliclibrary.com. Web Site: wamegopubliclibrary.com. *Dir,*

Leah Kulikowski; E-mail: director@wamegopubliclibrary.com; Staff 5 (Non-MLS 5)
Founded 1937. Pop 5,000; Circ 60,000
Library Holdings: Bk Titles 19,266; Per Subs 70
Subject Interests: Genealogy, Hist, Kansas
Automation Activity & Vendor Info: (Acquisitions) Follett Software; (Cataloging) Follett Software; (Circulation) Follett Software
Wireless access
Mem of North Central Kansas Libraries System
Open Mon-Thurs 10-7, Fri 9-5, Sat 9-1

WASHINGTON

P WASHINGTON PUBLIC LIBRARY*, 116 E Second St, 66968-1916. SAN 306-1744. Tel: 785-325-2114. E-mail: wpl@washingtonks.net. Web Site: washington.mykansaslibrary.org. *Librn,* Janet Keller
Founded 1909. Pop 5,683; Circ 10,739
Jan 2011-Dec 2011 Income $43,895, State $532, City $43,363. Mats Exp $5,475, Books $5,000, Per/Ser (Incl. Access Fees) $475
Library Holdings: Audiobooks 87; Large Print Bks 1,155; Bk Titles 18,080; Per Subs 14
Special Collections: Antique Doll Coll
Automation Activity & Vendor Info: (Acquisitions) Auto-Graphics, Inc; (Cataloging) Auto-Graphics, Inc; (Circulation) Auto-Graphics, Inc; (ILL) Auto-Graphics, Inc; (OPAC) Auto-Graphics, Inc
Wireless access
Mem of North Central Kansas Libraries System
Open Tues, Wed & Fri 10-5, Thurs 10-7, Sat 9-5
Friends of the Library Group

WATERVILLE

P WATERVILLE PUBLIC LIBRARY*, 129 E Commercial St, 66548. (Mail add: PO Box 132, 66548-0132), SAN 306-1752. Tel: 785-363-2769. FAX: 785-363-2778. E-mail: watlib@bluevalley.net. Web Site: www.waterville.mykansaslibrary.org. *Dir,* Tera Kindle
Founded 1914. Pop 900; Circ 5,490
Library Holdings: Audiobooks 100; DVDs 450; Large Print Bks 500; Bk Titles 8,500; Per Subs 40
Automation Activity & Vendor Info: (Cataloging) Auto-Graphics, Inc; (Circulation) Auto-Graphics, Inc
Wireless access
Open Mon, Wed & Fri 2-5, Tues 10-5, Thurs 5-8, Sat 10-1
Friends of the Library Group

WEIR

P WEIR PUBLIC LIBRARY*, 612 S Jefferson, 66781. (Mail add: PO Box 248, 66781-0248), SAN 306-1779. Tel: 620-396-8899. FAX: 620-356-8899. E-mail: weirlib@weir-ks.org. *Dir,* Stef Arbuckle; Staff 1 (Non-MLS 1)
Founded 1896. Pop 770; Circ 8,500
Library Holdings: Audiobooks 570; DVDs 500; Large Print Bks 200; Bk Vols 9,300; Per Subs 35; Videos 1,000
Wireless access
Mem of Southeast Kansas Library System
Open Mon, Wed & Fri 1-5, Tues 10-12 & 1-4, Thurs 1-6, Sat 1-4

WELLINGTON

P WELLINGTON PUBLIC LIBRARY*, 121 W Seventh St, 67152-3898. SAN 306-1787. Tel: 620-326-2011. FAX: 620-326-8193. Web Site: www.wellingtonpubliclibrary.org. *Dir,* Sara Dixon; E-mail: wpl@sutv.com
Founded 1916. Pop 8,535; Circ 60,081
Library Holdings: Bk Vols 53,000; Per Subs 105
Automation Activity & Vendor Info: (Acquisitions) Horizon; (Cataloging) Horizon; (Circulation) Horizon; (OPAC) Horizon
Mem of South Central Kansas Library System
Open Mon & Wed 9:30-6, Tues & Thurs 9:30-8:30, Fri 9:30-5, Sat 9:30-4
Friends of the Library Group

WELLSVILLE

P WELLSVILLE CITY LIBRARY*, 115 W Sixth St, 66092. (Mail add: PO Box 517, 66092-0517), SAN 306-1795. Tel: 785-883-2870. FAX: 785-883-2870. E-mail: wclibrary@wellsvillelibrary.org. *Librn,* Becky Dodd; *Asst Librn,* Robin Avers
Pop 1,722; Circ 19,000
Library Holdings: Bk Vols 14,500; Per Subs 33
Special Collections: Wellsville Globes, newsp
Automation Activity & Vendor Info: (Cataloging) Winnebago Software Co
Mem of Northeast Kansas Library System
Partic in Kansas Info Circuit
Open Mon-Wed & Fri 8-5:30, Sat 8:30-12:30
Friends of the Library Group

WETMORE

P WETMORE PUBLIC LIBRARY*, 333 Second St, 66550. (Mail add: PO Box 126, 66550), SAN 306-1809. Tel: 785-866-2250. FAX: 785-866-2250. Web Site: www.wetmorepubliclibrary.org. *Dir,* Misty Ballenger
Founded 1966. Pop 375; Circ 4,350
Library Holdings: AV Mats 95; Large Print Bks 160; Bk Titles 15,500; Talking Bks 120
Wireless access
Mem of Northeast Kansas Library System
Open Mon, Wed & Fri 12:30-5:30, Tues 8-1, Thurs 1-7, Sat 8-11
Friends of the Library Group

WHITE CITY

P WHITE CITY PUBLIC LIBRARY*, 111 E Mackenzie, 66872. (Mail add: PO Box 206, 66872-0206), SAN 306-1817. Tel: 785-349-5551. FAX: 785-349-5551. E-mail: wclib@tctelco.net. *Dir,* Frank L Nelson
Founded 1933. Pop 900; Circ 7,500
Library Holdings: Bk Vols 10,000; Per Subs 30
Wireless access
Mem of North Central Kansas Libraries System
Open Tues, Thurs & Sat 8-4

WHITEWATER

P WHITEWATER MEMORIAL LIBRARY*, 118 E Topeka, 67154. (Mail add: PO Box 9, 67154-0009), SAN 306-1825. Tel: 316-799-2471. FAX: 316-799-1099. E-mail: whitelib@sbcglobal.net. Web Site: www.whitewaterlib.info. *Dir,* Jean Thiessen
Founded 1928. Pop 783; Circ 23,230
Jan 2012-Dec 2012 Income (Main Library Only) $49,945, State $6,901, City $38,848, Other $4,196. Mats Exp $7,618, Books $3,899, Per/Ser (Incl. Access Fees) $1,089. Sal $29,478
Library Holdings: Audiobooks 491; Bks on Deafness & Sign Lang 10; Braille Volumes 1; CDs 300; DVDs 1,244; e-books 149; High Interest/Low Vocabulary Bk Vols 100; Bk Titles 9,703; Bk Vols 11,000; Per Subs 55
Special Collections: Novelty Cake Pans
Automation Activity & Vendor Info: (Acquisitions) Innovative Interfaces, Inc; (Cataloging) Innovative Interfaces, Inc; (Circulation) Innovative Interfaces, Inc; (Course Reserve) Innovative Interfaces, Inc; (OPAC) Innovative Interfaces, Inc
Wireless access
Function: Accessibility serv available based on individual needs, Adult bk club, Audio & video playback equip for onsite use, Audiobks via web, Bks on CD, CD-ROM, Computer training, Computers for patron use, Digital talking bks, e-mail serv, Electronic databases & coll, Exhibits, Fax serv, Free DVD rentals, Homebound delivery serv, ILL available, Music CDs, Online cat, Photocopying/Printing, Preschool reading prog, Prog for adults, Prog for children & young adult, Pub access computers, Scanner, Story hour, Summer reading prog, Telephone ref, Web-catalog
Mem of South Central Kansas Library System
Partic in South Central Kansas Automation Network (SCKAN)
Special Services for the Deaf - Bks on deafness & sign lang; Closed caption videos; High interest/low vocabulary bks
Special Services for the Blind - Bks on CD; Braille bks; Large print bks; Talking bks
Open Mon 4-8, Tues & Fri 1:30-5, Wed & Sat 9:30-Noon, Thurs 1:30-8
Friends of the Library Group

WICHITA

C FRIENDS UNIVERSITY*, Edmund Stanley Library, 2100 W University St, 67213-3397. SAN 306-1868. Tel: 316-295-5880. Toll Free Tel: 800-794-6945. FAX: 316-295-5080. E-mail: askmax@friends.edu. Web Site: www.friends.edu/academics/library. *Dir, Pub Serv Librn,* Max M Burson; Tel: 316-295-5521, E-mail: mburson@friends.edu; *Asst Libr Dir, Instruction Coordr, Ref Librn,* Kathy Delker; Tel: 316-295-5808, E-mail: kdelker@friends.edu; *Circ Mgr,* Kathy Edwards; Tel: 316-295-5607, E-mail: edwardsk@friends.edu; *ILL Supvr,* Jan Tillotson; Tel: 316-295-5603, E-mail: tillotson@friends.edu; *Cat, Syst Adminr,* Anne Crane; Tel: 316-295-5610, E-mail: annec@friends.edu; *Ser,* Jeanette Parker; Tel: 316-295-5887, E-mail: parkerjea@freinds.edu. Subject Specialists: *Educ, Soc sci,* Max M Burson; *Bus,* Kathy Delker; *Computer, Music,* Anne Crane; *Relig, Soc sci,* Jeanette Parker; Staff 7 (MLS 4, Non-MLS 3)
Founded 1898. Enrl 2,222; Highest Degree: Master
Jul 2009-Jun 2010. Mats Exp $215,000, Books $51,000, Per/Ser (Incl. Access Fees) $62,000, Other Print Mats $22,000, Electronic Ref Mat (Incl. Access Fees) $80,000. Sal $279,000
Library Holdings: AV Mats 367; CDs 2,335; DVDs 1,389; e-journals 21,731; Microforms 269; Music Scores 528; Bk Titles 66,864; Bk Vols 76,940; Per Subs 816; Videos 1,520
Special Collections: Friends University Archives, bks, cassette tapes, cats, correspondence, letters, memorabilia, negatives, newsletters, reel-to-reel tapes, student newsp, yearbks; MAYM (Mid America Yearly Meeting

Coll), Quaker genealogies, meeting bks & photog; Quaker Room Coll, bks, journals, newsletters, newsp, pamphlets
Automation Activity & Vendor Info: (Acquisitions) SirsiDynix; (Cataloging) SirsiDynix; (Circulation) SirsiDynix; (Course Reserve) SirsiDynix; (ILL) OCLC FirstSearch; (OPAC) SirsiDynix; (Serials) SirsiDynix
Database Vendor: ACM (Association for Computing Machinery), Bowker, CQ Press, EBSCO Information Services, Gale Cengage Learning, H W Wilson, LexisNexis, OCLC FirstSearch, OCLC WorldShare Interlibrary Loan, Oxford Online, ProQuest, PubMed, SerialsSolutions, SirsiDynix, STN International, ValueLine, World Book Online
Wireless access
Function: Archival coll, Art exhibits, Computers for patron use, Copy machines, e-mail serv, Electronic databases & coll, ILL available, Online cat, Orientations, Ref serv available
Partic in OCLC Online Computer Library Center, Inc; Private Academic Libraries Section, Kansas Library Association
Open Mon-Thurs (Fall & Spring) 7:45am-10pm, Fri 7:45-4, Sat 9-5, Sun 1:15-5; Mon-Thurs (Summer) 7:45-7, Fri 9-Noon
Restriction: Limited access for the pub, Open to pub for ref & circ; with some limitations, Open to students, fac, staff & alumni

S MIDWEST HISTORICAL & GENEALOGICAL SOCIETY, INC LIBRARY*, 1203 N Main St, 67203. (Mail add: PO Box 1121, 67201-1121), SAN 326-4939. Tel: 316-264-3611.
Founded 1966
Library Holdings: Bk Titles 20,000; Per Subs 45
Subject Interests: Genealogy
Wireless access
Publications: MHGS Register
Open Tues & Sat 9-4

CR NEWMAN UNIVERSITY, Dugan Library, 3100 McCormick Ave, 67213-2097. SAN 306-1884. Tel: 316-942-4291. FAX: 316-942-1747. Web Site: www.newmanu.edu. *Dir,* Steven L Hamersky; Tel: 316-942-4291, Ext 2108, E-mail: hamerskys@newmanu.edu; *Bibliog Instr, ILL,* Jeanette Parker; Tel: 316-942-4291, Ext 2104, E-mail: parkerj@newmanu.edu; Staff 2 (MLS 2)
Founded 1933. Enrl 2,700; Highest Degree: Master
Library Holdings: AV Mats 2,100; Bk Titles 106,429; Bk Vols 126,000; Per Subs 345
Special Collections: Cardinal Newman Coll
Subject Interests: Allied health, Catholicism, Nursing
Automation Activity & Vendor Info: (Acquisitions) Baker & Taylor; (Cataloging) EOS International; (Circulation) EOS International; (Course Reserve) EOS International; (Media Booking) EOS International; (OPAC) EOS International; (Serials) EOS International
Database Vendor: Amigos Library Services, CredoReference, EBSCOhost, LexisNexis, OCLC FirstSearch, OCLC WorldShare Interlibrary Loan, Oxford Online, ProQuest
Wireless access
Publications: Handbooks for faculty, students, graduate students (Newsletter); Video Catalog
Partic in Amigos Library Services, Inc
Open Mon-Thurs 8am-Midnight, Fri 8-5, Sat 11-3, Sun 2-Midnight
Restriction: Open to pub for ref & circ; with some limitations

L SEDGWICK COUNTY LAW LIBRARY*, 225 N Market St, Ste 210, 67202-2023. SAN 325-6081. Tel: 316-263-2251. FAX: 316-263-0629. Web Site: www.wichitabar.org. *Librn,* John Lewallen; Tel: 316-263-2251, Ext 120, E-mail: jlewallen@wichitabar.org
Library Holdings: Bk Titles 1,500; Bk Vols 30,000
Database Vendor: LexisNexis
Partic in BRS
Open Mon-Thurs 8-7, Fri 8-5, Sat 11-3

A UNITED STATES AIR FORCE*, Air Mobility Command, McConnell Air Force Base Library, McConnell AFB, 53476 Wichita St, Bldg 412, 67221. SAN 342-1171. Tel: 316-759-4207. FAX: 316-759-4254. Web Site: mcconnellafblibrary.com. *Dir,* Darla Cooper; E-mail: darla.cooper@mcconnell.af.mil; Staff 8 (MLS 2, Non-MLS 6)
Founded 1953
Library Holdings: Bk Vols 30,000; Per Subs 50
Special Collections: Chief of Staff Reading List; Kansas Coll; Military Aviation History Coll
Automation Activity & Vendor Info: (Acquisitions) SirsiDynix; (Cataloging) SirsiDynix; (Circulation) SirsiDynix; (OPAC) SirsiDynix; (Serials) SirsiDynix
Database Vendor: EBSCOhost, Gale Cengage Learning, Jane's, OCLC FirstSearch, Overdrive, Inc, ProQuest
Wireless access
Function: ILL available
Partic in OCLC Online Computer Library Center, Inc
Open Mon-Thurs 9-9, Fri 11-4, Sat 10-3

GL UNITED STATES COURTS LIBRARY*, B55 US Courthouse, 401 N Market St, 67202-2011. SAN 372-1256. Tel: 316-269-6162. FAX: 316-269-6168. *In Charge,* Lynda R Miller
Library Holdings: Bk Vols 10,000; Per Subs 12
Automation Activity & Vendor Info: (Cataloging) SirsiDynix
Open Mon-Fri 8-5
Restriction: Staff use only

C UNIVERSITY OF KANSAS, Kansas Geological Survey-Wichita Well Sample Library, 4150 W Monroe St, 67209. SAN 374-9576. Tel: 316-943-2343. FAX: 316-943-1261. E-mail: wwsl@kgs.ku.edu. Web Site: www.kgs.ku.edu. *Mgr,* Michael T Dealy; Tel: 316-943-2343, Ext 203, E-mail: mdealy@kgs.ku.edu. Subject Specialists: *Hydrogeology,* Michael T Dealy; Staff 3 (MLS 1, Non-MLS 2)
Founded 1938
Library Holdings: Bk Vols 2,000
Special Collections: Oil & Gas Well Data; Rock Samples from Gas & Oil Wells
Function: Computers for patron use, Copy machines, Electronic databases & coll, Online ref, Ref & res
Open Mon-Fri 8-5

CM UNIVERSITY OF KANSAS SCHOOL OF MEDICINE-WICHITA*, George J Farha Medical Library, 1010 N Kansas, 67214-3199. SAN 373-2770. Tel: 316-293-2629. FAX: 316-293-2608. Web Site: wichita.kumc.edu/library/. *Dir,* Position Currently Open; *Actg Dir,* Jane Griffith; E-mail: jgriffit@kumc.edu; *Coordr, ILL,* Patty Shay; E-mail: pshay@kumc.edu; *Acq, Cataloger,* Susan Clark; E-mail: sclark3@kumc.edu; *Admin Coordr,* Jeanie Moeder; E-mail: jmoeder@kumc.edu; Staff 6 (MLS 3, Non-MLS 3)
Founded 1981. Enrl 98; Fac 94; Highest Degree: Master
Library Holdings: Bk Vols 3,800; Per Subs 367
Automation Activity & Vendor Info: (Acquisitions) Ex Libris Group; (Cataloging) Ex Libris Group; (Circulation) Ex Libris Group; (OPAC) Ex Libris Group; (Serials) Ex Libris Group
Database Vendor: MD Consult, PubMed
Open Mon-Fri 8-5:30

M VIA CHRISTI LIBRARIES*, North Saint Francis Street, 929 N Saint Francis St, 67214-1315. SAN 306-1906. Tel: 316-268-5979. FAX: 316-268-8694. Web Site: www.viachristi.org/libraries. *Librn,* Camillia Gentry; Staff 5 (MLS 4, Non-MLS 1)
Founded 1938
Library Holdings: Bk Vols 5,000
Subject Interests: Allied health, Med, Nursing
Automation Activity & Vendor Info: (Cataloging) CyberTools for Libraries; (Circulation) CyberTools for Libraries; (OPAC) CyberTools for Libraries; (Serials) CyberTools for Libraries
Database Vendor: EBSCOhost, Elsevier, STAT!Ref (Teton Data Systems)
Wireless access
Function: Health sci info serv
Publications: Wichita Area Health Science Libraries Union List
Open Mon-Fri 8-4:30
Restriction: Circulates for staff only, Employees & their associates, Lending to staff only, Med staff only, Private libr

§J WICHITA AREA TECHNICAL COLLEGE, Southside Education Ctr, 4501 E 47th St S, 67210. Tel: 316-677-9492. Interlibrary Loan Service Tel: 316-677-1749. FAX: 316-554-2650. *Dir,* Rita Sevart; E-mail: rsevart@watc.edu
Function: Pub access computers
Open Mon-Thurs 7:30am-8pm, Fri 7:30-5, Sat 8:30-Noon

S WICHITA ART MUSEUM, The Emprise Bank Research Library, 1400 W Museum Blvd, 67203-3296. SAN 306-1965. Tel: 316-268-4918. FAX: 316-268-4980. E-mail: library@wichitaartmuseum.org. Web Site: www.wichitaartmuseum.org. *Librn,* Joyce Goering Norris; Staff 0.25 (MLS 0.25)
Founded 1963
Jan 2014-Dec 2014. Mats Exp $7,481, Books $3,500, Per/Ser (Incl. Access Fees) $3,981
Library Holdings: Bk Vols 13,486; Per Subs 30
Special Collections: Chris Paulsen Polk Papers; Elizabeth S Navas Archival Papers; Howard E Wooden Archival Papers
Automation Activity & Vendor Info: (Cataloging) Ex Libris Group; (OPAC) Ex Libris Group; (Serials) Ex Libris Group
Restriction: Open to pub for ref only

P WICHITA PUBLIC LIBRARY*, 223 S Main St, 67202. SAN 342-2135. Tel: 316-261-8500. Circulation Tel: 316-261-8508. Interlibrary Loan Service Tel: 316-261-8583. Reference Tel: 316-261-8510. Administration Tel: 316-261-8503. FAX: 316-262-4540. TDD: 316-262-3972. E-mail: admin@wichita.lib.ks.us. Web Site: www.wichita.lib.ks.us. *Dir of Libr,*

Cynthia Berner Harris; Tel: 316-261-8520, Fax: 316-219-6320, E-mail: cberner@wichita.gov; *Outreach Serv Librn, Prog Coordr,* Julie Linneman; Tel: 316-261-8590, E-mail: juliel@wichita.gov; *Customer Serv Mgr,* Jaime Prothro; Tel: 316-261-8530, E-mail: jprothro@wichita.gov; *Interim Digital Serv Mgr,* Rex Cornelius; Tel: 316-261-8522, E-mail: rcornelius@wichita.gov; *Mgr, Ref Serv & Coll Develop,* Larry Vos; Tel: 316-261-8540, E-mail: lvos@wichita.gov; *Support Serv Mgr,* Tammy Penland; Tel: 316-261-8534, Fax: 316-858-7321, E-mail: tpenland@wichita.gov; *Pub Relations Coordr,* Jennifer Heinicke; Tel: 316-261-8524, E-mail: jheinicke@wichita.gov; Staff 32 (MLS 28, Non-MLS 4)
Founded 1876. Pop 361,420; Circ 2,171,107
Jan 2008-Dec 2008 Income (Main Library and Branch(s)) $8,455,630, State $441,183, City $7,585,230, Federal $139,581, Other $289,636. Mats Exp $2,184,431. Sal $5,776,638
Library Holdings: Audiobooks 15,751; CDs 29,727; DVDs 22,405; High Interest/Low Vocabulary Bk Vols 1,317; Large Print Bks 11,352; Microforms 11,020; Music Scores 521; Bk Vols 665,772; Per Subs 7,667; Talking Bks 20,395; Videos 16,836
Special Collections: Motor Manuals; Mueller Philatelic Coll; Sullivan-Gagliardo Children's Literature Art Coll; Wichita Photo Archive (in cooperation with Wichita State University & the Wichita-Sedgwick County Historical Museum). State Document Depository
Subject Interests: Auto repair, Genealogy, Kansas, Local hist, Schematics
Automation Activity & Vendor Info: (Acquisitions) Innovative Interfaces, Inc; (Circulation) Innovative Interfaces, Inc; (OPAC) Innovative Interfaces, Inc
Database Vendor: EBSCO Information Services, Gale Cengage Learning, Grolier Online, LearningExpress, Newsbank, OCLC FirstSearch, OCLC WorldShare Interlibrary Loan, ProQuest, ReferenceUSA, World Book Online
Wireless access
Function: Handicapped accessible, Homebound delivery serv, ILL available, Magnifiers for reading, Photocopying/Printing, Prog for children & young adult, Ref serv available, Summer reading prog, Wheelchair accessible
Publications: Excerpts (Newsletter)
Mem of South Central Kansas Library System
Partic in OCLC Online Computer Library Center, Inc
Special Services for the Deaf - TTY equip
Special Services for the Blind - Assistive/Adapted tech devices, equip & products; BiFolkal kits; Bks on cassette; Bks on CD; Computer with voice synthesizer for visually impaired persons; Descriptive video serv (DVS); Extensive large print coll; Home delivery serv; Internet workstation with adaptive software; Talking bk & rec for the blind cat; Talking bks; Talking bks & player equip; Tel Pioneers equip repair group; ZoomText magnification & reading software
Open Mon-Thurs 10-9, Fri & Sat 10-5:30, Sun 1-5
Friends of the Library Group

Branches: 8

LIONEL ALFORD REGIONAL, 3447 S Meridian, 67217-2151. Tel: 316-337-9119. FAX: 316-337-9118. *Br Head,* Jean Hatfield
Founded 2003
Open Mon-Thurs 10-9, Fri & Sat 10-5, Sun (Winter) 1-5
Friends of the Library Group

MAYA ANGELOU NORTHEAST BRANCH, 3051 E 21st St, 67214, SAN 342-2283. Tel: 316-688-9580. *Br Mgr,* Position Currently Open
Open Tues 1-8, Wed-Sat 11-5:30, Sun 1-5
Friends of the Library Group

COMOTARA, 2244 N Rock Rd, 67226, SAN 328-7742. Tel: 316-688-9350. *Br Mgr,* Position Currently Open
Open Mon, Wed & Thurs 10-8, Tues, Fri & Sat 10-5:30, Sun 1-5
Friends of the Library Group

EVERGREEN, 2601 N Arkansas, 67204. Tel: 316-303-8181. *Br Mgr,* Anne Ethen; E-mail: aethen@wichita.gov
Founded 2002
Open Mon-Thurs 10-9, Fri & Sat 10-5, Sun (Winter) 1-5

LINWOOD PARK, 1901 S Kansas Ave, 67211, SAN 342-216X. Tel: 316-337-9125. *Br Mgr,* Jean Hatfield
Open Mon 12-8, Tues-Fri 10-5:30
Friends of the Library Group

ORCHARD PARK, 4808 W Ninth St, 67212, SAN 342-2291. Tel: 316-337-9084. *Br Mgr,* Tracie Partridge
Open Mon 1-8, Tues-Fri 11-5:30
Friends of the Library Group

FORD ROCKWELL BRANCH, 5939 E Ninth St, 67208, SAN 342-2194. Tel: 316-688-9361. *Br Mgr,* Position Currently Open
Open Mon-Thurs 10-9, Fri & Sat 10-5, Sun 1-5
Friends of the Library Group

WESTLINK BRANCH, 8515 Bekemeyer St, 67212, SAN 342-2402. Tel: 316-337-9456. *Br Mgr,* Tracie Partridge
Open Mon-Thurs 10-9, Fri & Sat 10-5, Sun 1-5
Friends of the Library Group

S WICHITA-SEDGWICK COUNTY HISTORICAL MUSEUM LIBRARY*, 204 S Main St, 67202. SAN 325-6103. Tel: 316-265-9314. FAX: 316-265-9319. E-mail: wschm@wichitahistory.org. Web Site: www.wichitahistory.org. *Dir,* Robert A Puckett; *Curator,* Jami Frazier Tracy; E-mail: jtracy@wichitahistory.org; Staff 1 (Non-MLS 1)
Founded 1939
Library Holdings: Bk Vols 330; Per Subs 10
Subject Interests: Local hist
Function: Archival coll
Restriction: Open by appt only

C WICHITA STATE UNIVERSITY LIBRARIES*, 1845 Fairmount, 67260-0068. SAN 306-1981. Tel: 316-978-3582. Interlibrary Loan Service Tel: 316-978-3167. Reference Tel: 316-978-3584. Administration Tel: 316-978-3586. FAX: 316-978-3048. Administration FAX: 316-978-3727. Web Site: libraries.wichita.edu. *Dean, Univ Libr,* Dr Donald L Gilstrap; E-mail: donald.gilstrap@wichita.edu; *Sr Assoc Dean, Univ Libr,* Kathy Downes; E-mail: kathy.downes@wichita.edu; *Asst Dean, Tech Serv,* Nancy Deyoe; Tel: 316-978-5140, E-mail: nancy.dayoe@wichita.edu; *Acq Librn,* Ginger Williams; Tel: 316-978-6442, E-mail: ginger.williams@wichita.edu; *Electronic Res Librn,* Mary Walker; Tel: 316-978-5792, E-mail: mary.walker@wichita.edu; *Metadata & Digital Initiatives Librn,* Lizzy Walker; Tel: 316-978-5138, E-mail: lizzy.walker@wichita.edu; *Ref Librn,* Angela Paul; Tel: 316-978-5084, E-mail: angela.paul@wichita.edu; *Res & Info Serv Librn,* Melissa Mallon; Tel: 316-978-5077, E-mail: melissa.mallon@wichita.edu; *Res & Info Serv Librn,* JJ Pionke; Tel: 316-978-5210, E-mail: jj.pionke@wichita.edu; *Coordr, Coll Develop,* Cathy Moore-Jansen; Tel: 316-978-5080, E-mail: cathy.moore-jansen@wichita.edu; *Curator, Spec Coll & Univ Archives,* Dr Lorraine Madway; Tel: 316-978-3590, E-mail: lorraine.madway@wichita.edu; *Cat & Metadata,* Susan Matveyeva; Tel: 316-978-5139, E-mail: susan.matveyeva@wichita.edu; *Info & Res Serv,* Janet Brown; Tel: 316-978-5075, E-mail: janet.brown@wichita.edu; *Info & Res Serv,* Rachel Crane; Tel: 316-978-5078, E-mail: rachel.crane@wichita.edu. Subject Specialists: *Bus, Humanities,* Melissa Mallon; *Eng, Nursing,* JJ Pionke; *Anthrop,* Cathy Moore-Jansen; *Educ,* Janet Brown; *Fine arts, Music,* Rachel Crane; Staff 18 (MLS 17, Non-MLS 1)
Founded 1895. Enrl 14,550; Fac 515; Highest Degree: Doctorate
Library Holdings: e-books 59,000; e-journals 56,647; Music Scores 33,840; Bk Vols 2,013,870; Per Subs 57,165
Special Collections: American Anti-Slavery Movement Coll; American Civil War Sanitary Commission Papers (Kantor Coll); Aviation History of World War I Coll; Congressional Papers of Members of Congress from Kansas & Seven Other States; Gordon Parks Papers; History of Books & Printing (Aitchison Coll); Hypnotism, Mesmerism & Animal Magnetism (Tinterow Coll); Kansas & the Great Plains (Historical Map Coll); Original Editorial Cartoons of Gene Bassett; Patent & Trademark Depository; W H Auden Coll; Wichita State University Archives; William Lloyd Garrison Papers; World War I & II Pamphlet Coll. State Document Depository; US Document Depository
Subject Interests: Eng, Hist, Manufacturing, Music, Psychol, Urban studies
Automation Activity & Vendor Info: (Acquisitions) Ex Libris Group; (Cataloging) Ex Libris Group; (Circulation) Ex Libris Group; (Course Reserve) Ex Libris Group; (ILL) OCLC ILLiad; (OPAC) Ex Libris Group; (Serials) Ex Libris Group
Wireless access
Friends of the Library Group

Departmental Libraries:

CHEMISTRY, 127 McKinley Hall, 67260-0051, SAN 324-3311. Tel: 316-978-3764. FAX: 316-978-3048. Web Site: library.wichita.edu/science/chemistry/chemlib.html.
Open Mon-Thurs 8-7, Fri 8-5, Sat & Sun 1-5

MUSIC LIBRARY, C 116 DFAC, 67260-0053, SAN 324-332X. Tel: 316-978-3029. FAX: 316-978-3584. Web Site: library.wichita.edu/music/mindex.html. *Librn,* Rachel Crane; E-mail: rachel.crane@wichita.edu
Library Holdings: CDs 5,797; Music Scores 24,585
Automation Activity & Vendor Info: (Acquisitions) Ex Libris Group; (Cataloging) Ex Libris Group; (Circulation) Ex Libris Group; (Course Reserve) Ex Libris Group; (ILL) Ex Libris Group; (Media Booking) Ex Libris Group; (OPAC) Ex Libris Group; (Serials) Ex Libris Group
Open Mon & Tues 8-8, Wed-Fri 8-5

WILLIAMSBURG

P WILLIAMSBURG COMMUNITY LIBRARY*, 107 S Louisa, 66095. (Mail add: PO Box 142, 66095-0142). Tel: 785-746-5407. E-mail: wmbglib@williamsburgcommunitylibrary.org. Web Site: www.williamsburgcommunitylibrary.org. *Dir,* Nancy Stover
Founded 1984
Library Holdings: Bk Vols 9,000
Wireless access

Mem of Northeast Kansas Library System
Open Mon & Thurs 3-7:30, Tues & Wed 10-5

WILSEY

P ELM CREEK TOWNSHIP LIBRARY, 213 N Fifth St, 66873-9768. SAN 306-199X. Tel: 785-497-2289. E-mail: books@tctelco.net. *Dir,* Marsha Filkin
Pop 359; Circ 3,500
Library Holdings: Bk Vols 8,000
Mem of North Central Kansas Libraries System
Open Wed (Winter) 9-12 & 2-6, Sat 1-4; Wed (Summer) 9-4:30, Sat 1-4

WILSON

P LANG MEMORIAL LIBRARY*, 2405 Ave F, 67490. (Mail add: PO Box 310, 67490-0310), SAN 320-4790. Tel: 785-658-3648. E-mail: langlib@wtciweb.com. *Head Librn,* Cheryl A Ptacek
Founded 1924. Pop 765; Circ 2,001
Library Holdings: AV Mats 315; DVDs 105; Bk Vols 14,000; Per Subs 24; Talking Bks 10; Videos 339
Automation Activity & Vendor Info: (Cataloging) Follett Software; (Circulation) Follett Software; (OPAC) Follett Software
Mem of Central Kansas Library System
Open Mon & Tues 2:30-8, Wed 10-1 & 2:30-8, Thurs & Fri 2:30-5:30, Sat 10-12

WINCHESTER

P WINCHESTER PUBLIC LIBRARY*, 203 Fourth St, 66097. (Mail add: PO Box 143, 66097-0143), SAN 376-5490. Tel: 913-774-4967. FAX: 913-774-4967. Web Site: www.winchesterlibrary.org. *Dir,* Cheryl Sylvester; E-mail: director@winchesterlibrary.org; *Asst Dir,* Raymond Riley; *ILL,* Kristie Scrivner; Staff 1 (MLS 1)
Pop 1,271
Jan 2006-Dec 2006 Income $36,000
Library Holdings: CDs 100; DVDs 100; Large Print Bks 500; Bk Titles 15,550; Bk Vols 16,000; Per Subs 15; Talking Bks 500; Videos 400
Automation Activity & Vendor Info: (Cataloging) SirsiDynix; (Circulation) SirsiDynix; (OPAC) SirsiDynix
Wireless access
Function: Adult bk club, Handicapped accessible, Homebound delivery serv, ILL available, Mail & tel request accepted, Music CDs, Photocopying/Printing, Prog for children & young adult, Senior computer classes, Summer reading prog, VHS videos
Partic in Kans City Mo Libr & Info Network
Special Services for the Deaf - Closed caption videos
Special Services for the Blind - Bks on cassette; Bks on CD; Home delivery serv; Large print bks
Open Mon & Thurs 10-7, Tues & Fri Noon-5, Wed 10-5:30, Sat 10-Noon

WINFIELD

S COWLEY COUNTY HISTORICAL SOCIETY MUSEUM LIBRARY*, 1011 Mansfield, 67156-3557. SAN 306-2007. Tel: 620-221-4811. Web Site: www.cchsm.com. *Dir,* Bruce Hedrick
Founded 1967
Library Holdings: Bk Vols 800
Special Collections: Military History of the Civil War; Winfield History, photog & newsp. Oral History
Subject Interests: Family hist, Local hist
Function: Res libr

C SOUTHWESTERN COLLEGE*, Memorial Library, 100 College St, 67156-2498. SAN 306-2031. Tel: 620-229-6225. Reference Tel: 620-229-6127. Toll Free Tel: 866-734-1275. FAX: 620-229-6382. Web Site: www.sckans.edu/library. *Dir,* Veronica Mc Asey; Tel: 620-229-6271, E-mail: veronica.mcasey@sckans.edu; *Circ, Ref,* Robert Peret; E-mail: robert.perret@sckans.edu. Subject Specialists: *Biblical studies, New Testament,* Veronica Mc Asey; Staff 3 (MLS 2, Non-MLS 1)
Founded 1885. Enrl 845; Fac 48; Highest Degree: Master
Library Holdings: Bk Vols 55,000; Per Subs 106
Special Collections: Black History & Literature (Ludgood-Walker Afro-American Studies Coll); East Asia (Sidney DeVere Brown Coll); Indian Studies (Watmull Coll)
Subject Interests: Liberal arts
Automation Activity & Vendor Info: (Acquisitions) EOS International; (Cataloging) EOS International; (Circulation) EOS International; (ILL) OCLC; (OPAC) EOS International; (Serials) EOS International
Database Vendor: EBSCOhost, Gale Cengage Learning, LexisNexis, OCLC FirstSearch, OVID Technologies, ProQuest
Function: Distance learning, Doc delivery serv, For res purposes, ILL available, Photocopying/Printing
Partic in CowlNet Library Consortium; Dialog Corp; New Mexico Consortium of Academic Libraries; OCLC Online Computer Library Center, Inc
Open Mon-Thurs 7:45am-Midnight, Fri 7:45-6, Sat 12-4, Sun 3pm-Midnight
Restriction: Open to pub for ref & circ; with some limitations, Open to students, fac & staff

P WINFIELD PUBLIC LIBRARY*, 605 College St, 67156-3199. SAN 306-204X. Tel: 620-221-4470. FAX: 620-221-6135. E-mail: library@wpl.org. Web Site: www.wpl.org. *Dir,* Joan Cales; E-mail: jcales@wpl.org; *Youth Serv Librn,* Joanna Brazil; E-mail: jbrazil@wpl.org; *Adult Serv, Pub Serv Spec,* Christina Salomon; E-mail: csalomon@wpl.org; Staff 12 (Non-MLS 12)
Founded 1912. Pop 11,900; Circ 189,000
Library Holdings: AV Mats 2,336; Large Print Bks 3,626; Bk Titles 59,930; Bk Vols 60,658; Per Subs 168
Subject Interests: Art, Genealogy, Kansas
Automation Activity & Vendor Info: (OPAC) Innovative Interfaces, Inc
Wireless access
Function: After school storytime, Art exhibits, Audio & video playback equip for onsite use, Audiobks via web, Bk club(s), Bks on CD, Children's prog, Computer training, Computers for patron use, Copy machines, e-mail & chat, e-mail serv, Electronic databases & coll, Exhibits, Family literacy, Fax serv, Free DVD rentals, Games & aids for the handicapped, Handicapped accessible, Holiday prog, Homebound delivery serv, ILL available, Large print keyboards, Magnifiers for reading, Music CDs, Online cat, Outreach serv, OverDrive digital audio bks, Photocopying/Printing, Preschool outreach, Prog for adults, Prog for children & young adult, Pub access computers, Ref serv available, Scanner, Senior computer classes, Senior outreach, Story hour, Summer reading prog, Tax forms, Teen prog, Telephone ref, Wheelchair accessible, Workshops, Writing prog
Publications: Newsletter (Monthly)
Open Mon-Thurs 9-8, Fri & Sat 10-6, Sun 1-5
Friends of the Library Group

YATES CENTER

P YATES CENTER PUBLIC LIBRARY*, 218 N Main, 66783-1424. SAN 306-2066. Tel: 620-625-3341. FAX: 620-625-3035. E-mail: yatescenterlib@ycl.kscoxmail.com. *Dir,* Janice Jones; Staff 4 (Non-MLS 4)
Founded 1908. Pop 1,998; Circ 16,667
Library Holdings: Bk Vols 15,500; Per Subs 41
Mem of Southeast Kansas Library System
Open Mon & Wed (Winter) 10:30-7:30, Tues, Thurs & Fri 10:30-5:30, Sat 10-1; Mon-Fri (Summer) 10:30-5:30, Sat 10-1

ZENDA

P ZENDA PUBLIC LIBRARY*, 215 N Main, 67159. (Mail add: PO Box 53, 67159-0053), SAN 306-2074. Tel: 620-243-5791. *Dir,* Delia Swingle
Founded 1967. Pop 248
Library Holdings: Bk Vols 7,905; Per Subs 11
Function: ILL available, Prog for children & young adult, Summer reading prog
Mem of South Central Kansas Library System
Open Thurs 10:30-5:30, Sat 8:30-12:30
Friends of the Library Group

KENTUCKY

Date of Statistics: FY 2013-2014
Population, 2010 U.S. Census: 4,339,367
Population, 2013 (est): 4,395,295
Population Served by Public Libraries & Bookmobiles: 4,395,295
Total Volumes in Public Libraries & Bookmobiles: 9,032,867
Volumes Per Capita (statewide): 2.06
Volumes Per Capita (population served): 2.06
Total Public Library Circulation (including Bookmobiles): 30,664,564
Circulation Per Capita (statewide): 6.98
Circulation Per Capita (population served): 6.98

Total Public Library Income: $176,636,123
Source of Income:
Public Funds: $168,120,537
State & Federal: $6,130,375
Expenditure Per Capita (population served): $31.71
Expenditure Per Capita (statewide): $31.71
Number of (Regional) Libraries: 8
Counties Unserved: 0
Number of Bookmobiles in State: 75
Grants-in-Aid to Public Libraries:
Federal (Library Services & Technology Act): $1,625,022

ALBANY

P CLINTON COUNTY PUBLIC LIBRARY*, 302 King Dr, 42602-1603. SAN 306-2082. Tel: 606-387-5989. FAX: 606-387-5989. E-mail: clintonlib@hotmail.com. Web Site: clintoncountypubliclibrary.org. *Dir,* Gayla Elizabeth Duvall; Staff 4 (MLS 2, Non-MLS 2)
Founded 1958. Pop 9,616; Circ 87,037
Library Holdings: Bk Titles 23,234; Bk Vols 32,981; Per Subs 24
Subject Interests: Kentucky
Automation Activity & Vendor Info: (Acquisitions) Follett Software; (Circulation) Follett Software
Open Mon, Wed & Fri 8-5, Tues 8-6:30, Sat 8-12

ASHLAND

J ASHLAND COMMUNITY & TECHNICAL COLLEGE, Mansbach Memorial Library, 1400 College Dr, 41101. SAN 306-2090. Tel: 606-326-2169. FAX: 606-326-2186. E-mail: as_reference@kctcs.edu. Web Site: www.ashland.kctcs.edu/library. *Dir,* Matthew Onion; Tel: 606-326-2113, E-mail: Matthew.Onion@kctcs.edu; *Acq/Ser Librn,* Pamela Klinepeter; Tel: 606-326-2254, E-mail: Pamela.Klinepeter@kctcs.edu, *Tech Serv,* Bettie George Frye; Tel: 606-326-2141, E-mail: BettieGeorge.Frye@kctcs.edu; Staff 5 (MLS 3, Non-MLS 2)
Founded 1938. Enrl 2,103, Fac 90; Highest Degree: Associate
Library Holdings: Bk Titles 42,197; Bk Vols 50,466; Per Subs 102
Special Collections: Fraley Memorial; Jesse Stuart Coll; Kentucky Authors Coll; Learning Disabilities (Ashworth Coll). US Document Depository
Automation Activity & Vendor Info: (Acquisitions) Ex Libris Group; (Cataloging) Ex Libris Group; (Circulation) Ex Libris Group; (Course Reserve) Ex Libris Group; (OPAC) Ex Libris Group
Database Vendor: EBSCOhost, Gale Cengage Learning, OCLC FirstSearch, ProQuest
Wireless access
Partic in OCLC Online Computer Library Center, Inc
Open Mon-Thurs 7:30-7, Fri 7:30-5
Departmental Libraries:
TECHNOLOGY DRIVE CAMPUS LIBRARY, 902 Technology Dr, Grayson, 41143. (Mail add: 1400 College Dr, 41101). Tel: 606-326-2000. Toll Free Tel: 800-928-4256. *Dir,* Matthew Onion; Tel: 606-326-2113, E-mail: Matthew.Onion@kctcs.edu
Library Holdings: Bk Titles 570; Bk Vols 650

P BOYD COUNTY PUBLIC LIBRARY*, 1740 Central Ave, 41101. SAN 306-2112. Tel: 606-329-0090. Administration Tel: 606-329-0518. FAX: 606-329-0578. Administration FAX: 606-325-4574. Web Site: www.thebookplace.org. *Libr Dir,* Debbie Cosper; E-mail: dcosper@thebookplace.org; *Circ Supvr,* Ben Nunley; E-mail: bnunley@thebookplace.org; *Supvr, Genealogy Serv,* James Kettel; E-mail: jkettel@thebookplace.org; *Tech Serv Supvr,* Kellie Nunley; E-mail: knunley@thebookplace.org; *Supvr, Youth Serv,* Denise Dillow; Staff 7 (MLS 5, Non-MLS 2)
Founded 1935. Pop 52,000; Circ 210,793
Jul 2010-Jun 2011 Income (Main Library and Branch(s)) $3,437,192, State $191,640, County $2,871,476, Locally Generated Income $271,183, Other $102,893. Mats Exp $668,957, Books $335,092, Per/Ser (Incl. Access Fees) $35,000, Micro $11,306, AV Mat $204,200, Electronic Ref Mat (Incl. Access Fees) $83,359. Sal $908,257 (Prof $554,626)
Library Holdings: Audiobooks 7,675; CDs 3,076; DVDs 15,880; e-books 6,588; Electronic Media & Resources 70; Large Print Bks 2,500; Bk Vols 136,297; Per Subs 500
Special Collections: Arnold Hanners Photo Coll; Genealogy & Local History (Minnie C Winder Coll), bks & micro; High Interest/Low Reading Coll; Ky Vital Records 1911-1995; Language Tape Coll; Records from Bellefonte, Buena Vista, Princess & Amanda Furnace Operations
Automation Activity & Vendor Info: (Acquisitions) Innovative Interfaces, Inc; (Cataloging) OCLC; (Circulation) Innovative Interfaces, Inc; (Serials) EBSCO Online
Database Vendor: EBSCO Auto Repair Reference, EBSCOhost, Facts on File, Gale Cengage Learning, infoUSA, LearningExpress, OCLC FirstSearch, OCLC WorldShare Interlibrary Loan, Overdrive, Inc, ProQuest, ReferenceUSA, Westlaw
Wireless access
Function: Adult bk club, Audiobks via web, Bk club(s), Bks on CD, Children's prog, Computers for patron use, Copy machines, e-mail & chat, e-mail serv, E-Reserves, Electronic databases & coll, Fax serv, Free DVD rentals, Handicapped accessible, Holiday prog, Homebound delivery serv, ILL available, Mail & tel request accepted, Notary serv, Online cat, Online ref, Online searches, Outreach serv, Outside serv via phone, mail, e-mail & web, OverDrive digital audio bks, Photocopying/Printing, Prog for adults, Prog for children & young adult, Pub access computers, Ref & res, Ref serv available, Ref serv in person, Story hour, Summer reading prog, Tax forms, Teen prog, Telephone ref, Web-catalog, Wheelchair accessible
Publications: Read All About It (Bi-monthly)
Partic in OCLC Online Computer Library Center, Inc; SE Ind Area Libr Servs Authority
Special Services for the Deaf - Assisted listening device; Closed caption videos
Special Services for the Blind - Accessible computers; Audio mat; Computer access aids; Copier with enlargement capabilities; Large print bks
Open Mon-Thurs 9-8, Fri & Sat 9-5, Sun 1-5
Restriction: Closed stack
Friends of the Library Group
Branches: 2
CATLETTSBURG BRANCH, 2704 Louisa St, Catlettsburg, 41129, SAN 324-296X. Tel: 606-739-8332. FAX: 606-739-5907. *Br Mgr,* Barbara Biggs
Open Mon-Thurs 9-6, Fri 9-5, Sat 1-5
Friends of the Library Group
KYOVA BRANCH, 10699 US Rte 60, Ste 920, 41102, SAN 321-8414. Tel: 606-929-5346. FAX: 606-929-5471. *Libr Dir,* Debbie Cosper; E-mail: dcosper@thebookplace.org
Open Mon-Sat 10-9, Sun 12-6

Friends of the Library Group
Bookmobiles: 1. Outreach Coordr, Nancy Stewart

R FIRST BAPTIST CHURCH LIBRARY*, 1701 Winchester Ave, 41101. (Mail add: PO Box 787, 41105-0787), SAN 306-2120. Tel: 606-324-3100. FAX: 606-324-4344. E-mail: fbcashlandky@gmail.com. Web Site: fbcashlandky.com. *Librn,* Lynn Hutchinson
Library Holdings: Bk Vols 8,000

AUBURN

S SOUTH UNION SHAKER VILLAGE*, Julia Neal Library, 850 Shaker Museum Rd, 42206. (Mail add: PO Box 177, 42206-0177), SAN 375-0736. Tel: 270-542-4167. Toll Free Tel: 800-811-8379. FAX: 270-542-7558. E-mail: shakmus@logantele.com. Web Site: www.shakermuseum.com. *Curator, Dir,* Thomas Collier Hines
Founded 1986
Library Holdings: Bk Titles 1,000
Special Collections: Historic Photographs; Manuscripts; Primary Materials
Subject Interests: Kentucky
Function: Archival coll
Open Mon-Sat 9-4, Sun (March-Dec) 1-4
Restriction: Non-circulating
Friends of the Library Group

AUGUSTA

P KNOEDLER MEMORIAL LIBRARY*, 315 Main St, 41002. SAN 306-2139. Tel: 606-756-3911. *Librn,* Karen Smithers
Founded 1928
Library Holdings: Bk Titles 12,000
Special Collections: Bracken County History; Kentuckiana (Walter Rankins Coll)
Open Mon, Tues, Thurs & Fri 11-5, Sat 10-2

BARBOURVILLE

P KNOX COUNTY PUBLIC LIBRARY*, 206 Knox St, 40906. SAN 306-2147. Tel: 606-546-5339. FAX: 606-546-3602. E-mail: knoxlibrary@barbourville.com. *Dir,* Lana Hale; Tel: 606-546-5339, Ext 5, E-mail: lana@barbourville.com; *Asst Dir,* George West; Tel: 606-546-5339, Ext 4, E-mail: jag@barbourville.com; Staff 1 (Non-MLS 1)
Founded 1964. Pop 30,239; Circ 74,309
Jul 2009-Jun 2010 Income $419,000, State $24,000, County $385,000, Other $10,000. Mats Exp $84,200, Books $43,000, Per/Ser (Incl. Access Fees) $2,800, Micro $1,400, AV Mat $12,000, Electronic Ref Mat (Incl. Access Fees) $25,000. Sal $515,000 (Prof $69,000)
Library Holdings: Audiobooks 698; AV Mats 135; Bks on Deafness & Sign Lang 15; CDs 492; DVDs 950; Large Print Bks 350; Microforms 175; Bk Titles 49,000; Bk Vols 52,000; Per Subs 48; Spec Interest Per Sub 5; Videos 500
Special Collections: Genealogy Coll; Kentucky Coll
Automation Activity & Vendor Info: (Cataloging) TLC (The Library Corporation); (Circulation) TLC (The Library Corporation); (OPAC) TLC (The Library Corporation)
Partic in Ky Libr Asn
Open Mon-Wed & Fri 9-5, Thurs 12-7, Sat 9-1
Bookmobiles: 1. Bkmobile Clerk, Adam Cavins

C UNION COLLEGE*, Weeks-Townsend Memorial Library, 310 College St, Campus Box D-21, 40906-1499. SAN 306-2155. Tel: 606-546-1240. Reference Tel: 606-546-1243. FAX: 606-546-1239. E-mail: library@unionky.edu, refdesk@unionky.edu. Web Site: www.unionky.edu/library. *Dir of Libr Serv,* Tara L Cooper; Tel: 606-546-1241, E-mail: tcooper@unionky.edu; *Asst Librn,* Bobbie Hamilton; *Circ Mgr,* Billie Daniels; Tel: 606-546-1630, E-mail: bdaniels@unionky.edu; *Coordr, Tech Serv,* Quetha Boles; Tel: 606-546-1627, E-mail: qboles@unionky.edu; Staff 3 (MLS 3)
Founded 1879. Enrl 1,108; Fac 55; Highest Degree: Master
Library Holdings: e-books 103,467; e-journals 15,211; Bk Vols 112,779; Per Subs 339; Videos 907
Special Collections: US Document Depository
Subject Interests: Civil War, Educ, Genealogy, State hist
Automation Activity & Vendor Info: (Acquisitions) Innovative Interfaces, Inc; (Cataloging) Innovative Interfaces, Inc; (Circulation) Innovative Interfaces, Inc; (Course Reserve) Innovative Interfaces, Inc; (ILL) OCLC; (OPAC) Innovative Interfaces, Inc; (Serials) Innovative Interfaces, Inc
Database Vendor: Alexander Street Press, American Chemical Society, American Psychological Association (APA), Annual Reviews, ARTstor, CredoReference, EBSCOhost, Greenwood Publishing Group, H W Wilson, Hoovers, Innovative Interfaces, Inc, JSTOR, Marcive, Inc, Newsbank, OCLC ArticleFirst, OCLC FirstSearch, OCLC WorldShare Interlibrary Loan, Oxford Online, ProQuest, SerialsSolutions, Westlaw
Wireless access
Function: Archival coll, Computers for patron use, Copy machines, E-Reserves, Fax serv, Govt ref serv, Handicapped accessible, Online cat
Partic in Appalachian Col Asn; Association of Independent Kentucky Colleges & Universities; Lyrasis; OCLC Online Computer Library Center, Inc
Open Mon-Thurs 7:30am-11pm, Fri 7:30-5:30, Sat 10-4, Sun 2-11

BARDSTOWN

S OSCAR GETZ MUSEUM OF WHISKEY HISTORY LIBRARY, 114 N Fifth St, 40004. SAN 329-8779. Tel: 502-348-2999. E-mail: whiskeymuseum@bardstowncable.net. Web Site: www.whiskeymuseum.com. *Curator,* Mary Hamilton
Founded 1979
Library Holdings: Bk Vols 300
Special Collections: Oral History
Open Mon-Fri (May-Oct) 10-5, Sat 10-4, Sun 12-4; Tues-Sat (Nov-April) 10-4, Sun 12-4

P NELSON COUNTY PUBLIC LIBRARY*, 201 Cathedral Manor, 40004-1515. SAN 342-2496. Tel: 502-348-3714. FAX: 502-348-5578. E-mail: nelsoncopublib@hotmail.com. Web Site: www.nelsoncopublib.org. *Dir,* Sharon Shanks; E-mail: sshanks@nelsoncopublib.org; *Asst Dir,* Carol Elliott; *Asst Dir,* Michael Greenwell; *Acq Librn,* Angela Howard; *Ch,* Stephanie King; E-mail: sking@nelsoncopublib.org; Staff 18 (MLS 4, Non-MLS 14)
Founded 1967. Pop 40,000; Circ 374,309
Jul 2011-Jun 2012 Income (Main Library and Branch(s)) $2,458,132, State $89,959, Locally Generated Income $2,368,173. Mats Exp $297,684, Books $189,330, Per/Ser (Incl. Access Fees) $5,884, AV Equip $16,840, AV Mat $8,424, Electronic Ref Mat (Incl. Access Fees) $77,206. Sal $781,654 (Prof $547,158)
Library Holdings: Audiobooks 12,497; CDs 670; DVDs 7,357; e-books 46,097; Large Print Bks 3,798; Bk Vols 94,942; Per Subs 47; Talking Bks 270
Special Collections: Genealogy Coll; Kentucky Coll
Function: Accelerated reader prog, Adult bk club, After school storytime, Art exhibits, Audio & video playback equip for onsite use, Audiobks via web, Bi-weekly Writer's Group, Bk club(s), Bks on cassette, Bks on CD, Children's prog, Computer training, Computers for patron use, Copy machines, Digital talking bks, e-mail serv, E-Reserves, Electronic databases & coll, Exhibits, Family literacy, Fax serv, Free DVD rentals, Genealogy discussion group, Handicapped accessible, Holiday prog, Home delivery & serv to Sr ctr & nursing homes, Homebound delivery serv, ILL available, Instruction & testing, Magnifiers for reading, Mail & tel request accepted, Microfiche/film & reading machines, Music CDs, Newsp ref libr, Notary serv, Online cat, Online info literacy tutorials on the web & in blackboard, Online searches, Outreach serv, Outside serv via phone, mail, e-mail & web, OverDrive digital audio bks, Photocopying/Printing, Preschool outreach, Prog for adults, Prog for children & young adult, Pub access computers, Ref & res, Ref serv available, Ref serv in person, Scanner, Senior outreach, Spanish lang bks, Spoken cassettes & CDs, Spoken cassettes & DVDs, Story hour, Summer & winter reading prog, Tax forms, Teen prog, VHS videos, Video lending libr, Web-catalog, Wheelchair accessible, Workshops, Writing prog
Open Mon, Fri & Sat 9-5, Tues-Thurs 9-8, Sun 1-5
Branches: 2
BLOOMFIELD BRANCH, 114 Fairfield Hill, Bloomfield, 40008. (Mail add: PO Box 249, Bloomfield, 40008-0024), SAN 342-2526. Tel: 502-252-9129. FAX: 502-252-8255. *Br Mgr,* Rhonda Olliges; E-mail: rolliges@nelsoncopublib.org; *Br Librn,* Glenda Owens; Staff 2 (Non-MLS 2)
Pop 1,000; Circ 6,994
Open Tues & Thurs 10-8, Wed 12-6, Fri 10-3, Sat 9-3
NEW HAVEN BRANCH, 318 Center St, New Haven, 40051, SAN 342-2615. Tel: 502-549-6735. FAX: 502-549-5668. *Br Mgr,* Catherine Williams; E-mail: cwilliams@nelsoncopublib.org; Staff 3 (Non-MLS 3)
Pop 900; Circ 30,963
Library Holdings: Bk Vols 2,600
Open Mon 10-1, Tues & Thurs 9-8, Wed 9-6, Sat 9-3
Bookmobiles: 1. Librn, Eileen Peterson. Bk Titles 4542

BARDWELL

P BALLARD-CARLISLE-LIVINGSTON COUNTY PUBLIC LIBRARY*, PO Box 428, 42023-0428. SAN 320-4804. Tel: 270-335-5059. *Head Librn,* Sonya Mainord; E-mail: sonya_bclpl@yahoo.com
Founded 1981
Library Holdings: AV Mats 2,563; Bk Vols 23,421; Per Subs 54
Subject Interests: Genealogy
Open Thurs & Fri 9-4
Friends of the Library Group

BEATTYVILLE

P LEE COUNTY PUBLIC LIBRARY, 123 Center St, 41311. (Mail add: PO Box V, 41311-2022), SAN 306-2163. Tel: 606-464-8014. FAX: 606-464-2052. E-mail: leecopublib@yahoo.com. Web Site: www.leecounty.ky.gov/departments.htm. *Dir,* Sonya Spencer
Pop 7,916; Circ 74,832
Library Holdings: Large Print Bks 250; Bk Vols 30,000; Per Subs 60
Special Collections: Genealogical Coll; Kentucky Coll; Quilt Coll
Wireless access
Open Mon-Fri 9-5, Sat 9-1
Friends of the Library Group

BEDFORD

P TRIMBLE COUNTY PUBLIC LIBRARY*, 35 Equity Dr, 40006-7622. (Mail add: PO Box 249, 40006-0249), SAN 306-2171. Tel: 502-255-7362. FAX: 502-255-7491. E-mail: help@trimblelibrary.org. *Dir,* Lisa Wegner; *Asst Dir,* Betsy Tweedy
Pop 7,800; Circ 41,998
Library Holdings: Bk Vols 20,000; Per Subs 50
Subject Interests: Children's fiction, Popular mat
Automation Activity & Vendor Info: (Acquisitions) TLC (The Library Corporation); (Cataloging) TLC (The Library Corporation); (Circulation) TLC (The Library Corporation); (Course Reserve) TLC (The Library Corporation); (ILL) TLC (The Library Corporation); (Media Booking) TLC (The Library Corporation); (OPAC) TLC (The Library Corporation); (Serials) TLC (The Library Corporation)
Wireless access
Open Mon, Wed & Thurs 9-5, Tues & Fri 9-8, Sat 9-1
Bookmobiles: 1

BENTON

P MARSHALL COUNTY PUBLIC LIBRARY SYSTEM*, 1003 Poplar St, 42025. SAN 342-264X. Tel: 270-527-9969. FAX: 270-527-0506. E-mail: mcpl@marshallcolibrary.org. Web Site: www.marshallcolibrary.org. *Dir,* Kristi Tucker; E-mail: ktucker@marshallcolibrary.org; *Ch,* Patricia Freeland; E-mail: tfreeland@marshallcolibrary.org; *Ch,* Beth Kerrick; E-mail: bkerrick@marshallcolibrary.org; *Ch,* Sarah Pace-McGowan; E-mail: smcgowan@marshallcolibrary.org; *YA Librn,* Tammy Blackwell; E-mail: tblackwell@marshallcolibrary.org; *Br Mgr,* Lenisa Jones; E-mail: ljones@marshallcolibrary.org; *ILL,* Debbie Medlock; Staff 1 (MLS 1)
Founded 1968. Pop 30,000
Special Collections: Local History. Oral History
Automation Activity & Vendor Info: (Acquisitions) Evergreen; (Cataloging) Evergreen; (Circulation) Evergreen; (OPAC) Evergreen
Database Vendor: Baker & Taylor, Booklist Online, Bowker, EBSCOhost, Gale Cengage Learning, Ingram Library Services, LearningExpress, OCLC FirstSearch, OCLC WebJunction, OCLC WorldShare Interlibrary Loan, Overdrive, Inc, ProQuest, TumbleBookLibrary, WebMD, Westlaw
Wireless access
Open Mon & Thurs 9-8, Tues, Wed, Fri & Sat 9-5
Branches: 2
CALVERT CITY, 23 Park Rd, Calvert City, 42029, SAN 342-2704. Tel: 270 395-5745. FAX: 270-252-7009. E-mail: ccpl@marshallcolibrary.org. *Br Mgr,* Nancy Petty
Open Mon 9-7, Tues-Sat 9-5
HARDIN, 4640 Murray Hwy, Hardin, 42048, SAN 342-2674. Tel: 270-437-4275. FAX: 270-437-4609. E-mail: hbpl@marshallcolibrary.org. *Br Mgr,* Kim Darnall
Open Mon 9-7, Tues-Fri 9-5
Bookmobiles: 1. Librn, Donna Jones

BEREA

C BEREA COLLEGE, Hutchins Library, 100 Campus Dr, 40404. (Mail add: CPO Library, 40404), SAN 342-2739. Tel: 859-985-3364. Interlibrary Loan Service Tel: 859-985-3275. Reference Tel: 859-985-3109. Administration Tel: 859-985-3266. Automation Services Tel: 859-985-3274. FAX: 859-985-3912. E-mail: reference_desk@berea.edu. Web Site: community.berea.edu/hutchinslibrary. *Dir,* Anne Chase; E-mail: chasea@berea.edu; *Assoc Dir, Libr Serv,* Calvin Gross; E-mail: calvin_gross@berea.edu; *Head, Spec Coll & Archives,* Rachel Vagts; Tel: 859-985-3267, E-mail: vagts@berea.edu; *Instrul Serv Librn,* Amanda Peach; Tel: 859-985-3279, E-mail: peacha@berea.edu; *Instrul Serv Librn,* Ed Poston; Tel: 859-985-3172, E-mail: postonp@berea.edu; *Acq, ILL,* Patty Tarter; E-mail: tarterp@berea.edu; *Coordr, Berea Digital,* Susan Henthorn; Tel: 859-985-3268, E-mail: susan_henthorn@berea.edu; *Coordr, Info Literacy,* Angel Rivera; Tel: 859-985-3372, E-mail: riveralopeza@berea.edu; *Coll Archivist,* Lori Myers-Steele; Tel: 859-985-3253, E-mail: myers-steelel@berea.edu; *Sound Rec Archivist,* Harry Rice; Tel: 859-985-3249, E-mail: riceh@berea.edu; *User Serv Spec,* Judy Gergen; Tel: 859-985-3285, E-mail: gergenj@berea.edu; Staff 16 (MLS 8, Non-MLS 8)
Founded 1870. Enrl 1,586; Fac 113; Highest Degree: Bachelor
Jul 2013-Jun 2014 Income $1,337,582. Mats Exp $452,993, Books $77,528, Per/Ser (Incl. Access Fees) $110,765, Other Print Mats $11,195, Micro $12,017, AV Mat $12,140, Electronic Ref Mat (Incl. Access Fees) $226,590, Presv $2,758. Sal $815,975 (Prof $540,238)
Library Holdings: AV Mats 11,900; e-books 198,160; e-journals 70,207; Microforms 149,400; Bk Vols 374,320; Per Subs 447
Special Collections: Appalachian Sound Archives; Berea Archives, ms; Shedd-Lincoln Coll; Weatherford-Hammond Appalachian Coll, bks & ms. Oral History
Automation Activity & Vendor Info: (Acquisitions) Ex Libris Group; (Cataloging) Ex Libris Group; (Circulation) Ex Libris Group; (Course Reserve) Ex Libris Group; (ILL) Atlas Systems; (OPAC) Ex Libris Group; (Serials) Ex Libris Group
Database Vendor: 3M Library Systems, ABC-CLIO, Agricola, Alexander Street Press, American Chemical Society, American Psychological Association (APA), ARTstor, Baker & Taylor, BioOne, Cinahl, CountryWatch, CQ Press, CRC Press/Taylor & Francis Group, EBSCO Information Services, EBSCOhost, Elsevier, Emerald, Gale Cengage Learning, Greenwood Publishing Group, Grolier Online, H W Wilson, Haworth Pres Inc, JSTOR, LexisNexis, McGraw-Hill, Modern Language Association, Nature Publishing Group, Newsbank, OCLC WorldShare Interlibrary Loan, Oxford Online, Project MUSE, ProQuest, PubMed, ScienceDirect, Scopus, Springer-Verlag, Springshare, LLC, STN International, Wiley InterScience, Wilson - Wilson Web
Wireless access
Partic in Appalachian Col Asn; Association of Independent Kentucky Colleges & Universities; Federation of Kentucky Academic Libraries (FoKAL); OCLC Online Computer Library Center, Inc
Open Mon-Thurs 8am-Midnight, Fri 8-7, Sat 10-6, Sun 2-Midnight

BOONEVILLE

P OWSLEY COUNTY PUBLIC LIBRARY*, Two Action Pl, 41314. (Mail add: PO Box 280, 41314-0280). Tel: 606-593-5700. FAX: 606-593-5708. *Dir,* Lisa Marcum; E-mail: marcum1@prtcnet.org; Staff 3 (Non-MLS 3)
Founded 1970. Pop 4,755; Circ 17,047
Library Holdings: Bk Titles 28,000; Per Subs 130; Videos 2,500
Special Collections: Kentucky Genealogy Coll
Subject Interests: Genealogy
Database Vendor: EBSCOhost, OCLC FirstSearch
Wireless access
Open Mon-Fri 9-5
Friends of the Library Group

BOWLING GREEN

P WARREN COUNTY PUBLIC LIBRARY*, 1225 State St, 42101. SAN 306-2198. Tel: 270-781-4882. FAX: 270-781-3699. Web Site: www.warrenpl.org. *Dir,* Lisa R Rice; E-mail: lisar@bgpl.org; *Asst Dir,* Ashley Fowlkes; Tel: 270-782-0252, E-mail: ashleyf@bgpl.org; *Outreach Mgr,* Monica Edwards; *Syst Adminr,* Alex Love; *Tech Serv,* Holly H Hedden; Staff 50 (MLS 7, Non-MLS 43)
Founded 1940. Pop 80,000; Circ 582,000
Library Holdings: Bk Vols 136,439; Per Subs 225
Automation Activity & Vendor Info: (Cataloging) SirsiDynix; (Circulation) SirsiDynix; (ILL) SirsiDynix; (OPAC) SirsiDynix
Database Vendor: OCLC FirstSearch, SirsiDynix
Function: ILL available
Partic in OCLC Online Computer Library Center, Inc
Open Mon-Thurs 8-8, Fri & Sat 9-5, Sun 1-5
Friends of the Library Group
Branches: 1
SMITHS GROVE BRANCH, 115 Second St, Smiths Grove, 42171. Tel: 270-563-6651. FAX: 270-563-1006. *Librn,* Ashley Fowkles
Library Holdings: Bk Titles 10,000; Per Subs 10
Open Mon 12-8, Tues, Wed, Fri & Sat 9-5, Thurs 9-8
Friends of the Library Group
Bookmobiles: 1

C WESTERN KENTUCKY UNIVERSITY LIBRARIES*, Helm-Cravens Library Complex, 1906 College Heights Blvd, No 11067, 42101-1067. SAN 342-2852. Tel: 270-745-2905. Circulation Tel: 270-745-3951. Interlibrary Loan Service Tel: 270-745-6118. Reference Tel: 270-745-6125. Automation Services Tel: 270-745-6122. FAX: 270-745-6422. Interlibrary Loan Service FAX: 270-745-5943. E-mail: library.web@wku.edu. Web Site: www.wku.edu/library. *Dean of Libr Serv,* Connie Foster; E-mail: connie.foster@wku.edu; *Head, Tech Serv,* Deana Groves; Tel: 270-745-4197, E-mail: deana.groves@wku.edu; *Art Librn,* Terri Baker; *Bus Librn,* John Gottfried; Tel: 270-745-6176, E-mail: john.gottfried@wku.edu; *Health Sci Librn,* Carol Watwood; *Humanities & Soc Sci Librn,* Sean Kinder; *Instrul Serv Librn, Ref Serv,* Dr Bryan Carson; *Spec Coll Librn,* Timothy Mullin; E-mail: timothy.mullins@wku.edu; *Acq, Coll Develop,* Jack Montgomery; *Circ, ILL,* Dan Forrest; *Govt Doc,* Rosemary Meszaros; *Pub Serv,* Dr Brian Coutts; E-mail: brian.coutts@wku.edu; *Sci,* Dr Charles Smith; *Webmaster,* Haiwang Yuan; Staff 31 (MLS 31)

Founded 1907. Enrl 19,761; Fac 1,120; Highest Degree: Doctorate
Library Holdings: Bk Titles 656,517; Bk Vols 783,803; Per Subs 3,912
Special Collections: Oral History; US Document Depository
Subject Interests: Folklore, Hist, Kentucky, Law, Shakers
Automation Activity & Vendor Info: (Acquisitions) Ex Libris Group; (Cataloging) Ex Libris Group; (Circulation) Ex Libris Group; (Course Reserve) Ex Libris Group; (ILL) Ex Libris Group; (Media Booking) Ex Libris Group; (OPAC) Ex Libris Group; (Serials) Ex Libris Group
Wireless access
Publications: Collections & Connections (Newsletter)
Partic in Center for Research Libraries; Lyrasis; OCLC Online Computer Library Center, Inc
Friends of the Library Group
Departmental Libraries:
EDUCATIONAL RESOURCES CENTER, Tate Page Hall, Rm 366, 1906 College Heights Blvd, No 31031, 42101. Tel: 270-745-4552, 270-745-4659. FAX: 270-745-4553. *Coordr,* Roxanne Spencer; E-mail: roxanne.spencer@wku.edu; Staff 1 (MLS 1)
Library Holdings: Bk Vols 12,000
Special Collections: Juvenile Literature; Textbook Adoption Review; Thematic Units
Subject Interests: Educ
Open Mon-Thurs 7:45-7:30, Fri 7:45-4:30, Sat 10-2
GLASGOW LIBRARY, 500 Hilltopper Way, Glasgow, 42141, SAN 370-5986. Tel: 270-659-6911. FAX: 270-659-6990. *Librn,* Katherine Pennavaria; Staff 1 (MLS 1)
Enrl 1,700
Library Holdings: Bk Vols 1,662; Per Subs 140
Open Mon-Thurs 8:30-6:30, Fri 8:30-1
KENTUCKY LIBRARY & MUSEUM, 1400 Kentucky St, 42101-3479. (Mail add: 1906 College Heights Blvd, No 11092, 42101-1092). Tel: 270-745-2592. Administration Tel: 270-745-6261. FAX: 270-745-6264. Web Site: www.wku.edu/library/kylm. *Dept Head,* Timothy J Mullin; E-mail: timothy.mullin@wku.edu; Staff 17 (MLS 9, Non-MLS 8)
Founded 1939. Enrl 18,000; Fac 9; Highest Degree: Master
Jul 2007-Jun 2008 Income $1,000,000, State $950,000, Locally Generated Income $50,000. Mats Exp $50,000. Sal $900,000
Library Holdings: Music Scores 700; Bk Vols 70,000; Per Subs 10
Special Collections: Civil War Coll, microfilm; History of Western Kentucky University (University Archives); Kentucky Authors (R P Warren Coll); Kentucky Coll, ephemera, maps, photog & recorded music; Kentucky Family Papers; Personal & Political Papers of Kentucky Congressmen, including Representative Natcher; Rare Books of Early America, Virginia & Kentucky; South Union Shakers Coll, account bks, diaries. Oral History
Function: Archival coll, Children's prog, Genealogy discussion group, Handicapped accessible, Holiday prog, Prog for adults, Prog for children & young adult, Wheelchair accessible, Workshops
Open Mon-Sat 9-4
Restriction: Closed stack, Non-circulating coll
Friends of the Library Group

BRANDENBURG

P MEADE COUNTY PUBLIC LIBRARY*, 966 Old Ekron Rd, 40108. SAN 306-2201. Tel: 270-422-2094. FAX: 270-422-3133. Web Site: www.meadereads.org. Staff 11 (MLS 1, Non-MLS 10)
Founded 1967. Pop 25,000
Library Holdings: Bk Vols 23,200; Per Subs 63
Special Collections: Oral History
Subject Interests: Genealogy, Local hist
Automation Activity & Vendor Info: (Acquisitions) Brodart; (Cataloging) Brodart; (Circulation) Brodart
Database Vendor: EBSCOhost, OCLC FirstSearch
Function: Accelerated reader prog, Adult bk club, Art exhibits, Audio & video playback equip for onsite use, Audiobks via web, Bks on cassette, Bks on CD, CD-ROM, Children's prog, Computer training, Computers for patron use, Copy machines, Digital talking bks, Equip loans & repairs, Fax serv, Free DVD rentals, Handicapped accessible, Holiday prog, Home delivery & serv to Sr ctr & nursing homes, ILL available, Jail serv, Music CDs, Notary serv, Online cat, Online searches, Prog for children & young adult, Pub access computers, Scanner, Serves mentally handicapped consumers, Story hour, Summer reading prog, Tax forms, Teen prog, VHS videos, Wheelchair accessible
Partic in Lyrasis
Open Mon-Thurs 9-8, Fri 9-5, Sat 9-3
Friends of the Library Group
Bookmobiles: 1

BROOKSVILLE

P BRACKEN COUNTY PUBLIC LIBRARY*, 310 W Miami St, 41004. (Mail add: PO Box 305, 41004-0305). Tel: 606-735-3620. FAX: 606-735-3378. Web Site: www.youseemore.com/bcpl. *Dir,* Valerie Clark; *Asst Librn,* Jean Blevins
Library Holdings: Bk Titles 22,000; Per Subs 78
Wireless access
Open Mon, Tues, Thurs & Fri 9-5, Wed 9-8, Sat 9-1
Bookmobiles: 1

BROWNSVILLE

P EDMONSON COUNTY PUBLIC LIBRARY*, 280 Ferguson St, 42210. (Mail add: PO Box 219, 42210-0219), SAN 306-221X. Tel: 270-597-2146. FAX: 270-597-3282, 270-597-9536. E-mail: ecplib@yahoo.com. Web Site: www.youseemore.com/Edmonson. *Dir,* Jeanie Munsee; Staff 6 (Non-MLS 6)
Founded 1956. Pop 11,644; Circ 50,883
Jul 2008-Jun 2009 Income $287,854, State $15,954, County $212,000, Other $59,900. Mats Exp $30,700, Books $23,000, Per/Ser (Incl. Access Fees) $1,200, AV Mat $4,500, Electronic Ref Mat (Incl. Access Fees) $2,000. Sal $126,361
Library Holdings: CDs 295; DVDs 280; Large Print Bks 600; Bk Titles 25,000; Per Subs 46; Talking Bks 378; Videos 425
Special Collections: Genealogy Coll; Local History Coll
Automation Activity & Vendor Info: (Cataloging) TLC (The Library Corporation); (Circulation) TLC (The Library Corporation); (ILL) OCLC
Database Vendor: OCLC FirstSearch, ProQuest, TLC (The Library Corporation)
Wireless access
Function: Home delivery & serv to Sr ctr & nursing homes, Homebound delivery serv, ILL available, Music CDs, Prog for children & young adult, Ref serv available, Summer reading prog, VCDs, VHS videos, Wheelchair accessible
Open Mon-Thurs 9-7, Fri 9-4:30, Sat 9-1
Bookmobiles: 1. Librn, Judy Renfro

BURGIN

G NORTHPOINT TRAINING CENTER*, Residents' Library, 710 Walter Reed Rd, 40310. (Mail add: PO Box 479, 40310-0479), SAN 325-0989. Tel: 859-239-7012, Ext 2070. FAX: 859-239-7173. *Librn,* James Dennis; Staff 11 (MLS 1, Non-MLS 10)
Founded 1983
Library Holdings: Bk Titles 3,000; Per Subs 130
Database Vendor: OCLC FirstSearch

BURKESVILLE

P CUMBERLAND COUNTY PUBLIC LIBRARY*, 114 W Hill St, 42717. (Mail add: PO Box 440, 42717-0440), SAN 306-2228. Tel: 270-864-2207. FAX: 270-864-5937. *Dir,* Liza Turner
Pop 7,200; Circ 57,536
Library Holdings: Bk Vols 25,000; Per Subs 25
Automation Activity & Vendor Info: (Cataloging) Book Systems; (Circulation) Book Systems
Open Mon-Fri 9-5, Sat 9-12

BURLINGTON

P BOONE COUNTY PUBLIC LIBRARY, 1786 Burlington Pike, 41005. SAN 306-2589. Tel: 859-342-2665. FAX: 859-689-0435. E-mail: info@bcpl.org. Web Site: www.bcpl.org. *Dir,* Carrie Herrmann; E-mail: director@bcpl.org; Staff 31 (MLS 29, Non-MLS 2)
Founded 1973. Pop 124,442; Circ 1,622,616
Jul 2013-Jun 2014 Income (Main Library and Branch(s)) $7,439,947, State $92,561, Federal $14,095, County $7,005,002. Mats Exp $954,633. Sal $3,499,994
Library Holdings: Audiobooks 32,048; DVDs 46,355; e-books 107,918; Bk Vols 257,197; Per Subs 667
Special Collections: Boone County Kentucky History
Automation Activity & Vendor Info: (Acquisitions) Innovative Interfaces, Inc; (Cataloging) Innovative Interfaces, Inc; (Circulation) Innovative Interfaces, Inc; (ILL) Clio; (OPAC) Innovative Interfaces, Inc
Database Vendor: Baker & Taylor, Career Guidance Foundation, EBSCOhost, Gale Cengage Learning, Ingram Library Services, LearningExpress, Newsbank, OCLC FirstSearch, OCLC WorldShare Interlibrary Loan, Overdrive, Inc, Oxford Online, ProQuest, ReferenceUSA, TumbleBookLibrary, ValueLine
Wireless access
Function: Adult bk club, Art exhibits, Bi-weekly Writer's Group, Bk club(s), Bks on CD, CD-ROM, Chess club, Children's prog, Computer training, Computers for patron use, Copy machines, e-mail serv, Electronic databases & coll, Exhibits, Fax serv, Free DVD rentals, Govt ref serv, Handicapped accessible, Holiday prog, Home delivery & serv to Sr ctr & nursing homes, Homebound delivery serv, Homework prog, ILL available, Magnifiers for reading, Mail & tel request accepted, Microfiche/film & reading machines, Music CDs, Online cat, Online ref, Online searches, Outreach serv, Outside serv via phone, mail, e-mail & web, OverDrive digital audio bks, Photocopying/Printing, Preschool outreach, Preschool reading prog, Prog for adults, Prog for children & young adult, Pub access

computers, Ref & res, Ref serv available, Ref serv in person, Senior computer classes, Senior outreach, Story hour, Summer reading prog, Telephone ref, Visual arts prog, Web-catalog, Workshops, Writing prog
Publications: Discover (Monthly newsletter)
Partic in Pub Libr Asn of N Ky; SouthWest Ohio & Neighboring Libraries
Special Services for the Deaf - Adult & family literacy prog; Bks on deafness & sign lang; Closed caption videos; High interest/low vocabulary bks; Sign lang interpreter upon request for prog
Special Services for the Blind - Bks on CD; Copier with enlargement capabilities; Extensive large print coll; Free checkout of audio mat; Home delivery serv; Large print bks; Magnifiers; Playaways (bks on MP3); Ref serv; Screen enlargement software for people with visual disabilities
Open Mon-Fri 9-9, Sat 9-5, Sun 1-5
Branches: 5
CHAPIN MEMORIAL, 6517 Market St, Petersburg, 41080. Tel: 859-342-2665. FAX: 859-689-4313. *Br Mgr,* Teresa Sayers; E-mail: tsayers@bcpl.org
Library Holdings: Bk Vols 6,000; Per Subs 12
Open Tues & Thurs 12-8, Wed 10-6, Fri 12-6, Sat 10-5
FLORENCE BRANCH, 7425 US 42, Florence, 41042. Tel: 859-342-2665. FAX: 859-371-0037. *Br Mgr,* Jasbir Chahal
Open Mon-Thurs 9-9, Fri 9-6, Sat 9-5, Sun 1-5
LENTS BRANCH, 3215 Cougar Path, Hebron, 41048-9642. Tel: 859-342-2665. FAX: 859-586-8215. *Br Mgr,* Sayers Teresa
Open Mon-Thurs 9-9, Fri 9-6, Sat 9-5
SCHEBEN BRANCH, 8899 US 42, Union, 41091. Tel: 859-342-2665. FAX: 859-384-5557. *Br Mgr,* Amy Foster
Open Mon-Fri 9-9, Sat 9-5, Sun 1-5
WALTON BRANCH, 21 S Main St, Walton, 41094-1135. Tel: 859-342-2665. FAX: 859-485-7049. *Br Mgr,* Sharon Franklin
Library Holdings: Bk Vols 40,000
Open Mon & Tues 9-9, Wed-Fri 9-6, Sat 9-5

CADIZ

P JOHN L STREET LIBRARY*, 244 Main St, 42211-9153. Tel: 270-522-6301. FAX: 270-522-1107. E-mail: johnlstreetlibrary@yahoo.com. Web Site: www.tclibrary.org. *Dir,* Pamela Thomas Metts
Founded 1954. Pop 12,593; Circ 110,011
Library Holdings: Bk Titles 45,000; Per Subs 120
Automation Activity & Vendor Info: (Acquisitions) Follett Software; (Cataloging) Follett Software; (Circulation) Follett Software; (Course Reserve) Follett Software; (ILL) Follett Software; (Media Booking) Follett Software; (OPAC) Follett Software; (Serials) Follett Software
Wireless access
Open Mon 9-8, Tues-Fri 9-5:30, Sat 9-12
Bookmobiles: 1. In Charge, Pam Underwood

CAMPBELLSVILLE

C CAMPBELLSVILLE UNIVERSITY*, Montgomery Library, One University Dr, 42718-2799. SAN 306-2252. Tel: 270-789-5024. FAX: 270-789-5336. E-mail: library@campbellsville.edu. Web Site: www.campbellsville.edu. *Dean of Libr Serv,* John R Burch, Jr; Tel: 270-789-5015, E-mail: jrburch@campbellsville.edu; *Pub Serv Librn,* Kay Alston; *Archivist,* Glen Taul; Staff 6 (MLS 2, Non-MLS 4)
Founded 1906. Enrl 1,365; Fac 92; Highest Degree: Master
Library Holdings: Bk Vols 86,000; Per Subs 900
Special Collections: College Archives
Subject Interests: Relig, US Civil War
Automation Activity & Vendor Info: (Cataloging) Ex Libris Group; (Circulation) Ex Libris Group; (OPAC) Ex Libris Group
Database Vendor: EBSCOhost, Gale Cengage Learning, JSTOR, LexisNexis, OCLC FirstSearch, Oxford Online, ProQuest, Wilson - Wilson Web
Publications: Policies & Procedures Handbook
Partic in Appalachian Col Asn; Association of Independent Kentucky Colleges & Universities; Kentucky Library Network, Inc
Open Mon-Thurs 8am-11pm, Fri 8-5, Sat 10-5

P TAYLOR COUNTY PUBLIC LIBRARY*, 1316 E Broadway, 42718. SAN 306-2260. Tel: 270-465-2562. FAX: 270-465-8026. E-mail: info@taylorcountypubliclibrary.org. Web Site: www.taylorcountypubliclibrary.org. *Dir,* Julia Turpin
Founded 1974. Pop 22,000
Library Holdings: Bk Vols 58,245; Per Subs 21
Automation Activity & Vendor Info: (Cataloging) Follett Software; (Circulation) Follett Software; (OPAC) Follett Software
Wireless access
Open Mon, Wed & Fri 9-5:20, Tues & Thurs 9-6:50, Sat 9-3:50

CAMPTON

P WOLFE COUNTY LIBRARY*, 176 Kentucky Hwy 15 N, 41301. (Mail add: PO Box 10, 41301-0010), SAN 306-2279. Tel: 606-668-6571. FAX: 606-668-6561. E-mail: books@mrtc.com. Web Site: www.wolfecountypubliclibrary.org. *Dir,* Debra Baker
Pop 7,000; Circ 48,193
Library Holdings: Bk Vols 22,700; Per Subs 49
Special Collections: Kentucky Genealogy Coll
Database Vendor: OCLC FirstSearch
Open Mon, Wed & Fri 9-4:30, Tues & Thurs 9-6, Sat 9-1
Friends of the Library Group

CARLISLE

P NICHOLAS COUNTY PUBLIC LIBRARY*, 223 N Broadway, 40311. SAN 306-2287. Tel: 859-289-5595. FAX: 859-289-4340. Web Site: www.nicholascountylibrary.com. *Dir,* Becky Reid; E-mail: becky@nicholascountylibrary.com; Staff 2 (Non-MLS 2)
Founded 1961. Pop 7,080
Library Holdings: Bks on Deafness & Sign Lang 31; Large Print Bks 420; Bk Vols 27,358; Per Subs 20; Talking Bks 360
Special Collections: Genealogy Reels, Census, Births, Marriages & Deaths, Bonds, Deeds, Wills from 1790
Automation Activity & Vendor Info: (Cataloging) Book Systems; (Circulation) Book Systems; (OPAC) Book Systems
Open Mon 9-8, Tues-Fri 9-5, Sat 9-12
Bookmobiles: 1. Librn, Susan Short

CARROLLTON

P CARROLL COUNTY PUBLIC LIBRARY*, 136 Court St, 41008. SAN 306-2295. Tel: 502-732-7020. FAX: 502-732-7122. E-mail: information@carrollcountylibrary.org. *Dir,* Hillary Arney; E-mail: hillary@carrollcountylibrary.org; *Asst Dir,* Patricia Hersey; *Circ Mgr,* Martha Noffsinger; E-mail: martha@carrollcountylibrary.org; *Outreach Serv Librn,* Sue Guelda; *Tech Serv,* Rita Stangle; E-mail: rita@carrollcountylibrary.org; *Youth Serv,* Leslie Sutherland; E-mail: leslie@carrollcountylibrary.org; Staff 1 (Non-MLS 1)
Founded 1978. Pop 10,000; Circ 90,000
Library Holdings: AV Mats 4,486; Bks on Deafness & Sign Lang 10; Large Print Bks 1,282; Bk Vols 24,854; Per Subs 76
Special Collections: Kentucky Coll
Subject Interests: Genealogy, Local hist, Spanish lang mat
Automation Activity & Vendor Info: (Cataloging) TLC (The Library Corporation); (Circulation) TLC (The Library Corporation); (OPAC) TLC (The Library Corporation)
Database Vendor: EBSCOhost
Wireless access
Partic in Kentucky Library Network, Inc; Pub Libr Asn of N Ky
Special Services for the Blind - Audio mat; Bks on cassette; Bks on CD; Talking bk & rec for the blind cat; Talking bks & player equip
Open Mon-Thurs 9:30-8, Fri & Sat 9:30-5

CLINTON

P HICKMAN COUNTY MEMORIAL LIBRARY*, 209 Mayfield Rd, 42031-1427. Tel: 270-653-2225. FAX: 270-653-2225. *Librn,* Laura Poole
Pop 5,146; Circ 12,481
Library Holdings: Bk Titles 11,000; Per Subs 23
Wireless access
Open Tues-Fri 2-5, Sat 9:30-12:30

COLD SPRING

P CAMPBELL COUNTY PUBLIC LIBRARY DISTRICT*, 3920 Alexandria Pike, 41076. SAN 306-3801. Tel: 859-781-6166. FAX: 859-572-5049. Web Site: www.cc-pl.org. *Libr Dir,* J C Morgan; E-mail: jcmorgan@cc-pl.org; *Br Mgr,* Dave Anderson; E-mail: danderson@cc-pl.org; Staff 57.5 (MLS 17.5, Non-MLS 40)
Founded 1978. Pop 90,000; Circ 853,519
Library Holdings: Bk Vols 200,000; Per Subs 300
Automation Activity & Vendor Info: (Acquisitions) Innovative Interfaces, Inc; (Cataloging) Innovative Interfaces, Inc; (Circulation) Innovative Interfaces, Inc; (OPAC) Innovative Interfaces, Inc
Wireless access
Function: Homebound delivery serv, ILL available, Prog for children & young adult, Ref serv available, Referrals accepted, Summer reading prog, Wheelchair accessible
Publications: Connections (Monthly)
Partic in Lyrasis; SouthWest Ohio & Neighboring Libraries
Open Mon-Thurs 9-9, Fri 9-7, Sat 9-5, Sun 1-5
Friends of the Library Group

Branches: 2
PHILIP N CARRICO BRANCH, 1000 Highland Ave, Fort Thomas, 41075. Tel: 859-572-5033. FAX: 859-572-5038. E-mail: ftinfo@cc-pl.org. *Br Mgr,* Pam Vincent; E-mail: pvincent@cc-pl.org
Open Mon-Thurs 9-9, Fri 9-7, Sat 9-5, Sun 1-5
NEWPORT BRANCH, 901 E Sixth St, Newport, 41071. Tel: 859-572-5035. FAX: 859-572-5036. E-mail: nwbranchmanager@cc-pl.org. *Br Mgr,* Chantelle Bentley Phillips; E-mail: cbentley@cc-pl.org
Library Holdings: Bk Titles 50,000; Per Subs 80
Open Mon-Thurs 9-9, Fri 9-7, Sat 9-5, Sun 1-5
Bookmobiles: 1

COLUMBIA

P ADAIR COUNTY PUBLIC LIBRARY*, 307 Greensburg St, 42728-1488. SAN 306-2309. Tel: 270-384-2472. FAX: 270-384-9446. *Dir,* Lee Ann Jessee; *Librn,* Jewel Kimbler; *Ch Serv,* Aleina Milligan
Pop 15,233; Circ 49,026
Library Holdings: Bk Vols 25,000; Per Subs 12
Special Collections: Janice Holt Giles Coll
Subject Interests: Kentucky
Automation Activity & Vendor Info: (Acquisitions) TLC (The Library Corporation); (Cataloging) TLC (The Library Corporation); (Circulation) TLC (The Library Corporation); (ILL) TLC (The Library Corporation); (Media Booking) TLC (The Library Corporation); (OPAC) TLC (The Library Corporation); (Serials) TLC (The Library Corporation)
Wireless access
Partic in OCLC Online Computer Library Center, Inc
Open Mon-Wed & Fri 8-5, Thurs 11-8, Sat 8-Noon
Bookmobiles: 1. Librn, Anita Riddle

CR LINDSEY WILSON COLLEGE*, Katie Murrell Library, 210 Lindsey Wilson St, 42728. SAN 306-2325. Tel: 270-384-8102. Administration Tel: 270-384-8250. Toll Free Tel: 800-264-6483. FAX: 270-384-4188. E-mail: library@lindsey.edu. Web Site: www.lindsey.edu/library. *Dir,* Philip Hanna; E-mail: hannap@lindsey.edu; *Pub Serv,* Brittany McDonald; Tel: 270-384-8251, E-mail: mcdonaldb@lindsey.edu; *Tech Serv,* Houston Barnes; Tel: 270-384-8252, E-mail: barnesh@lindsey.edu; Staff 6 (MLS 3, Non-MLS 3)
Founded 1902. Enrl 2,600; Highest Degree: Master
Jul 2012-Jun 2013 Income $443,515. Mats Exp $135,425, Books $27,066, Per/Ser (Incl. Access Fees) $77,156, AV Equip $2,864, AV Mat $4,300, Electronic Ref Mat (Incl. Access Fees) $23,889, Presv $150. Sal $193,343 (Prof $121,490)
Library Holdings: AV Mats 3,311; CDs 591; e-books 220,000; e-journals 30,000; Bk Titles 54,750; Bk Vols 61,600; Per Subs 200
Special Collections: Methodism on the Frontier (Methodist Coll). Oral History; US Document Depository
Subject Interests: Art, Children's lit, Counseling, Educ, Hist, Journalism, Kentucky
Automation Activity & Vendor Info: (Acquisitions) Innovative Interfaces, Inc; (Cataloging) Innovative Interfaces, Inc; (Circulation) Innovative Interfaces, Inc; (Course Reserve) Blackboard Inc; (ILL) Innovative Interfaces, Inc; (Media Booking) Innovative Interfaces, Inc; (OPAC) Innovative Interfaces, Inc; (Serials) Innovative Interfaces, Inc
Database Vendor: Alexander Street Press, American Psychological Association (APA), ARTstor, Baker & Taylor, BioOne, Brodart, EBSCOhost, Facts on File, Gale Cengage Learning, Greenwood Publishing Group, Grolier Online, Hoovers, infoUSA, Innovative Interfaces, Inc, JSTOR, Marcive, Inc, Medline, Mergent Online, Modern Language Association, OCLC FirstSearch, OCLC WorldShare Interlibrary Loan, Oxford Online, ProQuest, Wiley InterScience
Wireless access
Function: Computers for patron use, Copy machines, Distance learning, Doc delivery serv, E-Reserves, Electronic databases & coll, Equip loans & repairs, Exhibits, Fax serv, Free DVD rentals, Govt ref serv, ILL available, Instruction & testing, Microfiche/film & reading machines, Music CDs, Online cat, Online info literacy tutorials on the web & in blackboard, Online ref, Online searches, Orientations, Outside serv via phone, mail, e-mail & web, Photocopying/Printing, Ref serv available, Ref serv in person, Scanner, Spoken cassettes & CDs, VHS videos, Video lending libr, Wheelchair accessible
Partic in Appalachian Col Asn; Association of Independent Kentucky Colleges & Universities; Federation of Kentucky Academic Libraries (FoKAL); Lyrasis
Special Services for the Deaf - Accessible learning ctr
Special Services for the Blind - Recorded bks
Restriction: Open to pub by appt only

CORBIN

P CORBIN PUBLIC LIBRARY*, 215 Roy Kidd Ave, 40701. SAN 306-2333. Tel: 606-528-6366. FAX: 606-523-1895. E-mail: cplibrary@2geton.net. Web Site: www.corbinkylibrary.org. *Dir,* Brenda Huff
Founded 1916. Pop 22,472; Circ 56,233
Library Holdings: Bk Vols 30,000; Per Subs 52
Special Collections: Corbin Time Tribune, 1917-1970, micro
Open Mon, Tues, Thurs & Fri 10-7, Wed & Sat 10-2
Friends of the Library Group

COVINGTON

S BEHRINGER-CRAWFORD MUSEUM*, Lawrence Duba Research Library, 1600 Montague Rd, Devou Park, 41011. SAN 373-4579. Tel: 859-491-4003. E-mail: info@bcmuseum.org. Web Site: www.bcmuseum.org. *Exec Dir,* Laurie Risch; *Educ Dir,* Regina Siegrist; *Curator of Coll,* Tiffany Hoppenjans
Library Holdings: Bk Vols 1,250
Wireless access
Restriction: Open by appt only

P KENTON COUNTY PUBLIC LIBRARY*, Mary Ann Mongan Library, 502 Scott Blvd, 41011. SAN 342-300X. Tel: 859-962-4060. Reference Tel: 859-962-4071. FAX: 859-261-2676. Web Site: www.kentonlibrary.org. *Dir,* David E Schroeder; Tel: 859-962-4080; *Br Mgr,* Julia Allegrini; Tel: 859-962-4074, E-mail: julia.allegrini@kentonlibrary.org; *Coll Serv Mgr,* Becky Bowen; Tel: 859-962-4208; *Automation Syst Coordr,* Garry Collum; E-mail: garry.collum@kentonlibrary.org; Staff 94 (MLS 29, Non-MLS 65)
Founded 1967. Pop 151,464; Circ 2,128,503
Jul 2008-Jun 2009 Income (Main Library and Branch(s)) $10,911,112. Mats Exp $913,817, Books $583,723, AV Mat $212,094, Electronic Ref Mat (Incl. Access Fees) $118,000. Sal $5,759,401
Library Holdings: AV Mats 107,625; Bks on Deafness & Sign Lang 251; CDs 21,250; DVDs 36,253; e-books 7,574; Electronic Media & Resources 455; Large Print Bks 548; Bk Titles 221,621; Bk Vols 457,729; Per Subs 1,069; Talking Bks 15,675; Videos 9,450
Special Collections: Northern Kentucky Newspapers Index, 1835-1931, 1984-present
Subject Interests: Kentucky, Local hist
Automation Activity & Vendor Info: (Acquisitions) SirsiDynix; (Cataloging) SirsiDynix; (Circulation) SirsiDynix; (OPAC) SirsiDynix
Database Vendor: OCLC FirstSearch, SirsiDynix
Function: Homebound delivery serv, Preschool outreach
Publications: Calendar (Monthly)
Partic in SouthWest Ohio & Neighboring Libraries
Open Mon-Fri 9-9, Sat 10-5, Sun 1-5
Friends of the Library Group
Branches: 2
WILLIAM E DURR BRANCH, 1992 Walton-Nicholson Rd, Independence, 41051, SAN 376-916X. Tel: 859-962-4030. Circulation Tel: 859-962-4038. Interlibrary Loan Service Tel: 859-962-4081. Reference Tel: 859-962-4031. FAX: 859-962-4037. *Br Mgr,* Paul Duryea; Tel: 859-962-4036, E-mail: paul.duryea@kentonlibrary.org; *Adult Serv,* Kenny Lunceford; Tel: 859-962-4035, E-mail: kenny.lunceford@kentonlibrary.org; *Ch Serv,* Joel Caithamer; Tel: 859-962-4034, E-mail: joel.caithamer@kentonlibrary.org; *Circ Serv,* Position Currently Open; *ILL,* Jan Mueller; E-mail: jan.mueller@kentonlibrary.org
Library Holdings: Bk Vols 70,000; Per Subs 100
Open Mon-Fri 9-9, Sat 10-5, Sun 1-5
Friends of the Library Group
ERLANGER BRANCH, 401 Kenton Lands Rd, Erlanger, 41018, SAN 342-3034. Tel: 859-962-4000. FAX: 859-962-4010. *Br Mgr,* Angela Smith; Tel: 859-962-4001; *Circ Supvr,* Michael Richter
Library Holdings: Bk Vols 150,000; Per Subs 200
Open Mon-Fri 9-9, Sat 10-6, Sun 1-5
Friends of the Library Group
Bookmobiles: 2

R LATONIA BAPTIST CHURCH LIBRARY*, 38th & Church Sts, 41015. (Mail add: PO Box 15103, 41015-5103), SAN 306-2341. Tel: 859-431-8004. FAX: 859-757-2751. Web Site: www.latoniabaptist.org. *Librn,* Betty McCoy; Staff 6 (MLS 1, Non-MLS 5)
Library Holdings: Audiobooks 77; CDs 15; DVDs 58; Large Print Bks 149; Bk Vols 5,839; Videos 282
Automation Activity & Vendor Info: (Acquisitions) Book Systems; (Cataloging) Book Systems; (Circulation) Book Systems; (Media Booking) Book Systems

CRESTVIEW HILLS

C THOMAS MORE COLLEGE LIBRARY, 333 Thomas More Pkwy, 41017-2599. SAN 306-2597. Tel: 859-344-3300. FAX: 859-344-3342. E-mail: reference@thomasmore.edu. Web Site:

www.thomasmore.edu/library. *Dir,* Leoma Dunn; E-mail: leoma.dunn@thomasmore.edu; *Govt Doc/Ref Librn,* Alisha Copley; *Circ Supvr, ILL,* Joyce McKinley; *Coordr, Acq,* Sister Helen Wilke; Staff 3 (MLS 3)
Founded 1921. Enrl 1,197; Fac 66; Highest Degree: Master
Library Holdings: Bk Vols 113,056; Per Subs 601
Special Collections: Thomas More Coll. US Document Depository
Automation Activity & Vendor Info: (Cataloging) Ex Libris Group; (Circulation) Ex Libris Group; (Course Reserve) Ex Libris Group; (OPAC) Ex Libris Group
Database Vendor: EBSCOhost, ProQuest
Publications: Film & Video Catalog; Library Factsheets
Partic in Association of Independent Kentucky Colleges & Universities; Lyrasis; OCLC Online Computer Library Center, Inc; SouthWest Ohio & Neighboring Libraries
Open Mon-Thurs 8am-10pm, Fri 8-4:30, Sat 10-4, Sun 2-8

CUMBERLAND

J SOUTHEAST KENTUCKY COMMUNITY & TECHNICAL COLLEGE*, Gertrude Angel Dale Library, 207 Chrisman Hall, 700 College Rd, 40823. SAN 306-2384. Tel: 606-589-3099. Reference Tel: 606-589-3073. Administration Tel: 606-589-3070. Toll Free Tel: 888-274-3176. FAX: 606-589-4941. Web Site: www.secc.kctcs.edu/library/. *Dir,* Warren F Gray; E-mail: warren.gray@kctcs.edu; *Asst Librn,* Lynn M Cox; E-mail: lynn.cox@kctcs.edu; *Libr Spec,* Deanna Sherman; Tel: 606-589-3072, E-mail: dsherman0004@kctcs.edu; *Libr Spec,* Sherry McQueen; Staff 4 (MLS 2, Non-MLS 2)
Founded 1960. Fac 86
Library Holdings: Bk Vols 35,617; Per Subs 207
Special Collections: Kentucky Authors Coll
Subject Interests: Appalachia, Caribbean, Coal, Nursing, Pottery
Automation Activity & Vendor Info: (Cataloging) Ex Libris Group; (Circulation) Ex Libris Group; (Course Reserve) Ex Libris Group; (OPAC) Ex Libris Group
Database Vendor: CredoReference, EBSCOhost, Gale Cengage Learning, Newsbank, OCLC FirstSearch, Oxford Online, ProQuest
Function: ILL available
Partic in Lyrasis; OCLC Online Computer Library Center, Inc
Open Mon-Thurs 8-7:30, Fri 8-4:30

CYNTHIANA

P CYNTHIANA-HARRISON COUNTY PUBLIC LIBRARY*, 104 N Main St, 41031. SAN 342-3069. Tel: 859-234-4881. FAX: 859-234-0059. E-mail: info@cynthianalibrary.org. Web Site: www.cynthianalibrary.org. *Dir,* Patricia Barnes; E-mail: plbarnes@cynthianalibrary.org; *Youth Serv Librn,* Cindy Franklin; E-mail: cfranklin@cynthianalibrary.org; *Circ, ILL,* Terry Harris; E-mail: tharris@cynthianalibrary.org; *Tech Serv,* Starla Fields; E-mail: sfields@cynthianalibrary.org; Staff 10 (MLS 1, Non-MLS 9)
Founded 1932. Pop 18,227; Circ 108,600
Library Holdings: Bk Titles 45,000; Per Subs 97
Special Collections: Cissy Gregg Cookbook Coll; Civil War Coll; Kentucky & Local History; Whaley Photographic Coll. Oral History
Subject Interests: Econ, Genealogy, Health sci, Hist, Home econ
Wireless access
Function: After school storytime, Archival coll, Art exhibits, Audio & video playback equip for onsite use, CD-ROM, Computer training, Copy machines, e-mail serv, Electronic databases & coll, Equip loans & repairs, Fax serv, Handicapped accessible, Home delivery & serv to Sr ctr & nursing homes, Homebound delivery serv, Homework prog, ILL available, Mail & tel request accepted, Music CDs, Photocopying/Printing, Preschool outreach, Prog for adults, Prog for children & young adult, Spoken cassettes & CDs, Summer reading prog, Tax forms, Telephone ref, VHS videos, Video lending libr, Web-Braille, Wheelchair accessible, Workshops
Open Mon-Thurs 9-7, Fri 9-6, Sat 9-5
Bookmobiles: 1. Coordr, Ada Adair

DANVILLE

P BOYLE COUNTY PUBLIC LIBRARY*, 307 W Broadway, 40422. SAN 306-2406. Tel: 859-236-8466, 859-238-7323. FAX: 859-236-7692. TDD: 859-236-4921. E-mail: library@boylepublib.org. Web Site: www.boylepublib.org. *Dir,* Georgia de Araujo; E-mail: gdearaujo@boylepublib.org; *Ch,* Libby McWhorter; E-mail: lmcwhorter@boylepublib.org; *Circ Supvr,* Kathy Phillips; E-mail: kphillips@boylepublib.org; *Coordr, Info Tech,* Zachary Upton; E-mail: zupton@boylepublib.org; Staff 6 (MLS 3, Non-MLS 3)
Founded 1893. Pop 28,363; Circ 250,906
Jul 2006-Jun 2007 Income $983,649, State $40,710, County $833,191, Locally Generated Income $75,204, Other $34,544. Mats Exp $104,234, Books $70,020, Per/Ser (Incl. Access Fees) $4,615, AV Mat $21,719, Electronic Ref Mat (Incl. Access Fees) $7,880. Sal $526,615
Library Holdings: AV Mats 8,899; Bks on Deafness & Sign Lang 110; CDs 1,839; Electronic Media & Resources 48; Bk Titles 98,000; Bk Vols 104,972; Per Subs 145; Talking Bks 3,425
Subject Interests: Kentucky, Shakers
Automation Activity & Vendor Info: (Cataloging) Innovative Interfaces, Inc; (Circulation) Innovative Interfaces, Inc; (OPAC) Innovative Interfaces, Inc
Partic in KLN
Special Services for the Deaf - Staff with knowledge of sign lang; TTY equip; Videos & decoder
Open Mon & Thurs 9-8, Tues, Wed & Fri 9-5:30, Sat 9-5, Sun 1-5
Friends of the Library Group
Bookmobiles: 1

C CENTRE COLLEGE OF KENTUCKY*, Grace Doherty Library, 600 W Walnut St, 40422. SAN 306-2392. Tel: 859-238-5272. Circulation Tel: 859-238-5279. Interlibrary Loan Service Tel: 859-238-5275. Reference Tel: 859-238-5277. FAX: 859-236-7925. Web Site: www.centre.edu/web/library/homepage.html. *Dir, Libr Serv,* Stanley R Campbell; Tel: 859-238-5271, E-mail: stan.campbell@centre.edu; *Ref Librn,* Crystal Ellis; *Acq,* Crystal Wesley; Tel: 859-238-5273, E-mail: crystal.wesley@centre.edu; *Circ/Reserves,* Amy Watson; E-mail: amy.watson@centre.edu; *Tech Serv,* Beth Morgan; Staff 9 (MLS 4, Non-MLS 5)
Founded 1819. Enrl 1,130; Highest Degree: Bachelor
Library Holdings: CDs 3,334; e-books 30,757; e-journals 17,874; Bk Titles 225,841; Bk Vols 289,804; Per Subs 750
Special Collections: Centre College Archives; LeCompte Davis Coll. State Document Depository; US Document Depository
Automation Activity & Vendor Info: (Acquisitions) Innovative Interfaces, Inc; (Cataloging) Innovative Interfaces, Inc; (Circulation) Innovative Interfaces, Inc; (Course Reserve) Innovative Interfaces, Inc; (ILL) Innovative Interfaces, Inc; (OPAC) Innovative Interfaces, Inc; (Serials) Innovative Interfaces, Inc
Database Vendor: JSTOR, LexisNexis, OCLC FirstSearch, Wilson - Wilson Web
Partic in Asn of Colleges of the South; Association of Independent Kentucky Colleges & Universities; Lyrasis
Open Mon, Wed & Thurs 8:30am-10pm, Tues 8:30-4:30 & 7-10, Fri 8:30-4:30, Sat 12-6, Sun 12-4 & 7-10

DIXON

P WEBSTER COUNTY PUBLIC LIBRARY, 101 State Rte 132 E, 42409. (Mail add: PO Box 50, 42409-0050), SAN 342-3123. Tel: 270-639-9171. FAX: 270-639-6207. E-mail: libweb@bellsouth.net. Web Site: www.youseemore.com/webster. *Dir,* Erin Russelburg; *Cat Librn,* Shennon Sheridan; *Ch,* Michelle Brown; *Genealogist,* Mandee Franklin
Founded 1954. Pop 13,955; Circ 85,552
Library Holdings: Bk Titles 24,000; Per Subs 146
Special Collections: Webster County Authors (Rice Coll)
Subject Interests: Genealogy, Hist
Automation Activity & Vendor Info: (Cataloging) TLC (The Library Corporation); (Circulation) TLC (The Library Corporation)
Wireless access
Open Mon-Wed & Fri 9-4, Thurs 9-6, Sat 9-2
Branches: 1
PROVIDENCE BRANCH, 230 Willow St, Providence, 42450, SAN 342-3158. Tel: 270-667-5658. FAX: 270-667-6368. E-mail: publi100@bellsouth.net. *Librn,* Misty Layton
Open Mon-Fri 9-4, Sat 9-2

EDDYVILLE

S KENTUCKY STATE PENITENTIARY*, Inmate Library, 266 Water St, 42038. SAN 306-2430. Tel: 270-388-2211, Ext 355. *In Charge,* Michael Antosh; Tel: 270-388-2211, Ext 286
Founded 1958
Open Tues-Fri 8-5, Sat 7am-11am

P LYON COUNTY PUBLIC LIBRARY*, 261 Commerce St, 42038. (Mail add: PO Box 546, 42038-0546), SAN 306-2449. Tel: 270-388-7720. FAX: 270-388-7735. Web Site: www.lyoncountylibrary.com. *Dir,* Romona Engler
Founded 1970. Pop 8,200; Circ 45,556
Library Holdings: Bk Vols 29,000; Per Subs 30
Special Collections: Genealogy Coll; Indian Arrowhead Coll; Lyon County History Coll; Stamp & Foreign Money Coll. Oral History
Automation Activity & Vendor Info: (Acquisitions) Follett Software
Wireless access
Open Mon-Fri 8-6, Sat 9-12

EDGEWOOD

J GATEWAY COMMUNITY & TECHNICAL COLLEGE*, Edgewood Campus Library, 790 Thomas More Pkwy, Rm E 213, 41017. Tel: 859-442-4162. FAX: 859-341-6859. Web Site: www.gateway.kctcs.edu/library. *Interim Dir,* Kathy Driggers

Library Holdings: Bk Titles 672; Per Subs 90
Open Mon-Thurs 8am-9pm, Fri 8-5, Sat-Sun 8-1:30

Departmental Libraries:

BOONE CAMPUS LIBRARY, 500 Technology Way, Rm B09, Florence, 41042. Tel: 859-442-1682. *Dir, Knowledge Mgt,* Jeremy Berberich; E-mail: Jeremy.Berberich@kctcs.edu
Open Mon-Thurs 8-9, Fri 8-4:30, Sat 8-1

COVINGTON CAMPUS LIBRARY, 1025 Amsterdam Rd, Rm C 106, Covington, 41011. Tel: 859-442-4148. Web Site: www.gateway.kctcs.edu/Library.aspx. *Interim Dir,* Kathy Driggers; *Libr Spec,* Lori Jansson; E-mail: lorijansson@kctcs.edu
Open Mon-Thurs 8am-7pm, Fri 8-4:30

EDMONTON

P METCALFE COUNTY PUBLIC LIBRARY*, 200 S Main St, 42129. (Mail add: PO Box 626, 42129-0626), SAN 306-2457. Tel: 270-432-4981. FAX: 270-432-4981. E-mail: metcolib@scrtc.com. Web Site: www.youseemore.com/metcalfe. *Dir,* Rhonda Glass
Founded 1940
Library Holdings: Bk Titles 33,747; Per Subs 25
Subject Interests: Agr, Genealogy
Open Mon-Wed & Fri 8:30-4:30, Sat 9-2
Bookmobiles: 1

ELIZABETHTOWN

J ELIZABETHTOWN COMMUNITY & TECHNICAL COLLEGE LIBRARY*, 600 College Street Rd, 42701. SAN 306-2465. Tel: 270-706-8812. Circulation Tel: 270-706-8576. Interlibrary Loan Service Tel: 270-706-8441. Reference Tel: 270-706-8439. Administration Tel: 270-706-8444. FAX: 270-769-1618. Web Site: www.elizabethtown.kctcs.edu/services/library/index.htm. *Dir,* Ann B Thompson; E-mail: ann.thompson@kctcs.edu; *Acq,* Sarah Jones; E-mail: sarahs.jones@kctcs.edu; *ILL,* Robin Blair; Tel: 270-706-8445, E-mail: rblair0033@kctcs.edu; *Pub Serv,* Laurie MacKellar; E-mail: laurie.mackellar@kctcs.edu; *Pub Serv,* Callista M Meyer; Tel: 270-706-8443, E-mail: cmeyer0015@kctcs.edu; Staff 5 (MLS 3, Non-MLS 2)
Founded 1964. Enrl 6,000; Highest Degree: Associate
Library Holdings: Bk Vols 44,000; Per Subs 150
Special Collections: Hardin County Genealogical Coll (1793-1900), micro; Local Newspapers, micro
Subject Interests: Kentucky
Automation Activity & Vendor Info: (Cataloging) Ex Libris Group; (Circulation) Ex Libris Group; (Course Reserve) Ex Libris Group; (ILL) Ex Libris Group; (OPAC) Ex Libris Group
Database Vendor: EBSCOhost, Gale Cengage Learning, Newsbank, OCLC FirstSearch, OCLC WorldShare Interlibrary Loan, ProQuest
Wireless access
Partic in Lyrasis; Soline; Univ of Ky Commun Col Syst
Open Mon-Thurs 7:15-7, Fri 7:15-4

P HARDIN COUNTY PUBLIC LIBRARY*, 100 Jim Owen Dr, 42701. SAN 306-2473. Tel: 270-769-6337. FAX: 270-769-0437. Web Site: www.hcpl.info. *Dir,* Rene R Hutcheson; E-mail: director@hcpl.info; *Adult & Pub Serv,* Rebekah Akers; *Circ,* Charlotte Bragdon; *Youth Serv,* Gloria Stahl; Staff 22 (MLS 2, Non-MLS 20)
Founded 1958. Pop 107,025; Circ 236,122
Jul 2012-Jun 2013 Income $894,655, State $49,121, County $795,000, Locally Generated Income $50,534. Mats Exp $112,307, Books $79,258, AV Mat $14,714, Electronic Ref Mat (Incl. Access Fees) $13,839. Sal $600,295 (Prof $67,163)
Library Holdings: Audiobooks 5,335; AV Mats 10,069; CDs 216; e-books 319; Bk Vols 97,665; Per Subs 211; Videos 4,515
Automation Activity & Vendor Info: (Cataloging) Innovative Interfaces, Inc; (Circulation) Innovative Interfaces, Inc; (OPAC) Innovative Interfaces, Inc
Database Vendor: 3M Library Systems, Baker & Taylor, Bowker, Gale Cengage Learning, Newsbank, Overdrive, Inc
Wireless access
Open Mon, Tues & Thurs 9-8, Wed & Fri 9-6, Sat 9-3

Branches: 1

RADCLIFF BRANCH, 800 S Logston, Radcliff, 40160. Tel: 270-351-9999. *Br Mgr,* Tara Lewis-Tidwell; Fax: 270-351-5212, E-mail: hcpltaral@gmail.com
Open Mon, Tues & Thurs 9-8, Wed & Fri 9-6, Sat 9-3

Bookmobiles: 1. Librn, Lisa Waldeck-Huffer

M HARDIN MEMORIAL HOSPITAL*, William R Handley Health Sciences Library, 913 N Dixie Ave, 42701-2503. Tel: 270-706-1688. FAX: 270-706-1336. E-mail: library@hmh.net. Web Site: www.hmh.net. *Dir of Libr Serv,* Position Currently Open
Library Holdings: Bk Vols 600
Subject Interests: Allied health, Med, Nursing
Wireless access
Open Mon-Fri 8-4:30

ELKTON

P TODD COUNTY PUBLIC LIBRARY*, 302 E Main St, 42220. SAN 306-2503. Tel: 270-265-9071. FAX: 270-265-2599. E-mail: toddcountyof@bellsouth.net. *Dir,* Audrea Clairmont
Founded 1977. Pop 12,000
Library Holdings: Bk Titles 31,000; Bk Vols 33,638; Per Subs 23
Special Collections: Robert Penn Warren Coll
Subject Interests: Genealogy, Kentucky
Automation Activity & Vendor Info: (Cataloging) Innovative Interfaces, Inc; (Circulation) Innovative Interfaces, Inc; (OPAC) Innovative Interfaces, Inc
Database Vendor: OCLC FirstSearch
Partic in Lyrasis
Open Mon 9-7, Tues, Thurs & Fri 9-5, Wed 9-2, Sat 9-1
Friends of the Library Group
Bookmobiles: 1

EMINENCE

P HENRY COUNTY PUBLIC LIBRARY*, 172 Eminence Terrace, 40019-1146. SAN 306-2511. Tel: 502-845-5682. FAX: 502-845-4807. E-mail: info@henrylibrary.org. Web Site: www.henrylibrary.org. *Dir,* Joe Schweiss; *Tech Serv,* Sharon Aynes; Staff 9 (Non-MLS 9)
Pop 16,000; Circ 74,000
Library Holdings: Bk Vols 35,000; Per Subs 95
Automation Activity & Vendor Info: (Cataloging) TLC (The Library Corporation); (Circulation) TLC (The Library Corporation)
Wireless access
Open Mon-Wed, Fri & Sat 9-5, Thurs 9-8
Bookmobiles: 1

FALMOUTH

P PENDLETON COUNTY PUBLIC LIBRARY*, 228 Main St, 41040-1223. SAN 306-2546. Tel: 859-654-8535. FAX: 859-654-8538. Web Site: www.pcplibrary.org. *Dir,* Sherry Figgins
Founded 1953. Pop 14,000; Circ 99,427
Library Holdings: Bk Vols 31,000; Per Subs 36
Special Collections: E E Barton Genealogy Coll of Northern Kentucky Families; The Falmouth Outlook, microflm
Automation Activity & Vendor Info: (Cataloging) AmLib Library Management System; (Circulation) AmLib Library Management System; (OPAC) AmLib Library Management System
Wireless access
Open Mon-Thurs 9-8, Fri & Sat 9-5, Sun 1-5

FLEMINGSBURG

P FLEMING COUNTY PUBLIC LIBRARY*, 202 Bypass Blvd, 41041-7934. SAN 306-2570. Tel: 606-845-7851. FAX: 606-845-7045. E-mail: flemingcountylibrary@yahoo.com. Web Site: www2.youseemore.com/fleming. *Dir,* Mary Rushing; *Ch,* Charlotte Wagner; *Adult Serv, ILL,* Debbie Crump; *Cat & Adult Serv,* Connie Saunders; Staff 6 (Non-MLS 6)
Founded 1962. Pop 14,000; Circ 102,000
Jul 2006-Jun 2007 Income $358,000, State $23,500, County $296,000, Locally Generated Income $38,500. Mats Exp $45,900, Books $37,400, Per/Ser (Incl. Access Fees) $3,000, AV Mat $5,000, Electronic Ref Mat (Incl. Access Fees) $500. Sal $121,810
Library Holdings: Bks on Deafness & Sign Lang 20; Bk Vols 28,000; Per Subs 70
Special Collections: Frank Sousley Coll; Harriet Dudley Grannis Coll; Henry Chittison History/Music Coll. State Document Depository
Subject Interests: Genealogy
Automation Activity & Vendor Info: (Cataloging) TLC (The Library Corporation); (Circulation) TLC (The Library Corporation); (Course Reserve) TLC (The Library Corporation); (ILL) OCLC; (OPAC) TLC (The Library Corporation); (Serials) TLC (The Library Corporation)
Database Vendor: EBSCOhost
Open Mon & Wed 8-6, Tues & Thurs 8-8, Fri 8-5, Sat 8-3
Friends of the Library Group
Bookmobiles: 1. Librn, Barbara Faris

FORT CAMPBELL

A UNITED STATES ARMY*, R F Sink Memorial Library, 38 Screaming Eagle Blvd, 42223-5342. SAN 342-3182. Tel: 270-798-5729. Interlibrary Loan Service Tel: 270-956-3350. Reference Tel: 270-956-3344. Administration Tel: 270-798-1217. FAX: 270-798-0369. Web Site: www.fortcampbellmwr.com/library. *Librn,* James Moore; Staff 5 (MLS 5)
Founded 1941

Library Holdings: CDs 1,791; DVDs 1,146; Bk Titles 76,337; Bk Vols 88,216; Per Subs 315; Talking Bks 2,414; Videos 3,579
Special Collections: Local History, microfiche; Official Records of the Civil War; World War II Coll
Subject Interests: Mil hist
Automation Activity & Vendor Info: (Cataloging) Horizon; (Circulation) Horizon; (ILL) OCLC; (OPAC) Horizon
Publications: In house bibliographies
Partic in Dialog Corp; OCLC Online Computer Library Center, Inc
Open Tues-Thurs 10-8, Fri-Mon 9-5

FORT KNOX

UNITED STATES ARMY

A BARR MEMORIAL LIBRARY*, 62 W Spearhead Division Ave, Bldg 400, 40121-5187. Tel: 502-624-1232, 502-624-4636. E-mail: usarmy.knox.imcom-atlantic.mbx.dfmwr-barr-library@mail.mil. *Librn,* Cindy Arnold; Staff 11 (MLS 3, Non-MLS 8)
Library Holdings: AV Mats 8,000; Bk Vols 84,000; Per Subs 250; Talking Bks 1,000
Subject Interests: Kentucky, Mil sci
Automation Activity & Vendor Info: (Cataloging) TLC (The Library Corporation); (Circulation) TLC (The Library Corporation); (OPAC) TLC (The Library Corporation)
Publications: In-house bibliographies
Open Mon-Thurs 9-8, Fri & Sat 9-5

AM IRELAND ARMY HOSPITAL MEDICAL LIBRARY*, Bldg 851, Ireland Ave, 40121-5520, SAN 324-2358. Tel: 502-624-9550. FAX: 502-624-0280. Web Site: www.iach.knox.amedd.army.mil/iach. *Librn,* Craig Morrow; E-mail: craig.morrow@amedd.army.mil
Founded 1957
Library Holdings: Bk Vols 480; Per Subs 86
Partic in National Network of Libraries of Medicine
Open Mon-Fri 7-3:30
Restriction: Staff use only

A PATTON MUSEUM OF CAVALRY & ARMOR EMERT L DAVIS MEMORIAL LIBRARY*, 4554 Fayette Ave, 40121. (Mail add: PO Box 208, 40121-0208), SAN 342-3352. Tel: 502-624-6968. FAX: 502-624-2364. *Librn,* Candace L Fuller; E-mail: candy.fuller@us.army.mil
Founded 1975
Library Holdings: Bk Vols 13,000; Per Subs 20
Special Collections: General George S Patton, Jr Coll, photog; Robert J Icks' Photo & Manuscript Coll on Armored Equipment, bks, maps, photogs. Oral History
Partic in Tradoc

FORT MITCHELL

C BROWN MACKIE COLLEGE LIBRARY*, Northern Kentucky Campus, 309 Buttermilk Pike, 41017. SAN 376-5776. Tel: 859-486-2553. FAX: 859-341-6483. Web Site: www.librarybmc.com. *Head of Libr,* Karen Paxton; Staff 1.5 (MLS 1.5)
Enrl 750; Highest Degree: Bachelor
Jul 2009-Jun 2010. Mats Exp $58,000, Books $48,000, Per/Ser (Incl. Access Fees) $10,000
Library Holdings: DVDs 47; Electronic Media & Resources 50; Bk Titles 3,400; Per Subs 45
Automation Activity & Vendor Info: (Acquisitions) Baker & Taylor; (Cataloging) LibraryWorld, Inc; (Circulation) LibraryWorld, Inc; (OPAC) LibraryWorld, Inc; (Serials) EBSCO Online
Database Vendor: Bowker, EBSCOhost, Gale Cengage Learning, Grolier Online, ProQuest, Westlaw
Wireless access
Function: Adult bk club, Computers for patron use, Copy machines, Electronic databases & coll, Handicapped accessible, ILL available, Online cat, Orientations, Ref serv in person, Web-catalog
Partic in SouthWest Ohio & Neighboring Libraries
Open Mon, Tues & Thurs 8am-10pm, Wed & Fri 8-5

FRANKFORT

P KENTUCKY DEPARTMENT FOR LIBRARIES & ARCHIVES*, 300 Coffee Tree Rd, 40601. (Mail add: PO Box 537, 40602), SAN 342-3425. Tel: 502-564-8300. FAX: 502-564-5773. E-mail: kdla-referencedesk@ky.gov. Web Site: kdla.ky.gov. *State Librn,* Wayne Onkst; E-mail: wayne.onkst@ky.gov; *Mgr, User Serv,* Keith Knox; *Collection Access Mgt,* Bill Shrout; *Acq, Supvr,* Alicia McGrath; *Cat Supvr,* Cathy Crum; *Ref Supvr,* Jane Minder; Staff 170 (MLS 85, Non-MLS 85)
Founded 1834
Library Holdings: Audiobooks 4,594; AV Mats 570; CDs 110; DVDs 1,341; Large Print Bks 17,150; Microforms 1,061; Music Scores 343; Bk Titles 76,428; Per Subs 203; Videos 4,649
Special Collections: Civil War Records (Confederate & Union in Kentucky); Confederate Pensions; Kentuckiana Coll; Kentucky Public Records, Maps & Genealogy Coll; Local Government Depository Coll; Louisville Courier-Journal (1868-to-date), micro. State Document Depository; US Document Depository
Subject Interests: Art, Geol, Hist, Kentucky, Lit, Soc sci & issues
Automation Activity & Vendor Info: (Acquisitions) Ex Libris Group; (Cataloging) Ex Libris Group; (Circulation) Ex Libris Group; (Media Booking) Ex Libris Group; (OPAC) Ex Libris Group; (Serials) Ex Libris Group
Publications: Checklist of Kentucky State Publications; Statistical Report of Kentucky Public Libraries
Partic in Lyrasis; OCLC Online Computer Library Center, Inc; RLIN (Research Libraries Information Network)
Open Mon-Fri 8-4
Branches: 1
KENTUCKY REGIONAL LIBRARY FOR THE BLIND & PHYSICALLY HANDICAPPED
See Separate Entry
Bookmobiles: 76

S KENTUCKY HISTORICAL SOCIETY*, Martin F Schmidt Research Library, 100 W Broadway, 40601. SAN 306-2643. Tel: 502-564-1792. Reference Tel: 502-564-1792, Ext 4460. FAX: 502-564-4701. E-mail: khsrefdesk@ky.gov. Web Site: www.history.ky.gov. *Exec Dir,* Kent Whitworth; E-mail: kent.whitworth@ky.gov; *Functional Team Dir, Spec Coll & Libr,* Louise Jones; E-mail: louise.jones@ky.gov; *Ref & Digital Librn,* Jennifer Howard; E-mail: jennifer.howard2@ky.gov; *Sr Librn, Ref,* Cheri Daniels; *Oral Hist Adminr,* Sarah Milligan; E-mail: sarah.milligan@ky.gov; *Tech Serv Librn,* Shirley Ackerman; E-mail: shirley.ackerman@ky.gov; *Spec Coll Adminr,* Jennifer Duplaga; E-mail: jen.duplaga@ky.gov; Staff 10 (MLS 5, Non-MLS 5)
Founded 1836
Library Holdings: Bk Titles 48,539; Bk Vols 101,029; Per Subs 197; Spec Interest Per Sub 47
Special Collections: Oral History; State Document Depository
Subject Interests: Genealogy, Hist, Kentucky, Manuscripts, Maps, Rare bks
Automation Activity & Vendor Info: (Cataloging) Ex Libris Group; (Circulation) Ex Libris Group
Database Vendor: Ex Libris Group, OCLC FirstSearch, OCLC WorldShare Interlibrary Loan, ProQuest, Wilson - Wilson Web, WT Cox
Wireless access
Publications: Chronicle (Quarterly); Kentucky Ancestors (Quarterly); The Register (Quarterly)
Open Wed 10-4, Thurs 10-8, Fri & Sat 10-5
Restriction: Circulates for staff only

P KENTUCKY REGIONAL LIBRARY FOR THE BLIND & PHYSICALLY HANDICAPPED*, Kentucky Talking Book Library, 300 Coffee Tree Rd, 40601. (Mail add: PO Box 537, 40602-0537), SAN 306-2651. Tel: 502-564-8300, Ext 276. FAX: 502-564-5773. E-mail: ktbl.mail@ky.gov. Web Site: www.kdla.ky.gov/librarians/talkingbook. *Br Mgr,* Barbara Penegor; Tel: 502-564-8300, Ext 282; Staff 9 (MLS 3, Non-MLS 6)
Founded 1969. Pop 5,497; Circ 160,000
Library Holdings: AV Mats 500; Braille Volumes 14,000; Bk Titles 50,000; Bk Vols 141,000; Per Subs 84; Talking Bks 132,316; Videos 500
Publications: The Listening Post (Newsletter)
Special Services for the Blind - Bks & mags in Braille, on rec, tape & cassette; Descriptive video serv (DVS); Newsletter (in large print, Braille or on cassette); Newsline for the Blind; Spec cats; Talking bks; Volunteer serv
Open Mon-Fri 8-4:30

C KENTUCKY STATE UNIVERSITY, Paul G Blazer Library, 400 E Main St, 40601-2355. SAN 306-2678. Tel: 502-597-6852. Circulation Tel: 502-597-6851. Reference Tel: 502-597-6857. FAX: 502-597-5068. Circulation FAX: 502-597-6790. Web Site: www.kysu.edu/academics/library. *Dir, Libr Serv,* Sheila A Stuckey; E-mail: sheila.stuckey@kysu.edu; *Head, Archives & Spec Coll, Rec Librn,* Sharon McGee; Tel: 502-597-6824, E-mail: sharon.mcgee@kysu.edu; *Cat/ILL Librn, Head, Coll Mgt,* Margaret Hecker; E-mail: margaret.hecker@kysu.edu; *Coordr, Libr Instruction, Head, Pub Serv,* Nkechi Amadife; Tel: 502-597-6817, E-mail: nkechi.amadife@kysu.edu; *Acq Librn,* Debbra Tate; Tel: 502-597-6862, E-mail: debbra.tate@kysu.edu; *Circ Librn, Ref Librn,* Raphael Jackson; Tel: 502-597-5930; *Educ & Ref Librn,* Bobby Walter; E-mail: bobby.walter@kysu.edu; *Govt Doc/Ref Librn,* Bekele Tegegne; Tel: 502-597-6858, E-mail: bekele.tegegne@kysu.edu; *Per/Ref Librn,* Dantrea Hampton; Tel: 502-597-5946, E-mail: dantrea.hampton@kysu.edu; *Syst Librn,* Position Currently Open; Staff 15 (MLS 9, Non-MLS 6)
Founded 1886. Enrl 2,533; Fac 182; Highest Degree: Master
Library Holdings: e-books 23,412; Microforms 328,572; Bk Vols 346,399; Per Subs 418
Special Collections: Black Studies, bks, flm & micro. Oral History; US Document Depository

Automation Activity & Vendor Info: (Acquisitions) Ex Libris Group; (Cataloging) OCLC; (Circulation) Ex Libris Group; (Course Reserve) Ex Libris Group; (ILL) OCLC WorldShare Interlibrary Loan; (OPAC) Ex Libris Group; (Serials) Ex Libris Group
Database Vendor: 3M Library Systems, ABC-CLIO, Agricola, American Psychological Association (APA), Baker & Taylor, Bowker, Brodart, Cinahl, EBSCO Information Services, EBSCOhost, Elsevier, Ex Libris Group, Gale Cengage Learning, H W Wilson, JSTOR, LexisNexis, Medline, Newsbank-Readex, OCLC, OCLC FirstSearch, OCLC WorldShare Interlibrary Loan, Oxford Online, Project MUSE, ProQuest, Wilson - Wilson Web, WT Cox, YBP Library Services
Wireless access
Function: Archival coll, Computers for patron use, Copy machines, e-mail & chat, Electronic databases & coll, Fax serv, Govt ref serv, ILL available, Online cat, Online ref, Online searches, Orientations, Photocopying/Printing, Pub access computers, Ref & res, Ref serv in person, Tax forms, Telephone ref
Partic in Federation of Kentucky Academic Libraries (FoKAL); HBCU Library Alliance; Lyrasis; OCLC Online Computer Library Center, Inc; State Assisted Academic Library Council of Kentucky
Open Mon-Fri 8am-Midnight, Sat 2-Midnight, Sun 1-Midnight

P PAUL SAWYIER PUBLIC LIBRARY, 319 Wapping St, 40601-2605. SAN 306-2694. Tel: 502-352-2665. FAX: 502-227-2250. E-mail: director@pspl.org. Web Site: www.pspl.org. *Libr Dir,* Donna Riis Gibson; E-mail: donnag@pspl.org; *Adult Serv,* Jaci West; E-mail: jaci@pspl.org; *Youth Serv,* Erinn Conness; E-mail: erinn@pspl.org; Staff 28.24 (MLS 5.63, Non-MLS 22.61)
Founded 1908. Pop 49,648; Circ 516,329
Jul 2013-Jun 2014 Income $3,104,648, State $26,663, Locally Generated Income $2,957,431, Other $120,554. Mats Exp $2,616,141. Sal $1,716,237
Library Holdings: e-books 73,905; Bk Vols 126,401; Per Subs 184
Subject Interests: Local hist
Automation Activity & Vendor Info: (Cataloging) TLC (The Library Corporation); (Circulation) TLC (The Library Corporation); (OPAC) TLC (The Library Corporation); (Serials) TLC (The Library Corporation)
Database Vendor: ebrary, EBSCOhost, OCLC FirstSearch
Wireless access
Function: 24/7 Electronic res, 24/7 Online cat, Accessibility serv available based on individual needs, Activity rm, Adult bk club, Audiobks via web, Bk club(s), Bks on CD, Children's prog, Computer training, Computers for patron use, Copy machines, e-mail & chat, e-mail serv, eReaders, Exhibits, Fax serv, Free DVD rentals, Handicapped accessible, Home delivery & serv to Sr ctr & nursing homes, Homebound delivery serv, ILL available, Instruction & testing, Magazines, Magnifiers for reading, Mango lang, Music CDs, Notary serv, Online cat, Online ref, Online searches, Outreach serv, OverDrive digital audio bks, Photocopying/Printing, Preschool outreach, Printer for laptops & handheld devices, Prog for adults, Prog for children & young adult, Ref serv available, Ref serv in person, Scanner, Senior computer classes, Senior outreach, Story hour, Study rm, Summer reading prog, Teen prog, Telephone ref, Wheelchair accessible
Open Mon-Thurs 9-8, Fri 9-6, Sat 9-5, Sun 1-5
Friends of the Library Group

GL STATE LAW LIBRARY*, 700 Capital Ave, Ste 200, 40601-3489. SAN 306-2708. Tel: 502-564-4848. FAX: 502-564-5041. E-mail: statelawlibrary@kycourts.net. Web Site: www.kycourts.net. *Librn,* Jennifer Frazier; Staff 2 (MLS 1, Non-MLS 1)
Founded 1954
Library Holdings: e-journals 304; Bk Titles 10,500; Bk Vols 134,000
Special Collections: Kentucky Law
Subject Interests: Anglo-Am law
Database Vendor: Westlaw
Publications: Guide to Kentucky Legal Research: A State Bibliography (1985); Index to Kentucky Legal History, 18th & 19th Centuries (1983)
Partic in OCLC Online Computer Library Center, Inc
Special Services for the Deaf - TDD equip
Open Mon-Fri 8-4:30

FRANKLIN

P GOODNIGHT MEMORIAL LIBRARY*, 203 S Main St, 42134. SAN 306-2716. Tel: 270-586-8397. FAX: 270-586-8397. E-mail: goodmeml@bellsouth.net. Web Site: www.gmpl.org. *Dir,* Audrey Phillips; E-mail: audrey@gmpl.org; *Tech Coordr,* Jim Peterson; E-mail: jim@gmpl.org; *Ch Serv,* Gayle Foley; E-mail: gayle@gmpl.org; *ILL,* Stephanie Phippin; E-mail: stephanie@gmpl.org; *Teen Serv,* Athena Richardson; E-mail: athena@gmpl.org; Staff 2 (MLS 2)
Founded 1937. Pop 16,214; Circ 89,136
Library Holdings: Bk Vols 34,000; Per Subs 75
Automation Activity & Vendor Info: (Cataloging) TLC (The Library Corporation); (Circulation) TLC (The Library Corporation); (OPAC) TLC (The Library Corporation)
Open Mon & Tues 9-8, Wed-Sat 9-5:30
Friends of the Library Group
Bookmobiles: 1. Bkmobile Servs, Cheri Read

FRENCHBURG

P MENIFEE COUNTY PUBLIC LIBRARY*, 1585 Main St, 40322. (Mail add: PO Box 49, 40322-0049), SAN 306-2724. Tel: 606-768-2212. FAX: 606-768-9676. E-mail: library@mrtc.com. *Dir,* Melissa Wells
Pop 6,000; Circ 33,303
Library Holdings: AV Mats 404; Bk Vols 26,000; Per Subs 55; Talking Bks 787
Subject Interests: Genealogy, Kentucky
Automation Activity & Vendor Info: (Cataloging) TLC (The Library Corporation); (Circulation) TLC (The Library Corporation)
Wireless access
Open Mon, Wed & Fri 9-5, Tues & Thurs 9-7, Sat 9-3

FULTON

P FULTON COUNTY PUBLIC LIBRARY*, 312 Main St, 42041. SAN 342-3573. Tel: 270-472-3439. FAX: 270-472-6241. E-mail: fultonpl@bellsouth.net. Web Site: www.fultonlibrary.com. *Dir,* Heather Roberts
Founded 1965. Pop 14,382; Circ 83,680
Library Holdings: Bk Vols 70,000; Per Subs 150
Special Collections: Civil War Records
Subject Interests: Antiques, Genealogy, Hist
Partic in Kentucky Library Network, Inc
Open Mon & Sat 9-12:30, Tues 10:30-7, Wed-Fri 9-5
Friends of the Library Group
Branches: 1
HICKMAN PUBLIC, 902 Moscow Ave, Hickman, 42050, SAN 342-3603. Tel: 270-236-2464. FAX: 270-236-1442. E-mail: hickmanpl@bellsouth.net. *Librn,* Judy Reason
Open Tues 10:30-8, Wed, Fri & Sat 9-5
Friends of the Library Group
Bookmobiles: 1. Librn, Marda Pate

GEORGETOWN

C GEORGETOWN COLLEGE*, Ensor Learning Resource Center, 400 E College St, 40324. SAN 306-2732. Tel: 502-863-8400. Interlibrary Loan Service Tel: 502-863-8413. Reference Tel: 502-863-8401. FAX: 502-868-7740. Web Site: library.georgetowncollege.edu. *Dir,* Susan H Martin; Tel: 502-863-8407, E-mail: susan_martin@georgetowncollege.edu; *Cat Librn,* Greg Decker; Tel: 502-863-8409, E-mail: greg_decker@georgetowncollege.edu; *Coll Develop Librn,* Michele D Ruth; Tel: 502-863-8412, E-mail: michele_ruth@georgetowncollege.edu; *Electronic Res Librn,* Ben Rawlins; Tel: 502-863-8403, E-mail: ben_rawlins@georgetowncollege.edu; *Ref Librn,* Helen E Bischoff; Tel: 502-863-8405, E-mail: helen_bischoff@georgetowncollege.edu; *Mgr, ILL, Mgr, Per,* Ernie Heavin; E-mail: ernie_heavin@georgetowncollege.edu; *Day Circ Supvr,* Rachel Combs; Tel: 502-863-8404, E-mail: rachel_combs@georgetowncollege.edu; *Evening Circ Supvr,* Randall Myers; Tel: 502-863-8406, E-mail: randall_myers@georgetowncollege.edu; *Coordr, Archives & Spec Coll,* Sandy Baird; Tel: 502-863-8410, E-mail: sandra_baird@georgetowncollege.edu. Subject Specialists: *Chem, Kinesiology, Theatre,* Susan H Martin; *Art, Hist, Music,* Greg Decker; *Biol, Bus, Econ,* Michele D Ruth; *Communications, Polit sci, Relig,* Ben Rawlins; *Educ, Psychol,* Helen E Bischoff; Staff 9 (MLS 5, Non-MLS 4)
Founded 1829. Enrl 1,400; Fac 110; Highest Degree: Master
Library Holdings: Audiobooks 862; CDs 2,394; DVDs 4,255; e-books 113,331; e-journals 41,701; Electronic Media & Resources 10,261; Microforms 189,597; Bk Titles 146,316; Bk Vols 185,592; Per Subs 314; Videos 2,750
Special Collections: Christianity (Thompson Coll); Georgetown News & Georgetown Times, newsp; History Coll; Law (Smith Coll); Pre-1660 English Literature, microbk; Rankin Civil War Coll; Religion
Automation Activity & Vendor Info: (Acquisitions) Ex Libris Group; (Cataloging) Ex Libris Group; (Circulation) Ex Libris Group; (Course Reserve) Ex Libris Group; (Media Booking) Ex Libris Group; (OPAC) Ex Libris Group; (Serials) Ex Libris Group
Database Vendor: ABC-CLIO, Agricola, Cinahl, CredoReference, EBSCO Information Services, EBSCOhost, Ex Libris Group, H W Wilson, JSTOR, LexisNexis, Newsbank, OCLC FirstSearch, OVID Technologies, Oxford Online, ProQuest, STN International, Wilson - Wilson Web
Wireless access
Function: ILL available, Microfiche/film & reading machines, Music CDs, Online cat, Wheelchair accessible
Partic in Association of Independent Kentucky Colleges & Universities; Council of Independent Colleges (CIC); Federation of Kentucky Academic Libraries (FoKAL); OCLC Online Computer Library Center, Inc
Open Mon-Thurs 7:45am-1am, Fri 7:45-6, Sat 10-6, Sun 1-1
Restriction: ID required to use computers (Ltd hrs)

P SCOTT COUNTY PUBLIC LIBRARY, 104 S Bradford Lane, 40324-2335. SAN 306-2740. Tel: 502-863-3566. FAX: 502-863-9621. Web Site: www.scottpublib.org. *Dir,* Barbara O'Hara; *Asst Dir,* Patti Burnside; E-mail: patti@scottpublib.org; *Youth Serv Dir,* Roseann Polashek; *Adult Serv Mgr,* Melissa Gibson; E-mail: melissa@scottpublib.org; Staff 12.93 (MLS 3.81, Non-MLS 9.12)
Founded 1928. Pop 41,605; Circ 365,074
Jul 2014-Jun 2015 Income $2,486,500, State $22,500, County $2,400,000, Other $64,000. Mats Exp $343,000, Books $145,000, Per/Ser (Incl. Access Fees) $15,000, AV Equip $9,000, AV Mat $90,000, Electronic Ref Mat (Incl. Access Fees) $62,000, Presv $22,000. Sal $915,000 (Prof $450,000)
Library Holdings: CDs 2,438; DVDs 3,835; Bk Vols 91,577; Per Subs 167; Talking Bks 6,526
Subject Interests: Genealogy, Kentucky
Automation Activity & Vendor Info: (Cataloging) TLC (The Library Corporation); (Circulation) TLC (The Library Corporation); (OPAC) TLC (The Library Corporation); (Serials) TLC (The Library Corporation)
Wireless access
Function: Activity rm, Adult bk club, Adult literacy prog, Archival coll, Bilingual assistance for Spanish patrons, Bk club(s), Bks on CD, Children's prog, Computer training, Computers for patron use, Copy machines, Digital talking bks, e-mail & chat, e-mail serv, Electronic databases & coll, Exhibits, Family literacy, Fax serv, Free DVD rentals, Genealogy discussion group, Home delivery & serv to Sr ctr & nursing homes, Homebound delivery serv, ILL available, Instruction & testing, Magazines, Mango lang, Movies, Music CDs, Notary serv, Online cat, Online info literacy tutorials on the web & in blackboard, Online searches, Outreach serv, Outside serv via phone, mail, e-mail & web, Photocopying/Printing, Prog for adults, Prog for children & young adult, Pub access computers, Ref & res, Ref serv available, Ref serv in person, Referrals accepted, Scanner, Senior computer classes, Senior outreach, Spanish lang bks, Spoken cassettes & CDs, Story hour, Study rm, Summer & winter reading prog, Summer reading prog, Tax forms, Teen prog, Telephone ref, VHS videos, Workshops, Writing prog
Special Services for the Blind - Internet workstation with adaptive software; Large print & cassettes; Large print bks; Playaways (bks on MP3); Ref serv; Rental typewriters & computers
Open Mon-Thurs 9-9, Fri & Sat 9-6, Sun 1-5
Friends of the Library Group
Bookmobiles: 1. Lee Ray

GLASGOW

P MARY WOOD WELDON MEMORIAL LIBRARY*, 1530 S Green St, 42141. SAN 306-2759. Tel: 270-651-2824. FAX: 270-659-0367. E-mail: public_library@glasgow-ky.com. Web Site: www.weldonpubliclibrary.org. *Dir,* Lynn Andrew; *Head, Circ,* Angelina Clark; *Head of Outreach Serv,* Martha Nell Thomas; *Head, Tech Serv,* Deloris Flowers; *Head, Youth Serv,* Marla Ford; Staff 1 (MLS 1)
Founded 1925. Pop 34,000; Circ 117,000
Library Holdings: Bk Vols 61,000; Per Subs 115
Special Collections: Genealogy (Kentucky Coll), bks, micro
Automation Activity & Vendor Info: (Cataloging) TLC (The Library Corporation); (Circulation) TLC (The Library Corporation); (OPAC) TLC (The Library Corporation)
Database Vendor: EBSCOhost
Open Mon-Thurs 9-8, Fri & Sat 9-4
Friends of the Library Group
Bookmobiles: 1. Librn, Lenora Metcalfe

GRAYSON

CR KENTUCKY CHRISTIAN UNIVERSITY, Young Library, 100 Academic Pkwy, 41143. SAN 306-2767. Tel: 606-474-3240. FAX: 606-474-3123. E-mail: library@kcu.edu. Web Site: library.kcu.edu. *Dir,* Naulayne Enders; Tel: 606-474-3276, E-mail: nenders@kcu.edu; *Pub Serv Librn,* Heidi Wineland; Tel: 606-474-3241
Enrl 430
Library Holdings: e-books 100,000; e-journals 40,000; Bk Vols 100,000; Per Subs 11,000
Special Collections: Mission Papers (1969-present); Restoration Church History
Subject Interests: Educ, Relig
Automation Activity & Vendor Info: (Acquisitions) Innovative Interfaces, Inc; (Cataloging) Innovative Interfaces, Inc; (Circulation) Innovative Interfaces, Inc; (Course Reserve) Innovative Interfaces, Inc; (ILL) Innovative Interfaces, Inc; (OPAC) Innovative Interfaces, Inc; (Serials) Innovative Interfaces, Inc
Publications: Library News; Search Strategy Handbook; Your Library
Open Mon & Wed 8am-10pm, Tues & Thurs 8-11 & 12-10, Fri 8-5, Sat 11-4, Sun 2-5 & 7-10; Mon-Fri (Summer) 8-5

GREENSBURG

P GREEN COUNTY PUBLIC LIBRARY*, 112 W Court St, 42743. SAN 306-2775. Tel: 270-932-7081. FAX: 270-932-7081. *Dir,* Shelley Pruitt; E-mail: shelleypruitt@kyol.net; *Children's & YA Librn,* Debbie Harris; *Circ Mgr,* Missy Curry; *Outreach Serv,* Kayla Bradshaw; Staff 4 (Non-MLS 4)
Founded 1966. Pop 11,510; Circ 99,469
Library Holdings: Bk Vols 35,000; Per Subs 31
Special Collections: Genealogy & History of Original Green County
Open Mon 8-6, Tues, Wed & Fri 8-4:30, Sat 8:30-1

GREENUP

P GREENUP COUNTY PUBLIC LIBRARY*, 614 Main St, 41144-1036. SAN 342-3638. Tel: 606-473-6514. FAX: 606-473-6514. *Dir,* Dorothy K Griffith
Founded 1969. Pop 39,132; Circ 237,137
Library Holdings: Bk Vols 95,578; Per Subs 290
Special Collections: Jesse Stuart Coll, photogs. Oral History
Subject Interests: Genealogy, Hist, Kentucky, Local hist
Automation Activity & Vendor Info: (Cataloging) Marcive, Inc; (Circulation) Marcive, Inc; (OPAC) Marcive, Inc
Wireless access
Open Mon, Tues, Thurs & Fri 9-5, Wed 9-8, Sat 9-2
Branches: 2
FLATWOODS PUBLIC, 1705 Argillite Rd, Flatwoods, 41139, SAN 342-3662. Tel: 606-836-3771. FAX: 606-836-8674. *Librn,* Sharon Haines
Founded 1969
Library Holdings: Bk Titles 35,000; Bk Vols 45,000
Subject Interests: Kentucky
Open Mon, Tues & Thurs 10-8, Wed, Fri & Sat 10-5
MCKELL PUBLIC, 22 McKell Lane, South Shore, 41175, SAN 342-3697. Tel: 606-932-4478. FAX: 606-932-4478. *Librn,* Sue Evans
Subject Interests: Kentucky
Open Mon, Tues, Thurs & Fri 9-5, Wed 9-8, Sat 9-2
Bookmobiles: 1

GREENVILLE

P MUHLENBERG COUNTY LIBRARIES*, Harbin Memorial Library, 117 S Main St, 42345. SAN 342-3727. Tel: 270-338-4760. FAX: 270-338-4000. E-mail: hmlib@mcplib.org. Web Site: www.mcplib.org. *Libr Dir,* Janet Harrison; Staff 2 (Non-MLS 2)
Founded 1970. Pop 31,839; Circ 148,000
Library Holdings: Bk Vols 90,000; Per Subs 140; Talking Bks 2,200
Subject Interests: Genealogy, Local hist
Automation Activity & Vendor Info: (Cataloging) SirsiDynix; (Circulation) SirsiDynix
Open Mon 9-7, Tues-Fri 9-5, Sat 9-1
Branches: 1
CENTRAL CITY BRANCH, 108 E Broad St, Central City, 42330, SAN 342-3786. Tel: 270-754-4630. FAX: 270-754-2591. E-mail: cclib@mcplib.org
Open Mon 9-7, Tues-Fri 9-5, Sat 9-1

HARDINSBURG

P BRECKINRIDGE COUNTY PUBLIC LIBRARY, 308 Old Hwy 60, 40143. (Mail add: PO Box 248, 40143-0248), SAN 342-3816. Tel: 270-756-2323. FAX: 270-756-5634. Web Site: www.bcplibrary.org. *Dir,* Sarah Flood; E-mail: sarah_flood@bellsouth.net; *Asst Dir,* Position Currently Open; Staff 9.25 (MLS 2, Non-MLS 7.25)
Founded 1953. Pop 20,040; Circ 140,170
Jul 2013-Jun 2014 Income (Main Library and Branch(s)) $952,675. Mats Exp $124,883, Books $74,596, Per/Ser (Incl. Access Fees) $4,760, AV Mat $30,104, Electronic Ref Mat (Incl. Access Fees) $15,423. Sal $206,756 (Prof $84,543)
Library Holdings: Audiobooks 2,783; DVDs 5,868; e-books 73,901; Large Print Bks 6,000; Bk Titles 66,520; Per Subs 131
Automation Activity & Vendor Info: (Acquisitions) Evolve; (Cataloging) Evolve; (Circulation) Evolve; (Course Reserve) Evolve; (ILL) Evolve; (OPAC) Evolve; (Serials) Evolve
Database Vendor: EBSCOhost, Gale Cengage Learning, OCLC FirstSearch
Wireless access
Function: 24/7 Online cat, Accelerated reader prog, Activity rm, After school storytime, Bk club(s), Bks on CD, Children's prog, Computers for patron use, Copy machines, E-Reserves, Electronic databases & coll, Fax serv, Free DVD rentals, Handicapped accessible, Holiday prog, Home delivery & serv to Sr ctr & nursing homes, Homebound delivery serv, ILL available, Magazines, Online cat, Outreach serv, Photocopying/Printing, Preschool outreach, Prog for adults, Prog for children & young adult, Pub access computers, Scanner, Serves mentally handicapped consumers, Story hour, Study rm, Summer reading prog, Tax forms, Teen prog, Web-catalog, Wheelchair accessible

Special Services for the Blind - BiFolkal kits; Bks on cassette; Bks on CD; Large print bks; Large screen computer & software
Open Mon-Fri 8:30-6:30, Sat 9-2
Branches: 2
CLOVERPORT COMMUNITY, 101 Fourth St, Cloverport, 40111, SAN 342-3840. Tel: 270-788-3388, Ext 228. FAX: 270-788-6640. *Librn,* Bethaney Brent; Staff 1 (Non-MLS 1)
Function: Adult bk club, Bks on CD, Children's prog, Computers for patron use, Copy machines, Free DVD rentals, Handicapped accessible, ILL available, Prog for children & young adult, Story hour, Summer reading prog, Teen prog
Open Mon-Fri 12:30-5:30
IRVINGTON BRANCH, 212 E First St, Irvington, 40146. (Mail add: PO Box 381, Irvington, 40146-0381), SAN 342-3875. Tel: 270-547-7404. FAX: 270-547-7420. *Librn,* Angie Scott
Open Mon-Fri 11:30-4:30

HARLAN

P HARLAN COUNTY PUBLIC LIBRARIES*, Bryan W Whitfield Jr Public Library, 107 N Third St, 40831. SAN 342-3905. Tel: 606-573-5220. FAX: 606-573-5220. E-mail: harlanlibrary@gmail.com. Web Site: harlancountylibraries.org. *Dir,* Richard Haynes; Staff 2 (MLS 1, Non-MLS 1)
Founded 1968. Pop 32,095; Circ 78,454
Library Holdings: AV Mats 5,753; DVDs 1,000; Bk Vols 67,000; Per Subs 98; Talking Bks 2,562; Videos 400
Special Collections: Coal; Genealogy; Kentucky
Automation Activity & Vendor Info: (Cataloging) Innovative Interfaces, Inc; (Circulation) Innovative Interfaces, Inc; (OPAC) Innovative Interfaces, Inc
Wireless access
Open Mon, Wed, Fri & Sat 9-5, Tues & Thurs 9-8
Branches: 2
REBECCA CAUDILL PUBLIC LIBRARY, 310 W Main St, Cumberland, 40823, SAN 342-393X. Tel: 606-589-2409. FAX: 606-589-2409. *Br Mgr,* Luke Day
Open Mon, Wed & Fri 9-5, Tues & Thurs 9-7, Sat 9-2
EVARTS PUBLIC LIBRARY, 127A Yocum St, Evarts, 40828. Tel: 606-837-9703. FAX: 606-837-9703. *Br Mgr,* Lisa Adkisson
Founded 2011
Open Tues, Wed, Fri & Sat 9-5, Thurs 11-7
Bookmobiles: 1. Librn, Joanne Boggs. Bk vols 5,696

HARRODSBURG

S HARRODSBURG HISTORICAL SOCIETY*, Harrodsburg Mercer County Research Library, 220 S Chiles St, 40330-1631. (Mail add: PO Box 316, 40330-0316), SAN 375-1112. Tel: 859-734-5985. E-mail: library@harrodsburghistorical.org. Web Site: www.harrodsburghistorical.org. *In Charge,* Bonnie Moore
Library Holdings: Bk Vols 2,570; Per Subs 10
Special Collections: County Historical Archives
Open Tues 10-4, Wed-Sat 1-4

P MERCER COUNTY PUBLIC LIBRARY*, 109 W Lexington St, 40330-1542. SAN 306-2805. Tel: 859-734-3680. FAX: 859-734-7524. E-mail: webmistress@mcplib.info. Web Site: www.mcplib.info. *Dir,* Robin Singer Ison; E-mail: rsi@mcplib.info; *Acq Librn,* Carolyn Sue Patterson; E-mail: cwp@mcplib.info; *Tech Serv Coordr,* Natalie Cox Watts; Staff 16 (MLS 1, Non-MLS 15)
Founded 1970. Pop 20,817; Circ 177,838
Library Holdings: AV Mats 8,958; Bk Vols 62,557; Per Subs 121
Special Collections: Draper Manuscripts Coll; Joy's Toys Coll
Subject Interests: Genealogy, Kentucky
Automation Activity & Vendor Info: (Cataloging) Innovative Interfaces, Inc; (Circulation) Innovative Interfaces, Inc; (Course Reserve) Innovative Interfaces, Inc; (OPAC) Innovative Interfaces, Inc
Database Vendor: EBSCOhost, LearningExpress
Wireless access
Function: AV serv, Games & aids for the handicapped, Homebound delivery serv, ILL available, Magnifiers for reading, Photocopying/Printing, Prog for children & young adult, Ref serv available, Summer reading prog, Telephone ref, Wheelchair accessible
Open Mon-Thurs 9-7:30, Fri & Sat 9-5, Sun 1-5
Bookmobiles: 1

S SHAKER VILLAGE OF PLEASANT HILL MUSEUM LIBRARY*, 3501 Lexington Rd, 40330. SAN 373-4587. Tel: 859-734-5411. FAX: 859-734-7278. E-mail: library@shakervillageky.org. Web Site: www.shakervillageky.org. *Pres & Chief Exec Officer,* Maynard Crossland
Founded 1968
Library Holdings: Bk Vols 2,750; Spec Interest Per Sub 20
Special Collections: Shakers & the Village at Pleasant Hill, ephemera, mss, photographs
Subject Interests: 19th Century indust, Agr, Archit, Decorative art, Hist presv, Kentucky, Mus studies, Relig studies, Shakers
Function: Res libr
Restriction: Open by appt only

HARTFORD

P OHIO COUNTY PUBLIC LIBRARY*, 413 Main St, 42347. SAN 306-2813. Tel: 270-298-3790. FAX: 270-298-4214. E-mail: info@ohiocountypubliclibrary.org. Web Site: www.ohiocountypubliclibrary.org. *Dir,* Melissa Acquaviva
Founded 1967. Pop 23,500; Circ 130,250
Library Holdings: Bk Vols 59,100; Per Subs 85
Special Collections: Charles C Curran Coll, prints, VF; Ohio County History. Oral History
Automation Activity & Vendor Info: (Acquisitions) Follett Software
Wireless access
Open Mon & Tues 8:30-7:30, Wed-Fri 8:30-4:30, Sat 9-3

HAWESVILLE

P HANCOCK COUNTY PUBLIC LIBRARY*, 1210 Madison St, 42351. SAN 342-3964. Tel: 270-927-6760. FAX: 270-927-6847. E-mail: hcplky@gmail.com. Web Site: www.hcplky.org. *Dir,* Tina Snyder; *Ch,* Kendra Husk; *Teen Librn,* Britney White; *Circ Mgr,* Sherry Hagman; *Cataloger,* Tammy Sturgeon; E-mail: cataloger@hcplky.org
Founded 1954. Pop 9,000; Circ 60,000
Library Holdings: Bk Vols 32,700; Per Subs 63
Special Collections: Oral History
Automation Activity & Vendor Info: (Cataloging) TLC (The Library Corporation); (Circulation) TLC (The Library Corporation)
Open Mon-Wed & Fri 8:30-4:30, Thurs 8:30-7, Sat 8:30-12:00
Friends of the Library Group
Branches: 1
LEWISPORT BRANCH, 403 Second St, Lewisport, 42348, SAN 342-3999. Tel: 270-295-3765. *Br Mgr,* Kelley Richardson
Library Holdings: Bk Vols 5,000
Open Mon & Wed-Fri 8:30-4:30, Tues 8:30-7, Sat 8:30am-12:30pm
Friends of the Library Group
Bookmobiles: 1. Librn, Ann Jarboe

HAZARD

J HAZARD COMMUNITY & TECHNICAL COLLEGE LIBRARY, Stephens Library, One Community College Dr, 41701. SAN 306-2821. Tel: 606-487-3145. Toll Free Tel: 800-246-7521, Ext 73304. FAX: 606-439-1657. Web Site: www.hazard.kctcs.edu/en/Academics/Library.aspx. *Dir of Libr Serv,* Cathy Branson; E-mail: cathy.branson@kctcs.edu; *Ref Librn,* Patrick Davison; E-mail: patrick.davison@kctcs.edu; *Pub Serv,* Deirdre Campbell; E-mail: deirdre.campbell@kctcs.edu; *Tech Serv,* Marlene Conley; E-mail: marlene.conley@kctcs.edu; Staff 4 (MLS 2, Non-MLS 2)
Founded 1968. Highest Degree: Associate
Library Holdings: e-books 56,000; Bk Vols 42,249
Special Collections: US Document Depository
Subject Interests: Genealogy, Local hist
Automation Activity & Vendor Info: (Acquisitions) Ex Libris Group; (Cataloging) OCLC; (Circulation) Ex Libris Group; (Course Reserve) Ex Libris Group; (ILL) OCLC; (OPAC) Ex Libris Group
Database Vendor: EBSCOhost, Gale Cengage Learning
Wireless access
Partic in Federation of Kentucky Academic Libraries (FoKAL)
Open Mon-Thurs 8-5:30, Fri 8-4:30

P PERRY COUNTY PUBLIC LIBRARY*, 289 Black Gold Blvd, 41701. SAN 306-2848. Tel: 606-436-2475, 606-436-4747. FAX: 606-436-0191. E-mail: library@perrylib.org. Web Site: www.perrycountylibrary.org. *Dir,* Elaine Couch; E-mail: ecouch@perrylib.org; *Asst Dir,* Tina Williams; *Ad,* Leah Combs; *Ch,* Jennifer Young; *Circ Supvr,* Rayeanna Emery; *Tech Serv,* Rhonda Asher; Staff 2 (MLS 1, Non-MLS 1)
Founded 1970. Pop 28,751; Circ 188,142
Library Holdings: Audiobooks 3,387; DVDs 7,562; e-books 46,335; Electronic Media & Resources 8,559; Bk Vols 64,897; Per Subs 150
Special Collections: DVD Coll; Genealogy Coll; Large Print Coll; Music CD Coll; Newberry & Caldecott, Science Projects books
Automation Activity & Vendor Info: (ILL) OCLC FirstSearch
Database Vendor: EBSCOhost, Newsbank, Overdrive, Inc, World Book Online
Wireless access
Special Services for the Deaf - Bks on deafness & sign lang; Closed caption videos
Special Services for the Blind - Bks on CD; Copier with enlargement capabilities; Large print bks; PC for handicapped; Playaways (bks on MP3); Recorded bks; Screen enlargement software for people with visual disabilities; ZoomText magnification & reading software
Open Mon-Fri 9-7, Sat 8-4
Bookmobiles: 1. Librn, Terry Delph

M SOUTHEAST KENTUCKY AREA HEALTH EDUCATION CENTER*, Library Services, 100 Medical Center Dr, 41701-9429. SAN 370-5277. Tel: 606-439-6796. FAX: 606-439-6798. *Libr Spec,* Pansy Adams; E-mail: padams@arh.org
Founded 1985
Library Holdings: Bk Titles 2,000; Bk Vols 2,200; Per Subs 350
Special Collections: US Document Depository
Subject Interests: Med, Nursing, Rural health
Automation Activity & Vendor Info: (Cataloging) Marcive, Inc
Database Vendor: EBSCOhost, OCLC FirstSearch
Function: Doc delivery serv
Publications: Newsletter
Partic in Bluegrass Medical Libraries; Docline; Kentucky Library Network, Inc; Kentucky Medical Library Association; Nat AHEC Librns; Tennessee Health Science Library Association
Open Mon-Fri 8-4:30

HENDERSON

J HENDERSON COMMUNITY COLLEGE*, Hartfield Library, 2660 S Green St, 42420. SAN 306-2856. Tel: 270-831-9760. FAX: 270-831-9765. E-mail: hencclibrary@kctcs.edu. Web Site: www.henderson.kctcs.edu/library. *Asst Dean of Libr,* Michael Knecht; E-mail: mike.knecht@kctcs.edu; *Asst Dir/Ref Librn,* Kevin Reid; E-mail: kevin.reid@kctcs.edu; Staff 2 (MLS 2)
Founded 1960. Enrl 1,175; Fac 60
Library Holdings: Bk Vols 27,624; Per Subs 186
Automation Activity & Vendor Info: (Acquisitions) Ex Libris Group; (Cataloging) Ex Libris Group; (Circulation) Ex Libris Group; (Course Reserve) Ex Libris Group; (OPAC) Ex Libris Group
Database Vendor: EBSCOhost, Gale Cengage Learning, Newsbank, ProQuest
Partic in Kentucky Library Network, Inc; Lyrasis
Open Mon-Thurs 7:30am-7pm, Fri 7:30-4:30

P HENDERSON COUNTY PUBLIC LIBRARY*, 101 S Main St, 42420-3599. SAN 306-2864. Tel: 270-826-3712. FAX: 270-827-4226. Web Site: www.hcpl.org. *Dir,* Essy Day; Staff 10 (MLS 4, Non-MLS 6)
Founded 1904. Pop 45,000; Circ 310,207
Jul 2006-Jun 2007 Income $1,399,256, State $48,924, Locally Generated Income $1,350,332. Mats Exp $197,102, Books $116,677, Per/Ser (Incl. Access Fees) $5,710, AV Mat $33,694, Electronic Ref Mat (Incl. Access Fees) $41,021. Sal $808,658
Library Holdings: AV Mats 18,006; CDs 1,692; DVDs 4,008; Large Print Bks 7,328; Bk Vols 114,000; Per Subs 60; Talking Bks 5,586; Videos 6,660
Automation Activity & Vendor Info: (Cataloging) Innovative Interfaces, Inc; (Circulation) Innovative Interfaces, Inc; (OPAC) Innovative Interfaces, Inc
Wireless access
Partic in Kentucky Library Network, Inc; Lyrasis; OCLC Online Computer Library Center, Inc
Open Mon-Thurs 9-8, Fri & Sat 9-5, Sun 1:30-5
Friends of the Library Group
Bookmobiles: 1. Librn, Cheryl Mathias. Bk vols 3478

HIGHLAND HEIGHTS

C NORTHERN KENTUCKY UNIVERSITY, W Frank Steely Library, University Dr, 41099. (Mail add: Nunn Dr, 41099), SAN 342-4022. Tel: 859-572-5456. Circulation Tel: 859-572-5457. Interlibrary Loan Service Tel: 859-572-6365. Automation Services Tel: 859-572-6309. FAX: 859-572-5390. Web Site: library.nku.edu. *Assoc Provost,* Arne J Almquist, PhD; Tel: 859-572-5483, Fax: 859-572-6181, E-mail: almquista@nku.edu; *Head, Access Serv,* Craig Person; Tel: 859-572-6167, E-mail: personc1@nku.edu; *Head, Res & Instrul Serv,* Threasa Wesley; Tel: 859-572-5721, E-mail: wesley@nku.edu; *Head, Tech Serv, Librn,* Lois Schultz; Tel: 859-572-5275, E-mail: schultz@nku.edu; *Librn, Web Coordr,* Michael Providenti; Tel: 859-572-5936, E-mail: providenti@nku.edu; *Grants Coordr, Librn,* Laura Sullivan; Tel: 859-572-5724, E-mail: sullivanl@nku.edu; *Cat Librn,* Wendy Wood; Tel: 859-572-5480, E-mail: woodw@nku.edu; *Govt Doc Librn,* Philip Yannarella; Tel: 859-572-5455, E-mail: yannarella@nku.edu; *Intellectual Property Librn,* John Schlipp; Tel: 859-572-5723; *Res & Instruction Librn,* Mary Chesnut; Tel: 859-572-5826, E-mail: chesnutm@nku.edu; *Res & Instruction Librn,* Jennifer Smith, PhD; Tel: 859-572-6620, E-mail: smithjen@nku.edu; *SourceFinder Librn,* Justine Burchell; Tel: 859-572-7621, E-mail: burchellj1@nku.edu; *Syst Librn,* Mike Wells; Tel: 859-572-6026, E-mail: wellsm6@nku.edu; *Tech Serv Librn,* Donna Smith; Tel: 859-572-6140, E-mail: smithd@nku.edu; *Syst Mgr,* Perry Bratcher; E-mail: bratcher@nku.edu; *Coordr, Bachelor of Libr Info Prog,* Leslie Hammann; Tel: 859-572-6157, E-mail: hammannl1@nku.edu; *Acq,* Cheryl Edelen; *Univ Archivist,* Lois Hamill; Tel: 859-572-5863, E-mail: hamilll1@nku.edu; Staff 42 (MLS 22, Non-MLS 20)
Founded 1968. Enrl 15,816; Fac 530; Highest Degree: Doctorate
Jul 2012-Jun 2013. Mats Exp $1,399,517, Books $147,856, Per/Ser (Incl. Access Fees) $1,207,254, AV Mat $41,407, Presv $3,000. Sal $2,193,627 (Prof $1,090,886)
Library Holdings: AV Mats 19,759; CDs 5,328; e-books 37,528; e-journals 4,169; Microforms 599,034; Music Scores 9,992; Bk Titles 677,502; Bk Vols 773,658; Per Subs 4,093; Videos 5,971
Special Collections: Confederate Imprints; Kentucky One Thousand, ultra fiche; Library of American Civilization; Library of American Literature; Ohio River Materials. US Document Depository
Subject Interests: Kentucky
Automation Activity & Vendor Info: (Acquisitions) Ex Libris Group; (Cataloging) Ex Libris Group; (Circulation) Ex Libris Group; (Course Reserve) Blackboard Inc; (ILL) OCLC; (OPAC) Ex Libris Group; (Serials) EBSCO Online
Database Vendor: ARTstor, Baker & Taylor, Checkpoint Systems, Inc, Cinahl, CredoReference, EBSCOhost, Elsevier, Gale Cengage Learning, JSTOR, LexisNexis, Marcive, Inc, Medianet, Mergent Online, Newsbank, OCLC FirstSearch, OCLC WorldShare Interlibrary Loan, OVID Technologies, Project MUSE, ProQuest, PubMed, RefWorks, Safari Books Online, ScienceDirect, Wiley, Wilson - Wilson Web
Wireless access
Function: Archival coll, Art exhibits, Audio & video playback equip for onsite use, Computers for patron use, Copy machines, Distance learning, Doc delivery serv, e-mail & chat, E-Reserves, Electronic databases & coll, Exhibits, Govt ref serv, ILL available, Online cat, Online info literacy tutorials on the web & in blackboard, Online ref, Orientations, Outreach serv, Pub access computers, Ref serv in person, Scanner, Tax forms, Telephone ref, VHS videos, Video lending libr, Wheelchair accessible
Partic in Federation of Kentucky Academic Libraries (FoKAL); State Assisted Academic Library Council of Kentucky
Special Services for the Deaf - Assistive tech
Special Services for the Blind - Computer with voice synthesizer for visually impaired persons; PC for handicapped; Screen enlargement software for people with visual disabilities; Talking bks
Open Mon-Thurs 8am-2am, Fri 8-5:30, Sat 11-5, Sun 12:30-2am
Friends of the Library Group

CL NORTHERN KENTUCKY UNIVERSITY*, Salmon P Chase College of Law Library, Nunn Dr, 41099. SAN 306-2368. Tel: 859-572-5394. Circulation Tel: 859-572-6030. Reference Tel: 859-572-6484. Administration Tel: 859-572-5714. FAX: 859-572-6529, 859-572-6664. Web Site: chaselaw.nku.edu/library/index.php. *Assoc Dean, Law Libr Serv & Info Tech,* Michael Whiteman; Tel: 859-572-5717, E-mail: whiteman@nku.edu; *Assoc Dir,* Thomas Heard; Tel: 859-572-6482, E-mail: heard@nku.edu; *Head, Pub Serv,* Donna S Bennett; Tel: 859-572-5715, E-mail: dbennett@nku.edu; *Head, Ser Acq,* Jennifer Mart-Rice; Tel: 859-572-5712, E-mail: ricej2@nku.edu; *Fac Serv Librn,* Carol Bredemeyer; Tel: 859-572-5395, E-mail: bredemeyer@nku.edu; *Instrul Serv Librn, Outreach Serv Librn,* Carol Furnish; Tel: 859-572-5396, E-mail: furnish@nku.edu; *Res & Instruction Librn,* Donna Michelle Spears; Tel: 859-572-6035, E-mail: spearsd2@nku.edu; *Online Serv, Res Serv,* Jane Underwood; Tel: 859-572-6485. Staff 16 (MLS 7, Non-MLS 9)
Enrl 400; Fac 34; Highest Degree: Doctorate
Library Holdings: Bk Titles 85,000; Bk Vols 340,000; Per Subs 2,085
Automation Activity & Vendor Info: (Acquisitions) Ex Libris Group; (Cataloging) Ex Libris Group; (Circulation) Ex Libris Group; (OPAC) Ex Libris Group; (Serials) Ex Libris Group
Database Vendor: HeinOnline, JSTOR, LexisNexis, OCLC WorldShare Interlibrary Loan, ProQuest, Westlaw, Wilson - Wilson Web
Wireless access
Publications: Law Library Handbook
Partic in OCLC Online Computer Library Center, Inc
Open Mon-Thurs 8am-10pm, Fri 8-7, Sat 9-5, Sun 2-6

HINDMAN

P KNOTT COUNTY PUBLIC LIBRARY*, 238 Hwy 160 S, 41822. (Mail add: PO Box 667, 41822-0667), SAN 306-2880. Tel: 606-785-5412. FAX: 606-785-4299. E-mail: kclib9@hotmail.com. Web Site: www.knottcountylibrary.com. *Librn,* Tammie Owens
Pop 17,906; Circ 38,856
Library Holdings: Bk Vols 25,000; Per Subs 44
Special Collections: Appalachian; Genealogy
Automation Activity & Vendor Info: (Cataloging) TLC (The Library Corporation); (Circulation) TLC (The Library Corporation)
Open Mon-Fri 9-5
Friends of the Library Group
Bookmobiles: 1. Librn, Audrey Stone

HODGENVILLE

P LARUE COUNTY PUBLIC LIBRARY*, Lincoln Memorial Library, 201 S Lincoln Blvd, 42748. SAN 306-2899. Tel: 270-358-3851. FAX: 270-358-8647. E-mail: info@laruelibrary.org. Web Site: laruelibrary.org. *Dir,* Dana Jolley; *Ch Serv,* Katie Wheatley

Founded 1917. Pop 13,343; Circ 65,000
Library Holdings: AV Mats 2,400; Bks on Deafness & Sign Lang 45; CDs 200; DVDs 150; Large Print Bks 1,500; Music Scores 30; Bk Titles 41,527; Bk Vols 49,000; Per Subs 62; Talking Bks 850; Videos 900
Special Collections: Lincoln Coll. Municipal Document Depository; Oral History; State Document Depository
Subject Interests: Abraham Lincoln
Automation Activity & Vendor Info: (Cataloging) Book Systems; (Circulation) Book Systems; (Course Reserve) Book Systems; (ILL) OCLC; (OPAC) Book Systems; (Serials) OCLC FirstSearch
Special Services for the Blind - Bks on cassette
Open Mon, Wed & Fri 8-5:30, Tues & Thurs 8-7, Sat 9-2
Bookmobiles: 1. Librn, LaDana Jolly

S ABRAHAM LINCOLN BIRTHPLACE NATIONAL HISTORIC SITE LIBRARY*, 2995 Lincoln Farm Rd, 42748. SAN 370-2790. Tel: 270-358-3137, 270-358-3138. FAX: 270-358-3874. Web Site: www.nps.gov/abli. *In Charge,* Jennie Jones
Library Holdings: Bk Vols 717
Restriction: Restricted pub use

HOPKINSVILLE

P HOPKINSVILLE-CHRISTIAN COUNTY PUBLIC LIBRARY, 1101 Bethel St, 42240. SAN 306-2902. Tel: 270-887-4262. FAX: 270-887-4264. E-mail: director@hccpl.org. Web Site: hccpl.org. *Dir,* Jacqueline Saturley; E-mail: director@hccpl.org; *Asst Dir,* Martha White; Staff 3 (MLS 2, Non-MLS 1)
Founded 1874. Pop 69,502; Circ 179,498
Library Holdings: Bk Titles 99,743; Per Subs 104
Special Collections: Early Literacy; McCarroll Genealogy Coll
Automation Activity & Vendor Info: (Acquisitions) SirsiDynix; (Cataloging) SirsiDynix; (Circulation) SirsiDynix; (OPAC) SirsiDynix
Database Vendor: EBSCOhost, ProQuest, TumbleBookLibrary
Wireless access
Open Mon, Wed & Fri 9-6, Tues & Thurs 10-7, Sat 9-5

J HOPKINSVILLE COMMUNITY COLLEGE LIBRARY, 720 North Dr, 42240. (Mail add: PO Box 2100, 42241-2100), SAN 306-2910. Tel: 270-707-3760. Circulation Tel: 270-707-3764. Interlibrary Loan Service Tel: 270-707-3763. FAX: 270-885-6048. Web Site: www.hopkinsville.kctcs.edu/Academics/Library.aspx. *Dir,* Ann Nichols; E-mail: ann.nichols@kctcs.edu; *Cat,* Cynthia Atkins; E-mail: cynthia.atkins@kctcs.edu; Staff 5 (MLS 2, Non-MLS 3)
Founded 1965. Enrl 3,000; Fac 75; Highest Degree: Associate
Library Holdings: DVDs 955; e-books 43,713; Bk Vols 48,791; Per Subs 47
Special Collections: Kentucky Coll
Automation Activity & Vendor Info: (Cataloging) Ex Libris Group; (Circulation) Ex Libris Group; (Course Reserve) Ex Libris Group; (OPAC) Ex Libris Group
Database Vendor: 3M Library Systems, Alexander Street Press, CQ Press, CredoReference, EBSCOhost, Facts on File, H W Wilson, Hoovers, infoUSA, LearningExpress, OCLC FirstSearch, Oxford Communications, ProQuest, ReferenceUSA
Wireless access
Open Mon-Thurs 7:30-6:30, Fri 7:30-4:30

M WESTERN STATE HOSPITAL*, Professional Library, 2400 Russellville Rd, 42241. (Mail add: PO Box 2200, 42241-2200), SAN 306-2929. Tel: 270-889-6025. FAX: 270-885-5257. *Dir,* Steve Wiggins; Tel: 270-889-6025, Ext 436; *Librn,* Lindy Stumpff
Founded 1940
Library Holdings: Bk Titles 2,000
Subject Interests: Nursing, Psychiat, Soc serv (soc work)
Publications: Hospital Newsletter
Partic in Ky-Ohio-Mich Regional Med Libr
Open Mon-Fri 8:30-4:30
Restriction: Staff use only

HORSE CAVE

P HORSE CAVE FREE PUBLIC LIBRARY*, 111 Higbee St, 42749-1110. SAN 306-2937. Tel: 270-786-1130. FAX: 270-786-1131. *Dir,* Denise Ballard; *Asst Librn,* Doris Jones
Founded 1912. Pop 8,000; Circ 13,200
Library Holdings: Bk Vols 10,500; Per Subs 30
Special Collections: Kentucky Coll
Open Mon-Fri 8:30-5

HYDEN

C FRONTIER NURSING UNIVERSITY*, Alice E Whitman Memorial Library, 195 School St, 41749. (Mail add: PO Box 528, 41749-0528). Tel: 606-672-2312. FAX: 606-672-3779. E-mail: librarian@frontier.edu. Web Site: www.frontier.edu/student-services/library. *Dir of Libr Serv,* Billie Anne Gebb; *Info Serv Librn,* Zach Young
Library Holdings: e-journals 60; Bk Vols 1,700
Database Vendor: Medline
Wireless access
Open Mon-Fri 8-5

P LESLIE COUNTY PUBLIC LIBRARY*, 22065 Main St, 41749. (Mail add: PO Box 498, 41749-0498), SAN 306-2945. Tel: 606-672-2460. FAX: 606-672-4213. E-mail: books@leslielibrary.com. Web Site: www.leslielibrary.com. *Dir,* Clifford Hamilton; *Asst Dir,* Katherine Hamilton; *Librn,* Mason Collett; *Ch,* Leona Hamrick
Founded 1963. Pop 11,000; Circ 148,880
Library Holdings: Bk Vols 37,000; Per Subs 85
Special Collections: Genealogy (Leslie County Coll); Kentucky Coll
Automation Activity & Vendor Info: (Cataloging) TLC (The Library Corporation); (Circulation) TLC (The Library Corporation); (OPAC) TLC (The Library Corporation)
Wireless access
Special Services for the Deaf - Bks on deafness & sign lang; High interest/low vocabulary bks
Open Mon, Wed & Fri 8-5, Tues & Thurs 8-8, Sat 8-2
Bookmobiles: 1. Librn, Keith Collett

INEZ

P MARTIN COUNTY PUBLIC LIBRARY*, Central Library, 180 E Main St, 41224. (Mail add: PO Box 1318, 41224-1318). Tel: 606-298-7766. FAX: 606-298-0680. Web Site: www.martincolibrary.com. *Exec Dir,* Drema Jude
Jul 2009-Jun 2010 Income $496,200. Mats Exp $34,500, Books $22,000, Per/Ser (Incl. Access Fees) $1,000, AV Mat $11,500. Sal $166,200
Library Holdings: Bk Vols 22,966; Per Subs 25
Automation Activity & Vendor Info: (Acquisitions) TLC (The Library Corporation); (Cataloging) TLC (The Library Corporation); (Circulation) TLC (The Library Corporation); (Course Reserve) TLC (The Library Corporation); (ILL) TLC (The Library Corporation); (Media Booking) TLC (The Library Corporation); (OPAC) TLC (The Library Corporation); (Serials) TLC (The Library Corporation)
Database Vendor: OCLC FirstSearch
Wireless access
Open Mon, Wed & Fri 9-5, Tues & Thurs 9-7, Sat 9-12
Branches: 1
RUFUS M REED PUBLIC, 1442 River Front Rd, Lovely, 41231. (Mail add: PO Box 359, Lovely, 41231-0359). Tel: 606-395-6500. FAX: 606-395-6001. *Br Mgr,* Angela Begley
Library Holdings: Bk Vols 18,000; Per Subs 20
Open Mon-Wed & Fri 10-5, Thurs 10-7, Sat 9-12

IRVINE

P ESTILL COUNTY PUBLIC LIBRARY*, 246 Main St, 40336-1026. SAN 306-2953. Tel: 606-723-3030. FAX: 606-726-9971. E-mail: estillcolibrary@gmail.com. Web Site: www2.youseemore.com/estill. *Dir,* Glenn Kahmann; *Ch,* Virginia Owens; *Libr Asst,* Raymond Chaney
Founded 1969. Pop 14,500; Circ 81,700
Library Holdings: Bk Vols 36,500; Per Subs 86
Special Collections: Kentucky Coll
Automation Activity & Vendor Info: (Cataloging) TLC (The Library Corporation); (Circulation) TLC (The Library Corporation); (OPAC) TLC (The Library Corporation)
Database Vendor: Gale Cengage Learning, Overdrive, Inc
Publications: Bibliographies; Booklists; Newsletter
Open Mon, Tues & Fri 9-8, Wed 9-5, Thurs 12-8, Sat 9-2

JACKSON

P BREATHITT COUNTY PUBLIC LIBRARY*, 1024 College Ave, 41339. SAN 306-2961. Tel: 606-666-5541. FAX: 606-666-8166. E-mail: breathitt@bellsouth.net. Web Site: www.breathittcountylibrary.com. *Dir,* Stephen Bowling; *Asst Librn,* Susan Pugh
Founded 1967. Pop 17,000
Library Holdings: Bk Vols 52,000; Per Subs 50
Special Collections: Genealogical Research Library; History & Census Records (Breathitt and surrounding counties); Surname Information Files
Automation Activity & Vendor Info: (Acquisitions) Follett Software; (Cataloging) Follett Software; (Circulation) Follett Software; (Course Reserve) Follett Software; (ILL) Follett Software; (Media Booking) Follett Software; (OPAC) Follett Software; (Serials) Follett Software
Database Vendor: OCLC FirstSearch
Partic in Kentucky Library Network, Inc
Open Mon, Wed & Fri 8-5, Tues & Thurs 8-7, Sat 9-4

J HAZARD COMMUNITY & TECHNICAL COLLEGE, Lees College Campus Library, 601 Jefferson Ave, 41339. SAN 306-297X. Tel: 606-666-7521. Circulation Tel: 606-666-7521, Ext 73568. Toll Free Tel:

800-246-7521, Ext 73568. FAX: 606-487-3555. Web Site: www.hazard.kctcs.edu/en/Academics/Library.aspx. *Dir of Libr Serv,* Cathy Branson; E-mail: cathy.branson@kctcs.edu; *Pub Serv,* Donna Collins; *Tech Serv,* Barbara E Collins-Watts; E-mail: donna.collins@kctcs.edu; Staff 1 (MLS 1)
Founded 1883
Library Holdings: e-books 56,000; Bk Vols 50,000
Special Collections: Appalachia & Kentuckiana, bks, flm, cassettes & per. Oral History
Subject Interests: Local hist, Relig
Automation Activity & Vendor Info: (Cataloging) OCLC; (Circulation) Ex Libris Group; (ILL) OCLC; (OPAC) Ex Libris Group
Database Vendor: Cinahl, EBSCOhost, Gale Cengage Learning, Medline, OCLC FirstSearch, ProQuest
Wireless access
Partic in Federation of Kentucky Academic Libraries (FoKAL)
Open Mon-Thurs 8-5:30, Fri 8-4:30

R KENTUCKY MOUNTAIN BIBLE COLLEGE, Gibson Library, 855 Hwy 541, 41339-9433. SAN 306-4239. Tel: 606-693-5000. Circulation Tel: 606-693-5000, Ext 200. FAX: 606-693-4884. Web Site: www.kmbc.edu. *Librn,* Patricia Bowen; E-mail: pbowen@kmbc.edu; Staff 1 (MLS 1)
Founded 1931. Enrl 72; Fac 17; Highest Degree: Bachelor
Library Holdings: Bk Vols 28,700; Per Subs 191
Special Collections: Holiness, Missionary, Religious Biography
Wireless access
Open Mon-Thurs 7:30am-9pm, Fri 7:30-5, Sat 2-4

JAMESTOWN

P RUSSELL COUNTY PUBLIC LIBRARY, 94 N Main St, 42629. SAN 306-2988. Tel: 270-343-3545. FAX: 270-343-2019. Web Site: www.russellcountylibrary.com. *Dir,* Lindsey B Westerfield; Tel: 270-343-1691, E-mail: director@russellcountylibrary.com; *Br Librn,* Mildred Lawson; Tel: 270-866-5200; *Ch,* Fillamay Cowell; *Ref Librn,* Glenda York; Tel: 270-343-1692
Founded 1967. Pop 17,000; Circ 72,359
Library Holdings: Bk Vols 49,371; Per Subs 56
Special Collections: Westerns
Subject Interests: Easy bks, Genealogy, Juv, Kentucky, Romance langs, Sci fict, Young adult lit
Automation Activity & Vendor Info: (Circulation) TLC (The Library Corporation)
Database Vendor: OCLC FirstSearch
Wireless access
Partic in Keystone Library Network
Open Mon-Fri 8-4:30, Sat 12-Noon
Branches: 1
RUSSELL SPRINGS BRANCH, 512 Main St, Russell Springs, 42642-4356. (Mail add: PO Box 244, Russell Springs, 42642-0244). Tel: 270-866-5200. FAX: 270-866-5201. *Br Librn,* Mildred Lawson; *Libr Asst,* Kim Burchett
Open Mon, Wed-Fri 8-4:30, Tues 11-7

LA GRANGE

S KENTUCKY STATE REFORMATORY LIBRARY*, 3001 W Hwy 146, 40032. SAN 306-3011. Tel: 502-222-9441. FAX: 502-222-9022. *Librn,* Linda Goble; Staff 1 (MLS 1)
Founded 1938
Library Holdings: Audiobooks 148; CDs 1,675; DVDs 407; High Interest/Low Vocabulary Bk Vols 50; Large Print Bks 75; Music Scores 275; Bk Vols 23,100; Per Subs 128
Subject Interests: Fiction
Automation Activity & Vendor Info: (ILL) OCLC
Wireless access
Friends of the Library Group

S LUTHER LUCKETT CORRECTIONAL COMPLEX LIBRARY*, 1612 Dawkins Rd, 40031. (Mail add: PO Box 6, 40031-0006). Tel: 502-222-0363, Ext 3580.
Library Holdings: Bk Vols 9,000; Per Subs 125
Automation Activity & Vendor Info: (Cataloging) LiBRARYSOFT; (Circulation) LiBRARYSOFT
Database Vendor: Westlaw
Partic in OCLC Online Computer Library Center, Inc

P OLDHAM COUNTY PUBLIC LIBRARY*, 308 Yager Ave, 40031. SAN 320-1902. Tel: 502-222-9713. FAX: 502-222-1141. Web Site: www.oldhampl.org. *Dir,* Susan Eubank; Tel: 502-222-9713, Ext 304; *Asst Dir,* Mary Mielczarek; E-mail: marym@oldhampl.org; Staff 39 (MLS 7, Non-MLS 32)
Founded 1968. Pop 55,000; Circ 453,725
Library Holdings: AV Mats 116,008; Bk Vols 96,507; Per Subs 216
Special Collections: Census Coll; Genealogy Coll, bks & films; Kentucky Coll; Large Type Coll; Video Cassette Coll
Automation Activity & Vendor Info: (Cataloging) TLC (The Library Corporation); (Circulation) TLC (The Library Corporation); (OPAC) TLC (The Library Corporation)
Wireless access
Partic in Lyrasis
Open Mon-Thurs 9:30-8, Fri & Sat 9:30-5
Friends of the Library Group
Branches: 2
MAHAN OLDHAM COUNTY PUBLIC, 12505 Harmony Landing Lane, Goshen, 40026. (Mail add: PO Box 145, Goshen, 40026-0145), SAN 377-7324. Tel: 502-228-1852. FAX: 502-228-1852. *Br Mgr,* Rhonda Burks; E-mail: rhondab@oldhampl.org
Automation Activity & Vendor Info: (Acquisitions) TLC (The Library Corporation); (Course Reserve) TLC (The Library Corporation); (ILL) TLC (The Library Corporation); (Media Booking) TLC (The Library Corporation); (Serials) TLC (The Library Corporation)
Open Mon-Thurs 10-8, Fri & Sat 10-5
Friends of the Library Group
SOUTH OLDHAM, 6720 W Hwy 146, Crestwood, 40014. (Mail add: PO Box 365, Crestwood, 40014-0365), SAN 377-7340. Tel: 502-241-1108. FAX: 502-241-1108. *Br Mgr,* Vicki Marsh; E-mail: vmarsh@oldhampl.org
Open Mon-Thurs 10-8, Fri & Sat 10-5

LANCASTER

P GARRARD COUNTY PUBLIC LIBRARY*, 101 Lexington St, 40444. SAN 306-302X. Tel: 859-792-3424. FAX: 859-792-2366. E-mail: garrardlibrary@gmail.com. Web Site: garrardpublib.state.ky.us. *Dir,* Laura McWilliams
Pop 10,853; Circ 84,000
Library Holdings: Bk Vols 30,000; Per Subs 40
Automation Activity & Vendor Info: (Acquisitions) AmLib Library Management System; (Cataloging) AmLib Library Management System; (Circulation) AmLib Library Management System; (Course Reserve) AmLib Library Management System; (ILL) AmLib Library Management System; (Media Booking) AmLib Library Management System; (OPAC) AmLib Library Management System; (Serials) AmLib Library Management System
Open Mon, Wed-Fri 9-5, Tues 9-8, Sat 9-3
Bookmobiles: 1

LAWRENCEBURG

P ANDERSON COUNTY PUBLIC LIBRARY*, 114 N Main St, 40342. SAN 306-3038. Tel: 502-839-6420. FAX: 502-839-7243. Web Site: www.andersonpubliclibrary.org. *Dir,* Pamella Mullins; E-mail: pmullins@andersonpubliclibrary.org; *Asst Dir,* Pam Marks; E-mail: pmarks@andersonpubliclibrary.org; *Outreach Librn,* Deborah Perry; *Youth Serv Librn,* Sherry Noon; Staff 3 (MLS 1, Non-MLS 2)
Founded 1908. Pop 20,000; Circ 60,000
Library Holdings: Bk Titles 45,000; Bk Vols 55,700; Per Subs 81
Automation Activity & Vendor Info: (Cataloging) Innovative Interfaces, Inc; (Circulation) Innovative Interfaces, Inc
Open Mon-Fri 9-8, Sat 9-4, Sun 1-5
Friends of the Library Group

LEBANON

P MARION COUNTY PUBLIC LIBRARY*, 201 E Main St, 40033-1133. SAN 306-3046. Tel: 270-692-4698. FAX: 270-692-9555. E-mail: marioncountypubliclibrary@yahoo.com. Web Site: www.marioncopublic.org. *Dir,* Amy Morgeson; *Asst Dir,* Sandy Nunley; *Ch,* Patty May Brown; *Circ Librn,* Wanda Hazelwood; *Genealogy Librn, Ref Librn,* Jama Watts; *Outreach Librn,* Amanda Morgeson; *Per Librn,* Patty May Brown; *YA Librn,* Eleane Rahn; *Cataloger,* Terry Brockman; *Cataloger,* Angela Selter; Staff 6 (Non-MLS 6)
Founded 1966. Pop 18,812; Circ 100,186
Library Holdings: AV Mats 4,058; DVDs 1,200; Large Print Bks 1,234; Bk Titles 46,383; Per Subs 90; Talking Bks 1,149; Videos 700
Special Collections: Local Genealogy Coll
Subject Interests: Genealogy, Hist, Kentucky
Automation Activity & Vendor Info: (Cataloging) Follett Software; (Circulation) Follett Software; (ILL) OCLC; (OPAC) Follett Software
Wireless access
Special Services for the Blind - Bks on cassette; Bks on CD; Talking bks
Open Mon, Wed & Fri 9-5:30, Tues & Thurs 9-7, Sat 9-3
Friends of the Library Group
Bookmobiles: 1. Librn, Flora Anne Foster

LEITCHFIELD

P GRAYSON COUNTY PUBLIC LIBRARY*, 130 E Market St, 42754-1439. SAN 325-187X. Tel: 270-259-5455. FAX: 270-259-4552. Web Site: www.graysoncountylibrary.org. *Dir,* Lisa Jones; E-mail: jones@graysoncountylibrary.org; *Asst Dir,* Melissa Decker; E-mail: decker@graysoncountylibrary.org; *Genealogy & Per,* Bettie Arndell; *ILL,* Kevin Small; E-mail: small@graysoncountylibrary.org; *Youth Serv,* Laura Lindsey; E-mail: lindsey@graysoncountylibrary.org
Founded 1976. Pop 25,746; Circ 111,219
Library Holdings: AV Mats 1,894; e-books 56,752; Large Print Bks 1,615; Bk Titles 7,067; Bk Vols 40,000; Per Subs 60; Talking Bks 501; Videos 650
Subject Interests: Genealogy, Kentucky, Local hist
Automation Activity & Vendor Info: (Cataloging) TLC (The Library Corporation); (Circulation) TLC (The Library Corporation); (OPAC) TLC (The Library Corporation)
Database Vendor: EBSCOhost, OCLC FirstSearch
Wireless access
Function: ILL available, Photocopying/Printing, Telephone ref
Partic in OCLC Online Computer Library Center, Inc; Soline
Open Mon & Thurs 9-7, Tues, Wed, Fri & Sat 9-5
Friends of the Library Group
Bookmobiles: 1. Librn, Michelle Childress

LEXINGTON

L BINGHAM GREENEBAUM DOLL LLP*, Law Library, 300 W Vine St, Ste 1100, 40507-1622. SAN 323-7222. Tel: 859-288-4717. FAX: 859-255-2742. E-mail: dlf@gdm.com. Web Site: www.bgdlegal.com. *Librn,* Lynn Fogle; E-mail: dlf@gdm.com
Library Holdings: Bk Titles 3,000; Bk Vols 10,000; Per Subs 150
Open Mon-Fri 9-5

S BLACKBURN CORRECTIONAL COMPLEX LIBRARY*, 3111 Spurn Rd, 40511. Tel: 859-246-2366. FAX: 859-246-2376. *Librn,* Art Gorman
Library Holdings: Bk Vols 4,000; Per Subs 55
Database Vendor: Westlaw

J BLUEGRASS COMMUNITY & TECHNICAL COLLEGE, Learning Resource Center, Oswald Bldg, 470 Cooper Dr, 40506-0235. SAN 306-3151. Tel: 859-246-6380. Interlibrary Loan Service Tel: 859-246-6388. FAX: 859-246-4675. Web Site: bluegrass.kctcs.edu/library.aspx. *Libr Dir,* Steve Stone; Tel: 859-246-6387, E-mail: steve.stone@kctcs.edu; *Electronic Res Librn,* Maureen Cropper; Tel: 859-246-6394, E-mail: maureen.cropper@kctcs.edu; *Pub Serv Librn, Cooper Libr,* Jennifer Link; Tel: 859 246-6528, E-mail: jennifer.link@kctcs.edu; *Pub Serv Librn, Newton Learning Commons,* Terry Buckner; Tel: 859-246-6397, E-mail: terry.buckner@kctcs.edu; *Tech Serv Librn,* Kathleen Richardson; Tel: 859-246-6386, E-mail: kathleen.richardson@kctcs.edu; *Circ Supvr,* Meagan Brock; Staff 6.5 (MLS 5, Non-MLS 1.5)
Founded 1976. Enrl 8,775; Fac 654; Highest Degree: Associate
Library Holdings: AV Mats 4,052; Bk Titles 40,636; Bk Vols 42,823; Per Subs 165
Automation Activity & Vendor Info: (Acquisitions) Ex Libris Group; (Cataloging) Ex Libris Group; (Circulation) Ex Libris Group; (Course Reserve) Ex Libris Group; (ILL) OCLC FirstSearch; (OPAC) Ex Libris Group
Database Vendor: ARTstor, Booklist Online, ebrary, EBSCOhost, Gale Cengage Learning, JSTOR, Newsbank, OCLC FirstSearch, Oxford Online, SerialsSolutions
Wireless access
Function: Art exhibits, Audio & video playback equip for onsite use, AV serv, Bks on CD, CD-ROM, Computers for patron use, Copy machines, Distance learning, e-mail serv, E-Reserves, Electronic databases & coll, Equip loans & repairs, Free DVD rentals, Handicapped accessible, ILL available, Magnifiers for reading, Mail & tel request accepted, Music CDs, Online cat, Online info literacy tutorials on the web & in blackboard, Online ref, Online searches, Orientations, Ref serv available, Scanner, VHS videos
Partic in Lyrasis; OCLC Online Computer Library Center, Inc

S CARRIAGE MUSEUM OF AMERICA LIBRARY, 3915 Jay Trump Rd, 40511. (Mail add: 4089 Iron Works Pkwy, 40511), SAN 372-7823. Tel: 859-259-2933. FAX: 859-231-0973. E-mail: cmalibrary@windstream.net. Web Site: www.carriagemuseumlibrary.org. *Dir, Operations,* Mindy Groff; Staff 1 (MLS 1)
Founded 1978
Library Holdings: Bk Titles 3,000
Special Collections: Ken Sowles Coll; Paul Downing Coll; Richard B Harrington Coll; Thomas Ryder Coll
Subject Interests: Horse drawn transportation
Function: Archival coll, Online searches, Ref serv available
Restriction: Non-circulating, Open by appt only
Friends of the Library Group

M CENTRAL BAPTIST HOSPITAL LIBRARY*, 1740 Nicholasville Rd, 40503. Tel: 859-260-6297. FAX: 859-260-6442. *Dir,* Lonnie Wright; E-mail: lwright@bhsi.com; *Librn,* Carla Townsend; E-mail: carla.townsend@bhsi.com
Founded 1954
Library Holdings: Bks on Deafness & Sign Lang 10; Bk Titles 2,750; Bk Vols 3,000; Per Subs 275
Database Vendor: Agricola, Cinahl, CISTI Source, DynaMed, EBSCO Information Services, EBSCOhost, OCLC FirstSearch, PubMed, UpToDate
Wireless access
Open Mon-Fri 8-4:30

R CENTRAL CHRISTIAN CHURCH LIBRARY*, 205 E Short St, 40507. SAN 306-3089. Tel: 859-233-1551. FAX: 859-252-9287. Web Site: www.centralchristianlex.org/library.html. *Librn,* Debbie Rice; Staff 1 (MLS 1)
Library Holdings: Bk Vols 8,500
Subject Interests: Bible study, Ethics, Philos, Relig, Theol

M EASTERN STATE HOSPITAL*, Resource Library, 1350 Bull Lea Rd, 40511. SAN 306-3100. Tel: 859-246-7538. FAX: 859-246-7018. *Librn,* Shane Shoemaker; E-mail: rsshoemaker@bluegrass.org
Founded 1951
Library Holdings: Bk Vols 5,000; Per Subs 150
Subject Interests: Med, Psychiat, Psychol, Pub health
Open Mon-Fri 8:30-4

L FAYETTE COUNTY LAW LIBRARY*, 120 N Limestone, 40507-1137. Tel: 859-246-2143. *In Charge,* Vincent Riggs; Tel: 854-246-2240
Library Holdings: Bk Vols 6,000
Database Vendor: LexisNexis, Westlaw
Wireless access
Open Mon-Fri 8:30-4:30

S HEADLEY-WHITNEY MUSEUM LIBRARY*, 4435 Old Frankfort Pike, 40510. SAN 325-545X. Tel: 859-255-6653. FAX: 859-255-8375. E-mail: curator@headley-whitney.org. Web Site: www.headley-whitney.org. *Chief Adminr/Curator of Coll & Exhibitions,* Amy Greene
Library Holdings: Bk Vols 1,500; Per Subs 12
Subject Interests: Art, Ceramics, Furniture, Glassware, Jewels, Silver
Restriction: Non-circulating to the pub, Open by appt only

S KEENELAND ASSOCIATION*, Keeneland Library, Keeneland Race Course, 4201 Versailles Rd, 40510. (Mail add: PO Box 1690, 40588-1690), SAN 306-3135. Tel: 859-254-3412, Ext 4223. Toll Free Tel: 800-456-3412. FAX: 859-255-2484. E-mail: library@keeneland.com. Web Site: www.keeneland.com. *Librn,* Cathy Schenck; E-mail: cschenck@keeneland.com
Founded 1939
Library Holdings: Bk Vols 10,000; Per Subs 45; Videos 1,500
Special Collections: American Racing Coll, photog negative
Subject Interests: Horses
Wireless access
Open Mon-Fri 8:30-4:30
Restriction: Non-circulating to the pub

P LEXINGTON PUBLIC LIBRARY*, 140 E Main St, 40507-1376. SAN 342-4057. Tel: 859-231-5500. Administration Tel: 859-231-5504. FAX: 859-231-5598. Web Site: www.lexpublib.org. *Exec Dir,* Ann Hammond; Tel: 859-231-5599, E-mail: ahammond@lexpublib.org; *Dir, Libr Coll,* Tonya Head; *Dir of Libr Serv,* Susie Lawrence; Tel: 859-231-5533, E-mail: slawrence@lexpublib.org; Staff 169.5 (MLS 45, Non-MLS 124.5)
Founded 1898. Pop 260,512; Circ 2,825,384
Jul 2011-Jun 2012 Income (Main Library and Branch(s)) $14,893,048, State $236,837, Federal $52,185, County $13,583,126, Other $1,020,900. Mats Exp $1,362,953, Books $850,409, Other Print Mats $86,034, AV Mat $211,067, Electronic Ref Mat (Incl. Access Fees) $215,443. Sal $5,712,449 (Prof $2,398,158)
Library Holdings: e-books 4,344; Bk Vols 464,003
Special Collections: African-American Coll; Early Kentucky Books; Early Kentucky Newspapers; Grants Coll; Large Print Coll; Lexington Urban County Doc Coll
Automation Activity & Vendor Info: (Cataloging) TLC (The Library Corporation); (Circulation) TLC (The Library Corporation); (OPAC) TLC (The Library Corporation)
Database Vendor: SirsiDynix
Wireless access
Special Services for the Deaf - TTY equip
Open Mon-Thurs 9-9, Fri 9-6, Sat 9-5, Sun 1-5
Friends of the Library Group

Branches: 5

BEAUMONT, 3080 Fieldstone Way, 40513, SAN 342-4146. Tel: 859-231-5500. FAX: 859-422-6878. *Br Mgr,* William Biles; Staff 33 (MLS 8, Non-MLS 25)
Friends of the Library Group

EAGLE CREEK, 101 N Eagle Creek Dr, 40509, SAN 342-4081. Tel: 859-231-5500. FAX: 859-422-6868. Web Site: www.lexpublib.org/eaglecreek. *Br Mgr,* Karen Allen; Staff 13 (MLS 6, Non-MLS 7)
Function: Audiobks via web, Bks on cassette, Bks on CD, Chess club, Children's prog, Computer training, Computers for patron use, Copy machines, Handicapped accessible, ILL available, Music CDs, Online cat, Photocopying/Printing, Prog for adults, Prog for children & young adult, Pub access computers, Ref & res, Senior computer classes, Spoken cassettes & CDs, Spoken cassettes & DVDs, Story hour, Summer reading prog, Tax forms, Teen prog, Telephone ref, VHS videos, Web-catalog, Wheelchair accessible
Open Mon-Thurs 9:30-9, Fri 9:30-6, Sat 9:30-5, Sun 1-5
Friends of the Library Group

NORTHSIDE, 1737 Russell Cave Rd, 40505, SAN 322-6352. Tel: 859-231-5500. FAX: 859-422-6898. *Br Mgr,* Karen Davis; Staff 9.5 (MLS 4, Non-MLS 5.5)
Open Mon-Thurs 9:30-9, Fri & Sat 9:30-5, Sun 1-5
Friends of the Library Group

TATES CREEK, 3628 Walden Dr, 40517, SAN 342-4111. Tel: 859-231-5500. FAX: 859-422-6888. *Br Mgr,* Elliot Appelbaum; Staff 28 (MLS 9, Non-MLS 19)
Database Vendor: TLC (The Library Corporation)
Open Mon-Thurs 9:30-9, Fri & Sat 9:30-5, Sun 1-5
Friends of the Library Group

VILLAGE BRANCH, 2185 Versailles Rd, 40504. Tel: 859-231-5500. FAX: 859-422-6358. *Br Mgr,* Betty Abdmishani; E-mail: babdmishani@lexpublib.org; Staff 14 (MLS 4, Non-MLS 10)
Database Vendor: TLC (The Library Corporation)
Open Mon-Thurs 9:30-9, Fri 9:30-6, Sat 9:30-5, Sun 1-5
Friends of the Library Group

R LEXINGTON THEOLOGICAL SEMINARY*, Bosworth Memorial Library, 631 S Limestone St, 40508. SAN 306-316X. Tel: 859-280-1229. FAX: 859-281-6042. E-mail: libraryrefdesk@lextheo.edu. Web Site: library.lextheo.edu. *Dir,* Doloris Yilibuw; E-mail: dyilibuw@lextheo.edu; *Archival Librn,* J Charles Heaberlin; E-mail: cheaberlin@lextheo.edu; *Circ/Reserves Coordr,* Patty MacFarland; E-mail: pmacfarland@lextheo.edu; Staff 3 (MLS 2, Non-MLS 1)
Founded 1865. Enrl 85; Fac 6; Highest Degree: Doctorate
Library Holdings: Bk Vols 155,000; Per Subs 325
Special Collections: John Mason Neale, Disciples of Christ
Subject Interests: Biblical studies, Relig
Automation Activity & Vendor Info: (Acquisitions) Innovative Interfaces, Inc - Millenium; (Cataloging) Innovative Interfaces, Inc - Millenium; (Circulation) Innovative Interfaces, Inc - Millenium; (ILL) Innovative Interfaces, Inc - Millenium; (OPAC) Innovative Interfaces, Inc; (Serials) Innovative Interfaces, Inc - Millenium
Database Vendor: EBSCOhost, Gale Cengage Learning, JSTOR, OCLC FirstSearch
Wireless access
Publications: Guide to Cane Ridge; Lexington Theological (Quarterly); Occasional Papers
Partic in Lyrasis; Theological Education Association of Mid America
Open Mon-Fri 10-4

M SAINT JOSEPH HOSPITAL*, Medical Library, One Saint Joseph Dr, 40504. SAN 306-3186. Tel: 859-313-1677. FAX: 859-313-3065. Web Site: www.sjhlex.org. *Librn,* Laurie Henderson; E-mail: henderla@sjhlex.org
Library Holdings: Bk Vols 935; Per Subs 194
Subject Interests: Med, Nursing
Database Vendor: EBSCOhost, ProQuest
Partic in Bluegrass Medical Libraries; Tri-State Libr Consortium
Open Mon-Fri 8-4:30
Restriction: Open to students

L STOLL KEENON OGDEN PLLC*, Law Library, 300 W Vine St, Ste 2100, 40507-1801. SAN 372-1205. Tel: 859-231-3000. FAX: 859-253-1093. Web Site: www.skofirm.com. *Librn,* Jeffrey L Frey; E-mail: jeffrey.frey@skofirm.com
Library Holdings: Bk Vols 10,000; Per Subs 150
Restriction: Staff use only

C TRANSYLVANIA UNIVERSITY LIBRARY*, 300 N Broadway, 40508. SAN 306-3194. Tel: 859-233-8225. FAX: 859-233-8779. E-mail: library@transy.edu. Web Site: www.transy.edu/academics/library.htm. *Dir,* Susan M Brown; Tel: 859-246-5008, E-mail: subrown@transy.edu; *Pub Serv Librn,* Lisa Nichols; Tel: 859-246-5003, E-mail: lnichols@transy.edu; *Ref & Instruction Librn,* Robert Campbell; Tel: 859-246-5010, E-mail: rcampbell@transy.edu; *Spec Coll Librn,* B J Gooch; Tel: 859-246-5002, E-mail: bjgooch@transy.edu; *Tech Serv Librn,* Damon DeBorde; Tel: 859-246-5005, E-mail: ddeborde@transy.edu; *Acq/Ser Supvr,* Teresa Ann Long; E-mail: along@transy.edu; *Evening Supvr,* Phillip Ira Walker; Tel: 859-246-5006, E-mail: piwalker@transy.edu; *Cat Spec,* Elizabeth R Laumas; E-mail: elaumas@transy.edu; Staff 8 (MLS 5, Non-MLS 3)
Founded 1780. Enrl 1,100; Fac 90; Highest Degree: Bachelor
Library Holdings: AV Mats 3,100; e-books 84,000; e-journals 15,000; Microforms 61; Bk Titles 97,300; Bk Vols 107,300; Per Subs 500
Special Collections: Horse, Sporting & Natural History (Clara S Peck Coll); Kentucky History (J Winston Coleman Kentuckiana Coll), bks, photogs; Medicine to 1850 (Transylvania Medical Library); University archives & ms collection
Automation Activity & Vendor Info: (Acquisitions) Ex Libris Group; (Cataloging) Ex Libris Group; (Circulation) Ex Libris Group; (Course Reserve) Ex Libris Group; (ILL) OCLC ILLiad; (OPAC) Ex Libris Group; (Serials) Ex Libris Group
Database Vendor: American Chemical Society, Annual Reviews, Baker & Taylor, Cambridge Scientific Abstracts, ebrary, EBSCOhost, Gale Cengage Learning, JSTOR, Mergent Online, Nature Publishing Group, Newsbank, OCLC FirstSearch, ProQuest
Wireless access
Partic in Association of Independent Kentucky Colleges & Universities; Federation of Kentucky Academic Libraries (FoKAL); Lyrasis; OCLC Online Computer Library Center, Inc
Open Mon-Thurs (Winter) 8am-2am, Fri 8-6, Sat Noon-6, Sun Noon-2am; Mon-Fri (Summer) 8:30-5

C UNIVERSITY OF KENTUCKY LIBRARIES*, William T Young Library, I-85, 401 Hilltop Ave, 40506-0456. (Mail add: 500 S Limestone St, 40506-0456), SAN 342-4200. Tel: 859-218-1881. Interlibrary Loan Service Tel: 859-218-1880, 859-218-2027. Reference Tel: 859-218-2048. Administration Tel: 859-218-1939. Information Services Tel: 859-218-1831. Interlibrary Loan Service FAX: 859-257-0502. Reference FAX: 859-257-0505. Administration FAX: 859-257-8379. E-mail: lib.circdesk@email.uky.edu, refdesk@uky.edu. Web Site: libraries.uky.edu, libraries.uky.edu/WTYL. *Dean of Libr,* Dr Terry Birdwhistell; Tel: 859-218-1871, E-mail: tlbird@uky.edu; *Assoc Dean, Acad Affairs & Res,* Stacey Greenwell; Tel: 859-218-1322, E-mail: stacey@uky.edu; *Sr Assoc Dean for Coll, Digital Scholarship & Tech Serv,* Mary Beth Thomson; Tel: 859-218-1227, E-mail: mbthomson@uky.edu; *Assoc Dean, Spec Coll,* Deirdre Scaggs; Tel: 859-257-3653, Fax: 859-257-6311, E-mail: deirdre@uky.edu; *Assoc Dean, Libr Tech,* Mary Molinaro; Tel: 859-218-1329, E-mail: molinaro@uky.edu; *Asst Dean, Finance & Admin,* Stephen Sizemore; Tel: 859-218-1221, E-mail: stephen.sizemore@uky.edu; *Dir of Develop,* Greg Casey; Tel: 859-218-0707, E-mail: greg.casey@uky.edu; *Dir, Intl Prog,* Toni Greider; Tel: 859-218-0830, E-mail: Toni.Greider@uky.edu
Founded 1909. Highest Degree: Doctorate
Library Holdings: Bk Titles 3,213,176; Bk Vols 4,023,142
Special Collections: 17th-Century English Literature: Milton & Miltoniana; Appalachian Coll (Appalachian Regional Commission Archives, Frontier Nursing Service, archives, bks, ms); Applied Anthropology Documentation Coll; Broadcast & Audio-Visual Archives; Broadside Ballads & Chapbooks; Dime Novels; Early English Romantics: Wordsworth, Coleridge, Lamb (W Hugh Peal Coll); French English & Spanish Drama, 1600-1930; Graphic Arts; Kentuckiana (Breckinridge Family, Henry Clay, Cassius M Clay, Laura Clay, Zachary Taylor, Wickliffe-Preston Papers); Kentucky Imprints (Samuel M Wilson Coll); Medicine (Daniel Drake Coll); Modern Political Archives (incl Alben Barkley, A B Chandler, Earl Clements, John Sherman Cooper, Thruston & Rogers C B Morton, Stanley Reed, Jouett Shouse, Brent Spence, A O Stanley, Fred Vinson, Wilson Wyatt); Musicology (Alfred Cortot Library); Photographic Archives; Printing & Modern Fine Printing (King Library Press, Victor Hammer, Gravesend & Bur Presses); Spanish Manuscript Coll, 1139-1800; Urban Planning Coll; Western Travel. Can & Prov; Oral History; US Document Depository
Subject Interests: Agr, Appalachia, Coal, Educ, Eng, Hist, Humanities, Law, Med, Music
Automation Activity & Vendor Info: (Acquisitions) Ex Libris Group; (Cataloging) Ex Libris Group; (Circulation) Ex Libris Group; (OPAC) Ex Libris Group
Wireless access
Partic in Association of Research Libraries (ARL); Association of Southeastern Research Libraries; Center for Research Libraries; Federation of Kentucky Academic Libraries (FoKAL); Lyrasis; State Assisted Academic Library Council of Kentucky
Friends of the Library Group

Departmental Libraries:

AGRICULTURAL INFORMATION CENTER, N24 Agricultural Sciences Ctr N, 40546-0091, SAN 342-4235. Tel: 859-257-2758. FAX: 859-323-4719. Web Site: libraries.uky.edu/AIC. *Head of Libr,* Valerie Perry; Tel: 859-257-8360, E-mail: vperry@uky.edu; *Agr Librn,* Jason Keinsley; Tel: 859-218-1523, E-mail: jkeinsley@uky.edu; *Equine Librn,*

Gracie Hale; Tel: 859-218-1147, E-mail: ghale@email.uky.edu. Subject Specialists: *Agr, Biol sci,* Valerie Perry; *Equine,* Gracie Hale
Subject Interests: Agr, Botany, Entomology, Food indust & trade, Forestry, Hort, Landscape archit, Nutrition, Veterinary med
Friends of the Library Group

CENTER FOR APPLIED ENERGY RESEARCH LIBRARY, 2540 Research Park Dr, 40511-8410. Tel: 859-257-0309. FAX: 859-257-0302. Web Site: www.caer.uky.edu/library/home.shtml. *Libr Mgr,* Theresa Wiley; E-mail: theresa.wiley@uky.edu
Library Holdings: Bk Vols 8,500
Automation Activity & Vendor Info: (Cataloging) Inmagic, Inc.; (Circulation) Inmagic, Inc.
Open Mon-Fri 8-5

DESIGN LIBRARY, 200 Pence Hall, 40506-0041, SAN 342-426X. Tel: 859-257-4305. FAX: 859-257-4305. Web Site: libraries.uky.edu/Design. *Librn,* Faith Harders; E-mail: fharders@uky.edu
Special Collections: Le Corbusier
Subject Interests: Archit, Furniture, Interior design, Urban planning
Friends of the Library Group

EDUCATION, 205 Dickey Hall, 40506-0017, SAN 342-4413. Tel: 859-257-7977. E-mail: refdesk@uky.edu. Web Site: libraries.uky.edu/Educ. *Head of Libr,* Position Currently Open
Special Collections: Economic Education Coll; KERA Coll
Subject Interests: Children's lit, Educ, Kentucky
Friends of the Library Group

CL LAW LIBRARY, 620 S Limestone St, 40506-0048, SAN 342-4502. Tel: 859-257-8686. Reference Tel: 859-257-8131. FAX: 859-323-4906. E-mail: lawref@email.uky.edu. Web Site: library.law.uky.edu/home. *Libr Dir & Assoc Prof of Law,* James Donovan; Tel: 859-257-8351, E-mail: james.donovan@uky.edu; *Head, Pub Serv,* Ryan Valentin; Tel: 859-257-8346, E-mail: ravale2@uky.edu; *Head, Tech Serv,* Karen Nuckolls; Tel: 859-257-2437, E-mail: kanuck2@email.uky.edu; *Fac Serv Librn,* Franklin Runge; Tel: 859-257-1081, E-mail: franklin.runge@uky.edu; *Instrul Serv Librn,* Beau Steenken; Tel: 859-257-1578, E-mail: beau.steenken@uky.edu
Special Collections: Human Rights; International Primary & Legal Coll; Kentucky Supreme Court Briefs; US & Kentucky Legal Materials; US Supreme Court, briefs, rec
Subject Interests: Law, Legal mat
Partic in Lyrasis
Publications: Acquisitions List; Bibliographic Guides; Pathfinders
Friends of the Library Group

LEXMARK LIBRARY, 740 New Circle Rd NW, 40511, SAN 306-3127. Tel: 859-232-3783. FAX: 859-232-5728. E-mail: ilibrary@lexmark.com. Web Site: lexmark.kyvl.org. *Libr Mgr,* Alex Grigg; E-mail: agrigg@lexmark.com; *Librn,* Linda Niemi; Tel: 859-232-6042, E-mail: lniemi@lexmark.com; Staff 2 (MLS 1, Non-MLS 1)
Founded 1991
Special Collections: Patents; Products Manuals; Programming Trade Literature
Subject Interests: Bus & mgt, Chem, Electronic eng, Mechanical eng, Metallurgy, Physics
Database Vendor: LexisNexis, STN International
Restriction: Employee & client use only

LUCILLE LITTLE FINE ARTS LIBRARY & LEARNING CENTER, 160 Patterson Dr, 40506-0224, SAN 342-4294. Tel: 859-257-2800. FAX: 859-257-4662. E-mail: falib@email.uky.edu. Web Site: libraries.uky.edu/FAlib. *Head of Libr,* Meg Shaw; Tel: 859-257-4908, E-mail: megshaw@uky.edu; *Librn,* Paula Hickner; Tel: 859-257-4104, E-mail: paula.hickner@uky.edu; *Tech Serv,* Kerri Scannell; Tel: 859-257-4630, E-mail: kscannell@uky.edu. Subject Specialists: *Art, Photog, Theatre,* Meg Shaw; *Music,* Paula Hickner; *Music cat,* Kerri Scannell
Special Collections: Acting Editions of Plays; Early Music Treatises (Alfred Cortot Coll); Wilcox American Music Coll
Subject Interests: Art, Music, Photog
Friends of the Library Group

CM MEDICAL CENTER LIBRARY, 800 Rose St, 40536-0298, SAN 342-4561. Tel: 859-323-5300. Interlibrary Loan Service Tel: 859-323-6565. Administration Tel: 859-323-5727. FAX: 859-323-1040. E-mail: mclib@uky.edu. Web Site: libraries.uky.edu/MCL. *Dir & Asst Dir, Res, Educ & Clinical Serv, Interim Assoc Dean,* Rick Brewer; Tel: 859-323-5296, E-mail: rick.brewer@uky.edu; *Dir, Cat & Database Integrity,* Lynne Bowman; Tel: 859-323-8919, E-mail: lbowman@email.uky.edu; *Asst Dir, Access, Delivery & Outreach Serv,* Laura Davison; Tel: 859-323-6138, E-mail: davison@email.uky.edu; *Head, Ref Commons,* Frank Davis; Tel: 859-323-3983, E-mail: fldavi2@email.uky.edu; *Ref/Clinical Librn,* Bev Hilton; Tel: 859-323-8008, E-mail: bhilton@email.uky.edu. Subject Specialists: *Dentistry,* Rick Brewer
Founded 1957. Highest Degree: Doctorate
Subject Interests: Allied health, Dentistry, Med, Nursing, Pub health
Partic in National Network of Libraries of Medicine Greater Midwest Region; OCLC Online Computer Library Center, Inc
Friends of the Library Group

SCIENCE LIBRARY, 211 King Bldg, 40506-0039. Tel: 859-257-5730. FAX: 859-323-3225. Web Site: libraries.uky.edu/SciLib. *Head, Eng & Sci Libr,* Susan K Smith; Tel: 859-257-7176; 859-257-4364, Fax: 859-323-1911, E-mail: susan.smith@uky.edu; *Cat & Ref Librn, Maps Selector,* Gwen Curtis; Tel: 859-257-1853, E-mail: gwen.curtis@uky.edu; *Sci Librn,* Jan Carver; Tel: 859-257-4074, Fax: 859-323-4988, E-mail: jbcarv1@email.uky.edu; *Sci Librn,* Tom Hecker; Tel: 859-257-8343, E-mail: tom.hecker@uky.edu; *Sci Librn,* Mary Spencer; Tel: 859-257-8359, E-mail: mary.spencer@uky.edu; *Sr Libr Tech,* Alice Wasielewski; Tel: 859-257-6217, E-mail: alice.was@uky.edu. Subject Specialists: *Eng,* Susan K Smith; *Astronomy, Chem, Physics,* Jan Carver; *German, Math sci,* Tom Hecker
Subject Interests: Astronomy, Chem, Geol sci, Maps, Math, Physics, Statistics

SHAVER ENGINEERING LIBRARY, 355 Anderson Tower, 40506-0046, SAN 342-4448. Tel: 859-257-4364, 859-257-7176. FAX: 859-323-1911. Web Site: libraries.uky.edu/SEL. *Head, Eng & Sci Libr,* Susan K Smith; E-mail: susan.smith@uky.edu. Subject Specialists: *Computer sci, Eng, Sci,* Susan K Smith
Special Collections: Environmental Reports; Industry Standards; Robotics
Subject Interests: Coal, Energy, Environ eng, Transportation
Friends of the Library Group

SPECIAL COLLECTIONS RESEARCH CENTER, King Bldg, 40506-0039. Tel: 859-257-8611. FAX: 859-257-6311. E-mail: SCLREF@LSV.UKY.EDU. Web Site: libraries.uky.edu/SC. *Libr Dir,* Gordon Hogg; Tel: 859-257-1949, E-mail: gehogg01@uky.edu; *Dir, Louis B Nunn Ctr for Oral Hist,* Doug Boyd; Tel: 859-257-9672, E-mail: doug.boyd@uky.edu; *Assoc Dean, Spec Coll Res Ctr,* Deirdre Scaggs; Tel: 859-257-3653, E-mail: deirdre@uky.edu. Subject Specialists: *Oral hist,* Doug Boyd
Special Collections: Wendell H Ford Public Policy Research Center. Oral History
Subject Interests: Appalachian coll, Archives, Kentuckiana, Modern political archives, Oral hist prog

LIBERTY

P CASEY COUNTY PUBLIC LIBRARY*, 238 Middleburg St, 42539. SAN 320-8192. Tel: 606-787-9381. FAX: 606-787-7720. E-mail: info@caseylibrary.org. Web Site: www.caseylibrary.org. *Dir,* Jan J Banks; *Asst Dir,* Kathy Goode; *Asst Librn,* Donna Murrell; Staff 2 (MLS 1, Non-MLS 1)
Founded 1976. Pop 15,557; Circ 124,000
Library Holdings: Bk Vols 48,000; Per Subs 50
Special Collections: Genealogy Coll; Kentucky Coll; Large Print Coll. Oral History
Automation Activity & Vendor Info: (Cataloging) Follett Software; (Circulation) Follett Software
Open Mon, Tues, Wed & Fri 9-6, Sat 9-3
Friends of the Library Group
Bookmobiles: 1. Librn, Jim Tucker

LONDON

P LAUREL COUNTY PUBLIC LIBRARY DISTRICT*, 120 College Park Dr, 40741. SAN 306-3224. Tel: 606-864-5759. FAX: 606-862-8057. E-mail: mail@laurellibrary.org. Web Site: laurellibrary.org. *District Dir,* Peggy Mershon; *Ch Mgr,* Leah Rudder; *ILL Mgr,* Rachel Horton; *Mgr, Outreach Serv,* Eugenia Irvin; *Supvr, Circ,* Lisa Mynatt; *Syst Adminr,* Jamey Jeffrey; Staff 30 (MLS 5, Non-MLS 25)
Founded 1915. Pop 52,790; Circ 165,000
Library Holdings: Bk Vols 162,000; Per Subs 60
Automation Activity & Vendor Info: (Cataloging) Innovative Interfaces, Inc; (Circulation) Innovative Interfaces, Inc; (OPAC) Innovative Interfaces, Inc
Wireless access
Partic in Kentucky Library Network, Inc
Open Mon-Fri 9-8, Sat 9-5, Sun 1-5
Friends of the Library Group
Branches: 1

SOUTH BRANCH, 727 W Cumberland Gap Pkwy, Corbin, 40701. Tel: 606-258-7000. *Librn,* Wilma Smith
Library Holdings: Bk Vols 24,000
Open Mon-Fri 11-7, Sat 10-4

LOUISA

P LAWRENCE COUNTY PUBLIC LIBRARY*, 102 W Main & Jefferson, 41230. (Mail add: PO Box 600, 41230-0600), SAN 306-3259. Tel: 606-638-0544, 606-638-4497. FAX: 606-638-1293. Web Site: www.lcplky.org. *Dir,* Mary McGuire; E-mail: marymcguire1@yahoo.com; *Ch,* Deanna Nelson; *Ref Librn,* Clarice Kelly
Pop 15,800; Circ 61,025
Library Holdings: AV Mats 410; Bk Vols 35,000; Per Subs 110; Talking Bks 361

Special Collections: Genealogy Coll; Kentucky Coll
Automation Activity & Vendor Info: (Cataloging) Brodart; (Circulation) Brodart; (OPAC) Brodart
Special Services for the Blind - Talking bks
Open Mon, Wed & Fri 9-5, Tues 9-6, Thurs 9-7, Sat 9-1
Bookmobiles: 1. Librn, Elizabeth Parsons. Bk vols 2,500

LOUISVILLE

S AMERICAN PRINTING HOUSE FOR THE BLIND, INC*, M C Migel Library & Barr Research Library, 1839 Frankfort Ave, 40206. SAN 311-5798. Toll Free Tel: 800-223-1839, Ext 202. E-mail: library@aph.org. Web Site: www.migel.aph.org. *Librn,* Justin Gardner; Staff 1 (Non-MLS 1)
Founded 1921
Library Holdings: Bk Titles 125,000
Special Collections: Helen Keller Archives
Subject Interests: Blindness, Visual impairment
Automation Activity & Vendor Info: (Cataloging) OCLC; (ILL) OCLC
Function: Audio & video playback equip for onsite use, CD-ROM, Copy machines, Electronic databases & coll, Handicapped accessible, VHS videos, Wheelchair accessible
Publications: Bibliographies
Partic in Metropolitan New York Library Council; OCLC Online Computer Library Center, Inc
Special Services for the Blind - Assistive/Adapted tech devices, equip & products; Closed circuit TV; Computer with voice synthesizer for visually impaired persons; Photo duplicator for making large print; Reader equip; Scanner for conversion & translation of mats
Open Mon-Fri 8-4:30
Restriction: Access at librarian's discretion, Circulates for staff only, In-house use for visitors, Not a lending libr

M BAPTIST HOSPITAL EAST*, Hagan-Pedigo Library, 4000 Kresge Way, 40207-4676. SAN 324-5977. Tel: 502-897-8183. FAX: 502-897-8020. Web Site: www.baptisteast.com. *Librn,* Dina Burshteyn; E-mail: dburshteyn@bhsi.com
Founded 1978
Library Holdings: Bk Titles 1,200; Per Subs 160
Subject Interests: Med, Nursing
Automation Activity & Vendor Info: (Cataloging) EOS International
Database Vendor: OVID Technologies
Partic in Kentucky Medical Library Association; Lyrasis; National Network of Libraries of Medicine
Open Mon-Fri 8-4:30

C BELLARMINE UNIVERSITY*, W L Lyons Brown Library, 2001 Newburg Rd, 40205-0671. SAN 306-3291. Tel: 502-272-8140. Circulation Tel: 502-272-8141. Interlibrary Loan Service Tel: 502-272-8314. Reference Tel: 502-272-8317. FAX: 502-272-8038. Interlibrary Loan Service FAX: 502-272-8361. Web Site: www.bellarmine.edu/library. *Dir,* John Stemmer, PhD; *Ref & ILL Librn,* John Boyd; E-mail: jboyd@bellarmine.edu; *Ref Librn,* Kevin Peers; Tel: 502-272-8315, E-mail: kpeers@bellarmine.edu; *Supvr, Circ,* Tammy Uchida; Tel: 502-272-8308; *Libr Instruction,* Martha Lundgren Perry; Tel: 502-272 8139, E-mail: mperry@bellarmine.edu; Staff 11 (MLS 6, Non MLS 5)
Founded 1950. Enrl 2,400; Fac 115; Highest Degree: Doctorate
Library Holdings: Bk Titles 96,000; Bk Vols 113,500; Per Subs 541
Special Collections: Louisville Archdiocesan Coll, a-tapes; Louisville Historical League, a-tapes; Thomas Merton Coll. Oral History
Subject Interests: Health sci
Automation Activity & Vendor Info: (Acquisitions) Innovative Interfaces, Inc; (Cataloging) Innovative Interfaces, Inc; (Circulation) Innovative Interfaces, Inc; (Course Reserve) Innovative Interfaces, Inc; (ILL) OCLC ILLiad; (Media Booking) Innovative Interfaces, Inc; (OPAC) Innovative Interfaces, Inc; (Serials) Innovative Interfaces, Inc
Database Vendor: Bowker, Cambridge Scientific Abstracts, ebrary, EBSCOhost, Elsevier, Facts on File, Gale Cengage Learning, H W Wilson, Hoovers, JSTOR, LexisNexis, OCLC FirstSearch, OCLC WorldShare Interlibrary Loan, OVID Technologies, ProQuest
Wireless access
Publications: Student Library Handbook
Partic in Coun of Independent Ky Cols & Univs; Kentuckiana Metroversity, Inc; Lyrasis; OCLC Online Computer Library Center, Inc
Open Mon-Thurs 7:30am-Midnight, Fri 7:30am-10pm, Sat 7:45-5, Sun Noon-Midnight

L BINGHAM GREENEBAUM DOLL LLP*, Law Library, 101 S Fifth St, 40202-3140. SAN 372-1272. Tel: 502-589-4200. FAX: 502-587-3695. Web Site: www.bgdlegal.com. *Librn,* Tiana French
Library Holdings: Bk Vols 30,000; Per Subs 172
Automation Activity & Vendor Info: (Cataloging) EOS International
Open Mon-Fri 7:30-4

R DOUGLASS BOULEVARD CHRISTIAN CHURCH LIBRARY*, 2005 Douglass Blvd, 40205. SAN 306-3380. Tel: 502-452-2629. FAX: 502-452-2225.
Founded 1940
Library Holdings: Bk Titles 2,500
Subject Interests: Biblical studies, Fiction, Mental health, Missions & missionaries, Relig
Open Mon-Fri 7-3

S EMBROIDERERS GUILD OF AMERICA INC LIBRARY*, 1355 Bardstown Rd, Ste 157, 40204. SAN 325-5735. Tel: 502-589-6956. FAX: 502-584-7900. E-mail: egahq@egausa.org. Web Site: www.egausa.org. *Curator, Exec Dir,* Brad Cape
Library Holdings: Bk Titles 3,000
Special Collections: Clip Art Files; Needleart Videos; Rare Books
Subject Interests: Hist
Publications: Needle Arts Magazine & "How To" books
Open Mon-Fri 9-5

S FILSON HISTORICAL SOCIETY LIBRARY*, 1310 S Third St, 40208. SAN 306-3402. Tel: 502-635-5083. FAX: 502-635-5086. E-mail: research@filsonhistorical.org. Web Site: www.filsonhistorical.org. *Exec Dir,* Dr Mark V Wetherington; E-mail: markweth@filsonhistorical.org; *Head Librn,* Judith Partington; E-mail: Judithfc@filsonhistorical.org; *Ref Librn,* Jana Meyer; *Tech Serv Librn,* Kathryn Bratcher; *Curator,* James Holmberg; E-mail: holmberg@filsonhistorical.org; Staff 10 (MLS 7, Non-MLS 3)
Founded 1884
Library Holdings: Bk Titles 50,000; Per Subs 100
Special Collections: Ephemera; historical manuscripts; KY portraits; Maps; newspapers; photographs; Prints; Rare books; Sheet music; Silver (Kentucky Silversmiths Coll)
Subject Interests: Genealogy, Hist, Kentucky
Publications: Filson Club History Quarterly; Newsletter; Publication Series (history)
Partic in Lyrasis
Restriction: Non-circulating

L FROST BROWN TODD LLC*, Law Library, 400 W Market St, 32nd Flr, 40202-3363. SAN 372-1264. Tel: 502-589-5400. FAX: 502-581-1087. Web Site: www.fbtlaw.com. *Dir, Libr & Info Serv,* Tracie Tiegs; Tel: 513-651-6800; *Librn,* Kimberly Cage; Tel: 502-237-3831, E-mail: kcage@fbtlaw.com; *Asst Librn,* Lois Bullock; E-mail: lbullock@fbtlaw.com; *Law Librn,* Cam Stallard; Tel: 859-231-0000, Fax: 859-231-0011, E-mail: cstallard@fbtlaw.com; Staff 7 (MLS 4, Non-MLS 3)
Library Holdings: Bk Vols 40,000
Database Vendor: Checkpoint Systems, Inc, Factiva.com, LexisNexis, Westlaw
Function: For res purposes
Restriction: Staff use only

J JEFFERSON COMMUNITY & TECHNICAL COLLEGE*, John T Smith Learning Resource Center, 109 E Broadway, 40202. SAN 342-4626. Tel: 502 213-2154. Web Site: www.jefferson.kctcs.edu. *Dir, Libr Serv,* Sheree Huber Williams; Tel: 502 213-2156, E-mail: sheree.williams@kctcs.edu; *Pub Serv,* Lisa Eichholtz; Tel: 502-213-2281, E-mail: lisa.eichholtz@kctcs.edu; *Ref Serv,* Nancy Mollette; Tel: 502-213-2362, E-mail: nancy.mollette@kctcs.edu; *Tech Serv,* Nina Deeley; Tel: 502-213-2373, E-mail: nina.deeley@kctcs.edu
Founded 1968. Enrl 8,431; Fac 172; Highest Degree: Associate
Library Holdings: Bk Titles 50,321; Bk Vols 53,672; Per Subs 196
Automation Activity & Vendor Info: (Acquisitions) Ex Libris Group; (Cataloging) Ex Libris Group; (Circulation) Ex Libris Group; (Course Reserve) Ex Libris Group; (OPAC) Ex Libris Group; (Serials) Ex Libris Group
Database Vendor: EBSCOhost, Gale Cengage Learning
Function: Ref serv available
Partic in Lyrasis
Open Mon-Thurs 7:30am-8:30pm, Fri & Sat 9-1

Departmental Libraries:

CARROLLTON CAMPUS, 324 Main St, Carrollton, 41008. Tel: 502-213-4846. Toll Free Tel: 800-853-3887. *Coordr,* Jamie Beaven; E-mail: jamie.beaven@kctcs.edu
Library Holdings: Bk Titles 2,100; Per Subs 28
Open Mon-Thurs 9-6:30, Fri 9-Noon

SHELBY COUNTY CAMPUS LIBRARY, 1361 Frankfort Rd, Shelbyville, 40065. Tel: 502-213-3617. *Coordr,* Anne Sabetta; Tel: 502-213-3618, E-mail: anne.sabetta@kctcs.edu
Library Holdings: AV Mats 232; Bk Vols 3,152; Per Subs 28
Open Mon-Thurs (Winter) 8-7:30, Fri 8:30-1:30; Mon-Thurs (Summer) 8-4:30, Fri 8-Noon

SOUTHWEST CAMPUS LIBRARY, 1000 Community College Dr, 40272, SAN 342-4650. Tel: 502-213-7222. FAX: 502-935-8653. *Evening Librn,* Dan Bays; *Librn,* Krista Districh-Osiecki; *Librn,* Rafe Johnson; Tel:

502-213-7210; *Circ Mgr,* Kelly O'Hara; E-mail: kelly.o'hara@kctcs.edu; *Info Spec,* Jonathan Gass; Tel: 502-213-7388
Founded 1972
Library Holdings: Bk Titles 33,200; Per Subs 50
Partic in Lyrasis
Open Mon-Thurs 8am-9pm, Fri 9-2:30, Sat 10-2
TECHNICAL CAMPUS LIBRARY, 727 W Chestnut St, 40203. (Mail add: 1009E Broadway, 40402). Tel: 502-213-4167. *Coordr,* Geneva Jewell; E-mail: geneva.jewell@kctcs.edu
Library Holdings: AV Mats 26; Bk Vols 1,167; Per Subs 30
Open Mon-Thurs 9-5, Fri 9-1

L JEFFERSON COUNTY PUBLIC LAW LIBRARY*, Old Jail Bldg, Ste 240, 514 W Liberty St, 40202-2806. SAN 306-3429. Tel: 502-574-5943. FAX: 502-574-3483. E-mail: jcpll@bluegrass.net. Web Site: www.jcpll.net. *Exec Dir,* Linda Miller Robbins; Staff 1 (MLS 1)
Founded 1839
Library Holdings: Bk Vols 90,000
Special Collections: Indiana Coll; Kentucky Coll
Database Vendor: LexisNexis, Westlaw
Wireless access
Open Mon-Fri 8:30-4:30
Friends of the Library Group

R JEWISH COMMUNITY CENTER*, Israel T Naamani Library, 3600 Dutchmans Lane, 40205. SAN 306-3313. Tel: 502-459-0660, Ext 160. FAX: 502-459-6885. Web Site: www.jewishlouisville.org. *In Charge,* Slava Nelson; E-mail: snelson@jewishlouisville.org
Founded 1948
Library Holdings: Large Print Bks 50; Bk Vols 7,000; Per Subs 20
Special Collections: Jewish Music, Art, Theology, Crafts & Local Jewish History, Holocaust, Genealogy
Publications: Jewish Holiday Bibliographies; Newsletter (Monthly)
Open Mon-Wed 12-5, Tues 11:30-4:30

S KENTUCKY SCHOOL FOR THE BLIND LIBRARY*, 1867 Frankfort Ave, 40206. SAN 325-1853. Tel: 502-897-1583, Ext 6301. FAX: 502-897-2850. Web Site: www.ksb.k12.ky.us. *Sch Libr Media,* Heather Davis
Founded 1842
Library Holdings: Bk Titles 18,373; Per Subs 25
Special Collections: Braille, Talking Books
Subject Interests: Phys handicaps, Recreational reading
Automation Activity & Vendor Info: (Cataloging) Follett Software; (Circulation) Follett Software
Open Mon-Fri 7-2:30

S KENTUCKY SCIENCE CENTER*, 727 W Main St, 40202. SAN 373-0557. Tel: 502-561-6100, Ext 6571. FAX: 502-561-6145. Web Site: www.kysciencecenter.org. Staff 1 (Non-MLS 1)
Founded 1977
Library Holdings: Bk Vols 2,047; Spec Interest Per Sub 12
Function: Res libr
Restriction: Staff use only

S LOUISVILLE ACADEMY OF MUSIC LIBRARY*, 2740 Frankfort Ave, 40206-2669. SAN 306-3461. Tel: 502-893-7885. Web Site: www.laofm.org. *Pres & Dir,* Ruth S French
Founded 1954
Library Holdings: CDs 100; Bk Titles 8,000; Videos 95
Special Collections: 20th Century First Editions; Antique Piano Rolls; Biographies on Local Musicians; Kentucky Music History; Music by & about American Composers-Clifford Shaw, records & written mat; National Geographic Magazine
Subject Interests: Lit, Local hist, Music, Photog, World War II
Open Mon-Sat 3-9

P LOUISVILLE FREE PUBLIC LIBRARY*, 301 York St, 40203-2205. SAN 342-4685. Tel: 502-574-1611. Circulation Tel: 502-574-1781. Interlibrary Loan Service Tel: 502-574-1711. Reference Tel: 502-574-1616. Administration Tel: 502-574-1760. FAX: 502-574-1666, 502-574-1693. Reference FAX: 502-574-1657. Web Site: www.lfpl.org. *Dir,* Position Currently Open; *Asst Dir,* Nancye Browning; Tel: 502-574-1743, E-mail: nancye@lfpl.org; *Asst Dir,* Melanie Lilly; Tel: 502-574-1845, E-mail: melanie.lilly@lfpl.org; *Mgr, Br Serv,* Lisa Sizemore; Tel: 502-574-1718; *Mgr, Info Serv,* Carrick Arehart; Tel: 502-574-1712; Staff 67 (MLS 67)
Founded 1902. Pop 721,594; Circ 3,750,653
Special Collections: US Document Depository
Subject Interests: Patents
Wireless access
Open Mon-Thurs 9-9, Fri & Sat 9-5, Sun 1-5
Friends of the Library Group

Branches: 17
BON AIR REGIONAL, 2816 Del Rio Pl, 40220, SAN 342-474X. Tel: 502-574-1795. FAX: 502-454-0169. *Br Mgr,* Laura Kelleher; E-mail: laura.kelleher@lfpl.org
Open Mon-Thurs 9-9, Fri & Sat 9-5, Sun 1-5
Friends of the Library Group
CRESCENT HILL, 2762 Frankfort Ave, 40206, SAN 342-4774. Tel: 502-574-1793. FAX: 502-894-8505. *Br Mgr,* Sally Suter; *Asst Br Mgr,* Barbara Ledford
Open Mon-Thurs 10-9, Fri & Sat 10-5
Friends of the Library Group
FAIRDALE BRANCH, 10620 W Manslick Rd, Fairdale, 40118, SAN 378-0260. Tel: 502-375-2051. FAX: 502-375-2016. *Br Mgr,* Marci Reed
Open Mon, Wed & Thurs 12-8, Tues 10-8, Fri & Sat 10-5
FERN CREEK, 6768 Bardstown Rd, 40291, SAN 373-8132. Tel: 502-231-4605. FAX: 502-239-3336. *Br Mgr,* Brian Reynolds
Open Mon-Thurs 10-9, Fri & Sat 10-5
Friends of the Library Group
HIGHLANDS-SHELBY PARK, 1250 Bardstown Rd, Ste 4, 40204, SAN 342-4987. Tel: 502-574-1672. FAX: 502-451-0548. *Br Mgr,* Rachel Smith; *Asst Br Mgr,* Beth Nahinsky; *Ref Librn,* Ruth Ellen Flint
Open Mon-Thurs 10-9, Fri & Sat 10-5
Friends of the Library Group
IROQUOIS, 601 W Woodlawn Ave, 40215, SAN 342-5045. Tel: 502-574-1720. FAX: 502-367-1468. *Br Mgr,* Mike Jansen
Open Mon-Thurs 10-9, Fri & Sat 10-5, Sun 1-5
Friends of the Library Group
JEFFERSONTOWN BRANCH, 10635 Watterson Trail, Jeffersontown, 40299, SAN 342-507X. Tel: 502-267-5713. FAX: 502-266-6569. *Br Mgr,* Debra Anderson; *Librn,* James Falkenstine; E-mail: jim.falkenstine@LFPL.org; *Ch,* Melissa McCullough; E-mail: melissa.mccullough@LFPL.org; Staff 4 (MLS 3, Non-MLS 1)
Function: 24/7 Electronic res, 24/7 Online cat, Adult bk club, Audiobks via web, Bks on CD, Children's prog, Computer training, Computers for patron use, Copy machines, E-Reserves, Electronic databases & coll, Family literacy, Free DVD rentals, Handicapped accessible, ILL available, Life-long learning prog for all ages, Magazines, Music CDs, Online cat, Orientations, Outreach serv, Photocopying/Printing, Preschool outreach, Preschool reading prog, Prog for adults, Prog for children & young adult, Pub access computers, Ref & res, Ref serv available, Ref serv in person, Spanish lang bks, Story hour, Summer reading prog, Teen prog, Wheelchair accessible
Open Mon-Thurs 10-9, Fri & Sat 10-5
Friends of the Library Group
MIDDLETOWN, 200 N Juneau Dr, 40243, SAN 325-4135. Tel: 502-245-7332. FAX: 502-245-7038. *Br Mgr,* Lisa Dekker
Open Mon-Thurs 10-9, Fri & Sat 10-5
Friends of the Library Group
NEWBURG, 4800 Exeter Ave, 40218. Tel: 502-479-6163. FAX: 502-479-6160. *Br Mgr,* Kerry Hunter
Open Mon-Thurs 10-9, Fri & Sat 10-5
Friends of the Library Group
OKOLONA, 7709 Preston Hwy, 40219, SAN 342-5169. Tel: 502-964-3515. FAX: 502-964-7025. *Br Mgr,* Raechael Robertson; *Ch,* Theresa Lukas
Open Mon-Thurs 10-9, Fri & Sat 10-5, Sun 1-5
Friends of the Library Group
PORTLAND, 3305 Northwestern Pkwy, 40212, SAN 342-5258. Tel: 502-574-1744. FAX: 502-776-9947. *Br Mgr,* Luke Stifler
Open Mon, Tues & Thurs 12-8, Wed 10-8, Fri & Sat 10-5
Friends of the Library Group
ST MATTHEWS-ELINE BRANCH, 3940 Grandview Ave, 40207, SAN 342-4804. Tel: 502-574-1771. FAX: 502-894-8709. *Br Mgr,* Dustin Strong
Open Mon-Thurs 10-9, Fri & Sat 10-5,Sun 1-5
Friends of the Library Group
SHAWNEE, 3912 W Broadway, 40211, SAN 342-5282. Tel: 502-574-1722. FAX: 502-776-9983. *Br Mgr,* Beverly Imani; *Asst Br Mgr,* Katie Beach; *Ch,* Katy Grant
Open Mon-Thurs 10-9, Fri & Sat 10-5, Sun 1-5
Friends of the Library Group
SHIVELY, 3920 Dixie Hwy, 40216, SAN 342-5134. Tel: 502-574-1730. FAX: 502-449-3886.
Open Mon-Thurs 10-9, Fri & Sat 10-5
SOUTHWEST REGIONAL, 10375 Dixie Hwy, 40272, SAN 328-9028. Tel: 502-933-0029. FAX: 502-933-2782. *Br Mgr,* Rebecca Maddox; *Asst Br Mgr,* Lindsey Kokai
Open Mon-Thurs 9-9, Fri & Sat 9-5, Sun 1-5
Friends of the Library Group
WESTERN, 604 S Tenth St, 40203, SAN 342-5401. Tel: 502-574-1779. FAX: 502-589-9937. *Br Mgr,* Crystal Britton
Special Collections: Black History
Open Mon, Tues & Thurs 12-8, Wed 10-8, Fri & Sat 10-5
Friends of the Library Group

WESTPORT, 8100 Westport Rd, Ste B, 40222, SAN 376-8848. Tel: 502-394-0379. FAX: 502-394-0377. *Br Mgr,* Dustin Strong
Open Mon-Thurs 3-9, Sat 10-5
Friends of the Library Group
Bookmobiles: 1

S LOUISVILLE METRO PLANNING COMMISSION*, Louisville Metropolitan Planning Library, 444 S Fifth St, Ste 300, 40202. SAN 371-1714. Tel: 502-574-6230. FAX: 502-574-8129. Web Site: www.louisvilleky.gov. *Info Spec,* Jessica Wethington; Tel: 502-574-5174, E-mail: jessica.wethington@louisvilleky.gov
Library Holdings: Bk Vols 400

R LOUISVILLE PRESBYTERIAN THEOLOGICAL SEMINARY, Ernest Miller White Library, 1044 Alta Vista Rd, 40205-1798. SAN 306-3488. Circulation Tel: 502-992-9398. Toll Free Tel: 800-264-1839. FAX: 502-895-1096. Circulation E-mail: circdesk@lpts.edu. Web Site: www.lpts.edu/library. *Dir,* Matthew Collins; E-mail: mcollins@lpts.edu; *Head, Pub Serv,* Angela G Morris; E-mail: amorris@lpts.edu; *Tech Serv Librn,* Angeles Ramos-Ankrum; Tel: 502-895-3411, Ext 397, E-mail: aramosankrum@lpts.edu; *Tech Serv Spec,* Caren Nichter; E-mail: cnichter@lpts.edu; *Instrul Tech Adminr,* Carolyn Cardwell; Tel: 502-895-3411, Ext 422, E-mail: ccardwell@lpts.edu; Staff 5 (MLS 3, Non-MLS 2)
Founded 1853. Enrl 200; Fac 22; Highest Degree: Doctorate
Library Holdings: AV Mats 8,185; Microforms 11,892; Bk Vols 175,430; Per Subs 543
Special Collections: Reformation & Presbyterian History Coll
Subject Interests: Related disciplines, Relig, Theol
Automation Activity & Vendor Info: (Acquisitions) Ex Libris Group; (Cataloging) Ex Libris Group; (Circulation) Ex Libris Group; (OPAC) Ex Libris Group; (Serials) Ex Libris Group
Database Vendor: Alexander Street Press, EBSCOhost, OCLC FirstSearch
Wireless access
Function: Res libr
Partic in Federation of Kentucky Academic Libraries (FoKAL); Kentuckiana Metroversity, Inc; Lyrasis; Theological Education Association of Mid America
Special Services for the Blind - Accessible computers; Assistive/Adapted tech devices, equip & products; Computer with voice synthesizer for visually impaired persons; Internet workstation with adaptive software; Screen reader software
Open Mon-Thurs (Fall & Spring) 8am-10pm, Fri 8-5, Sat 12-5, Sun 5pm-10pm; Mon, Wed & Fri (Summer) 8:30-5, Tues & Thurs 8:30-8

S NATIONAL SOCIETY OF THE SONS OF THE AMERICAN REVOLUTION, Historical & Genealogical Research Library, 809 W Main St, 40202. Tel: 502-588-6138. FAX: 502-585-7674. E-mail: library@sar.org. Web Site: library.sar.org. *Librn,* Michael A Christian; E-mail: mchristi@sar.org; Staff 2 (MLS 1, Non-MLS 1)
Jan 2014-Dec 2014 Income $150,000
Library Holdings: Bk Vols 35,000; Per Subs 18
Special Collections: George Washington Coll
Subject Interests: Colonial period, Genealogy, Revolutionary war
Wireless access
Open Mon 9:30-Noon, Tues-Fri 9:30-4:30
Restriction: Non-circulating
Friends of the Library Group

M NORTON AUDUBON HOSPITAL*, R Dietz Wolfe Medical Library, One Audubon Plaza Dr, 40217. SAN 306-3569. Tel: 502-636-7296. FAX: 502-636-7257. *Librn,* Debra S Sullivan; Staff 1 (MLS 1)
Founded 1928
Library Holdings: Bk Titles 550; Per Subs 55
Subject Interests: Allied health, Med
Database Vendor: Gale Cengage Learning, OVID Technologies
Wireless access
Function: Ref serv available
Open Mon-Fri 7:30-2:30

M NORTON HEALTHCARE*, Medical Library, 200 E Chestnut St, 40202. (Mail add: PO Box 35070, 40232-5070), SAN 306-3526. Tel: 502-629-8125. FAX: 502-629-8138. E-mail: library@nortonhealthcare.org. *Librn,* Leslie Pancratz; *Librn,* Ann Schaap; Staff 3 (MLS 2, Non-MLS 1)
Founded 1959
Library Holdings: Bk Titles 3,200; Per Subs 275
Special Collections: Hospitals' Archives
Subject Interests: Allied health, Consumer health, Med, Nursing, Orthopedics, Pediatrics
Automation Activity & Vendor Info: (Cataloging) Ex Libris Group; (Circulation) Ex Libris Group; (OPAC) Ex Libris Group
Partic in Kentucky Medical Library Association; OCLC Online Computer Library Center, Inc

CR SIMMONS COLLEGE OF KENTUCKY LIBRARY*, 1018 S Seventh St, 40203. SAN 328-1221. Tel: 502-776-1443. FAX: 502-776-2227. Web Site: www.simmonscollegeky.edu. *Librn,* Betty Parish; Staff 1 (MLS 1)
Enrl 106; Highest Degree: Master
Library Holdings: Bk Vols 10,000
Special Collections: Oral History
Open Mon-Thurs 9-4
Friends of the Library Group

R SOUTHERN BAPTIST THEOLOGICAL SEMINARY, James P Boyce Centennial Library, 2825 Lexington Rd, 40280-0294. SAN 342-5436. Circulation Tel: 502-897-4713. Interlibrary Loan Service Tel: 502-897-4553. Reference Tel: 502-897-4071. Administration Tel: 502-897-4807. Administration FAX: 502-897-4600. Web Site: www.sbts.edu. *Librn,* C Berry Driver, Jr; E-mail: bdriver@sbts.edu; *Assoc Librn,* Ryan Vasut; *Assoc Librn, Res Serv & Archivist,* Jason Fowler; E-mail: jfowler@sbts.edu; *Dir, Tech Serv,* Martha C Powell; E-mail: mpowell@sbts.edu; *Tech Dir,* John Merritt; Tel: 502-897-4127, E-mail: jamerritt@sbts.edu; *Archivist,* Adam Winters; Staff 22 (MLS 5, Non-MLS 17)
Founded 1859. Enrl 3,600; Fac 76; Highest Degree: Doctorate
Library Holdings: Bk Vols 394,346; Per Subs 1,008
Special Collections: Archaeology (William F Albright Coll); Evangelism (Billy Graham Coll); Gospel Music (Ingersoll Coll); Hymnology (Converse Hymnology Coll); Missions (R Pierce Beaver Coll); Music (Everett Helm Coll)
Subject Interests: Archaeology, Bible, Educ, Ethics, Hist, Music, Psychol, Relig, Theol
Automation Activity & Vendor Info: (Acquisitions) Ex Libris Group; (Cataloging) Ex Libris Group; (Circulation) Ex Libris Group; (Course Reserve) Ex Libris Group; (ILL) Ex Libris Group; (OPAC) Ex Libris Group; (Serials) Ex Libris Group
Database Vendor: EBSCOhost, LexisNexis, OCLC FirstSearch, OCLC WorldShare Interlibrary Loan, ProQuest
Wireless access
Partic in Kentuckiana Metroversity, Inc; Lyrasis; Theological Education Association of Mid America
Open Mon-Thurs 7:45am-10pm, Fri 7:45-7, Sat 11-7

C SPALDING UNIVERSITY LIBRARY, 853 Library Lane, 40203-9986. SAN 306-3585. Tel: 502-585-7130. FAX: 502-585-7156. E-mail: library@spalding.edu. Web Site: www.spalding.edu/library. *Archivist, Libr Dir,* Jackie Young; E-mail: jyoung04@spalding.edu; *Libr Instruction, Ref Serv, User Experience Librn,* Alexa Clark; *Info Consult, ILL,* Linda Blandford; E-mail: ill@spalding.edu; *ILL,* Kim Wicke; *Learning Tech Translation Strategist,* Mimi O'Malley; *Ref Serv,* Janice Poston; E-mail: jposton@spalding.edu; Staff 4 (MLS 4)
Founded 1920. Enrl 1,650; Fac 128; Highest Degree: Doctorate
Special Collections: Edith Stein Coll; Kentucky Coll
Automation Activity & Vendor Info: (Acquisitions) Ex Libris Group; (OPAC) Ex Libris Group
Wireless access
Partic in Coun of Independent Ky Cols & Univs; Kentuckiana Metroversity, Inc; OCLC Online Computer Library Center, Inc

S SPEED ART MUSEUM LIBRARY*, 2035 S Third St, 40208. SAN 306-3593. Tel: 502-634-2710. FAX: 502-636-2899. Web Site: www.speedmuseum.org. *Dir of Coll,* Scott Erbes
Founded 1927
Library Holdings: Bk Titles 18,717; Per Subs 50; Spec Interest Per Sub 50
Special Collections: Indian (Weygold Coll); J B Speed's Lincoln Books
Subject Interests: Archit, Art, Decorative art, Films & filmmaking, Photog
Publications: Acquisitions List; Bibliographies; Gallery Publications Index; Index to the Scrapbooks; Speed Bulletin (In-house Index)
Restriction: Open by appt only

L STITES & HARBISON*, Law Library, 400 W Market St, Ste 1800, 40202. SAN 372-1280. Tel: 502-587-3400. FAX: 502-587-6391. Web Site: www.stites.com. *Librn,* Lynn H Fritsch; E-mail: lfritsch@stites.com
Library Holdings: Bk Vols 25,000
Special Collections: Historical Kentucky Statutes (back to 1800s)
Database Vendor: Westlaw
Restriction: Staff use only

C SULLIVAN UNIVERSITY LIBRARY*, 3101 Bardstown Rd, 40205. (Mail add: 2222 Wendell Ave, 40232-3308), SAN 324-1777. Tel: 502-456-6773. FAX: 502-456-0016. E-mail: libsul@sullivan.edu. Web Site: library.sullivan.edu. *Univ Librn,* Charles Brown; E-mail: cbrown@sullivan.edu; Staff 7 (MLS 6, Non-MLS 1)
Founded 1975. Enrl 2,500; Fac 80; Highest Degree: Doctorate
Library Holdings: DVDs 900; e-journals 32,000; Bk Titles 20,000; Bk Vols 28,000; Per Subs 150

Special Collections: Culinary Coll; Julia Child Cookbook Award Nominees 1991-Present; Pharmacy Coll
Subject Interests: Acctg, Bus mgt, Computer sci, Culinary, Paralegal, Travel
Automation Activity & Vendor Info: (Cataloging) TLC (The Library Corporation); (Circulation) TLC (The Library Corporation); (OPAC) TLC (The Library Corporation)
Database Vendor: EBSCOhost, Gale Cengage Learning, ProQuest
Partic in Kentucky Medical Library Association
Open Mon-Thurs 6:30am-9:45pm, Fri & Sat 8-4, Sun 12-5
Restriction: Not open to pub

Departmental Libraries:

LOUISVILLE TECHNICAL INSTITUTE CAMPUS, 3901 Atkinson Square Dr, 40218. Tel: 502-456-6509. *Librn,* Jill Sherman
Library Holdings: AV Mats 251; Bk Vols 2,695; Per Subs 70
Open Mon-Thurs 8am-9:30pm, Fri 8-Noon

SPENCERIAN COLLEGE LEXINGTON CAMPUS, 1575 Winchester Rd, Lexington, 40505-4520. Tel: 859-977-5465. FAX: 859-224-7744. *Librn,* James Seamans; E-mail: jseamans@spencerian.edu; Staff 2 (MLS 1, Non-MLS 1)
Founded 1892. Enrl 275; Fac 54; Highest Degree: Associate
Library Holdings: AV Mats 172; e-books 61,300; e-journals 45,000; Bk Titles 1,500; Bk Vols 2,100; Per Subs 58
Subject Interests: Allied health, Archit tech, Computer tech, Eng tech, Graphic arts
Automation Activity & Vendor Info: (Acquisitions) TLC (The Library Corporation); (Cataloging) TLC (The Library Corporation); (Circulation) TLC (The Library Corporation); (OPAC) TLC (The Library Corporation); (Serials) TLC (The Library Corporation)
Database Vendor: Cinahl, EBSCOhost, Hoovers, Medline, OCLC FirstSearch, OCLC WorldShare Interlibrary Loan, OHIONET, ProQuest, PubMed, WebMD, Westlaw
Function: AV serv, CD-ROM, Computer training, Computers for patron use, Copy machines, Learning ctr, Online cat, Online searches, Ref & res, Ref serv available
Open Mon-Fri 7:30am-9pm, Sat 8-1
Restriction: 24-hr pass syst for students only, Access at librarian's discretion, Authorized patrons, Borrowing privileges limited to fac & registered students, Limited access for the pub

C UNIVERSITY OF LOUISVILLE LIBRARIES*, 2215 S Third St, 40292. SAN 342-5495. Tel: 502-852-6745. FAX: 502-852-7394. Web Site: library.louisville.edu. *Dean,* Robert E Fox, Jr; E-mail: bob.fox@louisville.edu; *Assoc Dean, Assessment, Personnel & Res,* Melissa A Laning; Tel: 502-852-8726, E-mail: melissa.laning@louisville.edu; Staff 126 (MLS 42, Non-MLS 84)
Founded 1911. Enrl 22,293; Fac 2,316; Highest Degree: Doctorate
Jul 2012-Jun 2013. Mats Exp $9,671,768. Sal $6,379,626 (Prof $3,145,587)
Library Holdings: AV Mats 60,047; e-books 51,959; e-journals 66,761; Electronic Media & Resources 90,034; Microforms 2,297,563; Bk Titles 1,640,700; Bk Vols 2,341,521; Per Subs 70,666; Videos 18,310
Special Collections: Photographic Archives; Rare Books Coll. State Document Depository; US Document Depository
Automation Activity & Vendor Info: (Acquisitions) Ex Libris Group; (Cataloging) Ex Libris Group; (Circulation) Ex Libris Group; (Course Reserve) Ex Libris Group; (ILL) OCLC ILLiad; (Media Booking) Ex Libris Group; (OPAC) Ex Libris Group; (Serials) Ex Libris Group
Database Vendor: 3M Library Systems, ABC-CLIO, ACM (Association for Computing Machinery), Alexander Street Press, American Chemical Society, American Mathematical Society, American Physical Society, American Psychological Association (APA), ARTstor, BioOne, Bowker, BWI, Cambridge Scientific Abstracts, Cinahl, CQ Press, CRC Press/Taylor & Francis Group, Dun & Bradstreet, ebrary, EBSCO Information Services, EBSCOhost, Elsevier, Elsevier MDL, Emerald, EOS International, Ex Libris Group, Foundation Center, Gale Cengage Learning, Greenwood Publishing Group, Grolier Online, H W Wilson, Haworth Pres Inc, Hoovers, IEEE (Institute of Electrical & Electronics Engineers), infoUSA, Inspire, ISI Web of Knowledge, Jane's, JSTOR, LexisNexis, Marcive, Inc, Marquis Who's Who, McGraw-Hill, MD Consult, Medlib, Medline, Mergent Online, Modern Language Association, Newsbank, Newsbank-Readex, OCLC, OCLC FirstSearch, OCLC WorldShare Interlibrary Loan, OVID Technologies, Project MUSE, ProQuest, PubMed, ReferenceUSA, Safari Books Online, Sage, ScienceDirect, SerialsSolutions, Springshare, LLC, Standard & Poor's, Swets Information Services, Thomson - Web of Science, WebMD, Westlaw, Wiley, Wiley InterScience, YBP Library Services
Wireless access
Function: Accessibility serv available based on individual needs, Archival coll, Art exhibits, Computers for patron use, Copy machines, Digital talking bks, Distance learning, Doc delivery serv, e-mail & chat, E-Reserves, Electronic databases & coll, Equip loans & repairs, Exhibits, Free DVD rentals, ILL available, Microfiche/film & reading machines, Online cat, Online info literacy tutorials on the web & in blackboard, Online ref, Online searches, Outreach serv, Photocopying/Printing, Printer for laptops & handheld devices, Pub access computers, Ref & res, Ref serv available, Ref serv in person, Res libr, Telephone ref, Wheelchair accessible
Partic in Association of Research Libraries (ARL); Association of Southeastern Research Libraries; Coalition for Networked Information (CNI); Federation of Kentucky Academic Libraries (FoKAL); Kentuckiana Metroversity, Inc; Lyrasis; State Assisted Academic Library Council of Kentucky
Restriction: 24-hr pass syst for students only
Friends of the Library Group

Departmental Libraries:

DWIGHT ANDERSON MUSIC LIBRARY, 105 W Brandeis Ave, 40208. (Mail add: University of Louisville, 40292), SAN 342-5649. Tel: 502-852-5659. FAX: 502-852-7701. *Dir,* Karen Little; E-mail: krlitt01@louisville.edu; *Asst Dir,* James Procell; Tel: 502-852-0528, E-mail: jjproc01@exchange.louisville.edu; Staff 6 (MLS 2, Non-MLS 4)
Founded 1947
Jul 2011-Jun 2012 Income $521,837. Mats Exp $156,640, Books $25,214, Per/Ser (Incl. Access Fees) $44,463, Other Print Mats $18,493, AV Mat $6,230, Electronic Ref Mat (Incl. Access Fees) $27,067, Presv $35,173. Sal $279,633 (Prof $117,102)
Library Holdings: AV Mats 36,475; Music Scores 45,620; Bk Vols 126,067; Per Subs 266; Videos 3
Special Collections: 18th-19th Century Plorodine Music (Ricasoli Coll); 20th Century Music (Grawemeyer Coll)
Function: For res purposes

CL BRANDEIS SCHOOL OF LAW LIBRARY, 2301 S Third St, 40208. (Mail add: Law Library, University of Louisville, 40292), SAN 342-5584. Tel: 502-852-6392. FAX: 502-852-8906. Web Site: www.law.louisville.edu/library. *Dir,* David Ensign; E-mail: david.ensign@louisville.edu; *Pub Serv Librn,* Robin Harris; Tel: 502-852-6083, E-mail: rrharr01@louisville.edu; *Tech Serv Librn,* Scott Campbell; Tel: 502-852-6074, E-mail: pscamp01@louisville.edu; *Prof,* Kurt X Metzmeier; Tel: 502-852-6082, E-mail: kxmetz01@exchange.louisville.edu; *Asst Prof, Ref,* Will Hilyerd; Tel: 502-852-6080, E-mail: wahily01@louisville.edu; Staff 15 (MLS 6, Non-MLS 9)
Fac 30; Highest Degree: Doctorate
Jul 2011-Jun 2012 Income $2,511,551. Mats Exp $1,464,438, Books $161,360, Per/Ser (Incl. Access Fees) $1,049,310, Manu Arch $110, Micro $44,607, AV Mat $684, Electronic Ref Mat (Incl. Access Fees) $195,289, Presv $13,003. Sal $752,075 (Prof $475,886)
Special Collections: Justice (Louis D Brandeis Coll & John M Harlan Sr Coll), ms. US Document Depository
Function: Res libr
Restriction: Circ limited

MARGARET BRIDWELL ART LIBRARY, Schneider Hall, Belknap Campus, 40292, SAN 342-5525. Tel: 502-852-6741. Web Site: louisville.edu/library/art. *Dir,* Gail Gilbert; E-mail: gail.gilbert@louisville.edu; Staff 2 (MLS 1, Non-MLS 1)
Founded 1956
Jul 2012-Jun 2013. Mats Exp $158,399, Books $96,635, Per/Ser (Incl. Access Fees) $47,684, Other Print Mats $1,215, AV Mat $1,520, Electronic Ref Mat (Incl. Access Fees) $11,345
Library Holdings: CDs 323; DVDs 598; Microforms 2,961; Bk Vols 92,617; Per Subs 340

WILLIAM F EKSTROM LIBRARY, Belknap Campus, 2215 S Third St, 40292. (Mail add: William F Ekstrom Library, University of Louisville, 40292). Tel: 502-852-6745. Circulation Tel: 502-852-6757. Reference Tel: 502-852-6747. FAX: 502-852-7394. *Assoc Dean & Dir,* Bruce L Keisling; Tel: 508-852-8707; *Assoc Dean, Assessment, Personnel & Res,* Melissa Laning; Tel: 502-852-8726, E-mail: malani01@louisville.edu; *Head, Ref & Info Literacy Serv,* Anna Marie F Johnson; Tel: 502-852-1491, E-mail: amjohn01@louisville.edu; *Head, Coll Develop,* James Manasco; Tel: 502-852-8731, E-mail: james.manasco@louisville.edu; *Head, Spec Coll,* Delinda Stephens Buie; Tel: 502-852-6762, E-mail: dsbuie01@louisville.edu; *Head, Tech Serv,* Tyler Goldberg; Tel: 502-852-8723, E-mail: stgold01@louisville.edu; *Head, Web Serv,* Terri Holtze; Tel: 502-852-4477, E-mail: tlholt02@louisville.edu; *Coordr, Learning Commons,* Position Currently Open; Staff 87 (MLS 30, Non-MLS 57)
Founded 1911. Enrl 22,249; Fac 2,309; Highest Degree: Doctorate
Jul 2011-Jun 2012 Income $13,581,558. Mats Exp $5,980,229, Books $412,508, Per/Ser (Incl. Access Fees) $893,200, Manu Arch $29,196, Other Print Mats $134, Micro $39,024, AV Equip $3,025, AV Mat $11,254, Electronic Ref Mat (Incl. Access Fees) $4,553,405, Presv $32,061. Sal $3,603,875 (Prof $1,533,540)
Library Holdings: AV Mats 12,410; e-books 47,236; e-journals 66,761; Electronic Media & Resources 277; Microforms 2,244,637; Bk Vols 1,537,785; Per Subs 3,271
Special Collections: Arthur Rackham (Evelyn Parks Rymer Memorial Coll); Astronomy & Mathematics (William Marshall Bullitt Coll); Edgar Rice Burroughs (Neil Dismukes McWhorter Memorial Coll); H L Mencken (Victor Reno Coll); Irish Literature; Joyce & Yeats (Richard M Kain Coll). US Document Depository

Database Vendor: 3M Library Systems, ABC-CLIO, Agricola, American Chemical Society, American Psychological Association (APA), ARTstor, BioOne, Bowker, Cambridge Scientific Abstracts, Cinahl, ebrary, EBSCO Information Services, EBSCOhost, Elsevier, Emerald, Ex Libris Group, Facts on File, Haworth Pres Inc, IEEE (Institute of Electrical & Electronics Engineers), infoUSA, JSTOR, Knovel, LexisNexis, Marcive, Inc, Marquis Who's Who, McGraw-Hill, Medlib, Medline, Modern Language Association, Newsbank, OCLC, OCLC FirstSearch, OCLC WorldShare Interlibrary Loan, OVID Technologies, Project MUSE, ProQuest, PubMed, ReferenceUSA, Sage, ScienceDirect, SerialsSolutions, SirsiDynix, Springer-Verlag, Standard & Poor's, Swets Information Services, Thomson - Web of Science, Westlaw, Wiley, Wiley InterScience, YBP Library Services
Function: Archival coll, Art exhibits, Audio & video playback equip for onsite use, Audiobks via web, AV serv, Computers for patron use, Copy machines, Distance learning, Doc delivery serv, e-mail & chat, e-mail serv, E-Reserves, Electronic databases & coll, Equip loans & repairs, Exhibits, For res purposes, Govt ref serv, Handicapped accessible, ILL available, Learning ctr, Libr develop, Newsp ref libr, Online cat, Online info literacy tutorials on the web & in blackboard, Online ref, Online searches, Orientations, Outreach serv, Photocopying/Printing, Printer for laptops & handheld devices, Pub access computers, Ref & res, Ref serv available, Ref serv in person, Scanner, Telephone ref, VCDs, VHS videos, Video lending libr, Web-Braille, Web-catalog, Wheelchair accessible
Special Services for the Deaf - Assistive tech
Special Services for the Blind - Assistive/Adapted tech devices, equip & products
Restriction: 24-hr pass syst for students only, Badge access after hrs, ID required to use computers (Ltd hrs), In-house use for visitors, Open to pub for ref & circ; with some limitations, Open to students, fac, staff & alumni, Secured area only open to authorized personnel
Friends of the Library Group

CM KORNHAUSER HEALTH SCIENCES LIBRARY, Health Sciences Ctr, 500 S Preston St, 40202. (Mail add: University of Louisville, Health Sciences Library, 40292). Tel: 502-852-5775. Circulation Tel: 502-852-5771. FAX: 502-852-1631. Web Site: www.louisville.edu/library/kornhauser. *Dir,* Neal Dean Nixon; Tel: 502-852-8540, E-mail: ndnixo01@louisville.edu; *Asst Dir,* Elizabeth Smigielski; Tel: 502-852-0754, E-mail: emsmig01@exchange.louisville.edu; *Dep Dir,* Nancy Utterback; Tel: 502-852-1627, E-mail: n0utte01@exchange.louisville.edu; *Outreach Librn, Prof,* Carol Brinkman; Tel: 502-852-1008, E-mail: csbrin01@exchange.louisville.edu; *Prof, Ref Librn,* Michelle Cohen Atlas; Tel: 502-852-8534, E-mail: mcatla01@exchange.louisville.edu; *Assoc Prof, Ref Librn,* John Chenault; Tel: 502 852-3901, E-mail: jochen05@exchange.louisville.edu. Subject Specialists: *Med libr,* Elizabeth Smigielski; *Med libr,* Nancy Utterback; *Med libr,* Michelle Cohen Atlas; Staff 19 (MLS 6, Non-MLS 13)
Founded 1837. Highest Degree: Doctorate
Jul 2011-Jun 2012 Income $3,049,015. Mats Exp $1,543,022, Books $53,303, Per/Ser (Incl. Access Fees) $33,468, Manu Arch $22, Electronic Ref Mat (Incl. Access Fees) $1,453,102, Presv $810. Sal $902,267 (Prof $480,886)
Library Holdings: Bk Vols 267,383; Per Subs 510
Special Collections: Anesthesia Coll; History Coll; Kentucky Medicine Coll; Neurology Coll, Neurosurgery Coll; Pherenology Coll; Psychiatry Coll
Subject Interests: Allied health, Dentistry, Med, Nursing
Database Vendor: Springer-Verlag
Function: Accelerated reader prog
Partic in Greater Midwest Regional Medical Libr Network
Friends of the Library Group

SPECIAL COLLECTIONS/PHOTOGRAPHIC ARCHIVES, Belknap Campus, 2215 S Third St, 40208, SAN 342-5703. Tel: 502-852-6752. FAX: 502-852-8734. *Curator of Rare Bks & Ms, Head, Spec Coll,* Delinda Buie; Tel: 502-852-6762, E-mail: dsbuie01@louisville.edu; *Curator,* Elizabeth Reilly; Tel: 502-852-8730, E-mail: elizabeth.reilly@louisville.edu; Staff 6 (MLS 3, Non-MLS 3)
Function: Ref serv available

UNIVERSITY ARCHIVES & RECORDS CENTER, Ekstrom Library, 2215 S Third St, 40208. Tel: 502-852-6674. FAX: 502-852-7394. *Univ Archivist,* Caroline Daniels; Tel: 502-852-6676, E-mail: c0dani01@louisville.edu; *Assoc Archivist, Prof,* Dr Thomas Louis Owen; Tel: 502-852-8790, Fax: 502-852-6673, E-mail: tlowen01@exchange.louisville.edu; *Assoc Prof,* Chadwick Brice Owen; Fax: 502-852-6673, E-mail: c0owen03@exchange.louisville.edu; *Archivist, Assoc Prof, Curator,* Dr Katherine Burger Johnson; Fax: 502-852-6673, E-mail: kbjohn01@exchange.louisville.edu. Subject Specialists: *Local hist,* Dr Thomas Louis Owen; *Rec mgt,* Chadwick Brice Owen
Jul 2011-Jun 2012 Income $521,837. Sal $261,045 (Prof $211,035)
Library Holdings: Bk Vols 4,659; Per Subs 31
Special Collections: Oral History

GM VETERANS AFFAIRS MEDICAL CENTER LIBRARY*, 800 Zorn Ave, 40206-1499. SAN 306-3615. Tel: 502-287-6240. FAX: 502-287-6134. *Librn,* Maure Shelton; *Tech Support,* Sue Tomes; Staff 2 (MLS 1, Non-MLS 1)
Founded 1952
Library Holdings: DVDs 250; e-books 625; e-journals 5,000; Bk Titles 1,600; Per Subs 362
Automation Activity & Vendor Info: (Circulation) CyberTools for Libraries; (OPAC) CyberTools for Libraries; (Serials) EBSCO Online
Database Vendor: Cinahl, DynaMed, EBSCOhost, Elsevier, McGraw-Hill, MD Consult, Micromedex, Natural Standard, OCLC FirstSearch, OCLC WorldShare Interlibrary Loan, OVID Technologies, ProQuest, PubMed, Sage, ScienceDirect, SerialsSolutions, Springer-Verlag, STAT!Ref (Teton Data Systems), Swets Information Services, UpToDate, Wiley InterScience
Function: ILL available, Online searches, Photocopying/Printing, Ref serv available
Partic in Kentucky Medical Library Association
Restriction: Not open to pub

MADISONVILLE

P HOPKINS COUNTY-MADISONVILLE PUBLIC LIBRARY*, 455 Madison Square Dr, 42431. SAN 342-5762. Tel: 270-825-2680. FAX: 270-452-2451. E-mail: library@publiclibrary.org. Web Site: www.publiclibrary.org. *Dir,* Joel Meador; *Ch,* Angel Killough
Founded 1974. Pop 47,300; Circ 189,714
Library Holdings: AV Mats 45; Electronic Media & Resources 16; Large Print Bks 1,000; Bk Vols 85,000; Per Subs 108; Talking Bks 800
Special Collections: Kentucky Coll; Rare Book Coll
Automation Activity & Vendor Info: (Circulation) Mandarin Library Automation
Partic in Kentucky Library Network, Inc
Open Mon-Fri 10-7, Sat 10-5
Friends of the Library Group
Branches: 1
DAWSON SPRINGS BRANCH, 103 W Ramsey St, Dawson Springs, 42408-1738, SAN 342-5797. Tel: 270-797-8990. FAX: 270-797-8990. E-mail: branchlibrary@publiclibrary.org. *Br Mgr,* Mary Adams
Library Holdings: Bk Vols 30,000
Open Tues-Fri 10-5:30, Sat Noon-3
Friends of the Library Group
Bookmobiles: 1. Librn, Shanna Turner

J MADISONVILLE COMMUNITY COLLEGE*, Loman C Trover Library, 2000 College Dr, 42431. SAN 306-364X. Tel: 270-824-1722. FAX: 270-825-8553. Web Site: www.madisonville.kctcs.edu/library. *Dir,* Cherry Berges; Tel: 270-824-8677, E-mail: cherry.berges@kctcs.edu; *Librn,* Colin Magee; *Asst Librn,* Camille Richmond; Tel: 270-824-1721, E-mail: camille.richmond@kctcs.edu; *Libr Spec,* Tim Stutler; Tel: 270-824-8678, E-mail: tim.stutler@kctcs.edu
Founded 1968
Library Holdings: Bk Titles 24,000; Bk Vols 28,099, Per Subs 233
Subject Interests: Nursing, Phys therapy
Automation Activity & Vendor Info: (Acquisitions) Ex Libris Group; (Cataloging) Ex Libris Group; (OPAC) Ex Libris Group
Wireless access
Partic in Federation of Kentucky Academic Libraries (FoKAL); Kentucky Library Network, Inc; State Assisted Academic Library Council of Kentucky
Open Mon-Thurs 8-6, Fri 8-4, Sat 9-2

M REGIONAL MEDICAL CENTER*, Medical Library, 900 Hospital Dr, 42431-1694. SAN 323-6331. Tel: 270-825-5252. FAX: 270-825-3411. *Librn,* Teresa C Ruddell; E-mail: truddell@trover.org
Library Holdings: Bk Vols 1,500; Per Subs 220
Subject Interests: Consumer health info, Med
Wireless access
Partic in Kentucky Library Network, Inc; Ky Area Health Educ Ctr Consortium

MANCHESTER

P CLAY COUNTY PUBLIC LIBRARY*, 211 Bridge St, 40962. SAN 306-3658. Tel: 606-598-2617. FAX: 606-598-4671. E-mail: ccpublic@windstream.net. Web Site: www.claycountypubliclibrary.org. *Dir,* Linda Sandlin; *Asst Dir, Ch Serv, Dir of Outreach,* Donna Gillahan; *Outreach Librn,* Karen Burkholder; *Acq & Cat,* Olivia Dezarn
Founded 1954. Pop 24,000; Circ 53,470
Library Holdings: Bk Vols 20,000; Per Subs 67
Special Collections: Kentucky Coll; Large Print Books & Magazines; Local History Coll
Automation Activity & Vendor Info: (Cataloging) TLC (The Library Corporation); (Circulation) TLC (The Library Corporation); (OPAC) TLC (The Library Corporation)
Open Mon & Thurs 9-8, Tues, Wed & Fri 9-5, Sat 9-1

Friends of the Library Group
Bookmobiles: 1. Librn, Ryan Cornett

MARION

P CRITTENDEN COUNTY PUBLIC LIBRARY*, 204 W Carlisle St, 42064-1727. SAN 306-3666. Tel: 270-965-3354. FAX: 270-965-3354. Web Site: www.crittendenlibrary.org. *Dir,* Regina Merrick; E-mail: rmerrick@crittendenlibrary.org; *Children & Youth Serv Librn,* Kathleen Guess; *Circ Librn,* Casey Farmer; E-mail: ccplcirc@live.com; Staff 1 (Non-MLS 1)
Founded 1953. Pop 9,207; Circ 58,376
Library Holdings: Bk Vols 30,000; Per Subs 92
Special Collections: Oral History
Subject Interests: Local hist
Automation Activity & Vendor Info: (Cataloging) Follett Software; (Circulation) Follett Software
Function: Alaskana res
Open Mon, Tues, Thurs & Fri 9-5, Wed & Sat 9-1
Friends of the Library Group
Bookmobiles: 1. Librn, Nancy Brock

MAYFIELD

P GRAVES COUNTY PUBLIC LIBRARY*, 601 N 17th St, 42066. SAN 306-3674. Tel: 270-247-2911. FAX: 270-247-2991. Web Site: www.gcpl.org. *Interim Dir,* Susie Cain; *Children's & Youth Serv,* Susie Cain; *Circ/Per,* Deana Hopper
Founded 1940
Library Holdings: Bk Titles 53,934; Per Subs 108
Automation Activity & Vendor Info: (Acquisitions) Innovative Interfaces, Inc; (Circulation) Innovative Interfaces, Inc
Wireless access
Partic in Kentucky Library Network, Inc
Open Mon & Tues 9-8, Wed-Sat 9-5
Friends of the Library Group
Bookmobiles: 1. Librn, Sandy Hennessee

CR MID-CONTINENT UNIVERSITY*, Anne Parrish-Markham Library, 99 E Powell Rd, 42066-9007. SAN 325-0709. Tel: 270-247-8521, Ext 275. FAX: 270-247-3115. Web Site: www.midcontinent.edu. *Dean,* Ben Graves; Tel: 270-247-8521, Ext 634, E-mail: bgraves@midcontinent.edu; *Asst Librn,* Kim Scott; E-mail: kscott@midcontinent.edu; Staff 2 (MLS 1, Non-MLS 1)
Founded 1968. Enrl 180; Fac 12
Library Holdings: Bk Titles 32,756; Bk Vols 40,000; Per Subs 200
Special Collections: Bible Studies Coll. Oral History
Subject Interests: Bus, Hist, Psychol, Shakespeare
Automation Activity & Vendor Info: (Cataloging) Follett Software; (Circulation) Follett Software
Partic in Kentucky Library Network, Inc
Special Services for the Deaf - Bks on deafness & sign lang
Open Mon, Tues & Thurs 8:30am-9pm, Wed 8:30-4, Fri 8:30-5

MAYSVILLE

P MASON COUNTY PUBLIC LIBRARY*, 218 E Third St, 41056. SAN 306-3690. Tel: 606-564-3286. FAX: 606-564-5408. E-mail: masoncolibrary@bellsouth.net. Web Site: www.masoncountylibrary.com. *Dir,* Valerie Zempter; *Asst Librn,* Pam Erskine; *Ch,* Melissa Fulton; Staff 5 (MLS 1, Non-MLS 4)
Founded 1876. Pop 17,765
Jul 2006-Jun 2007 Income $637,009, State $21,548, County $565,662. Mats Exp $53,615, Books $40,884, Per/Ser (Incl. Access Fees) $5,000, AV Equip $3,231, AV Mat $3,000, Electronic Ref Mat (Incl. Access Fees) $1,500. Sal $125,167 (Prof $38,000)
Library Holdings: Bks on Deafness & Sign Lang 14; High Interest/Low Vocabulary Bk Vols 1,700; Bk Vols 52,000; Per Subs 58; Talking Bks 2,377; Videos 1,586
Special Collections: Music
Subject Interests: Kentucky
Automation Activity & Vendor Info: (Cataloging) Innovative Interfaces, Inc; (Circulation) Innovative Interfaces, Inc; (OPAC) Innovative Interfaces, Inc
Wireless access
Partic in Ky Libr Asn
Special Services for the Blind - Accessible computers; Audio mat; Bks available with recordings
Open Mon 9-8, Tues-Fri 9-6, Sat 9-5
Friends of the Library Group
Bookmobiles: 1. Librn, Heaven Greene. Bk vols 3,500

J MAYSVILLE COMMUNITY & TECHNICAL COLLEGE*, Maysville Campus Library, 1755 US Hwy 68, 41056. SAN 306-3682. Tel: 606-759-7141, Ext 66206. FAX: 606-759-7176. Web Site: www.maysville.kctcs.edu/Academics/library.aspx. *Dir of Libr Serv,* Sonja R Eads; Tel: 606-759-7141, Ext 66126, E-mail: sonja.eads@kctcs.edu; *Librn,* Carla Redden; Tel: 606-759-7141, Ext 66125, E-mail: carla.redden@kctcs.edu; *Libr Spec,* Garon Overley; Tel: 606-759-7141, Ext 66276, E-mail: garon.overley@kctcs.edu; *Libr Spec,* Seth Sisler; Tel: 606-759-7141, Ext 66124, E-mail: ssisler0002@kctcs.edu; Staff 7 (MLS 3, Non-MLS 4)
Founded 1968. Enrl 3,543; Fac 95; Highest Degree: Associate
Library Holdings: e-books 33,488; Bk Vols 37,423; Per Subs 32; Videos 2,939
Special Collections: Career Coll, AV, bks, micro; Kentuckiana Historical Coll; Rare Books
Subject Interests: Hist, Kentucky, Nursing, Tech subjects
Automation Activity & Vendor Info: (Cataloging) Ex Libris Group; (Circulation) Ex Libris Group; (Course Reserve) Ex Libris Group; (ILL) OCLC; (OPAC) Ex Libris Group
Database Vendor: CredoReference, Ex Libris Group, Gale Cengage Learning, Newsbank, OCLC FirstSearch, ProQuest
Wireless access
Publications: On A Roll (Monthly bulletin)
Partic in Lyrasis; OCLC Online Computer Library Center, Inc
Open Mon-Thurs (Fall & Spring) 8-7, Fri 8-4:30); Mon-Fri (Summer) 8-4:30

Departmental Libraries:

LICKING VALLEY CAMPUS LIBRARY, 319 Webster Ave, Cynthiana, 41031. Tel: 859-234-8626, Ext 66417. *Libr Spec,* Carla Keller
Automation Activity & Vendor Info: (Cataloging) Ex Libris Group; (Circulation) Ex Libris Group; (Course Reserve) Ex Libris Group; (OPAC) Ex Libris Group
Database Vendor: EBSCOhost, Gale Cengage Learning, OCLC WorldShare Interlibrary Loan, ProQuest
Open Mon, Thurs & Fri 8-4:30, Tues & Wed 8-7

ROWAN CAMPUS LIBRARY, 609 Viking Dr, Morehead, 40351. Tel: 606-783-1538, Ext 66366. *Libr Spec,* Kathy Riddle; E-mail: kriddle0004@kctcs.edu
Automation Activity & Vendor Info: (Cataloging) Ex Libris Group; (Circulation) Ex Libris Group; (Course Reserve) Ex Libris Group; (OPAC) Ex Libris Group
Database Vendor: EBSCOhost, Gale Cengage Learning, OCLC WorldShare Interlibrary Loan, ProQuest
Open Mon & Thurs-Fri 8-4:30, Tues & Wed 8-7

MCKEE

P JACKSON COUNTY PUBLIC LIBRARY, 338 N Main St, 40447. (Mail add: PO Box 160, 404447-0160), SAN 306-3631. Tel: 606-287-8113. FAX: 606-287-7774. E-mail: jcplib@prtcnet.org. *Dir,* Betty L Bingham; *Asst Dir, Youth Serv,* Malta Flannery; *Tech Serv,* Arlie Kay Morgan
Founded 1973. Pop 13,495; Circ 36,438
Library Holdings: Bk Vols 23,432; Per Subs 25
Automation Activity & Vendor Info: (Cataloging) Book Systems; (Circulation) Book Systems; (OPAC) Book Systems
Wireless access
Partic in Ky Libr Asn
Open Mon & Thurs 8:30-6, Tues, Wed & Fri 8:30-5, Sat 9-1
Bookmobiles: 1. Librn, Linda Croucher

MIDDLESBORO

S CUMBERLAND GAP NATIONAL HISTORICAL PARK LIBRARY*, 91 Bartlett Park Rd, 40965-1848. SAN 370-3088. Tel: 606-248-2817. FAX: 606-248-7276. Web Site: www.nps.gov/cuga. *Historian,* Martha Evans Wiley; Tel: 606-246-1051, E-mail: martha_wiley@nps.gov
Library Holdings: Bk Vols 200
Special Collections: Appalachian Culture (Hensley Settlement Oral History Coll); Robert Kincaid Coll. Oral History
Restriction: Open by appt only

P MIDDLESBOROUGH-BELL COUNTY PUBLIC LIBRARY*, 126 S 20th St, 40965-1212. (Mail add: PO Box 1677, 40965-3677), SAN 306-3704. Tel: 606-248-4812. FAX: 606-248-8766. E-mail: mborolib@bellcolib.org. Web Site: www.bellcolib.org. *Dir,* Beverly Greene; Tel: 606-248-5304; *Br Mgr, Tech Serv,* Michele B Lawson; E-mail: binglaw@hotmail.com; *Youth Serv Librn,* Cindy McGeorge; Staff 6 (MLS 1, Non-MLS 5)
Founded 1912. Pop 35,000; Circ 81,867
Library Holdings: Bk Vols 88,879; Per Subs 1,600
Special Collections: Oral History
Subject Interests: Genealogy for local families, Kentucky, Local hist
Automation Activity & Vendor Info: (Cataloging) Innovative Interfaces, Inc; (Circulation) Innovative Interfaces, Inc; (OPAC) Innovative Interfaces, Inc
Open Mon-Fri 9-6, Sat 10-4
Friends of the Library Group

J SOUTHEAST KENTUCKY COMMUNITY & TECHNICAL COLLEGE*, Middlesboro Campus Library, 1300 Chichester Ave, 40965. SAN 371-957X. Tel: 606-248-0442. FAX: 606-248-3268. Web Site: www.secc.kctcs.edu/library. *Dir,* Kevin Murphy; Tel: 606-248-0469, E-mail: kevin.murphy@kctcs.edu; *Librn,* Lisa Ahlstedt; Tel: 606-248-0470, E-mail: lisa.ahlstedt@kctcs.edu; *Tech Serv,* Mike Justice; Tel: 606-248-0443, E-mail: mike.justice@kctcs.edu; Staff 3 (MLS 2, Non-MLS 1)
Library Holdings: e-books 14,000; Bk Vols 15,000; Per Subs 90
Automation Activity & Vendor Info: (Cataloging) Ex Libris Group; (Circulation) Ex Libris Group; (Course Reserve) Ex Libris Group; (OPAC) Ex Libris Group
Open Mon-Thurs 7:30-7, Fri 8-4:30

MIDWAY

C MIDWAY COLLEGE*, Little Memorial Library, 512 E Stephens St, 40347-1120. SAN 306-3712. Tel: 859-846-5316. E-mail: library@midway.edu. Web Site: www.midway.edu/library. *Dir of Libr Serv,* Catherine L Reilender; Tel: 859-846-5315, E-mail: creilender@midway.edu; *Ref Librn,* Carrie Lewis; Tel: 859-846-5744, E-mail: clewis@midway.edu; Staff 2 (MLS 2)
Founded 1847. Enrl 1,200; Fac 120; Highest Degree: Master
Library Holdings: Bk Titles 56,000
Automation Activity & Vendor Info: (Acquisitions) Ex Libris Group; (Cataloging) Ex Libris Group; (Circulation) Ex Libris Group; (ILL) OCLC FirstSearch; (OPAC) Ex Libris Group; (Serials) Ex Libris Group
Database Vendor: EBSCOhost, LexisNexis, OCLC FirstSearch, ProQuest
Wireless access
Partic in Association of Independent Kentucky Colleges & Universities; Federation of Kentucky Academic Libraries (FoKAL); KLN
Restriction: Open by appt only

MONTICELLO

P WAYNE COUNTY PUBLIC LIBRARY*, 150 S Main St, 42633. SAN 306-3720. Tel: 606-348-8565. FAX: 606-348-3829. E-mail: staff@waynecountylibrary.org. Web Site: www.waynecountylibrary.org. *Libr Dir,* Anne Garner; *Asst Librn,* Barbara York; *Ch,* Donna Tuggle; *YA Librn,* Marlene Bass
Founded 1949. Pop 20,969; Circ 201,237
Library Holdings: Audiobooks 2,052; CDs 259; DVDs 1,803; Bk Vols 53,189; Per Subs 146
Special Collections: Genealogy Coll
Automation Activity & Vendor Info: (Cataloging) Follett Software; (Circulation) Follett Software
Wireless access
Mem of Marshes of Glynn Libraries
Open Mon, Wed, Fri & Sat 8:30-4:30, Tues & Thurs 8:30-6:30
Bookmobiles: 1. Librn, Debbie Marcum

MOREHEAD

C MOREHEAD STATE UNIVERSITY, Camden-Carroll Library, 150 University Blvd, 40351. SAN 306 3739. Tel: 606-783-2200. Circulation Tel: 606-783-5490. Interlibrary Loan Service Tel: 606-783-5107. Reference Tel: 606-783-5491. Administration Tel: 606-783-5169. Toll Free Tel: 800-423-0884. FAX: 606-783-5037. Interlibrary Loan Service FAX: 606-783-2799. E-mail: library@moreheadstate.edu. Web Site: www.moreheadstate.edu/library. *Dean, Libr Serv,* David Gregory; Tel: 606-783-5100, E-mail: d.gregory@moreheadstate.edu; *Dir, Instrul Serv,* Ray Bailey; Tel: 606-783-5106, E-mail: ra.bailey@moreheadstate.edu; *Head, Cat, Head, Tech Serv,* Pamela Colyer; Tel: 606-783-5118, E-mail: p.colyer@moreheadstate.edu; *Head, Spec Coll & Archives,* Dieter Ullrich; E-mail: d.ullrich@moreheadstate.edu; *Head, User Serv,* Jennifer Little; Tel: 606-783-5352, E-mail: j.little@moreheadstate.edu; *Cat Librn,* Jason Griffith; E-mail: jmgriffith@moreheadstate.edu; *Distance Instruction Librn,* Karla Aleman; Tel: 606-783-5114, E-mail: k.aleman@moreheadstate.edu; *Instruction & Outreach Librn,* Position Currently Open; *Ser/Govt Doc Librn,* Mykie Howard; Tel: 606-783-5116, E-mail: my.howard@moreheadstate.edu; *Syst Librn,* Ophelia Chapman; Tel: 606-783-5119, E-mail: o.chapman@moreheadstate.edu; *Coordr of Res Serv,* Tom Kmetz; Tel: 606-783-5111, E-mail: t.kmetz@moreheadstate.edu; *Coordr, Instrul Tech,* Rodney Watkins; Tel: 606-783-9343, E-mail: rlwatk01@moreheadstate.edu; Staff 37.5 (MLS 12, Non-MLS 25.5)
Founded 1922. Enrl 10,971; Fac 381; Highest Degree: Doctorate
Jul 2012-Jun 2013. Mats Exp $2,775,410, Books $216,363, Per/Ser (Incl. Access Fees) $527,812, AV Mat $40,775, Presv $3,201. Sal $1,557,210 (Prof $590,025)
Library Holdings: Audiobooks 825; AV Mats 26,900; CDs 36,574; DVDs 6,705; e-books 40,374; e-journals 72,804; Microforms 48,477; Music Scores 8,148; Bk Titles 442,652; Bk Vols 510,652; Per Subs 1,350; Videos 2,613
Special Collections: Adron & Mignon Doran Coll; Appalachian Coll; James Still Coll; Jesse Stuart Coll; Roger W Barbour Coll; University Archives. US Document Depository
Subject Interests: Appalachia, Educ, Math, Music, Nursing, Philos, Phys sci, Psychol, Soc serv (soc work)
Automation Activity & Vendor Info: (Acquisitions) Ex Libris Group; (Cataloging) Ex Libris Group; (Circulation) Ex Libris Group; (Course Reserve) Ex Libris Group; (ILL) OCLC ILLiad; (OPAC) Ex Libris Group; (Serials) Ex Libris Group
Database Vendor: ACM (Association for Computing Machinery), Alexander Street Press, American Chemical Society, American Mathematical Society, Annual Reviews, Bowker, CIOS (Communication Institute for Online Scholarship), CQ Press, EBSCOhost, Elsevier, Ex Libris Group, Facts on File, Gale Cengage Learning, Grolier Online, H W Wilson, ISI Web of Knowledge, JSTOR, LexisNexis, Mergent Online, Newsbank, OCLC WorldShare Interlibrary Loan, Oxford Online, Paratext, Project MUSE, ProQuest, PubMed, Sage, SBRnet (Sports Business Research Network), ScienceDirect, Standard & Poor's, ValueLine, Westlaw, Wiley InterScience
Wireless access
Function: Archival coll, Copy machines, E-Reserves, Electronic databases & coll, Handicapped accessible, ILL available, Online ref, Ref & res, Tax forms
Partic in Federation of Kentucky Academic Libraries (FoKAL); Lyrasis; National Network of Libraries of Medicine; OCLC Online Computer Library Center, Inc; State Assisted Academic Library Council of Kentucky
Open Mon-Wed 7am-Midnight, Thurs 7am-11pm, Fri 7-6, Sat 11-7, Sun 1-Midnight

P ROWAN COUNTY PUBLIC LIBRARY*, 175 Beacon Hill Dr, 40351. SAN 306-3747. Tel: 606-784-7137. FAX: 606-784-2130. *Dir,* Helen E Williams; Tel: 606-784-3528; *Pub Serv Librn,* Cynthia J Leach; *Circ Mgr,* Steven Oney; *Prog Coordr,* Sandra Fleshman; *Tech Coordr,* Michael Thornsbury; Staff 11 (MLS 2, Non-MLS 9)
Founded 1952. Pop 22,872; Circ 112,000
Library Holdings: Audiobooks 5,719; AV Mats 10,500; Large Print Bks 2,605; Bk Titles 43,493; Bk Vols 49,413; Per Subs 217
Special Collections: Rowan County Cemetery Records
Subject Interests: Cemetery, Genealogy, Kentucky, Obituary info
Automation Activity & Vendor Info: (Cataloging) TLC (The Library Corporation); (Circulation) TLC (The Library Corporation); (OPAC) TLC (The Library Corporation)
Database Vendor: EBSCOhost, Hoovers, LearningExpress, Newsbank, OCLC FirstSearch, ProQuest, TLC (The Library Corporation), WebMD, Wilson - Wilson Web
Function: Homebound delivery serv, Photocopying/Printing, Prog for children & young adult, Ref serv available, Serves mentally handicapped consumers, Summer reading prog, Wheelchair accessible
Partic in OCLC
Open Mon-Thurs 9-8, Fri & Sat 9-5, Sun 1-5
Friends of the Library Group
Bookmobiles: 1. Librn, Donna Christian

M SAINT CLAIRE REGIONAL MEDICAL CENTER LIBRARY*, 222 Medical Circle, 40351. SAN 320-3786. Tel: 606-783-6861. FAX: 606-784-2178. Web Site: www.st claire.org. *In Charge,* Cathy Mettey
Founded 1966
Library Holdings: Bk Titles 1,250; Per Subs 150
Database Vendor: EBSCOhost
Open Mon-Fri 8-4:30

MORGANTOWN

P BUTLER COUNTY PUBLIC LIBRARY*, 116 W Ohio St, 42261. (Mail add: PO Box 247, 42261-0247), SAN 306-3755. Tel: 270-526-4722. FAX: 270-526-9974. Web Site: www.bcplky.org. *Librn,* Kenna Martin; E-mail: kenna.martin@bcplky.org; *Asst Librn,* Connie Embry
Founded 1954. Pop 13,010; Circ 37,959
Library Holdings: DVDs 30; Bk Vols 29,000; Per Subs 42; Talking Bks 518; Videos 1,000
Automation Activity & Vendor Info: (Cataloging) AmLib Library Management System; (Circulation) AmLib Library Management System; (OPAC) AmLib Library Management System
Open Mon, Wed-Fri 8:30-4:30, Tues 8:30-7, Sat 8-4
Bookmobiles: 1. Librn, Sharon Nabours

MOUNT OLIVET

P ROBERTSON COUNTY PUBLIC LIBRARY*, 207 N Main St, 41064. (Mail add: PO Box 282, 41064-0282), SAN 320-8206. Tel: 606-724-5746. Administration Tel: 606-724-2015. FAX: 606-724-5746. E-mail: robertsoncountylibrary@yahoo.com. *Dir,* Carol Mitchell; E-mail: carol.mitchell@ky.gov; *Ch Serv, Circ,* Christy Haywood; E-mail: christy1haywood@yahoo.com
Founded 1979. Pop 2,266; Circ 30,737
Library Holdings: Bk Vols 15,206; Per Subs 22
Automation Activity & Vendor Info: (Cataloging) Triple B Technologies; (Circulation) Triple B Technologies

Wireless access
Special Services for the Blind - Bks on cassette
Open Mon, Tues, Thurs & Fri 10-5, Wed 9-6, Sat 9-Noon
Bookmobiles: 1. Librn, Dian Oaks

MOUNT STERLING

P MOUNT STERLING MONTGOMERY COUNTY LIBRARY*, 241 W Locust St, 40353. SAN 376-5806. Tel: 859-498-2404. FAX: 859-498-7477. E-mail: askmtsterlinglibrary@yahoo.com. Web Site: www.mstlib.com. *Dir,* Melissa Smathers-Barnes; *Ad, Circ Supvr,* Lori McAlister; *Ch Serv Librn,* Betty Trump; Staff 6 (MLS 1, Non-MLS 5)
Founded 1871. Pop 24,000; Circ 125,000
Library Holdings: AV Mats 2,675; Bks on Deafness & Sign Lang 25; CDs 300; DVDs 600; Electronic Media & Resources 50; Bk Vols 45,000; Per Subs 106; Talking Bks 835; Videos 1,000
Automation Activity & Vendor Info: (Acquisitions) TLC (The Library Corporation); (Cataloging) TLC (The Library Corporation); (Circulation) TLC (The Library Corporation); (Course Reserve) TLC (The Library Corporation); (ILL) TLC (The Library Corporation); (Media Booking) TLC (The Library Corporation); (OPAC) TLC (The Library Corporation); (Serials) TLC (The Library Corporation)
Open Mon, Tues & Thurs 8:30-8, Wed & Fri 8:30-6:30, Sat 8:30-3
Bookmobiles: 1. Librn, Nena Donovan

MOUNT VERNON

P ROCKCASTLE COUNTY PUBLIC LIBRARY*, 60 Ford Dr, 40456. SAN 306-3763. Tel: 606-256-2388. FAX: 606-256-5460. Web Site: www.rockcastlelibrary.org. *Dir,* Pamela Chaliff; E-mail: pam@rockcastlelibrary.org
Founded 1954. Pop 13,973; Circ 81,014
Library Holdings: Bk Vols 24,155; Per Subs 40
Subject Interests: Genealogy
Automation Activity & Vendor Info: (Acquisitions) Brodart; (Cataloging) Brodart; (Circulation) Brodart
Open Mon-Fri 9:30-6, Sat 9:30-2

MUNFORDVILLE

P HART COUNTY PUBLIC LIBRARY*, 500 E Union St, 42765. SAN 306-3771. Tel: 270-524-1953. FAX: 270-524-7323. E-mail: library@hartcountypubliclibrary.org. Web Site: www.hartcountypubliclibrary.org. *Dir,* Vicki Logsdon
Founded 1968. Pop 17,000; Circ 93,652
Library Holdings: Bk Vols 31,000; Per Subs 55
Special Collections: Oral History
Subject Interests: Genealogy
Automation Activity & Vendor Info: (Cataloging) Follett Software; (Circulation) Follett Software; (OPAC) Follett Software
Open Mon & Thurs 8:30-6, Tues, Wed & Fri 8:30-4:30, Sat 8:30-12

MURRAY

P CALLOWAY COUNTY PUBLIC LIBRARY*, 710 Main St, 42071. SAN 306-378X. Tel: 270-753-2288. FAX: 270-753-8263. Web Site: www.callowaycountylibrary.org. *Dir,* Mignon Pittman; Staff 3 (MLS 3)
Founded 1967. Pop 33,000; Circ 350,000
Library Holdings: Bk Vols 63,000; Per Subs 150
Special Collections: Calloway County Antique Photographs Coll; Kentucky Authors & Titles (Kentucky Coll). Oral History
Automation Activity & Vendor Info: (Cataloging) Follett Software; (Circulation) Follett Software; (ILL) OCLC; (OPAC) Follett Software
Wireless access
Publications: Pot Pouri-Calloway County
Open Mon-Fri 8-8, Sat 9-5, Sun 1-5

M MURRAY-COLLOWAY COUNTY HOSPITAL*, Houston Memorial Library, 803 Poplar St, 42071-2467. Tel: 270-762-1572. FAX: 270-762-1770. Web Site: www.murrayhospital.org.
Library Holdings: Bk Vols 200
Database Vendor: EBSCOhost, OVID Technologies
Wireless access
Open Mon-Fri 8-4:30

C MURRAY STATE UNIVERSITY*, Harry Lee Waterfield Library, 205 Waterfield Library, Dean's Office, 42071-3307. SAN 342-5916. Tel: 270-809-2291. Circulation Tel: 270-809-4990. Interlibrary Loan Service Tel: 270-809-4298, 270-809-4420. Reference Tel: 270-809-2053. FAX: 270-809-3736. Web Site: www.murraystate.edu/msml/msml.htm. *Dean,* Adam Murray; Fax: 270-809-5604, E-mail: amurray@murraystate.edu; *Dir, Archives & Spec Coll,* Dieter Ullrich; Tel: 270-809-4295, E-mail: dullrich@murraystate.edu; *Dir, Tech Serv & e-Res,* Cris Ferguson; Tel: 270-809-5607; *Head, Ref,* Becky Richardson; Tel: 270-809-4151; *Res & Instruction Librn,* Caitlin Bagley; Tel: 270-809-6221, E-mail: cbagley1@murraystate.edu; *Res & Instruction Librn,* Katherine Farmer; Tel: 270-809-6180, E-mail: kfarmer10@murraystate.edu; *Res & Instruction Librn,* Ashley Ireland; Tel: 270-809-4819, E-mail: aireland@murraystate.edu; *Res & Instruction Librn,* Julie Robinson; Tel: 270-809-2846, E-mail: jrobinson1@murraystate.edu; *Tech Serv Librn,* Leslie Engelson; Tel: 270-809-4818, E-mail: lengelson@murraystate.edu; Staff 11 (MLS 10, Non-MLS 1)
Founded 1923. Enrl 10,156; Fac 395; Highest Degree: Master
Jul 2010-Jun 2011 Income $3,521,552. Mats Exp $1,388,675, Books $147,617, Per/Ser (Incl. Access Fees) $565,256, Micro $23,721, AV Mat $41,628. Sal $1,180,603 (Prof $497,345)
Library Holdings: AV Mats 36,421; CDs 3,356; DVDs 2,281; e-books 40,222; e-journals 715; Microforms 205,593; Music Scores 5,902; Bk Titles 407,735; Bk Vols 409,441; Per Subs 1,306; Videos 5,537
Special Collections: Forrest Pogue Coll; Irvin S Cobb Coll; Jackson Purchase History & Genealogy; Jesse Stuart Coll, bks, memorabilia, ms; National, State & Regional Political Records. US Document Depository
Automation Activity & Vendor Info: (Acquisitions) Ex Libris Group; (Cataloging) Ex Libris Group; (Circulation) Ex Libris Group; (Course Reserve) Ex Libris Group; (ILL) OCLC; (OPAC) Ex Libris Group; (Serials) Ex Libris Group
Database Vendor: ABC-CLIO, Agricola, Alexander Street Press, American Mathematical Society, American Physical Society, ARTstor, Baker & Taylor, Bowker, Cambridge Scientific Abstracts, CredoReference, EBSCOhost, Elsevier, Ex Libris Group, Gale Cengage Learning, Grolier Online, H W Wilson, IEEE (Institute of Electrical & Electronics Engineers), ISI Web of Knowledge, JSTOR, LexisNexis, Mergent Online, OCLC, OCLC FirstSearch, OCLC WorldShare Interlibrary Loan, OVID Technologies, Oxford Online, ProQuest, ScienceDirect, Thomson - Web of Science, WebMD, Westlaw, Wiley, Wiley InterScience, Wilson - Wilson Web
Wireless access
Publications: MSU Inform (Newsletter)
Partic in Federation of Kentucky Academic Libraries (FoKAL); Lyrasis; OCLC Online Computer Library Center, Inc; State Assisted Academic Library Council of Kentucky
Special Services for the Blind - Reader equip; ZoomText magnification & reading software
Open Mon-Thurs 7am-12:30am, Fri 7am-8pm, Sat 10-8, Sun Noon-12:30am
Friends of the Library Group

NICHOLASVILLE

P JESSAMINE COUNTY PUBLIC LIBRARY*, 600 S Main St, 40356-1839. SAN 306-3828. Tel: 859-885-3523. FAX: 859-885-5164. E-mail: jcplcirculation@jesspublib.org. Web Site: www.jesspublib.org. *Exec Dir,* Dr Ron Critchfield; Tel: 859-885-3523, Ext 223; *Ch Serv Librn,* Juliana Gaddis; *Coll Serv Librn,* Mary Ann Abner; *Tech Librn,* David Powell; *User Serv Librn,* Sara King; Staff 26 (MLS 4, Non-MLS 22)
Founded 1968. Pop 40,016; Circ 386,182
Library Holdings: AV Mats 4,365; Bk Vols 60,682; Per Subs 115; Talking Bks 4,216
Special Collections: Jessamine County Genealogy; Kentucky Coll
Subject Interests: Kentucky
Automation Activity & Vendor Info: (Cataloging) SirsiDynix
Database Vendor: EBSCOhost, OCLC FirstSearch
Special Services for the Deaf - Assistive tech
Special Services for the Blind - Computer with voice synthesizer for visually impaired persons
Open Mon-Wed 9-9, Thurs 11:30-9, Fri 9-6, Sat 9-5, Sun 1:30-5
Friends of the Library Group
Bookmobiles: 1

OWENSBORO

CR BRESCIA UNIVERSITY*, Father Leonard Alvey Library, 717 Frederica St, 42301. SAN 306-3836. Tel: 270-686-4212. FAX: 270-686-4266. Web Site: www.brescia.edu/bu_library. *Dir, Libr & Info Serv,* Sister Judith N Riney; Tel: 270-686-4288, E-mail: judith.riney@brescia.edu; *Asst Librn,* Kathy Eby; Tel: 270-686-4213, E-mail: kathy.eby@brescia.edu; *Pub Serv Mgr,* Carrie Mann; Staff 4 (MLS 2, Non-MLS 2)
Founded 1950. Enrl 750; Highest Degree: Master
Library Holdings: e-books 120,000; e-journals 14,000; Bk Titles 79,000; Bk Vols 86,000
Special Collections: Kentuckiana
Subject Interests: Lit, Relig
Automation Activity & Vendor Info: (Acquisitions) Ex Libris Group; (Cataloging) Ex Libris Group; (Circulation) Ex Libris Group; (OPAC) Ex Libris Group
Database Vendor: CountryWatch, EBSCOhost, Ex Libris Group, Facts on File, Gale Cengage Learning, Grolier Online, JSTOR, OCLC FirstSearch, OCLC WorldShare Interlibrary Loan, Oxford Online, ProQuest, WT Cox
Wireless access
Publications: Faculty Handbook; List of Acquisitions; Student Handbook

Partic in Association of Independent Kentucky Colleges & Universities; Federation of Kentucky Academic Libraries (FoKAL); OCLC Online Computer Library Center, Inc
Open Mon-Thurs 7:30am-10pm, Fri 7:30-4, Sun 5-10

P DAVIESS COUNTY PUBLIC LIBRARY, 2020 Frederica St, 42301. SAN 306-3860. Tel: 270-684-0211. FAX: 270-684-0218. Administration FAX: 270-691-1890. Web Site: www.dcplibrary.org. *Dir,* James Blanton; *Accounts Mgr,* Debbie Young; E-mail: dyoung@dcplibrary.org; *Circ,* Brandon Hagan; *Info Tech,* Brian Lashbrook; *ILL,* Rhonda Schell; *Pub Serv, Youth Serv,* Shannon Sandefur; *Ref & Info Serv,* Christy Temple; *Spec Coll,* Leslie McCarty; *Tech Serv,* Irene Hatcher; *Web Serv,* Alicia Harrington; Staff 44 (MLS 6, Non-MLS 38)
Founded 1909. Pop 98,218; Circ 797,963
Jul 2013-Jun 2014 Income $4,113,216, State $109,563, Federal $9,896, Locally Generated Income $3,780,720, Other $213,037. Mats Exp $499,950, Books $237,275, Per/Ser (Incl. Access Fees) $85,710, Other Print Mats $168, AV Mat $70,475, Electronic Ref Mat (Incl. Access Fees) $106,322. Sal $1,512,880 (Prof $105,060)
Library Holdings: AV Mats 28,683; CDs 12,675; DVDs 15,591; e-books 78,343; Large Print Bks 16,353; Microforms 203; Bk Vols 215,366; Per Subs 3,615
Subject Interests: Genealogy, Hist, Kentucky, Local hist
Automation Activity & Vendor Info: (Acquisitions) Baker & Taylor; (Cataloging) OCLC; (Circulation) Innovative Interfaces, Inc; (ILL) OCLC; (OPAC) Innovative Interfaces, Inc
Database Vendor: 3M Library Systems, Baker & Taylor, Booksite, Bowker, Brodart, Dun & Bradstreet, EBSCO - WebFeat, EBSCO Auto Repair Reference, EBSCO Discovery Service, EBSCO Information Services, Facts on File, Gale Cengage Learning, Grolier Online, H W Wilson, infoUSA, Ingram Library Services, Library Automation Technologies, Inc. (LAT), Library Ideas, LLC, LibraryWorld, Inc, McGraw-Hill, Newsbank, OCLC, OCLC WebJunction, OCLC WorldShare Interlibrary Loan, Overdrive, Inc, ProQuest, ReferenceUSA, Sage, Tech Logic, TumbleBookLibrary, ValueLine, Westlaw, World Book Online, WT Cox
Wireless access
Open Mon-Thurs 9-9, Fri 9-8, Sat 9-6, Sun 1-5
Friends of the Library Group

C KENTUCKY WESLEYAN COLLEGE*, Library Learning Center, 3000 Frederica St, 42301. SAN 306-3852. Tel: 270-852-3259. Interlibrary Loan Service Tel: 270-852-3258. FAX: 270-926-3196. Web Site: kwcweb.kwc.edu/library. *Dir,* Pat McFarling; E-mail: patmc@kwc.edu; *Info Serv,* Deborah Russell; E-mail: drussell@kwc.edu; *Tech Serv,* Julie Gilmore; E-mail: juliegi@kwc.edu; Staff 2.75 (MLS 2, Non-MLS 0.75)
Founded 1858. Enrl 741; Fac 43; Highest Degree: Bachelor
Library Holdings: e-books 40,011; Bk Vols 90,120; Per Subs 119
Special Collections: Dan M King Architecture Coll; First Editions-American & English Literature (Dr & Mrs M David Orrahood Coll); Kentuckiana; Kentucky United Methodist Heritage Center Coll, bks, mss, pamphlets & pictures; KWC Archives; Toraichi Matsumoto Memorial Coll. US Document Depository
Automation Activity & Vendor Info: (OPAC) Ex Libris Group
Wireless access
Publications: Catalog of the Dan M King Architecture Coll; Catalog of the Dr & Mrs M David Orrahood Coll; KWC Non-Graduates 1866-1949, Millersburg-Winchester
Partic in Lyrasis; OCLC Online Computer Library Center, Inc

S OWENSBORO AREA MUSEUM OF SCIENCE & HISTORY LIBRARY*, 122 E Second St, 42301. SAN 323-4800. Tel: 270-687-2732. FAX: 270-687-2738. Web Site: www.owensboromuseum.org. *Exec Dir,* Kathy Olson
Founded 1966
Library Holdings: Bk Vols 450; Per Subs 12
Subject Interests: Kentucky, Mus studies, Native Am, Natural hist
Wireless access
Open Mon 10-8, Tues-Sat 10-5, Sun 1-5

J OWENSBORO COMMUNITY & TECHNICAL COLLEGE*, Learning Resources Center, 4800 New Hartford Rd, 42303. SAN 323-584X. Tel: 270-686-4574. Circulation Tel: 270-686-4590. FAX: 270-686-4594. Web Site: www.octc.kctcs.edu/library. *Dir of Libr Serv,* Donna Abell; Tel: 270-686-4575, E-mail: donna.abell@kctcs.edu; *Pub Serv Librn,* John Lutzel; E-mail: john.lutzel@kctcs.edu; *Acq,* Larry Waters; Tel: 270-686-4657; Staff 6 (MLS 2, Non-MLS 4)
Founded 1986. Enrl 2,827; Fac 100; Highest Degree: Associate
Library Holdings: AV Mats 1,261; e-books 45,000; Bk Titles 21,981; Bk Vols 23,440; Per Subs 59
Automation Activity & Vendor Info: (Cataloging) Ex Libris Group; (Circulation) Ex Libris Group; (Course Reserve) Ex Libris Group; (OPAC) Ex Libris Group
Database Vendor: EBSCOhost, Gale Cengage Learning, OCLC FirstSearch, ProQuest, Wilson - Wilson Web
Partic in Lyrasis; OCLC Online Computer Library Center, Inc
Open Mon-Thurs 7:45-7, Fri 7:45-4

M OWENSBORO MEDICAL HEALTH SYSTEM*, Threlkel Health Sciences Library, 811 E Parish Ave, 42303. Tel: 270-688-2167. FAX: 270-688-2168. *Librn,* Virginia Marx; E-mail: vmarx@omhs.org; *Librn,* Carol Taylor; E-mail: ctaylor@omhs.org
Library Holdings: Bk Vols 1,000
Database Vendor: MD Consult, PubMed
Wireless access
Open Mon-Fri 8-4:30

OWENTON

P OWEN COUNTY PUBLIC LIBRARY*, 1370 Hwy 22 E, 40359. SAN 306-3887. Tel: 502-484-3450. FAX: 502-484-3463. Web Site: www.owencountylibrary.org. *Dir,* Jennifer Nippert
Pop 11,300; Circ 89,000
Library Holdings: Bk Vols 28,600; Per Subs 64
Subject Interests: Kentucky
Automation Activity & Vendor Info: (Acquisitions) TLC (The Library Corporation); (Cataloging) TLC (The Library Corporation); (Circulation) TLC (The Library Corporation); (Course Reserve) TLC (The Library Corporation); (ILL) TLC (The Library Corporation); (OPAC) TLC (The Library Corporation); (Serials) TLC (The Library Corporation)
Database Vendor: Gale Cengage Learning
Wireless access
Open Mon-Thurs 9:30-8, Fri & Sat 9:30-5

OWINGSVILLE

P BATH COUNTY MEMORIAL LIBRARY*, 24 W Main St, 40360. (Mail add: PO Box 380, 40360-0380), SAN 306-3895. Tel: 606-674-2531. FAX: 606-674-2531. E-mail: bcml@bathcountylibrary.com. Web Site: www.bathcountylibrary.com. *Dir,* Brenda Vance; *Cataloger, Librn,* Lois Crump; *ILL, Librn,* Julia D Jones; *Circ Librn,* Vicki Browning; Staff 4.8 (Non-MLS 4.8)
Pop 11,707; Circ 62,604
Library Holdings: AV Mats 261; CDs 211; Large Print Bks 1,060; Bk Vols 23,587; Per Subs 79; Talking Bks 733; Videos 1,586
Special Collections: Kentucky Genealogy
Automation Activity & Vendor Info: (Cataloging) TLC (The Library Corporation); (Circulation) TLC (The Library Corporation); (OPAC) TLC (The Library Corporation)
Wireless access
Function: Copy machines, Fax serv, Handicapped accessible, Homebound delivery serv, ILL available, Magnifiers for reading, Prog for children & young adult, Spoken cassettes & CDs, Summer reading prog, Tax forms, VHS videos
Special Services for the Blind - Bks on cassette; Large print bks
Open Mon 9-6, Tues, Wed & Fri 9-5, Thurs 9-8, Sat 9-3
Bookmobiles: 1

PADUCAH

P MCCRACKEN COUNTY PUBLIC LIBRARY*, 555 Washington St, 42003-1735. SAN 306-3917. Tel: 270-442-2510, Ext 13. Circulation Tel: 270-442-2510, Ext 110. FAX: 270-443-9322. Web Site: www.mclib.net. *Libr Dir,* Julie Hart; E-mail: jhart@mclib.net; *Adult Serv Mgr,* Sarah Pace-McGowan; E-mail: smcgowan@mclib.net; *Bus Mgr,* Kim Hunt; *Tech Serv Mgr,* Patricia Sallee; E-mail: psallee@mclib.net; *Youth Serv Mgr,* Linda Bartley; E-mail: lbartley@mclib.net; *Tech Coordr,* Jay Hite; E-mail: jhite@mclib.net; Staff 3.5 (MLS 2, Non-MLS 1.5)
Founded 1901. Pop 64,950; Circ 336,367
Jul 2011-Jun 2012 Income $3,187,364, State $33,167, Federal $14,595, County $2,973,623, Locally Generated Income $165,979. Mats Exp $612,684, Books $302,897, Per/Ser (Incl. Access Fees) $12,500, AV Equip $42,047, AV Mat $207,623, Electronic Ref Mat (Incl. Access Fees) $47,617. Sal $937,587 (Prof $91,297)
Library Holdings: CDs 7,527; DVDs 38,672; e-books 57,093; Bk Titles 113,491; Bk Vols 127,542; Per Subs 218
Special Collections: Genealogy, bks, ms; History (Kentucky Coll), bks, ms; Literature (Irvin S Cobb Coll), bks, ms
Automation Activity & Vendor Info: (Acquisitions) Innovative Interfaces, Inc; (Circulation) Innovative Interfaces, Inc; (ILL) OCLC ILLiad
Database Vendor: EBSCOhost, Gale Cengage Learning, Innovative Interfaces, Inc, LexisNexis, OCLC FirstSearch, OCLC WorldShare Interlibrary Loan, ReferenceUSA, Westlaw
Wireless access
Function: Accelerated reader prog, Bk reviews (Group), Bks on cassette, Bks on CD, Children's prog, Computers for patron use, Copy machines, Fax serv, Free DVD rentals, Games & aids for the handicapped,

Handicapped accessible, ILL available, Jail serv, Preschool outreach, Prog for adults, Prog for children & young adult, Tax forms, Telephone ref
Partic in Lyrasis
Open Mon-Thurs 9-9, Fri & Sat 9-6, Sun 1-6
Friends of the Library Group

J WEST KENTUCKY COMMUNITY & TECHNICAL COLLEGE, Matheson Library, 4810 Alben Barkley Dr, 42001. (Mail add: PO Box 7380, 42002-7380), SAN 306-3909. Tel: 270-534-3197. Interlibrary Loan Service Tel: 270-534-3189. FAX: 270-554-6218. Web Site: www.westkentucky.kctcs.edu/academics/library.aspx. *Libr Dir,* Ken Bradshaw; Tel: 270-534-3169, E-mail: ken.bradshaw@kctcs.edu; *Res Serv Librn,* Amy Sullivan; Tel: 270-534-3171, E-mail: amy.sullivan@kctcs.edu; *User Serv Librn,* Carol Driver; Tel: 270-534-3170, E-mail: carol.driver@kctcs.edu; Staff 3 (MLS 3)
Founded 1932. Enrl 5,577; Fac 134; Highest Degree: Associate
Library Holdings: AV Mats 610; e-books 175,000; Bk Titles 19,523; Bk Vols 20,807; Per Subs 60; Videos 1,078
Automation Activity & Vendor Info: (Cataloging) Ex Libris Group; (Circulation) Ex Libris Group; (ILL) OCLC; (OPAC) Ex Libris Group
Database Vendor: Checkpoint Systems, Inc, EBSCO Auto Repair Reference, EBSCOhost, Ex Libris Group, Gale Cengage Learning, JSTOR, Medline, OCLC, ProQuest
Wireless access
Function: Orientations
Open Mon-Thurs 7:30am-8:30pm, Fri 7:30-4

M WESTERN BAPTIST HOSPITAL LIBRARY*, 2501 Kentucky Ave, 42003-3200. Tel: 270-575-2108. FAX: 270-575-2164. Web Site: www.westernbaptist.com. *Librn,* Carmen Davidson
Library Holdings: Bk Vols 1,000
Database Vendor: OCLC WorldShare Interlibrary Loan, PubMed
Wireless access
Open Mon-Fri 7:30-4

PAINTSVILLE

P JOHNSON COUNTY PUBLIC LIBRARY*, 444 Main St, 41240. SAN 306-3933. Tel: 606-789-4355. FAX: 606-789-6758. E-mail: johnsonlibrary@bellsouth.net. Web Site: www.johnsoncountypubliclibrary.org. *Dir,* Karen Daniel
Pop 23,827; Circ 207,863
Library Holdings: Audiobooks 1,199; AV Mats 172; DVDs 856; Microforms 120; Bk Vols 55,000; Per Subs 63; Talking Bks 973; Videos 391
Automation Activity & Vendor Info: (Cataloging) AmLib Library Management System; (Circulation) AmLib Library Management System; (Course Reserve) AmLib Library Management System; (OPAC) AmLib Library Management System
Database Vendor: Gale Cengage Learning
Open Mon, Wed & Fri 9:30-5, Tues & Thurs 9:30-8, Sat 9-2
Bookmobiles: 1. Librn, Ryan Skaggs

PARIS

P PARIS-BOURBON COUNTY LIBRARY*, 701 High St, 40361. SAN 306-395X. Tel: 859-987-4419. FAX: 859-987-2421. Web Site: www.bourbonlibrary.org. *Dir,* Mark Adler; E-mail: madler@bourbonlibrary.org; Staff 11 (MLS 3, Non-MLS 8)
Founded 1904. Pop 19,729; Circ 132,732
Jul 2009-Jun 2010 Income $975,710, State $19,392, Federal $12,661, Locally Generated Income $850,636, Other $93,021. Mats Exp $114,119, Books $82,416, AV Mat $24,157, Electronic Ref Mat (Incl. Access Fees) $7,546. Sal $303,352 (Prof $54,732)
Library Holdings: Bk Vols 42,283; Per Subs 98
Automation Activity & Vendor Info: (Acquisitions) AmLib Library Management System; (Cataloging) AmLib Library Management System; (Circulation) AmLib Library Management System; (ILL) AmLib Library Management System; (OPAC) AmLib Library Management System
Database Vendor: OCLC FirstSearch
Wireless access
Open Mon, Wed & Fri 9:30-5:30, Tues & Thurs 9:30-8, Sat 9:30-3
Friends of the Library Group
Bookmobiles: 1

PEWEE VALLEY

S KENTUCKY CORRECTIONAL INSTITUTION FOR WOMEN LIBRARY*, 3000 Ash Ave, 40056. (Mail add: PO Box 337, 40056-0337), SAN 306-3968. Tel: 502-241-8454, Ext 2224. E-mail: kciw.library@ky.gov. Web Site: www.corrections.ky.gov/kciw. *Librn,* Sarah Reed; Staff 1 (MLS 1)
Founded 1973
Library Holdings: High Interest/Low Vocabulary Bk Vols 400; Large Print Bks 450; Bk Titles 22,000; Per Subs 85

PIKEVILLE

P PIKE COUNTY PUBLIC LIBRARY DISTRICT*, 119 College St, 41502-1787. (Mail add: PO Box 1197, 41502-1197), SAN 306-249X. Tel: 606-432-9977. FAX: 606-432-9908. E-mail: pcpldao@pikelibrary.org. Web Site: www.pikelibrary.org. *Dir,* Leean L Allen
Founded 1970
Library Holdings: Bk Vols 168,472; Per Subs 296
Automation Activity & Vendor Info: (Cataloging) TLC (The Library Corporation); (Circulation) TLC (The Library Corporation); (OPAC) TLC (The Library Corporation)
Open Mon-Fri 8:30-5
Branches: 5
BELFRY PUBLIC, 24371 US Hwy 119 N, Belfry, 41514. (Mail add: PO Box 340, Belfry, 41514), SAN 342-6394. Tel: 606-353-9429. FAX: 330-408-0015. *Head Librn,* Delania Adkins
Open Tues & Thurs 10:30-7, Wed & Fri 9:30-6, Sat 9-5
ELKHORN CITY PUBLIC, 150 E Main St, Elkhorn City, 41522, SAN 375-541X. Tel: 606-754-5451. FAX: 330-248-0020. *Head Librn,* Delania Adkins
Open Tues & Thurs 10:30-7, Wed & Fri 9:30-6, Sat 9-5
PHELPS PUBLIC, 38575 State Hwy 194 E, Phelps, 41553, SAN 328-8773. Tel: 606-456-7860. FAX: 330-248-0027.
Open Tues & Thurs 10-7, Wed & Fri 9:30-6, Sat 9-5
PIKEVILLE PUBLIC, 119 College St, 41501-1787, SAN 376-9941. Tel: 606-432-1285. FAX: 330-838-0023. *Librn,* Delania Adkins
Open Mon-Thurs 9-7, Fri & Sat 9-5
VESTA ROBERTS-JOHNSON MEMORIAL LIBRARY, 180 Hwy 610 W, Virgie, 41572. (Mail add: PO Box 548, Virgie, 41572-0548), SAN 321-3331. Tel: 606-639-9839. FAX: 330-247-0035. *Head Librn,* Delania Adkins
Founded 1980
Open Tues & Thurs 10:30-7, Wed & Fri 9:30-6, Sat 9-5
Bookmobiles: 1. Librn, Brenda Griffin. Bk vols 4,000

C UNIVERSITY OF PIKEVILLE*, Frank M Allara Library, 147 Sycamore St, 41501-9118. SAN 306-3976. Tel: 606-218-5605. FAX: 606-218-5613. Web Site: www.upike.edu/Library. *Dir,* Karen S Evans; Tel: 606-218-5606, E-mail: KarenEvans@upike.edu; *Assoc Librn,* Mary A Harmon; Tel: 606-218-5610; *Ref & Instruction Librn,* Jane E Hammons; Tel: 606-218-5609; Staff 11 (MLS 4, Non-MLS 7)
Founded 1920. Enrl 1,169; Fac 54; Highest Degree: Bachelor
Library Holdings: Bk Titles 61,071; Bk Vols 70,883; Per Subs 357
Special Collections: Pike County Historical Society Coll
Subject Interests: Appalachia, Genealogy, Kentucky
Automation Activity & Vendor Info: (Acquisitions) Ex Libris Group; (Cataloging) Ex Libris Group; (OPAC) Ex Libris Group
Database Vendor: EBSCOhost, OCLC FirstSearch, ProQuest
Partic in Appalachian Col Asn; Coun of Independent Ky Cols & Univs; Lyrasis; OCLC Online Computer Library Center, Inc
Open Mon-Thurs 7:30am-11pm, Fri 7:30-5, Sat 10-5, Sun 3-11

PINEVILLE

S BELL COUNTY FORESTRY LIBRARY*, 560 Correctional Dr, 40977. Tel: 606-337-7065. FAX: 606-337-1312, Ext 243. *Librn,* Terry Partin
Library Holdings: Bk Vols 300; Per Subs 11
Open Mon-Sun 10-8

CR CLEAR CREEK BAPTIST BIBLE COLLEGE, Carolyn Boatman Brooks Memorial Library, 300 Clear Creek Rd, 40977. Tel: 606-337-3196. FAX: 606-337-2372. E-mail: library@ccbbc.edu. Web Site: www.ccbbc.edu. *Dir, Libr Serv,* Marge Cummings; *Asst Dir, Libr Serv,* Lynn Kahkola; *Cat Librn,* Hughes Bronwynn; Staff 2 (MLS 1, Non-MLS 1)
Founded 1926. Enrl 150; Highest Degree: Bachelor
Library Holdings: e-books 17,000; Bk Titles 43,945; Per Subs 256
Automation Activity & Vendor Info: (Cataloging) TLC (The Library Corporation); (Circulation) TLC (The Library Corporation); (Course Reserve) TLC (The Library Corporation); (ILL) OCLC; (OPAC) TLC (The Library Corporation)
Database Vendor: EBSCOhost, ProQuest
Wireless access
Partic in Christian Library Consortium; KLN
Open Mon, Tues & Thurs 7:30am-10pm, Wed & Fri 7:30-4, Sat 10-2

P PINEVILLE-BELL COUNTY PUBLIC LIBRARY*, 214 Walnut St, 40977. (Mail add: PO Box 1490, 40977-1490), SAN 306-3992. Tel: 606-337-3422. FAX: 606-337-9862. E-mail: pinevillelib@bellcolib.org. Web Site: www.bellcolib.org. *Dir,* Beverly Greene; *Br Mgr,* Elizabeth Warren; *Youth Serv Librn,* Christina Partin; E-mail: christinan2@hotmail.com; Staff 5 (Non-MLS 5)
Founded 1933. Pop 20,300
Library Holdings: Bk Vols 39,000; Per Subs 84
Special Collections: Oral History

Subject Interests: Genealogy, Hist, Local hist
Automation Activity & Vendor Info: (Cataloging) Innovative Interfaces, Inc; (Circulation) Innovative Interfaces, Inc; (ILL) Innovative Interfaces, Inc; (OPAC) Innovative Interfaces, Inc
Open Mon-Fri 10-6, Sat 10-4
Friends of the Library Group
Bookmobiles: 1

PIPPA PASSES

C ALICE LLOYD COLLEGE, McGaw Library & Learning Center, 100 Purpose Rd, 41844. SAN 306-400X. Tel: 606-368-6132. Reference Tel: 606-368 6117. FAX: 606-368-6212. E-mail: mcgaw_library@hotmail.com. Web Site: www.alc.edu. *Dir,* Andrew Busroe; E-mail: andrewbusroe@alc.edu; *Pub Serv,* Jeannie G Galloway; E-mail: jeanniegalloway@alc.edu; Staff 2 (MLS 2)
Founded 1923. Enrl 600; Highest Degree: Bachelor
Library Holdings: e-books 120,000; Bk Vols 74,218; Per Subs 219
Special Collections: Appalachian Oral History; Appalachian Photographic Coll; Children's Literature Coll
Automation Activity & Vendor Info: (Acquisitions) Innovative Interfaces, Inc; (Cataloging) Innovative Interfaces, Inc; (Circulation) Innovative Interfaces, Inc; (Course Reserve) Innovative Interfaces, Inc; (OPAC) Innovative Interfaces, Inc; (Serials) Innovative Interfaces, Inc
Database Vendor: EBSCOhost, JSTOR, Newsbank, OCLC FirstSearch, Oxford Online, Wilson - Wilson Web
Partic in Appalachian Col Asn; Association of Independent Kentucky Colleges & Universities; Lyrasis
Open Mon-Thurs (Winter) 8am-11pm, Fri 8-4:30, Sat 11:30-4:30, Sun 6pm-11pm; Mon-Fri (Summer) 8-4:30
Friends of the Library Group

PRESTONSBURG

J BIG SANDY COMMUNITY & TECHNICAL COLLEGE*, One Bert T Combs Dr, 41653. SAN 306-4034. Tel: 606-889-4749. Toll Free Tel: 888-641-4132, Circulation Toll Free Tel: 888-641-4132, Ext 67210. FAX: 606-886-8683. Web Site: www.bigsandy.kctcs.edu. *Dir,* Melissa M Forsyth; E-mail: melissa.forsyth@kctcs.edu; *Asst Librn,* Kathy Lowe; Tel: 606-889-4748, E-mail: kathy.lowe@kctcs.edu; *Ref,* Judy K Howell; Tel: 606-889-4750, E-mail: judy.howell@kctcs.edu; Staff 9 (MLS 3, Non MLS 6)
Founded 1964. Enrl 3,900; Fac 100; Highest Degree: Associate
Jul 2010-Jun 2011. Mats Exp $100,000
Library Holdings: AV Mats 1,432; e-books 64,722; Bk Titles 43,273; Per Subs 178
Special Collections: Eastern Kentucky History Coll
Automation Activity & Vendor Info: (Cataloging) OCLC; (Circulation) Ex Libris Group; (Course Reserve) Ex Libris Group; (ILL) Ex Libris Group; (OPAC) Ex Libris Group
Database Vendor: Gale Cengage Learning, Newsbank, Oxford Online, ProQuest
Wireless access
Function: Archival coll, Bk club(s), Computers for patron use, Copy machines, Distance learning, Doc delivery serv, e-mail serv, Electronic databases & coll, Handicapped accessible, ILL available, Wheelchair accessible
Publications: User's Guide
Partic in Lyrasis
Special Services for the Blind - Magnifiers; ZoomText magnification & reading software
Open Mon-Thurs 8-8, Fri 8-3, Sat 9-4:30

Departmental Libraries:

MAYO-PAINTSVILLE CAMPUS, Bldg F, 513 Third St, Rm 206A, Paintsville, 41240. Tel: 606-789-5321, Ext 82831. *Libr Tech,* Carol Talbert; E-mail: carol.talbert@kctcs.edu
Library Holdings: AV Mats 191; Bk Vols 25,000; Per Subs 30
Open Mon-Wed 8-6:30, Thurs 8-6, Fri 8-4:30

P FLOYD COUNTY PUBLIC LIBRARY*, 161 N Arnold Ave, 41653-1281. SAN 306-4026. Tel: 606-886-2981. FAX: 606-886-2284. Web Site: www.fclib.org. *Libr Dir,* Jonathan Campbell
Founded 1957. Pop 42,379; Circ 123,450
Library Holdings: Bk Vols 71,270; Per Subs 50
Special Collections: Kentucky Coll
Automation Activity & Vendor Info: (Cataloging) Innovative Interfaces, Inc; (Circulation) Innovative Interfaces, Inc; (OPAC) Innovative Interfaces, Inc
Open Mon & Wed-Fri 8:30-5, Tues 8:30-7:30, Sat 8:30-1
Bookmobiles: 1

PRINCETON

P GEORGE COON PUBLIC LIBRARY*, 114 S Harrison St, 42445-1946. (Mail add: PO Box 230, 42445-0230), SAN 306-4042. Tel: 270-365-2884. FAX: 270-365-2892. *Librn,* Judy Boaz; E-mail: jboaz@georgecoonpubliclibrary.com; *Ch Serv,* Kim Brown; Staff 1 (Non-MLS 1)
Founded 1913. Pop 12,898; Circ 55,229
Library Holdings: AV Mats 1,786; Bk Titles 26,622; Per Subs 41; Talking Bks 504
Special Collections: Genealogy (Ira Fears Coll), microfilm, bks; Rare Book Coll. Oral History
Automation Activity & Vendor Info: (Cataloging) TLC (The Library Corporation); (Circulation) TLC (The Library Corporation)
Database Vendor: TLC (The Library Corporation)
Open Mon-Fri 9-5, Sat 9-12
Friends of the Library Group

RICHMOND

C EASTERN KENTUCKY UNIVERSITY LIBRARIES*, 103 Crabbe Library, 521 Lancaster Ave, 40475-3102. SAN 342-6068. Tel: 859-622-1778. Circulation Tel: 859-622-1790. Interlibrary Loan Service Tel: 859-622-1415. Reference Tel: 859-622-6594. FAX: 859-622-1174. Web Site: www.library.eku.edu. *Dean of Libr,* Betina Gardner; E-mail: betina.gardner@eku.edu; *Univ Archivist,* Jackie Couture; *Coordr, Pub Serv,* Julie George; Staff 26 (MLS 22, Non-MLS 4)
Founded 1906. Enrl 12,184; Fac 663; Highest Degree: Master
Jul 2007-Jun 2008 Income $4,952,901. Mats Exp $1,300,000. Sal $2,601,438 (Prof $1,444,900)
Library Holdings: Audiobooks 614; AV Mats 14,467; Bks on Deafness & Sign Lang 177; Braille Volumes 74; CDs 5,144; DVDs 714; e-books 4,436; e-journals 18,819; Large Print Bks 143; Microforms 1,330,422; Bk Titles 571,175; Bk Vols 659,342; Per Subs 1,566; Videos 4,858
Special Collections: Learning Resources Center; Madison County-Eastern Kentucky University Law Library Coll; University Archives (Kentuckiana; bks; microfiche; mss). US Document Depository
Subject Interests: Educ, Humanities, Music, Nursing, Occupational therapy
Automation Activity & Vendor Info: (Acquisitions) Ex Libris Group; (Cataloging) Ex Libris Group; (Circulation) Ex Libris Group; (Course Reserve) Ex Libris Group; (ILL) OCLC ILLiad; (OPAC) Ex Libris Group; (Serials) Ex Libris Group
Database Vendor: 3M Library Systems, Agricola, ARTstor, Baker & Taylor, Blackwell, BWI, Cambridge Scientific Abstracts, EBSCOhost, Elsevier MDL, Gale Cengage Learning, Grolier Online, JSTOR, Newsbank, OCLC FirstSearch, OVID Technologies, ProQuest, ScienceDirect, Westlaw, Wiley, Wilson - Wilson Web
Wireless access
Partic in Lyrasis; OCLC Online Computer Library Center, Inc
Special Services for the Deaf - Assistive tech; Bks on deafness & sign lang; High interest/low vocabulary bks; TDD equip
Special Services for the Blind - Assistive/Adapted tech devices, equip & products
Open Mon-Thurs 7:30am-1am, Fri 7:30-6, Sat 11-6, Sun 11am-1am
Friends of the Library Group

Departmental Libraries:

THE ELIZABETH K BAKER MUSIC LIBRARY, Foster Bldg, 521 Lancaster Ave, 40475, SAN 342-6122. Tel: 859-622-1795. FAX: 859-622-1174. Web Site: www.library.eku.edu/music. *Librn,* Dr Greg Engstrom
Library Holdings: AV Mats 7,064; Music Scores 9,248; Bk Vols 12,182; Per Subs 129
Subject Interests: Music
Partic in Lyrasis
Open Mon-Thurs 8-8, Fri 8-4:30

P MADISON COUNTY PUBLIC LIBRARY*, 507 W Main St, 40475. SAN 375-3093. Tel: 859-623-6704. FAX: 859-623-2032. E-mail: richmond@madisonlibrary.org. Web Site: madisonlibrary.org. *Libr Dir,* Ruthie Maslin; E-mail: rmaslin@madisonlibrary.org; *Youth Serv Librn,* Bethany Halbert; *Br Serv Supvr,* Danny Jacobs; Staff 17 (MLS 3, Non-MLS 14)
Founded 1988. Pop 84,786; Circ 221,325
Library Holdings: CDs 2,856; DVDs 2,360; Bk Vols 94,731; Per Subs 217; Talking Bks 4,502; Videos 6,864
Subject Interests: Genealogy, Kentucky, Spanish
Automation Activity & Vendor Info: (Cataloging) SirsiDynix; (Circulation) SirsiDynix; (OPAC) SirsiDynix
Database Vendor: EBSCOhost
Open Mon-Thurs 9-8, Fri & Sat 9-6
Friends of the Library Group
Branches: 1
BEREA BRANCH, 319 Chestnut St, Berea, 40403, SAN 375-3107. Tel: 859-986-7112. FAX: 859-986-7208. E-mail: berea@madisonlibrary.org. *Br Serv Supvr,* Kathy V Hamblin; E-mail: kathyh@madisonlibrary.org; *Youth Serv Librn,* Pat Acevedo; E-mail: patacevedo@madisonlibrary.org
Founded 1988. Pop 72,408
Open Mon-Thurs 9-8, Fri & Sat 9-6

Friends of the Library Group
Bookmobiles: 1. Librn, Beth Madden

RUSSELLVILLE

P LOGAN COUNTY PUBLIC LIBRARY, 225 Armory Dr, 42276. (Mail add: PO Box 357, 42276), SAN 306-4093. Tel: 270-726-6129. FAX: 270-726-6127. E-mail: librarian@loganlibrary.org. Web Site: loganlibrary.org. *Dir,* King Simpson; E-mail: king@loganlibrary.org; *Bus Mgr,* Wanda Gower; *Acq,* Shelly Turner; *Adult Prog,* Tracy Houchens; E-mail: tracy@loganlibrary.org; *Cat, Tech,* Sherryl Appling; *Ch Serv,* Carole Faulkner; *Pub Serv,* Mark Griffin; *Pub Serv,* Ruth Mazour; *Pub Serv,* Beverly Terry; Staff 3 (MLS 1, Non-MLS 2)
Founded 1966. Pop 28,000; Circ 350,000
Jul 2007-Jun 2008 Income (Main Library and Branch(s)) $943,584, State $27,916, County $748,636, Locally Generated Income $167,032. Mats Exp $132,488. Sal $384,468
Library Holdings: Bk Vols 42,991; Per Subs 32
Special Collections: Oral History
Subject Interests: Census, Family hist, Genealogy, Local newsp, Photog hist
Automation Activity & Vendor Info: (Acquisitions) Evolve; (Cataloging) Evolve; (Circulation) Evolve; (Course Reserve) Evolve; (ILL) OCLC FirstSearch; (OPAC) Evolve
Database Vendor: Baker & Taylor, Gale Cengage Learning, Ingram Library Services, LearningExpress, WT Cox
Wireless access
Special Services for the Blind - Bks on CD; Large print bks; Large screen computer & software
Open Mon-Thurs 9-8, Fri 9-5, Sat 10-5, Sun 2-5
Friends of the Library Group
Branches: 2
ADAIRVILLE BRANCH, 101 Church St, Adairville, 42202, SAN 320-8141. Tel: 270-539-4601. FAX: 270-539-4601. *Librn,* Sharon Fuller
Library Holdings: Bk Vols 2,027
Open Mon & Wed 1:30-5:30, Fri 2-5:30
Friends of the Library Group
AUBURN BRANCH, 433 W Main St, Auburn, 42206, SAN 320-8168. Tel: 270-542-8180. FAX: 270-542-8180. *Librn,* Erdene Hughes; E-mail: erdene@loganlibrary.org
Library Holdings: Bk Vols 2,129
Open Mon, Wed & Fri 12-5
Friends of the Library Group

SAINT CATHARINE

CR ST CATHARINE COLLEGE LIBRARY*, Emily W Hundley Library, 2735 Bardstown Rd, 40061. SAN 306-4107. Tel: 859-336-5082, Ext 1260. FAX: 859-336-5031. E-mail: library@sccky.edu. Web Site: aquinas.sccky.edu, www.sccky.edu/academics/library. *Dir of Libr Serv,* Ilona Burdette; E-mail: iburdette@sccky.edu; *Asst Dir,* Kaye Peterson; E-mail: kpeterson@sccky.edu; *ILL, Ref Serv,* Clara Logsdon; E-mail: clogsdon@sccky.edu; Staff 4 (MLS 2, Non-MLS 2)
Founded 1930. Enrl 800; Highest Degree: Master
Library Holdings: Bk Titles 25,000
Special Collections: Elizabeth Madox Roberts Coll
Automation Activity & Vendor Info: (Cataloging) Ex Libris Group; (Circulation) Ex Libris Group; (OPAC) Ex Libris Group
Database Vendor: EBSCOhost, Gale Cengage Learning, Grolier Online, JSTOR, McGraw-Hill, OCLC WorldShare Interlibrary Loan, ProQuest
Wireless access
Function: Computers for patron use, Copy machines, ILL available
Partic in Association of Independent Kentucky Colleges & Universities; Federation of Kentucky Academic Libraries (FoKAL)
Open Mon-Thurs 7:30am-9pm, Fri 8:30-5, Sun 4-8

SALYERSVILLE

P MAGOFFIN COUNTY LIBRARY*, 141 Church St, 41465. (Mail add: PO Box 435, 41465-0435), SAN 306-4115. Tel: 606-349-2411. FAX: 606-349-1120. E-mail: maglib@foothills.net. *Dir,* Melanie Cain
Pop 13,515; Circ 29,747
Library Holdings: Bk Vols 22,000; Per Subs 15
Wireless access
Open Mon-Thurs 9-5, Fri 9-4

SANDY HOOK

P ROCKY J ADKINS PUBLIC LIBRARY, Main St, 41171. (Mail add: PO Box 750, 41171-0750). Tel: 606-738-5796. FAX: 606-738-4980. E-mail: ellcolib@mrtc.com. *Dir,* Jasmyne Combs; Staff 1 (Non-MLS 1)
Library Holdings: Audiobooks 463; Braille Volumes 152; CDs 476; DVDs 1,657; e-journals 31; Bk Vols 18,492; Per Subs 21
Automation Activity & Vendor Info: (Acquisitions) Follett Software; (Cataloging) Follett Software; (Circulation) Follett Software; (OPAC) Follett Software
Database Vendor: EBSCOhost, Infotrieve
Wireless access
Open Mon-Fri 8:30-5

SCOTTSVILLE

P ALLEN COUNTY PUBLIC LIBRARY*, 106 W Public Sq, 42164. (Mail add: PO Box 1447, 42164-1447), SAN 306-4123. Tel: 270-237-3861. FAX: 270-237-4095. E-mail: info@allencountylibrary.com. Web Site: www.youseemore.com/allen. *Dir,* Sheila Stovall; E-mail: sstovall@allencountylibrary.com; *Ch,* Amanda Mcreynolds; *Tech Serv,* Joanne Meador; E-mail: joanne@allencountylibrary.com; Staff 6 (Non-MLS 6)
Founded 1953. Pop 17,128; Circ 115,876
Library Holdings: Bk Vols 27,891; Per Subs 101
Special Collections: Kentucky Coll; Large Christian Fiction Coll; Large Type Books
Automation Activity & Vendor Info: (Acquisitions) TLC (The Library Corporation); (Cataloging) TLC (The Library Corporation); (Circulation) TLC (The Library Corporation); (Course Reserve) TLC (The Library Corporation); (OPAC) TLC (The Library Corporation)
Database Vendor: OCLC FirstSearch
Partic in Barron County Libr Servs (BCLS)
Open Mon-Thurs 9-7, Fri & Sat 9-4
Friends of the Library Group
Bookmobiles: 1

SHELBYVILLE

P SHELBY COUNTY PUBLIC LIBRARY*, 309 Eighth St, 40065. SAN 306-4131. Tel: 502-633-3803. FAX: 502-633-4025. E-mail: admin@scplibrary.net. *Dir,* Pamela W Federspiel; *Outreach Librn,* Shana Schack; *Circ,* Ann Blansett; *Circ,* Nancy Kovach; *Circ,* Alice Ritchey; *Ref,* Deborah Magan; *Tech Serv,* Joyce Lancaster; Staff 5 (MLS 1, Non-MLS 4)
Founded 1899. Pop 34,000; Circ 155,000
Library Holdings: Bk Vols 52,000; Per Subs 63
Special Collections: Shelby County Historical Records, micro
Automation Activity & Vendor Info: (Cataloging) TLC (The Library Corporation); (Circulation) TLC (The Library Corporation); (OPAC) TLC (The Library Corporation)
Wireless access
Open Mon-Thurs 9-7, Fri 9-5:30, Sat 9-1:30
Friends of the Library Group
Bookmobiles: 1

SHEPHERDSVILLE

P BULLITT COUNTY PUBLIC LIBRARY*, Ridgway Memorial Library, 127 N Walnut St, 40165-6083. (Mail add: PO Box 99, 40165-0099), SAN 342-6157. Tel: 502-543-7675. Circulation Tel: 502-543-7675, Ext 3. Interlibrary Loan Service Tel: 502-543-7675, Ext 9. Reference Tel: 502-543-7675, Ext 4. Administration Tel: 502-543-7675, Ext 7. FAX: 502-543-5487. E-mail: bcpl@iglou.com. Web Site: www.bcplib.org. *Dir,* Position Currently Open; *Asst Libr Dir,* Judy Jackson; E-mail: judy_tj@bcplib.org; *Prog Supvr,* Allison White; E-mail: childserv@bcplib.org; *Tech Serv Supvr,* Judy Jones; E-mail: techservices@bcplib.org; Staff 51 (MLS 1, Non-MLS 50)
Founded 1954. Pop 75,653; Circ 346,000
Library Holdings: Bk Vols 129,167; Per Subs 131
Special Collections: Oral History
Automation Activity & Vendor Info: (Cataloging) TLC (The Library Corporation); (Circulation) TLC (The Library Corporation); (OPAC) TLC (The Library Corporation)
Database Vendor: EBSCOhost, Gale Cengage Learning, LearningExpress, Newsbank, OCLC FirstSearch, ReferenceUSA, Westlaw
Wireless access
Function: AV serv, Handicapped accessible, ILL available, Photocopying/Printing, Prog for children & young adult, Summer reading prog
Open Mon-Thurs 9-8, Fri & Sat 9-5, Sun 1-5
Branches: 3
LEBANON JUNCTION BRANCH, 11382 S Preston Hwy, Lebanon Junction, 40150, SAN 342-6181. Tel: 502-833-4648. FAX: 502-833-9877. E-mail: ljl@bcplib.org. *Librn,* Mary Yocum
Open Mon-Thurs 9-8, Fri & Sat 9-5
MOUNT WASHINGTON BRANCH, 311 Snapp St, Mount Washington, 40047-7627, SAN 342-6211. Tel: 502-538-7560. FAX: 502-538-2696. E-mail: mwl@bcplib.org. *Librn,* Nancy Dearmond
Open Mon-Thurs 9-8, Fri & Sat 9-5
DOROTHEA STOTTMAN BRANCH, 1251 Hillview Blvd, Louisville, 40229, SAN 342-6246. Tel: 502-957-5759. FAX: 502-957-5759. E-mail: dsl@bcplib.org. *Librn,* Mona Timberlake
Open Mon & Thurs 12-8, Tues, Wed, Fri & Sat 9-5

SOMERSET

P PULASKI COUNTY PUBLIC LIBRARY, 304 S Main St, 42501-1402. (Mail add: PO Box 36, 42502-0036), SAN 342-6270. Tel: 606-679-8401. FAX: 606-679-1779. E-mail: pulaski.library@pulaskilibrary.com. Web Site: www.pulaskipubliclibrary.org. *Dir,* Charlotte Kay Keeney; E-mail: charlotte.keeney@pulaskilibrary.com; *Ch,* Carol Sexton; E-mail: carol.sexton@pulaskilibrary.com; *Circ Librn,* Wanda Gossett; *Ref Librn,* Louann Hardy; E-mail: louann.hardy@pulaskilibrary.com; *Teen Librn,* Shawn Spaw; E-mail: shawn.spaw@pulaskilibrary.com; Staff 3 (Non-MLS 3)
Founded 1905. Pop 61,000; Circ 386,577
Library Holdings: AV Mats 18,112; Bk Vols 98,469; Per Subs 210
Special Collections: Oral History
Subject Interests: Genealogy
Automation Activity & Vendor Info: (Cataloging) TLC (The Library Corporation); (Circulation) TLC (The Library Corporation); (OPAC) TLC (The Library Corporation)
Wireless access
Open Mon-Fri 9-7, Sat 9-5
Restriction: Borrowing requests are handled by ILL
Friends of the Library Group
Branches: 4
BURNSIDE BRANCH, 85 E French Ave, Burnside, 42519. (Mail add: PO Box 7, Burnside, 42519-0007), SAN 342-6300. Tel: 606-561-5287. FAX: 606-561-5287. E-mail: burnside.library@pulaskilibrary.com. *Librn,* Joy Halcomb; E-mail: joy.halcomb@pulaskilibrary.com
Open Mon, Wed & Fri 10-5, Tues & Thurs 10-7, Sat 9-Noon
NANCY BRANCH, Mills Springs Plaza, Nancy, 42544. (Mail add: PO Box 88, Nancy, 42544-0088), SAN 342-6335. Tel: 606-636-4241. FAX: 606-636-4241. E-mail: nancy.library@pulaskilibrary.com. *Librn,* J Noelene Whitaker; E-mail: noelene.whitaker@pulaskilibrary.com
Open Mon, Wed & Fri 10-5, Tues & Thurs 10-7, Sat 9-Noon
SCIENCE HILL BRANCH, 215 Main St, Science Hill, 42553. (Mail add: PO Box 448, Science Hill, 42553-0448), SAN 342-636X. Tel: 606-423-4221. FAX: 606-423-4221. E-mail: sciencehill.library@pulaskilibrary.com. *Librn,* Maggie Miracle; E-mail: maggie.miracle@pulaskilibrary.com
Open Mon, Wed & Fri 10-5, Tues & Thurs 10-7, Sat 9-Noon
SHOPVILLE BRANCH, 144 Shopville Rd, 42503, SAN 377-6727. Tel: 606-274-1671. FAX: 606-274-1671. E-mail: shopville.library@newwavecomm.net. *Librn,* Melanie Taylor
Founded 1995
Open Mon, Wed & Fri 10-5, Tues & Thurs 10-7, Sat 9-Noon
Bookmobiles: 1. Librn, Lindsey Meade

J SOMERSET COMMUNITY COLLEGE LIBRARY*, Harold B Strunk Learning Resource Ctr, 808 Monticello St, 42501. SAN 306-414X. Tel: 606-451-6710. Interlibrary Loan Service Tel: 606-451-6713. Administration Tel: 606-451-6711. Toll Free Tel: 877-629-9722. FAX: 606-679-5139. Web Site: www.somerset.kctcs.edu/library. *Assoc Dean,* Margo Hamm; E-mail: margo.hamm@kctcs.edu; *Dir, Pub Serv,* Mary Taylor Huntsman; E-mail: mary.huntsman@kctcs.edu; *Circ Supvr,* Pam Turner; Staff 7 (MLS 3, Non-MLS 4)
Founded 1965. Enrl 3,292; Fac 310; Highest Degree: Associate
Jul 2008-Jun 2009. Mats Exp $87,800, Books $34,300, Per/Ser (Incl. Access Fees) $13,400, Other Print Mats $1,300, AV Mat $6,000, Electronic Ref Mat (Incl. Access Fees) $32,800. Sal $338,884 (Prof $229,158)
Library Holdings: Audiobooks 92; CDs 389; DVDs 1,263; e-books 52,219; Bk Titles 27,087; Bk Vols 32,535; Per Subs 144
Special Collections: Local Newspaper, microfilm
Automation Activity & Vendor Info: (Cataloging) Ex Libris Group; (Circulation) Ex Libris Group; (Course Reserve) Ex Libris Group; (OPAC) Ex Libris Group
Database Vendor: CredoReference, EBSCOhost, Gale Cengage Learning, JSTOR, McGraw-Hill, OCLC FirstSearch, OCLC WorldShare Interlibrary Loan, Oxford Online, ProQuest, SerialsSolutions
Wireless access
Partic in Lyrasis
Special Services for the Deaf - Staff with knowledge of sign lang
Open Mon-Thurs 7:45-7, Fri 7:45-4:30, Sat 10-4

SPRINGFIELD

P WASHINGTON COUNTY PUBLIC LIBRARY, 210 E Main St, 40069. SAN 306-4158. Tel: 859-336-7655. FAX: 859-336-0256. E-mail: info@wcplky.org. Web Site: www1.youseemore.com/washingtoncountypl. *Dir,* Tara O'Hagan; E-mail: director@wcplky.org; Staff 8 (MLS 1, Non-MLS 7)
Founded 1964. Pop 11,260; Circ 74,886
Special Collections: Elizabeth Madox Roberts Coll. Oral History
Automation Activity & Vendor Info: (Acquisitions) TLC (The Library Corporation); (Cataloging) TLC (The Library Corporation); (Circulation) TLC (The Library Corporation); (ILL) OCLC WorldShare Interlibrary Loan; (OPAC) TLC (The Library Corporation); (Serials) TLC (The Library Corporation)
Database Vendor: Overdrive, Inc, TumbleBookLibrary
Wireless access
Function: ILL available, Photocopying/Printing, Prog for children & young adult, Spoken cassettes & CDs, Summer reading prog, Telephone ref, VHS videos
Open Mon, Tues & Thurs 10-7, Wed & Fri 10-5, Sat 9-1
Friends of the Library Group
Bookmobiles: 1

STANFORD

P LINCOLN COUNTY PUBLIC LIBRARY*, 201 Lancaster St, 40484. SAN 306-4174. Tel: 606-365-7513. FAX: 606-365-5566. Web Site: www.lcplinfo.org. *Dir,* Amanda Gearhart; *Asst Dir,* Angela Hensley; *Children's & Teen Serv,* Ashley Crace; *Outreach Librn,* Bev Madden
Pop 19,000; Circ 136,000
Library Holdings: Bk Vols 30,000; Per Subs 66
Automation Activity & Vendor Info: (Cataloging) Book Systems; (Circulation) Book Systems
Wireless access
Mem of Gaston-Lincoln Regional Library
Open Mon, Wed & Fri 9-5, Tues & Thurs 9-8, Sat 9-3
Bookmobiles: 1. Librn, Beverly Madder

STANTON

P POWELL COUNTY PUBLIC LIBRARY*, 725 Breckenridge St, 40380. SAN 306-4182. Tel: 606-663-4511. FAX: 606-663-4346. E-mail: powell_library@bellsouth.net. Web Site: powellcolibrary.org. *Dir,* Mark Wetherington, Jr; *Asst Dir,* Janice Sipple; E-mail: janicesipple@lycas.com; *Ch,* Rose Benningfield; E-mail: rosiebenningfield@lycos.com; *Libr Tech, Ref Librn,* Teresa Means
Founded 1964. Pop 13,237; Circ 92,402
Library Holdings: Bk Vols 20,000; Per Subs 64
Special Collections: Genealogy Coll (Kentucky Room); New Readers, large print
Automation Activity & Vendor Info: (Cataloging) Book Systems
Open Mon, Wed & Fri 9-5, Tue & Thurs 9-8, Sat 9-4
Bookmobiles: 1. Librn, Patsy Roe

TAYLORSVILLE

P SPENCER COUNTY PUBLIC LIBRARY, 168 Taylorsville Rd, 40071. SAN 320-8214. Tel: 502-477-8137. FAX: 502-477-5033. E-mail: scpl@spencercolibrary.us. Web Site: www.spencercountylibrary.us. *Dir,* Debra Lawson; *Asst Dir,* Lisa Johnson; *Adult Serv,* Christina Sheppard; *Children's & Youth Serv,* Stacy Tiller
Pop 17,061; Circ 48,425
Library Holdings: Bk Vols 43,000; Per Subs 32
Automation Activity & Vendor Info: (Cataloging) Book Systems; (Circulation) Book Systems
Partic in Ky Libr Asn; Midwest Collaborative for Library Services (MCLS)
Open Mon, Wed & Fri 10-5:30, Tues & Thurs 10-8, Sat 10-2

TOMPKINSVILLE

P MONROE COUNTY PUBLIC LIBRARY*, William B Harlan Memorial Library, 500 W Fourth St, 42167. SAN 306-4190. Tel: 270-487-5301. FAX: 270-487-5309. E-mail: wbhmlib@windstream.net. Web Site: www.youseemore.com/harlanml/default.asp. *Dir,* Ami Sandell; *Cataloger, Ch,* Brandi Stewart; *Pub Serv Librn,* Cody Crowe; *Pub Serv Librn,* Stephanie Hestand; *Pub Serv Librn,* Cindy Strode
Founded 1966. Pop 12,353
Automation Activity & Vendor Info: (Cataloging) SirsiDynix; (Circulation) SirsiDynix
Function: Adult bk club, Bk club(s), Bks on CD, CD-ROM, Children's prog, Computers for patron use, Copy machines, e-mail & chat, e-mail serv, Electronic databases & coll, Exhibits, Family literacy, Fax serv, Free DVD rentals, Handicapped accessible, Holiday prog, Home delivery & serv to Sr ctr & nursing homes, Homebound delivery serv, ILL available, Mail & tel request accepted, Microfiche/film & reading machines, Newsp ref libr, Online ref, Online searches, Outreach serv, Photocopying/Printing, Preschool outreach, Preschool reading prog, Printer for laptops & handheld devices, Prog for children & young adult, Pub access computers, Ref serv available, Ref serv in person, Referrals accepted, Story hour, Summer reading prog, Tax forms, Telephone ref, Web-catalog, Wheelchair accessible, Workshops
Open Mon 8:30-6, Tues-Fri 8:30-5, Sat 8:30-2
Friends of the Library Group
Bookmobiles: 1. Librn, Tina Gearlds

TRAPPIST

SR THE ABBEY OF GETHSEMANI LIBRARY*, 3642 Monks Rd, 40051. SAN 306-4204. Tel: 502-549-3117. FAX: 502-549-4124. Web Site: www.monks.org. *In Charge,* Fr Gaetan Blanchette; Tel: 502-549-3117, Ext 152
Founded 1848
Library Holdings: Bk Vols 40,000
Special Collections: Cistercian Monastic History & Liturgy, rare bks; Saint Bernard & DeRance, rare bks; Thomas Merton Coll
Subject Interests: Philos, Relig, Theol

VANCEBURG

P LEWIS COUNTY PUBLIC LIBRARY*, 27 Third St, 41179. SAN 306-4220. Tel: 606-796-2532. FAX: 606-796-0760. E-mail: lewiscountylibrary@gmail.com. Web Site: www.lewiscountylibrary.net. *Dir,* Marilyn Conway; *Asst Dir,* Kathy Hartley; *Ch,* Alison Spangler; Staff 3 (Non-MLS 3)
Founded 1954. Pop 14,545; Circ 82,402
Library Holdings: Bk Vols 31,000; Per Subs 50
Special Collections: Oral History
Automation Activity & Vendor Info: (Acquisitions) Follett Software; (Cataloging) Follett Software; (Circulation) Follett Software; (Course Reserve) Follett Software; (ILL) OCLC WorldShare Interlibrary Loan; (OPAC) Follett Software
Wireless access
Partic in OCLC Online Computer Library Center, Inc
Open Mon & Fri 8:30-5, Tues & Thurs 8:30-6, Wed 10-2, Sat 8:30-12:30
Friends of the Library Group

VERSAILLES

S WOODFORD COUNTY HISTORICAL SOCIETY LIBRARY*, 121 Rose Hill, 40383-1221. Tel: 859-873-6786. E-mail: woodford@qx.net. Web Site: www.woodfordkyhistory.org. *Curator,* Martha Martin
Founded 1966
Library Holdings: Bk Titles 3,500
Subject Interests: Genealogy, Hist
Publications: Woodford Heritage News (Newsletter)
Open Tues-Sat 10-4

P WOODFORD COUNTY LIBRARY*, 115 N Main St, 40383-1289. SAN 306-4247. Tel: 859-873-5191. FAX: 859-873-1542. Web Site: www.woodfordcountylibrary.org. *Dir,* Karen Kasacavage; E-mail: kkasacavage@woodfordlibrary.org; *Asst Dir,* John Crawford; *Outreach Serv Librn,* Kate Noye; *Youth Serv Librn,* Rebecca Watson; *Adult Serv,* Emily Saderholm; Staff 14 (MLS 3, Non-MLS 11)
Founded 1967. Pop 23,000; Circ 150,000
Library Holdings: Bk Vols 39,744; Per Subs 110
Subject Interests: Local hist
Automation Activity & Vendor Info: (Cataloging) TLC (The Library Corporation); (Circulation) TLC (The Library Corporation)
Database Vendor: EBSCOhost, OCLC FirstSearch
Open Mon-Thurs 9-8, Fri 9-6, Sat 9-5, Sun 2-5
Friends of the Library Group
Branches: 1
MIDWAY BRANCH, 400 Northside Dr, Midway, 40347. (Mail add: PO Box 4588, Midway, 40347). Tel: 859-846-4014. FAX: 859-846-4035. *Br Mgr,* Laura Bostrom; E-mail: lbostrom@woodfordlibrary.org; Staff 1 (MLS 1)
Library Holdings: AV Mats 2,000; Bk Vols 15,000; Per Subs 40
Friends of the Library Group
Bookmobiles: 1

VILLA HILLS

SR ST WALBURG MONASTERY ARCHIVES*, 2500 Amsterdam Rd, 41017. SAN 375-6521. Tel: 859-331-6324. FAX: 859-331-2136. Web Site: www.stwalburg.org. *Archives Dir,* Sister Deborah Harmeling; Tel: 859-331-6771, E-mail: sdhosb@yahoo.com; *Archivist,* Sister Betty Cahill; E-mail: bcahillosb@yahoo.com; *Archivist,* Sister Margaret Mary Gough; E-mail: nunsrus@flash.net; Staff 3 (MLS 1, Non-MLS 2)
Founded 1859
Restriction: Open by appt only

WARSAW

P GALLATIN COUNTY PUBLIC LIBRARY*, 209 W Market St, 41095. (Mail add: PO Box 848, 41095-0848), SAN 321-0510. Tel: 859-567-2786. FAX: 859-567-4750. E-mail: info@gallatincountylibrary.org. Web Site: www.gallatincountylibrary.org. *Dir,* Shirley S Warnickl; Tel: 859-567-8333, E-mail: shirley@gallatincpl.org; *Ch,* Amy Dickerson; *Outreach Librn/Circ,* Ann Webster; *Asst Ch,* Darla Jones; *Librn Asst, Genealogy & Local Hist,* Judy Oliver; Staff 5 (Non-MLS 5)
Founded 1978. Pop 8,035; Circ 52,577
Jul 2007-Jun 2008 Income $538,425, State $14,899, Federal $12,300, County $493,210, Other $18,016. Mats Exp $38,044, Books $24,184, Per/Ser (Incl. Access Fees) $2,560, Other Print Mats $1,105, Micro $359, AV Mat $9,478, Electronic Ref Mat (Incl. Access Fees) $358. Sal $142,185 (Prof $42,269)
Library Holdings: Audiobooks 811; Bks on Deafness & Sign Lang 5; CDs 265; DVDs 1,600; Electronic Media & Resources 3; Large Print Bks 450; Microforms 180; Bk Titles 25,000; Bk Vols 26,000; Per Subs 89; Videos 800
Special Collections: Oral History
Automation Activity & Vendor Info: (Acquisitions) TLC (The Library Corporation); (ILL) OCLC Online
Database Vendor: Baker & Taylor, EBSCOhost, LearningExpress, OCLC FirstSearch, OCLC WorldShare Interlibrary Loan, TLC (The Library Corporation)
Wireless access
Function: Equip loans & repairs, Fax serv, Free DVD rentals, Handicapped accessible, Home delivery & serv to Sr ctr & nursing homes, Homebound delivery serv, ILL available, Instruction & testing, Large print keyboards, Magnifiers for reading, Music CDs, Newsp ref libr, Notary serv, Online cat, Online ref, Online searches, Outreach serv, Photocopying/Printing, Preschool outreach, Prog for adults, Prog for children & young adult, Pub access computers, Scanner, Senior computer classes, Senior outreach, Story hour, Summer reading prog, Tax forms, Teen prog, VHS videos, Wheelchair accessible
Special Services for the Blind - Accessible computers; Aids for in-house use; BiFolkal kits; Bks on cassette; Bks on CD; Cassettes; Computer access aids; Internet workstation with adaptive software; Large print bks; Large screen computer & software; Magnifiers; PC for handicapped; Photo duplicator for making large print
Open Mon, Wed & Fri 9:30-7, Tues & Thurs 9:30-7, Sat 9:30-2

WEST LIBERTY

S EASTERN KENTUCKY CORRECTIONAL COMPLEX LIBRARY*, 200 Road to Justice, 41472. Tel: 606-743-2800. FAX: 606-743-2811. *Librn,* Daryl Thompson; E-mail: darylw.thompson@ky.gov
Library Holdings: Bk Vols 18,000; Per Subs 35
Open Mon & Tues 9-10:20, 1-3:15 & 6-8:30, Wed-Sun 9-10:20 & 1-3:15

P MORGAN COUNTY PUBLIC LIBRARY*, 151 University Dr, 41472. SAN 306-4255. Tel: 606-743-4151. FAX: 606-743-2170. E-mail: youseemoremcpl@yahoo.com. Web Site: www.youseemore.com/mcpl. *Libr Dir,* Allison Ennis; *Libr Asst,* Jerria Cantrell
Founded 1965. Pop 11,406; Circ 76,576
Library Holdings: Bk Vols 30,000; Per Subs 29
Subject Interests: Genealogy
Automation Activity & Vendor Info: (Cataloging) TLC (The Library Corporation); (Circulation) TLC (The Library Corporation)
Partic in Bergen County Cooperative Library System
Open Mon, Tues, Thurs & Fri 9-7, Wed 9-5, Sat 10-3

WHITESBURG

P LETCHER COUNTY PUBLIC LIBRARY DISTRICT*, Harry Caudill Memorial Library, 220 Main St, 41858. SAN 342-6459. Tel: 606-633-7547. FAX: 606-633-3407. E-mail: letcolib@bellsouth.net. Web Site: www.lcld.org. *Dir,* Angelina Tidal; *Ch,* Tessa Fugate-Caudill; *Tech Serv Librn,* Vicki Hurst; *Circ Mgr,* Patty Hawkins
Founded 1952. Pop 25,277; Circ 124,667
Jul 2012-Jun 2013 Income (Main Library and Branch(s)) $1,083,093, State $27,315, Federal $1,980, County $1,037,630, Other $16,168. Mats Exp $112,307, Books $70,605, Per/Ser (Incl. Access Fees) $3,983, Other Print Mats $6,643, AV Equip $10,153, AV Mat $12,098, Electronic Ref Mat (Incl. Access Fees) $8,825. Sal $234,894 (Prof $65,605)
Library Holdings: Audiobooks 2,255; AV Mats 544; CDs 2,257; DVDs 5,938; e-books 57,093; Electronic Media & Resources 2; Large Print Bks 2,000; Bk Titles 96,000; Bk Vols 100,856; Per Subs 191; Videos 2,330
Subject Interests: Genealogy, Local hist
Automation Activity & Vendor Info: (Cataloging) TLC (The Library Corporation); (Circulation) TLC (The Library Corporation); (ILL) OCLC; (OPAC) TLC (The Library Corporation); (Serials) TLC (The Library Corporation)
Database Vendor: OCLC FirstSearch, OCLC WorldShare Interlibrary Loan
Wireless access
Open Mon & Wed-Fri 9-5, Tues 9-7, Sat 9-4
Branches: 3
BLACKEY BRANCH, 295 Main St Loop, Blackey, 41804. (Mail add: PO Box 337, Blackey, 41804), SAN 374-4566. Tel: 606-633-4013. FAX: 606-632-9808. *Head Librn,* Mary Grace Raglin; *Asst Librn,* Nettie Combs
Automation Activity & Vendor Info: (Acquisitions) TLC (The Library Corporation); (Course Reserve) TLC (The Library Corporation)
Open Mon-Fri 9-5, Sat 9-4

FLEMING NEON PUBLIC LIBRARY, 1008 Hwy 317, Neon, 41840. (Mail add: PO Box 236, Neon, 41840-0236), SAN 342-6513. Tel: 606-855-7913. FAX: 606-855-4565. E-mail: lwlib@lcld.org. *Head Librn,* Jenay Ellen Hall; *Asst Librn,* Patricia Brashear
Pop 1,600
Open Mon-Fri 9-5, Sat 9-1

JENKINS PUBLIC, 9543 Hwy 805, Jenkins, 41537. (Mail add: PO Box 687, Jenkins, 41537-0687), SAN 342-6483. Tel: 606-832-4101. FAX: 606-832-0040. E-mail: jplib@lcld.org. Web Site: www.lcld.org/libraries/jenkins.html. *Head Librn,* Peggy Bentley; *Libr Asst,* Missy Hall
Automation Activity & Vendor Info: (Course Reserve) TLC (The Library Corporation)
Open Mon 9-7, Tues-Fri 9-5, Sat 9-1
Bookmobiles: 1. Librn, Legina Adams

J SOUTHEAST KENTUCKY COMMUNITY & TECHNICAL COLLEGE*, Whitesburg Campus Library, Two Long Ave, 41858. SAN 372-6959. Tel: 606-633-0279. FAX: 606-633-7225. Web Site: www.southeast.kctcs.edu/library. *Dir,* Evelyn Hensley; *Libr Spec,* Mitchell Caudill; Staff 2 (MLS 1, Non-MLS 1)
Founded 1990
Library Holdings: Bk Vols 4,800; Per Subs 38
Automation Activity & Vendor Info: (Cataloging) Ex Libris Group; (Circulation) Ex Libris Group; (OPAC) Ex Libris Group
Database Vendor: EBSCOhost, Gale Cengage Learning, OCLC FirstSearch, ProQuest
Wireless access
Function: For res purposes
Open Mon-Thurs 8-7, Fri 8-4:30

WHITLEY CITY

P MCCREARY COUNTY PUBLIC LIBRARY DISTRICT, Six N Main St, 42653. (Mail add: PO Box 8, 42653-0008), SAN 320-4812. Tel: 606-376-8738. FAX: 606-376-3631. E-mail: mcpl@highland.net. Web Site: www.mccrearylibrary.org. *Dir,* Kay Morrow; *Head, Circ,* Debbie Lyons; *Ch Serv,* Tracy Lumley; Staff 1 (Non-MLS 1)
Founded 1975. Pop 17,190; Circ 80,821
Jul 2013-Jun 2014 Income $404,303, State $46,303, Federal $60, County $338,627, Locally Generated Income $19,313. Mats Exp $54,023, Books $31,198, Per/Ser (Incl. Access Fees) $1,160, AV Mat $6,065, Electronic Ref Mat (Incl. Access Fees) $15,600. Sal $190,196 (Prof $49,000)
Library Holdings: Bks on Deafness & Sign Lang 10; CDs 216; DVDs 3,555; Large Print Bks 1,550; Microforms 100; Bk Titles 51,595; Bk Vols 51,850; Per Subs 35; Talking Bks 883; Videos 1,276
Special Collections: Pictorial History of McCreary County. Oral History
Automation Activity & Vendor Info: (Acquisitions) Follett Software; (Cataloging) Follett Software; (Circulation) Follett Software; (ILL) OCLC FirstSearch
Database Vendor: Gale Cengage Learning, Newsbank, OCLC FirstSearch, World Book Online
Wireless access
Function: ILL available
Special Services for the Deaf - Video & TTY relay via computer
Special Services for the Blind - Audio mat
Open Mon & Thurs 9-7, Tues, Wed & Fri 9-5:30, Sat 9-4
Bookmobiles: 1

WILLIAMSBURG

C UNIVERSITY OF THE CUMBERLANDS/CUMBERLAND COLLEGE, Norma Perkins Hagan Memorial Library, 821 Walnut St, 40769. SAN 306-4263. Tel: 606-539-4329. Reference Tel: 606-539-4526. Administration Tel: 606-539-4328. FAX: 606-539-4317. *Libr Dir,* Jan Wren; E-mail: jan.wren@ucumberlands.edu; *Ref & Instruction Librn,* Carrie Byrd; Tel: 606-539-4160, E-mail: carrie.byrd@ucumberlands.edu; *Tech Serv Librn,* Sara Schumacher; Tel: 606-539-4464, E-mail: sara.schumacher@ucumberlands.edu; Staff 6 (MLS 3, Non-MLS 3)
Founded 1889. Enrl 2,522; Fac 95; Highest Degree: Doctorate
Library Holdings: AV Mats 3,748; e-books 299,234; e-journals 58,720; Electronic Media & Resources 98; Bk Vols 146,306
Special Collections: Children's Coll; Steele-Reese Appalachian Coll. US Document Depository
Automation Activity & Vendor Info: (Cataloging) Innovative Interfaces, Inc; (Circulation) Innovative Interfaces, Inc; (OPAC) Innovative Interfaces, Inc
Database Vendor: ACM (Association for Computing Machinery), Alexander Street Press, American Chemical Society, American Psychological Association (APA), ARTstor, BioOne, Cinahl, CQ Press, CredoReference, EBSCOhost, Gale Cengage Learning, JSTOR, LexisNexis, Modern Language Association, OCLC WorldShare Interlibrary Loan, Oxford Online, Project MUSE, ProQuest, Sage, Springshare, LLC, STAT!Ref (Teton Data Systems)
Wireless access
Partic in Appalachian Col Asn; Association of Independent Kentucky Colleges & Universities

P WHITLEY COUNTY LIBRARY*, 285 S Third St, 40769. SAN 306-4271. Tel: 606-549-0818. FAX: 606-539-9242. E-mail: whitleylib@gmail.com. Web Site: www.youseemore.com/whitley/default.asp. *Dir,* Greg Meadors; *Ch,* Shonna Brown; *Circ Supvr,* Betty Croley
Founded 1960. Pop 33,396; Circ 124,937
Library Holdings: Bk Vols 25,000, Per Subs 65
Automation Activity & Vendor Info: (Acquisitions) TLC (The Library Corporation); (Cataloging) TLC (The Library Corporation); (Circulation) TLC (The Library Corporation); (Course Reserve) TLC (The Library Corporation); (OPAC) TLC (The Library Corporation)
Open Mon & Thurs 9-8, Tues, Wed & Fri 9-6, Sat 9-2
Bookmobiles: 1

WILLIAMSTOWN

P GRANT COUNTY PUBLIC LIBRARY DISTRICT, 201 Barnes Rd, 41097-9482. SAN 306-428X. Tel: 859-824-2080. FAX: 859-824-2083. E-mail: info@grantlib.org. Web Site: www.grantlib.org. *Dir,* Susan Nimersheim; E-mail: s.nimersheim@grantlib.org; *Pub Serv Librn,* Wynita Worley; E-mail: w.worley@grantlib.org; *Reader Serv Librn,* Angie Gabbard; E-mail: a.gabbard@grantlib.org; *Cat,* Kathy Dreifuss; E-mail: k.dreifuss@grantlib.org; *Youth Serv,* Cheryl Clemons; E-mail: c.clemons@grantlib.org. Subject Specialists: *Adult fiction, Ill,* Angie Gabbard; Staff 6 (MLS 4, Non-MLS 2)
Founded 1956. Pop 24,610; Circ 124,394
Library Holdings: AV Mats 3,004; CDs 793; DVDs 1,900; Large Print Bks 310; Bk Vols 35,132; Per Subs 96; Talking Bks 600; Videos 232
Special Collections: Genealogy Coll; Kentuckiana; Pedometers
Database Vendor: 3M Library Systems, Baker & Taylor, EBSCO Auto Repair Reference, EBSCO Information Services, EBSCOhost, Evanced Solutions, Inc, Gale Cengage Learning, Ingram Library Services, LearningExpress, Library Ideas, LLC, Newsbank, OCLC, Overdrive, Inc, ProQuest
Wireless access
Function: Bk club(s), Bks on CD, Children's prog, Computers for patron use, Copy machines, Doc delivery serv, Electronic databases & coll, eReaders, Free DVD rentals, Handicapped accessible, Home delivery & serv to Sr ctr & nursing homes, Homebound delivery serv, ILL available, Magazines, Mango lang, Microfiche/film & reading machines, Music CDs, Notary serv, Online cat, Outreach serv, OverDrive digital audio bks, Photocopying/Printing, Preschool outreach, Printer for laptops & handheld devices, Prog for adults, Prog for children & young adult, Pub access computers, Satellite serv, Senior outreach, Story hour, Summer & winter reading prog, Summer reading prog, Tax forms, Teen prog, Web-catalog, Wheelchair accessible, Winter reading prog
Open Mon-Thurs 9-8, Fri & Sat 9-6, Sun (Sept-May) 1-6

WILMORE

R ASBURY THEOLOGICAL SEMINARY*, B L Fisher Library, 204 N Lexington Ave, 40390-1199. SAN 306-4301. Tel: 859-858-2233. FAX: 859-858-2330. E-mail: information.commons@asburyseminary.edu. Web Site: www.asburyseminary.edu. *Dir of Libr Serv,* Paul Tippey; *Mgr, Info Tech,* Janice Huber; *Tech Serv Mgr,* Don Butterworth; *Spec Coll Librn,* Grace Yoder; Staff 16 (MLS 6, Non-MLS 10)
Founded 1939. Enrl 1,300; Fac 67; Highest Degree: Doctorate
Library Holdings: Bk Vols 260,000; Per Subs 1,054
Special Collections: Healing (Alfred E Price Coll); Wesleyan/Holiness; World Council of Churches (Faith & Order Papers Coll)
Subject Interests: Biblical studies, Missions, Theol
Automation Activity & Vendor Info: (Acquisitions) Horizon; (Cataloging) Horizon; (Circulation) Horizon; (Course Reserve) Horizon; (OPAC) Horizon; (Serials) Horizon
Database Vendor: EBSCOhost
Publications: Occasional Bibliographic Papers of the B L Fisher Library
Partic in Lyrasis; Theological Education Association of Mid America
Open Mon-Thurs 7:30am-Midnight, Fri 7:30-6, Sat 8-6

C ASBURY UNIVERSITY, Kinlaw Library, One Macklem Dr, 40390-1198. SAN 306-4298. Tel: 859-858-3511. Circulation Tel: 859-858-3511, Ext 2265. Interlibrary Loan Service Tel: 859-858-3511, Ext 2143. Reference Tel: 859-858-3511, Ext 2257. FAX: 859-858-3921. E-mail: reference@asbury.edu. Web Site: www.asbury.edu/library. *Dir of Libr Serv,* Morgan Tracy; Tel: 859-858-3511, Ext 2126, E-mail: morgan.tracy@asbury.edu; *Head, Archives & Instrul Serv,* Suzanne Gehring; Tel: 859-858-3511, Ext 2270, E-mail: suzanne.gehring@asbury.edu; *Head, Res & Distance Serv,* Jennifer Walz; Tel: 859-858-3511, Ext 2269, E-mail: jlwalz@asbury.edu; *Head, Tech Serv,* Doug Butler; Tel: 859-858-3511, Ext 2522, E-mail: doug.butler@asbury.edu; *Educ Librn,* Katrina Salley; Tel: 859-858-3511, Ext 2467, E-mail: katrina.salley@asbury.edu; *Instrul Serv Librn,* Amy

Bessin; E-mail: amy.bessin@asbury.edu; *ILL,* Bonnie Temple; E-mail: bonnie.temple@asbury.edu; Staff 11 (MLS 6, Non-MLS 5)
Founded 1890. Enrl 1,800; Fac 120; Highest Degree: Master
Special Collections: College Archives; Faculty & Alumni Publications; Missionary Coll. Oral History
Subject Interests: Holiness lit, Local hist
Automation Activity & Vendor Info: (Acquisitions) SirsiDynix; (Cataloging) SirsiDynix; (Circulation) SirsiDynix; (Course Reserve) SirsiDynix; (OPAC) SirsiDynix; (Serials) SirsiDynix
Database Vendor: ARTstor, Dialog, EBSCOhost, OCLC FirstSearch, ProQuest
Wireless access
Publications: Collegii Asburiensis Bibliotheca
Partic in Association of Independent Kentucky Colleges & Universities; Christian Libr Network; OCLC Online Computer Library Center, Inc
Special Services for the Blind - Assistive/Adapted tech devices, equip & products
Open Mon-Thurs 7:30am-11:50pm, Fri 7:30-6, Sat 10-10

WINCHESTER

P CLARK COUNTY PUBLIC LIBRARY*, 370 S Burns Ave, 40391-1876. SAN 306-431X. Tel: 859-744-5661. FAX: 859-744-5993. E-mail: clarkbooks@gmail.com. Web Site: www.clarkbooks.org. *Dir,* Julie Maruskin; *Ref Librn,* Andy Gary; *Ref Librn,* Angela Turner; *Adult Serv,* John Maruskin; *Youth Serv,* Renee Bush
Founded 1950. Pop 29,500; Circ 172,000
Library Holdings: Bk Vols 89,000; Per Subs 300
Special Collections: Heirloom Seal & Plant Materials Coll; Kentucky History (Doyle Coll & Kentucky Coll); Local Genealogy (Doyle Coll, Family File), bks, micro
Subject Interests: Out of print bks, Rare children's bks
Automation Activity & Vendor Info: (Acquisitions) TLC (The Library Corporation); (Cataloging) TLC (The Library Corporation); (Circulation) TLC (The Library Corporation)
Partic in Lyrasis
Open Mon-Thurs 9-8, Fri 9-5:30, Sat 9-5, Sun 1-5
Friends of the Library Group

LOUISIANA

Date of Statistics: FY 2013
Population, 2010 U.S. Census: 4,468,976
Population, 2014 U.S. Census (est.): 4,629,284
Population Served by Public Libraries: 4,629,284
Total Volumes in Public Libraries: 13,958,323
Volumes Per Capita: 3.00
Total Public Library Circulation: 20,286,867
Circulation Per Capita: 4.36
Total Public Library Income: $225,215,054
Median or Average Income: $3,311,986 (average); $1,293,994 (median)
Source of Income: Public Funds (Primarily property tax)
Expenditures Per Capita: $41.14
Number of County or Multi-county (Regional) Libraries: 68
Counties Served: 64

ABBEVILLE

P VERMILION PARISH LIBRARY, Abbeville Branch, 405 E Saint Victor, 70510-5101. (Mail add: PO Drawer 640, 70511-0640), SAN 342-6548. Tel: 337-893-2655. FAX: 337-898-0526. E-mail: abbeville@vermilion.lib.la.us. Web Site: www.vermilion.lib.la.us. *Dir,* Charlotte Trosclair; *Adult Serv, Prog Dir,* Sue Trahan; *Bus Mgr,* Amy Stelly; *Admin Mgr,* Dawn Hebert; *Br Mgr,* Susan Stelly; *IT Mgr,* Grant Domingue; *Ch Serv,* Sara Bailey-McDaniel; *ILL,* Elizabeth Stelly; Staff 16 (MLS 1, Non-MLS 15)
Founded 1941. Pop 53,044; Circ 299,077
Library Holdings: AV Mats 6,600; Bks on Deafness & Sign Lang 81; Large Print Bks 7,755; Bk Titles 136,294; Bk Vols 174,319; Per Subs 97; Talking Bks 4,957
Special Collections: Louisiana Coll
Automation Activity & Vendor Info: (Acquisitions) Book Systems; (Cataloging) Book Systems; (Circulation) Book Systems; (Course Reserve) Book Systems; (OPAC) Book Systems
Wireless access
Mem of Bayouland Library System
Special Services for the Blind - Bks on cassette; Bks on CD; Large print bks; Large screen computer & software; Low vision equip
Open Mon -Thurs 9-6:30, Fri 9-5:30, Sat 9-1
Friends of the Library Group
Branches: 5
DELCAMBRE BRANCH, 206 W Main St, Delcambre, 70528-2918, SAN 342-6602. Tel: 337-685-2388. FAX: 337-685-2388. E-mail: delcambre@vermilion.lib.la.us. *Br Supvr,* Bonnie Richard; Staff 2 (Non-MLS 2)
Library Holdings: AV Mats 115; Bk Vols 18,000; Per Subs 22
Open Mon-Thurs 10-5:30, Fri 10-5, Sat 9-12
ERATH BRANCH, 111 W Edwards St, Erath, 70533-4027, SAN 342-6637. Tel: 337-937-5628. FAX: 337-937-5656. E-mail: erath@vermilion.lib.la.us. *Br Mgr,* Patrice LeBlanc; E-mail: pleblanc@vermilion.lib.la.us; Staff 1 (Non-MLS 1)
Library Holdings: AV Mats 76; Bk Vols 16,904; Per Subs 22
Function: BA reader (adult literacy), Bks on cassette, Bks on CD, CD-ROM, Children's prog, Citizenship assistance, Computer training, Computers for patron use, Copy machines, Distance learning, e-mail serv, E-Reserves, Fax serv, Free DVD rentals, Govt ref serv, Handicapped accessible, Health sci info serv, Holiday prog, Home delivery & serv to Sr ctr & nursing homes, Homework prog, ILL available, Large print keyboards, Literacy & newcomer serv, Magnifiers for reading, Mail & tel request accepted, Newsp ref libr, Online ref, Online searches, Orientations, Outreach serv, Photocopying/Printing, Preschool outreach, Prof lending libr, Prog for adults, Prog for children & young adult, Pub access computers, Ref & res, Ref serv available, Senior outreach, Serves mentally handicapped consumers, Spoken cassettes & CDs, Spoken cassettes & DVDs, Story hour, Summer reading prog, Tax forms, Teen prog, Telephone ref, VHS videos, Video lending libr, Web-catalog, Wheelchair accessible, Workshops
Open Mon-Thurs 12-5:30, Fri 12-5, Sat 9-12
GUEYDAN BRANCH, 704 Tenth St, Gueydan, 70542-3806, SAN 342-6661. Tel: 337-536-6781. FAX: 337-536-0112. E-mail: gueydan@vermilion.lib.la.us. *Br Supvr,* Angela Touchet; Staff 1 (Non-MLS 1)
Library Holdings: AV Mats 110; Bk Vols 18,313; Per Subs 23
Open Mon-Fri 10-12:30 & 1-5, Sat 9-12
KAPLAN BRANCH, 815 N Cushing Ave, Kaplan, 70548-2614, SAN 342-6696. Tel: 337-643-7209. FAX: 337-643-7250. E-mail: kaplan@vermilion.lib.la.us. *Br Supvr,* Linda Leonard; Staff 2 (Non-MLS 2)
Library Holdings: AV Mats 75; Bk Vols 31,025; Per Subs 36
Open Mon, Wed & Thurs 9-5:30, Tues 9-8, Fri 9-5, Sat 9-Noon
MAURICE BRANCH, 8901 Maurice Ave, Maurice, 70555, SAN 342-6726. Tel: 337-893-5583. FAX: 337-893-5583. E-mail: maurice@vermilion.lib.la.us. *Br Mgr,* Cheryl Bergeron; Staff 2 (Non-MLS 2)
Library Holdings: AV Mats 90; Bk Vols 14,770; Per Subs 20
Open Mon-Thurs 12-5:30, Fri 12-5, Sat 9-12
Bookmobiles: 1. Mgr, Nella Efferson

ALEXANDRIA

S ALEXANDRIA DAILY TOWN TALK LIBRARY*, 1201 Third St, 71301. (Mail add: PO Box 7558, 71306-0558). Tel: 318-487-6330. FAX: 318-487-6488. Web Site: thetowntalk.com. *Librn,* Lynne Distefano
Library Holdings: Bk Vols 100
Restriction: Staff use only

GM DEPARTMENT OF VETERANS AFFAIRS*, Medical & Patient Library, VA Medical Center, 2495 Shreveport Hwy 71 N, 71360. (Mail add: PO Box 69004, 71306-9004), SAN 342-7056. Tel: 318-473-0010, Ext 2548. FAX: 318-473-9491. Web Site: www.alexandria.med.va.gov/lib.html. *Chief, Libr Serv,* Lola H Purvis; E-mail: lola.purvis@med.va.gov
Library Holdings: Bk Vols 5,247; Per Subs 444
Automation Activity & Vendor Info: (Cataloging) Ex Libris Group; (Circulation) Ex Libris Group; (OPAC) Ex Libris Group
Database Vendor: EBSCOhost
Partic in BRS; S Cent Regional Med Libr Program; Veterans Affairs Libr Network (VALNET)
Restriction: Staff & patient use

L GOLD, WEEMS, BRUSER, SUES & RUNDELL*, Law Library, 2001 MacArthur Dr, 71301. SAN 372-1299. Tel: 318-445-6471. FAX: 318-445-6476. Web Site: www.goldweems.com.
Library Holdings: Bk Titles 1,287; Per Subs 77
Database Vendor: Westlaw
Open Mon-Fri 8-5

C LOUISIANA STATE UNIVERSITY AT ALEXANDRIA, James C Bolton Library, 8100 Hwy 71 S, 71302. SAN 306-4344. Tel: 318-473-6438. Reference Tel: 318-473-6442. FAX: 318-473-6556. Web Site:

library.lsua.edu. *Dir, Libr Serv,* Bonnie Hines; *Archives & Spec Coll Librn,* Michelle Riggs; Tel: 318-619-2960, E-mail: mriggs@lsua.edu; *Ref & Instruction Librn,* Rusty Gaspard; E-mail: rgaspard@lsua.edu; *Cataloger & Acq, ILL,* Rachael Hunter; E-mail: rhunter@lsua.edu; *Ser,* Titus Belgard; Tel: 318-473-6440, E-mail: tbelgard@lsua.edu. Subject Specialists: *Hist,* Michelle Riggs; *Arts, English, Humanities,* Rusty Gaspard; Staff 5 (MLS 5)
Founded 1960. Enrl 2,574; Fac 1; Highest Degree: Bachelor
Jul 2014-Jun 2015 Income $310,294. Mats Exp $102,000, Books $35,000, Per/Ser (Incl. Access Fees) $5,000, Electronic Ref Mat (Incl. Access Fees) $58,000, Presv $4,000. Sal $227,024 (Prof $153,998)
Library Holdings: CDs 142; DVDs 162; e-books 202,444; e-journals 90,724; Electronic Media & Resources 77; Microforms 19,000; Bk Titles 121,161; Per Subs 57
Automation Activity & Vendor Info: (Acquisitions) SirsiDynix; (Cataloging) SirsiDynix; (Circulation) SirsiDynix; (Course Reserve) SirsiDynix; (ILL) OCLC ILLiad; (Media Booking) SirsiDynix; (OPAC) SirsiDynix; (Serials) SirsiDynix
Database Vendor: American Mathematical Society, American Psychological Association (APA), Cinahl, CQ Press, EBSCO Discovery Service, EBSCOhost, Gale Cengage Learning, JSTOR, LearningExpress, LexisNexis, Medline, OCLC FirstSearch, ProQuest, PubMed
Wireless access
Function: Archival coll, e-mail serv, Electronic databases & coll, ILL available, Instruction & testing, Online cat, Online info literacy tutorials on the web & in blackboard, Ref & res, Ref serv available
Partic in Louisiana Academic Library Information Network (LALINC); Lyrasis; The Louisiana Library Network
Open Mon-Thurs 7:45am-10pm, Fri 7:45-4:30, Sat 10-6, Sun 3-10
Restriction: In-house use for visitors, Internal use only
Friends of the Library Group

P RAPIDES PARISH LIBRARY*, 411 Washington St, 71301-8338. SAN 342-6785. Tel: 318-442-2411. Circulation Tel: 318-445-2411, Ext 1020. Interlibrary Loan Service Tel: 318-445-2411, Ext 1074. Reference Tel: 318-445-1840, Ext 1030. Administration Tel: 318-445-6436. Automation Services Tel: 318-445-2411, Ext 1050. FAX: 318-445-6478. Administration FAX: 318-445-6196. TDD: 318-445-8074. E-mail: info@rpl.org. Web Site: www.rpl.org. *Dir,* Laura-Ellen Ayres; Tel: 318-445-6436, Ext 1001, E-mail: lea@rpl.org; *Asst Dir, Direct Serv,* Laura-Ellen Ayres; Tel: 318-445-6436, Ext 1002, E-mail: lea@rpl.org; *Asst Dir, Support Serv,* Wesley Saunders; Tel: 318-445-2412, Ext 1044, E-mail: whsaunders@rpl.org; *Bus Mgr,* Jimmy Holsomback; Tel: 318-445-6436, Ext 1004, E-mail: joh@rpl.org; *Circ Mgr,* Brenda Harvey; E-mail: brenda@rpl.org; *Ref Mgr,* Linda Green; Tel: 318-445-2412, Ext 1030, E-mail: linda@rpl.org; *Coordr, Outreach Serv,* Tammy DiBartolo; Tel: 318-442-2483, Ext 1906; *Direct Serv Coordr,* Lenná Mouton; Staff 35 (MLS 7, Non-MLS 28)
Founded 1942. Pop 134,655; Circ 785,139
Jan 2012-Dec 2012 Income (Main Library and Branch(s)) $5,206,022, State $206,763, County $4,457,398, Locally Generated Income $393,476, Other $148,385. Mats Exp $388,241. Sal $2,115,466
Library Holdings: Audiobooks 2,887; AV Mats 920; Bks on Deafness & Sign Lang 178; Braille Volumes 19; CDs 8,807; DVDs 10,231; e-books 769; High Interest/Low Vocabulary Bk Vols 658; Large Print Bks 8,473; Microforms 262; Bk Vols 281,186; Per Subs 145; Videos 7,497
Special Collections: Map Coll. State Document Depository
Subject Interests: Local hist
Automation Activity & Vendor Info: (Acquisitions) Innovative Interfaces, Inc; (Cataloging) Innovative Interfaces, Inc; (Circulation) Innovative Interfaces, Inc; (ILL) Innovative Interfaces, Inc; (OPAC) Innovative Interfaces, Inc; (Serials) Innovative Interfaces, Inc
Wireless access
Function: Accelerated reader prog, Adult bk club, After school storytime, Audiobks via web, AV serv, Bk club(s), Bk reviews (Group), Bks on cassette, Bks on CD, Children's prog, Computer training, Computers for patron use, Copy machines, Digital talking bks, Electronic databases & coll, Family literacy, Fax serv, Free DVD rentals, Govt ref serv, Handicapped accessible, Home delivery & serv to Sr ctr & nursing homes, Homebound delivery serv, Homework prog, ILL available, Magnifiers for reading, Mail & tel request accepted, Microfiche/film & reading machines, Music CDs, Newsp ref libr, Online cat, Online ref, Online searches, Outreach serv, Outside serv via phone, mail, e-mail & web, OverDrive digital audio bks, Photocopying/Printing, Preschool outreach, Prog for adults, Prog for children & young adult, Pub access computers, Ref serv available, Ref serv in person, Senior outreach, Serves mentally handicapped consumers, Spanish lang bks, Spoken cassettes & CDs, Spoken cassettes & DVDs, Story hour, Summer reading prog, Tax forms, Teen prog, Telephone ref, VHS videos, Web-catalog, Wheelchair accessible, Workshops
Publications: Friends of the Rapides Library (Newsletter); Ripple (Newsletter)
Special Services for the Deaf - Assisted listening device; Assistive tech; Bks on deafness & sign lang
Special Services for the Blind - Accessible computers; Assistive/Adapted tech devices, equip & products; Bks & mags in Braille, on rec, tape & cassette; Bks on cassette; Bks on CD; Braille bks; Cassettes; Copier with enlargement capabilities; Free checkout of audio mat; Internet workstation with adaptive software; Large print bks; PC for handicapped; Photo duplicator for making large print; Playaways (bks on MP3); Ref serv; Screen enlargement software for people with visual disabilities
Open Mon-Sat 9-6, Sun 1-5
Restriction: Circ to mem only, ID required to use computers (Ltd hrs), In-house use for visitors
Friends of the Library Group
Branches: 8
BOYCE BRANCH, 500 A Ulster Ave, Boyce, 71409. (Mail add: PO Box 792, Boyce, 71409-0792), SAN 342-6815. Tel: 318-793-2182. FAX: 318-793-2736. E-mail: bccirc@rpl.org. *Mgr,* Margaret Catherine Mealer; E-mail: mcmealer@rpl.org; Staff 2 (Non-MLS 2)
Library Holdings: AV Mats 1,920; CDs 399; DVDs 789; Large Print Bks 413; Bk Vols 15,092; Videos 711
Open Tues 9-12 & 1-6, Wed & Fri 1-6, Thurs & Sat 9-1
Friends of the Library Group
CARL N GUNTER SR BRANCH, 5630 Hwy 28 W, Pineville, 71360, SAN 342-684X. Tel: 318-443-7259. FAX: 318-443-1293. *Mgr,* Pamela Martin; Staff 4.2 (Non-MLS 4.2)
Library Holdings: Audiobooks 75; AV Mats 2,733; CDs 870; DVDs 1,324; Large Print Bks 765; Bk Vols 29,781; Per Subs 36; Videos 405
Open Mon-Sat 9-6
HINESTON BRANCH, 1810 Hwy 121, Hineston, 71438, SAN 342-6882. Tel: 318-793-8461. FAX: 318-793-0691. E-mail: hncirc@rpl.org. *Mgr,* Donna Crawford; Staff 2 (Non-MLS 2)
Founded 1984
Library Holdings: Audiobooks 153; AV Mats 2,687; CDs 292; DVDs 1,150; Large Print Bks 436; Bk Vols 16,419; Per Subs 32; Videos 1,075
Open Mon & Sat 9-1, Tues 1:30-5, Wed & Fri 9-1 & 2-6
GEORGIE G JOHNSON BRANCH, 1610 Veterans Dr, Lecompte, 71346. (Mail add: PO Box 1207, Lecompte, 71346-1207), SAN 342-6904. Tel: 318-776-5153. FAX: 318-776-6744. E-mail: jncirc@rpl.org. *Mgr,* Mary Mahoney Murry; Staff 2 (Non-MLS 2)
Library Holdings: Audiobooks 174; AV Mats 1,856; CDs 379; DVDs 855; Large Print Bks 194; Bk Vols 12,187; Per Subs 39; Videos 436
Open Tues 9-5, Wed-Fri 1-5, Sat 9-1
Friends of the Library Group
MARTIN BRANCH, 801 W Shamrock, Pineville, 71360, SAN 342-6963. Tel: 318-442-7575. FAX: 318-449-4946. E-mail: mrcirc@rpl.org. *Librn,* Donna LeBlanc; Staff 2.5 (Non-MLS 2.5)
Founded 1950
Library Holdings: Audiobooks 118; AV Mats 1,684; Braille Volumes 584; CDs 624; Large Print Bks 345; Bk Vols 26,546; Per Subs 43; Videos 325
Open Mon-Sat 9-6
J W MCDONALD BRANCH, 1075 Hwy 497, Glenmora, 71433. (Mail add: PO Box 1206, Glenmora, 71433). Tel: 318-748-4848. FAX: 318-748-4851. E-mail: mccirc@rpl.org. *Mgr,* Gail Goldberg; Staff 2.5 (Non-MLS 2.5)
Library Holdings: Audiobooks 334; AV Mats 3,195; CDs 620; DVDs 1,153; Large Print Bks 665; Bk Titles 17,809; Bk Vols 20,259; Per Subs 39; Videos 1,042
Open Mon & Fri 1-6, Tues 10-6, Wed 1-5, Thurs 9-6, Sat 9-1
Friends of the Library Group
J L ROBERTSON BRANCH, 809 Tioga High School Rd, Ball, 71405, SAN 342-7021. Tel: 318-640-3098. FAX: 318-640-8713. E-mail: rbcirc@rpl.org. *Mgr,* Mariann Strange; Staff 4 (Non-MLS 4)
Founded 1942
Library Holdings: Audiobooks 440; AV Mats 3,099; CDs 1,139; DVDs 1,057; Large Print Bks 729; Bk Vols 33,646; Per Subs 38; Videos 418
Open Mon-Sat 9-6
WESTSIDE REGIONAL, 5416 Provine Pl, 71303, SAN 342-6939. Tel: 318-442-2483. FAX: 318-442-7678. E-mail: wrcirc@rpl.org. *Mgr,* Brandon Beckham; Tel: 318-442-2483, Ext 1903, E-mail: brandon@rpl.org; *Presch Outreach Plus Mgr,* Yolanda Skinner; Tel: 318-442-2483, Ext 1905; *Coordr, Outreach Serv,* Tammy DiBartolo; Tel: 318-442-2483, Ext 1906, E-mail: youthservices@rpl.org; *Youth Serv - Prog,* Karla Kirby; Tel: 318-442-2483, Ext 1904, E-mail: kjkirby@rpl.org; Staff 15 (MLS 2, Non-MLS 13)
Library Holdings: Audiobooks 214; AV Mats 4,056; CDs 1,625; DVDs 1,437; Large Print Bks 1,040; Bk Vols 39,162; Per Subs 56; Videos 634
Open Mon-Sat 9-6
Bookmobiles: 2. In Charge, Londa Price

M RAPIDES REGIONAL MEDICAL CENTER*, Medical Library, 211 Fourth St, 71301-8421. (Mail add: PO Box 30101, 71301), SAN 306-4352. Tel: 318-473-3563. FAX: 318-473-3489. Web Site: www.rapidesregional.com. *Asst Librn,* Denise Bordelon; Tel: 318-769-5341, E-mail: denise.bordelon@hcahealthcare.com; Staff 1 (Non-MLS 1)
Founded 1963
Library Holdings: Bk Vols 1,800; Per Subs 141
Subject Interests: Allied health, Health sci, Med, Nursing
Open Mon-Fri 8:30-4:30
Restriction: Staff use only

AMITE

P TANGIPAHOA PARISH LIBRARY*, Administration Office, 200 E Mulberry St, 70422. SAN 342-7110. Tel: 985-748-7559. FAX: 985-748-2812. Web Site: www.tangilibrary.com. *Dir,* Barry Bradford; E-mail: bbradford@state.lib.la.us; *Asst Dir,* Bianca Roberts; *Acq Mgr,* Melissa Granger; *Mgr, ILL,* Laura Augello; *Syst Adminr,* Ramon Wheeler; Staff 40 (MLS 3, Non-MLS 37)
Founded 1944. Pop 113,000; Circ 272,624
Library Holdings: AV Mats 13,688; Bk Vols 195,022; Per Subs 622
Subject Interests: Genealogy, Local hist
Database Vendor: EBSCOhost, Newsbank, ProQuest
Wireless access
Function: Adult bk club, Adult literacy prog, Bk club(s), Bks on cassette, Bks on CD, Children's prog, Computers for patron use, Copy machines, Free DVD rentals, Holiday prog, ILL available, Online cat, Prog for adults, Prog for children & young adult, Pub access computers, Ref serv available, Summer reading prog, Tax forms, VHS videos
Open Mon-Fri 8-3:30
Branches: 6
AMITE BRANCH, 761 W Oak St, 70422. Tel: 985-748-7151. FAX: 985-748-5476. *Br Mgr,* Jessica Kemm; Staff 3 (Non-MLS 3)
Founded 1944. Pop 5,500
Library Holdings: AV Mats 360; Bk Vols 45,000; Per Subs 86
Open Mon & Tues 8:30-8, Wed-Fri 8:30-6:30, Sat 8:30-3
HAMMOND BRANCH, 314 E Thomas, Hammond, 70401, SAN 342-7234. Tel: 985-345-0937, 985-345-3909. FAX: 985-345-2188. *Br Mgr,* Bill Dorman; Staff 2 (Non-MLS 2)
Pop 17,639
Library Holdings: AV Mats 216; Bk Vols 48,757; Per Subs 52
Open Mon, Tues & Fri 8:30-6:30, Wed & Thurs 8:30-8, Sat 8:30-3
INDEPENDENCE BRANCH, 290 S Pine St, Independence, 70443. (Mail add: PO Box 439, Independence, 70443-0439), SAN 342-7269. Tel: 985-878-2970. FAX: 985-878-1996. *Br Mgr,* Virginia Patanella; Staff 2 (Non-MLS 2)
Pop 2,000
Library Holdings: Bk Vols 15,101; Per Subs 21
Open Mon-Fri 10-5:30, Sat 9-1
KENTWOOD BRANCH, 101 Ave F, Kentwood, 70444, SAN 342-7293. Tel: 985-229-3596. FAX: 985-229-4566. *Br Mgr,* Peggy Fortinberry; Staff 2 (Non-MLS 2)
Pop 2,805
Library Holdings: AV Mats 207; Bk Vols 22,211; Per Subs 37
Open Mon-Fri 10-5:30, Sat 9-1
Friends of the Library Group
LORANGER BRANCH, 19451 Hwy 40, Loranger, 70446. (Mail add: PO Box 515, Loranger, 70446-0515), SAN 342-7315. Tel: 985-878-6224. FAX: 985-878-3571. *Br Mgr,* Mary Ann Cutrer; Staff 2 (Non-MLS 2)
Pop 3,500
Library Holdings: Bk Vols 6,235; Per Subs 21
Open Mon-Fri 10-5:30, Sat 9-1
PONCHATOULA BRANCH, 380 N Fifth St, Ponchatoula, 70454, SAN 342-7358. Tel: 985-386-6554, 985-386-6593. FAX: 985-370-5019. *Br Mgr,* Brenda Neidhamer; Staff 3 (Non MLS 3)
Pop 5,700
Library Holdings: AV Mats 148; Bk Vols 49,544; Per Subs 72
Open Mon & Tues 8:30-8, Wed-Fri 8:30-6:30, Sat 8:30-3
Friends of the Library Group

ANGIE

S RAYBURN CORRECTIONAL CENTER LIBRARY*, 27268 Hwy 21, 70426. SAN 373-8574. Tel: 985-986-5000, 985-986-5054. FAX: 985-986-5071. *Educ & Libr Dir,* Deborah Cook; Tel: 985-986-5000, Ext 5070, E-mail: dcook2@corrections.state.la.us; *Prog Dir,* Wayne Cook; E-mail: wcook@corrections.state.la.us
Library Holdings: Bk Vols 12,800; Per Subs 36
Open Mon-Sun 9-10:30, 1-3:30 & 6-9

ANGOLA

S LOUISIANA STATE PENITENTIARY LIBRARY*, Main Prison Library, A Bldg, 70712. SAN 306-4379. Tel: 225-655-2031. FAX: 225-655-2585. Web Site: www.corrections.state.la.us. *Librn,* Linda Holmes
Founded 1968
Jan 2012-Dec 2012. Mats Exp $18,000, Books $5,000, Per/Ser (Incl. Access Fees) $13,000. Sal $8,000
Library Holdings: Audiobooks 329; AV Mats 298; Bks on Deafness & Sign Lang 3; CDs 78; DVDs 281; High Interest/Low Vocabulary Bk Vols 462; Bk Vols 43,161; Per Subs 116; Videos 465
Special Collections: Criminal Justice; Science Fiction
Automation Activity & Vendor Info: (Circulation) Follett Software
Open Mon-Sun 8-12, 1-3 & 6-9

ARCADIA

P BIENVILLE PARISH LIBRARY*, 2768 Maple St, 71001-3699. SAN 306-4387. Tel: 318-263-7410. Toll Free Tel: 888-285-6750. FAX: 318-263-7428. E-mail: admin.g1bv@pelican.state.lib.la.us. Web Site: www.bienville.lib.la.us. *Dir,* Peggy Walls; *Asst Dir,* Wanda Bell; Staff 9 (MLS 1, Non-MLS 8)
Founded 1964. Pop 15,979; Circ 150,945
Library Holdings: AV Mats 1,280; Bk Titles 65,497; Bk Vols 88,000; Per Subs 226
Special Collections: Large print books, Louisiana material
Subject Interests: Genealogy, La
Automation Activity & Vendor Info: (Acquisitions) Innovative Interfaces, Inc; (Cataloging) Innovative Interfaces, Inc; (Circulation) Innovative Interfaces, Inc; (Course Reserve) Innovative Interfaces, Inc; (ILL) Innovative Interfaces, Inc; (OPAC) Innovative Interfaces, Inc
Open Mon & Wed-Fri 8:15-6, Tues 8:15-7, Sat 8:15-12
Branches: 2
RINGGOLD BRANCH, 2078 Hall St, Ringgold, 71068, SAN 324-3001. Tel: 318-894-9770. FAX: 318-894-4339. *Br Mgr,* Annette McLemore; Staff 4 (Non-MLS 4)
Library Holdings: AV Mats 80; Bk Vols 11,400; Per Subs 35
Open Mon & Wed-Fri 8:15-5, Tues 8:15-7, Sat 8:15-12
SALINE BRANCH, 1434 Fourth St, Saline, 71070. Tel: 318-576-8990. FAX: 318-576-8780. *Br Mgr,* Jeannie Basinger
Open Mon, Wed & Fri 8:15-5, Sat 8:15-12

BARKSDALE AFB

A UNITED STATES AIR FORCE*, Barksdale Air Force Base Library, 744 Douhet Dr, Bldg 4244, 71110. SAN 342-7447. Tel: 318-456-4182. Circulation Tel: 318-456-4101. Reference Tel: 318-456-5993. FAX: 318-752-0509. E-mail: barksdale.library2@barksdale.af.mil. Web Site: www.barksdalelibrary.org. *Dir,* C Frances Morris; E-mail: coralie.morris@barksdale.af.mil; *Acq,* Anthony Bellucci; Tel: 318-456-2093, E-mail: anthony.bellucci@barksdale.af.mil; *Cat,* Sharon Noland; E-mail: sharon.noland@barksdale.af.mil; *Circ,* Chris Rhodes; *ILL,* Catherine Lanham; E-mail: catherine.lanham@barksdale.af.mil; *Tech Serv,* Kirk Fontenot. Subject Specialists: *Econ, Law,* C Frances Morris; *Computer,* Kirk Fontenot; Staff 5 (MLS 2, Non-MLS 3)
Founded 1933
Library Holdings: AV Mats 4,200; Bk Vols 38,500; Per Subs 79
Special Collections: Chief of Staff Reading Lists; Louisiana History & Culture; Project Warrior Coll
Subject Interests: Mil hist (US)
Automation Activity & Vendor Info: (Acquisitions) SirsiDynix; (Cataloging) SirsiDynix; (Circulation) SirsiDynix; (Course Reserve) SirsiDynix; (OPAC) SirsiDynix; (Serials) SirsiDynix
Database Vendor: EBSCOhost, Gale Cengage Learning, Newsbank, OCLC FirstSearch
Wireless access
Function: ILL available
Special Services for the Blind - Large print bks
Open Mon-Thurs 10am-8pm, Fri 10-6, Sat 11-6
Restriction: Open to govt employees only

BASTROP

P MOREHOUSE PARISH LIBRARY*, 524 E Madison Ave, 71220. SAN 342-7471. Tel: 318-281-3696. FAX: 318-281-3683. Web Site: www.youseemore.com/morehouse. *Dir,* Ellen M Highsmith; Staff 4 (MLS 1, Non-MLS 3)
Founded 1940. Pop 34,000; Circ 129,402
Library Holdings: AV Mats 3,873; Bk Vols 53,063; Per Subs 101
Subject Interests: Genealogy, Local hist
Automation Activity & Vendor Info: (Cataloging) TLC (The Library Corporation); (Circulation) TLC (The Library Corporation); (OPAC) TLC (The Library Corporation)
Wireless access
Open Mon-Fri 8-5:30, Sat 9-1
Branches: 5
BONITA BRANCH, 15004 Henry St, Bonita, 71223. (Mail add: 524 E Madison Ave, 71220), SAN 342-7536. Tel: 318-823-2154. *Br Mgr,* Sue Barthol; Staff 1 (Non-MLS 1)
Open Thurs 10-5
COLLINSTON BRANCH, 4620 Main St, Collinston, 71229, SAN 342-7560. Tel: 318-874-3531. *Br Mgr,* Martha Crymes; Staff 1 (Non-MLS 1)
Open Mon & Thurs 12-3
DUNBAR, 1102 Perry St, 71220, SAN 342-7595. Tel: 318-281-1137. *Br Mgr,* Maple Jones; Staff 1 (Non-MLS 1)
Open Mon-Fri 1-5
MER ROUGE BRANCH, 107 S 16th St, Mer Rouge, 71261, SAN 342-7625. Tel: 318-647-5639. *Br Mgr,* Sue Barthol; Staff 1 (Non-MLS 1)
Open Tues 9-5

OAK RIDGE BRANCH, 106 N Oak St, Oak Ridge, 71264, SAN 342-765X. Tel: 318-244-5329. *Br Mgr,* Carolyn Files; Staff 1 (Non-MLS 1)
Library Holdings: Bk Vols 4,500; Per Subs 16
Open Mon & Thurs 8-11

BATON ROUGE

J BATON ROUGE COMMUNITY COLLEGE*, Magnolia Library, 201 Community College Dr, 70806. Tel: 225-216-8303. Reference Tel: 225-216-8555. Administration Tel: 225-216-8186. FAX: 225-216-8712. E-mail: librarian@mybrcc.edu. Web Site: www.mybrcc.edu/index.php?option=com_content&view=article&id=147&Itemid=362. *Dean, Learning Res,* Joanie D Chavis; E-mail: chavisj@mybrcc.edu; *Assoc Dean, Learning Res,* Jacqueline L Jones; Tel: 225-216-8170, E-mail: jonesjl@mybrcc.edu; *Chair of Instruction, Ref Librn,* Amy Reese; Tel: 225-216-8621, E-mail: reesea@mybrcc.edu; *Cat Librn,* Jenny Wong; Tel: 225-216-8590, E-mail: wongj@mybrcc.edu; *Gen Serv Librn,* Shereen Marx; Tel: 225-216-8557, E-mail: marxs@mybrcc.edu; *Ref Librn,* Peter Klubek; Tel: 225-216-8505, E-mail: klubekp@mybrcc.edu; *Ref Librn,* Lauren Wade McAdams; Tel: 225-216-8552, E-mail: wadel2@mybrcc.edu; *Ref Librn,* Kathryn Seidel; Tel: 225-216-8553, E-mail: seidelk@mybrcc.edu; *Supvr, Ser,* Laddawan Kongchum; Tel: 225-216-8017, E-mail: kongchuml@mybrcc.edu. Subject Specialists: *African-Am hist,* Jacqueline L Jones; *Bus, Hist, Sci tech,* Amy Reese; *Computer sci, Math,* Jenny Wong; *Paralegal, Psychol, Sociol,* Shereen Marx; *Art, Educ,* Peter Klubek; *Biol, Chem, Nursing,* Lauren Wade McAdams; *Eng, Philos, Polit sci,* Kathryn Seidel; *Avionics, Phys sci, Proc tech,* Laddawan Kongchum; Staff 8.5 (MLS 8.5)
Founded 1998. Enrl 7,150; Fac 293; Highest Degree: Associate
Library Holdings: Audiobooks 541; AV Mats 168; CDs 360; DVDs 2,760; e-books 59,377; Bk Titles 37,292; Bk Vols 45,601; Per Subs 215; Videos 2,356
Special Collections: Carville V Earle Coll; Multicultural Children's Resource Coll
Automation Activity & Vendor Info: (Acquisitions) SirsiDynix; (Cataloging) SirsiDynix; (Circulation) SirsiDynix; (Course Reserve) SirsiDynix; (OPAC) SirsiDynix; (Serials) SirsiDynix
Database Vendor: CQ Press, CredoReference, EBSCOhost, Gale Cengage Learning, JSTOR, LearningExpress, LexisNexis, OCLC FirstSearch, OCLC WorldShare Interlibrary Loan, Oxford Online, ProQuest
Wireless access
Function: e-mail serv, Ref serv available
Partic in Louisiana Academic Library Information Network (LALINC); Lyrasis; The Louisiana Library Network
Open Mon-Thurs 7:30am-8pm, Fri 7:30-5, Sat 8-1
Friends of the Library Group

M BATON ROUGE GENERAL MEDICAL CENTER*, Health Sciences Library, 3600 Florida Blvd, 70806. (Mail add: PO Box 2511, 70821-2511). Tel: 225-387-7012. FAX: 225-381-6116. *Dir,* Melissa Fahrmann; *Librn,* Wendy Pesch
Library Holdings: Bk Vols 450; Per Subs 200
Wireless access
Restriction: Staff use only

S CAPITAL CITY PRESS*, The Advocate Library, 7290 Bluebonnet Blvd, 70810. (Mail add: PO Box 588, 70821-0588), SAN 306-4395. Tel: 225-388-0328. Circulation Tel: 225-388-0222. Administration Tel: 225-388-0304, 225-388-0330. Automation Services Tel: 225-388-0169. FAX: 225-388-0329. Circulation FAX: 225-388-0362. Administration FAX: 225-388-0237. Automation Services FAX: 225-388-0206. E-mail: refdesk@theadvocate.com. Web Site: www.theadvocate.com. *Dir,* Judy Jumonville; E-mail: jjumonville@theadvocate.com; Staff 6 (MLS 1, Non-MLS 5)
Founded 1922
Library Holdings: Bk Vols 1,500; Per Subs 120
Special Collections: Newspaper Clipping Files (1922-1985)
Database Vendor: Newsbank
Wireless access
Function: Ref serv available
Restriction: Staff use only

P EAST BATON ROUGE PARISH LIBRARY*, Main Library, 7711 Goodwood Blvd, 70806-7625. SAN 342-7684. Tel: 225-231-3700. Circulation Tel: 225-231-3740. Interlibrary Loan Service Tel: 225-231-3755. Reference Tel: 225-231-3750. Automation Services Tel: 225-231-7520. FAX: 225-231-3788. E-mail: admin.c1eb@pelican.state.lib.la.us. Web Site: www.ebrpl.com. *Dir,* Spencer Watts; Fax: 225-231-3759, E-mail: spencerwatts@brgov.com; *Asst Dir, Adm Serv,* Mary Stein; Tel: 225-231-3710, E-mail: mstein@ebrpl.com; *Asst Dir, Br Serv,* Patricia Husband; Tel: 225-231-3785, E-mail: phusband@ebrpl.com; *Head, YA,* Barbara Roos; Tel: 225-231-3770, E-mail: broos@ebrpl.com; *Bus Mgr,* Rhonda Pinsonat; Tel: 225-231-3705, E-mail: rpinsonat@brgov.com; *Br Serv Coordr,* Cobb Mercedes; Tel: 225-231-3780, E-mail: mcobb@ebrpl.com; *Children's Serv Coordr,* Pabby Arnold; Tel: 225-231-3760, E-mail: parnold@ebrpl.com; *Circ Serv Coordr,* Elizabeth Myers; Tel: 225-231-3745, E-mail: emyers@ebrpl.com; *Ref & Computer Serv Coordr,* Emilie Smart; Tel: 225-231-3735, E-mail: esmart@ebrpl.com; *Tech Serv Coordr,* Andi Abraham; Fax: 225-231-3718, E-mail: aabraham@brgov.com; *Acq,* Jenny Wong; E-mail: jwong@ebrpl.com; *Coll Develop,* Carol Marcks; E-mail: cmarcks@ebrpl.com; *Commun Prog & Outreach Serv,* Chaundra Carroccio; Tel: 225-939-3896, E-mail: dfreyou@ebrpl.com; *ILL,* April Armstrong; Fax: 225-231-3736, E-mail: ill@ebrpl.com; Staff 108 (MLS 108)
Founded 1939. Pop 444,526; Circ 2,338,802
Jan 2012-Dec 2012 Income (Main Library and Branch(s)) $39,333,251, State $7,032, County $38,900,443, Other $425,776. Mats Exp $3,426,723, Books $1,404,957, Per/Ser (Incl. Access Fees) $171,336, Micro $49,300, AV Mat $342,672, Electronic Ref Mat (Incl. Access Fees) $1,336,422. Sal $17,019,745
Library Holdings: Audiobooks 17,579; AV Mats 1,227; Braille Volumes 495; CDs 28,949; DVDs 41,996; e-books 13,268; e-journals 3; Electronic Media & Resources 2,921; High Interest/Low Vocabulary Bk Vols 2,938; Large Print Bks 55,000; Microforms 47,821; Bk Titles 625,000; Bk Vols 1,618,168; Per Subs 3,100; Talking Bks 17,579; Videos 19,424
Special Collections: Oral History
Subject Interests: Genealogy, Grants, La
Automation Activity & Vendor Info: (Acquisitions) Infor Library & Information Solutions; (Cataloging) Infor Library & Information Solutions; (Circulation) Infor Library & Information Solutions; (ILL) TLC (The Library Corporation); (OPAC) Infor Library & Information Solutions; (Serials) Infor Library & Information Solutions
Database Vendor: 3M Library Systems, ABC-CLIO, Alexander Street Press, ALLDATA Online, AudioBookCloud, Backstage Library Works, Baker & Taylor, Bowker, Brodart, BWI, Career Guidance Foundation, Checkpoint Systems, Inc, Cinahl, CredoReference, EBSCO Auto Repair Reference, EBSCO Discovery Service, EBSCO Information Services, EBSCOhost, Evanced Solutions, Inc, Facts on File, Foundation Center, Gale Cengage Learning, Greenwood Publishing Group, H W Wilson, Infor Library & Information Solutions, Ingram Library Services, LearningExpress, McGraw-Hill, Newsbank, OCLC FirstSearch, OCLC WorldShare Interlibrary Loan, Overdrive, Inc, P4 Performance Management, Inc, ProQuest, PubMed, ReferenceUSA, Safari Books Online, Standard & Poor's, TumbleBookLibrary, ValueLine, Westlaw, Wilson - Wilson Web, World Book Online
Wireless access
Function: Adult bk club, Adult literacy prog, Art exhibits, AV serv, Bk club(s), Chess club, Computer training, Copy machines, Digital talking bks, e-mail serv, E-Reserves, Electronic databases & coll, Family literacy, Games & aids for the handicapped, Govt ref serv, Handicapped accessible, Health sci info serv, Home delivery & serv to Sr ctr & nursing homes, ILL available, Jazz prog, Magnifiers for reading, Mail & tel request accepted, Music CDs, Online ref, Orientations, Outside serv via phone, mail, e-mail & web, Photocopying/Printing, Preschool outreach, Prog for adults, Prog for children & young adult, Provide serv for the mentally ill, Ref & res, Ref serv available, Referrals accepted, Satellite serv, Senior computer classes, Serves mentally handicapped consumers, Spoken cassettes & CDs, Spoken cassettes & DVDs, Summer reading prog, Tax forms, Telephone ref, VHS videos, Wheelchair accessible, Workshops
Publications: Community Information Directory (Online only); The Source (Monthly newsletter)
Special Services for the Deaf - Adult & family literacy prog; Bks on deafness & sign lang; High interest/low vocabulary bks
Special Services for the Blind - Accessible computers; Audio mat; BiFolkal kits; Bks & mags in Braille, on rec, tape & cassette; Bks available with recordings; Bks on cassette; Bks on CD; Braille bks; Cassettes; Children's Braille; Computer with voice synthesizer for visually impaired persons; Copier with enlargement capabilities; Extensive large print coll; Internet workstation with adaptive software; Large print bks; Local mags & bks recorded; Magnifiers; Open bk software on pub access PC; PC for handicapped; Screen reader software; Videos on blindness & phys handicaps; ZoomText magnification & reading software
Friends of the Library Group
Branches: 13
BAKER BRANCH, 3501 Groom Rd, Baker, 70714, SAN 342-7714. Tel: 225-778-5940. Administration Tel: 225-778-5980. FAX: 225-778-5949. *Br Head,* Allison Broussard
Library Holdings: Bk Vols 92,554
BLUEBONNET REGIONAL, 9200 Bluebonnet Blvd, 70810, SAN 373-1243. Tel: 225-763-2240. Reference Tel: 225-763-2250. Administration Tel: 225-763-2280. FAX: 225-763-2253. *Br Head,* Melinda Newman
Library Holdings: Bk Vols 240,623
Special Collections: Genealogy Coll
CARVER, 720 Terrace St, 70802, SAN 342-7749. Tel: 225-389-7450. FAX: 225-389-7449. *Br Head,* Cynthia Watanabe; Tel: 225-389-7480, E-mail: cwatanabe@ebrpl.com
Library Holdings: Bk Vols 42,220

CENTRAL, 11260 Joor Rd, 70818, SAN 342-7773. Tel: 225-262-2640. Information Services Tel: 225-262-2650. FAX: 225-262-2649. *Br Mgr,* Heather Harrison; Tel: 225-262-2655
Library Holdings: Bk Vols 105,749
DELMONT GARDENS, 3351 Lorraine St, 70805, SAN 342-7838. Tel: 225-354-7050. FAX: 225-354-7049. *Br Mgr,* Charlotte Pringle; Tel: 225-354-7080
Library Holdings: Bk Vols 103,911
Open Mon-Thurs 9-8, Fri & Sat 9-6, Sun 2-6
EDEN PARK, 5131 Greenwell Springs Rd, 70806, SAN 342-7811. Tel: 225-231-3240. FAX: 225-231-3289. *Br Head,* Dorothy Thomas
Library Holdings: Bk Vols 39,411
FAIRWOOD BRANCH, 12910 Old Hammond Hwy, 70816. Tel: 225-924-9384. *Br Mgr,* Lauren Tomlin; Tel: 225-924-9380
GREENWELL SPRINGS ROAD REGIONAL, 11300 Greenwell Springs Rd, 70814, SAN 376-964X. Tel: 225-274-4440. Information Services Tel: 225-274-4450. FAX: 225-274-4454. *Br Mgr,* Geralyn Davis
Library Holdings: Bk Vols 164,218
JONES CREEK REGIONAL, 6222 Jones Creek Rd, 70817, SAN 370-1301. Tel: 225-756-1140. Reference Tel: 225-756-1150. FAX: 225-756-1153. *Br Head,* Yvonne Hull; Tel: 225-756-1180
Library Holdings: Bk Vols 237,051
PRIDE-CHANEYVILLE BRANCH, 11360 Pride-Port Hudson Rd, Pride, 70770, SAN 342-7862. Tel: 225-658-1550. FAX: 225-658-1549. *Br Coordr,* Jeanne Mixson; Tel: 225-658-1580
Library Holdings: Bk Vols 39,395
RIVER CENTER, 120 St Louis St, 70802. (Mail add: PO Box 1471, 70821-1471), SAN 342-7803. Tel: 225-389-4967. Information Services Tel: 225-389-4964. FAX: 225-389-8910. *Br Head,* Allison Cooper
Library Holdings: Bk Vols 128,384
Special Collections: Baton Rouge History Coll; Career Center; Foundation Center Cooperating Coll. Oral History
SCOTLANDVILLE, 7373 Scenic Hwy, 70807, SAN 342-7897. Tel: 225-354-7540. Information Services Tel: 225-354-7550. FAX: 225-354-7551. *Br Mgr,* Chaundra Carroccio; Tel: 225-354-7580
Library Holdings: Bk Vols 91,952
ZACHARY BRANCH, 1900 Church St, Zachary, 70791, SAN 342-7927. Tel: 225-658-1840. Reference Tel: 225-658-1850. FAX: 225-658-1844. *Br Mgr,* Lula Pride; Tel: 225-658-1880, E-mail: lpride@ebr.lib.la.us
Library Holdings: Bk Vols 97,747
Bookmobiles: 2. Bk titles 18,000

L HUEY P LONG MEMORIAL LAW LIBRARY*, State Capitol, 900 N Third St, 14th Flr, 70802. (Mail add: PO Box 94183, 70804). Tel: 225-342-2414. FAX: 225 342-2725. *Librn,* Arthur E McEnany
Library Holdings: Bk Vols 10,000; Per Subs 50

GL LOUISIANA DEPARTMENT OF JUSTICE, OFFICE OF THE ATTORNEY GENERAL*, Law Library, 1885 N Third St, 4th Flr, 70802. (Mail add: PO Box 94005, 70804-9005), SAN 327-4829. Tel: 225-326-6422. FAX: 225-326-6495. *Librn,* Mary Adams; E-mail: adamsm@ag.state.la.us
Library Holdings: Bk Vols 9,500; Per Subs 10
Database Vendor: Westlaw
Restriction: Not open to pub

S LOUISIANA ECONOMIC DEVELOPMENT LIBRARY*, 1051 N Third St, 70802. (Mail add: PO Box 94185, 70804-9185), SAN 306-4476. Tel: 225-342-3071. FAX: 225-342-5349. Web Site: www.led.state.la.us. *Librn,* Paula Bryars; E-mail: bryars@la.gov; Staff 1 (MLS 1)
Library Holdings: Per Subs 50
Special Collections: Business Reference; Current Economic Development Material; DED Publications, Economic Development Research Studies, Parish & Port Profiles, Louisiana International Trade; Manufacturing Directories from Most States
Subject Interests: Econ, La

GL LOUISIANA HOUSE OF REPRESENTATIVES*, David R Poynter Legislative Research Library, PO Box 94012, 70804-9012. SAN 306-4468. Tel: 225-342-2430. FAX: 225-342-2431. TDD: 888-850-6489. E-mail: drplibrary@legis.la.gov. Web Site: www.legis.state.la.us. *Dir,* Frances Thomas; *Librn,* Robyn Cockerham; *Librn,* Marilyn Kitchell; *Librn,* Kate Lemon; *Librn,* Elisa Naquin; Staff 5 (MLS 5)
Founded 1952
Library Holdings: Bk Vols 10,000; Per Subs 150
Special Collections: Legislative Archival Coll, committee reports; Legislative Documents & Research Publications, per, clippings
Automation Activity & Vendor Info: (Cataloging) Inmagic, Inc.
Publications: Membership in the Louisiana House of Representatives, 1812-2008 (Local historical information); Resume (Annual summary of enactments)
Special Services for the Deaf - TTY equip
Restriction: Not open to pub

G LOUISIANA OFFICE OF THE SECRETARY OF STATE*, Division of Archives, Records Management & History Library, 3851 Essen Lane, 70809-2137. (Mail add: PO Box 94125, 70804-9125), SAN 326-5463. Tel: 225-922-1208. FAX: 225-922-0433. E-mail: library@sos.la.gov, library@sos.louisiana.gov. Web Site: www.sos.la.gov. *Adminr,* Bill Stafford; E-mail: bstafford@sos.louisiana.gov; Staff 1 (MLS 1)
Founded 1956
Library Holdings: Bk Titles 6,400; Bk Vols 7,000; Per Subs 50
Special Collections: Louisiana Confederate Government (Rebel Archives Coll), doc; Louisiana Death Certificates, 1912 1960; Lumber Industry (Louisiana Longleaf Lumber Co Coll); Orleans Parish Birth Certificates, 1790-1910; Orleans Parish Death Certificates, 1804-1960; Orleans Parish Marriage Certificates, 1831-1960. Oral History; US Document Depository
Subject Interests: Genealogy, Mil hist
Publications: Legacy (Newsletter)
Open Mon-Fri 8-4
Friends of the Library Group

C LOUISIANA STATE UNIVERSITY LIBRARIES*, 295 Middleton Library, 70803. SAN 342-8133. Tel: 225-578-2217. Circulation Tel: 225-578-2058. Interlibrary Loan Service Tel: 225-578-2138. Reference Tel: 225-578-5652. FAX: 225-578-9432. Circulation FAX: 225-578-8612. Interlibrary Loan Service FAX: 225-578-5723. Web Site: www.lib.lsu.edu. *Dean of Libr,* Stanley Wilder; E-mail: wilder@lsu.edu; *Asst Dean, Libr,* Elaine Smyth; Fax: 225-578-6825, E-mail: esmyth@lsu.edu; *Head, Circ,* Elissa Plank; Tel: 225-578-3216, E-mail: esp1061@lsu.edu; *Head, Ref & Coll Develop,* Tom Diamond; Tel: 225-578-6572, E-mail: notted@lsu.edu; *Coll Develop Coordr,* William Armstrong; Tel: 225-578-2738, E-mail: notwwa@lsu.edu; *Instruction Coordr,* Mike Russo; Tel: 225-578-6823, E-mail: mrusso1@lsu.edu; *ILL,* Catherine Michael; Tel: 225-578-8560, Fax: 225-578-6992, E-mail: cmichael@lsu.edu; Staff 131 (MLS 41, Non-MLS 90)
Founded 1860. Enrl 28,985; Fac 1,415; Highest Degree: Doctorate
Library Holdings: AV Mats 21,242; e-books 43,295; e-journals 17,265; Bk Vols 3,213,314; Per Subs 18,695
Special Collections: Louisiana & Lower Mississippi Coll; McIlhenny Natural History Coll; Rare Book Coll. Oral History; State Document Depository; UN Document Depository; US Document Depository
Automation Activity & Vendor Info: (Acquisitions) SirsiDynix; (Cataloging) OCLC; (Circulation) SirsiDynix; (ILL) OCLC; (Media Booking) SirsiDynix; (OPAC) SirsiDynix; (Serials) SirsiDynix
Database Vendor: Dialog, Gale Cengage Learning, LexisNexis, OVID Technologies
Wireless access
Publications: Guide to Oral History Collections in Louisiana; Guide to the Russell B Long Coll; Historical Collections of Louisiana (CD-ROM Edition)
Partic in La Acad Libr Info Network Consortium; Lyrasis; National Network of Libraries of Medicine South Central Region; OCLC Online Computer Library Center, Inc; USDA SW Regional Doc Delivery Syst

Departmental Libraries:

CARTER MUSIC RESOURCES CENTER, 202 Middleton Library, 70803-3300, SAN 376-8538. Tel: 225-578-4674. Interlibrary Loan Service Tel: 225-578-2138. FAX: 225-578-6825. Web Site: www.lib.lsu.edu/music. *Head of Libr,* Lois Kuyper-Rushing; E mail: lkuyper@lsu.edu; *Libr Assoc,* Mikel Ledee; E-mail: mledee1@lsu.edu; *Libr Assoc,* Glenn Walden; E-mail: gwalden@lsu.edu; Staff 3 (MLS 1, Non-MLS 2)
Library Holdings: Bk Vols 57,600; Per Subs 90
Subject Interests: Hist, Music
CARTOGRAPHIC INFORMATION CENTER, Dept of Geography & Anthropology, Howe-Russell Geoscience Complex, Rm 313, 70803-4100. Tel: 225-578-6247. FAX: 225-578-4420. Web Site: www.cic.lsu.edu. *Dir, Maps Librn,* John Anderson; E-mail: janders@lsu.edu; Staff 1 (MLS 1)
Founded 1954
Library Holdings: CDs 1,680; Bk Vols 4,065
Special Collections: Robert C West Photographs. US Document Depository
Subject Interests: La, Latin Am, Miss river
Function: For res purposes, Govt ref serv, Handicapped accessible, Magnifiers for reading, Res libr
Open Mon-Fri 7:30-12 & 12:30-4
Restriction: Closed stack, Restricted borrowing privileges
EDUCATION RESOURCES, 227 Middleton Library, 70803-3300, SAN 376-852X. Tel: 225-578-2349. Interlibrary Loan Service Tel: 225-578-2138. FAX: 225-578-6992. Web Site: www.lib.lsu.edu/edu/er/. *Dept Head,* Peggy Chalaron; E-mail: pchalar@lsu.edu; Staff 2 (MLS 1, Non-MLS 1)
Library Holdings: Bk Titles 28,568
Subject Interests: Educ, Juv lit
Friends of the Library Group

CL PAUL M HEBERT LAW CENTER, One E Campus Dr, 70803-1000. Tel: 225-578-4042. Circulation Tel: 225-578-8814. Interlibrary Loan Service Tel: 225-578-4041. FAX: 225-578-5773. TDD: 225-388-4706. E-mail: info@law.lsu.edu. Web Site: www.law.lsu.edu/library. *Libr Dir,* Beth

Williams; Tel: 225-578-5770, E-mail: Beth.Williams@law.lsu.edu; *Head, Access Serv,* Charlene Cain; Tel: 225-578-4957, E-mail: charlene.cain@law.lsu.edu; *Head, Instrul Tech,* Will Monroe; Tel: 225-578-7838, E-mail: will.monroe@law.lsu.edu; *Acq Librn,* Ajaye Bloomstone; Tel: 225-578-4044, E-mail: ajaye.bloomstone@law.lsu.edu; *Cat Librn,* Susan Morrison; Tel: 225-578-4048, E-mail: susan.morrison@law.lsu.edu; *Circ Librn,* Kevin Baggett; E-mail: kevin.baggett@law.lsu.edu; *Electronic Serv Librn,* Mary Johns; Tel: 225-578-6530, E-mail: mary.johns@law.lsu.edu; *Media Serv Librn,* Rita Parham; Tel: 225-578-4043, E-mail: rita.parham@law.lsu.edu; *Ref Librn,* Phillip Gragg; Tel: 225-578-4952, E-mail: phillip.gragg@law.lsu.edu; Staff 19 (MLS 8, Non-MLS 11)
Founded 1906. Enrl 650; Fac 36; Highest Degree: Doctorate
Library Holdings: Bk Titles 139,589; Bk Vols 826,519; Per Subs 12,229
Special Collections: Foreign, Comparative & International Law
Automation Activity & Vendor Info: (Acquisitions) SirsiDynix; (Cataloging) SirsiDynix; (Circulation) SirsiDynix; (Course Reserve) SirsiDynix; (ILL) SirsiDynix; (OPAC) SirsiDynix; (Serials) SirsiDynix
Function: Doc delivery serv, ILL available, Photocopying/Printing, Ref serv available, Res libr
Partic in Association of Southeastern Research Libraries

CM LSU SCHOOL OF VETERINARY MEDICINE LIBRARY, Skip Bertman Dr, 70803-8414, SAN 342-8222. Tel: 225-578-9800. Administration Tel: 225-578-9796. FAX: 225-578-9798. E-mail: library@vetmail.lsu.edu. Web Site: www.vetmed.lsu.edu/library. *Dir,* Christine Russell; E-mail: crussell@lsu.edu; *Head, Tech Serv, Ser,* Corrie Hess; Tel: 225-578-9799, E-mail: clong2@lsu.edu; *Acq & Cat,* Angela Alleman; Tel: 225-578-9794, E-mail: aalleman@lsu.edu; *Circ,* Milton Chatelain; Tel: 225-578-9795, E-mail: peguita@lsu.edu; *Circ,* Lisa Lovello; *Pub Serv & ILL,* Holly Kerr; Tel: 225-578-9797, E-mail: hkerr@lsu.edu; Staff 6 (MLS 2, Non-MLS 4)
Founded 1974. Enrl 350; Highest Degree: Doctorate
Library Holdings: Bk Vols 47,000; Per Subs 600
Special Collections: Reprint Coll on Parasitology, 1865-1972
Subject Interests: Veterinary med
Automation Activity & Vendor Info: (Acquisitions) SirsiDynix; (Cataloging) OCLC; (Circulation) SirsiDynix; (OPAC) SirsiDynix; (Serials) SirsiDynix
Database Vendor: Blackwell, EBSCOhost, Elsevier, Nature Publishing Group, PubMed, ScienceDirect

C OUR LADY OF THE LAKE COLLEGE LIBRARY*, 5329 Didesse St, 70808. SAN 378-4533. Tel: 225-768-1730. Interlibrary Loan Service Tel: 225-490-1657. FAX: 225-761-7303. E-mail: library@ololcollege.edu. Web Site: ololcollege.edu/offices-services/library. *Co-Dir,* Lucas Huntington; Tel: 225-768-1732, E-mail: lucas.huntington@ololcollege.edu; *Co-Dir,* Maggie McCann; Tel: 225-768-1783, E-mail: maggie.mccann@ololcollege.edu; *Cat Librn,* Fatima Zamin; E-mail: fzamin@ololcollege.edu; Staff 9.5 (MLS 3.5, Non-MLS 6)
Founded 1923. Enrl 2,000; Fac 120; Highest Degree: Master
Library Holdings: CDs 300; DVDs 150; e-books 14,000; e-journals 100; Bk Titles 30,000; Per Subs 150; Videos 1,000
Special Collections: Historical Nursing Coll (Some materials date in the 1800's)
Database Vendor: EBSCOhost, Gale Cengage Learning, JSTOR, LexisNexis, OCLC FirstSearch, OCLC WorldShare Interlibrary Loan, ProQuest, YBP Library Services
Wireless access
Function: Audio & video playback equip for onsite use, CD-ROM, Computers for patron use, Copy machines, Electronic databases & coll, Exhibits, ILL available, Online cat, Online info literacy tutorials on the web & in blackboard, Online ref, Orientations, Photocopying/Printing, Ref & res, Ref serv in person, Telephone ref, VHS videos, Web-catalog
Partic in Lyrasis; The Louisiana Library Network
Open Mon-Thurs 8am-9pm, Fri 8-4:30, Sat & Sun 10-6

C SOUTHERN UNIVERSITY*, John B Cade Library, 167 Roosevelt Steptoe Ave, 70813-0001. SAN 342-8257. Tel: 225-771-4990. Circulation Tel: 225-771-2855. Interlibrary Loan Service Tel: 225-771-2869. Reference Tel: 225-771-2875. Information Services Tel: 225-771-2841. FAX: 225-771-4113. Web Site: www.lib.subr.edu. *Dean of Libr,* Emma Bradford Perry; Tel: 225-771-4991, E-mail: emmaperry@subr.edu; *Chair, Tech Serv,* Mildred Brown; Tel: 225-771-2862, E-mail: mildred@lib.subr.edu; *Head, Pub Serv,* Janice Bell; Tel: 225-771-2844, E-mail: janiceb@lib.subr.edu; *Head, Ref,* Jane Robinson; Tel: 225-771-2875, E-mail: jane@lib.subr.edu; *Mgr, Syst & Tech,* Dawn Kight; Tel: 225-771-4934, E-mail: dawn@lib.subr.edu; Staff 39 (MLS 13, Non-MLS 26)
Founded 1880. Enrl 8,572; Fac 425; Highest Degree: Doctorate
Library Holdings: AV Mats 42,734; e-books 16,325; e-journals 200; Electronic Media & Resources 593; Bk Titles 308,156; Bk Vols 406,815; Per Subs 1,675
Special Collections: Archives & Shade Coll. State Document Depository; US Document Depository
Subject Interests: African-Am, Agr, Art & archit, Bus & mgt, Econ, Educ
Automation Activity & Vendor Info: (Acquisitions) SirsiDynix; (Cataloging) SirsiDynix; (Circulation) SirsiDynix; (Course Reserve) SirsiDynix; (ILL) Infotrieve; (OPAC) SirsiDynix; (Serials) SirsiDynix
Database Vendor: EBSCOhost, Gale Cengage Learning, JSTOR, LexisNexis
Publications: Cade Books & Bytes (Newsletter)
Partic in Lyrasis; OCLC Online Computer Library Center, Inc
Open Mon-Thurs (Winter) 7:30am-Midnight, Fri 7:30-5, Sat 1-5, Sun 2-Midnight; Mon-Thurs (Summer) 7:30am-8pm, Fri 7:30-5, Sun 4pm-10pm

Departmental Libraries:

ART & ARCHITECTURE LIBRARY, School of Architecture, Engineering West Bldg, 2nd Flr, 70813. Tel: 225-771-3290. FAX: 225-771-4113, 225-771-4709. *In Charge,* Vanissa Gosserand; E-mail: vanissa_ely@subr.edu; Staff 1 (Non-MLS 1)
Library Holdings: AV Mats 19,520; Bk Titles 7,457; Bk Vols 8,295; Per Subs 40
Subject Interests: Archit

CL OLIVER B SPELLMAN LAW LIBRARY, 56 Roosevelt Steptoe, 70813. (Mail add: PO Box 9294, 70813-9294). Tel: 225-771-2139, 225-771-2315. Circulation Tel: 225-771-2146. Reference Tel: 225-771-2316. FAX: 225-771-6254. Web Site: www.sulc.edu/library/library.htm. *Dir, Libr Serv,* Ruth J Hill; E-mail: rhill@sulc.edu; *Acq,* Janice Williams; Tel: 225-771-2189, E-mail: jwilliams@sulc.edu; *Cat,* Valinda D LeDoux; Tel: 225-771-2196, E-mail: vledoux@sulc.edu; *Cat,* Marie Louis; E-mail: mlouis@sulc.edu; *Circ/Reserves,* Ollie M Lewis; E-mail: olewis@sulc.edu; *Circ/Reserves,* William M Lockhart, Jr; E-mail: wlockhart@sulc.edu; *Computer Serv,* Angela S Gaines; Tel: 225-771-4922, E-mail: angela@sulc.edu; *Govt Doc, Micro,* Rose Herbert; Tel: 225-771-2194, E-mail: rherbert@sulc.edu; *Ref Serv,* Harold Isadore; E-mail: hisadore@sulc.edu; *Ref Serv,* Adrienne Shields; E-mail: ashields@sulc.edu. Subject Specialists: *Advan legal res, Legal res,* Ruth J Hill; Staff 17 (MLS 6, Non-MLS 11)
Founded 1947. Enrl 450; Fac 45; Highest Degree: Doctorate
Library Holdings: Bk Titles 91,924; Bk Vols 475,081; Per Subs 989
Special Collections: South Africa Law. State Document Depository; US Document Depository
Subject Interests: Civil rights
Automation Activity & Vendor Info: (Acquisitions) SirsiDynix; (Cataloging) SirsiDynix; (Circulation) SirsiDynix; (Course Reserve) SirsiDynix; (OPAC) SirsiDynix; (Serials) SirsiDynix
Database Vendor: HeinOnline, JSTOR, LexisNexis, OCLC FirstSearch, Westlaw, YBP Library Services
Partic in Dialog Corp; Lyrasis; OCLC Online Computer Library Center, Inc; Westlaw
Publications: Library Newsletter; Reflections; Southern Univ Law Review
Open Mon-Thurs (Winter) 7am-Midnight, Fri 7-5, Sat 9-5, Sun 2-10; Mon-Thurs (Summer) 8am-9pm, Fri 8-5, Sat 10-4, Sun 2-10

P STATE LIBRARY OF LOUISIANA, 701 N Fourth St, 70802-5232. (Mail add: PO Box 131, 70821-0131), SAN 342-8044. Tel: 225-342-4923. Circulation Tel: 225-342-4915. Interlibrary Loan Service Tel: 225-342-4918. Reference Tel: 225-342-4913. Automation Services Tel: 225-342-6759. FAX: 225-219-4804. Circulation FAX: 225-342-7962. Interlibrary Loan Service FAX: 225-219-4725. TDD: 225-219-1696. E-mail: admin@state.lib.la.us. Web Site: www.state.lib.la.us. *State Librn,* Rebecca Hamilton; E-mail: rhamilton@crt.state.la.us; *Dep State Librn,* Diane M Brown; E-mail: dbrown@crt.state.la.us; *Assoc State Librn,* Margaret Placke; Tel: 225-342-4951, E-mail: mplacke@crt.state.la.us; *Dir, Communications,* Paulita Chartier; Tel: 225-342-9713, E-mail: pchartier@slol.lib.la.us; *Dir, Louisiana Ctr for the Bk,* Jim Davis; Tel: 225-342-9714, E-mail: jdavis@slol.lib.la.us; *Head, Access Serv,* Kytara Gaudin; Tel: 225-342-4920, E-mail: kgaudin@slol.lib.la.us; *Head, Acq & Ser,* Lesli Gray; Tel: 225-342-4937, E-mail: lgray@slol.lib.la.us; *Head, Info Tech,* Bryan Babin; E-mail: bbabin@slol.lib.la.us; *Head, Ref,* Michael Golrick; Tel: 225-219-4726, E-mail: mgolrick@slol.lib.la.us; *Bus Mgr,* Beverly Dugas; E-mail: bdugas@crt.state.la.us; *Outreach Serv,* Sheila Coleman; Tel: 225-342-4942, Fax: 225-342-6817, E-mail: scoleman@slol.lib.la.us; Staff 51 (MLS 18, Non-MLS 33)
Founded 1925
Jul 2014-Jun 2015 Income $8,834,983, State $5,645,470, Federal $3,099,513, Locally Generated Income $90,000
Library Holdings: AV Mats 28,413; Large Print Bks 21,037; Bk Vols 543,181; Per Subs 374; Talking Bks 278,381
Special Collections: Huey Long Photographs; Louisiana History, Politics, Economics, Literature. State Document Depository; US Document Depository
Subject Interests: La
Automation Activity & Vendor Info: (Acquisitions) Horizon; (Cataloging) Horizon; (Circulation) Horizon; (ILL) OCLC; (OPAC) Horizon; (Serials) Horizon
Database Vendor: Auto-Graphics, Inc, Baker & Taylor, CredoReference, EBSCOhost, Gale Cengage Learning, H W Wilson, Keystone Systems, Inc (KLAS), LearningExpress, Marcive, Inc, Medline, Newsbank, OCLC,

OCLC WorldShare Interlibrary Loan, ProQuest, SirsiDynix, TumbleBookLibrary
Wireless access
Publications: Library Laws of Louisiana; Louisiana Libraries-Economic Impact; Official Publications: Lists of the Public Documents of Louisiana; Public Documents; Public Libraries in Louisiana Statistical Report; Quick Facts-Louisiana Libraries; Searching for Your Louisiana Ancestors & All That Jazz
Partic in Lyrasis; OCLC Online Computer Library Center, Inc; The Louisiana Library Network
Special Services for the Deaf - ADA equip; Captioned film dep; High interest/low vocabulary bks
Special Services for the Blind - Accessible computers; Bks & mags in Braille, on rec, tape & cassette; Bks on cassette; Bks on flash-memory cartridges; Braille bks; Cassette playback machines; Cassettes; Closed circuit TV magnifier; Descriptive video serv (DVS); Digital talking bk; Digital talking bk machines; Extensive large print coll; Home delivery serv; Internet workstation with adaptive software; Large print bks; Large screen computer & software; Low vision equip; Machine repair; Newsletter (in large print, Braille or on cassette); Recorded bks; Screen enlargement software for people with visual disabilities; Screen reader software; Talking bks; Talking bks & player equip; Tel Pioneers equip repair group
Open Mon-Thurs 8-4:30
Friends of the Library Group

P STATE LIBRARY OF LOUISIANA*, Talking Books & Braille Library, 701 N Fourth St, 70802. (Mail add: PO Box 131, 70821-0131), SAN 306-4492. Tel: 225-342-0035. Toll Free Tel: 800-543-4702. FAX: 225-342-6817. E-mail: tbbl@state.lib.la.us. Web Site: www.state.lib.la.us. *Coordr, Spec Serv, Regional Librn,* Sheila Coleman; E-mail: scoleman@slol.lib.la.us; Staff 14 (MLS 4, Non-MLS 10)
Founded 1933
Library Holdings: Large Print Bks 18,000; Bk Titles 60,000; Talking Bks 200,000
Subject Interests: La
Publications: Louisiana Hotlines (Newsletter)
Special Services for the Blind - Cassettes; Descriptive video serv (DVS); Large print bks
Open Mon-Fri 8-5
Friends of the Library Group

R UNIVERSITY BAPTIST CHURCH LIBRARY*, 5775 Highland Rd, 70808. SAN 306-4522. Tel: 225-766-9474. FAX: 225-766-9101. Web Site: www.ubc-br.org. *Librn,* Dr Patsy Perritt
Founded 1955
Library Holdings: Bk Titles 6,250; Bk Vols 6,500
Special Collections: Children's Literature (Jim Smith Memorial Coll)
Subject Interests: Church hist
Open Wed 3:30-6

M WOMAN'S HOSPITAL*, Health Sciences Library, 100 Woman's Way, 70817. (Mail add: PO Box 95009, 70895-9009). Tel: 225-924-8462. FAX: 225-924-8467. E-mail: hslibrary@womans.org. Web Site: www.womans.com. *Info Spec,* Louise McLaughlin
Library Holdings: Bk Vols 1,600; Per Subs 150
Wireless access
Restriction: Staff use only

C WORLD EVANGELISM BIBLE COLLEGE LIBRARY*, 8919 World Ministry Ave, 70810-9000. (Mail add: PO Box 262550, 70826-2550). Tel: 225-768-3890. FAX: 225-768-4533. E-mail: info@webc.edu. *Dir,* Chanell Berg
Library Holdings: Bk Titles 25,000
Wireless access
Open Mon-Thurs 7:30-5, Fri 7:30-2:30

BELLE CHASSE

P PLAQUEMINES PARISH LIBRARY, 8442 Hwy 23, 70037. SAN 342-8583. Tel: 504-398-7302. FAX: 504-398-4580. Web Site: plaqueminesppl.booksys.net/opac/plaqueminesppl/index.html. *Dir,* Position Currently Open; *Asst Libr Dir,* Patrisha Walker; E-mail: pwalker@ppgov.net; Staff 1 (MLS 1)
Founded 1959
Special Collections: J Ben Meyer Historical Plaquemines Parish Coll; Louisiana Census Coll, microfilm; Video Cassette Coll
Automation Activity & Vendor Info: (Cataloging) Book Systems; (Circulation) Book Systems; (OPAC) Book Systems
Database Vendor: EBSCOhost, Newsbank
Function: Audio & video playback equip for onsite use, AV serv, Bks on cassette, Children's prog, Computers for patron use, Copy machines, E-Reserves, Electronic databases & coll, Fax serv, Handicapped accessible, ILL available, Newsp ref libr, Online searches, Photocopying/Printing, Preschool outreach, Prog for children & young adult, Ref & res, Scanner, Summer reading prog, Tax forms, VHS videos, Video lending libr, Wheelchair accessible
Open Mon, Wed & Fri 8:30-5, Tues & Thurs 8:30-7, Sat 8:30-12:30
Restriction: Residents only
Branches: 2
BELLE CHASSE BRANCH, 8442 Hwy 23, 70037, SAN 342-8613. Tel: 504-394-3570. FAX: 504-394-6102. *Librn,* Brigette Bolton; E-mail: bbolton@plaqueminesparish.com; *Librn,* Marie Martin; E-mail: mmartin@plaqueminesparish.com; *Librn,* Barbara Nash; E-mail: bnash@plaqueminesparish.com; *Librn,* Claire Paradelas; E-mail: cparadelas@plaqueminesparish.com
Pop 26,049; Circ 18,546
Library Holdings: AV Mats 1,112; Bks on Deafness & Sign Lang 25; Large Print Bks 112; Bk Titles 24,121; Bk Vols 26,624; Per Subs 91; Talking Bks 62; Videos 889
Function: Audio & video playback equip for onsite use, Bks on cassette, Children's prog, Computers for patron use, Copy machines, E-Reserves, Electronic databases & coll, Fax serv, Handicapped accessible, ILL available, Newsp ref libr, Prog for children & young adult, Scanner, Spoken cassettes & CDs, Summer reading prog, Tax forms, VHS videos, Wheelchair accessible
Open Mon, Wed & Fri 8:30-5, Tues & Thurs 8:30-7, Sat 8:30-12:30
Restriction: Residents only
PORT SULPHUR BRANCH, 139 Delta St, Port Sulphur, 70083, SAN 342-8702. Tel: 504-564-3681, 504-564-3682. FAX: 504-564-3274. *Librn,* Quiana Gibson; E-mail: qgibson@plaqueminesparish.com; *Librn,* Peggy Lytell; E-mail: plytell@plaqueminesparish.com
Open Mon-Fri 8:30-5
Bookmobiles: 1. Librn, Donna Pobrica

BLANCHARD

R FIRST BAPTIST CHURCH OF BLANCHARD*, FBC Media Center, 201 Attaway St, 71009. (Mail add: PO Box 65, 71009-0065), SAN 374-826X. Tel: 318-929-2346. FAX: 318-929-4680. E-mail: fbcblanchard@bellsouth.net. Web Site: www.fbcblanchard.com. *In Charge,* Kevin Sandifer
Library Holdings: AV Mats 112; Bk Vols 2,700

BOSSIER CITY

P BOSSIER PARISH CENTRAL LIBRARY*, 2206 Beckett St, 71111. SAN 342-8400. Tel: 318-746-1693. FAX: 318-746-7768. Administration E-mail: admin.g1bs@pelican.state.lib.la.us. Web Site: www.bossierlibrary.org. *Dir,* Heather McEntee; E-mail: hmcentee@state.lib.la.us; *Cent Libr Mgr,* Anne Madison; *Outreach Coordr,* Vickie Hardin; *Ch Serv,* Jessica McCart; E-mail: jmccart@state.lib.la.us; *IT Spec,* Jaketha Farmer; *Ref,* Connie Ammons; *Tech Serv,* Tedy Pesnell; Staff 14 (MLS 11, Non-MLS 3)
Founded 1940. Pop 119,732; Circ 530,701
Library Holdings: AV Mats 18,640; Bk Titles 199,749; Per Subs 14,477
Special Collections: Bossier Parish Police Jury Minutes, 1881-present, microfilm; County Newspaper, 1859-present, bd vols, microfilm
Subject Interests: Local hist archives
Automation Activity & Vendor Info: (Cataloging) TLC (The Library Corporation); (Circulation) TLC (The Library Corporation); (ILL) Auto-Graphics, Inc; (OPAC) TLC (The Library Corporation)
Wireless access
Function: Accelerated reader prog, Adult bk club, After school storytime, Archival coll, Art exhibits, Audiobks via web, AV serv, Bk club(s), Bks on CD, CD-ROM, Children's prog, Computer training, Computers for patron use, Copy machines, e-mail serv, Electronic databases & coll, Exhibits, Family literacy, Fax serv, Free DVD rentals, Handicapped accessible, Home delivery & serv to Sr ctr & nursing homes, Homebound delivery serv, ILL available, Instruction & testing, Mail & tel request accepted, Newsp ref libr, Online cat, Online ref, Online searches, Outreach serv, Outside serv via phone, mail, e-mail & web, OverDrive digital audio bks, Photocopying/Printing, Preschool outreach, Printer for laptops & handheld devices, Prog for adults, Prog for children & young adult, Pub access computers, Ref serv available, Ref serv in person, Senior outreach, Story hour, Summer reading prog, Tax forms, Teen prog, Telephone ref, Video lending libr, Web-catalog, Wheelchair accessible, Workshops, Writing prog
Open Mon-Thurs 9-8, Fri 9-6, Sat 9-5, Sun 2-5
Friends of the Library Group
Branches: 7
HENRY L AULDS MEMORIAL, 3950 Wayne Ave, 71112, SAN 342-8494. Tel: 318-742-2337. Administration Tel: 318-742-5819. FAX: 318-752-4034. *Br Mgr,* Diane Bundy; Staff 1 (Non-MLS 1)
Founded 1971
Function: Bks on CD, Children's prog, Computer training, Computers for patron use, Copy machines, Electronic databases & coll, Exhibits, Handicapped accessible, ILL available, Online cat, OverDrive digital audio bks, Photocopying/Printing, Printer for laptops & handheld devices, Prog for adults, Prog for children & young adult, Pub access computers, Ref serv available, Story hour, Summer reading prog, Tax forms, Teen prog

Open Mon-Wed 9-8, Thurs & Fri 9-6, Sat 9-5, Sun 2-5
Friends of the Library Group
BENTON BRANCH, 115 Courthouse Dr, Benton, 71006. (Mail add: PO Box 400, Benton, 71006-0400), SAN 342-8435. Tel: 318-965-2751. FAX: 318-965-4379. *Br Mgr,* Kristin Kennedy; *Financial Serv,* Theresa Allen; Staff 2 (MLS 1, Non-MLS 1)
Function: After school storytime, Bks on CD, Children's prog, Computer training, Computers for patron use, Copy machines, Electronic databases & coll, Exhibits, Handicapped accessible, ILL available, Online cat, OverDrive digital audio bks, Photocopying/Printing, Preschool outreach, Printer for laptops & handheld devices, Prog for adults, Prog for children & young adult, Pub access computers, Ref serv available, Story hour, Summer reading prog, Tax forms, Teen prog, Workshops
Open Mon-Fri 9-6, Sat 9-5
Friends of the Library Group
BOSSIER PARISH HISTORICAL CENTER, 2206 Beckett St, 71111. Tel: 318-746-7717. *Dir,* Ann Middleton; *Outreach/Educ,* Pam Carlisle; Staff 3 (MLS 1, Non-MLS 2)
Special Collections: Oral History
Automation Activity & Vendor Info: (Acquisitions) TLC (The Library Corporation)
Function: Archival coll, Computers for patron use, Copy machines, Electronic databases & coll, Exhibits, Outreach serv, Photocopying/Printing, Pub access computers, Ref serv available, Scanner, Wheelchair accessible
Open Mon-Fri 9-9, Sat 9-5, Sun 2-5
Restriction: Non-circulating coll
Friends of the Library Group
EAST 80, 1050 Bellevue Rd, Haughton, 71037, SAN 329-661X. Tel: 318-949-1959, 318-949-2665. Administration Tel: 318-390-6424. FAX: 318-949-2067. *Br Mgr,* Beverly Miles
Library Holdings: Bk Vols 15,000; Per Subs 31
Open Mon-Thurs 9-8, Fri 8:30-5:30 & Sat 9-5
Friends of the Library Group
HAUGHTON BRANCH, 116 E McKinley Ave, Haughton, 71037, SAN 342-8524. Tel: 318-949-0196. FAX: 318-949-0195. *Br Mgr,* Audra Bartholomew; Staff 2 (Non-MLS 2)
Function: Bks on CD, Children's prog, Computers for patron use, Copy machines, Electronic databases & coll, Free DVD rentals, ILL available, Online cat, OverDrive digital audio bks, Photocopying/Printing, Preschool outreach, Printer for laptops & handheld devices, Prog for adults, Prog for children & young adult, Pub access computers, Ref serv available, Story hour, Summer reading prog, Tax forms, Teen prog, Telephone ref, Wheelchair accessible
Open Mon-Fri 8:30-5:30
Friends of the Library Group
KORAN STATION, 5413 Hwy 627, Haughton, 71037, SAN 342-8508. Tel: 318-987-3915. *Br Mgr,* Nita Wilson; Staff 1 (Non-MLS 1)
Function: Bks on CD, Children's prog, Computers for patron use, Copy machines, Electronic databases & coll, Free DVD rentals, ILL available, Online cat, OverDrive digital audio bks, Photocopying/Printing, Pub access computers, Ref serv available, Story hour, Summer reading prog, Tax forms
Open Wed 8-12 & 1-5
Friends of the Library Group
PLAIN DEALING BRANCH, 208 E Mary Lee St, Plain Dealing, 71064, SAN 342-8559. Tel: 318-326-4233. *Br Mgr,* Linda Stanford; Staff 1 (Non-MLS 1)
Function: Bks on CD, Children's prog, Computers for patron use, Copy machines, Electronic databases & coll, Exhibits, Free DVD rentals, Handicapped accessible, ILL available, Online cat, OverDrive digital audio bks, Photocopying/Printing, Preschool outreach, Printer for laptops & handheld devices, Prog for children & young adult, Pub access computers, Ref serv available, Story hour, Summer reading prog, Tax forms, VHS videos
Open Mon-Fri 8:30-5:30, Sat 8-12
Friends of the Library Group

J BOSSIER PARISH COMMUNITY COLLEGE LIBRARY*, 6220 E Texas St, 71111. SAN 306-4530. Tel: 318-678-6042. FAX: 318-678-6400. E-mail: refdesk@bpcc.edu. Web Site: www.bpcc.edu/library. *Dean, Learning Res,* Brenda Brantley; Tel: 318-678-6068, E-mail: bbrantley@bpcc.edu; *Cat Librn,* Timothy Osteen; Tel: 318-678-6543, E-mail: tosteen@bpcc.edu; *Ref Librn,* Katie Jones; Tel: 318-678-6077, E-mail: kjones@bpcc.edu; *Syst Librn,* Debra Harmon; Tel: 318-678-6143, E-mail: dharmon@bpcc.edu; Staff 11 (MLS 5, Non-MLS 6)
Founded 1968. Enrl 4,700; Fac 111; Highest Degree: Associate
Library Holdings: AV Mats 2,600; Bk Titles 45,000; Per Subs 230
Special Collections: Local Newspaper, micro, vertical file
Subject Interests: Hist
Automation Activity & Vendor Info: (Acquisitions) Mandarin Library Automation; (Cataloging) SirsiDynix; (Circulation) SirsiDynix; (Course Reserve) SirsiDynix; (Serials) SirsiDynix
Database Vendor: Cambridge Scientific Abstracts, CQ Press, EBSCOhost, Gale Cengage Learning, JSTOR, LearningExpress, LexisNexis, OCLC FirstSearch, Oxford Online, ProQuest
Wireless access
Function: Distance learning, Doc delivery serv, ILL available, Photocopying/Printing, Ref serv available
Partic in The Louisiana Library Network
Open Mon-Thurs (Fall & Spring) 8-8, Fri 8-4:30; Mon-Fri (Summer) 8-4:30
Restriction: Open to students, fac & staff

BRIDGE CITY

S BRIDGE CITY CORRECTIONAL CENTER FOR YOUTH LIBRARY*, 3225 River Rd, 70094. (Mail add: PO Box 9098, 70094), SAN 326-4874. Tel: 504-436-4253. FAX: 504-342-8208. *Librn,* Gaynell Adams
Library Holdings: Bk Titles 2,200; Per Subs 25
Automation Activity & Vendor Info: (Acquisitions) Follett Software; (Cataloging) Follett Software; (Circulation) Follett Software; (OPAC) Follett Software
Open Mon-Fri 7:30-3:30

CAMERON

P CAMERON PARISH LIBRARY*, 501 Marshall St, 70631. (Mail add: PO Box 1130, 70631-1130), SAN 306-4549. Tel: 337-775-5421. FAX: 337-775-5346. Web Site: www.cameron.lib.la.us. *Asst Dir, Interim Mgr,* Dede Sanders; E-mail: dsanders@cameron.lib.la.us; *Dir,* Position Currently Open; *Financial Admin Officer,* Tina Boudreaux; E-mail: tboudrea@cameron.lib.la.us; *Cataloger,* Rhonda Duhoun; E-mail: rduhon@cameron.lib.la.us. Subject Specialists: *Ch, Mgt,* Position Currently Open; Staff 3 (Non-MLS 3)
Founded 1958. Pop 6,980; Circ 76,805
Library Holdings: Bk Vols 15,000; Per Subs 20
Special Collections: Cookbooks
Subject Interests: La
Automation Activity & Vendor Info: (Cataloging) Book Systems; (Circulation) Book Systems; (OPAC) Book Systems
Database Vendor: Baker & Taylor, BWI, Facts on File, Newsbank, Overdrive, Inc, ProQuest, TumbleBookLibrary
Wireless access
Function: Accelerated reader prog, Adult bk club, Art exhibits, Bks on CD, Children's prog, Computer training, Computers for patron use, Copy machines, e-mail & chat, Electronic databases & coll, Fax serv, Free DVD rentals, Handicapped accessible, ILL available, Music CDs, Online cat, Online searches, Outreach serv, OverDrive digital audio bks, Photocopying/Printing, Preschool outreach, Prog for adults, Prog for children & young adult, Pub access computers, Ref & res, Ref serv in person, Senior outreach, Spoken cassettes & CDs, Story hour, Summer reading prog, Tax forms, Teen prog, Telephone ref, VHS videos, Wheelchair accessible, Workshops
Partic in Libraries SouthWest
Open Mon-Thurs 8-6, Fri 8-4
Branches: 5
GRAND CHENIER BRANCH, 2867 Grand Chenier Hwy, Grand Chenier, 70643. Tel: 337-538-2214. FAX: 337-538-2216. *Br Mgr,* Beckie Primeaux
Library Holdings: Bk Titles 3,787
Open Mon-Thurs 8-6, Fri 8-4
GRAND LAKE, 961 Hwy 384, Lake Charles, 70607. Tel: 337-598-5950. *Br Mgr,* Jo Dee Roberts
Library Holdings: Bk Titles 10,364
Open Mon-Thurs 8-6, Fri 8-4
HACKBERRY BRANCH, 983 Main St, Hackberry, 70645. Tel: 337-762-3978. FAX: 337-762-4115. *Br Mgr,* Mae Simon
Library Holdings: Bk Titles 6,642
Open Mon-Thurs 8-6
JOHNSON BAYOU, 4586 Gulf Beach Hwy, 70631. Tel: 337-569-2892. FAX: 337-569-2905. *Br Mgr,* Julie Carlson; *Asst Mgr,* Chad Merritt
Library Holdings: Bk Titles 4,433
Open Mon-Thurs 8-6, Fri 8-4
LOWRY, 460 Lowry Hwy, Lake Arthur, 70549. Tel: 337-774-3030. FAX: 337-774-3032. *Br Mgr,* Alice Duhon
Library Holdings: Bk Titles 227
Open Mon & Thurs 8-6
Bookmobiles: 1

CHALMETTE

J NUNEZ COMMUNITY COLLEGE LIBRARY*, 3710 Paris Rd, 70043. Tel: 504-278-6230, 504-278-7498. Administration Tel: 504-680-2600. FAX: 504-680-2584. Web Site: www.nunez.edu/Library.htm, www.nunez.edu/Library/ncclib.htm. *Dir of Libr Serv,* Richard DeFoe; E-mail: RDeFoe@nunez.edu; *Ref Librn,* Caitlin Cooper; E-mail: CCooper@nunez.edu; *Libr Spec Supvr,* Jean Nunez; E-mail:

JNunez@nunez.edu; *Spec,* Rachel Monson; E-mail: rmonson@nunez.edu; Staff 5 (MLS 5)
Founded 1992. Enrl 2,000; Fac 50; Highest Degree: Associate
Library Holdings: Bks on Deafness & Sign Lang 30; Bk Titles 32,999; Bk Vols 37,626; Per Subs 326
Automation Activity & Vendor Info: (Acquisitions) SirsiDynix; (Cataloging) SirsiDynix; (Circulation) SirsiDynix; (Media Booking) SirsiDynix; (OPAC) SirsiDynix; (Serials) SirsiDynix
Database Vendor: EBSCOhost, Gale Cengage Learning, JSTOR, LexisNexis, OCLC WorldShare Interlibrary Loan, Westlaw
Publications: Information Source (Newsletter)
Partic in The Louisiana Library Network
Open Mon-Thurs 8am-9pm, Fri 8-4:30
Friends of the Library Group

CHAUVIN

G LOUISIANA UNIVERSITIES MARINE CONSORTIUM*, Lumcon Library, 8124 Hwy 56, 70344-2124. SAN 326-4815. Tel: 985-851-2800. FAX: 985-851-2874. Web Site: www.lumcon.edu/library. *Assoc Librn,* John Conover; Tel: 985-851-2875, E-mail: jconover@lumcon.edu; *Asst Librn,* Shanna Bonvillain; Tel: 985-851-2806, E-mail: sbonvillain@lumcon.edu; Staff 2 (MLS 1, Non-MLS 1)
Founded 1979
Library Holdings: Bk Titles 7,500; Bk Vols 5,800; Per Subs 200
Subject Interests: Geochemistry, Marine biol, Oceanography
Automation Activity & Vendor Info: (Cataloging) SirsiDynix; (OPAC) SirsiDynix
Publications: Effects of Offshore Oil & Gas Development: A Current Awareness Bibliography (Annotated, quarterly); US Minerals Management Service
Partic in Lyrasis; OCLC Online Computer Library Center, Inc; The Louisiana Library Network
Open Mon-Fri 8-4:30

CLINTON

P AUDUBON REGIONAL LIBRARY*, 12220 Woodville St, 70722. (Mail add: PO Box 8389, 70722-8389), SAN 342-8796. Tel: 225-683-8753. Interlibrary Loan Service Tel: 225-634 7408. Administration Tel: 225-683-4290. FAX: 225-683-4634. E-mail: admin.c1ar@state.lib.la.us. Web Site: www.youseemore.com/audubon. *Dir,* Patricia Boatman; E-mail: pboatman@state.lib.la.us; Staff 21 (MLS 1, Non-MLS 20)
Founded 1963. Pop 46,000; Circ 147,992
Library Holdings: AV Mats 1,000; Bk Vols 88,609; Per Subs 212
Subject Interests: Genealogy, Hist, La
Automation Activity & Vendor Info: (Cataloging) TLC (The Library Corporation); (Circulation) TLC (The Library Corporation); (ILL) TLC (The Library Corporation); (OPAC) TLC (The Library Corporation)
Open Mon-Thurs 9-5, Fri 9-3, Sat 8:30-12:30
Friends of the Library Group
Branches: 2
JACKSON BRANCH, 3312 College St, Jackson, 70748. (Mail add: PO Box 1830, Jackson, 70748-1830), SAN 342-8885. Tel: 225-634-7408. Interlibrary Loan Service Tel: 225-634-7508. FAX: 225-634-5896. *Br Mgr,* Londa L Matthews; Staff 3 (Non-MLS 3)
Library Holdings: AV Mats 242; Bk Vols 14,678; Per Subs 62
Open Mon-Thurs 9-5, Fri 9-3, Sat 9-1
Friends of the Library Group
ST HELENA BRANCH, 53 S Main St, Ste A, Greensburg, 70441. (Mail add: PO Box 368, Greensburg, 70441-0368), SAN 342-8850. Tel: 225-222-4328. FAX: 504-222-4335. *Br Mgr,* Jean Claxton; Staff 2 (Non-MLS 2)
Library Holdings: AV Mats 78; Bk Vols 13,055; Per Subs 32
Special Collections: St Helena Parish Information Coll, local genealogy & hist
Subject Interests: Genealogy, Local hist
Database Vendor: TLC (The Library Corporation)
Open Mon-Thurs 8:30-5, Fri 8:30-12:30, Sat 9-1
Friends of the Library Group
Bookmobiles: 1. Bk vols 6,100

COLFAX

P GRANT PARISH LIBRARY*, 300 Main St, 71417-1830. SAN 306-4565. Tel: 318-627-9920. FAX: 318-627-9900. Web Site: www.grant.lib.la.us. *Dir,* Doris Lively; E-mail: dlively@grant.lib.la.us; *Br Mgr,* Candace Whitstine; *ILL,* Bonnie Burch; Staff 5 (MLS 1, Non-MLS 4)
Founded 1959. Pop 17,495; Circ 90,600
Library Holdings: Bk Vols 62,137; Per Subs 131
Subject Interests: Genealogy, Hist, La
Automation Activity & Vendor Info: (Acquisitions) Auto-Graphics, Inc; (Cataloging) Auto-Graphics, Inc; (Circulation) Auto-Graphics, Inc; (Course Reserve) Auto-Graphics, Inc; (ILL) Auto-Graphics, Inc; (OPAC) Auto-Graphics, Inc; (Serials) Auto-Graphics, Inc
Wireless access
Open Mon 8-6, Tues-Fri 8-5, Sat 9-Noon
Branches: 4
DRY PRONG BRANCH, 605 Russell Hataway St, Dry Prong, 71423. Tel: 318-899-7588. FAX: 318-899-7588. *Br Mgr,* Tina Fox; Staff 1 (Non-MLS 1)
Library Holdings: Bk Vols 4,650; Per Subs 20
Open Mon & Thurs 1-5, Tues 1-7, Wed & Fri 8-Noon
GEORGETOWN BRANCH, 4570 Hwy 500, Georgetown, 71432, SAN 377-7561. Tel: 318-827-9427. FAX: 318-827-9427. *Br Mgr,* Judy Scott; Staff 1 (Non-MLS 1)
Library Holdings: Bk Vols 2,000; Per Subs 19
Open Tues-Thurs 1-5
MONTGOMERY BRANCH, 940 Caddo St, Montgomery, 71454. Tel: 318-646-3660. FAX: 318-646-3660. *Br Mgr,* Pat Dubois; Staff 1 (Non-MLS 1)
Library Holdings: Bk Vols 6,520; Per Subs 11
Open Mon & Tues 1-5, Thurs 8-12, Fri 8-12 & 1-5
POLLOCK BRANCH, 1316 Pine St, Pollock, 71467. (Mail add: 300 Main St, 71417). Tel: 318-765-9616. FAX: 318-765-9616. *Br Mgr,* Jeanie Tyler; Staff 1 (Non-MLS 1)
Library Holdings: Bk Vols 5,580; Per Subs 16
Open Mon, Wed & Fri 1-5, Tues 1-7, Thurs 8-12
Bookmobiles: 1

COLUMBIA

P CALDWELL PARISH LIBRARY*, 211 Jackson, 71418. (Mail add: PO Box 1499, 71418-1499), SAN 306-4573. Tel: 318-649-2259. FAX: 318-649-7768. E-mail: admin.t1cd@pelican.state.lib.la.us. Web Site: caldwelllibrary.com. *Dir,* Mary G Poole; E-mail: cal_lib71418@yahoo.com; Staff 3 (Non-MLS 3)
Founded 1953. Pop 9,810; Circ 53,096
Library Holdings: AV Mats 256; Bk Vols 40,275; Per Subs 160
Automation Activity & Vendor Info: (Acquisitions) Book Systems; (Cataloging) Book Systems; (Circulation) Book Systems; (OPAC) Book Systems
Wireless access
Open Mon-Fri 8-5, Sat 8:30-Noon

COTTONPORT

S AVOYELLES CORRECTIONAL CENTER LIBRARY*, 1630 Prison Rd, 71327. Tel: 318-876-2891, Ext 350. FAX: 318-876-4220. *In Charge,* Russell Clayton
Founded 1990
Library Holdings: Bk Vols 11,817; Per Subs 11
Subject Interests: Fantasy, Fiction, Westerns
Restriction: Restricted access

COUSHATTA

P RED RIVER PARISH LIBRARY*, 2022 Alonzo, 71019-9474. (Mail add: PO Box 1367, 71019-1367), SAN 306-4581. Tel: 318-932-5614. FAX: 318-932-6747. E-mail: admin.g1rr@pelican.state.lib.la.us. *Dir,* Marvin Lewis; E-mail: mlewis@pelican.state.lib.la.us; Staff 6 (MLS 1, Non-MLS 5)
Founded 1962. Pop 10,500; Circ 84,000
Library Holdings: AV Mats 4,000; Bk Vols 24,166
Automation Activity & Vendor Info: (Cataloging) Innovative Interfaces, Inc; (Circulation) Innovative Interfaces, Inc; (OPAC) Innovative Interfaces, Inc
Wireless access
Open Mon-Fri 8-5

COVINGTON

P SAINT TAMMANY PARISH LIBRARY*, 310 W 21st Ave, 70433. SAN 342-894X. Tel: 985-871-1219. Circulation Tel: 985-893-6280. Interlibrary Loan Service Tel: 985-809-5773. FAX: 985-871-1224. Circulation FAX: 985-893-6283. Web Site: www.sttammany.lib.la.us. *Dir,* Donald Westmoreland; Staff 84 (MLS 14, Non-MLS 70)
Founded 1950. Pop 191,268; Circ 1,167,914
Library Holdings: Bk Titles 250,000; Bk Vols 497,202; Per Subs 1,000
Subject Interests: Local hist
Automation Activity & Vendor Info: (Acquisitions) Innovative Interfaces, Inc; (Cataloging) Innovative Interfaces, Inc; (Circulation) Innovative Interfaces, Inc; (ILL) OCLC; (OPAC) Innovative Interfaces, Inc; (Serials) Innovative Interfaces, Inc
Database Vendor: EBSCOhost, Gale Cengage Learning, Newsbank
Special Services for the Deaf - Bks on deafness & sign lang; High interest/low vocabulary bks
Open Mon-Fri 8-5, Sat 9-5
Friends of the Library Group

Branches: 10
ABITA SPRINGS BRANCH, 71683 Leveson St, Abita Springs, 70420, SAN 342-8974. Tel: 985-893-6285. FAX: 985-893-1336. E-mail: abita@stpl.us. *Br Mgr,* Kay Redd
Open Mon, Tues, Thurs & Fri 10-6, Wed 12-8
BUSH BRANCH, 81597 Hwy 41, Bush, 70431, SAN 342-9008. Tel: 985-886-3588. FAX: 985-886-1054. E-mail: bush@stpl.us. *Br Mgr,* Marjie Jahncke
Open Mon, Tues, Thurs & Fri 10-6, Wed 12-8
CAUSEWAY BRANCH, 3457 Hwy 190, Mandeville, 70471. Tel: 985-626-9779. FAX: 985-626-9783. E-mail: causeway@stpl.us. *Br Mgr,* Sally Barringer; *Circ Mgr,* Adrienne Ivy
Open Mon-Thurs 9-8, Fri & Sat 9-5
COVINGTON BRANCH, 310 W 21st Ave, 70433. Tel: 985-893-6280. FAX: 985-893-1271. E-mail: covington@stpl.us. *Br Mgr,* Tamie Martin; *Circ Mgr,* Melanie Sharp
Library Holdings: Bk Vols 563,786
Open Mon-Thurs 9-8, Fri & Sat 9-5
Friends of the Library Group
FOLSOM BRANCH, 82393 Railroad Ave, Folsom, 70437, SAN 342-9091. Tel: 985-796-9728. FAX: 985-796-9304. E-mail: folsom@stpl.us. *Br Mgr,* Lynne Moore
Subject Interests: Gardening, Horses
Open Mon, Tues, Thurs & Fri 10-6, Wed 12-8
LACOMBE BRANCH, 28027 Hwy 190, Lacombe, 70445, SAN 342-9121. Tel: 985-882-7858. FAX: 985-882-8072. E-mail: lacombe@stpl.us. *Br Mgr,* Rhonda Spiess
Open Mon, Tues, Thurs & Fri 10-6, Wed 12-8
LEE ROAD BRANCH, 79213 Hwy 40, 70435, SAN 329-6512. Tel: 985-893-6284. FAX: 985-871-1349. E-mail: leeroad@stpl.us. *Br Mgr,* Lisa Haley
Open Mon, Tues, Thurs & Fri 10-6, Wed 12-8
MANDEVILLE BRANCH, 844 Girod St, Mandeville, 70448, SAN 342-9180. Tel: 985-626-4293. FAX: 985-624-4621. E-mail: mandeville@stpl.us. *Br Mgr,* Jennifer Mayer; *Circ Mgr,* Carra Rowland
Open Mon-Thurs 9-8, Fri & Sat 9-5
Friends of the Library Group
PEARL RIVER BRANCH, 64580 Hwy 41, Pearl River, 70452, SAN 342-9210. Tel: 985-863-5518. FAX: 985-863-1730. E-mail: pearlriver@stpl.us. *Br Mgr,* Adele Salzer
Open Mon, Tues, Thurs & Fri 10-6, Wed 12-8
SLIDELL BRANCH, 555 Robert Blvd, Slidell, 70458, SAN 342-9245. Tel: 985-646-6470. FAX: 985-645-3553. E-mail: slidell@stpl.us. *Br Mgr,* Nancy Little; *Circ Mgr,* Susan Taggart
Special Collections: Bayou Bonfouca Superfund Project Documents; Genealogy Coll; Louisiana Documents; Southern Shipbuilding Corporation Superfund Project Documents
Open Mon-Thurs 9-8, Fri & Sat 9-5
Friends of the Library Group

CROWLEY

P ACADIA PARISH LIBRARY*, 1125 N Parkerson Ave, 70526. (Mail add: PO Box 1509, 70527-1509), SAN 342-927X. Tel: 337-788-1880, 337-788-1881. FAX: 337-788-3759. E-mail: admin.b1ac@pelican.state.lib.la.us. Web Site: www.acadia.lib.la.us. *Dir,* Lyle C Johnson; *Asst Dir,* Ted Landry; *Acq, Ref Serv,* Ann Mire; Staff 29 (MLS 4, Non-MLS 25)
Founded 1945. Pop 59,600
Library Holdings: AV Mats 1,115; Bk Vols 150,000; Per Subs 310
Special Collections: Paul Freeland's Crowley Coll
Automation Activity & Vendor Info: (Cataloging) TLC (The Library Corporation); (Circulation) TLC (The Library Corporation); (OPAC) TLC (The Library Corporation)
Wireless access
Mem of Bayouland Library System
Open Mon-Fri 8-5:30, Sat 9-1
Branches: 6
CHURCH POINT BRANCH, 311 N Vista St, Church Point, 70525, SAN 342-9334. Tel: 337-684-5774. FAX: 337-684-1593. *Bus Mgr,* Linda Wills; Staff 1 (Non-MLS 1)
Pop 4,477
Library Holdings: AV Mats 112; Bk Vols 5,290; Per Subs 52
Open Mon-Fri 8-5, Sat 9-12
ESTHERWOOD BRANCH, 116 N LeBlanc St, Estherwood, 70534. (Mail add: PO Box 230, Estherwood, 70534-0230), SAN 342-9423. Tel: 337-785-1090. *Librn,* Katrina Benoit; Staff 1 (Non-MLS 1)
Pop 900
Library Holdings: AV Mats 88; Bk Vols 1,769; Per Subs 19
Open Mon & Wed 3-5
IOTA BRANCH, 119 Duson, Iota, 70543. (Mail add: PO Box 950, Iota, 70543-0950), SAN 342-9482. Tel: 337-779-2770. FAX: 337-779-2770. *Br Mgr, Librn,* Anne Ritter; Staff 1 (Non-MLS 1)
Pop 1,256
Library Holdings: AV Mats 110; Bk Vols 5,340; Per Subs 31
Open Mon-Fri 1-5
MERMENTAU BRANCH, 107 Second St, Mermentau, 70556. (Mail add: PO Box 369, Mermentau, 70556-0369), SAN 342-9512. Tel: 318-824-0690. FAX: 318-824-0690. *Librn,* Katrina Benoit; Staff 1 (Non-MLS 1)
Pop 801
Library Holdings: AV Mats 56; Bk Vols 2,109; Per Subs 11
Open Tues & Thurs 1-5
MORSE BRANCH, 209 S Jules Ave, Morse, 70559. (Mail add: PO Box 369, Morse, 70559-0369), SAN 342-9520. Tel: 337-783-0784. FAX: 337-783-0784. *Librn,* Mary Sonnier; Staff 1 (Non-MLS 1)
Pop 782
Library Holdings: AV Mats 49; Bk Vols 2,098
Open Mon & Wed 1-5, Fri 8-12 & 1-5
RAYNE BRANCH, 109 W Perrodin, Rayne, 70578, SAN 342-9547. Tel: 337-334-3188. FAX: 337-334-1181. *Librn,* Trudy Ronkartz; Staff 5 (Non-MLS 5)
Pop 8,502
Library Holdings: AV Mats 234; Bk Vols 35,191; Per Subs 70
Open Mon-Thurs 8-5:30, Fri 8-5, Sat 9-12

DERIDDER

P BEAUREGARD PARISH LIBRARY*, 205 S Washington Ave, 70634. Tel: 337-463-6217. Toll Free Tel: 800-524-6239 (Beauregard Parish only). FAX: 337-462-5434. E-mail: admin@beau.org. Administration E-mail: w1bg@beau.org. Web Site: www.beau.lib.la.us. *Dir,* Lilly F Smith; Staff 5 (Non-MLS 5)
Pop 35,000; Circ 381,017
Library Holdings: AV Mats 7,771; Bk Vols 83,154; Per Subs 210; Videos 6,300
Wireless access
Partic in Libraries SouthWest
Open Mon-Wed & Fri 9-5:30, Thurs 9-7:30, Sat 9-1
Branches: 5
EAST BEAUREGARD, 7580 Hwy 26, Wye Community, Dry Creek, 70634. (Mail add: 205 S Washington Ave, 70634). Tel: 337-463-6217. FAX: 337-462-5434. *In Charge,* Linda Harper; Staff 2 (Non-MLS 2)
Library Holdings: AV Mats 50; Bk Vols 4,000; Per Subs 16
Open Mon 1:30-5:30, Wed 9-5:30, Sat 9-1
FIELDS BRANCH, 13287 Hwy 389, Fields, 70653. Tel: 337-463-6217. FAX: 337-462-5434. E-mail: admin@beau.org. *In Charge,* Lenore Pickering; Staff 2 (Non-MLS 2)
Library Holdings: AV Mats 56; Bk Vols 4,000; Per Subs 16
Open Tues & Sat 9-1, Fri 2-5:30
MERRYVILLE BRANCH, 1007 Hwy 110, Merryville, 70653. (Mail add: 205 S Washington Ave, 70634). Tel: 337-463-6217. FAX: 337-462-5434. *Br Mgr,* Tess Yeager; Staff 1 (Non-MLS 1)
Library Holdings: AV Mats 60; Bk Vols 4,281; Per Subs 17
Open Mon & Thurs 1-5, Tues, Fri & Sat 9-1
SINGER BRANCH, 9130 Hwy 27, Singer, 70660. (Mail add: 205 S Washington Ave, 70634). Tel: 337-463-6217. FAX: 337-462-5434. *Br Mgr,* Position Currently Open
Library Holdings: AV Mats 68; Bk Vols 3,100; Per Subs 15
Open Tues 1:30-5:30, Fri & Sat 9-1
SOUTH BEAUREGARD, 6713 Hwy 12, Ragley, 70657. Tel: 337-463-6217. FAX: 337-462-5434. *In Charge,* Stephanie Gibbs
Library Holdings: AV Mats 63; Bk Vols 3,412; Per Subs 18
Open Mon 9-5, Wed & Thurs 1-5, Sat 9-1

DESTREHAN

P SAINT CHARLES PARISH LIBRARY*, East Regional Branch, 160 W Campus Dr, 70047. (Mail add: PO Box 1029, 70047-1029), SAN 343-1436. Tel: 985-764-2366. Administration Tel: 985-764-9643. FAX: 985-764-0447. Administration FAX: 985-764-1744. *Libr Dir,* Leann Benedict; E-mail: leann.benedict@myscpl.org; *Asst Dir, Pub Serv,* Vicki Nesting; E-mail: vicki.nesting@myscpl.org; *Asst Dir, Tech Serv,* Position Currently Open; *Br Librn,* Lauren Pitz; E-mail: lauren.pitz@myscpl.org; *Ch,* Marci Saucier; E-mail: marci.saucier@myscpl.org; *Tech Serv Librn,* Denise Wilson; E-mail: denise.wilson@myscpl.org; *YA Librn,* Amy Boling; E-mail: amy.boling@myscpl.org; Staff 31 (MLS 7, Non-MLS 24)
Wireless access
Open Mon-Thurs 9-8, Fri & Sat 9-5
Friends of the Library Group
Branches: 5
HAHNVILLE BRANCH, 14996 River Rd, Hahnville, 70057-2100. (Mail add: PO Box 444, Hahnville, 70057-0444), SAN 343-1460. Tel: 985-783-2341. *Br Supvr,* Robin Bourgeois; E-mail: robin.bourgeois@myscpl.org; Staff 2 (Non-MLS 2)
Open Mon-Fri 9-5

NORCO BRANCH, 197 Good Hope St, Norco, 70079-2516, SAN 343-1495. Tel: 985-764-6581. *Br Supvr,* Phyllis Smith; Staff 2 (Non-MLS 2)
Open Mon-Fri 9-5, Sat 10-2

PARADIS BRANCH, 307 Audubon St, Paradis, 70080. Tel: 985-758-1868. FAX: 985-758-1869. *Br Supvr,* Anne St Pierre; E-mail: anne.stpierre@myscpl.org; Staff 2 (Non-MLS 2)

SAINT ROSE BRANCH, 90 E Club Dr, Saint Rose, 70087. Tel: 504-465-0646. FAX: 504-465-0629. *Br Mgr,* Eva Fife; Staff 2 (Non-MLS 2)
Open Mon 10-8, Tues & Thurs 10-6, Fri 9-5, Sat 10 2

WEST REGIONAL BRANCH, 105 Lakewood Dr, Luling, 70070. (Mail add: PO Box 949, Luling, 70070-0949), SAN 343-1401. Tel: 985-785-8471. FAX: 985-785-8499. Web Site: www.stcharles.lib.la.us. *Br Librn,* Julie Cancienne; E-mail: julie.cancienne@myscpl.org; Staff 16 (MLS 1, Non-MLS 15)
Founded 1955. Pop 48,000; Circ 325,000
Subject Interests: Hist, La
Open Mon-Thurs 9-8, Fri & Sat 9-5

Bookmobiles: 1

DONALDSONVILLE

P ASCENSION PARISH LIBRARY*, Donaldsonville Branch, 500 Mississippi St, 70346-2535. SAN 342-9660. Tel: 225-473-8052. FAX: 225-473-9522. E-mail: admin.c1ac@pelican.state.lib.la.us. Web Site: www.ascension.lib.la.us. *Dir,* Angelle Deshautelles; Fax: 225-644-0063, E-mail: adeshaut@pelican.state.lib.la.us; *Assoc Dir,* Larie Myers; Tel: 225-647-8924; *Asst Dir,* John Stelly; *Ad,* Mimi Foster; *Cat Librn,* Vivian Solar; *Youth Serv Librn,* Jennifer Seneca; Staff 62 (MLS 12, Non-MLS 50)
Founded 1960. Pop 88,000; Circ 310,481
Library Holdings: Bk Vols 224,000; Per Subs 540
Special Collections: US Army Corps of Engineers, Lower Mississippi Valley Flood Control, doc
Automation Activity & Vendor Info: (Cataloging) TLC (The Library Corporation); (Circulation) TLC (The Library Corporation); (OPAC) TLC (The Library Corporation)
Open Mon, Wed & Fri 8:30-5:30, Tues & Thurs 8:30-8, Sat 8:30-12:30

Branches: 2

GALVEZ BRANCH, 40300 Hwy 42, Prairieville, 70769, SAN 325-397X. Tel: 225-622-3339. FAX: 225-622-2550. *Br Librn,* Joe Dolgos
Open Mon, Wed & Fri 8:30-5:30, Tues & Thurs 8:30-8, Sat 8:30-12:30

GONZALES BRANCH, 708 S Irma Blvd, Gonzales, 70737, SAN 342-9695. Tel: 225-647-3955. FAX: 225-644-0063. *Br Librn,* Chriselle Henry
Open Mon-Thurs 8:30-8, Fri & Sat 8:30-5:30

EUNICE

C LOUISIANA STATE UNIVERSITY*, LeDoux Library, 2048 Johnson Hwy, 70535. (Mail add: PO Box 1129, 70535-1129), SAN 306-4611. Tel: 337-550-1380. Interlibrary Loan Service Tel: 337-550-1384. Reference Tel: 337-550-1385. FAX: 337-550-1455. Web Site: www.lsue.edu. *Dir,* Gerald Patout; *Govt Doc,* Denise Foret; *Ref,* Shelby Anfenson Comeau; Staff 3 (MLS 2, Non-MLS 1)
Founded 1967. Enrl 3,300, Fac 75; Highest Degree: Associate
Library Holdings: Audiobooks 100; CDs 200; DVDs 200; e-books 50,000; e-journals 200; Microforms 300; Bk Vols 89,923; Per Subs 218; Videos 1,000
Special Collections: Rare Louisiana History (Sabatier Coll). State Document Depository; US Document Depository
Subject Interests: Genealogy, La
Automation Activity & Vendor Info: (Acquisitions) SirsiDynix; (Cataloging) SirsiDynix; (Circulation) SirsiDynix; (OPAC) SirsiDynix; (Serials) SirsiDynix
Partic in Lyrasis; OCLC Online Computer Library Center, Inc; The Louisiana Library Network
Open Mon-Fri 8-4:30
Friends of the Library Group

FARMERVILLE

P UNION PARISH LIBRARY*, 202 W Jackson St, 71241-2799. SAN 306-462X. Tel: 318-368-9226, 318-368-9288. FAX: 318-368-9224. E-mail: admin.t1un@pelican.state.lib.la.us. Web Site: www.youseemore.com/unionparish. *Dir,* Stephanie Herrmann; E-mail: sherrman@state.lib.la.us; *Asst Dir,* Thalia Williams
Founded 1956. Pop 20,690; Circ 62,068
Library Holdings: AV Mats 692; Large Print Bks 1,253; Bk Titles 46,876; Bk Vols 55,359; Per Subs 61; Talking Bks 856
Automation Activity & Vendor Info: (Cataloging) TLC (The Library Corporation); (Circulation) TLC (The Library Corporation); (OPAC) TLC (The Library Corporation)
Publications: Beacon Bulletin (Monthly)
Open Mon-Fri 8-5, Sat 8-12
Bookmobiles: 1. Bkmobile Serv Dir, JoAnn Buggs

FERRIDAY

P CONCORDIA PARISH LIBRARY*, 1609 Third St, 71334-2298. SAN 342-975X. Tel: 318-757-3550. FAX: 318-757-1941. E-mail: admin.t1cn@pelican.state.lib.la.us. Web Site: www.concordia.lib.la.us. *Dir,* Amanda Taylor; E-mail: ataylor@pelican.state.lib.la.us; Staff 3 (Non-MLS 3)
Founded 1928
Library Holdings: AV Mats 210; Bk Vols 85,000; Per Subs 95
Automation Activity & Vendor Info: (Cataloging) Innovative Interfaces, Inc; (Circulation) Innovative Interfaces, Inc; (OPAC) Innovative Interfaces, Inc
Open Mon & Fri 8-5, Tues-Thurs 8-6

Branches: 2

CLAYTON BRANCH, 8723 Hwy 566, Clayton, 71326, SAN 342-9784. Tel: 318-757-6460. *Br Mgr,* Dorothy Davis; Staff 2 (Non-MLS 2)
Library Holdings: AV Mats 58; Bk Vols 15,000; Per Subs 12
Open Mon-Thurs 2-5, Fri 8-5

VIDALIA BRANCH, 408 Texas St, Vidalia, 71373, SAN 342-9814. Tel: 318-336-5043. FAX: 318-336-0904. *Br Mgr,* Hattie Neil; E-mail: hneal@state.lib.la.us; Staff 2 (Non-MLS 2)
Library Holdings: Bk Vols 20,000; Per Subs 45
Open Mon & Fri 8-5, Tues-Thurs 8-6

Bookmobiles: 1

FORT POLK

S FORT POLK MILITARY MUSEUM LIBRARY*, 7881 Mississippi Ave, 71459. (Mail add: PO Box 3916, 71459-0916), SAN 374-8286. Tel: 337-531-7905. *Dir/Curator,* Frederick R Adolphus; E-mail: frederick.r.adolphus.civ@mail.mil
Founded 1972
Library Holdings: Bk Vols 500; Per Subs 100
Function: Ref serv available
Open Tues-Sat 10-5:30

UNITED STATES ARMY

A ALLEN MEMORIAL LIBRARY*, Bldg 660, 7460 Colorado Ave, 71459-5000, SAN 342-9849. Tel: 337-531-2665. FAX: 337-531-6687. *Dir,* Kelly Herbert
Library Holdings: Bk Vols 70,000; Per Subs 260
Subject Interests: La, Mil hist
Automation Activity & Vendor Info: (Cataloging) Horizon; (Circulation) Horizon; (OPAC) Horizon
Partic in OCLC Online Computer Library Center, Inc
Open Mon-Thurs 10-7, Fri 10-5, Sat 10-6, Sun 2-6

AM USA MEDDAC MEDICAL LIBRARY, FORT POLK - BAYNE-JONES ARMY COMMUNITY HOSPITAL*, 1585 Third St, Bldg 285, 71459-5110, SAN 342-9873. Tel: 337-531-3725, 337-531-3726. FAX: 337-531 3082. E-mail: usarmy.polk.medcom-bjach.mbx.library@mail.mil. *Librn,* Cecelia Higginbotham; Staff 1 (MLS 1)
Founded 1961
Library Holdings: Microforms 2,500; Bk Vols 2,000; Per Subs 63
Automation Activity & Vendor Info: (Acquisitions) OCLC; (Cataloging) OCLC; (Circulation) OCLC; (ILL) OCLC; (OPAC) OCLC WorldShare Interlibrary Loan; (Serials) OCLC
Database Vendor: EBSCOhost, Elsevier, Ingenta, MD Consult, Medline, OCLC Worldshare Management Services, OVID Technologies, PubMed, STAT!Ref (Teton Data Systems), TDNet, UpToDate, Wiley, WT Cox
Partic in Army Medical Department - Medical Library & Information Network (AMEDD MEDLI-NET); National Network of Libraries of Medicine; OCLC Online Computer Library Center, Inc; S Cent Regional Libr Prog
Open Mon-Fri 8-4:30

FRANKLIN

P SAINT MARY PARISH LIBRARY*, 206 Iberia St, 70538-4906. SAN 342-9903. Tel: 337-828-1624. Reference Tel: 337-828-5364. Toll Free Tel: 800-732-8698. FAX: 337-828-2329. E-mail: admin.b1my@pelican.state.lib.la.us. Web Site: www.stmary.lib.la.us. *Dir,* Julie Champagne; *Br Mgr,* Patty Robicheaux; Staff 39 (MLS 1, Non-MLS 38)
Founded 1953. Pop 48,669; Circ 321,828
Library Holdings: Bk Vols 178,155; Per Subs 239
Subject Interests: Genealogy
Automation Activity & Vendor Info: (Cataloging) TLC (The Library Corporation); (Circulation) TLC (The Library Corporation); (OPAC) TLC (The Library Corporation)
Publications: Library Lagniappe
Mem of Bayouland Library System
Open Mon-Fri 8-5
Friends of the Library Group

Branches: 5
AMELIA BRANCH, 625 Lake Palourde, Amelia, 70360, SAN 342-9911. Tel: 985-631-2262. FAX: 985-631-2632. *Interim Br Mgr,* Leisha Babin
Library Holdings: Bk Vols 16,138
Open Mon-Fri 8:30-5:30, Sat 9-12
BAYOU VISTA BRANCH, 1325 Bellview Dr, Bayou Vista, 70380, SAN 377-9998. Tel: 985-399-9866. FAX: 985-399-4232. *Br Mgr,* Leisha Babin
Founded 1998
Open Mon-Fri 8:30-5:30, Sat 9-12
BERWICK BRANCH, 3527 Fourth St, Berwick, 70342, SAN 342-9938. Tel: 985-385-2943. FAX: 985-385-6474. *Br Mgr,* Diane Matherne
Library Holdings: Bk Vols 31,406
Open Mon-Fri 8:30-5:30, Sat 9-12
PATTERSON BRANCH, 529 Catherine St, Patterson, 70392, SAN 342-9997. Tel: 985-395-2777. FAX: 985-399-4469. *Br Mgr,* Lisa Wilson
Library Holdings: Bk Vols 23,415
Open Mon-Fri 8:30-5:30, Sat 9-12
WEST END, 100 Charenton Rd, Baldwin, 70514. (Mail add: PO Box 309, Baldwin, 70514-0309), SAN 374-4175. Tel: 337-923-6205. FAX: 337-923-4507. *Br Mgr,* Connie Durocher
Open Mon-Fri 8:30-5:30, Sat 9-12
Bookmobiles: 1. Bk vols 18,511

FRANKLINTON

P WASHINGTON PARISH LIBRARY SYSTEM*, Headquarters, 825 Free St, 70438. SAN 343-0022. Tel: 985-839-7806. FAX: 985-839-7808. Web Site: www.washington.lib.la.us. *Dir,* Allison B Barron; E-mail: abarron@state.lib.la.us; Staff 5 (MLS 1, Non-MLS 4)
Founded 1946. Pop 48,185; Circ 153,776
Library Holdings: Bk Vols 109,405
Special Collections: Washington Parish & Local History
Automation Activity & Vendor Info: (Circulation) Innovative Interfaces, Inc
Database Vendor: EBSCOhost, infoUSA
Wireless access
Function: Bks on cassette, Bks on CD, Computer training, Computers for patron use, Copy machines, e-mail & chat, e-mail serv, Electronic databases & coll, Fax serv, Free DVD rentals, ILL available, Magnifiers for reading, Mail & tel request accepted, Online cat, Photocopying/Printing, Prog for adults, Prog for children & young adult, Pub access computers, Ref serv in person, Satellite serv, Scanner, Spoken cassettes & CDs, Spoken cassettes & DVDs, Summer reading prog, Tax forms, Telephone ref, VHS videos, Wheelchair accessible
Open Mon-Fri 9-5, Sat 9-2
Friends of the Library Group
Branches: 4
BOGALUSA BRANCH, 304 Ave F, Bogalusa, 70427, SAN 343-0081. Tel: 985-735-1961. FAX: 985-735-1996. Web Site: www.washington.lib.la.us/_overlay/bogalusa.htm. *Br Mgr,* Emmett Guy, Jr; E-mail: eguy@state.lib.la.us; Staff 1 (Non-MLS 1)
Library Holdings: Bk Vols 40,000; Per Subs 16
Function: Art exhibits, Copy machines, e-mail & chat, Ref serv in person, Summer reading prog, Tax forms
Open Mon-Fri 9-5, Sat 9-2
ENON, 14140 Hwy 16, 70438, SAN 343-0146. Tel: 985-839-9385. Web Site: www.washington.lib.la.us/Enon.htm. *Br Mgr,* Rebecca Dugas; E-mail: rdugas@state.lib.la.us; Staff 1 (Non-MLS 1)
Library Holdings: Bk Vols 2,640
Function: After school storytime, AV serv, Computers for patron use, ILL available, Pub access computers, Ref serv available, Summer reading prog, Tax forms
Open Tues-Fri 7:30-4:30
FRANKLINTON BRANCH, 825 Free St, 70438, SAN 343-0170. Tel: 985-839-7805. FAX: 985-839-7808. Web Site: www.washington.lib.la.us/franklinton.htm. *Br Mgr,* Bobbie Jones; E-mail: bjones@state.lib.la.us; Staff 1 (Non-MLS 1)
Library Holdings: Bk Vols 39,000; Per Subs 20
Automation Activity & Vendor Info: (Cataloging) Innovative Interfaces, Inc; (OPAC) Innovative Interfaces, Inc
Function: Bks on cassette, Bks on CD, Computers for patron use, Copy machines, e-mail & chat, Fax serv, ILL available, Pub access computers, Ref serv in person
Open Mon 9-8, Tues, Wed & Fri 9-5, Sat 9-2
THOMAS, 30369 Hwy 424, 70438, SAN 343-0235. Tel: 985-848-7061. Web Site: www.washington.lib.la.us/Thomas.htm. *Br Mgr,* Sylvia Ledet; E-mail: sledet@state.lib.la.us
Library Holdings: Bk Vols 3,678
Automation Activity & Vendor Info: (Acquisitions) Innovative Interfaces, Inc; (Cataloging) Innovative Interfaces, Inc
Open Mon-Thurs 9:30-5

GRAMBLING

C GRAMBLING STATE UNIVERSITY*, A C Lewis Memorial Library, 403 Main St, 71245. (Mail add: PO Box 4256, 71245-2761), SAN 306-4638. Tel: 318-274-3354. Circulation Tel: 318-274-2161. Interlibrary Loan Service Tel: 318-274-7732. Reference Tel: 318-274-2227. Administration Tel: 318-274-2568. Toll Free Tel: 800-569-4714. FAX: 318-274-3268. Interlibrary Loan Service FAX: 318-274-4085. Web Site: www.gram.edu/research/library. *Dir of Libr Serv,* Position Currently Open; *Head, Acq & Ser,* Dr Rosemary N Mokia; Tel: 318-274-2213, E-mail: mokiar@gram.edu; *Coordr, Tech Serv, Head Cataloger,* Position Currently Open; *Head, Circ,* Position Currently Open; *Acq Librn,* Sarah Hassen; Tel: 318-274-3145, E-mail: hassens@gram.edu; *Ref Librn,* Maraine Hall; Tel: 318-274-2229, E-mail: hallm@gram.edu; *Ser & Electronic Res Librn,* Rhonda Rolen; Tel: 318-274-2757, E-mail: rolenr@gram.edu; *Syst Librn,* Cecilia Iwala; Tel: 318-274-7367, E-mail: iwalac@gram.edu; *Circ, Ref Asst,* Mary Boden Harris; Tel: 318-274-2472, E-mail: harrism@gram.edu; Staff 9 (MLS 8, Non-MLS 1)
Founded 1935. Enrl 5,207; Fac 248; Highest Degree: Doctorate
Jul 2011-Jun 2012. Mats Exp $692,258, Books $41,382, Per/Ser (Incl. Access Fees) $115,134, Other Print Mats $2,935, AV Mat $2,935, Electronic Ref Mat (Incl. Access Fees) $529,872. Sal $953,996 (Prof $483,772)
Library Holdings: Audiobooks 666; AV Mats 3,559; e-books 20,483; Electronic Media & Resources 261,704; Microforms 122,298; Bk Titles 1,614,155; Bk Vols 280,015
Special Collections: Afro-American Rare Books, fiche; Crime & Juvenile Delinquency, fiche; Education (ERIC 1970-1980), fiche; English Literature, fiche; Housing & Urban Affairs 1965-1972, fiche; Library of American Civilization, fiche; Mary Watson Hymon Afro-American Coll; National Woman's Party Papers, micro; Schomburg Coll (partial); Sociology (Black Culture), micro; The Adams' Papers, micro; Update, fiche
Automation Activity & Vendor Info: (Cataloging) SirsiDynix; (Circulation) SirsiDynix; (OPAC) SirsiDynix
Database Vendor: CQ Press, EBSCO - WebFeat, EBSCOhost, Facts on File, IEEE (Institute of Electrical & Electronics Engineers), JSTOR, LexisNexis, Newsbank, ProQuest
Wireless access
Publications: Brochures; Handbooks; Newsletters
Partic in Dialog Corp; Lyrasis
Open Mon-Thurs 7:30am-10pm (7:30am-9pm Summer), Fri 7:30-2, Sat 10-2, Sun 4-10

HAMMOND

C SOUTHEASTERN LOUISIANA UNIVERSITY*, Linus A Sims Memorial Library, SLU Box 10896, 1211 SGA Dr, 70402. SAN 306-4646. Tel: 985-549-3860. Circulation Tel: 985-549-3968. Interlibrary Loan Service Tel: 985-549-5318. Automation Services Tel: 985-549-3954. FAX: 985-549-3995. Interlibrary Loan Service FAX: 985-549-3490. Web Site: www.selu.edu/library. *Dir,* Eric Johnson; E-mail: ejohnson@selu.edu; *Asst Dir,* Lynette Ralph; E-mail: lynette.ralph@selu.edu; Staff 20 (MLS 19, Non-MLS 1)
Founded 1925. Enrl 15,662; Fac 715; Highest Degree: Master
Library Holdings: AV Mats 49,138; CDs 512; e-books 38,829; Bk Vols 376,894; Per Subs 2,381; Videos 5,920
Special Collections: State Document Depository; US Document Depository
Subject Interests: Genealogy
Automation Activity & Vendor Info: (Acquisitions) SirsiDynix; (Cataloging) SirsiDynix; (Circulation) SirsiDynix; (OPAC) SirsiDynix; (Serials) SirsiDynix
Partic in Lyrasis
Open Mon-Thurs 7:30am-11pm, Fri 7:30-4:30, Sat 9-4, Sun 2-11
Friends of the Library Group

HARRISONBURG

P CATAHOULA PARISH LIBRARY, 300 Bushley St, 71340. (Mail add: PO Box 218, 71340-0218), SAN 343-0324. Tel: 318-744-5271. FAX: 318-744-5251. E-mail: admin.h1ct@pelican.state.lib.la.us. *Dir,* Wayne Spence; E-mail: wspence@state.lib.la.us; *Mgr,* Shelly McLendon; Staff 4 (MLS 1, Non-MLS 3)
Founded 1949. Pop 11,992; Circ 91,688
Library Holdings: Bk Titles 38,792; Bk Vols 39,219; Per Subs 86
Special Collections: Catahoula Parish History Coll
Subject Interests: Genealogy
Automation Activity & Vendor Info: (Cataloging) Book Systems; (Circulation) Book Systems; (OPAC) Book Systems
Wireless access
Open Mon-Fri 8:30-4:30
Branches: 2
JONESVILLE BRANCH, 205 Pond St, Jonesville, 71343, SAN 343-0359. Tel: 318-339-7070. FAX: 318-339-7073. E-mail: jonesvillelibrary@gmail.com. *Br Mgr,* Amy Lavoie; Staff 2 (Non-MLS 2)

Library Holdings: Bk Vols 15,000; Per Subs 21
Open Mon-Fri 8-4:30
SICILY ISLAND BRANCH, PO Box 266, Sicily Island, 71368, SAN 343-0383. Tel: 318-389-5804. FAX: 318-389-5804. *Br Mgr,* Vicki Trisler; Staff 1 (MLS 1)
Library Holdings: Bk Vols 19,000; Per Subs 11
Open Mon-Wed 8-4:30
Bookmobiles: 1

HOMER

P CLAIBORNE PARISH LIBRARY*, 909 Edgewood Dr, 71040. SAN 343-0413. Tel: 318-927-3845. FAX: 318-927-2016. Web Site: www.youseemore.com/claiborne. *Dir,* Pamela Suggs; E-mail: psuggs@state.lib.la.us; Staff 15 (MLS 1, Non-MLS 14)
Founded 1951. Pop 17,095; Circ 89,809
Library Holdings: AV Mats 560; Bk Titles 50,000; Per Subs 250
Subject Interests: La
Automation Activity & Vendor Info: (Cataloging) TLC (The Library Corporation); (Circulation) TLC (The Library Corporation); (OPAC) TLC (The Library Corporation)
Open Mon & Wed-Fri 8-6, Tues 8-7, Sat 9-1
Friends of the Library Group
Branches: 1
JOE W WEBB MEMORIAL, 1919 Main St, Haynesville, 71038, SAN 343-0448. Tel: 318-624-0364. FAX: 318-624-2624. *Br Libn,* Sandra Bower; Staff 4 (MLS 1, Non-MLS 3)
Library Holdings: AV Mats 119; Bk Vols 16,883; Per Subs 76
Open Mon-Fri 8-12 & 1-4:45
Friends of the Library Group
Bookmobiles: 1

S DAVID WADE CORRECTIONAL CENTER*, Wade Library, 670 Bell Hill Rd, 71040. Tel: 318-927-0424, Ext 427. FAX: 318-927-0423, 318-927-0459. *Dir,* Jamie Fussell
Library Holdings: Bk Vols 10,056
Open Mon-Sun 8-10:30, 12:30-3:30 & 5:30-8

HOUMA

CM LOUISIANA STATE UNIVERSITY, MEDICAL CENTER HOSPITALS*, Leonard J Chabert Medical Center Library, Health Care Services Division, 1978 Industrial Blvd, 70363. Tel: 985-873-1257. FAX: 985-873-1219. Web Site: www.lsuhospitals.org/hospitals/ljc/default.htm. *Libr Spec II,* Amanda Voisin; E-mail: avoisi@lsuhsc.edu
Founded 1978
Library Holdings: Bk Vols 750; Per Subs 75
Restriction: Open to students, fac & staff

P TERREBONNE PARISH LIBRARY*, 151 Library Dr, 70360. SAN 343-0502. Tel: 985-876-5861. Administration Tel: 985-876-5158. Information Services Tel: 985-876-1733. FAX: 985-917-0582. Administration FAX: 985-876-5864. Web Site: www.mytpl.org. *Dir,* Mary Cosper LeBoeuf; E-mail: mcleboeuf@mytpl.org; *Asst Dir,* Tracy Guyan; E-mail: tguyan@mytpl.org; *Acq Librn,* Keisa Arceneaux; E-mail: karceneaux@mytpl.org; *Adult Serv, Commun Librn,* Jennifer Hamilton; E-mail: jhamilton@mytpl.org; *Br Mgr,* Gina Hebert; E-mail: ghebert@mytpl.org; *Pub Relations Coordr,* Rachel LeCompte; E-mail: rlecompte@mytpl.org; *Ref Supvr,* Mays Ross; E-mail: rmays@mytpl.org; Staff 18 (MLS 7, Non-MLS 11)
Founded 1939. Pop 111,917; Circ 436,882
Jan 2012-Dec 2012 Income (Main Library and Branch(s)) $6,124,539, County $5,971,372, Locally Generated Income $116,770, Other $36,397. Mats Exp $642,404, Books $322,155, Per/Ser (Incl. Access Fees) $37,636, AV Equip $86,756, AV Mat $117,824, Electronic Ref Mat (Incl. Access Fees) $78,023. Sal $1,964,947
Library Holdings: Audiobooks 14,019; DVDs 26,453; e-books 4,507; Bk Vols 292,566; Per Subs 990
Subject Interests: Petroleum
Automation Activity & Vendor Info: (Cataloging) TLC (The Library Corporation); (Circulation) TLC (The Library Corporation); (ILL) TLC (The Library Corporation); (Serials) TLC (The Library Corporation)
Database Vendor: EBSCOhost, Gale Cengage Learning, Haworth Pres Inc, LexisNexis, ProQuest, Westlaw
Wireless access
Friends of the Library Group
Branches: 7
BAYOU DULARGE, 837 Bayou Dularge Rd, 70363, SAN 375-460X. Tel: 985-851-1752. FAX: 985-851-0287. E-mail: dularge@mytpl.org. *Br Mgr,* Martha Guidry
Library Holdings: Bk Vols 15,483
Open Mon-Thurs 10-6, Fri 10-5
Friends of the Library Group
BOURG BRANCH, 4405 Saint Andrew St, Bourg, 70343-5431, SAN 343-0537. Tel: 985-594-4717. FAX: 985-594-8392. E-mail: bourg@mytpl.org. *Mgr,* Stephanie Mahaffey
Library Holdings: Bk Vols 15,689
Open Mon-Thurs 10-6, Fri 10-5
Friends of the Library Group
CHAUVIN BRANCH, 5500 Hwy 56, Chauvin, 70344, SAN 343-0596. Tel: 985-594-9771. FAX: 985-594-7506. E-mail: chauvin@mytpl.org. *Br Mgr,* Tina Freeman
Library Holdings: Bk Vols 16,771
Open Mon-Thurs 10-6, Fri 10-5
Friends of the Library Group
EAST HOUMA, 778 Grand Caillou Rd, 70363, SAN 343-0626. Tel: 985-876-7072. FAX: 985-876-9658. E-mail: easthouma@mytpl.org. *Br Mgr,* Rhonda Madison
Founded 1968
Library Holdings: Bk Vols 43,894
Open Mon-Thurs 9-9, Fri & Sat 9-6
Friends of the Library Group
GIBSON BRANCH, 6363 S Bayou Black Dr, Gibson, 70356, SAN 326-7512. Tel: 985-575-2639. FAX: 985-575-3069. E-mail: gibson@mytpl.org. *Br Mgr,* Charlotte Celestin
Library Holdings: Bk Vols 6,279
Open Mon-Thurs 10-6, Fri 10-5
Friends of the Library Group
MONTEGUT BRANCH, 1135 Hwy 55, Montegut, 70377, SAN 343-0650. Tel: 985-594-4390. FAX: 985-594-9512. E-mail: montegut@mytpl.org. *Br Mgr,* Margaret Ann Hebert
Library Holdings: Bk Vols 9,935
Open Mon-Thurs 10-6, Fri 10-5
Friends of the Library Group
NORTH TERREBONNE, 4130 W Park Ave, Gray, 70359. (Mail add: 151 Library Dr, 70360), SAN 343-0669. Tel: 985-868-3050. FAX: 985-868-9404. E-mail: north@mytpl.org. *Br Mgr,* Lisa Cotton; Fax: 985-868-3051, E-mail: lcotton@mytpl.org; Staff 1 (MLS 1)
Library Holdings: Bk Vols 43,885
Open Mon-Thurs 9-9, Fri & Sat 9-6, Sun 2-6
Friends of the Library Group

JACKSON

S DIXON CORRECTIONAL INSTITUTE*, Law Library, PO Box 788, 70748. Tel: 225-634-1200, Ext 213. FAX: 225-634-4400. *Dir,* Ivy Miller
Library Holdings: Bk Vols 3,600; Per Subs 10
Database Vendor: LexisNexis
Open Mon-Fri 7-5:30

EASTERN LOUISIANA MENTAL HEALTH SYSTEMS
M CHAPMAN MEMORIAL LIBRARY*, 4502 Hwy 951, 70748. (Mail add: PO Box 498, 70748-0498). Tel: 225-634-0560. FAX: 225-634-0188. E-mail: elmhs-library@la.gov. Web Site: www.dhh.louisiana.gov. *In Charge,* Ada Lord, E-mail: alord@dhh.la.gov
Library Holdings: Bk Vols 3,000
Partic in Docline
Open Mon-Fri 8-4:30
Restriction: Access at librarian's discretion
M MEDICAL LIBRARY*, 4502 Hwy 951, 70748. (Mail add: PO Box 498, 70748), SAN 373-9031. Tel: 225-634-0560.
Library Holdings: Bk Titles 157; Bk Vols 163; Per Subs 11
Subject Interests: Psychiat
Restriction: Staff use only

JENA

P LASALLE PARISH LIBRARY*, 3108 N First St, 71342. (Mail add: PO Box 3199, 71342-3199), SAN 343-0715. Tel: 318-992-5675. FAX: 318-992-7374, 318-992-7394. E-mail: admin.h1ls@state.lib.la.us. Web Site: www.lasalle.lib.la.us. *Dir,* Andrea Book; *Outreach Serv Librn,* Becky Davidson; *AV, Cat, Per,* Barbara Murphy; *Ch Serv, ILL & Distance Libr Serv Spec,* Donna Estis; *Circ,* Kristi Proffer; Staff 5 (Non-MLS 5)
Founded 1952. Pop 14,040
Library Holdings: AV Mats 5,436; Bks on Deafness & Sign Lang 57; Electronic Media & Resources 60; Large Print Bks 387; Bk Vols 59,175; Per Subs 109
Subject Interests: La
Automation Activity & Vendor Info: (Cataloging) Book Systems; (Circulation) Book Systems; (OPAC) Book Systems
Database Vendor: EBSCOhost, ProQuest
Wireless access
Function: Copy machines, Online searches, Preschool outreach
Partic in IAC Searchbank
Open Mon & Wed-Fri 8-5, Tues 8-7, Sat 9-1
Friends of the Library Group

Branches: 1
OLLA BRANCH, 1449 Blake St, Olla, 71465. (Mail add: PO Box 1417, Olla, 71465-1417), SAN 343-074X. Tel: 318-495-5570. FAX: 318-495-5593. *Br Mgr,* Kristie Proffer; E-mail: kproffer@state.lib.la.us; Staff 1 (Non-MLS 1)
Library Holdings: AV Mats 300; Bks on Deafness & Sign Lang 20; Per Subs 44
Open Mon-Fri 9-5
Friends of the Library Group
Bookmobiles: 1

JENNINGS

P JEFFERSON DAVIS PARISH LIBRARY*, 118 W Plaquemine St, 70546-5856. SAN 343-0774. Tel: 337-824-1210. FAX: 337-824-5444. Web Site: www.jefferson-davis.lib.la.us. *Dir,* Linda LeBert-Corbello, PhD; *Br Mgr,* Suzanne Young; Staff 15 (Non-MLS 15)
Founded 1968. Pop 32,000; Circ 101,878
Library Holdings: Electronic Media & Resources 760; Bk Vols 100,950; Per Subs 254; Talking Bks 2,317; Videos 2,064
Subject Interests: Indians, La
Automation Activity & Vendor Info: (Cataloging) SirsiDynix; (Circulation) SirsiDynix; (ILL) TLC (The Library Corporation); (OPAC) SirsiDynix
Publications: Christmas Cookbook
Partic in Libraries SouthWest
Open Mon-Fri 9-6, Sat 9-1
Branches: 4
ELTON BRANCH, 813 Main St, Elton, 70532, SAN 343-0804. Tel: 318-584-2640. FAX: 318-584-2236. *Mgr,* Kitty Marsh
Library Holdings: Bk Vols 9,034
Special Collections: Coushatta Indian Coll
Open Mon 9-6, Tues-Fri 11:30-6, Sat 9-12
JENNINGS HEADQUARTER BRANCH, 118 W Plaquemine, 70546-0356, SAN 322-5755. Tel: 318-824-1210. Toll Free Tel: 800-735-0746. FAX: 318-824-5444. *Br Mgr,* Susanne Young; Staff 1 (Non-MLS 1)
Founded 1968. Pop 31,435; Circ 68,878
Library Holdings: Bk Vols 23,564
Open Mon-Fri 9-6, Sat 9-1
LAKE ARTHUR BRANCH, 600 Fourth St, Lake Arthur, 70549, SAN 343-0839. Tel: 337-774-3661. FAX: 337-774-3657. *Br Mgr,* Deanna LeMarie
Library Holdings: Bk Vols 18,841
Open Mon & Wed-Fri 11:30-6, Tues 9-6, Sat 9-12
MCBURNEY MEMORIAL, 301 S Sarah St, Welsh, 70591, SAN 343-0863. Tel: 337-734-3262. FAX: 337-734-4540. *Mgr,* Denice Sonnier
Library Holdings: Bk Vols 15,577
Open Mon & Wed-Fri 11:30-6, Tues 9-6, Sat 9-12
Bookmobiles: 1. Bk Courier, Kathy LeJeune

P JENNINGS CARNEGIE PUBLIC LIBRARY*, 303 Cary Ave, 70546-5223. (Mail add: PO Box 1249, 70546-1249), SAN 306-4654. Tel: 337-821-5517. FAX: 337-821-5527. E-mail: jcpl303@yahoo.com. Web Site: www.cityofjennings.com/depts/library/index.htm. *Dir,* Harriet Shultz
Founded 1885. Pop 12,500; Circ 39,157
Library Holdings: Audiobooks 835; AV Mats 891; Large Print Bks 2,759; Bk Vols 54,664; Per Subs 64; Talking Bks 156; Videos 220
Automation Activity & Vendor Info: (Cataloging) Book Systems; (Circulation) Book Systems
Open Mon-Thurs 10-6, Fri & Sat 9-5

JONESBORO

P JACKSON PARISH LIBRARY*, 614 S Polk Ave, 71251-3442. SAN 306-4662. Tel: 318-259-5697, 318-259-5698. FAX: 318-259-8984. Web Site: www.jackson.lib.la.us, www.jacksonparishlibrary.org. *Dir,* Crystal Gates; E-mail: cgates@myjpl.org; *Outreach Serv Mgr,* Vickie Yates; *Libr Res Coordr,* Gail Faircloth; Staff 10 (MLS 2, Non-MLS 8)
Founded 1960. Pop 16,240; Circ 107,944
Library Holdings: AV Mats 580; Bk Vols 63,316; Per Subs 162
Special Collections: Jennifer Blake Coll
Subject Interests: La, Local hist
Automation Activity & Vendor Info: (Cataloging) TLC (The Library Corporation); (Circulation) TLC (The Library Corporation); (ILL) Auto-Graphics, Inc; (OPAC) TLC (The Library Corporation)
Database Vendor: Brodart, EBSCO - WebFeat, EBSCO Auto Repair Reference, EBSCOhost, Ingram Library Services, LearningExpress, OCLC WorldShare Interlibrary Loan, TLC (The Library Corporation), World Book Online, WT Cox
Wireless access
Function: Ref serv available
Open Mon & Wed 8-5:30, Tues & Thurs 8-7, Sat 8-12
Bookmobiles: 1. Bkmobile Mgr, Vickie Yates. Bk titles 10,204

KROTZ SPRINGS

P KROTZ SPRINGS MUNICIPAL PUBLIC LIBRARY*, 216 Park St, 70570. (Mail add: PO Box 218, 70750). Tel: 337-566-8190. FAX: 337-566-2233. *Dir,* Suzanne Belleau; *Librn,* Jo Anne Johnson
Founded 2008
Library Holdings: Bk Titles 2,726
Automation Activity & Vendor Info: (Cataloging) Book Systems; (Circulation) Book Systems
Open Mon-Fri 9-5

LAFAYETTE

P LAFAYETTE PUBLIC LIBRARY*, 301 W Congress, 70501-6866. (Mail add: PO Box 3427, 70502), SAN 306-4700. Tel: 337-261-5784. Interlibrary Loan Service Tel: 337-261-5757. Reference Tel: 337-261-5787. Administration Tel: 337-261-5781. FAX: 337-261-5782. E-mail: admin.b1lf@pelican.state.lib.la.us. Web Site: www.lafayette.lib.la.us. *Dir,* Sona J Dombourian; E-mail: sdombour@state.lib.la.us; *Adminr,* Teresa Elberson; E-mail: telberso@state.lib.la.us; *Librn IV,* Daniel Gillane; Tel: 337-261-5799, E-mail: dgillane@state.lib.la.us; *Info Serv Librn,* Rebecca Libersat; *Regional Br Mgr,* Peggy Thibodeaux; Tel: 337-896-6323, E-mail: pthibode@state.lib.la.us; *Ch Serv,* Katherine Mulloy; Tel: 337-261-5786, E-mail: kmulloy@state.lib.la.us; *ILL,* Janice Cring; *YA Serv,* Amy Wander; Tel: 337-261-5789; Staff 11 (MLS 11)
Founded 1946. Pop 172,193; Circ 1,017,698
Library Holdings: AV Mats 1,011; Bk Vols 337,627; Per Subs 501
Special Collections: Adult New Readers; Dolls; Genealogy Coll; Jobs Coll; Large Print; Louisiana Coll
Automation Activity & Vendor Info: (Cataloging) SirsiDynix; (Circulation) SirsiDynix; (OPAC) SirsiDynix; (Serials) SirsiDynix
Wireless access
Function: Homebound delivery serv
Mem of Bayouland Library System
Partic in Lyrasis
Open Mon-Thurs 8:30-6:30, Fri 8:30-6, Sat 10-4, Sun 1-5
Friends of the Library Group
Branches: 9
BROUSSARD BRANCH, 100 W Main St, Broussard, 70518, SAN 377-7235. Tel: 337-837-3936. *Librn,* Cheryl Dugas; Staff 3 (Non-MLS 3)
Library Holdings: Bk Vols 9,338; Per Subs 10
Open Mon 10-7, Tues-Fri 9-6
BUTLER MEMORIAL & MARTIN LUTHER KING CENTER, 309 Cora St, 70501, SAN 376-981X. Tel: 337-234-0363. *In Charge,* David Mingo; Staff 1 (Non-MLS 1)
Library Holdings: Bk Vols 1,394
Open Mon-Thurs 3-7, Fri 3-6
CHENIER CENTER, 220-B W Willow St, 70501. Tel: 337-291-2941. *In Charge,* Shirley Auzenne; Staff 2 (Non-MLS 2)
Library Holdings: Bk Vols 5,377; Per Subs 12
Open Mon-Thurs 9-7, Fri 9-6, Sat 11-3
DUSON BRANCH, 708 First St, Duson, 70529, SAN 376-9836. Tel: 337-873-3521. *In Charge,* Dominique Ducote; Staff 1 (Non-MLS 1)
Library Holdings: Bk Vols 6,995; Per Subs 11
Open Mon 10-2 & 3-7, Tues-Fri 8-12 & 1-5
MILTON BRANCH, Cedar Village Shopping Ctr, Hwy 92, Milton, 70558, SAN 376-7353. Tel: 337-856-5261. *In Charge,* Henrietta Schilling
Library Holdings: Bk Vols 10,145; Per Subs 23
Open Mon 10-7, Tues-Fri 8-5
NORTH REGIONAL BRANCH, 5101 N University Ave, Carencro, 70520-3004, SAN 376-9828. Tel: 337-896-6323. *Regional Br Mgr,* Margaret Thibodeaux; Staff 11 (MLS 3, Non-MLS 8)
Library Holdings: Bk Vols 10,926; Per Subs 11
Open Mon-Thurs 9-8, Fri 9-6, Sat 10-5, Sun 1-5
SCOTT BRANCH, 5808 W Cameron St, Scott, 70583, SAN 376-9844. Tel: 337-232-9321. *Librn,* Eloise Dotson; Staff 1 (Non-MLS 1)
Library Holdings: Bk Vols 8,331; Per Subs 16
Open Mon 10-7, Tues-Fri 9-6
SOUTH REGIONAL LIBRARY, 6101 Johnston St, 70503. Tel: 337-981-1028. *Regional Libr Mgr,* Theresa Roy; Staff 21 (MLS 6, Non-MLS 15)
Open Mon-Thurs 9-9, Fri 9-7, Sat 9-5, Sun 1-5
YOUNGSVILLE BRANCH, Twin Oaks Plaza, 506 Lafayette St, Hwy 89, Ste C, Youngsville, 70592, SAN 376-9852. Tel: 337-856-9385. *In Charge,* Katie Martin; Staff 1 (Non-MLS 1)
Library Holdings: Bk Vols 8,972; Per Subs 14
Open Mon 10-7, Tues-Fri 9-6

S LAFAYETTE SCIENCE MUSEUM*, Research Library, 433 Jefferson St, 70501-7013. SAN 374-941X. Tel: 337-291-5420. Administration Tel: 337-291-5544. FAX: 337-291-5464. Web Site: lafayettesciencemuseum.orglnhmp_homepage.html. *Coll Curator, Librn,* Dr Deborah J Clifton, PhD; Tel: 337-291-5415, E-mail: dclifton@lafayettela.gov; *Libr Assoc,* Edi Gilbert; E-mail:

egilbert@lafayettela.gov. Subject Specialists: *Children's lit*, Edi Gilbert; Staff 3 (MLS 1, Non-MLS 2)
Library Holdings: AV Mats 360; Bk Titles 4,000; Bk Vols 8,000; Spec Interest Per Sub 50
Special Collections: Archives; Rare Book Coll. Municipal Document Depository; Oral History
Subject Interests: Astronomy, Environ sci, Nat hist, Natural sci, Phys sci
Wireless access
Function: Ref & res
Restriction: Non-circulating coll, Open to pub by appt only, Open to researchers by request

L ONEBANE LAW FIRM APC*, Law Library, 1200 Camellia Blvd, Ste 300, 70508. SAN 372-0837. Tel: 337-237-2660. FAX: 337-266-1232. Web Site: www.onebane.com. *Librn*, Shelly LeBlanc; Tel: 337-237-2660, Ext 1152
Library Holdings: Bk Vols 13,000; Per Subs 60
Database Vendor: LexisNexis, Westlaw
Restriction: Staff use only

C REMINGTON COLLEGE LIBRARY*, 303 Rue Louis XIV, 70508. Tel: 337-981-4010. Reference Tel: 337-983-7111. FAX: 337-983-7130. Web Site: www.remingtoncollege.edu. *Dir*, Greg Melton; Staff 2 (Non-MLS 2)
Enrl 400; Fac 30
Library Holdings: AV Mats 300; Bk Vols 6,600; Per Subs 65; Talking Bks 10
Automation Activity & Vendor Info: (Cataloging) Book Systems; (Circulation) Book Systems
Open Mon-Thurs 7:30am-10pm, Fri 8-4

C UNIVERSITY OF LOUISIANA AT LAFAYETTE*, Edith Garland Dupre Library, 400 E St Mary Blvd, 70504. (Mail add: PO Box 40199, 70504-0199), SAN 343-0898. Tel: 337-482-6396. Circulation Tel: 337-482-6025. Interlibrary Loan Service Tel: 337-482-6035. Reference Tel: 337-482-6030. FAX: 337-482-6399. Interlibrary Loan Service FAX: 337-482-1176. Web Site: library.louisiana.edu. *Dean of Libr*, Dr Charles W Triche, III; E-mail: ctriche@louisiana.edu; *Assoc Dean*, Susan Marshall Richard; E-mail: smr@louisiana.edu; *Asst Dean, Pub Serv*, Betsy Miguez; Tel: 337-482-1173, Fax: 337-482-5841, E-mail: bbmiguez@louisiana.edu; *Asst Dean, Spec Coll*, Dr I Bruce Turner; Tel: 337-482-5702, Fax: 337-482-5841, E-mail: bturner@louisiana.edu; *Asst Dean, Tech, Web & IT Serv*, Barbara Flynn; Tel: 337-482-6041, Fax: 337-482-5841, E-mail: bjf1855@louisiana.edu; *Head, Cat*, Position Currently Open; *Head, Coll Develop*, Andrea Flockton; Tel: 337-482-6677, Fax: 337-482-5841, E-mail: aflockton@louisiana.edu; *Head, E-Res & Ser*, Allison Gallaspy; Tel: 337-482-6033, Fax: 337-482-5841, E-mail: agallaspy@louisiana.edu; *Head, Ref & Res Serv*, Cara Chance; Tel: 337-482-2948, Fax: 337-482-5841, E-mail: cara@louisiana.edu; *Head, Web & IT Serv*, Sheryl Moore Curry; Tel: 337-482-5704, Fax: 337-482-5841, E-mail: sherry@louisiana.edu; *Distance Learning & Virtual Serv Librn*, Emily Deal; Tel: 337-482-1171, Fax: 337-482-5841, E-mail: emily.deal@louisiana.edu; *Instrul Serv Librn*, Jeremiah Paschke-Wood; Tel: 337-482-1160, Fax: 337-482-5841, E-mail: jpaschkewood@louisiana.edu; *ILL*, Deborah Lazare Johnson; Tel: 337-482-6036, E-mail: djohnson@louisiana.edu; Staff 52 (MLS 17, Non-MLS 35)
Founded 1901. Enrl 15,693; Fac 826; Highest Degree: Doctorate
Jul 2012-Jun 2013 Income $1,160,000. Mats Exp $1,160,000, Per/Ser (Incl. Access Fees) $704,702, Electronic Ref Mat (Incl. Access Fees) $455,298. Sal $2,054,939 (Prof $1,098,554)
Library Holdings: AV Mats 16,799; CDs 3,174; DVDs 1,023; e-books 8,075; e-journals 31; Electronic Media & Resources 25; Microforms 1,356,128; Bk Titles 6,077,050; Bk Vols 1,038,056; Per Subs 1,836; Videos 1,902
Special Collections: Acadian & Creole Folklore; Cajun & Creole Music Coll; Louisiana History (Jefferson Caffery Louisiana Room); Regional Photographic Coll. Oral History
Automation Activity & Vendor Info: (Cataloging) SirsiDynix; (Circulation) SirsiDynix; (Course Reserve) SirsiDynix; (ILL) OCLC ILLiad; (OPAC) SirsiDynix; (Serials) SirsiDynix
Database Vendor: ABC-CLIO, ACM (Association for Computing Machinery), Agricola, American Chemical Society, American Mathematical Society, American Physical Society, ARTstor, Baker & Taylor, Blackwell, Bowker, Cinahl, CQ Press, EBSCO Discovery Service, EBSCOhost, Gale Cengage Learning, IEEE (Institute of Electrical & Electronics Engineers), IOP, ISI Web of Knowledge, JSTOR, LearningExpress, LexisNexis, Marcive, Inc, Medline, Modern Language Association, Newsbank-Readex, OCLC WorldShare Interlibrary Loan, OVID Technologies, Oxford Online, Project MUSE, ProQuest, ScienceDirect, SirsiDynix, UpToDate, WT Cox
Wireless access
Function: Res libr
Publications: Bayou State Periodical Index (Index to periodicals)
Partic in Lyrasis; The Louisiana Library Network
Special Services for the Deaf - ADA equip
Special Services for the Blind - Accessible computers; Audio mat; Bks on cassette; Bks on CD; Computer access aids
Open Mon-Thurs 7:30am-Midnight, Fri 7:30-4:30, Sat 10-5, Sun 2-11
Friends of the Library Group

G USGS NATIONAL WETLANDS RESEARCH CENTER*, USGS Lafayette Branch Library, 700 Cajundome Blvd, 70506-3152. SAN 373-6237. Tel: 337-266-8692. FAX: 337-266-8841. E-mail: nwrclibrary@usgs.gov. Web Site: www.nwrc.usgs.gov/library. *Lead Librn*, Linda Broussard; E-mail: broussardl@usgs.gov; Staff 1 (MLS 1)
Founded 1978
Library Holdings: Bk Titles 14,000; Per Subs 250
Special Collections: Wetlands Ecology & Limnology (Robert G Wetzel Coll); Wetlands Research (NWRC Main Coll)
Subject Interests: Animal ecology & habitat protection, Forested wetlands, Geospatial analysis, Limnology, Remote sensing, Statistical analysis, Wetland ecology, Wetland loss, Wetland plants
Automation Activity & Vendor Info: (Cataloging) OCLC Connexion; (Circulation) Cuadra Associates, Inc; (ILL) OCLC FirstSearch; (OPAC) Cuadra Associates, Inc
Function: Res libr
Partic in OCLC-LVIS
Open Mon-Fri 8-4
Restriction: Circulates for staff only, Pub use on premises

LAKE CHARLES

P CALCASIEU PARISH PUBLIC LIBRARY*, 301 W Claude St, 70605-3457. SAN 306-4727. Tel: 337-721-7147. FAX: 337-475-8806. Web Site: www.calcasieulibrary.org. *Dir*, Michael Sawyer; E-mail: msawyer@calcasieu.lib.la.us; *Dir, Human Res*, Angela Stutes; Tel: 337-721-7155, E-mail: astutes@calcasieu.lib.la.us; *Assoc Librn, Coll & Computing Serv*, Loretta Gharst; Tel: 337-721-7150, E-mail: lgharst@calcasieu.lib.la.us; *Assoc Librn, Pub Serv*, Pamela Edwards; Tel: 337-721-7149, E-mail: pam@calcasieu.lib.la.us; *Bus Mgr*, Peggy Dupuis; Tel: 337-721-7154, E-mail: peggyd@calcasieu.lib.la.us; *Fac Mgr*, David Comeaux; Tel: 337-721-7151, E-mail: dcomeaux@calcasieu.lib.la.us; *Pub Info Officer*, Judy Davidson; Tel: 337-721-7148, E-mail: judy@calcasieu.lib.la.us; Staff 155 (MLS 12, Non-MLS 143)
Founded 1944. Pop 192,768; Circ 1,061,485
Jan 2011-Dec 2011 Income (Main Library and Branch(s)) $8,480,098. Mats Exp $1,017,250, Books $575,668, Per/Ser (Incl. Access Fees) $48,000, Micro $5,582, AV Mat $250,000, Electronic Ref Mat (Incl. Access Fees) $138,000. Sal $3,621,150 (Prof $426,132)
Library Holdings: AV Mats 61,851; e-books 4,577; Large Print Bks 13,601; Microforms 4,477; Bk Vols 275,873; Per Subs 841
Subject Interests: Genealogy, Local hist
Automation Activity & Vendor Info: (Acquisitions) SirsiDynix; (Cataloging) SirsiDynix; (Circulation) SirsiDynix; (ILL) Auto-Graphics, Inc; (OPAC) SirsiDynix; (Serials) SirsiDynix
Database Vendor: Baker & Taylor, Career Guidance Foundation, EBSCO Auto Repair Reference, EBSCO Information Services, EBSCOhost, Gale Cengage Learning, Overdrive, Inc, ProQuest, SirsiDynix, TumbleBookLibrary, World Book Online
Wireless access
Publications: Staff Intranet (Online only)
Partic in Libraries SouthWest
Open Mon-Fri 8-5
Friends of the Library Group
Branches: 13
CARNEGIE MEMORIAL, 411 Pujo St, 70601-4254. Tel: 337-721-7084. FAX: 337-437-3480. *Br Mgr*, Guillory Verdine
Founded 1901. Pop 11,732; Circ 31,482
Library Holdings: AV Mats 1,866; Large Print Bks 354; Bk Vols 9,917; Per Subs 30
Open Mon-Fri 9-6
Friends of the Library Group
CENTRAL LIBRARY, 301 W Claude St, 70605. Tel: 337-721-7116. FAX: 337-475-8797. *Br Mgr*, Claire Coleman
Pop 71,993; Circ 403,648
Library Holdings: AV Mats 23,015; Large Print Bks 4,542; Bk Vols 90,072; Per Subs 250
Open Mon-Thurs 9-8, Fri 9-6, Sat 9-5, Sun 2-6
Friends of the Library Group
DEQUINCY BRANCH, 102 W Harrison St, DeQuincy, 70633, SAN 374-6925. Tel: 337-721-7087. FAX: 337-786-4213. *Br Mgr*, Janet Jordy
Pop 7,603; Circ 54,596
Library Holdings: AV Mats 3,260; Large Print Bks 1,107; Bk Vols 17,146; Per Subs 40
Open Mon-Fri 9-6
Friends of the Library Group
EPPS MEMORIAL, 1320 N Simmons St, 70601, SAN 374-6933. Tel: 337-721-7090. FAX: 337-433-0033. *Br Mgr*, Felicia Oliver
Pop 11,732; Circ 24,861
Library Holdings: AV Mats 2,269; Large Print Bks 388; Bk Vols 10,677; Per Subs 30

Open Mon-Thurs 9-8, Fri 9-6, Sat 9-5
Friends of the Library Group
FONTENOT MEMORIAL, 1402 Center St, Vinton, 70668, SAN 374-6941. Tel: 337-721-7095. FAX: 337-589-3336. *Br Mgr,* Theresa Watson
Pop 6,469; Circ 30,835
Library Holdings: AV Mats 1,624; Large Print Bks 378; Bk Vols 6,982; Per Subs 40
Open Mon-Fri 9-6
Friends of the Library Group
HAYES BRANCH, 7709 Perier St, Hayes, 70646, SAN 374-695X. Tel: 337-721-7098. FAX: 337-622-3605. *Br Mgr,* Angel Trahan
Pop 950; Circ 10,237
Library Holdings: AV Mats 975; Large Print Bks 259; Bk Vols 4,147; Per Subs 15
Open Mon-Fri 2-6
Friends of the Library Group
IOWA BRANCH, 107 First St, Iowa, 70647, SAN 374-6968. Tel: 337-721-7101. FAX: 337-582-3597. *Br Mgr,* Cornell Thomas
Pop 3,000; Circ 43,679
Library Holdings: AV Mats 3,157; Large Print Bks 944; Bk Vols 13,403; Per Subs 40
Open Mon-Fri 9-6
Friends of the Library Group
MAPLEWOOD, 91 Center Circle, Sulphur, 70663, SAN 374-6976. Tel: 337-721-7104. FAX: 337-625-5692. E-mail: mwd@calcasieu.lib.la.us. *Br Mgr,* Esther Pennington; E-mail: esther@calcasieu.lib.la.us
Pop 6,793; Circ 14,204
Library Holdings: AV Mats 1,353; Large Print Bks 346; Bk Vols 11,871; Per Subs 30
Open Mon-Fri 1-5
Friends of the Library Group
MOSS BLUFF, 261 Parish Rd, 70611, SAN 374-6909. Tel: 337-721-7128. FAX: 337-855-1827. E-mail: mb@calcasieu.lib.la.us. *Br Mgr,* Vicky Staton; E-mail: vicky@calcasieu.lib.la.us
Pop 11,557; Circ 129,045
Library Holdings: AV Mats 6,988; Large Print Bks 1,051; Bk Vols 27,490; Per Subs 80
Open Mon-Thurs 9-8, Fri 9-6, Sat 9-5
Friends of the Library Group
SOUTHWEST LOUISIANA GENEALOGICAL & HISTORICAL LIBRARY, 411 Pujo St, 70601-4254, SAN 374-700X. Tel: 337-721-7110. FAX: 337-437-3490. *Br Mgr,* Linda Gill; E-mail: lgill@calcasieu.lib.la.us
Library Holdings: AV Mats 4; Microforms 4,477; Bk Vols 8,358; Per Subs 11
Open Mon-Fri 9-6, Sat 9-5
STARKS BRANCH, 113 S Hwy 109, Starks, 70661-4362, SAN 374-6992. Tel: 337-721-7107. FAX: 337-743-6560. E-mail: st@calcasieu.lib.la.us. *Br Mgr,* Janet Jordy; E-mail: janet@calcasieu.lib.la.us
Pop 2,505; Circ 21,313
Library Holdings: AV Mats 1,491; Large Print Bks 634; Bk Vols 7,414; Per Subs 35
Open Mon, Tues, Thurs & Fri 2-6, Wed 9-6
Friends of the Library Group
SULPHUR REGIONAL, 1160 Cypress St, Sulphur, 70663, SAN 373-7365. Tel: 337-721-7141. FAX: 337-527-7200. E-mail: sul@calcasieu.lib.la.us. *Br Mgr,* Esther Pennington; E-mail: esther@calcasieu.lib.la.us
Pop 20,410; Circ 229,377
Library Holdings: AV Mats 12,528; Large Print Bks 2,516; Bk Vols 54,019; Per Subs 200
Open Mon-Thurs 9-8, Fri 9-6, Sat 9-5, Sun 2-6
Friends of the Library Group
WESTLAKE BRANCH, 937 Mulberry St, Westlake, 70669, SAN 374-7018. Tel: 337-721-7113. FAX: 337-437-3571. E-mail: wl@calcasieu.lib.la.us. *Br Mgr,* Kathy Jones; E-mail: kjones@calcasieu.lib.la.us
Pop 4,568; Circ 48,995
Library Holdings: AV Mats 3,203; Large Print Bks 968; Bk Vols 15,763; Per Subs 40
Open Mon-Fri 9-6
Friends of the Library Group

M LAKE CHARLES MEMORIAL HOSPITAL*, Walter O Moss Medical Library, 1701 Oak Park Blvd, 70601-3713. SAN 370-5161. Tel: 337-494-3127. FAX: 337-430-6966, 337-494-3231. Web Site: www.lcmh.com. *Dir,* Lezlie Fletcher
Founded 1980
Library Holdings: Bk Vols 780; Per Subs 125
Restriction: Not open to pub

C MCNEESE STATE UNIVERSITY*, Lether E Frazar Memorial Library, 4205 Ryan St, 70609. (Mail add: PO Box 91445, 70609), SAN 306-4735. Tel: 337-475-5716. Circulation Tel: 337-475-5723. Interlibrary Loan Service Tel: 337-475-5726. Reference Tel: 337-475-5725. Toll Free Tel: 800-622-3352. FAX: 337-475-5719, 337-475-5727. Web Site: www.library.mcneese.edu. *Asst Prof, Dir,* Debbie Delafoisse Johnson-Houston; E-mail: djohnsonhouston@mcneese.edu; *Acq Librn, Asst Prof,* Lonnie Beene; Tel: 337-475-5724, E-mail: lbeene@mcneese.edu; *Archives & Spec Coll Librn, Asst Prof,* Pati Threatt; Tel: 337-475-5731, E-mail: pthreatt@mcneese.edu; *Cat Librn, ILL Librn,* David Guillory; E-mail: dguilroy@mcneese.edu; *Asst Prof, Circ Librn,* Mary Jane Bloomquist; Tel: 337-475-5718, E-mail: mbloomquist@mcneese.edu; *Govt Info Librn,* Position Currently Open; *Asst Prof, Info Res Librn,* Jerome Marcantel; Tel: 337-475-5728, E-mail: jmarcantel@mcneese.edu; *Asst Prof, Ref Librn,* Walt Fontane; Tel: 337-475-5729, E-mail: wfontane@mcneese.edu; *Asst Prof, Res Librn,* Barbara Houssiere; Tel: 337-475-5732, E-mail: bhoussie@mcneese.edu; *Asst Prof, Res Librn,* Jessica Hutchings; Tel: 337-475-5546, E-mail: jhutchings@mcneese.edu; *Asst Prof, Syst Librn,* Michael Sartori; Tel: 337-475-5720, E-mail: msartori@mcneese.edu; Staff 18 (MLS 10, Non-MLS 8)
Founded 1939. Enrl 8,295; Fac 369; Highest Degree: Master
Library Holdings: e-books 112,202; e-journals 140,487; Microforms 269,482; Bk Vols 155,000; Per Subs 457
Special Collections: 20th Century American First Editions; Fore-Edge Paintings; Lake Charles, Southwestern Louisiana Archives. Oral History; State Document Depository; US Document Depository
Subject Interests: Educ
Automation Activity & Vendor Info: (Acquisitions) SirsiDynix; (Cataloging) SirsiDynix; (Circulation) SirsiDynix; (Course Reserve) SirsiDynix; (ILL) SirsiDynix; (Media Booking) SirsiDynix; (OPAC) SirsiDynix; (Serials) SirsiDynix
Database Vendor: EBSCOhost
Wireless access
Publications: Friends of the Library (Online only)
Partic in La Acad Libr Info Network Consortium; Libraries SouthWest; Lyrasis; The Louisiana Library Network
Friends of the Library Group
Departmental Libraries:
CURRICULUM MATERIALS CENTER, PO Box 91380, 70609, SAN 322-6271. Tel: 337-475-5410. FAX: 337-475-5398. *Admin Officer,* Marcella Miller; E-mail: mmiller@mcneese.edu
Founded 1970. Enrl 8,295; Fac 369
Library Holdings: Bk Vols 8,500
Special Collections: Curriculum Materials; Library Science
Restriction: Open to students, fac & staff

LAKE PROVIDENCE

P EAST CARROLL PARISH LIBRARY*, 109 Sparrow St, 71254-2645. SAN 306-4751. Tel: 318-559-2615. FAX: 318-559-4635. E-mail: t1ec@pelican.state.lib.la.us. Web Site: www.ecarroll.lib.la.us. *Dir,* Christina Engel; E-mail: cengel@state.lib.la.us; Staff 5 (MLS 1, Non-MLS 4)
Founded 1954. Pop 8,166; Circ 43,085
Library Holdings: AV Mats 3,151; Bk Vols 29,861; Per Subs 48
Special Collections: Caldecott Coll; Coretta S King Coll; Newbery Coll
Subject Interests: African-Am hist, Hist, La
Automation Activity & Vendor Info: (Cataloging) TLC (The Library Corporation); (Circulation) TLC (The Library Corporation); (ILL) Auto-Graphics, Inc; (OPAC) TLC (The Library Corporation)
Database Vendor: TumbleBookLibrary
Wireless access
Open Mon-Fri 8-5, Sat 8-12
Friends of the Library Group
Bookmobiles: 1

LAPLACE

P SAINT JOHN THE BAPTIST PARISH LIBRARY*, 2920 New Hwy 51, 70068. SAN 343-0952. Tel: 985-652-2225, 985-652-6857. FAX: 985-652-8005. Web Site: www.stjohn.lib.la.us. *Dir,* Randy A De Soto; *Asst Dir, Cat,* Kay D McKey; E-mail: kay.mckey@email.address; *Ch,* Margaret Carlson; E-mail: mcarlson@stjohn.lib.la.us; *ILL Librn,* Karen Tassin; E-mail: ktassin@email.address; *Circ Supvr,* Joan Paisant; E-mail: jpaisant@email.address; *Admin Serv Coordr,* Tammy Houston; E-mail: thouston@email.address; *Youth Serv Coordr,* Roberta Z August; E-mail: raugust@email.address; *Syst Adminr,* Edward L Sims; E-mail: your@email.address; Staff 39 (MLS 5, Non-MLS 34)
Founded 1966. Pop 46,393
Library Holdings: AV Mats 9,249; Bks on Deafness & Sign Lang 30; CDs 444; DVDs 63; Large Print Bks 5,669; Bk Vols 143,817; Per Subs 186; Videos 3,666
Special Collections: Parish History, photos
Subject Interests: Genealogy, La, Local hist
Automation Activity & Vendor Info: (Cataloging) Innovative Interfaces, Inc; (Circulation) Innovative Interfaces, Inc; (OPAC) Innovative Interfaces, Inc
Database Vendor: Innovative Interfaces, Inc
Open Mon-Thurs 9-9, Fri & Sat 9-5:30, Sun 1:30-5:30
Friends of the Library Group

Branches: 3
GARYVILLE BRANCH, 111 Historic Front St, Garyville, 70051. Tel: 985-535-6868. FAX: 985-535-6868. *Br Supvr,* Delores Anderson
Library Holdings: Bk Vols 9,255
Open Mon & Thurs 10-7, Tues, Wed & Fri 8:30-5:30
RESERVE BRANCH, 170 W Tenth St, Reserve, 70084, SAN 329-6202. Tel: 985-536-4107. FAX: 985-536-4116. *Br Supvr,* Gloria Smith
Library Holdings: Bk Vols 31,040
Open Mon & Thurs 8:30-12:30 & 1:30-8, Tues, Wed, Fri & Sat 8:30-12:30 & 1:30-5:30
WEST, 2979 Hwy 18, Edgard, 70049, SAN 343-0987. Tel: 985-497-3453. FAX: 985-497-3453. *Br Supvr,* Jennifer Pierre
Library Holdings: Bk Vols 14,684
Open Mon-Wed 8:30-12:30 & 1:30-7, Thurs & Fri 8:30-12:30 & 1:30-5, Sat 8:30-12:30
Friends of the Library Group

LEESVILLE

C NORTHWESTERN STATE UNIVERSITY LIBRARIES*, Leesville Library, 3329 University Pkwy, 71446. Tel: 337-392-3126. FAX: 337-392-3184. Web Site: library.nsula.edu/leesville-library. *Libr Assoc II,* Anna T MacDonald; E-mail: macdonalda@nsula.edu; *Libr Spec,* Linda West; E-mail: westl@nusla.edu
Library Holdings: AV Mats 989; Bk Titles 11,388; Bk Vols 12,652
Automation Activity & Vendor Info: (Cataloging) SirsiDynix; (Circulation) SirsiDynix; (OPAC) SirsiDynix
Wireless access
Open Mon-Thurs 7:30-5, Fri 8-Noon
Friends of the Library Group

P VERNON PARISH LIBRARY*, 1401 Nolan Trace, 71446. SAN 343-1010. Tel: 337-239-2027. Toll Free Tel: 800-737-2231. FAX: 337-238-0666. E-mail: w1vr@state.lib.la.us. Administration E-mail: admin.w1vr@pelican.state.lib.la.us. Web Site: www.vernon.lib.la.us. *Dir,* Howard L Coy, Jr; E-mail: hcoy@state.lib.la.us
Founded 1956. Pop 55,000; Circ 264,612
Library Holdings: CDs 873; DVDs 4,888; e-books 31,200; Bk Vols 92,460; Videos 4,952
Special Collections: Fishing Rods; Local History Archives; School Yearbooks. State Document Depository; US Document Depository
Subject Interests: Archives, Civil War, Genealogy, La, World War II
Automation Activity & Vendor Info: (Acquisitions) Baker & Taylor; (Cataloging) TLC (The Library Corporation); (Circulation) TLC (The Library Corporation); (ILL) TLC (The Library Corporation); (Serials) EBSCO Online
Database Vendor: EBSCO Auto Repair Reference, EBSCOhost, Gale Cengage Learning, LexisNexis, Overdrive, Inc, ProQuest, TumbleBookLibrary, World Book Online
Wireless access
Function: Online cat
Open Mon-Thurs 9-8, Fri & Sat 9-5:30
Branches: 2
PAUL LAWRENCE DUNBAR BRANCH, 1003 N Gladys, 71446. (Mail add: 1401 Nolan Trace, 71446), SAN 343-1045. Tel: 337-239-7037. *Br Mgr,* Betty Stokes
Founded 1956
Special Collections: Archives; Federals Depository; Genealogy Coll
Database Vendor: TLC (The Library Corporation)
Open Mon, Wed & Fri 3:30-7, Sat 1:30-6
PITKIN BRANCH, 7277 Hwy 463, Pitkin, 70656, SAN 370-1190. Tel: 318-358-3294. FAX: 318-358-3294. *Br Mgr,* Donna Strother
Open Mon 2-6, Wed 9-1, Fri 1-5, Sat 9-12
Friends of the Library Group
Bookmobiles: 1

LIVINGSTON

P LIVINGSTON PARISH LIBRARY*, 13986 Florida Blvd, 70754-6340. (Mail add: PO Box 397, 70754-0397), SAN 343-107X. Tel: 225-686-2436. FAX: 225-686-3888. Web Site: www.livingston.lib.la.us. *Dir,* Giovanni Tairov; *Asst Dir,* Jennifer Seneca; E-mail: jseneca@mylpl.info; Staff 8 (MLS 2, Non-MLS 6)
Founded 1946. Pop 87,311; Circ 281,195
Jan 2006-Dec 2006 Income (Main Library and Branch(s)) $2,422,000. Mats Exp $300,000. Sal $1,000,000
Library Holdings: AV Mats 780; Bk Titles 153,831; Per Subs 434
Automation Activity & Vendor Info: (Cataloging) TLC (The Library Corporation); (Circulation) TLC (The Library Corporation); (OPAC) TLC (The Library Corporation)
Wireless access
Publications: Free State
Open Mon & Wed 9-6, Tues & Thurs 9-8, Fri 9-5, Sat 9-3
Friends of the Library Group
Branches: 4
ALBANY SPRINGFIELD, 26941 Louisiana Hwy 43, Hammond, 70403. (Mail add: PO Box 1256, Albany, 70711), SAN 343-110X. Tel: 225-567-1441. FAX: 225-567-3768. *Br Mgr,* Connie Shipp; Staff 1 (Non-MLS 1)
Circ 12,705
Library Holdings: Bk Vols 40,000; Per Subs 30
Open Mon & Wed 9-6, Tues & Thurs 9-8, Fri 9-5, Sat 10-2
DENHAM SPRINGS - WALKER BRANCH, 8101 US Hwy 190, Denham Springs, 70726, SAN 343-1134. Tel: 225-665-8118. FAX: 225-791-6325. *Br Mgr,* Felecia Walker
Circ 136,261
Library Holdings: AV Mats 300; Bk Vols 55,000; Per Subs 75
Open Mon-Thurs 9-9, Fri & Sat 9-5, Sun 2-6
Friends of the Library Group
SOUTH, 23477 Louisiana Hwy 444, 70754. Tel: 225-698-3015. FAX: 225-686-9979. *Br Mgr,* Robb Webb
Library Holdings: Bk Vols 35,000; Per Subs 25
Open Mon & Wed 9-6, Tues & Thurs 9-8, Fri 9-5, Sat 9-1
WATSON BRANCH, 36581 Outback Rd, Denham Springs, 70706. Tel: 225-664-3963. FAX: 225-664-1949. *Br Mgr,* Layne Johnson; Staff 3 (MLS 1, Non-MLS 2)
Circ 36,848
Library Holdings: Bk Vols 50,000; Per Subs 60
Open Mon-Thurs 9-8, Fri & Sat 9-5

LUTCHER

P ST JAMES PARISH LIBRARY*, 1879 W Main St, 70071-5140. SAN 343-1525. Tel: 225-869-3618. FAX: 225-869-8435. Web Site: www.stjames.lib.la.us. *Libr Supvr-Popular Libr,* Margaret Simon; Staff 8 (Non-MLS 8)
Founded 1966. Pop 22,000; Circ 85,000
Library Holdings: AV Mats 1,323; Bk Vols 86,000; Per Subs 151
Special Collections: Louisiana Coll; St James File (parish hist)
Automation Activity & Vendor Info: (Cataloging) Horizon; (Circulation) Horizon; (OPAC) Horizon; (Serials) Horizon
Wireless access
Open Mon-Thurs 8:30-6, Fri 8:30-5, Sat 8:30-1
Branches: 1
VACHERIE LIBRARY, 2593 Hwy 20, Vacherie, 70090-5601. (Mail add: PO Box 190, Vacherie, 70090-0190), SAN 343-155X. Tel: 225-265-9066. FAX: 225-265-4691. *Libr Supvr-Popular Libr,* Margaret Simon; Staff 2 (Non-MLS 2)
Library Holdings: Bk Vols 21,000; Per Subs 62
Special Collections: Parish History (St James Parish File), bks, clippings, microflm, newsp
Open Mon-Thurs 8-5:30, Fri 8-4, Sat 8-12:30
Bookmobiles: 1

MANDEVILLE

M SOUTHEAST LOUISIANA HOSPITAL*, Resource Center, 23515 Hwy 190, 70470. (Mail add: PO Box 3850, 70470-3850), SAN 324-5535. Tel: 985-626-6596. FAX: 985-626-6424. *Librn,* Alison Dillmann; E-mail: alison.dillmann@la.gov; Staff 2 (MLS 1, Non-MLS 1)
Library Holdings: Bk Titles 2,000; Per Subs 20
Subject Interests: Mental health
Database Vendor: Dialog
Partic in Docline
Open Mon-Fri 8-4:30
Restriction: Staff use only

MANSFIELD

P DESOTO PARISH LIBRARY, 109 Crosby St, 71052. SAN 321-7485. Tel: 318-872-6100. FAX: 318-872-6120. *Dir,* Linn Landis; *Asst Dir, Syst Adminr,* William Smith; E-mail: bsmith@state.lib.la.us; *Adult Serv Coordr, Outreach Librn,* Delbert Terry; E-mail: dterry@state.lib.la.us; *Chief Cataloger, Mgr,* Doris Ross; E-mail: dross@state.lib.la.us; *Ch Serv,* Darron Spencer; E-mail: dspencer@state.lib.la.us; Staff 5 (MLS 2, Non-MLS 3)
Founded 1941. Pop 27,083
Special Collections: Louisiana History
Subject Interests: Civil War, World War I, World War II
Automation Activity & Vendor Info: (Acquisitions) SirsiDynix; (Cataloging) SirsiDynix; (Circulation) SirsiDynix; (OPAC) SirsiDynix
Publications: Informational Brochure
Open Mon-Thurs 9-6, Fri 9-5, Sat 9-1
Friends of the Library Group
Branches: 3
LOGANSPORT BRANCH, 203 Hwy 5, Logansport, 71049. (Mail add: PO Box 970, Logansport, 71049-0970), SAN 321-7493. Tel: 318-697-2311. FAX: 318-697-4081. *Br Mgr,* Linda Foreman; *Ch Serv,* Terri Hawsey; E-mail: thawsey@state.lib.la.us; *Libr Assoc,* Patricia Murray; E-mail: pmurray@state.lib.la.us; *Libr Assoc,* Angela Toney; E-mail:

atoney@state.lib.la.us; *Libr Assoc,* Josh Wolf; E-mail: jwolf@state.lib.la.us; Staff 5 (Non-MLS 5)
Library Holdings: Bk Vols 20,900
Subject Interests: Local hist
Open Mon-Thurs 9-6, Fri 9-5, Sat 9-1
Friends of the Library Group

PELICAN BRANCH, 145 Jackson Ave, Pelican, 71063-2803. (Mail add: PO Box 109, Pelican, 71063-0109), SAN 324-2501. Tel: 318-755-2353. FAX: 318-755-2031. *Mgr,* Sarah Crump; E-mail: sabraham@state.lib.la.us; *Ch Serv,* Kriston Newsom; E-mail: knewsom@state.lib.la.us; *Libr Assoc,* Carol Crump; E-mail: ccrump@state.lib.la.us; *Libr Assoc,* Barbara Jones; E-mail: bjones@state.lib.la.us; Staff 4 (Non-MLS 4)
Open Mon 9-6, Tues-Fri 9-5, Sat 9-1
Friends of the Library Group

STONEWALL BRANCH, 808 Hwy 171, Stonewall, 71078, SAN 321-7507. Tel: 318-925-9191. FAX: 318-925-3392. *Br Mgr,* Tammy Overton; *Ch Serv,* Delores Cole; E-mail: dcole@state.lib.la.us; *Libr Assoc,* Sharon Bogan; Fax: 318-915-1694, E-mail: sbogan@state.lib.la.us; *Libr Assoc,* Robert Gullion; E-mail: rgullion@state.lib.la.us; *Libr Assoc,* Nell Holder; E-mail: nholder@state.lib.la.us; *Libr Assoc,* Carol Tolliver; E-mail: ktolliver@state.lib.la.us; Staff 6 (Non-MLS 6)
Open Mon 9-6, Tues-Fri 9-5, Sat 9-1
Friends of the Library Group

MANY

P SABINE PARISH LIBRARY, 705 Main St, 71449-3199. SAN 343-1649. Tel: 318-256-4150. FAX: 318-256-4154. Web Site: www.sabine.lib.la.us. *Dir,* Deborah Anderson; Staff 4 (MLS 1, Non-MLS 3)
Founded 1933. Pop 23,460; Circ 123,956
Library Holdings: AV Mats 4,048; Bk Vols 63,527; Per Subs 249
Special Collections: Sabine Parish History Coll
Automation Activity & Vendor Info: (Cataloging) TLC (The Library Corporation); (Circulation) TLC (The Library Corporation); (OPAC) TLC (The Library Corporation)
Database Vendor: TLC (The Library Corporation)
Wireless access
Mem of Green Gold Library System
Partic in SOQUIJ
Open Mon & Tues 8-6, Wed-Fri 8-5, Sat 8-Noon
Branches: 4

CONVERSE BRANCH, 400 Wildcat Dr, Converse, 71419. (Mail add: PO Box 69, Converse, 71419), SAN 343-1673. Tel: 318-567-3121. *Br Mgr,* Jerri Walker
Open Mon & Thurs 12-5

PLEASANT HILL BRANCH, 8434 Bridges St, Pleasant Hill, 71065. (Mail add: PO Box 277, Pleasant Hill, 71065-0277), SAN 343-1851. Tel: 318-796-2595. *Br Mgr,* Renee Layton
Open Mon & Thurs 12-5

TOLEDO BRANCH, 12350 Texas Hwy, 71449, SAN 328-7378. Tel: 318-256-4152. *Br Mgr,* Betty Fields
Open Mon-Thurs 12-5

ZWOLLE BRANCH, 2218 Port Arthur St, Zwolle, 71486. (Mail add: PO Box 536, Zwolle, 71486), SAN 343-1886. Tel: 318-645-6955. *Br Mgr,* Erma Jean Martinez
Open Mon-Wed 11-5, Thurs & Fri 12-5

MARKSVILLE

P AVOYELLES PARISH LIBRARY*, Marksville Branch, 104 N Washington St, 71351-2496. SAN 343-1916. Tel: 318-253-7559. FAX: 318-253-6361. Web Site: www.avoyelles.lib.la.us. *Dir,* Theresa Thevenote; E-mail: ttheveno@pelican.state.lib.la.us; *Assoc Librn,* Susan Guidry; E-mail: sguidry2@pelican.state.lib.la.us; Staff 5 (Non-MLS 5)
Founded 1949. Pop 40,801; Circ 95,608
Library Holdings: AV Mats 356; Bk Vols 79,860; Per Subs 200
Special Collections: Louisiana Room
Automation Activity & Vendor Info: (Cataloging) Book Systems; (Circulation) Book Systems; (ILL) Book Systems; (OPAC) Book Systems
Database Vendor: Bowker, EBSCOhost, Facts on File, Newsbank, World Book Online
Partic in The Louisiana Library Network
Open Mon, Tues, Thurs & Fri 8-5, Wed 9-6, Sat 9-1
Friends of the Library Group
Branches: 6

BUNKIE BRANCH, 107 W Oak St, Bunkie, 71322-1782. (Mail add: PO Box 80, Bunkie, 71322-0080), SAN 343-1940. Tel: 318-346-6122. FAX: 318-346-4301. E-mail: bunkie.h1av@pelican.state.lib.la.us. *Br Mgr,* Betty Williams; Staff 2 (Non-MLS 2)
Open Mon, Tues, Thurs & Fri 8-5, Wed 9-6, Sat 9-1

COTTONPORT BRANCH, 209 Cottonport Ave, Cottonport, 71327, SAN 343-1975. Tel: 318-876-3411. FAX: 318-876-2404. E-mail: cottonport.h1av@pelican.state.lib.la.us. *Br Mgr,* Karen Gisclair
Open Mon, Tues, Thurs & Fri 7:30-4, Wed 9:30-6, Sat 9-1

MOREAUVILLE BRANCH, Community Ctr, Tassin St, Moreauville, 71355. (Mail add: PO Box 130, Moreauville, 71355-0130), SAN 343-2092. Tel: 318-985-2767. E-mail: moreauville.h1av@pelican.state.lib.la.us. *Br Mgr,* Carol Couvillion
Library Holdings: Bk Vols 4,604; Per Subs 33
Open Tues 10-5, Fri 10-3

OUTREACH, 2111 Cleco Rd, Mansura, 71350. (Mail add: PO Box 448, Mansura, 71350-0448). Tel: 318-964-2118. FAX: 318-964-5701. *Br Mgr,* Annette Rabalais; Staff 2 (Non-MLS 2)
Library Holdings: AV Mats 54; Bk Vols 1,112; Per Subs 20
Open Mon-Fri 8:30-5

PLAUCHEVILLE BRANCH, Town Hall, Gin St, Plaucheville, 71362. (Mail add: PO Box 27, Plaucheville, 71362-0027), SAN 343-2122. Tel: 318-359-1016. E-mail: plaucheville.h1av@pelican.state.lib.la.us. *Br Mgr,* Roxanna Honea; Staff 2 (Non-MLS 2)
Library Holdings: AV Mats 91; Bk Vols 4,033; Per Subs 23
Open Tues 8-1 & 3-5, Fri 8-1

SIMMESPORT BRANCH, 461 Main St, Simmesport, 71369. (Mail add: PO Box 155, Simmesport, 71369-0155), SAN 343-2157. Tel: 318-941-2822. FAX: 318-941-5880. E-mail: simmesport.h1av@pelican.state.lib.la.us. *Br Mgr,* Merion Rabalais; Staff 2 (Non-MLS 2)
Open Mon, Tues, Thurs & Fri 8-5, Wed 9-6, Sat 9-1
Friends of the Library Group

METAIRIE

P JEFFERSON PARISH LIBRARY*, East Bank Regional Library, 4747 W Napoleon Ave, 70001. SAN 343-2181. Tel: 504-838-1190. Interlibrary Loan Service Tel: 504-838-1114. Reference Tel: 504-838-1111. Administration Tel: 504-838-1100. Automation Services Tel: 504-838-1101. FAX: 504-838-1117. Interlibrary Loan Service FAX: 504-838-1121. Reference FAX: 504-849-8800; 504-457-4659. Administration FAX: 504-838-1110. Automation Services FAX: 504-457-0198. Web Site: www.jefferson.lib.la.us. *Dir,* Marylyn Haddican; Tel: 504-838-1133, E-mail: mhaddican@jefferson.lib.la.us
Founded 1949. Pop 436,181
Library Holdings: Bk Titles 307,991
Subject Interests: Genealogy
Wireless access
Open Mon-Thurs 9-9, Fri & Sat 9-5, Sun 1-5
Friends of the Library Group
Branches: 14

BELLE TERRE, 5550 Belle Terre Rd, Marrero, 70072, SAN 343-219X. Tel: 504-349-5910. FAX: 504-349-5914. *Br Mgr, Librn II,* Thomas Giroir
Open Mon-Wed 11-7, Thurs-Sat 10-6
Friends of the Library Group

JANE O'BRIEN CHATELAIN WEST BANK REGIONAL, 2751 Manhattan Blvd, Harvey, 70058, SAN 370-9493. Tel: 504-364-2660. Reference Tel: 504-364-3720. FAX: 540-364-3739. *Br Mgr,* Position Currently Open
Founded 1990
Open Mon-Thurs 9-9, Fri & Sat 9-5, Sun 1-5
Friends of the Library Group

GRAND ISLE BRANCH, 2757 La Hwy 1, Grand Isle, 70358-9727, SAN 343-2211. Tel: 985-787-3450. FAX: 985-787-2715. *Br Mgr,* Tim Kirby
Open Tues & Wed 10-6, Fri & Sat 10-4
Friends of the Library Group

GRETNA BRANCH, 102 Willow Dr, Gretna, 70053, SAN 343-2246. Tel: 504-364-2716. FAX: 504-364-2710. *Br Mgr,* William McKee
Open Mon, Wed, Thurs & Sat 10-6
Friends of the Library Group

HARAHAN BRANCH, 219 Soniat Ave, Harahan, 70123, SAN 343-2270. Tel: 504-736-8745. FAX: 504-736-8746. *Br Mgr,* Janet Perry
Open Mon, Wed, Thurs & Sat 10-6
Friends of the Library Group

LAFITTE BRANCH, 4917 City Park Dr, Ste B, Lafitte, 70067, SAN 343-236X. Tel: 504-689-5097. FAX: 504-689-3354. *Br Mgr, Librn II,* Steven Hammel
Founded 1982
Open Mon-Wed & Sat 10-6
Friends of the Library Group

LAKESHORE, 1100 W Esplanade, 70005, SAN 376-9429. Tel: 504-838-4375. FAX: 504-838-4379. *Br Mgr,* Alison Williams
Open Tues-Sat 10-6
Friends of the Library Group

EDITH S LAWSON LIBRARY (WESTWEGO BRANCH), 635 Fourth St, Westwego, 70094, SAN 343-2513. Tel: 504-349-5912. FAX: 504-349-5920. *Br Mgr,* Daniel Cangelosi
Open Mon-Sat 10-6
Friends of the Library Group

LIVE OAK, 125 Acadia Dr, Waggaman, 70094, SAN 329-6644. Tel: 504-736-8475. FAX: 504-431-0653. *Br Mgr,* Eric Krieger
Founded 1989

Open Mon-Thurs 11-7
Friends of the Library Group
NORTH KENNER, 630 W Esplanade Ave, Kenner, 70065, SAN 343-2335. Tel: 504-736-8730. FAX: 504-736-8732. *Br Mgr,* Allison Williams
Open Mon-Thurs 9-9, Fri & Sat 9-5, Sun 1-5
Friends of the Library Group
OLD METAIRIE, 2350 Metairie Rd, 70001, SAN 343-2424. Tel: 504-838-4353. FAX: 504-838-1014. *Br Mgr,* Suzanne Upshaw
Open Mon-Wed 9-8, Thurs-Sat 10-6, Sun 1-5
Friends of the Library Group
ROSEDALE, 4036 Jefferson Hwy, Jefferson, 70121, SAN 329-3173. Tel: 504-838-4350. FAX: 504-838-1129. *Br Mgr,* Gwen Kelley
Open Mon-Sat 10-6
Friends of the Library Group
TERRYTOWN BRANCH, 680 Heritage Ave, Terrytown, 70056, SAN 343-2459. Tel: 504-364-2717. FAX: 504-364-2718. *Br Mgr,* Smith Nathan
Open Mon-Sat 10-6
Friends of the Library Group
CHARLES A WAGNER BRANCH, 6646 Riverside Dr, 70003, SAN 343-2483. Tel: 504-838-1193. *Br Mgr,* Joanna Sufic
Founded 1963
Open Mon-Wed & Fri-Sat 10-6
Friends of the Library Group

MINDEN

P WEBSTER PARISH LIBRARY*, 521 East & West St, 71055. SAN 343-2548. Tel: 318-371-3080. FAX: 318-371-3081. Administration E-mail: admin.g1wb@pelican.state.lib.la.us. Web Site: www.webster.lib.la.us. *Dir,* Beverly Hammett; E-mail: bhammett@state.lib.la.us; Staff 4 (MLS 3, Non-MLS 1)
Founded 1929. Pop 41,456; Circ 165,862
Library Holdings: Bk Vols 85,058; Per Subs 203
Subject Interests: La
Automation Activity & Vendor Info: (Acquisitions) Innovative Interfaces, Inc; (Cataloging) Innovative Interfaces, Inc; (Circulation) Innovative Interfaces, Inc; (Course Reserve) Innovative Interfaces, Inc; (ILL) Innovative Interfaces, Inc; (OPAC) Innovative Interfaces, Inc; (Serials) Innovative Interfaces, Inc
Wireless access
Function: Art exhibits, Audio & video playback equip for onsite use, CD-ROM, Handicapped accessible, Home delivery & serv to Sr ctr & nursing homes, Homebound delivery serv, ILL available, Music CDs, Online searches, Outside serv via phone, mail, e-mail & web, Photocopying/Printing, Prog for adults, Prog for children & young adult, Serves mentally handicapped consumers, Spoken cassettes & CDs, Summer reading prog, Telephone ref, VCDs, VHS videos, Wheelchair accessible
Special Services for the Deaf - Spec interest per
Open Mon-Thurs 8:15-8, Fri & Sat 8:15-5
Branches: 6
COTTON VALLEY BRANCH, 256 Main St, Cotton Valley, 71018, SAN 343-2572. Tel: 318-832-4290. FAX: 318-832-5335. E-mail: cottonvalley.g1wb@pelican.state.lib.la.us. *Br Mgr,* Nancy Windham
Library Holdings: Bk Vols 6,032
Open Mon-Fri 1-5
DOYLINE BRANCH, 333 Main St, Doyline, 71023. (Mail add: PO Box 8, Doyline, 71023-0008), SAN 343-2637. Tel: 318-745-3800. FAX: 318-745-2170. E-mail: doyline.g1wb@pelican.state.lib.la.us. *Br Mgr,* Joyce Cook
Library Holdings: Bk Vols 6,446
Open Mon, Tues, Thurs & Fri 2-5, Sat 9-12
HEFLIN BRANCH, 7041 Hwy 531, Heflin, 71039. (Mail add: PO Box 177, Heflin, 71039-0177), SAN 343-2661. Tel: 318-371-1027. FAX: 318-382-9613. E-mail: heflin.g1wb@pelican.state.lib.la.us. *Br Mgr,* Edna Coleman
Library Holdings: Bk Vols 3,720
Open Mon, Wed & Fri 2-5
MINDEN MAIN, 521 East & West St, 71055, SAN 343-2726. Tel: 318-371-3080. FAX: 318-371-3081. *Br Mgr,* Shelia Phenix
Library Holdings: Bk Vols 36,686
Open Mon-Thurs 8:15-8, Fri & Sat 8:15-5
SAREPTA BRANCH, 24522 Hwy 371, Sarepta, 71071. (Mail add: PO Box 127, Sarepta, 71071-0127). Tel: 318-847-4992. FAX: 318-847-4826. E-mail: sarepta.g1wb@pelican.state.lib.la.us. *Br Mgr,* Renee Andrews McCluskey
Library Holdings: Bk Vols 4,855
Open Mon, Wed & Fri 2-5
SPRINGHILL BRANCH, 217 N Main, Springhill, 71075, SAN 343-2815. Tel: 318-539-4117. FAX: 318-539-3718. E-mail: springhill.g1wb@pelican.state.lib.la.us. *Br Mgr,* Kathy Miller
Library Holdings: Bk Vols 21,036
Open Mon, Tues & Thurs 8:15-8, Wed & Fri 8:15-5, Sat 8:15-12

MONROE

M LSU HEALTH SCIENCES CENTER, E A Conway Medical Center Library, 4864 Jackson St, 71202. (Mail add: PO Box 1881, 71210-8005), SAN 306-4778. Tel: 318-330-7644. FAX: 318-330-7649. E-mail: eac-library@lsuhsc.edu. Web Site: www.lsuhscshreveport.edu/ConwayMedicalLibrary/ConwayMedicalLibraryHome.aspx. *Dir, Libr Serv,* Lesley Arnott; Staff 1 (MLS 1)
Library Holdings: e-journals 500; Bk Vols 612; Per Subs 200
Subject Interests: Clinical med
Database Vendor: DynaMed, Elsevier, OVID Technologies, PubMed
Open Mon-Fri 8-4:30

P OUACHITA PARISH PUBLIC LIBRARY*, 1800 Stubbs Ave, 71201. SAN 343-284X. Tel: 318-327-1490. FAX: 318-327-1373. Web Site: www.oplib.org. *Libr Dir,* Robin Toms; E-mail: rtoms@oplib.org; *Asst Dir,* Gloria Reeves; E-mail: greeves@oplib.org; *Head, Automation,* Eileen R Kontrovitz; E-mail: eileenk@oplib.org; *Head, Genealogy/Spec Coll,* Larry Foreman; E-mail: lforeman@oplib.org; *Head, Tech Serv,* Aleta Copeland; E-mail: acopeland@oplib.org; *Br Mgr, Main Libr,* Julie Crump; E-mail: jcrump@oplib.org; *Bus Mgr,* Marilyn Binford; E-mail: mbinford@oplib.org; *Children's Coordr,* LaKeisha Bosworth; E-mail: lbosworth@oplib.org; *Young Adult Serv Coordr,* Stephanie Wilkes; Staff 120 (MLS 8, Non-MLS 112)
Founded 1940. Pop 147,898; Circ 834,964
Library Holdings: Audiobooks 16,469; AV Mats 69,854; Bks on Deafness & Sign Lang 253; CDs 7,775; DVDs 16,635; e-books 4,961; Large Print Bks 19,902; Bk Vols 377,139; Per Subs 1,209; Videos 19,376
Special Collections: Genealogy, bks, microflm, microfiche, clippings, photog, original source mat. Oral History; State Document Depository
Subject Interests: La
Automation Activity & Vendor Info: (Acquisitions) Innovative Interfaces, Inc; (Cataloging) Innovative Interfaces, Inc; (Circulation) Innovative Interfaces, Inc; (Serials) Innovative Interfaces, Inc
Wireless access
Function: After school storytime, Archival coll, Copy machines, Digital talking bks, Handicapped accessible, Home delivery & serv to Sr ctr & nursing homes, Homework prog, ILL available, Music CDs, Online searches, Preschool outreach, Prog for adults, Prog for children & young adult, Spoken cassettes & CDs, Summer reading prog, Video lending libr
Open Mon-Thurs (Winter) 9-9, Fri 9-6, Sat 9-5, Sun 2-5; Mon-Thurs (Summer) 9-8, Fri 9-5, Sat 10-2, Sun 2-5
Friends of the Library Group
Branches: 9
OLLIE BURNS BRANCH, 5601 Hwy 165 S, Richwood, 71202. Tel: 318-327-1235. FAX: 318-329-8255. *Br Mgr,* Robert Tanzy
Library Holdings: CDs 600; DVDs 500; Bk Vols 15,000; Per Subs 87; Talking Bks 500; Videos 100
Open Mon-Thurs 9-8, Fri 9-6, Sat 9-5
Friends of the Library Group
CARVER MCDONALD BRANCH, 2941 Renwick St, 71201, SAN 343-2874. Tel: 318-327-1477. FAX: 318-329-4061. *Br Mgr,* Nora Collins; Staff 7 (Non-MLS 7)
Library Holdings: AV Mats 3,824; CDs 405; DVDs 846; Large Print Bks 110; Bk Titles 29,993; Bk Vols 30,634; Per Subs 110; Talking Bks 412; Videos 1,574
Open Mon-Fri (Winter) 9-6, Sat 9-5; Mon-Thurs (Summer) 9-6, Fri 9-5, Sat 10-2
Friends of the Library Group
ANNA MEYER BRANCH, 1808 Hwy 165 S, 71202, SAN 343-2904. Tel: 318-327-1351. FAX: 318-329-4059. *Br Mgr,* Terrie Wright; E-mail: twright@oplib.org; Staff 11 (Non-MLS 11)
Library Holdings: AV Mats 2,682; CDs 522; DVDs 753; Large Print Bks 465; Bk Titles 26,850; Bk Vols 28,231; Per Subs 42; Talking Bks 512; Videos 1,491
Open Mon-Thurs (Winter) 9-8, Fri 9-6, Sat 9-5; Mon & Thurs (Summer) 9-8, Tues & Wed 9-6, Fri 9-5, Sat 10-2
Friends of the Library Group
OUACHITA VALLEY BRANCH, 581 McMillian Rd, West Monroe, 71294, SAN 343-2939. Tel: 318-327-1471. FAX: 318-327-1473. *Br Mgr,* Chely Cantrell; Staff 19 (Non-MLS 19)
Library Holdings: AV Mats 12,404; CDs 1,072; DVDs 1,516; Large Print Bks 5,218; Bk Vols 79,213; Per Subs 125; Talking Bks 4,197; Videos 4,981
Open Mon-Thurs (Winter) 9-8, Fri 9-6, Sat 9-5, Sun 2-5; Mon-Thurs (Summer) 9-8, Fri 9-5, Sat 10-2, Sun 2-5
Friends of the Library Group
CPL J R SEARCY MEMORIAL LIBRARY, 5775 Jonesboro Rd, West Monroe, 71292. Tel: 318-327-1240. FAX: 318-323-1565. *Br Mgr,* Kayla Hebert
Library Holdings: CDs 327; DVDs 2,007; Bk Vols 9,896; Per Subs 76; Talking Bks 690
Open Mon-Thurs 9-8, Fri 9-6, Sat 9-5
Friends of the Library Group

STERLINGTON MEMORIAL BRANCH, 305 Keystone Rd, 71203. Tel: 318-327-1382. FAX: 318-665-9476. *Br Mgr,* Holly Priestley
Library Holdings: CDs 700; DVDs 2,600; Bk Vols 15,550; Per Subs 85; Talking Bks 1,450; Videos 450
Open Mon-Thurs 9-8, Fri 9-6, Sat 9-5
Friends of the Library Group

WEST MONROE BRANCH, 315 Cypress, West Monroe, 71291, SAN 343-2963. Tel: 318-327-1365. FAX: 318-329-4062. *Br Mgr,* Barbara Dunn; Staff 2 (Non-MLS 2)
Library Holdings: AV Mats 4,332; CDs 332; DVDs 696; Large Print Bks 2,583; Bk Vols 52,622; Per Subs 89; Talking Bks 653; Videos 2,082
Open Mon-Fri (Winter) 9-6, Sat 9-5; Mon-Thurs (Summer) 9-6, Fri 9-5, Sat 10-2
Friends of the Library Group

WEST OUACHITA BRANCH, 188 Hwy 546, West Monroe, 71291. Tel: 318-397-5414. FAX: 318-397-8659. *Br Mgr,* Nancy Green; Staff 9 (MLS 1, Non-MLS 8)
Library Holdings: AV Mats 5,613; CDs 638; DVDs 1,158; Large Print Bks 1,535; Bk Vols 28,778; Per Subs 42; Talking Bks 1,388; Videos 2,718
Open Mon-Thurs (Winter) 9-8, Fri 9-6, Sat 9-5; Mon & Thurs (Summer) 9-8, Tues & Wed 9-6, Fri 9-5, Sat 10-2
Friends of the Library Group

LOUISE WILLIAMS BRANCH, 140 Bayou Oaks Dr, 71203. Tel: 318-327-5422. FAX: 318-343-3476. *Br Mgr,* Robert Kelley, PhD; Staff 7 (MLS 2, Non-MLS 5)
Library Holdings: AV Mats 4,120; CDs 461; DVDs 1,300; Large Print Bks 1,351; Bk Vols 18,004; Talking Bks 1,283; Videos 930
Open Mon-Thurs (Winter) 9-8, Fri 9-6, Sat 9-5; Mon & Thurs (Summer) 9-8, Tues & Wed 9-6, Fri 9-5, Sat 10-2
Bookmobiles: 1. Bkmobile Mgr, Karen DeMoss. Bk titles 9,889

C UNIVERSITY OF LOUISIANA AT MONROE LIBRARY*, 700 University Ave, 71209-0720. SAN 306-4794. Tel: 318-342-1051. Circulation Tel: 318-342-1063. Interlibrary Loan Service Tel: 318-342-1067. Administration Tel: 318-342-1050. Information Services Tel: 318-342-1071. FAX: 318-342-1075. Web Site: www.ulm.edu/library. *Dean of Libr,* Donald R Smith; E-mail: dosmith@ulm.edu; *Asst Dean of Libr, Coordr, Spec Coll,* Cyndy Robertson; Tel: 318-342-1054, E-mail: crobertson@ulm.edu; *Pharm Librn,* Carita Alexander; Tel: 318-342-3042, E-mail: calexander@ulm.edu; *Ref Librn,* Karen Niemla; Tel: 318-342-3045, E-mail: niemla@ulm.edu; *Ref Librn,* Heather Pilcher; Tel: 318-342-1060, E-mail: pilcher@ulm.edu; *Ref Librn,* Maren Williams; Tel: 318-342-1065, E-mail: mawilliams@ulm.edu; *Coordr, Pub Serv,* Megan Lowe; Tel: 318-342-3041, E-mail: lowe@ulm.edu; *Coordr, Tech Serv,* Charles Hughes; Tel: 318-342-3051, E-mail: hughes@ulm.edu; *Acq, Coll Develop,* Lila Jefferson; Tel: 318-342-1053, E-mail: jefferson@ulm.edu; *ILL,* Melinda Matthews; E-mail: matthews@ulm.edu; Staff 10 (MLS 10)
Founded 1931. Enrl 8,500; Highest Degree: Doctorate
Jul 2012-Jun 2013 Income $1,297,174. Mats Exp $116,000. Sal $934,886 (Prof $473,281)
Library Holdings: e-books 71,000; Bk Titles 380,149; Bk Vols 423,659; Per Subs 153
Special Collections: Civil War (Gilhula Coll); Governor James Noe Papers; Griffin Photograph Coll; Regional History (Otto E Passman Papers). State Document Depository; US Document Depository
Subject Interests: Educ, Family counseling, Gerontology, Health sci, Marriage counseling, Pharm
Automation Activity & Vendor Info: (Acquisitions) SirsiDynix; (Cataloging) SirsiDynix; (Circulation) SirsiDynix; (Course Reserve) SirsiDynix; (ILL) OCLC ILLiad; (OPAC) SirsiDynix; (Serials) SirsiDynix
Database Vendor: ACM (Association for Computing Machinery), BioOne, EBSCO - WebFeat, EBSCOhost, ISI Web of Knowledge, JSTOR, LexisNexis, Medline, Mergent Online, OCLC FirstSearch, OCLC WorldShare Interlibrary Loan, ProQuest, SirsiDynix
Wireless access
Partic in BRS; Louisiana Academic Library Information Network (LALINC); OCLC Online Computer Library Center, Inc; The Louisiana Library Network
Restriction: ID required to use computers (Ltd hrs), In-house use for visitors
Friends of the Library Group

MORGAN CITY

P MORGAN CITY PUBLIC LIBRARY*, 220 Everett St, 70380-3619. (Mail add: PO Box 988, 70381-0988), SAN 306-4816. Tel: 985-380-4646. FAX: 985-380-4699. *Librn,* Malisa Mayon; Staff 3 (Non-MLS 3)
Founded 1934. Pop 16,114; Circ 44,616
Library Holdings: AV Mats 326; Bk Vols 48,000; Per Subs 135
Automation Activity & Vendor Info: (Cataloging) Follett Software; (Circulation) Follett Software; (OPAC) Follett Software
Open Mon Thurs 9 6, Fri 9 5, Sat 9 Noon

NAPOLEONVILLE

P ASSUMPTION PARISH LIBRARY*, 293 Napoleon Ave, 70390-2123. SAN 306-4824. Tel: 985-369-7070. E-mail: assumptionlib1@msn.com. Web Site: www.assumption.lib.la.us. *Dir,* Dr Teri Maggio; Staff 13 (MLS 1, Non-MLS 12)
Founded 1968. Pop 24,328; Circ 68,845
Library Holdings: AV Mats 1,000; Bk Vols 65,000; Per Subs 125
Special Collections: Assumption Pioneer (1850), micro; French Language Materials Coll (childrens & adult); Southern Louisiana Genealogy
Automation Activity & Vendor Info: (Cataloging) TLC (The Library Corporation); (Circulation) TLC (The Library Corporation); (OPAC) TLC (The Library Corporation)
Open Mon & Wed-Fri 8:30-5:30, Tues 8:30-7, Sat 8:30-12:30
Friends of the Library Group
Branches: 3

BAYOU L'OURSE BRANCH, 1214 Hwy 662, Morgan City, 70380. Tel: 985-631-3200. FAX: 985-631-3200. E-mail: bayoulourselibrary@yahoo.com. *Br Mgr,* Betsy Theriot
Library Holdings: Bk Vols 6,000
Open Mon, Wed & Thurs 1-5:30, Tues 1-7, Sat 8:30-12:30

LABADIEVILLE BRANCH, 105 Cherry St, Labadieville, 70372. Tel: 985-526-7055. FAX: 985-526-0278. *Br Mgr,* Lenore Carter; Staff 2 (Non-MLS 2)
Library Holdings: AV Mats 91; Bk Vols 15,000; Per Subs 25
Open Mon & Wed-Fri 1-5:30, Tues 1-7
Friends of the Library Group

PIERRE PART BRANCH, 2800 Hwy 70 S, Pierre Part, 70390. Tel: 985-252-4220. FAX: 985-252-1476. *Br Mgr,* Alicia Aucoin; Staff 2 (Non-MLS 2)
Library Holdings: AV Mats 88; Bk Vols 10,000; Per Subs 20
Open Mon-Thurs 10-5:30, Sat 8:30-12:30
Friends of the Library Group

NATCHITOCHES

P NATCHITOCHES PARISH LIBRARY, 450 Second St, 71457-4649. SAN 343-2998. Tel: 318-357-3280. FAX: 318-357-7073. E-mail: info@natchitoches.lib.la.us. Web Site: www.youseemore.com/natchitoches. *Libr Dir,* Robert E Black; Fax: 318-357-2449, E-mail: bblack@natchitoches.lib.la.us; *Dir of Libr Operations,* Vallery B Washington; E-mail: vallery@natchitoches.lib.la.us; *Ch,* Annabel Jones; Fax: 318-357-2458, E-mail: annabel@natchitoches.lib.la.us; *Circ Mgr,* Rosalind LaCour; Fax: 318-357-7073, E-mail: rosalind@natchitoches.lib.la.us; *Tech Serv Adminr,* Deborah Ransome; E-mail: deborah@natchitoches.lib.la.us; *Outreach Coordr,* Amy Walmsley; E-mail: amy@natchitoches.lib.la.us. Subject Specialists: *Pub relations,* Amy Walmsley; Staff 21 (MLS 1, Non-MLS 20)
Founded 1939. Pop 39,000; Circ 150,890
Jan 2014-Dec 2014 Income (Main Library Only) $2,274,720, State $26,432, Federal $21,875, County $2,200,000, Locally Generated Income $26,413. Mats Exp $225,000, Books $110,000, Per/Ser (Incl. Access Fees) $10,000, AV Mat $55,000, Electronic Ref Mat (Incl. Access Fees) $50,000. Sal $750,000 (Prof $70,000)
Library Holdings: Bk Vols 90,000; Per Subs 120
Special Collections: Louisiana History; Natchitoches Authors
Subject Interests: La, Local hist
Automation Activity & Vendor Info: (Cataloging) TLC (The Library Corporation); (Circulation) TLC (The Library Corporation); (ILL) TLC (The Library Corporation); (OPAC) TLC (The Library Corporation)
Wireless access
Mem of Green Gold Library System
Partic in The Louisiana Library Network
Open Mon-Fri 9-6, Sat 9-5
Friends of the Library Group
Bookmobiles: 1

C NORTHWESTERN STATE UNIVERSITY LIBRARIES, Eugene P Watson Memorial Library, 913 University Pkwy, 71497. SAN 343-3234. Tel: 318-357-4477. Interlibrary Loan Service Tel: 318-357-5465. Reference Tel: 318-357-4574. Administration Tel: 318-357-4403. Toll Free Tel: 888-540-9657. FAX: 318-357-4470. Interlibrary Loan Service FAX: 318-357-5201. Web Site: www.nsula.edu/watson_library. *Dir of Libr,* Abbie V Landry; E-mail: landry@nsula.edu; *Head Archivist,* Mary Linn Wernet; Tel: 318-357-4585, E-mail: wernet@nsula.edu; *Govt Doc, Head, Ref, Ref Librn,* Gail S Kwak; E-mail: kwak@nsula.edu; *Head, Ser & Media, ILL,* Michael E Matthews; Tel: 318-357-4406, E-mail: matthewsm@nsula.edu; *Coordr of Tech Processes,* Elizabeth Graves; E-mail: gravese@nsula.edu. Subject Specialists: *State hist,* Mary Linn Wernet; *Govt doc,* Gail S Kwak; Staff 21 (MLS 5, Non-MLS 16)
Founded 1884. Enrl 8,900; Fac 309; Highest Degree: Doctorate
Jul 2014-Jun 2015. Mats Exp $647,532, Books $88,041, Per/Ser (Incl. Access Fees) $454,536, Micro $35,508, Electronic Ref Mat (Incl. Access Fees) $60,265, Presv $9,182. Sal $889,984

Library Holdings: AV Mats 7,000; e-books 23,000; Bk Vols 312,324; Per Subs 1,271
Special Collections: Carl F Gauss (Dunnington Coll); Isthmian Canal, United States & Louisiana History (Owen Coll); Literature (Aswell Coll); Louisiana Folklore (Saucier Coll); Louisiana History & Folklore (Melrose Coll); Louisiana History (Egan, Safford, Harris & Cloutier Coll); Louisiana History, Indians & Botany (Dormon Coll); Mexican Revolution (Grass Coll); Poetry (Bancroft Coll). Oral History; State Document Depository; US Document Depository
Subject Interests: Bus, Educ, Nursing
Automation Activity & Vendor Info: (Acquisitions) SirsiDynix; (Cataloging) SirsiDynix; (Circulation) SirsiDynix; (ILL) OCLC; (OPAC) SirsiDynix; (Serials) SirsiDynix
Database Vendor: EBSCOhost, JSTOR, LexisNexis, OVID Technologies, ProQuest
Wireless access
Publications: Index & Abstracts of Colonial Documents in the Eugene P Watson Memorial Library; LibGuides; Library Handbook; User Guides
Partic in The Louisiana Library Network
Open Mon-Thurs 8am-10pm (8am-9pm Summer), Fri 8-Noon, Sun 2-10

NEW IBERIA

P IBERIA PARISH LIBRARY, 445 E Main St, 70560-3710. SAN 343-3269. Tel: 337-364-7024, 337-364-7074. Reference Tel: 337-364-7305. Administration Tel: 337-364-7150, 337-364-7188. FAX: 337-364-7042. Administration FAX: 337-364-7622. E-mail: newiberialib@yahoo.com. Administration E-mail: newiberialib@yahoo.com. Web Site: www.iberia.lib.la.us. *Dir,* Kathleen Miles; E-mail: kmiles@iberialibrary.org; *Asst Dir,* Cheryl Braud; E-mail: cbraud@iberialibrary.org; *Ch,* Sarah Boatman; Tel: 337-364-7134, E-mail: sboatman@iberialibrary.org; *Circ Supvr,* Jacqui Giovinazzo; E-mail: newiberialib@yahoo.com; *Circ Supvr,* Charlene Judice; E-mail: newiberialib@yahoo.com; *Commun Relations Coordr,* Sami Haggood; E-mail: shaggood@iberialibrary.org; *Cataloger,* Don Crook; E-mail: dcrook@iberialibrary.org; *ILL, Ref Serv,* Susan Naquin; E-mail: snaquin@iberialibrary.org; *IT Spec,* Edie Boudreaux; E-mail: eboudrea@iberialibrary.org; Staff 7 (MLS 5, Non-MLS 2)
Founded 1947. Pop 73,400; Circ 218,726
Jan 2011-Dec 2011 Income (Main Library and Branch(s)) $2,449,389, State $124,169, County $2,209,018, Locally Generated Income $116,202. Mats Exp $224,309, Books $143,347, Per/Ser (Incl. Access Fees) $12,714, AV Mat $34,293, Electronic Ref Mat (Incl. Access Fees) $33,955. Sal $892,938 (Prof $283,295)
Library Holdings: Audiobooks 5,617; AV Mats 8,411; CDs 352; DVDs 2,839; e-books 4,902; Electronic Media & Resources 75; Large Print Bks 9,315; Bk Titles 174,470; Bk Vols 249,763; Per Subs 355; Talking Bks 3,161; Videos 6,499
Special Collections: Bunk Johnson Coll; I A & Carroll Martin Photo Coll. Oral History
Automation Activity & Vendor Info: (Cataloging) Innovative Interfaces, Inc; (Circulation) Innovative Interfaces, Inc; (ILL) Auto-Graphics, Inc; (OPAC) Innovative Interfaces, Inc
Database Vendor: CredoReference, EBSCOhost, Facts on File, LearningExpress, Overdrive, Inc, ProQuest, ReferenceUSA, TumbleBookLibrary, World Book Online
Wireless access
Open Mon-Thurs 8:30-8, Fri & Sat 8:30-5:30, Sun 1:30-5:30
Friends of the Library Group
Branches: 7
COTEAU BRANCH, 6308 Coteau Rd, 70560, SAN 375-5746. Tel: 337-364-7430. FAX: 337-364-7430. E-mail: cotlib@yahoo.com. *Br Mgr,* Jean Segura; Staff 1 (Non-MLS 1)
Founded 1992
Open Mon-Fri 1-6
Friends of the Library Group
DELCAMBRE BRANCH, 206 W Main St, Delcambre, 70528-2918. Tel: 337-685-2388. FAX: 337-685-2388. E-mail: delcambre@vermilion.lib.la.us. *Br Mgr,* Bonnie Richard; Staff 1 (Non-MLS 1)
Open Mon-Thurs 10-11:30 & 12:30-5:30, Fri 10-11:30 & 12:30-5, Sat 9-12
Friends of the Library Group
JEANERETTE BRANCH, 411 Kentucky St, Jeanerette, 70544, SAN 343-3358. Tel: 337-276-4014. FAX: 337-276-9595. E-mail: jeanerettebranch@yahoo.com. *Br Mgr,* John Braud; *Libr Asst,* Jenny Switzer; Staff 1 (Non-MLS 1)
Founded 1979
Open Mon-Fri 9-6, Sat 10-3
Friends of the Library Group
LOREAUVILLE BRANCH, 510 N Main St, Loreauville, 70552, SAN 343-3382. Tel: 337-229-6348. FAX: 337-229-6348. E-mail: loreauvillebranch@yahoo.com. *Br Mgr,* Cynthia Sherman; Staff 1 (Non-MLS 1)
Founded 1961
Open Mon-Fri 1-6, Wed 9-12 & 1-6
Friends of the Library Group
LYDIA BRANCH, 4800 Freyou Rd, 70560, SAN 343-3412. Tel: 337-364-7808. FAX: 337-364-7808. E-mail: lydia_branch@yahoo.com. *Br Co-Mgr,* JoAnn Clay; *Br Co-Mgr,* Lauren Salkowitz; Staff 2 (Non-MLS 2)
Open Mon-Fri 9-6, Sat 10-3
Friends of the Library Group
PARKVIEW BRANCH, 500 Grand Pre Blvd, 70563. Tel: 337-364-7480. FAX: 337-364-7714. E-mail: parkviewlib@yahoo.com. *Br Mgr,* Linda Thronson
Special Collections: Genealogy
Special Services for the Blind - Computer with voice synthesizer for visually impaired persons; Large print bks; Low vision equip; Magnifiers
Open Mon-Fri 9-6, Sat 10-3
ST PETER STREET BRANCH, 1111 W Saint Peter St, 70560. Tel: 337-364-7670. FAX: 337-364-7261. E-mail: stp_lib@yahoo.com. *Br Mgr,* Nancy Guidry; Staff 1 (Non-MLS 1)
Founded 2005
Open Mon-Fri 9-6, Sat 10-3
Friends of the Library Group

NEW ORLEANS

L ADAMS & REESE LAW LIBRARY*, One Shell Sq, 701 Poydras, Ste 4500, 70139. SAN 372-0888. Tel: 504-581-3234. FAX: 504-566-0210. Web Site: www.adamsandreese.com. *Dir, Libr Serv,* Brent Hightower; E-mail: brent.hightower@arlaw.com; Staff 1 (MLS 1)
Library Holdings: Bk Vols 15,500; Per Subs 200

S AMISTAD RESEARCH CENTER*, Tulane University, Tilton Hall, 6823 St Charles Ave, 70118. SAN 306-4840. Tel: 504-862-3222. Administration Tel: 504-862-3225. FAX: 504-862-8961. Administration FAX: 504-862-8741. E-mail: reference@amistadresearchcenter.org. Web Site: www.amistadresearchcenter.org. *Exec Dir,* Dr Lee Hampton; E-mail: lhampto3@amistadresearchcenter.org; *Archives Dir,* Position Currently Open; *Dir, Ref & Libr Serv,* Christopher Harter; Tel: 504-862-3229, E-mail: charter@tulane.edu; *Dir of Proc,* Laura Thomson; Tel: 504-314-2137, E-mail: thomsonl@tulane.edu; *Archivist,* Shannon Burrell; E-mail: sburrel@tulane.edu; *AV Archivist,* Brenda Flora; E-mail: bflora@tulane.edu; *Ref Archivist,* Andrew Salinas; Tel: 504-862-3228, E-mail: asalinas@tulane.edu; Staff 7 (MLS 5, Non-MLS 2)
Founded 1966
Library Holdings: Bk Titles 25,000; Per Subs 30
Special Collections: Aaron Douglas Coll; American Missionary Association Archives; Countee Cullen Papers; Harlem Renaissance Authors Coll
Subject Interests: African-Am, Appalachian Whites, Latino studies, Minorities
Wireless access
Function: Archival coll, Online cat
Publications: Amistad E-Newsletter (Online only)
Partic in OCLC Online Computer Library Center, Inc
Open Mon-Fri 8:30-4:30
Restriction: Closed stack, Non-circulating
Friends of the Library Group

M CHILDREN'S HOSPITAL*, Medical Library, 200 Henry Clay Ave, 70118. SAN 322-8533. Tel: 504-896-9264. FAX: 504-896-3932. Web Site: www.chnola.org.
Library Holdings: Bk Titles 700; Bk Vols 3,000; Per Subs 92
Subject Interests: Abused children, Congenital, Developmental anatomy, Malformations, Pediatric emergency, Pediatric intensive care, Pediatric neonatal intensive care, Pediatric neurology, Pediatric neurosurgery, Pediatric oncology, Pediatric surgery, Pediatrics orthopedics
Partic in Health Sciences Library Association of Louisiana; National Network of Libraries of Medicine

J DELGADO COMMUNITY COLLEGE*, Moss Memorial Library, Bldg 10, Rm 116, 615 City Park Ave, 70119. SAN 306-493X. Tel: 504-671-5317. E-mail: cpref@dcc.edu. Web Site: www.dcc.edu/library. *Dean of Libr Serv,* Timothy Stamm; *Coll Develop, Head, Acq,* Caitlin Cooper; *Librn,* Gera J Bridgewater; E-mail: gbridg@dcc.edu; *Bibliog Instr, Ref,* Courtney Rimes; Tel: 504-671-5315, E-mail: crimes@dcc.edu; Staff 15 (MLS 6, Non-MLS 9)
Founded 1921. Enrl 16,670
Library Holdings: Bk Vols 123,000; Per Subs 981
Special Collections: State Document Depository
Subject Interests: La
Automation Activity & Vendor Info: (Cataloging) SirsiDynix; (Circulation) SirsiDynix; (Course Reserve) SirsiDynix; (ILL) OCLC; (OPAC) SirsiDynix
Database Vendor: ebrary, EBSCOhost, JSTOR, LexisNexis, OCLC WorldShare Interlibrary Loan, Oxford Online, ProQuest

Partic in The Louisiana Library Network
Open Mon-Thurs 8-8, Fri 8-4:30

Departmental Libraries:

JM CHARITY SCHOOL OF NURSING LIBRARY, 450 S Claiborne Ave, 70112, SAN 306-4913. Tel: 504-571-1274. FAX: 504-568-5494.
Founded 1895. Enrl 600
Library Holdings: Bk Titles 5,105; Bk Vols 7,700; Per Subs 115
Subject Interests: Med, Nursing
Automation Activity & Vendor Info: (Cataloging) SirsiDynix; (Circulation) SirsiDynix; (OPAC) SirsiDynix
Open Mon-Fri 8-5:30

L DEUTSCH, KERRIGAN & STILES*, Law Library, 755 Magazine St, 70130-3672. SAN 306-4948. Tel: 504-581-5141, Ext 465. FAX: 504-566-1201. Web Site: www.dkslaw.com. *Librn,* Jean Barney; Tel: 504-593-0779, E-mail: jbarney@dkslaw.com
Founded 1926
Library Holdings: Bk Vols 30,000; Per Subs 25
Subject Interests: Great Britain
Database Vendor: Westlaw
Restriction: Staff use only

C DILLARD UNIVERSITY, Will W Alexander Library, 2601 Gentilly Blvd, 70122-3097. SAN 306-4956. Tel: 504-816-4786. E-mail: dulibrary@dillard.edu. Web Site: www.dillard.edu/index.php?option=com_content&view=article&id=1301&Itemid=102. *Dir,* Cynthia Charles; Tel: 504-816-4263, E-mail: ccharles@dillard.edu; *Access Serv,* Malik Bartholomew; Tel: 504-816-4209, E-mail: mbartholomew@dillard.edu; *Archives, Spec Coll,* Beverly Harris; Tel: 504-816-4881, E-mail: bharris@dillard.edu; *Cat,* Melissa Dellihoue; Tel: 504-816-4537, E-mail: mdellihoue@dillard.edu; *Info Literacy,* Germaine Palmer; Tel: 504-816-4254, E-mail: gpalmer@dillard.edu. Subject Specialists: *Libr admin,* Cynthia Charles; Staff 6 (MLS 4, Non-MLS 2)
Founded 1961. Enrl 1,300; Fac 140; Highest Degree: Bachelor
Library Holdings: e-books 88,000; Bk Vols 106,000; Per Subs 100
Special Collections: Howard Patton (African American Authors Coll); Literature & Architecture (McPherson Memorial Freedom Coll); Spitz (David), Beale (Howard Kennedy), Goldstein (Moise) & Richards (E V) Coll. State Document Depository
Subject Interests: African-Am studies, Humanities, Nursing, Soc sci & issues
Automation Activity & Vendor Info: (Acquisitions) Ex Libris Group; (Cataloging) Ex Libris Group; (Circulation) Ex Libris Group; (ILL) Ex Libris Group; (OPAC) Ex Libris Group; (Serials) Ex Libris Group
Database Vendor: American Psychological Association (APA), CQ Press, CredoReference, EBSCO Discovery Service, EBSCO Information Services, EBSCOhost, H W Wilson, JSTOR, OCLC ArticleFirst, OCLC FirstSearch, OCLC WorldShare Interlibrary Loan, Oxford Online, ProQuest, ScienceDirect
Wireless access
Publications: Acquisitions list (Quarterly); Bibliographies; Gifts & Exchange List
Partic in Louisiana Academic Library Information Network (LALINC); Lyrasis; OCLC Online Computer Library Center, Inc; The Louisiana Library Network
Open Mon-Thurs 7:30am-11pm, Fri 7:30-5, Sat 10-4, Sun 1-8

S GALLIER HOUSE LIBRARY*, 1132 Royal St, 70116. (Mail add: 820 Saint Louis St, 70112). Tel: 504-525-5661. FAX: 504-568-9735. E-mail: hgrimagallier@aol.com. Web Site: hgghh.org. *Exec Dir,* Mamie Gasperecz; E-mail: mamieg@hgghh.org; *Dep Dir,* Carolyn Bercier; E-mail: carolynb@hgghh.org
Library Holdings: Bk Vols 1,000
Restriction: Private libr, Staff use only

L GORDON, ARATA, MCCOLLAM, DUPLANTIS & EGAN LLP*, Law Library, 201 Saint Charles Ave, Ste 4000, 70170. SAN 326-2596. Tel: 504-582-1111, Ext 4039. FAX: 504-582-1121. Web Site: www.gamde.com. *Librn,* Edward Benefiel; E-mail: ebenefiel@gamde.com; Staff 1 (MLS 1)
Library Holdings: Bk Vols 10,000; Per Subs 50
Wireless access
Restriction: Staff use only

S HERMANN-GRIMA HOUSE LIBRARY*, 820 Saint Louis St, 70112. SAN 374-8324. Tel: 504-525-5661. FAX: 504-568-9735. E-mail: hgrimagallier@aol.com. Web Site: www.hgghh.org. *Exec Dir,* Mamie Gaspercz; E-mail: mamieg@hgghh.org; *Dep Dir,* Carolyn Bercier; E-mail: carolynb@hgghh.org
Library Holdings: Bk Vols 700; Per Subs 10
Special Collections: New Orleans Coll 1830-1860
Restriction: Private libr, Staff use only

S HISTORIC NEW ORLEANS COLLECTION*, William Research Center, 410 Chartres St, 70130-2102. SAN 306-4980. Tel: 504-598-7171. FAX: 504-598-7168. E-mail: wrc@hnoc.org. Web Site: www.hnoc.org. *Dir,* Alfred E Lemmon; Tel: 504-598-7124, E-mail: alfredl@hnoc.org; *Asst Dir,* Jason Wiese; Tel: 504-598-7183, E-mail: jasonw@hnoc.org; *Head, Reader Serv,* Daniel Hammer; Tel: 504-598-7112, E-mail: danielh@hnoc.org; *Curator, Rare Bks, Sr Librn,* Pamela D Arceneaux; Tel: 504-598-7118, E-mail: pamela@hnoc.org; *Curator of Ms,* Mark Cave; Tel: 504-598-7132, E-mail: markc@hnoc.org; *Cataloger,* Anita Kazmierczak-Hoffman; Tel: 504-556-7610, E-mail: AnitaH@hnoc.org; Staff 9 (MLS 4, Non-MLS 5)
Founded 1966
Library Holdings: Bk Vols 16,000; Per Subs 30
Special Collections: Battle of New Orleans Coll; Manuscript Coll; Maps; New Orleans broadsides, directories, imprints, sheet music, selected ephemera; Photographic Coll; Ursuline Nuns Library Coll; Vieux Carre Survey (information on property in the French Quarter of New Orleans)
Subject Interests: La
Automation Activity & Vendor Info: (OPAC) MINISIS Inc
Publications: Bibliography of New Orleans Imprints, 1764-1864; Bound to Please (Collection catalog); Charting Louisiana; Guide to Research at the Historic New Orleans Coll; Guide to the Vieux Carre Survey
Partic in Lyrasis; OCLC Online Computer Library Center, Inc
Open Tues-Sat 9:30-4:30
Friends of the Library Group

S JEAN LAFITTE NATIONAL HISTORICAL PARK & PRESERVE*, Chalmette Battlefield Library, 419 Decatur St, 70130. SAN 321-4486. Tel: 504-589-2636. FAX: 504-589-3851. Web Site: www.nps.gov/jela. *Curator,* Kathy Lang; E-mail: kathy_lang@nps.gov
Founded 1939
Library Holdings: Bk Titles 300
Special Collections: Battle of New Orleans, bks, mss; War of 1812 History
Subject Interests: Cultural hist, La, State hist
Restriction: Open by appt only, Open to pub for ref only

GL LAW LIBRARY OF LOUISIANA*, Louisiana Supreme Court, 2nd Flr, 400 Royal St, 70130-2104. SAN 306-5014. Tel: 504-310-2400. Reference Tel: 504-310-2515. Toll Free Tel: 800-820-3038 (Louisiana only). FAX: 504-310-2419. E-mail: library@lasc.org. Reference E-mail: reference@lasc.org. Web Site: www.lasc.org. *Dir, Law Libr,* Georgia Chadwick; Tel: 504-310-2402, E-mail: gchadwick@lasc.org; *Head, Pub Serv,* Marie Erickson; *Head, Tech Serv,* Miriam Childs; *Acq/Ser Librn,* Jennifer Creevy; *Coll Develop/Ref Librn,* Tara Lombardi; *Ref/Electronic Serv Librn,* Katherine Nachod; *Libr Assoc,* Ruth Mahoney; *Libr Assoc,* Daphine Tassin; Staff 5 (MLS 5)
Founded 1838
Jul 2007-Jun 2008 Income $1,641,483. Mats Exp $874,218. Sal $636,483
Library Holdings: Bk Vols 175,000; Per Subs 600
Special Collections: 19th Century American, British & French Law, Louisiana Law. State Document Depository; US Document Depository
Automation Activity & Vendor Info: (Acquisitions) EOS International; (Cataloging) EOS International; (Circulation) EOS International; (OPAC) EOS International; (Serials) EOS International
Database Vendor: LexisNexis, Westlaw
Publications: De Novo (Newsletter)
Partic in Lyrasis
Open Mon-Thurs 9-6, Fri 9-5
Restriction: Non-circulating to the pub
Friends of the Library Group

S LOUISIANA STATE MUSEUM*, Louisiana Historical Center, 751 Chartres St, 70176. (Mail add: PO Box 2448, 70176-2448), SAN 306-5022. Tel: 504-568-7882, 504-568-8214. Toll Free Tel: 800-568-6968. FAX: 504-599-1950. E-mail: lsm@crt.state.la.us. Web Site: lsm.crt.state.la.us. *Dir of Coll,* Greg Lambousy; Staff 1 (Non-MLS 1)
Founded 1930
Library Holdings: Bk Titles 30,000
Special Collections: Colonial Judicial Documents, maps, mss, sheet music
Subject Interests: La, Local hist
Restriction: Non-circulating to the pub, Open by appt only

Branches:

NEW ORLEANS JAZZ CLUB COLLECTION, Old US Mint, 400 Esplanade Ave, 70176. (Mail add: PO Box 2448, 70165-2448). Tel: 504-568-6968. Toll Free Tel: 800-568-6968. FAX: 504-568-4995. Web Site: lsm.crt.state.la.us/collections/jazz.htm. *Dir of Coll,* Greg Lambousy; Staff 1 (Non-MLS 1)
Library Holdings: Bk Vols 28,500
Special Collections: New Orleans Jazz Club Coll. Oral History
Subject Interests: Jazz music
Function: Archival coll, For res purposes, Ref serv available
Restriction: Authorized scholars by appt, Closed stack, Not a lending libr, Pub ref by request

CM LOUISIANA STATE UNIVERSITY HEALTH SCIENCES CENTER, John P Ische Library, 433 Bolivar St, Box B3-1, 70112-2223. SAN 343-3471. Tel: 504-568-6100. Interlibrary Loan Service Tel: 504-568-6101. Reference Tel: 504-568-6102, 504-568-8339. Administration Tel: 504-568-6105. FAX: 504-568-7718. Web Site: www.lsuhsc.edu/no/library. *Dir, Libr Serv,* Debbie Sibley; Tel: 504-568-7698, E-mail: dsibl2@lsuhsc.edu; *Head, Acq, Head, Coll Develop,* Marlene Bishop; Tel: 504-568-6109, E-mail: mbisho@lsuhsc.edu; *Head, Cat, Head, Ser,* Hanna Kwasik; Tel: 504-568-6106, E-mail: hkwasi@lsuhsc.edu; *Head, ILL, Head, Info Tech,* Jennifer Lloyd; Tel: 504-568-5550, E-mail: jlloyd@lsuhsc.edu; *Br Coordr,* Julie Schiavo; Tel: 504-941-8162, E-mail: jschia@lsuhsc.edu; *Ref,* Carolyn Bridgewater; E-mail: cbridg@lsuhsc.edu; *Ref,* Jessica Brooks; *Ref,* Kathryn E Kerdolff; E-mail: kkerdo@lsuhsc.edu; *Ref,* Mary L Marix; E-mail: mmarix@lsuhsc.edu; *Ref,* Rita Premo; E-mail: rpremo@lsuhsc.edu; *Ser,* Rebecca Bealer; Tel: 504-568-6108, E-mail: rbeale@lsuhsc.edu. Subject Specialists: *Dental,* Julie Schiavo; Staff 12 (MLS 11, Non-MLS 1)
Founded 1931
Library Holdings: Bk Titles 60,798; Bk Vols 254,721; Per Subs 7,375
Subject Interests: Allied health, Dentistry, Med, Nursing, Pub health
Automation Activity & Vendor Info: (Acquisitions) Innovative Interfaces, Inc; (Cataloging) Innovative Interfaces, Inc; (Circulation) Innovative Interfaces, Inc; (ILL) OCLC ILLiad; (OPAC) Innovative Interfaces, Inc; (Serials) Innovative Interfaces, Inc
Database Vendor: Dialog, Gale Cengage Learning, LexisNexis, OVID Technologies, ProQuest, Wilson - Wilson Web
Wireless access
Partic in SCAMeL; The Louisiana Library Network
Restriction: Open to fac, students & qualified researchers

Departmental Libraries:

SCHOOL OF DENTISTRY LIBRARY, 1100 Florida Ave, 70119-2799, SAN 343-3501. Tel: 504-941-8158. FAX: 504-941-8161. *Head of Libr,* Elizabeth Strother; E-mail: estrot@lsuhsc.edu; *Ref,* Julie Schiavo; E-mail: jschia@lsuhsc.edu

C LOYOLA UNIVERSITY NEW ORLEANS*, J Edgar & Louise S Monroe Library, 6363 Saint Charles Ave, 70118-6195. (Mail add: Campus Box 198, 6363 Saint Charles Ave, 70118), SAN 343-3536. Tel: 504-864-7111. Interlibrary Loan Service Tel: 504-864-7144. Reference Tel: 504-864-7155. Administration Tel: 504-864-7051. Toll Free Tel: 877-614-0633. FAX: 504-864-7247. E-mail: libref@loyno.edu. Web Site: library.loyno.edu. *Dean of Libr,* Michael Olson; *Assoc Dean, Pub Serv,* Deborah Poole; *Assoc Dean, Tech Serv,* Laurie Phillips; *Coll Develop Librn,* Richard Snow; *Digital Initiatives Librn,* Elizabeth Kelly; *Coordr, Acq,* Denise Ammons; *Circ Coordr,* Evonne Kelly Lawrence; *Coordr, Media Serv,* Susan Brower; *ILL Coordr,* Pat Doran; *Libr Syst & Web Coordr,* Teri Oaks Gallaway; *Online Serv Coordr,* Jim Hobbs; Staff 34 (MLS 14, Non-MLS 20)
Founded 1912. Enrl 5,600; Fac 300; Highest Degree: Master
Library Holdings: AV Mats 14,872; e-books 14,330; Bk Vols 342,833; Per Subs 1,339
Special Collections: History (Spanish Documents & French Documents), micro, Louisiana Coll; New Orleans Province of Society of Jesus, archives; University Archives. US Document Depository
Subject Interests: English lit, Philos
Automation Activity & Vendor Info: (Acquisitions) SirsiDynix; (Cataloging) SirsiDynix; (Circulation) SirsiDynix; (Course Reserve) SirsiDynix; (ILL) SirsiDynix; (Media Booking) SirsiDynix; (OPAC) SirsiDynix; (Serials) SirsiDynix
Wireless access
Partic in Louisiana Academic Library Information Network (LALINC); Lyrasis

Departmental Libraries:

CL LOYOLA LAW LIBRARY, School of Law, 7214 St Charles Ave, 70118, SAN 343-3625. Tel: 504-861-5539. Circulation Tel: 504-861-5545. Reference Tel: 504-861-5692. FAX: 504-861-5895. Web Site: law.loyno.edu/library. *Dir,* P Michael Whipple; E-mail: pmwhippl@loyno.edu; *Cat Librn,* Cathy Wagar; *Foreign & Intl Law Librn,* Nona Beisenherz; *Sr Ref Librn,* Brian Huddleston; *Ref Librn,* Francis X Norton; *Ref Librn,* Etheldra Scoggin; *Ser/Doc Librn,* Michele Pope. Subject Specialists: *Foreign law, Intl law,* Nona Beisenherz; Staff 7 (MLS 7)
Founded 1914. Enrl 745; Fac 59
Library Holdings: Bk Vols 195,000; Per Subs 3,574
Special Collections: GATT; US Supreme Court Records & Briefs. State Document Depository; US Document Depository
Automation Activity & Vendor Info: (Acquisitions) Innovative Interfaces, Inc; (Cataloging) Innovative Interfaces, Inc; (Circulation) Innovative Interfaces, Inc; (Course Reserve) Innovative Interfaces, Inc; (OPAC) Innovative Interfaces, Inc; (Serials) Innovative Interfaces, Inc
Database Vendor: LexisNexis, Westlaw
Partic in Lyrasis; OCLC Online Computer Library Center, Inc; Westlaw
Open Mon-Fri 7:30am-Midnight, Sat & Sun 9am-10pm

L MILLING, BENSON, WOODWARD LLP*, Law Library, 909 Poydras St, Ste 2300, 70112-1017. SAN 326-100X. Tel: 504-569-7000, 504-569-7308. FAX: 504-569-7001. Web Site: www.millinglaw.com. *Managing Librn,* Vanessa Odems; E-mail: vodems@millinglaw.com
Library Holdings: Bk Titles 210

M NEW ORLEANS ADOLESCENT HOSPITAL*, Patient Library, 210 State St, 70118. Tel: 504-897-4639. FAX: 504-896-2652. *Dir,* Alison Dillmann
Library Holdings: Bk Vols 3,000
Restriction: Not open to pub

CR NEW ORLEANS BAPTIST THEOLOGICAL SEMINARY, John T Christian Library, 4110 Seminary Pl, 70126. SAN 343-365X. Tel: 504-282-4455. FAX: 504-816-8429. E-mail: library@nobts.edu. Web Site: www.nobts.edu/Library/Default.html. *Dean of Libr,* Dr Jeff Griffin; Tel: 504-282-4455, Ext 3288, E-mail: jgriffin@nobts.edu; *Dir, Tech Serv,* Kyara St Amant; Tel: 504-282-4455, Ext 3227, E-mail: kstamant@nobts.edu; *Head, Circ & Reserves,* Michele McClellan; Tel: 504-816-8018, E-mail: circ1@nobts.edu; *Coll Develop Librn, Media Librn, Ref Librn,* Eric Benoy; Tel: 504-282-4455, Ext 3336, E-mail: ebenoy@nobts.edu; *Extn Serv Librn,* Helen Shin; Tel: 770-321-1606, Fax: 770-321-5363, E-mail: hshin@nobts.edu; *Spec Coll Librn,* Connie Pong; Tel: 504-282-4455, Ext 8454, E-mail: cpong@nobts.edu; *Ser,* Cindy Ennis; E-mail: cennis@nobts.edu. Subject Specialists: *Educ, Music, Theol,* Eric Benoy; Staff 10.5 (MLS 4.5, Non-MLS 6)
Founded 1917. Enrl 1,400; Fac 70; Highest Degree: Doctorate
Aug 2013-Jul 2014 Income (Main Library and Branch(s)) $850,000. Mats Exp $318,500, Books $70,000, Per/Ser (Incl. Access Fees) $95,000, Manu Arch $500, Micro $1,000, AV Mat $2,000, Electronic Ref Mat (Incl. Access Fees) $140,000, Presv $10,000
Library Holdings: AV Mats 13,100; CDs 350; DVDs 196; e-books 127,000; Electronic Media & Resources 12; Microforms 18,824; Bk Titles 265,000; Bk Vols 344,000; Per Subs 800; Videos 2,000
Special Collections: C Penrose St Amant Coll; Institutional Archives; Pastor R G Lee Library; Rare Books, 15th-19th Century; Rare Pamphlets, 18th-19th Century; Southern Baptist Convention (SBC) Coll; V L Stanfield Papers
Automation Activity & Vendor Info: (Acquisitions) Horizon; (Cataloging) Horizon; (Circulation) Horizon; (ILL) OCLC WorldShare Interlibrary Loan; (OPAC) Horizon; (Serials) Horizon
Database Vendor: Alexander Street Press, Baker & Taylor, Blackwell, ebrary, EBSCOhost, Gale Cengage Learning, H W Wilson, Ingenta, OCLC, OCLC WorldShare Interlibrary Loan, Overdrive, Inc, Oxford Online, ProQuest, SirsiDynix, YBP Library Services
Wireless access
Function: Archival coll, Audio & video playback equip for onsite use, Computers for patron use, Copy machines, Doc delivery serv, Electronic databases & coll, ILL available, Microfiche/film & reading machines, Music CDs, Online cat, Photocopying/Printing, Pub access computers, Ref & res, VCDs, VHS videos
Partic in GALILEO (Georgia Library Learning Online); Louisiana Academic Library Information Network (LALINC); Lyrasis
Open Mon Thurs 7:30am-11pm, Fri 7:30-7:30, Sat 10-7
Restriction: Borrowing privileges limited to fac & registered students, Borrowing requests are handled by ILL, In-house use for visitors, Non-circulating of rare bks

Departmental Libraries:

CR MARTIN MUSIC LIBRARY, 4110 Seminary Pl, 70126. Tel: 504-282-4455, Ext 3289. Administration Tel: 504-282-4455, Ext 3336. FAX: 504-816-8429. E-mail: musiclibrary@nobts.edu. Web Site: www.nobts.edu/library/martin/default.html. *Dir,* Eric Benoy; E-mail: ebenoy@nobts.edu; Staff 2 (MLS 1, Non-MLS 1)
Founded 1920. Enrl 1,400; Highest Degree: Doctorate
Aug 2013-Jul 2014 Income $32,000. Mats Exp $24,000, Books $10,000, Per/Ser (Incl. Access Fees) $8,000, AV Mat $1,000, Electronic Ref Mat (Incl. Access Fees) $5,000. Sal $8,000 (Prof $2,400)
Library Holdings: AV Mats 6,800; CDs 3,535; DVDs 200; Electronic Media & Resources 3; Music Scores 17,400; Bk Vols 21,400; Per Subs 80; Videos 440
Special Collections: Martin & Keith Rare Hymnal Coll, 17th-20th Century
Automation Activity & Vendor Info: (Acquisitions) Horizon; (Cataloging) Horizon; (Circulation) Horizon; (ILL) OCLC WorldShare Interlibrary Loan; (OPAC) Horizon; (Serials) Horizon
Database Vendor: Alexander Street Press, Baker & Taylor, ebrary, EBSCOhost, OCLC WorldShare Interlibrary Loan, Overdrive, Inc, Oxford Online
Function: Archival coll, Distance learning, Doc delivery serv, Electronic databases & coll, Microfiche/film & reading machines, Music CDs, Online cat, Ref serv available, VCDs, VHS videos
Open Mon-Thurs 7:30am-11pm, Fri 7:30-7:30, Sat 10-7
Restriction: Borrowing requests are handled by ILL, In-house use for visitors, Non-circulating of rare bks, Non-circulating to the pub, Open to students, fac & staff, Restricted borrowing privileges

S NEW ORLEANS-BIRMINGHAM PSYCHOANALYTIC CENTER LIBRARY*, 3624 Coliseum St, 70115. SAN 371-2680. Tel: 504-899-5815. FAX: 504-899-5886. Web Site: www.nobpc.org/Page_Center/Library.html. *Librn,* Alvin Burstein
Library Holdings: Bk Vols 2,000; Per Subs 5
Wireless access

S NEW ORLEANS MUSEUM OF ART*, Felix J Dreyfous Library, One Collins Diboll Circle City Park, 70124. (Mail add: PO Box 19123, 70179-0123), SAN 306-5057. Tel: 504-658-4117. FAX: 504-658-4199. Web Site: www.noma.org. *Librn,* Sheila A Cork; E-mail: scork@noma.org; Staff 1 (MLS 1)
Founded 1972
Library Holdings: Bk Vols 20,000; Per Subs 70; Spec Interest Per Sub 70
Special Collections: WPA Index to New Orleans Artists, 1805-1940
Subject Interests: Art (19th Century), Art (20th Century), Glass technology, La, Oriental art, Paintings, Photog, Pottery, Pre-Columbian art, Prints
Wireless access
Function: Ref & res
Publications: Arts Quarterly; Handbook of the Collection
Partic in OCLC Online Computer Library Center, Inc
Restriction: Open to pub by appt only

P NEW ORLEANS PUBLIC LIBRARY*, 219 Loyola Ave, 70112-2044. SAN 343-3714. Tel: 504-529-7323, 504-596-2570. Circulation Tel: 504-596-2560. FAX: 504-596-2609. Web Site: www.nutrias.org. *Exec Dir,* Charles Brown; *Dep Dir,* Charles McMorran; E-mail: CMcmorran@neworleanspubliclibrary.org; *Dir, Initiatives & Stragegies,* Kim-Uyen Tran; E-mail: KTran@neworleanspubliclibrary.org; *IT Dir,* Jerry Pinkston; E-mail: JPinkston@neworleanspubliclibrary.org; *Assoc Dir, Br Serv,* Jessica Styons; E-mail: JStyons@neworleanspubliclibrary.org; *Assoc Dir, Cent Pub Serv,* Valencia Hawkins; E-mail: VHawkins@neworleanspubliclibrary.org; *Human Res Dir,* Linda Copeland; E-mail: LCopeland@neworleanspubliclibrary.org; *Bus Mgr,* Michel Thompson; E-mail: MThompson@neworleanspubliclibrary.org
Founded 1896. Pop 496,938; Circ 1,168,633
Library Holdings: Bk Vols 794,830; Per Subs 999
Special Collections: City Archives, microflm & mss; Foundation Center Coop Coll; Louisiana Division, bks, micro, audio & video tapes, news reels, slides, maps, pictures. US Document Depository
Automation Activity & Vendor Info: (Acquisitions) SirsiDynix; (Circulation) SirsiDynix
Wireless access
Partic in OCLC Online Computer Library Center, Inc
Open Mon-Thurs 10-6, Fri & Sat 10-5
Friends of the Library Group
Branches: 13
ALGIERS REGIONAL, 3014 Holiday Dr, 70131, SAN 343-3773. Tel: 504-596-2641. FAX: 504-596-2661. *Br Mgr,* B Strother
Founded 1966
Library Holdings: Bk Vols 55,958
Open Mon-Thurs 10-7, Sat 10-5
ALVAR BRANCH, 913 Alvar St, 70117-5409, SAN 343-3803. Tel: 504-596-2667. FAX: 504-596-2667. *Br Mgr,* Mary Ann Marx; E-mail: MMarx@neworleanspubliclibrary.org
Library Holdings: Bk Vols 17,957
Open Mon-Thurs 10-7, Sat 10-5
CENTRAL CITY BRANCH, 2405 Jackson Ave, Bldg C, Rm 235, 70113. Tel: 504-596-3112. *Br Mgr,* S Prevost
CHILDREN'S RESOURCE CENTER, 913 Napoleon Ave, 70115-2862, SAN 343-3951. Tel: 504-596-2628. FAX: 504-596-2669. *Br Mgr,* Sharon Kohl; E-mail: SKohl@neworleanspubliclibrary.org
Library Holdings: Bk Vols 19,443
Open Mon-Thurs 10-7, Fri 10-5
EAST NEW ORLEANS BRANCH, 5641 Read Blvd, 70127-3105, SAN 343-3862. Tel: 504-596-0200. *Br Mgr,* L Lagraize
Library Holdings: Bk Vols 57,057
Open Mon-Thurs 10-7, Sat 10-5
CITA DENNIS HUBBELL BRANCH, 725 Pelican Ave, 70114, SAN 343-3749. Tel: 504-596-2640. FAX: 504-596-2666. *Librn,* Seale Paterson
Library Holdings: Bk Vols 23,468
Open Mon-Thurs 10-7, Sat 10-5
ROSA KELLER BRANCH, 4300 S Broad, 70125, SAN 374-6836. Tel: 504-596-2660. FAX: 504-596-2678. *Br Mgr,* D Rhodes; E-mail: DRhodes@neworleanspubliclibrary.org
Library Holdings: Bk Vols 37,200
MARTIN LUTHER KING JR BRANCH, 1611 Caffin Ave, 70117, SAN 376-9410. Tel: 504-942-0834. FAX: 504-234-2699. *Br Mgr,* L Gielec; E-mail: LGielec@neworleanspubliclibrary.org
Library Holdings: Bk Vols 20,000
Open Mon-Fri 9-5
LAKEVIEW BRANCH, 6317 Argonne Blvd (@ Harrison Ave), 70124. Tel: 504-596-2638. *Br Mgr,* R Schultz; E-mail: RSchultz@neworleanspubliclibrary.org
Library Holdings: CDs 2,196; DVDs 2,883; Bk Vols 39,312; Per Subs 36; Talking Bks 1,165
Open Mon-Thurs 10-7, Sat 10-5
MILTON H LATTER MEMORIAL BRANCH, 5120 St Charles Ave, 70115-4941, SAN 343-3927. Tel: 504-596-2625. FAX: 504-596-2665. *Br Mgr,* Missy Abbott; Tel: 504-596-2626, E-mail: MAbbott@neworleanspubliclibrary.org; Staff 12 (MLS 2, Non-MLS 10)
Founded 1948
Library Holdings: Bk Vols 60,000; Per Subs 20
Open Mon & Wed 9-8, Tues & Thurs 9-6, Sat 10-5, Sun 12-5
Friends of the Library Group
NORMAN MAYER BRANCH, 3001 Gentilly Blvd, 70122, SAN 343-3897. Tel: 504-596-3100. *Br Mgr,* A Riley; E-mail: ARiley@neworleanspubliclibrary.org
Library Holdings: Bk Vols 34,653
Open Mon-Thurs 10-7, Sat 10-5
MID-CITY BRANCH, 3700 Orleans Ave, 70119. Tel: 504-596-2654. *Br Mgr,* R Smith; E-mail: RSmith@neworleanspubliclibrary.org
Open Mon-Thurs 10-7, Sat 10-5
NIX BRANCH, 1401 S Carrollton Ave, 70118-2809, SAN 343-401X. Tel: 504-596-2630. FAX: 504-596-2672. *Br Mgr,* Damian Lambert; E-mail: DLambert@neworleanspubliclibrary.org
Library Holdings: Bk Vols 22,978
Open Mon-Thurs 10-7, Sat 10-5

R NOTRE DAME SEMINARY GRADUATE SCHOOL OF THEOLOGY*, Reverend Robert J Stahl S M Memorial Library, 2901 S Carrollton Ave, 70118-4391. SAN 306-5065. Tel: 504-866-7426, Ext 3700. FAX: 504-866-6260. E-mail: Library@nds.edu. Web Site: nds.edu/notre-dame-seminary-library. *Dir,* Thomas B Bender, IV; Staff 1 (MLS 1)
Founded 1923. Enrl 173; Fac 22; Highest Degree: Master
Library Holdings: AV Mats 847; Electronic Media & Resources 8; Bk Vols 86,524; Per Subs 161
Subject Interests: Philos, Theol
Automation Activity & Vendor Info: (Acquisitions) Follett Software; (Cataloging) Follett Software; (Circulation) Follett Software; (ILL) OCLC FirstSearch
Database Vendor: CredoReference, EBSCOhost, Gale Cengage Learning, JSTOR, OCLC FirstSearch, OCLC WorldShare Interlibrary Loan, Sage, Swets Information Services, Wiley
Wireless access
Function: e-mail serv, Electronic databases & coll
Partic in Louisiana Academic Library Information Network (LALINC); The Louisiana Library Network
Special Services for the Blind - Aids for in-house use; Bks & mags in Braille, on rec, tape & cassette; Braille bks; Cassette playback machines; Digital talking bk machines
Restriction: Open to pub by appt only, Open to pub for ref only, Open to pub upon request, Open to pub with supv only, Open to qualified scholars, Open to researchers by request, Open to students, fac, staff & alumni

M OCHSNER CLINIC FOUNDATION, Ochsner Medical Library & Archives, 1514 Jefferson Hwy, 1st Flr, 70121-2429. SAN 306-5073. Tel: 504-842-3760. FAX: 504-842-5339. E-mail: medicallibrary@ochsner.org. Web Site: academics.ochsner.org/library.aspx. *Librn,* Thomas Bell; *Coll Librn,* Barbara Attebery; E-mail: battebery@ochsner.org; *Mgr,* Kelly Fogarty; *Archivist,* Courtney Master; Staff 4 (MLS 4)
Founded 1944
Special Collections: Ochsner Historical Archives. Oral History
Automation Activity & Vendor Info: (Circulation) Inmagic, Inc.; (ILL) OCLC ILLiad; (OPAC) SirsiDynix; (Serials) SirsiDynix
Wireless access
Function: Bilingual assistance for Spanish patrons, Computers for patron use, Copy machines, Exhibits, Handicapped accessible, ILL available, Pub access computers, Wheelchair accessible
Partic in Docline; Lyrasis; National Network of Libraries of Medicine; OCLC Online Computer Library Center, Inc
Open Mon-Fri 7:30-5
Restriction: Badge access after hrs, Circulates for staff only, Lending to staff only, Open to pub for ref & circ; with some limitations

C OUR LADY OF HOLY CROSS COLLEGE LIBRARY*, Blaine S Kern Library, 4123 Woodland Dr, 70131. SAN 306-5081. Tel: 504-394-7744. Interlibrary Loan Service Tel: 504-398-2103. Administration Tel: 504-398-2100. FAX: 504-391-2421. Web Site: www.olhcc.edu. *Dir,* Sister Helen Fontenot; E-mail: hfontenot@olhcc.edu; *Acq, Cat, Coll Develop,* Katharine Rubin; Tel: 504-398-2119, E-mail: krubin@olhcc.edu; *Coll Develop, ILL, Ser,* Diana Schaubhut; E-mail: dschaubhut@olhcc.edu; *Govt Doc, Ref Serv,* Ramesh Parikh; Tel: 504-398-2102, E-mail: rparikh@olhcc.edu; *Libr Asst,* Keisha Hawthorne; Tel: 504-398-2101, E-mail: khawthorne@olhcc.edu; Staff 4 (MLS 4)

Founded 1916. Enrl 1,220; Fac 110; Highest Degree: Master
Library Holdings: AV Mats 3,887; DVDs 301; e-books 70,865; Bk Vols 57,031; Per Subs 846; Videos 2,022
Special Collections: US Document Depository
Subject Interests: Children's lit, Educ, Genealogy, Humanities, La, Natural sci, Nursing, Soc sci & issues
Automation Activity & Vendor Info: (Cataloging) Innovative Interfaces, Inc; (Circulation) Follett Software; (OPAC) Follett Software
Database Vendor: Alexander Street Press, Bowker, EBSCOhost, Gale Cengage Learning, JSTOR, LearningExpress, LexisNexis, Newsbank-Readex, Oxford Online, ProQuest, Wilson - Wilson Web
Wireless access
Partic in Call; Louisiana Academic Library Information Network (LALINC); Lyrasis; The Louisiana Library Network
Open Mon-Thurs 8-8, Fri 8-3, Sat 9-2
Friends of the Library Group

L PHELPS DUNBAR LLP*, Law Library, 365 Canal St, Ste 2000, 70130-6534. SAN 372-087X. Tel: 504-566-1311, Ext 1287. FAX: 504-568-9130. *Dir,* Cynthia Jones; E-mail: jonesc@phelps.com
Library Holdings: Bk Vols 50,000; Per Subs 75
Automation Activity & Vendor Info: (Cataloging) SydneyPlus; (Serials) SydneyPlus
Database Vendor: LexisNexis, Westlaw
Restriction: Staff use only

L SESSIONS, FISHMAN, NATHAN & ISRAEL LLP LIBRARY*, 201 St Charles Ave, Ste 3500, 70170-3500. SAN 326-0127. Tel: 504-582-1500. FAX: 504-582-1555. Web Site: www.sessions-law.com. *Librn,* Jeanne Claudel-Simoneaux; Tel: 504-582-1563, E-mail: jclaudel@sessions-law.com
Founded 1958
Library Holdings: Bk Titles 5,000; Bk Vols 15,000; Per Subs 75
Publications: Now Hear This (internal newsletter)

L SIMON, PERAGINE, SMITH & REDFEARN LLP*, Law Library, Energy Ctr, 1100 Poydras St, 30th Flr, 70163. SAN 372-090X. Tel: 504-569-2030. FAX: 504-569-2999. Web Site: www.spsr-law.com. *Librn,* Frank Schiavo; E-mail: fschiavo@spsr-law.com; Staff 1 (MLS 1)
Founded 1979
Library Holdings: Bk Vols 9,100; Per Subs 36
Database Vendor: LexisNexis, Westlaw
Open Mon-Fri 9-5:30

M TOURO INFIRMARY*, Hospital Library, 1401 Foucher St, 70115. SAN 343-4079. Tel: 504-897-2640. FAX: 504-897-8228. Web Site: www.touro.com.
Founded 1947
Library Holdings: Bk Titles 1,000; Bk Vols 1,500; Per Subs 20
Subject Interests: Clinical med, Nursing
Database Vendor: EBSCOhost
Partic in BRS; S Cent Regional Med Libr Program
Open Mon-Fri 7:30-4

C TULANE UNIVERSITY*, Howard-Tilton Memorial Library, 7001 Freret St, 70118-5682. SAN 343-4133. Tel: 504-865-5131. Interlibrary Loan Service Tel: 504-865-5610. FAX: 504-865-6773. Web Site: library.tulane.edu. *Dean of Libr,* Lance Query; E-mail: lquery@tulane.edu; *Assoc Dean,* Andy Corrigan; Tel: 504-865-5679, E-mail: andyc@tulane.edu; *Head, Pub Serv,* Anne Houston; Tel: 504-314-7822, E-mail: ahouston@tulane.edu; *Ref Librn,* Johannah White; Tel: 504-314-7823, E-mail: jwhite1@tulane.edu; *Spec Coll Librn,* Wilbur E Meneray; Tel: 504-247-1832, E-mail: meneray@tulane.edu; *Bibliographer,* Eric Wedig; Tel: 504-865-5644, E-mail: wedig@tulane.edu; *ILL,* Arely Del Martinez; E-mail: amartin1@tulane.edu; *ILL,* Gaile Thomas; Tel: 504-865-5683, E-mail: gthomas@tulane.edu; Staff 33 (MLS 33)
Founded 1834. Enrl 11,487; Fac 927; Highest Degree: Doctorate
Library Holdings: Bk Vols 2,330,750; Per Subs 14,141
Special Collections: Architecture Library; Latin American Library; Louisiana History Coll; Rare Books; Southeastern Architectural Archive; University Archives; William Ranson Hogan Jazz Archive. US Document Depository
Automation Activity & Vendor Info: (Acquisitions) Ex Libris Group; (Cataloging) Ex Libris Group; (Circulation) Ex Libris Group; (Course Reserve) Ex Libris Group; (ILL) OCLC; (OPAC) Ex Libris Group; (Serials) Ex Libris Group
Database Vendor: OVID Technologies, ProQuest, Wilson - Wilson Web
Publications: The Jazz Archivist, Annual Report
Partic in Association of Research Libraries (ARL); Dialog Corp; Lyrasis
Open Mon-Thurs 7:30am-1:45am, Fri 7:30am-9:45pm, Sat 9am-9:45pm, Sun 9am-1:45am
Friends of the Library Group

Departmental Libraries:

ARCHITECTURE LIBRARY, Richardson Memorial Bldg, Rm 202, 6823 St Charles Ave, 70118, SAN 343-4168. Tel: 504-865-5391. FAX: 504-862-8966. *Head Librn,* Alan Velasquez; E-mail: avelasqu@tulane.edu
Library Holdings: Bk Vols 30,000; Per Subs 330

A H CLIFFORD MATHEMATICS RESEARCH LIBRARY, 430 Gibson Hall, 6823 St Charles Ave, 70118, SAN 343-4257. Tel: 504-862-3455. FAX: 504-865-5063. E-mail: awatts@tulane.edu. Web Site: tulane.edu/sse/math/library. *Librn,* Cammy Watts; E-mail: awatts@tulane.edu
Library Holdings: e-journals 245; Bk Vols 35,000; Per Subs 350
Special Collections: Alexander Doniphan Wallace Coll; Edward Daire Conway Coll; Frank Douglas Quigley Coll
Subject Interests: Math
Open Mon-Fri 8-4:30

CL LAW LIBRARY, 6329 Freret St, 70118-6231, SAN 343-4222. Tel: 504-865-5952. Interlibrary Loan Service Tel: 504-862-8896. Reference Tel: 504-865-8872. Administration Tel: 504-865-5950. FAX: 504-865-5917. E-mail: lawlib@tulane.edu. Web Site: www.law.tulane.edu/tlslibrary/index.aspx. *Dir, Law Libr & Assoc Prof of Law,* James E Duggan; E-mail: duggan@tulane.edu; *Assoc Dir,* Amanda Watson; Tel: 504-865-5955, E-mail: awatson3@tulane.edu; *Acq Librn,* Claire Ruswick; Tel: 504-862-8866, E-mail: cruswick@tulane.edu; *Cat Librn,* Cynthia Barrilleaux; Tel: 504-862-8867, E-mail: cbarril@tulane.edu; *Foreign, Comparative & Intl Law/Ref Librn,* Roy Sturgeon; Tel: 504-865-5953, E-mail: rsturgeo@tulane.edu; *Govt Doc/Micro Ref Librn,* Carla Pritchett; Tel: 504-865-5994, E-mail: cpritch@tulane.edu; *Sr Ref Librn,* Kimberly Koko Glorioso; Tel: 504-865-5902, E-mail: kglorioso@tulane.edu; *Instruction Coordr, Ref Librn,* Megan Garton; Tel: 504-865-5941, E-mail: mgarton@tulane.edu; Staff 16 (MLS 8, Non-MLS 8)
Founded 1847. Enrl 714; Fac 41; Highest Degree: Doctorate
Special Collections: French Civil Law Coll; Maritime Law Coll; Roman Law Coll
Automation Activity & Vendor Info: (Acquisitions) Innovative Interfaces, Inc; (Cataloging) Innovative Interfaces, Inc; (Circulation) Innovative Interfaces, Inc; (Course Reserve) Innovative Interfaces, Inc; (OPAC) Innovative Interfaces, Inc; (Serials) Innovative Interfaces, Inc
Database Vendor: Baker & Taylor, Gale Cengage Learning, H W Wilson, LexisNexis, Newsbank, Westlaw
Partic in OCLC Online Computer Library Center, Inc

CM RUDOLPH MATAS LIBRARY OF THE HEALTH SCIENCES, Tulane Health Sciences Campus, 1430 Tulane Ave, SL-86, 70112-2699, SAN 343-4281. Tel: 504-988-5155. Circulation Tel: 504-988-2405. FAX: 504-988-7417. E-mail: medref@tulane.edu. Web Site: matas.tulane.edu. *Dir,* Neville Prendergast; Tel: 504-988-2060, E-mail: nprender@tulane.edu; *Educ & Outreach Librn,* Elaine Hicks; Tel: 504-988-2785, E-mail: ehicks2@tulane.edu; *Monographs Librn,* Barbara Volo; Tel: 504-988-2404, E-mail: bvolo@tulane.edu; *Ref & Educ Librn,* Molly Knapp; E-mail: medref@tulane.edu; *Ref & Educ Librn,* Keith Pickett; Tel: 504-988-2406, E-mail: kpickett1@tulane.edu; *Coordr, Coll Mgt, Ser Librn,* Millie Moore; Tel: 504-988-2063, E-mail: millie@tulane.edu; *Mgr, ILL,* Josie Patton, Tel: 504-988-2413, E-mail: jpatton1@tulane.edu; *Coordr, Info Serv,* Mary Holt; Tel: 504-988-2062, E-mail: maryholt@tulane.edu; *Coordr, Syst & Digital Initiatives,* Mike Jennings; Tel: 504-988-5157, E-mail: wjenning@tulane.edu. Subject Specialists: *Pub health,* Elaine Hicks; Staff 14 (MLS 7, Non-MLS 7)
Founded 1844. Enrl 13,486; Highest Degree: Doctorate
Library Holdings: e-books 25,000; e-journals 8,174; Bk Titles 54,601; Bk Vols 157,758
Special Collections: Louisiana Medicine & Medical Biography
Subject Interests: Med, Pub health
Automation Activity & Vendor Info: (Cataloging) OCLC Connexion; (ILL) OCLC ILLiad; (OPAC) Ex Libris Group
Database Vendor: ebrary, EBSCOhost, Elsevier, McGraw-Hill, Micromedex, OCLC WorldShare Interlibrary Loan, OVID Technologies, PubMed, RefWorks, Sage, ScienceDirect, Springer-Verlag, Thomson - Web of Science, Wiley
Function: Health sci info serv, ILL available, Outreach serv
Partic in Coop Libr Agency for Syst & Servs; SCAMEL/NLM
Publications: Library News @ TUHSC (Online only)
Open Mon-Fri 8-6
Restriction: Badge access after hrs, Open to students, fac & staff

MUSIC & MEDIA LIBRARY, 7001 Freret St, 70118-5682. Tel: 504-865-5642. FAX: 504-865-6773. *Dir,* Leonard Bertrand; E-mail: lennyb@tulane.edu
Library Holdings: Bk Vols 21,744; Per Subs 90
Open Mon-Thurs (Winter) 8:30am-10pm, Fri 8-5, Sat 10-5, Sun 2-10; Mon-Thurs (Summer) 8:30-5, Fri 8:30-4:45, Sat 10-1

TURCHIN LIBRARY, Goldring/Woldenberg Hall I, 3rd Flr, Seven McAlister Dr, 70118, SAN 343-4370. Tel: 504-865-5376. FAX: 504-862-8953. E-mail: turchin@tulane.edu. Web Site: www.freeman.tulane.edu/lib-tech/turchin. *In Charge,* John Brandao
Library Holdings: Bk Vols 30,000; Per Subs 200

Subject Interests: Acctg, Finance, Organizational behavior
Database Vendor: EBSCOhost, ProQuest
Open Mon-Thurs 8:30am-11pm, Fri 8:30-6, Sat Noon-6, Sun Noon-11

A UNITED STATES ARMY*, Corps of Engineers New Orleans District Technical Library, 7400 Leake Ave, Rm 108, 70118. SAN 343-4400. Tel: 504-862-2559. FAX: 504-862-1721. Web Site: www.mvn.usace.army.mil/imo/iss/mgt_info_sec/library/library.htm. *Librn,* Sandra Brown; E-mail: sandra.a.brown@usace.army.mil; Staff 1 (MLS 1)
Founded 1974
Library Holdings: Bk Titles 14,000; Per Subs 500
Special Collections: Environmental Impact Statements; Government Reports; Standards & Specifications
Subject Interests: Archaeology, Biol, Civil eng, Eng, Environ studies, Flood control, Navigation, Water res
Partic in Dialog Corp; OCLC Online Computer Library Center, Inc
Open Mon-Fri 7:30-3:30
Restriction: Off-site coll in storage - retrieval as requested

GL UNITED STATES COURT OF APPEALS*, Fifth Circuit Library, 600 Camp St, Rm 106, 70130. SAN 306-5154. Tel: 504-310-7797. FAX: 504-310-7578. E-mail: library_mailbox@ca5.uscourts.gov. Web Site: www.lb5.uscourts.gov. *Circuit Librn,* Position Currently Open; *Head, Ref,* Amy Hale-Janeke; E-mail: ahjaneke@ca5.uscourts.gov; *Head, Tech Serv,* Anne G Middleton; E-mail: anne_middleton@ca5.uscourts.gov; *Libr Syst Mgr,* Paul Wallace; E-mail: paul_wallace@ca5.uscourts.gov; *Librn,* Victor L Buccola; E-mail: victor_buccola@ca5.uscourts.gov; *Librn,* Cassandra Hyer; E-mail: cassandra_hyer@ca5.uscourts.gov; *Librn,* Peggy Mitts; E-mail: peggy_mitts@ca5.uscourts.gov; *Librn,* Todd R St Pe; E-mail: todd_st_pe@ca5.uscourts.gov
Founded 1920
Special Collections: Government Documents Coll
Automation Activity & Vendor Info: (Cataloging) SirsiDynix
Database Vendor: LexisNexis, Westlaw
Restriction: Staff & mem only

G UNITED STATES DEPARTMENT OF AGRICULTURE*, Southern Regional Research Center, 1100 Robert E Lee Blvd, 70124. (Mail add: PO Box 19687, 70179-0687), SAN 306-5162. Tel: 504-286-4288. FAX: 504-286-4396. Web Site: www.ars.usda.gov. *Librn,* Suhad Wojkowski; E-mail: suhad@srrc.ars.usda.gov; *ILL,* Suzanne Martin
Founded 1941
Library Holdings: Bk Vols 25,000; Per Subs 500
Subject Interests: Bacteriology, Chem, Entomology, Food sci, Microbiology, Textiles
Automation Activity & Vendor Info: (Cataloging) SirsiDynix; (OPAC) SirsiDynix
Publications: Post Harvest News from the Library
Partic in OCLC Online Computer Library Center, Inc
Open Mon-Fri 8-4:30

G US DEPARTMENT OF THE INTERIOR*, Minerals Management Service - Regional Technical Library, 1201 Elmwood Park Blvd, MS-5031, 70123-2394. SAN 306-4905. Tel: 504-736-0057, 504-736-2521. FAX: 504-736-2525. *Libr Dir,* Stephen V Pomes; E-mail: stephen.pomes@mms.gov; Staff 1 (MLS 1)
Library Holdings: CDs 300; e-books 5,000; e-journals 1,000; Per Subs 30; Videos 20
Subject Interests: Environ law, Geol, Geophysics, Marine biol, Oceanography, Paleontology, Petroleum eng
Automation Activity & Vendor Info: (Cataloging) Follett Software; (Circulation) Follett Software; (ILL) OCLC; (OPAC) Follett Software
Database Vendor: Agricola, EBSCOhost, Gale Cengage Learning, IHS, JSTOR, Medline, OCLC FirstSearch, OCLC WorldShare Interlibrary Loan, PubMed, ScienceDirect
Partic in Fedlink; OCLC Online Computer Library Center, Inc; OCLC-LVIS; Soline
Restriction: Employees only

C UNIVERSITY OF NEW ORLEANS*, Earl K Long Library, 2000 Lakeshore Dr, 70148. SAN 306-5200. Tel: 504-280-6556. Circulation Tel: 504-280-6355. Reference Tel: 504-280-6549. FAX: 504-280-7277. Web Site: library.uno.edu. *Dean of Libr Serv,* Dr Sharon Mader; E-mail: smader@uno.edu; *Assoc Dean, Libr Serv,* Marilyn Hankel; Tel: 504-280-5563, E-mail: mhankel@uno.edu; *Chair, Spec Coll,* Florence Jumonville; Tel: 504-280-7275, E-mail: fjumonvi@uno.edu; *Humanities Librn,* Jeanne Pavy; Tel: 504-280-6547, E-mail: jpavy@uno.edu; *Asst Librn, Access Serv,* Janet Crane; E-mail: jmurphy@uno.edu; Staff 55 (MLS 25, Non-MLS 30)
Founded 1958. Enrl 17,040; Fac 727; Highest Degree: Doctorate
Library Holdings: Bk Vols 918,932; Per Subs 3,679
Special Collections: Egyptology (Judge Pierre Crabites Coll); European Community; Louisiana History; Nuclear Regulatory Commission; Orleans Parish School Board; Supreme Court of Louisiana Archives; William Faulkner (Frank A Von der Haar Coll). State Document Depository; US Document Depository
Subject Interests: Econ, Educ, Law, Natural sci, Soc sci & issues
Automation Activity & Vendor Info: (Acquisitions) SirsiDynix; (Cataloging) SirsiDynix; (Circulation) SirsiDynix; (Course Reserve) SirsiDynix; (OPAC) SirsiDynix; (Serials) SirsiDynix
Publications: Guide to Photographic Collections in New Orleans; Long View (Newsletter)
Partic in Lyrasis; OCLC Online Computer Library Center, Inc
Open Mon-Thurs 7:45am-10pm, Fri 7:45-4:30, Sat 10-6, Sun 12-8
Friends of the Library Group

C WILLIAM CAREY UNIVERSITY LIBRARIES*, New Orleans Learning Resource Center Library, 3939 Gentilly Blvd, Box 308, 70126. Tel: 504-286-3292. *Librn,* Janet Landrum

NEW ROADS

P POINTE COUPEE PARISH LIBRARY*, New Roads (Main Branch), 201 Claiborne St, 70760-3403. SAN 343-4524. Tel: 225-638-7593. Administration Tel: 225-638-9841. FAX: 225-638-9847. Web Site: www.pointe-coupee.lib.la.us. *Dir,* Melissa Hymel; E-mail: mkhymel@yahoo.com; Staff 5 (Non-MLS 5)
Pop 22,002; Circ 149,478
Library Holdings: AV Mats 1,152; Bk Vols 80,000; Per Subs 216
Special Collections: Louisiana Studies
Subject Interests: Art & archit, Geol, Humanities
Database Vendor: Gale Cengage Learning
Wireless access
Open Mon-Thurs 8:30-7:30, Fri & Sat 8:30-5, Sun 1-5
Friends of the Library Group
Branches: 4
INNIS BRANCH, 4306 Nichols Ave, Innis, 70747. (Mail add: PO Box 978, Innis, 70747-0978), SAN 343-4559. Tel: 225-492-2632. FAX: 225-492-2632. *Br Mgr,* Bennie Rice; Staff 2 (Non-MLS 2)
Library Holdings: AV Mats 150; Bk Vols 6,000; Per Subs 37
Open Mon-Fri 1-6
Friends of the Library Group
LIVONIA BRANCH, 3100 Hwy 78, Livonia, 70755. (Mail add: PO Box 510, Livonia, 70755-0510), SAN 343-4583. Tel: 225-637-2987. FAX: 225-637-2987. *Br Mgr,* Roye Chenever; Staff 2 (Non-MLS 2)
Library Holdings: Bk Vols 6,000; Per Subs 27
Open Mon-Fri 1-6
Friends of the Library Group
MORGANZA BRANCH, 221 S Louisiana, Hwy 1, Morganza, 70759. (Mail add: PO Box 309, Morganza, 70759-0309), SAN 343-4613. Tel: 225-694-2428. FAX: 225-694-2428. *Br Mgr,* Miriam Hodge; *Asst Br Mgr,* Stephanie Savoy; Staff 2 (Non-MLS 2)
Library Holdings: Bk Vols 6,000; Per Subs 18
Open Mon-Fri 1-6
Friends of the Library Group
JULIAN POYDRAS BRANCH, 4985 Poydras Lane, Rougon, 70773, SAN 343-4648. Tel: 225-627-5846. FAX: 225-627-5846. *Br Mgr,* Debra Soileau; *Asst Br Mgr,* Bonnie Bonaventure; Staff 2 (Non-MLS 2)
Library Holdings: Bk Vols 6,000; Per Subs 22
Open Mon-Fri 9:30-2:30
Friends of the Library Group

OAK GROVE

P WEST CARROLL PARISH LIBRARY*, 101 Marietta St, 71263. (Mail add: PO Box 703, 71263-0703), SAN 306-5235. Tel: 318-428-4100. Administration Tel: 318-428-2697. FAX: 318-428-9887. E-mail: admin.t1wc@pelican.state.lib.la.us. *Dir,* Clay Robertson; Staff 6 (MLS 1, Non-MLS 5)
Founded 1967. Pop 12,100; Circ 75,000
Library Holdings: AV Mats 814; Large Print Bks 2,500; Bk Titles 23,000; Bk Vols 25,209; Per Subs 126; Talking Bks 200; Videos 700
Special Collections: Louisiana Coll
Automation Activity & Vendor Info: (Cataloging) TLC (The Library Corporation); (Circulation) TLC (The Library Corporation); (ILL) TLC (The Library Corporation); (OPAC) TLC (The Library Corporation)
Open Mon-Fri 8-5, Sat 8-12
Bookmobiles: 1. Librn, Melody Harris. Bk titles 2,000

OBERLIN

P ALLEN PARISH LIBRARIES*, 320 S Sixth St, 70655. (Mail add: PO Box 400, 70655-0400), SAN 343-4702. Tel: 337-639-4315. Toll Free Tel: 800-960-3015. FAX: 337-639-2654. Web Site: www.allen.lib.la.us. *Dir,* Geraldine Harris; Staff 11 (MLS 2, Non-MLS 9)
Founded 1957. Pop 24,242; Circ 137,936
Library Holdings: CDs 47; Bk Vols 90,000; Per Subs 181; Talking Bks 1,886; Videos 3,393
Special Collections: Oral History

Automation Activity & Vendor Info: (Cataloging) Innovative Interfaces, Inc; (Circulation) Innovative Interfaces, Inc; (OPAC) Innovative Interfaces, Inc
Database Vendor: EBSCOhost
Mem of Bayouland Library System
Partic in Libraries SouthWest
Open Mon-Thurs 8-6, Fri 8-5, Sat 9-Noon
Friends of the Library Group
Branches: 2
KINDER BRANCH, 833 Fourth Ave, Kinder, 70648. (Mail add: PO Drawer 1990, Kinder, 70648), SAN 343-4761. Tel: 318-491-4514. FAX. 337-738-4213. *Br Mgr,* Lashandalyn Bracy; Staff 1 (Non-MLS 1)
Library Holdings: Bk Vols 19,000; Per Subs 81; Talking Bks 179
Open Mon-Thurs 8-6, Fri 8-5, Sat 9-12
Friends of the Library Group
OAKDALE BRANCH, 405 E Sixth Ave, Oakdale, 71463, SAN 343-4737. Tel: 318-335-2690. FAX: 318-335-4743. *Br Mgr,* Brenda Tichy; Staff 2 (MLS 1, Non-MLS 1)
Library Holdings: AV Mats 82; Bk Vols 30,000; Per Subs 56
Open Mon-Thurs 8-7, Fri 8-5, Sat 9-3
Friends of the Library Group
Bookmobiles: 1. Mgr, Renee Berry

OPELOUSAS

P OPELOUSAS-EUNICE PUBLIC LIBRARY*, 212 E Grolee St, 70570. (Mail add: PO Box 249, 70571-0249), SAN 343-4796. Tel: 337-948-3693. FAX: 337-948-5200. E-mail: admin.b1oe@state.lib.la.us. Web Site: www.opelousas.lib.la.us. *Br Mgr,* Angela Zachery; *Admin Librn,* Walter O Stubbs; Staff 12 (MLS 1, Non-MLS 11)
Founded 1967. Pop 89,116
Library Holdings: AV Mats 680; Bk Vols 41,593; Per Subs 150
Special Collections: Large print bks
Subject Interests: Genealogy, Hist, La
Automation Activity & Vendor Info: (Cataloging) Book Systems; (Circulation) Book Systems; (OPAC) Book Systems
Database Vendor: ProQuest
Mem of Bayouland Library System
Partic in The Louisiana Library Network
Open Mon-Fri 8-5:30, Sat 8-5
Branches: 1
EUNICE PUBLIC, 222 S Second St, Eunice, 70535, SAN 343-4826. Tel: 337-457-7120. FAX: 337-457-7114. *Br Mgr,* Lettie Marcantel; Staff 3 (Non-MLS 3)
Library Holdings: AV Mats 130; Bk Vols 33,407; Per Subs 56
Open Mon-Wed 8-5:30, Thurs-Sat 8-5

PINEVILLE

CENTRAL LOUISIANA STATE HOSPITAL
M DISTEFANO MEMORIAL LIBRARY*, 242 W Shamrock St, 71361. (Mail add: PO Box 5031, 71360-5031), SAN 343-4850. Tel: 318-484-6363. FAX: 318-484-6284. *Librn,* Deborah Boerdoom; Staff 3 (MLS 1, Non-MLS 2)
Founded 1958
Library Holdings: Bk Titles 3,000; Bk Vols 5,000; Per Subs 150
Subject Interests: Mental health, Neurology, Psychiat, Psychol, Psychotherapy, Soc serv (soc work)
Partic in S Cent Regional Med Libr Program
Restriction: Med staff only

M FOREST GLEN PATIENT'S LIBRARY*, 242 W Shamrock St, 71361. (Mail add: PO Box 5031, 71360-5031), SAN 343-4885. Tel: 318-484-6364. FAX: 318-484-6284. *Librn,* Deborah Boerdoom
Library Holdings: Bk Vols 10,000; Per Subs 20

C LOUISIANA COLLEGE*, Richard W Norton Memorial Library, 1140 College Blvd, 71359. SAN 306-5243. Tel: 318-487-7201. Reference Tel: 318-487-7184. FAX: 318-487-7143. Web Site: www2.youseemore.com/lacollege. *Dir,* W Terry Martin; Tel: 318-487-7110, E-mail: martin@lacollege.edu; *User Serv Librn,* Elizabeth Parish; *Mgr, Acq Serv, Mgr, Ser,* Penny Hollingsworth; *Access Serv Coordr,* Julie Crews; Tel: 318-487-7109, E-mail: crews@lacollege.edu; Staff 4 (MLS 2, Non-MLS 2)
Founded 1906. Enrl 1,173; Fac 72; Highest Degree: Master
Aug 2011-Jul 2012 Income $403,236. Mats Exp $212,155. Sal $139,783
Library Holdings: e-books 47,000; Microforms 134,130; Bk Vols 353,582; Per Subs 402
Special Collections: Baptist History Coll. State Document Depository; US Document Depository
Automation Activity & Vendor Info: (Acquisitions) TLC (The Library Corporation); (Cataloging) TLC (The Library Corporation); (Circulation) TLC (The Library Corporation); (OPAC) TLC (The Library Corporation); (Serials) TLC (The Library Corporation)
Wireless access
Partic in Lyrasis
Open Mon-Thurs 7:45am-11pm, Fri 7:45-4, Sat 9-4, Sun 3-11

PLAQUEMINE

S GEORGIA GULF CORP LIBRARY*, 26100 Hwy 405, 70764. (Mail add: PO Box 629, 70765-0629). Tel: 225-298-2785. FAX: 225-687-8630. Web Site: www.ggc.com. *Librn,* Donna Purpera; E-mail: purperad@ggc.com
Library Holdings: Bk Vols 2,000; Per Subs 4
Special Collections: Plant Process, Process Safety & Technology; Technical Records, Codes & Standards
Restriction: Staff use only

P IBERVILLE PARISH LIBRARY*, 24605 J Gerald Berret Blvd, 70764. (Mail add: PO Box 736, 70765-0736), SAN 343-4915. Tel: 225-687-2520, 225-687-4397. FAX: 225-687-9719. E-mail: admin.c1il@pelican.state.lib.la.us. Web Site: www.iberville.lib.la.us. *Dir,* Dannie J Ball; E-mail: dball@state.lib.la.us; *Cat, Tech Serv Adminr,* Audrey Devillier; E-mail: adevilli@state.lib.la.us; *Adult Serv,* Laura Stewart; E-mail: lstewart@state.lib.la.us; *Ch Serv,* Anne Reeves; E-mail: areeves@state.lib.la.us; *Circ,* Sandra Gilbert; E-mail: sgilbert@state.lib.la.us; *Ser,* Julie Simoneaux; E-mail: jsimonea@state.lib.la.us; Staff 10 (MLS 4, Non-MLS 6)
Founded 1951. Pop 33,000; Circ 242,536
Jan 2008-Dec 2008 Income (Main Library and Branch(s)) $1,544,500. Mats Exp $271,171, Books $154,000, Per/Ser (Incl. Access Fees) $22,500, Other Print Mats $5,000, AV Equip $4,036, AV Mat $10,000, Electronic Ref Mat (Incl. Access Fees) $73,135. Sal $692,000 (Prof $202,000)
Library Holdings: DVDs 380; Large Print Bks 3,855; Bk Vols 174,803; Per Subs 594; Talking Bks 2,205; Videos 4,555
Special Collections: Oral History
Subject Interests: La, Local authors, Local hist
Automation Activity & Vendor Info: (Acquisitions) TLC (The Library Corporation); (Cataloging) TLC (The Library Corporation); (Circulation) TLC (The Library Corporation); (ILL) Auto-Graphics, Inc; (OPAC) TLC (The Library Corporation); (Serials) TLC (The Library Corporation)
Database Vendor: EBSCOhost, Facts on File, Gale Cengage Learning, Newsbank
Wireless access
Open Mon-Thurs 8:30-6:30, Fri 8:30-5, Sat 9-4
Friends of the Library Group
Branches: 7
BAYOU PIGEON, 36625 Hwy 75, 70764, SAN 343-4974. Tel: 225 545-8567. FAX: 225-545-8567. E-mail: bayoupigeon.c1il@state.lib.la.us. *Br Mgr,* Joy Mullins; Staff 1 (Non-MLS 1)
Pop 33,000
Library Holdings: Bk Vols 6,441; Per Subs 12
Open Mon & Wed 12-6, Fri 10-1 & 2-5
Friends of the Library Group
BAYOU SORREL, 33415 Hwy 75, 70764. (Mail add: 32983 Gracie Lane, 70764), SAN 343 494X. Tel. 225-659-7055. FAX: 225-659-7055. E-mail: bayousorrel.c1il@pelican.state.lib.la.us. *Br Mgr,* Jo Ann Mendoza; Staff 1 (Non-MLS 1)
Library Holdings: AV Mats 30; Bk Vols 5,113; Per Subs 16
Open Mon & Wed 12-6, Fri 10-1 & 2-5
EAST IBERVILLE, 5715 Monticello St, Saint Gabriel, 70776, SAN 343-5008. Tel: 225-642-8380. FAX: 225-642-8381. E-mail: eastiberville.c1il@pelican.state.lib.la.us. *Br Mgr,* Lydia Haydel; Staff 1 (Non-MLS 1)
Pop 33,000
Library Holdings: AV Mats 160; Bk Vols 29,569; Per Subs 42
Open Mon-Wed 9-5, Thurs 9-6, Sat 8-12
Friends of the Library Group
GROSSE TETE BRANCH, 18135 Willow Rd, Grosse Tete, 70740. (Mail add: PO Box 218, Grosse Tete, 70740), SAN 343-5016. Tel: 225-648-2667. FAX: 225-648-2667. E-mail: grossetete.c1il@pelican.state.lib.la.us. *Br Mgr,* Anna Angelloz; Staff 1 (Non-MLS 1)
Pop 33,000
Library Holdings: Bk Vols 6,124; Per Subs 10
Open Mon, Wed & Fri 10-1 & 2-5
Friends of the Library Group
MARINGOUIN BRANCH, 77175 Ridgewood Dr, Maringouin, 70757. (Mail add: PO Box 37, Maringouin, 70757), SAN 343-5032. Tel: 225-625-2743. FAX: 225-625-2743. E-mail: maringouin.c1il@pelican.state.lib.la.us. *Br Mgr,* Debra Lewis; Staff 1 (Non-MLS 1)
Pop 33,000
Library Holdings: Bk Vols 10,027; Per Subs 26
Open Mon & Wed 10-1 & 2-6:30, Fri 10-1 & 2-5
ROSEDALE BRANCH, 15695 Rosedale Rd, Rosedale, 70772. (Mail add: PO Box 410, Rosedale, 70772-0410), SAN 343-5067. Tel: 225-648-2213. FAX: 225-648-2213. E-mail: rosedale.c1il@pelican.state.lib.la.us. *Br Mgr,* Brenda Coles; Staff 1 (Non-MLS 1)

Library Holdings: Bk Vols 7,084; Per Subs 14
Open Tues 9-12 & 2-6, Thurs 9-12 & 1-5, Sat 12-4
Friends of the Library Group
WHITE CASTLE BRANCH, 32835 Bowie St, White Castle, 70788, SAN 343-5121. Tel: 225-545-8424. FAX: 225-545-4536. E-mail: whitecastle.c1il@pelican.state.lib.la.us. *Br Mgr,* Kitty Wood; Staff 1 (Non-MLS 1)
Library Holdings: AV Mats 110; Bk Vols 20,668; Per Subs 40
Open Mon, Tues & Thurs 8:30-5, Wed 8:30-6, Sat 9-1
Friends of the Library Group

PORT ALLEN

P WEST BATON ROUGE PARISH LIBRARY, 830 N Alexander Ave, 70767-2327. SAN 306-526X. Tel: 225-342-7920. FAX: 225-342-7918. Web Site: www.wbrpl.com. *Dir,* Beth Vandersteen; E-mail: bvandersteen@wbrplibrary.us; *Ad,* Luis Interiano; *Youth Serv Librn,* Judy Boyce; *Circ Mgr,* James D Bridges; *Cat,* Jacqueline Brown; *ILL & Ser,* Cyndi Jones; Staff 4 (MLS 4)
Founded 1965. Pop 24,600; Circ 93,784
Library Holdings: AV Mats 3,000; Bk Vols 90,000; Per Subs 180; Talking Bks 1,400
Special Collections: Louisiana Material
Automation Activity & Vendor Info: (Cataloging) TLC (The Library Corporation); (Circulation) TLC (The Library Corporation); (OPAC) TLC (The Library Corporation)
Database Vendor: AudioBookCloud, Auto-Graphics, Inc, Baker & Taylor, CredoReference, EBSCO Auto Repair Reference, EBSCO Information Services, EBSCOhost, McGraw-Hill, Medline, Overdrive, Inc, ProQuest, ReferenceUSA, TLC (The Library Corporation), TumbleBookLibrary, World Book Online
Wireless access
Special Services for the Deaf - Accessible learning ctr
Special Services for the Blind - Accessible computers; Assistive/Adapted tech devices, equip & products; Bks on CD; Children's Braille; Closed circuit TV magnifier; Computer access aids; Computer with voice synthesizer for visually impaired persons; Digital talking bk; Extensive large print coll; IBM screen reader; Large print bks; Large screen computer & software; Low vision equip; PC for handicapped; Screen enlargement software for people with visual disabilities; Screen reader software; Talking bk serv referral; Talking bks
Open Mon, Wed & Fri 8:30-5:30, Tues & Thurs 8:30-8, Sat 9-5
Bookmobiles: 1. Libr Tech, Amy Hebert

RAYVILLE

P RICHLAND PARISH LIBRARY*, 1410 Louisa St, 71269-3299. SAN 343-5156. Tel: 318-728-4806. FAX: 318-728-6108. *Dir,* Amanda Stewart; *Asst Librn,* Margie Parks; Staff 3 (Non-MLS 3)
Founded 1926. Pop 21,774; Circ 110,051
Library Holdings: AV Mats 256; Bk Vols 66,281; Per Subs 118
Special Collections: 1927 Flood Coll; Literature (Ruth Hatch Coll); Reference (Innis Morris Ellis Coll). Oral History
Automation Activity & Vendor Info: (Cataloging) TLC (The Library Corporation); (Circulation) TLC (The Library Corporation); (OPAC) TLC (The Library Corporation)
Partic in Loan SHARK; Lyrasis
Open Mon-Fri 8:30-5:30, Sat 9-1
Branches: 2
DELHI BRANCH, 520 Main St, Delhi, 71232, SAN 343-5180. Tel: 318-878-5121. FAX: 318-878-0674. *Br Mgr,* Kim Fryer; Staff 2 (Non-MLS 2)
Library Holdings: Bk Vols 19,101; Per Subs 47
Open Mon-Fri 8:30-5, Sat 8:30-Noon
MANGHAM BRANCH, 302 Hixon St, Mangham, 71259, SAN 343-5210. Tel: 318-248-2493. FAX: 318-248-3912. *Br Mgr,* Kathryn Berry; Staff 1 (Non-MLS 1)
Library Holdings: AV Mats 80; Bk Vols 7,900; Per Subs 21
Open Mon-Fri 9-5, Sat 8:30-Noon

RUSTON

P LINCOLN PARISH LIBRARY*, 910 N Trenton St, 71270-3328. SAN 306-5286. Tel: 318-251-5030. Administration Tel: 318-513-6409. FAX: 318-251-5045. Administration FAX: 318-513-6446. Administration E-mail: administrator@mylpl.org. Web Site: www.mylpl.org. *Dir,* Vivian McCain; Tel: 318-513-6408, Fax: 318-513-6446, E-mail: vmccain@mylpl.org; *Head, Ch,* Virginia Ham; Tel: 318-513-6413, E-mail: vham@mylpl.org; *Head, Circ,* Sharon Hancock; Tel: 318-513-6406, E-mail: shancock@mylpl.org; *Head, Mat Mgt,* Theresa Spivey; Tel: 318-513-6426, E-mail: tspivey@mylpl.org; *Head, Outreach Serv,* Micah Foreman; Tel: 318-513-6428, E-mail: mforeman@mylpl.org; *Head, Pub Serv,* Jeremy Bolom; Tel: 318-513-6412, E-mail: jbolom@mylpl.org; Staff 13 (MLS 2, Non-MLS 11)
Founded 1962. Pop 42,935; Circ 378,000
Jan 2007-Dec 2007 Income $2,069,700. Mats Exp $1,786,816. Sal $731,851
Library Holdings: DVDs 13,359; Bk Vols 98,016; Per Subs 279; Talking Bks 5,004
Subject Interests: Genealogy, Local hist
Automation Activity & Vendor Info: (Cataloging) Auto-Graphics, Inc; (Circulation) Auto-Graphics, Inc; (OPAC) Auto-Graphics, Inc
Wireless access
Publications: Library Pages (Newsletter)
Partic in Green Gold Libr Syst
Special Services for the Deaf - Assistive tech
Special Services for the Blind - Assistive/Adapted tech devices, equip & products
Open Mon-Thurs 9-8, Fri & Sat 9-6, Sun 1-5
Friends of the Library Group

C LOUISIANA TECH UNIVERSITY*, Prescott Memorial Library, Everett St at The Columns, 71272. (Mail add: PO Box 10408, 71272-0046), SAN 306-5294. Tel: 318-257-3555. Interlibrary Loan Service Tel: 318-257-2926. Administration Tel: 318-257-2577. Information Services Tel: 318-257-2231. FAX: 318-257-2579. Interlibrary Loan Service FAX: 318-257-2447. Web Site: www.latech.edu/library. *Dean of Libr Serv,* Michael A DiCarlo; E-mail: miked@latech.edu; *Dir, Acad Serv,* Position Currently Open; *Dir, Coll Serv,* Mary McCorkle; *Head, Spec Coll, Ms & Archives,* Peggy Carter; *Electronic Serv Librn,* Rebecca Brantley; *Govt Pub Librn,* Rita Franks; *User Educ Librn,* Boris Teske; *User Serv Librn,* Robert Bremer; *Bibliog Mgt,* Daniel Bates; *Coll Develop,* John Calhoun; *IT Spec,* William Lancaster; *ILL,* Laura Ogden; *Ref,* Lynell Buckley; *Ref,* Kevin Cuccia; *Ref,* Sue McFadden; Staff 27 (MLS 11, Non-MLS 16)
Founded 1895. Enrl 11,257; Fac 390; Highest Degree: Doctorate
Jul 2007-Jun 2008 Income $3,464,357. Mats Exp $1,268,088, Books $92,401, Per/Ser (Incl. Access Fees) $1,157,448, Presv $18,239. Sal $1,265,520 (Prof $791,040)
Library Holdings: AV Mats 553; CDs 7,874; e-books 57,154; e-journals 57,419; Microforms 574,891; Bk Vols 456,152; Per Subs 2,654
Special Collections: State Document Depository; US Document Depository
Automation Activity & Vendor Info: (Acquisitions) SirsiDynix; (Cataloging) SirsiDynix; (Circulation) SirsiDynix; (OPAC) SirsiDynix; (Serials) SirsiDynix
Partic in La Acad Libr Info Network Consortium; Lyrasis

SAINT BENEDICT

CR SAINT JOSEPH SEMINARY COLLEGE*, Rouquette Library, 75376 River Rd, 70457-9900. SAN 306-5308. Tel: 985-867-2237. FAX: 985-867-2270. E-mail: rouquette@sjasc.edu. Web Site: www.sjasc.edu. *Dir,* Bonnie Bess Wood; Staff 6 (MLS 3, Non-MLS 3)
Founded 1891. Enrl 120; Highest Degree: Bachelor
Library Holdings: Bk Vols 60,000; Per Subs 155
Special Collections: Howze Philosophy Coll
Subject Interests: Educ, Fine arts, Hist, Lit, Philos, Relig
Automation Activity & Vendor Info: (Cataloging) Mandarin Library Automation; (Circulation) Mandarin Library Automation; (OPAC) Mandarin Library Automation
Database Vendor: EBSCOhost
Open Mon-Sun 8am-10:30pm

SAINT FRANCISVILLE

P WEST FELICIANA PARISH LIBRARY*, 11865 Ferdinand St, 70775-4341. (Mail add: PO Box 3120, 70775-3120), SAN 342-8915. Tel: 225-635-3364. FAX: 225-635-4986. Web Site: www.wfplibrary.org. *Libr Dir,* Glenna Clark Fallin; E-mail: gfallin@wfplibrary.org; *Libr Mgr,* Penny Graham; E-mail: pgraham@wfplibrary.org; Staff 6 (MLS 3, Non-MLS 3)
Founded 2003. Pop 15,000
Library Holdings: Per Subs 75
Special Collections: Genealogy (Louisiana & West Feliciana Parish)
Automation Activity & Vendor Info: (Acquisitions) Baker & Taylor; (Cataloging) TLC (The Library Corporation); (Circulation) TLC (The Library Corporation); (ILL) OCLC; (OPAC) TLC (The Library Corporation); (Serials) EBSCO Online
Database Vendor: 3M Library Systems, TLC (The Library Corporation), TumbleBookLibrary
Wireless access
Function: Adult bk club, Art exhibits, Bilingual assistance for Spanish patrons, Bk club(s), Bks on CD, Children's prog, Computer training, Computers for patron use, Copy machines, Digital talking bks, Electronic databases & coll, Free DVD rentals, Genealogy discussion group, Govt ref serv, Home delivery & serv to Sr ctr & nursing homes, ILL available, Jail serv, Music CDs, Online cat, Online ref, Photocopying/Printing, Preschool outreach, Printer for laptops & handheld devices, Pub access computers, Ref serv available, Story hour, Summer reading prog, Tax forms, Teen prog, Wheelchair accessible

Open Mon-Fri 8:30-6, Sat 9-1
Friends of the Library Group

SAINT GABRIEL

S HUNT CORRECTIONAL CENTER LIBRARY*, 6925 Hwy 74, 70776. (Mail add: PO Box 174, 70776-0174). Tel: 225-319-4513. FAX: 225-319-4596. *Librn,* Warren Hubert; Tel: 225-319-4507
Library Holdings: Bk Vols 7,000; Per Subs 40

S LOUISIANA CORRECTIONAL INSTITUTE FOR WOMEN LIBRARY*, Hwy 74, 70776. (Mail add: PO Box 26, 70776-0026), SAN 306-5316. Tel: 225-642-5529. FAX: 225-319-2757. *Coordr,* Paula Chong
Founded 1969
Library Holdings: Bk Vols 6,900; Per Subs 14
Database Vendor: Westlaw
Open Mon-Fri 8-8, Sat & Sun 8-2:30
Friends of the Library Group

SAINT JOSEPH

P TENSAS PARISH LIBRARY*, 135 Plank Rd, 71366. (Mail add: PO Box 228, 71366-0228), SAN 306-5324. Tel: 318-766-3781. FAX: 318-766-0098. E-mail: admin.t1tn@pelican.state.lib.la.us. *Dir,* Elizabeth Waggoner; Staff 4 (Non-MLS 4)
Founded 1952. Pop 7,200; Circ 37,453
Library Holdings: AV Mats 300; Bk Vols 25,600; Per Subs 32
Special Collections: Louisiana Section
Automation Activity & Vendor Info: (Cataloging) Book Systems
Open Mon-Wed & Fri 8-5, Thurs 8-12

SAINT MARTINVILLE

P SAINT MARTIN PARISH LIBRARY*, St Martinville Branch, 201 Porter St, 70582. SAN 306-5332. Tel: 337-394-2207, Ext 23. FAX: 337-394-2248. Web Site: www.stmartin.lib.la.us. *Dir,* Charlar Brew; *Br Mgr,* Theresa Williams; *Automation Librn, Ref Librn,* Paul Ardoin; *Coll Develop,* Teresa Thibodeaux; *Coordr, Ch Serv,* Sandra Solomon; *ILL,* Serhania Mitchell; Staff 19 (MLS 2, Non-MLS 17)
Founded 1955. Pop 46,262; Circ 199,003
Library Holdings: AV Mats 900; Bk Vols 142,883; Per Subs 278
Subject Interests: Genealogy, Hist, La
Automation Activity & Vendor Info: (Cataloging) TLC (The Library Corporation); (Circulation) TLC (The Library Corporation); (OPAC) TLC (The Library Corporation)
Publications: Genealogy catalog, microfilm catalog
Open Mon-Thurs 8-8, Fri & Sat 8-5
Friends of the Library Group
Branches: 4
ARNAUDVILLE BRANCH, 1021 Overton St, Arnaudville, 70512-3226, SAN 377-6107. Tel: 337-754-5037. FAX: 337-754-5037. *Libr Asst I,* Maureen DeVillier; Staff 1 (Non-MLS 1)
Library Holdings: Bk Vols 20,000; Per Subs 41
Open Mon & Wed 1-6
Friends of the Library Group
BREAUX BRIDGE BRANCH, 102 Courthouse St, Breaux Bridge, 70517, SAN 329-6962. Tel: 337-332-2733. FAX: 337-332-2733. *Br Mgr,* Lester Latiolais; Staff 2 (Non-MLS 2)
Library Holdings: AV Mats 310; Bk Vols 25,000; Per Subs 46
Open Mon-Thurs 8-8, Fri & Sat 8-5
Friends of the Library Group
CECILIA BRANCH, 2460 Cecilia Sr High School Hwy, Cecilia, 70521, SAN 329-6989. Tel: 337-667-7411. FAX: 337-667-7411. *Br Mgr,* Mary Jones; Staff 2 (Non-MLS 2)
Library Holdings: Bk Vols 11,000; Per Subs 27
Open Mon-Thurs 10-6, Fri & Sat 8-4
Friends of the Library Group
PARKS BRANCH, 1012 Martin St, Parks, 70582, SAN 377-614X. Tel: 337-845-4693. FAX: 337-845-4693. *Libr Asst I,* Maureen DeVillier; Staff 2 (Non-MLS 2)
Library Holdings: Bk Vols 16,000; Per Subs 29
Open Tues & Thurs 1-6
Friends of the Library Group

SHREVEPORT

S AMERICAN ROSE SOCIETY LIBRARY*, 8877 Jefferson Paige Rd, 71119-8817. (Mail add: PO Box 30000, 71130-0030), SAN 327-4616. Tel: 318-938-5402. FAX: 318-938-5405. E-mail: ars@ars-hq.org. Web Site: www.ars.org. *Librn,* Peggy Spivey
Library Holdings: Bk Titles 1,000
Subject Interests: Gardening

R B'NAI ZION CONGREGATION*, B'Nai Zion Memorial Library, 245 Southfield Rd, 71105. SAN 306-5359. Tel: 318-861-2122. FAX: 318-861-7961. E-mail: bnaizion@bellsouth.net. Web Site: www.bnaizioncongregation.org. *Librn,* Judith Grunes
Founded 1952
Library Holdings: Bk Titles 4,200
Subject Interests: Art, Hist, Judaica (lit or hist of Jews), Lit, Philos
Open Mon-Fri 9-4

C CENTENARY COLLEGE OF LOUISIANA, John F Magale Memorial Library, 2834 Woodlawn St, 71104-3335. (Mail add: 2911 Centenary Blvd, PO Box 41188, 71134-1188), SAN 306-5367. Tel: 318-869-5047. Interlibrary Loan Service Tel: 318-869-5202. Administration Tel: 318-869-5057, 318-869-5220. FAX: 318-869-5004. E-mail: ref@centenary.edu. Web Site: www.centenary.edu/library. *Dir of Libr Serv,* Christy Jordan Wrenn; E-mail: cwrenn@centenary.edu; *Dir, Hurley Music Libr,* Thomas Hundemer; Tel: 318-689-5247, Fax: 318-869-5248, E-mail: thundemer@centenary.edu; *Pub Access Librn,* Jeannette Curtis; E-mail: jcurtis@centenary.edu; *Cat, Ref/Electronic Res/Web Librn,* Kristi Kohl; E-mail: kkohl@centenary.edu; *Ser Coll Mgr & Acq,* Marcia M Alexander; E-mail: malexand@centenary.edu; *Archivist, Res,* Chris Brown; Tel: 318-869-5462, Fax: 318-869-5462, E-mail: archives@centenary.edu; *Circ, Doc Delivery, ILL,* Sharon K Chevalier; E-mail: schevali@centenary.edu. Subject Specialists: *Music hist,* Thomas Hundemer; *Info literacy,* Kristi Kohl; *Ill,* Sharon K Chevalier; Staff 7 (MLS 4, Non-MLS 3)
Founded 1825. Enrl 617; Fac 133; Highest Degree: Master
Library Holdings: AV Mats 29,789; Bks-By-Mail 2,315; Bks on Deafness & Sign Lang 10; CDs 4,644; DVDs 7,470; e-books 88,661; e-journals 11,332; Electronic Media & Resources 329,002; Microforms 362,333; Music Scores 14,592; Bk Titles 173,802; Bk Vols 254,708; Per Subs 204; Videos 7,470
Special Collections: Bill Corrington Papers & Personal Library; Centenary College Archives; Jack London Papers; North Louisiana Historical Association Archives; Pierce Cline Archive; Rare Books; Religious Studies Coll; United Methodist Church Archives
Subject Interests: Am lit, Geol, Music educ, Relig
Automation Activity & Vendor Info: (Acquisitions) SIRSI WorkFlows; (Cataloging) SIRSI WorkFlows; (Circulation) SIRSI WorkFlows; (Course Reserve) SIRSI WorkFlows; (ILL) OCLC FirstSearch; (Media Booking) SIRSI WorkFlows; (OPAC) SIRSI WorkFlows; (Serials) SIRSI WorkFlows
Database Vendor: 3M Library Systems, Agricola, American Chemical Society, American Mathematical Society, Amigos Library Services, Annual Reviews, ARTstor, Cambridge Scientific Abstracts, CredoReference, EBSCOhost, Gale Cengage Learning, IOP, JSTOR, LearningExpress, LexisNexis, Nature Publishing Group, OCLC FirstSearch, OCLC WorldShare Interlibrary Loan, ProQuest, Sage, SirsiDynix, Springer-Verlag Wireless access
Function: Art exhibits, ILL available
Publications: Archives & Special Coll (Archives guide); Information Literacy Handbook (Research guide); Magale Library Annual Report (Research guide); Magale Library Welcomes Centernary College Alumni (Reference guide); Online Information Literacy Subject Research Guides (Research guide); Student Worker Guidelines & Evaluation (Reference guide); The Magale Message (Monthly newsletter); Welcome to John F Magale Memorial Library (Research guide); Welcome to Non-Centenary College Patrons (Reference guide)
Partic in Amigos Library Services, Inc; ARIEL; Associated Colleges of the South; Louisiana Academic Library Information Network (LALINC); Lyrasis; OCLC Online Computer Library Center, Inc; OCLC-LVIS; Tex Independent Cols & Univ Librs; The Louisiana Library Network
Special Services for the Deaf - Bks on deafness & sign lang
Open Mon-Thurs 8am-Midnight, Fri 8-4:30, Sun 4-Midnight
Restriction: Authorized patrons, Authorized scholars by appt, Borrowing privileges limited to fac & registered students, ID required to use computers (Ltd hrs), Lending libr only via mail, Private libr

M CHRISPUS SCHEMPERT HEALTH SYSTEM*, Medical Library, One Saint Mary Pl, 71120. (Mail add: PO Box 21976, 71101-1976), SAN 324-5683. Tel: 318-681-4500, 318-681-4501. FAX: 318-681-4514. Web Site: www.christusschumpert.org.
Library Holdings: Bk Vols 500
Restriction: Staff use only

GM DEPARTMENT OF VETERANS AFFAIRS, Overton Brooks Medical Center Library, 510 E Stoner Ave, 71101-4295. SAN 306-5502. Tel: 318-990-5181. Interlibrary Loan Service Tel: 318-990-5061. FAX: 318-990-5570. E-mail: vhashrvalib@va.gov. *Librn,* Mary Virginia Taylor; E-mail: maryvirginia.taylor1@va.gov; *Libr Tech,* Sarah Logan; E-mail: sarah.logan@va.gov. Subject Specialists: *Health sci,* Mary Virginia Taylor; Staff 2 (MLS 1, Non-MLS 1)
Founded 1950
Oct 2012-Sept 2013 Income $175,711. Mats Exp $176,061, Books $91,080, Per/Ser (Incl. Access Fees) $42,318, AV Mat $1,000, Electronic Ref Mat (Incl. Access Fees) $41,663. Sal $129,356 (Prof $90,344)

Library Holdings: e-journals 1,500; Electronic Media & Resources 1,700; Bk Titles 1,000; Bk Vols 1,100; Per Subs 117
Subject Interests: Clinical med
Automation Activity & Vendor Info: (Acquisitions) CyberTools for Libraries; (Cataloging) CyberTools for Libraries; (Circulation) CyberTools for Libraries; (OPAC) CyberTools for Libraries; (Serials) CyberTools for Libraries
Database Vendor: Cinahl, CyberTools for Libraries, DynaMed, ebrary, EBSCOhost, Lexi-Comp, MD Consult, Natural Standard, Nature Publishing Group, OVID Technologies, ProQuest, PubMed, RefWorks, ScienceDirect, SerialsSolutions, STAT!Ref (Teton Data Systems), UpToDate
Function: Audio & video playback equip for onsite use, Bks on cassette, Bks on CD, Computers for patron use, Copy machines, Doc delivery serv, e-mail serv, Electronic databases & coll, For res purposes, ILL available, Online cat, Online ref, Online searches, Orientations, Photocopying/Printing, Prof lending libr, Provide serv for the mentally ill, Ref & res, Ref serv in person, Scanner, Spoken cassettes & CDs, Telephone ref, VHS videos
Partic in Docline
Open Mon-Fri 8-4:30

R FIRST PRESBYTERIAN CHURCH LIBRARY*, 900 Jordan St, 71101. SAN 306-5383. Tel: 318-222-0604. FAX: 318-221-8589. Web Site: www.fpcshreveport.org.
Founded 1952
Library Holdings: Bk Titles 7,500
Special Collections: A-Tapes, Sermons & Lectures
Open Mon-Fri 9-Noon, Sun 9am-11am

R FIRST UNITED METHODIST CHURCH*, Bliss Memorial Library, 500 Common St, 71101. (Mail add: PO Box 1567, 71165-1567), SAN 306-5375. Tel: 318-424-7771, Ext 113. FAX: 318-429-6888. Web Site: www.fumcshreveport.org. *Librn,* Ellen Caverlee; Tel: 318-865-4706; Staff 20 (MLS 3, Non-MLS 17)
Founded 1946
Library Holdings: Large Print Bks 75; Bk Titles 12,000; Bk Vols 12,500
Subject Interests: Fiction, Relig
Special Services for the Blind - Large print bks
Restriction: Mem only, Not open to pub

C LOUISIANA STATE UNIVERSITY, Noel Memorial Library, One University Pl, 71115-2399. SAN 306-5405. Tel: 318-798-5069. Interlibrary Loan Service Tel: 318-797-5225. Reference Tel: 318-798-5068. Administration Tel: 318-798-4131. FAX: 318-797-5156. Administration FAX: 318-798-4138. Web Site: www.lsus.edu/library. *Dean,* Dr Alan D Gabehart; *Head, Access Serv & Syst,* Brian Sherman; Tel: 318-797-5382; *Head, Res Serv,* Dr Julienne Wood; Tel: 318-797-5072; *Head, Tech Serv & Cat,* James Evans; Tel: 318-797-5070; *Archivist,* Dr Laura McLemore; Tel: 318-797-5378; *Acq,* Becky Dean; Tel: 318-798-4157; *Circ & ILL,* Susan Davison; Tel: 318-797-5225; *Curator, James Smith Noel Coll,* Dr Robert Leitz; Tel: 318-798-4161; *Govt Doc,* Rachael Green; Tel: 318-798-4158; *Ser,* Jacqueline Brooks; Tel: 318-798-4159; Staff 11 (MLS 8, Non-MLS 3)
Founded 1967. Enrl 4,000; Fac 160; Highest Degree: Doctorate
Jul 2014-Jun 2015 Income $1,387,933. Sal $731,570 (Prof $443,757)
Library Holdings: AV Mats 4,550; e-books 254,056; e-journals 73,943; Microforms 413,534; Bk Vols 396,348; Per Subs 298
Special Collections: James Smith Noel Coll; Northwest Louisiana & Lower Red River Region (Archives & Special Coll). Oral History; State Document Depository; US Document Depository
Automation Activity & Vendor Info: (Acquisitions) SirsiDynix; (Cataloging) SirsiDynix; (Circulation) SirsiDynix; (Course Reserve) SirsiDynix; (ILL) OCLC; (OPAC) SirsiDynix; (Serials) SirsiDynix
Database Vendor: ACM (Association for Computing Machinery), American Psychological Association (APA), EBSCO Discovery Service, EBSCOhost, JSTOR, LexisNexis, Marcive, Inc, Mergent Online, OCLC WorldShare Interlibrary Loan, SirsiDynix, Thomson - Web of Science, Westlaw
Wireless access
Function: 24/7 Electronic res, 24/7 Online cat
Partic in Amigos Library Services, Inc; OCLC Online Computer Library Center, Inc; The Louisiana Library Network
Open Mon-Thurs 7:30am-9pm, Fri 7:30-4:30, Sun 1-9

CM LOUISIANA STATE UNIVERSITY HEALTH SCIENCES CENTER*, Medical Library, 1501 Kings Hwy, 71130. (Mail add: PO Box 33932, 71130-3932), SAN 306-5413. Tel: 318-675-5445. Reference Tel: 318-675-5477. FAX: 318-675-5442. Web Site: lib-sh.lsuhsc.edu. *Dir,* Marianne L Comegys; Tel: 318-675-5449, E-mail: mcomeg@lsuhsc.edu; *Asst Dir, Syst,* Mararia Adams; Tel: 318-675-5448, E-mail: madams@lsuhsc.edu; *Head, Cat,* Dee Jones; Tel: 318-675-5458, E-mail: djone4@lsuhsc.edu; *Head, Coll Mgt,* Betty Tucker; Tel: 318-675-5457, E-mail: btucke@lsuhsc.edu; *Head, Ref,* Kerri Christopher; Tel: 318-675-5393, E-mail: kchris@lsuhsc.edu; *Head, User Access Serv,* Dawn Southwell; Tel: 318-675-4712, E-mail: dsouth@lsuhsc.edu; *Head, User Educ/Outreach,* Donna Timm; Tel: 318-675-5474, E-mail: dtimm@lsuhsc.edu; *ILL,* Barbara Reilly; Tel: 318-675-5452, E-mail: breill@lsuhsc.edu; Staff 22 (MLS 16, Non-MLS 6)
Founded 1968. Enrl 400; Highest Degree: Doctorate
Library Holdings: Bk Vols 190,623; Per Subs 325
Special Collections: Archives; History of Medicine; Medical Fiction
Subject Interests: Allied health, Med, Nursing
Automation Activity & Vendor Info: (Acquisitions) Innovative Interfaces, Inc; (Cataloging) Innovative Interfaces, Inc; (Circulation) Innovative Interfaces, Inc; (OPAC) Innovative Interfaces, Inc; (Serials) Innovative Interfaces, Inc
Database Vendor: EBSCOhost, OVID Technologies
Function: Doc delivery serv
Publications: Library Bulletin (Bi-monthly); Library Newsletter; LSUMC Faculty Publications (ann)
Partic in South Central Academic Medical Libraries Consortium; The Louisiana Library Network
Open Mon-Fri 7:30am-11pm, Sat 9am-11pm, Sun 1-11

CM NORTHWESTERN STATE UNIVERSITY LIBRARIES*, Shreveport Nursing Library, 1800 Line Ave, 71101. SAN 306-5421. Tel: 318-677-3007. Interlibrary Loan Service Tel: 318-677-3008. FAX: 318-676-7087. Web Site: www.nsula.edu/watson_library/shreve/default.htm. *Head Librn,* Paula Craig; E-mail: craigp@nsula.edu; *Libr Assoc,* Dorthy Fernandez; E-mail: fernandezd@nsula.edu; *Libr Assoc,* Sandra Rufty; E-mail: ruftys@nsula.edu; Staff 3 (MLS 1, Non-MLS 2)
Founded 1949. Enrl 1,100; Fac 52; Highest Degree: Master
Library Holdings: AV Mats 317; e-journals 239; Electronic Media & Resources 15; Bk Titles 8,114; Bk Vols 8,190; Per Subs 198
Special Collections: Historical Nursing Texts, microfilm
Subject Interests: Nursing, Radiologic tech
Automation Activity & Vendor Info: (Acquisitions) SirsiDynix; (Cataloging) SirsiDynix; (Circulation) SirsiDynix; (OPAC) SirsiDynix; (Serials) SirsiDynix
Database Vendor: Cambridge Scientific Abstracts, EBSCOhost, Gale Cengage Learning, JSTOR, LexisNexis, OVID Technologies, ProQuest
Partic in Docline; Louisiana Academic Library Information Network (LALINC); National Network of Libraries of Medicine; OCLC; The Louisiana Library Network
Open Mon-Thurs 8-8, Fri 8-4:30, Sat 10-5
Friends of the Library Group

S R W NORTON ART GALLERY, Reference & Research Library, 4747 Creswell Ave, 71106-1899. SAN 306-543X. Tel: 318-865-4201. FAX: 318-869-0435. E-mail: gallery@rwnaf.org. Web Site: www.rwnaf.org. *Cat,* Melisa Elrod; E-mail: me@rwnaf.org
Founded 1946
Library Holdings: Bk Titles 10,000; Per Subs 10
Special Collections: Early US, State & Local History, especially Virginia (James M Owens Memorial)
Subject Interests: Fine arts, Genealogy, Ornithology
Restriction: Non-circulating to the pub

P SHREVE MEMORIAL LIBRARY*, 424 Texas St, 71101. (Mail add: PO Box 21523, 71120-1523), SAN 343-5245. Tel: 318-226-5897. Interlibrary Loan Service Tel: 318-226-5887. Reference Tel: 318-226-5894. Administration Tel: 318-226-5871. Automation Services Tel: 318-226-5865. FAX: 318-226-4780. Reference FAX: 318-226-4782. Administration E-mail: admin.g1sh@pelican.state.lib.la.us. Web Site: www.shreve-lib.org. *Dir,* Dr Ron Heezen; Tel: 318-226-5870; *Asst Dir, Coordr, Br Serv,* Cindy Ortego; Tel: 318-226-5881, E-mail: cortego@shreve-lib.org; *Spec Coll Librn,* Pat Ferguson; Tel: 318-226-5888, E-mail: patf@shreve-lib.org; *Acq Mgr,* Peggy Evans; Tel: 318-226-5876, Fax: 318-429-4387, E-mail: pevans@shreve-lib.org; *Cat Mgr,* Belverly White; *Circ Mgr,* Dionci Sutton; *Human Res Mgr,* Jennie Paxton; Tel: 318-226-4789, E-mail: jpaxton@shreve-lib.org; *Mgr, ILL,* Linda McCrary; E-mail: lmmcrary@shreve-lib.org; *Tech Serv Mgr,* Grace Simmons; Tel: 318-226-4975, E-mail: gsimmons@shreve-lib.org; *Automation Syst Coordr,* Greg Frith; E-mail: gfrith@shreve-lib.org; *Coordr, Ch Serv,* Mary Ann Skarda; Tel: 318-226-5880, E-mail: maskarda@shreve-lib.org; *Ref Serv Coordr,* Barbara Moore; *Acq,* Susan Wise; Tel: 318-226-4980, E-mail: swise@shreve-lib.org; *Admin Serv,* Kathy Tuminello; E-mail: ktuminello@shreve-lib.org; *Financial Serv Assoc,* Carol Brossette; Tel: 318-226-5873, E-mail: cbrossette@shreve-lib.org; *Pub Relations,* Ivy Woodard-Latin; Tel: 318-226-4976, E-mail: ilatin@shreve-lib.org; Staff 48 (MLS 18, Non-MLS 30)
Founded 1923. Pop 250,342; Circ 1,037,046
Library Holdings: AV Mats 65,527; CDs 12,708; DVDs 18,946; Large Print Bks 15,181; Bk Titles 325,443; Bk Vols 725,184; Per Subs 660; Talking Bks 5,896; Videos 27,977
Special Collections: Louisiana Coll. State Document Depository; US Document Depository
Subject Interests: Geol, Petroleum

Automation Activity & Vendor Info: (Acquisitions) SirsiDynix; (Cataloging) SirsiDynix; (Circulation) SirsiDynix; (ILL) TLC (The Library Corporation); (OPAC) SirsiDynix
Database Vendor: SirsiDynix
Wireless access
Function: Adult bk club, Adult literacy prog, Archival coll, AV serv, Bus archives, Computer training, Copy machines, Doc delivery serv, e-mail serv, Electronic databases & coll, Fax serv, Handicapped accessible, Home delivery & serv to Sr ctr & nursing homes, ILL available, Music CDs, Newsp ref libr, Online searches, Outside serv via phone, mail, e-mail & web, Photocopying/Printing, Prog for children & young adult, Ref serv available, Res libr, Summer reading prog, Tax forms, Telephone ref, VHS videos, Video lending libr, Wheelchair accessible
Publications: Area Agencies & Organizations Directory (Annual); Creating Literacy: Literacy Specialist Training Manual (Library handbook); LITstART: The Art of Family Literacy; Magazine List (Serials catalog); PALS Club: Peer Advocates for Learning & Success (Library handbook); Read for Your Life: Early Childhood Literacy & Family Learning Initiative (Library handbook)
Partic in Green Gold Libr Syst
Special Services for the Blind - Audio mat; Bks on cassette; Bks on CD; Copier with enlargement capabilities; Large print bks; Ref serv; Talking bks
Open Mon-Thurs 9-9 Fri & Sat 9-6, Sun 1-5
Friends of the Library Group
Branches: 20
ATKINS BRANCH, 3704 Greenwood Rd, 71109, SAN 343-527X. Tel: 318-635-6222. FAX: 318-635-6912. E-mail: publicatkins@shreve-lib.org. *Br Mgr,* Wolanda Hall; E-mail: whall@shreve-lib.org; Staff 1 (Non-MLS 1)
Founded 1965
Library Holdings: Bk Vols 20,871
Function: Adult bk club, Music CDs, Online searches, Prog for adults, Prog for children & young adult, Summer reading prog, VHS videos, Wheelchair accessible
Open Mon-Wed 9-8, Thurs-Sat 9-6
Friends of the Library Group
BELCHER-WYCHE BRANCH, 409 Charles St, Belcher, 71004. (Mail add: PO Box 121, Belcher, 71004-0121), SAN 343-530X. Tel: 318-378-4567. FAX: 318-378-4567. *Br Mgr,* Lesa Miller; Staff 1 (Non-MLS 1)
Pop 270
Library Holdings: Audiobooks 48; CDs 89; DVDs 1,008; Bk Vols 5,500; Per Subs 24
Special Collections: Louisana Fiction & Nonfiction Coll
Open Tues 1-7, Thurs 3-6, Fri 10-12 & 1-5
Friends of the Library Group
BLANCHARD BRANCH, 344 Alexander St, Blanchard, 71009, SAN 343-5334. Tel: 318-929-3163. FAX: 318-929-3163. *Br Mgr,* Grace Harr; E-mail: gharr@shreve-lib.org; Staff 1 (Non-MLS 1)
Library Holdings: Bk Vols 7,088
Open Mon & Wed 11-5, Tues & Thurs 12-6, Fri 11-4
Friends of the Library Group
BROADMOOR BRANCH, 1212 Captain Shreve Dr, 71105, SAN 343-5369. Tel: 318-869-0120. FAX: 318-868-9464. *Br Mgr,* Maria Colon; Staff 5 (MLS 3, Non-MLS 2)
Founded 1948
Library Holdings: Bk Vols 79,122
Subject Interests: Genealogy
Function: Handicapped accessible, Music CDs, Online searches, Photocopying/Printing, Prog for children & young adult, Ref serv available, Summer reading prog
Open Mon-Thurs 9-9, Fri & Sat 9-6, Sun 1-5
Friends of the Library Group
CEDAR GROVE-LINE AVENUE BRANCH, 8303 Line Ave, 71106, SAN 343-5393. Tel: 318-868-3890. FAX: 318-868-2071. *Br Mgr,* MaryAnne Coppersmith; Staff 1 (MLS 1)
Founded 1929
Library Holdings: Bk Vols 32,821
Function: Adult literacy prog, Music CDs, Online searches, Photocopying/Printing, Prog for children & young adult, Summer reading prog, Wheelchair accessible
Open Mon-Wed 9-8, Thurs-Sat 9-6
Friends of the Library Group
GILLIAM BRANCH, 12797 Main St, Gilliam, 71029, SAN 343-5407. Tel: 318-296-4227. FAX: 318-296-4227. *Br Mgr,* Betty Hall; Staff 1 (Non-MLS 1)
Library Holdings: Bk Vols 6,532
Open Tues 1-6, Thurs 9-2
Friends of the Library Group
HAMILTON/SOUTH CADDO BRANCH, 2111 Bert Kouns Industrial Loop, 71118, SAN 343-5423. Tel: 318-687-6824. FAX: 318-686-0971. *Br Mgr,* Catherine Beaird; *Head, Ch,* Julie Grice; E-mail: jgrice@shreve-lib.org; *Circ Supvr,* Pam Charles; *Ref Serv Coordr,* Barbara Skains; E-mail: bskains@shreve-lib.org; Staff 2 (MLS 2)
Founded 1961
Library Holdings: Bk Vols 75,215
Function: Art exhibits, Handicapped accessible, Online searches, Photocopying/Printing, Prog for children & young adult, Ref serv available, Summer reading prog, VHS videos, Wheelchair accessible
Special Services for the Blind - Audio mat; Bks on cassette; Bks on CD; Large print bks; Talking bks
Open Mon-Thurs 9-9 (9-7 Jun-Aug), Fri & Sat 9-6, Sun 1-5
Friends of the Library Group
HIGGINBOTHAM/BRYSON BRANCH, 9359 Greenwood Rd, Greenwood, 71033, SAN 343-5458. Tel: 318-938-1451. FAX: 318-938-1451. *Br Mgr,* Cathy Key; Staff 1 (Non-MLS 1)
Library Holdings: Bk Vols 6,842
Function: Online searches, Summer reading prog, VHS videos, Wheelchair accessible
Open Mon, Fri & Sat 9-1, Tues & Thurs 3-7, Wed 1-5
Friends of the Library Group
HOLLYWOOD/UNION AVENUE, 2105 Hollywood Ave, 71108, SAN 328-8986. Tel: 318-636-5520. *Br Mgr,* Dawn Solomon; E-mail: dsolomon@shreve-lib.org; *Asst Br Mgr,* Pam Perry; Staff 1 (Non-MLS 1)
Founded 1965
Library Holdings: Bk Vols 24,728
Function: Handicapped accessible, Home delivery & serv to Sr ctr & nursing homes, Homebound delivery serv, Music CDs, Online searches, Photocopying/Printing, Prog for children & young adult, Summer reading prog, VHS videos, Wheelchair accessible
Open Mon-Wed 9-8, Thurs-Sat 9-6
Friends of the Library Group
HOSSTON BRANCH, 15487 US Hwy 71, Hosston, 71043, SAN 343-5482. Tel: 318-287-3265. FAX: 318-287-3265. *Br Mgr,* Rebecca Dean; Staff 1 (Non-MLS 1)
Library Holdings: Bk Vols 5,702
Open Mon & Fri 1-5, Wed 9-5
Friends of the Library Group
MEANS/IDA BRANCH, 7016 E Magnolia Lane, Ida, 71044, SAN 343-5547. Tel: 318-284-3416. *Br Mgr,* Wanda Dial; Staff 1 (Non-MLS 1)
Library Holdings: Bk Vols 6,249
Open Tues & Fri 1-5, Sat 12-4
Friends of the Library Group
MOORETOWN, 4360 Hollywood Ave, 71109. Tel: 318-636-5524. FAX: 318-636-6438. *Br Mgr,* Rose Davis; Staff 1 (MLS 1)
Founded 2003
Library Holdings: Bk Vols 18,256
Function: Handicapped accessible, Music CDs, Online searches, Photocopying/Printing, Prog for children & young adult, Summer reading prog, Wheelchair accessible
Open Mon-Wed 9-8, Thurs-Sat 9-6
Friends of the Library Group
MOORINGSPORT BRANCH, 603 Latimer St, Mooringsport, 71060, SAN 343-5571. Tel: 318-996-6720. FAX: 318-996-6720. *Br Mgr,* Cynthia Clark; Staff 1 (Non-MLS 1)
Library Holdings: Bk Vols 7,411
Function: Handicapped accessible, Music CDs, Online searches, Prog for children & young adult, Summer reading prog, Wheelchair accessible
Open Mon & Wed 12-6, Tues & Thurs 10:30-6
Friends of the Library Group
NORTH CADDO BRANCH, 615 N Pine St, Vivian, 71082, SAN 343-5601. Tel: 318-375-3975. FAX: 318-375-4597. E-mail: publicnc@shreve-lib.org. *Br Mgr,* Sonia McCrary; E-mail: smccrary@shreve-lib.org; Staff 1 (Non-MLS 1)
Founded 1923
Library Holdings: Bk Vols 35,958
Function: Handicapped accessible, Music CDs, Online searches, Photocopying/Printing, Prog for children & young adult, Summer reading prog, VHS videos, Wheelchair accessible
Open Mon-Wed 9-8, Thurs-Sat 9-6
Friends of the Library Group
NORTH SHREVEPORT BRANCH, 4844 N Market St, 71107. Tel: 318-674-8172. FAX: 318-868-9464. *Br Mgr,* Ronald R Heezen; Staff 1 (Non-MLS 1)
Founded 2003. Circ 78,205
Library Holdings: Bk Vols 21,100
Function: Handicapped accessible, Music CDs, Online searches, Photocopying/Printing, Prog for children & young adult, Summer reading prog, VHS videos, Wheelchair accessible
Open Mon-Wed 9-8, Thurs-Sat 9-6
Friends of the Library Group
OIL CITY BRANCH, 102 Allen, Oil City, 71061, SAN 343-5636. Tel: 318-995-7975. FAX: 318-995-7975. *Br Mgr,* Rose M Hopkins; Staff 1 (Non-MLS 1)
Library Holdings: Bk Vols 13,164
Function: Handicapped accessible, Music CDs, Online searches, Summer reading prog, VHS videos, Wheelchair accessible
Open Mon 12-6, Tues & Thurs 11:30-6

DAVID RAINES BRANCH, 2855 Martin Luther King Jr Dr, 71107, SAN 343-5660. Tel: 318-222-0824. FAX: 318-222-9154. *Br Mgr,* Catherine Collins; Staff 1 (MLS 1)
Founded 1972
Library Holdings: Bk Vols 21,696
Function: Handicapped accessible, Music CDs, Online searches, Photocopying/Printing, Prog for children & young adult, Summer reading prog, VHS videos, Wheelchair accessible
Open Mon-Wed 9-8, Thurs-Sat 9-6
Friends of the Library Group

RODESSA BRANCH, 10093 Main St, Rodessa, 71069, SAN 343-5695. Tel: 318-223-4211. FAX: 318-223-4211. *Br Mgr,* Susan McKenny; Staff 1 (Non-MLS 1)
Library Holdings: Bk Vols 7,091
Function: Handicapped accessible, Music CDs, Online searches, Summer reading prog, VHS videos, Wheelchair accessible
Open Mon 12:30-7, Wed 12:30-5:30
Friends of the Library Group

MAVICE COLLEY WALLETTE BRANCH, 363 Hearne Ave, 71103, SAN 343-5512. Tel: 318-425-3630. FAX: 318-226-8311. *Br Mgr,* Wyolanda Hall; E-mail: whall@shreve-lib.org; Staff 1 (Non-MLS 1)
Founded 1951
Library Holdings: Bk Vols 23,930
Function: Adult literacy prog, Handicapped accessible, Music CDs, Online searches, Photocopying/Printing, Prog for children & young adult, Summer reading prog, VHS videos, Wheelchair accessible
Open Mon-Wed 9-8, Thurs-Sat 9-6
Friends of the Library Group

WEST SHREVEPORT BRANCH, 4380 Pines Rd, 71119, SAN 370-4491. Tel: 318-635-0883. FAX: 318-621-1056. *Br Mgr,* Audrey Manning; Staff 1 (Non-MLS 1)
Founded 1989
Library Holdings: Bk Vols 43,011
Function: Handicapped accessible, Music CDs, Online searches, Photocopying/Printing, Prog for children & young adult, Summer reading prog, VHS videos, Wheelchair accessible
Open Mon-Wed 9-9, Thurs-Sat 9-6
Friends of the Library Group

Bookmobiles: 1. Br Mgr, Dawn Solomon

J SOUTHERN UNIVERSITY AT SHREVEPORT*, Shreveport Campus Library, 3050 Martin Luther King Jr Dr, 71107. SAN 306-5480. Tel: 318-670-6392. Circulation Tel: 318-674-3392. Interlibrary Loan Service Tel: 318-674-3396. FAX: 318-674-3403. Web Site: www.susla.edu. *Univ Librn,* Dr Orella Brazile; Tel: 318-670-6401, E-mail: obrazile@susla.edu; *Ref/Acq,* Jane O'Riley; Tel: 318-670-6482, E-mail: joriley@susla.edu; *Archivist,* Nitisue Edwards; E-mail: nedwards@susla.edu; *Cataloger, Syst Adminr,* Rose M Powell; E-mail: rmpowell@susla.edu; Staff 9 (MLS 3, Non-MLS 6)
Founded 1967. Enrl 2,538; Fac 168
Library Holdings: e-books 11,079; Bk Titles 36,140; Bk Vols 51,421; Per Subs 240
Special Collections: Black Studies, bks, pictures; Louisiana Coll
Subject Interests: Ethnic studies, Natural sci
Automation Activity & Vendor Info: (Cataloging) SirsiDynix; (Circulation) SirsiDynix; (OPAC) SirsiDynix; (Serials) EBSCO Online
Partic in The Louisiana Library Network
Open Mon-Thurs (Winter) 8-9, Fri 8-5, Sat 9-1; Mon-Fri (Summer) 8-5

L UNITED STATES COURTS LIBRARY*, 300 Fannin St, Rm 5012, 71101-6305. SAN 372-0934. Tel: 318-676-3230. FAX: 318-934-4866. E-mail: 5satlib-shreveport@ca5.uscourts.gov. *Librn,* Marian Drey
Library Holdings: Bk Vols 10,000; Per Subs 40
Automation Activity & Vendor Info: (OPAC) SirsiDynix
Database Vendor: LexisNexis, Westlaw
Restriction: Not open to pub

SORRENTO

J RIVER PARISHES COMMUNITY COLLEGE LIBRARY*, 7384 John LeBlanc Blvd (Hwy 22), 70778. (Mail add: PO Box 310, 70778-0310). Tel: 225-675-0218, 225-675-0231. FAX: 225-675-8595. E-mail: lrc@rpcc.edu. Web Site: library.rpcc.edu. *Dir, Libr Serv,* Wendy Johnson; Tel: 225-675-0230, E-mail: wjohnson@rpcc.edu; *Head, Pub Serv,* Connie Chemay; E-mail: cchemay@rpcc.edu; *Head, Tech Serv,* Victor Sanchez; E-mail: vsanchez@rpcc.edu; *Libr Spec III,* Siva Blake; Tel: 226-675-0201, E-mail: sblake@rpcc.edu; Staff 4 (MLS 3, Non-MLS 1)
Founded 1999. Enrl 3,500; Fac 55; Highest Degree: Associate
Library Holdings: AV Mats 2,800; e-books 90,000; e-journals 30,000; Bk Titles 17,000; Bk Vols 18,000; Per Subs 30
Automation Activity & Vendor Info: (Cataloging) SirsiDynix; (Circulation) SirsiDynix; (Course Reserve) SirsiDynix; (ILL) OCLC Online; (OPAC) SirsiDynix; (Serials) SirsiDynix
Database Vendor: Agricola, Alexander Street Press, American Mathematical Society, CQ Press, CredoReference, EBSCO Discovery Service, EBSCOhost, Gale Cengage Learning, H W Wilson, JSTOR, LearningExpress, LexisNexis, Medline, Newsbank-Readex, OCLC WorldShare Interlibrary Loan, Oxford Online, ProQuest, World Book Online
Function: Computers for patron use, Copy machines, Online cat, Photocopying/Printing, Scanner
Partic in La Acad Libr Info Network Consortium; Lyrasis; The Louisiana Library Network
Open Mon-Thurs 7:30-7:30, Fri 7:30-5
Restriction: Authorized patrons, Borrowing privileges limited to fac & registered students, In-house use for visitors

SUNSET

P SOUTH ST LANDRY COMMUNITY LIBRARY*, 235 Marie St, 70584. SAN 373-7659. Tel: 337-662-3442, 337-662-3544. FAX: 337-662-3475. Web Site: www.southstlandrylibrary.com. *Dir,* Barbara A Malbrue; E-mail: bmalbrue2@pelican.state.lib.la.us; Staff 7 (Non-MLS 7)
Founded 1989. Pop 8,500
Library Holdings: Bks on Deafness & Sign Lang 54; CDs 144; DVDs 350; Large Print Bks 150; Bk Vols 31,672; Per Subs 65; Talking Bks 163; Videos 1,569
Special Collections: The Louisiana Coll
Automation Activity & Vendor Info: (Acquisitions) Book Systems; (Cataloging) Book Systems; (Circulation) Book Systems; (OPAC) Book Systems
Function: CD-ROM, ILL available, Music CDs, Photocopying/Printing, Prog for adults, Prog for children & young adult, Summer reading prog, VHS videos, Workshops
Publications: Library Log (Quarterly)
Open Tues 10-8, Wed-Fri 10-6, Sat 10-4
Friends of the Library Group

TALLULAH

P MADISON PARISH LIBRARY*, 403 N Mulberry St, 71282. SAN 343-575X. Tel: 318-574-4308. FAX: 318-574-4312. E-mail: admin.t1md@pelican.state.lib.la.us. *Dir,* Kizzy Bynum; E-mail: kbynum@yahoo.com; Staff 4 (MLS 1, Non-MLS 3)
Founded 1945. Pop 12,930; Circ 19,625
Library Holdings: Bk Titles 26,800; Bk Vols 28,000; Per Subs 80
Subject Interests: Art & archit, Econ, Hort, Music, Relig, World War II
Automation Activity & Vendor Info: (Cataloging) Book Systems; (Circulation) Book Systems; (OPAC) Book Systems
Open Mon 11:30-8, Tues-Fri 8:30-5:30, Sat 8:30-12:30

THIBODAUX

P LAFOURCHE PARISH PUBLIC LIBRARY*, 303 W Fifth St, 70301-3123. SAN 343-5814. Tel: 985-446-1163. FAX: 985-446-3848. Web Site: www.lafourche.org. *Dir,* Susanna LeBouef; *Asst Dir,* Regina Lauland; E-mail: rlauland@lafourche.org; Staff 51 (MLS 3, Non-MLS 48)
Founded 1947. Pop 92,157; Circ 338,480
Library Holdings: Bk Titles 124,220; Bk Vols 234,403; Per Subs 400
Subject Interests: Genealogy, La
Automation Activity & Vendor Info: (Acquisitions) TLC (The Library Corporation); (Cataloging) TLC (The Library Corporation); (Circulation) TLC (The Library Corporation); (ILL) TLC (The Library Corporation); (OPAC) TLC (The Library Corporation); (Serials) TLC (The Library Corporation)
Wireless access
Friends of the Library Group
Branches: 9

BAYOU BLUE BRANCH, 198 Mazerac St, Houma, 70364. Tel: 985-580-0634. FAX: 985-580-0634. *Br Mgr,* Tangella Bergeron
Open Mon & Thurs 10-6, Tues & Wed 11-7, Fri 9-5

CHOCTAW BRANCH, 1887 Choctaw Rd, 70301. Tel: 985-633-6453. FAX: 985-633-6453. *Br Mgr,* Luticia Cortez
Library Holdings: Bk Titles 12,000
Open Mon-Thurs 10-6, Fri 9-5

GHEENS BRANCH, 153 N Leon Dr, Gheens, 70355. Tel: 985-532-2288. FAX: 985-532-2288. *Br Mgr,* Sally Guidroz; E-mail: sguidroz@lafourche.org
Library Holdings: Bk Titles 9,000
Open Mon-Thurs 2-6, Fri 1-5

GOLDEN MEADOW BRANCH BIBLIOTECA HISPANA BRANCH, 1403 N Bayou Dr, Golden Meadow, 70357-2513, SAN 343-5903. Tel: 985-475-5660. FAX: 985-475-5660. E-mail: GoldenMeadow@lafourche.org. Web Site: www.lafourche.org/newsite/golden_meadow.html. *Br Librn,* Katina Gaudet; Staff 2 (Non-MLS 2)
Pop 18,200; Circ 226,953
Library Holdings: Bk Titles 19,776; Per Subs 43
Open Mon-Thurs 10-6, Fri 9-5
Friends of the Library Group

LAROSE BRANCH, 305 E Fifth St, Larose, 70373, SAN 343-5938. Tel: 985-693-3336. FAX: 985-693-3336. *Br Mgr,* Mrs Daryle Hamblin; Staff 4 (Non-MLS 4)
Founded 1947. Pop 9,000
Library Holdings: Bk Titles 20,199; Per Subs 50
Function: Accelerated reader prog, After school storytime, Art exhibits, Children's prog, Computer training, Computers for patron use, Copy machines, Free DVD rentals, Holiday prog, Home delivery & serv to Sr ctr & nursing homes, Music CDs, Preschool outreach, Prog for adults, Prog for children & young adult, Story hour, Summer reading prog, Teen prog, VHS videos
Friends of the Library Group

LOCKPORT BRANCH, 518 Sixth St, Lockport, 70374, SAN 343-5997. Tel: 985-532-3158. FAX: 985-532-0270. *Br Mgr,* Brenda Bascle; E-mail: bbascle@lafourche.org; Staff 6 (Non-MLS 6)
Library Holdings: Bk Titles 21,859; Per Subs 49
Open Mon-Thurs 10-7, Fri & Sat 9-5
Friends of the Library Group

RACELAND BRANCH, 177 Recreation Dr, Raceland, 70394-2915, SAN 343-6020. Tel: 985-537-6875. FAX: 985-537-6875. *Supvr,* Jessica Casseo; Staff 3 (Non-MLS 3)
Library Holdings: Bk Titles 21,804; Per Subs 53
Open Mon & Thurs 10-6, Tues & Wed 11-7, Fri 9-5
Friends of the Library Group

SOUTH LAFOURCHE PUBLIC LIBRARY, 16241 East Main St, CutOff, 70345, SAN 343-5873. Tel: 985-632-7140. FAX: 985-632-4963. *Br Mgr,* Tammi Blanchard; *Ref Librn,* Katina Gaudet; E-mail: kgaudet@lafourche.org; *Youth Serv Coordr,* Trinna Holcomb; E-mail: tholcomb@lafourche.org; Staff 7 (Non-MLS 7)
Library Holdings: Bk Titles 31,250; Per Subs 50
Subject Interests: Genealogy, La
Open Mon-Thurs 9-7, Fri & Sat 9-5
Friends of the Library Group

MARTHA SOWELL UTLEY MEMORIAL (MAIN LIBRARY), 314 St Mary St, 70301-2620, SAN 343-6055. Tel: 985-447-4119. FAX: 985-449-4128. *Br Mgr,* Patricia Boatman; E-mail: pboatman@lafourche.org; *Ref Librn,* Naomi Hurtienne; E-mail: nhurtienne@lafourche.org; Staff 8 (MLS 2, Non-MLS 6)
Library Holdings: Bk Titles 46,670; Per Subs 145
Subject Interests: Genealogy, La
Open Mon & Tues 10-7, Wed & Thurs 10-6, Fri & Sat 9-5
Friends of the Library Group

C NICHOLLS STATE UNIVERSITY*, Allen J Ellender Memorial Library, 906 E First St, 70310. (Mail add: PO Box 2028, 70310), SAN 306-5529. Tel: 985-448-4646, 985-448-4660. Circulation Tel: 985-448-4654. Interlibrary Loan Service Tel: 985-448-4633. Reference Tel: 985-448-4625. FAX: 985-448-4925. Web Site: www.nicholls.edu/library. *Dir,* Carol Mathias; E-mail: carol.mathias@nicholls.edu; *Head, Acq,* Bonita L Herbert; E-mail: benita.herbert@nicholls.edu; *Head, Archives,* Clifton Theriot; Tel: 985-448-4621, E-mail: clifton.theriot@nicholls.edu; *Head, Automation,* Jeremy A Landry; E-mail: jeremy.landry@nicholls.edu; *Head, Cat,* Sherrill A Faucheaux, Tel: 985-448-4635, E-mail: sherrill.faucheaux@nicholls.edu; *Head, Circ & Reserves,* Geraldine Eusea; E-mail: deannie.eusea@nicholls.edu; *Head, Coll Develop,* Jean-Mark Sens; E-mail: jean-mark.sens@nicholls.edu; *Head, Doc,* Cynthia Dubois; E-mail: cynthia.dubois@nicholls.edu; *Head, ILL,* Anke Tonn; E-mail: anke.tonn@nicholls.edu; *Head, Multimedia,* Jolene M Knight; E-mail: jolene.knight@nicholls.edu; *Head, Ser,* Anthony Fonseca; E-mail: tony.fonseca@nicholls.edu; *Ref Librn,* Melissa Goldsmith; E-mail: melissa.goldsmith@nicholls.edu; *Info Literacy/Ref,* Van P Viator; E-mail: van.viator@nicholls.edu; Staff 29 (MLS 10, Non-MLS 19)
Founded 1948. Enrl 7,345; Fac 301; Highest Degree: Master
Library Holdings: Bk Titles 301,477; Bk Vols 532,948; Per Subs 1,650
Special Collections: Cajun & Zydeco Music Heritage; Center for Traditional Louisiana Boat Building; Local History (Historic Thibodaux & Historic Lafourche Parish); Sugar Cane Plantations (J Wilson Lepine Coll & Laurel Valley Coll), diaries, mss; United States Senators' Papers (Allen J Ellender Archives). State Document Depository; US Document Depository
Subject Interests: Agr, Bus & mgt, Culinary arts, Econ, Educ, Marine biol, Nursing
Automation Activity & Vendor Info: (Acquisitions) SirsiDynix; (Cataloging) SirsiDynix; (Circulation) SirsiDynix; (OPAC) SirsiDynix; (Serials) SirsiDynix
Database Vendor: Gale Cengage Learning, LexisNexis, OCLC FirstSearch, OVID Technologies
Partic in La Acad Libr Info Network Consortium
Open Mon-Thurs 7:30am-9pm, Fri 7:30-4:30, Sun 4-Midnight

VILLE PLATTE

P EVANGELINE PARISH LIBRARY*, 242 W Main St, 70586. SAN 306-5537. Tel: 337-363-1369. FAX: 337-363-2353. E-mail: admin.b1ev@pelican.state.lib.la.us. Web Site: www.evangeline.lib.la.us. *Dir,* Mary Foster-Galasso; E-mail: mfoster2@state.lib.la.us; *Asst Dir,* Hope Demoruelle; Staff 12 (MLS 2, Non-MLS 10)
Founded 1948. Pop 33,274; Circ 131,715
Library Holdings: AV Mats 3,979; Bk Vols 64,871; Per Subs 655
Special Collections: Louisiana, Cajuns & Cajun Music Coll
Subject Interests: Genealogy
Automation Activity & Vendor Info: (Cataloging) Innovative Interfaces, Inc; (Circulation) Innovative Interfaces, Inc; (OPAC) Innovative Interfaces, Inc
Partic in Libraries SouthWest
Open Mon, Thurs & Fri 8-6, Tues 8-8, Wed 10-6, Sat 8-12
Friends of the Library Group

Branches: 5

BASILE BRANCH, 3036 Stagg Ave, Basile, 70515. (Mail add: PO Box A, Basile, 70515). Tel: 337-432-6794. FAX: 337-432-6794. *Br Mgr,* Sherry Bergeron; Staff 2 (Non-MLS 2)
Library Holdings: Bk Titles 3,000; Per Subs 22
Open Mon-Fri 9-12 & 1-5

CHATAIGNIER BRANCH, 6215 Charles Armand Jr St, Chataignier, 70524. (Mail add: PO Box 94, Chataignier, 70524-0094). Tel: 337-885-2028. FAX: 337-885-2028. *Br Mgr,* Patrola Savoy; *Asst Br Mgr,* Yvonne Lavergne; Staff 1 (Non-MLS 1)
Founded 1995
Library Holdings: AV Mats 50; Bk Titles 2,936; Bk Vols 2,949; Per Subs 44
Open Mon-Fri 2:30-5:30
Friends of the Library Group

MAMOU BRANCH, 317 Second St, Ste A, Mamou, 70554. Tel: 337-468-5750. FAX: 337-468-5750. *Br Mgr,* Floretta Deshotel; Staff 1 (Non-MLS 1)
Founded 1976
Library Holdings: Bk Titles 5,000; Per Subs 33
Open Mon-Fri 8-12 & 1-5
Friends of the Library Group

REVEREND LESLIE T H PRESCOTT BRANCH, 111 Walnut St, Pine Prairie, 70576. (Mail add: PO Box 680, Pine Prairie, 70576-0680). Tel: 337-599-3179. FAX: 337-599-3188. *Br Mgr,* Pamela Guillory; Staff 2 (Non-MLS 2)
Founded 2000
Open Mon, Wed & Fri 8-5, Tues 8-3, Thurs 8-12
Friends of the Library Group

TURKEY CREEK, 13951 Veterans Memorial Hwy, 70586. (Mail add: PO Box 340, Turkey Creek, 70585). Tel: 337-461-2304. *Br Mgr,* Tina King; *Asst Br Mgr,* Angela Henry
Founded 2005
Library Holdings: Bk Vols 3,000
Open Tues & Thurs 8-1 & 2-6, Wed 10-1 & 2-6

WASHINGTON

P WASHINGTON MUNICIPAL LIBRARY*, 418 N Main St, 70589. (Mail add: PO Box 249, 70589-0249). Tel: 337-826-7336. FAX: 337-826-7521. *Dir,* Delilah Jackson; E-mail: delimore@bellsouth.net
Library Holdings: Bk Vols 8,051
Automation Activity & Vendor Info: (Cataloging) Book Systems; (Circulation) Book Systems
Open Tues & Wed 10-6, Thurs 9-5, Fri & Sat 9-1

WINNFIELD

S WINN CORRECTIONAL CENTER LIBRARY*, PO Box 1260, 71483-1260. Tel: 318-628-3971. *In Charge,* Francis Prince
Library Holdings: Bk Vols 6,922; Per Subs 13
Open Mon-Fri 1-8, Sat 8am-11am
Friends of the Library Group

P WINN PARISH LIBRARY, 200 N St John St, 71483-2718. SAN 343-608X. Tel: 318-628-4478. FAX: 318-628-9820. Web Site: www.winn.lib.la.us. *Dir,* Mary Doherty; E-mail: mdoherty@state.lib.la.us; *Asst Librn,* Scarlette Bolds; E-mail: sbold@state.lib.la.us; Staff 10 (MLS 1, Non-MLS 9)
Founded 1937. Pop 16,397; Circ 101,995
Library Holdings: AV Mats 460; Bk Vols 98,000; Per Subs 250
Subject Interests: Genealogy, La
Automation Activity & Vendor Info: (Acquisitions) Auto-Graphics, Inc; (Cataloging) Auto-Graphics, Inc; (Circulation) Auto-Graphics, Inc; (ILL) Auto-Graphics, Inc; (OPAC) Auto-Graphics, Inc
Wireless access
Special Services for the Blind - Large screen computer & software
Open Mon-Fri 8:30-5:30, Sat 8-Noon

Branches: 4
ATLANTA BRANCH, 110 School Rd, Atlanta, 71404. (Mail add: PO Box 231, Atlanta, 71404-0231), SAN 343-611X. Tel: 318-628-7657. *Br Mgr,* Carolyn Washington; Staff 1 (Non-MLS 1)
Library Holdings: AV Mats 40; Bk Vols 3,200; Per Subs 10
Open Mon-Thurs 9-4
CALVIN BRANCH, 255 Second St, Calvin, 71410. (Mail add: PO Box 150, Calvin, 71410-0150), SAN 343-6144. Tel: 318-727-9644. FAX: 318-727-9644. *Br Mgr,* Jan Collins; Staff 1 (Non-MLS 1)
Library Holdings: AV Mats 30; Bk Vols 3,600; Per Subs 10
DODSON BRANCH, 206 E Gresham, Dodson, 71422, SAN 343-6179. Tel: 318-628-2821. *Br Mgr,* Tonya LeBaron; Staff 1 (Non-MLS 1)
Library Holdings: AV Mats 45; Bk Vols 3,600; Per Subs 10
Open Mon-Thurs 8-4
SIKES BRANCH, 125 Fifth St, Sikes, 71473-0125. (Mail add: PO Box 60, Sikes, 71473-0060), SAN 343-6209. Tel: 318-628-2824. *Br Mgr,* Karla Wroten; Staff 1 (Non-MLS 1)
Library Holdings: AV Mats 30; Bk Vols 3,600; Per Subs 12
Open Mon, Wed & Thurs 9-4

WINNSBORO

P FRANKLIN PARISH LIBRARY*, 705 Prairie St, 71295-2629. SAN 343-6233. Tel: 318-435-4336. FAX: 318-435-1990. E-mail: admin.t1fr@pelican.state.lib.la.us. Web Site: www.franklinparishlibrary.org. *Dir,* Carolyn Flint; E-mail: carolyn@franklinparishlibrary.org; Staff 6 (MLS 1, Non-MLS 5)
Founded 1950. Pop 22,387; Circ 74,046
Library Holdings: AV Mats 3,000; Bk Vols 80,000; Per Subs 87
Special Collections: Louisiana Coll
Automation Activity & Vendor Info: (Cataloging) Innovative Interfaces, Inc; (Circulation) Innovative Interfaces, Inc; (OPAC) Innovative Interfaces, Inc
Wireless access
Open Mon-Fri 8:30-5:30, Sat 8-12:30
Friends of the Library Group
Branches: 1
WISNER BRANCH, 129 Fort Scott St, Wisner, 71378. (Mail add: PO Box 260, Wisner, 71378-0260), SAN 343-6268. Tel: 318-724-7399. FAX: 318-724-7399. *Br Mgr,* Dale Berry; Staff 2 (Non-MLS 2)
Library Holdings: AV Mats 88; Bk Vols 10,010; Per Subs 52
Open Tues & Thurs 8:30-5:30

MAINE

Date of Statistics: FY 2013
Population, 2010 U.S. Census: 1,326,361
Population, 2013 U.S. Census (est.): 1,345,012
Population Served by Public Libraries Reporting: 1,340,024
Total Volumes in Public Libraries Reporting: 6,342,505
Volumes Per Capita: 5
Total Public Library Circulation: 9,540,829
Circulation Per Capita: 7
Total Public Library Expenditures: $43,282,816
Expenditures Per Capita: $32.30
Number of Regional Districts: 3

ACTON

P ACTON PUBLIC LIBRARY, 33 H Rd, 04001. SAN 306-5545. Tel: 207-636-2781. E-mail: actionpublib@gmail.com. Web Site: actionmaine.org/library.cfm. *Exec Dir,* Elise Miller
Founded 1920. Pop 2,400; Circ 3,000
Library Holdings: Audiobooks 60; CDs 50; DVDs 50; Large Print Bks 75; Bk Vols 7,115
Wireless access
Mem of Southern Maine Library District
Open Tues 2pm-7pm, Wed 9-2, Fri 9-3, Sat 9-Noon

ALBION

P ALBION PUBLIC LIBRARY*, 18 Main St, 04910. (Mail add: PO Box 355, 04910-0355), SAN 376-3803. Tel: 207-437-2220. E-mail: albion@albion.lib.me.us. *Librn,* Martha M Doore
Pop 8,000
Library Holdings: AV Mats 80; Bk Vols 7,650
Automation Activity & Vendor Info: (Cataloging) Follett Software; (Circulation) Follett Software
Wireless access
Open Mon & Thurs 2-8, Wed & Sat 9-11
Friends of the Library Group

ALFRED

P PARSONS MEMORIAL LIBRARY*, 27 Saco Rd, 04002. (Mail add: PO Box 1065, 04002-1065), SAN 306-5561. Tel: 207-324-2001. FAX: 207-324-2001. E-mail: alflib@roadrunner.com. Web Site: www.alfredme.us. *Dir,* Gus Hedden; *Ch,* Gus Spiliopoulos; Staff 1 (Non-MLS 1)
Pop 1,850; Circ 5,417
Library Holdings: Bk Vols 24,000; Per Subs 25
Database Vendor: EBSCOhost
Wireless access
Mem of Southern Maine Library District
Open Mon & Wed 3-8, Tues & Sat 10-3, Sun 11-4
Friends of the Library Group

ANDOVER

P ANDOVER PUBLIC LIBRARY*, 46 Church St, 04216. (Mail add: PO Box 393, 04216-0393), SAN 306-557X. Tel: 207-392-4841. *Dir,* Janet Farrington; E-mail: janetf@andover.lib.me.us; Staff 1 (Non-MLS 1)
Pop 971; Circ 7,014
Library Holdings: Bk Vols 11,000; Per Subs 24
Automation Activity & Vendor Info: (Cataloging) Readerware
Mem of South Central Kansas Library System
Open Tues, Wed & Sat 1-4:30, Thurs 1-4:30 & 6-8

APPLETON

P MILDRED STEVENS WILLIAMS MEMORIAL LIBRARY*, 2916 Sennebec Rd, 04862. SAN 306-5588. Tel: 207-785-5656. E-mail: appletonlibraryangie@gmail.com. Web Site: www.appleton.lib.me.us. *Librn,* Angie McKenna; Staff 1 (Non-MLS 1)
Founded 1946. Pop 1,271; Circ 1,000
Library Holdings: Bk Vols 6,500
Special Collections: Maine Coll
Database Vendor: EBSCOhost
Function: Prog for children & young adult
Mem of Northeastern Maine Library District
Open Tues 12-5, Wed 3-6, Thurs 10-3 & 7-9, Sat 10-1
Friends of the Library Group

ASHLAND

P ASHLAND COMMUNITY LIBRARY*, 57 Exchange St, 04732. (Mail add: PO Box 639, 04732-0639), SAN 306-5596. Tel: 207-435-6532. *Librn,* Gladys Craig; E-mail. gcraig@ashland.lib.me.us; Staff 1 (Non-MLS 1)
Founded 1960. Pop 2,248; Circ 9,561
Jan 2008 Dec 2008 Income $37,158. Mats Exp $11,500, Books $6,000, AV Mat $500. Sal $22,820
Library Holdings: AV Mats 800; DVDs 300; Bk Vols 2,354; Talking Bks 50; Videos 200
Special Collections: Aroostook. Oral History
Mem of Northeastern Maine Library District
Open Mon 9-4, Wed & Fri 9-4 & 6-8

AUBURN

S ANDROSCOGGIN HISTORICAL SOCIETY*, Clarence E March Library, Two Turner St, Unit 8, 04210-5978. SAN 306-5618. Tel: 207-784-0586, 207-784-2129. Web Site: www.rootsweb.ancestry.com. *Pres,* David Colby Young; E-mail: davidcolbyyoung@androscogginhistorical.com
Founded 1923
Jun 2007-May 2008 Income $6,760. Mats Exp $200
Library Holdings: Bk Vols 3,900; Per Subs 15; Spec Interest Per Sub 15
Special Collections: Historical Diaries & Photographs (Local Coll); Local Maps; Local Vital & Church Record Coll
Subject Interests: Genealogy, Local hist
Function: Archival coll, For res purposes, Newsp ref libr, Photocopying/Printing, Ref serv available, Referrals accepted, Res libr, Telephone ref
Publications: Androscoggin History (Newsletter)
Open Wed-Fri 1:30-5
Restriction: Not a lending libr, Open to pub for ref only, Open to pub with supv only, Pub use on premises
Friends of the Library Group

P AUBURN PUBLIC LIBRARY, 49 Spring St, 04210. SAN 306-5626. Tel: 207-333-6640. FAX: 207-333-6644. E-mail: email@auburnpubliclibrary.org. Web Site: www.auburn.lib.me.us. *Dir,*

Mamie Anthoine Ney; Tel: 207-333-6640, Ext 6, E-mail: mmaney@auburnpubliclibrary.org; *Asst Dir, Head, Coll Serv,* Suzanne Sullivan; *Head, Ch,* Debbie Cleveland; *Head, Lending Serv,* John Kelley; *Head, Ref & Adult Serv,* Martin Gagnon; *Ref & Teen Librn,* Donna Wallace; *Info Syst Coordr,* Brian Usher; Staff 21 (MLS 4, Non-MLS 17)
Founded 1890. Pop 24,000; Circ 244,800
Library Holdings: AV Mats 7,100; Bk Vols 70,000; Per Subs 150
Subject Interests: Genealogy, Local hist
Automation Activity & Vendor Info: (Acquisitions) Baker & Taylor
Database Vendor: EBSCOhost
Wireless access
Publications: News from the Auburn Public Library (Newsletter)
Open Mon & Thurs 9-8, Tues, Wed & Fri 9-6, Sat 9-5

CM CENTRAL MAINE COMMUNITY COLLEGE LIBRARY*, 1250 Turner St, 04210-6498. SAN 377-9785. Tel: 207-755-5218. Interlibrary Loan Service Tel: 207-755-5335. FAX: 207-755-5494. Web Site: www.cmcc.edu/library. *Dir, Libr Serv,* Judith G Frost; Tel: 207-755-5266, E-mail: jfrost@cmcc.edu; *Pub Serv Librn,* Judi H Moreno; Tel: 207-755-5265, E-mail: jmoreno@cmcc.edu; *Assoc Librn, ILL,* Valerie O Frechette; E-mail: vfrechette@cmcc.edu; Staff 3 (MLS 2, Non-MLS 1)
Library Holdings: e-books 300; Bk Vols 14,100; Per Subs 130
Automation Activity & Vendor Info: (Acquisitions) Innovative Interfaces, Inc; (Cataloging) Innovative Interfaces, Inc; (Circulation) Innovative Interfaces, Inc; (Course Reserve) Innovative Interfaces, Inc; (ILL) OCLC FirstSearch; (OPAC) Innovative Interfaces, Inc; (Serials) Innovative Interfaces, Inc
Database Vendor: CQ Press, OCLC FirstSearch, ProQuest
Wireless access
Partic in Lyrasis; Maine Health Sci Librs & Info Consortium

AUGUSTA

GM DEPARTMENT OF VETERANS AFFAIRS*, Learning Resources Center, Togus VA Medical Ctr, One VA Center, 04330. SAN 306-5758. Tel: 207-623-5773. FAX: 207-623-5766. *Librn,* June Roullard; E-mail: june.roullard@med.va.gov; *Libr Tech,* Gary Pelletier; E-mail: gary.pelletier@med.va.gov; Staff 2 (MLS 1, Non-MLS 1)
Founded 1943
Library Holdings: Bk Vols 2,000; Per Subs 200
Subject Interests: Health sci
Partic in Health Sci Libr & Info Coop; Veterans Affairs Libr Network (VALNET)
Open Mon-Fri 8-3:30

P LITHGOW PUBLIC LIBRARY, 45 Winthrop St, 04330-5599. SAN 306-5669. Tel: 207-626-2415. FAX: 207-626-2419. Web Site: www.lithgow.lib.me.us. *Dir,* Elizabeth L Pohl; E-mail: betsy@lithgow.lib.me.us; *Asst Dir, Youth Serv Librn,* Sarah C Schultz-Nielsen; E-mail: saraho@lithgow.lib.me.us; *Ad,* Shelby Monroe; E-mail: shelby@lithgow.lib.me.us; *Syst Librn,* Wynter Giddings; E-mail: wynter.giddings@lithgow.lib.me.us; Staff 4 (MLS 4)
Founded 1896. Pop 19,136; Circ 173,440
Jul 2014-Jun 2015 Income $661,121, City $647,121, Other $14,000. Mats Exp $62,200, Books $48,000, AV Mat $14,200. Sal $454,928
Library Holdings: Audiobooks 3,181; DVDs 3,139; e-books 2,241; Electronic Media & Resources 63; Bk Vols 58,756; Per Subs 105
Automation Activity & Vendor Info: (Cataloging) Innovative Interfaces, Inc; (Circulation) Innovative Interfaces, Inc; (OPAC) Innovative Interfaces, Inc
Wireless access
Partic in Maine InfoNet
Open Mon-Thurs 9-8, Fri 9-5, Sat 9-12
Friends of the Library Group

S MAINE DEPARTMENT OF TRANSPORTATION LIBRARY*, 16 State House Sta, 04333-0016. Tel: 207-624-3230. FAX: 207-624-3221. *Librn,* Pamela Shofner; Staff 1 (MLS 1)
Library Holdings: CDs 200; DVDs 10; Bk Vols 12,000; Per Subs 60; Videos 340
Automation Activity & Vendor Info: (Cataloging) Inmagic, Inc.
Open Mon-Fri 7:30-3:30

M MAINE GENERAL MEDICAL CENTER LIBRARY*, Six E Chestnut St, 04330. SAN 343-6322. Tel: 207-626-1325. FAX: 207-626-1537. *Dir, Med Libr,* Kristen Murphy; Staff 1 (MLS 1)
Library Holdings: Bk Vols 3,000; Per Subs 52
Subject Interests: Consumer health, Hist of med
Automation Activity & Vendor Info: (Acquisitions) Innovative Interfaces, Inc; (Cataloging) Innovative Interfaces, Inc; (Circulation) Innovative Interfaces, Inc; (OPAC) Innovative Interfaces, Inc; (Serials) Innovative Interfaces, Inc
Partic in Basic Health Sciences Library Network; National Network of Libraries of Medicine
Open Mon-Fri 7-3:30

P MAINE REGIONAL LIBRARY FOR THE BLIND & PHYSICALLY IMPAIRED*, c/o Maine State Library, 64 State House Sta, 04333-0064. SAN 306-5685. Tel: 207-287-5650. Toll Free Tel: 800-762-7106. FAX: 207-287-5654. *Librn,* Chris Ranney Boynton; Tel: 207-287-5653, E-mail: chris.boynton@maine.gov; Staff 3 (MLS 3)
Founded 1972
Library Holdings: Bk Vols 135,000
Special Collections: French Language, cassette
Publications: Talking Books (Newsletter); Talking Books Borrower's Handbook
Open Mon-Fri 8-5

GL MAINE STATE LAW & LEGISLATIVE REFERENCE LIBRARY*, 43 State House Sta, 04333-0043. SAN 306-5731. Tel: 207-287-1600. FAX: 207-287-6467. TDD: 207-287-6431. E-mail: Lawlib.Reference@legislature.maine.gov. Web Site: www.maine.gov/legis/lawlib. *Dir,* John R Barden; E-mail: john.barden@legislature.maine.gov; *Dep Dir,* Elaine Apostola; *Sr Law Librn,* Nicole Dyszlewski; *Sr Law Librn,* Sue Wright; *Assoc Law Librn,* Alex Burnett; *Assoc Law Librn,* Julie Olson; *Libr Assoc,* Ryan Jones; *Libr Assoc,* Jennifer Locke; *Libr Assoc,* Donna Sullivan; *Libr Asst,* Gianine Lupo; *Libr Asst,* Amanda Ouellette; *Libr Asst,* Jon Williams; Staff 12.7 (MLS 5.7, Non-MLS 7)
Founded 1971
Jul 2005-Jun 2006 Income $1,558,924. Mats Exp $257,079
Library Holdings: Bk Vols 114,035; Per Subs 480
Special Collections: Legislative Committee Master Files (111th Legislative to present). State Document Depository; US Document Depository
Automation Activity & Vendor Info: (Acquisitions) Innovative Interfaces, Inc; (Cataloging) Innovative Interfaces, Inc; (Circulation) Innovative Interfaces, Inc; (ILL) OCLC; (OPAC) Innovative Interfaces, Inc; (Serials) Innovative Interfaces, Inc
Database Vendor: HeinOnline, LexisNexis, Westlaw
Wireless access
Publications: Legislative Reference Bibliographies
Open Mon-Fri 8-5

P MAINE STATE LIBRARY, LMA Bldg, 230 State St, 04333. (Mail add: LMA Bldg, 64 State House Sta, 04333-0064), SAN 343-6357. Tel: 207-287-5600. Interlibrary Loan Service Tel: 207-287-5641. Reference Tel: 207-287-5608. Administration Tel: 207-287-5620. FAX: 207-287-5615. Interlibrary Loan Service FAX: 207-287-5638. Administration FAX: 207-287-5624. E-mail: reference.desk@maine.gov. Web Site: www.maine.gov/msl. *State Librn,* Linda H Lord; E-mail: linda.lord@maine.gov; *Dir of Develop,* Janet McKenney; Tel: 207-287-5620, E-mail: janet.mckenney@maine.gov; *Dir, Reader & Info Services,* James Ritter; Tel: 207-287-5604, E-mail: james.ritter@maine.gov; *Coordr, Outreach Serv,* Chris Boynton; Tel: 207-287-5653, E-mail: chris.boynton@maine.gov; *Coordr, Ref & Res,* Peggy O'Kane; Tel: 207-287-5605, E-mail: peggy.o'kane@maine.gov; *Pub Info Coordr,* Adam Fisher; Tel: 207-287-5629, E-mail: adam.fisher@maine.gov; Staff 19 (MLS 17, Non-MLS 2)
Founded 1839. Circ 188,768
Jul 2012-Jun 2013 Income $4,826,978, State $2,882,776, Federal $1,254,225, Other $689,977. Mats Exp $346,500, Books $55,000, Per/Ser (Incl. Access Fees) $55,000, Manu Arch $1,500, AV Equip $5,000, AV Mat $5,000, Electronic Ref Mat (Incl. Access Fees) $225,000. Sal $2,182,068
Library Holdings: Audiobooks 1,071; AV Mats 1,445; Bks-By-Mail 43,818; Bks on Deafness & Sign Lang 4; Large Print Bks 222,480; Bk Vols 349,948; Per Subs 410; Talking Bks 92,893; Videos 1,890
Special Collections: Maine Authors; Maine Counties, Towns, Boundaries & Rivers (Map Coll); Maine Genealogy Coll; Maine Government, Baxter State Park & Conservation (Baxter Coll), letters, scrapbks, personal rec; Mt Katahdin, Lumbering in Northern Maine 1876-1936 & the Appalachian Trail (Avery Coll). Oral History; State Document Depository
Subject Interests: Genealogy, Hist
Automation Activity & Vendor Info: (Acquisitions) Innovative Interfaces, Inc; (Cataloging) Innovative Interfaces, Inc; (Circulation) Innovative Interfaces, Inc; (ILL) Innovative Interfaces, Inc; (OPAC) Innovative Interfaces, Inc; (Serials) Innovative Interfaces, Inc
Database Vendor: 3M Library Systems, Bowker, EBSCOhost, Gale Cengage Learning, infoUSA, Mergent Online, Nature Publishing Group, Newsbank, OCLC FirstSearch, OCLC WorldShare Interlibrary Loan, ReferenceUSA, TLC (The Library Corporation), ValueLine
Wireless access
Partic in OCLC Online Computer Library Center, Inc
Special Services for the Deaf - Bks on deafness & sign lang; Video & TTY relay via computer
Special Services for the Blind - Bks on CD; Extensive large print coll; Large print bks & talking machines; Machine repair; Rec & flexible discs;

Talking bk & rec for the blind cat; Talking bks & player equip; Tel Pioneers equip repair group
Open Mon, Wed & Thurs 9-6, Tues 9-7, Fri 9-5, Sat 9-2
Branches: 1
LIBRARY FOR THE BLIND & PHYSICALLY IMPAIRED
See Separate Entry under Maine Regional Library for the Blind & Physically Impaired

C UNIVERSITY OF MAINE AT AUGUSTA LIBRARIES, Bennett D Katz Library, 46 University Dr, 04330-9410. SAN 306-574X. Tel: 207-621-3349. Toll Free Tel: 877-862-1234, Ext 3349. FAX: 207-621-3311. Web Site: www.uma.maine.edu/libraries.html. *Interim Dir, Libr Serv,* Ben Treat; Tel: 207-621-3385, E-mail: treatb@maine.edu; *Head, Coll Develop & Copyright Serv,* Position Currently Open; *Acad Librn, User Experience Spec,* Jessica Isler; E-mail: jessica.isler@maine.edu; *Coordr, Off-Campus Libr Serv,* Shiva Darbandi; Tel: 207-621-3347, Fax: 207-621-3354, E-mail: shiva.darbandi@maine.edu; *Libr Assoc,* Brenda Sevigny-Killen; Fax: 207-621-3354, E-mail: brenda.sevigny@maine.edu. Subject Specialists: *Arts, Humanities,* Jessica Isler; Staff 7.5 (MLS 4, Non-MLS 3.5)
Founded 1965. Enrl 5,500; Fac 278; Highest Degree: Bachelor
Library Holdings: CDs 637; DVDs 104; e-books 7,885; Bk Vols 55,000; Per Subs 250; Videos 1,720
Special Collections: Maine Related Materials; Research Materials
Subject Interests: Archit, Art, Bus, Liberal arts, Maine, Nursing
Automation Activity & Vendor Info: (Acquisitions) Innovative Interfaces, Inc; (Cataloging) Innovative Interfaces, Inc; (Circulation) Innovative Interfaces, Inc; (Course Reserve) Innovative Interfaces, Inc; (ILL) Innovative Interfaces, Inc; (Media Booking) Innovative Interfaces, Inc; (OPAC) Innovative Interfaces, Inc; (Serials) Innovative Interfaces, Inc
Database Vendor: Alexander Street Press, Altarama Systems & Services, ARTstor, Bowker, CredoReference, ebrary, EBSCO Information Services, Gale Cengage Learning, H W Wilson, InfoWorks Technology, Innovative Interfaces, Inc, JSTOR, LexisNexis, OCLC, OCLC FirstSearch, OCLC WorldShare Interlibrary Loan, Overdrive, Inc, OVID Technologies, Project MUSE, ProQuest, RefWorks, ScienceDirect, SerialsSolutions, Wilson - Wilson Web
Wireless access
Partic in Central Maine Libr District; OCLC Online Computer Library Center, Inc; OCLC-LVIS
Open Mon-Thurs (Winter) 8-8, Fri 8-5, Sun 1-5; Mon-Fri (Summer) 8-5

BAILEYVILLE

P WOODLAND PUBLIC LIBRARY*, 169 Main St, 04694. (Mail add: PO Box 549, 04694-0549), SAN 306-7912. Tel: 207-427-3235. FAX: 207-427-3673. *Librn,* Sylvia Brown; *Librn,* Beverly Ober
Founded 1912. Pop 2,200; Circ 2,365
Jul 2009-Jun 2010. Mats Exp $6,168, Books $6,000, Per/Ser (Incl. Access Fees) $168. Sal $10,550
Library Holdings: CDs 10; Large Print Bks 400; Bk Vols 19,998; Per Subs 25; Talking Bks 400; Videos 40
Special Collections: Maine Authors Coll
Database Vendor: EBSCOhost
Wireless access
Mem of Northeastern Maine Library District
Open Tues-Thurs 12:30-5:30, Fri 11:30-4:30

BANGOR

S BANGOR HISTORICAL SOCIETY LIBRARY*, 159 Union St, 04401. SAN 371-6651. Tel: 207-942-1900, 207-942-5766. FAX: 207-942-1910. E-mail: info@bangormuseum.org. Web Site: bangormuseum.org. *Curator,* Dana Lippitt; E-mail: curator@bangormuseum.org; Staff 5 (Non-MLS 5)
Founded 1864
Library Holdings: Bk Titles 1,000
Subject Interests: Local hist
Wireless access
Function: Archival coll, Exhibits
Restriction: Non-circulating coll, Not a lending libr

P BANGOR PUBLIC LIBRARY*, 145 Harlow St, 04401-1802. SAN 343-6470. Tel: 207-947-8336. Toll Free Tel: 800-427-8336. FAX: 207-945-6694. E-mail: bplill@bpl.lib.me.us. Web Site: www.bpl.lib.me.us. *Dir,* Barbara Rice McDade; E-mail: bmcdade@bpl.lib.me.us; *Head, Children's Dept, Teen Librn,* Christine Erickson; E-mail: cerickson@bpl.lib.me.us; *Head, Tech Serv,* Judith Leighton; E-mail: judiel@bpl.lib.me.us; Staff 34 (MLS 10, Non-MLS 24)
Founded 1883. Pop 31,431; Circ 441,206
Library Holdings: Bk Vols 465,515; Per Subs 597
Special Collections: Aroostook War of 1839; Genealogy & Town History; Mountaineering; Ornithology; Penobscot Expedition of 1779; World War II Unit History. State Document Depository; US Document Depository
Subject Interests: Hist
Automation Activity & Vendor Info: (Acquisitions) Innovative Interfaces, Inc; (Cataloging) Innovative Interfaces, Inc; (Circulation) Innovative Interfaces, Inc; (ILL) Innovative Interfaces, Inc; (OPAC) Innovative Interfaces, Inc; (Serials) Innovative Interfaces, Inc
Database Vendor: EBSCOhost, Gale Cengage Learning, OCLC FirstSearch, OVID Technologies
Wireless access
Mem of Northeastern Maine Library District
Partic in Lyrasis; Maine State Libr Network
Open Mon-Thurs (Winter) 10-8, Fri & Sat 10-5; Mon-Thurs (Summer) 10-7, Fri 10-5
Friends of the Library Group

J BEAL COLLEGE LIBRARY, 99 Farm Rd, 04401-6831. SAN 306-5774. Tel: 207-947-4591. FAX: 207-947-0208. E-mail: librarian@bealcollege.edu. Web Site: www.bealcollege.edu. *Librn,* Tegan Mills; Staff 1.5 (MLS 1, Non-MLS 0.5)
Founded 1891. Enrl 500; Fac 25; Highest Degree: Associate
Library Holdings: Bk Vols 10,000; Per Subs 100
Subject Interests: Allied med professions, Bus, Law enforcement
Automation Activity & Vendor Info: (Cataloging) Book Systems; (Circulation) Book Systems; (OPAC) Book Systems
Wireless access
Function: Computers for patron use, ILL available, Online cat, OverDrive digital audio bks, Photocopying/Printing, Ref serv in person
Partic in Maine InfoNet
Restriction: Access at librarian's discretion, Borrowing requests are handled by ILL, Open to students, fac & staff

M DOROTHEA DIX PSYCHIATRIC CENTER*, Behavioral Health Library, 656 State St, 04402. (Mail add: PO Box 926, 04402-0926), SAN 343-6411. Tel: 207-941-4226. FAX: 207-941-4444. *Librn,* Ruth Mare; E-mail: ruth.mare@maine.gov
Founded 1972
Library Holdings: Bk Vols 1,000; Per Subs 80
Subject Interests: Consumer health, Geriatrics & gerontology, Nursing, Psychiat, Psychol
Mem of Northeastern Maine Library District
Partic in Health Science Library Information Consortium; Maine Libr Asn
Open Mon-Fri 8-3:45
Branches:
PATIENT LIBRARY, 656 State St, 04402. (Mail add: PO Box 926, 04402-0926). Tel: 207-941-4226. FAX: 207-941-4228. *Librn,* Ruth Mare
Library Holdings: Bk Vols 9,000; Per Subs 35
Open Mon-Fri 1-4

J EASTERN MAINE COMMUNITY COLLEGE LIBRARY*, Katahdin Hall, 354 Hogan Rd, 04401-4280. SAN 306-5782. Tel: 207-974-4640. Reference Tel: 207-974-4740. Administration Tel: 207-974-4606. FAX: 207-974-4641. E-mail: library@emcc.edu. Web Site: www.emcc.edu/library. *Assoc Dean, Libr Serv,* Janet Blood, E-mail: jblood@emcc.edu; *Pub Serv Librn,* Dian Stratton; E-mail: dstratton@emcc.edu; *Assoc Librn, Circ & Tech Serv,* Kara Schwartz; E-mail: kschwartz@emcc.edu; Staff 2.5 (MLS 2, Non-MLS 0.5)
Founded 1968. Enrl 1,365; Fac 173; Highest Degree: Associate
Library Holdings: AV Mats 235; e-books 300; Electronic Media & Resources 42; Bk Titles 16,211; Bk Vols 16,274; Per Subs 212; Videos 235
Special Collections: American Welding Society-Reference Coll
Subject Interests: Automotive eng, Construction, Electronics, Nursing, Radiology
Automation Activity & Vendor Info: (Acquisitions) Innovative Interfaces, Inc; (Cataloging) Innovative Interfaces, Inc; (Circulation) Innovative Interfaces, Inc; (Course Reserve) Innovative Interfaces, Inc; (ILL) Innovative Interfaces, Inc; (OPAC) Innovative Interfaces, Inc; (Serials) Innovative Interfaces, Inc
Database Vendor: 3M Library Systems, CQ Press, EBSCOhost, Innovative Interfaces, Inc, McGraw-Hill, OCLC FirstSearch, OCLC WorldShare Interlibrary Loan, ProQuest, STAT!Ref (Teton Data Systems), Wilson - Wilson Web
Wireless access
Function: Art exhibits, Computers for patron use, Copy machines, Distance learning, Doc delivery serv, e-mail serv, Electronic databases & coll, Online cat, Online ref, Online searches, Orientations, Outside serv via phone, mail, e-mail & web, Pub access computers, Ref & res, Scanner, Telephone ref
Partic in NE Libr Network
Special Services for the Deaf - Bks on deafness & sign lang
Special Services for the Blind - Magnifiers
Open Mon-Thurs (Winter) 8am-9pm, Fri 8-5, Sun 1-5; Mon-Fri (Summer) 8-5
Restriction: Open to pub for ref only, Open to students, fac & staff, Pub ref by request
Friends of the Library Group

M EASTERN MAINE MEDICAL CENTER, Hadley Parrot Health Sciences Library, 489 State St, 04401. (Mail add: PO Box 404, 04402-0404), SAN 320-4502. Tel: 207-973-8228. Interlibrary Loan Service Tel: 207-973-8236. FAX: 207-973-8233. E-mail: library@emhs.org. Web Site: library.emmc.org. *Dir,* Lucinda White; E-mail: lwhite@emhs.org; *ILL,* Megan McNichol; E-mail: mmcnichol@emhs.org; *Tech Serv,* Pat Bishop; Tel: 207-973-8232, E-mail: pbishop@emhs.org; Staff 5 (MLS 3, Non-MLS 2)
Founded 1892
Library Holdings: e-books 50; e-journals 700; Bk Titles 7,541; Per Subs 225
Special Collections: Hospital Annual Reports & Archives
Subject Interests: Consumer health, Med, Nursing
Automation Activity & Vendor Info: (Cataloging) Innovative Interfaces, Inc; (Circulation) Innovative Interfaces, Inc; (OPAC) Innovative Interfaces, Inc; (Serials) Innovative Interfaces, Inc
Database Vendor: Cinahl, EBSCOhost, Elsevier, Gale Cengage Learning, OVID Technologies, ProQuest, PubMed, STAT!Ref (Teton Data Systems), UpToDate, Wiley
Wireless access
Partic in Health Sci Libr & Info Coop; Maine School & Library Network
Open Mon-Fri 7:30-5

C HUSSON UNIVERSITY*, W Tom & Bonnie Sawyer Library, One College Circle, 04401-2999. SAN 306-5790. Tel: 207-941-7187, 207-941-7188. FAX: 207-941-7989. Web Site: www.husson.edu. *Dir,* Amy Averre; E-mail: averrea@husson.edu; *Cat,* Diane Hanscom
Founded 1947. Highest Degree: Doctorate
Library Holdings: Bk Vols 40,000; Per Subs 500
Automation Activity & Vendor Info: (Cataloging) Innovative Interfaces, Inc; (Circulation) Innovative Interfaces, Inc; (Course Reserve) Innovative Interfaces, Inc; (OPAC) Innovative Interfaces, Inc; (Serials) Innovative Interfaces, Inc
Database Vendor: EBSCOhost, OCLC FirstSearch
Wireless access
Mem of Northeastern Maine Library District
Partic in Health Science Library Information Consortium; Lyrasis; National Network of Libraries of Medicine
Open Mon-Thurs 8am-10pm, Fri 8-5, Sat 10-5, Sun 10-10

C UNIVERSITY OF MAINE AT AUGUSTA*, Nottage Library (Bangor Campus), 85 Texas Ave, Belfast Hall, 04401. SAN 306-5812. Tel: 207-262-7900. Administration Tel: 207-262-7902. FAX: 207-262-7901. *Libr Dir,* Ben Treat; E-mail: treatb@maine.edu; Staff 1 (MLS 1)
Founded 1968. Enrl 950; Fac 30; Highest Degree: Bachelor
Library Holdings: Bk Vols 23,500; Per Subs 195
Subject Interests: Dental health, Veterinary tech
Wireless access
Open Mon-Thurs 8-7, Fri 8-4, Sat & Sun 12:30-4:30

BAR HARBOR

C COLLEGE OF THE ATLANTIC*, Thorndike Library, 109 Eden St, 04609-1198. SAN 306-5820. Tel: 207-288-5015. Circulation Tel: 207-288-5015, Ext 275. FAX: 207-288-2328. Web Site: www.coa.edu/thorndikelibrary. *Dir,* Jane Hultberg; Tel: 207-288-5015, Ext 210, E-mail: jhultberg@coa.edu; *Assoc Dir,* Patricia Keene Cantwell; Tel: 207-288-5015, Ext 211, E-mail: tcantwell@coa.edu; *AV Tech Spec,* Zach Soares; Tel: 207-288-5015, Ext 213, E-mail: zsoares@coa.edu; Staff 2 (MLS 2)
Founded 1972. Enrl 300; Fac 26; Highest Degree: Master
Library Holdings: Bk Vols 40,000; Per Subs 250
Special Collections: Evolution (Philip Darlington Coll); Humanities (R Amory Thorndike Coll); Science & History of Science (Thomas S & Mary T Hall Coll)
Subject Interests: Botany, Environ studies, Evolution, Hort, Philos, Pub policy
Automation Activity & Vendor Info: (Cataloging) Follett Software; (Circulation) Follett Software; (Course Reserve) Follett Software; (ILL) Follett Software; (OPAC) Follett Software
Database Vendor: ARTstor, Gale Cengage Learning, JSTOR, LexisNexis, OCLC FirstSearch
Mem of Northeastern Maine Library District
Partic in Lyrasis
Open Mon-Thurs 7:30am-11pm, Fri 7:30am-10pm, Sat 10-10, Sun Noon-Midnight

M JACKSON LABORATORY*, Joan Staats Library, 600 Main St, 04609-1500. SAN 306-5839. Tel: 207-288-6146. FAX: 207-288-6079. E-mail: library@jax.org. Web Site: www.library.jax.org. *Dir,* Douglas Macbeth; E-mail: douglas.macbeth@jax.org; Staff 4 (MLS 2, Non-MLS 2)
Founded 1929
Library Holdings: Bk Titles 4,000; Per Subs 310
Special Collections: Historical archives of the Jackson Laboratory
Subject Interests: Biol, Cancer
Wireless access
Mem of Northeastern Maine Library District
Partic in BRS; Dialog Corp; Health Science Library Information Consortium; NRML; OCLC Online Computer Library Center, Inc
Open Mon-Fri 7:30-4

P JESUP MEMORIAL LIBRARY, 34 Mount Desert St, 04609-1727. SAN 306-5847. Tel: 207-288-4245. E-mail: info@jesuplibrary.org. Web Site: www.jesuplibrary.org. *Dir,* Ruth A Eveland; E-mail: reveland@jesuplibrary.org; *Asst Dir, Ch,* Mae Corrion; E-mail: mcorrion@jesuplibrary.org; Staff 6 (MLS 1, Non-MLS 5)
Founded 1875. Pop 5,235; Circ 64,877
Jan 2013-Dec 2013 Income $347,344, City $17,867, Other $329,477. Mats Exp $29,714, Books $24,943, AV Mat $2,741, Electronic Ref Mat (Incl. Access Fees) $2,030. Sal $228,136
Library Holdings: Bk Vols 31,000; Per Subs 50
Special Collections: Genealogy Coll; Local Newspapers from 1881-1968, microfilm
Automation Activity & Vendor Info: (Cataloging) Innovative Interfaces, Inc; (Circulation) Innovative Interfaces, Inc; (OPAC) Innovative Interfaces, Inc
Database Vendor: EBSCOhost
Wireless access
Function: 24/7 Online cat, Adult bk club, Art exhibits, Audiobks via web, Bks on cassette, Bks on CD, Children's prog, Computer training, Computers for patron use, Copy machines, e-mail & chat, E-Reserves, Electronic databases & coll, Equip loans & repairs, Exhibits, Free DVD rentals, Home delivery & serv to Sr ctr & nursing homes, ILL available, Magazines, Mail & tel request accepted, Mango lang, Microfiche/film & reading machines, Music CDs, Online cat, OverDrive digital audio bks, Photocopying/Printing, Prog for adults, Prog for children & young adult, Pub access computers, Ref & res, Ref serv available, Ref serv in person, Spoken cassettes & CDs, Spoken cassettes & DVDs, Story hour, Summer reading prog, Tax forms, Telephone ref, VHS videos, Writing prog
Mem of Northeastern Maine Library District
Partic in Maine Libr Asn
Open Tues, Fri & Sat 10-5, Wed & Thurs 10-8

BAR MILLS

P BERRY MEMORIAL LIBRARY*, 93 Main St, 04004. (Mail add: PO Box 25, 04004-0025), SAN 306-5855. Tel: 207-929-5484. Web Site: www.berrylibrary.com. *Dir,* Claudine Emerson; E-mail: claudine@berrylibrary.com; Staff 1 (Non-MLS 1)
Founded 1929. Pop 8,000
Library Holdings: Bk Titles 6,500; Per Subs 12
Special Collections: Genealogy (Downeast Ancestry; Histories of Several Maine Towns; Maine Authors (Kate D Wiggin Coll); Narragansett & Buxton Town Histories; Saco Valley Settlements & Families
Mem of Southern Maine Library District
Open Tues 11-5, Thurs 4-8, Sat 9-11

BATH

S MAINE MARITIME MUSEUM*, Library Archives, 243 Washington St, 04530. SAN 306-5863. Tel: 207-443-1316, Ext 328. Reference Tel: 207-443-1316, Ext 336. FAX: 207-443-1665. Web Site: www.mainemaritimemuseum.org. *Sr Curator,* Nathan Lipfert; E-mail: lipfert@maritimeme.org; Staff 2 (Non-MLS 2)
Founded 1964
Library Holdings: Bk Titles 10,000; Bk Vols 12,546; Per Subs 25
Special Collections: Bath, Maine Built Vessels (Photograph Coll); Ship Logs Coll, original doc in bk form; Ship Papers (Sewall Coll), original doc
Subject Interests: Maritime hist
Partic in Solar-net
Open Mon-Fri 9:30-3
Restriction: Closed stack, Fee for pub use, Non-circulating coll, Not a lending libr

P PATTEN FREE LIBRARY*, 33 Summer St, 04530. SAN 306-5871. Tel: 207-443-5141. Web Site: www.patten.lib.me.us. *Dir,* Lesley Dolinger; E-mail: lesley.dolinger@patten.lib.me.us; *Develop Dir,* Ellen Dyer; E-mail: edyer@patten.lib.me.us; *Head, Tech Serv,* Adam Bohanan; E-mail: adambohanan@patten.lib.me.us; *Outreach & Instruction Librn,* Roberta Jordan; E-mail: rjordan@patten.lib.me.us; *Adult Serv Mgr,* Leslie Mortimer; E-mail: lmortimer@patten.lib.me.us; *ILL Coordr,* Elizabeth McDorr; E-mail: emcdorr@patten.lib.me.us; *Ch Serv,* Carol McFadden; E-mail: ccmcfadden@patten.lib.me.us; Staff 10 (MLS 6, Non-MLS 4)
Founded 1847. Pop 17,500; Circ 143,259
Jul 2007-Jun 2008 Income $667,036, City $263,872, Locally Generated Income $403,164. Mats Exp $66,000, Books $44,500, Per/Ser (Incl. Access Fees) $7,800, AV Mat $9,900. Sal $487,473
Library Holdings: Bk Vols 56,165; Per Subs 243

Special Collections: Historic Preservation (Sagadahoc Preservation Inc Coll); Maine History & Genealogy Coll; Maritime (Whitmore, Stevens, Bath Iron Works Colls); Native American (Staton Coll)
Subject Interests: Genealogy, Local hist, Maritime hist
Database Vendor: Innovative Interfaces, Inc
Wireless access
Publications: Good Times & Hard Times in Bath, 1936-1986; I Am Now a Soldier: The Civil War Diaries of Lorenzo Vanderhoeff; Maine Odyssey; Pattens of Bath, a Seagoing Dynasty
Open Tues & Wed 10-8, Thurs & Fri 10-5, Sat 10-4
Friends of the Library Group

BELFAST

P BELFAST FREE LIBRARY, 106 High St, 04915. SAN 306-588X. Tel: 207-338-3884. FAX: 207-338-3895. E-mail: info@belfastlibrary.org. Web Site: www.belfastlibrary.org. *Libr Dir,* Steve Norman; E-mail: snorman@belfastlibrary.org; *Youth Serv Dir,* Jane Thompson; E-mail: jthompson@belfastlibrary.org; *Adult Prog Coordr,* Brenda Harrington; E-mail: bharrington@belfastlibrary.org; *Ref, Spec Coll,* Betsy Paradis; E-mail: bparadis@belfastlibrary.org; Staff 9 (MLS 5, Non-MLS 4)
Founded 1887. Pop 8,188; Circ 131,311
Jul 2013-Jun 2014 Income $626,529, City $534,769, Locally Generated Income $91,760. Mats Exp $46,535, Books $34,200, Per/Ser (Incl. Access Fees) $5,000, Manu Arch $500, AV Mat $4,500, Electronic Ref Mat (Incl. Access Fees) $2,335. Sal $354,455
Library Holdings: AV Mats 9,257; e-books 7,310; Bk Vols 48,252; Per Subs 117
Subject Interests: Genealogy, Local hist
Automation Activity & Vendor Info: (Cataloging) Innovative Interfaces, Inc; (Circulation) Innovative Interfaces, Inc; (ILL) Innovative Interfaces, Inc; (OPAC) Innovative Interfaces, Inc
Database Vendor: EBSCOhost, ValueLine
Wireless access
Function: Archival coll, Art exhibits, Audiobks via web, Bk club(s), Bks on CD, Children's prog, Copy machines, Genealogy discussion group, Handicapped accessible, ILL available, Microfiche/film & reading machines, OverDrive digital audio bks, Pub access computers, Story hour, Summer reading prog
Mem of Northeastern Maine Library District
Special Services for the Blind - Large print bks; Talking bks
Open Mon 9:30-8, Tues, Thurs & Fri 9:30-6, Wed 12-8, Sat 10-2
Friends of the Library Group

M WALDO COUNTY GENERAL HOSPITAL*, Health Sciences Library, 118 Northport Ave, 04915. SAN 377-9246. Tel: 207-338-2500, Ext 4154. FAX: 207-338-6029. Web Site: www.wchi.com. *Librn,* Lois Dutch
Library Holdings: Bk Titles 250; Per Subs 25
Partic in Health Science Library Information Consortium

BELGRADE

P BELGRADE PUBLIC LIBRARY*, One Center Dr, 04917-4407. Tel: 207-495-3508. FAX: 207-495 3508. E-mail: belgrade@belgrade.lib.me.us. Web Site: www.belgrade.lib.me.us. *Dir,* Marcia Haigh; E-mail: mhaigh@belgrade.lib.me.us
Founded 2000. Pop 2,978
Library Holdings: AV Mats 50; CDs 100; Bk Vols 6,000; Per Subs 30; Talking Bks 50
Special Collections: Local History Coll
Automation Activity & Vendor Info: (Cataloging) CASPR; (Circulation) CASPR; (OPAC) CASPR
Wireless access
Function: ILL available, Ref serv available
Special Services for the Blind - Audio mat; Large print bks
Open Tues & Thurs 10-7, Wed 3-7, Fri 10-1
Friends of the Library Group

BERNARD

P BASS HARBOR MEMORIAL LIBRARY*, 89 Bernard Rd, 04612. (Mail add: PO Box 99, 04612-0099), SAN 376-351X. Tel: 207-244-3798. E-mail: librarian@bassharborlibrary.com. Web Site: www.bassharborlibrary.com/. *Dir,* Clara Baker; *Librn,* Amanda Crafts; Staff 1 (Non-MLS 1)
Library Holdings: Bk Titles 8,700; Per Subs 30
Database Vendor: EBSCOhost
Wireless access
Mem of Northeastern Maine Library District
Open Tues & Thurs 1-7, Wed & Sat 9-1
Friends of the Library Group

BERWICK

P BERWICK PUBLIC LIBRARY*, 103 Old Pine Hill Rd, 03901. (Mail add: PO Box 838, 03901-0838), SAN 376-3889. Tel: 207-698-5737. FAX: 207-698-5737. Web Site: www.berwick.lib.me.us. *Dir,* Sandy Broomfield; E-mail: sbroomfield@berwick.lib.me.us; *Asst Librn,* Lyn Rouff; E-mail: lrouff@berwick.lib.me.us; Staff 2 (MLS 1, Non-MLS 1)
Founded 1987. Pop 7,548; Circ 21,867
Jul 2010-Jun 2011 Income $88,000, City $63,000, Parent Institution $25,000. Mats Exp $5,500
Library Holdings: AV Mats 500; High Interest/Low Vocabulary Bk Vols 100; Large Print Bks 150; Bk Titles 24,552; Bk Vols 24,614; Per Subs 15; Talking Bks 200
Special Collections: Local History Coll; Maine Coll
Automation Activity & Vendor Info: (Acquisitions) Follett Software; (Cataloging) Follett Software; (Circulation) Follett Software; (OPAC) Follett Software
Wireless access
Function: Adult bk club, Art exhibits, Bks on cassette, Bks on CD, Children's prog, Computer training, Computers for patron use, Copy machines, e-mail serv, Electronic databases & coll, Free DVD rentals, Genealogy discussion group, Handicapped accessible, Holiday prog, Homebound delivery serv, ILL available, Mail & tel request accepted, Mus passes, Music CDs, Online cat, Photocopying/Printing, Prog for adults, Prog for children & young adult, Pub access computers, Ref serv available, Ref serv in person, Spoken cassettes & CDs, Spoken cassettes & DVDs, Story hour, Summer reading prog, Tax forms, Telephone ref, VHS videos
Mem of Southern Maine Library District
Partic in Maine School & Library Network
Open Tues 10-8, Wed 10-6, Fri & Sat 10-2
Restriction: Authorized patrons, Circ to mem only, In-house use for visitors
Friends of the Library Group

BETHEL

P BETHEL LIBRARY ASSOCIATION*, Five Broad St, 04217. (Mail add: PO Box 130, 04217-0130), SAN 306-5898. Tel: 207-824-2520. *Librn,* Michelle Conroy; E-mail: mconroy@bethel.lib.me.us; Staff 1 (Non-MLS 1)
Pop 6,000; Circ 20,000
Library Holdings: AV Mats 1,000; Bk Titles 19,000; Bk Vols 20,000; Per Subs 56; Talking Bks 1,000
Special Collections: Maine History Coll
Automation Activity & Vendor Info: (Cataloging) Winnebago Software Co; (Circulation) Winnebago Software Co; (OPAC) Winnebago Software Co
Database Vendor: EBSCOhost
Wireless access
Open Mon & Sat 9-1, Tues, Thurs & Fri 1-5, Wed 1-8

BIDDEFORD

P MCARTHUR PUBLIC LIBRARY, 270 Main St, 04005. (Mail add: PO Box 346, 04005-0346), SAN 306-591X. Tel: 207-284-4181. FAX: 207-284-6761. E-mail: reference@mcarthur.lib.me.us. Web Site: www.mcarthurpubliclibrary.org. *Dir,* Jeff Cabral; E-mail: jcabral@mcarthur.lib.me.us; Staff 13.6 (MLS 4, Non-MLS 9.6)
Founded 1863. Pop 21,386; Circ 131,732
Jul 2011-Jun 2012 Income $911,981, City $280,000, Locally Generated Income $631,981. Mats Exp $75,300, Books $40,000, Per/Ser (Incl. Access Fees) $6,200, Micro $800, AV Mat $21,000, Electronic Ref Mat (Incl. Access Fees) $6,300, Presv $1,000. Sal $475,320 (Prof $167,735)
Library Holdings: AV Mats 7,059; e-books 2,370; Bk Vols 55,319; Per Subs 114
Automation Activity & Vendor Info: (Cataloging) Innovative Interfaces, Inc; (Circulation) Innovative Interfaces, Inc; (ILL) Innovative Interfaces, Inc; (OPAC) Innovative Interfaces, Inc; (Serials) Innovative Interfaces, Inc
Database Vendor: Gale Cengage Learning, ProQuest
Wireless access
Function: Accessibility serv available based on individual needs, Adult bk club, Archival coll, Art exhibits, Audiobks via web, Bk club(s), Bks on CD, Bus archives, Children's prog, Computer training, Computers for patron use, Copy machines, Digital talking bks, e-mail & chat, e-mail serv, E-Reserves, Electronic databases & coll, Equip loans & repairs, Exhibits, Family literacy, Free DVD rentals, Games & aids for the handicapped, Govt ref serv, Handicapped accessible, Holiday prog, ILL available, Literacy & newcomer serv, Magnifiers for reading, Mail & tel request accepted, Microfiche/film & reading machines, Mus passes, Music CDs, Newsp ref libr, Online cat, Online ref, Online searches, Orientations, Outreach serv, Outside serv via phone, mail, e-mail & web, OverDrive digital audio bks, Photocopying/Printing, Preschool outreach, Preschool reading prog, Printer for laptops & handheld devices, Prog for adults, Prog for children & young adult, Pub access computers, Ref & res, Ref serv available, Ref serv in person, Story hour, Summer & winter reading prog, Tax forms, Teen prog, Telephone ref, VHS videos, Video lending libr, Web-catalog, Wheelchair accessible, Workshops
Mem of Southern Maine Library District
Partic in Maine School & Library Network

Special Services for the Blind - Aids for in-house use; Bks available with recordings; Bks on cassette; Bks on CD; Large print bks; Magnifiers; Talking bks
Open Mon-Thurs 9:30-8, Fri 9:30-5, Sat 9:30-3:30

M SOUTHERN MAINE MEDICAL CENTER*, Health Sciences Library, One Medical Center Dr, 04005. (Mail add: PO Box 626, 04005-0626), SAN 328-4476. Tel: 207-283-7289. FAX: 207-283-7063. *Health Sci Librn,* Susan Bloomfield; E-mail: librarian1@southport.lib.me.us; Staff 1 (MLS 1)
Library Holdings: Bk Titles 700; Per Subs 85
Wireless access
Mem of Southern Maine Library District
Partic in Health Science Library Information Consortium

C UNIVERSITY OF NEW ENGLAND LIBRARIES*, Jack S Ketchum Library, 11 Hills Beach Rd, 04005. SAN 322-8142. Tel: 207-602-2361. Interlibrary Loan Service Tel: 207-602-2386. Reference Tel: 207-602-2363. Administration Tel: 207-602-2319. FAX: 207-602-5922. E-mail: library@une.edu. Web Site: www.une.edu/library. *Dean of Libr Serv,* Andrew J Golub; E-mail: agolub@une.edu; *Dir, Libr Syst,* Stew MacLehose; Tel: 207-221-4535, E-mail: smaclehose@une.edu; *Dir, Pub Serv,* Barbara Swartzlander; Tel: 207-602-2315, E-mail: bswartzlander@une.edu; *Dir, Tech Serv,* Sharon Eckert; Tel: 207-602-2364, E-mail: seckert@une.edu; *Pub Serv Librn,* Cadence Atchinson; Tel: 207-602-2497, E-mail: catchinson@une.edu; *Archivist, New England Osteopathic Heritage Ctr,* Zachary Enright; Tel: 207-602-2131, E-mail: zenright@une.edu; Staff 15 (MLS 11, Non-MLS 4)
Founded 1831. Enrl 3,804; Highest Degree: Doctorate
Library Holdings: e-books 130,000; e-journals 75,000; Bk Vols 135,000
Special Collections: Maine Women Writers Coll; New England Osteopathic Heritage Center
Subject Interests: Allied health, Educ, Life sci, Marine biol, Med
Automation Activity & Vendor Info: (Acquisitions) Innovative Interfaces, Inc; (Cataloging) Innovative Interfaces, Inc; (Circulation) Innovative Interfaces, Inc; (ILL) Innovative Interfaces, Inc
Database Vendor: Cambridge Scientific Abstracts, EBSCOhost, JSTOR, LexisNexis, OCLC FirstSearch, OVID Technologies, ProQuest
Wireless access
Mem of Southern Maine Library District
Partic in Health Science Library Information Consortium; National Network of Libraries of Medicine New England Region; OCLC Online Computer Library Center, Inc

Departmental Libraries:

JOSEPHINE S ABPLANALP LIBRARY, Portland Campus, 716 Stevens Ave, Portland, 04103, SAN 306-7262. Tel: 207-221-4330. Reference Tel: 207-221-4363. FAX: 207-221-4893. *Dean of Libr Serv,* Andrew J Golub; Tel: 207-602-2319, E-mail: agolub@une.edu; *Access Serv Librn,* Bethany Kenyon; Tel: 207-221-4325, E-mail: bkenyon@une.edu; *Pub Serv Librn,* Elizabeth Dyer; Tel: 207-221-4333, E-mail: edyer@une.edu; *Pub Serv Librn,* Roberta Gray; Tel: 207-221-4323, E-mail: rgray@une.edu; *Acq,* Chris McKinnon; Tel: 207-221-4327, E-mail: cmckinnon@une.edu; *Cat,* Robin Sanford; Tel: 207-221-4328, E-mail: rsanford@une.edu; *Curator,* Cally Gurley; Tel: 207-221-4324, E-mail: cgurley@une.edu; Staff 15 (MLS 11, Non-MLS 4)
Founded 1831. Enrl 1,373; Fac 66; Highest Degree: Master
Library Holdings: e-books 130,000; e-journals 75,000; Bk Vols 135,000
Special Collections: George & Barbara Bush Legacy Coll; Maine Women Writers Coll; New England Osteopathic Heritage Center; UNE Art Gallery; Westbrook College History Coll
Subject Interests: Anesthesiology, Nursing
Automation Activity & Vendor Info: (OPAC) Innovative Interfaces, Inc

BLUE HILL

S BAGADUCE MUSIC LENDING LIBRARY, Five Music Library Lane, 04614. (Mail add: PO Box 829, 04614-0829), SAN 373-0573. Tel: 207-374-5454. FAX: 207-374-2733. E-mail: library@bagaducemusic.org. Web Site: www.bagaducemusic.org. *Exec Dir,* Martina Herries; E-mail: martina@bagaducemusic.org; *Music Dir,* Mary Cheyney Gould; E-mail: mary.gould@bagaducemusic.org; *Operations Mgr,* Lynette Woods; E-mail: lynette@bagaducemusic.org; Staff 3 (Non-MLS 3)
Founded 1983
Library Holdings: Music Scores 250,000; Bk Titles 215,000
Special Collections: State of Maine Music Coll
Subject Interests: Music, Music scores, Sheet music
Function: Archival coll, Art exhibits, Mail & tel request accepted, Online cat, Online searches
Publications: Collection Catalogs
Mem of Northeastern Maine Library District
Open Mon-Fri 10-4
Restriction: Circ to mem only
Friends of the Library Group

P BLUE HILL PUBLIC LIBRARY*, Five Parker Point Rd, 04614-0821. SAN 306-5944. Tel: 207-374-5515. FAX: 207-374-5254. Web Site: www.bluehill.lib.me.us. *Dir,* Richard Boulet; Tel: 207-374-5515, Ext 13; *Asst Dir,* Karen Wyatt; E-mail: kwatt@bhpl.net; *Youth Serv Librn,* Pat Horton; *Bus Mgr,* Susan Farrar; Staff 7.25 (MLS 1.25, Non-MLS 6)
Founded 1796. Pop 2,599; Circ 105,000
Library Holdings: Bk Titles 39,000; Bk Vols 41,500; Per Subs 100
Special Collections: Large Print Books; Maine Local History Coll
Automation Activity & Vendor Info: (Cataloging) Follett Software; (Circulation) Follett Software; (OPAC) Follett Software
Wireless access
Mem of Northeastern Maine Library District
Open Mon-Wed & Fri 10-6, Thurs 10-8, Sat 10-2
Friends of the Library Group

BOOTHBAY HARBOR

P BOOTHBAY HARBOR MEMORIAL LIBRARY*, Four Oak St, 04538. SAN 306-5952. Tel: 207-633-3112. E-mail: bbhlibrary@bmpl.lib.me.us. Web Site: www.bmpl.lib.me.us. *Exec Dir,* Timothy McFadden; E-mail: tmcfadden@bmpl.lib.me.us; *Ch,* Mary Pinkham; Staff 4 (MLS 1, Non-MLS 3)
Founded 1924. Pop 6,000; Circ 45,000
Library Holdings: Bk Vols 27,000; Per Subs 45
Special Collections: Maine (Osgood Coll); Military History (Farmer Coll)
Automation Activity & Vendor Info: (Cataloging) Innovative Interfaces, Inc; (Circulation) Innovative Interfaces, Inc; (ILL) Innovative Interfaces, Inc; (OPAC) Innovative Interfaces, Inc
Wireless access
Special Services for the Blind - Bks on cassette; Bks on CD; Large print bks
Open Tues, Thurs, Fri & Sat 10-4:30, Wed 10-7
Friends of the Library Group

BOWDOINHAM

P BOWDOINHAM PUBLIC LIBRARY*, 13A School St, 04008. SAN 306-5960. Tel: 207-666-8405. Web Site: www.bowdoinham.lib.me.us. *Librn,* Kate Cutko; E-mail: kcutko@bowdoinham.lib.me.us; Staff 1 (Non-MLS 1)
Founded 1929. Pop 2,192; Circ 12,808
Library Holdings: Bk Titles 13,000; Bk Vols 13,676; Per Subs 30
Special Collections: Maine Coll
Wireless access
Open Tues 10-12, 2-5 & 7-8, Wed 2-6, Fri 2-5, Sat 10-3
Friends of the Library Group

BRADFORD

P JOHN B CURTIS FREE PUBLIC LIBRARY*, 435 Main Rd, 04410. (Mail add: 187 Wilder Davis Rd, 04410-3428), SAN 378-1283. Tel: 207-327-2923. Web Site: www.maine.gov/msl/mainelibs/displaypub.shtml?id=36888. *Dir,* Brenda S Mowdy
Founded 1913. Pop 1,186; Circ 3,331
Library Holdings: Large Print Bks 25; Bk Vols 9,300; Per Subs 12; Talking Bks 24
Subject Interests: Genealogy, Local hist
Wireless access
Mem of Northeastern Maine Library District
Open Wed (Winter) 5-7, Sat 10-3; Mon (Summer) 5-7, Wed 9-11 & 5-7, Sat 10-3
Friends of the Library Group

BREMEN

P BREMEN PUBLIC LIBRARY*, 204 Waldoboro Rd, 04551. (Mail add: PO Box 163, 04551-0163), SAN 376-379X. Tel: 207-529-5572. E-mail: bremen@bremen.lib.me.us. *Librn,* Sue Trouwhorst; Staff 1 (Non-MLS 1)
Library Holdings: Bk Vols 11,000
Wireless access
Function: Computers for patron use, Copy machines, ILL available, Story hour
Open Mon 10-7, Wed & Fri 10-3, Sat 10-12

BREWER

P BREWER PUBLIC LIBRARY*, 100 S Main St, 04412. SAN 306-5979. Tel: 207-989-7943. FAX: 207-989-8426. Web Site: www.brewer.lib.me.us. *Dir,* Donna Rasche; E-mail: drasche@brewerme.org; Staff 4 (Non-MLS 4)
Founded 1908. Pop 9,200; Circ 61,000
Library Holdings: AV Mats 3,400; Bk Vols 41,000; Per Subs 67
Special Collections: Fannie Hardy Eckstorm Coll, 1865-1946; Joshua Chamberlain Coll
Automation Activity & Vendor Info: (Cataloging) Follett Software; (Circulation) Follett Software; (OPAC) Follett Software

Wireless access
Mem of Northeastern Maine Library District
Open Mon & Wed 9-7, Tues, Thurs & Fri 9-5, Sat 9-1

BRIDGTON

P BRIDGTON PUBLIC LIBRARY*, One Church St, 04009. SAN 306-5987. Tel: 207-647-2472. FAX: 207-647-5660. Web Site: www.bridgton.lib.me.us. *Dir,* Holly Hancock; E-mail: hollyh@bridgton.lib.me.us; Staff 2 (MLS 1, Non-MLS 1)
Founded 1895. Pop 5,400; Circ 28,000
Library Holdings: Bk Vols 27,000; Per Subs 65
Special Collections: Local History Coll
Automation Activity & Vendor Info: (Cataloging) Follett Software; (Circulation) Follett Software
Wireless access
Mem of Southern Maine Library District
Open Tues 10-7, Wed & Fri 10-6, Sat 10-3
Friends of the Library Group

BROOKLIN

P FRIEND MEMORIAL PUBLIC LIBRARY*, One Reach Rd, 04616. (Mail add: PO Box 57, 04616-0057), SAN 306-6010. Tel: 207-359-2276. Web Site: www.friendml.org. *Dir,* Stephanie Atwater; E-mail: director@friend.lib.me.us; Staff 3 (MLS 1, Non-MLS 2)
Founded 1912. Circ 18,200
Library Holdings: Audiobooks 370; CDs 93; DVDs 882; Large Print Bks 190; Bk Vols 16,000; Per Subs 50
Wireless access
Mem of Northeastern Maine Library District
Open Tues, Fri & Sat (Winter) 10-4, Thurs 10-6; Tues-Sat (Summer) 10-6
Friends of the Library Group

BROOKSVILLE

P BROOKSVILLE FREE PUBLIC LIBRARY, INC*, Townhouse Bldg, One Townhouse Rd, 04617-3647. (Mail add: PO Box 38, 04617-0038), SAN 306-6029. Tel: 207-326-4560. FAX: 207-326-4560. E-mail: bfpl-df@bfpl.lib.me.us. Web Site: www.brooksvillelibrary.org. *Librn,* Sylvia Tapley; Staff 2 (Non-MLS 2)
Founded 1953. Pop 753; Circ 3,960
Library Holdings: Bk Vols 12,500; Per Subs 37
Subject Interests: Genealogy, Local hist
Wireless access
Publications: Newsletter
Mem of Northeastern Maine Library District
Partic in Scoop Purchasing Coop
Open Mon & Wed 9-5, Thurs 6pm-8pm, Sat 9-12
Friends of the Library Group

BROWNFIELD

P BROWNFIELD PUBLIC LIBRARY*, 216 Main St, 04010. (Mail add: PO Box 215, 04010-0215), SAN 374-5473. Tel: 207-935-3003. E-mail: librarian@brownfieldlibrary.com. Web Site: www.brownfieldlibrary.com. *Dir,* Rebecca Fuller; *Librn,* Susan Eland; *Librn,* Judi Schenstorm; Staff 1 (Non-MLS 1)
Founded 1908. Pop 1,421; Circ 2,784
Library Holdings: Audiobooks 36; DVDs 133; Large Print Bks 20; Bk Vols 6,571; Per Subs 1
Database Vendor: EBSCOhost
Wireless access
Mem of Southern Maine Library District
Open Mon 2-7, Tues & Wed 10-1, Thurs 3-7, Fri 2-6, Sat 10-2

BROWNVILLE

P BROWNVILLE FREE PUBLIC LIBRARY*, 27 Church St, 04414-3235. (Mail add: PO Box 687, 04414-0687), SAN 321-513X. Tel: 207-965-8318. *Librn,* Caryl Wagg
Pop 1,540
Jan 2010-Dec 2010 Income $4,700, City $4,600, Other $100. Mats Exp $700, Books $400, Per/Ser (Incl. Access Fees) $300. Sal $2,730
Library Holdings: Large Print Bks 10; Bk Vols 15,000; Per Subs 16; Spec Interest Per Sub 5
Open Tues 1-4, Sat 10-2

BRUNSWICK

C BOWDOIN COLLEGE LIBRARY*, 3000 College Sta, 04011-8421. SAN 306-6037. Circulation Tel: 207-725-3280. Interlibrary Loan Service Tel: 207-725-3283. Reference Tel: 207-725-3227. Administration Tel: 207-725-3155. Administration FAX: 207-725-3083. TDD: 207-798-7115. Web Site: library.bowdoin.edu. *Libr Dir,* Marjorie Hassen; E-mail: mhassen@bowdoin.edu; *Actg Librn,* Judith Montgomery; Tel: 207-725-3749; *Art Librn,* Anne Haas; *Cat Librn,* Mary Macul; *Coll Librn,* Joan Campbell; Tel: 207-725-3285; *Digital Tech Integration Librn,* Mike McDermott; *Govt Doc Librn,* Lucy Cunningham; *Instrul Media Serv Librn,* Carmen Greenlee; Tel: 207-725-3286; *Music Librn,* Karen Jung; *Pub Serv Librn,* Leanne Pander; *Ref Librn,* Katie Sasser; *Res & Instruction Librn,* Barbara Levergood; *Res & Web Develop Librn,* Carr Ross; *Sci Librn,* Sue O'Dell; *Syst & Digital Initiatives Librn,* Karl Fattig; *Tech Serv Mgr,* Roberta Schwartz; Tel: 207-725-3134; *ILL Supvr,* Guy Saldanha; Staff 32.07 (MLS 16.15, Non-MLS 15.92)
Founded 1794. Enrl 1,773; Fac 185; Highest Degree: Bachelor
Library Holdings: AV Mats 29,864; e-books 299,661; e-journals 29,543; Bk Vols 1,034,168; Per Subs 1,275
Special Collections: Abbot Coll; Arctic Coll; Carlyle Coll; Hawthorne Coll; Huguenot Coll; Longfellow Coll; Maine Coll; Senator George J Mitchell Papers. US Document Depository
Automation Activity & Vendor Info: (Acquisitions) Innovative Interfaces, Inc - Millenium; (Cataloging) Innovative Interfaces, Inc - Millenium; (Circulation) Innovative Interfaces, Inc - Millenium; (Course Reserve) Innovative Interfaces, Inc - Millenium; (OPAC) Innovative Interfaces, Inc - Millenium; (Serials) Innovative Interfaces, Inc - Millenium
Wireless access
Publications: From the Library (Newsletter)
Partic in Lyrasis; OCLC Online Computer Library Center, Inc
Special Services for the Deaf - TDD equip
Open Mon-Wed 8:30am-1:30am, Thurs 8:30am-Midnight, Fri 8:30am-11pm, Sat 10am-11pm, Sun 10am-1:30am

Departmental Libraries:

BECKWITH MUSIC LIBRARY, Gibson Hall, 1st Flr, 9210 College Sta, 04011. Tel: 207-725-3570. *Music Librn,* Karen Jung; Tel: 207-725-3311
Open Mon-Wed 9am-1:30am, Thurs 9am-Midnight, Fri 9-5, Sat 11-5, Sun Noon-1:30

HATCH SCIENCE LIBRARY, Hatch Science Bldg, 2nd Flr, 3100 College Sta, 04011. Tel: 207-725-3004. FAX: 207-725-3095. *Librn,* Sue O'Dell; E-mail: sodell@bowdoin.edu
Open Mon-Thurs 8:30am-Midnight, Fri 8:30-8, Sat Noon-8, Sun Noon-Midnight

LANGUAGE MEDIA CENTER, Sills Hall, 1st Flr, 8200 College Sta, 04011-8242. Tel: 207-725-3702. *Instrul Media Serv Librn,* Carmen Greenlee; E-mail: cgreenle@bowdoin.edu
Open Mon-Thurs 9am-11pm, Fri 9-5, Sat 1-5, Sun 2-11

PIERCE ART LIBRARY, Visual Arts Ctr, 9301 College Sta, 04011-8493. Tel: 207-725-3690. *Art Librn,* Anne Haas; E-mail: ahaas@bowdoin.edu
Open Mon-Thurs 9am-11pm, Fri 9-5, Sat 12-5, Sun Noon-11

P BRUNSWICK PUBLIC LIBRARY ASSOCIATION*, Captain John Curtis Memorial Library, 23 Pleasant St, 04011-2295. SAN 306-6045. Tel: 207-725-5242. Interlibrary Loan Service Tel: 207-725 5242, Ext 205. Reference Tel: 207-725-5242, Ext 204. FAX: 207-725-6313. E-mail: info@curtislibrary.com. Web Site: www.curtislibrary.com. *Dir,* Elisabeth Doucett; Tel: 207-725-5242, Ext 211, E-mail: edoucett@curtislibrary.com; *Asst Libr Dir, Youth Serv Mgr,* Pamela Jenkins; Staff 20 (MLS 11, Non-MLS 9)
Founded 1883. Pop 26,000; Circ 359,695
Jul 2007-Jun 2008 Income $1,220,085, City $1,135,378, Locally Generated Income $84,700. Mats Exp $92,682
Library Holdings: Bk Vols 146,625
Wireless access
Function: Art exhibits, Bks on cassette, Bks on CD, Children's prog, Computers for patron use, Copy machines, Digital talking bks, e-mail serv, E-Reserves, Electronic databases & coll, Free DVD rentals, Handicapped accessible, Health sci info serv, Homebound delivery serv, Homework prog, ILL available, Magnifiers for reading, Mail & tel request accepted, Mus passes, Music CDs, Online searches, Prog for children & young adult, Ref & res, Ref serv available, Summer reading prog, Tax forms, Telephone ref, VHS videos, Wheelchair accessible, Writing prog
Publications: Cornerstones of Science Newlsetter (Bi-annually); Library Newsletter
Special Services for the Blind - Assistive/Adapted tech devices, equip & products; Bks on cassette; Bks on CD; Closed circuit TV magnifier; Home delivery serv; Internet workstation with adaptive software; Large print bks; Low vision equip; Magnifiers; Open bk software on pub access PC; Volunteer serv; ZoomText magnification & reading software
Open Mon-Thurs 9:30-8, Fri 9:30-6, Sat 9:30-5, Sun Noon-4
Friends of the Library Group

M MID-COAST HOSPITAL*, Health Sciences Library, 123 Medical Center Dr, 04011. SAN 306-6061. Tel: 207-373-6571. FAX: 207-373-6572. E-mail: library@midcoasthealth.com. Web Site: www.midcoasthealth.com/library. *Librn,* Christina Stuntz; E-mail: cstuntz@midcoasthealth.com; Staff 1 (MLS 1)
Founded 1973
Oct 2009-Sept 2010 Income $53,000. Mats Exp $1,500. Sal $33,500
Library Holdings: Bk Titles 200; Bk Vols 325; Per Subs 48
Database Vendor: Cinahl, EBSCOhost, MD Consult, Micromedex, UpToDate

Wireless access
Mem of Southern Maine Library District
Partic in Basic Health Sciences Library Network; Health Science Library Information Consortium; North Atlantic Health Sciences Libraries, Inc
Open Mon, Wed & Fri 8-4

S PEJEPSCOT HISTORICAL SOCIETY, Research Library, 159 Park Row, 04011. SAN 306-6053. Tel: 207-729-6606. FAX: 207-729-6012. E-mail: info@pejepscothistorical.org. Web Site: pejepscothistorical.org. *Exec Dir,* Jennifer Blanchard; E-mail: director@pejepscothistorical.org
Founded 1888
Library Holdings: Bk Titles 500; Bk Vols 700
Special Collections: History of Brunswick Coll, 1803-59 Lincoln, Isaac, LC MS 65-20001, papers; Joshua Lawrence Chamberlain Coll; Local Franco-American History, Local Industrial History Colls. Oral History
Subject Interests: Local hist
Wireless access
Open Wed-Fri (Winter) 10-4; Tues-Sat (Summer) 10-4

BRYANT POND

P WHITMAN MEMORIAL LIBRARY*, Main St, 04219. (Mail add: PO Box 307, 04219-0307), SAN 306-7920. Tel: 207-665-2505. E-mail: whitmanlibrary@roadrunner.com. *Librn,* Althea Hathaway; Staff 1 (Non-MLS 1)
Founded 1908. Pop 1,194; Circ 2,456
Library Holdings: AV Mats 50; Bk Vols 11,219; Per Subs 21
Automation Activity & Vendor Info: (Cataloging) Follett Software; (Circulation) Follett Software
Open Tues & Thurs 1-5

BUCKFIELD

P ZADOC LONG FREE LIBRARY*, Five Turner St, Rte 117, 04220. (Mail add: PO Box 158, 04220-0158). Tel: 207-336-2171. E-mail: zadoc@zadoc.lib.me.us. Web Site: www.zadoc.lib.me.us. *Dir,* Ann Varney; Staff 0.7 (Non-MLS 0.7)
Founded 1901. Pop 3,944; Circ 3,002
Jul 2006-Jun 2007 Income $22,390. Mats Exp $24,190, Books $1,800. Sal $12,690
Library Holdings: Audiobooks 190; DVDs 30; Large Print Bks 60; Bk Titles 6,000; Per Subs 15; Videos 150
Special Collections: 23rd Maine Company C Reports; Long Diaries; Long Family Photos
Automation Activity & Vendor Info: (Cataloging) JayWil Software Development, Inc; (Circulation) JayWil Software Development, Inc
Database Vendor: JayWil Software Development, Inc
Function: Adult bk club
Open Mon & Wed 1-7, Tues 9-7, Sat 9-3
Friends of the Library Group

BUCKSPORT

P BUCK MEMORIAL LIBRARY*, 47 Main St, 04416. (Mail add: PO Box DD, 04416), SAN 306-607X. Tel: 207-469-2650. E-mail: buckmemorial@buck.lib.me.us. *Librn,* Geraldine Spooner
Founded 1887. Pop 4,345; Circ 10,233
Library Holdings: Bk Vols 27,000; Per Subs 20
Mem of Northeastern Maine Library District
Open Mon-Fri 10-5, Sat 10-12

BUXTON

P WEST BUXTON PUBLIC LIBRARY*, 34 River Rd, S R 112, 04093-0348. (Mail add: PO Box 348, 04093-0348), SAN 306-6088. Tel: 207-727-5898. Web Site: www.westbuxtonpubliclibrary.org. *Libr Dir,* Sharleen A Fields; E-mail: director@westbuxtonpubliclibrary.org; Staff 1 (Non-MLS 1)
Founded 1925. Pop 9,300
Jul 2007-Jun 2008 Income $29,800, City $10,000, Locally Generated Income $10,000, Other $9,800. Mats Exp $3,250, Books $3,000, Electronic Ref Mat (Incl. Access Fees) $250. Sal $1,200
Library Holdings: AV Mats 150; Bks-By-Mail 30; CDs 10; DVDs 25; Large Print Bks 30; Bk Titles 6,350; Per Subs 5; Videos 50
Wireless access
Function: Art exhibits, Bks on cassette, Bks on CD, Computers for patron use, Copy machines, e-mail serv, E-Reserves, Free DVD rentals, Games & aids for the handicapped, Handicapped accessible, Holiday prog, ILL available, Magnifiers for reading, Music CDs, Notary serv, Photocopying/Printing, Prof lending libr, Prog for adults, Prog for children & young adult, Summer reading prog, Tax forms, VHS videos, Wheelchair accessible
Mem of Southern Maine Library District
Open Tues & Thurs 4-8, Sat 9-1

CALAIS

P CALAIS FREE LIBRARY*, Nine Union St, 04619. SAN 306-6096. Tel: 207-454-2758. FAX: 207-454-2765. Web Site: www.calais.lib.me.us. *Dir,* Kathleen Staples; E-mail: kstaples@calais.lib.me.us; *Youth & Adult Serv Librn,* Greg Williams; E-mail: gregw@calais.lib.me.us; Staff 5 (MLS 2, Non-MLS 3)
Founded 1892. Pop 3,963; Circ 49,420
Library Holdings: AV Mats 350; Bk Vols 33,000; Per Subs 49
Special Collections: Champlain Coll; James S Pike Coll; Maine & Genealogy Coll, microfiche; State of Maine Coll
Automation Activity & Vendor Info: (Cataloging) Innovative Interfaces, Inc; (Circulation) Innovative Interfaces, Inc; (OPAC) Innovative Interfaces, Inc
Database Vendor: EBSCOhost
Wireless access
Mem of Northeastern Maine Library District
Open Mon, Wed & Fri 9-5, Tues Noon-8, Thurs 9-6
Friends of the Library Group

J WASHINGTON COUNTY COMMUNITY COLLEGE LIBRARY*, One College Dr, 04619. SAN 322-8452. Tel: 207-454-1000. FAX: 207-454-1053. Web Site: www.wccc.me.edu/library. *Dir, Libr Serv,* James Fein; Tel: 207-454-1050, E-mail: jfein@wccc.me.edu; *Librn,* John Leavitt; E-mail: jleavitt@wccc.me.edu; Staff 2 (MLS 1, Non-MLS 1)
Enrl 375; Fac 27; Highest Degree: Associate
Library Holdings: Bk Vols 11,000; Per Subs 140
Automation Activity & Vendor Info: (Acquisitions) Innovative Interfaces, Inc; (Cataloging) Innovative Interfaces, Inc; (Circulation) Innovative Interfaces, Inc; (Course Reserve) Innovative Interfaces, Inc; (ILL) Innovative Interfaces, Inc; (OPAC) Innovative Interfaces, Inc; (Serials) Innovative Interfaces, Inc
Database Vendor: EBSCOhost, ProQuest
Wireless access
Partic in Maine InfoNet; Maine State Libr Network
Open Mon-Thurs 8-7, Fri 8-4:30

CAMDEN

P CAMDEN PUBLIC LIBRARY*, 55 Main St, 04843-1703. SAN 306-610X. Tel: 207-236-3440. FAX: 207-236-6673. E-mail: info@librarycamden.org. Web Site: www.librarycamden.org. *Dir,* Nikki Maounis; *Asst Dir,* Ken Gross; *Ch,* Amy Hand; Staff 12 (MLS 4, Non-MLS 8)
Founded 1896. Pop 5,050; Circ 257,786
Library Holdings: AV Mats 6,354; e-books 890; Large Print Bks 686; Bk Vols 60,186; Per Subs 114
Special Collections: Edna St Vincent Millay Coll. Oral History
Automation Activity & Vendor Info: (Acquisitions) Innovative Interfaces, Inc; (Cataloging) Innovative Interfaces, Inc; (Circulation) Innovative Interfaces, Inc; (OPAC) Innovative Interfaces, Inc; (Serials) Innovative Interfaces, Inc
Database Vendor: EBSCOhost, OCLC FirstSearch
Wireless access
Publications: Library Underground (Newsletter)
Mem of Northeastern Maine Library District
Open Mon, Wed, Fri & Sat 9-6, Tues & Thurs 9-8, Sun 1-5

CANAAN

P CANAAN PUBLIC LIBRARY*, 288 Main St, 04924. (Mail add: PO Box 280, 04924-0280). Tel: 207-474-6397. E-mail: canplib@canaan.lib.me.us. *Dir,* Karen Fournier
Founded 1878. Pop 2,400
Library Holdings: AV Mats 10; Bk Vols 8,000; Per Subs 14; Talking Bks 150
Special Collections: Maine Coll
Automation Activity & Vendor Info: (Cataloging) ComPanion Corp; (Circulation) ComPanion Corp
Open Mon & Wed 10-6, Fri 9-5, Sat 9-2
Friends of the Library Group

CAPE ELIZABETH

P THOMAS MEMORIAL LIBRARY*, Six Scott Dyer Rd, 04107. SAN 322-6786. Tel: 207-799-1720. *Dir,* Jay Scherma; E-mail: jscherma@thomas.lib.me.us; *Ch Serv,* Rachel Q Davis; E-mail: rdavis@thomas.lib.me.us; *Ref,* Joyce Lourie; E-mail: jlourie@thomas.lib.me.us; *YA Serv,* Kevin Goody; E-mail: kgoody@thomas.lib.me.us; Staff 12 (MLS 4, Non-MLS 8)
Founded 1919. Pop 9,130; Circ 123,373
Jul 2005-Jun 2006 Income $477,739, City $460,183, Other $17,556. Mats Exp $44,089, Books $33,741, Per/Ser (Incl. Access Fees) $4,849, AV Mat $5,499. Sal $389,099
Library Holdings: Electronic Media & Resources 1; Large Print Bks 678; Bk Vols 48,303; Per Subs 86; Talking Bks 2,110; Videos 1,814

Special Collections: Gabriel A Zimpritch Coll; Maine Coll
Subject Interests: Contemporary lit, Contemporary poetry, Experimental lit, Experimental poetry
Automation Activity & Vendor Info: (Cataloging) Innovative Interfaces, Inc; (Circulation) Innovative Interfaces, Inc; (OPAC) Innovative Interfaces, Inc
Database Vendor: EBSCOhost
Wireless access
Mem of Southern Maine Library District
Open Mon, Wed, Fri & Sat (Winter) 9-5, Tues & Thurs 9-8:30; Mon, Wed & Fri (Summer) 9-5, Tues & Thurs 9-8:30, Sat 9-1
Friends of the Library Group

CAPE PORPOISE

P CAPE PORPOISE LIBRARY*, Kennebunkport, Atlantic Hall, 04014. (Mail add: PO Box 7248, 04014). Tel: 207-967-5668. FAX: 207-967-5668. E-mail: cplibrary@cape-porpoise.lib.me.us. *Dir,* Suzanne Perkins; Staff 1 (Non-MLS 1)
Pop 4,054; Circ 24,173
Library Holdings: Bk Titles 6,500; Per Subs 20
Mem of Southern Maine Library District
Open Tues & Thurs 1-4, Fri & Sat 9-12

CARIBOU

L CARIBOU LAW LIBRARY*, 144 Sweden, 04736. Tel: 207-762-2244. *In Charge,* Sarah LeClaire
Library Holdings: Bk Vols 1,000
Database Vendor: LexisNexis
Open Mon-Fri 9-1

P CARIBOU PUBLIC LIBRARY*, 30 High St, 04736. SAN 306-6126. Tel: 207-493-4214. FAX: 207-493-4654. Web Site: www.caribou-public.lib.me.us. *Dir,* Diane C Dubois; E-mail: ddubois@caribou-public.lib.me.us; *Asst Librn, Young Adult Serv,* Mona Martin; *Ch,* Jean Shaw; *Circ Librn,* Mary Anderson; *Circ Librn,* Barbara Finley; *Circ Librn,* Cassie Germain; *Tech Coordr,* Brian Levesque; Staff 3 (Non-MLS 3)
Founded 1911. Pop 9,920; Circ 65,700
Library Holdings: Bk Vols 48,000; Per Subs 105
Special Collections: Local History Coll; Local Newspapers 1887-1976, microfilm. Oral History
Automation Activity & Vendor Info: (Cataloging) Follett Software; (Circulation) Follett Software; (OPAC) Follett Software
Wireless access
Mem of Northeastern Maine Library District
Open Mon-Thurs 10-7, Fri 10-6, Sat 10-2
Friends of the Library Group

M CARY MEDICAL CENTER*, Health Science Library, 163 Van Buren Rd, Ste 1, 04736-2599. SAN 306-6134. Tel: 207-498-3111, Ext 1365. FAX: 207-498-1272. Web Site: www.carymed.org. *Coordr,* Jennifer Carlow
Library Holdings: Bk Vols 600; Per Subs 100
Subject Interests: Health sci
Wireless access

CARMEL

P SIMPSON MEMORIAL LIBRARY*, Eight Plymouth Rd, 04419. (Mail add: PO Box 186, 04419-0186), SAN 376-3544. Tel: 207-848-7145. FAX: 207-848-7145. Web Site: www.simpsonmemorial.org. *Dir,* Becky Ames; Staff 1 (Non-MLS 1)
Pop 2,850; Circ 4,005
Library Holdings: Audiobooks 192; Bks-By-Mail 30; Bks on Deafness & Sign Lang 5; CDs 96; DVDs 92; Large Print Bks 200; Bk Titles 6,068; Per Subs 11; Videos 315
Database Vendor: EBSCOhost
Wireless access
Function: Bks on cassette, Bks on CD, Children's prog, Computer training, Computers for patron use, Copy machines, e-mail serv, Family literacy, Fax serv, Free DVD rentals, Handicapped accessible, ILL available, Music CDs, Online searches, Photocopying/Printing, Ref serv in person, Story hour, Summer reading prog, VCDs, VHS videos, Wheelchair accessible
Mem of Northeastern Maine Library District
Open Tues & Thurs 11-7, Sat 9-1
Restriction: Access at librarian's discretion

CARRABASSETT

P CARRABASSETT VALLEY LIBRARY*, 3209 Carrabassett Dr, 04947-9724. Tel: 207-235-3535. FAX: 207-237-3536. *Dir,* Andrea DeBiase; E-mail: adebiase@carrabassett.lib.me.us
Founded 1989
Library Holdings: Bk Vols 2,000
Wireless access
Friends of the Library Group

CASCO

P CASCO PUBLIC LIBRARY*, Five Leach Hill Rd, 04015-3229. (Mail add: PO Box 420, 04015-0420), SAN 306-6142. Tel: 207-627-4541. E-mail: cascolib@casco.lib.me.us. Web Site: www.casco.lib.me.us. *Dir,* Carolyn Paradise; Staff 3 (MLS 1, Non-MLS 2)
Founded 1946. Pop 3,450; Circ 28,000
Library Holdings: Audiobooks 2,241; CDs 231; DVDs 1,928; e-books 5,388; Large Print Bks 116; Bk Vols 17,280; Per Subs 17
Database Vendor: EBSCOhost
Wireless access
Mem of Southern Maine Library District
Partic in Maine School & Library Network
Special Services for the Deaf - Adult & family literacy prog
Open Tues, Thurs & Sun 10-8

CASTINE

C MAINE MARITIME ACADEMY*, Nutting Memorial Library, Pleasant St, Box C-1, 04420. SAN 306-6150. Tel: 207-326-2263. FAX: 207-326-2261. Web Site: library.mma.edu. *Dir,* Wendy Girven; Tel: 207-326-2260, E-mail: wendy.girven@mma.edu; *Asst Librn,* Lauren Blanchard; E-mail: lauren.blanchard@mma.edu; *Asst Librn,* Sarah Danser; Tel: 207-326-2262, E-mail: sarah.danser@mma.edu; Staff 5 (MLS 3, Non-MLS 2)
Founded 1941. Enrl 820; Fac 65; Highest Degree: Master
Library Holdings: Bk Titles 66,000; Per Subs 250
Special Collections: Federal Maritime Commission Papers (Kanuk Coll); Military History (Schieffelin Coll); Oceanography (Gilmartin Coll). US Document Depository
Subject Interests: Marine tech, Maritime hist, Mil hist
Automation Activity & Vendor Info: (Acquisitions) Innovative Interfaces, Inc; (Cataloging) Innovative Interfaces, Inc; (Circulation) Innovative Interfaces, Inc; (Course Reserve) Innovative Interfaces, Inc; (ILL) OCLC; (OPAC) Innovative Interfaces, Inc; (Serials) Innovative Interfaces, Inc
Database Vendor: EBSCOhost, Newsbank, OCLC FirstSearch, OVID Technologies
Wireless access
Function: ILL available
Partic in Lyrasis

P WITHERLE MEMORIAL LIBRARY*, 41 School St, 04421. (Mail add: PO Box 202, 04421-0202), SAN 306-6169. Tel: 207-326-4375. E-mail: refdesk@witherle.lib.me.us. Web Site: www.witherle.lib.me.us. *Dir,* Anne Francis Romans; Staff 4 (MLS 1, Non-MLS 3)
Founded 1801. Pop 1,740; Circ 31,142
Jul 2012-Jun 2013 Income $142,344. Mats Exp $19,880, Books $14,459, AV Mat $5,059, Electronic Ref Mat (Incl. Access Fees) $362. Sal $91,435
Library Holdings: Audiobooks 1,232; Bks on Deafness & Sign Lang 11; DVDs 1,988; e-books 5,644; Electronic Media & Resources 66; Large Print Bks 273; Microforms 20; Bk Vols 13,161; Per Subs 26
Special Collections: Castine Newspapers on Microfilm 1800s & 1900s
Automation Activity & Vendor Info: (Acquisitions) Innovative Interfaces, Inc; (Cataloging) Innovative Interfaces, Inc; (Circulation) Innovative Interfaces, Inc; (ILL) Innovative Interfaces, Inc; (Media Booking) Innovative Interfaces, Inc; (OPAC) Innovative Interfaces, Inc; (Serials) Innovative Interfaces, Inc
Database Vendor: Agricola, EBSCOhost, Innovative Interfaces, Inc, ProQuest, ValueLine
Wireless access
Function: Adult bk club, Archival coll, Art exhibits, Audiobks via web, AV serv, Bk club(s), Bks on CD, Children's prog, Computer training, Computers for patron use, Copy machines, e-mail serv, Electronic databases & coll, Free DVD rentals, Handicapped accessible, Holiday prog, Homebound delivery serv, ILL available, Microfiche/film & reading machines, Mus passes, Music CDs, Online cat, Outreach serv, OverDrive digital audio bks, Photocopying/Printing, Preschool outreach, Prog for adults, Prog for children & young adult, Pub access computers, Ref & res, Ref serv available, Ref serv in person, Scanner, Senior computer classes, Summer & winter reading prog, Summer reading prog, Tax forms, Telephone ref, Wheelchair accessible, Winter reading prog
Mem of Northeastern Maine Library District
Special Services for the Deaf - Bks on deafness & sign lang
Special Services for the Blind - Large print bks; Talking bks
Friends of the Library Group

CENTER LOVELL

P LEWIS DANA HILL MEMORIAL LIBRARY*, 2079 Main St, 04231-9702. (Mail add: PO Box 92, 04016-0092), SAN 376-3757. Tel: 207-928-2301. *Head Librn,* Dennis Hodge; *Librn,* Susan Campo; *Asst Librn,* Deborah Bullard; Staff 1 (Non-MLS 1)
Pop 3,000

Library Holdings: CDs 100; DVDs 100; Large Print Bks 50; Bk Titles 9,000; Bk Vols 10,000; Per Subs 20; Talking Bks 300; Videos 300
Database Vendor: EBSCOhost
Open Tues & Thurs 5-7, Sat 9-12

CHARLESTON

P CHARLESTON PUBLIC LIBRARY*, 13 Atkinson Rd, 04422. (Mail add: PO Box 120, 04422-0120), SAN 372-6800. Tel: 207-285-3680. E-mail: charleston@charleston.lib.me.us. Web Site: www.charleston.lib.me.us. *Dir,* Ann Moore; Staff 1 (Non-MLS 1)
Founded 1900. Pop 1,523; Circ 2,409
Library Holdings: Bk Titles 7,000; Per Subs 10
Wireless access
Mem of Northeastern Maine Library District
Open Tues-Thurs 4-7
Friends of the Library Group

S MAINE DEPARTMENT OF CORRECTIONS*, Charleston Correctional Facility Library, 1202 Dover Rd, 04422. Tel: 207-285-0876. FAX: 207-285-0815. *Librn,* Paul Robbins
Founded 1980
Library Holdings: Bk Vols 3,000; Per Subs 15
Open Mon & Wed 5:50-8

S MOUNTAIN VIEW YOUTH DEVELOPMENT CENTER LIBRARY*, 1182 Dover Rd, 04422. Tel: 207-285-0780. *Librn,* Position Currently Open
Library Holdings: Bk Titles 5,674; Per Subs 15

CHEBEAGUE ISLAND

P CHEBEAGUE ISLAND LIBRARY*, 247 South Rd, Unit 3, 04017-3200. SAN 306-6207. Tel: 207-846-4351. FAX: 207-846-4358. E-mail: cheblib@hotmail.com. Web Site: chebeague.chebeague.lib.me.us. *Dir,* Deborah A Bowman
Founded 1965. Pop 2,000; Circ 13,450
Library Holdings: AV Mats 2,000; Large Print Bks 180; Bk Vols 16,000; Per Subs 32; Talking Bks 584
Subject Interests: Genealogy, Local hist, Maine
Wireless access
Mem of Southern Maine Library District
Open Mon 6pm-8pm, Tues & Thurs 10-4 & 6-8, Wed & Sat 10-1, Fri 10-4
Friends of the Library Group

CHERRYFIELD

P CHERRYFIELD FREE PUBLIC LIBRARY*, 35 Main St, 04622. (Mail add: PO BOx 121, 04622-4201), SAN 321-5989. Tel: 207-546-4228. FAX: 207-546-4228. E-mail: cherryfield@cherryfield.lib.me.us, cherryfield@msln.net. *Head Librn,* Cara Elizabeth Sawyer; Staff 1 (MLS 1)
Founded 1837. Pop 1,320; Circ 2,106
Oct 2005-Sept 2006 Income $38,096, City $3,500, Other $34,596. Mats Exp $1,500. Sal $4,059
Library Holdings: DVDs 11; Large Print Bks 350; Bk Titles 5,917; Talking Bks 138; Videos 327
Mem of Northeastern Maine Library District
Open Tues & Fri (Winter) 2-7, Wed & Thurs 2-6, Sat 11-3; Tues (Summer) Noon-8, Wed-Fri Noon-6, Sat 9-3

CHINA

P ALBERT CHURCH BROWN MEMORIAL LIBRARY*, 37 Main St, 04358. (Mail add: PO Box 6146, China Village, 04926-0146), SAN 376-687X. Tel: 207-968-2926. Web Site: www.acbrown.lib.me.us. *Librn,* Mary Grow; Staff 1 (Non-MLS 1)
Pop 4,328
Library Holdings: AV Mats 110; Bk Vols 16,500; Per Subs 13
Wireless access
Open Tues 2-6:30, Thurs 2-5:30, Sat 10-Noon

CLINTON

P BROWN MEMORIAL LIBRARY*, 53 Railroad St, 04927-3200. SAN 376-7434. Tel: 207-426-8686. FAX: 207-426-8686. E-mail: brownmemorial@roadrunner.com. *Libr Dir,* Cheryl Dickey-Whitish; *Asst Dir,* Cindy Lowell
Pop 3,636; Circ 5,840
Library Holdings: AV Mats 171; Bk Vols 13,478; Per Subs 36; Videos 100
Open Mon (Winter) 10-5, Tues & Wed 10-6, Thurs 12-8, Sat 9-1; Mon & Wed (Summer) 9-4, Tues 10-6, Thurs 12-8, Fri 9-3, Sat 9-1

CORINNA

P STEWART FREE LIBRARY, Eight Levi Stewart Dr, 04928. SAN 306-6185. Tel: 207-278-2454. FAX: 207-278-5200. E-mail: stewartdirector@stewart.lib.me.us. Web Site: www.corinna.govoffice.com. *Dir,* Jamie Irving; Staff 1 (Non-MLS 1)
Pop 2,196; Circ 7,228
Library Holdings: AV Mats 402; Large Print Bks 70; Bk Titles 12,516; Per Subs 18; Talking Bks 160
Special Collections: Abraham Lincoln, Napoleon & Civil War (Levi Stewart Private Library Room)
Wireless access
Mem of Northeastern Maine Library District
Open Tues 9-2, Wed & Thurs 1-7, Sat 9-12

CORINTH

P ATKINS MEMORIAL LIBRARY*, 419 Hudson Rd, 04427-3215. Tel: 207-285-7226. *Librn,* Christine McCorrison
Founded 1937. Pop 2,793; Circ 1,615
Library Holdings: AV Mats 25; Bk Vols 12,000
Special Collections: Annuals (Academy Rocket, Central High School Rocket) (Coll mostly of ECA Rockets); Local Interest (Limited coll of history of town)
Function: Archival coll, Children's prog, Computers for patron use
Open Mon 6pm-8pm, Thurs 12:30-6
Restriction: Non-circulating of rare bks, Residents only

CORNISH

P BONNEY MEMORIAL LIBRARY*, 36 Main St, 04020. (Mail add: PO Box 857, 04020-0857), SAN 306-6193. Tel: 207-625-8083. FAX: 207-625-8083. Web Site: www.bonney.lib.me.us. *Dir,* Cheryl Beth Hevey; E-mail: chevey@bonney.lib.me.us; Staff 1 (MLS 1)
Founded 1928. Pop 1,403
Nov 2010-Oct 2011 Income $46,889, City $12,000, Federal $373, Other $34,516. Mats Exp $6,456, Books $6,406, AV Mat $50. Sal $26,000
Library Holdings: Audiobooks 532; CDs 160; DVDs 85; Bk Titles 14,758; Per Subs 15; Videos 310
Automation Activity & Vendor Info: (Cataloging) LibraryWorld, Inc; (Circulation) LibraryWorld, Inc; (OPAC) LibraryWorld, Inc
Wireless access
Mem of Southern Maine Library District
Open Mon & Wed 10-7, Tues & Thurs 12-6, Sat (Sept-June) 10-1
Friends of the Library Group

CRANBERRY ISLES

P GREAT CRANBERRY LIBRARY*, 251 Cranberry Rd, 04625. (Mail add: PO Box 89, 04625-0013). Tel: 207-244-7358. FAX: 207-244-7358. E-mail: greatcranberrylibrary@yahoo.com. Web Site: www.cranberryisles.com. *Dir,* Ingrid Gaither; Staff 1 (Non-MLS 1)
Founded 1977. Circ 2,402
Jul 2005-Jun 2006 Income $32,300. Mats Exp $2,500. Sal $10,800
Library Holdings: Large Print Bks 20; Bk Vols 7,556; Per Subs 16; Talking Bks 80
Special Collections: Municipal Document Depository
Database Vendor: EBSCOhost
Wireless access
Open Tues & Fri (Oct-May) 10-2; Mon-Fri (June-Aug) 10-2

CUMBERLAND

P PRINCE MEMORIAL LIBRARY*, 266 Main St, 04021-9754. SAN 306-6215. Tel: 207-829-2215. FAX: 207-829-2221. E-mail: inquiry@princememorial.lib.me.us. Web Site: www.princememorial.lib.me.us. *Dir,* Thomas C Bennett; Tel: 207-829-2216, E-mail: tbennett@cumberlandmaine.com; *Circ Mgr,* Sandy McGowan; E-mail: smcgowan@princememorial.lib.me.us; *Ref Librn,* Elizabeth Tarasevich; E-mail: etarasevich@princememorial.lib.me.us; *Youth Serv Librn,* Jan Hamilton; E-mail: jhamilton@princememorial.lib.me.us; Staff 4 (MLS 2, Non-MLS 2)
Founded 1923. Pop 10,300; Circ 72,500
Library Holdings: AV Mats 2,344; Large Print Bks 983; Bk Titles 52,000; Per Subs 98
Special Collections: Maine Coll
Automation Activity & Vendor Info: (Cataloging) Follett Software; (Circulation) Follett Software; (OPAC) Follett Software
Database Vendor: EBSCOhost
Wireless access
Mem of Southern Maine Library District
Open Mon-Thurs 9-8, Fri 9-5, Sat 9-2
Friends of the Library Group

CUSHING

P CUSHING PUBLIC LIBRARY, 39 Cross Rd, 04563. (Mail add: PO Box 25, 04563-0025). Tel: 207-354-8860. E-mail: cushinglibrary@cushing.lib.me.us. Web Site: www.cushing.lib.me.us. *Dir,* Angel Bernardo
Founded 1995. Pop 1,400
Library Holdings: AV Mats 200; Bk Vols 3,000; Talking Bks 200
Wireless access
Open Mon & Wed 10-4, Fri 10:30-12:30, Sat 10-Noon
Friends of the Library Group

DAMARISCOTTA

P SKIDOMPHA PUBLIC LIBRARY*, 184 Main St, 04543-4670. (Mail add: PO Box 70, 04543-0070), SAN 306-6223. Tel: 207-563-5513. Circulation Tel: 207-563-1058. FAX: 207-563-1941. E-mail: skid@msln.net. Web Site: www.skidompha.org. *Dir,* Pam Gormley; E-mail: pgormley@msln.net; *Asst Librn,* Anne Holmes; Staff 3 (Non-MLS 3)
Founded 1905. Pop 9,000; Circ 68,000
Library Holdings: Large Print Bks 250; Bk Vols 30,000; Per Subs 20
Subject Interests: Genealogy, Local hist
Automation Activity & Vendor Info: (Acquisitions) Innovative Interfaces, Inc; (Cataloging) Innovative Interfaces, Inc; (Circulation) Innovative Interfaces, Inc; (ILL) Innovative Interfaces, Inc
Wireless access
Open Tues, Wed & Fri 9-5, Thurs 9-7, Sat 9-1
Friends of the Library Group

DANFORTH

P DANFORTH PUBLIC LIBRARY*, 46 Central St, 04424. (Mail add: PO Box 218, 04424-0218). Tel: 207-448-2055. E-mail: danforth@danforth.lib.me.us. Web Site: www.danforth.lib.me.us. *In Charge,* Barbara Bonner
Pop 600
Library Holdings: DVDs 100; Large Print Bks 95; Bk Vols 2,500
Wireless access
Open Tues & Sat 10-2

DEER ISLE

S DEER ISLE-STONINGTON HISTORICAL SOCIETY LIBRARY, ARCHIVES & MUSEUM*, Rte 15A/416 Sunset Rd, 04627. (Mail add: PO Box 652, 04627-0652), SAN 370-2162. Tel: 207-348-6400. Web Site: dis-historicalsociety.org. *Pres,* Tinker Crouch
Founded 1959
Library Holdings: Bk Vols 789
Special Collections: Oral History
Subject Interests: Genealogy, Island Indians, Marine hist, Marine vessels, Steamboats, Yachts
Open Wed & Fri 1-4

P CHASE EMERSON MEMORIAL LIBRARY*, 17 Main St, 04627. (Mail add: PO Box 9, 04627-0009), SAN 306-6231. Tel: 207-348-2899. *Librn,* Candace Hall; E-mail: candacel.hall2@gmail.com; Staff 1 (Non-MLS 1)
Founded 1922. Pop 1,985; Circ 5,552
Library Holdings: Bk Titles 24,000; Per Subs 12; Talking Bks 500; Videos 300
Special Collections: Merchant Sail (William A Fairburn Coll); Official Records of the Union & Confederate Armies (War of the Rebellion Coll)
Database Vendor: EBSCOhost
Wireless access
Mem of Northeastern Maine Library District
Open Mon 5pm-7pm, Wed 11-3, Sat 9-12

DENMARK

P DENMARK PUBLIC LIBRARY*, 121 E Main St, 04022. (Mail add: PO Box 50, 04022-0050), SAN 376-3811. Tel: 207-452-2200. E-mail: denmarklib@denmark.lib.me.us. *Librn,* Robin B Gosbee; Staff 1 (Non-MLS 1)
Founded 1987. Pop 2,008
Jul 2010-Jun 2011 Income $9,000. Mats Exp $4,000
Library Holdings: Bk Vols 6,500
Database Vendor: EBSCOhost
Wireless access
Mem of Southern Maine Library District
Open Tues 3-6, Wed 9-12, Thurs 3-8, Sat 12-4
Friends of the Library Group

DENNYSVILLE

P DENNYSVILLE-LINCOLN MEMORIAL LIBRARY*, 17 King St, 04628. (Mail add: PO Box 53, 04628-0053). Tel: 207-726-4750. E-mail: lincmem@lincolnd.lib.me.us. *Dir,* Dr Colin Windhorst; *Ch Serv, Coordr,* Ann Carter
Library Holdings: AV Mats 66; Large Print Bks 10; Bk Vols 5,000; Per Subs 10; Talking Bks 26
Special Collections: Local History & Genealogy Coll
Open Mon 4-7, Tues & Fri 1:30-4, Wed 2-4
Friends of the Library Group

DETROIT

P ANNA FIELD FERNALD LIBRARY*, 35 S Main St, 04929-3252. Tel: 207-257-4488. FAX: 207-257-2434. E-mail: fernald@fernald.lib.me.us. Web Site: www.fernald.lib.me.us. *Dir,* Bonnie Ross
Founded 1988. Pop 833; Circ 219
Library Holdings: Bk Vols 2,500
Open Mon-Wed & Fri 8:30-6:30

DEXTER

P ABBOTT MEMORIAL LIBRARY*, One Church St, 04930. SAN 306-6258. Tel: 207-924-7292. Web Site: abbott-library.com. *Dir,* Liz Breault; E-mail: liz@abbott-library.com; Staff 1 (MLS 1)
Founded 1894. Pop 3,580; Circ 24,764
Library Holdings: AV Mats 1,780; Bk Titles 19,225; Bk Vols 26,217; Per Subs 72
Special Collections: Maine History Coll, bks, cht, maps
Automation Activity & Vendor Info: (Cataloging) Winnebago Software Co; (Circulation) Winnebago Software Co
Database Vendor: EBSCOhost
Wireless access
Mem of Northeastern Maine Library District
Open Tues, Thurs & Fri 10-6, Wed 10-8, Sat 9-2

DIXFIELD

P LUDDEN MEMORIAL LIBRARY, 42 Main St, 04224. (Mail add: PO Box 805, 04224-0805), SAN 306-6266. Tel: 207-562-8838. FAX: 207-562-4311. Web Site: www.dixfield.org/library.html. *Dir,* Peggy Malley; E-mail: peggy.malley@ludden.lib.me.us
Founded 1939. Pop 5,000; Circ 28,663
Jul 2010-Jun 2011 Income $90,000. Mats Exp $10,500
Library Holdings: Bk Vols 20,000; Per Subs 33
Special Collections: Maine Town Histories & Geneologies
Automation Activity & Vendor Info: (Cataloging) Innovative Interfaces, Inc; (Circulation) Innovative Interfaces, Inc; (ILL) Innovative Interfaces, Inc; (OPAC) Innovative Interfaces, Inc
Database Vendor: EBSCOhost, Innovative Interfaces, Inc
Wireless access
Function: Bks on cassette, Bks on CD, Children's prog, Computers for patron use, Copy machines, Electronic databases & coll, Free DVD rentals, Games & aids for the handicapped, Handicapped accessible, Homebound delivery serv, ILL available, Online cat, OverDrive digital audio bks, Prog for children & young adult, Pub access computers, Spoken cassettes & CDs, Spoken cassettes & DVDs, Story hour, Summer reading prog, Tax forms, VHS videos, Video lending libr, Wheelchair accessible
Special Services for the Blind - Large print bks
Open Mon-Fri 9:30-5:30, Sat 9-12

DOVER-FOXCROFT

P THOMPSON FREE LIBRARY*, 186 E Main St, 04426. SAN 306-6274. Tel: 207-564-3350. FAX: 207-564-3531. E-mail: df@thompson.lib.me.us. Web Site: www.thompson.lib.me.us. *Librn,* Helen Fogler; *Asst Librn,* Jeannie Tabor; Staff 3 (MLS 1, Non-MLS 2)
Founded 1898. Pop 4,200; Circ 60,000
Jul 2011-Jun 2012 Income $188,000, City $148,000, Other $40,000. Mats Exp $18,500, Books $15,000, Per/Ser (Incl. Access Fees) $1,500, AV Mat $2,000
Library Holdings: CDs 21; DVDs 70; Bk Vols 30,365; Per Subs 30; Talking Bks 1,300; Videos 1,700
Special Collections: Maine Town Histories
Subject Interests: Gardening, Genealogy, Hist
Automation Activity & Vendor Info: (Cataloging) Evergreen; (Circulation) Evergreen; (OPAC) Evergreen
Wireless access
Mem of Northeastern Maine Library District
Open Tues & Thurs 10-8, Wed & Fri 10-5, Sat 10-2
Friends of the Library Group

DRESDEN

P BRIDGE ACADEMY PUBLIC LIBRARY*, 44 Middle Rd, 04342. Tel: 207-737-8810. FAX: 207-737-8810. E-mail: BALibrarian@Bridge-Academy.lib.me.us. Web Site: www.bapl.us. *Dir,* Susan Schroeder; Staff 1 (Non-MLS 1)
Pop 1,750; Circ 1,400
Library Holdings: Large Print Bks 25; Bk Titles 8,000; Per Subs 12; Talking Bks 150
Special Collections: Maine Books
Automation Activity & Vendor Info: (Acquisitions) LibraryWorld, Inc
Wireless access
Function: Copy machines, Electronic databases & coll, Online ref, Prog for adults, Prog for children & young adult
Partic in Maine State Libr Network
Special Services for the Deaf - Assisted listening device; Bks on deafness & sign lang
Open Tues & Thurs 2-7, Sat 9-Noon

EAST BALDWIN

P BROWN MEMORIAL LIBRARY*, Two Norton Pl, 04024. (Mail add: PO Box 24, 04024-0024), SAN 372-7548. Tel: 207-787-3155. E-mail: bml@brown.lib.me.us. Web Site: www.brown.lib.me.us. *Librn,* Norma Haines; Staff 1 (MLS 1)
Founded 1906. Pop 1,300; Circ 3,500
Library Holdings: Bks on Deafness & Sign Lang 10; CDs 90; DVDs 25; Electronic Media & Resources 4; Large Print Bks 50; Bk Vols 10,000; Videos 450
Special Collections: Baldwin History, bks, photogs; Baldwin Town Records
Automation Activity & Vendor Info: (Acquisitions) Baker & Taylor; (Cataloging) Winnebago Software Co; (Circulation) Winnebago Software Co
Wireless access
Special Services for the Deaf - Bks on deafness & sign lang
Open Mon 4:30-7, Wed 2-6, Sat 10-2
Friends of the Library Group

EAST MACHIAS

P STURDIVANT PUBLIC LIBRARY*, 963 Main St, 04630. SAN 306-6290. Tel: 207-255-0070. *Librn,* Paula Maker
Founded 1934. Pop 1,200
Library Holdings: Bk Vols 7,500
Wireless access
Open Tues 4-6, Sat 9:30-Noon

EAST MILLINOCKET

P EAST MILLINOCKET PUBLIC LIBRARY*, 53 Main St, 04430-1199. SAN 306-6304. Tel: 207-746-3554. FAX: 207-746-3550. *Vols Librn,* Brenda Brit; Staff 1 (Non-MLS 1)
Library Holdings: Large Print Bks 300; Bk Titles 22,700
Automation Activity & Vendor Info: (Cataloging) LS 2000; (Circulation) LS 2000
Database Vendor: EBSCOhost
Mem of Northeastern Maine Library District
Open Mon 9-Noon, Tues 5-8, Wed 1-4

EAST VASSALBORO

P VASSALBORO PUBLIC LIBRARY*, 930 Bog Rd, 04935. (Mail add: PO Box 62, 04935-0062), SAN 306-6312. Tel: 207-923-3233. E-mail: vplibrary@gmail.com. *Librn,* Dawn Thistle; *Asst Librn,* Russell Smith; Staff 1 (Non-MLS 1)
Founded 1910. Pop 4,000; Circ 23,031
Library Holdings: Bk Titles 27,584; Bk Vols 37,000; Per Subs 20
Subject Interests: Local hist
Wireless access
Open Mon & Wed 12:30-8, Sat 10-6

EAST WATERBORO

P WATERBORO PUBLIC LIBRARY*, 187 Main St, 04030. (Mail add: PO Box 308, 04030-0308), SAN 376-3854. Tel: 207-247-3363. FAX: 207-247-3363. E-mail: librarian@waterborolibrary.org. Web Site: www.waterborolibrary.org. *Dir,* Ruth A Blake; *Asst Librn,* Jean Rundgren
Founded 1985. Pop 6,800
Library Holdings: CDs 50; DVDs 50; Bk Titles 21,000; Per Subs 20; Talking Bks 800; Videos 650
Automation Activity & Vendor Info: (Cataloging) Follett Software; (Circulation) Follett Software; (OPAC) Follett Software
Wireless access
Function: CD-ROM, ILL available, Music CDs, Photocopying/Printing, Prog for children & young adult, Spoken cassettes & CDs, Summer reading prog, Telephone ref, Wheelchair accessible
Mem of Southern Maine Library District
Open Mon, Tues & Thurs 2-8, Wed 9-8, Sat 9-3
Friends of the Library Group

EASTPORT

P PEAVEY MEMORIAL LIBRARY*, 26 Water St, 04631. SAN 306-6320. Tel: 207-853-4021. FAX: 207-853-4021. E-mail: peaveymemoriallibrary@yahoo.com. *Librn,* Dana Chevalier
Founded 1893. Pop 4,100; Circ 7,384
Feb 2005-Jan 2006 Income $56,824. Mats Exp $6,911. Sal $26,075
Library Holdings: CDs 400; Bk Vols 33,000; Per Subs 40; Talking Bks 450; Videos 1,000
Special Collections: Civil War Coll; Genealogy Coll; Local Artists Coll, paintings, prints; Local Authors Coll; Local History Coll; Maine Coll; Newspaper, 1819-1915 (Eastport Sentinel Coll), micro & bd vols
Database Vendor: EBSCOhost
Mem of Northeastern Maine Library District
Special Services for the Blind - Braille bks; Large print bks; Talking bks
Open Mon 12-8, Tues & Thurs 12-5, Wed & Fri 10-5, Sat 10-3
Friends of the Library Group

S QUODDY TIDES FOUNDATION MARINE LIBRARY*, 123 Water St, 04631-1333. (Mail add: PO Box 213, 04631-0213), SAN 372-7270. Tel: 207-853-2366, 207-853-4806. FAX: 207-853-4095. E-mail: qtides@midmaine.com. *Librn,* Serena A Wilson; Staff 1 (Non-MLS 1)
Founded 1968
Library Holdings: Bk Titles 1,000; Per Subs 10
Subject Interests: Local hist
Mem of Northeastern Maine Library District
Open Mon-Fri 9-5

ELIOT

P WILLIAM FOGG LIBRARY*, 116 Old Rd, 03903. (Mail add: PO Box 359, 03903-0359), SAN 306-6339. Tel: 207-439-9437. FAX: 207-439-9437. Web Site: www.william-fogg.lib.me.us. *Adult Serv, Dir,* Mary P Class; *Ch Serv,* Nicole LaBranch; Staff 5 (MLS 2, Non-MLS 3)
Founded 1907. Pop 6,000; Circ 20,000
Library Holdings: Bk Titles 22,000; Bk Vols 23,000; Per Subs 40
Subject Interests: Genealogy, Local hist
Automation Activity & Vendor Info: (Cataloging) Follett Software; (Circulation) Follett Software; (OPAC) Follett Software
Database Vendor: EBSCOhost
Mem of Southern Maine Library District
Special Services for the Blind - Large print & cassettes
Open Mon & Wed 1-8, Tues & Thurs 10-5, Sat 9-1
Friends of the Library Group

ELLSWORTH

P ELLSWORTH PUBLIC LIBRARY*, 20 State St, 04605. SAN 306-6347. Tel: 207-667-6363. FAX: 207-667-4901. Web Site: www.ellsworth.lib.me.us. *Dir,* Charlene E Churchill; E-mail: director@ellsworth.lib.me.us; *Asst Dir,* Charlene Clemons; *Circ Librn,* Mary McKillop; *Youth Serv Librn,* Keli Gancos; *ILL,* Marie Davis; *Ref,* Irene Whitney; *Youth Serv,* Martha Dodge; *Youth Serv,* Abby Morrow; Staff 10.5 (MLS 2, Non-MLS 8.5)
Founded 1897. Pop 24,000; Circ 174,000
Jul 2005-Jun 2006 Income $555,715, City $508,323, Locally Generated Income $34,345, Other $13,047. Mats Exp $34,500, Books $25,000, Per/Ser (Incl. Access Fees) $6,500, AV Mat $3,000. Sal $251,078
Library Holdings: AV Mats 2,640; Bk Vols 37,929; Per Subs 140; Talking Bks 1,450; Videos 1,329
Special Collections: Whitmore Genealogy Coll
Subject Interests: Local hist
Wireless access
Mem of Northeastern Maine Library District
Open Mon, Tues & Fri 9-5, Wed & Thurs 9-8, Sat 9-2
Friends of the Library Group

ENFIELD

P COLE MEMORIAL LIBRARY*, 789 Hammett Rd, 04493-4347. SAN 325-2698. Tel: 207-732-4270. FAX: 207-732-5335. *Librn,* Theresa Thurlow; E-mail: thurlow@colemem.lib.me.us
Founded 1974. Pop 1,664
Jul 2005-Jun 2006 Income $500. Mats Exp $500, Books $141, Electronic Ref Mat (Incl. Access Fees) $359
Library Holdings: AV Mats 296; Large Print Bks 61; Bk Titles 3,072; Bk Vols 3,098
Special Collections: Genealogy Coll

Wireless access
Open Mon-Thurs 7-5

FAIRFIELD

J KENNEBEC VALLEY COMMUNITY COLLEGE*, Lunder Library, 92 Western Ave, 04937-1367. SAN 321-5636. Tel: 207-453-5004. Interlibrary Loan Service Tel: 207-453-5195. FAX: 207-453-5194. TDD: 207-453-5163. E-mail: library@kvcc.me.edu. Web Site: www.kvcc.me.edu/library. *Dir,* Stephen LaRochelle; *Pub Serv Librn,* Barbara Bartley; *Tech Serv Librn,* David Smith; Staff 3 (MLS 3)
Founded 1979. Enrl 2,000; Fac 50; Highest Degree: Associate
Library Holdings: Bk Vols 17,000; Per Subs 30; Videos 2,500
Subject Interests: Allied health, Bus, Computers, Nursing
Database Vendor: Agricola, Baker & Taylor, EBSCOhost, Innovative Interfaces, Inc, Medline, OCLC FirstSearch, OCLC WorldShare Interlibrary Loan, Oxford Online, ProQuest, PubMed, WebMD
Wireless access
Partic in Health Science Library Information Consortium; Lyrasis; OCLC Online Computer Library Center, Inc
Open Mon-Thurs 8am-9pm, Fri 8-4

P LAWRENCE PUBLIC LIBRARY*, 33 Lawrence Ave, 04937. SAN 306-6355. Tel: 207-453-6867. FAX: 207-453-6867. Web Site: www.lawrence.lib.me.us. *Dir,* Louella Bickford; E-mail: loubic@yahoo.com; Staff 1 (Non-MLS 1)
Founded 1901. Pop 6,113; Circ 15,597
Library Holdings: Bk Titles 26,000; Per Subs 60
Special Collections: Fairfield Historical Society Coll
Automation Activity & Vendor Info: (Cataloging) Winnebago Software Co; (Circulation) Winnebago Software Co; (OPAC) Winnebago Software Co
Wireless access
Open Mon & Thurs 12-6, Tues, Wed & Fri 10-5, Sat 9-2
Friends of the Library Group

FALMOUTH

P FALMOUTH MEMORIAL LIBRARY*, Five Lunt Rd, 04105-1292. SAN 306-6363. Tel: 207-781-2351. FAX: 207-781-4094. E-mail: library@falmouth.lib.me.us. Web Site: www.falmouth.lib.me.us. *Libr Dir,* Andi Jackson-Darling; Staff 5 (MLS 5)
Founded 1944. Pop 12,000; Circ 172,000
Jul 2005-Jun 2006 Income $426,000, City $326,000, Other $100,000. Mats Exp $33,100, Books $23,600, Per/Ser (Incl. Access Fees) $3,700, AV Mat $5,300, Electronic Ref Mat (Incl. Access Fees) $500. Sal $312,599 (Prof $140,109)
Library Holdings: CDs 1,106; DVDs 700; Large Print Bks 320; Bk Titles 42,588; Per Subs 90; Talking Bks 1,189; Videos 1,200
Special Collections: Crafts & Needlepoint Coll; Gardening Coll; Maine Coll
Subject Interests: Local hist
Automation Activity & Vendor Info: (Cataloging) Innovative Interfaces, Inc; (Circulation) Innovative Interfaces, Inc; (OPAC) Innovative Interfaces, Inc
Database Vendor: EBSCOhost, ProQuest
Wireless access
Function: Adult bk club, Art exhibits, Bk club(s), Handicapped accessible, Home delivery & serv to Sr ctr & nursing homes, Homebound delivery serv, ILL available, Magnifiers for reading, Music CDs, Online searches, Photocopying/Printing, Prog for adults, Prog for children & young adult, Ref serv available, Spoken cassettes & CDs, Spoken cassettes & DVDs, Summer reading prog, VHS videos, Video lending libr, Wheelchair accessible
Mem of Southern Maine Library District
Open Mon, Fri & Sat 9:30-5, Tues-Thurs 9:30-8, Sat (July & Aug) 9:30-12:30
Friends of the Library Group

S MAINE EDUCATION CENTER FOR THE DEAF & HARD OF HEARING*, Governor Baxter School for the Deaf Library, One Mackworth Island, 04105-1951. SAN 328-1973. Tel: 207-781-6237. FAX: 207-781-6240. Web Site: www.mecdhh.org. *Vols Librn,* Leona Anderson; Staff 2 (MLS 1, Non-MLS 1)
Library Holdings: Bk Titles 9,000; Per Subs 30
Subject Interests: Am sign lang, Audiology, Deaf culture, Deaf educ, Deafness
Automation Activity & Vendor Info: (Cataloging) Follett Software; (Circulation) Follett Software; (Course Reserve) Follett Software
Wireless access
Function: ILL available, Outside serv via phone, mail, e-mail & web, Photocopying/Printing, Prof lending libr, Telephone ref
Special Services for the Deaf - Am sign lang & deaf culture; Coll on deaf educ; Staff with knowledge of sign lang; TTY equip
Restriction: Circ limited

FARMINGTON

P FARMINGTON PUBLIC LIBRARY, 117 Academy St, 04938. SAN 306-6371. Tel: 207-778-4312. Web Site: www.farmington.lib.me.us. *Dir,* Maurie Stockford; E-mail: mstockford@farmington.lib.me.us; *Asst Libr Dir,* Jen Scott; E-mail: jenscott@farmington.lib.me.us; *Ch,* Joanne Moloney; E-mail: jmoloney@farmington.lib.me.us; Staff 4 (MLS 1, Non-MLS 3)
Founded 1890. Pop 7,430; Circ 75,000
Jan 2005-Dec 2005 Income $140,105, City $92,830, Locally Generated Income $47,275. Mats Exp $24,000
Library Holdings: Large Print Bks 1,000; Bk Titles 30,000; Per Subs 75; Talking Bks 900
Special Collections: Genealogy Coll; History Coll
Automation Activity & Vendor Info: (Cataloging) Evergreen; (Circulation) Evergreen; (OPAC) Evergreen
Database Vendor: EBSCOhost
Wireless access
Partic in Maine State Libr Network
Open Tues-Fri 10-6:30, Sat 10-2 (10-12 Summer)

M FRANKLIN MEMORIAL HOSPITAL*, Ben Franklin Center Library, 111 Franklin Health Commons, 04938. SAN 325-7525. Tel: 207-779-2554. FAX: 207-779-2749. E-mail: librarian@fchn.org. Web Site: www.fchn.org/ben-franklin-center/library. *Librn,* Meagan Carr; Staff 2 (MLS 1, Non-MLS 1)
Library Holdings: Bk Vols 700; Per Subs 60; Videos 800
Subject Interests: Med, Nursing
Database Vendor: EBSCOhost, Lexi-Comp, UpToDate
Function: Health sci info serv
Partic in Health Science Library Information Consortium; National Network of Libraries of Medicine; North Atlantic Health Sciences Libraries, Inc
Open Mon-Fri 8-4:30
Restriction: Hospital staff & commun, Restricted borrowing privileges

C UNIVERSITY OF MAINE AT FARMINGTON*, Mantor Library, 116 South St, 04938-1990. SAN 306-638X. Tel: 207-778 7210. FAX: 207-778-7223. Web Site: www.umf.maine.edu. *Dir,* Franklin D Roberts; Tel: 207-778-7215, E-mail: froberts@maine.edu; *Access Serv,* Janet Brackett; *Info Tech,* Jeanne Roy; *ILL,* Nancy Walters; *Ref,* Laurie MacWhinnie; *Tech Serv,* Richelle Davis; Staff 4 (MLS 4)
Founded 1933. Enrl 2,000; Fac 125; Highest Degree: Bachelor
Library Holdings: Bk Vols 99,474; Per Subs 1,800
Special Collections: University of Maine at Farmington Archives
Automation Activity & Vendor Info: (Acquisitions) Innovative Interfaces, Inc; (Cataloging) Innovative Interfaces, Inc; (Circulation) Innovative Interfaces, Inc; (Course Reserve) Innovative Interfaces, Inc; (ILL) Innovative Interfaces, Inc; (Media Booking) Innovative Interfaces, Inc; (OPAC) Innovative Interfaces, Inc; (Serials) Innovative Interfaces, Inc
Database Vendor: EBSCOhost
Partic in Central Maine Libr District; Lyrasis; OCLC Online Computer Library Center, Inc
Open Mon-Thurs (Winter) 8am-11pm, Fri 8-5, Sat 9-5, Sun 1-11; Mon-Thurs (Summer) 8-6, Fri 8-4:30

FAYETTE

P UNDERWOOD MEMORIAL LIBRARY*, 2006 Main St, 04349. SAN 306-6398. Tel: 207-685-3778. *Dir,* Suzanne Rich
Founded 1954. Pop 1,155; Circ 4,393
Library Holdings: Bk Titles 16,000; Per Subs 10; Talking Bks 65
Subject Interests: Maine
Wireless access
Partic in Lyrasis
Open Tues 9-Noon, Wed 5-8, Thurs 1-4

FORT FAIRFIELD

P FORT FAIRFIELD PUBLIC LIBRARY*, 339 Main St, 04742-1199. SAN 306-6401. Tel: 207-472-3880. *Dir,* Sharon Nadeau; E-mail: snadeau@fortfairfield.org; Staff 1 (Non-MLS 1)
Founded 1895. Pop 3,880; Circ 20,869
Library Holdings: Bk Titles 21,000; Per Subs 50
Special Collections: Civil War (Drew Coll). Oral History
Mem of Northeastern Maine Library District
Open Tues-Fri 10-5:30, Sat 10-4
Friends of the Library Group

FORT KENT

P FORT KENT PUBLIC LIBRARY*, One Monument Sq, 04743. SAN 306-641X. Tel: 207-834-3048. FAX: 207-834-2630. *Head of Libr,* Michelle Raymond; E-mail: mray@fort-kent.lib.me.us
Founded 1936. Pop 4,268; Circ 22,596

Jan 2006-Dec 2006 Income $22,500
Library Holdings: Bk Vols 22,000
Open Mon, Tues & Thurs 12-5, Wed & Fri 12-8

C UNIVERSITY OF MAINE AT FORT KENT*, Blake Library, 23 University Dr, 04743. SAN 306-6428. Tel: 207-834-7525. Circulation Tel: 207-834-7526. Reference Tel: 207-834-7527. FAX: 207-834-7518. Web Site: www.umfk.edu/library. *Dir, Info Serv,* Leslie Kelly; Tel: 207-834-7522, E-mail: lesliek@maine.edu; *Assoc Dir, Ref Librn,* Sofia Birden; E-mail: sbirden@maine.edu; *Asst Dir, Archives & Libr,* Kathryn Donahue; E-mail: kathryn.donahue@maine.edu; *Acq, Cat,* Asita Albert; E-mail: asita.albert@maine.edu; *Circ & ILL,* Debra Durkin; E-mail: debra.durkin@maine.edu; *Ser,* Brenda Pelletier; Tel: 207-834-7523, E-mail: brenda.m.pelletier@maine.edu; Staff 6 (MLS 3, Non-MLS 3)
Founded 1878. Enrl 1,100; Fac 41; Highest Degree: Bachelor
Library Holdings: Audiobooks 200; DVDs 1,007; Bk Vols 48,280; Per Subs 183; Videos 1,763
Special Collections: Aroostook Coll; Maine Coll; University Coll
Automation Activity & Vendor Info: (Cataloging) Innovative Interfaces, Inc; (Circulation) Innovative Interfaces, Inc; (Serials) Innovative Interfaces, Inc
Database Vendor: EBSCOhost
Wireless access
Function: Art exhibits, Audio & video playback equip for onsite use, Audiobks via web, Bks on cassette, Bks on CD, Computers for patron use, Copy machines, e-mail & chat, E-Reserves, Electronic databases & coll, Fax serv, Free DVD rentals, Handicapped accessible, ILL available, Music CDs, Online cat, Online info literacy tutorials on the web & in blackboard, Online ref, Orientations, Outside serv via phone, mail, e-mail & web, OverDrive digital audio bks, Photocopying/Printing, Printer for laptops & handheld devices, Pub access computers, Ref serv available, Ref serv in person, Scanner, Tax forms, VHS videos, Web-catalog, Wheelchair accessible
Open Mon-Thurs (Fall & Spring) 8am-11pm, Fri 8-4:30, Sat 10-5, Sun 1-9; Mon-Fri (Summer) 8-4:30

FREEPORT

P FREEPORT COMMUNITY LIBRARY*, Ten Library Dr, 04032. SAN 306-6436. Tel: 207-865-3307. FAX: 207-865-1395. Web Site: www.freeportlibrary.com. *Dir,* Beth Edmonds; Staff 7 (MLS 1, Non-MLS 6)
Founded 1904. Pop 8,200; Circ 150,440
Jul 2009-Jun 2010 Income $373,425. Mats Exp $53,250, Books $42,750, AV Mat $10,500. Sal $273,705
Library Holdings: Audiobooks 3,343; DVDs 3,914; Large Print Bks 552; Bk Titles 54,270; Bk Vols 55,547; Per Subs 157; Talking Bks 1,965; Videos 2,688
Special Collections: Maine (State & Local Historical Records); Sportman's Coll
Automation Activity & Vendor Info: (Acquisitions) Follett Software
Wireless access
Mem of Southern Maine Library District
Open Mon & Wed 11:30-8, Tues & Thurs 9:30-5, Fri 11:30-5, Sat 9-3

FRENCHBORO

P FRENCHBORO LIBRARY*, Schoolhouse Hill, 04635. Tel: 207-334-2924. *Librn,* Ruth Davis; Tel: 207-334-2948
Founded 1850. Pop 6,000
Library Holdings: DVDs 20; Bk Vols 6,000; Talking Bks 60; Videos 300
Special Collections: Biographies Coll; Crafts Coll; Maine Coll; Sea Stories
Friends of the Library Group

FRIENDSHIP

P FRIENDSHIP PUBLIC LIBRARY*, Three Main St, 04547-0039. (Mail add: PO Box 39, 04547-0039). Tel: 207-832-5332. *Librn,* Celia Briggs; E-mail: cbriggs@friendship-public.lib.me.us
Founded 1915. Circ 2,982
Library Holdings: Large Print Bks 120; Bk Vols 17,000; Per Subs 23; Talking Bks 75
Special Collections: Oral History
Open Wed (Winter) 2-6, Sat 9-12; Wed (Summer) 2-8, Fri 1-4, Sat 9-12

FRYEBURG

P FRYEBURG PUBLIC LIBRARY, 515 Main St, 04037. SAN 306-6452. Tel: 207-935-2731. FAX: 207-935-7217. E-mail: library@fryeburgmaine.org. *Dir,* Donnette Barnes; Staff 1 (Non-MLS 1)
Founded 1890. Pop 3,124; Circ 16,251
Library Holdings: Bk Vols 15,800; Per Subs 10
Special Collections: Clarence E Mulford Coll
Database Vendor: EBSCOhost
Wireless access
Mem of Southern Maine Library District
Open Mon-Wed 9-4, Thurs 9-1 & 1:30-4, Sat 9-Noon
Friends of the Library Group

GARDINER

P GARDINER PUBLIC LIBRARY*, 152 Water St, 04345. SAN 306-6460. Tel: 207-582-3312. FAX: 207-582-6104. Web Site: www.gpl.lib.me.us. *Dir,* Anne Davis; E-mail: adavis@gardinermaine.com; *Asst Dir,* Scott Handville; *Ch,* Charlene M Wagner; *Spec Coll Librn,* Dawn Thistle; *Tech Librn,* Ann Russell; *YA Librn,* Ginni Nichols; *Libr Asst,* Audrey Littlefield; *Libr Asst,* Claire Parker; Staff 4 (Non-MLS 4)
Founded 1881. Pop 16,588; Circ 141,882
Library Holdings: Bk Vols 42,364; Per Subs 89
Special Collections: E A Robinson Coll; Laura E Richards Coll; The Yellow House Papers
Database Vendor: EBSCOhost
Wireless access
Publications: Who Reads What List (Annual)
Open Mon, Wed & Thurs 10:30-5:30, Tues 10:30-7:30, Fri 9:30-5, Sat 9:30-12:30
Friends of the Library Group

GEORGETOWN

P LAURA E RICHARDS LIBRARY*, 863 Five Islands Rd, 04548-3306. (Mail add: 32 First Beach Rd, 04548-0456), SAN 372-6339. Tel: 207-371-9995. FAX: 207-371-2134. *Dir,* Nancy D Barney; Tel: 207-371-2134, E-mail: dbarney@nycap.rr.com; Staff 1 (MLS 1)
Founded 1937. Pop 1,020; Circ 2,905
Oct 2005-Sept 2006 Income $4,000, City $1,700, Other $2,300
Library Holdings: Bk Vols 5,327
Special Collections: Maine Coll
Function: Spoken cassettes & CDs

GORHAM

P BAXTER MEMORIAL LIBRARY*, 71 South St, 04038. SAN 306-6479. Tel: 207-222-1190. FAX: 207-839-7749. Web Site: www.baxter-memorial.lib.me.us. *Dir,* Pamela E Turner; E-mail: pturner@baxter-memorial.lib.me.us; *Pub Serv Librn,* James Rathbun; *Youth Serv Librn,* Kathy Stevens; *Sr Libr Asst,* Linda Straw; *Libr Asst,* Carol Robinson
Founded 1908. Pop 14,141; Circ 106,518
Library Holdings: Bk Vols 33,000; Per Subs 87
Special Collections: James Phinney Baxter Coll, papers & mss
Automation Activity & Vendor Info: (Cataloging) Innovative Interfaces, Inc; (Circulation) Innovative Interfaces, Inc; (OPAC) Innovative Interfaces, Inc
Wireless access
Mem of Southern Maine Library District
Open Mon & Wed 1-7, Tues & Thurs 9-7, Fri 9-4, Sat 9-1
Friends of the Library Group

P NORTH GORHAM PUBLIC LIBRARY*, Two Standish Neck Rd, 04038-2469. Tel: 207-892-2575. FAX: 207-892-2573. E-mail: libng@north-gorham.lib.me.us. *Dir,* Kathy Corbett
Founded 1897
Library Holdings: AV Mats 250; Bk Vols 9,500; Per Subs 13; Talking Bks 350
Automation Activity & Vendor Info: (Cataloging) Follett Software; (Circulation) Follett Software
Mem of Southern Maine Library District
Open Mon & Thurs 3-5:30, Wed 6-8, Sat 10-1

GRAY

P GRAY PUBLIC LIBRARY*, Five Hancock St, 04039. SAN 306-6495. Tel: 207-657-4110. FAX: 207-657-4138. E-mail: graylib@gray.lib.me.us. Web Site: www.gray.lib.me.us. *Dir,* Marie Morey; E-mail: mmorey@gray.lib.me.us; *Ad,* Cassie Comora; *Ch,* Kathy George; *Circ Mgr,* Darcel Devou; Staff 4 (MLS 2, Non-MLS 2)
Founded 1906. Pop 6,820; Circ 57,000
Library Holdings: Bk Titles 29,374; Per Subs 37
Special Collections: Maine Coll
Subject Interests: Agr, Humanities, Med, Natural sci
Automation Activity & Vendor Info: (Cataloging) Follett Software; (Circulation) Follett Software; (OPAC) Follett Software
Database Vendor: EBSCOhost
Wireless access
Mem of Southern Maine Library District
Open Tues & Wed 10-8, Thurs 10-6, Fri 10-5, Sat 10-3
Friends of the Library Group

GREENE

P JULIA ADAMS MORSE MEMORIAL LIBRARY*, 105 Main St, 04236. (Mail add: 279 Sprague Mill Rd, 04236-3220), SAN 306-6509. Tel: 207-946-5544. Web Site: www.maine.gov/msl/mainelibs/displaypub.shtml?id=40976. *Dir,* Patricia Rose; Staff 1 (Non-MLS 1)
Founded 1955. Pop 3,037; Circ 4,620
Library Holdings: Bk Vols 10,000
Database Vendor: EBSCOhost
Wireless access
Open Mon 2-7, Tues & Thurs 12-7, Sat 9-3
Friends of the Library Group

GREENVILLE

P SHAW PUBLIC LIBRARY*, Nine Lily Bay Rd, 04441. (Mail add: PO Box 510, 04441-0510), SAN 306-6517. Tel: 207-695-3579. FAX: 207-695-0310. E-mail: splibrary@shaw-greenville.lib.me.us. Web Site: www.greenvilleme.com. *Asst Librn,* Etta Hubbard; *Asst Librn,* Linda Wohlforth
Pop 2,037; Circ 15,379
Library Holdings: Bk Vols 20,000; Per Subs 50
Database Vendor: EBSCOhost
Wireless access
Mem of Northeastern Maine Library District
Open Tues & Fri 10-6, Wed 1-5, Thurs 5-7, Sat 9-1

GUILFORD

P GUILFORD MEMORIAL LIBRARY, Four Library St, 04443. (Mail add: PO Box 177, 04443-0177), SAN 306-6525. Tel: 207-876-4547. *Dir,* Heidi Dow; Staff 3 (MLS 1, Non-MLS 2)
Founded 1903
Library Holdings: Large Print Bks 1,500; Bk Vols 16,000; Per Subs 27; Talking Bks 350
Automation Activity & Vendor Info: (Cataloging) Follett Software; (Circulation) Follett Software
Database Vendor: EBSCOhost
Wireless access
Mem of Northeastern Maine Library District
Open Tues-Fri 10-5, Sat 9-1

HALLOWELL

P HUBBARD FREE LIBRARY*, 115 Second St, 04347. SAN 306-6533. Tel: 207-622-6582. E-mail: hfl@msln.net. Web Site: www.hubbardfree.org. *Dir,* Melody Norman-Camp; *ILL Coordr,* Sue Moseley; *Prog Coordr,* Robert Fagan; *Cataloger,* Doreen Judge; *Libr Asst,* Stacie Linkle; *Libr Asst,* Barbara Rohrbaugh
Founded 1880. Pop 5,072; Circ 23,320
Library Holdings: AV Mats 2,929; Bk Titles 29,083; Per Subs 45
Subject Interests: Local hist
Automation Activity & Vendor Info: (Acquisitions) Baker & Taylor; (Cataloging) Mandarin Library Automation; (Circulation) Mandarin Library Automation; (OPAC) Mandarin Library Automation
Wireless access
Function: Adult bk club, Archival coll, Audiobks via web, Bks on cassette, Bks on CD, Children's prog, Computers for patron use, Copy machines, Electronic databases & coll, Exhibits, Handicapped accessible, Home delivery & serv to Sr ctr & nursing homes, ILL available, Music CDs, Online cat, OverDrive digital audio bks, Prog for adults, Summer reading prog, VHS videos, Wheelchair accessible
Partic in Maine School & Library Network
Special Services for the Blind - Large print bks
Open Mon & Wed 10-5:30, Tues & Thurs 2-8, Fri 2-5:30, Sat 10-2
Friends of the Library Group

HAMPDEN

P EDYTHE L DYER COMMUNITY LIBRARY*, 269 Main Rd N, 04444. SAN 306-6541. Tel: 207-862-3550. Web Site: www.edl.lib.me.us. *Dir, Libr Serv,* Debora Lozito; E-mail: debbie.lozito@edythedyer.lib.me.us; *Youth Serv,* Mary Beckett; E-mail: mbeckett@edythedyer.lib.me.us; Staff 5 (MLS 2, Non-MLS 3)
Founded 1982. Pop 7,257; Circ 84,655
Jul 2011-Jun 2012 Income $253,104, City $237,583, Locally Generated Income $4,521, Other $11,000. Mats Exp $27,762, Books $16,917, Per/Ser (Incl. Access Fees) $1,692, AV Mat $8,853, Electronic Ref Mat (Incl. Access Fees) $300. Sal $150,124 (Prof $53,389)
Library Holdings: Audiobooks 246; CDs 1,792; DVDs 1,492; e-books 1,650; Large Print Bks 1,239; Bk Titles 20,713; Bk Vols 23,357; Per Subs 62
Automation Activity & Vendor Info: (Cataloging) Innovative Interfaces, Inc; (Circulation) Innovative Interfaces, Inc; (ILL) Innovative Interfaces, Inc; (OPAC) Innovative Interfaces, Inc; (Serials) Innovative Interfaces, Inc
Database Vendor: EBSCOhost, OCLC WebJunction
Wireless access
Function: Adult bk club, Art exhibits, Audiobks via web, Bk club(s), Bks on cassette, Bks on CD, Children's prog, Computer training, Computers for patron use, Copy machines, e-mail serv, E-Reserves, Fax serv, Free DVD rentals, Handicapped accessible, Homebound delivery serv, ILL available, Mail & tel request accepted, Mus passes, Music CDs, Online searches, OverDrive digital audio bks, Photocopying/Printing, Preschool reading prog, Pub access computers, Ref serv in person, Spoken cassettes & CDs, Spoken cassettes & DVDs, Story hour, Summer reading prog, Tax forms, VHS videos, Video lending libr
Special Services for the Blind - Bks on CD
Open Mon & Wed 9-8, Tues, Thurs & Fri 9-5, Sat (Fall-Spring) 9-2
Friends of the Library Group

HARPSWELL

P CUNDY'S HARBOR LIBRARY*, 935 Cundy's Harbor Rd, 04079-4511. Tel: 207-725-1461. Web Site: www.cundysharbor.lib.me.us. *Dir,* Linn Caroleo; E-mail: director@cundysharbor.lib.me.us
Founded 1953
Library Holdings: AV Mats 100; Bk Vols 5,700; Talking Bks 50
Special Collections: Maine, Local History & Genealogy Coll
Wireless access
Mem of Southern Maine Library District
Open Tues & Thurs 2-8
Friends of the Library Group

HARRINGTON

P GALLISON MEMORIAL LIBRARY*, 1292 Main St, 04643. (Mail add: PO Box 176, 04643-0176). Tel: 207-483-4547. E-mail: gallisonlibrary@gallison.lib.me.us. Web Site: www.gallison.lib.me.us. *Dir,* Gweneth Strout
Pop 1,000
Library Holdings: Bk Vols 6,000; Talking Bks 60; Videos 120
Special Collections: Antiquarian Books & Novels; Local History Coll; Maine Coll
Wireless access
Open Mon-Fri 2-6

HARRISON

P BOLSTERS MILLS VILLAGE LIBRARY*, 659 Bolsters Mills Rd, 04040. Tel: 207-583-6421. Administration Tel: 207-583-6284. *Librn,* Charna Katz
Founded 1859
Library Holdings: Large Print Bks 35; Bk Vols 9,702; Talking Bks 70; Videos 49
Special Collections: Children's Biographies Coll; Local History Coll; Maine Coll
Wireless access
Mem of Southern Maine Library District
Open Wed 7pm-9pm, Sat 2-4
Friends of the Library Group

P HARRISON VILLAGE LIBRARY*, Four Front St, 04040. (Mail add: PO Box 597, 04040-0597), SAN 306-6568. Tel: 207-583-2970. Web Site: www.harrison.lib.me.us. *Librn,* Kathleen Kramer; E-mail: kkramer@harrison.lib.me.us; Staff 1 (Non-MLS 1)
Founded 1908. Pop 2,315; Circ 7,469
Library Holdings: Bk Vols 7,500; Per Subs 15
Automation Activity & Vendor Info: (Cataloging) Follett Software; (Circulation) Follett Software
Database Vendor: EBSCOhost
Wireless access
Open Mon & Wed 1-7, Thurs 11-5, Sat 10-2
Friends of the Library Group

HARTLAND

P HARTLAND PUBLIC LIBRARY*, 16 Mill St, 04943-3736. SAN 306-6576. Tel: 207-938-4702. Web Site: www.hartland.lib.me.us. *Librn,* John R Clark, IV; E-mail: wizard@hartland.lib.me.us; Staff 1 (MLS 1)
Founded 1902. Pop 5,700; Circ 24,000
Library Holdings: Audiobooks 600; CDs 2,500; DVDs 4,700; Large Print Bks 175; Bk Titles 23,500; Bk Vols 24,000; Per Subs 40; Talking Bks 400; Videos 2,000
Special Collections: Local History Coll
Automation Activity & Vendor Info: (Acquisitions) Evergreen; (Cataloging) Evergreen; (Circulation) Evergreen; (OPAC) Evergreen
Wireless access
Function: Adult bk club, Bks on cassette, Bks on CD, Computers for patron use, Copy machines, Free DVD rentals, Handicapped accessible, ILL available, Music CDs, Online cat, Photocopying/Printing, Serves mentally handicapped consumers

Partic in Maine Balsam Library Consortium
Open Tues-Thurs 10-6, Fri 10-5, Sat 10-1

HIRAM

P SOLDIERS MEMORIAL LIBRARY*, 85 Main St, 04041-3208. (Mail add: PO Box 281, 04041-0281), SAN 372-7696. Tel: 207-625-4650. E-mail: hiramlibrary@soldiers.lib.me.us. Web Site: www.soldiers.lib.me.us. *Librn,* Pamela Slattery-Thomas; E-mail: pslattery65@yahoo.com; Staff 1 (Non-MLS 1)
Founded 1915. Pop 1,260; Circ 1,818
Library Holdings: Bk Titles 10,000
Special Collections: Maine Coll
Subject Interests: Fiction, Genealogy, Local hist
Automation Activity & Vendor Info: (Cataloging) LEX Systems Inc; (Circulation) LEX Systems Inc
Mem of Southern Maine Library District
Partic in Scoop Coop
Special Services for the Deaf - Bks on deafness & sign lang
Special Services for the Blind - Audio mat; Bks on cassette; Bks on CD; Cassettes; Copier with enlargement capabilities; Large print bks; Talking bk & rec for the blind cat
Open Tues 2-5, Wed & Thurs 10-5, Sat 9:30-12:30

HOLLIS

P SALMON FALLS LIBRARY*, 322 Old Alfred Rd, 04042. SAN 376-6489. Tel: 207-929-3990. FAX: 207-929-3990. *Librn,* Mary Weyer; E-mail: mweyer1@gmail.com; Staff 1 (Non-MLS 1)
Library Holdings: Bk Vols 10,000; Per Subs 17
Mem of Southern Maine Library District
Open Mon 3-6, Wed 4-7, Thurs 3-8, Sat 9-12
Friends of the Library Group

HOULTON

P CARY LIBRARY*, 107 Main St, 04730. SAN 343-6659. Tel: 207-532-1302. FAX: 207-532-4350. Web Site: www.cary.lib.me.us. *Dir,* Linda Faucher; E-mail: faucherl@cary.lib.me.us; Staff 4 (Non-MLS 4)
Founded 1903. Pop 14,000; Circ 83,841
Library Holdings: Bk Vols 50,000; Per Subs 120
Special Collections: Aroostook County Oral History; Aroostook Newspapers (1859-1938), micro. Oral History
Automation Activity & Vendor Info: (Cataloging) Follett Software; (Circulation) Follett Software; (OPAC) Follett Software
Database Vendor: EBSCOhost
Wireless access
Mem of Northeastern Maine Library District
Open Mon-Wed & Fri 9-5, Thurs 9-8, Sat 9-1

ISLAND FALLS

P KATAHDIN PUBLIC LIBRARY*, 20 Library St, 04747. (Mail add: PO Box 148, 04747-0148), SAN 306-6592, *Librn,* Rebecca J Drew; Tel: 207-463-2372, E-mail: rdrew@katahdin.lib.me.us; Staff 1 (Non-MLS 1)
Founded 1866. Pop 1,100; Circ 1,200
Jan 2006-Dec 2006 Income $7,600, City $6,000, Locally Generated Income $1,200, Other $400. Mats Exp $4,800, Books $4,100, Other Print Mats $700. Sal $2,400
Library Holdings: Bks on Deafness & Sign Lang 11; CDs 24; DVDs 16; Large Print Bks 210; Bk Vols 14,260; Per Subs 18; Talking Bks 164; Videos 120
Special Collections: Oral History
Subject Interests: Town hist
Mem of Northeastern Maine Library District
Partic in Maine State Libr Network
Special Services for the Blind - Talking bks

ISLE AU HAUT

P REVERE MEMORIAL LIBRARY*, Revere Memorial Hall, Ten Main St, 04645. (Mail add: PO Box 8, 04645-0008), SAN 374-4876. Tel: 207-335-5001. FAX: 207-335-5001. E-mail: reverememorial.library@gmail.com. *Librn,* Brenda Clark; Tel: 207-335-2979
Founded 1906. Pop 300
Library Holdings: CDs 30; DVDs 20; Bk Vols 2,500; Per Subs 10; Talking Bks 25; Videos 200
Special Collections: Founding Families & Isle Au Haut Oral History Coll. Oral History
Wireless access
Open Mon-Sat (Winter) 10-5; Mon, Wed & Fri (Summer) 10-12

ISLESBORO

P ALICE L PENDLETON LIBRARY*, 309 Main Rd, 04848-4505. (Mail add: PO Box 77, 04848-0077), SAN 306-6606. Tel: 207-734-2218. Web Site: www.alpl.lib.me.us. *Librn,* Linda Graf; E-mail: lgraf@alpl.lib.me.us; Staff 1 (Non-MLS 1)
Founded 1918. Pop 599; Circ 8,962
Library Holdings: AV Mats 200; Bk Vols 20,000; Per Subs 54; Talking Bks 500
Special Collections: Local Authors Coll; Maine Genealogy Books; Oil Paintings; Ship Models
Automation Activity & Vendor Info: (Cataloging) Follett Software; (Circulation) Follett Software
Wireless access
Mem of Northeastern Maine Library District
Special Services for the Blind - Bks on cassette; Descriptive video serv (DVS)
Open Mon & Wed (Winter) 10-12 & 1:30-4:30, Sat & Sun 1:30-4:30; Mon (Summer) 10-12 & 1:30-4:30, Wed 10-12 & 1:30-7, Sat & Sun 1:30-4:30
Friends of the Library Group

JACKMAN

P JACKMAN PUBLIC LIBRARY*, 604 Main St, 04945. (Mail add: PO Box 8, 04945-0008), SAN 321-0383. Tel: 207-668-2110. *Dir,* Lucinda Lacasse; Staff 2 (Non-MLS 2)
Founded 1917. Pop 967
Library Holdings: Large Print Bks 35; Bk Vols 7,097; Talking Bks 167
Special Collections: Maine Authors Coll
Open Mon, Wed & Sat 2-4

JEFFERSON

P JEFFERSON PUBLIC LIBRARY*, 48 Washington Rd, 04348. (Mail add: PO Box 226, 04348-0226). Tel: 207-549-7491. *Librn,* Kathy Stone
Founded 1984. Pop 2,400
Library Holdings: Bk Vols 4,000; Talking Bks 30
Open Tues & Thurs 4-7

JONESPORT

P PEABODY MEMORIAL LIBRARY, 162 Main St, 04649. (Mail add: PO Box 210, 04649-0210), SAN 376-3536. Tel: 207-497-3003. E-mail: peabodylibrarian@peabody.lib.me.us. Web Site: www.peabody.lib.me.us. *Librn,* Heidi Lynn Hinkley; Staff 1 (Non-MLS 1)
Founded 1915. Pop 1,800
Automation Activity & Vendor Info: (Acquisitions) Biblionix; (Cataloging) Biblionix; (Circulation) Biblionix
Wireless access
Mem of Northeastern Maine Library District
Open Tues-Thurs 10-4, Sat 10-2
Friends of the Library Group

KENDUSKEAG

P CASE MEMORIAL LIBRARY*, 911 Stetson Rd, 04450. (Mail add: PO Box 312, 04450-0312), SAN 306-6622. Tel: 207-884-8598. FAX: 207-884-3043. E-mail: casememorial@roadrunner.com. *Librn,* Diane Smith
Pop 1,210; Circ 1,300
Library Holdings: Bk Vols 6,000
Database Vendor: EBSCOhost
Mem of Northeastern Maine Library District
Open Mon & Thurs 6-8

KENNEBUNK

S THE BRICK STORE MUSEUM*, Edith Cleaves Barry Library, 117 Main St, 04043. SAN 326-615X. Tel: 207-985-4802. FAX: 207-985-6887. Web Site: www.brickstoremuseum.org. *Exec Dir,* Tracy L Baetz; E-mail: director@brickstoremuseum.org; *Archivist,* Rosalind Magnuson; E-mail: archives@brickstoremuseum.org
Library Holdings: Bk Vols 3,000
Special Collections: Oral History; State Document Depository
Subject Interests: Archit, Decorative art, Local hist
Function: Archival coll, For res purposes, Handicapped accessible, Homebound delivery serv, Photocopying/Printing, Ref serv available
Restriction: Non-circulating, Open to pub by appt only, Open to pub with supv only

P KENNEBUNK FREE LIBRARY*, 112 Main St, 04043. SAN 306-6649. Tel: 207-985-2173. FAX: 207-985-4730. E-mail: kfl@kennebunk.lib.me.us. Web Site: www.kennebunklibrary.org. *Libr Dir,* Jill E LeMay; *Asst Dir, Head, Adult Serv,* Janet Cate; *Head, Youth Serv,* Bernie Alie; Staff 12 (MLS 2, Non-MLS 10)
Founded 1882. Pop 10,000; Circ 121,436

Library Holdings: Bks on Deafness & Sign Lang 25; Large Print Bks 1,700; Bk Titles 38,655; Bk Vols 41,097; Per Subs 130; Talking Bks 1,250
Special Collections: Bolton Travel Library; Kenneth Joy Photographic Coll; Walker Diaries. Oral History
Automation Activity & Vendor Info: (Cataloging) Follett Software; (Circulation) Follett Software; (OPAC) Follett Software
Database Vendor: EBSCOhost
Wireless access
Function: Home delivery & serv to Sr ctr & nursing homes, Homebound delivery serv, ILL available, Large print keyboards, Online searches, Photocopying/Printing, Prog for adults, Prog for children & young adult, Ref serv available, Summer reading prog, Wheelchair accessible
Publications: History of Kennebunk
Mem of Southern Maine Library District
Open Mon & Tues 9:30-8, Wed 12:30-8, Thurs-Sat 9:30-5
Friends of the Library Group

KENNEBUNKPORT

P LOUIS T GRAVES MEMORIAL PUBLIC LIBRARY*, 18 Maine St, 04046-6173. (Mail add: PO Box 391, 04046-0391), SAN 306-6657. Tel: 207-967-2778. E-mail: graveslib@graves.lib.me.us. Web Site: www.graves.lib.me.us. *Dir,* Mary Lou Boucouvalas; E-mail: ml@graves.lib.me.us; *Librn,* Rosalind S Wade; Staff 3 (MLS 1, Non-MLS 2)
Founded 1921. Pop 3,500; Circ 6,000
Library Holdings: CDs 100; DVDs 30; Bk Vols 33,000; Per Subs 105; Talking Bks 1,422; Videos 1,282
Special Collections: Booth Tarkington Coll; Kenneth Roberts Coll; Margaret Deland Coll. Oral History
Automation Activity & Vendor Info: (OPAC) Follett Software
Wireless access
Mem of Southern Maine Library District
Partic in OCLC Online Computer Library Center, Inc
Open Mon-Thurs 11-7, Fri 10-5, Sat 9-12

S THE NEW ENGLAND ELECTRIC RAILWAY HISTORICAL SOCIETY*, Seashore Trolley Museum Library, 195 Log Cabin Rd, 04046. (Mail add: PO Box A, 04046), SAN 377-4503. Tel: 207-967-2712. FAX: 207-967-0867. E-mail: seashorelibrary@ramsdell.com. Web Site: www.trolleymuseum.org. *Librn,* Edward L Ramsdell
Library Holdings: Bk Vols 10,000
Subject Interests: Electric railway, Motor bus, Transit
Restriction: Open by appt only
Friends of the Library Group

KINGFIELD

P WEBSTER FREE LIBRARY*, 22 Depot St, 04947. (Mail add: PO Box 518, 04947-0518), SAN 306-6673. Tel: 207-265-2052. E-mail: websterfree@yahoo.com. *Librn,* Barbara Stewart
Pop 1,083; Circ 7,610
Library Holdings: Bk Vols 13,000; Per Subs 22
Special Services for the Blind - Audio mat; Large print bks
Open Wed 10-12 & 1-6, Sat 9-12

KITTERY

P RICE PUBLIC LIBRARY*, Eight Wentworth St, 03904. SAN 306-6681. Tel: 207-439-1553. FAX: 207-439-1765. E-mail: arabella@rice.lib.me.us. Web Site: www.rice.lib.me.us. *Dir,* Lee Perkins; Staff 8 (MLS 1, Non-MLS 7)
Founded 1875. Pop 9,687; Circ 99,246
Jul 2005-Jun 2006 Income $413,076, City $396,230, Locally Generated Income $16,846. Mats Exp $51,870, Books $44,354, Per/Ser (Incl. Access Fees) $5,000, AV Mat $2,516. Sal $229,721
Library Holdings: AV Mats 2,900; Bks on Deafness & Sign Lang 34; Large Print Bks 712; Bk Titles 54,041; Bk Vols 57,500; Per Subs 123
Special Collections: Kittery History & Genealogy, bks, photog
Automation Activity & Vendor Info: (Cataloging) Innovative Interfaces, Inc; (Circulation) Innovative Interfaces, Inc; (ILL) Innovative Interfaces, Inc; (OPAC) Innovative Interfaces, Inc
Wireless access
Function: Home delivery & serv to Sr ctr & nursing homes, Homebound delivery serv, ILL available, Photocopying/Printing, Prog for adults, Prog for children & young adult, Spoken cassettes & CDs, Summer reading prog, VHS videos
Mem of Southern Maine Library District
Special Services for the Deaf - Bks on deafness & sign lang; High interest/low vocabulary bks
Open Tues & Fri 10-5, Wed & Thurs 12-8, Sat 10-2
Friends of the Library Group

LEVANT

P LEVANT HERITAGE LIBRARY*, 1132 Union St, 04456. (Mail add: PO Box 1, 04456-0001). Tel: 207-884-8988. E-mail: levantheritagelibrary@yahoo.com. *Libr Dir,* Holly Williams
Founded 2005
Library Holdings: Bk Vols 3,437
Automation Activity & Vendor Info: (Cataloging) LibraryWorld, Inc; (Circulation) LibraryWorld, Inc; (OPAC) LibraryWorld, Inc
Open Mon, Wed & Thurs 4:30-7:30, Sat 10-2
Friends of the Library Group

LEWISTON

C BATES COLLEGE, George & Helen Ladd Library, 48 Campus Ave, 04240. SAN 306-6703. Tel: 207-786-6264. Interlibrary Loan Service Tel: 207-786-6471. Reference Tel: 207-786-6271. Administration Tel: 207-786-6261. FAX: 207-786-6055. Web Site: www.bates.edu/library. *Col Librn, VPres, Info & Libr Serv,* Eugene L Wiemers; E-mail: ewiemers@bates.edu; *Dir, Archives & Spec Coll,* Pat Webber; Tel: 207-786-6428, Fax: 207-755-5911, E-mail: jwebber@bates.edu; *Assoc Col Librn, Coll Mgt,* Rebecca Albitz; Tel: 207-786-6270, E-mail: ralbitz@bates.edu; *Assoc Col Librn, Ref Serv,* Laura Juraska; Tel: 207-786-8324, E-mail: ljuraska@bates.edu; *Assoc Col Librn, Syst & Bibliog Serv,* Sharon K Saunders; Tel: 207-786-8327, E-mail: ssaunder@bates.edu; *Asst Col Librn for Access Serv,* Julie A Retelle; Tel: 207-786-6265, E-mail: jretelle@bates.edu; Staff 25 (MLS 12.5, Non-MLS 12.5)
Founded 1855. Enrl 1,753; Fac 218; Highest Degree: Bachelor
Jul 2012-Jun 2013 Income $3,810,604. Mats Exp $1,658,000, Books $488,000, Per/Ser (Incl. Access Fees) $1,078,000, AV Mat $44,800
Library Holdings: AV Mats 38,600; e-journals 68,200; Bk Vols 593,000
Special Collections: Bates College Archives Coll; Books from the Library of Marsden Hartley; Dorothy Freeman Coll; Edmund S Muskie Coll; Freewill Baptist Coll; Jonathan Stanton Natural History Coll; Judaica (Berent Coll); Nineteenth Century Works in French & German (Rice Coll); Signed First Editions (Phelps Coll). Oral History; US Document Depository
Automation Activity & Vendor Info: (Acquisitions) Innovative Interfaces, Inc; (Cataloging) Innovative Interfaces, Inc; (Circulation) Innovative Interfaces, Inc; (ILL) OCLC ILLiad; (OPAC) Innovative Interfaces, Inc; (Serials) Innovative Interfaces, Inc
Wireless access
Partic in CBB Librs; Maine InfoNet; NExpress Consortium

M CENTRAL MAINE MEDICAL CENTER*, Gerrish-True Health Sciences Library, 300 Main St, 04240. (Mail add: PO Box 4500, 04240), SAN 306-6711. Tel: 207-795-2560. FAX: 207-795-2569. Web Site: www.cmmc.org. *Interim Dir,* Janet Bolduc; Staff 2 (MLS 2)
Library Holdings: Bk Vols 2,500; Per Subs 280
Special Collections: Health Information Coll
Automation Activity & Vendor Info: (Cataloging) Evergreen; (Circulation) Evergreen; (ILL) Innovative Interfaces, Inc - Millenium; (OPAC) Evergreen; (Serials) Evergreen
Database Vendor: Cinahl, DynaMed, ebrary, EBSCOhost, Lexi-Comp, Marcive, Inc, McGraw-Hill, MD Consult, Natural Standard, OVID Technologies, PubMed, ScienceDirect, UpToDate
Wireless access
Partic in Health Science Library Information Consortium; National Network of Libraries of Medicine; North Atlantic Health Sciences Libraries, Inc
Open Mon-Thurs 8-4:30, Fri 8-3:30

P LEWISTON PUBLIC LIBRARY, 200 Lisbon St, 04240. SAN 343-6713. Tel: 207-513-3004. Circulation Tel: 207-513-3134. FAX: 207-784-3011. TDD: 207-784-3123. Reference E-mail: lplreference@lewistonmaine.gov. Web Site: www.lplonline.org. *Dir,* Richard A Speer; E-mail: rspeer@lewistonmaine.gov; *Librn, Adult Serv,* Marcela Peres; E-mail: mperes@lewistonmaine.gov; *Ch,* David Moorhead; E-mail: dmoorhead@lewistonmaine.gov; *Tech Serv Librn,* Karen Jones; E-mail: kjones@lewistonmaine.gov; *Circ Supvr,* Beth Martel; E-mail: bmartel@lewistonmaine.gov; *ILL,* Irene Landry; E-mail: ilandry@lewistonmaine.gov; Staff 19.2 (MLS 4, Non-MLS 15.2)
Founded 1902. Pop 36,000; Circ 223,500
Jul 2005-Jun 2006 Income $1,102,175, State $5,100, City $1,086,073, Locally Generated Income $11,002. Mats Exp $122,907, Books $106,654, AV Mat $13,031, Electronic Ref Mat (Incl. Access Fees) $3,222. Sal $582,806
Library Holdings: AV Mats 5,400; Bk Vols 128,300; Per Subs 292
Special Collections: Bates Manufacturing Company Coll; Franklin Company Coll; French Literature (Dr Eustache N Giguere Memorial); Lewiston History Coll; W S Libbey Company Coll
Automation Activity & Vendor Info: (Cataloging) Innovative Interfaces, Inc; (Circulation) Innovative Interfaces, Inc; (ILL) Innovative Interfaces, Inc; (OPAC) Innovative Interfaces, Inc; (Serials) Innovative Interfaces, Inc

Database Vendor: EBSCOhost, Gale Cengage Learning, LearningExpress
Wireless access
Open Mon-Thurs 10-7, Fri & Sat 10-5
Friends of the Library Group

M SAINT MARY'S REGIONAL MEDICAL CENTER*, Health Sciences Library, PO Box 291, 04243-0291. SAN 321-5520. Tel: 207-777-8775. FAX: 207-777-8773. *Librn,* Happy Copley; Staff 2 (MLS 1, Non-MLS 1)
Founded 1970
Library Holdings: Bk Titles 1,100; Bk Vols 1,500; Per Subs 110
Subject Interests: Med, Nursing, Psychiat
Wireless access
Partic in Health Sci Libr & Info Coop
Open Mon-Fri 8-4:30

LIBERTY

P LIBERTY LIBRARY*, Ivan O Davis Library, 59 Main St, 04949. (Mail add: PO Box 280, 04949-0280). Tel: 207-589-3161. FAX: 207-589-3161. Web Site: www.liberty.lib.me.us. *Dir,* Barbara Worcester; E-mail: bworcester@liberty.lib.me.us
Founded 1995. Pop 2,500
Library Holdings: AV Mats 80; Bk Vols 7,500; Talking Bks 80
Special Collections: Native American Coll
Automation Activity & Vendor Info: (Cataloging) Follett Software; (Circulation) Follett Software
Wireless access
Open Mon 10-12 & 6-8, Tues 10-12 & 4-6, Wed 12-4, Thurs 7pm-9pm, Fri 10-4, Sat 10-12
Friends of the Library Group

LIMERICK

P LIMERICK PUBLIC LIBRARY*, 55 Washington St, 04048-3500. SAN 376-3870. Tel: 207-793-8975. FAX: 207-793-8443. E-mail: ll-cs@limerick.lib.me.us. *Dir,* Cynthia Smith; Staff 2 (Non-MLS 2)
Library Holdings: Bk Vols 14,000; Per Subs 20
Database Vendor: EBSCOhost
Wireless access
Mem of Southern Maine Library District
Open Mon & Fri 1-5, Tues 9-12 & 3-6, Wed 9-12 & 3-8, Thurs 5-8, Sat 9-1
Friends of the Library Group

LIMESTONE

P ROBERT A FROST MEMORIAL LIBRARY*, 42 Main St, 04750-1399. SAN 306-672X. Tel: 207-325-4706. FAX: 207-325-3035. E-mail: fml@limestonemaine.org. *Librn,* Rea Caldwell; Staff 2 (Non-MLS 2)
Founded 1899. Pop 3,000; Circ 20,000
Library Holdings: AV Mats 78; Bk Titles 24,542; Bk Vols 27,312; Per Subs 31
Special Collections: Aroostook History, bks, pamphlets; State & Local History, bks, maps, pamphlets, scrapbks. Oral History
Database Vendor: EBSCOhost
Wireless access
Publications: Booklist
Mem of Northeastern Maine Library District
Open Mon, Wed & Fri 12-5, Tues & Thurs 12-6
Friends of the Library Group

LIMINGTON

P DAVIS MEMORIAL LIBRARY*, 928 Cape Rd, 04049-3907. SAN 306-6738. Tel: 207-637-2422. FAX: 207-637-2422. E-mail: davismemoriallibrary@yahoo.com. Web Site: www.davismemoriallibrary.com/. *Dir,* Kay Deal; Staff 2 (Non-MLS 2)
Founded 1912. Pop 3,400; Circ 13,900
Library Holdings: AV Mats 400; Large Print Bks 25; Bk Vols 12,500; Per Subs 40; Talking Bks 360
Special Collections: Town Histories & Genealogy
Wireless access
Function: Adult bk club, Bk club(s), Copy machines, Fax serv, ILL available, Mail & tel request accepted, Music CDs, Photocopying/Printing, Prog for children & young adult, Summer reading prog, VHS videos
Publications: Davis Memorial Library Newsletter (Monthly)
Mem of Southern Maine Library District
Partic in Maine School & Library Network
Special Services for the Deaf - Bks on deafness & sign lang; High interest/low vocabulary bks
Special Services for the Blind - Bks on cassette; Bks on CD; Copier with enlargement capabilities; Large print bks
Open Mon & Tues 2-8, Thurs 10-6, Fri 2-6, Sat 10-1
Friends of the Library Group

LINCOLN

P LINCOLN MEMORIAL LIBRARY*, 21 W Broadway, 04457. SAN 306-6746. Tel: 207-794-2765. FAX: 207-794-2606. *Dir,* Linda Morrill; E-mail: Lindamorrill2@lincolnmaine.org; *Ch Serv,* Mary Jo Hammond; Staff 2 (Non-MLS 2)
Founded 1879. Pop 5,221
Library Holdings: Bks on Deafness & Sign Lang 10; Bk Vols 30,000; Per Subs 30
Automation Activity & Vendor Info: (Cataloging) Follett Software; (Circulation) Follett Software
Database Vendor: EBSCOhost, WT Cox
Wireless access
Function: Adult bk club, After school storytime, Archival coll, Bks on cassette, Bks on CD, Children's prog, Computer training, Computers for patron use, Copy machines, Exhibits, Free DVD rentals, Handicapped accessible, Holiday prog, Home delivery & serv to Sr ctr & nursing homes, ILL available, Libr develop, Music CDs, Preschool outreach, Prog for adults, Prog for children & young adult, Pub access computers, Ref & res, Ref serv in person, Spoken cassettes & CDs, Spoken cassettes & DVDs, Story hour, Summer reading prog, Tax forms, Teen prog, VHS videos, Wheelchair accessible
Mem of Northeastern Maine Library District
Open Mon-Fri 10-6, Sat 10-2
Friends of the Library Group

LISBON FALLS

P LISBON FALLS COMMUNITY LIBRARY*, 28 Main St, 04252-0028. SAN 306-6762. Tel: 207-353-6564. *Dir,* Diane Nadeau; Staff 3 (MLS 1, Non-MLS 2)
Founded 1920. Pop 13,000; Circ 32,621
Library Holdings: Bks on Deafness & Sign Lang 60; Bk Vols 41,000; Per Subs 45
Special Collections: Maine Coll
Database Vendor: EBSCOhost
Wireless access
Publications: Newsletter
Friends of the Library Group

LIVERMORE

P LIVERMORE PUBLIC LIBRARY*, 22 Church St, 04253-3699. (Mail add: PO Box 620, 04253-0620). Tel: 207-897-7173. Web Site: www.livermore.lib.me.us. *Librn,* Penny Brown; E-mail: pbrown@livermore.lib.me.us; Staff 1 (Non-MLS 1)
Founded 1913. Circ 2,322
Library Holdings: Bk Vols 9,785
Database Vendor: EBSCOhost
Wireless access
Open Tues 1-7, Thurs 1-5:30

LIVERMORE FALLS

P TREAT MEMORIAL LIBRARY*, 56 Main St, 04254. SAN 306-6770. Tel: 207-897-3631. Web Site: www.treat.lib.me.us. *Dir,* Elaine Smith; E-mail: elainesmith@treat.lib.me.us; *Asst Dir,* Myra Rosenbaum; Staff 2 (Non-MLS 2)
Founded 1900. Pop 3,572; Circ 24,100
Library Holdings: CDs 70; DVDs 50; Large Print Bks 200; Bk Titles 19,000; Per Subs 30; Talking Bks 75; Videos 400
Automation Activity & Vendor Info: (Cataloging) Winnebago Software Co; (Circulation) Winnebago Software Co; (OPAC) Winnebago Software Co
Database Vendor: EBSCOhost, OCLC FirstSearch
Open Tues & Thurs 1-7, Wed 10-3, Fri 1-5, Sat 10-2

LONG ISLAND

P LONG ISLAND COMMUNITY LIBRARY*, Seven Gorham St, 04050. (Mail add: PO Box 252, 04050-9710). Tel: 207-766-2530. FAX: 207-766-2530. Web Site: library.long-island.lib.me.u. *Dir,* Nancy Jordan; E-mail: njordan@long-island.lib.me.us
Founded 1986
Library Holdings: AV Mats 200; CDs 60; Bk Vols 8,300
Special Collections: Maine Authors; Maine Coll
Automation Activity & Vendor Info: (Cataloging) Follett Software; (Circulation) Follett Software; (OPAC) Follett Software
Wireless access
Mem of Southern Maine Library District
Open Mon 9:30-12, 1-4 & 7-8:30, Tues & Wed 9:30-12 & 7-8:30, Thurs 1-4 & 7-8:30, Fri & Sat (Summer) 9:30-12, Sun 11:30-1:30

LOVELL

P CHARLOTTE E HOBBS MEMORIAL LIBRARY*, 227 Main St, 04051. (Mail add: PO Box 105, 04051-0105), SAN 306-6789. Tel: 207-925-3177. FAX: 207-925-3177. Web Site: hobbslibrary.org. *Libr Dir,* Anne Romer; *Librn,* Rosie White; Staff 3 (Non-MLS 3)
Founded 1900. Pop 1,900; Circ 18,800
Jan 2005-Dec 2005 Income $102,000. Mats Exp $8,415, Books $7,000, Per/Ser (Incl. Access Fees) $1,065, Other Print Mats $350. Sal $75,000 (Prof $35,000)
Library Holdings: Large Print Bks 145; Bk Vols 16,155; Per Subs 20
Special Collections: Children's Room; Maine Books
Wireless access
Function: Adult bk club, After school storytime, Copy machines, Fax serv, Home delivery & serv to Sr ctr & nursing homes, ILL available, Prog for adults, Prog for children & young adult, Summer reading prog, VHS videos
Mem of Southern Maine Library District
Open Mon 9-8, Wed, Thurs & Fri 9-4, Sat 9-1; Mon & Thurs (July-Aug) 9-8, Tues, Wed & Fri 9-4, Sat 9-1

LYMAN

P COMMUNITY LIBRARY*, 10 John St, 04002-7312. Tel: 207-499-7114. E-mail: librarian@lymanlibrary.org. Web Site: www.lymanlibrary.org. *Head Librn,* Leila Roy; Staff 2 (Non-MLS 2)
Pop 6,642; Circ 12,661
Library Holdings: Bk Vols 16,000; Per Subs 32
Database Vendor: EBSCOhost
Wireless access
Open Mon & Wed 9-8, Tues 2-6, Thurs 4-8, Sat 9:30-2:30

MACHIAS

P PORTER MEMORIAL LIBRARY*, 92 Court St, 04654-2102. SAN 306-6797. Tel: 207-255-3933. E-mail: librarian@porter.lib.me.us. Web Site: www.porter.lib.me.us. *Dir,* Lee McBride; *IT Spec, Librn,* Ben Noeske; *Ch,* Becky McKenna; Staff 4 (Non-MLS 4)
Founded 1891. Pop 2,458; Circ 17,300
Library Holdings: Bk Titles 17,500; Per Subs 10
Special Collections: Maine Coll
Automation Activity & Vendor Info: (Acquisitions) Biblionix; (Cataloging) Biblionix; (Circulation) Biblionix
Database Vendor: EBSCOhost
Wireless access
Mem of Northeastern Maine Library District
Open Tues-Fri 10-6, Sat 10-2
Friends of the Library Group

C UNIVERSITY OF MAINE AT MACHIAS*, Merrill Library, 116 O'Brien Ave, 04654-1397. SAN 306-6800. Tel: 207-255-1234, Administration Tel: 207-255-1254. FAX: 207-255-1356. Web Site: machias.edu/merrill-library. *Dir,* Angelynn King; E-mail: angelynn.king@maine.edu; *Asst Librn,* Amy Wisehart; Tel: 207-255-1256, E-mail: amy.wisehart@maine.edu; *Libr Asst I,* Craig Chalone; Tel: 207-255-1362, E-mail: craig.chalone@maine.edu; *Libr Asst II,* Jeanne Vose; E-mail: jeannep@maine.edu; Staff 3 (MLS 2, Non-MLS 1)
Founded 1909. Enrl 670; Fac 30; Highest Degree: Bachelor
Automation Activity & Vendor Info: (Acquisitions) Innovative Interfaces, Inc; (Cataloging) Innovative Interfaces, Inc; (Circulation) Innovative Interfaces, Inc; (Course Reserve) Innovative Interfaces, Inc; (ILL) OCLC ILLiad; (OPAC) Innovative Interfaces, Inc; (Serials) Innovative Interfaces, Inc
Wireless access
Function: ILL available, Online cat
Open Mon-Thurs (Fall-Spring) 8am-10pm, Fri 8-5, Sat 1-6, Sun 1-10; Mon-Fri (Summer) 8-4:30
Restriction: Open to pub for ref & circ; with some limitations, Open to qualified scholars, Open to students, fac & staff

MACHIASPORT

S DEPARTMENT OF CORRECTIONS*, Down East Correctional Facility Library, 64 Base Rd, 04655-0428. SAN 371-666X. Tel: 207-255-1100, Ext 50262. FAX: 207-255-1176. *Librn,* Ann Hayword; Staff 4 (Non-MLS 4)
Founded 1987
Library Holdings: Bk Titles 8,000
Mem of Northeastern Maine Library District
Special Services for the Deaf - Bks on deafness & sign lang; High interest/low vocabulary bks; Spec interest per
Restriction: Staff & inmates only

MADAWASKA

P MADAWASKA PUBLIC LIBRARY*, 393 Main St, 04756-1126. SAN 306-6819. Tel: 207-728-3606. Web Site: www.madawaskalibrary.org. *Dir,* Ken Theriault
Founded 1939. Pop 4,800; Circ 22,622
Library Holdings: Bk Vols 20,000; Per Subs 40
Special Collections: Local Census (including US Census of the Madawaska Settlement of the St John Valley, 1820 & 1830; New Brunswick Family & Crop Enumeration of 1833; US Census of Aroostook County, 1840-1900; Canadian Census of Madawaska & Victoria Counties, 1851-1901); Local History (Family Genealogies-St John Valley & Canada, Photographic Coll & Oral History Coll, 1972); Marriage Registers/Repertoires (Leon Guimond Extracts of Marriages for St John Valley; Langlois Repertoire, mid 1600's-mid 1900's; Poitras Marriages of Northwest New Brunswick, 1792-2001)
Subject Interests: Genealogy
Database Vendor: EBSCOhost
Wireless access
Mem of Northeastern Maine Library District
Open Mon-Fri 10-7, Sat 10-2

MADISON

P MADISON PUBLIC LIBRARY*, 12 Old Point Ave, 04950. SAN 306-6827. Tel: 207-696-5626. E-mail: madison@madison.lib.me.us. Web Site: www.madison.lib.me.us. *Head Librn,* Julie Forbus; E-mail: julie@madison.lib.me.us; *Asst Librn,* Margot Rushton; *Asst Librn,* Jane Shaw; Staff 3 (Non-MLS 3)
Founded 1906. Pop 9,900; Circ 15,500
Library Holdings: Large Print Bks 125; Bk Titles 16,415; Per Subs 15; Talking Bks 65
Automation Activity & Vendor Info: (Acquisitions) Follett Software; (Cataloging) Follett Software; (Circulation) Follett Software
Database Vendor: EBSCOhost
Wireless access
Function: Handicapped accessible, Homebound delivery serv, ILL available, Photocopying/Printing, Prog for children & young adult, Summer reading prog, Tax forms
Open Mon-Wed 10-7:30, Thurs & Fri 10-5:30, Sat 10-3

MARS HILL

P WALTER T A HANSEN MEMORIAL LIBRARY*, Ten Hansen St, 04758. (Mail add: PO Box 1008, 04758-1008), SAN 306-6843. Tel: 207-429-9625. Web Site: www.wtahansenlibrary.com. *Librn,* Tina Field
Pop 2,898; Circ 5,543
Library Holdings: Bk Vols 18,500; Per Subs 35
Special Collections: Local History Coll
Automation Activity & Vendor Info: (Cataloging) Follett Software; (Circulation) Follett Software
Database Vendor: EBSCOhost
Wireless access
Mem of Northeastern Maine Library District
Open Mon, Tues & Thurs 1:30-5:30, Wed 6:30-8:30, Fri & Sat 9-12

MATTAWAMKEAG

P MATTAWAMKEAG PUBLIC LIBRARY*, 327 Main St, 04459. (Mail add: PO Box 259, 04459-0259), SAN 306-6851. Tel: 207-736-7013. FAX: 207-736-2545. *Librn,* Denise Day; Staff 1 (Non-MLS 1)
Pop 1,000; Circ 8,725
Library Holdings: Bk Titles 14,317; Bk Vols 15,000; Per Subs 15
Special Collections: Indian Arrowhead Coll
Database Vendor: EBSCOhost
Mem of Northeastern Maine Library District
Open Mon & Fri 6:30-8:30, Wed 1-4 & 6:30-8:30

MECHANIC FALLS

P MECHANIC FALLS PUBLIC LIBRARY*, 108 Lewiston St, 04256. SAN 306-686X. Tel: 207-345-9450. *Librn,* Connie Cushing-Sefcik; E-mail: ccushing@mechanicfalls.lib.me.us
Founded 1897
Library Holdings: Bk Vols 11,000
Wireless access
Open Mon & Wed 9-5:30, Tues & Thurs 3-7, Sat 9-2

MERCER

P SHAW LIBRARY*, Main St, 04957. (Mail add: RR 2, Box 900, 04957-9607). Tel: 207-587-2529. FAX: 207-587-2529. *Librn,* Mary Harris; *Librn,* Ethel Herbert; *Librn,* Bea LaPlante
Founded 1875. Pop 700
Library Holdings: Bk Vols 7,397
Open Mon & Wed 5-8, Tues 9-Noon, Thurs & Sat 1-5

MEXICO

P MEXICO FREE PUBLIC LIBRARY*, 134 Main St, 04257. SAN 306-6886. Tel: 207-364-3281. FAX: 207-364-5685. E-mail: library@mexicomaine.net. Web Site: www.mexico.lib.me.us. *Libr Dir,* Valerie Messana
Founded 1926. Pop 3,344; Circ 11,019
Library Holdings: AV Mats 720; Large Print Bks 175; Bk Vols 14,000; Per Subs 20; Talking Bks 200
Special Collections: Maine Coll
Wireless access
Open Mon & Thurs 11-5, Tues 10-5, Wed 11-6, Fri 9-4
Friends of the Library Group

MILBRIDGE

P MILBRIDGE PUBLIC LIBRARY*, 22 School St, 04658. (Mail add: PO Box 128, 04658), SAN 376-3552. Tel: 207-546-3066. FAX: 207-546-3066. Web Site: milbridgelibrary.org. *Librn,* Melissa Smith-Rapa; Staff 1 (Non-MLS 1)
Founded 1977
Library Holdings: CDs 30; DVDs 45; Large Print Bks 160; Bk Titles 6,500; Bk Vols 7,000; Talking Bks 500; Videos 275
Wireless access
Mem of Northeastern Maine Library District
Special Services for the Blind - Bks on cassette; Large print bks
Open Tues-Fri 8-5, Sat 8-12
Friends of the Library Group

MILLINOCKET

P MILLINOCKET MEMORIAL LIBRARY, Five Maine Ave, 04462. SAN 306-6894. Tel: 207-723-7020. FAX: 207-723-7020. Web Site: www.millinocket.lib.me.us. *Dir,* Lori Fitzgerals; E-mail: lfitz@millinocket.lib.me.us; *Libr Asst,* Billie Jean Brilliant; *Ch,* Martha Frost; Staff 6 (MLS 1, Non-MLS 5)
Founded 1919. Pop 4,698; Circ 25,000
Jul 2006-Jun 2007 Income $165,936, City $161,936, Locally Generated Income $4,000. Mats Exp $20,100, Books $16,500, Per/Ser (Incl. Access Fees) $3,000, Electronic Ref Mat (Incl. Access Fees) $600. Sal $121,571 (Prof $42,668)
Library Holdings: CDs 375; DVDs 35; Large Print Bks 1,250; Bk Vols 30,000; Per Subs 60; Talking Bks 350; Videos 560
Special Collections: Millinocket & Northern Maine History Coll. Oral History
Automation Activity & Vendor Info: (Cataloging) Innovative Interfaces, Inc; (Circulation) Innovative Interfaces, Inc; (ILL) Innovative Interfaces, Inc
Database Vendor: EBSCOhost, Gale Cengage Learning, Ingram Library Services, Innovative Interfaces, Inc
Wireless access
Function: Adult literacy prog, Archival coll, Art exhibits, AV serv, CD-ROM, Doc delivery serv, Govt ref serv, Handicapped accessible, Homebound delivery serv, ILL available, Music CDs, Newsp ref libr, Online searches, Outside serv via phone, mail, e-mail & web, Photocopying/Printing, Prog for children & young adult, Ref serv available, Spoken cassettes & CDs, Summer reading prog, Telephone ref, VHS videos, Wheelchair accessible, Workshops
Mem of Northeastern Maine Library District
Open Mon & Thurs 1-5, Tues 10-5
Restriction: Non-resident fee
Friends of the Library Group

MILO

P MILO FREE PUBLIC LIBRARY*, Four Pleasant St, 04463-1327. SAN 306-6908. Tel: 207-943-2612. FAX: 207-943-2785. E-mail: milo1@milo.lib.me.us. Web Site: www.milo.lib.me.us. *Dir,* Pamela Flanagan; *Asst Librn,* Rochelle Williams; Staff 2 (Non-MLS 2)
Founded 1921. Pop 2,650; Circ 7,000
Library Holdings: Large Print Bks 80; Bk Vols 18,000; Per Subs 25
Subject Interests: Gardening, Genealogy, Hist
Function: Ref serv available
Publications: Library News & Book Reviews Published in a Local Paper
Mem of Northeastern Maine Library District

MONHEGAN

P MONHEGAN MEMORIAL LIBRARY*, One Library Lane, 04852. Tel: 207-596-0549. E-mail: monlib@monhegan.lib.me.us. Web Site: monheganlibrary.com. *Librn,* Mia Boynton; *Librn,* Tara Hire; *Librn,* Matthew Holtzman; Staff 2 (Non-MLS 2)
Founded 1926. Pop 500
Library Holdings: Bk Vols 11,000; Per Subs 10
Special Collections: Archival Local History Coll; Monhegan History Coll
Open Tues & Fri (Nov-Apr) 1-3; Mon-Fri (May) 1-3; Mon-Sat (June-Aug) 1-3 & 5-7; Mon-Fri (Sept-Oct) 1-3

MONMOUTH

P CUMSTON PUBLIC LIBRARY*, 796 Main St, 04259. (Mail add: PO Box 239, 04259), SAN 306-6916. Tel: 207-933-4788. FAX: 207-933-3413. Web Site: www.cumston.lib.me.us. *Dir,* Julie Sawtelle; E-mail: jsawtelle@cumston.lib.me.us; *Children's Prog Dir,* Sarah Pedersen-Faria; Staff 4 (Non-MLS 4)
Founded 1900. Pop 3,800; Circ 23,473
Library Holdings: AV Mats 1,754; Electronic Media & Resources 54; High Interest/Low Vocabulary Bk Vols 50; Large Print Bks 519; Bk Titles 16,497; Per Subs 70; Talking Bks 702
Special Collections: Maine (Biographies, History, Authors)
Automation Activity & Vendor Info: (Cataloging) Mandarin Library Automation; (Circulation) Mandarin Library Automation
Wireless access
Partic in Solar-net
Open Mon & Wed 1-8, Tues 10-1, Fri 1-5, Sat 9-1
Friends of the Library Group

MONROE

P MONROE COMMUNITY LIBRARY*, Eight Swan Lake Ave, 04951. (Mail add: PO Box 749, 04951-0749). Tel: 207-525-3515. FAX: 207-525-6602. *Librn,* Martha Goodale
Pop 890
Library Holdings: CDs 45; DVDs 75; Bk Vols 4,500; Talking Bks 35; Videos 75
Open Mon & Thurs 9-5, Tues 1-5, Wed 9-2 & 5-8, Fri 9-1

MONSON

P MONSON FREE PUBLIC LIBRARY*, Ten Tenney Hill Rd, 04464-6432. (Mail add: PO Box 282, 04464-0282), SAN 321-5040. Tel: 207-997-3641. FAX: 207-997-3785. *Librn,* Van Wentworth; Staff 1 (Non-MLS 1)
Pop 600
Library Holdings: Large Print Bks 35; Bk Titles 3,400; Bk Vols 3,678; Talking Bks 51; Videos 67
Special Collections: Berenice Abbot Coll
Database Vendor: EBSCOhost
Mem of Northeastern Maine Library District
Open Mon & Wed 1-5, Fri 9-1

MOUNT DESERT

P SOMESVILLE LIBRARY ASSOCIATION*, 116 Main St, 04660. (Mail add: PO Box 280, 04660-0280). Tel: 207-244-7404. *Librn,* Thomas Lange; E-mail: tlange@acadia.net
Founded 1884
Library Holdings: Bk Vols 4,000
Open Wed 1-6, Sat 9-2

MOUNT VERNON

P DR SHAW MEMORIAL LIBRARY*, 344 Pond Rd, 04352. (Mail add: 35 DeMariano Rd, 04352-9705), SAN 322-8592. Tel: 207-293-2565. *Librn,* Alice Olson; Staff 3 (MLS 2, Non-MLS 1)
Founded 1943. Pop 1,083; Circ 12,000
Jan 2012-Dec 2013 Income $12,500, State $200, Locally Generated Income $10,500. Mats Exp $9,000, Books $8,500, Per/Ser (Incl. Access Fees) $200, Other Print Mats $300. Sal $6,000
Library Holdings: Audiobooks 635; CDs 100; DVDs 100; Large Print Bks 50; Bk Titles 12,000; Per Subs 25; Videos 1,000
Database Vendor: EBSCOhost
Wireless access
Partic in Maine State Libr Network
Open Mon 3-6, Wed 9-12 & 3-8, Sat 10-3
Friends of the Library Group

NAPLES

P NAPLES PUBLIC LIBRARY*, 940 Roosevelt Trail, 04055. Tel: 207-693-6841. FAX: 207-693-7098. Web Site: www.naples.lib.me.us. *Dir,* Christine Powers; E-mail: director@naples.lib.me.us; *Ch,* Kate Johnston; E-mail: childrenslib@naples.lib.me.us; *Libr Asst,* Regina Tremblay. Subject Specialists: *Ill,* Regina Tremblay; Staff 3 (MLS 1, Non-MLS 2)
Founded 1907. Pop 3,149; Circ 19,331
Library Holdings: Audiobooks 432; Bks on Deafness & Sign Lang 24; DVDs 1,241; Large Print Bks 1,016; Music Scores 155; Bk Titles 39,000; Bk Vols 41,000; Per Subs 32
Special Collections: Maine Historical Coll
Automation Activity & Vendor Info: (Cataloging) ByWater Solutions; (Circulation) ByWater Solutions; (OPAC) ByWater Solutions

Wireless access
Function: Bk club(s), Prog for adults, Prog for children & young adult, Workshops
Publications: Booklist
Mem of Southern Maine Library District
Open Tues & Thurs 10-7, Wed 2-7, Fri & Sat (July-Sept) 9-1

NEW GLOUCESTER

P NEW GLOUCESTER PUBLIC LIBRARY*, 379 Intervale Rd, 04260. (Mail add: PO Box 105, 04260-0105), SAN 306-6940. Tel: 207-926-4840. Web Site: www.newgloucesterlibrary.org. *Librn,* Suzan Hawkins; E-mail: srhawkins@maine.rr.com; *Asst Librn,* Carla McAllister; E-mail: carlamcallister@maine.rr.com; Staff 3 (Non-MLS 3)
Founded 1897. Pop 3,180; Circ 14,400
Library Holdings: Bk Titles 20,415; Bk Vols 20,500; Per Subs 27
Automation Activity & Vendor Info: (Cataloging) Follett Software; (Circulation) Follett Software
Database Vendor: EBSCOhost
Wireless access
Mem of Southern Maine Library District
Open Tues-Thurs 9-12 & 1-8, Fri 9-12 & 1-5, Sat 9-12
Friends of the Library Group

R SHAKER LIBRARY, 707 Shaker Rd, 04260. SAN 306-7149. Tel: 207-926-4597. E-mail: shakerlibrary@shaker.lib.me.us. Web Site: www.shaker.lib.me.us/library.html. *Dir,* Michael S Graham; E-mail: usshakers@aol.com; *Librn & Archivist,* Charles Edwin Rand; Staff 0.5 (MLS 0.5)
Founded 1882
Library Holdings: AV Mats 500; Bk Titles 14,044; Bk Vols 16,500
Special Collections: The Koreshan Unity; The Religious Society of Friends & Other Radical & Communal Groups; Thomsonian Medicine
Subject Interests: Shakers
Wireless access
Function: Archival coll, Ref & res, Ref serv available
Mem of Southern Maine Library District
Restriction: Non-circulating coll, Not a lending libr, Open to pub by appt only

NEW PORTLAND

P NEW PORTLAND COMMUNITY LIBRARY*, 899 River Rd, 04961. Tel: 207-628-6561. FAX: 207-628-6561.
Pop 800; Circ 363
Library Holdings: Bk Vols 3,500; Per Subs 2
Automation Activity & Vendor Info: (Acquisitions) LibraryWorld, Inc; (Cataloging) LibraryWorld, Inc; (Circulation) LibraryWorld, Inc; (ILL) LibraryWorld, Inc; (Media Booking) LibraryWorld, Inc; (OPAC) LibraryWorld, Inc
Wireless access
Function: Adult bk club, Audio & video playback equip for onsite use, Bks on cassette, Bks on CD, CD-ROM, Computers for patron use, Electronic databases & coll, Free DVD rentals, ILL available, Music CDs, Online cat, Online searches, Pub access computers, Tax forms, VHS videos, Video lending libr, Web-catalog
Open Mon, Wed & Thurs 4-6, Sat 10-12
Friends of the Library Group

NEW SHARON

P NEW SHARON JIM DITZLER MEMORIAL LIBRARY*, 37 Library Rd, 04955. (Mail add: PO Box 61, 04955-0061), SAN 376-7426. Tel: 207-779-1128. Web Site: www.newsharon.lib.me.us. *Librn,* Diana Oliver; E-mail: nsl-do@newsharon.lib.me.us; Staff 1 (Non-MLS 1)
Pop 1,250; Circ 2,863
Library Holdings: Bk Vols 8,500
Database Vendor: EBSCOhost
Wireless access
Open Tues 4-7, Thurs & Sat 10-1

NEW VINEYARD

P NEW VINEYARD PUBLIC LIBRARY*, 20 Lake St, 04956. (Mail add: PO Box 255, 04956-0255), SAN 306-6959. Tel: 207-652-2250. E-mail: newvineyardlibrary@yahoo.com. *Dir,* Sandy Bestwick; Staff 1 (Non-MLS 1)
Pop 607
Library Holdings: Bk Titles 3,631; Bk Vols 4,200; Per Subs 11
Database Vendor: EBSCOhost
Open Mon 5-8, Tues & Sat 10-12, Thurs 2-5
Friends of the Library Group

NEWPORT

P NEWPORT PUBLIC LIBRARY*, 154 Main St, 04953-1139. SAN 306-6967. Tel: 207-368-5074. E-mail: librarian@newportculturalcenter.org. Web Site: newportculturalcenter.net. *Librn,* Joanne Elwell; E-mail: jelwell@newportculturalcenter.org; *Librn,* Lee McCartin; *Libr Asst,* Nellie Rudder
Founded 1899. Pop 20,701
Library Holdings: Bk Vols 14,500; Per Subs 20
Automation Activity & Vendor Info: (Cataloging) Evergreen; (Circulation) Evergreen; (OPAC) Evergreen
Database Vendor: EBSCOhost
Mem of Northeastern Maine Library District
Open Tues-Fri 9:30-5:30, Sat 9:30-1:30

NORRIDGEWOCK

P NORRIDGEWOCK PUBLIC LIBRARY*, 40 Mercer Rd, 04957. (Mail add: PO Box 7, 04957-0007), SAN 306-6975. Tel: 207-634-2828. *Dir,* Kent Sinclair
Pop 3,105; Circ 4,007
Library Holdings: Bks on Deafness & Sign Lang 10; Large Print Bks 200; Bk Titles 15,000; Per Subs 12; Talking Bks 150
Special Services for the Deaf - Bks on deafness & sign lang
Special Services for the Blind - Bks on cassette; Large print bks
Open Tues & Thurs 10-6, Sat 10-2

NORTH ANSON

P STEWART PUBLIC LIBRARY*, 37 Elm St, 04958. (Mail add: PO Box 177, 04958-0177). Tel: 207-635-3212. E-mail: stewlib@stewartpub.lib.me.us. Web Site: www.stewartpub.lib.me.us. *Librn,* Emily Quint
Founded 1899. Pop 2,014
Library Holdings: Bk Vols 15,474; Per Subs 20
Open Wed 2:30-6, Sat 2:30-4:30

NORTH BERWICK

P D A HURD LIBRARY*, 41 High St, 03906. SAN 306-6983. Tel: 207-676-2215. FAX: 207-676-7976. E-mail: hurdlibrarian@da-hurd.lib.me.us. Web Site: www.da-hurd.lib.me.us. *Dir,* Beth Sweet; E-mail: hurddirector@da-hurd.lib.me.us; *Asst Dir,* Pamela Smart; *Ch Serv,* Corinne Feehan; E-mail: hurdchild@da-hurd.lib.me.us; Staff 2 (Non-MLS 2)
Founded 1927. Pop 8,475
Jul 2005-Jun 2006 Income $167,239, City $157,239, Locally Generated Income $10,000. Mats Exp $31,125, Books $29,560, Per/Ser (Incl. Access Fees) $1,565. Sal $88,967
Library Holdings: AV Mats 78; Bks-By-Mail 50; CDs 140; Large Print Bks 1,426; Bk Vols 26,892; Per Subs 81; Talking Bks 861; Videos 1,067
Special Collections: Local Genealogy, town reports, maps, regional history
Automation Activity & Vendor Info: (Cataloging) Winnebago Software Co; (Circulation) Winnebago Software Co
Database Vendor: EBSCOhost
Mem of Southern Maine Library District
Open Mon & Fri 9:30-5, Tues-Thurs 1-7, Sat 9:30-1

NORTH BRIDGTON

S BRIDGTON ACADEMY LIBRARY*, Chadbourne Hill Rd, 04057. (Mail add: PO Box 292, 04057-0292). Tel: 207-647-2121. FAX: 207-647-3146. Web Site: www.bridgtonacademy.org. *Head of Libr,* Milagros Katz; E-mail: mkatz@bridgtonacademy.org
Library Holdings: Bk Vols 8,000

P NORTH BRIDGTON PUBLIC LIBRARY*, 113 Waterford Rd, 04057. (Mail add: PO Box 268, 04057-0268), SAN 306-5995. Tel: 207-647-8563. Web Site: www.nbridgton.lib.me.us. *Dir,* Heather Silvia; E-mail: nbpldirector@nbridgton.lib.me.us; Staff 1 (MLS 1)
Founded 1917. Pop 534; Circ 4,042
Library Holdings: Bk Vols 7,000; Per Subs 13
Database Vendor: EBSCOhost
Wireless access
Mem of Southern Maine Library District
Open Mon 9-Noon, Thurs 1-5, Sat 9-1
Friends of the Library Group

NORTH HAVEN

P NORTH HAVEN LIBRARY*, 33 Main St, 04853. (Mail add: PO Box 486, 04853-0486), SAN 306-6991. Tel: 207-867-9797. FAX: 207-867-9797. *Librn,* Kathryn Quinn; E-mail: kquinn@sad7.k12.me.us; Staff 1 (Non-MLS 1)
Pop 373; Circ 4,367

Library Holdings: AV Mats 400; Bk Titles 14,000; Bk Vols 15,489; Per Subs 20
Automation Activity & Vendor Info: (Cataloging) ComPanion Corp; (Circulation) ComPanion Corp; (ILL) ComPanion Corp; (Serials) ComPanion Corp
Wireless access
Mem of Northeastern Maine Library District
Open Wed (Winter) 2-5, Sat 10-5; Mon-Sat (Summer) 1-5
Friends of the Library Group

NORTH JAY

P JAY-NILES MEMORIAL LIBRARY*, 983 Main St, 04262. (Mail add: PO Box 5008, 04262-5008), SAN 306-6614. Tel: 207-645-4062. E-mail: info@jaynileslibrary.com. Web Site: www.jaynileslibrary.com. *Head Librn,* Tamara Hoke; E-mail: thoke@jaynileslibrary.com; *Ch,* Priscilla Pineau; Staff 1 (Non-MLS 1)
Founded 1917. Pop 5,086
Library Holdings: AV Mats 180; Bk Titles 33,000; Per Subs 71
Automation Activity & Vendor Info: (Cataloging) Winnebago Software Co; (Circulation) Winnebago Software Co
Open Mon-Wed 3-8, Thurs & Fri 12-5, Sat (Sept-June) 10-3

NORTHEAST HARBOR

P NORTHEAST HARBOR LIBRARY*, One Joy Rd, 04662. (Mail add: PO Box 279, 04662-0279), SAN 306-7017. Tel: 207-276-3333. FAX: 207-276-3315. E-mail: info@nehlibrary.org. Web Site: www.nehlibrary.org. *Dir,* Brook Minner; E-mail: bminner@nehlibrary.org; *Asst Dir,* Anna Carr; Staff 5 (MLS 1, Non-MLS 4)
Pop 2,063; Circ 42,000
Library Holdings: Bk Vols 55,000; Per Subs 62
Special Collections: Architectural Drawings of Local Structures (Gerrish Coll); Collected Works of Samuel Eliot Morison; Horticulture (R Gwynne Stout Coll); Local History (I T Moore Coll), photog. Oral History
Automation Activity & Vendor Info: (Cataloging) Winnebago Software Co; (Circulation) Winnebago Software Co
Database Vendor: EBSCOhost
Wireless access
Function: Art exhibits, AV serv, ILL available, Prog for adults, Prog for children & young adult, Ref serv available, Summer reading prog
Mem of Northeastern Maine Library District
Open Mon, Tues & Thurs-Fri 9-5, Wed 10-7, Sat 9-1

NORWAY

P NORWAY MEMORIAL LIBRARY*, 258 Main St, 04268. SAN 306-7025. Tel: 207-743-5309. Circulation Tel: 207-743-5309, Ext 3. Reference Tel: 207-743-5309, Ext 1. Administration Tel: 207-743-5309, Ext 2. FAX: 207-744-0111. E-mail: norlib@norway.lib.me.us. Web Site: www.norway.lib.me.us. *Libr Dir,* Beth Kane; E-mail: nordir@norway.lib.me.us
Founded 1885. Pop 4,042; Circ 37,539
Library Holdings: Bk Vols 35,000; Per Subs 80
Automation Activity & Vendor Info: (Cataloging) Innovative Interfaces, Inc; (Circulation) Innovative Interfaces, Inc; (OPAC) Innovative Interfaces, Inc
Database Vendor: EBSCOhost
Wireless access
Open Mon & Fri 10-5, Tues & Thurs 12-5, Wed 10-8, Sat 10-3
Friends of the Library Group

OAKLAND

P OAKLAND PUBLIC LIBRARY*, 18 Church St, 04963. SAN 306-7033. Tel: 207-465-7533, 207-465-9554. FAX: 207-465-9554. *Librn,* Sarah Roy; E-mail: oaklandpubliclibrary@gmail.com; Staff 4 (MLS 1, Non-MLS 3)
Founded 1913. Pop 6,071; Circ 26,878
Library Holdings: Large Print Bks 600; Bk Vols 23,272; Per Subs 49
Special Collections: Maine Coll, bks on tape
Subject Interests: Hist
Automation Activity & Vendor Info: (Cataloging) Follett Software; (Circulation) Follett Software
Wireless access
Open Tues 10-7, Wed-Fri 10-6
Friends of the Library Group

OCEAN PARK

P OCEAN PARK MEMORIAL LIBRARY*, 11 Temple Ave, 04063. (Mail add: PO Box 7248, 04063-7248). Tel: 207-934-9068. FAX: 207-934-2823. E-mail: opa@oceanpark.org. Web Site: www.oceanpark.org/programs/education/library.html. *Dir,* Penny Gagnon; Staff 2 (Non-MLS 2)
Library Holdings: Bk Vols 10,000
Mem of Southern Maine Library District
Open Mon, Tues, Thurs & Fri 10-7, Sat 10-1

OGUNQUIT

P OGUNQUIT MEMORIAL LIBRARY*, 166 Shore Rd, 03907. (Mail add: PO Box 753, 03907-0753), SAN 306-7769. Tel: 207-646-9024. *Dir,* Mary W Littlefield; *Asst Librn,* Terri Neill; *Asst Librn,* Jane Staples; Staff 3 (Non-MLS 3)
Founded 1897. Pop 1,500; Circ 15,000
Library Holdings: Bks on Deafness & Sign Lang 10; CDs 100; DVDs 20; Large Print Bks 350; Bk Vols 10,000; Per Subs 25; Talking Bks 400; Videos 170
Special Collections: Municipal Document Depository
Mem of Southern Maine Library District
Open Mon-Sat 9-12 & 2-5

OLD ORCHARD BEACH

P LIBBY MEMORIAL LIBRARY*, 27 Staples St, 04064. SAN 306-7041. Tel: 207-934-4351. Web Site: www.ooblibrary.org. *Dir, ILL,* Lee Koenigs; E-mail: director@ooblibrary.org; *Asst Dir,* Eileen McNally; *Ch,* Kim McLaughlin; *Circ Librn,* Sheila Lauzon; *Libr Asst,* Jim Henry; *Computer Tech,* John P Griffin; Staff 3 (MLS 1, Non-MLS 2)
Pop 10,071; Circ 26,338
Library Holdings: Bk Titles 27,000; Per Subs 58
Special Collections: Chess Book Coll; Local History Coll
Automation Activity & Vendor Info: (Cataloging) Follett Software; (Circulation) Follett Software
Wireless access
Mem of Southern Maine Library District
Special Services for the Blind - Large print bks
Open Tues & Wed 10-8, Thurs & Fri 10-5:30, Sat 10-3
Friends of the Library Group

OLD TOWN

P OLD TOWN PUBLIC LIBRARY, 46 Middle St, 04468. SAN 306-705X. Tel: 207-827-3972. Administration Tel: 207-827-3973. FAX: 207-827-3978. E-mail: otpl@old-town.lib.me.us. Web Site: old-town.lib.me.us. *Dir,* Cynthia Jennings; E-mail: cindy.jennings@old-town.org; *Ch,* Cindy Seger; E-mail: cindy.seger@old-town.org
Founded 1904. Pop 8,130; Circ 156,000
Library Holdings: Bk Vols 48,000; Per Subs 100
Special Collections: Local Newspaper, microfilm (100 yrs)
Database Vendor: EBSCOhost
Wireless access
Publications: Booklist; Bulletin (for the Center for children's books); Hornbook; The Web
Mem of Northeastern Maine Library District
Special Services for the Deaf - TTY equip
Open Mon & Tues 10-7, Wed-Fri 10-5, Sat 10-1
Friends of the Library Group

ORONO

P ORONO PUBLIC LIBRARY*, 39 Pine St, 04473. SAN 306-7068. Tel: 207-866-5060. E-mail: opl@orono.lib.me.us. Web Site: www.orono.lib.me.us. *Dir,* Laurie Carpenter; E-mail: lauriec@orono.lib.me.us; *Youth Serv Librn,* Louise Jolliffe; E-mail: ljolliffe@orono.lib.me.us; Staff 3 (Non-MLS 3)
Founded 1880. Pop 10,573; Circ 43,017
Library Holdings: Bk Vols 40,000; Per Subs 100
Automation Activity & Vendor Info: (Cataloging) Innovative Interfaces, Inc; (Circulation) Innovative Interfaces, Inc; (OPAC) Innovative Interfaces, Inc
Database Vendor: EBSCOhost
Wireless access
Mem of Northeastern Maine Library District
Open Tues & Thurs 10-7, Wed & Fri 10-5, Sat 9-1
Friends of the Library Group

C UNIVERSITY OF MAINE, Raymond H Fogler Library, 5729 Fogler Library, 04469-5729. SAN 306-7076. Circulation Tel: 207-581-1666. Interlibrary Loan Service Tel: 207-581-1671. Reference Tel: 207-581-1673. Administration Tel: 207-581-1655. FAX: 207-581-1653. Web Site: www.library.umaine.edu. *Dean of Libr,* Joyce Rumery; *Dept Head, Regional Dep Librn & ILL Librn,* Greg Curtis; *Head, Coll Serv,* Deborah Rollins; *Head, Ref (Info Serv),* Jim Bird; *Head, Ref (Info Serv),* Nancy Lewis; *Head, Spec Coll,* Richard Hollinger; *Dept Head, Tech Serv,* Sharon Fitzgerald; Staff 20 (MLS 15, Non-MLS 5)
Founded 1865. Enrl 9,356; Fac 544; Highest Degree: Doctorate
Jul 2013-Jun 2014. Mats Exp $5,835,981, Books $397,489, Per/Ser (Incl. Access Fees) $5,190,257, Other Print Mats $177,656, Micro $53,849, Presv $16,730. Sal $2,192,192 (Prof $1,109,230)
Library Holdings: Bk Vols 1,199,476

Special Collections: Abolition & Antislavery (O'Brien Coll); Cole Maritime Coll; Hannibal Hamlin Family Papers; Indian Lore & Etymology (Eckstorm Coll); Senator William S Cohen Coll; State of Maine Coll, University Archives. State Document Depository; US Document Depository
Subject Interests: Can Am studies, Maine studies
Automation Activity & Vendor Info: (Serials) Innovative Interfaces, Inc
Wireless access
Publications: The Olive Tree
Partic in Lyrasis; Maine InfoNet; Northeast Research Libraries Consortium (NERL); OCLC Online Computer Library Center, Inc; Westchester Academic Library Directors Organization (WALDO)
Friends of the Library Group

ORRINGTON

P ORRINGTON PUBLIC LIBRARY*, 15 School St, 04474. SAN 376-3528. Tel: 207-825-4938. Web Site: orringtonlibrary.wordpress.com. *Librn,* Audrey Snowden; Staff 1 (Non-MLS 1)
Founded 1978. Pop 3,309
Library Holdings: Bk Titles 14,400; Per Subs 25
Automation Activity & Vendor Info: (Circulation) Follett Software
Database Vendor: EBSCOhost
Wireless access
Mem of Northeastern Maine Library District
Open Mon, Wed & Fri 9-5, Tues & Thurs 11-7

ORR'S ISLAND

P ORR'S ISLAND LIBRARY*, 1699 Harpswell Islands Rd, 04066. (Mail add: PO Box 175, 04066-0175), SAN 376-3846. Tel: 207-833-7811. Web Site: www.orrsislandlibrary.org. *Librn,* Joanne Rogers; Staff 1 (Non-MLS 1)
Pop 3,013
Library Holdings: AV Mats 1,300; Bk Titles 9,000; Per Subs 10; Talking Bks 1,000; Videos 1,300
Database Vendor: EBSCOhost
Open Mon & Wed 1-6, Fri 3-6, Sat 9-4
Friends of the Library Group

OWLS HEAD

S OWLS HEAD TRANSPORTATION MUSEUM LIBRARY*, Lang Center, PO Box 277, 04854-0277. Tel: 207-594-4418. FAX: 207-594-4410. Web Site: www.ohtm.org, www.owlshead.org. *Librn,* Ethan Yankura; E-mail: cyankura@ohtm.org
Library Holdings: Bk Vols 5,000; Per Subs 15
Automation Activity & Vendor Info: (Cataloging) Winnebago Software Co
Wireless access
Function: Res libr
Publications: Strut & Axle (Quarterly)
Open Tues 10-4
Restriction: Non-circulating

OXFORD

P FREELAND HOLMES LIBRARY*, 109 Pleasant St, 04270-4206. (Mail add: PO Box 197, 04270-0197), SAN 376-382X. Tel: 207-539-4016. E-mail: freeland@freeland-holmes.lib.me.us. Web Site: www.freeland-holmes.lib.me.us. *Librn,* Glenda Drapeau; Staff 1 (Non-MLS 1)
Library Holdings: Bk Vols 37,000
Wireless access
Open Tues & Thurs 1-5, Wed 6-8, Fri & Sat 9-Noon

PALERMO

P PALERMO COMMUNITY LIBRARY*, Rte 3, 04354. (Mail add: PO Box 102, 04354-0102). Tel: 207-993-6088. E-mail: palermo@palermo.lib.me.us. Web Site: www.palermo.lib.me.us. *In Charge,* Ellie Budzko
Founded 2000
Library Holdings: AV Mats 55; DVDs 55; Bk Vols 7,000; Talking Bks 90
Special Collections: Maine Coll
Function: ILL available
Open Tues 2-8, Thurs 3-5, Sat 10-2
Friends of the Library Group

PARKMAN

P HARVEY MEMORIAL LIBRARY*, 771 State Hwy 150, 04443-3201. Tel: 207-876-3730. *Librn,* Brenda Hartford
Founded 1963. Pop 840
Library Holdings: AV Mats 10; Bk Vols 400; Talking Bks 15
Open Mon & Fri 9-5, Tues-Thurs 9-1

PARSONSFIELD

P KEZAR FALLS CIRCULATING LIBRARY*, Two Wadleigh St, 04047. (Mail add: PO Box 11, 04047-0011). Tel: 207-625-2424. *Dir,* Erika Jordon
Pop 3,280; Circ 2,899
Library Holdings: AV Mats 75; Bk Vols 11,375; Talking Bks 60
Special Collections: Local Genealogy Coll
Wireless access
Mem of Southern Maine Library District
Open Tues 10-2, Wed 2:30-7, Thurs 2:30-5, Sat 10 12

PATTEN

P VETERANS MEMORIAL LIBRARY*, 30 Main St, 04765. (Mail add: PO Box 695, 04765-0695), SAN 306-7106. Tel: 207-528-2164. E-mail: vetmemlib@yahoo.com. Web Site: www.veterans-memorial.lib.me.us. *Librn,* Doris DeRespino
Pop 1,368; Circ 14,600
Library Holdings: Large Print Bks 150; Bk Titles 17,000; Bk Vols 18,000; Per Subs 30; Talking Bks 100
Automation Activity & Vendor Info: (Cataloging) Follett Software; (Circulation) Follett Software; (OPAC) Follett Software
Database Vendor: EBSCOhost
Mem of Northeastern Maine Library District
Special Services for the Blind - Bks on cassette
Open Mon 10-12, 1-4 & 6-8, Tues 9-12 & 1-4, Thurs 9-12, 1-4 & 6-8

PEMAQUID

P BRISTOL AREA LIBRARY*, 619 Old County Rd, Rte 130, 04458. (Mail add: PO Box 173, New Harbor, 04554-0173), SAN 376-3773. Tel: 207-677-2115. E-mail: libra@msln.net. *Librn,* Jackie Bennett; Staff 1 (Non-MLS 1)
Library Holdings: Bk Titles 10,000; Bk Vols 17,000; Per Subs 10
Wireless access
Open Mon, Wed & Fri 10-5, Thurs 2-6, Sat 10-12
Friends of the Library Group

PEMBROKE

P PEMBROKE LIBRARY*, 221 Old County Rd, 04666. (Mail add: 857 Leighton Point Rd, 04666-4507). Tel: 207-726-4745. FAX: 207-726-4745. E-mail: pemlib@pembroke.lib.me.us. *Dir,* Frederick Gralenski
Founded 2005. Pop 883; Circ 4,500
Library Holdings: Bk Vols 9,000
Wireless access
Open Tues 9-12 & 3-5, Wed 3-8, Thurs 3-5, Fri 3-6, Sat 9-12
Friends of the Library Group

PHILLIPS

P PHILLIPS PUBLIC LIBRARY*, 96 Main St, 04966. (Mail add: PO Box O, 04966-1514), SAN 306-7114. Tel: 207-639-2665. FAX: 207-639-2665. Web Site. www.phillips.lib.me.us. *Librn,* Hedy Langdon; Staff 2 (Non-MLS 2)
Founded 1910. Pop 1,885; Circ 2,975
Library Holdings: Bk Titles 12,000; Per Subs 14
Special Collections: Local History Coll; Maine Coll
Database Vendor: EBSCOhost
Wireless access
Open Wed 10-7, Thurs & Fri 10-5, Sat 10-2
Friends of the Library Group

PHIPPSBURG

P ALBERT F TOTMAN PUBLIC LIBRARY*, 28 Parker Head Rd, 04562-4576. Tel: 207-389-2309. FAX: 207-389-2309. E-mail: librarian@totman.lib.me.us. Web Site: www.totman.lib.me.us. *Librn,* Michele Morong; Staff 1 (Non-MLS 1)
Founded 1929. Pop 2,106
Library Holdings: AV Mats 700; CDs 60; DVDs 536; Large Print Bks 85; Bk Vols 10,100; Per Subs 23; Talking Bks 325; Videos 750
Automation Activity & Vendor Info: (Acquisitions) Book Systems; (Cataloging) Book Systems; (Circulation) Book Systems; (OPAC) Book Systems
Database Vendor: EBSCOhost, Overdrive, Inc, ProQuest
Wireless access
Function: Audiobks via web
Open Mon-Fri 10-5, Sat 10-1
Friends of the Library Group

PITTSFIELD

P PITTSFIELD PUBLIC LIBRARY*, 110 Library St, 04967. SAN 306-7122. Tel: 207-487-5880. Web Site: www.pittsfield.lib.me.us. *Dir,* Lyn Smith; E-mail: lsmith@pittsfield.lib.me.us; Staff 4 (MLS 1, Non-MLS 3)
Founded 1904. Pop 4,200; Circ 41,697

Jan 2005-Dec 2005 Income $127,419. Mats Exp $16,500, Books $13,000, Per/Ser (Incl. Access Fees) $2,000, AV Mat $1,500. Sal $60,727 (Prof $29,224)
Library Holdings: Large Print Bks 200; Bk Vols 21,000; Per Subs 70
Subject Interests: Local hist
Automation Activity & Vendor Info: (Cataloging) Follett Software; (Circulation) Follett Software
Database Vendor: EBSCOhost
Wireless access
Open Mon-Fri 10-6, Sat 10-1

POLAND

P ALVAN BOLSTER RICKER MEMORIAL LIBRARY, 1211 Maine St, 04274. SAN 306-7130. Tel: 207-998-4390. FAX: 207-998-2120. Web Site: www.rickerlibrary.org. *Adminr,* Joanne Messer; E-mail: jmesser@rickerlibrary.org; *Asst Librn,* Barbara Johnson; E-mail: barbj@rickerlibrary.org; *Asst Librn,* Terri LaClaire; E-mail: tlaclaire@rickerlibrary.org; Staff 7 (MLS 1, Non-MLS 6)
Founded 1963. Pop 4,866; Circ 22,000
Library Holdings: Bk Titles 25,000; Per Subs 35
Special Collections: Local History Coll; Maine Coll
Automation Activity & Vendor Info: (Cataloging) Follett Software; (Circulation) Follett Software
Wireless access
Partic in Maine InfoNet; Maine State Libr Network
Open Mon & Tues 9-8, Wed-Fri 9-5, Sat 10-2
Friends of the Library Group

PORTLAND

L PIERCE ATWOOD LLP*, Law Library, 254 Commercial St, 04101. SAN 372-0969. Tel: 207-791-1142. FAX: 207-791-1350. Web Site: www.pierceatwood.com. *Mgr, Libr Serv,* Kami Bedard; Tel: 207-791-1100; Staff 2 (MLS 1, Non-MLS 1)
Library Holdings: Bk Vols 20,000; Per Subs 120
Automation Activity & Vendor Info: (Acquisitions) Inmagic, Inc.; (Cataloging) Inmagic, Inc.; (Circulation) Inmagic, Inc.
Database Vendor: LexisNexis, Westlaw
Restriction: Staff use only

L BERNSTEIN, SHUR, SAWYER & NELSON*, Law Library, 100 Middle St, 04104. (Mail add: PO Box 9729, 04104-5029), SAN 329-1251. Tel: 207-228-7281. FAX: 207-774-1127. Web Site: www.bernsteinshur.com. *Librn,* Christine Bertsch; E-mail: cbertsch@bernsteinshur.com; Staff 2 (MLS 1, Non-MLS 1)
Founded 1981
Library Holdings: Bk Vols 8,000; Per Subs 200
Wireless access
Mem of Southern Maine Library District

L NATHAN & HENRY B CLEAVES LAW LIBRARY*, 142 Federal St, 04101. SAN 306-7165. Tel: 207-773-9712. Toll Free FAX: 866-894-9612. E-mail: info@cleaves.org. Web Site: www.cleaves.org. *Librn,* Nancy Rabasca; Staff 2 (MLS 1, Non-MLS 1)
Founded 1811
Library Holdings: DVDs 40; Bk Vols 30,000
Special Collections: Legal Photography Archives; Records & Briefs of the Supreme Judicial Court of the State of Maine. Oral History
Wireless access
Mem of Southern Maine Library District

S GREATER PORTLAND LANDMARKS, INC*, Frances W Peabody Research Library, 93 High St, 04101. SAN 306-7181. Tel: 207-774-5561. FAX: 207-774-2509. E-mail: info@portlandlandmarks.org. Web Site: www.portlandlandmarks.org. *Exec Dir,* Hilary Bassett; E-mail: hbassett@portlandlandmarks.org; Staff 3 (MLS 1, Non-MLS 2)
Founded 1971
Library Holdings: Bk Titles 1,250; Per Subs 5
Special Collections: Biography of Architects in Maine; Buildings & Architectural Detail, microprint; Scientific American Building Monthly, 1885-1905
Subject Interests: Local hist
Wireless access
Mem of Southern Maine Library District
Restriction: Open to pub by appt only

S MAINE CHARITABLE MECHANIC ASSOCIATION LIBRARY*, 519 Congress St, 04101. SAN 306-7203. Tel: 207-773-8396. Web Site: www.mainecharitablemechanicassociation.com. *Librn,* Pat Larrabee
Founded 1815
Library Holdings: DVDs 60; Large Print Bks 62; Bk Vols 32,500; Per Subs 2; Spec Interest Per Sub 1; Videos 132
Special Collections: 20th Century Fiction Coll; Maine Coll
Subject Interests: Fiction, Hist, Travel
Wireless access
Mem of Southern Maine Library District
Open Tues-Thurs 10-3
Restriction: Mem only

S MAINE COLLEGE OF ART*, Joanne Waxman Library, 522 Congress St, 04101. SAN 321-0391. Tel: 207-775-5153. Toll Free Tel: 800-639-4808. FAX: 207-772-5069. E-mail: library@meca.edu. Web Site: library.meca.edu. *Dir,* Moira Steven; Tel: 207-775-5153, Ext 5090, E-mail: msteven@meca.edu; *Circ Mgr,* Heather Dawn Driscoll; Tel: 207-775-5153, Ext 5091, E-mail: hdriscoll@meca.edu. Subject Specialists: *Art hist, Artists bks, Design,* Moira Steven; *Jewelry manufacturing, Metals,* Heather Dawn Driscoll; Staff 3 (MLS 1, Non-MLS 2)
Founded 1974. Enrl 330; Fac 50; Highest Degree: Master
Library Holdings: CDs 35; DVDs 500; e-journals 51; Bk Titles 33,000; Bk Vols 41,000; Per Subs 101
Special Collections: Bill Caldwell Rare Book Room, artist bks & rare bks; Visual Resource Coll
Subject Interests: Applied arts, Art hist, Design, Fine arts, Liberal arts
Automation Activity & Vendor Info: (Acquisitions) Innovative Interfaces, Inc - Millenium; (Cataloging) Innovative Interfaces, Inc - Millenium; (Circulation) Innovative Interfaces, Inc - Millenium; (Course Reserve) Innovative Interfaces, Inc - Millenium; (OPAC) Innovative Interfaces, Inc - Millenium; (Serials) Innovative Interfaces, Inc - Millenium
Database Vendor: 3M Library Systems, ARTstor, EBSCOhost, Innovative Interfaces, Inc, OCLC WebJunction, OCLC WorldShare Interlibrary Loan, ProQuest, Wilson - Wilson Web
Wireless access
Function: Archival coll, Art exhibits, CD-ROM, Computers for patron use, Copy machines, Exhibits, Handicapped accessible, ILL available, Online cat, Photocopying/Printing, Ref serv available, Scanner, VHS videos, Wheelchair accessible
Mem of Southern Maine Library District
Partic in Lyrasis; OCLC Online Computer Library Center, Inc
Open Mon-Thurs (Winter) 8-8, Fri 8-5, Sat 12-5; Mon-Fri (Summer) 9-5
Restriction: Fee for pub use, In-house use for visitors, Limited access for the pub, Non-circulating of rare bks

S MAINE HISTORICAL SOCIETY*, Brown Research Library, 489 Congress St, 04101-3498. SAN 306-7211. Tel: 207-774-1822. Reference Tel: 207-774-1822, Ext 209. FAX: 207-775-4301. E-mail: research@mainehistory.org. Web Site: www.mainehistory.org. *Head, Libr Serv,* Nicholas Noyes; E-mail: nnoyes@mainehistory.org; *Res Librn,* Jamie Kingman Rice; E-mail: jrice@mainehistory.org; Staff 6 (MLS 4, Non-MLS 2)
Founded 1822
Library Holdings: Bk Titles 65,000
Special Collections: Fogg Autograph Coll; Northeast Boundary Coll; Papers of Governor William King; Portland Company Records; Records of Kennebec Proprietors
Subject Interests: Early New England, Genealogy, Maine hist
Automation Activity & Vendor Info: (Cataloging) Innovative Interfaces, Inc
Wireless access
Function: Archival coll, Res libr
Publications: Maine Historical Society (Newsletter); Maine History
Mem of Southern Maine Library District
Open Tues-Sat 10-4
Restriction: Not a lending libr
Friends of the Library Group

M MAINE MEDICAL CENTER LIBRARY*, 22 Bramhall St, 04102. SAN 306-722X. Tel: 207-662-2202. FAX: 207-761-3027. E-mail: library@mmc.org. Web Site: www.mmc.org/library. *Libr Mgr,* Maryanne Lamont; Staff 5.7 (MLS 2, Non-MLS 3.7)
Founded 1874
Library Holdings: Bk Titles 4,000; Per Subs 700
Subject Interests: Hospital admin, Med, Nursing
Wireless access
Mem of Southern Maine Library District
Partic in Health Sci Libr & Info Coop; National Network of Libraries of Medicine New England Region; North Atlantic Health Sciences Libraries, Inc
Open Mon-Fri 7:30-5:30

P PORTLAND PUBLIC LIBRARY*, Five Monument Sq, 04101. SAN 343-6802. Tel: 207-871-1700. Circulation Tel: 207-871-1700, Ext 730. Interlibrary Loan Service Tel: 207-871-1700, Ext 735. Reference Tel: 207-871-1700, Ext 725. Administration Tel: 207-871-1700, Ext 756. Toll Free Tel: 800-649-7696. FAX: 207-871-1703. E-mail: Reference@portland.lib.me.us. Web Site: www.portlandlibrary.com. *Exec Dir,* Stephen J Podgajny; E-mail: podgajny@portland.lib.me.us; *Dir of Finance,* George Cooper; Tel: 207-871-1700, Ext 760, E-mail: cooper@portland.lib.me.us; *Br Adminr, Outreach Serv Librn,* Brian

Damien; Tel: 207-871-1700, Ext 716, E-mail: damien@portland.lib.me.us; *Ch Serv, YA Serv,* Mary Peverada; Tel: 207-871-1700, Ext 707, E-mail: peverada@portland.lib.me.us; *Circ, Syst Tech, Tech Serv,* Sarah Campbell; Tel: 207-871-1700, Ext 736, E-mail: campbell@portland.lib.me.us; *Ref,* Linda Putnam; Tel: 207-871-1725, E-mail: putnam@portland.lib.me.us; Staff 59 (MLS 14, Non-MLS 45)
Founded 1867. Pop 70,080; Circ 742,779
Library Holdings: AV Mats 38,967; Bk Titles 295,337; Bk Vols 311,069; Per Subs 1,700
Special Collections: Hugh Thomson (Antique Children's Books); Jacob Abbott Coll; Jewish Bi-Centennial Oral History Program; Music by Maine Composers; Newspapers from 1785; Portland Coll; Press Books (Dun Emer, Mosher, Southworth-Anthoensen, Cuala Shagbark); Sarah Orne Jewett Coll; State of Maine (Maine Authors, Maine & Portland Imprints). Oral History; State Document Depository; US Document Depository
Subject Interests: Art, Consumer health, Ireland
Automation Activity & Vendor Info: (Acquisitions) Innovative Interfaces, Inc; (Circulation) Innovative Interfaces, Inc; (OPAC) Innovative Interfaces, Inc; (Serials) Innovative Interfaces, Inc
Database Vendor: OCLC FirstSearch
Wireless access
Function: Adult bk club, Audio & video playback equip for onsite use, Audiobks via web, Bks on cassette, Bks on CD, CD-ROM, Children's prog, Computer training, Computers for patron use, Copy machines, Electronic databases & coll, Free DVD rentals, Handicapped accessible, Holiday prog, Home delivery & serv to Sr ctr & nursing homes, ILL available, Instruction & testing, Magnifiers for reading, Mail & tel request accepted, Mus passes, Music CDs, Newsp ref libr, Online cat, Orientations, Photocopying/Printing, Prog for adults, Prog for children & young adult, Pub access computers, Ref & res, Senior computer classes, Senior outreach, Summer reading prog, Tax forms, Teen prog, Telephone ref, VHS videos, Video lending libr, Web-catalog, Wheelchair accessible, Workshops, Writing prog
Publications: Annual Report; Seasonal Newsletter; Services Guide
Mem of Southern Maine Library District
Partic in Lyrasis
Special Services for the Deaf - Bks on deafness & sign lang; High interest/low vocabulary bks; TDD equip
Special Services for the Blind - Closed circuit TV
Open Mon-Thurs 10-7, Fri 10-6, Sat 10-5
Friends of the Library Group
Branches: 3
BURBANK, 377 Stevens Ave, 04103, SAN 376-1096. Tel: 207-774-4229. FAX: 207-871-1721. E-mail: burbank@portland.lib.me.us. *Mgr,* Ellen Gilliam; Staff 1 (Non-MLS 1)
Founded 1940. Circ 214,672
Library Holdings: Bk Vols 11,604; Per Subs 34
Open Tues 12-7, Wed & Fri 10-6, Thurs 10-7, Sat 9-5
Friends of the Library Group
PEAKS ISLAND BRANCH, 129 Island Ave, Peaks Island, 04108, SAN 343-6926. Tel: 207-766-5540. FAX: 207-766-5540. E-mail: peaks@portland.lib.me.us. *Mgr,* Priscilla Webster; E mail: webster@portland.lib.me.us; Staff 1 (Non-MLS 1)
Founded 1978. Circ 36,872
Library Holdings: Bk Vols 22,299; Per Subs 35
Open Tues 2-8, Wed 10-4, Fri 10-2, Sat 8-Noon
Friends of the Library Group
RIVERTON, 1600 Forest Ave, 04103-1399, SAN 343-6985. Tel: 207-797-2915. FAX: 207-756-8864. E-mail: riverton@portland.lib.me.us. *Mgr,* Steven Weigle; E-mail: weigle@portland.lib.me.us; Staff 1 (Non-MLS 1)
Founded 1977. Circ 54,788
Library Holdings: Bk Vols 32,327; Per Subs 20
Open Mon & Wed 1-6, Thurs 1-8, Fri 9-Noon, Sat 10-1
Friends of the Library Group
Bookmobiles: 1

L PRETI FLAHERTY BELIVEAU & PACHIOS*, One City Ctr, 04112. (Mail add: PO Box 9546, 04112). Tel: 207-791-3000. FAX: 207-791-3111. Web Site: www.preti.com. *Law Librn,* Rita P Bouchard; E-mail: rbouchard@preti.com
Library Holdings: Bk Vols 1,500; Per Subs 15
Database Vendor: LexisNexis, Westlaw
Wireless access
Restriction: Staff use only

P SOUTHERN MAINE LIBRARY DISTRICT*, Five Monument Sq, 04101-4072. SAN 306-7238. Tel: 207-871-1766. Web Site: www.maine.gov/msl/libs/districts/councils/smldboard.htm, www.maine.gov/msl/mrls/index.shtml. *Chair,* Jodi Breau; E-mail: breaujo@spsd.org; Staff 2 (MLS 1, Non-MLS 1)
Founded 1974. Pop 62,686; Circ 629,789
Library Holdings: Bk Vols 200; Per Subs 3
Subject Interests: Libr & info sci
Publications: News Notes
Member Libraries: Acton Public Library; Bangor Theological Seminary; Baxter Memorial Library; Bernstein, Shur, Sawyer & Nelson; Berry Memorial Library; Berwick Public Library; Bolsters Mills Village Library; Bonney Memorial Library; Bridgton Hospital; Bridgton Public Library; Brownfield Public Library; Cape Porpoise Library; Casco Public Library; Charlotte E Hobbs Memorial Library; Chebeague Island Library; Cundy's Harbor Library; D A Hurd Library; Davis Memorial Library; Denmark Public Library; Dorothy Fish Coastal Resource Library at Wells Reserve; Dyer Library; Falmouth Memorial Library; Foundation for Blood Research Library; Freeport Community Library; Fryeburg Public Library; Gray Public Library; Greater Portland Landmarks, Inc; Kaplan University; Kennebunk Free Library; Kezar Falls Circulating Library; Libby Memorial Library; Limerick Public Library; Long Island Community Library; Louis B Goodall Memorial Library; Louis T Graves Memorial Public Library; Maine Charitable Mechanic Association Library; Maine College of Art; Maine Department of Corrections; Maine Historical Society; Maine Medical Center Library; McArthur Public Library; Mercy Hospital; Merrill Memorial Library; Mid-Coast Hospital; Naples Public Library; Nathan & Henry B Cleaves Law Library; New England Bible College Library; New Gloucester Public Library; Newfield Village Library & Reading Room; North Bridgton Public Library; North Gorham Public Library; Ocean Park Memorial Library; Ogunquit Memorial Library; Old York Historical Society Library; Parsons Memorial Library; Perkins, Thompson Library; Portland Public Library; Prince Memorial Library; Raymond Village Library; Rice Public Library; Richville Library; Saint Joseph's College; Salmon Falls Library; Sappi Fine Paper North America; Scarborough Public Library; Shaker Library; Shapleigh Community Library; Soldiers Memorial Library; South Berwick Public Library; South Portland Public Library; Southern Maine Community College Library; Southern Maine Medical Center; Spaulding Memorial Library; Springvale Public Library; Steep Falls Public Library; Thomas Memorial Library; University of Maine School of Law; University of New England Libraries; Walker Memorial Library; Warren Memorial Library; Waterboro Public Library; Wells Public Library; West Buxton Public Library; William Fogg Library; Windham Public Library; York County Community College Library; York Public Library

CL UNIVERSITY OF MAINE SCHOOL OF LAW*, Donald L Garbrecht Law Library, 246 Deering Ave, 04102. SAN 306-7254. Tel: 207-780-4829. Circulation Tel: 207-780-4350. Interlibrary Loan Service Tel: 207-780-4818. Reference Tel: 207-780-4351. FAX: 207-780-4913. E-mail: lawlib@usm.maine.edu. Web Site: www.mainclaw.maine.edu/library. *Interim Dir,* Christine I Hepler; Tel: 207-780-4827, E-mail: christine.hepler@maine.edu; *Cat Librn, Ser,* Stephen R Salhany; *Govt Doc Law Librn, Ref Serv,* Maureen P Quinlan; *Ref Law Librn,* Johanna Julie Welch; *Coll Develop,* Suzanne Parent; *Tech Serv,* Lynn Wilcox; Staff 10 (MLS 6, Non-MLS 4)
Founded 1962. Enrl 300; Fac 16; Highest Degree: Doctorate
Library Holdings: Bk Vols 325,000; Per Subs 1,175
Special Collections: US Document Depository
Automation Activity & Vendor Info: (Acquisitions) Innovative Interfaces, Inc; (Cataloging) Innovative Interfaces, Inc; (Circulation) Innovative Interfaces, Inc; (Course Reserve) Innovative Interfaces, Inc; (ILL) Innovative Interfaces, Inc; (Media Booking) Innovative Interfaces, Inc
Database Vendor: EBSCOhost, Gale Cengage Learning, OVID Technologies, OVID Technologies
Publications: Law Library Guide
Mem of Southern Maine Library District
Partic in New England Law Library Consortium, Inc; OCLC Online Computer Library Center, Inc
Friends of the Library Group

C UNIVERSITY OF SOUTHERN MAINE*, University Libraries, 314 Forest Ave, 04104. (Mail add: PO Box 9301, 04104-9301), SAN 306-6487. Tel: 207-780-4270. Interlibrary Loan Service Tel: 207-228-8449. Reference Tel: 207-780-4272. FAX: 207-780-4042. TDD: 207-780-5646. Web Site: library.usm.maine.edu. *Dir, Univ Librn,* David J Nutty; Tel: 207-780-4276, E-mail: dnutty@usm.maine.edu; *Head, Access Serv,* Casandra Fitzherbert; Tel: 207-780-4279, E-mail: casandra@usm.maine.edu; *Head, Cat,* Elizabeth Phipps; Tel: 207-780-4990, E-mail: ephipps@usm.maine.edu; *Head, Coll Mgt Serv,* Lanier Lumbert; Tel: 207-780-4670, E-mail: lumbert@usm.maine.edu; *Head, Spec Coll,* Susie Bock; Tel: 207-780-4269, E-mail: bocks@usm.maine.edu; *Coll Mgt Librn,* Carolyn C Hughes; Tel: 207-780-4671, E-mail: hughes@usm.maine.edu; *Curator, Osher Map Libr,* Yolanda Theunissen; Tel: 207-780-4616, E-mail: curator@usm.maine.edu. Subject Specialists: *Cartography,* Yolanda Theunissen; Staff 24 (MLS 15, Non-MLS 9)
Founded 1878. Enrl 9,500; Fac 345; Highest Degree: Doctorate
Library Holdings: AV Mats 7,349; e-books 373,571; Microforms 24,284; Music Scores 1,637; Bk Vols 385,818; Per Subs 5,470; Videos 2,522
Special Collections: Antique Cartographic Materials; Jean Byers Sampson Center for Diversity; Maine Nursing Association Archives; Osher Map Library & Smith Center for Cartographic Education
Subject Interests: Interdisciplinary

Automation Activity & Vendor Info: (Acquisitions) Innovative Interfaces, Inc; (Cataloging) Innovative Interfaces, Inc; (Circulation) Innovative Interfaces, Inc; (Course Reserve) Innovative Interfaces, Inc; (ILL) Innovative Interfaces, Inc; (Media Booking) Innovative Interfaces, Inc; (OPAC) Innovative Interfaces, Inc; (Serials) Innovative Interfaces, Inc
Wireless access
Function: Doc delivery serv, For res purposes, Govt ref serv, Handicapped accessible, ILL available, Photocopying/Printing, Ref serv available
Publications: Reference LibGuides
Partic in Maine InfoNet; OCLC Online Computer Library Center, Inc
Open Mon-Thurs 8am-11pm, Fri 8-6, Sat 10-6, Sun 10-10

Departmental Libraries:

LEWISTON-AUBURN COLLEGE LIBRARY, 51 Westminster St, Lewiston, 04240. (Mail add: PO Box 1937, Lewiston, 04241-1937), SAN 377-9432. Tel: 207-753-6540. Interlibrary Loan Service Tel: 207-753-6526. FAX: 207-753-6543. *Head of Libr,* Evelyn Greenlaw; Tel: 207-753-6541, E-mail: evelyng@usm.maine.edu; *Circ, ILL,* Dale Kuczinski; E-mail: dalek@usm.maine.edu; *Ref Serv,* Maureen Perry; E-mail: mperry@usm.maine.edu; Staff 2 (MLS 2)
Founded 1988. Enrl 1,600; Fac 45; Highest Degree: Master
Library Holdings: Bk Titles 18,000; Per Subs 210
Special Collections: Franco-American Heritage Coll
Subject Interests: Behav sci, Franco-Am hist, Interdisciplinary, Leadership mgt, Occupational therapy
Automation Activity & Vendor Info: (Circulation) Innovative Interfaces, Inc; (Course Reserve) Innovative Interfaces, Inc; (ILL) Innovative Interfaces, Inc; (OPAC) Innovative Interfaces, Inc; (Serials) Innovative Interfaces, Inc
Database Vendor: EBSCOhost, OCLC FirstSearch, ProQuest
Partic in ARIEL; Maine Health Sci Librs & Info Consortium; OCLC Online Computer Library Center, Inc
Open Mon-Fri 8-8

L VERRILL DANA LIBRARY*, One Portland Sq, 04112. (Mail add: PO Box 586, 04112-0586), SAN 328-4417. Tel: 207-774-4000, Ext 4856. FAX: 207-774-7499. Web Site: www.verrilldana.com. *Librn,* Sally Caras; Tel: 207-253-4964; *Librn,* Anne M Reiman; Tel: 207-253-4856, E-mail: areiman@verrilldana.com; Staff 1 (Non-MLS 1)
Library Holdings: Bk Titles 13,000; Per Subs 100
Wireless access
Partic in Cas; LexisNexis; LOIS; Westlaw
Friends of the Library Group

S VICTORIA MANSION LIBRARY*, 109 Danforth St, 04101. SAN 320-8605. Tel: 207-772-4841. FAX: 207-772-6290. Web Site: www.victoriamansion.org. *Dir,* Robert Wolterstorff; Tel: 207-772-4841, Ext 11
Founded 1943
Library Holdings: Bk Titles 453
Subject Interests: Art & archit, Art (19th Century), Decorative art
Restriction: Open by appt only

PRESQUE ISLE

J NORTHERN MAINE COMMUNITY COLLEGE LIBRARY*, 33 Edgemont Dr, 04769-2016. SAN 306-7289. Tel: 207-768-2718. FAX: 207-768-2823. *Asst Dean,* Gail Roy; Tel: 207-768-2734, E-mail: groy@nmcc.edu; *Librn II,* Kim Ferguson; Tel: 207-768-2735, E-mail: kferguson@nmcc.edu; Staff 3 (MLS 1, Non-MLS 2)
Founded 1968. Fac 60; Highest Degree: Associate
Library Holdings: Bk Titles 14,000; Per Subs 250
Subject Interests: Bus, Computer, Med
Automation Activity & Vendor Info: (Acquisitions) Innovative Interfaces, Inc; (Cataloging) Innovative Interfaces, Inc; (Circulation) Innovative Interfaces, Inc; (Course Reserve) Innovative Interfaces, Inc; (ILL) Innovative Interfaces, Inc; (Media Booking) Innovative Interfaces, Inc; (OPAC) Innovative Interfaces, Inc; (Serials) Innovative Interfaces, Inc
Database Vendor: EBSCOhost
Publications: Acquisition List
Mem of Northeastern Maine Library District
Partic in Docline; Lyrasis; OCLC Online Computer Library Center, Inc
Open Mon-Thurs (Winter) 7:30am-9:30pm, Fri 7:30-4:30, Sat 12-5, Sun 3-7; Mon-Fri (Summer) 7:30-4:30

P MARK & EMILY TURNER MEMORIAL LIBRARY*, 39 Second St, 04769. SAN 306-7297. Tel: 207-764-2571. FAX: 207-768-5756. Web Site: www.presqueislelibrary.org. *Librn,* Sonja Morgan; *Ch Serv,* Diana Leighton. Subject Specialists: *Youth prog,* Diana Leighton; Staff 10 (MLS 1, Non-MLS 9)
Founded 1908. Pop 10,000; Circ 97,000
Jan 2010-Dec 2010. Mats Exp $20,000
Library Holdings: Bk Vols 65,000; Per Subs 98; Talking Bks 1,400
Special Collections: Local History Coll; Local Newspapers, microfilm, archives. Oral History
Automation Activity & Vendor Info: (Cataloging) Follett Software; (Circulation) Follett Software; (OPAC) Follett Software
Database Vendor: EBSCOhost
Wireless access
Function: ILL available
Special Services for the Blind - Closed circuit TV magnifier
Open Mon, Tues & Thurs 9-7, Wed & Fri 9-5:30, Sat 9-2, Sun 10-2

C UNIVERSITY OF MAINE AT PRESQUE ISLE LIBRARY*, 181 Main St, 04769-2888. SAN 306-7300. Tel: 207-768-9599. Interlibrary Loan Service Tel: 207-768-9595. Reference Tel: 207-768-9602. FAX: 207-768-9644. Web Site: www.umpi.maine.edu/library. *Dir,* Joanne Wallingford; *Cat, Circ, ILL,* Nancy Fletcher; *Doc, Reader Serv,* Virginia Fischer; Staff 4.75 (MLS 3, Non-MLS 1.75)
Founded 1903. Enrl 1,344; Fac 70; Highest Degree: Bachelor
Library Holdings: Bk Titles 70,336; Bk Vols 162,377; Per Subs 300
Special Collections: Aroostook County History Coll; Maine Coll; Rare bks. State Document Depository; US Document Depository
Subject Interests: Art, Educ
Automation Activity & Vendor Info: (Acquisitions) Innovative Interfaces, Inc; (Cataloging) Innovative Interfaces, Inc; (Circulation) Innovative Interfaces, Inc; (Course Reserve) Innovative Interfaces, Inc; (ILL) OCLC; (OPAC) Innovative Interfaces, Inc; (Serials) Innovative Interfaces, Inc
Wireless access
Publications: Faculty Staff Guide; Library Resources & Services Guide
Mem of Northeastern Maine Library District
Partic in Lyrasis; OCLC Online Computer Library Center, Inc
Open Mon-Thurs (Winter) 8am-10pm, Fri 8-4:30, Sat 12-4:30, Sun 2-10; Mon-Fri (Summer) 8-4:30

PRINCETON

P PRINCETON PUBLIC LIBRARY*, 40 Main St, 04668. (Mail add: PO Box 408, 04668-0408). Tel: 207-796-5333. E-mail: princetonlibrary@hotmail.com. *Librn,* Elizabeth Mitchell; Staff 1 (Non-MLS 1)
Circ 2,976
Library Holdings: Bk Vols 11,049; Per Subs 16
Wireless access
Mem of Northeastern Maine Library District
Open Mon & Tues 10-2, Wed-Fri 12-4
Friends of the Library Group

PROSPECT HARBOR

P DORCAS LIBRARY*, 28 Main St, 04669. (Mail add: PO Box 167, 04669-0167), SAN 376-3501. Tel: 207-963-4027, 207-963-4147. E-mail: dorcas@dorcas.lib.me.us, farmingdowneast@roadrunner.com. Web Site: www.dorcas.lib.me.us. *Chmn of Libr Board,* Alison Johnson; *Tech Consult,* Pauline V Angione; Tel: 207-963-2023, Fax: 800-851-1374, E-mail: pangione@gmail.com; Staff 1 (MLS 1)
Pop 1,600
Library Holdings: Audiobooks 612; Bks-By-Mail 112; DVDs 950; Electronic Media & Resources 1,988; Bk Titles 10,364; Bk Vols 15,000; Per Subs 28
Automation Activity & Vendor Info: (Acquisitions) LibraryWorld, Inc
Database Vendor: EBSCOhost, LibraryWorld, Inc
Wireless access
Mem of Northeastern Maine Library District
Open Mon 4-8, Wed 1:30-4 & 6-8, Sat 1:30-4
Friends of the Library Group

RANGELEY

P RANGELEY PUBLIC LIBRARY*, Seven Lake St, 04970. (Mail add: PO Box 1150, 04970-1150), SAN 306-7319. Tel: 207-864-5529. FAX: 207-864-2523. E-mail: info@rangeleylibrary.com. Web Site: www.rangeleyme.com/library. *Libr Dir,* Janet Wilson; *Asst Dir,* Cheryl Curris
Founded 1909. Pop 6,400; Circ 21,407
Library Holdings: Bk Vols 21,830; Per Subs 35
Special Collections: Wilhelm Reich Coll
Subject Interests: Lit
Automation Activity & Vendor Info: (Cataloging) Follett Software; (Circulation) Follett Software; (OPAC) Follett Software
Wireless access
Open Tues 10-7, Wed-Fri 10-4:30, Sat 10-2
Friends of the Library Group

RAYMOND

P RAYMOND VILLAGE LIBRARY*, Three Meadow Rd, 04071-6461. (Mail add: PO Box 297, 04071-0297), SAN 306-7327. Tel: 207-655-4283. E-mail: rlibrar1@maine.rr.com. Web Site: www.raymondvillagelibrary.org. *Dir,* Barbara Thorpe; Staff 1 (Non-MLS 1)
Founded 1914. Pop 4,299; Circ 24,866

Library Holdings: Bk Vols 18,167; Per Subs 20; Talking Bks 608; Videos 1,200
Special Collections: Maine Coll
Wireless access
Mem of Southern Maine Library District
Open Mon, Wed & Sun 10-7

READFIELD

P READFIELD COMMUNITY LIBRARY*, 1151 Main St, 04355-3512. (Mail add: PO Box 246, 04355-0246), SAN 374-6267. Tel: 207-685-4089. E-mail: readfieldlibrarian@readfield.lib.me.us. *Librn,* Nancy O'Toole; Staff 1 (MLS 1)
Pop 2,033; Circ 10,898
Library Holdings: Bk Vols 10,000; Per Subs 13
Database Vendor: EBSCOhost
Wireless access
Open Mon 6pm-8pm, Wed 2-8, Thurs 10-Noon, Sat 10-4

RICHMOND

P ISAAC F UMBERHINE LIBRARY*, 164 Main St, Ste 3, 04357. SAN 306-7343. Tel: 207-737-2770. Web Site: www.umberhine.lib.me.us/index.html. *Librn,* Donna McCluskey; Staff 1 (Non-MLS 1)
Pop 2,168; Circ 6,968
Library Holdings: AV Mats 600; Bk Vols 23,000; Per Subs 16; Talking Bks 600
Database Vendor: EBSCOhost
Function: Homebound delivery serv, Prog for children & young adult, Referrals accepted
Open Mon & Fri 2-6, Tues 1-5, Wed 9-12 & 6-8, Thurs 4-8, Sat 9-Noon

ROCKLAND

P ROCKLAND PUBLIC LIBRARY*, 80 Union St, 04841. SAN 306-7378. Tel: 207-594-0310. FAX: 207-594-0333. Web Site: www.rocklandlibrary.org. *Dir,* Amy Levine; E-mail: alevine@ci.rockland.me.us; *Dep Dir,* Linda Barnes; E-mail: lfairfield@ci.rockland.me.us; *Ch,* Jean Young; E-mail: jyoung@ci.rockland.me.us; *Circ Librn,* Patricia King; Staff 7 (MLS 1, Non-MLS 6)
Founded 1892. Pop 12,500; Circ 180,000
Library Holdings: AV Mats 8,410; Bk Vols 51,868, Per Subs 79; Videos 2,300
Special Collections: Children's Coll; Literacy Volunteers Coll; Maine Coll
Automation Activity & Vendor Info: (Cataloging) Innovative Interfaces, Inc; (Circulation) Innovative Interfaces, Inc; (OPAC) Innovative Interfaces, Inc
Database Vendor: EBSCOhost
Wireless access
Mem of Northeastern Maine Library District
Open Mon, Tues & Thurs 9-8, Wed, Fri & Sat 9-5
Friends of the Library Group

ROCKPORT

M PEN BAY MEDICAL CENTER*, Niles Perkins Health Science Library, Six Glen Cove Dr, 04856. SAN 377-9459. Tel: 207-596-8456. FAX: 207-593-5281. Web Site: www.pbmc.org/library. *Librn,* Patricia Kahn; E-mail: pkahn@penbayhealthcare.org; Staff 1 (MLS 1)
Library Holdings: Bk Titles 2,000; Per Subs 224
Wireless access
Partic in Basic Health Sciences Library Network; Maine Health Sci Librs & Info Consortium; North Atlantic Health Sciences Libraries, Inc
Open Mon-Fri 8:30-5

P ROCKPORT PUBLIC LIBRARY*, One Limerock St, 04856-6141. (Mail add: PO Box 8, 04856-0008), SAN 306-7386. Tel: 207-236-3642. E-mail: rpl@rockport.lib.me.us. Web Site: www.rockport.lib.me.us. *Interim Dir,* Ann Filley; *Tech Serv,* Jane G Babbitt; *Youth Serv,* Kim Slocomb; Staff 3 (Non-MLS 3)
Founded 1914. Pop 2,854; Circ 63,000
Library Holdings: AV Mats 2,500; Bk Vols 30,000; Per Subs 52
Subject Interests: Maritime hist
Automation Activity & Vendor Info: (Cataloging) Innovative Interfaces, Inc; (Circulation) Innovative Interfaces, Inc; (OPAC) Innovative Interfaces, Inc
Wireless access
Function: ILL available, Photocopying/Printing, Ref serv available
Mem of Northeastern Maine Library District
Open Mon, Tues & Thurs-Sat 9-5:30, Wed 11-8
Friends of the Library Group

RUMFORD

P RUMFORD PUBLIC LIBRARY*, 56 Rumford Ave, 04276-1919. SAN 306-7394. Tel: 207-364-3661. FAX: 207-364-7296. Web Site: www.rumford.lib.me.us. *Dir,* Luke E Sorensen; E-mail: lsorensen@rumford.lib.me.us; *Ch,* Ginny Todd; *Circ Librn,* Susan Brooke; *Ref Librn,* Claudia Reynolds; E-mail: creynolds@rumford.lib.me.us; Staff 8 (MLS 1, Non-MLS 7)
Founded 1903. Pop 9,439; Circ 62,000
Library Holdings: AV Mats 403; Large Print Bks 700; Bk Vols 38,000; Per Subs 68; Talking Bks 300
Special Collections: Maine History & Fiction
Automation Activity & Vendor Info: (Cataloging) Innovative Interfaces, Inc; (Circulation) Innovative Interfaces, Inc; (OPAC) Innovative Interfaces, Inc
Database Vendor: EBSCOhost
Wireless access
Open Mon & Sat 9-2, Tues, Wed & Fri 9-5, Thurs 9-8
Friends of the Library Group

SACO

P DYER LIBRARY*, 371 Main St, 04072. SAN 306-7408. Tel: 207-283-3861. FAX: 207-283-0754. Web Site: www.dyerlibrarysacomuseum.org. *Exec Dir,* Leslie L Rounds; E-mail: lrounds@dyer.lib.me.us; *Automation/Pub Serv Librn,* Stephanie Hicks; E-mail: srichard@dyer.lib.me.us; *Children's Coordr,* Laura Vickery; *Circ Coordr,* Cheryl Spaulding; Staff 1 (Non-MLS 1)
Founded 1881. Pop 20,700; Circ 117,896
Library Holdings: Bk Titles 60,000; Per Subs 120
Special Collections: Bureau of the Census; History (Maine Coll), bks, newspapers & photos (18th & 19th centuries), pamphlets, doc, town hist rec
Automation Activity & Vendor Info: (Cataloging) Follett Software; (Circulation) Follett Software; (OPAC) Follett Software
Database Vendor: EBSCOhost, Gale Cengage Learning
Wireless access
Function: Archival coll, Art exhibits, Copy machines, Electronic databases & coll, Family literacy, Fax serv, Home delivery & serv to Sr ctr & nursing homes, ILL available, Music CDs, Newsp ref libr, Online searches, Orientations, Preschool outreach, Prog for adults, Prog for children & young adult, Summer reading prog, Tax forms, Telephone ref, VHS videos, Workshops
Publications: Newsletter
Mem of Southern Maine Library District
Open Mon, Wed & Fri 9:30-5, Tues & Thurs 9:30-8, Sat 9:30-12:30

M SWEETSER CHILDREN'S SERVICES*, Professional Library, 50 Moody St, 04072-0892. SAN 378-0864. Tel: 207-294-4945. Toll Free Tel: 800-434-3000. FAX: 207-294-4940. *Librn,* Jan Wertheim; E-mail: jwertheim@sweetser.org
Library Holdings: Bk Titles 2,500; Per Subs 25
Database Vendor: EBSCOhost
Partic in Health Science Library Information Consortium
Open Mon-Fri 8-3:30

SANFORD

P LOUIS B GOODALL MEMORIAL LIBRARY*, 952 Main St, 04073. SAN 343-7078. Tel: 207-324-4714. FAX: 207-324-5982. E-mail: info@lbgoodall.org. Web Site: www.lbgoodall.org. *Dir,* Jackie McDougal; *Asst Dir,* Jean Collins; *Head, Ch,* Deidre Walsh; *Ref Librn,* Jason Fenimore; Staff 3 (MLS 2, Non-MLS 1)
Founded 1898. Pop 18,040; Circ 125,067
Library Holdings: Bk Vols 69,984; Per Subs 127
Special Collections: US Document Depository
Automation Activity & Vendor Info: (Cataloging) Follett Software; (Circulation) Follett Software
Database Vendor: EBSCOhost
Wireless access
Mem of Southern Maine Library District
Open Mon-Thurs 10-8, Fri 10-5, Sat 10-4

SANGERVILLE

P SANGERVILLE PUBLIC LIBRARY*, One Town Hall Ave, 04479. (Mail add: PO Box 246, 04479-0246), SAN 376-7582. Tel: 207-876-3491. Web Site: www.sangerville.lib.me.us. *Librn,* Linda Hall; E-mail: ljhall@msln.net; *Asst Librn,* Thelma Dufault
Founded 1923. Pop 700; Circ 3,760
Library Holdings: Bk Vols 11,200; Per Subs 10
Database Vendor: EBSCOhost
Wireless access
Mem of Northeastern Maine Library District
Partic in Scoop Coop
Open Mon-Thurs 2-7, Fri 11-4

SARGENTVILLE

P SARGENTVILLE LIBRARY ASSOCIATION*, 653 Reach Rd, 04673. (Mail add: PO Box 233, Sedgwick, 04676). Tel: 207-359-8086. *Librn, Libr Asn Pres,* Cathy Marshall; Tel: 207-348-6404
Founded 1905. Pop 1,300
Jan 2009-Dec 2009 Income $2,090, City $500, Locally Generated Income $590, Other $1,000. Mats Exp $2,050, Books $30
Library Holdings: Bk Vols 3,000
Subject Interests: Sargentville hist & genealogy
Function: Archival coll, Ref & res, Scanner
Open Sat (June-Sept) 10-Noon, Tues (July-Aug) 6-8

SCARBOROUGH

M FOUNDATION FOR BLOOD RESEARCH LIBRARY*, Eight Science Park Rd, 04070. (Mail add: PO Box 190, 04070-0190), SAN 324-5993. Tel: 207-883-4131. FAX: 207-885-0807. E-mail: librarian@fbr.org. Web Site: www.fbr.org/research/library.html. *Librn,* Nancy Cohen-Spiegel; Staff 0.5 (MLS 0.5)
Founded 1978
Library Holdings: Bk Vols 500; Per Subs 100
Subject Interests: Genetics, Immunology, Prenatal diagnosis
Mem of Southern Maine Library District
Partic in Health Sci Libr & Info Coop
Open Mon, Wed & Thurs 10-3

P SCARBOROUGH PUBLIC LIBRARY, 48 Gorham Rd, 04074. SAN 306-7432. Tel: 207-883-4723. FAX: 207-883-9728. E-mail: askspl@scarboroughlibrary.org. Web Site: www.scarboroughlibrary.org. *Dir,* Nancy E Crowell; Tel: 207-396-6266, E-mail: ncrowell@scarboroughlibrary.org; *Ref Librn,* Catherine Morrison; Tel: 207-396-6276, E-mail: cmorrison@scarboroughlibrary.org; *Syst Librn,* Thomas B Corbett; Tel: 207-396-6271, E-mail: tcorbett@scarboroughlibrary.org; *Youth Serv Librn,* Louise Capizzo; Tel: 207-396-6278, E-mail: lcapizzo@scarboroughlibrary.org; *Circ Mgr,* Michael Windsor; Tel: 207-396-6268, E-mail: mwindsor@scarboroughlibrary.org; *Tech Serv Mgr,* Denise M Menard; Tel: 207-396-6274, E-mail: dmenard@scarboroughlibrary.org; Staff 20 (MLS 7, Non-MLS 13)
Founded 1899. Pop 19,500; Circ 215,770
Automation Activity & Vendor Info: (Circulation) Innovative Interfaces, Inc - Millenium; (ILL) Innovative Interfaces, Inc - Millenium; (OPAC) Innovative Interfaces, Inc - Millenium
Database Vendor: EBSCOhost, ProQuest
Wireless access
Function: 24/7 Electronic res, 24/7 Online cat, Adult bk club, Adult literacy prog, Audio & video playback equip for onsite use, Audiobks via web, AV serv, Bks on CD, Children's prog, Computer training, Computers for patron use, Copy machines, Electronic databases & coll, eReaders, Free DVD rentals, Handicapped accessible, Home delivery & serv to Sr ctr & nursing homes, Homebound delivery serv, ILL available, Magazines, Magnifiers for reading, Monthly prog for perceptually impaired adults, Movies, Mus passes, Music CDs, Online cat, Online ref, Outreach serv, OverDrive digital audio bks, Preschool outreach, Preschool reading prog, Printer for laptops & handheld devices, Prog for adults, Prog for children & young adult, Pub access computers, Ref serv available, Ref serv in person, Serves mentally handicapped consumers, Spoken cassettes & CDs, Story hour, Study rm, Summer reading prog, Tax forms, Teen prog, VHS videos, Web-catalog, Wheelchair accessible
Publications: Footnotes (Newsletter)
Mem of Southern Maine Library District
Open Mon, Fri & Sat 10-5, Tues-Thurs 10-8, Sun 1-5
Restriction: Non-resident fee
Friends of the Library Group

SEARSMONT

P SEARSMONT TOWN LIBRARY*, 37 Main St S, 04973. (Mail add: PO Box 105, 04973-0105), SAN 374-7069. Tel: 207-342-5549. FAX: 207-342-3495. E-mail: stlme@searsmont.lib.me.us. *Libr Dir,* Tom Heely; Staff 11 (MLS 1, Non-MLS 10)
Founded 1990. Pop 1,250; Circ 4,000
Library Holdings: AV Mats 292; Bk Titles 8,860; Per Subs 30
Special Collections: Oral History
Database Vendor: EBSCOhost
Special Services for the Deaf - High interest/low vocabulary bks
Open Tues 9-7, Thurs 4-8, Fri 1-5, Sat 10-2
Friends of the Library Group

SEARSPORT

S PENOBSCOT MARINE MUSEUM, Stephen Phillips Memorial Library, Nine Church St, 04974. (Mail add: PO Box 498, 04974-0498), SAN 306-7459. Tel: 207-548-2529, Ext 212. FAX: 207-548-2520. E-mail: libraryresearcher@pmm-maine.org. Web Site: www.penobscotmarinemuseum.org, www.pmm-maine.org. *Coll Mgr,* Cipperly Good; E-mail: cgood@pmm-maine.org; Staff 1 (MLS 1)
Founded 1936
Library Holdings: Bk Titles 12,000; Per Subs 10
Special Collections: Maritime (Logbooks, Journals, Maritime Navigation & Law, Ship Registers)
Subject Interests: Genealogy, Local hist, Maritime hist
Function: Res libr
Partic in Maine Libr Asn
Open Tues-Fri 9am-1pm
Restriction: Non-circulating to the pub

SEBAGO

P SPAULDING MEMORIAL LIBRARY, 282 Sebago Rd, 04029-3732. (Mail add: PO Box 300, 04029-0300), SAN 306-7467. Tel: 207-787-2321. E-mail: directors@spaulding.lib.me.us. Web Site: www.spaulding.lib.me.us. *Dir,* Susan Newton; Staff 2 (Non-MLS 2)
Founded 1925. Pop 1,700; Circ 6,000
Library Holdings: Bk Titles 8,000
Subject Interests: Maine
Automation Activity & Vendor Info: (Cataloging) LibLime Koha; (Circulation) LibLime Koha
Wireless access
Function: 24/7 Online cat, Adult bk club, Bks on CD, Computer training, Computers for patron use, Copy machines, Fax serv, Free DVD rentals, Handicapped accessible, ILL available, Magazines, Mail & tel request accepted, Online cat, OverDrive digital audio bks, Prog for adults, Prog for children & young adult, Pub access computers, Scanner, Summer reading prog, Tax forms, VHS videos, Wheelchair accessible
Mem of Southern Maine Library District
Open Mon & Wed 8:30-7, Sat 9-1, Sun 2-4

SEDGWICK

P SEDGWICK LIBRARY ASSOCIATION*, 45 Main St, 04676. (Mail add: 284 Reach Rd, 04676). Tel: 207-359-2177. *Librn,* Mary Ellen Ashman
Pop 1,300
Library Holdings: AV Mats 100; Bk Vols 4,000; Talking Bks 100; Videos 40
Special Collections: Genealogy & Mystery (Maine Coll)
Open Thurs (Winter) 3-5, Sat 10-Noon; Wed (Summer) 5-7, Thurs 3-5, Sat 10-Noon

SHAPLEIGH

P SHAPLEIGH COMMUNITY LIBRARY*, Shapleigh Corner Rd, 04076. (Mail add: PO Box 97, 04076-0097). Tel: 207-636-3630. *Dir,* Gene Smith
Founded 1980. Pop 2,400; Circ 5,000
Jan 2009-Dec 2009 Income $32,000. Mats Exp $9,000. Sal $12,350
Library Holdings: AV Mats 400; Bks on Deafness & Sign Lang 4; CDs 150; DVDs 260; Large Print Bks 100; Bk Vols 18,000; Per Subs 19; Videos 30
Special Collections: Genealogy Coll; Local History Coll
Database Vendor: EBSCOhost
Mem of Southern Maine Library District
Open Tues (Winter) 1-4, Thurs & Sat 10-2; Tues (Summer) 3-8, Thurs 10-2 & 6-8, Sat 9-2

SHERMAN

P SHERMAN PUBLIC LIBRARY*, Nine Church St, 04776. (Mail add: 36 School St, Ste 1, 04776-3428), SAN 306-7475. Tel: 207-365-4882. Interlibrary Loan Service Tel: 207-947-8336. E-mail: shermanpl276@yahoo.com. *Librn,* Denise Tapley; Staff 1 (Non-MLS 1)
Pop 1,021; Circ 2,549
Library Holdings: Bk Vols 7,280
Special Collections: Local History Coll. Oral History
Database Vendor: EBSCOhost
Wireless access
Mem of Northeastern Maine Library District
Open Mon-Fri 1:30-3:30
Friends of the Library Group

SKOWHEGAN

M REDINGTON-FAIRVIEW GENERAL HOSPITAL*, Health Sciences Library, 46 Fairview Ave, 04976. (Mail add: PO Box 468, 04976-0468), SAN 377-984X. Tel: 207-474-5121, Ext 419. FAX: 207-858-2314. *Librn,* Rebecca Jordan; E-mail: rjordan@rfgh.net
Library Holdings: Bk Titles 200; Per Subs 160
Partic in Maine Health Sci Librs & Info Consortium
Open Mon, Wed & Fri 7:30-4

P SKOWHEGAN PUBLIC LIBRARY*, Nine Elm St, 04976. SAN 306-7483. Tel: 207-474-9072. E-mail: skowlib@skowhegan.lib.me.us. Web Site: www.skowhegan.lib.me.us. *Dir,* Dale Jandreau; Staff 3 (Non-MLS 3)
Founded 1889. Pop 10,121; Circ 51,700
Library Holdings: AV Mats 101; Bk Vols 45,000; Per Subs 52
Database Vendor: EBSCOhost
Wireless access
Function: Art exhibits, Audiobks via web, Bks on cassette, Bks on CD, Children's prog, Computer training, Computers for patron use, Copy machines, e-mail & chat, Electronic databases & coll, Exhibits, Fax serv, Free DVD rentals, Genealogy discussion group, Holiday prog, Homebound delivery serv, ILL available, Jazz prog, Mail & tel request accepted, Microfiche/film & reading machines, Online cat, Online ref, Online searches, OverDrive digital audio bks, Photocopying/Printing, Preschool outreach, Prog for adults, Prog for children & young adult, Pub access computers, Ref & res, Scanner, Story hour, Summer reading prog, Tax forms, Telephone ref, VHS videos, Workshops
Open Mon-Fri 10-6, Sat (Winter) 10-2
Restriction: Authorized patrons, Circ to mem only, Non-resident fee
Friends of the Library Group

C UNIVERSITY OF MAINE, Margaret Chase Smith Library, 56 Norridgewock Ave, 04976. Tel: 207-474-7133. FAX: 207-474-8878. E-mail: mcsl@mcslibrary.org. Web Site: www.mcslibrary.org. *Dir,* Dr David L Richards, PhD; E-mail: davidr@mcslibrary.org; *Coll Spec,* Angela N Stockwell; E-mail: angies@mcslibrary.org; Staff 5 (MLS 4, Non-MLS 1)
Founded 1982
Library Holdings: AV Mats 473; Bk Vols 3,300; Videos 342
Special Collections: Congressional Library of Senator Margaret Chase Smith's Career from 1940 to 1973; Scrapbooks, early 1900s to date; Statements & Speeches; Syndicated Column, Washington & You, 1941-1954
Subject Interests: Polit sci, Political hist
Wireless access
Function: Res libr
Publications: Friends of the Library (Newsletter)
Open Mon-Fri 10-4
Restriction: Non-circulating, Open to qualified scholars, Open to researchers by request, Open to students

SOLON

P COOLIDGE LIBRARY*, 17 S Main St, 04979. (Mail add: PO Box 238, 04979-0238), SAN 306-7491. Tel: 207-643-2562. *Librn,* Sally Foster; Staff 1 (Non-MLS 1)
Pop 966; Circ 1,524
Library Holdings: Bk Vols 5,000; Per Subs 10
Database Vendor: EBSCOhost
Wireless access
Open Tues 1-6:30, Sat 11-2

SOUTH BERWICK

P SOUTH BERWICK PUBLIC LIBRARY, 27 Young St, 03908. SAN 306-7505. Tel: 207-384-3308. Web Site: www.southberwicklibrary.org. *Librn,* Position Currently Open
Founded 1971. Pop 7,000; Circ 41,436
Library Holdings: Bk Vols 32,000; Per Subs 9
Automation Activity & Vendor Info: (Cataloging) Follett Software; (Circulation) Follett Software
Database Vendor: EBSCOhost
Wireless access
Function: 24/7 Electronic res, 24/7 Online cat, Activity rm, Adult bk club, Audio & video playback equip for onsite use, Audiobks via web, Bks on CD, Children's prog, Computers for patron use, Copy machines, E-Reserves, Electronic databases & coll, eReaders, Free DVD rentals, Handicapped accessible, Magazines, Movies, Mus passes, OverDrive digital audio bks, Photocopying/Printing, Preschool reading prog, Pub access computers, Story hour, Study rm, Summer reading prog, Web-catalog, Wheelchair accessible
Mem of Southern Maine Library District
Open Tues & Thurs 10-5, Wed 2-9, Fri 1-5, Sat 9-12:45
Friends of the Library Group

SOUTH BRISTOL

P RUTHERFORD LIBRARY*, 2000 State Rte 129, 04568. (Mail add: PO Box 145, 04568-0145). Tel: 207-644-1882. *Dir,* Ellen Shew; E-mail: ellenshew@gmail.com
Founded 1903. Pop 900; Circ 5,719
Jan 2005-Dec 2005 Income $55,837, City $4,000, Locally Generated Income $51,837. Mats Exp $4,485, Books $3,192, AV Mat $1,293. Sal $5,000
Library Holdings: AV Mats 786; DVDs 20; Large Print Bks 75; Bk Vols 14,000; Per Subs 17; Talking Bks 419
Special Collections: Local History Coll
Wireless access
Open Tues-Sat 2-5

SOUTH CHINA

P SOUTH CHINA PUBLIC LIBRARY*, 247 Village St, 04358. (Mail add: PO Box 417, 04358-0417), SAN 376-3765. Tel: 207-445-3094. E-mail: southchinalibrary@gmail.com. Web Site: www.southchina.lib.me.us *Librn,* Cheryl Baker; E-mail: cbaker@fairpoint.net
Library Holdings: Bk Vols 11,100; Per Subs 14
Special Collections: Quaker (Rufus Jones Coll)
Database Vendor: EBSCOhost
Open Wed 10-12 & 3-7, Sat 10-2

SOUTH PARIS

P HAMLIN MEMORIAL LIBRARY-PARIS HILL, 16 Hannibal Hamlin Dr, 04281. (Mail add: PO Box 43, Paris, 04271-0043), SAN 306-7092. Tel: 207-743-2980. E-mail: hamlinstaff@hamlin.lib.me.us. Web Site: www.hamlin.lib.me.us. *Librn,* Jennifer Lewis; Staff 1 (Non-MLS 1)
Founded 1902. Pop 300; Circ 1,700
Library Holdings: Bk Titles 5,900; Bk Vols 6,000; Per Subs 2
Special Collections: Hamlin Family Records; Town of Paris History
Database Vendor: EBSCOhost
Wireless access
Open Tues 11-5, Thurs 1-6, Sat 10-2

P PARIS PUBLIC LIBRARY*, 37 Market Sq, 04281. SAN 306-7513. Tel: 207-743-6994. E-mail: paris.public.library@msln.net. Web Site: www.paris.lib.me.us. *Dir,* Michael F Dignan; E-mail: mdignan@paris.lib.me.us; Staff 6 (MLS 1, Non-MLS 5)
Founded 1926. Pop 5,015; Circ 110,000
Jul 2012-Jun 2013 Income $168,000. Mats Exp $31,000, Books $27,000, AV Mat $3,000, Electronic Ref Mat (Incl. Access Fees) $1,000. Sal $89,000 (Prof $32,500)
Library Holdings: Audiobooks 1,397; DVDs 3,692; Large Print Bks 726; Bk Vols 29,172; Per Subs 32; Videos 3,088
Special Collections: Advertiser-Democrat Newspaper Coll; Town Histories; Youth's Companion Magazine Coll
Automation Activity & Vendor Info: (Cataloging) Follett Software; (Circulation) Follett Software; (OPAC) Follett Software
Database Vendor: EBSCOhost
Wireless access
Function: Adult bk club, Bks on CD, Computers for patron use, Free DVD rentals, Holiday prog, Homebound delivery serv, ILL available, Online cat, Story hour, Summer reading prog, Tax forms
Open Mon, Wed & Fri 9-6, Tues & Thurs 9-8, Sat 9-3
Friends of the Library Group

SOUTH PORTLAND

C KAPLAN UNIVERSITY*, South Portland Campus, 265 Western Ave, 04106. SAN 306-7157. Tel: 207-221-8745. FAX: 207-774-1715. *Dir,* Martha T Ott; Tel: 207-774-6126, Ext 8745, E-mail: mott@kaplan.edu; Staff 4 (MLS 4)
Founded 1967. Enrl 1,000; Fac 33; Highest Degree: Associate
Library Holdings: Bk Titles 12,000; Per Subs 125; Talking Bks 900; Videos 1,000
Subject Interests: Acctg, Bus, Computer sci, Criminal justice, Early childhood, Legal, Med asst, Off admin, Travel & tourism
Automation Activity & Vendor Info: (Cataloging) Innovative Interfaces, Inc; (Circulation) Innovative Interfaces, Inc; (ILL) Innovative Interfaces, Inc; (OPAC) Innovative Interfaces, Inc; (Serials) Innovative Interfaces, Inc
Mem of Southern Maine Library District
Open Mon-Thurs 7:30am-9:30pm, Fri 8-4

S MAINE DEPARTMENT OF CORRECTIONS*, Long Creek Youth Development Center Library, 675 Westbrook St, 04106. SAN 321-5075. Tel: 207-822-2679. FAX: 207-822-2775. *Librn,* Lisa Wojcik
Library Holdings: Bk Titles 8,000; Per Subs 23
Automation Activity & Vendor Info: (Acquisitions) Follett Software; (Cataloging) Follett Software; (Circulation) Follett Software; (Course Reserve) Follett Software; (ILL) Follett Software; (Media Booking) Follett Software; (OPAC) Follett Software; (Serials) Follett Software
Database Vendor: EBSCOhost
Mem of Southern Maine Library District
Restriction: Internal circ only

CR NEW ENGLAND BIBLE COLLEGE LIBRARY*, 879 Sawyer St, 04116. (Mail add: PO Box 2886, 04116-2886). Tel: 207-799-5979. Toll Free Tel: 800-286-1859. FAX: 207-799-6586. Web Site: www.nebc.edu. *Fac Supvr,* David Lambertson
Founded 1979
Library Holdings: Bk Titles 13,058; Bk Vols 15,489; Per Subs 16
Wireless access

Mem of Southern Maine Library District
Open Mon-Thurs 8-5

P SOUTH PORTLAND PUBLIC LIBRARY*, 482 Broadway, 04106. SAN 343-7132. Tel: 207-767-7660. FAX: 207-767-7626. Web Site: www.southportlandlibrary.com. *Dir,* Kevin Davis; *Adult Serv,* Marie Chenevert; *Ch Serv,* Tom Werley; *Tech Serv,* Charlotte Spear; *YA Serv,* Reta Nappi; Staff 13 (MLS 2, Non-MLS 11)
Founded 1965. Pop 23,163; Circ 228,806
Jul 2006-Jun 2007 Income (Main Library and Branch(s)) $764,598. Mats Exp $86,569, Books $71,455, Per/Ser (Incl. Access Fees) $5,000, AV Mat $10,114. Sal $602,671
Library Holdings: Bk Titles 73,228; Bk Vols 80,000; Per Subs 50
Special Collections: Cape Elizabeth Historical Records; Early American Children's Books (James Otis Kaler Coll); South Portland
Automation Activity & Vendor Info: (Cataloging) Innovative Interfaces, Inc; (Circulation) Innovative Interfaces, Inc; (OPAC) Innovative Interfaces, Inc
Wireless access
Function: Adult bk club, AV serv, BA reader (adult literacy), Bks on cassette, Bks on CD, Children's prog, Computers for patron use, Copy machines, e-mail serv, Electronic databases & coll, Free DVD rentals, Handicapped accessible, Home delivery & serv to Sr ctr & nursing homes, Homebound delivery serv, ILL available, Mail & tel request accepted, Mus passes, Music CDs, Online cat, Outreach serv, Photocopying/Printing, Preschool outreach, Prog for adults, Prog for children & young adult, Pub access computers, Ref serv available, Senior outreach, Spoken cassettes & CDs, Spoken cassettes & DVDs, Story hour, Summer reading prog, Tax forms, Teen prog, VHS videos, Video lending libr, Wheelchair accessible
Mem of Southern Maine Library District
Open Tues & Thurs 10-8, Wed, Fri & Sat 10-6
Restriction: Non-resident fee
Friends of the Library Group
Branches: 1
MEMORIAL BRANCH, 155 Wescott Rd, 04106, SAN 343-7167. Tel: 207-775-1835. FAX: 207-773-1036. *Dir,* Kevin M Davis
Circ 32,000
Library Holdings: Bk Vols 20,000; Per Subs 10
Open Mon 10-8, Wed & Fri 2-6, Sun 12-5
Friends of the Library Group

J SOUTHERN MAINE COMMUNITY COLLEGE LIBRARY*, Two Fort Rd, 04106. SAN 306-7521. Tel: 207-741-5521. FAX: 207-741-5522. E-mail: library@smccme.edu. Web Site: www.smccme.edu. *Assoc Dean,* Grasky Staci; *Head, Access & Coll Serv,* Carin Dunay; *Head, Ref & Res Serv,* Susan Nester; *Patron Serv,* Joanne Langerman; *Ref & Instrul Serv Librn,* Bryan Strniste; Staff 5 (MLS 4, Non-MLS 1)
Founded 1964. Enrl 4,000; Fac 81; Highest Degree: Associate
Library Holdings: DVDs 100; Bk Titles 16,000; Bk Vols 16,300; Per Subs 300; Videos 40
Subject Interests: Allied health, Culinary arts, Electronics, Law enforcement, Liberal arts, Nursing, Plants
Automation Activity & Vendor Info: (Cataloging) Innovative Interfaces, Inc; (Circulation) Innovative Interfaces, Inc; (OPAC) Innovative Interfaces, Inc; (Serials) Innovative Interfaces, Inc
Database Vendor: EBSCOhost, ProQuest, Wilson - Wilson Web
Mem of Southern Maine Library District
Partic in Health Science Library Information Consortium; Maine Libr Asn
Open Mon-Thurs 8-8, Fri 8-3:30, Sat 9-1

SOUTH THOMASTON

P SOUTH THOMASTON PUBLIC LIBRARY*, Eight Dublin Rd, 04858. (Mail add: PO Box 3, 04858-0003). Tel: 207-596-0022. FAX: 207-596-7529. E-mail: library@south-thomaston.lib.me.us. Web Site: www.south-thomaston.lib.me.us. *Dir,* Tina Branco; Staff 1 (MLS 1)
Library Holdings: Bk Vols 5,000; Per Subs 12
Automation Activity & Vendor Info: (Acquisitions) LibraryWorld, Inc; (Circulation) LibraryWorld, Inc; (OPAC) LibraryWorld, Inc
Database Vendor: Overdrive, Inc
Wireless access
Function: Adult bk club, Audiobks via web, Bks on CD, Children's prog, Computers for patron use, Copy machines, Handicapped accessible, ILL available, Online cat, Online searches, OverDrive digital audio bks, Photocopying/Printing, Preschool outreach, Prog for adults, Prog for children & young adult, Pub access computers, Story hour
Open Mon 11-4, Wed 2-7, Sat 10-2
Restriction: Co libr

SOUTHPORT

P SOUTHPORT MEMORIAL LIBRARY, 1032 Hendricks Hill Rd, 04576-3309. (Mail add: PO Box 148, 04576-0148), SAN 376-3781. Tel: 207-633-2741, E-mail: librarian1@southport.lib.me.us. *Librn,* Linda Brewer; *Asst Librn,* Sandy Larsen; *Asst Librn,* Ann R Roche; E-mail: annroche@southport.lib.me.us; Staff 3 (Non-MLS 3)
Founded 1906. Pop 3,000; Circ 13,500
Library Holdings: Bk Vols 36,000; Per Subs 30
Special Collections: Butterfly Coll. Oral History
Automation Activity & Vendor Info: (Acquisitions) LibraryWorld, Inc
Wireless access
Open Tues & Thurs 9-4 & 7-9, Sat 9-4
Friends of the Library Group

SOUTHWEST HARBOR

P SOUTHWEST HARBOR PUBLIC LIBRARY, 338 Main St, 04679. (Mail add: PO Box 157, 04679-0157), SAN 306-7556. Tel: 207-244-7065. FAX: 207-244-7065. E-mail: circulation@swharbor.lib.me.us. Web Site: www.swharbor.lib.me.us. *Dir,* Candy Emlen; E-mail: candy@swharbor.lib.me.us; *Asst Dir,* Kate Pickup-McMullin; E-mail: kpmcmullin@swharbor.lib.me.us; *Ch,* Susan Plimpton; E-mail: splimpton@swharbor.lib.me.us
Founded 1895. Pop 2,000; Circ 70,000
Library Holdings: Bk Vols 41,500; Per Subs 125
Special Collections: Genealogy; Historic Photo Coll; Maine History. Oral History
Subject Interests: Oral hist tapes
Wireless access
Mem of Northeastern Maine Library District
Open Mon, Tues, Thurs & Fri 9-5, Wed 9-8, Sat 9-1
Friends of the Library Group

SPRINGVALE

P SPRINGVALE PUBLIC LIBRARY*, 443 Main St, 04083. SAN 306-7424. Tel: 207-324-4624. Circulation FAX: 207-324-0550. E-mail: spl@springvalelibrary.org. Web Site: www.springvalelibrary.org. *Dir,* Karen McCarthy Eger; *Asst Dir,* Dawn M Brown; *Ch,* Sheila Dube; Staff 7 (MLS 1, Non-MLS 6)
Founded 1906. Pop 20,000; Circ 84,635
Library Holdings: Bk Vols 33,852; Per Subs 65
Special Collections: Genealogy & Local History Room
Subject Interests: Genealogy
Automation Activity & Vendor Info: (Cataloging) Follett Software; (Circulation) Follett Software; (OPAC) Follett Software
Wireless access
Function: Handicapped accessible, Homebound delivery serv, ILL available, Photocopying/Printing, Prog for children & young adult, Ref serv available, Serves mentally handicapped consumers, Summer reading prog, Telephone ref, Wheelchair accessible
Mem of Southern Maine Library District
Partic in Maine School & Library Network
Special Services for the Blind - Audio mat
Open Mon-Wed 9:30-7, Thurs 9:30-5, Sat 9-2

STANDISH

P RICHVILLE LIBRARY*, 743 Richville Rd, 04084. Tel: 207-776-4698. E-mail: richvillelibrary@gmail.com. *Dir,* Karen McNutt
Library Holdings: AV Mats 400; Bk Vols 4,000
Wireless access
Mem of Southern Maine Library District
Open Thurs 2-5, Sat 9-Noon
Friends of the Library Group

CR SAINT JOSEPH'S COLLEGE*, Wellehan Library, 278 Whites Bridge Rd, 04084-5263. SAN 306-7009. Tel: 207-893-7725. FAX: 207-893-7883. E-mail: library@sjcme.edu. Web Site: www.sjcme.edu/library. *Dir of Libr Serv,* Shelly Davis; Tel: 207-893-7726, E-mail: sdavis@sjcme.edu; *Head, Ref, Info Literacy,* Lynn Bivens; Tel: 207-893-7724, E-mail: lbivens@sjcme.edu; *Ref & Info Literacy Librn,* Lia Horton; Tel: 207-893-7725, E-mail: lhorton@sjcme.edu; Staff 6.2 (MLS 3, Non-MLS 3.2)
Founded 1912. Highest Degree: Master
Library Holdings: Bk Vols 75,000
Automation Activity & Vendor Info: (Cataloging) OCLC; (Circulation) Innovative Interfaces, Inc - Millenium; (OPAC) Innovative Interfaces, Inc; (Serials) Innovative Interfaces, Inc - Millenium
Database Vendor: Cambridge Scientific Abstracts, EBSCOhost, Gale Cengage Learning, Innovative Interfaces, Inc, JSTOR, LexisNexis, Modern Language Association, Nature Publishing Group, ProQuest, SerialsSolutions, ValueLine, Wilson - Wilson Web
Wireless access
Mem of Southern Maine Library District

STEEP FALLS

P STEEP FALLS PUBLIC LIBRARY*, 1128 Pequawket Trail, 04085. (Mail add: PO Box 140, 04085-0140), SAN 306-7572. Tel: 207-675-3132. E-mail: sflib@adelphia.net. Web Site: www.steepfallslibrary.org. *Librn,* Paula Paul; Staff 1 (Non-MLS 1)
Founded 1916. Pop 7,500; Circ 23,208
Library Holdings: Bk Vols 24,000; Per Subs 19
Special Collections: Hobson Coll; Pierce & Maine Colls
Subject Interests: Hist
Automation Activity & Vendor Info: (Cataloging) Follett Software
Mem of Southern Maine Library District
Open Mon, Tues & Wed 10-7, Sat 9-12
Friends of the Library Group

STETSON

P STETSON PUBLIC LIBRARY*, 70 Village Rd, 04488. (Mail add: PO Box 154, 04488-0154), SAN 376-3498. Tel: 207-296-2020. E-mail: volunteer@stetson.lib.me.us. Web Site: www.stetson.lib.me.us. *Librn,* Laura Ward; Staff 1 (Non-MLS 1)
Library Holdings: Bks on Deafness & Sign Lang 6; Large Print Bks 30; Bk Titles 4,500; Per Subs 8
Automation Activity & Vendor Info: (Cataloging) LibraryWorld, Inc; (Circulation) LibraryWorld, Inc
Database Vendor: EBSCOhost, LibraryWorld, Inc
Wireless access
Mem of Northeastern Maine Library District
Special Services for the Blind - Bks on CD; Large print bks
Open Mon & Sat 9am-11am, Tues 9-Noon, Wed 3-5, Thurs 5-7
Friends of the Library Group

STEUBEN

P HENRY D MOORE LIBRARY*, 22 Village Rd, 04680. (Mail add: PO Box 127, 04680-0127), SAN 325-2183. Tel: 207-546-7301. *Dir,* Jeanne Benedict; E-mail: jbenedict@msln.net; Staff 1 (Non-MLS 1)
Pop 1,084; Circ 5,202
Library Holdings: AV Mats 500; Bk Vols 11,000
Database Vendor: EBSCOhost
Wireless access
Mem of Northeastern Maine Library District
Open Mon (Winter) 5:30-8:30, Tues 1-4, Wed 10-6, Thurs 10-4, Sat 10-1; Mon (Summer) 5:30-8:30, Tues & Thurs 10-4, Wed 10-6, Sat 10-1

STOCKTON SPRINGS

P STOCKTON SPRINGS COMMUNITY LIBRARY*, Six Station St, 04981. (Mail add: PO Box 293, 04981-0293). Tel: 207-567-4147. FAX: 207-567-4147. E-mail: stocktonstaff@stocktonsprings.lib.me.us. Web Site: www.stocktonspringsme.com/pages/community.html. *Dir,* Patricia Curley
Founded 2001
Library Holdings: Bk Vols 7,000; Per Subs 10
Automation Activity & Vendor Info: (Cataloging) Follett Software; (Circulation) Follett Software
Wireless access
Open Tues 4-7, Wed 3-5, Thurs 9:30-12:30 & 6:30-8:30, Sat 9-12

STONINGTON

P STONINGTON PUBLIC LIBRARY*, Main St, 04681. (Mail add: PO Box 441, 04681-0441). Tel: 207-367-5926. E-mail: stoningtonlibrary@stonington.lib.me.us. *Librn,* Vicki Zelnick; Staff 0.33 (Non-MLS 0.33)
Founded 1955. Pop 1,500
Library Holdings: Bk Vols 10,000; Talking Bks 50; Videos 100
Special Collections: Art Coll; Local & State Authors (Maine Coll); Ocean & Sea Related Fiction & Non-Fiction (Sea Coll)
Wireless access
Open Tues (Winter) 12:30-4:30, Fri 11-3, Sat 10-12; Tues (Summer) 12:30-5:30, Fri 11-3, Sat 10-12
Friends of the Library Group

STRATTON

P STRATTON PUBLIC LIBRARY*, 88 Main St, 04982. (Mail add: PO Box 350, 04982-0350), SAN 372-6711. Tel: 207-246-4401. FAX: 207-246-3267. Web Site: www.stratton.lib.me.us/index.htm. *Actg Librn,* Wendy Boyle; E-mail: wboyle@stratton.lib.me.us; Staff 1 (Non-MLS 1)
Founded 1921. Pop 778; Circ 1,669
Jan 2012-Dec 2012 Income $34,498, City $28,000, Locally Generated Income $5,927, Other $571. Mats Exp $1,791, Books $1,556, Per/Ser (Incl. Access Fees) $235. Sal $18,662
Library Holdings: Audiobooks 178; Braille Volumes 1; Large Print Bks 55; Bk Vols 5,503; Per Subs 15; Videos 278
Database Vendor: Baker & Taylor, EBSCOhost, OCLC WebJunction, OCLC WorldShare Interlibrary Loan
Wireless access
Partic in Maine School & Library Network
Open Mon, Wed & Fri 10-5, Tues & Thurs 1-5, Sat 9-1

STRONG

P STRONG PUBLIC LIBRARY*, Foster Memorial Library, 14 S Main St, 04983. (Mail add: PO Box 629, 04983-0629), SAN 376-7825. Tel: 207-684-4003. FAX: 207-684-4004. E-mail: stronglibrary@yahoo.com. *Libr Dir,* Cheryl McCleery; Staff 1 (Non-MLS 1)
Pop 1,200
Library Holdings: AV Mats 88; Bk Titles 7,000; Bk Vols 7,300
Database Vendor: EBSCOhost
Open Tues & Thurs 1-7, Sat 10-2

SULLIVAN

P FRENCHMAN'S BAY LIBRARY*, 1776 US Hwy, No 1, 04664. (Mail add: PO Box 215, 04664-0215). Tel: 207-422-2307. E-mail: fblibrarian@frenchman.lib.me.us. Web Site: www.frenchman.lib.me.us. *Librn,* Barbara Sawyer
Pop 100
Library Holdings: Audiobooks 22; Bks-By-Mail 45; DVDs 30; Large Print Bks 12; Bk Vols 200; Talking Bks 150; Videos 175
Wireless access
Open Mon 5-8, Tues & Thurs 1-5, Sat 10-2
Friends of the Library Group

SWANS ISLAND

P SWANS ISLAND EDUCATIONAL SOCIETY*, Swans Island Public Library, 451 Atlantic Rd, 04685. (Mail add: PO Box 12, 04685-0012). Tel: 207-526-4330. E-mail: swanslib@msln.net. Web Site: www.swansisland.org. *Dir,* Candis Joyce; Staff 1 (Non-MLS 1)
Founded 1965. Pop 350; Circ 3,433
Jan 2007-Dec 2007 Income $17,000, City $10,000, Locally Generated Income $7,000. Sal $7,200
Library Holdings: AV Mats 50; CDs 25; DVDs 300; Large Print Bks 100; Music Scores 7; Bk Vols 10,000; Per Subs 11; Talking Bks 300; Videos 500
Special Collections: Maine Coll
Wireless access
Function: Archival coll, Art exhibits, Bks on cassette, Bks on CD, Children's prog, Computers for patron use, Copy machines, Distance learning, e-mail serv, E-Reserves, Fax serv, Free DVD rentals, Genealogy discussion group, ILL available, Online cat, Photocopying/Printing, Preschool outreach, Pub access computers, Scanner, Story hour, Summer reading prog, Tax forms, VHS videos, Video lending libr
Open Tues & Fri 1-4, Thurs 1-7, Sat 9-12

TENANTS HARBOR

P JACKSON MEMORIAL LIBRARY*, 38 Main St, 04860. (Mail add: PO Box 231, 04860-0231), SAN 306-7416. Tel: 207-372-8961. Web Site: www.jacksonmem.lib.me.us. *Dir,* Yvonne Gloede; *Assoc Dir,* Devin Burritt; Staff 2 (MLS 2)
Founded 1935. Pop 2,600
Library Holdings: DVDs 100; Large Print Bks 1,000; Bk Vols 15,000; Per Subs 50; Talking Bks 600; Videos 200
Database Vendor: EBSCOhost, LibLime
Wireless access
Mem of Northeastern Maine Library District
Open Tues-Thurs 10-6, Fri 12-5, Sat 9-2
Friends of the Library Group

THOMASTON

P THOMASTON PUBLIC LIBRARY*, 60 Main St, 04861. SAN 306-7599. Tel: 207-354-2453. E-mail: tpl@thomaston.lib.me.us. Web Site: www.thomaston.lib.me.us/. *Actg Dir,* Joanna Hynd
Founded 1898. Pop 7,901; Circ 89,382
Jul 2005-Jun 2006 Income $41,330, City $25,000, Locally Generated Income $3,804, Other $12,526. Mats Exp $25,900, Books $21,000, Per/Ser (Incl. Access Fees) $2,500, AV Mat $2,400
Library Holdings: Bks-By-Mail 312; CDs 400; DVDs 325; Large Print Bks 400; Music Scores 150; Bk Vols 34,000; Per Subs 55; Talking Bks 500; Videos 924
Special Collections: Municipal Document Depository; Oral History; State Document Depository
Subject Interests: Maine
Automation Activity & Vendor Info: (Acquisitions) Surpass; (Cataloging) Surpass; (Circulation) Surpass; (Course Reserve) Surpass; (ILL) Surpass
Database Vendor: Baker & Taylor, EBSCOhost, Gale Cengage Learning
Wireless access

Mem of Northeastern Maine Library District
Partic in Maine School & Library Network
Special Services for the Blind - Talking bks
Open Mon & Fri 11-7, Tues, Wed & Thurs 11-5, Sat 11-3
Friends of the Library Group
Bookmobiles: 1

TOPSHAM

P TOPSHAM PUBLIC LIBRARY*, 25 Foreside Rd, 04086. SAN 306-7602. Tel: 207-725-1727. FAX: 207-725-1735. Web Site: www.topshamlibrary.org. *Dir,* Susan M Preece; E-mail: director@topshamlibrary.org; Staff 5 (MLS 1, Non-MLS 4)
Founded 1931. Pop 10,000; Circ 58,000
Jul 2005-Jun 2006 Income $207,504. Mats Exp $15,150, Books $14,000, Per/Ser (Incl. Access Fees) $1,150. Sal $143,924
Library Holdings: Bk Vols 35,000; Per Subs 60
Automation Activity & Vendor Info: (Cataloging) Innovative Interfaces, Inc; (Circulation) Innovative Interfaces, Inc; (OPAC) Innovative Interfaces, Inc
Database Vendor: EBSCOhost
Wireless access
Function: ILL available
Open Mon & Wed 10-6, Tues & Thurs 10-8, Fri 12-6, Sat 9:30-2:30
Friends of the Library Group

TURNER

P TURNER PUBLIC LIBRARY*, 98 Matthews Way, 04282-3930. SAN 306-7610. Tel: 207-225-2030. E-mail: tplv@megalink.net. Web Site: www.turnerpubliclibrary.org. *Librn,* Vicki Varney; Staff 1 (Non-MLS 1)
Pop 3,539
Library Holdings: Bk Vols 12,000
Wireless access
Open Tues & Thurs 12-7, Sat 9:30-12
Friends of the Library Group

UNION

P VOSE LIBRARY*, 392 Common Rd, 04862-4249. (Mail add: PO Box 550, 04862-0550), SAN 306-7629. Tel: 207-785-4733. E-mail: voselibrarian@voselibrary.org. Web Site: www.voselibrary.org. *Dir,* Sue McClintock; Staff 1 (Non-MLS 1)
Founded 1932. Pop 2,400; Circ 9,000
Library Holdings: AV Mats 15; Bk Vols 15,000; Per Subs 40; Talking Bks 750; Videos 150
Automation Activity & Vendor Info: (Cataloging) ComPanion Corp
Database Vendor: EBSCOhost
Wireless access
Function: ILL available, Photocopying/Printing
Mem of Northeastern Maine Library District
Open Tues 10-8, Wed & Fri 10-6, Sat 9-12
Friends of the Library Group

UNITY

C UNITY COLLEGE, Dorothy Webb Quimby Library, 90 Quaker Hill Rd, 04988. (Mail add: PO Box 167, 04988-0167), SAN 306-7637. Tel: 207-509-7178. Reference Tel: 207-509-7234. Information Services Tel: 207-948-3131, Ext 328. FAX: 207-512-1218. E-mail: library@unity.edu. Web Site: unity.libguides.com/home. *Instrul Serv Librn, Interim Dir, Ref Serv,* Sandra Abbott-Stout; Staff 6 (MLS 2, Non-MLS 4)
Founded 1966. Highest Degree: Bachelor
Library Holdings: AV Mats 1,760; Bk Titles 54,600; Bk Vols 61,000; Per Subs 325
Subject Interests: Environ sci, Natural hist, Wildlife
Automation Activity & Vendor Info: (Cataloging) Follett Software; (Circulation) Innovative Interfaces, Inc; (ILL) OCLC; (OPAC) Innovative Interfaces, Inc
Database Vendor: BioOne, EBSCOhost, JSTOR, LexisNexis, ProQuest, Wiley
Wireless access
Partic in Lyrasis
Open Mon-Thurs (Winter) 8am-10pm, Fri 8-6, Sat 10-6, Sun 10-10; Mon (Summer) 9-7, Tues-Thurs 9-4

VAN BUREN

P ABEL J MORNEAULT MEMORIAL LIBRARY*, 153 Main St, 04785. SAN 306-7645. Tel: 207-868-5076. E-mail: nmt@morneault.lib.me.us. Web Site: www.morneault.lib.me.us/. *Dir,* Nancy Troeger
Founded 1974. Pop 3,000; Circ 13,500
Library Holdings: Bks on Deafness & Sign Lang 10; CDs 300; DVDs 250; Large Print Bks 350; Bk Titles 20,000; Per Subs 40; Talking Bks 200; Videos 600
Special Collections: Oral History
Subject Interests: Genealogy
Automation Activity & Vendor Info: (Acquisitions) Follett Software; (Cataloging) Follett Software; (Circulation) Follett Software; (ILL) Follett Software
Wireless access
Mem of Northeastern Maine Library District
Open Tues, Thurs & Fri 10-6, Wed 10-8, Sat 8-1
Friends of the Library Group

VINALHAVEN

P VINALHAVEN PUBLIC LIBRARY*, Six Carver St, 04863. (Mail add: PO Box 384, 04863-0384), SAN 306-7653. Tel: 207-863-4401. E-mail: vpl@vhaven.lib.me.us. *Libr Dir,* Valerie Morton; E-mail: vpl@vhaven.lib.me.us; Staff 2 (Non-MLS 2)
Founded 1887. Pop 1,225; Circ 19,902
Library Holdings: Bks on Deafness & Sign Lang 10; Large Print Bks 278; Bk Vols 18,759; Per Subs 22; Talking Bks 510
Automation Activity & Vendor Info: (Cataloging) Follett Software; (Circulation) Follett Software
Database Vendor: EBSCOhost
Wireless access
Function: Prog for children & young adult
Mem of Northeastern Maine Library District
Special Services for the Blind - Audio mat; Home delivery serv; Large print bks
Open Tues & Thurs 1-5 & 6-8, Wed & Fri 9-12 & 1-5, Sat 9-1
Friends of the Library Group

WALDOBORO

P WALDOBORO PUBLIC LIBRARY*, 908 Main St, 04572-0768. (Mail add: PO Box 768, 04572-6036), SAN 306-7661. Tel: 207-832-4484. FAX: 207-832-4484. E-mail: info@waldoboro.lib.me.us. Web Site: www.waldoborolibrary.org. *Dir,* Catherine Skov
Founded 1916. Pop 5,000; Circ 22,642
Library Holdings: AV Mats 2,000; Bk Vols 15,000; Per Subs 20
Automation Activity & Vendor Info: (Cataloging) LibraryWorld, Inc; (Circulation) LibraryWorld, Inc
Database Vendor: EBSCOhost
Wireless access
Function: ILL available
Publications: Newsletter (Quarterly)
Special Services for the Blind - Large print & cassettes
Open Mon & Thurs Noon-7, Wed & Fri 10-5, Sat 9-1
Friends of the Library Group

WALPOLE

C UNIVERSITY OF MAINE*, Darling Marine Center Library, 193 Clarks Cove Rd, 04573. SAN 306-767X. Tel: 207-563-8193. FAX: 207-563-3119. Web Site: server.dmc.maine.edu/library.html. *Librn,* Randy Lackovic; Staff 1 (Non-MLS 1)
Founded 1966. Fac 12; Highest Degree: Doctorate
Library Holdings: Bk Titles 10,000; Per Subs 300
Special Collections: Darling Marine Center History Coll; Reprint Coll; Sea Grant Coll
Subject Interests: Aquaculture, Marine biol, Marine geol, Marine zool, Oceanography
Wireless access
Open Mon-Thurs 9-4, Fri 8-2:30

WARREN

MAINE DEPARTMENT OF CORRECTIONS

S BOLDUC CORRECTIONAL FACILITY LIBRARY*, 516 Cushing Rd, 04864. Tel: 207-273-2036. FAX: 207-273-5124. *Actg Librn,* Brent Elwell
Library Holdings: Bk Vols 2,500; Per Subs 20
Open Mon, Tues & Fri 11:15-12:15 & 2-3, Wed & Thurs 11:15-12:15, 2-3 & 7-8, Sat & Sun 5:15-6:15

S MAINE STATE PRISON LIBRARY*, 807 Cushing Rd, 04864, SAN 306-7688. Tel: 207-273-5300. *Librn,* Jackie Weddle
Library Holdings: Bk Vols 7,000; Per Subs 20
Special Collections: State & Federal Criminal Law
Subject Interests: Art hist, Natural hist, Vocational info
Mem of Northeastern Maine Library District
Open Mon-Fri 8-11 & 1-4

P WARREN FREE PUBLIC LIBRARY*, 282 Main St, 04864. (Mail add: 167 Western Rd, 04864), SAN 306-7696. Tel: 207-273-2900. Web Site: www.warrenfreepubliclibrary.org. *Dir,* Cindy Norwood; *Asst Dir,* Russell Cloutier; Staff 1 (Non-MLS 1)
Founded 1927. Pop 3,500; Circ 12,506
Library Holdings: DVDs 148; Large Print Bks 225; Bk Vols 14,487; Per Subs 10; Talking Bks 100; Videos 200

Automation Activity & Vendor Info: (Cataloging) LibraryWorld, Inc; (Circulation) LibraryWorld, Inc
Database Vendor: EBSCOhost
Wireless access
Open Mon, Tues & Thurs 4-8, Wed Noon-6, Fri 10-6, Sat 9-Noon
Friends of the Library Group

WASHBURN

P WASHBURN MEMORIAL LIBRARY*, 1290 Main St, 04786. (Mail add: PO Box 571, 04786-0571), SAN 306-770X. Tel: 207-455-4814. *Librn,* Katherine D Corey; Staff 2 (Non-MLS 2)
Pop 2,240; Circ 17,643
Library Holdings: Bk Titles 16,289; Bk Vols 20,565; Per Subs 26; Talking Bks 800; Videos 500
Special Collections: Aroostook County Coll. Oral History
Mem of Northeastern Maine Library District
Open Mon & Wed 1-7, Tues & Thurs 10:30-4:30, Fri 12-4:30

WASHINGTON

P GIBBS LIBRARY*, 40 Old Union Rd, 04574. (Mail add: PO Box 348, 04574-0348), SAN 376-348X. Tel: 207-845-2663. E-mail: gibbslibrary@hotmail.com. Web Site: www.gibbslibrary.org. *Librn,* Madelon Kelly; *Asst Librn,* Liane Chapma
Founded 1993. Pop 1,500; Circ 1,200
Jul 2006-Jun 2007 Income $10,000. Mats Exp $10,000
Library Holdings: Bk Titles 10,000
Special Collections: College Level Great Courses, CDs, DVDs; Stephen & Tabitha King Language Arts Audios
Automation Activity & Vendor Info: (Acquisitions) Follett Software; (Cataloging) Follett Software; (Circulation) Follett Software
Database Vendor: EBSCOhost
Wireless access
Function: Senior computer classes
Partic in Maine School & Library Network
Open Mon 4-7, Tues 9-12 & 4-7, Thurs 3-6, Sat 9-3, Sun 2-5
Friends of the Library Group

WATERFORD

P WATERFORD LIBRARY ASSOCIATION*, 663 Waterford Rd, 04088. (Mail add: PO Box 176, 04088-0176). Tel: 207-583-2050. E-mail. wla@waterford.lib.me.us. Web Site: www.waterford.lib.me.us. *Dir,* Dorthe Hillquist
Pop 1,250
Library Holdings: Bk Vols 5,000; Talking Bks 100; Videos 50
Wireless access
Open Mon 2-6, Wed 3-8, Fri 10-Noon, Sat 10-2, Sun (Summer) 10-Noon
Friends of the Library Group

WATERVILLE

C COLBY COLLEGE LIBRARIES*, Miller Library, 5100 Mayflower Hill, 04901. SAN 343-7191. Tel: 207-859-5100, 207-859-5101. Interlibrary Loan Service Tel: 207-859-5125. Administration Tel: 207-859-5108. FAX: 207-859-5105. E-mail: refmill@colby.edu. Web Site: libguides.colby.edu. *Dir,* Clem P Guthro; E-mail: cpguthro@colby.edu; *Asst Dir, Digital & Spec Coll, Digital Coll Librn,* Martin Kelly; Tel: 207-859-5162, E-mail: mfkelly@colby.edu; *Asst Dir, Digital & Spec Coll, Spec Coll Librn,* Patricia Burdick; Tel: 207-859-5151, E-mail: Patricia.Burdick@colby.edu; *Asst Dir, Coll Mgt,* Toni Katz; Tel: 207-859-5142, E-mail: tdkatz@colby.edu; *Asst Dir, Scholarly Res & Serv/Sci Librn,* Suzi Cole; Tel: 207-859-5791, E-mail: swcole@colby.edu; *Asst Dir, Syst, Web & Emerging Tech,* Darylyne Provost; Tel: 207-859-5117, E-mail: dprovost@colby.edu; *Scholarly Res & Serv/Arts Librn,* Margaret Ericson; Tel: 207-859-5662, E-mail: mericson@colby.edu; *Scholarly Res & Serv/Humanities Librn,* Karen Gillum; Tel: 207-859-5123, E-mail: kjgillum@colby.edu; *Scholarly Res & Serv/Soc Sci & Humanities Librn,* Marilyn R Pukkila; Tel: 207-859-5145, E-mail: mrpukkil@colby.edu; *Scholarly Res & Serv/Soc Sci Librn,* Margaret Menchen; Tel: 207-859-5144, E-mail: mpmenche@colby.edu; *Syst & Emerging Tech Librn,* Michael C McGuire; Tel: 207-859-5161, E-mail: mcmcguir@colby.edu. Subject Specialists: *Knowledge mgt,* Clem P Guthro; *Gender studies, Women studies,* Marilyn R Pukkila; Staff 27 (MLS 12, Non-MLS 15)
Founded 1813. Enrl 1,850; Fac 175; Highest Degree: Bachelor
Jul 2012-Jun 2013 Income (Main and Other College/University Libraries) $4,708,494. Mats Exp $2,646,643, Books $400,000, Per/Ser (Incl. Access Fees) $1,125,000, Electronic Ref Mat (Incl. Access Fees) $475,000, Presv $16,000. Sal $1,354,845 (Prof $892,290)
Library Holdings: Audiobooks 1,264; DVDs 9,319; e-books 503,925; e-journals 86,472; Music Scores 9,848; Bk Titles 469,252; Per Subs 400; Videos 4,000
Special Collections: A E Housman Coll; Colby Archives; Contemporary Letters (Bern Porter Coll); Henry James Coll; Maine Authors (Jacob Abbot, Sarah Orne Jewett, Edna St Vincent Millay, Kenneth Roberts, Ben Ames Williams, Edwin Arlington Robinson); Modern Irish Literature (Lord Dunsany, Lady Gregory, Seamus Heaney, James Joyce, Cuala Press, J M Synge, William Trevor, W B Yeats); Thomas Hardy Coll; Thomas Mann Coll; Violet Paget Coll (Vernon Lee). US Document Depository
Automation Activity & Vendor Info: (Acquisitions) Innovative Interfaces, Inc - Millenium; (Cataloging) Innovative Interfaces, Inc - Millenium; (Circulation) Innovative Interfaces, Inc - Millenium; (Course Reserve) Innovative Interfaces, Inc - Millenium; (ILL) OCLC ILLiad; (Media Booking) Innovative Interfaces, Inc - Millenium; (OPAC) Innovative Interfaces, Inc - Millenium; (Serials) Innovative Interfaces, Inc - Millenium
Wireless access
Function: Archival coll, ILL available, Online searches, Photocopying/Printing, Ref serv available
Partic in Amigos Library Services, Inc
Open Mon-Sun (Winter) 8am-1am; Mon-Fri (Summer) 8:30-4:30
Restriction: Open to pub for ref & circ; with some limitations, Open to students, fac & staff

Departmental Libraries:

BIXLER ART & MUSIC LIBRARY, 5660 Mayflower Hill, 04901. Tel: 207-859-5660. FAX: 207-859-5105. E-mail: refbix@colby.edu. Web Site: libguides.colby.edu/bixler. *Scholarly Res & Serv/Arts Librn,* Margaret D Ericson; Tel: 207-859-5602, E-mail: mericson@colby.edu; Staff 1 (MLS 1)
Library Holdings: AV Mats 12,000; Bk Vols 53,000; Per Subs 100
Database Vendor: Alexander Street Press, ARTstor, CredoReference, Luna Imaging/Insight, Oxford Online, YBP Library Services
Open Mon-Thurs (Winter) 8:30am-Midnight, Fri 8:30-6, Sat 10-6, Sun 10am-Midnight; Tues-Fri (Summer) 8:30-4:30

SCIENCE LIBRARY, 5791 Mayflower Hill, 04901-4799. Tel: 207-859-5790. Administration Tel: 207-859-5791. FAX: 207-859-5105. E-mail: scilib@colby.edu. Web Site: libguides.colby.edu/olin. *Sci Librn,* Susan W Cole; E-mail: swcole@colby.edu; Staff 1 (MLS 1)
Library Holdings: CDs 460; Microforms 1,300; Bk Vols 41,000; Videos 604
Automation Activity & Vendor Info: (OPAC) Innovative Interfaces, Inc
Database Vendor: American Chemical Society, American Mathematical Society, Annual Reviews, BioOne, Elsevier, Gale Cengage Learning, JSTOR, Safari Books Online, ScienceDirect, SerialsSolutions, STN International, YBP Library Services
Open Mon-Thurs (Winter) 8am-Midnight, Fri 8am-10pm, Sat 10-10, Sun 10am-Midnight; Mon-Fri (Summer) 9-4

M INLAND HOSPITAL, Medical Library, 200 Kennedy Memorial Dr, 04901. SAN 378-0619. Tel: 207-861-3018. FAX: 207-861-3025. *Librn,* Position Currently Open
Library Holdings: Bk Titles 250; Bk Vols 310; Per Subs 40
Subject Interests: Osteopathy
Partic in Docline; Health Sci Libr Info Consortium
Restriction: Open by appt only

M MAINE GENERAL MEDICAL CENTER*, Health Sciences Library, 149 North St, 04901-1000. SAN 320-1929. Tel: 207-872-1224. FAX: 207-872-1460. *Librn,* Cora M Damon; E-mail: cora.damon@mainegeneral.org
Library Holdings: e-journals 1,000; Bk Titles 1,000; Bk Vols 3,000; Per Subs 175
Subject Interests: Allied health, Lit, Med
Automation Activity & Vendor Info: (Cataloging) Innovative Interfaces, Inc; (Circulation) Innovative Interfaces, Inc; (ILL) Innovative Interfaces, Inc; (OPAC) Innovative Interfaces, Inc; (Serials) Innovative Interfaces, Inc
Database Vendor: EBSCOhost, MD Consult, OVID Technologies, STAT!Ref (Teton Data Systems), UpToDate
Partic in BRS; Docline; Health Science Library Information Consortium; National Network of Libraries of Medicine
Open Mon-Fri 8-4:30

C THOMAS COLLEGE LIBRARY*, 180 W River Rd, 04901. SAN 306-7718. Tel: 207-859-1204. Web Site: www.thomas.edu/library. *VPres for Info Serv,* Christopher Rhoda; Staff 3 (MLS 1, Non-MLS 2)
Founded 1894. Enrl 650; Fac 30; Highest Degree: Master
Library Holdings: Bk Vols 24,000
Subject Interests: Bus & mgt, Criminal justice, Educ, Liberal arts
Database Vendor: Cambridge Scientific Abstracts, EBSCOhost, Gale Cengage Learning, LexisNexis, ProQuest, Westlaw
Wireless access
Open Mon-Thurs (Winter) 7:45am-10pm, Fri 7:45-4:30, Sat 1-4, Sun 5-10; Mon-Thurs (Summer) 8am-10pm, Fri 8-4

S WATERVILLE HISTORICAL SOCIETY LIBRARY*, 62 Silver St, Unit B, 04901. SAN 306-7726. Tel: 207-872-9439. Web Site: www.redingtonmuseum.org. *Pres,* Frederic P Johnson; Tel: 207-872-6286; *Librn,* Diane Johnson
Founded 1903

Library Holdings: Bk Titles 2,500
Special Collections: Coll of Waterville Mail (Newspaper Printed 1846-1906), microfilm
Subject Interests: Civil War, Local hist
Restriction: Open by appt only

P WATERVILLE PUBLIC LIBRARY*, 73 Elm St, 04901-6078. SAN 306-7734. Tel: 207-872-5433. FAX: 207-873-4779. E-mail: info@watervillelibrary.org. Web Site: www.watervillelibrary.org. *Dir,* Sarah Sugden; E-mail: ssugden@watervillelibrary.org; *Bus & Career Ctr Coordr,* Tammy Rabideau; E-mail: trabideau@watervillelibrary.org; *Cat, Tech Serv,* Cathy Perkins; E-mail: catperkins@watervillelibrary.org; *Ch Serv,* Kathleen Kenny; E-mail: kkenny@watervillelibrary.org; *Circ Supvr,* Lee Folsom; E-mail: lfolsom@watervillelibrary.org; *ILL,* Meta Vigue; E-mail: mvigue@watervillelibrary.org
Founded 1896. Pop 15,605; Circ 98,765
Library Holdings: AV Mats 6,438; Large Print Bks 1,599; Bk Vols 92,000; Per Subs 76
Special Collections: Franco-Americans & Lebanese-Americans in Waterville; Waterville-Area Genealogy & Local History. Oral History
Automation Activity & Vendor Info: (Cataloging) Innovative Interfaces, Inc; (Circulation) Innovative Interfaces, Inc; (ILL) Innovative Interfaces, Inc; (OPAC) Innovative Interfaces, Inc
Database Vendor: EBSCOhost
Wireless access
Open Mon-Fri 10-7, Sat 10-3

WAYNE

P CARY MEMORIAL LIBRARY*, 17 Old Winthrop Rd, 04284. (Mail add: PO Box 127, 04284-0127), SAN 306-7742. Tel: 207-685-3612. Web Site: www.cary-memorial.lib.me.us. *Librn,* Janet H Adelberg; E-mail: jadelberg@cary-memorial.lib.me.us; Staff 1 (Non-MLS 1)
Pop 1,100; Circ 14,500
Library Holdings: Bk Vols 12,280; Per Subs 40
Special Collections: Annie Louise Cary Memorabilia (Opera Star 1841-1921); Bookplates
Wireless access
Open Mon (Winter) 9-1 & 3-7, Tues & Thurs 3-7, Wed 2-7, Sat 9-3; Mon (Summer) 9-1 & 3-8, Tues & Thurs 3-8, Wed 1-8, Sat 9-3
Friends of the Library Group

WELD

P WELD FREE PUBLIC LIBRARY*, 25 Church St, 04285. (Mail add: PO Box 120, 04285-0120), SAN 306-7750. Tel: 207-585-2439. FAX: 207-585-2439. *Librn,* Judith Rogers
Founded 1905. Pop 400; Circ 4,848
Library Holdings: AV Mats 350; Large Print Bks 55; Bk Vols 10,000; Per Subs 15; Talking Bks 50
Open Tues & Thurs 2-7

WELLS

S DOROTHY FISH COASTAL RESOURCE LIBRARY AT WELLS RESERVE*, Wells Reserve Library, 342 Laudholm Farm Rd, 04090. Tel: 207-646-1555. Administration Tel: 207-646-1555, Ext 118. FAX: 207-646-2930. Web Site: www.wellsreserve.org/visit/library. *Educ Dir,* Suzanne Kahn Eder; Tel: 207-646-1555, Ext 116; Staff 0.3 (MLS 0.3)
Founded 1986
Library Holdings: AV Mats 150; Bk Vols 3,500
Subject Interests: Ecology, Estuary studies, Mgt
Database Vendor: Agricola, EBSCOhost, Medline, ProQuest, ValueLine
Wireless access
Mem of Southern Maine Library District
Open Tues 10-1, Wed 1-4

P WELLS PUBLIC LIBRARY*, 1434 Post Rd, 04090-4508. (Mail add: PO Box 699, 04090-0699), SAN 372-6320. Tel: 207-646-8181. FAX: 207-646-5636. E-mail: Libstaff@wellstown.org. Web Site: www.wells.lib.me.us. *Dir,* Cindy Schilling; Tel: 207-646-8181, Ext 206, E-mail: cschilling@wellstown.org; *Asst Libr Dir, Youth Serv Librn,* Devin Burritt; Tel: 207-646-8181, Ext 202; *Ref/Tech Support Librn,* Kristi Bryant; Tel: 207-646-8181, Ext 205; *Coordr, Circ,* Sandy Patrick; Tel: 207-646-8181, Ext 203; *Cataloger,* Anne Mosey; Tel: 207-646-8181, Ext 207; Staff 8 (MLS 2, Non-MLS 6)
Founded 1979. Pop 10,000; Circ 75,000
Library Holdings: Bk Titles 43,000; Bk Vols 44,000; Per Subs 91
Special Collections: Municipal Document Depository
Automation Activity & Vendor Info: (Cataloging) Innovative Interfaces, Inc; (Circulation) Innovative Interfaces, Inc; (OPAC) Innovative Interfaces, Inc
Database Vendor: EBSCOhost
Wireless access
Mem of Southern Maine Library District
Open Mon 10-6, Tues 1-8, Wed 10-8, Thurs 1-6, Fri 10-5, Sat 10-1
Friends of the Library Group

J YORK COUNTY COMMUNITY COLLEGE LIBRARY*, 112 College Dr, 04090. Tel: 207-646-9282. FAX: 207-641-2770. E-mail: library@yccc.edu. Web Site: www.yccc.edu. *Dir,* Amber Tatnall; E-mail: atatnall@yccc.edu; *Librn,* Annette Tanguay; Staff 2 (MLS 2)
Founded 1998
Library Holdings: Bk Vols 8,300
Automation Activity & Vendor Info: (Acquisitions) Innovative Interfaces, Inc; (Cataloging) Innovative Interfaces, Inc; (Circulation) Innovative Interfaces, Inc; (ILL) Innovative Interfaces, Inc; (OPAC) Innovative Interfaces, Inc; (Serials) Innovative Interfaces, Inc
Database Vendor: EBSCOhost, ProQuest
Mem of Southern Maine Library District
Open Mon-Thurs 8-8, Fri 9-4

WEST BOOTHBAY HARBOR

G MAINE DEPARTMENT OF MARINE RESOURCES*, Bigelow Laboratory for Ocean Sciences Library, 180 McKown Point Rd, 04575. (Mail add: PO Box 475, 04575-0475), SAN 306-7777. Tel: 207-633-9500, 207-633-9600. FAX: 207-633-9641. E-mail: library@bigelow.org. Web Site: www.bigelow.org. *Librn,* Pamela Shephard-Lupo; Tel: 207-633-9551
Founded 1957
Library Holdings: Bk Titles 3,500; Per Subs 252
Special Collections: fishing gear; Foreign Countries Documents; State & Federal Government Publications
Subject Interests: Biochem, Botany, Environ studies, Marine biol, Oceanography, Zoology
Publications: Department of Marine Resources, Scientific & Technical Publications Index 1946-1983
Partic in Dialog Corp; OCLC Online Computer Library Center, Inc
Open Mon-Fri 8-4:30

WEST NEWFIELD

P NEWFIELD VILLAGE LIBRARY & READING ROOM*, 637 Water St, 04095. (Mail add: PO Box 55, Newfield, 04056-0055), SAN 376-3862. Tel: 207-793-4348. FAX: 207-793-2162. *Librn,* Cheryl Cause; Staff 1 (Non-MLS 1)
Library Holdings: Audiobooks 25; CDs 9; DVDs 101; Electronic Media & Resources 49; Bk Titles 4,244; Bk Vols 4,744
Database Vendor: EBSCOhost
Mem of Southern Maine Library District
Open Tues 9-11:45, 1-4:45 & 6-7:45, Wed Noon-4:45, Thurs 9-11:45 & 1-4:45

WEST PARIS

P WEST PARIS PUBLIC LIBRARY*, Arthur L Mann Memorial Library, 226 Main St, 04289. (Mail add: PO Box 307, 04289-0307), SAN 321-0529. Tel: 207-674-2004. FAX: 207-674-2804. Web Site: www.westparis.lib.me.us. *Dir,* Patricia Makley
Pop 1,725
Library Holdings: DVDs 300; Large Print Bks 275; Bk Vols 12,000
Wireless access
Open Mon & Fri 1:30-6, Wed 1:30-7, Sat 10-2
Friends of the Library Group

WESTBROOK

S SAPPI FINE PAPER NORTH AMERICA*, Technology Center Library, 300 Warren Ave, 04092. (Mail add: PO Box 5000, 04098-1597), SAN 306-7785. Tel: 207-856-3538. FAX: 207-856-3770. *Librn,* Lynne Palmer
Library Holdings: Bk Titles 2,950; Per Subs 80
Subject Interests: Chem, Eng, Papermaking, Physics, Printing
Mem of Southern Maine Library District
Open Mon-Fri 8-5

P WALKER MEMORIAL LIBRARY*, 800 Main St, 04092. SAN 306-7793. Tel: 207-854-0630. FAX: 207-854-0629. E-mail: walkerlibrary@westbrook.me.us. Web Site: www.walker.lib.me.us. *Dir,* Karen Valley; E-mail: kvalley@westbrook.me.us; *Asst Dir,* Position Currently Open; *Youth Serv Librn,* Corinne Henning-Sachs; E-mail: chenningsachs@westbrook.me.us; *Curator,* Julie Peterson; E-mail: jpeter@westbrook.me.us; Staff 12 (MLS 4, Non-MLS 8)
Founded 1894. Pop 16,142; Circ 118,153
Library Holdings: AV Mats 3,647; Large Print Bks 2,701; Bk Vols 54,218; Per Subs 93
Special Collections: Large Print Coll; Local History Coll. Oral History
Automation Activity & Vendor Info: (Cataloging) Innovative Interfaces, Inc; (Circulation) Innovative Interfaces, Inc; (OPAC) Innovative Interfaces, Inc
Database Vendor: Innovative Interfaces, Inc
Wireless access

Publications: Monthly Calendar; Monthy e-newsletter
Mem of Southern Maine Library District
Open Tues & Thurs 10-7, Wed, Fri, & Sat 9-5
Friends of the Library Group

WHITNEYVILLE

P WHITNEYVILLE LIBRARY ASSOCIATION, INC*, 51 School St, 04654. SAN 306-7815. Tel: 207-255-8077. E-mail: whitstaff@msln.net. Web Site: www.whitneyville.lib.me.us. *Chief Librn, Ch, ILL Librn,* Patricia Brightly; *Asst Cat Librn, Asst Librn,* Renee Brightly; Staff 2 (Non-MLS 2)
Founded 1966. Pop 900; Circ 13,165
Library Holdings: Bk Titles 11,991; Bk Vols 15,310; Per Subs 4
Special Collections: All Newberry & Caldecott Medal Winners 1928-97; Children's Books (Lucy Stanton Bodger Coll); Memorial Children's Book Coll (1956-1963)
Subject Interests: Art & archit, Biol, Fiction, Hist, Lit, Music, Sports
Database Vendor: EBSCOhost
Wireless access
Function: Children's prog
Mem of Northeastern Maine Library District
Open Mon-Thurs & Sat 1-4
Friends of the Library Group

WILTON

P WILTON FREE PUBLIC LIBRARY*, Six Goodspeed St, 04294. (Mail add: PO Box 454, 04294-0454), SAN 306-7823. Tel: 207-645-4831. FAX: 207-645-9417. Web Site: www.wilton-free.lib.me.us. *Dir,* David L Olson; E-mail: director@wilton-free.lib.me.us; *Adult Serv,* Lynne Hunter; *Ch Serv,* Sandy Warren; Staff 4 (MLS 1, Non-MLS 3)
Founded 1901. Pop 4,242; Circ 35,000
Jul 2006-Jun 2007 Income $105,460, City $92,934, Locally Generated Income $7,000, Other $5,526. Mats Exp $12,816, Books $10,000, Per/Ser (Incl. Access Fees) $700, AV Equip $350, AV Mat $1,266, Electronic Ref Mat (Incl. Access Fees) $500. Sal $58,657 (Prof $24,000)
Library Holdings: AV Mats 1,615; Bks-By-Mail 375; Bks on Deafness & Sign Lang 10; CDs 427; DVDs 345; Electronic Media & Resources 60; Large Print Bks 504; Bk Titles 20,596; Bk Vols 21,000; Per Subs 63; Talking Bks 644; Videos 318
Special Collections: Genealogy Coll
Automation Activity & Vendor Info: (Acquisitions) Main Library Systems; (Cataloging) Main Library Systems; (Circulation) Main Library Systems
Wireless access
Function: Homebound delivery serv, ILL available, Photocopying/Printing, Prog for children & young adult, Summer reading prog
Special Services for the Deaf - Bks on deafness & sign lang; Staff with knowledge of sign lang
Special Services for the Blind - Large print & cassettes
Open Tues & Fri 10-5, Wed Noon-7, Thurs 10-7, Sat 10-1
Friends of the Library Group

WINDHAM

S MAINE DEPARTMENT OF CORRECTIONS*, Maine Correctional Center Library, 17 Mallison Falls Rd, 04062. Tel: 207-893-7000. FAX: 207-893-7001. *Librn,* Francine Bowden
Library Holdings: Bk Vols 11,500; Per Subs 30; Talking Bks 25
Special Collections: Law Coll
Automation Activity & Vendor Info: (Cataloging) Follett Software; (Circulation) Follett Software; (ILL) OCLC
Open Mon-Fri 9-11 & 1-4

P WINDHAM PUBLIC LIBRARY*, 217 Windham Center Rd, 04062. SAN 306-784X. Tel: 207-892-1908. FAX: 207-892-1915. E-mail: windham.public.library@msln.net. Web Site: www.windham.lib.me.us. *Dir,* Jen Leo; E-mail: jaleo@windhammaine.us; *Ch,* Laurel Parker; *Ad,* Sally Bannen; *Ref/Info Tech Serv Librn,* Barbara Keef; Staff 4 (MLS 3, Non-MLS 1)
Founded 1971. Pop 17,000; Circ 114,000
Jul 2010-Jun 2011 Income $302,000. Mats Exp $32,900, Books $24,300, Per/Ser (Incl. Access Fees) $3,000, AV Mat $5,600. Sal $263,000 (Prof $210,000)
Library Holdings: AV Mats 5,000; Bks on Deafness & Sign Lang 10; CDs 400; DVDs 500; Bk Vols 45,000; Per Subs 105; Talking Bks 1,000; Videos 1,000
Automation Activity & Vendor Info: (Cataloging) LibLime; (Circulation) LibLime; (OPAC) LibLime
Wireless access
Mem of Southern Maine Library District
Open Mon & Wed 9:30-8, Tues & Thurs 9:30-6, Fri & Sat 9:30-5
Friends of the Library Group

WINSLOW

P WINSLOW PUBLIC LIBRARY*, 136 Halifax St, 04901. SAN 372-6347. Tel: 207-872-1978. FAX: 207-872-1979. E-mail: wplill@winslow.lib.me.us. Web Site: www.winslow.lib.me.us. *Dir,* Pamela Fesq Bonney; E-mail: pbonney@winslow.lib.me.us; Staff 2 (MLS 1, Non-MLS 1)
Founded 1905. Pop 8,000; Circ 45,000
Library Holdings: Audiobooks 1,500; AV Mats 3,500; Bks on Deafness & Sign Lang 60; CDs 775; DVDs 930; Electronic Media & Resources 4; High Interest/Low Vocabulary Bk Vols 1,050; Large Print Bks 1,587; Bk Titles 43,379; Per Subs 67; Videos 2,360
Automation Activity & Vendor Info: (Acquisitions) Winnebago Software Co; (Cataloging) Winnebago Software Co; (Circulation) Winnebago Software Co; (OPAC) Winnebago Software Co
Database Vendor: EBSCOhost
Wireless access
Partic in Maine State Libr Network
Special Services for the Deaf - Accessible learning ctr; Adult & family literacy prog; Bks on deafness & sign lang; High interest/low vocabulary bks
Special Services for the Blind - Home delivery serv; Large print & cassettes; Large print bks
Open Mon, Tues & Fri 9-8, Wed & Thurs 1-8, Sat (Sept-June) 9-1
Friends of the Library Group

WINTER HARBOR

P WINTER HARBOR PUBLIC LIBRARY*, 18 Chapel Lane, 04693. (Mail add: PO Box 310, 04693-0310), SAN 306-7866. Tel: 207-963-7556. E-mail: winterharbor@winterharbor.lib.me.us. Web Site: www.winterharbor.lib.me.us. *Libr Dir,* Leslie Walton; Staff 0.375 (Non-MLS 0.375)
Founded 1918. Pop 1,120; Circ 4,185
Library Holdings: Audiobooks 200; DVDs 75; Bk Titles 4,991; Bk Vols 6,000; Videos 200
Database Vendor: EBSCOhost
Wireless access
Mem of Northeastern Maine Library District
Open Wed & Sat 1-5, Fri 10-5

WINTERPORT

P WINTERPORT MEMORIAL LIBRARY*, 229 Main St, 04496. (Mail add: PO Box 650, 04496-0650), SAN 306-7874. Tel: 207-223-5540. Web Site: www.winterportmaine.gov/library.htm. *Librn,* Mary Lester; E-mail: mlester@winterport.lib.me.us; Staff 1 (Non-MLS 1)
Pop 2,675; Circ 8,506
Library Holdings: Bk Titles 11,244; Bk Vols 12,000; Per Subs 40
Database Vendor: EBSCOhost
Mem of Northeastern Maine Library District
Open Tues Noon-5, Thurs 2-7, Sat 9-2

WINTHROP

P CHARLES M BAILEY PUBLIC LIBRARY*, 39 Bowdoin St, 04364. SAN 306-7882. Tel: 207-377-8673. Web Site: www.baileylibrary.org. *Dir,* Richard Fortin; E-mail: director@baileylibrary.org; *Ad,* Shane Malcolm Billings; E-mail: smbillings@baileylibrary.org; *Ch,* Cindy Hinkley; E-mail: chinkley@baileylibrary.org; Staff 5 (MLS 1, Non-MLS 4)
Founded 1916. Pop 6,500; Circ 65,000
Jul 2009-Jun 2010 Income $165,708. Mats Exp $24,250, Books $17,500, Per/Ser (Incl. Access Fees) $2,000, AV Mat $4,750. Sal $106,500 (Prof $39,000)
Library Holdings: Audiobooks 1,400; AV Mats 2,000; Bks on Deafness & Sign Lang 50; CDs 1,000; DVDs 1,400; e-books 36; Electronic Media & Resources 52; Large Print Bks 560; Bk Titles 26,575; Bk Vols 27,181; Per Subs 25; Talking Bks 1,400; Videos 600
Automation Activity & Vendor Info: (Acquisitions) Baker & Taylor; (Cataloging) Innovative Interfaces, Inc - Millenium; (Circulation) Innovative Interfaces, Inc - Millenium; (ILL) Innovative Interfaces, Inc - Millenium; (OPAC) Innovative Interfaces, Inc - Millenium; (Serials) Innovative Interfaces, Inc - Millenium
Database Vendor: Baker & Taylor, Booklist Online, EBSCOhost, H W Wilson, Innovative Interfaces, Inc, Innovative Interfaces, Inc, PubMed
Wireless access
Function: Adult bk club, After school storytime, Audiobks via web, Bk club(s), Bk reviews (Group), Bks on cassette, Bks on CD, CD-ROM, Children's prog, Computers for patron use, Copy machines, e-mail & chat, Electronic databases & coll, Free DVD rentals, Handicapped accessible, Holiday prog, ILL available, Mus passes, Music CDs, Online cat, Online ref, Online searches, Orientations, OverDrive digital audio bks, Photocopying/Printing, Prog for adults, Prog for children & young adult, Pub access computers, Ref & res, Ref serv available, Ref serv in person, Story hour, Summer reading prog, Tax forms, Teen prog, Telephone ref, VCDs, VHS videos, Video lending libr, Web-catalog, Wheelchair accessible

Partic in Central Maine Libr District
Open Mon, Wed & Fri 10-6, Tues 10-8, Sat 10-3
Friends of the Library Group

WISCASSET

GL LINCOLN COUNTY LAW LIBRARY*, Lincoln County Courthouse, 32 High St, 04578. (Mail add: PO Box 249, 04578-0249), SAN 306-7890. Tel: 207-882-7517. Administration Tel: 207-563-8900. *Head of Libr,* Dan Purdy
Library Holdings: Bk Vols 10,000
Open Mon-Fri 8-4

P WISCASSET PUBLIC LIBRARY*, 21 High St, 04578-4119. SAN 306-7904. Tel: 207-882-7161. FAX: 207-882-6698. E-mail: wpl@wiscasset.lib.me.us. Web Site: www.wiscasset.lib.me.us. *Dir,* Pamela Dunning; E-mail: pdunning@wiscasset.lib.me.us; *Ch Serv,* Judy Flanagan
Founded 1920. Pop 5,865
Jan 2012-Dec 2012 Income $171,199, City $88,213, Locally Generated Income $6,244, Other $33,167. Mats Exp $18,381. Sal $104,137
Library Holdings: AV Mats 1,648; CDs 270; DVDs 97; Large Print Bks 356; Bk Vols 30,777; Per Subs 77; Talking Bks 748; Videos 533
Special Collections: Art Coll; Local History Archives
Automation Activity & Vendor Info: (Cataloging) Follett Software; (Circulation) Follett Software; (OPAC) Follett Software
Wireless access
Function: Archival coll, Art exhibits, Audiobks via web, Bks on cassette, Bks on CD, Children's prog, Computers for patron use, Distance learning, e-mail serv, Electronic databases & coll, Home delivery & serv to Sr ctr & nursing homes, ILL available, Mus passes, Music CDs, Notary serv, OverDrive digital audio bks, Passport agency, Photocopying/Printing, Prog for adults, Pub access computers, Summer reading prog, Tax forms, Web-catalog
Open Tues, Thurs & Fri 10-5, Wed 10-7, Sat 9-2
Friends of the Library Group

YARMOUTH

P MERRILL MEMORIAL LIBRARY*, 215 Main St, 04096. SAN 306-7939. Tel: 207-846-4763. FAX: 207-846-2422. Web Site: www.yarmouth.me.us. *Dir,* Heidi Grimm; *Circ Librn,* Jo Adamo; *Children's & Youth Serv,* Melissa Madigan; *Syst/Tech Serv,* Nissa Flanagan; Staff 1 (Non-MLS 1)
Founded 1904. Pop 7,400; Circ 68,541
Library Holdings: Bk Vols 44,000; Per Subs 96
Subject Interests: Genealogy, Hist
Automation Activity & Vendor Info: (Cataloging) Follett Software; (Circulation) Follett Software; (OPAC) Follett Software
Database Vendor: EBSCOhost
Wireless access
Publications: Monthly Newsletter
Mem of Southern Maine Library District
Partic in OCLC Online Computer Library Center, Inc
Open Mon & Thurs-Sat 10-5, Tues & Wed 10-8
Friends of the Library Group

YORK

S OLD YORK HISTORICAL SOCIETY LIBRARY*, 207 York St, 03909. (Mail add: PO Box 312, 03909-0312), SAN 306-7947. Tel: 207-363-4974. FAX: 207-363-4021. E-mail: library@oldyork.org. Web Site: www.oldyork.org. *Librn,* Virginia Spiller
Library Holdings: Bk Titles 6,000
Special Collections: Local Photographs & Genealogies; Rare Books & Manuscripts from Local 18th Century Private Libraries & the York Social Library, estab 1796
Subject Interests: Am folk art, Decorative art, Genealogy, Local hist
Mem of Southern Maine Library District
Open Thurs & Fri 9-4, Sat 10-2:30

P YORK PUBLIC LIBRARY*, 15 Long Sands Rd, 03909. SAN 306-7955. Tel: 207-363-2818. FAX: 207-363-7250. E-mail: ypl@york.lib.me.us. Web Site: www.york.lib.me.us. *Dir,* Robert Waldman; *Asst Dir,* Sudie Blanchard; *Ch Serv,* Kathleen Whalin; *Circ,* Frank Dehler; Staff 4 (MLS 3, Non-MLS 1)
Founded 1912. Pop 15,000; Circ 86,370
Library Holdings: AV Mats 1,699; Large Print Bks 1,500; Bk Titles 39,000; Bk Vols 40,017; Per Subs 50; Talking Bks 599
Automation Activity & Vendor Info: (Cataloging) Innovative Interfaces, Inc; (Circulation) Innovative Interfaces, Inc; (ILL) Innovative Interfaces, Inc; (OPAC) Innovative Interfaces, Inc; (Serials) Innovative Interfaces, Inc
Database Vendor: EBSCOhost, ProQuest
Wireless access
Function: Handicapped accessible, Homebound delivery serv, ILL available, Photocopying/Printing, Prog for adults, Prog for children & young adult, Summer reading prog, Wheelchair accessible
Mem of Southern Maine Library District
Special Services for the Blind - Bks on cassette; Bks on CD; Home delivery serv; Large print bks
Open Tues-Thurs 10-8, Fri 10-5, Sat 10-2
Friends of the Library Group

MARYLAND

Date of Statistics: FY 2013
Population, 2010 U.S. Census: 5,773,552
Population Served: 5,773,552
Total Volumes in Public Libraries: 15,465,436
Volumes Per Capita: 2.88
Total Public Library Circulation: 57,538,130
Circulation Per Capita: 9.97
Total Public Library Income (including Grants-in-Aid): $258,698,515
Income per capita: $44.67
Source of Income: Public funds
Grants-in-Aid to Public Libraries:
Federal: $770,921
State Aid: $35,477,480
Library Operations: $245,312,482
Library Network: $9,641,832
Number of Bookmobiles: 16

ABERDEEN PROVING GROUND

UNITED STATES ARMY

A ABERDEEN AREA GARRISON LIBRARY*, Bldg 3326, 21005-5001, SAN 370-0992. Tel: 410-278-3417. FAX: 410-278-5684. *Librn,* Mike Lacomb
Library Holdings: Bk Titles 30,000; Per Subs 70
Subject Interests: Mil hist, World War II
Automation Activity & Vendor Info: (Cataloging) SirsiDynix; (Circulation) SirsiDynix
Function: ILL available, Ref serv available
Open Mon-Fri 11-6, Sat 9-2

A ORDNANCE CENTER & ORDNANCE MUSEUM LIBRARY*, 2221 Adams Bldg 5020, Fort Lee, 23801, SAN 343-7345. Tel: 804-734-4878. FAX: 410-278-7473. E-mail: usarmy.lee.tradoc.mbx.ordnance-museum@mail.mil. Web Site: www.ordmusfound.org.
Founded 1973
Library Holdings: Bk Vols 1,460
Special Collections: US Army Technical Manuals Coll
Subject Interests: Mat culture
Restriction: Not a lending libr

A PUBLIC HEALTH COMMAND LIBRARY*, 5158 Blackhawk Rd, BLDG E-5158, 21010-5403, SAN 343-7434. Tel: 410-436-4236. FAX: 410-436-4602. *Libr Tech,* Claudia A Coleman; *Libr Tech,* Letitia M Matthews
Founded 1945
Library Holdings: Bk Titles 13,000; Bk Vols 21,000; Per Subs 200
Subject Interests: Chem, Eng, Med, Occupational safety, Physics, Pub health, Toxicology
Partic in Dialog Corp; OCLC Online Computer Library Center, Inc; US National Library of Medicine
Publications: Journal Holdings List
Restriction: Access for corporate affiliates

AM UNITED STATES ARMY MEDICAL RESEARCH INSTITUTE OF CHEMICAL DEFENSE*, Wood Technical Library, 3100 Ricketts Point Rd, 21010-5400. SAN 343-7396. Tel: 410-436-4135. FAX: 410-436-3176. *Libr Dir,* Pamela Mesite; *Libr Tech,* Leanna Bush; Staff 2 (MLS 1, Non-MLS 1)
Founded 1979
Library Holdings: e-journals 25; Bk Vols 5,258; Per Subs 76
Subject Interests: Pharmacology, Toxicology
Automation Activity & Vendor Info: (Cataloging) Ex Libris Group; (Circulation) Ex Libris Group; (OPAC) Ex Libris Group; (Serials) TDNet
Database Vendor: American Chemical Society, Dialog, Ingenta, ISI Web of Knowledge, Nature Publishing Group, PubMed, Sage, TDNet, Thomson - Web of Science, Wiley
Function: ILL available, Res libr
Partic in National Network of Libraries of Medicine; OCLC Online Computer Library Center, Inc
Open Mon-Fri 7 5:30
Restriction: Restricted access

ACCOKEEK

S ACCOKEEK FOUNDATION LIBRARY*, 3400 Bryan Point Rd, 20607. SAN 371-2826. Tel: 301-283-2113. FAX: 301-283-2049. E-mail: info@accokeek.org. Web Site: www.accokeek.org. *Educ & Outreach Coordr,* Molly Meehan
Library Holdings: Bk Vols 2,600; Per Subs 20
Restriction: Authorized personnel only

ADELPHI

S UNITED STATES ARMY RESEARCH LABORATORY*, Technical Library, 2800 Powder Mill Rd, 20783-1197. SAN 306-7963. Tel: 301-394-2536. FAX: 301-394-1465. E-mail: libraryALC@arl.army.mil. *Librn,* Position Currently Open; *Tech Serv,* Louise McGovern; Staff 5 (MLS 1, Non-MLS 4)
Library Holdings: Bk Vols 36,000; Per Subs 800
Special Collections: DOD Publications
Subject Interests: Chem, Econ, Electrical eng, Electronics, Mechanical eng
Automation Activity & Vendor Info: (Acquisitions) SirsiDynix; (Cataloging) SirsiDynix; (Circulation) SirsiDynix; (OPAC) SirsiDynix; (Serials) SirsiDynix
Database Vendor: OCLC FirstSearch
Partic in Dialog Corp; OCLC Online Computer Library Center, Inc; SDC Info Servs
Special Services for the Deaf - Staff with knowledge of sign lang
Open Mon-Fri 9-4

ANDREWS AFB

AM UNITED STATES AIR FORCE*, 89th Malcolm Grow Medical Group, 1050 W Perimeter Rd, Bldg 1053, 20762-6601. SAN 337-0860. Tel: 240-857-2354. FAX: 240-857-8608. *Librn,* Tina Pinnix-Broome
Founded 1958
Library Holdings: Bk Vols 8,000; Per Subs 285
Automation Activity & Vendor Info: (OPAC) EOS International
Database Vendor: OVID Technologies
Partic in Fedlink; OCLC Online Computer Library Center, Inc
Restriction: Med staff only

ANNAPOLIS

GL ANNE ARUNDEL COUNTY CIRCUIT COURT*, Anne Arundel County Public Law Library, Seven Church Circle, Ste 303, 21401. (Mail add: PO Box 2395, 21404-2395), SAN 321-7701. Tel: 410-222-1387. FAX: 410-268-9762. E-mail: library@circuitcourt.org. Web Site: www.circuitcourt.org. *Librn,* Joan Bellistri; *Asst Librn,* Nancy Wallace; Staff 2 (MLS 1, Non-MLS 1)
Library Holdings: Bk Titles 2,157; Bk Vols 20,263; Per Subs 30

Special Collections: Law (Maryland Coll)
Database Vendor: HeinOnline, LexisNexis, OCLC WorldShare Interlibrary Loan, Westlaw
Partic in Law Libr Asn of Md
Open Mon-Fri 9-4:30
Restriction: Open to pub for ref only

P ANNE ARUNDEL COUNTY PUBLIC LIBRARY*, Headquarters, Five Harry S Truman Pkwy, 21401. SAN 343-7469. Tel: 410-222-7371. FAX: 410-222-7188. Web Site: www.aacpl.net. *Exec Dir,* Hampton Auld; Tel: 410-222-7234, E-mail: sauld@aacpl.net; *Chief Financial Officer,* Scott A Sedmak; Tel: 410-222-7236, E-mail: ssedmak@aacpl.net; *Chief, Info Tech Serv,* Randy Rice; E-mail: rrice@aacpl.net; *Chief, Pub Serv,* Nancy J Choice; Tel: 410-222-7287, E-mail: nchoice@aacpl.net; *Head, Mat Mgt,* Cynthia Bischoff; E-mail: cbischoff@aacpl.net; Staff 261 (MLS 53, Non-MLS 208)
Founded 1936. Pop 503,300; Circ 5,302,767
Library Holdings: Bk Vols 1,225,198
Subject Interests: Maryland
Automation Activity & Vendor Info: (Circulation) SirsiDynix
Database Vendor: SirsiDynix
Wireless access
Publications: Library Happenings; Seniors Brochure; Small Business Handbook; Staff Newsletter; Story Time; Welcome Flyer
Open Mon-Fri 8-4
Branches: 15
ANNAPOLIS REGIONAL LIBRARY, 1410 West St, 21401, SAN 343-7493. Tel: 410-222-1750. FAX: 410-222-1116. E-mail: ann@aacpl.net. *Br Mgr,* Gloria Harberts; E-mail: gharberts@aacpl.net
Library Holdings: Bk Vols 162,800
Open Mon-Thurs 9-9, Fri & Sat 9-5, Sun 1-5
BROADNECK COMMUNITY LIBRARY, 1275 Green Holly Dr, 21401, SAN 343-7507. Tel: 410-222-1905. FAX: 410-222-1908. E-mail: bdn@aacpl.net. *Br Mgr,* Debra Mattingly; E-mail: dmattingly@aacpl.net
Open Mon-Thurs 9-9, Fri & Sat 9-5
BROOKLYN PARK COMMUNITY LIBRARY, One E 11th Ave, Baltimore, 21225, SAN 343-7523. Tel: 410-222-6260. FAX: 410-222-6263. E-mail: bpk@aacpl.net. *Mgr,* Catherine McNamara; E-mail: cmcnamara@aacpl.net
Open Mon-Thurs 9-9, Fri & Sat 9-5
CROFTON COMMUNITY LIBRARY, 1681 Riedel Rd, Crofton, 21114, SAN 343-7558. Tel: 410-222-7915. FAX: 410-222-7269. *Mgr,* Ruby Jaby; E-mail: rjaby@aacpl.net
Open Mon-Thurs 9-9, Fri & Sat 9-5, Sun (Sept-May) 1-5
DEALE COMMUNITY LIBRARY, 5940 Deale-Churchton Rd, Deale, 20751, SAN 343-7825. Tel: 410-222-1925, 410-867-4164. FAX: 410-222-1910. E-mail: sco@aacpl.net. Web Site: www.aacpl.net/branch_info/sco.htm. *Br Mgr,* Rachel Myers; E-mail: rmyers@aacpl.net
Open Mon-Thurs 9-9, Fri & Sat 9-5
EASTPORT-ANNAPOLIS NECK BRANCH, 269 Hillsmere Dr, 21403, SAN 343-7582. Tel: 410-222-1770. FAX: 410-222-1973. *Br Mgr,* Michele Noble; E-mail: mnoble@aacpl.net
Open Mon-Thurs 9-9, Fri & Sat 9-5
EDGEWATER COMMUNITY LIBRARY, 25 Stepneys Lane, Edgewater, 21037, SAN 371-9758. Tel: 410-222-1538. FAX: 410-222-1543. E-mail: edg@aacpl.net. *Br Mgr,* Marc Gluck; E-mail: mgluck@aacpl.net
Open Mon-Thurs 9-9, Fri & Sat 9-5
GLEN BURNIE REGIONAL LIBRARY, 1010 Eastway, Glen Burnie, 21061, SAN 343-7701. Tel: 410-222-6270. FAX: 410-222-6276. E-mail: nco@aacpl.net. *Br Mgr,* Wanda Wagner; E-mail: wwagner@aacpl.net
Open Mon-Thurs 9-9, Fri & Sat 9-5, Sun (Sept-May) 1-5
LINTHICUM COMMUNITY LIBRARY, 400 Shipley Rd, Linthicum, 21090, SAN 343-7647. Tel: 410-222-6265. FAX: 410-222-6269. E-mail: lin@aacpl.net. *Br Mgr,* Adam Mazurek; E-mail: amazurek@aacpl.net
Open Mon-Thurs 9-9, Fri & Sat 9-5
MARYLAND CITY AT RUSSETT COMMUNITY LIBRARY, 3501 Russett Common, Laurel, 20724, SAN 343-7671. Tel: 301-725-2390. FAX: 301-498-5749. E-mail: mdc@aacpl.net. *Br Mgr,* Gail Vernon; E-mail: gvernon@aacpl.net
Open Mon-Thurs 9-9, Fri & Sat 9-5
MOUNTAIN ROAD COMMUNITY LIBRARY, 4730 Mountain Rd, Pasadena, 21122, SAN 374-5260. Tel: 410-222-6699. FAX: 410-222-6705. E-mail: mtr@aacpl.net. *Br Mgr,* Jennifer Adams; E-mail: jadams@aacpl.net
Open Mon-Thurs 9-9, Fri & Sat 9-5
ODENTON REGIONAL LIBRARY, 1325 Annapolis Rd, Odenton, 21113. Tel: 410-222-6277. FAX: 410-222-6279. E-mail: wco@aacpl.net. Web Site: www.aacpl.net/branch_info/wco.htm. *Br Mgr & Western Area Supvr,* Natalie Edington; E-mail: nedington@aacpl.net
Founded 2004
Open Mon-Thurs 9-9, Fri & Sat 9-5, Sun (Sept-May) 1-5
RIVIERA BEACH COMMUNITY LIBRARY, 1130 Duvall Hwy, Pasadena, 21122, SAN 343-7760. Tel: 410-222-6285. FAX: 410-222-6287. E-mail: riv@aacpl.net. *Br Mgr,* Timothy Burall; E-mail: tburall@aacpl.net
Open Mon-Thurs 9-9, Fri & Sat 9-5
SEVERN COMMUNITY LIBRARY, 2624 Annapolis Rd, Rte 175, Severn, 21144, SAN 328-6673. Tel: 410-222-6280. FAX: 410-222-6283. E-mail: pro@aacpl.net. *Br Mgr,* Carol Brothers; E-mail: cbrothers@aacpl.net
Open Mon-Thurs 9-9, Fri & Sat 9-5
SEVERNA PARK COMMUNITY LIBRARY, 45 McKinsey Rd, Severna Park, 21146, SAN 343-7795. Tel: 410-222-6290. FAX: 410-222-6297. E-mail: spk@aacpl.net. *Br Mgr,* Karen Mansbridge; E-mail: kmansbridge@aacpl.net
Open Mon-Thurs 9-9, Fri & Sat 9-5, Sun (Sept-May) 1-5

M ANNE ARUNDEL MEDICAL CENTER LIBRARY*, 2001 Medical Pkwy, 21401. SAN 306-7998. Tel: 443-481-1000, Ext 4877. Web Site: www.aahs.org. *Librn,* Joyce Cortright Miller
Founded 1970
Library Holdings: e-journals 1,250; Bk Vols 300; Per Subs 150
Automation Activity & Vendor Info: (Acquisitions) Follett Software; (Cataloging) Follett Software; (Circulation) Follett Software
Database Vendor: Cinahl, EBSCOhost, MD Consult, OVID Technologies, PubMed, UpToDate
Wireless access
Partic in US National Library of Medicine
Restriction: Employees only

S CENTER FOR PUBLIC JUSTICE LIBRARY*, 2444 Solomon's Island Rd, Ste 201, 21401. SAN 376-1789. Tel: 410-571-6300. FAX: 410-571-6365. Web Site: www.cpjustice.org. *Pres,* James W Skillen
Founded 1977
Library Holdings: Bk Vols 4,000; Per Subs 15
Open Mon-Fri 9-5

GL MARYLAND DEPARTMENT OF LEGISLATIVE SERVICES LIBRARY*, 90 State Circle, 21401. SAN 306-8048. Tel: 410-946-5400. FAX: 410-946-5405. E-mail: libr@mlis.state.md.us. *Dir, Libr & Info Serv,* Johanne Greer; *Cat Librn,* Lehmkuhl Karen; *Acq Mgr,* Cynthia Stiverson; Staff 11 (MLS 11)
Founded 1966
Jul 2005-Jun 2006. Mats Exp $370,000, Books $265,000, Per/Ser (Incl. Access Fees) $93,000
Library Holdings: Bk Titles 30,000; Bk Vols 100,000; Per Subs 150
Special Collections: Codes of Fifty States; Maryland County Codes Coll; Maryland History Coll; State Publications. State Document Depository
Subject Interests: State govt
Automation Activity & Vendor Info: (Acquisitions) SirsiDynix; (Cataloging) SirsiDynix; (Circulation) SirsiDynix; (OPAC) SirsiDynix; (Serials) SirsiDynix
Publications: Maryland Documents
Partic in OCLC Online Computer Library Center, Inc
Special Services for the Deaf - TTY equip
Open Mon-Fri 8-5:30
Restriction: Open to pub for ref only

G MARYLAND DEPARTMENT OF NATURAL RESOURCES*, Carter Library & Information Resource Center, 580 Taylor Ave, B3, 21401. Tel: 410-260-8830. FAX: 410-260-8951. E-mail: library@dnr.state.md.us. Web Site: www.dnr.state.md.us/irc. *Librn,* Ann Wheeler
Founded 1998
Library Holdings: AV Mats 3,000; Bk Vols 10,000; Per Subs 60
Special Collections: Grey Literature on the Chesapeake Bay; Maryland Department of Natural Resources Publications
Subject Interests: Chesapeake Bay, Land mgt, Land resources, Natural res, Resource mgt, Water mgt, Water res
Automation Activity & Vendor Info: (Cataloging) OCLC; (Circulation) Book Systems; (ILL) OCLC; (OPAC) Book Systems
Database Vendor: OCLC FirstSearch
Function: Res libr
Open Mon-Fri 8-4:30
Restriction: Non-circulating to the pub

L MARYLAND STATE LAW LIBRARY*, Courts of Appeal Bldg, 361 Rowe Blvd, 21401-1697. SAN 306-8064. Tel: 410-260-1430. Toll Free Tel: 888-216-8156. FAX: 410-260-1572. E-mail: lawlibrary@mdcourts.gov. Web Site: mdcourts.gov/lawlib, www.peoples-law.org. *Dir,* Steven Paul Anderson; E-mail: steve.anderson@courts.state.md.us; *Dep Dir,* James Durham; *Head, Ref & Outreach,* Catherine McGuire; *Head, Coll Mgt,* Mary Jo Lazun; *Head, Tech Serv,* Jessie Tam; *Cat & Ref Librn,* Jessica Nhem; *Ref Librn,* Elizabeth Simmons; *Ref Librn,* Tanya Thomas; *State Publ Librn,* Shirley Aronson; *Fiscal Serv Coordr,* Sara Marks; *Web Content Coordr,* Dave Pantzer; *Coll Mgt Spec,* Cindy Terry; *Ref Asst,* Maureen Della Barba; *Tech Asst,* Scott Ashlin; Staff 10.5 (MLS 10.5)

Founded 1826
Jul 2009-Jun 2010 Income $2,694,773. Mats Exp $1,029,000, Books $799,000, Electronic Ref Mat (Incl. Access Fees) $230,000
Library Holdings: Bk Titles 75,000; Bk Vols 400,000; Per Subs 700
Special Collections: Audubon's Birds of America Original Havell Edition Prints; Historic Legal Materials. State Document Depository; US Document Depository
Subject Interests: Govt, Law, State hist
Automation Activity & Vendor Info: (Acquisitions) Innovative Interfaces, Inc; (Cataloging) Innovative Interfaces, Inc; (ILL) OCLC; (OPAC) Innovative Interfaces, Inc; (Serials) Innovative Interfaces, Inc
Database Vendor: EBSCOhost, Gale Cengage Learning, H W Wilson, HeinOnline, Innovative Interfaces, Inc, Loislaw, OCLC FirstSearch, Progressive Technology Federal Systems, Inc (PTFS), ProQuest, SerialsSolutions, Westlaw, Wilson - Wilson Web
Wireless access
Function: Art exhibits, Audio & video playback equip for onsite use, AV serv, Computer training, Computers for patron use, Copy machines, Doc delivery serv, e-mail serv, Electronic databases & coll, Govt ref serv, ILL available, Online cat, Outreach serv, Scanner
Publications: Maryland State Law Library Annual Highlights (Annual report); Maryland State Selected New Booklist (Acquisition list); The People's Law Library (Online only)
Partic in Law Library Microform Consortium (LLMC); Legal Information Preservation Alliance (LIPA); OCLC Online Computer Library Center, Inc
Open Mon, Wed & Fri 8-4:30, Tues & Thurs 8am-9pm, Sat 9-4
Restriction: Non-circulating to the pub

A THE NAVAL INSTITUTE*, History, Reference & Preservation Department Library, 291 Wood Rd, 21402-5035. SAN 324-1033. Tel: 410-295-1024. FAX: 410-269-7940. E-mail: library@usni.org. Web Site: www.usni.org. *Mgr,* E T Woolridge; *Archivist,* Dewitt Roseborough
Library Holdings: Bk Titles 5,000
Special Collections: Photograph Archives. Oral History
Subject Interests: Mil hist
Open Mon-Fri 8-4:30

C ST JOHN'S COLLEGE LIBRARY*, Greenfield Library, 60 College Ave, 21401. (Mail add: PO Box 2800, 21404-2800), SAN 306-8080. Tel: 410-626-2548. Reference Tel: 410-295-6928. FAX: 410-295-6936. Web Site: www.stjohnscollege.edu/admin/AN/library/main.shtml. *Libr Dir,* Catherine Dixon; Tel: 410-626-2550, E-mail: catherine.dixon@sjca.edu; *Pub Serv Librn,* Cara Sabolcik; Tel: 410-295-6927, E-mail: cara.sabolcik@sjca.edu; *Tech Serv Librn,* Michael Waller; Tel: 410-626-2549, E-mail: michael.waller@sjca.edu; Staff 3 (MLS 3)
Founded 1793. Enrl 500; Highest Degree: Master
Library Holdings: CDs 200; DVDs 800; Bk Vols 115,000; Per Subs 120
Special Collections: Annapolitan Library (Bray Coll, Rev Thomas); Douglas Allanbrook Coll, musical scores; Prettyman Coll of Inscribed Books
Subject Interests: Classical studies, Hist of sci, Philos
Automation Activity & Vendor Info: (Cataloging) SirsiDynix; (Circulation) SirsiDynix; (OPAC) SirsiDynix
Database Vendor: ARTstor, Coutts Information Service, JSTOR, OCLC ArticleFirst, OCLC WorldShare Interlibrary Loan, Oxford Online, SirsiDynix, YBP Library Services
Wireless access
Function: Computers for patron use, Copy machines, Exhibits, Free DVD rentals, Handicapped accessible, ILL available, Mail & tel request accepted, Online cat, Orientations, Pub access computers, Ref serv available, Spoken cassettes & CDs, Telephone ref, VHS videos, Web-catalog
Partic in OCLC Online Computer Library Center, Inc

C UNITED STATES NAVAL ACADEMY*, Nimitz Library, 589 McNair Rd, 21402-5029. SAN 321-3404. Tel: 410-293-6900. Interlibrary Loan Service Tel: 410-293-6959. FAX: 410-293-6909. Interlibrary Loan Service FAX: 410-293-3669. Web Site: www.usna.edu/library. *Dir & Assoc Dean for Info Serv,* James Rettig; E-mail: rettig@usna.edu; *Assoc Libr Dir,* Patricia R Patterson; *Head, Acq,* Margaret J Danchik; *Head, Cat,* Laura R Nauta; *Head, Coll Develop & Media Serv,* Lawrence E Clemens; *Head, Ref & Instruction,* Barbara E Kemp; E-mail: bkemp@usna.edu; *Head, Spec Coll & Archives,* Jennifer A Bryan; *Head, Syst,* William Murray; *Actg Head, Circ,* Katherine Lang; Staff 36 (MLS 20, Non-MLS 16)
Founded 1845. Enrl 4,500; Fac 570; Highest Degree: Bachelor
Oct 2008-Sept 2009 Income $4,637,369, Federal $4,612,263, Other $25,106. Mats Exp $2,299,858, Books $412,826, Per/Ser (Incl. Access Fees) $1,802,420, Manu Arch $11,761, Other Print Mats $4,809, Micro $1,042, AV Mat $22,000, Presv $45,000. Sal $2,305,233
Library Holdings: Audiobooks 719; AV Mats 7,605; CDs 653; DVDs 2,865; Bk Vols 622,104; Per Subs 1,484; Videos 6,648
Special Collections: Albert A Michelson Coll; Electricity & Magnetism (Benjamin Coll); Naval Academy Archives; Naval History & Seapower; Paine Submarine Coll; Somers Submarine Coll; Steichen Photography Coll, bks & photogs; United States Navy Manuscript Colls. Oral History; US Document Depository
Subject Interests: Mil sci, Naval hist, Naval sci
Automation Activity & Vendor Info: (Acquisitions) Innovative Interfaces, Inc; (Cataloging) Innovative Interfaces, Inc; (Circulation) Innovative Interfaces, Inc; (OPAC) Innovative Interfaces, Inc; (Serials) Innovative Interfaces, Inc
Wireless access
Publications: Annual Report; Newsletter
Partic in National Research Library Alliance (NRLA); OCLC Online Computer Library Center, Inc

ARNOLD

J ANNE ARUNDEL COMMUNITY COLLEGE*, Andrew G Truxal Library, 101 College Pkwy, 21012-1895. SAN 306-8110. Tel: 410-777-2211. Circulation Tel: 410-777-2238. Interlibrary Loan Service Tel: 410-777-2536. Reference Tel: 410-777-2456. FAX: 410-777-2652. E-mail: library@aacc.edu. Web Site: www.aacc.edu/library. *Dir,* Cynthia Steinhoff; *Automation Librn,* Michelle Robertson; *Instrul Serv Librn,* Brandy Whitlock; *Access Serv,* Julia Woodward; *Cat, Distance Educ, ILL,* Vicki Cone; *Ref,* Janice Lathrop; Staff 18 (MLS 6, Non-MLS 12)
Founded 1961. Enrl 9,000; Fac 198; Highest Degree: Associate
Library Holdings: AV Mats 8,000; Bk Vols 140,000; Per Subs 375
Automation Activity & Vendor Info: (Cataloging) SirsiDynix; (Circulation) SirsiDynix; (ILL) OCLC; (OPAC) SirsiDynix; (Serials) SirsiDynix
Database Vendor: Gale Cengage Learning, OCLC FirstSearch, ProQuest, Westlaw
Partic in OCLC Online Computer Library Center, Inc
Open Mon-Thurs 8am-10pm, Fri 8-5, Sat 9-5, Sun 12-5
Friends of the Library Group

BALTIMORE

S ALTERNATIVE PRESS CENTER LIBRARY, 2239 Kirk Ave, 21218. (Mail add: PO Box 13127, 21203). Tel: 312-451-8133. E-mail: altpress@altpress.org. Web Site: www.altpress.org. *Exec Coordr,* Charles D'Adamo; E-mail: cdadamo@altpress.org; *Head Cataloger, Librn,* Kevin Jones; *Indexer, Production Coordr,* Graham Stephenson; *Indexer,* Kathleene Kunkle. Subject Specialists: *Humanities, Soc sci,* Charles D'Adamo; *Latin Am culture & politics, Spanish culture & politics,* Graham Stephenson; *Humanities,* Kathleene Kunkle; Staff 4 (MLS 3, Non-MLS 1)
Library Holdings: Bk Vols 2,000
Function: Archival coll
Restriction: Open by appt only

GL ATTORNEY GENERAL'S OFFICE*, Law Library, 200 Saint Paul Pl, 18th Flr, 21202. SAN 306-8641. Tel: 410-576-6400. FAX: 410-576-7002. Web Site: www.oag.state.md.us. *Chief Librn,* Natalie P Ellis; E-mail: nellis@oag.state.md.us; Staff 2 (MLS 1, Non-MLS 1)
Founded 1917
Library Holdings: Bk Vols 25,000; Per Subs 25
Automation Activity & Vendor Info: (Acquisitions) Inmagic, Inc.; (Cataloging) Inmagic, Inc.; (ILL) Inmagic, Inc.; (Serials) Inmagic, Inc.
Publications: Library Brief (Newsletter)

J BALTIMORE CITY COMMUNITY COLLEGE*, Bard Library, 2901 Liberty Heights Ave, 21215. SAN 343-7973. Tel: 410-462-8400. Reference Tel: 410-462-8240. FAX: 410-462-8233. Web Site: www.bccc.edu. *Dir, Libr Serv,* Stephanie Reidy; Staff 7 (MLS 5, Non-MLS 2)
Founded 1947. Enrl 4,460; Fac 120; Highest Degree: Associate
Jul 2010-Jun 2011. Mats Exp $220,000, Books $70,000, Per/Ser (Incl. Access Fees) $18,000, AV Mat $2,000, Electronic Ref Mat (Incl. Access Fees) $130,000
Library Holdings: Bk Vols 65,000; Per Subs 140
Special Collections: Baltimore Coll; Black History Coll; Maryland Coll. Oral History
Subject Interests: Allied health, Electronics, Ethnic studies, Nursing
Automation Activity & Vendor Info: (Cataloging) SIRSI Unicorn; (OPAC) SIRSI Unicorn; (Serials) SIRSI Unicorn
Publications: Baltimore Is Best
Open Mon-Thurs 7:45am-9pm, Fri 7:45-6, Sat 8-4:30

G BALTIMORE CITY DEPARTMENT OF LEGISLATIVE REFERENCE LIBRARY*, City Hall, Rm 626, 100 N Holliday St, 21202-3468. SAN 306-8196. Tel: 410-396-4730. FAX: 410-396-8483. *Dep Dir,* Nikki Fleming; Staff 8 (MLS 4, Non-MLS 4)
Founded 1874
Library Holdings: Bk Vols 500
Special Collections: Baltimore City Directories 1796-1964; Baltimore City Ordinances 1774-current; Court Proceedings (Maryland Reports 1780-current); Laws of Maryland 1692-current; Niles Register 1811-1848

Publications: Baltimore Charter; Baltimore City Building & Fire Codes; Baltimore City Code; Baltimore Municipal Handbook; Book Beat (Newsletter); Public Local Laws
Open Mon-Fri 8:30-4:30
Restriction: Open to pub for ref only

C BALTIMORE INTERNATIONAL COLLEGE*, George A Piendak Library, 17 Commerce St, 21202-3230. SAN 373-658X. Tel: 410-752-4710, Ext 137 or 138. FAX: 410-752-6720. *Dir,* Gwendolyn Baker; E-mail: wbaker@bic.edu; *Ref Librn,* Elizabeth Madero; Tel: 410-752-4710, Ext 210; *Tech Serv Librn,* Paul Edward McAdam; Tel: 410-752-4710, Ext 145, E-mail: pmcadam@bic.edu; *Circ Tech,* Nina Baker Lucas; E-mail: nbaker@bic.edu; Staff 4 (MLS 3, Non-MLS 1)
Founded 1987. Enrl 800; Fac 45; Highest Degree: Master
Library Holdings: AV Mats 1,000; DVDs 100; Bk Vols 18,000; Per Subs 120
Special Collections: Culinary/Hospitality Coll
Automation Activity & Vendor Info: (Acquisitions) Baker & Taylor; (Cataloging) Ex Libris Group; (Circulation) Ex Libris Group; (Course Reserve) Ex Libris Group; (ILL) OCLC Connexion; (OPAC) Ex Libris Group
Database Vendor: ebrary, EBSCOhost, Hoovers, LexisNexis, Medline, OCLC FirstSearch, OCLC WorldShare Interlibrary Loan
Wireless access
Function: Res libr
Partic in Maryland Interlibrary Consortium (MIC); Md Independent Cols & Univs Alliance
Open Mon, Tues & Thurs 8-5, Wed 8-6, Fri 8-4
Restriction: Authorized patrons

S BALTIMORE METROPOLITAN COUNCIL*, Regional Information Center, 1500 Whetstone Way, Ste 300, 21230. SAN 306-8692. Tel: 410-732-9570. FAX: 410-732-9488. E-mail: ric@baltometro.org. Web Site: www.baltometro.org/regional-information-center/regional-information-center. *Mgr,* Amy Swackhamer; E-mail: aswackhamer@baltometro.org; Staff 1 (MLS 1)
Founded 1963
Library Holdings: Bk Titles 8,000; Bk Vols 10,000; Per Subs 150
Subject Interests: Demographics, Econ, Environ studies, Finance, Govt, Transportation, Urban planning
Function: Ref serv available
Publications: Acquisitions List
Partic in Maryland Interlibrary Loan Organization
Restriction: Open by appt only

S BALTIMORE MUSEUM OF ART*, E Kirkbride Miller Art Research Library, Ten Art Museum Dr, 21218-3898. SAN 306-8218. Tel: 443-573-1778. FAX: 443-573-1781. Web Site: www.artbma.org. *Libr Dir,* Linda Tompkins-Baldwin; Tel: 443-573-1779, E-mail: ltompkins@artbma.org; *Archivist, Assoc Librn,* Emily Rafferty; Tel: 443-573-1780, E-mail: erafferty@artbma.org; *Project Archivist,* Anna Clarkson; Tel: 443-573-1782, E-mail: aclarkson@artbma.org; Staff 3 (MLS 3)
Founded 1929
Library Holdings: Bk Vols 50,000; Per Subs 300
Special Collections: American Decorative Arts; Artists' Books & Artists' Illustrated Books; Cone Coll, mss & papers; Cone Library; Dunton Papers; Lucas Library
Subject Interests: Africa, Art, Decorative art, Modern art, Photog, Prints
Automation Activity & Vendor Info: (Cataloging) SirsiDynix; (OPAC) SirsiDynix; (Serials) SirsiDynix
Database Vendor: ARTstor, H W Wilson, JSTOR, OCLC CAMIO, OCLC FirstSearch, OCLC WorldShare Interlibrary Loan, SirsiDynix
Wireless access
Function: For res purposes
Partic in OCLC Online Computer Library Center, Inc
Restriction: Non-circulating, Open by appt only

S BALTIMORE MUSEUM OF INDUSTRY, Research Center, 1415 Key Hwy, 21230. SAN 371-8581. Tel: 410-727-4808, Ext 110. FAX: 410-727-4869. Web Site: www.thebmi.org. *Librn,* Matthew Jones; E-mail: matthewwheelerjones@gmail.com; Staff 1 (MLS 1)
Founded 1990
Special Collections: Archival & Manuscript Colls; Business & Industry in Baltimore & Environs, AV, bks, flm, negatives, per, photogs, rare bks, tapes, trade cats, vf; Non-Current Periodicals. Oral History
Subject Interests: Indust hist, Soc hist, Urban studies
Function: Ref & res, Ref serv available
Publications: Research Center Brochure
Restriction: Non-circulating coll, Open by appt only, Open to pub by appt only, Open to researchers by request

M BON SECOURS HOSPITAL*, Health Science Library, 2000 W Baltimore St, 21223. SAN 306-8285. Tel: 410-362-3000, Ext 3581. FAX: 410-947-3210. Web Site: www.bonsecours.org/baltimore.
Founded 1970
Library Holdings: Bk Vols 3,000; Per Subs 38
Restriction: Employees only

SR CARMELITE MONASTERY*, Library & Archives, 1318 Dulaney Valley Rd, 21286-1399. SAN 327-5922. Tel: 410-823-7415. FAX: 410-823-7418. E-mail: info@baltimorecarmel.org. Web Site: www.baltimorecarmel.org/. *Sr Librn,* Leah Hargis; *Archivist,* Constance Fitzgerald
Library Holdings: Bk Titles 30,000
Special Collections: Archives of Oldest Community of Religious Women in 13 Original Colonies (1649-); Durham Coll - Maryland Law Suit (1820-1830); Rare Books from 1582
Subject Interests: Theol
Automation Activity & Vendor Info: (Cataloging) Mandarin Library Automation
Restriction: Mem only

M CARNEGIE INSTITUTION OF WASHINGTON*, Department of Embryology Library, 3520 San Marten Dr, 21218. SAN 375-2690. Tel: 410-246-3001. FAX: 410-243-6311. Web Site: www.ciwemb.edu.
Library Holdings: Bk Vols 800; Per Subs 10
Restriction: Mem only

C COPPIN STATE COLLEGE*, Parlett Moore Library, 2500 W North Ave, 21216-3698. SAN 306-8331. Tel: 410-951-3400. Circulation Tel: 410-951-3424. Reference Tel: 410-951-3425. FAX: 410-951-3430. Web Site: www.coppin.edu/library. *Dir,* Mary Wanza; *Circ,* Alice Smith; *Ref,* Robernette Smith; Staff 13 (MLS 7, Non-MLS 6)
Founded 1900. Enrl 3,400; Fac 111; Highest Degree: Master
Library Holdings: Bk Titles 68,178; Bk Vols 78,285; Per Subs 705
Special Collections: Black Studies; Maryland
Subject Interests: Biol, Educ, Nursing, Soc sci & issues
Automation Activity & Vendor Info: (Acquisitions) Ex Libris Group; (Cataloging) Ex Libris Group; (Circulation) Ex Libris Group; (Course Reserve) Ex Libris Group; (ILL) Ex Libris Group; (Media Booking) Ex Libris Group; (OPAC) Ex Libris Group; (Serials) Ex Libris Group
Database Vendor: OCLC FirstSearch
Wireless access
Partic in Colorado Alliance of Research Libraries; Maryland Interlibrary Loan Organization; OCLC Online Computer Library Center, Inc; Univ Syst of Md
Open Mon-Thurs 8am-11pm, Fri 8-5, Sat 10-4:30, Sun 2pm-7pm

S CYLBURN ARBORETUM ASSOCIATION LIBRARY*, 4915 Greenspring Ave, 21209. SAN 328-1493. Tel: 410-367-2217. FAX: 410-367-8039. E-mail: info@cas.org. Web Site: www.cylburnassociation.org. *Librn,* Adelaide C Rackemann
Founded 1955
Library Holdings: Bk Titles 2,000
Special Collections: Rock Gardening Coll; Wildflower Coll
Subject Interests: Hort
Automation Activity & Vendor Info: (Circulation) Ex Libris Group; (Course Reserve) Ex Libris Group
Function: Ref serv available
Restriction: Mem only

GM DEPARTMENT OF VETERANS AFFAIRS - VA MARYLAND HEALTH CARE SYSTEM*, Baltimore Medical Center Library, Ten N Greene St, BT/142D/LIB, 21201. SAN 306-8889. Tel: 410-605-7092. Administration Tel: 410-605-7093. FAX: 410-605-7905. *Librn,* Joanna Lin; Staff 2 (MLS 1, Non-MLS 1)
Founded 1952
Library Holdings: AV Mats 700; Bk Vols 12,000; Per Subs 300
Subject Interests: Educ, Hospital admin, Med, Nursing, Psychiat, Psychol, Soc serv (soc work)
Partic in Valpac; Veterans Affairs Libr Network (VALNET)
Open Mon-Fri 8-4:30

L DLA PIPER US LLP*, Law Library, 6225 Smith Ave, 21209-3600. SAN 306-8668. Tel: 410-580-3010. FAX: 410-580-3261. Web Site: www.dlapiper.com. *Librn,* Ronelle Manger; Tel: 410-580-4655, Fax: 410-580-3655, E-mail: ronelle.manger@dlapiper.com; Staff 6 (MLS 2, Non-MLS 4)
Library Holdings: Bk Vols 27,800; Per Subs 70
Subject Interests: Admin law, Banks & banking, Labor, Securities
Wireless access
Partic in Westlaw
Restriction: Not open to pub

P ENOCH PRATT FREE LIBRARY*, 400 Cathedral St, 21201-4484. SAN 343-8570. Tel: 410-396-5430. Administration Tel: 410-396-5395. FAX: 410-396-1441. Administration FAX: 410-396-1321. TDD: 410-396-3761. E-mail: GenInfo@prattlibrary.org. Web Site: www.prattlibrary.org. *Chief Exec Officer,* Dr Carla D Hayden; E-mail: chayden@prattlibrary.org; *Chief, Neighborhood Libr Serv,* Patricia Costello; *Chief, State Libr Res Ctr,* Wesley Wilson; E-mail: wwesley@prattlibrary.org; *Coord, Ad Serv,* Deborah Taylor; *Coordr, Ch Serv,* Ellen Riordan; *Circ,* Brandi Delly; *Coll Develop,* Lynn Stonesifer; *Res Sharing Spec,* Emma Beaven; Tel: 410-396-5498, Fax: 410-396-5837, E-mail: milo@prattlibrary.org
Founded 1886
Jul 2007-Jun 2008 Income (Main Library and Branch(s)) $34,844,215
Library Holdings: Audiobooks 33,945; AV Mats 125,402; CDs 35,483; DVDs 32,064; e-books 12,758; Electronic Media & Resources 83; Large Print Bks 12,212; Microforms 547; Music Scores 21,912; Bk Titles 1,141,436; Bk Vols 1,899,421; Per Subs 3,447; Videos 23,910
Special Collections: Adalbert Volck Civil War Etchings; African-American Rare Books Coll; African-American Sheet Music Coll; Baltimore Artist (Aaron Sopher Coll), drawings & prints; Baltimore Food & Wine Society Archives & Manuscripts; Baltimore Sculptor (Reuben Kramer Archives & Manuscripts); Baltimore Views, 1752-1930 (George Cator Coll); Bevan Bookplate Coll; Broadside Verses; Cookery, Gastronomy & Wines (Steiff Coll); Edgar Allen Poe Archives & Manuscripts; H L Mencken Archives & Manuscripts; Maryland Election/Campaign Literature Coll; Maryland Ephemera Coll; Maryland Imprints; Maryland Sheet Music Coll; Mencken's Saturday Night Club Sheet Music Coll; Richard Malcolm Johnston Archives & Manuscripts; Theater/Opera/Music Programs; United States Department Stores Mail Order Catalogs; Woman's Suffrage in Maryland Archives & Manuscripts; World War I & World War II Posters. State Document Depository; US Document Depository
Automation Activity & Vendor Info: (Acquisitions) SirsiDynix; (Cataloging) SirsiDynix; (Circulation) SirsiDynix; (ILL) SirsiDynix; (OPAC) SirsiDynix; (Serials) SirsiDynix
Wireless access
Publications: Cator Prints; Literacy Resources Bibliography; Menckeniana; Menckeniana; Reference Books; Selection Policies
Partic in OCLC Online Computer Library Center, Inc
Special Services for the Deaf - Bks on deafness & sign lang; Spec interest per; Staff with knowledge of sign lang; TTY equip
Special Services for the Blind - Reader equip; VisualTek equip
Friends of the Library Group
Branches: 20
BROOKLYN, 300 E Patapsco Ave, 21225-1828, SAN 343-8724. Tel: 410-396-1120. FAX: 410-396-1698. E-mail: brk@prattlibrary.org *Mgr,* Linda Schwaltz
CANTON, 1030 S Ellwood Ave, 21224-4930, SAN 343-902X. Tel: 410-396-8548. FAX: 410-396-7491. E-mail: cnt@prattlibrary.org. *Mgr,* Mariellen Baxter
Friends of the Library Group
CHERRY HILL, 606 Cherry Hill Rd, 21225, SAN 343-947X. Tel: 410-396-1168. FAX: 410-396-1174. E-mail: chr@prattlibrary.org. *Br Mgr,* Zandra Campbell
CLIFTON, 2001 N Wolfe St, 21213-1477, SAN 343-950X. Tel: 410-396-0984. FAX: 410-396-0985. E-mail: clf@prattlibrary.org. *Br Mgr,* Juanita Pilgrim
EDMONDSON AVENUE, 4330 Edmondson Ave, 21229-1615, SAN 343-9232. Tel: 410-396-0946. FAX: 410-396-0947. E-mail: edm@prattlibrary.org. *Br Mgr,* Shirley Johnson
Friends of the Library Group
FOREST PARK BRANCH, 3023 Garrison Blvd, 21216, SAN 343-9267. Tel: 410-396-0942. FAX: 410-396-0945. E-mail: frs@prattlibrary.org. *Br Mgr,* Marilyn Jones
Friends of the Library Group
GOVANS, 5714 Bellona Ave, 21212-3508, SAN 343-8813. Tel: 410-396-6098. FAX: 410-396-6291. E-mail: gvn@prattlibrary.org. *Br Mgr,* Jan Westervelt
Friends of the Library Group
HAMILTON, 5910 Harford Rd, 21214-1845, SAN 343-8848. Tel: 410-396-6088. FAX: 410-396-6097. E-mail: hml@prattlibrary.org. *Br Mgr,* Nancy Yob
HAMPDEN, 3641 Falls Rd, 21211-1815, SAN 343-9119. Tel: 410-396-6043. FAX: 410-396-7152. E-mail: hmp@prattlibrary.org. *Br Mgr,* Devon Ellis
HERRING RUN, 3801 Erdman Ave, 21213-2099, SAN 343-8872. Tel: 410-396-0996. FAX: 410-396-0997. E-mail: hrr@prattlibrary.org. *Br Mgr,* Doris Lynn Distance
Friends of the Library Group
LIGHT STREET, 1251 Light St, 21230-4305, SAN 343-8902. Tel: 410-396-1096. FAX: 410-396-1097. E-mail: lgh@prattlibrary.org. *Br Mgr,* Mary Triandafilou
Friends of the Library Group
NORTHWOOD BRANCH, 4420 Loch Raven Blvd, 21218-1553, SAN 343-8937. Tel: 410-396-6076. FAX: 410-396-6547. E-mail: nrt@prattlibrary.org. *Br Mgr,* Sylvia Coker
Friends of the Library Group
ORLEANS STREET, 1303 Orleans St, 21231, SAN 343-9208. Tel: 410-396-0970. FAX: 410-396-0979. E-mail: orl@prattlibrary.org. *Br Mgr,* Virginia Fore; Staff 5 (MLS 1, Non-MLS 4)
PATTERSON PARK, 158 N Linwood Ave, 21224-1255, SAN 343-8961. Tel: 410-396-0983. FAX: 410-396-5215. E-mail: ptt@prattlibrary.org. *Br Mgr,* Willie J Johnson
Friends of the Library Group
PENNSYLVANIA AVENUE, 1531 W North Ave, 21217-1735, SAN 343-9321. Tel: 410-396-0399. FAX: 410-396-0025. E-mail; pnn@prattlibrary.org. *Br Mgr,* Shirley Johnson
Subject Interests: Statistics
ROLAND PARK, 5108 Roland Ave, 21210-2132, SAN 343-8996. Tel: 410-396-6099. FAX: 410-396-6116. E-mail: rln@prattlibrary.org. Web Site: www.pratt.lib.md.us. *Br Mgr,* Julie Johnson; Staff 5 (MLS 2, Non-MLS 3)
Friends of the Library Group
SOUTHEAST ANCHOR, 3601 Eastern Ave, 21224-4109, SAN 343-9143. Tel: 410-396-1580. FAX: 443-984-3941. E-mail: sel@prattlibrary.org. *Br Mgr,* Cynthia Kleback
WALBROOK, 3203 W North Ave, 21216-3015, SAN 343-9410. Tel: 410-396-0935. FAX: 410-396-0256. E-mail: wlb@prattlibrary.org. *Br Mgr,* Stanley Butler
WASHINGTON VILLAGE, 856 Washington Blvd, 21230, SAN 377-6824. Tel: 410-396-1099. FAX: 410-396-1115. E-mail: wsh@prattlibrary.org. Web Site: www.pratt.lib.md.us/branches/wsh. *Br Mgr,* Romaine Chase Bobbitt
Library Holdings: Bk Titles 10,000; Bk Vols 15,000
WAVERLY, 400 E 33rd St, 21218-3401, SAN 343-9445. Tel: 410-396-6053. FAX: 410-396-6150. E-mail: wvr@prattlibrary.org. *Br Mgr,* Anne Marie Lalmansingh
Friends of the Library Group

R FAITH PRESBYTERIAN CHURCH LIBRARY*, 5400 Loch Raven Blvd, 21239. SAN 306-8366. Tel: 410-435-4330. FAX: 410-435-8449. *In Charge,* Misty Rossbottom
Founded 1951
Library Holdings: Bk Titles 620; Bk Vols 1,000; Per Subs 22
Subject Interests: Church hist, Theol
Open Mon-Sat 8:30-6

R FAITH THEOLOGICAL SEMINARY LIBRARY*, 529-531 Walker Ave, 21212-2624. SAN 314-4828. Tel: 410-323-6211. FAX: 410-323-6331. E-mail: fts@faiththeological.org. Web Site: www.faiththeological.org. *Head Librn,* Katherine Finnegan
Founded 1937
Library Holdings: Bk Vols 28,000; Per Subs 20
Open Mon-Sat 9-8

L GORDON FEINBLATT LLC*, Law Library, 233 E Redwood St, 21202. SAN 372-1019. Tel: 410-576-4255. FAX: 410-576-4246. Web Site: www.gfrlaw.com *Dir, Libr & Info Serv,* Sara Witman; E-mail: switman@gfrlaw.com; Staff 3 (MLS 2, Non-MLS 1)
Library Holdings: AV Mats 20; Bk Titles 2,000; Bk Vols 10,000; Per Subs 100
Automation Activity & Vendor Info: (Cataloging) Inmagic, Inc.
Database Vendor: LexisNexis, Westlaw
Function: For res purposes
Publications: Newsletter (Monthly)
Restriction: Co libr

S FORT MCHENRY NATIONAL MONUMENT & HISTORIC SHRINE LIBRARY*, Historical & Archeological Research Project Library, 2400 E Fort Ave, 21230-5393. SAN 306-8595. Tel: 410-962-4290, Ext 244. FAX: 410-962-2500. Web Site: www.nps.gov/fomc. *Head Archivist,* Scott S Sheads; E-mail: scott_sheads@nps.gov. Subject Specialists: *Civil War, War of 1812,* Scott S Sheads
Founded 1958
Library Holdings: Bk Vols 827
Special Collections: Fort McHenry History; Star Spangled Banner; War of 1812
Function: Res libr
Restriction: By permission only, Not open to pub

M FRIEDENWALD-ROMANO LIBRARY*, Johns Hopkins Hospital, Woods Res Bldg, 600 N Wolfe St, Rm 3B-50, 21287-9105. SAN 343-8309. Tel: 410-955-3127. FAX: 410-955-0046. Web Site: www.wilmer.jhu.edu. *Librn,* Michael Piorunski; E-mail: mprunski@jhmi.edu. Subject Specialists: *Ophthalmology,* Michael Piorunski; Staff 2 (Non-MLS 2)
Founded 1925
Library Holdings: AV Mats 1,000; Bk Titles 275; Bk Vols 20,000; Per Subs 115
Special Collections: History of Medicine (Wilmer Coll), rare bks; Ophthalmological Drawings (Annette Burgess Art Coll), original art
Subject Interests: Hist of med, Ophthalmology

Automation Activity & Vendor Info: (Cataloging) SirsiDynix; (Circulation) SirsiDynix; (Serials) SirsiDynix
Database Vendor: EBSCOhost, SirsiDynix
Function: Archival coll, For res purposes, Photocopying/Printing, Res libr, Telephone ref
Open Mon-Fri 9-4:30
Restriction: In-house use for visitors, Non-circulating to the pub, Open to pub with supv only

M GOOD SAMARITAN HOSPITAL*, Dr Samuel Morrison Medical Library, 5601 Loch Raven Blvd, 21239-2905. SAN 306-8412. Tel: 410-532-3891. FAX: 410-532-4381. *Librn,* Kathleen Curry; E-mail: kathy.curry@medstar.net
Founded 1968
Special Collections: Stroke Club Library
Database Vendor: OVID Technologies
Partic in Basic Health Sciences Library Network; Long Island Library Resources Council
Open Mon-Fri 8:30-5

C GOUCHER COLLEGE LIBRARY*, 1021 Dulaney Valley Rd, 21204. SAN 307-059X. Tel: 410-337-6360. Interlibrary Loan Service Tel: 410-337-6365. Reference Tel: 410-337-6212. Administration Tel: 410-337-6362. Automation Services Tel: 410-337-6370. FAX: 410-337-6419. E-mail: jrogers@goucher.edu. Web Site: www.goucher.edu/x643.xml. *Dir, Libr Serv,* Nancy Magnuson; Tel: 410-337-6364, E-mail: nmagnuso@goucher.edu; *Dir, Libr Presv,* Melissa Straw; Tel: 410-337-6368; *Assoc Librn, Coll,* Barbara Snead; Tel: 410-337-6366, E-mail: bsnead@goucher.edu; *Cat/Metadata Librn,* Margaret Dull; Tel: 410-337-6371, E-mail: margaret.dull@goucher.edu; *Digital Syst & Serv Librn,* Kristen Welzenbach; E-mail: kristen.welzenbach@goucher.edu; *Distance Learning Librn,* Yvonne Lev; *Instruction Librn,* James Huff; Tel: 410-337-6340, E-mail: jhuff@goucher.edu; *Ref Librn,* Muriel Jones; Tel: 410-337-3289; *Spec Coll & Archives Librn,* Tara Olivero; Tel: 410-337-6347, E-mail: taoli001@goucher.edu; *Spec Coll & Archives Librn,* Randy Smith; E-mail: rsmith@goucher.edu; *User Serv Librn,* Elizabeth DeCoster; Tel: 410-337-6361, E-mail: elizabeth.decoster@goucher.edu; *Circ Mgr,* Tom Minnema; Tel: 410-337-6356; *ILL Mgr,* Thomasin LaMay; Tel: 410-337-6031; *Coordr, Acq,* Sharon Hartmann; Tel: 410-337-6409; *Ref Serv,* Muriel Jones; *Libr Tech,* Lara Justis; Staff 13 (MLS 9, Non-MLS 4)
Founded 1885. Enrl 1,865; Fac 96; Highest Degree: Master
Library Holdings: AV Mats 3,945; e-books 1,410; e-journals 25,000; Electronic Media & Resources 100; Bk Vols 301,792; Per Subs 300
Special Collections: BS Corrin & CI Winslow Political Memorablia & Political Humor Coll; Goucher College Archives; H L & Sara Haardt Mencken Coll; History of Costume; HL Mencken Coll; Jane Austen (Alberta H Burke Coll); JW Bright Coll; Mark Twain (Eugene Oberdorfer Coll); Southern Women During the Civil War (Passano Coll)
Automation Activity & Vendor Info: (Acquisitions) Innovative Interfaces, Inc; (Cataloging) Innovative Interfaces, Inc; (Circulation) Innovative Interfaces, Inc; (ILL) OCLC FirstSearch; (OPAC) Innovative Interfaces, Inc; (Serials) SerialsSolutions
Database Vendor: Alexander Street Press, American Chemical Society, American Psychological Association (APA), Annual Reviews, Backstage Library Works, BioOne, EBSCOhost, Elsevier, Gale Cengage Learning, Innovative Interfaces, Inc, JSTOR, LexisNexis, Nature Publishing Group, OCLC, OCLC FirstSearch, OCLC WorldShare Interlibrary Loan, Oxford Online, Project MUSE, ProQuest, RefWorks, Sage, ScienceDirect, SerialsSolutions, WT Cox, YBP Library Services
Wireless access
Publications: Focus (Newsletter)
Partic in Baltimore Acad Libr Consortium; Lyrasis; OCLC Online Computer Library Center, Inc
Special Services for the Deaf - ADA equip
Restriction: Open to fac, students & qualified researchers
Friends of the Library Group

M GREATER BALTIMORE MEDICAL CENTER, John E Savage Medical Library, 6701 N Charles St, 21204. SAN 306-8420. Tel: 443-849-2530. FAX: 443-849-2664. E-mail: library@gbmc.org. Web Site: gbmc.org. *Dir,* Dianne Deck; Staff 2 (MLS 1, Non-MLS 1)
Founded 1965
Jul 2005-Jun 2006 Income $276,000
Library Holdings: DVDs 50; e-journals 1,000; Bk Titles 3,000; Per Subs 165
Subject Interests: Consumer health, Obstetrics & gynecology, Ophthalmology, Otolaryngology
Automation Activity & Vendor Info: (Acquisitions) LibraryWorld, Inc; (Cataloging) LibraryWorld, Inc; (Circulation) LibraryWorld, Inc; (OPAC) LibraryWorld, Inc
Database Vendor: Cinahl, DynaMed, ebrary, EBSCO Information Services, EBSCOhost, Elsevier, LibraryWorld, Inc, MD Consult, Medline, Micromedex, Natural Standard, OVID Technologies, PubMed, RefWorks, Sage, ScienceDirect, UpToDate, Wiley InterScience
Wireless access
Partic in Docline

M HARBOR HOSPITAL CENTER*, Health Sciences Library, S Main Bldg, Rm 112, 3001 S Hanover St, 21225-1290. SAN 306-8781. Tel: 410-350-3419. FAX: 410-350-2032. *Librn,* Shirley Lay; E-mail: shirley.s.lay@medstar.net; Staff 2 (MLS 1, Non-MLS 1)
Founded 1913
Library Holdings: Bk Vols 3,000; Per Subs 155
Special Collections: Education Media Coll
Subject Interests: Internal med, Obstetrics & gynecology, Surgery
Publications: Newsletter (Quarterly)
Partic in National Network of Libraries of Medicine
Restriction: Staff use only
Friends of the Library Group

S JEWISH MUSEUM OF MARYLAND*, Library & Archives, 15 Lloyd St, 21202. SAN 326-6028. Tel: 410-732-6400, Ext 18. FAX: 410-732-6451. Web Site: www.jewishmuseummd.org. *Archivist, Librn,* Rachel Kassman; *Spec Coll & Archives Librn,* Dr Deb Weiner; E-mail: dweiner@jewishmuseummd.org. Subject Specialists: *Family hist, Genealogy,* Dr Deb Weiner; Staff 3 (Non-MLS 3)
Founded 1960
Library Holdings: Bk Titles 3,000; Per Subs 20
Special Collections: Genealogy & Family History (Robert L Weinberg Family History Center); Organization, Business, Congregational & Personal Papers of the Maryland Jewish Community. Oral History
Restriction: Non-circulating to the pub, Open by appt only

JOHNS HOPKINS UNIVERSITY LIBRARIES

C JOHN WORK GARRETT LIBRARY*, Evergreen House, 4545 N Charles St, 21210, SAN 343-8066. Tel: 410-516-0889. FAX: 410-516-7202. Web Site: archives.mse.jhu.edu.
Library Holdings: Bk Vols 28,670
Special Collections: 17th Century Maryland (Books Printed Before 1700 Relating to Maryland); Architecture (Laurence H Fowler Coll); Bibles (Hoffmann Coll); Incunabula; Literature, Travel & Exploration, Natural History
Subject Interests: Rare bks
Partic in Association of Research Libraries (ARL)
Restriction: Open by appt only

CM CAROL J GRAY NURSING INFORMATION RESOURCE CENTER*, 525 N Wolfe St, Rm 313, 21202. Tel: 410-955-7559. E-mail: jhuson@son.jhmi.edu. Web Site: www.welch.jhu.edu/about/nirc.html. *Assoc Dir,* Jayne Campbell; *Librn,* Holly Harden
Library Holdings: Bk Titles 500
Partic in Maryland Interlibrary Loan Organization
Open Mon-Thurs 8am-9pm, Fri 8-4:30, Sat 10-4, Sun 1-7

C ADOLF MEYER LIBRARY*, 600 N Wolfe St, 21205. (Mail add: 1900 E Monument St, 21205-2113). Tel: 410-955-5819. FAX: 410-955-0860. Web Site: www.welch.jhu.edu/about/meyer.html. *Librn,* Ivy Garner; E-mail: ilg@jhmi.edu; *Librn,* James Tucker; E-mail: jmt@jhmi.edu
Library Holdings: Bk Titles 21,300; Per Subs 104
Open Mon-Fri 8-5:30

C GEORGE PEABODY LIBRARY*, 17 E Mount Vernon Pl, 21202, SAN 343-8635. Tel: 410-659-8179. FAX: 410-659-8137. Web Site: archives.mse.jhu.edu:8000.
Founded 1857
Library Holdings: Bk Vols 252,310; Per Subs 20; Spec Interest Per Sub 30
Special Collections: Cervantes: Editions of Don Quixote; General reference coll 19th Century Art & Architecture
Subject Interests: British hist, Decorative art, Geog, Maps, Relig, Travel
Partic in Association of Research Libraries (ARL)
Open Mon-Fri 9-3
Restriction: Circ limited

C SCHOOL OF PROFESSIONAL STUDIES IN BUSINESS & EDUCATION*, Ten N Charles St, 21201. Tel: 410-516-0700. FAX: 410-659-8210. *Librn,* Michael Houck
Library Holdings: Bk Titles 600
Open Mon-Fri 8:30-9, Sat 8:30-5

C THE SHERIDAN LIBRARIES*, 3400 N Charles St, 21218, SAN 343-8031. Tel: 410-516-8325. Circulation Tel: 410-516-8370. Reference Tel: 410-516-8335. FAX: 410-516-5080. Web Site: www.library.jhu.edu. *Dean,* Winston Tabb; Tel: 410-516-8328; *Assoc Dean,* Sayeed Choudhury; *Assoc Dir,* Kenneth Flower; E-mail: ken.flower@jhu.edu; *Assoc Dir,* Deborah Slingluff; Tel: 410-516-8254, E-mail: slingluff@jhu.edu; *Head, Coll Mgt,* Elizabeth Mengel; Staff 51 (MLS 39, Non-MLS 12)
Founded 1876. Enrl 17,881; Highest Degree: Doctorate
Library Holdings: AV Mats 6,000; e-journals 7,000; Bk Vols 2,619,190; Per Subs 17,757
Special Collections: 17th Century English Literature; 19th & 20th Century American; Economic Classics (Hutzler Coll); Edmund Spenser

(Tudor & Stuart Club Coll); French Drama (Couet Coll); German Literature (Kurrelmeyer Coll); Lord Byron; Louis Zukofsky; Manuscripts, including Sidney Lanier, Francis Lieber, D C Gilman, John Banister Tabb, Edward Lucas White, Arthur O Lovejoy Coll; Modern German Drama (Loewenberg Coll); Sheet Music (Levy Coll); Slavery (Birney Coll); Southey (Havens Coll); Trade Unions (Barnett Coll). US Document Depository
Automation Activity & Vendor Info: (Acquisitions) SirsiDynix; (Cataloging) SirsiDynix; (Circulation) SirsiDynix
Function: Res libr
Partic in Association of Research Libraries (ARL); Baltimore Acad Libr Consortium; Chesapeake Information & Research Library Alliance (CIRLA); Digital Libr Fedn; Md Independent Cols & Univs Alliance; Md Libr Asn
Publications: Ex Libris
Open Mon-Thurs 8-2, Fri & Sat 8-12, Sun 10-2
Friends of the Library Group

CM WILLIAM H WELCH MEDICAL LIBRARY*, 1900 E Monument St, 21205, SAN 343-8090. Tel: 410-955-3028. FAX: 410-955-0200. Web Site: www.welch.jhu.edu. *Mgr,* Donna D Hesson; E-mail: dhesson@jhmi.edu; *Librn,* Susan Rohner
Founded 1963
Library Holdings: Bk Vols 32,000; Per Subs 174
Automation Activity & Vendor Info: (Circulation) Horizon
Partic in Association of Research Libraries (ARL); OCLC Online Computer Library Center, Inc; RLIN (Research Libraries Information Network)
Publications: Library Bulletin (Quarterly)
Open Mon-Thurs 8am-9pm, Fri 8-6:30, Sat 10-5, Sun 1-7
Friends of the Library Group

S JOHNS HOPKINS UNIVERSITY-PEABODY CONSERVATORY OF MUSIC*, Arthur Friedheim Library, 21 E Mount Vernon Pl, 21202-2397. SAN 343-8511. Tel: 410-659-8100, Ext 1159. FAX: 410-685-0657. Web Site: www.peabody.jhu.edu/lib. *Head Librn,* Jennifer Ottervik; Tel: 410-234-4594, E-mail: ottervik@jhu.edu; *Acq, Ser,* Bozena Jedrzejczak; *AV,* Christopher Lobringier; Tel: 410-659-8100, Ext 1164; *Reader Serv,* Elizabeth N Nelson; E-mail: betsyn@peabody.jhu.edu; *Ref,* Ursula McLean; Tel: 410-659-8100, Ext 1162; Staff 5 (MLS 3, Non-MLS 2)
Founded 1866. Enrl 710; Fac 70; Highest Degree: Doctorate
Library Holdings: Bk Vols 114,000; Per Subs 240
Special Collections: Asgar Hamerik & Gustav Strube Coll, mss, published works; Barringer Jazz Coll; Brick Fleagle/Luther Henderson Jazz Recordings Coll; Franz Bornschein, George Boyle, Louis Cheslock, Robert L Paul, Ronald Roxbury, Bernhard Scholz, Howard Thatcher, Timothy Spelman, Vladimir Padwa & W L Hubbard Colls; Friedman Record Coll; John Charles Thomas & Enrico Caruso Coll; Joseph Schillinger Papers
Subject Interests: Dance, Music
Database Vendor: ProQuest, SirsiDynix
Partic in Maryland Interlibrary Loan Organization
Friends of the Library Group

L LIBRARY COMPANY OF THE BALTIMORE BAR*, Baltimore Bar Library, 100 N Calvert St, Rm 618, 21202-1723. SAN 306-8455. Tel: 410-727-0280. FAX: 410-685-4791. Web Site: www.barlib.org. *Asst Librn,* Joseph W Bennett; E-mail: jwbennett@barlib.org; *Tech Serv,* Barbara E Karpel; E-mail: bkarpel@barlib.org; Staff 2 (MLS 2)
Founded 1840
Library Holdings: Bk Vols 200,000; Per Subs 314
Subject Interests: Law
Automation Activity & Vendor Info: (Cataloging) SirsiDynix; (OPAC) SirsiDynix; (Serials) SirsiDynix
Publications: Bar Library Advance Sheet
Open Mon-Thurs 8:30-4, Fri 9-4
Restriction: Mem only

C LOYOLA-NOTRE DAME LIBRARY, INC*, 200 Winston Ave, 21212. SAN 306-8463. Tel: 410-617-6800. Circulation Tel: 410-617-6801. Interlibrary Loan Service Tel: 410-617-6804. Reference Tel: 410-617-6802. Administration Tel: 410-617-6814. Automation Services Tel: 410-617-6861. FAX: 410-617-6895. Interlibrary Loan Service FAX: 410-617-6896. E-mail: askemail@loyola.edu. Web Site: www.loyola.edu/library. *Dir,* John W McGinty; E-mail: jmcginty@loyola.edu; *Assoc Dir,* Jack G Ray; E-mail: ray@loyola.edu; *Head, Tech Serv,* Nancy Hanks; E-mail: nhanks@loyola.edu; *Acq,* Joseph Turkos; E-mail: jturkos@loyola.edu; *Bibliog Instr,* Susan Cooperstein; E-mail: cooperstein@loyola.edu; *Circ,* Gail Breyer; E-mail: breyer@loyola.edu; *Digital Serv,* Charles Lockwood; E-mail: clockwood@loyola.edu; *ILL & Distance Libr Serv Spec,* Peggy Feild; E-mail: mfeild@loyola.edu; *Media Spec,* Philip Fryer; E-mail: pdf@loyola.edu; *Ref,* Patricia MacDonald; E-mail: pmacdonald@loyola.edu; Staff 13 (MLS 12, Non-MLS 1)
Founded 1973. Enrl 9,250; Fac 375; Highest Degree: Doctorate
Library Holdings: DVDs 2,197; e-books 255,710; e-journals 23,988; Bk Titles 359,353; Bk Vols 463,042; Per Subs 989; Videos 10,076
Special Collections: Book Decoration (Henry A Knott Fore-Edge; English Literature (Gerard Manley Hopkins Coll), bks, per; Painting Coll)
Automation Activity & Vendor Info: (Acquisitions) Ex Libris Group; (Cataloging) Ex Libris Group; (Circulation) Ex Libris Group; (Course Reserve) Ex Libris Group; (ILL) Ex Libris Group; (Media Booking) Ex Libris Group; (OPAC) Ex Libris Group; (Serials) Ex Libris Group
Database Vendor: EBSCOhost, Gale Cengage Learning, LexisNexis, OCLC FirstSearch, OVID Technologies
Publications: The Bridge (Newsletter)
Partic in Baltimore Acad Libr Consortium
Open Mon-Thurs 8am-2am, Fri 8-7, Sat 8-8, Sun 10am-2am

G MARYLAND DEPARTMENT OF PLANNING LIBRARY*, 301 W Preston St, Rm 1101, 21201-2365. SAN 306-8498. Tel: 410-767-4500. FAX: 410-767-4480. Web Site: www.mdp.state.md.us/info/lib/html. *Librn,* Elizabeth Smith; E-mail: esmith@mdp.state.md.us
Founded 1959
Library Holdings: Bk Titles 9,550; Per Subs 140
Special Collections: Maryland Counties & Municipalities Central Depository of Plans. State Document Depository
Subject Interests: Census, Housing, Land use, Planning, Zoning
Publications: Acquisitions list (bi-monthly)
Open Mon-Fri 8-4:30

S MARYLAND HISTORICAL SOCIETY LIBRARY*, H Furlong Baldwin Library, 201 W Monument St, 21201. SAN 321-4508. Tel: 410-685-3750. Reference Tel: 410-685-3750, Ext 358. FAX: 410-385-0487. E-mail: library_dept@mdhs.org. Web Site: www.mdhs.org. *Dir,* Patricia Anderson; E-mail: panderson@mdhs.org; *Sr Ref Librn,* Francis O'Neill; E-mail: foneill@mdhs.org. Subject Specialists: *State hist,* Patricia Anderson; *Genealogy, Local hist,* Francis O'Neill; Staff 2.6 (MLS 1.6, Non-MLS 1)
Founded 1844
Library Holdings: Bk Titles 60,000; Per Subs 250
Special Collections: Historic Prints & Photographs, mss, maps, ephemera & broadsides
Subject Interests: Maryland
Database Vendor: EOS International
Wireless access
Open Wed-Sat 10-4:30
Restriction: Non-circulating, Photo ID required for access

C MARYLAND INSTITUTE COLLEGE OF ART, Decker Library, 1401 Mount Royal Ave, 21217. (Mail add: 1300 Mount Royal Ave, 21217), SAN 306-851X. Tel: 410-225-2304, 410-225-2311. Circulation Tel: 410-225-2272. Reference Tel: 410-225-2273. FAX: 410-225-2316. E-mail: refer@mica.edu. Web Site: www.mica.edu/academic_services_and_libraries.html. *Libr Dir,* Anthony White; E-mail: awhite03@mica.edu; *Cat Librn,* Kelly Swickard; Tel: 410-225-2248; *Digital Media Librn,* Michael Scott; Tel: 410-225-7005; *Instruction Librn,* Marianne Sade; *Sr Ref Librn,* Kathy Cowan; *Ref Librn,* Chris Drolsum; *Acq Mgr,* Deborah Viles; E-mail: dviles@mica.edu; *Circ Supvr,* Aaron Blickenstaff; *Cat Asst, Digital Res Coordr,* Mary Alessi; *Media Coordr,* Arthur Soontornsaratool; *Syst Coordr,* Sherri Faaborg; *Circ Asst,* John Dornberger; *Circ Asst,* Allison Fischbach; Staff 13 (MLS 6, Non-MLS 7)
Founded 1826. Enrl 2,150; Highest Degree: Master
Library Holdings: DVDs 5,000; e-books 100,000; e-journals 5,500; Bk Titles 64,000; Per Subs 325
Subject Interests: Art & archit
Automation Activity & Vendor Info: (Cataloging) SIRSI WorkFlows; (Circulation) SIRSI WorkFlows; (ILL) OCLC; (OPAC) SirsiDynix; (Serials) SIRSI WorkFlows
Database Vendor: 3M Library Systems, ACM (Association for Computing Machinery), Alexander Street Press, ARTstor, CredoReference, EBSCOhost, Gale Cengage Learning, H W Wilson, Ingram Library Services, JSTOR, Material ConneXion, Medline, OCLC, OCLC FirstSearch, OCLC WorldShare Interlibrary Loan, Oxford Online, ProQuest, SirsiDynix, YBP Library Services
Wireless access
Function: Art exhibits, Audio & video playback equip for onsite use, Computers for patron use, Copy machines, Doc delivery serv, Electronic databases & coll, Free DVD rentals, ILL available, Online cat, Orientations, Photocopying/Printing, Pub access computers, Ref & res, Scanner, Web-catalog
Partic in Association of Independent Colleges of Art & Design (AICAD); Lyrasis
Open Mon-Thurs 8:30am-9pm, Fri 8:30-4:30, Sat & Sun Noon-6
Restriction: Open to students, fac, staff & alumni
Friends of the Library Group

S MARYLAND PHARMACISTS ASSOCIATION LIBRARY, 1800 Washington Blvd, Ste 333, Montgomery Park, 21230. SAN 327-814X. Tel: 410-727-0746. FAX: 410-727-2253. *Interim Exec Dir,* Dixie Leikach; E-mail: dixie.leikach@mdpha.com

Library Holdings: Bk Titles 1,200; Per Subs 40
Restriction: Open by appt only

P MARYLAND STATE DEPARTMENT OF EDUCATION*, Division of Library Development & Services, 200 W Baltimore St, 21201-2595. SAN 343-8392. Tel: 410-767-0444. FAX: 410-333-2507. Web Site: marylandpublicschools.org/MSDE/divisions/library. *Asst State Superintendent,* Irene Padilla; Tel: 410-767-0435, E-mail: ipadilla@msde.state.md.us; *Fac Projects Mgr,* Renee Croft; Tel: 410-767-0445, E-mail: rcroft@msde.state.md.us; Staff 16 (MLS 10, Non-MLS 6)
Wireless access
Open Mon-Fri 8-5
Branches: 1
LIBRARY FOR THE BLIND & PHYSICALLY HANDICAPPED
See Separate Entry under Maryland State Library for the Blind & Physically Handicapped

P MARYLAND STATE LIBRARY FOR THE BLIND & PHYSICALLY HANDICAPPED*, 415 Park Ave, 21201-3603. SAN 306-8544. Tel: 410-230-2424. Toll Free Tel: 800-964-9209 (Baltimore Metro Area). FAX: 410-333-2095. TDD: 410-333-8679, 800-934-2541. Reference E-mail: referenc@lbph.lib.md.us. Web Site: www.lbph.lib.md.us. *Dir,* Position Currently Open; Staff 21 (MLS 5, Non-MLS 16)
Library Holdings: Large Print Bks 10,134; Bk Titles 67,000; Bk Vols 271,773
Special Collections: Marylandia, in-house produced a-tapes
Wireless access
Publications: Adult Newsletter (Quarterly); Annual Report; Bibliographies; Children's Newsletter (Bi-annually)
Special Services for the Deaf - TDD equip; Videos & decoder
Open Mon-Fri 8-5
Restriction: Registered patrons only
Friends of the Library Group

M MCGLANNAN HEALTH SCIENCES LIBRARY*, Mercy Medical Ctr, 301 Saint Paul Pl, 21202. SAN 343-8457. Tel: 410-332-9189. FAX: 410-332-0324. Web Site: www.mdmercy.com. *Dir, Libr Serv,* Holly Willis; Staff 2 (MLS 1, Non-MLS 1)
Founded 1874
Library Holdings: CDs 50; e-books 50; e-journals 3,000; High Interest/Low Vocabulary Bk Vols 200; Bk Titles 5,000; Per Subs 190
Special Collections: Consumer Health Coll; Medicine, Nursing & Allied Health Coll
Database Vendor: Gale Cengage Learning, Lexi-Comp, OVID Technologies
Function: Archival coll, Doc delivery serv, ILL available, Mail loans to mem, Ref serv available, Telephone ref
Partic in National Network of Libraries of Medicine
Open Mon-Fri 8-4:30
Restriction: Access at librarian's discretion, In-house use for visitors, Lending to staff only, Non-circulating to the pub, Open to pub with supv only

M MEDSTAR FRANKLIN SQUARE MEDICAL CENTER*, Health Sciences Library, 9000 Franklin Square Dr, 21237. SAN 306-8390. Tel: 443-777-7363. Administration Tel: 443-777-7463. FAX: 410-687-1742. E-mail: fshc_medical_library@medstar.net. *Librn,* Kristin Chapman; E-mail: kristin.m.chapman@medstar.net; *Libr Asst,* Donna Neukam; E-mail: donna.j.neukam@medstar.net; Staff 2 (MLS 1, Non-MLS 1)
Subject Interests: Nursing, Obstetrics & gynecology
Automation Activity & Vendor Info: (Acquisitions) EOS International; (Cataloging) EOS International; (Circulation) EOS International; (ILL) TDNet; (OPAC) EOS International; (Serials) EOS International
Database Vendor: Booksite, DynaMed, EBSCOhost, Elsevier, Elsevier MDL, Emerald, EOS International, Ex Libris Group, Ingenta, McGraw-Hill, MD Consult, Medlib, Medline, OVID Technologies, PubMed, Sage, ScienceDirect, Springer-Verlag, Swets Information Services, TDNet, WebMD, Wiley, Wiley InterScience
Wireless access
Function: Computer training, Computers for patron use, Copy machines, e-mail serv, Electronic databases & coll, Handicapped accessible, Health sci info serv, ILL available, Instruction & testing, Learning ctr, Mail & tel request accepted, Mail loans to mem, Online cat, Online searches, Photocopying/Printing, Printer for laptops & handheld devices, Pub access computers, Ref & res, Ref serv available, Ref serv in person, Res libr, Scanner, Serves mentally handicapped consumers, Spoken cassettes & CDs, Spoken cassettes & DVDs, Telephone ref, VHS videos, Video lending libr, Wheelchair accessible
Open Mon-Fri 8-5
Restriction: Badge access after hrs, Hospital employees & physicians only, Open to researchers by request, Open to staff, patients & family mem, Open to students, Photo ID required for access

S METROPOLITAN TRANSITION CENTER LIBRARY*, 954 Forrest St, 21202. Tel: 410-230-1472. FAX: 410-230-1472. *Librn,* Ruth Mewborn; Staff 1 (MLS 1)
Library Holdings: Bk Vols 8,299; Per Subs 22
Automation Activity & Vendor Info: (Cataloging) Follett Software; (Circulation) Follett Software
Database Vendor: Westlaw
Open Mon-Fri 9-11:45 & 12-1:45

L MILES & STOCKBRIDGE PC LIBRARY*, Ten Light St, 21202. SAN 325-4887. Tel: 410-385-3671. FAX: 410-385-3700. *Head Librn,* Sara Thomas; E-mail: sthomas@milesstockbridge.com; Staff 4 (MLS 1, Non-MLS 3)
Jan 2008-Dec 2008. Mats Exp $727,000, Books $25,000, Per/Ser (Incl. Access Fees) $700,000, Presv $2,000
Library Holdings: Bk Titles 12,000; Bk Vols 15,000; Per Subs 200
Subject Interests: Law
Automation Activity & Vendor Info: (Acquisitions) Inmagic, Inc.; (Cataloging) Inmagic, Inc.; (Circulation) Inmagic, Inc.; (ILL) Inmagic, Inc.; (OPAC) Inmagic, Inc.; (Serials) Inmagic, Inc.
Publications: A Guide to the Miles & Stockbridge Library

S HENRY LEE MOON LIBRARY & CIVIL RIGHTS ARCHIVES*, NAACP National Civil Rights Archives, 4805 Mount Hope Dr, 21215-3297. SAN 374-8669. Tel: 410-358-8900. FAX: 410-358-3386. Web Site: www.naacp.org. *Librn,* James Murray
Library Holdings: Bk Vols 1,500
Restriction: Open by appt only

C MORGAN STATE UNIVERSITY*, Earl S Richardson Library, 1700 E Cold Spring Lane, 21251. SAN 306-8579. Tel: 443-885-3477. Interlibrary Loan Service Tel: 443-885-1722. Reference Tel: 443-885-3450. Administration Tel: 443-885-3488. Administration FAX: 443-885-8246. Web Site: www.morgan.edu/library. *Dir of Libr Serv,* Dr Richard Bradberry; E-mail: richard.bradberry@morgan.edu; *Assoc Dir, Pub Serv,* Michelle Hammond; Tel: 443-885-3478, E-mail: michelle.hammond@morgan.edu; *Assoc Dir, Tech Serv,* Maggie Wanza; Tel: 443-885-1708, E-mail: maggie.wanza@morgan.edu; *Asst Dir, Info Tech,* Raul Valdez; Tel: 443-885-3930, E-mail: raul.valdez@morgan.edu; *Acq/Ser Librn,* Position Currently Open; *Circ Librn,* Alan Poulson; Tel: 443-885-1703; *Info Literacy Librn,* Felecia Tyler; E-mail: felecia.tyler@morgan.edu; *Instruction/Digital Initiatives Librn,* Position Currently Open; *Ref Librn,* Chris Iweha; Tel: 443-885-1721, E-mail: chris.iweha@morgan.edu; *Ref/Fed Doc Librn,* Position Currently Open; *Asst Spec Coll Librn,* Edith Murungi; Tel: 443-885-4294; *Univ Archivist,* Position Currently Open. Subject Specialists: *Bus, Music, Nursing,* Michelle Hammond; *Hist,* Maggie Wanza; *Computer sci, Eng,* Raul Valdez; *Humanities,* Alan Poulson; Staff 27 (MLS 11, Non-MLS 16)
Founded 1867. Enrl 7,900; Fac 450; Highest Degree: Doctorate
Jul 2013-Jun 2014 Income $3,326,120, Federal $132,445, Parent Institution $3,193,675. Sal $1,709,885 (Prof $1,482,330)
Library Holdings: AV Mats 18,300; Electronic Media & Resources 110; Bk Vols 310,000; Per Subs 650
Special Collections: African-American History & Life (Beulah M Davis Special Colls Room); Correspondence of Late Poet & Editor (W S Braithwaite Coll), letters; Negro Employment in WWII (Emmett J Scott Coll), letters; Papers of Emeritus President (D O W Holmes Papers, Martin D Jenkins Papers), letters; Quaker & Slavery (Forbush Coll), bk, ms. US Document Depository
Subject Interests: Educ, Ethnic studies
Automation Activity & Vendor Info: (Acquisitions) Ex Libris Group; (Cataloging) Ex Libris Group; (Circulation) Ex Libris Group; (Course Reserve) Ex Libris Group; (ILL) OCLC; (OPAC) Ex Libris Group; (Serials) Ex Libris Group
Database Vendor: 3M Library Systems, ACM (Association for Computing Machinery), Alexander Street Press, American Chemical Society, American Mathematical Society, American Psychological Association (APA), Bowker, Cambridge Scientific Abstracts, College Source, CredoReference, ebrary, EBSCO Discovery Service, EBSCO Information Services, EBSCOhost, Elsevier, Emerald, Ex Libris Group, Gale Cengage Learning, Hoovers, IEEE (Institute of Electrical & Electronics Engineers), ISI Web of Knowledge, JSTOR, LexisNexis, Marcive, Inc, Mergent Online, Modern Language Association, OCLC, OCLC ArticleFirst, OCLC FirstSearch, OCLC WorldShare Interlibrary Loan, Oxford Online, Project MUSE, ProQuest, Sage, ScienceDirect, Springer-Verlag, Springshare, LLC, ValueLine, Wiley, Wilson - Wilson Web, YBP Library Services
Wireless access
Function: Archival coll
Open Mon-Thurs 8am-Midnight, Fri 8am-9pm; Sat 9-6, Sun 1pm-Midnight

S NATIONAL AQUARIUM IN BALTIMORE*, A Carter Middendorf Library, 501 E Pratt St, 21202-3194. SAN 370-6397. Tel: 410-659-4257. FAX: 410-576-1080. Web Site: www.aqua.org. *Sci Res Mgr,* Valerie Lounsbury; Staff 0.3 (Non-MLS 0.3)

Founded 1980
Library Holdings: Bk Titles 3,600; Per Subs 12
Subject Interests: Aquatic animals, Conserv, Ecology
Automation Activity & Vendor Info: (ILL) OCLC
Function: ILL available
Restriction: Staff use only

G NATIONAL INSTITUTE ON AGING*, Gerontology Research Center Library & Information Services Section, 5600 Nathan Shock Dr, 21224-6825. Tel: 410-558-8125. FAX: 410-558-8224. *Librn,* Carmen Harris; Staff 4 (MLS 1, Non-MLS 3)
Founded 1977
Library Holdings: Bk Titles 10,000; Bk Vols 25,000; Per Subs 20
Subject Interests: Biological sci, Biomed res, Cardiovascular med, Cognitive sci, Genetics, Immunology, Neuropsychology, Personalities
Automation Activity & Vendor Info: (Acquisitions) OCLC Online; (Cataloging) OCLC Online; (ILL) OCLC Online
Database Vendor: Dialog, OVID Technologies
Partic in BRS; Dialog Corp; OCLC Online Computer Library Center, Inc; US National Library of Medicine
Open Mon-Fri 9-5
Restriction: Mem only

G NATIONAL INSTITUTE ON DRUG ABUSE*, Addiction Research Center Library, 5500 Nathan Shock Dr, 21224-6823. (Mail add: PO Box 5180, 21224-0180), SAN 306-3178. Tel: 410-550-1488. FAX: 410-550-1438. *Librn,* Mary Pfeiffer; E-mail: mpfeiffe@irp.nida.nih.gov; *Assoc Librn,* Denise Byrd; Staff 2 (MLS 1, Non-MLS 1)
Founded 1935
Library Holdings: Bk Titles 8,700; Bk Vols 10,000; Per Subs 250
Subject Interests: Biochem, Drug (chemistry), Neurology, Pharmacology, Physiology, Psychiat, Psychol
Automation Activity & Vendor Info: (Acquisitions) Innovative Interfaces, Inc; (Cataloging) Innovative Interfaces, Inc; (Circulation) Innovative Interfaces, Inc; (OPAC) Innovative Interfaces, Inc
Partic in Dialog Corp; National Network of Libraries of Medicine; OCLC Online Computer Library Center, Inc
Open Mon-Fri 9-4:30

S NATURAL HISTORY SOCIETY OF MARYLAND, INC LIBRARY*, 6908 Belair Rd, 21206. (Mail add: PO Box 18750, 21206), SAN 326-0194. Tel: 410-882-5376. Web Site: www.marylandnature.org. *Pres,* McSharry Joe; Staff 1 (MLS 1)
Founded 1929
Library Holdings: Bk Titles 20,200
Subject Interests: Natural hist

R NER ISRAEL RABBINICAL COLLEGE LIBRARY*, 400 Mount Wilson Lane, 21208. SAN 306-8609. Tel: 410-484-7200. FAX: 410-484-3060. *Librn,* Avrohom S Shnidman
Founded 1933
Library Holdings: Bk Vols 23,000; Per Subs 18
Special Collections: Biblical Commentaries, Hebrew Newspapers of European Communities 1820-1937; Responsa; Talmudic Laws
Open Sun-Thurs 9-5, Fri 9-Noon

L NILES, BARTON & WILMER LAW LIBRARY*, 111 S Calvert St, Ste 1400, 21202. SAN 327-8182. Tel: 410-783-6300. FAX: 410-783-6363. Web Site: www.niles-law.com. *Librn,* Thea Warner; Tel: 410-783-6386; Staff 1 (Non-MLS 1)
Library Holdings: Bk Vols 10,000
Database Vendor: LexisNexis, Westlaw
Restriction: Staff use only

S NORTHROP GRUMMAN CORP*, Electronic Sensors & Systems Division, PO Box 1693, MS-1138, 21203-1693. SAN 322-4961. Tel: 410-765-5565. FAX: 410-993-7675. E-mail: library.baltimore@ngc.com. *Mgr,* Rebekah Cerame; Staff 5 (MLS 5)
Library Holdings: DVDs 103; e-books 7,000; Electronic Media & Resources 30; Bk Titles 8,000; Per Subs 100
Subject Interests: Eng, Mil sci, Mkt
Automation Activity & Vendor Info: (Cataloging) EOS International; (Circulation) EOS International; (OPAC) EOS International; (Serials) EOS International
Database Vendor: ACM (Association for Computing Machinery), Carroll Publishing, Dialog, Dun & Bradstreet, EBSCOhost, Elsevier, Emerald, EOS International, Factiva.com, Gale Cengage Learning, IEEE (Institute of Electrical & Electronics Engineers), IHS, Jane's, LexisNexis, Marquis Who's Who, ReferenceUSA, ScienceDirect, Swets Information Services
Function: Bks on CD, Computers for patron use, Copy machines, Distance learning, Doc delivery serv, Electronic databases & coll, Handicapped accessible, ILL available, Mail loans to mem, Online cat, Online ref, Online searches, Orientations, Photocopying/Printing, Pub access computers, Ref & res, Ref serv available, Ref serv in person, Res libr, Telephone ref, Video lending libr, Wheelchair accessible
Restriction: Authorized personnel only

L OBER/KALER LAW LIBRARY, 100 Light St, Ste B2, 21202-1643. SAN 327-8204. Tel: 410-230-7181, 410-685-1120. FAX: 410-547-0699. Web Site: www.ober.com. *Dir,* Kumar H Jayasuriya; E-mail: hkpjayasuriya@ober.com
Library Holdings: Bk Vols 3,500; Per Subs 300
Automation Activity & Vendor Info: (Cataloging) EOS International; (Circulation) EOS International; (OPAC) EOS International
Database Vendor: LexisNexis, Westlaw
Partic in Dialog Corp; Dow Jones News Retrieval; Westlaw
Restriction: Staff use only

M SAINT AGNES HEALTHCARE*, Lewis P Gundry Health Sciences Library, 900 Caton Ave, 21229. SAN 306-8714. Tel: 410-368-3123, 410-368-3124. FAX: 410-368-3298. Web Site: www.stagnas.org. *Dir,* Joanne Sullivan; Staff 3 (MLS 1, Non-MLS 2)
Library Holdings: Bk Vols 3,500; Per Subs 210
Special Collections: Medicine - Historical (Cohn-Bloodgood Coll)
Subject Interests: Admin law, Allied health, Med, Nursing
Automation Activity & Vendor Info: (Acquisitions) EOS International; (Cataloging) EOS International; (Circulation) EOS International; (OPAC) EOS International; (Serials) EOS International
Database Vendor: OVID Technologies
Publications: Newsletter (quarterly)
Restriction: Staff use only

CR SAINT MARY'S SEMINARY & UNIVERSITY*, Knott Library, 5400 Roland Ave, 21210-1994. SAN 306-8722. Tel: 410-864-3621. FAX: 410-435-8571. Web Site: www.stmarys.edu. *Dir,* David Carter; Staff 3 (MLS 3)
Founded 1791. Enrl 157; Fac 25; Highest Degree: Master
Library Holdings: Bk Vols 120,000; Per Subs 325
Special Collections: Early Catholic Americana; Scripture/Orientalia (Arbez Coll); Semitics
Subject Interests: Relig, Theol
Automation Activity & Vendor Info: (Acquisitions) TLC (The Library Corporation); (Cataloging) TLC (The Library Corporation); (Circulation) TLC (The Library Corporation); (OPAC) TLC (The Library Corporation); (Serials) TLC (The Library Corporation)
Database Vendor: EBSCOhost
Partic in OCLC Online Computer Library Center, Inc
Open Mon-Thurs 8:15am-10pm, Fri 8:15-4, Sat 9-4, Sun 1-8

L SAUL EWING LLP*, 500 E Pratt St, 9th Flr, 21202. SAN 306-8900. Tel: 410-332-8832. FAX: 410-332-8862. Web Site: www.saul.com. *Librn,* Stacey Digan; E-mail: sdigan@saul.com; Staff 1 (MLS 1)
Library Holdings: Bk Vols 10,000; Per Subs 40
Subject Interests: Banks & banking, Commercial law, Corporate law, Labor, Litigation, Real estate, Securities
Function: For res purposes, ILL available, Online searches
Restriction: Staff use only

L SEMMES, BOWEN & SEMMES LIBRARY, 25 S Charles St, Ste 1400, 21201. SAN 306-8757. Tel: 410-385-3936. FAX: 410-539-5223. *Dir,* Kathleen Sweeney; E-mail: ksweeney@semmes.com
Subject Interests: Gen law
Automation Activity & Vendor Info: (Acquisitions) Inmagic, Inc.; (Cataloging) Inmagic, Inc.; (Serials) Inmagic, Inc.
Wireless access

M SINAI HOSPITAL OF BALTIMORE*, Eisenberg Medical Staff Library, 2401 W Belvedere, 21215-5271. SAN 306-8765. Tel: 410-601-5015. FAX: 410-664-7432. *Dir,* Lee Cook; E-mail: lcook@lifebridgehealth.org; Staff 4 (MLS 2, Non-MLS 2)
Library Holdings: Bk Vols 4,100; Per Subs 300
Special Collections: Jewish Medicine & Health Coll; Management Coll
Subject Interests: Med, Nursing
Database Vendor: EBSCOhost, OVID Technologies
Partic in National Network of Libraries of Medicine
Restriction: Staff use only

C SOJOURNER-DOUGLASS COLLEGE*, Walter P Carter Library, 500 N Caroline St, 21205. SAN 325-0660. Tel: 410-276-0306, Ext 269. FAX: 410-675-1810. E-mail: oali@host.sdc.edu. Web Site: www.sdc.edu. *Librn,* Sadiq Omowali Ali; Staff 1 (MLS 1)
Founded 1976
Library Holdings: Bk Titles 22,000; Bk Vols 22,500; Per Subs 80
Special Collections: Africa & African American History (Old Rare Books Coll)
Database Vendor: Wilson - Wilson Web
Open Mon-Thurs 10-10, Fri 10-6, Sat 10-5

S SPACE TELESCOPE SCIENCE INSTITUTE LIBRARY*, 3700 San Martin Dr, 21218. SAN 323-7729. Tel: 410-338-4961. FAX: 410-338-4767. E-mail: library@stsci.edu. Web Site: www.sesame.stsci.edu/library.html. *Chief Librn,* Jill Lagerstrom; Staff 3 (MLS 2, Non-MLS 1)
Founded 1983
Oct 2007-Sept 2008. Mats Exp $164,000, Books $22,000, Per/Ser (Incl. Access Fees) $130,000, Electronic Ref Mat (Incl. Access Fees) $12,000
Library Holdings: Bk Titles 7,769; Bk Vols 8,863; Per Subs 207
Special Collections: Sky Survey Photographs
Subject Interests: Astrophysics
Automation Activity & Vendor Info: (Acquisitions) SirsiDynix; (Cataloging) SirsiDynix; (Circulation) SirsiDynix; (OPAC) SirsiDynix; (Serials) SirsiDynix
Wireless access
Publications: Acquisitions List; STEPsheet (preprint listing)
Restriction: Open by appt only

S TRIBUNE CO*, Baltimore Sun Library, 501 N Calvert St, 21202-3604. SAN 306-8242. Tel: 410-332-6255. Toll Free Tel: 800-829-8000, Ext 6255. FAX: 410-332-6918. E-mail: research@baltsun.com. Web Site: www.baltimoresun.com. *Res Librn,* Paul McCardell; Tel: 410-332-6933, E-mail: paul.mccardell@baltsun.com; Staff 2 (MLS 1, Non-MLS 1)
Founded 1840
Library Holdings: Bk Vols 5,000; Per Subs 80
Special Collections: A Aubrey Bodine Coll, black & white photogs; H L Mencken Clipping Coll; Index to The Evening Sun, 1910-1951, flm; Index to The Sun & Sunday Sun, 1891-1951, flm; John F Kennedy Memorial Coll, flm; Maryland Laws Coll
Subject Interests: Hist, Journalism
Automation Activity & Vendor Info: (Cataloging) Inmagic, Inc.; (Serials) Inmagic, Inc.
Database Vendor: Dialog, Factiva.com, LexisNexis, Newsbank, ProQuest
Function: Archival coll, Res libr
Restriction: Internal circ only

L TYDINGS & ROSENBERG LLP*, Law Library, 100 E Pratt St, 26th Flr, 21202. SAN 372-0993. Tel: 410-752-9700, 410-752-9804. FAX: 410-727-5460. Web Site: www.tydingslaw.com. *Dir,* Jean Hessenauer; E-mail: jhessenauer@tydingslaw.com; Staff 1 (MLS 1)
Library Holdings: Bk Vols 10,000; Per Subs 50
Database Vendor: LexisNexis, Westlaw
Restriction: Staff use only

M UNION MEMORIAL HOSPITAL*, Library & Information Resources, 201 E University Pkwy, 21218. SAN 343-9801. Tel: 410-554-2294. FAX: 410-554-2166. *Mgr,* Carole Lever; Staff 2 (MLS 1, Non-MLS 1)
Founded 1935
Library Holdings: Bk Vols 3,000; Per Subs 300
Subject Interests: Clinical med, Med, Orthopedics, Sports, Surgery
Database Vendor: OVID Technologies
Partic in National Network of Libraries of Medicine
Restriction: Not open to pub

SR UNITED METHODIST HISTORICAL SOCIETY*, Lovely Lane Museum & Archives, 2200 St Paul St, 21218-5897. SAN 306-8838. Tel: 410-889-4458. FAX: 410-889-1501. E-mail: lovlnmus@cavtel.net. Web Site: www.lovelylanemuseum.com. *Dir,* James E Reaves; *Assoc Dir,* Wanda B Hall. Subject Specialists: *Genealogy,* Wanda B Hall; Staff 2 (Non-MLS 2)
Founded 1855
Jan 2009-Dec 2009 Income $98,000, Locally Generated Income $19,000, Parent Institution $79,000. Mats Exp $1,500, Books $150, Per/Ser (Incl. Access Fees) $150. Sal $53,000
Library Holdings: Bk Vols 4,857; Spec Interest Per Sub 15
Special Collections: Archives of Baltimore-Washington Conference; Journals of Preachers
Subject Interests: Hist
Publications: Methodist Union Catalog; Union List of Methodist Serials
Open Thurs & Fri 10-4
Restriction: Fee for pub use, Non-circulating
Friends of the Library Group

L UNITED STATES COURTS LIBRARY*, US Courthouse, Rm 3625, 101 W Lombard St, 21201. SAN 372-1000. Tel: 410-962-0997. FAX: 410-962-9313. *Librn,* Charmaine Metallo
Library Holdings: Bk Vols 38,000; Per Subs 125
Automation Activity & Vendor Info: (Acquisitions) SirsiDynix; (Cataloging) SirsiDynix; (Circulation) SirsiDynix; (ILL) SirsiDynix; (OPAC) SirsiDynix; (Serials) SirsiDynix
Database Vendor: LexisNexis, Westlaw
Open Mon-Fri 8:30-5

C UNIVERSITY OF BALTIMORE, Langsdale Library, 1420 Maryland Ave, 21201. SAN 343-9925. Tel: 410-837-4260. Interlibrary Loan Service Tel: 410-837-4283. Reference Tel: 410-837-4274. Administration Tel: 410-837-4290. Automation Services Tel: 410-837-4204. Toll Free Tel: 888-526-4733. FAX: 410-837-4319. Administration FAX: 410-837-4319. TDD: 410-837-4297. E-mail: langcirc@ubalt.edu, langref@ubalt.edu. Web Site: langsdale.ubalt.edu. *Dir,* Lucy Holman; Tel: 410-837-4333, E-mail: lholman@ubalt.edu; *Assoc Dir, Pub Serv,* Jeffrey Hutson; Tel: 410-837-4298, E-mail: jhutson@ubalt.edu; *Head, Ref,* Michael Shochet; Tel: 410-837-4277, E-mail: mshochet@ubalt.edu; *Head, Tech Serv & Content Mgt,* Betty Landesman; E-mail: blandesman@ubalt.edu; *Integrated Digital Serv Librn,* Bill Helman; Tel: 410-837-4209, E-mail: whelman@ubalt.edu; *Bk & Doc Delivery Supvr,* Carol Vaeth; E-mail: cvaeth@ubalt.edu; *Circ Supvr,* Tammy Taylor; Tel: 410-837-4263, E-mail: ttaylor@ubalt.edu; *Electronic Res,* Susan Wheeler; Tel: 410-837-4299, E-mail: swheeler@ubalt.edu; Staff 15 (MLS 13, Non-MLS 2)
Founded 1926. Enrl 6,265; Fac 123; Highest Degree: Doctorate
Library Holdings: Bk Vols 181,000; Per Subs 450
Special Collections: Society of Colonial Wars Archives; WMAR-TV Film Archives. Oral History; State Document Depository; US Document Depository
Automation Activity & Vendor Info: (Acquisitions) Ex Libris Group; (Cataloging) Ex Libris Group; (Circulation) Ex Libris Group; (ILL) OCLC ILLiad; (Media Booking) Ex Libris Group; (OPAC) Ex Libris Group; (Serials) Ex Libris Group
Database Vendor: 3M Library Systems, ABC-CLIO, ACM (Association for Computing Machinery), Annual Reviews, Atlas Systems, Coutts Information Service, CQ Press, Dun & Bradstreet, EBSCOhost, Elsevier, Ex Libris Group, Gale Cengage Learning, HeinOnline, Hoovers, IBISWorld, infoUSA, ISI Web of Knowledge, JSTOR, LexisNexis, Mergent Online, OCLC FirstSearch, OCLC WorldShare Interlibrary Loan, OVID Technologies, ProQuest, ReferenceUSA, SerialsSolutions, Springshare, LLC, Thomson - Web of Science, Wiley InterScience
Wireless access
Publications: Langsdale Library Link
Partic in Baltimore Acad Libr Consortium; Lyrasis; OCLC Online Computer Library Center, Inc; Univ Syst of Md
Special Services for the Deaf - ADA equip; Assisted listening device; Closed caption videos
Special Services for the Blind - Assistive/Adapted tech devices, equip & products; Audio mat; Computer with voice synthesizer for visually impaired persons; Dragon Naturally Speaking software; Internet workstation with adaptive software; Large print & cassettes; Magnifiers
Open Mon-Thurs 8:30am-10pm, Fri 8:30-6, Sat & Sun 10-7

Departmental Libraries:

CL LAW LIBRARY, 1415 Maryland Ave, 21201, SAN 343-995X. Tel: 410-837-4554. Reference Tel: 410-837-4559. FAX: 410-837-4570. Web Site: law.ubalt.edu/lawlib. *Dir,* Will Tress; *Asst Dir, Pub Serv,* Joanne Colvin; *Govt Doc,* Pat Behles; *Info Tech,* Harvey Morrell; *Tech Serv,* Clement Chu-Sing Lau; Staff 17 (MLS 10.5, Non-MLS 6.5)
Founded 1925. Enrl 1,000; Fac 45; Highest Degree: Master
Library Holdings: Bk Titles 27,130; Bk Vols 305,000; Per Subs 3,500
Special Collections: State Document Depository; US Document Depository
Automation Activity & Vendor Info: (ILL) OCLC
Database Vendor: JSTOR, Westlaw
Partic in Cap Area Libr Consortium; Maryland Interlibrary Loan Organization; OCLC Online Computer Library Center, Inc
Publications: Anglo-American law (Research guide)
Open Mon-Fri 8am-Midnight, Sat & Sun 9am-Midnight

UNIVERSITY OF MARYLAND, BALTIMORE

CM HEALTH SCIENCES & HUMAN SERVICES LIBRARY*, 601 W Lombard St, 21201, SAN 344-001X. Tel: 410-706-7545. Circulation Tel: 410-706-7928, 410-706-7995. Interlibrary Loan Service Tel: 410-706-3239. Information Services Tel: 410-706-7996. FAX: 410-706-3101. Web Site: www.hshsl.umaryland.edu/. *Exec Dir,* M J Tooey; E-mail: mjtooey@hshsl.umaryland.edu; *Exec Dir, NN/LM SE/ARMLS,* Janice Kelly; Tel: 410-706-2855; *Assoc Dir, Res,* Beverly Gresehover; Tel: 410-706-1784, E-mail: bgreseho@hshsl.umaryland.edu; *Assoc Dir, Serv, Pub Serv,* Alexa Mayo; Tel: 410-706-1316, E-mail: amayo@hshsl.umaryland.edu; *Asst Dir, Bus Develop & Operations,* Aphrodite Bodycomb; Tel: 410-706-8853, E-mail: abodycomb@hshsl.umaryland.edu. Subject Specialists: *Consulting, Educ,* Alexa Mayo; Staff 66 (MLS 29, Non-MLS 37)
Founded 1813. Enrl 5,875; Fac 1,600; Highest Degree: Doctorate
Library Holdings: Bk Vols 365,000; Per Subs 2,400
Special Collections: History of Dentistry (Grieves Coll), bks, pictures; History of Medicine (Crawford, Cordell Coll); History of Nursing; History of Pharmacy
Subject Interests: Dentistry, Med, Nursing, Pharm, Soc serv (soc work)
Automation Activity & Vendor Info: (Acquisitions) Ex Libris Group; (Cataloging) Ex Libris Group; (Circulation) Ex Libris Group; (Course Reserve) Docutek; (OPAC) Ex Libris Group; (Serials) Ex Libris Group
Database Vendor: SirsiDynix

Partic in Lyrasis; OCLC Online Computer Library Center, Inc; Univ Syst of Md
Open Mon-Fri 8am-10:30pm, Sat 8-5, Sun 11-8
Friends of the Library Group

CL THURGOOD MARSHALL LAW LIBRARY, 501 W Fayette St, 21201-1768, SAN 344-0044. Tel: 410-706-7270. Interlibrary Loan Service Tel: 410-706-3240. Reference Tel: 410-706-6502. FAX: 410-706-8354. Interlibrary Loan Service FAX: 410-706-0554. Web Site: www.law.umaryland.edu/marshall. *Assoc Dean,* Barbara Gontrum; E-mail: bgontrum@law.umaryland.edu; *Dir, Info Policy & Mgt,* Nathan Robertson; Tel: 410-706-1213, E-mail: nrobertson@law.umaryland.edu; *Actg Dir,* Camilla Tubbs; Tel: 410-706-0792, E-mail: ctubbs@law.umaryland.edu; *Assoc Dir,* David Grahek; Tel: 410-706-2025, E-mail: dgrahek@law.umaryland.edu; *Digital Legal Res & Syst Librn,* Joseph Neumann; Tel: 410-706-2736, E-mail: jneumann@law.umaryland.edu; *Res Librn,* Maxine Grosshans; Tel: 410-706-0791, E-mail: mgross@law.umaryland.edu; *Res Librn,* Jason Hawkins; Tel: 410-706-0735, E-mail: jhawkins@law.umaryland.edu; *Res Librn,* Susan Herrick; Tel: 410-706-3213, E-mail: sherrick@law.umaryland.edu; *Res Librn,* Charles Pipins; Tel: 410-706-9784, E-mail: cpipins@law.umaryland.edu; *Res Librn,* Jenny Rensler; Tel: 410-706-2466, E-mail: jrensler@law.umaryland.edu; *Res Acq & Metadata Serv Librn,* Stephanie Bowe; Tel: 410-706-0783, E-mail: sbowe@law.umaryland.edu; Staff 24 (MLS 11, Non-MLS 13)
Founded 1843
Special Collections: East Asian Legal Studies Coll; German & French Civil Law Coll. US Document Depository
Automation Activity & Vendor Info: (Acquisitions) Ex Libris Group; (Cataloging) Ex Libris Group; (Circulation) Ex Libris Group; (ILL) Ex Libris Group; (OPAC) Ex Libris Group; (Serials) Ex Libris Group
Database Vendor: 3M Library Systems, Backstage Library Works, Bowker, Dialog, EBSCOhost, Ex Libris Group, Gale Cengage Learning, HeinOnline, Ingenta, LexisNexis, OCLC FirstSearch, OCLC WorldShare Interlibrary Loan, Project MUSE, Westlaw, Wiley, YBP Library Services
Partic in Lyrasis; New England Law Library Consortium, Inc; OCLC Online Computer Library Center, Inc; University System of Maryland & Affiliated Institutions (USMAI)
Open Mon-Thurs 7:30am-Midnight, Fri 7:30-6, Sat 9am-10pm, Sun 10am-11pm

C UNIVERSITY OF MARYLAND, BALTIMORE COUNTY, Albin O Kuhn Library & Gallery, 1000 Hilltop Circle, 21250. SAN 306-8854. Tel: 410-455-2356. Circulation Tel: 410-455-2354. Interlibrary Loan Service Tel: 410-455-2234. Reference Tel: 410-455 2346. Circulation FAX: 410-455-1153. Interlibrary Loan Service FAX: 410-455-1061. Reference FAX: 410-455-1906. Administration FAX: 410-455-1078. E-mail: aok@umbc.edu. Web Site: www.umbc.edu/library. *Dir,* Position Currently Open; *Actg Dir,* Joyce Tenney; Fax: 410-455-1138, E-mail: tenney@umbc.edu; *Assoc Dir,* Robin Moskal; Fax: 410-455-1598, E-mail: moskal@umbc.edu; *Head, Spec Coll,* Tom Beck; Fax: 410-455-1567, E-mail: beck@umbc.edu; *Head, Tech Serv,* Lynda Aldana; Fax: 410-455-1598, E-mail: laldana@umbc.edu; *Asst Head, Ref Serv,* Kathryn Sullivan; E-mail: sullivan@umbc.edu; *Acq Librn,* Michelle Flinchbaugh; Fax: 410-455-1598, E mail: flinchba@umbc.edu; *Cat Librn,* Vicki Sipe; Fax: 410-455-1598, E-mail: sipe@umbc.edu; *Cat Librn,* Tiffany Wilson; Fax: 410-455-1598, E-mail: twilson@umbc.edu; *Digital Media Librn,* Jodi Hoover; E-mail: hooverj@umbc.edu; *IT Librn,* James Stephens; E-mail: jstephen@umbc.edu; *Ref Librn,* Drew Alfgren; E-mail: alfgren@umbc.edu; *Ref & Instruction Librn,* Joanna Gadsby; E-mail: gadsby@umbc.edu; *Ref & Instruction Librn,* Gergana Kostova; E-mail: g.kostova@umbc.edu; *Ref & Web Serv Librn,* Janet Hack; E-mail: jhack@umbc.edu; *Sci Ref Instruction Librn,* Shu Qian; E-mail: qian@umbc.edu; *Ser & Electronic Res Librn,* Kelly Shipp; Fax: 410-455-1138, E-mail: kshipp@umbc.edu; *Serv Develop & Spec Projects Librn,* Simmona Simmons; E-mail: simmons@umbc.edu; *Spec Coll Librn,* Susan Graham; Fax: 410-455-1567, E-mail: sgraha1@umbc.edu; *Bus Mgr,* Melissa S Button; E-mail: mbutton@umbc.edu; *Circ Mgr,* Michael Dick; E-mail: michaed@umbc.edu; *IT Serv Mgr,* Stephen Jones; E-mail: stjones@umbc.edu; *Archivist,* Lindsey Loeper; Fax: 410-455-1567, E-mail: lloepe1@umbc.edu; *Curator,* Emily Hauver; Fax: 410-455-1567, E-mail: emilyh2@umbc.edu. Subject Specialists: *Photog,* Tom Beck; Staff 23.5 (MLS 19.5, Non-MLS 4)
Founded 1966. Enrl 13,637; Fac 740; Highest Degree: Doctorate
Jul 2011-Jun 2012. Mats Exp $3,799,040, Books $503,088, Per/Ser (Incl. Access Fees) $3,295,952. Sal $2,900,831 (Prof $1,415,448)
Library Holdings: CDs 7,888; DVDs 7,282; e-books 61,548; e-journals 2,285; Microforms 1,018,693; Bk Vols 654,758; Per Subs 4,917; Videos 4,064
Special Collections: 19th Century English Graphic Satire (Merkle Coll); American Society for Microbiology Archives, bks, pers, mss; Baltimore Sun Photo Archives; Children's Science Books; Marylandia (Howard Coll); Photography, bks, pers, photo apparatus; Popular Culture; Tissue Culture Association Archives; University Archives, photog. Oral History; State Document Depository; US Document Depository
Automation Activity & Vendor Info: (Acquisitions) Ex Libris Group; (Cataloging) Ex Libris Group; (Circulation) Ex Libris Group; (Course Reserve) Ex Libris Group; (ILL) OCLC ILLiad; (Media Booking) Ex Libris Group; (Serials) Ex Libris Group
Database Vendor: EBSCOhost, OCLC FirstSearch
Wireless access
Publications: Exhibition Catalogs; From the Stacks (Newsletter)
Partic in ARIEL; OCLC Online Computer Library Center, Inc; Univ of Md Libr Info Mgt Syst
Open Mon-Thurs 7:30am Midnight, Fri 7:30-7, Sat 10-6, Sun Noon-Midnight
Friends of the Library Group

A USACE BALTIMORE DISTRICT LIBRARY*, Ten S Howard St, 21201. (Mail add: PO Box 1715, 21203-1715), SAN 343-9860. Tel: 410-962-3423. FAX: 410-962-1889. *Libr Tech,* Stephen L Brooks; E-mail: stephen.l.brooks@usace.army.mil; Staff 1 (Non-MLS 1)
Founded 1974
Library Holdings: AV Mats 78; Bk Vols 20,000; Per Subs 150
Special Collections: Corps of Army Engineers (Annual Reports 1800-); Waterway Legislation (Rivers & Harbors 1800-)
Subject Interests: Civil eng, Environ studies, Law, Soil mechanics, Water res
Function: Outside serv via phone, mail, e-mail & web
Publications: Library Bulletin
Partic in OCLC Online Computer Library Center, Inc
Open Mon-Fri 7-3:30
Restriction: Authorized patrons

L VENABLE LLP LIBRARY*, 750 E Pratt St, 9th Flr, 21202. SAN 306-8870. Tel: 410-244-7502. Administration Tel: 410-244-7689. FAX: 410-244-7742. E-mail: lib01@venable.com. Web Site: www.venable.com. *Dir,* Barbara Folensbee-Moore; E-mail: bfolensbee-moore@venable.com; *Ref Librn,* Katherine Bare; E-mail: kbare@venable.com; *Computer Serv,* Mark R Desierto; Tel: 410-244-7840, E-mail: mrdesierto@venable.com; *Ref Serv,* Vivian V Shern; Tel: 410-244-7843, E-mail: vvshern@venable.com; Staff 4 (MLS 3, Non-MLS 1)
Founded 1900
Library Holdings: e-journals 20; Electronic Media & Resources 100; Bk Vols 30,000; Per Subs 25
Subject Interests: Bankruptcy, Banks & banking, Corporate law, Employee benefits, Employment law, Environ law, Estates, Finance, Govt, Law, Litigation, Real property, Securities, Taxation, Transportation, Trusts
Automation Activity & Vendor Info: (Cataloging) Sydney; (Circulation) Sydney; (OPAC) Sydney; (Serials) Sydney
Wireless access
Restriction: By permission only

Branches:

DC OFFICE
See Separate Entry in Washington, DC
ROCKVILLE OFFICE, One Church St, Ste 500, Rockville, 20850, SAN 370-937X. Tel: 301-217-5600. FAX: 301-217-5617.
Founded 1967
Library Holdings: e-journals 20; Electronic Media & Resources 25; Bk Vols 1,250
Subject Interests: Employment law, Labor law, Litigation, Municipal corp, Real estate law
Restriction: Staff use only
TOWSON OFFICE, 210 W Pennsylvania Ave, Ste 500, Towson, 21204, SAN 370-9388. Tel: 410-494-6200. FAX: 410-821-0147. E-mail: lib01@venable.com. *Dir,* Barbara Folensbee-Moore
Founded 1962
Library Holdings: Bk Vols 1,250
Subject Interests: Civil litigation, Construction law, Govt, Law, Real estate law
VIRGINIA OFFICE
See Separate Entry in Vienna, VA

S WALTERS ART MUSEUM LIBRARY*, 600 N Charles St, 21201-5185. SAN 306-8897. Tel: 410-547-9000, Ext 297. FAX: 410-752-4797. E-mail: info@thewalters.org. Web Site: www.thewalters.org. *Archivist/Librn,* Diane Bockrath; E-mail: dbockrath@thewalters.org; Staff 1 (Non-MLS 1)
Founded 1934
Library Holdings: Bk Vols 120,000; Per Subs 100
Special Collections: Art Auction Catalogs
Subject Interests: Hist
Automation Activity & Vendor Info: (Acquisitions) SirsiDynix; (Cataloging) SirsiDynix; (OPAC) SirsiDynix; (Serials) SirsiDynix
Wireless access
Function: Res libr
Partic in OCLC Online Computer Library Center, Inc
Restriction: Closed stack, Non-circulating, Not a lending libr, Open by appt only

L WHITEFORD, TAYLOR & PRESTON, LLP*, Law Library, Seven St Paul St, Ste 1500, 21202-1636. SAN 372-0616. Tel: 410-347-8700. FAX: 410-752-7092. Web Site: www.wtplaw.com. *Librn,* Mary Longchamp; E-mail: mlongchamp@wtplaw.com; Staff 4 (MLS 1, Non-MLS 3)
Library Holdings: Bk Vols 8,000; Per Subs 125
Automation Activity & Vendor Info: (Acquisitions) TLC (The Library Corporation); (Cataloging) TLC (The Library Corporation)
Database Vendor: LexisNexis, Westlaw
Restriction: Staff use only

BEL AIR

J HARFORD COMMUNITY COLLEGE LIBRARY*, 401 Thomas Run Rd, 21015. SAN 306-8935. Tel: 410-836-4268. Reference Tel: 410-836-4131. Administration Tel: 410-836-4316. FAX: 410-836-4198. E-mail: referenc@harford.edu. Web Site: www.harford.edu/library. *Dean of Libr & Instrul Serv,* Lucy Holman Rector; Tel: 410-836-4144, Fax: 410-836-4481; *Assoc Dir,* Christel Vonderscheer; Tel: 410-836-4145; *Ref,* Mary Somers; Tel: 410-836-4232; Staff 10 (MLS 9, Non-MLS 1)
Founded 1957. Enrl 5,500; Fac 85
Library Holdings: Bk Vols 54,000; Per Subs 428
Special Collections: Maryland Constitutional Convention File; Maryland History; Rosenburg Report. US Document Depository
Subject Interests: Art
Automation Activity & Vendor Info: (Acquisitions) SirsiDynix; (Circulation) SirsiDynix; (Course Reserve) SirsiDynix; (OPAC) SirsiDynix
Database Vendor: OCLC FirstSearch
Open Mon-Thurs 7:30am-10pm, Fri 7:30-4:30, Sat 10-4, Sun 12-4

BELCAMP

P HARFORD COUNTY PUBLIC LIBRARY*, 1221-A Brass Mill Rd, 21017-1209. SAN 344-0079. Tel: 410-273-5600, 410-575-6761. Reference Tel: 410-638-3151. FAX: 410-273-5606. Web Site: www.hcplonline.org. *Dir,* Mary L Hastler; Tel: 410-273-5600, Ext 2252, E-mail: hastler@hcplonline.org; *Assoc Dir,* Steve D Kirchner; Tel: 410-273-5600, Ext 2250, E-mail: kirchner@hcplonline.org; *Assoc Dir,* Daria A Parry; Tel: 410-273-5600, Ext 2246, E-mail: parry@hcplonline.org; *Found Dir,* Amber Shrodes; Tel: 410-273-5600, Ext 2283, E-mail: shrodes@hcplonline.org; *Human Res Sr Adminr,* Terri Schell; Tel: 410-273-5600, Ext 2223, E-mail: schell@hcplonline.org; *Sr Adminr, Pub Serv,* Joseph Thompson; *Mat Mgt Adminr,* Jennifer Ralston; Tel: 410-273-5600, Ext 2273, E-mail: ralston@hcplonline.org; *Tech Adminr,* Gia Wilhelm; Tel: 410-273-5600, Ext 2248, E-mail: wilhelm@hcplonline.org; *Mkt Mgr,* Janine Lis; Tel: 410-273-5600, Ext 2256, E-mail: lis@hcplonline.org; *Commun Relations Spec,* Bethany Hacker; Tel: 410-273-5600, Ext 2243, E-mail: hacker@hcplonline.org; Staff 132 (MLS 41, Non-MLS 91)
Founded 1946. Pop 244,826; Circ 4,814,696
Jul 2010-Jun 2011 Income (Main Library and Branch(s)) $18,837,328, State $2,690,400, Federal $8,000, County $15,112,147, Locally Generated Income $1,007,166, Other $19,615. Mats Exp $2,710,623, Books $1,600,410, Per/Ser (Incl. Access Fees) $70,634, AV Mat $864,124, Electronic Ref Mat (Incl. Access Fees) $175,455. Sal $9,336,411 (Prof $5,916,004)
Library Holdings: AV Mats 221,469; CDs 42,157; DVDs 108,225; e-books 14,338; Large Print Bks 20,228; Bk Vols 797,732; Per Subs 1,338; Talking Bks 62,215
Special Collections: Juvenile Historical Coll; Learning, Sharing & Caring; Project LEAP; PTC Coll; Ripken Literacy Coll; Rolling Reader Coll; Silver Reader; Spanish (Juvenile & Adult). Oral History
Subject Interests: Maryland
Automation Activity & Vendor Info: (Acquisitions) Innovative Interfaces, Inc; (Cataloging) Innovative Interfaces, Inc; (Circulation) Innovative Interfaces, Inc; (ILL) Innovative Interfaces, Inc; (Media Booking) Innovative Interfaces, Inc; (OPAC) Innovative Interfaces, Inc; (Serials) Innovative Interfaces, Inc
Database Vendor: SirsiDynix
Wireless access
Publications: Harford County Public Library (Annual report); Headlines & Happenings (Newsletter)
Partic in Marynet
Special Services for the Deaf - Assistive tech; Closed caption videos; Sign lang interpreter upon request for prog; TTY equip
Special Services for the Blind - Audio mat; Bks on CD; Copier with enlargement capabilities; Digital talking bk; Large print bks; Magnifiers; Recorded bks
Open Mon, Tues & Thurs 10-8, Wed 1-8, Fri & Sat 10-5
Friends of the Library Group
Branches: 11
ABERDEEN BRANCH, 21 Franklin St, Aberdeen, 21001-2495, SAN 344-0109. Tel: 410-273-5608. FAX: 410-273-5610. *Br Mgr,* Jennifer Jones; E-mail: jonesj@hcplonline.org
Special Collections: African-American Coll; Parent-Teacher Coll; Ripken Literacy Center
Subject Interests: Maryland
Open Mon, Tues & Thurs 10-8, Wed 1-8, Fri & Sat 10-5
Friends of the Library Group
ABINGDON BRANCH, 2510 Tollgate Rd, Abingdon, 21009. Tel: 410-638-3990. FAX: 410-638-3995. *Br Mgr,* Lisa Mittman; E-mail: mittman@hcplonline.org
Founded 2003
Open Mon, Tues & Thurs 10-8, Wed 1-8, Fri & Sat 10-5
Friends of the Library Group
BEL AIR BRANCH, 100 E Pennsylvania Ave, Bel Air, 21014-3799, SAN 344-0133. Tel: 410-638-3151. FAX: 410-638-3155. *Br Mgr,* Beth LaPenotiere; E-mail: lapenotiere@hcplonline.org
Special Collections: Juvenile Historical Coll; LSC Coll; Parent-Teacher Coll
Subject Interests: Maryland
Special Services for the Deaf - TTY equip
Open Mon, Tues & Thurs 10-9, Wed 12-9, Fri & Sat 10-5
Friends of the Library Group
DARLINGTON BRANCH, 1134 Main St, Darlington, 21034-1418, SAN 344-0168. Tel: 410-638-3750. FAX: 410-638-3752. *Br Mgr,* Mrs Gregory Wollon; E-mail: wollon@hcplonline.org
Special Collections: Parent-Teacher Coll
Subject Interests: Maryland
Open Mon, Tues & Wed 3-8, Thurs 12-5, Fri 1-5, Sat 10-2
Friends of the Library Group
EDGEWOOD BRANCH, 629 Edgewood Rd, Edgewood, 21040-2607, SAN 344-0192. Tel: 410-612-1600. FAX: 410-612-1602. *Br Mgr,* Susan Deeney; E-mail: deeney@hcplonline.org
Special Collections: AF-AM Coll; Parent-Teacher Coll
Subject Interests: Maryland
Open Mon, Tues & Thurs 10-8, Wed 1-8, Fri & Sat 10-5
Friends of the Library Group
FALLSTON BRANCH, 1461 Fallston Rd, Fallston, 21047-1699, SAN 326-7059. Tel: 410-638-3003. FAX: 410-638-3005. *Br Mgr,* Joyce Wemer; E-mail: wemer@hcplonline.org
Special Collections: Parent-Teacher Coll
Subject Interests: Maryland
Open Mon, Tues & Thurs 10-8, Wed 1-8, Fri & Sat 10-5
Friends of the Library Group
HAVRE DE GRACE BRANCH, 120 N Union Ave, Havre de Grace, 21078-3000, SAN 344-0222. Tel: 410-939-6700. FAX: 410-939-6702. *Br Mgr,* Irmgarde Brown; E-mail: brown@hcplonline.org
Special Collections: African-American Coll; Learn to Earn; Parent-Teacher Coll
Subject Interests: Maryland
Open Mon, Tues & Thurs 10-8, Wed 1-8, Fri & Sat 10-5
Friends of the Library Group
JARRETTSVILLE BRANCH, 3722 Norrisville Rd, Jarrettsville, 21084. *Br Mgr,* Linda Lupro; Tel: 410-692-7887, E-mail: lupro@hcplonline.org
Open Mon, Tues & Thurs 10-8, Wed 1-8, Fri & Sat 10-5
JOPPA BRANCH, 655 Towne Center Dr, Joppa, 21085-4497, SAN 344-0214. Tel: 410-612-1660. FAX: 410-612-1662. *Br Mgr,* Pam Taylor; Tel: 410-612-1600, E-mail: taylor@hcplonline.info
Special Collections: Parent-Teacher Coll
Subject Interests: Maryland
Open Mon & Wed 10-8, Tues & Thurs 1-8, Fri & Sat 10-5
Friends of the Library Group
NORRISVILLE BRANCH, 5310 Norrisville Rd, White Hall, 21161-8924, SAN 328-7661. Tel: 410-692-7850. FAX: 410-692-7851. *Br Mgr,* Joan Stiffler; E-mail: stiffler@hcplonline.org
Open Mon, Tues & Thurs 10-8, Wed 1-8, Fri & Sat 10-5
Friends of the Library Group
WHITEFORD BRANCH, 2407 Whiteford Rd, Whiteford, 21160-1218, SAN 344-0249. Tel: 410-638-3608. FAX: 410-638-3610. *Br Mgr,* Heidi Richardson; Tel: 410-452-8831, E-mail: richardson@hcplonline.org
Special Collections: Parent-Teacher Coll
Subject Interests: Maryland
Open Mon, Tues & Thurs 10-8, Wed 1-8, Fri & Sat 10-5
Friends of the Library Group
Bookmobiles: 2. Bk titles 9,554

BELTSVILLE

G UNITED STATES BUREAU OF ALCOHOL, TOBACCO, FIREARMS & EXPLOSIVES*, National Laboratory Center Library, 6000 Ammendale Rd, 20705-1250. SAN 371-1315. Tel: 202-648-6074. FAX: 202-648-6073. *Librn,* Susan B Wright; E-mail: susan.wright@atf.gov; Staff 1 (MLS 1)
Oct 2012-Sept 2013. Mats Exp $42,000, Books $5,000, Per/Ser (Incl. Access Fees) $37,000
Library Holdings: AV Mats 25; Bk Titles 3,200; Bk Vols 4,041; Per Subs 60
Subject Interests: Analytical chem, Forensic sci
Automation Activity & Vendor Info: (Cataloging) Horizon; (Circulation) SirsiDynix; (OPAC) SirsiDynix

Database Vendor: Dialog, EBSCOhost, HeinOnline, LAC Group, LexisNexis, Medlib, OCLC FirstSearch, ProQuest, PubMed, WT Cox
Restriction: Staff use only

G UNITED STATES DEPARTMENT OF AGRICULTURE, National Agricultural Library, 10301 Baltimore Ave, 20705-2351. SAN 344-0257. Tel: 301-504-5755. Interlibrary Loan Service Tel: 301-504-5717. Administration Tel: 301-504-5248. Information Services Tel: 301-504-5788. FAX: 301-504-5472. Administration FAX: 301-504-7042. Information Services FAX: 301-504-6927. *Dir,* Simon Liu, PhD
Founded 1862
Library Holdings: Bk Vols 2,455,950; Per Subs 17,299
Automation Activity & Vendor Info: (Acquisitions) Ex Libris Group; (Cataloging) Ex Libris Group; (Circulation) Ex Libris Group; (ILL) Ex Libris Group; (OPAC) Ex Libris Group; (Serials) Ex Libris Group
Partic in Association of Research Libraries (ARL); Fedlink; OCLC Online Computer Library Center, Inc
Open Mon-Fri 9-4:30

BETHESDA

S AMERICAN OCCUPATIONAL THERAPY FOUNDATION*, Wilma L West Occupational Therapy Library, 4720 Montgomery Lane, 20814-5385. (Mail add: PO Box 31220, 20824-1220), SAN 324-6795. Tel: 301-652-6611, Ext 2557. Administration Toll Free Tel: 800-729-2682 (Members only). FAX: 301-656-3620. E-mail: wlwlib@aotf.org. Web Site: www.aotf.org/html/library.shtml. *Dir, Libr & Info Serv,* Mary Binderman; E-mail: mbinderman@aotf.org; *Mgr, Info Tech,* Kreg Williams; E-mail: kwilliams@aotf.org; *Ref,* Mindy Hecker; E-mail: mhecker@aotf.org; Staff 2 (MLS 2)
Founded 1980
Library Holdings: AV Mats 1,005; Bk Vols 5,466; Per Subs 60
Special Collections: A Jean Ayres Coll; AOTA Archives Coll; Gail Fidler Coll; Mary Reilly Coll
Subject Interests: Human occupation, Occupation sci, Occupational therapy, Rehabilitation
Publications: Occupational Therapy Library Brochure
Partic in District of Columbia Area Health Science Libraries; National Network of Libraries of Medicine
Restriction: Open by appt only, Restricted pub use

M AMERICAN SOCIETY OF HEALTH-SYSTEM PHARMACISTS*, Library, 7272 Wisconsin Ave, 20814. SAN 377-1636. Tel: 301-657-3000. Web Site: www.ashp.org. *Archivist, Librn, Rec Mgr,* Anne Callas; E-mail: acallas@ashp.org; Staff 1 (MLS 1)
Library Holdings: Bk Vols 1,200; Per Subs 500
Function: Archival coll
Restriction: By permission only, Circulates for staff only, Visitors must make appt to use bks in the libr

R BETHESDA UNITED METHODIST CHURCH LIBRARY*, 8300 Old Georgetown Rd, 20814. SAN 306-8978. Tel: 301-652-2990. FAX: 301-652-1965. E-mail: bethesdaum@aol.com. *Librn,* Donna Runyan
Founded 1956
Library Holdings: Bk Vols 4,000
Subject Interests: Biblical studies, Child welfare, Church hist, Relig
Publications: Library News (Newsletter)
Open Mon-Fri 10-5, Sun 12-2
Friends of the Library Group

S CAMBRIDGE SCIENTIFIC ABSTRACTS LIBRARY*, 7200 Wisconsin Ave, 20814. SAN 307-0026. Tel: 301-961-6795. FAX: 301-961-6720. E-mail: info@proquest.com. Web Site: www.csa.com. *VPres,* Anthea Gotto
Founded 1952
Subject Interests: Aquatic sci, Biological sci, Eng, Linguistics, Mat sci, Sociol
Publications: ASFA Thesaurus; Life Sciences Thesaurus; Thesaurus of Linguistics Indexing Terms; Thesaurus of Metallurgical Terms; Thesaurus of Sociological Indexing Terms
Open Mon-Fri 10-6

S EDITORIAL PROJECTS IN EDUCATION LIBRARY*, Education Week Library, 6935 Arlington Rd, 20814. SAN 377-1237. Tel: 301-280-3100. FAX: 301-280-3200. E-mail: library@epe.org. Web Site: www.edweek.org. *Dir, Libr & Info Serv,* Kathryn Dorko; E-mail: kdorko@epe.org; Staff 2 (MLS 1, Non-MLS 1)
Founded 1995
Library Holdings: Bk Titles 3,898; Bk Vols 3,898; Per Subs 223
Wireless access
Function: Newsp ref libr

S FOSTER ASSOCIATES, INC LIBRARY*, 4550 Montgomery Ave, Ste 350N, 20814. SAN 302-6574. Tel: 301-664-7800. FAX: 301-664-7810. E-mail: fainfo@foster-fa.com. Web Site: www.foster-fa.com. *Librn,* Peter McArthur
Founded 1956
Library Holdings: Bk Vols 18,000; Per Subs 150
Subject Interests: Energy
Open Mon-Fri 8-4

SR FOURTH PRESBYTERIAN CHURCH*, Media Center, 5500 River Rd, 20816-3399. SAN 371-7321. Tel: 301-320-3434. FAX: 301-320-6315. Web Site: www.4thpres.org. *Dir,* Jeri Weaver; *Ch Serv,* Holly Gochnaur; Staff 5 (Non-MLS 5)
Library Holdings: Bk Titles 10,000; Per Subs 50
Automation Activity & Vendor Info: (Cataloging) Book Systems; (Circulation) Book Systems; (OPAC) Book Systems
Open Mon-Thurs 9-5, Sun 9-12:30

L LERCH, EARLY & BREWER*, Law Library, Three Bethesda Metro Ctr, Ste 460, 20814. SAN 372-1035. Tel: 301-986-1300. FAX: 301-986-0332. Web Site: www.lerchearly.com. *Librn,* Belinda Cain; E-mail: bcain@lerchearly.com
Library Holdings: Bk Vols 5,000; Per Subs 35
Open Mon-Fri 8:30-5:30

L LINOWES & BLOCHER LLP*, Law Library, 7200 Wisconsin Ave, Ste 800, 20814. SAN 372-0608. Tel: 301-961-5163. FAX: 301-654-2801. Web Site: www.linowes-law.com. *Librn,* Deborah Cannon; E-mail: dcannon@linowes-law.com; Staff 2 (MLS 1, Non-MLS 1)
Library Holdings: Bk Vols 3,000; Per Subs 35
Subject Interests: Real estate
Automation Activity & Vendor Info: (Cataloging) Inmagic, Inc.; (Serials) Inmagic, Inc.
Database Vendor: LexisNexis
Restriction: Staff use only

GM NATIONAL CANCER INSTITUTE*, Office of Communications Library, 6116 Executive Blvd, Rm 3068, 20892. SAN 377-4805. Tel: 301-496-6756. FAX: 301-496-7096. *Librn,* Judy Grosberg; E-mail: grosberj@mail.nih.gov
Library Holdings: Bk Vols 300; Per Subs 20
Database Vendor: Dialog, LexisNexis
Restriction: Not open to pub

G NATIONAL INSTITUTE OF ARTHRITIS & MUSCULOSKELETAL & SKIN DISEASES INFORMATION CLEARINGHOUSE*, One AMS Circle, 20892-3675. SAN 326-3312. Tel: 301-495-4484. Toll Free Tel: 877-226-4267. FAX: 301-718-6366. TDD: 301-565-2966. E-mail: niamsinfo@mail.nih.gov. Web Site: www.niams.nih.gov.
Subject Interests: Arthritis, Related musculoskeletal, Rheumatic diseases, Skin diseases, Sports injuries
Publications: Bibliographies; Brochures & Info Packages
Special Services for the Deaf - TTY equip
Restriction: Staff use only

GM NATIONAL INSTITUTES OF HEALTH LIBRARY*, 10 Center Dr, Rm 1L25A, 20892. SAN 344-0400. Tel: 301-496-1080. Administration Tel: 301-496 2448. FAX: 301-402-0254. E-mail: nihlibrary@nih.gov. Web Site: nihlibrary.nih.gov. *Dir,* Dr Keith Cogdill; E-mail: keith.cogdill@nih.gov; *Br Chief,* Ben Hope; Tel: 301-594-6473, E-mail: tallguy@nih.gov; *Br Chief,* Terrie Wheeler; Tel: 301-496-1157, E-mail: terrie.wheeler@nih.gov; Staff 50 (MLS 40, Non-MLS 10)
Founded 1903
Library Holdings: e-books 700; e-journals 8,500; Electronic Media & Resources 50; Bk Titles 63,000; Per Subs 8,620
Subject Interests: Biol, Chem, Health sci, Med, Physiology, Pub health
Automation Activity & Vendor Info: (Acquisitions) Innovative Interfaces, Inc; (Cataloging) Innovative Interfaces, Inc; (Circulation) Innovative Interfaces, Inc; (ILL) Relais International; (OPAC) Innovative Interfaces, Inc; (Serials) Innovative Interfaces, Inc
Database Vendor: Agricola, American Chemical Society, American Mathematical Society, American Physical Society, American Psychological Association (APA), Annual Reviews, BioOne, Blackwell, Cinahl, Dialog, Elsevier, Elsevier MDL, IEEE (Institute of Electrical & Electronics Engineers), Ingenta, Innovative Interfaces, Inc, IOP, ISI Web of Knowledge, JSTOR, LexisNexis, MD Consult, Medline, Micromedex, Natural Standard, Nature Publishing Group, OVID Technologies, PubMed, ScienceDirect, Springer-Verlag, STN International, UpToDate, Westlaw, Wiley InterScience, YBP Library Services
Wireless access
Partic in Fedlink; OCLC Online Computer Library Center, Inc; Ser Holdings Network
Restriction: Non-circulating to the pub, Pub use on premises

GM NATIONAL LIBRARY OF MEDICINE, Bldg 38, Rm 2E-17B, 8600 Rockville Pike, 20894. SAN 306-9079. Tel: 301-496-6308. Interlibrary Loan Service Tel: 301-496-5511. Toll Free Tel: 888-346-3656. FAX: 301-496-4450. E-mail: custserv@nlm.nih.gov. Web Site: www.nlm.nih.gov.

Dir, Dr Donald A B Lindberg; E-mail: lindberg@nlm.nih.gov; *Coll,* Lee Hammond; *Ms, Rare Bks,* Karen Pitts; *Pub Serv,* Martha Fishel; E-mail: fishelm@mail.nlm.nih.gov; *Pub Serv,* Ruth Hill; *Ref Serv, Web Serv,* Lenora Burts; *Ref Serv,* Lori Klien; *Ref Serv, Web Serv,* Marcia Zorn
Founded 1836
Library Holdings: Bk Vols 2,500,000; Per Subs 22,500
Special Collections: Manuscripts. Oral History; US Document Depository
Subject Interests: Health sci, Med
Database Vendor: LexisNexis
Partic in Association of Research Libraries (ARL); National Network of Libraries of Medicine; US National Library of Medicine
Open Mon-Fri 8:30-5, Sat 8:30-12:30
Friends of the Library Group

CM UNIFORMED SERVICES UNIVERSITY OF THE HEALTH SCIENCES*, James A Zimble Learning Resource Center, 4301 Jones Bridge Rd, 20814-4799. SAN 324-2226. Tel: 301-295-3350. Circulation Tel: 301-295-3189. FAX: 301-295-3795. E-mail: lrc.services@usuhs.edu. Web Site: www.lrc.usuhs.edu. *Dir,* Linda Spitzer; *Head, Ref Serv,* Alison Rollins; Staff 15 (MLS 4, Non-MLS 11)
Founded 1976. Enrl 1,100; Fac 1,000; Highest Degree: Doctorate
Library Holdings: e-books 17,000; e-journals 9,900; Bk Vols 28,000
Special Collections: US Document Depository
Subject Interests: Mil med
Automation Activity & Vendor Info: (Acquisitions) Innovative Interfaces, Inc; (Circulation) Innovative Interfaces, Inc; (Course Reserve) Innovative Interfaces, Inc; (OPAC) Innovative Interfaces, Inc; (Serials) Innovative Interfaces, Inc
Database Vendor: EBSCOhost, OVID Technologies
Wireless access
Publications: Learning Resource Center Guides; Research Guide Series
Partic in National Network of Libraries of Medicine
Special Services for the Deaf - Staff with knowledge of sign lang
Open Mon-Thurs 7am-11pm, Fri 7-5, Sat 9-5, Sun Noon-11
Friends of the Library Group

G UNITED STATES CONSUMER PRODUCT SAFETY COMMISSION LIBRARY, 4330 East W Hwy, Rm 519, 20814. SAN 306-9001. Tel: 301-504-7570. FAX: 301-504-0124. E-mail: library@cpsc.gov. Web Site: www.cpsc.gov. *Chief Librn,* Deborah C Inyamah; Staff 2 (MLS 2)
Founded 1973
Library Holdings: Bk Titles 3,000; Per Subs 20
Special Collections: Indexed Documents Coll; Technical Standards (Standards Coll), doc, bk & micro
Subject Interests: Admin law, Bus & mgt, Econ, Eng, Health sci, Law, Med, Safety, Standards (government), Toxicology
Publications: Information Update (Newsletter); New Accessions List; User's Guide to Library & Information Services
Partic in Docline; Dun & Bradstreet Info Servs; LexisNexis; OCLC-LVIS; Westlaw
Open Mon-Fri 10-2
Restriction: Restricted access

BOWIE

C BOWIE STATE UNIVERSITY*, Thurgood Marshall Library, 14000 Jericho Park Rd, 20715. SAN 306-9141. Tel: 301-860-3850. FAX: 301-860-3848. Web Site: www.bowiestate.edu. *Dean of Libr,* Dr Richard Bradberry; *Assoc Dean,* Marian Rucker-Shamu; *Asst Dean,* Cynthia Coleman
Founded 1937
Library Holdings: Bk Vols 244,000; Per Subs 732
Special Collections: Afro-American Experience, Slave Doc; Maryland subject; Rare books; University history
Subject Interests: Art
Automation Activity & Vendor Info: (Acquisitions) Ex Libris Group; (Cataloging) Ex Libris Group; (Circulation) Ex Libris Group; (Course Reserve) Ex Libris Group; (ILL) Ex Libris Group; (OPAC) Ex Libris Group
Database Vendor: EBSCOhost
Partic in Canadian Association of Research Libraries; Dialog Corp; OCLC Online Computer Library Center, Inc
Open Mon-Thurs 8-11, Fri 8-5, Sat 9-6, Sun 1-9

CALIFORNIA

G NAVAL AIR WARFARE CENTER*, MPRA Library, 22560 Epic Dr, Ste 100, 20619. SAN 326-176X. Tel: 301-862-0337. FAX: 301-862-5499. *Librn,* Shirley A Sharrow; Staff 4 (MLS 2, Non-MLS 2)
Founded 1977
Library Holdings: Bk Vols 94,000
Special Collections: P-3 Airplane Information (VP Program Library); S-3 Airplane Information (VS Program Library). US Document Depository
Publications: Lists of holdings
Open Mon-Thurs 7-4:30, Fri 7-3:30
Restriction: Authorized personnel only

CAMBRIDGE

GL DORCHESTER COUNTY CIRCUIT COURT*, Law Library, 206 High St, 21613. Tel: 410-228-6300. FAX: 410-221-5003. *Librn,* Mitchelle Upchurch
Library Holdings: Bk Titles 40; Bk Vols 3,000
Database Vendor: LexisNexis
Open Mon-Fri 1-3

P DORCHESTER COUNTY PUBLIC LIBRARY, 303 Gay St, 21613. SAN 344-0524. Tel: 410-228-7331. FAX: 410-228-6313. TDD: 410-228-0454. E-mail: dcpl@dorchesterlibrary.org. Reference E-mail: infodesk@dorchesterlibrary.org. Web Site: www.dorchesterlibrary.org. *Dir,* Frances Cresswell; E-mail: fcresswell@dorchesterlibrary.org; Staff 7 (MLS 3, Non-MLS 4)
Founded 1922. Pop 30,400; Circ 88,657
Library Holdings: AV Mats 2,944; Electronic Media & Resources 37; Bk Titles 74,329; Bk Vols 97,329; Per Subs 153
Special Collections: Dorchester County History & Genealogy; Drama Coll; Maryland Coll
Automation Activity & Vendor Info: (Acquisitions) Innovative Interfaces, Inc - Millenium; (Cataloging) Innovative Interfaces, Inc - Millenium; (Circulation) Innovative Interfaces, Inc - Millenium; (ILL) Relais International; (OPAC) Innovative Interfaces, Inc - Millenium
Wireless access
Partic in Eastern Shore Regional Library
Special Services for the Deaf - Sign lang interpreter upon request for prog; Video relay serv
Special Services for the Blind - Assistive/Adapted tech devices, equip & products; Bks on CD; Children's Braille; Copier with enlargement capabilities; Large print bks; Recorded bks; Text reader
Open Mon, Wed & Fri 10-6, Tues & Thurs 10-8, Sat 9-5
Friends of the Library Group
Branches: 1
HURLOCK BRANCH, 222 S Main St, Hurlock, 21643. (Mail add: PO Box 114, Hurlock, 21643), SAN 344-0559. Tel: 410-943-4331. FAX: 410-943-0293. *Br Mgr,* Charlotte Bradley
Founded 1900. Circ 37,000
Special Collections: Maryland History Coll
Partic in Lower Shore Library Consortium
Special Services for the Blind - Audio mat; Children's Braille; Large print bks
Open Mon, Wed & Fri 10-6, Tues & Thurs 10-8, Sat 9-12
Friends of the Library Group

M EASTERN SHORE HOSPITAL CENTER PROFESSIONAL LIBRARY*, Estella C Clendaniel Library, 5262 Woods Rd, 21613-3796. (Mail add: PO Box 800, 21613-0800), SAN 306-915X. Tel: 410-221-2485. Toll Free Tel: 888-216-8110. FAX: 410-221-2475. *In Charge,* Dolores Jean Slyter; E-mail: dslyter@dhmh.state.md.us; Staff 1 (Non-MLS 1)
Founded 1953
Library Holdings: Bk Titles 1,000; Bk Vols 2,669; Per Subs 39
Subject Interests: Med, Nursing, Psychiat, Psychol
Function: ILL available
Partic in Docline; SE-Atlantic Regional Med Libr Servs; US National Library of Medicine
Restriction: Med staff only, Not open to pub

C UNIVERSITY OF MARYLAND*, Center for Environmental Science, Horn Point Library, PO Box 775, 21613-0775. SAN 328-8439. Tel: 410-221-8450. FAX: 410-221-8490. Web Site: www.umces.edu/hpl. *Librn,* Susie Hines; E-mail: hines@umces.edu; Staff 1 (MLS 1)
Founded 1972. Fac 25; Highest Degree: Doctorate
Jul 2007-Jul 2008. Mats Exp $104,618, Books $6,150, Per/Ser (Incl. Access Fees) $81,729, Other Print Mats $1,400, Electronic Ref Mat (Incl. Access Fees) $15,339
Library Holdings: Bk Titles 3,000; Bk Vols 3,350; Per Subs 97
Subject Interests: Aquaculture, Marine biol, Oceanography, Wetland ecology
Automation Activity & Vendor Info: (Serials) EBSCO Online
Database Vendor: EBSCOhost, TLC (The Library Corporation)
Function: ILL available
Partic in Maryland Interlibrary Loan Organization; Univ Syst of Md

CAMP SPRINGS

S TRANSPORTATION INSTITUTE*, Information Resources Center, 5201 Auth Way, 5th Flr, 20746. SAN 302-7902. Tel: 301-423-3335, Ext 21. FAX: 301-423-0634. Web Site: www.trans-inst.org. *Mgr,* Robyn Farrell
Founded 1968
Library Holdings: AV Mats 82; Bk Titles 1,289; Per Subs 34
Subject Interests: Water transportation
Open Mon-Fri 9-5

CAPITOL HEIGHTS

C MAPLE SPRINGS BAPTIST BIBLE COLLEGE & SEMINARY LIBRARY*, Instructional Resources Center, 4130 Belt Rd, 20743. Tel: 301-736-3631. FAX: 301-735-6507. *Dir,* Darren Jones; *Librn,* Valerie Foster; *Cat,* Geraldine Nelson
Founded 1986. Enrl 253; Highest Degree: Doctorate
Library Holdings: Bk Titles 6,000
Partic in OCLC Online Computer Library Center, Inc
Open Mon-Fri 8:30-5:30

CATONSVILLE

J COMMUNITY COLLEGE OF BALTIMORE COUNTY*, Catonsville Library, Y Bldg, 800 S Rolling Rd, 21228. SAN 343-7949. Circulation Tel: 443-840-2710. Reference Tel: 443-840-2730. FAX: 410-455-6436. E-mail: crefdesk@ccbcmd.edu. Web Site: library.ccbcmd.edu. *Dir of Libr Serv,* Cynthia Roberts; Tel: 443-840-4589, E-mail: croberts@ccbcmd.edu; Staff 22 (MLS 7, Non-MLS 15)
Founded 1957. Enrl 10,500; Fac 200; Highest Degree: Associate
Library Holdings: e-books 187; Bk Titles 105,246; Bk Vols 110,481; Per Subs 450
Subject Interests: Automotive tech, Computer graphics, Construction mgt, Construction tech, Criminal justice, Environ sci, Info tech, Mortuary sci, Network tech, Nursing, Teacher educ, Visual communications
Automation Activity & Vendor Info: (Acquisitions) Innovative Interfaces, Inc; (Cataloging) Innovative Interfaces, Inc; (Circulation) Innovative Interfaces, Inc; (Course Reserve) Innovative Interfaces, Inc; (ILL) Innovative Interfaces, Inc; (Media Booking) Innovative Interfaces, Inc; (OPAC) Innovative Interfaces, Inc; (Serials) Innovative Interfaces, Inc
Wireless access
Function: Computers for patron use, Copy machines, Doc delivery serv, Electronic databases & coll, ILL available, Magnifiers for reading, Online cat, Photocopying/Printing, Pub access computers, Ref & res, VHS videos
Partic in Md Commun Col Libr Consortium
Special Services for the Deaf - Videos & decoder
Special Services for the Blind - Audio mat; Reader equip; Talking bk & rec for the blind cat; Variable speed audiotape players; VisualTek equip
Restriction: Open to pub upon request
Departmental Libraries:
DUNDALK LIBRARY, 100 College Community Ctr, Bldg 700, Sollers Point Rd, Baltimore, 21222, SAN 306-834X. Circulation Tel: 443-840-2591. Reference Tel: 443-840-2592. FAX: 443-840-3559. E-mail: dlibrary@ccbcmd.edu. *Dir, Libr Serv,* Cynthia Roberts; E-mail: croberts@ccbcmd.edu
Founded 1971. Enrl 1,600; Fac 125; Highest Degree: Associate
Library Holdings: Bk Vols 36,000; Per Subs 125
Subject Interests: Chem dependency, Criminal justice, Dental hygiene, Nursing, Sustainable horticulture
Automation Activity & Vendor Info: (Acquisitions) Innovative Interfaces, Inc - Millenium; (Cataloging) Innovative Interfaces, Inc - Millenium; (Circulation) Innovative Interfaces, Inc - Millenium; (Course Reserve) Innovative Interfaces, Inc - Millenium; (Media Booking) Innovative Interfaces, Inc - Millenium; (OPAC) Innovative Interfaces, Inc - Millenium; (Serials) Innovative Interfaces, Inc - Millenium
Database Vendor: Cinahl, CQ Press, CredoReference, EBSCO Discovery Service, EBSCOhost, Elsevier, Gale Cengage Learning, Innovative Interfaces, Inc, JSTOR, LexisNexis, McGraw-Hill, PubMed, ScienceDirect
Partic in Maryland Interlibrary Loan Organization
Open Mon-Thurs (Fall & Spring) 7:45am-10pm, Fri 7:45-4:30, Sat 10-3; Mon-Thurs (Summer) 8:30-7:30, Fri 8:30-4:30

M SPRING GROVE HOSPITAL CENTER*, Sulzbacher Memorial Staff Library, Isidore Tuerk Bldg, 55 Wade Ave, 21228. SAN 306-9168. Tel: 410-402-7824. FAX: 410-402-7732. *Librn,* Hannah Johnston
Founded 1938
Library Holdings: Bk Titles 2,100; Per Subs 26
Special Collections: American Journal of Insanity, 1846-1921; Hospital Reports from 1897
Restriction: Staff use only

CENTREVILLE

P QUEEN ANNE'S COUNTY FREE LIBRARY*, 121 S Commerce St, 21617. SAN 306-9176. Tel: 410-758-0980. FAX: 410-758-0614. Web Site: www.quan.lib.md.us. *Dir,* John Walden; E-mail: jwalden@quan.lib.md.us; *ILL,* Patricia Houghton; E-mail: phoughto@quan.lib.md.us; Staff 21 (MLS 7, Non-MLS 14)
Founded 1909. Pop 47,000; Circ 400,000
Library Holdings: Bk Vols 100,305; Per Subs 10
Subject Interests: Local hist
Automation Activity & Vendor Info: (Circulation) SirsiDynix
Wireless access
Partic in Eastern Shore Regional Library; Maryland Interlibrary Loan Organization
Open Mon-Thurs 10-8, Fri & Sat 9-5
Branches: 1
KENT ISLAND BRANCH, 200 Library Circle, Stevensville, 21666-4026, SAN 376-9860. Tel: 410-643-8161. FAX: 410-643-7098. *Mgr,* Peggy Ranson; E-mail: pransom@quan.lib.md.us
Automation Activity & Vendor Info: (Circulation) SirsiDynix
Open Mon-Thurs 10-8, Fri & Sat 9-5

CHARLOTTE HALL

P SOUTHERN MARYLAND REGIONAL LIBRARY ASSOCIATION, INC*, 37600 New Market Rd, 20622-3041. (Mail add: PO Box 459, 20622-0459), SAN 306-9826. Tel: 301-843-3634, 301-884-0436, 301-934-9442. FAX: 301-884-0438. E-mail: smrla@somd.lib.md.us. Web Site: cosmos.somd.lib.md.us. *Dir,* Sharan D Marshall; E-mail: smarshall@somd.lib.md.us; *Head, Info Serv,* David J Paul; E-mail: dpaul@somd.lib.md.us; *Head, Tech Serv,* Susan Grant; E-mail: sgrant@somd.lib.md.us; *Training Coordr,* Jennifer Falkowski; E-mail: jfalkowski@somd.lib.md.us. Subject Specialists: *Tech innovation,* David J Paul; Staff 8 (MLS 4, Non-MLS 4)
Founded 1959. Pop 329,045
Special Collections: State Document Depository
Automation Activity & Vendor Info: (Acquisitions) SirsiDynix; (Cataloging) SirsiDynix; (Circulation) SirsiDynix; (ILL) SirsiDynix; (OPAC) SirsiDynix
Database Vendor: EBSCO Auto Repair Reference, EBSCOhost, Gale Cengage Learning, OCLC WorldShare Interlibrary Loan, ProQuest, PubMed, SirsiDynix, WebMD
Wireless access
Function: ILL available
Publications: Community Information Directory
Member Libraries: Calvert County Public Library; Charles County Public Library; Saint Mary's County Memorial Library
Open Mon-Fri 8:30-4:30

CHESTERTOWN

P KENT COUNTY PUBLIC LIBRARY*, 408 High St, 21620-1312. SAN 306-9184. Tel: 410-778-3636. FAX: 410-778-6756. Web Site: www.kentcountylibrary.org. *Dir,* Jackie Adams; Staff 12 (MLS 4, Non-MLS 8)
Founded 1961. Pop 19,200; Circ 140,000
Automation Activity & Vendor Info: (Acquisitions) Evergreen; (Cataloging) Evergreen; (Circulation) Evergreen; (ILL) Relais International; (OPAC) Evergreen; (Serials) Evergreen
Wireless access
Partic in Eastern Shore Regional Library; Maryland Interlibrary Loan Organization
Open Mon-Thurs 9-6, Fri 9-5, Sat 9-3
Friends of the Library Group
Branches: 2
NORTH COUNTY, 111-B1 N Main St, Galena, 21635. Tel: 410-648-5380. *Mgr,* Jeanne Geibel
Open Tues & Thurs 10-6, Fri 10-5, Sat 10-2
Friends of the Library Group
ROCK HALL, 5585 Main St Municipal Bldg, 21661, SAN 376-8090. Tel: 410-639-7162. *Mgr,* Jeanne Geibel
Open Mon, Wed & Fri 9-3, Sat 9-1
Friends of the Library Group

C WASHINGTON COLLEGE*, Clifton M Miller Library, 300 Washington Ave, 21620-1197. SAN 306-9192. Tel: 410-778-7292. Circulation Tel: 410-778-7280. FAX: 410-778-7288. Web Site: libraryweb.washcoll.edu. *Dir,* Dr Ruth C Shoge; E-mail: rshoge2@washcoll.edu; *Dir, Access Serv,* Amanda Kramer; *Dir, Tech Serv,* Judith I Hymes; Tel: 410-778-7278, E-mail: judith.hymes@washcoll.edu; *Head, Circ & Reserves,* Cynthia Suttton; Staff 10 (MLS 4, Non-MLS 6)
Founded 1782. Enrl 1,350; Fac 116; Highest Degree: Master
Library Holdings: e-books 2,000; e-journals 15,076; Bk Titles 157,263; Bk Vols 171,830; Per Subs 602
Special Collections: Maryland Coll. US Document Depository
Automation Activity & Vendor Info: (Acquisitions) Innovative Interfaces, Inc; (Cataloging) Innovative Interfaces, Inc; (Circulation) Innovative Interfaces, Inc; (Course Reserve) Docutek; (ILL) OCLC WorldShare Interlibrary Loan; (Media Booking) Innovative Interfaces, Inc; (OPAC) Innovative Interfaces, Inc; (Serials) Innovative Interfaces, Inc
Database Vendor: Dialog, EBSCOhost, Gale Cengage Learning, JSTOR, LexisNexis, OCLC FirstSearch, OCLC WorldShare Interlibrary Loan, ProQuest, SerialsSolutions, Wilson - Wilson Web
Publications: Miller Library (Newsletter); Reference Guide Brochures
Partic in OCLC Online Computer Library Center, Inc
Special Services for the Blind - Assistive/Adapted tech devices, equip & products

Open Mon-Thurs 8:15am-11pm, Fri 8:15am-10pm, Sat 10-10, Sun Noon-Midnight
Friends of the Library Group

CHEVERLY

M PRINCE GEORGE'S HOSPITAL CENTER*, Saul Schwartzbach Memorial Library, 3001 Hospital Dr, 20785-1193. SAN 306-9206. Tel: 301-618-2490. FAX: 301-618-2493. *Librn,* Penny Martin
Founded 1944
Library Holdings: Bk Titles 1,500; Bk Vols 5,500; Per Subs 160
Automation Activity & Vendor Info: (Acquisitions) CyberTools for Libraries; (Cataloging) CyberTools for Libraries; (ILL) CyberTools for Libraries
Partic in National Network of Libraries of Medicine
Restriction: Staff use only

CHEVY CHASE

S AUDUBON NATURALIST SOCIETY LIBRARY*, 8940 Jones Mill Rd, 20815. SAN 372-6258. Tel: 301-652-9188. FAX: 301-951-7179. Web Site: www.audubonnaturalist.org. *Librn,* Karen Voight
Library Holdings: Bk Titles 1,000; Per Subs 115
Restriction: Mem only

M HOWARD HUGHES MEDICAL INSTITUTE*, Purnell W Choppin Library, 4000 Jones Bridge Rd, 20815-6789. SAN 323-7087. Tel: 301-215-8661. FAX: 301-215-8663. *Mgr, Libr Serv,* Megumi Saito Lincoln; Staff 1 (MLS 1)
Library Holdings: Bk Titles 5,000; Per Subs 500
Subject Interests: Finance, Genetics, Immunology, Law
Automation Activity & Vendor Info: (Acquisitions) Ex Libris Group; (Cataloging) Ex Libris Group; (Circulation) Ex Libris Group; (OPAC) Ex Libris Group; (Serials) Ex Libris Group
Database Vendor: Dialog, EBSCOhost, LexisNexis
Function: ILL available, Res libr
Restriction: Not open to pub

R OHR KODESH CONGREGATION*, Salzberg Library, 8300 Meadowbrook Dr, 20815. SAN 373-059X. Tel: 301-589-3880. FAX: 301-495-4801. Web Site: www.ohrkodesh.org. *Librn,* Brenda Sislen Bergstein
Library Holdings: DVDs 100; Bk Vols 4,300
Subject Interests: Jewish hist, Judaica
Open Mon-Fri 8-6

CLINTON

S MARYLAND NATIONAL CAPITAL PARK & PLANNING COMMISSION, James O Hall Research Center Library, 9118 Brandywine Rd, 20735. SAN 371-8697. Tel: 301-868-1121. Administration Tel: 301-868-6185. FAX: 301-868-8177. Web Site: www.surrattmuseum.org/research. *Dir,* Laurie Verge; E-mail: laurie.verge@pgparks.com; *Librn,* Sandra Walia; E-mail: sandra.walia@pgparks.com; Staff 1 (MLS 1)
Founded 1975
Library Holdings: Bk Vols 1,500
Special Collections: Lincoln Assassination Study Materials
Subject Interests: Civil War, Local hist
Wireless access

M SOUTHERN MARYLAND HOSPITAL CENTER LIBRARY*, 7503 Surratts Rd, 20735. SAN 377-4236. Tel: 301-877-4536. FAX: 301-856-0911. *Coordr,* Judy Woodburn
Library Holdings: Bk Vols 500; Per Subs 85
Restriction: Staff use only

COLLEGE PARK

S AMERICAN INSTITUTE OF PHYSICS, Niels Bohr Library, One Physics Ellipse, 20740-3843. SAN 311-5844. Tel: 301-209-3177. FAX: 301-209-3144. E-mail: nbl@aip.org. Web Site: aip.org/history-programs/niels-bohr-library. *Dir,* Joseph Anderson; *Asst Dir,* Melanie Mueller; *Librn,* Elaina Vitale; *Photo Librn,* Savannah Gignac; *Archivist,* Chip Calhoun; *Archivist,* Amanda Nelson; Staff 8 (MLS 6, Non-MLS 2)
Founded 1962
Library Holdings: Bk Titles 16,400; Per Subs 75
Special Collections: History of Astronomy, 1850-1960, misc; History of Physics, 1850-1950, archives, autobiog, bks, dissertations, ms, notebks, oral hist mat, per, photog
Subject Interests: Astronomy, Hist of physics, Physics
Automation Activity & Vendor Info: (Acquisitions) SirsiDynix; (Cataloging) SirsiDynix; (OPAC) SirsiDynix; (Serials) SirsiDynix
Publications: Guide to the Archival Collection of the AIP Niels Bohr Library; National Catalog of Sources for History of Physics; Newsletter
Open Mon-Fri 8:30-5
Friends of the Library Group

G FDA BIOSCIENCES LIBRARY*, Center for Food Safety & Applied Nutrition Library, 5100 Paint Branch Pkwy, 20740. SAN 374-4647. Tel: 240-402-2163. FAX: 301-436-2653. E-mail: cfsanlib@fda.hhs.gov. *Br Head, Pub Serv,* Lee S Bernstein; Tel: 240-402-1882, E-mail: lee.bernstein@fda.hhs.gov; *Librn,* Christine Baker; Tel: 240-402-1878, E-mail: christine.baker@fda.hhs.gov; Staff 2 (MLS 2)
Library Holdings: Bk Vols 5,000; Per Subs 200
Database Vendor: Dialog, EBSCOhost, JSTOR, LexisNexis, OCLC FirstSearch, OCLC WorldShare Interlibrary Loan, PubMed, ScienceDirect, STAT!Ref (Teton Data Systems), STN International, Wiley
Partic in OCLC Online Computer Library Center, Inc
Restriction: Not open to pub
Friends of the Library Group

G NATIONAL ARCHIVES & RECORDS ADMINISTRATION*, Archives Library Information Center, 8601 Adelphi Rd, Rm 2380, 20740. SAN 336-9064. Tel: 301-837-2000, 301-837-3415. FAX: 301-837-0459. E-mail: alic@nara.gov. Web Site: www.archives.gov. *Dir,* Jeffery Hartley; Tel: 301-837-1795; Staff 2 (MLS 2)
Founded 1934
Library Holdings: Bk Titles 102,200; Bk Vols 170,000; Per Subs 300
Special Collections: Archival Record Set of Publications of the United States Government; Archives & Records Management Literature; Federal Government Publications Issued by the Government Printing Office; United States History, bks, per
Automation Activity & Vendor Info: (Acquisitions) Cuadra Associates, Inc; (Cataloging) Cuadra Associates, Inc; (Circulation) Cuadra Associates, Inc
Wireless access
Partic in Fedlink; OCLC Online Computer Library Center, Inc
Open Mon-Fri 9-4

C UNIVERSITY OF MARYLAND LIBRARIES*, 20742. SAN 344-0583. Tel: 301-405-9128. FAX: 301-314-9408. Web Site: www.lib.umd.edu. *Dean,* Patricia A Steele; E-mail: pasteele@umd.edu; Staff 207 (MLS 78, Non-MLS 129)
Founded 1813. Enrl 37,631; Fac 4,248; Highest Degree: Doctorate
Library Holdings: AV Mats 289,839; e-books 599,198; e-journals 22,497; Bk Vols 4,094,341; Per Subs 12,808
Special Collections: Books in Many Scholarly Fields; Broadcast Pioneers Library; East Asia Coll, misc; Gordon W Prange Coll, archives & ms; International Piano Archives at Maryland; Katherine Anne Porter Coll, bks, ms, memorabilia; Maryland State Documents; Marylandia, bks, ms; Music Educators' National Conference Historical Center Coll, misc; National & International Music Organizations Coll; National Public Broadcasting Archives; National Trust for Historic Preservation Library Coll; Official Records & Publications of the University of Maryland at College Park; Oral History Records, memorabilia; Personal Papers & Textual Manuscripts of American & English Authors of the Modern Period; Personal/Family Papers; Rare Bks; Records of Organizations, photog; Special Coll of Papers of Maryland Political Figures. Oral History; State Document Depository; US Document Depository
Automation Activity & Vendor Info: (Acquisitions) Ex Libris Group; (Cataloging) Ex Libris Group; (Circulation) Ex Libris Group; (ILL) Ex Libris Group; (OPAC) Ex Libris Group; (Serials) Ex Libris Group
Database Vendor: Cambridge Scientific Abstracts, EBSCOhost, Gale Cengage Learning, JSTOR, LexisNexis, Newsbank, OCLC FirstSearch, OCLC WorldShare Interlibrary Loan, OVID Technologies, ProQuest, Swets Information Services
Wireless access
Function: Archival coll
Publications: Library Bulletin; Library Issues
Partic in Association of Research Libraries (ARL); Association of Southeastern Research Libraries; Center for Research Libraries; Chesapeake Information & Research Library Alliance (CIRLA); Northeast Research Libraries Consortium (NERL)
Open Mon-Thurs 8am-11pm, Fri 8-8, Sat 10-8, Sun Noon-11
Friends of the Library Group

Departmental Libraries:

ARCHITECTURE LIBRARY, 20742-7011. Tel: 301-405-6317. FAX: 301-314-9583. Web Site: www.lib.umd.edu/ARCH/architecture.html. *Head of Libr,* Alan Mattlage; E-mail: mattlage@umd.edu; *Librn,* Patricia Kosco Cossard; *Art Librn, Ref Librn,* Louise Greene; *Circ/Reserves, Ser,* Cindy Larimer; *Tech Serv,* Warren Stephenson
Founded 1967
Library Holdings: Bk Vols 41,294; Per Subs 158
Special Collections: World Expositions from 1851-1937
Subject Interests: Archit, Landscape archit

Automation Activity & Vendor Info: (Cataloging) Ex Libris Group; (Circulation) Ex Libris Group; (OPAC) Ex Libris Group
Open Mon-Thurs 8:30am-10pm, Fri 8:30-5, Sat 1-5, Sun 1-10

ART LIBRARY, Art/Sociology Bldg, 20742. Tel: 301-405-9061. Interlibrary Loan Service Tel: 301-405-9178. Interlibrary Loan Service FAX: 301-314-9416. Web Site: www.lib.umd.edu/art. *Art Librn,* Patricia Kosco Cossard; Tel: 301-405-9065, E-mail: pcossard@umd.edu; *Coordr,* Amrita Jit Kaur; Tel: 301-405-9062. Subject Specialists: *Art hist, Studio art,* Patricia Kosco Cossard; Staff 2 (MLS 1, Non-MLS 1)
Founded 1979. Highest Degree: Doctorate
Library Holdings: Bk Vols 84,441; Per Subs 394
Special Collections: Art Exhibition Catalog Coll; Decimal Index Art of Low Countries; Emblem Books; Index Photographique de l'art de France; Marburg Index
Automation Activity & Vendor Info: (Acquisitions) Ex Libris Group; (Cataloging) Ex Libris Group; (Circulation) Ex Libris Group; (OPAC) Ex Libris Group
Database Vendor: ARTstor, CredoReference, ebrary, H W Wilson, Ingenta, JSTOR, OCLC, OCLC FirstSearch, Oxford Online, Project MUSE, ProQuest, RefWorks, YBP Library Services

BROADCAST PIONEERS LIBRARY OF AMERICAN BROADCASTING, Hornbake Library, 20742, SAN 302-6000. Tel: 301-405-9160. FAX: 301-314-2634. E-mail: labcast@umd.edu. Web Site: www.lib.umd.edu/lab/. *Curator,* Charles Howell; *Archivist, Asst Curator,* Karen Fishman; Staff 4 (MLS 3, Non-MLS 1)
Founded 1971
Library Holdings: Bk Titles 5,768; Bk Vols 9,550; Per Subs 382
Special Collections: "Wisdom" Coll; Alois Havrilla Coll, photog; Arthur Godfrey Coll; BMI Coll, a-tapes; Edythe J Meserand Coll; Elmo Neale Pickerill Coll; Jane Barton Coll, photog; Joseph E Baudino Coll; National Association of Broadcasters Coll; Peter H Bontsema Coll; Radio Advertising Bureau Coll, recording; Ray Stanich Coll; Robert E Lee Coll; Rod E Phillips Coll; St Louis Post-Dispatch Coll, photog; Westinghouse Broadcasting News Coll, a-tapes; William S Hedges Coll. Oral History
Subject Interests: Radio, Television
Open Mon, Tues, Thurs & Fri 10-5, Wed 10-8, Sat 12-5

ENGINEERING & PHYSICAL SCIENCES LIBRARY, 20742-7011. Tel: 301-405-9157. Interlibrary Loan Service Tel: 301-405-9178. Interlibrary Loan Service FAX: 301-314-9416. Web Site: www.lib.umd.edu/epsl. *Head of Libr,* Nevenka Zdravkovska; Tel: 301-405-9144, E-mail: nevenka@umd.edu; *Agr & Natural Res Librn,* Alex Carroll; Tel: 301-405-9153, E-mail: ajcarrol@umd.edu; *Eng/Res Data Librn,* Robin Dasler; Tel: 301-405-9155, E-mail: rdasler@umd.edu; *Ref,* Jim Miller; Tel: 301-405-9152, E-mail: jmiller2@umd.edu; *Ref,* Nedelina Tchangalova; Tel: 301-405-9151, E-mail: nedelina@umd.edu. Subject Specialists: *Environ sci, Food sci, Nutrition,* Alex Carroll; *Eng,* Robin Dasler; Staff 7 (MLS 3, Non-MLS 4)
Founded 1953
Library Holdings: Bk Vols 397,125; Per Subs 1,450
Special Collections: Rand Corp Coll, Technical Reports (NASA & NACA, its predecessor); US Patent & Trademark Coll
Subject Interests: Eng, Phys sci

R LEE HORNBAKE LIBRARY, 0300 Hornbake Library Bldg, North Wing, 20742-7011, SAN 344-0788. Tel: 301-405-9236. FAX: 301-314-9419. E-mail: nonprint@umd.edu. Web Site: www.lib.umd.edu/nonprint/. *Head, Nonprint Media Serv,* Carleton L Jackson; Tel: 301-405-9226, E-mail: carleton@umd.edu. Subject Specialists: *Media, Tech,* Carleton L Jackson
Special Collections: Public Television Archives Colls include: Maryland Public Television, Corporation for Public Broadcasting & NAEB Radio Programs
Function: AV serv, Computers for patron use, Electronic databases & coll, Spoken cassettes & CDs, Spoken cassettes & DVDs, VHS videos
Restriction: Borrowing privileges limited to fac & registered students

THEODORE R MCKELDIN LIBRARY, 20742-7011. Tel: 301-314-9046. Circulation Tel: 301-405-9095. Interlibrary Loan Service Tel: 301-405-9178. FAX: 301-314-9408. Interlibrary Loan Service FAX: 301-314-9416. TDD: 301-405-9076. Web Site: www.lib.umd.edu/mckeldin. *Dean of Libr,* Patricia A Steele; Tel: 301-405-9128, E-mail: pasteele@umd.edu; *Acq,* Lila Angie Ohler; Tel: 301-405-9306, E-mail: lohler@umd.edu; *Metadata Serv,* Kathy Glennan; *Terrapin Learning Commons & Student Support Serv,* Cinthya Ippoliti; Tel: 301-314-7224, E-mail: ctodd@umd.edu
Special Collections: Delaware, DC & Maryland Regional Document Depository; East Asia (Chinese, Japanese & Korean Language Publications); Gordon W Prange Coll; Katherine Ann Porter Room, bks, memorabilia, photogs; Marylandia; National Trust for Historic Preservation
Subject Interests: Rare bks
Special Services for the Deaf - TDD equip

MICHELLE SMITH PERFORMING ARTS LIBRARY, 2511 Clarice Smith Performing Arts Center, 20742-1630. Tel: 301-405-9217. Reference Tel: 301-314-1316 (Theatre & Dance), 301-405-9256 (Music). FAX: 301-314-7170. Web Site: www.lib.umd.edu/mspal. *Head of Libr,* Stephen P Henry; E-mail: shenry@umd.edu; *Music Librn,* Stephen Henry; E-mail: shenry@umd.edu; *Theatre, Dance & Performance Studies Librn,* Felicity Brown; Tel: 301-405-9117, E-mail: fabrown@umd.edu; *Circ & Reserves Supvr,* Mary Scott; Tel: 301-405-9223, E-mail: mscott1@umd.edu; *Evening/Weekend Supvr,* Bruce Tennant; Tel: 301-405-9218, E-mail: btennant@umd.edu; *Curator,* Vincent J Novara; Tel: 301-405-9220, E-mail: vnovara@umd.edu; *Curator, Intl Piano Archives at Maryland,* Donald Manildi; Tel: 301-405-9224, E-mail: godowsky@umd.edu. Subject Specialists: *Music,* Stephen Henry; *Spec coll,* Vincent J Novara; Staff 4 (MLS 2, Non-MLS 2)
Founded 1982. Fac 4; Highest Degree: Doctorate
Library Holdings: Bk Vols 101,162; Per Subs 345
Special Collections: Arts Education (Charles Fowler Papers); Handeliana (Jacob Coppersmith Coll); International Piano Archives at Maryland; Musical Americana (Irving & Magery Lowens Coll); National & International Music Organization Coll

WHITE MEMORIAL CHEMISTRY LIBRARY, 1526 Chemistry Bldg, 20742-7011. Tel: 301-405-9078. Interlibrary Loan Service Tel: 301-405-9178. Reference Tel: 301-405-9080. FAX: 301-405-9164. Web Site: www.lib.umd.edu/chem/chemistry.html. *Head Librn,* Svetla Baykoucheva; E-mail: sbaykouc@umd.edu; *Librn,* Thomas Harrod; E-mail: tharrod@umd.edu; *Libr Tech,* Alla Ballanik; Tel: 301-405-9081. Subject Specialists: *Genetics,* Thomas Harrod; Staff 4 (MLS 2, Non-MLS 2)
Founded 1975
Library Holdings: Bk Vols 85,380; Per Subs 455
Subject Interests: Biochem, Chem, Microbiology, Molecular genetics
Open Mon-Thurs 8am-Midnight, Fri 8-8, Sat 10-8, Sun Noon-Midnight
Friends of the Library Group

COLUMBIA

S W R GRACE & CO*, Information Center, 7500 Grace Dr, 21044. SAN 306-9311. Tel: 410-531-4146. FAX: 410-531-4546. *Mgr,* Theo S Jones-Quartey; Staff 3 (MLS 1, Non-MLS 2)
Founded 1953
Library Holdings: Bk Titles 15,000; Per Subs 40
Subject Interests: Chem eng, Inorganic chem, Organic chem, Polymer chem
Automation Activity & Vendor Info: (Acquisitions) SirsiDynix; (Cataloging) SirsiDynix; (Circulation) SirsiDynix; (Serials) SirsiDynix
Database Vendor: Dialog, EBSCOhost, LexisNexis, SirsiDynix
Function: Res libr
Publications: InfoSource (Newsletter)
Restriction: Staff use only

J HOWARD COMMUNITY COLLEGE LIBRARY, 10901 Little Patuxent Pkwy, 21044. SAN 306-9338. Tel: 443-518-4812. Circulation Tel: 443-518-1460. Reference Tel: 443-518-1450. FAX: 443-518-4993. Web Site: www.howardcc.edu. *Dir,* Alesia McManus; E-mail: amcmanus@howardcc.edu; *Asst Dir, Info Literacy Librn,* Gail Hollander; Tel: 443-518-4633, E-mail: ghollander@howardcc.edu; *Archives Librn, Electronic Res Librn,* Amy Krug; Tel: 443-518-4788, E-mail: akrug@howardcc.edu; *Libr Assoc/Acq Section,* Sharon Frey; Tel: 443-518-4813, E-mail: sfrey@howardcc.edu; *Libr Tech & Syst Spec,* Apichart Chalungsooth; Tel: 443-518-4683, E-mail: chalungsooth@howardcc.edu; *Ref Asst,* Christina Pabon-Buck; Tel: 443-518-4917, E-mail: cpabon-buck@howardcc.edu; Staff 13 (MLS 6, Non-MLS 7)
Founded 1970. Enrl 2,932; Fac 730; Highest Degree: Associate
Jul 2012-Jun 2013 Income $882,462. Mats Exp $267,117, Books $47,494, Per/Ser (Incl. Access Fees) $3,100, Electronic Ref Mat (Incl. Access Fees) $216,066. Sal $577,079 (Prof $413,389)
Library Holdings: AV Mats 5,281; CDs 1,457; DVDs 751; e-books 2,406; e-journals 51,602; Bk Titles 39,260; Bk Vols 45,776; Per Subs 51,669; Videos 1,875
Subject Interests: Art, Nursing
Automation Activity & Vendor Info: (Acquisitions) SirsiDynix; (Cataloging) SirsiDynix; (Circulation) SirsiDynix; (Course Reserve) SirsiDynix; (OPAC) SirsiDynix; (Serials) SirsiDynix
Database Vendor: ABC-CLIO, Alexander Street Press, ARTstor, Baker & Taylor, Blackwell, Booklist Online, Bowker, Cinahl, CQ Press, CRC Press/Taylor & Francis Group, CredoReference, ebrary, EBSCOhost, Elsevier, Facts on File, Gale Cengage Learning, Greenwood Publishing Group, Grolier Online, JSTOR, LexisNexis, McGraw-Hill, Micromedex, Nature Publishing Group, OCLC WorldShare Interlibrary Loan, OVID Technologies, Oxford Online, ProQuest, ScienceDirect, SerialsSolutions, SirsiDynix, Wiley, WT Cox, YBP Library Services
Wireless access
Function: Archival coll, Audio & video playback equip for onsite use, Bk club(s), Computers for patron use, Copy machines, E-Reserves, Electronic databases & coll, Handicapped accessible, ILL available, Magnifiers for reading, Music CDs, Online cat, Online ref, Online searches, Orientations, Photocopying/Printing, Pub access computers, Ref & res, Ref serv available, Telephone ref, VHS videos, Web-catalog, Wheelchair accessible

Partic in Lyrasis; Md Commun Col Libr Consortium; OCLC Online Computer Library Center, Inc
Special Services for the Blind - Accessible computers; Aids for in-house use; ZoomText magnification & reading software
Open Mon-Thurs 8am-11pm, Fri 8-5, Sat 1-5, Sun (Sept-May) 1-5

P HOWARD COUNTY LIBRARY SYSTEM*, Administrative Offices, 6600 Cradlerock Way, 21045-4912. SAN 344-0850. Tel: 410-313-7750. FAX: 410-313-7742. TDD: 410-313-7883. Web Site: www.hclibrary.org. *Pres & Chief Exec Officer,* Valerie J Gross; E-mail: valerie.gross@hclibrary.org; *Dir, Human Res,* Stacey Fields; E-mail: stacey.fields@hclibrary.org; *Dir IT, Data Serv & Mat Proc,* Holly A Johnson; E-mail: holly.johnson@hclibrary.org; *Dir, Pub Relations,* Christie P Lassen; E-mail: christie.lassen@hclibrary.org; *Chief Opearting Officer, Pub Serv,* Ann T Gilligan; E-mail: ann.gilligan@hclibrary.org; *Chief Operating Officer, Support Serv,* Angela Brade; E-mail: angela.brade@hclibrary.org; *Head, Children's & Teen Curric,* Cari A Gast; E-mail: cari.gast@hclibrary.org; *Head, Customer Serv,* Lew Belfont; E-mail: lew.belfont@hclibrary.org; *Head, Mat Mgt,* Cindy Jones; E-mail: cindy.jones@hclibrary.org; *Events & Seminars Mgr,* Lisa Bankman; E-mail: lisa.bankman@hclibrary.org
Founded 1940. Pop 282,000; Circ 7,439,154
Special Collections: Adult Basic Education Materials; Toys
Subject Interests: Health educ
Automation Activity & Vendor Info: (Acquisitions) Innovative Interfaces, Inc; (Cataloging) Innovative Interfaces, Inc; (Circulation) Innovative Interfaces, Inc; (OPAC) Innovative Interfaces, Inc; (Serials) Innovative Interfaces, Inc
Wireless access
Function: Wheelchair accessible
Publications: Source (Newsletter)
Special Services for the Deaf - High interest/low vocabulary bks; Staff with knowledge of sign lang; TDD equip; TTY equip
Special Services for the Blind - Screen enlargement software for people with visual disabilities
Open Mon-Thurs 10-9, Fri & Sat 10-6, Sun 1-5
Friends of the Library Group
Branches: 7
CENTRAL BRANCH, 10375 Little Patuxent Pkwy, 21044-3499, SAN 344-0915. Tel: 410-313-7800. FAX: 410-313-7864. TDD: 410-313-7883. *Br Mgr,* Nina Krzysko; E-mail: nina.krzysko@hclibrary.org; *Adult Literacy Coordr,* Emma Ostendorp; Tel: 410-313-7900, E-mail: emma.ostendorp@hclibrary.org
Special Services for the Deaf - TDD equip
EAST COLUMBIA, 6600 Cradlerock Way, 21045-4912, SAN 374-647X. Tel: 410-313-7700. TDD: 410-313-7740. *Br Mgr,* Suki Lee
Library Holdings: Bk Vols 166,664
Special Services for the Deaf - TDD equip
ELKRIDGE BRANCH, 6540 Washington Blvd, Elkridge, 21075, SAN 328-5049. Tel: 410-313-5077. FAX: 410-313-5090. *Br Mgr,* Phil Lord; E-mail: phil.lord@hclibrary.org
Special Services for the Deaf - TDD equip
GLENWOOD BRANCH, 2350 State Rte 97, Cooksville, 21723. Tel: 410-313-5575. *Br Mgr,* Tanya Malveaux; E-mail: tanya.malveaux@hclibrary.org
HOWARD COUNTY DETENTION CENTER, 7301 Waterloo Rd, 20794. Tel: 410-313-5239. FAX: 410-313-5216. *Res Spec,* J Alan Simpson; E-mail: alan.simpson@hclibrary.org
Library Holdings: Bk Vols 4,500; Per Subs 20
Special Collections: Law Coll
Open Tues & Thurs 8-12, Wed & Fri 8-4
MILLER BRANCH & HISTORICAL CENTER, 9421 Frederick Rd, Ellicott City, 21042-2119, SAN 344-0885. Tel: 410-313-1950. FAX: 410-313-1999. TDD: 410-313-1957. *Br Mgr,* Susan Stonesifer; Tel: 410-313-1978
Special Services for the Deaf - TDD equip
SAVAGE BRANCH, 9125 Durness Lane, Laurel, 20723-5991, SAN 328-5022. Tel: 410-880-5975. FAX: 410-880-5999. TDD: 410-880-5979. *Br Mgr,* Diane Li; E-mail: diane.li@hclibrary.org
Special Services for the Deaf - TDD equip

C JOHNS HOPKINS UNIVERSITY LIBRARIES*, School of Professional Studies in Business & Education Library, 6740 Alexander Bell Dr, 21040. Tel: 301-621-3377, 410-290-1777. FAX: 410-290-0007. *Librn,* Michael Houck
Library Holdings: Bk Titles 500; Per Subs 51
Open Mon-Thurs 8:30am-10pm, Fri & Sat 8:30-5

CUMBERLAND

J ALLEGANY COLLEGE OF MARYLAND LIBRARY*, Donald L Alexander Library, 12401 Willowbrook Rd SE, 21502-2596. SAN 306-9354. Tel: 301-784-5268. Circulation Tel: 301-784-5269. Interlibrary Loan Service Tel: 301-784-5241. Reference Tel: 301-784-5138. FAX: 301-784-5017. Web Site: www.allegany.edu/library. *Dir, Learning Res,* Robert Baldwin; *Coordr, Libr Serv/Libr Instruction/Ref,* Teresa Wilmes; Tel: 301-784-5294; *Cat/Ref/Libr Instruction,* Barbara Browning; Tel: 301-784-5240; *Cat/Ref/Libr Instruction,* Matthew Hay; Tel: 301-784-5366; Staff 4 (MLS 4)
Founded 1961. Enrl 3,905; Fac 227; Highest Degree: Associate
Library Holdings: Bk Titles 49,081; Bk Vols 56,554; Per Subs 182
Special Collections: Local Hist (Appalachian Coll). Oral History; US Document Depository
Subject Interests: Allied health, Criminal law & justice, Soc sci & issues
Automation Activity & Vendor Info: (Acquisitions) Infor Library & Information Solutions; (Cataloging) Infor Library & Information Solutions; (Circulation) Infor Library & Information Solutions; (Course Reserve) Infor Library & Information Solutions; (OPAC) Infor Library & Information Solutions; (Serials) Infor Library & Information Solutions
Database Vendor: Baker & Taylor, Cinahl, CQ Press, EBSCOhost, Facts on File, Gale Cengage Learning, LexisNexis, Marcive, Inc, Medline, Newsbank, Oxford Online, ProQuest, TLC (The Library Corporation), WT Cox
Wireless access
Function: Audio & video playback equip for onsite use, CD-ROM, Computers for patron use, Copy machines, Electronic databases & coll, Fax serv, ILL available, Photocopying/Printing, Ref serv available, Telephone ref, VHS videos, Web-catalog, Wheelchair accessible
Publications: Bibliographies & User Guides; Western Maryland Materials Union List
Partic in Md Commun Col Libr Consortium
Open Mon-Thurs 8am-9pm, Fri 8:30-4:30, Sat 11-5, Sun 1-7

L ALLEGANY COUNTY CIRCUIT COURT LAW LIBRARY, Allegany County Circuit Courthouse, 30 Washington St, 21502. SAN 306-9362. Tel: 301-777-5925. FAX: 301-777-2055. *Court Adminr,* Anne M SanGiovanni
Subject Interests: Law
Open Mon-Fri 8:30-4:30

P ALLEGANY COUNTY PUBLIC LIBRARY SYSTEM*, 31 Washington St, 21502. SAN 344-0974. Tel: 301-777-1200. FAX: 301-777-7299. Web Site: www.alleganycountylibrary.info. *Dir,* John Taube; *Admin Coordr,* Cheryl Willis; E-mail: cwillis@allconet.org; *Network Serv Coordr,* Jason Armstrong; E-mail: jarmstrong@allconet.org; *Pub Serv Coordr,* Lisa McKenney; E-mail: lmckenney@allconet.org; *Circ Supvr,* Maryland Appel; E-mail: mappel@allconet.org
Founded 1924. Pop 75,500; Circ 393,223
Library Holdings: Bk Vols 56,179; Per Subs 144
Special Collections: Western Maryland (Maryland History & Genealogy)
Automation Activity & Vendor Info: (Cataloging) Brodart; (Circulation) TLC (The Library Corporation)
Mem of Western Maryland Regional Library
Open Mon-Thurs 9-9, Fri & Sat 9-5, Sun 1-5
Branches: 5
FROSTBURG PUBLIC, 65 E Main St, Frostburg, 21532, SAN 344-1008. Tel: 301-687-0790. FAX: 301-687-0791. *Br Mgr,* Patricia Merrbach; *Children's Coordr,* Constance Wilson
Library Holdings: Bk Vols 30,587; Per Subs 54
Open Mon-Thurs 9-9, Fri & Sat 9-5
Friends of the Library Group
GEORGE'S CREEK, 76 Main St, Lonaconing, 21539. Tel: 301-463-2629. FAX: 301-463-2485. E-mail: gcreekpl@allconet.org. *Br Mgr,* Deborah Hartman
Library Holdings: Bk Vols 15,133; Per Subs 58
Open Mon-Thurs 9-9, Fri & Sat 9-5
LAVALE BRANCH, 815 National Hwy, LaVale, 21502, SAN 344-1032. Tel: 301-729-0855. FAX: 301-729-3490. E-mail: lavalepl@allconet.org. *Br Mgr,* Pamela K Neder; *Tech Serv Coordr,* Carol Waugerman
Library Holdings: Bk Vols 43,377; Per Subs 76
Open Mon-Thurs 9-9, Fri & Sat 9-5
SOUTH CUMBERLAND, 100 Seymour St, 21502, SAN 344-1067. Tel: 301-724-1607. FAX: 301-724-1504. E-mail: southlibrary@allconet.org. *Br Mgr,* Nora Drake; *Ch,* Tammy Fearon
Library Holdings: Bk Vols 37,828; Per Subs 81
Open Mon-Thurs 10-8, Fri & Sat 10-5
Friends of the Library Group
WESTERNPORT BRANCH, 66 Main St, Westernport, 21562, SAN 344-1091. Tel: 301-359-0455. FAX: 301-359-0046. *Br Mgr,* Nancy L Sudine
Library Holdings: Bk Vols 26,164; Per Subs 57
Bookmobiles: 1

S WESTERN CORRECTIONAL INSTITUTION LIBRARY*, 13800 McMullen Hwy SW, 21502. Tel: 301-729-7184. FAX: 301-729-7150.
Library Holdings: Bk Vols 14,200; Per Subs 34
Automation Activity & Vendor Info: (Cataloging) Follett Software; (Circulation) Follett Software
Database Vendor: Westlaw

DENTON

P CAROLINE COUNTY PUBLIC LIBRARY, 100 Market St, 21629. SAN 344-1121. Tel: 410-479-1343. Administration Tel: 410-479-2254. FAX: 410-479-1443. Administration FAX: 410-479-4935. E-mail: info@carolib.org. Web Site: www.carolib.org. *Exec Dir,* Deborah A Bennett; E-mail: dbennett@carolib.org; *Br Mgr,* Ann M Reinecke; E-mail: areinecke@carolib.org; *Mgr, Ad Serv,* Laura Powell; E-mail: lpowell@carolib.org; *Mgr, Libr Syst,* John Courie; E-mail: jcourie@carolib.org; *Mgr, Youth Serv,* Amanda M Courie; E-mail: acourie@carolib.org; Staff 20 (MLS 4, Non-MLS 16)
Founded 1961. Pop 32,985; Circ 197,949
Jul 2013-Jun 2014 Income (Main Library and Branch(s)) $1,659,787, State $388,236, County $1,090,000, Other $181,551. Sal $821,425
Library Holdings: Audiobooks 17,295; DVDs 6,364; e-books 20,829; Bk Vols 75,531; Per Subs 219
Special Collections: Caroline County Genealogy Coll
Automation Activity & Vendor Info: (Cataloging) SirsiDynix; (Circulation) SirsiDynix; (OPAC) SirsiDynix; (Serials) SirsiDynix
Database Vendor: Baker & Taylor, EBSCO Auto Repair Reference, EBSCOhost, Newsbank, Overdrive, Inc, ProQuest, SirsiDynix, TumbleBookLibrary
Wireless access
Partic in Eastern Shore Regional Library; Maryland Interlibrary Loan Organization
Open Mon-Wed 10-6, Thurs 10-8, Fri 12-6, Sat 10-3
Friends of the Library Group
Branches: 2
FEDERALSBURG BRANCH, 123 Morris Ave, Federalsburg, 21632, SAN 344-1156. Tel: 410-754-8397. FAX: 410-754-3058. *Br Mgr,* Jeanne Trice; E-mail: jtrice@carolib.org
Library Holdings: Bk Titles 5,000; Bk Vols 6,000
Open Mon, Wed & Thurs 10-6, Tues 12-8
NORTH COUNTY BRANCH, 101 Cedar Lane, Greensboro, 21639. (Mail add: PO Box 336, Greensboro, 21639-0336), SAN 377-7421. Tel: 410-482-2173. FAX: 410-482-2634. *Br Mgr,* Tara Hill-Coursey; E-mail: thill-coursey@carolib.org
Open Mon, Tues & Thurs 10-6, Wed 12-8

EASTON

S ACADEMY ART MUSEUM*, Art Resource Center & Library, 106 South St, 21601. SAN 306-9397. Tel: 410-822-2787. FAX: 410-822-5997. *Dir,* Erik H Neil
Founded 1958
Library Holdings: Bk Vols 3,000; Per Subs 10
Special Collections: Fine Art Books
Subject Interests: Art & archit, Arts & crafts, Music, Photog
Database Vendor: LIBRARYSOFT
Restriction: Mem only

M MEMORIAL HOSPITAL*, Health Sciences Library, 219 S Washington St, 21601. SAN 306-9400. Tel: 410-822-1000, Ext 5776. FAX: 410-820-4020. *Mgr, Libr Serv,* Lois Sanger; Staff 1 (MLS 1)
Founded 1929
Library Holdings: Bk Titles 3,000; Per Subs 250
Subject Interests: Med, Nursing, Obstetrics & gynecology, Orthopedics, Pediatrics, Surgery
Open Mon-Fri 8-4:30

P TALBOT COUNTY FREE LIBRARY*, 100 W Dover St, 21601-2620. SAN 306-9419. Tel: 410-822-1626. FAX: 410-820-8217. TDD: 410-822-1916. E-mail: askus@talb.lib.md.us. Web Site: www.talb.lib.md.us. *Dir,* Robert T Horvath; E-mail: rhorvath@tcfl.org; *Head, ILL,* Christine Eareckson; E-mail: chrise@tcfl.org; *Ch & Youth Librn,* Rosemary Morris; E-mail: rmorris@tcfl.org; *Ref Librn,* Diana Hastings; *Circ Mgr,* Mia Y Clark; E-mail: mclark@tcfl.org; *Asst Admin,* Frankie Bauer; E-mail: fbauer@tcfl.org; Staff 12 (MLS 7, Non-MLS 5)
Founded 1925. Pop 32,400; Circ 179,206
Library Holdings: AV Mats 6,900; Large Print Bks 1,600; Bk Titles 78,517; Bk Vols 107,127; Per Subs 150
Subject Interests: Maryland
Automation Activity & Vendor Info: (Circulation) SirsiDynix
Publications: Talbot County Free Library's Weathervane
Partic in Eastern Shore Regional Library
Special Services for the Deaf - TTY equip
Open Mon & Thurs (Winter) 9-8, Tues & Wed 9-6, Fri & Sat 9-5; Mon (Summer) 9-8, Tues & Wed 9-6, Fri 9-5, Sat 9-1
Friends of the Library Group
Branches: 2
SAINT MICHAELS BRANCH, 106 N Fremont St, Saint Michaels, 21663, SAN 376-8198. Tel: 410-745-5877. FAX: 410-745-6937. *Head of Libr,* Shauna Beulah; E-mail: sbeulah@tcfl.org
Library Holdings: Bk Titles 5,000; Bk Vols 10,000; Per Subs 105
Open Mon & Tues 10-6, Wed 2-6, Thurs 10-7, Fri & Sat 10-5
TILGHMAN BRANCH, 21374 Foster Ave, Tilghman, 21671. Tel: 410-886-9816. *Br Mgr,* Betty Dorbin; E-mail: bdorbin@talb.lib.md.us
Library Holdings: AV Mats 218; CDs 91; DVDs 20; Bk Vols 3,519; Per Subs 10; Videos 294
Open Mon & Fri 10-6, Thurs 3-8
Bookmobiles: 1

ELKTON

GL CECIL COUNTY CIRCUIT COURT LIBRARY*, Courthouse, 2nd Flr, 129 E Main St, 21921. Tel: 410-996-5325. FAX: 410-996-5120. E-mail: lawlibrary@mdcourts.gov. Web Site: www.lawlib.state.md.us. *Librn,* Jason Allison; *Librn,* Shelly Patterson
Library Holdings: Bk Titles 150; Bk Vols 5,000
Automation Activity & Vendor Info: (Circulation) Ex Libris Group; (ILL) Ex Libris Group; (Serials) Ex Libris Group
Open Mon-Fri 9-5

P CECIL COUNTY PUBLIC LIBRARY*, Elkton Central Library, 301 Newark Ave, 21921-5441. SAN 344-1180. Tel: 410-996-5600. Administration Tel: 410-996-1055. FAX: 410-996-5604. TDD: 410-996-5609. E-mail: cecilref@ccplnet.org. Web Site: www.cecil.ebranch.info. *Dir,* Denise Davis; E-mail: ddavis@ccplnet.org; *Assoc Dir,* Position Currently Open; *Asst Dir,* Morgan Miller; E-mail: mmiller@ccplnet.org; *Bus Librn,* Laura Metzler; E-mail: lmetzler@ccplnet.org; *Digital & Training Serv Librn,* Kevin Urian; E-mail: kurian@ccplnet.org; *Cent Libr Mgr,* Position Currently Open; *Mat Mgr,* Nikki Bigley; E-mail: nbigley@ccplnet.org; *Tech Syst & Proc Mgr,* Frieda Jack; E-mail: fjack@ccplnet.org; *Web Serv Mgr,* Erica Jesonis; E-mail: webmaster@ccplnet.org; *Commun Relations Spec,* Frazier Walker; E-mail: fwalker@ccplnet.org; *Staff Develop,* Lisa Yarnall; E-mail: lyarnall@ccplnet.org; Staff 45 (MLS 11, Non-MLS 34)
Founded 1947. Pop 97,796; Circ 1,050,893
Library Holdings: AV Mats 45,386; Bk Vols 266,938; Per Subs 694
Automation Activity & Vendor Info: (Cataloging) OCLC Connexion; (Circulation) SirsiDynix; (ILL) SirsiDynix; (OPAC) SIRSI-iBistro
Wireless access
Publications: Library Link (Newsletter)
Partic in Maryland ILL Org
Open Mon-Thurs 10-9, Fri & Sat 10-5
Friends of the Library Group
Branches: 6
CECILTON BRANCH, 215 E Main St, Cecilton, 21913-1000, SAN 344-1210. Tel: 410-275-1091. FAX: 410-275-1092.
Open Mon & Tues 10-8, Wed & Thurs 10-6, Sat 10-5
CHESAPEAKE CITY BRANCH, 2527 Augustine Herman Hwy, Chesapeake City, 21915, SAN 344-1229. Tel: 410-996-1134.
Open Mon & Tues 10-8, Wed & Thurs 10-6, Fri & Sat 10-5
NORTH EAST BRANCH, 106 W Cecil Ave, North East, 21901, SAN 344-1245. Tel: 410-996-6269. FAX: 410-996-6268.
Open Mon & Tues 10-8, Wed & Thurs 10-6, Fri & Sat 10-5
PERRYVILLE BRANCH, 500 Coudon Blvd, Perryville, 21903, SAN 344-1253. Tel: 410-996-6070.
Open Mon-Thurs 10-9, Fri & Sat 10-5
PORT DEPOSIT BRANCH, 13 S Main St, Port Deposit, 21904, SAN 328-7963. Tel: 410-996-6055. FAX: 410-996-1047.
Open Mon-Wed 12-6, Sat 10-2
RISING SUN BRANCH, 111 Colonial Way, Rising Sun, 21911, SAN 344-127X. Tel: 410-658-4025. FAX: 410-658-4024.
Open Mon-Thurs 10-8, Fri & Sat 10-5
Friends of the Library Group
Bookmobiles: 1

EMMITSBURG

C MOUNT SAINT MARY'S UNIVERSITY*, Hugh J Phillips Library, 16300 Old Emmitsburg Rd, 21727-7799. SAN 306-9435. Tel: 301-447-5244. FAX: 301-447-5099. Web Site: www.msmary.edu/studentsandstaff/library. *Dean, Libr Serv,* D Stephen Rockwood; E-mail: rockwood@msmary.edu; *Bibliog Instr, Ref,* Laurel Thrasher; E-mail: thrasher@msmary.edu; *Online Serv, Pub Serv,* Joy Allison; E-mail: jallison@msmary.edu; *Syst Coordr,* Bruce Yelovich; E-mail: yelovich@msmary.edu; *Tech Serv,* Kathleen Sterner; E-mail: sterner@msmary.edu; Staff 9 (MLS 5, Non-MLS 4)
Enrl 1,710; Fac 120; Highest Degree: Master
Library Holdings: Bk Vols 210,875; Per Subs 910
Special Collections: 16th & 17th Century Religions; Early Catholic Americana
Automation Activity & Vendor Info: (Acquisitions) Ex Libris Group; (Cataloging) Ex Libris Group; (Circulation) Ex Libris Group; (Course Reserve) Ex Libris Group; (ILL) Ex Libris Group; (Media Booking) Ex Libris Group; (OPAC) Ex Libris Group; (Serials) Ex Libris Group
Partic in OCLC Online Computer Library Center, Inc
Friends of the Library Group

G US FIRE ADMINISTRATION*, National Emergency Training Center Learning Resource Center, 16825 S Seton Ave, 21727. SAN 325-8939. Tel: 301-447-1030. Toll Free Tel: 800-638-1821. FAX: 301-447-3217. *Head Librn,* Edward J Metz; E-mail: edward.metz@dhs.gov; Staff 10.5 (MLS 5, Non-MLS 5.5)
Oct 2007-Sept 2008 Income $880,000. Mats Exp $177,000, Books $88,000, Per/Ser (Incl. Access Fees) $66,000, Other Print Mats $11,800, AV Mat $7,700, Presv $3,500. Sal $632,000 (Prof $300,000)
Library Holdings: AV Mats 800; CDs 350; DVDs 100; Bk Titles 48,000; Bk Vols 85,000; Per Subs 300; Videos 4,377
Subject Interests: Arson, Disaster mgt, Emergency med care, Emergency response, Fire prevention, Fire serv admin, Homeland security
Automation Activity & Vendor Info: (Acquisitions) Cuadra Associates, Inc; (Cataloging) Cuadra Associates, Inc; (Circulation) Cuadra Associates, Inc; (ILL) OCLC; (OPAC) Cuadra Associates, Inc; (Serials) Cuadra Associates, Inc
Function: ILL available, Ref serv available
Partic in Fedlink
Restriction: Not open to pub, Open to students, fac & staff

FORT GEORGE G MEADE

G SSG PAUL D SAVANUCK MEMORIAL LIBRARY, Defense Information School, 6500 Mapes Rd, Rm 1161, 20755. (Mail add: 6500 Mapes Rd, Ste 5620, 20755-5620). Tel: 301-677-4692. FAX: 301-677-4697. E-mail: dma.meade.dinfos.list.library@mail.mil. Web Site: www.dinfos.dma.mil. *Librn,* Mary Hickey; *Libr Tech,* Janet Curtis; Staff 3 (MLS 1, Non-MLS 2)
Founded 1975
Library Holdings: Audiobooks 800; DVDs 1,800; Electronic Media & Resources 450; Bk Vols 15,000; Per Subs 137
Special Collections: Photography & Photojournalism (Savanuck Coll)
Subject Interests: Broadcasting, Distance learning, Journalism, Multimedia, Photog, Videography
Automation Activity & Vendor Info: (Acquisitions) TLC (The Library Corporation); (Cataloging) TLC (The Library Corporation); (Circulation) TLC (The Library Corporation); (OPAC) TLC (The Library Corporation); (Serials) TLC (The Library Corporation)
Database Vendor: Baker & Taylor, EBSCOhost, Gale Cengage Learning, Ingram Library Services, Newsbank, OCLC, Sage, TLC (The Library Corporation)
Partic in Fedlink; OCLC Online Computer Library Center, Inc
Restriction: Authorized patrons, Mil only, Not a lending libr, Not open to pub, Open to students, fac & staff, Photo ID required for access, Use of others with permission of librn

UNITED STATES ARMY

AM KIMBROUGH AMBULATORY CARE CENTER MEDICAL LIBRARY*, 2480 Llewellyn Ave, Ste 5800, 20755-5800, SAN 344-1326. Tel: 301-677-8228. FAX: 301-677-8108. *In Charge,* Patricia L Passaro
Library Holdings: Bk Titles 2,057; Per Subs 140
Subject Interests: Nursing, Primary health care, Surgery
Automation Activity & Vendor Info: (Acquisitions) Ex Libris Group; (Cataloging) Ex Libris Group; (Circulation) Ex Libris Group; (Course Reserve) Ex Libris Group; (ILL) Ex Libris Group; (Serials) Ex Libris Group
Partic in SE-Atlantic Regional Med Libr Servs
Open Mon-Fri 9-5

A THE MEDAL OF HONOR MEMORIAL LIBRARY*, 4418 Llewellyn Ave, Ste 5068, Fort George G. Meade, 20755-5068, SAN 344-130X. Tel: 301-677-4509, 301-677-5522. Administration Tel: 301-677-3594. FAX: 301-677-2694. E-mail: ftmeade.lib@us.army.mil. Web Site: www.ftmeademwr.com/library.htm. *Supvry Librn,* Karen L Hayward; E-mail: karen.hayward@us.army.mil; Staff 3 (MLS 1, Non-MLS 2)
Founded 1952
Library Holdings: Bk Vols 25,000; Per Subs 100
Automation Activity & Vendor Info: (Acquisitions) Baker & Taylor; (Cataloging) OCLC; (Circulation) Innovative Interfaces, Inc - Millenium; (ILL) OCLC; (OPAC) Innovative Interfaces, Inc - Millenium; (Serials) Innovative Interfaces, Inc - Millenium
Database Vendor: Baker & Taylor, CountryWatch, CredoReference, EBSCO Auto Repair Reference, EBSCOhost, Facts on File, Gale Cengage Learning, Innovative Interfaces, Inc, OCLC, OCLC FirstSearch, OCLC WorldShare Interlibrary Loan, Overdrive, Inc, ProQuest, Safari Books Online, WT Cox
Partic in Fedlink; OCLC Online Computer Library Center, Inc
Open Tues & Thurs 11-7, Wed & Fri 11-6, Sat 10-2

G US ENVIRONMENTAL PROTECTION AGENCY, Environmental Science Center Library, 701 Mapes Rd, 20755-5350. SAN 306-8005. Tel: 410-305-2603, 410-305-3031. FAX: 410-305-3092. Web Site: www.epa.gov/region3/esc/library. *Librn,* Kim Waidelich; E-mail: waidelich.kim@epa.gov; Staff 1 (MLS 1)
Founded 1964
Library Holdings: AV Mats 87; Bk Titles 6,000; Per Subs 40
Special Collections: Chesaspeake Bay Coll; Delaware Coll; District of Columbia Coll; EPA Region 3 Coll; Maryland Coll; Pennsylvania Coll; Virginia Coll; West Virginia Coll
Subject Interests: Analytical chem, Environment
Automation Activity & Vendor Info: (ILL) OCLC FirstSearch
Database Vendor: ScienceDirect
Open Mon-Thurs 9:30-4
Restriction: External users must contact libr, In-house use for visitors

FREDERICK

J FREDERICK COMMUNITY COLLEGE LIBRARY*, 7932 Opossumtown Pike, 21702. SAN 306-946X. Tel: 301-846-2444. FAX: 301-624-2877. Web Site: www.frederick.edu/library. *Exec Dir,* Mick O'Leary; E-mail: moleary@frederick.edu; Staff 4 (MLS 2, Non-MLS 2)
Founded 1957. Enrl 5,000; Fac 80; Highest Degree: Associate
Library Holdings: Bks on Deafness & Sign Lang 20; High Interest/Low Vocabulary Bk Vols 200; Bk Titles 32,000; Bk Vols 35,000; Per Subs 100
Subject Interests: Nursing
Automation Activity & Vendor Info: (Acquisitions) Innovative Interfaces, Inc; (Cataloging) Innovative Interfaces, Inc; (Circulation) Innovative Interfaces, Inc; (Course Reserve) Innovative Interfaces, Inc; (ILL) OCLC; (OPAC) Innovative Interfaces, Inc
Database Vendor: EBSCOhost, Gale Cengage Learning, OCLC FirstSearch, ProQuest
Wireless access
Partic in OCLC Online Computer Library Center, Inc
Open Mon-Thurs 8am-9pm, Fri 8-4, Sat 10-4

S FREDERICK COUNTY ARCHIVES & RESEARCH CENTER LIBRARY*, 24 E Church St, 21701. SAN 371-778X. Tel: 301-663-1188. FAX: 301-663-0526. E-mail: library@hsfcinfo.org. Web Site: www.hsfcinfo.org. *Archivist, Dept Head, Ref,* Rebecca Crago; E-mail: rcrago@hsfcinfo.org; Staff 1 (MLS 1)
Founded 1984
Library Holdings: Bk Titles 5,000; Bk Vols 7,000
Special Collections: History of Frederick County Coll, diaries, ms, scrapbks. Oral History
Subject Interests: Genealogy, Local hist
Automation Activity & Vendor Info: (Cataloging) Inmagic, Inc.
Function: Archival coll, Audio & video playback equip for onsite use, Electronic databases & coll, Exhibits, Genealogy discussion group, Newsp ref libr, Online cat, Outside serv via phone, mail, e-mail & web, Photocopying/Printing, Workshops
Publications: Historical Society of Frederick County (Newsletter); Journal
Open Tues-Sat 10-4
Restriction: Non-circulating

P FREDERICK COUNTY PUBLIC LIBRARIES*, 110 E Patrick St, 21701. SAN 306-9494. Tel: 301-600-1613. FAX: 301-600-3789. Web Site: www.fcpl.org. *Dir,* Darrell Batson; E-mail: dbatson@frederickcountymd.gov; *Assoc Dir,* Dolores Maminski; E-mail: dmaminski@frederickcountymd.gov; *Mgr, Ch & Youth Serv,* Leslie Gincley; E-mail: lgincley@frederickcountymd.gov; *Mgr, Ch & Youth Serv,* Cathy Link; E-mail: clink@frederickcountymd.gov; *Coll Develop, Tech Serv Mgr,* Position Currently Open; *ILL Spec,* Jane Spear; E-mail: jspear@frederickcountymd.gov; Staff 157 (MLS 2, Non-MLS 155)
Founded 1937. Pop 225,721; Circ 2,325,040
Library Holdings: AV Mats 41,227; e-books 12,868; Bk Vols 445,677; Per Subs 923
Special Collections: Maryland Hist (Maryland Coll), bks, micro
Automation Activity & Vendor Info: (Cataloging) SirsiDynix; (Circulation) SirsiDynix; (OPAC) SirsiDynix; (Serials) SirsiDynix
Wireless access
Special Services for the Deaf - Staff with knowledge of sign lang
Open Mon-Fri 8:30-4:30
Friends of the Library Group
Branches: 7
C BURR ARTZ PUBLIC LIBRARY, 110 E Patrick St, 21701, SAN 374-7506. Tel: 301-600-1630. FAX: 301-600-2905. *Br Mgr,* Sydney McCoy; E-mail: smccoy@frederickcountymd.gov
Open Mon-Thurs 10-8, Fri & Sat 10-5, Sun 1-5
Friends of the Library Group
BRUNSWICK BRANCH, 915 N Maple Ave, Brunswick, 21716, SAN 320-2844. Tel: 301-600-7250. FAX: 301-834-8763. *Br Mgr,* Michael Carlson; Tel: 301-600-7251, E-mail: mcarlson@frederickcountymd.gov
Open Mon & Wed 10-6, Tues & Thurs 10-8, Sat 10-5
Friends of the Library Group
EMMITSBURG BRANCH, 300-A S Seton Ave, Unit 2 J, Emmitsburg, 21727, SAN 320-2852. Tel: 301-600-6329. FAX: 301-600-6330. *Br Mgr,* Erin Dingle; E-mail: edingle@frederickcountymd.gov
Open Mon & Wed 10-6, Tues & Thurs 10-8, Sat 10-5
Friends of the Library Group

MIDDLETOWN BRANCH, 101 Prospect, Middletown, 21769, SAN 320-2860. Tel: 301-371-7560. *Br Mgr,* Sharon Lauchner; E-mail: slauchner@frederickcountymd.gov
Open Mon & Wed 10-6, Tues & Thurs 10-8, Sat 10-5
Friends of the Library Group

THURMONT BRANCH, 76 E Moser Rd, Thurmont, 21788, SAN 320-2879. Tel: 301-600-7200. *Librn,* Erin Dingle; E-mail: edingle@frederickcountymd.gov
Open Mon-Thurs 10-8, Fri & Sat 10 5, Sun 1-5
Friends of the Library Group

URBANA, 9020 Amelung St, 21704. Tel: 301-600-7000. *Br Mgr,* Amy Whitney
Open Mon-Thurs 10-8, Fri & Sat 10-5, Sun 1-5
Friends of the Library Group

WALKERSVILLE BRANCH, 57 W Frederick St, Walkersville, 21793, SAN 329-6024. Tel: 301-845-8880. FAX: 301-845-5759. *Br Adminr,* Sharon Lauchner; E-mail: slauchner@frederickcountymd.gov
Open Mon & Wed 10-6, Tues & Thurs 10-8, Sat 10-5
Friends of the Library Group

Bookmobiles: 2

M FREDERICK MEMORIAL HOSPITAL*, Walter F Prior Medical Library, 400 W Seventh St, 21701. SAN 306-9508. Tel: 240-566-3459. FAX: 240-566-3650. E-mail: medlib@fmh.org. *Librn,* Lucy Koscielniak; Staff 1 (Non-MLS 1)
Founded 1962
Library Holdings: Bk Vols 1,000; Per Subs 50
Subject Interests: Med, Nursing, Obstetrics & gynecology, Ophthalmology, Orthopedics, Pediatrics, Psychiat, Radiology, Surgery
Automation Activity & Vendor Info: (Serials) EBSCO Online
Partic in National Network of Libraries of Medicine
Restriction: Staff use only

C HOOD COLLEGE, Beneficial-Hodson Library, 401 Rosemont Ave, 21701. SAN 306-9524. Tel: 301-696-3909. Circulation Tel: 301-696-3709. Interlibrary Loan Service Tel: 301-696-3921. Reference Tel: 301-696-3915. FAX: 301-696-3796. Web Site: www.hood.edu/library. *Acq of Monographs & Journals, Coll Develop, Dir,* Jan Samet O'Leary; Tel: 301-696-3934, E-mail: jsamet@hood.edu; *Head, Access Serv,* Toby Peterson; Tel: 301-696-3924, E-mail: peterson@hood.edu; *Head, Ref,* Mary Champagne; Tel: 301-696-3917, E-mail: champagne@hood.edu; *Ref & Instruction Librn,* Aimee Gee; Tel: 301-696-3975, E-mail: gee@hood.edu; *Cat Mgr,* Sherry Davids; Tel: 301-696-3874, E-mail: davids@hood.edu; *Access Serv,* Megan Mannes; E-mail: mannes@hood.edu; *Access Serv,* Cathy Martino; E-mail: martino@hood.edu; *Access Serv,* David Salner; E-mail: salner@hood.edu; *Acq of Monographs & Journals,* Phyllis Townsend; Tel: 301-696-3933, E-mail: townsend@hood.edu; *Info Tech,* John Urian; Tel: 301-696-3858, E-mail: urian@hood.edu; *ILL,* Kaitlyn May; Tel: 301-696-3695, E-mail: may@hood.edu; *Curator of Archives,* Mary Atwell; Tel: 301-696-3873, E-mail: atwell@hood.edu; Staff 12 (MLS 7, Non-MLS 5)
Founded 1893. Enrl 2,500; Fac 107; Highest Degree: Master
Jul 2011-Jun 2012. Mats Exp $409,649, Books $118,699, Per/Ser (Incl. Access Fees) $155,997, Electronic Ref Mat (Incl. Access Fees) $134,953. Sal $469,477
Library Holdings: Audiobooks 400; AV Mats 5,500; e-books 310,000; e-journals 24,500; Bk Vols 211,000; Per Subs 305
Special Collections: Landauer Civil War Coll; Sylvia Meagher (Kennedy Assassination Archives); Weisberg Kennedy Assassination Archives Coll
Subject Interests: Biol, Civil War, Thanatology
Automation Activity & Vendor Info: (Acquisitions) Ex Libris Group; (Cataloging) Ex Libris Group; (Circulation) Ex Libris Group; (ILL) OCLC; (OPAC) Ex Libris Group; (Serials) Ex Libris Group
Database Vendor: ABC-CLIO, ACM (Association for Computing Machinery), Alexander Street Press, American Chemical Society, American Mathematical Society, American Psychological Association (APA), BioOne, Cambridge Scientific Abstracts, Cinahl, CRC Press/Taylor & Francis Group, Dun & Bradstreet, ebrary, EBSCO Discovery Service, EBSCO Information Services, EBSCOhost, Elsevier, Ex Libris Group, Gale Cengage Learning, IEEE (Institute of Electrical & Electronics Engineers), JSTOR, LexisNexis, McGraw-Hill, Medline, Mergent Online, Modern Language Association, Newsbank, OCLC, OCLC FirstSearch, OVID Technologies, Oxford Communications, ProQuest, PubMed, Sage, ScienceDirect, SerialsSolutions, Springshare, LLC, Standard & Poor's, TLC (The Library Corporation)
Wireless access
Function: 24/7 Online cat, Archival coll, Audio & video playback equip for onsite use, Bks on CD, Computers for patron use, Copy machines, Doc delivery serv, e-mail & chat, eReaders, Exhibits, Free DVD rentals, ILL available, Magazines, Microfiche/film & reading machines, Movies, Music CDs, Online cat, Online ref, Orientations, Photocopying/Printing, Ref & res, Ref serv available, Ref serv in person, Scanner, Spoken cassettes & CDs, Study rm, Telephone ref, Video lending libr, Web-catalog, Wheelchair accessible, Workshops
Partic in Lyrasis; Maryland Interlibrary Loan Organization
Special Services for the Deaf - Bks on deafness & sign lang; Closed caption videos; Coll on deaf educ; Deaf publ; Spec interest per
Special Services for the Blind - Bks on CD; Reader equip; Ref serv
Open Mon-Thurs 8am-12:30am, Fri 8-5, Sat 11-5, Sun 1:30pm-12:30am
Restriction: Authorized patrons, In-house use for visitors, Limited access for the pub, Non-circulating of rare bks, Pub use on premises, Restricted pub use

S NATIONAL CANCER INSTITUTE AT FREDERICK SCIENTIFIC LIBRARY*, Bldg 549, Sultan St, 21702-8255. SAN 306-9451. Tel: 301-846-1093. Interlibrary Loan Service Tel: 301-846-5843. FAX: 301-846-6332. E-mail: ncifredlibrary@mail.nih.gov. Web Site: www-library.ncifcrf.gov. *Mgr,* Susan W Wilson
Founded 1972
Library Holdings: Bk Vols 15,500; Per Subs 700
Subject Interests: Biol, Biological physics, Cancer, Chem
Automation Activity & Vendor Info: (Cataloging) Innovative Interfaces, Inc - Millenium; (Circulation) Innovative Interfaces, Inc - Millenium; (ILL) OCLC FirstSearch; (OPAC) Innovative Interfaces, Inc - Millenium; (Serials) Innovative Interfaces, Inc - Millenium
Database Vendor: American Chemical Society, Dialog, Gale Cengage Learning, Innovative Interfaces, Inc, Nature Publishing Group, OCLC FirstSearch, OCLC WorldShare Interlibrary Loan, OVID Technologies, PubMed, ScienceDirect, Scopus, SerialsSolutions, Springer-Verlag, Swets Information Services, Thomson - Web of Science, Wiley, YBP Library Services
Wireless access
Publications: Accessions list; Serial holdings list
Open Mon-Fri 9-5

UNITED STATES ARMY

A FORT DETRICK POST LIBRARY*, Fort Detrick, 1520 Freedman Dr, 21702, SAN 324-2331. Tel: 301-619-7519. FAX: 301-619-2884. *Librn,* Doug Markin
Library Holdings: Bk Vols 32,857; Per Subs 90
Automation Activity & Vendor Info: (Cataloging) Ex Libris Group; (Circulation) Ex Libris Group; (OPAC) Ex Libris Group
Partic in OCLC Online Computer Library Center, Inc
Open Mon-Fri 9-5

AM MEDICAL RESEARCH INSTITUTE OF INFECTIOUS DISEASES LIBRARY, Fort Detrick, 1425 Porter, 21702-5011. Tel: 301-619-2717. FAX: 301-619-6059. *Dir,* Denise Lupp; E-mail: denise.lupp@us.army.mil; Staff 3 (MLS 2, Non-MLS 1)
Library Holdings: Bk Titles 4,000; Bk Vols 10,000; Per Subs 220
Subject Interests: Communicable diseases
Partic in Dialog Corp; OCLC Online Computer Library Center, Inc; US National Library of Medicine
Restriction: Not open to pub

FROSTBURG

C FROSTBURG STATE UNIVERSITY*, Lewis J Ort Library, One Stadium Dr, 21532. SAN 306-9532. Tel: 301 687-4396. Circulation Tel: 301-687-4395. Interlibrary Loan Service Tel: 301-687-4886. Reference Tel: 301-687-4424. FAX: 301-687-7069. Interlibrary Loan Service FAX: 301-687-3009. Web Site: www.frostburg.edu/dept/library. *Dir,* Dr David M Gillespie; E-mail: dgillespie@frostburg.edu; *Assoc Dir,* Dr Lea Messman-Mandicott; Tel: 301-687-4890, E-mail: lmessman@frostburg.edu; *Assoc Dir,* Pamela S Williams; Tel: 301-687-4887, E-mail: pwilliams@frostburg.edu; *Access Serv Librn,* Amanda L Bena; Tel: 301-687-7012, E-mail: albena@frostburg.edu; *Acq, Coll Develop & Ser,* Randall A Lowe; Tel: 301-687-4313, E-mail: rlowe@frostburg.edu; *Spec Coll Librn,* MaryJo Price; Tel: 301-687-4889, E-mail: mprice@frostburg.edu; *Coordr of First Year Libr Instruction,* Theresa M Mastrodonato; Tel: 301-687-4425, E-mail: tmmastrodonato@frostburg.edu; *Coordr, Libr Instruction, Webmaster,* Dr Sean Henry; Tel: 301-687-4888, E-mail: shenry@frostburg.edu; *Govt Doc Coordr,* Lisa A Hartman; Tel: 301-687-4734; *Syst Coordr,* Position Currently Open; *Cat,* Virginia Williams; Tel: 301-687-4884, E-mail: vwilliams@frostburg.edu. Subject Specialists: *Educ,* Dr Lea Messman-Mandicott; *Humanities,* Pamela S Williams; *Humanities,* MaryJo Price; *Computer sci,* Theresa M Mastrodonato; *German, Hist,* Dr Sean Henry; *Maps,* Virginia Williams; Staff 24 (MLS 10, Non-MLS 14)
Founded 1898. Enrl 4,372; Fac 247; Highest Degree: Doctorate
Jul 2011-Jun 2012 Income $2,342,530, State $2,335,795, Federal $6,735. Mats Exp $797,267, Books $46,191, Per/Ser (Incl. Access Fees) $140,881, Micro $11,605, AV Mat $3,787, Electronic Ref Mat (Incl. Access Fees) $388,010, Presv $11,902. Sal $1,146,928 (Prof $641,529)
Library Holdings: AV Mats 60,133; CDs 773; DVDs 950; e-books 7,053; e-journals 73; Electronic Media & Resources 64; Microforms 516,917; Bk Titles 202,070; Bk Vols 294,994; Per Subs 413; Videos 2,893
Special Collections: George Meyers American Communist Party & Labor Materials Coll; Railroad Photography (William Price Coll); Selected US Survey Maps; Senator J Glenn Beall Papers. State Document Depository; US Document Depository

Automation Activity & Vendor Info: (Acquisitions) Ex Libris Group; (Cataloging) Ex Libris Group; (Circulation) Ex Libris Group; (Course Reserve) Ex Libris Group; (ILL) OCLC ILLiad; (OPAC) Ex Libris Group; (Serials) Ex Libris Group
Database Vendor: ACM (Association for Computing Machinery), American Chemical Society, American Psychological Association (APA), Cambridge Scientific Abstracts, Children's Literature Comprehensive Database Company (CLCD), Cinahl, CQ Press, Dialog, EBSCOhost, Elsevier, Ex Libris Group, Gale Cengage Learning, ISI Web of Knowledge, JSTOR, LexisNexis, Medline, Mergent Online, Modern Language Association, OCLC ArticleFirst, OCLC CAMIO, OCLC FirstSearch, OCLC WorldShare Interlibrary Loan, Project MUSE, ProQuest, PubMed, Sage, ScienceDirect, Standard & Poor's, Thomson - Web of Science, ValueLine, Wiley InterScience
Wireless access
Publications: LibGuides; Library Blog; Library Handouts
Partic in Lyrasis; OCLC Online Computer Library Center, Inc; Univ Syst of Md; University System of Maryland & Affiliated Institutions (USMAI)
Open Mon-Thurs 7:30am-Midnight, Fri 7:30-6, Sat 11-6, Sun 1-Midnight

GAITHERSBURG

S FOI SERVICES INC LIBRARY*, 704 Quince Orchard Rd, Ste 275, 20878-1751. SAN 329-8744. Tel: 301-975-9400. FAX: 301-975-0702. E-mail: infofoi@foiservices.com. Web Site: www.foiservices.com. *Pres,* John E Carey; E-mail: jcarey@foiservices.com; *VPres,* Marlene S Bobka; E-mail: mbobka@foiservices.com
Founded 1975
Library Holdings: Bk Vols 16,000
Special Collections: FDA Records
Subject Interests: Approval of pharmaceuticals, Regulation of pharmaceuticals
Open Mon-Fri 9-5

S LOCKHEED MARTIN CORP*, Information Resource Center, 700 N Frederick Ave, 20879. SAN 306-9559. Tel: 301-240-5500. FAX: 301-240-6855. *Mgr,* P Paul Power; *Librn,* Henry Courtney
Founded 1960
Library Holdings: Bk Vols 7,000; Per Subs 100
Subject Interests: Math
Publications: On-Line Bulletin (Monthly)
Restriction: Staff use only

G NATIONAL INSTITUTE OF STANDARDS & TECHNOLOGY RESEARCH LIBRARY*, Information Services Office Research Library & Information Program, 100 Bureau Dr, Stop 2500, 20899-2500. SAN 306-9567. Tel: 301-975-2784. Circulation Tel: 301-975-2793. Interlibrary Loan Service Tel: 301-975-3060. Reference Tel: 301-975-3052. FAX: 301-869-8071. Interlibrary Loan Service FAX: 301-869-6787. E-mail: library@nist.gov. Web Site: nvl.nist.gov. *Mgr, Res Libr & Info Prog,* Rosa Liu; Tel: 301-975-2787, E-mail: rosa.liu@nist.gov; *Ref Serv,* Keith Martin; Tel: 301-975-2789, E-mail: keith.martin@nist.gov; Staff 15 (MLS 8, Non-MLS 7)
Founded 1901
Library Holdings: Per Subs 1,500
Special Collections: Artifacts of the National Bureau of Standards (Historical Museum Coll), congressional mats, legal refs; Biographical Files on NBS & NIST Scientists & Managers; National Bureau of Standards Personalities; Old & Rare 17th & 18th Century Scientific Meterology Treaties (Historical Coll), bks, mss, tech rpts; Significant Compilations of Atomic & Molecular Properties, Chemical Kinetics (Colloid & Surface), Fundamental Particles, Mechanical, Nuclear, Solid State, Thermodynamic & Transport Properties (National Standard Reference Data Coll); Weights & Measures Historical Coll. Oral History
Subject Interests: Chem, Computer sci, Eng, Libr & info sci, Math, Physics, Statistics
Automation Activity & Vendor Info: (Acquisitions) SirsiDynix; (Circulation) SirsiDynix; (Serials) SirsiDynix
Wireless access
Publications: Abstract & Index Collection in the NIST Research Library of the National Institute of Standards & Technology; An Annotated List of Historically & Scientifically Important Works Published Before 1900 in the Library of the National Bureau of Standards; Data Bases Available at the National Institute of Standards & Technology Research Library (Annual); Foundations of Metrology: Important Early Works on Weights & Measures in the Library of the National Bureau of Standards; National Institute of Standards & Technology Research Library Handbook; National Institute of Standards & Technology, Research Library Serial Holdings (Annual); Science-Technology Information, OIS (Monthly bulletin)
Partic in Fedlink; Nat Res Libr Alliance (NRLA); OCLC Online Computer Library Center, Inc; Upcounty Libraries Roundtable (ULR)
Restriction: Authorized scholars by appt, In-house use for visitors, Lending to staff only, Non-circulating to the pub, Open to researchers by request

GLEN BURNIE

S CDI MARINE SYSTEMS DEVELOPMENT DIVISION*, Technical Library, 6960 Aviation Blvd, No A, 21061-2531. SAN 370-3924. Tel: 410-544-2800. FAX: 410-647-3411. *Dir,* Shirley Wilson
Library Holdings: Bk Titles 15,500; Per Subs 25
Open Mon-Fri 8-4
Restriction: Not open to pub

S CRISTAL USA, INC, 6752 Baymeadow Dr, 21060. Tel: 410-762-1117. FAX: 410-762-1030. E-mail: librarian@cristal.com. *Sr Analyst - Knowledge Serv, R&D,* Dawn S French; E-mail: dawn.french@cristal.com; Staff 1 (MLS 1)
Founded 1944
Subject Interests: Analytical chem, Ceramics, Chem eng, Inorganic chem, Polymer chem
Database Vendor: American Chemical Society, Dialog, Knovel, ScienceDirect, STN International
Function: Res libr
Restriction: Open to pub upon request

GLEN ECHO

S UNITED STATES NATIONAL PARK SERVICE*, Clara Barton National Historic Site Library, 5801 Oxford Rd, 20812. SAN 373-1561. Tel: 301-320-1410. FAX: 301-320-1415. Web Site: www.nps.gov/clba. *Curator,* Kim Robinson; Tel: 301-320-1411
Library Holdings: Bk Vols 500
Restriction: Open by appt only

GREENBELT

G NASA*, Goddard Space Flight Center Library-Homer E Newell Memorial, Library, Bldg 21, Code 272, 20771. (Mail add: Bldg 21, Rm L200, 8800 Greenbelt Rd, 20771), SAN 306-9648. Tel: 301-286-7218. Interlibrary Loan Service Tel: 301-286-7217. FAX: 301-286-1755. E-mail: library@listserv.gsfc.nasa.gov. Web Site: library.gsfc.nasa.gov. *Br Head,* Robin Miller Dixon; Tel: 301-286-9230, E-mail: robin.m.dixon@nasa.gov; *Digital Projects Librn,* Patrick Healey; Tel: 301-286-0884; *Electronic Res Mgt Librn,* Mitzi Cole; Tel: 301-286-9348; *Ref Librn,* Charles Early; Tel: 301-286-0887; *Acq,* Bridget Burns; Tel: 301-286-6245; *Ref Serv,* Tonia Reynolds-Pope; Tel: 301-286-4746; *Tech Info Spec,* Gordon Bonholzer; Tel: 301-286-6244; Staff 14 (MLS 12, Non-MLS 2)
Founded 1959
Library Holdings: CDs 1,574; Bk Titles 83,846; Bk Vols 103,933; Per Subs 2,371; Videos 1,279
Subject Interests: Astrophysics, Communications & navigation systs, Earth sci, Exploration systs, Heliophysics, Solar syst exploration
Automation Activity & Vendor Info: (Acquisitions) SirsiDynix; (Cataloging) SirsiDynix; (Circulation) SirsiDynix; (ILL) OCLC; (OPAC) SirsiDynix
Database Vendor: Dialog, OCLC FirstSearch
Wireless access
Partic in National Research Library Alliance (NRLA)
Special Services for the Deaf - TDD equip
Restriction: Govt use only

HAGERSTOWN

GL CIRCUIT COURT FOR WASHINGTON COUNTY LAW LIBRARY*, Circuit Court House, 95 W Washington St, 21740. SAN 306-9702. Tel: 240-313-2570. Web Site: www.courts.state.md.us.
Library Holdings: Bk Vols 20,000; Per Subs 10
Open Mon-Fri 8:30-4:30

J HAGERSTOWN COMMUNITY COLLEGE LIBRARY*, 11400 Robinwood Dr, 21742-6590. SAN 306-9664. Tel: 301-790-2800, Ext 237. FAX: 301-393-3681. Web Site: www.hagerstowncc.edu. *Dir,* James Feagin; *Librn,* Alice Yang; *Bibliog Instr,* LuAnn Fisher; E-mail: fisherl@hagerstowncc.edu
Founded 1946. Enrl 1,200
Library Holdings: Bk Vols 44,872; Per Subs 225
Automation Activity & Vendor Info: (Cataloging) SirsiDynix; (Circulation) SirsiDynix; (Course Reserve) SirsiDynix; (OPAC) SirsiDynix
Database Vendor: EBSCOhost, LexisNexis, ProQuest
Open Mon-Thurs 8:30-4:30, Fri 9-4:30

C KAPLAN UNIVERSITY HAGERSTOWN LIBRARY*, Kiracofe-Lewis Memorial Library, 18618 Crestwood Dr, 21742. SAN 326-9329. Tel: 301-766-3600, 301-766-3653. FAX: 301-791-7661. Web Site: www.youseemore.com/kaplanu. *Dir of Libr Serv,* Thomas M Statton; E-mail: tstatton@kaplan.edu; Staff 2 (MLS 1, Non-MLS 1)
Founded 1938. Enrl 800; Fac 63; Highest Degree: Bachelor
Library Holdings: AV Mats 550; DVDs 200; Bk Vols 10,000; Per Subs 80; Spec Interest Per Sub 35; Videos 250

Automation Activity & Vendor Info: (Acquisitions) TLC (The Library Corporation); (Cataloging) TLC (The Library Corporation); (Circulation) TLC (The Library Corporation); (OPAC) TLC (The Library Corporation); (Serials) EBSCO Online
Database Vendor: EBSCO Discovery Service, EBSCOhost, Facts on File, Medline, PubMed, ReferenceUSA, Springshare, LLC, TLC (The Library Corporation), Westlaw
Wireless access
Function: Computer training, Computers for patron use, Copy machines, e-mail & chat, Electronic databases & coll, Online cat, Online ref, Online searches, Orientations, Photocopying/Printing, Workshops
Open Mon-Thurs 7:30am-10pm, Fri 8-1
Restriction: Access at librarian's discretion, Borrowing privileges limited to fac & registered students

S MARYLAND CORRECTIONAL INSTITUTION-HAGERSTOWN LIBRARY*, 18601 Roxbury Rd, 21746. Tel: 240-420-1000, Ext 2347, 301-733-2800, Ext 2347. FAX: 301-797-8448. *Librn,* Mary Stevanus; E-mail: mstevanus@dllr.state.md.us; Staff 1 (MLS 1)
Library Holdings: Bk Vols 8,467; Per Subs 39
Automation Activity & Vendor Info: (Cataloging) Follett Software; (Circulation) Follett Software
Database Vendor: Westlaw
Open Mon, Tues, Thurs & Fri 8-9:40, 10-11:40 & 1-2:10, Wed 8-9:40, 10-11:40, 1-2:10 & 7-8:45

S MARYLAND CORRECTIONAL TRAINING CENTER LIBRARY*, 18800 Roxbury Rd, 21746. Tel: 240-420-1607. FAX: 301-665-1813. *Librn,* Shirley Smith; Staff 1 (Non-MLS 1)
Library Holdings: Bk Vols 7,542; Per Subs 41
Automation Activity & Vendor Info: (Cataloging) Follett Software; (Circulation) Follett Software
Database Vendor: Westlaw
Open Mon-Fri 8:20-11 & 12:10-2:40

S NATIONAL PARK SERVICE*, Chesapeake & Ohio Canal National Historical Park Library, 1850 Dual Hwy, Ste 100, 21740. SAN 371-6228. Tel: 301-739-4200. Web Site: www.nps.gov/choh.
Library Holdings: Bk Titles 500
Restriction: Open by appt only

S REVIEW & HERALD PUBLISHING ASSOCIATION*, Editorial Library, 55 W Oak Ridge Dr, 21740. SAN 302-7619. Tel: 301-393-4141. FAX: 301-393-4055. E-mail: info@rhpa.org. Web Site: www.rhpa.org. *Dir, Libr Serv,* Jocelyn Fay
Founded 1903
Library Holdings: Bk Titles 40,000; Per Subs 90
Special Collections: Early Seventh-day Adventist Publications; Millerite Coll
Subject Interests: Church hist, Rare bks, Theol
Restriction: Staff use only

S ROXBURY CORRECTIONAL INSTITUTION LIBRARY*, 18701 Roxbury Rd, 21746. Tel: 240-420-3000, Ext 5290. FAX: 301-733-2672. *Librn,* Addis Kambule; Staff 1 (MLS 1)
Library Holdings: Bk Vols 10,399; Per Subs 39
Automation Activity & Vendor Info: (Cataloging) Follett Software; (Circulation) Follett Software
Database Vendor: Westlaw
Open Mon & Wed-Fri 8:30-11:30 & 12:30-2:30, Tues 8:30-11:30, 12:30-2:30 & 7-9

P WASHINGTON COUNTY FREE LIBRARY*, 100 S Potomac St, 21740. SAN 344-1458. Tel: 301-739-3250. FAX: 301-739-7603. Web Site: www.washcolibrary.org. *Dir,* Mary Catherine Baykan; E-mail: baykanm@washcolibrary.org; *Asst Dir,* Kathleen Mary O'Connell; E-mail: ko01@washcolibrary.org; *Assoc Dir, Western Md Regional Libr,* Joseph Thompson; E-mail: jthompson@washcolibrary.org; *Head, Tech Proc,* William Taylor; E-mail: wtaylor@washcolibrary.org; *Head, Adult Serv,* Elizabeth Hulett; E-mail: ehulett@washcolibrary.org; *Hed, Bkmobile Dept,* Laura Schnackenberg; E-mail: lschnackenberg@washcolibrary.org; *Head, Ch,* Jeff Ridgeway; E-mail: pr01@washcolibrary.org; *Head, Circ,* Delissa Key; Tel: 301-739-3250, Ext 126, E-mail: lk01@washcolibrary.org; *Head, County Serv,* Janlee Viands; E-mail: jv01@washcolibrary.org; *Head, Prog & PR,* Patricia Wishard; E-mail: pwishard@washcolibrary.org; *Head, YA,* Angela Garcia; E-mail: agarcia@washcolibrary.org; *Coll Develop,* Barbara Kronewitter; E-mail: bkronewitter@washcolibrary.org
Founded 1898. Pop 147,050; Circ 946,291
Library Holdings: Bks on Deafness & Sign Lang 200; High Interest/Low Vocabulary Bk Vols 500; Large Print Bks 5,000; Bk Vols 329,105; Per Subs 580; Talking Bks 3,000
Special Collections: Government Reference Service; Historical Lectures, video; Western Maryland (Western Maryland Rm), bks, AV. Oral History; State Document Depository
Subject Interests: Bus, Genealogy, Govt, Local hist
Automation Activity & Vendor Info: (Acquisitions) Innovative Interfaces, Inc; (Cataloging) Innovative Interfaces, Inc; (Circulation) Innovative Interfaces, Inc
Wireless access
Function: Audio & video playback equip for onsite use, Audiobks via web, AV serv, BA reader (adult literacy), Bi-weekly Writer's Group, Bilingual assistance for Spanish patrons, Bk club(s), Bk reviews (Group), Bks on cassette, Bks on CD, Bus archives, CD-ROM, Chess club, Children's prog, Citizenship assistance, Computer training, Computers for patron use, Copy machines, Digital talking bks, Distance learning, Doc delivery serv, e-mail & chat, e-mail serv, E-Reserves, Electronic databases & coll, Equip loans & repairs, Exhibits, Family literacy, Fax serv, For res purposes, Free DVD rentals, Games & aids for the handicapped, Genealogy discussion group, Govt ref serv, Handicapped accessible, Health sci info serv, Holiday prog, Home delivery & serv to Sr ctr & nursing homes, Homebound delivery serv, Homework prog, ILL available, Instruction & testing, Jail serv, Jazz prog, Large print keyboards, Learning ctr, Legal assistance to inmates, Libr develop, Literacy & newcomer serv, Magnifiers for reading, Mail & tel request accepted, Mail loans to mem, Masonic res mat, Microfiche/film & reading machines, Monthly prog for perceptually impaired adults, Mus passes, Music CDs, Newsp ref libr, Notary serv, Online cat, Online info literacy tutorials on the web & in blackboard, Online ref, Online searches, Orientations, Outreach serv, Outside serv via phone, mail, e-mail & web, OverDrive digital audio bks, Passport agency, Photocopying/Printing, Preschool outreach, Preschool reading prog, Printer for laptops & handheld devices, Prof lending libr, Prog for adults, Prog for children & young adult, Provide serv for the mentally ill, Pub access computers, Ref & res, Ref serv available, Ref serv in person, Referrals accepted, Res libr, Res performed for a fee, Satellite serv, Scanner, Senior computer classes, Senior outreach, Serves mentally handicapped consumers, Spanish lang bks, Specialized serv in classical studies, Spoken cassettes & CDs, Spoken cassettes & DVDs, Story hour, Summer & winter reading prog, Summer reading prog, Tax forms, Teen prog, Telephone ref, VCDs, VHS videos, Video lending libr, Visual arts prog, Web-Braille, Web-catalog, Wheelchair accessible, Winter reading prog, Words travel prog, Workshops
Publications: A Newspaper History of Washington County; Index to Hagerstown Newspapers
Mem of Western Maryland Regional Library
Special Services for the Deaf - Assistive tech; Bks on deafness & sign lang; Captioned film dep; Closed caption videos; Deaf publ
Special Services for the Blind - Assistive/Adapted tech devices, equip & products; Audio mat; Bks available with recordings; Bks on cassette; Bks on CD; Braille alphabet card; Braille bks; Closed circuit TV magnifier; Copier with enlargement capabilities; Home delivery serv; Large print & cassettes; Large print bks; Large screen computer & software; Low vision equip; Magnifiers; Reading & writing aids; Talking bks; Videos on blindness & phys handicaps; Volunteer serv
Friends of the Library Group
Branches: 7
BOONSBORO FREE LIBRARY, 401 Potomac St, Boonsboro, 21713, SAN 344-1482. Tel: 301-432-5723. *Librn,* Melissa Foltz; E-mail: mfoltz@washcolibrary.org
Library Holdings: Bk Vols 12,350
HANCOCK WAR MEMORIAL, Park Rd, Hancock, 21750, SAN 344-1512. Tel: 301-678-5300. *Librn,* Marilyn Pontius; E-mail: mp01@washcolibrary.org
Library Holdings: Bk Vols 16,197
KEEDYSVILLE BRANCH, 22 Taylor Dr, Keedysville, 21756, SAN 373-8094. Tel: 301-432-6641. Administration Tel: 301-739-3250. E-mail: kee@washcolibrary.org. *Br Mgr,* Adryana Billotti; E-mail: abillotti@washcolibrary.org
SHARPSBURG PUBLIC, 106 E Main St, Sharpsburg, 21782, SAN 344-1547. Tel: 301-432-8825. *Br Mgr,* Barb Twigg
Library Holdings: Bk Vols 10,790
SMITHSBURG BRANCH, 66 W Water St, Smithsburg, 21783-1604. (Mail add: PO Box 648, Smithsburg, 21783-0648), SAN 344-1571. Tel: 301-824-7722. E-mail: smi@washcolibrary.org. *Br Mgr,* Ashley Hutson
Library Holdings: Bk Vols 21,500
Open Mon-Fri 10-7, Sat 10-2
Friends of the Library Group
LEONARD P SNYDER MEMORIAL, 12624 Broadfording Rd, Clear Spring, 21722. Tel: 301-842-2730. FAX: 301-842-2829. *Librn,* Angie Garcia; E-mail: agarcia@washcolibrary.org
WILLIAMSPORT MEMORIAL, 104 E Potomac St, Williamsport, 21795, SAN 344-1601. Tel: 301-223-7027. *Librn,* Susan Schnebly; E-mail: sschnebly@washcolibrary.org
Library Holdings: Bk Vols 17,512
Bookmobiles: 1

S WASHINGTON COUNTY HISTORICAL SOCIETY*, Jamieson Memorial Library, 135 W Washington St, 21740. SAN 371-5183. Tel: 301-797-8782. FAX: 240-625-9498. Web Site: www.washcomdhistoricalsociety.org. *Exec*

Dir, Linda Irvin-Craig; E-mail: linda@washcomdhistoricalsociety.org; *Genealogist,* Albert Werking
Founded 1962
Library Holdings: Bk Vols 1,200
Subject Interests: Genealogy, Local hist
Open Tues-Fri 9-4
Restriction: Non-circulating to the pub

S WASHINGTON COUNTY MUSEUM OF FINE ARTS LIBRARY*, City Park, 91 Key St, 21741. (Mail add: PO Box 423, 21741-0423), SAN 325-8858. Tel: 301-739-5727. FAX: 301-745-3741. E-mail: info@wcmfa.org. Web Site: www.wcmfa.org. *Actg Librn,* Virginia Bryan
Library Holdings: Bk Vols 6,000
Subject Interests: Art
Open Tues-Fri 9-5, Sat 9-4, Sun 1-5

P WESTERN MARYLAND REGIONAL LIBRARY*, 100 S Potomac St, 21740. SAN 306-9729. Tel: 301-739-3250, Ext 140. FAX: 301-739-7603. Web Site: www.westmdlib.info. *Assoc Dir,* Position Currently Open; Staff 4 (MLS 4)
Founded 1968. Pop 229,900
Library Holdings: Bk Vols 61,743
Automation Activity & Vendor Info: (Cataloging) SirsiDynix; (Circulation) SirsiDynix
Database Vendor: EBSCOhost, Gale Cengage Learning
Publications: Western Maryland Public Libraries Sign System Manual
Member Libraries: Allegany County Public Library System; Ruth Enlow Library of Garrett County; Washington County Free Library
Open Mon-Fri 8-4:30

HUNT VALLEY

S BALTIMORE COUNTY HISTORICAL SOCIETY LIBRARY*, 9811 Van Buren Lane, 21030. SAN 371-9979. Tel: 410-666-1876. FAX: 410-666-5276. Web Site: www.hsobc.org. *Dir, Libr & Archives, Dir, Libr Serv,* Kevin T Clement; Tel: 410-666-1976, Ext 102; Staff 1 (MLS 1)
Founded 1959
Library Holdings: Bk Titles 2,500
Special Collections: Tombstone Inscriptions, bks & mss. Oral History
Subject Interests: Genealogy, Local hist
Publications: History Trails (Quarterly)
Open Tues-Sat 10-4
Restriction: Not a lending libr

S MCCORMICK & CO, INC*, Information Resource Center, 204 Wight Ave, 21031. SAN 306-9737. Tel: 410-771-7707. FAX: 410-785-7439. Web Site: www.mccormick.com. *Mgr,* Alice F Tramontana; Tel: 410-771-7983. Subject Specialists: *Chem, Food indust, Patents,* Alice F Tramontana; Staff 3 (Non-MLS 3)
Founded 1970
Library Holdings: Bk Titles 2,500; Bk Vols 4,000; Per Subs 300
Special Collections: Flavor Chemistry; Spices & Herbs
Subject Interests: Chem
Database Vendor: Dialog, EBSCOhost
Function: For res purposes
Restriction: Staff use only

HYATTSVILLE

SR FIRST UNITED METHODIST CHURCH LIBRARY*, 6201 Belcrest Rd, 20782. SAN 306-9753. Tel: 301-927-6133. FAX: 301-927-7368. Web Site: www.fumchy.org. *In Charge,* Falvia Brown
Founded 1949
Library Holdings: Bk Vols 2,500
Automation Activity & Vendor Info: (Acquisitions) SirsiDynix; (Cataloging) SirsiDynix
Open Mon-Fri 8:30-6

P PRINCE GEORGE'S COUNTY MEMORIAL LIBRARY SYSTEM, 6532 Adelphi Rd, 20782-2098. SAN 344-1636. Tel: 301-699-3500. FAX: 301-985-5494. TDD: 301-808-2061. Web Site: www.pgcmls.info. *Chief Exec Officer,* Kathleen Teaze; E-mail: kathleen.teaze@pgcmls.info; *Chief Financial Officer,* Lamont Corprew; Fax: 301-699-0668, E-mail: lamont.corprew@pgcmls.info; *Chief Opearting Officer, Pub Serv,* Michelle Hamiel; Fax: 301-699-0122, E-mail: michelle.hamiel@pgcmls.info; *Chief Operating Officer, Support Serv,* Michael Gannon; Fax: 301-699-1368, E-mail: michael.gannon@pgcmls.info; *Dir, Human Res,* Koven Roundtree; Fax: 301-927-6516, E-mail: koven.roundtree@pgcmls.info
Founded 1946. Pop 890,081; Circ 5,105,120
Library Holdings: Bk Titles 2,248,189; Per Subs 559
Special Collections: American Blacks (Sojourner Truth Room); Horses & Horse Racing (Selima Room); Maryland Room; Planned Communities & Consumers Cooperatives (Rexford G Tugwell Room)
Automation Activity & Vendor Info: (Acquisitions) Innovative Interfaces, Inc; (Circulation) Innovative Interfaces, Inc; (OPAC) Innovative Interfaces, Inc
Database Vendor: 3M Library Systems, ABC-CLIO, Alexander Street Press, Auto-Graphics, Inc, Baker & Taylor, Bowker, BWI, Dun & Bradstreet, EBSCO - WebFeat, EBSCO Auto Repair Reference, EBSCO Discovery Service, EBSCO Information Services, EBSCOhost, Elsevier, Evanced Solutions, Inc, Facts on File, Gale Cengage Learning, Greenwood Publishing Group, Grolier Online, H W Wilson, infoUSA, Ingram Library Services, Innovative Interfaces, Inc, LearningExpress, LexisNexis, McGraw-Hill, Medline, Mergent Online, Newsbank, OCLC, OCLC FirstSearch, OCLC WorldShare Interlibrary Loan, Overdrive, Inc, ProQuest, ReferenceUSA, Sage, Standard & Poor's, ValueLine, WebMD, Westlaw, Wiley, World Book Online
Wireless access
Publications: Friends Handbook; Selection Policy for Library Materials; Service Code for Information Services; Volunteer's Handbook
Special Services for the Deaf - TTY equip
Friends of the Library Group
Branches: 19
ACCOKEEK BRANCH, 15773 Livingston Rd, Accokeek, 20607-2249, SAN 344-1660. Tel: 301-292-2880. FAX: 301-292-0984. *Area Mgr,* Deena-Marie Beresford; E-mail: Deena-Marie.Beresford@pgcmls.info
Special Services for the Deaf - TTY equip
Open Mon & Wed 1-9, Tues & Thurs 10-6, Sat 10-5
Friends of the Library Group
BADEN BRANCH, 13603 Baden-Westwood Rd, Brandywine, 20613-8167, SAN 344-1695. Tel: 301-888-1152. *Area Mgr,* Deena-Marie Beresford
Open Mon-Thurs 10-6
BELTSVILLE BRANCH, 4319 Sellman Rd, Beltsville, 20705-2543, SAN 344-1725. Tel: 301-937-0294. FAX: 301-595-3455. *Area Mgr,* Blaine Halliday; E-mail: Blaine.Halliday@pgcmls.info
Special Services for the Deaf - TTY equip
Open Mon & Tues 1-9, Wed-Fri 10-6, Sat 10-5
Friends of the Library Group
BLADENSBURG BRANCH, 4820 Annapolis Rd, Bladensburg, 20710-1250, SAN 344-175X. Tel: 301-927-4916. FAX: 301-454-0324. *Area Mgr,* Catherine Hollerbach; E-mail: catherine.hollerbach@pgcmls.info
Special Services for the Deaf - TTY equip
Open Mon-Thurs 11-7, Sat 10-5
Friends of the Library Group
BOWIE BRANCH, 15210 Annapolis Rd, Bowie, 20715, SAN 344-1784. Tel: 301-262-7000. FAX: 301-809-2792. *Area Mgr,* Blaine Halliday; E-mail: Blaine.Halliday@pgcmls.info
Special Collections: Selima Room (horses & horse racing)
Special Services for the Deaf - TTY equip
Open Mon-Wed 10-9, Thurs & Fri 10-6, Sat 10-5
Friends of the Library Group
FAIRMOUNT HEIGHTS BRANCH, 5904 Kolb St, Fairmount Heights, 20743-6595, SAN 344-1873. Tel: 301-883-2650. FAX: 301-925-7936. *Area Mgr,* Victoria Johnson; E-mail: victoria.johnson@pgcmls.info
Special Services for the Deaf - TTY equip
Open Mon-Thurs 11-7, Sat 10-5
Friends of the Library Group
GLENARDEN BRANCH, 8724 Glenarden Pkwy, Glenarden, 20706-1646, SAN 344-1903. Tel: 301-772-5477. FAX: 301-322-3410. *Area Mgr,* Victoria Johnson; E-mail: victoria.johnson@pgcmls.info
Open Mon & Tues 12-8, Wed & Thurs 10-6, Sat 10-5
Friends of the Library Group
GREENBELT BRANCH, 11 Crescent Rd, Greenbelt, 20770-1898, SAN 344-1938. Tel: 301-345-5800. FAX: 301-982-5018. *Area Mgr,* Blaine Halliday; E-mail: Blaine.Halliday@pgcmls.info
Special Collections: Tugwell Room (Planned Communities & Consumers Cooperatives)
Special Services for the Deaf - TTY equip
Open Mon & Tues 1-9, Wed-Fri 10-6, Sat 10-5
Friends of the Library Group
HILLCREST HEIGHTS BRANCH, 2398 Iverson St, Temple Hills, 20748-6850, SAN 344-1962. Tel: 301-630-4900. *Area Mgr,* Victoria Johnson; E-mail: victoria.johnson@pgcmls.info
Special Services for the Deaf - TTY equip
Open Mon & Wed 12-8, Tues & Thurs 10-6, Sat 10-5
Friends of the Library Group
HYATTSVILLE BRANCH, 6530 Adelphi Rd, 20782-2098, SAN 344-1997. Tel: 301-985-4690. *Area Mgr,* Catherine Hollerbach; E-mail: catherine.hollerbach@pgcmls.info
Special Collections: Maryland Room (Maryland & Prince George's County History)
Special Services for the Deaf - TTY equip
Open Mon-Wed 10-9, Thurs & Fri 10-6, Sat 10-5, Sun 1-5
Friends of the Library Group

LARGO-KETTERING, 9601 Capital Lane, Largo, 20774, SAN 329-6431. Tel: 301-336-4044. FAX: 301-333-8857. *Area Mgr,* Luis Labra; E-mail: luis.labra@pgcmls.info
Special Services for the Deaf - TTY equip
Open Mon & Tues 1-9, Wed-Fri 10-6, Sat 10-5
Friends of the Library Group

LAUREL BRANCH, 507 Seventh St, Laurel, 20707-4013, SAN 344-2020. Tel: 301-497-4223, 301-776-6790. *Area Mgr,* Blaine Halliday; E-mail: blaine.halliday@pgcmls.info
Special Services for the Deaf - TTY equip
Open Mon-Wed 10-9, Thurs & Fri 10-6, Sat 10-5
Friends of the Library Group

MOUNT RAINIER BRANCH, 3409 Rhode Island Ave, Mount Rainier, 20712-2073, SAN 344-211X. Tel: 301-864-8937. FAX: 301-779-6207. *Area Mgr,* Catherine Hollerbach; E-mail: catherine.hollerbach@pgcmls.info
Special Services for the Deaf - TTY equip
Open Mon-Wed 11-7, Sat 10-5
Friends of the Library Group

NEW CARROLLTON BRANCH, 7414 Riverdale Rd, New Carrollton, 20784-3799, SAN 344-2144. Tel: 301-459-6900. FAX: 301-577-5085. *Area Mgr,* Kelley Perkins; E-mail: kelley.perkins@pgcmls.info
Special Services for the Deaf - TTY equip
Open Mon-Wed 10-9, Thurs & Fri 10-6, Sat 10-5
Friends of the Library Group

OXON HILL BRANCH, 6200 Oxon Hill Rd, Oxon Hill, 20745-3091, SAN 344-2179. Tel: 301-749-1784, 301-839-2400. *Area Mgr,* Kelley Perkins; E-mail: kelley.perkins@pgcmls.info
Special Collections: Sojourner Truth Room (African American Hist)
Special Services for the Deaf - TTY equip
Open Mon-Wed 10-9, Thurs & Fri 10-6, Sat 10-5, Sun 1-5
Friends of the Library Group

SOUTH BOWIE BRANCH, 15301 Hall Rd, Bowie, 20721. Tel: 301-850-0475. FAX: 240-206-8047. *Area Mgr,* Luis Labra; E-mail: luis.labra@pgcmls.info
Open Mon, Wed & Fri 10-6, Sat 10-5, Sun 1-5
Friends of the Library Group

SPAULDINGS BRANCH, 5811 Old Silver Hill Rd, District Heights, 20747-2108, SAN 328-7513. Tel: 301-817-3750. FAX: 301-967-7087. *Area Mgr,* Victoria Johnson; E-mail: victoria.johnson@pgcmls.info
Special Services for the Deaf - TTY equip
Open Mon & Tues 1-9, Wed-Fri 10-6, Sat 10-5
Friends of the Library Group

SURRATTS-CLINTON BRANCH, 9400 Piscataway Rd, Clinton, 20735-3632, SAN 344-2268. Tel: 301-868-9200. FAX: 301-856-9369. TDD: 301-856-2067. *Area Mgr,* Kelley Perkins; E-mail: kelley.perkins@pgcmls.info
Special Services for the Deaf - TTY equip
Open Mon-Wed 10-9, Thurs & Fri 10-6, Sat 10-5
Friends of the Library Group

UPPER MARLBORO, 14730 Main St, Upper Marlboro, 20772-3053, SAN 344-208X. Tel: 301-627-9330. FAX: 301-627-9332. *Area Mgr,* Luis Labra; E-mail: luis.labra@pgcmls.info
Special Services for the Deaf - TTY equip
Open Mon-Thurs 11-7, Sat 10-5
Friends of the Library Group

INDIAN HEAD

UNITED STATES NAVY

A ALBERT T CAMP TECHNICAL LIBRARY, Naval Surface Warfare Ctr IHD-Technical Library, 4171 Fowler Rd, Bldg 299, Ste 101, 20640-5110. (Mail add: Albert T Camp Technical Library, 4171 Fowler Road, Bldg 299, Ste 101, 20640-5110). Tel: 301-744-4742. FAX: 301-744-4192. E-mail: ihdivtechnicallibrary@navy.mil. Web Site: www.ih.navy.mil. *Tec Data Librn,* Eugene Bruce; Staff 2 (Non-MLS 2)
Library Holdings: Bk Titles 5,000; Bk Vols 12,150; Per Subs 50
Special Collections: Ordnance; Research; Rocketry; Test & Evaluation Reports
Subject Interests: Chem, Eng
Database Vendor: EOS International
Function: Copy machines, Doc delivery serv, Electronic databases & coll, Fax serv, Govt ref serv, ILL available, Online ref, Online searches, Outside serv via phone, mail, e-mail & web, Photocopying/Printing, Ref serv available, Res libr, Scanner, Telephone ref
Partic in OCLC Online Computer Library Center, Inc
Restriction: Authorized personnel only, Borrowing requests are handled by ILL, Circ limited, Employee & client use only, Employees & their associates, External users must contact libr, Not open to pub, Open to mil & govt employees only, Private libr

A GENERAL LIBRARY*, Naval Support Facility-S Potomac, Strauss Ave, Bldg 620, 20640, SAN 344-2322. Tel: 301-744-4747. FAX: 301-744-4386. Web Site: www.ih.navy.mil. *In Charge,* Janet Ferrell; E-mail: janetferrell@navy.mil; Staff 1 (Non-MLS 1)
Jul 2005-Jun 2006. Mats Exp $20,000. Sal $46,000
Library Holdings: Bk Titles 7,000; Per Subs 116
Special Collections: Maryland & Charles County History Books; Navy Biographical & Historical Books
Open Mon-Fri 8-4

A NAVAL EXPLOSIVE ORDNANCE DISPOSAL TECHNOLOGY DIVISION TECHNICAL LIBRARY*, 2008 Stump Neck Rd, Code 2011, 20640-5070, SAN 344-2381. Tel: 301-744-6817. FAX: 301-744-6902. *Br Head,* William Wilson; E-mail: william.r.wilson@navy.mil; Staff 6 (MLS 1, Non-MLS 5)
Founded 1956
Library Holdings: Bk Titles 120,000; Per Subs 100
Partic in Consortium of Naval Libraries (CNL); Fedlink
Publications: Accession List
Restriction: Closed stack, Not open to pub, Secured area only open to authorized personnel

JESSUP

S BROCKBRIDGE CORRECTIONAL FACILITY LIBRARY*, PO Box 537, 20794. Tel: 410-799-1363, Ext 5310. FAX: 410-799-3170. Staff 1 (MLS 1)
Library Holdings: Bk Vols 4,852; Per Subs 23
Automation Activity & Vendor Info: (Cataloging) Follett Software; (Circulation) Follett Software
Database Vendor: Westlaw
Open Tues & Fri 8:30-10:45 & 12:30-3

S MARYLAND CORRECTIONAL INSTITUTION FOR WOMEN LIBRARY*, Rte 175, Box 535, 20794. Tel: 410-379-3828. FAX: 410-799-8867. Web Site: www.dllr.state.md.us. *Librn,* Malveaux Herbert; E-mail: hmalveaux@dllr.state.md.us; *Evening Librn,* Beverly Bowles; Staff 1 (MLS 1)
Library Holdings: Bk Vols 7,686; Per Subs 25
Automation Activity & Vendor Info: (Cataloging) Follett Software; (Circulation) Follett Software
Database Vendor: Westlaw
Open Mon & Thurs 9:15-2:45 & 6-8, Tues, Wed & Fri 9:15-2:45

S MARYLAND CORRECTIONAL INSTITUTION-JESSUP LIBRARY*, 7803 House of Corrections Rd, Rte 175, 20794. (Mail add: PO Box 549, 20794). Tel: 410-799-7610. FAX: 410-799-7527. *Librn,* Patricia Smart; Staff 1 (MLS 1)
Library Holdings: Bk Vols 4,000; Per Subs 25
Automation Activity & Vendor Info: (Cataloging) Follett Software; (Circulation) Follett Software
Open Mon-Fri 8:30-10:30 & 1-2:15

S MARYLAND HOUSE OF CORRECTION LIBRARY*, Rte 175, Box 534, 20794. Tel: 410-799-0100, Ext 1446. FAX: 410-799-3013. *Librn,* Grace Schroeder; E-mail: gschroeder@dllr.state.md.us; Staff 1 (MLS 1)
Library Holdings: Bk Vols 7,838; Per Subs 38
Automation Activity & Vendor Info: (Cataloging) Follett Software; (Circulation) Follett Software
Database Vendor: Westlaw

S PATUXENT INSTITUTION LIBRARY*, 7555 Old Waterloo Rd, 20794. (Mail add: PO Box 700, 20794-0700). Tel: 410-799-3400, Ext 4226. FAX: 410-799-1137. *Librn,* Ruth Mewborn; E-mail: rmewborn@dllr.state.md.us; Staff 1 (MLS 1)
Library Holdings: Bk Vols 5,466; Per Subs 23
Automation Activity & Vendor Info: (Cataloging) Follett Software; (Circulation) Follett Software
Database Vendor: Westlaw

LA PLATA

L CHARLES COUNTY CIRCUIT COURT*, Charles County Public Law Library, 200 Charles St, 20646. (Mail add: PO Box 3060, 20646-3060), SAN 329-8574. Tel: 301-932-3322. FAX: 301-932-3324. Web Site: www.charlescountylawlibrary.com/index.html. *Librn,* Mary Rice; E-mail: ricem@charlescounty.org; Staff 1 (MLS 1)
Library Holdings: Bk Vols 8,000
Subject Interests: Law
Automation Activity & Vendor Info: (Cataloging) LibraryWorld, Inc
Database Vendor: LexisNexis, Westlaw
Function: Electronic databases & coll, Online ref
Open Mon-Fri 8:30-4:30
Restriction: Non-circulating, Not a lending libr

P CHARLES COUNTY PUBLIC LIBRARY, La Plata Branch, Two Garrett Ave, 20646-5959. SAN 344-2411. Tel: 301-934-9001. FAX: 301-934-2297. TDD: 301-934-9090. Web Site: www.ccplonline.org. *Actg Dir,* Diane Johnson; E-mail: djohnson@ccplonline.org; *Interim Asst Dir,* Janet Salazar; E-mail: jsalazar@ccplonline.org; *Br Mgr,* Lloyd Jansen; E-mail: ljansen@ccplonline.org; Staff 42 (MLS 11, Non-MLS 31)
Founded 1923. Pop 146,551; Circ 799,110

Library Holdings: Audiobooks 8,312; DVDs 18,644; Bk Titles 134,787; Bk Vols 201,125; Per Subs 195
Subject Interests: Local genealogy, Spanish
Automation Activity & Vendor Info: (Acquisitions) Innovative Interfaces, Inc; (Cataloging) Innovative Interfaces, Inc; (Circulation) Innovative Interfaces, Inc; (ILL) Relais International; (OPAC) Innovative Interfaces, Inc
Database Vendor: EBSCOhost, Gale Cengage Learning, Overdrive, Inc, TumbleBookLibrary, World Book Online
Wireless access
Function: Adult bk club, Bk club(s), Bks on cassette, Bks on CD, Children's prog, Computer training, Computers for patron use, Copy machines, e-mail & chat, Electronic databases & coll, Fax serv, Handicapped accessible, Holiday prog, Home delivery & serv to Sr ctr & nursing homes, Homebound delivery serv, ILL available, Online cat, Online ref, Outreach serv, Outside serv via phone, mail, e-mail & web, OverDrive digital audio bks, Photocopying/Printing, Preschool outreach, Prog for adults, Prog for children & young adult, Pub access computers, Ref serv available, Senior outreach, Spanish lang bks, Spoken cassettes & CDs, Story hour, Summer reading prog, Tax forms, Teen prog, Telephone ref, VHS videos
Mem of Southern Maryland Regional Library Association, Inc
Special Services for the Deaf - TDD equip
Special Services for the Blind - Audio mat
Open Mon-Thurs 9-8, Fri 1-5, Sat 9-5
Friends of the Library Group
Branches: 3
P D BROWN MEMORIAL, 50 Village St, Waldorf, 20602-1837, SAN 344-2500. Tel: 301-645-2864. FAX: 301-843-4869. *Br Mgr,* Cynthia Thornley; E-mail: cthornley@ccplonline.org
Open Mon-Thurs 9-8, Fri 1-5, Sat 9-5
Friends of the Library Group
POTOMAC BRANCH, 3225 Ruth B Swann Dr, Indian Head, 20640-3038. Tel: 301-375-7375. *Br Mgr,* Alyssa Williams; E-mail: awilliams@ccplonline.org
Open Mon-Thurs 9-8, Fri 1-5, Sat 9-5
Friends of the Library Group
WALDORF WEST BRANCH, 10405 O'Donnell Pl, Waldorf, 20603-7207. Tel: 301-645-1395. *Br Mgr,* Janet Salazar; E-mail: jsalazar@ccplonline.org
Bookmobiles: 1

J COLLEGE OF SOUTHERN MARYLAND LIBRARY*, 8730 Mitchell Rd, 20646. (Mail add: PO Box 910, 20646-0910), SAN 306-9818. Tel: 301-934-7626. Toll Free Tel: 800-933-9177, Ext 7626. FAX: 301-934-7699. E-mail: library@csmd.edu. Web Site: www.csmd.edu/library. *Dir,* Thomas Repenning; Tel: 301-934-7630, E-mail: tomr@csmd.edu; *Ref,* Vince Doblos; Staff 4 (MLS 3, Non-MLS 1)
Founded 1958. Enrl 11,211; Fac 204; Highest Degree: Associate
Library Holdings: AV Mats 13,615; Bk Titles 37,260; Bk Vols 45,430; Per Subs 73; Talking Bks 229
Special Collections: Southern Maryland Manuscripts & Genealogy. Oral History
Subject Interests: Local hist
Automation Activity & Vendor Info: (Cataloging) TLC (The Library Corporation); (Circulation) Follett Software; (Course Reserve) Docutek; (OPAC) Follett Software
Database Vendor: EBSCOhost, Gale Cengage Learning, OCLC WorldShare Interlibrary Loan, ProQuest, PubMed, SerialsSolutions, TLC (The Library Corporation), Westlaw
Wireless access
Partic in Md Commun Col Libr Consortium

LANDOVER

M EPILEPSY FOUNDATION, National Epilepsy Library®, 8301 Professional Pl-East, Ste 200, 20785. SAN 302-6469. Toll Free Tel: 800-332-4050. FAX: 301-577-4941. E-mail: nel@efa.org. Web Site: www.epilepsy.com. *Sr Dir, Info Serv,* Paul Scribner; Tel: 301-918-3729; *Sr Info Spec,* Tom Buckley; Tel: 301-918-3770; *Prog Coordr,* Carmen Fletcher; Tel: 301-918-3733; Staff 2 (MLS 1, Non-MLS 1)
Founded 1982
Library Holdings: e-journals 6; Bk Vols 1,200; Per Subs 37
Special Collections: Albert & Ellen Grass Archives
Database Vendor: EBSCOhost
Function: For res purposes
Restriction: Open by appt only

R FIRST BAPTIST CHURCH OF HIGHLAND PARK LIBRARY*, 6801 Sheriff Rd, 20785. Tel: 301-773-6655, Ext 236. FAX: 301-773-1347. Web Site: www.fbhp.org. *Librn,* Ruby Alexander; Staff 2 (MLS 2)
Founded 1998
Library Holdings: Bk Titles 2,100; Per Subs 25
Subject Interests: Children's lit, Christianity
Automation Activity & Vendor Info: (Cataloging) Book Systems; (Circulation) Book Systems; (OPAC) Book Systems
Function: Ref serv available
Restriction: Mem only

S NATIONAL REHABILITATION INFORMATION CENTER, 8400 Corporate Dr, Ste 500, 20785. SAN 371-263X. Tel: 301-459-5900. Toll Free Tel: 800-346-2742. FAX: 301-459-4263. TDD: 301-459-5984. E-mail: naricinfo@heitechservices.com. Web Site: www.naric.com. *Dir,* Mark X Odum; Staff 9 (MLS 1, Non-MLS 8)
Founded 1977
Library Holdings: Bks on Deafness & Sign Lang 5,120; Bk Vols 20,000; Per Subs 108
Subject Interests: Disability, Rehabilitation, Spec educ
Function: Archival coll, Doc delivery serv, e-mail & chat, Electronic databases & coll, Govt ref serv, Handicapped accessible, Online searches, Referrals accepted, Wheelchair accessible
Special Services for the Deaf - TTY equip
Special Services for the Blind - Braille servs
Open Mon-Fri 8:30-5:30
Restriction: Non-circulating to the pub

LANHAM

M DOCTORS COMMUNITY HOSPITAL*, Medical Library, 8118 Good Luck Rd, 20706. SAN 377-3841. Tel: 301-552-8072. E-mail: library@dchweb.org. Web Site: www.dchweb.org. *In Charge,* Andrea Castrogiovanni; Staff 1 (MLS 1)
Founded 1975
Library Holdings: Bk Titles 100; Per Subs 35
Function: Doc delivery serv, Health sci info serv, Online searches, Ref & res
Partic in Medical Library Association (MLA); Mid-Atlantic Med Librs
Open Mon-Fri 8-4:30
Restriction: Pub use on premises

CR WASHINGTON BIBLE COLLEGE-CAPITAL BIBLE SEMINARY*, Oyer Memorial Library, 6511 Princess Garden Pkwy, 20706. SAN 306-9834. Tel: 301-552-1400, Ext 1231. FAX: 301-552-2775. Web Site: www.bible.edu. *Dir,* William Banks; E-mail: bbanks@bible.edu; Staff 2 (MLS 2)
Library Holdings: Bk Titles 68,570; Per Subs 258
Subject Interests: Rare bks, Theol
Automation Activity & Vendor Info: (Acquisitions) EOS International; (Cataloging) EOS International; (Circulation) EOS International; (Course Reserve) EOS International; (OPAC) EOS International; (Serials) EOS International
Partic in OCLC Online Computer Library Center, Inc
Open Mon-Thurs 7:30am-10pm, Fri 7:30-6:30, Sat 10-5

LARGO

C PRINCE GEORGE'S COMMUNITY COLLEGE LIBRARY*, 301 Largo Rd, 20774-2199. SAN 306-9842. Tel: 301-322-0462. Circulation Tel: 301-322-0475. Interlibrary Loan Service Tel: 301-322-0021. Reference Tel: 301-322-0476. FAX: 301-808-8847. Web Site: www.pgcc.edu/library/index.htm. *Dean,* Dr Lynda Byrd Logan; Tel: 301-322-0466, E-mail: loganlb@pgcc.edu; *Coll Develop Librn,* Norma A Schmidt; Tel: 301-322-0471, E-mail: nschmidt@pgcc.edu; *Electronic Res,* Imogene Zachery; Tel: 301-322-0138, E-mail: izachery@pgcc.edu; *Info Literacy,* Jean McEvoy; Tel: 301-322-0467, E-mail: mcevoyjl@pgcc.edu; *Pub Serv,* Priscilla C Thompson; Tel: 301-322-0468, E-mail: pthompson@pgcc.edu; *Tech Serv,* John D Bartles; Tel: 301-322-0469, E-mail: jbartles@pgcc.edu; Staff 48 (MLS 12, Non-MLS 36)
Founded 1958. Enrl 6,451; Fac 369
Library Holdings: Bk Titles 93,500; Per Subs 250
Special Collections: Municipal
Automation Activity & Vendor Info: (Acquisitions) Ex Libris Group; (Cataloging) Ex Libris Group; (Circulation) Ex Libris Group; (Course Reserve) Ex Libris Group; (ILL) Ex Libris Group; (Media Booking) Ex Libris Group; (OPAC) Ex Libris Group; (Serials) Ex Libris Group
Database Vendor: Gale Cengage Learning, OCLC FirstSearch, ProQuest, Westlaw
Partic in Md Commun Col Libr Consortium
Open Mon-Thurs 8am-10pm, Fri 8-6, Sat 9-5, Sun 12-5
Friends of the Library Group

LAUREL

C CAPITOL COLLEGE*, John G & Beverly A Puente Library, 11301 Springfield Rd, 20708. SAN 306-9796. Tel: 301-369-2800. FAX: 301-369-2552. Web Site: www.capitol-college.edu. *Dir, Libr Serv,* Rick A Sample; E-mail: rsample@capitol-college.edu; *Assoc Dir, Libr Operations,* Sandy Pisano; E-mail: spisano@capitol-college.edu; Staff 2 (MLS 2)
Founded 1966. Enrl 680; Fac 22; Highest Degree: Master
Library Holdings: Bk Titles 9,700; Bk Vols 9,817; Per Subs 87

Subject Interests: Archives, Computer sci, Electronics, Eng, Info tech
Automation Activity & Vendor Info: (Acquisitions) EOS International; (Cataloging) EOS International; (Circulation) EOS International; (OPAC) EOS International; (Serials) EOS International
Publications: Road Map to Borrowing
Partic in Maryland Interlibrary Loan Organization

S FREEDOM FORUM WORLD CENTER LIBRARY*, 9893 Brewers Ct, 20723. SAN 375-5193. Tel: 301-957-3210. FAX: 301-957-3280. *Mgr, Libr Serv,* Rick Mastroianni; E-mail: rmastroianni@freedomforum.org; *Sr Librn,* Sage Hulsebus; Tel: 301-957-3215, E-mail: shulsebus@freedomforum.org; Staff 7 (MLS 5, Non-MLS 2)
Founded 1990
Library Holdings: Bk Titles 12,000; Per Subs 150
Special Collections: First Amendment & Journalism Coll
Automation Activity & Vendor Info: (Cataloging) Inmagic, Inc.

S JOHNS HOPKINS UNIVERSITY, APPLIED PHYSICS LABORATORY*, R E Gibson Library & Information Center, 11100 Johns Hopkins Rd, 20723-6099. SAN 306-9850. Tel: 443-778-5151. Interlibrary Loan Service Tel: 443-778-5152. FAX: 443-778-5353. Web Site: www.jhuapl.edu. *Librn,* Susan Singerman; Staff 25 (MLS 13, Non-MLS 12)
Founded 1945
Library Holdings: Bk Titles 60,000; Per Subs 500
Subject Interests: Aerospace sci, Electronics, Math, Physics
Automation Activity & Vendor Info: (Acquisitions) Horizon; (Cataloging) Horizon; (Circulation) Horizon; (OPAC) Horizon
Publications: Information Exchange
Open Mon-Thurs 8:30am-9pm

GL MARYLAND STATE DIVISION OF LABOR & INDUSTRY*, Occupational Safety & Health Library, 312 Marshall Ave, Ste 600, 20707. SAN 370-1565. Tel: 410-880-4970. FAX: 301-483-8332. Web Site: www.dllr.state.md.us/labor/mosh.html. *Librn,* Arathi Kemparaju
Library Holdings: Bk Titles 500
Subject Interests: Occupational health, Occupational safety
Open Mon-Fri 9-4

G USGS PATUXENT WILDLIFE RESEARCH CENTER LIBRARY*, 12100 Beech Forest Rd, 20708-4030. SAN 306-9869. Tel: 301-497-5550. FAX: 301-497-5545. E-mail: pwrclibrary@usgs.gov. Web Site: www.pwrc.usgs.gov/library. *Librn,* Lynda Garrett; E-mail: lgarrett@usgs.gov. Subject Specialists: *Wildlife,* Lynda Garrett; Staff 1 (Non-MLS 1)
Founded 1942
Library Holdings: e-journals 14; Bk Titles 9,000; Per Subs 20
Special Collections: Pesticides & Pollution, reprints
Subject Interests: Biometrics, Environ pollution, Ornithology
Automation Activity & Vendor Info: (Cataloging) OCLC Connexion; (ILL) OCLC
Database Vendor: BioOne, Elsevier, Ingenta, ISI Web of Knowledge, JSTOR, OCLC FirstSearch, OCLC WorldShare Interlibrary Loan, ProQuest, PubMed, ScienceDirect, Scopus, SerialsSolutions, Springer-Verlag, Thomson - Web of Science, Wiley
Wireless access
Function: ILL available, Wheelchair accessible
Publications: Journal & Serial Holdings List
Partic in Maryland Interlibrary Loan Organization; OCLC Online Computer Library Center, Inc
Open Mon-Fri 8-4:30
Restriction: In-house use for visitors, Open to pub for ref only, Photo ID required for access, Restricted pub use

LEONARDTOWN

S ST MARY'S COUNTY HISTORICAL SOCIETY, Research Center, 41680 Tudor Pl, 20650. (Mail add: PO Box 212, 20650-0212), SAN 306-9885. Tel: 301-475-2467. FAX: 301-475-2467. Web Site: www.stmaryshistory.org. *Exec Dir,* Susan J Wolfe; E-mail: smchsdirector@md.metrocast.net; Staff 2 (MLS 1, Non-MLS 1)
Founded 1951
Library Holdings: AV Mats 45; CDs 20; DVDs 3; Electronic Media & Resources 3; Music Scores 2; Bk Titles 2,000; Bk Vols 3,500; Per Subs 35
Special Collections: Chronicles of St Mary's Coll; Early Maryland & English History Coll; Local Authors Coll. Oral History
Subject Interests: Genealogy, Local hist, Relig
Wireless access
Open Tues & Wed 9-4, Thurs & Fri 11-4
Restriction: Non-circulating to the pub

P SAINT MARY'S COUNTY MEMORIAL LIBRARY*, 23250 Hollywood Rd, 20650. SAN 344-2535. Tel: 301-475-2846. FAX: 301-884-4415. Web Site: www.stmalib.org. *Dir,* Kathleen Reif; E-mail: kreif@stmalib.org
Founded 1950. Pop 89,000
Library Holdings: Bk Vols 176,958; Per Subs 444
Special Collections: Genealogy Society Coll
Automation Activity & Vendor Info: (Cataloging) SirsiDynix; (Circulation) SirsiDynix; (OPAC) SirsiDynix
Mem of Southern Maryland Regional Library Association, Inc
Partic in Maryland Interlibrary Loan Organization
Open Mon-Thurs 9-8, Fri 11-5, Sat 9-5
Friends of the Library Group
Branches: 2
CHARLOTTE HALL BRANCH, 37600 New Market Rd, Charlotte Hall, 20622, SAN 344-2543. Tel: 301-884-2211. FAX: 301-884-2113. *Br Mgr,* Mary Anne Bowman; E-mail: mabowman@stmalib.org
Open Mon-Thurs 9-8, Fri 11-5, Sat 9-5
LEXINGTON PARK BRANCH, 21677 FDR Blvd, Lexington Park, 20653, SAN 344-256X. Tel: 301-863-8188. FAX: 301-863-2550. E-mail: lexi.manager@stmalib.org. *Head of Libr,* Teresa Tresp; Tel: 301-863-8188, Ext 1012; *Youth Serv Coordr,* Janis Cooker; Tel: 301-863-8188, Ext 1006, E-mail: coordinator@stmalib.org
Open Mon & Tues 9-8, Wed 12-8, Thurs & Sat 9-5, Fri 11-5
Bookmobiles: 1

MCHENRY

J GARRETT COLLEGE, Library Resource Center, (Formerly Garrett College), 687 Mosser Rd, 21541. SAN 306-9923. Tel: 301-387-3009. FAX: 301-387-3720. Web Site: www.garrettcollege.edu/services/lrc. *Interim Dir,* Ellen Sheaffer; Tel: 301-387-3003, E-mail: ellen.sheaffer@garrettcollege.edu; *Instruction & Ref Librn,* Krista McKenzie; Tel: 301-387-3022; *Cat,* Teresa Feather; Tel: 301-387-3002; *Circ/Acq, ILL,* Linda Tomblin; E-mail: ltomblin@garrettcollege.edu; Staff 2 (Non-MLS 2)
Founded 1971. Enrl 620; Fac 18
Library Holdings: Bk Titles 24,803; Bk Vols 27,592; Per Subs 70
Special Collections: Coal Talk Oral Hist; Western Maryland. Oral History
Subject Interests: Natural res
Automation Activity & Vendor Info: (Cataloging) Follett Software; (Circulation) Follett Software; (OPAC) Follett Software
Database Vendor: ProQuest
Wireless access
Open Mon-Wed 8am-9pm, Thurs 8-7, Fri 8:30-4:30, Sun 2-8

MILLERSVILLE

S ECOSYSTEMS INTERNATIONAL INC LIBRARY*, 1107 Dicus Mill Rd, 21108. (Mail add: PO Box 225, Gambrills, 21054-0225), SAN 373-1588. Tel: 410-987-4976. FAX: 410-729-1960. E-mail: wdc101@aol.com. *Librn,* Darlene Barckley
Founded 1972
Library Holdings: Bk Titles 30,000; Bk Vols 38,000; Per Subs 88

NORTH EAST

J CECIL COLLEGE, Veterans Memorial Library, One Seahawk Dr, 21901-1904. SAN 306-9931. Tel: 410-287-1005. Interlibrary Loan Service Tel: 410-287-6060, Ext 576. Reference Tel: 410-287-6060, Ext 577. FAX: 410-287-1607. E-mail: library@cecil.edu. Web Site: www.cecil.edu/library. *Dir,* Lorraine Martorana; E-mail: lmartorana@cecil.edu; *Cat & Acq,* Paula Bartlett; E-mail: pbartlett@cecil.edu; *Instrul Librn,* Melissa A D'Agostino; E-mail: mdagostino@cecil.edu; Staff 4.5 (MLS 2.5, Non-MLS 2)
Founded 1968. Enrl 1,916; Fac 40; Highest Degree: Associate
Library Holdings: Audiobooks 32; e-books 57,982; Bk Titles 26,130; Per Subs 39; Videos 554
Special Collections: Bridges of Cecil County (Photographs from the depression era)
Subject Interests: Genealogy, Maryland
Automation Activity & Vendor Info: (Acquisitions) SirsiDynix; (Cataloging) SirsiDynix; (Circulation) SirsiDynix; (Course Reserve) SirsiDynix; (ILL) SirsiDynix; (OPAC) SirsiDynix; (Serials) SirsiDynix
Database Vendor: CredoReference, EBSCOhost, Newsbank, OCLC FirstSearch, OVID Technologies, Oxford Online, ProQuest, PubMed, SirsiDynix, Springshare, LLC
Wireless access
Open Mon-Fri 7:30am-8pm, Sat & Sun 11-4

OAKLAND

P RUTH ENLOW LIBRARY OF GARRETT COUNTY, Six N Second St, 21550-1393. SAN 344-2659. Tel: 301-334-3996. FAX: 301-334-4152. TDD: 301-334-3997. E-mail: info@relib.net. Web Site: www.relib.net. *Dir,* Cathy A Ashby; Tel: 301-334-3996, Ext 102, E-mail: cashby@relib.net; *Br Mgr,* Ann Leighton; Tel: 301-334-3996, Ext 104, E-mail: ann@relib.net; Staff 2 (MLS 2)
Founded 1946. Pop 29,250; Circ 225,000
Special Collections: Garrett County; Garrett County Families; Western Maryland
Subject Interests: Local hist

Automation Activity & Vendor Info: (Cataloging) Innovative Interfaces, Inc; (Circulation) Innovative Interfaces, Inc; (OPAC) Innovative Interfaces, Inc; (Serials) EBSCO Online
Database Vendor: EBSCOhost, Gale Cengage Learning
Wireless access
Mem of Western Maryland Regional Library
Partic in Maryland Interlibrary Loan Organization
Special Services for the Deaf - TDD equip
Open Mon & Wed 9:15-8, Tues, Thurs & Fri 9:15-5:30, Sat 9-4
Friends of the Library Group
Branches: 4
ACCIDENT BRANCH, 106 S North St, Accident, 21520. (Mail add: PO Box 154, Accident, 21520-0154), SAN 344-2683. Tel: 301-746-8792. FAX: 301-746-8399. E-mail: accident.branch@relib.net. *Br Mgr,* Susan Haydel
Founded 1977. Pop 349
Open Mon, Tues, Thurs & Fri 11-5:30, Wed 11-7, Sat 9-1
Friends of the Library Group
FRIENDSVILLE BRANCH, PO Box 57, Friendsville, 21531-0057, SAN 344-2748. Tel: 301-746-5663. FAX: 301-746-5663. *Br Mgr,* Michele Liston; E-mail: michele@relib.net; Staff 1 (Non-MLS 1)
Friends of the Library Group
GRANTSVILLE BRANCH, PO Box 237, Grantsville, 21536-0237, SAN 344-2772. Tel: 301-895-5298. FAX: 301-245-4411. *Br Mgr,* Kimberly Lishia; E-mail: kim@relib.net
Friends of the Library Group
KITZMILLER BRANCH, PO Box 100, Kitzmiller, 21538-0100, SAN 344-2802. Tel: 301-453-3368. FAX: 301-453-3368. *Br Mgr,* Diane Kisner; E-mail: diane@relib.net
Friends of the Library Group

GL GARRETT COUNTY CIRCUIT COURT LIBRARY*, Courthouse, Rm 107B, 203 S Fourth St, 21550. Tel: 301-334-1934. FAX: 301-334-5042. *In Charge,* Bill Graham
Library Holdings: Bk Vols 500
Restriction: Not open to pub

OXFORD

G COOPERATIVE OXFORD LABORATORY LIBRARY*, 904 S Morris St, 21654-9724. SAN 306-9966. Tel: 410-226-5193. FAX: 410-226-5925. Web Site: mrl.cofc.edu/oxford. *Librn,* Position Currently Open
Founded 1961
Library Holdings: Bk Vols 23,540; Per Subs 75
Subject Interests: Marine biol
Database Vendor: Dialog
Publications: Annual Publications List; Dissertations; Serial & Journal Holdings; Theses List
Partic in Dialog Corp; OCLC Online Computer Library Center, Inc
Open Mon-Fri 8-4:30

PATUXENT RIVER

A UNITED STATES NAVY*, NAVAIR Scientific & Technical Library, 22269 Cedar Point Rd B407, 20670-1120. SAN 344-2837. Tel: 301-342-1927. Interlibrary Loan Service Tel: 301-342-5286. Reference Tel: 301-342-1925, 301-342-1930. FAX: 301-342-1933. E-mail: technical.library.fct@navy.mil. *Libr Team Lead,* Moira E Zelechoski; E-mail: moira.zelechoski@navy.mil; Staff 6 (MLS 3, Non-MLS 3)
Founded 1952
Library Holdings: Bk Vols 15,113; Per Subs 30
Special Collections: NAVAIR Technical Manuals & Directives; NAWCAD Technical Reports; Technical Coll. US Document Depository
Subject Interests: Aeronaut, Computer sci, Eng, Phys sci
Automation Activity & Vendor Info: (Cataloging) SirsiDynix; (Circulation) SirsiDynix; (ILL) OCLC; (OPAC) SirsiDynix
Database Vendor: Cambridge Scientific Abstracts, EBSCOhost, Elsevier, IEEE (Institute of Electrical & Electronics Engineers), Jane's, Knovel, OCLC ArticleFirst, OCLC FirstSearch, OCLC WorldShare Interlibrary Loan, ProQuest, Thomson - Web of Science
Function: Bks on CD, Computers for patron use, Doc delivery serv, e-mail serv, Electronic databases & coll, Exhibits, Fax serv, Govt ref serv, ILL available, Online cat, Online ref, Online searches, Orientations, Outreach serv, Ref & res, Ref serv available, Ref serv in person, Res libr, Tax forms
Partic in Consortium of Naval Libraries (CNL); Fedlink
Open Mon-Thurs 7:30-4:30, Fri 10-2
Restriction: Open to mil & govt employees only, Photo ID required for access

PERRY POINT

GM VA MARYLAND HEALTH CARE SYSTEM*, Perry Point VA Medical Center Library, 21902 Circle Dr, Bldg 3H, 21902. SAN 306-9974. Tel: 410-642-2411, Ext 5716. Toll Free Tel: 800-949-1003. FAX: 410-642-1103.
Founded 1924
Library Holdings: Bk Vols 5,000; Per Subs 250
Subject Interests: Geriatrics & gerontology, Nursing, Psychiat, Psychol
Automation Activity & Vendor Info: (Acquisitions) Ex Libris Group; (Circulation) Ex Libris Group
Partic in National Network of Libraries of Medicine
Open Mon-Fri 8-4:30

PINEY POINT

S SEAFARER'S HARRY LUNDEBERG SCHOOL OF SEAMANSHIP*, Paul Hall Library & Maritime Museum, PO Box 75, 20674-0075. SAN 306-9982. Tel: 301-994-0010, Ext 5353. *Dir,* Janice M Smolek; Staff 3 (MLS 2, Non-MLS 1)
Founded 1970
Library Holdings: Bk Vols 19,000; Per Subs 100
Subject Interests: Hist, Maritime hist

PRINCE FREDERICK

P CALVERT COUNTY PUBLIC LIBRARY*, 850 Costley Way, 20678. SAN 307-000X. Tel: 410-535-0291. FAX: 410-535-3022. Web Site: www.calvert.lib.md.us. *Dir,* Carrie Plymire; *Br Mgr,* Marcia Hammett; E-mail: mhammett@somd.lib.md.us; *Info Serv Coordr,* Sheila Hejl; E-mail: shejl@somd.lib.md.us; *Pub Relations Coordr,* Robyn Truslow; E-mail: rtruslow@somd.lib.md.us; *Youth Serv Coordr,* Beverly Izzi; E-mail: bizzi@somd.lib.md.us; Staff 8 (MLS 8)
Founded 1959. Pop 84,000; Circ 962,246
Jul 2006-Jun 2007 Income (Main Library and Branch(s)) $3,211,552, State $539,006, Federal $11,500, County $2,429,503, Locally Generated Income $231,543. Mats Exp $348,620, Books $223,255, Per/Ser (Incl. Access Fees) $14,703, AV Mat $110,662. Sal $1,964,970
Library Holdings: AV Mats 27,293; e-books 1,000; Bk Vols 153,443; Per Subs 221
Subject Interests: Maryland
Automation Activity & Vendor Info: (Acquisitions) SirsiDynix; (Circulation) SirsiDynix; (OPAC) SirsiDynix
Wireless access
Function: Adult bk club, Adult literacy prog, After school storytime, Computer training, Copy machines, E-Reserves, Electronic databases & coll, Family literacy, Fax serv, Homebound delivery serv, ILL available, Magnifiers for reading, Online ref, Photocopying/Printing, Preschool outreach, Prog for adults, Prog for children & young adult, Ref serv available, Spoken cassettes & CDs, Spoken cassettes & DVDs, Summer reading prog, Tax forms, Telephone ref, VHS videos, Workshops
Mem of Southern Maryland Regional Library Association, Inc
Special Services for the Deaf - TTY equip
Special Services for the Blind - Bks on cassette; Bks on CD; Large print bks
Open Mon-Thurs 9-9, Fri 12-5, Sat 9-5
Friends of the Library Group
Branches: 3
FAIRVIEW, 8120 Southern Maryland Blvd, Owings, 20736, SAN 321-9585. Tel: 410-257-2101. FAX: 410-257-0662. *Br Mgr,* Lisa Tassa; E-mail: ltassa@somd.lib.md.us
Open Mon-Thurs 9-9, Fri 12-5, Sat 9-5
SOUTHERN BRANCH, 20 Appeal Lane, Lusby, 20657. (Mail add: PO Box 599, Lusby, 20657-0599), SAN 329-5516. Tel: 410-326-5289. FAX: 410-326-8370. *Br Mgr,* Trudy Mihalcik; E-mail: tmihalcik@somd.lib.md.us
Open Mon-Thurs 9-9, Fri 12-5, Sat 9-5
TWIN BEACHES BRANCH, 3819 Harbor Rd, Chesapeake Beach, 20732, SAN 321-9593. Tel: 410-257-2411. FAX: 410-257-0663. *Br Mgr,* Joan Kilmon; E-mail: jkilmon@somd.lib.md.us
Open Mon-Thurs 9-9, Fri 12-5, Sat 9-5
Bookmobiles: 1

PRINCESS ANNE

GL SOMERSET COUNTY CIRCUIT COURT LIBRARY*, Courthouse, 30512 Prince William St, 21853. (Mail add: PO Box 279, 21853-0279). Tel: 410-621-7581. FAX: 410-621-7595. *Librn,* Nancy Selby
Library Holdings: Bk Vols 1,500

P SOMERSET COUNTY LIBRARY SYSTEM, 11767 Beechwood St, 21853. SAN 344-2861. Tel: 410-651-0852. FAX: 410-651-1388. Web Site: www.somelibrary.org. *Dir,* Gail Sheldon; E-mail: gsheldon@somelibrary.org; *Head, Circ,* Joan Terry; *Br Mgr, ILL,* Rose Donoway; *Acq & Cat,* Lynn Windsor; *Ch Serv,* Mary Zimmermann; *Tech Serv,* Gabriel Stucky
Founded 1967. Pop 26,500
Library Holdings: Bk Vols 104,672; Per Subs 67
Subject Interests: Hist, Maryland
Automation Activity & Vendor Info: (Acquisitions) Innovative Interfaces, Inc; (Cataloging) Innovative Interfaces, Inc; (OPAC) Innovative Interfaces, Inc; (Serials) Innovative Interfaces, Inc

Database Vendor: EBSCOhost, ProQuest
Partic in Eastern Shore Regional Library
Open Mon-Thurs 10-7, Fri & Sat 10-5
Branches: 1
CORBIN MEMORIAL LIBRARY, Four E Main St, Crisfield, 21817, SAN 344-2896. Tel: 410-968-0955. FAX: 410-968-2363. *Librn,* Gabriel Stuckey; E-mail: gstuckey@some.lib.md.us
Open Mon, Wed & Fri 1-7, Tues & Thurs 11-7, Sat 10-5

C UNIVERSITY OF MARYLAND-EASTERN SHORE, Frederick Douglass Library, 11868 Academic Oval, 21853. SAN 344-2926. Tel: 410-651-2200, 410-651-6621. FAX: 410-651-6269. Web Site: www.umes.edu/fdl. *Dean of Libr Serv,* Ellis B Beteck, PhD; *Head of Ref & Instrul Serv,* Marvella Rounds; *Access Serv Librn,* Joseph D Bree; *Cat & Ref Librn,* Fanuel Chirombo; *Electronic Res & Ser Mgt Librn,* Cynthia I Nyirenda; *Media Serv Librn,* Sharon D Brooks; *Outreach & Spec Coll Librn,* Position Currently Open; *Ref & Instrul Serv Librn,* Renise M Johnson; *Ref & Instrul Serv Librn,* Ann Cober Reed; *Acq, Coll Develop,* Theresa Dadson; Staff 10 (MLS 10)
Founded 1968. Enrl 4,443; Fac 220; Highest Degree: Doctorate
Library Holdings: Audiobooks 797; DVDs 192; e-books 36,939; e-journals 5,889; Electronic Media & Resources 44,015; Microforms 500,000; Bk Titles 199,508; Bk Vols 271,310; Per Subs 937
Special Collections: African American History (Black Coll), culture & lit, out-of-print, rare & first editions; Maryland Eastern Shore Coll (Somerset, Wicomico & Worcester Counties), bks, clippings, photog, correspondence, reports & maps; University Archives. State Document Depository
Subject Interests: Agr, Allied health, Arts, Bus, Golf course mgt, Hospitality, Sci, Tourism
Automation Activity & Vendor Info: (Acquisitions) Ex Libris Group; (Cataloging) Ex Libris Group; (Circulation) Ex Libris Group; (Course Reserve) Ex Libris Group; (ILL) Ex Libris Group; (OPAC) Ex Libris Group; (Serials) Ex Libris Group
Database Vendor: Agricola, American Chemical Society, BioOne, LexisNexis
Wireless access
Publications: A Mini Guide; Departmental Brochures (Reference guide); Douglass Notes (Newsletter); Library Aides (Research guide); New Acquisitions List; Periodical Holdings (Union list of serials)
Partic in HBCU Library Alliance; OCLC Online Computer Library Center, Inc
Open Mon-Thurs 8am-Midnight, Fri 8-5, Sat 10-7, Sun 3pm-Midnight
Departmental Libraries:
MUSIC LEARNING RESOURCES, PAC Bldg, 21853, SAN 344-2950. Tel: 410-651-2200, Ext 6570. FAX: 410-651-7688. *Dir,* John R Lamkin, II; E-mail: jrlamkin@mail.umes.edu
Partic in OCLC Online Computer Library Center, Inc
Publications: Annual Report; Douglass Notes; DOUGNET; Mini Library Guide; New Acquisitions; Serials-Documents; State Publications

RANDALLSTOWN

S NORTHWEST HOSPITAL CENTER*, Health Sciences Library, 5401 Old Court Rd, 21133. SAN 325-8815. Tel: 410-521-2200, Ext 55682. FAX: 410-496-7549. *Actg Adminr,* Darcie Cote-Rumsey; E-mail: drumsey@lifebridgehealth.org; Staff 1 (MLS 1)
Library Holdings: Bk Vols 500; Per Subs 105
Database Vendor: EBSCOhost
Restriction: Med staff only, Open to others by appt

ROCKVILLE

S AMERICAN RED CROSS HOLLAND LABORATORY*, Ann I Harnsberger Biomedical Sciences Library, 15601 Crabbs Branch Way, 20855-2743. SAN 377-1725. Tel: 301-738-0640. FAX: 301-738-0660. *Med Librn,* Shali Y Jiang; Staff 1 (Non-MLS 1)
Founded 1987
Library Holdings: Bk Vols 5,000; Per Subs 37
Automation Activity & Vendor Info: (Acquisitions) EOS International; (Cataloging) EOS International; (Circulation) EOS International; (Course Reserve) EOS International; (OPAC) EOS International; (Serials) EOS International
Wireless access
Partic in Docline; Medical Library Association (MLA); National Network of Libraries of Medicine Southeastern Atlantic Region
Restriction: Not open to pub, Staff use only

R JEWISH COMMUNITY CENTER OF GREATER WASHINGTON*, Kass Judaic Library, 6125 Montrose Rd, 20852. SAN 307-0085. Tel: 301-881-0100. FAX: 301-881-5512. Web Site: www.jccgw.org. *Coordr, Literary Prog,* Debby Goldberg; Tel: 301-348-3816, E-mail: dgoldberg@jccgw.org; Staff 21 (MLS 1, Non-MLS 20)
Founded 1970
Library Holdings: DVDs 70; Bk Vols 2,000; Per Subs 15

C JOHNS HOPKINS UNIVERSITY LIBRARIES*, Montgomery Library Resource Center, 9601 Medical Center Dr, 20850. Tel: 301-294-7030. FAX: 301-294-7032. Web Site: library.jhu.edu. *Mgr,* Sharon Morris; Tel: 301-294-7033
Founded 1988
Library Holdings: Bk Vols 3,500
Open Mon-Thurs 12-9, Fri 12-6, Sat 9-5

J MONTGOMERY COLLEGE*, 51 Mannakee St, 20850. Tel: 240-567-7101. FAX: 240-567-7141. Web Site: www.montgomerycollege.edu/library. *Dir, Col Libr & Info Serv,* Tanner Wray; E-mail: tanner.wray@montgomerycollege.edu; *Tech Serv Mgr,* Kari Schmidt; Tel: 240-567-4135, E-mail: kari.schmidt@montgomerycollege.edu
Highest Degree: Associate
Library Holdings: Bk Titles 192,384; Bk Vols 211,924; Per Subs 1,604
Automation Activity & Vendor Info: (Acquisitions) Ex Libris Group; (Cataloging) Ex Libris Group; (Circulation) Ex Libris Group; (Course Reserve) Docutek; (ILL) Clio; (OPAC) Ex Libris Group; (Serials) Ex Libris Group
Wireless access
Function: ILL available, Ref serv available
Partic in Lyrasis; Maryland Interlibrary Loan Organization; OCLC Online Computer Library Center, Inc
Special Services for the Deaf - ADA equip; Closed caption videos; Sorenson video relay syst; TTY equip
Special Services for the Blind - Accessible computers; Assistive/Adapted tech devices, equip & products; Bks on CD; Computer with voice synthesizer for visually impaired persons; Copier with enlargement capabilities; HP Scan Jet with photo-finish software; Large screen computer & software; Magnifiers; PC for handicapped; Reader equip; Screen reader software; ZoomText magnification & reading software
Open Mon-Fri 8-5
Departmental Libraries:
GERMANTOWN CAMPUS LIBRARY, 20200 Observation Dr, Germantown, 20876, SAN 321-0804. Tel: 240-567-7858. Reference Tel: 240-567-7853. Administration Tel: 240-567-7849. FAX: 240-567-7859. TDD: 301-353-1971. *Libr Mgr,* Alex Moyer; E-mail: alex.moyer@montgomerycollege.edu
Founded 1978. Enrl 4,720; Fac 73; Highest Degree: Associate
Open Mon-Thurs 8-8, Fri 8-5, Sat 9-5
ROCKVILLE CAMPUS LIBRARY, 51 Mannakee St, Macklin Tower, 20850, SAN 307-0093. Tel: 240-567-7117. Interlibrary Loan Service Tel: 240-567-7118. Reference Tel: 240-567-7130. Administration Tel: 240-567-4244. FAX: 240-567-7153. *Libr Mgr,* Del Hornbuckle; E-mail: del.hornbuckle@montgomerycollege.edu
Founded 1965. Enrl 13,965; Fac 250; Highest Degree: Associate
Open Mon-Thurs 8-8, Fri 8-5, Sat 9-5
SCHOOL OF ART & DESIGN, 7600 Takoma Ave, Takoma Park, 20912, SAN 307-0379. Tel: 240-567-5813. *Libr Mgr,* Sarah Fisher; Tel: 240-567-1544
Founded 1977
Open Mon-Fri 8-4:30
TAKOMA PARK CAMPUS LIBRARY, 7600 Takoma Ave, Takoma Park, 20912, SAN 307-0506. Tel: 240-567-1540. Reference Tel: 240-567-1536. FAX: 240-567-1550. *Libr Mgr,* Sarah Fisher; Tel: 240-567-1544
Founded 1946. Fac 125; Highest Degree: Associate
Open Mon-Thurs 8-8, Fri 8-5, Sat 9-5

GL MONTGOMERY COUNTY CIRCUIT COURT, Law Library, Judicial Ctr, 50 Maryland Ave, Ste 3420, 20850. SAN 307-0107. Tel: 240-777-9120. FAX: 240-777-9126. E-mail: lawlibrary@mcccourt.com. Web Site: www.courts.state.md.us/montgomery. *Dir,* Kathleen Martin; Tel: 240-777-9121, E-mail: kmartin@mcccourt.com; *Asst Librn,* Julia Viets; Tel: 240-777-9122. Subject Specialists: *Admin law,* Kathleen Martin; *Cataloging, Law,* Julia Viets; Staff 3 (MLS 2, Non-MLS 1)
Library Holdings: Bk Vols 80,000; Per Subs 110
Special Collections: How To Books for self-represented patrons; Maryland, DC & Virginia Legal & Federal Materials
Subject Interests: Continuing educ, Legal
Automation Activity & Vendor Info: (Cataloging) EOS International; (OPAC) EOS International
Database Vendor: HeinOnline, LexisNexis, Westlaw
Wireless access
Function: ILL available
Open Mon-Fri 8-5:30
Restriction: Open to pub for ref only

S MONTGOMERY COUNTY HISTORICAL SOCIETY LIBRARY*, Jane C Sween Library, 111 W Montgomery Ave, 20850. SAN 326-0402. Tel: 301-340-2974. FAX: 301-340-2871. E-mail: info@montgomeryhistory.org. Web Site: www.montgomeryhistory.org. *Librn,* Patricia A Andersen; E-mail: pandersen@montgomeryhistory.org; *Archivist,* Linda M Kennedy; Staff 10 (MLS 2, Non-MLS 8)
Founded 1965

Library Holdings: Bk Titles 4,100; Per Subs 10
Special Collections: Montgomery Mutual Insurance Papers. Oral History
Subject Interests: Genealogy, Local hist, Local newsp, Manuscripts
Publications: Montgomery County Story (Quarterly)
Open Tues-Sat 10-4
Restriction: Open to pub for ref only

P MONTGOMERY COUNTY PUBLIC LIBRARIES, Central Offices, 21 Maryland Ave, Ste 310, 20850. SAN 344-2985. Tel: 240-777-0002. Interlibrary Loan Service Tel: 240-777-0063. Interlibrary Loan Service FAX: 240-777-0064. Web Site: www.montgomerycountymd.gov/library. *Dir of Libr,* B Parker Hamilton; E-mail: parker.hamilton@montgomerycountymd.gov; *Pub Serv Adminr, Strategic Mgt, Fac & Cap Projects,* Rita Gale; Fax: 240-777-0008, E-mail: rita.gale@montgomerycountymd.gov; *Chief, Coll & Tech Mgt,* Mary Louise Daneri; Tel: 240-777-0031, E-mail: marylouise.daneri@montgomerycountymd.gov; *Bus & Finance Mgr,* Eric Carzon; Tel: 240-777-0048, Fax: 240-777-0047, E-mail: eric.carzon@montgomerycountymd.gov; *Human Res Mgr,* Carol Legarreta; Tel: 240-777-0030, E-mail: carol.legarreta@montgomerycountymd.org
Founded 1951
Special Collections: Business Resource Center (Rockville); Health Information Center (Wheaton). Oral History; US Document Depository
Subject Interests: Govt
Automation Activity & Vendor Info: (Cataloging) SirsiDynix
Partic in Md State Libr Network; OCLC Online Computer Library Center, Inc
Special Services for the Deaf - TTY equip
Special Services for the Blind - Newsline for the Blind; SNL for registered users
Friends of the Library Group

Branches: 22

ASPEN HILL LIBRARY, 4407 Aspen Hill Rd, 20853-2899, SAN 344-3019. Tel: 240-773-9410. FAX: 301-871-0443. TDD: 301-871-2097. *Mgr,* Nancy Savas; Tel: 240-773-9401, E-mail: nancy.savas@montgomerycountymd.gov
Special Collections: Foreign Language (Spanish) Coll; Literacy Coll
Special Services for the Deaf - TTY equip
Special Services for the Blind - Closed circuit TV; Computer with voice synthesizer for visually impaired persons; Copier with enlargement capabilities; Large print bks; Magnifiers; Screen enlargement software for people with visual disabilities
Friends of the Library Group

BETHESDA LIBRARY, 7400 Arlington Rd, Bethesda, 20814, SAN 344-3043. Tel: 240-777-0970. FAX: 301-657-0841. TDD: 301-657-0840. *Br Mgr,* Kay Bowman; Tel: 240-773-0934, E-mail: kay.bowman@montgomerycountymd.gov
Circ 550,000
Special Services for the Deaf - TTY equip
Friends of the Library Group

CHEVY CHASE LIBRARY, 8005 Connecticut Ave, Chevy Chase, 20815-5997, SAN 344-3078. Tel: 240-773-9590. TDD: 301-657-0830. *Mgr,* Barbara McClayton; Staff 16 (MLS 7, Non-MLS 9)
Special Collections: Glass Coll
Function: Wheelchair accessible
Special Services for the Deaf - TTY equip
Special Services for the Blind - Computer with voice synthesizer for visually impaired persons; Copier with enlargement capabilities; Large print bks; Screen enlargement software for people with visual disabilities
Open Mon & Wed 1-8, Tues & Thurs-Sat 10-6
Friends of the Library Group

DAMASCUS LIBRARY, 9701 Main St, Damascus, 20872, SAN 344-3108. Tel: 240-773-9444. TDD: 301-253-0148. *Mgr,* Karen Miller; Tel: 240-773-9440, E-mail: karen.miller@montgomerycountymd.gov; Staff 11.5 (MLS 4, Non-MLS 7.5)
Special Collections: Damascus Local History
Special Services for the Deaf - Video & TTY relay via computer
Special Services for the Blind - Audio mat; Computer with voice synthesizer for visually impaired persons; Copier with enlargement capabilities; Large print bks; Magnifiers; Screen enlargement software for people with visual disabilities
Open Mon & Wed 1-8, Tues & Thurs-Sat 10-6
Friends of the Library Group

DAVIS LIBRARY, 6400 Democracy Blvd, Bethesda, 20817-1638, SAN 344-3132. Tel: 240-777-0922. FAX: 301-564-5055. TDD: 301-897-2203. *Br Mgr,* Joseph Eagan
Founded 1964
Special Services for the Deaf - TTY equip
Special Services for the Blind - Audio mat; Computer with voice synthesizer for visually impaired persons; Copier with enlargement capabilities; Large print bks; Screen enlargement software for people with visual disabilities
Open Mon & Tues 1-8, Wed & Thurs 10-8, Fri & Sat 10-6
Friends of the Library Group

GAITHERSBURG INTERIM LIBRARY, Lakeforest Mall, 701 Russell Ave D201, Gaithersburg, 20879, SAN 344-3191. Tel: 240-773-9490. TDD: 301-840-2641. *Mgr,* Kay Bowman; Tel: 240-773-9494, E-mail: kay.bowman@montgomerycountymd.gov
Special Collections: Foreign Language Coll (Chinese, French, German, Korean, Spanish, Vietnamese); Literacy Coll
Special Services for the Deaf - TTY equip
Special Services for the Blind - Computer with voice synthesizer for visually impaired persons; Copier with enlargement capabilities; Large print bks; Magnifiers; Screen enlargement software for people with visual disabilities
Friends of the Library Group

GERMANTOWN LIBRARY, 19840 Century Blvd, Germantown, 20874, SAN 328-9966. Tel: 240-777-0110. FAX: 240-777-0129. TDD: 240-777-0901. E-mail: comments@montgomerycountymd.gov. *Mgr,* Karen Miller; Tel: 240-773-0126, E-mail: Karen.miller@montgomerycountymd.gov
Special Collections: Foreign Language (Spanish) Coll
Special Services for the Deaf - TTY equip
Special Services for the Blind - Audio mat; Computer with voice synthesizer for visually impaired persons; Copier with enlargement capabilities; Large print bks; Magnifiers; Screen enlargement software for people with visual disabilities
Friends of the Library Group

KENSINGTON PARK LIBRARY, 4201 Knowles Ave, Kensington, 20895-2408, SAN 344-3221. Tel: 240-773-9510. FAX: 301-897-2238. TDD: 301-897-2250. *Mgr,* Kathie Meizner; Tel: 240-773-9505, E-mail: kathie.meizner@montgomerycountymd.gov; Staff 7 (MLS 4, Non-MLS 3)
Special Services for the Deaf - TTY equip
Special Services for the Blind - Audio mat; Computer with voice synthesizer for visually impaired persons; Copier with enlargement capabilities; Large print bks; Screen enlargement software for people with visual disabilities

LITTLE FALLS LIBRARY, 5501 Massachusetts Ave, Bethesda, 20816, SAN 344-3256. Tel: 240-773-9520. FAX: 301-320-0164. TDD: 301-320-8813. *Br Mgr,* Ken Lewis; Tel: 240-773-9526, E-mail: kenneth.lewis@montgomerycountymd.gov
Special Services for the Deaf - TTY equip
Special Services for the Blind - Computer with voice synthesizer for visually impaired persons; Copier with enlargement capabilities; Large print bks; Magnifiers; Screen enlargement software for people with visual disabilities
Friends of the Library Group

LONG BRANCH, 8800 Garland Ave, Silver Spring, 20901. Tel: 240-777-0910. *Br Mgr,* Ed Trever

MONTGOMERY COUNTY CORRECTIONAL FACILITY, 22880 Whelan Lane, Boyds, 20841, SAN 344-3000. Tel: 240-773-9914. FAX: 240-773-9939. *Librn,* Andrea Castrogiovanni; E-mail: andrea.castrogiovanni@montgomerycountymd.gov
Database Vendor: Westlaw

NOYES CHILDREN'S LIBRARY, 10237 Carroll Pl, Kensington, 20895-3361, SAN 344-3310. Tel: 240-773-9575. Administration Tel: 301-929-5533. FAX: 301-929-5470. *Librn,* Susan Modak; *Mgr,* Kathie Meizner
Special Services for the Blind - Computer with voice synthesizer for visually impaired persons; Screen enlargement software for people with visual disabilities

OLNEY LIBRARY, 3500 Olney-Laytonsville Rd, Olney, 20832-1798, SAN 344-340X. Tel: 240-773-9545, 301-774-7260 TTY. *Actg Br Mgr,* Tina Rawhouser
Special Services for the Deaf - TTY equip
Special Services for the Blind - Computer with voice synthesizer for visually impaired persons; Copier with enlargement capabilities; Large print bks; Screen enlargement software for people with visual disabilities

POOLESVILLE LIBRARY, 19633 Fisher Ave, Poolesville, 20837-2071, SAN 344-3493. Tel: 240-773-9550. TDD: 301-972-7825. *Mgr,* Steve Warrick; Tel: 240-773-9552, E-mail: steven.warrick@montgomerycountymd.gov
Special Services for the Deaf - TTY equip
Special Services for the Blind - Computer with voice synthesizer for visually impaired persons; Copier with enlargement capabilities; Large print bks; Screen enlargement software for people with visual disabilities

POTOMAC LIBRARY, 10101 Glenolden Dr, Potomac, 20854-5052, SAN 344-3345. Tel: 240-777-0690. FAX: 301-983-4479. TDD: 301-765-4083. *Mgr,* Lindsey Hundt; E-mail: lindsey.hundt@montgomerycountymd.gov
Special Collections: Chinese Language Coll
Special Services for the Deaf - TTY equip
Special Services for the Blind - Audio mat; Computer with voice synthesizer for visually impaired persons; Copier with enlargement capabilities; Large print bks; Screen enlargement software for people with visual disabilities
Friends of the Library Group

MARILYN J PRAISNER BRANCH, 14910 Old Columbia Pike, Burtonsville, 20866, SAN 374-7964. Tel: 240-773-9430. FAX: 301-421-5407. *Mgr,* James Stewart; E-mail: james.stewart@montgomerycountymd.gov
Special Collections: Foreign Language (Chinese & Korean Coll)
Special Services for the Deaf - TTY equip
Special Services for the Blind - Audio mat; Computer with voice synthesizer for visually impaired persons; Copier with enlargement capabilities; Large print bks; Screen enlargement software for people with visual disabilities
Friends of the Library Group

QUINCE ORCHARD LIBRARY, 15831 Quince Orchard Rd, Gaithersburg, 20878. Tel: 240-777-0200. FAX: 240-777-0202. TDD: 240-777-0903. *Mgr,* Ann Stillman; Tel: 240-777-0212, E-mail: ann.stillman@montgomerycountymd.gov
Special Collections: Foreign Language (Chinese) Coll
Special Services for the Deaf - TTY equip
Special Services for the Blind - Audio mat; Computer with voice synthesizer for visually impaired persons; Copier with enlargement capabilities; Large print bks; Screen enlargement software for people with visual disabilities
Open Mon-Thurs 9-9, Fri & Sat 10-6

ROCKVILLE LIBRARY, 21 Maryland Ave, 20850-2371, SAN 344-337X. Tel: 240-777-0140. Reference Tel: 240-777-0001. FAX: 240-777-0157. TDD: 240-777-0902. *Mgr,* Nancy Benner; E-mail: nancy.benner@montgomerycountymd.gov
Special Collections: Business Resource Center (Business Counselling); Children's Resource Center; County Government Archives; Foreign Language Coll (Chinese, Korean & Vietnamese); Local. US Document Depository
Special Services for the Deaf - TTY equip
Special Services for the Blind - Computer with voice synthesizer for visually impaired persons; Copier with enlargement capabilities; Large print bks; Screen enlargement software for people with visual disabilities
Friends of the Library Group

SILVER SPRING LIBRARY, 8901 Colesville Rd, Silver Spring, 20910-4339, SAN 344-3434. Tel: 240-773-9420. TDD: 301-565-7505. *Mgr,* Fran Ware; E-mail: fran.ware@montgomerycountymd.gov
Special Collections: Chinese Language Coll; Literacy Coll; Spanish Language Coll
Special Services for the Deaf - TTY equip
Special Services for the Blind - Computer with voice synthesizer for visually impaired persons; Copier with enlargement capabilities; Large print bks; Screen enlargement software for people with visual disabilities
Friends of the Library Group

TWINBROOK LIBRARY, 202 Meadow Hall Dr, 20851-1551, SAN 344-3469. Tel: 240-777-0240. FAX: 240-777-0258. TDD: 240-777-0904. *Libr Mgr,* Will Wheeler; Tel: 240-777-0249, E-mail: william.wheeler@montgomerycountymd.gov
Special Collections: Foreign Language Coll (Chinese, Korean, Spanish, Vietnamese)
Special Services for the Deaf - TTY equip
Special Services for the Blind - Computer with voice synthesizer for visually impaired persons; Copier with enlargement capabilities; Large print bks; Screen enlargement software for people with visual disabilities

WHEATON LIBRARY, 11701 Georgia Ave, Wheaton, 20902-1997, SAN 344-3523. Tel: 240-777-0678. FAX: 301-929-5525. TDD: 301-929-5524. *Mgr,* Dianne Whitaker; Tel: 240-777-0686, E-mail: dianne.whitaker@montgomerycountymd.gov
Special Collections: Foreign Language (Chinese, French, German, Korean, Spanish & Vietnamese) Coll; Health Information Center; Literacy Coll; Science & Technology
Special Services for the Deaf - TTY equip
Special Services for the Blind - Audio mat; Closed circuit TV; Computer with voice synthesizer for visually impaired persons; Copier with enlargement capabilities; Large print bks; Magnifiers; Screen enlargement software for people with visual disabilities

WHITE OAK LIBRARY, 11701 New Hampshire Ave, Silver Spring, 20904-2898, SAN 344-3558. Tel: 240-773-9565. FAX: 301-989-1921. TDD: 301-622-6596. *Mgr,* Jan Baird-Adams; Tel: 240-777-9558, E-mail: jan.baird-adams@montgomerycountymd.gov
Special Collections: Foreign Language (Spanish) Coll; Literacy Coll
Special Services for the Deaf - TTY equip
Special Services for the Blind - Computer with voice synthesizer for visually impaired persons; Copier with enlargement capabilities; Large print bks; Magnifiers; Screen enlargement software for people with visual disabilities
Friends of the Library Group

M SHADY GROVE ADVENTIST HOSPITAL*, Medical Library, 9901 Medical Center Dr, 20850. SAN 377-4589. Tel: 240-826-6101. FAX: 240-826-6500. Web Site: extranetapps.adventisthealthcare.com/librarysgah. *Librn,* Carol Chandler; E-mail: cchandle@ahm.com; Staff 1 (MLS 1)
Library Holdings: e-books 80; e-journals 170; Bk Titles 1,200; Per Subs 230
Automation Activity & Vendor Info: (Acquisitions) CyberTools for Libraries; (Cataloging) CyberTools for Libraries; (Circulation) CyberTools for Libraries; (OPAC) CyberTools for Libraries; (Serials) CyberTools for Libraries
Database Vendor: OVID Technologies
Wireless access
Function: ILL available
Open Mon-Thurs 8:30-5, Fri 8:30-4:30

UNITED STATES DEPARTMENT OF HEALTH & HUMAN SERVICES

GM NATIONAL CENTER FOR HEALTH STATISTICS STAFF RESEARCH LIBRARY*, 3311 Toledo Rd, Rm 2403, Hyattsville, 20782, SAN 306-9788. Tel: 301-458-4775. FAX: 301-458-4019. Web Site: www.library.psc.gov. *ILL,* Charlene Brock; *Ref,* Harnethia Cousar; Staff 3 (MLS 1, Non-MLS 2)
Founded 1977
Library Holdings: Bk Vols 1,500; Per Subs 120
Subject Interests: Epidemiology, Health statistics, Pub health
Automation Activity & Vendor Info: (Acquisitions) EBSCO Online; (Circulation) EBSCO Online; (OPAC) EBSCO Online; (Serials) EBSCO Online
Database Vendor: OVID Technologies
Function: Res libr
Partic in Dialog Corp; OCLC Online Computer Library Center, Inc
Publications: Guide to Library Resources; Recent Acquisitions List
Open Mon-Fri 9-5
Restriction: Pub use on premises

GM FDA LIBRARY, WO2, Rm 3302, 10903 New Hampshire Ave, Silver Spring, 20993, SAN 344-3760. Reference Tel: 301-796-2039. Interlibrary Loan Service FAX: 301-796-9852. Reference FAX: 301-796-9756. *Dir,* Kathrin L McConnell; Tel: 301-796-2387, E-mail: kathrin.mcconnell@fda.hhs.gov; *Div Dir, Pub Serv,* Position Currently Open; *Div Dir, Tech Serv,* Colleen Pritchard; Tel: 301-796-2373, E-mail: colleen.pritchard@fda.hhs.gov; Staff 23 (MLS 17, Non-MLS 6)
Founded 1948
Library Holdings: e-books 1,200; e-journals 3,000; Bk Vols 10,000; Per Subs 850
Special Collections: Adverse Drug Effects; FDA Publications
Subject Interests: Biologics, Chem, Drug laws & legislation, Drug safety, Food safety, Med device, Nutrition, Pharm, Pharmacology, Pub health, Radiology, Toxicology, Veterinary med
Restriction: Non-circulating to the pub, Open to mil & govt employees only, Open to others by appt, Photo ID required for access, Pub by appt only

UNITED STATES NUCLEAR REGULATORY COMMISSION

G LAW LIBRARY*, 11555 Rockville Pike, 20852. (Mail add: MS 0-15D21, Washington, 20555), SAN 377-4260. Tel: 301-415-1526. FAX: 301-415-3725. *Law Librn,* Bertus Lee; E-mail: bert.lee@nrc.gov; *Legis Spec,* Anne Frost; Tel: 301-415-1613, E-mail: Anne.Frost@nrc.gov.
Subject Specialists: *Admin, Environ law, Nuclear energy,* Bertus Lee
Library Holdings: Bk Vols 5,000; Per Subs 50
Function: ILL available
Restriction: Staff use only

G TECHNICAL LIBRARY*, 11545 Rockville Pike, T2C8, 20852-2738, SAN 320-6300. Tel: 301-415-6239, 301-415-7204. FAX: 301-415-5365. E-mail: library.resource@nrc.gov. *Chief, User Serv Br,* Anna Therese McGowan; E-mail: anna.mcgowan@nrc.gov; Staff 5 (MLS 3, Non-MLS 2)
Founded 1975
Library Holdings: Bk Titles 25,000; Per Subs 700
Special Collections: International Atomic Energy Agency Publications
Subject Interests: Energy, Nuclear sci, Radiation
Partic in Fedlink; OCLC Online Computer Library Center, Inc
Restriction: Open to pub by appt only
Friends of the Library Group

S WESTAT, INC LIBRARY*, 1650 Research Blvd, 20850. SAN 307-0190. Tel: 301-251-1500. FAX: 301-294-2034. *Head Librn,* Maureen Stawick; *Librn,* Ken Vaughan; *Librn,* Rebekah Zanditon
Library Holdings: Bk Vols 10,000; Per Subs 250
Subject Interests: Econ, Educ, Health sci, Labor, Mkt, Psychol, Soc sci & issues, Statistics
Open Mon-Fri 8:30-5

SAINT MARY'S CITY

S HISTORIC SAINT MARY'S CITY*, Research Library, 18401 Rosecroft Rd, 20686. (Mail add: PO Box 39, 20686-0039), SAN 329-3920. Tel: 240-895-4974. FAX: 240-895-4968. Web Site: www.saintmaryscity.org. *Dir,* Henry Miller; *Res,* Patricia Dance; E-mail: pridance@smcm.edu
Library Holdings: Bk Vols 375; Per Subs 10
Restriction: Open by appt only

C SAINT MARY'S COLLEGE OF MARYLAND LIBRARY, 18952 E Fisher Rd, 20686-3001. SAN 307-0204. Tel: 240-895-4256. Circulation Tel: 240-895-4264. Interlibrary Loan Service Tel: 240-895-4437. Reference Tel: 240-895-4272. FAX: 240-895-4914. Circulation FAX: 240-895-4400. Interlibrary Loan Service FAX: 240-895-4492. E-mail: libfeedback@smcm.edu. Web Site: www.smcm.edu/library. *Interim Dir,* Katherine H Ryner; Tel: 240-895-4260, E-mail: khryner@smcm.edu; *Col Archivist/Ref Librn,* Kent D Randell; Tel: 240-895-4196, E-mail: kdrandell@smcm.edu; *Circ,* Linda A Russell; E-mail: larussell@smcm.edu; *ILL,* Brenda Rodgers; E-mail: blrodgers@smcm.edu; *Patron Serv,* Conrad A Helms; Tel: 240-895-3214, E-mail: cahelms@smcm.edu; *Ref,* Veronica I Arellano Douglas; Tel: 240-895-4265, E-mail: viarellano@smcm.edu; *Ref,* Alana M Verminski; Tel: 240-895-4268, E-mail: amverminski@smcm.edu; *Ref/Instruction/Outreach,* Pamela E Mann; Tel: 240-895-4285, E-mail: pemann@smcm.edu. Subject Specialists: *Archives, Hist, Maryland,* Kent D Randell; *Anthrop, Polit sci, Psychol,* Veronica I Arellano Douglas; *Environ studies, Math, Sciences,* Alana M Verminski; *Art, English, Media studies,* Pamela E Mann; Staff 15 (MLS 6, Non-MLS 9)
Founded 1840. Enrl 1,878; Fac 142; Highest Degree: Master
Jul 2012-Jun 2013. Mats Exp $714,086, Books $125,380, AV Mat $16,250, Electronic Ref Mat (Incl. Access Fees) $225,337. Sal $934,238 (Prof $719,870)
Library Holdings: CDs 1,430; DVDs 3,000; Bk Titles 218,000
Special Collections: College Archives; Maryland History (especially Saint Mary's County). Oral History
Automation Activity & Vendor Info: (Acquisitions) Ex Libris Group; (Cataloging) Ex Libris Group; (Circulation) Ex Libris Group; (Course Reserve) Ex Libris Group; (ILL) OCLC ILLiad; (Media Booking) Ex Libris Group; (OPAC) Ex Libris Group; (Serials) Ex Libris Group
Database Vendor: ACM (Association for Computing Machinery), American Chemical Society, American Mathematical Society, American Psychological Association (APA), Annual Reviews, ARTstor, Baker & Taylor, BioOne, Brodart, Cambridge Scientific Abstracts, Checkpoint Systems, Inc, CredoReference, ebrary, EBSCO Discovery Service, EBSCOhost, Elsevier, Ex Libris Group, Gale Cengage Learning, JSTOR, LexisNexis, Medline, Modern Language Association, OCLC FirstSearch, OCLC WorldShare Interlibrary Loan, Paratext, Project MUSE, ProQuest, Sage, Springshare, LLC, YBP Library Services
Wireless access
Function: 24/7 Electronic res, 24/7 Online cat, Archival coll, Audio & video playback equip for onsite use, AV serv, Computers for patron use, Copy machines, Doc delivery serv, e-mail & chat, E-Reserves, Electronic databases & coll, eReaders, Free DVD rentals, Handicapped accessible, ILL available, Magazines, Microfiche/film & reading machines, Music CDs, Online cat, Online ref, Photocopying/Printing, Pub access computers, Ref serv available, Scanner, Study rm, VHS videos
Partic in Lyrasis; OCLC Online Computer Library Center, Inc; University System of Maryland & Affiliated Institutions (USMAI)
Open Mon-Wed 8am-1am, Thurs 8am-Midnight, Fri 8am-9pm, Sat 9-9, Sun 11am-1am

SAINT MICHAELS

S CHESAPEAKE BAY MARITIME MUSEUM LIBRARY, 213 N Talbot St, 21663. (Mail add: PO Box 636, 21663-0636), SAN 307-0212. Tel: 410-745-2916. FAX: 410-745-6088. E-mail: library@cbmm.org. Web Site: www.cbmm.org. *Chief Curator,* Pete Lesher; Tel: 410-745-4971, E-mail: plesher@cbmm.org; *Coll Mgr,* Lynne Phillips; Tel: 410-745-4972, E-mail: lphillips@cbmm.org; Staff 3 (Non-MLS 3)
Founded 1967
Library Holdings: Bk Vols 9,800; Per Subs 17
Special Collections: Chesapeake Bay (Constance Stuart Larrabee Coll), photog; Howard I Chapelle Papers; Manuscript Coll, 1800-; Photograph Coll, 1880-; Ships Plans (Chesapeake Indigenous Watercraft, circa 1880-). Oral History
Subject Interests: Hist, Maritime hist, Maryland, Va
Restriction: Open by appt only

SALISBURY

M PENINSULA REGIONAL MEDICAL CENTER, Charles Long-Ulman Health Sciences Library, 100 E Carroll St, 21801. SAN 329-2177. Tel: 410-543-7094. FAX: 410-543-7156. *Librn,* Valerie Ruark; E-mail: valerie.ruark@peninsula.org; Staff 1 (MLS 1)
Library Holdings: Bk Vols 1,750; Per Subs 100
Subject Interests: Med, Nursing
Wireless access

C SALISBURY UNIVERSITY, Blackwell Library, 1101 Camden Ave, 21801-6863. SAN 307-0239. Tel: 410-543-6130. Interlibrary Loan Service Tel: 410-543-6077. Reference Tel: 410-548-5988. FAX: 410-543-6203. Web Site: www.salisbury.edu/library. *Dean of Libr, Instrul Res,* Dr Beatriz B Hardy; *Assoc Dean, Dir, Tech Serv,* Martha Zimmerman; *Dir, Pub Serv,* Moushumi Chakraborty; *Bus Instrul Librn,* Sarah Loudenslager; *Res & Instruction Librn,* Angeline Prichard; *Res & Instruction Librn,* Gaylord Robb; *Res & Instruction Librn/Chair, Ref,* Susan Brazer; *Scholarly Communications Librn,* Laura Hanscom; *Tech Librn,* Christopher Woodall; *Coordr, Curric Res Ctr,* Stephen Ford; *Info Literacy/Instruction Coordr,* James Parrigin; *Cat,* Audrey Schadt; Staff 22 (MLS 14, Non-MLS 8)
Founded 1925. Enrl 8,643; Fac 662; Highest Degree: Doctorate
Jul 2013-Jun 2014 Income $3,034,909. Mats Exp $937,903, Books $87,256, Per/Ser (Incl. Access Fees) $553,879, Micro $6,247, Electronic Ref Mat (Incl. Access Fees) $282,131, Presv $8,390. Sal $1,153,688 (Prof $794,267)
Library Holdings: CDs 143; DVDs 807; Microforms 757,125; Bk Vols 226,417; Per Subs 873
Special Collections: Civil War (Les Callette Memorial Coll); Movie Press Kits; Special Collections Room, bks, press kits; Teacher Education (Educational Resources Coll), AV, bks, micro. State Document Depository; US Document Depository
Automation Activity & Vendor Info: (Acquisitions) Ex Libris Group; (Cataloging) Ex Libris Group; (Circulation) Ex Libris Group; (Course Reserve) Ex Libris Group; (ILL) OCLC; (OPAC) Ex Libris Group; (Serials) Ex Libris Group
Database Vendor: Alexander Street Press, Annual Reviews, ARTstor, Cambridge Scientific Abstracts, CIOS (Communication Institute for Online Scholarship), CQ Press, EBSCOhost, Elsevier MDL, JSTOR, OCLC FirstSearch, ProQuest
Wireless access
Partic in Lyrasis; Maryland Interlibrary Loan Organization; OCLC Online Computer Library Center, Inc; Univ Syst of Md

P WICOMICO PUBLIC LIBRARY, 122 S Division St, 21801. SAN 307-0247. Tel: 410-749-3612. FAX: 410-548-2968. E-mail: askus@wicomico.org. Web Site: www.wicomicolibrary.org. *Exec Dir,* Andrea Berstler; Tel: 410-749-3612, Ext 113, E-mail: aberstler@wicomico.org; *Dir, Prog & Serv,* Linda Parry; Tel: 410-749-3612, Ext 140, E-mail: lparry@wicomico.org; *Dir, Operations,* Jennifer Neumyer; Tel: 410-749-3612, Ext 116, E-mail: jneumyer@wicomico.org; *Circ Mgr,* Bernadette Cannady; Tel: 410-749-3612, Ext 133, E-mail: bcannady@wicomico.org; *Tech Serv Mgr,* Charlotte Hotton; Tel: 410-749-3612, Ext 118, E-mail: chotton@wicomico.org; Staff 9 (MLS 4, Non-MLS 5)
Founded 1927. Pop 91,987
Library Holdings: Audiobooks 8,217; DVDs 13,134; e-books 124; Bk Vols 138,911; Per Subs 217
Automation Activity & Vendor Info: (Acquisitions) Innovative Interfaces, Inc; (Cataloging) Innovative Interfaces, Inc; (Circulation) Innovative Interfaces, Inc; (OPAC) Innovative Interfaces, Inc
Database Vendor: EBSCOhost, Gale Cengage Learning, Newsbank, ProQuest
Wireless access
Function: Audiobks via web, Bks on CD, CD-ROM, Children's prog, Citizenship assistance, Computer training, Computers for patron use, Copy machines, e-mail & chat, Electronic databases & coll, Exhibits, Free DVD rentals, ILL available, Mail & tel request accepted, Music CDs, Online cat, Online ref, Outreach serv, Outside serv via phone, mail, e-mail & web, OverDrive digital audio bks, Photocopying/Printing, Preschool outreach, Prog for adults, Prog for children & young adult, Pub access computers, Ref & res, Ref serv in person, Story hour, Summer reading prog, Tax forms, Teen prog, Web-catalog, Wheelchair accessible
Partic in Eastern Shore Regional Library; Lower Shore Library Consortium
Special Services for the Deaf - Sign lang interpreter upon request for prog; Video & TTY relay via computer
Special Services for the Blind - Bks on CD; Computer with voice synthesizer for visually impaired persons; Large print bks
Open Mon, Wed, Fri & Sat 10-5, Tues & Thurs 10-8, Sun 1-5
Friends of the Library Group
Branches: 2
CENTRE BRANCH, N Salisbury Blvd, 21801. Tel: 410-546-5397. *Outreach Serv Librn,* Linda Parry; E-mail: lparry@wicomico.org
Library Holdings: Audiobooks 106; DVDs 55; Bk Vols 3,898; Per Subs 8
Automation Activity & Vendor Info: (Circulation) Innovative Interfaces, Inc; (OPAC) Innovative Interfaces, Inc - Millenium
Open Mon & Wed 10-9, Fri & Sat 10-6, Sun 12-6
PITTSVILLE BRANCH, 34372 Old Ocean City Rd, Pittsville, 21850-2008. Tel: 410-835-2353. *Outreach Librn,* Linda Parry
Library Holdings: Bk Titles 1,000
Open Mon & Wed 10-6, Tues & Thurs 2-8, Sat 10-4
Bookmobiles: 1. Bkmobile Mgr, Barbara Prevento

E WOR-WIC COMMUNITY COLLEGE, Library Services, 32000 Campus Dr, 21804. Tel: 410-334-2883, 410-334-2884. FAX: 410-334-2956. Web Site: www.worwic.edu/students/learningresources/libraryresources.aspx. *Dir,* Cheryl Michael; E-mail: cmichael@worwic.edu; Staff 6 (MLS 3, Non-MLS 3)
Founded 1994. Highest Degree: Associate
Library Holdings: Electronic Media & Resources 72
Wireless access

Function: For res purposes, Newsp ref libr, Online searches, Photocopying/Printing, Ref serv available, Res libr, Telephone ref
Restriction: Open to students, fac & staff, Pub use on premises

SANDY SPRING

S SANDY SPRING MUSEUM LIBRARY*, 17901 Bentley Rd, 20860. SAN 375-6807. Tel: 301-774-0022. FAX: 301 774-8149. E-mail: contactus@sandyspringmuseum.org. Web Site: www.sandyspringmuseum.org. *Exec Dir,* Dr Sharon Ann Holt
Library Holdings: Bk Titles 150; Bk Vols 400
Special Collections: Local African American History; Underground Railroad. Oral History
Subject Interests: Genealogy, Quakers
Wireless access
Publications: Sandy Spring Legacy, 1999
Open Mon, Wed & Thurs 9-4, Sat & Sun 12-4

SEVERNA PARK

R WOODS MEMORIAL PRESBYTERIAN CHURCH LIBRARY*, 611 Baltimore-Annapolis Blvd, 21146. SAN 307-0255. Tel: 410-647-2550. FAX: 410-647-2781. Web Site: woodschurch.com. *Dir,* Elizabeth McLean
Library Holdings: Bk Vols 2,400
Subject Interests: Children's lit, Marriage, Relig, Women's studies
Open Mon-Fri 9am-9:30pm

SHARPSBURG

S NATIONAL PARK SERVICE*, Antietam National Battlefield Library, PO Box 158, 21782. SAN 307-0263. Tel: 301-432-8674. FAX: 301-432-4590. Web Site: www.nps.gov/antietam. *Librn,* Ted Alexander; E-mail: ted_alexander@nps.gov
Founded 1940
Library Holdings: Bk Titles 3,500
Special Collections: Battle of Antietam Coll; Civil War Regimental Histories; Civil War Soldiers' Letters & Diaries; Info on Civil War Artillery; National Tribune on microfilm; Park History; Research Reports; War of the Rebellion, Official Records of the Union & Confederate Armies
Subject Interests: Civil War, Local hist
Restriction: Open by appt only

SILVER SPRING

S AMERICAN INSTITUTES FOR RESEARCH LIBRARY*, 10720 Columbia Pike, Ste 500, 20901. Tel: 301-592-3347. FAX: 301-592-8602. *Librn,* Liz Scalia; E-mail: escalia@air.org; Staff 1 (MLS 1)
Subject Interests: Educ, Health, Psychol, Soc sci
Restriction: Co libr, Employee & client use only, Not open to pub

S RACHEL CARSON COUNCIL, INC LIBRARY*, PO Box 10779, 20914-0779. SAN 327-0467. Tel: 301-593-7507. FAX: 301-593-7508. E-mail: rccouncil@aol.com. Web Site: www.rachelcarsoncouncil.org. *Pres,* Dr Diana Post
Founded 1965
Library Holdings: Bk Vols 1,500; Per Subs 12
Special Collections: Rachel Carson Coll
Subject Interests: Low-risk pest mgt, Pesticides, Rachel Carson
Restriction: Open by appt only

SR GENERAL CONFERENCE OF SEVENTH-DAY ADVENTISTS*, Rebok Memorial Library, 12501 Old Columbia Pike, 20904. SAN 325-5115. Tel: 301-680-6495. FAX: 301-680-6090. *Dir,* Alan S Hecht; E-mail: hechta@gc.adventist.org
Founded 1983
Library Holdings: Bk Vols 14,000
Special Collections: Religion (Seventh-Day Adventists & Other Religions)
Automation Activity & Vendor Info: (Cataloging) Follett Software; (OPAC) Follett Software
Database Vendor: Dialog, OCLC FirstSearch
Publications: Check It Out (Newsletter)
Restriction: Open by appt only

M HOLY CROSS HOSPITAL OF SILVER SPRING*, Medical Library, 1500 Forest Glen Rd, 20910. SAN 325-8734. Tel: 301-754-7245. FAX: 301-754-7247. *Librn,* Cynthia Phyillaier
Library Holdings: Bk Vols 1,000; Per Subs 185
Database Vendor: OVID Technologies
Restriction: Med staff only

G NATIONAL GEODETIC SURVEY LIBRARY*, 1315 East West Hwy, N/NGS43, SSMC III, No 8200, 20910. SAN 328-1876. Tel: 301-713-3249, Ext 130. FAX: 301-713-4327. *Chief Librn,* Clyde Dean
Founded 1970
Library Holdings: Bk Vols 500; Per Subs 1,500
Special Collections: 3500 Technical Papers
Subject Interests: Geodesy
Automation Activity & Vendor Info: (Cataloging) TLC (The Library Corporation); (Circulation) TLC (The Library Corporation); (ILL) TLC (The Library Corporation)
Publications: C & GS Special Publication; FGCC Publication; NOAA Manual; NOAA Professional Paper; NOAA Technical Memorandum; NOAA Technical Report
Restriction: Open by appt only

G NATIONAL OCEANIC & ATMOSPHERIC ADMINISTRATION*, Library & Information Services Division, 1315 East West Hwy, 2nd Flr, 20910. SAN 344-3582. Tel: 301-713-2600, Ext 157. Interlibrary Loan Service Tel: 301-713-2607, Ext 113. FAX: 301-713-4598. Interlibrary Loan Service FAX: 301-713-4599. E-mail: library.reference@noaa.gov. Web Site: www.lib.noaa.gov. *Dir, Libr & Info Serv,* Neal Kaske; *Coll Develop,* Steven Quillen; *ILL,* Sarah Davis
Founded 1809
Library Holdings: Bk Vols 1,500,000
Special Collections: Climatology (Daily Weather Maps), bks, flm; Coast & Geodetic Survey Coll; Marine Fisheries Technical Reports, micro. US Document Depository
Subject Interests: Atmospheric sci, Climatology, Ecosystems, Marine biol, Nautical charting, Ocean eng, Oceanography, Rare bks
Automation Activity & Vendor Info: (Cataloging) SirsiDynix; (Circulation) SirsiDynix; (OPAC) SirsiDynix; (Serials) SirsiDynix
Partic in Dialog Corp; OCLC Online Computer Library Center, Inc
Open Mon-Fri 9-4
Friends of the Library Group

SR PRESBYTERIAN CHURCH OF THE ATONEMENT LIBRARY*, 10613 Georgia Ave, 20902. SAN 327-0505. Tel: 301-649-4131. FAX: 301-649-9633. Web Site: www.atonement-arp.org. *In Charge,* Rick Plasterer
Founded 1953
Library Holdings: Bk Titles 4,500; Bk Vols 4,800; Per Subs 11
Special Collections: religious bks
Partic in Churchline Coun; Prof Libr Asn

R WOODSIDE UNITED METHODIST CHURCH LIBRARY*, 8900 Georgia Ave, 20910-2739. SAN 307-0441. Tel: 301-587-1215. FAX: 301-589-6338. E-mail: woodsideumc@verizon.net. Web Site: www.gbgm-umc.org. *Librn,* Margaret Madert
Founded 1962
Library Holdings: Bk Vols 1,200
Open Mon-Fri 4-8

SNOW HILL

P WORCESTER COUNTY LIBRARY*, 307 N Washington St, 21863. SAN 344-3884. Tel: 410-632-2600. FAX: 410-632-1159. E-mail: worc@worc.lib.md.us. Web Site: www.worcesterlibrary.org. *Dir,* Mark Thomas; E-mail: mthomas@worc.lib.md.us; *Asst Dir,* Karen Neville; E-mail: kneville@worc.lib.md.us; *Youth Serv Mgr,* Kathy Breithut; Tel: 443-235-5597, E-mail: kbreithut@worc.lib.md.us; *ILL,* Lori Staton; Tel: 410-632-5622; *Tech Serv,* Lorna Hinds; E-mail: lhinds@worc.lib.md.us; Staff 18 (MLS 2, Non-MLS 16)
Founded 1959. Pop 49,274; Circ 543,522
Jul 2010-Jun 2011 Income (Main Library and Branch(s)) $2,247,595, Federal $12,000, County $1,980,348, Locally Generated Income $37,000, Other $218,247
Subject Interests: Real estate
Automation Activity & Vendor Info: (Cataloging) Innovative Interfaces, Inc; (Circulation) Innovative Interfaces, Inc; (OPAC) Innovative Interfaces, Inc
Function: Audiobks via web, Bks on cassette, Bks on CD, Children's prog, Computer training, Computers for patron use, Copy machines, Digital talking bks, Free DVD rentals, Handicapped accessible, ILL available, Music CDs, OverDrive digital audio bks, Photocopying/Printing, Prog for adults, Prog for children & young adult, Ref serv available, Senior computer classes, Summer reading prog, Tax forms
Publications: Agriculture Directory Program Resources Handbook; Program Schedules (Quarterly)
Partic in Eastern Shore Regional Library; Maryland Interlibrary Loan Organization
Open Mon-Fri 8-4:30
Friends of the Library Group
Branches: 5
BERLIN BRANCH, 220 N Main St, Berlin, 21811. SAN 344-3914. Tel: 410-641-0650. FAX: 410-641-9566. E-mail: worc-b@worc.lib.md.us. *Librn,* Alice Paterra; E-mail: apaterra@worc.lib.md.us
Open Mon & Wed 10-8, Tues, Thurs & Fri 10-6, Sat 9-1
Friends of the Library Group

OCEAN CITY BRANCH, 10003 Coastal Hwy, Ocean City, 21842, SAN 344-3949. Tel: 410-524-1818. FAX: 410-289-5577. E-mail: oceancity@worcesterlibrary.org. *Br Mgr, Dep Libr Dir,* Jennifer Ranck; E-mail: jranck@worcesterlibrary.org; *Asst Br Mgr,* Meg Arnold; E-mail: marnold@worcesterlibrary.org; *Asst Br Mgr,* Goolcher Grazier; E-mail: cgrazier@worc.lib.md.us
Open Mon & Wed-Fri 10-6, Tues 10-7, Sat 10-3
Friends of the Library Group

OCEAN PINES BRANCH, 11107 Cathell Rd, Berlin, 21811. Tel: 410-208-4014. E-mail: worc-op@worc.lib.md.us. *Br Mgr,* Patti Hall; E-mail: phall@worc.lib.md.us; *Youth Serv Mgr,* Kathy Breithut; E-mail: kbreithut@worc.lib.md.us
Open Mon & Thurs 10-8, Tues, Wed & Fri 10-6, Sat 9-3
Friends of the Library Group

POCOMOKE CITY BRANCH, 301 Market St, Pocomoke City, 21851, SAN 344-3973. Tel: 410-957-0878. FAX: 410-957-4773. E-mail: worc-p@worc.lib.md.us. *Librn,* Dawn Ingrassia; E-mail: dawn@worc.lib.md.us
Open Mon, Wed & Fri 10-6, Tues & Thurs 10-8, Sat 9-1

SNOW HILL BRANCH, 307 N Washington St, 21863, SAN 344-4007. Tel: 410-632-3495. FAX: 410-632-1159. E-mail: worc-sh@worc.lib.md.us. *Librn,* Carol Howe; E-mail: chowe@worc.lib.md.us
Open Mon & Wed 10-8, Tues, Thurs & Fri 10-6, Sat 9-1
Friends of the Library Group

SOLOMONS

S CALVERT MARINE MUSEUM LIBRARY, 14150 Solomons Island Rd, 20688. (Mail add: PO Box 97, 20688-0097), SAN 324-1122. Tel: 410-326-2042, Ext 14. FAX: 410-326-6691. TDD: 410-535-6355. E-mail: information@calvertmarinemuseum.com. Web Site: www.calvertmarinemuseum.com. *Curator,* Richard Dodds; E-mail: doddsrj@co.cal.md.us
Founded 1970
Jul 2012-Jun 2013 Income $1,700, County $1,500, Locally Generated Income $200. Mats Exp $1,450, Books $1,000, Per/Ser (Incl. Access Fees) $300, Manu Arch $50, Presv $100
Library Holdings: AV Mats 5; CDs 50; DVDs 125; Bk Titles 8,000; Bk Vols 8,250; Per Subs 35; Videos 200
Special Collections: B B Wills Steamboat Research Files; Boat Building (M M Davis & Son Coll), blueprints, clippings, correspondence; Chesapeake Bay History (M V Brewington Research Coll); History of Solomons Island (Patuxent River Seafood Industries); Seafood Processing (J C Lore & Sons Coll & Warren Denton Oysterhouse Coll); Tobacco Culture in Calvert County; Tom Wisner Archive (Chesapeake Bay education). Oral History
Subject Interests: Ecology, Local hist, Maritime hist, Paleontology
Function: Res libr
Special Services for the Deaf - TDD equip
Open Mon, Wed & Fri 9-4:30
Restriction: Not a lending libr

C UNIVERSITY OF MARYLAND CENTER FOR ENVIRONMENTAL SCIENCE*, Chesapeake Biological Laboratory Library, Farren Ave, 146 Williams St, 20688. (Mail add: PO Box 38, 20688-0038), SAN 328-8625. Tel: 410-326-7287. Interlibrary Loan Service Tel: 410-326-7301. FAX: 410-326-7430. E-mail: ill@cbl.umces.edu, librarian@umces.edu. Web Site: www.cbl.umces.edu/library/index.html. *Librn,* Kathy Heil; E-mail: heil@cbl.umces.edu; Staff 1 (MLS 1)
Founded 1927. Enrl 42; Fac 20; Highest Degree: Doctorate
Jul 2012-Jun 2013 Income $100,000. Mats Exp $103,500, Books $1,000, Per/Ser (Incl. Access Fees) $60,000, Manu Arch $500, Electronic Ref Mat (Incl. Access Fees) $40,000, Presv $2,000. Sal $75,000
Library Holdings: CDs 10; DVDs 5; e-journals 24,000; Bk Titles 12,000; Bk Vols 18,000; Per Subs 500
Special Collections: Chesapeake Bay; Shellfish, early reprints
Subject Interests: Aquatic biol, Chem, Ecology, Fisheries, Marine biol
Automation Activity & Vendor Info: (Acquisitions) Ex Libris Group; (Cataloging) Ex Libris Group; (Circulation) Ex Libris Group; (ILL) OCLC ILLiad; (OPAC) Ex Libris Group; (Serials) Ex Libris Group
Database Vendor: American Chemical Society, BioOne, Cambridge Scientific Abstracts, EBSCO Discovery Service, EBSCOhost, ISI Web of Knowledge, JSTOR, OCLC WorldShare Interlibrary Loan, ProQuest, PubMed, Springer-Verlag, Wiley
Wireless access
Function: Electronic databases & coll, ILL available, Photocopying/Printing, Pub access computers, Ref serv available, Scanner
Partic in Maryland Interlibrary Loan Organization; OCLC-LVIS; Univ Syst of Md
Open Mon-Fri 8-5
Restriction: Authorized patrons, Authorized scholars by appt, Borrowing privileges limited to fac & registered students, Circ to mem only, In-house use for visitors, Non-circulating to the pub, Open to fac, students & qualified researchers, Open to pub for ref only, Pub use on premises

STEVENSON

C STEVENSON UNIVERSITY LIBRARY*, 1525 Greenspring Valley Rd, 21153-0641. SAN 307-0468. Tel: 410-486-7000, 443-334-2233. FAX: 410-486-7329. Web Site: stevensonlibrary.org. *Dir, Libr Serv,* Maureen Anne Beck; Tel: 443-334-2231, E-mail: mbeck@stevenson.edu; *Chief Pub Serv Librn,* Susan H Bonsteel; Tel: 443-334-2320, E-mail: shbonsteel@stevenson.edu; *Coll Develop Librn, Tech Serv,* Steven M Williams; Tel: 443-334-2346, E-mail: smwilliams@stevenson.edu; *Pub Serv Librn,* Sandra A Marinaro; E-mail: smarinaro@stevenson.edu; *Cat, Ser Librn,* Christina J Hipsley; Tel: 443-334-2766, E-mail: chipsley@stevenson.edu; *Syst Librn,* Robin A Findeisen; Tel: 443-334-2218, E-mail: rfindeisen@stevenson.edu; *Coordr, Info Literacy,* Virginia J Polley; Tel: 443-334-2688, E-mail: vpolley@stevenson.edu; *Historian, Univ Archivist,* Dr Glenn T Johnston; Tel: 443-334-2196, E-mail: gjohnston@stevenson.edu. Subject Specialists: *Bus,* Maureen Anne Beck; Staff 12 (MLS 8, Non-MLS 4)
Founded 1953. Enrl 1,820; Fac 120; Highest Degree: Master
Library Holdings: Bk Titles 65,000; Bk Vols 75,000; Per Subs 689
Subject Interests: Educ, Nursing, Paralegal
Automation Activity & Vendor Info: (Acquisitions) Ex Libris Group; (Cataloging) Ex Libris Group; (Circulation) Ex Libris Group; (Course Reserve) Docutek; (ILL) OCLC Connexion; (OPAC) Ex Libris Group; (Serials) Ex Libris Group
Database Vendor: ACM (Association for Computing Machinery), American Chemical Society, American Psychological Association (APA), Cinahl, College Source, EBSCOhost, Elsevier, Gale Cengage Learning, Hemscott Data, Hoovers, LexisNexis, Modern Language Association, OCLC WorldShare Interlibrary Loan, ProQuest, PubMed, Safari Books Online, ScienceDirect, SirsiDynix, Westlaw
Wireless access
Partic in Baltimore Acad Libr Consortium; Lyrasis
Special Services for the Blind - ZoomText magnification & reading software
Open Mon-Thurs 8am-10pm, Fri 8-6, Sat 11-5; Mon-Thurs (Summer) 8-6, Fri 8-5

STEVENSVILLE

S HISTORICAL EVALUATION & RESEARCH ORGANIZATION*, Hero Library, 1407 Love Point Rd, 21666. SAN 324-1297. Tel: 410-643-8807. FAX: 410-643-8469. E-mail: hero_library@msn.com. Web Site: www.herolibrary.org. *Dir,* Charles Hawkins
Founded 1962
Library Holdings: Bk Titles 4,350
Special Collections: Military Law (Wiener Coll)
Subject Interests: Mil hist
Restriction: Open by appt only

SYKESVILLE

M THE LIBRARY AT SPRINGFIELD HOSPITAL CENTER*, 6655 Sykesville Rd, 21784. SAN 307-0484. Tel: 410-970-7000, Ext 3481. FAX: 410-970-7197. *Mgr,* Janet Short; Staff 2.5 (Non-MLS 2.5)
Founded 1953
Library Holdings: AV Mats 300; Bks on Deafness & Sign Lang 60; High Interest/Low Vocabulary Bk Vols 57; Large Print Bks 20; Bk Titles 6,000; Per Subs 34; Spec Interest Per Sub 100; Talking Bks 20
Subject Interests: Addictions, Art therapy, Dance movement therapy, Deafness, Dietary, Forensic sci, Gerontology, Mental health, Mental illness, Music therapy, Neurology, Nursing, Occupational therapy, Phys therapy, Psychiat, Psychol, Recreational therapy, Rehabilitation, Soc serv (soc work), Speech therapy
Automation Activity & Vendor Info: (Cataloging) SirsiDynix
Function: ILL available, Photocopying/Printing
Special Services for the Blind - Bks & mags in Braille, on rec, tape & cassette
Open Mon-Fri 8:30-5

TAKOMA PARK

S LTG ASSOCIATES LIBRARY*, 6930 Carrol Ave, Ste 700, 20912. SAN 377-1466. Tel: 301-270-0882. FAX: 301-270-1966. Web Site: www.ltgassociates.com. *Librn,* Matthew Jones
Library Holdings: Bk Vols 200
Open Mon-Fri 9-5

P TAKOMA PARK MARYLAND LIBRARY*, 101 Philadelphia Ave, 20912. SAN 307-0514. Tel: 301-891-7259. FAX: 301-270-0814. Web Site: www.takomapark.info/library/. *Dir,* Ellen Arnold-Robbins; *Ch Serv, Youth Serv,* Karen MacPherson; *Pub Serv Coordr,* Rebecca Brown; *Tech Serv Coordr,* Nic Fontem; Staff 8.25 (MLS 4, Non MLS 4.25)
Founded 1935. Pop 17,299; Circ 143,898
Library Holdings: Bk Vols 63,242; Per Subs 201

Automation Activity & Vendor Info: (Cataloging) Auto-Graphics, Inc; (Circulation) Auto-Graphics, Inc; (OPAC) Auto-Graphics, Inc
Database Vendor: Auto-Graphics, Inc, Brodart, BWI, ebrary, EBSCOhost, Facts on File, ProQuest
Wireless access
Function: Adult bk club, Adult literacy prog, Bilingual assistance for Spanish patrons, Bk club(s), Bk reviews (Group), Bks on CD, Children's prog, Computer training, Computers for patron use, Copy machines, E-Reserves, Handicapped accessible, Holiday prog, Home delivery & serv to Sr ctr & nursing homes, ILL available, Large print keyboards, Magnifiers for reading, Music CDs, Online cat, Online searches, Photocopying/Printing, Preschool outreach, Prog for adults, Prog for children & young adult, Pub access computers, Ref serv in person, Senior computer classes, Story hour, Summer reading prog, Tax forms, Teen prog, Telephone ref, Wheelchair accessible, Workshops
Partic in Maryland Interlibrary Loan Organization
Open Mon & Wed 1-9, Tues & Thurs 10-9, Fri 12-6, Sat 10-5
Friends of the Library Group

M WASHINGTON ADVENTIST HOSPITAL*, Health Sciences Library, 7600 Carroll Ave, 20912. SAN 307-0530. Tel: 301-891-5260. FAX: 301-891-6087. *Librn*, Cathy Cumbo; E-mail: ccumbo@ahm.com; Staff 1 (Non-MLS 1)
Founded 1956
Jan 2007-Dec 2007. Mats Exp $99,500, Books $10,000, Per/Ser (Incl. Access Fees) $84,500, AV Mat $5,000. Sal $55,923
Library Holdings: CDs 26; DVDs 18; e-journals 300; Bk Vols 1,500; Per Subs 323; Videos 271
Subject Interests: Clinical med, Hospital admin, Nursing
Automation Activity & Vendor Info: (Cataloging) Professional Software; (Circulation) Professional Software; (OPAC) Professional Software; (Serials) Professional Software
Database Vendor: OVID Technologies
Partic in District of Columbia Area Health Science Libraries
Open Mon-Thurs 7:30-4:30, Fri 7:30-2
Restriction: Circulates for staff only, Open to pub for ref only

CR WASHINGTON ADVENTIST UNIVERSITY*, Weis Library, 7600 Flower Ave, 20912-7796. SAN 307-0492. Tel: 301-891-4217. Circulation Tel: 301-891-4220. Interlibrary Loan Service Tel: 301-891-4223. Administration Tel: 301-891-4218, 301-891-4222. FAX: 301-891-4204. E-mail: library@wau.edu. Web Site: www.wau.edu/library. *Dir, Ref*, Lee Marie Wisel; E-mail: lwisel@wau.edu; *Access Serv*, Jane Ogora; E-mail: janogora@wau.edu; *Cat*, Genevieve Singh; Tel: 301-891-4221, E-mail: gsingh@wau.edu; *Ser*, Kathy Hecht; Tel: 301-891-4216, E-mail: khecht@wau.edu; *Acq Tech*, Debby Szasz; E-mail: dszasz@wau.edu; Staff 5 (MLS 2, Non-MLS 3)
Founded 1904. Highest Degree: Master
Special Collections: Seventh-day Adventists History & Publications, bks, per
Automation Activity & Vendor Info: (Acquisitions) Ex Libris Group; (Cataloging) Ex Libris Group; (Circulation) Ex Libris Group; (Course Reserve) Ex Libris Group; (ILL) Ex Libris Group; (OPAC) Ex Libris Group; (Serials) Ex Libris Group
Database Vendor: Atlas Systems, Cambridge Scientific Abstracts, Cinahl, College Source, ebrary, EBSCOhost, Gale Cengage Learning, Mergent Online, Modern Language Association, OCLC FirstSearch, OCLC WorldShare Interlibrary Loan, Springshare, LLC
Wireless access
Partic in Maryland Interlibrary Consortium (MIC)
Open Mon-Thurs 8:30am-11pm, Fri 8:30-1, Sun 11-11
Restriction: Authorized patrons, Authorized scholars by appt, Borrowing privileges limited to fac & registered students, Borrowing requests are handled by ILL

TOWSON

GL BALTIMORE COUNTY CIRCUIT COURT LIBRARY, 401 Bosley Ave, 21204. SAN 307-0565. Tel: 410-887-3086. FAX: 410-887-4807. *Dir*, Stephanie Levasseur; *Assoc Librn*, Errin Roby; E-mail: ekroby@baltimorecountymd.gov; *Assoc Librn*, Scott Stevens; E-mail: sstevens@baltimorecountymd.gov
Library Holdings: CDs 60; DVDs 100; Bk Titles 2,800; Bk Vols 50,000; Per Subs 30
Automation Activity & Vendor Info: (Acquisitions) Inmagic, Inc.; (Cataloging) Inmagic, Inc.
Database Vendor: Bloomberg, EBSCOhost, HeinOnline, LexisNexis, Westlaw
Wireless access
Open Mon, Tues & Fri 8:30-4:30, Wed & Thurs 8:30-7

P BALTIMORE COUNTY PUBLIC LIBRARY, 320 York Rd, 21204-5179. SAN 344-4031. Tel: 410-887-6100. FAX: 410-887-6103. TDD: 410-284-0160. Web Site: www.bcpl.info. *Dir*, Paula Miller; *Asst Dir, Pub Serv*, Irene Briggs; *Asst Dir, Support Serv*, James Cooke; *Fiscal Serv Mgr*, John Santora; *Mgr, Human Res*, Cindy Pol; *Mgr, Mkt & Develop*, Position Currently Open; *Media Support Serv Mgr*, Carl Birkmeyer; *Operations Support Mgr*, Ed Cook; *Planning & Projects Mgr*, Position Currently Open; *Coordr, Coll Develop*, Jamie Watson; *Coordr, Info Serv*, Jim DeArmey; *Coordr, Tech Serv*, Jody Sharp; *Coordr, Youth Serv*, Marisa Conner; Tel: 410-887-0517; Staff 184.4 (MLS 82, Non-MLS 102.4)
Founded 1948. Pop 805,029; Circ 11,287,133
Jul 2013-Jun 2014 Income (Main Library and Branch(s)) $45,686,042. Mats Exp $7,581,058. Sal $21,485,847
Library Holdings: AV Mats 212,744; DVDs 114,960; e-books 45,342; Bk Vols 1,433,343; Per Subs 4,290
Special Collections: African-American Coll; Children's Picture Book Spanish Language Coll; Historical Coll; Historical Photograph Coll; Korean Coll; Local History Coll; Maryland Coll; Russian Coll; Spanish Coll
Automation Activity & Vendor Info: (Acquisitions) Innovative Interfaces, Inc; (Cataloging) Innovative Interfaces, Inc; (Circulation) Innovative Interfaces, Inc; (ILL) OCLC FirstSearch
Wireless access
Publications: Baltimore County Directory of Organizations; Branching Out; Day By Day; Your Library Programs & News
Special Services for the Deaf - TDD equip
Open Mon-Thurs 9-9, Fri & Sat 9-5:30, Sun 1-5
Friends of the Library Group
Branches: 19
ARBUTUS, 855 Sulphur Spring Rd, Baltimore, 21227-2598, SAN 344-4066. Tel: 410-887-1451. FAX: 410-536-0328. *Mgr*, Robert Maranto; E-mail: rmaranto@bcpl.net
Circ 476,840
Library Holdings: Bk Vols 99,142
Open Mon-Thurs 9-9, Fri & Sat 9-5:30, Sun 1-5
Friends of the Library Group
CATONSVILLE, 1100 Frederick Rd, Baltimore, 21228-5092, SAN 344-4090. Tel: 410-887-0951. FAX: 410-788-8166. E-mail: catonsville@bcpl.net. *Mgr*, Melissa Gotsch; E-mail: mgotsch@bcpl.net
Circ 774,523
Library Holdings: Bk Vols 136,598
Open Mon-Thurs 9-9, Fri & Sat 9-5:30, Sun 1-5
Friends of the Library Group
COCKEYSVILLE BRANCH, 9833 Greenside Dr, Cockeysville, 21030-2188, SAN 344-4120. Tel: 410-887-7750. FAX: 410-666-0325. E-mail: cockeysville@bcpl.net. *Mgr*, Darcy Cahill; E-mail: darcy@bcpl.net
Circ 1,511,568
Library Holdings: Bk Vols 178,752
Open Mon-Thurs 9-9, Fri & Sat 9-5:30, Sun 1-5
Friends of the Library Group
ESSEX, 1110 Eastern Blvd, Baltimore, 21221-3497, SAN 344-421X. Tel: 410 887-0295. FAX: 410-687-0075. E-mail: essex@bcpl.net. *Mgr*, Yvette May; E-mail: ymay@bcpl.net
Circ 383,074
Library Holdings: Bk Vols 82,640
Open Mon-Thurs 9-9, Fri & Sat 9-5:30, Sun 1-5
HEREFORD, 16940 York Rd, Monkton, 21111, SAN 378-0473. Tel: 410-887-1919. FAX: 410-329-8203. *Asst Br Mgr*, Samantha O'Heren; E-mail: soheren@bcpl.net
Circ 287,505
Library Holdings: Bk Vols 47,961
Open Mon-Thurs 9-9, Fri & Sat 9-5:30, Sun 1-5
Friends of the Library Group
LANSDOWNE, 500 Third Ave, Baltimore, 21227. Tel: 410-887-5602. FAX: 410-887-5633. E-mail: lansdowne@bcpl.net. *Asst Libr Mgr*, Cindy Swanson-Farmarco
Circ 68,012
Library Holdings: Bk Vols 19,979
Open Mon-Thurs 9-9, Fri & Sat 9-5:30, Sun 1-5
LOCH RAVEN, 1046 Taylor Ave, 21286, SAN 378-049X. Tel: 410-887-4444. FAX: 410-296-4339. *Librn*, Melissa Hepler; E-mail: mhepler@bcpl.net
Circ 123,782
Library Holdings: Bk Vols 21,057
Open Mon-Thurs 9-9, Fri & Sat 9-5:30, Sun 1-5
Friends of the Library Group
NORTH POINT, 1716 Merritt Blvd, Baltimore, 21222-3295, SAN 344-4368. Tel: 410-887-7255. FAX: 410-282-3272. *Mgr*, Joanie Bradford; E-mail: jbradford@bcpl.net
Circ 570,085
Library Holdings: Bk Vols 116,486
Open Mon-Thurs 9-9, Fri & Sat 9-5:30, Sun 1-5
OWINGS MILLS BRANCH, 10302 Grand Central Ave, Owings Mills, 21117. Tel: 410-887-2092. FAX: 410-356-5935. E-mail: owingsmills@bcpl.net. *Br Mgr*, Barbara Salit-Mischel; E-mail: bmischel@bcpl.net
Circ 593,721

Library Holdings: Bk Vols 118,340
Open Mon-Thurs 9-9, Fri & Sat 9-5:30, Sun 1-5
PARKVILLE-CARNEY, 9509 Harford Rd, Baltimore, 21234-3192, SAN 344-4392. Tel: 410-887-5353. FAX: 410-668-3678. *Mgr,* Elizabeth Storms; E-mail: estorms@bcpl.net
Circ 525,058
Library Holdings: Bk Vols 82,071
Open Mon-Thurs 9-9, Fri & Sat 9-5:30, Sun 1-5
PERRY HALL, 9685 Honeygo Blvd, Baltimore, 21128, SAN 344-4422. Tel: 410-887-5195. FAX: 410-529-9430. E-mail: perryhall@bcpl.net. *Mgr,* Cynthia Kleback; E-mail: ckleback@bcpl.net
Circ 714,487
Library Holdings: Bk Vols 119,510
Open Mon-Thurs 9-9, Fri & Sat 9-5:30, Sun 1-5
Friends of the Library Group
PIKESVILLE, 1301 Reisterstown Rd, Baltimore, 21208-4195, SAN 344-4457. Tel: 410-887-1234. FAX: 410-486-2782. E-mail: pikesville@bcpl.net. *Mgr,* Judith Kaplan; E-mail: jkaplan@bcpl.net
Circ 1,421,998
Library Holdings: Bk Vols 159,508
Open Mon-Thurs 9-9, Fri & Sat 9-5:30, Sun 1-5
Friends of the Library Group
RANDALLSTOWN BRANCH, 8604 Liberty Rd, Randallstown, 21133-4797, SAN 344-4481. Tel: 410-887-0770. FAX: 410-521-3614. E-mail: randallstown@bcpl.net. *Mgr,* Sarah Smith; E-mail: sjsmith@bcpl.net
Circ 383,301
Library Holdings: Bk Vols 87,648
Open Mon-Thurs 9-9, Fri & Sat 9-5:30, Sun 1-5
Friends of the Library Group
REISTERSTOWN BRANCH, 21 Cockeys Mill Rd, Reisterstown, 21136-1285, SAN 344-4511. Tel: 410-887-1165. FAX: 410-833-8756. E-mail: reisterstown@bcpl.net. *Mgr,* Abby Cooley; E-mail: acooley@bcpl.net
Circ 451,234
Library Holdings: Bk Vols 83,597
Open Mon-Thurs 9-9, Fri & Sat 9-5:30, Sun 1-5
Friends of the Library Group
ROSEDALE, 6105 Kenwood Ave, Baltimore, 21237-2097, SAN 344-4546. Tel: 410-887-0512. FAX: 410-866-4299. E-mail: rosedale@bcpl.net. *Mgr,* Theresa Murphy; E-mail: tmurphy@bcpl.net
Circ 328,903
Library Holdings: Bk Vols 73,563
Open Mon-Thurs 9-9, Fri & Sat 9-5:30, Sun 1-5
SOLLERS POINT BRANCH, 323 Sollers Point Rd, Baltimore, 21222-6169. Tel: 410-288-3123. FAX: 410-288-3125. E-mail: sollerspoint@bcpl.net. *Mgr,* Yvette May; E-mail: ymay@bcpl.net
Circ 29,399
Library Holdings: Bk Vols 17,033
Open Mon-Thurs 9-9, Fri & Sat 9-5:30, Sun 1-5
TOWSON BRANCH, 320 York Rd, 21204-5179, SAN 344-4570. Tel: 410-887-6166. FAX: 410-887-3170. E-mail: towson@bcpl.net. *Mgr,* Lisa Hughes; E-mail: lhughes@bcpl.net
Circ 1,052,145
Library Holdings: Bk Vols 179,017
Open Mon-Thurs 9-9, Fri & Sat 9-5:30, Sun 1-5
Friends of the Library Group
WHITE MARSH, 8133 Sandpiper Circle, Baltimore, 21236-4973, SAN 329-6725. Tel: 410-887-5097. FAX: 410-931-9229. E-mail: whitemarsh@bcpl.net. *Mgr,* Sandra Lombardo; E-mail: slombard@bcpl.net
Circ 590,394
Library Holdings: Bk Vols 100,653
Open Mon-Thurs 9-9, Fri & Sat 9-5:30, Sun 1-5
WOODLAWN, 1811 Woodlawn Dr, Baltimore, 21207-4074, SAN 344-466X. Tel: 410-887-1336. FAX: 410-281-9584. E-mail: woodlawn@bcpl.net. *Mgr,* Ashley Rogers; E-mail: arogers@bcpl.net
Circ 374,995
Library Holdings: Bk Vols 85,355
Open Mon-Thurs 9-9, Fri & Sat 9-5:30, Sun 1-5
Bookmobiles: 3

M SAINT JOSEPH MEDICAL CENTER*, Otto C Brantigan Medical Library, 7601 Osler Dr, 21204. SAN 343-9747. Tel: 410-337-1210. FAX: 410-337-1116. *Librn,* Marianne Prenger; E-mail: marianneprenger@umm.org
Founded 1940
Library Holdings: Bk Vols 2,000; Per Subs 170
Database Vendor: Cinahl, MD Consult, UpToDate
Wireless access

M SHEPPARD PRATT HEALTH SYSTEMS*, Lawrence S Kubie Medical Library, 6501 N Charles St, 21204. (Mail add: PO Box 6815, Baltimore, 21285-6815), SAN 344-4694. Tel: 410-938-4594. FAX: 410-938-4596. E-mail: info@sheppardpratt.org. Web Site: www.sheppardpratt.org. *Dir,* Donald R Ross
Founded 1891
Library Holdings: Bk Vols 3,000; Per Subs 17
Subject Interests: Psychiat, Psychotherapy, Soc serv (soc work)
Partic in Dialog Corp; US National Library of Medicine
Open Mon-Thurs 8-4, Fri 8-2
Restriction: Staff use only

C TOWSON UNIVERSITY*, Albert S Cook Library, 8000 York Rd, 21252-0001. SAN 307-0611. Tel: 410-704-2450. Circulation Tel: 410-704-2456. Interlibrary Loan Service Tel: 410-704-3292. Reference Tel: 410-704-2462. FAX: 410-704-3760. Interlibrary Loan Service FAX: 410-704-3829. Web Site: cooklibrary.towson.edu. *Univ Librn,* Deborah A Nolan; E-mail: dnolan@towson.edu; *Assoc Univ Librn, Admin Serv,* Patricia MacDonald; Tel: 410-704-2445, E-mail: pmacdonald@towson.edu; *Asst Univ Librn, Coll Mgt,* Mary Gilbert; Tel: 410-704-4926, E-mail: mgilbert@towson.edu; *Asst Univ Librn, Pub Serv,* Mary Ranadive; Tel: 410-704-2618, E-mail: mranadive@towson.edu; *Circ Mgr,* Paula Langley; Tel: 410-704-3442, E-mail: plangley@towson.edu; *Mgr, Info Tech & Media Serv,* Paul Peeling; Tel: 410-704-4895, Fax: 410-704-5246, E-mail: ppeeling@towson.edu; Staff 30 (MLS 21, Non-MLS 9)
Founded 1866. Enrl 21,117; Fac 822; Highest Degree: Doctorate
Jul 2009-Jun 2010 Income $5,928,624. Mats Exp $2,312,857, Books $191,621, Per/Ser (Incl. Access Fees) $2,087,953, Manu Arch $2,665, AV Mat $25,222, Electronic Ref Mat (Incl. Access Fees) $5,396. Sal $2,515,819 (Prof $1,512,444)
Library Holdings: AV Mats 1,548; CDs 66; DVDs 2,498; e-books 190,182; e-journals 39,438; Microforms 886,912; Bk Vols 622,485; Per Subs 7,108; Videos 7,641
Special Collections: Baltimore Hebrew Institute Coll
Subject Interests: Art, Educ, Ethnic studies, Fine arts, Health professions, Music, Women's studies
Automation Activity & Vendor Info: (Acquisitions) Ex Libris Group; (Cataloging) Ex Libris Group; (Circulation) Ex Libris Group; (Course Reserve) Docutek; (ILL) OCLC ILLiad; (OPAC) Ex Libris Group; (Serials) Ex Libris Group
Database Vendor: ABC-CLIO, ACM (Association for Computing Machinery), Alexander Street Press, American Chemical Society, American Mathematical Society, Annual Reviews, ARTstor, BioOne, Bowker, Cambridge Scientific Abstracts, Checkpoint Systems, Inc, CISTI Source, CQ Press, ebrary, EBSCOhost, Elsevier MDL, Emerald, Ex Libris Group, Factiva.com, Gale Cengage Learning, Haworth Pres Inc, Hoovers, IEEE (Institute of Electrical & Electronics Engineers), ISI Web of Knowledge, JSTOR, LexisNexis, Majors, Medline, Mergent Online, Nature Publishing Group, OCLC FirstSearch, OCLC WorldShare Interlibrary Loan, OVID Technologies, Oxford Online, Project MUSE, ProQuest, PubMed, RefWorks, Safari Books Online, Sage, SBRnet (Sports Business Research Network), ScienceDirect, SerialsSolutions, Springer-Verlag, Standard & Poor's, Thomson - Web of Science, ValueLine
Wireless access
Function: Archival coll, AV serv, Bk club(s), Computers for patron use, Copy machines, Distance learning, Doc delivery serv, e-mail & chat, E-Reserves, Electronic databases & coll, ILL available, Jazz prog, Online cat, Online info literacy tutorials on the web & in blackboard, Online ref, Orientations, Outreach serv, Pub access computers, Ref & res, Ref serv available, Ref serv in person, Telephone ref, VHS videos
Partic in Lyrasis; OCLC Online Computer Library Center, Inc; Univ Syst of Md
Special Services for the Deaf - Assistive tech
Special Services for the Blind - Assistive/Adapted tech devices, equip & products
Open Mon-Thurs 8am-2am, Fri 8-8, Sat 10-8, Sun Noon-2am

UPPER MARLBORO

GL PRINCE GEORGE'S COUNTY*, Law Library, 14735 Main St, M4100, 20772. (Mail add: PO Box 1696, 20773-1696), SAN 307-062X. Tel: 301-952-3438. FAX: 301-952-2770. E-mail: lawlibrary@co.pg.md.us. Web Site: www.co.pg.md.us. *Librn,* Tonya Baroudi; Staff 2 (MLS 1, Non-MLS 1)
Founded 1900
Library Holdings: Bk Titles 37,000; Per Subs 50
Subject Interests: Criminal law & justice, Law, Maryland
Publications: Acquisitions list
Partic in Westlaw
Open Mon-Fri 8:30-4:30
Friends of the Library Group

WEST BETHESDA

G NAVAL SURFACE WARFARE CENTER*, Carderock Division Technical Information Center, 9500 MacArthur Blvd, 20817-5700. SAN 337 2065. Tel: 301 227-1433. FAX: 301-227-5307. *Head, Tech Serv,* David Glenn; E-mail: david.glenn@navy.mil

Library Holdings: Bk Vols 38,500; Per Subs 10
Database Vendor: Dialog, OCLC FirstSearch
Partic in Dialog Corp
Restriction: Not open to pub, Staff use only

WESTMINSTER

J CARROLL COMMUNITY COLLEGE*, Library & Media Center, 1601 Washington Rd, 21157-6944. SAN 373-2827. Tel: 410-386-8330. Reference Tel: 410-386-8340. Toll Free Tel: 888-221-9748. FAX: 410-386-8331. E-mail: ref_desk@carrollcc.edu. Web Site: www.carrollcc.edu/library. *Dir, Libr Serv,* Alan Bogage; Tel: 410-386-8339, E-mail: abogage@carrollcc.edu; *Head, Tech Serv,* Christi Karman; Tel: 410-386-8337, E-mail: ckarman@carrollcc.edu; *Pub Serv Librn,* Jeremy Green; Tel: 410-386-8335, E-mail: jgreen@carrollcc.edu; *Pub Serv Librn,* Wanda Meck; Tel: 410-386-8342, E-mail: wmeck@carrollcc.edu; *Electronic Res,* Elizabeth Beere; Tel: 410-386-8333, E-mail: ebeere@carrollcc.edu; Staff 5 (MLS 5)
Founded 1976. Enrl 2,518; Fac 342; Highest Degree: Associate
Jul 2011-Jun 2012. Mats Exp $174,000, Books $64,000, Per/Ser (Incl. Access Fees) $20,000, AV Mat $10,000, Electronic Ref Mat (Incl. Access Fees) $80,000. Sal $655,578 (Prof $196,000)
Library Holdings: CDs 372; DVDs 1,039; e-books 77,928; Electronic Media & Resources 29; Music Scores 92; Bk Titles 44,000; Per Subs 200; Videos 1,266
Automation Activity & Vendor Info: (Acquisitions) Innovative Interfaces, Inc; (Cataloging) Innovative Interfaces, Inc; (Circulation) Innovative Interfaces, Inc; (Course Reserve) Innovative Interfaces, Inc; (OPAC) Innovative Interfaces, Inc; (Serials) Innovative Interfaces, Inc
Database Vendor: ABC-CLIO, ARTstor, Baker & Taylor, Checkpoint Systems, Inc, CQ Press, ebrary, EBSCOhost, Gale Cengage Learning, Greenwood Publishing Group, Hoovers, OCLC, Oxford Online, ProQuest, SerialsSolutions, Springshare, LLC, STAT!Ref (Teton Data Systems)
Wireless access
Function: Audio & video playback equip for onsite use, AV serv, Bks on CD, Computers for patron use, Copy machines, e-mail & chat, Electronic databases & coll, ILL available, Music CDs, Online info literacy tutorials on the web & in blackboard, Online ref, Orientations, Ref serv in person
Partic in Carroll Librs in Partnership; Md Commun Col Libr Consortium
Open Mon-Thurs 8am-10pm, Fri & Sat 8:30-4:30

S CARROLL COUNTY FARM MUSEUM*, Landon Burns Memorial Library, 500 S Center St, 21157. SAN 371-201X. Tel: 410-386-3880. Toll Free Tel: 800-654-4645. FAX: 410-876-8544. E-mail: ccfarm@ccg.carr.org. Web Site: www.carrollcountyfarmmuseum.org. *Adminr,* Dottie Freeman; *Curator,* Victoria Fowler
Founded 1966
Library Holdings: Bk Vols 650; Per Subs 12
Restriction: Not open to pub, Open by appt only

P CARROLL COUNTY PUBLIC LIBRARY*, 115 Airport Dr, 21157. SAN 344-4759. Tel: 410-386-4500. Reference Tel: 410-386-4488. FAX: 410-386-4509. Reference FAX: 410-386-4489. Web Site: library.carr.org. *Dir,* K Lynn Wheeler; Tel: 410-386-4500, Ext 136, E-mail: lwheeler@carr.org; *Dep Dir, Ref,* Gail L Griffith; Tel: 410-386-4500, Ext 131, E-mail: gailg@carr.org; *Asst Dir, Operations,* Scott Reinhart; Tel: 410-386-4500, Ext 137, E-mail: scottr@carr.org; *Mgr, Info Tech, Web Librn,* Robert Kuntz; *Ref Mgr,* Greg Becker; *Coll Develop,* Concetta Pisano; Tel: 410-386-4500, Ext 142, E-mail: cpisano@carr.org; *ILL,* Sharon Hayes; *Outreach Serv Librn, Prog Serv,* Dorothy Stoltz; Tel: 410-386-4450, Ext 733, Fax: 410-386-4497, E-mail: dstoltz@carr.org; *Tech Serv,* Elaine Adkins; Staff 144 (MLS 22, Non-MLS 122)
Founded 1958. Pop 161,700; Circ 3,579,244
Library Holdings: AV Mats 80,558; Bk Vols 584,167; Per Subs 1,461
Subject Interests: Local hist
Automation Activity & Vendor Info: (Acquisitions) SirsiDynix; (Cataloging) SirsiDynix; (Circulation) SirsiDynix; (OPAC) SirsiDynix; (Serials) SirsiDynix
Database Vendor: EBSCOhost, SirsiDynix
Wireless access
Publications: Directory of Community Services for Carroll County, Maryland; Ghosts & Legends of Carroll County, Maryland
Partic in Carroll Librs in Partnership
Special Services for the Deaf - TTY equip
Open Mon-Thurs 8am-9pm, Fri & Sat 8-5
Branches: 5
ELDERSBURG BRANCH, 6400 W Hemlock Dr, Eldersburg, 21784-6538, SAN 344-4872. Tel: 410-386-4460. FAX: 410-386-4466. *Br Mgr,* Nadine Rosendale
Open Mon-Thurs 9-8:45, Fri & Sat 9-5
MOUNT AIRY BRANCH, 705 Ridge Ave, Mount Airy, 21771-3911, SAN 344-4813. Tel: 410-386-4470. FAX: 410-386-4477. *Br Mgr,* Patricia Sandberg
Open Mon-Thurs 9-8:45, Fri & Sat 9-5
NORTH CARROLL, 2255 Hanover Pike, Greenmount, 21074, SAN 344-4783. Tel: 410-386-4480. FAX: 410-386-4486. *Br Mgr,* Cindy Ahman; E-mail: cindya@carr.org
Open Mon-Thurs 9-8:45, Fri & Sat 9-5
TANEYTOWN BRANCH, 10 Grand Dr, Taneytown, 21787-2421, SAN 344-4848. Tel: 410-386-4510. FAX: 410-386-4515. *Br Mgr,* Jillian Dittrich; E-mail: jdittrich@carr.org; Staff 8 (MLS 2, Non-MLS 6)
Circ 383,570
Automation Activity & Vendor Info: (OPAC) Innovative Interfaces, Inc
Open Mon-Thurs 9-8:45, Fri 9-5, Sat 9-5
WESTMINSTER BRANCH, 50 E Main St, 21157-5097, SAN 375-6297. Tel: 410-386-4490. FAX: 410-386-4487. *Br Mgr,* Christina Kuntz; E-mail: cogle@carr.org
Special Services for the Deaf - TTY equip
Open Mon-Thurs 9:30-8:45, Fri 9:30-6, Sat 9:30-5
Bookmobiles: 3. In Charge, Connie Wilson. Bk vols 11,000

GL CIRCUIT COURT FOR CARROLL COUNTY*, Law Library, Historic Court House, Court & Willis Sts, 21157. SAN 307-0638. Tel: 410-386-2672. FAX: 410-751-5240. E-mail: lawlib@ccg.carr.org. Web Site: ccgovernment.carr.org/ccg/circuit-court/law-lib.aspx. *Librn,* Position Currently Open
Database Vendor: LexisNexis, Westlaw
Open Mon-Fri 9-4:30

S HISTORICAL SOCIETY OF CARROLL COUNTY LIBRARY, 210 E Main St, 21157. SAN 371-6694. Tel: 410-848-6494. FAX: 410-848-3596. E-mail: Library@HSCCmd.org. Web Site: www.hsccmd.org. *Exec Dir,* Dr Gainor Davis; E-mail: gainor@hsccmd.org; *Curator,* Catherine Baty; E-mail: cathy@hsccmd.org; Staff 2 (Non-MLS 2)
Founded 1939
Library Holdings: Bk Titles 750; Bk Vols 1,000; Per Subs 10
Special Collections: Carroll County History, bks, ms, maps, newsp, photos; Family Files (Genealogy Typescripts, Monographs & Special Research); Land Patent Records (Tracey Coll); Taneytown Community History (Crapster Coll)
Subject Interests: Local hist
Wireless access
Open Tues-Fri 9:30-4

C MCDANIEL COLLEGE*, Hoover Library, Two College Hill, 21157. SAN 307-0646. Tel: 410-857-2281. Circulation Tel: 410-857-2744. Interlibrary Loan Service Tel: 410-857-2288. Reference Tel: 410-857-2282. FAX: 410-857-2748. Web Site: hoover.mcdaniel.edu. *Dir,* Jessame Ferguson; E-mail: jferguson@mcdaniel.edu; *Coll Res Mgt Librn,* Mary Wilson; Tel: 410-857-2284, E-mail: mwilson@mcdaniel.edu; *Pub Serv Mgt Librn,* Brynne Norton; Tel: 410-857-2278, E-mail: bnorton@mcdaniel.edu; *Res & Instruction Librn/Info Literacy,* Marla Beebe; Tel: 410-857-2287, E-mail: mbeebe@mcdaniel.edu; *Res & Instruction Librn/Sci & Online Tech,* Janet Hack; Tel: 410-857-2283, E-mail: jhack@mcdaniel.edu; *Res & Instruction Librn/User Experience,* Jordan Sly; Tel: 410-386-4679, E-mail: jsly@mcdaniel.edu; *Acq Mgr,* Linda Garber; Tel: 410-857-2285, E-mail: lgarber@mcdaniel.edu; *Circ & Reserves Mgr,* Angie Bachtel; Tel: 410-857-2744, E-mail: arasche@mcdaniel.edu; *Cat Supvr,* Roxane Brewer; Tel: 410-857-2847, E-mail: mbrewer@mcdaniel.edu; *ILL Supvr,* Lisa Russell; Tel: 410-857-2788, E-mail: lmrussel@mcdaniel.edu; *Col Archivist,* Barbara O'Brien; Tel: 410-857-2793, E-mail: bobrien@mcdaniel.edu; *Ser & Govt Doc Spec,* Lorri Pickett; Tel: 410-857-2789, E-mail: lpickett@mcdaniel.edu; Staff 13 (MLS 6, Non-MLS 7)
Founded 1867. Enrl 3,284; Fac 103; Highest Degree: Master
Library Holdings: Bk Titles 200,000; Bk Vols 234,319; Per Subs 32,675
Special Collections: US Document Depository
Automation Activity & Vendor Info: (Acquisitions) Innovative Interfaces, Inc; (Cataloging) Innovative Interfaces, Inc; (Circulation) Innovative Interfaces, Inc; (Course Reserve) Innovative Interfaces, Inc; (ILL) OCLC ILLiad; (OPAC) Innovative Interfaces, Inc; (Serials) Innovative Interfaces, Inc
Database Vendor: ABC-CLIO, ACM (Association for Computing Machinery), Alexander Street Press, Annual Reviews, ARTstor, BioOne, CQ Press, ebrary, EBSCO Discovery Service, EBSCOhost, Elsevier, Gale Cengage Learning, JSTOR, LexisNexis, Project MUSE, ProQuest, Sage, ScienceDirect, YBP Library Services
Partic in Carroll Librs in Partnership; Lyrasis; OCLC Online Computer Library Center, Inc
Special Services for the Deaf - Bks on deafness & sign lang; Spec interest per
Open Mon-Thurs 8am-Midnight, Fri 8-7, Sat 9-7, Sun Noon-Midnight

WESTOVER

EASTERN CORRECTIONAL INSTITUTION
S EAST LIBRARY*, 30420 Revells Neck Rd, 21890-3358. Tel: 410-845-4000, Ext 6227. FAX: 410-845-4208. *Librn,* Liam Kennedy; E-mail: lkennedy@dllr.state.md.us; *Evening Librn,* Sharon Brooks; Staff 1 (MLS 1)

Library Holdings: Bk Vols 5,565; Per Subs 40
Automation Activity & Vendor Info: (Cataloging) Follett Software; (Circulation) Follett Software
Database Vendor: Westlaw
Open Mon & Thurs 7:45am-10am, 11:30-1:45 & 6:30-8:30

S WEST LIBRARY*, 30420 Revells Neck Rd, 21890-3358. Tel: 410-845-4000, Ext 6423. FAX: 410-845-4206. *Librn,* June Brittingham; E-mail: jbrittingham@dllr.state.md.us; *Evening Librn,* Indira Cropper; Staff 1 (MLS 1)
Founded 1989
Library Holdings: CDs 30; High Interest/Low Vocabulary Bk Vols 45; Large Print Bks 25; Bk Vols 9,262; Per Subs 21; Talking Bks 20
Automation Activity & Vendor Info: (Cataloging) Follett Software; (Circulation) Follett Software
Database Vendor: LexisNexis
Restriction: Staff & inmates only

WYE MILLS

C CHESAPEAKE COLLEGE*, Learning Resource Center, PO Box 8, 21679. SAN 307-0654. Tel: 410-827-5860. FAX: 410-827-5257. Web Site: www.chesapeake.edu/library. *Dir,* Chandra Gigliotti-Guridi; *Librn,* Virginia Capute; E-mail: vcapute@chesapeake.edu; *Cat Tech,* Kim Green; Tel: 410-827-5860, Ext 292, E-mail: kgreen@chesapeake.edu
Founded 1967
Library Holdings: Bk Titles 40,000; Bk Vols 45,000; Per Subs 232
Special Collections: Eastern Shore Literature (Chesapeake Room)
Automation Activity & Vendor Info: (Cataloging) SirsiDynix; (Circulation) SirsiDynix; (OPAC) SirsiDynix
Database Vendor: EBSCOhost, Gale Cengage Learning, ProQuest
Publications: Directory of Community Services
Open Mon-Thurs 8am-9pm, Fri 8-4, Sat 10-4, Sun 1-5

MASSACHUSETTS

Date of Statistics: FY 2013
Population, 2010 U.S. Census: 6,547,629
Population Served by Public Libraries: 6,645,917
Unserved: 227
Number of Cities & Towns: 351
Total Public Library Holdings (Print & Nonprint): 48,924,670
Holdings (Print & Nonprint) Per Capita: 7.36
Total Public Library Operating Income: $269,778,605
Source of Income: Municipal appropriation: $241,357,099
Expenditures Per Capita (excluding Fed. Grants): $46.35
Number of Regional Library Systems: 1
Counties Served: All 351 cities & towns (systems not developed on county basis)
Grants-in-Aid to Public Libraries:
State Aid: $6,823,657
State Funding for one Regional Library System & Library of The Commonwealth: $9,231,475
State Expenditures for Public Library Construction: $20 million

ABINGTON

P ABINGTON PUBLIC LIBRARY*, 600 Gliniewicz Way, 02351. SAN 307-5737. Tel: 781-982-2139. FAX: 781-878-7361. E-mail: ablib@ocln.org. Web Site: abingtonpl.org. *Actg Dir,* Deborah Grimmett; *Asst Librn,* Sandy Bumpus; *Asst Librn,* Susan Durand; *Asst Librn,* Linda Sampson; *Ch,* Position Currently Open; *Ref Librn,* Judy Condon; Staff 6 (MLS 2, Non-MLS 4)
Founded 1878. Pop 16,351; Circ 87,643
Jul 2006-Jun 2007 Income $436,403, State $21,945, City $409,105, Locally Generated Income $5,353. Mats Exp $68,191, Books $57,829, Per/Ser (Incl. Access Fees) $4,784, AV Mat $4,678, Electronic Ref Mat (Incl. Access Fees) $900. Sal $249,310 (Prof $59,804)
Library Holdings: AV Mats 3,268; Bk Vols 61,206; Per Subs 88
Special Collections: Civil War (Arnold Coll); Large Print Coll
Function: Computer training
Mem of Massachusetts Libr Syst
Partic in Old Colony Libr Network (OCLN)
Friends of the Library Group

ACTON

P ACTON MEMORIAL LIBRARY*, 486 Main St, 01720. SAN 307-0670. Tel: 978-264-9641. FAX: 978-635-0073. TDD: 978-635-0072. Web Site: www.actonmemoriallibrary.org. *Dir,* Marcia Rich; E-mail: Mrich@acton-ma.gov; *Asst Dir,* Ellen Clark; *Cat,* Stephanie Knowland; *Ch Serv,* Lee Donohue; *Circ,* Gloria Reid; *ILL,* Julia Glendon; *Ref,* Susan Paju; *YA Serv,* Pamela Parenti; Staff 34 (MLS 10, Non-MLS 24)
Founded 1890. Pop 20,300; Circ 595,000
Jul 2007-Jun 2008 Income $950,000. Mats Exp $160,000. Sal $723,000
Library Holdings: AV Mats 5,400; DVDs 5,900; Electronic Media & Resources 137; Bk Vols 128,000; Per Subs 215
Special Collections: Arthur Davis Paintings; Civil War Artifacts; Literacy Coll. Municipal Document Depository; Oral History
Subject Interests: Local hist
Automation Activity & Vendor Info: (Cataloging) Innovative Interfaces, Inc; (Circulation) Innovative Interfaces, Inc; (OPAC) Innovative Interfaces, Inc
Wireless access
Publications: Good Word (Newsletter)
Special Services for the Deaf - Bks on deafness & sign lang
Special Services for the Blind - Accessible computers; Assistive/Adapted tech devices, equip & products; Audio mat; Bks on cassette; Bks on CD; Closed circuit TV magnifier; Copier with enlargement capabilities; Home delivery serv; Large print bks; Talking bks
Open Mon-Thurs 9-9, Fri & Sat 9-5, Sun (Winter) 2-5
Friends of the Library Group

ACUSHNET

P RUSSELL MEMORIAL LIBRARY*, 88 Main St, 02743. SAN 307-0700. Tel: 508-998-0270. FAX: 508-998-0271. Web Site: www.sailsinc.org/acushnet. *Dir,* Jayme Z Viveiros; Staff 1 (MLS 1)
Founded 1930. Pop 10,582; Circ 24,623
Library Holdings: Bk Vols 19,000; Per Subs 203
Special Collections: History Coll; Joseph Lincoln Books
Automation Activity & Vendor Info: (Cataloging) SirsiDynix, (Circulation) SirsiDynix; (OPAC) SirsiDynix
Mem of Massachusetts Libr Syst
Partic in SAILS Library Network
Open Mon & Wed 10-8, Tues & Thurs 1-8, Sat 9-3
Friends of the Library Group

ADAMS

P ADAMS FREE LIBRARY*, 92 Park St, 01220-2096. SAN 307-0719. Tel: 413-743-8345. FAX: 413-743-8344. Web Site: town.adams.ma.us. *Dir,* Deborah G Bruneau; *Cataloger,* Lyn Wilson; *Ch Serv,* Holli Jayko; *ILL,* Lorraine M Kalisz; Staff 5.5 (MLS 1.5, Non-MLS 4)
Founded 1883. Pop 9,311; Circ 70,089
Jul 2006-Jun 2007 Income $292,723, State $16,934, City $257,504, Locally Generated Income $4,330, Other $13,955. Mats Exp $49,165, Books $35,820, Per/Ser (Incl. Access Fees) $4,053, Other Print Mats $540, Micro $1,076, AV Mat $3,327, Electronic Ref Mat (Incl. Access Fees) $4,349. Sal $176,052 (Prof $153,967)
Library Holdings: Audiobooks 880; AV Mats 25; Bks on Deafness & Sign Lang 47; CDs 308; DVDs 503; Electronic Media & Resources 3; Large Print Bks 605; Bk Titles 39,349; Bk Vols 43,633; Per Subs 74; Videos 708
Subject Interests: Genealogy, Local hist
Automation Activity & Vendor Info: (Cataloging) Follett Software; (Circulation) Follett Software; (ILL) Innovative Interfaces, Inc; (OPAC) Follett Software
Database Vendor: Bowker, Innovative Interfaces, Inc
Wireless access
Function: Adult bk club, Bk club(s), Bks on cassette, Bks on CD, Children's prog, Computers for patron use, Copy machines, Free DVD rentals, Handicapped accessible, Home delivery & serv to Sr ctr & nursing homes, Homebound delivery serv, ILL available, Magnifiers for reading, Mail & tel request accepted, Mus passes, Photocopying/Printing, Prog for adults, Prog for children & young adult, Spoken cassettes & CDs, Summer reading prog, Tax forms, VHS videos, Wheelchair accessible
Partic in Central-Western Mass Automated Resource Sharing
Special Services for the Deaf - ADA equip; Assisted listening device; Assistive tech; Bks on deafness & sign lang; TTY equip; Videos & decoder
Special Services for the Blind - Aids for in-house use; Assistive/Adapted tech devices, equip & products; Audio mat; Bks on cassette; Bks on CD; Cassette playback machines; Cassettes; Large print & cassettes; Large print

bks; Large print bks & talking machines; Magnifiers; Recorded bks; Talking bks & player equip
Open Mon & Fri 9-6, Tues & Thurs 12-8, Wed 9-4, Sat 9-12

AGAWAM

P AGAWAM PUBLIC LIBRARY*, 750 Cooper St, 01001. SAN 307-0727. Tel: 413-789-1550. FAX: 413-789-1552. Web Site: www.agawamlibrary.org. *Dir,* Judith M Clini; E-mail: jclini@agawamlibrary.org; *Asst Dir,* Jolene Mercadante; E-mail: jmercada@agawamlibrary.org; *Head, Ref,* Jerome Walczak; E-mail: jwalczak@cwmars.org; *Circ Supvr,* Laura Paul; E-mail: lpaul@agawamlibrary.org; *Adult Serv,* Joanne Szelag; *ILL,* Maria Yacovone; E-mail: myacovon@agawamlibrary.org; *Youth Serv,* Cynthia Sutter; Staff 5 (MLS 4, Non-MLS 1)
Pop 29,000; Circ 324,198
Library Holdings: AV Mats 18,276; Bk Vols 124,078; Per Subs 243
Automation Activity & Vendor Info: (Acquisitions) Innovative Interfaces, Inc; (Cataloging) Innovative Interfaces, Inc; (Circulation) Innovative Interfaces, Inc; (OPAC) Innovative Interfaces, Inc; (Serials) Innovative Interfaces, Inc
Wireless access
Partic in Central & Western Massachusetts Automated Resource Sharing
Open Mon-Thurs 9-9, Fri 10-6, Sat 10-5
Friends of the Library Group

AMESBURY

P AMESBURY PUBLIC LIBRARY*, 149 Main St, 01913. SAN 307-0743. Tel: 978-388-8148. E-mail: mam@mvlc.org. Web Site: www.amesburylibrary.org. *Dir,* Patty DiTullio; E-mail: pditullio@mvlc.org; *Asst Dir,* Erin Matlin; E-mail: ematlin@mvlc.org; *Head, Tech Serv,* Suzanne Cote; *Ref Librn,* Pam Schwotzer; E-mail: pschwotzer@mvlc.org; *Ch Serv,* Clare Dombrowski; E-mail: cdombrowski@mvlc.org; *Circ,* Michaela Pelletier; *YA Serv,* Margie Walker; E-mail: mwalker@mvlc.org; Staff 3.95 (MLS 3.95)
Founded 1856. Pop 16,429; Circ 146,240
Library Holdings: Audiobooks 3,250; CDs 104; DVDs 2,470; Microforms 1,026; Bk Vols 70,127; Per Subs 110
Special Collections: Amesbury Carriage History Material; Charles H Davis Painting Coll; John Greenleaf Whittier Material
Automation Activity & Vendor Info: (Cataloging) Horizon; (Circulation) Horizon; (ILL) Horizon; (OPAC) Horizon
Wireless access
Function: Adult bk club, Archival coll, Art exhibits, Audiobks via web, Bk club(s), Bks on CD, CD-ROM, Children's prog, Computer training, Computers for patron use, Copy machines, Electronic databases & coll, Free DVD rentals, Holiday prog, Home delivery & serv to Sr ctr & nursing homes, Homebound delivery serv, ILL available, Mus passes, Music CDs, Online cat, Online ref, OverDrive digital audio bks, Photocopying/Printing, Preschool outreach, Prog for adults, Prog for children & young adult, Pub access computers, Ref & res, Ref serv available, Ref serv in person, Senior outreach, Story hour, Summer reading prog, Tax forms, Teen prog, Telephone ref, Writing prog
Partic in Merrimack Valley Library Consortium
Open Mon-Wed 10-8, Thurs, Fri & Sat 10-5 (Sat July & Aug 10-1)
Friends of the Library Group

AMHERST

C AMHERST COLLEGE*, Robert Frost Library, 61 Quadrangle Dr, 01002. SAN 344-4902. Circulation Tel: 413-542-2373. Interlibrary Loan Service Tel: 413-542-2666. Reference Tel: 413-542-2319. Administration Tel: 413-542-2212. FAX: 413-542-2662. E-mail: library@amherst.edu. Web Site: www.amherst.edu/library. *Librn of the Col,* Bryn Geffert; E-mail: bgeffert@amherst.edu; *Head, Archives & Spec Coll,* Mike Kelly; *Head, Cat,* Jane Beebe; *Head, Info Tech,* Jan Jourdain; *Head, Pub Serv,* Margaret Adams Groesbeck; *Head, Ser,* Paul Trumble; *Head, Tech Serv,* Susan Sheridan; *Access Serv Librn,* Odelia Levanovsky; *Cat Librn,* Kate Gerrity; *Cat Librn,* Rebecca Henning; *Cat Librn,* Marjorie Hess; *Digital Res Librn,* Catherine Winston; *Coordr, Coll Develop, Ref Librn,* Michael Kasper; *Sci & Electronic Serv Librn,* Susan J Kimball; *Tech Serv Librn,* Erin Loree; Staff 17 (MLS 15, Non-MLS 2)
Enrl 1,648; Fac 201; Highest Degree: Bachelor
Jul 2005-Jun 2006. Mats Exp $2,310,280. Sal $2,060,649 (Prof $1,120,042)
Library Holdings: Bk Vols 1,078,161; Per Subs 5,798
Special Collections: Augustine Daly Coll; Clyde Fitch Coll; Dylan Thomas Coll; Emily Dickinson Coll; John J McCloy Coll; Richard Mann Coll; Richard Wilbur Coll; Robert Frost Coll; Rolfe Humphreys Coll; Walt Whitman Coll; William Wordsworth Coll. US Document Depository
Automation Activity & Vendor Info: (Acquisitions) Ex Libris Group; (Cataloging) Ex Libris Group; (Circulation) Ex Libris Group; (Course Reserve) Ex Libris Group; (ILL) OCLC ILLiad; (Media Booking) Ex Libris Group; (OPAC) Ex Libris Group; (Serials) Ex Libris Group
Wireless access
Publications: Friends of the Amherst College Library (Newsletter)
Partic in Nylink
Restriction: Open to fac, students & qualified researchers
Friends of the Library Group
Departmental Libraries:
KEEFE SCIENCE LIBRARY, 01002. Tel: 413-542-2076. Reference Tel: 413-542-8112. Web Site: www.amherst.edu/library/depts/science. *Sci Librn,* Kristen Greenland; Staff 2 (MLS 1, Non-MLS 1)
Founded 1996
Library Holdings: Bk Vols 52,518
VINCENT MORGAN MUSIC LIBRARY, 01002. Tel: 413-542-2387. Web Site: www.amherst.edu/library/depts/music. *Music Librn,* Jane Beebe; Tel: 413-542-2667, E-mail: jabeebe@amherst.edu
Library Holdings: CDs 14,105; Music Scores 20,880; Bk Vols 30,962

C HAMPSHIRE COLLEGE LIBRARY*, Harold F Johnson Library Center, 893 West St, 01002-5001. SAN 307-0751. Tel: 413-559-5440. Interlibrary Loan Service Tel: 413-559-5475. Reference Tel: 413-559-5758. Administration Tel: 413-559-6691. FAX: 413-559-5419. E-mail: library@hampshire.edu. Web Site: www.hampshire.edu/library. *Libr Dir,* Jennifer Gunter King; Tel: 413-559-5761, E-mail: jking@hampshire.edu; *Access & Art Librn,* Rachel Beckwith; E-mail: rbeckwith@hampshire.edu; *Critical Soc Inquiry & Digital Pedagogy Librn,* Alana Kumbier; Tel: 413-559-5704, E-mail: aklLO@hampshire.edu; *Interdisciplinary Sci Librn,* Thea Atwood; E-mail: tatwood@hampshire.edu; *Archivist,* Jimi Jones; E-mail: jljLO@hampshire.edu; *Bibliog Instr, Ref,* Bonnie Vigeland; E-mail: bvigeland@hampshire.edu; *Online Serv, Ser,* Abigail Baines; E-mail: asbLO@hampshire.edu. Subject Specialists: *Soc sci,* Alana Kumbier; *Cognitive sci, Natural sci,* Thea Atwood; *Humanities,* Bonnie Vigeland; Staff 8 (MLS 6, Non-MLS 2)
Founded 1970. Enrl 1,450; Fac 140; Highest Degree: Bachelor
Jul 2007-Jun 2008 Income $450,000. Mats Exp $325,582, Books $47,915, Per/Ser (Incl. Access Fees) $215,667, AV Equip $47,000, AV Mat $15,000. Sal $826,934 (Prof $375,832)
Library Holdings: AV Mats 42,100; e-books 64,469; Microforms 99; Bk Vols 134,544; Per Subs 56,041
Subject Interests: Environ studies, Films & filmmaking, Gender studies, Pub policy, Sustainable agr, Third World
Automation Activity & Vendor Info: (Acquisitions) Ex Libris Group; (Cataloging) OCLC Connexion; (Circulation) Ex Libris Group; (Course Reserve) Ex Libris Group; (ILL) OCLC FirstSearch; (Media Booking) Ex Libris Group; (OPAC) Ex Libris Group; (Serials) Ex Libris Group
Database Vendor: Agricola, Alexander Street Press, American Psychological Association (APA), Annual Reviews, ARTstor, Backstage Library Works, BioOne, Cambridge Scientific Abstracts, Cinahl, EBSCO Information Services, EBSCOhost, Elsevier, Ex Libris Group, Gale Cengage Learning, Greenwood Publishing Group, H W Wilson, Haworth Pres Inc, HeinOnline, Ingenta, ISI Web of Knowledge, JSTOR, LexisNexis, Marquis Who's Who, Modern Language Association, Nature Publishing Group, OCLC FirstSearch, OCLC WorldShare Interlibrary Loan, OVID Technologies, Oxford Online, Project MUSE, ProQuest, PubMed, Sage, ScienceDirect, Springer-Verlag, Thomson - Web of Science, Wiley InterScience
Wireless access
Function: Art exhibits, Audio & video playback equip for onsite use, Computers for patron use, Copy machines, E-Reserves, Electronic databases & coll, Music CDs, Online cat, Online searches, Photocopying/Printing, Pub access computers, Ref serv in person, Spoken cassettes & CDs
Mem of Massachusetts Libr Syst
Partic in Five Colleges, Inc; Lyrasis; OCLC Online Computer Library Center, Inc
Open Mon-Fri 8:30am-Midnight, Sat & Sun 10am-Midnight

P JONES LIBRARY, INC*, 43 Amity St, 01002-2285. SAN 344-502X. Tel: 413-259-3090. Circulation Tel: 413-259-3091. Reference Tel: 413-259-3096. Administration Tel: 413-259-3106. FAX: 413-256-4096. E-mail: info@joneslibrary.org. Web Site: www.joneslibrary.org. *Dir,* Sharon A Sharry; E-mail: sharrys@joneslibrary.org; *Head, Prog & Outreach,* Janet Ryan; Tel: 413-259-3223, E-mail: ryanj@joneslibrary.org; *Head, Borrower Serv,* Amy Anaya; Tel: 413-259-3132, E-mail: anayaa@joneslibrary.org; *Head, Coll,* Linda Wentworth; Tel: 413-259-3168, E-mail: wentworthl@joneslibrary.org; *Head, Info Serv,* Matthew Berube; Tel: 413-259-3195, E-mail: berubem@joneslibrary.org; *Head, Tech Serv,* Carolyn Platt; Tel: 413-259-3214; *Head, Youth Serv,* Sondra M Radosh; Tel: 413-259-3219, E-mail: radoshs@joneslibrary.org; *Br Head,* Susan Hugus; Tel: 413-259-3095, E-mail: e.hugus@gmail.com; *Br Head,* Maggie Spiegel; Tel: 413-259-3099, E-mail: spiegelm@joneslibrary.org; *Fac Supvr,* George Hicks; Tel: 413-259-3174, E-mail: hicksg@joneslibrary.org; *Curator, Spec Coll,* Tevis Kimball; Tel: 413-259-3182, E-mail: kimballt@joneslibrary.org; Staff 30 (MLS 10, Non-MLS 20)
Founded 1919. Pop 37,000; Circ 540,000
Jul 2008-Jun 2009 Income (Main Library and Branch(s)) $2,143,347, State $100,000, City $1,490,385, Locally Generated Income $80,550, Other

$472,412. Mats Exp $239,408, Books $158,688, Per/Ser (Incl. Access Fees) $21,420, AV Mat $39,300, Electronic Ref Mat (Incl. Access Fees) $20,000. Sal $1,352,965
Library Holdings: AV Mats 24,400; Bk Vols 209,300; Per Subs 316
Special Collections: Early Textbooks & Children's Books (Clifton Johnson Coll); Emily Dickinson Coll; Genealogy (Boltwood Coll); Harlan Fiske Stone Coll; Julius Lester Coll; Local History; Ray Stannard Baker Coll; Robert Frost Coll; Sidney Waugh Coll
Subject Interests: English (Lang)
Automation Activity & Vendor Info: (Acquisitions) Evergreen; (Cataloging) OCLC CatExpress; (Circulation) Evergreen; (OPAC) Evergreen
Wireless access
Publications: Annual Report; Tales of Amherst; The Library in North Amherst
Partic in Central & Western Massachusetts Automated Resource Sharing
Special Services for the Deaf - TDD equip; TTY equip
Special Services for the Blind - Closed circuit TV magnifier; Descriptive video serv (DVS)
Open Mon 1-5:30, Tues & Thurs 9am-9:30pm, Wed, Fri & Sat 9-5:30, Sun 1-5
Friends of the Library Group
Branches: 2
MUNSON MEMORIAL, 1046 S East St, South Amherst, 01002, SAN 344-5089. Tel: 413-259-3095. *Br Head,* Susan Hugus; E-mail: e.hugus@gmail.com
Open Mon, Tues & Thurs 2-5:30, Wed 2-7:30, Sat 9-1
NORTH AMHERST BRANCH, Eight Montague Rd, 01002, SAN 344-5054. Tel: 413-259-3099. *Br Head,* Maggie Spiegel; E-mail: spiegelm@joneslibrary.org
Open Mon 10-1:30, Tues 2-7:30, Wed-Fri 2-5:30, Sat 10-2

S NATIONAL YIDDISH BOOK CENTER, Harry & Jeanette Weinberg Bldg, 1021 West St, 01002-3375. SAN 370-5056. Tel: 413-256-4900. FAX: 413-256-4700. Web Site: www.yiddishbookcenter.org. *Bibliographer,* Catherine Madsen; E-mail: cmadsen@bikher.org; Staff 1 (Non-MLS 1)
Library Holdings: Bk Titles 20,000; Bk Vols 1,500,000
Automation Activity & Vendor Info: (Cataloging) OCLC WorldShare Interlibrary Loan
Wireless access
Publications: Steven Spielberg Digital Yiddish Library

C UNIVERSITY OF MASSACHUSETTS AMHERST LIBRARIES*, W E B Du Bois Library, 154 Hicks Way, University of Massachusetts, 01003-9275. SAN 344-5119. Circulation Tel: 413-545-2622. Interlibrary Loan Service Tel: 413-545-0553. Reference Tel: 413-545-0150. Administration Tel: 413-545-0284. Interlibrary Loan Service FAX: 413-577-1536. Administration FAX: 413-545-6873. Web Site: www.library.umass.edu. *Dir of Libr,* Jay Schafer; E-mail: jschafer@library.umass.edu; *Dir of Libr Develop & Communications,* Carol Connare; Tel: 413-545-0995, E-mail: cconnare@library.umass.edu; *Assoc Dir, Libr Serv,* Leslie Horner Button; Tel: 413-545-6845, E-mail: button@library.umass.edu; *Head, Access Serv,* Kathryn Leigh; Tel: 413-577-0175, E-mail: kathrynr@library.umass.edu; *Head, Image Coll,* Brian Shelburne; Tel: 413-545-4061, E-mail: bps@library.umass.edu; *Head, Info Res Mgt,* Gary Hough; Tel: 413-545-6856, E-mail: ghough@library.umass.edu; *Head, Res & Liaison Serv,* Beth Lang; Tel: 413-545-6890, E-mail: bwlang@library.umass.edu; *Head, Sci & Eng,* Maxine Schmidt; Tel: 413-545-6739, E-mail: mschmidt@library.umass.edu; *Head, Spec Coll & Archives,* Robert Cox; Tel: 413-545-2780, E-mail: rscox@library.umass.edu; *Head, Syst & Web Mgt,* MJ Canavan; Tel: 413-545-6824, E-mail: mjcanavan@library.umass.edu; *Head, Undergrad Teaching & Learning Serv,* Sarah Hutton; Tel: 413-545-6740, E-mail: shutton@library.umass.edu; *Assessment Librn,* Rachel Lewellen; Tel: 413-545-3343, E-mail: rlewellen@library.umass.edu; *Scholarly Communications Librn,* Marilyn Billings; Tel: 413-545-6891, E-mail: mbillings@library.umass.edu; *Mgr, Circ Serv,* Thomas Paige; Tel: 413-577-2103, E-mail: tpaige@library.umass.edu; *Coordr, Learning Commons,* Carol Will; Tel: 413-545-6795, E-mail: cwill@library.umass.edu; *Coordr, Multimedia Ctr,* Jeanne Antill; Tel: 413-545-6959, E-mail: jantill@library.umass.edu; *Curator of Ms & Univ Archivist,* Danielle Kovacs; Tel: 413-545-2784; Staff 124 (MLS 42, Non-MLS 82)
Founded 1865. Enrl 24,000; Fac 1,182; Highest Degree: Doctorate
Library Holdings: Bk Vols 5,900,000; Per Subs 15,427
Special Collections: Benjamin Smith Lyman Papers & Japanese Coll; Broadside Press; County Atlases of New England, New York & New Jersey (Farm Credit Bank's Coll); French Revolution (Binet Coll); Harvey Swados Papers; Horace Mann Bond Papers; Massachusetts Government Publications; Massachusetts Labor & Business Records; Massachusetts Social Action & Peace Organizations; Massachusetts Social Service Agencies Records; Robert Francis Coll; Silvio O Conte Congressional Papers; Slavery & Anti-Slavery Pamphlets 1725-1911; Travel & Tourism in the Northeast; W B Yeats (R K Alspach Coll); W E B Du Bois Papers; Wallace Stevens Coll. State Document Depository; US Document Depository
Subject Interests: African-Am, Agr, Ethnic studies, Geog, Latin Am, Massachusetts, Natural hist, New England
Automation Activity & Vendor Info: (Acquisitions) Ex Libris Group; (Cataloging) Ex Libris Group; (Circulation) Ex Libris Group; (Course Reserve) Ex Libris Group; (OPAC) Ex Libris Group; (Serials) Ex Libris Group
Wireless access
Open Mon-Thurs 8am-Midnight, Fri 8-6, Sat 10-6, Sun 1-Midnight
Friends of the Library Group

ANDOVER

S ANDOVER HISTORICAL SOCIETY LIBRARY*, Caroline M Underhill Research Center, 97 Main St, 01810. SAN 325-8696. Tel: 978-475-2236. FAX: 978-470-2741. E-mail: info@andoverhistorical.org. Web Site: www.andoverhistorical.org. *Exec Dir,* Elaine Clements; E-mail: eclements@andoverhistorical.org
Library Holdings: Bk Vols 3,240
Special Collections: 19th & 20th Century Photographs of Andover People, Events, Buildings & Sites; Andover Imprints
Subject Interests: Decorative art
Wireless access
Publications: Andover Century of Change 1896-1996; Andover Townswomen by Bessie Goldsmith; Historical Sketches of Andover

CL MASSACHUSETTS SCHOOL OF LAW LIBRARY*, Information Resource Center, 500 Federal St, 01810. SAN 371-5892. Tel: 978-681-0800. FAX: 978-681-6330. Web Site: www.mslaw.edu/directory_library.htm. *Dir,* Judith Wolfe; E-mail: wolfe@mslaw.edu; *Ref Serv,* Edward A Becker; E-mail: ebecker@mslaw.edu; *Ref Serv,* Mary Kilpatrick; E-mail: kilpatrick@mslaw.edu; *Tech Serv,* Shukla Biswas; E-mail: biswas@mslaw.edu; Staff 5 (MLS 4, Non-MLS 1)
Enrl 600; Fac 17; Highest Degree: Doctorate
Library Holdings: Bk Titles 11,529; Bk Vols 81,627; Per Subs 276
Automation Activity & Vendor Info: (Acquisitions) OCLC; (Cataloging) OCLC; (Circulation) OCLC
Mem of Massachusetts Libr Syst
Partic in Lyrasis
Open Mon-Fri 8am-11pm, Sat 8-6:30, Sun 11-6:30

P MEMORIAL HALL LIBRARY*, Two N Main St, 01810. SAN 344-5208. Tel: 978-623-8401. FAX: 978-623-8407. E-mail: rdesk@mhl.org. Web Site: www.mhl.org. *Dir,* Beth Mazin; *Asst Dir,* Susan Katzenstein; E-mail: skatzenstein@mhl.org; *Head, Ch,* Beth Kerrigan; *Head, Circ, Head, Tech Serv,* Nancy Richards; E-mail: nrichards@mhl.org; *Commun Serv Librn,* Emily Classon; E-mail: eclasson@mhl.org; *Ref,* Eleanor Sathan; E-mail: esathan@mhl.org; Staff 15 (MLS 15)
Founded 1873. Pop 32,296; Circ 530,425
Jul 2009-Jun 2010. Mats Exp $312,000. Sal $2,011,489
Automation Activity & Vendor Info: (Cataloging) SirsiDynix; (Circulation) SirsiDynix; (ILL) SirsiDynix; (OPAC) SirsiDynix
Database Vendor: Baker & Taylor, EBSCOhost, ReferenceUSA, SirsiDynix, Westlaw
Wireless access
Mem of Massachusetts Libr Syst
Partic in Merrimack Valley Library Consortium
Open Mon-Thurs 9-9, Fri & Sat 9-5, Sun 1-5
Friends of the Library Group

S PHILLIPS ACADEMY*, Robert S Peabody Museum of Archaeology, 180 Main St, 01810. Tel: 978-749-4490. FAX: 978-749-4495. Web Site: www.andover.edu/rspeabody/index.html. *Dir,* Malinda Blustain
Founded 1901
Library Holdings: Bk Vols 6,000; Per Subs 15
Open Mon-Fri 8-5
Restriction: Non-circulating to the pub, Open by appt only

AQUINNAH

P AQUINNAH PUBLIC LIBRARY*, One Church St, 02535. SAN 375-4367. Tel: 508-645-2314. FAX: 508-645-2188. E-mail: aquilib@vineyard.net. Web Site: www.aquinnah-ma.gov/content/aquinnah-public-library. *Libr Dir,* Catherine A Thompson; Staff 2 (MLS 1, Non-MLS 1)
Founded 1901. Pop 311; Circ 11,584
Library Holdings: AV Mats 1,340; Bk Vols 7,319; Per Subs 34
Automation Activity & Vendor Info: (Cataloging) Follett Software; (Circulation) Follett Software
Wireless access
Open Tues & Thurs 2-7, Sat 10-4
Friends of the Library Group

ARLINGTON

S ARMENIAN CULTURAL FOUNDATION LIBRARY*, 441 Mystic St, 02474-1108. SAN 373-0654. Tel: 781-646-3090. FAX: 781-646-3090. *Curator,* Ara Ghazarian
Founded 1945
Library Holdings: CDs 10; Music Scores 186; Bk Vols 33,000; Per Subs 10
Open Mon-Fri 9-2
Friends of the Library Group

P PUBLIC LIBRARY OF ARLINGTON*, Robbins Library, 700 Massachusetts Ave, 02476. SAN 344-5267. Tel: 781-316-3200, 781-316-3233. FAX: 781-316-3209. Web Site: www.robbinslibrary.org. *Dir,* Ryan Livergood; *Adult Serv,* Jennifer DeRemer; *Tech Serv,* Susan Neubauer; Staff 11 (MLS 11)
Founded 1807. Pop 42,389; Circ 525,791
Jul 2005-Jun 2006 Income $1,934,610, State $56,803, City $1,734,462, Federal $9,815, Locally Generated Income $133,530. Mats Exp $275,893, Books $179,691, Per/Ser (Incl. Access Fees) $16,988, Other Print Mats $6,410, Micro $10,269, AV Mat $44,791, Electronic Ref Mat (Incl. Access Fees) $17,744
Library Holdings: AV Mats 23,377; Electronic Media & Resources 223; Bk Vols 205,351; Per Subs 296
Special Collections: Robbins Print Coll, etchings, lithographs, prints. Oral History
Automation Activity & Vendor Info: (Cataloging) Innovative Interfaces, Inc; (Circulation) Innovative Interfaces, Inc; (OPAC) Innovative Interfaces, Inc
Wireless access
Partic in Minuteman Library Network
Open Mon-Wed 9-9, Thurs 1-9, Fri & Sat 9-5
Friends of the Library Group
Branches: 1
EDITH M FOX LIBRARY & COMMUNITY CENTER, 175 Massachusetts Ave, 02474, SAN 344-5321. Tel: 781-316-3198. Web Site: www.robbinslibrary.org/about/fox_branch. *Librn,* Laura Lintz; Tel: 781-316-3196, E-mail: llintz@minlib.net; Staff 2.5 (MLS 1, Non-MLS 1.5)
Library Holdings: Bk Vols 27,483
Open Tues, Thurs & Fri 9-5, Wed 12-8
Friends of the Library Group

ASHBURNHAM

P STEVENS MEMORIAL LIBRARY*, 20 Memorial Dr, 01430. SAN 307-0808. Tel: 978-827-4115. FAX: 978-827-4116. E-mail: ashlibrary@net1plus.com. *Dir,* Cheryl Bradley; *Asst Librn,* Melissa Walker
Pop 5,733; Circ 27,000
Library Holdings: Bk Vols 35,000; Per Subs 35
Open Mon-Thurs 10-8, Fri 10-5, Sat (Sept-May) 10-2
Friends of the Library Group

ASHBY

P ASHBY FREE PUBLIC LIBRARY*, 812 Main St, 01431. (Mail add: PO Box 279, 01431-0279), SAN 307-0816. Tel: 978-386-5377. FAX: 978-386-5377. E-mail: ashby@cwmars.org. Web Site: www.ashbylibrary.org. *Librn,* Marja-Leena LePoer
Pop 2,740; Circ 18,500
Library Holdings: Bk Vols 25,000
Mem of Massachusetts Libr Syst
Open Tues & Fri 1:30-9, Wed 2-7, Sat 9-12
Friends of the Library Group

ASHFIELD

P BELDING MEMORIAL LIBRARY, 344 Main St, 01330. (Mail add: PO Box 407, 01330-0407), SAN 307-0824. Tel: 413-628-4414. Web Site: beldingmemoriallibrary.org. *Librn,* Martha Cohen; E-mail: mcohen@cwmars.org; Staff 1 (MLS 1)
Founded 1914. Pop 1,739; Circ 18,608
Library Holdings: Audiobooks 228; DVDs 908; Bk Titles 12,690; Per Subs 23
Wireless access
Open Mon & Wed 2-8, Sat 10-3
Friends of the Library Group

ASHLAND

S ASHLAND HISTORICAL SOCIETY LIBRARY*, Two Myrtle St, 01721. (Mail add: PO Box 145, 01721-0145), SAN 329-8698. Tel: 508-881-8183. E-mail: ashlandhistsoc@msn.com. *Pres,* Cliff Wilson
Founded 1990
Library Holdings: Bk Vols 500
Subject Interests: Genealogy, Hist, Local hist
Restriction: Non-circulating, Open by appt only

P ASHLAND PUBLIC LIBRARY*, 66 Front St, 01721-1606. SAN 307-0832. Tel: 508-881-0134. FAX: 508-881-0135. E-mail: library@ashlandmass.com. Web Site: www.ashlandmass.com/library/index.htm. *Dir,* Paula Bonetti; E-mail: pbonetti@ashlandmass.com; *Ch Serv,* Lois McAuliffe; *ILL,* J Dee Clark
Pop 11,604; Circ 48,500
Library Holdings: Bk Vols 30,808; Per Subs 70
Automation Activity & Vendor Info: (Cataloging) Innovative Interfaces, Inc; (Circulation) Innovative Interfaces, Inc; (Media Booking) Innovative Interfaces, Inc
Open Tues-Thurs 10-8, Fri 2-5, Sat 10-5
Friends of the Library Group

ATHOL

P ATHOL PUBLIC LIBRARY*, 568 Main St, 01331. SAN 307-0840. Tel: 978-249-9515. FAX: 978-249-7636. E-mail: info@athollibrary.org. Web Site: athollibrary.org. *Dir,* Debra Blanchard; E-mail: dblanchard@mass.rr.com; *Asst Dir,* Robin Shtulman; E-mail: rshtulman@cwmars.org; *ILL & Distance Libr Serv Spec,* Marie Lehmann; *Cat, Webmaster,* Libby Lipin; E-mail: llipin@cwmars.org; *Ch Serv,* Jean Shaughnessy; *Genealogy Serv,* Karen McNiff; Staff 8 (MLS 4, Non-MLS 4)
Founded 1882. Pop 1,451; Circ 147,869
Jul 2009-Jun 2010. Mats Exp $398,787, Books $49,515, Per/Ser (Incl. Access Fees) $5,000, Electronic Ref Mat (Incl. Access Fees) $3,000. Sal $271,768
Library Holdings: Bk Vols 53,497; Per Subs 58; Talking Bks 1,843; Videos 3,371
Special Collections: Local Art Originals; Local History Archives
Automation Activity & Vendor Info: (Cataloging) Follett Software; (Circulation) Follett Software
Wireless access
Mem of Massachusetts Libr Syst
Partic in Central & Western Massachusetts Automated Resource Sharing
Open Mon & Wed-Fri 9:30-5:30, Tues 9:30-7
Friends of the Library Group

ATTLEBORO

P ATTLEBORO PUBLIC LIBRARY*, 74 N Main St, 02703. SAN 344-5356. Tel: 508-222-0157. Reference Tel: 508-222-0157, Ext 14. FAX: 508-226-3326. E-mail: apl_ref@sailsinc.org. Web Site: attleborolibrary.org. *Dir,* Joan Pilkington-Smyth; *Ch,* Krystal Brown; *Ref,* Kathleen Hibbert; *Tech Serv,* Heidi Cauley
Founded 1885. Pop 42,185
Library Holdings: Bk Vols 90,000; Per Subs 120
Special Collections: Attleboro History, bks, mss & papers
Subject Interests: Genealogy, Local hist
Automation Activity & Vendor Info: (Cataloging) SirsiDynix; (Circulation) SirsiDynix; (OPAC) SirsiDynix
Wireless access
Partic in SAILS Library Network
Open Mon, Wed & Thurs 8:30-8:30, Tues & Fri 8:30-4:30, Sat (Sept-May) 8:30-4:30
Friends of the Library Group

M STURDY MEMORIAL HOSPITAL*, Health Sciences Library, 211 Park St, 02703. SAN 307-0859. Tel: 508-236-7920. FAX: 508-236-7909. E-mail: medlib@sturdymemorial.org. *Librn,* Joseph Holland
Founded 1960
Library Holdings: Bk Titles 500; Bk Vols 1,950; Per Subs 40
Subject Interests: Cardiology, Obstetrics & gynecology, Pediatrics, Surgery, Urology
Partic in North Atlantic Health Sciences Libraries, Inc; Southeastern Massachusetts Consortium of Health Science Libraries

AUBURN

P AUBURN PUBLIC LIBRARY*, 369 Southbridge St, 01501. SAN 307-0867. Tel: 508-832-7790. FAX: 508-832-7792. Web Site: www.auburnlibrary.org. *Dir,* Diane Ramsay; *Asst Dir,* Donna Galonek; *Ch,* Renee Bichan; *ILL,* Marie Carbone; Staff 8 (MLS 3, Non-MLS 5)
Founded 1872. Pop 15,870; Circ 182,080
Jul 2011-Jun 2012 Income $556,879. Mats Exp $89,540
Library Holdings: CDs 6,140; DVDs 4,594; e-books 9,754; Electronic Media & Resources 3,999; Microforms 2,900; Bk Vols 82,542; Per Subs 111
Special Collections: Local History Coll
Automation Activity & Vendor Info: (Cataloging) Evergreen; (Circulation) Evergreen; (OPAC) Evergreen
Wireless access

Mem of Massachusetts Libr Syst
Partic in Central-Western Mass Automated Resource Sharing
Open Mon-Thurs 9:30-8:30, Fri 9:30-5:30, Sat 9-1
Friends of the Library Group

R FIRST CONGREGATIONAL CHURCH LIBRARY*, 128 Central St, 01501. SAN 307 0875. Tel: 508-832-2845. FAX: 508-721-2539. *In Charge,* Gloria Whitehead
Founded 1959
Library Holdings: Large Print Bks 60; Bk Titles 3,300
Subject Interests: Arts, Drama, Family, Fiction, Health, Hist, Nature, Non-fiction, Poetry, Travel
Restriction: Not open to pub

AVON

P AVON PUBLIC LIBRARY*, 280 W Main St, 02322. SAN 307-0905. Tel: 508-583-0378. FAX: 508-580-2757. E-mail: avlib@ocln.org. Web Site: www.avonpubliclibrary.org. *Dir,* Karen A Johnson; E-mail: kjohnson@ocln.org; *Asst Librn, Circ Supvr,* Ann Marie Fogg; E-mail: afogg@ocln.org. Subject Specialists: *Children's lit,* Karen A Johnson; Staff 6 (Non-MLS 6)
Founded 1892. Pop 4,300; Circ 42,693
Jul 2006-Jun 2007 Income $324,264. Mats Exp $70,000
Library Holdings: High Interest/Low Vocabulary Bk Vols 100; Bk Vols 31,000; Per Subs 103; Talking Bks 1,358
Special Collections: Childrens' Coll
Subject Interests: Antiques, Restoration
Automation Activity & Vendor Info: (Acquisitions) SirsiDynix; (Cataloging) SirsiDynix; (Circulation) SirsiDynix; (OPAC) SirsiDynix
Database Vendor: SirsiDynix
Wireless access
Function: Handicapped accessible, ILL available, Prog for children & young adult, Ref serv available, Summer reading prog, Wheelchair accessible
Mem of Massachusetts Libr Syst
Partic in Old Colony Libr Network (OCLN)
Special Services for the Blind - Audio mat; Bks on CD
Open Mon & Wed 10-5, Tues & Thurs 10-7:30, Fri 10-3, Sat 10-2
Friends of the Library Group

AYER

P AYER LIBRARY*, 26 E Main St, 01432. SAN 307-0913. Tel: 978-772-8250. FAX: 978-772-8251. Web Site: www.ayerlibrary.org. *Dir,* Mary Anne Lucht; *Ch Serv,* Mona Blanchette; *Ref,* Jean Henry
Pop 7,000; Circ 24,000
Library Holdings: Bk Vols 50,000; Per Subs 70
Automation Activity & Vendor Info: (Cataloging) Innovative Interfaces, Inc; (Circulation) Innovative Interfaces, Inc; (OPAC) Innovative Interfaces, Inc
Wireless access
Mem of Massachusetts Libr Syst
Open Tues & Wed 10-8, Thurs & Fri 10-6, Sat 10-2
Friends of the Library Group

BABSON PARK

C BABSON COLLEGE*, Horn Library, 231 Forest St, 02457-0310. SAN 307-0921. Tel: 781-239-4596. Interlibrary Loan Service Tel: 781-239-4574. FAX: 781-239-5226. E-mail: library@babson.edu. Web Site: library.babson.edu. *Dir,* Position Currently Open; *Assoc Dir, Access Serv,* Dee Stonberg; Tel: 781-239-4391, E-mail: stonberg@babson.edu; *Mgr, Coll Mgt,* Martha Burk; Tel: 781-239-4988, E-mail: burk@babson.edu; *Mgr, Info Desks,* Sarah Pawlek; Tel: 781-239-5604, E-mail: spawlek@babson.edu; *Archivist,* Ron Rybnikar; Tel: 781-239-4570, E-mail: rybnikar@babson.edu. Subject Specialists: *Mgt,* Dee Stonberg; *Arts, Humanities,* Sarah Pawlek; Staff 18 (MLS 16, Non-MLS 2)
Founded 1919. Enrl 2,723; Fac 208; Highest Degree: Master
Library Holdings: AV Mats 4,153; e-books 57,578; e-journals 217; Bk Titles 91,488; Bk Vols 114,006; Per Subs 409
Special Collections: Sailing & Transportation (Hinckley Coll); Sir Isaac Newton Coll
Subject Interests: Bus & mgt, Econ
Automation Activity & Vendor Info: (Acquisitions) SirsiDynix; (Cataloging) SirsiDynix; (Circulation) SirsiDynix; (Course Reserve) SirsiDynix; (ILL) SirsiDynix; (OPAC) SirsiDynix; (Serials) SirsiDynix
Database Vendor: EBSCOhost, Factiva.com, IBISWorld, JSTOR, LexisNexis, ProQuest, Standard & Poor's, Westlaw, World Book Online
Wireless access
Publications: Infobits (Consumer guide); ITSD Update (Newsletter)
Mem of Massachusetts Libr Syst
Partic in Lyrasis; OCLC Online Computer Library Center, Inc; WEBnet Libr Consortium
Open Mon-Thurs 7:30am-Midnight, Fri 7:30-7:30, Sat 8:30-5:30, Sun 9am-Midnight

BARNSTABLE

L MASSACHUSETTS TRIAL COURT LAW LIBRARIES*, Barnstable Law Library, First District Court House, 02630. (Mail add: PO Box 427, 02630-0427), SAN 325-8653. Tel: 508-362-8539. FAX: 508-362-1374. E-mail: barnstablelawlibrary@gmail.com. Web Site: www.lawlib.state.ma.us. *Law Librn,* Margaret J Hill
Library Holdings: Bk Vols 15,000; Per Subs 30
Automation Activity & Vendor Info: (Cataloging) SirsiDynix; (Circulation) SirsiDynix
Wireless access
Open Mon-Fri 8:30-4:30

P STURGIS LIBRARY*, 3090 Main St, 02630. (Mail add: PO Box 606, 02630-0606), SAN 307-093X. Tel: 508-362-6636. FAX: 508-362-5467. E-mail: sturgislibrary@comcast.net. Web Site: www.sturgislibrary.org. *Dir,* Lucy E Loomis; Tel: 508-362-8448; *Ad, Asst Dir,* Antonia Stephens; *Tech Serv Librn,* Julie French; E-mail: jfrench@clamsnet.org; *Circ Supvr,* Karen Horn; E-mail: khorn@clamsnet.org; Staff 10 (MLS 2, Non-MLS 8)
Founded 1863. Pop 48,000; Circ 74,000
Library Holdings: Bk Titles 65,000; Bk Vols 68,000; Per Subs 55
Special Collections: Early Cape Cod Land Deeds, Some Indian (Stanley W Smith Coll); Genealogy & Local History (Hooper Room); Local Authors (Cape Cod Coll); Maritime History (Kittredge Room), bks, micro; Nineteenth Century Literature
Subject Interests: Genealogy, Geog, Hist, Maritime hist
Automation Activity & Vendor Info: (Acquisitions) Innovative Interfaces, Inc; (Cataloging) Innovative Interfaces, Inc; (Circulation) Innovative Interfaces, Inc; (Course Reserve) Innovative Interfaces, Inc; (ILL) Innovative Interfaces, Inc; (Media Booking) Innovative Interfaces, Inc; (OPAC) Innovative Interfaces, Inc; (Serials) Innovative Interfaces, Inc
Mem of Massachusetts Libr Syst
Partic in Cape Libraries Automated Materials Sharing Network
Open Mon, Wed, Thurs & Fri 10-5, Tues 1-8, Sat 10-4
Friends of the Library Group

BARRE

P WOODS MEMORIAL LIBRARY*, 19 Pleasant St, 01005. (Mail add: PO Box 489, 01005-0489), SAN 307-0948. Tel: 978-355-2533. FAX: 978-355-2511. Web Site: www.barrelibrary.org. *Dir,* Stephanie Young; *Youth Serv,* Mary Ellen Radziewicz; Staff 5 (MLS 1, Non-MLS 4)
Founded 1857. Pop 4,900; Circ 35,967
Library Holdings: Bks on Deafness & Sign Lang 20; Bk Titles 21,000; Per Subs 80
Special Collections: Local History Coll
Automation Activity & Vendor Info: (Cataloging) Follett Software; (Circulation) Follett Software
Mem of Massachusetts Libr Syst
Partic in Central-Western Mass Automated Resource Sharing
Open Tues & Thurs 10-8, Wed 2-8, Fri 2-6, Sat 10-2

BECKET

P BECKET ATHENAEUM, INC LIBRARY*, 3367 Main St, 01223. SAN 307-0956. Tel: 413-623-5483. E-mail: BecketAthenaeum@gmail.com. Web Site: www.BecketAthenaeum.org/. *Dir,* Zina Jayne; *Librn,* Nancy Wilson; Staff 1 (Non-MLS 1)
Founded 1888. Pop 2,350
Library Holdings: DVDs 45; Bk Titles 18,000; Per Subs 15; Talking Bks 300; Videos 800
Automation Activity & Vendor Info: (Cataloging) Follett Software; (Circulation) Follett Software; (ILL) OCLC
Function: Adult bk club, Bks on CD, Children's prog, Computer training, Computers for patron use, Copy machines, Electronic databases & coll, Free DVD rentals, Homework prog, ILL available, Large print keyboards, Mus passes, Music CDs, Online cat, Prog for adults, Prog for children & young adult, Pub access computers, Tax forms, Workshops
Open Tues & Thurs 1-7, Wed 3-7, Sat 10-4

BEDFORD

P BEDFORD FREE PUBLIC LIBRARY*, Seven Mudge Way, 01730-2168. SAN 307-0980. Tel: 781-275-9440. FAX: 781-275-3590. TDD: 781-275-6347. E-mail: bedford@minlib.net. Web Site: www.bedfordlibrary.net. *Dir,* Richard Callaghan; *Asst Dir,* Vanessa Abraham; *Head, Ch,* Sharon McDonald; *Head, Circ,* Lisa Baylis; *Head, Circ,* Jennifer Dalrymple; *Head, Ref,* Joanne Poage; *Head, Tech Serv,* Kathleen Ruggeri; *Teen Librn,* Dee Clarke; Staff 16 (MLS 6, Non-MLS 10)
Founded 1876. Pop 12,571; Circ 284,622
Jul 2006-Jun 2007 Income $1,050,171. Mats Exp $201,662, Books $144,189, Per/Ser (Incl. Access Fees) $14,773. Sal $655,789

Library Holdings: CDs 2,892; DVDs 1,437; Electronic Media & Resources 144; Large Print Bks 1,022; Bk Titles 94,497; Per Subs 261; Talking Bks 2,684; Videos 2,314
Special Collections: Local History (Bedford Coll), multi-media; Parent's Coll. Oral History
Automation Activity & Vendor Info: (Acquisitions) Innovative Interfaces, Inc; (Cataloging) Innovative Interfaces, Inc; (Circulation) Innovative Interfaces, Inc; (OPAC) Innovative Interfaces, Inc
Database Vendor: Innovative Interfaces, Inc
Wireless access
Function: Art exhibits, Copy machines, Digital talking bks, Electronic databases & coll, Handicapped accessible, ILL available, Magnifiers for reading, Mail & tel request accepted, Music CDs, Prog for adults, Prog for children & young adult, Ref serv available, Spoken cassettes & CDs, Spoken cassettes & DVDs, Summer reading prog, Tax forms, Telephone ref, VCDs, VHS videos, Wheelchair accessible
Publications: Bedford Flag Unfurled; History of the Town of Bedford
Mem of Massachusetts Libr Syst
Partic in Minuteman Library Network
Special Services for the Blind - Bks on cassette; Bks on CD; Copier with enlargement capabilities; Digital talking bk; Magnifiers
Open Mon-Thurs 9-9, Fri & Sat 9-5, Sun (Sept-May) 12-5
Friends of the Library Group

GM DEPARTMENT OF VETERANS AFFAIRS*, Medical Library Service, 200 Springs Rd, 01730. SAN 344-5410. Tel: 781-687-2504, Ext 2077. FAX: 781-687-2507. *Libr Mgr,* Bob Bottino
Founded 1928
Library Holdings: Large Print Bks 300; Bk Vols 5,500; Per Subs 245
Subject Interests: Med, Nursing, Psychol, Soc serv (soc work)
Wireless access

J MIDDLESEX COMMUNITY COLLEGE*, Academic Resources Division, Bldg 1-ARC, Springs Rd, 01730. (Mail add: 591 Springs Rd, 01730-1197), SAN 307-1014. Tel: 781-280-3708. Reference Tel: 781-280-3706. FAX: 781-280-3771. E-mail: mcc@noblenet.org. Web Site: www.middlesex.cc.ma.us. *Dir,* Mary Ann Niles; Tel: 781-280-3703; *Syst Coordr,* Laura Horgan; Tel: 781-280-3702; *Pub Serv,* Tamara Anderson; *Ref Serv,* Richard Allen; *Ref Serv,* Shelley Quezada
Founded 1970. Enrl 3,810; Fac 181; Highest Degree: Associate
Library Holdings: Bk Vols 53,000; Per Subs 300
Automation Activity & Vendor Info: (Cataloging) Innovative Interfaces, Inc
Database Vendor: OCLC FirstSearch
Publications: Annual Reports; Film & Video List (Annual); MCC Libraries Newsletter (Occasional); Middlesex Community College Library Periodicals

S MITRE CORP, Information Services, 202 Burlington Rd, 01730-1420. SAN 317-3399. Tel: 781-271-7667. FAX: 781-271-2452. E-mail: infodesk@mitre.org. Web Site: www.mitre.org. *Dept Head,* Ethel M Salonen; Staff 23 (MLS 21, Non-MLS 2)
Founded 1959
Library Holdings: e-books 4,000; e-journals 2,500; Bk Vols 50; Per Subs 50
Subject Interests: Aviation, Civil info systs, Communications, Cyber security, Data analysis, Defense communications, Energy
Database Vendor: ACM (Association for Computing Machinery), American Chemical Society, American Mathematical Society, American Physical Society, Cambridge Scientific Abstracts, Carroll Publishing, CQ Press, Dun & Bradstreet, ebrary, Elsevier, IEEE (Institute of Electrical & Electronics Engineers), IHS, ISI Web of Knowledge, JSTOR, LexisNexis, Nature Publishing Group, OCLC FirstSearch, OCLC WorldShare Interlibrary Loan, ProQuest, Safari Books Online, ScienceDirect, SerialsSolutions, Wiley InterScience
Wireless access
Partic in Interlibrary Users Association
Restriction: Authorized personnel only, Co libr, Internal use only, Not open to pub

BELCHERTOWN

P CLAPP MEMORIAL LIBRARY*, 19 S Main St, 01007-0627. (Mail add: PO Box 627, 01007-0627), SAN 307-1057. Tel: 413-323-0417. Administration Tel: 413-323-0478. FAX: 413-323-0453. E-mail: clapp@cwmars.org. Web Site: www.clapplibrary.org/. *Dir,* Sheila McCormick; *Head, Automated Libr Serv,* Nancy Bronner; *Head, Circ & Ref,* Ann Kuchieski; *Head, Ch,* Jennifer Whitehead; *Libr Tech,* Nina Mulligan; *Libr Tech,* Mary Senecal; Staff 8 (MLS 1, Non-MLS 7)
Founded 1887. Pop 14,000; Circ 138,333
Library Holdings: Bk Titles 22,729; Bk Vols 25,000; Per Subs 82; Talking Bks 2,000; Videos 3,000
Automation Activity & Vendor Info: (Circulation) Innovative Interfaces, Inc
Partic in Central & Western Massachusetts Automated Resource Sharing
Open Mon & Fri 10-6, Tues-Thurs 10-7, Sat 9-1
Friends of the Library Group

BELLINGHAM

P BELLINGHAM PUBLIC LIBRARY*, 100 Blackstone St, 02019. SAN 307-1065. Tel: 508-966-1660. FAX: 508-966-3189. E-mail: library@bellinghamlibrary.org. Web Site: www.bellinghamlibrary.org. *Dir,* Bernadette D Rivard; E-mail: brivard@bellinghamma.org; *Ref Librn,* Cecily Christensen; *YA Librn,* Amanda Maclure; *Youth Serv Librn,* Steven Fowler; Staff 8 (MLS 3, Non-MLS 5)
Founded 1894. Pop 16,332; Circ 108,204
Jul 2012-Jun 2013 Income $468,640. Mats Exp $79,717. Sal $302,885 (Prof $145,125)
Library Holdings: Bk Titles 53,156; Per Subs 78
Automation Activity & Vendor Info: (Cataloging) Evergreen; (Circulation) Evergreen; (OPAC) Evergreen
Database Vendor: Gale Cengage Learning, Overdrive, Inc
Wireless access
Mem of Massachusetts Libr Syst
Partic in Central-Western Mass Automated Resource Sharing
Open Mon & Thurs 10-8, Tues & Wed 10-6, Fri 10-5, Sat (Sept-June) 10-5
Friends of the Library Group

BELMONT

P BELMONT PUBLIC LIBRARY*, 336 Concord Ave, 02478-0904. (Mail add: PO Box 125, 02478-0125), SAN 344-547X. Tel: 617-489-2000, 617-993-2850. Circulation Tel: 617-993-2855. Interlibrary Loan Service Tel: 617-993-2887. Reference Tel: 617-993-2871. Administration Tel: 617-993-2852. Information Services Tel: 617-993-2870. FAX: 617-993-2893. Administration FAX: 617-993-2894. Web Site: www.belmont.lib.ma.us. *Dir,* Maureen Conners; Tel: 617-489-2000, Ext 2852, E-mail: mconners@minlib.net; *Circ Supvr,* Lisa Cassidy; *Ch Serv,* Denise Shaver; *ILL,* Carol Baer; *Ref Serv,* Emily Reardon; *Tech Serv,* Frederick C Dooe; Staff 11 (MLS 9, Non-MLS 2)
Founded 1868. Pop 24,762; Circ 566,872
Jul 2009-Jun 2010 Income $1,866,210, State $29,560, Locally Generated Income $1,738,080, Other $98,570. Mats Exp $1,765,191, Books $169,152, Per/Ser (Incl. Access Fees) $12,912, Other Print Mats $17,194, AV Mat $36,722, Electronic Ref Mat (Incl. Access Fees) $38,348. Sal $1,077,583 (Prof $598,132)
Library Holdings: AV Mats 14,419; e-books 261; Bk Vols 131,065; Per Subs 273
Automation Activity & Vendor Info: (Cataloging) Innovative Interfaces, Inc; (Circulation) Innovative Interfaces, Inc; (OPAC) Innovative Interfaces, Inc
Wireless access
Partic in Minuteman Library Network
Open Mon-Thurs 9-9, Fri & Sat 9-5, Sun 2-5
Friends of the Library Group

P EVERETT C BENTON LIBRARY*, 75 Oakley Rd, 02478-0125. SAN 344-550X. Tel: 617-489-0988. E-mail: ecbentonlibrary@gmail.com. Web Site: www.ecbentonlibrary.org. *Pres,* Elizabeth Gibson
Library Holdings: Bk Vols 13,000
Wireless access
Open Tues 10-3, Wed & Thurs 2-6
Friends of the Library Group

R BETH-EL TEMPLE CENTER*, Carl Kales Memorial Library, Two Concord Ave, 02478-4075. SAN 307-1073. Tel: 617-484-6668. FAX: 617-484-6020. Web Site: www.urj.org/ma/betc. *Librn,* Robin Zeitz
Library Holdings: Bk Vols 2,400
Open Mon-Thurs 9-5

M MCLEAN HOSPITAL, Mental Health Sciences Library, 115 Mill St, Mail Stop 203, 02478. SAN 307-109X. Tel: 617-855-2460. FAX: 617-855-2414. E-mail: mcleanlibrary@partners.org. Web Site: www.mcleanhospital.org/education-training/library. *Mgr, Libr & Info Res,* Pam Hastings; Staff 1 (MLS 1)
Founded 1836
Library Holdings: e-books 100; e-journals 120; Bk Titles 7,000; Per Subs 120; Videos 75
Subject Interests: Drug dependence, Mental health, Psychiat, Psychoanalysis, Psychol, Psychopharmacology, Psychotherapy, Soc sci & issues
Automation Activity & Vendor Info: (Cataloging) OCLC; (Circulation) SydneyPlus; (OPAC) SydneyPlus
Database Vendor: EBSCOhost, OCLC, OCLC FirstSearch, OCLC WorldShare Interlibrary Loan, OVID Technologies, PubMed, TDNet
Wireless access

Partic in Docline; Massachusetts Health Sciences Libraries Network; North Atlantic Health Sciences Libraries, Inc; OCLC Online Computer Library Center, Inc; Partners Library Network
Open Mon-Fri 8:30-4:45
Friends of the Library Group

BERKLEY

P BERKLEY PUBLIC LIBRARY*, Three N Main St, 02779. SAN 307-1103. Tel: 508-822-3329. FAX: 508-824-2471. E-mail: berpl@sailsinc.org. *Dir,* William Schneller; *Cat,* Vicki Dawson; *Ch Serv,* Melissa Kimmer; *Circ,* Carla Paiva; Staff 4 (MLS 1, Non-MLS 3)
Founded 1893. Circ 6,100
Library Holdings: Bk Vols 16,000; Per Subs 30
Automation Activity & Vendor Info: (Acquisitions) SIRSI WorkFlows; (Cataloging) SIRSI WorkFlows; (Circulation) SIRSI WorkFlows; (ILL) SIRSI WorkFlows; (OPAC) SIRSI-iBistro
Wireless access
Mem of Massachusetts Libr Syst
Partic in The Library Network
Open Tues 9-5, Wed & Thurs 1-8, Fri & Sat 9-12
Friends of the Library Group

BERLIN

P BERLIN PUBLIC LIBRARY*, 23 Carter St, 01503-1219. SAN 307-1111. Tel: 978-838-2812. FAX: 978-838-2812. Web Site: www.townofberlin.com/library. *Dir,* Bob Hodge; E-mail: rhodge@cwmars.org; Staff 3 (MLS 1, Non-MLS 2)
Pop 2,700; Circ 18,000
Library Holdings: Bk Vols 16,000; Per Subs 60
Automation Activity & Vendor Info: (Cataloging) Evergreen; (Circulation) Evergreen; (OPAC) Evergreen
Wireless access
Mem of Winnefox Library System
Partic in Central & Western Massachusetts Automated Resource Sharing
Open Mon-Thurs 11-6:30, Sat 10-1
Friends of the Library Group

BERNARDSTON

P CUSHMAN LIBRARY*, 28 Church St, 01337. (Mail add: PO Box 248, 01337-0248), SAN 307-112X. Tel: 413-648-5402. FAX: 413-648-0168. E-mail: cushmanlibrary@gmail.com. Web Site: www.cushmanlibrary.org. *Dir,* Karen Stinchfield; *Asst Libm,* Bonnie Delcamp
Founded 1863. Pop 2,800; Circ 15,600
Library Holdings: AV Mats 1,035; Bk Titles 14,384; Bk Vols 18,000; Per Subs 28
Special Collections: Oral History
Partic in Central & Western Massachusetts Automated Resource Sharing
Open Mon 2-6, Wed 10-7:30, Sat 10-3.30
Friends of the Library Group

BEVERLY

S BEVERLY HISTORICAL SOCIETY*, Charles W Galloupe Memorial Library, 117 Cabot St, 01915-5107. SAN 307-1138. Tel: 978-922-1186. FAX: 978-922-7387. E-mail: info@beverlyhistory.org. Web Site: www.beverlyhistory.org. *Curator of Coll,* Darren Brown; E-mail: dbrown@beverlyhistory.org
Founded 1891
Library Holdings: Bk Vols 2,000
Special Collections: 17th Century Essex County Settlement History; New England History (Charles W Galloupe Memorial Library); Salem & Beverly Ship Logs, 1750's to late early 20th Century; Walker Transportation Coll, photog
Subject Interests: Genealogy, Maritime, New England, Transportation
Publications: Beverly High Football in the 20th Century; Beverly Men in the War of Independence; History of Beverly; North Beverly Remembered; Reflections of Mid-20th Century Beverly; Ryal Side From Early Days of Salem Colony; Thieves, Cow Beaters & Other True Tales of Colonial Beverly; Treasures of a Seaport Town
Open Tues & Sat 10-4, Wed 1-9
Restriction: Non-circulating to the pub

M BEVERLY HOSPITAL LIBRARY*, 85 Herrick St, 01915-1777. SAN 344-5569. Tel: 978-922-3000, Ext 2920. *Librn,* Ann M Tomes; E-mail: atomes@nhs-healthlink.org
Founded 1900
Library Holdings: Bk Vols 1,000; Per Subs 100
Special Collections: Medical Incunabula (Beverly Hospital Historical Library)
Partic in Northeastern Consortium for Health Information
Restriction: Staff use only

P BEVERLY PUBLIC LIBRARY*, 32 Essex St, 01915-4561. SAN 344-5593. Tel: 978-921-6062. FAX: 978-922-8329. E-mail: beverly_library@noblenet.org. Web Site: www.noblenet.org/beverly. *Dir,* Patricia Cirone; E-mail: cirone@noblenet.org; *Asst Dir,* Anna L Langstaff; E-mail: langstaff@noblenet.org; *Ch Serv,* Nancy Bonne; *Ref,* Suzanne Nichelson; *Tech Serv,* Laurie Formichella; Staff 19 (MLS 14, Non-MLS 5)
Founded 1855. Pop 40,235; Circ 288,380
Jul 2005-Jun 2006 Income $1,300,000. Mats Exp $215,000. Sal $850,000 (Prof $635,800)
Library Holdings: Bk Vols 180,058; Per Subs 125
Special Collections: Original Lithographs (Will Barnet Coll)
Automation Activity & Vendor Info: (Circulation) Innovative Interfaces, Inc
Database Vendor: EBSCOhost, Gale Cengage Learning, OCLC FirstSearch
Publications: Beverly Public Library (Newsletter)
Mem of Massachusetts Libr Syst
Partic in North of Boston Library Exchange, Inc
Open Mon-Thurs 9-9, Fri & Sat 9-5, Sun 1-5
Friends of the Library Group
Branches: 1
BEVERLY FARMS, 24 Vine St, 01915-2208, SAN 344-5623. Tel: 978-921-6066. FAX: 978-927-9239. E-mail: beverlyfarms_library@noblenet.org. *Librn,* Kate Ingalls; *Librn,* Brenda Wettergreen
Library Holdings: Bk Vols 20,756; Per Subs 30
Open Mon & Wed 10-6, Tues & Thurs 10-9, Fri 10-5, Sat 9-5
Friends of the Library Group
Bookmobiles: 1. Librn, Linda Caravaggio

S COMMUNICATION & POWER INDUSTRIES*, Technical Library, 150 Sohier Rd, 01915-5595. SAN 307-1170. Tel: 978 922-6000. FAX: 978-922-8914. Web Site: www.cpii.com/bmd. *Dir,* Gene Spirko
Founded 1963
Library Holdings: Bk Titles 1,400; Per Subs 60
Subject Interests: Electronics, Eng

C ENDICOTT COLLEGE LIBRARY*, Diane M Halle Library, 376 Hale St, 01915. SAN 307-1146. Tel: 978-232-2279. Reference Tel: 978-232-2268. Administration Tel: 978-232-2278. FAX: 978-232-2700. E-mail: end@noblenet.org. Web Site: www.endicott.edu. *Dir,* Brian Courtemanche; E-mail: bcourtem@endicott.edu; *Ref Librn,* Bridget Cunio; Tel: 978-232-2285, E-mail: bcunio@endicott.edu; *Ref Librn,* Audrey M Koke; Tel: 978-232-2273, E-mail: akoke@endicott.edu; *Ref Librn,* Elizabeth Roland; Tel: 978-232-2275, E-mail: broland@endicott.edu; *Coordr, Libr User Serv,* Alison Barry; Tel: 978-232 2276, E-mail: abarry@endicott.edu; Staff 6 (MLS 4, Non-MLS 2)
Founded 1939. Enrl 2,220; Fac 173; Highest Degree: Master
Library Holdings: Electronic Media & Resources 67,548; Bk Vols 120,520; Per Subs 95
Automation Activity & Vendor Info: (Acquisitions) Innovative Interfaces, Inc; (Cataloging) Innovative Interfaces, Inc; (Circulation) Innovative Interfaces, Inc; (Course Reserve) Innovative Interfaces, Inc; (ILL) Innovative Interfaces, Inc; (OPAC) Innovative Interfaces, Inc
Database Vendor: ACM (Association for Computing Machinery), ARTstor, EBSCOhost, Emerald, Gale Cengage Learning, H W Wilson, Innovative Interfaces, Inc, LexisNexis, ProQuest
Wireless access
Publications: New Acquisition List
Partic in North of Boston Library Exchange, Inc; Northeast Consortium of Colleges & Universities In Massachusetts
Open Mon-Thurs 7:30am-Midnight, Fri 7:30am-8pm, Sat 11-5, Sun Noon-Midnight

C MONTSERRAT COLLEGE OF ART, Paul M Scott Library, 23 Essex St, 01915. SAN 328-6231. Circulation Tel: 978-921-4242, Ext 1203. FAX: 978-922-4268. Web Site: www.montserrat.edu/academics/library.php. *Col Librn,* Cheri Coe; Tel: 978-921-4242, Ext 1208, E-mail: cheri.coe@montserrat.edu
Founded 1979
Library Holdings: Bk Titles 11,000; Bk Vols 12,000; Per Subs 75
Special Collections: Paul M Scott Archives
Automation Activity & Vendor Info: (Circulation) Evergreen
Database Vendor: EBSCOhost, Gale Cengage Learning
Wireless access
Mem of Massachusetts Libr Syst
Partic in North of Boston Library Exchange, Inc
Open Mon-Thurs 8am-9pm, Fri 8:30-6, Sun 12-6

S OSRAM SYLVANIA*, R & D Library, 71 Cherry Hill Dr, 01915. SAN 307-3432. Tel: 978-750-1725. FAX: 978-750-1797. *Librn,* Dave Jelley; E-mail: dave.jelly@sylvania.com
Library Holdings: Bk Titles 9,000; Per Subs 150
Subject Interests: Eng, Optics, Phys chem

BILLERICA

S AERODYNE RESEARCH, INC*, Technical Information Center, 45 Manning Rd, 01821-3976. SAN 307-0964. Tel: 978-663-9500, Ext 257. FAX: 978-663-4918. Web Site: www.aerodyne.com. *Info Spec,* Susan B Mast; E-mail: mast@aerodyne.com; Staff 1 (MLS 1)
Founded 1975
Jan 2007-Dec 2007 Income $105,000. Mats Exp $73,000
Library Holdings: Bk Vols 2,000; Per Subs 210
Subject Interests: Atmospheric chem, Optics
Publications: Journal List; Technical Information Center Bytes
Partic in SLA
Open Mon-Fri 9-5

P BILLERICA PUBLIC LIBRARY*, 15 Concord Rd, 01821. SAN 307-1189. Tel: 978-671-0948. FAX: 978-667-4242. Web Site: www.billericalibrary.org. *Dir,* Position Currently Open; *Asst Dir,* Priscilla Vaughn; E-mail: pvaughn@mvlc.org
Pop 38,000; Circ 232,000
Jul 2006-Jun 2007 Income $1,152,932. Mats Exp $129,820. Sal $829,941
Library Holdings: AV Mats 8,000; Large Print Bks 1,500; Bk Vols 120,000; Per Subs 230
Special Collections: Oral History
Automation Activity & Vendor Info: (Cataloging) SirsiDynix; (Circulation) SirsiDynix; (OPAC) SirsiDynix
Partic in Merrimack Valley Library Consortium
Open Mon-Thurs (Winter) 9-9, Fri & Sat 9-5, Sun 1-5; Mon-Thurs (Summer) 9-9, Fri 9-5
Friends of the Library Group

BLACKSTONE

P BLACKSTONE PUBLIC LIBRARY*, 86 Main St, 01504-2277. SAN 307-1200. Tel: 508-883-1931. FAX: 508-883-1531. *Actg Dir, Ch,* Tressy Collier; E-mail: tressy@blackstonepubliclibrary.org; *Dir,* Position Currently Open; *Head, Circ,* Donna Ansell; E-mail: donna@blackstonepubliclibrary.org; Staff 9 (MLS 1, Non-MLS 8)
Founded 1889. Pop 8,804
Library Holdings: Audiobooks 1,421; Braille Volumes 4; CDs 393; DVDs 2,452; Electronic Media & Resources 1; Large Print Bks 1,718; Bk Vols 36,510; Per Subs 79; Videos 2,443
Automation Activity & Vendor Info: (Cataloging) Innovative Interfaces, Inc; (Circulation) Innovative Interfaces, Inc; (ILL) Innovative Interfaces, Inc - Millenium; (OPAC) Innovative Interfaces, Inc
Database Vendor: World Book Online
Wireless access
Function: Adult bk club, Computers for patron use, Copy machines, Electronic databases & coll, Family literacy, Fax serv, Free DVD rentals, Handicapped accessible, Home delivery & serv to Sr ctr & nursing homes, Homebound delivery serv, ILL available, Mus passes, Music CDs, Notary serv, OverDrive digital audio bks, Photocopying/Printing, Prog for adults, Prog for children & young adult, Pub access computers, Spoken cassettes & CDs, Story hour, Summer reading prog, Tax forms, Telephone ref, VHS videos, Web-catalog
Mem of Massachusetts Libr Syst
Partic in Central & Western Massachusetts Automated Resource Sharing
Open Mon 9-8, Tues & Thurs 12-8, Fri & Sat 10-2
Friends of the Library Group

BLANDFORD

P PORTER MEMORIAL LIBRARY*, 87 Main St, 01008-9518. (Mail add: PO Box 797, 01008-0797), SAN 307-1219. Tel: 413-848-2853. FAX: 413-848-2853. *Dir,* Eileen Gates; E-mail: eileengates@verizon.net; *Asst Dir,* Michele Crane; *Librn,* Pamela Darrow; Staff 3 (Non-MLS 3)
Founded 1892. Pop 1,264; Circ 10,399
Library Holdings: Bk Vols 9,000; Per Subs 10
Subject Interests: Genealogy
Open Mon 5-9, Tues & Thurs 1-9, Sat 10-4
Friends of the Library Group

BOLTON

P BOLTON PUBLIC LIBRARY*, 738 Main St, 01740-1202. (Mail add: PO Box 188, 01740-0188), SAN 307-1227. Tel: 978-779-2839. FAX: 978-779-2293. E-mail: library@townofbolton.com. Web Site: www.townofbolton.com. *Dir,* Kelly Collins; Staff 7 (MLS 1, Non-MLS 6)
Founded 1856. Pop 4,500; Circ 38,500
Library Holdings: Bk Vols 25,000; Per Subs 75
Subject Interests: Local hist
Automation Activity & Vendor Info: (Cataloging) Innovative Interfaces, Inc; (Circulation) Innovative Interfaces, Inc; (ILL) Innovative Interfaces, Inc; (OPAC) Innovative Interfaces, Inc
Mem of Massachusetts Libr Syst
Open Tues-Thurs 10-8, Fri 10-5, Sat 10-3
Friends of the Library Group

BOSTON

SR AMERICAN CONGREGATIONAL ASSOCIATION, Congregational Library & Archives, 14 Beacon St, 2nd Flr, 02108-9999. SAN 307-1235. Tel: 617-523-0470. FAX: 617-523-0491. E-mail: info@14beacon.org. Web Site: www.congregationallibrary.org. *Exec Dir,* Dr Margaret Lamberts Bendroth; E-mail: mbendroth@14beacon.org; *Dir of Develop,* Cary Hewitt; E-mail: chewitt@14beacon.org; *Librn,* Claudette Newhall; E-mail: cnewhall@14beacon.org; *Asst Librn, Ref/Cat,* Steve Picazio; E-mail: spicazio@14beacon.org; *Archivist,* Jessica Steytler; E-mail: jsteytler@14beacon.org; *Digital Archivist,* Sari Mauro; E-mail: smauro@14beacon.org; Staff 6 (MLS 4, Non-MLS 2)
Founded 1853
Library Holdings: Bk Titles 225,000; Per Subs 40
Special Collections: Church Records, micro, ms, rec; Mather Family Coll, ms, printed; Monographs, ms & printed; Newspapers & Periodicals, printed originals & micro; Theology & Sermons, 17th-19th centuries
Automation Activity & Vendor Info: (Cataloging) Softlink America; (OPAC) Softlink America; (Serials) Softlink America
Wireless access
Function: Mail & tel request accepted, Ref serv available, Workshops
Publications: Bulletin
Open Mon-Fri 9-5
Restriction: Closed stack

S APPALACHIAN MOUNTAIN CLUB, Library & Archives, Five Joy St, 02108. SAN 307-1243. Tel: 617-391-6629. FAX: 617-523-0722. E-mail: amclibrary@outdoors.org. Web Site: www.outdoors.org. *Archivist, Librn,* Rebecca Fullerton; Staff 1 (Non-MLS 1)
Founded 1876
Library Holdings: DVDs 50; Bk Titles 3,000; Bk Vols 3,500; Per Subs 20
Special Collections: Appalachian Mountain Club Records, 1876-present; Outdoor Recreation in Northeast US (Appalachian Mountain Club Photographic Colls); Vittorio Sella Photographic Coll, 1859-1943, prints; White Mountains Coll, bks, images
Subject Interests: Environ conserv, Mountaineering, Outdoor educ, Outdoor recreation
Automation Activity & Vendor Info: (Acquisitions) LibraryWorld, Inc; (Cataloging) LibraryWorld, Inc; (OPAC) LibraryWorld, Inc; (Serials) LibraryWorld, Inc
Function: Archival coll
Restriction: Open to pub by appt only

J BAY STATE COLLEGE LIBRARY*, 35 Commonwealth Ave, 02116. (Mail add: 122 Commonwealth Ave, 02116), SAN 307-1278. Tel: 617-217-9296. FAX: 617-236-8023. Web Site: www.baystate.edu. *Dir,* Jessica Neave; Staff 1 (MLS 1)
Founded 1946
Library Holdings: Bk Titles 5,300; Per Subs 100
Subject Interests: Acctg, Allied health, Bus, Early childhood, Educ, Fashion, Hotel admin, Legal, Occupational therapy, Phys therapy, Tourism, Travel
Automation Activity & Vendor Info: (Circulation) EOS International
Database Vendor: LexisNexis, ProQuest
Partic in Boston Regional Library System; Lyrasis
Open Mon-Thurs 8-8, Fri 8-4:30

C BENJAMIN FRANKLIN INSTITUTE OF TECHNOLOGY*, Lufkin Memorial, Franklin Union Blg., Rm. 114, 41 Berkeley St, 02116. SAN 307-1707. Tel: 617-423-4630, Ext 123. Web Site: www.bfit.edu. *Dir, Libr Serv,* Sharon B Bonk; E-mail: sbonk@bfit.edu; *Cat,* Julie Hankinson; E-mail: jhankinson@bfit.edu; Staff 2 (MLS 2)
Founded 1908. Enrl 400
Library Holdings: e-books 15,000; Bk Titles 23,000; Per Subs 120
Special Collections: Benjamin Franklin Coll; Photographic Science (Dr Leonard E Ravich Coll)
Subject Interests: Archit, Civil eng, Computer sci, Electronic eng, Mechanical eng
Automation Activity & Vendor Info: (Circulation) LibraryWorld, Inc; (OPAC) LibraryWorld, Inc
Database Vendor: Dialog, EBSCOhost, Gale Cengage Learning, ProQuest, Wilson - Wilson Web
Publications: Guide to the Library
Partic in Boston Library Consortium, Inc; Boston Regional Library System; Lyrasis; Mass Libr & Info Network
Open Mon-Thurs 7:30-6:30, Fri 7:30-6

C BERKLEE COLLEGE OF MUSIC LIBRARY*, Stan Getz Media Center & Library, 150 Massachusetts Ave, 02115. (Mail add: 1140 Boylston St, 02215-3631), SAN 307-1286. Tel: 617-747-2258. Reference Tel: 617-747-8002. FAX: 617-747-2050. E-mail: library@berklee.edu. Web Site: library.berklee.edu. *Dean, Learning Res,* Gary Haggerty; Tel: 617-747-2603, E-mail: ghaggerty@berklee.edu; *Dir, Libr Serv,* Paul Engle;

Tel: 617-747-8683, E-mail: pengle@berklee.edu; *Libr Syst Adminr,* Yamil Suarez; Tel: 617-747-2617, E-mail: ysuarez@berklee.edu; *Cat Librn,* Jenee Morgan; Tel: 617-747-8684, E-mail: jemorgan@berklee.edu; *Asst Cat Librn,* Swartz Amy; Tel: 617-747-3194, E-mail: aswartz@berklee.edu; *Outreach Librn,* Erica Charis; Tel: 617-747-8465, E-mail: echaris@berklee.edu; *Ref Librn,* Marci Cohen; Tel: 617-747-8525, E-mail: mcohen2@berklee.edu; *Ref Librn,* Zoe Rath; Tel: 617-747-8143, E-mail: zrath@berklee.edu; *Media Ctr Mgr,* Ralph Rosen; Tel: 617-747-8338, E-mail: rrosen@berklee.edu; *Circ/ILL Asst,* Dhyana Berry; E-mail: dberry1@berklee.edu; *Per Asst,* Anna Esty; Tel: 617-747-2599, E-mail: aesty@berklee.edu; Staff 13 (MLS 7, Non-MLS 6)
Founded 1964. Enrl 4,200; Fac 500; Highest Degree: Master
Library Holdings: AV Mats 5,100; CDs 34,545; e-books 10,000; Music Scores 24,009; Bk Titles 27,072; Per Subs 217
Special Collections: Jazz & Rock Music Coll, scores with matching recordings
Subject Interests: Humanities, Music
Automation Activity & Vendor Info: (Cataloging) Evergreen; (Circulation) Evergreen; (OPAC) Evergreen
Database Vendor: EBSCOhost, Elsevier, Gale Cengage Learning, JSTOR, Medline, OCLC FirstSearch
Wireless access
Open Mon-Thurs 9am-11:45pm, Fri 9am-9:45pm, Sat 10-9:45, Sun 1-11:45
Friends of the Library Group

L BINGHAM MCCUTCHEN LLP*, Law Library, 150 Federal St, 02110. SAN 307-1308. Tel: 617-951-8313. Circulation Tel: 617-951-8106. Reference Tel: 617-951-4911. FAX: 617-951-8543. Web Site: www.bingham.com. *Dir,* Gina Lynch; *Librn, Ref,* Jeanette Silic; *Spec Projects,* Heather Bragdon; Staff 10 (MLS 4, Non-MLS 6)
Library Holdings: Bk Vols 30,000; Per Subs 150
Automation Activity & Vendor Info: (Acquisitions) Inmagic, Inc.; (Cataloging) Inmagic, Inc.; (Circulation) Inmagic, Inc.
Function: ILL available
Restriction: Staff use only

C BOSTON ARCHITECTURAL COLLEGE, Shaw & Stone Library, 320 Newbury St, 02115. SAN 307-1324. Tel: 617-585-0155. FAX: 617-585-0151. E-mail: library@the-bac.edu. Web Site: www.the-bac.edu/library. *Dir,* Susan Lewis; Tel: 617-585-0234, E-mail: susan.lewis@the-bac.edu; *Assoc Dir,* Whitney Vitale; Tel: 617 585-7337, E-mail: whitney.vitale@the-bac.edu; *Ref Librn, Visual Res,* Sheri L Rosenzweig; Tel: 617-585-0257, E-mail: sheri.rosenzweig@the-bac.edu; *Syst & Distance Educ Librn,* Toshika Suzuki; E-mail: toshika.suzuki@the-bac.edu; *Coordr, Acq, Reserves,* Robert Adams; *Archivist,* Kris Kobialka; Tel: 617-585-0133, E-mail: kris.kobialka@the-bac.edu; *Cataloger,* Chris Leshock; E-mail: christine.leshock@the-bac.edu; Staff 6 (MLS 6)
Founded 1966. Enrl 1,200; Fac 250; Highest Degree: Master
Library Holdings: e-journals 5,000; Bk Vols 50,000; Per Subs 120; Videos 150
Special Collections: Architectural History (Memorial Library Coll)
Subject Interests: Archit, Conserv, Interior design, Landscape archit, Photog, Solar energy, Urban planning
Automation Activity & Vendor Info: (Acquisitions) Ex Libris Group; (Cataloging) Ex Libris Group; (Circulation) Ex Libris Group; (Course Reserve) Ex Libris Group; (OPAC) Ex Libris Group; (Serials) Ex Libris Group
Database Vendor: Cambridge Scientific Abstracts, JSTOR, ProQuest, YBP Library Services
Wireless access
Function: Web-catalog
Open Mon-Thurs 10-10:30, Fri & Sat 10-5, Sun 12-7
Restriction: Open to pub for ref only
Friends of the Library Group

S BOSTON ATHENAEUM*, 10 1/2 Beacon St, 02108-3777. SAN 307-1332. Tel: 617-227-0270. FAX: 617-227-5266. Web Site: www.bostonathenaeum.org. *Pres,* George Marshall Moriarty; *Dir,* Richard Wendorf; *Assoc Dir,* John Lannon; E-mail: lannon@bostonathenaeum.org; *Circ,* James Feeney, Jr; E-mail: feeney@bostonathenaeum.org; *Reader Serv,* Stephen Z Nonack; E-mail: nonack@bostonathenaeum.org; *Tech Serv,* Robert Kruse; E-mail: kruse@bostonathenaeum.org; Staff 26 (MLS 11, Non-MLS 15)
Founded 1807
Library Holdings: Bk Vols 603,000; Per Subs 450
Special Collections: 18th & 19th Century Tracts; American 19th Century Photographs; American Prints & Drawings; Books from the Library of George Washington; Byroniana; Confederate Imprints, bk, micro; European & American 19th Century paintings & sculpture; General Henry Knox Library; Gypsy Literature; Henry Rowe Schoolcraft Coll; John Fowles; John Masefield; Merrymount Press Coll; TS Eliot. US Document Depository
Subject Interests: Archives, Fine arts, Hist, Manuscripts
Automation Activity & Vendor Info: (Acquisitions) Ex Libris Group; (Cataloging) Ex Libris Group; (Circulation) Ex Libris Group; (OPAC) Follett Software
Function: For res purposes, ILL available, Mail loans to mem, Ref serv available, Res libr, Telephone ref
Publications: Athenaeum Items (Newsletter)
Partic in Boston Regional Library System; OCLC Online Computer Library Center, Inc; RLIN (Research Libraries Information Network)
Open Mon 8:30-8, Tues-Fri 8.30-5:30, Sat 9-4

CR BOSTON BAPTIST COLLEGE LIBRARY*, 950 Metropolitan Ave, 02136. Tel: 617-364-3510, Ext 216. Web Site: www.boston.edu. *Dir,* Fred Tatro; E-mail: ftatro@boston.edu; Staff 1 (MLS 1)
Founded 1976. Enrl 120; Highest Degree: Bachelor
Library Holdings: e-journals 4,000; Bk Titles 54,072; Bk Vols 57,139
Special Collections: Religious Resources 1800's to present, bks, microfiche
Automation Activity & Vendor Info: (Cataloging) Follett Software; (Circulation) Follett Software; (OPAC) Follett Software
Partic in Boston Regional Library System
Open Mon-Thurs 8am-10pm, Fri 8-5, Sun 9pm-11pm

M BOSTON CHILDREN'S HOSPITAL LIBRARY*, Fegan Plaza, 300 Longwood Ave, 02115. SAN 377-9173. Tel: 617-355-7232. FAX: 617-730 0983. *Mgr, Libr & Info Serv,* Alison Clapp; E-mail: alison.clapp@childrens.harvard.edu. Subject Specialists: *Pediatrics,* Alison Clapp; Staff 2.25 (MLS 2, Non-MLS 0.25)
Founded 1994
Library Holdings: e-books 75; e-journals 2,000; Bk Titles 3,000; Per Subs 200
Subject Interests: Pediatrics
Automation Activity & Vendor Info: (OPAC) Softlink America
Database Vendor: EBSCO Information Services
Wireless access
Function: Handicapped accessible, Health sci info serv, ILL available, Online searches, Photocopying/Printing, Ref serv available
Partic in Boston Biomedical Library Consortium; National Network of Libraries of Medicine New England Region
Open Mon-Fri 8-6
Restriction: Circulates for staff only, Non-circulating to the pub

C THE BOSTON CONSERVATORY*, Albert Alphin Music Library, Eight The Fenway, 02215-4099. SAN 307-1359. Tel: 617-912-9131. FAX: 617-912-9101. Web Site: www.bostonconservatory.edu/programs/library.html. *Dir,* Jennifer Hunt; Tel: 617-912-9132, E-mail: jhunt@bostonconservatory.edu; *Evening Librn, Metadata Librn,* Rachel Fox Von Swearingen; *Acq, Cat,* Reginald A Didham; Tel: 617-912-9130, E-mail: rdidham@bostonconservatory.edu; *Pub Serv, Spec Coll,* Jenny Smilovitz; E-mail: jsmilovitz@bostonconservatory.edu
Founded 1867. Highest Degree: Master
Library Holdings: Bk Vols 40,000; Per Subs 85
Special Collections: James Pappoutsakis Memorial Coll; Jan Veen - Katrine Amory Hooper Memorial Art Coll
Subject Interests: Dance, Drama, Music, Opera
Automation Activity & Vendor Info: (Cataloging) Follett Software; (Circulation) Follett Software; (ILL) OCLC; (OPAC) Follett Software
Partic in OCLC Online Computer Library Center, Inc
Open Mon-Thurs 8am-11pm, Fri 8-6, Sat 10-5, Sun 2-10

S BOSTON GLOBE*, Newspaper Library, 135 Morrissey Blvd, 02107. (Mail add: PO Box 55819, 02205-5819), SAN 307-3491. Tel: 617-929-2540. FAX: 617-929-3314. Web Site: www.boston.com. *Librn,* Lisa Tuite
Founded 1887
Library Holdings: Bk Titles 4,500; Bk Vols 6,500; Per Subs 50
Special Collections: Boston History
Automation Activity & Vendor Info: (Acquisitions) Inmagic, Inc.; (Cataloging) Inmagic, Inc.; (Circulation) Inmagic, Inc.
Database Vendor: EBSCOhost, LexisNexis
Publications: Boston Globe Library; Library News (Acquisition list)
Partic in Dow Jones News Retrieval
Open Mon-Fri 7am-9pm

P BOSTON PUBLIC LIBRARY*, 700 Boylston St, 02116-2813. SAN 344-5712. Tel: 617-536-5400. FAX: 617-236-4306. E-mail: ask@bpl.org. Web Site: www.bpl.org. *Pres,* Amy Ryan; E-mail: aeryan@bpl.org; *Dir, Libr Serv,* Michael Colford; Staff 425 (MLS 150, Non-MLS 275)
Founded 1852. Pop 574,283; Circ 3,116,540
Jul 2008-Jun 2009 Income (Main Library and Branch(s)) $46,859,614, City $31,230,179, Other $15,629,435. Mats Exp $8,794,416
Library Holdings: Audiobooks 65,948; AV Mats 113,633; Electronic Media & Resources 9,177; Microforms 6,943,617; Bk Vols 8,895,168; Per Subs 4,673

Special Collections: Albert H Wiggin Print Coll; American & English History & Biography incl Fine Editions (Thayer Coll), Spanish & Portuguese (Ticknor Coll); American & English History & Literature, Jurists, Artists, Men of Letters, Anti-slavery; American & Foreign Authors & Rare Editions incl Longfellow Memorial known as Artz Coll; American Accounting to 1900 (Bentley Coll); Astronomy, Mathematics & Navigation (Bowditch Coll); Books By & About Women (Galatea Coll); Books Printed in England before 1640, Newspapers, City of Boston Records & Government Documents, microfilm; Christian Science (Works of Mary Baker Eddy); Dance (Lilla Viles Wyman Coll); Defoe & Defoeana (Trent Coll); Drama (Barton, Gilbert & Ticknor Colls); Early & Important Children's Books; Early Boston Imprints (John A Lewis Coll); English & American Literature; Engravings & Early Rare Impressions (Tosti Coll); Frankliniana; Fred Allen Papers; Genealogy (New England Families, English Parish Records); German 18th & 19th Century Poetry (Sears-Freiligrath Coll); Government Documents; Great Britain, Ireland, Scotland & United States Colls; Heraldry Coll; Imprints before 1850 (Charlotte Harris Coll); James Brendan Connolly Coll (First Editions); Joan of Arc Coll; Landscape Architecture (Codman Coll); Literature Coll; Manuscript Coll; Maps & Atlases; Medieval Manuscripts; Military Science & History & Civil War (20th Regiment); Music (Brown Coll); Newspapers (Early American & Current from all over the World); Patents (Early American to present, British, German); Periodicals & Serials (Boston Imprints, Learned Societies, Literary, Foreign Language); Photographs, Early & Civil War, Baseball Players (Michael T McGreevy Coll); Picture Coll; President John Adams Library; Prince Coll; Printing Coll, 16th Century to Present; Religion & Theology Coll; Robert & Elizabeth Browning Coll; Sacco-Vanzetti Papers; Statistics; The Book of Common Prayer (Benton Coll); Theatre (Brown Coll); Theodore Parker Library; Walt Whitman Coll; Washingtoniana (Lewisson Coll); West Indies (Benjamin P Hunt Coll); Wilfred Beaulieu Papers; William Peterson Trent Coll; Works Printed by John Baskerville (Benton Coll); World War I (Mary Boyle O'Reilly Coll). UN Document Depository; US Document Depository
Automation Activity & Vendor Info: (Acquisitions) Horizon; (Cataloging) Horizon; (Circulation) Horizon
Wireless access
Function: Adult bk club, Adult literacy prog, After school storytime, Archival coll, Art exhibits, Audiobks via web, AV serv, Bk club(s), Bks on cassette, Bks on CD, Bus archives, Chess club, Children's prog, Computers for patron use, Copy machines, E-Reserves, Electronic databases & coll, Exhibits, Family literacy, Govt ref serv, Handicapped accessible, Homework prog, ILL available, Mus passes, Music CDs, Online cat, Online ref, Online searches, OverDrive digital audio bks, Photocopying/Printing, Prog for adults, Pub access computers, Ref & res, Ref serv in person, Story hour, Summer reading prog, Teen prog, Telephone ref
Publications: Armstrong & Co Artistic Lithographers; BPL Press/Catalogue of Publications; Catalog of the Large Print Collection; Childs Gallery, Boston, 1937-1980; Evolution of a Catalogue: From Folio to Fiche; Irwin D Hoffman, an Artist's Life; Small Talk About Great Books (Bromsen lecture VII); The Sacco-Vanzetti Case: Developments & Reconsiderations, 1979; The Society of Arts & Crafts: Boston Exhibition Record, 1897-1928
Partic in Boston Library Consortium, Inc; Lyrasis; Metro Boston Libr Network
Open Mon-Thurs 9-9, Fri & Sat 9-5
Friends of the Library Group

Branches: 26

ADAMS STREET, 690 Adams St, Dorchester, 02122-1907, SAN 344-5836. Tel: 617-436-6900. *Librn,* Kate Brown
Founded 1951. Circ 96,323
Library Holdings: Bk Vols 30,000; Per Subs 35
Open Mon & Wed 12-8, Tues & Thurs 10-6, Fri & Sat 9-5
Friends of the Library Group

BRIGHTON BRANCH, 40 Academy Hill Rd, Brighton, 02135-3316, SAN 344-5895. Tel: 617-782-6032. *Br Librn,* Uma Murthy
Founded 1969. Circ 71,539
Library Holdings: Bk Vols 75,000; Per Subs 50
Open Mon & Thurs 12-8, Tues & Wed 10-6, Fri & Sat 9-5
Friends of the Library Group

CHARLESTOWN BRANCH, 179 Main St, Charlestown, 02129-3208, SAN 344-5925. Tel: 617-242-1248. *Br Librn,* Maureen Marx
Founded 1970. Circ 83,574
Library Holdings: Bk Vols 43,000; Per Subs 71
Open Mon & Thurs 12-8, Tues & Wed 10-6, Fri 9-5, Sat 9-2
Friends of the Library Group

CODMAN SQUARE, 690 Washington St, Dorchester, 02124-3511, SAN 344-595X. Tel: 617-436-8214. *Librn,* Janice Knight
Founded 1978. Circ 55,117
Library Holdings: Large Print Bks 800; Bk Vols 84,390; Per Subs 70; Talking Bks 1,500; Videos 500
Open Mon & Thurs 12-8, Tues & Wed 10-6, Fri & Sat 9-5
Friends of the Library Group

CONNOLLY, 433 Centre St, Jamaica Plain, 02130-1831, SAN 344-5984. Tel: 617-522-1960. *Br Librn,* Jane Bickford
Founded 1932. Circ 77,651
Library Holdings: Bk Vols 30,000; Per Subs 42
Open Mon 12-8, Tues-Thurs 10-6, Fri 9-5, Sat 9-2
Friends of the Library Group

DUDLEY BRANCH, 65 Warren St, Roxbury, 02119-3206. Tel: 617-442-6186. *Br Librn,* Allen Knight
Founded 1978. Circ 48,859
Library Holdings: Bk Vols 11,000
Open Mon & Thurs 12-8, Tues & Wed 10-6, Fri & Sat 9-5

DUDLEY LITERACY CENTER, 65 Warren St, Roxbury, 02119-3206, SAN 344-6018. Tel: 617-859-2446. *Spec,* Michael Murray
Founded 2002. Circ 2,234
Library Holdings: Bk Vols 77,642; Per Subs 40
Friends of the Library Group

EAST BOSTON, 365 Bremen St, East Boston, 02128-1451, SAN 344-6042. Tel: 617-569-0271. *Br Librn,* Margaret Kelly
Founded 1914. Circ 79,150
Library Holdings: Bk Vols 39,000; Per Subs 50
Open Mon & Thurs 12-8, Tues & Wed 10-6, Fri & Sat 9-5
Friends of the Library Group

EGLESTON SQUARE, 2044 Columbus Ave, Roxbury, 02119-1123, SAN 344-6077. Tel: 617-445-4340. *Br Librn,* Audrey Leppanen
Founded 1953. Circ 27,800
Library Holdings: Bk Vols 24,426
Open Mon, Tues & Thurs 10-6, Wed 12-8, Fri 9-5, Sat 9-2
Friends of the Library Group

FANEUIL, 419 Faneuil St, Brighton, 02135-1629, SAN 344-6107. Tel: 617-782-6705. *Br Librn,* Dorothy Keller
Founded 1932. Circ 125,604
Library Holdings: Bk Vols 22,416; Per Subs 15
Open Mon, Wed & Thurs 10-6, Tues 12-8, Fri 9-5, Sat 9-2
Friends of the Library Group

FIELDS CORNER, 1520 Dorchester Ave, Dorchester, 02122-1327, SAN 344-6131. Tel: 617-436-2155. *Br Librn,* Kimberly McCleary
Founded 1969. Circ 72,518
Library Holdings: Bk Vols 33,000; Per Subs 20; Videos 400
Open Mon, Wed & Thurs 10-6, Tues 12-8, Fri 9-5, Sat 9-2

GROVE HALL, 41 Geneva Ave, Dorchester, 02121-3109, SAN 344-6166. Tel: 617-427-3337. *Br Librn,* Paul Edwards
Library Holdings: Bk Vols 32,167
Open Mon-Wed 10-6, Thurs 12-8, Fri & Sat 9-5
Friends of the Library Group

HONAN-ALLSTON BRANCH, 300 N Harvard St, Allston, 02134-1530. Tel: 617-787-6313. *Br Librn,* Carin O'Connor
Founded 2001. Circ 140,007
Library Holdings: Large Print Bks 200; Bk Vols 50,000; Per Subs 65; Talking Bks 300
Open Mon & Wed 12-8, Tues & Thurs 10-6, Fri & Sat 9-5
Friends of the Library Group

HYDE PARK BRANCH, 35 Harvard Ave, Hyde Park, 02136-2831, SAN 344-6190. Tel: 617-361-2524. *Br Librn,* Mary Margaret Pitts
Founded 1912. Circ 106,476
Library Holdings: Large Print Bks 1,000; Bk Vols 50,000; Per Subs 100
Open Mon & Thurs 12-8, Tues & Wed 10-6, Fri & Sat 9-5
Friends of the Library Group

JAMAICA PLAIN BRANCH, 12 Sedgwick St, Jamaica Plain, 02130-2835, SAN 344-6220. Tel: 617-524-2053. *Br Librn,* Laura Pattison
Founded 1911. Circ 152,254
Library Holdings: Bk Vols 40,000; Per Subs 50
Open Mon-Wed 10-6, Thurs 12-8, Fri 9-5, Sat 9-2
Friends of the Library Group

KIRSTEIN BUSINESS, 700 Boylston St, Concourse Level, 02117, SAN 344-5771. Tel: 617-859-2142. *Communications Mgr,* Gina Perille
Founded 1930. Circ 39,092
Library Holdings: Bk Vols 40,000; Per Subs 480
Open Mon-Thurs 8-5, Fri & Sat 9-5

LOWER MILLS, 27 Richmond St, Dorchester, 02124-5610, SAN 344-6255. Tel: 617-298-7841. *Br Librn,* Margaret Phillibert
Founded 1981. Circ 59,614
Library Holdings: Large Print Bks 500; Bk Vols 45,000; Per Subs 30; Talking Bks 300
Open Mon & Thurs 12-8, Tues & Wed 10-6, Fri 9-5, Sat 10-3
Friends of the Library Group

MATTAPAN, 1350 Blue Hill Ave, Mattapan, 02126-1843, SAN 344-628X. Tel: 617-298-9218. *Br Librn,* Maurice Gordon
Founded 1931. Circ 58,901
Library Holdings: AV Mats 200; Large Print Bks 200; Bk Vols 23,000; Per Subs 35
Open Mon & Wed 10-6, Tues & Thurs 12-8, Fri & Sat 9-5
Friends of the Library Group

NORTH END, 25 Parmenter St, 02113-2306, SAN 344-631X. Tel: 617-227-8135. *Br Librn,* Susan Voloshin
Founded 1965. Circ 70,099
Library Holdings: Bk Vols 30,000; Per Subs 34
Open Mon, Tues & Thurs 10-6, Wed 12-8, Fri 9-5, Sat 10-3
Friends of the Library Group

PARKER HILL, 1497 Tremont St, Roxbury, 02120-2909, SAN 344-6379. Tel: 617-427-3820. *Br Librn,* Rebecca Manos
Library Holdings: Bk Vols 29,000; Per Subs 46
Open Mon-Wed 10-6, Thurs 12-8, Fri 9-5, Sat 9-2
Friends of the Library Group

ROSLINDALE BRANCH, 4246 Washington St, Roslindale, 02131-2517, SAN 344-6409. Tel: 617-323-2343. *Br Librn,* Catherine Clancy
Founded 1961. Circ 90,165
Library Holdings: Bk Vols 45,000; Per Subs 70; Talking Bks 200
Open Mon-Wed 10-6, Thurs 12-8, Fri 9-5, Sat 9-2
Friends of the Library Group

SOUTH BOSTON, 646 E Broadway, 02127-1502, SAN 344-6433. Tel: 617-268-0180. *Br Librn,* Frances Francis
Founded 1957. Circ 90,159
Library Holdings: Bk Vols 39,000; Per Subs 45; Talking Bks 300
Open Mon & Thurs 12-8, Tues & Wed 10-6, Fri & Sat 9-5
Friends of the Library Group

SOUTH END, 685 Tremont St, 02118-3144, SAN 344-6468. Tel: 617-536-8241. *Br Librn,* Anne Smart
Founded 1971. Circ 86,452
Library Holdings: Bk Vols 50,000; Per Subs 20; Talking Bks 300
Open Mon, Wed & Thurs 10-6, Tues 12-8, Fri 9-5, Sat 9-2
Friends of the Library Group

UPHAMS CORNER, 500 Columbia Rd, Dorchester, 02125-2322, SAN 344-6492. Tel: 617-265-0139. *Br Librn,* Georgia Titonis
Founded 1907. Circ 32,298
Library Holdings: Bk Vols 32,000; Per Subs 25
Open Mon-Wed 10-6, Thurs 12-8, Fri 9-5, Sat 9-2

WEST END, 151 Cambridge St, 02114-2704, SAN 344-6522. Tel: 617-523-3957. *Br Librn,* Helen Bender
Founded 1968. Circ 143,588
Library Holdings: Bk Vols 25,000; Per Subs 25; Talking Bks 100
Open Mon-Wed 10-6, Thurs 12-8, Fri 9-5, Sat 10-3
Friends of the Library Group

WEST ROXBURY BRANCH, 1961 Centre St, West Roxbury, 02132-2534, SAN 344-6557. Tel: 617-325-3147. *Br Librn,* Sheila G Scott
Founded 1922. Circ 155,565
Library Holdings: Bk Vols 105,000; Per Subs 50
Open Mon & Thurs 12-8, Tues & Wed 10-6, Fri & Sat 9-5
Friends of the Library Group

BOSTON UNIVERSITY LIBRARIES

C AFRICAN STUDIES LIBRARY*, 771 Commonwealth Ave, 02215, SAN 344-6611. Tel: 617-353-3726. FAX: 617-358-1729. Web Site: www.bu.edu/library/asl/index.html. *Librn,* David Westley; E-mail: dwestley@bu.edu; Staff 5 (MLS 3, Non-MLS 2)
Library Holdings: Bk Titles 150,000; Bk Vols 200,000; Per Subs 425
Special Collections: African Government Documents; African Studies
Open Mon-Fri 9-5

CM ALUMNI MEDICAL LIBRARY*, 715 Albany St L-12, 02118-2394, SAN 344-6670. Tel: 617-638-4232. Circulation Tel: 617-638-4244. Interlibrary Loan Service Tel: 617-638-4270. Reference Tel: 617-638-4228. Automation Services Tel: 617-638-4230. FAX: 617-638-4233. Administration FAX: 617-638-4478. Web Site: medlib.bu.edu. *Dir,* David S Ginn, PhD; E-mail: dginn@bu.edu; Staff 18 (MLS 7, Non-MLS 11)
Founded 1848
Library Holdings: AV Mats 256; e-books 190; Bk Titles 150,000; Bk Vols 160,000; Per Subs 4,000
Subject Interests: Dentistry, Med, Mental health, Pub health
Automation Activity & Vendor Info: (Acquisitions) Innovative Interfaces, Inc; (Cataloging) Innovative Interfaces, Inc; (Circulation) Innovative Interfaces, Inc; (Course Reserve) Innovative Interfaces, Inc; (ILL) Innovative Interfaces, Inc; (Media Booking) Innovative Interfaces, Inc; (OPAC) Innovative Interfaces, Inc; (Serials) Innovative Interfaces, Inc
Open Mon-Thurs 7:30am-Midnight, Fri 7:30am-10pm, Sat 10-10, Sun 10am-Midnight

C GEORGE H BEEBE COMMUNICATIONS LIBRARY*, College of Communication, 640 Commonwealth Ave, Rm B31, 02215, SAN 325-8025. Tel: 617-353-9240. Web Site: www.bu.edu/library/beebe. *Coordr,* Diane D'Almeida; E-mail: dalmeida@bu.edu; Staff 1 (Non-MLS 1)
Library Holdings: Bk Titles 45; Bk Vols 96; Per Subs 85
Special Collections: Boston Herald Newspaper Clippings, late 19th century-mid 1970's
Subject Interests: Advertising, Films & filmmaking, Journalism, Mass communications
Partic in Association of Research Libraries (ARL)
Open Mon-Fri 10-5

C MUGAR MEMORIAL LIBRARY*, 771 Commonwealth Ave, 02215, SAN 344-6581. Tel: 617-353-3710. Circulation Tel: 617-353-3708. Interlibrary Loan Service Tel: 617-353-3706. Reference Tel: 617-353-3704. FAX: 617-353-2084. Web Site: www.bu.edu/library. *Univ Librn,* Robert Hudson; E-mail: rehuds@bu.edu; *Assoc Univ Librn, Digital Initiatives & Open Access,* Jackie Ammerman; E-mail: jwa@bu.edu; *Assoc Univ Librn, Grad & Res Serv,* Linda Plunket; E-mail: plunket@bu.edu; *Assoc Univ Librn, Undergrad & Distance Serv,* Thomas Casserly; E-mail: casserly@bu.edu; *Institutional Repository Librn,* Vika Zafrin; E-mail: vzafrin@bu.edu; Staff 89 (MLS 89)
Founded 1839. Enrl 29,000; Fac 2,312; Highest Degree: Doctorate
Library Holdings: Bk Vols 2,396,362; Per Subs 34,214; Talking Bks 52,224
Special Collections: African Studies; Americana to 1920 (Mark & Llora Bortman Coll); Art of the Printed Book; Browning Coll; Endowment for Biblical Research; G B Shaw Coll; H G Wells Coll; History of Nursing; Lincolniana (Edward C Stone & F Lauriston Bullard Colls); Liszt Coll; Military History; Mystery & Suspense Novel Coll; Nineteenth Century English Literature; Pascal Coll; Paul C Richards Literary & Hi Manuscript Holdings in Contemporary Literature; Private Press Books; Public Affairs, Theater, Film, Music, Journalism; Robert Frost Coll; Theodore Roosevelt Coll; Whitman Coll. Oral History
Subject Interests: Art & archit, Bus & mgt, Law, Med, Music, Relig, Soc sci & issues
Automation Activity & Vendor Info: (Acquisitions) Innovative Interfaces, Inc; (Cataloging) Innovative Interfaces, Inc; (Circulation) Innovative Interfaces, Inc; (OPAC) Innovative Interfaces, Inc; (Serials) Innovative Interfaces, Inc
Open Mon-Thurs 8am-Midnight, Fri & Sat 8am-11pm, Sun 10am-Midnight
Friends of the Library Group

C MUSIC LIBRARY*, 771 Commonwealth Ave, 02215, SAN 325-3279. Tel: 617-353-3705. FAX: 617-353-2084. E-mail: musiclib@bu.edu. Web Site: www.bu.edu/library/music. *Head Librn,* Holly E Mockovak; *Asst Head, Music Libr,* Sarah P Hunter; *Instrul & Reserves Coordr,* Anya Brodrick; *Pub Serv, Student Asst Coordr,* Donald Denniston; *Cat, Metadata Serv,* Marc Benador; Staff 5 (MLS 2, Non-MLS 3)
Highest Degree: Doctorate
Automation Activity & Vendor Info: (Cataloging) Ex Libris Group

CL PAPPAS LAW LIBRARY*, 765 Commonwealth Ave, 02215. Tel: 617-353-3151. FAX: 617-353-5995. Web Site: www.bu.edu/lawlibrary. *Libr Dir,* Marlene Alderman; Tel: 617-353-8870, E-mail: alderman@bu.edu; *Assoc Dir,* Russell Sweet; Tel: 617-353-8877, E-mail: rlsweet@bu.edu; *Asst Dir,* Stefanie Weigmann; Tel: 617-358-4997, E-mail: sweig@bu.edu
Founded 1872
Library Holdings: Bk Vols 650,000
Subject Interests: Anglo-Am law, Banking & financial law, Health law, Intellectual property, Intl law, Tax law
Automation Activity & Vendor Info: (Acquisitions) Innovative Interfaces, Inc - Millenium; (Cataloging) Innovative Interfaces, Inc - Millenium; (Circulation) Innovative Interfaces, Inc - Millenium; (Course Reserve) Innovative Interfaces, Inc - Millenium; (ILL) OCLC; (OPAC) Innovative Interfaces, Inc - Millenium; (Serials) Innovative Interfaces, Inc - Millenium
Database Vendor: Innovative Interfaces, Inc, OCLC WorldShare Interlibrary Loan
Partic in Boston Library Consortium, Inc; New England Law Library Consortium, Inc
Publications: Law Review Table of Contents; Recent Acquisitions
Open Mon-Thurs 8am-11:30pm, Fri 8am-10pm, Sat 9-9, Sun 10am-11:30pm

C FREDERIC S PARDEE MANAGEMENT LIBRARY, Boston University School of Management, 595 Commonwealth Avenue, 02215, SAN 377-8126. Tel: 617-353-4301. Reference Tel: 617-353-4303, 617-353-4304. FAX: 617-353-4307. Web Site: www.bu.edu/library/management. *Head of Libr,* Arlyne Ann Jackson; Tel: 617-353-4310, E-mail: ajac@bu.edu; *Asst Librn, Access Serv,* Brock Edmunds; Tel: 617-353-4311, E-mail: edmundsb@bu.edu; *Asst Librn, Info serv,* Kathleen M Berger; Tel: 617-353-4312, E-mail: bergerkm@bu.edu; Staff 13 (MLS 5, Non-MLS 8)
Founded 1997. Highest Degree: Doctorate
Library Holdings: e-journals 50,000; Bk Vols 60,000
Subject Interests: Acctg, Advertising, Bus, Econ, Human resources, Mgt, Mkt
Automation Activity & Vendor Info: (Acquisitions) Ex Libris Group; (Cataloging) Ex Libris Group; (Circulation) Ex Libris Group; (Course Reserve) Ex Libris Group; (ILL) OCLC ILLiad; (OPAC) Ex Libris Group; (Serials) Ex Libris Group
Database Vendor: ABC-CLIO, ACM (Association for Computing Machinery), Agricola, Blackwell, Bloomberg, Bowker, Dun & Bradstreet, ebrary, EBSCOhost, Elsevier, Emerald, Ex Libris Group, Factiva.com, Gale Cengage Learning, H W Wilson, Haworth Pres Inc, HeinOnline, IBISWorld, infoUSA, Ingenta, ISI Web of Knowledge, JSTOR, LexisNexis, Medline, Mergent Online, OCLC, OCLC FirstSearch, OCLC

WorldShare Interlibrary Loan, Oxford Online, Project MUSE, ProQuest, PubMed, ReferenceUSA, RefWorks, Safari Books Online, Sage, ScienceDirect, SerialsSolutions, Springer-Verlag, Standard & Poor's, Thomson - Web of Science, Wiley, Wiley InterScience, Wilson - Wilson Web, YBP Library Services
Function: Computers for patron use, Copy machines, Electronic databases & coll, ILL available, Pub access computers, Scanner
Partic in Boston Library Consortium, Inc; Northeast Research Libraries Consortium (NERL); OCLC Research Library Partnership
Open Mon-Thurs 8am-11pm, Fri 8-8, Sat 10-6, Sun 10am-11pm

C PICKERING EDUCATIONAL RESOURCES LIBRARY*, Two Sherborn St, 02215, SAN 344-6646. Tel: 617-353-3734. FAX: 617-353-6105. Web Site: www.bu.edu/library/education. *Librn,* Linda Plunket; Tel: 617-353-3735, E-mail: plunket@bu.edu; Staff 1 (MLS 1)
Library Holdings: Bk Vols 20,000; Per Subs 100; Videos 90
Special Collections: Curriculum Guides; Standardized Psychological and Educational Tests
Subject Interests: Educ
Partic in Association of Research Libraries (ARL); OCLC Online Computer Library Center, Inc
Open Mon-Thurs 8:30am-9pm, Fri 8:30-5, Sat 10-5

CR SCHOOL OF THEOLOGY LIBRARY*, 745 Commonwealth Ave, 2nd Flr, 02215, SAN 344-676X. Tel: 617-353-3034. Reference Tel: 617-353-5357. FAX: 617-358-0699. E-mail: sthlib@bu.edu. Web Site: www.bu.edu/sth/sthlibrary. *Head Librn,* Amy Limpitlaw; E-mail: ael23@bu.edu; *Head, Pub Serv,* James R Skypeck; *Access Serv Librn,* Stacey Battles De Ramos; *Acq Librn,* Olga Potap; *Archivist & Spec Coll Librn,* Kara Jackman; *Cat Librn,* Janet Russell; Tel: 617-353-1353, E-mail: janetr@bu.edu. Subject Specialists: *Bus,* Olga Potap; *Methodist hist,* Kara Jackman; Staff 7 (MLS 5, Non-MLS 2)
Founded 1839. Enrl 450; Fac 24; Highest Degree: Doctorate
Library Holdings: Bk Vols 145,576; Per Subs 545
Special Collections: American Guild of Organists Library; History of Christian Missions Coll; Hymnals (Metcalf-Nutter Coll); Kimball Bible Coll; Liturgy and Worship Coll; Massachusetts Bible Society Coll; New England Methodist Hist Soc Coll; Nutter-Metcalf Hymnal Coll; Oriental Art Objects (Woodward Coll)
Subject Interests: Biblical studies, Music, Philos, Relig hist, Theol
Database Vendor: Innovative Interfaces, Inc
Partic in Association of Research Libraries (ARL)
Open Mon-Thurs (Winter) 8am-9pm, Fri 8-5, Sat 10-6; Mon-Fri (Summer) 8:30-4:30

C SCIENCE & ENGINEERING LIBRARY*, 38 Cummington St, 02215, SAN 325-3716. Tel: 617-353-3733. Reference Tel: 617-353-9474. FAX: 617-353-3470. E-mail: selill@bu.edu. Web Site: www.bu.edu/library/sel. *Ref Librn,* Paula Carey; Tel: 617-358-3963, E-mail: pac@bu.edu; Staff 18 (MLS 4, Non-MLS 14)
Founded 1983. Enrl 25,000; Highest Degree: Doctorate
Library Holdings: Bk Titles 80,000; Bk Vols 85,000; Per Subs 1,800
Subject Interests: Aerospace sci, Biol, Chem, Cognitive sci, Computer eng, Computer sci, Earth sci, Electrical eng, Manufacturing eng, Math, Mechanical eng, Physics
Automation Activity & Vendor Info: (Circulation) Innovative Interfaces, Inc; (Course Reserve) Innovative Interfaces, Inc; (OPAC) Innovative Interfaces, Inc; (Serials) Innovative Interfaces, Inc
Database Vendor: OVID Technologies
Function: Res libr
Partic in Lyrasis; National Network of Libraries of Medicine New England Region; Northeast Research Libraries Consortium (NERL)
Open Mon-Thurs 8am-Midnight, Fri 8-7, Sat 11-7
Restriction: Open to pub for ref only

C STONE SCIENCE LIBRARY*, 771 Commonwealth Ave, 02215, SAN 370-6451. Tel: 617-353-5679. FAX: 617-353-5358. *Head Librn,* Nasim Parveen; E-mail: momen@bu.edu; Staff 2 (MLS 2)
Founded 1988. Enrl 35,000
Library Holdings: Bk Titles 10,000; Per Subs 225
Special Collections: Balloon Aerial Photographs; Geography (George K Lewis Coll); Math (Brad Washburn Coll)
Subject Interests: Archaeology, Geog, Geol, Remote sensing
Partic in BRS
Open Mon-Thurs 9-9, Fri 9-5, Sun Noon-8

M BRIGHAM & WOMEN'S FAULKNER HOSPITAL*, Ingersoll Bowditch Library, 1153 Centre St, 02130. SAN 307-4595. Tel: 617-983-7443. FAX: 617-983-7555. Web Site: www.brighamandwomensfaulkner.org/default.aspx#.UlbzvtJON8E. *Dir,* Cara Marcus; E-mail: cmarcus@partners.org; Staff 4 (MLS 1, Non-MLS 3)
Founded 1940
Library Holdings: Bk Vols 578; Per Subs 212
Special Collections: Patient/Family Resource Center
Subject Interests: Consumer health, Hospital admin, Med, Nursing, Orthopedics, Pathology, Psychiat, Radiology, Surgery
Automation Activity & Vendor Info: (Serials) CyberTools for Libraries
Database Vendor: EBSCOhost, OVID Technologies
Partic in Boston Biomedical Library Consortium; Massachusetts Health Sciences Libraries Network; North Atlantic Health Sciences Libraries, Inc
Open Mon-Fri 8:30-5

M BRIGHAM & WOMEN'S HOSPITAL*, Medical Library, Thorn 127, 75 Francis St, 02115. SAN 377-9157. Tel: 617-732-5684. FAX: 617-975-0890. *Dir,* Anne Sladger
Library Holdings: Bk Vols 1,000; Per Subs 300
Automation Activity & Vendor Info: (Cataloging) Inmagic, Inc.; (Circulation) Inmagic, Inc.; (Serials) EBSCO Online
Database Vendor: OVID Technologies
Function: ILL available, Res libr
Partic in Massachusetts Health Sciences Libraries Network; North Atlantic Health Sciences Libraries, Inc
Restriction: Staff use only

L BROWN, RUDNICK LLP, Research Services, One Financial Ctr, 02111. SAN 372-0748. Tel: 617-856-8213. Reference Tel: 617-856-8111. FAX: 617-856-8201. E-mail: research@brownrudnick.com. Web Site: www.brownrudnick.com. *Co-Dir,* Kathleen Gerwatowski; E-mail: kgerwatowski@brownrudnick.com; *Co-Dir,* Diana Pierce; *Res Spec,* Alison Rutley; *Res Spec,* Helen Vlachos; *Tech Serv Spec,* Pat Killeen; Staff 6 (MLS 4, Non-MLS 2)
Library Holdings: Bk Vols 10,000; Per Subs 400
Automation Activity & Vendor Info: (Cataloging) Inmagic, Inc.; (Circulation) Inmagic, Inc.; (OPAC) Inmagic, Inc.
Database Vendor: LexisNexis, Westlaw
Wireless access
Restriction: Staff use only

J BUNKER HILL COMMUNITY COLLEGE*, Library & Learning Commons, E Bldg, 3rd Flr, Rm E300, 250 New Rutherford Ave, 02129-2925. SAN 307-1456. Tel: 617-228-2213. Reference Tel: 617-228-3479. FAX: 617-228-3288. E-mail: BHCCLibrary@bhcc.mass.edu. Web Site: www.bhcc.mass.edu/library. *Dir, Libr & Learning Commons,* Vivica Smith Pierre; Tel: 617-228-3240, E-mail: vdpierre@bhcc.mass.edu; *Coordr, Libr Serv,* Elizabeth Fields; Tel: 617-228-2307, E-mail: erfields@bhcc.mass.edu; *Coordr, Libr Serv,* Anicia Kuchesky; Tel: 617-936-1961, E-mail: arkuches@bhcc.mass.edu; *Coordr, Libr Serv,* Svetlana Ordian; Tel: 617-228-2211, E-mail: sordian@bhcc.mass.edu; *Coordr, Libr Serv,* Cecilia Roberts; Tel: 617-228-2423, E-mail: cfrobert@bhcc.mass.edu; Staff 5 (MLS 4, Non-MLS 1)
Founded 1973. Enrl 14,000; Fac 123; Highest Degree: Associate
Library Holdings: AV Mats 156; Bks on Deafness & Sign Lang 214; CDs 225; DVDs 347; e-books 37,892; e-journals 65,906; Electronic Media & Resources 232; Large Print Bks 84; Music Scores 130; Bk Titles 53,811; Bk Vols 65,000; Per Subs 130; Talking Bks 14; Videos 300
Subject Interests: Allied health, Bus, Careers, Citizenship, Criminal justice, Diversity, Econ, Educ, Eng, Legal studies, Math, Nursing, Paralegal studies, Sci, Tech
Automation Activity & Vendor Info: (Acquisitions) Innovative Interfaces, Inc; (Cataloging) Innovative Interfaces, Inc; (Circulation) Innovative Interfaces, Inc; (ILL) Innovative Interfaces, Inc; (OPAC) Innovative Interfaces, Inc; (Serials) Innovative Interfaces, Inc
Database Vendor: EBSCOhost, Gale Cengage Learning, JSTOR, LexisNexis, OCLC FirstSearch, ProQuest
Wireless access
Function: ILL available, Photocopying/Printing
Partic in Massachusetts Commonwealth Consortium of Libraries in Public Higher Education Institutions (MCCLPHEI); North of Boston Library Exchange, Inc
Special Services for the Blind - Talking bks & player equip
Open Mon-Fri 8am-9pm, Sat & Sun 8-4
Restriction: Open to pub for ref & circ; with some limitations, Open to students, fac & staff

L BURNS & LEVINSON*, Law Library, 125 Summer St, 02110-1624. SAN 372-073X. Tel: 617-345-3000. FAX: 617-345-3299. Web Site: www.burnslev.com. *Mgr, Libr Serv,* Abbi Maher; E-mail: amaher@burnslev.com
Library Holdings: Bk Vols 7,000; Per Subs 50
Open Mon-Fri 9-5

M CARITAS ST ELIZABETH'S MEDICAL CENTER*, Stohlman Library, 736 Cambridge St, 02135. Tel: 617-789-2177. FAX: 617-789-5081. E-mail: sem_lib@cchcs.org. *Librn,* Catherine Guarcello; *ILL,* Marybeth Edwards; Staff 2 (MLS 2)
Library Holdings: Bk Titles 2,000; Per Subs 200
Automation Activity & Vendor Info: (Cataloging) CyberTools for Libraries; (Circulation) CyberTools for Libraries
Partic in Boston Biomedical Library Consortium; Massachusetts Health Sciences Libraries Network; National Network of Libraries of Medicine New England Region; North Atlantic Health Sciences Libraries, Inc
Restriction: Circulates for staff only

L CHOATE, HALL & STEWART LLP LIBRARY*, Two International Pl, 02110. SAN 307-1510. Tel: 617-248-5202. FAX: 617-248-4000. *Dir, Libr Serv,* Mary E Rogalski; Staff 5 (MLS 2, Non-MLS 3)
Library Holdings: Bk Vols 15,000
Subject Interests: Law
Restriction: Private libr

S CHRISTIAN SCIENCE MONITOR LIBRARY*, One Norway St, 02115. SAN 307-1529. Tel: 617-450-2688. FAX: 617-450-2689. E-mail: csmlibrary@csps.com. Web Site: www.csmonitor.com. *Librn,* Leigh Montgomery; E-mail: montgomeryl@csps.com; Staff 1 (MLS 1)
Founded 1909
Library Holdings: Bk Titles 3,000; Per Subs 30
Subject Interests: Current events
Partic in Dialog Corp; Dow Jones News Retrieval
Restriction: Not open to pub

GL COMMONWEALTH OF MASSACHUSETTS*, Office of the Attorney General Library, One Ashburton Pl, 02108. SAN 307-1537. Tel: 617-693-2060, 617-693-2098. FAX: 617-727-6016. *Law Librn,* Kevin Coakley-Welch; *Ref Spec,* Laurel Davis; Staff 2 (MLS 1, Non-MLS 1)
Founded 1975
Library Holdings: Bk Titles 2,000; Bk Vols 10,000; Per Subs 200
Database Vendor: Dun & Bradstreet, Loislaw, Westlaw
Wireless access
Publications: Index to Opinions of Attorney General
Restriction: By permission only

S CRA INTERNATIONAL LIBRARY*, 200 Clarendon St T-33, 02116. SAN 307-1499. Tel: 617-425-3000. FAX: 617-425-3132. Web Site: www.crai.com. *Librn,* Doug Southard
Founded 1975
Library Holdings: Bk Vols 20,000; Per Subs 300
Subject Interests: Econ, Energy, Environ studies, Metal working, Transportation
Partic in Lyrasis

M DANA-FARBER CANCER INSTITUTE*, Baruj Benacerraf Library, 44 Binney St, 02115-6084. SAN 325-2787. Tel: 617-632-3508. Administration Tel: 617-632-2489. FAX: 617-632-2488. E-mail: dfcilib@dfci.harvard.edu. *Librn,* Christine W Fleuriel; Staff 2 (MLS 1, Non-MLS 1)
Founded 1981
Library Holdings: Bk Titles 1,300; Per Subs 265
Subject Interests: AIDS, Alternative med, Cancer res, Clinical oncology, Immunology, Nursing, Pharmacology
Automation Activity & Vendor Info: (Acquisitions) EOS International; (Cataloging) EOS International; (OPAC) EOS International; (Serials) EOS International
Database Vendor: EBSCOhost, OVID Technologies
Partic in Boston Biomedical Library Consortium; Massachusetts Health Sciences Libraries Network
Restriction: Staff use only

L DAY PITNEY LLP*, Information Resource Center, One International Pl, 02110. Tel: 617-345-4600. FAX: 617-345-4745. Web Site: www.daypitney.com. *Info Res Spec,* Carol S Wellington; Staff 1 (MLS 1)
Library Holdings: Bk Vols 5,000; Per Subs 50

L DECHERT LAW LIBRARY*, 200 Clarendon St, 27th Flr, 02116. SAN 372-0659. Tel: 617-728-7100, Ext 7198. FAX: 617-426-6567. Web Site: www.dechert.com. *Librn,* Christine Dubuque
Library Holdings: Bk Vols 6,000; Per Subs 68

S THE MARY BAKER EDDY LIBRARY, Research & Reference Services, 200 Massachusetts Ave, P02-10, 02115-3017. SAN 326-3525. Tel: 617-450-7218. FAX: 617-450-7048. E-mail: librarymail@mbelibrary.org. Web Site: www.mbelibrary.org/research. *Exec Dir,* Michael Hamilton; Tel: 617-450-7400, E-mail: hamiltonm@mbelibrary.org; *Ref Librn,* Mark Montgomery; Tel: 617-450-7315, E-mail: montgomerym@mbelibrary.org; *Fel Coordr, Res,* Dr Darling Sherry; Tel: 617-450-7316; *Archivist,* Position Currently Open; *Curator,* Pam Winstead; Tel: 617-450-7127, E-mail: winsteadp@mbelibrary.org; *Sr Res Archivist,* Judith A Huenneke; Tel: 617-450-7111, E-mail: huennekej@mbelibrary.org; *Sr Researcher,* Mike Davis; Tel: 617-450-7121; *Res,* Kurt Morris; Tel: 617-450-7124, E-mail: morrisk@mbelibrary.org; *Res,* Dorothy Rivera; Tel: 617-450-7002; Staff 6 (MLS 2, Non-MLS 4)
Founded 2002
Library Holdings: CDs 25; DVDs 100; Bk Titles 10,000; Bk Vols 18,000; Per Subs 25; Spec Interest Per Sub 15; Videos 75
Special Collections: Organizational Records for The First Church of Christ, Scientist; The life and works of Mary Baker Eddy; The Mary Baker Eddy Archive (Includes letters, manuscripts, photographs, artifacts, books, periodicals, and other materials)
Subject Interests: 19th Century hist, Bible studies, Contemporary, Cultural studies, Relig hist, Spirituality, Women in lit, Women in theol
Automation Activity & Vendor Info: (Acquisitions) Re:discovery Software, Inc; (Cataloging) OCLC Connexion; (Circulation) Re:discovery Software, Inc; (ILL) OCLC Online; (OPAC) Re:discovery Software, Inc
Database Vendor: OCLC FirstSearch, OCLC WorldShare Interlibrary Loan, ProQuest
Wireless access
Function: Archival coll, Art exhibits, Doc delivery serv, ILL available, Online searches, Orientations, Outside serv via phone, mail, e-mail & web, Photocopying/Printing, Ref serv available, Res libr, Spoken cassettes & CDs
Mem of Massachusetts Libr Syst
Partic in Lyrasis; OCLC-LVIS
Open Tues-Fri 10-4
Restriction: Open to pub for ref & circ; with some limitations, Res pass required for non-affiliated visitors

L EDWARDS ANGELL PALMER & DODGE LLP*, Law Library, 111 Huntington Ave, 02199. SAN 372-0632. Tel: 617-239-0254. FAX: 617-227-4420. Web Site: www.eapdlaw.com. *Head, Firmwide Libr Serv,* Nuchine Nobari; Tel: 617-239-0104, E-mail: nnobari@eapdlaw.com; *Ref,* Wilfred Lawrence Pollender; Tel: 617-239-0610. Subject Specialists: *Bus, Law,* Nuchine Nobari; Staff 7 (MLS 4, Non-MLS 3)
Library Holdings: Bk Vols 35,000; Per Subs 425
Automation Activity & Vendor Info: (Acquisitions) EOS International; (Cataloging) EOS International
Database Vendor: American Chemical Society, Bloomberg, Cambridge Scientific Abstracts, GalleryWatch, LexisNexis, Westlaw, Westlaw Business
Wireless access
Partic in Mass Libr & Info Network

C EMERSON COLLEGE*, Iwasaki Library, 120 Boylston St, 02116-4624. SAN 307-1588. Tel: 617-824-8668. Interlibrary Loan Service Tel: 617-824-8333. Reference Tel: 617-824-8674. Administration Tel: 617-824-8670. Automation Services Tel: 617-824-8339. Information Services Tel: 617-824-8675. FAX: 617-824-7817. Automation Services FAX: 617-824-8549. E-mail: circulation@emerson.edu. Web Site: www.emerson.edu/library. *Exec Dir,* Robert Fleming; E-mail: robert_fleming@emerson.edu; *Assoc Dir, Info Serv,* Beth Joress; Tel: 617-824-8331, E-mail: beth_joress@emerson.edu; *Asst Dir, Tech & Access Serv,* Elena O'Malley; E-mail: elena_omalley@emerson.edu; *Head, Archives & Spec Coll,* Christina Zamon; Tel: 617-824-8679, E-mail: christina_zamon@emerson.edu; *Head, Info Res,* Kerry Adams; Tel: 617-824 8338, E-mail: kerry_adams@emerson.edu; *Instruction Librn,* Christina Dent; Tel: 617-824-8364, E-mail: christina_dent@emerson.edu; *Media Librn,* Maureen Tripp; Tel: 617-824-8407, E-mail: maureen_tripp@emerson.edu; *Coordr, Electronic Res, Ref Librn,* Daniel Crocker; Tel: 617-824 8332, E-mail: daniel_crocker@emerson.edu; *Coordr, Instruction, Ref Librn,* Karla Fribley; Tel: 617-824-8330, E-mail: karla_fribley@emerson.edu; *Coordr, Outreach Serv, Ref Librn,* Mary Hirschbiel; Tel: 617-824-8340, E mail: mary_Hirschbiel@emerson.edu; *Ref Librn,* Esther Roth-Katz; Tel: 617-824-8334, E-mail: esther_rothkatz@emerson.edu; Staff 22 (MLS 12, Non-MLS 10)
Founded 1880. Enrl 4,376; Fac 267; Highest Degree: Master
Library Holdings: AV Mats 15,214; e-books 87,130; e-journals 57,126; Bk Vols 144,059; Per Subs 381
Special Collections: American Comedy Archives; Bill Dana papers; Jan Murray papers; Janis Paige papers; Variety Vaudeville Protection Agency Coll. Oral History
Subject Interests: Comedy, Mass communications, Performing arts
Automation Activity & Vendor Info: (Acquisitions) Ex Libris Group; (Cataloging) Ex Libris Group; (Circulation) Ex Libris Group; (Course Reserve) Ex Libris Group; (ILL) OCLC; (Media Booking) Dymaxion; (OPAC) Ex Libris Group; (Serials) Ex Libris Group
Wireless access
Partic in Fenway Libraries Online, Inc; Fenway Library Consortium (FLC)
Open Mon-Thurs 7:45am-11pm, Fri 7:45am-9pm, Sat 10-6, Sun Noon-11

C EMMANUEL COLLEGE*, Cardinal Cushing Library, 400 The Fenway, 02115. SAN 307-1596. Tel: 617-735-9927. FAX: 617-735-9763. Web Site: www1.emmanuel.edu/library. *Dir,* Dr Susan E von Daum Tholl; Tel: 617-264-7659, E-mail: tholl@emmanuel.edu; *Asst Dir, Technology & Tech Serv,* Catherine Tuohy; Tel: 617-264-7658, E-mail: tuohyc@emmanuel.edu; *Head, Ref,* Diane Zydlewski; Tel: 617-264-7654, E-mail: zydlewsd@emmanuel.edu; *Cataloger/Distribution Librn,* Jennifer Woodall; Tel: 617-264-7653, E-mail: woodall@emmanuel.edu; Staff 6.75 (MLS 4.75, Non-MLS 2)
Founded 1919. Enrl 2,802; Fac 76; Highest Degree: Master
Library Holdings: AV Mats 800; Bk Vols 96,000; Per Subs 800
Special Collections: Church History
Subject Interests: Art, Art therapy, Lit, Theol, Women's studies
Automation Activity & Vendor Info: (Acquisitions) Ex Libris Group; (Cataloging) Ex Libris Group; (Circulation) Ex Libris Group; (Course

Reserve) Ex Libris Group; (ILL) Ex Libris Group; (OPAC) Ex Libris Group; (Serials) Ex Libris Group
Database Vendor: Agricola, Alexander Street Press, American Chemical Society, American Psychological Association (APA), ARTstor, CountryWatch, EBSCOhost, Elsevier, Gale Cengage Learning, JSTOR, LexisNexis, Mergent Online, Newsbank, ProQuest, PubMed, ScienceDirect, TDNet, ValueLine, Wiley InterScience, Wilson - Wilson Web
Wireless access
Partic in Fenway Libraries Online, Inc; Fenway Library Consortium (FLC)
Special Services for the Deaf - Assistive tech; Bks on deafness & sign lang
Special Services for the Blind - Aids for in-house use
Open Mon-Thurs 7:30am-1am, Fri 7:30am-8pm, Sat 9-8, Sun Noon-1am

R EPISCOPAL DIOCESE OF MASSACHUSETTS*, Diocesan Library & Archives, 138 Tremont St, 02111. SAN 307-1618. Tel: 617-482-4826, Ext 488. FAX: 617-482-4826. E-mail: archivist@diomass.org. Web Site: www.diomass.org.
Founded 1884
Library Holdings: Bk Vols 3,500
Special Collections: 18th & 19th Century Americana, pamphlets & SPG publications; Books of Common Prayer
Subject Interests: Church hist
Wireless access
Function: Archival coll
Publications: Guide to the Parochial Archives of the Episcopal Church in Boston, 1981; Littera Scripta Manet (Newsletter)
Restriction: Authorized patrons
Friends of the Library Group

S FEDERAL RESERVE BANK OF BOSTON*, Research Library, 600 Atlantic Ave, 02210-2204. SAN 307-1634. Tel: 617-973-3397. Circulation Tel: 617-973-3396. Interlibrary Loan Service Tel: 617-973-3668. FAX: 617-973-4221. E-mail: boston.library@bos.frb.org. Web Site: www.bos.frb.org. *Dir,* Joyce Hannan; *ILL, Ref, Sr Info Res Spec,* Teresa Huie; E-mail: teresa.huie@bos.frb.org; *Ref, Sr Info Res Spec,* Catherine Spozio; Tel: 617-973-3393, E-mail: catherine.spozio@bos.frb.org; Staff 5.5 (MLS 3, Non-MLS 2.5)
Founded 1921
Library Holdings: Bk Vols 70,000
Special Collections: Federal Reserve System Materials
Subject Interests: Econ, Finance
Publications: Booknews (Newsletter)
Mem of Massachusetts Libr Syst
Open Mon-Fri 10-4
Restriction: Access at librarian's discretion, Borrowing requests are handled by ILL

C FISHER COLLEGE LIBRARY*, 118 Beacon St, 02116. SAN 307-1677. Tel: 617-236-8875. FAX: 617-670-4426. E-mail: library@fisher.edu. Web Site: www.fisher.edu/library. *Col Librn, Libr Dir,* Joshua Van Kirk McKain; E-mail: jmckain@fisher.edu; *Assoc Col Librn,* Cara Parkoff; E-mail: cparkoff@fisher.edu; Staff 4 (MLS 4)
Founded 1903. Enrl 1,474; Fac 104; Highest Degree: Bachelor
Jul 2012-Jun 2013 Income $2,910. Mats Exp $108,944, Books $16,202, Per/Ser (Incl. Access Fees) $4,544, AV Mat $8,753, Electronic Ref Mat (Incl. Access Fees) $79,445. Sal $170,852
Library Holdings: DVDs 2,505; Bk Titles 26,533; Bk Vols 26,667; Per Subs 77; Videos 674
Automation Activity & Vendor Info: (Acquisitions) Innovative Interfaces, Inc; (Cataloging) Innovative Interfaces, Inc; (Circulation) Innovative Interfaces, Inc; (Course Reserve) Innovative Interfaces, Inc; (ILL) OCLC FirstSearch; (OPAC) Innovative Interfaces, Inc
Database Vendor: BiblioCommons, College Source, CredoReference, EBSCOhost, Gale Cengage Learning, LexisNexis, Newsbank, OCLC FirstSearch, OCLC WorldShare Interlibrary Loan, ProQuest
Wireless access
Function: Copy machines, Electronic databases & coll, Free DVD rentals, ILL available, Instruction & testing, Mus passes, Online info literacy tutorials on the web & in blackboard, Orientations, Ref serv available, Ref serv in person, VHS videos
Partic in Lyrasis; Metro Boston Libr Network
Open Mon-Thurs 8am-10pm, Fri 8-4, Sat 12-8, Sun 2-10
Restriction: Open to pub for ref & circ; with some limitations, Open to students, fac, staff & alumni

L FOLEY & HOAG LLP LIBRARY*, 155 Seaport Blvd, 02210. SAN 307-1685. Tel: 617-832-7070. Reference Tel: 617-832-7098. FAX: 617-832-7000. *Dir, Libr Serv,* Jeannette Tracy; *Asst Dir,* Allen Rines; E-mail: arines@fhe.com; *Ref Librn,* Joanne Blinn; *Tech Serv,* Bridget Lonergan; Staff 5 (MLS 4, Non-MLS 1)
Library Holdings: Bk Vols 50,000; Per Subs 250
Subject Interests: Corporate law, Environ law, Intellectual property, Labor, Litigation
Wireless access
Restriction: Authorized personnel only

M FORSYTH INSTITUTE*, Percy R Howe Memorial Library, 140 The Fenway, 02115-3799. SAN 307-1693. Tel: 617-892-8245. FAX: 617-892-8470. Web Site: www.forsyth.org. *Dir,* Susan Orlando; E-mail: sorlando@forsyth.org; *Librn,* Dan McCloskey; E-mail: dmccloskey@forsyth.org; Staff 4 (MLS 2, Non-MLS 2)
Founded 1913
Library Holdings: Bk Vols 6,900; Per Subs 180
Special Collections: Forsyth Institute Archives, bks, memorabilia, photogs. Oral History
Subject Interests: Bacteriology, Dentistry, Immunology, Microbiology, Molecular biol, Pharmacology
Automation Activity & Vendor Info: (Cataloging) EOS International; (Circulation) EOS International; (Serials) EOS International
Publications: Collected Reprints of Forsyth Dental Center (Newsletter)
Partic in Boston Biomedical Library Consortium; Docline; Massachusetts Health Sciences Libraries Network; North Atlantic Health Sciences Libraries, Inc
Open Mon-Fri 9-5
Friends of the Library Group

S ISABELLA STEWART GARDNER MUSEUM LIBRARY*, 280 The Fenway, 02115-5897. SAN 328-6134. Tel: 617-278-5121. FAX: 617-278-5177. E-mail: collection@isgm.org. Web Site: www.gardnermuseum.org. *Curator,* Joseph Saravo; Staff 1 (Non-MLS 1)
Founded 1903
Library Holdings: Bk Titles 2,300; Per Subs 10
Special Collections: Isabella Stewart Gardner Coll, bks, binding, mss, letters, autographs, music scores, archives
Subject Interests: Art hist, Conserv
Database Vendor: OCLC FirstSearch
Function: Archival coll
Restriction: Non-circulating, Open by appt only

J GIBBS COLLEGE OF BOSTON*, William F Reilly Library, 126 Newbury St, 02116. SAN 326-1123. Tel: 617-578-7100, 617-578-7178. FAX: 617-578-7163. E-mail: library@gibbsboston.edu. Web Site: www.gibbsboston.edu. *Librn,* William Grealish; E-mail: bgrealish@gibbsboston.edu; Staff 1 (MLS 1)
Founded 1982
Library Holdings: e-books 5,000; e-journals 11,000; Bk Vols 1,000; Per Subs 25
Wireless access
Partic in Boston Regional Library System
Open Mon & Wed 8-6, Tues & Thurs 8-7, Fri 8-4
Restriction: Authorized patrons

L GOODWIN PROCTER*, Law Library, Exchange Pl, 53 State St, 02109. SAN 328-4654. Tel: 617-570-1994, 617-570-6868. FAX: 617-523-1231. Web Site: www.goodwinprocter.com.
Library Holdings: Bk Vols 40,000; Per Subs 2,500
Partic in Dialog Corp; Westlaw

L GOULSTON & STORRS, PC*, Library Services, 400 Atlantic Ave, 02110. SAN 372-0772. Tel: 617-482-1776. Web Site: www.goulstonstorrs.com. *Mgr, Libr Serv,* Robert DeFabrizio; *Asst Librn,* Jennifer Meger; *Libr Tech,* James Mudge; Staff 2 (MLS 1, Non-MLS 1)
Library Holdings: Bk Vols 10,000; Per Subs 200
Subject Interests: Health, Law, Real estate, Securities
Automation Activity & Vendor Info: (Cataloging) EOS International; (OPAC) EOS International; (Serials) EOS International
Wireless access
Function: ILL available, Online searches, Photocopying/Printing
Partic in OCLC Online Computer Library Center, Inc
Restriction: Co libr, Employee & client use only, Not open to pub

S GRAND LODGE OF MASONS IN MASSACHUSETTS*, Samuel Crocker Lawrence Library, 186 Tremont St, 02111. SAN 307-1774. Tel: 617-426-6040, Ext 4221. FAX: 617-426-6115. E-mail: library@massfreemasonry.org. Web Site: www.massfreemasonry.org. *Librn,* Cynthia Alcorn; Staff 3 (MLS 1, Non-MLS 2)
Founded 1814
Library Holdings: Bk Vols 50,000; Per Subs 60
Special Collections: Freemasonry (John Paul Jones Coll), mss; Histories; New England Towns & Cities
Function: Res libr
Open Mon-Fri 8:30-4:30

L HALE & DORR LIBRARY*, 60 State St, 02109. SAN 307-1782. Tel: 617-526-5900. FAX: 617-526-5000. *Librn,* Donna Lombardo
Library Holdings: Bk Vols 21,000
Subject Interests: Govt, Law

S HALEY & ALDRICH INC, LIBRARY*, 465 Medford St, Ste 2200, 02129. SAN 373-0670. Tel: 617-886-7426. FAX: 617-886-7726. Web Site: www.haleyaldrich.com. *Librn,* Rich Oliver; E-mail: roliver@haleyaldrich.com
Library Holdings: Bk Titles 5,000; Bk Vols 5,500; Per Subs 15
Subject Interests: Environ eng, Geotechnical
Automation Activity & Vendor Info: (Acquisitions) Inmagic, Inc.; (Cataloging) Inmagic, Inc.; (Circulation) Inmagic, Inc.
Wireless access
Restriction: Clients only, Open by appt only, Staff use only

S HARVARD MUSICAL ASSOCIATION LIBRARY*, 57A Chestnut St, 02108. SAN 307-1812. Tel: 617-523-2897. FAX: 617-523-2897. E-mail: info@hmaboston.org. Web Site: www.hmaboston.org. *Mgr,* Craig Hanson
Founded 1837
Library Holdings: Bk Titles 12,000
Special Collections: Chamber Music Parts; Two-Piano Music

L HEMENWAY & BARNES*, Law Library, 60 State St, 02109. SAN 372-0667. Tel: 617-227-7940. FAX: 617-227-0781. *Librn,* Jane Huston; E-mail: jhuston@hembar.com; Staff 1 (Non-MLS 1)
Founded 1863
Special Collections: Massachusetts Statutes Back to 1694

S HISTORIC NEW ENGLAND*, Library & Archives, 141 Cambridge St, 02114-2702. SAN 307-1928. Tel: 617-994-5946. FAX: 617-249-1597. E-mail: archives@historicnewengland.org. Web Site: www.historicnewengland.org. *Librn & Archivist,* Abigail Cramer; E-mail: acramer@historicnewengland.org; *Libr & Archives Spec,* Jeanne Gamble; Tel: 617-994-5945, E-mail: jgamble@historicnewengland.org; *Mus Historian,* Jennifer Pustz; Tel: 617-994-5947, E-mail: jpustz@historicnewengland.org; *Sr Curator, Libr & Archives,* Lorna Condon; Tel: 617-994-5944, E-mail: lcondon@historicnewengland.org; Staff 4 (MLS 2, Non-MLS 2)
Founded 1910
Library Holdings: Bk Titles 13,000; Bk Vols 15,000
Special Collections: Architectural Drawings, 19th & 20th Centuries (Asher Benjamin, Luther Briggs, Frank Chouteau Brown, Herbert Browne, George Clough, Ogden Codman, Jr, Robert Allen Cook, Arland Dirlam, Halfdan Hanson, Arthur Little, J Luippold, Richard Upjohn); Architecture & Design (Rare Books Coll); Builders Guides & Account Books, 19th & 20th Centuries; Edwin Whitefield Coll, sketchbks, watercolors; Ephemera Coll, advertisements, billheads, trade cards, trade cats; Family Papers & Manuscripts (Casey, Codman, Jewett, Marrett, Rundlet-May & Sayward Families); Harrison Gray Otis Business Papers; Historic American Buildings Survey, Massachusetts; Historic New England/SPNEA Institutional Records; New England Maps & Atlases; New England/Regional & Boston, pamphlets; Photographic Colls (Boston & Albany Railroad, Boston Elevated Railroad & Boston Transit Commission, Emma Coleman, Baldwin Coolidge, Alfred Cutting, Domestic Interiors, Geographic, Halliday Historic Photograph, Arthur Haskell, Mary Northend, Wallace Nutting, Henry Peabody, Fred Quimby, Soule Art Photo Company, N L Stebbins, Thompson & Thompson/New England News, Yankee Magazine)
Subject Interests: Archit, Decorative art, Photog
Wireless access
Function: Archival coll
Restriction: Open by appt only
Friends of the Library Group

S INSTITUTE OF CONTEMPORARY ART LIBRARY*, 955 Boylston St, 02115. SAN 374-9533. Tel: 617-266-5152. FAX: 617-266-4021. E-mail: info@icaboston.org. *Dir,* Jill Medvedow
Library Holdings: Bk Vols 500
Subject Interests: Archit
Open Wed & Fri 12-5, Thurs 12-9, Sat & Sun 11-5
Restriction: Open to pub for ref only, Private libr

S INSURANCE LIBRARY ASSOCIATION OF BOSTON*, 156 State St, 02109. SAN 307-1855. Tel: 617-227-2087. FAX: 617-723-8524. Web Site: www.insurancelibrary.org. *Dir,* Jean Lucey; E-mail: jlucey@insurancelibrary.org; *Librn,* Sarah Hart; *Librn,* Meagan Stefanow
Founded 1887
Library Holdings: Bk Titles 15,000; Bk Vols 30,000; Per Subs 200
Special Collections: Sanborn Fire Maps
Publications: Membership Newsletter (Quarterly)
Open Mon-Fri 9-5

S CAROL R JOHNSON & ASSOCIATES, INC LIBRARY*, 115 Broad St, 02110-3032. SAN 327-7216. Tel: 617-896-2500, Ext 2653. FAX: 617-896-2340. Web Site: www.crja.com. *Librn,* Desiree Goodwin; Tel: 617-896-2653, E-mail: dgoodwin@crja.com. Subject Specialists: *Archit, Landscaping, Urban planning,* Desiree Goodwin; Staff 1 (MLS 1)
Library Holdings: Bk Vols 2,000; Per Subs 125
Subject Interests: Landscaping, Urban planning
Restriction: Access for corporate affiliates

L K&L GATES LLP*, Law Library, State Street Financial Ctr, One Lincoln St, 02111-2950. SAN 327-6082. Tel: 617-951-9160. FAX: 617-261-3175. Web Site: www.klgates.com. *Libr Mgr,* Elizabeth Labedz; E-mail: betsy.labedz@klgates.com; *Ref Asst,* Katherine R Bradley; Tel: 617-951-9048, E-mail: kate.bradley@klgates.com. Subject Specialists: *Law,* Elizabeth Labedz; *Law,* Katherine R Bradley; Staff 1 (MLS 1)
Library Holdings: Bk Vols 8,000; Per Subs 100
Automation Activity & Vendor Info: (Acquisitions) SirsiDynix; (Cataloging) SirsiDynix; (Circulation) SirsiDynix
Restriction: Not open to pub

CL LABOURE COLLEGE*, Helen Stubblefield Law Library, 2120 Dorchester Ave, 02124. SAN 307-191X. Tel: 617-296-8300, Ext 4012. FAX: 617-296-7947. Web Site: www.laboure.edu. *Dir,* Andrew M Calo; Staff 1 (MLS 1)
Founded 1971. Enrl 600
Library Holdings: Bk Vols 11,000; Per Subs 155
Subject Interests: Nursing
Database Vendor: Gale Cengage Learning, OCLC FirstSearch, PubMed
Partic in Massachusetts Health Sciences Libraries Network
Open Mon-Thurs 8am-10pm, Fri 8-9, Sat 9-8, Sun 10-8
Friends of the Library Group

S LESLEY UNIVERSITY, Art Institute of Boston Library, 700 Beacon St, 02215-2598. SAN 307-1251. Tel: 617-585-6670. FAX: 617-585-6655. Web Site: www.lesley.edu/aib/studentlife/services_lib.html, www.lesley.edu/library. *Head Librn,* Carrie McDade; Tel: 617-585-6671, E-mail: cmcdade@lesley.edu; *Visual Res Curator,* Carrie Salazar; Tel: 617-585-6673; *Libr Asst,* Raye Yankauskas; Tel: 617-585-6672; Staff 3 (MLS 1, Non-MLS 2)
Highest Degree: Master
Library Holdings: DVDs 300; Bk Vols 12,000; Per Subs 75; Videos 300
Special Collections: Artist's Books Coll; Bradbury Thompson Coll, bks, pamphlets, posters
Subject Interests: Art hist, Design, Visual arts
Automation Activity & Vendor Info: (Acquisitions) Ex Libris Group; (Circulation) Ex Libris Group
Partic in Fenway Libraries Online, Inc; Fenway Library Consortium (FLC)
Open Mon-Thurs (Sept-May) 8:30am-9:30pm, Fri 8:30-5:30, Sat 12-6, Sun 2-8

L LIBERTY MUTUAL GROUP*, Law Library, 175 Berkeley St, 7th Flr, 02116-5066. SAN 344-6883. Tel: 617-357-9500, Ext 44192. FAX: 617-574-5830. *Dir, Law Libr,* Chris Laut, III; E-mail: chris.laut@libertymutual.com. Subject Specialists: *Ins, Rec mgt, Securities law,* Chris Laut, III; Staff 4 (MLS 2, Non-MLS 2)
Founded 1918
Library Holdings: Bk Vols 130,000; Per Subs 120
Subject Interests: Admin law, Ethics, Ins
Automation Activity & Vendor Info: (Acquisitions) Softlink America; (Cataloging) Softlink America; (Circulation) Softlink America; (ILL) Softlink America; (OPAC) Softlink America; (Serials) Softlink America
Database Vendor: Bloomberg, Dun & Bradstreet, Factiva.com, Hoovers, LexisNexis, Sage, Westlaw
Wireless access
Restriction: Authorized personnel only

S THE LIBRARY OF THE FRENCH CULTURAL CENTER ALLIANCE FRANCAISE OF BOSTON*, 53 Marlborough St, 02116-2099. SAN 307-1715. Tel: 617-912-0400, Ext 419. Circulation Tel: 617-912-0417. FAX: 617-912-0450. E-mail: librarian@frenchculturalcenter.org. Web Site: www.frenchculturalcenter.org. *Head Librn,* Marie Lalevee; Staff 1.5 (MLS 0.5, Non-MLS 1)
Founded 1945
Library Holdings: Audiobooks 400; CDs 1,500; DVDs 1,050; e-books 570; Music Scores 20; Bk Vols 21,200; Per Subs 30; Videos 650
Special Collections: Children's Literature Coll; Cultures and literature of the francophone world; Films; Francophone Music & Books on CD; French Culture Coll; French language; History & Literature of France & French-Speaking Countries
Subject Interests: Humanities
Automation Activity & Vendor Info: (Cataloging) ByWater Solutions; (Circulation) ByWater Solutions; (OPAC) ByWater Solutions; (Serials) ByWater Solutions
Wireless access
Function: Adult bk club, Bks on CD, Electronic databases & coll, ILL available, Music CDs, Online cat, Online searches, Outside serv via phone, mail, e-mail & web, Ref serv available, VHS videos, Video lending libr
Special Services for the Blind - Bks on CD
Open Mon, Tues & Thurs 10-6, Wed 10-8, Sat 10-5
Restriction: Circ to mem only

S LYMAN LIBRARY*, Educator Resource Center, Museum of Science, One Science Park, 02114-1099. SAN 307-2150. Tel: 617-589-0170. FAX: 617-589-0494. E-mail: library@mos.org. Web Site: www.mos.org/library. *Sr Curator, Mus Coll,* Carolyn Kirdahy; *Coordr,* Jeff Mehigan; Staff 2 (MLS 2)
Founded 1831
Library Holdings: Bk Vols 17,000; Per Subs 75
Special Collections: 19th Century Natural History, bk, journal & mss; Archives of the Boston Society of Natural History founded 1830, the predecessor of the Museum of Science; Technology & Engineering Curriculum
Subject Interests: Educ
Wireless access

S MASSACHUSETTS BOARD OF LIBRARY COMMISSIONERS*, 98 N Washington St, Ste 401, 02114. SAN 307-1952. Tel: 617-725-1860. FAX: 617-725-0140. Web Site: mblc.state.ma.us/. *Actg Dir,* Dianne L Carty; Staff 22 (MLS 11, Non-MLS 11)
Founded 1890
Library Holdings: Bk Vols 3,000
Special Collections: Agency Archival Coll
Publications: Annual Report of Board of Library Commissioners; Data for Massachusetts Series (Public Library Statistics & Personnel Data); Directory of Free Public Libraries in Massachusetts; Library Services & Technology Act Massachusetts Long Range Plan 2013-2017; Strategic Plan for the Future of Library Services in Massachusetts
Partic in North of Boston Library Exchange, Inc

C MASSACHUSETTS COLLEGE OF ART & DESIGN*, Morton R Godine Library, 621 Huntington Ave, 02115-5882. SAN 307-1960. Tel: 617-879-7150. Interlibrary Loan Service Tel: 617-879-7113. Reference Tel: 617-879-7101. FAX: 617-879-7110. Web Site: www.massart.edu/library. *Dir,* Paul Dobbs; *Instrul Serv Librn, Ref Librn,* Greg Wallace; E-mail: greg.wallace@massart.edu; *Access Serv, Visual Res,* Gabrielle Reed; Tel: 617-879-7199, E-mail: gabrielle.reed@massart.edu; *Acq, Ser,* Richard McElroy; Tel: 617-879-7112;879-7106, E-mail: rmcelroy@massart.edu; *Circ, Computer Serv,* Leslie Everett; E-mail: leverett@massart.edu; *Tech Serv,* Rachel Resnik; Tel: 617-879-7115, E-mail: rresnik@massart.edu; *Visual Res,* Pereira Caitlin; Tel: 617-879-7116, E-mail: caitlin.pereira@massart.edu; Staff 12 (MLS 4, Non-MLS 8)
Founded 1873. Enrl 2,000; Highest Degree: Master
Jul 2006-Jun 2007. Mats Exp $95,310
Library Holdings: Bk Titles 85,000; Per Subs 280; Videos 3,100
Special Collections: Art Educ; College Archives; Design
Subject Interests: Art, Art hist, Design, Films & filmmaking
Automation Activity & Vendor Info: (Cataloging) Ex Libris Group; (Circulation) Ex Libris Group
Database Vendor: SirsiDynix
Partic in Fenway Libraries Online, Inc; Fenway Library Consortium (FLC); Lyrasis; OCLC Online Computer Library Center, Inc
Open Mon-Thurs 8am-9pm, Fri 8-6, Sat 11-5, Sun 2-8

CM MASSACHUSETTS COLLEGE OF PHARMACY & HEALTH SCIENCES*, Henrietta DeBenedictis Library, 179 Longwood Ave, 02115-5896. SAN 307-1979. Tel: 617-732-2803. Reference Tel: 617-732-2813. FAX: 617-278-1566. Web Site: www.mcphs.edu/libraries. *Dir,* Richard Kaplan; E-mail: richard.kaplan@mcphs.edu; *Head, Ref,* Sarah McCord; Tel: 617-735-1439, E-mail: sarah.mccord@mcphs.edu; *Access Serv, Head, Tech Serv,* Joanne Doucette; Tel: 617-732-2805, E-mail: joanne.doucette@mcphs.edu; Staff 15 (MLS 7, Non-MLS 8)
Founded 1823. Highest Degree: Doctorate
Library Holdings: Bk Titles 15,000; Bk Vols 20,000; Per Subs 700
Subject Interests: Med, Pharmacology
Automation Activity & Vendor Info: (Acquisitions) Ex Libris Group; (Cataloging) Ex Libris Group; (Circulation) Ex Libris Group
Publications: Acquisitions List (Quarterly); Annual Report; Current Serials; Library Guide
Partic in Fenway Library Consortium (FLC); Lyrasis
Open Mon-Thurs 7:30am-11pm, Fri 7:30-7, Sat 11-9, Sun Noon-11

G MASSACHUSETTS DEPARTMENT OF PUBLIC HEALTH*, Central Library, Central Library Bldg, 3rd Flr, 250 Washington St, 02108-4619. SAN 307-2002. Tel: 617-624-5190. FAX: 617-624-5185. Web Site: www.mass.gov/dph.
Library Holdings: Bk Vols 1,200; Per Subs 150
Subject Interests: Pub health
Partic in Docline; OCLC Online Computer Library Center, Inc
Open Mon-Fri 8:30-5

M MASSACHUSETTS EYE & EAR INFIRMARY LIBRARIES*, 243 Charles St, 02114. SAN 328-400X. Tel: 617-573-3196. Reference Tel: 617-573-3664. FAX: 617-573-3370. Web Site: www.meei.harvard.edu. *Dir,* Chris Nims; E-mail: jcnims@meei.harvard.edu; *Ref Librn,* Kathleen Kennedy; E-mail: kathy_kennedy@meei.harvard.edu
Library Holdings: Bk Vols 5,500; Per Subs 150
Automation Activity & Vendor Info: (Acquisitions) Innovative Interfaces, Inc; (Cataloging) Innovative Interfaces, Inc; (Circulation) Innovative Interfaces, Inc
Partic in Asn for Vision Sci Librns; Massachusetts Health Sciences Libraries Network; Medical Library Association (MLA)
Open Mon-Thurs 8:30-7, Fri 8:30-5
Friends of the Library Group

MASSACHUSETTS GENERAL HOSPITAL

M TRACY BURR MALLORY MEMORIAL LIBRARY*, Dept of Pathology, 55 Fruit St, 02114, SAN 344-6948. Tel: 617-726-8892. FAX: 617-726-7474. *Dir,* Dr Robert H Young; Staff 2 (MLS 1, Non-MLS 1)
Founded 1952
Library Holdings: Bk Titles 400; Bk Vols 500; Per Subs 20
Subject Interests: Pathology
Open Mon-Fri 9-5

M TREADWELL LIBRARY, Bartlett Hall Ext-I, 55 Fruit St, 02114-2696, SAN 344-6972. Tel: 617-726-8600. Reference Tel: 617-726-8605. FAX: 617-726-6784. E-mail: treadwellqanda@partners.org. Web Site: www.massgeneral.org/library. *Dir,* Elizabeth Schneider; *Ref,* Martha Stone; Staff 20 (MLS 9, Non-MLS 11)
Founded 1858
Library Holdings: Bk Titles 15,000; Bk Vols 50,000; Per Subs 1,600
Subject Interests: Biochem, Biol, Med, Nursing
Automation Activity & Vendor Info: (Acquisitions) SydneyPlus; (Cataloging) SydneyPlus; (Circulation) SydneyPlus; (Course Reserve) SydneyPlus; (Serials) SydneyPlus
Database Vendor: Dialog, EBSCOhost, OVID Technologies
Partic in Dialog Corp; Docline; Lyrasis; OCLC Online Computer Library Center, Inc
Restriction: Staff & patient use

M WARREN LIBRARY*, 55 Fruit St, 02114-2622, SAN 344-7006. Tel: 617-726-2253. *Librn,* Nancy Marshall
Founded 1841
Library Holdings: Bk Vols 10,000; Per Subs 25
Open Mon-Fri 9:30-4:15

S MASSACHUSETTS HISTORICAL SOCIETY LIBRARY*, 1154 Boylston St, 02215-3695. SAN 307-2037. Tel: 617-536-1608. Reference Tel: 617-646-0532. FAX: 617-859-0074. E-mail: library@masshist.org. Web Site: www.masshist.org. *Librn,* Peter Drummey; Tel: 617-646-0501, E-mail: pdrummey@masshist.org; *Coll Serv,* Brenda Lawson; Tel: 617-646-0502, E-mail: blawson@masshist.org; *Reader Serv,* Elaine Heavey; Tel: 617-646-0509, E-mail: eheavey@masshist.org; *Sr Cataloger,* Mary Yacovone; Tel: 617-646-0504, E-mail: myacovone@masshist.org. Subject Specialists: *Manuscripts,* Brenda Lawson; *Rare bks,* Mary Yacovone; Staff 14 (MLS 11, Non-MLS 3)
Founded 1791
Library Holdings: Bk Vols 200,000; Per Subs 160
Special Collections: Historical Coll, broadsides, maps, ms, photos, prints, rare bks
Subject Interests: Colonial period, Massachusetts, New England, Revolutionary period
Automation Activity & Vendor Info: (Acquisitions) Ex Libris Group; (Cataloging) Ex Libris Group
Database Vendor: OCLC FirstSearch
Wireless access
Function: Archival coll, Ref serv available
Partic in OCLC Online Computer Library Center, Inc
Open Mon & Wed-Fri 9-4:45, Tues 9-7:45
Restriction: Non-circulating, Photo ID required for access

C MASSACHUSETTS SCHOOL OF PROFESSIONAL PSYCHOLOGY LIBRARY*, 221 Rivermoor St, 02132. Tel: 617-327-6777, Ext 220. FAX: 617-327-4447. E-mail: library@mspp.edu. Web Site: www.mspp.edu. *Librn,* Matthew Kramer; Staff 1 (MLS 1)
Founded 1974. Enrl 300; Highest Degree: Doctorate
Library Holdings: AV Mats 100; Bk Vols 10,000; Per Subs 25
Special Collections: School Archives; Testing Kits
Subject Interests: Assessment, Clinical psychol, Counseling, Psychopharmacology, Psychotherapy, Sch psychol
Automation Activity & Vendor Info: (Cataloging) Follett Software; (Circulation) Follett Software; (ILL) OCLC; (OPAC) Follett Software
Database Vendor: EBSCOhost
Partic in Boston Regional Library System
Open Mon-Thurs 9-9, Fri 9-5

S MASSACHUSETTS SOCIETY FOR THE PREVENTION OF CRUELTY TO ANIMALS LIBRARY*, 350 S Huntington Ave, 02130. SAN 327-3253. Tel: 617-522-7400. FAX: 617-522-4885. Web Site: www.mspca.org. *Librn,* Jen Holmquist
Library Holdings: Bk Titles 1,000; Bk Vols 1,500; Per Subs 65

Special Collections: Archives of George Angel I
Restriction: Staff use only

S MASSACHUSETTS TAXPAYERS FOUNDATION LIBRARY*, 333 Washington St, Ste 853, 02108. SAN 307-2088. Tel: 617-720-1000. FAX: 617-720-0799. Web Site: www.masstaxpayers.org. *Mgr,* Kris Mullen
Founded 1948
Library Holdings: Bk Vols 6,800; Per Subs 100
Special Collections: Massachusetts Taxpayers Foundation Archives
Publications: Annual Report; Ballot Questions (Annual); Budget Analysis (Annual); Library List (Quarterly); Massachusetts Legislative Directory; Municipal Financial Data (Annual)
Open Mon-Fri 8:30-5

L MINTZ, LEVIN, COHN, FERRIS, GLOVSKY & POPEO*, Law Library, One Financial Ctr, 02111. SAN 307-2118. Tel: 617-542-6000, Ext 4852. Circulation Tel: 617-348-4846. FAX: 617-542-2241. Web Site: www.mintz.com. *Dir, Libr Serv,* Lori Tarpinian; Tel: 617-348-4851, E-mail: ltarpinian@mintz.com; *Dir, Info Serv,* Fred Pretorius
Library Holdings: Bk Vols 5,000; Per Subs 600
Partic in Dialog Corp

L MORRISON, MAHONEY LLP*, Law Library, 250 Summer St, 02210. SAN 372-0780. Tel: 617-439-7507. FAX: 617-439-7590. Web Site: www.morrisonmahoney.com. *Librn,* Mary Boudreau; E-mail: mboudrea@morrisonmahoney.com
Library Holdings: Bk Titles 1,000; Per Subs 25
Database Vendor: LexisNexis, Westlaw
Restriction: Staff use only

S MUSEUM OF FINE ARTS, BOSTON*, William Morris Hunt Memorial Library, 300 Massachusetts Ave, 02115. (Mail add: 465 Huntington Ave, 02115), SAN 307-2126. Tel: 617-369-3385. Interlibrary Loan Service Tel: 617-369-3971. FAX: 617-369-4257. Web Site: www.mfa.org. *Dir,* Maureen Melton; *Head Librn,* Deborah Barlow Smedstad; *Head, Tech Serv,* Lee-Anne Famolare; Staff 4 (MLS 3, Non-MLS 1)
Founded 1879
Library Holdings: Bk Titles 256,000; Bk Vols 423,261; Per Subs 1,000
Subject Interests: Archaeology, Egypt, Fine arts, Museology
Automation Activity & Vendor Info: (Acquisitions) Ex Libris Group; (Cataloging) Ex Libris Group; (Circulation) Ex Libris Group; (ILL) OCLC WorldShare Interlibrary Loan; (OPAC) Ex Libris Group; (Serials) Ex Libris Group
Database Vendor: EBSCO Information Services, Gale Cengage Learning, ProQuest
Partic in Fenway Libraries Online, Inc; Fenway Library Consortium (FLC); OCLC Research Library Partnership
Open Mon-Fri 1-5
Restriction: Closed stack, Open to pub for ref only
Branches:
W VAN ALAN CLARK JR LIBRARY, 230 The Fenway, 02115, SAN 307-2134. Tel: 617-369-3650. *Dir, Libr Serv,* Darin Murphy; Staff 3 (Non-MLS 3)
Founded 1928
Library Holdings: Bk Vols 21,000
Subject Interests: 20th Century art, Contemporary art
Function: AV serv, ILL available
Open Mon-Thurs 9-9, Fri 9-5, Sat 10-5, Sun 1-5
Restriction: Non-circulating, Open to students, fac & staff

S MUSEUM OF NATIONAL CENTER OF AFRO-AMERICAN ARTISTS*, Slide Library, 300 Walnut Ave, 02119. SAN 307-2142. Tel: 617-442-8614. FAX: 617-445-5525. Web Site: www.ncaaa.org. *Chief Curator, Exec Dir,* Edmund B Gaither; E-mail: bgaither@mfa.org
Founded 1969
Library Holdings: Bk Vols 450

S NATIONAL ARCHIVES & RECORDS ADMINISTRATION*, John F Kennedy Presidential Library & Museum, Columbia Point, 02125. SAN 307-7438. Tel: 617-514-1600. Toll Free Tel: 866-535-1960. FAX: 617-514-1593. Web Site: www.jfklibrary.org. *Dir,* Thomas Putnam; *Librn,* Erica Boudreau; *Chief Archivist,* Allan Goodrich; *Archivist,* Stephen Plotkin; *Curator,* Stacey Bredhoff; Staff 45 (MLS 18, Non-MLS 27)
Founded 1963
Library Holdings: Bk Titles 32,000; Bk Vols 35,000; Per Subs 10
Special Collections: Ernest Hemingway Coll, film, mss, photog, printed mat; Mid-Twentieth Century American Politics & Government,; The Life & Times of John F Kennedy. Oral History
Publications: Historical Materials in the John F Kennedy Library
Open Mon-Fri 8:30-4:30
Friends of the Library Group

M NEW ENGLAND BAPTIST HOSPITAL*, Paul E Woodard Health Sciences Library, 125 Parker Hill Ave, 02120-2847. SAN 344-7030. Tel: 617-754-5155. FAX: 617-754-6414. Web Site: www.nebh.org/display.asp?node_id=4356. *Librn,* Olga Lyczmanenko; Staff 1 (MLS 1)
Founded 1963
Library Holdings: Bk Titles 2,200; Per Subs 150
Special Collections: Orthopaedics & History of Medicine (Morton Smith-Petersen Coll); Otto Aufranc Coll
Subject Interests: Orthopedics
Database Vendor: EBSCOhost
Partic in Boston Biomedical Library Consortium; Massachusetts Health Sciences Libraries Network; National Network of Libraries of Medicine
Open Mon-Fri 8-4:30

CM NEW ENGLAND COLLEGE OF OPTOMETRY LIBRARY, 424 Beacon St, 02115. SAN 307-2185. Tel: 617-587-5589. FAX: 617-587-5573. E-mail: library@neco.edu. Web Site: www.neco.edu/library. *Dir of Libr Serv,* Kristin Motte; Tel: 617-589-5658, E-mail: mottek@neco.edu; *Asst Dir, Libr Serv,* Heather Edmonds; Tel: 617-587-5579, E-mail: edmondsh@neco.edu; *Educ Media Coordr,* Marek Jacisin; Tel: 617-587-5654, E-mail: jacisinm@neco.edu; *Pub Serv Coordr,* Patricia McIvor; Tel: 617-587-5657, E-mail: mcivorp@neco.edu; *Libr Asst,* Alexandria Cronin; Tel: 617-587-5623, E-mail: cronina@neco.edu; Staff 5 (MLS 2, Non-MLS 3)
Founded 1894. Enrl 500; Fac 120; Highest Degree: Doctorate
Library Holdings: Bk Titles 7,284; Bk Vols 17,665; Per Subs 238
Special Collections: History of Optometry
Subject Interests: Ophthalmology, Optometry
Automation Activity & Vendor Info: (Acquisitions) SirsiDynix; (Cataloging) SirsiDynix; (Circulation) SirsiDynix; (Course Reserve) SirsiDynix; (OPAC) SirsiDynix; (Serials) SirsiDynix
Database Vendor: Blackwell, EBSCOhost, Elsevier, JSTOR, OCLC WorldShare Interlibrary Loan, OVID Technologies, PubMed, ScienceDirect, STAT!Ref (Teton Data Systems), Wiley
Wireless access
Mem of Massachusetts Libr Syst
Partic in Association of Vision Science Librarians (AVSL); Basic Health Sciences Library Network; Boston Biomedical Library Consortium; OCLC-LVIS
Open Mon-Thurs (Winter) 8:30am-9pm, Fri 8:30-7, Sat & Sun 11-6; Mon-Fri (Summer) 8:30-7, Sat 11-6

S NEW ENGLAND CONSERVATORY OF MUSIC*, Harriet M Spaulding Library, 33 Gainsborough St, 02115. SAN 344-712X. Tel: 617-585-1250. FAX: 617-585-1245. Web Site: www.necmusic.edu/libraries. *Head of Libr,* Jean Morrow; Tel: 617-585-1247, E-mail: jean.morrow@necmusic.edu; *Archivist,* Maryalice Perrin-Mohr; Tel: 617-585-1252, E-mail: mperrin-mohr@necmusic.edu; *Cat,* Damian Iseminger; Tel: 617-585-1254, E-mail: damian.iseminger@necmusic.edu; *ILL,* Mary Jane Loizou; Tel: 617-585-1248, E-mail: ill@necmusic.edu; *Pub Serv,* Richard Vallone; Tel: 617-585-1251, E-mail: richard.vallone@necmusic.edu; *Tech Serv,* Patrick Maxfield; Tel: 617-585-1256, E-mail: patrick.maxfield@necmusic.edu; Staff 10 (MLS 6, Non-MLS 4)
Founded 1867
Library Holdings: CDs 65,000; Music Scores 65,000; Bk Vols 30,000; Per Subs 295
Special Collections: Firestone Hour Music Coll, rec, v-tapes; New England Composers, ms; Preston Coll of Musicians' Letters; Vaughn Monroe Coll of Camel Caravan, scores
Automation Activity & Vendor Info: (Acquisitions) Ex Libris Group; (Cataloging) Ex Libris Group; (Circulation) Ex Libris Group; (Course Reserve) Ex Libris Group; (OPAC) Ex Libris Group; (Serials) Ex Libris Group
Database Vendor: EBSCOhost, OCLC WorldShare Interlibrary Loan, Oxford Online
Wireless access
Mem of Massachusetts Libr Syst
Partic in Fenway Libraries Online, Inc; Fenway Library Consortium (FLC); Lyrasis; OCLC Online Computer Library Center, Inc
Branches:
IDABELLE FIRESTONE AUDIO LIBRARY, 290 Huntington Ave, 02115, SAN 344-7154. Tel: 617-585-1255. FAX: 617-585-1245. Web Site: www.newenglandconservatory.edu/libraries. *Librn,* Jean Morrow; Staff 9.7 (MLS 6, Non-MLS 3.7)
Founded 1867. Enrl 750; Fac 200; Highest Degree: Doctorate
Library Holdings: AV Mats 65,000; Music Scores 65,000; Bk Vols 30,000; Per Subs 300
Special Collections: American Composers' Manuscripts; Early Jazz Recordings; New England Conservatory Concerts
Automation Activity & Vendor Info: (Acquisitions) Ex Libris Group; (Cataloging) Ex Libris Group; (Circulation) Ex Libris Group; (Course Reserve) Ex Libris Group; (OPAC) Ex Libris Group; (Serials) Ex Libris Group

S NEW ENGLAND HISTORIC GENEALOGICAL SOCIETY LIBRARY*, 99-101 Newbury St, 02116-3007. SAN 307-2193. Tel: 617-536-5740. Reference Tel: 617-226-1234. FAX: 617-536-7307. E-mail: nehgs@nehgs.org. Web Site: www.newenglandancestors.org. *Dir, Libr Serv,* Marie Daly; Tel: 617-226-1231, E-mail: mdaly@nehgs.org; *Dir, Tech Serv,* Lynne Burke; Tel: 617-226-1225, E-mail: lburke@nehgs.org; *Ref Librn,* David Curtis Dearborn; E-mail: dcdearborn@nehgs.org; *Tech Serv Librn,* Jean Maguire; Tel: 617-226-1229, E-mail: jmaguire@nehgs.org; *Ref Serv,* Julie Otto; E-mail: jotto@nehgs.org; *Tech Serv,* Olga Tugarina; Tel: 617-226-1228, E-mail: otugarina@nehgs.org; *Virtual Ref,* David Allen Lambert; Tel: 617-226-1239, E-mail: dalambert@nehgs.org; *Archivist,* Timothy Salls; Tel: 617-536-5740, Ext 232, E-mail: tsalls@nehgs.org; *Asst Archivist,* Judith Lucey; Tel: 617-226-1223, E-mail: jlucey@nehgs.org; Staff 14 (MLS 5, Non-MLS 9)
Founded 1845
Library Holdings: CDs 500; Bk Titles 100,000; Bk Vols 200,000; Per Subs 700
Special Collections: Manuscripts of Family Histories; town & church records, diaries, heraldry, census records, probate records & deeds of New England states; Microtext: Census records, vital records
Subject Interests: Genealogy, Heraldry, Local hist
Automation Activity & Vendor Info: (Acquisitions) Innovative Interfaces, Inc; (Cataloging) Innovative Interfaces, Inc; (Circulation) Innovative Interfaces, Inc; (OPAC) Innovative Interfaces, Inc; (Serials) Innovative Interfaces, Inc
Database Vendor: Newsbank, OCLC FirstSearch, OCLC WorldShare Interlibrary Loan, ProQuest
Wireless access
Function: CD-ROM, Copy machines, Electronic databases & coll, Handicapped accessible, Online ref, Orientations, Photocopying/Printing, Prog for adults, Ref serv available
Publications: New England Ancestors Magazine; New England Historical & Genealogical Register
Partic in Boston Regional Library System; Lyrasis
Special Services for the Blind - Closed circuit TV magnifier
Open Tues & Thurs-Sat 9-5, Wed 9-9
Restriction: Fee for pub use, Limited access for the pub, Non-circulating

CL NEW ENGLAND SCHOOL OF LAW LIBRARY*, 154 Stuart St, 02116-5687. SAN 307-2231. Tel: 617-422-7282. Circulation Tel: 617-422-7288. Interlibrary Loan Service Tel: 617-422-7418. Reference Tel: 617-422-7299, Ext 299. FAX: 617-422-7303. Web Site: www.nesl.edu/library. *Dir,* Anne M Acton; Tel: 617-422-7290, E-mail: aacton@library.nesl.edu; *Assoc Dir,* Kristin McCarthy; E-mail: kmccarth@nesl.edu; *Acq, Coll Mgt,* Anne Lynch; Tel: 617-422-7293, E-mail: alynch@library.nesl.edu; *Cat, Presv,* Tim Devin; E-mail: tdevin@library.nesl.edu; *Circ, ILL,* Anita Chase; Tel: 617-422-7307, E-mail: achase@library.nesl.edu; *Coll Develop,* Helen Litwack; *Computer Serv,* Sandra Lamar; *Govt Doc,* James Gage; Tel: 617-422-7310, E-mail: jgage@library.nesl.edu; *Per,* Mary J Gadbois; Tel: 617-422-7202, E-mail: mgadbois@library.nesl.edu; *Ref Serv,* Barry Stearns; *Tech Serv,* Kyle Kelly; Tel: 617-422-7214, E-mail: kkelly@library.nesl.edu; Staff 11 (MLS 9, Non-MLS 2)
Founded 1917. Enrl 1,100; Fac 76; Highest Degree: Doctorate
Library Holdings: Bk Vols 340,000; Per Subs 3,100
Special Collections: Standard American Law Library Coll, bks, micro, AV & on line resources
Automation Activity & Vendor Info: (Acquisitions) Innovative Interfaces, Inc; (Cataloging) Innovative Interfaces, Inc; (Circulation) Innovative Interfaces, Inc; (Serials) Innovative Interfaces, Inc
Publications: Library Guide; Library Newsletter; Selected List of Recent Acquisitions
Partic in Lyrasis; New England Law Library Consortium, Inc; Westlaw
Special Services for the Deaf - TTY equip
Open Mon-Fri 7:30am-11pm, Sat 9am-10pm, Sun 10am-11pm

S NICHOLS HOUSE MUSEUM*, 55 Mount Vernon St, 02108. SAN 377-516X. Tel: 617-227-6993. FAX: 617-723-8026. E-mail: info@nicholshousemuseum.org. Web Site: nicholshousemuseum.org. *Exec Dir,* Flavia Cigliano
Founded 1961
Library Holdings: Bk Vols 1,000
Special Collections: Nichols Family Papers; Nichols Family Photograph Coll; Rose Standish Nichols Postcard Coll. Oral History
Subject Interests: European, Gardens
Restriction: Open by appt only

L NIXON PEABODY LLP*, Law Library, 100 Summer St, 02110-1832. SAN 372-0721. Tel: 617-345-1000. FAX: 617-345-1300. Web Site: www.nixonpeabody.com. *Libr Mgr,* Joanne Santino; Tel: 617-345-1360
Library Holdings: Bk Vols 8,500; Per Subs 150
Open Mon-Fri 9-5

NORTHEASTERN UNIVERSITY LIBRARIES
C SNELL LIBRARY*, 360 Huntington Ave, 02115. SAN 344-7243. Tel: 617-373-8778. Interlibrary Loan Service Tel: 617-373-8276. Reference Tel: 617-373-2356. Administration Tel: 617-373-5001. Automation Services Tel: 617-373-7088. Toll Free Tel: 855-618-7512. Interlibrary Loan Service FAX: 617-373-8681. Administration FAX: 617-373-5409. Web Site: library.northeastern.edu. *Dean, Univ Libr,* William M Wakeling; E-mail: w.wakeling@neu.edu; *Assoc Dean, Digital Strategies & Serv,* Patrick Yott; E-mail: p.yott@neu.edu; *Assoc Dean, Scholarly Res,* Amira Aaron; Tel: 617-373-4961, E-mail: a.aaron@neu.edu; *Assoc Dean, User Serv,* Lesley Milner; Tel: 617-373-4920, E-mail: l.milner@neu.edu; *Dir, Admin & Finance,* Elizabeth C Habich; Tel: 617-373-4924, E-mail: e.habich@neu.edu; *Head, Access Serv,* Brian Greene; Tel: 617-373-2401, E-mail: br.greene@neu.edu; *Head, Res & Instruction,* James Dendy; Tel: 617-373-3344, E-mail: j.dendy@neu.edu; *Head, Res Mgt,* Janet Belanger Morrow; Tel: 617-373-4959, Fax: 617-373-8396, E-mail: j.morrow@neu.edu; *Head, Spec Coll,* Position Currently Open; *Coll Develop Librn,* Amy Lewontin; Tel: 617-373-2001, E-mail: a.lewontin@neu.edu; *Metadata Librn,* Daniel Jergovic; Tel: 617-373-7102, E-mail: d.jergovic@neu.edu; *Metadata Librn,* Sarah Sweeney; Tel: 617-373-5062, E-mail: sj.sweeney@neu.edu; *Res & Instruction Librn,* Rebecca Bailey; Tel: 617-373-2344, E-mail: re.bailey@neu.edu; *Res & Instruction Librn,* Sandra Dunphy; Tel: 617-373-5322, E-mail: s.dunphy@neu.edu; *Res & Instruction Librn,* Katherine Herrlich; Tel: 617-373-5305, E-mail: k.herrlich@neu.edu; *Res & Instruction Librn,* Julie Jersyk; Tel: 617-373-2458, E-mail: j.jersyk@neu.edu; *Res & Instruction Librn,* Donna Kennedy; Tel: 617-373-3197, E-mail: d.kennedy@neu.edu; *Res & Instruction Librn,* Joan Omoruyi; Tel: 617-373-2806, E-mail: j.omoruyi@neu.edu; *Res & Instruction Librn,* Diann Smothers; Tel: 617-373-2363, E-mail: d.smothers@neu.edu; *Scholarly Communications Librn,* Hillary Corbett; Tel: 617-373-2352, E-mail: h.corbett@neu.edu; *Soc Sci & Govt Info Librn,* Roxanne B Palmatier; Tel: 617-373-4968, E-mail: r.palmatier@neu.edu; *Archives, Staff Librn,* Mia Guem; Tel: 617-373-2351; *Syst Librn,* Ernesto Valencia; Tel: 617-373-3398, E-mail: e.valencia@neu.edu; *User Engagement & Assessment Librn,* Gayane Karen Merguerian; Tel: 617-373-2747, E-mail: g.merguerian@neu.edu; *Circ Supvr,* Tricia Reinhart; Tel: 617-373-4970, E-mail: t.reihnhart@neu.edu; *Res Mgt Supvr,* Stacy Maubourquette; Tel: 617-373-4974, E-mail: s.maubourquette@neu.edu; *Circ/Reserves Coordr,* Anita Bennett; Tel: 617-373-4646, E-mail: a.bennett@neu.edu; *Syst Coordr,* Karl Yee; Tel: 617-373-4904, E-mail: k.yee@neu.edu. Subject Specialists: *Jewish studies,* Amira Aaron; *Philos, Relig,* Brian Greene; *Agr, Geol, Hist,* James Dendy; *Children's lit,* Janet Belanger Morrow; *Computer sci,* Amy Lewontin; *Art & archit, Foreign lang, Sports,* Rebecca Bailey; *Allied health fields, Med, Nursing,* Sandra Dunphy; *Chem, Pharmacology, Psychol,* Katherine Herrlich; *Communication studies, Journalism, Librarianship,* Julie Jersyk; *Educ, Math,* Donna Kennedy; *Environ studies, Latin Am studies, Nanotechnologies,* Joan Omoruyi; *Bus, Econ, Transportation,* Diann Smothers; *Criminal justice, Mil sci, Polit sci,* Roxanne B Palmatier; Staff 39.3 (MLS 31, Non-MLS 8.3)
Founded 1898. Enrl 26,761; Fac 2,313; Highest Degree: Doctorate
Jul 2011-Jun 2012. Mats Exp $5,865,211, Books $228,018, Per/Ser (Incl. Access Fees) $153,415, AV Mat $42,859, Electronic Ref Mat (Incl. Access Fees) $5,359,479, Presv $81,440
Library Holdings: AV Mats 18,210; e-books 365,520; e-journals 58,559; Electronic Media & Resources 43,769; Bk Titles 677,357; Bk Vols 896,213; Per Subs 69,468
Special Collections: Boston Historical Coll; Digital Repository Service; Northeastern University Archives & Historical Coll, audio, course cats, doctoral dissertations, master theses, newsp, photog, publs, rare bks, videos, yearbks. Oral History; US Document Depository
Subject Interests: Allied health, Biol, Bus, Computer sci, Criminal law & justice, Econ, Educ, Humanities, Pharmacology
Automation Activity & Vendor Info: (Acquisitions) Innovative Interfaces, Inc; (Cataloging) Innovative Interfaces, Inc; (Circulation) Innovative Interfaces, Inc; (Course Reserve) Innovative Interfaces, Inc; (ILL) OCLC ILLiad; (Media Booking) Innovative Interfaces, Inc; (OPAC) Innovative Interfaces, Inc; (Serials) TDNet
Function: Archival coll, Computers for patron use, e-mail & chat, Electronic databases & coll, Handicapped accessible, ILL available, Online cat, Ref serv in person
Partic in Boston Library Consortium, Inc; Lyrasis; NExpress Consortium; Northeast Research Libraries Consortium (NERL); OCLC Online Computer Library Center, Inc
Special Services for the Deaf - Bks on deafness & sign lang; Closed caption videos; Sign lang interpreter upon request for prog
Special Services for the Blind - Assistive/Adapted tech devices, equip & products; Computer with voice synthesizer for visually impaired persons; Digital talking bk machines; Dragon Naturally Speaking software; Magnifiers; Scanner for conversion & translation of mats; Screen enlargement software for people with visual disabilities; Screen reader software; Text reader; Videos on blindness & phys handicaps

Open Mon-Thurs 7:45am-Midnight, Fri 7:45-9, Sat 9am-10pm, Sun 10-Midnight
Friends of the Library Group

CL NORTHEASTERN UNIVERSITY SCHOOL OF LAW LIBRARY*, 400 Huntington Ave, 02115. SAN 344-7367. Tel: 617-373-3552. Circulation Tel: 617-373-3332. Reference Tel: 617-373-3594. FAX: 617-373-8705. Web Site: www.northeastern.edu/law/library/index.html. *Asst Dean, Dir,* Sarah Hooke Lee; Tel: 617-373-3394, E-mail: sa.lee@neu.edu; *Assoc Dir,* Lydia Lafionatis; Tel: 617-373-5482, E-mail: l.lafionatis@neu.edu; *Head, Res & Instruction,* Sharon Persons; Tel: 617-373-3883, E-mail: s.persons@neu.edu; *Head, Tech Serv,* Susan More; Tel: 617-373-3691, E-mail: slaw_publcorr@neu.edu; *Metadata Librn,* Stephanie Hudner; Tel: 617-373-3716, E-mail: shudner@neu.edu; *Sr Law Librn,* Alfreda Russell; Tel: 617-373-3589, E-mail: al.russell@neu.edu; *Supvr, Access Serv,* Warren Yee; Tel: 617-373-3350, E-mail: w.yee@neu.edu; *Tech Serv Supvr,* Rachel Bates; Tel: 617-373-3553, E-mail: ra.bates@neu.edu; *Budget Analyst/Journal Ed,* Joseph Miranda; Tel: 617-373-3552, E-mail: j.miranda@neu.edu; Staff 16 (MLS 8, Non-MLS 8)
Founded 1898. Enrl 600; Fac 30; Highest Degree: Doctorate
Library Holdings: Bk Vols 397,000
Special Collections: Pappas Public Interest Law Coll
Automation Activity & Vendor Info: (Acquisitions) Innovative Interfaces, Inc; (Cataloging) Innovative Interfaces, Inc; (Circulation) Innovative Interfaces, Inc; (Course Reserve) Innovative Interfaces, Inc; (ILL) Innovative Interfaces, Inc; (OPAC) Innovative Interfaces, Inc; (Serials) Innovative Interfaces, Inc
Database Vendor: 3M Library Systems, Cassidy Cataloguing Services, Inc, Gale Cengage Learning, HeinOnline, Innovative Interfaces, Inc, JSTOR, LexisNexis, OCLC FirstSearch, Sage, Westlaw, Wilson - Wilson Web, YBP Library Services
Wireless access
Function: Res libr
Partic in Boston Library Consortium, Inc; Lyrasis; New England Law Library Consortium, Inc; NExpress Consortium
Open Mon-Thurs 7:30am-10pm, Fri 7:30-9, Sat 9-5, Sun 2-10
Restriction: Badge access after hrs, Open to students, fac & staff, Pub use on premises

L NUTTER MCCLENNEN & FISH LLP*, Law Library, World Trade Center W, 155 Seaport Blvd, 02210. SAN 307-2266. Tel: 617-439-2000. FAX: 617-310-9000. E-mail: librarian@nutter.com. Web Site: www.nutter.com. *Dir, Libr Serv,* Susan M Cleary; *Acq & Cat,* Sean C Thibodeau; *Ref,* Lila J Abraham; Staff 4 (MLS 3, Non-MLS 1)
Wireless access

S PAYETTE ASSOCIATES*, David J Rowan Library, 285 Summer St, 02210. SAN 327-3458. Tel: 617-895-1000. FAX: 617-895-1002. Web Site: www.payette.com. *Dir,* Nora B Zaldivar; E-mail: nzaldivar@payette.com; *Ref,* Eric Crockwell
Founded 1979
Library Holdings: Bk Titles 4,000; Per Subs 75
Special Collections: Healthcare
Subject Interests: Archit
Partic in Dialog Corp
Restriction: Not open to pub

L PEABODY & ARNOLD LLP*, Law Library, Federal Reserve Plaza, 600 Atlantic Ave, 02110. SAN 372-0713. Tel: 617-261-5051, Ext 7157. FAX: 617-951-2125. Web Site: www.peabodyarnold.com. *Mgr, Libr Serv,* Brian Treanor; Staff 1 (Non-MLS 1)
Library Holdings: Bk Vols 12,000

L RACKEMANN, SAWYER & BREWSTER LIBRARY*, 160 Federal St, 02110-1700. SAN 323-7478. Tel: 617-542-2300. Administration Tel: 617-897-2287. FAX: 617-542-7437. Web Site: www.rackemann.com. *Librn,* Amanda Merk; E-mail: amerk@accufile.com; Staff 2 (MLS 1, Non-MLS 1)
Founded 1886
Library Holdings: Bk Vols 12,000; Per Subs 100
Special Collections: Zoning Coll
Subject Interests: Estates, Real estate, Trusts
Open Mon-Fri 8-5

S RITTNERS SCHOOL OF FLORAL DESIGN LIBRARY*, The Augusta Rittner Floral Library, 345 Marlborough St, 02115. SAN 328-2198. Tel: 617-267-3824. FAX: 617-267-3824. Web Site: www.floralschool.com/library-new.htm. *Librn,* Stephen Rittner; E-mail: stevrt@tiac.net
Library Holdings: Bk Vols 4,000
Subject Interests: Floral design, Mgt

L ROPES & GRAY LLP LIBRARY*, Prudential Tower, 800 Boylston St, 02199. SAN 329-0468. Tel: 617-951-7855. FAX: 617-951-7050. *Librn,* Andrea Rasmussen; *Pub Serv,* Kimberly Sweet; Staff 9 (MLS 7, Non-MLS 2)
Library Holdings: Bk Titles 10,000; Bk Vols 40,000; Per Subs 300
Subject Interests: Law
Automation Activity & Vendor Info: (Acquisitions) Softlink America; (OPAC) Softlink America; (Serials) Softlink America
Restriction: Staff use only

J ROXBURY COMMUNITY COLLEGE LIBRARY*, Academic Bldg, Rm 211, 1234 Columbus Ave, 02120-3400. SAN 307-6466. Tel: 617-541-5323. FAX: 617-933-7476. Web Site: www.rcc.mass.edu/lib. *Dir,* William Hoag; E-mail: whoag@rcc.mass.edu; Staff 3 (MLS 3)
Founded 1973. Enrl 2,368; Fac 45; Highest Degree: Associate
Jul 2006-Jun 2007 Income $387,400. Mats Exp $103,500
Library Holdings: Bk Titles 30,389; Bk Vols 38,210; Per Subs 115
Special Collections: Black United Front Archives; Mel King Papers
Automation Activity & Vendor Info: (Cataloging) SirsiDynix; (Circulation) SirsiDynix; (Course Reserve) SirsiDynix; (ILL) SirsiDynix; (OPAC) SirsiDynix
Database Vendor: EBSCOhost, Gale Cengage Learning, LexisNexis
Wireless access
Mem of Massachusetts Libr Syst
Partic in Lyrasis; OCLC Online Computer Library Center, Inc
Open Mon-Thurs 8:30am-9pm, Fri 8:30-4:30, Sat 8:30-3

C SIMMONS COLLEGE*, Beatley Library, 300 The Fenway, 02115-5898. SAN 307-2312. Tel: 617-521-2000. Circulation Tel: 617-521-2786. Interlibrary Loan Service Tel: 617-521-2746. Reference Tel: 617-521-2784. Administration Tel: 617-521-2741. Administration FAX: 617-521-3093. E-mail: library@simmons.edu. Web Site: www.simmons.edu/library. *Dir,* Daphne Harrington; Tel: 617-521-2754, E-mail: daphne.harrington@simmons.edu; *Dep Dir,* Vivienne Piroli; Tel: 617-521-2752, E-mail: vivienne.piroli@simmons.edu; *Head, Libr Info Serv,* Rex Krajewski; Tel: 617-521-2756, E-mail: krajewsk@simmons.edu; *Col Archivist & Head, Discovery Serv,* Jason Wood; Tel: 617-521-2441, E-mail: jason.wood@simmons.edu; Staff 23.6 (MLS 14.6, Non-MLS 9)
Founded 1899. Enrl 3,982; Fac 310; Highest Degree: Doctorate
Jul 2011-Jun 2012 Income $3,090,836. Mats Exp $1,096,004, Books $204,000, Per/Ser (Incl. Access Fees) $275,000, Manu Arch $36,000, Electronic Ref Mat (Incl. Access Fees) $617,004. Sal $1,239,102 (Prof $972,038)
Library Holdings: AV Mats 7,122; e-books 26,472; e-journals 56,543; Microforms 13,515; Bk Titles 198,315; Bk Vols 214,200; Per Subs 1,413
Special Collections: Career Resource Materials; Children's Literature (Knapp Coll); Simmons College Archives
Subject Interests: Libr & info sci, Soc serv (soc work), Women's studies
Automation Activity & Vendor Info: (Acquisitions) Innovative Interfaces, Inc; (Cataloging) Innovative Interfaces, Inc; (Circulation) Innovative Interfaces, Inc; (Course Reserve) Atlas Systems; (ILL) OCLC ILLiad; (OPAC) Innovative Interfaces, Inc; (Serials) Innovative Interfaces, Inc
Database Vendor: ABC-CLIO, ACM (Association for Computing Machinery), Alexander Street Press, American Chemical Society, American Psychological Association (APA), Amigos Library Services, ARTstor, Atlas Systems, Baker & Taylor, Booklist Online, Bowker, Cambridge Scientific Abstracts, Coutts Information Service, CQ Press, CRC Press/Taylor & Francis Group, CredoReference, Dun & Bradstreet, ebrary, EBSCOhost, Elsevier, Emerald, Facts on File, Gale Cengage Learning, H W Wilson, Infotrieve, infoUSA, Innovative Interfaces, Inc, ISI Web of Knowledge, JSTOR, Lexi-Comp, LexisNexis, McGraw-Hill, Modern Language Association, Nature Publishing Group, OCLC FirstSearch, OCLC WorldShare Interlibrary Loan, OneSource, OVID Technologies, Oxford Online, Paratext, Project MUSE, ProQuest, PubMed, ReferenceUSA, RefWorks, Sage, ScienceDirect, SerialsSolutions, Springshare, LLC, Standard & Poor's, STAT!Ref (Teton Data Systems), Thomson - Web of Science, Wiley InterScience, Wilson - Wilson Web
Wireless access
Partic in Fenway Library Consortium (FLC)

M JOHN SNOW, INC*, JSI Research & Training Institute Library, 44 Farnsworth St, 02210-1211. SAN 377-9130. Tel: 617-482-9485. FAX: 617-482-0617. E-mail: jsinfo@jsi.com. Web Site: www.jsi.com. *In Charge,* John Carper; Staff 1 (MLS 1)
Library Holdings: Bk Vols 10,000; Per Subs 200
Subject Interests: Pub health
Automation Activity & Vendor Info: (Acquisitions) Inmagic, Inc.; (Cataloging) Inmagic, Inc.
Partic in Boston Regional Library System
Restriction: Staff use only

P THE STATE LIBRARY OF MASSACHUSETTS*, George Fingold Library, State House, Rm 341, 24 Beacon St, 02133. SAN 307-2339. Tel: 617-727-2590. FAX: 617-727-9730. Web Site: www.mass.gov/lib. *State*

Librn, Elvernoy Johnson; Tel: 617-727-2592, E-mail: elvernoy.johnson@state.ma.us; *Assoc Dir,* Alix Quan; Tel: 617-727-2403, E-mail: alix.quan@state.ma.us; *Spec Coll Librn,* Elizabeth Carroll-Horacks; Tel: 617-727-2595, E-mail: elizabeth.carroll-horacks@state.ma.us; *Govt Doc,* Bette Siegel; Tel: 617-727-6279, E-mail: bette.siegel@state.ma.us; *Tech Serv,* Judith Carlstrom; Tel: 617-727-2590, Ext 272, E-mail: judith.carlstrom@state.ma.us; Staff 14 (MLS 13, Non-MLS 1)
Founded 1826
Library Holdings: Bk Vols 500,000; Per Subs 1,845
Special Collections: Americana, early Massachusetts imprints; Massachusetts History & Biography, atlases, city directories, ms, maps; Massachusetts Legislators' Private Papers; Massachusetts State House Coll, doc, photog & prints; New England History; Revolutionary War Broadsides. State Document Depository; US Document Depository
Subject Interests: Law, Legis hist, Polit sci
Automation Activity & Vendor Info: (Cataloging) Innovative Interfaces, Inc; (Circulation) Innovative Interfaces, Inc; (OPAC) Innovative Interfaces, Inc; (Serials) Innovative Interfaces, Inc
Database Vendor: EBSCOhost, Innovative Interfaces, Inc, LexisNexis, ProQuest
Wireless access
Function: Res libr
Publications: Annual Checklist of State Publications; Quarterly Checklist of State Publications
Partic in Boston Library Consortium, Inc; Boston Regional Library System; Central & Western Massachusetts Automated Resource Sharing; Lyrasis
Special Services for the Deaf - TTY equip
Open Mon-Fri 9-5
Restriction: Lending to staff only

S STATE TRANSPORTATION LIBRARY*, Ten Park Plaza, 02116. SAN 321-9720. Tel: 617-973-8000. FAX: 617-973-7153. TDD: 617-973-8005. E-mail: library@mbta.com. Web Site: www.stlibrary.org. *Dir,* Lynn Matis; *Asst Librn,* Valerie Thomas; *Ref,* George Sanborn; *Tech Serv,* Stephanie Chester. Subject Specialists: *Law,* Lynn Matis; Staff 4 (MLS 3, Non-MLS 1)
Founded 1983
Library Holdings: Bk Vols 20,000; Per Subs 200
Special Collections: Boston Transportation Planning Review Archives, files, publications, MBTA History; Massachusetts Highway History
Subject Interests: Transportation, Urban planning
Publications: Computer-Assisted Research Services (Brochure); List of Selected Acquisitions; Transportation Library (Brochure)
Partic in Dialog Corp; OCLC Online Computer Library Center, Inc
Open Mon-Fri 9-5
Restriction: Non-circulating to the pub

C SUFFOLK UNIVERSITY*, Mildred F Sawyer Library, 73 Tremont St, 02108. SAN 344-7391. Tel: 617-573-8535. Interlibrary Loan Service Tel: 617-573-8427. Reference Tel: 617-573-8532. FAX: 617-573-8756. E-mail: sawlib@suffolk.edu. Web Site: www.suffolk.edu/sawlib/sawyer.htm. *Dir,* Sharon Britton; E-mail: sbritton@suffolk.edu; *Asst Dir, Head, Tech Serv,* Beata Panagopoulos; *Sr Ref Librn,* Sonia Didriksson; *Sr Ref Librn,* Lindsay Nichols; *Sr Ref Librn,* Connie Sellers; *Sr Ref Librn,* Ellen Yen; *Electronic Res Librn,* Amy Dumouchel; Staff 9 (MLS 9)
Founded 1936. Enrl 6,573; Highest Degree: Doctorate
Library Holdings: e-books 93,175; e-journals 21,709; Bk Vols 142,047; Per Subs 756
Special Collections: Afro-American Literature Coll
Automation Activity & Vendor Info: (Acquisitions) Innovative Interfaces, Inc - Millenium; (Cataloging) OCLC WorldShare Interlibrary Loan; (Circulation) Innovative Interfaces, Inc - Millenium; (OPAC) Innovative Interfaces, Inc - Millenium; (Serials) Innovative Interfaces, Inc - Millenium
Database Vendor: ABC-CLIO, ACM (Association for Computing Machinery), Alexander Street Press, American Chemical Society, American Psychological Association (APA), ARTstor, BioOne, CountryWatch, CQ Press, CredoReference, Dun & Bradstreet, ebrary, EBSCOhost, Elsevier, Emerald, Gale Cengage Learning, HeinOnline, Hoovers, IEEE (Institute of Electrical & Electronics Engineers), Innovative Interfaces, Inc, ISI Web of Knowledge, LexisNexis, Mergent Online, OCLC WorldShare Interlibrary Loan, Oxford Online, Project MUSE, ProQuest, PubMed, ReferenceUSA, RefWorks, Sage, ScienceDirect, SerialsSolutions, Springer-Verlag, Standard & Poor's, Thomson - Web of Science, ValueLine, Wiley InterScience
Wireless access
Publications: Help & Research Guides
Partic in Fenway Library Consortium (FLC); Lyrasis; New England Law Library Consortium, Inc; Northeast Research Libraries Consortium (NERL)
Open Mon-Thurs 8am-11pm, Fri & Sat 8-8, Sun 11-11
Restriction: Mem organizations only, Open to students, fac & staff

Departmental Libraries:

CL JOHN JOSEPH MOAKLEY LAW LIBRARY, 120 Tremont St, 02108-4977, SAN 344-7421. Tel: 617-573-8177. Interlibrary Loan Service Tel: 617-305-1614. Web Site: www.law.suffolk.edu/library. *Dir,* Elizabeth McKenzie; *Assoc Dir,* Susan Sweetgall; *Tech Serv,* Larry Flynn; Staff 26 (MLS 12, Non-MLS 14)
Enrl 1,671; Fac 61; Highest Degree: Doctorate
Library Holdings: Bk Titles 78,431; Bk Vols 210,690; Per Subs 6,620
Special Collections: Congressman J Joseph Moakley Archives
Automation Activity & Vendor Info: (Acquisitions) Innovative Interfaces, Inc; (Cataloging) Innovative Interfaces, Inc; (Circulation) Innovative Interfaces, Inc; (Course Reserve) Innovative Interfaces, Inc; (ILL) Innovative Interfaces, Inc; (OPAC) Innovative Interfaces, Inc; (Serials) Innovative Interfaces, Inc
Partic in OCLC Online Computer Library Center, Inc
Publications: Browsing The Library; Faculty Research Materials; Law Library Research Series
Open Mon-Fri 8am-11pm, Sat & Sun 9am-11pm

L SULLIVAN & WORCESTER, LLP*, Law Library, One Post Office Sq, 02109. SAN 372-0675. Tel: 617-338-2800. FAX: 617-338-2880. Web Site: www.sandw.com. *Mgr, Libr Serv,* Sarah Bennett; E-mail: sbennett@sandw.com; *Tech Serv Librn,* Jessica A Sullivan; Staff 3 (MLS 2, Non-MLS 1)
Founded 1943
Library Holdings: Bk Titles 3,000; Bk Vols 25,000; Per Subs 100
Subject Interests: Corp law
Automation Activity & Vendor Info: (Cataloging) Softlink America; (Circulation) Softlink America; (OPAC) Softlink America; (Serials) Softlink America
Database Vendor: Cassidy Cataloguing Services, Inc, Dun & Bradstreet, HeinOnline, Westlaw
Publications: Brochures; Newsletter
Restriction: Not open to pub

R TEMPLE ISRAEL LIBRARY*, Beit Midrash Library-Dr Arnold L Segel Library Center, 477 Longwood Ave, 02215. SAN 307-2371. Tel: 617-566-3960. FAX: 617-731-3711. Web Site: www.tisrael.org. *Librn,* Ann Abrams; E-mail: aabrams@tisrael.org
Library Holdings: Bk Titles 10,000; Per Subs 12
Subject Interests: Judaica (lit or hist of Jews)
Open Mon 10-8:30, Tues 10-9, Thurs 10-5, Fri 9-5:45, Sat 9-12, Sun 9-2
Friends of the Library Group

CM TUFTS UNIVERSITY*, Health Sciences Library, 145 Harrison Ave, 02111-1843. SAN 307-238X. Reference Tel: 617-636-6705. Administration Tel: 617-636-2481. FAX: 617-636-4039. E-mail: hhsl@tufts.edu. Web Site: www.library.tufts.edu/hsl/about. *Dir,* Eric Albright; *Dep Dir,* Cora C Ho; E-mail: cora.ho@tufts.edu; *Head, Coll Mgt,* Frances Burke-Foret; Tel: 617-636-0319, E-mail: frances.foret@tufts.edu; *Head, Info Serv,* Kate Kelly; *Head, Pub Serv,* Barbara Hefler; Tel: 617-636-2956, E-mail: bhefler@opal.tufts.edu; *Info Serv Librn,* Jane Ichord; *Info Serv Librn,* Amy Lapidow; E-mail: amy.lapidow@tufts.edu; *Info Serv Librn,* Eileen Moyer; Tel: 617-636-2466, E-mail: eileen.moyer@tufts.edu; *Info Serv Librn,* Judy Musnikow; *Info Serv Librn,* Anne Nou; E-mail: anne.nou@tufts.edu; *Info Serv Librn,* Elizabeth J Richardson; E-mail: elizabeth.richardson@tufts.edu; *Ser Librn,* JoAnne Griffin; Tel: 617-636-2452, E-mail: jgriffin@emerald.tufts.edu; *Mgr,* Paul Anderson; Tel: 617-636-2961; *Supvr, Pub Serv,* John Hanlin; Tel: 617-636-6706, E-mail: john.hanlin@tufts.edu; *Admin Coordr,* Lydia Quirk; *ILL Coordr,* Connie Wong; Tel: 617-636-3787, E-mail: connie.wong@tufts.edu; Staff 31 (MLS 18, Non-MLS 13)
Founded 1906. Enrl 1,500; Highest Degree: Doctorate
Library Holdings: Bk Titles 52,128; Bk Vols 158,400; Per Subs 972
Subject Interests: Dentistry, Hist of med, Med, Nutrition, Veterinary med
Automation Activity & Vendor Info: (Acquisitions) SirsiDynix; (Cataloging) SirsiDynix; (Circulation) SirsiDynix; (ILL) SirsiDynix; (OPAC) SirsiDynix; (Serials) SirsiDynix
Database Vendor: OVID Technologies
Function: Doc delivery serv
Publications: Bibliographies; Brochures; Health Science Link (Newsletter); Online Library Guide
Partic in OCLC Online Computer Library Center, Inc; UCMP
Open Mon-Thurs 7:45am-11pm, Fri 7:45-7, Sat 10-7, Sun Noon-10
Friends of the Library Group

GL UNITED STATES COURTS*, First Circuit Library, John Joseph Moakley US Courthouse, Ste 9400, One Courthouse Way, 02210. SAN 307-2401. Tel: 617-748-9044. FAX: 617-748-9358. *Librn,* Susan C Sullivan; E-mail: susan_sullivan@ca1.uscourts.gov; Staff 11 (MLS 7, Non-MLS 4)
Library Holdings: Bk Vols 40,000; Per Subs 170
Special Collections: US Document Depository
Subject Interests: Law
Automation Activity & Vendor Info: (Acquisitions) SirsiDynix; (Cataloging) SirsiDynix; (ILL) OCLC
Publications: Library Handbook; Newsletter (Bi-monthly)
Partic in OCLC Online Computer Library Center, Inc
Open Mon-Fri 8:30-4:30

C UNIVERSITY OF MASSACHUSETTS AT BOSTON*, Joseph P Healey Library, 100 Morrissey Blvd, 02125-3300. SAN 344-7456. Tel: 617-287-5900. Interlibrary Loan Service Tel: 617-287-5931. Reference Tel: 617-287-5940. Administration Tel: 617-287-5910. Interlibrary Loan Service FAX: 617-287-5955. Administration FAX: 617-287-5950. E-mail: library.admin@umb.edu, library.circulation@umb.edu. Web Site: www.lib.umb.edu. *Univ Librn,* Daniel Ortiz; Tel: 617-287-5916, E-mail: daniel.ortiz@umb.edu; *Assoc Univ Librn,* George Hart; Tel: 617-287 5923, E-mail: george.hart@umb.edu; *Assoc Univ Librn,* Joanne Riley; Tel: 617-287-5927, E-mail: joanne.riley@umb.edu; *Archives & Spec Coll Librn,* Elizabeth Mock; Tel: 617-287-5944, E-mail: elizabeth.mock@umb.edu; *Digital Librn,* I Jeremy Seiferth; Tel: 617-287-5938, E-mail: jeremy.seiferth@umb.edu; *Instrul Serv Librn,* Janet DiPaolo; Tel: 617-287-5939, E-mail: janet.dipaolo@umb.edu; *Ref Librn,* Frances Schlesinger; Tel: 617-287-5943, E-mail: frances.schlesinger@umb.edu; *Ref Librn,* Louisa Tseng; Tel: 617-287-5924, E-mail: louisa.tseng@umb.edu; *Ref, Outreach & Instruction Librn,* Christina Mullins; Tel: 617-287-5933, E-mail: tina.mullins@umb.edu; *Bus Operations & Res Mgr,* Sallyann Lopez; Tel: 617-287-5917, E-mail: sallyann.lopez@umb.edu; *Circ Mgr,* Robert Conway; Tel: 617-287-5948, E-mail: robert.conway@umb.edu; *Outreach & Develop Mgr,* Kim Trauceniek; Tel: 617-287-5921, E-mail: kim.trauceniek@umb.edu; *Libr Syst Spec,* Terry MacAskill; Tel: 617-287-5914, E-mail: terry.macaskill@umb.edu; Staff 17 (MLS 11, Non-MLS 6)
Founded 1965. Enrl 13,232; Fac 462; Highest Degree: Doctorate
Library Holdings: Bk Vols 586,667
Database Vendor: Cambridge Scientific Abstracts, Dialog, EBSCOhost, Gale Cengage Learning, JSTOR, LexisNexis, Newsbank, OCLC FirstSearch, OVID Technologies, ProQuest, SirsiDynix
Wireless access
Function: Archival coll, Computers for patron use, Distance learning, Doc delivery serv, E-Reserves, Electronic databases & coll, ILL available, Online cat, Online searches, Ref & res
Partic in Boston Library Consortium, Inc; Fenway Library Consortium (FLC); Massachusetts Commonwealth Consortium of Libraries in Public Higher Education Institutions (MCCLPHEI)
Friends of the Library Group

C WENTWORTH INSTITUTE OF TECHNOLOGY*, Alumni Library, 550 Huntington Ave, 02115-5998. SAN 307-2460. Tel: 617-989-4040. FAX: 617-989-4091. Web Site: www.wit.edu/Library/. *Dir,* Walter T Punch; Tel: 617-989-4097; *Asst Dir, Head, Info Serv,* Kristin Motte; Tel: 617-989-4092; *Evening/Weekend Librn,* Priscilla Biondi; *Mgr, Access Serv,* Kurt Oliver; *Mgr, Libr Recs,* Linda Gallagher; *Archivist,* C Anthony Reed; *Circ,* Dan O'Connell; *Info Serv,* Pia Romano; *Info Serv, Info Tech,* Rachel Zyirek; *Ref Serv, Visual Res,* Thomas Fulda; *Tech Serv,* Dennis Berthiaume; Staff 9.5 (MLS 6, Non-MLS 3.5)
Founded 1904. Enrl 3,000; Highest Degree: Bachelor
Library Holdings: Bk Vols 75,000, Per Subs 500
Special Collections: Archives Coll; ASEE/ET Archives; Edward Kingman Coll; Mechanical Engineering (Richard H Lufkin Coll), bks, per
Subject Interests: Archit, Electrical eng, Electronics, Manufacturing, Mechanical eng
Automation Activity & Vendor Info: (Circulation) Ex Libris Group
Publications: Accessions List; Library Handbooks (Student, staff & faculty); Research Guide
Partic in Dialog Corp; Fenway Library Consortium (FLC); Lyrasis
Open Mon-Thurs 7:45am-10pm, Fri 7:45-5:30, Sat 7:45-6, Sun 1-9

C WHEELOCK COLLEGE LIBRARY*, 132 The Riverway, 02215-4815. SAN 307-2479. Tel: 617-879-2220. Reference Tel: 617-879-2222. Administration Tel: 617-879-2092. FAX: 617-879-2408. E-mail: reference@wheelock.edu. Web Site: www.wheelock.edu/library. *Dir, Acad Res,* Brenda Ecsedy; Tel: 617-879-2225, E-mail: becsedy@wheelock.edu; *Assoc Dir, Coll Mgt Librn,* Ann Glannon; Tel: 617-879-2251, E-mail: aglannon@wheelock.edu; *Access Serv Librn,* Ashley Peterson; Tel: 617-879-2398, E-mail: apeterson@wheelock.edu; *Digital Serv Librn,* Louisa Choy; Tel: 617-879-2213, E-mail: lchoy@wheelock.edu; *E-Learning & Ref Librn,* Marie Kramer; Tel: 617-879-1141, E-mail: mkramer@wheelock.edu; *Res & Instruction Librn,* Adam Williams; Tel: 617-879-2279, E-mail: awilliams@wheelock.edu; *Tech Serv Librn,* Anne Moore; Tel: 617-879-2221, E-mail: amoore@wheelock.edu; *Res Ctr Mgr,* Cortney Tunis; Tel: 617-879-2142, E-mail: ctunis@wheelock.edu; Staff 7.5 (MLS 6.5, Non-MLS 1)
Founded 1889. Enrl 1,069; Fac 65; Highest Degree: Master
Library Holdings: AV Mats 3,596; e-books 10,309; e-journals 10,345; Bk Vols 92,000; Per Subs 536
Special Collections: Early Childhood Curriculum Resource Coll; History of Kindergarten in the United States; Rare & Historical Children's Literature (US & Great Britian)
Subject Interests: Early childhood educ, Educ, Soc serv (soc work), Spec educ
Automation Activity & Vendor Info: (Acquisitions) Ex Libris Group; (Cataloging) Ex Libris Group; (Circulation) Ex Libris Group; (Course Reserve) Ex Libris Group; (ILL) Ex Libris Group; (OPAC) Ex Libris Group; (Serials) Ex Libris Group
Database Vendor: ARTstor, Cambridge Scientific Abstracts, ebrary, EBSCOhost, Gale Cengage Learning, JSTOR, LexisNexis, Newsbank, OCLC FirstSearch, OVID Technologies, ProQuest, Sage, ScienceDirect
Wireless access
Publications: Bibliographies; Information Handbook; Library Guide (Library handbook)
Partic in Fenway Libraries Online, Inc; Fenway Library Consortium (FLC); OCLC Online Computer Library Center, Inc
Open Mon-Thurs 7:30am-11pm, Fri 7:30am-8pm, Sun Noon-11

BOURNE

P JONATHAN BOURNE PUBLIC LIBRARY*, 19 Sandwich Rd, 02532-3699. SAN 344-7545. Tel: 508-759-0644. Reference Tel: 508-759-0644, Ext 109. FAX: 508-759-0647. Web Site: www.bournelibrary.org. *Dir,* Patrick W Marshall; Tel: 508-759-0644, Ext 107, E-mail: pmarshall@bournelibrary.org; *Asst Dir,* Diane M Ranney; Tel: 508-759-0644, Ext 103, E-mail: dranney@bournelibrary.org; *Cat,* Randall Mason; Tel: 508-759-0644, Ext 104, E-mail: rmason@bournelibrary.org; *Ch Serv,* Judith Blaisdell; Tel: 508-759-0644, Ext 106, E-mail: jblaisdell@bournelibrary.org; Staff 9 (MLS 3, Non-MLS 6)
Founded 1896. Pop 18,873
Jul 2005-Jun 2006 Income $506,272. Mats Exp $105,250, Books $62,500, Per/Ser (Incl. Access Fees) $6,000, Micro $250, Electronic Ref Mat (Incl. Access Fees) $36,500. Sal $353,463 (Prof $234,797)
Library Holdings: AV Mats 8,000; Bks on Deafness & Sign Lang 15; Large Print Bks 5,600; Bk Titles 46,000; Bk Vols 53,000; Per Subs 107
Special Collections: Army National Guard Base (Otis) Hazardous Waste Cleanup; Cape Cod Coll; EPA Materials on Massachusetts; Genealogy Coll; Large Print Coll; Young Adult Coll
Automation Activity & Vendor Info: (Acquisitions) Innovative Interfaces, Inc; (Cataloging) Innovative Interfaces, Inc; (Circulation) Innovative Interfaces, Inc; (Course Reserve) Innovative Interfaces, Inc; (ILL) Innovative Interfaces, Inc; (OPAC) Innovative Interfaces, Inc; (Serials) Innovative Interfaces, Inc
Database Vendor: EBSCOhost, Gale Cengage Learning, ProQuest
Mem of Massachusetts Libr Syst
Partic in Cape Libraries Automated Materials Sharing Network
Special Services for the Deaf - Bks on deafness & sign lang; High interest/low vocabulary bks; TTY equip
Special Services for the Blind - Bks on cassette
Open Tues-Thurs 9-8, Fri & Sat 9-5:30
Friends of the Library Group

BOXBOROUGH

P SARGENT MEMORIAL LIBRARY*, 427 Massachusetts Ave, 01719. SAN 307-2487. Tel: 978-263-4680. FAX: 978-263-1275. Web Site: www.boxlib.org. *Dir,* Maureen Strapko; E-mail: mstrapko@cwmars.org; *Youth Serv,* Heather Wilkinson; E-mail: hwilkins@cwmars.org; Staff 2 (MLS 1, Non-MLS 1)
Founded 1891
Library Holdings: Bk Vols 40,000; Per Subs 85
Automation Activity & Vendor Info: (Cataloging) Innovative Interfaces, Inc; (Circulation) Innovative Interfaces, Inc; (OPAC) Innovative Interfaces, Inc
Mem of Massachusetts Libr Syst
Open Mon & Wed 10-6, Tues & Thurs 10-8, Sat 10-3
Friends of the Library Group

BOXFORD

P BOXFORD TOWN LIBRARY*, Ten Elm St, 01921. SAN 344-7669. Tel: 978-887-7323. FAX: 978-887-6352. E-mail: boxford@mvlc.org. Web Site: www.boxfordlibrary.org. *Dir,* Nancy Milone Hill; E-mail: nhill@mvlc.org; *Head, Circ,* Winifred Flint; *Head, Ref,* Anna Call; *Ch,* Joshua Kennedy
Founded 1966. Pop 8,550; Circ 85,963
Library Holdings: AV Mats 16,839; DVDs 3,371; Electronic Media & Resources 7; Bk Vols 54,617; Per Subs 311
Automation Activity & Vendor Info: (Cataloging) SirsiDynix; (Circulation) SirsiDynix; (OPAC) SirsiDynix
Database Vendor: EBSCOhost, LearningExpress, ProQuest
Wireless access
Function: Art exhibits, Bks on cassette, Bks on CD, Children's prog, Computers for patron use, Copy machines, E-Reserves, Electronic databases & coll, Fax serv, Genealogy discussion group, Holiday prog, ILL available, Mus passes, Music CDs, Online cat, OverDrive digital audio bks, Photocopying/Printing, Prog for adults, Prog for children & young adult, Pub access computers, Ref serv available, Story hour, Summer reading prog, Tax forms, Teen prog, Telephone ref, VHS videos, Web-catalog
Mem of Massachusetts Libr Syst
Partic in Merimack Valley Libr Consortium
Open Mon-Thurs 10-8, Fri 12-5, Sat 10-3
Friends of the Library Group

BOYLSTON

P BOYLSTON PUBLIC LIBRARY*, 695 Main St, 01505. SAN 307-2495. Tel: 508-869-2371. FAX: 508-869-6195. E-mail: publiclibrary@boylston-ma.gov. Web Site: www.boylstonlibrary.org. *Dir,* Jennifer Carrico; *Asst Dir,* Lynn Clermont; E-mail: lclermont@boylston-ma.gov; *Ch,* Judy Friebert; E-mail: jmfriebert1@hotmail.com; Staff 2.31 (MLS 0.68, Non-MLS 1.63)
Founded 1880. Pop 4,200; Circ 24,227
Jul 2005-Jun 2006 Income $147,588, State $4,522, City $141,471, Locally Generated Income $1,045, Other $550. Mats Exp $29,696, Books $13,119, Per/Ser (Incl. Access Fees) $3,366, AV Mat $13,175, Electronic Ref Mat (Incl. Access Fees) $36. Sal $93,911 (Prof $81,911)
Library Holdings: AV Mats 4,037; Bk Vols 26,848; Per Subs 77
Automation Activity & Vendor Info: (Acquisitions) Innovative Interfaces, Inc; (Cataloging) Innovative Interfaces, Inc; (Circulation) Innovative Interfaces, Inc; (ILL) Innovative Interfaces, Inc
Database Vendor: Innovative Interfaces, Inc
Publications: Binder (Newsletter)
Mem of Massachusetts Libr Syst
Partic in Central & Western Massachusetts Automated Resource Sharing
Open Tues & Wed 10-8, Thurs 2-8, Fri 2-5, Sat 10-2
Friends of the Library Group

S WORCESTER COUNTY HORTICULTURAL SOCIETY*, Tower Hill Botanic Garden Library, 11 French Dr, 01505. (Mail add: PO Box 598, 01505-0598), SAN 307-8337. Tel: 508-869-6111, Ext 116. FAX: 508-869-0314. E-mail: librarian@towerhillbg.org. Web Site: www.towerhillbg.org/thweblibrary.html. *Librn,* Kathy Bell; Staff 1 (MLS 1)
Founded 1842
Library Holdings: Bk Vols 8,700; Per Subs 26
Subject Interests: Fruit, Garden hist, Hort, Landscape design
Automation Activity & Vendor Info: (Cataloging) OCLC; (Circulation) CyberTools for Libraries; (OPAC) CyberTools for Libraries
Database Vendor: Newsbank
Wireless access
Function: Archival coll, Prof lending libr
Mem of Massachusetts Libr Syst
Open Tues, Thurs & Sat 10-4
Restriction: Circ to mem only

BRAINTREE

S BRAINTREE HISTORICAL SOCIETY, INC LIBRARY*, 85 Quincey Ave, 02184-4416. SAN 327-5523. Tel: 781-843-1518. FAX: 781-380-0731. *Archivist, Dir,* Jim Fahey; *Librn,* Marjorie P Maxham
Library Holdings: Bk Vols 3,000
Special Collections: Military History Archive; Photo Archive
Subject Interests: Antiques, Genealogy, Local hist, Shipbuilding
Restriction: Not open to pub, Private libr

P THAYER PUBLIC LIBRARY*, 798 Washington St, 02184. SAN 344-7723. Tel: 781-848-0405. Circulation Tel: 781-848-0405, Ext 4410. Reference Tel: 781-848-0405, Ext 4417. Administration Tel: 781-848-0405, Ext 4420. FAX: 781-356-5447. Administration FAX: 781-356-0672. E-mail: referencedesk@braintreema.gov. Web Site: www.thayerpubliclibrary.net, www.thayerpubliclibrary.org. *Dir,* Terri Stano; E-mail: tstano@braintreema.gov; *Asst Dir,* Position Currently Open; *Ch Serv,* Elisabeth Strachan; Tel: 781-848-0405, Ext 4426, E-mail: estrachan@braintreema.gov; *Ref Serv,* Moira Cavanagh; Tel: 781-848-0405, Ext 4434, E-mail: mcavanagh@braintreema.gov; *Ref Serv,* Priscilla Crane; Tel: 781-848-0405, Ext 4407, E-mail: pcrane@braintreema.gov; *Tech Serv,* Constance Collier; Tel: 781-848-0405, Ext 4418, E-mail: ccollier@braintreema.gov; Staff 25 (MLS 8, Non-MLS 17)
Founded 1874. Pop 34,598
Special Collections: Braintree Historical Coll
Automation Activity & Vendor Info: (Acquisitions) SirsiDynix; (Cataloging) SirsiDynix; (Circulation) SirsiDynix
Database Vendor: Gale Cengage Learning, TLC (The Library Corporation)
Wireless access
Partic in Old Colony Libr Network (OCLN)
Open Mon-Thurs (Fall-Spring) 9-9, Fri & Sat 9-5; Mon-Thurs (Summer) 9-8, Fri 9-5
Friends of the Library Group

BREWSTER

P BREWSTER LADIES' LIBRARY*, 1822 Main St, 02631. SAN 307-2509. Tel: 508-896-3913. Administration Tel: 508-896-2297. FAX: 508-896-9372. E-mail: bll@brewsterladieslibrary.org. Web Site: www.brewsterladieslibrary.org. *Dir,* Kathy Cockcroft; E-mail: kcockcroft@brewsterladieslibrary.org; *Asst Dir, Youth Serv Librn,* Claire Gradone; E-mail: cgradone@brewsterladieslibrary.org; *Adult Serv, Ref Librn,* Kathleen Remillard; E-mail: kremillard@brewsterladieslibrary.org; *Circ Mgr,* Christine Lord; E-mail: clord@brewsterladieslibrary.org; Staff 5 (MLS 2, Non-MLS 3)
Founded 1852. Pop 10,043; Circ 140,557
Library Holdings: AV Mats 48,951; Bk Titles 89,126; Per Subs 166
Special Collections: Brewster History Coll; Cape Cod Coll; Joseph Lincoln Novels; Plays. Oral History
Automation Activity & Vendor Info: (Acquisitions) Innovative Interfaces, Inc; (Cataloging) Innovative Interfaces, Inc; (Circulation) Innovative Interfaces, Inc; (ILL) Innovative Interfaces, Inc; (OPAC) Innovative Interfaces, Inc; (Serials) EBSCO Online
Database Vendor: CredoReference, EBSCOhost, ProQuest, World Book Online
Wireless access
Function: Adult bk club, Archival coll, Art exhibits, Bks on cassette, Bks on CD, Children's prog, Computer training, Computers for patron use, Copy machines, Electronic databases & coll, Fax serv, Free DVD rentals, Handicapped accessible, Home delivery & serv to Sr ctr & nursing homes, Homebound delivery serv, ILL available, Magnifiers for reading, Mus passes, Music CDs, Online cat, Online searches, Photocopying/Printing, Prog for adults, Prog for children & young adult, Ref serv available, Summer reading prog, Tax forms, Teen prog, Telephone ref, VHS videos, Wheelchair accessible, Writing prog
Publications: Library Update (Newsletter)
Partic in Cape Libraries Automated Materials Sharing Network
Special Services for the Deaf - Assisted listening device
Special Services for the Blind - Large print bks
Open Tues & Thurs 10-8, Wed, Fri & Sat 10-5
Friends of the Library Group

S CAPE COD MUSEUM OF NATURAL HISTORY*, Clarence L Hay Library, 869 Main St, 02631. SAN 307-2517. Tel: 508-896-3867. FAX: 508-896-8844. Web Site: www.ccmnh.org. *Librn,* Susan Carr; Staff 1 (Non-MLS 1)
Founded 1958
Library Holdings: Bk Vols 10,000; Per Subs 35
Special Collections: Scientific Specimens
Subject Interests: Archaeology, Botany, Conserv, Ecology, Entomology, Geol, Marine biol, Ornithology, Zoology
Wireless access
Publications: Newsletter
Open Mon-Sun 9:30-4
Friends of the Library Group

BRIDGEWATER

P BRIDGEWATER PUBLIC LIBRARY, 15 South St, 02324-2593. SAN 307-2525. Tel: 508-697-3331. FAX: 508-279-1467. E-mail: bwpl@sailsinc.org. Web Site: www.bridgewaterpubliclibrary.org. *Dir,* Sean Daley; *Ch,* Christine Stefani; *Circ Librn,* Ann Gerald; *Ref Librn,* Mary O'Connell; Staff 5 (MLS 4, Non-MLS 1)
Founded 1881. Pop 25,802; Circ 96,436
Library Holdings: Bk Vols 139,459; Per Subs 110
Automation Activity & Vendor Info: (Acquisitions) SirsiDynix; (Cataloging) SirsiDynix; (Circulation) SirsiDynix; (Media Booking) SirsiDynix; (OPAC) SirsiDynix; (Serials) SirsiDynix
Wireless access
Function: e-mail & chat, e-mail serv, E-Reserves, Electronic databases & coll, Exhibits, Fax serv, Free DVD rentals, Handicapped accessible, Mus passes, Music CDs, Online ref, Online searches, OverDrive digital audio bks, Photocopying/Printing, Prog for adults, Prog for children & young adult, Pub access computers, Ref serv in person, Story hour, Summer reading prog, Tax forms, Wheelchair accessible
Partic in SAILS Library Network
Special Services for the Deaf - TDD equip
Special Services for the Blind - Assistive/Adapted tech devices, equip & products
Open Mon-Wed 9-8, Thurs 10-5, Fri & Sat 10-2
Friends of the Library Group

C BRIDGEWATER STATE UNIVERSITY, Clement C Maxwell Library, 10 Shaw Rd, 02325. SAN 307-2533. Tel: 508-531-1392. Interlibrary Loan Service Tel: 508-697-1706. FAX: 508-531-1349, 508-531-6103. E-mail: libraryweb@bridgew.edu. Web Site: www.bridgew.edu/library. *Dir,* Michael Somers; E-mail: msomers@bridgew.edu; *Head, Educ Res Ctr,* Christine Brown; Tel: 508-531-2023, E-mail: c4brown@bridgew.edu; *Head, Ref Serv,* Marcia Dinneen; Tel: 508-531-1742, E-mail: m.dinneen@bridgew.edu; *Archivist, Head, Spec Coll,* Orson Kingsley; Tel: 508-531-1389, E-mail: orson.kingsley@bridgew.edu; *Head, Tech Serv,* Sarah Wallbank; Tel: 508-531-2665, E-mail: sarah.wallbank@bridgew.edu; *Ref Librn,* Pamela Hayes-Bohanan; Tel: 508-531-2893, E-mail: phayesboh@bridgew.edu; *Circ,* Kevin Manning; Tel: 508-531-2005, E-mail: kmanning@bridgew.edu; *Ref, Ref Serv, Ad,* Cynthia J W Svoboda; Tel: 508-531-1256. Subject Specialists: *Educ res,* Christine Brown; *Music, Psychol, Sociol,* Sarah Wallbank; Staff 27 (MLS 10, Non-MLS 17)
Founded 1840. Enrl 11,500; Highest Degree: Master

Library Holdings: Bk Titles 242,644; Bk Vols 299,645; Per Subs 1,100
Special Collections: Abraham Lincoln Coll; Albert G Boyden Coll of Early American Textbooks; Bridgewaterana; Children's Coll; Dicken's Coll; Educational Resources Information Center, micro; Library of American Civilization, micro; Library of English Literature, micro; Standardized Tests; Tests in Microfiche; Theodore Roosevelt Coll. State Document Depository; US Document Depository
Subject Interests: Art, Educ
Automation Activity & Vendor Info: (Acquisitions) Ex Libris Group; (Cataloging) Ex Libris Group; (Circulation) Ex Libris Group; (Course Reserve) Ex Libris Group; (OPAC) Ex Libris Group; (Serials) Ex Libris Group
Database Vendor: Dialog, EBSCOhost, Gale Cengage Learning, LexisNexis, OCLC FirstSearch, ProQuest, TLC (The Library Corporation)
Wireless access
Publications: SE Mass Cooperating Libraries Union List of Serials
Partic in Lyrasis

MASSACHUSETTS DEPARTMENT OF CORRECTIONS

S INSTITUTIONAL LIBRARY AT MASSACHUSETTS TREATMENT CENTER*, One Administration Rd, 02324. Tel: 508-279-8100, Ext 8443. *Librn,* Natalya Pushkina
Library Holdings: Bk Vols 9,250; Per Subs 31
Open Mon, Tues & Fri 8-4, Wed & Thurs 8-4 & 7-9

S INSTITUTIONAL LIBRARY AT OLD COLONY CORRECTIONAL CENTER*, One Administration Rd, 02324. Tel: 508-279-6006, Ext 6803. *Librn,* Ann Cowell
Library Holdings: Bk Vols 5,000; Per Subs 38
Automation Activity & Vendor Info: (Circulation) Follett Software
Mem of Massachusetts Libr Syst

S STATE HOSPITAL LIBRARY*, 20 Administration Rd, 02324, SAN 307-2541. Tel: 508-279-4500, Ext 4600. FAX: 508-279-4502. *Librn,* Kurt Eichner; Staff 1 (MLS 1)
Founded 1975
Library Holdings: Bk Titles 9,000; Per Subs 23
Subject Interests: Law
Restriction: Staff & inmates only

BRIGHTON

S NATIONAL TAY-SACHS & ALLIED DISEASES ASSOCIATION LIBRARY*, 2001 Beacon St, Ste 204, 02135. SAN 372-6312. Tel: 617-277-4463. Toll Free Tel: 800-906-8723. FAX: 617-277-0134. E-mail: info@ntsad.org. Web Site: www.ntsad.org. *Exec Dir,* Susan Kahn; E-mail: skahn@ntsad.org
Founded 1957
Library Holdings: Bk Vols 300
Subject Interests: Bereavement, Diseases, Human genetics
Restriction: Circ limited

BRIMFIELD

P BRIMFIELD PUBLIC LIBRARY*, 25 Main St, 01010-9701. SAN 307-2584. Tel: 413-245-3518. FAX: 413-245-3468. *Dir,* Rebecca Wells; E-mail: rebecca@brimfieldpubliclibrary.org; *Webmaster,* Michael DeFalco
Founded 1877. Pop 3,136; Circ 20,179
Library Holdings: Bk Vols 15,000; Per Subs 70
Special Collections: Oral History
Subject Interests: Genealogy, Local hist
Automation Activity & Vendor Info: (Cataloging) Innovative Interfaces, Inc; (Circulation) Innovative Interfaces, Inc; (OPAC) Innovative Interfaces, Inc
Mem of Massachusetts Libr Syst
Open Mon 10-1 & 6-9, Tues & Thurs 3-8, Wed 2-6, Sat 9-1
Friends of the Library Group

BROCKTON

M BROCKTON HOSPITAL LIBRARY*, 680 Centre St, 02302. SAN 371-2028. Tel: 508-941-7207. FAX: 508-941-6412. E-mail: library@brocktonhospital.org. Web Site: www.brocktonhospital.com. *Mgr, Libr Serv,* Mary Conners; Staff 4 (MLS 1, Non-MLS 3)
Library Holdings: e-journals 45; Bk Titles 2,500; Bk Vols 9,000; Per Subs 268
Subject Interests: Med, Nursing
Publications: Brochures
Partic in Basic Health Sciences Library Network; Southeastern Massachusetts Consortium of Health Science Libraries

P BROCKTON PUBLIC LIBRARY SYSTEM*, 304 Main St, 02301-5390. SAN 344-7812. Tel: 508-580-7890. FAX: 508-580-7898. Web Site: www.brocktonpubliclibrary.org. *Dir,* Elizabeth Marcus; *Asst Dir,* Keith Choquette; E-mail: keithc@ocln.org; *Head, Tech Serv,* Michelle Poor; E-mail: mpoor@ocln.org; *Ch Serv,* Sharon Quint; E-mail: squint@ocln.org; *ILL,* John Reardon; E-mail: btill@ocln.org; *Ref,* Lucia Shannon; E-mail: lshannon@ocln.org; Staff 45 (MLS 5, Non-MLS 40)
Founded 1867. Pop 94,304; Circ 241,610
Library Holdings: Bk Vols 139,692; Per Subs 120
Automation Activity & Vendor Info: (Cataloging) SirsiDynix; (Circulation) SirsiDynix; (OPAC) SirsiDynix
Partic in Old Colony Libr Network (OCLN)
Friends of the Library Group
Branches: 2
EAST, 54 Kingman St, 02302, SAN 344-7871. Tel: 508-580-7892. FAX: 508-580-7861. E-mail: bteast@ocln.org. *Dir,* Elizabeth Marcus
Founded 1969
Library Holdings: Bk Vols 22,618
Partic in Old Colony Libr Network (OCLN)
Friends of the Library Group
WEST, 540 Forest Ave, 02301, SAN 344-7936. Tel: 508-580-7894. FAX: 508-580-7863. E-mail: btwest@ocln.org.
Founded 1969
Library Holdings: Bk Vols 25,841
Partic in Old Colony Libr Network (OCLN)
Friends of the Library Group

GL COMMONWEALTH OF MASSACHUSETTS - TRIAL COURT*, Brockton Law Library, 72 Belmont St, 02301. SAN 307-2630. Tel: 508-586-7110. FAX: 508-588-8483. E-mail: brocklaw72@hotmail.com. Web Site: www.lawlib.state.ma.us. *Dir,* Jean Smith; Staff 2 (MLS 1, Non-MLS 1)
Jul 2005-Jun 2006. Mats Exp $69,868, Books $46,036, Electronic Ref Mat (Incl. Access Fees) $23,832. Sal $114,500
Library Holdings: Bk Vols 24,532
Automation Activity & Vendor Info: (Cataloging) SirsiDynix; (Circulation) SirsiDynix; (OPAC) SirsiDynix; (Serials) SirsiDynix
Database Vendor: Gale Cengage Learning, LexisNexis, Westlaw
Partic in New England Law Library Consortium, Inc
Open Mon-Fri 8:30-4

S ENTERPRISE LIBRARY*, 60 Main St, 02303. (Mail add: PO Box 1450, 02303-1450), SAN 307-2606. Tel: 508-586-6200. FAX: 508-586-6506. E-mail: newsroom@enterprisenews.com. Web Site: www.southofboston.com. *Librn,* Beth Gould
Founded 1880
Special Collections: News clippings
Subject Interests: Hist
Restriction: Staff use only

J MASSASOIT COMMUNITY COLLEGE LIBRARY*, One Massasoit Blvd, 02302. SAN 307-2622. Tel: 508-588-9100, Ext 1941. FAX: 508-427-1265. Web Site: www.massasoit.mass.edu/library/library.cfm. *Dir,* Joanne E Jones; Tel: 508-588-9100, Ext 1944, E-mail: jjones@massasoit.mass.edu; *Coordr, Pub Serv & Instruction,* Jennifer Rudolph; Tel: 508-588-9100, Ext 1946, E-mail: jrudolph@massasoit.mass.edu; *Archives, Coordr, Tech Serv, ILL,* Mary C Nelson; Tel: 508-588-9100, Ext 1943, E-mail: mnelson@massasoit.mass.edu; *Ref Librn,* Pauline Aiello; Tel: 508-588-9100, Ext 1948, E-mail: paiello@massasoit.mass.edu; *Ref Librn,* Neal Carney; E-mail: ncarney@massasoit.mass.edu; *Ref Librn,* Lorna Rodio; E-mail: lrodio@massasoit.mass.edu; *Ref Librn,* Jim Sacchetti; E-mail: jsacchetti@massasoit.mass.edu; *Per,* M Lou Nesson; Tel: 508-588-9100, Ext 1932, E-mail: mlnesson@massasoit.mass.edu
Founded 1966
Library Holdings: Bk Vols 63,764; Per Subs 175
Special Collections: Allied Health Resources; New York Times, 1851-date
Automation Activity & Vendor Info: (Acquisitions) SirsiDynix; (Cataloging) SirsiDynix; (Circulation) SirsiDynix
Wireless access
Open Mon-Fri 8am-9pm, Sat 8:30-4:30

GM VA MEDICAL CENTER*, Medical Library 142D, 940 Belmont St, 02301. SAN 307-2649. Tel: 774-826-1142. FAX: 774-826-1537. *Librn,* Martha Roberts
Founded 1953
Library Holdings: Bk Vols 4,000; Per Subs 60
Subject Interests: Alcohol & drugs, Drug abuse, Med, Nursing, Psychiat, Psychol, Soc sci & issues
Partic in Boston Biomedical Library Consortium; Southeastern Massachusetts Consortium of Health Science Libraries
Open Mon-Fri 8-4

BROOKFIELD

P MERRICK PUBLIC LIBRARY*, Two Lincoln St, 01506. (Mail add: PO Box 528, 01506-0528), SAN 307-2657. Tel: 508-867-6339. FAX: 508-867-2981. *Dir,* Brenda Metterville
Pop 3,100; Circ 13,355

Library Holdings: Bk Vols 20,000; Per Subs 50
Subject Interests: Local hist
Automation Activity & Vendor Info: (Cataloging) Follett Software; (Circulation) Follett Software
Mem of Massachusetts Libr Syst
Open Tues & Thurs 1-8, Wed & Fri 11-5, Sat 10-1
Friends of the Library Group

BROOKLINE

S LARZ ANDERSON AUTO MUSEUM LIBRARY & ARCHIVES*, Larz Anderson Park, 15 Newton St, 02445. SAN 375-1538. Tel: 617-522-6547. FAX: 617-524-0170. Web Site: www.mot.org. *Dir,* Michael Iandoli; *Educ Mgr,* Molly Niemy; Staff 1 (Non-MLS 1)
Founded 1948
Library Holdings: Bk Vols 2,000; Per Subs 12
Special Collections: Larry Wineman Coll (GM); Larz and Isabel Anderson Coll; Roderick Blood Coll (Packard)
Subject Interests: Automobiles
Function: Res libr
Publications: Carriage House Notes (Newsletter)
Restriction: Non-circulating, Open by appt only

CR HELLENIC COLLEGE-HOLY CROSS GREEK ORTHODOX SCHOOL OF THEOLOGY*, Archbishop Iakovos Library, 50 Goddard Ave, 02445-7496. SAN 307-2673. Tel: 617-850-1223. FAX: 617-850-1470. Web Site: holycross.hchc.edu/holycross/campus_life/library.html. *Dir,* Joachim Cotsonis; Tel: 617-850-1243, E-mail: jcotsonis@hchc.edu; *Syst Librn,* Richard Vanderhoef; Tel: 617-850-1245, E-mail: rvanderhoef@hchc.edu; *Acq, Cat,* Anne Reece; Tel: 617-850-1367, E-mail: areece@hchc.edu; *Circ, ILL, Per,* Hilary Rogler; Tel: 617-850-1244, E-mail: hrogler@hchc.edu; Staff 4 (MLS 4)
Founded 1937. Enrl 200; Fac 23; Highest Degree: Master
Library Holdings: AV Mats 71; CDs 73; DVDs 38; e-journals 519; Microforms 883; Music Scores 310; Bk Titles 62,032; Per Subs 730; Videos 516
Special Collections: Archbishop Iakovos Coll, rare bks; Archive
Subject Interests: Archival, Greek, Hist, Orthodox theol
Automation Activity & Vendor Info: (Acquisitions) SirsiDynix; (Cataloging) SirsiDynix; (Circulation) SirsiDynix; (ILL) OCLC Connexion; (OPAC) SirsiDynix; (Serials) EBSCO Online
Database Vendor: EBSCOhost, Gale Cengage Learning, OCLC, OCLC ArticleFirst, OCLC FirstSearch, OCLC WorldShare Interlibrary Loan, SirsiDynix
Wireless access
Publications: Archbishop Iakovos Library Acquisitions List (Quarterly)
Mem of Massachusetts Libr Syst
Partic in OCLC Online Computer Library Center, Inc
Open Mon-Fri 9-5 & 7-12, Sat 10-4, Sun 7-12

C NEWBURY COLLEGE LIBRARY*, 150 Fisher Ave, 02445-5796. (Mail add: 129 Fisher Ave, 02445-5796), SAN 307-2258. Tel: 617-730-7070. Circulation Tel: 617-738-2443. Reference Tel: 617-730-7071. Administration Tel: 617-730-7255. Automation Services Tel: 617-738-2429. Information Services Tel: 617-730-7008. Toll Free Tel: 800-755-7071. FAX: 617-730-7239. E-mail: library@newbury.edu. Web Site: www.newbury.edu/library. *Coll Mgt Librn,* Norma Gahl; E-mail: ngahl@newbury.edu; *Info Serv Librn,* Janet Hayashi; E-mail: jhayashi@newbury.edu; Staff 5 (MLS 4, Non-MLS 1)
Founded 1970. Enrl 950; Fac 35; Highest Degree: Bachelor
Jul 2009-Jun 2010 Income $518,229. Mats Exp $518,229, Books $30,000, Per/Ser (Incl. Access Fees) $16,000, AV Mat $1,500, Electronic Ref Mat (Incl. Access Fees) $47,783. Sal $369,929
Library Holdings: Audiobooks 700; AV Mats 350; CDs 47; DVDs 197; e-books 7,000; e-journals 14,472; Bk Titles 33,601; Bk Vols 36,432; Per Subs 151; Videos 282
Subject Interests: Bus, Communications, Criminal justice, Culinary, Design, Hotel mgt, Psychol, Restaurant mgt
Automation Activity & Vendor Info: (Acquisitions) Innovative Interfaces, Inc; (Cataloging) Innovative Interfaces, Inc; (Circulation) Innovative Interfaces, Inc; (Course Reserve) Innovative Interfaces, Inc; (ILL) OCLC; (Media Booking) Innovative Interfaces, Inc; (OPAC) Innovative Interfaces, Inc; (Serials) Innovative Interfaces, Inc
Database Vendor: American Psychological Association (APA), ARTstor, CQ Press, CredoReference, Gale Cengage Learning, Grolier Online, Hoovers, Innovative Interfaces, Inc, JSTOR, LexisNexis, Newsbank, OCLC FirstSearch, OCLC WorldShare Interlibrary Loan, ProQuest, SerialsSolutions, Westlaw
Wireless access
Mem of Massachusetts Libr Syst
Partic in Lyrasis; Minuteman Library Network; National Network of Libraries of Medicine; OCLC Online Computer Library Center, Inc

P PUBLIC LIBRARY OF BROOKLINE*, 361 Washington St, 02445. SAN 344-7960. Tel: 617-730-2370. Reference Tel: 617-730-2369. FAX: 617-730-2160. Web Site: www.brooklinelibrary.com. *Dir,* Sara F Slymon; Tel: 617-730-2360; *Asst Dir,* Dalija P Karoblis; Staff 22 (MLS 22)
Founded 1857. Pop 54,700; Circ 729,718
Library Holdings: Bk Vols 319,779; Per Subs 820
Automation Activity & Vendor Info: (Cataloging) Innovative Interfaces, Inc; (Circulation) Innovative Interfaces, Inc; (OPAC) Innovative Interfaces, Inc
Wireless access
Partic in Minuteman Library Network
Open Mon-Thurs 10-9, Fri & Sat 10-5, Sun (Fall & Winter) 1-5
Friends of the Library Group
Branches: 2
COOLIDGE CORNER, 31 Pleasant St, 02446, SAN 344-7995. Tel: 617-730-2380. FAX: 617-734-4565. *Librn,* Catherine Dooley
Library Holdings: Bk Vols 93,984
Open Mon & Wed 10-6, Tues & Thurs 10-9, Fri & Sat 9:30-5, Sun (Fall & Winter) 1-5
Friends of the Library Group
PUTTERHAM, 959 W Roxbury Pkwy, Chestnut Hill, 02467, SAN 344-8029. Tel: 617-730-2385. FAX: 617-469-3947. *Librn,* Barbara Warner
Library Holdings: Bk Vols 40,997
Open Mon & Wed 1-9, Tues & Thurs 10-6, Fri & Sat (Fall & Winter) 10-5

R TEMPLE SINAI LIBRARY*, 50 Sewall Ave, 02446. SAN 307-2703. Tel: 617-277-5888. FAX: 617-277-5842. E-mail: sinaibrook@aol.com. Web Site: uahcweb.org/ma/sinai-brookline. *Librn,* Leann Shamash
Founded 1960
Library Holdings: Bk Vols 500
Subject Interests: Israel, Judaica (lit or hist of Jews), Middle East

BURLINGTON

P BURLINGTON PUBLIC LIBRARY*, 22 Sears St, 01803. SAN 307-2738. Tel: 781-270-1690. FAX: 781-229-0406. Web Site: www.burlingtonpubliclibrary.org. *Dir,* Lori Hodgson; E-mail: lhodgson@burlmass.org; *Circ,* Cara Thissell; *Ref,* Marnie Smith; Staff 10 (MLS 7, Non-MLS 3)
Founded 1857. Pop 23,694; Circ 240,515
Library Holdings: Bk Vols 90,687; Per Subs 168
Subject Interests: Bus & mgt, Law
Automation Activity & Vendor Info: (Cataloging) SirsiDynix; (Circulation) SirsiDynix; (OPAC) SirsiDynix
Function: ILL available, Photocopying/Printing
Open Mon-Thurs 10-9, Fri 10-6, Sat 10-5, Sun 1-5
Friends of the Library Group

M LAHEY HOSPITAL & MEDICAL CENTER, Cattell Memorial Library, 41 Mall Rd, 01805. SAN 320-5827. Tel: 781-744-2409. FAX: 781-744-3615. Web Site: www.lahey.org/library. *Dir,* Carol Spencer; E-mail: carol.spencer@lahey.org; Staff 1 (MLS 1)
Founded 1965
Library Holdings: Bk Titles 1,200; Bk Vols 8,000; Per Subs 150
Subject Interests: Med
Automation Activity & Vendor Info: (Cataloging) EOS International; (OPAC) EOS International
Database Vendor: DynaMed, OVID Technologies, PubMed, UpToDate
Wireless access
Function: For res purposes
Partic in Boston Biomedical Library Consortium; Massachusetts Health Sciences Libraries Network; National Network of Libraries of Medicine New England Region
Open Mon-Fri 8:30-5
Restriction: Hospital staff & commun, Non-circulating to the pub

G VISIDYNE, INC LIBRARY*, Ten Corporate Pl, Ste 10, 99 S Bedford St, 01803-5168. SAN 329-9961. Tel: 781-273-2820. FAX: 781-272-1068. E-mail: villa@visidyne.com. Web Site: www.visidyne.com. *Librn,* Elise Robitallie; E-mail: elise@visidyne.com
Library Holdings: Bk Vols 200; Per Subs 12
Subject Interests: Atmospheric optics, Govt, Naval, Rpts, Surface analysis

BUZZARDS BAY

S MASSACHUSETTS MARITIME ACADEMY, ABS Information Commons, ABS IC-123, 101 Academy Dr, 02532. SAN 307-2878. Tel: 508-830-5034. FAX: 508-830-5074. Web Site: library.maritime.edu. *Dir,* Susan Berteaux; E-mail: sberteaux@maritime.edu; *Assoc Dir,* Liz Novak; E-mail: lnovak@maritime.edu; Staff 4 (MLS 2, Non-MLS 2)
Founded 1970. Enrl 1,200; Highest Degree: Master
Library Holdings: e-books 120,000; e-journals 45,000; Bk Vols 44,000; Per Subs 48

Subject Interests: Emergency response, Law, Maritime studies, Nautical hist, Ocean eng, Oceanography
Automation Activity & Vendor Info: (Acquisitions) SirsiDynix; (Cataloging) SirsiDynix; (Circulation) SirsiDynix
Function: Archival coll, Exhibits, Handicapped accessible
Publications: Acquisitions List
Partic in Lyrasis
Open Mon-Thurs 7:30am-10pm, Fri 7.30-4
Restriction: Borrowing privileges limited to fac & registered students, Borrowing requests are handled by ILL, Circ privileges for students & alumni only

BYFIELD

P NEWBURY TOWN LIBRARY*, 0 Lunt St, 01922-1232. SAN 307-5605. Tel: 978-465-0539. FAX: 978-465-1071. E-mail: mnb@mvlc.org. Web Site: www.newburylibrary.org. *Dir,* Amy Sadkin; E-mail: asadkin@mvlc.org; *Asst Dir,* Jean Ackerly; E-mail: jackerly@mvlc.org; *Circ Librn,* Susanne Monier; *Youth Serv Librn,* Olivia Gatti; Staff 9 (MLS 1, Non-MLS 8)
Founded 1926. Pop 6,900; Circ 76,901
Library Holdings: AV Mats 1,737; Electronic Media & Resources 188; Bk Vols 44,030; Per Subs 89; Videos 2,854
Automation Activity & Vendor Info: (Cataloging) SirsiDynix; (Circulation) SirsiDynix; (OPAC) SirsiDynix
Partic in Merrimack Valley Library Consortium
Open Wed & Thurs 10-7, Fri 10-5, Sat (Sep-May) 10-2
Restriction: Access at librarian's discretion
Friends of the Library Group

CAMBRIDGE

S AMERICAN ASSOCIATION OF VARIABLE STAR OBSERVERS*, Charles Y McAteer Library, 25 Birch St, 02138. SAN 323-4894. Tel: 617-354-0484. FAX: 617-354-0665. E-mail: aavso@aavso.org. Web Site: www.aavso.org. *Dir,* Dr Janet A Mattei
Library Holdings: Bk Vols 2,500; Per Subs 200
Subject Interests: Astronomy
Open Mon-Fri 9-5

S CAMBRIDGE HISTORICAL COMMISSION ARCHIVE*, 831 Massachusetts Ave, 2nd Flr, 02139. SAN 329-0905. Tel: 617-349-4683. FAX: 617-349-3116. E-mail: histcomm@cambridgema.gov. Web Site: www.cambridgema.gov/historic. *Exec Dir,* Charles M Sullivan; *Asst Dir,* Kathleen L Rawlins; Staff 0.5 (MLS 0.5)
Founded 1964
Library Holdings: Bk Titles 500
Special Collections: Building Permits Index, 1886-1937; Cambridge City Directories, 1848-1972; Cambridge Historical Commission Photo Coll; Cambridge Historical Society Proceedings; Cambridge Subway Construction, photos 1909-1912; Maps & Atlases, 1830-1997; Survey of Architectural History in Cambridge, inventory with photo of every Cambridge building 1965-present. Oral History
Subject Interests: Archit, Local hist, Photog
Wireless access
Open Tues-Fri 9:30-11:30 & 2-4
Restriction: Non-circulating

M CAMBRIDGE HOSPITAL-CAMBRIDGE HEALTH ALLIANCE*, Bor Medical Library, 1493 Cambridge St, 02139. SAN 372-6274. Tel: 617-665-1439. FAX: 617-665-1424. *Dir, Libr Serv,* Jenny Olsen; E-mail: jolsen@challiance.org; Staff 2 (MLS 1, Non-MLS 1)
Library Holdings: Bk Titles 1,000; Bk Vols 1,200; Per Subs 82
Subject Interests: Med, Med humanities, Podiatry, Psychiat
Database Vendor: DynaMed, EBSCOhost, Lexi-Comp, PubMed, UpToDate, WebMD
Wireless access
Publications: Blog/Newsletter (Online only)
Mem of Massachusetts Libr Syst
Partic in Boston Biomedical Library Consortium; Massachusetts Health Sciences Libraries Network; Medical Library Association (MLA); Northeastern Consortium for Health Information
Friends of the Library Group

P CAMBRIDGE PUBLIC LIBRARY*, 449 Broadway, 02138. SAN 344-8053. Tel: 617-349-4040. Interlibrary Loan Service Tel: 617-349-6970. Reference Tel: 617-349-4044. Administration Tel: 617-349-4032. Information Services Tel: 617-349-4030. FAX: 617-349-4028. TDD: 617-349-4421. Web Site: www.cambridgema.gov/~cpl. *Dir,* Susan Flannery; E-mail: sflannery@minlib.net; *Asst Dir,* Karen Brown; *Asst Dir,* Bertha Chandler; *Bus & Finance Mgr,* William Courier; Tel: 617-349-4413, Fax: 617-349-3108; *Fac Mgr,* Warren Pearson; *IT Mgr,* Jule O'Donnell; *Acq,* Stephanie Zabriskie; *Ch Serv,* Julie Roach; *Circ,* Jennifer Blakely; *Ref,* Mark Freed. Subject Specialists: *Human resources,* Bertha Chandler; *Finance,* William Courier; Staff 97 (MLS 42, Non-MLS 55)
Pop 105,000; Circ 1,397,593
Jun 2010-May 2011 Income (Main Library and Branch(s)) $8,135,070, State $88,685, City $8,046,385. Mats Exp $772,497, Books $445,666, Per/Ser (Incl. Access Fees) $58,581, Other Print Mats $13,988, AV Mat $201,243, Electronic Ref Mat (Incl. Access Fees) $53,019. Sal $6,162,898
Library Holdings: AV Mats 18,539; DVDs 27,415; Bk Vols 298,758; Per Subs 1,387
Database Vendor: Booksite, Ingram Library Services, Newsbank, OCLC, ReferenceUSA, ValueLine, World Book Online, WT Cox
Wireless access
Mem of Massachusetts Libr Syst; South Central Library System
Partic in Minuteman Library Network
Special Services for the Deaf - TTY equip
Special Services for the Blind - Bks on CD
Open Mon-Thurs 9-9, Fri & Sat 9-5, Sun (Oct-April) 1-5
Restriction: Circ limited
Friends of the Library Group
Branches: 6
BOUDREAU (OBSERVATORY HILL) BRANCH, 245 Concord Ave, 02138, SAN 344-8231. Tel: 617-349-4017. FAX: 617-349-4424. *Br Mgr,* Linda Haines; E-mail: lhaines@cambridgema.gov; Staff 2 (MLS 1, Non-MLS 1)
Circ 83,818
Library Holdings: AV Mats 3,011; Bk Vols 80,807
Open Mon, Wed & Fri 10-6, Tues & Thurs 10-8
Friends of the Library Group
CENTRAL SQUARE BRANCH, 45 Pearl St, 02139, SAN 344-8118. Tel: 617-349-4010. FAX: 617-349-4418. *Br Mgr,* Position Currently Open
Circ 16,640
Library Holdings: AV Mats 4,450; Bk Vols 35,356
Open Mon, Wed & Fri 10-6, Tues & Thurs 10-9, Sat (Sept-June) 10-2
Friends of the Library Group
COLLINS BRANCH, 64 Aberdeen Ave, 02138, SAN 344-8177. Tel: 617-349-4021. FAX: 617-349-4423. *Br Mgr,* Joseph Logue; Staff 2 (MLS 1, Non-MLS 1)
Founded 1940
Library Holdings: AV Mats 2,076; Bk Vols 45,283
Open Mon 1-8, Tues, Wed & Fri 10-5:30, Thurs 1-5:30
Friends of the Library Group
O'CONNELL BRANCH, 48 Sixth St, 02141, SAN 344-8142. Tel: 617-349-4019. FAX: 617-349-4420. *Br Mgr,* Yan Qu; E-mail: yanqu@cambridgema.gov; Staff 2 (MLS 2)
Circ 63,584
Library Holdings: AV Mats 1,723; Bk Vols 12,840
Open Mon, Wed & Thurs 10-5, Tues 10-7:30
Friends of the Library Group
O'NEILL BRANCH, 70 Rindge Ave, 02140, SAN 344-8207. Tel: 617-349-4023. FAX: 617-349-4422. *Br Mgr,* Lyndsay Forbes; E-mail: lforbes@cambridgema.gov; Staff 2 (MLS 2)
Circ 106,840
Library Holdings: AV Mats 2,624; Bk Vols 22,922
Open Mon, Wed & Thurs 9-8, Tues & Fri 9-5:30
VALENTE BRANCH, 826 Cambridge St, 02141, SAN 344-8088. Tel: 617-349-4015. FAX: 617-349-4416. *Br Mgr,* Ardemis Kilroy; E-mail: akilroy@cambridgema.gov; Staff 2 (MLS 1, Non-MLS 1)
Circ 55,570
Library Holdings: AV Mats 2,447; Bk Vols 23,107
Open Mon & Wed 10-8, Tues & Fri 10-6
Friends of the Library Group

S CDM SMITH INFOCENTER*, 50 Hampshire St, 02139. SAN 307-1472. Tel: 617-452-6778. FAX: 617-452-6778. E-mail: infocenter@cdmsmith.com. *Librn,* Alex Lumb; Tel: 617-452-6822; *Librn,* Cohen B Stacie; Tel: 617-452-6824, Fax: 617-452-8824; Staff 2 (MLS 2)
Founded 1963
Library Holdings: Bk Titles 2,000; Bk Vols 28,000; Per Subs 52
Subject Interests: Environ eng, Wastewater treatment
Automation Activity & Vendor Info: (Acquisitions) EOS International; (Cataloging) EOS International; (Circulation) EOS International; (OPAC) EOS International; (Serials) EOS International
Database Vendor: Elsevier, EOS International, Knovel, OCLC FirstSearch, ScienceDirect
Function: Res libr
Mem of Massachusetts Libr Syst
Partic in Lyrasis

S CULTURAL SURVIVAL INC, LIBRARY*, 215 Prospect St, 02139. SAN 326-8977. Tel: 617-441-5400. FAX: 617-441-5417. E-mail: culturalsurvival@culturalsurvival.org. Web Site: www.culturalsurvival.org. *Coordr,* Mark Camp; Tel: 617-441-5400, Ext 11, E-mail: mcamp@culturalsurvival.org
Library Holdings: Bk Vols 3,500; Per Subs 100
Subject Interests: Anthrop, Educ, Human rights
Publications: Cultural Survival (Quarterly); Cultural Survival Voices (Newsletter); World Indigenous News
Restriction: Open by appt only

R EPISCOPAL DIVINITY SCHOOL - SHERRILL LIBRARY, 99 Brattle St, 02138. SAN 307-3165. Tel: 617-349-8850. Interlibrary Loan Service Tel: 617-349-8824. Reference Tel: 617-682-1523. FAX: 617-349-8849. E-mail: library@eds.edu. Web Site: www.eds.edu/library. *Sr Asst Dir, Libr Serv,* Aura A Fluet; E-mail: afluet@eds.edu; *Coll Serv Librn,* Anne-Marie Mulligan; E-mail: amulligan@eds.edu. Subject Specialists: *Theol,* Aura A Fluet; *Cataloging,* Anne-Marie Mulligan; Staff 9 (MLS 7, Non-MLS 2)
Founded 1867. Enrl 300; Fac 29; Highest Degree: Doctorate
Library Holdings: Bk Vols 70,000; Per Subs 225
Subject Interests: Biblical studies, Church hist, Contemporary soc, Ethics, Liturgics, Ministry
Automation Activity & Vendor Info: (Acquisitions) Ex Libris Group; (Cataloging) Ex Libris Group; (Circulation) Ex Libris Group; (Course Reserve) Ex Libris Group; (ILL) OCLC WorldShare Interlibrary Loan; (OPAC) Ex Libris Group; (Serials) Ex Libris Group
Database Vendor: 3M Library Systems, CredoReference, ebrary, EBSCO Information Services, EBSCOhost, OCLC FirstSearch, Oxford Online, RefWorks
Wireless access
Function: Archival coll, Audio & video playback equip for onsite use, Computers for patron use, Copy machines, E-Reserves, Electronic databases & coll, ILL available
Mem of Massachusetts Libr Syst
Open Mon-Thurs 8am-10pm, Fri 8am-9pm, Sat 9-6, Sun 1-9

S W R GRACE & CO LIBRARY*, 62 Whittemore Ave, 02140. SAN 307-2991. Tel: 617-498-4595. FAX: 617-864-7198. *Librn,* Jennifer L Umali; Staff 1 (MLS 1)
Founded 1955
Library Holdings: Bk Titles 3,000; Per Subs 125
Subject Interests: Chem, Polymer chem, Rubber chem
Automation Activity & Vendor Info: (Acquisitions) SirsiDynix; (Cataloging) SirsiDynix; (Circulation) SirsiDynix; (OPAC) SirsiDynix; (Serials) SirsiDynix
Database Vendor: Dialog, OCLC FirstSearch, SirsiDynix
Partic in Lyrasis
Restriction: Open by appt only

S GRADIENT*, Information Resource Center, 20 University Ave, 02138. SAN 370-8764. Tel: 617-395-5000. FAX: 617-395-5001. Web Site: www.gradientcorp.com. *Mgr,* Marcia Olson; Tel: 617-395-5562, E-mail: molson@gradientcorp.com; Staff 4 (MLS 3, Non-MLS 1)
Founded 1986
Subject Interests: Environ sci, Risk assessment, Toxicology
Automation Activity & Vendor Info: (OPAC) Inmagic, Inc.
Database Vendor: American Chemical Society, Bloomberg, Dialog, Elsevier, HeinOnline, Infotrieve, OCLC WorldShare Interlibrary Loan, PubMed, ScienceDirect, Scopus
Restriction: Co libr, Employee & client use only, Not open to pub, Staff use only

C HARVARD LIBRARY*, 1341 Massachusetts Ave, Wadsworth House, 02138. SAN 344-8266. Tel: 617-495-3650. Circulation Tel: 617-495-2413. Interlibrary Loan Service Tel: 617-495-2972. Reference Tel: 617-495-2411. FAX: 617-495-0370. Circulation FAX: 617-496-3692. Reference FAX: 617-495-2129. E-mail: Library_Admin@Harvard.edu. Web Site: library.harvard.edu. *VPres,* Sarah Thomas; *Dir,* Robert Darnton; *Assoc Dir,* Dale P Flecker; *Assoc Dir,* Barbara Graham
Founded 1638. Enrl 25,778; Fac 2,520; Highest Degree: Doctorate
Jul 2006-Jun 2007. Mats Exp $147,408,623. Sal $61,027,990
Library Holdings: Bk Vols 15,943,078
Automation Activity & Vendor Info: (Acquisitions) Ex Libris Group; (Cataloging) Ex Libris Group; (Circulation) Ex Libris Group; (Serials) Ex Libris Group
Wireless access
Publications: Harvard Librarian; Harvard Library Bulletin; HUL Notes
Partic in Association of Research Libraries (ARL); Coun of Libr Info Resources; Digital Libr Fedn; Northeast Research Libraries Consortium (NERL); OCLC Online Computer Library Center, Inc; OCLC Research Library Partnership
Special Services for the Deaf - Bks on deafness & sign lang; Spec interest per
Friends of the Library Group

Departmental Libraries:

CR ANDOVER-HARVARD THEOLOGICAL LIBRARY, Divinity School, 45 Francis Ave, 02138, SAN 344-8622. Tel: 617-495-5788. Interlibrary Loan Service Tel: 617-495-7738. Reference Tel: 617-496-2485. Administration Tel: 617-495-5770. FAX: 617-496-4111. Web Site: www.hds.harvard.edu/library. *Archivist, Curator,* Frances O'Donnell; *Coll Mgt,* Russell O Pollard; Staff 7 (MLS 7)
Founded 1816. Enrl 550; Fac 41; Highest Degree: Doctorate
Library Holdings: Bk Vols 485,000; Per Subs 2,000
Special Collections: Religion of Liberal Churches
Partic in Boston Theological Institute Library Program; New England Law Library Consortium, Inc; OCLC Online Computer Library Center, Inc
Open Mon-Thurs 8:30am-11pm, Fri 8:30am-9pm, Sat 9-9, Sun Noon-11

ARNOLD ARBORETUM HORTICULTURAL LIBRARY, 125 Arborway, Jamaica Plain, 02130, SAN 344-8657. Tel: 617-522-1086. FAX: 617-524-1418. E-mail: hortlib@arnarb.harvard.edu. Web Site: arboretum.harvard.edu. *Librn,* Larissa Glasser; *Interim Libr Supvr,* Lisa E Pearson; Staff 2.3 (MLS 2, Non-MLS 0.3)
Founded 1872
Library Holdings: Bk Vols 40,000
Subject Interests: Botany, Dendrology, Garden hist, Hort, Landscape design
Function: Archival coll, Online cat, Online searches, Photocopying/Printing, Pub access computers, Ref & res, Ref serv available, Res libr, Scanner
Open Mon-Sat 10-3:45
Restriction: Circ limited

BAKER LIBRARY, Harvard Business School, Ten Soldiers Field Rd, Boston, 02163, SAN 344-8681. Tel: 617-495-6040. FAX: 617-496-6909. Web Site: www.library.hbs.edu. *Exec Dir,* Deb Wallace; Staff 56 (MLS 27, Non-MLS 29)
Founded 1908. Enrl 1,994; Fac 217; Highest Degree: Doctorate
Library Holdings: Bk Vols 649,142; Per Subs 2,056
Special Collections: Adam Smith (Vanderblue Coll); Business & Economics from 1484 to 1850 (Kress Coll); Credit Reports from 1840's to 1880's (R G Dun & Co Coll); Harvard Business School Archives; Historical Corporate Reports; South Sea Bubble
Partic in RLIN (Research Libraries Information Network)
Publications: Baker Books (Online only); HBS Working Knowledge (Online only)

BELFER CENTER FOR SCIENCE & INTERNATIONAL AFFAIRS LIBRARY, John F Kennedy School of Government, 79 John F Kennedy St, 02138, SAN 345-0600. Tel: 617-495-1408. FAX: 617-495-8963. E-mail: bcsia_library@ksg.harvard.edu. Web Site: belfercenter.ksg.harvard.edu/about/library.html. *Librn,* Anne Cushing Jenkins
Founded 1973
Library Holdings: Bk Vols 4,500; Per Subs 250
Subject Interests: Environ sci, Security
Publications: Aquisitions List
Open Mon-Fri 9-5

BIOCHEMICAL SCIENCES TUTORIAL LIBRARY, Seven Divinity Ave, 02138-2092, SAN 344-9947. Tel: 617-495-4106. FAX: 617-496-6148. E-mail: biochsci@mcb.harvard.edu.
Library Holdings: Bk Vols 946

GEORGE DAVID BIRKHOFF MATHEMATICAL LIBRARY, Science Ctr 337, One Oxford St, 02138, SAN 344-9971. Tel: 617-495-2147. *Head Librn,* Nancy Milller; Staff 1 (Non-MLS 1)
Library Holdings: Bk Vols 13,000; Per Subs 40
Open Mon-Fri 9-5
Restriction: Non-circulating

BLUE HILL METEOROLOGICAL OBSERVATORY LIBRARY, Pierce Hall, 29 Oxford St, 02138, SAN 344-9289. Tel: 617-495-2836. FAX: 617-495-9837. Web Site: library.deas.harvard.edu. *Librn,* Martha F Wooster; *Coll Coordr, Syst Coordr,* Heidi Letko; *Circ,* Gideon Wu; *Doc Delivery, ILL,* Casey Maniscalco; *Pub Serv,* Diane Pochini
Library Holdings: e-journals 364; Bk Vols 115,000; Per Subs 583
Subject Interests: Atmospheric sci, Climatology, Earth sci, Geophysics, Meteorology, Oceanography
Publications: New Acquisitions (Monthly)
Open Mon-Thurs 9am-10pm, Fri 9-6, Sat 10-6, Sun Noon-6

GODFREY LOWELL CABOT SCIENCE LIBRARY, Science Center, One Oxford St, 02138, SAN 344-8355. Tel: 617-495-5353. FAX: 617-495-5324. E-mail: cabref@fas.harvard.edu. Web Site: hcl.harvard.edu/cabot. *Librn,* Lynne M Schmelz; Tel: 617-495-5351; *Circ, Tech Serv,* Allen Bourque; Tel: 617-496-8805; *Coll Develop,* Michael Leach; Tel: 617-495-7091; *Ref,* Elaine Clement; Tel: 617-496-8442
Library Holdings: Bk Vols 400,000
Open Mon-Thurs 8:30am-Midnight; Fri 8:30-6; Sat Noon-10; Sun 10am-Midnight

CENTER FOR HELLENIC STUDIES LIBRARY, 3100 Whitehaven St NW, Washington, 20008. Tel: 202-745-4414. Interlibrary Loan Service Tel: 202-745-4416. FAX: 202-797-1540. E-mail: library@chs.harvard.edu. Web Site: chs.harvard.edu. *Acq, Ref Serv,* Thomas Temple Wright
Founded 1961
Library Holdings: Bk Vols 61,000; Per Subs 300
Subject Interests: Ancient Greek lang & lit, Archaeology, Classical art, Classical hist, Classical Latin lit, Classical philos, Hellenic civilization
Automation Activity & Vendor Info: (ILL) OCLC
Restriction: By permission only, Not open to pub

CHEMISTRY & CHEMICAL BIOLOGY, Department of Chemistry & Chemical Biology, 12 Oxford St, 02138, SAN 344-8770. Tel: 617-495-4076. FAX: 617-495-0788. Web Site: www.chem.harvard.edu/library. *Head Librn,* Marcia L Chapin
Library Holdings: AV Mats 300; Bk Vols 57,000; Per Subs 250
Open Mon-Fri 9-5

CHILD MEMORIAL & ENGLISH TUTORIAL LIBRARY, Widener, Rm Z, 02138, SAN 344-9556. Tel: 617-495-4681. *In Charge,* Eric Idsvoog
Library Holdings: Bk Vols 17,319
Open Mon-Thurs 9am-9:45pm, Fri 9-7
Restriction: Non-circulating

CM FRANCIS A COUNTWAY LIBRARY OF MEDICINE, Boston Med Libr-Harvard Med Libr, Ten Shattuck St, Boston, 02115, SAN 344-8835. Tel: 617-432-4807. Circulation Tel: 617-432-2136. Interlibrary Loan Service Tel: 617-432-2631. Reference Tel: 617-432-2134. Administration Tel: 617-432-2142. Information Services Tel: 617-432-2147. Circulation FAX: 617-432-4739. Interlibrary Loan Service FAX: 617-432-1833. Reference FAX: 617-432-0693. Web Site: www.countway.med.harvard.edu. *Dir,* Isaac Kohane, PhD; E-mail: isaac_kohane@hms.harvard.edu; *Dep Dir,* Alexa T McCray; E-mail: alexa_mccray@hms.harvard.edu; *Libr Operations,* Rebecca Graham; *Access Serv,* David Osterbur; E-mail: david_osterbur@hms.harvard.edu; *Ref Serv,* Paul Bain; E-mail: paul_bain@hms.harvard.edu. Subject Specialists: *Educ,* Paul Bain; Staff 21 (MLS 14, Non-MLS 7)
Founded 1964
Library Holdings: DVDs 23; e-books 177; e-journals 2,247; Bk Titles 246,951; Bk Vols 694,701; Per Subs 2,428
Special Collections: Americana (before 1821), Emphasis on Items Bearing New England Imprints; Chinese & Japanese Medicine, 1650-1850; Dissertations, 1498-; English & Other Foreign Imprints before 1701; Incunabula of Medical Interest (William Norton Bullard Coll); Jewish Medicine (Solomon M Hymans Coll); Legal Medicine; Medical Medals (Horatio Robinson Storer Coll); Medieval & Renaissance Manuscripts of Medical Interest; Oliver Wendell Holmes Coll; Paintings of Boston Physicians; Physicians' Account Books & Case Books, 1729-1850; Spanish Imprints, including Mexico & South America before 1826
Subject Interests: Anatomy, Biochem, Biol, Cytology (study of cells), Dermatology, Genetics, Geriatrics & gerontology, Immunology, Microscopy, Molecular biol, Obstetrics & gynecology, Oncology, Pediatrics, Pharmacology, Physiology, Psychiat, Pub health, Radiology, Statistics
Open Mon-Thurs 8am-11pm, Fri 8-8, Sat Noon-7, Sun Noon-11
Friends of the Library Group

DAVIS CENTER FOR RUSSIAN & EURASIAN STUDIES FUNG LIBRARY, Knafel Bldg, Concourse Level, 1737 Cambridge St, 02138, SAN 344-9408. Tel: 617-496-0485. FAX: 617-496-0091. Web Site: hcl.harvard.edu/libraries/#fung. *Librn,* Hugh K Truslow; E-mail: truslow@fas.harvard.edu
Library Holdings: Bk Vols 20,000; Per Subs 115
Function: Archival coll, CD-ROM, Electronic databases & coll, ILL available, Orientations, Ref & res, VHS videos
Open Mon-Fri 9-5

DEVELOPMENT OFFICE LIBRARY, University Pl, 4th Flr, 124 Mount Auburn St, 02138-5762, SAN 345-0058. Tel: 617-495-9750. FAX: 617-496-9140. *Librn,* Jennifer Beauregard; Staff 1 (MLS 1)
Founded 1964
Library Holdings: Bk Vols 6,000; Per Subs 100
Restriction: Non-circulating, Open by appt only

DUMBARTON OAKS RESEARCH LIBRARY, 1703 32nd St NW, Washington, 20007, SAN 344-886X. Tel: 202-339-6400. FAX: 202-625-0279. Web Site: www.doaks.org. *Dir,* Sheila Klos; *Acq/Ser Librn,* Sarah Pomerantz; *ILL Librn,* Ingrid Gibson; *Rare Bk Librn,* Linda Lott; *Ref/Spec Projects Librn,* Sarah Burke Cahalan; *Head Cataloger,* Sandra Parker Provenzano; *Cataloger,* Kimball Clark; *Res Serv,* Deborah Brown; *Res Serv,* Bridget Gazzo. Subject Specialists: *Byzantine studies,* Deborah Brown; *Pre-Columbian studies,* Bridget Gazzo; Staff 15 (MLS 11, Non-MLS 4)
Founded 1936
Library Holdings: Bk Vols 222,000; Per Subs 1,130
Subject Interests: Byzantine studies, Garden design, Garden hist, Landscape archit, Medieval studies, Pre-Columbian studies
Automation Activity & Vendor Info: (ILL) OCLC; (OPAC) Ex Libris Group
Restriction: By permission only, Not open to pub

FACULTY OF ARTS & SCIENCES OFFICE OF CAREER SERVICES LIBRARY, 54 Dunster St, 02138, SAN 345-0007. Tel: 617-495-2595. FAX: 617-495-3584. Web Site: www.ocs.fas.harvard.edu. *Dir,* Robin Mount
Subject Interests: Career develop
Restriction: Not open to pub

FINE ARTS LIBRARY, Fogg Art Museum, 32 Quincy St, 02138, SAN 344-838X. Tel: 617-495-3374. Reference Tel: 617-496-3592. FAX: 617-496-4889. Web Site: hcl.harvard.edu/libraries/#fal. *Librn,* Katharine Martinez; *Head, Coll,* Amanda Bowen; E-mail: abowen@fas.harvard.edu; *Head, Pub Serv, Head, Res Serv,* Mary Clare Altenhofen; E-mail: altenhof@fas.harvard.edu; *Head, Tech Serv,* Linda Takata; E-mail: ltakata@fas.harvard.edu
Library Holdings: Bk Vols 330,000
Friends of the Library Group

FUNG LIBRARY, 625 Massachusetts Ave, 02139. (Mail add: Coolidge Hall, 1737 Cambridge St, 02138), SAN 345-0120. Tel: 617-495-5753. FAX: 617-495-9976. Web Site: hcl.harvard.edu/libraries/#fung. *Librn,* Nancy Hearst, E-mail: hearst@fas.harvard.edu
Library Holdings: Bk Vols 40,000; Per Subs 200
Subject Interests: Chinese lang, English (Lang)
Open Mon-Fri 9:30-4:30
Restriction: Non-circulating

HAMILTON A R GIBB ISLAMIC SEMINAR LIBRARY, Widener Library, Rm Q, Harvard University, 02138, SAN 344-9580. Tel: 617-495-2437, 617-495-4310. FAX: 617-496-2902. Web Site: lib.harvard.edu/libraries/0038.html. *In Charge,* Wolfhart P Heinrichs; *Librn,* Michael Hopper
Founded 1981
Library Holdings: Bk Vols 7,656

GROSSMAN LIBRARY FOR UNIVERSITY EXTENSION, 311 Sever Hall, Harvard Yard, 02138, SAN 345-0244. Tel: 617-495-4163. FAX: 617-495-9438. E-mail: grossman@dcemail.harvard.edu. Web Site: isites.harvard.edu/icb/icb.do?keyword=k11950. *Librn,* Mary Frances Angelini; Staff 4 (MLS 1, Non-MLS 3)
Founded 1967. Enrl 14,000; Fac 600; Highest Degree: Master
Library Holdings: Bk Vols 5,000
Open Mon-Thurs 10-10, Fri & Sat 10-6, Sun 12-8
Restriction: Non-circulating

GUTMAN LIBRARY-RESEARCH CENTER, Graduate School of Educ, Six Appian Way, 02138, SAN 344-9041. Tel: 617-495-4225. Circulation Tel: 617-495-3423. Reference Tel: 617-495-3421. FAX: 617-495-0540. Web Site: www.gse.harvard.edu/library. *Interim Dir,* Marcella Flaherty; E-mail: marcella_flaherty@gse.harvard.edu; *Head, Libr Syst, Head, Tech Serv,* Joseph Gabriel; E-mail: joe_gabriel@gse.harvard.edu; *Head, Res & Instruction,* Deborah Garson; E-mail: deborah_garson@gse.harvard.edu
Library Holdings: Bk Vols 202,000; Per Subs 1,300
Special Collections: Action for Children's Television Coll; Curriculum Materials; Early American Textbooks; Educational Software; Jeanne Chall Coll; Private School Catalogs; Public School Reports
Subject Interests: Educ
Partic in BRS; Dialog Corp; OCLC Online Computer Library Center, Inc
Open Mon-Thurs 8am-11pm, Fri 8-7, Sat 9-7, Sun 12-9

HARVARD COLLEGE LIBRARY (HEADQUARTERS IN HARRY ELKINS WIDENER MEMORIAL LIBRARY), Widener Library, Rm 110, 02138. Tel: 617-495-2401. Reference Tel: 617-495-2425. FAX: 617-496-4750. Web Site: www.hcl.harvard.edu, www.hcl.harvard.edu/widener. *Assoc Librn, Res, Teaching & Learning, Interim Librn,* Susan M Fliss; *Assoc Librn, Coll Develop,* Dan C Hazen; *Res Librn,* Cheryl LaGuardia; Fax: 617-496-4226, E-mail: claguard@fas.harvard.edu
Library Holdings: Bk Vols 10,000,000
Special Collections: Author Coll: Achebe, Alcott Family, Ariosto, Aristophanes, Bacon, Beerbohm, Blake, Bossuet, Byron, Caldecott, Camoes, Carlyle, Carman, Carroll, Cervantes, Chaucer, Coleridge, Walter Crane, Cruikshank, E E Cummings, Dante, Dickens, Emily Dickinson, Donne, Dryden, T S Eliot, Emerson, Erasmus, Faulkner, Fielding, Galsworthy, John Gay, Goethe, Hearn, Heine, Herbert, Hofmannsthal, Horace, Henry James, William James, Johnson, Kipling, T E Lawrence, Lear, Levi, Longfellow, Amy Lowell, Masefield, Melville, Milton, Moliere, Montaigne, Nabokov, Persius, Petrach, Alexander Pope, Rilke, Rousseau, Schiller, Shakespeare, Shelley, Robert E Sherwood, Soyinka, Steinbeck, Stevenson, Strindberg, Tasso, Thackeray, Trotsky, Updike, Villard Family, Gilbert White, Thomas Wolfe; Farnsworth Recreational Reading Room Coll; Harry Elkins Widener Memorial Coll; John Keats & His Circle Coll; John Keats Coll; Printing & Graphic Arts Coll; The Science Fiction Coll; Theatre Coll; Theodore Roosevelt Coll; Winsor Memorial Map Room Coll; Woodberry Poetry Room Coll. UN Document Depository; US Document Depository
Subject Interests: Am hist, Arabic lang, Art, Canadiana, Cartography, Church hist, Dutch (Lang), Educ, European hist, Folklore, German (Lang), Hist, Hist of sci, Italian (Lang), Judaica (lit or hist of Jews), Latin (Lang), Lit, Local hist, Maps, Mormons, Music, New England, Numismatics, Persian (Lang), Photog, Portuguese (Lang), Quakers, Siam, Slavic hist & lit, Spanish (Lang), Typography, Yiddish (Lang)
Partic in OCLC Online Computer Library Center, Inc; RLIN (Research Libraries Information Network)
Friends of the Library Group

HARVARD FOREST LIBRARY, 324 N Main St, Petersham, 01366, SAN 344-9076. Tel: 978-724-3302. FAX: 978-724-3595. E-mail: hflib@fas.harvard.edu. Web Site: harvardforest.fas.harvard.edu. *Res Asst,* Elaine D Doughty
Founded 1907
Library Holdings: Bk Vols 29,326
Subject Interests: Ecology, Forestry

CL HARVARD LAW SCHOOL LIBRARY, Langdell Hall, 1545 Massachusetts Ave, 02138, SAN 344-919X. Tel: 617-495-3170. Interlibrary Loan Service Tel: 617-495-3176. FAX: 617-495-4449. Web Site: www.law.harvard.edu/library. *Vice Dean, Libr & Info Res,* Jonathan Zittrain; E-mail: zittrain@law.harvard.edu; *Exec Dir,* Suzanne Wones; E-mail: swones@law.harvard.edu; *Assoc Dir, Coll Develop & Digitization,* Kim Dulin; E-mail: kdulin@law.harvard.edu; *Asst Dir, Admin,* Pamela Peifer; E-mail: peifer@law.harvard.edu; Staff 50 (MLS 28, Non-MLS 22)
Founded 1817. Enrl 2,000; Fac 150; Highest Degree: Doctorate
Library Holdings: Bk Titles 723,096; Bk Vols 868,619; Per Subs 49,070
Special Collections: English Common Law (Dunn Coll); French Legal History (Violett Coll); International Law (Olivart Coll); Japanese Law (de Becker Coll)
Partic in Center for Research Libraries; Lyrasis; OCLC Online Computer Library Center, Inc
Open Mon-Thurs 8am-Midnight, Fri 8am-9pm, Sat 9-9, Sun 9am-Midnight

HARVARD-MIT DATA CENTER, CGIS Knafel Bldg, 1737 Cambridge St, 02138, SAN 345-0279. Tel: 617-495-4734. FAX: 617-496-5149. E-mail: support@help.hmdc.harvard.edu. Web Site: www.hmdc.harvard.edu. *Dir,* Gary King
Open Mon-Fri 9-5
Restriction: Open to students, fac & staff

HARVARD-YENCHING LIBRARY, Two Divinity Ave, 02138, SAN 344-8444. Tel: 617-495-2756. FAX: 617-496-6008. Web Site: hcl.harvard.edu/harvard-yenching/. *Head of Libr,* James Cheng; *Head, Access Serv,* Sharon-Lishiuan Yang; *Librn,* Phan Thi Ngoc Chan; *Librn,* Mikyung Kang; *Librn,* Raymond Lum; *Librn,* Xiao-He Ma; *Librn,* Kuniko McVey; *Cat,* James K Lin; *Curator, Rare Bks,* Chun Shum. Subject Specialists: *Vietnamese,* Phan Thi Ngoc Chan; *Korean,* Mikyung Kang; *Western,* Raymond Lum; *Chinese,* Xiao-He Ma; *Japanese,* Kuniko McVey
Library Holdings: Bk Vols 952,000; Per Subs 5,000
Subject Interests: Japanese (Lang), Tibetan (Lang), Vietnam
Publications: Harvard-Yenching Library Bibliographical Services; Harvard-Yenching Library Occasional Reference Notes
Open Mon-Fri 9am-10pm, Sat 9-5, Sun 12-5
Friends of the Library Group

HISTORY DEPARTMENT LIBRARY, Robinson Hall, 02138, SAN 345-0368. Tel: 617-495-2556. FAX: 617-496-3425. E-mail: history@fas.harvard.edu. Web Site: lib.harvard.edu/libraries/0045.html. *In Charge,* Michael McCormick
Library Holdings: Bk Vols 9,623; Per Subs 33
Open Mon-Fri 10-6
Restriction: Non-circulating

HISTORY OF SCIENCE LIBRARY - CABOT SCIENCE LIBRARY, Science Center, One Oxford St, 02138. Tel: 617-495-5355. FAX: 617-495-5324. E-mail: cabref@fas.harvard.edu. Web Site: www.hcl.harvard.edu/cabot. *Head, Circ, Head, Coll Mgt,* Alan Borque; *Head, Coll Develop,* Michael Leach; *Head, Ref & Res Serv,* Ellie Clement; *Head, Tech Serv,* Jindra Miller; *Librn,* Lynne Schmelz; *Ref Librn, Sci Librn,* Reed Lowrie; *ILL, Ref Librn, Sci Librn,* Ann Robinson; *Coordr, Electronic Res,* Kristin Stoklosa
Founded 1973
Library Holdings: Bk Vols 24,312

HOUGHTON LIBRARY-RARE BOOKS & MANUSCRIPTS, Houghton Library, 02138. Tel: 617-495-2441. FAX: 617-495-1376. Web Site: www.hcl.harvard.edu/houghton. *Head Librn,* William P Stoneman; E-mail: stoneman@fas.harvard.edu; *Assoc Librn,* Position Currently Open; *Assoc Librn, Pub Serv,* Rachel Howarth; *Assoc Librn, Tech Serv,* Susan Pyzinski
Library Holdings: AV Mats 50,000; Bk Vols 600,000; Per Subs 200
Open Mon-Fri 9-5, Sat 9-1

JOHN F KENNEDY SCHOOL OF GOVERNMENT LIBRARY, 79 John F Kennedy St, 02138, SAN 344-8924. Tel: 617-495-1300. Reference Tel: 617-495-1302. FAX: 617-495-1972. E-mail: library@hks.harvard.edu. Web Site: www.hks.harvard.edu/library. *Dir & Mgr, Coll & Digital Content,* Leslie Donnell; E-mail: leslie_donnell@harvard.edu; *Asst Mgr,* Timothy Bove; *Res & Instruction Librn,* Luke Gaudreau; *Res & Knowledge Serv Librn,* Valerie Weis; *Res & Instruction Librn,* Keely Wilczek; *Mgr, Res, Instruction & Knowledge Serv,* Heather McMullen; Tel: 617-495-1304, E-mail: heather_mcmullen@ksg.harvard.edu; Staff 5 (MLS 5)
Library Holdings: Bk Vols 60,000; Per Subs 1,500
Subject Interests: Govt, Nonprofit mgt, Pub policy
Open Mon-Thurs 8:30am-11pm, Fri 8:30-7, Sat 9-6, Sun Noon-11

LAMONT LIBRARY-UNDERGRADUATE, Harvard Yard, Harvard University, 02138. Tel: 617-495-2450. Circulation Tel: 617-495-2452. FAX: 617-496-3692. E-mail: lamref@fas.harvard.edu. Web Site: hcl.harvard.edu/libraries/#lamont. *Interim Librn,* Martin Schreiner; E-mail: schrein@fas.harvard.edu; *Head, Access Serv,* Linda Collins; E-mail: lcollins@fas.harvard.edu
Library Holdings: Bk Vols 200,000
Friends of the Library Group

EDA KUHN LOEB MUSIC LIBRARY, Music Bldg, Harvard University, 02138. Tel: 617-495-2794. FAX: 617-496-4636. E-mail: muslib@fas.harvard.edu. Web Site: lib.harvard.edu/mus. *Librn,* Sarah Adams; *Head, Media Presv Serv,* David Ackerman; *Access Serv Librn,* Andrew Wilson; *Rec Librn,* Robert Dennis; *Res Serv Librn,* Liza Vick; *Spec Coll Librn,* Sarah Adams; *Coll Develop,* Sandi-Jo Malmon; *Music & Media Cataloger,* Beth Iseminger; E-mail: biseming@fas.harvard.edu; Staff 20 (MLS 6, Non-MLS 14)
Founded 1956. Enrl 100; Fac 21; Highest Degree: Doctorate
Library Holdings: CDs 60,000; DVDs 1,900; e-journals 110; Electronic Media & Resources 30; Microforms 40,000; Music Scores 200,000; Bk Vols 90,000; Per Subs 1,000; Videos 700
Special Collections: Archive of World Music, sound rec; Isham Memorial Library
Subject Interests: Music
Automation Activity & Vendor Info: (ILL) OCLC; (OPAC) Ex Libris Group
Function: Audio & video playback equip for onsite use, Music CDs, Ref serv available
Special Services for the Deaf - ADA equip
Special Services for the Blind - Aids for in-house use
Open Mon-Thurs 9am-10pm, Fri 9-5, Sat 1-5, Sun 1-10
Restriction: Open to fac, students & qualified researchers

FRANCES LOEB LIBRARY, Harvard Graduate School of Design, 48 Quincy St, Gund Hall, 02138, SAN 344-922X. Tel: 617-495-9163. Web Site: library.harvard.edu/des, www.gsd.harvard.edu/#/loeblibrary/index.html. *Dir,* Ann Whiteside; *Head, Instrul Tech & Libr Info Serv,* Kevin Lau; E-mail: klau@gsd.harvard.edu; *Digital Initiatives Librn,* Alix Reiskind; E-mail: areiskind@gsd.harvard.edu; *Instrul Serv & Res Librn,* Sarah Dickinson; E-mail: sdickenson@gsd.harvard.edu; *Archivist,* Ines Zalduendo; E-mail: izalduendo@gsd.harvard.edu; Staff 7 (MLS 5, Non-MLS 2)
Founded 1900. Enrl 550; Fac 100; Highest Degree: Doctorate
Library Holdings: Bk Vols 282,000; Per Subs 1,650
Special Collections: Le Corbusier Coll; Papers of Charles Eliot II, Daniel Kiley, J C Olmsted, Josep L Luis Sert, Arthur Shurcliff, Hugh Stubbins
Subject Interests: Archit, Landscape archit, Urban planning

GORDON MCKAY LIBRARY, School of Engineering & Applied Sciences, Pierce Hall, 29 Oxford St, 02138, SAN 344-9254. Tel: 617-495-2836. FAX: 617-495-9837. E-mail: library@seas.harvard.edu. Web Site: library.seas.harvard.edu. *Librn,* Martha F Wooster; *Ser,* Heidi Simon; *Tech Serv,* Suzanne Meunier
Library Holdings: Bk Vols 106,241
Special Collections: Division Publications
Subject Interests: Computer sci, Electrical eng, Mechanical eng, Microbiology, Optics, Water res
Partic in OCLC Online Computer Library Center, Inc
Publications: New Acquisitions (Monthly)
Open Mon-Thurs 9am-10pm, Fri 9-6, Sat 10-6, Sun Noon-6

NIEMAN FOUNDATION-BILL KOVACH COLLECTION OF CONTEMPORARY JOURNALISM LIBRARY, One Francis Ave, 02138, SAN 345-0481. Tel: 617-495-2237. FAX: 617-495-8976. E-mail: niemanweb@harvard.edu. Web Site: www.nieman.harvard.edu, www.niemanwatchdog.org.
Library Holdings: AV Mats 1,000; Bk Vols 2,500; Per Subs 30
Special Collections: Financial Files of PM; Herman Obermeyer American Nazi Party Coll; Herman Obermeyer Rape & Sexual Assault Coll; Nieman Alumni Coll; Roland Steel Walter Lippmann Coll
Subject Interests: Journalism
Open Mon-Fri 10-4

MILMAN PARRY COLLECTION OF ORAL LITERATURE, Widener, Rm C, 02138. Tel: 617-496-2499. Web Site: www.chs119.harvard.edu/mpc. *In Charge,* Stephen Mitchell; *Curator,* Gregory Nagy; *Asst Curator,* David Elmer; E-mail: delmer@fas.harvard.edu
Library Holdings: Bk Vols 1,200; Talking Bks 3,700
Restriction: Open by appt only

PHYSICS RESEARCH LIBRARY, 450 Jefferson Laboratory, 17 Oxford St, 02138, SAN 344-9343. Tel: 617-495-2878. FAX: 617-495-0416. E-mail: library@physics.harvard.edu. Web Site: www.physics.harvard.edu/prl/. *Librn,* Marina D Werbeloff; Staff 2 (MLS 1, Non-MLS 1)
Founded 1931. Fac 63; Highest Degree: Doctorate
Library Holdings: Bk Vols 29,340
Restriction: Open to students, fac & staff

ROBBINS LIBRARY OF PHILOSOPHY, Emerson Hall 211, Harvard University, Dept of Philosophy, 25 Quincy St, 02138, SAN 345-0570. Administration Tel: 617-495-2194. FAX: 617-495-2192. Web Site: www.fas.harvard.edu/~phildept/robbins.html. *Librn,* Eric Johnson-DeBaufre; E-mail: ejohnsondebaufre@fas.harvard.edu; Staff 1 (MLS 1)
Founded 1905. Fac 30; Highest Degree: Doctorate

Library Holdings: Bk Vols 10,000; Per Subs 51
Special Collections: Kierkegaard Coll in Danish
Subject Interests: Aesthetics, Analytical philos, Ethics, Hist of philosophy, Logic, Philos of mind, Philos of sci, Pragmatism, Psychol
Function: Copy machines, For res purposes, Online ref, Orientations, Photocopying/Printing, Ref & res, Ref serv available, Telephone ref
Open Mon 12-10, Tues-Thurs 12-8, Fri 12-4
Restriction: Non-circulating, Open to fac, students & qualified researchers, Open to pub for ref only

ARTHUR & ELIZABETH SCHLESINGER LIBRARY ON THE HISTORY OF WOMEN IN AMERICA, Three James St, 02138-3766. (Mail add: Ten Garden St, 02138), SAN 307-3106. Tel: 617-495-8647. FAX: 617-496-8340. E-mail: slref@radcliffe.edu. Web Site: www.radcliffe.edu/schles. *Exec Dir,* Marilyn Dunn; E-mail: mdunn@radcliffe.edu; *Dir,* Nancy F Cott; Tel: 617-495-8263; *Curator,* Marylene Altieri; Tel: 617-495-8651; *Curator,* Kathryn Jacob; Tel: 617-495-8530; *Archivist,* Jane Knowles; Tel: 617-495-8662; *Pub Serv,* Ellen Shea; Tel: 617-495-8549. Subject Specialists: *Manuscripts,* Kathryn Jacob; Staff 28 (MLS 15, Non-MLS 13)
Founded 1943
Library Holdings: Bk Vols 80,000; Per Subs 230; Videos 50
Special Collections: Culinary History; Women's Studies. Oral History
Subject Interests: Women's hist, Women's rights
Partic in OCLC Online Computer Library Center, Inc; RLIN (Research Libraries Information Network)
Publications: 40th Anniversary Report; A Bibliography for Culinary Historians; Annual Newsletters; Innocent Documents; New Viewpoints in Women's History: Working Papers from the Schlesinger Library 50th Anniversary Conference; The Black Women Oral History Project, A Guide to the Transcripts; Women of Courage Exhibition Catalogue
Open Mon-Fri 9-5
Restriction: Non-circulating to the pub
Friends of the Library Group

HERBERT WEIR SMYTH CLASSICAL LIBRARY, Widener, Rm E, 02138. Tel: 617-495-4027. FAX: 617-496-6720. *Librn,* Kathleen Coleman
Library Holdings: Bk Vols 8,000
Open Mon-Thurs 9am-10pm, Fri 9-7, Sat 9-5, Sun 12-8
Restriction: Non-circulating, Restricted access

SOCIAL SCIENCES PROGRAM, Lamont Library, Level B, Harvard University, 02138, SAN 344-8479. Tel: 617-495-2106. FAX: 617-496-5570. Web Site: hcl.harvard.edu/libraries/#ssp. *Head Librn,* Diane Geraci; Tel: 617-496-2532; *Head, Coll Mgt,* Jan Voogd; *Head, Map Coll,* David Cobb; *Head, Numeric Data Serv,* Meghan Dolan; *Environ Res Librn/Govt Info Serv Mgr,* George Clark
Library Holdings: Bk Vols 427,707; Per Subs 894
Special Collections: Manpower & Industrial Relations
Open Mon-Thurs 10-8, Fri 10-6, Sat 12-5, Sun 12-8

STATISTICS LIBRARY, Science Ctr, Rm 300F, One Oxford St, 02138-2901. (Mail add: Science Ctr, Rm 703, One Oxford St, 02138), SAN 345-066X. Tel: 617-496 1402. FAX: 617-496-8057. Web Site: www.stat.harvard.edu.
Highest Degree: Doctorate
Library Holdings: Bk Vols 2,000; Per Subs 19; Spec Interest Per Sub 24
Open Mon-Fri 9-5
Restriction: Circ limited, In-house use for visitors, Internal circ only, Open to fac, students & qualified researchers

TOZZER LIBRARY, 21 Divinity Ave, 02138, SAN 344-8568. Tel: 617-495-1481, 617-495-2253. FAX: 617-496-2741. Web Site: hcl.harvard.edu/tozzer. *Assoc Librn, Pub Serv, Head, Ref,* Gregory A Finnegan; *Cat Librn, Head, Tech Serv,* Isabel Quintana; *Acq Librn,* Lars Klint; *Assoc Librn, Coll,* Janet L Steins; Staff 4 (MLS 4)
Library Holdings: Bk Vols 272,275; Per Subs 1,521
Subject Interests: Anthrop, Archaeology
Automation Activity & Vendor Info: (Course Reserve) Ex Libris Group; (ILL) Ex Libris Group; (OPAC) Ex Libris Group
Database Vendor: OCLC FirstSearch
Publications: Anthropological Literature (Online only)
Open Mon-Thurs 9-9, Fri 9-5, Sat & Sun 1-5

UKRAINIAN RESEARCH INSTITUTE REFERENCE LIBRARY, 34 Kirkland St, 02138, SAN 345-0724. Tel: 617-496-5891. Administration Tel: 617-495-4053. FAX: 617-495-8097. E-mail: huri@fas.harvard.edu. Web Site: www.huri.harvard.edu/. *Bibliographer,* Olha Aleksic; E-mail: oaleksic@fas.harvard.edu. Subject Specialists: *Ukraine,* Olha Aleksic; Staff 2 (MLS 1, Non-MLS 1)
Founded 1973
Library Holdings: Bk Vols 3,500; Per Subs 145
Special Collections: Archives of Ukrainian Cultural Institutions & Ukrainian Civic, Cultural & Political Figures
Subject Interests: Ukraine, Ukrainian diaspora
Function: Ref serv available
Open Mon-Fri 9-5

S HARVARD-SMITHSONIAN CENTER FOR ASTROPHYSICS LIBRARY*, John G Wolbach Library, 60 Garden St, MS-56, 02138. SAN 307-3122. Tel: 617-496-5769. FAX: 617-495-7199. E-mail: library@cfa.harvard.edu. Web Site: www.cfa.harvard.edu/lib. *Adminr,* Amy L Cohen; Tel: 617-496-7808; *Asst Librn, Digital Res Librn,* Position Currently Open; *Head Librn,* Christopher Erdmann; Tel: 617-495-7289, E-mail: cerdmann@cfa.harvard.edu; *Doc Delivery, ILL,* Maria McEachern; Tel: 617-495-7266, E-mail: mmceachern@cfa.harvard.edu; *Tech Serv,* William Graves; Tel: 617-496-7550, E-mail: wgraves@cfa.harvard.edu; Staff 5 (MLS 3, Non-MLS 2)
Founded 1959
Library Holdings: Per Subs 850
Special Collections: Astronomical Institutes Coll: Early Observatory Publications from Around the World; Early Observatory Publications (Al Coll)
Subject Interests: Astronomy, Astrophysics, Space sci
Automation Activity & Vendor Info: (Cataloging) Ex Libris Group; (Circulation) Ex Libris Group; (OPAC) Ex Libris Group; (Serials) Ex Libris Group
Wireless access
Publications: Acquisition List (Quarterly)
Open Mon-Fri 10-4
Restriction: Open to others by appt, Open to students, fac & staff

S INSTITUTE FOR FOREIGN POLICY ANALYSIS, INC*, International Relations Library, 675 Massachusetts Ave, 10th flr, 02139-3396. SAN 325-0067. Tel: 617-492-2116. FAX: 617-492-8242. E-mail: mail@ifpa.org. Web Site: www.ifpa.org. *Pres,* Dr Robert L Paltzgraff
Library Holdings: Bk Titles 1,000; Per Subs 50
Subject Interests: Arms control, Intl relations, Intl security studies, NATO, US Foreign policy
Publications: Foreign Policy Reports, National Security Papers & Conference Reports; Special Reports

C LESLEY UNIVERSITY, Sherrill Library, 89 Brattle St, 02138-2790. (Mail add: 29 Everett St, 02138-2790), SAN 307-3025. Tel: 617-349-8840. Circulation Tel: 617-349-8850. Interlibrary Loan Service Tel: 617-349-8845. Reference Tel: 617-349-8872. FAX: 617-349-8849. E-mail: library@lesley.edu. Web Site: www.lesley.edu/library. *Dir,* Patricia Payne; E-mail: ppayne@lesley.edu; *Assoc Dir,* Constance Vrattos; E-mail: cvrattos@lesley.edu; *Asst Dir,* Katherine Holmes; *Head, Access Serv,* Robyn Ferrero; *Head, Coll Serv,* Lee Sullivan; *Coll Mgt Librn,* Marilyn Geller; *Ref & Instruction Librn,* Dianne Brown; *Ref & Instruction Librn,* Tamar Brown; *Ref & Instruction Librn,* Karen Storz; *Univ Archivist,* Marie Wasnock; Staff 18 (MLS 11, Non-MLS 7)
Founded 1909. Enrl 3,580; Fac 81; Highest Degree: Doctorate
Special Collections: Curriculum Materials; Educational Test
Subject Interests: Art, Educ, Feminism, Psychol, Spec educ, Therapy
Automation Activity & Vendor Info: (Acquisitions) Ex Libris Group; (Cataloging) Ex Libris Group; (Circulation) Ex Libris Group; (Course Reserve) Ex Libris Group; (ILL) OCLC ILLiad; (Media Booking) Dymaxion; (OPAC) Ex Libris Group; (Serials) Ex Libris Group
Wireless access
Partic in Fenway Libraries Online, Inc; Fenway Library Consortium (FLC), Lyrasis; OCLC Online Computer Library Center, Inc
Open Mon-Thurs 8am-10pm, Fri 8-6, Sat 9-6, Sun 11-9

C LONGY SCHOOL OF MUSIC*, Bakalar Library, One Follen St, 02138. SAN 324-2846. Tel: 617-876-0956, Ext 540. Administration Tel: 617-876-0956, Ext 541. FAX: 617-354-8841. Web Site: www.longy.edu/about/library.htm. *Libr Dir,* Roy Rudolph; E-mail: rrudolph@longy.edu; *Circ Supvr,* Catherine Klenov; E-mail: cklenov@longy.edu; Staff 2 (MLS 1, Non-MLS 1)
Founded 1915. Enrl 1,350; Fac 148
Library Holdings: AV Mats 115; CDs 6,600; DVDs 47; Music Scores 11,000; Bk Titles 24,330; Per Subs 30; Videos 69
Special Collections: Baroque Dance (Margaret Daniels-Girard Coll); Nadia Baulanger, E Power Biggs & other 20th Century Longy Faculty (Longy Archives Coll), correspondence, photogs
Subject Interests: Music
Automation Activity & Vendor Info: (Acquisitions) Inmagic, Inc.; (Cataloging) Inmagic, Inc.; (Circulation) Inmagic, Inc.; (Course Reserve) Inmagic, Inc.; (OPAC) Inmagic, Inc.
Database Vendor: JSTOR
Wireless access
Mem of Massachusetts Libr Syst
Partic in Lyrasis
Open Mon-Thurs 9-9, Fri 9-6, Sat 10-5, Sun 1-5
Restriction: Open to students, fac & staff, Use of others with permission of librn

C MASSACHUSETTS INSTITUTE OF TECHNOLOGY LIBRARIES*, Office of the Director, 160 Memorial Dr, 02142. (Mail add: Office of the Director, Bldg 14S-216, 77 Massachusetts Ave, 02139-4307), SAN 345-0783. Tel: 617-253-5651, 617-253-5655. Interlibrary Loan Service Tel:

617-253-5668. Reference Tel: 617-324-2275. FAX: 617-253-8894. Interlibrary Loan Service FAX: 617-253-1690. Web Site: libraries.mit.edu. *Dir of Libr,* Dr Chris Bourg; *Dir, Develop & Communications,* Sharon Stanczak; Tel: 617-452-2123, E-mail: stanczak@mit.edu; *Assoc Dir, Admin Serv,* Keith Glavash; Tel: 617-253-7059, Fax: 617-253-0583, E-mail: kglavash@mit.edu; *Assoc Dir, Coll Serv,* Carol Fleishauer; *Assoc Dir, Info Res,* Diane Geraci; Tel: 617-253-5962, E-mail: dgeraci@mit.edu; *Assoc Dir, Pub Serv,* Steven Gass; Tel: 617-253-7058, E-mail: sgass@mit.edu; *Assoc Dir, Tech,* Position Currently Open; Staff 191 (MLS 96, Non-MLS 95)

Founded 1862. Enrl 9,998; Fac 974; Highest Degree: Doctorate

Library Holdings: AV Mats 31,546; Bk Vols 2,741,944; Per Subs 22,312

Special Collections: 19th Century Glass Manufacture in US (Gaffield Coll); Architecture & Planning, photostats, slides, pamphlets; Charles Bulfinch & Benjamin Latrobe Coll, drawings; Civil Engineering (Baldwin Coll); Early History of Aeronautics (Vail Coll); Early Works in Mathematics & Physics (Louis Derr Coll); Linguistics (Roman Jakobson Coll); Maps; Microscopy, 17th-19th Century (Melville Eastham Coll); Spectroscopy (Kayser Coll). Oral History; UN Document Depository; US Document Depository

Automation Activity & Vendor Info: (Acquisitions) Ex Libris Group

Publications: Bibliotech (Newsletter)

Partic in Association of Research Libraries (ARL); Boston Library Consortium, Inc; BRS; Dialog Corp; Lyrasis; RLIN (Research Libraries Information Network); SDC Search Serv

Departmental Libraries:

BARKER ENGINEERING, Bldg 10-500, 77 Massachusetts Ave, 02139-4307, SAN 345-0937. Tel: 617-253-5663. Circulation Tel: 617-253-5661. Interlibrary Loan Service Tel: 617-253-5668. Reference Tel: 617-324-2275. FAX: 617-258-5623. Interlibrary Loan Service FAX: 617-253-1689. Web Site: www.libraries.mit.edu/barker. *Head Librn,* Tracy Gabridge; Tel: 617-253-8971, E-mail: tag@mit.edu; *Head Librn,* Howard Silver; Tel: 617-253-9319, E-mail: hsilver@mit.edu; *Librn,* Remlee Green; Tel: 617-253-4088, E-mail: remlee@mit.edu; *Librn,* Anne Graham; Tel: 617-253-7744, E-mail: grahama@mit.edu; *Supvr, Access Serv,* Cassandra Fox; Tel: 617-324-6212, E-mail: cassfox@mit.edu; *Eng Librn, Instruction Coordr,* Angela Locknar; Tel: 617-253-9230, E-mail: locknar@mit.edu; *Coll Mgr,* Carol Robinson; Tel: 617-253-7749, E-mail: csrobins@mit.edu; *Info Serv,* Stephanie Hartman; Tel: 617-253-9361, E-mail: hartman@mit.edu; *Tech Serv,* Darcy Duke; Tel: 617-253-9370, E-mail: darcy@mit.edu. Subject Specialists: *Civil eng, Environ eng,* Anne Graham; *Eng, Mat sci,* Angela Locknar; Staff 15 (MLS 8, Non-MLS 7)

Subject Interests: Applied math, Bioeng, Civil, Computer sci, Energy, Eng electrical, Environ, Mechanical, Ocean, Transportation

Function: ILL available, Res libr

DEWEY LIBRARY FOR MANAGEMENT & SOCIAL SCIENCES, MIT Bldg, Rm E53-100, 30 Wadsworth St, 02139. (Mail add: 77 Massachusetts Ave, 02139), SAN 345-0872. Tel: 617-253-5676. Interlibrary Loan Service Tel: 617-253-5668. FAX: 617-253-0642. Interlibrary Loan Service FAX: 617-253-1690. Web Site: www.libraries.mit.edu/dewey. *Head Librn,* michelle Baildon; Staff 6 (MLS 6)

Founded 1938

Special Collections: Historical Corporate Financial Reports; Industrial Relation Historical Documents; OECD Publications; United Nations Historical Documents; World Bank Publications. UN Document Depository; US Document Depository

Subject Interests: Econ, Law, Mgt & finance, Polit sci, Psychol, Sociol

Function: Bus archives, ILL available, Res libr

HUMANITIES, Bldg 14S-200, Hayden Library Bldg, 77 Massachusetts Ave, 02139-4307, SAN 345-0996. Tel: 617-253-5683. Circulation Tel: 617-253-5671. FAX: 617-253-3109. Interlibrary Loan Service FAX: 617-253-1690. Web Site: www.libraries.mit.edu/humanities. *Head Librn,* Theresa A Tobin; Tel: 617-253-5674, E-mail: tat@mit.edu; Staff 28 (MLS 10, Non-MLS 18)

Highest Degree: Doctorate

Subject Interests: Anthrop, Archeology, Educ, Foreign lang, Hist, Hist of sci & tech, Libr & info sci, Linguistics, Lit, Media studies, Philos, Psychol, Relig, Women's & men's studies

Function: ILL available, Res libr

INSTITUTE ARCHIVES & SPECIAL COLLECTIONS, Bldg 14N-118, Hayden Library, 160 Memorial Dr, 02139-4307. (Mail add: Bldg 14N-118, 77 Massachusetts Ave, 02139-4307), SAN 345-102X. Tel: 617-253-5136. FAX: 617-258-7305. E-mail: mithistory@mit.edu. Web Site: libraries.mit.edu/archives. *Archivist, Head of Libr,* Tom Rosko; Tel: 617-253-5688, E-mail: rosko@mit.edu; *Archivist for Coll & Assoc Head,* Elizabeth Andrews; Tel: 617-253-4323; *Archivist for Ref, Outreach & Instruction,* Nora Murphy; Tel: 617-253-8066; Staff 8 (MLS 7, Non-MLS 1)

Founded 1961. Highest Degree: Doctorate

Special Collections: Animal Magnetism, Chemistry, Electricity, Engineering & Other Branches of Science & Technology (Rare Book Coll); Books & Periodicals About or By MIT Alumni, Staff; MIT & Science & Technology in the 19th & 20th Centuries (Archival & Manuscript Colls). Oral History

Function: Archival coll

Restriction: Non-circulating, Open by appt only, Open to researchers by request

LEWIS MUSIC LIBRARY, Bldg 14E-109, 77 Massachusetts Ave, 02139-4307, SAN 345-1054. Tel: 617-253-5689. Interlibrary Loan Service Tel: 617-253-5668. Reference Tel: 617-253-5636. FAX: 617-253-3109. Interlibrary Loan Service FAX: 617-253-1690. Web Site: libraries.mit.edu/music. *Librn,* Peter Munstedt; E-mail: pmunsted@mit.edu; Staff 3 (MLS 1, Non-MLS 2)

Special Collections: Music & Recordings of Composers Associated with MIT

Function: ILL available

Publications: Whats the Score? (Newsletter)

Open Mon-Thurs 8:30am-10pm, Fri 8:30-7, Sat 11-6, Sun 1-10

LINDGREN LIBRARY-EARTH, ATMOSPHERIC & PLANETARY SCIENCES, Bldg 54-200, 77 Massachusetts Ave, 02139-4307, SAN 345-0902. Tel: 617-253-5679. Interlibrary Loan Service Tel: 617-253-5668. Reference Tel: 617-324-2275. FAX: 617-252-1621. Interlibrary Loan Service FAX: 617-253-1690. Web Site: libraries.mit.edu/lindgren. *Librn,* Chris Sherratt; Tel: 617-253-5648, E-mail: gcsherra@mit.edu; Staff 3 (MLS 1, Non-MLS 2)

Founded 1964

Subject Interests: Environment, Geochemistry, Geol, Geophysics, Meteorology, Oceanography, Planetary sci

Function: ILL available, Res libr

Open Mon-Thurs 9-9, Fri 9-6, Sat 11-6, Sun 1-9

ROTCH LIBRARY-ARCHITECTURE & PLANNING, Bldg 7-238, 77 Massachusetts Ave, 02139-4307, SAN 345-0848. Tel: 617-258-5590. Circulation Tel: 617-258-5592. Reference Tel: 617-258-5599. FAX: 617-253-9331. Web Site: libraries.mit.edu/rotch/. *Head of Libr,* Christine Quirion; Tel: 617-258-5594; *Coll Mgr, Pub Serv,* Jennifer Friedman; Tel: 617-258-5595, E-mail: jrfried@mit.edu; *Pub Serv, Ref Coordr,* Heather McCann; Tel: 617-253-7098, E-mail: hmccann@mit.edu; *Circ Supvr,* Kevin Sheehan; Tel: 617-253-1837, E-mail: ksheehan@mit.edu; *Supvr,* Jonah Jenkins; Tel: 617-258-5588, E-mail: jjjenkin@mit.edu

Special Collections: Architecture; Art; Geographic Information Systems; Housing; Islamic Architecture; Real Estate; Regional Planning & Development; Urban Planning

SCIENCE, Bldg 14S-134, 77 Massachusetts Ave, 02139-4307, SAN 345-1089. Tel: 617-253-5685. FAX: 617-253-6365. Web Site: www.libraries.mit.edu/science/index.html. *Head Librn,* Tracy Gabridge; Tel: 617-253-8971, E-mail: tag@mit.edu; *Head Librn,* Howard Silver; Tel: 617-253-9319, E-mail: hsilver@mit.edu; *Librn,* Remlee Green; Tel: 617-253-4088, E-mail: remlee@mit.edu; *Coll Mgr,* Michael Noga; Tel: 617-253-1290, E-mail: mnoga@mit.edu; *Info Serv,* Stephanie Hartman; Tel: 617-253-9361, E-mail: hartman@mit.edu

Subject Interests: Chem eng, Math, Nuclear eng, Physics

Open Mon-Thurs 8am-Midnight, Fri 8am-10pm, Sat 10-10, Sun 10am-Midnight

SCIENCE FICTION SOCIETY LIBRARY, 84 Massachusetts Ave, W20-473, 02139-4307, SAN 324-1149. Tel: 617-258-5126. E-mail: mitsfs@mit.edu. Web Site: www.mit.edu/~mitsfs/. *Pres,* T C Skinner

Founded 1949

Library Holdings: Bk Titles 22,533; Bk Vols 60,000; Per Subs 14

Special Collections: Foreign Language Materials

Subject Interests: Fantasy, Sci fict

Publications: Twilight Zine (Irregularly Published Almost-fanzine)

VISUAL COLLECTIONS, 77 Massachusetts Ave, 7-238, 02139-4307, SAN 345-1143. Tel: 617-253-7087. Web Site: libraries.mit.edu/rotch. *Access Serv Asst,* Rosemary Hanley

Special Collections: Aga Khan Visual Archive; Architecture Studios Student Archive; Kidder Smith Slide Archives: American Architecture

GL MIDDLESEX LAW LIBRARY AT CAMBRIDGE*, Superior Courthouse, 40 Thorndike St, 02141. SAN 307-3068. Tel: 617-494-4148. FAX: 617-225-0026. E-mail: midlawlib@yahoo.com. Web Site: www.lawlib.state.ma.us. *Head Law Librn,* Linda Hom; *Law Librn,* Andrew Montalto; Staff 5 (MLS 2, Non-MLS 3)

Founded 1815

Jul 2005-Jun 2006. Mats Exp $201,000, Books $149,000, Electronic Ref Mat (Incl. Access Fees) $44,500, Presv $7,500

Library Holdings: Bk Titles 4,250; Bk Vols 90,000; Per Subs 500

Special Collections: Massachusetts, United States & Federal Law. State Document Depository

Automation Activity & Vendor Info: (Acquisitions) SirsiDynix; (Cataloging) SirsiDynix; (Circulation) SirsiDynix; (ILL) SirsiDynix; (Serials) SirsiDynix

Mem of Massachusetts Libr Syst

Partic in New England Law Library Consortium, Inc; OCLC Online Computer Library Center, Inc

Open Mon-Fri 8:45-4:45

Friends of the Library Group

M MOUNT AUBURN HOSPITAL*, Tartakoff Library, 330 Mount Auburn St, 02238. SAN 307-3076. Tel: 617-499-5109. FAX: 617-499-5433. *Dir,* M Cherie Haitz; Staff 1 (MLS 1)
Library Holdings: Bk Vols 1,800; Per Subs 120
Special Collections: Classics in Medicine
Subject Interests: Health sci
Database Vendor: EBSCOhost, OVID Technologies, PubMed
Function: Doc delivery serv, ILL available, Photocopying/Printing, Ref serv available
Partic in Boston Biomedical Library Consortium; National Network of Libraries of Medicine
Restriction: Open to pub by appt only

S SCHLUMBERGER-DOLL RESEARCH*, One Hampshire St, 02139. SAN 302-3354. Tel: 617-768-2110. FAX: 617-768-2380. *Mgr, Libr Serv,* Josephine P M Ndinyah; E-mail: jndinyah@slb.com
Founded 1947
Library Holdings: Bk Titles 30,000; Per Subs 130
Subject Interests: Geochemistry, Geophysics, Math, Nuclear sci, Petroleum, Physics
Automation Activity & Vendor Info: (Cataloging) SirsiDynix; (Circulation) SirsiDynix; (ILL) OCLC; (Serials) SirsiDynix
Wireless access
Partic in Lyrasis; OCLC Online Computer Library Center, Inc
Restriction: Staff use only

S TIBETAN BUDDHIST RESOURCE CENTER, INC, 1430 Massachusetts Ave, 5th Flr, 02138. Tel: 617-354-7900. FAX: 617-354-7911. E-mail: info@tbrc.org. Web Site: tbrc.org. *Exec Dir,* Jeff Wallman; Staff 6 (MLS 1, Non-MLS 5)
Founded 1998
Library Holdings: Bk Vols 12,000; Spec Interest Per Sub 40
Special Collections: Tibetan Literature
Function: Ref serv available
Open Mon-Fri 9-6
Restriction: Access at librarian's discretion
Friends of the Library Group

G JOHN A VOLPE NATIONAL TRANSPORTATION SYSTEMS CENTER*, Technical Reference Center Library, 55 Broadway, Bldg 1, 2nd Flr, 02142-1093. SAN 307-3149. Tel: 617-494-2306. Administration Tel: 617-494-2117. FAX: 617-494-3125. E-mail: volpelibrary@dot.gov. Web Site: www.volpe.dot.gov/library/index.html. *Dir,* Susan C Dresley; E-mail: susan.dresley@dot.gov; Staff 3 (MLS 3)
Founded 1970
Library Holdings: Bk Titles 25,000; Bk Vols 32,000; Per Subs 250
Special Collections: Fed Aviation Administration Documents; Motor Vehicle Specifications; Transportation Statistics Documents; Volpe Center Technical Reports
Subject Interests: Aviation, Eng, Transportation
Automation Activity & Vendor Info: (Circulation) Sydney; (OPAC) Sydney; (Serials) Sydney
Database Vendor: Dialog, EBSCOhost, Gale Cengage Learning, Newsbank, OCLC FirstSearch, OVID Technologies
Publications: Conference Newsletter; Published & Presented; Transportation Systems Center Bibliography of Technical Reports; TRC Bulletin (Monthly acquisitions)
Partic in Fedlink; OCLC Online Computer Library Center, Inc
Restriction: Open to pub by appt only

M WHITEHEAD INSTITUTE FOR BIOMEDICAL RESEARCH*, Elizabeth Augustus Whitehead Library, Nine Cambridge Ctr, 02142. SAN 377-9076. Tel: 617-258-5132. FAX: 617-324-0266. Web Site: web.wi.mit.edu/library. *Mgr, Libr Serv,* David Richardson; E-mail: richardson@wi.mit.edu
Founded 1984
Library Holdings: Bk Titles 300; Per Subs 100
Wireless access
Partic in National Network of Libraries of Medicine New England Region
Open Mon-Fri 9-6

CANTON

S CANTON HISTORICAL SOCIETY LIBRARY*, 1400 Washington St, 02021. SAN 375-2615. Tel: 781-828-8537. E-mail: historical@canton.org. Web Site: www.canton.org. *Pres,* James Roache
Founded 1893
Library Holdings: Bk Vols 500
Restriction: Open by appt only

P CANTON PUBLIC LIBRARY*, 786 Washington St, 02021-3029. SAN 307-3173. Tel: 781-821-5027. FAX: 781-821-5029. Interlibrary Loan Service FAX: 781-821-5028. E-mail: caill@ocln.org. Web Site: www.town.canton.ma.us/library. *Dir,* Mark Lague; *Asst Librn,* Lisa Quinn; *Ch Serv,* Ann Woodman; *Circ,* Ilene Kramer; *Ref,* Patty Ryburn; Staff 6 (MLS 6)
Founded 1902. Pop 21,306; Circ 230,136
Library Holdings: AV Mats 6,422; Electronic Media & Resources 388; Bk Vols 98,770; Per Subs 147
Special Collections: Municipal Document Depository
Subject Interests: Art & archit
Automation Activity & Vendor Info: (Cataloging) SirsiDynix; (Circulation) SirsiDynix; (OPAC) SirsiDynix
Function: Audio & video playback equip for onsite use, Handicapped accessible, Homebound delivery serv, Prog for children & young adult
Partic in Old Colony Libr Network (OCLN)
Open Mon 1-9, Tues-Thurs 10-9, Fri & Sat 10-5:30
Friends of the Library Group

M MASSACHUSETTS HOSPITAL SCHOOL*, Dr Paul L Norton Medical Library, Three Randolph St, 02021. SAN 326-1085. Tel: 781-830-8441. FAX: 781-830-8498. *Librn,* Helen McCormick
Library Holdings: Bk Titles 500
Partic in Southeastern Massachusetts Consortium of Health Science Libraries
Restriction: Non-circulating to the pub

CARLISLE

P GLEASON PUBLIC LIBRARY, 22 Bedford Rd, 01741-1857. SAN 307-3181. Tel: 978-369-4898. FAX: 978-371-1268. E-mail: mca@mvlc.org. Web Site: www.gleasonlibrary.org. *Dir,* Katie Huffman; E-mail: khuffman@mvlc.org; *Asst Dir,* Marty Seneta
Founded 1872. Pop 4,828; Circ 134,121
Library Holdings: AV Mats 5,066; Bk Vols 42,847; Per Subs 187
Special Collections: Local History (Wilkins Coll)
Automation Activity & Vendor Info: (Cataloging) Evergreen; (Circulation) Evergreen; (OPAC) Evergreen
Wireless access
Function: Ref serv available
Mem of Massachusetts Libr Syst
Partic in Merrimack Valley Library Consortium
Open Mon, Tues & Thurs 10-9, Wed 1-9, Fri 10-5, Sat (Sept-Jun) 10-5; Sat (July-Aug) 10-1
Friends of the Library Group

CARVER

P CARVER PUBLIC LIBRARY*, Two Meadowbrook Way, 02330-1278. SAN 307-319X. Tel: 508-866-3415. FAX: 508-866-3416. Web Site: www.carverpl.org. *Dir,* Carole A Julius; E-mail: cjulius@carverpl.org; *Head, Circ,* Patricia Martin; E-mail: pmartin@sailsinc.org; *Ch Serv,* Melissa MacLeod; E-mail: mmacleod@sailsinc.org; *Ref,* Amy Sheperdson; E-mail: asheperd@sailsinc.org; Staff 10 (MLS 2, Non-MLS 8)
Founded 1895. Pop 11,500; Circ 80,000
Library Holdings: Large Print Bks 300; Bk Vols 54,000; Per Subs 100; Talking Bks 300
Special Collections: Local Genealogy
Automation Activity & Vendor Info: (Acquisitions) SirsiDynix; (Cataloging) SirsiDynix; (Circulation) SirsiDynix; (Course Reserve) SirsiDynix; (ILL) SirsiDynix; (Media Booking) SirsiDynix; (OPAC) SirsiDynix; (Serials) SirsiDynix
Partic in SAILS Library Network
Open Mon & Wed 10-6, Tues & Thurs 10-8, Fri & Sat 10-4
Friends of the Library Group

CENTERVILLE

P CENTERVILLE PUBLIC LIBRARY ASSOCIATION, INC*, 585 Main St, 02632. SAN 307-3203. Tel: 508-790-6220. FAX: 508-790-6218. Web Site: www.centervillelibrary.org. *Dir,* Elizabeth M Butler; *Asst Libr Dir,* Jacqueline Dager; *Youth Serv Dir,* Penelope Terkelsen
Circ 49,937
Library Holdings: Bk Vols 32,000; Per Subs 75
Special Collections: Walter Lippmann Coll, non-fiction bks
Automation Activity & Vendor Info: (Cataloging) Innovative Interfaces, Inc; (Circulation) Innovative Interfaces, Inc; (OPAC) Innovative Interfaces, Inc
Partic in Cape Libraries Automated Materials Sharing Network
Open Mon, Wed & Fri 9:30-5, Tues & Thurs 9:30-7, Sat 10-2
Friends of the Library Group

CHARLEMONT

P TYLER MEMORIAL LIBRARY*, Town Hall, 157 Main St, 01339-9703. (Mail add: PO Box 518, 01339-0518), SAN 307-3211. Tel: 413-339-0301. FAX: 413-339-0320. *Librn,* Bambi Miller
Pop 1,250; Circ 12,274
Library Holdings: Bk Vols 9,700; Per Subs 12

Special Collections: Local History Coll
Open Tues 5:30-8, Thurs 1-5, Sat 9-12:30

CHARLESTOWN

S CHARLESTOWN BOYS & GIRLS CLUB*, Charles Hayden Memorial Library, 15 Green St, 02129. SAN 307-1448. Tel: 617-242-1775. FAX: 617-241-3847. Web Site: www.bgcb.org. *Dir,* Jenny Atkinson
Founded 1893
Library Holdings: Bk Vols 8,000; Per Subs 15
Open Mon-Fri 1-6
Restriction: Mem only

M SPAULDING REHABILITATION HOSPITAL*, Dr Walter R Frontera Medical Library, 300 First Ave, Rm 1262, 02129. Tel: 617-952-5171. Information Services Tel: 617-952-5000. FAX: 617-952-5932. E-mail: srhmedlib@partners.org. Web Site: www.spauldingrehab.org/education/medical-libraries-and-resources.aspx. *In Charge,* John Solomon
Library Holdings: Bk Vols 1,100; Per Subs 35
Wireless access
Open Mon-Fri 9-5:30
Restriction: Non-circulating to the pub

CHARLTON

P CHARLTON PUBLIC LIBRARY*, 40 Main St, 01507. SAN 307-322X. Tel: 508-248-0452. FAX: 508-248-0456. Web Site: www.charltonlibrary.org. *Dir,* Cheryl Hansen; E-mail: chansen@cwmars.org; *Asst Dir, Head, Youth Serv,* Molly Johnson; E-mail: mjohnson@cwmars.org; *Head, Circ/ILL,* Marie Beesley; *Head, Tech Serv,* Kathryn Webber
Founded 1905. Pop 11,400; Circ 100,000
Library Holdings: Bk Vols 40,000; Per Subs 100
Automation Activity & Vendor Info: (Cataloging) Innovative Interfaces, Inc - Millenium; (Circulation) Innovative Interfaces, Inc - Millenium
Wireless access
Mem of Massachusetts Libr Syst
Partic in Central-Western Mass Automated Resource Sharing
Open Mon & Wed 9:30-5, Tues & Thurs 9:30-8, Sat 9:30-3
Friends of the Library Group

CHATHAM

P ELDREDGE PUBLIC LIBRARY*, 564 Main St, 02633-2296. SAN 307-3238. Tel: 508-945-5170. FAX: 508-945-5173. Web Site: www.eldredgelibrary.org. *Dir,* Irene B Gillies; E-mail: igillies@clamsnet.org; Staff 4 (MLS 3, Non-MLS 1)
Founded 1895. Pop 6,700; Circ 163,000
Jul 2009-Jun 2010 Income $689,357. Mats Exp $81,989. Sal $483,730
Library Holdings: Audiobooks 4,468; DVDs 3,902; e-books 562; Electronic Media & Resources 194; Microforms 123; Bk Titles 48,338; Per Subs 126
Special Collections: Genealogy (Edgar Francis Waterman Coll)
Database Vendor: Innovative Interfaces, Inc
Wireless access
Mem of Massachusetts Libr Syst
Partic in Cape Libraries Automated Materials Sharing Network
Special Services for the Deaf - Assistive tech
Special Services for the Blind - Closed circuit TV magnifier; Copier with enlargement capabilities; Home delivery serv; Large print bks; Lending of low vision aids; Playaways (bks on MP3); Recorded bks; Text reader; ZoomText magnification & reading software
Open Mon, Wed, Fri & Sat 10-5, Tues & Thurs 1-9
Friends of the Library Group

CHELMSFORD

P CHELMSFORD PUBLIC LIBRARY*, 25 Boston Rd, 01824-3088. SAN 345-1208. Tel: 978-256-5521. FAX: 978-256-8511. Web Site: www.chelmsfordlibrary.org. *Dir,* Becky Herrmann; *Asst Libr Dir,* Christopher Kupec; *Asst Dir, Tech,* Barbara Morrison; *Head, Ch,* Maureen Foley; *Head, Circ,* Linda Robinson; *Head, Ref,* Brian Herzog; *Head, Tech Serv,* Vickie Turcotte; *Head, YA,* Roberta Barricelli; *Commun Relations Librn,* Kathy Cryan-Hicks; *ILL,* Linda Webb; Staff 23 (MLS 6, Non-MLS 17)
Founded 1894. Pop 32,383; Circ 380,313
Library Holdings: Bk Titles 111,244; Bk Vols 117,885; Per Subs 238
Subject Interests: Local hist
Automation Activity & Vendor Info: (Cataloging) Horizon; (Circulation) Horizon; (OPAC) Horizon
Database Vendor: Booksite, College Source, EBSCOhost, Gale Cengage Learning, Grolier Online, LearningExpress, Marquis Who's Who, Newsbank, Overdrive, Inc, ProQuest, ReferenceUSA, SirsiDynix, ValueLine
Wireless access
Publications: Handbook of Chelmsford Organizations; Library Lines (Newsletter); Poetry: Community Connections
Partic in Merrimack Valley Library Consortium
Friends of the Library Group
Branches: 1
MACKAY, 43 Newfield St, North Chelmsford, 01863-1799, SAN 345-1232. Tel: 978-251-3212. FAX: 978-251-8782. Web Site: www.chelmsfordlibrary.org/mackay/index.html. *Ch Serv,* Bonnie Rankin
Library Holdings: Bk Vols 30,000; Per Subs 60
Open Mon & Wed 10-8, Fri 10-5, Sat 10-3
Friends of the Library Group

CHELSEA

P CHELSEA PUBLIC LIBRARY*, 569 Broadway, 02150-2991. SAN 307-3254. Tel: 617-466-4350. Administration Tel: 617-466-4355. FAX: 617-466-4359. E-mail: coclibrary@chelseama.gov. Web Site: www.chelseama.gov. *Dir,* Robert E Collins; *Cat,* George Athas; *Ch Serv,* Dennis Cooper; *ILL,* Draica Ivanis; *Ref,* Adelaide Sexton; Staff 4 (MLS 1, Non-MLS 3)
Founded 1870. Pop 35,100; Circ 61,000
Library Holdings: AV Mats 6,000; Large Print Bks 1,000; Bk Titles 74,000; Bk Vols 75,000; Per Subs 75
Subject Interests: Local hist archives, Spanish
Automation Activity & Vendor Info: (Acquisitions) SirsiDynix; (Cataloging) SirsiDynix; (Circulation) SirsiDynix; (OPAC) SirsiDynix; (Serials) SirsiDynix
Partic in Metro Boston Libr Network
Open Mon & Tues 9-9, Wed & Thurs 9-8, Fri 9-Noon
Friends of the Library Group

G MASSACHUSETTS WATER RESOURCES AUTHORITY LIBRARY*, Two Griffin Way, 02150. (Mail add: 100 First Ave, Boston, 02129), SAN 371-7682. Tel: 617-305-5584. FAX: 617-371-1610. E-mail: mwralib@mwra.state.ma.us. Web Site: www.mwra.state.ma.us. *Librn,* Mary Lydon; Staff 3 (MLS 1, Non-MLS 2)
Founded 1986
Library Holdings: Bk Titles 4,000; Bk Vols 5,000; Per Subs 75
Special Collections: Massachusetts Water Resources Authority Publications
Publications: Information Services (Quarterly)

CHESHIRE

P CHESHIRE PUBLIC LIBRARY*, 23 Depot St, 01225. (Mail add: PO Box 740, 01225-0740), SAN 307-3262. Tel: 413-743-4746. E-mail: cheshire@cwmars.org. Web Site: cheshirepubliclibrary.wordpress.com. *Dir,* Katharine Westwood; Staff 1 (MLS 1)
Pop 3,418; Circ 15,000
Library Holdings: Bk Vols 7,000; Per Subs 30
Wireless access
Partic in Central-Western Mass Automated Resource Sharing

CHESTER

P HAMILTON MEMORIAL LIBRARY*, 195 Rte 20, 01011-9648. (Mail add: 15 Middlefield Rd, 01011), SAN 307-3270. Tel: 413-354-7808. E-mail: chesterlibrary@gmail.com. *Librn,* Gale LaScala
Pop 1,114; Circ 5,269
Library Holdings: Bk Vols 6,000; Per Subs 22
Open Mon & Fri 2-8, Wed 6-8
Friends of the Library Group

CHESTERFIELD

P CHESTERFIELD PUBLIC LIBRARY*, 408 Main Rd, 01012-9708. (Mail add: PO Box 305, 01012-0305), SAN 307-3289. Tel: 413-296-4735. E-mail: chesterfieldpubliclibrary@gmail.com. *Dir,* Cynthia Squier-Klein
Pop 1,138; Circ 9,757
Library Holdings: Bk Vols 6,154; Per Subs 20
Special Collections: Hampshire County & Chesterfield
Subject Interests: Local hist
Wireless access
Open Mon 2-7, Wed 10-4, Sat 9-1
Friends of the Library Group

CHESTNUT HILL

C BOSTON COLLEGE LIBRARIES, 140 Commonwealth Ave, 02467. SAN 345-1267. Circulation Tel: 617-552-8038. Interlibrary Loan Service Tel: 617-552-3209. Reference Tel: 617-552-4472. Administration Tel: 617-552-4470. Interlibrary Loan Service FAX: 617-552-2600. Administration FAX: 617-552-0599. Web Site: www.bc.edu/libraries. *Univ Librn,* Thomas Wall; E-mail: thomas.wall.2@bc.edu; *Assoc Univ Librn, Coll & Admin Serv,* Christine Conroy; Tel: 617-552-1942, E-mail: christine.conroy@bc.edu; *Assoc Univ Librn, Digital Initiatives & Serv,*

Position Currently Open; *Assoc Univ Librn, Pub Serv,* Scott Britton; Tel: 617-552-3155, E-mail: scott.britton@bc.edu; Staff 141 (MLS 72, Non-MLS 69)
Founded 1863. Enrl 13,214; Fac 814; Highest Degree: Doctorate
Jun 2012-May 2013. Mats Exp $11,697,021. Sal $9,563,101 (Prof $5,949,244)
Library Holdings: e-books 494,112; Bk Titles 2,191,660; Bk Vols 3,072,624
Special Collections: Balkan Studies; Bookbuilders of Boston Archives, 1938-; Boston History; British Catholic Authors; Caribbeana; Catholic Liturgy & Life in America, 1925-1975; Eire Society of Boston Archives; Flann O'Brien Papers; Francis Thomson Coll, 1859-1907; Gilbert Keith Chesterton Coll, 1874-1936; Graham Greene Library & Archive; Hillaire Belloc Coll & Archives; Irish Coll; Irish Music Center; Jane Jacobs Coll; Jesuitana Coll, 1540-1773; Rex Stout Coll & Archives; S J Papers; Samuel Beckett Coll; Seamus Heaney Coll; The Honorable Margaret Heckler Papers; The Reverend Robert F Drinan; Theodore Dreiser Coll; Thomas Merton Coll; William Butler Yeats Coll. US Document Depository
Automation Activity & Vendor Info: (Acquisitions) Ex Libris Group; (Cataloging) Ex Libris Group; (Circulation) Ex Libris Group; (Course Reserve) Ex Libris Group; (ILL) OCLC ILLiad; (OPAC) Ex Libris Group; (Serials) Ex Libris Group
Wireless access
Partic in Boston Library Consortium, Inc; Greater NE Regional Med Libr Program; Northeast Research Libraries Consortium (NERL)

Departmental Libraries:

BAPST ART LIBRARY, 140 Commonwealth Ave, 02467-3810, SAN 323-5297. Tel: 617-552-3200. E-mail: bapst@bc.edu. Web Site: www.bc.edu//libraries/collections/bapst.html. *Librn,* Adeane Bregman; Tel: 617-552-3136, E-mail: adeane.bregman@bc.edu
Open Mon-Thurs 8am-Midnight, Fri 8-5, Sat 10-6, Sun 11am-Midnight

JOHN J BURNS LIBRARY OF RARE BOOKS & SPECIAL COLLECTIONS, 140 Commonwealth Ave, 02467. Tel: 617-552-3282. FAX: 617-552-2465. E-mail: burns.reference@bc.edu. Web Site: www.bc.edu//libraries/collections/burns.html. *Burns Librn & Assoc Univ Librn, Spec Coll,* Christian Dupont; Tel: 617-552-8297, E-mail: christian.dupont@bc.edu; *Sr Ref Librn,* Justine Sundaram; Tel: 617-552-4832, E-mail: justine.sundaram@bc.edu; *Head Archivist,* Amy Braitsch; Tel: 617-552-3249, E-mail: amy.braitsch@bc.edu; *Sr Cataloger,* David Richtmyer; Tel: 617-552-0543, E-mail: david.richtmyer@bc.edu
Special Collections: Balkan Coll; British Catholic Authors Coll; Burns & Oates Coll; Congregationalism (1629-1829); Congressional Archives (Edward P Boland, Robert F Drinan, Margaret Heckler, Thomas P O'Neill Jr); Coventry Kersy Dighton Patmore (1823-1896); David Jones (1895-1973); DeFacto School Segregation; Detective Fiction Coll; Eire Society of Boston; Ethnology; Evelyn Waugh (1903-1966); Fallon Funeral Home; Fatherless Children of France (WW I); Fine Print Coll; Flann O'Brien Papers; Folklore, Jamaica & West Africa; Foulis Press; Freemasons; Golden Cockerel Press; Graham Greene (1904); Graham Greene Coll; Hibernia Bank; Hilaire Belloc Coll; Irish Authors; Irish Coll (Samuel Becket, William Butler Yeats, Seamus Heaney); Irish Land League; Irish Literature; Irish Music Center, Jamaica; Japanese Prints; Jesuitana Coll; John Henry Newman (1801-1890); Judaica; Liturgy & Life Coll; Nativism; Nero Wolfe Attractions; New England Theology; Nicholas M Williams Ethnological Coll; Nicholas M Williams Ethnological Coll; Nonesuch Press (London); Nursing; Oriole Press; Peppercannister Press; Playbills; Publishers & Publishing; Rare Books; Rita P Kelleher Nursing Coll; Salem Divines Coll; Samuel Beckett; St Dominic's Press; St Vincent DePaul Society; Stanbrook Abbey Press; Theater Programs; Thomas P O'Neill Jr Papers; Type Designers; Union Warren Savings Bank Archives; US Congressional Archives; Viola (Dallyn) Meynell (1886-1956); West Indies; William Butler Yeats (1865-1939); Women's History (Janet Wilson James Coll); World War I & II
Subject Interests: Catholic Church, Jesuit, Manuscripts, Medieval mss, Nursing
Publications: Art of the Book (Collection catalog); Catalogue of Books, Manuscripts, etc in the Caribbeana Section of the Nicholas M Williams Memorial Ethnological Collection; Jesuitana at Boston College
Open Mon, Tues, Thurs & Fri 9-5, Wed 9-8, Sat 10-2
Restriction: Non-circulating

EDUCATIONAL RESOURCE CENTER, 140 Commonwealth Ave, 02467, SAN 323-5319. Tel: 617-552-4920. FAX: 617-552-1769. E-mail: erc@bc.edu. Web Site: www.bc.edu/libraries/collections/erc.html. *Head Librn,* Margaret Cohen; Tel: 617-552-4919, E-mail: margaret.cohen@bc.edu; *Sr Cataloger,* Trina Soderquist; Tel: 617-552-4619, E-mail: trina.soderquist@bc.edu. Subject Specialists: *Educ K-12,* Margaret Cohen
Subject Interests: Educ K-12, Psychol
Open Mon-Thurs 9am-10pm, Fri 9-5, Sat Noon-5, Sun Noon-8

CATHERINE B O'CONNOR LIBRARY, Weston Observatory, 381 Concord Rd, Weston, 02193-1340, SAN 307-7934. Tel: 617-552-8321. FAX: 617-552-8388. Web Site: www.bc.edu/libraries/collections/weston.html. *Sr Res Librn,* Enid Karr; Tel: 617-552-4477, E-mail: enid.karr@bc.edu; Staff 1 (Non-MLS 1)
Founded 1946
Subject Interests: Geol, Geophysics
Function: Res libr
Restriction: Open to fac, students & qualified researchers, Open to pub by appt only

CR THOMAS P O'NEILL JR LIBRARY (CENTRAL LIBRARY), 140 Commonwealth Ave, 02467. Circulation Tel: 617-552-8038. Interlibrary Loan Service Tel: 617-552-3209. Administration Tel: 617-552-4470. Interlibrary Loan Service FAX: 617-552-2600. Administration FAX: 617-552-0599. *Head, Access Serv,* Connie Strittmatter; Tel: 617-552-4834, E-mail: connie.strittmatter@bc.edu; *Head, Coll Develop & Res,* Jonas Barciauskas; Tel: 617-552-4447, E-mail: jonas.barciauskas.1@bc.edu; *Head, Continuing & E-Res,* Young Moon; Tel: 617-552-3207, E-mail: young.moon@bc.edu; *Head, Digital Libr Prog,* Betsy Post; Tel: 617-552-1989, E-mail: betsy.post@bc.edu; *Head, Libr Syst & Applications,* Kevin Kidd; Tel: 617-552-1359, E-mail: kevin.kidd@bc.edu; *Head, Metadata Serv,* Kelly Webster; Tel: 617-552-0164, E-mail: kelly.webster@bc.edu; *Head, Outreach & Digital Res,* Este Pope; Tel: 617-552-2081, E-mail: este.pope@bc.edu; *Head Scholarly Communication & Res,* Jane Morris; Tel: 617-552-4481, E-mail: jane.morris@bc.edu; *ILL Mgr,* Anne Kenny; Tel: 617-552-6937, E-mail: ann.kenny.1@bc.edu

SOCIAL WORK LIBRARY, McGuinn Hall 038, 140 Commonwealth Ave, 02467-3810, SAN 345-147X. Tel: 617-552-3233. Circulation Tel: 617-552-0109. FAX: 617-552-3199. Web Site: www.bc.edu/libraries/collections/socialwork.html. *Head Librn,* Hannah Ha; Tel: 617-552-3234, E-mail: hannah.ha@bc.edu; *Sr Ref Librn,* Kate Silfen; Tel: 617-552-0792, E-mail: kate.silfen@bc.edu
Subject Interests: Child welfare, Geriatrics & gerontology
Open Mon-Thurs 8am-10pm, Fri 8-5, Sat 10-6, Sun 1-9

THEOLOGY & MINISTRY LIBRARY, 117 Lake St, Brighton, 02135. Tel: 617-552-0549. FAX: 617-552-6549. Web Site: www.bc.edu//libraries/collections/theology.html. *Head Librn,* Esther Griswold; Tel: 617-552-6540, E-mail: esther.griswold@bc.edu; *Coll Develop/Ref Librn,* Stephen Dalton; Tel: 617-552-6541, E-mail: stephen.dalton@bc.edu

SR CONGREGATION MISHKAN TEFILA*, Harry & Anna Feinberg Library, 300 Hammond Pond Pkwy, 02167. SAN 326-033X. Tel: 617-332-7770. FAX: 617-332-2871. E-mail: librarian@mishkantefila.org. *Librn,* Barbara Mende; Staff 1 (MLS 1)
Library Holdings: Bk Vols 5,000; Per Subs 10
Mem of Massachusetts Libr Syst
Special Services for the Deaf - Accessible learning ctr

S LONGYEAR MUSEUM LIBRARY, 1125 Boylston St, 02467. SAN 370-1506. Tel: 617-278-9000. Interlibrary Loan Service Tel: 617-278-9000, Ext 350. Toll Free Tel: 800-277-8943. FAX: 617-278-9003. E-mail: administrator@longyear.org. Web Site: www.longyear.org. *Exec Dir,* Sandra J Houston; *Mgr, Mus Coll,* Laurie Coleman
Library Holdings: Bk Vols 6,000
Special Collections: History of Christian Science 1821-1910; Life of Mary Baker Eddy & Her Early Followers, diaries, journals, letters, logbks, photog
Subject Interests: Christian sci
Database Vendor: ProQuest
Wireless access
Open Mon & Wed-Sat 10-4, Sun 1-4
Restriction: Non-circulating

C PINE MANOR COLLEGE*, Annenberg Library & Communications Center, 400 Heath St, 02467. SAN 307-3297. Tel: 617-731-7081. FAX: 617-731-7045. Web Site: www.pmc.edu/library. *Actg Dir, Head, Ref,* Sarah Woolf; Tel: 617-731-7080, E-mail: woolfsar@pmc.edu; *Cataloger, Ref,* Panit Satyasai-Crimmin; Tel: 617-731-7082, E-mail: satyasaipanit@pmc.edu; *Circ, ILL & Ser,* Corinne Griffiths; E-mail: griffithcorinne@pmc.edu; Staff 8 (MLS 5, Non-MLS 3)
Founded 1911. Enrl 400; Fac 59; Highest Degree: Bachelor
Library Holdings: Bk Titles 55,967; Bk Vols 63,000; Per Subs 250
Special Collections: First Editions of Noted American Women Authors
Subject Interests: Educ, Psychol
Automation Activity & Vendor Info: (Acquisitions) SirsiDynix; (Cataloging) SirsiDynix; (Circulation) SirsiDynix; (Course Reserve) SirsiDynix; (OPAC) SirsiDynix; (Serials) SirsiDynix
Mem of Massachusetts Libr Syst
Partic in Lyrasis; OCLC Online Computer Library Center, Inc; Webnet
Open Mon-Thurs 8am-10pm, Fri 8-5, Sat & Sun 1-5

CHICOPEE

P CHICOPEE PUBLIC LIBRARY*, 449 Front St, 01013. SAN 345-150X. Tel: 413-594-1800. FAX: 413-594-1819. E-mail: cpl@chicopeepubliclibrary.org. Web Site: www.chicopeepubliclibrary.org. *Dir,* Nancy M Contois; E-mail: ncontois@cwmars.org; *Asst Dir,* Mary Jane Trybulski; E-mail: mtrybuls@cwmars.org; *Sr Ref Librn,* Carol Lynne

Bagley; Tel: 413-594-1800, Ext 125, E-mail: cbagley@cwmars.org; *Electronic Ref Librn,* Amber Clooney; Tel: 413-594-1800, Ext 114, E-mail: aclooney@chicopeelibrary.org; *Syst Librn,* Diane Robillard; E-mail: drobilla@cwmars.org; *Youth Serv Coordr,* Diane Ramsay; Tel: 413-594-1800, Ext 120, E-mail: dramsay@cwmars.org; *Acq,* Maureen Geoffrey; *Cat,* Eileen Cullinan; E-mail: ecullina@cwmars.org; *Commun Serv,* Anne Gancarz; E-mail: agancarz@cwmars.org; Staff 41 (MLS 8, Non-MLS 33)
Founded 1853. Pop 55,000; Circ 431,806
Jul 2011-Jun 2012 Income (Main Library and Branch(s)) $1,517,442. Mats Exp $183,112. Sal $1,182,854
Library Holdings: AV Mats 15,346; Bk Vols 89,827; Per Subs 211
Subject Interests: Local hist, Polish (Lang)
Automation Activity & Vendor Info: (Acquisitions) Evergreen; (Cataloging) Evergreen; (Circulation) Evergreen; (OPAC) Evergreen; (Serials) Evergreen
Wireless access
Function: Accessibility serv available based on individual needs, Adult bk club, After school storytime, Art exhibits, Audiobks via web, Bks on CD, Children's prog, Computer training, Computers for patron use, Copy machines, Electronic databases & coll, Exhibits, Genealogy discussion group, Handicapped accessible, Holiday prog, Home delivery & serv to Sr ctr & nursing homes, ILL available, Magnifiers for reading, Microfiche/film & reading machines, Mus passes, Music CDs, Newsp ref libr, Online cat, Outreach serv, OverDrive digital audio bks, Photocopying/Printing, Preschool reading prog, Prog for adults, Prog for children & young adult, Pub access computers, Ref serv available, Senior outreach, Spanish lang bks, Story hour, Summer & winter reading prog, Summer reading prog, Tax forms, Teen prog, Telephone ref, Web-catalog, Wheelchair accessible
Partic in Central-Western Mass Automated Resource Sharing
Open Mon-Thurs 9-9, Fri 9-5, Sat 9-4 & Sun 12-4
Friends of the Library Group
Branches: 2
CHICOPEE FALLS, 216 Broadway, 01020, SAN 345-1569. Tel: 413-594-1820. *Dir,* Nancy Contois; Staff 2 (Non-MLS 2)
Founded 1884
Library Holdings: Bk Vols 17,781
Function: After school storytime
Open Tues-Fri 10-5
Friends of the Library Group
FAIRVIEW, 402 Britton St, 01020, SAN 345-1593. Tel: 413-533-8218. *Dir,* Nancy Contois; Staff 2 (Non-MLS 2)
Founded 1910. Circ 19,552
Library Holdings: Bk Vols 8,659
Function: Computers for patron use, Handicapped accessible
Open Mon, Wed & Fri 10-5, Tues 1-8, Thurs 4-8
Friends of the Library Group

C COLLEGE OF OUR LADY OF THE ELMS*, Alumnae Library, 291 Springfield St, 01013-2839. SAN 307-3300. Tel: 413-265-2280. Interlibrary Loan Service Tel: 413-265-2280, Ext 2286. Reference Tel: 413-265-2280, Ext 2297. FAX: 413-594-7418. Web Site: www.elms.edu/departments/library. *Dir,* Patricia Bombardier; Tel: 413-265-2281, E-mail: bombardierp@elms.edu; *Circ,* Michael Smith; E-mail: smithm@elms.edu; *Archivist, Spec Coll Librn,* Sister Mary E Gallagher; Tel: 413-265-2280, Ext 2354, E-mail: gallagherm@elms.edu; *Ser, Syst Coordr,* Debra Gomes; Tel: 413-265-2280, Ext 2316; *ILL,* Sister Elizabeth Sullivan; E-mail: sullivanel@elms.edu; *Acq, Cat,* Lynn Gamble; E-mail: gamblel@elms.edu; *Ref,* Mary E Courtney; E-mail: courtneym@elms.edu; *Tech Serv,* Elaine Pinkos; Tel: 413-265-2280, Ext 2285, E-mail: pinkose@elms.edu; Staff 7 (MLS 5, Non-MLS 2)
Founded 1928. Enrl 750; Highest Degree: Master
Library Holdings: AV Mats 8,324; Bk Vols 11,947; Per Subs 823
Special Collections: 18th Century Editions of English Authors; Ecclesiology, 16th & 17th Century Editions; Sir Walter Scott Coll, First Editions. US Document Depository
Subject Interests: Irish, Philos, Relig, Theatre
Automation Activity & Vendor Info: (Cataloging) Innovative Interfaces, Inc; (Circulation) Innovative Interfaces, Inc; (Course Reserve) Innovative Interfaces, Inc; (ILL) Innovative Interfaces, Inc; (OPAC) Innovative Interfaces, Inc; (Serials) Innovative Interfaces, Inc
Database Vendor: EBSCOhost, Gale Cengage Learning, OCLC FirstSearch
Publications: Barry Collection Catalog; Serials Catalog
Partic in Central & Western Massachusetts Automated Resource Sharing; Cooperating Libraries of Greater Springfield
Open Mon-Thurs 8am-11pm, Fri 8-7, Sat 9-5, Sun Noon-11

CHILMARK

P CHILMARK FREE PUBLIC LIBRARY*, 522 South Rd, 02535. (Mail add: PO Box 180, 02535-0180), SAN 307-3319. Tel: 508-645-3360. Administration Tel: 508-645-3360, Ext 103. FAX: 508-645-3737. E-mail: chillib@vineyard.net. Web Site: www.library.chilmark.ma.us. *Dir,* Catherine A Thompson; Staff 2 (Non-MLS 2)
Founded 1882. Pop 948
Library Holdings: AV Mats 7,607; Bk Vols 29,080; Per Subs 92
Special Collections: Brickner Poetry Corner; Martha's Vineyard Room
Automation Activity & Vendor Info: (Cataloging) Follett Software; (Circulation) Follett Software
Database Vendor: EBSCOhost, Gale Cengage Learning
Mem of Massachusetts Libr Syst
Open Mon & Sat 10:30-5:30, Tues 9:30-12:30, Wed 11-7:30, Thurs 3:30-6:30
Friends of the Library Group

CLARKSBURG

P CLARKSBURG TOWN LIBRARY*, 711 W Cross Rd, 01247. SAN 376-7124. Tel: 413-664-6050. FAX: 413-664-6384. E-mail: clarksburg@cwmars.org. *Dir,* Lynn Depaoli; Staff 3 (MLS 1, Non-MLS 2)
Founded 1898. Pop 1,650; Circ 17,000
Library Holdings: AV Mats 2,000; Bk Titles 14,000; Per Subs 53; Talking Bks 92
Automation Activity & Vendor Info: (Cataloging) Innovative Interfaces, Inc; (Circulation) Innovative Interfaces, Inc; (OPAC) Innovative Interfaces, Inc
Open Mon-Fri 10-4, Wed 10-7:30, Sat 10-2
Friends of the Library Group

CLINTON

P BIGELOW FREE PUBLIC LIBRARY*, 54 Walnut St, 01510. SAN 307-3335. Tel: 978-365-4160. Circulation Tel: 978-365-4160, Ext 221. Administration Tel: 978-365-4160, Ext 222. FAX: 978-365-4161. E-mail: bigelowlibrary@yahoo.com. Web Site: www.bigelowlibrary.org. *Dir,* Erin Klemm
Pop 12,978; Circ 72,455
Library Holdings: Bk Vols 137,748; Per Subs 60
Mem of Massachusetts Libr Syst
Partic in Central & Western Massachusetts Automated Resource Sharing
Open Tues-Fri 9-6, Sat 9-1
Friends of the Library Group

COHASSET

S COHASSET HISTORICAL SOCIETY LIBRARY*, 106 S Main St, 02025. (Mail add: PO Box 627, 02025-0627), SAN 372-6428. Tel: 781-383-1434. FAX: 781-383-1190. E-mail: cohassethistory@yahoo.com. Web Site: www.cohassethistoricalsociety.org. *Exec Adminr,* Lynne DeGiacomo; *Asst Dir, Coll Develop,* Laura Abrams; *Historian,* David H Wadsworth; Staff 1 (MLS 1)
Founded 1928
Library Holdings: Bk Titles 1,000
Special Collections: Local & Area History (includes Henry F Howe Coll); Local & Area Theater (Arthur Mahoney Coll); Maritime History
Function: Res libr
Publications: Historical Highlights (Newsletter)
Open Mon-Fri 10-4
Restriction: In-house use for visitors

P PAUL PRATT MEMORIAL LIBRARY*, 35 Ripley Rd, 02025-2097. SAN 307-3343. Tel: 781-383-1348. FAX: 781-383-1698. E-mail: library@cohassetlibrary.org. Web Site: www.cohassetlibrary.org. *Libr Dir,* Jackie Rafferty; *Head, Circ,* Paul Gailunas; E-mail: gailunas@ocln.org; *Ch,* Sharon Moody; E-mail: smoody@ocln.org; *Ref Librn,* Gayle Walsh; E-mail: gwalsh@ocln.org; Staff 9 (MLS 3, Non-MLS 6)
Founded 1879. Pop 7,823; Circ 85,500
Library Holdings: Bk Vols 54,428; Per Subs 164
Automation Activity & Vendor Info: (Acquisitions) SirsiDynix; (Cataloging) SirsiDynix; (Circulation) SirsiDynix
Partic in Old Colony Libr Network (OCLN)
Open Mon, Tues & Thurs 10-8, Wed & Fri 10-5, Sat 9-5, Sun 2-5
Friends of the Library Group

COLRAIN

P GRISWOLD MEMORIAL LIBRARY*, 12 Main St, 01340. (Mail add: PO Box 33, 01340-0033), SAN 307-3351. Tel: 413-624-3619. E-mail: biblib3@aol.com. *Dir,* Betty Johnson
Founded 1908. Pop 1,850
Library Holdings: Large Print Bks 200; Bk Vols 10,000; Per Subs 16
Automation Activity & Vendor Info: (Cataloging) Evergreen; (Circulation) Evergreen; (ILL) Evergreen; (OPAC) Evergreen
Open Mon & Fri 3-8, Wed 10-8, Sat 10-1
Friends of the Library Group

CONCORD

S LOUISA MAY ALCOTT MEMORIAL ASSOCIATION LIBRARY*, 399 Lexington Rd, 01742. (Mail add: PO Box 343, 01742-0343), SAN 371-1552. Tel: 978-369-4118. FAX: 978-369-1367. Web Site: www.louisamayalcott.org. *Exec Dir,* Jan Turnquist
Library Holdings: Bk Vols 550
Special Collections: The Alcott Coll
Function: Res libr
Restriction: Not open to pub, Open by appt only

P CONCORD FREE PUBLIC LIBRARY*, 129 Main St, 01742-2494. SAN 345-1658. Tel: 978-318-3300. Circulation Tel: 978-318-3301. Reference Tel: 978-318-3347. FAX: 978-318-3344. TDD: 978-318-3340. E-mail: concord@minlib.net. Web Site: www.concordlibrary.org. *Dir,* Kerry Cronin; Tel: 978-318-3377; *Asst Libr Dir,* Deborah Ervin; *Dir of Develop,* Susan Gladstone; *Head, Ch,* Karen Ahearn; Tel: 978-318-3358; *Head, Circ,* Robin Demas; *Head, Ref Serv,* Judith Gray; *Head, Tech Serv,* Caroline Nie; Tel: 978-318-3368; *Curator, Spec Coll Librn,* Leslie Wilson; Tel: 978-318-3342; *Ch, YA Librn,* Fayth Chamberland; *Staff Librn,* Jane Misslin
Founded 1873. Pop 15,551; Circ 400,000
Library Holdings: AV Mats 16,462; Bks on Deafness & Sign Lang 30; Large Print Bks 3,331; Bk Titles 225,300; Bk Vols 232,395; Per Subs 570
Special Collections: Alcott Family; Concord History; Henry David Thoreau Coll; Nathaniel Hawthorne Coll; Ralph Waldo Emerson Coll. Oral History
Subject Interests: Am lit, Hist
Automation Activity & Vendor Info: (Acquisitions) Innovative Interfaces, Inc - Millenium; (Cataloging) Innovative Interfaces, Inc - Millenium; (Circulation) Innovative Interfaces, Inc - Millenium
Wireless access
Publications: Library eNewsletter (Monthly newsletter)
Partic in Minuteman Library Network
Special Services for the Deaf - TTY equip
Open Mon-Thurs (Winter) 9-9, Fri 9-6, Sat 9-5, Sun 1-5; Mon-Thurs (Summer) 9-9, Fri 9-6, Sat 9-1
Friends of the Library Group
Branches: 1
FOWLER MEMORIAL, 1322 Main St, 01742, SAN 345-1682. Tel: 978-318-3350. FAX: 978-318-0906. *Librn,* Sharon McCarrell; *Librn,* Pat Pluskal
Library Holdings: Bk Titles 30,000
Open Mon 9-7, Tues & Wed 9-6, Thurs 1-6, Fri & Sat 9-5; Mon (Summer) 9-7, Tues & Wed 9-6, Thurs 1-6, Fri 9-5

S CONCORD MUSEUM LIBRARY*, 200 Lexington Rd, 01742. (Mail add: PO Box 146, 01742-0146), SAN 373-1677. Tel: 978-369-9763. FAX: 978-369-9660. E-mail: cm1@concordmuseum.org. Web Site: www.concordmuseum.org. *Dir, Pub Relations,* Carol Haines; *Curator,* David Wood
Library Holdings: Bk Vols 950; Per Subs 12
Special Collections: Concord History Coll
Subject Interests: Decorative art
Function: Res libr
Restriction: Open by appt only

M EMERSON HOSPITAL MEDICAL LIBRARY*, Lund Consumer Health Information Center, 133 Old Rd to Nine Acre Corner, 01742. SAN 307-3378. Tel: 978-287-3090. FAX: 978-287-3651. *Mgr, Libr Serv,* Melinda Marchand; E-mail: msaffer@emersonhosp.org
Library Holdings: e-books 30; e-journals 532; Bk Vols 700; Per Subs 150
Database Vendor: Cinahl, DynaMed, EBSCO Information Services, Gale Cengage Learning, Lexi-Comp, MD Consult, Medline, OCLC WorldShare Interlibrary Loan, PubMed, UpToDate, WebMD
Wireless access
Open Mon-Fri 8:30-4:30

S MASSACHUSETTS CORRECTIONAL INSTITUTION-CONCORD LIBRARY*, 965 Elm St, 01742-2119. (Mail add: PO Box 9106, 01742-9106), SAN 307-3386. Tel: 978-369-3220, Ext 292. FAX: 978-405-6108. *Librn,* Margaret Mubiru-Musoke
Library Holdings: Large Print Bks 300; Bk Vols 8,000; Per Subs 20
Special Collections: Spanish Coll
Subject Interests: Law
Automation Activity & Vendor Info: (Acquisitions) Follett Software; (Cataloging) Follett Software; (Circulation) Follett Software
Open Mon-Fri 9-4

A UNITED STATES ARMY*, Corps of Engineers New England District Library, 696 Virginia Rd, 01742-2751. SAN 345-7206. Tel: 978-318-8349. Circulation Tel: 978-318-8118. Information Services Tel: 978-318-8045. FAX: 978-318-8693. E-mail: library@nae02.usace.army.mil. Web Site: www.nae.usace.army.mil/library/libhp.html. *Chief Librn,* Timothy Hays; E-mail: timothy.p.hays@usace.army.mil
Founded 1947
Library Holdings: Bk Titles 4,000; Bk Vols 4,500; Per Subs 12
Special Collections: New England District Documents
Subject Interests: Civil eng, Ecology, Natural sci, Real estate, Soil mechanics, Structural eng, Water res
Automation Activity & Vendor Info: (Cataloging) OCLC; (ILL) OCLC; (OPAC) OCLC
Partic in Dialog Corp; OCLC Online Computer Library Center, Inc
Open Mon-Fri 8-4:30

CONWAY

P FIELD MEMORIAL LIBRARY, One Elm St, 01341. (Mail add: PO Box 189, 01341-0189), SAN 307-3394. Tel: 413-369-4646. E-mail: conwayfml@gmail.com. *Dir,* Carol Jean Baldwin; Tel: 413-369-4646, E-mail: conwayfmld@gmail.com; Staff 3 (MLS 1, Non-MLS 2)
Founded 1901. Pop 1,897; Circ 12,050
Library Holdings: Bk Vols 15,500; Per Subs 20
Wireless access
Mem of Massachusetts Libr Syst
Partic in Central & Western Massachusetts Automated Resource Sharing
Open Wed 3-8, Sat 10-3
Friends of the Library Group

COTUIT

S CAHOON MUSEUM OF AMERICAN ART*, American Painting Research Library, 4676 Falmouth Rd, 02635-2521. (Mail add: PO Box 1853, 02635-1853), SAN 375-8338. Tel: 508-428-7581. FAX: 508-420-3709. Web Site: www.cahoonmuseum.org. *Dir,* Richard Waterhouse; E-mail: rwaterhouse@cahoonmuseum.org. Subject Specialists: *Symbolism,* Richard Waterhouse
Founded 1984
Library Holdings: Bk Titles 2,000
Function: Res libr
Open Tues-Sat 10-4
Restriction: Staff use only

P COTUIT LIBRARY*, 871 Main St, 02635. (Mail add: PO Box 648, 02635-0648), SAN 307-3408. Tel: 508-428-8141. FAX: 508-428-4636. E-mail: cotuitlibrarian@gmail.com, librarian@cotuitlibrary.org. Web Site: www.cotuitlibrary.org. *Dir,* Jennie Wiley; E-mail: jwiley@clamsnet.org; *Asst Dir, Youth Serv,* Lenora Levine; *Circ Supvr, ILL,* Melissa Cavill; *Cat,* Kathleen Pratt; *Circ Asst,* Diane Farry; *Circ Asst,* Laurie Hadley; *Circ Asst,* Valerie Mogan; E-mail: vmorgan@clamsnet.org; *Homebound Outreach & Prog,* Frances Bausman; E-mail: fbausman@clamsnet.org; Staff 8 (MLS 3, Non-MLS 5)
Founded 1874. Circ 56,365
Jul 2012-Jul 2013 Income $306,953, State $3,125, City $144,394, Locally Generated Income $159,434. Mats Exp $36,420, Books $29,171, Per/Ser (Incl. Access Fees) $2,717, Electronic Ref Mat (Incl. Access Fees) $4,532. Sal $144,005
Library Holdings: Bk Titles 48,322; Per Subs 90
Special Collections: Art Books; Classic Mysteries; Kirkman Coll of Fine Books
Automation Activity & Vendor Info: (Acquisitions) Innovative Interfaces, Inc; (Cataloging) Innovative Interfaces, Inc; (Circulation) Innovative Interfaces, Inc; (Course Reserve) Innovative Interfaces, Inc; (ILL) Innovative Interfaces, Inc; (Media Booking) Innovative Interfaces, Inc; (OPAC) Innovative Interfaces, Inc; (Serials) Innovative Interfaces, Inc
Wireless access
Mem of Massachusetts Libr Syst
Partic in Cape Libraries Automated Materials Sharing Network
Special Services for the Blind - Assistive/Adapted tech devices, equip & products; Home delivery serv
Open Mon & Wed 1:30-8, Tues, Thurs & Fri 9:30-5, Sat 9:30-4
Friends of the Library Group

CUMMINGTON

P BRYANT FREE LIBRARY*, 455 Berkshire Trail, Rte 9, 01026-9610. SAN 307-3416. Tel: 413-634-0109. *Chair,* John Maruskin; *Dir,* Mark DeMaranville
Founded 1872. Pop 994; Circ 5,857
Library Holdings: Bk Vols 7,700; Per Subs 11
Open Mon & Wed 6-9, Sat 8:30-12:30

DALTON

P DALTON FREE PUBLIC LIBRARY*, 462 Main St, 01226. SAN 307-3424. Tel: 413-684-6112. FAX: 413-684-4750. E-mail: dalton@cwmars.org. Web Site: www.daltonlibrary.org. *Dir,* Position Currently Open; *Asst Librn,* Katherine Hoag; Staff 1 (MLS 1)
Founded 1861. Pop 6,874; Circ 42,754
Jul 2011-Jun 2012 Income $194,151, State $8,633, City $173,372, Locally Generated Income $3,694, Other $8,452. Mats Exp $44,522, Books

$29,675, Per/Ser (Incl. Access Fees) $4,002, AV Equip $2,717, AV Mat $7,771, Electronic Ref Mat (Incl. Access Fees) $357. Sal $118,694 (Prof $54,518)
Library Holdings: Audiobooks 1,055; DVDs 1,831; e-books 7,573; Electronic Media & Resources 31; Microforms 18; Bk Titles 37,845; Per Subs 77
Special Collections: Dalton Education Plan
Subject Interests: Local hist
Automation Activity & Vendor Info: (Circulation) Evergreen; (ILL) Evergreen; (OPAC) Evergreen
Database Vendor: Gale Cengage Learning, ProQuest
Wireless access
Function: Adult bk club, Bks on CD, Computers for patron use, Copy machines, Distance learning, Electronic databases & coll, Handicapped accessible, Mus passes, Online cat, OverDrive digital audio bks, Photocopying/Printing, Pub access computers, Story hour, Summer reading prog, Tax forms
Mem of Massachusetts Libr Syst
Partic in Central & Western Massachusetts Automated Resource Sharing
Special Services for the Deaf - Bks on deafness & sign lang
Special Services for the Blind - Bks on CD; Copier with enlargement capabilities; Large print bks; Playaways (bks on MP3); Recorded bks
Open Mon & Wed 12-8, Tues 10-4, Thurs & Fri 12-5:30, Sat 10-2
Friends of the Library Group

DANVERS

J NORTH SHORE COMMUNITY COLLEGE LIBRARY*, One Ferncroft Rd, 01923-4093. SAN 307-1154. Tel: 978-762-4000. Circulation Tel: 978-739-5526. Interlibrary Loan Service Tel: 978-739-5426. Reference Tel: 978-739-5525. Administration Tel: 978-739-5524. FAX: 978-739-5500. E-mail: library@northshore.edu. Web Site: library.northshore.edu. *Dir,* Karen Pangallo; E-mail: kpangall@northshore.edu; *Head, Circ Serv,* Kerrie Mangione; Tel: 978-739-6251, E-mail: kmangion@northshore.edu; *Ref Librn,* Christine Goodchild; Tel: 978-739-5532, E-mail: cgoodchi@northshore.edu; *Coordr, Pub Serv,* Dava Davainis; Tel: 978-739-6245, E-mail: ddavaini@northshore.edu; *Coordr, Pub Serv,* William J Meunier; Tel: 978-739-5540, E-mail: wmeunier@northshore.edu; *Coordr, Tech Serv,* John Koza; Tel: 978-739-5413, E-mail: jkoza@northshore.edu; *Ref Serv,* Torrey Dukes; Tel: 978-739-6244, E-mail: tdukes@northshore.edu; Staff 6 (MLS 6)
Enrl 4,610; Highest Degree: Associate
Wireless access
Function: Art exhibits, Audiobks via web, Computers for patron use, Copy machines, Distance learning, e-mail & chat, E-Reserves, Exhibits, Handicapped accessible, ILL available, Magnifiers for reading, Mus passes, Online cat, Online info literacy tutorials on the web & in blackboard, Orientations, OverDrive digital audio bks, Photocopying/Printing, Pub access computers, Ref & res, Ref serv available, Ref serv in person, Scanner, Telephone ref, Web-catalog, Wheelchair accessible
Mem of Massachusetts Libr Syst
Partic in Massachusetts Commonwealth Consortium of Libraries in Public Higher Education Institutions (MCCLPHEI); North of Boston Library Exchange, Inc; Northeast Consortium of Colleges & Universities In Massachusetts
Open Mon-Thurs 8am-8:30pm, Fri 8-4, Sat 8:30-12:30

P PEABODY INSTITUTE LIBRARY*, 15 Sylvan St, 01923. SAN 345-1712. Tel: 978-774-0554. FAX: 978-762-0251. E-mail: dan@noblenet.org. Web Site: www.danverslibrary.org. *Dir,* Alan Thibeault; *Asst Dir,* Suzanne MacLeod; *Head, Ch,* JoAnne Powell; *Head, Circ Serv,* Patricia Arrington; *Head, Ref (Info Serv),* Donna Maturi; *Head, Tech Serv,* Frances Hegarty; *Archivist,* Richard Trask; Staff 4 (MLS 4)
Founded 1866. Pop 25,000; Circ 204,826
Library Holdings: AV Mats 8,966; Large Print Bks 1,674; Bk Vols 119,169; Per Subs 240
Special Collections: Anti Slavery (Parker Pillsbury Coll), bks, pamphlets; Danvers (Town Records Coll), ms; Witchcraft (Ellerton J Brehart Coll), bks, pamphlets, photog, ms
Automation Activity & Vendor Info: (Cataloging) Innovative Interfaces, Inc; (Circulation) Innovative Interfaces, Inc; (ILL) Innovative Interfaces, Inc
Wireless access
Open Mon-Thurs 9-9, Fri 12-5, Sat 9-5, Sun (Sept-May) 1-5
Friends of the Library Group

DARTMOUTH

P DARTMOUTH PUBLIC LIBRARIES*, Southworth Library, 732 Dartmouth St, 02748. SAN 345-5971. Tel: 508-999-0726. FAX: 508-992-9914. Web Site: www.dartmouthpubliclibraries.org. *Actg Dir,* Lynne Antuns; E-mail: lantunes@sailsinc.org; *Ch,* Kathleen Redfearn; *Ref Librn,* Sharani Robins; E-mail: srobins@sailsinc.org; *Ref Librn,* Brian Walsh; E-mail: bwalsh@sailsinc.org
Pop 32,000; Circ 246,903
Library Holdings: Bk Vols 118,339; Per Subs 200
Automation Activity & Vendor Info: (Acquisitions) SirsiDynix; (Cataloging) SirsiDynix; (Circulation) SirsiDynix; (OPAC) SirsiDynix; (Serials) SirsiDynix
Partic in SAILS Library Network
Open Mon-Thurs 9-8, Fri & Sat 9-5
Friends of the Library Group
Branches: 1
NORTH DARTMOUTH, 1383 Tucker Rd, 02747, SAN 345-6005. Tel: 508-999-0728. FAX: 508-999-0795. *Actg Dir,* Lynne Antunes
Library Holdings: Bk Vols 24,000
Open Mon, Wed & Fri 5-8, Tues & Thurs 9-1

DEDHAM

S DEDHAM HISTORICAL SOCIETY, 612 High St, 02027. (Mail add: PO Box 215, 02027-0215), SAN 327-3482. Tel: 781-326-1385. FAX: 781-326-5762. E-mail: library@dedhamhistorical.org. Web Site: www.dedhamhistorical.org. *Archivist, Librn,* Sandra Waxman; Staff 2 (MLS 1, Non-MLS 1)
Founded 1859
Library Holdings: Bk Titles 20,000; Per Subs 5
Special Collections: Ames Family Coll; Church Records 1638-1890; Mann Family Coll; Original Dedham Grant Area Residents & Artifacts (incl Nathaniel Ames-father & son); Records of Firms & Associations
Subject Interests: Genealogy, Town hist
Open Tues-Fri 9-4

P DEDHAM PUBLIC LIBRARY*, 43 Church St, 02026. SAN 345-1771. Tel: 781-751-9284. Reference Tel: 781-751-9287. FAX: 781-751-9289. Web Site: library.dedham-ma.gov. *Dir,* Mary Ann Tricarico; Staff 6 (MLS 6)
Founded 1872. Pop 24,729; Circ 140,195
Library Holdings: AV Mats 6,648; CDs 9,590; DVDs 32,159; e-books 1,449; Bk Vols 88,477
Special Collections: Dedham Historical Coll
Subject Interests: Archit, Art, Bus & mgt, Hist, Soc sci & issues
Automation Activity & Vendor Info: (Acquisitions) Innovative Interfaces, Inc; (Cataloging) Innovative Interfaces, Inc; (Circulation) Innovative Interfaces, Inc; (ILL) Innovative Interfaces, Inc; (OPAC) Innovative Interfaces, Inc; (Serials) Innovative Interfaces, Inc
Function: Adult bk club, Bks on cassette, Bks on CD, Children's prog, Computers for patron use, Copy machines, Handicapped accessible, Homebound delivery serv, ILL available, Mus passes, Music CDs, Online searches, Prog for children & young adult, Ref serv available, Summer reading prog, Tax forms, Telephone ref, VHS videos, Wheelchair accessible
Partic in Minuteman Library Network
Open Mon & Wed 10-9, Tues, Thurs & Fri 10-5
Friends of the Library Group
Branches: 1
ENDICOTT, 257 Mount Vernon St, 02026, SAN 345-1801. Tel: 781-751-9178. *Circ,* Janice Crowley; E-mail: jcrowley@dedham-ma.gov; Staff 1 (MLS 1)
Founded 1970. Circ 47,282
Library Holdings: Bk Vols 22,000
Open Mon & Wed-Sat 10-5, Tues 1-9
Friends of the Library Group

GL MASSACHUSETTS TRIAL COURT*, Norfolk Law Library, 649 High St, Ste 210, 02026-1831. SAN 307-3459. Tel: 781-329-1401, Ext 2. FAX: 781-329-1404. E-mail: norfolklawlibrary@hotmail.com. Web Site: www.lawlib.state.ma.us. *Head Law Librn,* Agnes Leathe
Founded 1898
Library Holdings: Bk Vols 40,000
Special Collections: Legal Videos for Laypeople
Subject Interests: State law
Database Vendor: OCLC FirstSearch
Wireless access
Mem of Massachusetts Libr Syst
Open Mon-Fri 8:30-4:30
Restriction: Non-circulating coll
Friends of the Library Group

DEERFIELD

S HISTORIC DEERFIELD INC & POCUMTUCK VALLEY MEMORIAL ASSOCIATION LIBRARIES*, Six Memorial St, 01342-9736. (Mail add: PO Box 53, 01342-0053), SAN 371-6058. Tel: 413-775-7125. FAX: 413-775-7223. E-mail: library@historic-deerfield.org. Web Site: www.historic-deerfield.org/library. *Librn,* David C Bosse; E-mail: dbosse@historic-deerfield.org; *Asst Librn,* Heather Harrington; E-mail: hharrington@historic-deerfield.org; Staff 2 (MLS 2)
Founded 1970
Library Holdings: CDs 10; Bk Titles 50,350; Per Subs 40; Videos 20

Special Collections: History & Application of Color (Stephen L Wolf Coll)
Subject Interests: Archit, Decorative art, Genealogy, Hist of color, Local hist, Mat culture
Automation Activity & Vendor Info: (Cataloging) Ex Libris Group; (Circulation) Ex Libris Group; (OPAC) Ex Libris Group
Wireless access
Publications: Brochure; Research at Deerfield
Partic in Lyrasis; OCLC Online Computer Library Center, Inc
Open Tues-Fri 9-12 & 1-5

DENNIS

P DENNIS MEMORIAL LIBRARY ASSOCIATION*, 1020 Old Bass River Rd, 02638. SAN 307-3475. Tel: 508-385-2255. FAX: 508-385-7322. E-mail: dennismemorial@gmail.com. *Dir,* Nancy Symington; E-mail: nsymington@clamsnet.org; *Ref Librn,* Barbara Wells; *Cataloger, Ch,* Susan Parker; *Libr Asst,* Alice Halvorsen
Founded 1924. Pop 14,000; Circ 60,000
Jul 2007-Jun 2008. Mats Exp $30,000. Sal $26,300
Library Holdings: Large Print Bks 300; Bk Vols 15,000; Per Subs 27; Talking Bks 2,500; Videos 1,500
Automation Activity & Vendor Info: (Cataloging) Innovative Interfaces, Inc; (Circulation) Innovative Interfaces, Inc; (OPAC) Innovative Interfaces, Inc
Wireless access
Open Mon-Thurs 1-8, Fri & Sat 1-5

DENNISPORT

P DENNIS PUBLIC LIBRARY*, Five Hall St, 02639. Tel: 508-760-6219. FAX: 508-760-6101. E-mail: den_mail@clamsnet.org. *Dir,* Jessica Langlois; *Asst Dir, Ref Serv,* Cindy Cullen; *Ch Serv,* Zoe McInerney; *Circ,* Kathy Pedini; *Circ,* Julie Remie; *Ref Serv,* Susan Henken; *Tech Serv,* Lisa Cunningham
Open Tues-Thurs 10-8, Fri & Sat 10-2

DIGHTON

S DIGHTON HISTORICAL SOCIETY MUSEUM LIBRARY*, 1217 Williams St, 02715-1013. (Mail add: PO Box 655, 02715-0655), SAN 372-6738. Tel: 508-669-5514. *Curator,* Elaine Varley
Founded 1962
Library Holdings: Bk Titles 100
Special Collections: Dighton Area Pictures & Scrapbooks; Indian Artifacts; Military & Children's Clothing; Old School Books

P DIGHTON PUBLIC LIBRARY*, 395 Main St, 02715. SAN 307-3483. Tel: 508-669-6421. FAX: 508-669-6963. E-mail: di@sailsinc.org. Web Site: www.dightonlibrary.org. *Dir,* Jocelyn Tavares; E-mail: jtavares@sailsinc.org; *Ch,* Lorie Van Hook; E-mail: landrews@sailsinc.org; *Circ Librn,* Phyllis Haskell; E-mail: phaskell@sailsinc.org; *Tech Librn,* Brenda Carr; E-mail: bcarr@sailsinc.org; Staff 4 (MLS 1, Non-MLS 3)
Founded 1894. Pop 7,030; Circ 35,000
Library Holdings: CDs 200; e-books 661; Bk Vols 22,200; Per Subs 62; Talking Bks 1,200; Videos 1,500
Special Collections: Births & Deaths; Town Documents
Automation Activity & Vendor Info: (Acquisitions) SirsiDynix; (Cataloging) SirsiDynix; (Circulation) SirsiDynix; (OPAC) SirsiDynix
Database Vendor: EBSCOhost, Gale Cengage Learning, Newsbank
Function: Audio & video playback equip for onsite use, AV serv, Doc delivery serv, Homebound delivery serv, ILL available, Magnifiers for reading, Online searches, Photocopying/Printing, Prog for adults, Prog for children & young adult, Ref serv available, Summer reading prog, Workshops
Publications: Friend's (Newsletter)
Mem of Massachusetts Libr Syst
Partic in SAILS Library Network
Open Mon & Fri 10-4, Tues-Thurs 12-8, Sat (Sept-May) 10-2
Friends of the Library Group

DORCHESTER

M CARITAS CARNEY HOSPITAL*, Colpoys Library, 2100 Dorchester Ave, 02124-5666. SAN 307-3513. Tel: 617-296-4000, Ext 2050. FAX: 617-474-3861. *Librn,* Charles Severens; E-mail: charles.severens@caritaschristi.org; Staff 1 (MLS 1)
Founded 1953
Oct 2007-Sept 2008 Income $100,000. Sal $50,000
Library Holdings: Bk Titles 2,300; Per Subs 125
Subject Interests: Med
Automation Activity & Vendor Info: (Serials) EBSCO Online
Function: Res libr
Partic in Boston Biomedical Library Consortium; Massachusetts Health Sciences Libraries Network; North Atlantic Health Sciences Libraries, Inc
Restriction: Not open to pub

DOVER

P DOVER TOWN LIBRARY*, 56 Dedham St, 02030-2214. (Mail add: PO Box 669, 02030-0669), SAN 307-3521. Tel: 508-785-8113. FAX: 508-785-0138. Web Site: library.doverma.org. *Dir,* Cheryl Abdullah; E-mail: cabdullah@minlib.net; *Asst Dir,* Ryan Livergood; *Head, Ch,* Bonnie Peirce-Roalsen; *Head, Circ,* Joan Howland; *Head, Tech Serv,* Ellie Herd; *YA Librn,* Aimee Gagnon; Staff 12 (MLS 6, Non-MLS 6)
Founded 1894. Pop 5,907; Circ 127,608
Library Holdings: Audiobooks 816; CDs 2,330; DVDs 3,563; e-books 261; Electronic Media & Resources 881; Bk Vols 58,733; Per Subs 248
Special Collections: Diverse Technologies Coll
Automation Activity & Vendor Info: (Cataloging) Innovative Interfaces, Inc; (Circulation) Innovative Interfaces, Inc
Wireless access
Function: Art exhibits, Audiobks via web, Bk club(s), Computer training, Copy machines, Exhibits, Handicapped accessible, Instruction & testing, Mail loans to mem, Mus passes, OverDrive digital audio bks, Prog for adults, Prog for children & young adult, Pub access computers, Senior computer classes, Story hour, Summer reading prog, Tax forms, Teen prog, Wheelchair accessible
Mem of Massachusetts Libr Syst
Partic in Minuteman Library Network
Open Mon-Wed 10-8, Thurs & Fri 10-6, Sat 10-4
Friends of the Library Group

DRACUT

P MOSES GREELEY PARKER MEMORIAL LIBRARY*, 28 Arlington St, 01826. SAN 307-3548. Tel: 978-454-5474. FAX: 978-454-9120. Web Site: www.dracutlibrary.org. *Dir,* Dana Mastroianni; E-mail: dmastroianni@mvlc.org; *Youth/Young Adult Librn,* Carole Hamilton; E-mail: chamilton@mvlc.org; *Adult Serv,* Jeanne Roy; *Ch Serv,* Penny Berube; E-mail: pberube@mvlc.org; *Tech Serv,* Lee Doyle; E-mail: ldoyle@mvlc.org
Founded 1922. Pop 28,000; Circ 155,000
Library Holdings: Bk Vols 80,000; Per Subs 105
Subject Interests: Local hist
Automation Activity & Vendor Info: (Cataloging) SirsiDynix; (Circulation) SirsiDynix; (OPAC) SirsiDynix
Partic in Merrimack Valley Library Consortium
Open Mon-Thurs 8:30-8:30, Fri & Sat 8:30-4:30
Friends of the Library Group

DUDLEY

P PEARLE L CRAWFORD MEMORIAL LIBRARY*, 40 Schofield Ave, 01571. SAN 307-3556. Tel: 508-949-8021. FAX: 508-949-8026. E-mail: pearle@cwmars.org. Web Site: crawfordlibrary.org. *Libr Dir,* Nancy Barta Norton; *Ch,* Kathryn Dunton; Staff 6 (MLS 1, Non-MLS 5)
Founded 1897. Pop 10,057; Circ 49,000
Library Holdings: Bk Vols 21,000; Per Subs 16
Mem of Massachusetts Libr Syst
Partic in Central & Western Massachusetts Automated Resource Sharing
Open Mon & Thurs 10-8, Tues, Wed & Fri 10-5, Sat 10-2
Friends of the Library Group

C NICHOLS COLLEGE*, Conant Library, 124 Center Rd, 01571. (Mail add: PO Box 5000, 01571-5000), SAN 307-3564. Tel: 508-213-2334. Reference Tel: 508-213-2222. Toll Free Tel: 877-266-2681. FAX: 508-213-2323. E-mail: reference@nichols.edu. Web Site: www.nichols.edu/library/. *Dir,* Jim Douglas; Tel: 508-213-2333, E-mail: jim.douglas@nichols.edu; *Coordr, Patron Serv,* Sandra Lobo; Tel: 508-213-2234, E-mail: sandra.lobo@nichols.edu; *Coordr, Ser, Coordr, Tech Serv,* Donna DeNardis; Tel: 508-213-2229, E-mail: donna.denardis@nichols.edu; *Acq,* Evelyn Nieszczezewski; Tel: 508-213-2220, E-mail: evelyn.nieszczezewski@nichols.edu; *Instrul Serv/Ref Librn,* Matthew Haggard; Tel: 508-213-2437, E-mail: matthew.haggard@nichols.edu; Staff 6 (MLS 2, Non-MLS 4)
Founded 1815. Enrl 877; Fac 53; Highest Degree: Master
Library Holdings: Bk Vols 43,495; Per Subs 211
Special Collections: History of Dudley, Webster & Nichols Academy
Subject Interests: Econ, Finance, Mgt
Automation Activity & Vendor Info: (Cataloging) Follett Software; (Circulation) Follett Software; (OPAC) Follett Software
Database Vendor: EBSCOhost, Gale Cengage Learning, LexisNexis, Mergent Online, OCLC FirstSearch, OCLC WorldShare Interlibrary Loan, ProQuest, SBRnet (Sports Business Research Network)
Wireless access
Publications: Newsletter (Bi-annually)
Mem of Massachusetts Libr Syst
Partic in Lyrasis; OCLC Online Computer Library Center, Inc
Open Mon-Wed (Winter) 7:45am-11:30pm, Thurs 7:45am-10:30pm, Fri 7:45-4:30, Sat 1-5, Sun 12:30-11:30; Mon-Thurs (Summer) 8am-8:30pm, Fri 8-3

DUNSTABLE

P DUNSTABLE FREE PUBLIC LIBRARY*, 588 Main St, 01827. (Mail add: PO Box 219, 01827-0219), SAN 307-3572. Tel: 978-649-7830. FAX: 978-649-4215. *Dir,* Mary Beth Pallis
Pop 3,000; Circ 30,000
Library Holdings: Bk Vols 26,000; Per Subs 56
Automation Activity & Vendor Info: (Cataloging) SirsiDynix; (Circulation) SirsiDynix; (OPAC) SirsiDynix
Publications: Dunstable Village; Nason's History of Dunstable, Massachusetts
Partic in Merrimack Valley Library Consortium
Open Tues 5-9, Wed, Fri & Sat 10-2, Thurs 10-8
Friends of the Library Group

DUXBURY

S ART COMPLEX MUSEUM*, Carl A Weyerhaeuser Library, 189 Alden St, 02331. (Mail add: PO Box 2814, 02331-2814), SAN 325-318X. Tel: 781-934-6634, Ext 35. Administration Tel: 781-934-6634, Ext 10. FAX: 781-934-5117. Web Site: www.artcomplex.org. *Librn,* Cheryl O'Neill; E-mail: cheryl.oneill@artcomplex.org. Subject Specialists: *Art,* Cheryl O'Neill; Staff 1 (MLS 1)
Library Holdings: Bk Vols 6,500; Per Subs 15
Special Collections: American Art Coll; Asian Art (Japanese Prints & Pottery Coll); Prints; Shaker Furniture
Subject Interests: Art hist
Publications: Acquisition List; Museum Catalogues; Shaped with a Passion
Open Wed-Sun 1-4
Restriction: Open to pub for ref only
Friends of the Library Group

P DUXBURY FREE LIBRARY*, 77 Alden St, 02332. SAN 307-3599. Tel: 781-934-2721. Interlibrary Loan Service Tel: 781-934-2721, Ext 131. FAX: 781-934-0663. Web Site: www.duxburyfreelibrary.org. *Dir,* Carol Jankowski; Tel: 781-934-2721, Ext 104, E-mail: carolj@ocln.org; *Ch Serv,* Nancy Denman; Tel: 781-934-2721, Ext 116, E-mail: ndenman@ocln.org; *Circ,* Denise Garvin; Tel: 781-934-2721, Ext 107, E-mail: dgarvin@ocln.org; *Ref Serv,* David Murphy; Tel: 781-934-2721, Ext 103, E-mail: dmurphy@ocln.org; Staff 19 (MLS 9, Non-MLS 10)
Founded 1889. Pop 14,248; Circ 235,680
Library Holdings: AV Mats 8,000; CDs 1,000; Bk Vols 105,581; Per Subs 250; Talking Bks 3,600; Videos 4,600
Subject Interests: Local hist
Automation Activity & Vendor Info: (Cataloging) SirsiDynix; (Circulation) SirsiDynix; (OPAC) SirsiDynix
Wireless access
Mem of Massachusetts Libr Syst
Partic in Old Colony Libr Network (OCLN)
Open Mon 2-8, Tues-Thurs 10-8, Fri & Sat 10-5
Friends of the Library Group

EAST BRIDGEWATER

P EAST BRIDGEWATER PUBLIC LIBRARY*, 32 Union St, 02333-1598. SAN 307-3602. Tel: 508-378-1616. FAX: 508-378-1617. E-mail: ebpl@sailsinc.org. Web Site: www.sailsinc.org/ebpl. *Dir,* Manny Leite; E-mail: mleite@sailsinc.org; *Asst Dir,* Marilyn Greeley; E-mail: mgreeley@sailsinc.org; *Ch,* Anne Vantran; E-mail: avantran@sailsinc.org; *Tech Serv Librn,* Janice Allman; E-mail: jallman@sailsinc.org; Staff 13 (MLS 2, Non-MLS 11)
Pop 13,526; Circ 93,205
Library Holdings: CDs 1,398; DVDs 544; e-books 361; Electronic Media & Resources 142; Large Print Bks 673; Bk Vols 50,840; Per Subs 105; Talking Bks 1,106; Videos 1,992
Special Collections: F D Millet Archive
Subject Interests: Local hist
Automation Activity & Vendor Info: (Cataloging) SirsiDynix; (Circulation) SirsiDynix; (OPAC) SirsiDynix
Database Vendor: EBSCOhost, Gale Cengage Learning
Mem of Massachusetts Libr Syst
Partic in SAILS Library Network
Special Services for the Blind - Scanner for conversion & translation of mats
Open Mon & Tues 9-8, Wed & Thurs 9-5, Fri 1-5, Sat 9-2
Friends of the Library Group

EAST BROOKFIELD

P EAST BROOKFIELD PUBLIC LIBRARY*, Memorial Town Complex, 122 Connie Mack Dr, 01515. SAN 307-3610. Tel: 508-867-7928. FAX: 508-867-4181. *Dir,* Wendy Payette
Pop 2,000; Circ 18,343
Jul 2012-Jun 2013 Income $69,500. Mats Exp $14,000
Library Holdings: Audiobooks 375; CDs 100; DVDs 1,228; Large Print Bks 250; Bk Vols 16,347; Per Subs 18
Automation Activity & Vendor Info: (Acquisitions) Follett Software; (Cataloging) Follett Software; (Circulation) Follett Software
Wireless access
Function: ILL available
Mem of Massachusetts Libr Syst
Open Mon 2-8, Tues & Thurs 9:30-12:30 & 1:30-5:30, Wed 1:30-5:30, Sat 9-1
Friends of the Library Group

EAST DENNIS

P JACOB SEARS MEMORIAL LIBRARY*, 23 Center St, 02641. (Mail add: PO Box 782, 02641-0782), SAN 307-3629. Tel: 508-385-8151. FAX: 508-385-8661. Web Site: www.jacobsearsmemoriallibrary.org. *Dir,* Phillip Inman; Staff 1 (Non-MLS 1)
Founded 1896. Pop 4,000; Circ 27,000
Library Holdings: Audiobooks 100; DVDs 2,200; Large Print Bks 1,000; Bk Vols 14,500
Subject Interests: Antiques, Hist, Natural sci
Automation Activity & Vendor Info: (Acquisitions) Innovative Interfaces, Inc; (Cataloging) Innovative Interfaces, Inc; (Circulation) Innovative Interfaces, Inc; (Course Reserve) Innovative Interfaces, Inc; (OPAC) Innovative Interfaces, Inc; (Serials) Innovative Interfaces, Inc
Wireless access
Open Mon-Sat 9-1
Friends of the Library Group

EAST DOUGLAS

P SIMON FAIRFIELD PUBLIC LIBRARY*, 290 Main St, 01516. (Mail add: PO Box 607, 01516-0607), SAN 307-3637. Tel: 508-476-2695. FAX: 508-476-2695. *Dir,* Ann D Carlsson; Staff 1 (Non-MLS 1)
Founded 1903. Pop 5,021; Circ 20,315
Library Holdings: Bk Titles 25,000; Per Subs 52
Special Collections: Douglas History Coll
Automation Activity & Vendor Info: (Cataloging) Follett Software; (Circulation) Follett Software
Mem of Massachusetts Libr Syst
Open Mon 12-5, Tues & Thurs 12-8, Wed 10-5, Sat 9-1

EAST FREETOWN

P JAMES WHITE MEMORIAL LIBRARY*, Five Washburn Rd, 02717-1220. SAN 307-3645. Tel: 508-763-5344. Web Site: www.sailsinc.org/freetown. *Dir,* Vicki L Dawson; *Ch Serv, Sr Librn,* Althea H Brady; Staff 4 (Non-MLS 4)
Circ 18,003
Library Holdings: Bk Vols 24,524; Per Subs 121
Subject Interests: Local hist
Automation Activity & Vendor Info: (Acquisitions) SirsiDynix; (Cataloging) SirsiDynix; (Circulation) SirsiDynix
Function: Doc delivery serv, Homebound delivery serv, ILL available, Photocopying/Printing, Prog for children & young adult, Ref serv available, Summer reading prog, Telephone ref, Wheelchair accessible
Partic in SAILS Library Network
Open Tues & Thurs 10-9, Sat 1-5
Friends of the Library Group
Branches: 1
G H HATHAWAY LIBRARY, Six N Main St, Assonet, 02702, SAN 307-4013. Tel: 508-644-2385. *Librn,* Althea H Brady
Pop 8,600
Subject Interests: Local hist
Open Mon 3-7, Wed 3-5, Fri 1-5, Sat 10-12
Friends of the Library Group

EAST LONGMEADOW

P EAST LONGMEADOW PUBLIC LIBRARY*, 60 Center Sq, 01028-2459. SAN 307-3653. Tel: 413-525-5400. Circulation Tel: 413-525-5400, Ext 1511. Administration Tel: 413-525-5400, Ext 1501. Information Services Tel: 413-525-5400, Ext 1508. FAX: 413-525-0344. Web Site: www.eastlongmeadow.org/library. *Dir,* Susan M Peterson; E-mail: speterson@eastlongmeadowma.gov; *Asst Dir, Ref Librn,* Susan Teale; E-mail: steale@cwmars.org; *Ch Serv,* MacNaught Cynthia; E-mail: cmacnaught@eastlongmeadowma.gov; *Tech Serv,* Kristen Savaria; E-mail: ksavaria@wmars.org; Staff 13 (MLS 3, Non-MLS 10)
Founded 1896. Pop 15,300; Circ 232,688
Jul 2005-Jun 2006 Income $565,373, State $20,509, City $526,501, Other $18,363. Mats Exp $88,407, Books $69,500, Per/Ser (Incl. Access Fees) $4,500, AV Mat $12,025, Electronic Ref Mat (Incl. Access Fees) $2,382. Sal $412,845
Library Holdings: Bk Vols 82,217; Per Subs 106

Automation Activity & Vendor Info: (Cataloging) Innovative Interfaces, Inc; (Circulation) Innovative Interfaces, Inc; (ILL) Innovative Interfaces, Inc; (OPAC) Innovative Interfaces, Inc
Database Vendor: Innovative Interfaces, Inc
Wireless access
Function: Audiobks via web, Bks on cassette, Bks on CD, Children's prog, Computers for patron use, Copy machines, Electronic databases & coll, Free DVD rentals, Handicapped accessible, Mus passes, Music CDs, Online cat, OverDrive digital audio bks, Prog for adults, Prog for children & young adult, Pub access computers, Story hour, Summer reading prog, Tax forms, Teen prog, Wheelchair accessible
Partic in Central & Western Massachusetts Automated Resource Sharing
Open Mon-Wed 9:30-8, Thurs & Fri 9:30-5, Sat 9:30-4
Friends of the Library Group

EAST SANDWICH

S ROBERT S SWAIN NATURAL HISTORY LIBRARY, Green Briar Nature Center, Six Discovery Hill Rd, 02537. SAN 329-7845. Tel: 508-888-6870. FAX: 508-888-1919. E-mail: info@thorntonburgess.org. Web Site: www.thorntonburgess.org/green%20briar.htm.
Founded 1979
Library Holdings: Bk Vols 1,800; Per Subs 10
Subject Interests: Natural hist
Function: Archival coll
Special Services for the Deaf - Spec interest per
Open Tues-Sat (Jan-March) 10-4; Mon-Sat (April-Dec) 10-4, Sun 1-4
Restriction: Circ limited
Friends of the Library Group

EASTHAM

P EASTHAM PUBLIC LIBRARY, 190 Samoset Rd, 02642. SAN 307-3661. Tel: 508-240-5950. FAX: 508-240-0786. Web Site: www.easthamlibrary.org. *Dir,* Debra DeJonker-Berry; E-mail: ddejonkerberry@clamsnet.org; *Ad,* Karen MacDonald; *Youth Serv Librn,* Fran McLoughlin; E-mail: franm@easthamlibrary.org; *Tech Serv,* Connie Wells; Staff 6 (MLS 3, Non-MLS 3)
Founded 1878. Pop 5,646; Circ 101,779
Jul 2014-Jun 2015 Income $327,115, State $5,182, City $304,233, Other $17,700. Mats Exp $69,100, Books $32,700, Per/Ser (Incl. Access Fees) $6,400, AV Mat $13,000, Electronic Ref Mat (Incl. Access Fees) $16,500, Presv $500. Sal $226,500
Library Holdings: Audiobooks 4,344; DVDs 3,671; Large Print Bks 1,300; Bk Vols 40,714; Per Subs 118
Special Collections: Cape Cod Coll. Oral History
Subject Interests: Genealogy, Local hist
Automation Activity & Vendor Info: (Acquisitions) Innovative Interfaces, Inc; (Cataloging) Innovative Interfaces, Inc; (Circulation) Innovative Interfaces, Inc; (ILL) Innovative Interfaces, Inc; (OPAC) Innovative Interfaces, Inc; (Serials) Innovative Interfaces, Inc
Database Vendor: EBSCOhost, Gale Cengage Learning, Newsbank
Wireless access
Function: 24/7 Online cat, Adult bk club, Art exhibits, Bks on CD, Children's prog, Computers for patron use, Copy machines, Digital talking bks, Fax serv, Free DVD rentals, ILL available, Magazines, Mus passes, Music CDs, Online cat, OverDrive digital audio bks, Photocopying/Printing, Preschool reading prog, Prog for adults, Prog for children & young adult, Pub access computers, Scanner, Story hour, Summer reading prog, Tax forms, Wheelchair accessible
Publications: History of the Eastham Library
Mem of Massachusetts Libr Syst
Partic in Cape Libraries Automated Materials Sharing Network
Open Tues & Thurs 10-8, Wed, Fri & Sat 10-4
Friends of the Library Group

EASTHAMPTON

P EMILY WILLISTON MEMORIAL LIBRARY*, Nine Park St, 01027. SAN 307-367X. Tel: 413-527-1031. FAX: 413-527-3765. E-mail: ehampton@cwmars.org. Web Site: www.ewmlibrary.org. *Dir,* Position Currently Open
Founded 1869. Pop 16,000; Circ 124,000
Library Holdings: Audiobooks 2,000; CDs 929; DVDs 2,056; Large Print Bks 586; Bk Vols 58,736; Per Subs 100; Videos 1,067
Special Collections: Local History (Museum Coll), area city & town directories, photog & print archives
Automation Activity & Vendor Info: (Cataloging) Innovative Interfaces, Inc; (Circulation) Innovative Interfaces, Inc; (OPAC) Innovative Interfaces, Inc
Wireless access
Partic in Central & Western Massachusetts Automated Resource Sharing
Open Mon 10-8, Tues & Wed 9-8, Thurs & Fri 9-6
Friends of the Library Group

EASTON

C STONEHILL COLLEGE*, MacPhaidin Library, 320 Washington St, 02357-4015. SAN 307-5958. Tel: 508-565-1313. Interlibrary Loan Service Tel: 508-565-1538. Reference Tel: 508-565-1203. FAX: 508-565-1424. Web Site: www.stonehill.edu/library. *Interim Dir,* Susan Conant; Tel: 508-565-1289, E-mail: sconant@stonehill.edu; *Head, Ref,* Joseph Middleton; Tel: 508-565-1433, E-mail: jmiddleton@stonehill.edu; *Head, Syst,* Jennifer Macaulay; Tel: 508-565-1238, E-mail: jmacaulay@stonehill.edu; *Cat,* Cheryl Brigante; Tel: 505-565-1151, E-mail: cbrigante@stonehill.edu; *Coll Develop,* Betsy Dean; Tel: 508-565-1329, E-mail: bdean@stonehill.edu; *Govt Doc, Ref Serv,* Jane Swiszcz; Tel: 508-565-1452, E-mail: jswiszcz@stonehill.edu; *ILL, Ref Serv,* Heather Perry; E-mail: hperry@stonehill.edu; *Per,* Geri Sheehan; Tel: 508-565-1293, E-mail: gsheehan@stonehill.edu; *Ref,* Patricia McPherson; Tel: 508-565-1844, E-mail: pmcpherson@stonehill.edu; *Spec Coll & Archives Librn,* Nicole Casper; Tel: 508-565-1396; *Syst Tech,* Katie Conklin; Tel: 508-565-1213; Staff 19 (MLS 9, Non-MLS 10)
Founded 1948. Enrl 2,410; Fac 192; Highest Degree: Bachelor
Library Holdings: CDs 3,093; DVDs 447; e-journals 1,282; Bk Vols 225,300; Per Subs 928; Videos 3,045
Special Collections: Michael Novak Papers; Rep Joseph W Martin Jr Papers & Memorabilia; Tofias Business Archives
Subject Interests: Bus & mgt, Relig
Automation Activity & Vendor Info: (Acquisitions) Innovative Interfaces, Inc; (Cataloging) Innovative Interfaces, Inc; (Circulation) Innovative Interfaces, Inc; (Course Reserve) Innovative Interfaces, Inc; (OPAC) Innovative Interfaces, Inc; (Serials) Innovative Interfaces, Inc
Database Vendor: Dialog, Gale Cengage Learning, LexisNexis, OCLC FirstSearch, TLC (The Library Corporation)
Mem of Massachusetts Libr Syst
Partic in Lyrasis; OCLC Online Computer Library Center, Inc
Special Services for the Deaf - Assistive tech; Closed caption videos
Special Services for the Blind - Assistive/Adapted tech devices, equip & products
Open Mon-Thurs 8am-1am, Fri 8am-10pm, Sat 10-9, Sun 10am-1am

EDGARTOWN

L DUKES LAW LIBRARY*, PO Box 1267, 02539. SAN 373-1650. Tel: 508-627-4668. *Adminr,* Paula Devaney
Library Holdings: Bk Vols 2,000; Per Subs 20
Open Mon-Fri 8:30-4

P EDGARTOWN FREE PUBLIC LIBRARY*, 58 N Water St, 02539. (Mail add: PO Box 5249, 02539-5249), SAN 307-3688. Tel: 508-627-1373. E-mail: edg_mail@clamsnet.org. Web Site: www.edpublib.vineyard.net. *Dir,* Felicia Cheney; *Asst Dir,* Deborah A MacInnis
Founded 1892. Pop 2,900; Circ 47,117
Library Holdings: Bk Vols 40,000; Per Subs 150
Automation Activity & Vendor Info: (Cataloging) Innovative Interfaces, Inc; (Circulation) Innovative Interfaces, Inc; (OPAC) Innovative Interfaces, Inc
Partic in Cape & Islands Interlibrary Asn; Cape Libraries Automated Materials Sharing Network
Open Mon & Thurs 10-5, Tues & Wed 12-8, Fri & Sat 12-5
Friends of the Library Group

S MARTHA'S VINEYARD MUSEUM*, Gale Huntington Library of History, Pease House, 59 School St, 02539. (Mail add: PO Box 1310, 02539-1310), SAN 321-0731. Tel: 508-627-4441. FAX: 508-627-4436. Web Site: www.marthasvineyardhistory.org. *Librn,* Position Currently Open; *Asst Librn,* Linda Wilson; Tel: 508-627-4441, Ext 115, E-mail: lwilson@mvmuseum.org; *Genealogy Serv,* Catherine Mayhew; E-mail: cmayhew@mvmuseum.org
Founded 1922
Library Holdings: Bk Titles 3,000; Per Subs 30
Special Collections: Account Books from Island Businesses & Individuals; Logbooks; Martha's Vineyard Genealogy; Photographs; Wampanoag Indian History & Genealogy. Oral History
Subject Interests: Agr, Archit, Fishing, Geol, Hist of Martha's Vineyard, Methodist histl mat, Oral hist, Seafaring, Steamboats, Whaling
Publications: The Dukes County Intelligencer (Local historical information)
Open Mon-Sat (mid-June to mid-October) 10-5; Wed-Sat (mid-October to mid-June) 11-4
Restriction: Open to pub for ref only

ERVING

P ERVING PUBLIC LIBRARY, 17 Moore St, 01344. SAN 307-3696. Tel: 413-423-3348. Web Site: www.erving-ma.org/library. *Libr Dir,* Barbara Friedman; E-mail: library.barbara.friedman@erving-ma.org
Pop 1,800; Circ 15,879
Library Holdings: Bk Vols 9,452; Per Subs 20
Wireless access

Open Mon & Thurs 1-7, Wed 10-4, Sun 1-4
Friends of the Library Group

ESSEX

S ESSEX HISTORICAL SOCIETY & SHIPBUILDING MUSEUM, INC*, Archives & Library, 28 Main St, 01929. (Mail add: PO Box 277, 01929-0277), SAN 371-6902. Tel: 978-768-3866. FAX: 978-768-2541. E-mail: info@essexshipbuildingmuseum.org. Web Site: essexshipbuildingmuseum.org. *Dir of Educ,* Randy Robar; *Archivist, Coll Develop, Curator,* Courtney Ellis Peckham
Founded 1976
Library Holdings: Bk Vols 900; Per Subs 10
Special Collections: Choate Papers; Essex History, bks, doc & photos; Maritime History, bks, doc & photos; Shipbuilding, bks, doc, drawings & photos
Subject Interests: Maritime hist
Function: Res libr
Publications: List of Watercraft Built in Essex 1860-1980
Restriction: Open by appt only

P T O H P BURNHAM PUBLIC LIBRARY, 30 Martin St, 01929. SAN 307-370X. Tel: 978-768-7410. FAX: 978-768-3370. E-mail: mes@mvlc.org. Web Site: www.essexma.org/Pages/EssexMA_Library/Index. *Dir,* Deborah French
Founded 1894. Pop 3,400; Circ 26,500
Library Holdings: DVDs 525; Bk Vols 22,000; Per Subs 24; Talking Bks 250
Wireless access
Mem of Massachusetts Libr Syst
Partic in Merrimack Valley Library Consortium
Open Mon & Wed 1-7, Tues, Thurs & Fri 1-5, Sat 10-Noon
Friends of the Library Group

EVERETT

P EVERETT PUBLIC LIBRARIES*, Frederick E Parlin Memorial Library, 410 Broadway, 02149. SAN 345-1895. Tel: 617-394-2300. Reference Tel: 617-394-2302. FAX: 617-389-1230. TDD: 617-389-0784. E-mail: eve@noblenet.org. Web Site: www.noblenet.org/everett. *Dir,* Deborah V Abraham; Tel: 617-394-2303, E-mail: abraham@noblenet.org; *Asst Dir,* Mary Puleo; Tel: 617-394-2304; *Cat,* Sharon Morita; Tel: 617-394-2307, E-mail: morita@noblenet.org; *Ch Serv,* Ellen VandaLinda; Tel: 617-394-2305, E-mail: vandalinda@noblenet.org; *Circ,* Lisa Navarro; E-mail: navarro@noblenet.org; *Circ, Ch,* Anna Pisano; Tel: 617-394-2306, E-mail: pisano@noblenet.org; *Ref Serv, Ad,* Mark Parisi; E-mail: parisi@noblenet.org; *YA Serv,* Stacy DeBole; E-mail: debole@noblenet.org; Staff 35 (MLS 9, Non-MLS 26)
Founded 1879. Pop 34,773; Circ 111,239
Library Holdings: Bks on Deafness & Sign Lang 115; High Interest/Low Vocabulary Bk Vols 50; Bk Vols 85,000; Per Subs 120
Subject Interests: City hist
Automation Activity & Vendor Info: (Cataloging) Innovative Interfaces, Inc; (Circulation) Innovative Interfaces, Inc; (ILL) Innovative Interfaces, Inc; (OPAC) Innovative Interfaces, Inc
Database Vendor: EBSCOhost, Gale Cengage Learning
Publications: Children's Brochure; General Brochure; Internet Services Brochure; Young Adult Brochure
Partic in North of Boston Library Exchange, Inc
Special Services for the Deaf - TDD equip
Special Services for the Blind - Internet workstation with adaptive software
Open Mon-Thurs 9-9, Fri & Sat 9-5
Friends of the Library Group
Branches: 1
SHUTE MEMORIAL, 781 Broadway, 02149, SAN 307-3742. Tel: 617-394-2308. FAX: 617-394-2354. *Dir,* Deborah Abraham; E-mail: abraham@noblenet.org; Staff 5 (MLS 2, Non-MLS 3)
Library Holdings: Bk Vols 30,000; Per Subs 30
Publications: Shute Memorial Library: A Short History (Local historical information)
Open Mon-Thurs 10-6, Fri 10-5
Friends of the Library Group

FAIRHAVEN

P MILLICENT LIBRARY*, 45 Centre St, 02719. (Mail add: PO Box 30, 02719-0030), SAN 307-3769. Tel: 508-992-5342. FAX: 508-993-7288. Web Site: www.millicentlibrary.org. *Dir,* Carolyn Longworth; E-mail: clongworth@sailsinc.org; *Asst Dir,* Juanita Goulart; E-mail: jgoulart@sailsinc.org; *Archivist,* Debbie Charpentier; E-mail: dcharpentier@sailsinc.org; *Youth Serv,* Lee Engwall; E-mail: lengwall@sailsinc.org; Staff 10 (MLS 3, Non-MLS 7)
Founded 1893. Pop 16,279; Circ 124,025
Library Holdings: AV Mats 7,334; Bk Vols 64,785; Per Subs 175
Special Collections: Manjiro Nakahama (Journal of His Voyages 1840); Mark Twain (Letters to the Rogers Family)
Subject Interests: Art & archit
Automation Activity & Vendor Info: (Cataloging) SirsiDynix; (Circulation) SirsiDynix; (OPAC) SirsiDynix
Publications: Booklets on Fairhaven's History; Henry Huttleson Rogers; Mark Twain & Henry Huttleson Rogers, An Odd Couple; Mark Twain Letter to the Rogers Family
Partic in SAILS Library Network
Friends of the Library Group

FALL RIVER

J BRISTOL COMMUNITY COLLEGE*, Eileen T Farley Learning Resources Center, 777 Elsbree St, 02720. SAN 307-3777. Tel: 508-678-2811. Circulation Tel: 508-678-2811, Ext 2105. Interlibrary Loan Service Tel: 508-678-2811 Ext 2106. Reference Tel: 508-678-2811, Ext 2108. Administration Tel: 508-678-2811, Ext 2102. FAX: 508-730-3270. Web Site: bristolcc.edu/academics/library/index.cfm. *Dean, Learning Res,* Sainath Chinnaswamy; Tel: 508-678-2811, Ext 2675; *Librn,* Gabriela Adler; Tel: 508-678-2811, Ext 2104; *Librn,* James Emond; Tel: 508-678-2811, Ext 2316; *Access Serv Librn,* Robert Rezendes; *Ser Librn,* Melanie Johnson; Tel: 508-678-2811, Ext 2458; *Coordr, Acq,* Maryellen Pettine; Tel: 508-678-2811, Ext 2281; Staff 7 (MLS 4, Non-MLS 3)
Founded 1966. Enrl 5,059; Fac 106; Highest Degree: Associate
Library Holdings: Audiobooks 888; Bks on Deafness & Sign Lang 215; CDs 1,537; DVDs 923; e-books 395; Electronic Media & Resources 17; Microforms 12,640; Bk Titles 54,800; Bk Vols 63,200; Per Subs 220; Videos 4,946
Special Collections: Lizzie Borden Coll
Automation Activity & Vendor Info: (Cataloging) SirsiDynix; (Circulation) SirsiDynix; (Course Reserve) SirsiDynix; (OPAC) SirsiDynix; (Serials) SirsiDynix
Database Vendor: EBSCOhost, Gale Cengage Learning, LexisNexis, OCLC FirstSearch
Wireless access
Function: ILL available
Mem of Massachusetts Libr Syst
Partic in Lyrasis; SAILS Library Network
Special Services for the Blind - Computer with voice synthesizer for visually impaired persons; Screen enlargement software for people with visual disabilities
Open Mon-Thurs 8-9, Fri 8-7, Sat 9-5, Sun 11-6

M CHARLTON MEMORIAL HOSPITAL*, Ida S Charlton Medical Library, 363 Highland Ave, 02720. SAN 307-3831. Tel: 508-679-7196. FAX: 508-679-7458. Web Site: www.southcoast.org/library. *Med Librn,* Jennifer Lanouette
Founded 1949
Library Holdings: e-books 60; e-journals 5,000; Bk Vols 450; Per Subs 60
Special Collections: Rare Books
Database Vendor: OVID Technologies
Mem of Massachusetts Libr Syst
Partic in Southeastern Massachusetts Consortium of Health Science Libraries
Open Mon, Wed & Fri 7:30-4

S FALL RIVER HISTORICAL SOCIETY MUSEUM*, Archives & Research, 451 Rock St, 02720. SAN 370-8500. Tel: 508-679-1071. FAX: 508-675-5754. Web Site: www.lizzieborden.org. *Curator,* Michael Martins; *Archivist,* Marie-Claire Lajoie
Library Holdings: Bk Vols 7,500
Open Tues-Fri 9-4:30

P FALL RIVER PUBLIC LIBRARY, 104 N Main St, 02720. SAN 345-2018. Tel: 508-324-2700. Web Site: www.fallriverlibrary.org. *Adminr,* Laurel Ann Clark; Fax: 508-327-2707, E-mail: lclark@sailsinc.org; *Asst Admin,* Liane Verville; E-mail: lverville@sailsinc.org; *Ch Serv,* David Mello; E-mail: dmello@sailsinc.org; *Ref Serv,* Kulpa Kathryn; E-mail: kkulpa@sailsinc.org; *Tech Serv,* Kimberly Silva; E-mail: ksilva@sailsinc.org; Staff 19 (MLS 4, Non-MLS 15)
Founded 1860. Pop 88,945; Circ 206,114
Jul 2013-Jun 2014 Income (Main Library and Branch(s)) $1,295,668, State $138,637, City $1,055,906, Federal $101,125. Mats Exp $146,237, Books $106,899, Per/Ser (Incl. Access Fees) $24,478, AV Mat $14,860. Sal $734,269
Library Holdings: AV Mats 4,000; CDs 1,912; DVDs 8,181; e-books 8,002; Electronic Media & Resources 4,230; Large Print Bks 6,000; Bk Titles 161,710; Bk Vols 200,235; Per Subs 245; Talking Bks 3,000; Videos 3,200
Special Collections: Dr David S Greer Coll for Peace, Science & Education; Estes Coll of Books by Individuals Born & Who Have Lived in Fall River; Lizzie Borden Coll; Portuguese Language Materials Coll
Subject Interests: Local hist

Automation Activity & Vendor Info: (Acquisitions) SirsiDynix; (Cataloging) SirsiDynix; (Circulation) SirsiDynix; (OPAC) SirsiDynix
Database Vendor: Gale Cengage Learning
Wireless access
Mem of Massachusetts Libr Syst
Partic in SAILS Library Network
Special Services for the Blind - Audio mat; Bks on cassette; Bks on CD
Open Mon-Thurs 9-9, Fri 9-5, Sat (Sept-June) 9-5
Friends of the Library Group
Branches: 2
EAST END, 1386 Pleasant St, 02723, SAN 345-2042. Tel: 508-324-2709. FAX: 508-324-2709. *Br Mgr,* Conor Murray; E-mail: cmurray@sailsinc.org; Staff 3 (Non-MLS 3)
Open Mon-Wed 9-5, Thurs 12:30-8, Fri 9-4:30, Sat (Fall-Spring) 9-4:30
Friends of the Library Group
SOUTH, 1310 S Main St, 02724, SAN 345-2077. Tel: 508-324-2708. FAX: 508-324-2708. *Br Mgr,* Elizabeth Washburn; E-mail: bwashbur@sailsinc.org; Staff 3 (Non-MLS 3)
Library Holdings: AV Mats 290; Large Print Bks 150; Bk Vols 20,000; Per Subs 36
Open Mon, Tues & Thurs 9-5, Wed 11-7, Fri & Sat 9-4:30
Friends of the Library Group

S MARINE MUSEUM AT FALL RIVER, INC LIBRARY*, 70 Water St, 02721. SAN 307-3807. Tel: 508-674-3533. FAX: 508-674-3534. *Librn,* Carol Gafford
Founded 1968
Library Holdings: Bk Vols 2,000
Wireless access
Restriction: Open by appt only

GL MASSACHUSETTS TRIAL COURT LAW LIBRARIES*, Fall River Law Library, Superior Courthouse, 186 S Main St, 02721. SAN 307-3793. Tel: 508-491-3475. FAX: 508-491-3482. E-mail: fallriver.lawlib@verizon.net. Web Site: www.lawlib.state.ma.us/locations.html. *Head Librn,* Madlyn Correa; *Asst Librn,* Robin Perry
Library Holdings: Bk Vols 31,000; Per Subs 37
Database Vendor: OCLC FirstSearch, Westlaw
Wireless access
Partic in OCLC Online Computer Library Center, Inc
Open Mon-Fri 8:30-4:30

R TEMPLE BETH EL*, Ziskind Memorial Library, 385 High St, 02720. SAN 307-3823. Tel: 508-674-3529. FAX: 508-674-3058. *Librn,* Robin Fielding
Founded 1955
Library Holdings: Bk Vols 6,500; Per Subs 35

S USS MASSACHUSETTS MEMORIAL COMMITTEE, INC*, Archives & Technical Library, Battleship Cove, Five Water St, 02721-1540. SAN 370-3258. Tel: 508-678-1100. Toll Free Tel: 800-533-3194 (New England only). FAX: 508-674-5597. E-mail: battleship@battleshipcove.org, curator@battleshipcove.org. Web Site: www.battleshipcove.com. *Curator,* Donald R Shannon; Tel: 508-678-1100, Ext 116, E-mail: dshannon@battleshipcove.org; *Coll Develop,* Christopher J Nardi; Tel: 508-678-1100, Ext 108
Library Holdings: Bk Vols 2,000
Special Collections: Blue Prints of Ships & Equipment, Machinery of US Navy
Subject Interests: World War II
Wireless access
Restriction: Open by appt only

FALMOUTH

S FALMOUTH HISTORICAL SOCIETY*, Resources Center History & Genealogy Archives Library, Palmer Ave at the Village Green, 02541. (Mail add: PO Box 174, 02541-0174), SAN 326-5080. Tel: 508-548-4857. FAX: 508-540-0968. E-mail: fhs@cape.com. Web Site: www.falmouthhistoricalsociety.org. *Dir,* Carolyn T Powers; *Archivist,* Mary E Sicchio
Library Holdings: Bk Vols 1,020
Special Collections: Katharine Lee Bates Coll. Oral History
Subject Interests: Genealogy, Local hist
Publications: Arnold W Dyer Hotels & Inns of Falmouth (1993); Arnold W Dyer Residential Falmouth: an 1897 Souvenir brought up-to-date (c1897, 1992); Charlotte S Price Compilation (guide to manuscripts & special coll in the archives of Falmouth Historial Society); Geoffrey Theodate Suckanesset: Reprint with index (c1928, 1992)

M FALMOUTH HOSPITAL*, Medical Library, 100 Ter Heun Dr, 02540. SAN 377-9092. Tel: 508-457-3521. FAX: 508-457-3997. *Librn,* Susan Hanley
Library Holdings: Bk Vols 800; Per Subs 150
Partic in Massachusetts Health Sciences Libraries Network; National Network of Libraries of Medicine New England Region; Southeastern Massachusetts Consortium of Health Science Libraries

P FALMOUTH PUBLIC LIBRARY*, 300 Main St, 02540. SAN 345-2107. Tel: 508-457-2555. FAX: 508-457-2559. E-mail: info@falmouthpubliclibrary.org. Web Site: www.falmouthpubliclibrary.org. *Dir,* Leslie Morrissey; *Asst Dir,* Linda Collins; E-mail: lcollins@falmouthpubliclibrary.org; *Ad, Ref Supvr,* Jill Erickson; *Ch,* Laura Ford; *Circ Librn,* Tammy Amon; *Syst Librn,* Peter Cook; *Tech Serv Librn,* Frances Bordonaro; Staff 35 (MLS 10, Non-MLS 25)
Founded 1901. Pop 33,123; Circ 452,535
Jul 2010-Jun 2011 Income (Main Library and Branch(s)) $1,621,866. Sal $1,240,879
Library Holdings: Audiobooks 7,602; CDs 7,602; DVDs 11,516; e-books 20,317; Electronic Media & Resources 135; Microforms 7,183; Bk Titles 128,993; Per Subs 417; Spec Interest Per Sub 18
Special Collections: Genealogy Coll; Local Author (Katharine Lee Bates Coll); Local History Coll
Subject Interests: Local hist, Poetry
Automation Activity & Vendor Info: (Acquisitions) Innovative Interfaces, Inc; (Cataloging) Innovative Interfaces, Inc; (Circulation) Innovative Interfaces, Inc; (Course Reserve) Innovative Interfaces, Inc; (ILL) Innovative Interfaces, Inc; (Media Booking) Innovative Interfaces, Inc; (OPAC) Innovative Interfaces, Inc; (Serials) Innovative Interfaces, Inc
Wireless access
Function: Summer reading prog
Mem of Massachusetts Libr Syst
Partic in Cape Libraries Automated Materials Sharing Network
Special Services for the Deaf - Bks on deafness & sign lang; Closed caption videos; High interest/low vocabulary bks; Sign lang interpreter upon request for prog; TTY equip
Special Services for the Blind - Accessible computers; Bks available with recordings; Bks on cassette; Bks on CD; Cassettes; Computer with voice synthesizer for visually impaired persons; Copier with enlargement capabilities; Descriptive video serv (DVS); Extensive large print coll; Home delivery serv; Internet workstation with adaptive software; Large print & cassettes; Large print bks; Magnifiers; PC for handicapped; Recorded bks; Screen enlargement software for people with visual disabilities; Screen reader software; Sound rec; ZoomText magnification & reading software
Open Mon, Thurs & Fri 9:30-5:30, Tues & Wed 9:30-9, Sat 9:30-5, Sun (Sept-June) 12-4
Friends of the Library Group
Branches: 2
EAST FALMOUTH BRANCH, 310 E Falmouth Hwy, East Falmouth, 02536, SAN 345-2131. Tel: 508-548-6340. FAX: 508-543-6340. E-mail: efal_mail@clamsnet.org. *Librn,* Margaret Borden
Library Holdings: Bk Vols 20,000
Database Vendor: Newsbank, ProQuest, ReferenceUSA
Open Mon & Wed 10-5, Tues 1-5, Thurs 1-7
Friends of the Library Group
NORTH FALMOUTH BRANCH, Six Chester St, North Falmouth, 02556-2408. (Mail add: PO Box 370, North Falmouth, 02556-0370), SAN 345-2166. Tel: 508-563-2922. *Librn,* Laurie McNee
Open Mon & Fri 2-7, Wed 9-12
Friends of the Library Group

FITCHBURG

P FITCHBURG PUBLIC LIBRARY*, 610 Main St, 01420-3146. SAN 307-3866. Tel: 978-829-1780. FAX: 978-345-9631. E-mail: fplref@cwmars.org. Web Site: www.fitchburgpubliclibrary.org. *Dir,* Sharon A Bernard; E-mail: sbernard@fitchburgma.gov; *Youth Serv Librn,* Marcia Ladd; Tel: 978-829-1789, E-mail: mladd@cwmars.org; Staff 6 (MLS 4.5, Non-MLS 1.5)
Founded 1859. Pop 40,000; Circ 142,687
Jul 2012-Jun 2013 Income $727,498, City $662,498, Other $65,000. Mats Exp $97,332. Sal $409,435 (Prof $267,479)
Library Holdings: Audiobooks 9,666; AV Mats 7,030; DVDs 9,520; e-books 17,026; Bk Vols 118,369; Per Subs 53
Automation Activity & Vendor Info: (Cataloging) Evergreen; (Circulation) Evergreen; (ILL) Evergreen; (OPAC) Evergreen
Database Vendor: Gale Cengage Learning, Newsbank, ProQuest
Wireless access
Function: Adult bk club, Adult literacy prog, Archival coll, Audiobks via web, Bk club(s), Bks on cassette, Bks on CD, Children's prog, Computers for patron use, Copy machines, e-mail serv, Electronic databases & coll, Exhibits, Free DVD rentals, Genealogy discussion group, Magnifiers for reading, Mail & tel request accepted, Microfiche/film & reading machines, Mus passes, Music CDs, Online cat, Online ref, OverDrive digital audio

bks, Photocopying/Printing, Preschool outreach, Preschool reading prog, Prog for adults, Prog for children & young adult, Pub access computers, Ref serv available, Ref serv in person, Res libr, Scanner, Spanish lang bks, Spoken cassettes & CDs, Spoken cassettes & DVDs, Story hour, Summer reading prog, Tax forms, Teen prog, Telephone ref, VHS videos, Wheelchair accessible, Writing prog
Mem of South Central Library System
Partic in Central-Western Mass Automated Resource Sharing
Special Services for the Deaf - TTY equip
Special Services for the Blind - Magnifiers
Open Mon & Tues 10-8, Wed & Thurs 12-8, Fri 10-5, Sat 10-3
Friends of the Library Group

C FITCHBURG STATE UNIVERSITY*, Amelia V Galucci-Cirio Library, 160 Pearl St, 01420. SAN 307-3874. Tel: 978-665-3194, 978-665-3196. Circulation Tel: 978-665-3063. Interlibrary Loan Service Tel: 978-665-3065. Reference Tel: 978-665-3223. FAX: 978-665-3069. E-mail: circulation@fitchburgstate.edu. Web Site: www.fitchburgstate.edu/academics/library. *Dir,* Robert Foley; E-mail: rfoley@fitchburgstate.edu; *Ref Librn,* Jennifer Fielding; Tel: 978 665-3197; *Ref Librn,* Mark Melchior; Tel: 978 665-4869; *Tech Serv Librn,* Nancy Tunrbill; Tel: 978 665-4338; *Access Serv,* Linda LeBlanc; Tel: 978-665-3062; Staff 12 (MLS 6, Non-MLS 6)
Founded 1894. Enrl 6,768; Fac 177; Highest Degree: Master
Jul 2008-Jun 2009 Income $571,785. Mats Exp $430,574, Books $87,840, Per/Ser (Incl. Access Fees) $177,722, Other Print Mats $1,374, Micro $424, AV Mat $2,455, Electronic Ref Mat (Incl. Access Fees) $160,000, Presv $358. Sal $636,715 (Prof $367,615)
Library Holdings: AV Mats 2,455; e-journals 47,000; Electronic Media & Resources 140; Microforms 130,860; Bk Vols 220,018; Per Subs 1,861; Spec Interest Per Sub 8
Special Collections: College Archives; John van Cortland Moon Coll; Rice Art Coll; Robert Cormier Coll; Robert Salvatore Coll
Subject Interests: Bus, Communications, Computer sci, Media, Nursing
Automation Activity & Vendor Info: (Acquisitions) Ex Libris Group; (Cataloging) Ex Libris Group; (Circulation) Ex Libris Group; (Course Reserve) Docutek; (ILL) OCLC; (OPAC) Ex Libris Group; (Serials) Ex Libris Group
Database Vendor: ACM (Association for Computing Machinery), American Psychological Association (APA), Annual Reviews, Backstage Library Works, BioOne, Career Guidance Foundation, Cinahl, College Source, CRC Press/Taylor & Francis Group, CredoReference, Dialog, EBSCOhost, Facts on File, Gale Cengage Learning, Grolier Online, Ingenta, JSTOR, LexisNexis, OCLC FirstSearch, OCLC WorldShare Interlibrary Loan, Paratext, Project MUSE, ProQuest, PubMed, RefWorks, SerialsSolutions, Wilson - Wilson Web, YBP Library Services
Wireless access
Publications: Annual Reports; Directories; LibGuides (Library instruction); Newsletter
Partic in Dialog Corp; Lyrasis; OCLC Online Computer Library Center, Inc
Open Mon-Thurs 8am-11pm, Fri 8-5, Sat Noon-5, Sun 1-11

L MASSACHUSETTS TRIAL COURT*, Fitchburg Law Library, Superior Court House, 84 Elm St, 01420-3296. SAN 307-3858. Tel: 978-345-6726. FAX: 978-345-7334. *Librn,* Peter Anderegg; E-mail: peter.anderegg@verizon.net; *Asst Librn,* Donna Wilkin
Founded 1871
Subject Interests: Law
Partic in OCLC Online Computer Library Center, Inc
Open Mon-Fri 8:30-4:30

FLORENCE

P LILLY LIBRARY*, 19 Meadow St, 01062. SAN 322-7626. Tel: 413-587-1500. Reference Tel: 413-587-1501. Administration Tel: 413-587-1503. FAX: 413-587-1504. E-mail: lillylibrary@cwmars.org. Web Site: www.lillylibrary.org. *Dir,* Mary Anne Tourjee; *Asst Dir, Cat,* Charlotte Carver; *Ch Serv,* Kimberly Evans-Perez; Staff 11 (MLS 2, Non-MLS 9)
Founded 1890. Pop 30,000; Circ 79,000
Library Holdings: AV Mats 812; DVDs 182; Large Print Bks 174; Bk Vols 22,185; Per Subs 109; Talking Bks 364; Videos 798
Automation Activity & Vendor Info: (Cataloging) Follett Software; (Circulation) Follett Software; (OPAC) Follett Software
Function: ILL available, Photocopying/Printing, Prog for children & young adult, Ref serv available, Summer reading prog, Wheelchair accessible
Friends of the Library Group

FLORIDA

P FLORIDA FREE LIBRARY*, 56 N County Rd, 01247-9614. SAN 307-3890. Tel: 413-664-0153. FAX: 413-663-3593. *Actg Dir,* Alicia Daniels; E-mail: danielsmill@netzero.com
Pop 779; Circ 14,965
Library Holdings: DVDs 25; Bk Titles 9,000; Per Subs 36; Videos 400
Open Mon & Fri 9-3, Tues & Thurs 5-8

FOXBOROUGH

P BOYDEN LIBRARY*, Ten Bird St, 02035. SAN 307-3904. Tel: 508-543-1245. FAX: 508-543-1193. Web Site: www.boydenlibrary.org. *Dir,* Jerry Cirillo; *Adult Serv,* Diane Monahan; *Cat,* Timothy Golden; *Ch Serv,* Margaret Rossetti; *Circ,* Deborah Volpini; *Ref,* Kathy Bell-Harney; Staff 6 (MLS 6)
Founded 1870. Pop 16,813; Circ 196,042
Jul 2007-Jun 2008 Income $876,891. Mats Exp $117,250. Sal $658,441
Library Holdings: AV Mats 10,642; Bk Vols 91,066; Per Subs 194
Special Collections: Genealogy & Local History Coll
Automation Activity & Vendor Info: (Cataloging) SirsiDynix; (Circulation) SirsiDynix; (ILL) SirsiDynix; (OPAC) SirsiDynix
Mem of Massachusetts Libr Syst
Partic in SAILS Library Network
Open Mon-Thurs 10-8, Fri 10-6, Sat 10-5
Friends of the Library Group

FRAMINGHAM

S DANFORTH MUSEUM OF ART*, Marks Fine Arts Library, 123 Union Ave, 01702. SAN 373-1618. Tel: 508-620-0050. FAX: 508-872-5542. Web Site: www.danforthmuseum.org. *Dir,* Katherine French
Founded 1975
Library Holdings: Bk Vols 10,000
Restriction: Limited access for the pub, Open by appt only

P FRAMINGHAM PUBLIC LIBRARY*, 49 Lexington St, 01702-8278. SAN 345-2344. Tel: 508-532-5570. FAX: 508-820-7210. TDD: 508-872-2775. Web Site: www.framinghamlibrary.org. *Dir,* Mark Contois; Tel: 508-879-5570, Ext 4358, E-mail: mcontois@minlib.net; *Asst Dir,* Jane Peck; *Ch Serv,* Lucy Loveridge; Tel: 508-879-5570, Ext 4334, E-mail: lloverridge@minlib.net; *Circ,* Kelly Sprague; Tel: 508-879-5570, Ext 4345; *Coll Develop Librn,* Christine Hunnefeld; Tel: 508-879-5570, Ext 4359, E-mail: hunnefeld@minlib.net; *Commun Serv,* Michelle LeMonde-McIntyre; Tel: 508-879-5570, Ext 4347, E-mail: mlemonde-mcintyre@minlib.net; *ILL,* Laraine Warby; Tel: 508-879-3570, Ext 224; *Tech Serv,* Linda Benjaminsen; Tel: 508-879-5570, Ext 4319, E-mail: lbenjaminsen@minlib.net; Staff 87 (MLS 26, Non-MLS 61)
Founded 1855. Pop 64,462; Circ 872,067
Jul 2006-Jun 2007 Income $2,326,743. Mats Exp $361,250. Sal $1,861,989
Library Holdings: Bk Titles 239,718; Per Subs 394
Subject Interests: Educ, Employment, Local hist, Portuguese (Lang), Spanish (Lang)
Automation Activity & Vendor Info: (Acquisitions) Innovative Interfaces, Inc; (Cataloging) Innovative Interfaces, Inc; (Circulation) Innovative Interfaces, Inc; (OPAC) Innovative Interfaces, Inc; (Serials) Innovative Interfaces, Inc
Database Vendor: Gale Cengage Learning, OCLC FirstSearch, SirsiDynix
Mem of Massachusetts Libr Syst
Partic in Minuteman Library Network
Special Services for the Deaf - TTY equip
Open Mon-Thurs 9-9, Fri & Sat 9-5, Sun 2-5
Friends of the Library Group
Branches: 1
CHRISTA CORRIGAN MCAULIFFE BRANCH, Ten Nicholas Rd, 01701-3469, SAN 345-2409. Tel: 508-532-5636. FAX: 508-788-1930. *Br Mgr,* Jane Peck; E-mail: jpeck@minlib.net; *Ch Serv,* Robin Frank
Open Mon-Thurs 9-9, Fri & Sat 9-5
Friends of the Library Group

C FRAMINGHAM STATE COLLEGE*, Henry Whittemore Library, 100 State St, 01701. (Mail add: PO Box 9101, 01701-9101), SAN 307-3955. Tel: 508-626-4651. Circulation Tel: 508-626-4650. Reference Tel: 508-626-4654. FAX: 508-626-4006. E-mail: reference@framingham.edu. Web Site: www.framingham.edu/henry-whittemore-library. *Dir of Libr Serv,* Bonnie Mitchell; E-mail: bmitchell@framingham.edu; *Access Serv Librn,* Peg Snyder; Tel: 508-626-4027, E-mail: msnyder@framingham.edu; *Acq Librn,* Shin Freedman; Tel: 508-626-4666, E-mail: sfreedman@framingham.edu; *Cat Librn,* Suzanne Meunier; Tel: 508-626-4656, E-mail: smeunier@framingham.edu; *Curric Librn,* Kim Cochrane; Tel: 508-626-4657, E-mail: kcochrane1@framingham.edu; *Electronic Res Librn, Ref Serv Librn,* Millie Gonzalez; Tel: 508-626-4655, E-mail: vgonzalez@framingham.edu; *Ref Librn,* Marion Slack; E-mail: mslack@framingham.edu; *Ref & Instruction Librn,* Sandra Rothenberg; Tel: 508-626-4083, E-mail: srothenberg@framingham.edu; *Archivist, Spec Coll Librn,* Colleen Previte; Tel: 508-626-4648, E-mail: cprevite@framingham.edu; *Tech Serv Librn,* Richard Clare; E-mail: rclare@framingham.edu; Staff 11 (MLS 10, Non-MLS 1)
Founded 1969. Enrl 3,445; Fac 221; Highest Degree: Master
Library Holdings: Bk Titles 169,000; Bk Vols 205,000; Per Subs 400

Special Collections: College & Local History Coll; Curriculum Materials; Eric Documents Coll; Faculty Publications; Modern American Poetry
Subject Interests: Biol, Chem, Computer sci, Educ, Natural sci, Nursing, Phys sci, Psychol, Soc sci & issues
Automation Activity & Vendor Info: (Acquisitions) Innovative Interfaces, Inc; (Cataloging) Innovative Interfaces, Inc; (Circulation) Innovative Interfaces, Inc; (ILL) Innovative Interfaces, Inc; (OPAC) Innovative Interfaces, Inc; (Serials) Innovative Interfaces, Inc
Publications: Staff Newsletter; Student & Faculty Handbooks; Student Employee Manual
Partic in Lyrasis; Minuteman Library Network; OCLC Online Computer Library Center, Inc
Open Mon-Thurs 8am-11pm, Fri 8-5, Sat 9-5, Sun 1-11

M METROWEST MEDICAL CENTER*, Tedeschi Library & Information Center, 115 Lincoln St, 01702. SAN 307-3963. Tel: 508-383-1591. FAX: 508-879-0471. *Dir,* Sandra R Clevesy; Staff 3 (MLS 1, Non-MLS 2)
Founded 1960
Library Holdings: Bk Vols 3,200; Per Subs 126
Subject Interests: Clinical med, Hospital admin, Nursing
Database Vendor: OVID Technologies
Partic in Boston Biomedical Library Consortium; Dialog Corp; Massachusetts Health Sciences Libraries Network; National Network of Libraries of Medicine; OCLC Online Computer Library Center, Inc
Open Mon-Fri 8-4:30

S NEW ENGLAND WILD FLOWER SOCIETY, INC*, Lawrence Newcomb Library, 180 Hemenway Rd, 01701-2699. SAN 324-6892. Tel: 508-877-7630. FAX: 508-877-3658. Web Site: www.newfs.org. *Librn,* Nancy Webb; Staff 6 (MLS 2, Non-MLS 4)
Founded 1969
Library Holdings: Bk Titles 4,000
Special Collections: Comprehensive Coll of books on Wildflowers; Native Plant Slides; Newsletters of US Native Plant Societies
Subject Interests: Botany, Conserv of native plants, Ecology, Hort, Native plants, Natural hist, New England
Publications: Bibliography of Publications About Gardening with Native Plants; List of Botanical Clubs & Native Plants Societies in the US; Readsources: Book Review Section of Wild Flower Society Magazine

FRANKLIN

C DEAN COLLEGE*, E Ross Anderson Library, 99 Main St, 02038-1994. SAN 307-3998. Tel: 508-541-1771. FAX: 508-541-1918. Web Site: www.dean.edu/academics/library.cfm. *Dir,* Rick Barr; *Librn,* Judy Tobey; *Circ,* Karline Wild; *Instrul Tech,* Ted Burke; Staff 4 (MLS 3, Non-MLS 1)
Founded 1865. Enrl 1,400
Jun 2007-May 2008. Mats Exp $61,819, Books $31,449, Per/Ser (Incl. Access Fees) $10,720, AV Mat $1,381, Electronic Ref Mat (Incl. Access Fees) $18,269
Library Holdings: Bk Titles 32,500; Per Subs 110
Automation Activity & Vendor Info: (Cataloging) Innovative Interfaces, Inc; (Circulation) Innovative Interfaces, Inc; (Course Reserve) Innovative Interfaces, Inc; (OPAC) Innovative Interfaces, Inc; (Serials) Innovative Interfaces, Inc
Database Vendor: CQ Press, Gale Cengage Learning, H W Wilson, LexisNexis, ProQuest
Wireless access
Mem of Massachusetts Libr Syst
Partic in Minuteman Library Network; SE Asn of Coop Higher Educ Mass Consortium

P FRANKLIN PUBLIC LIBRARY*, 118 Main St, 02038. SAN 307-4005. Tel: 508-520-4940. Web Site: www.franklin.ma.us/auto/town/library. *Dir,* Betsy Ferry; *Asst Dir,* Felicia Oti; *Circ Mgr,* Jane Whiton; *Ch,* Elaine Fort Weischedel; *Ref,* Vicki Buchanio; Staff 18 (MLS 4, Non-MLS 14)
Founded 1790. Pop 29,560
Library Holdings: Bk Vols 87,000; Per Subs 230
Special Collections: Benjamin Franklin Special Coll; First Books of the Franklin Library
Subject Interests: Local hist
Publications: History of the Franklin Library
Open Mon-Thurs 9-9, Fri & Sat 9-5, Sun (Oct-April) 2-5
Friends of the Library Group

GARDNER

P LEVI HEYWOOD MEMORIAL LIBRARY*, 55 W Lynde St, 01440. SAN 307-4021. Tel: 978-632-5298. FAX: 978-630-2864. *Dir,* Gail P Landy; Staff 9 (MLS 2, Non-MLS 7)
Founded 1886. Pop 19,000
Library Holdings: Bk Vols 100,000; Per Subs 155
Subject Interests: Furniture
Automation Activity & Vendor Info: (Cataloging) Innovative Interfaces, Inc; (Circulation) Innovative Interfaces, Inc; (OPAC) Innovative Interfaces, Inc
Mem of Massachusetts Libr Syst
Open Mon & Wed 12-8, Tues, Thurs & Sat 9-5
Friends of the Library Group

S MASSACHUSETTS DEPARTMENT OF CORRECTIONS*, North Central Correctional Institute Library, 500 Colony Rd, 01440. SAN 372-4913. Tel: 978-632-2000, Ext 325. FAX: 978-630-6044. *Librn,* Carolyn Murphy
Library Holdings: Bk Vols 6,995; Per Subs 95
Open Mon-Sun 9-10:50, 1-2:40 & 6-8:40

J MOUNT WACHUSETT COMMUNITY COLLEGE LIBRARY*, LaChance Library, 444 Green St, 01440. SAN 307-403X. Tel: 978-630-9125. Reference Tel: 978-630-9338. Toll Free Tel: 888-884-6922. FAX: 978-630-9556. E-mail: library@mwcc.mass.edu. Web Site: library.mwcc.mass.edu. *Dean of Libr Serv,* Heidi McCann; Tel: 978-630-9126, E-mail: hmccann@mwcc.mass.edu; *Acq,* Nancy Boucher; *Cat,* Jess Mynes; *Circ,* Carla Morrissey; *Ref & Instrul Serv Librn,* Suzanne Levasseur; Staff 8 (MLS 6, Non-MLS 2)
Founded 1964. Enrl 6,282; Fac 73; Highest Degree: Associate
Jul 2008-Jun 2009 Income $515,374, Federal $1,870, Locally Generated Income $1,536, Parent Institution $511,968. Mats Exp $89,674, Books $10,394, Per/Ser (Incl. Access Fees) $20,367, Other Print Mats $26,045, AV Mat $4,969, Electronic Ref Mat (Incl. Access Fees) $27,899. Sal $384,993 (Prof $338,318)
Library Holdings: AV Mats 2,490; Bk Vols 53,763; Per Subs 146
Automation Activity & Vendor Info: (Acquisitions) Innovative Interfaces, Inc; (Cataloging) Innovative Interfaces, Inc; (Circulation) Innovative Interfaces, Inc; (Course Reserve) Innovative Interfaces, Inc; (ILL) OCLC Online; (OPAC) Innovative Interfaces, Inc; (Serials) Innovative Interfaces, Inc
Database Vendor: ALLDATA Online, Bowker, College Source, CredoReference, EBSCOhost, Facts on File, Gale Cengage Learning, Grolier Online, LexisNexis, OCLC FirstSearch, OCLC WorldShare Interlibrary Loan, Oxford Online, ProQuest, Westlaw
Wireless access
Mem of Massachusetts Libr Syst
Partic in Central & Western Massachusetts Automated Resource Sharing; Lyrasis; OCLC Online Computer Library Center, Inc; Westchester Academic Library Directors Organization (WALDO)
Special Services for the Deaf - Assistive tech
Special Services for the Blind - Assistive/Adapted tech devices, equip & products
Open Mon-Thurs (Sept-June) 7:30-7:30, Fri 7:30-4; Mon-Thurs (July & Aug) 8-4:30, Fri 8-4

GEORGETOWN

P GEORGETOWN PEABODY LIBRARY*, Lincoln Park, 01833. SAN 307-4056. Tel: 978-352-5728. FAX: 978-352-7415. Web Site: www.georgetownpl.org. *Dir, Libr Serv,* Ruth Eifert; E-mail: reifert@mvlc.org; *Ch Serv,* Catherine DeWitt; E-mail: cdewitt@mvlc.org; *Sr Libr Tech,* Michael Williams; E-mail: mwilliams@mvlc.org; Staff 5.3 (MLS 1, Non-MLS 4.3)
Founded 1869. Pop 7,377; Circ 43,865
Jul 2007-Jun 2008 Income $278,943. Mats Exp $61,653. Sal $161,643 (Prof $46,000)
Library Holdings: Audiobooks 1,150; DVDs 1,600; Bk Titles 43,000; Per Subs 95
Special Collections: Historical Newspapers; Local Town Reports
Automation Activity & Vendor Info: (Cataloging) SirsiDynix; (Circulation) SirsiDynix; (OPAC) SirsiDynix
Database Vendor: EBSCOhost, Wilson - Wilson Web
Wireless access
Partic in Merrimack Valley Library Consortium
Open Mon & Wed 2-8, Tues 10-8, Fri 10-5:30, Sat 9-1
Friends of the Library Group

GILL

P SLATE MEMORIAL LIBRARY*, 332 Main Rd, 01376. SAN 376-7515. Tel: 413-863-2591. FAX: 413-863-9347. E-mail: gill.slate.library@gmail.com. *Librn,* Jocelyn Castro-Santos
Pop 1,392; Circ 5,314
Library Holdings: Bk Titles 2,500; Bk Vols 3,000; Per Subs 10
Open Mon 2-6, Thurs 2-8, Sat 10-2
Friends of the Library Group

GLOUCESTER

S CAPE ANN MUSEUM LIBRARY/ARCHIVES*, 27 Pleasant St, 01930. SAN 307-4080. Tel: 978-283-0455. FAX: 978-283-4141. Web Site: www.capeannmuseum.org. *Dir,* Ronda Faloon; *Archivist/Librn,* Stephanie Buck; Staff 2 (MLS 1, Non-MLS 1)

Founded 1875
Library Holdings: Bk Titles 3,800; Per Subs 25; Videos 54
Special Collections: Manuscript Coll; Rare Book Coll; Turn of the Century Documentary Photography. Municipal Document Depository
Subject Interests: Decorative art, Fine arts, Genealogy, Local hist, Maritime hist, Photog
Wireless access
Open Wed-Sat 10-1
Restriction: Open to pub for ref only

M ADDISON GILBERT HOSPITAL*, Medical Library, 298 Washington St, 01930. SAN 377-9114. Tel: 978-283-4001, Ext 608. FAX: 978-281-1129. *Librn,* Charlotte Minasian
Library Holdings: Bk Titles 800; Per Subs 54
Partic in Massachusetts Health Sciences Libraries Network; Medical Library Association (MLA); Northeastern Consortium for Health Information

P GLOUCESTER, LYCEUM & SAWYER FREE LIBRARY*, Two Dale Ave, 01930-5906. SAN 345-2468. Tel: 978-281-9763. FAX: 978-281-9770. E-mail: sflib@sawyerfreelibrary.org. Web Site: www.sawyerfreelibrary.org. *Dir,* David McArdle; *Asst Dir,* Carol Gray; E-mail: gray@noblenet.org; *Librn,* Sharon Cohen; *Ref,* Judith Oski; *Ch Serv,* Catherine Talty; *Cat,* Helen Freeman; *Circ,* Gail Mondello; *YA Serv,* Cynthia Williams; Staff 17 (MLS 5, Non-MLS 12)
Founded 1830. Pop 30,000; Circ 202,100
Library Holdings: Bk Vols 118,369; Per Subs 194
Special Collections: Charles Olson Coll; T S Eliot Coll; US Census. Oral History
Subject Interests: Art & archit
Automation Activity & Vendor Info: (Cataloging) Innovative Interfaces, Inc; (Circulation) Innovative Interfaces, Inc; (OPAC) Innovative Interfaces, Inc
Database Vendor: Dialog, EBSCOhost, Gale Cengage Learning, OCLC FirstSearch, Wilson - Wilson Web
Publications: Annual Report; Newsletter (Monthly)
Mem of Massachusetts Libr Syst
Special Services for the Deaf - TTY equip
Open Mon-Thurs 8:30-8, Fri & Sat 8:30-5, Sun 1-5
Friends of the Library Group
Bookmobiles: 1. Librn, Sharon Cohen

P MAGNOLIA LIBRARY CENTER*, One Lexington Ave, 01930-3915. (Mail add: PO Box 5552, 01930-0007), SAN 307-4099. Tel: 978-525-3343. Web Site: www.maglib.org. *Chair,* Michele Brooks
Pop 27,209
Library Holdings: Bk Vols 1,500
Wireless access
Open Mon-Wed (Winter) 2-4, Sat 10-12; Mon-Fri (Summer) 10-12
Friends of the Library Group

GOSHEN

P GOSHEN FREE PUBLIC LIBRARY, 42 Main St, 01032-9608. (Mail add: 40 Main St, 01032), SAN 307-4110. Tel: 413-268-8236, Ext 111. E-mail: goshenfreelibrary@gmail.com. *Dir,* Martha N Noblick; Staff 1 (MLS 1)
Founded 1910. Pop 1,054; Circ 1,351
Library Holdings: Bk Titles 7,500; Bk Vols 8,000; Per Subs 15
Wireless access
Open Mon 4-8, Wed 3-6, Sat 10-1

GRAFTON

P GRAFTON PUBLIC LIBRARY*, 35 Grafton Common, 01519. (Mail add: PO Box 387, 01519-0387), SAN 345-2557. Tel: 508-839-4649. FAX: 508-839-7726. Web Site: www.graftonlibrary.org. *Dir,* Beth Gallaway; E-mail: bgallaway@cwmars.org; *Ref Librn,* Heidi Fowler; *Ch Serv,* Jennifer Mentzer; *Circ,* Susan Leto; *YA Serv,* Suzanne Witham; Staff 6 (MLS 3, Non-MLS 3)
Founded 1858. Pop 17,765; Circ 106,618
Library Holdings: AV Mats 5,789; e-books 1; Bk Vols 30,862; Per Subs 102
Automation Activity & Vendor Info: (Cataloging) Evergreen; (Circulation) Evergreen; (OPAC) Evergreen
Database Vendor: Facts on File, Gale Cengage Learning, Overdrive, Inc, ReferenceUSA, World Book Online
Wireless access
Function: Adult bk club, Audiobks via web, Bks on CD, Copy machines, Free DVD rentals, Homebound delivery serv, ILL available, Magnifiers for reading, Music CDs, Online searches, Photocopying/Printing, Prog for children & young adult, Pub access computers, Ref & res, Story hour, Summer reading prog, Tax forms, Telephone ref
Mem of Massachusetts Libr Syst
Partic in Cent Mass Automated Resource Sharing Network, Inc
Open Mon-Thurs 10-9, Fri & Sat 10-5
Friends of the Library Group

GRANBY

P GRANBY PUBLIC LIBRARY*, One Library Lane, 01033-9416. SAN 307-4137. Tel: 413-467-3320. FAX: 413-467-3320. Web Site: www.granbylibrary.com. *Dir,* Jennifer Crosby; E-mail: jennifer.crosby@cwmars.org; *Youth Serv Librn,* Janice McArdle; E-mail: jmcardle302@yahoo.com; *Cataloger,* Jeanne Crosby; E-mail: jcrosby@cwmars.org; Staff 3 (MLS 1, Non-MLS 2)
Founded 1891. Pop 5,850; Circ 25,853
Jul 2006-Jun 2007. Mats Exp $12,000
Library Holdings: AV Mats 1,900; Large Print Bks 170; Bk Titles 20,000; Bk Vols 22,000; Per Subs 75
Special Collections: Church Records (microfiche); Town Records
Subject Interests: Genealogy, Local hist, Math
Automation Activity & Vendor Info: (Cataloging) Innovative Interfaces, Inc; (Circulation) Innovative Interfaces, Inc; (OPAC) Innovative Interfaces, Inc
Partic in Connecticut Library Consortium
Open Tues, Wed & Fri 10:30-7, Sat 10:30-1
Friends of the Library Group

GRANVILLE

P GRANVILLE PUBLIC LIBRARY*, Two Granby Rd, 01034-9539. SAN 307-4153. Tel: 413-357-8531. FAX: 413-357-8531. *Dir,* Mary Short
Founded 1900. Pop 1,183; Circ 11,707
Library Holdings: Bk Vols 8,900
Open Mon 10-12 & 3-8, Wed 3-8, Thurs 5-8, Sat 10-12
Friends of the Library Group

GREAT BARRINGTON

S AMERICAN INSTITUTE FOR ECONOMIC RESEARCH, E C Harwood Library, 250 Division St, 01230-1119. (Mail add: PO Box 1000, 01230-1000), SAN 322-7928. Tel: 413-528-1216. FAX: 413-528-0103. E-mail: info@aier.org, library@aier.org. Web Site: www.aier.org. *Librn,* Suzanne Hermann; Staff 1 (MLS 1)
Founded 1975
Library Holdings: Bk Titles 15,000; Per Subs 70
Special Collections: AIER's Economic Education Bulletins 1961-present; AIER'S Research Reports 1934-present; Commercial & Financial Chronicle, 1923-1974; File of E C Harwood's Papers; The Annalist, 1923-1940
Subject Interests: Bus, Econ, Finance
Automation Activity & Vendor Info: (Cataloging) Inmagic, Inc.; (OPAC) Inmagic, Inc.; (Serials) Inmagic, Inc.
Wireless access
Publications: Business Cycle Monthly; Inflation Report (Monthly)

C BARD COLLEGE AT SIMON'S ROCK, Alumni Library, 84 Alford Rd, 01230. SAN 307-417X. Tel: 413-528-7370. FAX: 413-528-7380. E-mail: library@simons-rock.edu. Web Site: library.simons-rock.edu. *Dir,* Brian Mikesell; Tel: 413-528-7274, E-mail: bmikesell@simons-rock.edu; *ILL, Supvr, Access Serv,* Beth Sack; Tel: 413-528-7361, E-mail: bsack@simons-rock.edu; *ILL, Supvr, Tech Serv,* Beth Moser; Tel: 413-528-7356, E-mail: bbmoser@simons-rock.edu; *Coordr, Electronic Res,* Dana Cummings; Tel: 413-528-7284, E-mail: cummings@simons-rock.edu; Staff 4 (MLS 2, Non-MLS 2)
Founded 1966. Enrl 380; Fac 40; Highest Degree: Bachelor
Special Collections: Artist Book Coll; Early Music Scores (Bernard Krainus Coll); Social Movement Pamphlets; W E B DuBois Coll on the Black Experience
Automation Activity & Vendor Info: (Acquisitions) SirsiDynix; (Cataloging) SirsiDynix; (Circulation) SirsiDynix; (ILL) OCLC; (OPAC) SirsiDynix; (Serials) SirsiDynix
Wireless access
Restriction: Open to pub for ref & circ; with some limitations

P MASON LIBRARY*, 231 Main St, 01230. SAN 307-4161. Tel: 413-528-2403. *Dir,* Anne Just; *Asst Dir,* Linda Santos; *Ch Serv,* Karen Ball; Staff 8 (MLS 2, Non-MLS 6)
Founded 1861. Pop 7,441; Circ 12,648
Jul 2007-Jun 2008 Income $436,478, State $9,518, City $408,470, Locally Generated Income $18,490. Mats Exp $78,803, Books $49,891, Per/Ser (Incl. Access Fees) $7,066, AV Mat $21,846. Sal $279,692 (Prof $50,100)
Library Holdings: AV Mats 4,000; Large Print Bks 5,000; Bk Vols 35,000; Per Subs 70
Subject Interests: Genealogy
Automation Activity & Vendor Info: (Cataloging) Innovative Interfaces, Inc; (Circulation) Innovative Interfaces, Inc
Partic in Central & Western Massachusetts Automated Resource Sharing
Open Mon-Wed 10-6, Thurs 1-6, Fri 10-8, Sat 9-1
Friends of the Library Group

GREENFIELD

M FRANKLIN MEDICAL CENTER*, Health Sciences Library, 164 High St, 01301. SAN 377-9270. Tel: 413-773-2211. FAX: 413-773-2094. *Libr Serv Rep,* Adrienne Racz
Library Holdings: Bk Titles 800; Per Subs 60
Automation Activity & Vendor Info: (OPAC) SirsiDynix
Database Vendor: EBSCOhost, OVID Technologies
Wireless access
Partic in Basic Health Sciences Library Network; Massachusetts Health Sciences Libraries Network; Western Mass Health Info Consortium
Open Tues-Fri 8-4

J GREENFIELD COMMUNITY COLLEGE LIBRARY*, One College Dr, 01301-9739. SAN 307-4196. Tel: 413-775-1830. Circulation Tel: 413-775-1837. Reference Tel: 413-775-1831. Administration Tel: 413-775-1832. FAX: 413-775-1838. E-mail: reference@gcc.mass.edu. Web Site: web.gcc.mass.edu/library. *Libr Dir,* Deborah S Chown; E-mail: chown@gcc.mass.edu; *Librn,* Liza Harrington; Tel: 413-775-1836, E-mail: harringtonl@gcc.mass.edu; *Evening/Weekend Librn,* Jeri Moran; E-mail: moranj@gcc.mass.edu; *Coordr, Libr Serv,* Eric Poulin; Tel: 413-775-1834, E-mail: pouline@gcc.mass.edu; *Circ,* Terry Smith; E-mail: smitht@gcc.mass.edu; *Tech Serv,* Judi Ketchum; Tel: 413-775-1859, E-mail: ketchumj@gcc.mass.edu; *Tech Serv,* Hope Schneider; Tel: 413-775-1833, E-mail: schneide@gcc.mass.edu; Staff 6 (MLS 3.5, Non-MLS 2.5)
Founded 1962. Enrl 1,500; Highest Degree: Associate
Library Holdings: Electronic Media & Resources 60; Bk Vols 50,000; Per Subs 176
Special Collections: Archibald MacLeish Coll
Automation Activity & Vendor Info: (Cataloging) Innovative Interfaces, Inc; (Circulation) Innovative Interfaces, Inc; (OPAC) Innovative Interfaces, Inc; (Serials) Innovative Interfaces, Inc
Database Vendor: CQ Press, EBSCOhost, Facts on File, Gale Cengage Learning, LexisNexis, Newsbank, OCLC, Oxford Online, ProQuest, Springshare, LLC
Wireless access
Partic in Central-Western Mass Automated Resource Sharing; Lyrasis; OCLC Online Computer Library Center, Inc
Special Services for the Deaf - Assistive tech
Open Mon-Thurs 8am-8:30pm, Fri 8-5, Sat 10-4

P GREENFIELD PUBLIC LIBRARY, 402 Main St, 01301. SAN 307-420X. Tel: 413-772-1544. FAX: 413-772-1589. E-mail: librarian@greenfieldpubliclibrary.org. Web Site: www.greenfieldpubliclibrary.org. *Libr Dir,* Ellen Boyer; *Actg Head, Info Serv, Asst Libr Dir,* Lisa Prolman; *Head, Borrower Serv,* Jane Buchanan; *Head, Youth Serv,* Kay Lyons; *Tech Serv,* Cynthia Clifford; Staff 12 (MLS 3, Non-MLS 9)
Founded 1881. Pop 17,400; Circ 314,309
Library Holdings: AV Mats 8,550; e-books 32,468; Electronic Media & Resources 2,046; Microforms 693; Bk Vols 43,647; Per Subs 64
Special Collections: Genealogy Coll; Town Histories-Franklin County
Subject Interests: Local hist
Automation Activity & Vendor Info: (Cataloging) Evergreen; (Circulation) Evergreen; (OPAC) Evergreen
Database Vendor: Baker & Taylor, BWI, EBSCOhost, Gale Cengage Learning, Ingram Library Services, Medline, Newsbank, Overdrive, Inc
Wireless access
Function: 24/7 Online cat, Bks on CD, Chess club, Children's prog, Computers for patron use, Copy machines, Electronic databases & coll, eReaders, Free DVD rentals, Homebound delivery serv, ILL available, Magazines, Mus passes, Music CDs, Photocopying/Printing, Prog for adults, Prog for children & young adult, Pub access computers, Ref serv available, Scanner, Summer reading prog, Tax forms, Telephone ref
Publications: Bulletin (Online only); Newsletter (Quarterly)
Mem of Massachusetts Libr Syst
Partic in Central-Western Mass Automated Resource Sharing
Open Mon-Wed 9:30-8, Thurs & Fri 9:30-5, Sat 9:30-2
Friends of the Library Group

GL MASSACHUSETTS TRIAL COURT LAW LIBRARIES*, Franklin Law Library, Court House, 425 Main St, 01301. SAN 307-4188. Tel: 413-772-6580. FAX: 413-772-0743. E-mail: franklinlawlib@hotmail.com. Web Site: www.lawlib.state.ma.us. *Law Librn,* Susan Wells; Staff 1 (MLS 1)
Founded 1812
Library Holdings: Bk Titles 1,600; Bk Vols 30,000; Per Subs 200
Subject Interests: Fed law, State law
Automation Activity & Vendor Info: (Cataloging) SirsiDynix; (Circulation) SirsiDynix; (ILL) OCLC; (OPAC) SirsiDynix; (Serials) SirsiDynix
Database Vendor: HeinOnline, Loislaw, OCLC FirstSearch, OCLC WorldShare Interlibrary Loan, SirsiDynix, Westlaw
Wireless access
Function: Archival coll, ILL available, Online ref, Photocopying/Printing, Ref serv available, Telephone ref
Partic in Lyrasis; New England Law Library Consortium, Inc
Open Mon-Fri 8:30-4:30

S NORTHEAST SUSTAINABLE ENERGY ASSOCIATION*, Resource Center, 50 Miles St, 01301. SAN 321-7590. Tel: 413-774-6051. FAX: 413-774-6053. E-mail: nesea@nesea.org. Web Site. www.nesea.org. *Exec Dir,* Jennifer Marrapese; E-mail: jmarrapese@nesea.org; *Mgr,* Daniel Gronwald; Tel: 413-774-6051, Ext 10, E-mail: dgronwald@nesea.org
Founded 1974
Library Holdings: Bk Vols 2,000; Per Subs 50
Restriction: Open to pub for ref only

GROTON

P GROTON PUBLIC LIBRARY*, 99 Main St, 01450. SAN 307-4218. Tel: 978-448-8000. Circulation Tel: 978-448-1167. FAX: 978-448-1169. E-mail: info@gpl.org. Web Site: www.gpl.org. *Dir,* Vanessa Abraham; E-mail: vabraham@gpl.org; *Cat, Tech & Ref,* Jeffrey Pike; E-mail: jpike@gpl.org; *Ch Serv,* Karen Dunham; Tel: 978-448-1168; *ILL,* Karen L Bolduc; E-mail: kbolduc@gpl.org; *Ref Serv, Webmaster,* Susanne Olson; E-mail: solson@gpl.org; Staff 14 (MLS 3, Non-MLS 11)
Founded 1854. Pop 10,013; Circ 202,710
Jul 2005-Jun 2006 Income $642,134. Mats Exp $108,600. Sal $345,696 (Prof $151,921)
Library Holdings: AV Mats 8,460; Large Print Bks 386; Bk Titles 52,629; Bk Vols 57,260; Per Subs 147; Talking Bks 1,833
Automation Activity & Vendor Info: (Cataloging) TLC (The Library Corporation); (Circulation) TLC (The Library Corporation); (OPAC) TLC (The Library Corporation)
Database Vendor: Baker & Taylor, EBSCOhost, Facts on File, Gale Cengage Learning, Library Ideas, LLC, ProQuest, TLC (The Library Corporation)
Wireless access
Open Tues-Thurs 10-9, Fri 10-5, Sat 10-3, Sun (Jan-Apr) 1-5

GROVELAND

P LANGLEY-ADAMS LIBRARY*, 185 Main St, 01834-1314. SAN 307-4226. Tel: 978-372-1732. FAX: 978-374-6590. Web Site: www.langleyadamslib.org. *Dir,* Nathalie Harty; E-mail: nharty@mvlc.org; *Libr Serv Mgr,* Gail Ouellet; E-mail: gouellet@mvlc.org; *Youth Serv Librn,* Susan Lord; *Adult Serv & Outreach Coordr,* Diana Cummings; E-mail: dcummingslt@mvlc.org; Staff 4 (MLS 1, Non-MLS 3)
Pop 6,700; Circ 3,000
Library Holdings: Bk Vols 27,488; Per Subs 35
Automation Activity & Vendor Info: (Acquisitions) Horizon; (Cataloging) Horizon; (Circulation) Horizon; (OPAC) SirsiDynix
Database Vendor: EBSCOhost, Ingram Library Services, ProQuest
Wireless access
Partic in Merrimack Valley Library Consortium
Open Mon & Wed 1-8, Tues & Thurs 10-5:30, Fri 10-5, Sat 10-2
Friends of the Library Group

HADLEY

P GOODWIN MEMORIAL LIBRARY*, 50 Middle St, 01035-9544. SAN 307-4234. Tel: 413-584-7451. FAX: 413-584-9137. E-mail: goodwinlibrary@hadleyma.org. Web Site: www.hadley-goodwin.org. *Dir,* Jane Babcock; Staff 2 (MLS 1, Non-MLS 1)
Pop 5,000; Circ 23,000
Library Holdings: Audiobooks 200; CDs 150; Bk Vols 26,808; Per Subs 70; Videos 2,100
Wireless access
Open Tues & Thurs 11-5, Wed 3-8, Fri 3-7, Sat 1-4
Friends of the Library Group

HALIFAX

P HOLMES PUBLIC LIBRARY*, 470 Plymouth St, 02338. SAN 307-4242. Tel: 781-293-2271. FAX: 781-294-8518. E-mail: hfxpl@sailsinc.org. Web Site: www.sailsinc.org/halifax. *Dir, Libr Serv,* Elizabeth Randall; Fax: 781-294-8515; *Tech Coordr,* Darcy Klooster; *Adult Serv,* Jean Gallant; *Ch Serv,* Marie Coady; *Ref Serv,* Patricia Killeen; *Tech Serv,* Margaret Benoit; Staff 7 (MLS 1, Non-MLS 6)
Founded 1876. Pop 7,781; Circ 55,000
Library Holdings: Bk Titles 35,000; Per Subs 40
Automation Activity & Vendor Info: (Cataloging) SirsiDynix; (Circulation) SirsiDynix; (OPAC) SirsiDynix
Database Vendor: EBSCOhost, Gale Cengage Learning, OCLC FirstSearch, SirsiDynix
Wireless access
Partic in SAILS Library Network

Special Services for the Blind - Large print bks; Talking bks & player equip
Open Mon & Wed 12-8, Tues, Thurs & Fri 10-5, Sat 10-2
Friends of the Library Group

HANCOCK

P TAYLOR MEMORIAL LIBRARY*, Main St, 01237. (Mail add: 2832 Hancock Rd, Williamstown, 01267), SAN 307-4269. Tel: 413-738-5326. Interlibrary Loan Service FAX: 413-738-5310. *Chair,* Julie Bourassa
Pop 1,012; Circ 2,064
Library Holdings: Large Print Bks 200; Bk Vols 7,525; Talking Bks 20
Open Fri 2-4:30 & 6:30-8

HANOVER

P JOHN CURTIS FREE LIBRARY*, 534 Hanover St, 02339-2228. SAN 307-4277. Tel: 781-826-2972. FAX: 781-826-3130. E-mail: halib@ocln.org. Web Site: www.hanovermass.com/library. *Chair,* Lawrence Bandoni; *Dir,* Lorraine Welsh; E-mail: lwelsh@ocln.org; *Ref Librn,* Tara Grosso; E-mail: tgrosso@ocln.org; *Circ Supvr,* Lynne Goodwin; E-mail: lgoodwin@ocln.org; *Ch Serv,* Lynne Campbell; E-mail: lcampbell@ocln.org; Staff 8 (MLS 3, Non-MLS 5)
Founded 1907. Pop 13,472; Circ 149,169
Jul 2005-Jun 2006 Income $493,324, State $15,756, Locally Generated Income $477,568. Mats Exp $100,631, Books $50,859, Per/Ser (Incl. Access Fees) $5,100, AV Mat $18,210, Electronic Ref Mat (Incl. Access Fees) $26,462
Library Holdings: CDs 3,277; DVDs 4,371; Electronic Media & Resources 42; Bk Titles 56,023; Per Subs 119
Special Collections: Historical Coll
Automation Activity & Vendor Info: (Cataloging) SirsiDynix; (Circulation) SirsiDynix; (OPAC) SirsiDynix; (Serials) SirsiDynix
Publications: New Books at JCFL
Partic in Old Colony Libr Network (OCLN)
Open Mon & Wed 10-8, Tues 1-8, Thurs-Sat 10-5
Friends of the Library Group

HANSCOM AFB

UNITED STATES AIR FORCE

A AIR FORCE RESEARCH LABORATORY LIBRARY*, Five Wright St, 01731-3004, SAN 345-2646. Tel: 781-377-4742. Circulation Tel: 781-377-4768. Reference Tel: 781-377-4619. FAX: 781-377-4896. *Dir,* John F Griffin; E-mail: john.griffin@hanscom.af.mil; Staff 8 (MLS 3, Non-MLS 5)
Founded 1945
Library Holdings: Bk Titles 100,000; Bk Vols 252,663; Per Subs 425
Special Collections: Air Flight Coll; Early Ballooning & Aeronautics; Geophysics of Space Coll; Oriental Science Library; Rare Books Coll; Science Manuscripts of Lords Rayleigh III & IV
Subject Interests: Astronomy, Astrophysics, Chem, Electronics, Eng, Geol, Geophysics, Math, Meteorology, Phys sci, Physics
Database Vendor: Dialog, OCLC FirstSearch, OVID Technologies, ProQuest, TLC (The Library Corporation)
Partic in BRS; Dialog Corp; OCLC Online Computer Library Center, Inc
Publications: Accessions List (weekly); Recurrent Bibliographies
Friends of the Library Group

A HANSCOM AIR FORCE BASE LIBRARY FL2835*, 66 SVS/SVMG, 98 Barksdale St, Bldg 1530, 01731-1807, SAN 345-2670. Tel: 781-377-2177. FAX: 781-377-4482. Web Site: www.hanscomservices.com/library.html. *Librn,* Teresa Hathaway; E-mail: teresa.hathaway@hanscom.af.mil; Staff 5 (MLS 1, Non-MLS 4)
Founded 1952
Library Holdings: Bk Vols 21,000; Per Subs 110
Special Collections: Air War Coll; Military History Coll; Project Warrior
Automation Activity & Vendor Info: (Cataloging) SirsiDynix; (Circulation) SirsiDynix
Partic in OCLC Online Computer Library Center, Inc
Open Tues-Thurs 9-8, Fri & Sat 10-5
Restriction: Employees only, Mil only

HANSON

P HANSON PUBLIC LIBRARY*, 132 Maquan St, 02341. SAN 307-4285. Tel: 781-293-2151. FAX: 781-293-6801. Reference E-mail: hansonref@sailsinc.org. Web Site: www.sailsinc.org/hansonpl. *Dir,* Nancy Cappellini; E-mail: ncappell@sailsinc.org; *Acq, Cat,* Sue Olsen; *Ch Serv,* Kathryn Godwin; *Circ,* Donald Colon; *Circ, ILL,* Jean Kelly; *Ref Serv,* Karen Stolfer; *Syst Serv, Tech Serv,* Antonia Leverone; *Youth Serv,* Ann Marie Pokaski
Pop 9,690; Circ 58,052
Library Holdings: Bk Titles 50,125; Per Subs 45
Subject Interests: Local hist
Wireless access
Function: Children's prog, Fax serv, Homework prog, ILL available, Meeting rooms, Photocopying/Printing
Partic in SAILS Library Network
Open Mon & Fri 10-5, Tues 12-8, Thurs 1-8, Sat 9-3
Friends of the Library Group

HARDWICK

P PAIGE MEMORIAL LIBRARY*, 87 Petersham Rd, 01037. (Mail add: PO Box 128, 01037-0128), SAN 307-4293. Tel: 413-477-6704. *Librn,* Sonja Craig
Pop 2,379; Circ 3,592
Library Holdings: Bk Vols 12,000; Per Subs 20
Automation Activity & Vendor Info: (Cataloging) Follett Software; (Circulation) Follett Software
Open Tues 7-9, Wed 11:30-3:30, Thurs 1-7, Sat 9-12
Friends of the Library Group

HARVARD

S FRUITLANDS MUSEUMS LIBRARY*, 102 Prospect Hill Rd, 01451. SAN 307-4307. Tel: 978-456-3924. FAX: 978-456-8078. Web Site: www.fruitlands.org.
Founded 1914
Library Holdings: Bk Vols 11,200; Per Subs 15
Special Collections: American Indians Coll; American Literature & History Coll; American Paintings Coll; Shaker History Coll
Restriction: Open by appt only

P HARVARD PUBLIC LIBRARY*, Four Pond Rd, 01451-1647. SAN 307-4315. Tel: 978-456-4114. Circulation Tel: 978-456-4114, Ext 221. Interlibrary Loan Service Tel: 978-456-4114, Ext 225. Reference Tel: 978-456-4114, Ext 229. FAX: 978-456-4115. Web Site: www.harvardpubliclibrary.org. *Dir,* Mary Wilson
Founded 1886. Pop 5,400
Library Holdings: Bk Vols 56,000; Per Subs 158
Subject Interests: Local hist, Shakers
Automation Activity & Vendor Info: (Cataloging) Innovative Interfaces, Inc; (Circulation) Innovative Interfaces, Inc; (OPAC) Innovative Interfaces, Inc
Database Vendor: Gale Cengage Learning, Newsbank
Mem of Massachusetts Libr Syst
Open Mon, Tues & Thurs 10-9, Wed & Fri 10-5, Sat 10-4 (10-2 June-Aug)
Friends of the Library Group

HARWICH

P BROOKS FREE LIBRARY*, 739 Main St, 02645. SAN 307-4323. Tel: 508-430-7562. FAX: 508-430-7564. E-mail: bfl_mail@clamsnet.org. Web Site: www.vsg.cape.com/~brooks. *Dir,* Virginia A Hewitt; *Pub Serv Librn,* Suzanne Martell; *Ref Librn,* Jennifer Pickett; *Ch,* Ann Bower; Staff 3 (MLS 3)
Founded 1885. Pop 12,858; Circ 145,212
Library Holdings: AV Mats 2,665; Bk Titles 50,398; Per Subs 174; Talking Bks 1,848
Special Collections: Local History Room
Automation Activity & Vendor Info: (Acquisitions) Innovative Interfaces, Inc; (Cataloging) Innovative Interfaces, Inc; (Circulation) Innovative Interfaces, Inc; (ILL) Innovative Interfaces, Inc; (OPAC) Innovative Interfaces, Inc; (Serials) Innovative Interfaces, Inc
Database Vendor: Dialog, EBSCOhost, Gale Cengage Learning, SirsiDynix, TLC (The Library Corporation)
Wireless access
Function: Homebound delivery serv, Ref serv available
Mem of Massachusetts Libr Syst
Partic in Cape Libraries Automated Materials Sharing Network
Special Services for the Blind - Braille equip; Reader equip; Screen reader software; Vera Arkenstone
Open Tues-Thurs 11-7, Fri & Sat 11-5
Friends of the Library Group

HARWICH PORT

P HARWICH PORT LIBRARY ASSOCIATION*, 49 Lower Bank St, 02646. (Mail add: PO Box 175, 02646-0175), SAN 307-4331. Tel: 508-432-3320. *Dir,* Maryanne Desmareis
Founded 1923. Pop 12,000; Circ 31,632
Library Holdings: Bk Titles 14,000
Special Collections: Mystery Coll
Mem of Massachusetts Libr Syst
Partic in Cape Libraries Automated Materials Sharing Network
Open Mon & Fri Noon-6

HATFIELD

P HATFIELD PUBLIC LIBRARY*, 39 Main St, 01038. SAN 307-434X. Tel: 413-247-9097. FAX: 413-247-9237. E-mail: hatfieldpubliclibrary@gmail.com. Web Site: hatfieldpubliclibrary.org. *Dir,* Eliza Langhans; E-mail: elanghan@cwmars.org; *Asst Dir, Children's Prog,* Cheri Hardy; E-mail: arhwana.arts@gmail.com; Staff 1 (MLS 1)
Founded 1874. Pop 3,600; Circ 21,000
Jul 2007-Jun 2008 Income $86,000. Mats Exp $17,163
Library Holdings: AV Mats 1,249; Large Print Bks 100; Bk Titles 22,254; Per Subs 50; Talking Bks 224
Subject Interests: Local hist, Poland
Automation Activity & Vendor Info: (Cataloging) Innovative Interfaces, Inc; (ILL) Innovative Interfaces, Inc; (OPAC) Innovative Interfaces, Inc
Wireless access
Open Tues & Thurs 10-5, Wed & Fri 5-8, Sat 9-1
Friends of the Library Group

HAVERHILL

P HAVERHILL PUBLIC LIBRARY*, 99 Main St, 01830-5092. SAN 345-2700. Tel: 978-373-1586. Circulation Tel: 978-373-1586, Ext 603. Reference Tel: 978-363-1586, Ext 606, 978-373-1586, Ext 608. Administration Tel: 978-373-1586, Ext 617. Automation Services Tel: 978-373-1586, Ext 619. FAX: 978-372-8508. Reference FAX: 978-373-8466. Web Site: www.haverhillpl.org. *Dir,* Carol Verny; Tel: 978-373-1586, Ext 621, E-mail: cverny@mvlc.org; *Asst Dir,* Sarah Moser; Tel: 978-373-1586, Ext 641; *Head, Circ,* Catherine Page; Tel: 978-373-1586, Ext 602, E-mail: cpage@mvlc.org; *Head, Info Serv, Head, Ref,* Rand Hall; *Head, Youth Serv,* Nancy Chase; Tel: 978-373-1586, Ext 626; *Automation Librn, Syst Adminr,* Stephen Berezansky; E-mail: sberezansky@mvlc.org; Staff 21 (MLS 7, Non-MLS 14)
Founded 1873. Pop 60,176; Circ 459,286
Jul 2008-Jun 2009 Income $1,680,019, State $70,488, City $1,253,968, Locally Generated Income $169,955, Other $164,764. Mats Exp $224,948, Books $116,100, Per/Ser (Incl. Access Fees) $16,660, Other Print Mats $13,824, AV Mat $61,034, Electronic Ref Mat (Incl. Access Fees) $17,330. Sal $929,821
Library Holdings: Electronic Media & Resources 170; Bk Titles 170,535; Per Subs 390; Talking Bks 13,366; Videos 11,608
Special Collections: Fine Arts Coll; Genealogy Coll; Haverhill & New England Towns History Coll; John Greenleaf Whittier Coll; New England States Coll; US Topo Maps
Automation Activity & Vendor Info: (Cataloging) SirsiDynix; (Circulation) SirsiDynix; (ILL) SirsiDynix; (OPAC) SirsiDynix
Database Vendor: Checkpoint Systems, Inc, EBSCOhost, Electric Library, Newsbank, OCLC WorldShare Interlibrary Loan, Overdrive, Inc, SirsiDynix
Wireless access
Publications: Architectural Heritage of Haverhill; Holdings of the HPL-J G Whittier Collection; HPL Technical Services Department-Procedures Manual; Internet Information; Northeast Early Childhood Resource News Center
Partic in Merrimack Valley Library Consortium
Special Services for the Blind - Computer with voice synthesizer for visually impaired persons
Open Mon, Tues & Thurs 9-9, Wed, Fri & Sat 9-5, Sun 1-5
Friends of the Library Group

M MERRIMACK VALLEY HOSPITAL*, Medical Library, 140 Lincoln Ave, 01830. SAN 307-4382. Tel: 978-374-2000, 978-521-8542. *In Charge,* Janice Fleming
Library Holdings: Bk Titles 1,680; Per Subs 95
Subject Interests: Allied health, Med, Nursing
Partic in Haverhill Libr Res Consortium; Northeastern Consortium for Health Information

J NORTHERN ESSEX COMMUNITY COLLEGE*, Bentley Library, 100 Elliott St, 01830. SAN 307-4390. Tel: 978-556-3400. FAX: 978-556-3738. Web Site: www.necc.mass.edu/departments/library. *Dir,* Linda Hummel-Shea; Tel: 978-556-3423, E-mail: lshea@necc.mass.edu; *Coordr, Electronic Res,* Ann Grandmaison; Tel: 978-556-3426, E-mail: agrandmaison@necc.mass.edu; *Coordr, Ref (Info Serv),* Gail Stuart; Tel: 978-556-3421, E-mail: gstuart@necc.mass.edu; *Circ,* Louise Bevilacqua; Tel: 978-556-3422, E-mail: lbevilacqua@necc.mass.edu; *Tech Serv,* Helen Mansur; Tel: 978-556-3425, E-mail: hmansur@necc.mass.edu; Staff 7 (MLS 5, Non-MLS 2)
Founded 1961. Enrl 3,200; Highest Degree: Associate
Library Holdings: Bk Vols 64,000; Per Subs 350
Automation Activity & Vendor Info: (Cataloging) Innovative Interfaces, Inc; (Circulation) Innovative Interfaces, Inc; (Course Reserve) Innovative Interfaces, Inc; (ILL) Innovative Interfaces, Inc; (OPAC) Innovative Interfaces, Inc
Database Vendor: Innovative Interfaces, Inc
Publications: NECC Periodicals Holdings List
Partic in Lyrasis; North of Boston Library Exchange, Inc
Special Services for the Deaf - Bks on deafness & sign lang; Spec interest per
Open Mon-Thurs 8am-9pm, Fri 8-5, Sat 9-1
Departmental Libraries:
LAWRENCE CAMPUS LIBRARY, 45 Franklin St, Lawrence, 01841, SAN 376-0308. Tel: 978-738-7400. FAX: 978-738-7114. Web Site: www.necc.mass.edu/departments/library/index.htm. *Dir, Libr Serv,* Linda Hummel-Shea; Tel: 978-556-3423, E-mail: lshea@necc.mass.edu; *Coordr, Libr Serv,* Mike Hearn; E-mail: mhearn@necc.mass.edu; Staff 2 (MLS 2)
Library Holdings: Bk Vols 6,736; Per Subs 87
Subject Interests: Law, Nursing
Mem of Massachusetts Libr Syst
Open Mon-Wed 9-8, Thurs 9-5, Fri 9-3, Sat 9-1

CR NORTHPOINT BIBLE COLLEGE LIBRARY*, 320 S Main St, 01835. SAN 320-7358. Tel: 978-478-3417. Administration Tel: 978-478-3416. Toll Free Tel: 800-356-4014. FAX: 978-478-3406. Web Site: www.northpoint.edu/academics/library. *Librn,* Ginger R McDonald; E-mail: gmcdonald@northpoint.edu; *Asst Librn,* Elaine Martell; Tel: 978-478-3415, E-mail: emartell@northpoint.edu; Staff 4 (MLS 2, Non-MLS 2)
Founded 1956. Enrl 375; Fac 35; Highest Degree: Master
May 2013-Apr 2014 Income $250,000. Mats Exp $39,000, Books $22,000, Per/Ser (Incl. Access Fees) $17,000. Sal $90,000 (Prof $85,000)
Library Holdings: Bk Vols 41,000; Per Subs 100
Subject Interests: Rare bks
Automation Activity & Vendor Info: (Acquisitions) Follett Software; (Cataloging) Follett Software; (Circulation) Follett Software; (ILL) OCLC; (OPAC) Follett Software
Database Vendor: EBSCOhost
Wireless access
Partic in Lyrasis
Open Mon-Thurs 9am-10pm, Fri & Sat 9-8, Sun 6pm-10pm

HAYDENVILLE

P HAYDENVILLE PUBLIC LIBRARY*, Main St, 01039-0516. (Mail add: PO Box 772, Williamsburg, 01096-0772), SAN 376-7116. Tel: 413-268-8406. Reference Tel: 413-268-7472. FAX: 413-268-8406. E-mail: meekins@cwmars.org. Web Site: www.meekins-library.org. *Dir,* Lisa Wenner; E-mail: lwenner@cwmars.org
Library Holdings: Bk Titles 4,000
Wireless access
Open Tues 4-6, Thurs 5-7
Friends of the Library Group

HEATH

P HEATH PUBLIC LIBRARY*, One E Main St, 01346. SAN 307-4404. Tel: 413-337-4934. FAX: 413-337-8542. E-mail: heath@cwmars.org. *Dir,* Charlene Churchill; *Asst Librn,* Donald Purington
Founded 1894. Pop 805; Circ 16,525
Library Holdings: AV Mats 15,000, Large Print Bks 200; Bk Titles 10,000; Per Subs 35
Open Mon 4-8, Wed Noon-7, Sat 9-1
Friends of the Library Group

HINGHAM

P HINGHAM PUBLIC LIBRARY*, 66 Leavitt St, 02043. SAN 307-4412. Tel: 781-741-1405. FAX: 781-749-0956. E-mail: hiref@ocln.org. Web Site: www.hingham-ma.com/library. *Dir,* Dennis Corcoran; E-mail: dennisc@ocln.org; *Head, Ref,* Kathleen Leahy; E-mail: kleahy@ocln.org; *Cat,* Juliana Holbrook; *Circ,* Linda Harper; *ILL, Ref,* Ann Dalton; Staff 29 (MLS 6, Non-MLS 23)
Founded 1869. Pop 19,500; Circ 402,062
Library Holdings: Bk Vols 174,519; Per Subs 348
Special Collections: Typography (W A Dwiggins Coll)
Subject Interests: Local hist
Automation Activity & Vendor Info: (Cataloging) SirsiDynix; (Circulation) SirsiDynix; (OPAC) SirsiDynix
Database Vendor: SirsiDynix
Partic in Old Colony Libr Network (OCLN)

HINSDALE

P HINSDALE PUBLIC LIBRARY*, 58 Maple St, 01235. (Mail add: PO Box 397, 01235-0397), SAN 307-4420. Tel: 413-655-2303. FAX: 413-655-2303. E-mail: hinsdale@hinsdalelibrary.org. Web Site: www.hinsdalelibrary.org. *Dir,* Thomas A Butler, Jr; *Ch,* Lauren Paro; *Adult Serv,* Mary Lunsford; *Cat, Reader Serv,* Sue Shelsy
Founded 1866. Pop 1,780; Circ 29,745
Library Holdings: Bk Vols 10,000; Per Subs 52
Special Collections: First Congregational Church Records (1790-1980); Handwritten records of Burials of Maple Street Cemetary (1790-1912); Israel Bissell Coll; Local Newspaper Clippings (1890-to date)

Open Mon & Sat 9-1, Tues & Fri 2-6, Wed & Thurs 4-8
Friends of the Library Group

HOLBROOK

P HOLBROOK PUBLIC LIBRARY*, Two Plymouth St, 02343. SAN 307-4439. Tel: 781-767-3644. FAX: 781-767-5721. E-mail: holib@ocln.org. *Dir & Head Librn,* Ruth A Hathaway; E-mail: rhathawa@ocln.org; *Asst Dir,* Debra Clifton; E-mail: dclifton@ocln.org; Staff 2 (MLS 2)
Founded 1872. Pop 10,785; Circ 70,455
Library Holdings: Bk Vols 38,820
Automation Activity & Vendor Info: (Cataloging) SirsiDynix; (Circulation) SirsiDynix; (OPAC) SirsiDynix; (Serials) SirsiDynix
Database Vendor: Gale Cengage Learning, SirsiDynix
Wireless access
Mem of Massachusetts Libr Syst
Partic in Old Colony Libr Network (OCLN)
Friends of the Library Group

HOLDEN

P GALE FREE LIBRARY*, 23 Highland St, 01520-2599. SAN 307-4447. Tel: 508-210-5560. Circulation Tel: 508-210-5562. Reference Tel: 508-210-5569. FAX: 508-829-0232. Web Site: www.galefreelibrary.org. *Dir,* Susan Scott; Tel: 508-210-5566; *Asst Dir,* Paul Korstvedt; *Head, Circ,* JoAnn Avdette; *Ch Serv,* Beverly Dinneen; Tel: 508-210-4191, E-mail: bdinneen@cwmars.org; *Tech Serv,* Kathy Major; Staff 16 (MLS 4, Non-MLS 12)
Founded 1888. Pop 16,000; Circ 302,000
Library Holdings: Bk Titles 65,000; Per Subs 142
Special Collections: Local Newspapers, micro. Oral History
Automation Activity & Vendor Info: (Cataloging) Evergreen; (Circulation) Evergreen; (OPAC) Evergreen
Wireless access
Mem of Massachusetts Libr Syst
Partic in Central & Western Massachusetts Automated Resource Sharing
Special Services for the Blind - Bks on CD; Large print bks; Magnifiers; ZoomText magnification & reading software
Open Mon, Wed & Fri 9:30-5:30, Tues & Thurs 9:30-8, Sat 9-4 (9-1 Summer)
Friends of the Library Group

HOLLAND

P HOLLAND PUBLIC LIBRARY*, 27 Sturbridge Rd, Unit 9, 01521. SAN 307-6873. Tel: 413-245-3607. E-mail: holland@cwmars.org. *Dir,* Joan W Markert
Founded 1912. Pop 2,185; Circ 8,384
Library Holdings: Bk Vols 8,000
Open Mon & Wed 3-9, Tues 10-12 & 6-8, Sat 10-1

HOLLISTON

P HOLLISTON PUBLIC LIBRARY*, 752 Washington St, 01746. SAN 307-4455. Tel: 508-429-0617. FAX: 508-429-0625. Web Site: www.hollistonlibrary.org. *Dir,* Leslie McDonnell; *Asst Dir, Head, Tech Serv, YA Librn,* Jennifer Keen; *Head, Circ,* Laura Kurzontkowski; E-mail: lkurzontkowski@minlib.net; *Ref Librn, Tech Coordr,* Margaret Perkins; *Ch,* Tenna Foale; E-mail: tfoale@minlib.net
Founded 1879. Pop 14,000; Circ 176,000
Library Holdings: Bk Titles 65,032; Per Subs 109
Automation Activity & Vendor Info: (Cataloging) Innovative Interfaces, Inc; (Circulation) Innovative Interfaces, Inc; (OPAC) Innovative Interfaces, Inc
Open Mon, Tues & Thurs 11-9, Wed 11-6, Fri 11-5, Sat 10-5
Friends of the Library Group

HOLYOKE

J HOLYOKE COMMUNITY COLLEGE LIBRARY*, Donahue Bldg, 2nd Flr, 303 Homestead Ave, 01040-1099. SAN 307-4463. Tel: 413-538-7000, Ext 2261. Circulation Tel: 413-552-2372. Reference Tel: 413-552-2424. FAX: 413-552-2729. Web Site: www.hcc.mass.edu. *Dean, Libr Serv,* Judith Campbell; Tel: 413-552-2260, E-mail: jcampbell@hcc.mass.edu; *Acq,* Robert Stoddard; Tel: 413-552-2376, E-mail: rstoddard@hcc.mass.edu; *ILL,* Claire Wheeler; Tel: 413-552-2187, E-mail: cwheeler@hcc.mass.edu; *Ref,* Kathleen McDonough; Tel: 413-552-2598, E-mail: kmcdonough@hcc.mass.edu; *Tech Serv,* Carl Todd; Tel: 413-552-2374, E-mail: ctodd@hcc.mass.edu; Staff 3 (MLS 3)
Founded 1946. Highest Degree: Associate
Library Holdings: AV Mats 7,000; Bk Vols 75,000; Per Subs 400
Special Collections: Library of English Literature, ultrafiche
Automation Activity & Vendor Info: (Cataloging) OCLC; (ILL) OCLC
Partic in Central & Western Massachusetts Automated Resource Sharing; Lyrasis; OCLC Online Computer Library Center, Inc
Open Mon-Thurs 8am-8:30pm, Fri 8-4:30, Sat 10-2

P HOLYOKE PUBLIC LIBRARY, 250 Chestnut St, 01040-4858. SAN 345-276X. Tel: 413-420-8101. FAX: 413-532-4230. E-mail: library@holyoke.org. Web Site: www.holyokelibrary.org. *Dir,* Maria G Pagan
Founded 1870. Pop 39,947; Circ 100,000
Library Holdings: Bk Vols 76,500; Per Subs 110
Special Collections: US Volleyball Association
Automation Activity & Vendor Info: (Cataloging) Evergreen; (Circulation) Evergreen; (ILL) Evergreen; (OPAC) Evergreen
Database Vendor: EBSCO Auto Repair Reference, Gale Cengage Learning, LearningExpress, Newsbank
Wireless access
Function: Adult bk club, Bilingual assistance for Spanish patrons, Bk club(s), Bks on cassette, Bks on CD, Children's prog, Computer training, Computers for patron use, Copy machines, Electronic databases & coll, Fax serv, Free DVD rentals, ILL available, Mus passes, Music CDs, Outside serv via phone, mail, e-mail & web, OverDrive digital audio bks, Preschool outreach, Prog for adults, Prog for children & young adult, Pub access computers, Ref & res, Ref serv available, Ref serv in person, Spoken cassettes & CDs, Spoken cassettes & DVDs, Story hour, Summer reading prog, Tax forms, Teen prog, VHS videos, Video lending libr, Web-catalog
Partic in Central & Western Massachusetts Automated Resource Sharing
Open Mon-Thurs (Winter) 8:30-8:30, Fri & Sat 8:30-4; Mon-Wed (Summer) 8:30-6, Thurs & Fri 8:30-5
Friends of the Library Group

HOPEDALE

P BANCROFT MEMORIAL LIBRARY*, 50 Hopedale St, 01747-1799. SAN 307-4471. Tel: 508-634-2209. FAX: 508-634-8095. *Dir,* Ann Fields; E-mail: afields@cwmars.org; *Ch Serv,* Elaine Kraimer; E-mail: ekraimer@cwmars.org; Staff 3.6 (MLS 1, Non-MLS 2.6)
Founded 1898. Pop 6,142; Circ 36,351
Jul 2012-Jun 2013 Income $244,072, State $5,620, City $237,242, Locally Generated Income $1,210. Mats Exp $43,526, Books $25,866, Per/Ser (Incl. Access Fees) $2,724, AV Mat $8,255, Electronic Ref Mat (Incl. Access Fees) $6,681. Sal $137,458 (Prof $54,101)
Library Holdings: AV Mats 3,622; DVDs 1,765; Bk Vols 28,965; Per Subs 51
Special Collections: Adin Ballou Coll; Draper Corporation Coll
Automation Activity & Vendor Info: (Cataloging) Evergreen; (Circulation) Evergreen; (ILL) Evergreen; (OPAC) Evergreen
Database Vendor: CredoReference, Grolier Online, ProQuest, World Book Online
Wireless access
Mem of Massachusetts Libr Syst
Partic in Central & Western Massachusetts Automated Resource Sharing
Open Mon & Wed 1-8, Tues & Thurs 10-5, Fri 1-5, Sat 10-2
Friends of the Library Group

HOPKINTON

P HOPKINTON PUBLIC LIBRARY*, 13 Main St, 01748. SAN 307-448X. Tel: 508-497-9777. FAX: 508-497-9778. Web Site: www.hopkintonlibrary.org. *Dir,* Rownak P Hussain; *Ad,* Rebecca McCaffery; *Youth Serv Librn,* Denise Kofron
Founded 1890
Jul 2006-Jun 2007. Mats Exp $63,000. Sal $200,000
Library Holdings: AV Mats 4,000; Large Print Bks 200; Bk Vols 35,000; Per Subs 224
Special Collections: Local History Vital Records Coll
Automation Activity & Vendor Info: (Cataloging) Innovative Interfaces, Inc; (Circulation) Innovative Interfaces, Inc; (OPAC) Innovative Interfaces, Inc
Wireless access
Mem of Massachusetts Libr Syst
Open Mon, Wed & Fri 10-9, Tues & Thurs 10-5, Sat (Sept-June) 10-1
Friends of the Library Group

HOUSATONIC

P RAMSDELL PUBLIC LIBRARY*, 1087 Main St, 01236-9730. (Mail add: PO Box 568, 01236-0568), SAN 307-4498. Tel: 413-274-3738. E-mail: ramsdellpublic@hotmail.com. Web Site: www.gblibraries.net. *Dir,* Marlene Drew; *Tech Serv,* Dawn Barbieri
Circ 15,000
Library Holdings: Bk Vols 33,000; Per Subs 46
Open Mon, Tues, Thurs & Fri 1-6, Sat 9-1
Friends of the Library Group

HUBBARDSTON

P HUBBARDSTON PUBLIC LIBRARY*, Seven Main St, Unit 8, 01452. (Mail add: PO Box D, 01452-0225), SAN 307-4501. Tel: 978-928-4775. FAX: 978-928-1273. E-mail: library@hubbardstonma.us. Web Site: www.hubbardstonpubliclibrary.org. *Librn,* Jayne Arata; *Asst Librn,* Christine Barbera
Founded 1872. Pop 2,400; Circ 11,612
Library Holdings: DVDs 300; Large Print Bks 100; Bk Vols 10,000; Per Subs 30; Videos 500
Wireless access
Mem of Massachusetts Libr Syst
Open Mon & Thurs 1-7, Wed 10-4, Sat 9-Noon
Friends of the Library Group

HUDSON

P HUDSON PUBLIC LIBRARY*, Three Washington St at The Rotary, 01749-2499. SAN 307-451X. Tel: 978-568-9644. FAX: 978-568-9646. Web Site: www.hudsonpubliclibrary.com. *Dir,* Patricia Desmond; E-mail: tdesmond@cwmars.org; *Asst Dir, Tech Serv,* Deborah Kane; E-mail: dkane@cwmars.org; *Circ Mgr, ILL,* Nancy DelVecchio; E-mail: ndelvecc@cwmars.org; *Ch Serv,* Deborah Backman; Tel: 978-568-9645, E-mail: dbackman@cwmars.org; *Circ,* Susan Ramsbottom; E-mail: sramsbot@cwmars.org; *Circ, Ch,* Tina Craig; E-mail: tcraig@cwmars.org; *Ref,* Nicole Kramer; E-mail: nkramer@cwmars.org; Staff 8 (MLS 3, Non-MLS 5)
Founded 1868. Pop 19,063; Circ 237,456
Jul 2013-Jun 2014 Income $703,483. Mats Exp $104,400. Sal $506,895
Library Holdings: CDs 1,513; Electronic Media & Resources 47; Large Print Bks 850; Bk Vols 65,000; Per Subs 149; Talking Bks 2,000; Videos 4,061
Automation Activity & Vendor Info: (Acquisitions) Evergreen; (Cataloging) Evergreen; (Circulation) Evergreen
Database Vendor: Gale Cengage Learning, LibraryInsight, Newsbank, Overdrive, Inc, Westlaw, World Book Online
Wireless access
Function: ILL available, Prog for children & young adult, Ref serv available, Summer reading prog
Publications: Library Newsletter (Bi-monthly)
Mem of Massachusetts Libr Syst
Partic in Central-Western Mass Automated Resource Sharing
Open Mon-Thurs 9-8:30, Fri 9-6, Sat 9-5
Friends of the Library Group

HULL

P HULL PUBLIC LIBRARY*, Nine Main St, 02045-1199. SAN 307-4528. Tel: 781-925-2295. FAX: 781-925-0867. Web Site: www.hullpubliclibrary.org. *Dir,* Daniel J Johnson, E-mail: djohnson@ocln.org; *Ch Serv,* Anne Masland
Founded 1913. Pop 9,600; Circ 32,000
Library Holdings: Bk Vols 30,000; Per Subs 100
Special Collections: Local History Hull & Boston Harbor Islands
Automation Activity & Vendor Info: (Cataloging) SirsiDynix; (Circulation) SirsiDynix; (OPAC) SirsiDynix
Open Mon, Tues & Thurs 10-8, Fri 2-5, Sat 10-3
Friends of the Library Group

HUNTINGTON

P HUNTINGTON PUBLIC LIBRARY*, Seven E Main St, 01050. (Mail add: PO Box 597, 01050-0597), SAN 307-4536. Tel: 413-667-3506. FAX: 413-667-0088. E-mail: huntingtonlib@comcast.net. *Libr Dir,* Margaret Nareau; *Asst Dir,* Bethany Sorrell
Pop 2,095; Circ 10,295
Library Holdings: Bk Vols 12,000; Per Subs 50
Open Mon & Thurs 1-4 & 5-8, Tues 1-4, Wed 3-8, Sat 10-3
Friends of the Library Group

HYANNIS

M CAPE COD HOSPITAL, Medical Library, 27 Park St, 02601-5230. (Mail add: PO Box 640, 02601-0640), SAN 377-9122. Tel: 508-862 5443. FAX: 774-552-6904. E-mail: medlib@capecodhealth.org. *Dir,* Jeanie M Vander Pyl; Tel: 508-862-5866, E-mail: jvanderpyl@capecodhealth.org; *Cat,* Deborah Tustin; *ILL & Ser,* June Bianchi; Tel: 508-862-5867; Staff 3 (MLS 2, Non-MLS 1)
Oct 2013-Sept 2014. Mats Exp $94,500, Books $3,000, Per/Ser (Incl. Access Fees) $43,000, Electronic Ref Mat (Incl. Access Fees) $47,000, Presv $1,500
Library Holdings: AV Mats 720; e-journals 195; Bk Titles 7,977; Bk Vols 7,713; Per Subs 147
Automation Activity & Vendor Info: (Cataloging) LibLime; (OPAC) LibLime; (Serials) Basch Subscriptions, Inc
Database Vendor: Gale Cengage Learning, Medline, Micromedex, Newsbank, OVID Technologies, PubMed, ScienceDirect, STAT!Ref (Teton Data Systems), UpToDate
Wireless access
Function: ILL available
Mem of Massachusetts Libr Syst
Partic in Massachusetts Health Sciences Libraries Network; North Atlantic Health Sciences Libraries, Inc; Southeastern Massachusetts Consortium of Health Science Libraries
Open Mon-Fri 8:30-4:30

P HYANNIS PUBLIC LIBRARY ASSOCIATION*, 401 Main St, 02601-3019. SAN 307-4544. Tel: 508-775-2280. FAX: 508-790-0087. Web Site: www.hyannislibrary.org. *Dir,* Position Currently Open; *Interim Dir, Ref Librn,* Carol J Saunders; *Ch Serv,* Mary Bianco
Founded 1865. Pop 12,000; Circ 150,000
Library Holdings: Bk Vols 60,000; Per Subs 175
Automation Activity & Vendor Info: (Cataloging) Innovative Interfaces, Inc; (Circulation) Innovative Interfaces, Inc; (OPAC) Innovative Interfaces, Inc
Wireless access
Open Tues & Wed 11-8, Thurs-Sat 11-5

IPSWICH

P IPSWICH PUBLIC LIBRARY, 25 N Main St, 01938-2217. SAN 307-4560. Tel: 978-356-6648. FAX: 978-356-6647. E-mail: ipswich@mvlc.org. Web Site: www.ipswichlibrary.org. *Dir,* Victor Dyer; Tel: 978-356-6649, E-mail: vdyer@mvlc.org; *Asst Dir,* Genevieve Picard; *Ch Serv,* Laurie Collins; Tel: 978-412-8713; *ILL, Ref & Info Serv,* Paula Grillo; Staff 4.36 (MLS 3.43, Non-MLS 0.93)
Founded 1868. Pop 13,175; Circ 166,503
Jul 2013-Jun 2014 Income $604,220, State $10,620, City $593,600. Mats Exp $104,430, Books $62,991, Per/Ser (Incl. Access Fees) $18,563, AV Mat $13,107, Electronic Ref Mat (Incl. Access Fees) $9,769
Library Holdings: AV Mats 9,634; Microforms 283; Bk Vols 96,782; Per Subs 216
Subject Interests: Genealogy, Local hist
Automation Activity & Vendor Info: (Cataloging) Evergreen; (Circulation) Evergreen; (ILL) Evergreen; (OPAC) Evergreen
Database Vendor: EBSCO Auto Repair Reference, EBSCOhost, Gale Cengage Learning, Grolier Online, Overdrive, Inc, Safari Books Online
Wireless access
Function: Adult bk club, Adult literacy prog, Archival coll, Audiobks via web, AV serv, Bks on cassette, Bks on CD, CD-ROM, Chess club, Children's prog, Copy machines, e-mail serv, Electronic databases & coll, Free DVD rentals, Handicapped accessible, Holiday prog, Homebound delivery serv, ILL available, Magnifiers for reading, Mus passes, Music CDs, Online cat, Online ref, Online searches, OverDrive digital audio bks, Photocopying/Printing, Preschool outreach, Prog for adults, Prog for children & young adult, Pub access computers, Ref serv available, Summer reading prog, Tax forms, Teen prog, Telephone ref, VHS videos, Wheelchair accessible
Publications: Ipswich Public Library: The Newsletter
Partic in Merrimack Valley Library Consortium
Open Mon-Thurs (Winter) 10-8, Fri 10-5:30, Sat 9-4, Sun 1-4; Mon & Wed (Summer) 9-8, Tues, Thurs & Fri 9-5
Friends of the Library Group

JAMAICA PLAIN

GM MASSACHUSETTS STATE LABORATORY INSTITUTE LIBRARY*, Dept of Public Health, 305 South St, 02130. SAN 377-922X. Tel: 617-983-6290. FAX: 617-983-6292. *Librn,* Jennifer D Mann; E-mail: jennifer.mann@state.ma.us; Staff 1 (MLS 1)
Library Holdings: Bk Titles 750; Per Subs 110
Subject Interests: Clinical labs, Infectious diseases, Laboratory med, Med, Pub health med
Database Vendor: OCLC FirstSearch
Function: ILL available
Partic in Boston Regional Library System; National Network of Libraries of Medicine; OCLC Online Computer Library Center, Inc
Open Mon-Fri 8:30-5

M LEMUEL SHATTUCK HOSPITAL*, Bettencourt Medical Library, 170 Morton St, 02130. SAN 345-2859. Tel: 617-971-3225. FAX: 617-971-3850. *Dir, Libr Serv,* Kathryn Noonan; E-mail: kathryn.noonan@state.ma.us; Staff 2 (MLS 1, Non-MLS 1)
Founded 1954
Library Holdings: Bk Titles 500; Per Subs 110
Function: ILL available
Mem of Massachusetts Libr Syst
Partic in Massachusetts Health Sciences Libraries Network; National Network of Libraries of Medicine
Open Mon-Fri 8:30-5

KINGSTON

P KINGSTON PUBLIC LIBRARY*, Six Green St, 02364. SAN 307-4617. Tel: 781-585-0517. Circulation Tel: 781-585-0517, Ext 112. Reference Tel: 781-585-0517, Ext 121. FAX: 781-585-0521. E-mail: kilib@kingstonpubliclibrary.org. Web Site: www.kingstonpubliclibrary.org. *Dir,* Sia Stewart; E-mail: sstewart@ocln.org; Staff 4 (MLS 4)
Founded 1898. Pop 12,204; Circ 192,333
Library Holdings: e-books 1,648; Bk Vols 62,216
Special Collections: History of Kingston; History of Plymouth County
Automation Activity & Vendor Info: (Cataloging) SirsiDynix; (Circulation) SirsiDynix; (OPAC) SirsiDynix
Open Mon 1-8, Tues-Thurs 10-8, Sat 10-5
Friends of the Library Group

LAKEVILLE

P LAKEVILLE PUBLIC LIBRARY*, Four Precinct St, 02347. SAN 307-4625. Tel: 508-947-9028. FAX: 508-923-9934. Web Site: www.lakevillelibrary.org. *Dir,* Olivia Melo; E-mail: omelo@sailsinc.org; *Youth Serv,* Teresa Mirra
Founded 1914. Pop 10,000; Circ 86,000
Jul 2005-Jun 2006 Income $256,000. Mats Exp $40,000, Books $26,000, Per/Ser (Incl. Access Fees) $2,000, Other Print Mats $2,000, AV Mat $10,000. Sal $145,500 (Prof $88,000)
Library Holdings: e-books 500; Large Print Bks 500; Bk Titles 28,000; Per Subs 55
Automation Activity & Vendor Info: (Cataloging) SirsiDynix; (Circulation) SirsiDynix; (OPAC) SirsiDynix
Partic in SAILS Library Network
Open Tues & Thurs 10-8, Wed & Fri 10-6, Sat (Oct-May) 10-2
Friends of the Library Group

LANCASTER

P THAYER MEMORIAL LIBRARY*, 717 Main St, 01523-2248. (Mail add: PO Box 5, 01523-0005), SAN 307-4633. Tel: 978-368-8928. FAX: 978-368-8929. *Dir,* Joseph J Mule; E-mail: jmule@cwmars.org; Staff 7 (MLS 1, Non-MLS 6)
Founded 1862. Pop 7,380; Circ 58,369
Library Holdings: AV Mats 3,228; e-books 6,548; Bk Vols 51,071; Per Subs 55
Subject Interests: Am Indians, Botany, Civil War, Local hist, Rare bks
Automation Activity & Vendor Info: (Cataloging) Innovative Interfaces, Inc; (Circulation) Innovative Interfaces, Inc; (ILL) Innovative Interfaces, Inc; (OPAC) Innovative Interfaces, Inc
Mem of Massachusetts Libr Syst
Partic in Central & Western Massachusetts Automated Resource Sharing
Open Mon 12-6, Tues 12-8, Wed & Thurs 10-8, Sat (Sept-May) 10-2
Friends of the Library Group

LANESBOROUGH

P LANESBOROUGH PUBLIC LIBRARY*, 83 N Main St, 01237. (Mail add: PO Box 352, 01237-0352), SAN 307-4641. Tel: 413-442-0222. FAX: 413-443-5811. E-mail: lanesborough@gmail.com. Web Site: www.lanesborough-ma.gov. *Dir,* Kathy Adams; *Asst Librn,* Alyssa Griffin
Founded 1871. Pop 3,170
Library Holdings: Bk Titles 15,000
Automation Activity & Vendor Info: (Cataloging) Follett Software; (Circulation) Follett Software
Open Mon, Wed & Thurs 2-7, Tues 10-7, Sat 10-1
Friends of the Library Group

LAWRENCE

M LAWRENCE GENERAL HOSPITAL*, Medical Library, One General St, 01841-2997. (Mail add: PO Box 189, 01842-0389), SAN 307-465X. Tel: 978-683-4000, Ext 2221.
Library Holdings: Bk Vols 1,100; Per Subs 50
Partic in Northeastern Consortium for Health Information
Open Mon-Fri 7:30-2

L LAWRENCE LAW LIBRARY*, Two Appleton St, 01840-1525. SAN 307-4668. Tel: 978-687-7608. FAX: 978-688-2346. E-mail: lawrencelawlibrary@yahoo.com. Web Site: www.lawlib.state.ma.us. *Librn,* Brian J Archambault
Founded 1905
Library Holdings: Bk Vols 50,000
Open Mon, Wed & Fri 8:30-4:30, Tues & Thurs 8:30am-9:30pm, Sat 9-1
Friends of the Library Group

P LAWRENCE PUBLIC LIBRARY*, 51 Lawrence St, 01841. SAN 345-2913. Tel: 978-620-3600. Administration Tel: 978-620-3621. FAX: 978-688-3142. Web Site: www.lawrencefreelibrary.org. *Dir,* Maureen L Nimmo; *Asst Dir,* Ana Santos; *Dir, Ch Serv,* Solanyi Munoz; *Spec Coll Librn,* Louise Sandberg; *Circ Supvr,* Lois Elliott; Staff 32 (MLS 4, Non-MLS 28)
Founded 1872. Pop 70,000; Circ 150,000
Library Holdings: Large Print Bks 2,000; Bk Vols 150,000; Per Subs 300
Special Collections: Adult Basic Education; Career Opportunity Center Computerized Info & Referral; Funding Resources Center; Literacy; Local Historical Archives (1912 Labor Strike - Lawrence Historical Materials); Old Radio Shows (Kelly Tape Coll); Spanish Language Materials
Automation Activity & Vendor Info: (Cataloging) SirsiDynix; (Circulation) SirsiDynix; (ILL) SirsiDynix; (OPAC) SirsiDynix
Database Vendor: EBSCOhost, OCLC WorldShare Interlibrary Loan, SirsiDynix
Function: Adult bk club, Archival coll, AV serv, CD-ROM, Computer training, Copy machines, Electronic databases & coll, Handicapped accessible, ILL available, Online searches, Orientations, Photocopying/Printing, Prog for adults, Prog for children & young adult, Spoken cassettes & CDs, Summer reading prog, Tax forms, Telephone ref, VHS videos, Wheelchair accessible
Publications: English & Spanish; ESL Writing Curriculum Guide; Friends (Brochure); General Information (Brochure)
Mem of Massachusetts Libr Syst
Open Mon-Thurs 9-9, Fri 9-5
Friends of the Library Group
Branches: 1
SOUTH LAWRENCE BRANCH, 135 Parker St, South Lawrence, 01843, SAN 345-2948. Tel: 978-794-5789. FAX: 978-688-3142. *Dir,* Maureen Nimmo; Tel: 978-682-1727; Staff 3 (MLS 1, Non-MLS 2)
Function: AV serv, CD-ROM, Copy machines, Electronic databases & coll, Online searches, Photocopying/Printing, Preschool outreach, Prog for children & young adult, Spoken cassettes & CDs, Summer reading prog, Telephone ref, VHS videos
Open Mon, Wed & Sat 10-5
Friends of the Library Group

LEE

P LEE LIBRARY ASSOCIATION*, 100 Main St, 01238-1688. SAN 307-4676. Tel: 413-243-0385. FAX: 413-243-0381. E-mail: lee@cwmars.org. Web Site: www.leelibrary.org. *Dir, Libr Serv,* Georgia A Massucco; *Supvr, Circ,* Patricia Richard; *Pub Serv,* Rosemarie Borsody; *Tech Serv,* Mary DeVarennes; Staff 10 (MLS 1, Non-MLS 9)
Founded 1874. Pop 5,865; Circ 42,280
Jul 2009-Jun 2010 Income $256,804, State $6,646, City $250,158. Mats Exp $42,663. Sal $164,805 (Prof $54,325)
Library Holdings: Audiobooks 617; DVDs 245; e-books 1,145; Bk Titles 50,410; Per Subs 101; Videos 494
Special Collections: Oral History
Subject Interests: Local hist
Automation Activity & Vendor Info: (Cataloging) Innovative Interfaces, Inc; (Circulation) Innovative Interfaces, Inc; (OPAC) Innovative Interfaces, Inc
Wireless access
Partic in Central & Western Massachusetts Automated Resource Sharing
Open Mon, Tues & Thurs 10-8, Wed & Fri 10-5, Sat 10-2

LEEDS

GM DEPARTMENT OF VETERANS AFFAIRS*, Medical Center Library, 421 N Main St, 01053-9714. SAN 307-5923. Tel: 413-584-4040, Ext 2432. FAX: 413-582-3039. *Libr Tech,* Jim Mias
Library Holdings: Bk Vols 5,000; Per Subs 75
Special Collections: Patient Health Coll
Subject Interests: Psychiat, Psychol
Partic in Medical Library Association (MLA)
Open Mon-Fri 7:30-4
Restriction: Open to pub for ref only

LEICESTER

C BECKER COLLEGE, Paul Swan Library, 13 Washburn Sq, 01524. (Mail add: 61 Sever St, Worcester, 01609-2165), SAN 307-4684. Tel: 774-354-0655. E-mail: library@becker.edu. Web Site: www.becker.edu/academics/libraries-2. *Dir of Libr,* Garrett Eastman; Tel: 508-373-9709, E-mail: garrett.eastman@becker.edu
Enrl 1,000
Library Holdings: Bk Vols 31,000; Per Subs 104
Special Collections: Samuel May Coll
Subject Interests: Equine studies, Philos, Psychol, Sport mgt, Veterinary sci, Veterinary tech
Automation Activity & Vendor Info: (Cataloging) Innovative Interfaces, Inc - Millenium; (Circulation) Innovative Interfaces, Inc - Millenium; (Course Reserve) Innovative Interfaces, Inc - Millenium; (ILL) OCLC FirstSearch; (Media Booking) Innovative Interfaces, Inc; (OPAC) Innovative Interfaces, Inc; (Serials) EBSCO Online
Wireless access
Mem of Massachusetts Libr Syst

Partic in OCLC Online Computer Library Center, Inc
Open Mon-Thurs 8am-9pm, Fri 8-4, Sun 4-9

P LEICESTER PUBLIC LIBRARY*, 1136 Main St, 01524-0389. SAN 345-2972. Tel: 508-892-7020. FAX: 508-892-7045. Web Site: www.leicesterma.org. *Interim Dir,* Patricia M Grady; E-mail: gradyp@leicesterma.org; *Cat,* Donna Johnson; *Ch Serv,* Jennifer Carey-Robinson
Pop 10,000; Circ 35,655
Jul 2005-Jun 2006 Income $141,000. Mats Exp $29,000
Library Holdings: AV Mats 2,500; Bk Vols 37,000; Per Subs 55; Talking Bks 763
Automation Activity & Vendor Info: (Cataloging) Follett Software; (Circulation) Follett Software
Mem of Massachusetts Libr Syst
Open Tues-Thurs (Winter) 10-8, Fri 10-5, Sat 10-2; Tues & Thurs (Summer) 10-8, Wed & Fri 10-5
Friends of the Library Group

LENOX

P LENOX LIBRARY ASSOCIATION*, 18 Main St, 01240. SAN 307-4706. Tel: 413-637-0197. FAX: 413-637-2115. Web Site: lenoxlib.org. *Exec Dir,* Denis J Lesieur; Tel: 413-637-2630, E-mail: dlesieur@lenoxlib.org; *Asst Dir,* Sherry Gaherty; E-mail: sgaherty@cwmars.org; *Youth Serv Librn,* Ruth LaFrance; E-mail: rlafrance@cwmars.org; Staff 19 (MLS 5, Non-MLS 14)
Founded 1856. Pop 5,070; Circ 93,418
Library Holdings: Bk Vols 67,289; Per Subs 137
Special Collections: Art Exhibits; Elizabeth MacKinstry Coll; Fanny Kemble Coll; Historic Photographs; Judge Julius Rockwell Coll; Music Study Scores; Thomas Egelston Coll
Subject Interests: Local hist, Music
Function: ILL available
Publications: Photographs by Edwin Hale Lincoln (Local historical information); Pride of Palaces (Local historical information)
Partic in Central & Western Massachusetts Automated Resource Sharing
Open Tues-Sat 10-5

LEOMINSTER

M HEALTHALLIANCE HOSPITAL-LEOMINSTER CAMPUS*, Medical Library, Hospital Rd, 01453-8004. SAN 307-4722. Tel: 978-466-4035. FAX: 978-466-4038. E-mail: library@healthalliance.com. *AV Coordr, Med Librn & Coordr Med Educ,* Francis R Landry; Staff 1 (MLS 1)
Founded 1950
Library Holdings: e-books 35; Bk Titles 500; Per Subs 100
Subject Interests: Allied health, Consumer health, Gen med, Nursing
Automation Activity & Vendor Info: (Serials) SERHOLD
Database Vendor: EBSCOhost, Gale Cengage Learning, Marquis Who's Who, MD Consult, Medlib, Medline, OVID Technologies, PubMed, UpToDate, WebMD
Wireless access
Function: Computers for patron use, Electronic databases & coll, Health sci info serv, Notary serv, Online ref, Online searches, Outreach serv, Ref & res, Res libr, Wheelchair accessible
Publications: User Guide
Partic in Basic Health Sciences Library Network; Massachusetts Health Sciences Libraries Network; National Network of Libraries of Medicine; North Atlantic Health Sciences Libraries, Inc
Open Tues-Thurs 7:30-3
Restriction: Badge access after hrs, Borrowing privileges limited to fac & registered students, External users must contact libr, Hospital staff & commun, Med & nursing staff, patients & families

P LEOMINSTER PUBLIC LIBRARY*, 30 West St, 01453. SAN 307-4730. Tel: 978-534-7522. FAX: 978-840-3357. E-mail: leomref@cwmars.org. Web Site: www.leominsterlibrary.org. *Dir,* Susan Theriault Shelton; *Asst Dir,* Meredith Foley; *Hist Coll Librn,* Jeannine Levesque; *Adult Serv,* Edward Bergman; *Ch Serv,* Linda Peterson; *Circ,* Nancy Tourigny; *ILL, Media Spec,* Ann Finch; *YA Serv,* Diane Sanabria
Founded 1856. Pop 38,258; Circ 234,965
Library Holdings: Bk Vols 105,486; Per Subs 203
Special Collections: Career Information Center; Local Historical & Genealogical Coll; Parent Resource Center
Automation Activity & Vendor Info: (Cataloging) Innovative Interfaces, Inc; (Circulation) Innovative Interfaces, Inc; (OPAC) Innovative Interfaces, Inc
Publications: Friend's (Newsletter)
Mem of Massachusetts Libr Syst
Partic in Central & Western Massachusetts Automated Resource Sharing
Open Mon-Thurs 9-9, Fri & Sat 9-5, Sun 1-5
Friends of the Library Group

LEVERETT

P LEVERETT LIBRARY*, 75 Montague Rd, 01054-9701. (Mail add: PO Box 250, 01054-0250), SAN 307-4749. Tel: 413-548-9220. FAX: 413-548-9034. Web Site: www.leverettlibrary.org. *Librn,* Linda Wentworth
Pop 1,900; Circ 38,000
Library Holdings: Bk Vols 9,500; Per Subs 24
Automation Activity & Vendor Info: (Cataloging) Evergreen; (Circulation) Evergreen
Wireless access
Partic in Cent Mass Automated Resource Sharing Network, Inc
Open Tues & Thurs 3-8, Wed & Sat 10-3, Sun (Sept-May) 12-5
Friends of the Library Group

LEXINGTON

P CARY MEMORIAL LIBRARY, 1874 Massachusetts Ave, 02420. SAN 345-3030. Tel: 781-862-6288. FAX: 781-862-7355. Web Site: www.carylibrary.org. *Dir,* Koren Stembridge; Tel: 781-862-6288, Ext 312, E-mail: kstembridge@lexingtonma.gov; *Asst Dir,* Cynthia Johnson; Tel: 781-862-6288, Ext 314, E-mail: cjohnson@minlib.net; *Head, Ch,* Alissa Lauzon; Tel: 781-862-6288, Ext 172, E-mail: alauzon@minlib.net; *Head, Circ,* Peggy Bateson; Tel: 781-862-6288, Ext 212, E-mail: pbateson@minlib.net; *Head, Ref,* Cathie Ghorbani; Tel: 781-862-6288, Ext 232, E-mail: cghorbani@minlib.net; *Tech Coordr,* Emily Smith; Tel: 781-862-6288, Ext 152, E-mail: esmith@minlib.net; Staff 61 (MLS 26, Non-MLS 35)
Founded 1868. Pop 32,272; Circ 814,678
Library Holdings: Bk Vols 207,013; Per Subs 225
Special Collections: American Revolutionary War Coll; Lexington History (Worthen Coll). Oral History
Subject Interests: Local hist
Automation Activity & Vendor Info: (Acquisitions) Innovative Interfaces, Inc; (Cataloging) Innovative Interfaces, Inc; (Circulation) Innovative Interfaces, Inc; (Course Reserve) Innovative Interfaces, Inc; (ILL) Innovative Interfaces, Inc; (Media Booking) Innovative Interfaces, Inc; (OPAC) Innovative Interfaces, Inc; (Serials) Innovative Interfaces, Inc
Wireless access
Partic in Minuteman Library Network
Open Mon-Thurs 9-9, Fri & Sat 9-5, Sun (Sept-May) 1-5
Friends of the Library Group

S LEXINGTON HISTORICAL SOCIETY, INC*, Library Archives, 1332 Massachusetts Ave, 02420-3809. (Mail add: PO Box 514, 02420-0005), SAN 375-1015. Tel: 781-862-1703. FAX: 781-862-4920. E-mail: director@lexingtonhistory.org, info@lexingtonhistory.org. Web Site: www.lexingtonhistory.org. *Dir,* Susan Bennett
Library Holdings: Bk Titles 200

S MASSACHUSETTS INSTITUTE OF TECHNOLOGY*, Lincoln Laboratory Knowledge Services, 244 Wood St, 02420-9176. SAN 307-482X. Tel: 781-981-5500. E-mail: library@ll.mit.edu. *Sector Mgr,* Suellen Green; Tel: 781-981-3221, Fax: 781-981-0345; *Archives Team Lead,* Nora Zaldivar; Tel: 781-981-3985; *Info Mgt & Metadata Team Lead,* Bobb Menk; Tel: 781-981-5354; *Res Team Lead,* Rob Seidel; Tel: 781-981-3440; Staff 23 (MLS 18, Non-MLS 5)
Founded 1952
Library Holdings: e-books 10,000; e-journals 4,000; Bk Titles 127,000; Bk Vols 130,000; Per Subs 963
Subject Interests: Aerospace sci, Electronics, Eng, Optics, Solid state physics
Automation Activity & Vendor Info: (Acquisitions) SirsiDynix; (Cataloging) SirsiDynix; (Circulation) SirsiDynix; (OPAC) SirsiDynix; (Serials) SirsiDynix
Database Vendor: Dialog, ProQuest
Function: Archival coll, Bus archives, Doc delivery serv, For res purposes, Govt ref serv, ILL available, Online searches, Res libr
Publications: DoD Update; Management Focus; Scanner; Technical Reports Announcement
Partic in OCLC Online Computer Library Center, Inc
Restriction: Not open to pub

S SCOTTISH RITE MASONIC MUSEUM & LIBRARY, INC*, Van Gorden-Williams Library & Archives (National Heritage Museum), 33 Marrett Rd, 02421. Tel: 781-457-4109, 781-457-4125. FAX: 781-861-9846 (call first). E-mail: library@monh.org. Web Site: vgwcatalog.nationalheritagemuseum.org, www.nationalheritagemuseum.org. *Mgr, Libr & Archives,* Jeff Croteau; E-mail: jcroteau@monh.org; *Archivist,* Catherine Swanson; Tel: 781-457-4116, E-mail: cswanson@monh.org; Staff 2 (MLS 2)
Founded 1975
Library Holdings: Bk Vols 60,000; Per Subs 50
Special Collections: Archives of Scottish Rite Northern Masonic Supreme Council
Subject Interests: Am Revolution, Americana, Freemasonry

Automation Activity & Vendor Info: (Cataloging) TLC (The Library Corporation); (Circulation) TLC (The Library Corporation); (OPAC) TLC (The Library Corporation); (Serials) TLC (The Library Corporation)
Wireless access
Function: Archival coll, Exhibits, For res purposes, Handicapped accessible, ILL available, Online cat, Ref serv available, Res libr, Telephone ref, Web-catalog, Wheelchair accessible
Mem of Massachusetts Libr Syst
Open Tues-Fri 10-4:30
Restriction: Closed stack, Open to pub for ref only, Restricted borrowing privileges

S TIAX LLC LIBRARY*, 35 Hartwell Ave, 02421-3102. SAN 307-3033. Tel: 781-879-1200. FAX: 781-879-1201. Web Site: www.tiaxllc.com. *Dir,* Position Currently Open
Founded 1886
Library Holdings: Bk Vols 3,000; Per Subs 150
Special Collections: Arthur D Little Coll
Subject Interests: Chem, Energy, Eng, Environ, Food indust, Info sci, Mgt safety
Publications: Acquisitions List; Union List of Serials
Partic in Lyrasis; OCLC Online Computer Library Center, Inc

LEYDEN

P ROBERTSON MEMORIAL LIBRARY*, 849 Greenfield Rd, 01301-9419. SAN 307-4862. Tel: 413-773-9334. FAX: 413-772-0146. *Dir,* Christine Johnston
Founded 1913. Pop 720; Circ 8,850
Library Holdings: AV Mats 150; Bk Titles 3,762
Friends of the Library Group

LINCOLN

P LINCOLN PUBLIC LIBRARY*, Three Bedford Rd, 01773. SAN 307-4889. Tel: 781-259-8465. FAX: 781-259-1056. E-mail: lincoln@minlib.net. Web Site: www.lincolnpl.org. *Dir,* Barbara Myles; *Asst Dir,* Ellen Sisco; E-mail: esisco@minlib.net; *Ch,* Jane Flanders; E-mail: jflanders@minlib.net; *Ch,* Amy Gavalis; E-mail: agavalis@minlib.net; *Ref Librn,* Jeanne Munn Bracken; E-mail: jbracken@minlib.net; *Cataloger,* Lisa Rothenberg; E-mail: lrothenberg@minlib.net; *ILL,* Nadine Rebovich; E-mail: nrebovich@minlib.net; Staff 7 (MLS 6, Non-MLS 1)
Founded 1883. Pop 8,056; Circ 157,781
Jul 2005-Jun 2006 Income $691,254. Mats Exp $102,000. Sal $503,689
Library Holdings: Bk Vols 87,036; Per Subs 216
Subject Interests: Local hist
Automation Activity & Vendor Info: (Acquisitions) Innovative Interfaces, Inc; (Cataloging) Innovative Interfaces, Inc; (Circulation) Innovative Interfaces, Inc; (ILL) Innovative Interfaces, Inc; (OPAC) Innovative Interfaces, Inc
Database Vendor: Gale Cengage Learning
Open Mon (Winter) 1-8:30, Tues, Thurs & Fri 9-6, Wed 9-8:30, Sat 10-5, Sun 1-5; Mon (Summer) 1-8:30, Tues, Thurs & Fri 9-6, Wed 9-8:30
Friends of the Library Group

LITTLETON

P REUBEN HOAR LIBRARY*, 41 Shattuck St, 01460-4506. SAN 307-4900. Tel: 978-486-4046. FAX: 978-952-2323. E-mail: mli@mvlc.org. Web Site: www.littletonlibrary.org. *Libr Dir,* Laura Zalewski; E-mail: lzalewski@mvlc.org; Staff 15 (MLS 2, Non-MLS 13)
Founded 1887. Pop 8,000; Circ 180,583
Jul 2007-Jun 2008 Income $502,230, State $14,897, City $417,613, Federal $19,956, Locally Generated Income $46,180, Other $3,584. Mats Exp $77,679, Books $50,764, Per/Ser (Incl. Access Fees) $9,937, Other Print Mats $593, AV Mat $15,436, Electronic Ref Mat (Incl. Access Fees) $949. Sal $339,906
Library Holdings: DVDs 4,995; Microforms 116; Bk Titles 75,843; Per Subs 183
Subject Interests: Local hist, Sci fict
Automation Activity & Vendor Info: (Cataloging) SirsiDynix; (Circulation) SirsiDynix; (OPAC) SirsiDynix
Database Vendor: EBSCOhost, Electric Library, Grolier Online, OCLC WorldShare Interlibrary Loan, ProQuest, ValueLine
Wireless access
Function: After school storytime, Art exhibits, Audiobks via web, Bks on cassette, Bks on CD, Children's prog, Computers for patron use, Copy machines, Electronic databases & coll, Free DVD rentals, Handicapped accessible, Home delivery & serv to Sr ctr & nursing homes, Homebound delivery serv, ILL available, Mail & tel request accepted, Mus passes, Music CDs, Notary serv, Online cat, Online ref, OverDrive digital audio bks, Preschool outreach, Prog for children & young adult, Pub access computers, Ref serv in person, Story hour, Summer reading prog, Tax forms, Teen prog, Telephone ref, VHS videos, Web-catalog, Wheelchair accessible
Publications: Reuben's Notes (Newsletter)
Mem of Massachusetts Libr Syst
Partic in MVLC
Open Mon & Sat 10-4, Tues & Thurs 2-9, Wed 10-9, Fri 10-1
Friends of the Library Group

LONGMEADOW

C BAY PATH COLLEGE*, Hatch Library, 539 Longmeadow St, 01106. (Mail add: 588 Longmeadow St, 01106), SAN 307-4927. Tel: 413-565-1376. FAX: 413-567-8345. E-mail: library@baypath.edu. Web Site: library.baypath.edu. *Dir, Libr & Info Serv,* Michael J Moran; Tel: 413-565-1284, E-mail: mmoran@baypath.edu; *Ref & Instrul Serv Librn,* Position Currently Open; *Syst, Ref & Instruction Librn,* Sandra Cahillane; E-mail: scahilla@baypath.edu; *Tech Serv,* Kathleen Staron; E-mail: kstaron@baypath.edu; Staff 5 (MLS 5)
Founded 1897. Enrl 1,689; Fac 175; Highest Degree: Master
Jul 2009-Jun 2010 Income $284,644. Mats Exp $284,644, Books $47,845, Per/Ser (Incl. Access Fees) $36,322, Micro $1,260, AV Mat $10,494, Electronic Ref Mat (Incl. Access Fees) $156,068
Library Holdings: Audiobooks 26; AV Mats 4,451; CDs 201; DVDs 612; e-books 11,894; e-journals 52; Electronic Media & Resources 85; Microforms 4,380; Bk Titles 50,958; Bk Vols 69,987; Per Subs 140; Videos 2,810
Subject Interests: Bus, Info tech, Legal, Occupational therapy, Psychol
Automation Activity & Vendor Info: (Cataloging) SirsiDynix; (OPAC) SirsiDynix
Partic in Cooperating Libraries of Greater Springfield; Lyrasis; OCLC-LVIS
Open Mon-Thurs 8am-10pm, Fri 8-5, Sat 7-7, Sun 1-10

P RICHARD SALTER STORRS LIBRARY*, 693 Longmeadow St, 01106. SAN 307-4935. Tel: 413-565-4181. FAX: 413-565-4183. Web Site: www.longmeadowlibrary.wordpress.com. *Dir,* Karen Kappenman; E-mail: kkappenman@longmeadow.org; *Adult Serv,* Barbara Fitzgerald; *Ref,* Andrea LeClair
Founded 1908. Pop 17,000; Circ 213,216
Library Holdings: Bk Vols 100,000; Per Subs 130
Special Collections: Genealogy Coll; Local History Coll
Automation Activity & Vendor Info: (Cataloging) Innovative Interfaces, Inc; (Circulation) Innovative Interfaces, Inc; (OPAC) Innovative Interfaces, Inc
Database Vendor: Innovative Interfaces, Inc
Wireless access
Mem of Massachusetts Libr Syst
Partic in Central & Western Massachusetts Automated Resource Sharing
Open Mon-Wed 10-8, Thurs & Fri 10-5, Sat 10-4
Friends of the Library Group

LOWELL

M LOWELL GENERAL HOSPITAL*, Health Sciences Library, 295 Varnum Ave, 01854. SAN 307-4951. Tel: 978-937-6247. FAX: 978-937-6855. Web Site: www.lowellgeneral.org/go/library. *Dir,* Donna Beales; E-mail: dbeales@lowellgeneral.org
Library Holdings: Bk Titles 1,000; Bk Vols 1,100; Per Subs 120
Special Collections: Obstetrics Coll
Partic in Massachusetts Health Sciences Libraries Network; Medical Library Association (MLA); Northeastern Consortium for Health Information
Open Mon-Fri 7:30-4

L MASSACHUSETTS TRIAL COURT*, Lowell Law Library, Superior Court House, 360 Gorham St, 01852. SAN 307-496X. Tel: 978-452-9301. FAX: 978-970-2000. E-mail: lowlaw@meganet.net. Web Site: www.lawlib.state.ma.us/lowell.html. *Librn,* Catherine Mello Alves; Staff 2 (MLS 1, Non-MLS 1)
Founded 1815
Library Holdings: Bk Vols 35,000; Per Subs 53
Special Collections: Law books - Legal Periodicals Statutes, Case Reporters, Digests, Legal Treatises
Automation Activity & Vendor Info: (Cataloging) SirsiDynix; (Circulation) Horizon; (ILL) OCLC FirstSearch; (OPAC) Horizon; (Serials) Horizon
Database Vendor: Gale Cengage Learning, HeinOnline, LexisNexis, Loislaw, OCLC, OCLC WorldShare Interlibrary Loan, ProQuest, SirsiDynix, Westlaw
Wireless access
Partic in New England Law Library Consortium, Inc
Open Mon-Fri 8:30-4:30
Friends of the Library Group

J MIDDLESEX COMMUNITY COLLEGE*, City Campus Library, Federal Bldg, E Merrimack St, 01852. (Mail add: 33 Kearney Sq, 01852-1987), SAN 372-4093. Tel: 978-937-5454. Circulation Tel: 978-656-3004.

Reference Tel: 978-656-3005. FAX: 978-656-3031. *Dir,* Mary Ann Niles; Tel: 781-280-3703; *Coordr,* Laura Horgan; *Librn,* Allyson O'Brien; *Ref Serv,* Paula Cross; *Ref Serv,* Mary Fardy
Library Holdings: Bk Vols 16,000; Per Subs 200
Automation Activity & Vendor Info: (Acquisitions) Innovative Interfaces, Inc; (Cataloging) Innovative Interfaces, Inc; (Circulation) Innovative Interfaces, Inc
Open Mon Thurs (Winter) 8:30-8, Fri 8;30-4:30, Sat 9-1; Mon-Fri (Summer) 8:30-4:30

P POLLARD MEMORIAL LIBRARY, 401 Merrimack St, 01852. SAN 307-4943. Tel: 978-674-4120. Reference Tel: 978-674-4121. FAX: 978-970-4117. TDD: 978-970-4129. Web Site: www.pollardml.org. *Dir,* Victoria B Woodley; Tel: 978-674-1525, E-mail: vwoodley@lowellma.gov; *Asst Dir, Head, Ref,* Susan Fougstedt; Tel: 978-674-1537, E-mail: sfougstedt@lowellma.gov; *Literacy Prog Dir,* Julie Iatron; Tel: 978-674-1541, E-mail: jiatron@mvlc.org; *Ch,* Lauren Eldred; Tel: 978-674-1528, E-mail: leldred@mvlc.org; *Circ Librn,* Pam Colt; Tel: 978-674-1535, E-mail: pcolt@mvlc.org; *Commun Planning Librn,* Winifred Flint; Tel: 978-674-1548, E-mail: wflint@lowellma.gov; *Ref Librn,* Monica McDermott; Tel: 978-674-1536, E-mail: mmcdermott@mvlc.org; *YA Librn,* Beth Brassel; Tel: 978-674-1543, E-mail: ebrassel@mvlc.org; *Coordr, Automation & Tech Serv,* Dory Lewis; Tel: 978-674-1539, E-mail: dlewis@mvlc.org; *Commun Planning Coordr,* Sean Thibodeau; Tel: 978-674-1542, E-mail: sthibodeau@mvlc.org; *Coordr, Youth Serv,* Molly Hancock; Tel: 978-674-1527, E-mail: mhancock@mvlc.org; *IT Spec,* Jessica McCarthy; Tel: 978-674-1547, E-mail: jmccarthy@mvlc.org; Staff 12 (MLS 11, Non-MLS 1)
Founded 1844. Pop 105,167; Circ 212,401
Library Holdings: AV Mats 3,981; Bk Vols 166,217; Per Subs 580
Special Collections: History of Lowell Coll
Subject Interests: Genealogy
Automation Activity & Vendor Info: (Cataloging) Evergreen; (Circulation) Evergreen; (OPAC) Evergreen
Database Vendor: EBSCOhost, Gale Cengage Learning, LibraryInsight, OCLC FirstSearch, Overdrive, Inc, ProQuest
Wireless access
Function: 24/7 Online cat, Activity rm, Adult bk club, Adult literacy prog, Archival coll, Audiobks via web, BA reader (adult literacy), Bks on CD, CD-ROM, Children's prog, Citizenship assistance, Computer training, Computers for patron use, Copy machines, Digital talking bks, E-Reserves, Electronic databases & coll, Free DVD rentals, Handicapped accessible, Holiday prog, ILL available, Large print keyboards, Magazines, Magnifiers for reading, Microfiche/film & reading machines, Movies, Mus passes, Music CDs, Newsp ref libr, Online cat, OverDrive digital audio bks, Photocopying/Printing, Prog for adults, Prog for children & young adult, Pub access computers, Ref serv available, Ref serv in person, Res performed for a fee, Spanish lang bks, Spoken cassettes & CDs, Story hour, Study rm, Summer reading prog, Tax forms, Teen prog, Telephone ref, Web-catalog, Wheelchair accessible
Mem of Massachusetts Libr Syst
Partic in Merrimack Valley Library Consortium
Special Services for the Deaf - TTY equip
Special Services for the Blind - Accessible computers; Assistive/Adapted tech devices, equip & products; Bks on CD; Computer access aids; Computer with voice synthesizer for visually impaired persons; Copier with enlargement capabilities
Open Mon-Thurs (Winter) 9-9, Fri & Sat 9-5; Mon-Thurs (Summer) 9-9, Fri 9-5
Friends of the Library Group
Branches: 1
SENIOR CENTER BRANCH, 276 Broadway St, 01854. Administration Tel: 978-970-4186. *Dir,* Victoria Woodley
Library Holdings: Bk Vols 2,200
Function: Computers for patron use, Copy machines, Photocopying/Printing
Open Mon-Fri 9-4

M SAINTS MEMORIAL MEDICAL CENTER*, Health Sciences Library, Hospital Dr, 01852-1389. (Mail add: PO Box 30, 01853-0030), SAN 327-3016. Tel: 978-934-8308. FAX: 978-934-8241. *Librn,* Bette Bissonnette
Library Holdings: Bk Vols 800; Per Subs 200
Automation Activity & Vendor Info: (Cataloging) Auto-Graphics, Inc
Partic in Boston Biomedical Library Consortium; Mashlin; National Network of Libraries of Medicine; Northeastern Consortium for Health Information
Open Mon-Fri 8-4:30

C UNIVERSITY OF MASSACHUSETTS LOWELL LIBRARIES*, O'Leary Library, 61 Wilder St, 01854-3098. SAN 345-312X. Tel: 978-934-4550, 978-934-4551. Circulation Tel: 978-934-4585. Interlibrary Loan Service Tel: 978-934-4573. Reference Tel: 978-934-4554. Administration Tel: 978-934-4575. Automation Services Tel: 978-923-4570. FAX: 978-934-3015. Administration FAX: 978-934-3020. Web Site: www.uml.edu/libraries. *Dir,* Patricia Noreau; E-mail: patricia_noreau@uml.edu; *Head, Access Serv,* Ellen Keane; Tel: 978-934-4594, E-mail: ellen_keane@uml.edu; *Head, Media Serv,* Mitch Shuldman; Tel: 978-934-4561, E-mail: mitchell_shuldman@uml.edu; *Head, Pub Serv,* Rosanna Kowalewski; Tel: 978-934-4580, E-mail: rosanna_kowalewski@uml.edu; *Acq & Cat Librn,* Suzanne Nault; Tel: 978-934-4592, E-mail: suzanne_nault@uml.edu; *Ref Librn,* Helen Jones; Tel: 978-934-4581, E-mail: helen_jones@uml.edu; *Ref Librn,* Ronald Karr; Tel: 978-934-4590, E-mail: ronald_karr@uml.edu; *Ref Librn,* Richard Slapsys; Tel: 978-934-4593, E-mail: richard_slapsys@uml.edu; *Coordr, Access Serv,* Deborah Friedman; Tel: 978-934-4572, E-mail: deborah_friedman@uml.edu; *Media Serv,* John Callahan; Tel: 978-934-4571, E-mail: john_callahan@uml.edu. Subject Specialists: *Educ, Psychol, Sociol,* Rosanna Kowalewski; *Health, Med,* Helen Jones; *Criminal justice, Hist, Polit sci,* Ronald Karr; *Art, Lit, Music,* Richard Slapsys; Staff 24 (MLS 14, Non-MLS 10)
Enrl 8,125; Fac 453; Highest Degree: Doctorate
Library Holdings: AV Mats 7,656; e-books 4,289; e-journals 12,498; Bk Vols 397,652; Per Subs 520; Videos 6,168
Special Collections: ERIC Microfiche Coll (1972-2002). US Document Depository
Subject Interests: Allied health, Educ, Fine arts, Humanities, Nursing
Automation Activity & Vendor Info: (Acquisitions) Ex Libris Group; (Cataloging) Ex Libris Group; (Circulation) Ex Libris Group; (Course Reserve) Ex Libris Group; (ILL) OCLC; (OPAC) Ex Libris Group; (Serials) Ex Libris Group
Database Vendor: Cambridge Scientific Abstracts, EBSCOhost, Gale Cengage Learning, LexisNexis, Newsbank, OCLC WorldShare Interlibrary Loan, OVID Technologies, ProQuest, ScienceDirect
Wireless access
Function: AV serv, Handicapped accessible, Health sci info serv, ILL available, Music CDs, Orientations, Photocopying/Printing, Ref serv available, Telephone ref, VHS videos, Wheelchair accessible
Mem of Massachusetts Libr Syst
Partic in Boston Library Consortium, Inc; Lyrasis
Special Services for the Blind - Assistive/Adapted tech devices, equip & products
Open Mon-Thurs (Winter) 7:30am-Midnight, Fri 7:30-5, Sat 10-6, Sun 1-Midnight; Mon-Thurs (Summer) 7:30am-10pm, Fri 7:30-5
Friends of the Library Group
Departmental Libraries:
CENTER FOR LOWELL HISTORY, Patrick J Mogan Cultural Ctr, 40 French St, 01852, SAN 329-6369. Tel: 978-934-4997. FAX: 978-934-4995. *Dir, Spec Coll,* Martha Mayo; Tel: 978-934-4998, E-mail: martha_mayo@uml.edu; *Archives Mgr,* Janine Whitcomb; E-mail: janine_whitcomb@uml.edu; Staff 2 (MLS 1, Non-MLS 1)
Founded 1971
Special Collections: Boston & Maine Railroad Historical Society Coll; Lowell Historical Society Coll; Lowell Museum Coll; Manning Family Coll, Middlesex Canal Assoc Coll; Proprietors of the Locks Canal Co Coll; Senator Paul E Tsongas Coll, papers; Textiles (Olney Coll); University of Lowell Archives. Oral History
Function: ILL available
Open Mon, Wed-Fri 9-5, Tues 9-9, Sat 10-3
Restriction: Non-circulating coll
LYDON LIBRARY, 84 University Ave, 01854-2896, SAN 345-309X. Tel: 978-934-3205. Interlibrary Loan Service Tel: 978-934-3206. Reference Tel: 978-934-3213. Administration Tel: 978-934-3216. FAX: 978-934-3014. *Head, Access Serv,* Ellen Keane; Tel: 978-934-3203, E-mail: ellen_keane@uml.edu; *Ref Librn,* Margaret Manion; Tel: 978-934-3211, E-mail: margaret_manion@uml.edu; *Ref Librn,* Marion Muskiewicz; Tel: 978-934-3209, E-mail: marion_muskiewicz@uml.edu; *Coordr, Access Serv,* Judith Barnes-Long; Tel: 978-934-3552, E-mail: judith_barnes@uml.edu; *Access Serv,* Denise Chandonnet; Tel: 978-934-3215, E-mail: denise_chandonnet@uml.edu; *Access Serv,* Donna Tanguay; Tel: 978-934-3204, E-mail: donna_tanguay@uml.edu. Subject Specialists: *Eng,* Margaret Manion; Staff 5 (MLS 4, Non-MLS 1)
Special Collections: University of Lowell Archives. Oral History
Subject Interests: Bus & mgt, Chem, Computer sci, Electrical eng, Eng, Environ studies, Indust eng, Nuclear eng, Physics, Software eng
Function: AV serv, Govt ref serv, Handicapped accessible, ILL available, Orientations, Ref serv available, Wheelchair accessible
Open Mon-Thurs 7:30am-Midnight, Fri 7:30-5, Sat 10-6, Sun 1-Midnight

LUDLOW

P HUBBARD MEMORIAL LIBRARY*, 24 Center St, 01056-2795. SAN 307-4986. Tel: 413-583-3408. FAX: 413-583-5646. E-mail: info@hubbardlibrary.org. Web Site: www.hubbardlibrary.org. *Dir,* Judy Kelly; E-mail: jkelly@cwmars.org; Staff 8 (MLS 2, Non-MLS 6)
Founded 1891. Pop 22,000; Circ 107,657
Library Holdings: AV Mats 4,255; Bk Vols 56,862; Per Subs 95
Special Collections: Jack Alves Vietnam Coll
Subject Interests: World War II

Automation Activity & Vendor Info: (Circulation) Innovative Interfaces, Inc; (ILL) Innovative Interfaces, Inc; (OPAC) Innovative Interfaces, Inc
Database Vendor: Gale Cengage Learning, Newsbank
Partic in Central & Western Massachusetts Automated Resource Sharing
Open Mon, Wed & Fri 9-5, Tues & Thurs 9-8, Sat (Sept-June) 9-1
Friends of the Library Group

LUNENBURG

P LUNENBURG PUBLIC LIBRARY*, 1023 Massachusetts Ave, 01462. SAN 307-4994. Tel: 978-582-4140. FAX: 978-582-4141. E-mail: lunenburglibrary@gmail.com. Web Site: www.lunenburg.gov. *Dir,* Martha Moore; E-mail: mmoore@cwmars.org; *Asst Dir,* Patricia Dupont; *Ch Serv,* Karen Kemp; Staff 7 (Non-MLS 7)
Founded 1909. Pop 9,400
Library Holdings: Bk Titles 29,643; Per Subs 80
Automation Activity & Vendor Info: (Cataloging) Evergreen; (Circulation) Evergreen; (ILL) Evergreen; (OPAC) Evergreen
Database Vendor: Gale Cengage Learning
Wireless access
Partic in Central & Western Massachusetts Automated Resource Sharing
Special Services for the Blind - Closed circuit TV magnifier; Magnifiers
Open Mon-Thurs 10-8, Sat 10-2
Friends of the Library Group

LYNN

P LYNN PUBLIC LIBRARY*, Five N Common St, 01902. SAN 345-3154. Tel: 781-595-0567. FAX: 781-592-5050. E-mail: lynnq@noblenet.org. Web Site: www.noblenet.org/lynn. *Chief Librn,* Position Currently Open; *Archives Mgr, Hist Coll Dir, Ref,* Lisa Bourque; *Bus & Finance Mgr,* Paula Joyal; *Circ Mgr, Computer Serv, ILL,* Eileen Kearney; *Ch Serv,* Theresa Hurley; Staff 5 (MLS 2, Non-MLS 3)
Founded 1815. Pop 89,050
Library Holdings: Bk Titles 110,000; Per Subs 210
Special Collections: Shoe Industry Coll
Subject Interests: Civil War, Genealogy, Hist, Law
Automation Activity & Vendor Info: (Cataloging) Innovative Interfaces, Inc; (Circulation) Innovative Interfaces, Inc; (OPAC) Innovative Interfaces, Inc
Database Vendor: EBSCOhost, Facts on File, Ingram Library Services, LearningExpress
Wireless access
Function: After school storytime, Archival coll, CD-ROM, Copy machines, E-Reserves, Electronic databases & coll, Handicapped accessible, Home delivery & serv to Sr ctr & nursing homes, Homework prog, ILL available, Magnifiers for reading, Mail & tel request accepted, Music CDs, Photocopying/Printing, Prog for adults, Prog for children & young adult, Ref serv available, Spoken cassettes & CDs, Spoken cassettes & DVDs, Summer reading prog, Tax forms, Telephone ref, VHS videos, Wheelchair accessible
Partic in North of Boston Library Exchange, Inc
Special Services for the Deaf - Assisted listening device; Interpreter on staff; TTY equip
Special Services for the Blind - Audiovision-a radio reading serv; Bks on cassette; Bks on CD
Open Mon-Thurs 9-9, Fri & Sat 9-5
Friends of the Library Group

M NSMC*, Union Hospital Health Sciences Library, 500 Lynnfield St, 01904. SAN 320-3816. Tel: 781-581-9200, Ext 4123. FAX: 781-581-0720. *Dir,* Deborah Almquist; E-mail: dalmquist@partners.org; Staff 3 (MLS 1, Non-MLS 2)
Library Holdings: Bk Titles 1,179; Per Subs 90
Special Collections: Consumer Health Coll
Subject Interests: Med, Nursing, Surgery
Partic in Docline; Essex County Libr Consortium; Northeastern Consortium for Health Information; Regional Med Libr Network
Open Mon-Fri 7:30-3:30

LYNNFIELD

P LYNNFIELD PUBLIC LIBRARY*, 18 Summer St, 01940-1837. SAN 345-3278. Tel: 781-334-5411. FAX: 781-334-2164. E-mail: lfd@noblenet.org. Web Site: www.noblenet.org/lynnfield. *Dir,* Nancy D Ryan; *Head, Ref Serv,* Patricia Kelly; *Tech Serv,* Laurel Toole; *Head, Youth Serv,* Laura Bruynell; *Circ Mgr,* Hollin Elizabeth Pagos; Staff 19 (MLS 4, Non-MLS 15)
Founded 1892. Pop 11,903; Circ 113,229
Library Holdings: AV Mats 4,494; Bk Vols 55,281; Per Subs 173
Special Collections: Oral History
Subject Interests: Local hist
Automation Activity & Vendor Info: (Acquisitions) Innovative Interfaces, Inc; (Cataloging) Innovative Interfaces, Inc; (Circulation) Innovative Interfaces, Inc; (ILL) Innovative Interfaces, Inc; (OPAC) Innovative Interfaces, Inc; (Serials) Innovative Interfaces, Inc
Database Vendor: Innovative Interfaces, Inc
Function: Handicapped accessible, Homebound delivery serv, ILL available, Photocopying/Printing, Prog for children & young adult, Ref serv available, Summer reading prog, Telephone ref, Wheelchair accessible
Publications: Library Link
Mem of Massachusetts Libr Syst
Open Mon-Thurs 9-9, Fri & Sat 9-5
Friends of the Library Group

MALDEN

P MALDEN PUBLIC LIBRARY*, 36 Salem St, 02148-5291. SAN 345-3332. Tel: 781-324-0218. Interlibrary Loan Service Tel: 781-324-0220. FAX: 781-324-4467. Web Site: www.maldenpubliclibrary.org. *Dir,* Dina G Malgeri; E-mail: dmalgeri@maldenpubliclibrary.org; *Asst Dir,* Donna Alger; E-mail: dalger@maldenpubliclibrary.org; *Sr Librn,* Julia Ierardi; E-mail: jierardi@maldenpubliclibrary.org; *Ref, Syst Librn,* Stephen Nedell; E-mail: snedell@maldenpubliclibrary.org; *Adult Serv,* Stacy Holder; E-mail: sholder@maldenpubliclibrary.org; *Adult Serv,* Sothy Orn; *Adult Serv,* Kenneth Pease; E-mail: kpease@maldenpubliclibrary.org; *Ch Serv,* Rebecca Smith; Tel: 781-388-0803, E-mail: rsmith@maldenpubliclibrary.org; *Tech Serv,* Wendy Kung; E-mail: wkung@maldenpubliclibrary.org; *YA Serv,* Keri Lynn Adams; Staff 10 (MLS 10)
Founded 1879. Pop 53,313; Circ 168,328
Library Holdings: Bk Titles 194,740; Per Subs 200
Special Collections: Abraham Lincoln (Pierce Coll)
Subject Interests: Art & archit, Hist, Local hist, Relig
Automation Activity & Vendor Info: (Cataloging) SirsiDynix; (Circulation) SirsiDynix; (ILL) SirsiDynix; (OPAC) SirsiDynix; (Serials) SirsiDynix
Database Vendor: SirsiDynix
Publications: Annual Report; Booklet
Partic in Metro Boston Libr Network
Open Mon-Thurs 9-9, Fri & Sat 9-6
Friends of the Library Group
Branches: 1
LINDEN BRANCH, Oliver & Clapp Sts, 02148, SAN 329-3157. Tel: 781-397-7067. *Librn,* Martha Van Riddle; E-mail: mvanriddle@maldenpubliclibrary.org; Staff 1 (MLS 1)
Library Holdings: Bk Vols 9,524
Open Tues 11-8, Wed-Fri 11-7, Sat 12-4

MANCHESTER-BY-THE-SEA

P MANCHESTER-BY-THE-SEA PUBLIC LIBRARY*, 15 Union St, 01944. SAN 307-5036. Tel: 978-526-7711. FAX: 978-526-2018. Web Site: www.manchesterpl.org. *Dir,* Dorothy Sieradzki; *Asst Dir,* Michael O'Connor; *Ch Serv,* Sara Collins; *Circ,* Lori Dumont; Staff 4 (MLS 3, Non-MLS 1)
Founded 1886. Pop 5,305; Circ 55,509
Jul 2007-Jun 2008 Income $325,628. Mats Exp $62,000. Sal $210,943
Library Holdings: AV Mats 5,047; Bk Titles 45,000; Bk Vols 44,953; Per Subs 125
Automation Activity & Vendor Info: (Cataloging) SirsiDynix; (Circulation) SirsiDynix; (OPAC) SirsiDynix
Wireless access
Mem of Massachusetts Libr Syst
Partic in Merrimack Valley Library Consortium
Open Mon & Wed 10-8, Tues & Thurs 1-8, Fri & Sat 10-5
Friends of the Library Group

S MANCHESTER HISTORICAL MUSEUM*, Ten Union St, 01944. SAN 329-7403. Tel: 978-526-7230. FAX: 978-526-6060. E-mail: manchesterhistorical@verizon.net. Web Site: manchesterhistorical.com. *Archivist,* Esther Proctor
Library Holdings: Bk Titles 500
Special Collections: Local Deeds Depository Coll
Subject Interests: Doc, Genealogy, Local hist, Manuscripts, Photog
Restriction: Open by appt only

MANOMET

S MANOMET CENTER FOR CONSERVATION SCIENCES LIBRARY*, PO Box 1770, 02345. SAN 371-2281. Tel: 508-224-6521. FAX: 508-224-9220. Web Site: www.manomet.org. *In Charge,* Jack Halloran
Library Holdings: Bk Vols 12,000
Open Mon-Fri 9-5

MANSFIELD

P MANSFIELD PUBLIC LIBRARY*, 255 Hope St, 02048-2353. SAN 307-5044. Tel: 508-261-7380. FAX: 508-261-7422. E-mail: mansfieldlibrary2001@yahoo.com. Web Site: www.sailsinc.org/mansfield. *Dir,* Janet Campbell; E-mail: jcampbel@sailsinc.org; *Asst Dir, Youth Serv*

Librn, Katherine Schacht; *Circ,* Barbara Sheffield; *Ref,* Mary Tynan; Staff 3 (MLS 3)
Founded 1884. Pop 22,400
Jul 2008-Jun 2009 Income $678,768, State $31,000, City $640,937, Locally Generated Income $6,831. Mats Exp $132,947, Books $84,076, Per/Ser (Incl. Access Fees) $11,748, Micro $450, AV Equip $3,297, AV Mat $18,620, Electronic Ref Mat (Incl. Access Fees) $10,392. Sal $428,578 (Prof $197,950)
Library Holdings: Audiobooks 4,039; CDs 1,580; e-books 361; Microforms 733; Bk Vols 90,979; Per Subs 191; Videos 5,091
Subject Interests: Local hist
Automation Activity & Vendor Info: (Acquisitions) SIRSI Unicorn
Database Vendor: Booklist Online, EBSCOhost, Electric Library, Gale Cengage Learning, Newsbank, Overdrive, Inc, ProQuest
Wireless access
Mem of Massachusetts Libr Syst
Special Services for the Deaf - Assistive tech; Bks on deafness & sign lang; Closed caption videos
Special Services for the Blind - Assistive/Adapted tech devices, equip & products; Computer with voice synthesizer for visually impaired persons
Open Mon-Thurs 10-8, Fri 10-5, Sat 1-4
Friends of the Library Group

MARBLEHEAD

P ABBOT PUBLIC LIBRARY*, 235 Pleasant St, 01945. SAN 307-5052. Tel: 781-631-1481. Reference Tel: 781-631-1481, Ext 213. FAX: 781-639-0558. E-mail: mar@noblenet.org. Web Site: www.abbotlibrary.org. *Dir,* Patricia J Rogers; E-mail: rogers@noblenet.org; *Asst Dir, Head, Ref,* Ann E Connolly; E-mail: aconnoll@nobletnet.org; *Ch Serv,* Marcia Cannon; E-mail: cannon@noblenet.org; *ILL,* Jonathan Randolph; E-mail: randolph@noblenet.org; *Ref Serv, YA,* Mary Farrell; E-mail: farrell@noblenet.org; *Tech Serv,* Christine Evans; E-mail: evans@noblenet.org; Staff 24 (MLS 6, Non-MLS 18)
Founded 1878. Pop 19,971; Circ 219,458
Library Holdings: Bk Vols 115,895; Per Subs 258
Special Collections: Yachts & Yachting
Automation Activity & Vendor Info: (Cataloging) Innovative Interfaces, Inc; (Circulation) Innovative Interfaces, Inc; (Course Reserve) Innovative Interfaces, Inc; (OPAC) Innovative Interfaces, Inc; (Serials) Innovative Interfaces, Inc
Mem of Massachusetts Libr Syst
Partic in North of Boston Library Exchange, Inc
Open Mon-Wed 9:30-9, Thurs 1-6, Fri & Sat 9:30-5, Sun 1-5
Friends of the Library Group

S MARBLEHEAD MUSEUM & HISTORICAL SOCIETY LIBRARY*, 170 Washington St, 01945-3340. SAN 320-8613. Tel: 781-631-1069. FAX: 781-631-0917. Web Site: www.marbleheadmuseum.org. *Curator,* Karen MacInnis; E-mail: karenmac@marbleheadmuseum.org
Founded 1898
Library Holdings: Bk Vols 1,000
Special Collections: Diary & Genealogy Coll; Ledger & Log Book Coll; Unbound Document Coll
Open Tues-Fri 10-4

MARION

P ELIZABETH TABER LIBRARY*, Eight Spring St, 02738. SAN 307-5060. Tel: 508-748-1252. Web Site: www.elizabethtaberlibrary.org. *Dir,* Elisabeth O'Neill; E-mail: eoneill@sailsinc.org; *Ch,* Rosemary Grey; E-mail: rgrey@sailsinc.org; Staff 4 (MLS 2, Non-MLS 2)
Founded 1852. Pop 8,000
Library Holdings: AV Mats 2,500; Large Print Bks 200; Bk Titles 37,000; Per Subs 75
Special Collections: Maritime History Coll, Marion History Coll
Automation Activity & Vendor Info: (Cataloging) SirsiDynix; (Circulation) SirsiDynix; (ILL) SirsiDynix; (OPAC) SirsiDynix; (Serials) SirsiDynix
Wireless access
Publications: Newsletter
Open Mon, Wed & Fri 10-5, Tues & Thurs 10-8, Sat 10-3, Sun (Oct-April) 1-4
Friends of the Library Group

MARLBOROUGH

P MARLBOROUGH PUBLIC LIBRARY, 35 W Main St, 01752-5510. SAN 307-5095. Tel: 508-624-6900. Reference Tel: 508-624-6992. Administration Tel: 508-624-6996. FAX: 508-485-1494. Web Site: www.marlboroughpubliclibrary.org. *Dir,* Margaret Cardello; Tel: 508-624-6901, E-mail: mcardello@marlborough-ma.gov; *Head, Circ, Head, Tech,* Katherine Gurbanov; Tel: 508-624-6998, E-mail: kgurbanov@cwmars.org; *Head, Tech Serv,* Karen Mattes; E-mail: kmattes@cwmars.org; *Ch Serv,* Position Currently Open; *Ref,* Position Currently Open; *YA Serv,* Jessica Bacon; Tel: 508-460-3796, E-mail: jbacon@cwmars.org; Staff 33 (MLS 5, Non-MLS 28)
Founded 1871. Pop 38,500
Library Holdings: Bk Vols 130,000; Per Subs 275
Special Collections: Horatio Alger Coll
Automation Activity & Vendor Info: (Cataloging) Evergreen; (Circulation) Evergreen; (OPAC) Evergreen
Wireless access
Partic in Central & Western Massachusetts Automated Resource Sharing
Open Mon-Thurs 9-8:30, Fri & Sat 9-5, Sun 1-5
Friends of the Library Group

S RAYTHEON CO*, Research Library, 1001 Boston Post Rd, 01752-3789. SAN 329-112X. Tel: 508-490-2288. FAX: 508-490-2017. Web Site: www.raytheon.com. *Librn,* Steve McCulloch; Staff 1 (Non-MLS 1)
Founded 1988
Library Holdings: AV Mats 125; CDs 50; e-books 150; e-journals 50; Bk Titles 30,000; Per Subs 400; Talking Bks 300
Special Collections: ICAO Documents; IEEE Conference Proceedings
Subject Interests: Air traffic control, Computer sci, Electronics, Homeland security, Math, Transportation
Automation Activity & Vendor Info: (Acquisitions) SirsiDynix; (Cataloging) SirsiDynix; (Circulation) SirsiDynix; (ILL) SirsiDynix; (OPAC) SirsiDynix; (Serials) SirsiDynix
Wireless access
Publications: Bulletin
Partic in Dialog Corp; Lyrasis; NASA Libraries Information System-NASA Galaxie; OCLC Online Computer Library Center, Inc
Restriction: Not open to pub, Staff use only

MARSHFIELD

P VENTRESS MEMORIAL LIBRARY*, 15 Library Plaza, 02050. SAN 307-5117. Tel: 781-834-5535. FAX: 781-837-8362. E-mail: malib@ocln.org. Web Site: www.ventresslibrary.org. *Dir,* Ellen Riboldi; *Ref,* Christine Woods; *Ch Serv,* Wendy Ward; *Cat,* Nancy Kelly; *Circ,* Robin Hall; Staff 7 (MLS 5, Non-MLS 2)
Founded 1895. Pop 21,531; Circ 240,000
Library Holdings: Bk Titles 81,539; Per Subs 200
Special Collections: Local History, prints, photogs
Subject Interests: New England
Database Vendor: Facts on File, ReferenceUSA
Partic in Old Colony Libr Network (OCLN)
Open Mon-Wed 9:30-9:00, Thurs-Sat 9:30-5:30
Friends of the Library Group

MARSTONS MILLS

P MARSTONS MILLS PUBLIC LIBRARY*, 2160 Main St, 02648. (Mail add: PO Box 9, 02648-0009), SAN 307-5125. Tel: 508-428-5175. FAX: 508-420-5194. E-mail: mmpl@cape.com. Web Site: www.mmpl.org. *Dir,* Renee Voorhees; *Ad,* Ann Flynn; *Tech Serv, Youth Serv Librn,* Lindsey Hughes; *Libr Spec, Webmaster,* Sue Martin; Staff 2 (Non-MLS 2)
Founded 1891. Pop 9,500; Circ 47,000
Library Holdings: Bks on Deafness & Sign Lang 10; CDs 65; DVDs 250; Large Print Bks 250; Bk Vols 19,639; Per Subs 53; Talking Bks 748; Videos 1,100
Special Collections: Cape Cod Coll; Contemporary American Women Poets Coll
Subject Interests: Landscape design, Mysteries
Automation Activity & Vendor Info: (Acquisitions) Innovative Interfaces, Inc - Millenium; (Cataloging) Innovative Interfaces, Inc; (Circulation) Innovative Interfaces, Inc; (ILL) Innovative Interfaces, Inc; (OPAC) Innovative Interfaces, Inc
Database Vendor: Baker & Taylor, EBSCOhost
Wireless access
Function: ILL available, Prog for children & young adult, Spoken cassettes & CDs, Summer reading prog, Telephone ref, VHS videos, Wheelchair accessible
Publications: Marstons Mills Public Library Newsletter (Quarterly)
Mem of Massachusetts Libr Syst
Partic in Cape Libraries Automated Materials Sharing Network
Special Services for the Blind - Bks on cassette; Bks on CD; Large print bks
Open Mon, Thurs & Fri 10-5, Tues 10-8, Wed 10-6, Sat 10-2

MASHPEE

P MASHPEE PUBLIC LIBRARY*, 64 Steeple St, 02649. (Mail add: PO Box 657, 02649-0657), SAN 376-7868. Tel: 508-539-1435. FAX: 508-539-1437. Web Site: www.ci.mashpee.ma.us, www.clamsnet.org. *Dir,* Kathleen Mahoney; E-mail: kmahoney@clamsnet.org; *Ch Serv,* Janet Burke; E-mail: jburke@clamsnet.org; *Tech Serv,* Bridget Bontrager; E-mail: bbontrager@clamsnet.org; Staff 2.75 (MLS 1.75, Non-MLS 1)
Pop 14,300; Circ 128,000

Jul 2006-Jun 2007 Income $261,487, State $16,192, City $243,459, Locally Generated Income $1,836. Mats Exp $55,425, Books $25,000, Per/Ser (Incl. Access Fees) $4,000, Other Print Mats $2,600, AV Mat $23,000, Electronic Ref Mat (Incl. Access Fees) $825
Library Holdings: AV Mats 5,600; Bk Vols 30,000; Per Subs 60
Special Collections: Native American Coll
Automation Activity & Vendor Info: (Acquisitions) Innovative Interfaces, Inc; (Cataloging) Innovative Interfaces, Inc; (Circulation) Innovative Interfaces, Inc; (ILL) Innovative Interfaces, Inc; (OPAC) Innovative Interfaces, Inc; (Serials) Innovative Interfaces, Inc
Database Vendor: EBSCOhost
Wireless access
Mem of Massachusetts Libr Syst
Partic in Cape Libraries Automated Materials Sharing Network
Open Mon, Wed, Fri & Sat 10-5, Tues & Thurs 12-7
Friends of the Library Group

MATTAPOISETT

P MATTAPOISETT FREE PUBLIC LIBRARY*, Seven Barstow St, 02739-0475. (Mail add: PO Box 475, 02739). Tel: 508-758-4171. FAX: 508-758-4783. E-mail: mfpl@sailsinc.org. Web Site: www.mattapoisettlibrary.org. *Dir,* Judith E Wallace
Founded 1882. Pop 6,048; Circ 52,000
Library Holdings: AV Mats 9,942; Bks on Deafness & Sign Lang 10; Bk Vols 30,000; Per Subs 94
Automation Activity & Vendor Info: (Acquisitions) SirsiDynix; (Cataloging) SirsiDynix; (Circulation) SirsiDynix
Mem of Massachusetts Libr Syst
Partic in SAILS Library Network
Open Tues & Wed 10-8, Thurs & Fri 10-5, Sat 10-4
Friends of the Library Group

MAYNARD

P MAYNARD PUBLIC LIBRARY, 77 Nason St, 01754-2316. SAN 307-515X. Tel: 978-897-1010. FAX: 978-897-9884. E-mail: mayill@minlib.net. Web Site: www.maynardpubliclibrary.org. *Dir,* Stephen Weiner; *Asst Dir,* Cynthia C Howe; *Circ Librn,* Carol Casey; *Ch Serv, Youth Serv,* Mark A Malcolm; *ILL, Ref,* Jeremy Robichaud; *Tech Serv,* Karen Weir; Staff 5.5 (MLS 3, Non-MLS 2.5)
Founded 1881. Pop 10,305; Circ 45,000
Library Holdings: AV Mats 7,000; Bk Vols 50,000; Per Subs 126
Special Collections: Maynard History
Automation Activity & Vendor Info: (Cataloging) Innovative Interfaces, Inc; (Circulation) Innovative Interfaces, Inc; (OPAC) Innovative Interfaces, Inc
Function: 24/7 Electronic res, 24/7 Online cat, Bk club(s), Bks on CD, Computer training, Computers for patron use, Copy machines, Electronic databases & coll, Fax serv, Free DVD rentals, Homebound delivery serv, ILL available, Magazines, Magnifiers for reading, Microfiche/film & reading machines, Movies, Mus passes, Music CDs, OverDrive digital audio bks, Prog for adults, Prog for children & young adult, Ref serv available, Scanner, Story hour, Study rm, Summer reading prog, Tax forms, Teen prog, Telephone ref, VCDs, Video lending libr, Web-catalog, Workshops
Partic in Minuteman Library Network
Open Mon, Fri & Sat 10-5, Tues & Thurs 2-9, Wed 10-6
Friends of the Library Group

MEDFIELD

S MEDFIELD HISTORICAL SOCIETY LIBRARY*, Six Pleasant St, 02052. (Mail add: PO Box 233, 02052-0233), SAN 375-152X. Tel: 508-359-4773. *Pres,* George Gray
Founded 1891
Library Holdings: Bk Titles 200
Subject Interests: Genealogy, Local hist
Open Sat 10-12

P MEDFIELD MEMORIAL PUBLIC LIBRARY*, 468 Main St, 02052-2008. SAN 307-5168. Tel: 508-359-4544. FAX: 508-359-8124. E-mail: info@medfieldlibrary.org. Web Site: www.medfieldlibrary.org. *Libr Dir,* Deborah Kelsey; E-mail: dkelsey@minlib.net; *Ad,* Andrea Fiorillo; E-mail: afiorillo@minlib.net; *Ad,* Mare Parker-O'Toole; E-mail: mare@minlib.net; *Ch Serv Librn,* Ann Russo; E-mail: arusso@minlib.net; *Teen Serv Librn,* Jen Forgit; E-mail: jforgit@minlib.net; Staff 8.5 (MLS 4, Non-MLS 4.5)
Founded 1872. Pop 12,275; Circ 213,178
Jul 2010-Jun 2011 Income $612,000. Mats Exp $98,000. Sal $385,000
Library Holdings: CDs 7,631; DVDs 8,801; e-books 261; e-journals 1; Bk Vols 60,271; Per Subs 125
Automation Activity & Vendor Info: (Acquisitions) Innovative Interfaces, Inc; (Cataloging) Innovative Interfaces, Inc; (Circulation) Innovative Interfaces, Inc; (Course Reserve) Innovative Interfaces, Inc; (ILL) Innovative Interfaces, Inc; (Media Booking) Innovative Interfaces, Inc; (OPAC) Innovative Interfaces, Inc; (Serials) Innovative Interfaces, Inc
Wireless access
Function: Adult bk club, Bk club(s), Bks on CD, Children's prog, Computer training, Computers for patron use, Copy machines, Electronic databases & coll, Fax serv, Free DVD rentals, Handicapped accessible, ILL available, Mus passes, Music CDs, Online cat, Outside serv via phone, mail, e-mail & web, OverDrive digital audio bks, Photocopying/Printing, Prog for adults, Prog for children & young adult, Pub access computers, Ref serv available, Ref serv in person, Story hour, Summer reading prog, Tax forms, Teen prog, Telephone ref, Web-catalog, Wheelchair accessible, Workshops
Partic in Minuteman Library Network
Open Mon, Wed & Fri 10:30-6, Tues & Thurs 10:30-9, Sat 10:30-5, Sun 2-5
Friends of the Library Group

MEDFORD

M LAWRENCE MEMORIAL HOSPITAL OF MEDFORD*, Robert J Fahey Health Sciences Library, 170 Governors Ave, 02155-1698. SAN 307-5176. Tel: 781-306-6606. FAX: 781-306-6655. *Librn,* Terri Niland; E-mail: tniland@hallmarkhealth.org; Staff 1 (MLS 1)
Founded 1977
Library Holdings: Bk Titles 3,000; Bk Vols 4,000; Per Subs 105
Special Collections: Helene Fuld Media Network Coll
Subject Interests: Nursing
Database Vendor: EBSCOhost
Partic in CinaHL
Open Mon-Fri 8-4

P MEDFORD PUBLIC LIBRARY*, 111 High St, 02155. SAN 307-5184. Tel: 781-395-7950. FAX: 781-391-2261. Web Site: www.medfordlibrary.org. *Dir,* Brian G Boutilier; E-mail: bboutilier@minlib.net; *Asst Dir, Media Spec,* Barbara E Kerr; *Adult Serv, ILL,* Barbara DelDuca; *Cat,* Maryalyce Pastorello; *Ch Serv,* Phyllis Breslow; *Ch Serv,* Susan Tomeo; *Commun Serv,* Mary Gallant; *Pub Serv,* Kathleen Kane; *Ref,* Victoria Schneiderman; *YA Serv,* Gay Hyson; Staff 12 (MLS 9, Non-MLS 3)
Founded 1825. Pop 58,076; Circ 283,115
Library Holdings: AV Mats 1,000; Large Print Bks 500; Bk Vols 150,000; Per Subs 250
Special Collections: Medford History. Oral History
Automation Activity & Vendor Info: (Cataloging) Innovative Interfaces, Inc; (Circulation) Innovative Interfaces, Inc; (OPAC) Innovative Interfaces, Inc
Publications: This Month at Medford Public Library
Partic in Minuteman Library Network
Special Services for the Deaf - High interest/low vocabulary bks; TTY equip
Open Mon-Thurs 9-9, Fri 9-6, Sat 9-5
Friends of the Library Group

C TUFTS UNIVERSITY*, Tisch Library, 35 Professors Row, 02155-5816. (Mail add: 35 Packard Ave, 02155), SAN 345-3545. Tel: 617-627-3345. Circulation Tel: 617-627-3347. Reference Tel: 617-627-3460. FAX: 617-627-3002. E-mail: tischref@tufts.edu. Web Site: www.library.tufts.edu/tisch. *Dir,* Laura Wood; E-mail: laura.wood@tufts.edu; *Assoc Dir of Teaching, Res & Info Resources,* Laura Walters; Tel: 617-627-2098, E-mail: laura.walters@tufts.edu; *Head, Access Serv,* Position Currently Open; *Head, Res & Instruction,* Evan Simpson; Tel: 617-627-6253, E-mail: evan.simpson@tufts.edu; *Head, Tech Serv,* Alicia Morris; Tel: 617-627-2399, E-mail: alicia.morris@tufts.edu; *Music Librn,* Michael Rogan; Tel: 617-627-2846, E-mail: michael.rogan@tufts.edu; *Acq Mgr,* Anthony Kodzis; Tel: 617-627-3595, E-mail: anthony.kodzis@tufts.edu; *Admin Officer,* Paulette Johnson; E-mail: paulette.johnson@tufts.edu; *Info Tech,* Thomas Cox; Tel: 617-627-4318, E-mail: thomas.cox@tufts.edu; *Univ Archivist,* Anne Sauer; Tel: 617-627-2696, E-mail: anne.sauer@tufts.edu; Staff 55.57 (MLS 16.5, Non-MLS 39.07)
Founded 1852. Enrl 5,522; Fac 550; Highest Degree: Doctorate
Jul 2009-Jun 2010 Income (Main Library Only) $10,812,716. Mats Exp $6,250,295, Books $851,484, Per/Ser (Incl. Access Fees) $5,235,202, AV Mat $113,609, Presv $50,000. Sal $3,988,159 (Prof $1,194,764)
Library Holdings: CDs 27,507; e-books 42,000; e-journals 44,814; Bk Vols 927,192; Per Subs 1,162; Videos 26,301
Special Collections: Asa Alfred; Tufts Center for Health, Environment & Justice (Love Canal); Confederate Archives; Edwin Bolles Coll; Henri Gioiran Coll; Hosea Ballou Coll; John Holmes Coll; Musicology Coll; P T Barnum Coll; Ritter Coll; Ryder Coll; Stearus Coll; University Archives; William Bentley Sermon Coll. US Document Depository
Automation Activity & Vendor Info: (Acquisitions) Innovative Interfaces, Inc; (Cataloging) Innovative Interfaces, Inc; (Circulation) Innovative Interfaces, Inc; (Course Reserve) Innovative Interfaces, Inc; (ILL)

Innovative Interfaces, Inc; (OPAC) Innovative Interfaces, Inc; (Serials) Innovative Interfaces, Inc
Database Vendor: Gale Cengage Learning, JSTOR, LexisNexis, OCLC FirstSearch, SirsiDynix
Wireless access
Function: Handicapped accessible, ILL available, Music CDs, Online cat, Online info literacy tutorials on the web & in blackboard, Online ref, Orientations, Photocopying/Printing, Ref & res, Scanner, VHS videos, Video lending libr, Web-catalog, Workshops
Publications: Bibliotech Connections
Mem of Massachusetts Libr Syst
Partic in OCLC Online Computer Library Center, Inc
Restriction: In-house use for visitors
Friends of the Library Group

Departmental Libraries:

CL EDWIN GINN LIBRARY, Mugar Bldg, 1st Flr, 160 Packard St, 02155-7082, SAN 345-3669. Tel: 617-627-3273. Circulation Tel: 617-627-3852. Interlibrary Loan Service Tel: 617-627-6421. Reference Tel: 617-627-5021. FAX: 617-627-3736. E-mail: ginnref@tufts.edu. Web Site: www.library.tufts.edu/ginn. *Dir,* Barbara Boyce; Tel: 617-627-2175; *Assoc Librn,* Miriam Seltzer; Tel: 617-627-2974; *Assoc Librn, IT Mgr,* Evviva Weineaub; Tel: 617-627-3023; *Circ/Reserves,* Paula Cammarata; *Ref,* Ellen McDonald; Tel: 617-627-3858
Founded 1933. Enrl 320
Library Holdings: Bk Vols 113,741; Per Subs 900
Special Collections: Ambassador John Moors Cabot Papers; Ambassador Phillip K Crowe Papers; Edward R Murrow Papers; International Labor Office; League of Nations; Permanent Court of International Justice; United Nations Coll
Subject Interests: Intl law
Partic in Boston Library Consortium, Inc; Lyrasis

LILLY MUSIC LIBRARY, Granoff Music Ctr, Rm M030 Lower Level, 20 Talbot Ave, 02155, SAN 328-7726. Tel: 617-627-3594. FAX: 617-627-3002. Web Site: tischlibrary.tufts.edu/use-library/music-library. *Music Librn,* Michael Rogan; Tel: 617-627-2846, E-mail: michael.rogan@tufts.edu; Staff 2 (MLS 1, Non-MLS 1)
Highest Degree: Master
Library Holdings: CDs 19,100; DVDs 80; Electronic Media & Resources 20; Music Scores 16,300; Bk Titles 14,500

MEDWAY

P MEDWAY PUBLIC LIBRARY, 26 High St, 02053. SAN 345-3693. Tel: 508-533-3217. FAX: 508-533-3219. Web Site: medwaylib.org. *Dir,* Margaret Y Perkins; E-mail: mperkins@minlib.net; *Ch,* Position Currently Open; Staff 2.5 (MLS 0.5, Non-MLS 2)
Founded 1860. Pop 12,864; Circ 102,333
Library Holdings: AV Mats 7,300; Bk Vols 61,978; Per Subs 127
Special Collections: Medway Coll. Oral History
Automation Activity & Vendor Info: (Cataloging) Innovative Interfaces, Inc, (Circulation) Innovative Interfaces, Inc; (OPAC) Innovative Interfaces, Inc
Wireless access
Mem of Massachusetts Libr Syst
Open Mon & Wed 10-8, Tues & Thurs 2-8, Fri & Sat 10-2
Friends of the Library Group

MELROSE

M AMERICAN SOCIETY OF ABDOMINAL SURGEONS, Donald Collins Memorial Library, 824 Main St, 2nd Flr, Ste 1, 02176. SAN 328-6215. Tel: 781-665-6102. FAX: 781-665-4127. E-mail: office@abdominalsurg.org. Web Site: www.abdominalsurg.org. *Pres/Trustee,* Dr Louis F Alfano, Jr
Library Holdings: Bk Vols 1,000; Per Subs 62

R FIRST BAPTIST CHURCH LIBRARY*, 561 Main St, 02176. SAN 307-5192. Tel: 781-665-4470. FAX: 781-665-3050. E-mail: melrose1bc@aol.com.
Library Holdings: Bk Titles 1,025
Subject Interests: Art, Educ, Relig

P MELROSE PUBLIC LIBRARY*, 69 W Emerson St, 02176. SAN 345-3758. Tel: 781-665-2313. FAX: 781-662-4229. E-mail: mel@noblenet.org. Web Site: www.melrosepubliclibrary.org. *Dir,* Linda C Walsh; *Asst Dir, Tech Serv Librn,* Diane R Wall; *Ref Librn, YA Serv,* Shelley L O'Brien; *Ch Serv,* Marianne J Stanton; *Circ,* Christine A Morrissey; *Ref Serv,* Andrew E McLaughlin; Staff 21 (MLS 5, Non-MLS 16)
Founded 1871. Pop 27,503; Circ 257,500
Library Holdings: Bk Titles 109,000; Bk Vols 110,000; Per Subs 95
Special Collections: Fine Arts (Felix A Gendrot Coll); Sadie & Alex Levine Coll
Subject Interests: Art, Genealogy, Local hist

Automation Activity & Vendor Info: (Acquisitions) Innovative Interfaces, Inc; (Cataloging) Innovative Interfaces, Inc; (Circulation) Innovative Interfaces, Inc
Database Vendor: EBSCOhost, Innovative Interfaces, Inc
Publications: Friends of Library (Newsletter)
Partic in North of Boston Library Exchange, Inc
Open Mon-Thurs 10-9, Fri & Sat 10-5, Sun 2-5
Friends of the Library Group

MENDON

P TAFT PUBLIC LIBRARY, 18 Main St, 01756. (Mail add: PO Box 35, 01756-0035), SAN 307-5214. Tel: 508-473-3259. FAX: 508-473-7049. E-mail: librarydirector@mendonma.gov. *Dir,* Andrew Jenrich
Founded 1881. Pop 5,876; Circ 34,076
Library Holdings: Bk Vols 34,577; Per Subs 82
Special Collections: History Coll
Automation Activity & Vendor Info: (Cataloging) Evergreen; (Circulation) Evergreen
Wireless access
Open Tues & Wed 10-7, Thurs 3-7, Fri 12-5, Sat 9-Noon
Friends of the Library Group

MERRIMAC

P MERRIMAC PUBLIC LIBRARY*, Thomas H Hoyt Memorial, 34 W Main St, 01860. SAN 307-5222. Tel: 978-346-9441. FAX: 978-346-8272. Web Site: www.merrimaclib.org. *Dir,* Donald MacMillan; *Ch Serv,* Cathy Fowler
Founded 1930. Pop 5,400; Circ 36,008
Library Holdings: Bk Vols 28,000; Per Subs 67
Special Collections: Local History (Thomas H Hoyt Family Coll), bks & papers. State Document Depository
Automation Activity & Vendor Info: (Cataloging) SirsiDynix; (Circulation) SirsiDynix; (OPAC) SirsiDynix
Open Mon, Wed & Fri 10-5, Tues & Thurs 10-7, Sat (Sept-May) 10-2
Friends of the Library Group

METHUEN

M CARITAS HOLY FAMILY HOSPITAL & MEDICAL CENTER*, Health Sciences Library, 70 East St, 01844-4597. SAN 307-5230. Tel: 978-687-0151, Ext 2392. FAX: 978-688-7689. *Librn,* Fredella Sally; E-mail: sally.fredella@caritaschristi.org
Founded 1950
Library Holdings: e-books 55; e-journals 120; Bk Titles 1,200; Per Subs 52
Subject Interests: Allied health, Med, Nursing
Automation Activity & Vendor Info: (Cataloging) Marcive, Inc; (OPAC) Auto-Graphics, Inc; (Serials) EBSCO Online
Database Vendor: Cinahl, EBSCO Information Services, EBSCOhost, Gale Cengage Learning, Grolier Online, Infotrieve, Lexi-Comp, Marcive, Inc, Medlib, Medline, Micromedex, Newsbank, OCLC WorldShare Interlibrary Loan, OVID Technologies, ScienceDirect, UpToDate, WebMD
Partic in Massachusetts Health Sciences Libraries Network; Medical Library Association (MLA); North Atlantic Health Sciences Libraries, Inc; Northeastern Consortium for Health Information
Restriction: Staff use only
Friends of the Library Group

P NEVINS MEMORIAL LIBRARY*, 305 Broadway, 01844-6898. SAN 307-5249. Tel: 978-686-4080. FAX: 978-686-8669. E-mail: mme@mvlc.org. Web Site: www.nevinslibrary.org. *Dir,* Krista I McLeod; E-mail: kmcleod@mvlc.org; *Head, Ch,* Kathleen Moran-Wallace; E-mail: kmoranwallace@mvlc.org; *Head, Reader Serv,* Nanci Hill; E-mail: nhill@mvlc.org; *Head, Ref,* Kirsten Underwood; E-mail: kunderwood@mvlc.org; *Head, Tech Serv,* Beverly Winn; E-mail: bwinn@mvlc.org; Staff 45 (MLS 8, Non-MLS 37)
Founded 1883. Pop 44,000; Circ 189,000
Library Holdings: AV Mats 6,600; Bk Titles 85,024; Per Subs 182
Special Collections: Elise Nevins Morgan Meditation Series, mss & bks
Automation Activity & Vendor Info: (Cataloging) SirsiDynix; (Circulation) SirsiDynix
Database Vendor: EBSCO Information Services, Gale Cengage Learning, LearningExpress, ProQuest
Wireless access
Mem of Massachusetts Libr Syst
Partic in Merrimack Valley Library Consortium
Open Mon-Thurs 9-9, Fri & Sat 9-5; Mon-Thurs (Summer) 9-9, Fri 9-5
Friends of the Library Group

MIDDLEBOROUGH

S MASSACHUSETTS ARCHAEOLOGICAL SOCIETY RESEARCH LIBRARY*, 17 Jackson St, 02346-2413. (Mail add: PO Box 700, 02346-0700), SAN 370-1573. Tel: 508-947-9005. FAX: 508-947-9005.

E-mail: info@massarchaeology.org. Web Site: www.massarchaeology.org. *Librn,* Kathryn Fairbanks; E-mail: kfairbanks@verizon.net
Founded 1939
Jul 2009-Jun 2010 Income $200
Library Holdings: High Interest/Low Vocabulary Bk Vols 40; Bk Titles 3,500; Per Subs 50; Spec Interest Per Sub 50; Videos 40
Subject Interests: Anthrop, Archaeology, Ethnography, Local hist
Function: Children's prog, Copy machines, e-mail serv, Handicapped accessible, Res libr, Wheelchair accessible
Publications: Bulletin of the Massachusetts Archaelogical Society; Newsletter; 'Round Robbins'
Open Wed 10-2
Restriction: Access at librarian's discretion, Closed stack, Not a lending libr
Friends of the Library Group

P MIDDLEBOROUGH PUBLIC LIBRARY*, 102 N Main St, 02346. SAN 307-5257. Tel: 508-946-2470. FAX: 508-946-2473. Web Site: www.midlib.org. *Dir,* Danielle Bowker; *Asst Dir, Tech Serv,* Christine Dargelis; *Adult Serv, Ref Librn,* Betty Brown; *Info Syst,* Dale Irving; *Youth Serv,* Marilyn Thayer; Staff 5 (MLS 3, Non-MLS 2)
Founded 1875. Pop 21,085; Circ 130,549
Library Holdings: Bk Vols 77,308; Per Subs 214
Special Collections: Cranberry Culture Coll
Automation Activity & Vendor Info: (Acquisitions) SirsiDynix; (Cataloging) SirsiDynix; (Circulation) SirsiDynix; (OPAC) SirsiDynix
Partic in SAILS Library Network
Special Services for the Blind - Bks on cassette
Open Mon-Thurs (Winter) 10-8, Sat 10-3; Mon-Thurs (Summer) 10-8, Fri 10-3
Friends of the Library Group

MIDDLEFIELD

P MIDDLEFIELD PUBLIC LIBRARY*, 188 Skyline Trail, 01243. (Mail add: PO Box 128, 01243-0128), SAN 307-5265. Tel: 413-623-6421. *Dir,* Cynthia Oligny
Library Holdings: Bk Vols 12,000
Open Mon 4-8, Wed 4-7, Sat 9-12

MIDDLETON

P FLINT PUBLIC LIBRARY*, One S Main St, 01949. (Mail add: PO Box 98, 01949-0198), SAN 307-5273. Tel: 978-774-8132. FAX: 978-777-3270. E-mail: flint3@comcast.net. Web Site: www.flintlibrary.org. *Dir,* Adela B Carter; Staff 11 (MLS 1, Non-MLS 10)
Founded 1891. Pop 7,744; Circ 55,624
Library Holdings: AV Mats 1,473; Electronic Media & Resources 59; Large Print Bks 400; Bk Vols 38,068; Per Subs 161; Talking Bks 1,045
Special Collections: Local Author Coll
Automation Activity & Vendor Info: (Cataloging) SirsiDynix; (Circulation) SirsiDynix; (ILL) SirsiDynix; (OPAC) SirsiDynix
Database Vendor: EBSCOhost, Gale Cengage Learning, TLC (The Library Corporation)
Wireless access
Function: Homebound delivery serv, ILL available, Photocopying/Printing, Prog for adults, Prog for children & young adult, Ref serv available, Summer reading prog, Telephone ref
Mem of Massachusetts Libr Syst
Partic in Merrimack Valley Library Consortium
Open Mon-Thurs (Winter) 10-8, Fri 10-5, Sun 1-5; Tues-Thurs (Summer) 10-8, Fri 10-2
Friends of the Library Group

MILFORD

P MILFORD TOWN LIBRARY*, 80 Spruce St, 01757. SAN 307-5281. Tel: 508-473-0651, 508-473-2145. FAX: 508-473-8651. E-mail: milfref@cwmars.org. Web Site: www.milfordtownlibrary.org. *Dir,* Susan Edmonds; E-mail: sedmonds@cwmars.org; *Circ Supvr,* Kathleen Kirchner; E-mail: kkirchne@cwmars.org; *Supvr, Tech Serv,* Jay Campbell; *YA Librn,* Jacque Gorman; Staff 20 (MLS 4, Non-MLS 16)
Founded 1986. Pop 27,033; Circ 204,315
Library Holdings: AV Mats 6,086; e-books 6,547; Electronic Media & Resources 4,364; Large Print Bks 2,814; Bk Vols 107,019; Per Subs 147; Talking Bks 3,053
Special Collections: Local History (Milford Room)
Automation Activity & Vendor Info: (Acquisitions) Innovative Interfaces, Inc; (Cataloging) Innovative Interfaces, Inc; (Circulation) Innovative Interfaces, Inc; (OPAC) Innovative Interfaces, Inc; (Serials) Innovative Interfaces, Inc
Database Vendor: Gale Cengage Learning
Function: AV serv, Handicapped accessible, Homebound delivery serv, ILL available, Magnifiers for reading, Photocopying/Printing, Prog for children & young adult, Ref serv available, Summer reading prog, Wheelchair accessible
Mem of Massachusetts Libr Syst
Partic in Central & Western Massachusetts Automated Resource Sharing
Special Services for the Blind - Assistive/Adapted tech devices, equip & products; Audio mat; Bks & mags in Braille, on rec, tape & cassette; Large print bks; Large screen computer & software; Low vision equip; Magnifiers; Ref serv; Talking bks & player equip
Open Mon-Thurs 9-9, Fri 9-6, Sat 9-5
Friends of the Library Group

S WATERS CORP*, Information Center, 34 Maple St, 01757. SAN 325-2981. Tel: 508-478-2000. FAX: 508-482-2417. Web Site: www.waters.com. *Librn,* Carla Clayton; E-mail: carla_clayton@waters.com; *Asst Librn,* Maureen Eplite; Staff 3 (MLS 1, Non-MLS 2)
Library Holdings: Bk Titles 2,000; Per Subs 150
Subject Interests: Liquid chromatography
Partic in Dialog Corp; OCLC Online Computer Library Center, Inc
Restriction: Restricted pub use

MILL RIVER

P NEW MARLBOROUGH TOWN LIBRARY*, One Mill River Great Barrington Rd, 01244-0239. (Mail add: PO BOX 239, MILL RIVER, 01244), SAN 318-1375. Tel: 413-229-6668. FAX: 413-229-6668. E-mail: newmarlborough@gmail.com. Web Site: www.new-marlborough.ma.us. *Librn,* Debora O'Brien
Pop 1,078; Circ 8,456
Library Holdings: Bk Vols 10,000; Per Subs 30
Automation Activity & Vendor Info: (Cataloging) Follett Software; (Circulation) Follett Software
Open Tues & Thurs (Winter) 1:30-5:30, Wed, Fri & Sat 10-5:30; Tues & Fri (Summer) 1:30-7:30, Wed & Sat 10-5:30, Thurs 1:30-5:30
Friends of the Library Group

MILLBURY

P MILLBURY PUBLIC LIBRARY*, 128 Elm St, 01527. SAN 307-5311. Tel: 508-865-1181. FAX: 508-865-0795. *Dir,* Elizabeth Valero; Staff 13 (MLS 2, Non-MLS 11)
Founded 1869. Pop 12,121; Circ 70,000
Jul 2006-Jun 2007 Income $352,818. Sal $209,000 (Prof $55,000)
Library Holdings: AV Mats 6,668; Large Print Bks 400; Bk Vols 40,000; Per Subs 100
Automation Activity & Vendor Info: (Cataloging) Follett Software; (Circulation) Follett Software
Wireless access
Mem of Massachusetts Libr Syst
Open Tues-Thurs 10-8, Fri 10-6, Sat 9-12
Friends of the Library Group

MILLIS

P MILLIS PUBLIC LIBRARY, 961 Main St, 02054. SAN 307-5338. Tel: 508-376-8282. FAX: 508-376-1278. Web Site: www.millislibrary.org. *Interim Dir,* Maria Neville; *Children & Youth Serv Librn,* Rachel Silverman; *Circ Supvr,* Nancy Doyle; *Sr Libr Asst,* Rena Romano; *Libr Asst,* Donna Brooks; *Cataloger,* Joan Dikun; *Circ,* Esther Davis; Staff 8 (MLS 2, Non-MLS 6)
Founded 1887. Pop 8,000; Circ 188,801
Library Holdings: Audiobooks 1,285; AV Mats 2,413; Bks on Deafness & Sign Lang 6; Braille Volumes 2; CDs 1,967; DVDs 2,426; Large Print Bks 786; Bk Titles 44,189; Per Subs 95; Talking Bks 10; Videos 446
Automation Activity & Vendor Info: (Cataloging) Innovative Interfaces, Inc - Sierra; (Circulation) Innovative Interfaces, Inc - Sierra; (OPAC) Innovative Interfaces, Inc - Sierra
Wireless access
Mem of Massachusetts Libr Syst
Partic in Minuteman Library Network
Special Services for the Deaf - Bks on deafness & sign lang; Closed caption videos; Spec interest per; Staff with knowledge of sign lang
Special Services for the Blind - Audio mat; Bks available with recordings; Bks on cassette; Bks on CD; Braille alphabet card; Braille bks; Cassette playback machines; Copier with enlargement capabilities; Descriptive video serv (DVS); Handicapped awareness prog; Large print bks; Sub-lending agent for Braille Inst Libr; Talking bks & player equip
Open Mon 12-8, Tues & Wed 10-8, Thurs & Fri 10-4, Sat (Sept-June) 10-3
Friends of the Library Group

MILLVILLE

P MILLVILLE FREE PUBLIC LIBRARY*, 169 Main St, 01529. (Mail add: PO Box 726, 01529-0726), SAN 376-7736. Tel: 508-883-1887. FAX: 508-883-1887. *Dir,* Rose Flaherty
Library Holdings: Large Print Bks 150; Bk Titles 12,500; Per Subs 20
Mem of Massachusetts Libr Syst
Open Mon & Wed 6-8, Tues & Thurs 1:30-5:30, Sat 10-2

MILTON

C CURRY COLLEGE*, Louis R Levin Memorial Library, 1071 Blue Hill Ave, 02186-9984. SAN 307-5346. Tel: 617-333-2177. FAX: 617-333-2164. Web Site: www.curry.edu. *Dir,* Jane Lawless; Tel: 617-333-2245, E-mail: jlawless@curry.edu; *Head, Coll Serv,* Mary Ryan; Tel: 617-333-2937, E-mail: mryan@curry.edu; *Circ,* Leslie Becker; Tel: 617-333-2102, E-mail: lbecker@curry.edu; *ILL,* Kathy Russell; Tel: 617-333-2100, E-mail: krussell@curry.edu; *Reader Serv,* Gail Shank; Tel: 617-333-2170, E-mail: gshank@curry.edu; *Tech Serv,* David Miller; Tel: 617-333-2101, E-mail: dmiller@curry.edu; Staff 12 (MLS 7, Non-MLS 5)
Founded 1952. Enrl 1,880; Fac 100; Highest Degree: Master
Library Holdings: AV Mats 1,114; Bks on Deafness & Sign Lang 48; Bk Vols 94,300; Per Subs 725; Talking Bks 60
Special Collections: US Document Depository
Subject Interests: Learning disabilities
Automation Activity & Vendor Info: (Acquisitions) Innovative Interfaces, Inc; (Cataloging) Innovative Interfaces, Inc; (Circulation) Innovative Interfaces, Inc; (OPAC) Innovative Interfaces, Inc; (Serials) Innovative Interfaces, Inc
Database Vendor: EBSCOhost, Gale Cengage Learning, LexisNexis, OCLC FirstSearch, OVID Technologies, ProQuest
Function: For res purposes, ILL available, Telephone ref, Wheelchair accessible
Mem of Massachusetts Libr Syst
Partic in Lyrasis
Open Mon-Thurs 8am-11pm, Fri 8-6, Sat 10-6, Sun 1:30-11

P MILTON PUBLIC LIBRARY*, 476 Canton Ave, 02186-3299. SAN 345-3847. Tel: 617-698-5757. FAX: 617-698-0441. E-mail: miref@ocln.org. Web Site: www.miltonlibrary.org. *Dir,* William Adamcyk; *Asst Dir,* Dan Haacker; *Adult Serv,* Jean Hlady; *Ch Serv,* Elaine Weischedel; *Tech Serv,* Shirley Pyne; Staff 6 (MLS 6)
Founded 1871. Pop 26,062; Circ 167,352
Jul 2012-Jun 2013 Income $1,142,354, State $22,000, City $1,050,354, Locally Generated Income $70,000. Mats Exp Books $155,000. Sal $804,939
Library Holdings: DVDs 7,704; Bk Vols 95,498
Subject Interests: Local hist
Automation Activity & Vendor Info: (Cataloging) SirsiDynix; (Circulation) SirsiDynix; (OPAC) SirsiDynix; (Serials) SirsiDynix
Wireless access
Partic in Old Colony Libr Network (OCLN)
Open Mon-Wed 9-9, Thurs 1-9, Fri 9-5:30, Sat 9-5 , Sun (Oct-May) 1-5
Friends of the Library Group

MONROE BRIDGE

P MONROE PUBLIC LIBRARY*, 3B School St, 01350. (Mail add: PO Box 35, 01350-0035), SAN 307-5362. Tel: 413-424-5272. *Librn,* Carla Davis-Little
Pop 120; Circ 1,581
Library Holdings: Bk Vols 3,000
Open Mon 6-7

MONSON

P MONSON FREE LIBRARY*, Two High St, 01057-1095. SAN 307-5370. Tel: 413-267-3866. FAX: 413-267-5496. E-mail: monsonfl@cwmars.org. Web Site: www.monsonlibrary.com. *Dir,* Katie Krol; Tel: 413-267-9035, E-mail: kkrol@cwmars.org; *Ch,* Betsy Rajotte; E-mail: brajotte@cwmars.org
Founded 1878. Pop 8,400; Circ 60,000
Library Holdings: Bk Vols 39,000; Per Subs 144
Automation Activity & Vendor Info: (Cataloging) Innovative Interfaces, Inc; (Circulation) Innovative Interfaces, Inc; (OPAC) Innovative Interfaces, Inc
Partic in Central & Western Massachusetts Automated Resource Sharing
Open Tues & Thurs 2-8, Wed 10-6, Fri 10-2
Friends of the Library Group

MONTEREY

P MONTEREY LIBRARY*, 452 Main Rd, 01245. (Mail add: PO Box 172, 01245-0172), SAN 307-5397. Tel: 413-528-3795. E-mail: montereylibrary@gmail.com. *Dir,* Mark Makuc
Founded 1890. Pop 970; Circ 11,371
Library Holdings: Bk Titles 8,000; Per Subs 14
Subject Interests: Local hist
Automation Activity & Vendor Info: (Cataloging) Innovative Interfaces, Inc; (Circulation) Innovative Interfaces, Inc
Database Vendor: Innovative Interfaces, Inc
Wireless access
Function: Bks on cassette, Bks on CD, Children's prog, Computer training, Computers for patron use, Copy machines, Homebound delivery serv, ILL available, Mus passes, Online cat, OverDrive digital audio bks, Photocopying/Printing, Prog for adults, Prog for children & young adult, Pub access computers, Spoken cassettes & CDs, Spoken cassettes & DVDs, Summer reading prog, VHS videos, Web-catalog
Partic in Central-Western Mass Automated Resource Sharing
Open Mon 7-9, Tues 9:30-12, Wed 3-5, Thurs 4-6, Sat 9:30-12:30 & 7-9

MONTGOMERY

P GRACE HALL MEMORIAL LIBRARY*, 161 Main Rd, 01085-9525. SAN 307-5400. Tel: 413-862-3894. E-mail: gracehall_lib@yahoo.com. Web Site: www.community.masslive.com/cc/gracehall. *Librn,* Paula Long
Pop 780
Library Holdings: Bk Vols 5,000; Per Subs 15
Automation Activity & Vendor Info: (Cataloging) Follett Software; (Circulation) Follett Software
Open Tues 11-5:30, Thurs 3-8, Sat 10-12:30
Friends of the Library Group

MOUNT WASHINGTON

P MOUNT WASHINGTON PUBLIC LIBRARY*, Town Hall, 118 East St, 01258. SAN 307-5419. Tel: 413-528-1798, 413-528-2839. FAX: 413-528-2839. *Librn,* Ellie Lovejoy
Pop 130; Circ 1,860
Library Holdings: Bk Titles 2,500; Videos 26
Open Mon-Wed 9:30-3:30

NAHANT

P NAHANT PUBLIC LIBRARY, 15 Pleasant St, 01908. (Mail add: PO Box 76, 01908-0076), SAN 307-5427. Tel: 781-581-0306. E-mail: nahantlibrarydirector@gmail.com. Web Site: www.nahant.org. *Dir,* Sheridan Montgomery
Founded 1819. Pop 3,900; Circ 30,000
Library Holdings: Bk Titles 42,000; Per Subs 22
Special Collections: Nahant Historical
Wireless access
Publications: Newsletter (Occasionally)
Open Mon-Thurs 10-8, Fri 10-5, Sat & Sun 2-5
Friends of the Library Group

C NORTHEASTERN UNIVERSITY LIBRARIES*, Marine Science Center, 430 Nahant Rd, 01908. SAN 344-7383. Tel: 781-581-7370. FAX: 781-581-6076. Web Site: www.marinescience.neu.edu. *Librn,* Liza Genovese
Library Holdings: Bk Vols 5,000
Automation Activity & Vendor Info: (Circulation) Innovative Interfaces, Inc; (OPAC) Innovative Interfaces, Inc
Restriction: Staff use only

NANTUCKET

P NANTUCKET ATHENEUM*, One India St, 02554-3519. (Mail add: PO Box 808, 02554-0808), SAN 307-5435. Tel. 508-228-1110. FAX: 508-228-1973. E-mail: info@nantucketatheneum.org. Web Site: www.nantucketatheneum.org. *Dir,* Molly Anderson; Tel: 508-228-1974; Staff 7 (MLS 6, Non-MLS 1)
Founded 1834. Circ 113,068
Library Holdings: AV Mats 2,126; Bk Vols 38,864; Per Subs 194
Special Collections: 19th Century American Coll; Nantucket Coll
Automation Activity & Vendor Info: (Cataloging) Innovative Interfaces, Inc; (Circulation) Innovative Interfaces, Inc; (OPAC) Innovative Interfaces, Inc
Database Vendor: Innovative Interfaces, Inc
Partic in Cape Libraries Automated Materials Sharing Network
Open Tues & Thurs (Winter) 9:30-8, Wed, Fri & Sat 9:30-5; Mon, Wed, Fri & Sat (Summer) 9:30-5, Tues & Thurs 9:30-8
Friends of the Library Group

S NANTUCKET HISTORICAL ASSOCIATION, Research Library, Seven Fair St, 02554-3737. (Mail add: PO Box 1016, 02554-1016), SAN 327-3091. Tel: 508-228-1655. FAX: 508-325-7968. E-mail: library@nha.org. Web Site: www.nha.org. *Chief Curator,* Michael R Harrison; E-mail: mharrison@nha.org; Staff 4 (MLS 2, Non-MLS 2)
Founded 1894
Library Holdings: Bk Titles 5,000
Special Collections: Architectural Drawings; Log Books & Account Books; Manuscript & Audio-Visual Colls; Maps. Oral History
Subject Interests: Maritime hist, Quaker hist, Rare bks, Whaling
Mem of Massachusetts Libr Syst
Open Mon, Thurs & Fri 10-4, Tues 11-4
Restriction: Non-circulating

S NANTUCKET MARIA MITCHELL ASSOCIATION, Maria Mitchell Science Library & Archives, Two Vestal St, 02554-2699. (Mail add: Four Vestal St, 02554), SAN 307-5443. Tel: 508-228-9219. Administration Tel:

505-228-9198. FAX: 508-228-1031. Web Site: mariamitchell.org. *Curator,* J Finger
Founded 1902
Library Holdings: Bk Titles 9,000; Per Subs 42
Special Collections: Maria Mitchell Association Archives; Original Notebooks & Papers (Maria Mitchell Memorabilia Coll), journals, lecture notes, micro
Subject Interests: Astronomy, Biol, Botany, Chem, Geol, Oceanography, Ornithology, Physics, Zoology
Wireless access
Function: Archival coll, Res libr
Restriction: Non-circulating, Open by appt only

NATICK

P BACON FREE LIBRARY, 58 Eliot St, 01760. SAN 372-7602. Tel: 508-653-6730. E-mail: bfl@minlib.net. Web Site: www.baconfreelibrary.net. *Dir,* Meena Jain; E-mail: mjain@minlib.net; *Asst Dir/Ch,* Holley C Meyer; E-mail: hmeyer@minlib.net; *Sr Libr Asst,* Frances Daneault; E-mail: fdaneault@minlib.net; *Libr Asst,* Graziella Lesellier; E-mail: glesellier@minlib.net; *Libr Asst,* Casey Stirling; E-mail: cstirling@minlib.net; Staff 5 (MLS 2, Non-MLS 3)
Founded 1870. Pop 9,000
Special Collections: Early Christian Native Americans of South Natick; Natick Historical Coll
Automation Activity & Vendor Info: (Circulation) Innovative Interfaces, Inc
Database Vendor: EBSCOhost
Wireless access
Function: 24/7 Online cat, Adult bk club, After school storytime, Archival coll, Art exhibits, Audiobks via web, Bk club(s), Bk reviews (Group), Bks on CD, CD-ROM, Children's prog, Computer training, Computers for patron use, Copy machines, e-mail serv, Electronic databases & coll, eReaders, Exhibits, Family literacy, Free DVD rentals, Holiday prog, ILL available, Life-long learning prog for all ages, Literacy & newcomer serv, Magazines, Movies, Mus passes, Music CDs, Newsp ref libr, Online cat, Online ref, Online searches, Outreach serv, Outside serv via phone, mail, e-mail & web, OverDrive digital audio bks, Photocopying/Printing, Preschool outreach, Preschool reading prog, Prog for adults, Prog for children & young adult, Provide serv for the mentally ill, Pub access computers, Ref serv in person, Scanner, Senior outreach, Spoken cassettes & CDs, Spoken cassettes & DVDs, Story hour, Summer reading prog, Web-catalog
Partic in Minuteman Library Network
Open Mon 2-5:30, Tues 9:30-8:30, Wed-Fri 9:30-5:30, Sat (Sept-May) 9-1
Friends of the Library Group

S CARR RESEARCH LABORATORY, INC LIBRARY*, 251 W Central St, Ste D-36, 01760. (Mail add: 17 Waban St, Wellelsey, 02482), SAN 371-5248. Tel: 508-651-7027. FAX: 508-647-4737. Web Site: www.carr-research-lab.com. *Pres,* Jerome B Carr
Founded 1974
Jan 2007-Dec 2007. Mats Exp $6,391
Library Holdings: CDs 40; Bk Titles 5,500; Per Subs 58
Subject Interests: Ecology, Geol, Geophysics, Oceanography, Wetlands
Restriction: Co libr

P MORSE INSTITUTE LIBRARY*, 14 E Central St, 01760. SAN 307-5451. Tel: 508-647-6520. Reference Tel: 508-647-6521. FAX: 508-647-6527. Web Site: www.morseinstitute.org. *Dir,* Linda Stetson; Tel: 508-647-6523, E-mail: lstetson@minlib.net; *Asst Dir,* Jane A Finlay; Tel: 508-647-6526, Fax: 508-647-6526, E-mail: jfinlay@minlib.net; *Head, Circ,* Paula Welch; E-mail: pwelch@minlib.net; *Head, Mat Mgt,* Martha Jones; Tel: 508-647-6400, Ext 1534, E-mail: mjones@minlib.net; *Head, Ref,* Demetri Kyriakis; Tel: 508-647-6400, Ext 1527, E-mail: dkyriakis@minlib.net; *Commun Relations Coordr,* Marie Nardi; Tel: 508-647-6524, E-mail: mnardi@minlib.net; *AV,* Susan Barnicle; Tel: 508-647-6522; *Ch Serv,* Dale Smith; E-mail: dsmith@minlib.net; *Literacy Serv,* Laurie Christie; Tel: 508-647-6400, Ext 1583, E-mail: lchristie@minlib.net; Staff 30.79 (MLS 10.4, Non-MLS 20.39)
Founded 1873. Pop 33,006; Circ 567,076
Library Holdings: Bk Vols 183,701; Per Subs 234
Special Collections: Natick Historical Coll
Automation Activity & Vendor Info: (Cataloging) Innovative Interfaces, Inc; (Circulation) Innovative Interfaces, Inc; (OPAC) Innovative Interfaces, Inc
Database Vendor: Dun & Bradstreet, EBSCO Information Services, EBSCOhost, Gale Cengage Learning, LearningExpress, Newsbank, OCLC WorldShare Interlibrary Loan, ProQuest
Wireless access
Publications: Off the Shelf (Newsletter)
Mem of Massachusetts Libr Syst
Partic in Lyrasis; Minuteman Library Network
Special Services for the Blind - Extensive large print coll; Screen enlargement software for people with visual disabilities; Talking bk serv referral; Talking bks; ZoomText magnification & reading software
Open Mon-Thurs 10-9, Fri & Sat 10-5, Sun 2-5
Friends of the Library Group
Bookmobiles: 1. Bkmobile Coordr, Rose Huling. Bk titles 2,000

S NATICK HISTORICAL SOCIETY*, Historical Natural History & Library Society of South Natick, 58 Eliot St, 01760. SAN 371-2567. Tel: 508-647-4841. E-mail: info@natickhistoricalsociety.org. Web Site: www.natickhistoricalsociety.org. *Dir,* Jennifer Hance; E-mail: jennifer@natickhistoricalsociety.org; *Curator,* Anne Schaller; Staff 1 (Non-MLS 1)
Founded 1870
Library Holdings: Bk Vols 1,800; Per Subs 34
Special Collections: Indian Artifacts; Vice-President Henry Wilson
Subject Interests: Local hist
Wireless access
Function: Archival coll, For res purposes, Handicapped accessible, Mail & tel request accepted, Photocopying/Printing, Prog for adults, Ref & res, Wheelchair accessible
Publications: From Many Backgrounds: The Heritage of the Eliot Church of South Natick (Local historical information); Images of America-Natick-Arcadia Pub Co (Local historical information); The Arrow (Newsletter)
Open Tues (Winter) 2-8:30, Wed 2-4:30, Sat 10-12:30; Tues (Summer) 2-8:30, Wed 2-4:30
Restriction: Open to pub for ref only

A UNITED STATES ARMY*, Alvin O Ramsley Technical Library, AMSRD-NSC-OC-T, 20 Kansas St, 01760-5056. SAN 345-3936. Tel: 508-233-4306. Interlibrary Loan Service Tel: 508-233-4542. FAX: 508-233-4248. Web Site: www.ssc.army.mil. *Doc,* Patricia E Bremner; *ILL,* Denice M Czedik; Staff 2 (MLS 1, Non-MLS 1)
Founded 1946
Library Holdings: Bk Titles 42,490; Bk Vols 47,890; Per Subs 100
Subject Interests: Biochem, Biol, Chem, Eng, Math, Med, Phys sci, Psychol, Soc sci & issues, Textiles
Automation Activity & Vendor Info: (Cataloging) Auto-Graphics, Inc; (Circulation) Auto-Graphics, Inc
Database Vendor: OCLC FirstSearch
Publications: Annual Bibliography of Technical Publications; Papers & List of Patents
Partic in Dialog Corp; OCLC Online Computer Library Center, Inc
Open Mon-Fri 9-5:30
Restriction: Employees only, Mil only

NEEDHAM

P NEEDHAM FREE PUBLIC LIBRARY, 1139 Highland Ave, 02494-3298. SAN 345-3960. Tel: 781-455-7559. FAX: 781-455-7591. TDD: 781-453-5617. E-mail: neemail1@minlib.net. Web Site: www.needhamma.gov/library. *Dir,* Ann C MacFate; *Asst Dir,* Dana Mastroianni; *Head, Ref,* April Asquith; *Archivist, Tech,* Danielle Tawa; *Tech Serv,* Diane Browne; Staff 15 (MLS 15)
Founded 1888. Pop 30,457; Circ 525,798
Jul 2013-Jun 2014 Income $1,419,551. Mats Exp $211,051, Books $126,858, Per/Ser (Incl. Access Fees) $17,313, Micro $6,321, AV Mat $45,705, Electronic Ref Mat (Incl. Access Fees) $14,854. Sal $1,103,803
Library Holdings: AV Mats 30,005; e-books 19,383; Electronic Media & Resources 14; Large Print Bks 6,000; Bk Vols 149,130; Per Subs 240
Special Collections: Benjamin Franklin Coll; N C Wyeth Art Coll; Needham Archives; Needham History Coll
Subject Interests: Bus & mgt
Automation Activity & Vendor Info: (Cataloging) Innovative Interfaces, Inc; (Circulation) Innovative Interfaces, Inc; (ILL) Innovative Interfaces, Inc; (OPAC) Innovative Interfaces, Inc
Wireless access
Mem of Massachusetts Libr Syst
Partic in Minuteman Library Network
Special Services for the Deaf - TTY equip
Open Mon-Thurs 9-9, Fri 9-5:30, Sat 9-5, Sun (Sept-June) 1-5
Friends of the Library Group

NEW BEDFORD

P NEW BEDFORD FREE PUBLIC LIBRARY*, 613 Pleasant St, 02740-6203. SAN 345-4029. Tel: 508-991-6275. Reference Tel: 508-991-6278, 508-991-6280. Administration Tel: 508-991-6338. FAX: 508-991-6368. E-mail: nbmref@sailsinc.org. Web Site: www.new-bedford.ma.gov/library/library.html. *Dir,* Stephen Fulchino; Tel: 508-961-3044; *Commun Serv,* Dale Easton; *Ref,* Paul Cyr; *Youth Serv,* Janice Pina; Staff 43 (MLS 7, Non-MLS 36)
Founded 1852. Pop 99,922; Circ 240,178

Library Holdings: AV Mats 18,559; Electronic Media & Resources 843; Bk Titles 407,132; Per Subs 762; Spec Interest Per Sub 28,504
Special Collections: Melville Whaling Room, ms, microfilm; Portuguese Coll. Oral History; US Document Depository
Subject Interests: Genealogy
Automation Activity & Vendor Info: (Cataloging) SirsiDynix; (Circulation) SirsiDynix; (OPAC) SirsiDynix
Special Services for the Deaf - TDD equip
Open Mon-Thurs 9-9, Fri & Sat 9-5
Friends of the Library Group
Branches: 4
CASA DA SAUDADE, 58 Crapo St, 02740, SAN 345-4088. Tel: 508-991-6218. FAX: 508-979-1705. Web Site: www.newbedford-ma.gov/library/casa.html. *Dir,* Stephen Fulchino; Tel: 508-961-3044; *Librn,* Judith Downey; Staff 4 (MLS 1, Non-MLS 3)
Founded 1971
Library Holdings: Bk Vols 34,000; Per Subs 40
Open Mon, Wed, Fri & Sat 9-5, Tues & Thurs 12-8
Friends of the Library Group
HOWLAND-GREEN, Three Rodney French Blvd, 02744, SAN 345-4118. Tel: 508-991-6212. FAX: 508-979-1774. Web Site: www.newbedford-ma.gov/library/howland.html. *Actg Dir,* Geoffrey Dickinson; Tel: 508-961-3044; *Mgr,* Kathleen Paroline Vernon; Tel: 508-991-6213, E-mail: kvernon@sailsinc.org; Staff 3 (MLS 1, Non-MLS 2)
Founded 1964
Library Holdings: Bk Vols 24,000
Special Collections: Spanish Language Coll
Automation Activity & Vendor Info: (Acquisitions) SIRSI WorkFlows; (Cataloging) SIRSI WorkFlows
Friends of the Library Group
FRANCIS J LAWLER BRANCH, 745 Rockdale Ave, 02740, SAN 345-4053. Tel: 508-991-6216. FAX: 508-961-3077. Web Site: www.newbedford-ma.gov/library/buttonwood.html. *Dir,* Stephen Fulchino; Tel: 508-961-3044; *Librn,* Denise Plaskon
Founded 1960
Library Holdings: Large Print Bks 120; Bk Vols 40,000
Open Mon & Fri 10-6, Tues & Thurs Noon-8, Sat 9-5,
Friends of the Library Group
WILKS, 1911 Acushnet Ave, 02746, SAN 345-4142. Tel: 508-991-6214. FAX: 508-998-6039. Web Site: www.newbedford-ma.gov/library/wilks.html. *Dir,* Stephen Fulchino; Tel: 508-961-3044; *Mgr,* Dale Easton
Founded 1958
Library Holdings: Bk Vols 24,000
Open Mon, Wed, Fri & Sat 9-5, Tues & Thurs 12-8
Friends of the Library Group
Bookmobiles: 1

GL NEW BEDFORD LAW LIBRARY*, Superior Courthouse, 441 County St, 02740. SAN 307-5532. Tel: 508-992-8077. FAX: 508 991-7411. Web Site: www.lawlib.state.ma.us/newbedford.html. *Librn,* Jane E Callahan; E-mail: jane.callahan@verizon.net; *Coordr,* Marnie Warner; Tel: 617-878-0338, Fax: 617-723-8821, E-mail: margaret.warner@jud.state.ma.us; *Electronic Res Librn,* Meg Hayden; E-mail: meg.hayden@gmail.com
Founded 1894
Jan 2006-Dec 2006. Mats Exp $78,000. Sal $119,766
Library Holdings: Bk Vols 25,000; Per Subs 25
Automation Activity & Vendor Info: (Acquisitions) SirsiDynix; (Cataloging) SirsiDynix; (Circulation) SirsiDynix
Open Mon-Fri 8:30-4:30

S OLD DARTMOUTH HISTORICAL SOCIETY*, New Bedford Whaling Museum Research Library, 791 Purchase St, 02740-6398. (Mail add: 18 Johnny Cake Hill, 02740), SAN 307-5540. Tel: 508-997-0046. FAX: 508-207-1064. E-mail: research@whalingmuseum.org. Web Site: www.whalingmuseum.org/library/index.html. *Librn,* Laura Pereira; E-mail: lpereira@whalingmuseum.org; *Sr Curator,* Stuart M Frank, PhD; *Maritime Curator,* Michael Dyer; Tel: 508-997-0046, Ext 137, E-mail: mdyer@whalingmuseum.org. Subject Specialists: *Rare bks,* Stuart M Frank, PhD; Staff 3 (MLS 1, Non-MLS 2)
Founded 1956
Library Holdings: Bk Vols 20,000; Spec Interest Per Sub 10
Special Collections: International Marine Archives, micro; Maritime History (Charles A Goodwin Coll); Whaling (Charles F Batchelder Coll); Whaling Museum Logbook Coll. Oral History
Subject Interests: Fine arts, Hist, Manuscripts, Navigation, Voyages, Whaling
Publications: 100 Highlights; 100 Years, 100 Curiosities; American Landscape & Seascape Paintings; Fifty States: America's Whaling Heritage; Kendall Whaling Museum Monograph Series; The Africa Connection; The Kendall Whaling Museum (Newsletter)
Open Tues-Fri 12-4

M SOUTHCOAST MEDICAL LIBRARIES*, 101 Page St, 02740. SAN 307-5559. Tel: 508-961-5267. FAX: 508-961-5263. E-mail: slh_library@southcoast.org. Web Site: www.southcoast.org/library. *Mgr, Libr Serv,* Judy Donn; Staff 2 (MLS 2)
Founded 1954
Library Holdings: Bk Vols 1,500; Per Subs 110
Special Collections: Hospital Archives
Subject Interests: Allied health, Med, Nursing, Patient educ
Database Vendor: EBSCOhost, OVID Technologies, PubMed
Wireless access
Partic in Massachusetts Health Sciences Libraries Network; Medical Library Association (MLA); North Atlantic Health Sciences Libraries, Inc; Southeastern Massachusetts Consortium of Health Science Libraries
Open Mon-Fri 8-4
Restriction: Badge access after hrs, Pub use on premises

NEW BRAINTREE

P NEW BRAINTREE PUBLIC LIBRARY*, 45 Memorial Dr, 01531. SAN 307-5583. Tel: 508-867-7650. FAX: 508-867-7650. *Librn,* Alice Webb
Pop 834; Circ 5,814
Library Holdings: Bk Vols 11,000
Mem of Massachusetts Libr Syst
Open Mon 12-8:30, Thurs 12-4
Friends of the Library Group

NEW SALEM

P NEW SALEM PUBLIC LIBRARY, 23 S Main St, 01355. SAN 307-5591. Tel: 978-544-6334. FAX: 978-544-6334. E-mail: n_salem@cwmars.org. *Dir,* Diana Smith
Founded 1890. Pop 920; Circ 14,820
Library Holdings: Bk Vols 8,000; Per Subs 40
Automation Activity & Vendor Info: (Cataloging) Evergreen
Database Vendor: Gale Cengage Learning
Wireless access
Open Tues 12-8, Thurs 10-6, Sat 10-2
Friends of the Library Group

NEWBURYPORT

S HISTORICAL SOCIETY OF OLD NEWBURY LIBRARY*, Cushing House Museum, 98 High St, 01950. SAN 328 2813. Tel: 978-462-2681. FAX: 978-462-0134. E-mail: info@newburyhist.org. Web Site: www.newburyhist.com. *Curator,* Jay Williamson
Library Holdings: Bk Vols 2,500
Special Collections: Local History; Newbury, Newburyport & West Newbury
Open Tues-Fri 9-4, Sat (May-Oct) 11-2

P NEWBURYPORT PUBLIC LIBRARY, 94 State St, 01950-6619. SAN 307-5621. Tel: 978-465-4428. Circulation Tel: 978-465-4428, Ext 236. Reference Tel: 978-465-4428, Ext 226. Administration Tel: 978-465 4428, Ext 221. FAX: 978-463-0394. E-mail: npl@mvlc.org. Web Site: www.newburyportpl.org. *Head Librn,* Cynthia Dadd; Tel: 978-465-4428, Ext 222; *Asst Head Librn,* Giselle Stevens; Tel: 978-465-4428, Ext 224; *Circ Mgr,* Lynn Marks; Tel: 978-465-4428, Ext 243; *Archivist,* Jessica Gill; Tel: 978-465-4428, Ext 229; *Ch Serv,* Allison Driscoll; Tel: 978-465-4428, Ext 235; *Info Serv,* Jessica Atherton; *Tech Serv,* Dan Tremblay; Tel: 978-465-4428, Ext 230; *YA Serv,* Jessica Hilbun; Tel: 978-465-4428, Ext 228; Staff 21 (MLS 7, Non-MLS 14)
Founded 1854. Pop 17,500; Circ 345,000
Jul 2006-Jun 2007 Income $1,216,588, State $24,588, City $1,167,000, Locally Generated Income $25,000. Mats Exp $180,300, Books $118,000, Per/Ser (Incl. Access Fees) $8,700, Other Print Mats $4,000, Micro $800, AV Mat $36,000, Electronic Ref Mat (Incl. Access Fees) $9,800, Presv $3,000. Sal $130,500 (Prof $832,787)
Library Holdings: AV Mats 9,668; Large Print Bks 1,900; Bk Vols 101,661; Per Subs 174
Special Collections: Genealogy Coll; Newburyport History, bks, doc, maps, photog
Automation Activity & Vendor Info: (Cataloging) Evergreen; (Circulation) Evergreen; (OPAC) Evergreen
Database Vendor: EBSCOhost, Gale Cengage Learning, Newsbank, OCLC FirstSearch, Overdrive, Inc, ProQuest, ReferenceUSA
Wireless access
Function: Games & aids for the handicapped, Handicapped accessible, ILL available, Large print keyboards, Magnifiers for reading, Outside serv via phone, mail, e-mail & web, Photocopying/Printing, Prog for children & young adult, Ref serv available, Summer reading prog, Telephone ref, Wheelchair accessible
Mem of Massachusetts Libr Syst
Partic in Merrimack Valley Library Consortium
Open Mon-Thurs 9-9, Fri & Sat 9-5, Sun (Oct-April) 1-5
Friends of the Library Group

NEWTON

S BOSTON PSYCHOANALYTIC SOCIETY & INSTITUTE, INC*, The Hanns Sachs Medical Library, 169 Herrick Rd, 02459. SAN 307-1391. Tel: 617-266-0953, Ext 104. FAX: 857-255-3253. E-mail: library@bpsi.org. Web Site: www.bpsi.org/library. *Dir,* Dr Daniel Jacobs; *Dir, Archives,* Dr Sanford Gifford; *Librn & Archivist,* Olga Umansky; Staff 1 (MLS 1)
Founded 1933
Library Holdings: Bk Titles 9,000; Per Subs 95
Special Collections: Archives (History of Psychoanalysis)
Subject Interests: Psychoanalysis
Automation Activity & Vendor Info: (Acquisitions) Mandarin Library Automation; (Cataloging) Mandarin Library Automation; (Circulation) Mandarin Library Automation; (Course Reserve) Mandarin Library Automation; (ILL) Mandarin Library Automation; (Media Booking) Mandarin Library Automation; (OPAC) Mandarin Library Automation; (Serials) Mandarin Library Automation
Open Mon-Fri 9-5
Friends of the Library Group

C LASELL COLLEGE*, Brennan Library, 80 A Maple Ave, 02466. SAN 307-0891. Tel: 617-243-2244. FAX: 617-243-2458. Web Site: www.lasell.edu/studentlife/brennan_library.asp. *Dir,* Marilyn Negip; Tel: 617-243-2243, E-mail: mnegip@lasell.edu; *Ref,* Jill Shoemaker; E-mail: jshoemaker@lasell.edu; *Tech Serv,* Lydia Pittman; Tel: 617-243-2207, E-mail: jpittman@lasell.edu; Staff 7 (MLS 4, Non-MLS 3)
Founded 1851. Enrl 1,200; Fac 120; Highest Degree: Master
Library Holdings: AV Mats 1,888; Bk Titles 55,928; Bk Vols 58,000; Per Subs 193
Special Collections: Lasell Historical Coll
Subject Interests: Bus, Child studies, Educ, Fashion, Hotel admin, Phys therapy, Physiology, Retailing, Travel
Automation Activity & Vendor Info: (Cataloging) Innovative Interfaces, Inc; (Circulation) Innovative Interfaces, Inc
Database Vendor: EBSCOhost, Gale Cengage Learning, LexisNexis, OCLC FirstSearch, ProQuest
Function: ILL available, Photocopying/Printing
Partic in Minuteman Library Network
Open Mon-Thurs 8am-Midnight, Fri 8-5, Sat 12-5, Sun Noon-Midnight

MOUNT IDA COLLEGE

J NATIONAL CENTER FOR DEATH EDUCATION LIBRARY*, 777 Dedham St, 02459, SAN 325-4836. Tel: 617-928-4552. FAX: 617-928-4713. E-mail: ncde@mountida.edu. Web Site: www.mountida.edu/ncde. *Coordr,* Judith Harding; E-mail: jharding@mountida.edu; Staff 1 (MLS 1)
Founded 1984
Library Holdings: Bk Titles 3,000; Per Subs 47
Partic in Minuteman Library Network

J WADSWORTH LIBRARY*, 777 Dedham St, 02459, SAN 307-5699. Tel: 617-928-4552. FAX: 617-928-4038. E-mail: reference@mountida.edu. Web Site: www.mountida.edu. *Dean, Info Tech & Learning Res,* Marge Lippincott; Tel: 617-928-4596, E-mail: mmlippincott@mountida.edu; *Assoc Dir, Libr Serv,* Judy Harding; E-mail: jharding@mountida.edu; *Ref Librn,* Tim Gerolami; E-mail: tgerolami@mountida.edu; *Asst Librn,* Sarah Dolan; E-mail: sdolan@mountida.edu; *Asst Librn,* Diane Post; E-mail: dpost@mountida.edu; *Asst Librn, Tech Serv,* Donna Dodson; E-mail: ddodson@mountida.edu; *Coordr, Tech Serv,* Clemencia Aramburo; E-mail: caramburo@mountida.edu; Staff 11 (MLS 11)
Founded 1939. Enrl 18; Fac 47
Library Holdings: Bk Titles 60,000; Per Subs 530
Special Collections: History of Mount Ida College Archives; National Center for Death Education Library
Subject Interests: Art, Fashion, Literary criticism, Med, Veterinary med
Automation Activity & Vendor Info: (Cataloging) Innovative Interfaces, Inc
Open Mon-Thurs 7:30am-11pm, Fri 7:30-5, Sat 10-5, Sun 2-Midnight

S NEWTON HISTORY MUSEUM AT THE JACKSON HOMESTEAD*, Manuscript & Photograph Collection Library, 527 Washington St, 02458. SAN 307-5656. Tel: 617-796-1450. FAX: 617-552-7228. Web Site: www.ci.newton.ma.us/jackson/. *Dir,* Cynthia Stone; E-mail: cstone@newtonma.gov; *Curator,* Susan D Abele; Tel: 617-796-1462, E-mail: sabele@newtonma.gov. Subject Specialists: *Local hist,* Susan D Abele; Staff 1 (MLS 1)
Founded 1950
Library Holdings: Bk Vols 1,000
Special Collections: Manuscript & Photograph Coll
Subject Interests: Abolitionism, African-Am (ethnic), Architectural hist, Decorative art, Genealogy, Local hist, Slavery, State hist for genealogy
Function: Ref serv available
Open Tues-Fri 11-5, Sat & Sun 12-5

NEWTON CENTRE

R ANDOVER NEWTON THEOLOGICAL SCHOOL, Franklin Trask Library, 169 Herrick Rd, 02459. SAN 307-5680. Tel: 617-831-2415. FAX: 617-831-1643. Web Site: www.ants.edu/library. *Co-Dir, Pub Serv Librn,* Nancy Lois; Tel: 617-831-2416, E-mail: nlois@ants.edu; *Co-Dir, Tech Serv Librn,* Jeffrey Brigham; Tel: 617-831-2417, E-mail: jbrigham@ants.edu; *Pub Serv Asst,* Kristen Watson; Tel: 617-831-2443, E-mail: kwatson@ants.edu; *Tech Serv Asst,* Bruno Leung; Tel: 617-831-2418, E-mail: bleung@ants.edu; Staff 4 (MLS 2, Non-MLS 2)
Founded 1807. Enrl 350; Fac 16; Highest Degree: Doctorate
Library Holdings: Bk Vols 130,000; Per Subs 257
Special Collections: Baptist & Congregational Church Records Coll, ms; Isaac Backus Coll, ms; Jonathan Edwards Coll, ms; New England Baptist History Coll
Automation Activity & Vendor Info: (Cataloging) SirsiDynix; (Circulation) SirsiDynix; (Course Reserve) SirsiDynix; (ILL) OCLC; (OPAC) SirsiDynix
Database Vendor: EBSCOhost, Gale Cengage Learning, Oxford Online, SirsiDynix
Wireless access
Partic in Lyrasis; OCLC Online Computer Library Center, Inc
Open Mon-Thurs 8:30am-10pm, Fri 8:30-4:30, Sat 1-5

CL BOSTON COLLEGE, Law Library, 885 Centre St, 02459. SAN 345-1321. Tel: 617-552-4405. Interlibrary Loan Service Tel: 617-552-4066. FAX: 617-552-2889. Web Site: www.bc.edu/lawlibrary. *Prof of Law & Assoc Dean, Libr & Tech Serv,* Filippa Marullo Anzalone; Tel: 617-552-6809, E-mail: filippa.anzalone@bc.edu; *Assoc Dir, Admin & Tech Serv,* Michael I Mitsukawa; Tel: 617-552-2355, E-mail: michael.mitsukawa@bc.edu; *Assoc Law Librn, Access & Organization,* Helen Lacouture; Tel: 617-552-8609, E-mail: helen.lacouture@bc.edu; *Assoc Law Librn, Educ & Ref,* Mary Ann Neary; Tel: 617-552-8612, E-mail: maryann.neary@bc.edu; *Access Serv Librn,* Lily Olson; Tel: 617-552-8610, E-mail: lily.olson@bc.edu; *Coll Serv Librn,* Deena Frazier; Tel: 617-552-4409, E-mail: deena.frazier@bc.edu; *Digital Initiatives & Scholarly Communication Librn,* Nick Szydlowski; Tel: 617-552-4474, E-mail: nick.szydlowski@bc.edu; *Legal Info Librn,* Karen S Breda; Tel: 617-552-4407, E-mail: karen.breda@bc.edu; *Legal Info Librn,* Xin Sherry Chen; Tel: 617-552-2897, E-mail: sherry.xin.chen@bc.edu; *Curator, Spec Coll, Legal Info Librn,* Laurel Davis; Tel: 617-552-4410, E-mail: laurel.davis.2@bc.edu; *Legal Info Librn,* Joan A Shear; Tel: 617-552-2895, E-mail: joan.shear@bc.edu; *Legal Info Librn,* Susan Vaughn; Tel: 617-552-8607, E-mail: susan.vaughn@bc.edu; *Weekend Ref Librn,* Connie Sellers; Tel: 617-552-4434, E-mail: connie.sellers@bc.edu; *Educ Tech Spec,* Chester G Kozikowski, III; Tel: 617-552-8606, E-mail: chester.kozikowski@bc.edu. Subject Specialists: *Advan legal res, Art law,* Filippa Marullo Anzalone; Staff 15.2 (MLS 11.2, Non-MLS 4)
Founded 1929. Enrl 760; Fac 56; Highest Degree: Doctorate
Library Holdings: Bk Vols 501,875; Per Subs 2,482
Automation Activity & Vendor Info: (Acquisitions) Ex Libris Group; (Cataloging) Ex Libris Group; (Circulation) Ex Libris Group; (Course Reserve) Ex Libris Group; (ILL) OCLC ILLiad; (OPAC) Ex Libris Group; (Serials) Ex Libris Group
Database Vendor: Bloomberg, HeinOnline, JSTOR, LexisNexis, Loislaw, OCLC FirstSearch, OCLC WorldShare Interlibrary Loan, RefWorks, Westlaw
Wireless access
Function: Archival coll, CD-ROM, Computers for patron use, Copy machines, E-Reserves, Electronic databases & coll, Exhibits, Govt ref serv, Handicapped accessible, ILL available, Online cat, Online ref, Wheelchair accessible
Partic in Association of Jesuit Colleges & Universities (AJCU); Legal Information Preservation Alliance (LIPA); New England Law Library Consortium, Inc
Open Mon-Thurs 7:30am-11:45pm, Fri 7:30am-10pm, Sat 9am-10pm, Sun 10am-11:45pm
Restriction: Borrowing privileges limited to fac & registered students, Non-circulating coll, Non-circulating of rare bks, Non-circulating to the pub, Restricted access, Restricted borrowing privileges

CR HEBREW COLLEGE, The Rae & Joseph Gann Library, 160 Herrick Rd, 02459. SAN 307-2665. Tel: 617-559-8750. FAX: 617-559-8751. E-mail: library@hebrewcollege.edu. Web Site: www.hebrewcollege.edu/library. *Libr Dir,* Harvey Sukenic; E-mail: hsukenic@hebrewcollege.edu; *Circ,* Robert Listernick; Staff 2 (MLS 1, Non-MLS 1)
Founded 1918. Enrl 250; Fac 66; Highest Degree: Doctorate
Library Holdings: Bks on Deafness & Sign Lang 46; CDs 264; DVDs 286; Bk Vols 95,000; Per Subs 180
Special Collections: Canadian Jewry (Norman Tasgal Coll); Children's Hebrew Literature (Helen Sarna Coll); Eastern European Jewish History (Philip Lief Coll); Finkel Video Coll; Hebrew College Women's Association, Jewish Women's Studies; Holocaust (Birnbaum & Motzkin Coll); Japanese-Judaica Coll; Jewish Communal Service (Simon & Sylvia Krakow Fund); Jewish Education (Herman & Peggy Vershbow Pedagogic

Center); Jewish Genealogy; Jewish Medical Ethics (Harry A & Beatrice Savitz Coll); John S & Florence G Lawrence Coll, micro; Large Print Books of Jewish Interest (Bessie Berkowitz Coll); Modern Hebrew Literature (Katz Coll)
Subject Interests: Jewish educ, Jewish lit, Judaica, Rabbinics
Automation Activity & Vendor Info: (Cataloging) OPALS (Open-source Automated Library System); (Circulation) OPALS (Open-source Automated Library System), (OPAC) OPALS (Open-source Automated Library System)
Database Vendor: ebrary, EBSCO Information Services, EBSCOhost, ProQuest, SerialsSolutions
Wireless access
Function: Distance learning, Doc delivery serv, For res purposes, Handicapped accessible, ILL available, Ref serv available
Publications: Bibliography of Japanese-Judaica; Bibliography of Russian - Judaica in the Hebrew College Library 2nd Ed; Jewish Genealogical Resources in the Hebrew College Library; Jewish Reference Books 1980-1990; Manuscripts in the Hebrew College Library
Open Mon, Wed & Thurs 9-7, Tues 9-9, Fri 9-12, Sun 9-3
Restriction: Open to fac, students & qualified researchers, Open to pub for ref & circ; with some limitations, Photo ID required for access

P NEWTON FREE LIBRARY, 330 Homer St, 02459-1429. SAN 345-4231. Tel: 617-796-1360. Reference Tel: 617-796-1380. Administration Tel: 617-796-1400. FAX: 617-965-8457. Web Site: www.newtonfreelibrary.net/. *Dir,* Phil McNulty; E-mail: pmcnulty@minlib.net; *Asst Dir,* Jill Graboski; *Ch,* Jane Malmberg; Staff 73 (MLS 33, Non-MLS 40)
Founded 1870. Pop 86,307; Circ 1,658,948
Library Holdings: Audiobooks 35,041; AV Mats 66,457; DVDs 30,554; e-books 20,451; e-journals 35; Electronic Media & Resources 862; Large Print Bks 9,553; Microforms 603; Music Scores 8,805; Bk Vols 452,318; Per Subs 4,325; Talking Bks 234
Special Collections: Newton Historical Coll. Oral History
Automation Activity & Vendor Info: (Acquisitions) Innovative Interfaces, Inc; (Cataloging) Innovative Interfaces, Inc; (Circulation) Innovative Interfaces, Inc; (OPAC) Innovative Interfaces, Inc; (Serials) Innovative Interfaces, Inc
Wireless access
Publications: Booklists in Subject Fields; History of Newton Free Library; Newsletter (Monthly); Newtoniana
Mem of Massachusetts Libr Syst
Partic in Minuteman Library Network
Special Services for the Deaf - Bks on deafness & sign lang; Captioned film dep; Spec interest per; TTY equip
Special Services for the Blind - Assistive/Adapted tech devices, equip & products; Audio mat; BiFolkal kits; Bks & mags in Braille, on rec, tape & cassette; Closed circuit TV magnifier; Computer with voice synthesizer for visually impaired persons; Large print bks; Large screen computer & software; Magnifiers; Playaways (bks on MP3); Reader equip; Talking bks
Open Mon-Thurs 9-9, Fri 9-6, Sat 9-5, Sun (Sept-June) 1-5
Friends of the Library Group

NEWTON LOWER FALLS

M NEWTON-WELLESLEY HOSPITAL*, Paul Talbot Babson Memorial Library, 2014 Washington St, 02462-1699. SAN 307-5702. Tel: 617-243-6279. FAX: 617-243-6595. Web Site: www.nwh.org. *Dir, Libr Serv,* Christine L Bell; E-mail: clbell@partners.org; *Coordr, Libr Serv,* Ross Sharp
Founded 1945
Library Holdings: Bk Vols 11,000; Per Subs 220
Special Collections: Newton-Wellesley Hospital Archives
Subject Interests: Health sci, Hospital admin, Med, Nursing, Psychiat
Partic in Boston Biomedical Library Consortium; Massachusetts Health Sciences Libraries Network
Open Mon-Fri 8:30-5

NORFOLK

P NORFOLK PUBLIC LIBRARY*, 139 Main St, 02056. SAN 307-5729. Tel: 508-528-3380. FAX: 508-528-6417. E-mail: norfolkpl@sailsinc.org. Web Site: library.virtualnorfolk.org. *Dir,* Robin Glasser; E-mail: rglasser@sailsinc.org; *Assoc Dir,* Sarina Bluhm; E-mail: sbluhm@virtualnorfolk.org; *Electronic Res, Ref Serv,* John Spinney; E-mail: jspinney@virtualnorfolk.org; *Youth Serv Librn,* Marissa Antosh; Staff 10 (MLS 4, Non-MLS 6)
Founded 1880. Pop 10,000
Jul 2006-Jun 2007 Income $528,000. Mats Exp $75,000. Sal $330,000 (Prof $190,000)
Library Holdings: Bk Titles 49,000; Per Subs 150
Automation Activity & Vendor Info: (Acquisitions) SirsiDynix; (Cataloging) SirsiDynix
Database Vendor: Gale Cengage Learning
Open Mon 2-7:30, Tues-Thurs 10-7:30, Fri & Sat 10-4, Sun Noon-4
Friends of the Library Group

NORTH ADAMS

C MASSACHUSETTS COLLEGE OF LIBERAL ARTS*, Eugene L Freel Library, 375 Church St, Ste 9250, 01247. SAN 307-5753. Tel: 413-662-5321. Reference Tel: 413-662-5325. FAX: 413-662-5286. Web Site: www.mcla.edu/library. *Assoc Dean, Libr Serv,* Maureen Horak; E-mail: M.Horak@mcla.edu; *Pub Serv Librn,* Linda Kaufmann; *Ref Librn,* Susan Denault; *Circ,* Glenn Lawson; Staff 14 (MLS 3, Non-MLS 11)
Founded 1894. Enrl 1,400; Fac 92; Highest Degree: Master
Library Holdings: Bk Vols 170,000; Per Subs 75
Special Collections: Hoosac Valley Coll for Local History; Teacher Resources Coll. Oral History
Subject Interests: Educ, Liberal arts
Automation Activity & Vendor Info: (Cataloging) Innovative Interfaces, Inc; (Circulation) Innovative Interfaces, Inc
Database Vendor: EBSCOhost, Gale Cengage Learning
Partic in Central & Western Massachusetts Automated Resource Sharing; Dialog Corp; Lyrasis

P NORTH ADAMS PUBLIC LIBRARY, 74 Church St, 01247. SAN 307-3327. Tel: 413-662-3133. FAX: 413-662-3039. Web Site: www.naplibrary.com. *Dir,* Mindy Hackner; E-mail: mhackner@northadams-ma.gov; *Adult Serv,* Robin Martin; Staff 10 (MLS 4, Non-MLS 6)
Founded 1884. Pop 13,000; Circ 120,000
Jul 2013-Jun 2014 Income $296,751, Federal $20,597. Mats Exp $52,190, Books $32,127, Per/Ser (Incl. Access Fees) $5,775, Micro $150, AV Mat $8,488, Electronic Ref Mat (Incl. Access Fees) $5,600. Sal $254,157
Library Holdings: Bks on Deafness & Sign Lang 27; CDs 2,200; DVDs 5,740; e-books 24,552; High Interest/Low Vocabulary Bk Vols 1,070; Large Print Bks 3,500; Microforms 1,137; Music Scores 21; Bk Vols 47,561; Per Subs 180; Spec Interest Per Sub 21; Talking Bks 3,920
Special Collections: Hoosac Tunnel
Automation Activity & Vendor Info: (Acquisitions) Evergreen; (Cataloging) Evergreen; (Circulation) Evergreen; (ILL) Evergreen; (OPAC) Evergreen; (Serials) Evergreen
Database Vendor: Baker & Taylor, Booklist Online, Bowker, Brodart, BWI, CQ Press, Dun & Bradstreet, EBSCO - WebFeat, EBSCO Auto Repair Reference, Facts on File, Foundation Center, Gale Cengage Learning, Greenwood Publishing Group, Grolier Online, infoUSA, Ingram Library Services, Innovative Interfaces, Inc, Jane's, LearningExpress, McGraw-Hill, Medline, Newsbank, Overdrive, Inc, ProQuest, Standard & Poor's, ValueLine, WebMD, Westlaw, World Book Online
Wireless access
Function: Archival coll, Art exhibits, Audio & video playback equip for onsite use, Audiobks via web, Bks on cassette, Bks on CD, Chess club, Children's prog, Computer training, Computers for patron use, Copy machines, E-Reserves, Fax serv, Free DVD rentals, Handicapped accessible, Holiday prog, Homebound delivery serv, Mail & tel request accepted, Mus passes, Music CDs, Newsp ref libr, Online cat, Online ref, Online searches, Photocopying/Printing, Preschool outreach, Prog for adults, Prog for children & young adult, Pub access computers, Ref serv available, Referrals accepted, Scanner, Senior computer classes, Serves mentally handicapped consumers, Spoken cassettes & CDs, Spoken cassettes & DVDs, Story hour, Summer reading prog, Tax forms, Teen prog, VHS videos, Video lending libr, Web-catalog, Wheelchair accessible, Workshops
Mem of Massachusetts Libr Syst
Partic in Central & Western Massachusetts Automated Resource Sharing
Special Services for the Deaf - Accessible learning ctr; Bks on deafness & sign lang; Coll on deaf educ; High interest/low vocabulary bks
Special Services for the Blind - Accessible computers; Audio mat; Bks available with recordings; Bks on cassette; Bks on CD; Cassettes; Home delivery serv; Large print & cassettes; Large print bks; PC for handicapped; Recorded bks; Screen enlargement software for people with visual disabilities; Sound rec
Open Mon, Tues, Wed & Fri 9-5, Thurs 12-8, Sat 10-1
Restriction: In-house use for visitors
Friends of the Library Group

M NORTH ADAMS REGIONAL HOSPITAL*, Dr Robert Carpenter Memorial Library, 71 Hospital Ave, 01247. SAN 377-9025. Tel: 413-663-3701. FAX: 413-664-5016. Web Site: www.nbhealth.org/narh/narh1.html. *Librn,* Deborah Lipa; E-mail: dlipa@nbhealth.org
Library Holdings: Bk Titles 300; Per Subs 100
Partic in Basic Health Sciences Library Network; National Network of Libraries of Medicine South Central Region; Western Mass Health Info Consortium

NORTH ANDOVER

C MERRIMACK COLLEGE*, McQuade Library, 315 Turnpike St, 01845. SAN 307-580X. Tel: 978-837-5215. FAX: 978-837-5434. E-mail: mcquade@merrimack.edu. Web Site: www.merrimack.edu/library. *Dir,*

Kathryn Geoffrion Scannell; *Dir, Media Instrul Serv,* Kevin Salemme; *Head, Access Serv,* Christina Condon; *Head, Instruction & Outreach,* Lyena Chavez; *Head, Res Mgt,* Frances Nilsson; Staff 13.95 (MLS 5.25, Non-MLS 8.7)
Founded 1947. Enrl 2,279; Fac 140; Highest Degree: Master
Library Holdings: AV Mats 3,897; e-books 82,521; e-journals 33,220; Bk Vols 101,801; Per Subs 150
Special Collections: Augustinian Studies; Education Resource Coll
Automation Activity & Vendor Info: (OPAC) Evergreen
Wireless access
Mem of Massachusetts Libr Syst
Partic in Northeast Research Libraries Consortium (NERL); Westchester Academic Library Directors Organization (WALDO)
Restriction: 24-hr pass syst for students only, Access at librarian's discretion, Borrowing requests are handled by ILL, ID required to use computers (Ltd hrs), Restricted pub use

S NORTH ANDOVER HISTORICAL SOCIETY LIBRARY, 153 Academy Rd, 01845. SAN 373-1626. Tel: 978-686-4035. FAX: 978-686-6616. E-mail: archives.nahistory@gmail.com. Web Site: essexheritage.org/sites/north_andover_hist_soc.shtm, www.northandoverhistoricalsociety.org. *Dir,* Carol Majahad; E-mail: director.nahistory@gmail.com; *Curator,* Inga C Larson; Staff 1 (Non-MLS 1)
Founded 1913
Library Holdings: Bk Vols 1,500
Special Collections: Local Architectural History Coll, doc, maps & photog
Subject Interests: Genealogy
Wireless access
Function: Magnifiers for reading
Restriction: Non-circulating, Open by appt only

P STEVENS MEMORIAL LIBRARY, 345 Main St, 01845. SAN 307-5826. Tel: 978-688-9505. FAX: 978-688-9507. E-mail: msm@mvlc.org. Web Site: www.stevensmemlib.org. *Dir,* Mary Rose Quinn; E-mail: mquinn@mvlc.org; *Asst Dir,* Kathleen Keenan; *Head, Circ,* Marie McAndrew-Taylor; *Ch Serv,* Marina Salenikas; *Ref Serv, Ad,* Irja Finn; Staff 15 (MLS 5, Non-MLS 10)
Founded 1907. Pop 27,196; Circ 201,961
Jul 2013-Jun 2014 Income $887,066, State $23,379, City $863,687. Mats Exp $157,722, Books $87,415, Per/Ser (Incl. Access Fees) $7,000, AV Mat $31,915, Electronic Ref Mat (Incl. Access Fees) $31,392. Sal $611,300
Library Holdings: CDs 4,285; DVDs 3,903; e-books 11,843; Bk Vols 86,857
Special Collections: Essex County, Massachusetts; Poetry (Anne Bradstreet Coll)
Automation Activity & Vendor Info: (Cataloging) Evergreen; (Circulation) Evergreen; (OPAC) Evergreen; (Serials) EBSCO Online
Database Vendor: Baker & Taylor, ebrary, EBSCOhost, Evanced Solutions, Inc, Facts on File, Gale Cengage Learning, Grolier Online, Ingram Library Services, LearningExpress, Library Ideas, LLC, Newsbank, Overdrive, Inc, ProQuest, Safari Books Online, ValueLine, World Book Online
Wireless access
Mem of Massachusetts Libr Syst
Partic in Merimack Valley Libr Consortium
Special Services for the Blind - Accessible computers; Bks available with recordings; Closed circuit TV magnifier; Extensive large print coll
Open Mon-Thurs 10-9, Fri & Sat 10-5, Sun 2-5
Friends of the Library Group

NORTH ATTLEBORO

P RICHARDS MEMORIAL LIBRARY*, North Attleboro Public Library, 118 N Washington St, 02760. SAN 307-5834. Tel: 508-699-0122. FAX: 508-699-8075. Web Site: www.rmlonline.org. *Dir,* Francis Ward; E-mail: fward@sailsinc.org; *Assoc Dir, Ref,* Cynthia Edson; *Dir of Circ,* Ellen Casaccio; *Tech Serv,* David Lockhart
Founded 1878. Pop 28,000; Circ 103,000
Library Holdings: AV Mats 2,565; Bk Vols 45,113; Per Subs 137; Talking Bks 1,075
Automation Activity & Vendor Info: (Cataloging) SirsiDynix; (Circulation) SirsiDynix; (OPAC) SirsiDynix
Open Mon-Thurs (Winter) 9-9, Fri & Sat 9-5; Mon & Thurs (Summer) 9-8, Tues, Wed, Fri & Sat 9-5
Friends of the Library Group

NORTH BROOKFIELD

P HASTON FREE PUBLIC LIBRARY*, North Brookfield Library, 161 N Main St, 01535. SAN 307-5842. Tel: 508-867-0208. FAX: 508-867-0216. Web Site: northbrookfieldlibrary.org. *Dir,* Ann L Kidd; E-mail: akidd@cwmars.org; *Asst Librn,* Regina Allen-Davis; *Ch Serv,* Rosemary Mackenzie; *Tech Serv Librn,* Helen Foyle; Staff 1.9 (Non-MLS 1.9)
Founded 1879. Pop 4,817; Circ 36,554
Jul 2012-Jun 2013 Income $111,742, State $5,646, City $96,714, Locally Generated Income $500, Other $8,882. Mats Exp $22,127, Books $14,756, Per/Ser (Incl. Access Fees) $999, AV Mat $5,922, Electronic Ref Mat (Incl. Access Fees) $450. Sal $56,408
Library Holdings: Audiobooks 1,115; Braille Volumes 2; CDs 500; DVDs 1,427; e-books 17,026; Electronic Media & Resources 3; Large Print Bks 395; Microforms 10; Bk Vols 20,393; Per Subs 30; Videos 10
Special Collections: Local History (North Brookfield Journals)
Automation Activity & Vendor Info: (Cataloging) Evergreen; (Circulation) Evergreen; (ILL) Evergreen; (OPAC) Evergreen
Database Vendor: EBSCO Information Services, ProQuest
Wireless access
Function: Adult bk club, After school storytime, Art exhibits, Bk club(s), Bks on CD, Children's prog, Computer training, Computers for patron use, Copy machines, e-mail serv, Electronic databases & coll, Exhibits, Fax serv, Free DVD rentals, Handicapped accessible, Holiday prog, Homebound delivery serv, ILL available, Magnifiers for reading, Microfiche/film & reading machines, Mus passes, Music CDs, Online cat, Online ref, Online searches, Photocopying/Printing, Preschool reading prog, Prog for adults, Prog for children & young adult, Pub access computers, Ref serv available, Spanish lang bks, Story hour, Summer reading prog, Tax forms, Teen prog, Wheelchair accessible, Writing prog
Mem of Massachusetts Libr Syst
Partic in Central & Western Massachusetts Automated Resource Sharing
Special Services for the Blind - Bks on cassette; Bks on CD; Home delivery serv; Large print & cassettes; Low vision equip; Magnifiers; Videos on blindness & phys handicaps
Open Mon & Wed 1-7, Tues 10-5, Thurs 1-6, Sat 9-Noon
Friends of the Library Group

NORTH DARTMOUTH

L SOUTHERN NEW ENGLAND SCHOOL OF LAW LIBRARY*, 333 Faunce Corner Rd, 02747. SAN 372-0314. Tel: 508-998-9888. *Dir,* Spencer Clough; *Acq, Cat,* Abby Davis; *Pub Serv,* Howard Senzel; *Ref Serv,* Cathy O'Neill; Staff 4 (MLS 4)
Automation Activity & Vendor Info: (Serials) Auto-Graphics, Inc
Database Vendor: HeinOnline, LexisNexis, Westlaw
Wireless access
Partic in Lyrasis; OCLC Online Computer Library Center, Inc
Open Mon-Thurs 8am-11pm, Fri & Sat 8-6, Sun 11-9

C UNIVERSITY OF MASSACHUSETTS DARTMOUTH LIBRARY*, Claire T Carney Library, 285 Old Westport Rd, 02747-2300. SAN 307-5850. Tel: 508-999-8678. Circulation Tel: 508-999-8750. Interlibrary Loan Service Tel: 508-999-6951. Administration Tel: 508-999-8157. Automation Services Tel: 508-999-8680. Information Services Tel: 508-999-8951. FAX: 508-999-8987. Interlibrary Loan Service FAX: 508-999-9142. Reference FAX: 508-999-9240. E-mail: libweb@umassd.edu. Web Site: www.lib.umassd.edu. *Vice Chancellor, Libr Serv, Info Res & Tech,* Robert W Green; Tel: 508-999-8260, E-mail: rgreen@umassd.edu; *Dean, Libr Serv,* Sharon Weiner; Tel: 508-999-8664; *Head, Access Serv,* Catherine A Fortier-Barnes; Tel: 508-999-8665, E-mail: cfortier@umassd.edu; *Head, Info Serv,* Linda Zieper; Tel: 508-999-8526; *Head, Libr Syst,* Charles A McNeil; E-mail: cmcneil@umassd.edu; *Coll Develop, Head, Tech Serv,* Bruce Barnes; Tel: 508-999-8666, E-mail: bbarnes@umassd.edu; *Assoc Librn, Archives & Spec Coll,* Judith Farrar; Tel: 508-999-8686, Fax: 508-999-8424, E-mail: jfarrar@umassd.edu; *Info Serv Librn,* Kathleen Randall Haley; Tel: 508-999-8670, E-mail: krandall@umassd.edu. Subject Specialists: *Polit sci,* Bruce Barnes; Staff 15 (MLS 14, Non-MLS 1)
Founded 1960. Enrl 8,299; Fac 350; Highest Degree: Doctorate
Jul 2005-Jun 2006 Income $4,222,697, State $2,251,010, Locally Generated Income $135,762, Parent Institution $1,809,372, Other $26,553. Mats Exp $1,224,735, Books $88,900, Per/Ser (Incl. Access Fees) $804,753, Micro $38,091, AV Mat $2,592, Electronic Ref Mat (Incl. Access Fees) $282,371, Presv $8,028. Sal $2,251,010 (Prof $1,463,156)
Library Holdings: AV Mats 9,699; e-books 243; Bk Titles 271,274; Bk Vols 468,216; Per Subs 2,754
Special Collections: Alfred Lewis manuscripts and papers; American Imprints Coll; Archives of the Center for Jewish Culture; Archives of the Franco American League of Fall River; Can; Franco-American Coll; Hansard Parliamentary Debates; Portuguese-American Historical Coll; Robert Kennedy Assassination Archives. US Document Depository
Subject Interests: Lit, Portuguese (Lang)
Automation Activity & Vendor Info: (Cataloging) Ex Libris Group; (Circulation) Ex Libris Group; (Course Reserve) Ex Libris Group; (Media Booking) Ex Libris Group; (OPAC) Ex Libris Group
Database Vendor: Dialog, EBSCOhost, Gale Cengage Learning, LexisNexis, OCLC FirstSearch, OVID Technologies, ProQuest, SirsiDynix, Wilson - Wilson Web
Function: Archival coll, AV serv, Distance learning, Handicapped accessible, ILL available, Photocopying/Printing
Publications: Library News (Newsletter)

Partic in Boston Library Consortium, Inc; Lyrasis; Southeastern Massachusetts Consortium of Health Science Libraries
Special Services for the Blind - Assistive/Adapted tech devices, equip & products
Open Mon-Thurs (Feb-May) 7:30am-11pm, Fri 7:30-5, Sat 9:30-5, Sun 12-9; Mon-Thurs (June-Aug) 7:30am-10pm, Fri 7:30-5
Friends of the Library Group

NORTH EASTON

P AMES FREE LIBRARY*, Easton's Public Library, 53 Main St, 02356. SAN 307-594X. Tel: 508-238-2000. FAX: 508-238-2980. Web Site: amesfreelibrary.org. *Exec Dir,* Dr Uma Hiremath; E-mail: uhiremath@easton.ma.us; *Assoc Dir, Head, Tech & User Experience,* Jason Bloom; E-mail: jbloom@easton.ma.us; *Asst Dir, Head, Youth Serv,* Catherine Coyne; E-mail: ccoyne@easton.ma.us; *Ref & Ad Serv Librn,* Ian Dunbar; E-mail: idunbar@easton.ma.us; *Circ Supvr,* Joan Roan; E-mail: jroan@easton.ma.us; *Ref & Info Serv,* Steve Somerdin; E-mail: ssomerdin@easton.ma.us; Staff 13 (MLS 6, Non-MLS 7)
Founded 1877. Pop 22,299; Circ 183,891
Jul 2011-Jun 2012 Income $1,080,800, State $20,000, City $443,500, Locally Generated Income $591,000, Other $26,300. Mats Exp $75,000. Sal $607,000
Library Holdings: Audiobooks 988; CDs 2,888; DVDs 4,646; e-books 5,176; Electronic Media & Resources 2,963; Bk Titles 52,948; Per Subs 826
Special Collections: 19th Century Periodicals; Easton Journal, bd; H H Richardson Materials; Massachusetts Town Reports
Automation Activity & Vendor Info: (Acquisitions) SirsiDynix; (Cataloging) SirsiDynix; (Circulation) SirsiDynix; (ILL) SirsiDynix; (OPAC) SirsiDynix; (Serials) SirsiDynix
Database Vendor: EBSCOhost, Gale Cengage Learning, Ingram Library Services, Newsbank, OCLC FirstSearch, ProQuest, SirsiDynix
Wireless access
Function: Adult bk club, Art exhibits, Bk club(s), Bk reviews (Group), Bks on CD, Children's prog, Computer training, Computers for patron use, Copy machines, Electronic databases & coll, Exhibits, Free DVD rentals, Handicapped accessible, Homebound delivery serv, ILL available, Magnifiers for reading, Mail & tel request accepted, Mus passes, Music CDs, Online cat, Photocopying/Printing, Preschool outreach, Preschool reading prog, Prog for adults, Prog for children & young adult, Provide serv for the mentally ill, Pub access computers, Ref serv available, Ref serv in person, Scanner, Senior computer classes, Senior outreach, Spoken cassettes & CDs, Spoken cassettes & DVDs, Story hour, Summer reading prog, Tax forms, Teen prog, Telephone ref, Wheelchair accessible, Writing prog
Publications: The First Century (A Centennial History of Ames Free Library of Easton, Inc)
Mem of Massachusetts Libr Syst
Partic in SAILS Library Network
Special Services for the Deaf - Bks on deafness & sign lang
Special Services for the Blind - Bks on CD; Home delivery serv; Large print bks; Low vision equip; Playaways (bks on MP3)
Open Mon-Thurs 10-8, Fri 10-5, Sat (Summer) 10-5
Friends of the Library Group

NORTH READING

P FLINT MEMORIAL LIBRARY*, 147 Park St, 01864. SAN 307-5869. Tel: 978-664-4942. FAX: 978-664-0812. E-mail: mnr@mvlc.org. Web Site: www.flintmemoriallibrary.org. *Dir,* Helena Minton; *Asst Dir,* Judith Ann Segur; *Ch Serv,* Kate Bell; *Ref,* Debra Hindes; Staff 4 (MLS 4)
Founded 1872. Pop 14,518; Circ 100,836
Library Holdings: Bk Vols 78,000; Per Subs 200
Special Collections: Genealogy & History (Clara Burnham, North Reading & George Root Colls) bks, mss, maps. Oral History
Subject Interests: Local hist
Automation Activity & Vendor Info: (Cataloging) SirsiDynix; (Circulation) SirsiDynix; (OPAC) SirsiDynix
Wireless access
Mem of Massachusetts Libr Syst
Partic in Merrimack Valley Library Consortium
Open Mon 1-8, Tues & Thurs 10-8, Wed 1-5, Fri 10-5, Sat (Sept-May) 10-5
Friends of the Library Group

NORTH TRURO

P TRURO PUBLIC LIBRARY*, Five Library Lane, 02652. (Mail add: PO Box 357, 02652-0357), SAN 307-5877. Tel: 508-487-1125. FAX: 508-487-3571. Web Site: www.trurolibrary.org. *Dir,* Margaret A Royka; E-mail: mroyka@clamsnet.org; *Adult Serv, Ref,* Sharon Sullivan
Founded 1894. Pop 2,000; Circ 28,000
Library Holdings: Bk Titles 25,300; Per Subs 98
Special Collections: Oral History
Automation Activity & Vendor Info: (Acquisitions) Innovative Interfaces, Inc; (Cataloging) Innovative Interfaces, Inc; (Circulation) Innovative Interfaces, Inc; (ILL) Innovative Interfaces, Inc; (OPAC) Innovative Interfaces, Inc
Wireless access
Function: Adult literacy prog, Handicapped accessible, Homebound delivery serv, ILL available, Large print keyboards, Magnifiers for reading, Music CDs, Online searches, Orientations, Photocopying/Printing, Prog for adults, Prog for children & young adult, Ref serv available, Spoken cassettes & CDs, Summer reading prog, Telephone ref, VHS videos, Wheelchair accessible, Workshops
Mem of Massachusetts Libr Syst
Special Services for the Deaf - Closed caption videos
Special Services for the Blind - Assistive/Adapted tech devices, equip & products; Audio mat; Bks available with recordings; Bks on cassette; Bks on CD; Computer with voice synthesizer for visually impaired persons; Copier with enlargement capabilities; Descriptive video serv (DVS); Home delivery serv; Large print bks; Large screen computer & software; Low vision equip; Magnifiers; Talking bks
Open Tues & Wed 9:30-8, Thurs 9:30-6, Fri 9:30-4, Sat 9:30-2
Friends of the Library Group

NORTHAMPTON

M COOLEY DICKINSON HOSPITAL*, Richard H Dolloff Medical Library, 30 Locust St, 01060. SAN 345-4592. Tel: 413-582-2291. FAX: 413-582-2985. *Librn,* Elaine Aldrich; Staff 2 (MLS 1, Non-MLS 1)
Founded 1969
Library Holdings: Bk Titles 800; Per Subs 185
Subject Interests: Clinical med
Database Vendor: OVID Technologies
Function: Prof lending libr
Partic in Basic Health Sciences Library Network; Docline; Massachusetts Health Sciences Libraries Network; Western Mass Health Info Consortium
Restriction: Open by appt only

P FORBES LIBRARY*, 20 West St, 01060-3798. SAN 307-5885. Tel: 413-587-1011. Reference Tel: 413-587-1012. Administration Tel: 413-587-1017 FAX: 413-587-1015. E-mail: director@forbeslibrary.org. Web Site: www.forbeslibrary.org. *Dir,* Janet Moulding; Tel: 413-587-1016, E-mail: jmoulding@forbeslibrary.org; *Adult Serv, Asst Dir,* Lisa Downing; E-mail: ldowning@forbeslibrary.org; *Head, Art & Music, Info Serv Supvr, Webmaster,* Faith Kaufmann; Tel: 413 587-1013, E-mail: fkaufmann@forbeslibrary.org; *Head, Ref, Info Serv Librn,* Molly Moss; E-mail: mmoss@forbeslibrary.org; *Archivist, Info Serv Librn,* Julie Bartlett Nelson; Tel: 413-587-1014, E-mail: jbartlett@forbeslibrary.org; *Ch Serv, YA Serv,* Jude McGowan; Tel: 413-587-1010, E-mail: jmcgowan@forbeslibrary.org; *Tech Serv,* Paula Elliot; E-mail: pelliot@forbeslibrary.org. Subject Specialists: *Arts, Music,* Faith Kaufmann; *Local hist,* Julie Bartlett Nelson; Staff 37 (MLS 12, Non-MLS 25)
Founded 1894. Pop 30,000; Circ 396,808
Library Holdings: Audiobooks 6,250; Braille Volumes 25; CDs 6,250; DVDs 12,370; e-books 17,026; Large Print Bks 4,000; Music Scores 3,000; Bk Vols 156,063; Per Subs 1,809; Videos 12,370
Special Collections: Calvin Coolidge; Connecticut Valley History; Genealogy Coll
Subject Interests: Art & archit, Music
Automation Activity & Vendor Info: (Acquisitions) Evergreen; (Cataloging) Evergreen; (Circulation) Evergreen; (ILL) Evergreen; (OPAC) Evergreen; (Serials) Evergreen
Wireless access
Function: Adult bk club, Archival coll, Art exhibits, Audio & video playback equip for onsite use, Audiobks via web, Bk club(s), Bks on CD, Chess club, Children's prog, Computer training, Computers for patron use, Copy machines, Digital talking bks, e-mail & chat, e-mail serv, E-Reserves, Electronic databases & coll, Exhibits, Free DVD rentals, Games & aids for the handicapped, Genealogy discussion group, Handicapped accessible, Home delivery & serv to Sr ctr & nursing homes, Homebound delivery serv, ILL available, Magnifiers for reading, Mail & tel request accepted, Microfiche/film & reading machines, Mus passes, Music CDs, Newsp ref libr, Online cat, Online ref, Online searches, Outside serv via phone, mail, e-mail & web, OverDrive digital audio bks, Photocopying/Printing, Prog for adults, Prog for children & young adult, Pub access computers, Ref & res, Ref serv available, Ref serv in person, Scanner, Senior computer classes, Spanish lang bks, Spoken cassettes & CDs, Spoken cassettes & DVDs, Story hour, Summer reading prog, Tax forms, Teen prog, Telephone ref, Video lending libr, Visual arts prog, Wheelchair accessible, Workshops, Writing prog
Partic in Central & Western Massachusetts Automated Resource Sharing
Special Services for the Blind - Reader equip
Open Mon & Wed 9-9, Tues & Thurs 1-5, Fri & Sat 9-5
Friends of the Library Group

S HISTORIC NORTHAMPTON*, Archives & Library, 46 Bridge St, 01060. SAN 329-9112. Tel: 413-584-6011. FAX: 413-584-7956. Web Site: www.historic-northampton.org. *Exec Dir,* Kerry W Buckley
Founded 1905
Library Holdings: Bk Titles 2,500
Special Collections: Houses & People (Howes Brothers Coll), docs, ephemera, maps, mss & photog from 19th-20th centuries, archives from 17th-20th centuries. Oral History
Subject Interests: Local hist
Publications: History of Northampton; Newsletters; Weathervane Series (Booklets on local subjects)
Restriction: Authorized scholars by appt
Friends of the Library Group

GL MASSACHUSETTS TRIAL COURT, Hampshire Law Library, Courthouse, 99 Main St, Ste 1, 01060. SAN 307-5893. Tel: 413-586-2297. FAX: 413-584-0870. E-mail: hampshirelawlibrary@hotmail.com. Web Site: www.lawlib.state.ma.us. *Head Law Librn,* Kathleen Ludwig; *Law Librn,* Susan Wells; Staff 1.5 (MLS 1, Non-MLS 0.5)
Founded 1894
Library Holdings: CDs 372; e-books 100; e-journals 1,500; Bk Titles 3,000; Bk Vols 16,000; Per Subs 20
Special Collections: Massachusetts Legislative Documents (paper 1871-1988, online 1994-present)
Automation Activity & Vendor Info: (Cataloging) SirsiDynix; (Circulation) SirsiDynix; (ILL) OCLC FirstSearch; (OPAC) SirsiDynix
Database Vendor: HeinOnline, LexisNexis, Loislaw, OCLC WorldShare Interlibrary Loan, Westlaw
Wireless access
Partic in Lyrasis; OCLC Online Computer Library Center, Inc
Open Mon-Fri 8:30-4:30
Friends of the Library Group

S NEW SONG LIBRARY, PO Box 295, 01061-0295. SAN 323-7141. Tel: 413-586-9485. Web Site: www.newsonglibrary.org. *Dir,* Johanna Halbeisen; E-mail: jh@newsonglibrary.org
Founded 1974
Library Holdings: CDs 2,000; Bk Titles 200
Special Collections: Civil Rights songs & songs of other freedom movement around the world; Coll of songs about parenting, growing older, family violence, addictions & spiritual growth; Labor songs (contemporary & historical); Recordings by gay & lesbian artists; Tapes of workshops & songsharings from People's Music Network (1977-1989); Weavers, Malvina Reynolds, Phil Ochs, Pete Seeger, Joan Baez & 60's era recordings
Function: Res libr
Restriction: Non-circulating, Open by appt only

C SMITH COLLEGE LIBRARIES*, William Allan Neilson Library, 01063. SAN 345-4657. Tel: 413-585-2910. Interlibrary Loan Service Tel: 413-585-2962. Reference Tel: 413-585-2960. Administration Tel: 413-585-2902. FAX: 413-585-2904. Interlibrary Loan Service FAX: 413-585-4485. Web Site: www.smith.edu/libraries. *Dir of Libr,* Christopher B Loring; E-mail: cloring@email.smith.edu; *Dep Dir,* Christine Hannon; Tel: 413-585-2911, E-mail: channon@email.smith.edu; *Assoc Dir, Coll Serv,* James Montgomery; Tel: 413-585-2921, E-mail: jmontgom@email.smith.edu; *Assoc Dir, Coll Develop,* Mia Brazill; Tel: 413-585-2922, E-mail: mbrazill@email.smith.edu; *Libr Syst Mgr,* Eric Loehr; Tel: 413-585-2969, E-mail: eloehr@email.smith.edu; *ILL Supvr,* Christina Ryan; E-mail: cryan@email.smith.edu; *Coordr, Info Literacy,* Bruce Sajdak; Tel: 413-585-2967, E-mail: bsajdak@email.smith.edu; Staff 50 (MLS 18, Non-MLS 32)
Founded 1878. Enrl 3,571; Fac 285; Highest Degree: Doctorate
Library Holdings: Bk Vols 1,338,734; Per Subs 2,345
Special Collections: Sylvia Plath, Virginia Woolf & Bloomsbury Colls
Subject Interests: Art & archit, Feminism, Fr Can, Hist, Printing, Women's hist
Automation Activity & Vendor Info: (Acquisitions) Ex Libris Group; (Cataloging) Ex Libris Group; (Circulation) Ex Libris Group; (Course Reserve) Ex Libris Group; (ILL) OCLC ILLiad; (OPAC) Ex Libris Group; (Serials) Ex Libris Group
Wireless access
Publications: News From the Libraries
Partic in Lyrasis; OCLC Online Computer Library Center, Inc; RLIN (Research Libraries Information Network); The Five Colleges of Ohio
Open Mon-Thurs (Fall & Spring) 7:30am-1am, Fri 7:30am-9pm, Sat 10-9, Sun 10am-1am; Mon-Thurs (Summer) 8am-Midnight, Fri 8-6, Sat 10-6, Sun 10am-Midnight
Friends of the Library Group

Departmental Libraries:

COLLEGE ARCHIVES, Seven Neilson Dr, 01063. Tel: 413-585-2970. Web Site: www.smith.edu/libraries/libs/archives. *Archivist,* Nanci Young; Tel: 413-585-2976, E-mail: nyoung@email.smith.edu; Staff 1 (Non-MLS 1)
Founded 1921
Special Collections: College Records (Cambridge School of Landscape Architecture other college offices & departments); Faculty Papers (Mary Ellen Chase, John Duke, William Allan Neilson & Harris Hawthorne Wilder Colls); Institute for the Coordination of Women's Interests; Photographs; School for Social Work; Smith College Relief Unit; Student Diaries & Letters
Subject Interests: Educ, Hist, Landscape archit, Soc serv (soc work)
Open Mon, Tues, Thurs & Fri 10-5, Wed 1-9
Restriction: Non-circulating to the pub

HILLYER ART LIBRARY, Brown Fine Arts Ctr, Smith College, 01063, SAN 345-4681. Tel: 413-585-2940, 413-585-2946. FAX: 413-585-6975. Web Site: www.smith.edu/libraries/libs/hillyer. *Head of Libr,* Barbara Polowy; Tel: 413-585-2941, E-mail: bpolowy@smith.edu; *Circ Coordr,* Lisa DeCarolis; Tel: 413-585-2942, E-mail: ldecarol@smith.edu; *Tech Serv/Circ Assoc,* Matthew Durand; Tel: 413-585-2843, E-mail: mdurand@smith.edu; Staff 3 (MLS 1, Non-MLS 2)
Library Holdings: CDs 275; DVDs 150; Microforms 1,025; Bk Titles 105,600; Bk Vols 119,000; Per Subs 200
Subject Interests: Archit, Art, Art hist, Landscaping
Automation Activity & Vendor Info: (Acquisitions) Ex Libris Group; (Cataloging) Ex Libris Group; (Circulation) Ex Libris Group; (Course Reserve) Ex Libris Group; (ILL) OCLC ILLiad; (OPAC) Ex Libris Group
Database Vendor: ABC-CLIO, Alexander Street Press, American Psychological Association (APA), ARTstor, ebrary, EBSCO Discovery Service, EBSCO Information Services, ISI Web of Knowledge, LexisNexis, Luna Imaging/Insight, Marquis Who's Who, Medline, Newsbank-Readex, OCLC, Oxford Online, Project MUSE, ProQuest, RefWorks, Sage, ScienceDirect, Springer-Verlag, Springshare, LLC, Wiley, WT Cox, YBP Library Services
Partic in Five Colleges, Inc
Open Mon-Thurs (Fall-Spring) 9am-11pm, Fri 9-9, Sat 10-9, Sun Noon-Midnight; Mon-Fri (Summer) 9-4

WERNER JOSTEN PERFORMING ARTS LIBRARY, Mendenhall Ctr for the Performing Arts, 01063, SAN 345-4711. Tel: 413-585-2930, 413-585-2935. FAX: 413-585-3930. Web Site: www.smith.edu/libraries/libs/josten. *Head Librn,* Marlene M Wong; Tel: 413-585-2931, E-mail: mmwong@email.smith.edu; *Circ Coordr,* Janet Spongberg; Tel: 413-585-2932, E-mail: jspongbe@email.smith.edu; Staff 1 (MLS 1)
Special Collections: Einstein Coll (music of the 16th & 17th Centuries copied in score by Alfred Einstein); Music & correspondence of Werner Josten
Subject Interests: Dance, Music
Open Mon-Thurs (Fall-Spring) 8am-11pm, Fri 8am-9pm, Sat 10am-9pm, Sun Noon-11; Mon-Fri (Summer) 10-4

MORTIMER RARE BOOK ROOM, 01063. Tel: 413-585-2906. FAX: 413-585-4486. Web Site: www.smith.edu/libraries/libs/rarebook. *Curator,* Martin Antonetti; Tel: 413-585-2907, E-mail: mantonet@email.smith.edu; *Assoc Curator,* Karen Kukil; Tel: 413-585-2908, E-mail: kkukil@email.smith.edu; Staff 2 (MLS 2)
Founded 1942
Library Holdings: Bk Vols 31,364
Special Collections: Book Arts; Botany; English & American Children's Books, 17th-20th Centuries (Ernest Hemingway, Rudyard Kipling & George Bernard Shaw Colls); Iconography (Bloomsbury, Sylvia Plath & Virginia Woolf Colls)
Subject Interests: Am lit, English lit, Printing
Open Mon-Fri 9-12 & 1-5
Restriction: Non-circulating to the pub

SOPHIA SMITH COLLECTION, Seven Neilson Dr, 01063. Tel: 413-585-2970. FAX: 413-585-2886. E-mail: ssc-wmhist@email.smith.edu. Web Site: www.smith.edu/libraries/libs/ssc. *Dir,* Sherrill Redmon; Tel: 413-585-2978, E-mail: sredmon@email.smith.edu; *Outreach Coordr,* Maida Goodwin; Tel: 413-585-2996, E-mail: mgoodwin@email.smith.edu; *Curator,* Amy Hague; Tel: 413-585-2977, E-mail: ahague@email.smith.edu; *Coll Develop Spec,* Joyce Follet; Tel: 413-585-2979, E-mail: jfollett@email.smith.edu; *Accessioning Archivist,* Burd Schlessinger; Tel: 413-585-4884, E-mail: bschless@email.smith.edu; *Digital Serv Archivist,* Margaret Jessup; Tel: 413-585-2985, E-mail: mjessup@email.smith.edu; *Ref Archivist,* Susan Boone; Tel: 413-585-2974, E-mail: sboone@email.smith.edu; *Ref Archivist,* Karen Kukil; Tel: 413-585-2988, E-mail: kkukil@email.smith.edu; Staff 7 (MLS 3, Non-MLS 4)
Founded 1942
Library Holdings: Per Subs 950
Special Collections: 19th & 20th Century Social Reform Movements (Steinem, Timpson, etc); Birth Control (Margaret Sanger, Planned Parenthood), mss; Suffrage & Peace, mss; United States 19th Century Social, Economic & Political Reforms (Garrison & Ames Family Papers), mss; Women in Industry (Mary van Kleeck Papers), mss; YWCA of the USA Records. Oral History
Subject Interests: Birth control, Feminism, Reform movements, Women's hist
Publications: Imposing Evidence (Newsletter)

Open Mon, Tues, Thurs & Fri 10-5, Wed 1-9
Restriction: Non-circulating to the pub
ANITA O'K & ROBERT R YOUNG SCIENCE LIBRARY, Clark Science Center, Bass Hall, 01063, SAN 345-4746. Tel: 413-585-2950. FAX: 413-585-4480. Web Site: www.smith.edu/libraries/libs/young/. *Head Librn,* Rocco Piccinino; Tel: 413-585-2951, E-mail: rpiccini@email.smith.edu; *Circ Coordr,* Josephine Hernandez; Tel: 413-585-2881, E-mail: jhernand@email.smith.edu; Staff 1 (MLS 1)
Founded 1966
Library Holdings: Bks on Deafness & Sign Lang 100; Bk Titles 154,560; Per Subs 707
Special Collections: Maps, printed, mss, wall, raised relief & gazetteers
Subject Interests: Astronomy, Biol, Chem, Computer sci, Eng, Environ sci, Exercise, Geol, Hist of sci, Math, Physics, Psychol, Sci hist, Sports
Open Mon-Thurs (Fall-Spring) 7:45am-Midnight, Fri 7:45am-11pm, Sat 10am-11pm, Sun 10am-Midnight; Mon-Fri (Summer) 8-5, Sat 10-6

NORTHBOROUGH

P NORTHBOROUGH FREE LIBRARY*, 34 Main St, 01532-1942. SAN 307-5931. Tel: 508-393-5025. FAX: 508-393-5027. E-mail: library@town.northborough.ma.us. Web Site: www.northboroughlibrary.org/northborough. *Dir,* Jean M Langley; E-mail: jlangley@town.northborough.ma.us; *Ch,* Laura Brennan; E-mail: lbrennan@cwmars.org; *Ref Librn,* Deborah Hersh; E-mail: reference@northboroughlibrary.org; *Youth/Young Adult Librn,* Sandra Stafford; *Supvr, Circ,* Julie Brownlee; Staff 4.275 (MLS 4.275)
Founded 1868. Pop 14,632; Circ 224,073
Library Holdings: AV Mats 3,198; Bks on Deafness & Sign Lang 10; DVDs 3,745; e-books 9,778; Electronic Media & Resources 290; Microforms 16,017; Bk Vols 62,859; Per Subs 111
Automation Activity & Vendor Info: (Cataloging) Evergreen; (Circulation) Evergreen; (ILL) Evergreen; (OPAC) Evergreen
Database Vendor: EBSCO Auto Repair Reference, Facts on File, Gale Cengage Learning, Newsbank, Overdrive, Inc, ProQuest
Wireless access
Function: Adult bk club, Audiobks via web, Bk club(s), Bks on CD, Children's prog, Computers for patron use, Copy machines, E-Reserves, Electronic databases & coll, Free DVD rentals, Handicapped accessible, ILL available, Magnifiers for reading, Mail & tel request accepted, Mus passes, Music CDs, Online cat, Online searches, OverDrive digital audio bks, Photocopying/Printing, Preschool reading prog, Prog for adults, Prog for children & young adult, Pub access computers, Ref serv available, Ref serv in person, Spoken cassettes & CDs, Story hour, Summer reading prog, Tax forms, Teen prog, Telephone ref
Publications: Gale Forecast (Newsletter)
Mem of Massachusetts Libr Syst
Partic in Central & Western Massachusetts Automated Resource Sharing
Special Services for the Blind - Magnifiers; Talking bks
Open Mon 12-8:30, Tues & Wed 9:30-8:30, Thurs, Fri & Sat 9:30-5
Friends of the Library Group

NORTHFIELD

P DICKINSON MEMORIAL LIBRARY*, 115 Main St, 01360. SAN 307-5966. Tel: 413-498-2455. FAX: 413-498-5111. E-mail: dmemlib@cwmars.org. Web Site: www.mynorthfield.org. *Dir,* Deb Kern
Founded 1878. Pop 3,000; Circ 33,000
Library Holdings: Bk Vols 19,000; Per Subs 40
Automation Activity & Vendor Info: (Cataloging) Innovative Interfaces, Inc; (Circulation) Innovative Interfaces, Inc; (OPAC) Innovative Interfaces, Inc
Open Tues 1-8, Wed & Thurs 1-6, Fri 10-6, Sat 10-3
Friends of the Library Group

P FIELD LIBRARY*, 243 Millers Falls Rd, 01360. SAN 307-5974. Tel: 413-498-0220. *Librn,* Linda Chapin
Pop 457; Circ 1,950
Library Holdings: AV Mats 399; Bk Vols 9,448; Per Subs 60; Videos 66
Open Fri 4-8

NORTON

P NORTON PUBLIC LIBRARY*, L G & Mildred Balfour Memorial, 68 E Main St, 02766. SAN 307-5982. Tel: 508-285-0265. Interlibrary Loan Service Tel: 508-286-2695. Administration Tel: 508-286-2694. FAX: 508-285-0266. Web Site: www.nortonlibrary.org. *Libr Dir,* Lee Parker; *Circ Librn,* Molly Klenowski; *Info Serv Librn,* Amanda Viana; *Youth Serv Librn,* Leslianne Costello; Staff 14 (MLS 3, Non-MLS 11)
Founded 1886. Pop 18,036; Circ 116,000
Library Holdings: Bk Vols 54,246; Per Subs 137
Subject Interests: Local hist
Open Mon & Fri 10-5, Tues-Thurs 10-8, Sat 9-3
Friends of the Library Group

C WHEATON COLLEGE LIBRARY*, Madeleine Clark Wallace Library, 26 E Main St, 02766-2322. SAN 345-4770. Interlibrary Loan Service Tel: 508-286-3701. Web Site: wheatoncollege.edu/library/library-research/. *Assoc VPres, Libr & Info Serv,* Susan V Wawrzaszek; *Dir, Commun & Tech Serv,* Gloria Barker; Tel: 508-286-3723, E-mail: gbarker@wheatonma.edu; *Ser & Electronic Res Librn,* Jean Callaghan; Tel: 508-286-3715, E-mail: jcallagh@wheatonma.edu; *Coordr, Circ,* Mary Savolainen; Tel: 508-286-3708, E-mail: msavolai@wheatonma.edu; *ILL Coordr,* Kimberly A Guarino; Tel: 508-286-5821, E-mail: kguarino@wheatonma.edu; *Col Archivist/Spec Coll Curator,* Zephorene L Stickney; Tel: 508-286-3712, E-mail: zstickne@wheatonma.edu; *Cataloger,* Deryl Freeman; Staff 8 (MLS 8)
Founded 1840. Enrl 1,572; Fac 152; Highest Degree: Bachelor
Special Collections: History of Women; Lucy Larcom Coll; Wheaton Family Coll
Automation Activity & Vendor Info: (Acquisitions) Innovative Interfaces, Inc; (Cataloging) Innovative Interfaces, Inc; (Circulation) Innovative Interfaces, Inc; (Course Reserve) Docutek; (ILL) Clio; (OPAC) Innovative Interfaces, Inc; (Serials) Innovative Interfaces, Inc
Database Vendor: ABC-CLIO, ACM (Association for Computing Machinery), American Chemical Society, Annual Reviews, ARTstor, BioOne, Blackwell, Cambridge Scientific Abstracts, CQ Press, Dialog, ebrary, EBSCOhost, Elsevier, Facts on File, Gale Cengage Learning, Haworth Pres Inc, JSTOR, LexisNexis, Nature Publishing Group, OCLC FirstSearch, OCLC WorldShare Interlibrary Loan, OCLC-RLG, OVID Technologies, ProQuest, PubMed, ScienceDirect, SerialsSolutions, Springer-Verlag, Swets Information Services, Wiley, Wilson - Wilson Web
Wireless access
Function: Audio & video playback equip for onsite use, Computers for patron use, Copy machines, E-Reserves, Electronic databases & coll, Equip loans & repairs, Handicapped accessible, ILL available, Magnifiers for reading, Online cat, Online ref, Online searches, Pub access computers, Ref serv in person
Partic in Helin; Northeast Research Libraries Consortium (NERL)
Special Services for the Blind - Bks on cassette; Closed circuit TV magnifier; Reader equip
Open Mon-Thurs 8am-2am, Fri 8am-10pm, Sat 10-10, Sun 10am-2am
Restriction: Open to fac, students & qualified researchers, Pub use on premises

NORWELL

SR FIRST PARISH CHURCH OF NORWELL*, The James Library Center for the Arts, 24 West St, 02061. (Mail add: PO Box 164, 02061). Tel: 781-659-7100. E-mail: jameslibrary@verizon.net. Web Site: jameslibrary.org. *Dir,* Caroline D Chapin; Staff 1 (MLS 1)
Founded 1874
Library Holdings: Bk Titles 20,000
Special Collections: First Parish Church, Norwell; Local History; North River Ship Building
Mem of Massachusetts Libr Syst
Open Tues-Fri 1-5, Sat (Sept-June) 10-1
Friends of the Library Group

P NORWELL PUBLIC LIBRARY*, 64 South St, 02061-2433. SAN 321-0812. Tel: 781-659-2015. FAX: 781-659-6755. E-mail: noref@ocln.org. Web Site: www.norwellpubliclibrary.org. *Dir,* Rebecca Freer; E-mail: rfreer@ocln.org; *Ad,* Jeanne Ryer; E-mail: jryer@ocln.org; *Tech Serv Librn,* Barbara Sullivan; E-mail: bsullivan@ocln.org; *Ch Serv,* Nancy Perry; E-mail: nperry@ocln.org; Staff 7 (MLS 4, Non-MLS 3)
Pop 10,166; Circ 127,569
Library Holdings: Bk Vols 62,000; Per Subs 115
Automation Activity & Vendor Info: (Acquisitions) SirsiDynix; (Cataloging) SirsiDynix; (Circulation) SirsiDynix
Database Vendor: infoUSA, LearningExpress, Overdrive, Inc, ReferenceUSA
Wireless access
Function: Accelerated reader prog, Adult bk club, Audiobks via web, Bk club(s), Bks on CD, Children's prog, Computer training, Computers for patron use, Copy machines, E-Reserves, Electronic databases & coll, Exhibits, Fax serv, Free DVD rentals, Games & aids for the handicapped, Holiday prog, Home delivery & serv to Sr ctr & nursing homes, Homebound delivery serv, Homework prog, ILL available, Instruction & testing, Large print keyboards, Magnifiers for reading, Mail & tel request accepted, Mus passes, Music CDs, Notary serv, Online cat, Orientations, Outreach serv, Photocopying/Printing, Preschool outreach, Prof lending libr, Prog for adults, Prog for children & young adult, Pub access computers, Ref serv available, Ref serv in person, Senior computer classes, Spoken cassettes & CDs, Spoken cassettes & DVDs, Story hour, Summer reading prog, Tax forms, Teen prog, VHS videos, Video lending libr, Workshops, Writing prog
Mem of Massachusetts Libr Syst
Partic in Old Colony Libr Network (OCLN)
Open Mon 10-8, Tues & Wed Noon-8, Thurs & Fri 10-5, Sat 10-3
Friends of the Library Group

S SOUTH SHORE NATURAL SCIENCE CENTER*, Vinal Library, 48 Jacob's Lane, 02061-1149. (Mail add: PO Box 429, 02061-0429), SAN 371-7259. Tel: 781-659-2559. FAX: 781-659-5924. Web Site: www.ssnsc.org. *Exec Dir,* Debbie Edelstein
Founded 1976
Library Holdings: Bk Titles 600
Special Collections: William Gould Vinal Coll
Subject Interests: Natural sci

NORWOOD

S FM GLOBAL*, Technical Information Center, 1151 Boston-Providence Tpk, 02062. SAN 307-6008. Tel: 781-762-4300. FAX: 781-762-9375. Web Site: www.fmglobal.com. *Librn, Mgr,* Janet B Green; E-mail: janet.green@fmglobal.com; Staff 8 (MLS 3, Non-MLS 5)
Founded 1968
Library Holdings: DVDs 120; e-journals 78; Bk Titles 17,000; Per Subs 167; Videos 20
Special Collections: Corporate Historical Coll, docs, rare bks, visual mats
Subject Interests: Eng, Fire res, Loss prevention
Automation Activity & Vendor Info: (Acquisitions) Inmagic, Inc.; (Cataloging) Inmagic, Inc.; (ILL) Inmagic, Inc.; (OPAC) Inmagic, Inc.; (Serials) Inmagic, Inc.
Database Vendor: Dialog, ScienceDirect
Function: Bus archives, Doc delivery serv, For res purposes, Govt ref serv, Res libr
Open Mon-Fri 8-4:30
Restriction: Access for corporate affiliates, Circulates for staff only, Co libr, Open to researchers by request, Restricted access

P MORRILL MEMORIAL LIBRARY*, 33 Walpole St, 02062-1206. (Mail add: PO Box 220, 02062-0220), SAN 345-486X. Tel: 781-769-0200. Circulation Tel: 781-769-0200, Ext 224. Reference Tel: 781-769-0200, Ext 223. Information Services Tel: 781-769-0200, Ext 111. FAX: 781-769-6083. E-mail: norwood@minlib.net. Web Site: www.norwoodlibrary.org. *Dir,* Charlotte Canelli; Tel: 781-769-0200, Ext 101, E-mail: ccanelli@minlib.net; *Adult Serv,* April Cushing; E-mail: acushing@minlib.net; *Ch Serv,* Kelly Unsworth; E-mail: kunsworth@minlib.net; *Literacy Serv,* Norma Logan; E-mail: nlogan@minlib.net; *Literacy Serv,* Bonnie Wyler; E-mail: bwyler@minlib.net; *Outreach Serv,* Nancy Ling; E-mail: nling@minlib.net; *Ref Serv,* Marie Lydon; E-mail: mlydon@minlib.net; *Tech Serv,* Diane Phillips; E-mail: dphillips@minlib.net; *Tech Serv,* Brian Samek; E-mail: bsamek@minlib.net; Staff 22 (MLS 10, Non-MLS 12)
Founded 1873. Pop 28,000; Circ 330,026
Library Holdings: AV Mats 12,176; Electronic Media & Resources 12,135; Bk Vols 98,916; Per Subs 1,064
Special Collections: Norwood Coll
Automation Activity & Vendor Info: (Acquisitions) Innovative Interfaces, Inc; (Cataloging) Innovative Interfaces, Inc; (Circulation) Innovative Interfaces, Inc; (ILL) Innovative Interfaces, Inc; (OPAC) Innovative Interfaces, Inc
Publications: Calendar (Monthly); New At Your Library
Partic in Minuteman Library Network
Special Services for the Blind - Computer with voice synthesizer for visually impaired persons
Open Mon-Thurs 9-9, Fri 10-5, Sat 9-5, Sun 2-5
Friends of the Library Group

OAK BLUFFS

P OAK BLUFFS PUBLIC LIBRARY, 56R School St, 02557. (Mail add: PO Box 2039, 02557-2039), SAN 307-6032. Tel: 508-693-9433. FAX: 508-693-5377. E-mail: oakbluffslibrary@gmail.com. Web Site: oakbluffslibrary.org. *Libr Dir,* Sondra Murphy; E-mail: smurphy@clamsnet.org; *Ch,* Zoe Pechter; *Circ Mgr,* Anna Marie D'Addarie; E-mail: adaddarie@clamsnet.org; Staff 3 (MLS 3)
Founded 1906. Pop 3,713; Circ 110,934
Library Holdings: CDs 1,682; Bk Vols 26,052; Per Subs 80; Videos 4,518
Automation Activity & Vendor Info: (Acquisitions) Innovative Interfaces, Inc - Millenium; (Cataloging) Innovative Interfaces, Inc - Millenium; (Circulation) Innovative Interfaces, Inc - Millenium; (ILL) Innovative Interfaces, Inc - Millenium; (OPAC) Innovative Interfaces, Inc
Database Vendor: EBSCOhost, ProQuest
Wireless access
Partic in Cape Libraries Automated Materials Sharing Network
Open Tues & Thurs 10-8, Wed & Fri 10-5, Sat 10-4
Friends of the Library Group

OAKHAM

P FOBES MEMORIAL LIBRARY*, Four Maple St, 01068. SAN 307-6040. Tel: 508-882-3372. FAX: 508-882-3372. *Librn,* Maude M Stone; *Asst Librn,* Sharon Lirocco
Pop 1,079; Circ 14,000
Library Holdings: Bk Vols 15,885; Per Subs 20
Mem of Massachusetts Libr Syst
Open Tues & Thurs 10-4:30 & 7-9, Sat 9-11
Friends of the Library Group

ORANGE

P WHEELER MEMORIAL LIBRARY*, 49 E Main St, 01364-1267. SAN 307-6067. Tel: 978-544-2495. FAX: 978-544-1116. Web Site: www.orangelib.org. *Dir,* Walt Owens; Tel: 978-544-2495, Ext 101, E-mail: wowens@cwmars.org; *Br Librn, Tech Serv,* Dianne Salcedo; *Coordr, ILL,* Candace Curran; Staff 6 (MLS 1, Non-MLS 5)
Founded 1847. Pop 7,312; Circ 43,820
Library Holdings: Bk Vols 42,698; Per Subs 30
Special Collections: Local History Coll
Automation Activity & Vendor Info: (Cataloging) Innovative Interfaces, Inc; (Circulation) Innovative Interfaces, Inc; (OPAC) Innovative Interfaces, Inc
Partic in Central & Western Massachusetts Automated Resource Sharing
Open Mon & Tues 10-6, Wed & Thurs 1-8, Sat 10-2
Friends of the Library Group

ORLEANS

P SNOW LIBRARY*, 67 Main St, 02653-2413. SAN 307-6075. Tel: 508-240-3760. FAX: 508-255-5701. Web Site: www.snowlibrary.org. *Dir,* Tavi Prugno; E-mail: tprugno@clamsnet.org; *Youth Serv,* Susan Kelley; Staff 2 (MLS 2)
Founded 1876. Pop 6,911; Circ 151,453
Library Holdings: AV Mats 2,058; Bk Vols 55,293; Per Subs 92; Talking Bks 2,401
Special Collections: H K Cummings Coll of Historical Photographs (1870-1900's)
Automation Activity & Vendor Info: (Acquisitions) Innovative Interfaces, Inc; (Cataloging) Innovative Interfaces, Inc; (Circulation) Innovative Interfaces, Inc; (ILL) Innovative Interfaces, Inc; (OPAC) Innovative Interfaces, Inc; (Serials) Innovative Interfaces, Inc
Partic in Cape Libraries Automated Materials Sharing Network
Open Mon, Thurs & Fri 10-5, Tues & Wed 10-8, Sat 10-4, Sun 2-4
Friends of the Library Group

OXFORD

P OXFORD FREE LIBRARY*, 339 Main St, 01540. SAN 345-4924. Tel: 508-987-6003. FAX: 508-987-3896. *Dir,* Timothy A Kelley; E-mail: tkelley@town.oxford.ma.us; *Asst Dir, Ref Serv,* Brenna Pomeroy; E-mail: bpomeroy@cwmars.org; Staff 12 (MLS 3, Non-MLS 9)
Founded 1903. Pop 13,100; Circ 125,322
Jul 2010-Jun 2011 Income $408,850, State $22,121, City $386,729. Mats Exp $72,200, Books $58,000, Per/Ser (Incl. Access Fees) $3,000, AV Mat $11,000, Presv $200. Sal $257,918 (Prof $58,968)
Library Holdings: AV Mats 4,221; Large Print Bks 555; Bk Vols 53,000; Per Subs 111; Talking Bks 1,084
Special Collections: Local History (Records to 1850)
Automation Activity & Vendor Info: (Circulation) Innovative Interfaces, Inc
Wireless access
Mem of Massachusetts Libr Syst
Partic in Central & Western Massachusetts Automated Resource Sharing
Special Services for the Blind - Computer with voice synthesizer for visually impaired persons; Reader equip
Friends of the Library Group

PALMER

P PALMER PUBLIC LIBRARY*, 1455 N Main St, 01069. SAN 307-6091. Tel: 413-283-3330. FAX: 413-283-9970. Web Site: www.palmer.lib.ma.us. *Dir,* Dorene Miller; E-mail: director@palmer.lib.ma.us; *Asst Dir, Ref Serv,* Mary Bernat; E-mail: mbernat@palmer.lib.ma.us; *Borrower Serv Librn,* Michelle Soares; E-mail: msoares@palmer.lib.ma.us; *Coll Develop Librn,* Helene O'Connor; E-mail: hoconner@palmer.lib.ma.us; *Outreach Serv Librn,* Sandra Burke; E-mail: sburke@palmer.lib.ma.us; *YA Librn,* Matthew DeCara; E-mail: mdecara@palmer.lib.ma.us; *Youth Serv Librn,* Stephanie Maher; E-mail: smaher@palmer.lib.ma.us; *Cataloger,* Amy Golenski; E-mail: agolenski@palmer.lib.ma.us
Founded 1878. Pop 12,112; Circ 201,398
Library Holdings: Bk Vols 111,245
Special Collections: Palmer Coll; Palmer Journal-Register
Subject Interests: Genealogy, Local hist
Automation Activity & Vendor Info: (Acquisitions) Evergreen; (Cataloging) Evergreen; (Circulation) Evergreen; (ILL) Evergreen; (OPAC) Evergreen
Wireless access
Partic in Central-Western Mass Automated Resource Sharing
Special Services for the Deaf - TTY equip

Open Mon 10-5, Tues-Thurs 10-8, Fri & Sat 10-2
Friends of the Library Group

PAXTON

CR ANNA MARIA COLLEGE*, Mondor-Eagen Library, 50 Sunset Lane, 01612-1198. SAN 307-6105. Tel: 508-849-3405, Interlibrary Loan Service Tel: 508-849-3407. Reference Tel: 508-849-3473. FAX: 508-849-3408. Web Site: www.annamaria.edu/library/index.php. *Dir, Libr Serv,* Ruth Pyne; Tel: 508-849-3406, E-mail: rpyne@annamaria.edu; Staff 6 (MLS 3, Non-MLS 3)
Founded 1946. Enrl 933; Fac 165; Highest Degree: Master
Library Holdings: Bk Vols 75,000; Per Subs 290
Subject Interests: Art, Bus, Criminal justice, Educ, English lit, Music, Psychol, Relig, Sociol
Automation Activity & Vendor Info: (Acquisitions) Innovative Interfaces, Inc - Millenium; (Cataloging) Innovative Interfaces, Inc - Millenium; (Circulation) Innovative Interfaces, Inc - Millenium; (OPAC) Innovative Interfaces, Inc; (Serials) Innovative Interfaces, Inc - Millenium
Database Vendor: Facts on File, Gale Cengage Learning, JSTOR, LexisNexis, Modern Language Association, OCLC FirstSearch, OVID Technologies, ValueLine
Wireless access
Function: Ref serv available
Publications: Introduction to the Library; Library Guides
Mem of Massachusetts Libr Syst
Partic in Central & Western Massachusetts Automated Resource Sharing; Lyrasis
Open Mon-Thurs 8am-11pm, Fri 8-4:30, Sat 12-5, Sun 1-11

P RICHARDS MEMORIAL LIBRARY*, 44 Richards Ave, 01612. SAN 307-6113. Tel: 508-754-0793. FAX: 508-754-0793. Web Site: www.rmlpaxton.org. *Librn,* Deborah Bailey; E-mail: dbailey@cwmars.org; Staff 1 (Non-MLS 1)
Founded 1926. Pop 4,400; Circ 51,000
Library Holdings: Bk Vols 25,795; Per Subs 70
Automation Activity & Vendor Info: (Cataloging) Follett Software; (Circulation) Follett Software
Function: Computers for patron use
Partic in Central-Western Mass Automated Resource Sharing; SAILS Library Network
Open Tues & Thurs (Winter) 1-8, Wed & Fri 9-12 & 1-5, Sat 10-4; Tues & Thurs (Summer) 1-8, Wed & Fri 9-12 & 1-5
Friends of the Library Group

PEABODY

S PEABODY HISTORICAL SOCIETY & MUSEUM*, Library & Archives, 35 Washington St, 01960-5520. SAN 329-8892. Tel: 978-531-0805. FAX: 978-531-7292. Web Site: www.peabodyhistorical.org. *Pres,* William R Power; *Librn,* Daniel Doucette
Founded 1896
Library Holdings: Bk Titles 420
Special Collections: Historical Documents
Subject Interests: Genealogy
Open Tues 7pm-9pm, Wed 1-4

P PEABODY INSTITUTE LIBRARY*, 82 Main St, 01960-5592. SAN 345-4983. Tel: 978-531-0100. FAX: 978-532-1797. Web Site: www.peabodylibrary.org. *Dir,* Martha H Holden; E-mail: holden@noblenet.org; *Asst Dir,* Gerri Guyote; *Adult Serv,* Kelley Rae Unger; *Ref,* Gwendolyn Charter; Staff 55 (MLS 6, Non-MLS 49)
Founded 1852. Pop 48,000; Circ 251,665
Jul 2005-Jun 2006 Income (Main Library and Branch(s)) $1,429,748, State $56,000, City $1,342,294, Federal $7,100, Parent Institution $24,354. Mats Exp $200,000. Sal $1,045,000 (Prof $808,000)
Library Holdings: Bk Vols 162,703; Per Subs 331
Wireless access
Publications: Annual Report; Library News (Monthly); Special Pamphlets
Partic in North of Boston Library Exchange, Inc
Special Services for the Blind - Reader equip
Friends of the Library Group
Branches: 2
SOUTH, 78 Lynn St, 01960, SAN 345-5017. Tel: 978-531-3380. FAX: 978-531-9113. E-mail: sbl@noblenet.org. *Librn,* Renee Wood
Library Holdings: Bk Vols 22,277
Friends of the Library Group
WEST, 603 Lowell St, 01960, SAN 345-5041. Tel: 978-535-3354. FAX: 978-535-0147. *Librn,* Kathy Walsh
Library Holdings: Bk Vols 24,143
Open Mon & Wed 9-6, Tues & Thurs 12-9, Sat 9-5
Friends of the Library Group

PELHAM

P PELHAM LIBRARY*, Two S Valley Rd, 01002. SAN 307-6121. Tel: 413-253-0657. FAX: 413-253-0594. E-mail: pelhamlibrary@arps.org. Web Site: www.pelham-library.org. *Dir,* Adam Novitt; *Asst Dir,* Ashley Rodkey; *Librn,* Sally Goldin; *Archivist,* Robert Lord Keyes; *Ch Serv,* Jodi Levine; *Circ,* Betty Hawley. Subject Specialists: *City hist, Genealogy,* Robert Lord Keyes; Staff 4 (MLS 1, Non-MLS 3)
Founded 1893. Pop 1,403; Circ 4,876
Jul 2006-Jun 2007 Income $55,000, State $4,500, City $43,310. Mats Exp $10,400, Books $9,000, Per/Ser (Incl. Access Fees) $1,400
Library Holdings: AV Mats 3,000; Bk Vols 29,000; Per Subs 76
Special Collections: Local Historical Books & Pamphlets. Oral History
Database Vendor: Gale Cengage Learning, Newsbank
Wireless access
Function: Archival coll, AV serv, ILL available, Photocopying/Printing, Prog for children & young adult, Ref serv available, Summer reading prog, Telephone ref, Wheelchair accessible
Publications: Gneiss News (Newsletter)
Special Services for the Deaf - Bks on deafness & sign lang
Special Services for the Blind - Talking bks
Open Mon, Tues & Thurs 3-8, Wed 1-8, Fri 10-12, Sat 10-2
Friends of the Library Group

PEMBROKE

P PEMBROKE PUBLIC LIBRARY*, 142 Center St, 02359-2613. SAN 307-613X. Tel: 781-293-6771. FAX: 781-294-0742. Web Site: www.pembrokepubliclibrary.org. *Dir,* Deborah Wall; Tel: 781-293-6771, Ext 13; Staff 8 (MLS 2, Non-MLS 6)
Founded 1878. Pop 18,000; Circ 145,445
Library Holdings: Large Print Bks 8,540; Bk Vols 69,000; Per Subs 117; Talking Bks 22
Special Services for the Deaf - Closed caption videos
Special Services for the Blind - Bks & mags in Braille, on rec, tape & cassette; Bks available with recordings; Bks on cassette; Bks on CD; Talking bks
Open Mon-Thurs 10-8, Fri & Sat 10-5, Sun (Oct-May) 12-4
Friends of the Library Group

PEPPERELL

P LAWRENCE LIBRARY*, 15 Main St, 01463. SAN 307-6148. Tel: 978-433-0330. FAX: 978-433-0317. Web Site: lawrencelibrary.org. *Dir,* Debra Spratt; E-mail: dspratt@cwmars.org; *Asst Dir, Dir, Adult Serv,* Tina McEvoy; E-mail: tmcevoy@cwmars.org; *Circ,* Myra Lane; E-mail: mlane@cwmars.org; *Youth Serv,* Jo Ann Pierce; E-mail: jpierce@cwmars.org; Staff 3 (MLS 3)
Founded 1900. Pop 11,435; Circ 164,187
Library Holdings: AV Mats 2,775; Bks on Deafness & Sign Lang 15; Large Print Bks 600; Bk Vols 44,354; Per Subs 137; Talking Bks 2,436
Subject Interests: Genealogy, Local hist
Automation Activity & Vendor Info: (Circulation) Innovative Interfaces, Inc
Database Vendor: Gale Cengage Learning
Publications: Clipboard - Friend of the Library (Newsletter)
Mem of Massachusetts Libr Syst
Partic in Central & Western Massachusetts Automated Resource Sharing
Open Tues-Thurs 10-8, Fri 10-5, Sat 10-4
Friends of the Library Group

PERU

P PERU LIBRARY INC, Six W Main Rd, 01235-9254. (Mail add: PO Box 1190, Hinsdale, 01235-1190), SAN 376-7531. Tel: 413-655-8650. E-mail: perulibrary@gmail.com. *Dir,* Ruth Calaycay
Library Holdings: Bk Vols 3,800; Talking Bks 100; Videos 1,250
Wireless access
Open Wed 1-7, Sat 9-1

PETERSHAM

P PETERSHAM MEMORIAL LIBRARY*, 23 Common St, 01366. SAN 307-6172. Tel: 978-724-3405. FAX: 978-724-0089. Web Site: www.petershamlibrary.net. *Dir,* Jayne Arata; *Asst Dir,* Jeanne Forand; Staff 2 (MLS 1, Non-MLS 1)
Founded 1890. Pop 1,100; Circ 9,170
Library Holdings: DVDs 218; Bk Titles 12,000; Per Subs 42; Videos 535
Subject Interests: Local hist
Automation Activity & Vendor Info: (Circulation) Innovative Interfaces, Inc; (ILL) Innovative Interfaces, Inc; (OPAC) Innovative Interfaces, Inc
Mem of Massachusetts Libr Syst
Partic in Central & Western Massachusetts Automated Resource Sharing
Open Tues 10-5, Wed 2-7, Fri 2-5, Sat 9-1

PHILLIPSTON

P PHILLIPS FREE PUBLIC LIBRARY*, 25 Templeton Rd, 01331-9704. SAN 307-6180. Tel: 978-249-1734. FAX: 978-249-3356. E-mail: Phillipstonlibrary@comcast.net. Web Site: www.phillipstonlibrary.org. *Dir,* Jacqueline Prime
Pop 962; Circ 6,325
Library Holdings: Bk Vols 9,000
Mem of Massachusetts Libr Syst
Open Mon 5-8, Tues 9-2, Sat 9-11
Friends of the Library Group

PITTSFIELD

P BERKSHIRE ATHENAEUM*, Pittsfield's Public Library, One Wendell Ave, 01201-6385. SAN 345-5076. Tel: 413-499-9480. Circulation Tel: 413-399-9480, Ext 201. Reference Tel: 413-499-9480, Ext 202. Administration Tel: 413-499-9480, Ext 205. FAX: 413-499-9489. E-mail: pittsref@cwmars.org. Web Site: www.pittsfieldlibrary.org. *Dir,* Ronald B Latham; E-mail: rlatham@cwmars.org; *Tech Serv Supvr,* Alex Reczkowski; Tel: 413-499-9480, Ext 115, E-mail: areczkowski@cwmars.org; *Ch Serv,* Joanne Pearson; E-mail: jpearson@cwmars.org; *Circ,* Catherine Congelosi; E-mail: ccongelo@cwmars.org; *Ref,* Madeline Kelly; E-mail: mkelly@cwmars.org; Staff 9 (MLS 9)
Founded 1871. Pop 46,437; Circ 275,000
Library Holdings: Bk Vols 219,993; Per Subs 1,233
Special Collections: Berkshire Authors Room; Herman Melville Memorial Room; Morgan Ballet Coll
Subject Interests: Genealogy
Automation Activity & Vendor Info: (Cataloging) Evergreen; (Circulation) Evergreen; (OPAC) Evergreen
Wireless access
Partic in Central & Western Massachusetts Automated Resource Sharing
Open Mon & Fri (Winter) 9-5, Tues-Thurs 9-9, Sat 10-5; Mon, Wed & Fri (Summer) 9-5, Tues & Thurs 9-9, Sat 10-5
Friends of the Library Group

J BERKSHIRE COMMUNITY COLLEGE*, Jonathan Edwards Library, 1350 West St, 01201. SAN 307-6199. Tel: 413-236-2150. FAX: 413-448-2700. Web Site: www.berkshirecc.edu/library/index.html. *Dir,* Nancy A Walker; Tel: 413-236-2151, E-mail: nwalker@berkshirecc.edu; *Coordr, Libr Serv,* Karen Carreras-Hubbard; Tel: 413-236-2153, E-mail: khubbard@berkshirecc.edu; Staff 1 (MLS 1)
Founded 1960. Enrl 1,551; Fac 100
Library Holdings: Bk Vols 58,400; Per Subs 350
Subject Interests: Art, Environ studies, Soc sci & issues
Automation Activity & Vendor Info: (Acquisitions) Innovative Interfaces, Inc; (Cataloging) Innovative Interfaces, Inc; (Circulation) Innovative Interfaces, Inc
Open Mon-Thurs 8-8, Fri 8-4

M BERKSHIRE MEDICAL CENTER*, Health Science Library, 725 North St, 01201. SAN 307-6202. Tel: 413-447-2734. *Librn,* Martha Prescott; *Libr Tech,* Kathy Gordon; Staff 2 (MLS 1, Non-MLS 1)
Founded 1968
Library Holdings: Bk Titles 1,500; Bk Vols 1,800; Per Subs 165
Subject Interests: Med
Wireless access
Partic in Basic Health Sciences Library Network; Cooperating Libraries of Greater Springfield; Western Mass Health Info Consortium
Open Mon-Fri 9-3

L MASSACHUSETTS TRIAL COURT*, Berkshire Law Library, Court House, 76 East St, 01201. SAN 324-346X. Tel: 413-442-5059. FAX: 413-448-2474. E-mail: berkshirelawlib@hotmail.com. Web Site: www.lawlib.state.ma.us. *Head Librn,* Barbara D Schneider; *Librn,* Gary Smith; Staff 2 (MLS 2)
Founded 1842
Library Holdings: Bk Titles 10,000; Per Subs 40
Subject Interests: Law for layman, Mass legal mat
Automation Activity & Vendor Info: (Cataloging) OCLC Connexion; (Circulation) Horizon; (OPAC) Horizon
Database Vendor: LexisNexis, Westlaw
Wireless access
Open Mon-Fri 8:30-4:30

PLAINFIELD

P SHAW MEMORIAL LIBRARY, 312 Main St, 01070-9709. SAN 307-6245. Tel: 413-634-5406. FAX: 413-634-5683. E-mail: plainfieldsml@gmail.com. *Librn,* Denise Sessions
Founded 1926. Pop 609; Circ 9,000
Library Holdings: Bk Titles 9,000; Per Subs 14
Wireless access
Open Tues 2-8, Thurs 6-8, Sat 9-12
Friends of the Library Group

PLAINVILLE

P PLAINVILLE PUBLIC LIBRARY, 198 South St, 02762-1512. SAN 307-6253. Tel: 508-695-1784. FAX: 508-695-6359. E-mail: info@plainvillepubliclibrary.org. Web Site: www.plainvillepubliclibrary.org. *Dir,* Melissa M Campbell; E-mail: mcampbel@sailsinc.org; *Head, Circ,* Paul Cutler; *Ch,* Position Currently Open; *Tech Serv,* Keely Penny; Staff 4.5 (MLS 1, Non-MLS 3.5)
Pop 8,200; Circ 85,000
Jul 2011-Jun 2012 Income $201,608, State $12,500, City $183,108, Locally Generated Income $6,000. Mats Exp $39,600, Books $26,000, Per/Ser (Incl. Access Fees) $2,600, Other Print Mats $2,000, AV Mat $9,000
Library Holdings: AV Mats 4,900; Bk Vols 33,376; Per Subs 74; Talking Bks 2,000
Wireless access
Function: Free DVD rentals
Open Mon 1-8, Tues 10-5, Wed 10-8, Thurs & Sat 10-2
Friends of the Library Group

PLYMOUTH

S GENERAL SOCIETY OF MAYFLOWER DESCENDANTS, Mayflower Society Library, Four Winslow St, 02360. (Mail add: PO Box 3297, 02361-3297), SAN 373-1669. Tel: 508-746-3188. FAX: 508-746-2488. E-mail: library@themayflowersociety.org. Web Site: www.themayflowersociety.org/library.htm. *Librn/Head, Ref Coll Develop,* Carolyn Freeman Travers. Subject Specialists: *Genealogy, Hist,* Carolyn Freeman Travers; Staff 5 (MLS 1, Non-MLS 4)
Founded 1897
Library Holdings: Bk Titles 2,500; Bk Vols 3,400; Per Subs 70
Special Collections: Pilgrims Coll
Subject Interests: Genealogy, Hist, Massachusetts
Wireless access
Open Mon-Fri 10-3:30
Restriction: Non-circulating to the pub

M JORDAN HOSPITAL*, Daryl A Lima Memorial Library, 275 Sandwich St, 02360. SAN 377-9319. Tel: 508-830-2157. FAX: 508-830-2887. *Librn,* Marian A De la Cour; E-mail: mdelacour@jordanhospital.org; Staff 1 (MLS 1)
Library Holdings: Bk Titles 100; Per Subs 84
Function: Telephone ref
Partic in Massachusetts Health Sciences Libraries Network; National Network of Libraries of Medicine; North Atlantic Health Sciences Libraries, Inc; Southeastern Massachusetts Consortium of Health Science Libraries
Restriction: Non-circulating

S PILGRIM SOCIETY*, Pilgrim Hall Museum, 75 Court St, 02360-3891. SAN 307-6261. Tel: 508-746-1620. FAX: 508-746-3396. Web Site: www.pilgrimhall.org/library.htm. *Dir,* Ann Berry; E-mail: director@pilgrimhall.org; Staff 8 (MLS 1, Non-MLS 7)
Founded 1820
Library Holdings: Bk Titles 6,000
Special Collections: Manuscript Coll; Plymouth, Massachusetts & Pilgrim History Coll
Subject Interests: Decorative art, Hist
Publications: Pilgrim Society News
Restriction: Open by appt only

S PLIMOTH PLANTATION*, Research Library, 137 Warren Ave, 02360-2436. (Mail add: PO Box 1620, 02362-1620), SAN 327-3199. Tel: 508-746-1622, Ext 8379. FAX: 508-746-4978. Web Site: www.plimoth.org. *Curator of Coll & Libr,* Karin J Goldstein; E-mail: kgoldstein@plimoth.org
Founded 1968
Library Holdings: e-journals 1; Bk Titles 6,000; Bk Vols 6,400; Per Subs 50
Subject Interests: 17th Century hist
Wireless access
Function: Res libr
Restriction: Non-circulating, Open by appt only

P PLYMOUTH PUBLIC LIBRARY*, 132 South St, 02360-3309. SAN 345-522X. Tel: 508-830-4250. FAX: 508-830-4258. TDD: 508-747-5882. Web Site: www.plymouthpubliclibrary.org. *Dir,* Dinah L O'Brien; E-mail: do'brien@townhall.plymouth.ma.us; *Asst Dir,* Jennifer Harris; E-mail: jharris@townhall.plymouth.ma.us; *Br Librn,* Jessica Connelly; *Outreach Serv Librn,* Sharon LaRosa; E-mail: slarosa@ocln.org; *Ref Librn,* M Lee Regan; *Circ Supvr,* Linda Fitzgerald; *Literacy Coordr,* Jeanne Annino; Tel: 508-830-4260, E-mail: plymouthlit@comcast.net; *Ch Serv,* Margaret

McGrath; E-mail: mcgrathm13@yahoo.com; *Tech Serv,* Danielle Savin; Staff 31 (MLS 9, Non-MLS 22)
Founded 1857. Pop 56,000; Circ 392,739
Jul 2007-Jun 2008 Income (Main Library and Branch(s)) $1,637,507, State $138,759, City $1,417,151, Locally Generated Income $31,597, Other $50,000. Mats Exp $213,646, Books $137,249, Per/Ser (Incl. Access Fees) $19,623, Other Print Mats $19,737, AV Mat $24,840, Electronic Ref Mat (Incl. Access Fees) $12,197. Sal $1,060,380
Library Holdings: Audiobooks 1,083; AV Mats 415; CDs 9,726; e-books 2; Microforms 114,863; Bk Titles 271,866; Bk Vols 135,748; Per Subs 294; Videos 10,814
Special Collections: Irish Coll; Plymouth Coll
Subject Interests: Genealogy
Automation Activity & Vendor Info: (Acquisitions) SirsiDynix; (Cataloging) SirsiDynix; (Circulation) SirsiDynix; (ILL) SirsiDynix; (OPAC) SirsiDynix
Database Vendor: Baker & Taylor
Wireless access
Function: Adult literacy prog
Publications: Connections
Partic in Old Colony Libr Network (OCLN)
Special Services for the Deaf - Assisted listening device; TTY equip
Special Services for the Blind - Talking bk serv referral
Open Mon-Wed 10-9, Thurs 10-6, Fri & Sat 10-5:30, Sun 12:30-5
Branches: 1
MANOMET BRANCH, 12 Strand Ave, Manomet, 02345. (Mail add: PO Box 1035, Manomet, 02345-1035), SAN 345-5254. Tel: 508-830-4185. E-mail: plmlib@ocln.org, Web Site: www.plymouthpubliclibrary.org/manometbranch.htm. *Librn,* Jessica Connelly; *Youth Serv Librn,* Jennifer Jones
Open Mon & Thurs 9-9, Wed & Sat 9-5
Friends of the Library Group

PLYMPTON

P PLYMPTON PUBLIC LIBRARY*, 248 Main St, 02367-1114. SAN 307-627X. Tel: 781-585-4551. FAX: 781-585-7660. Web Site: www.plymptonlibrary.org. *Dir,* Debra L Batson; E mail: dbatson@sailsinc.org; Staff 1.75 (Non MLS 1.75)
Founded 1894. Pop 2,800; Circ 20,450
Library Holdings: Bk Vols 24,000; Per Subs 35
Automation Activity & Vendor Info: (Cataloging) SirsiDynix; (Circulation) SirsiDynix; (OPAC) SirsiDynix
Wireless access
Function: Adult bk club, Bks on CD, Story hour
Mem of Massachusetts Libr Syst
Partic in SAILS Library Network
Open Tues & Thurs 10-8, Sat 10-4

PRINCETON

P PRINCETON PUBLIC LIBRARY*, Two Town Hall Dr, 01541. SAN 307-6288. Tel: 978-464-2115. FAX: 978-464-2116. E-mail: library@town.princeton.ma.us. Web Site: www.princetonpubliclibrary.org. *Dir,* Wendy F Pape; E-mail: wpape@cwmars.org; Staff 5 (Non-MLS 5)
Founded 1884. Pop 3,700; Circ 33,956
Jun 2011-Jul 2012 Income $170,842, State $3,000, City $151,842, Locally Generated Income $12,000, Other $4,000. Mats Exp $33,060, Books $22,000, Per/Ser (Incl. Access Fees) $2,160, AV Mat $8,900. Sal $97,985
Library Holdings: AV Mats 1,184; CDs 5; DVDs 1,314; e-books 4,318; Electronic Media & Resources 2,460; Bk Vols 16,601; Per Subs 68
Subject Interests: Arts, Cookery, Gardening, Hist
Automation Activity & Vendor Info: (Acquisitions) Innovative Interfaces, Inc; (Cataloging) Innovative Interfaces, Inc; (Circulation) Innovative Interfaces, Inc - Millenium
Database Vendor: Facts on File, Gale Cengage Learning, Newsbank, OCLC WorldShare Interlibrary Loan, ProQuest, World Book Online
Wireless access
Function: Adult bk club, After school storytime, Bk club(s), Bks on cassette, Bks on CD, Children's prog, Computers for patron use, Copy machines, Electronic databases & coll, Fax serv, Free DVD rentals, Handicapped accessible, Holiday prog, Home delivery & serv to Sr ctr & nursing homes, Homebound delivery serv, ILL available, Mus passes, Music CDs, Online cat, OverDrive digital audio bks, Photocopying/Printing, Preschool outreach, Prog for adults, Prog for children & young adult, Pub access computers, Spoken cassettes & CDs, Story hour, Summer reading prog, VHS videos, Wheelchair accessible
Mem of Massachusetts Libr Syst
Open Tues & Thurs 10-8, Wed 10-5, Fri 12-5, Sat 10-3
Restriction: Authorized patrons
Friends of the Library Group

PROVINCETOWN

P PROVINCETOWN PUBLIC LIBRARY*, 356 Commercial St, 02657-2209. SAN 307-6296. Tel: 508-487-7094. FAX: 508-487-7096. Web Site: www.ptownlib.com. *Dir,* Cheryl Napsha; E-mail: cnapsha@provincetown-ma.gov; Staff 5 (MLS 2, Non-MLS 3)
Founded 1873. Pop 3,741; Circ 56,387
Library Holdings: AV Mats 3,495; Bks on Deafness & Sign Lang 20; Bk Vols 26,886; Per Subs 176
Subject Interests: Am art, Local hist, Modern art, Paintings
Automation Activity & Vendor Info: (Acquisitions) Innovative Interfaces, Inc; (Cataloging) Innovative Interfaces, Inc; (Circulation) Innovative Interfaces, Inc; (ILL) Innovative Interfaces, Inc; (OPAC) Innovative Interfaces, Inc; (Serials) Innovative Interfaces, Inc
Mem of Massachusetts Libr Syst
Partic in Cape Libraries Automated Materials Sharing Network
Special Services for the Blind - Closed circuit TV
Open Mon & Fri 10-5, Tues & Thurs Noon-8, Wed 10-8, Sat 10-2, Sun 1-5
Friends of the Library Group

QUINCY

P THOMAS CRANE PUBLIC LIBRARY*, 40 Washington St, 02269-9164. SAN 345-5289. Tel: 617-376-1300. Circulation Tel: 617-376-1301. Interlibrary Loan Service Tel: 617-376-1319. Reference Tel: 617-376-1316. FAX: 617-376-1313. TDD: 617-689-8324. E-mail: quref@ocln.org. Web Site: thomascranelibrary.org. *Asst Dir,* Megan Allen; Tel: 617-376-1331, E-mail: mallen@ocln.org; *Syst Librn,* Deborah Rich; E-mail: drich@ocln.org; *Acq,* Rita Seegraber; Tel: 617-376-1306, Fax: 617-376-1438, E-mail: ritas@ocln.org; *Ch Serv,* Julie M Rines; Tel: 617-376-1332, E-mail: jrines@ocln.org; *Circ,* Will Adamczyk; E-mail: wadamczyk@ocln.org; *ILL,* James Jaquette; E-mail: jjaquett@ocln.org; *Ref Serv,* Linda Beeler; Tel: 617-376-1310, Fax: 617-376-1308, E-mail: lbeeler@ocln.org; Staff 28 (MLS 16, Non-MLS 12)
Founded 1871. Pop 92,271; Circ 737,906
Jul 2011-Jun 2012 Income (Main Library and Branch(s)) $2,507,222, State $97,958, City $2,361,811, Other $47,453. Mats Exp $324,149, Books $196,296, Per/Ser (Incl. Access Fees) $32,191, Other Print Mats $7,600, AV Mat $63,469, Electronic Ref Mat (Incl. Access Fees) $24,594. Sal $1,940,610
Library Holdings: Audiobooks 14,685; e-books 3,633; Electronic Media & Resources 1,936; Microforms 8,089; Bk Vols 240,159; Per Subs 442; Videos 16,189
Subject Interests: Art, Local hist
Automation Activity & Vendor Info: (Acquisitions) SirsiDynix; (Cataloging) SirsiDynix; (Circulation) SirsiDynix; (ILL) SirsiDynix; (OPAC) SirsiDynix; (Serials) SirsiDynix
Wireless access
Mem of Massachusetts Libr Syst
Partic in OCLC Online Computer Library Center, Inc; Old Colony Libr Network (OCLN)
Special Services for the Deaf - TDD equip
Special Services for the Blind - Assistive/Adapted tech devices, equip & products
Open Mon-Thurs 9-9, Fri & Sat 9-5, Sun 1-5
Friends of the Library Group
Branches: 3
ADAMS SHORE BRANCH, 519 Sea St, 02169, SAN 345-5319. Tel: 617-376-1325, 617-376-1326. FAX: 617-376-1437. E-mail: quacirc@ocln.org. *Ch Serv, Librn,* Lori Seegraber; Staff 2 (MLS 1, Non-MLS 1)
Founded 1970. Circ 34,354
NORTH QUINCY BRANCH, 381 Hancock St, 02171, SAN 345-5408. Tel: 617-376-1320, 617-376-1321. FAX: 617-376-1432. E-mail: quncirc@ocln.org. *Librn,* Jessie Thuma; Staff 2 (MLS 1, Non-MLS 1)
Founded 1963. Circ 53,277
WOLLASTON BRANCH, 41 Beale St, 02170, SAN 345-5491. Tel: 617-376-1330. FAX: 617-376-1430. E-mail: quwcirc@ocln.org. *Librn,* Barbara Glod; Staff 2 (Non-MLS 2)
Founded 1923. Circ 29,452

C EASTERN NAZARENE COLLEGE*, Nease Library, 23 E Elm Ave, 02170. SAN 307-8159. Tel: 617-745-3850. FAX: 617-745-3913. Web Site: library.enc.edu. *Dir,* Susan J Watkins; *Acq,* Angela Gerica; *Circ,* Erin McCoy; *Info Serv,* Amy Hwang; *Instrul Res,* Joanna Taylor; *Tech Serv,* Terttu Savoie; Staff 5 (MLS 3, Non-MLS 2)
Enrl 862; Fac 57; Highest Degree: Master
Library Holdings: AV Mats 4,250; Bk Vols 137,000; Per Subs 500
Special Collections: Theology Coll
Automation Activity & Vendor Info: (Cataloging) SirsiDynix; (Circulation) SirsiDynix
Database Vendor: Gale Cengage Learning
Mem of Massachusetts Libr Syst

Partic in Lyrasis; OCLC Online Computer Library Center, Inc; Old Colony Libr Network (OCLN)
Open Mon-Thurs 7:30am-Midnight, Fri 7:30-5, Sat 10-8, Sun 2-10

S MARINE PRODUCTS LIBRARY*, Ten Furnace Brook Pkwy, 02169. SAN 307-1936. Tel: 617-268-0758. FAX: 617-472-9359. *Dir,* Edward J Iorio
Founded 1929
Library Holdings: Bk Titles 5,000; Per Subs 10
Subject Interests: Pharmaceuticals
Restriction: Staff use only

S NATIONAL FIRE PROTECTION ASSOCIATION, Charles S Morgan Technical Library, One Batterymarch Park, 02169-7471. SAN 307-2169. Tel: 617-984-7445. FAX: 617-984-7060. E-mail: library@nfpa.org. Web Site: www.nfpa.org/library. *Head Librn,* Mary Elizabeth Woodruff; *Librn, Rec Mgr,* Nicole Dutton; Tel: 617-984-7475, E-mail: ndutton@nfpa.org; *Archivist, Taxonomy Librn,* Jacob Ratliff; Tel: 617-984-7447, E-mail: jratliff@nfpa.org. Subject Specialists: *Taxonomy,* Jacob Ratliff; Staff 3 (MLS 3)
Founded 1945
Library Holdings: CDs 353; DVDs 100; e-books 3; Microforms 1,528; Bk Titles 14,270; Bk Vols 17,730; Per Subs 253; Videos 453
Special Collections: National Fire Codes, 1896-present; National Fire Protection Association Published Archives Coll; US Fire History (FIDO Coll)
Subject Interests: Codes & standards, Fires & fire protection, Safety
Automation Activity & Vendor Info: (Cataloging) Surpass; (OPAC) Surpass; (Serials) Surpass
Wireless access
Function: CD-ROM, Copy machines, Doc delivery serv, e-mail serv, ILL available, Online cat, Photocopying/Printing, Res libr, Scanner, VHS videos, Web-catalog, Wheelchair accessible
Mem of Massachusetts Libr Syst
Open Mon-Fri 8:30-4:30
Restriction: Circulates for staff only, Non-circulating coll, Open to pub for ref only

J QUINCY COLLEGE*, Anselmo Library, Newport Hall, Rm 103, 150 Newport Ave, 02171. (Mail add: 24 Saville Ave, 02169), SAN 307-6326. Tel: 617-984-1680. FAX: 617-984-1782. E-mail: help@quincycollegelibrary.org. Web Site: www.quincycollegelibrary.org. *Fac Librn,* Dava Davainis; E-mail: ddavainis@quincycollege.edu; *Fac Librn,* Patrick Dillon; E-mail: pdillon@quincycollege.edu; *Fac Librn,* Janet Lanigan; E-mail: jlanigan@quincycollege.edu
Founded 1958. Enrl 2,800; Fac 44
Library Holdings: Bk Vols 50,000; Per Subs 145
Subject Interests: Allied health, Computer sci, Criminal law & justice, Environ studies, Nursing, Psychol
Automation Activity & Vendor Info: (Acquisitions) Ex Libris Group; (Cataloging) Ex Libris Group; (Circulation) Ex Libris Group; (Course Reserve) Ex Libris Group; (OPAC) Ex Libris Group; (Serials) Ex Libris Group
Open Mon-Thurs (Fall & Spring) 8-8, Fri 8-4, Sat 8-1; Mon-Thurs (Summer) 12-6, Fri 10-4

S QUINCY HISTORICAL SOCIETY LIBRARY*, Adams Academy Bldg, Eight Adams St, 02169. SAN 328-1256. Tel: 617-773-1144. FAX: 617-773-1872. E-mail: quincyhistory@verizon.net. Web Site: www.quincyma.gov/index.cfm. *Dir,* Dr Edward Fitzgerald
Founded 1893
Library Holdings: Bk Titles 5,000; Per Subs 14
Special Collections: Adams Family Coll, bks; Shipbuilding Coll, bks, ms & photog
Function: Res libr
Open Mon-Fri 9-Noon
Restriction: Non-circulating

M QUINCY MEDICAL CENTER LIBRARY*, 114 Whitwell St, 02169. SAN 307-6318. Tel: 617-773-6100, Ext 4094. FAX: 617-376-1650. Web Site: www.quincymc.org. *Librn,* Joanne Donovan; E-mail: jdonovan@quincymc.org
Library Holdings: Bk Vols 300; Per Subs 14
Partic in SE Mass Health Sci Librs Consortium
Open Mon 8-2:30, Tues & Wed 7-2:30

RANDOLPH

P TURNER FREE LIBRARY*, Two N Main St, 02368. SAN 307-6342. Tel: 781-961-0932. FAX: 781-961-0933. *Libr Dir,* Position Currently Open; Staff 3 (MLS 3)
Founded 1874. Pop 30,600; Circ 236,567
Jul 2008-Jun 2009 Income $671,450. Mats Exp $92,925, Books $62,925, AV Mat $30,000. Sal $485,466 (Prof $174,126)
Library Holdings: Bk Vols 59,400; Per Subs 110; Talking Bks 2,300; Videos 6,970
Automation Activity & Vendor Info: (Cataloging) SirsiDynix; (Circulation) SirsiDynix
Partic in Old Colony Libr Network (OCLN)
Open Mon-Thurs 9-8, Fri & Sat 9-5
Friends of the Library Group

RAYNHAM

P RAYNHAM PUBLIC LIBRARY*, 760 S Main St, 02767. SAN 307-6350. Tel: 508-823-1344. FAX: 508-824-0494. Web Site: raynhampubliclibrary.org. *Dir,* Eden Fergusson; E-mail: efergusson@sailsinc.org; *Head, Tech Serv,* Lorna Sylvia; Staff 8 (MLS 1, Non-MLS 7)
Founded 1888. Pop 10,340; Circ 36,788
Library Holdings: Bk Titles 33,398; Bk Vols 29,000; Per Subs 44
Mem of Massachusetts Libr Syst
Partic in SAILS Library Network
Open Mon-Thurs 10-8, Fri 10-5, Sat (Sept-May) 10-3
Friends of the Library Group

READING

P READING PUBLIC LIBRARY, 64 Middlesex Ave, 01867-2550. SAN 307-6377. Tel: 781-944-0840. FAX: 781-942-9106. E-mail: readingpl@noblenet.org. Web Site: www.readingpl.org. *Dir,* Ruth Urell; Tel: 781-942-6725, Fax: 781-942-9113, E-mail: urell@noblenet.org; *Asst Dir,* Amy Lannon; Tel: 781-942-6711, Fax: 781-942-9113, E-mail: lannon@noblenet.org; *Head, Ch,* Corinne Fisher; Tel: 781-942-6705, E-mail: fisher@noblenet.org; *Head, Circ,* Michelle Filleul; Tel: 781-942-6702, E-mail: filleul@noblenet.org; *Head, Info Serv,* Lorraine Barry; Tel: 781-942-6703, E-mail: barry@noblenet.org; *Head, Tech Serv,* Jamie Penney; Fax: 781-942-6704, E-mail: jamie@noblenet.org; *Ch, Local Hist Librn,* Rachel Baumgartner; E-mail: rdgref@noblenet.org; *Ch,* Ashley Waring; E-mail: waring@noblenet.org; *Ch,* Brenda Wettergreen; E-mail: rdgchild@noblenet.org; *Promotional Serv Librn,* Kathleen Miksis; E-mail: miksis@noblenet.org; *Ref Librn,* Eileen Barrett; E-mail: barrett@noblenet.org; *Ref & Ad Serv Librn,* Andrea Fiorillo; E-mail: fiorillo@noblenet.org; *Ref Librn/YA,* Susan Beauregard; E-mail: rdgteen@noblenet.org; *Ref/YA,* Renee Smith; E-mail: rsmith@noblenet.org; *ILL,* Allison DaSilva; Tel: 781-942-6721, E-mail: dasilva@noblenet.org; Staff 38 (MLS 15, Non-MLS 23)
Founded 1867. Pop 25,000; Circ 484,610
Library Holdings: CDs 9,134; DVDs 12,700; e-books 8,302; Electronic Media & Resources 3,023; Microforms 2,507; Bk Titles 85,703; Per Subs 363
Subject Interests: Local hist
Automation Activity & Vendor Info: (OPAC) Evergreen
Database Vendor: EBSCOhost, Gale Cengage Learning, LibraryInsight, OCLC FirstSearch, OCLC WorldShare Interlibrary Loan, Overdrive, Inc, ProQuest, Standard & Poor's, TumbleBookLibrary, ValueLine, WT Cox
Wireless access
Publications: Off the Shelf (Newsletter)
Mem of Massachusetts Libr Syst
Open Mon-Wed 9-9, Thurs 1-9, Fri & Sat 9-5, Sun (Oct-May) 2-5
Friends of the Library Group

REHOBOTH

P BLANDING PUBLIC LIBRARY*, 124 Bay State Rd, 02769. SAN 307-6385. Tel: 508-252-4236. FAX: 508-252-5834. Web Site: www.blandinglibrary.org. *Dir,* Laura Bennett; E-mail: lbennett@sailsinc.org
Founded 1886. Pop 11,000
Library Holdings: AV Mats 1,200; Large Print Bks 60; Bk Titles 14,000; Per Subs 20; Talking Bks 200
Subject Interests: Art & archit, Genealogy, Music
Automation Activity & Vendor Info: (Cataloging) SirsiDynix; (Circulation) SirsiDynix; (OPAC) SirsiDynix
Open Mon-Thurs 11:30-8, Fri & Sat 10-4
Friends of the Library Group

REVERE

P REVERE PUBLIC LIBRARY*, 179 Beach St, 02151. SAN 307-6393. Tel: 781-286-8380. FAX: 781-286-8382. Web Site: www.noblenet.org/revere. *Dir,* John Cronim; Staff 12 (MLS 3, Non-MLS 9)
Founded 1880. Pop 48,398; Circ 48,635
Library Holdings: Bk Vols 48,265; Per Subs 80
Special Collections: Horatio Alger Coll
Subject Interests: Local hist
Automation Activity & Vendor Info: (Cataloging) Innovative Interfaces, Inc; (Circulation) Innovative Interfaces, Inc; (OPAC) Innovative Interfaces, Inc
Partic in North of Boston Library Exchange, Inc

Open Mon-Thurs 9-9, Fri & Sat 9-5
Friends of the Library Group

RICHMOND

P RICHMOND FREE PUBLIC LIBRARY*, 2821 State Rd, 01254-9472. SAN 307-6407. Tel: 413-698-3834. *Dir,* Kristin Smith; *Asst Dir,* Candace Mountain
Pop 1,689; Circ 10,000
Library Holdings: Bk Vols 12,100; Per Subs 24
Automation Activity & Vendor Info: (Cataloging) Innovative Interfaces, Inc; (Circulation) Innovative Interfaces, Inc; (OPAC) Innovative Interfaces, Inc
Partic in Central-Western Mass Automated Resource Sharing
Open Tues & Thurs 10-8, Sat 10-2
Friends of the Library Group

ROCHESTER

P JOSEPH H PLUMB MEMORIAL LIBRARY*, 17 Constitution Way, 02770. (Mail add: PO Box 69, 02770-0069), SAN 307-6415. Tel: 508-763-8600. FAX: 508-763-9593. E-mail: info@plumblibrary.com. Web Site: www.plumblibrary.com. *Librn,* Olivia Melo
Pop 5,000; Circ 53,000
Library Holdings: AV Mats 938; Bk Vols 17,849
Special Collections: Rochester Historical Coll
Automation Activity & Vendor Info: (Cataloging) SirsiDynix; (Circulation) SirsiDynix; (OPAC) SirsiDynix
Partic in SAILS Library Network
Open Mon & Thurs 1-8, Tues & Wed 10-6, Fri 10-5, Sat 10-2
Friends of the Library Group

ROCKLAND

P ROCKLAND MEMORIAL LIBRARY*, 20 Belmont St, 02370-2232. SAN 307-6423. Tel: 781-878-1236. FAX: 781-878-4013. E-mail: info@rocklandmemoriallibrary.org. Web Site: www.rocklandmemoriallibrary.org. *Dir,* Beverly C Brown; *Circ Chief,* Jane Long; *Ref Librn,* Robin Hall; *Youth Serv Librn,* Geralyn Schultz; *Cataloger,* Janis Chandler; Staff 5 (MLS 3, Non-MLS 2)
Founded 1878. Pop 17,780; Circ 76,423
Jul 2008-Jun 2009 Income $377,237, State $26,734, City $341,000, Locally Generated Income $4,293, Other $5,210. Mats Exp $44,175, Books $20,828, Per/Ser (Incl. Access Fees) $9,076, Other Print Mats $658, AV Mat $9,884, Electronic Ref Mat (Incl. Access Fees) $3,729. Sal $271,508 (Prof $133,567)
Library Holdings: Electronic Media & Resources 30; Microforms 376; Bk Vols 43,808; Per Subs 117
Special Collections: Municipal Document Depository
Subject Interests: Local hist
Automation Activity & Vendor Info: (Cataloging) SirsiDynix; (Circulation) SirsiDynix; (OPAC) SIRSI-iBistro; (Serials) SirsiDynix
Database Vendor: Baker & Taylor, EBSCOhost, Ingram Library Services, Newsbank
Function: Adult bk club, Archival coll, Bks on cassette, Bks on CD, Computers for patron use, Copy machines, Handicapped accessible, ILL available, Magnifiers for reading, Music CDs, Prog for adults, Prog for children & young adult, Ref serv available, Summer reading prog, Tax forms, Telephone ref, VHS videos, Wheelchair accessible
Partic in Old Colony Libr Network (OCLN)
Special Services for the Deaf - Bks on deafness & sign lang
Special Services for the Blind - Large print bks; Magnifiers
Open Mon, Thurs & Fri 10-5, Tues & Wed 10-8

ROCKPORT

L EDWIN T HOLMES LAW LIBRARY*, 146 South St, 01966. SAN 372-0330. Tel: 978-546-3478. FAX: 978-546-6785. *Librn,* Edwin Holmes
Library Holdings: Bk Vols 800

P ROCKPORT PUBLIC LIBRARY, 17 School St, 01966. SAN 307-6431. Tel: 978-546-6934. FAX: 978-546-1011. E-mail: mrc@mvlc.org. Web Site: www.rockportlibrary.org. *Libr Dir,* Cindy Grove; *Outreach Serv Librn,* Andrea Nichols; *Ch Serv,* Carol Bender; E-mail: cbender@mvlc.org; *Tech Serv,* Rosemary Bigelow; Staff 12 (MLS 2, Non-MLS 10)
Founded 1871. Pop 7,000; Circ 73,300
Library Holdings: Bk Vols 64,422; Per Subs 969
Subject Interests: Art, Local hist
Automation Activity & Vendor Info: (Cataloging) Evergreen; (Circulation) Evergreen; (ILL) Clio; (OPAC) Evergreen
Database Vendor: EBSCOhost, Electric Library, Gale Cengage Learning, Ingram Library Services, OCLC FirstSearch, ProQuest
Wireless access
Mem of Massachusetts Libr Syst
Partic in Merimack Valley Libr Consortium
Open Mon, Wed & Thurs 1-8, Tues & Sun 1-5, Sat 10-5
Friends of the Library Group

S SANDY BAY HISTORICAL SOCIETY & MUSEUMS LIBRARY*, 40 King St, 01966. (Mail add: PO Box 63, 01966-0063), SAN 329-0913. Tel: 978-546-9533. Web Site: www.sandybayhistorical.org.
Founded 1926
Library Holdings: Bk Vols 1,000
Special Collections: Cape Ann Hist; Genealogical Coll by Family
Subject Interests: Massachusetts
Function: Res libr
Publications: Quarterly Bulletin, Ad Hoc Brochures, Pamphlets
Open Mon 9-1
Restriction: Fee for pub use, Mem only, Non-circulating

ROWE

P ROWE TOWN LIBRARY*, 318 Zoar Rd, 01367-9998. SAN 307-644X. Tel: 413-339-4761. FAX: 413-339-4761. E-mail: rowelibrary@gmail.com. *Dir,* Lane A Molly; Staff 1 (MLS 1)
Founded 1787. Pop 380; Circ 12,000
Library Holdings: Bk Vols 12,069; Per Subs 51
Subject Interests: Local hist
Automation Activity & Vendor Info: (Cataloging) Follett Software; (Circulation) Follett Software
Open Tues & Sat 10-5, Wed 10-8

ROWLEY

P ROWLEY PUBLIC LIBRARY*, 141 Main St, 01969. SAN 307-6458. Tel: 978-948-2850. FAX: 978-948-2266. E-mail: iro@mvlc.org. Web Site: www.rowleylibrary.org. *Dir,* Pamela Jacobson; *Adult Serv,* Eileen Fitzgerald; E-mail: efitzgerald@mvlc.org; *Ch Serv,* Xenda Laramie; Staff 11 (MLS 1, Non-MLS 10)
Founded 1894. Pop 5,393
Library Holdings: AV Mats 6,330; Bk Vols 22,000; Per Subs 50
Subject Interests: Genealogy
Automation Activity & Vendor Info: (Cataloging) Follett Software; (Circulation) Follett Software; (OPAC) SirsiDynix
Mem of Massachusetts Libr Syst
Partic in Merimack Valley Libr Consortium
Special Services for the Blind - Audio mat; Bks on CD; Home delivery serv; Talking bks
Open Mon & Wed (Winter) 9-12 & 3-8, Tues & Thur 1-8, Sat 1-5; Mon & Wed (Summer) 9-12 & 3-8, Tues & Thurs 1-8, Fri 1-5
Friends of the Library Group

ROXBURY

S METROPOLITAN COUNCIL FOR EDUCATIONAL OPPORTUNITY LIBRARY*, 40 Dimock St, 02119. SAN 328-4077. Tel: 617-427-1545. FAX: 617-541-0550. Web Site: www.metcoinc.org. *Dir,* Jean McGuire
Library Holdings: Bk Vols 10,000; Per Subs 50
Open Mon-Fri 8-8

ROYALSTON

P PHINEHAS S NEWTON LIBRARY*, 19 On the Common, 01368. (Mail add: PO Box 133, 01368-0133), SAN 307-6474. Tel: 978-249-3572. FAX: 978-249-3572. E-mail: royalstonlibrary@gmail.com. Web Site: www.royalstonlibrary.org. *Dir,* Kathy Morris; *Asst Dir,* Gina Verrilli
Pop 1,012; Circ 2,326
Library Holdings: Bk Vols 9,400
Mem of Massachusetts Libr Syst
Open Mon 10-8:30, Thurs 1-5 & 6:30-8:30, Sat 9-Noon
Friends of the Library Group

RUSSELL

P RUSSELL PUBLIC LIBRARY*, 162 Main St, 01071. (Mail add: PO Box 438, 01071-0438), SAN 307-6482. Tel: 413-862-3102. FAX: 413-862-3106. *Librn,* Gail Duso
Pop 1,713; Circ 5,405
Library Holdings: Bk Vols 6,255
Open Mon, Wed & Fri 3-8, Tues & Thurs 3-5
Friends of the Library Group

RUTLAND

P RUTLAND FREE PUBLIC LIBRARY*, 280 Main St, 01543. SAN 307-6490. Tel: 508-886-4108. FAX: 508-886-4141. E-mail: contact@rutlandlibrary.org. Web Site: www.rutlandlibrary.org. *Dir,* Kerry J Remington; *Asst Dir,* Susan Liimatainen; *Ch,* Maureen Lynch; Staff 3 (Non-MLS 3)
Founded 1866. Pop 6,591; Circ 58,623
Library Holdings: Bk Vols 50,000; Per Subs 100

Automation Activity & Vendor Info: (Cataloging) Follett Software; (Circulation) Follett Software
Database Vendor: Dialog, Gale Cengage Learning, Innovative Interfaces, Inc, OCLC FirstSearch
Mem of Massachusetts Libr Syst
Partic in Central & Western Massachusetts Automated Resource Sharing
Open Tues & Wed 10-8, Thurs 1-8, Sat (Sept-May) 10-1
Friends of the Library Group

SALEM

GL ESSEX LAW LIBRARY, J Michael Ruane Judicial Ctr, 56 Federal St, 01970. SAN 307-6512. Tel: 978-741-0674. FAX: 978-745-7224. E-mail: essexlawlibrary@hotmail.com. Web Site: www.lawlib.state.ma.us. *Head Law Librn,* Robin W Bates; Staff 2 (MLS 2)
Founded 1856
Library Holdings: Bk Vols 30,000; Per Subs 200
Open Mon-Fri 8-4
Friends of the Library Group

M NORTH SHORE MEDICAL CENTER, SALEM HOSPITAL*, Health Sciences Library, 81 Highland Ave, 01970. SAN 324-6647. Tel: 978-354-4950. FAX: 978-744-9110. *Dir, Libr Serv,* Deborah Almquist; *Assoc Librn,* Carolee Pelletier; Staff 3 (MLS 2, Non-MLS 1)
Founded 1928
Library Holdings: Bk Titles 4,400; Per Subs 250
Subject Interests: Med
Database Vendor: Gale Cengage Learning, OCLC FirstSearch, OVID Technologies
Publications: Newsletter
Partic in Dialog Corp; National Network of Libraries of Medicine
Open Mon-Fri 8-4:30
Restriction: Employees & their associates, Med staff only, Staff & patient use

S PEABODY ESSEX MUSEUM*, Phillips Library, East India Sq, 161 Essex St, 01970-3783. SAN 323-8520. Tel: 978-745-9500. Reference Tel: 978-745-9500, Ext 3053. Toll Free Tel: 800-745-4054, Ext 3053. FAX: 978-741-9012. TDD: 978-740-3649. Web Site: www.pem.org/museum/library.php. *Dir,* Sidney E Berger; *Head, Ref,* Kathy Flynn; Staff 8 (MLS 4, Non-MLS 4)
Founded 1799
Library Holdings: Bk Vols 400,000; Per Subs 200
Special Collections: Chinese History (Frederick T Ward Coll), bks, mss, broadsides, photogs. Oral History
Subject Interests: Am folk art, Archaeology, Archit, Art, Decorative art, Ethnology, Fine arts, Maritime hist, Massachusetts, Natural hist, New England
Database Vendor: EBSCOhost
Publications: Peabody Essex Museum Collections (Annual); The American Neptune (Quarterly)
Partic in Lyrasis
Open Wed 10-5, Thurs 1-5
Restriction: Non-circulating to the pub
Friends of the Library Group

S SALEM ATHENAEUM*, 337 Essex St, 01970. SAN 371-8344. Tel: 978-744-2540. FAX: 978-744-7536. E-mail: info@salemathenaeum.net. Web Site: www.salemathenaeum.net. *Dir,* Jean Marie Procious; Staff 1 (MLS 1)
Founded 1760
Library Holdings: Bk Titles 54,202; Per Subs 31
Special Collections: Personal Library of Dr Edward Holyoke, 18th to early 19th century; Philosophical Library 1781; Social Library of 1760
Wireless access
Function: Bi-weekly Writer's Group, Children's prog, ILL available, Prog for adults, Ref serv available
Mem of Massachusetts Libr Syst
Open Tues, Wed & Fri 1-5, Thurs 5-9, Sat 10-2
Restriction: Circ to mem only, Open to researchers by request, Private libr, Pub use on premises

P SALEM PUBLIC LIBRARY*, 370 Essex St, 01970-3298. SAN 345-5521. Tel: 978-744-0860. FAX: 978-745-8616. E-mail: sal@noblenet.org. Web Site: www.noblenet.org. *Dir,* Lorraine Jackson; *Asst Dir,* Nancy Tracy; *Ch Serv,* Cheryl Opolski; *Circ,* Christine Morin; *Ref,* Jane Walsh
Founded 1888. Pop 40,407; Circ 490,204
Library Holdings: Bk Vols 128,569; Per Subs 150
Partic in Essex County Coop Librs; North of Boston Children's Libr Servs Asn

C SALEM STATE UNIVERSITY LIBRARY*, 352 Lafayette St, 01970-5353. SAN 307-6547. Tel: 978-542-6230. Interlibrary Loan Service Tel: 978-542-6501. Reference Tel: 978-542-6766. Administration Tel: 978-542-6232. Automation Services Tel: 978-542-6813. FAX: 978-542-6596. Administration FAX: 978-542-2132. Web Site: www.salemstate.edu/library. *Dean, Libr & Acad Support,* Dr Susan E Cirillo; E-mail: scirillo@salemstate.edu; *Acq Librn,* Elizabeth Dole; Tel: 978-542-6477, E-mail: elizabeth.dole@salemstate.edu; *Cat Librn,* Stephen C Pew; Tel: 978-542-6769, E-mail: spew@salemstate.edu; *Educ Res Librn,* Jason Soohoo; Tel: 978-542-6967, E-mail: jsoohoo@salemstate.edu; *Electronic Res Librn,* Nancy George; Tel: 978-542-7182, E-mail: ngeorge@salemstate.edu; *Humanities Librn,* Cathy Fahey; Tel: 978-542-7203, E-mail: cfahey@salemstate.edu; *Humanities Librn,* Zachary Newell; Tel: 978-542-7406, E-mail: znewell@salemstate.edu; *Sci & Tech Librn,* Nancy Dennis; Tel: 978-542-6218, E-mail: ndennis@salemstate.edu; *Soc Sci Librn,* Tara Fitzpatrick; Tel: 978-542-6765, E-mail: tfitzpatrick@salemstate.edu; *Soc Sci Librn,* Carol Zoppel; Tel: 978-542-6811, E-mail: carol.zoppel@salemstate.edu; *Syst Librn,* Glenn Macnutt; E-mail: gmacnutt@salemstate.edu; *Access Serv Mgr,* Jill Hennessey; Tel: 978-542-6368, E-mail: henness@noblenet.org; *Archivist,* Susan Edwards; Tel: 978-542-6781, E-mail: sedwards@salemstate.edu. Subject Specialists: *Educ,* Jason Soohoo; *Nursing,* Nancy George; *Communications, English,* Cathy Fahey; *Interdisciplinary studies, Sci, Tech,* Nancy Dennis; *Criminal justice, Psychol, Sociol,* Tara Fitzpatrick; *Geog, Hist, Polit sci,* Carol Zoppel; Staff 15 (MLS 13, Non-MLS 2)
Founded 1854. Enrl 10,125; Fac 566; Highest Degree: Master
Jul 2011-Jun 2012 Income $2,869,803. Mats Exp $1,096,511, Books $123,028, Per/Ser (Incl. Access Fees) $175,085, Micro $1,550, AV Mat $10,148, Electronic Ref Mat (Incl. Access Fees) $783,700, Presv $3,000. Sal $1,490,555
Library Holdings: Audiobooks 483; AV Mats 6,739; e-books 308,454; e-journals 57,642; Electronic Media & Resources 10,931; Microforms 584,195; Bk Vols 299,210; Per Subs 400
Special Collections: Historic Geography; History of Education (19th Century Normal School Texts Coll); Music Coll; North Shore Political Archives; Salem History
Subject Interests: Bus, Educ, Humanities, Nursing, Soc sci
Automation Activity & Vendor Info: (Acquisitions) Evergreen; (Cataloging) Evergreen; (Circulation) Evergreen; (Course Reserve) Evergreen; (ILL) Evergreen; (OPAC) Evergreen; (Serials) Evergreen
Database Vendor: 3M Library Systems, ACM (Association for Computing Machinery), Alexander Street Press, American Chemical Society, ARTstor, Career Guidance Foundation, CQ Press, CredoReference, Dun & Bradstreet, EBSCO Information Services, EBSCOhost, Elsevier, Emerald, Gale Cengage Learning, Grolier Online, Hoovers, ISI Web of Knowledge, JSTOR, LexisNexis, Medline, Mergent Online, Newsbank, OCLC, OCLC WorldShare Interlibrary Loan, Overdrive, Inc, OVID Technologies, Oxford Online, Project MUSE, ProQuest, ReferenceUSA, RefWorks, Sage, ScienceDirect, SerialsSolutions, Standard & Poor's, Thomson - Web of Science, ValueLine, Westlaw, Wiley
Wireless access
Function: Accessibility serv available based on individual needs, Archival coll, Audio & video playback equip for onsite use, Bks on cassette, Bks on CD, Computers for patron use, Copy machines, E-Reserves, Electronic databases & coll, Handicapped accessible, Microfiche/film & reading machines, Online cat, Online ref, Pub access computers, Ref serv available, Wheelchair accessible
Publications: Bookmark (Bi-annually); Brochure (Bi-annually); Periodical List; Research Guides (Online only)
Partic in Massachusetts Commonwealth Consortium of Libraries in Public Higher Education Institutions (MCCLPHEI); North of Boston Library Exchange, Inc; Northeast Consortium of Colleges & Universities In Massachusetts; Northeastern Consortium for Health Information; OCLC Online Computer Library Center, Inc
Special Services for the Deaf - ADA equip; Assisted listening device; Assistive tech
Special Services for the Blind - Assistive/Adapted tech devices, equip & products
Open Mon-Thurs 7:45am-2am, Fri 7:45-7, Sat Noon-4, Sun 2-11
Restriction: In-house use for visitors, Lending limited to county residents, Non-circulating of rare bks, Off-site coll in storage - retrieval as requested

G US NATIONAL PARK SERVICE*, Salem Maritime National Historic Site Library, 160 Derby St, 01970. SAN 323-7451. Tel: 978-740-1680. FAX: 978-740-1685. Web Site: www.nps.gov/sama. *Curator,* David Kayser; *Hist Coll Librn, Ref Serv,* Emily Murphy; E-mail: emily_murphy@nps.gov
Founded 1937
Library Holdings: Bk Titles 975; Bk Vols 1,150
Special Collections: Essex County Coll; New England Maritime History Coll; Salem History Coll
Subject Interests: Maritime hist
Function: Res libr
Restriction: Non-circulating, Open by appt only

SALISBURY

P SALISBURY PUBLIC LIBRARY*, 17 Elm St, 01952. SAN 307-6555. Tel: 978-465-5071. *Dir,* Terry Kyrios
Founded 1895. Pop 7,170; Circ 27,284
Library Holdings: Bk Titles 23,839; Per Subs 51
Subject Interests: Genealogy, Local hist
Automation Activity & Vendor Info: (Cataloging) SirsiDynix; (Circulation) SirsiDynix; (OPAC) SirsiDynix
Open Mon & Wed 10-5, Tues 12-8, Thurs 10-6
Friends of the Library Group

SANDISFIELD

P SANDISFIELD FREE PUBLIC LIBRARY*, 23 Sandisfield Rd, 01255. (Mail add: PO Box 183, 01255-0183), SAN 307-6563. Tel: 413-258-4966. *Librn,* Pat Richard
Pop 660; Circ 3,040
Library Holdings: AV Mats 24; Bk Titles 3,750; Per Subs 12
Publications: Fact sheet for town
Partic in Central-Western Mass Automated Resource Sharing
Open Mon & Tues 9-12, Wed 6:30-8:30, Thurs 9-1, Sat 9:30-11:30
Friends of the Library Group

SANDWICH

S THE SANDWICH GLASS MUSEUM LIBRARY*, 129 Main St, 02563-2233. (Mail add: PO Box 103, 02563-0103), SAN 323-8679. Tel: 508-888-0251. FAX: 508-888-4941. Web Site: www.sandwichglassmuseum.org. *Dir,* Katie Campbell; E-mail: katie.campbell@sandwichglassmuseum.org; *Curator,* Dorothy Schofield; E-mail: dorothy.schofield@sandwichglassmuseum.org
Founded 1907
Library Holdings: Bk Titles 1,700; Per Subs 2
Special Collections: B & S Correspondence, Demming Jarves Letters, archival doc; Town of Sandwich Families, archival doc, letters
Subject Interests: Antiques
Restriction: Non-circulating to the pub, Open by appt only

P SANDWICH PUBLIC LIBRARY*, 142 Main St, 02563. SAN 307-658X. Tel: 508-888-0625. FAX: 508-833-1076. E-mail: spllib@comcast.net. Web Site: www.sandwichpubliclibrary.com. *Dir,* Joanne Lamothe; *Acq, Media Spec,* Pat Vineis; *Cat, Tech Serv,* Jo Ann Latimer; *Ch Serv,* Stu Parsons; *Ref,* Lauren Robinson; Staff 5 (MLS 5)
Founded 1891. Pop 20,000; Circ 214,000
Jul 2011-Jun 2012 Income $892,196. Mats Exp $127,598. Sal $708,463
Library Holdings: Bk Titles 58,000; Per Subs 288
Special Collections: Glass Books
Subject Interests: Glass technology
Wireless access
Partic in Old Colony Libr Network (OCLN)
Open Tues-Thurs 9:30-8:30, Fri & Sat 9:30-4, Sun (Sept-May) 1-5
Friends of the Library Group

SAUGUS

G NATIONAL PARK SERVICE DEPARTMENT OF INTERIOR*, Saugus Iron Works National Historic Site Library, 244 Central St, 01906. SAN 323-7613. Tel: 781-233-0050. FAX: 781-231-7345. Web Site: www.nps.gov/sair. *In Charge,* Curtis White
Library Holdings: Bk Titles 1,000
Restriction: Open by appt only

SAVOY

P SAVOY HOLLOW LIBRARY*, Town Off Bldg, 720 Main St, 01256-9387. SAN 307-6598. Tel: 413-743-4290. Reference Tel: 413-743-4542. FAX: 413-743-4292. *Dir,* Ronna Brandt; E-mail: ronnabrandt@yahoo.com; *Chair,* Susan O'Grady
Founded 1890. Pop 720; Circ 3,669
Library Holdings: Bk Vols 520
Open Tues 1-4 & 7-9, Thurs 1-4, Sat 10-12

SCITUATE

S SCITUATE HISTORICAL SOCIETY LIBRARY*, 43 Cudworth Rd, 02066-3802. (Mail add: PO Box 276, 02066-0276), SAN 326-7814. Tel: 781-545-1083. FAX: 781-544-1249. *Archives,* Carol Miles; Staff 1 (MLS 1)
Founded 1984
Library Holdings: Bk Titles 700
Special Collections: Thomas W Lawson Coll
Subject Interests: Genealogy, Hist
Function: Res libr
Open Mon-Sat 10-4
Restriction: Pub use on premises

P SCITUATE TOWN LIBRARY*, 85 Branch St, 02066. SAN 307-6601. Tel: 781-545-8727. FAX: 781-545-8728. E-mail: info@scituatetownlibrary.org. Web Site: www.scituatetownlibrary.org. *Dir,* Jessica Finnie; *Asst Dir,* Toni Snee; *Adult Serv,* Susan Pope; *Ch Serv,* Joey Von Iderstein
Founded 1893. Pop 17,829; Circ 137,466
Library Holdings: Bk Vols 74,948; Per Subs 121
Special Collections: Oral History
Automation Activity & Vendor Info: (Cataloging) SirsiDynix; (Circulation) SirsiDynix; (OPAC) SirsiDynix
Open Mon-Thurs 9-9, Fri & Sat 9-5, Sun (Oct-Apr) 1:30-5
Friends of the Library Group

SEEKONK

P SEEKONK PUBLIC LIBRARY*, 410 Newman Ave, 02771. SAN 345-570X. Tel: 508-336-8230. FAX: 508-336-6437. E-mail: library@seekonkpl.org. Web Site: www.seekonkpl.org. *Dir,* Peter Fuller; Tel: 508-336-8230, Ext 5101, E-mail: pfuller@seekonkpl.org; *Assoc Dir,* Cynthia Marcoux; *Adult Serv,* Sharon Fredette; E-mail: sfredette@seekonkpl.org; *Adult Serv,* Michelle Gario; Tel: 508-336-8230, Ext 5130, E-mail: mgario@seekonkpl.org; *Youth Serv,* Sharon Clarke; Tel: 508-336-8230, Ext 5140, E-mail: sclarke@seekonkpl.org; *Youth Serv,* Mary Ellen Siniak; E-mail: msiniak@seekonkpl.org; Staff 21 (MLS 6, Non-MLS 15)
Founded 1899. Pop 13,539; Circ 275,878
Jul 2005-Jun 2006 Income $680,700, State $24,692, City $637,758, Other $18,250. Mats Exp $114,689, Books $69,559, Per/Ser (Incl. Access Fees) $10,679, AV Mat $30,279, Electronic Ref Mat (Incl. Access Fees) $4,172. Sal $466,129
Library Holdings: AV Mats 17,251; CDs 7,782; DVDs 9,469; e-books 361; Electronic Media & Resources 457; Bk Vols 78,597; Per Subs 277
Automation Activity & Vendor Info: (Acquisitions) SirsiDynix; (Cataloging) SirsiDynix; (Circulation) SirsiDynix; (Course Reserve) SirsiDynix; (ILL) SirsiDynix; (Media Booking) SirsiDynix; (OPAC) SirsiDynix; (Serials) SirsiDynix
Database Vendor: Booksite, Overdrive, Inc, ValueLine, World Book Online
Wireless access
Partic in SAILS Library Network
Open Mon-Thurs 10-8, Fri 10-5, Sat 10-4
Friends of the Library Group

SHARON

P SHARON PUBLIC LIBRARY, 11 N Main St, 02067-1299. SAN 307-6628. Tel: 781-784-1578. Reference Tel: 781-784-1578, Ext 1422. Administration Tel: 781-784-1578, Ext 1424. FAX: 781-784-4728. Web Site: www.sharonpubliclibrary.org. *Dir,* Lee Ann Amend; E-mail: lamend@ocln.org; *Head, Youth Serv,* Danielle Margarida; E-mail: dmargarida@ocln.org; *Info Serv Librn,* Margret Branschofsky; Staff 19 (MLS 5, Non-MLS 14)
Pop 17,000; Circ 223,000
Library Holdings: Bk Vols 90,000; Per Subs 125
Special Collections: Deborah Sampson Coll
Subject Interests: Local hist
Automation Activity & Vendor Info: (Acquisitions) SirsiDynix; (Cataloging) SirsiDynix; (Circulation) SirsiDynix; (Serials) SirsiDynix
Database Vendor: Dialog, EBSCOhost, Gale Cengage Learning, TLC (The Library Corporation)
Wireless access
Function: Telephone ref
Publications: Between the Lines (Newsletter)
Mem of Massachusetts Libr Syst
Partic in Old Colony Libr Network (OCLN)
Open Mon & Fri 10-6, Tues-Thurs 10-8, Sat 10-5
Friends of the Library Group

SR TEMPLE ISRAEL*, Neipris Library, 125 Pond St, 02067-2049. (Mail add: PO Box 377, 02067-0377), SAN 307-6636. Tel: 781-784-3986. FAX: 781-784-0719. Web Site: www.tisharon.org.
Founded 1953
Library Holdings: Bk Vols 6,350
Subject Interests: Judaica (lit or hist of Jews)
Function: Res libr
Restriction: Mem only
Friends of the Library Group

SHEFFIELD

P BUSHNELL-SAGE LIBRARY*, 48 Main St, 01257. (Mail add: PO Box 487, 01257-0487), SAN 307-6644. Tel: 413-229-7004. FAX: 413-229-7003. Web Site: www.sheffieldma.gov. *Librn,* Nancy Hahn
Founded 1892. Pop 2,743; Circ 33,000
Library Holdings: Bk Vols 36,000; Per Subs 100

Automation Activity & Vendor Info: (Acquisitions) Innovative Interfaces, Inc; (Cataloging) Innovative Interfaces, Inc; (Circulation) Innovative Interfaces, Inc; (OPAC) Innovative Interfaces, Inc
Open Tues-Thurs & Sat 10-5, Fri 10-8, Sun 2-5
Friends of the Library Group

SHELBURNE FALLS

P ARMS LIBRARY ASSOCIATION*, Bridge & Main St, 01370. SAN 307-6652. Tel: 413-625-0306. Web Site: www.armslibrary.org. *Dir,* Laurie Wheeler
Founded 1854
Library Holdings: Bk Vols 22,840; Per Subs 48
Wireless access
Open Mon & Wed 1-8, Sat 11-3
Friends of the Library Group

P BUCKLAND PUBLIC LIBRARY*, 30 Upper St, 01370. (Mail add: PO Box 149, Buckland, 01338-0149), SAN 307-2711. Tel: 413-625-9412. FAX: 413-625-9412. E-mail: bucklandpubliclibrary@cwmars.org. Web Site: www.bucklandpubliclibrary.org. *Dir,* Liz Jacobson-Carroll; E-mail: ljacobson-carroll@cwmars.org
Pop 2,165; Circ 13,820
Library Holdings: Bk Vols 9,000; Per Subs 25
Automation Activity & Vendor Info: (Cataloging) Innovative Interfaces, Inc; (Circulation) Innovative Interfaces, Inc; (OPAC) Innovative Interfaces, Inc
Wireless access
Partic in Central-Western Mass Automated Resource Sharing
Open Tues 2-8, Fri 1-6, Sat 9-1

P SHELBURNE FREE PUBLIC LIBRARY*, 233 Shelburne Center Rd, 01370. SAN 307-6660. Tel: 413-625-0307. FAX: 413-625-0307. *Librn,* Elizabeth Burnham
Pop 8,000; Circ 8,648
Library Holdings: Bk Vols 12,000; Per Subs 33
Automation Activity & Vendor Info: (Cataloging) Innovative Interfaces, Inc; (Circulation) Innovative Interfaces, Inc; (OPAC) Innovative Interfaces, Inc
Open Wed 2-8, Fri 6-8, Sat 9-11

SHERBORN

P SHERBORN LIBRARY*, Four Sanger St, 01770-1499. SAN 307-6679. Tel: 508-653-0770. FAX: 508-650-9243. E-mail: referencelibrarian@comcast.net. Web Site: home.comcast.net/~sherbornlibrary. *Dir,* M Elizabeth Johnston; *Ch Serv,* Cheryl Stern Ouellette; *Pub Serv,* Donna Bryant; *Tech Serv,* Kathleen Rao; Staff 9 (MLS 4, Non-MLS 5)
Founded 1860. Pop 4,472; Circ 54,743
Library Holdings: Bk Titles 52,725; Per Subs 169
Automation Activity & Vendor Info: (Cataloging) EOS International; (Circulation) EOS International; (OPAC) EOS International
Publications: First Search
Mem of Massachusetts Libr Syst
Partic in OCLC Online Computer Library Center, Inc
Friends of the Library Group

SHIRLEY

P HAZEN MEMORIAL LIBRARY, Three Keady Way, 01464. SAN 307-6687. Tel: 978-425-2620. FAX: 978-425-2621. E-mail: shirley@cwmars.org. Web Site: www.shirleylibrary.org. *Dir,* Debra J Roy; Staff 2 (MLS 1, Non-MLS 1)
Founded 1893. Pop 6,373; Circ 33,929
Jul 2006-Jun 2007 Income $178,728. Mats Exp $33,900. Sal $120,803
Library Holdings: Bk Vols 36,000; Per Subs 94
Subject Interests: Local hist
Automation Activity & Vendor Info: (Cataloging) Evergreen; (Circulation) Evergreen; (OPAC) Evergreen
Wireless access
Mem of Massachusetts Libr Syst
Partic in Central & Western Massachusetts Automated Resource Sharing
Open Mon & Wed 10-6, Tues & Thurs 12-8, Sat 10-2
Friends of the Library Group

SHREWSBURY

P SHREWSBURY PUBLIC LIBRARY*, 609 Main St, 01545. SAN 307-6695. Tel: 508-841-8537. FAX: 508-841-8540. Web Site: www.shrewsbury-ma.gov/library. *Dir,* Ellen M Dolan; E-mail: edolan@th.ci.shrewsbury.ma.us; *Asst Dir,* George Brown; E-mail: gbrown@cwmars.org; *YA Librn,* Dan Barbour; E-mail: dbarbour@cwmars.org; *Ch Serv,* Linda Johnson Dashnaw; E-mail: ljohnson@cwmars.org; Staff 17 (MLS 4, Non-MLS 13)
Founded 1872. Pop 33,450; Circ 423,368
Library Holdings: AV Mats 16,054; e-books 1,145; Bk Vols 118,834; Per Subs 211
Special Collections: Early New England History & Biography (Artemas Ward Coll)
Automation Activity & Vendor Info: (Acquisitions) Innovative Interfaces, Inc; (Cataloging) Innovative Interfaces, Inc; (Circulation) Innovative Interfaces, Inc; (ILL) Innovative Interfaces, Inc; (OPAC) Innovative Interfaces, Inc; (Serials) Innovative Interfaces, Inc
Wireless access
Publications: Newsletter (Quarterly)
Mem of Massachusetts Libr Syst
Open Mon-Thurs (Winter) 10-9, Fri 10-5, Sat 9-5, Sun 1-5; Mon-Thurs (Summer) 10-9, Fri 10-5
Friends of the Library Group

SHUTESBURY

P MN SPEAR MEMORIAL LIBRARY, Ten Cooleyville Rd, 01072-9766. (Mail add: PO Box 256, 01072-0256), SAN 307-6717. Tel: 413-259-1213. FAX: 413-259-1107. E-mail: library.director@shutesbury.org. *Dir,* Mary Anne Antonellis
Pop 1,800; Circ 29,000
Library Holdings: DVDs 4,000; Bk Vols 8,000; Per Subs 31
Automation Activity & Vendor Info: (Cataloging) Follett Software; (Circulation) Follett Software
Partic in Central & Western Massachusetts Automated Resource Sharing
Open Mon & Wed 11-1 & 3-6, Tues & Thurs 3-7:30, Fri & Sun 3-6, Sat 10-1
Friends of the Library Group

SOMERSET

P SOMERSET PUBLIC LIBRARY, 1464 County St, 02726. SAN 345-5769. Tel: 508-646-2829. FAX: 508-646-2831. E-mail: somersetpl@sailsinc.org. Web Site: www.somersetpubliclibrary.org. *Libr Dir,* Bonnie Davis Mendes; E-mail: bmendes@sailsinc.org; *Head, Ref,* Susan Hughey; E-mail: shughey@sailsinc.org; *Ch Serv,* Chris Matos; E-mail: cmatos@sailsinc.org
Founded 1897. Pop 18,165; Circ 140,745
Library Holdings: Audiobooks 3,696; DVDs 3,792; e-books 1,759; Microforms 3,939; Bk Vols 61,203; Per Subs 210
Special Collections: Local History Coll
Automation Activity & Vendor Info: (Acquisitions) SIRSI-DRA; (Cataloging) SirsiDynix; (Circulation) SirsiDynix; (OPAC) SirsiDynix
Database Vendor: EBSCO Auto Repair Reference, ProQuest
Wireless access
Mem of Indianhead Federated Library System
Special Services for the Blind - Aids for in-house use
Open Mon & Tues 12-8, Wed & Thurs 10-5, Fri & Sat 10-3
Friends of the Library Group

SOMERVILLE

P SOMERVILLE PUBLIC LIBRARY*, 79 Highland Ave, 02143. SAN 345-5882. Tel: 617-623-5000. Circulation Tel: 617-623-5000, Ext 2900. Reference Tel: 617-623-5000, Ext 2955. FAX: 617-628-4052. Web Site: www.somervillepubliclibrary.org. *Dir,* Position Currently Open; *Head, AV,* Susan Lamphier; Tel: 617-623-5000, Ext 2836, E-mail: slamphier@minlib.net; *Head, Ref,* Ron Castile; Tel: 617-623-5000, Ext 2969, E-mail: rcastile@minlib.net; *Ch Serv,* Cathy Piantigini; Tel: 617-623-5000, Ext 2950, E-mail: cpiantigini@minlib.net; *Circ,* James A Ventura; Tel: 617-623-5000, Ext 2905, E-mail: jventura@minlib.net; *Tech Serv,* Wendy Wood; Tel: 617-623-5000, Ext 2945, E-mail: wwood@minlib.net; Staff 36 (MLS 18, Non-MLS 18)
Founded 1873. Pop 78,385; Circ 383,006
Library Holdings: AV Mats 14,846; Electronic Media & Resources 237; Bk Vols 217,286; Per Subs 819
Special Collections: New England & Somerville History Coll. Oral History
Subject Interests: Art, Genealogy, Travel, Women's studies
Automation Activity & Vendor Info: (Acquisitions) Innovative Interfaces, Inc; (Cataloging) Innovative Interfaces, Inc; (Circulation) Innovative Interfaces, Inc; (OPAC) Innovative Interfaces, Inc
Wireless access
Function: AV serv, Homebound delivery serv, ILL available
Mem of Massachusetts Libr Syst
Partic in Minuteman Library Network
Open Mon-Thurs 9-9, Fri 9-6, Sat 9-5, Sun 1-5
Friends of the Library Group
Branches: 2
EAST, 115 Broadway, 02145, SAN 345-5912. Tel: 617-623-5000, Ext 2970. FAX: 617-623-9403. *Br Head,* Marylin Eastwood; E-mail: meastwood@minlib.net; Staff 3 (MLS 2, Non-MLS 1)
Founded 1918. Circ 25,919
Library Holdings: Bk Vols 17,207

Open Mon & Thurs 10-9, Tues 2-6, Wed & Fri 10-6
Friends of the Library Group

WEST, 40 College Ave, 02144, SAN 345-5947. Tel: 617-623-5000, Ext 2975. Web Site: www.somervillepubliclibrary.org/westbranch.html. *Br Head,* Karen Kramer; E-mail: kkramer@minlib.net; Staff 3.4 (MLS 1.4, Non-MLS 2)
Founded 1909. Circ 75,450
Function: Adult bk club, Audiobks via web, Bks on cassette, Bks on CD, Children's prog, Computers for patron use, Copy machines, Electronic databases & coll, Free DVD rentals, ILL available, Mus passes, Music CDs, Online cat, Prog for adults, Pub access computers, Ref serv available, Story hour, Summer reading prog, Tax forms, VHS videos
Open Mon & Thurs 10-9, Tues & Wed 9-6, Fri 2-6
Friends of the Library Group

SOUTH CHATHAM

P SOUTH CHATHAM PUBLIC LIBRARY*, 2559 Main St, 02659. (Mail add: PO Box 218, 02659-0218), SAN 307-6725. Tel: 508-430-7989.
Founded 1874. Pop 5,000
Library Holdings: Bk Vols 4,500
Open Tues & Fri 1-4 (1-4:30 Summer)

SOUTH DEERFIELD

P TILTON LIBRARY, 75 N Main St, 01373. SAN 345-1860. Tel: 413-665-4683. FAX: 413-665-9118. E-mail: tiltonlibrary@cwmars.org. Web Site: www.tiltonlibrary.org. *Dir,* Sara Woodbury; E-mail: swoodbur@cwmars.org; *Ch,* Julie Cavacco; E-mail: jcavacco@cwmars.org; Staff 1 (MLS 1)
Founded 1915. Pop 5,119; Circ 51,561
Library Holdings: Audiobooks 975; DVDs 1,656; e-books 24,553; Bk Titles 17,866; Per Subs 90
Automation Activity & Vendor Info: (Cataloging) Innovative Interfaces, Inc - Millenium; (Circulation) Innovative Interfaces, Inc - Millenium; (OPAC) Innovative Interfaces, Inc
Wireless access
Function: 24/7 Electronic res, 24/7 Online cat, Adult bk club, Art exhibits, Audiobks via web, Children's prog, Computers for patron use, Copy machines, Electronic databases & coll, eReaders, Fax serv, Free DVD rentals, Homebound delivery serv, ILL available, Magazines, Mail & tel request accepted, Mus passes, Music CDs, Online cat, OverDrive digital audio bks, Photocopying/Printing, Preschool outreach, Preschool reading prog, Prog for adults, Prog for children & young adult, Pub access computers, Ref serv available, Serves mentally handicapped consumers, Story hour, Summer reading prog, Tax forms, Telephone ref, Web-catalog, Wheelchair accessible, Workshops
Partic in Central & Western Massachusetts Automated Resource Sharing
Open Mon & Thurs 1-8, Tues 1-5, Wed 10-5, Sat 9-1
Friends of the Library Group

SOUTH DENNIS

P SOUTH DENNIS FREE PUBLIC LIBRARY*, 389 Main St, 02660. (Mail add: PO Box 304, 02660), SAN 307-6733. Tel: 508-394-8954. FAX: 508-394-4392. Web Site: www.southdennislibrary.org. *Dir,* Anne Speyer; *Asst Dir,* Marcella Curry; *Circ Asst,* Patricia O'Neill; Staff 2 (MLS 1, Non-MLS 1)
Founded 1900
Library Holdings: AV Mats 400; Large Print Bks 100; Bk Titles 6,365; Per Subs 14
Wireless access
Mem of Massachusetts Libr Syst
Partic in Cape Libraries Automated Materials Sharing Network
Open Mon-Wed 10-4, Sat 10-12
Friends of the Library Group

SOUTH EGREMONT

P EGREMONT FREE LIBRARY*, One Buttonball Lane, 01258. (Mail add: PO Box 246, 01258-0246), SAN 307-6741. Tel: 413-528-1474. FAX: 413-528-6416. *Dir,* Sally Caldwell
Founded 1882. Pop 1,200; Circ 6,530
Library Holdings: Large Print Bks 100; Bk Vols 9,204; Per Subs 30; Talking Bks 131
Automation Activity & Vendor Info: (Cataloging) Follett Software; (Circulation) Follett Software; (OPAC) Follett Software
Open Mon, Tues & Thurs 2-6, Sat 9-12
Friends of the Library Group

SOUTH HADLEY

C MOUNT HOLYOKE COLLEGE LIBRARY*, Library, Information & Technology Services, 50 College St, 01075-1423. SAN 307-675X. Tel: 413-538-2225. Circulation Tel: 413-538-2230. Interlibrary Loan Service Tel: 413-538-2423. Reference Tel: 413-538-2212. FAX: 413-538-2370. Web Site: www.mtholyoke.edu/lits. *Chief Info Officer,* Alex R Wirth-Cauchon, PhD; E-mail: awirthca@mtholyoke.edu; *Dir, Discovery & Access,* Erin Stalberg; Tel: 413-538-2228, E-mail: estalber@mtholyoke.edu; *Head, Archives & Spec Coll,* Leslie Fields; Tel: 413-538-2441, E-mail: lfields@mthoyloke.edu; *Coll Develop,* Kathleen Norton; Tel: 413-538-2158, E-mail: knorton@mtholyoke.edu; Staff 21 (MLS 16, Non-MLS 5)
Founded 1837. Enrl 2,100; Fac 200; Highest Degree: Master
Library Holdings: AV Mats 7,206; e-books 4,598; e-journals 1,536; Bk Titles 477,668; Bk Vols 721,223; Per Subs 3,805
Special Collections: Alumnae Letters & Diaries; Faculty Papers; Illustrated Editions of Dante's Divine Comedy (Giamatti Dante Coll); Women's Education 1920
Subject Interests: Econ, Feminism, Hist, Natural sci
Automation Activity & Vendor Info: (Acquisitions) Ex Libris Group; (Cataloging) Ex Libris Group; (Circulation) Ex Libris Group; (Course Reserve) Ex Libris Group; (Media Booking) Ex Libris Group; (OPAC) Ex Libris Group; (Serials) Ex Libris Group
Database Vendor: EBSCOhost, Gale Cengage Learning, ISI Web of Knowledge, JSTOR, LexisNexis, Newsbank, OCLC FirstSearch, OCLC WorldShare Interlibrary Loan, OVID Technologies, ProQuest, ScienceDirect
Wireless access
Function: Computers for patron use
Restriction: Open to pub for ref & circ; with some limitations, Open to students, fac & staff, Pub use on premises

P SOUTH HADLEY PUBLIC LIBRARY*, 27 Bardwell St, 01075. SAN 345-6064. Tel: 413-538-5045. FAX: 413-539-9250. Web Site: www.shadleylib.org. *Dir,* Joseph Rodio; E-mail: jrodio@cwmars.org; *Head, Circ,* Rena Lapinski; E-mail: rlapinski@cwmars.org; *Head, Tech Serv,* Lorraine Ensor; E-mail: lensor@cwmars.org; *Ref & Ad Serv Librn,* Desiree Smelcer; E-mail: dsmelcer@cwmars.org; *Youth Serv,* Meg Clancy; E-mail: mclancy@cwmars.org; Staff 11 (MLS 4, Non-MLS 7)
Founded 1897. Pop 17,000; Circ 194,000
Jul 2012-Jun 2013 Income $515,520. Mats Exp $90,000. Sal $351,655
Subject Interests: Local hist
Automation Activity & Vendor Info: (Circulation) Evergreen; (OPAC) Evergreen
Database Vendor: ProQuest
Wireless access
Function: Bk club(s), Bks on CD, Children's prog, Computers for patron use, Copy machines, Electronic databases & coll, Fax serv, Free DVD rentals, ILL available, Mail & tel request accepted, Mus passes, Music CDs, Online cat, OverDrive digital audio bks, Photocopying/Printing, Preschool reading prog, Prog for adults, Prog for children & young adult, Pub access computers, Ref serv available, Story hour, Summer reading prog, Tax forms, Teen prog
Partic in Central-Western Mass Automated Resource Sharing
Open Mon-Wed 9:30-8, Thurs & Fri 9:30-5, Sat 9:30-1
Friends of the Library Group

SOUTH HAMILTON

R GORDON-CONWELL THEOLOGICAL SEMINARY*, Burton L Goddard Library, 130 Essex St, 01982-2317. SAN 307-6776. Tel: 978-646-4074. Interlibrary Loan Service Tel: 978-646-4075. Reference Tel: 978-646-4004. Administration Tel: 978-646-4076. FAX: 978-646-4567. E-mail: glibrary@gcts.edu, reference@gcts.edu. Web Site: onlinecatalog.gordonconwell.edu, www.gordonconwell.edu/library/Hamilton-Goddard.cfm. *Coordr, ILL, Dir, Head, Ser Acq,* Meredith Moyer Kline; E-mail: mmkine@gcts.edu; *Acq,* Pamela Gore; Tel: 978-646-4078, E-mail: pgore@gcts.edu; *Archives, Pub Serv,* Robert McFadden; E-mail: rmcfadden@gcts.edu; *Ref,* James Darlack; E-mail: jdarlack@gcts.edu; *Tech Serv,* Cynthia Bolshaw; Tel: 978-646-4079, E-mail: cbolshaw@gcts.edu. Subject Specialists: *Ecclesiastical hist, Hebrew,* Meredith Moyer Kline; *Biblical studies,* James Darlack; Staff 5 (MLS 4, Non-MLS 1)
Founded 1970. Highest Degree: Doctorate
Library Holdings: CDs 400; Electronic Media & Resources 250; Bk Vols 174,090; Per Subs 700; Videos 1,694
Special Collections: Assyro-Babylonian (Mercer Coll); Aston Coll-Judaism, Christianity 1615-1691 (Richard Babson Coll); John Bunyan Coll; Millerite-Adventual Coll; Rare Bibles (Babson Coll); Washburn Baptist Coll
Automation Activity & Vendor Info: (Acquisitions) TLC (The Library Corporation); (Cataloging) OCLC Connexion; (Circulation) TLC (The Library Corporation); (Course Reserve) TLC (The Library Corporation); (ILL) OCLC; (OPAC) TLC (The Library Corporation); (Serials) TLC (The Library Corporation)
Database Vendor: Alexander Street Press, EBSCOhost, Gale Cengage Learning, Ingenta, JSTOR, OCLC FirstSearch, OCLC WorldShare Interlibrary Loan, ProQuest, Sage, TLC (The Library Corporation)
Wireless access

Function: Audio & video playback equip for onsite use, AV serv, CD-ROM, Computers for patron use, Copy machines, Distance learning, Doc delivery serv, Electronic databases & coll, Free DVD rentals, Handicapped accessible, ILL available, Mail loans to mem, Microfiche/film & reading machines, Music CDs, Online cat, Online ref, Online searches, Orientations, Photocopying/Printing, Printer for laptops & handheld devices, Prof lending libr, Pub access computers, Ref & res, Ref serv available, Res libr, Satellite serv, Scanner, Spoken cassettes & CDs, Telephone ref, VHS videos, Web-catalog, Wheelchair accessible
Partic in Lyrasis
Open Mon-Thurs 7:45am-11pm, Fri 7:45-5, Sat 9-9
Restriction: Non-resident fee, Open to pub for ref & circ; with some limitations, Open to students, fac, staff & alumni

P HAMILTON-WENHAM PUBLIC LIBRARY*, 14 Union St, 01982. SAN 307-7691. Tel: 978-468-5577. Reference Tel: 978-468-5577, Ext 19. FAX: 978-468-5535. Web Site: www.hwlibrary.org. *Dir,* Jan Dempsey; Tel: 978-468-5577, Ext 21, E-mail: jdempsey@mvlc.org; *Head, Circ,* Tara Mansfield; *Head, Ref,* Sarah Lauderdale; *Head, Tech Serv,* Nancy Day; Tel: 978-468-5577, Ext 16, E-mail: nday@mvlc.org; *Ch,* Lorraine Der; Tel: 978-468-5577, Ext 13, E-mail: lder@mvlc.org; Staff 13 (MLS 1, Non-MLS 12)
Founded 2001. Pop 12,390; Circ 150,000
Library Holdings: Large Print Bks 8,000; Bk Vols 84,750; Per Subs 161
Subject Interests: Genealogy, Local hist
Automation Activity & Vendor Info: (Circulation) SirsiDynix
Database Vendor: ebrary, EBSCOhost, Gale Cengage Learning, Grolier Online, OCLC WorldShare Interlibrary Loan, ProQuest
Mem of Massachusetts Libr Syst
Partic in Merrimack Valley Library Consortium
Open Mon-Thurs 10-8, Fri 10-5, Sat 10-4
Friends of the Library Group

SOUTH LANCASTER

C ATLANTIC UNION COLLEGE*, G Eric Jones Library, 338 Main St, 01561. (Mail add: PO Box 1000, 01561-1000), SAN 307-6792. Tel: 978-368-2000. FAX: 978-368-2013. Web Site: www.auc.edu. *Chief Financial Officer,* Lloyd Brown; E-mail: lloyd.brown@auc.edu
Founded 1882. Enrl 603
Library Holdings: Bk Vols 109,744; Per Subs 533
Special Collections: 20th Cent British & American Poets (Stafford Poetry Coll); Career Reference Center; George H Reavis Education material; Seventh-Day Adventist Coll
Subject Interests: Literary criticism, Relig, Seventh Day Adventists, Theol
Automation Activity & Vendor Info: (Acquisitions) Innovative Interfaces, Inc; (Cataloging) Innovative Interfaces, Inc
Publications: Library Handbook; New Titles; Recent Accessions
Partic in Central-Western Mass Automated Resource Sharing; Lyrasis

SOUTH WALPOLE

S MASSACHUSETTS DEPARTMENT OF CORRECTIONS*, Institution Library at MCI Cedar Junction, PO Box 100, 02071-0100. SAN 307-7330. Tel: 508-668-2100. *Librn,* Beverly Veglas; Staff 10 (MLS 2, Non-MLS 8)
Founded 1956
Library Holdings: Bk Titles 4,300; Bk Vols 10,000
Special Collections: Law Library Coll
Open Mon-Fri 8:15am-8:30pm, Sat & Sun 8:15-3:30

SOUTH WEYMOUTH

M SOUTH SHORE HOSPITAL*, Medical Library, 55 Fogg Rd at Rte 18, 02190. Tel: 781-340-8000, 781-340-8528. FAX: 781-331-0834. Web Site: www.southshorehospital.org. *Librn,* Kathy McCarthy; E-mail: kathy_mccarthy@sshosp.org
Library Holdings: Bk Titles 1,000; Per Subs 135
Automation Activity & Vendor Info: (Cataloging) Auto-Graphics, Inc
Restriction: Med staff only

SOUTH YARMOUTH

P YARMOUTH TOWN LIBRARIES, 312 Old Main St, 02664. SAN 307-8450. Tel: 508-760-4820. Circulation Tel: 508-760-4820, Ext 1311. Administration Tel: 508-760-4820, Ext 1312. Web Site: www.yarmouthlibraries.org. *Libr Dir,* Jane Cain; E-mail: jcain@clamsnet.org; Staff 10 (MLS 2, Non-MLS 8)
Founded 1866. Pop 23,793; Circ 263,776
Library Holdings: CDs 3,466; DVDs 6,170; Electronic Media & Resources 612; Bk Vols 88,000; Per Subs 337
Automation Activity & Vendor Info: (Acquisitions) Innovative Interfaces, Inc; (Cataloging) Innovative Interfaces, Inc; (Circulation) Innovative Interfaces, Inc; (OPAC) Innovative Interfaces, Inc; (Serials) Innovative Interfaces, Inc
Database Vendor: Gale Cengage Learning, Innovative Interfaces, Inc, ProQuest
Wireless access
Partic in Cape Libraries Automated Materials Sharing Network
Friends of the Library Group
Branches: 2
SOUTH YARMOUTH BRANCH, 312 Old Main St, 02664, SAN 307-6822. Tel: 508-760-4820. FAX: 508-760-2699.
Founded 1866
Library Holdings: Audiobooks 3,305; AV Mats 535; e-books 24,904; Bk Titles 52,377; Per Subs 337; Talking Bks 1,831; Videos 6,580
Special Collections: Joseph C Lincoln Coll
Subject Interests: Hist
Open Mon & Wed 10-8, Tues, Thurs & Fri 10-5, Sat 10-4, Sun (Sept-May) 12-4
Friends of the Library Group
WEST YARMOUTH BRANCH, 391 Main St, Rte 28, West Yarmouth, 02673, SAN 307-7853. Tel: 508-775-5206.
Founded 1891
Open Mon, Wed & Fri 11-4, Tues & Thurs 3-8
Friends of the Library Group

SOUTHAMPTON

P EDWARDS PUBLIC LIBRARY*, 30 East St, 01073. SAN 307-6830. Tel: 413-527-9480. FAX: 413-527-9480. E-mail: edwards@cwmars.org. Web Site: www.southamptonlibrary.org. *Dir,* Barbara Goldin; E-mail: bgoldin@cwmars.org; *Ch Serv,* Berkeley McChesney; E-mail: bmcchesn@cwmars.org; *Tech Serv,* Carol Goulet; E-mail: cgoulet@cwmars.org; Staff 1 (MLS 1)
Founded 1904. Pop 5,736; Circ 33,044
Jul 2006-Jun 2007 Income $97,000. Mats Exp $24,180, Books $23,775, Per/Ser (Incl. Access Fees) $1,654, AV Mat $2,810, Electronic Ref Mat (Incl. Access Fees) $220. Sal $64,000
Library Holdings: AV Mats 2,188; e-books 796; Bk Titles 30,026; Per Subs 49
Special Collections: Local History Coll; Vocal Music Coll
Automation Activity & Vendor Info: (Cataloging) Innovative Interfaces, Inc; (Circulation) Innovative Interfaces, Inc; (OPAC) Innovative Interfaces, Inc
Partic in Central & Western Massachusetts Automated Resource Sharing
Open Mon & Wed 10-4, Tues & Thurs 10-8, Fri 1-4, Sat 10-1
Friends of the Library Group

SOUTHBOROUGH

P SOUTHBOROUGH PUBLIC LIBRARY*, 25 Main St, 01772. SAN 307-6849. Tel: 508-485-5031. FAX: 508-229-4451. Web Site: www.southboroughlibrary.org. *Dir,* Kimberley Ivers; E-mail: kivers@southboroughma.com; *Librn,* Patricia Ellis; *Librn,* Jean Infante; *Librn,* Heidi Lindsey; *Librn,* Naomi Magnoni; *Ch Serv,* Lisa Taranto
Founded 1852. Pop 6,326; Circ 76,156
Library Holdings: Bk Vols 63,000; Per Subs 100
Automation Activity & Vendor Info: (Cataloging) Innovative Interfaces, Inc; (Circulation) Innovative Interfaces, Inc; (OPAC) Innovative Interfaces, Inc
Wireless access
Mem of Massachusetts Libr Syst
Open Mon, Fri & Sat 10-5, Tues-Thurs 10-9
Friends of the Library Group

SOUTHBRIDGE

P JACOB EDWARDS LIBRARY*, 236 Main St, 01550-2598. SAN 307-6865. Tel: 508-764-5426. Interlibrary Loan Service Tel: 508-764-5426, Ext 103. Reference Tel: 508-764-5426, Ext 105. Administration Tel: 508-764-5426, Ext 101. FAX: 508-764-5428. Web Site: www.jacobedwardslibrary.org. *Dir,* Margaret Morrissey; E-mail: mmorriss@cwmars.org; *Ad,* Ashley Malouin; E-mail: amalouin@cwmars.org; *Circ Librn,* Corinna Tiberii; E-mail: ctiberii@cwmars.org; *Tech Serv Librn,* Lynn Wolstencroft; E-mail: lwolsten@cwmars.org; Staff 3 (MLS 1, Non-MLS 2)
Founded 1914. Pop 17,214; Circ 85,274
Library Holdings: AV Mats 9,367; Bk Titles 63,271; Per Subs 160
Subject Interests: Local hist
Automation Activity & Vendor Info: (Cataloging) Innovative Interfaces, Inc; (Circulation) Innovative Interfaces, Inc; (ILL) Innovative Interfaces, Inc
Mem of Massachusetts Libr Syst
Partic in Central & Western Massachusetts Automated Resource Sharing
Open Mon & Thurs 9-8, Tues, Wed & Fri 9-5, Sat (Sept-May) 9-1
Friends of the Library Group

SOUTHWICK

P SOUTHWICK PUBLIC LIBRARY*, 95 Feeding Hills Rd, 01077-9683. SAN 307-6881. Tel: 413-569-1221. FAX: 413-569-0440. E-mail: southwicklibrary@comcast.net. *Dir,* Anne M Murray; Staff 5 (Non-MLS 5)
Founded 1892. Pop 8,835; Circ 9,686
Library Holdings: Bk Titles 45,806
Publications: Links (Newsletter)
Special Services for the Blind - Talking bks
Open Mon-Wed 10-8, Thurs & Fri 10-5, Sat 10-1
Friends of the Library Group

SPENCER

SR SAINT JOSEPH'S ABBEY*, Monastic Library, 167 N Spencer Rd, 01562-1233. SAN 328-1302. Tel: 508-885-8700, Ext 524. FAX: 508-885-8701. *Adminr,* Timothy Scott; E-mail: timothy@spencerabbey.org
Library Holdings: Bk Titles 45,000; Per Subs 25
Automation Activity & Vendor Info: (Acquisitions) L4U Library Software; (Cataloging) L4U Library Software; (Circulation) L4U Library Software; (OPAC) L4U Library Software; (Serials) L4U Library Software
Database Vendor: Gale Cengage Learning, Grolier Online, ProQuest

P RICHARD SUGDEN LIBRARY*, Eight Pleasant St, 01562. SAN 307-689X. Tel: 508-885-7513. FAX: 508-885-7523. *Dir,* Mary Baker-Wood; E-mail: mbwood@cwmars.org
Pop 11,500; Circ 77,430
Library Holdings: Bk Vols 54,600; Per Subs 100
Special Collections: Historical Materials of Spencer & Massachusetts
Automation Activity & Vendor Info: (Cataloging) Follett Software; (Circulation) Follett Software
Mem of Massachusetts Libr Syst
Open Tues-Thurs 10-8, Fri 10-5, Sat 10-1
Friends of the Library Group

SPRINGFIELD

C AMERICAN INTERNATIONAL COLLEGE*, James J Shea Sr Memorial Library, 1000 State St, 01109. SAN 307-6903. Tel: 413-205-3225. Reference Tel: 413-205-3206. FAX: 413-205-3904. Web Site: www.aic.edu/library. *Dir of Libr Serv,* Heidi Spencer; Tel: 413-205-3461, E-mail: estelle.spencer@aic.edu; *ILL Librn, Ref Serv,* Katherine Deliso; E-mail: katherine.deliso@aic.edu; *Digital Res Librn, Instruction Librn,* Amber Kanner; Staff 4 (MLS 4)
Founded 1885. Enrl 1,800; Fac 94; Highest Degree: Doctorate
Library Holdings: Bk Titles 70,100; Bk Vols 75,436; Per Subs 525
Special Collections: Curriculum Libr, rare bks. Oral History
Subject Interests: Educ, Psychol
Automation Activity & Vendor Info: (Acquisitions) Innovative Interfaces, Inc; (Cataloging) Innovative Interfaces, Inc; (Circulation) Innovative Interfaces, Inc; (Course Reserve) Innovative Interfaces, Inc; (ILL) Innovative Interfaces, Inc; (Media Booking) Innovative Interfaces, Inc; (OPAC) Innovative Interfaces, Inc; (Serials) Innovative Interfaces, Inc
Database Vendor: Innovative Interfaces, Inc
Mem of Massachusetts Libr Syst
Partic in Central & Western Massachusetts Automated Resource Sharing; Cooperating Libraries of Greater Springfield
Open Mon-Thurs 8am-10pm, Fri 8-4, Sat 10-5, Sun Noon-10

M BAYSTATE MEDICAL CENTER*, Health Sciences Library, 759 Chestnut St, 01199. SAN 345-6153. Tel: 413-794-1865. FAX: 413-794-1974. E-mail: library@bhs.org. Web Site: libraryinfo.bhs.org. *Librn,* Ellen Brassil; Staff 8 (MLS 4, Non-MLS 4)
Library Holdings: Bk Titles 10,700; Per Subs 500
Subject Interests: Anesthesiology, Cardiology, Hist of med, Lit, Med, Nursing, Obstetrics & gynecology, Oncology, Orthopedics, Pediatrics, Surgery
Wireless access
Publications: What's New (Quarterly)

S CONNECTICUT VALLEY HISTORICAL MUSEUM*, Genealogy & Local History Library, The Quadrangle, Edwards St, 01103. (Mail add: 220 State St, 01103), SAN 307-6911. Tel: 413-263-6800, Ext 230. FAX: 413-263-6898. Web Site: www.springfieldmuseums.org/cvhm.htm. *Exec Dir, Pres,* Joseph Carvalho; Fax: 413-263-6875, E-mail: president@springfieldmuseums.org; *Dir,* Guy McLain; E-mail: gmclain@springfieldmuseums.org; *Head of Libr & Archives,* Margaret Humberston; Tel: 413-263-6800, Ext 311, E-mail: mhumberston@springfieldmuseums.org; Staff 4 (MLS 1, Non-MLS 3)
Founded 1876
Library Holdings: Bk Titles 24,000; Bk Vols 30,000; Per Subs 50
Special Collections: Business & Personal Records of Connecticut Valley (1650-present)
Subject Interests: Fr Can studies, Genealogy, Local hist, New England genealogy
Function: Res libr
Mem of Massachusetts Libr Syst
Open Wed-Sat 12-4
Restriction: Not a lending libr
Friends of the Library Group

GL MASSACHUSETTS TRIAL COURT*, Hampden Law Library, 50 State St, 01103-2021. (Mail add: PO Box 559, 01102-0559), SAN 307-692X. Tel: 413-748-7923. FAX: 413-734-2973. E-mail: hampdenlawlibrary@yahoo.com. Web Site: masslaw.library.net. *Head Librn,* Kathleen M Flynn; Staff 5 (MLS 2, Non-MLS 3)
Founded 1890
Library Holdings: Bk Vols 61,489; Per Subs 389
Special Collections: Massachusetts Law
Subject Interests: Fed law
Partic in Cooperating Libraries of Greater Springfield; Lyrasis; OCLC Online Computer Library Center, Inc
Open Mon-Fri 8-4
Friends of the Library Group

S NAISMITH MEMORIAL BASKETBALL HALL OF FAME*, Edward J & Gena G Hickox Library, 1000 W Columbus Ave, 01105. SAN 307-6954. Tel: 413-781-6500. FAX: 413-781-1939. Web Site: www.hoophall.com. *Librn,* Matt Zeysing
Founded 1968
Library Holdings: Bk Titles 2,300; Per Subs 23
Special Collections: Basketball (William G Mokray Coll); Complete Set of Basketball Rule Books (Spalding Coll)
Restriction: Open by appt only

S THE REPUBLICAN LIBRARY*, 1860 Main St, 01101. SAN 371-4357. Tel: 413-788-1018. FAX: 413-788-1301. Web Site: www.masslive.com. *Dir,* James S Gleason; Tel: 413-788-1151, E-mail: jgleason@repub.com; Staff 5 (MLS 1, Non-MLS 4)
Library Holdings: Bk Titles 500; Per Subs 10
Special Collections: Merlin Database of Articles from 1988; Microfilm of Newspapers to 1824-no index; Springfield Newspapers-1824 to present, database, microfilm
Database Vendor: LexisNexis
Function: Bus archives
Restriction: Not open to pub, Staff use only

P SPRINGFIELD CITY LIBRARY*, Central Branch, 220 State St, 01103. SAN 345-6218. Tel: 413-263-6828. Circulation Tel: 413-263-6828, Ext 218, 413-263-6828, Ext 239. Interlibrary Loan Service Tel: 413-263-6828, Ext 200. Reference Tel: 413-263-6828, Ext 213. FAX: 413-263-6817. TDD: 413-263-6835. Web Site: www.springfieldlibrary.org. *Dir,* Molly Fogarty; Tel: 413-263-6828, Ext 290, Fax: 413-263-6825; *Asst Dir,* John Ramsay; Tel: 413-263-6828, Ext 293; *Regional Ref Librn,* Donna Goldthwaite; Tel: 413-263-6828, Ext 437, E-mail: dgoldthwaite@springfieldlibrary.org; *Mgr, Borrower Serv,* Patti D'Amario; Tel: 413-263-6828, Ext 220; *Mgr, Coll Develop, Mgr, Tech Serv,* Ann Keefe; Tel: 413-263-6828, Ext 294, E-mail: akeefe@springfieldlibrary.org; *Mgr, Info Serv,* Mary Frederick; Tel: 413-263-6828, Ext 202; *Mgr, Pub Serv,* Jean Canosa-Albano; Tel: 413-263-65828, Ext 291, E-mail: jcanosa@springfieldlibrary.org; *Prog Coordr,* Matthew Jaquith; Tel: 413-263-6828, Ext 221, E-mail: mjaquith@springfieldlibrary.org; *Ch Serv,* Linda Lajoie; Tel: 413-263-6828, Ext 201, E-mail: llajoie@springfieldlibrary.org; *YA Serv,* Martha Coons; Tel: 413-263-6828, Ext 425, E-mail: mcoons@springfieldlibrary.org; Staff 65.5 (MLS 25.5, Non-MLS 40)
Founded 1857. Pop 150,000; Circ 569,199
Library Holdings: Electronic Media & Resources 3,980; Bk Vols 645,944; Talking Bks 3,549; Videos 34,456
Special Collections: American Wood Engravings (Aston Coll); Economics (David A Wells Coll); Holacaust Coll. US Document Depository
Automation Activity & Vendor Info: (Acquisitions) Evergreen; (Cataloging) Evergreen; (Circulation) Innovative Interfaces, Inc
Database Vendor: Gale Cengage Learning, Innovative Interfaces, Inc, OCLC FirstSearch
Wireless access
Special Services for the Deaf - Bks on deafness & sign lang; Captioned film dep; High interest/low vocabulary bks; Spec interest per; TDD equip
Open Mon & Wed 12-8, Tues, Thurs & Sat 9-5, Sun 12-5
Friends of the Library Group
Branches: 9
BRIGHTWOOD BRANCH, 359 Plainfield St, 01107, SAN 345-6242. Tel: 413-263-6805. FAX: 413-263-6810. Web Site: www.springfieldlibrary.org/branches/bw.html. *Mgr,* Maeleah Carlisle; *Supvr,* Haydee Hodis; E-mail: hhodis@springfieldlibrary.org
Library Holdings: Bk Vols 51,039
Open Tues 10-5, Thurs 1-8, Fri 9-1
Friends of the Library Group

EAST FOREST PARK BRANCH, 122-124 Island Pond Rd, 01118. Tel: 413-263-6836. FAX: 413-263-6838. Web Site: www.springfieldlibrary.org/branches/efp.html. *Mgr,* Reginald Wilson; E-mail: rwilson@springfieldlibrary.org; *Asst Mgr,* Maeleah Gorman
Library Holdings: Bk Vols 40,070
Open Mon 1-5, Tues 12-8, Thurs 9-5, Sat 11-3
Friends of the Library Group

EAST SPRINGFIELD BRANCH, 21 Osborne Terrace, 01104, SAN 345-6277. Tel: 413-263-6840. FAX: 413-263-6842. Web Site: www.springfieldlibrary.org/branches/es.html. *Mgr,* Haydee Hodis; E-mail: hhodis@springfieldlibrary.org; *Asst Mgr,* Linda Grodofsky
Library Holdings: Bk Vols 29,833
Open Mon & Thurs 1-5, Wed 11-7, Fri 9-5
Friends of the Library Group

FOREST PARK BRANCH, 380 Belmont Ave, 01108, SAN 345-6307. Tel: 413-263-6843. FAX: 413-263-6845. Web Site: www.springfieldlibrary.org/branches/fp.html. *Mgr,* Reginald Wilson; E-mail: rwilson@springfieldlibrary.org; *Asst Mgr,* Maeleah Gorman
Library Holdings: Bk Vols 68,035
Open Tues 9-5, Wed 11-7, Fri 1-5, Sat 11-3
Friends of the Library Group

INDIAN ORCHARD BRANCH, 44 Oak St, Indian Orchard, 01151, SAN 345-6331. Tel: 413-263-6846. FAX: 413-263-6848. Web Site: www.springfieldlibrary.org/branches/io.html. *Mgr,* Maeleah Carlisle; *Asst Mgr,* Haydee Hodis
Library Holdings: Bk Vols 40,515
Open Mon 10-5, Wed 1-8, Sat 11-3
Friends of the Library Group

LIBERTY BRANCH, 773 Liberty St, 01104, SAN 345-6366. Tel: 413-263-6849. FAX: 413-263-6851. Web Site: www.springfieldlibrary.org/branches/li.html. *Mgr,* Haydee Hodis; E-mail: hhodis@springfieldlibrary.org; *Asst Mgr,* Linda Grodofsky
Library Holdings: Bk Vols 29,889
Open Mon 1-5, Tues 11-7, Thurs 9-5, Sat 11-3
Friends of the Library Group

MASON SQUARE BRANCH, 765 State St, 01109, SAN 345-6455. Tel: 413-263-6853. FAX: 413-263-6854. Web Site: www.springfieldlibrary.org/branches/ms.html. *Mgr,* Reginald Wilson; E-mail: rwilson@springfieldlibrary.org; *Asst Mgr,* Maeleah Gorman
Library Holdings: Bk Vols 35,570
Open Mon & Wed 9-5, Thurs 11-7, Fri 9-1
Friends of the Library Group

PINE POINT BRANCH, 204 Boston Rd, 01109, SAN 345-6390. Tel: 413-263-6855. FAX: 413-263-6857. Web Site: www.springfieldlibrary.org/branches/pp.html. *Mgr,* Reggie Wilson; *Asst Mgr,* Linda Lajoie
Library Holdings: Bk Vols 62,279
Open Mon 1-5, Wed 1-8, Fri 10-5
Friends of the Library Group

SIXTEEN ACRES BRANCH, 1187 Parker St, 01129, SAN 345-6420. Tel: 413-263-6858. FAX: 413-263-6860. Web Site: www.springfieldlibrary.org/branches/sa.html. *Mgr,* Reggie Wilson; *Asst Mgr,* Linda Lajoie
Founded 1966
Library Holdings: Bk Vols 71,291
Open Tues 1-8, Thurs 10-5, Sat 11-3
Friends of the Library Group

C SPRINGFIELD COLLEGE*, Babson Library, 263 Alden St, 01109-3797. SAN 307-6997. Tel: 413-748-3315. Interlibrary Loan Service Tel: 413-748-3559. Administration Tel: 413-748-3609. FAX: 413-748-3631. Web Site: www.spfldcol.edu/library. *Dir,* Andrea S Taupier; E-mail: ataupier@springfieldcollege.edu; *ILL,* Lynn Martin; *Pub Serv, Ref & Info Serv,* Rachael Naismith; Tel: 413-748-3505; *Tech Serv,* Michael Stevens; Tel: 413-748-3360; Staff 16 (MLS 9, Non-MLS 7)
Founded 1885. Enrl 5,200; Fac 250; Highest Degree: Doctorate
Library Holdings: e-books 72,905; Microforms 803,743; Bk Titles 125,465
Special Collections: Sports Rules; US Volleyball Association Materials
Subject Interests: Allied health, Educ, Hist, Humanities, Natural sci, Soc sci & issues
Automation Activity & Vendor Info: (Acquisitions) Ex Libris Group; (Cataloging) Ex Libris Group; (Circulation) Ex Libris Group; (Course Reserve) Ex Libris Group; (ILL) Ex Libris Group; (OPAC) Ex Libris Group; (Serials) Ex Libris Group
Wireless access
Partic in CCGS; Cooperating Libraries of Greater Springfield; Lyrasis
Open Mon-Thurs 7:30am-Midnight, Fri 7:30am-9pm, Sat 9-9, Sun 9am-Midnight

J SPRINGFIELD TECHNICAL COMMUNITY COLLEGE LIBRARY, One Armory Sq, Ste 1, 01105-1685. (Mail add: PO Box 9000, 01102-9000), SAN 307-7012. Tel: 413-755-4845. Reference Tel: 413-755-4549. FAX: 413-755-6315. TDD: 413-746-0079. Web Site: library.stcc.edu. *Dean, Libr Serv,* Barbara Wurtzel; E-mail: bwurtzel@stcc.edu; *Info Literacy & Ref Librn,* Ruth Alcabes; Tel: 413-755-4550, E-mail: raalcabes@stcc.edu; *Syst/Ref Librn,* Erica Eynouf; Tel: 413-755-4064, E-mail: eweynouf@stcc.edu; *Circ Mgr,* Kim Noel; Tel: 413-755-4564, E-mail: knoel@stcc.edu; *Coordr, Instruction & Ref,* Eric Warren; Tel: 413-755-4555, E-mail: ewarren@stcc.edu; *Coordr, Tech Serv,* Lynn Coakley; Tel: 413-755-4565, E-mail: lcoakley@stcc.edu; Staff 8 (MLS 8)
Founded 1969. Enrl 4,600; Fac 255; Highest Degree: Associate
Jul 2013-Jun 2014. Mats Exp $99,551, Books $15,157, Per/Ser (Incl. Access Fees) $33,183, AV Mat $6,459, Electronic Ref Mat (Incl. Access Fees) $44,752. Sal $507,585 (Prof $395,966)
Library Holdings: AV Mats 9,435; e-books 36,588; Electronic Media & Resources 93; Bk Vols 53,000; Per Subs 209
Subject Interests: Allied health, Dental hygiene, Med, Nursing
Automation Activity & Vendor Info: (Acquisitions) Evergreen; (Cataloging) OCLC Connexion; (Circulation) Evergreen; (Course Reserve) Evergreen; (ILL) OCLC Online; (OPAC) Evergreen; (Serials) SerialsSolutions
Database Vendor: Cinahl, CredoReference, ebrary, EBSCO Information Services, EBSCOhost, Facts on File, Gale Cengage Learning, LexisNexis, McGraw-Hill, Newsbank, OCLC FirstSearch, OCLC WorldShare Interlibrary Loan, Oxford Online, ScienceDirect, Springshare, LLC
Wireless access
Publications: Audio-Visual Catalog; STCC Library Guide; STCC Library Home Page
Mem of Massachusetts Libr Syst
Partic in Central & Western Massachusetts Automated Resource Sharing; Lyrasis; OCLC Online Computer Library Center, Inc; Western Massachusetts Health Information Consortium
Open Mon-Thurs (Fall & Spring) 8am-9pm, Fri 8-4, Sat 9-1; Mon & Tues (Summer) 8-8, Wed-Fri 8-4

C WESTERN NEW ENGLAND UNIVERSITY, D'Amour Library, 1215 Wilbraham Rd, 01119. SAN 345-648X. Tel: 413-782-1535. Interlibrary Loan Service Tel: 413-782-1654. Reference Tel: 413-782-1655. Administration Tel: 413-782-1531, 413-782-1532. Toll Free Tel: 800-325-1122, Ext 1535. FAX: 413-796-2011. Web Site: libraries.wne.edu. *Dir,* Priscilla L Perkins; E-mail: pperkins@wne.edu; *Head, Access Serv & Electronic Res,* Lindsay Roberts; E-mail: lindsay.roberts@wne.edu; *Head, Info Literacy & Instruction Serv,* Mary Jane Sobinski-Smith; Tel: 413-782-1533, E-mail: msobinsk@wne.edu; *Cat Librn,* Damian Biagi; Tel: 413-782-1635, E-mail: damian.biagi@wne.edu; *Coll Develop Librn, Ref Coordr,* Vicky Ludwig; Tel: 413-796-2265, E-mail: vludwig@wne.edu; *Info Literacy Librn,* Joshua Becker; Tel: 413-782-1537, E-mail: jbecker@wne.edu; *Info Serv & Instrul Librn,* Eugenia Liu; Tel: 413-782-1534, E-mail: eugenia.liu@wne.edu; *Archivist,* Rosemary O'Donoghue; Tel: 413-782-1495, E-mail: rosemary.odonoghue@wne.edu; Staff 7.5 (MLS 7, Non-MLS 0.5)
Founded 1951. Enrl 3,387; Fac 363; Highest Degree: Doctorate
Library Holdings: Audiobooks 122; CDs 950; DVDs 4,181; e-books 26,015; Microforms 188,300; Bk Titles 113,141; Bk Vols 133,777; Videos 1,244
Subject Interests: Arts, Bus, Criminal justice, Educ, Eng
Automation Activity & Vendor Info: (Acquisitions) Innovative Interfaces, Inc; (Cataloging) Innovative Interfaces, Inc; (Circulation) Innovative Interfaces, Inc; (Course Reserve) Innovative Interfaces, Inc; (ILL) OCLC; (OPAC) Innovative Interfaces, Inc; (Serials) Innovative Interfaces, Inc
Database Vendor: ARTstor, College Source, CQ Press, EBSCO Discovery Service, EBSCOhost, Elsevier, Gale Cengage Learning, IBISWorld, JSTOR, Knovel, Lexi-Comp, LexisNexis, Medline, Micromedex, Natural Standard, Newsbank, Newsbank-Readex, OCLC FirstSearch, OVID Technologies, Project MUSE, ProQuest, PubMed, SBRnet (Sports Business Research Network), ScienceDirect, Springshare, LLC, UpToDate, ValueLine, Westlaw
Wireless access
Publications: Course Guides (Research guide); D'Amour Library Newsline (Newsletter); Subject Guides (Research guide)
Partic in CCGS; Cooperating Libraries of Greater Springfield; Lyrasis; OCLC Online Computer Library Center, Inc
Open Mon-Thurs 7:45am-Midnight, Fri 7:45am-8pm, Sat 9-8, Sun Noon-Midnight; Mon-Thurs (Summer) 8:30am-9pm, Fri 8:30-4, Sat & Sun Noon-6

CL WESTERN NEW ENGLAND UNIVERSITY*, School of Law Library, 1215 Wilbraham Rd, 01119-2689. SAN 345-651X. Tel: 413-782-1457. Reference Tel: 413-782-1458. FAX: 413-782-1745. Web Site: www.law.wne.edu/library. *Assoc Dir,* Pat Newcombe; Tel: 413-782-1616, E-mail: pnewcombe@law.wne.edu; *Head, Access Serv,* Nicole Belbin; Tel: 413-782-1484, E-mail: nbelbin@law.wne.edu; *Head, Res Serv,* Renee Rastorfer; Tel: 413-782-1459, E-mail: rrastorfer@law.wne.edu; *Head, Tech Serv,* Christine Archambault; Tel: 413-782-1474, E-mail: carchambault@law.wne.edu; *Cat Librn,* Steven Bobowicz; Tel: 413-782-1309, E-mail: sbobowicz@law.wne.edu; *Res/Fac Serv Librn,* Elliott Hibbler; Tel: 413-782-1454, E-mail: ehibbler@law.wne.edu; Staff 8 (MLS 8)

Founded 1973. Enrl 517; Fac 35; Highest Degree: Doctorate
Special Collections: Government Documents; Massachusetts Continuing Legal Education Material
Subject Interests: Estate planning, Health law, Labor, Tax
Automation Activity & Vendor Info: (Acquisitions) Innovative Interfaces, Inc; (Cataloging) Innovative Interfaces, Inc; (Circulation) Innovative Interfaces, Inc; (Course Reserve) Innovative Interfaces, Inc; (ILL) OCLC WorldShare Interlibrary Loan; (Media Booking) Innovative Interfaces, Inc; (OPAC) Innovative Interfaces, Inc; (Serials) Innovative Interfaces, Inc
Database Vendor: HeinOnline, Innovative Interfaces, Inc, LexisNexis, OCLC FirstSearch, OCLC WorldShare Interlibrary Loan, SerialsSolutions, Westlaw
Wireless access
Publications: Cybercites; Library Guide (Library handbook); Research Guides & Pathfinders; Self Guided Tour
Partic in New England Law Library Consortium, Inc

STERLING

P CONANT PUBLIC LIBRARY*, Four Meetinghouse Hill Rd, 01564. (Mail add: PO Box 428, 01564), SAN 307-7039. Tel: 978-422-6409. FAX: 978-422-6643. Web Site: www.sterlinglibrary.org. *Dir,* Patrica Campbell; E-mail: pcampbel@cwmars.org; *Head, Ch,* Danielle Mattei; E-mail: dmattei@cwmars.org; Staff 6 (MLS 3, Non-MLS 3)
Founded 1871. Pop 6,659
Library Holdings: Bk Titles 28,000; Per Subs 83
Automation Activity & Vendor Info: (Cataloging) Innovative Interfaces, Inc; (Circulation) Innovative Interfaces, Inc; (OPAC) Innovative Interfaces, Inc
Database Vendor: Facts on File
Publications: Sterling Business Directory (Bi-ennial); Sterling Factsheet: A Guide To Community Resources & Services (Irregular)
Mem of Massachusetts Libr Syst
Open Mon-Thurs 10-8, Sat 10-3 (10-1 Summer)
Friends of the Library Group

STOCKBRIDGE

G BERKSHIRE BOTANICAL GARDEN LIBRARY*, PO Box 826, 01262-0826. SAN 373-174X. Tel: 413-298 3926. FAX: 413-298-4897. Web Site: www.berkshirebotanical.org. *Exec Dir,* Molly Boxer
Library Holdings: Bk Vols 3,000; Per Subs 20
Restriction: Open to pub upon request

S NORMAN ROCKWELL MUSEUM*, Reference Center, Nine Glendale Rd, 01262. (Mail add: PO Box 308, 01262-0308), SAN 328-6177. Tel: 413-298-4100. FAX: 413-298-4145. Web Site: www.nrm.org. *Archivist,* Jessika Drmacich; *Curator of Archival Coll,* Kanzenberg Corry
Founded 1969
Library Holdings: Bk Vols 1,337; Per Subs 7; Videos 270
Special Collections: American Illustration (Norman Rockwell Coll); The Norman Rockwell Archive
Wireless access
Mem of Massachusetts Libr Syst
Open Tues, Thurs & Sat (Winter) 1-4; Tues, Thurs & Sat (Summer) 1-5

P STOCKBRIDGE LIBRARY ASSOCIATION*, 46 Main St, 01262. (Mail add: PO Box 119, 01262-0119), SAN 307-7055. Tel: 413-298-5501. FAX: 413-298-0218. E-mail: info@stockbridgelibrary.org. *Dir,* Katherine O'Neil; *Asst Dir,* Linda Brazeau
Founded 1868. Pop 2,312; Circ 59,441
Library Holdings: Bk Vols 27,000; Per Subs 70
Special Collections: Historical Coll
Partic in Central & Western Massachusetts Automated Resource Sharing
Open Tues & Fri 9-8, Wed & Thurs 9-5, Sat 9-2

STONEHAM

P STONEHAM PUBLIC LIBRARY*, 431 Main St, 02180. SAN 307-7063. Tel: 781-438-1324. FAX: 781-279-3836. E-mail: sto@noblenet.org. Web Site: www.stonehamlibrary.org. *Dir,* Mary P Todd; E-mail: todd@noblenet.org; *Asst Dir,* Mary Forkin; E-mail: forkin@noblenet.org; *Ch,* Janice L Chase; E-mail: chase@noblenet.org; *Ref Librn,* Maureen Saltzman; E-mail: saltzman@noblenet.org; *Circ Supvr,* Deborah Cunningham; E-mail: dcunning@noblenet.org; Staff 6 (MLS 6)
Founded 1859. Pop 22,203; Circ 115,000
Library Holdings: Bk Titles 80,592; Per Subs 226
Special Collections: 18th-20th Century (Stoneham Coll), docs on micro. Oral History
Automation Activity & Vendor Info: (Acquisitions) Innovative Interfaces, Inc; (Cataloging) Innovative Interfaces, Inc; (Circulation) Innovative Interfaces, Inc; (Course Reserve) Innovative Interfaces, Inc; (ILL) Innovative Interfaces, Inc; (Media Booking) Innovative Interfaces, Inc; (OPAC) Innovative Interfaces, Inc; (Serials) Innovative Interfaces, Inc
Wireless access
Mem of Massachusetts Libr Syst
Partic in North of Boston Library Exchange, Inc
Special Services for the Deaf - TTY equip
Open Mon, Tues & Thurs 10-9, Wed & Fri 10-5, Sat 10-2; Mon 1-9, Tues-Thurs 10-6, Fri 10-5, Sat 10-2
Friends of the Library Group

STOUGHTON

M NEW ENGLAND SINAI HOSPITAL & REHABILITATION CENTER*, Medical Library, 150 York St, 02072. SAN 377-9181. Tel: 781-344-0600, Ext 1172. FAX: 781-344-0128. TDD: 781-341-2395. Web Site: www.newenglandsinai.org.
Library Holdings: Bk Vols 600; Per Subs 20
Wireless access
Partic in Basic Health Sciences Library Network; Massachusetts Health Sciences Libraries Network; North Atlantic Health Sciences Libraries, Inc; Southeastern Massachusetts Consortium of Health Science Libraries

P STOUGHTON PUBLIC LIBRARY*, 84 Park St, 02072-2974. SAN 345-6544. Tel: 781-344-2711. FAX: 781-344-7340. E-mail: stlib@ocln.org. Web Site: www.stoughtonlibrary.org. *Dir,* Patricia Basler; *Asst Dir,* Diane Browne; E-mail: dbrowne@ocln.org; *Adult Serv, Ref Serv,* Josh Olshin; E-mail: jolshin@ocln.org; *Ch Serv,* Barbara Pally; E-mail: bpally@ocln.org; *YA Serv,* Dipti Mehta; E-mail: dmehta@ocln.org; Staff 4 (MLS 4)
Founded 1874. Pop 25,605; Circ 143,185
Library Holdings: Bk Vols 101,767; Per Subs 196
Special Collections: Stoughton Coll
Wireless access
Publications: Stoughton Houses: 100 Years; Stoughton Public Library: 100 Years
Mem of Massachusetts Libr Syst
Partic in Old Colony Libr Network (OCLN)
Open Mon-Thurs 9-9, Fri & Sat 9-5
Friends of the Library Group

STOW

P RANDALL LIBRARY*, 19 Crescent St, 01775. SAN 307-7071. Tel: 978-897-8572. FAX: 978-897-7379. *Dir,* Melissa Fournier; E-mail: mfournier@minlib.net; Staff 3 (MLS 1, Non-MLS 2)
Founded 1892. Pop 6,000; Circ 126,038
Jul 2008-Jun 2009 Income $241,003, State $9,673, City $194,450, Locally Generated Income $34,112, Other $2,768. Mats Exp $37,929, Books $23,836, Per/Ser (Incl. Access Fees) $2,490, Other Print Mats $1,250, AV Mat $7,598, Electronic Ref Mat (Incl. Access Fees) $2,755. Sal $134,412 (Prof $59,224)
Library Holdings: Audiobooks 2,371; DVDs 2,368; Large Print Bks 248; Bk Vols 42,422; Per Subs 63; Videos 329
Subject Interests: Local hist
Automation Activity & Vendor Info: (Cataloging) Innovative Interfaces, Inc; (Circulation) Innovative Interfaces, Inc; (OPAC) Innovative Interfaces, Inc
Database Vendor: Innovative Interfaces, Inc
Wireless access
Function: After school storytime, Audiobks via web, Bks on cassette, Bks on CD, Children's prog, Computers for patron use, Copy machines, Doc delivery serv, Electronic databases & coll, Free DVD rentals, Handicapped accessible, ILL available, Mus passes, Online cat, OverDrive digital audio bks, Pub access computers, Ref serv in person, Spoken cassettes & CDs, Spoken cassettes & DVDs, Story hour, Summer reading prog, Tax forms, Telephone ref, VHS videos, Wheelchair accessible
Partic in Minuteman Library Network
Open Tues-Thurs 10-8, Fri 10-2, Sat 10-5
Friends of the Library Group

STURBRIDGE

P JOSHUA HYDE PUBLIC LIBRARY*, 306 Main St, 01566-1242. SAN 307-708X. Tel: 508-347-2512. FAX: 508-347-2872. E-mail: library@town.sturbridge.ma.us. Web Site: www.sturbridgelibrary.org. *Dir,* Becky Plimpton; E-mail: bplimpton@cwmars.org; *Adult Serv,* Cheryl Zelazo; E-mail: czelazo@cwmars.org; *Ch Serv,* Patricia Lalli; E-mail: plalli@cwmars.org; Staff 12 (MLS 3, Non-MLS 9)
Founded 1896. Pop 9,000; Circ 135,000
Jul 2005-Jun 2006 Income $331,756. Mats Exp $63,041. Sal $214,602
Library Holdings: AV Mats 2,128; Bk Titles 36,830; Per Subs 91; Talking Bks 2,512
Subject Interests: Local hist
Automation Activity & Vendor Info: (Cataloging) Innovative Interfaces, Inc; (Circulation) Innovative Interfaces, Inc; (ILL) Innovative Interfaces, Inc
Mem of Massachusetts Libr Syst
Partic in Central & Western Massachusetts Automated Resource Sharing

Open Mon 1:30-5, Tues-Thurs 10:30-9, Fri & Sat 10:30-5; Sun (Oct-May)1:30-5
Friends of the Library Group

SUDBURY

P GOODNOW LIBRARY, 21 Concord Rd, 01776-2383. SAN 307-7101. Tel: 978-443-1035. Reference Tel: 978-440-5520. E-mail: goodnow@sudbury.ma.us. Web Site: goodnowlibrary.org. *Dir,* Esme Green; Tel: 978-440-5515, E-mail: greene@sudbury.ma.us; *Asst Dir,* Karen Tobin; Tel: 978-440-5525, E-mail: tobink@sudbury.ma.us; *Ch,* Kat Liddle; Tel: 978-443-5545, E-mail: kliddle@minlib.net; *Circ,* Michael Briody; *Tech Serv,* Elizabeth Rose; Staff 8 (MLS 4, Non-MLS 4)
Founded 1862. Pop 16,000; Circ 270,000
Library Holdings: Bk Vols 93,000; Per Subs 130
Subject Interests: Genealogy, Local hist
Automation Activity & Vendor Info: (Cataloging) Innovative Interfaces, Inc; (Circulation) Innovative Interfaces, Inc; (OPAC) Innovative Interfaces, Inc
Database Vendor: Gale Cengage Learning, LearningExpress, ProQuest, ReferenceUSA
Wireless access
Partic in Minuteman Library Network
Special Services for the Deaf - Staff with knowledge of sign lang
Open Mon-Thurs 9-9, Fri & Sat 9-5, Sun 2-5
Friends of the Library Group

S RAYTHEON CO*, Research Library, 528 Boston Post Rd, 01776-3375. SAN 307-711X. Tel: 978-440-2282. FAX: 978-440-4412. Web Site: www.raytheon.com. *Librn,* Cheryl Cove; Staff 1 (MLS 1)
Founded 1962
Library Holdings: Bk Titles 7,000; Per Subs 100
Subject Interests: Aerospace, Electronics
Automation Activity & Vendor Info: (Cataloging) Inmagic, Inc.
Publications: Union List of Book; Union List of Serials
Partic in BiblioTech
Restriction: Staff use only

SUNDERLAND

P SUNDERLAND PUBLIC LIBRARY*, 20 School St, 01375. SAN 307-7136. Tel: 413-665-2642. FAX: 413-665-1435. E-mail: director@sunderlandpubliclibrary.org. Web Site: www.sunderlandpubliclibrary.org. *Dir,* Sheila P McCormick; *YA Librn,* Moira Cranshaw; *Adult Serv,* Laura Williams; *Circ,* Tara Herzig; *Circ,* Vanessa Ryder; *Youth Serv,* Kelly Daniels Baker; Staff 4 (MLS 1, Non-MLS 3)
Founded 1869. Pop 3,777; Circ 62,000
Library Holdings: AV Mats 2,815; Bk Titles 19,340; Per Subs 99
Automation Activity & Vendor Info: (Cataloging) Innovative Interfaces, Inc; (Circulation) Innovative Interfaces, Inc; (OPAC) Innovative Interfaces, Inc
Database Vendor: Gale Cengage Learning
Wireless access
Function: Art exhibits, Audiobks via web, Bks on cassette, Bks on CD, Children's prog, Computers for patron use, Copy machines, e-mail & chat, Electronic databases & coll, Fax serv, Free DVD rentals, Handicapped accessible, Homebound delivery serv, ILL available, Mus passes, Online cat, OverDrive digital audio bks, Photocopying/Printing, Prog for adults, Prog for children & young adult, Pub access computers, Story hour, Summer reading prog, VHS videos
Open Mon 10-8, Tues & Wed 1-8, Fri 10-7, Sat 10-5
Friends of the Library Group

SUTTON

P SUTTON FREE PUBLIC LIBRARY*, Four Uxbridge Rd, 01590. SAN 345-6609. Tel: 508-865-8752. FAX: 508-865-8751. *Dir,* Carol Geary; E-mail: cgeary@cwmars.org; *Youth Serv Librn,* Amanda Thornton; *Circ Spec, ILL Spec,* Pamela Johnson; E-mail: pamelaj@cwmars.org; Staff 5 (MLS 1, Non-MLS 4)
Pop 9,800
Library Holdings: Audiobooks 306; AV Mats 3,638; CDs 697; DVDs 2,102; Electronic Media & Resources 106; Large Print Bks 532; Bk Vols 24,467; Per Subs 67; Videos 2,102
Automation Activity & Vendor Info: (Circulation) Innovative Interfaces, Inc - Millenium
Wireless access
Function: Adult bk club, Archival coll, Bk club(s), Bks on CD, CD-ROM, Children's prog, Computers for patron use, Fax serv, Genealogy discussion group, Holiday prog, ILL available, Mus passes, Music CDs, Online cat, Online ref, Prog for adults, Prog for children & young adult, Summer reading prog
Mem of Massachusetts Libr Syst
Open Tues & Thurs 10-8, Wed & Fri 10-6, Sat 10-3
Friends of the Library Group

SWAMPSCOTT

JR MARIAN COURT COLLEGE*, Lindsay Library, 35 Little's Point Rd, 01907-2896. SAN 370-5404. Tel: 781-309-5219. FAX: 781-595-3560. Web Site: www.mariancourt.edu. *Col Librn,* Mike Crockett; E-mail: mcrockett@mariancourt.edu; Staff 1 (MLS 1)
Founded 1964. Enrl 200; Fac 20; Highest Degree: Associate
Library Holdings: Audiobooks 10; DVDs 75; Bk Titles 10,000; Per Subs 50; Videos 75
Automation Activity & Vendor Info: (Cataloging) LibraryWorld, Inc
Mem of Massachusetts Libr Syst
Partic in Northeast Consortium of Colleges & Universities In Massachusetts
Open Mon, Tues & Thurs 9-5, Wed 10-7, Fri 9-4

P SWAMPSCOTT PUBLIC LIBRARY, 61 Burrill St, 01907. SAN 307-7144. Tel: 781-596-8867. FAX: 781-596-8826. E-mail: swa@noblenet.org. Web Site: www.noblenet.org/swampscott. *Dir,* Alyce Deveau; E-mail: deveau@noblenet.org; *Asst Dir, Head, Tech,* Susan Conner; *Head, Adult Serv, Head, Circ,* Maureen McCarthy; *Head, Ch,* Israela Abrams; *Head, Ch,* Elizabeth Coughlin; *Head, Ref (Info Serv), Head, YA,* Sandra Moltz; *Head, Tech Serv,* Marcia Harrison; Staff 19 (MLS 5, Non-MLS 14)
Founded 1853. Pop 14,412; Circ 172,360
Library Holdings: Bk Vols 92,488; Per Subs 100
Special Collections: Railroads & Model Railroads (Albert W Lalime Coll); Town History (Henry Sill Baldwin Coll)
Wireless access
Partic in North of Boston Library Exchange, Inc
Open Mon-Wed 10-8:30, Thurs 1-8:30, Fri 10-1, Sat 10-2
Friends of the Library Group

SWANSEA

P SWANSEA FREE PUBLIC LIBRARY*, 69 Main St, 02777. SAN 345-6668. Tel: 508-674-9609. FAX: 508-675-5444. E-mail: Library@swansealibrary.org. Web Site: www.swansealibrary.org. *Dir,* Cynthia St Amour; E-mail: camour@sailsinc.org; *Youth Serv Librn,* Carol Gafford; *Circ,* Persephone Alves; *Circ,* Kaija Gallucci; *Circ,* Maire Shea; *Circ,* Florina St Laurent; *Tech Serv,* Amy Lawton; *Tech Serv,* Mary Murphy
Founded 1896. Pop 16,000; Circ 82,226
Library Holdings: Bk Titles 52,000; Per Subs 117
Subject Interests: Genealogy, Hist
Wireless access
Open Mon-Thurs 10-5 & 6:30-8:30, Fri & Sat 10-5
Friends of the Library Group

TAUNTON

GL BRISTOL LAW LIBRARY*, Superior Court House, Nine Court St, 02780. SAN 307-7152. Tel: 508-824-7632. FAX: 508-824-4723. E-mail: bristollawlibrary@yahoo.com. Web Site: www.lawlib.state.ma.us. *Actg Adminr,* Cynthia Campbell
Founded 1858
Library Holdings: Bk Vols 28,000; Per Subs 24
Special Collections: Complete Massachusetts Laws, cases, regulations
Wireless access
Open Mon-Fri 8:30-4:30
Friends of the Library Group

S OLD COLONY HISTORICAL SOCIETY, 66 Church Green, 02780. SAN 307-7160. Tel: 508-822-1622. FAX: 508-880-6317. E-mail: oldcolony@oldcolonyhistoricalsociety.org. Web Site: www.oldcolonyhistoricalsociety.org. *Archivist, Libr Mgr,* Andrew D Boisvert; E-mail: adboisvert@oldcolonyhistoricalsociety.org. Subject Specialists: *Genealogy, Taunton regional hist,* Andrew D Boisvert; Staff 1 (Non-MLS 1)
Founded 1853
Library Holdings: Bk Titles 8,000; Spec Interest Per Sub 25
Special Collections: Original Manuscripts, Letters & Records
Subject Interests: Civil War, Genealogy, Local hist
Wireless access
Function: Microfiche/film & reading machines, Prog for adults, Scanner, Workshops
Open Tues-Sat 10-4
Restriction: Non-circulating
Friends of the Library Group

P TAUNTON PUBLIC LIBRARY*, 12 Pleasant St, 02780. SAN 345-6722. Tel: 508-821-1410. Circulation Tel: 508-821-1412 (Children's). Reference Tel: 508-821-1413. FAX: 508-821-1414. TDD: 508-821-1418. Web Site: www.tauntonlibrary.org. *Dir,* Susanne Costa Duquette; E-mail:

sduquette@taunton-ma.gov; *Commun Relations Librn,* Deborah Dutra; *Ref Librn,* Marguerite Jacinto; *Ref Librn,* Virginia Johnson; *Circ Supvr,* Helen Medeiros; *Tech Serv Supvr,* Gail Coelho; *Acq,* Carolyn Silva; *Acq,* Elizabeth Wheeler; *Cat,* Jamie MacDonald; *Cat,* Martha Palmer; *Ch Serv,* Mary Elizabeth Belanger; *Ch Serv,* Daisy Delano; *Circ,* Amy Boivin; *ILL,* Robyn Bryant; *Ref Serv,* Aaron Cushman; *Ser,* Mary Moitoso; *Tech Info Spec,* Michael Marcondes; *Tech Serv,* Karen Pereira; Staff 19 (MLS 6, Non-MLS 13)
Founded 1866. Pop 50,962; Circ 180,511
Library Holdings: CDs 302; DVDs 1,652; Electronic Media & Resources 92; Bk Vols 201,055; Per Subs 167; Talking Bks 3,829; Videos 2,485
Special Collections: American-Portuguese Genealogical Coll; History of Taunton File Reference Coll; Literacy Center; Portuguese Coll; Young Adult Coll
Subject Interests: Am lit, Art & archit, Genealogy, Hist, Local hist, World War II
Automation Activity & Vendor Info: (Acquisitions) SirsiDynix; (Cataloging) SirsiDynix; (Circulation) SirsiDynix; (Course Reserve) SirsiDynix; (ILL) SirsiDynix; (Media Booking) LAC Group; (OPAC) SirsiDynix; (Serials) SirsiDynix
Database Vendor: SirsiDynix
Publications: Newsletter (Monthly)
Mem of Massachusetts Libr Syst
Partic in SAILS Library Network
Special Services for the Deaf - TDD equip
Friends of the Library Group

M TAUNTON STATE HOSPITAL*, Medical Library, 60 Hodges Ave, 02780. (Mail add: PO Box 4007, 02780-0997), SAN 307-7179. Tel: 508-977-3000. *Librn,* Cedric Wright
Founded 1948
Library Holdings: Bk Vols 909; Per Subs 78
Partic in SE Mass Health Sci Librs Consortium
Restriction: Med staff only

TEMPLETON

P BOYNTON PUBLIC LIBRARY*, 27 Boynton Rd, 01468-1412. (Mail add: PO Box 296, 01468 0296), SAN 345-6846. Tel: 978-939-5582. FAX: 978-939-8755. *Dir,* Jacqueline Prime; jprime@cwmars.org; *Asst Librn,* Irene Young
Pop 6,079
Library Holdings: AV Mats 335; Bk Vols 13,000; Per Subs 25
Automation Activity & Vendor Info: (Acquisitions) Horizon; (Cataloging) Horizon
Mem of Massachusetts Libr Syst
Open Mon & Thurs 1-7, Tues 10-1, Wed 10-5, Sat 9-12
Friends of the Library Group

TEWKSBURY

P TEWKSBURY PUBLIC LIBRARY*, 300 Chandler St, 01876. SAN 307-7195. Tel: 978-640-4490. E-mail: mte@mvlc.org. Web Site: www.tewksburypl.org. *Dir,* Elisabeth Desmarais; Staff 22 (MLS 5, Non-MLS 17)
Founded 1877. Pop 29,500; Circ 35,000
Library Holdings: Bk Vols 90,000; Per Subs 175
Mem of Massachusetts Libr Syst
Partic in Merrimack Valley Library Consortium
Friends of the Library Group

TOLLAND

P TOLLAND PUBLIC LIBRARY*, 22 Clubhouse Rd, 01034-9551. SAN 376-7108. Tel: 413-258-4201. E-mail: tplibrary@verizon.net. Web Site: www.tolland-ma.gov/Public_Documents/TollandMA_Library/index. *Librn,* Jessica Kelmelis
Pop 295; Circ 2,771
Library Holdings: Bk Vols 7,100
Wireless access
Open Mon & Wed 3-6, Thurs 11-4, Sat 10-Noon

TOPSFIELD

P TOPSFIELD TOWN LIBRARY*, One S Common St, 01983-1496. SAN 307-7217. Tel: 978-887-1528. FAX: 978-887-0185. E-mail: mto@mvlc.org. Web Site: www.topsfieldtownlibrary.org. *Dir,* Laura Zalewski; *Head, Adult Serv,* Rebecca Rowlands; *Head, Tech Serv,* Sibyl Hezlett; *Ch,* Jane Johnson; *ILL, Ref Librn,* Wendy Thatcher; Staff 13 (MLS 2, Non-MLS 11)
Founded 1794. Pop 6,140; Circ 161,489
Library Holdings: AV Mats 3,617; Bk Titles 49,273; Per Subs 170; Talking Bks 3,557
Automation Activity & Vendor Info: (Cataloging) SirsiDynix; (Circulation) SirsiDynix
Mem of Massachusetts Libr Syst
Partic in Merrimack Valley Library Consortium
Open Mon & Thurs 10-8, Tues & Sat 10-5, Wed & Fri 12-5
Friends of the Library Group

TOWNSEND

P TOWNSEND PUBLIC LIBRARY*, 276 Main St, 01469-1513. (Mail add: PO Box 526, 01469-0526), SAN 307-7225. Tel: 978-597-1714. FAX: 978-597-2779. E-mail: library@townsendlibrary.org. Web Site: www.townsendlibrary.org. *Dir,* Heidi E Fowler; *Ch Serv,* Sheila Brown; *Ch Serv,* Diane Eaton; *Libr Tech,* Catherine Hill; *Libr Tech,* Lori V Stevenson; Staff 7 (MLS 1, Non-MLS 6)
Founded 1929. Pop 9,158
Library Holdings: Bk Vols 29,210; Per Subs 29
Subject Interests: Genealogy, Local hist
Database Vendor: Innovative Interfaces, Inc
Mem of Massachusetts Libr Syst
Partic in Central-Western Mass Automated Resource Sharing
Friends of the Library Group

TURNERS FALLS

P MONTAGUE PUBLIC LIBRARIES*, Carnegie Library-Main Branch, 201 Ave A, 01376-1989. SAN 307-7233. Tel: 413-863-3214. FAX: 413-863-3227. Web Site: www.montaguepubliclibraries.org. *Dir,* Linda Hickman; *Ch,* Angela Rovatti-Leonard; Staff 7 (MLS 2, Non-MLS 5)
Library Holdings: Bk Vols 35,000; Per Subs 100
Special Collections: Local History Materials
Automation Activity & Vendor Info: (Cataloging) Innovative Interfaces, Inc; (Circulation) Innovative Interfaces, Inc; (OPAC) Innovative Interfaces, Inc
Open Mon-Wed 1-8, Thurs 1-5, Fri 10-5, Sat 10-2
Friends of the Library Group
Branches: 2
MILLERS FALLS BRANCH, 23 Bridge St, Millers Falls, 01349, SAN 307-532X. Tel: 413-659-3801. *Br Mgr,* Jean Truckey
Pop 1,000; Circ 11,753
Special Collections: Early Town Histories, photogs
Open Tues & Thurs 2-5 & 6-8
Friends of the Library Group
MONTAGUE CENTER BRANCH, 17 Center St, Montague, 01351. (Mail add: PO Box 157, Montague, 01351-0157), SAN 307-5389. Tel: 413 367-2852.
Circ 9,870
Special Collections: Early Massachusetts Historical Information
Open Mon & Wed 2-5 & 6-8
Friends of the Library Group

TYNGSBORO

P TYNGSBOROUGH PUBLIC LIBRARY*, 25 Bryant Lane, 01879-1003. SAN 307-7241. Tel. 978-649 7361. FAX: 978-649-2578. Web Site: www.tynglib.org. *Dir,* Carol Bacon; *Asst Dir,* Terri Ducharme; Staff 9 (MLS 2, Non-MLS 7)
Founded 1878. Pop 11,300; Circ 84,000
Library Holdings: AV Mats 1,700; Bk Titles 32,000; Bk Vols 33,500; Per Subs 212
Special Collections: Puppets
Automation Activity & Vendor Info: (Cataloging) SirsiDynix; (Circulation) SirsiDynix; (ILL) SirsiDynix; (OPAC) SirsiDynix
Function: Archival coll, Bi-weekly Writer's Group, Handicapped accessible, ILL available, Photocopying/Printing, Prog for children & young adult, Ref serv available, Summer reading prog, Telephone ref, Wheelchair accessible
Mem of Massachusetts Libr Syst
Partic in Merrimack Valley Library Consortium
Open Mon & Wed 9-9, Tues, Thurs & Fri 9-5, Sat 9-2
Friends of the Library Group

TYRINGHAM

P TYRINGHAM FREE PUBLIC LIBRARY*, 118 Main Rd, 01264-9700. (Mail add: PO Box 440, 01264-0440), SAN 307-725X. Tel: 413-243-1373. *Librn,* Mary Garner
Founded 1891. Circ 355
Library Holdings: Bk Vols 7,000
Open Tues 3-5, Sat 10-Noon

UPTON

P UPTON TOWN LIBRARY*, Two Main St, 01568-1608. (Mail add: PO Box 1196, 01568-1196), SAN 307-7276. Tel: 508-529-6272. FAX: 508-529-2453. Web Site: webpages.charter.net/uptonlib. *Dir,* Matthew Bachtold; E-mail: mbachtol@cwmars.org; *Ch Serv, YA Serv,* Lisa Stratton
Founded 1871. Pop 3,884; Circ 24,000
Library Holdings: Bk Vols 24,000; Per Subs 105

Automation Activity & Vendor Info: (Cataloging) Innovative Interfaces, Inc; (Circulation) Innovative Interfaces, Inc; (OPAC) Innovative Interfaces, Inc
Mem of Massachusetts Libr Syst
Partic in Central-Western Mass Automated Resource Sharing
Open Tues-Thurs 10-8, Fri 10-4, Sat 10-2
Friends of the Library Group

UXBRIDGE

P UXBRIDGE FREE PUBLIC LIBRARY, 15 N Main St, 01569-1822. SAN 307-7284. Tel: 508-278-8624. FAX: 508-278-8618. Web Site: www.uxbridgelibrary.org. *Actg Dir,* Debra Young; Tel: 508-278-8624, Ext 101, E-mail: dyoung@uxbridge-ma.gov; *Head, Historical Coll,* Betsy Youngsma; *Head, ILL,* Carol Caffrey; Tel: 508-278-8624, Ext 100; Staff 2 (MLS 1, Non-MLS 1)
Founded 1894. Pop 13,100; Circ 61,000
Library Holdings: Bk Vols 40,000; Per Subs 40
Special Collections: Local History & Genealogy Coll
Automation Activity & Vendor Info: (Cataloging) Evergreen; (Circulation) Evergreen; (OPAC) Evergreen
Wireless access
Mem of Massachusetts Libr Syst
Partic in Central-Western Mass Automated Resource Sharing
Open Mon & Thurs (Winter) 10-8, Tues & Wed 10-5:30, Sat 9-2; Mon & Thurs (Summer) 10-8, Tues & Wed 10-5:30, Fri 9-2
Friends of the Library Group

VINEYARD HAVEN

P VINEYARD HAVEN PUBLIC LIBRARY*, 200 Main St, 02568-9710. SAN 375-3719. Tel: 508-696-4211. FAX: 508-696-7495. Web Site: www.vhlibrary.org. *Dir,* Amy Ryan; Tel: 508-696-4211, Ext 11, E-mail: amyryan@clamsnet.org; *Ch,* Sarah Hines; Tel: 508-696-4211, Ext 14; *Ref Librn,* Cecily Greenaway; Tel: 508-696-4211, Ext 15; *YA Librn,* Amy Diegelman; *Adult Prog,* Betty Burton; Tel: 508-696-4211, Ext 16; *ILL,* Hal Garneau; Tel: 508-696-4211, Ext 12; *Ser,* Jennifer Rapuano; Staff 7 (MLS 3, Non-MLS 4)
Founded 1878. Pop 10,000; Circ 127,000
Jul 2005-Jun 2006 Income $482,127, State $7,240, City $426,476, Locally Generated Income $2,411, Other $46,000. Mats Exp $80,438, Books $41,743, Per/Ser (Incl. Access Fees) $15,205, AV Mat $21,427, Electronic Ref Mat (Incl. Access Fees) $1,449. Sal $308,723
Library Holdings: CDs 1,918; DVDs 3,761; Bk Vols 33,902; Per Subs 150
Special Collections: Vineyard Coll
Automation Activity & Vendor Info: (Acquisitions) Innovative Interfaces, Inc - Millenium; (Cataloging) Innovative Interfaces, Inc - Millenium; (Circulation) Innovative Interfaces, Inc - Millenium; (Course Reserve) Innovative Interfaces, Inc - Millenium; (ILL) Innovative Interfaces, Inc - Millenium; (Media Booking) Innovative Interfaces, Inc - Millenium; (OPAC) Innovative Interfaces, Inc - Millenium; (Serials) Innovative Interfaces, Inc - Millenium
Wireless access
Function: Adult bk club, Art exhibits, Audiobks via web, Bks on CD, Children's prog, Computer training, Computers for patron use, Copy machines, Electronic databases & coll, Fax serv, Free DVD rentals, Handicapped accessible, ILL available, Literacy & newcomer serv, Magnifiers for reading, Microfiche/film & reading machines, Mus passes, Music CDs, OverDrive digital audio bks, Photocopying/Printing, Preschool outreach, Preschool reading prog, Prog for adults, Prog for children & young adult, Pub access computers, Ref serv available, Scanner, Spoken cassettes & CDs, Spoken cassettes & DVDs, Story hour, Summer reading prog, Tax forms, Teen prog, Wheelchair accessible
Partic in Cape Libraries Automated Materials Sharing Network
Open Mon, Wed & Sat 10-5:30, Tues & Thurs 10-8, Fri 1-5:30
Friends of the Library Group

WAKEFIELD

P LUCIUS BEEBE MEMORIAL LIBRARY*, 345 Main St, 01880-5093. SAN 345-6900. Tel: 781-246-6334. FAX: 781-246-6385. E-mail: wakefieldlibrary@noblenet.org. Web Site: www.wakefieldlibrary.org. *Dir,* Sharon A Gilley; Tel: 781-246-6335, E-mail: gilley@noblenet.org; *Asst Dir,* Catherine McDonald; E-mail: cmcdonal@noblenet.org; *Head, Circ,* Jaclyn Strycharz; E-mail: strycharz@noblenet.org; *Head, Info Serv,* Jeffrey M Klapes; E-mail: klapes@noblenet.org; *Head, Tech Serv,* Rebecca Rohr; E-mail: rohr@noblenet.org; *Youth Serv,* Nancy Sheehan; E-mail: sheehan@noblenet.org; Staff 31 (MLS 12, Non-MLS 19)
Founded 1856. Pop 25,000; Circ 301,877
Library Holdings: Bk Vols 110,250; Spec Interest Per Sub 220
Special Collections: Rifles, Riflery & Target Shooting (Keough Coll); Wakefield Authors
Subject Interests: Local hist
Automation Activity & Vendor Info: (Acquisitions) Innovative Interfaces, Inc; (Cataloging) Innovative Interfaces, Inc; (Circulation) Innovative Interfaces, Inc; (OPAC) Innovative Interfaces, Inc; (Serials) Innovative Interfaces, Inc
Database Vendor: Dialog, EBSCOhost, Gale Cengage Learning, Innovative Interfaces, Inc, OCLC FirstSearch
Mem of Massachusetts Libr Syst
Partic in North of Boston Library Exchange, Inc
Open Mon-Thurs 9-9, Fri 9-6, Sat 9-5
Friends of the Library Group

WALES

P WALES PUBLIC LIBRARY*, 77 Main St, 01081. (Mail add: PO Box 243, 01081-0243), SAN 307-7322. Tel: 413-245-9072. FAX: 413-245-9098. *Dir,* Nancy Baer; *Librn,* Jackie Figura
Pop 1,700; Circ 6,805
Library Holdings: Bk Vols 10,000; Per Subs 22
Open Mon & Wed 2:30-7, Sat 10-1
Friends of the Library Group

WALPOLE

P WALPOLE PUBLIC LIBRARY, 143 School St, 02081. SAN 345-6994. Tel: 508-660-7340. E-mail: info@walpolelibrary.org. Web Site: www.walpolelibrary.org. *Dir,* Salvatore Genovese; Tel: 508-660-7334; *Acq, Head, Adult Serv, Tech Serv,* Norma Jean Cauldwell; Tel: 508-660-6358; *Ref Librn,* Warren Smith; Tel: 508-660-7341; *Youth Serv Librn,* Kara Dean; Tel: 508-660-7384; Staff 4 (MLS 4)
Founded 1876. Pop 21,151; Circ 235,000
Library Holdings: Bk Vols 102,000; Per Subs 150
Automation Activity & Vendor Info: (Cataloging) SirsiDynix; (Circulation) SirsiDynix; (OPAC) SirsiDynix
Partic in Old Colony Libr Network (OCLN)
Open Mon-Thurs 10-9, Fri 10-5, Sat 10-3
Friends of the Library Group

WALTHAM

C BENTLEY COLLEGE*, Solomon R Baker Library, 175 Forest St, 02452-4705. SAN 307-7381. Tel: 781-891-2168. Interlibrary Loan Service Tel: 781-891-2301. Reference Tel: 781-891-2300. FAX: 781-891-2830. E-mail: library@bentley.edu. Web Site: ecampus.bentley.edu/dept/li. *Dir,* Phillip Knutel; *Head, Circ,* Catherine Cronin; *Head, Ref,* Sheila Ekman; *Head, Tech Serv,* Donna Bacchiocchi; *Bibliog Instr,* Lisa Scott; *Cat,* Ziping Wu; *Electronic Res,* Stephen Tracey; *Ref,* Kimberly Morin; *Ser,* Enza Rapatano; Staff 15 (MLS 7, Non-MLS 8)
Founded 1917. Enrl 5,500; Fac 215; Highest Degree: Master
Library Holdings: Bk Vols 225,000; Per Subs 624
Special Collections: Business Histories
Subject Interests: Acctg, Bus, Econ, Finance, Mgt, Mkt
Automation Activity & Vendor Info: (Acquisitions) SirsiDynix; (Cataloging) SirsiDynix; (Circulation) SirsiDynix; (Course Reserve) SirsiDynix; (ILL) SirsiDynix; (OPAC) SirsiDynix; (Serials) SirsiDynix
Partic in Lyrasis; WEBnet Libr Consortium

C BRANDEIS UNIVERSITY LIBRARIES*, Library & Technology Services, 415 South St, Mailstop 045, 02454-9110. SAN 345-7087. Tel: 781-736-7777. Circulation Tel: 781-736-4624. Interlibrary Loan Service Tel: 781-736-4676. Reference Tel: 781-736-4730. FAX: 781-736-4719. Web Site: lts.brandeis.edu. *Dir, Info Syst,* Lisa DeMings
Founded 1948. Enrl 5,311; Fac 511; Highest Degree: Doctorate
Jul 2007-Jun 2008. Mats Exp $3,300,000
Library Holdings: e-journals 33,137; Bk Vols 1,207,217
Special Collections: Louis D Brandeis Coll. US Document Depository
Subject Interests: Judaica
Automation Activity & Vendor Info: (Acquisitions) Ex Libris Group; (Cataloging) Ex Libris Group; (Circulation) Ex Libris Group; (Course Reserve) Ex Libris Group; (ILL) OCLC ILLiad; (OPAC) Ex Libris Group; (Serials) Ex Libris Group
Database Vendor: EBSCOhost, Elsevier MDL, Gale Cengage Learning, JSTOR, LexisNexis, ProQuest
Wireless access
Function: Res libr
Mem of Massachusetts Libr Syst
Partic in Boston Library Consortium, Inc; Coalition for Networked Information (CNI); OCLC Online Computer Library Center, Inc; OCLC Research Library Partnership; Scholarly Publ & Acad Resources Coalition
Open Mon-Thurs (Fall) 8:30am-2am, Fri 8:30-6, Sat Noon-6, Sun 12pm-2am; Mon-Fri (Winter) 8:30-5:30
Friends of the Library Group

S CHARLES RIVER MUSEUM OF INDUSTRY LIBRARY, 154 Moody St, 02453. SAN 375-7102. Tel: 781-893-5410. FAX: 781-891-4536. Web Site: www.crmi.org. *Exec Dir,* Katherine Davis
Founded 1980
Library Holdings: Bk Titles 3,000

S GORE PLACE SOCIETY, INC LIBRARY*, 52 Gore St, 02453. SAN 327-3210. Tel: 781-894-2798. FAX: 781-894-5745. E-mail: goreplace@goreplace.org. Web Site: www.goreplace.org. *Dir,* Susan Robertson
Library Holdings: Bk Vols 2,000
Open Mon, Thurs, Sat & Sun 1-5

S SIMPSON, GUMPERTZ & HEGER, INC LIBRARY*, 41 Seyon St, Bldg No 1, Ste 500, 02453. SAN 373-0662. Tel: 781-907-9000. FAX: 781-907-9009. Web Site: www.sgh.com. *Mgr,* Evelyn Neuburger
Library Holdings: Bk Vols 20,000; Per Subs 45
Subject Interests: Structural eng
Restriction: Staff use only

S THE WALTHAM MUSEUM INC LIBRARY*, 25 Lexington St, 02452. SAN 373-0689. Tel: 781-893-8017, 781-893-9020. Web Site: www.walthammuseum.com. *Dir,* Albert Arena; E-mail: aaarena@hotmail.com
Library Holdings: Bk Vols 5,000
Subject Interests: City hist, Eng, Watchmaking
Wireless access
Restriction: Non-circulating, Open by appt only

P WALTHAM PUBLIC LIBRARY*, 735 Main St, 02451. SAN 345-7230. Tel: 781-314-3425. FAX: 781-314-3426. Web Site: www.waltham.library.ma.us. *Dir,* Katherine Tranquada; Tel: 781-314-3430, E-mail: ktranquada@city.waltham.ma.us; *Asst Dir, AV,* Deb Fasulo; Tel: 781-314-3432; *Ch Serv,* Nancy Rea; E-mail: nrea@city.waltham.ma.us; *Circ,* Louise Goldstein; *Computer Serv,* Todd Strauss; *Ref,* Laura Bernheim; Tel: 781-314-3435; *Tech Serv,* Marcia M Luce; Tel: 781-314-3436, E-mail: mluce@city.waltham.ma.us; *ILL,* Marialice Wade
Founded 1865. Pop 59,073; Circ 642,884
Library Holdings: Bk Vols 195,860; Per Subs 417
Partic in Minuteman Library Network
Open Mon-Thurs 9-9, Fri & Sat 9-5, Sun 1-4
Friends of the Library Group

WARE

M BAYSTATE MARY LANE HOSPITAL*, Community Health Information Center, 85 South St, 01082. SAN 377-9351. Tel: 413-967-2226. FAX: 413-967-2115. *Librn,* Janet Lussier; E-mail: janet.lussier@bhs.org
Library Holdings: Bk Vols 400
Partic in Massachusetts Health Sciences Libraries Network; North Atlantic Health Sciences Libraries, Inc; Western Mass Health Info Consortium
Open Mon-Fri 9-5:30

P YOUNG MEN'S LIBRARY ASSOCIATION*, Ware's Public Library, 37 Main St, 01082-1317. SAN 307-7535. Tel: 413-967-5491. FAX: 413-967-6060. Web Site: www.warelibrary.org. *Dir,* Heidi Reed; *Ch,* A Vessella; *Asst Librn,* Katheryn Nowak; Staff 4 (MLS 1, Non-MLS 3)
Founded 1872. Pop 9,824; Circ 40,532
Library Holdings: AV Mats 2,784; Bk Vols 43,962; Per Subs 91
Subject Interests: Local hist
Automation Activity & Vendor Info: (Cataloging) Innovative Interfaces, Inc - Millenium; (Circulation) Innovative Interfaces, Inc - Millenium; (OPAC) Innovative Interfaces, Inc - Millenium
Database Vendor: Gale Cengage Learning
Wireless access
Function: Art exhibits, Audiobks via web, Bks on cassette, Bks on CD, Computers for patron use, Copy machines, Fax serv, Free DVD rentals, ILL available, Mus passes, Music CDs, OverDrive digital audio bks, Photocopying/Printing, Prog for children & young adult, Summer reading prog, Tax forms, Telephone ref
Partic in Central & Western Massachusetts Automated Resource Sharing
Open Mon & Fri 1-8, Tues & Thurs 10-5, Sat (Sept-June) 9-Noon

WAREHAM

M TOBEY HOSPITAL*, Stillman Library, 43 High St, 02571. SAN 328-6150. Tel: 508-273-4037. FAX: 508-295-0910. Web Site: www.southcoast.org/library. *Librn,* Gaelen Adam
Founded 1956
Library Holdings: Bk Titles 300; Per Subs 40
Subject Interests: Health
Restriction: Open by appt only

P WAREHAM FREE LIBRARY*, 59 Marion Rd, 02571. SAN 307-7543. Tel: 508-295-2343. Circulation Tel: 508-295-2343, Ext 1011. Reference Tel: 508-295-2343, Ext 1012. FAX: 508-295-2678. Web Site: www.warehamfreelibrary.org. *Dir,* Denise Medeiros; Tel: 508-295-2343, Ext 1010; *Head, Ref Serv,* Laurie Cavanaugh; *Ch Serv,* Marcia Hickey; Tel: 508-295-2343, Ext 1014, E-mail: mhickey@sailsinc.org; *Ref,* Patty Neal; E-mail: pneal@sailsinc.org; *Tech Serv,* Kathy Murphy; Tel: 508-295-2343, Ext 1015, E-mail: kmurphy@sailsinc.org; Staff 7 (MLS 3, Non-MLS 4)
Founded 1891. Pop 20,340; Circ 245,000
Jul 2005-Jun 2006 Income $781,840, State $28,000, City $699,500, Locally Generated Income $54,340. Mats Exp $112,000. Sal $525,000
Library Holdings: Bk Vols 101,000; Per Subs 110
Special Collections: Wareham Coll. Municipal Document Depository; Oral History
Automation Activity & Vendor Info: (Cataloging) SirsiDynix; (Circulation) SirsiDynix; (OPAC) SirsiDynix
Wireless access
Partic in SAILS Library Network
Open Mon, Thurs & Fri 10-5, Tues 12-8, Wed 10-8, Sat 10-2
Friends of the Library Group

WARREN

P WARREN PUBLIC LIBRARY*, 934 Main St, 01083-0937. SAN 307-7551. Tel: 413-436-7690. FAX: 413-436-7690. *Dir,* Elaine Barrie; *Asst Dir,* Kim Kvaracein; Staff 1.375 (Non-MLS 1.375)
Founded 1879. Pop 5,000; Circ 23,357
Jul 2005-Jun 2006 Income $109,014, State $12,764, City $92,122, Locally Generated Income $4,128. Mats Exp $21,221, Books $11,799, Per/Ser (Incl. Access Fees) $1,489, AV Mat $7,827, Electronic Ref Mat (Incl. Access Fees) $106. Sal $53,528
Library Holdings: AV Mats 3,148; Electronic Media & Resources 26; Bk Titles 22,663; Per Subs 69
Special Collections: Genealogy Coll; Local History Coll
Wireless access
Mem of Massachusetts Libr Syst
Partic in Central & Western Massachusetts Automated Resource Sharing; Evergreen Indiana Consortium; Suburban Library Cooperative
Open Tues & Thurs 11-7, Wed & Sat 11-3
Friends of the Library Group

WARWICK

P WARWICK FREE PUBLIC LIBRARY*, Four Hotel Rd, 01378-9311. SAN 307-6059. Tel: 978-544-7866. FAX: 978-544-7866. E-mail: warwick@cwmars.org. *Dir,* Nancy Hickler
Founded 1870. Pop 780
Library Holdings: Bk Titles 8,000; Per Subs 22
Open Mon 10-4, Tues 1-8, Thurs 5-8, Sat 9-2

WATERTOWN

S ARMENIAN MUSEUM OF AMERICA, INC, Armenian Library, 65 Main St, 02472. SAN 325-8963. Tel: 617-926-2562. FAX: 617-926-0175. E-mail: info@almainc.org. *Dir,* Berj Chekijian; *Asst Dir,* Howayda Abu Affan; *Curator,* Gary Lind-Sinanian; *Curator,* Susan Lind-Sinanian
Founded 1971
Library Holdings: AV Mats 2,000; CDs 200; DVDs 300; Music Scores 400; Bk Titles 22,000; Bk Vols 25,000
Special Collections: Oral History
Automation Activity & Vendor Info: (Cataloging) Follett Software
Wireless access
Function: Res libr
Friends of the Library Group

P PERKINS SCHOOL FOR THE BLIND, Perkins Library, 175 N Beacon St, 02472. SAN 345-732X. Tel: 617-972-7240. Reference Tel: 617-972-7245. Toll Free Tel: 800-852-3133. FAX: 617-972-7363. TDD: 617-972-7610. E-mail: library@perkins.org. Web Site: www.perkinslibrary.org. *Dir,* Kim L Charlson; *Dep Dir,* James E Gleason; Staff 27 (MLS 7, Non-MLS 20)
Founded 1829. Pop 25,000; Circ 482,149
Library Holdings: Bk Titles 75,000
Special Collections: Foreign Language, cassettes; French, German, Italian, Polish, Portuguese & Massachusetts, cassettes; Reference Material on Blindness & Other Physical Handicaps
Automation Activity & Vendor Info: (Acquisitions) Keystone Systems, Inc (KLAS); (Cataloging) Keystone Systems, Inc (KLAS); (Circulation) Keystone Systems, Inc (KLAS); (OPAC) Keystone Systems, Inc (KLAS)
Wireless access
Function: Accessibility serv available based on individual needs, Bk club(s), Computers for patron use, Digital talking bks, e-mail serv, Magnifiers for reading, Mail & tel request accepted, Mus passes, Online cat, Online ref, Online searches, Summer reading prog, Web-Braille, Wheelchair accessible
Publications: Dots & Decibels (Newsletter); El Narrador (Newsletter); PerKids (Newsletter)
Special Services for the Deaf - TTY equip
Special Services for the Blind - Accessible computers; Assistive/Adapted tech devices, equip & products; Bks on flash-memory cartridges; Braille alphabet card; Braille bks; Braille equip; Braille servs; Cassette playback machines; Cassettes; Children's Braille; Closed circuit TV magnifier;

Computer with voice synthesizer for visually impaired persons; Descriptive video serv (DVS); Digital talking bk; Digital talking bk machines; Duplicating spec requests; Extensive large print coll; Home delivery serv; Internet workstation with adaptive software; Local mags & bks recorded; Machine repair; Mags & bk reproduction/duplication; Newsletter (in large print, Braille or on cassette); Newsline for the Blind; Scanner for conversion & translation of mats; Screen enlargement software for people with visual disabilities; Screen reader software; Sound rec; Soundproof reading booth; Spanish Braille mags & bks; Talking bks & player equip; Variable speed audiotape players; Web-Braille; ZoomText magnification & reading software
Open Mon, Wed & Fri 8:30-5, Tues & Thurs 8:30-7
Restriction: Circ limited
Friends of the Library Group
Branches: 1
SAMUEL P HAYES RESEARCH LIBRARY, 175 N Beacon St, 02472. Tel: 617-972-7250. FAX: 617-923-8076. E-mail: hayeslibrary@perkins.org. Web Site: www.perkins.org/researchlibrary. *Librn,* Jan Seymour-Ford; E-mail: jan.seymour-ford@perkins.org; Staff 2 (MLS 1, Non-MLS 1)
Founded 1880
Library Holdings: Bks on Deafness & Sign Lang 30; CDs 95; DVDs 90; e-books 20; Microforms 1,700; Bk Titles 8,000; Bk Vols 33,000; Per Subs 150
Special Collections: Correspondence Between Henney, Anne Sullivan & Helen Keller (Nella Braddy Henney Coll); Institutional History; International Music Braille (Bettye Krolick Coll); Laura Bridgman Coll, artifacts, journals, papers
Subject Interests: Blindness, Spec educ
Automation Activity & Vendor Info: (Cataloging) Inmagic, Inc.; (OPAC) Inmagic, Inc.; (Serials) EBSCO Online
Function: Res libr
Mem of Massachusetts Libr Syst
Special Services for the Blind - Assistive/Adapted tech devices, equip & products; Closed circuit TV; Computer with voice synthesizer for visually impaired persons; Reader equip
Restriction: Non-circulating

S SASAKI ASSOCIATES, INC LIBRARY*, 64 Pleasant St, 02472. SAN 307-7578. Tel: 617-923-7131. FAX: 617-924-2748. E-mail: librarian@sasaki.com. Web Site: www.sasaki.com. *Librn,* Deirdre Doran; Staff 1 (MLS 1)
Founded 1966
Library Holdings: Bk Vols 5,000; Per Subs 150
Special Collections: Company Archives
Subject Interests: Archit, Civil eng, Graphics, Landscape archit, Planning
Restriction: Staff use only

P WATERTOWN FREE PUBLIC LIBRARY*, 123 Main St, 02472. SAN 345-7508. Tel: 617-972-6431. Reference Tel: 617-972-6436. FAX: 617-926-4375. TDD: 617-926-4189. Web Site: www.watertownlib.org. *Dir,* Leone Cole; Tel: 617-972-6434, E-mail: lcole@watertown-ma.gov; *Asst Dir,* Beverly Shank; Tel: 617-972-6438, E-mail: bshank@watertown-ma.gov; *Ch,* Jenny Caron; Tel: 617-972-6435, E-mail: jcaron@watertown-ma.gov; *Teen Serv,* Carey Conkey; Tel: 617-972-6437, E-mail: cconkey@watertown-ma.gov; Staff 19 (MLS 19)
Founded 1868. Pop 33,284; Circ 378,518
Library Holdings: AV Mats 15,728; Bk Titles 129,204; Per Subs 346
Special Collections: Armenian Materials (in English & Armenian); Art of 19th Century Watertown Women Artists. Oral History
Subject Interests: Art & archit, Genealogy, Local hist
Automation Activity & Vendor Info: (Acquisitions) Innovative Interfaces, Inc; (Cataloging) Innovative Interfaces, Inc; (Circulation) Innovative Interfaces, Inc; (OPAC) Innovative Interfaces, Inc; (Serials) Innovative Interfaces, Inc
Database Vendor: Gale Cengage Learning, OCLC FirstSearch, SirsiDynix
Publications: Crossroads on the Charles; Images of America-Watertown
Partic in Minuteman Library Network
Special Services for the Deaf - Spec interest per
Open Mon-Thurs 9-9, Fri & Sat 9-5, Sun 1-5
Friends of the Library Group

WAYLAND

P WAYLAND FREE PUBLIC LIBRARY*, Five Concord Rd, 01778. SAN 345-7621. Tel: 508-358-2311. FAX: 508-358-5249. E-mail: wayland@waylandlibrary.org. Web Site: www.waylandlibrary.org. *Dir,* Ann Knight; *Asst Dir,* Kathleen Powers; E-mail: kpowers@minlib.net; *Head, Circ,* Jan Demeo; E-mail: jdemeo@minlib.net; *Bibliog Serv Librn,* Marjanneke Amare; *Ref Librn,* Andrew Moore; *Ref Librn,* Sandra Raymond; *Youth Serv Librn,* April Mazza; Tel: 508-358-2308, E-mail: amazza@minlib.net; *Youth Serv Librn,* Pamela Sway; E-mail: psway@minlib.net; Staff 13 (MLS 6, Non-MLS 7)
Founded 1848. Pop 13,800; Circ 237,141
Library Holdings: AV Mats 16,265; DVDs 8,768; Bk Titles 76,791; Per Subs 224
Special Collections: Wayland Local History Coll
Subject Interests: Gardening
Automation Activity & Vendor Info: (Acquisitions) Innovative Interfaces, Inc; (Cataloging) Innovative Interfaces, Inc - Millenium; (Circulation) Innovative Interfaces, Inc - Millenium; (OPAC) Innovative Interfaces, Inc
Database Vendor: Gale Cengage Learning, OCLC FirstSearch, Westlaw
Wireless access
Function: Adult literacy prog, Homebound delivery serv, ILL available, Magnifiers for reading, Online searches, Photocopying/Printing, Prog for adults, Prog for children & young adult, Ref serv available, Summer reading prog, Telephone ref, Wheelchair accessible
Publications: Wayland Public Library Update (Newsletter)
Mem of Massachusetts Libr Syst
Partic in Minuteman Library Network
Open Mon-Thurs 9-9, Fri 9-6, Sat 10-5, Sun 2-5
Friends of the Library Group

WEBSTER

P CHESTER C CORBIN PUBLIC LIBRARY*, Two Lake St, 01570. SAN 307-7594. Tel: 508-949-3880. FAX: 508-949-0537. Web Site: www.corbinlibrary.org. *Libr Dir,* Amanda Grenier; E-mail: agrenier@cwmars.org; *Ad,* Dan Gallagher; *Circ Serv Librn,* Riana Freytag; *Youth Serv Librn,* Andrew Tai; Staff 4 (MLS 3, Non-MLS 1)
Founded 1920. Pop 16,000; Circ 35,263
Special Collections: Historical Coll
Automation Activity & Vendor Info: (Cataloging) Evergreen; (Circulation) Evergreen; (OPAC) Evergreen
Wireless access
Function: Adult bk club, Archival coll, Audiobks via web, Bk club(s), Bks on cassette, Bks on CD, CD-ROM, Children's prog, Computer training, Computers for patron use, Copy machines, e-mail serv, Electronic databases & coll, Free DVD rentals, Handicapped accessible, Home delivery & serv to Sr ctr & nursing homes, ILL available, Mail & tel request accepted, Microfiche/film & reading machines, Mus passes, Music CDs, Newsp ref libr, Online cat, Online ref, OverDrive digital audio bks, Photocopying/Printing, Prog for adults, Prog for children & young adult, Pub access computers, Ref & res, Ref serv available, Ref serv in person, Spoken cassettes & CDs, Spoken cassettes & DVDs, Story hour, Summer reading prog, Tax forms, Teen prog, Telephone ref, VHS videos, Web-catalog, Wheelchair accessible, Workshops
Partic in Central & Western Massachusetts Automated Resource Sharing
Open Mon, Tues & Thurs 9-8, Wed 9-1, Fri 9-5, Sat 9-2
Friends of the Library Group

WELLESLEY

S MASSACHUSETTS HORTICULTURAL SOCIETY LIBRARY*, 900 Washington St, Rte 16, 02482. SAN 307-2045. Tel: 617-933-4900. FAX: 617-933-4901. Web Site: www.masshort.org/mhs-library. *Librn,* Maureen Horn; Tel: 617-933-4910, E-mail: mhorn@masshort.org
Founded 1829
Library Holdings: Bk Vols 20,000; Per Subs 10
Special Collections: Print Coll; Rare Book Coll; Seed & Nursery Catalogs
Subject Interests: Art, Hist
Mem of Massachusetts Libr Syst
Partic in Lyrasis; OCLC Online Computer Library Center, Inc
Open Mon-Fri 10-4

J MASSBAY COMMUNITY COLLEGE*, Perkins Library, 50 Oakland St, 02481. SAN 307-7616. Tel: 781-239-2610. FAX: 781-239-3621. Web Site: www.massbay.edu. *Dir, Learning Serv,* Timothy Rivard; Tel: 781-239-2631, E-mail: trivard@massbay.edu; *Ref,* Catherine Abraham; Tel: 781-239-2617, E-mail: cabraham@massbay.edu; Staff 6 (MLS 3, Non-MLS 3)
Founded 1961. Enrl 5,000; Fac 130; Highest Degree: Associate
Library Holdings: Bk Titles 42,146; Bk Vols 51,808; Per Subs 216
Automation Activity & Vendor Info: (Cataloging) Innovative Interfaces, Inc - Millenium; (Circulation) Innovative Interfaces, Inc - Millenium; (OPAC) Innovative Interfaces, Inc - Millenium
Database Vendor: Cinahl, CQ Press, EBSCOhost, Gale Cengage Learning, LexisNexis, SerialsSolutions, STAT!Ref (Teton Data Systems)
Wireless access
Partic in Minuteman Library Network
Open Mon-Thurs 7:45am-10pm, Fri 7:45-5, Sat 8-4, Sun 11-3
Departmental Libraries:
LEARNING RESOURCE CENTER, 19 Flagg Dr, Framingham, 01702-5928, SAN 373-2916. Tel: 508-270-4210. FAX: 508-270-4216. *Ref,* Karen Delorey; Tel: 508-270-4215, E-mail: kdelorey@massbay.edu; Staff 2 (MLS 2)
Highest Degree: Associate
Library Holdings: Bk Vols 11,000
Open Mon-Thurs 8am-10pm, Fri 8-5, Sat 8-Noon

C WELLESLEY COLLEGE*, Margaret Clapp Library, 106 Central St, 02481-8275. SAN 345-7680. Tel: 781-283-2166. Interlibrary Loan Service Tel: 781-283-2101. Reference Tel: 781-283-2097. Administration Tel: 781-283-2096. FAX: 781-283-3690. Web Site: www.wellesley.edu/library. *VPres for Info Serv,* Micheline Jedry; Fax: 781-283-3904; *Mgr,* Eileen Hardy; Tel: 781-283-3317, E-mail: ehardy@wellesley.edu; *Mgr,* Dale Katzif; Tel: 781-283-2109, E-mail: dkatzif@wellesley.edu; *Acq Mgr, Cat Mgr,* Ross Wood; Tel: 781-283-2104, E-mail: rwood@wellesley.edu; *Mgr, Res,* BethAnn Zambella; Tel: 781-283-3512, E-mail: bzambell@wellesley.edu; *Spec Coll Librn,* Ruth Rogers; *Archivist,* Wilma Slaight; Tel: 781-283-2128, Fax: 781-283-3796, E-mail: wslaight@wellesley.edu; Staff 38 (MLS 14, Non-MLS 24)
Founded 1875. Enrl 2,231; Fac 212; Highest Degree: Bachelor
Library Holdings: Bk Vols 100,000; Per Subs 2,305
Special Collections: Book Arts; First & Rare Editions of English & American Poetry; Italian Renaissance (Plimpton Coll), bks & mss; Ruskin; Slavery (Elbert Coll). US Document Depository
Automation Activity & Vendor Info: (Acquisitions) Innovative Interfaces, Inc; (Circulation) Innovative Interfaces, Inc; (Serials) Innovative Interfaces, Inc
Database Vendor: Dialog, LexisNexis, OCLC FirstSearch, SirsiDynix
Wireless access
Partic in Boston Library Consortium, Inc; OCLC Online Computer Library Center, Inc
Friends of the Library Group
Departmental Libraries:
ART LIBRARY, Jewett Arts Ctr, 106 Central St, 02481, SAN 345-7699. Tel: 781-283-2049. Reference Tel: 781-283-3258. FAX: 781-283-3647. *Art Librn,* Brooke Henderson
Open Mon-Thurs 8:15am-11pm, Fri 8:15-7, Sat 12-5, Sun 12-11
Restriction: Non-circulating to the pub
Friends of the Library Group
MUSIC LIBRARY, Jewett Arts Ctr, Rm 208, 106 Central St, 02481-8203, SAN 345-7702. Tel: 781-283-2075. Reference Tel: 781-283-2076. FAX: 781-283-2869. Web Site: www.wellesley.edu/library/music/musiclib.html. *Librn,* Pamela Bristah; E-mail: pbristah@wellesley.edu
Friends of the Library Group
SCIENCE LIBRARY, Science Ctr, 106 Central St, 02481, SAN 345-7710. Tel: 781-283-3084. Circulation Tel: 781-283-3083. Reference Tel: 781-283-3085. FAX: 781-283-3642. *Librn,* Lisa Brainard; *Librn,* Neil Nero; *Instrul Serv Librn, Res,* Irene Laursen
Library Holdings: Bk Vols 105,000; Per Subs 625
Open Mon-Fri 8:30-4:30
Friends of the Library Group
WELLESLEY CENTERS FOR WOMEN, Cheever House, 106 Central St, 02481, SAN 374-9886. Tel: 781-283-2500. FAX: 781-283-2504. E-mail: WCW@wellesley.edu. Web Site: wcwonline.org. *Exec Dir,* Layli Maparyan; E-mail: layli.maparyan@wellesley.edu
Library Holdings: Bk Vols 1,000
Restriction: Open to pub for ref only

P WELLESLEY FREE LIBRARY*, 530 Washington St, 02482. SAN 345-7745. Tel: 781-235-1610. Reference Tel: 781-235-1610, Ext 1117. FAX: 781-235-0495. E-mail: weldir@minlib.net. Web Site: www.wellesleyfreelibrary.org. *Dir,* Position Currently Open; *Asst Dir,* Helen Charbonneau; Tel: 781-235-1610, Ext 1130, E-mail: hcharbonneau@minlib.net; *Asst Dir,* Elise MacLennan; Tel: 781-235-1610, Ext 1107, E-mail: emaclennan@minlib.net; *Head, Circ,* Pearl Der; Tel: 781-235-1610, Ext 1131, E-mail: pder@minlib.net; *Head, Ref,* Sue Hamilos; Tel: 781-235-1610, Ext 1110, E-mail: shamilos@minlib.net; *Acq,* Elaine Schicitano; *Ch Serv,* Farouqua Abuzeit; Tel: 781-235-1610, Ext 1109, E-mail: fabouzeit@minlib.net; *ILL,* Sue Kaler; Tel: 781-235-1610, Ext 1112, E-mail: skaler@minlib.net; Staff 66 (MLS 16, Non-MLS 50)
Founded 1883. Pop 26,613; Circ 667,193
Jul 2009-Jun 2010 Income (Main Library Only) $2,067,164. Mats Exp $247,439, Books $135,439, Per/Ser (Incl. Access Fees) $17,000, Micro $13,500, AV Mat $66,500, Electronic Ref Mat (Incl. Access Fees) $15,000. Sal $1,504,418
Library Holdings: CDs 17,221; DVDs 14,533; e-books 4,246; Electronic Media & Resources 55; Bk Titles 239,862; Per Subs 330
Subject Interests: Bus
Automation Activity & Vendor Info: (Acquisitions) Innovative Interfaces, Inc - Millenium; (Cataloging) Innovative Interfaces, Inc - Millenium; (Circulation) Innovative Interfaces, Inc - Millenium; (ILL) Clio; (OPAC) Innovative Interfaces, Inc - Millenium; (Serials) Innovative Interfaces, Inc - Millenium
Database Vendor: Gale Cengage Learning, OCLC FirstSearch, ProQuest
Wireless access
Function: Ref serv available
Partic in Minuteman Library Network
Special Services for the Deaf - TTY equip
Open Mon-Thurs 9-9, Fri 9-6, Sat 9-5, Sun (Sept-June) 1-5
Friends of the Library Group
Branches: 2
FELLS BRANCH, 308 Weston Rd, 02482, SAN 345-777X. Tel: 781-237-0485. *Dir,* Janice G Coduri; Tel: 781-235-1610, Ext 1129, Fax: 781-235-0495; Staff 5 (MLS 1, Non-MLS 4)
Founded 1923
Jul 2009-Jun 2010 Income $35,000
Library Holdings: Bk Titles 4,783
Friends of the Library Group
WELLESLEY HILLS BRANCH, 210 Washington St, Wellesley Hills, 02481, SAN 345-780X. Tel: 781-237-0381. *Dir,* Janice G Coduri; Tel: 781-235-1610, Ext 1129, Fax: 781-235-0495, E-mail: jcoduri@minlib.net; Staff 5 (MLS 1, Non-MLS 4)
Founded 1928
Jul 2009-Jun 2010 Income $50,000
Library Holdings: Bk Titles 7,292
Automation Activity & Vendor Info: (Acquisitions) Innovative Interfaces, Inc - Millenium; (Cataloging) Innovative Interfaces, Inc - Millenium; (Circulation) Innovative Interfaces, Inc - Millenium; (OPAC) Innovative Interfaces, Inc - Millenium
Open Tues & Thurs 10-8, Wed, Fri & Sat 10-5
Friends of the Library Group

WELLESLEY HILLS

R WELLESLEY HILLS CONGREGATIONAL CHURCH LIBRARY*, 207 Washington St, 02481-3105. SAN 307-7632. Tel: 781-235-4424. FAX: 781-235-9838. Web Site: www.whcc-ucc.org. *Librn,* Dr Lorraine E Tolman
Founded 1956
Jan 2005-Dec 2005. Mats Exp Books $1,000
Library Holdings: Bk Vols 3,500
Special Collections: Children Coll
Subject Interests: Relig
Restriction: Mem only

WELLFLEET

S US NATIONAL PARK SERVICE*, Cape Cod National Seashore Library, 99 Marconi Site Rd, 02667. SAN 370-3061. Tel: 508-349-3785. FAX: 508-349-9052. Web Site: www.nps.gov/caco.
Library Holdings: Bk Titles 2,500; Per Subs 10
Function: Ref serv available
Open Wed 9:30-4
Restriction: Non-circulating

P WELLFLEET PUBLIC LIBRARY*, 55 W Main St, 02667. SAN 307-7659. Tel: 508-349-0310, 508-349-0311. FAX: 508-349-0312. Web Site: www.wellfleetlibrary.org. *Librn,* Elaine R McIlroy; E-mail: emcilroy@clamsnet.org; Staff 7 (MLS 1, Non-MLS 6)
Founded 1893. Pop 3,200; Circ 97,000
Jul 2006-Jun 2007 Income $348,920, State $4,220, City $300,000, Locally Generated Income $40,000, Other $4,700. Mats Exp $75,600, Books $45,900, Per/Ser (Incl. Access Fees) $5,800, Other Print Mats $3,500, AV Mat $18,000, Electronic Ref Mat (Incl. Access Fees) $2,400. Sal $236,267 (Prof $60,000)
Library Holdings: CDs 2,310; DVDs 1,500; Bk Vols 43,316; Per Subs 100; Videos 1,500
Special Collections: Cape Cod Coll
Subject Interests: Aquaculture, Art
Wireless access
Mem of Massachusetts Libr Syst
Open Mon, Wed & Thurs (Nov-April) 2-8, Tues 10-8, Fri & Sat 10-5, Sun 2-5
Friends of the Library Group

WENDELL

P WENDELL FREE LIBRARY*, Seven Wendell Depot Rd, 01379. (Mail add: PO Box 236, 01379-7910), SAN 307-7667. Tel: 978-544-3559. FAX: 978-544-3559. Web Site: www.wendellfreelibrary.org. *Dir,* Rosemary Heidkamp
Founded 1894. Pop 1,058; Circ 17,415
Jul 2011-Jun 2012. Mats Exp $5,500. Sal $27,000
Library Holdings: AV Mats 100; Bks on Deafness & Sign Lang 15; DVDs 500; Bk Titles 14,000; Per Subs 40; Videos 200
Partic in Central & Western Massachusetts Automated Resource Sharing
Open Tues 3-6, Wed 10-8, Sat 9:30-2:30, Sun 2-5:30
Friends of the Library Group

WENHAM

C GORDON COLLEGE*, Jenks Library, 255 Grapevine Rd, 01984-1899. SAN 307-7675. Tel: 978-867-4339. Interlibrary Loan Service Tel: 978-867-4416. Reference Tel: 978-867-4342. FAX: 978-867-4660. E-mail: library@gordon.edu. Web Site: www.gordon.edu/library/. *Dir of Libr Serv,* Dr Myron Schirer-Suter; Tel: 978-867-4083, E-mail: myron.schirer-suter@gordon.edu; *Asst Dir, Pub Serv,* Randall Gowman;

E-mail: randy.gowman@gordon.edu; *Acq, Cat,* Alec Li; Tel: 978-867-4341, E-mail: alec.li@gordon.edu; *Archivist,* John Beauregard; Tel: 978-867-4140, E-mail: john.beauregard@gordon.edu; *Bibliog Instr, ILL,* Martha Crain; E-mail: martha.crain@gordon.edu; *Govt Doc, Ser,* Janet Bjork; Tel: 978-867-4345, E-mail: janet.bjork@gordon.edu; Staff 5 (MLS 5)
Founded 1889. Enrl 1,530; Fac 100; Highest Degree: Master
Jul 2007-Jun 2008 Income $851,000. Mats Exp $175,117, Books $63,746, Per/Ser (Incl. Access Fees) $60,207, Other Print Mats $7,637, Electronic Ref Mat (Incl. Access Fees) $43,527. Sal $433,179
Library Holdings: CDs 1,730; DVDs 1,300; e-books 397; Microforms 31,736; Music Scores 2,008; Bk Vols 150,379; Per Subs 327; Videos 2,994
Special Collections: American Linguistics; Bibles; Global Circumnavigation; Northwest Exploration; Shakespeare (Vining Coll). US Document Depository
Subject Interests: Educ, Fine arts, Humanities, Natural sci, Soc sci & issues
Automation Activity & Vendor Info: (Acquisitions) Innovative Interfaces, Inc; (Cataloging) Innovative Interfaces, Inc; (Circulation) Innovative Interfaces, Inc; (Course Reserve) Innovative Interfaces, Inc; (ILL) Innovative Interfaces, Inc; (Media Booking) Innovative Interfaces, Inc; (OPAC) Innovative Interfaces, Inc; (Serials) Innovative Interfaces, Inc
Database Vendor: American Chemical Society, BioOne, Dialog, EBSCOhost, Facts on File, Gale Cengage Learning, LexisNexis, Modern Language Association, OCLC WorldShare Interlibrary Loan, Overdrive, Inc, Project MUSE, ProQuest, PubMed
Wireless access
Function: ILL available, Ref serv available
Mem of Massachusetts Libr Syst
Partic in Lyrasis; North of Boston Library Exchange, Inc; OCLC Online Computer Library Center, Inc
Open Mon-Thurs 7:45am-Midnight, Fri 7:45am-9pm, Sat 10-9, Sun 2pm-Midnight

S WENHAM MUSEUM*, Colonel Timothy Pickering Library, 132 Main St, 01984. SAN 307-7683. Tel: 978-468-2377. FAX: 978-468-1763. E-mail: info@wenhammuseum.org. Web Site: www.wenhammuseum.org. *Exec Dir,* Emily S Fertik
Founded 1953
Library Holdings: Bk Titles 1,100
Special Collections: Historical Association, account bks, deeds, diaries, papers; Massachusetts Society for Promoting Agriculture, medals, mementoes, paintings, publications
Subject Interests: Agr, Costume design, Genealogy, Hist
Function: Res libr
Publications: Annual Report of Museum; History of Claflin-Richards House, Allens History of Wenham
Mem of Massachusetts Libr Syst
Restriction: Non-circulating, Open by appt only

WEST ACTON

P WEST ACTON CITIZEN'S LIBRARY*, 21 Windsor Ave, 01720-2809. SAN 307-0697. Tel: 978-264-9652. E-mail: wacl@acton-ma.gov. Web Site: www.acton-ma.gov. *Dir,* Jennifer Friedman; E-mail: jfriedman@acton-ma.gov
Library Holdings: Bk Vols 11,700; Per Subs 25
Open Tues 10-7, Wed-Fri 10-5
Friends of the Library Group

WEST BARNSTABLE

J CAPE COD COMMUNITY COLLEGE*, Wilkens Library, 2240 Iyannough Rd, 02668-1599. SAN 307-7705. Tel: 508-362-2131. Circulation Tel: 508-362-2131, Ext 4342, 508-362-2131, Ext 4480. Interlibrary Loan Service Tel: 508-362-2131, Ext 4448. Reference Tel: 508-362-2131, Ext 4343. Toll Free Tel: 877-846-3672. FAX: 508-375-4020. E-mail: refdesk@capecod.edu. Web Site: www.capecod.edu/library. *Assoc Dean, Learning Res, Pub Serv,* Jeanmarie Fraser; Tel: 508-362-2131, Ext 4618, E-mail: jfraser@capecod.edu; *Ref & Instruction Librn,* Stephanie Turnbull; Tel: 508-362-2131, Ext 4753, E-mail: sturnbull@capecod.edu; *Spec Coll Librn,* Mary LaBombard; Tel: 508-362-2131, Ext 4445, E-mail: mlabombard@capecod.edu; *Circ Mgr,* Eileen Redfield; E-mail: ekearns@capecod.edu; *Pub Serv Coordr,* Tim Gerolami; Tel: 508-362-2131, Ext 4351, E-mail: tgerolami@capecod.edu. Subject Specialists: *Archives, Hist,* Mary LaBombard; *Ill,* Eileen Redfield; Staff 9.5 (MLS 5, Non-MLS 4.5)
Founded 1961. Enrl 5,000; Fac 75; Highest Degree: Associate
Jul 2006-Jun 2007 Income $706,000, Locally Generated Income $7,000, Parent Institution $699,000. Mats Exp $187,182, Books $101,795, Per/Ser (Incl. Access Fees) $28,295, AV Mat $11,463, Electronic Ref Mat (Incl. Access Fees) $45,629. Sal $470,701 (Prof $255,684)
Library Holdings: AV Mats 3,320; e-books 836; e-journals 49,097; Microforms 17,800; Bk Vols 19,963; Per Subs 178
Special Collections: Cape Cod History Coll; FC Cooperating Coll. Oral History
Automation Activity & Vendor Info: (Acquisitions) Innovative Interfaces, Inc - Millenium; (Cataloging) Innovative Interfaces, Inc - Millenium; (Circulation) Innovative Interfaces, Inc - Millenium; (Course Reserve) Innovative Interfaces, Inc - Millenium; (ILL) Innovative Interfaces, Inc; (Media Booking) Innovative Interfaces, Inc - Millenium; (OPAC) Innovative Interfaces, Inc; (Serials) Innovative Interfaces, Inc
Database Vendor: Checkpoint Systems, Inc, Cinahl, CredoReference, Dun & Bradstreet, ebrary, EBSCOhost, Electric Library, Elsevier, Facts on File, Foundation Center, Gale Cengage Learning, LexisNexis, Marquis Who's Who, McGraw-Hill, Medline, Mergent Online, Micromedex, Natural Standard, Newsbank, OCLC FirstSearch, OCLC WorldShare Interlibrary Loan, ProQuest, PubMed, ReferenceUSA, SerialsSolutions, Standard & Poor's, STAT!Ref (Teton Data Systems), TLC (The Library Corporation)
Wireless access
Function: Archival coll, Computers for patron use, Copy machines, Doc delivery serv, Electronic databases & coll, Equip loans & repairs, Handicapped accessible, ILL available, Learning ctr, Microfiche/film & reading machines, Online cat, Online info literacy tutorials on the web & in blackboard, Online searches, Orientations, Photocopying/Printing, Pub access computers, Ref & res, Ref serv available, Ref serv in person, Scanner, Telephone ref, Wheelchair accessible
Mem of Massachusetts Libr Syst
Partic in Cape & Islands Interlibrary Asn; Cape Libraries Automated Materials Sharing Network; Lyrasis; Southeastern Massachusetts Consortium of Health Science Libraries
Open Mon-Thurs 8am-9:30pm, Fri 8-4:30, Sat 9-1, Sun 1-5
Restriction: Non-circulating of rare bks, Open to pub for ref & circ; with some limitations

P WHELDEN MEMORIAL LIBRARY*, 2401 Meetinghouse Way, 02668-1403. (Mail add: PO Box 147, 02668-0147), SAN 307-7713. Tel: 508-362-2262. FAX: 508-362-1344. E-mail: whelden@comcast.net. Web Site: www.wheldenlibrary.org. *Dir,* Kathleen Swetish; E-mail: kswetish@clamsnet.org; Staff 4 (Non-MLS 4)
Founded 1899. Pop 2,206; Circ 25,249
Library Holdings: AV Mats 3,709; Bk Vols 16,921; Per Subs 22
Special Collections: Finnish History Coll
Subject Interests: Local hist
Database Vendor: Innovative Interfaces, Inc
Wireless access
Partic in Cape Libraries Automated Materials Sharing Network
Open Mon & Wed 2-8, Tues & Thurs-Sat 9-2
Friends of the Library Group

WEST BOYLSTON

P BEAMAN MEMORIAL PUBLIC LIBRARY, Eight Newton St, 01583. SAN 307-7721. Tel: 508-835-3711. FAX: 508-835-4770. E-mail: beaman@cwmars.org. Web Site: beamanlibrary.org. *Dir,* Louise Howland; *Asst Dir,* Anna Kanabay; *Ch Serv,* Susan Smith; Staff 4.5 (MLS 0.8, Non-MLS 3.7)
Founded 1878. Pop 7,669; Circ 73,736
Jul 2014-Jun 2015 Income $384,848, State $9,000, City $365,848, Locally Generated Income $10,000. Mats Exp $54,800, Books $31,400, Per/Ser (Incl. Access Fees) $6,000, AV Mat $5,000, Electronic Ref Mat (Incl. Access Fees) $12,400. Sal $237,085 (Prof $139,918)
Library Holdings: Bk Vols 77,754; Per Subs 89
Automation Activity & Vendor Info: (Cataloging) Evergreen; (Circulation) Evergreen; (OPAC) Evergreen
Database Vendor: EBSCOhost, Gale Cengage Learning
Wireless access
Function: Bk club(s), Bks on cassette, Bks on CD, Children's prog, Computers for patron use, Copy machines, Electronic databases & coll, Handicapped accessible, Home delivery & serv to Sr ctr & nursing homes, ILL available, Magnifiers for reading, Mus passes, Music CDs, Notary serv, Prog for adults, Prog for children & young adult, Pub access computers, Story hour, Tax forms, VHS videos
Publications: Beaman Browser (Newsletter)
Mem of Massachusetts Libr Syst
Partic in Central & Western Massachusetts Automated Resource Sharing
Open Tues, Wed & Thurs 10-8, Fri 1-5, Sat (Sept-June) 10-2
Friends of the Library Group

S WORCESTER COUNTY JAIL & HOUSE OF CORRECTION LIBRARY*, Five Paul X Tivnan Dr, 01583. SAN 372-7254. Tel: 508-854-1800, Ext 2344. FAX: 508-852-8754. *Librn,* Christina Moore; Staff 2 (MLS 1, Non-MLS 1)
Library Holdings: Bk Vols 8,000; Per Subs 17
Special Collections: Black History, bks, videotapes; Spanish Coll
Open Mon-Fri 7-3

WEST BRIDGEWATER

P WEST BRIDGEWATER PUBLIC LIBRARY*, 80 Howard St, 02379-1710. SAN 307-773X. Tel: 508-894-1255. FAX: 508-894-1258. Web Site: www.sailsinc.org/westbridgewater. *Libr Dir,* Beth Roll Smith; E-mail: bsmith@sailsinc.org; *Asst Dir,* April McDermott; *Ch,* Nanette Ryan; *Ref Serv,* Sherry Pinter; *Tech Serv,* Ellen Crawford; Staff 5 (MLS 1, Non-MLS 4)
Founded 1879. Pop 6,742; Circ 64,059
Jul 2009-Jun 2010 Income $362,687, State $9,789, City $342,992, Locally Generated Income $6,800, Other $3,106. Mats Exp $69,505, Books $61,402, Per/Ser (Incl. Access Fees) $3,000, Other Print Mats $1,000, AV Mat $3,100, Electronic Ref Mat (Incl. Access Fees) $1,003. Sal $219,464 (Prof $64,368)
Library Holdings: Audiobooks 500; AV Mats 457; Bks on Deafness & Sign Lang 30; Braille Volumes 2; CDs 1,294; DVDs 1,000; e-books 893; Electronic Media & Resources 20; High Interest/Low Vocabulary Bk Vols 200; Large Print Bks 2,000; Microforms 1; Music Scores 250; Bk Titles 61,402; Per Subs 180; Videos 500
Special Collections: West Bridgewater History Coll; World War II Autobiographies & Accounts. Oral History
Subject Interests: Local genealogy, W Bridgewater hist
Automation Activity & Vendor Info: (Acquisitions) SirsiDynix; (Cataloging) SirsiDynix; (Circulation) SirsiDynix; (Course Reserve) SirsiDynix; (OPAC) SirsiDynix; (Serials) SirsiDynix
Publications: Heddalines (Newsletter)
Mem of Massachusetts Libr Syst
Partic in SAILS Library Network
Open Mon, Thurs & Fri 10-5, Tues & Wed 10-7, Sat (Winter) 10-2
Friends of the Library Group

WEST BROOKFIELD

P MERRIAM-GILBERT PUBLIC LIBRARY, Three W Main St, 01585. (Mail add: PO Box 364, 01585-0364), SAN 307-7748. Tel: 508-867-1410. FAX: 508-867-1409. Web Site: www.wbrookfieldlibrary.org. *Dir,* Position Currently Open; *Adult Serv, Asst Librn,* Holly Takorian; E-mail: htakoria@cwmars.org; *Ch Serv,* Mary Beth Jackson; E-mail: mjackson@cwmars.org
Founded 1880. Pop 3,800; Circ 35,928
Jul 2011-Jun 2012. Mats Exp $37,089, Books $25,000, AV Mat $12,089. Sal $110,597
Library Holdings: CDs 1,062; DVDs 1,421; e-books 9,844; e-journals 3,549; Bk Titles 13,592; Per Subs 44; Videos 280
Special Collections: Massachusetts Genealogy Coll
Subject Interests: Archives, Local hist, Manuscripts
Wireless access
Mem of Central Massachusetts Regional Library System
Partic in Central & Western Massachusetts Automated Resource Sharing
Open Mon & Wed 9-5, Tues & Thurs 2-8, Sat 9-Noon
Friends of the Library Group

WEST DENNIS

P WEST DENNIS LIBRARY*, 260 Main St, Rte 28, 02670. (Mail add: PO Box 158, 02670-0158), SAN 307-7764. Tel: 508-398-2050. FAX: 508-394-6279. E-mail: dem_w_mail@clamsnet.org. Web Site: www.westdennis.library.org. *Dir,* Tiffany Turner; *Cataloger,* Belva Dudac; *Vols Coordr,* Joyce Oppen
Pop 5,000; Circ 15,183
Library Holdings: Bk Vols 14,000; Per Subs 42
Open Mon-Thurs 10-2, Fri 10-8, Sun 11-1
Friends of the Library Group

WEST FALMOUTH

P WEST FALMOUTH LIBRARY*, 575 W Falmouth Hwy, 02574. (Mail add: PO Box 1209, 02574-1209), SAN 307-7772. Tel: 508-548-4709. FAX: 508-457-9534. E-mail: westfallib@comcast.net. Web Site: westfalmouthlibrary.org. *Librn,* Pamela Thoits Olson
Pop 2,500; Circ 39,785
Library Holdings: Bk Vols 12,500; Per Subs 28
Automation Activity & Vendor Info: (Acquisitions) Innovative Interfaces, Inc - Millenium; (Cataloging) Innovative Interfaces, Inc - Millenium; (Circulation) Innovative Interfaces, Inc - Millenium
Wireless access
Open Tues, Wed & Fri 10-5, Thurs 2-8, Sat 10-1

WEST HARWICH

P CHASE LIBRARY*, Seven Main St, 02671-1041. (Mail add: PO Box 457, 02671-0457), SAN 307-7780. Tel: 508-432-2610. E-mail: chase.lib@verizon.net. *Dir,* Maryanne Desmarais
Founded 1907. Circ 10,000
Library Holdings: Bk Vols 20,000
Wireless access
Function: ILL available
Open Tues 10-4, Sat 12-2:30
Friends of the Library Group

WEST NEWBURY

P G A R MEMORIAL LIBRARY*, 490 Main St, 01985-1115. SAN 307-7799. Tel: 978-363-1105. FAX: 978-363-1116. *Dir,* Katharine M Gove; E-mail: kgove@mvlc.org, Staff 1 (Non-MLS 1)
Founded 1819. Pop 4,450; Circ 105,493
Jul 2006-Jun 2007 Income $285,874, State $6,570, City $255,114, Other $24,190. Mats Exp $79,608, Books $29,540, Per/Ser (Incl. Access Fees) $8,382, AV Mat $17,658, Electronic Ref Mat (Incl. Access Fees) $24,028. Sal $172,220 (Prof $64,359)
Library Holdings: AV Mats 17,658; CDs 238; DVDs 1,422; Electronic Media & Resources 9; Large Print Bks 164; Bk Titles 47,018; Per Subs 174; Talking Bks 2,155
Automation Activity & Vendor Info: (Cataloging) SirsiDynix; (Circulation) SirsiDynix; (ILL) SirsiDynix
Wireless access
Mem of Massachusetts Libr Syst
Partic in Merrimack Valley Library Consortium
Open Mon-Thurs 10-8, Fri 10-5, Sat 9-1
Friends of the Library Group

WEST ROXBURY

GM VA MEDICAL CENTER*, Medical Library, 1400 Veterans of Foreign Wars Pkwy, 02132. SAN 307-7802. Tel: 617-323-7700, Ext 35142. FAX: 857-203-5532. *Chief, Libr Serv,* Elaine Alligood; E-mail: elaine.alligood@va.gov; *Libr Tech,* Rebecca Ahmed; E-mail: rebecca.morton@va.gov; Staff 2 (MLS 1, Non-MLS 1)
Library Holdings: Bk Vols 3,850; Per Subs 300
Subject Interests: Allied health, Cardiology, Med, Surgery
Partic in Boston Biomedical Library Consortium
Open Mon-Fri 8:30-4:30

WEST SPRINGFIELD

S STORROWTON VILLAGE MUSEUM LIBRARY*, 1305 Memorial Ave, 01089. SAN 373 1758. Tel: 413-205-5051. FAX: 413-205-5054. E-mail: storrow@thebige.com. *Dir,* Dennis D Picard
Library Holdings: Bk Vols 750
Subject Interests: Local hist
Restriction: Non-circulating, Open by appt only

P WEST SPRINGFIELD PUBLIC LIBRARY*, 200 Park St, 01089. SAN 307-7810. Tel: 413-736-4561. FAX: 413-736-6469. TDD: 413-732-2599. Web Site: www.wspl.org. *Dir,* Antonia Golinski-Foisy; Tel: 413-736-4561, Ext 102, E-mail: agolinsk@cwmars.org; *Asst Dir,* Nancy Dellapenna; E-mail: ndellape@cwmars.org; *Adult Serv, Ref,* David Morrell; Tel: 413-736 4561, Ext 3, E-mail; dmorrell@cwmars.org; *Cat, Tech Serv Supvr,* Eileen Chapman; E-mail: echapman@cwmars.org; *Youth Serv,* Terri Mitus, Tel: 413-736-4561, Ext 4, E-mail: tmitus@cwmars.org; Staff 24 (MLS 10, Non-MLS 14)
Founded 1854. Pop 25,876; Circ 198,517
Library Holdings: Bk Vols 102,154; Per Subs 196
Automation Activity & Vendor Info: (Acquisitions) Innovative Interfaces, Inc; (Cataloging) Innovative Interfaces, Inc; (Circulation) Innovative Interfaces, Inc; (OPAC) Innovative Interfaces, Inc
Special Services for the Deaf - TDD equip; TTY equip
Special Services for the Blind - Descriptive video serv (DVS)
Open Mon-Thurs (Winter) 9-9, Fri & Sat 9-5; Mon-Thurs (Summer) 9-8, Fri 9-5
Friends of the Library Group

WEST STOCKBRIDGE

P WEST STOCKBRIDGE PUBLIC LIBRARY*, 21 State Line Rd, 01266. (Mail add: PO Box 60, 01266-0060), SAN 307-7829. Tel: 413-232-0300, Ext 308. E-mail: weststockbridgelibrary@gmail.com. Web Site: www.weststockbridgelibrary.org/home. *Dir,* Lee Appelbaum; *Libr Asst,* Jodi Magner
Founded 1890. Pop 1,400
Library Holdings: Bk Titles 7,500; Per Subs 15
Wireless access
Open Tues 12-5, Wed 1-5, Thurs & Fri 2-6, Sat 10-2
Friends of the Library Group

WEST TISBURY

P WEST TISBURY FREE PUBLIC LIBRARY, 1042 State Rd, 02575. (Mail add: 1042 State Rd, Vineyard Haven, 02568), SAN 307-7837. Tel: 508-693-3366. FAX: 508-696-0130. E-mail: circ@westtisburylibrary.org. Web Site: www.westtisburylibrary.org. *Dir,* Beth Kramer; *Asst Librn,* Nelia Decker; *Asst Librn,* Amy Hoff; Staff 1 (Non-MLS 1)

Founded 1893. Pop 5,700; Circ 173,000
Library Holdings: Audiobooks 2,000; Bks on Deafness & Sign Lang 50; DVDs 4,000; Large Print Bks 200; Bk Titles 54,000; Bk Vols 55,000; Per Subs 115; Talking Bks 1,371
Special Collections: Vineyard Authors
Automation Activity & Vendor Info: (Cataloging) Innovative Interfaces, Inc - Millenium; (Circulation) Innovative Interfaces, Inc - Millenium
Wireless access
Function: Adult bk club, After school storytime, Art exhibits, Bk reviews (Group), Children's prog, Computers for patron use, Copy machines, Digital talking bks, Doc delivery serv, e-mail & chat, E-Reserves, Exhibits, Fax serv, Free DVD rentals, Handicapped accessible, Health sci info serv, Holiday prog, Home delivery & serv to Sr ctr & nursing homes, ILL available, Instruction & testing, Jazz prog, Magnifiers for reading, Mail & tel request accepted, Online cat, Online searches, Outreach serv, Passport agency, Photocopying/Printing, Prog for adults, Prog for children & young adult, Pub access computers, Scanner, Senior computer classes, Senior outreach, Spoken cassettes & CDs, Spoken cassettes & DVDs, Story hour, Summer reading prog, Tax forms, Web-catalog, Wheelchair accessible, Workshops
Open Mon 10-9, Tues-Thurs 10-6, Fri & Sat 10-5, Sun (Winter) 1-5
Friends of the Library Group

WEST WARREN

P WEST WARREN LIBRARY*, 2370 Main St, 01092. (Mail add: PO Box 369, 01092-0369), SAN 307-7845. Tel: 413-436-9892. FAX: 413-436-5086. E-mail: wwpl@comcast.net. Web Site: www.westwarrenlibrary.org. *Librn,* Patricia Meleski
Circ 5,390
Library Holdings: Bk Vols 9,000; Per Subs 18
Mem of Massachusetts Libr Syst
Open Mon & Fri 12-5, Wed 12-7, Thurs 4-7, Sat 9-Noon
Friends of the Library Group

WESTBOROUGH

P WESTBOROUGH PUBLIC LIBRARY*, 55 W Main St, 01581. SAN 307-787X. Tel: 508-366-3050. FAX: 508-366-3049. E-mail: westboro@cwmars.org. Web Site: www.westboroughlib.org. *Libr Dir,* Maureen Ambrosino; *Circ Supvr,* Jennifer Schwartz; *Adult Serv,* Donna Martel; *Ch Serv,* Dorothy Hurley; Staff 17 (MLS 5, Non-MLS 12)
Founded 1908. Pop 18,000
Library Holdings: Audiobooks 5,202; DVDs 4,402; e-books 2,810; e-journals 8; Bk Titles 81,100; Per Subs 154
Special Collections: Local History (Reed Coll). Oral History
Automation Activity & Vendor Info: (Acquisitions) Innovative Interfaces, Inc - Millenium; (Cataloging) Innovative Interfaces, Inc - Millenium; (Circulation) Innovative Interfaces, Inc - Millenium; (OPAC) Innovative Interfaces, Inc - Millenium
Database Vendor: EBSCOhost, Evanced Solutions, Inc, Facts on File, Gale Cengage Learning, Grolier Online, Newsbank, ProQuest, ReferenceUSA, ValueLine
Wireless access
Function: Adult bk club, Archival coll, Audiobks via web, Bks on CD, CD-ROM, Children's prog, Computers for patron use, Copy machines, Electronic databases & coll, Family literacy, Free DVD rentals, Handicapped accessible, Homebound delivery serv, ILL available, Mus passes, Music CDs, Online cat, Online searches, OverDrive digital audio bks, Photocopying/Printing, Prog for adults, Prog for children & young adult, Pub access computers, Story hour, Summer reading prog, Tax forms, Teen prog, Telephone ref, Wheelchair accessible
Mem of Massachusetts Libr Syst
Partic in Central & Western Massachusetts Automated Resource Sharing
Open Mon-Thurs 10-9, Fri 10-6, Sat 10-5, Sun (Oct-May) 1-5
Friends of the Library Group

WESTFIELD

P WESTFIELD ATHENAEUM*, Six Elm St, 01085-2997. SAN 345-7834. Tel: 413-568-7833. Circulation Tel: 413-568-7833, Ext 3. Administration Tel: 413-568-0638, Ext 83. Information Services Tel: 413-562-0716, Ext 4. FAX: 413-568-0988. Web Site: www.westath.org. *Dir,* Christopher J Lindquist; Tel: 413-568-7833, Ext 81, E-mail: clindquist@westath.org; *Asst Dir,* Ralph Melnick; Tel: 413-568-7833, Ext 82, E-mail: rmelnick@westath.org; *Head, Tech Serv,* Jeanne T Peer; Tel: 413-568-7833, Ext 7, E-mail: jpeer@westath.org; *Ch Serv,* Kara Welch; *Info Serv,* Janice Gryszkiewicz; Staff 29 (MLS 1, Non-MLS 28)
Founded 1864. Pop 38,000; Circ 327,211
Library Holdings: Bk Vols 119,311; Per Subs 132
Special Collections: Edward Taylor Colonial Poetry Coll, mss
Automation Activity & Vendor Info: (Cataloging) Innovative Interfaces, Inc; (Circulation) Innovative Interfaces, Inc; (OPAC) Innovative Interfaces, Inc
Partic in Central-Western Mass Automated Resource Sharing
Open Mon-Thurs 8:30-8, Fri 8:30-5, Sat (Sept-June) 8:30-5
Friends of the Library Group

C WESTFIELD STATE UNIVERSITY*, Ely Library, 577 Western Ave, 01085-2580. (Mail add: PO Box 1630, 01086-1630), SAN 307-7896. Tel: 413-572-5251. Circulation Tel: 413-572-5231. Interlibrary Loan Service Tel: 413-572-5655. Reference Tel: 413-572-5234. Administration Tel: 413-572-5233, 413-572-5639. FAX: 413-572-5520. Web Site: lib.westfield.ma.edu. *Libr Dir,* Thomas Raffensperger; E-mail: traffensperger@westfield.ma.edu; *Head, Access Serv,* Carolyn Schwartz; Tel: 413-572-5327, E-mail: cschwartz@westfield.ma.edu; *Head, Archives, Head, Tech Serv,* Judith Carlson; Tel: 413-572-5252, E-mail: jcarlson@westfield.ma.edu; *Head, Ref (Info Serv),* Brian Hubbard; Tel: 413-572-5482, E-mail: bhubbard@westfield.ma.edu; *Head, Res,* Corinne Ebbs; E-mail: cebbs@westfield.ma.edu; *Info & Instruction Librn, Ref Librn,* Teri Shiel; *Info & Instruction Librn, Ref Librn,* Laura Wilson; *Coordr, Info Serv, Coordr, Instruction,* Oliver Zeff; Staff 13 (MLS 8, Non-MLS 5)
Founded 1839. Enrl 4,871; Fac 222; Highest Degree: Master
Library Holdings: Bk Titles 120,685; Bk Vols 159,126; Per Subs 638
Subject Interests: Criminal law & justice, Educ
Automation Activity & Vendor Info: (Acquisitions) Ex Libris Group; (Cataloging) Ex Libris Group; (Circulation) Ex Libris Group; (Course Reserve) Ex Libris Group; (ILL) Ex Libris Group; (Media Booking) Ex Libris Group; (OPAC) Ex Libris Group; (Serials) Ex Libris Group
Wireless access
Publications: Student Guide
Partic in Cooperating Libraries of Greater Springfield; Lyrasis; OCLC Online Computer Library Center, Inc
Special Services for the Deaf - Assisted listening device; Assistive tech
Special Services for the Blind - Accessible computers; Assistive/Adapted tech devices, equip & products; Copier with enlargement capabilities; Duplicating spec requests; Networked computers with assistive software; Scanner for conversion & translation of mats; Screen enlargement software for people with visual disabilities; Screen reader software
Open Mon-Thurs (Fall & Spring) 8am-Midnight, Fri 8-5, Sat 10-6, Sun 1-Midnight; Mon & Tues (Summer) 9-9, Wed & Thurs 9-6, Fri 9-5

WESTFORD

P J V FLETCHER LIBRARY*, 50 Main St, 01886-2599. SAN 307-790X. Tel: 978-692-5555. Circulation Tel: 978-399-2301. Interlibrary Loan Service Tel: 978-399-2309. Reference Tel: 978-399-2304. Administration Tel: 978-692-5557. FAX: 978-692-4418. Administration FAX: 978-692-0287. E-mail: westfordlibrary@westfordma.gov. Web Site: www.westfordlibrary.org. *Dir,* Ellen Downey Rainville; Tel: 978-399-2312, E-mail: erainville@westfordma.gov; *Asst Dir,* India Nolen; Tel: 978-399-2311, E-mail: inolen@westfordma.gov; *Head, Circ,* Holly Pritchard; Tel: 978-399-2313; *Head, Tech Serv, Syst Programmer,* Dina Kanabar; Tel: 978-399-2308, E-mail: dkanabar@westfordma.gov; *Ref,* Kristina Leedberg; *Youth Serv,* Nancy Boutet; Tel: 978-399-2307, E-mail: nboutet@westfordma.gov; Staff 20.17 (MLS 9, Non-MLS 11.17)
Founded 1797. Pop 21,951; Circ 322,509
Jul 2011-Jun 2012 Income $1,443,575, State $19,037, City $1,424,538. Mats Exp $237,088, Books $104,068, Per/Ser (Incl. Access Fees) $16,402, AV Mat $50,800, Electronic Ref Mat (Incl. Access Fees) $59,000. Sal $1,083,226 (Prof $384,414)
Library Holdings: Audiobooks 8,149; CDs 1,560; DVDs 8,165; e-books 3,856; Electronic Media & Resources 2,688; Microforms 19,208; Bk Vols 99,393; Per Subs 342
Special Collections: Chinese Foreign Language Titles; Genealogical Data Coll; Merrimack Valley Historic Document Coll; Textile Mill Histories Coll
Automation Activity & Vendor Info: (Cataloging) Evergreen; (Circulation) Evergreen
Database Vendor: EBSCOhost, Gale Cengage Learning, Newsbank, Overdrive, Inc, ProQuest
Wireless access
Function: Adult bk club, Adult literacy prog, After school storytime, Archival coll, Audiobks via web, AV serv, Bk club(s), Bks on cassette, Bks on CD, CD-ROM, Computer training, Computers for patron use, Copy machines, Distance learning, Doc delivery serv, e-mail serv, Electronic databases & coll, Fax serv, Handicapped accessible, Homebound delivery serv, ILL available, Microfiche/film & reading machines, Mus passes, Music CDs, Online cat, Online ref, Online searches, Outside serv via phone, mail, e-mail & web, OverDrive digital audio bks, Photocopying/Printing, Preschool reading prog, Prog for adults, Prog for children & young adult, Pub access computers, Ref serv available, Spoken cassettes & CDs, Summer reading prog, Telephone ref, VHS videos, Wheelchair accessible, Workshops
Publications: Bi-Annual Town Wide Mailing of Programs & Events; J V Fletcher Library e-News; Library Latest Byline; Online Library Website
Mem of Massachusetts Libr Syst
Partic in Merrimack Valley Library Consortium

Open Mon-Thurs 10-9, Fri 1-5, Sat 10-5; Sun (Jan-Apr) 2-5
Friends of the Library Group

WESTHAMPTON

P WESTHAMPTON PUBLIC LIBRARY*, One North Rd, 01027. SAN 307-7918. Tel: 413-527-5386. E-mail: westhampton@cwmars.org. *Dir,* Carolyn A Keating
Founded 1866. Pop 1,750; Circ 24,000
Automation Activity & Vendor Info: (Cataloging) Innovative Interfaces, Inc; (Circulation) Innovative Interfaces, Inc; (OPAC) Innovative Interfaces, Inc
Wireless access
Open Mon & Thurs 2-8, Tues & Wed 9-12 & 1-5, Sat (Oct-May) 10-1
Friends of the Library Group

WESTMINSTER

P FORBUSH MEMORIAL LIBRARY*, Westminster Public Library, 118 Main St, 01473. (Mail add: PO Box 468, 01473-0468), SAN 307-7926. Tel: 978-874-7416. FAX: 978-874-7424. Web Site: www.forbushlibrary.org. *Dir,* Nick Langhart; *Ch,* Geraldine Manning; *Ref Librn,* Jason Cavanaugh; Staff 3 (MLS 2, Non-MLS 1)
Founded 1901. Pop 7,600; Circ 76,000
Jul 2008-Jun 2009 Income $632,000, State $12,000, City $310,000, Locally Generated Income $310,000. Mats Exp $60,000, Books $41,000, Per/Ser (Incl. Access Fees) $3,000, AV Mat $16,000. Sal $189,000 (Prof $122,000)
Library Holdings: CDs 300; DVDs 1,500; Large Print Bks 1,000; Bk Titles 42,500; Bk Vols 50,000; Per Subs 75; Videos 100
Special Collections: Local History & Genealogy Coll
Automation Activity & Vendor Info: (Cataloging) Innovative Interfaces, Inc; (Circulation) Innovative Interfaces, Inc; (ILL) Innovative Interfaces, Inc; (OPAC) Innovative Interfaces, Inc; (Serials) EBSCO Online
Mem of Massachusetts Libr Syst
Partic in Central & Western Massachusetts Automated Resource Sharing
Open Tues-Thurs 10-8, Fri 10-6, Sat 9-1
Friends of the Library Group

S WESTMINSTER HISTORICAL SOCIETY LIBRARY, 110 Main St, 01473. (Mail add: PO Box 177, 01473-0177), SAN 375-1872. Tel: 978-874-5569. FAX: 978-874-5569. E-mail: westminsterhistory@verizon.net. Web Site: www.westminsterhistory.org. *Coll Develop, Curator,* Betsy Hannula; E-mail: betsyhannula@gmail.com
Founded 1921
Library Holdings: Bk Titles 1,000
Special Collections: General Nelson A Miles Coll
Subject Interests: Local hist

WESTON

R BLESSED POPE JOHN XXIII NATIONAL SEMINARY LIBRARY*, 558 South Ave, 02493. SAN 307-7950. Tel: 781-899-5500, Ext 20. FAX: 781-899-9057. Web Site: www.blessedjohnxxiii.edu.
Founded 1963. Enrl 62; Fac 20; Highest Degree: Doctorate
Library Holdings: Bk Vols 65,904
Special Collections: Comprehensive English Language Theology, 1958 to date
Database Vendor: OCLC FirstSearch
Mem of Massachusetts Libr Syst

C REGIS COLLEGE LIBRARY*, 235 Wellesley St, 02493. SAN 307-7969. Tel: 781-768-7300. Reference Tel: 781-768-7303. FAX: 781-768-7323. Web Site: www.regiscollege.edu. *Libr Dir,* Lynn Triplett; Tel: 781-768-7000, Ext 7307; *Circ,* Deborah Lovett; *Coll Develop,* Julie Merrill; *Info Serv Dir/Ref,* Cecilia Roberts; *ILL,* Armine Bagdasarian; *Ref,* S Eleanor Deady; Staff 12 (MLS 6, Non-MLS 6)
Founded 1927. Enrl 1,590; Fac 129; Highest Degree: Doctorate
Library Holdings: e-journals 19,140; Bk Titles 113,108; Bk Vols 135,458; Per Subs 607
Special Collections: Cardinal Newman Coll; Madeleine Doran Coll
Subject Interests: Art, Econ, Hist, Lit, Music, Natural sci, Nursing, Women's studies
Automation Activity & Vendor Info: (Acquisitions) SirsiDynix; (Cataloging) SirsiDynix; (Circulation) SirsiDynix; (Course Reserve) SirsiDynix; (OPAC) SirsiDynix; (Serials) SirsiDynix
Database Vendor: EBSCOhost, Gale Cengage Learning, LexisNexis, OCLC FirstSearch, OCLC WorldShare Interlibrary Loan
Mem of Massachusetts Libr Syst
Partic in OCLC Online Computer Library Center, Inc; WEBnet Libr Consortium

S SPELLMAN MUSEUM OF STAMPS & POSTAL HISTORY LIBRARY*, 235 Wellesley St, 02493. SAN 307-7942. Tel: 781-768-8367. E-mail: info@spellman.org. Web Site: www.spellman.org. *Curator,* George Norton; E-mail: george.norton@spellman.org
Founded 1960
Library Holdings: Bk Titles 15,000; Per Subs 25
Subject Interests: Philately
Open Thurs-Sun 12-5
Restriction: Non-circulating

P WESTON PUBLIC LIBRARY, 87 School St, 02493. SAN 307-7977. Tel: 781-786-6150. Circulation Tel: 781-786-6163. Reference Tel: 781-786-6165. Administration Tel: 781-768-6155. FAX: 781-786-6159. E-mail: weston@minlib.net. Web Site: www.westonlibrary.org. *Dir,* Susan Brennan; *Asst Dir,* Jennifer Warner; *Adult Serv, Coll Develop,* Donna Davies; *Ch Serv,* Kelly Wood; *Ref Serv,* Tatanya Flannery; *Tech Serv,* Jaclyn Degrace; Staff 8 (MLS 8)
Founded 1857. Pop 11,469; Circ 222,463
Library Holdings: Bk Vols 91,500; Per Subs 221
Special Collections: Local History
Wireless access
Partic in Minuteman Library Network
Open Mon-Thurs 9-9, Sat 10-5, Sun 1-5
Friends of the Library Group

WESTPORT

P WESTPORT FREE PUBLIC LIBRARY*, 408 Old County Rd, 02790. (Mail add: PO Box N-157, 02790-0630), SAN 307-7985. Tel: 508-636-1100. FAX: 508-636-1102. Web Site: www.westport-ma.com/library/index.html. *Dir,* Susan R Branco; E-mail: sbranco@sailsinc.org; *Asst Dir,* Linda R Cunha
Founded 1891. Pop 14,594; Circ 57,521
Library Holdings: Bk Titles 38,965; Per Subs 73
Mem of Massachusetts Libr Syst
Partic in SAILS Library Network
Open Mon & Thurs 12:30-8:30, Tues, Wed & Fri 10-5, Sat 10-4
Friends of the Library Group

WESTWOOD

P WESTWOOD PUBLIC LIBRARY*, 668 High St, 02090. SAN 345-7893. Tel: 781-326-7562. Circulation Tel: 781-320-1048. Reference Tel: 781-320-1045. Automation Services Tel: 781-320-1041. FAX: 781-326-5383. Web Site: www.westwoodlibrary.org/home. *Dir,* Thomas P Viti; E-mail: tviti@minlib.net; *Adult Serv,* Margaret Reucroft, *Ch Serv,* Loretta Eysie; Tel: 781-320-1043; *ILL,* Nancy Hogan; Tel: 781-320-1049; *Tech Serv,* Caroline Nie; Tel: 781-320-1047; Staff 28 (MLS 8, Non-MLS 20)
Founded 1898. Pop 14,200; Circ 247,000
Library Holdings: AV Mats 8,780; Electronic Media & Resources 206; Bk Vols 96,630; Per Subs 196
Special Collections: Sautter Art Coll
Database Vendor: Innovative Interfaces, Inc
Partic in Minuteman Library Network
Open Mon-Wed 10-9, Thurs 1-9, Fri 10-6, Sat 10-5 (July Aug 10-1)
Friends of the Library Group
Branches: 1
ISLINGTON, 280 Washington St, 02090, SAN 345-7923. Tel: 781-326-5914. *Librn,* Claire Connors
Library Holdings: Bk Vols 16,000; Per Subs 75
Open Tues & Thurs 10-5, Wed 1-8, Sat (Sept-June) 10-1
Friends of the Library Group

WEYMOUTH

P WEYMOUTH PUBLIC LIBRARIES*, Tufts Library, 46 Broad St, 02188. SAN 345-7958. Tel: 781-337-1402. FAX: 781-682-6123. *Dir,* Robert MacLean; Staff 11 (MLS 11)
Founded 1879. Pop 55,137; Circ 215,006
Library Holdings: Bk Vols 155,151; Per Subs 400
Special Collections: Local History Coll; Teachers' Professional Library. Oral History
Automation Activity & Vendor Info: (Acquisitions) SirsiDynix; (Cataloging) SirsiDynix; (Circulation) SirsiDynix; (ILL) SirsiDynix; (OPAC) SirsiDynix; (Serials) SirsiDynix
Database Vendor: Newsbank, ProQuest
Open Mon-Thurs 9-9, Fri & Sat 9-5
Friends of the Library Group
Branches: 3
FOGG LIBRARY, One Columbian Sq, South Weymouth, 02190, SAN 345-7982. Tel: 781-337-0410.
Library Holdings: Bk Vols 25,000
Open Mon 9-5, Tues 9-1, Wed 1-5
NORTH BRANCH, 220 North St, 02191, SAN 375-2968. Tel: 718-340-5036.
Open Mon & Thurs 1-5, Wed 9-5
Friends of the Library Group

FRANKLIN N PRATT LIBRARY, 1400 Pleasant St, East Weymouth, 02189, SAN 345-8016. Tel: 781-337-1677.
Library Holdings: Bk Vols 14,000
Open Tues 9-5, Wed 9-1, Thurs 1-5

WHATELY

P S WHITE DICKINSON MEMORIAL LIBRARY*, 202 Chestnut Plain Rd, 01093. (Mail add: PO Box 187, 01093-0187), SAN 307-8000. Tel: 413-665-2170. FAX: 413-665-9560. E-mail: library@whately.org. Web Site: www.whately.org/library. *Dir,* Tiffany Hilton; *Asst Librn,* Betsy Cook
Founded 1951. Pop 1,400; Circ 9,380
Library Holdings: Bk Vols 11,000
Special Collections: New England History of towns, Genealogy books - gift of Stuart Waite
Subject Interests: Local hist
Open Mon-Wed 1-8, Sat 10-3
Friends of the Library Group

WHITINSVILLE

P WHITINSVILLE SOCIAL LIBRARY, INC*, 17 Church St, 01588. SAN 345-8075. Tel: 508-234-2151. E-mail: books@northbridgemass.org. Web Site: www.northbridgemass.org/WSL/wslhome.htm. *Dir,* Christine McLaughlin
Founded 1844. Pop 13,685; Circ 62,031
Library Holdings: Bk Vols 37,000; Per Subs 90
Special Collections: Northbridge Historical Coll
Automation Activity & Vendor Info: (Cataloging) Follett Software; (Circulation) Follett Software
Mem of Massachusetts Libr Syst
Open Wed 2-8, Thurs 10-4
Friends of the Library Group

WHITMAN

P WHITMAN PUBLIC LIBRARY*, 100 Webster St, 02382. SAN 307-8019. Tel: 781-447-7613. FAX: 781-447-7678. Web Site: www.whitmanpubliclibrary.org. *Dir,* Andrea Rounds; E-mail: arounds@ocln.org; *Ad, Ref Librn,* Samantha Duckworth; E-mail: sduckworth@ocln.org; *Supvr, Circ,* Barbara Bryant; E-mail: barbarab@ocln.org; *Sr Libr Tech,* Rebecca Rogers; Staff 5 (MLS 2, Non-MLS 3)
Founded 1879. Pop 14,381; Circ 71,078
Library Holdings: AV Mats 4,787; Bk Vols 45,536; Per Subs 113
Subject Interests: Local hist
Automation Activity & Vendor Info: (Cataloging) SirsiDynix; (Circulation) SirsiDynix; (OPAC) SirsiDynix
Wireless access
Partic in Old Colony Libr Network (OCLN)
Open Mon-Thurs 10-8, Fri 1-5, Sat (Sept-June) 10-4
Friends of the Library Group

WILBRAHAM

P WILBRAHAM PUBLIC LIBRARY*, 25 Crane Park Dr, 01095-1799. SAN 307-8027. Tel: 413-596-6141. FAX: 413-596-5090. E-mail: reference@wilbrahamlibrary.org. Web Site: www.wilbrahamlibrary.org. *Libr Dir,* Karen Demers; E-mail: karendemers@wilbrahamlibrary.org; *Head, Ch,* Elaine Wrubel; E-mail: elaine@wilbrahamlibrary.org; *Ref Librn,* Mary Bell; E-mail: mbell@wilbrahamlibrary.org; *IT Tech, Webmaster,* Wayne Wrubel; E-mail: wayne@wilbrahamlibrary.org; Staff 17 (MLS 4, Non-MLS 13)
Founded 1892. Pop 13,500; Circ 165,262
Library Holdings: Audiobooks 4,623; AV Mats 7,775; Bk Vols 48,059; Per Subs 1,733; Videos 3,749
Special Collections: Local History (Wilbraham Coll)
Automation Activity & Vendor Info: (Circulation) Innovative Interfaces, Inc; (OPAC) Innovative Interfaces, Inc
Function: ILL available, Outside serv via phone, mail, e-mail & web, Photocopying/Printing, Telephone ref
Publications: Library News (Newsletter)
Partic in Central & Western Massachusetts Automated Resource Sharing
Open Mon-Wed 10-8, Thurs & Fri 10-5, Sat 10-2
Friends of the Library Group

WILLIAMSBURG

P MEEKINS LIBRARY*, Two Williams St, 01096. (Mail add: PO Box 772, 01096-0772), SAN 307-8035. Tel: 413-268-7472. FAX: 413-268-7488. E-mail: meekins@cwmars.org. Web Site: www.meekins-library.org. *Librn,* Lisa Wenner; E-mail: lwenner@cwmars.org
Pop 2,515; Circ 57,700
Library Holdings: Bk Titles 25,000; Per Subs 32
Automation Activity & Vendor Info: (Cataloging) Innovative Interfaces, Inc; (Circulation) Innovative Interfaces, Inc; (OPAC) Innovative Interfaces, Inc
Publications: Abridged Readers Guide to Periodical Literature
Open Tues 12-5, Wed 10-8, Thurs 3-8, Sat 10-3
Friends of the Library Group

WILLIAMSTOWN

P DAVID & JOYCE MILNE PUBLIC LIBRARY*, 1095 Main St, 01267-2627. SAN 345-813X. Tel: 413-458-5369. FAX: 413-458-3085. Web Site: www.milnelibrary.org. *Dir,* Patricia McLeod; E-mail: pmcleod@williamstown.net; *Assoc Dir,* Deb Felix; E-mail: dfelix@williamstown.net; *Ch,* Position Currently Open; *Circ Mgr,* Juliana Haubrich; E-mail: julianav7@gmail.com; *Ref,* Fern Sann; E-mail: fsann@cwmars.org; Staff 16 (MLS 3, Non-MLS 13)
Founded 1876. Pop 8,220; Circ 212,923
Library Holdings: CDs 5,599; DVDs 5,229; e-books 5,448; Large Print Bks 2,419; Bk Titles 76,081; Per Subs 268; Talking Bks 2,970
Subject Interests: Local hist
Automation Activity & Vendor Info: (Cataloging) Evergreen; (Circulation) Evergreen; (OPAC) Evergreen
Database Vendor: EBSCOhost, Gale Cengage Learning, Newsbank
Wireless access
Function: Adult bk club, Adult literacy prog, Art exhibits, Audiobks via web, Chess club, Children's prog, Computers for patron use, Copy machines, e-mail serv, E-Reserves, Free DVD rentals, Handicapped accessible, Home delivery & serv to Sr ctr & nursing homes, ILL available, Mus passes, OverDrive digital audio bks, Prog for adults, Ref serv available, Spoken cassettes & CDs, Summer reading prog, Tax forms, Telephone ref, Web-catalog, Workshops, Writing prog
Publications: Biblio-File (Newsletter)
Partic in Central-Western Mass Automated Resource Sharing
Open Mon, Tues, Thurs & Fri 10-5:30, Wed 10-8, Sat 10-4
Friends of the Library Group

S STERLING & FRANCINE CLARK ART INSTITUTE LIBRARY*, 225 South St, 01267. SAN 307-8043. Tel: 413-458-9545. Reference Tel: 413-458-0532. FAX: 413-458-9542. E-mail: library@clarkart.edu. Web Site: www.clarkart.edu/library. *Chief Librn,* Susan Roeper; Tel: 413-458-0550, E-mail: sroeper@clarkart.edu; *Dept Head, Tech Serv,* Penny Baker; Tel: 413-458-0531, E-mail: pbaker@clarkart.edu; *Dept Head, User Serv,* Karen Bucky; E-mail: kbucky@clarkart.edu; *Acq,* Terri Boccia; Tel: 413-458-0437, E-mail: tboccia@clarkart.edu; Staff 7 (MLS 3, Non-MLS 4)
Founded 1962
Library Holdings: Bk Vols 230,000; Per Subs 650
Special Collections: Auction Catalogues; History of Photomechanical Reproduction (David A Hanson Coll); Mary Ann Beinecke Decorative Arts Coll; Robert Sterling Clark Coll of Rare & Illustrated Books
Subject Interests: Contemporary art, European art, Medieval art
Automation Activity & Vendor Info: (Acquisitions) Innovative Interfaces, Inc - Millenium; (Cataloging) Innovative Interfaces, Inc - Millenium; (Circulation) Innovative Interfaces, Inc - Millenium; (ILL) OCLC ILLiad; (OPAC) Innovative Interfaces, Inc - Millenium; (Serials) Innovative Interfaces, Inc - Millenium
Database Vendor: ARTstor, Innovative Interfaces, Inc, OCLC CAMIO, OCLC FirstSearch, OCLC WorldShare Interlibrary Loan, OCLC-RLG, Swets Information Services, Wilson - Wilson Web
Wireless access
Function: Res libr
Partic in Lyrasis; OCLC Research Library Partnership
Open Mon-Fri 9-5
Restriction: Non-circulating

C WILLIAMS COLLEGE*, Sawyer Library, 55 Sawyer Library Dr, 01267. SAN 345-8199. Tel: 413-597-2501. Interlibrary Loan Service Tel: 413-597-2005. Reference Tel: 413-597-2505. Administration Tel: 413-597-2504. FAX: 413-597-4106. Interlibrary Loan Service FAX: 413-597-2478. Web Site: www.library.williams.edu. *Dir,* David M Pilachowski; Tel: 413-597-2502, E-mail: david.pilachowski@williams.edu; *Head, Access Serv,* Jo-Ann Irace; Tel: 413-597-2920, E-mail: jo-ann.irace@williams.edu; *Head, Coll Mgt,* M Robin Kibler; Tel: 413-597-3047, E-mail: m.robin.kibler@williams.edu; *Head, Libr Syst,* Walter Komorowski; Tel: 413-597-2084, E-mail: walter.komorowski@williams.edu; *Head, Ref & Res Serv,* Christine Menard; Tel: 413-597-2515, E-mail: christine.menard@williams.edu; *Cat Librn,* Karen Benko; Tel: 413-597-4322, E-mail: karen.gorss.benko@williams.edu; *Cat Librn,* Christine Blackman; Tel: 413-597-4403, E-mail: christine.blackman@williams.edu; *Col Archivist & Spec Coll Librn,* Sylvia Kennick Brown; Tel: 413-597-2596, E-mail: sylvia.k.brown@williams.edu; *Ref/Govt Doc Librn,* Rebecca Ohm; Tel: 413-597-4321, E-mail: rebecca.ohm@williams.edu; *Ref & Instrul Serv Librn,* Lori DuBois; Tel: 413-597-4614, E-mail: lori.a.dubois@williams.edu; *Ref & Web Serv Librn,* Mercedea Shriver; Tel: 413-597-4716, E-mail: mercedea.shriver@williams.edu; Staff 18 (MLS 14, Non-MLS 4)
Founded 1793. Enrl 2,255; Fac 321; Highest Degree: Master

Library Holdings: AV Mats 43,337; CDs 570; DVDs 4,376; e-books 141,584; e-journals 35,472; Microforms 480,447; Bk Titles 565,521; Bk Vols 899,872; Per Subs 983
Special Collections: Paul Whiteman Coll, ms, rec & scores; Shaker Coll, bks, ms & pamphlets; William Cullen Bryant Coll, bks & ms. US Document Depository
Subject Interests: Humanities, Natural sci
Automation Activity & Vendor Info: (OPAC) Innovative Interfaces, Inc
Database Vendor: Innovative Interfaces, Inc
Wireless access
Partic in Boston Library Consortium, Inc; Center for Research Libraries; NExpress Consortium; OCLC Online Computer Library Center, Inc

Departmental Libraries:

CHAPIN LIBRARY, 26 Hopkins Hall Dr, 01267. (Mail add: PO Box 426, 01267-0426), SAN 345-8253. Tel: 413-597-4200. FAX: 413-597-2929. E-mail: chapin.library@williams.edu. Web Site: chapin.williams.edu. *Custodian of the Chapin Libr,* Robert L Volz; Tel: 413-597-2930, E-mail: rvolz@williams.edu; *Asst Chapin Librn,* Wayne G Hammond; Tel: 413-597-2462, E-mail: whammond@williams.edu; Staff 2 (MLS 2)
Founded 1923
Jul 2013-Jun 2014 Income $306,756, Parent Institution $302,283, Other $4,473. Mats Exp $317,779, Books $268,148, Per/Ser (Incl. Access Fees) $2,412, Manu Arch $29,794, Presv $17,425
Library Holdings: Bk Vols 55,000; Per Subs 10
Special Collections: Aldine Press Coll; Bees & Beekeeping Coll; Bibles & Liturgical Books; Breman Coll (African-American & Black culture); C B Falls Coll; Chesterwood Archives (Daniel Chester French papers); Daniel Press Coll; Daniel Webster Coll; Edwin Arlington Robinson (John T Snyder Coll); Field Family Coll; Frank Lloyd Wright Coll; Gelett Burgess Coll; Herman Rosse Coll; James Elroy Flecker (Hugh M MacMullan Coll); John DePol Coll; Joseph Conrad (Donald S Klopfer Coll); Leo Wyatt Coll; Oliver Herford Coll; Overbrook Press Coll; Pauline Baynes Coll; Rudyard Kipling Coll; Rupert Brooke (Hugh M MacMullan Coll); Samuel Butler (Carroll Atwood Wilson Coll), correspondence, first ed, music & memorabilia, notebks, photog; Sporting Books Coll; Stereos, Photographs Coll; T S Eliot (Hugh M MacMullan Coll); Theodore Roosevelt Coll; Walt Whitman (Julian K Sprague Coll); William Faulkner Coll; William Saroyan Coll; Winston S Churchill Coll
Subject Interests: Africa, African-Am studies, Am lit, Americana, Art, English lit, Fr (Lang), German (Lang), Hist of sci, Incunabula, Italian (Lang), Latin (Lang), Manuscripts, Performing arts, Printing, Spanish lang, Women's studies
Automation Activity & Vendor Info: (Cataloging) OCLC; (OPAC) Innovative Interfaces, Inc
Database Vendor: Innovative Interfaces, Inc, OCLC
Function: Res libr
Partic in OCLC Online Computer Library Center, Inc
Publications: British Book Illustration 1924-36; British Ecclesiastical Architecture; Catalogue of the Collection of Samuel Butler; Finished by Hand; Graphic Art of C B Falls; London: High Life & Low Life; Short-Title List
Open Mon-Fri 10-5
Restriction: Closed stack, Not a lending libr

S WILLIAMSTOWN HISTORICAL MUSEUM, 1095 Main St, 01267. SAN 373-1995. Tel: 413-458-2160. E-mail: info@williamstownhistoricalmuseum.org. Web Site: www.williamstownhistoricalmuseum.org. *Dir,* Sarah Currie; E-mail: sarah@williamstownhistoricalmuseum.org; Staff 1 (Non-MLS 1)
Founded 1941
Library Holdings: Bk Vols 1,805
Subject Interests: Genealogy, Local hist
Wireless access
Function: Res libr
Publications: Newsletter

WILMINGTON

P WILMINGTON MEMORIAL LIBRARY, 175 Middlesex Ave, 01887-2779. SAN 307-8086. Tel: 978-658-2967. Reference Tel: 978-694-2099. FAX: 978-658-9699. E-mail: mwlinfo@mvlc.org. Web Site: www.wilmlibrary.org. *Dir,* Christina A Stewart; E-mail: tstewart@mvlc.org; *Asst Libr Dir,* Charlotte Wood; E-mail: cwood@mvlc.org; *Adult Serv, Head, Ref,* Anna Call; E-mail: acall@mvlc.org; *Mkt Librn,* Pamela Gardner; E-mail: pgardner@mvlc.org; *Tech Librn,* Bradley McKenna; E-mail: bmckenna@mvlc.org; *Ch Serv,* Barbara Raab; E-mail: braab@mvlc.org; *Circ,* Linda Pavluk; E-mail: lpavluk@mvlc.org; *YA Serv,* Alison Schwartz; E-mail: aschwartz@mvlc.org; Staff 8 (MLS 7, Non-MLS 1)
Founded 1871. Pop 22,936; Circ 216,485
Jul 2012-Jun 2013 Income $1,038,859. Mats Exp $135,139, Books $71,049, Per/Ser (Incl. Access Fees) $7,103, AV Mat $23,442, Electronic Ref Mat (Incl. Access Fees) $33,545. Sal $831,543 (Prof $368,194)
Library Holdings: AV Mats 10,976; Bk Vols 42,552
Automation Activity & Vendor Info: (Acquisitions) Evergreen; (Cataloging) Evergreen; (Circulation) Evergreen; (ILL) Evergreen; (OPAC) Evergreen; (Serials) Evergreen
Database Vendor: EBSCO Information Services, EBSCOhost, Electric Library, Gale Cengage Learning, Grolier Online, H W Wilson, infoUSA, OCLC FirstSearch, Overdrive, Inc, ProQuest, ReferenceUSA, Safari Books Online, TumbleBookLibrary, WT Cox
Wireless access
Function: Adult bk club, Audiobks via web, Bk club(s), Bks on cassette, Bks on CD, Children's prog, Computer training, Computers for patron use, Copy machines, Digital talking bks, e-mail serv, E-Reserves, Electronic databases & coll, Fax serv, Handicapped accessible, Home delivery & serv to Sr ctr & nursing homes, Homebound delivery serv, ILL available, Mus passes, Music CDs, Newsp ref libr, Online cat, Online ref, Online searches, OverDrive digital audio bks, Photocopying/Printing, Prog for adults, Prog for children & young adult, Scanner, Spoken cassettes & CDs, Spoken cassettes & DVDs, Story hour, Summer reading prog, Tax forms, Teen prog, Telephone ref, Wheelchair accessible
Mem of Massachusetts Libr Syst
Partic in Merrimack Valley Library Consortium
Special Services for the Deaf - Bks on deafness & sign lang; Closed caption videos
Special Services for the Blind - Audio mat; Bks on cassette; Bks on CD; Copier with enlargement capabilities; Home delivery serv; Large print bks; Photo duplicator for making large print
Open Mon-Thurs 9-9, Fri & Sat (Winter) 9-5
Friends of the Library Group

WINCHENDON

P BEALS MEMORIAL LIBRARY*, 50 Pleasant St, 01475. SAN 307-8094. Tel: 978-297-0300. FAX: 978-297-2018. *Dir,* Julia White Cardinal
Founded 1867. Pop 10,000; Circ 43,000
Library Holdings: Bk Vols 40,000; Per Subs 80
Subject Interests: Local hist
Automation Activity & Vendor Info: (Cataloging) Innovative Interfaces, Inc; (Circulation) Innovative Interfaces, Inc; (OPAC) Innovative Interfaces, Inc
Mem of Massachusetts Libr Syst
Open Mon-Thurs 1-8, Fri 9-5, Sat (Sept-May) 9-1
Friends of the Library Group

WINCHESTER

G UNITED STATES FOOD & DRUG ADMINISTRATION DEPARTMENT OF HEALTH & HUMAN SERVICES*, Winchester Engineering & Analytical Center Library, 109 Holton St, 01890. SAN 307-8108. Tel: 781-729-5700. FAX: 781-729-3593.
Founded 1961
Library Holdings: Bk Titles 1,500; Per Subs 50
Subject Interests: Electronics, Eng, Med, Physics
Restriction: Staff use only

M WINCHESTER HOSPITAL*, Health Sciences Library, 41 Highland Ave, 01890. SAN 377-9378. Tel: 781-756-2165. FAX: 781-756-2059. Web Site: www.winchesterhospital.org. *Librn,* Mary Miller; E-mail: mmiller@winhosp.org
Library Holdings: e-books 76; Bk Vols 400; Per Subs 135
Subject Interests: Nursing
Wireless access
Partic in Basic Health Sciences Library Network; Massachusetts Health Sciences Libraries Network; North Atlantic Health Sciences Libraries, Inc; Northeastern Consortium for Health Information

P WINCHESTER PUBLIC LIBRARY*, 80 Washington St, 01890. SAN 307-8116. Tel: 781-721-7171. Administration Tel: 781-721-7177. FAX: 781-721-7170. Administration FAX: 781-721-7101. Web Site: winpublib.org. *Dir,* Ann Wirtanen; Tel: 781-721-7171, Ext 10, E-mail: awirtanen@minlib.net; *Asst Dir,* Barbara Yuan; Tel: 781-721-7171, Ext 18, E-mail: byuan@minlib.net; *Head, Ch,* Yvonne K Coleman; Tel: 781-721-7171, Ext 22, E-mail: ycoleman@minlib.net; *Head, Circ,* Karen Brown; Tel: 781-721-7171, Ext 16, E-mail: kbrown@minlib.net; *Head, Ref (Info Serv),* Julie A Kinchla; Tel: 781-721-7171, Ext 23, E-mail: jkinchla@minlib.net; *Head, Tech Serv,* Geraldine Pothier; Tel: 781-721-7171, Ext 27, E-mail: gpothier@minlib.net; *Commun Serv,* Janet Nelson; Tel: 781-721-7171, Ext 24, E-mail: jnelson@minlib.net; *YA Serv,* Molly Wiellette; Tel: 781-721-7171, Ext 20, E-mail: mwiellette@minlib.net
Founded 1858. Pop 20,652; Circ 511,244
Library Holdings: Bk Vols 107,357; Per Subs 382
Special Collections: Civil War History (Lincoln & Lee Coll)
Automation Activity & Vendor Info: (Circulation) Innovative Interfaces, Inc
Publications: Art in the Library; Guide to Winchester Public Library
Special Services for the Deaf - TTY equip
Special Services for the Blind - Closed circuit TV magnifier

Open Mon-Thurs 9:30-9, Fri & Sat 9:30-5:30, Sun 2-5
Friends of the Library Group

WINDSOR

P WINDSOR FREE PUBLIC LIBRARY*, 1890 Rte 9, 01270. (Mail add: PO Box 118, 01270-0118), SAN 376-7094. Tel: 413-684-3811. FAX: 413-684-3806. E-mail: windsorma@gmail.com. *Dir,* Margaret Birchfield; Staff 1 (MLS 1)
Library Holdings: Audiobooks 140; CDs 150; DVDs 1,100; Bk Vols 4,350; Videos 380
Wireless access
Open Mon 5-7, Wed 4:30-6:30, Fri 12-4, Sat 10-12
Friends of the Library Group

WINTHROP

P WINTHROP PUBLIC LIBRARY & MUSEUM*, Two Metcalf Sq, 02152-3157. SAN 307-8124. Tel: 617-846-1703. FAX: 617-846-7083. *Dir,* Peter Struzziero; E-mail: struzziero@noblenet.org; *Asst Dir, Head, Ref,* Catelyn Johnson; E-mail: cjohnson@noblenet.org; *Ch,* Ellen J Nickerson; *Circ Supvr,* Peter Solomon; *Tech Serv,* Richard Allen; Staff 6 (MLS 3, Non-MLS 3)
Founded 1885. Pop 18,263
Library Holdings: Audiobooks 3,031; CDs 52; e-books 114; Electronic Media & Resources 12; Microforms 100; Bk Vols 89,898; Per Subs 47; Videos 2,906
Special Collections: Lincoln Memorabilia; Local History (Museum Coll), bks, postcards, artifacts, pamphlets
Subject Interests: Local hist
Automation Activity & Vendor Info: (Cataloging) Evergreen; (Circulation) Evergreen; (ILL) Evergreen
Wireless access
Function: Adult bk club, Archival coll, Art exhibits, Audiobks via web, Bks on cassette, Bks on CD, Children's prog, Computers for patron use, Copy machines, Digital talking bks, Electronic databases & coll, Exhibits, Free DVD rentals, ILL available, Magnifiers for reading, Mus passes, Music CDs, Online cat, OverDrive digital audio bks, Prog for adults, Prog for children & young adult, Pub access computers, Ref serv available, Ref serv in person, Spoken cassettes & CDs, Spoken cassettes & DVDs, Story hour, Summer reading prog, VHS videos, Web-catalog
Partic in North of Boston Library Exchange, Inc
Friends of the Library Group

WOBURN

S CONCEPTS NREC LIBRARY*, 39 Olympia Ave, 01801-2073. SAN 307-3084. Tel: 781-935-9050. FAX: 781-935-9052. Web Site: www.conceptsnrec.com. *Sr Librn,* Jane B Waks; Staff 1 (MLS 1)
Founded 1965
Library Holdings: Bk Vols 800; Per Subs 65
Special Collections: NACA/NASA publications
Subject Interests: Aeronaut, Energy
Open Mon-Fri 9-5:30

P WOBURN PUBLIC LIBRARY*, 45 Pleasant St, 01801. (Mail add: PO Box 298, 01801-0298), SAN 307-8140. Tel: 781-933-0148. FAX: 781-938-7860. E-mail: woburn@minlib.net. Web Site: www.woburnpubliclibrary.org. *Dir,* Kathleen O'Doherty; E-mail: kodoherty@minlib.net; *Asst Dir,* Andrea Bunker; E-mail: abunker@minlib.net; *Acq,* Jessica Stitson; *Archivist,* Thomas Doyle; E-mail: tdoyle@minlib.net; *Cat, Tech Serv,* Beverly Thompson; *Ch Serv,* Cynthia Fordham; *Ref Serv, YA,* Christi Showman Farrar; E-mail: cfarrar@minlib.net
Founded 1856
Library Holdings: AV Mats 7,000; DVDs 1,500; Large Print Bks 1,800; Bk Vols 80,000; Per Subs 152; Videos 2,000
Subject Interests: Genealogy
Automation Activity & Vendor Info: (Acquisitions) Innovative Interfaces, Inc; (Cataloging) Innovative Interfaces, Inc; (Circulation) Innovative Interfaces, Inc; (ILL) Innovative Interfaces, Inc; (OPAC) Innovative Interfaces, Inc; (Serials) Innovative Interfaces, Inc
Database Vendor: EBSCO Information Services, Gale Cengage Learning, Newsbank, OCLC FirstSearch, ProQuest
Wireless access
Mem of Massachusetts Libr Syst
Partic in Minuteman Library Network
Special Services for the Blind - Aids for in-house use; Bks on cassette; Bks on CD; Closed circuit TV magnifier; Descriptive video serv (DVS); Home delivery serv; Large print bks; Magnifiers
Open Mon-Thurs 9-9, Fri 9-5:30, Sat (Sept-June) 9-5:30
Friends of the Library Group

WOODS HOLE

S MARINE BIOLOGICAL LABORATORY*, Woods Hole Oceanographic Institution Library, McLean MS 8, 360 Woods Hole Rd, 02543-1539. SAN 345-8288. Tel: 508-289-2269. FAX: 508-457-2156. E-mail: archives@whoi.edu. *Assoc Libr Dir,* Lisa Raymond; Staff 6 (MLS 2, Non-MLS 4)
Founded 1956
Special Collections: Institution Archives, charts, data, instruments, logs, maps. Oral History
Subject Interests: Chem, Geol, Geophysics, Meteorology, Ocean eng, Oceanography
Wireless access

G NORTHEAST FISHERIES SCIENCE CENTER*, Woods Hole Laboratory Library, 166 Water St, 02543-1097. SAN 307-8175. Tel: 508-495-2260. FAX: 508-495-2258. Web Site: www.nefsc.noaa.gov/nefsclibrary/. *Librn,* J Riley; E-mail: jacqueline.riley@noaa.gov
Founded 1885
Library Holdings: Bk Vols 1,000; Per Subs 20
Special Collections: Laboratory Research (Archives 1871-1979)
Subject Interests: Biol, Ecology
Automation Activity & Vendor Info: (Cataloging) SirsiDynix; (OPAC) SirsiDynix
Partic in BRS; Dialog Corp; OCLC Online Computer Library Center, Inc
Open Mon-Fri 7-3

P WOODS HOLE PUBLIC LIBRARY*, 581 Woods Hole Rd, 02543. (Mail add: PO Box 185, 02543-0185), SAN 307-8183. Tel: 508-548-8961. FAX: 508-540-1969. E-mail: info@woodsholepubliclibrary.org, whpl_mail@clamsnet.org. Web Site: www.woodsholepubliclibrary.org. *Dir,* Margaret McCormick; E-mail: mmccormick@clamsnet.org; Staff 2 (Non-MLS 2)
Founded 1910. Pop 5,000; Circ 37,000
Library Holdings: Bk Vols 29,000; Per Subs 50
Special Collections: Oral History
Subject Interests: Local hist
Automation Activity & Vendor Info: (Cataloging) Innovative Interfaces, Inc; (Circulation) Innovative Interfaces, Inc; (OPAC) Innovative Interfaces, Inc
Wireless access
Function: e-mail serv, Fax serv, ILL available, Mus passes, Music CDs, Online cat, OverDrive digital audio bks, Photocopying/Printing, Preschool outreach, Prog for adults, Prog for children & young adult, Pub access computers, Spoken cassettes & CDs, Story hour, Summer & winter reading prog, Summer reading prog, Workshops
Mem of Massachusetts Libr Syst
Open Mon 12-5:30 & 7-9, Tues, Thurs & Fri 3-5:30, Wed 10-5:30 & 7-9, Sat 12-5:30

WORCESTER

S AMERICAN ANTIQUARIAN SOCIETY LIBRARY*, 185 Salisbury St, 01609-1634. SAN 307-8191. Tel: 508-755-5221. FAX: 508-753-3311. E-mail: library@mwa.org. Web Site: www.americanantiquarian.org. *Pres,* Ellen S Dunlap
Founded 1812
Library Holdings: Bk Vols 690,000; Per Subs 1,200
Special Collections: Manuscripts relating to the history of the American book trades & New England families; Pre-1877 American & Canadian bks, pamphlets, almanacs, directories, children's lit, cook bks, genealogies, broadsides, graphic arts, printed ephemera, local & state histories, songsters, hymnals, sheet music, bibliographies, newspapers, & periodicals. US Document Depository
Subject Interests: Am hist, Lit
Automation Activity & Vendor Info: (Acquisitions) Ex Libris Group; (Cataloging) Ex Libris Group; (OPAC) Ex Libris Group; (Serials) Ex Libris Group
Publications: Bibliographies; Proceedings; Source Materials
Mem of Massachusetts Libr Syst
Partic in Academic & Research Collaborative (ARC); OCLC Research Library Partnership
Open Mon, Tues, Thurs & Fri 9-5, Wed 10-8
Friends of the Library Group

C ASSUMPTION COLLEGE, Emmanuel D'Alzon Library, 500 Salisbury St, 01609. SAN 307-8205. Tel: 508-767-7135. Reference Tel: 508-767-7273. FAX: 508-767-7374. E-mail: library@assumption.edu. Web Site: www.assumption.edu/dept/library. *Dir of Libr Serv,* Doris Ann Sweet; Tel: 508-767-7272, E-mail: dasweet@assumption.edu; *Head, Access Serv & Coll Mgt,* Robin Maddalena; Tel: 508-767-7271, E-mail: r.maddalena@assumption.edu; *Head, Libr Syst & Tech,* Mary Brunelle; Tel: 508-767-7002, E-mail: mbrunelle@assumption.edu; *Head, Res Support Serv,* Phillip Waterman; Tel: 508 767-7020, E-mail: pwaterman@assumption.edu; *Head, Tech Serv,* Elizabeth Maisey; Tel:

508-767-7384, E-mail: emaisey@assumption.edu; *Cataloger/Res Librn,* Elizabeth Lipin; Tel: 508-767-7136, E-mail: em.lipin@assumption.edu; *Res Serv Librn,* Kate Bejune; E-mail: ke.bejune@assumption.edu; *Res Serv Librn,* Barrie Mooney; Tel: 508-767-7036, E-mail: bmooney@assumption.edu; *Res Serv Librn,* Nancy O'Sullivan; E-mail: naosullivan@assumption.edu; *Evening Supvr,* Paul Johnson; E-mail: pjohnson@assumption.edu; *Weekend Supvr,* Renee Fratantonio; E-mail: r.frantantonio@assumption.edu; *Acq & Purchasing Coordr,* Joan O'Rourke; Tel: 508-767-7202, E-mail: jorourke@assumption.edu; *Circ/ILL Asst,* Vivienne Anthony; Tel: 508-767-7291, E-mail: vanthony@assumption.edu; *Coordr, Ser,* Julie O'Shea; Tel: 508-767-7137, E-mail: joshea@assumption.edu; Staff 12.3 (MLS 8, Non-MLS 4.3)
Founded 1904. Enrl 2,754; Fac 156; Highest Degree: Master
Jun 2013-May 2014 Income $1,556,650. Mats Exp $1,371,460, Books $71,800, Per/Ser (Incl. Access Fees) $306,000, Electronic Ref Mat (Incl. Access Fees) $224,450, Presv $20,000. Sal $836,650 (Prof $673,398)
Library Holdings: Audiobooks 100; DVDs 2,323; e-books 8,518; e-journals 51,050; Electronic Media & Resources 114; Microforms 23,416; Bk Titles 152,791; Bk Vols 227,234; Per Subs 1,076; Videos 2,323
Subject Interests: Fr Canadian, Franco-Am, Hist, Lit, Theol
Automation Activity & Vendor Info: (Acquisitions) Ex Libris Group; (Cataloging) Ex Libris Group; (Circulation) Ex Libris Group; (Course Reserve) Ex Libris Group; (ILL) OCLC ILLiad; (OPAC) Ex Libris Group; (Serials) Ex Libris Group
Database Vendor: ABC-CLIO, Alexander Street Press, American Chemical Society, ARTstor, Bowker, CQ Press, CredoReference, EBSCOhost, Elsevier, Ex Libris Group, Gale Cengage Learning, Grolier Online, H W Wilson, ISI Web of Knowledge, JSTOR, LexisNexis, Newsbank, Newsbank-Readex, OCLC FirstSearch, OCLC WorldShare Interlibrary Loan, OVID Technologies, Oxford Online, Project MUSE, ProQuest, PubMed, RefWorks, Sage, ScienceDirect, SerialsSolutions, Springshare, LLC, STN International, Thomson - Web of Science, Wilson - Wilson Web, YBP Library Services
Wireless access
Mem of Massachusetts Libr Syst
Partic in OCLC Online Computer Library Center, Inc; Westchester Academic Library Directors Organization (WALDO)
Special Services for the Blind - Braille equip; Closed circuit TV magnifier; Computer with voice synthesizer for visually impaired persons; Reader equip
Open Mon-Thurs 8am-1am, Fri 8-6, Sat 10-8, Sun 1-1

C BECKER COLLEGE*, William F Ruska Library, 61 Sever St, 01609. SAN 345-8377. Tel: 508-373-9710. Web Site: www.becker.edu/academics/libraries-2. *Dir of Libr,* Garrett Eastman; Tel: 508-373-9709, E-mail: garrett.eastman@becker.edu; *Asst Dir, Operations,* Donna Sibley; E-mail: donna.sibley@becker.edu
Enrl 1,900
Library Holdings: Bk Vols 40,000; Per Subs 117
Subject Interests: Criminal law & justice, Nursing, Philos, Psychol
Automation Activity & Vendor Info: (Acquisitions) Innovative Interfaces, Inc; (Circulation) Innovative Interfaces, Inc; (Course Reserve) Innovative Interfaces, Inc; (OPAC) Innovative Interfaces, Inc
Database Vendor: EBSCOhost, Gale Cengage Learning, Nature Publishing Group, ProQuest, Springshare, LLC
Publications: Acquisitions List; Faculty Handbook
Partic in Academic & Research Collaborative (ARC)
Open Mon-Thurs 7:30am-11pm, Fri 7:30-5, Sun 2-11

L BOWDITCH & DEWEY*, Law Library, 311 Main St, 01608. (Mail add: PO Box 15156, 01615-0156), SAN 372-0349. Tel: 508-926-3331. FAX: 508-929-3140. Web Site: www.bowditch.com. *Librn,* Leslie Bitman
Library Holdings: Bk Vols 5,000
Partic in New England Law Library Consortium, Inc

C CLARK UNIVERSITY*, Robert Hutchings Goddard Library, 950 Main St, 01610-1477. SAN 345-8407. Tel: 508-793-7711. Interlibrary Loan Service Tel: 508-793-7578. Reference Tel: 508-793-7579. Administration Tel: 508-793-7573. FAX: 508-793-8871. Web Site: www.clarku.edu/research/goddard. *Dir,* Gwen Arthur; Tel: 508-793-7384, E-mail: garthur@clarku.edu; *Head, Cat,* Joanne Palko; Tel: 508-793-7581, E-mail: jpalko@clarku.edu; *Head, Ref,* Irene Walch; E-mail: iwalch@clarku.edu; *Librn,* Beverly Presley; Tel: 508-793-7706, E-mail: bpresley@clarku.edu; *Assoc Librn, Pub Serv,* Mary Hartman; E-mail: mhartman@clarku.edu; *Syst Librn,* Edward McDermott; Tel: 508-793-7651, E-mail: emcdermott@clarku.edu; *Circ Supvr,* Anne Leroy; Tel: 508-793-7461, E-mail: aleroy@clarku.edu; *Coll Develop,* Michael Olson; Tel: 508-421-3804, E-mail: molson@clarku.edu. Subject Specialists: *Geog, Math,* Beverly Presley; Staff 30 (MLS 12, Non-MLS 18)
Founded 1889. Enrl 2,700; Fac 163; Highest Degree: Doctorate
Jun 2005-May 2006 Income $2,730,000. Mats Exp $1,256,000. Sal $971,000 (Prof $567,000)
Library Holdings: Bk Vols 613,000; Per Subs 1,303
Special Collections: Rare Books (Robert H Goddard Coll & G Stanley Hall Papers). US Document Depository
Automation Activity & Vendor Info: (Acquisitions) Ex Libris Group; (Cataloging) Ex Libris Group; (Circulation) Ex Libris Group; (Course Reserve) Ex Libris Group; (OPAC) Ex Libris Group; (Serials) Ex Libris Group
Database Vendor: Dialog, Gale Cengage Learning, LexisNexis, OCLC FirstSearch, OVID Technologies
Mem of Massachusetts Libr Syst
Partic in Lyrasis; OCLC Online Computer Library Center, Inc
Open Mon-Thurs 8am-Midnight, Fri 8am-10pm, Sat 10-10, Sun Noon-Midnight
Friends of the Library Group

Departmental Libraries:

ARCHIVES & SPECIAL COLLECTIONS, Downing & Woodland Sts, 01610-1477. (Mail add: 950 Main St, 01610-1477). Tel: 508-793-7572. FAX: 508-793-8871. E-mail: archives@clarku.edu. Web Site: www.clarku.edu/research/archives. *Archivist,* Mott Linn; E-mail: mlinn@clarku.edu
Open Mon-Fri 9:30-4

GUY H BURNHAM MAP & AERIAL PHOTOGRAPHY LIBRARY, 950 Main St, 01610-1477. Tel: 508-793-7322. FAX: 508-793-8881. Web Site: www.clarku.edu/research/maplibrary. *Librn,* Beverly Presley; Tel: 508-793-7706, E-mail: bpresley@clarku.edu
Open Mon-Fri 12:30-4:30

SCIENCE, 950 Main St, 01610. Tel: 508-793-7712. FAX: 508-793-8871. Web Site: www.clarku.edu/research/sciencelibrary. *Sci Librn,* Position Currently Open
Open Mon-Thurs 8am-10pm, Fri 8-5, Sat 9-5, Sun Noon-10

CR COLLEGE OF THE HOLY CROSS, Dinand Library, One College St, 01610. SAN 345-8466. Tel: 508-793-3372. Circulation Tel: 508-793-2642. Interlibrary Loan Service Tel: 508-793-2639. Reference Tel: 508-793-2259. FAX: 508-793-2372. Web Site: academics.holycross.edu/libraries. *Interim Dir, Libr Serv,* Karen J Reilly; Tel: 508-793-3371, E-mail: kreilly@holycross.edu; *Head, Access & Discovery Serv,* Eileen Cravedi; Tel: 508-793-2672, E-mail: ecravedi@holycross.edu; *Cat, Head, Acq,* Mary Moran; Tel: 508-793-2478, E-mail: mjmoran@holycross.edu; *Head, Archives & Spec Coll,* Mark Savolis; Tel: 508-793-2506, E-mail: msavolis@holycross.edu; *Head, Res & Instrul Serv,* Alicia Hansen; Tel: 508-793-3533, E-mail: ahansen@holycross.edu; *Cat Librn,* Theresa Huaman; Tel: 508-793-2638, E-mail: thuaman@holycross.edu; *Digital Scholarship Librn,* Lisa Villa; Tel: 508-793-2767, E-mail: lvilla@holycross.edu; *Ref & Instruction Librn,* Laura Hibbler; Tel: 508-793-3886, E-mail: lhibbler@holycross.edu; *Ref Librn,* Gudrun Krueger; Tel: 508-793-2640, E-mail: gkrueger@holycross.edu; *Res, Instruction & Outreach Librn,* Jennifer Adams; Tel: 508-793-2254, E-mail: jadams@holycross.edu; *Visual Arts Res Librn,* Janis DesMarais; Tel: 508-793-2453, E-mail: jdesmara@holycross.edu; *Asst Archivist,* Sarah Campbell; Tel: 508-793-2575, E-mail: scampbel@holycross.edu; *Electronic Res,* Robert Scheier; Tel: 508-793-3495, E-mail: rscheier@holycross.edu; *Per,* Diane Gallagher; Tel: 508-793-3543, E-mail: dgallagh@holycross.edu; Staff 19.7 (MLS 16.7, Non-MLS 3)
Founded 1843. Enrl 2,877; Fac 301; Highest Degree: Bachelor
Jul 2013-Jun 2014 Income (Main and Other College/University Libraries) $4,796,456, Locally Generated Income $3,294, Parent Institution $4,522,246, Other $270,916. Mats Exp $1,678,703, Books $258,476, Per/Ser (Incl. Access Fees) $1,101,170, Micro $1,304, AV Mat $32,614, Electronic Ref Mat (Incl. Access Fees) $262,690, Presv $22,449. Sal $1,818,091 (Prof $1,358,837)
Library Holdings: e-books 147,271; Bk Titles 547,069; Bk Vols 640,137; Per Subs 7,351
Special Collections: Americana up to 1840, Holocaust, bks; Early Christian Iberia (Roman-Visigothic-Hispania Coll, 50-711AD), bks, maps; History (David I Walsh Coll, 1872-1947), correspondence, papers, scrapbks; History (James M Curley Coll, 1874-1958), photog, scrapbks; Irish in Worcester, 1880-1890 (Richard O'Flynn Coll); Literature (Louise I Guiney Coll, 1861-1920), bks, letters, ms; Rare Books 16th-17th Century (Jesuitana Coll)
Automation Activity & Vendor Info: (Acquisitions) Innovative Interfaces, Inc; (Cataloging) Innovative Interfaces, Inc; (Circulation) Innovative Interfaces, Inc; (Course Reserve) Innovative Interfaces, Inc; (ILL) OCLC Online; (OPAC) Innovative Interfaces, Inc; (Serials) Innovative Interfaces, Inc
Database Vendor: American Chemical Society, American Mathematical Society, American Physical Society, American Psychological Association (APA), ARTstor, BioOne, Blackwell, CQ Press, Dialog, EBSCOhost, Elsevier, Gale Cengage Learning, Innovative Interfaces, Inc, ISI Web of Knowledge, JSTOR, LexisNexis, Newsbank, OCLC WorldShare Interlibrary Loan, OVID Technologies, Project MUSE, ProQuest, PubMed, ScienceDirect, Wiley
Wireless access
Publications: Handbook; Recent Acquisitions; Subject Reference Guides
Open Mon-Sun 8:30am-11pm

Departmental Libraries:
FENWICK MUSIC LIBRARY, Fenwick Bldg, 01610-2394, SAN 345-8482. Tel: 508-793-2295. *Librn,* Alan Karass; E-mail: akarass@holycross.edu; Staff 2 (MLS 1, Non-MLS 1)
Founded 1978
Library Holdings: Bk Vols 25,310; Per Subs 86
O'CALLAHAN SCIENCE LIBRARY, Swords Bldg, 01610, SAN 345-8490. Tel: 508-793-2643. Circulation Tel: 508-793-2739. *Sci Librn,* Barbara Merolli; E-mail: bmerolli@holycross.edu. Subject Specialists: *Biol, Chem, Physics,* Barbara Merolli; Staff 2 (MLS 1, Non-MLS 1)
Library Holdings: Bk Vols 101,972; Per Subs 3,962
Subject Interests: Astronomy, Biol, Chem, Computer sci, Hist of sci, Math, Med, Physics

S HIGGINS ARMORY MUSEUM*, Olive Higgins Prouty Library & Research Center, 100 Barber Ave, 01606-2444. SAN 307-8248. Tel: 508-853-6015. FAX: 508-852-7697. E-mail: higgins@higgins.org. Web Site: www.higgins.org. *Curator,* Dr Jeffrey L Forgeng; Tel: 508-853-6015, Ext 17, E-mail: jforgeng@higgins.org; *Asst Curator,* Heather Feland; Tel: 508-853-6015, Ext 23
Founded 1964
Library Holdings: Bk Vols 2,500
Special Collections: Museum Archives
Subject Interests: Armour, Arms, Art, Hist, Medieval, Mil hist, Renaissance
Function: For res purposes
Publications: John Woodman Higgins Memorial Library Catalogue of Books (circa 1970)
Open Wed 2-4
Restriction: Non-circulating

GL MASSACHUSETTS TRIAL COURT*, Worcester Law Library, 184 Main St, 01608. SAN 307-8345. Tel: 508-831-2525. FAX: 508-754-9933. E-mail: worcesterlaw@yahoo.com. Web Site: www.lawlib.state.ma.us. *Head Law Librn,* Suzanne M Hoey; Staff 3.5 (MLS 1.5, Non-MLS 2)
Founded 1842
Special Collections: History of Worcester County & its Cities & Towns; Legal Textbooks (Major Coll on General Law); Massachusetts & Federal Law Coll
Automation Activity & Vendor Info: (Acquisitions) SirsiDynix; (Cataloging) SirsiDynix; (Circulation) SirsiDynix
Wireless access
Open Mon-Fri 8-4:30
Friends of the Library Group

L MIRICK O'CONNELL*, Law Library, 100 Front St, 01608-1477. SAN 372-0357. Tel: 508-860-1520. FAX: 508-983-6230. *Librn,* Catherine Tucker
Library Holdings: Bk Vols 5,000; Per Subs 50
Restriction: Staff use only

J QUINSIGAMOND COMMUNITY COLLEGE*, George I Alden Library, 670 W Boylston St, 01606-2092. SAN 307-8272. Tel: 508-854-4366. Interlibrary Loan Service Tel: 508-854-7491. Administration Tel: 508-854-4461. Information Services Tel: 508-854-7492. FAX: 508-854-4204. E-mail: reference@qcc.mass.edu. Web Site: www.qcc.mass.edu/library. *Dean, Libr & Acad Support,* Andrea MacRitchie; E-mail: amacritchie@qcc.mass.edu; *Head, Circ, Head, ILL,* Paula McDonald; E-mail: paulam@qcc.mass.edu; *Ref & Instruction Librn,* Matthew Bejune; Tel: 508-854-4210, E-mail: mbejune@qcc.mass.edu; *Re/Ser Librn,* Dale LaBonte; Tel: 508-854-7472, E-mail: dlabonte@qcc.mass.edu; *Tech Serv & Syst Librn,* Denise Cross; Tel: 508-854-4480, E-mail: dcross@qcc.mass.edu; *Coll Develop,* Michael Stevenson; Tel: 508-854-2793, E-mail: mstevenson@qcc.mass.edu; Staff 7 (MLS 4, Non-MLS 3)
Founded 1963. Enrl 5,282; Fac 350; Highest Degree: Associate
Library Holdings: AV Mats 2,899; Bk Titles 45,641; Per Subs 294
Subject Interests: Bus, Criminal justice, Early childhood educ, Health sci
Automation Activity & Vendor Info: (Acquisitions) Innovative Interfaces, Inc; (Cataloging) Innovative Interfaces, Inc; (Circulation) Innovative Interfaces, Inc; (Course Reserve) Innovative Interfaces, Inc; (ILL) OCLC Online; (OPAC) Innovative Interfaces, Inc; (Serials) Innovative Interfaces, Inc
Database Vendor: EBSCOhost, Gale Cengage Learning, LexisNexis, Newsbank, OCLC FirstSearch
Function: Handicapped accessible, ILL available, Online searches, Photocopying/Printing, Ref serv available, Telephone ref
Mem of Massachusetts Libr Syst
Partic in Central & Western Massachusetts Automated Resource Sharing; Lyrasis; OCLC Online Computer Library Center, Inc
Special Services for the Deaf - TTY equip
Open Mon-Thurs (Fall & Spring) 8am-9pm, Fri 8-5, Sat 9-3; Mon-Thurs (Summer) 8am-9pm, Fri 8-5; Mon-Thurs (Winter) 8-7, Fri 8-5
Restriction: Open to students, fac & staff, Pub ref by request

M SAINT VINCENT HOSPITAL*, John J Dumphy Memorial Library, 123 Summer St, 01608. SAN 307-8280. Tel: 508-363-6117. FAX: 508-363-9118. E-mail: SVH-Library@StVincentHospital.com. Web Site: www.stvincenthospital.com/professionals/dumphy-library.aspx. *Mgr, Libr Serv,* Joan Yanicke; E-mail: joan.yanicke@StVincentHospital.com; Staff 2 (MLS 1, Non-MLS 1)
Founded 1900
Library Holdings: e-books 100; e-journals 6,000; Bk Titles 1,000; Per Subs 175
Special Collections: St Vincent Hospital History
Subject Interests: Med, Nursing
Automation Activity & Vendor Info: (Cataloging) CyberTools for Libraries; (OPAC) CyberTools for Libraries; (Serials) CyberTools for Libraries
Database Vendor: EBSCOhost, Gale Cengage Learning, OCLC FirstSearch, OCLC WorldShare Interlibrary Loan, OVID Technologies, PubMed, UpToDate
Mem of Massachusetts Libr Syst
Partic in Basic Health Sciences Library Network; Central Massachusetts Consortium of Health Related Libraries (CMCHRL); OCLC-LVIS

R TEMPLE EMANUEL LIBRARY*, 280 May St, 01602-2599. SAN 307-8302. Tel: 508-755-1257. FAX: 508-795-0417. Web Site: www.temple-emanuel.org. *Librn,* Melanie Ullman
Founded 1949
Library Holdings: Bk Vols 6,000; Per Subs 12
Subject Interests: Jewish hist & lit, Judaica (lit or hist of Jews), Relig
Automation Activity & Vendor Info: (Cataloging) Inmagic, Inc.
Open Mon 1-5, Tues 9:30-11:30, Wed 12:30-6:30

CM UNIVERSITY OF MASSACHUSETTS MEDICAL SCHOOL*, Lamar Soutter Library, 55 Lake Ave N, 01655-2397. SAN 307-8310. Tel: 508-856-6099. Interlibrary Loan Service Tel: 508-856-2080. Reference Tel: 508-856-6857. Administration Tel: 508-856-2205. FAX: 508-856-5039. Web Site: library.umassmed.edu. *Dir, Libr Serv,* Elaine Martin; Tel: 508-856-2399, E-mail: elaine.martin@umassmed.edu; *Assoc Dir,* Javier Crespo; Tel: 508-856-2223, E-mail: javier.crespo@umassmed.edu; *Assoc Dir, Educ & Res Serv,* James Comes; Tel: 508-856-6810, E-mail: james.comes@umassmed.edu; *Assoc Dir, Strategic Initiatives & Workforce Develop,* Barbara Ingrassia; Tel: 508-856-1041, E-mail: barbara.ingrassia@umassmed.edu; *Assoc Dir, Tech Initiatives & Res Mgt,* Mary Piorun; Tel: 508-856-2206, E-mail: mary.piorun@umassmed.edu; *Assoc Dir, User Serv,* Jane Fama; Tel: 508-856-2099, E-mail: jane.fama@umassmed.edu; Staff 23 (MLS 19, Non-MLS 4)
Founded 1973
Library Holdings: e-books 200; Bk Vols 280,000
Special Collections: Humanities in Medicine Coll; Massachusetts Medical History (Worcester Medical Library). US Document Depository
Automation Activity & Vendor Info: (Acquisitions) Ex Libris Group; (Cataloging) Ex Libris Group; (Circulation) Ex Libris Group; (Course Reserve) Ex Libris Group; (ILL) OCLC ILLiad; (OPAC) Ex Libris Group; (Serials) Ex Libris Group
Database Vendor: OVID Technologies
Partic in Academic & Research Collaborative (ARC); Boston Library Consortium, Inc; Lyrasis; OCLC Online Computer Library Center, Inc
Special Services for the Deaf - Assistive tech
Open Mon-Thurs 7:30am-11pm, Fri 7:30am-9pm, Sat 10am-9pm, Sun 10am-11pm

S WORCESTER ART MUSEUM LIBRARY*, 55 Salisbury St, 01609-3196. SAN 307-8329. Tel: 508-799-4406, Ext 3070. FAX: 508-798-5646. E-mail: library@worcesterart.org. Web Site: www.worcesterart.org. *Librn,* Debby Aframe; *Asst Librn,* Christine Clayton; Staff 3 (MLS 2, Non-MLS 1)
Founded 1909
Library Holdings: Bk Vols 45,000
Subject Interests: Asian art, European art, Prints
Mem of Massachusetts Libr Syst
Open Wed & Fri 11-5, Thurs 11-8, Sat 10-5
Restriction: Non-circulating
Friends of the Library Group

S WORCESTER HISTORICAL MUSEUM*, Research Library, 30 Elm St, 01605. SAN 307-8361. Tel: 508-753-8278, Ext 105. FAX: 508-753-9070. Web Site: www.worcesterhistory.org/library.html. *Exec Dir,* William D Wallace; Tel: 508-753-8278, Ext 106, E-mail: williamwallace@worcesterhistory.net; *Librn,* Robyn L Christensen; E-mail: robynchristensen@worcesterhistory.net; *Archivist,* William F Carrol; Staff 6 (MLS 3, Non-MLS 3)
Founded 1875
Library Holdings: Bk Titles 6,000; Bk Vols 10,000; Per Subs 20
Special Collections: Anti-Slavery (Kelley-Foster Coll), mss; Architectural Drawings Coll; City of Worcester, mss; Diner Industry; Howland Valentines; Local Information (Worcester Pamphlet Files); Out-of-Print Worcester Newspaper & Periodicals; Photographic & Graphic Coll

Subject Interests: Local hist
Open Tues-Sat 10-4, Thurs 10-8:30

C WORCESTER POLYTECHNIC INSTITUTE*, George C Gordon Library, 100 Institute Rd, 01609-2280. SAN 307-8396. Tel: 508-831-5410. Interlibrary Loan Service Tel: 508-831-5414. FAX: 508-831-5829. TDD: 508-831-6700. Web Site: www.wpi.edu/academics/library. *Asst VPres, Libr Serv,* Dr Tracey Leger-Hornby; *Assoc Libr Dir,* Matthew Hall; *Asst Dir, Coll Develop,* Lora Brueck; *Asst Dir, Ser,* Martha Gunnarson; *Asst Dir, Syst & Tech,* Donald Richardson; *Mgr, Access Serv,* Deborah Bockus; *Mgr, Instruction & Outreach,* Christine Drew; *Access Serv Librn,* Lynne Riley; *Conserv Librn,* Kathleen Markees; *Ref Coordr,* Joanne Beller; *User Serv,* Laura Hanlan; *Univ Archivist,* Rodney Obien; *Asst Archivist,* Margaret Anderson; Staff 17 (MLS 11, Non-MLS 6)
Founded 1867. Enrl 3,600; Fac 324; Highest Degree: Doctorate
Library Holdings: e-books 38,000; e-journals 35,000; Bk Vols 270,000; Per Subs 900
Special Collections: Charles Dickens (The Robert Fellman Coll); History of Science & Technology; NASA; Theo Brown Diaries
Subject Interests: Environ studies, Safety
Wireless access
Publications: Brochure; Calendar of Library Hours; Handbook; Monthly Acquisitions; Specialized Bibliographic Instruction Material
Mem of Massachusetts Libr Syst
Partic in Lyrasis; OCLC Online Computer Library Center, Inc; Westchester Academic Library Directors Organization (WALDO)

P WORCESTER PUBLIC LIBRARY*, Three Salem Sq, 01608. SAN 345-8644. Tel: 508-799-1655. Interlibrary Loan Service Tel: 508-799-1697. FAX: 508-799-1652. Web Site: www.worcpublib.org. *Head Librn,* Christopher J Korenowsky; *Assoc Head Librn,* John Weedon; Staff 27 (MLS 27)
Founded 1859. Pop 175,966; Circ 597,175
Library Holdings: AV Mats 33,014; e-books 796; Electronic Media & Resources 23,472; Bk Vols 588,958; Per Subs 1,148
Special Collections: US History (Library of American Civilization), micro. US Document Depository
Automation Activity & Vendor Info: (Acquisitions) Innovative Interfaces, Inc; (Cataloging) Innovative Interfaces, Inc; (Circulation) Innovative Interfaces, Inc; (ILL) Innovative Interfaces, Inc; (OPAC) Innovative Interfaces, Inc; (Serials) Innovative Interfaces, Inc
Database Vendor: Baker & Taylor, Booksite, EBSCOhost, Facts on File, infoUSA, Marcive, Inc, Mergent Online, OCLC WorldShare Interlibrary Loan, ProQuest, ReferenceUSA
Wireless access
Publications: Your Library (Quarterly)
Mem of Massachusetts Libr Syst
Partic in Academic & Research Collaborative (ARC); Central & Western Massachusetts Automated Resource Sharing; Lyrasis
Special Services for the Deaf - TTY equip
Friends of the Library Group
Branches: 3
GREAT BROOK VALLEY, 89 Tacoma St, 01605-3518, SAN 345-8725. Tel: 508-799-1729. *Librn,* Marilyn Rudolph; E-mail: mrudolph@worcpublib.org
Founded 1981
Library Holdings: Bk Vols 7,000
Open Mon-Fri 2-5
Friends of the Library Group
FRANCES PERKINS BRANCH, 470 W Boylston St, 01606-3226, SAN 345-8733. Tel: 508-799-1687. *Br Supvr,* Frank Sestokas
Founded 1914
Library Holdings: Bk Vols 48,000
Open Mon 9-9, Tues & Wed 9-5:30, Thurs & Fri 1-9
Friends of the Library Group

P WORCESTER TALKING BOOK LIBRARY, Three Salem Sq, 01608-2015, SAN 345-8679. Tel: 508-799-1655, 508-799-1730. Toll Free Tel: 800-762-0085 (Mass only). FAX: 508-799-1676, 508-799-1734. TDD: 508-799-1731. E-mail: talkbook@worcpublib.org. Web Site: www.worcpublib.org/talkingbook. *Librn,* James Izatt; Staff 2 (MLS 2)
Founded 1973
Automation Activity & Vendor Info: (Cataloging) Keystone Systems, Inc (KLAS); (Circulation) Keystone Systems, Inc (KLAS); (Media Booking) Keystone Systems, Inc (KLAS); (OPAC) Keystone Systems, Inc (KLAS)
Database Vendor: Keystone Systems, Inc (KLAS)
Function: Bks on cassette, Digital talking bks, e-mail serv, Handicapped accessible, Home delivery & serv to Sr ctr & nursing homes, Homebound delivery serv, Online cat, Senior outreach, VHS videos, Web-Braille, Web-catalog, Wheelchair accessible
Special Services for the Blind - Braille equip; Braille servs; Magnifiers; Reader equip
Open Tues-Thurs 9-9, Fri & Sat 9-5:30, Sun (Jan-May) 1:30-5:30
Friends of the Library Group

C WORCESTER STATE COLLEGE*, Learning Resources Center, 486 Chandler St, 01602-2597. SAN 307-840X. Tel: 508-929-8027. FAX: 508-929-8198. E-mail: library@worcester.edu. Web Site: www.worcester.edu/library. *Dir,* Dr Donald Hochstetler; Tel: 508-929-8511, E-mail: dhochstetler@worcester.edu; *Sr Librn, Electronic Res,* Betsey J Brenneman; Tel: 508-929-8801, E-mail: bbrenneman@worcester.edu; *Sr Librn, Ref,* Pamela R McKay; Tel: 508-929-8528, E-mail: pmckay@worcester.edu; *Sr Librn, Tech Serv,* Krishna DasGupta; Tel: 508-929-8802, E-mail: kdasgupta@worcester.edu; *Assoc Librn, Cat,* Ruth A Webber; Tel: 508-929-8676, E-mail: rwebber@worcester.edu; *Acq,* Carolyn Mathews; Tel: 508-929-8647, E-mail: cmathews@worcester.edu; *Ser,* Alison Majeau; Tel: 508-929-8531, E-mail: amajeau@worcester.edu; Staff 6 (MLS 6)
Founded 1874. Enrl 5,300; Fac 245; Highest Degree: Master
Library Holdings: e-books 16,000; Bk Vols 190,000; Per Subs 1,000
Special Collections: Dennis Brutus Coll
Subject Interests: Archives, Children's lit, Educ, Nursing
Automation Activity & Vendor Info: (Acquisitions) Ex Libris Group; (Cataloging) Ex Libris Group; (Circulation) Ex Libris Group; (Course Reserve) Ex Libris Group; (ILL) Ex Libris Group; (Media Booking) Ex Libris Group; (OPAC) Ex Libris Group; (Serials) Ex Libris Group
Partic in Academic & Research Collaborative (ARC); Lyrasis; OCLC Online Computer Library Center, Inc
Open Mon-Thurs (Fall & Spring) 8am-11pm, Fri 8-5, Sat 9-5, Sun 1-11; Mon-Thurs (Summer) 8am-9:30pm, Fri 8-4, Sun 1-9

S WORCESTER STATE HOSPITAL LIBRARY*, 305 Belmont St, 01604. SAN 345-8881. Tel: 508-368-3300, Ext 83540. *In Charge,* Eileen Melican; Staff 2 (MLS 1, Non-MLS 1)
Founded 1956
Library Holdings: Bk Titles 4,000; Per Subs 75

WORTHINGTON

P WORTHINGTON LIBRARY*, Frederick Sargent Huntington Memorial Library, One Huntington Rd, 01098. (Mail add: PO Box 598, 01098-0598), SAN 307-8434. Tel: 413-238-5565. E-mail: theworthingtonlibrary@gmail.com. Web Site: www.theworthingtonlibrary.org. *Dir,* Leona Arthen; Staff 1 (Non-MLS 1)
Founded 1915. Pop 1,210
Library Holdings: Large Print Bks 81; Bk Vols 8,467; Per Subs 50; Talking Bks 467; Videos 780
Special Collections: Russell H Conwell Coll
Wireless access
Open Tues 3-7, Thurs 10-12 & 3-7, Sat 10-4
Friends of the Library Group

WRENTHAM

P FISKE PUBLIC LIBRARY*, 110 Randall Rd, 02093. (Mail add: PO Box 340, 02093-0340), SAN 307-8442. Tel: 508-384-5440. FAX: 508-384-5443. Web Site: www.fiskelib.org. *Dir,* Mary Tobichuk; *Ref Librn,* Claudia Schumacher; *Ch Serv,* Elizabeth Nadow; *Circ,* Nancy Daniels
Founded 1892. Pop 9,166; Circ 51,500
Library Holdings: Bk Vols 55,000; Per Subs 110; Talking Bks 2,446; Videos 2,304
Automation Activity & Vendor Info: (Cataloging) SirsiDynix; (Circulation) SirsiDynix; (OPAC) SirsiDynix
Open Tues-Thurs 10-8, Fri 10-5, Sat 10-4
Friends of the Library Group

YARMOUTH PORT

S HISTORICAL SOCIETY OF OLD YARMOUTH LIBRARY*, 11 Strawberry Lane, 02675. (Mail add: PO Box 11, 02675-0011), SAN 373-2002. Tel: 508-362-3021. E-mail: hsoy@comcast.net. Web Site: hsoy.org. *Librn,* Daryl Marty
Library Holdings: Bk Vols 2,500
Subject Interests: Local hist
Open Tues & Thurs 9:30-3

P YARMOUTH PORT LIBRARY*, 297 Main St, Rte 6A, 02675. Tel: 508-362-3717. FAX: 508-362-6739. Web Site: www.yarmouthportlibrary.org. *Librn,* Anne Cifelli; *Assoc Librn,* Lynn Lesperance; Staff 2 (MLS 1, Non-MLS 1)
Founded 1866. Circ 46,831
Special Collections: Genealogy (New England Historic General Register & Amos Otis Papers); Histories of Cape Cod
Wireless access
Open Tues & Thurs 1-5, Wed 1-7, Fri 10-4, Sat 10-2
Friends of the Library Group

MICHIGAN

Date of Statistics: FY 2014
Population, 2010 U.S. Census: 9,883,640
STATE LIBRARY ACTIVITIES
Reference Requests: 8,634
Circulation: 1,145
Interlibrary Loan Transactions: 1,047
Total Number State Aid Grants Awarded: 382
STATE LIBRARY GRANT ACTIVITIES
Total Applications Reviewed: 386
State Aid Grants to Public Libraries: $5,738,272
State Aid Grants to Library Cooperatives: $3,137,727
State Aid to Subregionals (Blind/Handicapped): $451,800
Federal Grants Awarded: 31
Federal Library Services & Technology Act (LSTA): $4,251,300
PUBLIC LIBRARY ACTIVITIES
Total Income Reported by Public Libraries: $402,145,266
Average Income Per Capita: $40.69
Source of Income: Mainly local (approximately 98% local, 2% state & federal)
Expenditures Per Capita: $40.02
Total Number Public Library Employees: 4,768
Total Volumes Reported by Public Libraries: 33,389,784
Average Volumes Per Capita: 3.39
Total Items Available: 40,546,178
Total Circulation Reported by Public Libraries: 86,866,045
Average Circulation Per Capita: 8.79
Total Audiovisual Resources Available: 7,089,179

ADRIAN

C ADRIAN COLLEGE, Shipman Library, 110 S Madison St, 49221. SAN 345-8911. Tel: 517-264-3828. FAX: 517-264-3748. Web Site: www.adrian.edu/library. *Tech Serv Librn,* Noelle Keller; Tel: 517-265-5161, Ext 4229, E-mail: nkeller@adrian.edu; *Acq, Ser,* Elizabeth Maertens; Tel: 517-264-3900, E-mail: emaertens@adrian.edu; *Electronic Serv,* David Cruse; Tel: 517-265-5161, Ext 4241, E-mail: dcruse@adrian.edu; *Ref Serv,* Richard Geyer; Tel: 517-265-5161, Ext 4220, E-mail: rgeyer@adrian.edu; Staff 4 (MLS 3, Non-MLS 1)
Founded 1859. Enrl 1,658; Fac 101; Highest Degree: Master
Jul 2013-Jun 2014. Mats Exp $287,215, Books $14,833, Per/Ser (Incl. Access Fees) $181,272, AV Mat $101, Electronic Ref Mat (Incl. Access Fees) $88,211, Presv $2,798
Library Holdings: CDs 1,326; e-books 15,983; Bk Titles 112,579; Bk Vols 122,379; Per Subs 2,971; Videos 2,716
Special Collections: Lincolniana (Piotrowski-Lemke); United Methodist (Detroit Conference Archives)
Subject Interests: Liberal arts
Database Vendor: ARTstor, Gale Cengage Learning, JSTOR, LexisNexis, Medline, OCLC FirstSearch, ProQuest, SerialsSolutions, SirsiDynix
Wireless access
Partic in Midwest Collaborative for Library Services (MCLS)
Departmental Libraries:
EDUCATIONAL CURRICULUM CENTER, 110 S Michigan St, 49221. Tel: 517-265-5161, Ext 4485. Web Site: www.adrian.edu. *Dir,* Shirley McDaid; E-mail: smcdaid@adrian.edu
Library Holdings: Bk Vols 817

P ADRIAN PUBLIC LIBRARY, 143 E Maumee St, 49221-2773. SAN 307-8469. Tel: 517-265-2265. FAX: 517-265-8847. E-mail: adrianpubliclibrary@ci.adrian.mi.us. Web Site: www.adrian.lib.mi.us. *Dir,* Shirley A Ehnis; E-mail: sehnis@adrian.mi.gov; *Youth Serv Librn,* Cathy Chesher; E-mail: cchesher@adrian.mi.gov; Staff 7.5 (MLS 3, Non-MLS 4.5)
Founded 1868. Pop 21,333
Jul 2010-Jun 2011 Income $835,944, State $104,160, City $673,302, Locally Generated Income $58,544. Mats Exp $116,955, Books $99,893, Electronic Ref Mat (Incl. Access Fees) $17,062. Sal $349,455
Library Holdings: Audiobooks 6,511; e-books 540; Bk Vols 92,388; Per Subs 196
Special Collections: Local History Coll; Small Business Resource Center
Automation Activity & Vendor Info: (Cataloging) Innovative Interfaces, Inc; (Circulation) Innovative Interfaces, Inc; (ILL) Mel Cat; (OPAC) Innovative Interfaces, Inc
Database Vendor: Booksite, Gale Cengage Learning, ReferenceUSA
Wireless access
Mem of Woodlands Library Cooperative
Partic in Midwest Collaborative for Library Services (MCLS)
Open Mon, Tues & Thurs 10-8, Wed & Fri 10-5:30, Sat 10-3

P LENAWEE DISTRICT LIBRARY, 4459 W US HWY 223, 49221-1294. SAN 345-8970. Tel: 517-263-1011. FAX: 517-263-7109. Web Site: lenawee.lib.mi.us. *Dir,* Trevor Van Valkenburg; Staff 3 (MLS 3)
Founded 1935. Pop 42,000; Circ 180,000
Library Holdings: Bk Vols 100,000; Per Subs 144
Automation Activity & Vendor Info: (Acquisitions) Innovative Interfaces, Inc; (Cataloging) Innovative Interfaces, Inc; (Circulation) Innovative Interfaces, Inc; (OPAC) Innovative Interfaces, Inc
Wireless access
Mem of Woodlands Library Cooperative
Open Mon-Thurs 9:30-8, Fri & Sat 9:30-5:30
Branches: 5
ADDISON BRANCH, 102 S Talbot St, Addison, 49220. (Mail add: 4459 W US 223, 49221-1246), SAN 345-9004. Tel: 517-547-3414. FAX: 517-547-3414. *Librn,* Scott Culver
Open Mon 1-7, Wed & Fri 1-6, Sat 9:30-12:30
Friends of the Library Group
BRITTON BRANCH, 120 College Ave, Britton, 49229-9705. (Mail add: 4459 W US 223, 49221-1246), SAN 345-9039. Tel: 517-451-2860. FAX: 517-451-2860. *Librn,* Margaret Hans
Open Mon 1-7, Wed & Fri 1-6, Sat 9:30-12:30
Friends of the Library Group
CLAYTON BRANCH, 3457 State St, Clayton, 49235-9205. (Mail add: 4459 W US 223, 49221-1246), SAN 345-9063. Tel: 517-445-2619. FAX: 517-445-2619. *Librn,* Sarah Gebhert
Open Mon & Wed 5-8, Fri 4-8, Sat 9:30-1:30
Friends of the Library Group
DEERFIELD BRANCH, 170 Raisin St, Deerfield, 49238-9717. (Mail add: 4459 W US 223, 49221-1246), SAN 345-9152. Tel: 517-447-3400. FAX: 517-447-3400. *Librn,* Rose Piotter
Open Mon & Fri 1-6, Wed 1-7, Sat 9:30-12:30
Friends of the Library Group
ONSTED BRANCH, 261 S Main St, Onsted, 49265-9749. (Mail add: 4459 W US 223, 49221-1246), SAN 345-9098. Tel: 517-467-2623. FAX: 517-467-6298. *Librn,* Mary Jo Kokochak
Open Mon & Fri 1-6, Wed 1-7, Sat 9:30-12:30
Friends of the Library Group
Bookmobiles: 1

M LENAWEE HEALTH ALLIANCE*, Medical Staff Library, 818 Riverside Ave, 49221. SAN 327-6481. Tel: 517-265-0961. FAX: 517-265-0884. *Librn,* Kay Barber; E-mail: kay.barber@promedica.org
Library Holdings: Bk Titles 100

C SIENA HEIGHTS UNIVERSITY LIBRARY*, 1247 E Siena Heights Dr, 49221-1796. SAN 307-8485. Tel: 517-264-7150. Interlibrary Loan Service Tel: 517-264-7155. Reference Tel: 517-264-7205. FAX: 517-264-7711. Web Site: www.sienaheights.edu/library.aspx. *Dir, Libr & Res Serv,* Dr Robert W Gordon; Tel: 517-264-7152, E-mail: rgordon@sienaheights.edu; *Pub Serv Librn,* Melissa M Sissen; E-mail: msissen@sienaheights.edu; *Circ Serv Coordr,* Renee M Bracey; E-mail: rbracey@sienaheights.edu; *Coordr, Ser,* Elizabeth Brooks; Tel: 517-264-7153, E-mail:

ebrooks@sienaheights.edu; *Cataloger,* Bruce A Moore; Tel: 517-264-7151, E-mail: bmoore@sienaheights.edu; Staff 4 (MLS 2, Non-MLS 2)
Founded 1919. Enrl 1,000; Fac 65; Highest Degree: Master
Library Holdings: Bk Vols 112,895; Per Subs 352
Subject Interests: Archit, Art
Automation Activity & Vendor Info: (Acquisitions) SirsiDynix; (Cataloging) SirsiDynix; (Circulation) SirsiDynix; (Course Reserve) SirsiDynix; (OPAC) SirsiDynix; (Serials) SirsiDynix
Database Vendor: Dialog, EBSCOhost, Gale Cengage Learning, OCLC FirstSearch, OCLC WorldShare Interlibrary Loan, SirsiDynix
Wireless access
Partic in Midwest Collaborative for Library Services (MCLS)
Open Mon-Wed (Fall & Winter) 8:30am-11pm, Thurs 8:30am-9pm, Fri 8:30-5, Sat 12-5, Sun 1-11; Mon-Thurs (Summer) 8:30-8

S WACKER SILICONES CORP*, Technical Library, 3301 Sutton Rd, 49221. SAN 307-8493. Tel: 517-264-8500. FAX: 517-264-8246. *In Charge,* Kenny Fee
Founded 1964
Library Holdings: Bk Vols 4,000

ALANSON

P ALANSON AREA PUBLIC LIBRARY*, 7631 Burr Ave, 49706. (Mail add: PO Box 37, 49706-0037), SAN 376-7744. Tel: 231-548-5465. FAX: 231-548-5465. Web Site: alansonlibrary.com. *Dir,* Karen Walker; E-mail: alanson@racc2000.com
Library Holdings: Bk Titles 5,000
Partic in Northland Library Cooperative
Open Mon-Thurs 10-7, Fri 10-5, Sat 10-3

ALBION

C ALBION COLLEGE*, Stockwell-Mudd Libraries, 602 E Cass St, 49224-1879. (Mail add: Kellog Ctr 4692, 611 E Porter St, 49224), SAN 307-8507. Tel: 517-629-0285. Circulation Tel: 517-629-0489. Interlibrary Loan Service Tel: 517-629-0441. Reference Tel: 517-629-0382. Automation Services Tel: 517-629-0270. FAX: 517-629-0504. E-mail: library@albion.edu. Web Site: campus.albion.edu/library, www.albion.edu/library. *Co-Dir,* Claudia C Diaz; Tel: 517-629-0386, E-mail: cdiaz@albion.edu; *Co-Dir,* Michael VanHouten; Tel: 517-629-0293, E-mail: mvanhouten@albion.edu; *Head, Access Serv,* Alice Wiley Moore; E-mail: amoore@albion.edu; *Ref & Instrul Serv Librn,* Cheryl Blackwell; Tel: 517-629-0447, E-mail: cblackwell@albion.edu; *Web Serv & Emerging Tech Librn,* Megan O'Neill; Tel: 517-629-0270, E-mail: moneill@albion.edu; *Circ Serv Coordr,* Becky Markovich; E-mail: rmarkovich@albion.edu; *Coordr, Acq,* Patricia Engelter; E-mail: pengelter@albion.edu; *Coordr, Cat,* Beverly Brankovich; E-mail: bbrankovich@albion.edu; *Coordr, Ser,* Marion Meilaender; E-mail: mmeilaender@albion.edu; *Archivist,* Nicole Garrett; Tel: 517-629-0487, E-mail: ngarrett@albion.edu; Staff 12.2 (MLS 5.7, Non-MLS 6.5)
Founded 1835. Enrl 1,700; Fac 120; Highest Degree: Bachelor
Library Holdings: AV Mats 7,780; Bks on Deafness & Sign Lang 40; CDs 1,500; DVDs 2,000; e-books 6,331; e-journals 1,357; Music Scores 2,500; Bk Titles 278,967; Bk Vols 368,060; Per Subs 2,091; Videos 3,000
Special Collections: Albion Americana; Albion College Archives; Bible Coll; M F K Fisher; Modern Literary First Editions; Western Michigan Conference of United Methodist Church Archives, bks, letters. US Document Depository
Subject Interests: Liberal arts
Automation Activity & Vendor Info: (Acquisitions) Innovative Interfaces, Inc; (Cataloging) Innovative Interfaces, Inc; (Circulation) Innovative Interfaces, Inc; (Course Reserve) Innovative Interfaces, Inc; (ILL) Innovative Interfaces, Inc; (OPAC) Innovative Interfaces, Inc; (Serials) Innovative Interfaces, Inc
Database Vendor: Blackwell, Cambridge Scientific Abstracts, ebrary, EBSCOhost, Elsevier, Gale Cengage Learning, Innovative Interfaces, Inc, ISI Web of Knowledge, JSTOR, LexisNexis, Newsbank, OCLC, OCLC FirstSearch, OCLC WorldShare Interlibrary Loan, Project MUSE, ProQuest, SerialsSolutions, STN International, Wilson - Wilson Web
Wireless access
Function: Archival coll, Audio & video playback equip for onsite use, Computers for patron use, Copy machines, Doc delivery serv, e-mail & chat, E-Reserves, Electronic databases & coll, Exhibits, Free DVD rentals, Govt ref serv, Handicapped accessible, ILL available, Learning ctr, Music CDs, Online cat, Online info literacy tutorials on the web & in blackboard, Online ref, Online searches, Photocopying/Printing, Ref & res, Ref serv available, Ref serv in person, Scanner, Wheelchair accessible
Publications: Ex Libris (Newsletter)
Partic in Midwest Collaborative for Library Services (MCLS); Oberlin Group; OCLC Online Computer Library Center, Inc; Woodlands Interlibrary Loan
Special Services for the Deaf - Assisted listening device; Assistive tech, Bks on deafness & sign lang; Deaf publ
Special Services for the Blind - ABE/GED & braille classes for the visually impaired & print handicapped; Assistive/Adapted tech devices, equip & products; Audio mat; Braille bks; Braille equip; Braille servs; Computer with voice synthesizer for visually impaired persons; Large screen computer & software; Reader equip; Talking bks
Open Mon-Fri 7:30am-2am (8-5 Summer), Sat 9-9, Sun Noon-2am
Restriction: Open to pub for ref & circ; with some limitations, Open to students, fac & staff
Friends of the Library Group

P ALBION DISTRICT LIBRARY*, 501 S Superior St, 49224. SAN 307-8515. Tel: 517-629-3993. FAX: 517-629-5354. Web Site: www.albionlibrary.org. *Dir,* Colleen Richards Verge; *Ad,* Cindy Stanczak; *Ch,* Shelley Herron; *Hist Coll Librn,* Mary Houghton; Staff 9 (MLS 4, Non-MLS 5)
Founded 1919. Pop 12,300; Circ 68,400
Library Holdings: Audiobooks 1,212; CDs 200; e-books 5,482; Bk Vols 44,026; Per Subs 105; Talking Bks 1,502; Videos 5,499
Subject Interests: Local hist
Automation Activity & Vendor Info: (Circulation) Innovative Interfaces, Inc; (ILL) Innovative Interfaces, Inc; (Media Booking) Innovative Interfaces, Inc; (OPAC) Innovative Interfaces, Inc
Wireless access
Publications: A Michigan Childhood
Mem of Woodlands Library Cooperative
Open Mon-Thurs 10-8, Sat & Sun 1-5
Friends of the Library Group

P WOODLANDS LIBRARY COOPERATIVE*, 415 S Superior, Ste A, 49224-2174. SAN 307-8523. Tel: 517-629-9469. FAX: 517-629-3812. Web Site: woodlands.lib.mi.us/. *Dir,* Kate Pohjola Andrade; E-mail: kate.pohjolaandrade@monroe.lib.mi.us; Staff 2 (MLS 1, Non-MLS 1)
Founded 1978. Pop 855,034
Oct 2013-Sept 2014 Income $499,598, State $493,573, Other $6,025. Sal $85,700 (Prof $50,000)
Wireless access
Publications: News Notes (Quarterly)
Member Libraries: Adrian Public Library; Albion District Library; Bellevue Township Library; Branch District Library; Burr Oak Township Library; Camden Township Public Library; Charlotte Community Library; Colon Township Library; Constantine Township Library; Delta Township District Library; Delton District Library; Dorothy Hull Windsor Township Library; Dowling Public Library; East Lansing Public Library; Eaton Rapids Public Library; George W Spindler Memorial Library; Grand Ledge Area District Library; Hillsdale Community Library; Hudson Carnegie District Library; Jackson District Library; Jonesville District Library; Lenawee District Library; Litchfield District Library; Lyons Township District Library; Marshall District Library; Mendon Township Library; Mulliken District Library; North Adams Community Memorial Library; Nottawa Township Library; Pittsford Public Library; Portland District Library; Potterville Benton Township District Library; Putnam District Library; Reading Community Library; Schoolcraft Community Library; Stair Public Library; Sturgis Public Library; Sunfield District Library; Tecumseh District Library; Tekonsha Public Library; Van Buren District Library; Vermontville Township Library; Waldron District Library; White Pigeon Township Library
Open Mon-Fri 8-4:30

ALDEN

P HELENA TOWNSHIP PUBLIC LIBRARY*, 8751 Helena Rd, 49612. SAN 307-8531. Tel: 231-331-4318. FAX: 231-331-4245. E-mail: aldenlib@torchlake.com. Web Site: www.aldenlib.info. *Dir,* Sue Riegler; *Asst Dir,* Diane Nemeth
Circ 22,580
Library Holdings: Bk Vols 18,000; Per Subs 35
Wireless access
Partic in Mid-Michigan Library League
Open Mon & Wed-Fri 9-5, Tues 9-8, Sat 9-2
Friends of the Library Group

ALLEGAN

P ALLEGAN DISTRICT LIBRARY*, 331 Hubbard St, 49010. SAN 307-854X. Tel: 269-673-4625. FAX: 269-673-8661. E-mail: apl@alleganlibrary.org. Web Site: www.alleganlibrary.org. *Dir,* Ann Perrigo; E-mail: aperrigo@alleganlibrary.org; *Genealogy & Hist Librn, Ref Serv, Ad,* Linda Koch; E-mail: lkoch@alleganlibrary.org; *ILL, Music Librn, Tech Coordr,* P J Wilson; E-mail: pjwilson@alleganlibrary.org; *Network Adminr,* Alan Smith; *Ch Serv, Youth Serv,* Sharon Crotser-Toy; E-mail: scrotser-toy@alleganlibrary.org. Subject Specialists: *Allegan hist, Genealogy,* Linda Koch; *Music,* P J Wilson; Staff 6 (MLS 3, Non-MLS 3)
Founded 1843. Pop 16,165; Circ 86,892

Jul 2008-Jun 2009 Income $420,300, State $7,500, City $249,000, Locally Generated Income $133,100, Other $17,700. Mats Exp $38,900, Books $29,900, Per/Ser (Incl. Access Fees) $3,000, AV Mat $6,000. Sal $303,840
Library Holdings: Audiobooks 920; AV Mats 4,391; Bks on Deafness & Sign Lang 21; CDs 1,521; DVDs 614; e-books 1,932; Large Print Bks 1,708; Bk Titles 68,000; Per Subs 150; Talking Bks 920; Videos 843
Special Collections: Civil War Coll; Michigan Coll
Automation Activity & Vendor Info: (Acquisitions) ComPanion Corp; (Cataloging) ComPanion Corp; (Circulation) ComPanion Corp; (Course Reserve) ComPanion Corp; (ILL) Innovative Interfaces, Inc - Millenium; (OPAC) ComPanion Corp; (Serials) EBSCO Online
Database Vendor: 3M Library Systems, ABC-CLIO, Booklist Online, Booksite, Bowker, Brodart, BWI, ComPanion Corp, ebrary, EBSCO Information Services, EBSCOhost, Ex Libris Group, Facts on File, H W Wilson, Innovative Interfaces, Inc, McGraw-Hill, Medlib, OCLC FirstSearch, OCLC WebJunction, OCLC WorldShare Interlibrary Loan, ProQuest, WebMD
Wireless access
Function: Adult bk club, After school storytime, Audiobks via web, Bk club(s), Bks on cassette, Bks on CD, Children's prog, Computers for patron use, Copy machines, Digital talking bks, Fax serv, Free DVD rentals, Handicapped accessible, ILL available, Music CDs, Online cat, OverDrive digital audio bks, Photocopying/Printing, Prog for adults, Prog for children & young adult, Pub access computers, Scanner, Spoken cassettes & CDs, Story hour, Summer reading prog, Tax forms, Teen prog, VHS videos, Web-catalog, Wheelchair accessible
Partic in Southwest Michigan Library Cooperative
Open Mon-Thurs 10-9, Fri & Sat 9-5:30
Friends of the Library Group

ALLEN PARK

P ALLEN PARK PUBLIC LIBRARY*, 8100 Allen Rd, 48101. SAN 307-8558. Tel: 313-381-2425. FAX: 313-381-2124. Web Site: www.allen-park.lib.mi.us. *Dir,* Sandi Blakney; E-mail: sblakney@cityofallenpark.org; *YA Serv,* Karen M Smith; E-mail: ksmith@cityofallenpark.org; Staff 5 (MLS 2, Non-MLS 3)
Founded 1927. Pop 34,169; Circ 88,045
Library Holdings: Bk Vols 80,000; Per Subs 220
Special Collections: Local Newspapers, 1921-present
Automation Activity & Vendor Info: (Cataloging) SirsiDynix; (Circulation) SirsiDynix; (OPAC) SirsiDynix
Database Vendor: OCLC FirstSearch, ReferenceUSA
Open Mon-Thurs 12-8, Fri & Sat (Sept-May) 10-5
Friends of the Library Group

C BAKER COLLEGE*, Allen Park Campus Library, 4500 Enterprise Dr, 48101-3033. Tel: 313-425-3713. Toll Free Tel: 800-767-4120. FAX: 313-425-3777. E-mail: library-ap@baker.edu. Web Site: www.baker.edu. *Dir,* Fiona Brown; Tel: 313-425-3711; Staff 2 (MLS 1.5, Non-MLS 0.5)
Founded 1911. Enrl 2,000; Highest Degree: Master
Library Holdings: AV Mats 50; Bk Titles 5,000; Per Subs 50
Wireless access
Open Mon-Thurs 8:30am-9pm, Fri & Sat 8:30-5

R DETROIT BAPTIST THEOLOGICAL SEMINARY LIBRARY*, 4801 Allen Rd, 48101. SAN 373-2010. Tel: 313-381-0111. FAX: 313-381-0798. E-mail: library@dbts.edu. Web Site: library.dbts.edu. *Dir, Libr Serv,* Mark A Snoeberger; Tel: 313-381-0111, Ext 409, E-mail: msnoeberger@dbts.edu; *Acq Librn,* John Aloisi; E-mail: jaloisi@dbts.edu; *Ref/Cat Librn,* Andrea Miller; E-mail: amiller@dbts.edu; Staff 2 (MLS 1, Non-MLS 1)
Founded 1976. Enrl 120; Highest Degree: Master
Library Holdings: Bk Titles 40,000; Bk Vols 45,000; Per Subs 300
Subject Interests: Biblical studies, Church hist, Theol
Automation Activity & Vendor Info: (Acquisitions) LibLime; (Cataloging) LibLime; (Circulation) LibLime; (Course Reserve) LibLime; (ILL) LibLime; (Media Booking) LibLime; (OPAC) LibLime; (Serials) LibLime
Database Vendor: EBSCOhost, OCLC FirstSearch
Wireless access
Open Mon-Fri 8-4

ALLENDALE

P ALLENDALE TOWNSHIP LIBRARY*, 6175 Library Ln, 49401. SAN 307-8574. Tel: 616-895-4178. Circulation Tel: 616-895-4178, Ext 12. FAX: 616-895-5178. E-mail: all@llcoop.org. Web Site: www.allendalelibrary.org. *Dir,* Robert Bristow; Tel: 616-895-4178, Ext 10, E-mail: allrb@llcoop.org; *Asst Libr Dir,* Janice Sall; Tel: 616-895-4178, Ext 14; *Circ,* Joy Bos; *Circ,* Sara Rotman; *Circ,* Suzanne Stevens; *Youth Serv,* Sueann Posthumus; Tel: 616-895-4178, Ext 13, E-mail: allsp@llcoop.org; Staff 10.2 (MLS 1.2, Non-MLS 9)
Founded 1966. Pop 14,072
Automation Activity & Vendor Info: (Cataloging) Innovative Interfaces, Inc; (Circulation) Innovative Interfaces, Inc; (OPAC) Innovative Interfaces, Inc
Wireless access
Function: Adult bk club, Audiobks via web, Bk club(s), Bks on cassette, Bks on CD, CD-ROM, Children's prog, Computer training, Computers for patron use, Copy machines, e-mail serv, Electronic databases & coll, Fax serv, Free DVD rentals, Handicapped accessible, Holiday prog, Home delivery & serv to Sr ctr & nursing homes, Homebound delivery serv, ILL available, Instruction & testing, Mail & tel request accepted, Music CDs, Online cat, Online ref, Online searches, Orientations, Outreach serv, Photocopying/Printing, Prog for adults, Prog for children & young adult, Pub access computers, Ref serv available, Senior computer classes, Senior outreach, Spoken cassettes & CDs, Spoken cassettes & DVDs, Story hour, Summer reading prog, Tax forms, Teen prog, Telephone ref, VHS videos, Wheelchair accessible, Workshops
Partic in Lakeland Library Cooperative
Open Mon & Thurs 9-9, Tues & Wed 1-9, Fri 9-5, Sat 11-5

C GRAND VALLEY STATE UNIVERSITY LIBRARIES*, One Campus Dr, 49401-9403. SAN 307-8582. Tel: 616-331-3500. Toll Free Tel: 800-879-0581. E-mail: library@gvsu.edu. Web Site: www.gvsu.edu/library. *Dean, Univ Libr,* Lee VanOrsdel; Tel: 616-331-2621, E-mail: vanorsdl@gvsu.edu; *Assoc Dean, Res & Instruction,* Julie Garrison; Tel: 616-331-3636, E-mail: garrisoj@gvsu.edu; *Assoc Dean, Tech & Info Res,* Carlos Rodriguez; Tel: 616-331-2628, E-mail: rodriguc@gvsu.edu; *Dir, Planning & Organizational Res,* Lynell De Wind; Tel: 616-331-3005, E-mail: dewindl@gvsu.edu; *Dir, Spec Coll & Archives,* Robert Beasecker; Tel: 616-331-8556, E-mail: beaseckr@gvsu.edu
Founded 1960. Enrl 24,541; Highest Degree: Doctorate
Special Collections: Limited Edition Series; Lincoln & the Civil War Coll; Michigan Novels; US Geological Survey Maps
Wireless access

ALMA

C ALMA COLLEGE LIBRARY*, 614 W Superior St, 48801. SAN 307-8590. Tel: 989-463-7229. Interlibrary Loan Service Tel: 989-463-7128. Reference Tel: 989-463-7343. FAX: 989-463-8694. Web Site: library.alma.edu. *Dir,* Carol A Zeile; Tel: 989-463-7342, E-mail: zeile@alma.edu; *Head, Ref & Res Serv,* Steven Vest; Tel: 989-463-7344, E-mail: vest@alma.edu; *Ref & Instrul Serv Librn,* Jennifer Starkey; Tel: 989-463-7409, E-mail: starkey@alma.edu; *Circ Mgr,* Melissa Hovey; E-mail: hovey@alma.edu; *Access Serv,* Angie Kelleher; Tel: 989-463-7345, E-mail: kelleher@alma.edu; *Govt Doc, ILL,* Susan Cross; E-mail: cross@alma.edu; Staff 9 (MLS 4, Non-MLS 5)
Founded 1889. Enrl 1,261; Fac 102; Highest Degree: Bachelor
Library Holdings: AV Mats 8,377; Bk Titles 204,051; Bk Vols 251,641; Per Subs 1,200
Special Collections: College Archives
Automation Activity & Vendor Info: (Acquisitions) Innovative Interfaces, Inc; (Cataloging) Innovative Interfaces, Inc; (Circulation) Innovative Interfaces, Inc; (OPAC) Innovative Interfaces, Inc; (Serials) Innovative Interfaces, Inc
Database Vendor: Gale Cengage Learning, LexisNexis, OCLC FirstSearch, ProQuest
Partic in Midwest Collaborative for Library Services (MCLS)
Open Mon-Thurs (Winter) 8am-Midnight, Fri 8-8, Sat 10-8, Sun 12:30-Midnight; Mon-Fri (Summer) 8-5

P ALMA PUBLIC LIBRARY*, 351 N Court, 48801-1999. SAN 307-8604. Tel: 989-463-3966. FAX: 989-466-5901. E-mail: ill@alma.lib.mi.us. Web Site: www.alma.lib.mi.us. *Dir,* Bryan E Dinwoody; Tel: 989-463-3966, Ext 110; *Asst Dir, Head, Ch,* Tina Leonard; Tel: 989-463-3966, Ext 104, E-mail: tleonard@alma.lib.mi.us; *Head, Circ,* Lorrie Taylor; Tel: 989-463-3966, Ext 101, E-mail: ltaylor@alma.lib.mi.us; Staff 3 (MLS 1, Non-MLS 2)
Founded 1909. Circ 126,514
Library Holdings: Large Print Bks 354; Bk Vols 69,000; Per Subs 158; Talking Bks 2,061
Special Collections: Republic Truck Photography Coll
Automation Activity & Vendor Info: (Cataloging) SirsiDynix; (Circulation) SirsiDynix; (OPAC) SirsiDynix
Database Vendor: SirsiDynix
Publications: Annual Report; Subject Bibliographies
Mem of Capital Library Cooperative
Open Mon & Fri 12-9, Tues-Thurs 9:30-9, Sat 9:30-5:30

ALMONT

P ALMONT DISTRICT LIBRARY*, Henry Stephens Memorial Library, 213 W St Clair St, 48003-8476. (Mail add: PO Box 517, 48003-0517), SAN 307-8620. Tel: 810-798-3100. FAX: 810-798-2208. Web Site: www.adlmi.org. *Dir,* Kay Hurd; *Head, Reader Serv,* Linda Clouse
Founded 1916. Pop 6,041; Circ 22,950

Library Holdings: Bk Titles 28,000
Wireless access
Function: ILL available, Photocopying/Printing, Telephone ref
Partic in Mideastern Mich Libr Coop
Open Mon-Thurs 10-8, Fri 10-5, Sat 10-2

ALPENA

J ALPENA COMMUNITY COLLEGE*, Stephen H Fletcher Library, The Center Bldg, Rm 111, 665 Johnson St, 49707. SAN 307-8639. Tel: 989-358-7252. FAX: 989-358-7556. E-mail: acclrc@alpenacc.edu. Web Site: www.alpenacc.edu/library. *Dean, Learning Res, Media Serv,* Wendy Brooks; Tel: 989-358-7249, E-mail: brooksw@alpenacc.edu; *AV, Media Serv,* John Parris; Tel: 989-358-7244, E-mail: parrisj@alpenacc.edu
Founded 1952. Enrl 1,200; Fac 85; Highest Degree: Associate
Library Holdings: AV Mats 1,667; Large Print Bks 67; Bk Titles 37,748; Bk Vols 42,169; Per Subs 134; Talking Bks 199
Automation Activity & Vendor Info: (Cataloging) Follett Software; (Circulation) Follett Software; (ILL) Auto-Graphics, Inc; (Media Booking) Follett Software; (OPAC) Follett Software; (Serials) Follett Software
Database Vendor: Gale Cengage Learning, LexisNexis, Newsbank, OCLC FirstSearch, OCLC WorldShare Interlibrary Loan, ProQuest, SerialsSolutions
Publications: Guide to Library
Partic in Midwest Collaborative for Library Services (MCLS)
Open Mon-Thurs (Winter) 7:30am-8pm, Fri 7:30-4, Sat & Sun 12-4; Mon-Fri (Summer) 7:30-4

P ALPENA COUNTY LIBRARY*, George N Fletcher Public Library, 211 N First St, 49707. SAN 307-8647. Tel: 989-356-6188. FAX: 989-356-2765. Web Site: www.alpenalibrary.org. *Dir,* Eric Magness-Eubank; E-mail: emeacl@alpenalibrary.org; Staff 21 (MLS 2, Non-MLS 19)
Founded 1967. Pop 35,000; Circ 307,000
Library Holdings: AV Mats 3,800; Large Print Bks 750; Bk Titles 85,000; Per Subs 240
Special Collections: 19th Century Great Lakes Maritime Materials (Thunder Bay National Marine Sanctuary Research Coll); Adult Literacy Coll; Cooperating Coll for the Foundation of New York; Genealogy Center; Michigan Coll. State Document Depository; US Document Depository
Automation Activity & Vendor Info: (Cataloging) SirsiDynix; (Circulation) SirsiDynix; (OPAC) SirsiDynix; (Serials) SirsiDynix
Database Vendor: SirsiDynix
Wireless access
Function: Adult bk club, Adult literacy prog, Archival coll, Art exhibits, Bks on cassette, Bks on CD, Children's prog, Computer training, Computers for patron use, Copy machines, Electronic databases & coll, Family literacy, Holiday prog, ILL available, Music CDs, Photocopying/Printing, Prog for adults, Prog for children & young adult, Ref & res, Wheelchair accessible
Partic in Midwest Collaborative for Library Services (MCLS); Northland Library Cooperative
Open Mon-Thurs 9:30-9, Fri & Sat 9:30-5, Sun (Sept-May) 1-5
Friends of the Library Group

AMASA

P AMASA COMMUNITY LIBRARY*, 109 W Pine St, 49903. SAN 307-8663. Tel: 906-822-7291.
Pop 1,020; Circ 1,174
Library Holdings: AV Mats 23; Bk Vols 5,000

ANN ARBOR

S ACCESS-AIC SERVICES LIBRARY*, Liberty Sta, PO Box 8030, 48107-8030. Tel: 734-996-5553. FAX: 734-996-5570. E-mail: aicservices@provide.net.
Library Holdings: Bk Vols 100

P ANN ARBOR DISTRICT LIBRARY*, 343 S Fifth Ave, 48104. SAN 345-9217. Tel: 734-327-4200. Circulation Tel: 734-327-4219. Reference Tel: 734-327-4525. Administration Tel: 734-327-4263. Web Site: aadl.org. *Libr Dir,* Josie Parker; Fax: 734-327-8309, E-mail: parkerj@aadl.org; *Assoc Dir, Finance/HR & Operations,* Ken Nieman; Tel: 734-327-4517, Fax: 734-327-8324, E-mail: niemank@aadl.org; *Assoc Dir, IT & Product Develop,* Eli Neiburger; Tel: 734-327-4245, Fax: 734-327-8325, E-mail: neiburgere@aadl.org; *Assoc Dir, Serv, Coll & Access,* Position Currently Open; *Mgr, Circ Serv,* Diane Dahlem; Tel: 734-327-4281, Fax: 734-327-8305, E-mail: dahlemd@aadl.org; *Mgr, Commun Relations & Mkt,* Tim Grimes; Tel: 734-327-4265, Fax: 734-327-8355, E-mail: grimest@aadl.org; *Mgr, Human Res,* DeAnn Doll; Tel: 734-327-4273, E-mail: dolld@aadl.org; *Mgr, Outreach & Neighborhood Serv,* Terry Soave; Tel: 734-327-8327, Fax: 734-327-4255, E-mail: soavet@aadl.org; *Mgr, Youth & Adult Serv & Coll,* Sherlonya Turner; Tel: 734-327-4268, Fax: 734-327-8307, E-mail: turners@aadl.org; Staff 144 (MLS 21, Non-MLS 123)
Founded 1856. Pop 163,590; Circ 8,805,859
Jul 2012-Jun 2013 Income (Main Library and Branch(s)) $12,056,184. Mats Exp $1,848,599. Sal $5,695,993
Library Holdings: Audiobooks 27,575; CDs 58,241; DVDs 99,202; Bk Vols 410,125
Special Collections: Ann Arbor News Archive; Art Prints; Bi-Folkal Kits; Black Studies Coll; Book Clubs to Go (Youth & Adult); Energy Meters; Language Learning Coll; Music Tools; Musical Scores; Paperback Plays; Science to Go (Interactive Science Materials); Science Tools; Stories to Go (Storytime Kits); Telescopes; World Language Coll; Youth Kits (Print Book/Audio Book Pairs, Brainquest Cards, Fandex Cards)
Subject Interests: Art, Local hist, Music
Automation Activity & Vendor Info: (Acquisitions) Innovative Interfaces, Inc; (Cataloging) Innovative Interfaces, Inc; (Circulation) Innovative Interfaces, Inc; (OPAC) Innovative Interfaces, Inc; (Serials) Innovative Interfaces, Inc
Database Vendor: Baker & Taylor, BWI, EBSCOhost, Gale Cengage Learning, Ingram Library Services, LearningExpress, Newsbank, OCLC WorldShare Interlibrary Loan, Overdrive, Inc, ProQuest, ReferenceUSA, TumbleBookLibrary, ValueLine
Wireless access
Function: Archival coll, Art exhibits, Audiobks via web, Bks on cassette, Bks on CD, Computer training, Computers for patron use, Copy machines, Doc delivery serv, Electronic databases & coll, Exhibits, Free DVD rentals, Handicapped accessible, Holiday prog, Home delivery & serv to Sr ctr & nursing homes, Homebound delivery serv, Homework prog, ILL available, Large print keyboards, Magnifiers for reading, Mus passes, Music CDs, Online cat, Online ref, Outreach serv, OverDrive digital audio bks, Preschool outreach, Prog for adults, Prog for children & young adult, Pub access computers, Ref serv available, Ref serv in person, Scanner, Senior computer classes, Senior outreach, Spoken cassettes & CDs, Story hour, Summer reading prog, Tax forms, Telephone ref, VHS videos, Web-catalog, Wheelchair accessible
Publications: AADL News (Newsletter); Axis: Stuff for Teens Grades 6-12 (Newsletter); Jump: Fun Stuff Just for Kids (Newsletter); WLBPD@AAADL News (Newsletter)
Partic in Midwest Collaborative for Library Services (MCLS); OCLC Online Computer Library Center, Inc
Special Services for the Blind - Accessible computers; Assistive/Adapted tech devices, equip & products; BiFolkal kits; Bks on cassette; Bks on CD; Closed circuit TV magnifier; Descriptive video serv (DVS); Digital talking bk; Internet workstation with adaptive software; Large print bks; Magnifiers; Networked computers with assistive software; Newsletter (in large print, Braille or on cassette); PC for handicapped; Recorded bks; Ref serv; Scanner for conversion & translation of mats; Screen enlargement software for people with visual disabilities; Screen reader software; Talking bk serv referral; Talking bks; Talking bks & player equip; Variable speed audiotape players
Open Mon 10-9, Tues-Fri 9-9, Sat 9-6, Sun 12-6
Friends of the Library Group
Branches: 5
MALLETTS CREEK BRANCH, 3090 E Eisenhower Pkwy, 48108. FAX: 734-827-5128.
Special Services for the Blind - Accessible computers; Bks on CD; Large print bks; Magnifiers; Networked computers with assistive software
Open Mon 10-9, Tues-Fri 9-9, Sat 9-6, Sun 12-6
PITTSFIELD BRANCH, 2359 Oak Valley Dr, 48103. FAX: 734-332-3941.
Special Services for the Blind - Accessible computers; Bks on CD; Large print bks; Magnifiers; Networked computers with assistive software
Open Mon 10-9, Tues-Fri 9-9, Sat 10-6, Sun 12-6
TRAVERWOOD, 3333 Traverwood Dr, 48105. FAX: 734-213-2023.
Special Services for the Blind - Accessible computers; Bks on CD; Large print bks; Magnifiers; Networked computers with assistive software
Open Mon 10-9, Tues-Fri 9-9, Sat 9-6, Sun 12-6

P WASHTENAW LIBRARY FOR THE BLIND & PHYSICALLY DISABLED, 343 S Fifth Ave, 48104. Tel: 734-327-4224. Toll Free Tel: 800-460-0680. FAX: 734-327-8309. E-mail: wlbpd@aadl.org. Web Site: wlbpd.aadl.org. *Libr Dir,* Josie Parker; Tel: 734-327-4263, E-mail: parkerj@aadl.org
Library Holdings: DVDs 335; Large Print Bks 4,622; Talking Bks 14,220
Special Services for the Blind - Accessible computers; Assistive/Adapted tech devices, equip & products; Bks on CD; Bks on flash-memory cartridges; Closed caption display syst; Computer with voice synthesizer for visually impaired persons; Copier with enlargement capabilities; Descriptive video serv (DVS); Digital talking bk; Digital talking bk machines; Extensive large print coll; Free checkout of audio mat; Home delivery serv; Internet workstation with adaptive software; Large print bks; Large print bks & talking machines; Large screen computer & software; Low vision equip; Magnifiers; Networked computers with assistive software; PC for handicapped; Scanner for conversion & translation of mats; Screen enlargement software for people with visual disabilities; Screen reader software; Talking bks; Talking bks & player equip
Open Mon 10-9, Tues-Fri 9-9, Sat 9-6, Sun 12-6

WEST BRANCH, 2503 Jackson Rd, 48103, SAN 345-9276. FAX: 734-827-5115.
Special Services for the Blind - Accessible computers; Bks on CD; Large print bks; Magnifiers; Networked computers with assistive software
Open Mon 10-9, Tues-Fri 9-9, Sat 10-6, Sun 12-6

C CONCORDIA UNIVERSITY*, Zimmerman Library, 4090 Geddes Rd, 48105-2797. SAN 307-8698. Tel: 734-995-7353. Toll Free Tel. 888-734-4237. FAX: 734-995-7405. E-mail: library@cuaa.edu. Web Site: cuaa.edu/library. *Mgr, Libr Serv,* Michael O'Leary; E-mail: michael.oleary@cuaa.edu
Founded 1963. Enrl 625; Fac 46; Highest Degree: Master
Library Holdings: e-journals 14,411; Bk Titles 95,000; Bk Vols 113,000; Per Subs 146
Special Collections: Classics; ERIC depository; French Language & Literature (Denkinger); History of Science (Annual Volumes & Backfile Bound Periodicals for Creation Research Society Quarterly, vols 1 to date & Journal of Victoria Institute, 1861-1975). US Document Depository
Subject Interests: Educ, Hist, Music, Natural sci, Theol
Automation Activity & Vendor Info: (Cataloging) Follett Software; (Circulation) Follett Software; (Course Reserve) Follett Software; (OPAC) Follett Software
Database Vendor: OCLC FirstSearch
Partic in Libr Network of Mich; OCLC Online Computer Library Center, Inc
Open Mon-Thurs (Fall & Spring) 8am-Midnight, Fri 8-6, Sat 9-4, Sun 2-Midnight

GM DEPARTMENT OF VETERANS AFFAIRS*, VA Ann Arbor Healthcare System Medical Center Library, 2215 Fuller Rd, 48105. SAN 346-0207. Tel: 734-845-5408. FAX: 734-845-3110. *Libr Mgr,* Sara Peth; E-mail: sara.peth@va.gov; Staff 1 (MLS 1)
Library Holdings: AV Mats 323; Bk Titles 3,300; Per Subs 185
Subject Interests: Med, Nursing, Psychol
Automation Activity & Vendor Info: (Acquisitions) EOS International; (Cataloging) EOS International; (Circulation) EOS International; (OPAC) EOS International; (Serials) EOS International
Database Vendor: EBSCO Information Services, EBSCOhost, Elsevier, Gale Cengage Learning, OCLC FirstSearch, OCLC WorldShare Interlibrary Loan, OVID Technologies, ProQuest, PubMed, STAT!Ref (Teton Data Systems), Swets Information Services, UpToDate
Function: Doc delivery serv, Ref serv available
Partic in Midwest Collaborative for Library Services (MCLS)
Open Mon-Fri 8-4:30
Restriction: Circ limited, External users must contact libr, Restricted pub use

G ENVIRONMENTAL PROTECTION AGENCY, National Vehicle & Fuel Emissions Laboratory Library, 2000 Traverwood Dr, 48105. SAN 307-8701. Tel: 734-214-4311. FAX: 734-214-4525. E-mail: AALibrary@epa.gov. Web Site: epa.gov/natlibra/libraries/nvfel.htm. *Librn,* Kirk E Nims; Tel: 734-214-4434, E-mail: nims.kirk@epa.gov; *Web Librn,* Shan Liao; Tel: 734-214-4435, E-mail: liao.shan@epa.gov; Staff 2 (MLS 2)
Founded 1975
Library Holdings: Bk Vols 3,000; Per Subs 90
Special Collections: EPA Report Coll; Legislative Materials, Documents & Reports; Microfiche Federal Register, 1977-present; Society of Automotive Engineers Papers, 1962-present
Subject Interests: Air pollution, Automotive eng, Fuel
Automation Activity & Vendor Info: (Cataloging) OCLC Connexion
Database Vendor: Dialog, OCLC FirstSearch, OCLC WorldShare Interlibrary Loan, ScienceDirect
Function: CD-ROM, Doc delivery serv, Govt ref serv, ILL available, Online searches, Orientations, Photocopying/Printing, Ref serv available, Telephone ref
Open Mon-Fri 9-4
Restriction: Circulates for staff only, In-house use for visitors, Lending to staff only, Non-circulating to the pub, Open to pub upon request, Open to researchers by request, Pub use on premises, Restricted borrowing privileges

G MICHIGAN DEPARTMENT OF NATURAL RESOURCES, INSTITUTE FOR FISHERIES, Fisheries Division Library, NIB G250, 400 N Ingalls St, 48109-5480. SAN 307-8779. Tel: 734-663-3554, Ext 10555. FAX: 734-663-9399. Web Site: www.michigan.gov/dnr/0,7-153-10364_52259_19056—,00.html. *Librn,* Tina M Tincher; E-mail: tinchert@michigan.gov; Staff 0.6 (MLS 0.6)
Founded 1930
Library Holdings: Bk Vols 800; Per Subs 15
Subject Interests: Fisheries
Restriction: Non-circulating to the pub, Open by appt only

S MICHIGAN MUNICIPAL LEAGUE LIBRARY*, 1675 Green Rd, 48105. (Mail add: PO Box 1487, 48106-1487), SAN 321-5229. Tel: 734-662-3246. Toll Free Tel: 800-653-2483. FAX: 734-662-8083. E-mail: info@mml.org. Web Site: www.mml.org. *Dir,* Colleen Layton; Tel: 734-669-6320, E-mail: clayton@mml.org; Staff 5 (MLS 1, Non-MLS 4)
Founded 1899
Library Holdings: Bk Titles 3,000
Special Collections: Charters, Codes & Ordinances for Michigan Cities; Michigan Proposed Legislation
Automation Activity & Vendor Info: (Cataloging) Inmagic, Inc.
Publications: Subject List of MML Publications
Restriction: Non-circulating, Staff & mem only

G NATIONAL ARCHIVES & RECORDS ADMINISTRATION, Gerald R Ford Presidential Library, 1000 Beal Ave, 48109-2114. SAN 321-6497. Tel: 734-205-0555. FAX: 734-205-0571. E-mail: ford.library@nara.gov. Web Site: www.fordlibrarymuseum.gov. *Dir,* Dr Elaine Didier; Tel: 734-205-0566; *Supvry Archivist,* Geir Gundersen; Tel: 734-205-0556; *Computer Syst Adminr,* John Hurley; Tel: 734-205-0553; *Archivist,* Stacy Davis; Tel: 734-205-0563; *Archivist,* Mark Fischer; Tel: 734-205-0558; *Archivist,* Ken Hafeli; Tel: 734-205-0568; *Archivist,* Donna Lehman; Tel: 734-205-0560; *Archivist,* Jeremy Schmidt; Tel: 734-205-0578; *Archive Spec,* Tim Holtz; Tel: 734-205-0592; *Archives, Tech,* Elizabeth Druga; Tel: 734-205-0554; *Archives, Tech,* James Neel; Tel: 734-205-0557; *Archives, Tech,* John O'Connell; Tel: 734-205-0559; *Spec Events Coordr,* Kate Murray; Tel: 734-205-0567. Subject Specialists: *Digitization,* Stacy Davis; Staff 14 (MLS 6, Non-MLS 8)
Founded 1977
Library Holdings: Bk Titles 6,550; Bk Vols 9,618; Per Subs 25
Special Collections: Personal Papers of Gerald Ford & of His Associates in Politics & Government, 1950-2000; Presidential Papers & Government Records, 1974-77 (includes Archives of President Ford, White House Staff, & National Security Council). Oral History
Subject Interests: Cold War, Foreign affairs, Politics, Presidential elections, US domestic policy
Wireless access
Function: Archival coll, Distance learning, For res purposes, Govt ref serv, Mail & tel request accepted, Online ref, Photocopying/Printing, Ref serv available, Telephone ref
Open Mon-Fri 8:45-4:45
Restriction: Non-circulating coll
Friends of the Library Group

M ST JOSEPH MERCY HOSPITAL*, Riecker Memorial Library, 5301 E Huron River Dr, Rm 1712, 48106. (Mail add: PO Box 995, 48106-0995), SAN 307-8809. Tel: 734-712-3045. FAX: 734-712-2679. *Librn,* Jillah Biza; E-mail: bizaj@trinity-health.org; Staff 2 (MLS 1, Non-MLS 1)
Subject Interests: Consumer health info, Med, Nursing
Database Vendor: Dialog, EBSCOhost, Gale Cengage Learning, OCLC FirstSearch, OVID Technologies
Wireless access
Partic in Medical Library Association (MLA); Metrop Detroit Med Libr Group; Michigan Health Sciences Libraries Association; Midwest Collaborative for Library Services (MCLS), National Network of Libraries of Medicine; National Network of Libraries of Medicine Greater Midwest Region; OWLSnet
Restriction: Private libr

G UNITED STATES GEOLOGICAL SURVEY, GREAT LAKES SCIENCE CENTER*, John Van Oosten Library, 1451 Green Rd, 48105-2807. SAN 307-8817. Tel: 734-214-7210. FAX: 734-994-8780. Web Site: www.glsc.usgs.gov/library. *Librn,* Christine Schmuckal; E-mail: cschmuckal@usgs.gov; Staff 1 (MLS 1)
Founded 1966
Subject Interests: Biol, Environ studies, Great Lakes
Partic in Fedlink; Midwest Collaborative for Library Services (MCLS); OCLC Online Computer Library Center, Inc
Restriction: Borrowing requests are handled by ILL, Visitors must make appt to use bks in the libr

UNIVERSITY OF MICHIGAN

C BENTLEY HISTORICAL LIBRARY*, 1150 Beal Ave, 48109-2113, SAN 345-9489. Tel: 734-764-3482. FAX: 734-936-1333. E-mail: bentley.ref@umich.edu. Web Site: bentley.umich.edu. *Dir,* Terrence J McDonald; E-mail: tmcd@umich.edu; *Assoc Dir,* Position Currently Open; *Actg Assoc Dir,* Nancy Bartlett; E-mail: nbart@umich.edu; Staff 22 (MLS 12, Non-MLS 10)
Founded 1935
Library Holdings: Bk Vols 60,000; Per Subs 110
Special Collections: Architectural Coll; Papers of Frank Murphy, George Romney, Arthur Vandenburg, G Mennen Williams, Gerald L K Smith, William G Milliken, Detroit Urban League; Records of University of Michigan; Temperance & Prohibition (Women's Christian Temerance Union), ms, micro, printed; US & China Coll; US & Philippines Coll
Subject Interests: Mich
Partic in RLIN (Research Libraries Information Network)

Publications: Asn of Res Librs
Open Mon-Fri 9-5
Friends of the Library Group

C WILLIAM L CLEMENTS LIBRARY*, 909 S University Ave, 48109-1190, SAN 326-4343. Tel: 734-764-2347. FAX: 734-647-0716. Web Site: www.clements.umich.edu. *Dir,* J Kevin Graffagnino; E-mail: jkgraff@umich.edu; *Assoc Dir,* Brian Leigh Dunnigan; E-mail: briand@umich.edu; *Head, Reader Serv,* Clayton D Lewis; E-mail: clayclem@umich.edu; *Curator,* Barbara DeWolfe; E-mail: bdewolfe@umich.edu. Subject Specialists: *Manuscripts,* Barbara DeWolfe; Staff 8 (MLS 7, Non-MLS 1)
Founded 1923
Library Holdings: Bk Vols 77,000; Per Subs 34
Partic in RLIN (Research Libraries Information Network)
Publications: Exhibit Bulletins; The Quarto
Open Mon-Wed & Fri (Winter) 9-4:45, Thurs 9-7:45; Mon-Thurs (Summer) 9-5:45, Fri 9am-11:45am
Restriction: Non-circulating
Friends of the Library Group

C SUMNER & LAURA FOSTER LIBRARY*, 265 Lorch Hall, 48109-1220, SAN 345-9519. Tel: 734-763-6609. FAX: 734-763-2769. E-mail: foster.library@umich.edu. Web Site: www.lib.umich.edu/foster-library. *Mgr,* Brenda Fischer; E-mail: bsfische@umich.edu; *Econ Librn,* Pamela MacKintosh; E-mail: pmackin@umich.edu; Staff 2 (MLS 1, Non-MLS 1)
Founded 1986
Library Holdings: Bk Vols 2,500; Per Subs 100
Special Collections: Working Papers & Research Reports from other Universities & Research Institute
Subject Interests: Econ
Partic in Association of Research Libraries (ARL)
Open Mon-Thurs (Fall & Winter) 10-7, Fri 10-5

C KRESGE LIBRARY SERVICES, Stephen M Ross School of Business, 701 Tappan St, 48109-1234, SAN 345-9306. Circulation Tel: 734-764-1375. Reference Tel: 734-764-9464. E-mail: kresge_library@umich.edu. Web Site: www.bus.umich.edu/kresgelibrary. *Dir,* Corey Seeman; Tel: 734-764-9969, E-mail: cseeman@umich.edu; *Fac Res Serv/Ref Serv Librn,* Laura Berdish; Tel: 734-763-9360, E-mail: berdish@umich.edu; *Fac Res Serv/Ref Serv Librn,* Danguole Kviklys; Tel: 734-764-8424, E-mail: dkviklys@umich.edu; *Fac Res Serv/Ref Serv Librn,* Celia Ross; Tel: 734-763-5452, E-mail: caross@umich.edu; *Instrul Serv Librn,* Sally Ziph; Tel: 734-764-5532, E-mail: sweston@umich.edu; *Ref Serv Librn,* Position Currently Open; *Digital Serv,* Jennifer Lammers Zimmer; Tel: 734-764-6845; *Tech Serv,* John Sterbenz; Tel: 734-764-5746, E-mail: jsterben@umich.edu. Subject Specialists: *Acctg, Finance,* Celia Ross; Staff 19 (MLS 8, Non-MLS 11)
Founded 1925. Enrl 3,400; Fac 189; Highest Degree: Doctorate
Library Holdings: Bk Titles 150; Bk Vols 200; Per Subs 2,500
Subject Interests: Bus, Career info
Automation Activity & Vendor Info: (Acquisitions) Innovative Interfaces, Inc; (Cataloging) Innovative Interfaces, Inc; (Circulation) Innovative Interfaces, Inc; (Course Reserve) Innovative Interfaces, Inc; (ILL) Innovative Interfaces, Inc; (Media Booking) Innovative Interfaces, Inc; (OPAC) Innovative Interfaces, Inc; (Serials) Innovative Interfaces, Inc
Database Vendor: ebrary, EBSCOhost, Elsevier, Factiva.com, Faulkner Information Services, Gale Cengage Learning, HeinOnline, IBISWorld, IEEE (Institute of Electrical & Electronics Engineers), infoUSA, Innovative Interfaces, Inc, ISI Web of Knowledge, JSTOR, LexisNexis, Marquis Who's Who, Mergent Online, OneSource, Plunkett Research, Ltd, ProQuest, ReferenceUSA, RefWorks, Safari Books Online, Sage, SBRnet (Sports Business Research Network), ScienceDirect, Scopus, SerialsSolutions, Springer-Verlag, Standard & Poor's, Thomson - Web of Science, ValueLine
Function: Doc delivery serv, e-mail & chat, e-mail serv, Electronic databases & coll, Fax serv, ILL available, Mail & tel request accepted, Ref & res, Ref serv available, Ref serv in person, Web-catalog
Partic in Association of Research Libraries (ARL); OCLC Online Computer Library Center, Inc
Restriction: Not open to pub

CL LAW LIBRARY*, 801 Monroe St, 48109-1210, SAN 345-942X. Tel: 734-764-9324. Circulation Tel: 734-764-4252. Interlibrary Loan Service Tel: 734-763-7940. FAX: 734-615-0178. Circulation FAX: 734-936-3884. Reference FAX: 734-764-5863. Web Site: www.law.umich.edu/library/info/pages/default.aspx. *Dir,* Margaret A Leary; Tel: 734-764-9322, E-mail: mleary@umich.edu; *Asst Dir,* Barbara Garavaglia; Tel: 734-764-9338, E-mail: bvaccaro@umich.edu; *Asst Dir,* Barbara Snow; Tel: 734-763-3767, E-mail: barbsnow@umich.edu; Staff 57 (MLS 12, Non-MLS 45)
Founded 1859. Enrl 1,150; Fac 60; Highest Degree: Doctorate
Library Holdings: Bk Titles 305,352; Bk Vols 941,237; Per Subs 9,733
Automation Activity & Vendor Info: (Acquisitions) Innovative Interfaces, Inc; (Cataloging) Innovative Interfaces, Inc; (Circulation) Innovative Interfaces, Inc; (Course Reserve) Innovative Interfaces, Inc; (ILL) Innovative Interfaces, Inc; (OPAC) Innovative Interfaces, Inc; (Serials) Innovative Interfaces, Inc
Database Vendor: Dialog, Gale Cengage Learning, Innovative Interfaces, Inc, JSTOR, LexisNexis, OCLC FirstSearch, Westlaw
Partic in Center for Research Libraries; Committee on Institutional Cooperation; Law Library Microform Consortium (LLMC); Midwest Collaborative for Library Services (MCLS); National Network of Libraries of Medicine Greater Midwest Region; OCLC Research Library Partnership; RLIN (Research Libraries Information Network)
Restriction: Internal circ only, Restricted access

C TRANSPORTATION RESEARCH INSTITUTE LIBRARY*, 2901 Baxter Rd, 48109-2150, SAN 345-939X. Tel: 734-764-2171. FAX: 734-936-1081. E-mail: umtri-lib@umich.edu. Web Site: www.umtri.umich.edu. *Mgr,* Bob Sweet; Tel: 734-936-1073, E-mail: bsweet@umich.edu; Staff 5 (MLS 2, Non-MLS 3)
Founded 1965
Library Holdings: Bk Titles 110,000; Per Subs 300
Subject Interests: Automotive eng
Automation Activity & Vendor Info: (Circulation) Inmagic, Inc.
Partic in Dialog Corp
Publications: UMTRI Bibliography (cumulative); UMTRI Current Acquisitions - A Selected List (weekly - electronic & printed editions)
Open Mon-Fri 8-12 & 1-5

C UNIVERSITY OF MICHIGAN*, University Library, 818 Hatcher Graduate Library, 48109-1190. SAN 345-9578. Tel: 734-764-9356. Circulation Tel: 734-764-0401. Interlibrary Loan Service Tel: 734-764-8584. Reference Tel: 734-764-9373. FAX: 734-763-5080. Circulation FAX: 734-647-9557. Interlibrary Loan Service FAX: 734-936-3630. Web Site: www.lib.umich.edu. *Univ Librn & Dean of Libr,* James Hilton; E-mail: hilton@umich.edu; *Assoc Univ Librn, Coll Develop,* Bryan Skib; E-mail: bskib@umich.edu; *Assoc Univ Librn, Dir of the Taubman Health Sci Libr,* Jane Blumenthal; E-mail: janeblum@umich.edu; *Assoc Univ Librn, Learning & Teaching,* Laurie Alexander; E-mail: lauriea@umich.edu; *Assoc Univ Librn, Libr Operations,* Rebecca Dunkle; E-mail: rdunkle@umich.edu; *Assoc Univ Librn, Res Serv,* Elaine Westbrooks; E-mail: ewestbrk@umich.edu; Staff 488 (MLS 158, Non-MLS 330)
Founded 1817. Enrl 58,947; Fac 6,941; Highest Degree: Doctorate
Library Holdings: Bk Vols 7,290,793; Per Subs 63,329
Special Collections: American Society of Information Sciences, ms; Food & Agriculture Organizations; Human Relations Area Files; Organization of American States; World Health Organizations. Can & Prov; State Document Depository; UN Document Depository; US Document Depository
Subject Interests: Astronomy, Bibliographies, Botany, E Asia, English, Geog, Hist, Hist of sci, Hist of transportation, Math, Near East, Netherlands, S Asia, Slavic (Lang), Zoology
Automation Activity & Vendor Info: (Acquisitions) Ex Libris Group; (OPAC) Ex Libris Group
Partic in OCLC Online Computer Library Center, Inc

Departmental Libraries:

ART, ARCHITECTURE & ENGINEERING LIBRARY, Duderstadt Ctr, 2281 Bonnisteel Blvd, 48109-2094, SAN 345-9667. Tel: 734-647-5747. Reference Tel: 734-647-5735. FAX: 734-764-4487. Web Site: www.lib.umich.edu/aael/. *Dir,* Catherine B Soehner; Tel: 734-936-7274, E-mail: csoehner@umich.edu; *Librn,* David Carter; *Librn,* Paul Grochowski; *Librn,* Annette Haines; *Librn,* Rebecca Price; *Librn,* Robert Tolliver; *Coll Develop, Ref,* Leena Lalwani. Subject Specialists: *Eng,* David Carter; *Eng,* Paul Grochowski; *Arts, Design,* Annette Haines; *Archit, Urban planning,* Rebecca Price; *Eng,* Robert Tolliver; *Eng,* Leena Lalwani; Staff 27 (MLS 7, Non-MLS 20)
Library Holdings: Bk Vols 663,460
Special Collections: Charles Sawyer Papers; D H Burnham Papers; Geo Bringham Papers; Leonard Eaton Papers; Michigan Reports; Walter Sanders Papers. US Document Depository
Subject Interests: Archit, Art, Design, Eng, Urban planning
Function: Audio & video playback equip for onsite use, For res purposes, Handicapped accessible, ILL available, Ref serv available, Res libr
Restriction: Open to pub for ref only, Open to students, fac & staff
Friends of the Library Group

ASIA, Hatcher Library, 920 N University St, Rm 418, 48109-1205, SAN 345-987X. Tel: 734-764-0406. FAX: 734-647-2885. Web Site: www.lib.umich.edu/asia. *Head of Libr,* Dr Jidong Yang; Tel: 734-936-2354, E-mail: yangjd@umich.edu; *Coordr, Pub Serv,* Brian Vivier; Staff 11 (MLS 6, Non-MLS 5)
Founded 1948
Library Holdings: Bk Vols 689,508
Special Collections: Ch'ing Archives; Gaimosho Archives; GB PRO Files on China; Hussey Papers; Japanese Diet Proceedings; URI Files
Subject Interests: China, Far East, Japan, Korea
Publications: The Catalogs of the Asia Library, G K Hall, 1979

ASKWITH MEDIA LIBRARY, Shapiro Library, Rm 2002, 919 S University Ave, 48109-1185, SAN 370-3533. Tel: 734-764-5360. FAX: 734-764-7087. Web Site: www.lib.umich.edu/aml. *Head of Libr,* Jeffrey

Pearson; Tel: 734-763-3758, E-mail: jwpearso@umich.edu; Staff 4 (MLS 1, Non-MLS 3)
Founded 1939
Library Holdings: AV Mats 9,476; Talking Bks 135; Videos 19,413
Subject Interests: Film, Media, Video
Function: Audio & video playback equip for onsite use, AV serv, Digital talking bks
Open Mon-Thurs (Fall & Winter) 8am-9pm, Fri 8-5, Sun 1-6; Mon-Thurs (Spring) 8-8, Fri 8-5, Sun 1-5; Mon-Thurs (Summer) 8-7, Fri 8-5
Friends of the Library Group

FINE ARTS LIBRARY, 260 Tappan Hall, 519 S State St, 48109-1357, SAN 345-9934. Tel: 734-764-5405. FAX: 734-764-5408. E-mail: finearts@umich.edu. Web Site: www.lib.umich.edu/finearts/. *Head of Libr,* Deirdre Spencer; E-mail: deirdres@umich.edu. Subject Specialists: *Art hist,* Deirdre Spencer; Staff 4 (MLS 1, Non-MLS 3)
Library Holdings: Bk Vols 96,161
Subject Interests: Art hist
Open Mon-Thurs (Fall & Winter) 8am-10pm, Fri 8-5, Sat 1-6, Sun 1-10; Mon-Thurs (Spring & Summer) 8-8, Fri 8-5, Sun 1-5
Friends of the Library Group

HARLAN HATCHER GRADUATE LIBRARY, 209 Hatcher N, 920 N University, 48109-1205, SAN 371-4810. Tel: 734-764-0400. Reference Tel: 734-764-9373. Web Site: www.lib.umich.edu/grad. *Interim Head, Ref & Instruction,* Laurie Alexander; Tel: 734-763-1539, E-mail: lauriea@umich.edu
Founded 1838
Library Holdings: Bk Vols 3,605,791
Special Collections: UN Document Depository; US Document Depository
Subject Interests: Humanities

MUSEUMS, 2500 Museums Bldg, 1108 Geddes Rd, 48109-1079, SAN 346-0118. Tel: 734-764-0467. FAX: 734-764-3829. Web Site: www.lib.umich.edu/museums. *Librn,* Scott Martin; Tel: 734-936-2337, E-mail: samarti@umich.edu; *Supvr,* Charlene Stachnik; E-mail: sta@umich.edu
Library Holdings: Bk Vols 129,293
Subject Interests: Anthrop, Botany, Natural hist, Paleontology, Zoology
Friends of the Library Group

MUSIC LIBRARY, 3239 Moore Bldg, 3rd Flr, 1100 Baits Dr, 48109-2085, SAN 345-9756. Tel: 734 764 2512. FAX: 734-764-5097. E-mail: music.circ@umich.edu, music.library@umich.edu. Web Site: www.lib.umich.edu/music. *Head of Libr,* Kristen Castellana; E-mail: krismcc@umich.edu; *Music Librn,* Jason Imbesi; E-mail: imbesij@umich.edu. Subject Specialists: *Musicology,* Kristen Castellana; Staff 5 (MLS 2, Non-MLS 3)
Founded 1940
Library Holdings: Bk Vols 145,732
Special Collections: American Sheet Music; Ivan Galamin Coll; Michael Rabin Coll; Music & Musicology Coll (17th-19th Century); Radio Canada Int; Women Composers Coll
Subject Interests: Dance, Music, Music educ, Musicology
Function: Audio & video playback equip for onsite use, Photocopying/Printing, Ref serv available
Friends of the Library Group

SHAPIRO SCIENCE LIBRARY, 3175 Shapiro Library, 919 S University Ave, 48109-1185, SAN 345-9993. Circulation Tel: 734-764-7490. Reference Tel: 734-936-2327. FAX: 734-763-9813. E-mail: sciencelibrary@umich.edu. Web Site: www.lib.umich.edu/science/. *Head Librn,* Jacob Glenn; Tel: 734-936-2339, E-mail: jkglenn@umich.edu; *Coll Coordr,* JoAnn Sears; Tel: 734-936-2341, E-mail: josears@umich.edu. Subject Specialists: *Math, Statistics,* JoAnn Sears; Staff 16 (MLS 7, Non-MLS 9)
Library Holdings: Bk Vols 484,030
Special Collections: Astronomical Maps; Rare Book Coll
Subject Interests: Astronomy, Biol, Chem, Geol, Math, Natural res, Physics, Statistics
Publications: Newsletter
Friends of the Library Group

SHAPIRO UNDERGRADUATE LIBRARY, 919 S University Ave, 48109-1185. Tel: 734-764-7490. Reference Tel: 734-763-4141. FAX: 734-764-6849. E-mail: undergrad.library@umich.edu. Web Site: www.lib.umich.edu/ugl. *Dir,* Laurie Alexander; Staff 17 (MLS 8, Non-MLS 9)
Library Holdings: Bk Vols 150,000
Friends of the Library Group

SPECIAL COLLECTIONS LIBRARY, Hatcher Graduate Library, 913 S University Ave, 48109-1190, SAN 346-0002. Tel: 734-764-9377. E-mail: special.collections@umich.edu. Web Site: www.lib.umich.edu/special-collections-library. *Dir,* Martha O'Hara Conway

CM A ALFRED TAUBMAN HEALTH SCIENCES LIBRARY, 1135 E Catherine, 48109-2038, SAN 345-9721. Tel: 734-764-1210. E-mail: thlibrary@umich.edu. Web Site: www.lib.umich.edu/health-sciences-libraries. *Assoc Univ Librn,* Jane Blumenthal; E-mail: janeblum@umich.edu; *Dep Dir,* Nancy Allee; E-mail: nallee@umich.edu; *Coordr, Coll & Info Serv,* Nadia Lalla
Founded 1920
Library Holdings: Bk Vols 398,829
Special Collections: US Document Depository
Subject Interests: Dentistry, Homeopathy, Med, Nursing, Pharm, Pub health
Friends of the Library Group

J WASHTENAW COMMUNITY COLLEGE, Richard W Bailey Library, 4800 E Huron River Dr, 48105-4800. SAN 307-8841. Tel: 734-973-3379. Circulation Tel: 734-973-3731. Interlibrary Loan Service Tel: 734-973-3734. Reference Tel: 734-973-3431. FAX: 734-973-3446. E-mail: circdesk@wccnet.edu. Web Site: www.wccnet.edu/resources/library. *Dean, Learning Res,* Victor Liu; E-mail: vliu@wccnet.edu; *Dir, Access Serv,* Bethany Kennedy; Tel: 734-477-8723, E-mail: bakennedy@wccnet.edu; *Librn,* Alexa Azzopardi; Tel: 734-677-5294, E-mail: agazzopardi@wccnet.edu; *Librn,* Molly Ledermann; Tel: 734-973-3313, E-mail: mledermann@wccnet.edu; *Librn,* Sandy McCarthy; Tel: 734-677-5293, E-mail: mccarthy@wccnet.edu; *Librn,* Maureen Perault; Tel: 734-973-3407, E-mail: mperault@wccnet.edu; *Librn,* Kathleen Scott; Tel: 734-973-3430, E-mail: kscott@wccnet.edu; *Access Serv Tech-ILL,* Brooke Regensburg; E-mail: bregensburg@wccnet.edu; *Access Serv Tech-Reserves,* Catherine Karain; Tel: 734-477-8709, E-mail: ckarain@wccnet.edu; *Access Serv Tech-Spec Mat Coll,* Eyana Tooson; Tel: 734-477-8710, E-mail: etooson@wccnet.edu; *Access Serv-Tech Asst,* Position Currently Open; *Acq Asst,* Heather Bertke; Tel: 734-973-3402, E-mail: hbertke@wccnet.edu; *Acq Asst,* Irene Brock; Tel: 734-973-3399, E-mail: ibrock@wccnet.edu; *Cataloger,* Laura Zimbleman; Tel: 734-973-3401, E-mail: laurazim@wccnet.edu; Staff 12.5 (MLS 5.5, Non-MLS 7)
Founded 1965. Enrl 8,700; Fac 400; Highest Degree: Associate
Jul 2013-Jun 2014 Income $1,523,439. Mats Exp $241,000, Books $70,000, Per/Ser (Incl. Access Fees) $38,000, Other Print Mats $4,126, AV Mat $10,000, Electronic Ref Mat (Incl. Access Fees) $118,874. Sal $1,185,139
Library Holdings: AV Mats 3,599; CDs 360; DVDs 2,194; e-books 138,127; e-journals 64,851; Microforms 68; Bk Titles 66,760; Bk Vols 71,516; Per Subs 220; Videos 3,141
Automation Activity & Vendor Info: (Acquisitions) SirsiDynix; (Cataloging) SirsiDynix; (Circulation) SirsiDynix; (Course Reserve) SirsiDynix; (ILL) Mel Cat; (OPAC) SirsiDynix; (Serials) SirsiDynix
Database Vendor: ABC-CLIO, Bowker, CQ Press, Discovery Education, ebrary, EBSCO Discovery Service, EBSCOhost, Gale Cengage Learning, LearningExpress, LexisNexis, Medline, Micromedex, Newsbank, OCLC WorldShare Interlibrary Loan, ProQuest, PubMed, ReferenceUSA, SirsiDynix, Wiley
Wireless access
Partic in Midwest Collaborative for Library Services (MCLS); OCLC Online Computer Library Center, Inc
Special Services for the Deaf - Assistive tech
Special Services for the Blind - Assistive/Adapted tech devices, equip & products

S WASHTENAW COUNTY METROPOLITAN PLANNING COMMISSION LIBRARY*, 705 N Zeeb Rd, 48107. SAN 327-5108. Tel: 734-994-2435. FAX: 734-994-8284. *Librn,* Mechelle Hardy
Library Holdings: Bk Titles 2,000

S WILSON ORNITHOLOGICAL SOCIETY, Josselyn Van Tyne Memorial Library, Univ of Michigan Museum of Zoology, 1109 Geddes Ave, 48109-1079. SAN 327-4799. Tel: 734-764-0457. FAX: 734-763-4080. Web Site: www.wilsonsociety.org/wilsonsoc/library. *Librn,* Janet Hinshaw; E-mail: jhinshaw@umich.edu; Staff 1 (Non-MLS 1)
Founded 1930
Library Holdings: Bk Titles 3,000; Spec Interest Per Sub 210
Subject Interests: Ornithology
Wireless access
Function: Mail loans to mem

ARMADA

P ARMADA FREE PUBLIC LIBRARY*, 73930 Church St, 48005-3331. SAN 307-885X. Tel: 586-784-5921. Web Site: www.armadalib.org. *Dir,* Margaret Smith; E-mail: smithm@libcoop.net; Staff 4 (MLS 1, Non-MLS 3)
Founded 1901. Pop 5,334; Circ 44,610
Library Holdings: Bk Titles 27,799; Per Subs 82
Automation Activity & Vendor Info: (Acquisitions) SirsiDynix; (Cataloging) SirsiDynix; (Circulation) SirsiDynix; (ILL) SirsiDynix; (OPAC) SirsiDynix; (Serials) SirsiDynix
Wireless access
Open Mon & Tues 12-8, Wed & Thurs 9-8, Fri 9-5, Sat 10-2

ASHLEY

P ASHLEY DISTRICT LIBRARY*, 104 New St, 48806. (Mail add: PO Box 6, 48806-0006). Tel: 989-847-4283, Ext 6. FAX: 989-847-4204. *Dir,* Lynne Clark
Library Holdings: Bk Vols 8,500; Per Subs 15
Automation Activity & Vendor Info: (Cataloging) Follett Software; (Circulation) Follett Software
Wireless access
Mem of Capital Library Cooperative
Open Mon & Tues (Winter) 8-11 & 12-5, Thurs 12-5; Tues & Wed (Summer) 9-12 & 12:30-3, Thurs 1:30-7

ATHENS

P ATHENS COMMUNITY LIBRARY*, 106 E Burr Oak St, 49011-9793. (Mail add: PO Box 216, 49011-0216), SAN 307-8868. Tel: 269-729-4479. E-mail: athens_library@sbcglobal.net. *Dir,* Diane Garlets
Circ 1,316
Library Holdings: Bk Vols 3,505; Per Subs 34; Talking Bks 139
Open Tues 3-7, Wed-Fri 1-5, Sat 9-1
Friends of the Library Group

ATLANTA

P MONTMORENCY COUNTY PUBLIC LIBRARIES*, Atlanta Headquarters, 11901 Haymeadow Rd, 49709. (Mail add: PO Box 438, 49709-0438). Tel: 989-785-3941. FAX: 989-785-3941. E-mail: montmor1@nemichigan.com. Web Site: www.montmorencylibrary.com. *Dir,* Lori Weaver; *Librn,* Andrea Mellingen
Library Holdings: Bk Vols 12,196; Per Subs 15
Automation Activity & Vendor Info: (Cataloging) SirsiDynix; (Circulation) SirsiDynix
Wireless access
Function: Photocopying/Printing
Partic in Northland Library Cooperative
Open Mon-Wed 10-6, Thurs & Fri 10-5, Sat 9-12
Branches: 2
LEWISTON PUBLIC, 2851 Kneeland St, Lewiston, 49756. (Mail add: PO Box 148, Lewiston, 49756-0148). Tel: 989-786-2985. *Librn,* Mary Lou Barber
Open Tues, Thurs & Fri 10-5, Wed 12-6, Sat 10-3
Friends of the Library Group
HILLMAN WRIGHT BRANCH, 121 W Second St, Hillman, 49746-9024. (Mail add: PO Box 247, Hillman, 49746-0247). Tel: 989-742-4021. FAX: 989-742-4021. E-mail: hillmanlib@yahoo.com. *Librn,* Kim Wade
Library Holdings: Bk Vols 10,000; Per Subs 24
Special Services for the Blind - Computer with voice synthesizer for visually impaired persons; Large print bks
Open Tues, Wed & Fri 10-5, Thurs 10-7, Sat 10-2

AUBURN HILLS

P AUBURN HILLS PUBLIC LIBRARY*, 3400 E Seyburn Dr, 48326-2759. SAN 329-1332. Tel: 248-370-9466. FAX: 248-370-9364. Web Site: www.auburn-hills.lib.mi.us. *Dir,* Karrie Waarala; Tel: 248-364-6705; *Head, Adult Serv,* Maria Danna; *Head, Support Serv,* Denise Janus; *Head, Youth Serv,* Linda Coleman; *Tech Coordr,* Cheryl DeCovich; Staff 28 (MLS 10, Non-MLS 18)
Founded 1986. Pop 19,310
Jan 2006-Dec 2006 Income $1,384,810. Sal $561,200
Library Holdings: Bk Vols 60,380
Automation Activity & Vendor Info: (Acquisitions) SirsiDynix; (Cataloging) SirsiDynix; (Circulation) SirsiDynix
Database Vendor: Electric Library, LearningExpress, OCLC FirstSearch
Wireless access
Publications: Auburn Hills Highlights (quarterly newsletter)
Partic in OCLC Online Computer Library Center, Inc
Open Mon-Thurs 9:30-9, Fri & Sat 9:30-5

C BAKER COLLEGE OF AUBURN HILLS LIBRARY*, 1500 University Dr, 48326-2642. Tel: 248-276-8223. Toll Free Tel: 888-429-0410. FAX: 248-340-0607. E-mail: library-ah@baker.edu. Web Site: www.baker.edu. *Dir,* Michele Pratt; E-mail: michele.pratt@baker.edu
Library Holdings: Bk Vols 13,000; Per Subs 125
Automation Activity & Vendor Info: (Cataloging) SirsiDynix; (Circulation) SirsiDynix; (OPAC) SirsiDynix
Open Mon-Thurs 8:30am-9:30pm, Fri 8:30am-9pm

OAKLAND COMMUNITY COLLEGE
J AUBURN HILLS CAMPUS LIBRARY*, 2900 Featherstone Rd, Bldg D, 48326, SAN 320-9121. Tel: 248-232-4125. Information Services Tel: 248-232-4128. FAX: 248-232-4136. Web Site: www.oaklandcc.edu/library. *Librn,* Christine L Malmsten; Tel: 248-232-4131, E-mail: clmalmst@oaklandcc.edu; Staff 1 (MLS 1)
Founded 1965. Enrl 8,979; Fac 83; Highest Degree: Associate
Jul 2012-Jun 2013. Mats Exp $111,536, Books $45,358, Per/Ser (Incl. Access Fees) $28,911, Other Print Mats $19,585, Micro $13,107, AV Mat $279, Electronic Ref Mat (Incl. Access Fees) $2,165, Presv $2,131. Sal $276,972 (Prof $127,028)
Library Holdings: Audiobooks 315; AV Mats 5,778; Bks on Deafness & Sign Lang 98; CDs 690; DVDs 1,596; e-books 30,826; e-journals 5; Microforms 3,527; Bk Titles 51,264; Bk Vols 60,305; Per Subs 203; Talking Bks 315; Videos 2,934
Automation Activity & Vendor Info: (Acquisitions) SirsiDynix; (Cataloging) SirsiDynix; (Circulation) SirsiDynix; (Course Reserve) SirsiDynix; (ILL) OCLC; (OPAC) SirsiDynix; (Serials) SirsiDynix
Database Vendor: Alexander Street Press, ARTstor, Bowker, Children's Literature Comprehensive Database Company (CLCD), College Source, CQ Press, EBSCO Discovery Service, EBSCO Information Services, EBSCOhost, Elsevier, Gale Cengage Learning, JSTOR, LearningExpress, Micromedex, Oxford Online, ProQuest, ScienceDirect, SirsiDynix, Springshare, LLC, Standard & Poor's
Function: Accessibility serv available based on individual needs, Audio & video playback equip for onsite use, Bks on cassette, Bks on CD, CD-ROM, Computers for patron use, Copy machines, Digital talking bks, Distance learning, Doc delivery serv, Electronic databases & coll, Exhibits, Free DVD rentals, Handicapped accessible, ILL available, Magnifiers for reading, Mail & tel request accepted, Microfiche/film & reading machines, Music CDs, Online cat, Online info literacy tutorials on the web & in blackboard, Online ref, Online searches, Orientations, Outreach serv, Photocopying/Printing, Pub access computers, Ref & res, Ref serv available, Ref serv in person, Scanner, Spanish lang bks, Spoken cassettes & CDs, Spoken cassettes & DVDs, Tax forms, Telephone ref, VHS videos, Video lending libr, Web-catalog, Wheelchair accessible, Workshops
Special Services for the Deaf - Accessible learning ctr; ADA equip; Assistive tech; Bks on deafness & sign lang
Special Services for the Blind - Closed circuit TV magnifier; Computer with voice synthesizer for visually impaired persons; Copier with enlargement capabilities; Dragon Naturally Speaking software; Free checkout of audio mat; Internet workstation with adaptive software; Large print bks; Ref serv; Screen reader software
Open Mon-Thurs 8am-10pm, Fri 8-4:30, Sat 9-3

J LIBRARY SYSTEMS*, 2900 Featherstone Rd, MTEC A210, 48326, SAN 307-8876. Tel: 248-232-4478. Interlibrary Loan Service Tel: 248-232-4479. Administration Tel: 248-232-4476. FAX: 248-232-4089. Web Site: www.oaklandcc.edu/library. *Dean,* Mary Ann Sheble; Tel: 248-341-2053, E-mail: masheble@oaklandcc.edu; *Mgr, Tech Serv,* Elizabeth A Lindley; E-mail: ealindle@oaklandcc.edu; *Coordr, Electronic Res,* Jeffrey Zachwieja; Tel: 248-522-3488, E-mail: jxzachwi@oaklandcc.edu; *Tech Serv,* Susan Appelt; Tel: 248-232-4480, E-mail: smappelt@oaklandcc.edu; *Tech Serv,* Marianne Calunas; E-mail: mxcaluna@oaklandcc.edu; Staff 5 (MLS 3, Non-MLS 2)
Founded 1965. Enrl 28,984; Highest Degree: Associate
Jul 2009-Jun 2010. Mats Exp $168,039, Books $500, Electronic Ref Mat (Incl. Access Fees) $167,539
Library Holdings: e-books 15,802
Automation Activity & Vendor Info: (Acquisitions) SirsiDynix; (Cataloging) SirsiDynix; (Circulation) SirsiDynix; (ILL) OCLC; (OPAC) SirsiDynix; (Serials) SirsiDynix
Database Vendor: ARTstor, Bowker, College Source, EBSCO Information Services, EBSCOhost, Elsevier, Gale Cengage Learning, Ingenta, JSTOR, LearningExpress, McGraw-Hill, Micromedex, OCLC CAMIO, OCLC WorldShare Interlibrary Loan, ProQuest, ScienceDirect, SirsiDynix, ValueLine, Wilson - Wilson Web
Open Mon-Fri 7:30-5:30
Restriction: Restricted pub use

AUGUSTA

P MCKAY LIBRARY*, 105 S Webster St, 49012-9601. (Mail add: PO Box 308, 49012-0308), SAN 307-8884. Tel: 616-731-4000. FAX: 616-731-5323. E-mail: info@mckaylibrary.org. *Dir,* Linda Mony; E-mail: linda@mckaylibrary.org; *Librn,* Anne Terpstra
Pop 7,095; Circ 25,830
Library Holdings: Large Print Bks 200; Bk Vols 27,000; Per Subs 55
Special Collections: Local Newspaper Coll, Augusta Beacon 1902-1964, micro
Automation Activity & Vendor Info: (Cataloging) Follett Software; (Circulation) Follett Software
Partic in Southwest Michigan Library Cooperative
Friends of the Library Group

BAD AXE

P BAD AXE AREA DISTRICT LIBRARY*, 200 S Hanselman, 48413. SAN 307-8892. Tel: 989-269-8538. FAX: 989-269-2411. Web Site: www.badaxelibrary.org. *Dir,* Mimi Herrington; E-mail: mherrington@badaxelibrary.org; *Asst Dir,* Mary McIntyre

Pop 9,300; Circ 84,000
Library Holdings: Bk Vols 23,000; Per Subs 110
Special Collections: Huron Daily Tribune 1860's-present; Local History Coll
Automation Activity & Vendor Info: (Cataloging) Auto-Graphics, Inc; (Circulation) Auto-Graphics, Inc; (OPAC) Auto-Graphics, Inc
Wireless access
Open Mon-Fri 12-9, Sat 1-5
Friends of the Library Group

L HURON COUNTY LAW LIBRARY*, 250 E Huron Ave, 2nd Flr, 48413. Tel: 989-269-7112. FAX: 989-269-0005. *In Charge,* Mary Jo Risch; E-mail: rischm@co.huron.mi.us
Library Holdings: Bk Vols 2,950

BALDWIN

P PATHFINDER COMMUNITY LIBRARY*, 812 Michigan Ave, 49304. (Mail add: PO Box 880, 49304-0880), SAN 307-8906. Tel: 231-745-4010. FAX: 231-745-7681. *Dir,* Bonnie Povilaitis; E-mail: bpovilaitis@yahoo.com
Founded 1953. Pop 4,200; Circ 14,500
Library Holdings: Bk Vols 26,000; Per Subs 50
Partic in Mid-Michigan Library League

BARAGA

S MICHIGAN DEPARTMENT OF CORRECTIONS*, Baraga Maximum Facility Library, 13924 Wadaga Rd, 49908. Tel: 906-353-7070, Ext 1321. FAX: 906-353-7957. *Librn,* Joseph Bouchard; E-mail: bouchajj@michigan.gov; *Asst Librn,* Mary Aho
Library Holdings: Bk Vols 6,000; Per Subs 12

BARRYTON

P BARRYTON PUBLIC LIBRARY*, 198 Northern Ave, 49305. (Mail add: PO Box 215, 49305-0215), SAN 307-8914. Tel: 989-382-5288. FAX: 989-382-9073. E-mail: barrytonlibrary@yahoo.com. *Dir,* Ben Huffman; *Asst Librn,* Marcia Laughlin
Founded 1930. Pop 3,107; Circ 20,000
Library Holdings: Bk Vols 17,000; Per Subs 25
Partic in Mid-Michigan Library League
Open Tues-Fri 9-6, Sat 9-1

BATTLE CREEK

S ART CENTER OF BATTLE CREEK LIBRARY*, 265 E Emmett St, 49017. SAN 307-8922. Tel: 269-962-9511. FAX: 269-969-3838. E-mail: artcenterofbc@yahoo.com.
Library Holdings: Bk Vols 500
Special Collections: Michigan Art Coll & Archival Library
Subject Interests: Art, Art hist
Open Tues-Fri 10-5, Sat 11-3

M BATTLE CREEK HEALTH SYSTEM*, Professional Library, 300 N Ave, 49017. SAN 329-9139. Tel: 269-245-8000, 269-245-8331. *Librn,* Martin Krieger; E-mail: kriegerm@bronsonhg.org; Staff 1 (MLS 1)
Founded 1927
Library Holdings: Bk Vols 1,000; Per Subs 75
Subject Interests: Health sci
Automation Activity & Vendor Info: (Cataloging) EOS International; (Circulation) EOS International; (OPAC) EOS International
Open Mon-Fri 8-4:30
Restriction: Circ limited

GM DEPARTMENT OF VETERANS AFFAIRS*, Medical Center Library, 5500 Armstrong Rd, 49015. SAN 307-8981. Tel: 269-966-5600, Ext 6490. FAX: 269-660-6031. *Librn,* Linda S Polardino; E-mail: linda.polardino@med.va.gov; *Med Librn,* Brenda Newberry; Tel: 269-966-5600, Ext 6495, E-mail: brenda.newberry@med.va.gov; Staff 4 (MLS 2, Non-MLS 2)
Library Holdings: Bk Vols 3,000; Per Subs 180
Subject Interests: Psychiat
Automation Activity & Vendor Info: (Cataloging) EOS International; (Circulation) EOS International; (OPAC) EOS International; (Serials) EOS International
Open Mon & Fri 7:30-4:30 Tues-Thurs 7:30-5

J KELLOGG COMMUNITY COLLEGE*, Emory W Morris Learning Resource Center, 450 North Ave, 49017-3397. SAN 307-8965. Tel: 269-965-4122. Reference Tel: 269-965-4122, Ext 2373. FAX: 269-965-4133. TDD: 269-962-0898. Web Site: www.kellogg.edu/library. *Acq/Ref Serv, Dir,* Martha A Stilwell; Tel: 269-965-4122, Ext 2380, E-mail: stilwellm@kellogg.edu; *Mgr, Libr Serv,* Kassie Dunham; Tel: 269-965-4122, Ext 2613, E-mail: dunhamk@kellogg.edu; Staff 3 (MLS 3)
Founded 1956. Enrl 3,451; Fac 400; Highest Degree: Associate
Jul 2005-Jun 2006 Income $564,415. Mats Exp $160,812, Books $36,812, Per/Ser (Incl. Access Fees) $13,500, AV Equip $25,000, AV Mat $3,500, Electronic Ref Mat (Incl. Access Fees) $64,200. Sal $403,603 (Prof $278,298)
Library Holdings: e-books 21,000; Bk Vols 51,500; Per Subs 210
Special Collections: Law Reference Coll
Automation Activity & Vendor Info: (Acquisitions) Innovative Interfaces, Inc; (Cataloging) Innovative Interfaces, Inc; (Circulation) Innovative Interfaces, Inc; (Course Reserve) Innovative Interfaces, Inc; (ILL) Innovative Interfaces, Inc; (OPAC) Innovative Interfaces, Inc; (Serials) Innovative Interfaces, Inc
Database Vendor: EBSCOhost, Gale Cengage Learning, Newsbank, OCLC FirstSearch, ProQuest, Westlaw
Partic in Midwest Collaborative for Library Services (MCLS); OCLC Online Computer Library Center, Inc
Special Services for the Deaf - TDD equip
Open Mon-Thurs (Winter) 8am-9pm, Fri 8-5, Sat 11-3; Mon-Thurs (Summer) 7:45am-8pm

P WILLARD LIBRARY, Seven W Van Buren St, 49017-3009. SAN 307-899X. Tel: 269-968-8166. FAX: 269-968-3284. E-mail: infodesk@willard.lib.mi.us. Web Site: www.willard.lib.mi.us. *Dir,* Leah Dodd; E-mail: ldodd@willard.lib.mi.us; *Asst Dir,* Kathy Lucas; *Br Mgr,* Susan Schroeder; *Circ,* Sharon Kobs
Founded 1840. Pop 90,804; Circ 1,045,517
Library Holdings: Bk Vols 180,362
Subject Interests: Local hist
Wireless access
Partic in Southwest Michigan Library Cooperative
Open Mon-Thurs 9-9, Fri 9-6, Sat 9-5, Sun (Sept-May) 1-5
Branches: 1
HELEN WARNER BRANCH, 36 Minges Creek Pl, 49015. Tel: 269-968-8166, Ext 600. FAX: 269-979-8072. *Br Mgr,* Sue Steeby
Library Holdings: Bk Vols 43,251
Open Mon-Thurs 10-8, Fri & Sat 10-5, Sun 1-5

BAY CITY

S BAY COUNTY HISTORICAL SOCIETY*, Butterfield Memorial Research Library, 321 Washington Ave, 48708. SAN 327-0246. Tel: 989-893-5733. FAX: 989-893-5741. Web Site: www.bchsmuseum.org. *Dir,* Gay McInerney; *Curator,* Ron Bloomfield
Founded 1919
Library Holdings: Bk Titles 8,000
Special Collections: Corporate Archives (Monitor Sugar Co), Patrol Craft Sailors Assoc Archives - military, WWII; Research Materials on Bay County, 1830-present, photos. Municipal Document Depository; Oral History
Subject Interests: Agr, Archit, Genealogy, Great Lakes maritime hist, Local hist, Manufacturing, Politics, WWII
Function: Res libr
Open Tues-Thurs 11-5
Restriction: Non-circulating

P BAY COUNTY LIBRARY SYSTEM*, 500 Center Ave, 48708. SAN 346-0290. Tel: 989-894-2837. FAX: 989-894-2021. TDD: 989-893-7052. Web Site: www.baycountylibrary.org. *Interim Dir,* Kevin Ayala; E-mail: kayala@baycountylibrary.org; *Ch Serv,* Krista Pedersen; E-mail: kpedersen@baycountylibrary.org; *Ref,* Mary McManman; Tel: 989-893-9566, Fax: 989-893-9799, E-mail: mmcmanman@baycountylibrary.org; Staff 17 (MLS 14, Non-MLS 3)
Founded 1974. Pop 107,517; Circ 880,000
Library Holdings: Bk Vols 304,554; Per Subs 781
Special Collections: Local History (Michigan Coll). State Document Depository
Subject Interests: Local hist
Automation Activity & Vendor Info: (Acquisitions) OCLC Connexion; (Circulation) Horizon; (OPAC) OCLC WorldShare Interlibrary Loan
Database Vendor: OCLC FirstSearch
Wireless access
Publications: Library Tidings (Newsletter)
Partic in Mideastern Michigan Library Cooperative; OCLC Online Computer Library Center, Inc; Valley Libr Consortium
Special Services for the Deaf - TDD equip
Open Mon-Fri 8-5
Friends of the Library Group
Branches: 4
AUBURN AREA BRANCH LIBRARY, 235 W Midland Rd, Auburn, 48611, SAN 346-0320. Tel: 989-662-2381. FAX: 989-662-2647. *Managing Librn,* Kirsten Wellnitz; E-mail: kwellnitz@baycountylibrary.org
Founded 1973
Library Holdings: Bk Vols 36,103
Open Tues-Thurs 10-8, Fri & Sat 9-5

PINCONNING BRANCH LIBRARY, 218 S Kaiser St, Pinconning, 48650-0477, SAN 346-041X. Tel: 989-879-3283. FAX: 989-879-5669. *Managing Librn,* Kirsten Wellnitz; E-mail: kwellnitz@baycountylibrary.org
Founded 1947
Library Holdings: Bk Vols 29,692
Open Tues-Thurs 10-8, Fri & Sat 9-5

SAGE BRANCH LIBRARY, 100 E Midland St, 48706, SAN 346-0444. Tel: 989-892-8555. FAX: 989-892-1516. *Managing Librn,* Sarah Wohlschlag; E-mail: swohlschlag@baycountylibrary.org
Founded 1884. Pop 107,517
Open Mon, Tues & Fri 9-5, Wed & Thurs 12-8
Friends of the Library Group

ALICE & JACK WIRT PUBLIC LIBRARY, 500 Center Ave, 48708-5989, SAN 346-0355. Tel: 989-893-9566. FAX: 989-893-9799. *Managing Librn,* Jane Anderson; E-mail: janderson@baycountylibrary.org
Founded 1974. Pop 107,517
Library Holdings: Bk Vols 94,471
Open Mon-Thurs 10-8, Fri & Sat 9-5, Sun (Sept-May) 1-4
Friends of the Library Group

Bookmobiles: 1

M BAY REGIONAL MEDICAL CENTER LIBRARY*, 1900 Columbus Ave, 48708-6880. SAN 307-9015. Tel: 989-894-3783. FAX: 989-894-4862. E-mail: webcontact@mclaren.org.
Founded 1958
Library Holdings: Bk Titles 2,780; Per Subs 320
Subject Interests: Allied health
Database Vendor: OVID Technologies
Function: Doc delivery serv, ILL available, Photocopying/Printing, Prof lending libr, Ref serv available, Telephone ref
Publications: Union List of Serials
Partic in Greater Midwest Regional Medical Libr Network; Michigan Health Sciences Libraries Association; National Network of Libraries of Medicine; National Network of Libraries of Medicine South Central Region
Restriction: Circulates for staff only, Pub use on premises

BEAVER ISLAND

P BEAVER ISLAND DISTRICT LIBRARY*, 26400 Donegal Bay Rd, 49782. (Mail add: PO Box 246, 49782-0246). Tel: 231-448-2701. FAX: 231-448-2801. Web Site: www.beaverisland.michlibrary.org. *Dir,* Patrick S McGinnity; *Tech Serv,* Phyllis Moore
Library Holdings: Bk Vols 17,000; Per Subs 36
Wireless access
Open Mon-Fri 10-6, Sat 12-5

BELDING

P ALVAH N BELDING MEMORIAL LIBRARY*, 302 E Main St, 48809-1799. SAN 307-9031. Tel: 616-794-1450. FAX: 616-794-3510. TDD: 800-649-3777. E-mail: bel@llcoop.org. Web Site: www.belding.michlibrary.org. *Dir,* Deborah Jones; E-mail: beldrj@llcoop.org; *Youth Serv,* Carrie Roer; Staff 1 (Non-MLS 1)
Founded 1890. Pop 11,000; Circ 40,484
Library Holdings: Bk Titles 54,000; Per Subs 74
Special Collections: Michigan Coll
Subject Interests: Antiques, Arts & crafts, Genealogy, Local hist
Automation Activity & Vendor Info: (Circulation) Innovative Interfaces, Inc
Wireless access
Partic in Lakeland Library Cooperative
Open Mon & Wed 9-8, Tues, Thurs & Sat 9-1, Fri 9-5
Friends of the Library Group

BELLAIRE

P BELLAIRE PUBLIC LIBRARY*, 111 S Bridge St, 49615-9566. (Mail add: PO Box 477, 49615-0477), SAN 307-904X. Tel: 231-533-8814. FAX: 231-533-5064. E-mail: bellairelibrary@torchlake.com. Web Site: www.bellairelibrary.org. *Dir,* Linda Offenbecker
Pop 3,054; Circ 23,440
Library Holdings: AV Mats 1,258; Bk Vols 19,356; Per Subs 60
Partic in Mid-Michigan Library League
Open Tues-Thurs 10-6, Fri 10-5, Sat 10-2
Friends of the Library Group

BELLEVILLE

P FRED C FISCHER LIBRARY*, 167 Fourth St, 48111. SAN 307-9058. Tel: 734-699-3291. FAX: 734-699-6352. Web Site: www.belleville.lib.mi.us. *Dir,* Debra L Green; *Asst Dir,* Mary Jo Suchy; Staff 8 (MLS 4, Non-MLS 4)
Founded 1920. Pop 39,500; Circ 148,458
Library Holdings: AV Mats 6,972; Bk Vols 60,683; Per Subs 171
Automation Activity & Vendor Info: (Acquisitions) SirsiDynix; (Cataloging) SirsiDynix; (Circulation) SirsiDynix; (OPAC) SirsiDynix
Database Vendor: ProQuest
Wireless access
Open Mon-Thurs 10-9, Fri & Sat 10-5
Friends of the Library Group

BELLEVUE

P BELLEVUE TOWNSHIP LIBRARY*, 212 N Main St, 49021. SAN 307-9066. Tel: 269-763-3369. FAX: 269-763-3369. E-mail: bellvu@monroe.lib.mi.us. *Librn,* Brenda Harrison
Circ 5,948
Library Holdings: Bk Vols 10,000
Automation Activity & Vendor Info: (Cataloging) Auto-Graphics, Inc; (Circulation) Auto-Graphics, Inc; (OPAC) Auto-Graphics, Inc
Publications: Monthly Bulletin on Libr Activities
Mem of Woodlands Library Cooperative
Open Mon-Fri 1-6

BENTON HARBOR

P BENTON HARBOR PUBLIC LIBRARY*, 213 E Wall St, 49022-4499. SAN 346-0509. Tel: 269-926-6139. FAX: 269-926-1674. E-mail: staff@bentonharborlibrary.com. Web Site: www.bentonharborlibrary.com. *Dir,* Position Currently Open; *Cat, Tech Serv,* Sharon Holloway; E-mail: tech@bentonharborlibrary.com; *Ch Serv,* Sue Kading; *Doc, Ref,* Jill Rauh; Staff 16 (MLS 3, Non-MLS 13)
Founded 1898. Pop 27,586; Circ 88,158
Library Holdings: Bk Vols 100,510; Per Subs 80
Special Collections: Biological Sciences (Don Farnum Coll); Black Studies (Martin Luther King Jr Coll); Civil War (Randall Perry Coll); Indian Coll; Israelite House of David Coll; Judaica (Lillian Faber Coll); Theater (Helen Polly Klock Coll). State Document Depository; US Document Depository
Subject Interests: Ethnic studies
Wireless access
Partic in Midwest Collaborative for Library Services (MCLS); Southwest Michigan Library Cooperative
Open Mon & Wed 9-8, Tues, Thurs & Fri 9-6, Sat 9-5

J LAKE MICHIGAN COLLEGE*, William Hessel Library, 2755 E Napier Ave, 49022. SAN 307-9074. Tel: 269-927-8605. Interlibrary Loan Service Tel: 269-927-6281. Reference Tel: 269-927-6287. Automation Services Tel: 269-927-8100. FAX: 269-927-6656. E-mail: library@lakemichigancollege.edu. Web Site: www.lakemichigancollege.edu/lib. *Ref Librn,* Diane Baker; E-mail: baker@lakemichigancollege.edu; *Tech Serv Librn,* Tim Bishop; Tel: 269-927-6542, E-mail: bishop@lakemichigancollege.edu; *Circ & Ref Asst,* Vickie Semrinec; E-mail: vsemrinec@lakemichigancollege.edu; Staff 2.5 (MLS 1, Non-MLS 1.5)
Founded 1946. Enrl 3,961; Fac 66; Highest Degree: Associate
Library Holdings: Audiobooks 8; AV Mats 42; CDs 435; DVDs 800; e-books 25,000; e-journals 24,450; Large Print Bks 5; Microforms 1; Bk Vols 62,809; Per Subs 122; Videos 2,683
Special Collections: Lake Michigan College Archives
Automation Activity & Vendor Info: (Cataloging) OCLC Connexion; (Circulation) Auto-Graphics, Inc; (ILL) OCLC FirstSearch; (OPAC) Auto-Graphics, Inc
Database Vendor: CQ Press, EBSCOhost, Facts on File, Gale Cengage Learning, LearningExpress, LexisNexis, OCLC FirstSearch, OCLC WorldShare Interlibrary Loan, ProQuest, ScienceDirect, SerialsSolutions, Wilson - Wilson Web
Wireless access
Function: Art exhibits, Copy machines, ILL available, Online cat, Online ref, Online searches, Orientations
Partic in Midwest Collaborative for Library Services (MCLS); OCLC Online Computer Library Center, Inc
Open Mon-Thurs (Winter) 8am-9pm, Fri 8-4, Sat 10-2; Mon-Thurs (Spring & Summer) 8-6:30, Fri 8-4
Restriction: Borrowing privileges limited to fac & registered students, Limited access for the pub

BENZONIA

P BENZONIA PUBLIC LIBRARY*, 891 Michigan Ave, 49616-9784. (Mail add: PO Box 445, 49616-0445), SAN 307-9090. Tel: 231-882-4111. FAX: 231-882-4111. E-mail: benzoniapubliclibrary@gmail.com. Web Site: www.benzonia.lib.mi.us. *Dir,* Sara Boven; E-mail: bovens@benzonia.lib.mi.us; *Youth Serv,* Barbara McBride; E-mail: benzonia-library@att.net; *Libr Asst,* Kathy Johnson; Staff 1.25 (MLS 0.75, Non-MLS 0.5)
Founded 1925. Pop 4,158; Circ 20,000
Library Holdings: CDs 100; Large Print Bks 600; Bk Vols 16,900; Per Subs 61; Talking Bks 600; Videos 300

Special Collections: Benzie Banner-Record Patriot Local Newspapers, 1888-Present; Bruce Catton Coll, bks & mat
Subject Interests: Art & archit, Hist, Local hist, Relig
Automation Activity & Vendor Info: (ILL) OCLC Online
Wireless access
Function: Free DVD rentals, Handicapped accessible, ILL available, Literacy & newcomer serv, Mail & tel request accepted, Newsp ref libr, Prog for adults, Prog for children & young adult, Pub access computers, Ref serv in person, Spoken cassettes & CDs, Story hour, Summer & winter reading prog, Summer reading prog, Tax forms, Telephone ref
Publications: Newsletter
Partic in Mid-Michigan Library League
Open Mon & Wed 11-7, Tues, Thurs & Fri 11-5, Sat 11-3
Friends of the Library Group

BERKLEY

P BERKLEY PUBLIC LIBRARY, 3155 Coolidge Hwy, 48072. SAN 307-9104. Tel: 248-658-3440. FAX: 248-658-3441. E-mail: library@berkley.lib.mi.us. Web Site: www.berkley.lib.mi.us. *Dir,* Matt Church; E-mail: mchurch@berkley.lib.mi.us; Staff 5 (MLS 4, Non-MLS 1)
Founded 1928. Pop 14,970; Circ 149,803
Jul 2013-Jun 2014 Income $673,968, State $8,111, City $609,064, Federal $3,113, County $20,000, Locally Generated Income $33,680. Mats Exp $69,050, Books $35,654, Per/Ser (Incl. Access Fees) $9,862, AV Mat $19,334, Electronic Ref Mat (Incl. Access Fees) $4,200. Sal $338,982 (Prof $199,014)
Library Holdings: Audiobooks 2,414; CDs 3,293; DVDs 7,585; e-books 10,761; Electronic Media & Resources 4,224; High Interest/Low Vocabulary Bk Vols 250; Large Print Bks 2,974; Bk Vols 67,223; Per Subs 142
Automation Activity & Vendor Info: (Acquisitions) SirsiDynix; (Cataloging) SirsiDynix; (Circulation) SirsiDynix; (OPAC) SirsiDynix; (Serials) SirsiDynix
Database Vendor: Gale Cengage Learning, OCLC FirstSearch
Wireless access
Partic in The Library Network
Open Mon-Wed 10-8, Thurs-Sat 10-6
Friends of the Library Group

BERRIEN CENTER

M LAKELAND SPECIALTY HOSPITAL*, Health Sciences Library, 6418 Deans Hill Rd, 49102-9750. Tel: 269-982-4904. FAX: 269-982-4993. Web Site: www.lakelandhealth.org. *Coordr,* Mike Dill; E-mail: mdill@lakelandregional.org
Library Holdings: Bk Vols 70
Open Mon-Fri 7-1:30
Restriction: Staff use only

BERRIEN SPRINGS

C ANDREWS UNIVERSITY*, James White Library, 1400 Library Rd, 49104-1400. SAN 346-0568. Tel: 269-471-3264, 269-471-3275. Circulation Tel: 269-471-3267. Interlibrary Loan Service Tel: 269-471-3506. Reference Tel: 269-471-3283. FAX: 269-471-6166. Web Site: www.andrews.edu/library. *Dean of Libr,* Lawrence Onsager; Tel: 269-471-3379, E-mail: lonsager@andrews.edu; *Head, Bibliog Serv,* Sallie Alger; Tel: 269-471-6215, E-mail: salger@andrews.edu; *Head, Cat,* Felipe Tan; Tel: 269-471-6262, E-mail: tan@andrews.edu; *Head, Info Serv, Online Serv,* Cynthia Helms; Tel: 269-471-6260, E-mail: helmsc@andrews.edu; *Head, Syst & Media Serv,* Steve Sowder; Tel: 269-471-6242, E-mail: sowder@andrews.edu; *Instruction Librn,* Lauren Matacio; Tel: 269-471-6062, E-mail: matacio@andrews.edu; *Per/Acq Librn,* Bernard Helms; Tel: 269-471-3208, E-mail: helms@andrews.edu; *Sem Coll Librn,* Terry Robertson; Tel: 269-471-3269, E-mail: trobtsn@andrews.edu; *Circ Mgr,* Mildred McGrath; Tel: 269-471-3976, E-mail: mcgrath@andrews.edu; *Mgr, ILL,* Muritha Mutale; E-mail: mmutale@andrews.edu; *Syst Mgr,* Josip Horonic; Tel: 269-471-3865, E-mail: horonic@andrews.edu; *Mgr, Off of the Dean of Libr & Info Serv,* Wanda Cantrell; E-mail: lovice@andrews.edu; *Ref Serv,* Judith Nelson; Tel: 269-471-3639, E-mail: nelsonj@andrews.edu; Staff 21 (MLS 12, Non-MLS 9)
Founded 1874. Enrl 2,950; Fac 240; Highest Degree: Doctorate
Library Holdings: Bk Vols 750,000; Per Subs 2,800
Special Collections: Environmental Design Research (EDRA); Seventh Day Adventist Church History (Center for Adventist Research), bks, mss, personal papers. Oral History
Subject Interests: Art, Biol, Relig
Wireless access
Partic in Adventist Librs Info Coop; OCLC Online Computer Library Center, Inc; Southwest Michigan Library Cooperative
Open Mon-Thurs 8am-10:30pm, Fri 8-3, Sun 1-10:30
Friends of the Library Group

Departmental Libraries:
ARCHITECTURAL RESOURCE CENTER, 8435 E Campus Circle Dr, 49104-0450. Tel: 269-471-2417, 616-471-3027. FAX: 269-471-6261. *Assoc Prof, Dir,* Kathleen M Demsky; Tel: 269-471-2418, E-mail: demskyk@andrews.edu; Staff 1 (MLS 1)
Founded 1986
Library Holdings: CDs 202; DVDs 254; Electronic Media & Resources 44,000; Bk Titles 30,000; Per Subs 78; Videos 505
Special Collections: Archival Coll; Human Factor in Built & Unbuilt Environment - EDRA
Subject Interests: Archit
Open Mon-Thurs 8:30am-10:30pm, Fri 8:30-1:30, Sun 5:30-10:30
MUSIC MATERIALS CENTER, 10230 Hamel Hall Rd, 49104-0230. Tel: 269-471-6217. Web Site: www.andrews.edu/library/mmcindex.html. *Dir,* Linda Mack; Tel: 269-471-3114, E-mail: mack@andrews.edu; Staff 1 (MLS 1)
Library Holdings: Bk Titles 12,500
Open Mon-Wed 8:25am-8:30pm, Thurs 8:25-7:30, Fri 9-2, Sun 1:30-6:30

S BERRIEN COUNTY HISTORICAL ASSOCIATION LIBRARY*, 313 N Cass St, 49103-1038. (Mail add: PO Box 261, 49103-0261), SAN 373-2029. Tel: 269-471-1202. FAX: 269-471-7412. E-mail: bcha@berrienhistory.org. Web Site: www.berrienhistory.org. *Curator,* Robert C Myers; E-mail: rmyers@berrienhistory.org
Founded 1967
Library Holdings: Bk Vols 200
Special Collections: Clark Equipment Archives
Subject Interests: Local hist
Open Mon-Fri 10-5, Sat (Summer) 10-5

P BERRIEN SPRINGS COMMUNITY LIBRARY*, 215 W Union St, 49103-1077. SAN 307-9112. Tel: 269-471-7074. FAX: 269-471-4433. E-mail: bsclibrary@comcast.net. Web Site: bsclibrary.org. *Dir,* Judy Berry; Staff 7 (MLS 1, Non-MLS 6)
Founded 1906. Pop 9,843; Circ 134,000
Apr 2005-Mar 2006 Income $291,069, State $4,282, Locally Generated Income $185,026, Other $101,761. Mats Exp $42,752. Sal $155,687
Library Holdings: AV Mats 4,600; Bks on Deafness & Sign Lang 41; High Interest/Low Vocabulary Bk Vols 110; Large Print Bks 1,200; Bk Titles 54,000; Bk Vols 60,272; Per Subs 120; Talking Bks 2,051
Special Collections: Genealogy Coll of the Berrien County Genealogical Society; John Deere & other Tractor bks
Subject Interests: Local hist
Automation Activity & Vendor Info: (Cataloging) Follett Software; (Circulation) Follett Software; (OPAC) Follett Software
Partic in Southwest Michigan Library Cooperative
Open Mon-Thurs 10-8, Fri 10-6, Sat 10-4
Friends of the Library Group

BESSEMER

P BESSEMER PUBLIC LIBRARY*, 411 S Sophie St, 49911. SAN 307-9120. Tel: 906-667-0404. FAX: 906-667-0442. *Librn,* Sharon Baksic
Library Holdings: Audiobooks 1,328; DVDs 377; Large Print Bks 1,609; Bk Titles 20,963; Per Subs 54; Videos 1,391
Automation Activity & Vendor Info: (Cataloging) Follett Software; (Circulation) Follett Software
Wireless access
Partic in Superiorland Library Cooperative
Open Mon-Thurs 9:30-5:30, Fri 1-5:30, Sat 10-12

BEULAH

P DARCY LIBRARY OF BEULAH*, 7238 Commercial St, 49617. (Mail add: PO Box 469, 49617-0469), SAN 307-9139. Tel: 231-882-4037. E-mail: beulah_library@sbcglobal.net. Web Site: www.mmll.org/beulahpubliclibrary.htm. *Dir,* Heather Doran
Library Holdings: Bk Vols 12,000; Per Subs 27
Partic in Mid-Michigan Library League
Open Mon, Wed & Fri 12-5, Tues & Thurs 3-7, Sat 9-1
Friends of the Library Group

BEVERLY HILLS

SR OUR LADY QUEEN OF MARTYRS CHURCH*, Saint Lucian Library, 32340 Pierce St, 48025. SAN 307-9171. Tel: 248-644-8620. FAX: 248-644-8623. *Librn,* Jane King
Founded 1954
Library Holdings: Bk Vols 2,000

BIG RAPIDS

P BIG RAPIDS COMMUNITY LIBRARY*, 426 S Michigan Ave, 49307. SAN 307-9147. Tel: 231-796-5234. FAX: 231-796-1078. E-mail: librarian@bigrapids.lib.mi.us. Web Site: www.bigrapids.lib.mi.us. *Dir,* Helena Hayes; Staff 6 (MLS 1, Non-MLS 5)

Automation Activity & Vendor Info: (Cataloging) Innovative Interfaces, Inc; (Circulation) Innovative Interfaces, Inc; (OPAC) Innovative Interfaces, Inc
Wireless access
Partic in Mid-Michigan Library League
Open Tues-Thurs 10-8, Fri 10-5, Sat 10-1
Friends of the Library Group

C FERRIS STATE UNIVERSITY LIBRARY*, Ferris Library for Information, Technology & Education, 1010 Campus Dr, 49307-2279. SAN 307-9155. Tel: 231-591-3500. Circulation Tel: 231-591-2669. Interlibrary Loan Service Tel: 231-591-3540. Reference Tel: 231-591-3602. Administration Tel: 231-591-3728. FAX: 231-591-3724. Interlibrary Loan Service FAX: 231-591-2662. Reference TDD: 231-591-3603. E-mail: reference@ferris.edu. Web Site: www.ferris.edu/library. *Dean,* Scott Garrison; *Head, Pub Serv,* Position Currently Open; *Head, Tech Serv,* Leah Monger; *Automation Librn,* Rick Bearden; *Spec Coll & Archives Librn,* Melinda Isler; *Acq, Coll Develop,* Fran Rosen; *Cat,* Yuri Konovalov; *Distance Educ,* Stacy Anderson; *Doc Delivery, ILL,* David Scott; *Govt Doc,* Paul Kammerdiner; *Libr Instruction,* Kristen Motz; Staff 19 (MLS 16, Non-MLS 3)
Founded 1884. Enrl 14,533; Fac 940; Highest Degree: Doctorate
Jul 2012-Jun 2013 Income $4,579,602, Locally Generated Income $46,304, Parent Institution $4,395,130, Other $138,168. Mats Exp $1,028,114, Books $138,515, Per/Ser (Incl. Access Fees) $202,194, Electronic Ref Mat (Incl. Access Fees) $678,334, Presv $9,071. Sal $1,763,170 (Prof $1,322,015)
Library Holdings: CDs 377; DVDs 1,034; e-books 158,718; e-journals 74,452; Microforms 3,703,791; Bk Titles 197,098; Bk Vols 238,642; Per Subs 1,058; Videos 930
Special Collections: Michigan Coll; University Archives; US Patents & Trademarks; Woodbridge N Ferris Papers. US Document Depository
Subject Interests: Criminal justice, Educ, Health sci, Law, Optometry, Pharm, Tech
Automation Activity & Vendor Info: (Acquisitions) Innovative Interfaces, Inc; (Cataloging) Innovative Interfaces, Inc; (Circulation) Innovative Interfaces, Inc; (Course Reserve) Innovative Interfaces, Inc; (ILL) OCLC ILLiad; (Media Booking) Innovative Interfaces, Inc; (OPAC) Innovative Interfaces, Inc; (Serials) Innovative Interfaces, Inc
Database Vendor: 3M Library Systems, ACM (Association for Computing Machinery), ALLDATA Online, American Chemical Society, ARTstor, Bowker, Cambridge Scientific Abstracts, College Source, CredoReference, ebrary, EBSCOhost, Elsevier, Emerald, Ex Libris Group, Facts on File, Faulkner Information Services, Foundation Center, Gale Cengage Learning, Innovative Interfaces, Inc, JSTOR, LearningExpress, LexisNexis, Micromedex, Modern Language Association, Nature Publishing Group, Newsbank, OCLC FirstSearch, OCLC WorldShare Interlibrary Loan, OVID Technologies, Oxford Online, Project MUSE, ProQuest, PubMed, ReferenceUSA, Safari Books Online, Sage, ScienceDirect, Springer-Verlag, Springshare, LLC, Standard & Poor's, STAT!Ref (Teton Data Systems), Westlaw, Wiley, YBP Library Services
Wireless access
Function: Archival coll, Audio & video playback equip for onsite use, Computers for patron use, Copy machines, Distance learning, Doc delivery serv, E-Reserves, Electronic databases & coll, Fax serv, Govt ref serv, Handicapped accessible, Health sci info serv, ILL available, Magnifiers for reading, Microfiche/film & reading machines, Online cat, Online info literacy tutorials on the web & in blackboard, Online ref, Pub access computers, Ref serv available, Tax forms, Telephone ref, Wheelchair accessible
Partic in OCLC Online Computer Library Center, Inc
Special Services for the Blind - Assistive/Adapted tech devices, equip & products; Braille equip; Closed circuit TV; Computer with voice synthesizer for visually impaired persons; Dragon Naturally Speaking software; Reader equip; Talking calculator; ZoomText magnification & reading software
Open Mon-Thurs 7:30am-Midnight, Fri 7:30-6, Sat 12-5, Sun 1-12

BIRCH RUN

P THOMAS E FLESCHNER MEMORIAL LIBRARY*, 11935 Silver Creek Dr, 48415-9767. (Mail add: PO Box 152, 48415-0152), SAN 325-2655. Tel: 989-624-5171. FAX: 989-624-0120. E-mail: birchrun@vlc.lib.mi.us. *Dir,* Jeanette F Morrish; Tel: 989-624-9759, E-mail: j.morrish@vlc.lib.mi.us; Staff 3 (MLS 1, Non-MLS 2)
Founded 1979. Pop 6,349; Circ 32,000
Apr 2007-Mar 2008 Income $111,100, State $4,900, County $26,300, Locally Generated Income $59,900, Other $20,000. Mats Exp $17,300, Books $15,000, Per/Ser (Incl. Access Fees) $800, AV Mat $1,500. Sal $62,000
Library Holdings: AV Mats 200; DVDs 100; Large Print Bks 600; Bk Titles 28,000; Per Subs 21; Talking Bks 1,086
Automation Activity & Vendor Info: (Acquisitions) Follett Software; (Cataloging) Follett Software; (Circulation) Follett Software; (OPAC) SirsiDynix
Partic in White Pine Libr Coop
Open Mon (Winter) 10-6, Tues-Thurs 12-8, Wed 1-6, Fri 9-5, Sat 10-3; Mon (Summer) 10-6, Tues & Thurs 12-8, Wed 1-6, Fri 9-5

BIRMINGHAM

P BALDWIN PUBLIC LIBRARY*, 300 W Merrill St, 48009-1483. SAN 307-9163. Tel: 248-647-1700. Circulation Tel: 248-554-4630. Administration Tel: 248-647-7339. FAX: 248-647-6393. Web Site: www.baldwinlib.org. *Dir,* Douglas Koschik; Staff 29 (MLS 13, Non-MLS 16)
Founded 1869. Pop 35,350; Circ 721,380
Jul 2010-Jun 2011 Income $2,871,234, State $13,941, Locally Generated Income $2,650,035, Other $137,258. Mats Exp $395,509, Books $217,140, AV Equip $110,831, Electronic Ref Mat (Incl. Access Fees) $67,538. Sal $1,349,644
Library Holdings: AV Mats 28,991; e-books 7,821; Bk Vols 144,208; Per Subs 394
Special Collections: Oral History
Subject Interests: Genealogy, Local hist, Mich hist
Automation Activity & Vendor Info: (Acquisitions) SirsiDynix; (Cataloging) SirsiDynix; (Circulation) SirsiDynix; (ILL) Mel Cat; (Media Booking) SirsiDynix; (OPAC) SirsiDynix; (Serials) SirsiDynix
Database Vendor: EBSCOhost, Facts on File, Gale Cengage Learning, Grolier Online, infoUSA, LearningExpress, Newsbank, Overdrive, Inc, ProQuest
Wireless access
Function: Adult bk club, Audiobks via web, Bk club(s), Bks on CD, CD-ROM, Computer training, Computers for patron use, Copy machines, Digital talking bks, Doc delivery serv, e-mail serv, E-Reserves, Electronic databases & coll, Fax serv, Free DVD rentals, Handicapped accessible, Home delivery & serv to Sr ctr & nursing homes, Homebound delivery serv, ILL available, Instruction & testing, Magnifiers for reading, Mail & tel request accepted, Mus passes, Music CDs, Online searches, Photocopying/Printing, Printer for laptops & handheld devices, Prog for adults, Prog for children & young adult, Pub access computers, Ref serv in person
Publications: Books & Beyond (Newsletter)
Partic in Metro Net Libr Consortium; OCLC Online Computer Library Center, Inc
Special Services for the Blind - Audio mat; Bks on CD; Large print bks; Magnifiers
Open Mon-Thurs 9:30-9, Fri & Sat 9:30-5:30, Sun 12-5
Friends of the Library Group

BLOOMFIELD HILLS

S CRANBROOK ACADEMY OF ART LIBRARY*, 39221 Woodward Ave, 48304. (Mail add: PO Box 801, 48303-0801), SAN 307-9201. Tel: 248-645-3355. FAX: 248-645-3464. Web Site: www.cranbrookart.edu/library. *Dir, Libr Serv,* Judy Dyki; Tel: 248-645-3364, E-mail: jdyki@cranbrook.edu; *ILL, Librn,* Mary Beth Kreiner; Tel: 248-645-3477, E-mail: mkreiner@cranbrook.edu; *Libr Asst,* Elizabeth Dizik; E-mail: edizik@cranbrook.edu; Staff 3 (MLS 2, Non-MLS 1)
Founded 1928. Enrl 150; Fac 10; Highest Degree: Master
Library Holdings: DVDs 1,500; Bk Titles 28,000; Per Subs 190; Videos 1,400
Special Collections: Artist's Books; Booth Coll of Fine Arts Folios; Cranbrook Press Books; Exhibition Catalogs; Faculty Lectures, tapes; Fine Bindings; Folios; Theses
Subject Interests: Art & archit
Automation Activity & Vendor Info: (Cataloging) SirsiDynix; (Circulation) SirsiDynix; (ILL) OCLC; (OPAC) SirsiDynix
Database Vendor: ARTstor, Backstage Library Works, EBSCOhost, Gale Cengage Learning, JSTOR, Material ConneXion, OCLC FirstSearch, OCLC WorldShare Interlibrary Loan, Oxford Online, SirsiDynix
Wireless access
Partic in Midwest Collaborative for Library Services (MCLS); OCLC Online Computer Library Center, Inc; Southeastern Michigan League of Libraries
Open Mon-Thurs 9-8, Fri 9-5, Sat & Sun 1-5

L DYKEMA GOSSETT PLLC*, Law Library, 39577 N Woodward Ave, Ste 300, 48304-2820. SAN 372-0373. Tel: 248-203-0560. FAX: 248-203-0763. Web Site: www.dykema.com. *Ref Serv,* Baiba Seward; E-mail: bseward@dykema.com; Staff 1 (MLS 1)
Founded 1994
Library Holdings: Bk Vols 1,500
Subject Interests: Bankruptcy, Corporate practice, Intellectual property
Automation Activity & Vendor Info: (Acquisitions) EOS International; (Cataloging) EOS International; (Circulation) EOS International; (OPAC) EOS International; (Serials) EOS International
Database Vendor: Dialog, EBSCOhost, LexisNexis, OCLC FirstSearch
Wireless access

Function: ILL available
Partic in Midwest Collaborative for Library Services (MCLS); OCLC
Restriction: Staff use only

L PLUNKETT & COONEY*, Law Library, 38505 Woodward Ave, 48304. SAN 371-4101. Tel: 248-901-4099. FAX: 248-901-4040. *Libr Mgr,* Kevin Barry; Tel: 248-901-4094, E-mail: kbarry@plunkettcooney.com; *Ref Serv,* Kelly Klimmek; Tel: 248-901-4090, E-mail: kklimmek@plunkettcooney.com; Staff 4 (MLS 2, Non-MLS 2)
Library Holdings: Bk Vols 10,000
Wireless access

R TEMPLE BETH EL*, Prentis Memorial Library, 7400 Telegraph Rd, 48301-3876. SAN 307-918X. Tel: 248-851-1100, Ext 3138. FAX: 248-851-1187. Web Site: www.tbeonline.org. *Librn,* Eileen Polk
Founded 1878
Library Holdings: Bk Vols 10,000
Special Collections: 16th-19th Century Judaica (Leonard Simons Coll of Rare Judaica); Large Print Books (Goldman Coll); Older American Jewish Periodicals (Irving I Katz Coll of Jewish Americana)
Subject Interests: Jewish hist & lit, Judaica (lit or hist of Jews)
Automation Activity & Vendor Info: (Acquisitions) Follett Software; (Cataloging) Follett Software; (Circulation) Follett Software
Open Mon (Winter) 9:30-2:30, Tues 9:30-6:30, Wed 1-6:30, Sun 9-1; Mon-Thurs (Summer) 10-3
Friends of the Library Group

BLOOMFIELD TOWNSHIP

P BLOOMFIELD TOWNSHIP PUBLIC LIBRARY*, 1099 Lone Pine Rd, 48302-2410. SAN 307-9198. Tel: 248-642-5800. FAX: 248-258-2555. Web Site: www.btpl.org. *Dir,* Carol Mueller; *Asst Dir,* Position Currently Open; *Head, Adult Serv,* Ann M Williams; *Head, Circ,* Anna Pelepchuk; *Head, Syst,* Joan Wu; *Head, Tech Serv,* Marianne Abdoo; *Head, Youth Serv,* Marian Rafal; *ILL,* Deb Smith; Staff 60 (MLS 20, Non-MLS 40)
Founded 1964. Pop 41,070; Circ 908,115
Apr 2011-Mar 2012 Income $4,915,721. Mats Exp $8,304,070. Sal $3,268,714
Library Holdings: AV Mats 53,537; e-books 23,275; Bk Titles 272,552; Per Subs 635
Automation Activity & Vendor Info: (Acquisitions) Innovative Interfaces, Inc; (Cataloging) Innovative Interfaces, Inc; (Circulation) Innovative Interfaces, Inc; (ILL) Mel Cat; (Media Booking) Innovative Interfaces, Inc; (OPAC) Innovative Interfaces, Inc; (Serials) Innovative Interfaces, Inc
Database Vendor: TLC (The Library Corporation)
Wireless access
Publications: Discover (Quarterly)
Partic in Metro Net Libr Consortium; Midwest Collaborative for Library Services (MCLS); The Library Network
Special Services for the Deaf - TTY equip
Special Services for the Blind - Closed circuit TV
Open Mon-Thurs 9:30-9, Fri 9:30-6:30, Sat 9:30-5, Sun 12-5:30
Friends of the Library Group

BOYNE CITY

P BOYNE DISTRICT LIBRARY*, 201 E Main St, 49712. SAN 307-9236. Tel: 231-582-7861. FAX: 231-582-2998. E-mail: info@boynelibrary.org. Web Site: www.boynelibrary.org. *Dir,* Nannette Miller; *ILL, Ref Serv,* Nancy Fulkerson; Staff 8 (Non-MLS 8)
Founded 1918. Pop 7,031; Circ 41,096
Library Holdings: Bk Titles 20,115; Bk Vols 20,175; Per Subs 75
Subject Interests: Local hist
Automation Activity & Vendor Info: (Circulation) SirsiDynix; (OPAC) SirsiDynix
Database Vendor: Gale Cengage Learning, OCLC FirstSearch
Partic in Northland Library Cooperative
Open Mon-Thurs 9-8, Fri 9-5, Sat 9-3, Sun 1-5

BRECKENRIDGE

P HOWE MEMORIAL LIBRARY*, 128 E Saginaw St, 48615. (Mail add: PO Box 398, 48615-0398), SAN 307-9244. Tel: 989-842-3202. FAX: 989-842-3202. E-mail: brecklib128@yahoo.com. Web Site: howemempl@michlibrary.org. *Dir,* Glenda VanDenBosch; *Librn,* Cathy Finlan; *Librn,* Cherie Neitzke; *Librn,* Janice Pavlik
Founded 1938. Pop 6,180; Circ 23,756
Library Holdings: AV Mats 980; Bks on Deafness & Sign Lang 20; Large Print Bks 300; Bk Vols 16,997; Per Subs 81; Talking Bks 686
Automation Activity & Vendor Info: (Cataloging) Auto-Graphics, Inc; (Circulation) Auto-Graphics, Inc; (ILL) Auto-Graphics, Inc
Mem of Capital Library Cooperative
Open Mon 10-7, Tues & Thurs 11-5, Sat 11-1

BRIDGEPORT

P BRIDGEPORT PUBLIC LIBRARY*, 3399 Williamson Rd, 48601. SAN 376-6144. Tel: 989-777-6030. FAX: 989-777-6880. E-mail: bridgeportlibrary@vlc.lib.mi.us. Web Site: www.bridgeportlibrary.org. *Dir,* Rosemary D Rice-Gutierrez; E-mail: rrice@vlc.lib.mi.us
Library Holdings: Bk Vols 45,000; Per Subs 170
Automation Activity & Vendor Info: (Cataloging) SirsiDynix; (Circulation) SirsiDynix; (ILL) SirsiDynix; (OPAC) SirsiDynix; (Serials) SirsiDynix
Wireless access
Partic in White Pine Libr Coop
Open Mon-Thurs 9-9, Fri & Sat 9-5

BRIDGMAN

P BRIDGMAN PUBLIC LIBRARY*, 4460 Lake St, 49106-9510. SAN 307-9252. Tel: 269-465-3663. FAX: 269-465-3249. E-mail: bridgmanlibrary@comcast.net. *Dir,* Carol Richardson; E-mail: carol.a.richardson@comcast.net
Founded 1966. Pop 5,576; Circ 53,387
Library Holdings: Bk Vols 31,623; Per Subs 106
Special Collections: Oral History
Partic in Southwest Michigan Library Cooperative
Open Mon-Thurs 10-8, Fri 10-5, Sat 10-4
Friends of the Library Group

BRIGHTON

P BRIGHTON DISTRICT LIBRARY*, 100 Library Dr, 48116. SAN 307-9260. Tel: 810-229-6571. Administration Tel: 810-229-6571, Ext 206. Automation Services Tel: 810-229-6571, Ext 205. FAX: 810-229-3161. Web Site: brightonlibrary.info. *Dir,* Nancy B Johnson; Tel: 810-229-6571, Ext 203, E-mail: nbjohnson@brightonlibrary.info; *Asst Dir,* Ed Rutkowski; Tel: 810-229-6571, Ext 222, E-mail: erutkowski@brightonlibrary.info; *Head, Adult Serv,* Mary Ann Scott; Tel: 810-229-6571, Ext 225, E-mail: maryann@brightonlibrary.info; *Head, Youth Serv,* Carla Sharp; Tel: 810-229-6571, Ext 209, E-mail: csharp@brightonlibrary.info; *Circ Supvr,* Sandra Schulenburg; Tel: 810-229-6571, Ext 231, E-mail: schulenburg@brightonlibrary.info; *Tech Serv Supvr,* Diana Cunningham; Tel: 810-229-6571, Ext 220, E-mail: dlc@brightonlibrary.info; *Commun Relations Coordr,* Diana Dart; Tel: 810-229-6571, Ext 211, E-mail: ddart@brightonlibrary.info; *Teen Serv,* Jennifer Osborne; Tel: 810-229-6571, Ext 213, E-mail: klane@brightonlibrary.info; *Webmaster,* Sarah Neidert; E-mail: sarah@brightonlibrary.info; Staff 19 (MLS 11, Non-MLS 8)
Founded 1992. Pop 39,594; Circ 463,768
Dec 2007-Nov 2008 Income $1,719,134. Mats Exp $182,800. Sal $981,544
Special Collections: Career Coll
Subject Interests: Genealogy, Local hist
Automation Activity & Vendor Info: (Cataloging) SirsiDynix; (Circulation) SirsiDynix; (OPAC) SirsiDynix
Wireless access
Publications: Brighton District Library Newsletter
Partic in The Library Network
Open Mon-Thurs 10-9, Fri & Sat 10-5, Sun (Aug-June) 1-5
Friends of the Library Group

BRIMLEY

J BAY MILLS COMMUNITY COLLEGE*, Library & Heritage Center, 12214 W Lakeshore Dr, 49715-9320. Tel: 906-248-3354, Ext 4202. Toll Free Tel: 800-844-2622. FAX: 906-248-2432. E-mail: library@bmcc.edu. Web Site: www.bmcc.edu. *Dir, Libr Serv,* Megan Clarke; E-mail: meganparish@bmcc.edu; *Asst Dir, Libr Serv,* Patricia Croad-Teeple
Library Holdings: Bk Vols 8,000; Per Subs 30
Function: Fax serv
Open Mon-Thurs 8-8, Fri 8:30-4:30, Sat 10-2

BROWN CITY

P BROWN CITY PUBLIC LIBRARY*, 4207 Main St, 48416. (Mail add: PO Box 58, 48416-0058), SAN 307-9279. Tel: 810-346-2511. FAX: 810-346-2511. E-mail: bcplmi@greatlakes.net. *Dir,* Shirley K Wood
Circ 18,475
Library Holdings: Bk Vols 14,200; Per Subs 70
Partic in White Pine Libr Coop
Open Tues & Thurs 10-5:30, Wed 12-9, Fri 11-5:30, Sat 9:30-1

BUCHANAN

P BUCHANAN DISTRICT LIBRARY*, 128 E Front St, 49107. SAN 307-9287. Tel: 269-695-3681. FAX: 269-695-0004. Web Site: www.buchananlibrary.org. *Dir,* Kate Scheid; E-mail: k.scheid@buchananlibrary.com; *Asst Dir,* Pam Salo; E-mail: p.salo@buchananlibrary.com; *Cataloger,* Debbie VerValin; E-mail:

d.vervalin@buchananlibrary.com; *Youth Serv,* Sarah Gault; E-mail: s.gault@buchananlibrary.com; Staff 7 (Non-MLS 7)
Pop 9,285; Circ 105,682
Jul 2006-Jun 2007 Income $350,000. Mats Exp $44,000. Sal $135,000
Library Holdings: Bk Vols 52,000; Per Subs 100
Special Collections: Local History Coll
Automation Activity & Vendor Info: (Cataloging) Follett Software; (Circulation) Follett Software; (ILL) Auto-Graphics, Inc; (OPAC) Follett Software
Partic in Southwest Michigan Library Cooperative
Open Tues & Fri 9-6, Wed & Thurs 12-8, Sat 9-2

BURLINGTON

P BURLINGTON TOWNSHIP LIBRARY*, 135 Elm St, 49029. (Mail add: PO Box 39, 49029-0039), SAN 307-9309. Tel: 517-765-2702. FAX: 517-765-2702. *Dir,* Rosemary Claire Johnson; Staff 1 (Non-MLS 1)
Founded 1935. Pop 1,941; Circ 4,988
Library Holdings: CDs 26; DVDs 150; Bk Titles 10,488; Talking Bks 25; Videos 100
Function: Archival coll, Bks on CD, Computers for patron use, Copy machines, Fax serv, Free DVD rentals, ILL available, Music CDs, Photocopying/Printing, Spoken cassettes & DVDs, Summer reading prog, VHS videos
Open Tues 11-5, Wed & Thurs 1-6, Sat 9-Noon

BURNIPS

P SALEM TOWNSHIP LIBRARY*, 3007 142nd Ave, 49314. (Mail add: PO Box 58, 49314-0058), SAN 346-3532. Tel: 616-896-8170. FAX: 616-896-8035. E-mail: bur@llcoop.org. Web Site: burnips.llcoop.org. *Dir,* Sharon Engelsman; *Asst Librn,* Jan Parbos
Library Holdings: AV Mats 1,800; Bk Vols 22,000; Per Subs 82
Automation Activity & Vendor Info: (Cataloging) Innovative Interfaces, Inc; (Circulation) Innovative Interfaces, Inc
Partic in Lakeland Library Cooperative
Open Mon & Wed 10-8, Tues 1-5, Thurs 1-8, Fri 3-6, Sat 9-1

BURR OAK

P BURR OAK TOWNSHIP LIBRARY*, 220 S Second St, 49030-5133. (Mail add: PO Box 309, 49030-0309), SAN 307-9317. Tel: 269-489-2906. FAX: 269-489-2906. Web Site: woodlands.lib.mi.us/burr/Burr.html. *Dir,* Audrey Borkholder
Founded 1905. Pop 2,500; Circ 9,919
Library Holdings: Bk Vols 17,919; Per Subs 29
Automation Activity & Vendor Info: (Cataloging) Follett Software; (Circulation) Follett Software; (OPAC) Follett Software
Mem of Woodlands Library Cooperative
Open Mon 3-7, Tues 9-7, Thurs 12-6, Fri 12-5, Sat 9-12
Friends of the Library Group

BURT

P TAYMOUTH TOWNSHIP LIBRARY*, 2361 E Burt Rd, 48417-9426. (Mail add: PO Box 158, 48417-0158), SAN 376-706X. Tel: 989-770-4651. FAX: 989-770-4651. Interlibrary Loan Service E-mail: bur_ill@yahoo.com. Web Site: www.taymouthtwplibrary.org. *Dir,* Diane Snellenberger
Founded 1979. Pop 4,624; Circ 12,438
Jul 2006-Jun 2007 Income $65,064. Mats Exp $10,995, Books $8,500, Per/Ser (Incl. Access Fees) $2,495. Sal $32,450 (Prof $20,375)
Library Holdings: Large Print Bks 257; Bk Titles 19,248; Per Subs 38; Talking Bks 668
Subject Interests: Local hist
Partic in White Pine Libr Coop
Open Mon & Thurs 2-9, Tues 10-6, Fri 9-4
Friends of the Library Group

CADILLAC

C BAKER COLLEGE OF CADILLAC LIBRARY*, 9600 E 13th St, 49601-9169. Tel: 231-876-3112. Toll Free Tel: 888-313-3463. FAX: 231-775-6187. E-mail: library-ca@baker.edu. Web Site: www.baker.edu. *Dir, Acad Res,* Laurie Arrick
Library Holdings: Bk Vols 6,600; Per Subs 90
Automation Activity & Vendor Info: (Cataloging) Horizon; (Circulation) Horizon; (Serials) Horizon
Open Mon-Thurs 8am-9pm, Fri 8-5

P CADILLAC-WEXFORD PUBLIC LIBRARY*, 411 S Lake St, 49601. SAN 346-0622. Tel: 231-775-6541. Reference Tel: 231-775-6541, Ext 109. FAX: 231-775-6778. E-mail: liedekea@cadillaclibrary.org. Web Site: www.cadillaclibrary.org. *Dir,* Kathy Kirch; *Dir,* Cathy Tacoma; Staff 12 (MLS 3, Non-MLS 9)
Founded 1906. Pop 30,265; Circ 203,540
Library Holdings: Bk Vols 147,000; Per Subs 275
Automation Activity & Vendor Info: (Cataloging) Auto-Graphics, Inc; (Circulation) Auto-Graphics, Inc; (OPAC) Auto-Graphics, Inc
Database Vendor: Gale Cengage Learning
Wireless access
Partic in Mid-Michigan Library League; MLC
Open Mon-Thurs (Winter) 9-8, Fri & Sat 9-6; Mon-Thurs (Summer) 9-8, Fri 9-6, Sat 9-3
Friends of the Library Group
Branches: 3
BUCKLEY BRANCH, 305 S First St, Buckley, 49620-9526. Tel: 231-269-3325, Ext 3020. FAX: 231-269-3625. *Br Librn,* Susan Utter
Automation Activity & Vendor Info: (Cataloging) Brodart; (Circulation) Brodart
Open Mon-Thurs 3:30-6:30
Friends of the Library Group
MANTON BRANCH, 404 W Main St, Manton, 49663. (Mail add: PO Box F, Manton, 49663-0906), SAN 346-0681. Tel: 231-824-3584. FAX: 231-824-3584. *Br Librn,* Debra Letts; Staff 2 (Non-MLS 2)
Open Mon, Wed & Fri 10-5, Tues & Thurs 11:30-6:30, Sat 9-12
Friends of the Library Group
MESICK BRANCH, 117 Eugene St, Mesick, 49668, SAN 346-0657. Tel: 231-885-1120. FAX: 231-885-1120. *Br Librn,* Penny Carlson; *Br Librn,* Debbie Stanton
Open Mon 10-2, Tues & Wed 2-6, Thurs 2-8, Fri & Sat 10-2
Friends of the Library Group

CAMDEN

P CAMDEN TOWNSHIP PUBLIC LIBRARY*, 119 S Main St, 49232. (Mail add: PO Box 189, 49232-0189), SAN 307-9341. Tel: 517-368-5554. FAX: 517-368-5554. E-mail: camden@monroe.lib.mi.us. *Dir,* Laura Orlowski
Circ 13,947
Library Holdings: Bk Vols 8,000; Per Subs 15
Mem of Woodlands Library Cooperative
Open Mon & Thurs 10-5, Tues 1-7, Fri 3-7, Sat 9-12
Friends of the Library Group

CANTON

P CANTON PUBLIC LIBRARY, 1200 S Canton Center Rd, 48188-1600. SAN 321-2645. Tel: 734-397-0999. FAX: 734-397-1130. Web Site: www.cantonpl.org. *Dir,* Eva Davis; Tel: 734-397-0999, Ext 1065, E-mail: davise@cantonpl.org; *Head, Commun Relations,* Laurie Golden; E-mail: goldenl@cantonpl.org; *Head, Bus Serv,* Marian Nicholson; E-mail: nicholsonm@cantonpl.org; *Head, Circ Serv,* Nancy Szczepanski; E-mail: szczepan@cantonpl.org; *Head, Info Serv,* Rebecca Havenstein-Coughlin; E-mail: havensr@cantonpl.org; *Head, Info Tech,* Leo Papa; E-mail: papal@cantonpl.org; Staff 88 (MLS 26, Non-MLS 62)
Founded 1980. Pop 90,000; Circ 1,600,000
Library Holdings: e-books 19,000; Bk Titles 249,000; Bk Vols 296,000; Per Subs 750
Automation Activity & Vendor Info: (Acquisitions) Innovative Interfaces, Inc; (Cataloging) Innovative Interfaces, Inc; (Circulation) Innovative Interfaces, Inc; (ILL) Innovative Interfaces, Inc; (OPAC) Innovative Interfaces, Inc; (Serials) Innovative Interfaces, Inc
Wireless access
Function: 24/7 Electronic res, 24/7 Online cat, Activity rm, Adult bk club, Adult literacy prog, Audiobks via web, AV serv, Bk club(s), Bks on CD, Children's prog, Computer training, Computers for patron use, Copy machines, Electronic databases & coll, Fax serv, Free DVD rentals, Handicapped accessible, Homebound delivery serv, ILL available, Large print keyboards, Life-long learning prog for all ages, Magazines, Magnifiers for reading, Mango lang, Movies, Mus passes, Music CDs, OverDrive digital audio bks, Photocopying/Printing, Printer for laptops & handheld devices, Prog for adults, Prog for children & young adult, Pub access computers, Study rm, Summer reading prog, Tax forms, Telephone ref, Wheelchair accessible
Publications: Connections
Partic in The Library Network
Open Mon-Thurs 9-9, Fri & Sat 9-6, Sun 12-6
Friends of the Library Group

CARO

P CARO AREA DISTRICT LIBRARY, 840 W Frank St, 48723. SAN 307-935X. Tel: 989-673-4329. FAX: 989-673-4777. E-mail: info@carolibrary.org. Web Site: www.carolibrary.org. *Dir,* Erin Schmandt; Tel: 989-673-4329, Ext 102, E-mail: erin@carolibrary.org; *Asst Dir, Ch Serv,* Betty Gettel; Tel: 989-673-4329, Ext 103; Staff 7 (MLS 2, Non-MLS 5)
Founded 1904. Pop 11,837
Library Holdings: AV Mats 6,020; Bks on Deafness & Sign Lang 90; Braille Volumes 13; Electronic Media & Resources 1; High Interest/Low Vocabulary Bk Vols 139; Large Print Bks 2,037; Bk Vols 62,714; Per Subs 162; Talking Bks 1,527

Subject Interests: Genealogy, Local hist
Automation Activity & Vendor Info: (Cataloging) Horizon; (Circulation) Horizon; (ILL) Horizon; (OPAC) Horizon; (Serials) Horizon
Database Vendor: SirsiDynix
Wireless access
Publications: Indianfields Public Library History 1904-1975
Partic in Valley Library Consortium; White Pine Libr Coop
Open Mon-Fri 9-8, Sat 9-5
Friends of the Library Group

CARSON CITY

M CARSON CITY HOSPITAL*, Medical Library, 406 E Elm, 48811-9693. (Mail add: PO Box 879, 48811-0879), SAN 307-9368. Tel: 989-584-3131, Ext 243. FAX: 989-584-6165. Web Site: www.carsoncityhospital.com. *Librn,* Mary Ann Kapustka; Staff 1 (MLS 1)
Founded 1969
Library Holdings: Bk Vols 500; Per Subs 52
Partic in ILL Regional Med Libr, Western Mich Asn of Libr
Open Mon-Fri 7-5

P CARSON CITY PUBLIC LIBRARY*, 102 W Main St, 48811-0699. SAN 307-9376. Tel: 989-584-3680. FAX: 989-584-3680. E-mail: car@llcoop.org. Web Site: www.carsoncity.llcoop.org. *Dir,* Beth O'Grady; *Asst Librn,* Janette Kipp
Founded 1900. Pop 9,681; Circ 39,900
Library Holdings: Bk Vols 35,000; Per Subs 65
Subject Interests: Genealogy
Automation Activity & Vendor Info: (Cataloging) Innovative Interfaces, Inc; (Circulation) Innovative Interfaces, Inc; (OPAC) Innovative Interfaces, Inc
Partic in Lakeland Library Cooperative
Open Mon-Fri 10-6, Sat 10-2
Branches: 1
CRYSTAL COMMUNITY, 221 W Lake St, Crystal, 48818, SAN 376-9232. Tel: 989-235-6111. FAX: 989-235-6111. *Br Librn,* Brenda Geselman
Open Mon-Fri 11-6, Sat 10-2

MICHIGAN DEPARTMENT OF CORRECTIONS
S ERNEST C BROOKS CORRECTIONAL FACILITY LIBRARY*, 2500 S Sheridan Rd, Muskegon, 49444. Tel: 231-773-9200, Ext 1916. *Librn,* Elisia Hardiman; E-mail: hardimane@michigan.gov; *Libr Tech,* Geraldine Harris
Library Holdings: Bk Vols 20,000; Per Subs 15
Open Mon & Sun 12-4, Tues-Thurs 7am-9pm, Fri & Sat 7-4
S CARSON CITY CORRECTIONAL FACILITY LIBRARY*, PO Box 5000, 48811-5000. Tel: 989-584-3941, Ext 6332. FAX: 989-584-6535. *Libr Tech,* Amy Platte; Tel: 989-548-3941, Ext 6331, E-mail: plattea1@michigan.gov; Staff 3 (MLS 1, Non-MLS 2)
Founded 1987
Library Holdings: Bk Vols 10,000
Function: Audio & video playback equip for onsite use, Bks on cassette, Legal assistance to inmates, Photocopying/Printing, VHS videos
Restriction: Staff & inmates only

CASS CITY

C BAKER COLLEGE OF CASS CITY LIBRARY*, 6667 Main St, 48726-1558. SAN 377-1865. Tel: 989-872-6019. FAX: 989-872-6001. E-mail: library-cy@baker.edu. Web Site: www.baker.edu. *Libr Asst,* Dee Mulligan; E-mail: deeann.mulligan@baker.edu
Library Holdings: Bk Vols 10,000; Per Subs 45
Automation Activity & Vendor Info: (Cataloging) Horizon; (Circulation) Horizon; (OPAC) Horizon
Wireless access

P RAWSON MEMORIAL DISTRICT LIBRARY*, 6495 Pine St, 48726-4073. SAN 307-9384. Tel: 989-872-2856. FAX: 989-872-4073. E-mail: librarian@rawson.lib.mi.us. Web Site: www.rawson.lib.mi.us. *Dir,* Kate Van Auken; E-mail: kvanauken@rawson.lib.mi.us; *Asst Libr Dir,* Ruth Steele; Staff 5 (MLS 1, Non-MLS 4)
Founded 1910. Pop 8,589; Circ 70,648
Library Holdings: Bk Vols 34,800; Per Subs 86
Automation Activity & Vendor Info: (Acquisitions) Auto-Graphics, Inc; (Cataloging) Auto-Graphics, Inc; (Circulation) Auto-Graphics, Inc; (ILL) Auto-Graphics, Inc; (OPAC) Auto-Graphics, Inc
Wireless access
Partic in White Pine Libr Coop
Open Mon, Wed & Fri 9-9, Tues & Thurs 9-5:30, Sat 9-4
Friends of the Library Group

CASSOPOLIS

P CASS DISTRICT LIBRARY*, 319 M-62 N, 49031-1099. SAN 346-0711. Tel: 269-445-3400. Toll Free Tel: 800-595-4186. FAX: 269-445-8795. E-mail: cass@cass.lib.mi.us. Web Site: www.cass.lib.mi.us. *Dir,* Jennifer Ray; Tel: 269-445-3400, Ext 25, E-mail: jray@cass.lib.mi.us; *Syst Adminr,* Sue Pickar; Tel: 269-445-3400, Ext 33, E-mail: spickar@cass.lib.mi.us; Staff 11 (MLS 1, Non-MLS 10)
Founded 1940. Pop 39,204
Database Vendor: SirsiDynix
Partic in Southwest Michigan Library Cooperative
Open Mon-Thurs 9-8, Fri 9-6, Sat 9-3
Friends of the Library Group
Branches: 4
EDWARDSBURG BRANCH, 26745 Church St, Edwardsburg, 49112. (Mail add: PO Box 709, Edwardsburg, 49112-0710), SAN 346-0746. Tel: 269-663-5875. FAX: 269-663-6215. *Br Mgr,* Shirley Hartley
Founded 1932
Open Mon-Thurs 9-8, Fri 9-6, Sat 9-1
HOWARD, 2341 Yankee St, Niles, 49120, SAN 346-0770. Tel: 269-684-1680. FAX: 269-684-1680. *Br Mgr,* Toni Reynolds
Founded 1966
Open Mon-Thurs 11-7, Sat 9-1
Friends of the Library Group
LOCAL HISTORY, 145 N Broadway St, 49031, SAN 373-7233. Tel: 269-445-0412. FAX: 269-445-8795. *Br Mgr,* Jon Wuepper; E-mail: jwuepper@cass.lib.mi.us
Founded 1994
Open Mon-Thurs 9-4, Sat 10-2
MASON-UNION, 17049 US 12 E, Edwardsburg, 49112, SAN 346-0800. Tel: 269-641-7674. FAX: 269-641-7674. *Br Mgr,* Holly Spoor
Founded 1973
Open Mon-Thurs 11-7, Sat 9-1
Friends of the Library Group

CEDAR SPRINGS

P CEDAR SPRINGS PUBLIC LIBRARY*, 43 W Cherry St, 49319. SAN 307-9406. Tel: 616-696-1910. FAX: 616-696-1910. E-mail: ced@llcoop.org. Web Site: cedarsprings.llcoop.org. *Dir,* Donna Clark; E-mail: ceddc@llcoop.org
Founded 1936
Library Holdings: Bk Vols 23,000; Per Subs 15
Automation Activity & Vendor Info: (Cataloging) SirsiDynix; (Circulation) SirsiDynix; (OPAC) SirsiDynix
Partic in Lakeland Library Cooperative
Open Mon, Tues & Fri 12-6, Wed 10-7, Sat 10-1

CENTER LINE

P CENTER LINE PUBLIC LIBRARY*, 7345 Weingartz St, 48015-1462. SAN 307-9422. Tel: 586-758-8274. *Dir,* Heather Hames; E-mail: hhames@centerline.gov
Founded 1929. Pop 8,257; Circ 40,000
Jul 2012-Jun 2013 Income $249,293. Mats Exp $30,000. Sal $110,000
Library Holdings: Bk Vols 53,000; Per Subs 25
Automation Activity & Vendor Info: (Acquisitions) SirsiDynix; (Cataloging) SirsiDynix; (Circulation) SirsiDynix; (OPAC) SirsiDynix; (Serials) SirsiDynix
Wireless access
Partic in Suburban Library Cooperative
Open Mon & Wed 10-5, Tues & Thurs 10-7, Fri & Sat 12-5
Friends of the Library Group

CENTRAL LAKE

P CENTRAL LAKE DISTRICT LIBRARY*, 7900 Maple St, 49622. (Mail add: PO Box 397, 49622-0397), SAN 307-9430. Tel: 231-544-2517. FAX: 231-544-5016. Web Site: www.centrallakelibrary.com. *Dir,* Becky Graham; E-mail: director@centrallakelibrary.com; *Circ,* Carol Stoutjesdyk; Staff 1 (Non-MLS 1)
Pop 3,839; Circ 26,106
Library Holdings: Audiobooks 1,000; Bks on Deafness & Sign Lang 12; CDs 300; DVDs 500; Large Print Bks 1,500; Bk Vols 21,000; Per Subs 54; Videos 1,500
Special Collections: Michigan Coll
Partic in Mid-Michigan Library League
Open Mon, Tues, Thurs & Fri 10-6, Wed 10-8, Sat 10-3
Friends of the Library Group

CENTREVILLE

J GLEN OAKS COMMUNITY COLLEGE LIBRARY*, E J Shaheen Library, 62249 Shimmel Rd, 49032-9719. SAN 307-9449. Tel: 269-467-9945. Toll Free Tel: 888-994-7818. FAX: 269-467-4114. E-mail:

library@glenoaks.edu. Web Site: www.glenoaks.edu. *Librn,* Betsy Susan Morgan; Tel: 269-467-9945, Ext 202, E-mail: bmorgan@glenoaks.edu
Founded 1966. Enrl 1,200; Fac 91
Library Holdings: Bk Titles 36,431; Bk Vols 40,133; Per Subs 239
Partic in Southwest Michigan Library Cooperative
Open Mon-Thurs (Fall) 7:45-6:30, Fri 7:45-2; Mon-Thurs (Winter) 7:45am-8pm, Fri 7:45-2; Mon-Thurs (Spring & Summer) 8-6:30

P NOTTAWA TOWNSHIP LIBRARY*, 685 E Main St, 49032-9603. (Mail add: PO Box 398, 49032-0398), SAN 307-9457. Tel: 269-467-6289. FAX: 269-467-4422. E-mail: nottawa@monroe.lib.mi.us. Web Site: nottawatownshiplibrary.com. *Dir,* Bonnie Heflin; *Ch,* Karen Peterson
Founded 1871. Pop 6,394; Circ 47,185
Jul 2006-Jun 2007 Income $219,984, State $2,600, Locally Generated Income $171,784, Other $45,600. Mats Exp $32,000. Sal $99,000
Library Holdings: AV Mats 1,528; Bks on Deafness & Sign Lang 12; CDs 73; DVDs 616; Large Print Bks 280; Bk Titles 24,894; Bk Vols 26,252; Per Subs 48; Talking Bks 1,248; Videos 912
Special Collections: Amish Religion Coll
Automation Activity & Vendor Info: (Acquisitions) Follett Software; (Cataloging) Follett Software; (Circulation) Follett Software
Database Vendor: OCLC WorldShare Interlibrary Loan
Wireless access
Function: Copy machines, e-mail serv, Fax serv, Handicapped accessible, Homebound delivery serv, ILL available, Music CDs, Photocopying/Printing, Prog for children & young adult, Spoken cassettes & CDs, Summer reading prog, Tax forms, VHS videos, Wheelchair accessible, Workshops
Mem of Woodlands Library Cooperative
Partic in Mich Libr Asn
Open Mon & Wed-Fri 9-5, Tues 11-7, Sat 9-12
Friends of the Library Group

CHARLEVOIX

P CHARLEVOIX PUBLIC LIBRARY*, 220 W Clinton St, 49720. SAN 307-9465. Tel: 231-547-2651. Interlibrary Loan Service Tel: 231-237-7340. FAX: 231-547-0678. E-mail: info@charlevoixlibrary.org. Web Site: www.charlevoixlibrary.org. *Dir,* Valerie Meyerson; Tel: 231-237-7360, E-mail: val@charlevoixlibrary.org; Staff 13.5 (MLS 5, Non-MLS 8.5)
Founded 1907. Pop 9,405; Circ 120,000
Jul 2012-Jun 2013 Income $975,480, State $3,950, County $46,000, Locally Generated Income $925,530. Mats Exp $71,600, Books $42,500, Per/Ser (Incl. Access Fees) $7,500, AV Mat $14,500, Electronic Ref Mat (Incl. Access Fees) $7,100. Sal $434,000 (Prof $171,000)
Library Holdings: Audiobooks 3,700; CDs 1,893; DVDs 3,050; e-books 1,000; Large Print Bks 1,099; Bk Vols 41,109; Per Subs 130
Special Collections: Local History. Oral History
Automation Activity & Vendor Info: (Cataloging) SirsiDynix; (Circulation) SirsiDynix; (OPAC) SIRSI-iBistro
Database Vendor: Gale Cengage Learning, OCLC FirstSearch, SirsiDynix
Wireless access
Function: Adult bk club, Art exhibits, Audiobks via web, Bi-weekly Writer's Group, Bk club(s), Bks on cassette, Bks on CD, CD-ROM, Children's prog, Computer training, Computers for patron use, Copy machines, e-mail & chat, E-Reserves, Electronic databases & coll, Exhibits, Family literacy, Fax serv, Free DVD rentals, Genealogy discussion group, Handicapped accessible, Home delivery & serv to Sr ctr & nursing homes, Homebound delivery serv, ILL available, Jazz prog, Magnifiers for reading, Mail & tel request accepted, Microfiche/film & reading machines, Music CDs, Notary serv, Online cat, Online ref, Outreach serv, Outside serv via phone, mail, e-mail & web, OverDrive digital audio bks, Photocopying/Printing, Preschool outreach, Preschool reading prog, Printer for laptops & handheld devices, Prog for adults, Prog for children & young adult, Ref & res, Ref serv available, Ref serv in person, Scanner, Senior computer classes, Senior outreach, Spoken cassettes & CDs, Spoken cassettes & DVDs, Story hour, Summer reading prog, Tax forms, Teen prog, Telephone ref, VHS videos, Web-catalog, Wheelchair accessible, Workshops
Partic in Midwest Collaborative for Library Services (MCLS); Northland Library Cooperative; OCLC Online Computer Library Center, Inc; PAC2 Consortium
Open Mon-Thurs 10-8, Fri & Sat 10-5, Sun 1-5
Friends of the Library Group

CHARLOTTE

P CHARLOTTE COMMUNITY LIBRARY*, 226 S Bostwick St, 48813-1801. SAN 307-9473. Tel: 517-543-8859. FAX: 517-543-8868. Web Site: www.charlottelibrary.org. *Dir,* William D Siarny; E-mail: billsiarny@ameritech.net; *Dir, Finance & Gen Serv,* Marlena Arras; E-mail: marlenaarras@ameritech.net; *Ch Serv, Youth Serv Librn,* Sally Seifert; E-mail: sallyseifert@ameritech.net; *Coordr,* Ann Goeman; E-mail: agoeman36@gmail.com; *Access Serv, ILL Spec, Pub Serv,* Barbara Phlegar; *Acq of Monographs & Journals, AV Coll, ILL Spec,* Bridget Gregus; E-mail: bridgetgregus@ameritech.net; *Adult Serv,* Karen Lewis; E-mail: klkarma@yahoo.com; Staff 19 (MLS 2, Non-MLS 17)
Founded 1895. Pop 29,000; Circ 120,627
Library Holdings: Bk Titles 70,000; Per Subs 113
Special Collections: Local History Coll
Automation Activity & Vendor Info: (Acquisitions) Auto-Graphics, Inc; (Cataloging) Auto-Graphics, Inc; (Circulation) Auto-Graphics, Inc; (ILL) Mel Cat; (Media Booking) Auto-Graphics, Inc; (OPAC) Auto-Graphics, Inc; (Serials) Auto-Graphics, Inc
Wireless access
Function: Adult bk club, Adult literacy prog, Art exhibits, AV serv, Bk club(s), Bks on cassette, Bks on CD, CD-ROM, Children's prog, Computer training, Computers for patron use, Copy machines, Digital talking bks, E-Reserves, Exhibits, Fax serv, Home delivery & serv to Sr ctr & nursing homes, Homebound delivery serv, ILL available, Magnifiers for reading, Music CDs, Notary serv, Photocopying/Printing, Prog for adults, Prog for children & young adult, Pub access computers, Spoken cassettes & CDs, Spoken cassettes & DVDs, Summer reading prog, Tax forms, Teen prog, VHS videos, Video lending libr, Web-catalog, Wheelchair accessible
Mem of Woodlands Library Cooperative
Open Mon-Fri 9-8, Sat 9-5 (9-2 Summer)
Friends of the Library Group

CHASE

P CHASE TOWNSHIP PUBLIC LIBRARY*, Chase Library, 8400 E North St, 49623. (Mail add: PO Box 24, 49623), SAN 307-9481. Tel: 231-832-9511. FAX: 231-832-9511. E-mail: chaselibrary@yahoo.com. *Librn,* Roxanne Ware
Circ 1,906
Library Holdings: Bk Vols 11,044; Per Subs 12
Partic in Mid-Michigan Library League
Open Mon-Thurs 11-7, Fri 1-4

CHEBOYGAN

P CHEBOYGAN AREA PUBLIC LIBRARY*, 100 S Bailey St, 49721-1661. SAN 307-949X. Tel: 231-627-2381. FAX: 231-627-9172. E-mail: contactus@cheboyganlibrary.org. Web Site: cheboyganlibrary.org. *Dir,* Mark C Bronson; *ILL, Ref Serv,* Joyce Krawczak
Pop 14,624
Library Holdings: Bk Vols 41,000; Per Subs 150
Automation Activity & Vendor Info: (Cataloging) SirsiDynix; (Circulation) SirsiDynix; (OPAC) SirsiDynix
Wireless access
Function: Digital talking bks, Handicapped accessible, Magnifiers for reading, Music CDs, Photocopying/Printing, Prog for adults, Prog for children & young adult, Spoken cassettes & CDs, Summer reading prog, VCDs, VHS videos, Wheelchair accessible
Partic in Northland Library Cooperative
Open Mon-Thurs 10-8, Fri 10-5, Sat 10-3
Restriction: Non-resident fee
Friends of the Library Group

CHELSEA

P CHELSEA DISTRICT LIBRARY*, 221 S Main St, 48118-1267. SAN 307-9503. Tel: 734-475-8732. FAX: 734-475-6190. Web Site: chelsea.lib.mi.us. *Libr Dir,* William Harmer; *Asst Dir, Head, Circ,* Linda Ballard; Tel: 734-475-8732, Ext 202; *Head, Adult Serv,* Sara Wedell; *Head, Youth & Teen Serv,* Karen Persello; *Network Adminr,* Melanie Bell; Staff 21 (MLS 6, Non-MLS 15)
Founded 1998. Pop 15,000
Library Holdings: Bk Vols 42,549; Per Subs 98
Special Collections: Chelsea History, bk, ms, microfilm, pictures; Wastenaw County History Coll, pictures
Automation Activity & Vendor Info: (Acquisitions) SirsiDynix; (Cataloging) SirsiDynix; (Circulation) SirsiDynix; (OPAC) SirsiDynix; (Serials) SirsiDynix
Wireless access
Function: Adult bk club, Archival coll, Art exhibits, Bk club(s), CD-ROM, Chess club, Computer training, Digital talking bks, E-Reserves, Electronic databases & coll, Family literacy, Handicapped accessible, Health sci info serv, Home delivery & serv to Sr ctr & nursing homes, Homebound delivery serv, Homework prog, ILL available, Music CDs, Online searches, Photocopying/Printing, Preschool outreach, Prog for adults, Prog for children & young adult, Ref serv available, Senior computer classes, Summer reading prog, Telephone ref, Wheelchair accessible, Workshops
Partic in TLN
Open Mon-Thurs (Winter) 10-9, Fri 10-6, Sat 10-5, Sun 1-5; Mon-Thurs (Summer) 10-8, Fri 10-6, Sat 10-3, Sun 1-5
Friends of the Library Group

CHESANING

P RIVER RAPIDS DISTRICT LIBRARY, 227 E Broad St, 48616. SAN 307-9511. Tel: 989-845-3211. FAX: 989-845-2166. Web Site: www.riverrapidslibrary.org. *Dir,* Sally Alexander; E-mail: rrdl.director@vlc.lib.mi.us; Staff 2.8 (MLS 1, Non-MLS 1.8)
Founded 1936. Pop 4,861; Circ 29,600
Library Holdings: Bk Vols 43,392; Per Subs 60
Special Collections: Genealogy; Local History. Oral History
Automation Activity & Vendor Info: (Cataloging) Horizon; (Circulation) Horizon; (OPAC) Horizon
Wireless access
Function: Adult bk club, Audiobks via web, AV serv, Bk club(s), Bks on cassette, Bks on CD, Bus archives, Children's prog, Computer training, Computers for patron use, Copy machines, Digital talking bks, e-mail & chat, Fax serv, ILL available, Microfiche/film & reading machines, Mus passes, Music CDs, Online cat, OverDrive digital audio bks, Photocopying/Printing, Preschool outreach, Preschool reading prog, Prog for adults, Prog for children & young adult, Pub access computers, Ref serv available, Scanner, Senior computer classes, Spoken cassettes & CDs, Spoken cassettes & DVDs, Story hour, Summer & winter reading prog, Summer reading prog, Tax forms, Teen prog, Telephone ref, VHS videos, Winter reading prog
Partic in Valley Library Consortium; White Pine Libr Coop
Open Mon (Winter) 10-6, Tues & Thurs 10-8, Sat 12-4; Mon & Tues (Summer) 10-6, Thurs 10-8, Fri 10-2
Restriction: Pub use on premises
Friends of the Library Group

CHESTERFIELD

P CHESTERFIELD TOWNSHIP LIBRARY*, 50560 Patricia Ave, 48051-3804. SAN 377-7537. Tel: 586-598-4900. FAX: 586-598-7900. E-mail: chesterfieldlibrary@chelibrary.org. Web Site: www.chelibrary.org. *Dir,* Marion Ashen Lusardi; *Asst Dir,* Paulette Moran; E-mail: moranp@libcoop.net; *Head, Circ,* Jean Wilkins; E-mail: wilkinsj@libcoop.net; *Head, Youth Serv,* Holly Kirsten; E-mail: kirstenh@libcoop.net; *Bus Librn,* Susan Archambault; E-mail: archams@libcoop.net; *Syst Coordr,* Lynn Marie Minor; E-mail: minorl@libcoop.net; Staff 19 (MLS 7, Non-MLS 12)
Founded 1994. Pop 37,403; Circ 165,906
Library Holdings: Audiobooks 4,456; AV Mats 972; CDs 888; DVDs 3,344; Bk Vols 65,699; Per Subs 203; Videos 3,436
Automation Activity & Vendor Info: (Acquisitions) SirsiDynix; (Cataloging) SirsiDynix; (Circulation) SirsiDynix; (ILL) SirsiDynix; (OPAC) SirsiDynix; (Serials) SirsiDynix
Database Vendor: Gale Cengage Learning, OCLC FirstSearch
Partic in Suburban Library Cooperative
Open Mon-Thurs 10-8, Fri 10-5, Sat 10-4
Friends of the Library Group

CLARE

P PERE MARQUETTE DISTRICT LIBRARY*, 185 E Fourth St, 48617. SAN 307-952X. Tel: 989-386-7576. FAX: 989-386-3576. E-mail: pmdl@cityofclare.org. Web Site: www.pmdl.org. *Dir,* Sheila Bissonnette; *Pub Serv Librn,* Pamela McKnight; *Ch Serv,* Rachell Brownlee; Staff 3 (MLS 1, Non-MLS 2)
Founded 1962. Pop 10,801; Circ 27,000
Library Holdings: Bk Vols 36,000; Per Subs 80
Automation Activity & Vendor Info: (Cataloging) TLC (The Library Corporation); (Circulation) TLC (The Library Corporation); (OPAC) TLC (The Library Corporation)
Wireless access
Function: After school storytime, Homebound delivery serv, ILL available, Magnifiers for reading, Music CDs, Online searches, Photocopying/Printing, Prog for children & young adult, Ref serv available, Spoken cassettes & CDs, Summer reading prog, Telephone ref, VHS videos
Partic in Mideastern Mich Libr Coop
Open Tues & Wed 12-8, Thurs 10-6, Fri 10-5, Sat 10-2
Friends of the Library Group

CLARKSTON

P CLARKSTON INDEPENDENCE DISTRICT LIBRARY*, 6495 Clarkston Rd, 48346. SAN 307-9546. Tel: 248-625-2212. Automation Services Tel: 248-625-4633. Web Site: www.indelib.org. *Dir,* Julia Meredith; *Head, Children's & Teen Serv,* Andrea R Tietz; *Head, Adult Serv,* Lawrence Marble; *Head, Circ, IT Mgr,* Bill Bowman; *Head, Tech Serv,* Keegan Sulecki; Staff 4 (MLS 4)
Founded 1955. Pop 34,000; Circ 230,000
Library Holdings: High Interest/Low Vocabulary Bk Vols 200; Bk Vols 100,000; Per Subs 250
Partic in Metronet
Open Mon-Wed 10-9, Thurs-Sat 10-6
Friends of the Library Group

CLAWSON

P BLAIR MEMORIAL LIBRARY*, 416 N Main St, 48017-1599. SAN 307-9554. Tel: 248-588-5500. FAX: 248-588-3114. Web Site: www.clawson.lib.mi.us. *Libr Dir,* Jenni Gannod; *Youth Serv Librn,* Kristin Church
Founded 1929. Pop 12,732; Circ 105,891
Jul 2006-Jun 2007 Income $438,650. Mats Exp $57,500. Sal $195,570 (Prof $110,570)
Library Holdings: AV Mats 7,601; Bks on Deafness & Sign Lang 70; Large Print Bks 1,474; Bk Vols 65,223; Per Subs 130
Automation Activity & Vendor Info: (Cataloging) SirsiDynix; (Circulation) SirsiDynix; (ILL) SirsiDynix; (OPAC) SirsiDynix
Wireless access
Partic in The Library Network
Open Mon & Wed Noon-8, Tues & Thurs 10-6, Sat 9-5
Friends of the Library Group

CLIMAX

P LAWRENCE MEMORIAL PUBLIC LIBRARY*, 107 N Main St, 49034-9638. (Mail add: PO Box 280, 49034-0280), SAN 307-9562. Tel: 269-746-4125. FAX: 269-746-4125. *Dir,* Ralph Weessies
Founded 1882. Pop 2,881; Circ 5,470
Library Holdings: Large Print Bks 147; Bk Vols 17,300; Per Subs 19
Special Collections: Historical Society Coll
Partic in Southwest Michigan Library Cooperative
Open Mon 2-5, Tues-Thurs 2-7, Sat 9-12

CLINTON

P CLINTON TOWNSHIP PUBLIC LIBRARY*, 100 Brown St, 49236. (Mail add: PO Box 530, 49236-0530), SAN 307-9570. Tel: 517-456-4141. FAX: 517-456-4142. *Dir,* Grace Strauss; E-mail: gstrauss@monroe.lib.mi.us
Founded 1937. Pop 3,557; Circ 33,085
Library Holdings: Bk Vols 25,000; Per Subs 100
Automation Activity & Vendor Info: (Cataloging) Brodart; (Circulation) Brodart
Open Mon-Thurs 11-8, Fri 11-6, Sat 10-2
Friends of the Library Group

CLINTON TOWNSHIP

C BAKER COLLEGE OF CLINTON TOWNSHIP LIBRARY*, 34950 Little Mack Ave, 48035-4701. Tel: 586-790-9584. Toll Free Tel: 888-272-2842. FAX: 586-791-0967. E-mail: library-ct@baker.edu. Web Site: www.baker.edu. *Dir,* David Miller; E-mail: david.miller@baker.edu; *Asst Dir,* Hinde Fertig; E-mail: hinde.fertig@baker.edu
Library Holdings: Bk Vols 20,000; Per Subs 120
Automation Activity & Vendor Info: (Acquisitions) SirsiDynix; (Cataloging) SirsiDynix; (Circulation) SirsiDynix; (OPAC) SirsiDynix; (Serials) SirsiDynix
Open Mon-Thurs 8am-9:40pm, Fri 8-6:30, Sat 8-4

P CLINTON-MACOMB PUBLIC LIBRARY*, 40900 Romeo Plank Rd, 48038-2955. SAN 375-4251. Tel: 586-226-5000. Circulation Tel: 586-226-5020. Reference Tel: 586-226-5040. FAX: 586-226-5008. TDD: 586-226-5009. E-mail: info@cmpl.org. Web Site: www.cmpl.org. *Libr Dir,* Larry Neal; Tel: 586-226-5011, E-mail: lneal@cmpl.org; *Assoc Dir,* Juliane Morian; Tel: 586-226-5091; *Head, Circ,* Debbie Prykucki; Tel: 586-226-5021; *Head, Youth Serv,* Lisa Mulvenna; Tel: 586-226-5031; *Cat Mgr,* Andrea Tasker; Tel: 586-226-5061; *Circ Mgr,* Cathy Marshall; Tel: 586-226-5024; *Tech Mgr,* Aaron Green; Tel: 586-226-5017; Staff 35 (MLS 20, Non-MLS 15)
Founded 1992. Pop 170,000; Circ 1,676,552
Dec 2010-Nov 2011 Income (Main Library and Branch(s)) $5,782,531, State $67,414, City $5,123,405. Mats Exp $511,666, Books $405,124, Per/Ser (Incl. Access Fees) $20,177, Electronic Ref Mat (Incl. Access Fees) $86,365. Sal $2,220,583
Library Holdings: AV Mats 77,665; Bk Vols 277,684
Automation Activity & Vendor Info: (Acquisitions) Innovative Interfaces, Inc; (Cataloging) Innovative Interfaces, Inc; (Circulation) Innovative Interfaces, Inc; (ILL) Innovative Interfaces, Inc; (OPAC) Innovative Interfaces, Inc; (Serials) Innovative Interfaces, Inc
Database Vendor: Baker & Taylor, Gale Cengage Learning, OCLC FirstSearch, OCLC WorldShare Interlibrary Loan
Wireless access
Function: Accelerated reader prog, Accessibility serv available based on individual needs, Adult bk club, Adult literacy prog, After school storytime, Art exhibits, AV serv, Bk club(s), Bks on CD, CD-ROM, Children's prog, Computer training, Computers for patron use, Copy machines, Digital talking bks, e-mail & chat, e-mail serv, Electronic databases & coll, Fax serv, Free DVD rentals, Handicapped accessible,

Holiday prog, Homework prog, ILL available, Large print keyboards, Magnifiers for reading, Mail & tel request accepted, Mus passes, Music CDs, Online cat, Online ref, Orientations, OverDrive digital audio bks, Photocopying/Printing, Prog for adults, Prog for children & young adult, Ref serv available, Ref serv in person, Scanner, Serves mentally handicapped consumers, Spanish lang bks, Story hour, Summer & winter reading prog, Telephone ref, Web-catalog, Wheelchair accessible
Publications: Library Matters (Newsletter); Library Matters (Monthly newsletter)
Partic in Suburban Library Cooperative
Special Services for the Deaf - Assisted listening device; Closed caption videos; TDD equip; TTY equip
Special Services for the Blind - Accessible computers; Assistive/Adapted tech devices, equip & products; BiFolkal kits; Bks & mags in Braille, on rec, tape & cassette; Bks available with recordings; Bks on CD; Bks on flash-memory cartridges; Blind students ctr; Closed circuit TV; Closed circuit TV magnifier; Computer with voice synthesizer for visually impaired persons; Descriptive video serv (DVS); Digital talking bk; Digital talking bk machines; Free checkout of audio mat; Handicapped awareness prog; Large print bks; Large print bks & talking machines; Lending of low vision aids; Low vision equip; Magnifiers; Newsletter (in large print, Braille or on cassette); Playaways (bks on MP3); Screen enlargement software for people with visual disabilities; Screen reader software; Talking bks; Talking bks & player equip
Open Mon-Thurs 9-9, Fri & Sat 9-6, Sun (Sept-May) 1-6
Friends of the Library Group
Branches: 3

P MACOMB LIBRARY FOR THE BLIND & PHYSICALLY HANDICAPPED, 40900 Romeo Plank Rd, 48038-2955, SAN 324-2250. Tel: 586-286-1580. Toll Free Tel: 855-203-5274. FAX: 586-286-0634. E-mail: MLBPH@cmpl.org. Web Site: www.cmpl.org/MLBPH/default.asp. *Coordr, Ch Serv, Spec Serv Librn,* Anne Mandel; Staff 4 (MLS 2, Non-MLS 2)
Founded 1983. Pop 1,200; Circ 40,350
Library Holdings: Bks on Deafness & Sign Lang 250; Large Print Bks 7,500; Talking Bks 41,698; Videos 710
Special Collections: Bi-Folkal Kits; Descriptive Videos; Matchingbook & Tape Kits
Subject Interests: Handicaps
Function: Bks on cassette, Computer training, Computers for patron use, Handicapped accessible, Magnifiers for reading, Mail & tel request accepted, Mail loans to mem, Pub access computers, Summer reading prog, Wheelchair accessible
Publications: LBPH (Newsletter)
Special Services for the Deaf - TDD equip
Special Services for the Blind - Aids for in-house use; Assistive/Adapted tech devices, equip & products; BiFolkal kits; Bks on cassette; Braille equip; Braille servs; Cassette playback machines; Closed circuit TV; Computer with voice synthesizer for visually impaired persons; Internet workstation with adaptive software; Large print bks; Large screen computer & software; Newsletter (in large print, Braille or on cassette); Open bk software on pub access PC; Screen enlargement software for people with visual disabilities; ZoomText magnification & reading software
Open Mon-Thurs 9-9, Fri & Sat 9-6, Sun (Sept-May) 1-6
Restriction: Restricted access
Friends of the Library Group

NORTH, 16800 24 Mile Rd, Macomb Township, 48042. Tel: 586-226-5080. Reference Tel: 586-226-5083. Information Services Tel: 586-226-5088. FAX: 586-226-5088. *Br Mgr,* Gretchen Krug; Tel: 586-226-5081, E-mail: gkrug@cmpl.org; *Circ Mgr,* Cindy Fisher; Tel: 586-226-5084; Staff 7 (MLS 4, Non-MLS 3)
Library Holdings: AV Mats 13,601; Bk Vols 52,923
Open Mon-Thurs 9-9, Fri & Sat 9-6
Friends of the Library Group

SOUTH, 35891 S Gratiot Ave, 48035. Tel: 586-226-5070. Reference Tel: 586-226-5073. Information Services Tel: 586-226-5072. FAX: 586-226-5078. TDD: 586-226-5009. *Br Mgr,* Margaret Dekovich; Tel: 586-226-5071; *Circ Mgr,* Matthew Piper; Tel: 586-226-5074; Staff 7 (MLS 4, Non-MLS 3)
Library Holdings: AV Mats 9,663; Bk Vols 34,494
Open Mon-Thurs 9-9, Fri & Sat 9-6
Friends of the Library Group

COLDWATER

P BRANCH DISTRICT LIBRARY, Ten E Chicago St, 49036-1615. SAN 346-086X. Tel: 517-278-2341. Circulation Tel: 517-278-2341, Ext 19 or 20. Reference Tel: 517-278-2341, Ext 17. Web Site: www.branchdistrictlibrary.org. *Dir,* Evette Atkin; Tel: 517-278-2341, Ext 16, E-mail: director@branchdistrictlibrary.org; *Asst Dir, Coordr, Info Tech,* John Rucker; Tel: 517-278-2341, Ext 15, E-mail: automation@branchdistrictlibrary.org; Staff 34 (MLS 3, Non-MLS 31)
Founded 1991. Pop 44,900; Circ 138,000
Library Holdings: Bk Titles 71,464; Per Subs 95
Special Collections: Geneaological Research Materials. Oral History
Automation Activity & Vendor Info: (Cataloging) Evergreen; (Circulation) Evergreen; (ILL) Mel Cat
Database Vendor: OCLC FirstSearch, ProQuest
Wireless access
Function: ILL available
Mem of Woodlands Library Cooperative
Open Mon (Winter) 10-8, Tues-Thurs 9-8, Fri 9-5, Sat 9-3; Tues & Wed (Summer) 9-5
Friends of the Library Group
Branches: 5

ALGANSEE, 580-B S Ray Quincy Rd, Quincy, 49082-9530, SAN 346-0894. Tel: 517-639-9830. FAX: 517-639-9830. *Br Mgr,* Janice Clark
Founded 1938
Library Holdings: Bk Vols 1,700
Open Tues 12-6, Wed 1-6, Fri 10-6, Thurs 9-1, Sat 9-12
Friends of the Library Group

BRONSON BRANCH, 207 N Matteson St, Bronson, 49028-1308, SAN 346-0924. Tel: 517-369-3785. FAX: 517-369-3785. E-mail: bronson@branchdistrictlibrary.org. *Br Mgr,* Lynnell Eash
Founded 1888
Library Holdings: Bk Vols 4,750
Open Tues 12-6, Wed 10:30-6, Thurs 10:30-5, Fri 10:30-4, Sat 9-12
Friends of the Library Group

DEARTH UNION TOWNSHIP BRANCH, 195 N Broadway, Union City, 49094-1153, SAN 346-1017. Tel: 517-741-5061. FAX: 517-741-5061. E-mail: union@branchdistrictlibrary.org. *Br Mgr,* Patricia Kaniewski
Founded 1870
Open Tues & Wed 9:30-5, Fri 9:30-4:30, Sat 9-12
Friends of the Library Group

QUINCY BRANCH, 11 N Main St, Quincy, 49082-1163, SAN 346-0959. Tel: 517-639-4001. FAX: 517-639-4001. E-mail: quincy@branchdistrictlibrary.org. *Br Mgr,* Lisa Wood
Founded 1870
Open Tues & Fri 9-5, Wed & Thurs 12-5, Sat 9-12
Friends of the Library Group

SHERWOOD BRANCH, 118 E Sherman St, Sherwood, 49089, SAN 346-0983. Tel: 517-741-7976. FAX: 517-741-7976. *Br Coordr,* Traci Counterman
Founded 1947
Open Tues 2-6, Wed 9-2, Thurs 1-5, Sat 9-Noon
Friends of the Library Group

COLEMAN

P COLEMAN AREA LIBRARY*, 111 First St, 48618. (Mail add: PO Box 515, 48618-0515), SAN 307-9589. Tel: 989-465-6398. FAX: 989-465-1861. E-mail: library@tm.net. Web Site: www.colemanlibrary.org. *Dir,* Gale L Nelson
Pop 4,594; Circ 13,340
Library Holdings: Bk Vols 19,000; Per Subs 54; Videos 812
Automation Activity & Vendor Info: (Cataloging) TLC (The Library Corporation); (Circulation) TLC (The Library Corporation); (OPAC) TLC (The Library Corporation)
Open Tues, Wed & Fri 9-5, Thurs 12:30-8:30, Sat 8-12

COLOMA

P COLOMA PUBLIC LIBRARY*, 151 W Center St, 49038. (Mail add: PO Box 430, 49038-0430), SAN 307-9597. Tel: 269-468-3431. FAX: 269-468-8077. *Dir,* Charles Dickinson; E-mail: chuckcolomalibrary@yahoo.com; Staff 2 (MLS 1, Non-MLS 1)
Founded 1963. Pop 13,835; Circ 82,441
Jul 2005-Jun 2006 Income $250,000. Mats Exp $45,000
Library Holdings: Bk Vols 55,000; Per Subs 204
Subject Interests: Mich
Automation Activity & Vendor Info: (Cataloging) Follett Software; (Circulation) Follett Software; (ILL) Auto-Graphics, Inc; (OPAC) Auto-Graphics, Inc
Database Vendor: OCLC FirstSearch
Wireless access
Partic in Southwest Michigan Library Cooperative
Open Mon & Fri 10-5:30, Tues-Thurs 10-8, Sat 10-2

COLON

P COLON TOWNSHIP LIBRARY*, 128 S Blackstone Ave, 49040. (Mail add: PO Box 9, 49040-0009), SAN 307-9600. Tel: 269-432-3958. FAX: 269-432-4554. E-mail: colon@monroe.lib.mi.us. Web Site: www.colonlibrary.org. *Dir,* Patti A Miller; E-mail: pamiller@monroe.lib.mi.us; *Asst Dir,* Katie Bir; Staff 2 (MLS 1, Non-MLS 1)
Founded 1897. Pop 3,901; Circ 23,521
Library Holdings: Audiobooks 1,022; CDs 48; DVDs 399; Large Print Bks 228; Bk Vols 17,926; Per Subs 42; Videos 383

Automation Activity & Vendor Info: (Cataloging) Auto-Graphics, Inc; (Circulation) Auto-Graphics, Inc; (ILL) Innovative Interfaces, Inc - Millenium; (OPAC) Auto-Graphics, Inc
Wireless access
Function: Adult bk club, Bks on CD, Children's prog, Computers for patron use, Copy machines, Fax serv, Handicapped accessible, ILL available, Online cat, OverDrive digital audio bks, Photocopying/Printing, Prog for children & young adult, Pub access computers, Senior outreach, Spoken cassettes & CDs, Summer reading prog, Tax forms, VCDs, Web-catalog, Wheelchair accessible, Workshops
Mem of Woodlands Library Cooperative
Open Tues & Thurs 9-7, Wed 9-5, Fri & Sat 9-1
Friends of the Library Group

COMMERCE TOWNSHIP

§P COMMERCE TOWNSHIP COMMUNITY LIBRARY, 2869 N Pontiac Trail, 48390. SAN 760-8241. Tel: 248-669-8108. FAX: 248-669-3247. Web Site: www.commercelibrary.info. *Libr Dir,* Connie Jo Ozinga; Tel: 248-669-8101, Ext 101, E-mail: cjozinga@commercelibrary.info; *Dir of Tech,* Ben Sebrowski; Tel: 248-669-8101, Ext 107, E-mail: bsebrowski@commercelibrary.info; *Head, Circ & Tech Serv,* Bill Wines; Tel: 248-669-8101, Ext 102, E-mail: bwines@commercelibrary.info; *Ad,* José Argandoña; Tel: 248-669-8101, Ext 110, E-mail: jargandona@commercelibrary.info; *Ad,* Dustin Brown; Tel: 2408-669-8101, Ext 115, E-mail: dbrown@commercelibrary.info; *Teen Serv Librn,* Elizabeth Norton; Tel: 248-669-8101, Ext 109, E-mail: enorton@commercelibrary.info; *Youth Serv Librn,* Emily Dumas; Tel: 248-669-8101, Ext 112, E-mail: edumas@commercelibrary.info; *Youth Serv Librn,* Trista Reno; E-mail: treno@commercelibrary.info; *Adult Serv Mgr,* Marika Zemke; Tel: 248-669-8101, Ext 108, E-mail: mzemke@commercelibrary.info; *Youth & Teen Serv Mgr,* Abigail Daniels; Tel: 248-669-8101, Ext 106, E-mail: adaniels@commercelibrary.info
Open Mon-Thurs 10-9, Fri & Sat 10-5, Sun 1-5

COMSTOCK

P COMSTOCK TOWNSHIP LIBRARY*, 6130 King Hwy, 49041. (Mail add: PO Box 25, 49041-0025), SAN 307-9619. Tel: 269-345-0136. FAX: 269-345-0138. E-mail: adultlibrarian@yahoo.com. Web Site: www.comstocklibrary.org. *Dir,* Meg King-Sloan; E-mail: msloan@voyager.net; *Ad,* Rachel Wiegmann; *Adult Serv,* Joey Ives; *Ch Serv,* Myla Stuart; Staff 15 (MLS 7, Non-MLS 8)
Founded 1938. Pop 13,851; Circ 128,500
Library Holdings: Bk Titles 70,617; Bk Vols 78,643; Per Subs 125
Subject Interests: Local hist
Automation Activity & Vendor Info: (Cataloging) TLC (The Library Corporation); (Circulation) TLC (The Library Corporation); (ILL) Mel Cat; (OPAC) TLC (The Library Corporation); (Serials) TLC (The Library Corporation)
Wireless access
Function: Photocopying/Printing, Preschool outreach, Prog for children & young adult, Pub access computers, Ref serv available, Ref serv in person, Spoken cassettes & CDs, Spoken cassettes & DVDs, Story hour, Summer reading prog, Tax forms, Telephone ref, Web-catalog, Wheelchair accessible
Open Mon-Thurs 9:30-8:30, Fri 10-6, Sat 10-4

COMSTOCK PARK

P KENT DISTRICT LIBRARY*, 814 West River Center Dr NE, 49321. SAN 346-5489. Tel: 616-784-2007. Automation Services Tel: 616-453-2575. FAX: 616-647-3828. Web Site: www.kdl.org. *Dir,* Lance M Werner; Staff 192 (MLS 57, Non-MLS 135)
Founded 1927. Pop 395,660; Circ 5,586,894
Jan 2013-Dec 2013 Income (Main Library and Branch(s)) $15,122,563. Mats Exp $2,237,436. Sal $7,848,869
Library Holdings: Braille Volumes 187; CDs 86,105; DVDs 63,022; e-books 10,853; Bk Vols 828,654; Per Subs 2,467
Subject Interests: Antiques, Careers, Collectibles, Health
Automation Activity & Vendor Info: (Acquisitions) Innovative Interfaces, Inc; (Cataloging) Innovative Interfaces, Inc; (Circulation) Innovative Interfaces, Inc; (OPAC) Innovative Interfaces, Inc
Wireless access
Publications: What's Next: Books in Series
Friends of the Library Group
Branches: 19

ALPINE TOWNSHIP BRANCH, 5255 Alpine Ave NW, 49321, SAN 346-5608. *Br Mgr,* Shaunna Martz; E-mail: smartz@kdl.org
Founded 1934. Pop 13,336; Circ 55,051
Open Mon & Wed 12-8, Tues 9:30-5, Fri 1-5, Sat 9:30-1:30
Friends of the Library Group

ALTO BRANCH, 6071 Linfield Ave, Alto, 49302, SAN 346-5632. *Br Mgr,* Sandy Graham; E-mail: sgraham@kdl.org
Founded 1937. Pop 2,793; Circ 33,145
Open Mon & Sat 9:30-1:30, Tues & Wed 12-8, Thurs 1-5
Friends of the Library Group

BYRON TOWNSHIP BRANCH, 8191 Byron Center Ave SW, Byron Center, 49315, SAN 346-5667. *Br Mgr,* Eric DeHaan; E-mail: edehaan@kdl.org
Founded 1887. Pop 20,317; Circ 346,157
Open Mon & Thurs 12-8, Tues 9:30-8, Wed, Fri & Sat 9:30-5

CALEDONIA TOWNSHIP BRANCH, 6260 92nd St SE, Caledonia, 49316, SAN 346-5691. *Br Mgr,* Liz Guarino-Kozlowicz; E-mail: eguarino@kdl.org
Founded 1926. Pop 12,294; Circ 190,189
Subject Interests: Local hist
Open Mon, Wed & Sat 9:30-5, Tues & Thurs 12-8
Friends of the Library Group

CASCADE TOWNSHIP BRANCH, 2870 Jack Smith Ave SE, Grand Rapids, 49546, SAN 346-5721. *Br Mgr,* Diane Cutler; E-mail: dcutler@kdl.org
Founded 1965. Pop 17,134; Circ 589,629
Open Mon-Thurs 9:30-8, Fri & Sat 9:30-5, Sun (Sept-May) 1-5
Friends of the Library Group

COMSTOCK PARK BRANCH, 3943 West River Dr NE, 49321, SAN 346-5756. *Br Mgr,* Nancy Mulder; E-mail: nmulder@kdl.org
Founded 1961. Pop 30,952; Circ 151,804
Open Mon 9:30-8, Tues & Thurs 12-8, Wed 9:30-5, Fri & Sat 1-5

EAST GRAND RAPIDS BRANCH, 746 Lakeside Dr SE, East Grand Rapids, 49506, SAN 346-5780. *Br Mgr,* Dawn Lewis; E-mail: dlewis@kdl.org
Founded 1959. Pop 10,694; Circ 451,306
Open Mon-Thurs 9:30-8, Fri & Sat 9:30-5, Sun (Sept-May) 1-5
Friends of the Library Group

ENGLEHARDT BRANCH, 200 N Monroe St, Lowell, 49331, SAN 346-5969. *Br Mgr,* Josh Bernstein; E-mail: jbernstein@kdl.org
Founded 1878. Pop 3,783; Circ 182,055
Open Mon-Wed 12-8, Thurs & Fri 9:30-5, Sat 9:30-1:30
Friends of the Library Group

GAINES TOWNSHIP BRANCH, 421 68th St SE, Grand Rapids, 49548, SAN 346-5810. *Br Mgr,* Cathy Neis; E-mail: cneis@kdl.org
Founded 1969. Pop 25,146; Circ 280,853
Open Mon & Thurs 12-8, Tues 9:30-8, Wed, Fri & Sat 9:30-5

GRANDVILLE BRANCH, 4055 Maple St SW, Grandville, 49418, SAN 346-5845. *Br Mgr,* Patrice Vrona; E-mail: pvrona@kdl.org
Founded 1952. Pop 15,378; Circ 579,706
Open Mon-Thurs 9:30-8, Fri & Sat 9:30-5
Friends of the Library Group

KENTWOOD BRANCH, 4950 Breton SE, Kentwood, 49508, SAN 346-590X. *Br Mgr,* Cheryl Cammenga; E-mail: ccammenga@kdl.org
Founded 1955. Pop 48,707; Circ 547,211
Open Mon-Thurs 9:30-8, Fri & Sat 9:30-5, Sun (Sept-May) 1-5
Friends of the Library Group

KRAUSE MEMORIAL BRANCH, 140 E Bridge St, Rockford, 49341, SAN 346-5934. *Br Mgr,* Jennifer German; E-mail: jgerman@kdl.org
Founded 1937. Pop 5,719; Circ 395,196
Open Mon 9:30-8, Tues & Thurs 12-8, Wed, Fri & Sat 9:30-5
Friends of the Library Group

P LIBRARY FOR THE BLIND & PHYSICALLY HANDICAPPED, 3350 Michael Ave SW, Wyoming, 49509, SAN 346-5519. Tel: 616-647-3988. E-mail: lbphstaff@kdl.org. *Br Mgr,* Lori Holland; E-mail: lholland@kdl.org
Circ 47,315
Partic in Lakeland Library Cooperative
Open Mon-Thurs 9:30-8, Fri & Sat 9:30-5, Sun (Sept-May) 1-5

PLAINFIELD TOWNSHIP BRANCH, 2650 Five Mile Rd NE, Grand Rapids, 49525, SAN 346-5993. *Br Mgr,* Liz Breed; E-mail: lbreed@kdl.org
Founded 1968. Pop 30,952; Circ 615,398
Open Mon-Thurs 9:30-8, Fri & Sat 9:30-5, Sun (Sept-May) 1-5
Friends of the Library Group

SAND LAKE/NELSON TOWNSHIP BRANCH, 88 Eighth St, Sand Lake, 49343-9737, SAN 346-6027. *Br Mgr,* Craig Buno; E-mail: cbuno@kdl.org
Founded 1920. Pop 4,764; Circ 96,605
Open Mon & Wed 12-8, Tues & Sat 9:30-5, Fri 1-5
Friends of the Library Group

SPENCER TOWNSHIP BRANCH, 14960 Meddler Ave, Gowen, 49326, SAN 378-1615. *Br Mgr,* Heather Wood-Gramza; E-mail: hwood-gramza@kdl.org
Founded 1998. Pop 3,960; Circ 44,888
Open Tues & Thurs 12-8, Wed 1-5, Sat 9:30-1:30
Friends of the Library Group

TYRONE TOWNSHIP BRANCH, 43 S Main St, Kent City, 49330, SAN 346-587X. *Br Mgr,* Liz Knapp; E-mail: lknapp@kdl.org
Founded 1935. Pop 4,731; Circ 46,295
Open Tues 12-8, Wed 9:30-5, Thurs 4-8, Fri 1-5, Sat 9:30-1:30

WALKER BRANCH, 4293 Remembrance Rd NW, Walker, 49534-7502, SAN 346-6051. *Br Mgr,* Chris Lohman; E-mail: clohman@kdl.org
Founded 1991. Pop 23,537; Circ 284,478
Open Mon, Tues & Thurs 9:30-8, Wed, Fri & Sat 9:30-5
Friends of the Library Group

WYOMING BRANCH, 3350 Michael Ave SW, Wyoming, 49509, SAN 346-6086. *Br Mgr,* Lori Holland; E-mail: lholland@kdl.org
Founded 1940. Pop 72,125; Circ 597,746
Open Mon-Thurs 9:30-8, Fri & Sat 9:30-5, Sun (Sept-May) 1-5
Friends of the Library Group

CONSTANTINE

P CONSTANTINE TOWNSHIP LIBRARY*, 165 Canaris St, 49042-1015. SAN 307-9627. Tel: 269-435-7957. FAX: 269-435-5800. Web Site: www.woodlands.lib.mi.us/constantine. *Dir,* Jane Moe; E-mail: jmoe@monroe.lib.mi.us; Staff 4 (Non-MLS 4)
Founded 1915. Pop 5,030; Circ 32,000
Jan 2007-Dec 2007 Income $159,000. Mats Exp $22,700. Sal $75,000
Library Holdings: AV Mats 700; Large Print Bks 150; Bk Vols 18,000; Per Subs 61; Talking Bks 350
Automation Activity & Vendor Info: (Circulation) AmLib Library Management System; (ILL) Auto-Graphics, Inc
Mem of Woodlands Library Cooperative
Open Mon & Wed-Fri 10-5, Tues 10-8, Sat 10-3, Sun (Sept-June) 12-5

COOPERSVILLE

P COOPERSVILLE AREA DISTRICT LIBRARY*, 333 Ottawa St, 49404-1243. SAN 307-9635. Tel: 616-837-6809. FAX: 616-837-7689. *Dir,* Lavonne Marshall; Staff 3 (Non-MLS 3)
Founded 1915. Pop 11,862; Circ 91,528
Library Holdings: Bk Vols 36,537; Per Subs 72
Special Collections: Coopersville Observers 1880's-1970
Wireless access
Function: Adult bk club, Art exhibits, Audiobks via web, Bks on CD, CD-ROM, Children's prog, Computer training, Computers for patron use, Copy machines, Digital talking bks, Electronic databases & coll, Exhibits, Family literacy, Fax serv, Free DVD rentals, Handicapped accessible, Holiday prog, ILL available, Magnifiers for reading, Mail & tel request accepted, Microfiche/film & reading machines, Music CDs, Online cat, OverDrive digital audio bks, Photocopying/Printing, Preschool outreach, Preschool reading prog, Prog for adults, Prog for children & young adult, Scanner, Senior computer classes, Spanish lang bks, Spoken cassettes & CDs, Spoken cassettes & DVDs, Story hour, Summer & winter reading prog, Summer reading prog, Tax forms, Teen prog, Visual arts prog, Winter reading prog
Partic in Lakeland Library Cooperative
Open Mon & Thurs 12-8, Tues, Wed & Fri 10-5:30, Sat 10-2
Friends of the Library Group

CORUNNA

P COMMUNITY DISTRICT LIBRARY*, Administration Office, 210 E Corunna Ave, 48817. SAN 346-1041. Tel: 989-743-3287. FAX: 989-743-5496. E-mail: director@mycdl.org. Web Site: www.mycdl.org. *Dir,* Jami Cromley; Staff 10 (MLS 1, Non-MLS 9)
Founded 2004. Pop 23,617; Circ 94,772
Jul 2006-Jun 2007 Income (Main Library and Branch(s)) $402,475, Locally Generated Income $295,070, Other $107,405. Mats Exp $55,000. Sal $227,030 (Prof $42,000)
Library Holdings: Bk Vols 53,000
Special Collections: Corunna Journal 1887-1913
Automation Activity & Vendor Info: (Cataloging) Horizon; (Circulation) Horizon; (OPAC) Horizon
Database Vendor: OCLC FirstSearch
Wireless access
Partic in Midwest Collaborative for Library Services (MCLS)
Friends of the Library Group
Branches: 7

BANCROFT-SHIAWASSEE TOWNSHIP BRANCH, 625 Grand River Rd, Bancroft, 48414, SAN 346-1165. Tel: 989-634-5689. FAX: 989-634-5689. Web Site: www.communitydistrictlibrary.org. *Br Librn,* Mary Kalat; Tel: 989-743-5689, E-mail: mlklibrarian@yahoo.com
Pop 18,298
Partic in Mideastern Michigan Library Cooperative
Open Tues & Thurs 10-7, Wed 11-7
Friends of the Library Group

BENTLEY MEMORIAL, 135 S Main St, Perry, 48872-0017, SAN 308-3373. Tel: 517-625-3166. FAX: 517-625-7214. E-mail: perry@mycdl.org. *Br Librn,* Patricia Brown
Founded 1929. Pop 3,990; Circ 27,000
Jul 2006-Jun 2007 Income $97,623. Mats Exp $6,500
Library Holdings: AV Mats 847; Large Print Bks 469; Bk Vols 9,929; Per Subs 33; Talking Bks 300
Automation Activity & Vendor Info: (Cataloging) Follett Software; (Circulation) Follett Software; (OPAC) Follett Software
Partic in Mideastern Michigan Library Cooperative
Open Mon, Wed & Thurs 12-8, Fri & Sat 10-2
Friends of the Library Group

CORUNNA BRANCH, 210 E Corunna Ave, 48817, SAN 307-9643. Tel: 989-743-4800. FAX: 989-743-5502. E-mail: corunna@mycdl.org. *Br Librn,* Cathy Cramner; *Br Librn,* Sue Huff; *Br Librn,* Peggy Spring; Staff 1 (MLS 1)
Founded 2004
Open Mon, Wed & Fri 10-5, Tues & Thurs 10-8, Sat 10-2
Friends of the Library Group

LENNON-VENICE TOWNSHIP, 11904 Lennon Rd, Lennon, 48449. (Mail add: PO Box 349, Lennon, 48449-0349), SAN 346-1106. Tel: 810-621-3202. FAX: 810-621-3202. *Br Librn,* Lee Warren; E-mail: leedav6@yahoo.com
Open Mon 1-5, Tues & Wed 11-6, Thurs 11-7

MORRICE-PERRY TOWNSHIP, 300 Main St, Morrice, 48857, SAN 346-1130. Tel: 517-625-7911. FAX: 517-625-7911. *Br Librn,* Jeni Oliver
Open Mon & Tues 1-7, Wed & Fri 10-5
Friends of the Library Group

NEW LOTHROP-HAZELTON TOWNSHIP, 9387 Genesee St, New Lothrop, 48460. (Mail add: PO Box 279, New Lothrop, 48460-0279), SAN 346-1076. Tel: 810-638-7575. FAX: 810-638-7575. *Br Librn,* Agnes Andres; E-mail: aandres@newlothrop.k12.mi.us
Open Mon (Winter) 5-8, Tues-Thurs 8-5, Fri 8-3; Tues (Summer) 4-8, Wed & Thurs 10-6

BYRON COMMUNITY-BURNS TOWNSHIP GEORGE VINCE LIBRARY, 312 W Maple St, Byron, 48418, SAN 377-6042. Tel: 810-266-4620, Ext 445. FAX: 810-266-5010. E-mail: byroncommlib@yahoo.com. *Br Librn,* Karen Bowers
Partic in Mideastern Mich Libr Coop
Open Mon-Thurs (Winter) 3-8; Mon & Tues (Summer) 10-5, Wed 1-7
Friends of the Library Group

CROSWELL

P AITKIN MEMORIAL DISTRICT LIBRARY*, 111 N Howard Ave, 48422-1225. SAN 307-9651. Tel: 810-679-3627. FAX: 810-679-3392. E-mail: aitkinlibrary@sbcglobal.net. Web Site: www.croswell-library.com. *Dir,* Jennifer Walters; Staff 4 (MLS 1, Non-MLS 3)
Founded 1911. Pop 7,333; Circ 39,000
Library Holdings: Bk Vols 39,396; Per Subs 77
Automation Activity & Vendor Info: (Circulation) Follett Software
Wireless access
Function: Bks on cassette, Bks on CD, Children's prog, Computer training, Computers for patron use, Copy machines, Handicapped accessible, Homebound delivery serv, ILL available, Magnifiers for reading, Photocopying/Printing, Prog for adults, Prog for children & young adult, Pub access computers, Ref serv available, Story hour, Summer reading prog, Tax forms, Teen prog, VHS videos, Video lending libr, Web-catalog, Wheelchair accessible, Workshops
Partic in White Pine Libr Coop
Open Mon-Thurs 10-7, Fri 10-5, Sat 10-2
Friends of the Library Group

CRYSTAL FALLS

P CRYSTAL FALLS DISTRICT COMMUNITY LIBRARY*, 237 Superior Ave, 49920-1331. SAN 307-966X. Tel: 906-875-3344. FAX: 906-874-0077. E-mail: cflib@uproc.lib.mi.us. Web Site: www.uproc.lib.mi.us/CrystalFalls. *Dir,* Mary J Thoreson
Founded 1955. Pop 32,224
Automation Activity & Vendor Info: (Cataloging) SirsiDynix; (Circulation) SirsiDynix
Wireless access
Partic in Superiorland Library Cooperative
Open Mon-Thurs 9-7, Fri 9-4, Sat 9-1

DAVISBURG

P SPRINGFIELD TOWNSHIP LIBRARY*, 12000 Davisburg Rd, 48350. SAN 307-9678. Tel: 248-846-6550. FAX: 248-846-6555. Web Site: springfield.lib.mi.us. *Dir,* Catherine Phillips Forst; E-mail: cforst@tln.lib.mi.us; *Head, Tech Serv,* Kathryn Kraepel; *Circ Supvr,* Gretchen Mayville; Staff 5 (MLS 1, Non-MLS 4)
Founded 1976. Pop 13,338
Jan 2006-Dec 2006 Income $315,000. Mats Exp $35,000. Sal $235,000
Library Holdings: Bk Vols 40,000; Per Subs 105
Automation Activity & Vendor Info: (Acquisitions) SirsiDynix; (Cataloging) SirsiDynix; (Circulation) SirsiDynix; (OPAC) SirsiDynix; (Serials) SirsiDynix
Database Vendor: SirsiDynix
Partic in The Library Network
Open Mon, Tues & Thurs 10-8, Wed 12-8, Fri 10-6, Sat 10-4
Friends of the Library Group

DEARBORN

S DEARBORN HISTORICAL MUSEUM LIBRARY*, McFadden-Ross House, 915 Brady St, 48126. SAN 307-9708. Tel: 313-565-3000. FAX: 313-565-4848. Web Site: www.cityofdearborn.org. *Curator,* Kirt Gross; E-mail: kgross@ci.dearborn.mi.us; Staff 5 (MLS 2, Non-MLS 3)
Founded 1950
Library Holdings: Bk Titles 1,172; Bk Vols 2,556; Per Subs 10
Special Collections: Local Historical Records & Manuscripts
Publications: Dearborn Historian
Restriction: Open by appt only, Open to pub for ref only

P DEARBORN PUBLIC LIBRARY, Henry Ford Centennial Library, 16301 Michigan Ave, 48126. SAN 346-1289. Tel: 313-943-2330. Administration Tel: 313-943-2037. FAX: 313-943-2853. Administration FAX: 313-943-3063. TDD: 313-943-2193. E-mail: library@ci.dearborn.mi.us. Web Site: www.dearbornlibrary.org. *Dir of Libr,* Maryanne Bartles; *Dep Dir,* Julie Schaefer; *Admin Librn,* Steve Smith; *Br Serv Supvr,* James Knapp; Staff 29 (MLS 15, Non-MLS 14)
Founded 1919. Pop 98,153; Circ 874,771
Library Holdings: CDs 15,773; DVDs 25,949; Large Print Bks 2,731; Bk Vols 94,690; Talking Bks 6,141; Videos 6,060
Special Collections: City of Dearborn Coll; Ford Coll
Automation Activity & Vendor Info: (Acquisitions) SirsiDynix; (Cataloging) SirsiDynix; (Circulation) SirsiDynix; (OPAC) SirsiDynix
Database Vendor: ALLDATA Online, Booksite, Gale Cengage Learning, infoUSA, OCLC FirstSearch, ProQuest, SirsiDynix, Wilson - Wilson Web
Wireless access
Open Mon-Thurs 9:30-8:30, Fri & Sat 9:30-5:30, Sun (Sept-May) 1-5
Friends of the Library Group
Branches: 2
BRYANT BRANCH LIBRARY, 22100 Michigan Ave, 48124, SAN 346-1319. Tel: 313-943-4091. FAX: 313-943-3099. TDD: 313-943-2335.
Library Holdings: Bk Vols 29,430
Open Mon & Tues 12:30-8:30, Wed 10:30-5:30, Thurs 12:30-5:30, Fri (June-Aug) 12:30-5:30, Sat (Sept-May) 12:30-5:30
Friends of the Library Group
ESPER BRANCH LIBRARY, 12929 W Warren, 48126, SAN 346-1343. Tel: 313-943-4096. FAX: 313-943-4097. TDD: 313-943-2814.
Library Holdings: Bk Vols 26,486
Open Mon & Tues 12:30-8:30, Wed 10:30-5:30, Thurs 12:30-5:30, Fri (June-Aug) 12:30-5:30, Sat (Sept-May) 12:30-5:30
Friends of the Library Group

S THE HENRY FORD*, Benson Ford Research Center, 20900 Oakwood Blvd, 48121. (Mail add: PO Box 1970, 48121-1970), SAN 307-9716. Tel: 313-982-6020. FAX: 313-982-6244. Web Site: www.thehenryford.org. *Dir,* Marilyn Zoidis; E-mail: marilynz@thehenryford.org; *Mgr, Llbr & Archives,* Nardina Mein; E-mail: nardinam@thehenryford.org; *Head, Access Serv,* Kathy Steiner, Tel: 313-982-6100, Ext 2285, E-mail: kathys@thehenryford.org; *Head, Tech Serv,* Linda Choo; Tel: 313-982-6100, Ext 2509, E-mail: lindach@thehenryford.org; *Ref Librn,* Linda Skolarus; Tel: 313-982-6057, E-mail: lindas@thehenryford.org; *Archivist,* Rebecca Bizonet; Tel: 313-982-6100, Ext 2284, E-mail: rebeccab@thehenryford.org; *Archivist,* Terry Hoover; Tel: 313-982-6087, E-mail: terryh@thehenryford.org; *Archivist,* Peter Kalinski; Tel: 313-982-6100, Ext 2538, E-mail: peterk@thehenryford.org; Staff 11 (MLS 8, Non-MLS 3)
Founded 1929
Library Holdings: Bk Vols 45,000; Per Subs 200; Videos 380
Special Collections: Dave Friedman Racing Photogs; Detroit Publishing Company, archives, photogs; Edison Recording Artists; Ephemera Coll, trade lit; Fire Insurance Maps; Ford Motor Company Records; Gebelein Silversmiths; Henry & Clara Ford Papers; Henry Austin Clark Coll; HJ Heinz Co Records; Images Ford Motor Company; Industrial Design Coll; John Burroughs Papers; Stickley Furniture Co Records
Subject Interests: Hist, Mat culture
Automation Activity & Vendor Info: (Cataloging) Horizon; (Circulation) Horizon; (ILL) OCLC WorldShare Interlibrary Loan; (OPAC) Horizon
Wireless access
Partic in Detroit Area Library Network; Midwest Collaborative for Library Services (MCLS); OCLC Online Computer Library Center, Inc; The Library Network
Open Tues-Fri 9:30-5
Restriction: Circulates for staff only, Closed stack

J HENRY FORD COMMUNITY COLLEGE*, Eshleman Library, 5101 Evergreen Rd, 48128-1495. SAN 307-9724. Tel: 313-845-6375. Reference Tel: 313-845-6377. Information Services Tel: 313-845-9606. FAX: 313-845-9795. Web Site: clara.hfcc.edu. *Dir,* Barbara Lukasiewicz; Tel: 313-845-6379, E-mail: bluka@hfcc.edu; *Circ Mgr,* Terrence Potvin; Tel: 313-845-9760, E-mail: tpotvin@hfcc.edu; *Acq,* Janet Schneider; Tel: 313-845-9764, E-mail: jmschneider@hfcc.edu; *Cat,* Nancy Widman; Tel: 313-845-9786, E-mail: nwidman@hfcc.edu; *Govt Doc,* Vicki Morris; Tel: 313-845-9761, E-mail: vmorris@hfcc.edu; *Ref Serv,* Kathleen Cunningham; Tel: 313-845-9763, E-mail: kcunning@hfcc.edu; *Ref Serv,* Patricia Doline; Tel: 313-845-9762, E-mail: pdoline@hfcc.edu; *Ser,* Joann Billings; Tel: 313-845-6371, E-mail: jbillings@hfcc.edu; *Syst Adminr,* Daniel Harrison; Tel: 313-845-6376, E-mail: dharrisn@hfcc.edu; Staff 7 (MLS 7)
Founded 1938. Enrl 12,525; Fac 216; Highest Degree: Associate
Library Holdings: Bk Titles 67,510; Bk Vols 130,000; Per Subs 590
Subject Interests: Law, Nursing, Performing arts
Automation Activity & Vendor Info: (Acquisitions) Innovative Interfaces, Inc
Database Vendor: SirsiDynix
Open Mon-Thurs (Fall & Winter) 7:30am-9pm, Fri 7:30-4:30, Sat 9-5; Mon-Thurs (Spring & Summer) 7:30am-9pm

M OAKWOOD HOSPITAL MEDICAL LIBRARY*, Ernest & Kellie Sorini Medical Library, 18101 Oakwood Blvd, 48124-2500. SAN 307-9732. Tel: 313-593-7685. E-mail: medlibrary@oakwood.org. Web Site: www.oakwood.org/medical-library. *Librn,* Diane E LeBar; Tel: 313-593-8652, E-mail: diane.lebar@oakwood.org; *Mgr,* Valerie Reid; Tel: 313-593-7692, E-mail: valerie.reid@oakwood.org; *ILL,* Sally J Castillo; Tel: 313-593-7687, E-mail: sally.castillo@oakwood.org; *Pub Serv,* Kim Kelly; E-mail: kimberly.kelly@oakwood.org; Staff 4 (MLS 2, Non-MLS 2)
Founded 1953
Library Holdings: AV Mats 500; CDs 200; DVDs 100; e-books 275; e-journals 6,000; Bk Titles 5,500; Bk Vols 12,000; Per Subs 400
Special Collections: Bereavement Coll, bks, booklets; Complementary & Alternative Medicine Coll; Consumer Health Coll, AV mats, bks, online info; Management & Leadership Coll, AV, bks; National Alliance on Mental Illness Local Coll, AV mats, bks; Transcultural Resources Coll, AV mat, bks, govt doc, journals, teaching tools
Subject Interests: Clinical med, Health sci, Hospital admin, Nursing
Automation Activity & Vendor Info: (Cataloging) EOS International; (Circulation) EOS International; (OPAC) EOS International; (Serials) EOS International
Database Vendor: EBSCOhost, Elsevier, EOS International, LearningExpress, Lexi-Comp, Medline, Micromedex, Newsbank, OCLC ArticleFirst, OCLC FirstSearch, OCLC WorldShare Interlibrary Loan, OVID Technologies, PubMed, ScienceDirect, STAT!Ref (Teton Data Systems), UpToDate, Wilson - Wilson Web
Partic in Metrop Detroit Med Libr Group; Michigan Health Sciences Libraries Association; Midwest Collaborative for Library Services (MCLS)
Open Mon-Fri 7:30-5
Restriction: Badge access after hrs

C UNIVERSITY OF MICHIGAN-DEARBORN*, Mardigian Library, 4901 Evergreen Rd, 48128-2406. SAN 307-9759. Tel: 313-593-5445. Circulation Tel: 313-593-5598. Interlibrary Loan Service Tel: 313-593-3284. Reference Tel: 313-593-5563. Automation Services Tel: 313-593-5615. Information Services Tel: 313-593-5400. FAX: 313-593-5478. Reference FAX: 313-593-5561. Web Site: library.umd.umich.edu. *Dir,* Elaine M Logan; E-mail: loganem@umich.edu; *Assoc Dir,* Barbara Kriigel; Tel: 313-593-5614, E-mail: bkriigel@umich.edu; *Assoc Dir, Grad Prog, Res & Scholarly Publ,* Dr M Robert Fraser; Tel: 313-593-3740, E-mail: rfraser@umich.edu; *Head, Tech Serv, Librn,* Beth Taylor; Tel: 313-593-5402, E-mail: bjtaylor@umich.edu; *Archivist, Librn,* Karen Morgan; Tel: 313-593-5618, E-mail: kmissy@umich.edu; *Cat, Sr Assoc Librn,* Barbara Bolek; Tel: 313-593-5401, E-mail: bbolek@umich.edu; *Sr Assoc Librn,* Teague Orblych; Tel: 313-593-5562, E-mail: mtorblyc@umich.edu; *Sr Assoc Librn,* Joel Seewald; Tel: 313-583-6326, E-mail: seewaldj@umich.edu; *Assoc Librn, ILL Librn,* Lavada Smith; E-mail: lavadas@umich.edu; *Assoc Librn, Syst Coordr,* Julia Daniel Walkuski; E-mail: jcdaniel@umich.edu. Subject Specialists: *Gender studies, Lang, Lit,* Karen Morgan; *Soc sci,* Teague Orblych; *Eng, Sci, Tech,* Joel Seewald; Staff 25 (MLS 12, Non-MLS 13)
Founded 1959
Jul 2012-Jun 2013 Income $2,498,755. Mats Exp $307,566, Books $154,126, Per/Ser (Incl. Access Fees) $121,000, AV Mat $4,914, Electronic Ref Mat (Incl. Access Fees) $25,023, Presv $2,503. Sal $1,358,555 (Prof $753,679)
Library Holdings: AV Mats 4,148; e-books 352,282; e-journals 66,264; Microforms 544,495; Bk Titles 265,531; Bk Vols 300,501; Per Subs 350; Videos 3,397
Special Collections: Juvenile Historic Coll; Voice/Vision Holocaust Survivor Oral History Archive
Automation Activity & Vendor Info: (Acquisitions) Innovative Interfaces, Inc; (Cataloging) Innovative Interfaces, Inc; (Circulation) Innovative Interfaces, Inc; (Course Reserve) Innovative Interfaces, Inc; (ILL) OCLC ILLiad; (Media Booking) Innovative Interfaces, Inc; (OPAC) Innovative Interfaces, Inc; (Serials) Innovative Interfaces, Inc
Database Vendor: Alexander Street Press, ebrary, EBSCOhost, Gale Cengage Learning, JSTOR, OCLC FirstSearch, ProQuest, Sage, ScienceDirect, Springer-Verlag, Swets Information Services, Wiley
Wireless access
Publications: Occasional Bibliographic Series

Partic in OCLC Online Computer Library Center, Inc
Open Mon-Thurs (Fall & Winter) 8am-11:45pm, Fri 8-8, Sat 10-6, Sun Noon-11:45 (Noon-6 Summer)

DEARBORN HEIGHTS

DEARBORN HEIGHTS CITY LIBRARIES

P CAROLINE KENNEDY LIBRARY*, 24590 George St, 48127, SAN 307-9767. Tel: 313-791-3800. Administration Tel: 313-791-3804. FAX: 313-791-3801. *Dir, Libr Serv,* Michael McCaffery; E-mail: mmccaffery@ci.dearborn-heights.mi.us; *Supv Librn,* Mary Howard; Tel: 313-791-3824, E-mail: mhoward@ci.dearborn-heights.mi.us; *Head, Circ,* Emily Kleszcz; Tel: 313-791-3805, E-mail: ekleszcz@ci.dearborn-heights.mi.us; Staff 5 (MLS 5)
Founded 1961. Pop 59,600; Circ 83,092
Library Holdings: Bk Vols 59,000; Per Subs 120
Automation Activity & Vendor Info: (Cataloging) SirsiDynix; (Circulation) SirsiDynix; (OPAC) SirsiDynix
Partic in The Library Network
Open Mon-Thurs 10-9, Fri & Sat 10-5, Sun 12-5
Friends of the Library Group

P JOHN F KENNEDY JR LIBRARY*, 24602 Van Born Rd, 48125, SAN 307-9775. Tel: 313-791-6050. FAX: 313-791-6051. *Supv Librn,* Michael Wrona; Tel: 313-791-6053, E-mail: mwrona@ci.dearborn-heights.mi.us; *Head, Circ,* Janelle Martin; Tel: 313-791-6055, E-mail: jmartin@ci.dearborn-heights.mi.us; Staff 6.5 (MLS 1.5, Non-MLS 5)
Pop 59,600
Library Holdings: Bk Vols 55,000; Per Subs 120
Automation Activity & Vendor Info: (Cataloging) SirsiDynix; (Circulation) SirsiDynix; (OPAC) SirsiDynix
Open Mon-Thurs 12-8, Sat & Sun 12-5
Friends of the Library Group

DECATUR

P VAN BUREN DISTRICT LIBRARY*, Webster Memorial Library, 200 N Phelps St, 49045-1086. SAN 346-1491. Tel: 269-423-4771. FAX: 269-423-8373. Web Site: vbdl.org. *Dir,* Ryan S Wieber; E-mail: rwieber@vbdl.org; *Asst Dir, Tech Coordr,* Debby Stassek; E-mail: dstassek@vbdl.org; *Genealogy Librn, Local Hist Librn,* Toni Benson; E-mail: tbenson@vbdl.org; *Bus Mgr,* Molly Wunderlich; E-mail: mwunder@vbdl.org; *Br Serv Coordr,* Matt Weston; E-mail: mweston@vbdl.org; *Ch Serv,* Emily Burns; E-mail: eburns@vbdl.org; *ILL,* Janet Abshagen; Staff 41 (MLS 3, Non-MLS 38)
Founded 1941. Pop 44,711; Circ 266,136
Library Holdings: AV Mats 7,290; e-books 11,000; Large Print Bks 4,404; Bk Vols 154,169; Per Subs 303; Talking Bks 4,719
Subject Interests: Civil War, Genealogy, Mich
Automation Activity & Vendor Info: (Cataloging) TLC (The Library Corporation); (Circulation) TLC (The Library Corporation)
Database Vendor: Gale Cengage Learning, OCLC FirstSearch, TLC (The Library Corporation)
Wireless access
Function: Wheelchair accessible
Mem of Woodlands Library Cooperative
Open Mon-Thurs (Winter) 9-8, Fri 9-5, Sat 9-3; Mon-Thurs (Summer) 9-7, Fri 9-5, Sat 9-3
Friends of the Library Group
Branches: 6

ANTWERP SUNSHINE BRANCH, 24823 Front Ave, Mattawan, 49071, SAN 346-167X. Tel: 269-668-2534. FAX: 269-668-2534. *Librn,* Kay McAdams; E-mail: kmcadam@vbdl.org
Open Mon-Wed 10-7, Thurs & Fri 10-5, Sat 10-4
Friends of the Library Group

BANGOR BRANCH, 420 Division St, Bangor, 49013-1112, SAN 346-1521. Tel: 269-427-8810. FAX: 269-427-8810. *Librn,* Bobbi Martindale; E-mail: bmartindale@vbdl.org
Open Mon & Wed 9-7, Tues 12-5, Fri 9-6, Sat 9-2
Friends of the Library Group

BLOOMINGDALE BRANCH, 109 E Kalamazoo St, Bloomingdale, 49026. (Mail add: PO Box 218, Bloomingdale, 49026-0218), SAN 346-1556. Tel: 269-521-7601. FAX: 269-521-7601. *Librn,* Marianne Sipka; E-mail: asipka@vbdl.org
Open Mon, Thurs & Fri 10-5, Wed 10-8, Sat 10-3

COVERT BRANCH, 33680 M-140 Hwy, Covert, 49043. (Mail add: PO Box 7, Covert, 49043-0007), SAN 346-1580. Tel: 269-764-1298. FAX: 269-764-1298. *Br Librn,* Lois Brigham; E-mail: lbrigham@vbdl.org
Open Mon & Tues 10-7, Thurs 10-6, Fri 10-5, Sat 10-3

GOBLES BRANCH, 105 E Main St, Gobles, 49055. (Mail add: PO Box 247, Gobles, 49055-0247), SAN 346-1610. Tel: 269-628-4537. FAX: 269-628-4537. *Librn,* Shirley Whitt; E-mail: swhitt@vbdl.org
Open Mon & Fri 10-6, Tues 1 6, Wed 10-7, Sat 10-5
Friends of the Library Group

LAWRENCE COMMUNITY, 212 N Paw Paw St, Lawrence, 49064. (Mail add: PO Box 186, Lawrence, 49064-0186), SAN 346-1645. Tel: 269-674-3200. FAX: 269-674-3200. *Librn,* Denise Campagna; E-mail: dcampagna@vbdl.org
Open Mon 10-8, Tues & Thurs 10-7, Fri 10-5, Sat 10-3
Friends of the Library Group

DECKERVILLE

P DECKERVILLE PUBLIC LIBRARY*, 3542 N Main St, 48427-9638. SAN 307-9783. Tel: 810-376-8015. FAX: 810-376-8593. E-mail: deckervillelibrary@yahoo.com. Web Site: www.deckervillelibrary.com. *Dir,* Amanda J Morningstar; *Web Serv,* Kathy Wedyke
Founded 1924. Pop 4,908; Circ 106,279
Library Holdings: Bk Titles 18,793; Per Subs 80
Special Collections: Census of Sanilac County Cemeteries - Evergreen, Marion Twp, Mt Zion, Rosbury & Tucker; History of Sanilac County 1834-1984; Michigan Census Bk, 1904; Michigan Pioneer & Historical Coll (1881-1912); Sanilac County Atlas, 1906; Sanilac County Portrait & Biographical Album, 1884 & 1984
Automation Activity & Vendor Info: (Cataloging) Follett Software; (Circulation) Follett Software
Wireless access
Partic in White Pine Libr Coop
Open Tues 10-6, Wed 3:30-7:30, Fri 10-5, Sat 9-12

DELTON

P DELTON DISTRICT LIBRARY*, 330 N Grove St, 49046. (Mail add: PO Box 155, 49046-0155), SAN 307-9791. Tel: 269-623-8040. FAX: 269-623-6740. E-mail: deltonlib@mei.net. Web Site: www.deltonlib.org. *Dir,* Cheryl Bower; Staff 7 (MLS 1, Non-MLS 6)
Founded 1974. Pop 13,000; Circ 70,000
Apr 2005-Mar 2006 Income $156,155, State $10,400. Mats Exp $21,340, Books $15,390, Per/Ser (Incl. Access Fees) $868, AV Mat $5,082. Sal $106,360 (Prof $38,086)
Library Holdings: High Interest/Low Vocabulary Bk Vols 100; Large Print Bks 655; Bk Titles 29,325; Per Subs 30; Talking Bks 1,536; Videos 2,112
Special Collections: Tractor Manuals
Automation Activity & Vendor Info: (Cataloging) AmLib Library Management System; (Circulation) AmLib Library Management System; (ILL) Auto-Graphics, Inc
Wireless access
Function: Adult bk club, Art exhibits, CD-ROM, Computer training, Copy machines, Digital talking bks, Fax serv, Genealogy discussion group, Handicapped accessible, ILL available, Mail & tel request accepted, Online searches, Outside serv via phone, mail, e-mail & web, Photocopying/Printing, Preschool outreach, Prog for adults, Prog for children & young adult, Spoken cassettes & CDs, Spoken cassettes & DVDs, Summer reading prog, Tax forms, Telephone ref, VHS videos, Video lending libr, Wheelchair accessible
Mem of Woodlands Library Cooperative
Open Mon, Wed & Fri 10-5, Tues & Thurs 10-8, Sat 9-1
Friends of the Library Group

DETOUR VILLAGE

P DETOUR AREA SCHOOL & PUBLIC LIBRARY*, 202 S Division St, 49725. (Mail add: PO Box 429, 49725-0429), SAN 307-9686. Tel: 906-297-2011. FAX: 906-297-3403. Web Site: www.eup.k12.mi.us/eup/site/default.asp. *Dir,* Carole Hiney; E-mail: chiney@eup.k12.mi.us
Pop 1,829; Circ 11,449
Library Holdings: Bk Vols 21,000; Per Subs 55
Automation Activity & Vendor Info: (Cataloging) Follett Software; (Circulation) Follett Software
Wireless access
Open Mon, Tues, Thurs & Fri (Winter) 8-3:30, Wed 8-3:30 & 6-8, Sat 10-2; Tues & Thurs (Summer) 8-4, Wed 6-8, Sat 10-2
Friends of the Library Group

DETROIT

L BODMAN PLC LAW LIBRARY*, Ford Field, 6th Flr, 1901 Saint Antoine St, 48226. SAN 372-2902. Tel: 313-259-7777. FAX: 313-393-7579. Web Site: www.bodmanllp.com. Staff 1 (MLS 1)
Founded 1927
Library Holdings: Bk Vols 10,000; Per Subs 15
Function: ILL available
Restriction: Staff use only

SR BUSHNELL CONGREGATIONAL CHURCH LIBRARY*, 15000 Southfield Rd, 48223. Tel: 313-272-3550.
Library Holdings: Bk Vols 200

L CHARFOOS & CHRISTENSEN LAW LIBRARY*, Hecker-Smiley Mansion, 5510 Woodward Ave, 48202. SAN 327-2125. Tel: 313-875-8080. Toll Free Tel: 800-247-5974. FAX: 313-875-8522, 313-875-9857. E-mail: lawyers1@c2law.com. Web Site: c2law.com. *Dir,* Position Currently Open; Staff 1 (Non-MLS 1)
Founded 1929
Library Holdings: Bk Vols 500
Subject Interests: Law, Med

CHILDREN'S HOSPITAL OF MICHIGAN
M PHYLLIS ANN COLBURN MEMORIAL FAMILY LIBRARY*, 3901 Beaubien Blvd, 5th Flr, 48201. Tel: 313-745-5653. FAX: 313-993-0148. E-mail: cmedical@dmc.org. *Librn,* Patricia Supnick; Tel: 313-745-5437, E-mail: psupnick@dmc.org
Library Holdings: AV Mats 100; Bk Titles 1,000
Open Mon-Fri 9:30-4
M MEDICAL LIBRARY*, 3901 Beaubien Blvd, 1st Flr, 48201, SAN 307-9899. Tel: 313-745-0252, 313-745-5322. Toll Free Tel: 888-362-2500. E-mail: cmedical@dmc.org. Web Site: www.childrensdmc.org. *Head Librn,* Cathy Eames; *Librn,* Misa Mi; E-mail: mmi@dmc.org
Library Holdings: Bk Vols 3,300; Per Subs 200
Subject Interests: Pediatrics
Automation Activity & Vendor Info: (Cataloging) SirsiDynix; (Circulation) SirsiDynix; (OPAC) SirsiDynix
Open Mon-Thurs 8-7, Fri 8-6, Sat 9-1

L CITY OF DETROIT*, Law Department Library, First National Bldg, 660 Woodward Ave, Ste 1650, 48226. SAN 307-9902. Tel: 313-224-4550, Ext 23150. FAX: 313-224-5505. *Librn,* Thomas R Killian; E-mail: killtr@law.ci.detroit.mi.us
Founded 1935
Library Holdings: Bk Vols 35,000; Per Subs 30
Subject Interests: Law, Mich
Restriction: Staff use only

L CLARK HILL PLC, Law Library, 500 Woodward Ave, Ste 3500, 48226-3435. SAN 326-3851. Tel: 313-965-8300, Ext 8277, 412-394-7711, Ext 2358. FAX: 313-965-8252. *Librn,* Kathleen A Gamache; E-mail: kgamache@clarkhill.com; *Librn,* Donna Kielar; Tel: 412-394-2358, Fax: 412-394-2555, E-mail: dkielar@clarkhill.com; Staff 2 (MLS 2)
Wireless access

C COLLEGE FOR CREATIVE STUDIES LIBRARY*, Manoogian Visual Resource Ctr, 301 Frederick Douglass Dr, 48202-4034. SAN 307-9880. Tel: 313-664-7642. Reference Tel: 313-664-7803. FAX: 313-664-7880. Web Site: www.collegeforcreativestudies.edu. *Dir,* Beth E Walker; Tel: 313-664-7641, E-mail: bwalker@collegeforcreativestudies.edu. Subject Specialists: *Art hist,* Beth E Walker; Staff 5 (MLS 3, Non-MLS 2)
Founded 1966. Enrl 1,220; Highest Degree: Bachelor
Library Holdings: AV Mats 880; Bk Titles 35,700; Bk Vols 40,000; Per Subs 250
Subject Interests: Animation, Applied arts, Fine arts, Graphic design, Photog
Database Vendor: EBSCOhost, Gale Cengage Learning, Innovative Interfaces, Inc, OVID Technologies, ProQuest, Wilson - Wilson Web
Partic in Midwest Collaborative for Library Services (MCLS)
Open Mon-Thurs 8:30am-10pm, Fri 8:30-4:30, Sat 10-5, Sun 1-7
Restriction: Open to pub for ref & circ; with some limitations

GM DEPARTMENT OF VETERANS AFFAIRS LIBRARY SERVICE*, John D Dingell VA Medical Center, 4646 John R St, 48201. SAN 307-8566. Tel: 313-576-1000, Ext 3380. FAX: 313-576-1048. *Dir,* Karen Tubolino; Tel: 313-576-1085, E-mail: karen.tubolino@med.va.gov; *Librn,* Mary Jo Durivage; Staff 2 (MLS 2)
Library Holdings: Bk Vols 5,000; Per Subs 250
Automation Activity & Vendor Info: (Cataloging) Horizon; (Circulation) Horizon; (OPAC) Horizon; (Serials) Horizon
Database Vendor: EBSCOhost, OCLC FirstSearch
Partic in Detroit Area Library Network
Open Mon-Fri 7:30-5

S DETROIT GARDEN CENTER, INC LIBRARY*, 1900 E Jefferson Ave, Ste 227, 48207-1456. SAN 324-1017. Tel: 313-259-6363. FAX: 313-259-0107. E-mail: detroitgardenctr@yahoo.com. Web Site: www.detroitgardencenter.org. *Librn,* Beverly Donaldson
Library Holdings: Bk Titles 6,200
Subject Interests: Hort
Function: Photocopying/Printing, Telephone ref
Publications: Detroit Garden Center Bulletin
Open Tues-Thurs 9:30-4
Restriction: Circ to mem only, Non-circulating to the pub, Open to pub for ref only

S DETROIT HEALTH DEPARTMENT LIBRARY*, 1151 Taylor St, Rm 243-B, 48202. Tel: 313-876-4096. FAX: 313-871-9437. Web Site: www.dethealth.org/index.php?id=0. *Librn,* Nancy Rusin; E-mail: rusinn@health.ci.detroit.mi.us
Library Holdings: Bk Vols 700; Per Subs 31
Restriction: Staff use only

S DETROIT INSTITUTE OF ARTS*, Research Library & Archives, 5200 Woodward Ave, 48202. SAN 308-0005. Tel: 313-833-3460. Administration Tel: 313-833-7929. FAX: 313-833-6405. Web Site: www.dia.org/research/research_library/index.asp. *Dept Head,* Maria Ketcham; E-mail: mketcham@dia.org; Staff 5 (MLS 1, Non-MLS 4)
Founded 1905
Library Holdings: Bk Vols 180,000; Per Subs 200
Special Collections: Albert Kahn Architecture Library; Grace Whitney Hoff Coll, fine bindings; Puppetry (Paul McPharlin Coll)
Subject Interests: Art, Art hist, Conserv, Decorative art, Films & filmmaking, Furniture, Paintings, Sculpture
Automation Activity & Vendor Info: (Cataloging) OCLC Connexion; (OPAC) Horizon
Partic in Detroit Area Library Network; Midwest Collaborative for Library Services (MCLS); OCLC Online Computer Library Center, Inc
Restriction: Open by appt only

S THE DETROIT NEWS, INC*, George B Catlin Memorial Library, 615 W Lafayette Blvd, 48226. SAN 308-0072. Tel: 313-222-2090. FAX: 313-496-5255. Web Site: www.detroitnews.com. *Mgr, Digital Assets,* Danielle Kaltz; E-mail: dkaltz@detroitnews.com; Staff 1 (MLS 1)
Founded 1918
Library Holdings: Bk Vols 15,000
Special Collections: Detroit News 1873-present, micro, clips & digital photos
Subject Interests: Local hist
Restriction: By permission only, Staff use only

P DETROIT PUBLIC LIBRARY, 5201 Woodward Ave, 48202. SAN 346-1769. Tel: 313-481 1300. Circulation Tel: 313-481-1378. Interlibrary Loan Service Tel: 313-481-1376. Reference Tel: 313-481-1367. Administration Tel: 313-481-1302. FAX: 313-481-1477. Interlibrary Loan Service FAX: 313-481-1484. Web Site: www.detroitpubliclibrary.org. *Exec Dir,* Jo Anne Mondowney; E-mail: dir@detroitpubliclibrary.org; Staff 339 (MLS 94, Non-MLS 245)
Founded 1865. Pop 713,777
Jul 2013-Jun 2014 Income (Main Library and Branch(s)) $33,309,305. Mats Exp $1,087,309
Special Collections: Burton Historical Coll (Genealogy); E Azalia Hackley Coll (African Americans & Africans in the performing arts); Ernie Harwell Sports Coll; National Automotive History Coll (History of automobile). Municipal Document Depository
Subject Interests: Archit, Art, Bus & mgt, Econ, Ethnic studies, Hist, Maps, Music, Natural sci, Soc sci, Tech
Automation Activity & Vendor Info: (Cataloging) SirsiDynix; (Circulation) SirsiDynix; (OPAC) SirsiDynix
Database Vendor: Gale Cengage Learning, OCLC FirstSearch, SirsiDynix, Wilson - Wilson Web
Wireless access
Special Services for the Deaf - Staff with knowledge of sign lang; TTY equip
Special Services for the Blind - Assistive/Adapted tech devices, equip & products
Open Tues & Wed Noon-8, Thurs-Sat 10-6
Friends of the Library Group
Branches: 22
BOWEN, 3648 W Vernor, 48216-1441, SAN 346-1823. Tel: 313-481-1540. *Mgr,* Robbie Flowers; E-mail: rflowers@detroitpubliclibrary.org
Subject Interests: Spanish lang mat
Open Mon, Wed & Sat 10-6, Tues & Thurs 12-8
Friends of the Library Group
CAMPBELL BRANCH, 8733 W Vernor, 48209-1434. Tel: 313-481-1550.
Open Mon & Wed 12-8, Tues, Thurs & Sat 10-6
CHANDLER PARK, 12800 Harper Ave, 48213-1823, SAN 346-1912. Tel: 313-481-1560.
Open Wed & Fri 10-6, Thurs 12-8
Friends of the Library Group
CHANEY, 16101 Grand River, 48227-1821, SAN 346-1947. Tel: 313-481-1570.
Open Mon, Wed & Fri 10-6, Tues & Thurs 12-8
Friends of the Library Group
CHASE, 17731 W Seven Mile Rd, 48235-3050, SAN 346-1971. Tel: 313-481-1580.
Open Mon, Wed & Fri 10-6, Tues & Thurs 12-8
Friends of the Library Group

CONELY, 4600 Martin St, 48210-2343, SAN 346-2005. Tel: 313-481-1590.
Open Mon, Wed & Fri 10-6, Tues & Thurs 12-8
Friends of the Library Group

P DETROIT SUBREGIONAL LIBRARY FOR THE BLIND & PHYSICALLY HANDICAPPED, 3666 Grand River Ave, 48208-2880, SAN 346-1777. Tel: 313-481-1702. TDD: 313-833-5492.
Founded 1980
Subject Interests: Braille
Publications: In-Focus (Newsletter)
Special Services for the Deaf - TTY equip
Special Services for the Blind - Assistive/Adapted tech devices, equip & products; Audio mat; Bks & mags in Braille, on rec, tape & cassette; Bks on cassette; Bks on CD; Braille servs; Extensive large print coll; Large print bks; Ref serv
Open Mon-Fri 10-6
Friends of the Library Group

FREDERICK DOUGLASS BRANCH FOR SPECIALIZED SERVICES, 3666 Grand River, 48208-2880, SAN 346-203X. Tel: 313-481-1700.
Subject Interests: Children's bks
Open Mon-Fri 10-6
Friends of the Library Group

DUFFIELD, 2507 W Grand Blvd, 48208-1236, SAN 346-2099. Tel: 313-481-1710.
Open Mon, Wed & Sat 10-6, Tues & Thurs 12-8
Friends of the Library Group

EDISON, 18400 Joy Rd, 48228-3131, SAN 346-2129. Tel: 313-481-1720.
Open Mon & Wed 12-8, Tues, Thurs & Fri 10-6
Friends of the Library Group

ELMWOOD PARK, 550 Chene St, 48207, SAN 346-2153. Tel: 313-481-1730.
Open Mon, Wed & Fri 10-6, Tues & Thurs 12-8
Friends of the Library Group

FRANKLIN, 13651 E McNichols Rd, 48205-3457, SAN 346-2188. Tel: 313-481-1740.
Open Mon, Wed & Fri 10-6, Tues & Thurs 12-8
Friends of the Library Group

HUBBARD, 12929 W McNichols Rd, 48235-4106, SAN 346-2242. Tel: 313-481-1750.
Open Mon & Wed 12-8, Tues, Thurs & Sat 10-6
Friends of the Library Group

JEFFERSON, 12350 E Outer Dr, 48224, SAN 346-2277. Tel: 313-481-1760.
Open Mon & Wed 12-8, Tues, Thurs & Fri 10-6
Friends of the Library Group

KNAPP, 13330 Conant St, 48212, SAN 346-2307. Tel: 313-481-1770.
Open Mon & Wed 12-8, Tues, Thurs & Sat 10-6
Friends of the Library Group

LINCOLN, 1221 E Seven Mile Rd, 48203-2103, SAN 346-2331. Tel: 313-481-1780.
Open Mon 12-8, Tues 10-6
Friends of the Library Group

MONTEITH, 14100 Kercheval St, 48215-2810, SAN 346-2420. Tel: 313-481-1800.
Open Mon 12-8, Tues 10-6
Friends of the Library Group

PARKMAN, 1766 Oakman Blvd, 48238-2735, SAN 346-2455. Tel: 313-481-1810.
Open Mon & Wed 12-8, Tues, Thurs & Sat 10-6
Friends of the Library Group

REDFORD, 21200 Grand River/W McNichols, 48219-3851, SAN 346-248X. Tel: 313-481-1820.
Open Mon & Wed 12-8, Tues, Thurs & Sat 10-6
Friends of the Library Group

SHERWOOD FOREST, 7117 W Seven Mile Rd, 48221-2240, SAN 346-2544. Tel: 313-481-1840.
Open Mon, Wed & Fri 10-6, Tues & Thurs 12-8
Friends of the Library Group

SKILLMAN, 121 Gratiot Ave, 48226-2203, SAN 346-2064. Tel: 313-481-1850.
Special Collections: National Automotive History Coll
Open Mon-Fri 10-6
Friends of the Library Group

WILDER, 7140 E Seven Mile Rd, 48234-3065, SAN 346-2579. Tel: 313-481-1870.
Open Wed 12-8, Thurs & Sat 10-6
Friends of the Library Group
Bookmobiles: 1

S DETROIT SYMPHONY ORCHESTRA LIBRARY*, 3711 Woodward Ave, 48201. SAN 329-8876. Tel: 313-576-5100, 313-576-5172. FAX: 313-576-5593. Web Site: www.detroitsymphony.com. *Principal Librn,* Robert Stiles; E-mail: rstiles@dso.org; *Librn,* Ethan Allen; E-mail: eallen@dso.org
Library Holdings: Bk Vols 200
Special Collections: Rare Scores
Restriction: Not a lending libr

L DICKINSON WRIGHT PLLC LIBRARY*, 500 Woodward Ave, Ste 4000, 48226-3425. SAN 308-0048. Tel: 313-223-3500. FAX: 313-223-3598. Web Site: www.dickinson-wright.com. *Librn,* Mark A Heinrich; E-mail: mheinrich@dickinson-wright.com; *Tech Serv,* Carol M Darga; Staff 2 (MLS 2)
Founded 1878
Library Holdings: Bk Vols 25,000; Per Subs 4,000
Subject Interests: Law
Automation Activity & Vendor Info: (Cataloging) EOS International; (OPAC) EOS International; (Serials) EOS International
Database Vendor: Dun & Bradstreet, Fastcase, HeinOnline, OCLC ArticleFirst, OCLC WorldShare Interlibrary Loan, WestlaweCARSWELL
Wireless access
Publications: Current Awareness Bulletin; Library Guide; Research Guides (Bi-annually)
Partic in Dun & Bradstreet Info Servs; OCLC Online Computer Library Center, Inc; Westlaw
Restriction: Staff use only

S DOSSIN GREAT LAKES MUSEUM*, 100 Strand Dr on Belle Isle, 48207. SAN 327-0289. Tel: 313-852-4051. FAX: 313-833-5342. Web Site: www.detroithistorical.org. *Exec Dir,* Robert Bury; *Chief of Operations,* Michelle Wooddell
Founded 1960
Library Holdings: Bk Vols 1,000
Special Collections: Great Lakes Coll
Restriction: Open by appt only, Staff use only

L DYKEMA GOSSETT PLLC*, Law Library, 400 Renaissance Ctr, 38th Flr, 48243. SAN 308-0056. Tel: 313-568-6800. FAX: 313-568-6893. Web Site: www.dykema.com. *Libr Asst,* Sandra Suokas; Staff 8 (MLS 4, Non-MLS 4)
Founded 1929
Library Holdings: Bk Titles 2,945; Bk Vols 14,725; Per Subs 510
Subject Interests: Employment, Environ law, Labor, Law, Patents, Securities
Automation Activity & Vendor Info: (Acquisitions) EOS International; (Cataloging) EOS International; (Circulation) EOS International; (OPAC) EOS International; (Serials) EOS International
Database Vendor: Dialog, EBSCOhost, LexisNexis, OCLC FirstSearch
Wireless access
Mem of Reaching Across Illinois Library System (RAILS)
Partic in Midwest Collaborative for Library Services (MCLS); OCLC Online Computer Library Center, Inc
Restriction: Staff use only

SR ECUMENICAL THEOLOGICAL SEMINARY*, John E Biersdorf Library, 2930 Woodward Ave, 48201. SAN 371-1382. Tel: 313-831-5200, Ext 222. FAX: 313-831-1353. *Dir, Libr Serv,* Dianne Helene VanMarter; E-mail: dvanmarter@etseminary.edu; Staff 1 (MLS 1)
Founded 1997. Highest Degree: Doctorate
Library Holdings: Bk Titles 29,000; Bk Vols 32,000; Per Subs 76
Automation Activity & Vendor Info: (OPAC) Follett Software
Database Vendor: EBSCOhost, OCLC FirstSearch
Wireless access
Function: Res libr
Restriction: In-house use for visitors

M HENRY FORD HOSPITAL*, Sladen Library, 2799 W Grand Blvd, 48202. SAN 308-0080. Tel: 313-916-2550. FAX: 313-874-4730. Web Site: www.henryford.com/sladen. *Dir,* Gayle Williams; *Coll Develop,* Audrey Bondar; E-mail: abondar1@sladen.hfhs.org; Staff 8.4 (MLS 6.4, Non-MLS 2)
Founded 1915
Library Holdings: e-journals 1,773; Bk Vols 7,726; Per Subs 1,060
Special Collections: Archives of Henry Ford Health System; Medical History Coll
Subject Interests: Hospital admin, Med, Nursing
Automation Activity & Vendor Info: (Acquisitions) SirsiDynix; (Cataloging) SirsiDynix; (Circulation) SirsiDynix; (ILL) Relais International; (OPAC) SirsiDynix; (Serials) SirsiDynix
Database Vendor: Blackwell, Checkpoint Systems, Inc, Cinahl, Ex Libris Group, Majors, Micromedex, Nature Publishing Group, OCLC ArticleFirst, OCLC FirstSearch, OCLC WorldShare Interlibrary Loan, PubMed, ScienceDirect, SirsiDynix, Springer-Verlag, STAT!Ref (Teton Data Systems), Swets Information Services, UpToDate
Wireless access
Partic in Midwest Collaborative for Library Services (MCLS); OCLC Online Computer Library Center, Inc
Open Mon-Thurs 8:30am-9pm, Fri 8:30-5, Sat 9-1

GL RALPH M FREEMAN MEMORIAL LIBRARY FOR THE US COURTS*, 436 US Courthouse, 231 W Lafayette Blvd, 48226-2719. SAN 308-0420. Tel: 313-234-5255. FAX: 313-234-5383. *Satellite Librn,* Elise Keller; Staff 2 (MLS 1, Non-MLS 1)
Founded 1975
Subject Interests: Law
Partic in OCLC Online Computer Library Center, Inc

L HONIGMAN MILLER SCHWARTZ & COHN LLP*, Law Library, 2290 First National Bldg, 660 Woodward Ave, 48226-3583. SAN 321-8090. Tel: 313-465-7169. FAX: 313-465-8000. *Mgr,* Trish Webster; *Librn,* Kimberly Koscielniak; *Librn,* Patricia A McKanna; E-mail: tmckanna@honigman.com
Library Holdings: Bk Titles 8,000; Bk Vols 15,000; Per Subs 350
Restriction: Staff use only

C LEWIS COLLEGE OF BUSINESS*, Harris Learning Resource Center Library, 17370 Meyers Rd, 48235-1423. Tel: 313-862-6300, Ext 225. FAX: 313-862-1027. Web Site: www.lewiscollege.edu.
Founded 1928
Library Holdings: Bk Vols 7,000; Per Subs 79
Open Mon-Thurs 9-8:30, Fri & Sat 9-3

C MARYGROVE COLLEGE LIBRARY*, 8425 W McNichols Rd, 48221-2599. SAN 308-0188. Tel: 313-927-1300. Interlibrary Loan Service Tel: 313-927-1342. Reference Tel: 313-927-1346. Information Services Tel: 313-927-1355. FAX: 313-927-1366. Web Site: www.marygrove.edu. *Head of Ref & Instrul Serv, Head, Access Serv,* Linnea Dudley; Tel: 313-927-1349, E-mail: ldudley@marygrove.edu; *Head, Circ,* Dana Zurawski; E-mail: dpawloski@marygrove.edu; *IT Librn,* Crystal Agnew; Tel: 313-927-1340, E-mail: cagnew@marygrove.edu; *Coordr, Educ Tech, Online Serv Coordr,* Linda Brawner; E-mail: lbrawner@marygrove.edu; Staff 12 (MLS 7, Non-MLS 5)
Founded 1927. Enrl 5,600; Highest Degree: Master
Library Holdings: Bk Titles 82,350; Bk Vols 99,000; Per Subs 450
Database Vendor: Gale Cengage Learning, LexisNexis, OCLC FirstSearch, OCLC WorldShare Interlibrary Loan, OVID Technologies, ProQuest, Wilson - Wilson Web
Wireless access
Partic in Detroit Area Library Network; Midwest Collaborative for Library Services (MCLS); Southeastern Michigan League of Libraries

S MICHIGAN DEPARTMENT OF CORRECTIONS*, Mound Correctional Facility Library, 17601 Mound Rd, 48212. Tel: 313-368-8300, Ext 52327. FAX: 313-368-8972. *Librn,* Sharon Grossett; E-mail: grossetts@michigan.gov; Staff 1 (MLS 1)
Founded 1994
Library Holdings: Bk Vols 5,000; Per Subs 45
Open Mon & Fri Sun 7:30-4:30, Tues-Thurs 7:30am-9pm

L MILLER, CANFIELD, PADDOCK & STONE LIBRARY*, 150 W Jefferson, Ste 2500, 48226. SAN 327-0424. Tel: 313-963-6420. FAX: 313-496-8452. *Ref,* Penelope Damore; *Tech Serv,* Catherine Mulla
Library Holdings: Bk Vols 50,000; Per Subs 500
Subject Interests: Educ, Labor, Real estate, Securities

S PRICE WATERHOUSE COOPERS LLP*, Information Center, 1900 St Antione St, 48226. SAN 308-0293. Tel: 313-394-6000. FAX: 313-394-6010. *Info Spec,* John Monoco
Founded 1975
Library Holdings: Bk Titles 500; Per Subs 50
Subject Interests: Acctg, Taxes
Publications: Booklets on Tax, Accounting & Auditing
Partic in Dialog Corp; Westlaw

M REHABILITATION INSTITUTE OF MICHIGAN*, Learning Resources Center, 261 Mack Blvd, 48201-2417. SAN 308-0315. Tel: 313-745-9860. FAX: 313-745-9863. *Dir,* Daria Drobny; E-mail: ddrobny@dmc.org
Founded 1958
Library Holdings: Bk Titles 4,100; Per Subs 145
Subject Interests: Educ, Med, Phys therapy, Vocational educ

R SACRED HEART MAJOR SEMINARY*, Edmund Cardinal Szoka Library, 2701 Chicago Blvd, 48206. SAN 323-5793. Tel: 313-883-8650. Interlibrary Loan Service Tel: 313-883-8654. FAX: 313-868-8594. Web Site: www.shms.edu. *Dir,* Chris Spilker; Tel: 313-883-8651, E-mail: spilker.chris@shms.edu. Subject Specialists: *Theol,* Chris Spilker; Staff 6 (MLS 1, Non-MLS 5)
Founded 1921. Enrl 590; Fac 65; Highest Degree: Master
Library Holdings: Bk Titles 120,000; Bk Vols 122,800; Per Subs 500
Special Collections: Church History; Early Michigan (Gabriel Richard Coll), bks, mss
Subject Interests: Philos, Theol
Automation Activity & Vendor Info: (Cataloging) SirsiDynix; (Circulation) SirsiDynix; (OPAC) SirsiDynix; (Serials) SirsiDynix
Database Vendor: SirsiDynix
Publications: Accessions Lists; Brochure; Straight From the Heart (Newsletter)
Open Mon-Thurs 8:30am-10pm, Fri 8:30-7, Sat 12-5, Sun 2-10
Restriction: Circ limited

M SAINT JOHN HOSPITAL & MEDICAL CENTER LIBRARY*, 22101 Moross Rd, 48236. SAN 308-0358. Tel: 313-343-3733. FAX: 313-343-7598. *Dir,* Ellen O'Donnell; Staff 3 (MLS 1, Non-MLS 2)
Founded 1952
Library Holdings: Bk Titles 2,500; Per Subs 320
Subject Interests: Hospital admin, Med, Nursing

L THIRD JUDICIAL CIRCUIT COURT, WAYNE COUNTY*, Law Library, Two Woodward Ave, Ste 780, 48226-3461. SAN 308-0455. Tel: 313-224-5265. FAX: 313-967-3562. *Dep Librn,* Lynn Reeves
Library Holdings: Bk Vols 20,000
Partic in Mich Asn of Law Librs; Ohio Regional Asn of Law Librs

L THIRTY SIXTH DISTRICT COURT LAW LIBRARY*, 421 Madison Ave, 48226. SAN 372-0411. Tel: 313-965-2792. FAX: 313-965-4057. *Librn,* Theodosia Clemons
Library Holdings: Bk Vols 30,000; Per Subs 75
Wireless access

CR UNIVERSITY OF DETROIT MERCY LIBRARY*, McNichols Campus, 4001 W McNichols Rd, 48221-3038. SAN 346-3087. Tel: 313-993-1071. Circulation Tel: 313-993-1795. Interlibrary Loan Service Tel: 313-993-1072. Administration Tel: 313-993-1090. FAX: 313-993-1780. E-mail: refdesk@udmercy.edu. Web Site: research.udmercy.edu. *Dean, Univ Librs & Instrul Tech,* Margaret E Auer; E-mail: auerme@udmercy.edu; *Assoc Dean, Instrul Tech,* Russell Davidson, III; Tel: 313-578-0579, E-mail: davidsor@udmercy.edu; *Assoc Dean, Pub Serv,* George H Libbey; Tel: 313-993 1078, E-mail: libbeygh@udmercy.edu; *Assoc Dean, Tech Serv & Libr Syst,* Sara J K Martin; Tel: 313-993-1074, E-mail: martinsjk@udmercy.edu; *Head, Cat & Database Mgt,* Position Currently Open; *Head, Circ,* Betty Nelson; E-mail: nelsonbj@udmercy.edu; *Head, ILL,* Sandra Wilson; E-mail: wilsonsh@udmercy.edu; *Head, Ref,* Susan Homant; Tel: 313-578-0577, E-mail: homantsj@udmercy.edu; *Archives & Spec Coll Librn,* Patricia Higo; Tel: 313-578-0435, E-mail: higopa@udmercy.edu; *Syst Adminr,* Nathan Siva; Tel: 313-993-1794, E-mail: nanthasi@udmercy.edu; *Govt Doc,* Kris McLonis; Tel: 313-578-0457, E-mail: mclonika@udmercy.edu; Staff 28 (MLS 14, Non-MLS 14)
Founded 1877. Enrl 5,231; Fac 654; Highest Degree: Doctorate
Jul 2012-Jun 2013 Income (Main Library Only) $3,448,200, Locally Generated Income $16,837, Parent Institution $3,409,178, Other $22,185. Mats Exp $968,319, Books $145,724, Per/Ser (Incl. Access Fees) $798,526, AV Mat $8,797, Electronic Ref Mat (Incl. Access Fees) $11,329, Presv $3,943. Sal $1,630,477 (Prof $1,140,259)
Library Holdings: Audiobooks 441; AV Mats 2,940; CDs 2,734; DVDs 4,328; e-books 114,417; e-journals 41,952; Microforms 10,833; Bk Titles 378,666; Per Subs 200
Special Collections: Black Abolitionist Archives, digital; Carney Latin American Solidarity Archive, print; Celebrating Scholarly Achievement Coll, digital; Dichotomy: School of Architecture Student Journal, digital; Dudley Randall Broadside Press Coll, print; Father Charles E Coughlin Coll, digital; Father Edward J Dowling Marine Historical Coll, digital, print; Lawrence DeVine Playbill Coll, print; Marie Corelli Coll, print; Maurice Greenia Jr Coll, digital; Sisters of Mercy Coll, digital; Society of Jesus Publs, print; Student Arts Journal, digital; Theses, digital, print; University Archives, AV mats, publs, rec; University Commencement Coll; University Honors Coll, digital; University of Detroit Football Coll, digital; University of Detroit Yearbook Coll, digital; William Kienzle Manuscripts, print. US Document Depository
Subject Interests: Archit, Philos, Theol
Automation Activity & Vendor Info: (Acquisitions) SirsiDynix; (Cataloging) SirsiDynix; (Circulation) SirsiDynix; (Course Reserve) SirsiDynix; (ILL) OCLC; (OPAC) SirsiDynix; (Serials) SirsiDynix
Database Vendor: ACM (Association for Computing Machinery), Alexander Street Press, American Chemical Society, American Mathematical Society, American Psychological Association (APA), Annual Reviews, ARTstor, ASCE Research Library, Blackwell, Cambridge Scientific Abstracts, Children's Literature Comprehensive Database Company (CLCD), ebrary, EBSCOhost, Elsevier, Emerald, Faulkner Information Services, Gale Cengage Learning, H W Wilson, infoUSA, JSTOR, LexisNexis, Modern Language Association, Newsbank, OCLC FirstSearch, OCLC WorldShare Interlibrary Loan, OVID Technologies, Oxford Online, Project MUSE, ProQuest, PubMed, ReferenceUSA, RefWorks, Sage, ScienceDirect, Springshare, LLC, Standard & Poor's, Westlaw, Wiley, Wiley InterScience, Wilson - Wilson Web
Wireless access

Function: Archival coll, Bks on CD, Computers for patron use, Copy machines, Distance learning, Doc delivery serv, e-mail & chat, Electronic databases & coll, Exhibits, Free DVD rentals, Handicapped accessible, ILL available, Online cat, Online info literacy tutorials on the web & in blackboard, Online ref, Orientations, Photocopying/Printing, Ref & res, Ref serv available, Ref serv in person, Scanner, Telephone ref, Wheelchair accessible
Publications: User Guide
Partic in Association of Jesuit Colleges & Universities (AJCU); Detroit Area Consortium of Catholic Colleges; Midwest Collaborative for Library Services (MCLS)
Open Mon-Thurs 8am-10pm, Fri 8-5:30, Sat 9-5, Sun 12:30-7
Restriction: Access for corporate affiliates

Departmental Libraries:

CL KRESGE LAW LIBRARY, 651 E Jefferson, 48226, SAN 346-3206. Tel: 313-596-0239. Circulation Tel: 313-596-0241. Reference Tel: 313-596-0244. FAX: 313-596-0245. E-mail: lawlibrary@udmercy.edu. Web Site: www.law.udmercy.edu/lawlibrary. *Dir,* Patrick Meyer; E-mail: meyerpi@udmercy.edu; *Head, Tech Serv,* Latha Rangarajan; E-mail: rangarl@udmercy.edu; *Govt Doc, Ref Librn,* Gene P Moy; E-mail: moyg@udmercy.edu; *Syst Coordr,* Sally Moy; E-mail: sally@udmercy.edu; Staff 7 (MLS 4, Non-MLS 3)
Founded 1912. Enrl 410; Fac 25; Highest Degree: Doctorate
Library Holdings: Bk Titles 42,762; Bk Vols 346,972; Per Subs 1,500; Videos 45
Special Collections: US Document Depository
Subject Interests: Labor, Taxes
Automation Activity & Vendor Info: (Acquisitions) Innovative Interfaces, Inc; (Cataloging) OCLC; (Circulation) Innovative Interfaces, Inc; (Course Reserve) Innovative Interfaces, Inc; (ILL) OCLC; (OPAC) Innovative Interfaces, Inc; (Serials) Innovative Interfaces, Inc
Database Vendor: Dialog, Gale Cengage Learning, JSTOR, LexisNexis, OCLC FirstSearch, OCLC WorldShare Interlibrary Loan, Westlaw, Wilson - Wilson Web
Function: AV serv, For res purposes, Govt ref serv
Partic in Detroit Area Library Network; Dialog Corp; Midwest Collaborative for Library Services (MCLS); OCLC Online Computer Library Center, Inc; Southeastern Michigan League of Libraries
Publications: Acquisitions List (Monthly); Library Handbook (Bi-annually)
Open Mon-Thurs (Winter) 8am-9:50pm, Fri 8-5:50, Sat & Sun 10-5:50; Mon-Fri (Summer) 8-5:50
Restriction: Open to fac, students & qualified researchers

SCHOOL OF DENTISTRY, CORKTOWN CAMPUS, 2700 Martin Luther King Jr Blvd, 48208-2576. Tel: 313-494-6900. Interlibrary Loan Service Tel: 313-494-6901. Administration Tel: 313-494-6905. FAX: 313-494-6838. *Dir,* Marilyn Dow; Staff 5 (MLS 3, Non-MLS 2)
Founded 1877. Enrl 5,231; Fac 654; Highest Degree: Doctorate
Jul 2012-Jun 2013 Income $433,870, Locally Generated Income $213, Parent Institution $433,657. Mats Exp $108,350, Books $10,433, Per/Ser (Incl. Access Fees) $63,485, Electronic Ref Mat (Incl. Access Fees) $33,730, Presv $702. Sal $186,741 (Prof $133,289)
Library Holdings: AV Mats 1,175; CDs 193; DVDs 78; e-books 100,162; e-journals 41,449; Bk Titles 14,813; Per Subs 103
Special Collections: Antique Dental Instruments & Equipment Coll
Subject Interests: Dentistry
Automation Activity & Vendor Info: (OPAC) Horizon
Database Vendor: EBSCOhost, Haworth Pres Inc, Medline, YBP Library Services
Partic in Metrop Detroit Med Libr Group; Michigan Health Sciences Libraries Association
Restriction: Authorized patrons, Borrowing privileges limited to fac & registered students, Not open to pub

J WAYNE COUNTY COMMUNITY COLLEGE DISTRICT*, Learning Resource Center, 801 W Fort St, 48226-3010. SAN 308-0463. Tel: 313-496-2358. Web Site: www.wcccd.edu/dept/learning_resource_center.htm. *District Dean, LRC Serv,* Stephanie A Coffer; E-mail: scoffer1@wcccd.edu
Founded 1974
Library Holdings: Bk Titles 70,000; Per Subs 559
Automation Activity & Vendor Info: (Acquisitions) SirsiDynix; (Cataloging) SirsiDynix; (Circulation) SirsiDynix; (Course Reserve) SirsiDynix; (ILL) SirsiDynix; (Media Booking) SirsiDynix; (OPAC) SirsiDynix; (Serials) SirsiDynix
Database Vendor: 3M Library Systems, Brodart
Wireless access
Partic in Detroit Area Library Network
Open Mon-Thurs 8:30am-9pm, Fri 8:30-4:30, Sat 8:30-4

Departmental Libraries:

ARTHUR CARTWRIGHT LRC LIBRARY, 1001 W Fort St, 48226-3096. Tel: 313-496-2358, Ext 2063. FAX: 313-962-4506. E-mail: downtownlrc@wcccd.edu. *District Dean, LRC Serv,* Stephanie A Coffer; E-mail: scoffer1@wcccd.edu
Library Holdings: Bk Vols 29,000; Per Subs 100
Automation Activity & Vendor Info: (Cataloging) SirsiDynix; (Circulation) SirsiDynix; (OPAC) SirsiDynix
Open Mon-Thurs 7:30am-10pm, Fri 8-4:30, Sat & Sun 8-4

C WAYNE STATE UNIVERSITY LIBRARIES, 5150 Anthony Wayne Dr, Ste 3100, 48202. SAN 346-3230. Tel: 313-577-4023. FAX: 313-577-5525. Web Site: library.wayne.edu. *Dean,* Dr Sandra G Yee; Tel: 313-577-4020, E-mail: aj0533@wayne.edu; *Assoc Dean,* Dr Sharon Phillips; Tel: 313-577-4238, E-mail: ae7228@wayne.edu; Staff 132 (MLS 49, Non-MLS 83)
Enrl 26,894; Fac 2,790; Highest Degree: Doctorate
Library Holdings: e-books 819,540; Bk Vols 2,491,403; Per Subs 68,952
Special Collections: Arthur L Johnson African-American History Coll, bks, non-print mats, v-tapes; Curriculum Guide Coll; Florence Nightingale Coll (Purdy/Kresge Coll, items once owned by Florence Nightingale); Jeheskel (Hezy) Shoshani Library Endowed Coll; Judaic-Christian Heritage, Judaica, Hebraica & Yiddish Literature (Kasle Coll); Juvenile Coll; Leonard Simons Coll of Rare Michigan History Texts, mats; Literature for Young People 18th Century to Present (Ramsey Coll), rare bks, periodicals; Merril-Palmer Institute Coll early 1900s, bks, journals, monographs; Mildred Jeffrey Coll of Peace & Conflict Resolution; Urban Ethnic Materials (Millicent A Wills Coll); William Alfred Boyce Storytelling Coll. US Document Depository
Automation Activity & Vendor Info: (Acquisitions) Innovative Interfaces, Inc - Millenium; (Cataloging) Innovative Interfaces, Inc - Millenium; (Circulation) Innovative Interfaces, Inc - Millenium; (Course Reserve) Innovative Interfaces, Inc - Millenium; (ILL) OCLC ILLiad; (OPAC) Innovative Interfaces, Inc - Millenium; (Serials) Innovative Interfaces, Inc - Millenium
Wireless access
Publications: Annual report; Newsletters (Online only)
Partic in Association of Research Libraries (ARL); Midwest Collaborative for Library Services (MCLS); OCLC Online Computer Library Center, Inc
Special Services for the Deaf - ADA equip

Departmental Libraries:

DAVID ADAMANY UNDERGRADUATE LIBRARY, 5150 Anthony Wayne, 48202. Tel: 313-577-5121. Circulation Tel: 313-577-8854. Interlibrary Loan Service Tel: 313-577-4011. Reference Tel: 313-577-8852. Administration Tel: 313-577-4023. FAX: 313-577-5265. Administration FAX: 313-577-5525.
Founded 1997

CL ARTHUR NEEF LAW LIBRARY, 474 Gilmour Mall, 48202, SAN 346-332X. Tel: 313-577-3925. FAX: 313-577-5498. Web Site: library.wayne.edu/neef. *Dir,* Virginia C Thomas; Staff 8 (MLS 4, Non-MLS 4)
Special Collections: Law Libr Microform Consortium Publications; Social Studies; Women & the Law, flm. US Document Depository
Subject Interests: Bus & mgt, Hist
Partic in Westlaw
Publications: US Documents Information Guide

PURDY-KRESGE LIBRARY, 5265 Cass Ave, 48202, SAN 346-3389. Tel: 313-577-4042. Circulation Tel: 313-577-4043. Interlibrary Loan Service Tel: 313-577-4011. Reference Tel: 313-577-6423. FAX: 313-577-3436.
Special Collections: Children & Young People (Eloise Ramsey Coll); Peace & Conflict (Mildred Jeffrey Coll). State Document Depository; US Document Depository
Subject Interests: Bus, Educ, Humanities, Soc sci & issues

WALTER P REUTHER LIBRARY OF LABOR & URBAN AFFAIRS, 5401 Cass Ave, 48202, SAN 346-329X. Tel: 313-577-4024. FAX: 313-577-4300. Web Site: www.reuther.wayne.edu. *Dir,* Erik Nordberg; Tel: 313-577-2013, E-mail: ds2391@wayne.edu; Staff 18 (MLS 17, Non-MLS 1)
Founded 1960
Library Holdings: Bk Vols 9,000; Per Subs 650
Special Collections: Manuscript Coll; Metropolitan Detroit & University Archives; Photograph Coll. Oral History
Subject Interests: Archives, Labor
Publications: Reuther Library Newsletter
Open Mon-Fri 10-2

CM VERA P SHIFFMAN MEDICAL LIBRARY & LEARNING RESOURCES CENTERS, 320 East Canfield, 48201, SAN 346-3354. Tel: 313-577-1088. Circulation Tel: 313-577-1089. Interlibrary Loan Service Tel: 313-577-1100. Administration Tel: 313-577-1168. Information Services Tel: 313-577-1094. FAX: 313-577-6668. Interlibrary Loan Service FAX: 313-577-0706. Web Site: www.lib.wayne.edu/shiffman/index.php. *Dir,* Sandra Martin; Tel: 313-577-6665, E-mail: aa8801@wayne.edu; Staff 12 (MLS 2, Non-MLS 10)
Special Collections: Community Health Information Services; Detroit Community AIDS Library; Pharmacy & Allied Health Learning Resources Center Coll
Subject Interests: Allied health, Clinical med, Consumer health, Health sci, Med, Statistics
Automation Activity & Vendor Info: (Acquisitions) Innovative Interfaces, Inc; (Cataloging) Innovative Interfaces, Inc; (Circulation)

Innovative Interfaces, Inc; (Course Reserve) Docutek; (ILL) OCLC ILLiad; (OPAC) Innovative Interfaces, Inc; (Serials) Innovative Interfaces, Inc
Database Vendor: ABC-CLIO, ACM (Association for Computing Machinery), Agricola, American Chemical Society, American Psychological Association (APA), Annual Reviews, BioOne, Bowker, Cambridge Scientific Abstracts, Community of Science (COS), CQ Press, Dialog, ebrary, EBSCOhost, Elsevier, Emerald, Factiva.com, Facts on File, Gale Cengage Learning, H W Wilson, Haworth Pres Inc, HeinOnline, Hoovers, IEEE (Institute of Electrical & Electronics Engineers), Infotrieve, IOP, ISI Web of Knowledge, Jane's, JSTOR, Lexi-Comp, LexisNexis, McGraw-Hill, Natural Standard, Nature Publishing Group, Newsbank, OCLC FirstSearch, OCLC WorldShare Interlibrary Loan, OVID Technologies, Oxford Online, ProQuest, PubMed, SerialsSolutions, Springer-Verlag, STAT!Ref (Teton Data Systems), STN International, Swets Information Services, UpToDate, Wiley, Wilson - Wilson Web
Function: Computer training, Computers for patron use, Copy machines, Doc delivery serv, e-mail serv, E-Reserves, Electronic databases & coll, Handicapped accessible, Health sci info serv, ILL available, Magnifiers for reading, Online info literacy tutorials on the web & in blackboard, Online ref, Online searches, Orientations, Outside serv via phone, mail, e-mail & web, Photocopying/Printing, Ref & res, Ref serv available, Res libr, Scanner, Senior computer classes, Telephone ref, VHS videos, Workshops
Special Services for the Blind - Aids for in-house use; Assistive/Adapted tech devices, equip & products; Cassette playback machines; Copier with enlargement capabilities; ZoomText magnification & reading software
Restriction: Non-circulating of rare bks, Off-site coll in storage - retrieval as requested

DEWITT

P DEWITT DISTRICT LIBRARY, 13101 Schavey Rd, 48820-9008. Tel: 517-669-3156. FAX: 517-669-6408. E-mail: director@dewittlibrary.org. Web Site: www.dewittlibrary.org. *Dir,* Jennifer Balcom; Staff 18 (MLS 3, Non-MLS 15)
Founded 1934. Pop 34,000; Circ 225,000
Library Holdings: e-books 2,000; Bk Vols 58,000; Per Subs 124
Automation Activity & Vendor Info: (Acquisitions) SirsiDynix; (Cataloging) SirsiDynix; (Circulation) SirsiDynix; (OPAC) SirsiDynix
Wireless access
Open Mon-Thurs 10-8:30, Fri 1-7, Sat 10-4, Sun (Sept-May) 1-4
Friends of the Library Group
Branches: 1
COMMUNITY SATELLITE, 16101 Brook Rd, Lansing, 48906, SAN 346-122X. Tel: 517-702-9389. FAX: 517-702-9417. *Br Mgr,* Position Currently Open
Founded 2007
Special Collections: Local History
Automation Activity & Vendor Info: (Cataloging) SirsiDynix; (Circulation) SirsiDynix; (OPAC) SirsiDynix; (Serials) SirsiDynix
Open Tues-Thurs 2-5, Sat 10-2
Friends of the Library Group

DEXTER

P DEXTER DISTRICT LIBRARY*, 3255 Alpine St, 48130. SAN 308-048X. Tel: 734-426-4477. Administration Tel: 734-426-7731. FAX: 734-426-1217. Web Site: www.dexter.lib.mi.us. *Dir,* Paul McCann; E-mail: pmccann@dexter.lib.mi.us; *Head, Adult Serv,* Lisa Ryan; E-mail: lryan@dexter.lib.mi.us; *Head, Youth Serv,* Cathy Jurich; E-mail: cjurich@dexter.lib.mi.us; *Tech Librn,* Scott Wright; E-mail: swright@dexter.lib.mi.us; *Admin Serv Mgr,* Kim Swoverland; E-mail: kswoverland@dexter.lib.mi.us; *Circ Supvr,* Mary Graulich; E-mail: mgraulich@dexter.lib.mi.us; Staff 33 (MLS 10, Non-MLS 23)
Founded 1927. Pop 16,155; Circ 463,859
Oct 2011-Sept 2012 Income $1,308,257, State $8,774, City $1,193,124, Federal $4,317, County $26,269, Locally Generated Income $75,773. Mats Exp $148,112, Books $89,709, Per/Ser (Incl. Access Fees) $7,864, AV Mat $42,349, Electronic Ref Mat (Incl. Access Fees) $8,190. Sal $581,607 (Prof $404,000)
Library Holdings: Audiobooks 2,836; CDs 6,914; DVDs 7,727; e-books 3,859; Large Print Bks 370; Bk Vols 71,557; Per Subs 190; Videos 2,158
Automation Activity & Vendor Info: (Cataloging) SirsiDynix; (Circulation) SirsiDynix; (OPAC) SirsiDynix; (Serials) SirsiDynix
Database Vendor: Comprise Technologies Inc, EBSCO Information Services, Gale Cengage Learning, OCLC FirstSearch, Overdrive, Inc, SirsiDynix
Wireless access
Function: Adult bk club, Art exhibits, AV serv, Bk club(s), Bks on cassette, Bks on CD, Children's prog, Computer training, Computers for patron use, Copy machines, Digital talking bks, Electronic databases & coll, Fax serv, Free DVD rentals, Handicapped accessible, Holiday prog, ILL available, Magnifiers for reading, Mail & tel request accepted, Mus passes, Music CDs, Online cat, Online searches, OverDrive digital audio bks, Photocopying/Printing, Preschool reading prog, Prog for adults, Prog for children & young adult, Pub access computers, Ref serv available, Ref serv in person, Scanner, Senior computer classes, Spoken cassettes & CDs, Spoken cassettes & DVDs, Story hour, Summer reading prog, Tax forms, Teen prog, Telephone ref, VHS videos, Web-catalog, Wheelchair accessible, Workshops
Publications: Ex Libris (Newsletter)
Special Services for the Deaf - Video relay serv
Open Mon-Fri 9-9, Sat 9-5, Sun 1-5
Friends of the Library Group

DIMONDALE

P DOROTHY HULL WINDSOR TOWNSHIP LIBRARY*, 405 W Jefferson St, 48821. SAN 308-0498. Tel: 517-646-0633. FAX: 517-646-7061. Web Site: www.twp.windsor.mi.us/library/library.htm. *Librn,* Joy Slee; E-mail: sleejoy@gmail.com; *Asst Librn,* Sandy Moor
Pop 6,000; Circ 31,508
Library Holdings: Bk Vols 19,000; Per Subs 43
Wireless access
Mem of Woodlands Library Cooperative
Open Mon, Tues, Thurs & Fri 1-5:30, Wed 1-8, Sat 9-2:30

DOLLAR BAY

P OSCEOLA TOWNSHIP PUBLIC & SCHOOL LIBRARY*, 48475 Maple St, 49922. (Mail add: PO Box 371, 49922-0371), SAN 308-0501. Tel: 906-482-5800. FAX: 906-487-5931. *Librn,* Jennifer Strand
Founded 1924. Circ 5,000
Library Holdings: AV Mats 60; Bk Vols 5,800
Open Mon, Tues, Thurs & Fri 7:45-4:30, Wed 7:45-4:30 & 5:30-7:30

DORR

P DORR TOWNSHIP LIBRARY, 1804 Sunset Dr, 49323. SAN 346-3478. Tel: 616-681-9678. FAX: 616-681-5650. E-mail: dorrlibrary@hotmail.com. Web Site: www.dorrlibrary.org. *Dir,* Natalie Bazan; Staff 3.3 (Non-MLS 3.3)
Founded 1940. Pop 7,439; Circ 45,052
Apr 2011-Mar 2012 Income $169,277, State $2,595, Locally Generated Income $166,682. Mats Exp $17,520, Books $12,781, AV Mat $4,289. Sal $69,142
Library Holdings: Audiobooks 1,142; AV Mats 1,744; Bk Vols 25,037; Per Subs 61
Automation Activity & Vendor Info: (Acquisitions) OCLC; (Cataloging) Innovative Interfaces, Inc; (Circulation) Innovative Interfaces, Inc; (ILL) Innovative Interfaces, Inc; (OPAC) Innovative Interfaces, Inc
Database Vendor: Innovative Interfaces, Inc
Wireless access
Function: Adult bk club, Bks on CD, Children's prog, Computers for patron use, Copy machines, Fax serv, Free DVD rentals, Handicapped accessible, ILL available, Music CDs, Online cat, Photocopying/Printing, Preschool outreach, Prog for children & young adult, Story hour, Summer reading prog, Tax forms, Telephone ref, Web-catalog, Wheelchair accessible
Partic in Lakeland Library Cooperative
Open Mon & Thurs 12-8, Tues, Wed & Fri 10-5, Sat 10-2
Friends of the Library Group

DOUGLAS

P SAUGATUCK-DOUGLAS DISTRICT LIBRARY*, Ten Mixer St, 49406. (Mail add: PO Box 789, 49406-0789), SAN 308-4027. Tel: 269-857-8241. FAX: 269-857-3005. E-mail: std@llcoop.org. Web Site: www.sdlibrary.org. *Dir,* Martha M Boetcher; E-mail: mboetcher@llcoop.org
Founded 1965. Pop 7,202; Circ 28,223
Library Holdings: Bk Vols 20,000; Per Subs 62
Automation Activity & Vendor Info: (Cataloging) Innovative Interfaces, Inc; (Circulation) Innovative Interfaces, Inc
Wireless access
Partic in Lakeland Library Cooperative
Open Mon-Thurs 10-8, Fri 10-6, Sat 10-2, Sun 1-4
Friends of the Library Group

DOWAGIAC

P DOWAGIAC DISTRICT LIBRARY*, 211 Commercial St, 49047-1728. SAN 346-3567. Tel: 269-782-3826. FAX: 269-782-9798. Web Site: dowagiacdl.org. *Dir,* Katherine Johnson; *Ch Serv,* Alma Adams; *Circ,* Kay Gray; Staff 6 (MLS 1, Non-MLS 5)
Founded 1872. Pop 14,256; Circ 51,339
Library Holdings: Bk Vols 38,000; Per Subs 38
Subject Interests: Local hist
Automation Activity & Vendor Info: (Cataloging) Auto-Graphics, Inc; (Circulation) Auto-Graphics, Inc

Wireless access
Partic in Southwest Michigan Library Cooperative
Open Mon, Wed & Fri 9-5:30, Tues & Thurs 9-8:30, Sat 9-2
Friends of the Library Group

J SOUTHWESTERN MICHIGAN COLLEGE*, Fred L Mathews Library, 58900 Cherry Grove Rd, 49047. SAN 308-051X. Tel: 269-782-1339. Interlibrary Loan Service Tel: 269-782-1205. Toll Free Tel: 800-456-8675. FAX: 269-782-9575. Web Site: www.swmich.edu/library. *Dir, Libr Serv,* Dr Jane Spencer; Tel: 269-782-1204, E-mail: jspencer@swmich.edu; *AV,* Ernie Knapp; Tel: 269-782-1341; Staff 4 (MLS 1, Non-MLS 3)
Founded 1964. Enrl 3,600; Fac 53; Highest Degree: Bachelor
Library Holdings: Electronic Media & Resources 3,000; Bk Vols 37,000; Per Subs 1,000
Special Collections: American Civil War. State Document Depository; US Document Depository
Automation Activity & Vendor Info: (Cataloging) SirsiDynix; (Circulation) SirsiDynix; (OPAC) SirsiDynix
Database Vendor: Gale Cengage Learning, OCLC FirstSearch, ProQuest, SirsiDynix
Wireless access
Partic in Mich Libr Asn
Open Mon-Thurs (Winter) 8-8, Fri 8-5, Sun 1-5; Mon-Thurs (Summer) 8-7, Fri 8-5

DRYDEN

P DRYDEN TOWNSHIP LIBRARY*, 5480 Main St, 48428-9968. (Mail add: PO Box 280, 48428-0280), SAN 308-0528. Tel: 810-796-3586. FAX: 810-796-2634. Web Site: www.drydentownshiplibrary.org. *Dir,* Desta Ureel; E-mail: d.ureel@vlc.lib.mi.us; *Asst Librn,* Nancy Wagner; E-mail: nwagner@edcen.ehhs.cmich.edu
Founded 1975. Pop 3,399
Library Holdings: Large Print Bks 453; Bk Vols 19,495; Per Subs 105
Automation Activity & Vendor Info: (Cataloging) SirsiDynix; (Circulation) SirsiDynix; (OPAC) SirsiDynix
Partic in Mideastern Michigan Library Cooperative
Open Mon, Tues & Thurs 10-5 & 7-9, Wed 10-7, Fri & Sat 10-2

EAST JORDAN

P JORDAN VALLEY DISTRICT LIBRARY*, One Library Lane, 49727. (Mail add: PO Box 877, 49727-0877), SAN 308-0552. Tel: 231-536-7131. FAX: 231-536-3646. E-mail: dir@jvdl.info. Web Site: jvdl.info. *Dir,* Dawn Pringle; Staff 11 (MLS 1, Non-MLS 10)
Pop 6,997; Circ 45,233
Jul 2011-Jun 2012 Income $404,000, State $3,100, City $316,000, County $30,000, Other $54,900. Mats Exp $40,500, Books $25,500, Per/Ser (Incl. Access Fees) $4,000, Electronic Ref Mat (Incl. Access Fees) $10,000, Presv $1,000. Sal $150,000
Library Holdings: Audiobooks 2,354; AV Mats 884; CDs 2,139; DVDs 1,849; e-books 5,138; Large Print Bks 150; Microforms 50; Bk Titles 35,000; Per Subs 121; Videos 750
Automation Activity & Vendor Info: (Cataloging) Horizon; (Circulation) Horizon; (OPAC) Horizon
Database Vendor: SirsiDynix
Wireless access
Function: Art exhibits, Audiobks via web, Bks on cassette, Bks on CD, Children's prog, Computer training, Computers for patron use, Copy machines, Digital talking bks, e-mail & chat, e-mail serv, Electronic databases & coll, Exhibits, Fax serv, Free DVD rentals, Govt ref serv, Handicapped accessible, Homework prog, ILL available, Learning ctr, Magnifiers for reading, Mail & tel request accepted, Microfiche/film & reading machines, Music CDs, Online cat, Online ref, Online searches, OverDrive digital audio bks, Photocopying/Printing, Printer for laptops & handheld devices, Prog for adults, Prog for children & young adult, Pub access computers, Ref & res, Ref serv available, Story hour, Summer & winter reading prog, Summer reading prog, Tax forms, Teen prog, Telephone ref, VHS videos, Video lending libr, Visual arts prog, Web-catalog, Wheelchair accessible, Workshops
Publications: Jordan Valley Library News (Newsletter)
Partic in Northland Library Cooperative
Open Mon & Wed 9-7, Tues, Thurs & Fri 9-5, Sat 9-1, Sun 1-5
Restriction: Circ limited
Friends of the Library Group

EAST LANSING

P EAST LANSING PUBLIC LIBRARY*, 950 Abbott Rd, 48823-3105. SAN 308-0560. Tel: 517-351-2420. Circulation Tel: 517-351-2420, Ext 6898. Interlibrary Loan Service Tel: 517-351-2420, Ext 6962. Reference Tel: 517-351-2420, Ext 6845. Administration Tel: 517-319-6863. FAX: 517-351-9536. E-mail: elplcirc@cityofeastlansing.com. Web Site: www.elpl.org. *Dir,* Kristin Shelley; Tel: 517-319-6913, E mail: kshelley@cityofeastlansing.com; *Head, Pub Serv,* Jill Abood; Tel: 517-319-6939, E-mail: jabood@cityofeastlansing.com; *Head, Tech Serv,* Lauren Douglass; Tel: 517-351-2420, Ext 104, E-mail: ldougla@cityofeastlansing.com
Founded 1923. Pop 48,579; Circ 319,370
Jul 2011-Jun 2012 Income $1,814,222, State $19,464, City $1,478,040, County $111,072, Locally Generated Income $205,646. Mats Exp $210,167, Per/Ser (Incl. Access Fees) $9,817, Other Print Mats $166,517, Electronic Ref Mat (Incl. Access Fees) $33,833. Sal $1,062,745
Library Holdings: Bk Vols 130,000
Special Collections: Local History
Automation Activity & Vendor Info: (Cataloging) Innovative Interfaces, Inc; (Circulation) Innovative Interfaces, Inc; (OPAC) Innovative Interfaces, Inc
Wireless access
Mem of Woodlands Library Cooperative
Open Mon-Thurs 10-9, Fri 10-6, Sat 10-5:30, Sun (Sept-May) 1-5
Friends of the Library Group

CL MICHIGAN STATE UNIVERSITY COLLEGE OF LAW LIBRARY*, John F Schaefer Law Library, 648 N Shaw Lane, 48824-1300. SAN 307-9953. Tel: 517-432-6860. Reference Tel: 517-432-6870. FAX: 517-432-6861. E-mail: reference@law.msu.edu. Web Site: www.law.msu.edu. *Dir,* Charles Ten Brink; Tel: 517-432-6862, E-mail: cjtb@law.msu.edu; *Assoc Dir,* Hildur Hanna; Tel: 517-432-6863, E-mail: hannahi@law.msu.edu; *Asst Dir, Pub Serv,* Jane Meland; Tel: 517-432-6867; *Head, Tech Serv,* Brooke Moynihan; Tel: 517-432-6864, E-mail: moynihbr@law.msu.edu; *Ref Librn,* Barbara Bean; Tel: 517-432-6878; *Ref Librn,* Brent Domann; Tel: 517-432-6851, E-mail: domannbr@law.msu.edu; *Ref Librn,* Jane Hedin; Tel: 517-432-6957, E-mail: hedinj@law.msu.edu; *Tech Serv Librn,* James La Macchia, II; Tel: 517-432-6866, E-mail: lamacchi@law.msu.edu; *Circ Mgr,* Robin Doutre; Tel: 517-432-6869; Staff 7 (MLS 7)
Founded 1891. Enrl 1,000; Fac 38; Highest Degree: Doctorate
Library Holdings: Bk Titles 147,748; Bk Vols 284,804
Special Collections: US Document Depository
Automation Activity & Vendor Info: (Acquisitions) Innovative Interfaces, Inc; (Cataloging) Innovative Interfaces, Inc; (Circulation) Innovative Interfaces, Inc; (OPAC) Innovative Interfaces, Inc; (Serials) Innovative Interfaces, Inc
Database Vendor: HeinOnline, LexisNexis, Loislaw, Westlaw, YBP Library Services
Wireless access
Publications: Acquisitions List
Partic in Lexis, OCLC Online Computer Libr Ctr, Inc; Midwest Collaborative for Library Services (MCLS); Westlaw
Restriction: Pub use on premises

C MICHIGAN STATE UNIVERSITY LIBRARY*, Main Library, 366 W Circle Dr, 48824-1048. SAN 346-3621. Tel: 517-432-6123. Interlibrary Loan Service Tel: 517-884-6399. Toll Free Tel: 800-500-1554. FAX: 517-432-3532. Interlibrary Loan Service FAX: 517-432-1446. TDD: 517-353-9034. Web Site: www.lib.msu.edu. *Dir,* Clifford H Haka; Tel: 517-355-2341, E-mail: hakac@msu.edu; *Assoc Dir, Spec Coll & Presv,* Peter Berg; Tel: 517-884-6396, Fax: 517-532-0487, E-mail: berg@msu.edu; *Sr Assoc Dir, Text Mgt/Interlibrary Serv,* Colleen F Hyslop; Tel: 517-884-6390, E-mail: hyslop@mail.lib.msu.edu; *Assoc Dir, Coll,* Steven Sowards; Tel: 517-884-6391, Fax: 517-432-0487, E-mail: sowards@msu.edu; *Assoc Dir, Tech Serv & Syst,* Nancy Fleck; Tel: 517-884-6455, Fax: 517-353-8969, E-mail: fleckn@mail.lib.msu.edu; *Asst Dir, Digital Serv,* Shawn Nicholson; Tel: 517-884-6448, Fax: 517-432-4795, E-mail: nicho147@msu.edu; *Asst Dir, Pub Serv,* Arlene Weismantel; Tel: 517-884-6447, E-mail: weisman1@mail.lib.msu.edu. Subject Specialists: *Human resources,* Colleen F Hyslop; Staff 185 (MLS 73, Non-MLS 112)
Founded 1855. Enrl 49,343; Fac 2,577; Highest Degree: Doctorate
Library Holdings: e-books 1,329,222; Bk Titles 7,606,499; Bk Vols 6,295,758
Special Collections: American Popular Culture; American Radical History; Apiculture Coll; Changing Men Coll; Comic Art; Cookery Coll; Early Works in Criminology; Eighteenth Century English Studies; English & American Authors; Fencing Coll; History of the French Monarchy; Illuminated Manuscripts in Facsimile; Italian Risorgimento History; Natural Science, especially Botany & Entomology; Veterinary History
Automation Activity & Vendor Info: (Acquisitions) Innovative Interfaces, Inc; (Circulation) Innovative Interfaces, Inc; (Serials) Innovative Interfaces, Inc
Wireless access
Partic in Association of Research Libraries (ARL); National Network of Libraries of Medicine

Departmental Libraries:

AREA STUDIES, Main Library, 366 W Circle Dr, 48824, SAN 346-4075. Tel: 517-884-6392. FAX: 517-432-3532. *Librn,* Joseph Lauer; E-mail: lauer@msu.edu; *Librn,* Peter Limb; E-mail: limb@msu.edu; *Librn,* Xian Wu; E-mail: wuxian@msu.edu; *Coordr, Area Studies,* Mary Jo Zeter; E-mail: zeter@msu.edu

DIGITAL SOURCES & MULTIMEDIA CENTER, W432 Main Library, 366 W Circle Dr, 48824, SAN 346-377X. Tel: 517-884-6470. FAX: 517-432-4795. Web Site: www.digital.lib.msu.edu. *Asst Dir, Digital Serv,* Shawn Nicholson; Tel: 517-884-6448, E-mail: nicho147@msu.edu; *Librn,* Aaron Collie; Tel: 517-884-0867, E-mail: collie@mail.lib.msu.edu

ENGINEERING LIBRARY, 1515 Engineering Bldg, 428 S Shaw Lane, 48824, SAN 346-3982. Tel: 517-355-8536. FAX: 517-353-9041. Web Site: www.lib.msu.edu/coll/branches/engin. *Librn,* Tom Volkening; E-mail: volkenin@msu.edu; Staff 3 (MLS 1, Non-MLS 2)
Founded 1963

FINE ARTS-ART, W403 Main Library, 366 W Circle Dr, 48824, SAN 346-3745. Tel: 517-884-6469. FAX: 517-432-3532. Web Site: www.lib.msu.edu/coll/main/finearts. *Librn,* Terrie Wilson; E-mail: wilso398@msu.edu

FINE ARTS-MUSIC, W403 Main Library, 366 W Circle Dr, 48824, SAN 346-4164. Tel: 517-884-6469. FAX: 517-432-3532. Web Site: www.lib.msu.edu/coll/main/finearts. *Head Librn,* Mary Black-Junttonen; E-mail: blackma@mail.lib.msu.edu

WILLIAM C GAST BUSINESS LIBRARY, 50 Law College Bldg, 648 N Shaw Lane, 48824, SAN 346-380X. Tel: 517-355-3380. FAX: 517-353-6648. *Head Librn,* Nancy Lucas; E-mail: lucasn@msu.edu

MAP LIBRARY, W308 Main Library, 366 W Circle Dr, 48824, SAN 329-6423. Tel: 517-884-6467. FAX: 517-432-3532. *Librn,* Kathleen Weessies

MATHEMATICS, D-101 Wells Hall, 48824, SAN 346-413X. Tel: 517-353-8852. FAX: 517-353-7215. *Librn,* Ezzo Ania; E-mail: ezzoa@msu.edu

VOICE LIBRARY, W422 Library, 366 W Circle Dr, 48824, SAN 346-4318. Tel: 517-884-6470. FAX: 517-432-4795. *Asst Dir, Digital Serv,* Shawn Nicholson; E-mail: nicho147@msu.edu

EAST TAWAS

P IOSCO-ARENAC DISTRICT LIBRARY, 120 W Westover St, 48730. SAN 347-0822. Tel: 989-362-2651. FAX: 989-362-6056. Web Site: www.ioscoarenaclibrary.org. *Dir,* Stephanie Mallak Olson; E-mail: director@ioscoarenaclibrary.org; *Commun Liaison Librn,* Arleen Wood; *Tech Coordr,* John Cargo; *Ch Serv, Youth Serv,* Lynne Bigelow; *ILL,* Richard Marx; Staff 9 (MLS 2, Non-MLS 7)
Founded 1935. Pop 41,786; Circ 141,990
Library Holdings: Audiobooks 1,619; CDs 4,161; e-books 2,321; Electronic Media & Resources 4; Bk Vols 100,368; Per Subs 246
Special Collections: Business Resource Center
Subject Interests: Genealogy, Local hist, Mich
Automation Activity & Vendor Info: (Cataloging) SirsiDynix; (Circulation) SirsiDynix; (ILL) Mel Cat; (OPAC) SirsiDynix
Database Vendor: Baker & Taylor, Brodart, Gale Cengage Learning, Overdrive, Inc, ProQuest, SirsiDynix
Wireless access
Publications: Annual Report
Partic in Valley Libr Consortium; White Pine Libr Coop
Open Mon-Fri 8-4:30
Friends of the Library Group
Branches: 8

AU GRES COMMUNITY, 230 N MacKinaw, Au Gres, 48703. (Mail add: PO Box 146, Au Gres, 48703), SAN 347-0857. Tel: 989-876-8818. FAX: 989-876-8818. ; Staff 2 (Non-MLS 2)
Circ 12,154
Open Mon & Tues 12-7, Wed-Fri 9-5, Sat 9:30-12:30
Friends of the Library Group

EAST TAWAS BRANCH, 204 Sawyer St, 48730, SAN 347-0881. Tel: 989-362-6162. FAX: 989-362-1449. E-mail: libraryet@yahoo.com. *Librn,* Luann Elvey; Staff 1 (Non-MLS 1)
Circ 17,916
Open Mon, Thurs & Fri 8-11:30 & 12:30-5, Tues 12-4 & 5-8:30, Sat 8-12
Friends of the Library Group

MARY JOHNSTON MEMORIAL LIBRARY - STANDISH BRANCH, 114 N Court, Standish, 48658-9416. (Mail add: PO Box 698, Standish, 48658-0698), SAN 347-0970. Tel: 989-846-6611. FAX: 989-846-6611. *Librn,* Hilda Carruthers; Staff 2.4 (Non-MLS 2.4)
Circ 29,050
Open Mon & Tues 11-7:30, Wed & Thurs 1-7:30, Fri & Sat 10-3
Friends of the Library Group

OMER BRANCH, 205 E Center St, Omer, 48749. (Mail add: PO Box 186, Omer, 48749), SAN 325-4283. Tel: 989-653-2230. FAX: 989-653-2230. *Librn,* Charmaine Ploof; Staff 1 (Non-MLS 1)
Circ 4,862
Open Mon & Fri 1:30-6, Tues 12-6, Wed & Thurs 1:30-8, Sat 10-2

ROBERT J PARKS LIBRARY - OSCODA BRANCH, 6010 N Skeel Ave, Oscoda, 48750, SAN 347-0946. Tel: 989-739-9581. FAX: 989-739-9581. *Librn,* Diana London; Staff 2.15 (Non-MLS 2.15)
Circ 33,416
Open Mon, Fri & Sat 9-5, Tues-Thurs 9-8
Friends of the Library Group

PLAINFIELD TOWNSHIP, 220 N Washington, Hale, 48739-9578. (Mail add: PO Box 247, Hale, 48739-0247), SAN 347-0911. Tel: 989-728-4086. FAX: 989-728-6491. *Librn,* Cheryl Tyler; Staff 2 (Non-MLS 2)
Circ 13,149
Open Mon, Tues, Thurs & Fri 8-4, Wed 8-6:30, Sat 9-12
Friends of the Library Group

TAWAS CITY BRANCH, 208 North St, Tawas City, 48763, SAN 347-1004. Tel: 989-362-6557. FAX: 989-362-6557. *Librn,* Terri Stein; Staff 1 (Non-MLS 1)
Circ 18,013
Open Mon-Thurs 10-1 & 2-6, Sat 10-12
Friends of the Library Group

WHITTEMORE BRANCH, 483 Bullock St, Whittemore, 48770-5134. (Mail add: PO Box 247, Whittemore, 48770-0247), SAN 347-1039. Tel: 989-756-3186. FAX: 989-756-3186. *Librn,* Marie Burkholder; Staff 2 (Non-MLS 2)
Circ 6,603
Open Mon, Wed & Fri 10-6, Tues, Thurs & Sat 10-4
Friends of the Library Group

EASTPOINTE

P EASTPOINTE MEMORIAL LIBRARY*, 15875 Oak St, 48021-2390. SAN 308-0544. Tel: 586-445-5096. FAX: 586-775-0150. E-mail: eplweb@libcoop.net. Web Site: www.cityofeastpointe.net. *Dir,* Carol Sterling; E-mail: sterlinc@libcoop.net; *Asst Dir,* Sue Todd; E-mail: todds@libcoop.net; *Youth Serv Librn,* Abby Bond; E-mail: bonda@libcoop.net; Staff 4 (MLS 4)
Founded 1939. Pop 34,077; Circ 162,452
Library Holdings: AV Mats 5,164; Bk Vols 61,809; Per Subs 124
Special Collections: Automobile Manuals Coll
Automation Activity & Vendor Info: (Acquisitions) SirsiDynix; (Cataloging) SirsiDynix; (Circulation) SirsiDynix; (ILL) SirsiDynix; (OPAC) SirsiDynix; (Serials) SirsiDynix
Wireless access
Function: Accelerated reader prog
Partic in Suburban Library Cooperative
Open Mon-Thurs 10-8, Fri & Sat 12-5
Friends of the Library Group

EATON RAPIDS

P EATON RAPIDS PUBLIC LIBRARY, 220 S Main St, 48827-1256. SAN 308-0595. Tel: 517-663-8118, Ext 4. FAX: 517-663-1940. E-mail: erlibrary@cityofeatonrapids.com. *Dir,* Sandra L Porter; E-mail: sporter@cityofeatonrapids.com; Staff 2.88 (Non-MLS 2.88)
Founded 1876. Pop 5,214; Circ 29,156
Library Holdings: Audiobooks 284; AV Mats 32; CDs 135; DVDs 616; Bk Vols 21,096; Per Subs 27; Videos 485
Automation Activity & Vendor Info: (Circulation) Auto-Graphics, Inc
Wireless access
Function: 24/7 Online cat, Bks on CD, Children's prog, Computers for patron use, Copy machines, Fax serv, ILL available, Magazines, Microfiche/film & reading machines, OverDrive digital audio bks, Photocopying/Printing, Prog for children & young adult, Summer reading prog, Tax forms, VHS videos
Mem of Woodlands Library Cooperative
Open Mon & Wed 10-8, Tues, Thurs & Fri 10-5, Sat (Winter) 10-1
Restriction: Non-resident fee
Friends of the Library Group

EAU CLAIRE

P EAU CLAIRE DISTRICT LIBRARY*, 6528 E Main St, 49111. (Mail add: PO Box 328, 49111-0328), SAN 308-0609. Tel: 269-461-6241. FAX: 269-461-3721. Web Site: www.eauclairelibrary.org. *Dir,* Ann Greene; Staff 6 (MLS 1, Non-MLS 5)
Founded 1938. Pop 8,332; Circ 39,474
Library Holdings: Bk Vols 30,391; Per Subs 63
Subject Interests: Indians, Local hist, Spanish (Lang)
Automation Activity & Vendor Info: (Cataloging) Follett Software; (Circulation) Follett Software; (OPAC) Follett Software
Wireless access
Partic in Southwest Michigan Library Cooperative
Open Mon & Wed 12-9, Tues, Thurs & Fri 10-6, Sat 10-4

ECORSE

P ECORSE PUBLIC LIBRARY*, 4184 W Jefferson Ave, 48229. SAN 308-0617. Tel: 313-389-2030. FAX: 313-389-2032. Web Site: ecorse.lib.mi.us. *Dir,* Gurpreet Samra; E-mail: gsamra@ecorse.lib.mi.us; *ILL,* Blois Brown; E-mail: bbrown@ecorse.lib.mi.us
Founded 1948
Library Holdings: Bk Titles 25,000; Bk Vols 35,000; Per Subs 70

Automation Activity & Vendor Info: (Cataloging) SirsiDynix; (Circulation) SirsiDynix; (OPAC) SirsiDynix
Function: Fax serv, Homework prog, Notary serv, Photocopying/Printing, Summer reading prog
Open Mon, Tues & Thurs 10-6
Friends of the Library Group

EDMORE

P HOME TOWNSHIP LIBRARY*, 329 E Main St, 48829. (Mail add: PO Box 589, 48829-0589), SAN 308-0625. Tel: 989-427-5241. FAX: 989-427-3233. E-mail: edm@llcoop.org. Web Site: edmore.llcoop.org. *Dir,* Jonelle Ball
Pop 4,568; Circ 19,490
Jul 2006-Jun 2007 Income $114,975. Mats Exp $22,500, Books $17,500, Per/Ser (Incl. Access Fees) $1,000, AV Mat $4,000. Sal $44,000 (Prof $18,000)
Library Holdings: AV Mats 610; Large Print Bks 150; Bk Vols 17,600; Per Subs 38; Talking Bks 450
Automation Activity & Vendor Info: (Cataloging) Innovative Interfaces, Inc; (Circulation) Innovative Interfaces, Inc; (ILL) Innovative Interfaces, Inc
Partic in Lakeland Library Cooperative

ELK RAPIDS

P ELK RAPIDS DISTRICT LIBRARY*, 300 Isle of Pines, 49629. (Mail add: PO Box 337, 49629-0337), SAN 308-065X. Tel: 231-264-9979. FAX: 231-264-9975. E-mail: erdl@elkrapidsnet.com. Web Site: www.elkrapidslibrary.org. *Dir,* Nannette D Miller; Staff 1 (Non-MLS 1)
Founded 1939. Pop 5,393; Circ 34,163
Library Holdings: Bk Vols 20,000; Per Subs 42
Subject Interests: Local hist, Mich
Wireless access
Partic in Mid-Michigan Library League
Open Mon-Thurs 10-8, Fri & Sat 10-5, Sun 1-5
Friends of the Library Group

ELSIE

P ELSIE PUBLIC LIBRARY*, 145 W Main St, 48831. (Mail add: PO Box 545, 48831-0545), SAN 308-0676. Tel: 989-862-4633. FAX: 989-862-4633. E-mail: elsielibrary@mutualdata.com. *Dir,* Ann Trierweiler
Founded 1943. Pop 3,500; Circ 21,953
Library Holdings: CDs 500; DVDs 2,600; Bk Titles 25,000; Per Subs 89; Talking Bks 100; Videos 50
Automation Activity & Vendor Info: (Cataloging) Auto-Graphics, Inc; (Circulation) Auto-Graphics, Inc; (ILL) Auto-Graphics, Inc
Wireless access
Open Mon 11-5, Wed & Thurs 1-7, Sat 10-2

EMPIRE

P GLEN LAKE COMMUNITY LIBRARY*, 10115 W Front St, 49630-9418. Tel: 231-326-5361. FAX: 231-326-5361. Web Site: www.glenlakelibrary.net. *Dir,* David F Diller; E-mail: dfdiller@centurytel.net
Founded 1977
Library Holdings: Bks on Deafness & Sign Lang 15; Bk Vols 15,000; Per Subs 50; Talking Bks 800
Wireless access
Partic in Mid-Michigan Library League
Open Mon, Wed & Fri 10-5, Tues & Thurs 10-7, Sat 10-3
Friends of the Library Group

ESCANABA

J BAY DE NOC COMMUNITY COLLEGE*, Learning Resources Center/Library, 2001 N Lincoln Rd, 49829-2511. SAN 308-0684. Tel: 906-217-4055, 906-217-4076. Reference Tel: 906-217-4079. FAX: 906-789-6912. E-mail: lrchelp@baycollege.edu. Web Site: library.baycollege.edu. *Libr Dir,* Oscar T DeLong; Fax: 906-217-1657, E-mail: oscar.delong@baycollege.edu; *Bibliog Instr, Coll Develop, Ref,* Ann Bissell; Fax: 906-217-1682, E-mail: bissella@baycollege.edu; Staff 2 (Non-MLS 2)
Founded 1963. Enrl 2,000; Fac 140; Highest Degree: Associate
Library Holdings: Audiobooks 357; CDs 300; DVDs 1,745; e-books 26,000; Bk Titles 30,000; Bk Vols 40,000; Per Subs 92; Videos 2,310
Special Collections: Delta County Oral History. Oral History
Automation Activity & Vendor Info: (Acquisitions) OCLC; (Cataloging) OCLC; (Circulation) OCLC; (Course Reserve) OCLC; (ILL) OCLC; (OPAC) OCLC WorldShare Interlibrary Loan
Database Vendor: CredoReference, Gale Cengage Learning, LexisNexis, Newsbank, OCLC FirstSearch, OCLC WorldShare Interlibrary Loan, ProQuest
Wireless access
Partic in Mich Libr Asn; OCLC Online Computer Library Center, Inc
Open Mon-Thurs (Winter) 8-8, Fri 8-4:30; Mon-Fri (Summer) 8-4:30

P ESCANABA PUBLIC LIBRARY*, 400 Ludington St, 49829. SAN 308-0692. Tel: 906-789-7323. Reference Tel: 906-786-4463. FAX: 906-786-0942. E-mail: epl@uproc.lib.mi.us. Web Site: www.uproc.lib.mi.us/epl. *Dir,* Carolyn Stacey; *Ch Serv,* Patricia J Fittante; *ILL,* Jessica McLamb; *Ref,* Arlene Wood; Staff 4 (MLS 2, Non-MLS 2)
Founded 1903. Pop 13,140; Circ 104,802
Jul 2005-Jun 2006 Income $475,256, State $25,099, City $235,000, Federal $16,157, County $199,000. Mats Exp $66,483, Books $61,483, Per/Ser (Incl. Access Fees) $5,000. Sal $222,925
Library Holdings: AV Mats 500; Bk Vols 72,692; Per Subs 136; Talking Bks 800; Videos 628
Subject Interests: Genealogy, Local hist
Automation Activity & Vendor Info: (Circulation) SirsiDynix; (OPAC) SirsiDynix
Wireless access
Partic in Superiorland Library Cooperative
Special Services for the Blind - Reader equip
Open Mon-Thurs (Winter) 9-8:30, Fri & Sat 10-5; Mon-Thurs (Summer) 10-8, Fri 10-5
Friends of the Library Group

EVART

P EVART PUBLIC LIBRARY*, 104 N Main St, 49631. (Mail add: PO Box 576, 49631-0576), SAN 308-0714. Tel: 231-734-5542. FAX: 231-734-5542. E-mail: evartlibrary@yahoo.com. *Librn,* Lilas VanScoyoc; *Asst Librn,* Elsie Connor
Pop 6,000; Circ 34,580
Library Holdings: Bk Titles 24,000; Per Subs 65
Automation Activity & Vendor Info: (Cataloging) Auto-Graphics, Inc; (Circulation) Auto-Graphics, Inc
Wireless access
Partic in Mid-Michigan Library League
Open Mon-Fri 9-4:30, Sat 9-12

EWEN

P MCMILLAN TOWNSHIP LIBRARY*, 200 Cedar St, 49925. (Mail add: PO Box 49, 49925-0049), SAN 376-7078. Tel: 906-988-2515. FAX: 906-988-2255. *Dir,* Lorraine Sain
Library Holdings: Bk Titles 10,000; Per Subs 28
Automation Activity & Vendor Info: (Cataloging) Follett Software; (Circulation) Follett Software
Partic in Superiorland Library Cooperative
Open Tues & Thurs 10:30-7, Fri 11-5

FAIRGROVE

P FAIRGROVE DISTRICT LIBRARY*, 1959 Main St, 48733. (Mail add: PO Box 9, 48733-0009), SAN 308-0722. Tel: 989-693-6050. FAX: 989-693-6446. Web Site: www.fairgrove.lib.mi.us/library. *Dir,* Larry Haubenstricker
Founded 1884. Pop 5,500; Circ 18,000
Library Holdings: Bk Vols 22,000; Per Subs 50
Automation Activity & Vendor Info: (Cataloging) Follett Software; (Circulation) Follett Software
Function: Computers for patron use, Fax serv, Photocopying/Printing
Partic in OCLC Online Computer Library Center, Inc; White Pine Libr Coop
Open Mon, Wed & Fri 9-8, Tues 9-1, Sat 10-1
Friends of the Library Group

FALMOUTH

P FALMOUTH AREA LIBRARY*, 219 E Prosper Rd, 49632-0602. Tel: 231-826-3738. *Dir,* Margaret B Rosenbrook
Library Holdings: Bk Vols 13,000
Partic in Mid-Michigan Library League
Open Tues-Thurs 1-6, Sat 9-1

FARMINGTON HILLS

SR BIRMINGHAM TEMPLE LIBRARY*, 28611 W Twelve Mile Rd, 48334. SAN 308-0749. Tel: 248-477-1410. FAX: 248-477-9014. E-mail: info@birminghamtemple.org. Web Site: www.birminghamtemple.org. *Librn,* Pera Kane
Founded 1963
Library Holdings: Bk Vols 3,000; Per Subs 20
Subject Interests: Jewish hist & lit, Judaism (religion), Philos

M BOTSFORD HOSPITAL*, Library & Internet Services, 28050 Grand River Ave, 48336-5919. SAN 308-0757. Tel: 248-471-8434. FAX: 248-471-8060. E-mail: circ@botsford.org. Web Site: www.botsford.org/library. *Dir,* Deborah L Adams; E-mail: dadams@botsford.org; Staff 2 (MLS 2)
Founded 1970
Jan 2013-Dec 2013 Income $500,000. Mats Exp $217,000, Books $10,000, Electronic Ref Mat (Incl. Access Fees) $207,000. Sal $124,000
Library Holdings: DVDs 122; e-books 250; e-journals 2,400; Bk Titles 2,800; Per Subs 10
Subject Interests: Consumer health, Med, Nursing
Automation Activity & Vendor Info: (Cataloging) EOS International; (Circulation) EOS International; (OPAC) EOS International; (Serials) SerialsSolutions
Database Vendor: Checkpoint Systems, Inc, EBSCOhost, Elsevier, EOS International, Gale Cengage Learning, LearningExpress, McGraw-Hill, MD Consult, Micromedex, Natural Standard, OVID Technologies, PubMed, ScienceDirect, SerialsSolutions, STAT!Ref (Teton Data Systems), Thomson - Web of Science, UpToDate
Function: Audio & video playback equip for onsite use, AV serv, Computers for patron use, Copy machines, Doc delivery serv, Electronic databases & coll, Health sci info serv, ILL available, Online cat, Online searches, Orientations, Outside serv via phone, mail, e-mail & web, Prof lending libr, Ref serv available, VHS videos
Partic in Midwest Collaborative for Library Services (MCLS)
Open Mon-Fri 7:30-4
Restriction: 24-hr pass syst for students only

P FARMINGTON COMMUNITY LIBRARY*, 32737 W 12 Mile Rd, 48334-3302. SAN 346-4342. Tel: 248-553-0300. Reference Tel: 248-553-6880. Administration Tel: 248-848-4303. Automation Services Tel: 248-553-8678. FAX: 248-553-3228. Administration FAX: 248-553-6892. Web Site: www.farmlib.org. *Dir,* Tina M Theeke; Tel: 248-848-4301, E-mail: theeket@farmlib.org; *Asst Dir,* Gerald M Furi; Tel: 248-848-4302, E-mail: gmf@metronet.lib.mi.us; *Br Head,* Sharon Vincent; Tel: 248-848-4307, E-mail: vincents@farmlib.org; Staff 16 (MLS 16)
Founded 1955. Pop 92,534; Circ 1,167,623
Jul 2005-Jun 2006 Income (Main Library and Branch(s)) $7,480,847, State $66,587, City $7,157,380, Locally Generated Income $199,800, Other $123,667. Mats Exp $699,000, Books $390,000, Per/Ser (Incl. Access Fees) $43,000, AV Mat $126,000, Electronic Ref Mat (Incl. Access Fees) $140,000. Sal $2,469,537
Library Holdings: Bk Vols 260,428; Per Subs 395
Special Collections: Business, Law Grantsmanship, parent, teacher, professional; Entrepreneur Coll for Small Business
Automation Activity & Vendor Info: (Acquisitions) SirsiDynix; (Cataloging) SirsiDynix; (Circulation) SirsiDynix; (ILL) OCLC; (OPAC) SirsiDynix
Wireless access
Publications: Info Exchange (Quarterly); Quarterly Program Booklet
Partic in Metro Net Libr Consortium; The Library Network
Open Mon-Thurs 9-9, Fri & Sat 9-6, Sun 12-6
Friends of the Library Group
Branches: 1
FARMINGTON BRANCH, 23500 Liberty St, Farmington, 48335-3570, SAN 346-4407. Tel: 248-553-0300. FAX: 248-474-6915.
Library Holdings: Bk Vols 70,000; Per Subs 200
Open Mon-Thurs 9-9, Fri & Sat 9-6, Sun 12-6
Friends of the Library Group

S MICHIGAN PSYCHOANALYTIC INSTITUTE & SOCIETY*, Ira Miller Memorial Library, 32841 Middlebelt Rd, Ste 411, 48334. SAN 327-7615. Tel: 248-851-3380. FAX: 248-851-1806. E-mail: mpi1@ix.netcom.com. Web Site: www.mpi-mps.org.
Founded 1957
Library Holdings: Bk Titles 2,200; Per Subs 29
Subject Interests: Psychoanalysis, Psychol
Automation Activity & Vendor Info: (OPAC) Inmagic, Inc.
Database Vendor: OCLC FirstSearch
Function: For res purposes

J OAKLAND COMMUNITY COLLEGE, King Library, Orchard Ridge Campus, Bldg K, 27055 Orchard Lake Rd, 48334-4579. SAN 346-4431. Tel: 248-522-3525, 248-522-3526. Reference Tel: 248-522-3612. FAX: 248-522-3530. Web Site: www.oaklandcc.edu/library. *Librn, Ref,* Nadja Springer-Ali; Tel: 248-522-3531, E-mail: nmspring@oaklandcc.edu; *Librn, Ref,* Ann Walaskay; Tel: 248-522-3528, E-mail: aawalask@oaklandcc.edu. Subject Specialists: *Govt doc,* Nadja Springer-Ali; Staff 5.5 (MLS 2, Non-MLS 3.5)
Founded 1967. Enrl 7,450; Fac 83; Highest Degree: Associate
Jul 2013-Jun 2014. Mats Exp $139,984, Books $67,339, Per/Ser (Incl. Access Fees) $21,947, Other Print Mats $50,452, Micro $246. Sal $389,639 (Prof $203,897)
Library Holdings: AV Mats 106; CDs 363; e-books 30,836; Electronic Media & Resources 14,115; Microforms 6,810; Bk Vols 80,819; Per Subs 266; Videos 2,187
Special Collections: US Document Depository
Automation Activity & Vendor Info: (Cataloging) SirsiDynix; (Circulation) SirsiDynix; (Course Reserve) SirsiDynix; (ILL) OCLC; (OPAC) SirsiDynix; (Serials) SirsiDynix
Database Vendor: 3M Library Systems, Alexander Street Press, ARTstor, Bowker, College Source, CQ Press, EBSCO Discovery Service, EBSCO Information Services, EBSCOhost, Electric Library, Elsevier, Gale Cengage Learning, JSTOR, LexisNexis, OCLC WorldShare Interlibrary Loan, Oxford Online, ProQuest, SirsiDynix, Standard & Poor's
Wireless access
Function: Audio & video playback equip for onsite use, Copy machines, Distance learning, e-mail & chat, e-mail serv, Electronic databases & coll, Free DVD rentals, Govt ref serv, ILL available, Microfiche/film & reading machines, Online cat, Online ref, Orientations, Photocopying/Printing, Pub access computers, Wheelchair accessible
Special Services for the Blind - Computer with voice synthesizer for visually impaired persons; Reader equip
Open Mon-Thurs 8am-10pm, Fri 8-5, Sat 10-2

FARWELL

P SURREY TOWNSHIP PUBLIC LIBRARY*, 105 E Michigan, 48622. (Mail add: PO Box 189, 48622-0189), SAN 308-0773. Tel: 989-588-9782. FAX: 989-588-4488. E-mail: loveyourlibrary@yahoo.com. Web Site: www.stpl.org. *Dir,* Jean Gaskill; E-mail: director@stpl.org; *Asst Dir,* Summer Clark; *Circ,* Patty Ried; Staff 6 (MLS 1, Non-MLS 5)
Circ 24,227
Library Holdings: Bk Vols 35,000; Per Subs 80
Automation Activity & Vendor Info: (Acquisitions) Follett Software; (Cataloging) Follett Software; (Circulation) Follett Software; (OPAC) Follett Software
Database Vendor: Gale Cengage Learning, OCLC FirstSearch
Function: Adult literacy prog, Distance learning, ILL available, Magnifiers for reading, Newsp ref libr, Online searches, Outside serv via phone, mail, e-mail & web, Photocopying/Printing, Prog for children & young adult, Summer reading prog, Telephone ref, Wheelchair accessible
Partic in Mid-Michigan Library League
Special Services for the Deaf - Bks on deafness & sign lang; High interest/low vocabulary bks; Videos & decoder
Special Services for the Blind - Aids for in-house use; Audio mat; Bks on cassette; Braille bks; Children's Braille; Copier with enlargement capabilities; Extensive large print coll
Open Mon, Tues, Thurs & Fri 9-6, Wed 9-7, Sat 12-4
Friends of the Library Group

FENNVILLE

P FENNVILLE DISTRICT LIBRARY*, 400 W Main St, 49408. (Mail add: PO Box 1130, 49408-1130), SAN 308-0781. Tel: 269-561-5050. FAX: 269-561-5251. E-mail: fen@llcoop.org. Web Site: www.fennvilledl.michlibrary.org. *Dir,* Bob VandeVusse
Founded 1924. Pop 14,564; Circ 41,000
Library Holdings: Bk Vols 37,000; Per Subs 150
Subject Interests: Mich
Automation Activity & Vendor Info: (Cataloging) Innovative Interfaces, Inc; (Circulation) Innovative Interfaces, Inc; (OPAC) Innovative Interfaces, Inc
Wireless access
Partic in Lakeland Library Cooperative; OCLC Online Computer Library Center, Inc
Special Services for the Deaf - Bks on deafness & sign lang; High interest/low vocabulary bks
Open Mon-Thurs 10-8, Fri 10-5, Sat 10-2, Sun 2-4

FERNDALE

P FERNDALE PUBLIC LIBRARY*, 222 E Nine Mile Rd, 48220. SAN 308-0811. Tel: 248-546-2504. FAX: 248-545-5840. E-mail: info@ferndalepubliclibrary.org. Web Site: www.ferndale.lib.mi.us. *Dir,* Jessica Keyser; Staff 10 (MLS 4, Non-MLS 6)
Founded 1930. Pop 22,105; Circ 125,000
Jul 2007-Jun 2008 Income $1,295,000, State $15,000, City $1,200,000, County $30,000, Locally Generated Income $50,000. Mats Exp $100,000. Sal $227,955
Library Holdings: CDs 1,200; DVDs 1,600; Bk Vols 90,000; Per Subs 125; Talking Bks 1,000; Videos 5,000
Special Collections: Cookbook Coll
Automation Activity & Vendor Info: (Acquisitions) SirsiDynix; (Cataloging) SirsiDynix; (Circulation) SirsiDynix; (ILL) SirsiDynix; (OPAC) SirsiDynix
Wireless access
Partic in The Library Network
Open Mon-Thurs 10-8, Fri 10-5:30, Sat 12-4
Friends of the Library Group

FIFE LAKE

P FIFE LAKE PUBLIC LIBRARY*, 77 Lakecrest Lane, 49633. SAN 308-082X. Tel: 231-879-4101. FAX: 231-879-3360. E-mail: flpl@tadl.tcnet.org. Web Site: www.tadl.tcnet.org. *Librn,* Julie Gray
Founded 1887. Pop 1,517; Circ 12,000
Library Holdings: Large Print Bks 10; Bk Titles 16,000; Per Subs 52
Wireless access
Partic in Mid-Michigan Library League
Open Tues 3-8, Wed & Fri 12-5, Thurs 12-8, Sat 10-3
Friends of the Library Group

FLAT ROCK

P FLAT ROCK PUBLIC LIBRARY*, 25200 Gibraltar Rd, 48134. (Mail add: PO Box 160, 48134-0160), SAN 308-0838. Tel: 734-782-2430. Circulation Tel: 734-782-2430, Ext 106. Reference Tel: 734-782-2430, Ext 107. Administration Tel: 734-782-3444. FAX: 734-789-8265. Administration FAX: 734-789-8266. Web Site: www.frlib.org. *Dir,* Linda Mulder; *Ad,* David Maurer; E-mail: maurer@frlib.org; *Youth Serv Librn,* Connie Biccum
Founded 1999. Pop 11,930; Circ 62,545
Library Holdings: AV Mats 8,366; Bks on Deafness & Sign Lang 20; Large Print Bks 652; Bk Vols 29,896; Per Subs 72; Talking Bks 2,900
Special Collections: Local History Coll
Automation Activity & Vendor Info: (Acquisitions) SirsiDynix; (Cataloging) SirsiDynix; (Circulation) SirsiDynix; (ILL) SirsiDynix; (OPAC) SirsiDynix; (Serials) SirsiDynix
Partic in TLN
Open Mon-Wed 10-8, Thurs-Sun 12-5
Friends of the Library Group

FLINT

C BAKER COLLEGE OF FLINT LIBRARY*, 1050 W Bristol Rd, 48507-5508. SAN 308-0846. Tel: 810-766-4237. Reference Tel: 810-766-4236. Toll Free Tel: 888-854-1058. FAX: 810-766-2013. E-mail: library-fl@baker.edu. Web Site: www.baker.edu. *Dir,* Eric Palmer; Tel: 810-766-4050, E-mail: eric.palmer@baker.edu; *Dir, Ref & Libr Info Serv,* Lynn Stacey; Tel: 810-766-4240; *Ref Librn,* Bruce Childs; *Ref Librn,* Maragaret Forrest; *Ref Librn,* Sulbha Tendulkar; Tel: 810-766-2016; *Ref Librn,* Susan Wizinsky; Staff 16 (MLS 7, Non-MLS 9)
Founded 1912. Enrl 17,000
Library Holdings: Bk Vols 60,000; Per Subs 225
Subject Interests: Aviation, Bus & mgt, Computer sci, Electronics, Eng, Fashion, Interior design, Occupational safety, Phys therapy, Travel
Automation Activity & Vendor Info: (Acquisitions) SirsiDynix; (Cataloging) SirsiDynix; (Circulation) SirsiDynix; (OPAC) SirsiDynix
Wireless access
Partic in OCLC Online Computer Library Center, Inc
Open Mon-Thurs (Winter) 8am-10pm, Fri 8-6, Sat 9-2, Sun 12-5; Mon-Thurs (Summer) 8-8, Fri 8-3, Sat 9-2

SR FIRST PRESBYTERIAN CHURCH OF FLINT*, Pierce Memorial Library, 746 S Saginaw St, 48502-1508. SAN 329-8833. Tel: 810-234-8673. FAX: 810-234-1643. Web Site: www.fpcf.org. *Librn,* Steve Hill; E-mail: shill@fpcf.org
Founded 1841
Library Holdings: AV Mats 3,076; CDs 1,021; DVDs 226; Bk Titles 4,823; Bk Vols 5,208; Talking Bks 633; Videos 2,848
Automation Activity & Vendor Info: (Cataloging) LibraryWorld, Inc; (Circulation) LibraryWorld, Inc
Open Mon-Fri (Winter) 8:30-4:30, Sun 8:30-12; Mon-Fri (Summer) 8-4, Sun 9:30-11

S FLINT INSTITUTE OF ARTS*, Reference Library, 1120 E Kearsley St, 48503-1915. SAN 308-0927. Tel: 810-237-7386. FAX: 810-234-1692. E-mail: librarian@flintarts.org. Web Site: flintarts.org/collections_library.html. *Dir,* John B Henry, III; *Librn,* Judy Johnson; *Educ Curator,* Monique Desormeau
Founded 1928
Library Holdings: Bk Titles 8,000
Subject Interests: Art & archit
Publications: Exhibition Catalogues
Open Mon-Sat 12-5, Sun 1-5
Restriction: Non-circulating to the pub

P FLINT PUBLIC LIBRARY*, 1026 E Kearsley St, 48502-1994. SAN 346-4466. Tel: 810-232-7111. Reference Tel: 810-249-2569. FAX: 810-249-2635. Web Site: www.flint.lib.mi.us. *Dir,* Kathryn Schwartz; *Adult Serv, Teen Serv,* Leslie Acevedo; Tel: 810-249-2046, E-mail: lacevedo@fpl.info; *Ch Serv,* Janet Trosino; Tel: 810-249-2175, E-mail: jtrosino@fpl.info; Staff 31 (MLS 22, Non-MLS 9)
Founded 1851. Pop 124,943
Jul 2007-Jun 2008 Income $5,365,578, State $98,762, City $4,782,757, Locally Generated Income $142,445, Other $341,614. Mats Exp $425,302, Books $317,014. Sal $2,657,589
Library Holdings: AV Mats 34,233; e-books 300; Bk Vols 407,614; Per Subs 976
Special Collections: US Document Depository
Subject Interests: Children's lit, Genealogy, Local hist
Automation Activity & Vendor Info: (Circulation) SirsiDynix
Function: ILL available, Ref serv available
Publications: Ring A Ring O'Roses
Partic in Mideastern Michigan Library Cooperative
Special Services for the Deaf - High interest/low vocabulary bks; Staff with knowledge of sign lang; TTY equip
Open Tues-Sat 9-8
Friends of the Library Group
Bookmobiles: 1

L GENESEE COUNTY CIRCUIT COURT*, Law Library, County Court House, Ste 204, 900 S Saginaw St, 48502. SAN 329-7691. Tel: 810-257-3253. FAX: 810-239-9280. Web Site: co.genesee.mi.us. *Librn,* Trea Poe
Library Holdings: Bk Vols 10,000; Per Subs 10
Wireless access
Open Mon-Fri 8-5
Restriction: Limited access for the pub, Ref only

S GENESEE COUNTY METROPOLITAN PLANNING COMMISSION LIBRARY*, 1101 Beach St, Rm 223, 48502-1470. SAN 373-0727. Tel: 810-257-3010. FAX: 810-257-3185. E-mail: gcmpc@co.genesee.mi.us. *Asst Dir,* Thomas Goergen
Library Holdings: Bk Vols 300
Subject Interests: Housing, Transportation
Restriction: Staff use only

P GENESEE DISTRICT LIBRARY*, G-4195 W Pasadena Ave, 48504. SAN 346-4709. Tel: 810-732-5570. Circulation Tel: 810-732-0110. Interlibrary Loan Service Tel: 810-789-2800. Reference Tel: 810-732-0123. FAX: 810-732-1161. Web Site: www.thegdl.org. *Exec Dir,* Carolyn Nash; Tel: 810-230-3335, E-mail: cnash@thegdl.org; *IT Dept Head,* Ronnie Morgan; Tel: 810-230-3341, E-mail: rmorgan@thegdl.org; *Br Operations Mgr,* Kelly Richards; Tel: 810-230-3330; 810-230-3331, E-mail: krichards@thegdl.org; *Finance Mgr,* Amy Goldyn; Tel: 810-230-3334, E-mail: agoldyn@thegdl.org; *Human Res Mgr,* Heather Gill; Tel: 810-230-3340, E-mail: hgill@thegdl.org; *Tech Serv Mgr,* Darwin McGuire; Tel: 810-230-3329, E-mail: dmcguire@thegdl.org; *Commun Relations Officer,* Trenton Marcus Smiley; Tel: 810-230-9613, E-mail: tsmiley@thegdl.org; Staff 35 (MLS 33, Non-MLS 2)
Founded 1942. Pop 332,567; Circ 4,555,186
Jan 2011-Dec 2011 Income (Main Library and Branch(s)) $8,549,386, State $194,118, County $7,851,363, Other $503,905. Mats Exp $1,575,500, Books $960,000, Per/Ser (Incl. Access Fees) $65,000, Micro $5,000, AV Equip $30,000, AV Mat $410,000, Electronic Ref Mat (Incl. Access Fees) $105,000, Presv $500. Sal $3,492,000 (Prof $2,370,000)
Library Holdings: Audiobooks 4,828; AV Mats 253,292; Bks-By-Mail 7,000; Bks on Deafness & Sign Lang 80; Braille Volumes 21; CDs 8,142; DVDs 182,443; e-books 7,888; Electronic Media & Resources 52; High Interest/Low Vocabulary Bk Vols 30; Large Print Bks 137,999; Bk Vols 880,999; Per Subs 1,285; Talking Bks 14,011; Videos 11,004
Special Collections: American Indians Coll, bks, recs; Civil War (Robert L Calkins Memorial Coll); Genesee County Coll
Subject Interests: Genealogy
Automation Activity & Vendor Info: (Acquisitions) Innovative Interfaces, Inc; (Cataloging) Innovative Interfaces, Inc; (Circulation) Innovative Interfaces, Inc; (OPAC) Innovative Interfaces, Inc; (Serials) Innovative Interfaces, Inc
Database Vendor: Innovative Interfaces, Inc
Wireless access
Function: Words travel prog
Publications: Newsletter of the Genesee District Library
Special Services for the Deaf - Videos & decoder
Special Services for the Blind - Accessible computers; Aids for in-house use; Assistive/Adapted tech devices, equip & products; Audio mat; BiFolkal kits; Bks & mags in Braille, on rec, tape & cassette; Bks available with recordings; Bks on cassette; Blind Club (monthly newsletter); Braille bks; Braille Webster's dictionary; Cassette playback machines; Cassettes; Club for the blind; Computer access aids; Computer with voice synthesizer for visually impaired persons; Copier with enlargement capabilities; Descriptive video serv (DVS); Digital talking bk; Duplicating spec requests; Handicapped awareness prog; Home delivery serv; Info on spec aids & appliances; Internet workstation with adaptive software; Large print & cassettes; Large print bks; Large print bks & talking machines; Large screen computer & software; Lending of low vision aids; Low vision equip; Machine repair; Magnifiers; Networked computers with assistive software; Newsline for the Blind; Newsp on cassette; PC for handicapped; Playaways (bks on MP3); Sound rec; Spec

cats; Spec prog; Talking bks & player equip; Talking bks from Braille Inst; Text reader; Volunteer serv
Friends of the Library Group
Branches: 21
BAKER PARK, G-3410 S Grand Traverse, Burton, 48529, SAN 346-5128. Tel: 810-742-7860. FAX: 810-742-2927. *Librn,* Robert Gorney; Staff 1.6 (MLS 1, Non-MLS 0.6)
Open Mon, Tues & Thurs 12-8, Wed 10-6, Fri & Sat 9-5
BURTON MEMORIAL, G-4012 E Atherton Rd, Burton, 48519, SAN 346-4733. Tel: 810-742-0674. FAX: 810-742-2928. *Librn,* Amy Calmes; Staff 2 (MLS 1, Non-MLS 1)
Open Mon 9-9, Tues & Thurs 10-6, Wed 12-8, Sat 9-5
Friends of the Library Group
CLIO AREA, G-2080 W Vienna Rd, Clio, 48420, SAN 346-4768. Tel: 810-686-7130. FAX: 810-686-0071. *Librn,* Roy Soncrant; E-mail: rsoncrant@thegdl.org; Staff 1 (MLS 1)
Open Mon & Wed 12-8, Tues & Thurs 10-6, Sat 9-5
Friends of the Library Group
DAVISON AREA, 203 E Fourth St, Davison, 48423, SAN 346-4792. Tel: 810-653-2022. FAX: 810-653-7633. *Librn,* Mary Higginbottom; Staff 1 (MLS 1)
Special Collections: Calkins Civil War Coll
Open Mon-Thurs 9-9, Fri & Sat 9-5, Sun 12-6
FLUSHING AREA, 120 N Maple, Flushing, 48433, SAN 346-4881. Tel: 810-659-9755. FAX: 810-659-1781. *Librn,* Faye Gulley; Staff 2 (MLS 2)
Open Mon-Thurs 9-9, Fri & Sat 9-5
Friends of the Library Group
FOREST TOWNSHIP, 123 W Main St, Otisville, 48463, SAN 346-5098. Tel: 810-631-6330. FAX: 810-631-6076. *Librn,* Marya Gutek; Staff 1 (MLS 1)
Open Mon 10-6, Tues-Thurs 12-8, Sat 9-5
Friends of the Library Group
GAINES STATION, 103 E Walker, Gaines, 48436, SAN 378-133X. Tel: 989-271-8720. FAX: 989-271-8816.
Open Mon-Thurs 12-6, Sat 9-5
GENESEE VALLEY DEMONSTRATION LOCATION, 3293 S Linden Rd, 48507. Tel: 810-732-1822. FAX: 810-732-1726. *Librn,* Sarah Fiala; E-mail: sfiala@thegdl.org; Staff 1 (MLS 1)
Open Mon & Tue 10-9, Wed & Thurs 11-7, Fri & Sat 10-6, Sun 1-5
GOODRICH AREA, 10237 Hegel Rd, Goodrich, 48438, SAN 346-4911. Tel: 810-636-2489. FAX: 810-636-3304. *Librn,* Megan Brown; E-mail: mbrown@thegdl.org; Staff 1 (MLS 1)
Open Mon-Wed 12-8, Thurs 10-6, Fri & Sat 9-5
Friends of the Library Group
HEADQUARTERS, G-4195 W Pasadena Ave, 48504, SAN 346-4989. Tel: 810-732-0110. Interlibrary Loan Service Tel: 810-789-2800. FAX: 810-732-3146. *Sr Librn,* Tom Rohrer; *Librn,* Sue Misra; *Tech Serv Librn,* Kara Yater. Subject Specialists: *Blind, Bus, Libr,* Tom Rohrer; *Cataloging,* Kara Yater; Staff 3 (MLS 3)
Special Services for the Blind - Descriptive video serv (DVS); Talking bks
Open Mon & Tues 9-9, Wed & Thurs 12-8, Fri & Sat 9-5
HEADQUARTERS REFERENCE, G-4195 W Pasadena Ave, 48504. Tel: 810-732-0110. FAX: 810-732-3146. *Ref,* Tom Rohrer; Staff 1 (MLS 1)
Open Mon & Tues 9-9, Wed & Thurs 12-8, Fri & Sat 9-5
MONTROSE-JENNINGS LIBRARY, 241 Feher Dr, Montrose, 48457, SAN 346-5039. Tel: 810-639-6388. FAX: 810-639-3675. *Librn,* Susan Harshfield; E-mail: sharshfield@thegdl.org; Staff 1 (MLS 1)
Open Mon & Wed 10-6, Tues & Thurs 12-8, Sat 9-5
GENESEE TOWNSHIP (JOHNSON MEMORIAL LIBRARY), 7397 N Genesee Rd, Genesee, 48437, SAN 346-4970. Tel: 810-640-1410. FAX: 810-640-2413. *Librn,* Shari Suarez; Staff 1 (MLS 1)
Open Mon 10-6, Tues & Thurs 12-8, Fri & Sat 9-5
Friends of the Library Group

P LIBRARY FOR THE BLIND & PHYSICALLY HANDICAPPED, G-4195 W Pasadena Ave, 48504. Tel: 810-732-1120. FAX: 810-732-1715. *Librn,* Thomas Rohrer; E-mail: trohrer@thegdl.org; Staff 1 (MLS 1)
Partic in Mideastern Michigan Library Cooperative; Midwest Collaborative for Library Services (MCLS)
Special Services for the Blind - Bks on cassette; Descriptive video serv (DVS)
Open Mon-Fri 9-5

LINDEN AREA, 201 N Main, Linden, 48451, SAN 346-5004. Tel: 810-735-7700. FAX: 810-735-9163. *Librn,* Hans Norbotten; Staff 1 (MLS 1)
Open Mon, Wed & Thurs 12-8, Tues & Sat 9-5
FLINT TOWNSHIP (MCCARTY PUBLIC LIBRARY), 2071 S Graham Rd, 48532, SAN 346-4857. Tel: 810-732-9150. FAX: 810-732-0878. *Librn,* Cara Birmingham; E-mail: cbirmingham@thegdl.org; Staff 1 (MLS 1)
Open Mon & Wed 10-6, Tues & Thurs 12-8, Fri & Sat 9-5
GRAND BLANC-MCFARLEN PUBLIC LIBRARY, 515 Perry Rd, Grand Blanc, 48439, SAN 346-4946. Tel: 810-694-5310. FAX: 810-694-5313. *Sr Br Librn,* Kara Kvasnicka; *Bus Librn,* Trevor Winn; Staff 3 (MLS 3)
Open Mon-Thurs 9-9, Fri & Sat 9-5, Sun 12-6
Friends of the Library Group
MOUNT MORRIS AREA, 685 Van Buren Ave, Mount Morris, 48458, SAN 346-5063. Tel: 810-686-6120. FAX: 810-686-0661. *Librn,* Susan Badgley; E-mail: sbadgley@thegdl.org; Staff 1 (MLS 1)
Open Mon-Thurs 9-9, Fri & Sat 9-5
VERA B RISON-BEECHER LIBRARY, 1386 W Coldwater Rd, 48505. Tel: 810-789-2800. FAX: 810-789-2882. *Librn,* John Ekleberry; E-mail: jekleberry@thegdl.org; Staff 1 (MLS 1)
Open Mon, Wed, Fri & Sat 9-5, Tues & Thurs Noon-8
Friends of the Library Group
SWARTZ CREEK-PERKINS LIBRARY, 8095 Civic Dr, Swartz Creek, 48473, SAN 346-5152. Tel: 810-635-3900. FAX: 810-635-4179. *Librn,* Ivan Smith; Staff 1 (MLS 1)
Open Mon-Wed 12-8, Thurs & Sat 9-5
FENTON-JACK R WINEGARDEN LIBRARY, 200 E Caroline St, Fenton, 48430, SAN 346-4822. Tel: 810-629-7612. FAX: 810-629-0855. *Sr Br Librn,* Christine Heron; Staff 1 (MLS 1)
Open Mon & Wed 10-6, Tues & Thurs 12-8, Fri & Sat 9-5

M HURLEY MEDICAL CENTER*, Michael H & Robert M Hamady Health Sciences Library, One Hurley Plaza, 48503. SAN 308-0919. Tel: 810-257-9427. Interlibrary Loan Service Tel: 810-257-9055. Administration Tel: 810-257-9163. Information Services Tel: 810-257-9442. FAX: 810-762-7107. E-mail: library1@hurleymc.com. *Libr Dir,* Sharon Williams; Staff 3 (MLS 2, Non-MLS 1)
Founded 1928
Library Holdings: Bk Titles 4,000; Per Subs 300
Special Collections: Consumer Health Information
Subject Interests: Health sci, Hospital admin, Med, Nursing
Automation Activity & Vendor Info: (Cataloging) EOS International; (Circulation) EOS International; (Serials) EOS International
Partic in Docline; Michigan Health Sciences Libraries Association; National Network of Libraries of Medicine
Restriction: Not open to pub

C KETTERING UNIVERSITY LIBRARY*, 1700 W University Ave, 48504-4898. SAN 308-0900. Tel: 810-762-7814. Reference Tel: 810-762-9598. Administration Tel: 810-762-7812. FAX: 810-762 9744. Web Site: www.kettering.edu/library. *Dir,* Dr Charles Hanson; E-mail: chanson@kettering.edu; *Digital Tech/Ref Librn,* Jessica Sanchez; Tel: 810-762-7815, E-mail: jsanchez@kettering.edu; *Pub Serv Librn,* Jim Kangas; Tel: 810-762-7818, E-mail: jkangas@kettering.edu; *Pub Serv Librn,* Jessica Long; Tel: 810-762-9618, E-mail: jlong@kettering.edu; *Tech Serv Librn,* Dawn Olmsted-Swanson; Tel: 810-762-7817, E-mail: dswanson@kettering.edu; Staff 5 (MLS 5)
Founded 1928. Enrl 2,675; Fac 154; Highest Degree: Master
Library Holdings: e books 28,500; e-journals 3,400; Bk Titles 131,700; Bk Vols 147,900; Per Subs 400
Special Collections: ASTM Standards; NASA Technical Reports; SAE & SME Technical Papers
Subject Interests: Bus & mgt, Eng
Automation Activity & Vendor Info: (Acquisitions) SirsiDynix; (Cataloging) SirsiDynix; (Cataloging) OCLC; (Circulation) SirsiDynix; (Course Reserve) Blackboard Inc; (ILL) Clio; (OPAC) SirsiDynix; (Serials) EBSCO Online
Database Vendor: ACM (Association for Computing Machinery), American Chemical Society, American Mathematical Society, College Source, CRC Press/Taylor & Francis Group, EBSCOhost, Elsevier, Gale Cengage Learning, IEEE (Institute of Electrical & Electronics Engineers), Ingenta, IOP, LearningExpress, Marquis Who's Who, Newsbank, OCLC FirstSearch, ProQuest, RefWorks, ScienceDirect, SerialsSolutions, SirsiDynix, Springer-Verlag, Thomson - Web of Science, Wiley InterScience
Wireless access
Function: Res libr
Partic in PALnet
Open Mon-Thurs 7:45am-11pm, Fri 7:45-5:30, Sat 10-5, Sun 12-8
Restriction: Open to fac, students & qualified researchers
Friends of the Library Group

M MCLAREN REGIONAL MEDICAL CENTER*, Medical Library, 401 S Ballenger Hwy, 48532-3685. SAN 324-3907. Tel: 810-342-2141. FAX: 810-342-2269. E-mail: medlib@mclaren.org. *Mgr,* Diane Gardner; *Asst Librn,* Mary Fitzpatrick; E-mail: maryk@mclaren.org; *Tech Serv,* Diane Gardner; E-mail: dianeg@mclaren.org; Staff 3 (MLS 1, Non-MLS 2)
Founded 1951
Library Holdings: e-books 60; e-journals 2,500; Bk Titles 1,500; Per Subs 300
Subject Interests: Clinical med, Family practice, Health, Hospital admin, Nursing, Orthopedics, Radiology, Surgery

Automation Activity & Vendor Info: (Cataloging) EOS International; (Circulation) EOS International; (OPAC) EOS International; (Serials) EOS International
Partic in Docline; National Network of Libraries of Medicine; OCLC Online Computer Library Center, Inc
Open Mon-Fri 7-5

J MOTT COMMUNITY COLLEGE*, Mott Library, 1401 E Court St, 48503. SAN 308-0935. Tel: 810-762-0400. Circulation Tel: 810-762-0403. Reference Tel: 810-762-0411. Administration Tel: 810-762-0408. FAX: 810-762-0407. E-mail: library@mcc.edu. Web Site: library.mcc.edu. *Dir of Libr Serv,* Position Currently Open; *Coordr, Circ & Tech Serv, Interim Dir,* Linda Rutherford; Tel: 810-762-0402; *Coordr, Pub Serv,* Michael Ugorowski; Tel: 810-762-5662; Staff 9.5 (MLS 6.5, Non-MLS 3)
Founded 1923. Enrl 10,400; Fac 554; Highest Degree: Associate
Jul 2012-Jun 2013 Income $1,039,808. Mats Exp $137,000, Books $40,000, Per/Ser (Incl. Access Fees) $32,000, Electronic Ref Mat (Incl. Access Fees) $65,000. Sal $483,429 (Prof $348,429)
Library Holdings: e-books 25,000; Bk Vols 75,000; Per Subs 150
Special Collections: College History Archive
Automation Activity & Vendor Info: (Acquisitions) SirsiDynix; (Cataloging) SirsiDynix; (Circulation) SirsiDynix; (Course Reserve) SirsiDynix; (ILL) OCLC; (OPAC) SirsiDynix; (Serials) SirsiDynix
Database Vendor: Cinahl, CQ Press, ebrary, EBSCOhost, Gale Cengage Learning, JSTOR, LearningExpress, OCLC, SirsiDynix, Springshare, LLC
Wireless access
Function: Audio & video playback equip for onsite use, Computers for patron use, Copy machines, Electronic databases & coll, Online cat, Online ref, Orientations, Scanner
Partic in Mideastern Michigan Library Cooperative; PALnet
Restriction: ID required to use computers (Ltd hrs), Lending limited to county residents, Open to students, fac & staff
Friends of the Library Group

S SLOAN MUSEUM*, Perry Archives, Flint Cultural Ctr, 303 Walnut St, 48503. SAN 325-920X. Tel: 810-237-3440. Toll Free Tel: 866-756-2631. FAX: 810-237-3433. E-mail: sloan@sloanlongway.org. Web Site: sloanmuseum.org. *Curator,* Jeff Taylor; Tel: 810-237-3435
Library Holdings: Bk Vols 4,000
Special Collections: Archives Holdings for Flint & Genesee County
Restriction: Open by appt only

C UNIVERSITY OF MICHIGAN-FLINT*, Frances Willson Thompson Library, 303 E Kearsley St, 48502-1950. SAN 308-0951. Tel: 810-762-3400. Reference Tel: 810-762-3408. FAX: 810-762-3133. Web Site: umflint.edu/library. *Dir,* Robert L Houbeck, Jr; Tel: 810-762-3018, E-mail: rhoubeck@umflint.edu; *Head, Circ, Ref & Instruction Librn,* Mickey Doyle; Tel: 810-762-3401, E-mail: doylemd@umflint.edu; *Coll Develop Librn, Webmaster,* Paul Streby; Tel: 810-762-3405, E-mail: pgstreby@umflint.edu; *Syst Librn,* Kui-Bin Im; Tel: 810-762-3199, E-mail: kuibinim@umflint.edu; *Archivist,* Paul Gifford; Tel: 810-762-3402, E-mail: pgifford@umflint.edu; *Ser,* Anh Thach; Tel: 810-762-3414, E-mail: athach@umflint.edu; Staff 15 (MLS 10, Non-MLS 5)
Founded 1956. Enrl 7,200; Fac 333; Highest Degree: Master
Library Holdings: Bk Vols 235,000; Per Subs 905
Special Collections: Genesee Historical Coll Center
Automation Activity & Vendor Info: (Acquisitions) Ex Libris Group; (Cataloging) Ex Libris Group; (Circulation) Ex Libris Group; (Course Reserve) Ex Libris Group; (OPAC) Ex Libris Group; (Serials) Ex Libris Group
Database Vendor: Ex Libris Group
Wireless access
Function: Pub access computers
Partic in Midwest Collaborative for Library Services (MCLS)
Special Services for the Deaf - Closed caption videos

FOSTORIA

P WATERTOWN TOWNSHIP FOSTORIA LIBRARY*, 9405 Foster St, 48435. (Mail add: PO Box 39, 48435-0039), SAN 308-096X. Tel: 989-795-2794. FAX: 989-795-2892. *Librn,* Cathy Valentine
Founded 1964. Pop 2,100; Circ 4,800
Library Holdings: Bk Vols 7,000; Per Subs 10
Wireless access
Partic in White Pine Libr Coop
Open Mon-Thurs 12-5 & Sat 10-12

FOWLERVILLE

P FOWLERVILLE DISTRICT LIBRARY*, 131 Mill St, 48836. (Mail add: PO Box 313, 48836-0313), SAN 308-0978. Tel: 517-223-9089. FAX: 517-223-0781. E-mail: info@fowlervillelibrary.org. Web Site: www.fowlervillelibrary.org. *Dir,* Cheryl Poch; E-mail: c.poch@fowlervillelibrary.org; *Asst Dir,* Karin Pomeroy; E-mail: k.pomeroy@fowlervillelibrary.org; *Circ Mgr,* Cindy Peach; E-mail: c.peach@fowlervillelibrary.org; *Circ Serv Coordr,* Jessica Schell; E-mail: j.schell@fowlervillelibrary.org; Staff 1 (Non-MLS 1)
Circ 23,000
Library Holdings: AV Mats 3,913; High Interest/Low Vocabulary Bk Vols 774; Large Print Bks 421; Bk Titles 28,248; Bk Vols 29,368; Per Subs 65
Subject Interests: Holidays
Automation Activity & Vendor Info: (Cataloging) Follett Software; (Circulation) Follett Software; (ILL) Follett Software
Partic in The Library Network
Open Mon-Thurs 9:30-7, Fri 9:30-5, Sat 10-2
Friends of the Library Group

FRANKENMUTH

S FRANKENMUTH HISTORICAL ASSOCIATION, Frankenmuth Historical Museum Library, 613 S Main St, 48734. SAN 326-0690. Tel: 989-652-9701. FAX: 989-652-9390. E-mail: fharesearch@airadv.net. Web Site: www.frankenmuthmuseum.org. *Dir,* Jonathan T Webb; E-mail: fhadirector@airadv.net; *Curator of Coll, Curator of Res Serv,* Mary Nuechterlein; Staff 1 (MLS 1)
Founded 1972
Library Holdings: Bk Titles 2,000; Bk Vols 2,500
Special Collections: Wilhelm Loehe Memorial Library; Wm Loehe Mission Activities. Oral History
Publications: Annual Booklet on History of Local Business or Organization
Restriction: Open by appt only, Pub use on premises

P FRANKENMUTH JAMES E WICKSON DISTRICT LIBRARY*, 359 S Franklin St, 48734. SAN 308-0986. Tel: 989-652-8323. FAX: 989-652-3450. E-mail: wicksonlibrary@gmail.com. Web Site: www.wicksonlibrary.org. *Libr Dir,* Mary Chasseur; *Asst Libr Dir,* Kathy Wiese; *Ch,* Pam Williams; Staff 12 (MLS 1, Non-MLS 11)
Founded 1974. Pop 6,887; Circ 95,953
Library Holdings: AV Mats 3,749; CDs 351; DVDs 114; Large Print Bks 1,249; Bk Vols 46,863; Per Subs 92; Talking Bks 1,015; Videos 1,832
Subject Interests: Genealogy, German lang, Local hist, Women studies
Automation Activity & Vendor Info: (Cataloging) Auto-Graphics, Inc; (Circulation) Auto-Graphics, Inc; (OPAC) Auto-Graphics, Inc
Database Vendor: Gale Cengage Learning, OCLC FirstSearch
Wireless access
Publications: Newsletter (Quarterly)
Partic in White Pine Libr Coop
Open Mon-Thurs 9-9, Fri 9-5, Sat 10-5, Sun (Oct-Apr) 1-4
Friends of the Library Group

FRANKFORT

P BENZIE SHORES DISTRICT LIBRARY*, 630 Main St, 49635. (Mail add: PO Box 631, 49635-0631), SAN 308-0994. Tel: 231-352-4671. FAX: 231-352-4671. E-mail: bsdl@benzieshoreslibrary.org. Web Site: www.benzieshoreslibrary.org. *Dir,* Cathy Carter; *Libr Asst, Tech Serv,* Cindy Collier; *Ch,* Julie Morris; *Asst Librn,* Stacy Pasche; E-mail: spasche@benzieshoreslibrary.org; Staff 3 (MLS 1.5, Non-MLS 1.5)
Pop 4,000; Circ 64,253
Jul 2012-Jun 2013 Income $269,544. Mats Exp $269,555. Sal $138,400 (Prof $71,000)
Library Holdings: Audiobooks 800; DVDs 800; e-books 4,000; e-journals 50; Large Print Bks 2,000; Bk Vols 25,000; Per Subs 75; Talking Bks 1,114
Automation Activity & Vendor Info: (ILL) Mel Cat
Wireless access
Function: Adult bk club, Home delivery & serv to Sr ctr & nursing homes, Homebound delivery serv, ILL available, Libr develop, Online searches, Photocopying/Printing, Prog for children & young adult, Ref & res, Ref serv available, Spoken cassettes & CDs, Summer reading prog, Wheelchair accessible, Workshops
Partic in Mid-Michigan Library League
Open Mon & Wed 10-8, Tues, Thurs & Fri 10-5, Sat 10-3
Restriction: Circ to mem only
Friends of the Library Group

S PAUL OLIVER MEMORIAL HOSPITAL*, Caregiver Resource Center & Library, 224 Park Ave, 49635. Tel: 231-352-2312. E-mail: library-pomhcaregiverresourcecenter@mhc.net. Web Site: www.munsonhealthcare.org. *Coordr,* Sherri Dittman. Subject Specialists: *Gerontology,* Sherri Dittman; Staff 1 (Non-MLS 1)
Founded 2002
Library Holdings: AV Mats 200; Bk Titles 400; Bk Vols 450; Per Subs 11; Spec Interest Per Sub 11
Special Collections: Caregiving (Laylevel Resource Coll); Gerontology (Clinical Resource Coll)
Automation Activity & Vendor Info: (Cataloging) Follett Software; (Circulation) Follett Software; (OPAC) Follett Software

Function: For res purposes, Handicapped accessible, Homebound delivery serv, Mail loans to mem, Outside serv via phone, mail, e-mail & web, Photocopying/Printing, Prog for adults, Ref serv available, Referrals accepted, Telephone ref, Wheelchair accessible
Open Mon-Sun 8-8

FRANKLIN

P FRANKLIN PUBLIC LIBRARY*, 32455 Franklin Rd, 48025. SAN 308-1001. Tel: 248-851-2254. FAX: 248-851-5846. Web Site: www.franklin.lib.mi.us. *Dir,* Teresa Natzke; Staff 7 (MLS 1, Non-MLS 6)
Pop 3,000; Circ 24,000
Library Holdings: Bk Vols 14,000; Per Subs 50
Automation Activity & Vendor Info: (Cataloging) SirsiDynix; (Circulation) SirsiDynix; (OPAC) SirsiDynix
Wireless access
Function: Adult bk club, Bks on CD, Children's prog, Computers for patron use, Copy machines, Fax serv, Free DVD rentals, Handicapped accessible, ILL available, Large print keyboards, Mus passes, Online cat, Online searches, Photocopying/Printing, Preschool outreach, Prog for adults, Prog for children & young adult, Pub access computers, Ref serv in person, Story hour, Summer reading prog, Tax forms, Wheelchair accessible
Open Mon, Wed & Fri 11-6, Tues & Thurs 11-8, Sat 11-4
Friends of the Library Group

FRASER

P E C WEBER FRASER PUBLIC LIBRARY*, 16330 Fourteen Mile Rd, 48026-2034. SAN 308-101X. Tel: 586-293-2055. FAX: 586-294-5777. Web Site: www.micityoffraser.com. *Dir,* Regina Slivka; E-mail: slivkar@libcoop.net; Staff 6.5 (MLS 2, Non-MLS 4.5)
Founded 1963. Pop 14,400; Circ 111,382
Jul 2011-Jun 2012 Income $419,032, State $6,122, City $399,198, County $13,712. Mats Exp $30,871, Books $19,257, Per/Ser (Incl. Access Fees) $2,028, Other Print Mats $3,453, AV Mat $4,387, Electronic Ref Mat (Incl. Access Fees) $1,746. Sal $248,587
Library Holdings: Audiobooks 386; CDs 3,640; DVDs 6,158; e-books 1,286; Electronic Media & Resources 49; Large Print Bks 609; Bk Vols 60,807; Per Subs 100; Videos 90
Automation Activity & Vendor Info: (Acquisitions) SirsiDynix; (Cataloging) SirsiDynix; (Circulation) SirsiDynix
Database Vendor: Gale Cengage Learning, Overdrive, Inc, SirsiDynix
Wireless access
Function: Adult bk club, Art exhibits, Audiobks via web, AV serv, Bk club(s), Bks on CD, Children's prog, Computers for patron use, Copy machines, Electronic databases & coll, Exhibits, Free DVD rentals, Handicapped accessible, Holiday prog, ILL available, Mus passes, Music CDs, Online cat, Online searches, OverDrive digital audio bks, Prog for adults, Prog for children & young adult, Pub access computers, Ref & res, Ref serv available, Ref serv in person, Story hour, Summer reading prog, Tax forms, Telephone ref, Wheelchair accessible
Partic in Suburban Library Cooperative
Open Mon-Thurs 10-8, Fri & Sat 10-5
Restriction: Authorized patrons
Friends of the Library Group

FREELAND

S MICHIGAN DEPARTMENT OF CORRECTIONS*, Saginaw Correctional Facility Library, 9625 Pierce Rd, 48623. Tel: 989-695-9880. FAX: 989-695-6345. *Librn,* Ervin Bell; E-mail: belled@michigan.gov; *Libr Tech,* Dan Fortier
Library Holdings: Bk Vols 20,000; Per Subs 50
Automation Activity & Vendor Info: (Cataloging) Winnebago Software Co; (Circulation) Winnebago Software Co
Open Mon 8-4:30, Tues-Fri 8am-9pm, Sat 10:30-7

FREEPORT

P FREEPORT DISTRICT LIBRARY*, 208 S State St, 49325-9759. (Mail add: PO Box 5, 49325-0005), SAN 308-1028. Tel: 616-765-5181. FAX: 616-765-5181. E-mail: fre@lakeland.lib.mi.us. Web Site: freeport.llcoop.org. *Dir,* Joanne Hesselink; Staff 2 (Non-MLS 2)
Founded 1942. Pop 5,062; Circ 25,000
Library Holdings: AV Mats 920; Large Print Bks 210; Bk Titles 12,060; Per Subs 18; Talking Bks 570
Automation Activity & Vendor Info: (Cataloging) Innovative Interfaces, Inc; (Circulation) Innovative Interfaces, Inc; (ILL) Innovative Interfaces, Inc; (OPAC) Innovative Interfaces, Inc
Open Mon & Thurs 1-8, Wed 9-5, Fri 1-5, Sat (Sept-Apr) 9am-11am
Friends of the Library Group

FREMONT

P FREMONT AREA DISTRICT LIBRARY*, 104 E Main, 49412. SAN 308-1036. Tel: 231-924-3480. Circulation Tel: 231-928-0244. Reference Tel: 231-928-0256. Administration Tel: 231-928-0243. FAX: 231-924-2355. E-mail: fmt@llcoop.org. Web Site: www.fremontlibrary.net. *Dir,* Ray Arnett; E-mail: rarnett@fremontlibrary.net; *Adult Serv, Ref Serv,* Jill Hansen; Tel: 231-928-0253, E-mail: jhansen@fremontlibrary.net; *Circ,* Lois Beekman; E-mail: lbeekman@fremontlibrary.net; *Youth Serv,* Roxanne Landin; Tel: 231-928-2049, E-mail: rlandin@fremontlibrary.net; Staff 18 (MLS 3, Non-MLS 15)
Founded 1996. Pop 13,413; Circ 170,000
Library Holdings: Bk Vols 81,000; Per Subs 200
Special Collections: Local History (Harry L Spooner Coll)
Automation Activity & Vendor Info: (Acquisitions) Innovative Interfaces, Inc; (Cataloging) Innovative Interfaces, Inc; (Circulation) Innovative Interfaces, Inc; (ILL) Innovative Interfaces, Inc; (OPAC) Innovative Interfaces, Inc; (Serials) Innovative Interfaces, Inc
Database Vendor: Checkpoint Systems, Inc, Gale Cengage Learning, OCLC FirstSearch, ProQuest
Wireless access
Publications: Friends of the Library Newsletter (Quarterly)
Partic in Lakeland Library Cooperative
Special Services for the Blind - Audio mat; Bks on cassette; Bks on CD; Extensive large print coll
Open Mon, Tues & Thurs 10-7, Wed & Fri 10-5, Sat 10-1
Friends of the Library Group

GALESBURG

P GALESBURG CHARLESTON MEMORIAL DISTRICT LIBRARY, 188 E Michigan Ave, 49053. SAN 308-1052. Tel: 269-665-7839. FAX: 269-665-7788. E-mail: galesburglibrary@hotmail.com. *Dir,* Donna Kowalewski
Pop 8,100; Circ 18,500
Library Holdings: Audiobooks 683; Bk Vols 30,490; Per Subs 21; Videos 1,001
Special Collections: Michigan Coll; Michigan Nut Growers Association; Michigan Pioneer Coll
Subject Interests: Local hist
Automation Activity & Vendor Info: (Acquisitions) Biblionix/Apollo; (Cataloging) Biblionix/Apollo; (Circulation) Biblionix/Apollo; (ILL) Mel Cat
Wireless access
Partic in Southwest Michigan Library Cooperative
Open Tues & Wed 10:30-6:30, Thurs & Fri 10:30-4:30, Sat 10-2
Friends of the Library Group

GALIEN

P GALIEN TOWNSHIP PUBLIC LIBRARY*, 302 N Main St, 49113. (Mail add: PO Box 278, 49113-0278), SAN 308-1060. Tel: 269-545-8281. FAX: 269-545-8281. *Dir,* Sue Robinson
Library Holdings: Bk Vols 30,000; Per Subs 40
Automation Activity & Vendor Info: (Cataloging) Follett Software; (Circulation) Follett Software
Partic in Southwest Michigan Library Cooperative
Open Mon & Wed 12-8, Tues & Thurs 10-5:30, Fri 12-5:30, Sat 9-1

GARDEN CITY

P GARDEN CITY PUBLIC LIBRARY*, 31735 Maplewood Rd, 48135. SAN 308-1087. Tel: 734-793-1830. Automation Services Tel: 734-793-1836. FAX: 734-793-1831. Web Site: garden-city.lib.mi.us. *Dir,* James Lenze; E-mail: lenze@gardencitylib.org; *Ref Librn,* Dan Lodge; *Youth Librn,* Lindsay Fricke; Staff 12 (MLS 4, Non-MLS 8)
Founded 1923. Pop 30,047; Circ 75,000
Library Holdings: Bk Vols 50,000; Per Subs 80
Automation Activity & Vendor Info: (Circulation) SirsiDynix; (ILL) SirsiDynix; (OPAC) SirsiDynix
Function: AV serv, Handicapped accessible, ILL available, Magnifiers for reading, Online searches, Photocopying/Printing, Prog for children & young adult, Summer reading prog, Telephone ref, Wheelchair accessible
Special Services for the Blind - Bks on cassette; Bks on CD; Large print bks; Magnifiers; Screen enlargement software for people with visual disabilities
Open Mon-Thurs 12-6, Sat 10-2
Friends of the Library Group

GAYLORD

P OTSEGO COUNTY LIBRARY*, 700 S Otsego Ave, 49735-1723. SAN 308-1095. Tel: 989-732-5841. FAX: 989-732-9401. E-mail: ocl@otsego.org. Web Site: otsego.lib.mi.us. *Dir,* Maureen Derenzy; Tel: 989-732-5841, Ext 15; *Asst Dir,* Jackie Skinner; Tel: 989-732-5841, Ext

14; *Tech Coordr,* Chris Knight; *Ch Serv,* Cathy Campbell; *ILL,* Jean Brown; Staff 4 (MLS 2, Non-MLS 2)
Pop 23,301; Circ 152,451
Library Holdings: Bk Vols 59,280; Per Subs 355
Special Collections: State Document Depository
Subject Interests: Local hist
Automation Activity & Vendor Info: (Cataloging) SirsiDynix; (Circulation) SirsiDynix; (OPAC) SirsiDynix
Database Vendor: SirsiDynix
Partic in Northland Library Cooperative
Special Services for the Blind - Bks on cassette; Closed circuit TV; Reader equip
Open Mon-Wed 9-8, Thurs & Fri 9-5, Sat 9-1, Sun 1-5
Friends of the Library Group
Branches: 2
JOHANNESBURG BRANCH, 10900 East M-32, Johannesburg, 49751, SAN 329-3548. Tel: 989-732-3928. FAX: 989-731-3365. E-mail: ocl@otsego.org. *Br Mgr,* Vickie Hoecherl; E-mail: jbl@otsego.org; Staff 2 (Non-MLS 2)
Open Mon 2-6, Tues 9-1, Wed, Thurs & Fri 1-5
Friends of the Library Group
VANDERBILT BRANCH, 8170 Mill St, Vanderbilt, 49795, SAN 329-3564. Tel: 989-983-3600. FAX: 989-983-3105. *Br Mgr,* Tianne Jones; Staff 1 (Non-MLS 1)
Open Mon 3-7, Tues-Thurs 1-5, Fri 9-1

GLADSTONE

P GLADSTONE AREA SCHOOL & PUBLIC LIBRARY, 300 S Tenth St, 49837-1518. SAN 308-1109. Tel: 906-428-4224. FAX: 906-789-8452. Web Site: www.gladstoneschools.com/library/Main%20Library.htm. *Dir,* Lori Wells; E-mail: lwells@gladstone.k12.mi.us; Staff 3.75 (MLS 1, Non-MLS 2.75)
Founded 1913. Pop 9,500; Circ 99,884
Library Holdings: Bk Vols 45,000; Per Subs 150
Automation Activity & Vendor Info: (Cataloging) SirsiDynix; (Circulation) SirsiDynix; (OPAC) SirsiDynix
Wireless access
Function: 24/7 Electronic res, 24/7 Online cat, Accelerated reader prog, Accessibility serv available based on individual needs, Activity rm, Adult bk club
Open Mon-Thurs (Sept-May) 8-6:30, Fri 8-3:30; Mon-Thurs (June-Aug) 10-6
Friends of the Library Group

GLADWIN

P GLADWIN COUNTY DISTRICT LIBRARY*, 402 James Robertson Dr, 48624. SAN 308-1117. Tel: 989-426-8221. FAX: 989-426-6958. Web Site: www.gladwinlibrary.org. *Dir,* Bruce Guy; E-mail: director@gladwinlibrary.org; *Head, Ch,* Donna Frederick; E-mail: d.frederick@vlc.lib.mi.us; *Head, Circ,* Laura Rickord; E-mail: l.rickord@vlc.lib.mi.us; *Acq,* Laurel Breault; Staff 9 (MLS 1, Non-MLS 8)
Founded 1934. Pop 26,023; Circ 139,000
Jan 2006-Dec 2006. Mats Exp $65,000, Books $50,000, AV Mat $15,000
Library Holdings: Bk Vols 42,500; Per Subs 120
Special Collections: Genealogy room; Local History, local newsp on micro
Automation Activity & Vendor Info: (Cataloging) SirsiDynix; (Circulation) SirsiDynix; (OPAC) SirsiDynix
Wireless access
Publications: Annotated Catalog of Large Print Books; Index to Obituaries in the Gladwin County Record; Page 1 (newsletter)
Partic in Valley Libr Consortium
Open Mon-Thurs 9-8, Fri & Sat 9-5
Friends of the Library Group
Branches: 1
BEAVERTON BRANCH, 128 W Saginaw St, Beaverton, 48612. Tel: 989-435-3981. FAX: 989-435-2577.
Library Holdings: Bk Vols 11,500; Per Subs 28
Open Mon 9-8, Tues-Thurs 10-6, Fri 9-5, Sat 10-2
Friends of the Library Group

GLENNIE

P CURTIS TOWNSHIP LIBRARY*, 4884 Bamfield Rd, 48737. Tel: 989-735-2601. FAX: 989-735-2601. Web Site: www.curtistownship.org. *Libr Dir,* Deb Tacoma; E-mail: librarydirector@centurytel.net
Library Holdings: Bk Vols 9,000
Automation Activity & Vendor Info: (Cataloging) SirsiDynix; (Circulation) SirsiDynix; (OPAC) SirsiDynix
Partic in Northland Library Cooperative
Open Tues & Wed (Winter) 11-5, Thurs 1-5, Sat 11-3; Tues & Wed (Summer) 11-6, Thurs 1-6, Sat 11-3

GRAND BLANC

M GENESYS REGIONAL MEDICAL CENTER*, Medical Library, One Genesys Pkwy, 48439-1477. SAN 308-0943. Tel: 810-606-5260. FAX: 810-606-5270. E-mail: ilibrary@genesys.org. *Librn,* Doris Blauet; Staff 4 (MLS 1, Non-MLS 3)
Founded 1936
Library Holdings: Bk Titles 3,000; Per Subs 241
Subject Interests: Cardiology, Geriatrics & gerontology, Obstetrics & gynecology, Oncology
Partic in Flint Area Health Sci Libr Network

GRAND HAVEN

S COUNCIL OF MICHIGAN FOUNDATIONS*, Library & Information Services, One S Harbor Dr, Ste 3, 49417. SAN 377-1598. Tel: 616-842-7080. FAX: 616-842-1760. E-mail: info@michiganfoundations.org. *Info Serv Spec,* Barbara A Dryer
Founded 1972
Library Holdings: AV Mats 500; Bk Titles 2,500; Per Subs 20
Subject Interests: Foundations, Grants, Philanthropy
Automation Activity & Vendor Info: (OPAC) Inmagic, Inc.
Function: Mail loans to mem
Restriction: Circ limited, Pub use on premises

P LOUTIT DISTRICT LIBRARY*, 407 Columbus Ave, 49417. SAN 308-1125. Tel: 616-842-5560. Reference Tel: 616-842-5560, Ext 214. FAX: 616-847-0570. E-mail: gdh@llcoop.org. Web Site: www.loutitlibrary.org. *Dir,* John Martin; Tel: 616-842-5560, Ext 212, E-mail: jmartin@loutitlibrary.org; *Asst Dir,* Kerry Fitzgerald; Tel: 616-842-5560, Ext 233, E-mail: kfitzgerald@loutitlibrary.org; *Ref Librn,* Mary Mihovich; Tel: 616-842-5560, Ext 221; *Bus Mgr,* Gail Skruch; Tel: 616-842-5560, Ext 231; *Commun Relations Coordr,* Larry Halverson; Tel: 616-842-5560, Ext 222; *Adult Serv,* Laura J Kraly; Tel: 616-842-5560, Ext 220, E-mail: lkraly@loutitlibrary.org; *Local Hist/Genealogy,* Jeanette Weiden; Tel: 616-842-5560, Ext 225, E-mail: jweiden@loutitlibrary.org; *Youth Serv,* Allison Boyer; Tel: 616-842-5560, Ext 219; Staff 26 (MLS 5, Non-MLS 21)
Founded 1910. Pop 35,540; Circ 345,187
Library Holdings: Bk Vols 101,082; Per Subs 115
Special Collections: Genealogy & Local History Coll. Municipal Document Depository; Oral History
Automation Activity & Vendor Info: (Acquisitions) Innovative Interfaces, Inc; (Circulation) Innovative Interfaces, Inc; (OPAC) Innovative Interfaces, Inc
Database Vendor: Gale Cengage Learning, OCLC FirstSearch
Wireless access
Partic in Lakeland Library Cooperative; Midwest Collaborative for Library Services (MCLS)
Open Mon-Thurs 9-9, Fri 9-6, Sat 9-5, Sun (Sept-May) 1-5
Friends of the Library Group

S TRI-CITIES HISTORICAL MUSEUM*, 200 Washington Ave, 49417. SAN 373-2061. Tel: 616-842-0700. FAX: 616-842-3698. Web Site: www.tri-citiesmuseum.org. *Dir,* Steven Radtke; E-mail: sradtke@tri-citiesmuseum.org
Library Holdings: Bk Vols 500
Subject Interests: Local hist
Publications: Riverwinds (Newsletter)
Open Mon-Fri 10-5, Sat & Sun 12-5
Restriction: Not a lending libr

GRAND LEDGE

P GRAND LEDGE AREA DISTRICT LIBRARY*, 131 E Jefferson St, 48837-1534. SAN 308-1133. Tel: 517-627-7014. FAX: 517-627-6276. Web Site: grandledge.lib.mi.us. *Dir,* Suzanne E Bowles; E-mail: szbwgladlib@netscape.net; *Media Spec,* Judy Howard; *Tech Serv,* Suzanne Schramski; Staff 18 (MLS 1, Non-MLS 17)
Founded 1911. Pop 15,554
Library Holdings: Bk Vols 50,000; Per Subs 76
Subject Interests: Local hist
Automation Activity & Vendor Info: (Cataloging) SirsiDynix; (Circulation) SirsiDynix
Mem of Woodlands Library Cooperative
Open Mon-Thurs 10-9, Fri & Sat 10-5, Sun 1-5
Friends of the Library Group
Branches: 1
WACOUSTA BRANCH, 13080 Wacousta Rd, 48837. Tel: 517-626-6577. FAX: 517-626-6577. *Dir,* Suzanne Bowle
Automation Activity & Vendor Info: (Cataloging) Horizon; (Circulation) Horizon
Database Vendor: Overdrive, Inc
Open Mon & Wed 3-7, Tues, Thurs & Sat 10-2

GRAND RAPIDS

C AQUINAS COLLEGE, Grace Hauenstein Library, 1607 Robinson Rd SE, 49506-1799. SAN 308-1141. Tel: 616-632-2137. Reference Tel: 616-632-2140. Administration Tel: 616-632-2130, 616-632-2131. FAX: 616-732-4534. E-mail: library@aquinas.edu. Web Site: www.aquinas.edu/library. *Co-Dir, Electronic Serv,* Shellie Jeffries; E-mail: jeffrmic@aquinas.edu; *Co-Dir, Media Librn,* Francine Paolini; E mail: paolifra@aquinas.edu; *Circ,* Pam Luebke; Tel: 616-632-2127, E-mail: luebkpam@aquinas.edu; *Info Literacy,* Christina Radisauskas; Tel: 616-632-2124, E-mail: radischr@aquinas.edu; *Ref Serv, Ser,* Kristine Derks; Tel: 616-632-2133, E-mail: derkskri@aquinas.edu; *Tech Serv,* Susan Ponischil; Tel: 616-632-2134, E-mail: ponissus@aquinas.edu; Staff 9.5 (MLS 6, Non-MLS 3.5)
Founded 1936. Enrl 2,330; Fac 105; Highest Degree: Master
Jul 2013-Jun 2014. Mats Exp $353,643, Books $59,362, Per/Ser (Incl. Access Fees) $63,140, Micro $9,500, AV Mat $16,985, Electronic Ref Mat (Incl. Access Fees) $204,656. Sal $564,690 (Prof $346,257)
Library Holdings: CDs 2,252; DVDs 2,551; e-books 181,917; Electronic Media & Resources 99; Microforms 199,498; Bk Vols 102,649; Per Subs 237
Automation Activity & Vendor Info: (Acquisitions) Innovative Interfaces, Inc; (Cataloging) Innovative Interfaces, Inc; (Circulation) Innovative Interfaces, Inc; (OPAC) Innovative Interfaces, Inc; (Serials) Innovative Interfaces, Inc
Database Vendor: American Chemical Society, American Psychological Association (APA), ARTstor, CountryWatch, CQ Press, CredoReference, ebrary, EBSCOhost, Gale Cengage Learning, JSTOR, LexisNexis, Project MUSE, ProQuest, RefWorks, ScienceDirect, SerialsSolutions, Springshare, LLC
Wireless access
Partic in Lakenet, Mich Libr Consortium; OCLC Online Computer Library Center, Inc

C CALVIN COLLEGE & CALVIN THEOLOGICAL SEMINARY*, Hekman Library, 1855 Knollcrest Circle SE, 49546-4402. SAN 308-1168. Tel: 616-526-7197. Interlibrary Loan Service Tel: 616-526-8573. Reference Tel: 616-526-6307. Administration Tel: 616-526-6072. FAX: 616-526-6470. Administration FAX: 616-526-6146. Web Site: library.calvin.edu. *Dir,* Glenn A Remelts; E-mail: remelt@calvin.edu; *Theological Librn,* Lugene Schemper; *Circ Coordr,* Carla Mayer; Tel: 616-526-6256; *ILL Coordr,* Kathleen Struck; Tel: 616-526-8573, E-mail: kstruck@calvin.edu; *Cat,* Francene Lewis; Tel: 616-526-6308, E-mail: flewis@calvin.edu; *Coll Develop,* Katherine Swart; *Electronic Serv,* Dan Wells; *Instruction & Outreach,* Sarah McClure Kolk; Tel: 616-526-6014, E mail: smk23@calvin.edu; *Ref,* Kathleen DeMey; Tel: 616-526-6310, E-mail: kdemey@calvin.edu; Staff 22 (MLS 9, Non-MLS 13)
Founded 1892. Enrl 4,200; Fac 300; Highest Degree: Master
Library Holdings: Bk Titles 465,000; Bk Vols 765,000; Per Subs 2,658
Special Collections: Archives of Christian Reformed Church (Heritage Hall Archives), bk & microfilm; H Henry Meeter Calvinism Research Coll, bk & microfilm. State Document Depository; US Document Depository
Subject Interests: Humanities, Soc sci & issues, Theol
Automation Activity & Vendor Info: (Acquisitions) SirsiDynix; (Cataloging) SirsiDynix; (Circulation) SirsiDynix; (Course Reserve) SirsiDynix; (OPAC) SirsiDynix; (Serials) SirsiDynix
Database Vendor: SirsiDynix
Publications: Heritage Hall Publications; Origins
Partic in OCLC Online Computer Library Center, Inc
Restriction: Circ limited

CR CORNERSTONE UNIVERSITY*, Miller Library, 1001 E Beltline Ave NE, 49525. SAN 308-1265. Tel: 616-949-5300. Circulation Tel: 616-222-1458. Reference Tel: 616-254-1976. Administration Tel: 616-254-1662. FAX: 616-222-1405. E-mail: circulation@cornerstone.edu. Web Site: library.cornerstone.edu. *Dir,* Dr Fred Sweet; E-mail: fred.sweet@cornerstone.edu; *Assoc Dir, Access Serv,* Fay Bush; E-mail: fay.bush@cornerstone.edu; *Head, Tech Serv,* Jamie Tiemeyer; E-mail: jamie.tiemeyer@cornerstone.edu; *Librn,* Gail R Atwood; E-mail: gail.atwood@cornerstone.edu; *Circ Librn,* Laura Walton; E-mail: laura.walton@cornerstone.edu; *Instrul Serv Librn,* Brian Holda; E-mail: brian.holda@cornerstone.edu; *ILL/Doc Delivery/CMC Librn,* Gina Bolger; E-mail: gina.bolger@cornerstone.edu; *Res Librn,* Jessica Shuck; E-mail: jessica.shuck@cornerstone.edu. Subject Specialists: *Hist, Theol,* Dr Fred Sweet; *Arts, Kinesiology,* Gail R Atwood; *Theatre,* Laura Walton; *Bus,* Jessica Shuck; Staff 8.5 (MLS 7, Non-MLS 1.5)
Founded 1941. Enrl 2,561; Fac 83; Highest Degree: Master
Library Holdings: DVDs 392; e-books 25,318; e-journals 900; Bk Titles 99,635; Bk Vols 127,000; Per Subs 1,163
Subject Interests: Theol
Automation Activity & Vendor Info: (Acquisitions) Innovative Interfaces, Inc; (Cataloging) Innovative Interfaces, Inc; (Circulation) Innovative Interfaces, Inc; (Course Reserve) Innovative Interfaces, Inc; (ILL) OCLC Online; (OPAC) Innovative Interfaces, Inc; (Serials) Innovative Interfaces, Inc
Database Vendor: Cambridge Scientific Abstracts, CQ Press, CredoReference, ebrary, EBSCOhost, Gale Cengage Learning, JSTOR, LexisNexis, Project MUSE, ProQuest, Sage, SBRnet (Sports Business Research Network), SerialsSolutions, Wiley
Function: Archival coll, Doc delivery serv, ILL available, Ref serv available, Telephone ref
Partic in Christian Library Consortium; Midwest Collaborative for Library Services (MCLS)
Open Mon-Thurs (Fall & Winter) 7:30am-11pm, Fri 7:30-7, Sat 12-5, Sun 6pm-9pm; Mon-Thurs (Summer) 10-8, Fri & Sat 10-5

C DAVENPORT UNIVERSITY*, Margaret D Sneden Library, 6191 Kraft Ave SE, 49512. SAN 308-1192. Tel: 616-554-5612. Reference Toll Free Tel: 800-632-9569. Toll Free Tel: 866-925-3884. FAX: 616-554-5226. E-mail: main_library@davenport.edu. Web Site: www.davenport.edu. *Interim Exec Dir,* Karen McLaughlin; E-mail: karen.mclaughlin@davenport.edu; *Dir, Libr Syst & Tech Serv,* Julie Gotch; E-mail: julie.gotch@davenport.edu; Staff 39 (MLS 13.5, Non-MLS 25.5)
Founded 1866. Enrl 10,773; Highest Degree: Master
Library Holdings: AV Mats 89,391; e-books 15,740; Bk Titles 75,293; Bk Vols 83,371; Per Subs 307
Subject Interests: Acctg, Allied health, Bus mgt, Computing, Info tech, Nursing
Automation Activity & Vendor Info: (Cataloging) SirsiDynix; (Circulation) SirsiDynix; (ILL) OCLC; (OPAC) SirsiDynix; (Serials) SirsiDynix
Database Vendor: EBSCO - WebFeat, EBSCOhost, Gale Cengage Learning, Hoovers, LearningExpress, Mergent Online, Newsbank, OCLC FirstSearch, ProQuest, Safari Books Online, SerialsSolutions, SirsiDynix, Standard & Poor's, Westlaw
Wireless access
Partic in Midwest Collaborative for Library Services (MCLS); OCLC Online Computer Library Center, Inc; Southeastern Michigan League of Libraries

C FERRIS STATE UNIVERSITY*, Kendall College of Art & Design Library, 17 Fountain St NW, 2nd Flr, 49503-3002. SAN 308-1311. Tel: 616-451-2787, Ext 1121. Reference Tel: 616-451-1868, Ext 1123. Administration Tel: 616-451-2787, Ext 1122. Automation Services Tel: 616-451-2787, Ext 1126. Toll Free Tel: 800-676-2787. FAX: 616-831-9689. Web Site: libkcad.ferris.edu. *Dir,* Michael J Kruzich; Tel: 616-451-1868, Ext 1122, E-mail: michaelkruzich@ferris.edu; Staff 3 (MLS 3)
Founded 1928. Enrl 1,400; Fac 64; Highest Degree: Master
Library Holdings: Audiobooks 77; CDs 525; DVDs 1,117; Electronic Media & Resources 200; Bk Titles 24,000; Bk Vols 25,500; Per Subs 110
Special Collections: 19th & Early 20th Century History of Furniture Design, Interiors & Ornament, auction cats, bks, company cats, exhibition cats, portfolios, prints
Subject Interests: Art educ, Art hist, Digital media, Drawing, Fine arts, Functional art & sculpture, Graphic design, Illustration, Interior design, Jewelry design, Metals design, Painting, Photog
Automation Activity & Vendor Info: (Acquisitions) Innovative Interfaces, Inc - Millenium; (Cataloging) OCLC; (Circulation) Innovative Interfaces, Inc - Millenium; (Course Reserve) Innovative Interfaces, Inc - Millenium; (ILL) Innovative Interfaces, Inc - Millenium; (Media Booking) Innovative Interfaces, Inc - Millenium; (OPAC) Innovative Interfaces, Inc - Millenium; (Serials) Innovative Interfaces, Inc - Millenium
Database Vendor: ABC-CLIO, ARTstor, Cambridge Scientific Abstracts, CQ Press, CredoReference, Emerald, Facts on File, Gale Cengage Learning, H W Wilson, Ingenta, JSTOR, LearningExpress, LexisNexis, Marquis Who's Who, Material ConneXion, Newsbank, OCLC ArticleFirst, OCLC CAMIO, OCLC FirstSearch, OCLC WorldShare Interlibrary Loan, OVID Technologies, Oxford Online, Project MUSE, ProQuest, PubMed, ScienceDirect, Standard & Poor's, Wilson - Wilson Web
Wireless access
Function: Electronic databases & coll, ILL available, Orientations, Ref serv available
Partic in Midwest Collaborative for Library Services (MCLS)
Open Mon-Thurs (Fall & Spring) 8am-9:30pm, Fri 8-4:30, Sun 4-8; Mon-Thurs (Summer) 8-5, Fri 8-4:30
Restriction: In-house use for visitors

S FISHBECK, THOMPSON, CARR & HUBER*, Information Management Center, 1515 Arboretum Dr SE, 49546. Tel: 616-575-3824. FAX: 616-464-3993. E-mail: info@ftch.com. Web Site: www.ftch.com. *Info Res Spec,* Sandie Ross; E-mail: slross@ftch.com; Staff 1 (Non-MLS 1)
Founded 1956
Library Holdings: Bk Titles 7,000; Per Subs 164
Subject Interests: Archit, Eng

CR GRACE BIBLE COLLEGE*, Bultema Memorial Library, 1011 Aldon St SW, 49509. SAN 308-1249. Tel: 616-261-8575. FAX: 616-538-0599. *Dir,* Kathy Molenkamp; E-mail: kmolenkamp@gbcol.edu; Staff 2.5 (MLS 1, Non-MLS 1.5)

Founded 1945. Enrl 170; Fac 34; Highest Degree: Bachelor
Library Holdings: Bk Vols 40,000; Per Subs 150
Subject Interests: Bible, Educ, Music, Soc serv, Theol
Automation Activity & Vendor Info: (Acquisitions) Follett Software; (Cataloging) Follett Software; (Circulation) Follett Software; (OPAC) Follett Software
Database Vendor: OCLC ArticleFirst, OCLC FirstSearch, OCLC WorldShare Interlibrary Loan, Wilson - Wilson Web
Wireless access
Open Mon-Thurs 8am-Midnight, Fri 8-4, Sat 11-4, Sun 8pm-11pm
Restriction: Open to students, fac & staff

S GRAND RAPIDS ART MUSEUM*, McBride Art Reference Library, 101 Monroe Center, 49503. SAN 308-1257. Tel: 616-831-1000, 616-831-2901, 616-831-2909 (appt number). FAX: 616-559-0422. Web Site: www.gramonline.org. *Dir,* Celeste Adams; E-mail: cadams@artmuseumgr.org; *Assoc Curator,* Cindy Buckner; E-mail: curator@artmuseumgr.org
Founded 1910
Library Holdings: Bk Titles 6,310
Special Collections: Art History Coll; Museum Archival Material
Open Tues-Thurs & Sat 10-5, Fri 10-9, Sun 12-5

J GRAND RAPIDS COMMUNITY COLLEGE*, Arthur Andrews Memorial Library, 140 Ransom NE Ave, 49503. (Mail add: 143 Bostwick Ave NE, 49503), SAN 308-1281. Tel: 616-234-3868. Circulation Tel: 616-234-3872. Interlibrary Loan Service Tel: 616-234-3749. FAX: 616-234-3889. Web Site: www.grcc.edu/library. *Dir,* Pat Ingersoll; *Coll Develop Librn,* Sophia Brewer; *Ref & Instruction Librn,* Nan Schichtel; *Ref & Tech Librn,* Lori DeBie; *Archivist, Ref Librn,* Michael Klawitter; Tel: 616-234-3473, E-mail: mklawitt@grcc.edu; *Circ Coordr,* Kevin Lyons; Staff 10 (MLS 5, Non-MLS 5)
Founded 1914. Enrl 9,000; Fac 600; Highest Degree: Associate
Library Holdings: e-books 106,000; Bk Titles 81,000; Bk Vols 85,000
Automation Activity & Vendor Info: (Acquisitions) Innovative Interfaces, Inc; (Cataloging) Innovative Interfaces, Inc; (Circulation) Innovative Interfaces, Inc; (Course Reserve) Innovative Interfaces, Inc; (ILL) OCLC; (OPAC) Innovative Interfaces, Inc; (Serials) Innovative Interfaces, Inc
Wireless access
Partic in MeLCat
Open Mon-Thurs (Fall & Winter) 7:30am-9:45pm, Fri 7:30-5, Sat 10-2, Sun 1-5; Mon-Thurs (Summer) 8-8, Fri 8-5

P GRAND RAPIDS PUBLIC LIBRARY*, 111 Library St NE, 49503-3268. SAN 346-5306. Tel: 616-988-5400. Interlibrary Loan Service Tel: 616-988-5402, Ext 5561. FAX: 616-988-5419. Web Site: www.grpl.org. *Dir,* Marcia A Warner; Tel: 616-988-5402, Ext 5431, Fax: 616-988-5429; *Asst Libr Dir,* Marla Ehlers; E-mail: mehlers@grpl.org; *Circ Supvr,* Elaine Bosch; Tel: 616-988-5402, Ext 5452, E-mail: ebosch@grpl.org; *Coordr, Ref Serv-Adult,* Asante Cain; *Coordr, Youth Serv,* Sarah McCarville; E-mail: smccarville@grpl.org; Staff 35 (MLS 35)
Founded 1871. Pop 197,800; Circ 1,523,566
Library Holdings: AV Mats 76,199; Electronic Media & Resources 21; Bk Titles 388,006; Bk Vols 722,280; Per Subs 1,163
Special Collections: Foundation Center Regional Coll; Furniture Coll; Genealogy (Lawrence Fund); History of Old Northwest Territory (Campbell Fund); Landscape Architecture & Gardening (Richmond Fund); Michigan History (Stuart Fund); Picture Books (Butler Fund). Oral History; State Document Depository; US Document Depository
Subject Interests: Art & archit, Bus & mgt, Educ, Hist, Music, Soc sci & issues
Automation Activity & Vendor Info: (Circulation) Innovative Interfaces, Inc
Wireless access
Function: Adult bk club, After school storytime, Archival coll, Computer training, Copy machines, Electronic databases & coll, Govt ref serv, Handicapped accessible, Home delivery & serv to Sr ctr & nursing homes, ILL available, Newsp ref libr, Online ref, Online searches, Photocopying/Printing, Prog for adults, Prog for children & young adult, Ref serv available, Senior computer classes, Spoken cassettes & CDs, Spoken cassettes & DVDs, Summer reading prog, Tax forms, Telephone ref
Publications: Tree That Never Dies
Partic in OCLC Online Computer Library Center, Inc
Open Mon-Thurs 9-9, Fri & Sat 9-5:30, Sun (Sept-May) 1-5
Friends of the Library Group
Branches: 7
MADISON SQUARE, 1201 Madison SE, 49507, SAN 373-5362. Tel: 616-988-5411. FAX: 616-245-1403. E-mail: gms@grpl.org. *Librn,* Anjie Gleisner
Open Tues, Wed & Fri 10-6, Thurs 12-8, Sat 9:30-5:30
OTTAWA HILLS, 1150 Giddings Ave SE, 49506, SAN 346-5365. Tel: 616-988-5412. FAX: 616-241-1460. E-mail: gro@grpl.org. *Librn,* Catherine Page
Open Tues, Thurs & Fri 10-6, Wed 12-8, Sat 9:30-5:30
Friends of the Library Group
SEYMOUR, 2350 Eastern Ave SE, 49507, SAN 346-539X. Tel: 616-988-5413. FAX: 616-241-1445. E-mail: grs@grpl.org. *Librn,* Asante Cain
Open Mon & Tues 12-8, Wed & Thurs 10-6, Sat 9:30-5:30
Friends of the Library Group
VAN BELKUM BRANCH, 1563 Plainfield Ave NE, 49505, SAN 346-5330. Tel: 616-988-5410. FAX: 616-365-2615. E-mail: grc@grpl.org. *Librn,* Judith Stilley
Open Tues, Thurs & Fri 10-6, Wed 12-8, Sat 9:30-5:30
WEST LEONARD BRANCH, 1017 Leonard St NW, 49504. Tel: 616-988-5416. FAX: 616-301-9438. *Librn,* Liz Knapp; E-mail: lknapp@grpl.org
Open Mon & Tues 12-8, Wed, Thurs & Sat 10-6
WEST SIDE, 713 Bridge St NW, 49504, SAN 346-542X. Tel: 616-988-5414. FAX: 616-458-0103. E-mail: grw@grpl.org. *Librn,* Tim Sage; E-mail: tsage@grpl.org
Open Tues, Wed & Fri 10-6, Thurs 12-8, Sat 9:30-5:30
Friends of the Library Group
YANKEE CLIPPER, 2025 Leonard NE, 49505, SAN 346-5454. Tel: 616-988-5415. FAX: 616-235-8349. E-mail: gy@grpl.org. *Librn,* Kayne Ferrier
Open Mon & Tues 12-8, Wed & Thurs 10-6, Sat 9:30-5:30
Friends of the Library Group

J ITT TECHNICAL INSTITUTE LIBRARY*, Grand Rapids Campus, 4020 Sparks Dr SE, 49546-6192. SAN 377-1539. Tel: 616-956-1060. Toll Free Tel: 800-632-4676. FAX: 616-956-5606. Web Site: library.itt-tech.edu. *Librn,* John Potter; E-mail: jpotter@itt-tech.edu; Staff 2 (MLS 1, Non-MLS 1)
Founded 1969
Library Holdings: e-journals 3,000; Bk Titles 6,500; Bk Vols 6,600; Per Subs 70
Subject Interests: Bus admin, Computer, Computer design, Computer eng, Criminal justice, Drafting, Electronics, Multimedia, Networking systs, Prog, Web design
Automation Activity & Vendor Info: (Cataloging) LibraryWorld, Inc; (Circulation) LibraryWorld, Inc; (OPAC) LibraryWorld, Inc
Database Vendor: EBSCOhost, ProQuest
Partic in Mich Libr Asn
Restriction: Not open to pub, Open to students

CR KUYPER COLLEGE*, Zondervan Library, 3333 E Beltline NE, 49525. SAN 308-1362. Tel: 616-222-3000. Interlibrary Loan Service Tel: 616-988-3660. Information Services Tel: 616-988-3700. FAX: 616-222-3045, 616-988-3608. E-mail: library@kuyper.edu. Web Site: www.kuyper.edu/library. *Dir, Libr Serv,* Dianne Zandbergen; Tel: 616-988-3635, E-mail: dzandbergen@kuyper.edu; *Assoc Dir,* Michelle Norquist; E-mail: mnorquist@kuyper.edu; Staff 2 (MLS 2)
Founded 1940. Enrl 324; Fac 14; Highest Degree: Bachelor
Jul 2008-Jun 2009 Income $354,270, Mats Exp $354,270, Books $18,711, Per/Ser (Incl. Access Fees) $10,150, Micro $185, AV Mat $2,539, Electronic Ref Mat (Incl. Access Fees) $17,854. Sal $119,947 (Prof $105,633)
Library Holdings: AV Mats 3,049; e-books 13,827; Microforms 4,754; Bk Titles 42,678; Bk Vols 56,492; Per Subs 208
Special Collections: Zondervan Publishing House Coll
Subject Interests: Biblical studies, Educ, Hist, Relig, Theol
Automation Activity & Vendor Info: (Cataloging) Follett Software; (Circulation) Follett Software; (OPAC) Follett Software
Database Vendor: BCR: Christian Periodical Index, Bowker, Facts on File, Gale Cengage Learning, Grolier Online, H W Wilson, LexisNexis, OCLC FirstSearch, OCLC WorldShare Interlibrary Loan, ProQuest, SerialsSolutions
Wireless access
Publications: Library Handbook
Partic in Asn of Christian Librs; Midwest Collaborative for Library Services (MCLS)
Open Mon-Thurs (Winter) 8am-10pm, Fri 8-5, Sat 10-5; Mon-Thurs (Summer) 8-4:30, Fri 8-3

S MICHIGAN MASONIC MUSEUM & LIBRARY*, 233 E Fulton St, Ste 10, 49503-3270. Tel: 616-459-9336. Toll Free Tel: 888-748-4540. FAX: 616-459-9436. E-mail: library@gl-mi.org. Web Site: masonichistory.org. *Dir,* John A Wallsteadt
Library Holdings: Bk Vols 8,000; Per Subs 15; Videos 25
Special Collections: Oral History
Subject Interests: Fraternal movement, Masonic heritage, Mich hist, Philos, Symbolism
Publications: Masonic Resources (Quarterly)

Open Mon-Fri 1-6
Friends of the Library Group

L MILLER, JOHNSON, SNELL & CUMMISKEY, Law Library, 250 Monroe NW, Ste 800, 49503-2250. SAN 372-0446. Tel: 616-831-1875. FAX: 616-988-1875. Web Site: www.millerjohnson.com. *Info Serv Mgr,* Jessica M Fields; E-mail: library@millerjohnson.com; Staff 2 (MLS 1, Non-MLS 1)
Restriction: Private libr

S RIGHT TO LIFE OF MICHIGAN, State Central Resource Center, 2340 Porter St SW, 49509. (Mail add: PO Box 901, 49509-0901), SAN 375-1902. Tel: 616-532-2300. FAX: 616-532-3461. E-mail: info@rtl.org. Web Site: www.rtl.org. *Pub Relations,* Pam Sherstad
Library Holdings: Bk Vols 300
Subject Interests: Abortion, Euthanasia
Open Mon-Fri 8:30-5

M SAINT MARY'S HEALTH SCIENCES LIBRARY*, 200 Jefferson SE, 49503. SAN 308-1370. Tel: 616-752-6243. FAX: 616-752-6419. *Librn,* Mary A Hanson; Staff 2 (MLS 1, Non-MLS 1)
Founded 1920
Library Holdings: Bk Titles 2,000; Bk Vols 2,500; Per Subs 450
Subject Interests: Med, Nursing
Publications: Newsletter (Quarterly)

R SECOND CONGREGATIONAL UNITED CHURCH OF CHRIST LIBRARY*, 525 Cheshire Dr NE, 49505. SAN 308-1389. Tel: 616-361-2629. FAX: 616-361-8181. *Librn,* Gerry Klepser
Library Holdings: Bk Vols 2,050

L SMITH, HAUGHEY, RICE & ROEGGE*, Law Library, 200 Calder Plaza Bldg, 250 Monroe Ave NW, 49503. SAN 372-0454. Tel: 616-774-8000. FAX: 616-774-2461. Web Site: www.shrr.com. *Dir, Info Serv,* Penelope A Turner; Tel: 614-458-5315, E-mail: pturner@shrr.com; Staff 2 (Non-MLS 2)
Library Holdings: Bk Vols 6,000; Per Subs 101
Automation Activity & Vendor Info: (Cataloging) EOS International; (Serials) EOS International
Database Vendor: LexisNexis, Westlaw
Restriction: Co libr

M RICHARD R SMITH MEDICAL LIBRARY*, Spectrum Health Campus, 1840 Wealthy St SE, 49506. SAN 308-115X. Tel: 616-774-7931. FAX: 616-774-5290. *Librn,* Diane Hummel
Founded 1934
Library Holdings: Bk Vols 1,800; Per Subs 350
Subject Interests: Med, Surgery
Partic in Dialog Corp

M SPECTRUM HEALTH, Amberg Health Sciences Library, A Level West Bldg, 100 Michigan St NE, 49503-2560. SAN 346-5276. Tel: 616-391-1655. Interlibrary Loan Service Tel: 616-391-2061. FAX: 616-391-3527. Web Site: www.spectrum-health.org. *Mgr,* Diane Hummel; E-mail: diane.hummel@spectrum-health.org
Founded 1918
Library Holdings: e-books 100; e-journals 275; Bk Titles 6,000; Per Subs 650
Special Collections: American Nurse's Association Publications; National League for Nursing Publications Coll
Subject Interests: Med, Nursing
Automation Activity & Vendor Info: (Acquisitions) EOS International; (Cataloging) EOS International; (Circulation) EOS International; (Course Reserve) EOS International; (OPAC) EOS International; (Serials) EOS International
Database Vendor: OCLC FirstSearch
Publications: Ex Libris
Partic in Midwest Collaborative for Library Services (MCLS)
Open Mon-Thurs (Winter) 8:30-8, Fri 8:30-5; Mon-Thurs (Summer) 8:30-6, Fri 8:30-5

GL UNITED STATES DEPARTMENT OF JUSTICE*, United States Attorney's Office Library, 330 Ionia, Ste 501, 49503. (Mail add: PO Box 208, 49501-0208). Tel: 616-456-2404, Ext 2050. FAX: 616-456-2408. Web Site: www.usdoj.gov/usao/miw. *Librn,* June L Van Wingen; E-mail: june.vanwingen@usdoj.gov
Library Holdings: Bk Vols 7,500; Per Subs 20
Restriction: Staff use only

L WARNER, NORCROSS & JUDD, LLP LIBRARY*, 900 Fifth Third Ctr, 111 Lyon St NW, 49503-2487. SAN 308-1397. Tel: 616-752-2236. FAX: 616-752-2236. Web Site: www.wnj.com. *Dir, Libr Serv,* Mary Lou Wilker; Staff 4 (MLS 1, Non-MLS 3)
Founded 1931
Library Holdings: Bk Vols 15,000
Automation Activity & Vendor Info: (Cataloging) Inmagic, Inc.; (Circulation) Inmagic, Inc.
Function: ILL available
Partic in Midwest Collaborative for Library Services (MCLS)
Restriction: Employees & their associates

R WESTVIEW CHRISTIAN REFORMED CHURCH LIBRARY*, 2929 Leonard St NW, 49504. SAN 308-1400. Tel: 616-453-3105. FAX: 616-453-8891. *Librn,* Jan Bigelow; Staff 4 (MLS 1, Non-MLS 3)
Library Holdings: Bk Vols 3,590

GRANDVILLE

R THEOLOGICAL SCHOOL OF PROTESTANT REFORMED CHURCHES LIBRARY*, 4949 Ivanrest Ave SW, 49418-9709. Tel: 616-531-1490. FAX: 616-531-3033. Web Site: www.prca.org/seminary/seminary.html. *Dir,* Russell J Dykstra; E-mail: dykstra@prca.org; *Librn,* Darrel Huisken
Library Holdings: Bk Vols 8,000

GRANT

P GRANT AREA DISTRICT LIBRARY*, 122 Elder St, 49327. SAN 308-1419. Tel: 231-834-5713. FAX: 231-834-9705. E-mail: gnt@llcoop.org. Web Site: grantlibrary.net. *Dir,* Deborah Bose; Tel: 231-834-5713, Ext 103; Staff 1 (MLS 1)
Founded 1920. Pop 9,000; Circ 35,814
Library Holdings: Bk Titles 40,000; Per Subs 40
Special Collections: Oral History
Subject Interests: Local hist
Automation Activity & Vendor Info: (Cataloging) SirsiDynix; (Circulation) SirsiDynix; (OPAC) SirsiDynix
Wireless access
Publications: Grant Area, Yesterday-Today (local history book)
Partic in Lakeland Library Cooperative
Open Mon, Wed & Fri 9:30-5, Tues & Thurs 12-8, Sat 9:30-1
Friends of the Library Group

GRAYLING

P CRAWFORD COUNTY LIBRARY SYSTEM*, Devereaux Memorial Library, 201 Plum St, 49738. SAN 308-1427. Tel: 989-348-9214. FAX: 989-348-9294. Web Site: www.crawfordco.lib.mi.us. *Dir of Libr, Mgr Fac, Spec Coll Librn,* Bambi Mansfield; *Admin Librn, Cat Mgr, Head, ILL,* Mary Kay Hinkle; *Circ Mgr, Planning & Develop Librn,* JoAnne Yoder; *Br Supvr, Cat, Ch Serv,* Constance Meyer; Tel: 989-348-4067; *Prog Coordr, Pub Relations Coordr, Youth Serv Coordr,* Jane Gyulveszi; *Tech Support,* Karyn Ruley; Staff 10 (MLS 1, Non-MLS 9)
Founded 1927. Pop 14,273; Circ 67,690
Library Holdings: AV Mats 3,012; Bks on Deafness & Sign Lang 35; CDs 300; e books 14,000; Large Print Bks 1,205; Bk Vols 54,332; Per Subs 72; Talking Bks 4,024
Special Collections: Fly Fishing (George Griffith & Marion Wright Memorial Coll), prints; Local Newspaper Coll, 1879-present, micro & print
Subject Interests: Local hist, Popular mat
Automation Activity & Vendor Info: (Cataloging) SirsiDynix; (Circulation) SirsiDynix; (ILL) SirsiDynix; (OPAC) SirsiDynix
Database Vendor: Baker & Taylor, Bowker, Brodart, BWI, Medline, OCLC FirstSearch, OCLC WorldShare Interlibrary Loan, Overdrive, Inc, SirsiDynix, Westlaw
Wireless access
Partic in Superiorland Library Cooperative
Special Services for the Blind - Audio mat; Bks on cassette; Bks on CD; Home delivery serv; HP Scan Jet with photo-finish software; Large screen computer & software; Low vision equip; Magnifiers; PC for handicapped; Ref serv; Talking bks
Open Mon-Thurs 9-7, Fri 9-6, Sat 9-2
Restriction: Access for corporate affiliates
Friends of the Library Group
Branches: 1
FREDERIC TOWNSHIP LIBRARY, 6470 Manistee St, Frederic, 49733, SAN 376-0286. Tel: 989-348-4067. FAX: 989-348-0224. E-mail: frederic@crawfordco.lib.mi.us. *Br Mgr,* Connie Meyer
Library Holdings: Bk Vols 4,800; Per Subs 11
Special Services for the Blind - Computer with voice synthesizer for visually impaired persons
Open Mon 9-6, Wed & Fri 1-6, Thurs & Sat 9-2
Friends of the Library Group

GREENVILLE

P FLAT RIVER COMMUNITY LIBRARY*, 200 W Judd St, 48838-2225. SAN 308-1435. Tel: 616-754-6359. FAX: 616-754-1398. E-mail: gre@llcoop.org. Web Site: www.flatriverlibrary.org. *Dir,* Laura Powers; Tel: 616-754-6359, Ext 102, E-mail: grelp@llcoop.org; *Ch Serv, YA Serv,* Lisa

Watson; E-mail: grelw@llcoop.org; *Ref/Tech Serv,* Timothy J West; E-mail: gretjw@llcoop.org; Staff 6 (MLS 2, Non-MLS 4)
Founded 1868. Pop 17,626
Special Collections: Hans Christian Andersen Coll
Subject Interests: Local hist
Automation Activity & Vendor Info: (Cataloging) Innovative Interfaces, Inc; (Circulation) Innovative Interfaces, Inc; (OPAC) Innovative Interfaces, Inc; (Serials) Innovative Interfaces, Inc
Wireless access
Function: Art exhibits, AV serv, BA reader (adult literacy), Handicapped accessible, Home delivery & serv to Sr ctr & nursing homes, Homebound delivery serv, ILL available, Magnifiers for reading, Online searches, Outside serv via phone, mail, e-mail & web, Photocopying/Printing, Prog for adults, Prog for children & young adult, Ref serv available, Serves mentally handicapped consumers, Spoken cassettes & CDs, Summer reading prog, Telephone ref, VHS videos, Wheelchair accessible
Partic in Lakeland Library Cooperative
Open Mon-Thurs 9-8, Fri & Sat 9-5
Friends of the Library Group

GROSSE ILE

R GROSSE ILE PRESBYTERIAN CHURCH LIBRARY*, 7925 Horsemill Rd, 48138. SAN 308-1443. Tel: 734-676-8811. FAX: 734-676-2718. E-mail: gipc@gipc.org. Web Site: www.gipc.org.
Founded 1960
Library Holdings: Bk Vols 850

GROSSE POINTE

M BEAUMONT HOSPITAL*, Department of Library Services, 468 Cadieux Rd, 48230. SAN 320-3832. Tel: 313-343-1000, 313-343-1620. Administration Tel: 313-343-1919. FAX: 313-343-1947. Web Site: www.beaumonthospitals.com. *Librn,* Andrea Rogers
Founded 1970
Library Holdings: Bk Titles 3,000; Per Subs 250
Subject Interests: Allied health, Med, Nursing
Automation Activity & Vendor Info: (Cataloging) CyberTools for Libraries; (Circulation) CyberTools for Libraries; (OPAC) CyberTools for Libraries; (Serials) CyberTools for Libraries
Database Vendor: EBSCOhost, Gale Cengage Learning, OVID Technologies
Function: Doc delivery serv, ILL available, Ref serv available, Referrals accepted
Open Mon-Fri 8-4:30
Restriction: Open to pub for ref & circ; with some limitations

GROSSE POINTE FARMS

P GROSSE POINTE PUBLIC LIBRARY*, Ten Kercheval at Fisher Rd, 48236-3693. SAN 346-6116. Tel: 313-343-2074. FAX: 313-343-2437. Web Site: www.gp.lib.mi.us. *Dir,* Vickey Bloom; E-mail: vbloom@gp.lib.mi.us; *Asst Dir,* Cynthia Zurschmiede; Staff 18 (MLS 18)
Founded 1929. Pop 54,600
Jul 2006-Jun 2007 Income (Main Library and Branch(s)) $4,209,283. Mats Exp $542,090. Sal $2,218,951
Library Holdings: Bk Vols 173,076; Per Subs 276
Special Collections: Oral History
Subject Interests: Bus & mgt, Med, Music
Automation Activity & Vendor Info: (Acquisitions) Innovative Interfaces, Inc; (Cataloging) Innovative Interfaces, Inc; (Circulation) Innovative Interfaces, Inc; (OPAC) Innovative Interfaces, Inc
Database Vendor: Gale Cengage Learning, LearningExpress, ProQuest, ReferenceUSA
Wireless access
Publications: Library Pointes
Open Mon-Thurs (Winter) 9-9, Fri & Sat 9-5, Sun 1-5; Mon-Thurs (Summer) 9-9, Fri & Sat 9-5
Friends of the Library Group
Branches: 2
EWALD, 15175 E Jefferson, Grosse Pointe Park, 48230, SAN 346-6140. Tel: 313-343-2071. FAX: 313-821-8356. *Librn,* John Clexton; E-mail: jclexton@gp.lib.mi.us; Staff 3 (MLS 3)
Library Holdings: Bk Vols 30,544; Per Subs 129
Open Mon-Thurs 10-9, Fri & Sat 10-5
Friends of the Library Group
WOODS, 20680 Mack Ave, Grosse Pointe Woods, 48236, SAN 346-6175. Tel: 313-343-2072. FAX: 313-343-2486. *Librn,* Jame Moffet; Staff 4 (MLS 4)
Library Holdings: Bk Vols 45,816; Per Subs 135
Open Mon-Thurs 10-9, Fri & Sat 10-5, Sun (Winter) 1-5
Friends of the Library Group

GWINN

P FORSYTH TOWNSHIP PUBLIC LIBRARY*, 184 W Flint St, 49841. (Mail add: PO Box 1328, Gwin, 49841-1328), SAN 308-146X. Tel: 906-346-3433. FAX: 906-346-3433. E-mail: fyill@uproc.lib.mi.us. Web Site: www.uplibraries.org/forsyth.htm. *Dir,* Kathleen Holman; E-mail: kholman@uproc.lib.mi.us
Pop 4,824; Circ 12,500
Library Holdings: AV Mats 200; Bk Vols 12,000; Per Subs 52
Partic in Superiorland Library Cooperative
Open Mon & Wed 12-8, Tues & Thurs 9-5, Fri 12-5, Sat 10-1

HAMBURG

P HAMBURG TOWNSHIP LIBRARY, 10411 Merrill Rd, 48139. (Mail add: PO Box 247, 48139-0247), SAN 308-1478. Tel: 810-231-1771. FAX: 810-231-1520. E-mail: hamb@tln.lib.mi.us. Web Site: www.hamburglibrary.org. *Dir,* Holly Hentz; E-mail: hhentz@hamburglibrary.org; *Financial Mgr,* Christine Weber; E-mail: cweber@hamburglibrary.org; *Circ Librn,* Kim Roberts; E-mail: kroberts@hamburglibrary.org; *Adult Serv,* Bree Stokanovich; *Youth Serv,* Laura Strandt; E-mail: lstrandt@hamburglibrary.org; Staff 12 (MLS 3, Non-MLS 9)
Founded 1966. Pop 21,165; Circ 140,070
Library Holdings: Bk Vols 55,399; Per Subs 88
Special Collections: Arts & Crafts Coll; EPA Coll; Local History Coll; Michigan Coll; Speigleburg Rasmussen Sites
Automation Activity & Vendor Info: (Cataloging) Auto-Graphics, Inc; (Circulation) Auto-Graphics, Inc; (OPAC) Auto-Graphics, Inc
Wireless access
Function: 24/7 Electronic res, 24/7 Online cat, Accelerated reader prog, Activity rm, Adult bk club, Art exhibits, Audio & video playback equip for onsite use, AV serv, Bk club(s), Bks on CD, Children's prog, Computer training, Computers for patron use, Copy machines, e-mail serv, E-Reserves, Electronic databases & coll, Exhibits, Fax serv, Free DVD rentals, Handicapped accessible, ILL available, Laminating, Life-long learning prog for all ages, Literacy & newcomer serv, Magazines, Mail & tel request accepted, Movies, Mus passes, Music CDs, Online cat, Online ref, Photocopying/Printing, Preschool reading prog, Prog for adults, Prog for children & young adult, Pub access computers, Ref serv available, Ref serv in person, Scanner, Spoken cassettes & CDs, Story hour, Study rm, Summer reading prog, Tax forms, Teen prog, Telephone ref, Video lending libr, Web-catalog, Wheelchair accessible
Publications: Newsletter
Partic in Midwest Collaborative for Library Services (MCLS); The Library Network
Open Mon-Thurs 9-8, Fri 12-6, Sat 9-5

HAMTRAMCK

P HAMTRAMCK PUBLIC LIBRARY*, Albert J Zak Memorial Library, 2360 Caniff St, 48212. SAN 308-1486. Tel: 313-365-7050. FAX: 313-365-0160. Web Site: hamtramck.lib.mi.us. *Dir,* E Tamara Sochacka; E-mail: tamarasochacka@comcast.net; *Circ Mgr,* Ania Kosowski; E-mail: astachelek@hamtramck.lib.mi.us; *Asst Mgr, Coll Develop,* Oleksandr Boyko; *Syst Adminr,* Konrad Maziarz; E-mail: kmaziarz@hamtramck.lib.mi.us; Staff 3 (MLS 2, Non-MLS 1)
Founded 1918. Pop 18,000; Circ 60,000
Library Holdings: AV Mats 410; Bk Vols 60,000; Per Subs 200; Talking Bks 830
Special Collections: City of Hamtramck Historical File, bks, clippings, microfilm, newsp; Polish, Ukrainian, Russian (Foreign Language Coll); Svengali, Hindi, Urdu, Serbian, Croatian, Bosnian, Arabic & Albanian Colls
Automation Activity & Vendor Info: (Cataloging) SirsiDynix; (Circulation) SirsiDynix; (OPAC) SirsiDynix
Partic in The Library Network
Open Mon, Wed & Fri 9-5, Tues & Thurs 11-7, Sat 10-2
Friends of the Library Group

HANCOCK

C FINLANDIA UNIVERSITY*, Maki Library, 601 Quincy St, 49930-1882. SAN 346-6205. Tel: 906-487-7252. Interlibrary Loan Service Tel: 906-487-7503. Administration Tel: 906-487-7253. Toll Free Tel: 800-682-7604, Ext 252. FAX: 906-487-7297. E-mail: maki.library@finlandia.edu. Web Site: www.finlandia.edu/Maki-Library.html. *Interim Head Librn,* Rebecca Daly; E-mail: rebecca.daly@finlandia.edu; Staff 3 (MLS 2, Non-MLS 1)
Founded 1896. Enrl 580; Fac 35; Highest Degree: Bachelor
Library Holdings: Electronic Media & Resources 58; Bk Titles 37,296; Bk Vols 45,033; Per Subs 217
Special Collections: Finnish-American Life & Culture; Upper Peninsula of Michigan
Subject Interests: Art, Bus, Design, Educ, Nursing

Automation Activity & Vendor Info: (Acquisitions) Ex Libris Group; (Cataloging) Ex Libris Group; (Circulation) Ex Libris Group; (Course Reserve) Ex Libris Group; (ILL) Ex Libris Group; (OPAC) Ex Libris Group; (Serials) Ex Libris Group
Database Vendor: CredoReference, Gale Cengage Learning, H W Wilson, Hoovers, Medline, OCLC ArticleFirst, OCLC FirstSearch, OCLC WorldShare Interlibrary Loan, ProQuest, PubMed, SerialsSolutions
Wireless access
Partic in Midwest Collaborative for Library Services (MCLS); Upper Peninsula Region of Library Cooperation, Inc
Open Mon-Thurs (Fall & Spring) 8am-10pm, Fri 8-5, Sat 1-5, Sun 2-10; Mon-Fri (Summer) 8-5

HARBOR BEACH

P HARBOR BEACH AREA DISTRICT LIBRARY*, 105 N Huron Ave, 48441. SAN 308-1516. Tel: 989-479-3417. FAX: 989-479-6818. E-mail: librarian@hbadl.org. *Dir,* Vicki Mazure
Founded 1917. Circ 24,262
Library Holdings: Bk Vols 20,000; Per Subs 45
Open Mon, Wed & Fri 12-8, Tues, Thurs & Sat 9-5
Friends of the Library Group

HARPER WOODS

P HARPER WOODS PUBLIC LIBRARY*, 19601 Harper, 48225-2001. SAN 308-1524. Tel: 313-343-2575. FAX: 313-343-2127. E-mail: hwl@libcoop.net. *Dir,* Dale Parus; *Adult Serv,* Suzanne D Kent; *YA Serv,* Cate Fleming; *YA Serv,* Nancy Maxon
Pop 14,254; Circ 73,000
Library Holdings: Bk Vols 42,000; Per Subs 108
Partic in Suburban Library Cooperative
Open Mon-Thurs 9:30-8, Fri & Sat 10-5

HARRISON

P HARRISON COMMUNITY LIBRARY*, 105 E Main St, 48625. (Mail add: PO Box 380, 48625-0380), SAN 308-1532. Tel: 989-539-6711. FAX: 989-539-6301. Web Site: www.harrisondistrictlibrary.org. *Dir,* Shelia Bissonnette; E-mail: sbissonnette@harrisondistrictlibrary.org; *Pub Serv Librn,* Mary-Jane Ogg; E-mail: mogg@harrrisondistrictlibrary.org; Staff 4 (MLS 1, Non-MLS 3)
Founded 1948. Pop 13,415; Circ 50,000
Library Holdings: Bk Vols 32,000; Per Subs 90
Automation Activity & Vendor Info: (Cataloging) SirsiDynix; (Circulation) SirsiDynix; (ILL) SirsiDynix; (OPAC) SirsiDynix; (Serials) SirsiDynix
Database Vendor: SirsiDynix
Wireless access
Partic in Valley Libr Consortium; White Pine Libr Coop
Special Services for the Deaf - TDD equip
Open Mon 10-7, Tues-Fri 10-6, Sat 10-2
Friends of the Library Group

J MID MICHIGAN COMMUNITY COLLEGE*, Charles A Amble Library & Community Learning Center, 1375 S Clare Ave, 48625. SAN 346-6264. Tel: 989-386-6617. Circulation Tel: 989-386-6618. FAX: 989-386-2411. Web Site: www.midmich.edu/library. *Dir, Libr Serv,* Shawn R Troy; Tel: 989-386-6616, E-mail: stroy@midmich.edu; Staff 2 (MLS 1, Non-MLS 1)
Founded 1969. Enrl 2,200; Fac 59; Highest Degree: Associate
Library Holdings: Bk Titles 22,000; Per Subs 100
Special Collections: Mid-Michigan History (Meek Coll), still pictures
Automation Activity & Vendor Info: (Cataloging) Horizon; (Circulation) Horizon
Database Vendor: SirsiDynix
Partic in Valley Library Consortium; White Pine Libr Coop
Open Mon-Thurs 8-8, Fri 8-4:30

HARRISON TOWNSHIP

M SAINT JOHN NORTH SHORES HOSPITAL*, Medical Library, 26755 Ballard Rd, 48045. SAN 324-5578. Tel: 586-465-5501, Ext 45858. FAX: 586-466-5370. *Librn,* Deborah R Cicchini; E-mail: debra.cicchini@stjohn.org; Staff 1 (MLS 1)
Library Holdings: Bk Titles 350; Bk Vols 875; Per Subs 50
Subject Interests: Podiatry, Rehabilitation
Database Vendor: EBSCOhost, OVID Technologies

HARRISVILLE

P ALCONA COUNTY LIBRARY SYSTEM*, 312 W Main, 48740. (Mail add: PO Box 348, 48740-0348), SAN 308-1540. Tel: 989-724-6796. FAX: 989-724-6173. E-mail: alcona1@northland.lib.mi.us. Web Site: www.alcona.lib.mi.us. *Dir,* Carol Luck; Staff 5 (MLS 1, Non-MLS 4)
Founded 1940. Pop 11,719; Circ 30,545
Library Holdings: Bk Titles 38,000; Bk Vols 50,000; Per Subs 50
Subject Interests: Local hist, Mich
Automation Activity & Vendor Info: (Acquisitions) SirsiDynix; (Cataloging) SirsiDynix; (Circulation) SirsiDynix
Wireless access
Partic in Northland Library Cooperative
Open Mon-Thurs 10-7, Fri 10-5, Sat 10-3
Friends of the Library Group
Branches: 3
CALEDONIA TOWNSHIP, 1499 Hurbert Rd, Hubbard Lake, 49747-9611. (Mail add: PO Box 56, Hubbard Lake, 49747-0056), SAN 376-7949. Tel: 989-727-3105. FAX: 989-727-3105. *In Charge,* Helen Timm; Tel: 989-724-6796, Fax: 989-724-6173
Open Thurs 11-5:30, Fri (Summer) 12-4, Sat 10-2
Friends of the Library Group
LINCOLN BRANCH, 330 Traverse Bay Rd, Lincoln, 48742-0115. (Mail add: PO Box 115, Lincoln, 48742-0115), SAN 376-8058. Tel: 989-736-3388. FAX: 989-736-3388. *In Charge,* Sue Malski; Tel: 989-724-6796; Staff 1 (Non-MLS 1)
Open Mon-Thurs 12-6, Fri 10-4
MIKADO TOWNSHIP, 2291 S F-41, Mikado, 48745. (Mail add: PO Box 110, Mikado, 48745-0110), SAN 376-8066. Tel: 989-736-8389. FAX: 989-736-8389. *In Charge,* Mary Carpenter
Open Mon-Thurs 2-6
Friends of the Library Group

HART

P HART AREA PUBLIC LIBRARY*, 415 S State St, 49420-1228. SAN 308-1559. Tel: 231-873-4476. FAX: 231-873-4476. E-mail: librarian@hartpubliclibrary.org. Web Site: www.hart.lib.mi.us. *Dir,* Joan LundBorg; E-mail: hapl@hartpubliclibrary.org
Pop 8,465; Circ 90,000
Library Holdings: Bk Vols 35,000; Per Subs 120
Subject Interests: Hist
Automation Activity & Vendor Info: (Acquisitions) Auto-Graphics, Inc; (Cataloging) Auto-Graphics, Inc; (Circulation) Auto-Graphics, Inc
Wireless access
Function: Art exhibits, Bilingual assistance for Spanish patrons, Bk club(s), Bks on cassette, Bks on CD, Children's prog, Computers for patron use, Copy machines, Digital talking bks, E-Reserves, Electronic databases & coll, Free DVD rentals, Handicapped accessible, Health sci info serv, Holiday prog, Home delivery & serv to Sr ctr & nursing homes, Homebound delivery serv, ILL available, Mail & tel request accepted, Music CDs, Notary serv, Online cat, Online ref, Photocopying/Printing, Preschool outreach, Prog for adults, Prog for children & young adult, Ref serv available, Spoken cassettes & CDs, Spoken cassettes & DVDs, Summer reading prog, Tax forms, Teen prog, Telephone ref, VHS videos, Wheelchair accessible, Writing prog
Partic in Mid-Michigan Library League
Special Services for the Blind - Audio mat; Bks on cassette; Bks on CD; Digital talking bk; Large print bks
Open Mon & Thurs 9-8:30, Tues, Wed & Fri 9-5, Sat 9-2
Friends of the Library Group

HARTFORD

P HARTFORD PUBLIC LIBRARY*, 15 Franklin St, 49057. (Mail add: PO Box 8, 49057-0008), SAN 308-1567. Tel: 616-621-3408. FAX: 616-621-3073. E-mail: hartfordlibrary2000@yahoo.com. *Dir,* Stephanie Daniels
Pop 6,311; Circ 48,960
Library Holdings: Bk Vols 50,000; Per Subs 48; Talking Bks 575
Special Collections: Hartford Day Spring Newspaper 1881-1973, microflm
Partic in OCLC Online Computer Library Center, Inc; Southwest Michigan Library Cooperative
Open Mon & Wed 10-7, Tues & Thurs 1-5, Fri 9-5, Sat 10-2
Friends of the Library Group

HARTLAND

P CROMAINE DISTRICT LIBRARY*, 3688 N Hartland Rd, 48353. (Mail add: PO Box 308, 48353-0308), SAN 308-1575. Tel: 810-632-5200. E-mail: cromaine@cromaine.org. Web Site: www.cromaine.org. *Libr Dir,* Cecilia Ann Marlow; Tel: 810-632-5200, Ext 105, E-mail: cmarlow@cromaine.org; *Circ Mgr,* Sue Strouse; Tel: 810-632-5200, Ext 102, E-mail: sstrouse@cromaine.org; *Mrg/Youth & Adult Serv,* Jeanne Smith; Tel: 810-632-5200, Ext 107, E-mail: jsmith@cromaine.org; *Syst Mgr,* Renay Elve; Tel: 810-632-5200, Ext 100, E-mail: relve@cromaine.org; Staff 23.25 (MLS 7, Non-MLS 16.25)
Founded 1927. Pop 26,391; Circ 448,848
Special Collections: Historical Documents of Hartland & Livingston County (J R Crouse Coll), art works, autographed letters, bks, doc, photog
Automation Activity & Vendor Info: (Acquisitions) SirsiDynix; (Cataloging) SirsiDynix; (Circulation) SirsiDynix; (OPAC) SirsiDynix
Wireless access
Partic in The Library Network

Open Mon-Thurs 9-8, Fri 9-6, Sat 9-4
Friends of the Library Group
Branches: 1
CROSSROADS, 1788 N Old US 23, Howell, 48843. Tel: 810-632-7480. Administration Tel: 810-632-5200. *Circ Mgr,* Sue Strouse; E-mail: sstrouse@cromaine.org
Founded 2005
Library Holdings: Bk Vols 8,800
Open Mon-Thurs 9-8, Fri 9-6, Sat 9-4, Sun 1-5
Friends of the Library Group

HASTINGS

P DOWLING PUBLIC LIBRARY*, 1765 E Dowling Rd, 49058-9332. Tel: 269-721-3743. FAX: 269-721-3743. Web Site: www.dowlingpubliclibrary.com. *Dir,* Kris Miller
Circ 2,800
Library Holdings: AV Mats 132; CDs 35; DVDs 120; Bk Vols 12,000; Per Subs 20
Automation Activity & Vendor Info: (Cataloging) Auto-Graphics, Inc
Mem of Woodlands Library Cooperative
Open Mon, Tues & Fri (Winter) 11-6, Wed 11-7, Sat 10-2; Mon-Wed & Fri (Summer) 12-6
Friends of the Library Group

P HASTINGS PUBLIC LIBRARY*, 227 E State St, 49058-1817. SAN 308-1583. Tel: 269-945-4263. FAX: 269-948-3874. E-mail: has@llcoop.org. Web Site: hastings.llcoop.org. *Adminr,* Evelyn Holzwarth; *Adult Prog Coordr,* Michael Evans; *Circ Supvr,* Laura Gould; *Network Adminr,* Edward Englerth; Staff 10 (MLS 2, Non-MLS 8)
Founded 1896. Pop 13,033; Circ 106,000
Library Holdings: Bk Vols 37,781; Per Subs 110
Subject Interests: Genealogy, Local hist
Automation Activity & Vendor Info: (Circulation) Innovative Interfaces, Inc; (ILL) Innovative Interfaces, Inc; (OPAC) Innovative Interfaces, Inc
Database Vendor: Gale Cengage Learning, Innovative Interfaces, Inc, OCLC FirstSearch
Partic in Lakeland Library Cooperative
Open Mon-Thurs 9-8, Fri 9-6, Sat 9-3
Friends of the Library Group

S HISTORIC CHARLTON PARK VILLAGE & MUSEUM LIBRARY*, 2545 S Charlton Park Rd, 49058-8102. SAN 323-4169. Tel: 269-945-3775. FAX: 269-945-0390. Web Site: www.charltonpark.org. *Curator,* Claire Johnston; Tel: 269-945-3775, Ext 102, E-mail: claire_l_johnston@yahoo.com
Founded 1936
Library Holdings: Bk Vols 1,500
Special Collections: Museum Books & Journals, Historic Preservation Archival Coll, Archival Newspapers
Subject Interests: Agr, Barry County hist, Gas engines, Native Am hist, Steam engines
Function: Res libr
Restriction: Non-circulating, Open by appt only

M PENNOCK HOSPITAL*, Health Sciences Library, 1009 W Green St, 49058. SAN 327-0483. Tel: 269-945-3451, Ext 199. FAX: 269-945-3035. *In Charge,* Teresa McSall; Staff 1 (MLS 1)
Library Holdings: Bk Vols 300; Per Subs 50

HAZEL PARK

P HAZEL PARK MEMORIAL LIBRARY*, 123 E Nine Mile Rd, 48030. SAN 308-1591. Tel: 248-542-0940, 248-546-4095. FAX: 248-546-4083. Web Site: www.hazel-park.lib.mi.us. *Dir,* Joan E Ludlow; E-mail: ludlow@tln.lib.mi.us; *Adult Serv,* Gary Allen; E-mail: gallen@tln.lib.mi.us; *Adult Serv,* Corrine Boland; E-mail: cboland@tln.lib.mi.us; *Ch Serv,* Linda Sims; E-mail: lsims@tln.lib.mi.us; *Ref Serv,* David Stokes; E-mail: dstokes@tln.lib.mi.us; Staff 14 (MLS 5, Non-MLS 9)
Founded 1936. Pop 18,963; Circ 54,000
Library Holdings: Bk Vols 87,000; Per Subs 130
Automation Activity & Vendor Info: (Cataloging) SirsiDynix; (Circulation) SirsiDynix; (ILL) SirsiDynix; (OPAC) SirsiDynix; (Serials) SirsiDynix
Database Vendor: OCLC FirstSearch
Wireless access
Partic in Libr Network of Mich
Open Mon-Thurs 12-8, Fri 9-5, Sat 12-4, Sun (Sept-May) 12-4
Friends of the Library Group

HEMLOCK

P RAUCHHOLZ MEMORIAL LIBRARY*, 1140 N Hemlock Rd, 48626. SAN 308-1605. Tel: 989-642-8621. FAX: 989-642-5559. E-mail: library@rauchholzlibrary.org. Web Site: www.rauchholzlibrary.org. *Dir,* BillieJo Bluemer; Staff 2 (Non-MLS 2)
Founded 1942. Pop 6,380; Circ 63,629
Apr 2009-Mar 2010 Income $127,384, State $1,929, Locally Generated Income $125,455. Mats Exp $14,060, Books $9,318, Per/Ser (Incl. Access Fees) $1,506, AV Mat $2,000, Electronic Ref Mat (Incl. Access Fees) $1,236. Sal $90,038
Library Holdings: CDs 450; DVDs 604; Bk Titles 28,062; Per Subs 38; Talking Bks 1,068; Videos 730
Special Collections: Audio History, cassettes; Local History, slides. Oral History
Automation Activity & Vendor Info: (Cataloging) Follett Software; (Circulation) Follett Software; (OPAC) Follett Software
Wireless access
Function: AV serv, Home delivery & serv to Sr ctr & nursing homes, Homebound delivery serv, ILL available, Photocopying/Printing, Prog for children & young adult, Summer reading prog, Wheelchair accessible
Partic in White Pine Libr Coop
Open Mon, Tues & Fri 9-5, Wed & Thurs 1-8, Sat (Sept-May) 10-2
Friends of the Library Group

HESPERIA

P HESPERIA COMMUNITY LIBRARY*, 80 S Division St, 49421-9004. SAN 308-1613. Tel: 231-854-5125. FAX: 231-854-5125. E-mail: hes@hesperialibrary.org. Web Site: hesperialibrary.org. *Dir,* Kay Brennan
Circ 31,942
Library Holdings: Bk Vols 22,510; Per Subs 69
Wireless access
Partic in Lakeland Library Cooperative
Open Mon-Thurs 10-7, Fri 10-5, Sat 10-3
Friends of the Library Group

HIGHLAND

P HIGHLAND TOWNSHIP PUBLIC LIBRARY*, 444 Beach Farm Circle, 48357. (Mail add: PO Box 277, 48357-0277), SAN 308-163X. Tel: 248-887-2218. FAX: 248-887-5179. E-mail: htplreply@highland.lib.mi.us. Web Site: www.highlandlibrary.info. *Dir,* Jude Halloran; Tel: 248-887-2218, Ext 110, E-mail: jhalloran@highland.lib.mi.us; *Head, Adult Serv,* Cathy Buehner; *Youth Serv Dept Head,* Brenda Dunseth; *Teen Serv,* Dawn Dittmar; E-mail: ddittmar@highland.lib.mi.us; Staff 5 (MLS 5)
Founded 1856. Pop 19,202; Circ 187,103
Jan 2012-Dec 2012 Income $983,555. Mats Exp $983,555
Library Holdings: Audiobooks 2,637; CDs 2,083; DVDs 3,935; Large Print Bks 1,150; Bk Vols 76,549; Per Subs 165; Videos 2,030
Automation Activity & Vendor Info: (Circulation) SirsiDynix; (OPAC) SirsiDynix
Database Vendor: Gale Cengage Learning, OCLC FirstSearch
Wireless access
Partic in The Library Network
Open Mon-Thurs 10-8, Fri & Sat 10-5
Friends of the Library Group

HILLSDALE

C HILLSDALE COLLEGE, Michael Alex Mossey Library, 33 E College St, 49242. SAN 308-1672. Tel: 517-607-2701. Circulation Tel: 517-607-2404. Administration Tel: 517-607-2400. FAX: 517-607-2248. Web Site: lib.hillsdale.edu. *Libr Dir,* Daniel L Knoch; Tel: 517-607-2401, E-mail: dknoch@hillsdale.edu; *Pub Serv Librn,* Linda Moore; Tel: 517-607-2403, E-mail: lmoore@hillsdale.edu; *Pub Serv Librn,* Brenna Wade; Tel: 517-607-2606, E-mail: bwade@hillsdale.edu; *Tech Serv Librn,* Dr Maurine McCourry; Tel: 517-607-2402, E-mail: mmccourry@hillsdale.edu; *Tech Serv Librn,* LeAnne Rumler; Tel: 517-607-2405, E-mail: lrumler@hillsdale.edu; Staff 5 (MLS 5)
Founded 1971. Enrl 1,436; Fac 124; Highest Degree: Master
Jul 2014-Jun 2015. Mats Exp $667,500, Books $136,500, Per/Ser (Incl. Access Fees) $167,500, Manu Arch $20,000, Micro $20,000, AV Equip $10,000, AV Mat $13,500, Electronic Ref Mat (Incl. Access Fees) $300,000
Library Holdings: CDs 7,365; DVDs 6,504; e-books 642,489; e-journals 30,000; Microforms 507,393; Bk Vols 235,313; Per Subs 570; Videos 5,912
Special Collections: Ancient, Modern & US Currency (Alwin C Carus Coin Coll); Ludwig von Mises Library; Money, Banking & US Monetary Policy (George Edward Durell Coll); Richard Weaver Coll; Russell Kirk Library; Thomas Kimball Civil War Diary; Works by Founders of Western Civilization (Heritage Coll)
Subject Interests: Conservative movement, modern & traditional
Automation Activity & Vendor Info: (Acquisitions) Innovative Interfaces, Inc; (Cataloging) Innovative Interfaces, Inc; (Circulation) Innovative Interfaces, Inc; (ILL) OCLC; (OPAC) Innovative Interfaces, Inc; (Serials) Innovative Interfaces, Inc
Database Vendor: American Chemical Society, American Psychological Association (APA), Annual Reviews, BioOne, Dialog, EBSCO Discovery Service, Gale Cengage Learning, Innovative Interfaces, Inc, ISI Web of

Knowledge, JSTOR, LexisNexis, OCLC ArticleFirst, OCLC FirstSearch, OCLC WorldShare Interlibrary Loan, Olive Software, Inc, Oxford Online, Project MUSE, ProQuest, SerialsSolutions, Wilson - Wilson Web
Wireless access
Function: 24/7 Electronic res, Archival coll, Bks on cassette, Bks on CD, Computers for patron use, Copy machines, Electronic databases & coll, Exhibits, ILL available, Music CDs, Online cat, Printer for laptops & handheld devices, Pub access computers, Ref serv available, Ref serv in person, Spoken cassettes & CDs, Spoken cassettes & DVDs, Study rm, VHS videos
Partic in Midwest Collaborative for Library Services (MCLS)
Restriction: Borrowing privileges limited to fac & registered students, Limited access for the pub, Non-circulating of rare bks, Restricted pub use

P HILLSDALE COMMUNITY LIBRARY*, 11 E Bacon St, 49242. SAN 308-1680. Tel: 517-437-6470. Administration Tel: 517-437-6472. FAX: 517-437-6477. E-mail: info@hillsdale-library.org. Web Site: hillsdale-library.org. *Dir,* LeAnn Beckwith; *Ch,* Debera McCluer; Tel: 517-437-6473; Staff 2 (MLS 1, Non-MLS 1)
Founded 1879. Pop 15,571; Circ 56,355
Library Holdings: Audiobooks 1,250; Electronic Media & Resources 9,122; Large Print Bks 2,093; Bk Vols 45,587; Per Subs 55; Videos 542
Automation Activity & Vendor Info: (Acquisitions) Follett Software; (Cataloging) Follett Software
Database Vendor: OCLC FirstSearch
Wireless access
Function: Audiobks via web, Bks on cassette, Bks on CD, Children's prog, Computers for patron use, Copy machines, Electronic databases & coll, Fax serv, Handicapped accessible, ILL available, Online cat, OverDrive digital audio bks, Photocopying/Printing, Prog for children & young adult, Pub access computers, Summer reading prog, Tax forms, Teen prog, VHS videos, Video lending libr, Web-catalog, Wheelchair accessible
Mem of Woodlands Library Cooperative
Open Mon-Wed 10-8, Thurs & Fri 10-5, Sat 10-2

HOLLAND

P HERRICK DISTRICT LIBRARY*, 300 S River Ave, 49423-3290. SAN 346-6299. Tel: 616-355-3100. Reference Tel: 616-355-3720. Administration Tel: 616-355-3723, 616-355-3724. Reference FAX: 616 355-3083 Administration FAX: 616-355-1426. TDD: 616-355-3086. Web Site: www.herrickdl.org. *Dir,* Thomas J Genson; *Librn,* Mary Vanderkooy; *Pub Relations Mgr,* Hillary Hovinga; Tel: 616-355-3728, E-mail: hhovinga@herrickdl.org; *Automation Syst Coordr, Tech Serv,* Lin Light, *Acq,* Dianna Harrington; *Adult Serv, Circ,* Diane Corradini; *AV,* Susan Panasuk; *ILL,* Christine Abma; *Ref,* Kelli Perkins; *Youth Serv,* Marilyn Brown. Subject Specialists: *Genealogy,* Mary Vanderkooy; Staff 17.2 (MLS 17.2)
Founded 1867. Pop 102,212; Circ 1,307,639
Jul 2009-Jun 2010 Income (Main Library and Branch(s)) $5,372,804, State $20,270, Federal $26,642, Locally Generated Income $5,329,892, Other $52,912. Mats Exp $576,866, Books $300,968, Per/Ser (Incl. Access Fees) $28,579, AV Mat $104,436, Electronic Ref Mat (Incl. Access Fees) $142,913. Sal $2,123,960 (Prof $980,750)
Library Holdings: AV Mats 38,303; CDs 18,334; DVDs 14,886; e-books 5,083; Electronic Media & Resources 7,166; Bk Vols 256,698; Per Subs 500
Special Collections: Dutch, Spanish Periodicals; Indo-Chinese Language Coll; Local Genealogy Coll; Spanish Language Coll
Automation Activity & Vendor Info: (Cataloging) Innovative Interfaces, Inc; (Circulation) Innovative Interfaces, Inc; (OPAC) Innovative Interfaces, Inc
Wireless access
Function: Adult bk club, Audiobks via web, Bi-weekly Writer's Group, Bilingual assistance for Spanish patrons, Bk club(s), Bks on CD, Children's prog, Computer training, Computers for patron use, Copy machines, E-Reserves, Electronic databases & coll, Fax serv, Free DVD rentals, Handicapped accessible, ILL available, Magnifiers for reading, Music CDs, Online searches, OverDrive digital audio bks, Photocopying/Printing, Preschool outreach, Prog for adults, Prog for children & young adult, Pub access computers, Senior computer classes, Story hour, Summer & winter reading prog, Tax forms, Teen prog, Telephone ref
Partic in Lakeland Library Cooperative
Special Services for the Deaf - TDD equip
Open Mon-Thurs 9-9, Fri & Sat 9-6
Restriction: Restricted borrowing privileges
Friends of the Library Group
Branches: 1
NORTH SIDE, 155 Riley St, 49424-1884. Tel: 616-738-4360. FAX: 616-738-4359. E-mail: hnb@llcoop.org. *Br Mgr,* Diane Kooiker; Tel: 616-738-4364, E-mail: dkooiker@herrickdl.org
Founded 2000
Library Holdings: Bk Vols 20,000; Per Subs 60
Open Mon & Tues 12-8, Wed-Fri 10-5, Sat 10-2

M HOLLAND HOSPITAL*, Medical Library, 602 Michigan Ave, 3rd Flr, 49423. SAN 325-9145. Tel: 616-394-3107, 616-394-3109. FAX: 616-392-8448. E-mail: medlib@hollandhospital.org. Web Site: www.hoho.org.
Founded 1917
Library Holdings: Bk Vols 5,000; Per Subs 240
Subject Interests: Cultural diversity
Partic in Michigan Health Sciences Libraries Association
Open Mon-Fri 8-4:30
Branches:
HEALTH INFOSOURCE LIBRARY, 3235 N Wellness Dr, 49424, SAN 376-9364. Tel: 616-394-3795. Toll Free Tel: 800-304-5182. FAX: 616-394-3777. Web Site: www.hollandhospital.org.
Library Holdings: AV Mats 200; Bk Vols 1,000; Per Subs 20
Subject Interests: Consumer health

HOPE COLLEGE
C THE JOINT ARCHIVES OF HOLLAND*, Theil Research Ctr, Nine E Tenth St, 49423-3513. (Mail add: PO Box 9000, 49422-9000), SAN 327-5701. Tel: 616-395-7798. FAX: 616-395-7197. E-mail: archives@hope.edu. Web Site: www.jointarchives.org. *Dir,* Geoffrey D Reynolds; E-mail: reynoldsg@hope.edu; Staff 1 (MLS 1)
Founded 1988. Enrl 3,000; Highest Degree: Bachelor
Special Collections: Archival Coll of the Holland Historical Trust (Holland Museum); Coll of City of Holland, City of Saugatuck & Village of Douglas; Hope College & Western Theological Seminary
Subject Interests: Immigration, Oral hist, Reform church hist, Regional hist
Function: Archival coll
Publications: A C Van Raalte: Dutch Leader & American Patriot, 1997; Campus Alive: A Walking Tour of Hope College, 1999; Guide to Collections of The Joint Archives of Holland, 1989; Supplement to The Guide to the Collection, 1991; The Joint Archives Quarterly
Open Mon-Fri 8-12 & 1-5
Restriction: Non-circulating to the pub
Friends of the Library Group

C VAN WYLEN LIBRARY*, 53 Graves Pl, 49422. (Mail add: PO Box 9012, 49422-9012), SAN 308-1710. Tel: 616-395-7790. FAX: 616-395-7965. Web Site: www.hope.edu/lib. *Dir,* Kelly Jacobsma; E-mail: jacobsma@hope.edu; *Head, Access Serv,* David O'Brien; Tel: 616-395-7791, E-mail: obriend@hope.edu; *Head, Ref & Instruction,* Priscilla Atkins; Tel: 616-395-7986, E-mail: atkinsp@hope.edu; *Head, Tech Serv & Syst,* Brian Yost; Tel: 616-395-7492, E-mail: yostb@hope.edu; *Ref & Instrul Serv Librn,* Rachel Bishop; Tel: 616-395-7299, E-mail: bishop@hope.edu; *Ref & Instrul Serv Librn,* Jessica Hronchek; Tel: 616-395-7124, E-mail: hronchek@hope.edu; *Ref & Instrul Serv Librn,* Todd Wiebe; Tel: 616-395-7286, E-mail: wiebe@hope.edu; *Tech Serv Librn,* Colleen Conway; Tel: 616-395-7792, E-mail: conwayc@hope.edu; *Tech Serv Librn,* Gloria Slaughter; Tel: 616-395-7793, E-mail: slaughtcrg@hope.edu; *Circ Supvr,* Carla Kaminski; Tel: 616-395-7889, E-mail: kaminski@hope.edu; *TechLab Coordr,* Daphne Fairbanks; Tel: 616-395-7283, E-mail: fairbanks@hope.edu; *ILL Assoc,* Michelle Kelley; Tel: 616-395-7794, E-mail: kelley@hope.edu; *Music Libr Assoc,* John Hoyer; Tel: 616-395-7659, E-mail: hoyerj@hope.edu; *Media Serv,* Jan Zessin; Tel: 616-395-7463, E-mail: zessinj@hope.edu; Staff 9 (MLS 9)
Founded 1866. Enrl 3,075; Fac 239; Highest Degree: Bachelor
Jul 2005-Jun 2006 Income $2,135,661. Mats Exp $841,864, Books $207,215, Per/Ser (Incl. Access Fees) $357,435, Micro $32,811, Electronic Ref Mat (Incl. Access Fees) $234,783, Presv $9,619. Sal $864,961
Library Holdings: Bk Vols 366,783; Per Subs 1,548
Special Collections: Church History (Reformed Church in America); Dutch American History; Holland Joint Archives
Subject Interests: Art hist
Automation Activity & Vendor Info: (Acquisitions) Innovative Interfaces, Inc; (Cataloging) Innovative Interfaces, Inc; (Circulation) Innovative Interfaces, Inc; (Course Reserve) Docutek; (OPAC) Innovative Interfaces, Inc; (Serials) Innovative Interfaces, Inc
Database Vendor: 3M Library Systems, Agricola, ARTstor, Blackwell, Cambridge Scientific Abstracts, Dialog, Gale Cengage Learning, JSTOR, LexisNexis, Newsbank, OCLC FirstSearch, OCLC WorldShare Interlibrary Loan, ProQuest, PubMed, ScienceDirect, SerialsSolutions, Wilson - Wilson Web
Partic in OCLC Online Computer Library Center, Inc
Publications: Annual Bibliography of Faculty Scholarship (Bibliographies)
Special Services for the Deaf - Assistive tech
Special Services for the Blind - Assistive/Adapted tech devices, equip & products
Open Mon-Thurs (Winter) 8am-Midnight, Fri 8-6, Sat 10-6, Sun 1-Midnight; Mon-Fri (Summer) 8-6, Sun 4-7

R WESTERN THEOLOGICAL SEMINARY*, Beardslee Library, 101 E 13th St, 49423. SAN 308-1729. Tel: 616-392-8555. Circulation Tel: 616-392-8555, Ext 139. Administration Tel: 616-392-8555, Ext 143. Toll Free Tel: 800-392-8554. Web Site: www.westernsem.edu/library. *Dir,* Paul M Smith; E-mail: paul.smith@westernsem.edu; *Assoc Dir,* Ann E Nieuwkoop; Tel: 616-392-8555, Ext 141, E-mail: ann@westernsem.edu; *Electronic Serv, Syst Librn,* Steve Michaels; Tel: 616-392-8555, Ext 187, E-mail: steve.michaels@westernsem.edu; *Circ Supvr,* Glenda McKinley; E-mail: glenda.mckinley@westernsem.edu; Staff 4 (MLS 3, Non-MLS 1)
Founded 1866. Enrl 223; Fac 17; Highest Degree: Doctorate
Library Holdings: Bk Vols 110,665; Per Subs 442
Special Collections: 15th-18th Century; History of Reformed Church in America (Kolkman Memorial Archives), ms mat; Theology (Rare bks), bd vols
Subject Interests: Art & archit, Biblical studies, Church hist, Educ, Relig, Theol
Automation Activity & Vendor Info: (Acquisitions) Innovative Interfaces, Inc - Millenium; (Cataloging) Innovative Interfaces, Inc - Millenium; (Circulation) Innovative Interfaces, Inc - Millenium; (ILL) OCLC; (OPAC) Innovative Interfaces, Inc; (Serials) Innovative Interfaces, Inc - Millenium
Database Vendor: OCLC FirstSearch
Wireless access
Partic in Mich Libr Asn; Midwest Collaborative for Library Services (MCLS); OCLC Online Computer Library Center, Inc

HOLLY

P HOLLY TOWNSHIP LIBRARY, 1116 N Saginaw St, 48442-1395. SAN 308-1737. Tel: 248-634-1754. FAX: 248-634-8088. *Librn,* Shirley Roos; E-mail: sroos@comcast.net; *Ch Serv,* Lucy Summers; *YA Serv,* Evelyn Wheeler; Staff 1 (Non-MLS 1)
Founded 1852. Pop 23,088; Circ 81,391
Jul 2011-Jun 2012 Income $647,478, State $8,193, County $310,500, Locally Generated Income $299,049, Other $29,736. Mats Exp $34,020, Books $20,000, Per/Ser (Incl. Access Fees) $1,020, AV Mat $13,000. Sal $224,500
Library Holdings: Audiobooks 5,200; Bks on Deafness & Sign Lang 15; CDs 2,300; DVDs 1,500; High Interest/Low Vocabulary Bk Vols 65; Large Print Bks 3,200; Per Subs 52
Special Collections: Municipal Document Depository
Subject Interests: Mich
Automation Activity & Vendor Info: (Circulation) Follett Software; (ILL) Follett Software
Wireless access
Function: Bk club(s), Bks on CD, CD-ROM, Children's prog, Computer training, Computers for patron use, Copy machines, E-Reserves, Electronic databases & coll, Fax serv, Free DVD rentals, Handicapped accessible, Holiday prog, Home delivery & serv to Sr ctr & nursing homes, ILL available, Large print keyboards, Magnifiers for reading, Mail & tel request accepted, Microfiche/film & reading machines, Music CDs, Online cat, Online searches, Photocopying/Printing, Preschool outreach, Printer for laptops & handheld devices, Prog for adults, Prog for children & young adult, Pub access computers, Ref serv available, Ref serv in person, Scanner, Senior computer classes, Spanish lang bks, Story hour, Summer & winter reading prog, Tax forms, Wheelchair accessible
Partic in Mideastern Michigan Library Cooperative
Special Services for the Deaf - Staff with knowledge of sign lang
Open Mon-Thurs 9:30-8, Fri 9:30-5, Sat 9:30-3
Friends of the Library Group

HOMER

P HOMER PUBLIC LIBRARY*, 141 W Main St, 49245. SAN 376-7043. Tel: 517-568-3450. FAX: 517-568-4021. E-mail: hpl@wowway.biz. Web Site: homerpl.michlibrary.org. *Dir,* Trixie L McMeeking
Pop 3,901
Library Holdings: Bk Titles 16,000; Per Subs 20
Wireless access
Open Mon-Wed 10-5, Thurs 10-8, Fri 10-4, Sat 9-12

HOPKINS

P HOPKINS PUBLIC LIBRARY*, 118 E Main St, 49328-0366. SAN 308-1745. Tel: 269-793-7516. FAX: 269-793-7047. E-mail: hop@llcoop.org. Web Site: hopkins.llcoop.org. *Dir,* Alice Hazen
Circ 16,186
Library Holdings: Bk Vols 18,000; Per Subs 20
Partic in Lakeland Library Cooperative
Open Mon-Wed & Fri 10-5:30, Sat 9-12

HOUGHTON

C MICHIGAN TECHNOLOGICAL UNIVERSITY*, J Robert Van Pelt & John & Ruanne Opie Library, 1400 Townsend Dr, 49931-1295. SAN 308-1753. Tel: 906-487-2508. Interlibrary Loan Service Tel: 906-487-3207. Reference Tel: 906-487-2507. Administration Tel: 906-487-2500. Administration FAX: 906-487-1765. E-mail: library@mtu.edu, reflib@mtu.edu. Interlibrary Loan Service E-mail: ill@mtu.edu. Web Site: www.mtu.edu/library. *Libr Dir, Univ Librn,* Ellen Marks; E-mail: ebmarks@mtu.edu; *Head, Coll & Tech Serv,* Ellen Seidel; Tel: 906-487-3064, E-mail: eseidel@mtu.edu; *Head, Tech Strategy & Innovation,* Chad Arney; Tel: 906-487-4321, E-mail: caarney@mtu.edu; *Copyright Librn, Ref & ILL Librn,* Nora Allred; Tel: 906-487-3208, E-mail: nsallred@mtu.edu; *Instruction & Learning Librn,* Sarah Lucchesi; Tel: 906-487-3379, E-mail: slucches@mtu.edu; *Instruction & Learning Librn,* Margaret Phillips; Tel: 906-487-1443, E-mail: mphillip@mtu.edu; *Instruction & Learning Librn,* Jennifer Sams; Tel: 906-487-2698, E-mail: jsams@mtu.edu; *Ref & Instruction Librn,* Amanda Binoniemi; Tel: 906-487-1814, E-mail: abinonie@mtu.edu; *Ser Librn,* Pattie Luokkanen; Tel: 906-487-2484, E-mail: paluokka@mtu.edu; *Strategic Initiatives Librn,* Julia Blair; Tel: 906-487-3168, E-mail: jblair@mtu.edu; *Finance & Operations Mgr,* Carol Makkonen; Tel: 906-487-3535, E-mail: makkonen@mtu.edu; *Digital Res Coordr,* Mies Martin; Tel: 906-487-2135, E-mail: miesmart@mtu.edu; *Univ Archivist,* Erik Nordberg; Tel: 906-487-2505, E-mail: enordber@mtu.edu; *Archivist,* Elizabeth Russell; E-mail: earussel@mtu.edu; *Web Developer,* Randal Harrison; Tel: 906-487-1482, E-mail: rsharris@mtu.edu; Staff 14.75 (MLS 11.75, Non-MLS 3)
Founded 1887. Enrl 6,976; Fac 47; Highest Degree: Doctorate
Jul 2011-Jun 2012 Income $4,230,307. Mats Exp $5,445,992, Books $144,983, Per/Ser (Incl. Access Fees) $2,702,629, Electronic Ref Mat (Incl. Access Fees) $2,598,380. Sal $1,058,205 (Prof $711,560)
Library Holdings: Microforms 559,776; Bk Vols 796,179; Per Subs 30,226
Special Collections: Copper Country Historical; Copper Mining Company Records; University Archives; USBM Mine Maps of Michigan
Subject Interests: Eng
Automation Activity & Vendor Info: (Acquisitions) Ex Libris Group; (Cataloging) Ex Libris Group; (Circulation) Ex Libris Group; (Course Reserve) Ex Libris Group; (ILL) OCLC ILLiad; (OPAC) Ex Libris Group; (Serials) Ex Libris Group
Database Vendor: ACM (Association for Computing Machinery), Agricola, American Chemical Society, American Physical Society, Annual Reviews, ASCE Research Library, Baker & Taylor, BioOne, Blackwell, Cambridge Scientific Abstracts, Cinahl, CQ Press, CRC Press/Taylor & Francis Group, Elsevier, Elsevier MDL, Ex Libris Group, Facts on File, Gale Cengage Learning, H W Wilson, Haworth Pres Inc, IEEE (Institute of Electrical & Electronics Engineers), IOP, ISI Web of Knowledge, JSTOR, Knovel, LexisNexis, Marcive, Inc, McGraw-Hill, Modern Language Association, Nature Publishing Group, OCLC ArticleFirst, OCLC CAMIO, OCLC FirstSearch, OCLC WorldShare Interlibrary Loan, Project MUSE, ProQuest, PubMed, Sage, ScienceDirect, Springer-Verlag, Thomson - Web of Science, Wiley InterScience, Wilson - Wilson Web
Wireless access
Function: Archival coll, Audio & video playback equip for onsite use, Computers for patron use, Copy machines, Distance learning, Doc delivery serv, e-mail & chat, E-Reserves, Electronic databases & coll, Equip loans & repairs, Exhibits, Handicapped accessible, ILL available, Instruction & testing, Magnifiers for reading, Microfiche/film & reading machines, Online cat, Online info literacy tutorials on the web & in blackboard, Online ref, Online searches, Orientations, Photocopying/Printing, Pub access computers, Ref & res, Ref serv available, Ref serv in person, Scanner, Telephone ref, VHS videos, Web-catalog, Wheelchair accessible, Workshops
Partic in Midwest Collaborative for Library Services (MCLS); OCLC Online Computer Library Center, Inc; Upper Peninsula Region of Library Cooperation, Inc
Open Mon-Thurs 7:45am-Midnight, Fri 7:45-5, Sat Noon-5, Sun Noon-Midnight
Friends of the Library Group

P PORTAGE LAKE DISTRICT LIBRARY*, 58 Huron St, 49931-2194. SAN 308-1761. Tel: 906-482-4570. FAX: 906-482-2129. Web Site: www.pldl.org. *Dir,* Shawn Leche; Staff 22 (MLS 1, Non-MLS 21)
Founded 1910. Pop 14,243; Circ 101,200
Library Holdings: AV Mats 750; Bk Titles 50,000; Per Subs 100; Talking Bks 500
Automation Activity & Vendor Info: (Cataloging) SirsiDynix; (Circulation) SirsiDynix
Wireless access
Function: For res purposes, ILL available, Mail loans to mem, Photocopying/Printing, Prog for children & young adult, Ref serv available, Summer reading prog, Telephone ref
Partic in Superiorland Library Cooperative
Open Mon, Thurs & Fri 10-9, Tues & Wed 10-5, Sat 10-3
Friends of the Library Group

HOUGHTON LAKE

P HOUGHTON LAKE PUBLIC LIBRARY, 4431 W Houghton Lake Dr, 48629-8713. SAN 308-177X. Tel: 989-366-9230. E-mail: staff@hlpl.lib.mi.us. Web Site: www.hlpl.org. *Dir,* Donna J Alward; E-mail: dalward@hlpl.lib.mi.us; Staff 2 (MLS 2)
Founded 1964. Pop 15,325
Jul 2012-Jun 2013 Income $637,797, State $7,646, Locally Generated Income $630,151. Mats Exp $658,735, Books $24,936, Per/Ser (Incl. Access Fees) $6,685, Other Print Mats $4,000, AV Mat $11,519, Electronic Ref Mat (Incl. Access Fees) $5,676. Sal $305,558
Library Holdings: Audiobooks 1,284; CDs 1,869; DVDs 1,889; Large Print Bks 1,296; Bk Titles 43,081; Per Subs 109; Videos 1,669
Automation Activity & Vendor Info: (Cataloging) Innovative Interfaces, Inc; (Circulation) Innovative Interfaces, Inc; (ILL) Mel Cat; (OPAC) Innovative Interfaces, Inc
Database Vendor: EBSCOhost, Gale Cengage Learning, Overdrive, Inc, TumbleBookLibrary, World Book Online
Wireless access
Function: 24/7 Electronic res, 24/7 Online cat, Adult bk club, Bk club(s), Bks on CD, Children's prog, Computer training, Computers for patron use, Copy machines, e-mail & chat, E-Reserves, Fax serv, Free DVD rentals, Handicapped accessible, ILL available, Magazines, Magnifiers for reading, Microfiche/film & reading machines, Movies, Music CDs, Online cat, OverDrive digital audio bks, Photocopying/Printing, Preschool outreach, Preschool reading prog, Printer for laptops & handheld devices, Prog for adults, Prog for children & young adult, Pub access computers, Ref serv available, Scanner, Story hour, Summer & winter reading prog, Summer reading prog, Tax forms, Teen prog, Telephone ref, Wheelchair accessible, Winter reading prog
Partic in Mid-Michigan Library League; Midwest Collaborative for Library Services (MCLS)
Open Mon-Thurs 10-7, Fri & Sat 10-5

HOWARD CITY

P TIMOTHY C HAUENSTEIN REYNOLDS TOWNSHIP LIBRARY*, 117 W Williams St, 49329. (Mail add: PO Box 220, 49329-0220), SAN 308-1788. Tel: 231-937-5575. Reference Tel: 231-937-6175. FAX: 231-937-9240. E-mail: how@llcoop.org. Web Site: reynolds.llcoop.org. *Dir,* Janice Williams; E-mail: howjw@llcoop.org
Library Holdings: Bk Titles 22,393; Per Subs 65
Special Collections: Howard City Record, microfilm
Automation Activity & Vendor Info: (Cataloging) Innovative Interfaces, Inc; (Circulation) Innovative Interfaces, Inc; (OPAC) Innovative Interfaces, Inc
Database Vendor: EBSCOhost
Wireless access
Partic in Lakeland Library Cooperative; Mich Libr Asn
Open Mon, Wed & Fri 10-5, Tues & Thurs 10-7, Sat (Sept-May) 10-2
Friends of the Library Group

HOWELL

C CLEARY UNIVERSITY LIBRARY*, 3750 Cleary Dr, 48843. SAN 308-4930. Tel: 517-548-3670. Toll Free Tel: 800-686-1883. FAX: 517-548-2170. E-mail: librarian@cleary.edu. Web Site: www.cleary.edu. *Dir, Univ Libr,* Jane Ellen Innes; Tel: 734-332-4477, Ext 3320, E-mail: jeinnes@cleary.edu; Staff 1 (MLS 1)
Founded 1883. Enrl 1,011; Fac 48; Highest Degree: Master
Library Holdings: AV Mats 450; e-books 5,000; e-journals 20,000; Bk Titles 800; Bk Vols 1,000; Per Subs 20; Talking Bks 10
Subject Interests: Acctg, Mgt, Mkt
Database Vendor: Electric Library, Gale Cengage Learning, Hoovers, Infotrieve, LexisNexis, OCLC FirstSearch, OCLC WorldShare Interlibrary Loan, ProQuest, PubMed, SerialsSolutions, Wilson - Wilson Web
Wireless access
Function: Instruction & testing, Online ref, Online searches, Orientations
Partic in Midwest Collaborative for Library Services (MCLS)
Departmental Libraries:
WASHTENAW CAMPUS, 3601 Plymouth Rd, Ann Arbor, 48105-2659. Tel: 734-332-4477. Toll Free Tel: 800-589-1979. FAX: 734-332-4646. *Dir, Univ Libr,* Jane Ellen Innes; Tel: 734-332-4477, Ext 3320, E-mail: jeinnes@cleary.edu
Library Holdings: e-books 5,000; e-journals 20,000; Bk Titles 400; Bk Vols 500; Talking Bks 10; Videos 15

P HOWELL CARNEGIE DISTRICT LIBRARY*, 314 W Grand River Ave, 48843. SAN 308-1796. Tel: 517-546-0720. FAX: 517-546-1494. Web Site: www.howelllibrary.org. *Dir,* Kathleen Zaenger; *Adult Serv, Ref Serv,* Jerilee Cook; *Circ,* Emily DeJeagher; *Youth Serv,* Holly Ward Lamb; Staff 37 (MLS 8, Non-MLS 29)
Founded 1906. Pop 41,916; Circ 555,003
Library Holdings: Bk Vols 126,264; Per Subs 398
Special Collections: Livingston County Local History, photog
Automation Activity & Vendor Info: (Cataloging) Innovative Interfaces, Inc - Millenium; (Circulation) Innovative Interfaces, Inc - Millenium; (OPAC) Innovative Interfaces, Inc - Millenium
Database Vendor: Gale Cengage Learning, OCLC FirstSearch
Wireless access
Function: Adult literacy prog, Archival coll, Art exhibits, Bk club(s), Bks on cassette, Bks on CD, Bus archives, CD-ROM, Children's prog, Computer training, Computers for patron use, Copy machines, E-Reserves, Electronic databases & coll, Exhibits, Fax serv, Free DVD rentals, Handicapped accessible, ILL available, Music CDs, Online cat, Online ref, Online searches, OverDrive digital audio bks, Photocopying/Printing, Preschool outreach, Printer for laptops & handheld devices, Prog for adults, Prog for children & young adult, Pub access computers, Ref serv in person, Satellite serv, Scanner, Spoken cassettes & CDs, Spoken cassettes & DVDs, Story hour, Summer reading prog, Tax forms, Telephone ref, VHS videos, Web-catalog, Wheelchair accessible
Partic in The Library Network
Open Mon-Thurs 10-8, Fri & Sat 10-5, Sun (Sept-May) 12-4
Friends of the Library Group

HUDSON

P HUDSON CARNEGIE DISTRICT LIBRARY*, 205 S Market, 49247. SAN 308-1818. Tel: 517-448-3801. FAX: 517-448-5095. *Dir,* Joann Crater; E-mail: joannatthelibrary@yahoo.com; Staff 1 (Non-MLS 1)
Founded 1904. Pop 4,604; Circ 69,000
Library Holdings: Bk Vols 39,000; Per Subs 30
Special Collections: Carnegie Library; Hudson Historical Coll; Will Carleton Coll
Automation Activity & Vendor Info: (Cataloging) Follett Software; (Circulation) Follett Software; (ILL) Auto-Graphics, Inc
Wireless access
Mem of Woodlands Library Cooperative
Partic in OCLC Online Computer Library Center, Inc
Open Mon 1-6, Tues 9-6, Wed & Thurs 9-5, Fri 9-3, Sat 9-1

HUDSONVILLE

P GARY BYKER MEMORIAL LIBRARY*, 3338 Van Buren St, 49426. SAN 308-1826. Tel: 616-669-1255. FAX: 616-669-5150. Web Site: www.hudsonville.org/library. *Dir,* Melissa Ann Huisman; Tel: 616-669-7172, Ext 5; *Ch Serv,* Elizabeth Mazor; Tel: 616-669-7172, Ext 4; Staff 14 (MLS 1, Non-MLS 13)
Founded 1967. Pop 9,067; Circ 133,701
Library Holdings: CDs 1,212; DVDs 1,013; Large Print Bks 1,397; Bk Vols 46,852; Per Subs 95; Talking Bks 1,697; Videos 2,867
Subject Interests: Local hist
Automation Activity & Vendor Info: (Cataloging) Innovative Interfaces, Inc; (Circulation) Innovative Interfaces, Inc; (ILL) Innovative Interfaces, Inc; (OPAC) Innovative Interfaces, Inc; (Serials) Innovative Interfaces, Inc
Database Vendor: Gale Cengage Learning, OCLC FirstSearch, OCLC WorldShare Interlibrary Loan
Function: Adult bk club, Electronic databases & coll, Handicapped accessible, ILL available, Music CDs, Online searches, Photocopying/Printing, Prog for adults, Prog for children & young adult, Spoken cassettes & CDs, Summer reading prog, Telephone ref, VHS videos
Partic in Lakeland Library Cooperative
Open Mon, Tues & Thurs (Winter) 10-8, Wed & Fri 10-5, Sat 10-1; Mon, Wed & Fri (Summer) 10-5, Tues & Thurs 10-8, Sat 10-1
Restriction: Non-resident fee
Friends of the Library Group

HUNTINGTON WOODS

P HUNTINGTON WOODS PUBLIC LIBRARY*, 26415 Scotia, 48070-1198. SAN 308-1834. Tel: 248-543-9720. FAX: 248-543-2559. E-mail: htwd@huntington-woods.lib.mi.us. Web Site: www.huntington-woods.lib.mi.us. *Dir,* Anne Hage; E-mail: ahage@huntington-woods.lib.mi.us; *Head, Circ,* Sally Kohlenberg; E-mail: sbk@huntington-woods.lib.mi.us; *Head, Tech Serv,* Jesse Mitchell; E-mail: jmitchell@huntington-woods.lib.mi.us; *Librn,* Gail Gilman; *Librn,* Karen Tower; *Tech Coordr,* Jamie Richards; *Ch Serv,* Falenski Beth; E-mail: bfalenski@huntington-woods.lib.mi.us
Founded 1942. Pop 6,514; Circ 55,000
Library Holdings: Bks on Deafness & Sign Lang 50; High Interest/Low Vocabulary Bk Vols 100; Bk Vols 40,000; Per Subs 125
Special Collections: Early American Newspapers (Columbian Centinel of Boston 1792-1794)
Database Vendor: Electric Library, OCLC FirstSearch, ProQuest
Wireless access
Open Mon-Thurs (Fall & Winter) 10-9, Sat 10-5, Sun 1-5; Mon-Thurs (Summer) 10-9, Fri 10-5
Friends of the Library Group

IDLEWILD

P IDLEWILD PUBLIC LIBRARY*, 4713 E Baldwin Rd, 49642-9737. (Mail add: PO Box 148, 49642-0148), SAN 308-1842. Tel: 231-745-7652. FAX: 231-745-7652. E-mail: idlewildlibrary@yahoo.com. *Dir,* Susan K Dooley
Pop 585; Circ 2,985
Library Holdings: AV Mats 75; CDs 250; Bk Vols 6,900; Per Subs 20
Special Collections: Black Coll
Partic in Mid-Michigan Library League
Open Mon-Wed & Fri 2-6, Sat 10-2
Friends of the Library Group

IMLAY CITY

P RUTH HUGHES MEMORIAL DISTRICT LIBRARY*, 211 N Almont Ave, 48444-1004. SAN 308-1850. Tel: 810-724-8043. FAX: 810-724-2602. Web Site: ruthhughes.org. *Dir,* Tracy Harnish; Staff 4 (MLS 2, Non-MLS 2)
Founded 1923. Pop 11,480; Circ 110,000
Library Holdings: Bk Vols 49,000; Per Subs 80
Automation Activity & Vendor Info: (Cataloging) Horizon; (Circulation) Horizon; (OPAC) Horizon
Database Vendor: Gale Cengage Learning
Wireless access
Partic in Mideastern Michigan Library Cooperative
Open Mon-Thurs 10-8, Fri & Sat 10-5
Friends of the Library Group
Branches: 1
ATTICA TOWNSHIP LIBRARY, 4302 Peppermill Rd, Attica, 48412-9624. Tel: 810-724-2007. FAX: 810-724-2007. *Dir,* Tracy Harnish; E-mail: tharnish@ruthhughes.org; *Ch,* Megan Goedge
Library Holdings: Bk Vols 8,000
Open Mon & Thurs 2-7, Tues & Fri 9-2, Sat 10-3

INDIAN RIVER

P INDIAN RIVER AREA LIBRARY*, 3546 S Straits Hwy, 49749. (Mail add: PO Box 160, 49749-0160), SAN 321-0405. Tel: 231-238-8581. FAX: 231-238-9494. E-mail: indriv1@northland.lib.mi.us. Web Site: www.indianriverarealibrary.michlibrary.org. *Dir,* Cindy Lou Poquette; *Asst Librn,* Mary Smith; *Asst Librn,* Karen Vance; Staff 3 (MLS 1, Non-MLS 2)
Founded 1977. Pop 5,584; Circ 26,013
Jul 2013-Jun 2014 Income $118,969, State $2,266, City $62,398, County $29,644, Other $24,661. Mats Exp $26,840, Books $18,448, Per/Ser (Incl. Access Fees) $2,003, Other Print Mats $60, AV Mat $6,329. Sal $31,217
Library Holdings: AV Mats 3,191; Bks on Deafness & Sign Lang 18; CDs 1,769; DVDs 1,250; Large Print Bks 2,718; Bk Vols 43,094; Per Subs 146; Videos 1,941
Subject Interests: Careers, Dance, Music
Automation Activity & Vendor Info: (Circulation) Nugen Systems Inc; (ILL) Mel Cat
Publications: Newsletter
Partic in Northland Library Cooperative
Open Tues & Fri 11-8, Wed & Thurs 11-5:30
Friends of the Library Group

INKSTER

P LEANNA HICKS PUBLIC LIBRARY*, 2005 Inkster Rd, 48141. SAN 308-1869. Tel: 313-563-2822. FAX: 313-274-5130. Web Site: www.inkster.lib.mi.us. *Dir,* Suzanne Street; E-mail: sstreet@tln.lib.mi.us; *Asst Librn,* Laura Gregory; E-mail: lgregory@tln.lib.mi.us; *Asst Librn,* Sister Larry Mills
Founded 1960. Pop 35,190
Library Holdings: Bk Vols 38,000; Per Subs 75
Publications: The Roots of Inkster
Friends of the Library Group

INTERLOCHEN

INTERLOCHEN CENTER FOR THE ARTS

S BONISTEEL LIBRARY - SEABURY ACADEMIC LIBRARY*, 4000 M-137, 49643. (Mail add: PO Box 199, 49643), SAN 308-1877. Tel: 231-276-7420. FAX: 231-276-5232. Web Site: www.interlochen.org. *Dir of Libr,* Elizabeth Gourley; E-mail: beth.gourley@interlochen.org; *Academy Librn,* Carol Niemi; E-mail: carol.niemi@interlochen.org; *Archivist,* Byron Hanson; *Libr Asst,* Joe Doerfer; Staff 3 (MLS 1, Non-MLS 2)
Founded 1962
Library Holdings: Bk Vols 27,000; Per Subs 80
Special Collections: Music Library Coll
Subject Interests: Art & archit, Dance, Drama, Music
Automation Activity & Vendor Info: (Cataloging) SirsiDynix; (Circulation) SirsiDynix; (OPAC) SirsiDynix

S FREDERICK & ELIZABETH LUDWIG FENNELL MUSIC LIBRARY*, 4000 Hwy M-137, 49643. (Mail add: PO Box 199, 49643-0199). Tel: 231-276-7230. FAX: 231-276-7882. Web Site: library.interlochen.org. *Dir of Libr,* Elizabeth Gourley; E-mail: beth.gourley@interlochen.org; *Head Librn,* Eleanor Lange; E-mail: eleanor.lange@interlochen.org; *Access Serv Coordr, Asst Music Librn,* Jacey Kepich
Founded 1928
Special Collections: Performance Materials
Automation Activity & Vendor Info: (Cataloging) SirsiDynix; (Circulation) SirsiDynix; (OPAC) SirsiDynix

P INTERLOCHEN PUBLIC LIBRARY*, 9700 Riley Rd, 49643. Tel: 231-276-6767. FAX: 231-276-5172. E-mail: ipl@interlochenpubliclibrary.org. Web Site: www.interlochenpubliclibrary.org. *Dir,* Janette Grice; E-mail: jgrice@tadl.org; Staff 8 (MLS 1, Non-MLS 7)
Founded 1976. Pop 3,500
Library Holdings: Bks on Deafness & Sign Lang 10; Bk Vols 26,000; Per Subs 100
Special Collections: Interlochen History Coll
Automation Activity & Vendor Info: (Cataloging) Evergreen; (Circulation) Evergreen
Database Vendor: TumbleBookLibrary
Wireless access
Partic in Mid-Michigan Library League
Open Mon, Tues, Fri & Sat 9-5, Wed & Thurs 9-8
Friends of the Library Group

IONIA

P IONIA COMMUNITY LIBRARY*, 126 E Main St, 48846. SAN 308-1885. Tel: 616-527-3680. FAX: 616-527-6210. E-mail: ion@llcoop.org. Web Site: www.ioniacommunitylibrary.org. *Dir,* Denise McKernan; *Ch,* Mike Golczynski; *Teen Librn,* Sally Wilcox; Staff 8 (Non-MLS 8)
Founded 1903. Pop 21,871; Circ 86,902
Jul 2012-Jun 2013 Income $549,640. Mats Exp $46,900, Books $28,500, Per/Ser (Incl. Access Fees) $4,300, AV Mat $8,500, Electronic Ref Mat (Incl. Access Fees) $5,600. Sal $264,064
Library Holdings: AV Mats 1,747; Bk Vols 33,547; Per Subs 84
Special Collections: Civil War Coll
Automation Activity & Vendor Info: (Cataloging) Innovative Interfaces, Inc; (Circulation) Innovative Interfaces, Inc; (OPAC) Innovative Interfaces, Inc
Wireless access
Open Mon-Thurs 10-8, Fri 10-6, Sat 10-2
Friends of the Library Group

M IONIA COUNTY MEMORIAL HOSPITAL*, Health Science Library, 479 Lafayette St, 48846-1834. (Mail add: PO Box 1001, 48846-6001), SAN 373-9147. Tel: 616-527-4200, Ext 281. FAX: 616-527-5731.
Founded 1980
Library Holdings: Bk Vols 566; Per Subs 36
Partic in Lakeland Library Cooperative; Michigan Health Sciences Libraries Association; National Network of Libraries of Medicine
Restriction: Not open to pub

IRON MOUNTAIN

P DICKINSON COUNTY LIBRARY*, 401 Iron Mountain St, 49801-3435. SAN 346-6442. Tel: 906-774-1218. Administration Tel: 906-774-3862. FAX: 906-774-4079. E-mail: dcl@dcl-lib.org. Web Site: www.dcl-lib.org. *Dir,* Beth Baker; E-mail: beth@dcl-lib.org; *Ch Serv,* Virginia Adams; Staff 19 (MLS 3, Non-MLS 16)
Founded 1902. Pop 26,168; Circ 172,380
Library Holdings: AV Mats 11,060; Bk Titles 94,267; Per Subs 319
Subject Interests: Genealogy, Local hist, Mich
Automation Activity & Vendor Info: (Cataloging) SirsiDynix; (Circulation) SirsiDynix; (OPAC) SirsiDynix
Database Vendor: SirsiDynix
Wireless access
Function: Adult bk club, Audiobks via web, AV serv, Bks on cassette, Bks on CD, Children's prog, Computers for patron use, Copy machines, Digital talking bks, Electronic databases & coll, Exhibits, Free DVD rentals, Genealogy discussion group, Handicapped accessible, Homebound delivery serv, ILL available, Magnifiers for reading, Mail & tel request accepted, Music CDs, OverDrive digital audio bks, Prog for adults, Prog for children & young adult, Pub access computers, Ref serv in person, Summer reading prog, Tax forms, Teen prog, Telephone ref, VHS videos, Video lending libr, Wheelchair accessible, Workshops
Publications: Ford Comes to Kingsford; The Evolution of the Public Library in Michigan's Dickinson County
Mem of Superiorland Library Cooperative
Partic in Midwest Collaborative for Library Services (MCLS)

Open Mon-Thurs (Winter) 9-9, Fri 9-6, Sat 9-5, Sun 1-4; Mon-Thurs (Summer) 9-8, Fri 9-6, Sat 9-1
Friends of the Library Group
Branches: 2
NORTH DICKINSON, W6588 M-69, Felch, 49831. Tel: 906-542-7230. *Libr Assoc II,* Kara Nussbaumer
Open Mon-Thurs (Winter) 11-7; Mon & Thurs (Summer) 10-3
Friends of the Library Group
SOLOMONSON BRANCH, 620 Section St, Norway, 49870, SAN 346-6477. Tel: 906-563-8617. FAX: 906-563-7224. *In Charge,* Kay Boughner; Staff 2 (Non-MLS 2)
Open Mon & Wed 9:30-8, Tues, Thurs & Fri 9:30-5, Sat 9:30-1
Friends of the Library Group

GM OSCAR G JOHNSON VETERANS AFFAIRS MEDICAL CENTER*, Medical Library, 325 East H St, 49801. SAN 308-1907. Tel: 906-774-3300, Ext 32450, 906-779-3172. Toll Free Tel: 800-215-8262, Ext 32450. FAX: 906-779-3107. Web Site: www.ironmountain.va.gov. *Chief, Libr Serv,* Jeanne Marie Chouinard; E-mail: jeanne.chouinard@va.gov; Staff 1 (MLS 1)
Founded 1950
Oct 2011-Sept 2012 Income $35,000. Mats Exp $35,000. Sal $72,700
Library Holdings: CDs 15; DVDs 75; e-books 50; e-journals 500; Large Print Bks 25; Bk Titles 250; Bk Vols 275; Per Subs 6
Subject Interests: Allied health, Local authors, Local hist, Med, Mil, Nursing
Automation Activity & Vendor Info: (Cataloging) OCLC WorldShare Interlibrary Loan; (Circulation) EOS International; (OPAC) EOS International; (Serials) SerialsSolutions
Database Vendor: Cinahl, EOS International, Lexi-Comp, Library Systems & Services (LSSI), MD Consult, Micromedex, OCLC FirstSearch, OCLC WorldShare Interlibrary Loan, PubMed, ScienceDirect, SerialsSolutions, STAT!Ref (Teton Data Systems), UpToDate, WT Cox
Function: CD-ROM, Computer training, Copy machines, Electronic databases & coll, Fax serv, Health sci info serv, ILL available, Online cat, Online searches, Photocopying/Printing, Satellite serv, Scanner, Telephone ref, Web-catalog, Wheelchair accessible
Special Services for the Blind - Closed circuit TV
Open Mon-Thurs 8-4:30, Fri 7:30-4
Restriction: Borrowing requests are handled by ILL, Non-circulating to the pub, Open to pub for ref only

IRON RIVER

P WEST IRON DISTRICT LIBRARY*, 116 W Genesee St, 49935-1437. (Mail add: PO Box 328, 49935-0328), SAN 308-1915. Tel: 906-265-2831. FAX: 906-265-2062. E-mail: lbbartel@uproc.lib.mi.us. Web Site: rpa.uproc.lib.mi.us/westiron.htm, www.uproc.lib.mi.us/widl. *Dir,* Barbara Bartel
Founded 1967. Pop 8,341; Circ 38,000
Library Holdings: Bk Titles 38,000, Bk Vols 980,000; Per Subs 90
Special Collections: Large Print Books
Partic in Superiorland Library Cooperative
Open Mon-Wed & Fri 8:30-5, Thurs 8:30-7, Sat 10-2
Friends of the Library Group

IRONWOOD

J GOGEBIC COMMUNITY COLLEGE*, Alex D Chisholm Learning Resources Center, E4946 Jackson Rd, 49938. SAN 308-1931. Tel: 906-932-4231, Ext 270. Toll Free Tel: 800-682-5910, Ext 270. FAX: 906-932-0868. E-mail: library@gogebic.edu. Web Site: www.gogebic.edu/library. *Dir,* Walter Lessun, Jr; Tel: 906-932-4231, Ext 344, E-mail: waltl@gogebic.edu; *Asst Librn,* Kathryn Slizewski; E-mail: kathryns@gogebic.edu. Subject Specialists: *Bus,* Walter Lessun, Jr; Staff 2 (MLS 2)
Founded 1932. Enrl 1,050; Fac 67; Highest Degree: Associate
Jul 2012-Jun 2013 Income $244,470. Mats Exp $45,000, Books $15,000, Per/Ser (Incl. Access Fees) $15,000, Electronic Ref Mat (Incl. Access Fees) $15,000. Sal $114,000
Library Holdings: Audiobooks 24; DVDs 30; Bk Titles 21,000; Bk Vols 22,000; Per Subs 100; Videos 1,500
Special Collections: Mining Memorabilia
Subject Interests: Great Lakes, Hist, Local hist
Automation Activity & Vendor Info: (Acquisitions) Ex Libris Group; (Cataloging) Ex Libris Group; (Circulation) Ex Libris Group; (Course Reserve) Ex Libris Group; (ILL) Ex Libris Group; (OPAC) Ex Libris Group; (Serials) Ex Libris Group
Database Vendor: Baker & Taylor, Bowker, ebrary, EBSCO Information Services, EBSCOhost, Ex Libris Group, Gale Cengage Learning, H W Wilson, infoUSA, OCLC FirstSearch, Oxford Online, ProQuest
Wireless access
Function: Adult bk club
Partic in Upper Peninsula Region of Library Cooperation, Inc
Open Mon-Fri 8-4:30

P IRONWOOD CARNEGIE PUBLIC LIBRARY*, 235 E Aurora St, 49938-2178. SAN 308-1923. Tel: 906-932-0203. FAX: 906-932-2447. *Dir,* Joe Carlson; *Circ, ILL,* Mary Pat Baginski; Staff 4 (MLS 1, Non-MLS 3)
Founded 1901. Pop 9,629; Circ 54,607
Library Holdings: Bk Vols 29,152; Per Subs 85
Special Collections: Local newspapers on microfilm dating back to 1890; State of Michigan. State Document Depository
Subject Interests: Arts & crafts, Hist
Automation Activity & Vendor Info: (Cataloging) Follett Software; (Circulation) Follett Software
Database Vendor: Gale Cengage Learning, OCLC FirstSearch
Partic in Superiorland Library Cooperative
Friends of the Library Group

ISHPEMING

P ISHPEMING CARNEGIE PUBLIC LIBRARY*, 317 N Main St, 49849-1994. SAN 308-194X. Tel: 906-486-4381. FAX: 906-486-6226. Web Site: www.uproc.lib.mi.us/ish. *Dir,* John McNaughton; Staff 5 (MLS 2, Non-MLS 3)
Founded 1904. Pop 13,888; Circ 54,176
Library Holdings: AV Mats 620; Large Print Bks 175; Bk Vols 72,000; Per Subs 78; Talking Bks 270
Automation Activity & Vendor Info: (Cataloging) SirsiDynix; (Circulation) SirsiDynix; (OPAC) SirsiDynix
Wireless access
Partic in Superiorland Library Cooperative; Upper Peninsula Region of Library Cooperation, Inc
Open Mon, Tues & Fri 9-5, Wed & Thurs 9-7, Sat 9-4
Friends of the Library Group

S US NATIONAL SKI HALL OF FAME*, Roland Palmedo National Ski Library, 610 Palms Ave, 49849. (Mail add: PO Box 191, 49849-0191), SAN 308-1958. Tel: 906-485-6323. FAX: 906-486-4570. Web Site: www.skihall.com/ski-hall-of-fame-library.asp. *Chief Exec Officer,* J Thomas West; E-mail: twest@skihall.com
Founded 1956
Library Holdings: Bk Titles 1,500
Special Collections: Roland Palmedo Coll
Subject Interests: Hist
Publications: Midwest Skiing - A Glance Back; Nine Thousand Years of Skis: Norwegian Wood to French Plastic; Seventy-Five Years of Skiing, 1904-79; Skiing Then & Now; The Flying Norseman
Friends of the Library Group

ITHACA

P THOMPSON HOME PUBLIC LIBRARY*, 125 W Center St, 48847. SAN 308-1966. Tel: 989-875-4184. FAX: 989-875 3374. E-mail: thpl@edzone.net. Web Site: www.ithacalibrary.org. *Dir, Libr Serv,* Vicki Root; E-mail: thlibdir@edzone.net; *Asst Librn,* Peggy Kosek
Founded 1926. Pop 10,179
Library Holdings: Bk Vols 25,500; Per Subs 68
Subject Interests: Local hist, Mich
Automation Activity & Vendor Info: (Cataloging) Follett Software; (Circulation) Follett Software
Mem of Capital Library Cooperative
Open Mon & Wed 10-8, Tues, Thurs & Fri 10-5, Sat 10-2

JACKSON

C BAKER COLLEGE OF JACKSON LIBRARY*, 2800 Springport Rd, 49202-1255. Tel: 517-780-4572. Reference Tel: 517-780-4565. Administration Tel: 517-780-4571. Toll Free Tel: 888-343-3683. FAX: 517-789-3058. E-mail: library-jk@baker.edu. Web Site: www.baker.edu. *Dir, Libr Serv,* Melissa McPherson; E-mail: melissa.mcpherson@baker.edu; Staff 8 (MLS 2, Non-MLS 6)
Founded 1994. Enrl 1,600; Highest Degree: Master
Sept 2005-Aug 2006. Mats Exp $104,000, Books $62,000, Per/Ser (Incl. Access Fees) $12,000, Electronic Ref Mat (Incl. Access Fees) $30,000. Sal Prof $66,000
Library Holdings: Bk Vols 17,000; Per Subs 110
Automation Activity & Vendor Info: (Cataloging) Horizon; (Circulation) Horizon; (OPAC) Horizon; (Serials) Horizon
Database Vendor: Gale Cengage Learning, LexisNexis, OCLC FirstSearch, ProQuest, Westlaw
Partic in Lyrasis
Open Mon-Fri 9-9, Sat 9-3

CONSUMERS ENERGY
S CORPORATE LIBRARY*, One Energy Plaza, EP1-244, 49201, SAN 321-8104. Tel: 517-788-0541. FAX: 517-768-3804. *Dir,* Michele Morante Puckett; E-mail: michele.puckett@cmsenergy.com; *Asst Librn,* Joseph B Anteau; Tel: 517-788-2520, E-mail:

joseph.anteau@cmsenergy.com. Subject Specialists: *Bus, Eng, Utilities,* Michele Morante Puckett; Staff 2 (MLS 2)
Founded 1977
Library Holdings: Audiobooks 200; DVDs 50; Bk Titles 6,000; Per Subs 225
Special Collections: Company & Industry Historical Archival Coll; Electric & Gas Industry Reports; Industry Standards
Subject Interests: Diversity, Energy disciplines, Health & wellness, Leadership, Safety
Automation Activity & Vendor Info: (ILL) OCLC FirstSearch; (Serials) EBSCO Online
Function: Archival coll, Audio & video playback equip for onsite use, Audiobks via web, Bks on CD, Bus archives, CD-ROM, Computers for patron use, Doc delivery serv, e-mail & chat, e-mail serv, Electronic databases & coll, Fax serv, Handicapped accessible, ILL available, Instruction & testing, Learning ctr, Microfiche/film & reading machines, Online cat, Online ref, Online searches, Orientations, Outside serv via phone, mail, e-mail & web, Res libr, Scanner, Tax forms, Telephone ref, Wheelchair accessible
Restriction: Access at librarian's discretion, Access for corporate affiliates, Borrowing requests are handled by ILL, By permission only, Circulates for staff only, External users must contact libr, Lending to staff only, No access to competitors, Non-circulating of rare bks, Not open to pub, Secured area only open to authorized personnel, Use of others with permission of librn
Friends of the Library Group

S LEGAL LIBRARY*, One Energy Plaza, 49201, SAN 308-1974. Tel: 517-788-1088. FAX: 517-788-1682. *Librn,* Betsy S Domschot
Founded 1955
Library Holdings: Bk Vols 32,000; Per Subs 25
Restriction: Restricted pub use

S G ROBERT COTTON REGIONAL CORRECTIONAL FACILITY LIBRARY*, 3500 N Elm Rd, 49201. SAN 371-7585. Tel: 517-780-5172. FAX: 517-780-5100. *Librn,* Hatatu Elum; *Asst Librn,* Jackie Cooke; *Libr Tech,* Charley Pelkey; Staff 3 (MLS 1, Non-MLS 2)
Library Holdings: Bk Vols 10,000; Per Subs 14
Open Mon-Sun 8am-9pm

J JACKSON COMMUNITY COLLEGE*, Atkinson Library, 2111 Emmons Rd, 49201-8399. SAN 308-2016. Tel: 517-796-8622. FAX: 517-796-8623. E-mail: jcclibrary@jccmi.edu. Web Site: www.jccmi.edu/library. *Libr Dir,* Stephanie DeLano Davis; Tel: 517-796-8482, E-mail: davisstephand@jccmi.edu; *Coordr,* Debora Moyer; Tel: 517-796-8621, E-mail: moyerdeboraj@jccmi.edu; Staff 5 (MLS 2, Non-MLS 3)
Founded 1928. Enrl 6,328; Fac 95; Highest Degree: Associate
Library Holdings: Bk Vols 38,000; Per Subs 325
Special Collections: Historical Coll
Automation Activity & Vendor Info: (Cataloging) SirsiDynix; (Circulation) SirsiDynix; (Course Reserve) SirsiDynix; (ILL) OCLC; (OPAC) SirsiDynix; (Serials) SirsiDynix
Database Vendor: Children's Literature Comprehensive Database Company (CLCD), Cinahl, ebrary, EBSCOhost, Electric Library, Facts on File, Gale Cengage Learning, LearningExpress, OCLC, ProQuest, SerialsSolutions, SirsiDynix, WT Cox
Wireless access
Partic in Midwest Collaborative for Library Services (MCLS)
Open Mon-Thurs 7:30am-10pm, Fri 7:30-5, Sat 8-5

P JACKSON DISTRICT LIBRARY*, 290 W Michigan Ave, 49201. (Mail add: 244 W Michigan Ave, 49201), SAN 346-6507. Tel: 517-788-4087. Circulation Tel: 517-788-4087, Ext 230. Interlibrary Loan Service Tel: 517-788-4087, Ext 1483. Reference Tel: 517-788-4087, Ext 1339. Administration Tel: 517-788-4099. Information Services Tel: 517-788-4099, Ext 1307. FAX: 517-782-8635. Administration FAX: 517-788-6024. Web Site: www.myjdl.com. *Dir,* Ishwar Laxminarayan; Tel: 517-788-4099, Ext 1309, E-mail: ishwar@myjdl.com; *Pub Serv Adminr,* Sarilda Tackett; E-mail: tackettse@myjdl.com; *Cent Serv Coordr,* Melissa Peters; Tel: 517-788-4087, Ext 1333, E-mail: petersmm@myjdl.com; *Coordr, Circ,* Susan McGee; Tel: 517-788-4087, Ext 1345, E-mail: mcgesse@myjdl.com; *Ref Serv Coordr,* Deborah Sears; Tel: 517-788-4087, Ext 1344, E-mail: searsdd@myjdl.com; *Tech Serv Coordr,* Lorraine Butchart; Tel: 517-788-4673, Fax: 517-788-9987, E-mail: butchartlk@myjdl.com; Staff 23 (MLS 15, Non-MLS 8)
Founded 1978. Pop 158,422; Circ 806,445
Jan 2007-Dec 2007 Income (Main Library and Branch(s)) $4,813,018, State $125,240, County $479,237, Locally Generated Income $3,578,570, Other $629,971. Mats Exp $719,501, Books $409,164, Per/Ser (Incl. Access Fees) $37,609, AV Mat $149,518, Electronic Ref Mat (Incl. Access Fees) $122,608, Presv $602. Sal $2,584,350
Library Holdings: Audiobooks 11,981; Bks on Deafness & Sign Lang 68; Braille Volumes 12; CDs 9,304; DVDs 14,459; e-books 20,147; Electronic Media & Resources 8,689; High Interest/Low Vocabulary Bk Vols 79; Large Print Bks 8,547; Microforms 4,044; Bk Titles 247,161; Per Subs 756; Videos 6,465
Special Collections: African American Coll; Genealogy Coll; Jackson & Michigan History Coll; Large Print Coll; Literacy Coll; Spanish Coll. US Document Depository
Automation Activity & Vendor Info: (Acquisitions) SirsiDynix; (Cataloging) SirsiDynix; (Circulation) SirsiDynix; (ILL) OCLC ILLiad; (Media Booking) SirsiDynix; (OPAC) SirsiDynix; (Serials) SirsiDynix
Database Vendor: Alexander Street Press, Baker & Taylor, Booksite, Bowker, BWI, EBSCO Information Services, Gale Cengage Learning, Grolier Online, infoUSA, Ingram Library Services, Marquis Who's Who, OCLC FirstSearch, OCLC WorldShare Interlibrary Loan, Oxford Online, ProQuest, ReferenceUSA, SirsiDynix
Wireless access
Function: Adult bk club, Adult literacy prog, After school storytime, Art exhibits, Audio & video playback equip for onsite use, Audiobks via web, Bk club(s), Bks on cassette, Bks on CD, CD-ROM, Children's prog, Computer training, Computers for patron use, Copy machines, Distance learning, E-Reserves, Electronic databases & coll, Family literacy, Games & aids for the handicapped, Govt ref serv, Handicapped accessible, Health sci info serv, Home delivery & serv to Sr ctr & nursing homes, Homebound delivery serv, ILL available, Magnifiers for reading, Mail & tel request accepted, Music CDs, Notary serv, Online cat, Online ref, Online searches, Orientations, Outside serv via phone, mail, e-mail & web, Photocopying/Printing, Preschool outreach, Prog for adults, Prog for children & young adult, Ref serv available, Senior computer classes, Senior outreach, Serves mentally handicapped consumers, Spoken cassettes & CDs, Spoken cassettes & DVDs, Summer reading prog, Tax forms, Teen prog, Telephone ref, VHS videos, Video lending libr, Wheelchair accessible, Workshops
Mem of Woodlands Library Cooperative
Special Services for the Deaf - Bks on deafness & sign lang
Special Services for the Blind - Large print bks & talking machines
Open Mon-Thurs 9-9, Fri 9-6, Sat 10-5
Friends of the Library Group
Branches: 13
BROOKLYN BRANCH, 207 N Main St, Brooklyn, 49230. (Mail add: PO Box 490, Brooklyn, 49230), SAN 378-1577. Tel: 517-592-3406. FAX: 517-592-3054. E-mail: brooklyn@myjdl.com. *Br Mgr,* Erica Grimm
Founded 1918. Pop 10,156; Circ 53,535
Open Mon & Wed 10-7, Tues & Fri 10-6, Thurs 12-6, Sat 10-2
Friends of the Library Group
CARNEGIE, 244 W Michigan Ave, 49201, SAN 378-1593. Tel: 517-788-4087. Circulation Tel: 517-788-4087, Ext 1332. Interlibrary Loan Service Tel: 517-788-4087, Ext 1483. Reference Tel: 517-788-4087, Ext 1339. Automation Services Tel: 517-784-2280. Information Services Tel: 517-788-4673. FAX: 517-782-8635. *Br Mgr,* Melissa Peters; Tel: 517-788-4099, Ext 236, E-mail: petersmm@myjdl.com
Founded 1863. Pop 36,316; Circ 212,055
Special Services for the Deaf - Bks on deafness & sign lang
Open Mon-Thurs 9-9, Fri 9-6, Sat 10-5
Friends of the Library Group
CONCORD BRANCH, 108 S Main St, Concord, 49237. (Mail add: PO Box 458, Concord, 49237-0458), SAN 346-6590. Tel: 517-905-1379. FAX: 517-524-6971. E-mail: concord@myjdl.com. *Br Mgr,* Karen Veramay; E-mail: veramayka@myjdl.com
Founded 1903. Pop 5,641; Circ 25,307
Open Mon & Fri 1-6, Wed 10-7, Sat 10-2
Friends of the Library Group
EASTERN, 3125 E Michigan Ave, 49201, SAN 346-6620. Tel: 517-788-4074. FAX: 517-788-4645. E-mail: eastern@myjdl.com. *Br Mgr,* Steven George; E-mail: georgesm@myjdl.com
Founded 1914. Pop 30,278; Circ 105,004
Open Mon, Wed & Thurs 10-8, Tues & Fri 12-5, Sat 10-5, Sun 1-5
Friends of the Library Group
GRASS LAKE BRANCH, 130 W Michigan Ave, Grass Lake, 49240. (Mail add: PO Box 335, Grass Lake, 49240-0335), SAN 346-6655. Tel: 517-522-8211. FAX: 517-522-8215. E-mail: grasslake@myjdl.com. *Br Mgr,* Sue Weible; E-mail: weiblesm@myjdl.com
Founded 1935. Pop 5,353; Circ 38,244
Open Mon & Wed 10-7, Fri 10-6, Sat 10-2
Friends of the Library Group
HANOVER BRANCH, 118 W Main St, Hanover, 49241. (Mail add: PO Box 130, Hanover, 49241-0130), SAN 346-668X. Tel: 517-905-1399. FAX: 517-563-8346. E-mail: hanover@myjdl.com. *Br Mgr,* Christopher A Sadler; E-mail: sadlerca@myjdl.com
Founded 1927. Pop 7,661; Circ 19,659
Open Mon & Fri 1-6, Wed 10-7, Sat 10-2
Friends of the Library Group
HENRIETTA, 11744 Bunkerhill Rd, Pleasant Lake, 49272. (Mail add: PO Box 88, Pleasant Lake, 49272-0088), SAN 346-6698. Tel: 517-769-6537. FAX: 517-769-6537. E-mail: henrietta@myjdl.com. *Br Mgr,* Sarah Hashimoto; E-mail: hashimotos@myjdl.com
Founded 1982. Pop 12,277; Circ 20,849
Open Mon & Fri 1-6, Wed 10-7, Sat 10-2
Friends of the Library Group

MEIJER, 2699 Airport Rd, 49202, SAN 346-6736. Tel: 517-788-4480. FAX: 517-788-4481. E-mail: meijer@myjdl.com. *Br Mgr,* Patricia Snoblen; E-mail: snoblenpa@myjdl.com
Founded 1928. Pop 27,432; Circ 159,659
Open Mon-Thurs 9-8, Fri 9-6, Sat 9-5, Sun 1-5
Friends of the Library Group

NAPOLEON BRANCH, 6755 S Brooklyn Rd, Napoleon, 49261. (Mail add: PO Box 710, Napoleon, 49261-0476), SAN 346-6779. Tel: 517-536-4266. FAX: 517-536-0531. E-mail: napoleon@myjdl.com. *Br Mgr,* Nicole Gilbert; E-mail: gilbertnj@myjdl.com
Founded 1930. Pop 6,273; Circ 25,806
Open Mon, Tues & Thurs 1-6, Wed 10-6
Friends of the Library Group

PARMA BRANCH, 102 Church St, Parma, 49269. (Mail add: PO Box 227, Parma, 49269-0227), SAN 346-6809. Tel: 517-531-4908. FAX: 517-531-5085. E-mail: parma@myjdl.com. *Br Mgr,* Jackie Merritt; E-mail: merrittja@myjdl.com
Founded 1922. Pop 8,114; Circ 19,001
Open Mon & Fri 1-6, Wed 10-7, Sat 10-2
Friends of the Library Group

SPRING ARBOR BRANCH, 113 E Main St, Spring Arbor, 49283. (Mail add: PO Box 264, Spring Arbor, 49283-0264), SAN 346-6833. Tel: 517-750-2030. FAX: 517-750-2030. E-mail: springarbor@myjdl.com. *Br Mgr,* Diana Hill; E-mail: hilldl@myjdl.com
Founded 1965. Pop 9,198; Circ 39,040
Open Mon & Wed 10-7, Fri 10-6, Sat 10-2
Friends of the Library Group

SPRINGPORT BRANCH, 110 Mechanic St, Springport, 49284. (Mail add: PO Box 172, Springport, 49284-0172), SAN 346-6868. Tel: 517-857-3833. FAX: 517-857-3833. E-mail: springport@myjdl.com. *Br Mgr,* Jackie Merritt; E-mail: merrittja@myjdl.com
Founded 1901. Pop 5,612; Circ 10,644
Open Mon & Fri 1-6, Wed 10-7, Sat 10-2
Friends of the Library Group

SUMMIT, 104 Bird Ave, 49203, SAN 346-6892. Tel: 517-783-4030. FAX: 517-783-1788. E-mail: summit@myjdl.com. *Br Mgr,* Theresa Runyan; E-mail: runyant@myjdl.com
Founded 1939. Pop 26,640; Circ 63,601
Function: CD-ROM, Music CDs, Prog for adults, Prog for children & young adult, Ref serv available, Summer reading prog, VHS videos
Special Services for the Blind - Reader equip
Open Mon 9-8, Wed 10-8, Thurs & Fri 10-6, Sat 10-5
Friends of the Library Group

S MICHIGAN DEPARTMENT OF CORRECTIONS*, Parnall Correctional Facility Library, 1790 E Parnall Rd, 49201-9037. Tel: 517-780-6000. FAX: 517-780-6399. *Librn,* Louis Yonke
Library Holdings: Bk Vols 10,500

JAMESTOWN

P PATMOS LIBRARY*, 2445 Riley St, 49427. (Mail add: PO Box 87, 49427), SAN 346-6388. Tel: 616-896-9798. FAX: 616-896-7645. E-mail: jam@llcoop.org. Web Site: www.patmoslibrary.michlibrary.org. *Libr Dir,* Mary Ellen Van Stempvoort; E-mail: jammvs@llcoop.org; Staff 5 (MLS 1, Non-MLS 4)
Pop 7,034; Circ 57,947
Apr 2009-Mar 2010 Income $159,275, State $3,654, County $16,722, Locally Generated Income $138,899. Sal $26,000
Library Holdings: AV Mats 2,015; Large Print Bks 151; Bk Vols 46,318; Per Subs 90; Talking Bks 1,718
Special Collections: Local History Coll
Automation Activity & Vendor Info: (Cataloging) Innovative Interfaces, Inc; (Circulation) Innovative Interfaces, Inc; (ILL) Innovative Interfaces, Inc; (OPAC) Innovative Interfaces, Inc; (Serials) Innovative Interfaces, Inc
Database Vendor: OCLC FirstSearch
Wireless access
Function: Adult bk club, Audiobks via web, Bk club(s), Bks on cassette, Bks on CD, CD-ROM, Children's prog, Computers for patron use, Copy machines, Digital talking bks, E-Reserves, Fax serv, Handicapped accessible, Holiday prog, ILL available, Music CDs, Online cat, OverDrive digital audio bks, Photocopying/Printing, Prog for adults, Prog for children & young adult, Pub access computers, Ref & res, Scanner, Spoken cassettes & CDs, Spoken cassettes & DVDs, Story hour, Summer & winter reading prog, Summer reading prog, Tax forms, VHS videos, Video lending libr, Wheelchair accessible, Winter reading prog
Partic in Lakeland Library Cooperative
Open Mon & Thurs 12-8, Tues, Wed & Fri 10-4, Sat 10-1
Restriction: ID required to use computers (Ltd hrs)
Friends of the Library Group

JENISON

P GEORGETOWN CHARTER TOWNSHIP LIBRARY*, 1525 Baldwin St, 49428. SAN 308-2032. Tel: 616-457-9620. FAX: 616-457-3666. E-mail: jen@lakeland.lib.mi.us. Web Site: www.georgetown-mi.gov/library. *Dir, Head, Ref,* Pamela A Myers; E-mail: jenpam@lakeland.lib.mi.us; *Ch Serv,* Mary Griffith Reed; E-mail: jenmr@lakeland.lib.mi.us; *Ref Serv, Ad,* Susan Carlson; E-mail: jensc@lakeland.lib.mi.us; Staff 21 (MLS 4, Non-MLS 17)
Founded 1965. Pop 50,446; Circ 263,000
Library Holdings: AV Mats 8,345; Large Print Bks 1,100; Bk Titles 95,000; Bk Vols 98,366; Per Subs 313; Talking Bks 2,525
Automation Activity & Vendor Info: (Cataloging) Innovative Interfaces, Inc; (Circulation) Innovative Interfaces, Inc; (OPAC) Innovative Interfaces, Inc
Database Vendor: Gale Cengage Learning, Innovative Interfaces, Inc, OCLC FirstSearch
Function: ILL available
Partic in Lakeland Library Cooperative
Open Mon-Thurs (Winter) 10-9, Fri & Sat 10-5; Mon-Thurs (Summer) 9-9, Fri 9-5, Sat 9-1
Friends of the Library Group

JONESVILLE

P JONESVILLE DISTRICT LIBRARY*, 310 Church St, 49250-1087. (Mail add: PO Box 184, 49250-0184), SAN 308-2040. Tel: 517-849-9701. FAX: 517-849-0009. Web Site: woodlands.lib.mi.us/jonesville/jonesville.html. *Dir,* Mary Miller; E-mail: memiller@monroe.lib.mi.us; *Asst Librn,* Faith Popejoy
Pop 5,894; Circ 28,209
Library Holdings: Bk Vols 26,000; Per Subs 32
Mem of Woodlands Library Cooperative
Open Mon & Wed 11-8, Tues & Thurs 11-6, Fri 2-6, Sat 10-2
Friends of the Library Group

KALAMAZOO

M BORGESS MEDICAL CENTER LIBRARY*, 1521 Gull Rd, 49048-1666. SAN 314-4658. Tel: 269-226-7360. FAX: 269 226-6881. E-mail: librarystaff@borgess.com. Web Site: www.borgess.com. *Mgr,* Jennifer Barlow; *Libr Asst,* Heather Spence; Staff 1.2 (MLS 0.6, Non MLS 0.6)
Jul 2011-Jun 2012. Mats Exp $110,000, Books $15,000, Per/Ser (Incl. Access Fees) $20,000, Electronic Ref Mat (Incl. Access Fees) $75,000
Library Holdings: Bk Vols 3,000; Per Subs 120
Subject Interests: Consumer health, Hospital admin, Med, Nursing, Patient health info
Automation Activity & Vendor Info: (Cataloging) Softlink America; (Circulation) Softlink America; (OPAC) Softlink America; (Serials) Softlink America
Wireless access
Partic in Michigan Health Sciences Libraries Association; National Network of Libraries of Medicine Greater Midwest Region
Open Mon-Thurs 9-2:30, Fri 9-1

M BRONSON METHODIST HOSPITAL, Health Sciences Library, 601 John St, Box B, 49007. SAN 308-2067. Tel: 269-341-6318. FAX: 269-341-7043. E-mail: bronsonlibrary@bronsonhg.org. *Libr Serv Supvr,* Liz Colson; Tel: 269-341-8627, E-mail: colsone@bronsonhg.org; *Info Serv Spec,* Jennifer Herron; E-mail: Herronj@bronsonhg.org; Staff 4 (MLS 2, Non-MLS 2)
Founded 1961
Library Holdings: e-books 200; e-journals 280; Bk Titles 750; Bk Vols 900; Per Subs 65
Subject Interests: Allied health, Consumer health, Health sci, Hospital admin, Med, Nursing
Automation Activity & Vendor Info: (Cataloging) EOS International; (Circulation) EOS International; (OPAC) EOS International; (Serials) EOS International
Database Vendor: Cinahl, DynaMed, EBSCOhost, Lexi-Comp, McGraw-Hill, Natural Standard, PubMed, STAT!Ref (Teton Data Systems)
Wireless access
Function: Prof lending libr
Partic in Michigan Health Sciences Libraries Association; Midwest Collaborative for Library Services (MCLS); National Network of Libraries of Medicine; Southwest Michigan Library Cooperative
Open Mon-Fri 8-5

R HERITAGE CHRISTIAN REFORMED CHURCH LIBRARY*, 2857 S 11th, 49009. SAN 308-2075. Tel: 269-372-3830. FAX: 269-372-5939. *Librn,* Carol Bickle
Founded 1869
Library Holdings: Bk Titles 800; Bk Vols 1,000
Open Mon-Thurs 9-2

C KALAMAZOO COLLEGE LIBRARY, 1200 Academy St, 49006-3285. SAN 308-2091. Tel: 269-337-7153. Interlibrary Loan Service Tel: 269-337-7148. Reference Tel: 269-337-7152. FAX: 269-337-7143. Web Site: www.kzoo.edu/is/library. *Dir,* Dr Stacy Nowicki; Tel: 269-337-5750, E-mail: stacy.nowicki@kzoo.edu; *Circ & Syst Librn,* Kyle Schulz; Tel: 269-337-5731, E-mail: kyle.schulz@kzoo.edu; *Coll Develop & Digital Integration Librn,* Leslie Burke; Tel: 269-337-7144, E-mail: leslie.burke@kzoo.edu; *Ref & Instruction Librn,* Robin Rank; E-mail: robin.rank@kzoo.edu; *Ref & Instruction Librn,* Liz Smith; E-mail: liz.smith@kzoo.edu; *Tech Serv Librn,* Paul G Smithson; Tel: 269-337-7147, E-mail: paul.smithson@kzoo.edu; *ILL Spec,* Leatha Burris; E-mail: leatha.burris@kzoo.edu; *Acq Asst,* Renata Schnelker; Tel: 269-337-7150, E-mail: renata.schnelker@kzoo.edu; *Archivist,* Lisa Murphy; Tel: 269-337-7151, E-mail: lisa.murphy@kzoo.edu; Staff 7.5 (MLS 4.5, Non-MLS 3)

Founded 1833. Enrl 1,392; Fac 99; Highest Degree: Bachelor

Library Holdings: AV Mats 7,975; CDs 1,433; DVDs 1,851; Microforms 908; Bk Titles 283,439; Bk Vols 352,499

Special Collections: Fine Birds Coll; History of Books & Printing; History of Science; Michigan Baptist Coll; Private Presses

Automation Activity & Vendor Info: (Acquisitions) Innovative Interfaces, Inc; (Cataloging) Innovative Interfaces, Inc; (Circulation) Innovative Interfaces, Inc; (Course Reserve) Innovative Interfaces, Inc; (ILL) OCLC ILLiad; (Media Booking) Innovative Interfaces, Inc; (OPAC) Innovative Interfaces, Inc; (Serials) Innovative Interfaces, Inc

Database Vendor: ABC-CLIO, ACM (Association for Computing Machinery), Alexander Street Press, American Chemical Society, American Mathematical Society, American Psychological Association (APA), Annual Reviews, ARTstor, Atlas Systems, Baker & Taylor, BioOne, Blackwell, Cambridge Scientific Abstracts, EBSCOhost, Gale Cengage Learning, H W Wilson, Innovative Interfaces, Inc, ISI Web of Knowledge, JSTOR, LexisNexis, Nature Publishing Group, Newsbank-Readex, OCLC, OCLC ArticleFirst, OCLC FirstSearch, OCLC WorldShare Interlibrary Loan, Oxford Online, Project MUSE, ProQuest, PubMed, Sage, ScienceDirect, SerialsSolutions, Thomson - Web of Science, Westlaw

Wireless access

Function: Computers for patron use, E-Reserves, Electronic databases & coll, Fax serv, ILL available, Microfiche/film & reading machines, Music CDs, Online cat, Outside serv via phone, mail, e-mail & web, Photocopying/Printing, Pub access computers, Ref serv available, Scanner, VHS videos, Web-catalog, Wheelchair accessible

Partic in Midwest Collaborative for Library Services (MCLS); Oberlin Group; OCLC Online Computer Library Center, Inc

Open Mon-Thurs 8am-2am, Fri 8am-10pm, Sat 9am-10pm, Sun 11am-2am; Mon-Fri (Summer) 8-5

Restriction: Circ limited, In-house use for visitors, Non-circulating of rare bks, Off-site coll in storage - retrieval as requested, Open to fac, students & qualified researchers, Open to pub for ref & circ; with some limitations, Open to students, fac & staff, Registered patrons only

S KALAMAZOO INSTITUTE OF ARTS*, Mary & Edwin Meader Fine Arts Library, 314 S Park St, 49007. SAN 308-2113. Tel: 269-349-7775, Ext 3166. FAX: 269-349-9313. E-mail: library@kiarts.org. Web Site: www.kiarts.org/page.php?menu_id=68. *Librn,* Malcolm McBryde; Tel: 269-349-7775, Ext 3165, E-mail: malcolmm@kiarts.org

Founded 1956

Library Holdings: AV Mats 250; Bk Vols 11,000; Per Subs 52

Special Collections: 19th & 20th Century American Art; Local & Regional Artists Coll, vf; Teacher Resource Center

Subject Interests: Am Art 19th-20th Centuries, Fine arts, Photog

Automation Activity & Vendor Info: (Cataloging) Auto-Graphics, Inc; (Circulation) Auto-Graphics, Inc; (OPAC) Auto-Graphics, Inc

Publications: Exhibition Catalogs

Partic in Southwest Michigan Library Cooperative

Open Tues-Thurs 11-3, Sat 10-2

P KALAMAZOO PUBLIC LIBRARY*, 315 S Rose St, 49007-5264. SAN 346-6981. Tel: 269-342-9897. Circulation Tel: 269-553-7806. Interlibrary Loan Service Tel: 269-553-7892. Reference Tel: 269-553-7801. FAX: 269-553-7999. Web Site: www.kpl.gov. *Dir,* Ann Rohrbaugh; Tel: 269-553-7828, E-mail: annr@kpl.gov; *Asst Dir, Admin Serv,* Diane Schiller; Tel: 269-553-7856, E-mail: DianeS@kpl.gov; *Head, Adult Serv,* Michael Cockrell; Tel: 269-553-7841, E-mail: michaelh@kpl.gov; *Head, Br & IT Serv,* Kevin King; Tel: 269-553-7881, Fax: 269-553-7969, E-mail: kevink@kpl.gov; *Head, Circ & Tech Serv,* Gary Green; Tel: 269-553-7861, E-mail: gary@kpl.gov; *Head Fac Mgt,* Susan Lindemann; Tel: 269-553-7883, E-mail: SusanL@kpl.gov; *Head, Youth Serv,* Susan Warner; Tel: 269-553-7876, Fax: 269-553-7940, E-mail: susan@kpl.gov; *Human Res Mgr,* Terry New; Tel: 269-553-7931, E-mail: TerryN@kpl.gov; *Mkt & Communications Mgr,* Farrell Howe; Tel: 269-553-7879, E-mail: FarrellH@kpl.gov; Staff 20 (MLS 20)

Founded 1872. Pop 123,979; Circ 1,398,360

Jul 2011-Jun 2012 Income (Main Library and Branch(s)) $12,343,360, State $34,584, Locally Generated Income $12,308,776. Mats Exp $977,010, Books $605,832, AV Mat $237,647, Electronic Ref Mat (Incl. Access Fees) $133,531. Sal $4,494,478

Library Holdings: AV Mats 58,913; CDs 23,292; DVDs 22,964; e-books 22,999; Bk Vols 316,215; Per Subs 744

Special Collections: Michigan & Kalamazoo History. US Document Depository

Wireless access

Function: Adult bk club, After school storytime, Audiobks via web, AV serv, Bilingual assistance for Spanish patrons, Bk club(s), Bks on CD, Children's prog, Computers for patron use, Copy machines, Digital talking bks, e-mail & chat, e-mail serv, E-Reserves, Electronic databases & coll, Fax serv, Free DVD rentals, Govt ref serv, Handicapped accessible, Holiday prog, Home delivery & serv to Sr ctr & nursing homes, Homebound delivery serv, ILL available, Magnifiers for reading, Mail & tel request accepted, Microfiche/film & reading machines, Music CDs, Newsp ref libr, Notary serv, Online cat, Online ref, Online searches, Outreach serv, OverDrive digital audio bks, Photocopying/Printing, Preschool outreach, Printer for laptops & handheld devices, Prog for adults, Prog for children & young adult, Pub access computers, Ref serv available, Ref serv in person, Scanner, Senior outreach, Spanish lang bks, Spoken cassettes & CDs, Story hour, Summer reading prog, Tax forms, Teen prog, Telephone ref, VHS videos, Wheelchair accessible, Workshops

Publications: LINK (Newsletter)

Partic in Southwest Michigan Library Cooperative

Open Mon-Wed (Summer) 9-9, Thurs & Fri 9-6, Sat 9-5; Mon-Thurs (Winter) 9-9, Fri 9-6, Sat 9-5, Sun 1-5

Restriction: Non-resident fee

Friends of the Library Group

Branches: 4

EASTWOOD, 1112 Gayle St, 49048, SAN 346-7163. Tel: 269-553-7810. FAX: 269-345-6095. *Lead Librn,* Judi Rambow
Open Mon 12-6, Tues 1-8, Wed & Thurs 10-6, Fri 12-5, Sat 10-5
Friends of the Library Group

OSHTEMO, 7265 W Main St, 49009, SAN 346-7198. Tel: 269-553-7980. FAX: 269-375-6610. *Lead Librn,* Nancy Smith; Staff 2 (MLS 2)
Open Mon & Wed 10-9, Tues 12-9, Thurs 10-6, Fri & Sat 10-5
Friends of the Library Group

ALMA POWELL BRANCH, 1000 W Paterson St, 49007, SAN 346-7139. Tel: 269-553-7960. FAX: 269-344-0782. *Lead Librn,* Judi Rambow; Tel: 269-553-7961, E-mail: judir@kpl.gov
Open Mon & Wed 1-6, Tues 1-8, Thurs 10-6, Fri 10-5
Friends of the Library Group

WASHINGTON SQUARE, 1244 Portage Rd, 49001, SAN 346-7228. Tel: 269-553-7970. FAX: 269-342-9261. *Lead Librn,* Nancy Stern
Open Mon & Wed 1-6, Tues 1-8, Thurs 10-6, Fri 10-5, Sat 9-Noon
Friends of the Library Group

J KALAMAZOO VALLEY COMMUNITY COLLEGE LIBRARIES*, 6767 West O Ave, 49003. (Mail add: PO Box 4070, 49003-4070), SAN 308-213X. Tel: 269-488-4328, 269-488-4380. Circulation Tel: 269-488-5673. Interlibrary Loan Service Tel: 269-488-4331. Reference Tel: 269-488-4380. Administration Tel: 269-488-4326. FAX: 269-488-4488. E-mail: libref@kvcc.edu. Web Site: www.kvcc.edu/library. *Dir of Libr,* Dr Janet Alm; E-mail: jalm@kvcc.edu; *Librn, Arcadia Commons Campus,* Jim Ratliff; *Cataloger, Coll Develop Librn,* Jackie Howlett; *Ref & Instrul Serv Librn,* Irene Turcott; *Ref & Instrul Serv Librn,* Paula Willson; Staff 15 (MLS 6, Non-MLS 9)

Founded 1968. Enrl 15,000; Fac 136; Highest Degree: Associate

Library Holdings: AV Mats 22,767; Bks on Deafness & Sign Lang 300; Bk Titles 149,000; Per Subs 245

Special Collections: Alva Dorn Photography Coll; Mary Mace Spradling African American Coll; Michigan History (Ned Rubenstein Memorial Coll)

Subject Interests: Career res, Sign lang

Wireless access

Open Mon-Thurs (Fall & Winter) 7:45am-9pm, Fri 7:45-5, Sat 10-2, Sun Noon-5; Mon-Thurs (Summer) 8am-9pm, Fri 8-Noon

S KALSEC, INC*, Information Center, 3713 W Main St, 49006. (Mail add: PO Box 50511, 49005-0511), SAN 327-4012. Tel: 269-349-9711. FAX: 269-382-3060. E-mail: info@kalsec.com. Web Site: www.kalsec.com. *Res,* Bill Kaczmarski; Tel: 269-382-3342; *Tech Serv,* Patti Roberts; E-mail: proberts@kalsec.com. Subject Specialists: *Biol,* Bill Kaczmarski; Staff 3 (MLS 1, Non-MLS 2)

Library Holdings: Bk Vols 5,000; Per Subs 25

Subject Interests: Chem, Food sci

Database Vendor: Agricola, Dialog, EBSCOhost, Elsevier MDL, OCLC FirstSearch, PubMed, ScienceDirect, STN International

Function: Res libr

Partic in Midwest Collaborative for Library Services (MCLS)

Restriction: Staff use only

R SAINT LUKE'S EPISCOPAL CHURCH LIBRARY*, 247 W Lovell St, 49007. SAN 308-2148. Tel: 269-345-8553. FAX: 269-345-5559. *Librn,* Margaret Eiszner
Library Holdings: Bk Vols 1,600
Friends of the Library Group

S W E UPJOHN INSTITUTE FOR EMPLOYMENT RESEARCH, Information Center, 300 S Westnedge Ave, 49007-4686. SAN 371-8174. Tel: 269-343-5541, Ext 418. FAX: 269-343-3308. Web Site: www.upjohn.org. *Mgr,* Linda S Richer; E-mail: richer@upjohn.org; Staff 3.25 (MLS 1, Non-MLS 2.25)
Founded 1945
Library Holdings: CDs 96; e-books 541; e-journals 257; Electronic Media & Resources 2,416; Bk Titles 14,353; Bk Vols 25,791; Per Subs 250
Subject Interests: Educ, Employment, Labor econ, Poverty & income support, Unemployment
Automation Activity & Vendor Info: (Acquisitions) EOS International; (Cataloging) EOS International; (Circulation) EOS International; (ILL) OCLC; (OPAC) EOS International; (Serials) EOS International
Database Vendor: Dialog, EBSCOhost, Elsevier, JSTOR, LexisNexis, OCLC ArticleFirst, OCLC FirstSearch, OCLC WorldShare Interlibrary Loan, ReferenceUSA, ScienceDirect, Wiley InterScience
Function: Res libr
Partic in Midwest Collaborative for Library Services (MCLS)
Restriction: Staff use only

C WESTERN MICHIGAN UNIVERSITY*, Dwight B Waldo Library, Arcadia at Vande Giessen St, 49008-5353. (Mail add: 1903 W Michigan Ave, 49008-5353), SAN 346-7341. Tel: 269-387-5059. Circulation Tel: 269-387-5156. Interlibrary Loan Service Tel: 269-387-5172. Reference Tel: 269-387-5178. Administration Tel: 269-387-5202. Automation Services Tel: 269-387-5039. FAX: 269-387-5077. Circulation FAX: 269-387-4343. Interlibrary Loan Service FAX: 269-387-5124. Reference FAX: 269-387-5836. Web Site: www.wmich.edu/library. *Dean,* Joseph Reish; E-mail: joe.reish@wmich.edu; *Assoc Dean, Coll & Tech Serv,* Barbara Cockrell; Tel: 269-387-5143, E-mail: barbara.cockrell@wmich.edu; *Assoc Dean, Pub Serv & Tech,* Scott Garrison; Tel: 269-387-5239, E-mail: scott.garrison@wmich.edu; *Dir, Operational Serv,* Regina Buckner; Tel: 269-387-5204, E-mail: regina.buckner@wmich.edu; *Head, Cent Ref Serv,* Maria A Perez-Stable; Tel: 269-387-5322, E-mail: maria.perez-stable@wmich.edu; *Head, Govt Doc & Maps,* Michael McDonnell; Tel: 269-387-5187, Fax: 269-387-5012, E-mail: michael.mcdonnell@wmich.edu; *Monographic Acq Librn,* Randle J Gedeon; Tel: 269-387-5227, Fax: 269-387-5193, E-mail: randle.gedeon@wmich.edu. Subject Specialists: *Children's lit, Hist,* Maria A Perez-Stable; *Geog,* Michael McDonnell; *German,* Randle J Gedeon; Staff 82 (MLS 31, Non-MLS 51)
Founded 1903. Enrl 24,433; Fac 885; Highest Degree: Doctorate
Library Holdings: Bk Titles 970,038; Bk Vols 1,910,778; Per Subs 7,743
Special Collections: African Studies (Ann Kercher Memorial); Cistercian Manuscript & Rare Book Coll; D B Waldo Lincoln Coll; Haenicke American Women's Poetry Coll; Historical Children's Book Coll; History (Regional History); LeFevre Miniature Book Coll; Medieval Studies (Institute of Cistercian Studies), bks, mss. State Document Depository; US Document Depository
Automation Activity & Vendor Info: (Acquisitions) Ex Libris Group; (Cataloging) Ex Libris Group; (Circulation) Ex Libris Group; (ILL) Ex Libris Group; (Media Booking) Ex Libris Group; (OPAC) Ex Libris Group; (Serials) Ex Libris Group
Database Vendor: Ex Libris Group, Gale Cengage Learning, JSTOR, LexisNexis, Luna Imaging/Insight, Marcive, Inc, MD Consult, OCLC FirstSearch, OVID Technologies, ProQuest, RefWorks, SerialsSolutions, Wilson - Wilson Web
Wireless access
Function: Archival coll, Audio & video playback equip for onsite use, CD-ROM, Copy machines, Doc delivery serv, e-mail & chat, E-Reserves, Electronic databases & coll, Fax serv, Govt ref serv, Handicapped accessible, ILL available, Music CDs, Online cat, Online info literacy tutorials on the web & in blackboard, Online ref, Orientations, Photocopying/Printing, Ref & res, Ref serv available, Ref serv in person, Scanner, Tax forms, Telephone ref, Video lending libr, Wheelchair accessible
Publications: Gatherings (Newsletter)
Partic in Midwest Collaborative for Library Services (MCLS)
Special Services for the Blind - Computer with voice synthesizer for visually impaired persons; Large print bks
Restriction: Borrowing privileges limited to fac & registered students, Non-circulating coll, Non-circulating of rare bks, Off-site coll in storage - retrieval as requested
Friends of the Library Group

Departmental Libraries:

ARCHIVES & REGIONAL HISTORY COLLECTION, 111 East Hall, 1903 W Michigan Ave, 49008-5307, SAN 376-8864. Tel: 269-387-8490. FAX: 269-387-8484. E-mail: arch_collect@wmich.edu. Web Site: www.wmich.edu/library/archives. *Dir,* Dr Sharon Carlson; Tel: 269-387-8496, E-mail: sharon.carlson@wmich.edu. Subject Specialists: *Hist of libr, US hist, Women's hist,* Dr Sharon Carlson; Staff 5 (MLS 1, Non-MLS 4)
Founded 1958. Enrl 28,500; Highest Degree: Doctorate
Library Holdings: Bk Vols 17,114
Special Collections: Western Michigan University Archives
Subject Interests: Census data, County govt rec, Govt doc
Function: Archival coll
Open Tues-Fri (Sept-June) 8-5, Sat 9-4; Mon-Fri (July-Aug) 9-4
Restriction: Non-circulating, Not a lending libr
Friends of the Library Group

EDUCATION LIBRARY, 2800 Sangren Hall, 1903 W Michigan Ave, 49008, SAN 346-7430. Tel: 269-387-5223. FAX: 268-387-5231. *Head of Libr,* Dennis Strasser; Tel: 269-387-5230, E-mail: dennis.strasser@wmich.edu; *Coordr,* Brandon Meissner; Tel: 269-387-5167, E-mail: brandon.meissner@wmich.edu; Staff 5 (MLS 2, Non-MLS 3)
Enrl 28,500; Highest Degree: Doctorate
Library Holdings: Bk Titles 60,000; Bk Vols 70,003; Per Subs 600
Function: Ref serv available, Res libr
Friends of the Library Group

MUSIC & DANCE, 3006 Dalton Ctr, 3rd Flr, 49008. (Mail add: 1903 W Michigan Ave, 49008-5353), SAN 346-7465. Tel: 269-387-5237. FAX: 269-387-5809. *Head of Libr,* Gregory Fitzgerald; Tel: 269-387-5236, E-mail: gregory.fitzgerald@wmich.edu; Staff 2 (MLS 1, Non-MLS 1)
Enrl 28,500; Highest Degree: Doctorate
Library Holdings: Bk Titles 35,656; Bk Vols 43,684
Subject Interests: Dance, Music
Function: Ref serv available
Friends of the Library Group

VISUAL RESOURCES, 2213 Sangren Hall, 2nd Flr, 49008. (Mail add: 1903 W Michigan Ave, 49008-5353), SAN 377-743X. Tel: 269-387-4111. FAX: 269-387-4114. *Head of Libr,* Miranda Howard; Tel: 269-387-4113, E-mail: miranda.howard@wmich.edu. Subject Specialists: *Art, Costumes,* Miranda Howard; Staff 2 (MLS 1, Non-MLS 1)
Founded 1998. Enrl 28,500; Highest Degree: Doctorate
Function: Ref serv available
Friends of the Library Group

KALKASKA

P KALKASKA COUNTY LIBRARY*, 247 S Cedar St, 49646. SAN 308-2164. Tel: 231-258-9411. E-mail: kalkaskalibrary@yahoo.com. Web Site: www.kalkaskacounty.net/library.asp. *Dir,* Bradley Chaplin; E-mail: kcldirector@yahoo.com; *Ref Librn,* Bonnie Reed; Staff 4.5 (MLS 1.5, Non-MLS 3)
Founded 1934. Pop 17,500; Circ 32,305
Library Holdings: Audiobooks 1,150; Bks-By-Mail 200; Bks on Deafness & Sign Lang 10; Braille Volumes 8; CDs 415; DVDs 425; Large Print Bks 900; Bk Vols 40,200; Per Subs 20; Videos 800
Special Collections: Genealogy Coll; Northern Michigan History Coll
Wireless access
Function: Accelerated reader prog, Accessibility serv available based on individual needs, Adult bk club, Audio & video playback equip for onsite use, Audiobks via web, BA reader (adult literacy), Bi-weekly Writer's Group, Bilingual assistance for Spanish patrons, Bk club(s), Bks on cassette, Bks on CD, Children's prog, Computer training, Computers for patron use, Copy machines, Digital talking bks, e-mail & chat, E-Reserves, Electronic databases & coll, Equip loans & repairs, Exhibits, Free DVD rentals, Games & aids for the handicapped, Genealogy discussion group, Handicapped accessible, Holiday prog, Home delivery & serv to Sr ctr & nursing homes, Homebound delivery serv, ILL available, Instruction & testing, Jail serv, Magnifiers for reading, Mail & tel request accepted, Mail loans to mem, Microfiche/film & reading machines, Music CDs, Newsp ref libr, Online cat, Online info literacy tutorials on the web & in blackboard, Online searches, Orientations, Outreach serv, Outside serv via phone, mail, e-mail & web, OverDrive digital audio bks, Photocopying/Printing, Preschool outreach, Preschool reading prog, Prof lending libr, Prog for adults, Prog for children & young adult, Pub access computers, Ref & res, Ref serv available, Ref serv in person, Referrals accepted, Res libr, Scanner, Senior computer classes, Senior outreach, Story hour, Summer reading prog, Tax forms, Teen prog, Telephone ref, VHS videos, Web-catalog, Wheelchair accessible, Workshops
Partic in Dialog Corp; Mid-Michigan Library League; SDC Info Servs
Open Mon-Fri 9-8, Sat 9-3
Friends of the Library Group

KINGSLEY

S MICHIGAN DEPARTMENT OF CORRECTIONS*, Pugsley Correctional Facility Library, 7401 Walton Rd, 49649. Tel: 231-263-5253. FAX: 231-263-3944, 231-263-7606. *Librn,* Denise Bearre
Library Holdings: Bk Vols 10,000; Per Subs 20

Automation Activity & Vendor Info: (Cataloging) Follett Software; (Circulation) Follett Software
Open Mon-Fri 9-5

KINGSTON

P JACQUELIN E OPPERMAN MEMORIAL LIBRARY*, Kingston Community Public Library, 5790 State St, 48741. SAN 308-2180. Tel: 989-683-2500. FAX: 989-683-2081. Web Site: www.kingston.lib.mi.us. *Dir,* Glenna Ford; E-mail: gford@kingston.lib.mi.us; Staff 2 (MLS 1, Non-MLS 1)
Founded 1970. Pop 4,080; Circ 14,300
Library Holdings: Audiobooks 459; CDs 116; DVDs 712; e-books 14,751; Large Print Bks 45; Bk Titles 32,928; Per Subs 24; Videos 1,238
Automation Activity & Vendor Info: (Acquisitions) Winnebago Software Co; (Cataloging) Winnebago Software Co; (Circulation) Winnebago Software Co; (Course Reserve) Winnebago Software Co; (ILL) Innovative Interfaces, Inc - Millenium; (Media Booking) Winnebago Software Co; (OPAC) Winnebago Software Co
Wireless access
Partic in White Pine Libr Coop
Open Mon & Fri 8-3, Tues-Thurs 8-3 & 6-8, Sat 10-3

LAINGSBURG

P LAINGSBURG PUBLIC LIBRARY*, 255 E Grand River, 48848-8601. (Mail add: PO Box 280, 48848-0280), SAN 308-2210. Tel: 517-651-6282. FAX: 517-651-6371. *Dir,* Sandra Chavez; E-mail: schavez77@hotmail.com
Founded 1905. Pop 7,132; Circ 26,667
Library Holdings: Bk Vols 15,000; Per Subs 42
Subject Interests: Local hist
Partic in Mideastern Michigan Library Cooperative
Open Tues-Fri 9-6, Sat 9-1
Friends of the Library Group

LAKE CITY

P MISSAUKEE DISTRICT LIBRARY*, 210 S Canal St, 49651. (Mail add: PO Box 340, 49651-0340), SAN 308-2229. Tel: 231-839-2166. FAX: 231-839-3865. Web Site: www.missaukeelibrary.org. *Dir, Librn,* Michelle Moore; E-mail: moore@missaukeelibrary.org; Staff 7 (MLS 1, Non-MLS 6)
Founded 1907. Pop 14,000; Circ 42,000
Library Holdings: AV Mats 474; Bks on Deafness & Sign Lang 41; Large Print Bks 657; Bk Titles 31,537; Bk Vols 40,000; Per Subs 56; Talking Bks 1,350
Special Collections: Local History
Wireless access
Function: ILL available, Magnifiers for reading, Photocopying/Printing, Prog for children & young adult, Summer reading prog, Telephone ref
Partic in Mid-Michigan Library League
Special Services for the Deaf - Bks on deafness & sign lang
Special Services for the Blind - Bks on cassette; Bks on CD; Copier with enlargement capabilities; Extensive large print coll; VisualTek equip
Open Mon 9-8, Tues-Fri 9-6, Sat 9-12
Friends of the Library Group

LAKE ODESSA

P LAKE ODESSA COMMUNITY LIBRARY*, 1007 Fourth Ave, 48849-1023. SAN 376-3714. Tel: 616-374-4591. FAX: 616-374-3054. E-mail: lkocmt@lakeodessalibrary.org. Web Site: lakeodessalibrary.org. *Dir,* Connie Teachworth
Founded 1986. Pop 4,434; Circ 33,500
Library Holdings: AV Mats 240; Bk Vols 18,000; Per Subs 35; Talking Bks 300
Database Vendor: Baker & Taylor, BWI, Gale Cengage Learning, OCLC FirstSearch, ProQuest
Wireless access
Partic in Lakeland Library Cooperative
Special Services for the Blind - Braille bks; Talking bks
Open Tues & Thurs 9-7, Wed & Fri 9-5, Sat 9-12
Friends of the Library Group

LAKE ORION

P ORION TOWNSHIP PUBLIC LIBRARY*, 825 Joslyn Rd, 48362. SAN 346-752X. Tel: 248-693-3000. Reference Tel: 248-693-3001. FAX: 248-693-3009. Web Site: www.orionlibrary.org. *Dir,* Karen Knox; Tel: 248-693-3000, Ext 305, E-mail: kknox@orionlibrary.org; *Head, Adult/Teen/Outreach Serv,* Beth Sheridan; Tel: 248-693-3000, Ext 332, E-mail: sheridan@orionlibrary.org; *Head, Info Tech,* Judi Rudisill; Tel: 248-693-3000, Ext 322, E-mail: rudisill@orionlibrary.org; *Head, Support Serv,* Martha Lee; Tel: 248-693-3000, Ext 304, E-mail: mlee@orionlibrary.org; *Head, Youth Serv,* Debra Refior; Tel: 248-693-3000, Ext 341, E-mail: drefior@orionlibrary.org; *ILS Coordr,* Barnard Anne; Tel: 248-693-3000, Ext 339, E-mail: abarnard@orionlibrary.org; Staff 12 (MLS 12)
Founded 1926. Pop 35,394; Circ 505,910
Jan 2012-Dec 2012 Income $2,536,000. Mats Exp $171,000, Books $112,000, Per/Ser (Incl. Access Fees) $12,000, Other Print Mats $2,000, AV Mat $39,000, Electronic Ref Mat (Incl. Access Fees) $6,000. Sal $1,210,000
Library Holdings: Audiobooks 10,118; CDs 7,973; DVDs 9,069; e-books 4,732; Large Print Bks 5,540; Bk Titles 151,036; Per Subs 357; Videos 4,431
Subject Interests: Genealogy, Mich
Automation Activity & Vendor Info: (Acquisitions) Horizon; (Cataloging) Horizon; (Circulation) Horizon; (Serials) Horizon
Database Vendor: Baker & Taylor, BWI, OCLC FirstSearch, ProQuest
Wireless access
Function: Adult bk club, Art exhibits, Audio & video playback equip for onsite use, Audiobks via web, Bk club(s), Bks on cassette, Bks on CD, Chess club, Children's prog, Computer training, Computers for patron use, Copy machines, e-mail & chat, Electronic databases & coll, Exhibits, Fax serv, Free DVD rentals, Handicapped accessible, Home delivery & serv to Sr ctr & nursing homes, Homebound delivery serv, Homework prog, ILL available, Magnifiers for reading, Microfiche/film & reading machines, Monthly prog for perceptually impaired adults, Mus passes, Music CDs, Notary serv, Online cat, Online ref, Outreach serv, OverDrive digital audio bks, Photocopying/Printing, Preschool outreach, Preschool reading prog, Printer for laptops & handheld devices, Prog for adults, Prog for children & young adult, Provide serv for the mentally ill, Pub access computers, Ref serv available, Ref serv in person, Scanner, Senior computer classes, Senior outreach, Serves mentally handicapped consumers, Story hour, Summer reading prog, Tax forms, Teen prog, Telephone ref, Wheelchair accessible
Publications: Newsletter (Quarterly)
Partic in TLN
Special Services for the Deaf - Accessible learning ctr; Assisted listening device; Bks on deafness & sign lang; High interest/low vocabulary bks
Special Services for the Blind - BiFolkal kits; Bks on cassette; Bks on CD; Closed circuit TV magnifier; Extensive large print coll; Home delivery serv; Magnifiers; Reader equip
Open Mon-Thurs 9:30-9, Fri & Sat 9:30-5
Friends of the Library Group

LAKEVIEW

P TAMARACK DISTRICT LIBRARY, 832 S Lincoln Ave, 48850. (Mail add: PO Box 469, 48850-0469), SAN 308-2245. Tel: 989-352-6274. FAX: 989-352-7713. E-mail: lvw@llcoop.org. Web Site: tamaracklibrary.org. *Libr Dir,* Hope Nobel; Staff 5 (MLS 2, Non-MLS 3)
Founded 1965. Pop 10,485; Circ 59,239
Automation Activity & Vendor Info: (Cataloging) Innovative Interfaces, Inc; (Circulation) Innovative Interfaces, Inc; (ILL) Innovative Interfaces, Inc; (OPAC) Innovative Interfaces, Inc; (Serials) Innovative Interfaces, Inc
Wireless access
Function: Adult bk club, After school storytime, Audiobks via web, Bk club(s), Bks on cassette, Bks on CD, CD-ROM, Children's prog, Computer training, Computers for patron use, Copy machines, Electronic databases & coll, Fax serv, Holiday prog, ILL available, Magnifiers for reading, Mus passes, Music CDs, Notary serv, Online cat, Outreach serv, OverDrive digital audio bks, Photocopying/Printing, Preschool outreach, Prog for adults, Prog for children & young adult, Pub access computers, Ref serv available, Ref serv in person, Senior outreach, Story hour, Summer & winter reading prog, Summer reading prog, Tax forms, Teen prog, Telephone ref, VHS videos, Wheelchair accessible
Partic in Lakeland Library Cooperative
Open Mon-Thurs 9:30-6, Fri 9:30-5, Sat 9-12
Friends of the Library Group

L'ANSE

P L'ANSE AREA SCHOOL-PUBLIC LIBRARY*, 201 N Fourth St, 49946-1499. SAN 308-2199. Tel: 906-524-6213. FAX: 906-524-5331. Web Site: www.uplibraries.org. *Dir,* Chris Collins; E-mail: ccollins@laschools.k12.mi.us
Pop 9,140
Library Holdings: Bk Vols 16,500; Per Subs 63
Special Collections: Native American Coll
Automation Activity & Vendor Info: (Cataloging) SirsiDynix; (Circulation) SirsiDynix
Partic in Superiorland Library Cooperative
Open Mon & Wed 7:30-4 & 6:30-8:30, Tues, Thurs & Fri 7:30-4
Friends of the Library Group

LANSING

P CAPITAL AREA DISTRICT LIBRARIES, 401 S Capitol Ave, 48933. (Mail add: PO Box 40719, 48901-7919), SAN 346-8453. Tel: 517-367-6300. Circulation Tel: 517-367-6350. Information Services Tel:

517-367-6363. FAX: 517-374-1068. Web Site: www.cadl.org. *Dir,* Maureen Hirten; Tel: 517-367-6341, E-mail: hirtenm@cadl.org; *Dir of Finance,* Patrick Taylor; Tel: 517-367-6337, E-mail: taylorp@cadl.org; *Human Res Dir,* Julie Laxton; Tel: 517-367-6349, E-mail: laxtonj@cadl.org; *Dir, Mkt & Communications,* Trenton Smiley; Tel: 517-367-6348, E-mail: smileyt@cadl.org; *Tech Dir,* Sheryl Cormicle Knox; Tel: 517-367-6347, E-mail: knoxs@cadl.org; *Assoc Dir, Coll Serv,* Scott Duimstra; Tel: 517-367-0810, E-mail: duimstras@cadl.org; *Assoc Dir, Pub Serv,* Jolee Hamlin; Tel: 517-367-0813, E-mail: hamlinj@cadl.org; Staff 20 (MLS 13, Non-MLS 7)
Founded 1998. Pop 240,165; Circ 2,288,317
Jan 2011-Dec 2011 Income (Main Library and Branch(s)) $11,325,723. Mats Exp $1,248,976. Sal $5,501,361
Library Holdings: Audiobooks 24,418; CDs 33,256; DVDs 55,924; e-books 8,840; Large Print Bks 10,318; Music Scores 23; Bk Vols 440,406; Per Subs 534; Videos 1,416
Automation Activity & Vendor Info: (Acquisitions) Innovative Interfaces, Inc; (Cataloging) Innovative Interfaces, Inc; (Circulation) Innovative Interfaces, Inc; (ILL) Innovative Interfaces, Inc; (OPAC) Innovative Interfaces, Inc
Database Vendor: Innovative Interfaces, Inc
Wireless access
Function: Bks on CD, CD-ROM, Children's prog, Computer training, Computers for patron use, Copy machines, Digital talking bks, Free DVD rentals, Home delivery & serv to Sr ctr & nursing homes, Homebound delivery serv, Music CDs, Online cat, Online ref, OverDrive digital audio bks, Prog for adults, Prog for children & young adult, Ref serv available, Teen prog, Telephone ref, Video lending libr
Partic in Mideastern Michigan Library Cooperative; Midwest Collaborative for Library Services (MCLS)
Open Mon-Fri 9-5
Restriction: Non-resident fee
Friends of the Library Group
Branches: 13
AURELIUS LIBRARY, 1939 S Aurelius Rd, Mason, 48854-9763, SAN 346-8488. Tel: 517 628-3743. FAX: 517-628-2141. *Head Librn,* Jennifer DeGroat; Staff 1 (MLS 1)
Founded 1936
Special Services for the Blind - Audiovision-a radio reading serv
Open Mon & Wed 11-7, Tues, Thurs & Fri 3-6, Sat 10- 1
Friends of the Library Group
DANSVILLE LIBRARY, 1379 E Mason St, Dansville, 48819, SAN 346-8518. Tel: 517-623-6511. FAX: 517-623-0520. *Head Librn,* Melissa Cole; Staff 2 (MLS 2)
Open Mon & Wed 3-7, Tues & Thurs 11-6, Fri 3-6, Sat 10-2
Friends of the Library Group
DOWNTOWN LANSING LIBRARY, 401 S Capitol Ave, 48933. (Mail add: PO Box 40719, 48909-7919), SAN 377-7588. Tel: 517-367-6363. Reference Tel: 517-367-6346. FAX: 517-374-1068. *Head Librn,* Katherine Johnson; Tel: 517-367-6322, E-mail: johnsonk@cadl.org; *Head, Circ,* Deb Ketchum; Tel: 517-367-6315, E-mail: ketchumd@cadl.org; *Pub Serv,* Jessica Trotter; Tel: 517-367-6302, E-mail: trotterj@cadl.org; Staff 13 (MLS 13)
Open Mon-Thurs 9-9, Fri & Sat 9-6, Sun 1-6
Friends of the Library Group
FOSTER LIBRARY, 200 N Foster Ave, 48912, SAN 378-2425. Tel: 517-485-5185. FAX: 517-485-5239. *Head Librn,* Jean S Bolley; Staff 1 (MLS 1)
Open Mon-Wed 1-7, Thurs & Fri 12-5, Sat 11-3
Friends of the Library Group
HASLETT LIBRARY, 1590 Franklin St, Haslett, 48840, SAN 346-8534. Tel: 517-339-2324. FAX: 517-339-0349. *Head Librn,* Ann Chapman; Staff 2 (MLS 2)
Open Mon-Thurs 10-9, Fri & Sat 10-7, Sun (Sept-May) 1-5
Friends of the Library Group
HOLT-DELHI LIBRARY, 2078 Aurelius Rd, Holt, 48842, SAN 346-8542. Tel: 517-694-9351. FAX: 517-699-3865. *Head Librn,* Jolee Hamlin; Staff 2 (MLS 2)
Open Mon-Wed 10-9, Thurs-Sat 10-7, Sun 12-5
Friends of the Library Group
LESLIE LIBRARY, 201 Pennsylvania St, Leslie, 49251, SAN 346-8607. Tel: 517-589-9400. FAX: 517-589-0536. *Head Librn,* Barbara Keeler; Staff 2 (MLS 2)
Open Mon 1-7, Tues, Thurs & Fri 1-6, Wed 11-7, Sat 10-2
Friends of the Library Group
MASON LIBRARY, 145 W Ash St, Mason, 48854, SAN 346-8631. Tel: 517-676-9088. FAX: 517-676-3780. *Head Librn,* Cheryl Lyons; E-mail: lyonsc@cadl.org; Staff 2 (MLS 2)
Open Mon-Thurs 11-8, Fri 10-6, Sat 10-5, Sun 1-5
Friends of the Library Group
OKEMOS LIBRARY, 4321 Okemos Rd, Okemos, 48864, SAN 346-8666. Tel: 517-347-2021. Reference Tel: 517-347-2023. Administration Tel: 517-347-2031. FAX: 517-347-2034. *Head Librn,* Betsy Hull; E-mail: hullb@cadl.org; *Youth Serv Librn,* Thomas Shilts; E-mail: shiltst@cadl.org; Staff 4 (MLS 4)
Function: Adult bk club, After school storytime, Art exhibits, AV serv, Bk club(s), Bks on cassette, Bks on CD, Children's prog, Computer training, Computers for patron use, Copy machines, Digital talking bks, e-mail serv, E-Reserves, Electronic databases & coll, Free DVD rentals, Handicapped accessible, Holiday prog, ILL available, Mail & tel request accepted, Music CDs, Online cat, Online ref, Prog for adults, Prog for children & young adult, Spoken cassettes & CDs, Spoken cassettes & DVDs, Summer reading prog, Tax forms, Teen prog, Telephone ref, VCDs, VHS videos, Wheelchair accessible
Open Mon-Thurs 9-9, Fri & Sat 9-7, Sun 12-6
Friends of the Library Group
SOUTH LANSING LIBRARY, 3500 S Cedar St, Ste 108, 48910, SAN 378-2441. Tel: 517-272-9840. FAX: 517-272-9901. *Head Librn,* Michele Brussow; E-mail: brussowm@cadl.org; Staff 3 (MLS 3)
Open Mon-Thurs 10-8, Fri 10-7, Sat 10-6, Sun 12-5
Friends of the Library Group
STOCKBRIDGE LIBRARY, 200 Wood St, Stockbridge, 49285. (Mail add: PO Box 245, Stockbridge, 49285), SAN 346-8690. Tel: 517-851-7810. FAX: 517-851-8612. *Head Librn,* Paul Crandall; E-mail: crandallp@cadl.org; Staff 1 (MLS 1)
Partic in Southwest Michigan Library Cooperative
Open Mon-Fri 11-7, Sat 11-5, Sun (Sept-May) 1-5
Friends of the Library Group
WEBBERVILLE LIBRARY, 115 S Main St, Webberville, 48892. (Mail add: PO Box 689, Webberville, 48892-0689), SAN 346-8755. Tel: 517-521-3643. FAX: 517-521-1079. *Head Librn,* Peg Mawby; E-mail: mawbyp@cadl.org; Staff 1 (MLS 1)
Open Mon 1-6, Tues & Thurs 2-8, Wed 10-6, Fri 2-6, Sat 10-2
Friends of the Library Group
WILLIAMSTON LIBRARY, 201 School St, Williamston, 48895-1337, SAN 346-878X. Tel: 517-655-1191. FAX: 517-655-5243. *Head Librn,* Julie Chrisinske; E-mail: chrisinskej@cadl.org; Staff 1 (MLS 1)
Open Mon-Thurs 10-7, Fri 10-6, Sat 12-4, Sun (Sept-May) 12-4
Friends of the Library Group
Bookmobiles: 1. Outreach Coordinator, Bill Nelton

P DELTA TOWNSHIP DISTRICT LIBRARY*, 5130 Davenport Dr, 48917-2040. Tel: 517-321-4014. FAX: 517-321-2080. Web Site: www.dtdl.org. *Dir,* Cherry Hamrick; E-mail: chamrick@deltami.gov; *Asst Dir,* Mary Rzepczynski; E-mail: mrzepczynski@deltami.gov; *Ad,* Sara Wedell; E mail: swedell@deltami.gov; *Youth Serv Librn,* Becky Fermanich; E-mail: bleboeuf@deltami.gov; Staff 13 (MLS 2, Non-MLS 11)
Pop 30,056; Circ 162,802
Library Holdings: AV Mats 2,939; Bks on Deafness & Sign Lang 25; Large Print Bks 1,022; Bk Titles 24,471; Per Subs 110
Automation Activity & Vendor Info: (Cataloging) SirsiDynix; (Circulation) SirsiDynix; (ILL) Auto-Graphics, Inc; (OPAC) SirsiDynix; (Serials) SirsiDynix
Wireless access
Publications: @ Your Library (Newsletter)
Mem of Woodlands Library Cooperative
Partic in Capitol Area Librs Coop
Open Mon-Fri 10-8, Sat 10-4
Friends of the Library Group

S GANNETT CO INC*, Lansing State Journal Library, 120 E Lenawee, 48919. SAN 308-2350. Tel: 517-377-1008. FAX: 517-377-1298. Web Site: www.lsj.com. *Librn,* Diana Buchanan; *Librn,* Pam Gawronski; E-mail: pgawronski@lansing.gannett.com
Founded 1855
Library Holdings: Bk Vols 900
Restriction: Staff use only

CR GREAT LAKES CHRISTIAN COLLEGE*, Louis M Detro Memorial Library, 6211 W Willow Hwy, 48917. SAN 308-227X. Tel: 517-321-0242, Ext 237. FAX: 517-321-5902. E-mail: library@glcc.edu. Web Site: www.glcc.edu/library. *Dir, Libr & Info Serv,* James Orme; Tel: 517-321-0242, Ext 251, E-mail: jorme@glcc.edu; Staff 3 (MLS 1, Non-MLS 2)
Founded 1949. Enrl 220; Fac 13; Highest Degree: Bachelor
Library Holdings: Bk Vols 47,000; Per Subs 239
Special Collections: Bibles; C S Lewis
Subject Interests: Hist, Lang arts, Music, Theol
Automation Activity & Vendor Info: (Cataloging) Winnebago Software Co; (Circulation) Winnebago Software Co; (Course Reserve) Winnebago Software Co; (ILL) Winnebago Software Co; (OPAC) Winnebago Software Co; (Serials) Winnebago Software Co
Database Vendor: Gale Cengage Learning, OCLC FirstSearch, ProQuest, SerialsSolutions
Partic in Asn of Christian Librs; Midwest Collaborative for Library Services (MCLS); OCLC-LVIS
Open Mon (Winter) 9-9, Tues-Thurs 7:45-9, Fri 7:45-5, Sat 2-4; Mon-Fri (Summer) 9-12 & 1-4

S HISTORICAL SOCIETY OF MICHIGAN, 5815 Executive Dr, 48911. SAN 371-8778. Tel: 517-324-1828. FAX: 517-324-4370. E-mail: hsm@hsmichigan.org. Web Site: www.hsmichigan.org. *Exec Dir,* Larry J Wagenaar
Founded 1828
Library Holdings: Bk Titles 1,700
Special Collections: Michigan History Books
Subject Interests: Local hist, Mich hist
Wireless access
Publications: Historic Michigan Travel Guide (Bi-annually); Michigan History for Kids (Bi-monthly); Michigan History magazine (Bi-monthly); The Chronicle (Quarterly); The Michigan Historical Review; The Michigan History Directory (Reference guide)
Restriction: Mem only, Not a lending libr, Open by appt only

M INGHAM REGIONAL MEDICAL CENTER*, John W Chi Memorial Medical Library, 401 W Greenlawn Ave, 48910-2819. SAN 320-3840. Tel: 517-334-2270. Interlibrary Loan Service Tel: 517-334-2177. FAX: 517-334-2939. Interlibrary Loan Service FAX: 517-334-2181. E-mail: johnchilibrary@irmc.org. Web Site: www.irmc.org. *Med Librn,* Judy Barnes; E-mail: judith.barnes@irmc.org; Staff 5 (MLS 1, Non-MLS 4)
Founded 1913
Library Holdings: AV Mats 1,000; Bk Titles 8,000; Per Subs 500; Talking Bks 100
Subject Interests: Allied health, Consumer health, Med, Nursing, Osteopathy, Pharmacology
Automation Activity & Vendor Info: (ILL) OCLC
Database Vendor: EBSCOhost, OCLC FirstSearch
Publications: Acquisition List (Monthly)
Partic in Docline; Michigan Health Sciences Libraries Association; MLC; National Network of Libraries of Medicine; OCLC Online Computer Library Center, Inc
Open Mon-Fri 8-4:30

J LANSING COMMUNITY COLLEGE LIBRARY*, 200 Technology & Learning Ctr, 419 N Capitol Ave, 48933. (Mail add: 1510 Library, PO Box 40010, 48901-7210), SAN 346-7589. Tel: 517-483-1657. Circulation Tel: 517-483-1626. Interlibrary Loan Service Tel: 517-483-1665. Reference Tel: 517-483-1615. Administration Tel: 517-483-1647. Toll Free Tel: 800-644-4522. FAX: 517-483-5300. Web Site: www.lcc.edu/library. *Dir, Libr Serv,* Elenka Raschkow; Tel: 517-483-1639, E-mail: raschke@lcc.edu; *Electronic Res Librn,* Suzanne Sawyer; Tel: 517-483-9717, E-mail: sawyers@lcc.edu; *Instrul Serv Librn,* Kim Farley; Tel: 517-483-1662, E-mail: farleyk@lcc.edu; *Ref Serv Librn,* Karl Ericson; Tel: 517-483-1650, E-mail: ericsk@lcc.edu; Staff 21 (MLS 9, Non-MLS 12)
Founded 1959. Enrl 19,890; Highest Degree: Associate
Library Holdings: AV Mats 5,974; e-books 25,044; e-journals 8,199; Electronic Media & Resources 100; Bk Titles 120,494; Per Subs 413
Special Collections: Career Coll; Easy Reading Browsing
Subject Interests: Criminal justice, Nursing, Travel info
Automation Activity & Vendor Info: (Acquisitions) Innovative Interfaces, Inc; (Cataloging) Innovative Interfaces, Inc; (Circulation) Innovative Interfaces, Inc; (ILL) Innovative Interfaces, Inc; (Media Booking) Innovative Interfaces, Inc; (OPAC) Innovative Interfaces, Inc; (Serials) Innovative Interfaces, Inc
Database Vendor: Gale Cengage Learning, Innovative Interfaces, Inc, OCLC FirstSearch, ProQuest, SerialsSolutions, Wilson - Wilson Web
Wireless access
Publications: Link (Newsletter)
Partic in Midwest Collaborative for Library Services (MCLS)
Special Services for the Deaf - TDD equip
Special Services for the Blind - Computer with voice synthesizer for visually impaired persons; Reader equip

P LIBRARY OF MICHIGAN*, 702 W Kalamazoo St, 48915. (Mail add: PO Box 30007, 48909-0007), SAN 346-7708. Tel: 517-373-1580. Interlibrary Loan Service Tel: 517-373-8926. Reference Tel: 517-373-1300. Toll Free Tel: 877-479-0021. FAX: 517-373-5700. Interlibrary Loan Service FAX: 517-373-3381. Toll Free FAX: 800-292-2431 (MI only). E-mail: librarian@michigan.gov. Web Site: www.michigan.gov/libraryofmichigan. *State Librn,* Randy Riley; Tel: 517-373-9464, E-mail: rileyr@michigan.gov; *Dir, Statewide Libr Serv,* Sheryl Mase; Tel: 517-373-4331, E-mail: mases@michigan.gov; *Asst Dir,* Don Todaro; Tel: 517-373-1395, E-mail: todarod@michigan.gov; *Law Librn,* Kim Koscielniak; Tel: 517-373-4697, E-mail: koscielniakk@michigan.gov; *Electronic Res Coordr, Ref Librn,* Janice Murphy; Tel: 517-373-1302, E-mail: murphyj3@michigan.gov; *E-Library & Outreach Coordr, Notable Bk Coordr,* Position Currently Open; *Acq, Ser,* Mary Rumler; Fax: 517-373-8936, E-mail: rumlerm@michigan.gov; *Cat,* Tim Watters; Tel: 517-373-3071, E-mail: watterst@michigan.gov; *Mich Doc,* Bernadette Bartlett; Tel: 517-373-2971, E-mail: bartlettb@michigan.gov; *Rare Bks,* Carol Fink; Tel: 517-373-3765, E-mail: finkc2@michigan.gov; Staff 33 (MLS 22, Non-MLS 11)
Founded 1828
Special Collections: Federal & Michigan Document Coll; Michigan Resources Coll; Rare Book Room. State Document Depository; US Document Depository
Subject Interests: Law, Mich, Pub policy
Automation Activity & Vendor Info: (Acquisitions) Innovative Interfaces, Inc; (Cataloging) Innovative Interfaces, Inc; (Circulation) Innovative Interfaces, Inc; (ILL) OCLC; (OPAC) Innovative Interfaces, Inc; (Serials) Innovative Interfaces, Inc
Database Vendor: Gale Cengage Learning, HeinOnline, LexisNexis, Newsbank, ProQuest, Westlaw
Wireless access
Publications: Certification Handbook; Library Laws Handbook (Online only); Library of Michigan/Library of Michigan Foundation Annual Report; LM4X (Online only); LSTA 5-Year Plan; LSTA Report; Michigan Interactive Library Directory (Online only); Michigan Public Libraries Data Digest
Open Mon-Fri 10-5

L LIBRARY OF MICHIGAN*, State Law Library, 702 W Kalamazoo St, 48909. (Mail add: PO Box 30007, 48909-7507), SAN 370-9353. Tel: 517-373-0630. E-mail: lmlawlib@michigan.gov. Web Site: www.michigan.gov/lawlibrary. *Law Librn,* Kimberly Koscielniak; E-mail: koscielniakk@michigan.gov; *Ref Librn,* Timothy Watters; E-mail: watterst@michigan.gov. Subject Specialists: *Law,* Kimberly Koscielniak; *Law,* Timothy Watters; Staff 2.5 (MLS 2.5)
Library Holdings: Bk Vols 200,000; Per Subs 200
Automation Activity & Vendor Info: (Cataloging) Innovative Interfaces, Inc; (Circulation) Innovative Interfaces, Inc; (OPAC) Innovative Interfaces, Inc
Wireless access
Open Mon-Fri 10-5

P MICHIGAN COMMISSION FOR THE BLIND - BRAILLE & TALKING BOOK LIBRARY*, Michigan Library & Historical Ctr, 702 W Kalamazoo St, 48915-1703. (Mail add: PO Box 30007, 48909-7507), SAN 308-2334. Tel: 517-373-5614. Toll Free Tel: 800-992-9012. FAX: 517-373-5865. Toll Free FAX: 800-726-7323. E-mail: DLEG-BTBL@michigan.gov. Web Site: www.michigan.gov/mcb. *Mgr,* Sue Chinault; Tel: 517-373-5353, E-mail: chinaults@michigan.gov; Staff 9 (MLS 5, Non-MLS 4)
Founded 1931
Library Holdings: Bk Titles 15,000; Bk Vols 315,022; Talking Bks 60,000
Special Collections: Finnish Language, cassettes; Michigan History & Authors, cassettes
Publications: InFocus (Newsletter)
Partic in Consortium of User Libraries
Special Services for the Blind - Volunteer serv
Open Mon-Fri 8-5
Restriction: Restricted access

G MICHIGAN DEPARTMENT OF TRANSPORTATION LIBRARY*, 425 W Ottawa, 48909. (Mail add: PO Box 30050, Library B155, 48909-7550), SAN 308-2318. Tel: 517-373-8548. FAX: 517-241-3194. *Librn,* Alexandra Briseno; E-mail: brisenoa1@michigan.gov; Staff 1 (MLS 1)
Founded 1964
Library Holdings: Bk Titles 26,000; Bk Vols 31,000
Special Collections: Transportation Research Board
Subject Interests: Transportation
Automation Activity & Vendor Info: (Cataloging) OCLC Connexion; (Circulation) OCLC; (ILL) OCLC WorldShare Interlibrary Loan
Wireless access
Partic in Cap Area Libr Consortium; Midwest Collaborative for Library Services (MCLS); Midwest Transportation Knowledge Network (MTKN); OCLC Online Computer Library Center, Inc
Restriction: Govt use only, Staff use only

G MICHIGAN LEGISLATIVE SERVICE BUREAU LIBRARY*, Boji Tower, 4th Flr, 48909. (Mail add: PO Box 30036, 48909-7773), SAN 326-4203. Tel: 517-373-5200. FAX: 517-373-0171. *Dir,* Karen East; E-mail: keast@legislature.mi.gov; Staff 2 (Non-MLS 2)
Founded 1941
Library Holdings: Bk Titles 15,750; Bk Vols 17,350; Per Subs 115
Special Collections: Legislative Reports (docs); Michigan Law (bks)
Subject Interests: Govt, Law
Publications: Guide to Legal Research in the Legislative Service Bureau Library; Recent Acquisitions in the Legislative Service Bureau Library
Restriction: Not open to pub

G MICHIGAN STATE DEPARTMENT OF NATURAL RESOURCES & ENVIRONMENT LIBRARY*, Constitution Hall, 525 W Allegan, 48913. (Mail add: PO Box 30273, 48909-7773), SAN 371-733X. Tel: 517-241-9536. FAX: 517-241-2915. *Librn,* Emily Weingartz; E-mail: weingartze@michigan.gov
Founded 1981
Library Holdings: Bk Titles 5,000
Subject Interests: Great Lakes, Pollution, Toxicology

Open Mon-Fri 7-5
Restriction: Non-circulating to the pub

S RIGHT TO LIFE OF MICHIGAN, Mid-Michigan Resource Center, 233 N Walnut St, 48933-1121. SAN 373-210X. Tel: 517-487-3376. FAX: 517-487-6453. E-mail: info@rtl.org. Web Site: www.rtl.org. *Coordr,* Laura Hammes
Library Holdings: Bk Vols 200
Subject Interests: Abortion, Euthanasia
Open Mon-Fri 8:30-4:30

M SPARROW HEALTH SYSTEM*, Sparrow Health Sciences Library, 1200 E Michigan Ave, Ste 111, 48912. SAN 308-2342. Tel: 517-364-5660. Reference Tel: 517-364-5660, Ext 1. Administration Tel: 517-364-5656. FAX: 517-364-5665. E-mail: medical.library@sparrow.org. Web Site: www.sparrow.org/sparrowlibrary. *Mgr, Libr Serv,* Michael Simmons; E-mail: michael.simmons@sparrow.org; Staff 3 (MLS 1, Non-MLS 2)
Library Holdings: e-books 2,500; e-journals 25,000; Bk Titles 7,000; Bk Vols 3,780; Per Subs 2,500
Subject Interests: Evidence-based med, Nursing, Point-of-care res
Automation Activity & Vendor Info: (Cataloging) EOS International; (Circulation) EOS International; (OPAC) EOS International; (Serials) EOS International
Database Vendor: Blackwell, DynaMed, EBSCOhost, Elsevier, EOS International, Gale Cengage Learning, Ingenta, McGraw-Hill, MD Consult, Medline, Micromedex, OCLC, OVID Technologies, PubMed, SerialsSolutions, Springer-Verlag, STAT!Ref (Teton Data Systems), Wiley
Wireless access
Function: For res purposes, Health sci info serv, Online searches, Ref serv available
Partic in Michigan Health Sciences Libraries Association; Midwest Collaborative for Library Services (MCLS); National Network of Libraries of Medicine Greater Midwest Region
Open Mon-Fri 7-5
Restriction: Open to fac, students & qualified researchers, Open to pub for ref & circ; with some limitations

CL THOMAS M COOLEY LAW SCHOOL LIBRARIES*, Brennan Law Library, 300 S Capitol Ave, 48901. (Mail add: PO Box 13038, 48901 3038), SAN 308-2261. Tel: 517-371-5140. Circulation Tel: 517-371-5140, Ext 3100. Reference Tel: 517-371-5140, Ext 3111. Toll Free Tel: 866-733-3375. FAX: 517-334-5715, 517-334-5717. Web Site: www.cooley.edu/library. *Assoc Dean,* Duane Strojny; Tel: 517-371-5140, Ext 3401, E-mail: strojnyd@cooley.edu; *Assoc Dir,* Clare Membiela; Tel: 517-371-5140, Ext 3402, E-mail: membielc@cooley.edu; *Head, Circ,* Eric Hoheisel; Tel: 517-371-5140, Ext 3311, E-mail: hoheisee@cooley.edu; *Head, Tech Serv,* Pamela Bartlett; Tel: 517-371-5140, Ext 3410, E-mail: bartletp@cooley.edu; *Admin Librn,* Eric Kennedy; Tel: 517-371-5140, Ext 3306, E-mail: kennedye@cooley.edu; *Cat Librn,* Dennis Gliszczak, Tel: 517-371-5140, Ext 3412, E-mail: gliszczad@cooley.edu; *Ref Librn,* Randy Foreman; Tel: 517-371-5140, Ext 3305, E-mail: foremanr@cooley.edu; *Ref Librn,* Brian Van Pottelsberghe; Tel: 517-371-5140, Ext 3309, E-mail: vanpottb@cooley.edu; *Ref & Instrul Serv Librn,* John Michaud; Tel: 517-371-5140, Ext 3308, E-mail: michaudj@cooley.edu; *Ref & ILL Librn,* Ardena Walsh; Tel: 517-371-5140, Ext 3304, E-mail: walshal@cooley.edu; *Circ Supvr,* Elayne Lyne; Tel: 517-371-5140, Ext 3101, E-mail: lynee@cooley.edu; *Ref & Outreach,* Tim Innes; Tel: 517-371-5140, Ext 3303, E-mail: innest@cooley.edu; Staff 13 (MLS 12, Non-MLS 1)
Founded 1972. Enrl 2,000; Fac 63; Highest Degree: Doctorate
Library Holdings: e-books 6,332; Bk Titles 175,000; Bk Vols 535,000; Per Subs 4,335
Special Collections: Michigan Supreme Court Records & Briefs (1907-present), bound volumes. US Document Depository
Automation Activity & Vendor Info: (Acquisitions) Innovative Interfaces, Inc; (Cataloging) Innovative Interfaces, Inc; (Circulation) Innovative Interfaces, Inc; (Course Reserve) Innovative Interfaces, Inc; (OPAC) Innovative Interfaces, Inc; (Serials) Innovative Interfaces, Inc
Database Vendor: LexisNexis, OCLC FirstSearch, Westlaw
Wireless access
Publications: Library Research Guides (various subjects); User's Guide to the Thomas M Cooley Law School Library
Partic in Lexus; OCLC Online Computer Library Center, Inc; Westlaw
Open Mon-Thurs & Sun 7am-1am, Fri & Sat 7am-Midnight

LAPEER

P LAPEER DISTRICT LIBRARY*, 201 Village West Dr S, 48446-1699. SAN 346-7791. Tel: 810-664-9521. FAX: 810-664-8527. Web Site: www.library.lapeer.org. *Dir,* Melissa Malcolm; *Asst Dir, Tech Serv,* Ann Baker; *Head, Children's Dept,* Janet Curtis; *Head, Fiction Serv,* Janelle Martin; *Head, Ref,* Laura Fromwiller; Staff 19 (MLS 7, Non-MLS 12)
Founded 1939. Pop 62,378; Circ 177,293
Library Holdings: Bk Vols 102,148; Per Subs 246
Special Collections: Local History Coll, bks, news clippings; Marguerite de Angeli Coll
Partic in Mideastern Michigan Library Cooperative; Valley Library Consortium
Open Mon-Fri 8-5
Restriction: Access for corporate affiliates
Friends of the Library Group
Branches: 8
CLIFFORD, 9530 Main St, Clifford, 48727. (Mail add: PO Box 233, Clifford, 48727-0233), SAN 346-7821. Tel: 989-761-7393. FAX: 989-761-7541. *Dir,* Melissa Malcolm; *Librn,* Rachael Smyczak
Library Holdings: Bk Vols 4,966; Per Subs 10
Open Mon 11-5, Wed 2-8
COLUMBIAVILLE BRANCH, 4718 First St, Columbiaville, 48421-9143. (Mail add: PO Box 190, Columbiaville, 48421-0190), SAN 346-7856. Tel: 810-793-6100. FAX: 810-793-6243. *Librn,* Barbara Harris
Founded 1876
Library Holdings: Bk Vols 7,385; Per Subs 15
Open Mon & Wed 2-8, Fri 11-5
Friends of the Library Group
MARGUERITE DEANGELI BRANCH, 921 W Nepessing St, 48446, SAN 346-797X. Tel: 810-664-6971. FAX: 810-664-5581. *Dir,* Melissa Malcolm
Library Holdings: Bk Vols 79,659; Per Subs 121
Special Collections: Career Resource Center; Coll & Exhibit on Marguerite deAngeli; Genealogy Coll
Open Mon-Thurs 9-8, Fri & Sat 9-5, Sun 1-5
Friends of the Library Group
ELBA, 5508 Davison Rd, 48446, SAN 346-7880. Tel: 810-653-7200. FAX: 810-653-4267. *Librn,* Mary Ellen Thomas
Library Holdings: Bk Vols 3,214; Per Subs 10
Open Mon 9-3, Thurs 1-7
GOODLAND, 2370 N Van Dyke Rd, Imlay City, 48444, SAN 346-7910. Tel: 810-724-1970. FAX: 810-724-5612. *Librn,* Yvonne Brown; *Librn,* Linda Long
Library Holdings: Bk Vols 3,385; Per Subs 12
Subject Interests: Genealogy
Open Tues 2-8, Thurs 11-5
Friends of the Library Group
HADLEY BRANCH, 3556 Hadley Rd, Hadley, 48440. (Mail add: PO Box 199, Hadley, 48440-0199), SAN 346-7945. Tel: 810-797-4101. FAX: 810-797-2912. *Librn,* Debi Rasmussen; *Librn,* Jacalyn Woolbright
Library Holdings: Bk Vols 9,716; Per Subs 33
Friends of the Library Group
METAMORA BRANCH, 4018 Oak St, Metamora, 48455. (Mail add: PO Box 77, Metamora, 48455-0077), SAN 346-8003. Tel: 810-678-2991. FAX: 810-678-3253. *Librn,* Carol Kellerman; *Librn,* Pam Orr; *Librn,* Debi Rasmussen
Library Holdings: Bk Vols 9,618; Per Subs 27
Special Collections: Michigan Coll
Open Mon 9-5, Wed & Thurs 11-8, Fri 9-2
Friends of the Library Group
OTTER LAKE BRANCH, 6361 Detroit St, Otter Lake, 48464-9104. (Mail add: PO Box 185, Otter Lake, 48464-0185), SAN 346-8038. Tel: 810-793-6300. FAX: 810-793-7040. *Br Librn,* Gena Bunch; *Librn,* Barbara Harris
Library Holdings: Bk Vols 4,157; Per Subs 16
Open Tues 11-5, Thurs 2-8
Friends of the Library Group

LAWTON

P LAWTON PUBLIC LIBRARY*, 125 S Main St, 49065. (Mail add: PO Box 520, 49065-0520), SAN 308-2369. Tel: 269-624-5481. FAX: 269-624-1909. *Dir,* Chris Roussel; *Asst Librn,* Jo Ann Blum; Staff 4 (MLS 1, Non-MLS 3)
Pop 1,865; Circ 17,680
Library Holdings: Bks on Deafness & Sign Lang 15; Bk Titles 32,000; Per Subs 49
Automation Activity & Vendor Info: (Cataloging) Follett Software; (Circulation) Follett Software; (OPAC) Follett Software
Wireless access
Open Mon-Wed & Fri 10-7, Sat 10-2

LELAND

S LEELANAU HISTORICAL SOCIETY*, Leelanau Historical Museum Archives, 203 E Cedar St, 49654. (Mail add: PO Box 246, 49654-0246), SAN 371-5698. Tel: 231-256-7475. FAX: 231-256-7650. E-mail: info@leelanauhistory.org. Web Site: www.leelanauhistory.org. *Pres,* Francie Gits
Founded 1957
Library Holdings: Bk Vols 500
Special Collections: Oral History

P LELAND TOWNSHIP PUBLIC LIBRARY*, 203 E Cedar, 49654. (Mail add: PO Box 736, 49654-0736), SAN 308-2385. Tel: 231-256-9152. FAX: 231-256-8847. E-mail: lelandlibrary@lelandtownshiplibrary.org. Web Site: www.lelandtownshiplibrary.michlibrary.org. *Librn,* Sylvia Merz; *Asst Librn,* Donna Stowe
Circ 12,000
Library Holdings: AV Mats 10,100; Bk Vols 35,000; Per Subs 60
Special Collections: Michigan History Coll
Wireless access
Partic in Mid-Michigan Library League
Open Mon, Tues, Thurs & Fri 10-5, Wed 10-6, Sat 10-2
Friends of the Library Group

LEONARD

P ADDISON TOWNSHIP PUBLIC LIBRARY*, 1440 Rochester Rd, 48367-3555. SAN 376-6152. Tel: 248-628-7180. FAX: 248-628-6109. *Dir,* Michele Presley
Pop 6,439
Library Holdings: AV Mats 1,306; Bk Titles 27,000; Per Subs 52
Automation Activity & Vendor Info: (Cataloging) SirsiDynix; (Circulation) SirsiDynix; (OPAC) SirsiDynix
Open Mon, Tues & Thurs 10-8, Wed 10-6, Fri & Sat 10-4
Friends of the Library Group

LEROY

P LEROY COMMUNITY LIBRARY*, 104 W Gilbert St, 49655. (Mail add: PO Box 157, 49655-0157), SAN 308-2377. Tel: 231-768-4493. FAX: 231-768-5024. E-mail: leroylibrary@att.net. Web Site: www.leroylibrary.michlibrary.org. *Dir,* Denise Schmidt; *Asst Librn,* Tom Shook
Circ 5,736
Library Holdings: AV Mats 63; Bk Vols 18,222; Per Subs 49; Talking Bks 270
Subject Interests: Mich
Automation Activity & Vendor Info: (Circulation) Auto-Graphics, Inc
Wireless access
Partic in Mich Libr Asn; Mid-Michigan Library League
Open Mon & Fri 10-2, Tues & Thurs 1-6, Wed 12-5, Sat 10-1

LEWISTON

P LEWISTON PUBLIC LIBRARY*, 2851 Kneeland, 49756. (Mail add: PO Box 148, 49756-0148), SAN 376-5865. Tel: 989-786-2985. FAX: 989-786-2985. E-mail: lewistonlib@nemichigan.com. *Librn,* Mary Lou Barber
Library Holdings: Bk Vols 10,025; Per Subs 20
Automation Activity & Vendor Info: (Cataloging) SirsiDynix; (Circulation) SirsiDynix
Wireless access
Open Tues, Thurs & Fri 10-5, Wed 12-6, Sat 10-3
Friends of the Library Group

LEXINGTON

P MOORE PUBLIC LIBRARY*, 7239 Huron Ave, 48450. (Mail add: PO Box 189, 48450-0189), SAN 308-2393. Tel: 810-359-8267. FAX: 810-359-2986. E-mail: lexlibrary@yahoo.com. Web Site: www.lexingtonlibrary.net. *Dir,* Beth Schumacher
Founded 1903. Pop 5,125; Circ 25,000
Jan 2009-Dec 2009 Income $161,000, State $3,000, County $38,000, Locally Generated Income $120,000. Mats Exp $18,900, Books $17,000, Per/Ser (Incl. Access Fees) $1,500, AV Mat $400. Sal $80,000 (Prof $31,000)
Library Holdings: Audiobooks 607; Bks on Deafness & Sign Lang 2; CDs 75; DVDs 60; Large Print Bks 150; Bk Titles 16,703; Per Subs 50; Videos 500
Automation Activity & Vendor Info: (Circulation) Follett Software
Wireless access
Partic in White Pine Libr Coop
Open Mon & Thurs 10-7, Tues, Wed & Fri 10-5, Sat 10-1
Friends of the Library Group

LINCOLN PARK

P LINCOLN PARK PUBLIC LIBRARY*, 1381 Southfield Rd, 48146. SAN 308-2415. Tel: 313-381-0374. FAX: 313-381-2205. Web Site: www.lincoln-park.lib.mi.us. *Dir,* Theresa Powers
Founded 1925. Pop 40,008; Circ 89,500
Library Holdings: Bk Vols 56,000; Per Subs 120
Automation Activity & Vendor Info: (Cataloging) SirsiDynix; (Circulation) SirsiDynix
Partic in The Library Network
Open Mon-Thurs 12-8, Sat 12-5
Friends of the Library Group

LITCHFIELD

P LITCHFIELD DISTRICT LIBRARY, 108 N Chicago St, 49252-9738. (Mail add: PO Box 357, 49252-0357), SAN 308-2423. Tel: 517-542-3887. FAX: 517-542-3887. E-mail: litchfielddistrictlibrary@yahoo.com. Web Site: www.litchfieldddl.michlibrary.org. *Libr Dir,* Janet Barton; *Asst Dir,* Shelly Wykes
Library Holdings: Audiobooks 1,265; Bks-By-Mail 571; CDs 129; DVDs 2,993; Large Print Bks 635; Bk Titles 10,000; Bk Vols 16,912; Per Subs 12; Videos 104
Automation Activity & Vendor Info: (Acquisitions) Follett Software; (Cataloging) Follett Software; (Circulation) Follett Software; (Course Reserve) Follett Software
Database Vendor: Baker & Taylor
Wireless access
Mem of Woodlands Library Cooperative
Open Mon, Wed & Fri 10-6, Sat 9-1

LIVONIA

P LIVONIA PUBLIC LIBRARY*, 32777 Five Mile Rd, 48154-3045. SAN 346-8062. Tel: 734-466-2450. FAX: 734-458-6011. Web Site: livonia.lib.mi.us.
Founded 1958. Pop 100,545; Circ 761,307
Library Holdings: Bk Vols 256,442; Per Subs 672
Special Collections: US Document Depository
Automation Activity & Vendor Info: (Cataloging) SirsiDynix; (Circulation) SirsiDynix; (ILL) SirsiDynix
Database Vendor: Gale Cengage Learning, OCLC FirstSearch
Special Services for the Deaf - TTY equip
Special Services for the Blind - Braille bks; Magnifiers
Open Mon-Thurs 9-9, Fri & Sat 9-5, Sun (Winter) 1-5
Friends of the Library Group
Branches: 4
CIVIC CENTER, 32777 Five Mile Rd, 48154-3045, SAN 328-9796. Tel: 734-466-2450. Circulation Tel: 734-466-2491. Reference Tel: 734-466-2490. FAX: 734-458-6011. Web Site: livonia.lib.mi.us/civic.html. *Actg Dir,* Kathleen L Monroe; Tel: 734-466-2480, E-mail: kmonroe@tln.lib.mi.us; *Automation Syst Coordr,* Dolores Hayden; Tel: 734-466-2675, E-mail: dhayden@tln.lib.mi.us; *Ref Serv, Ad,* Carl Katafiasz; *Ref Serv, Ch,* Trinidad Turse; Tel: 734-466-2454, E-mail: tturse@tln.lib.mi.us; Staff 35 (MLS 15, Non-MLS 20)
Founded 1988. Circ 486,457
Library Holdings: Bk Vols 162,821; Per Subs 125
Special Services for the Blind - Braille bks; Magnifiers
Open Mon-Thurs 9-9, Fri-Sat 9-5, Sun (Winter) 1-5
Friends of the Library Group
ALFRED NOBLE BRANCH, 32901 Plymouth Rd, 48150-1793, SAN 346-8151. Tel: 734-421-6600. FAX: 734-421-6606. Web Site: livonia.lib.mi.us/noble.html. *Br Librn,* Toni LaPorte; E-mail: laporte@livonia.lib.mi.us; *Librn,* Patty Goonis; E-mail: pgoonis@livonia.lib.mi.us; *Ch Serv,* Michelle Stiennon; E-mail: msteinnon@livonia.lib.mi.us; *YA Serv,* Ken Bignotti; E-mail: bignotti@tln.lib.mi.us; Staff 7 (MLS 4, Non-MLS 3)
Founded 1958. Circ 115,909
Library Holdings: Bk Vols 51,450; Per Subs 162
Open Mon 12-8, Wed 10-6
Friends of the Library Group
CARL SANDBURG BRANCH, 30100 W Seven Mile Rd, 48152-1918, SAN 346-8127. Tel: 248-893-4010. FAX: 248-476-6230. Web Site: livonia.lib.mi.us/sandburg.html. *Br Librn,* Toni LaPorte; E-mail: laporte@tln.lib.mi.us; *Ch Serv,* Michelle Stiennon; E-mail: mstiennon@livonia.lib.mi.us; *YA Serv,* Patty Goonis; E-mail: pgoonis@livonia.lib.mi.us; Staff 6 (MLS 3, Non-MLS 3)
Founded 1961. Circ 158,941
Library Holdings: Bk Vols 42,171; Per Subs 125
Open Tues 12-8, Sat 9-5
Friends of the Library Group
VEST POCKET, 15128 Farmington Rd, 48154-5417. Tel: 734-466-2559. Web Site: livonia.lib.mi.us/vest.html. *Br Librn,* Toni LaPorte; E-mail: laporte@livonia.lib.mi.us; Staff 1 (MLS 1)
Founded 1972
Library Holdings: Bk Vols 6,475
Open Mon-Fri 9:30-3:30
Friends of the Library Group

C MADONNA UNIVERSITY LIBRARY*, 36600 Schoolcraft Rd, 48150-1173. SAN 346-8186. Tel: 734-432-5703. Interlibrary Loan Service Tel: 734-452-5679. Reference Tel: 734-432-5767. Toll Free Tel: 800-852-4951. FAX: 734-432-5687. Web Site: ww3.madonna.edu/library. *Dir,* Joanne Lumetta; Tel: 734-432-5689, E-mail: jlumetta@madonna.edu; *Coll Mgt Librn,* William A Vine; Tel: 734-432-5685, E-mail: wvine@madonna.edu; *Syst Mgr,* Elizabeth Bodenmiller; Tel: 734-432-5702; Staff 17 (MLS 7, Non-MLS 10)

Founded 1947
Library Holdings: e-journals 15,396; Bk Titles 95,300; Bk Vols 115,012; Per Subs 600
Special Collections: Artifacts from Diverse Ethnic Cultures; Institutional Archives; Transcultural Nursing Materials (Madeline Leininger Coll)
Subject Interests: Bus, Educ, Lang arts, Lit, Nursing, Paralegal studies, Sign lang
Automation Activity & Vendor Info: (Acquisitions) SirsiDynix; (Cataloging) SirsiDynix; (Circulation) SirsiDynix; (Course Reserve) SirsiDynix; (OPAC) SirsiDynix; (Serials) SirsiDynix
Database Vendor: EBSCOhost, Gale Cengage Learning, LexisNexis, Newsbank, OCLC FirstSearch, OVID Technologies, ProQuest, Westlaw, Wilson - Wilson Web
Publications: Information Guide Series; Library Handbook; New Book List; Reference Guide Series; Subject Guide Series
Partic in OCLC Online Computer Library Center, Inc; Southeastern Michigan League of Libraries
Open Mon-Thurs (Fall & Winter) 8am-10:30pm, Fri 8-7, Sat 9-5:30, Sun 1-5; Mon-Thurs (Spring & Summer) 8am-10pm, Fri 8-4:30, Sat 11-5
Friends of the Library Group

J SCHOOLCRAFT COLLEGE*, Eric J Bradner Library, 18600 Haggerty Rd, 48152-2696. SAN 308-244X. Tel: 734-462-4440. FAX: 734-462-4495. E-mail: library@schoolcraft.edu. Web Site: www.schoolcraft.edu/library. *Librn,* Roy Nuffer; Tel: 734-462-4400, Ext 5315, E-mail: rnuffer@schoolcraft.edu; *Ref & ILL Librn,* Wayne Pricer; Tel: 734-462-4400, Ext 5317, E-mail: wpricer@schoolcraft.edu; *Tech Serv Librn,* Diane Nesbit; Tel: 734-462-4400, Ext 5319, E-mail: dnesbit@schoolcraft.edu; *Circ Supvr,* Lissa McCarthy; Tel: 734-462-4400, Ext 5326
Founded 1964
Library Holdings: Bk Vols 70,000; Per Subs 300
Special Collections: US Document Depository
Automation Activity & Vendor Info: (Acquisitions) SirsiDynix; (Cataloging) SirsiDynix; (Circulation) SirsiDynix; (Course Reserve) SirsiDynix; (ILL) SirsiDynix; (Media Booking) SirsiDynix; (OPAC) SirsiDynix; (Serials) SirsiDynix
Wireless access
Departmental Libraries:
RADCLIFF LIBRARY, 1751 Radcliff St, Rm RC355, Garden City, 48135, SAN 329-2630. Tel: 734-462-4400, Ext 6020. FAX: 734-462-4743. *Librn,* Graham Burrell; Tel: 734-462-4400, Ext 6019, E-mail: gburrell@schoolcraft.edu
Library Holdings: Bk Vols 13,000; Per Subs 228

LUDINGTON

P MASON COUNTY DISTRICT LIBRARY*, Ludington Branch, 217 E Ludington Ave, 49431-2118. (Mail add: PO Box 549, 49431-0549), SAN 308-2458. Tel: 231-843-8465. FAX: 231-843-1491. Interlibrary Loan Service E-mail: librarian@masoncounty.lib.mi.us. Web Site: www.masoncounty.lib.mi.us. *Dir,* Robert T Dickson; E-mail: rdickson@masoncounty.lib.mi.us; *Asst Dir,* Susan Carlson; E-mail: scarlson@masoncounty.lib.mi.us; Staff 10 (MLS 1, Non-MLS 9)
Founded 1905. Pop 28,800; Circ 180,000
Library Holdings: Bk Vols 120,000; Per Subs 200
Special Collections: State Document Depository
Automation Activity & Vendor Info: (Acquisitions) Auto-Graphics, Inc; (Cataloging) Auto-Graphics, Inc; (Circulation) Auto-Graphics, Inc
Database Vendor: EBSCOhost
Wireless access
Publications: Friends of LPL Potpourri (Newsletter); Subject bibliographies
Partic in Mid-Michigan Library League; OCLC Online Computer Library Center, Inc
Open Mon-Wed 9-8, Thurs & Fri 9-6, Sat 9-5, Sun (Sept-May) 12-4
Friends of the Library Group
Branches: 1
SCOTTVILLE BRANCH, 204 E State St, Scottville, 49454-9506, SAN 308-406X. Tel: 231-757-2588. FAX: 231-757-3401.
Founded 1941. Pop 28,000; Circ 75,000
Automation Activity & Vendor Info: (Cataloging) Auto-Graphics, Inc; (Circulation) Auto-Graphics, Inc
Open Mon-Wed 9-8, Thurs & Fri 9-6, Sat 9-5, Sun (Sept-May) 12-4
Friends of the Library Group

S MASON COUNTY HISTORICAL SOCIETY*, Historic White Pine Village Research Library, 1687 S Lakeshore Dr, 49431. SAN 321-4702. Tel: 231-843-4808. FAX: 231-843-7089. E-mail: info@historicwhitepinevillage.org. Web Site: www.historicwhitepinevillage.org. *Exec Dir,* Ronald M Wood; E-mail: rmwood@historicwhitepinevillage.org; *Coordr, Coll Serv,* Neva Wood
Founded 1937
Library Holdings: Bk Titles 700; Per Subs 10
Special Collections: Business-Lumbering (Charles Mears Coll), diaries; Civil War (B S Mills Coll); Civil War (Hazel Oldt Coll), letters; Documentary on Wintertime Car Ferry Service across Lake Michigan, video; Lumbering (Jake Lunde Coll), a-tapes, microfilm of Mason County Papers, slides; Maritime Coll. Oral History
Subject Interests: Agr, Civil War, Genealogy, Local hist, Lumbering, Maritime
Function: Res libr
Publications: Centennial Farms of Mason County; Historic Mason County - 1980; Mason County Pictorial History - 1987; Mason Memories; Nature Power Then & Now
Open Tues-Sat (May-Sept) 10-5; Tues & Thurs (Oct-April) 11-4
Restriction: Non-circulating

LUTHER

P LUTHER AREA PUBLIC LIBRARY*, 115 State St, 49656. (Mail add: PO Box 86, 49656-0086). Tel: 231-797-8006. FAX: 231-797-8010. *Dir,* Gail Ganger; *Asst Librn,* Jody Lucas; *Children's Prog,* Carol Peel
Founded 1979. Pop 3,540; Circ 3,512
Library Holdings: Bk Vols 12,000
Wireless access
Partic in Mid-Michigan Library League
Open Mon, Wed & Fri 10:30-6, Thurs 2-6, Sat 10:30-1:30
Friends of the Library Group

LYONS

P LYONS TOWNSHIP DISTRICT LIBRARY*, 309 Bridge St, 48851. (Mail add: PO Box 185, 48851-0185). Tel: 989-855-3414. FAX: 989-855-2069. E-mail: lyonslib@hotmail.com. *Dir,* Vicki Reinhardt; *Asst Librn,* Nancy Maki; *Asst Librn,* Christina Russell; *Asst Librn,* Cindy Thayer
Library Holdings: Bk Vols 20,000; Per Subs 36
Mem of Woodlands Library Cooperative

MACKINAC ISLAND

P MACKINAC ISLAND PUBLIC LIBRARY*, 903 Main St, 49757. (Mail add: PO Box 903, 49757-0903), SAN 308-2466. Tel: 906-847-3421. FAX: 906-847-3368. *Dir,* Anne L St Onge
Founded 1936. Pop 469; Circ 6,500
Library Holdings: Bk Vols 12,000; Per Subs 28
Subject Interests: Hist
Partic in OCLC Online Computer Library Center, Inc
Open Tues-Sat 11-5:30
Friends of the Library Group

MACKINAW CITY

P MACKINAW AREA PUBLIC LIBRARY, 528 W Central Ave, 49701-9681. (Mail add: PO Box 67, 49701-0067), SAN 346-8240. Tel: 231-436-5451. FAX: 231-436-7344. Web Site: www.mackinawareapubliclibrary.org. *Dir,* Jolene E Michaels, E-mail: mackinaw3@gmail.com. Subject Specialists: *Local hist, Mich,* Jolene E Michaels; Staff 3 (Non-MLS 3)
Founded 1968. Pop 4,689; Circ 66,182
Jul 2009-Jun 2010 Income (Main Library and Branch(s)) $196,601, State $2,339, Locally Generated Income $165,381, Other $28,881. Mats Exp $168,197, Books $19,662, Per/Ser (Incl. Access Fees) $2,331, Micro $148, AV Mat $2,799. Sal $117,325 (Prof $20,800)
Library Holdings: Audiobooks 607; CDs 2,000; DVDs 1,643; Bk Titles 39,384; Per Subs 72; Videos 3,151
Special Collections: Durant Rolls; Extensive Michigan History Coll
Automation Activity & Vendor Info: (ILL) Mel Cat
Wireless access
Publications: Memories of Mackinaw by Judy Ranville & Nancy Campbell (Local historical information)
Partic in Northland Library Cooperative
Special Services for the Deaf - Bks on deafness & sign lang
Special Services for the Blind - Audio mat; Bks on cassette; Bks on CD; Cassettes; Large print bks; Talking bks
Open Mon, Tues, Thurs & Fri 11-5, Wed 12-8
Branches: 2
BLISS BRANCH, 265 Sturgeon Bay Trail, Levering, 49755, SAN 346-8259. Tel: 231-537-2927. *Br Head,* Mary Hohlbein; E-mail: blissbranch@gmail.com. Subject Specialists: *Local hist,* Mary Hohlbein; Staff 1 (Non-MLS 1)
Pop 572; Circ 6,106
Subject Interests: Local hist
Automation Activity & Vendor Info: (ILL) Mel Cat
Function: Prog for adults, Prog for children & young adult, Spoken cassettes & CDs, Summer reading prog, VHS videos
Special Services for the Blind - Audio mat; Bks on cassette; Bks on CD; Large print bks; Talking bks; Videos on blindness & phys handicaps
Open Tues 2-8, Fri 1-5
Restriction: Open to pub for ref & circ; with some limitations

PELLSTON BRANCH, 125 N Milton St, Pellston, 49769-9301. (Mail add: PO Box 456, Pellston, 49769-0456), SAN 346-8275. Tel: 231-539-8858. E-mail: pellstonbranch@gmail.com. *Br Head,* Tammy Gregory; Staff 1 (Non-MLS 1)
Circ 18,705
Function: ILL available, Photocopying/Printing, Prog for children & young adult, Spoken cassettes & CDs, Summer reading prog, VHS videos
Special Services for the Blind - Audio mat; Bks on cassette; Bks on CD; Large print bks; Talking bks; Videos on blindness & phys handicaps
Open Mon 11-4, Tues & Thurs 2-7
Restriction: Open to pub for ref & circ; with some limitations

MADISON HEIGHTS

P MADISON HEIGHTS PUBLIC LIBRARY*, 240 W 13 Mile Rd, 48071-1894. SAN 308-2474. Tel: 248-588-7763. Interlibrary Loan Service Tel: 248-837-2854. Administration Tel: 248-837-2852. Information Services Tel: 248-837-2851. FAX: 248-588-2470. E-mail: library@madison-heights.org. Web Site: www.madison-heights.org/library. *Libr Dir,* Roslyn Yerman; E-mail: ryerman@madison-hgts.lib.mi.us; *Head Ref Librn,* Sally Arrivee; E-mail: arrivee@madison-hgts.lib.mi.us; *Adult Ref Librn,* Krista Ghazar; Tel: 248-837-2850, E-mail: kghazar@madison-hgts.lib.mi.us; *Commun Serv Librn,* Jane Haigh; Tel: 248-837-2856, E-mail: jhaigh@madison-hgts.lib.mi.us; *Youth Serv Librn,* Amanda Gehrke; E-mail: gehrke@madison-hgts.lib.mi.us; *Libr Tech,* Rebecca Willemsen; E-mail: rebeccaw@madison-hgts.lib.mi.us; Staff 6.2 (MLS 3.1, Non-MLS 3.1)
Founded 1954. Pop 29,694; Circ 100,392
Jul 2012-Jun 2013 Income $584,233. Mats Exp $56,207, Books $40,707, Per/Ser (Incl. Access Fees) $6,500, AV Mat $9,000. Sal $310,893 (Prof $197,530)
Library Holdings: Audiobooks 2,957; CDs 3,097; DVDs 4,362; e-books 8,138; Bk Vols 95,760; Per Subs 100; Videos 4,362
Special Collections: Historical. US Document Depository
Automation Activity & Vendor Info: (Acquisitions) SirsiDynix; (Cataloging) SirsiDynix; (Circulation) SirsiDynix; (ILL) SirsiDynix; (OPAC) SirsiDynix; (Serials) SirsiDynix
Database Vendor: 3M Library Systems
Wireless access
Function: Archival coll, Audiobks via web, AV serv, Bk club(s), Bks on cassette, Bks on CD, Children's prog, Computers for patron use, Copy machines, Exhibits, Fax serv, Free DVD rentals, Govt ref serv, Handicapped accessible, Holiday prog, Homebound delivery serv, ILL available, Large print keyboards, Magnifiers for reading, Mail & tel request accepted, Music CDs, Online cat, Outreach serv, OverDrive digital audio bks, Photocopying/Printing, Preschool reading prog, Prog for children & young adult, Pub access computers, Ref & res, Ref serv available, Ref serv in person, Story hour, Summer reading prog, Tax forms, Telephone ref, VHS videos, Wheelchair accessible
Partic in The Library Network
Open Mon, Tues & Thurs 9-8, Wed & Fri 9-5, Sat 10-5
Friends of the Library Group

MANCELONA

P MANCELONA TOWNSHIP LIBRARY*, 202 W State St, 49659. (Mail add: PO Box 499, 49659-0499), SAN 308-2490. Tel: 231-587-9451. *Librn,* Kathy Pintcke
Circ 16,983
Library Holdings: Bk Vols 16,000; Per Subs 10
Wireless access
Partic in Mid-Michigan Library League
Open Tues, Wed & Fri 10-6, Thurs 12-8
Friends of the Library Group

MANCHESTER

P MANCHESTER DISTRICT LIBRARY*, 912 City Rd (M-52), 48158-0540. (Mail add: PO Box 540, 48158-5140), SAN 308-2504. Tel: 734-428-8045. Web Site: www.manchesterlibrary.info. *Dir,* Heather Sturm; Staff 4 (MLS 2, Non-MLS 2)
Founded 1838. Pop 7,300
Library Holdings: AV Mats 1,500; Large Print Bks 100; Bk Titles 28,000; Per Subs 83; Talking Bks 500
Special Collections: Manchester Michigan Area History
Automation Activity & Vendor Info: (OPAC) SirsiDynix
Database Vendor: Gale Cengage Learning, OCLC FirstSearch, Wilson - Wilson Web
Wireless access
Function: Archival coll, Handicapped accessible, ILL available, Prog for children & young adult, Ref serv available, Summer reading prog, Telephone ref, Wheelchair accessible
Partic in Midwest Collaborative for Library Services (MCLS); The Library Network
Special Services for the Blind - Bks on cassette; Bks on CD; Copier with enlargement capabilities; Large print bks; Ref serv; Videos on blindness & phys handicaps
Open Mon-Wed 10-8, Fri 10-6, Sat 10-2, Sun 1-5
Restriction: Open to pub for ref & circ; with some limitations
Friends of the Library Group

MANISTEE

S MANISTEE COUNTY HISTORICAL MUSEUM*, Fortier Memorial Library, 425 River St, 49660. SAN 323-5394. Tel: 231-723-5531. E-mail: manisteemuseum@yahoo.com. Web Site: www.manisteemuseum.org. *Dir,* Mark Fedder; Staff 1 (Non-MLS 1)
Library Holdings: Bk Titles 1,000
Subject Interests: Great Lakes maritime hist, Manistee County hist
Open Tues-Sat 10-5
Restriction: Ref only

P MANISTEE COUNTY LIBRARY SYSTEM, 95 Maple St, 49660. SAN 346-8305. Tel: 231-723-2510, 231-723-2519. FAX: 231-723-8270. Web Site: www.manisteelibrary.org. *Dir,* Charles Haemker; E-mail: chaemker@manisteelibrary.org; *Asst Admin, Head, Youth Serv,* Andrea Cosier; E-mail: cosiera@manisteelibrary.org; Staff 20 (MLS 2, Non-MLS 18)
Founded 1903. Pop 24,750
Oct 2014-Sept 2015 Income (Main Library and Branch(s)) $1,354,400. Mats Exp $155,300, Books $74,500, Per/Ser (Incl. Access Fees) $13,900, AV Mat $60,800, Electronic Ref Mat (Incl. Access Fees) $6,100. Sal $566,809 (Prof $126,800)
Library Holdings: Audiobooks 5,103; Bks on Deafness & Sign Lang 200; CDs 2,743; DVDs 11,879; Electronic Media & Resources 10; Large Print Bks 6,132; Microforms 515; Bk Vols 98,675; Per Subs 299; Videos 125
Subject Interests: Local hist, Victorian lit
Automation Activity & Vendor Info: (Cataloging) TLC (The Library Corporation); (Circulation) TLC (The Library Corporation); (OPAC) TLC (The Library Corporation)
Database Vendor: Baker & Taylor, EBSCOhost, Newsbank, TLC (The Library Corporation)
Wireless access
Function: 24/7 Electronic res, 24/7 Online cat, Activity rm, Adult literacy prog, Audiobks via web, Computer training, Computers for patron use, Copy machines, Electronic databases & coll, Fax serv, Home delivery & serv to Sr ctr & nursing homes, ILL available, Magazines, Magnifiers for reading, Music CDs, Online cat, Online info literacy tutorials on the web & in blackboard, OverDrive digital audio bks, Preschool outreach, Prog for adults, Prog for children & young adult, Pub access computers, Ref serv available, Spoken cassettes & CDs, Story hour, Summer reading prog, Tax forms, Teen prog, Telephone ref, Video lending libr
Partic in Mid-Michigan Library League
Special Services for the Blind - Accessible computers; Large print bks; Magnifiers; Playaways (bks on MP3); Talking bk serv referral
Open Mon & Tues 9:30-8, Wed-Fri 9:30-5, Sat 10-3
Friends of the Library Group
Branches: 5
ARCADIA BRANCH, 3586 Glovers Lake Rd, Arcadia, 49613. (Mail add: PO Box 109, Arcadia, 49613-0109), SAN 374-4582. Tel: 231-889-4230. FAX: 231-889-4230. *Br Mgr,* Deanna Draze
Open Tues 12-6, Thurs 12-4, Fri 10-4
Friends of the Library Group
BEAR LAKE LIBRARY, 12325 Virginia St, Bear Lake, 49614. (Mail add: PO Box 266, Bear Lake, 49614-0266), SAN 346-833X. Tel: 231-864-2700. *Br Mgr,* Marcella Guinan
Open Mon-Wed & Fri 11-5, Thurs 1-7, Sat (July & Aug) 9-12
KALEVA BRANCH, 14618 Walta St, Kaleva, 49645. (Mail add: PO Box 125, Kaleva, 49645-0125), SAN 346-8364. Tel: 231-362-3178. FAX: 231-362-3180. *Br Mgr,* Carolyn Tennant; Staff 1 (Non-MLS 1)
Open Mon, Tues & Thurs 11-5, Wed 12-6, Fri 10-4, Sat (June-Aug) 9-12
ONEKAMA BRANCH, 5283 Main St, Onekama, 49675-9701. (Mail add: PO Box 149, Onekama, 49675-0149), SAN 346-8399. Tel: 616-889-4041. *Br Mgr,* Jane Diesing
Pop 582
Open Mon & Tues 11-5, Wed & Thurs 12-6, Fri 10-4, Sat (July & Aug) 9-12
WELLSTON BRANCH, 1451 Seaman Rd, Wellston, 49689-9510. (Mail add: PO Box 162, Wellston, 49689-0162), SAN 346-8429. Tel: 231-848-4013. *Br Mgr,* Joyce Myers; Staff 1 (Non-MLS 1)
Open Mon 1-7, Tues 12-6, Thurs 11-5, Fri 10-4

S MICHIGAN DEPARTMENT OF CORRECTIONS*, Oaks Correctional Facility Library, 1500 Caberfae Way, 49660-0038. Tel: 231-723-8272. FAX: 231-723-8430. *Librn,* Danielle Straubel; E-mail: straubda@michigan.gov
Library Holdings: Bk Vols 15,000
Open Mon-Sun 7:45-10:45, 12:45-3:45 & 5:45-8:45

M WEST SHORE MEDICAL CENTER LIBRARY*, 1465 Parkdale Ave, 49660-9785. Tel: 231-398-1171. *Coordr,* Karen Miller
Library Holdings: Bk Vols 350
Restriction: Staff use only

MANISTIQUE

P MANISTIQUE SCHOOL & PUBLIC LIBRARY*, 100 N Cedar St, 49854-1293. SAN 308-2512. Tel: 906-341-4316. FAX: 906-341-6751. Web Site: www.manistique.k12.mi.us/library. *Dir,* Mary Hook; *Libr Asst,* Bonnie Hoedel
Pop 8,401; Circ 44,459
Library Holdings: Bk Vols 35,000; Per Subs 78
Automation Activity & Vendor Info: (Cataloging) SirsiDynix; (Circulation) SirsiDynix
Open Mon & Thurs 11:30-8, Tues, Wed & Fri 11:30-4
Friends of the Library Group

MAPLE RAPIDS

P MAPLE RAPIDS PUBLIC LIBRARY*, 130 S Maple Ave, 48853. (Mail add: PO Box 410, 48853-0410), SAN 321-4672. Tel: 989-682-4464. FAX: 989-682-4149. E-mail: mrlibrary@mutualdata.com. *Dir,* Marvia Nemetz; *Asst Librn,* Kim Salisbury
Founded 1935. Circ 3,935
Library Holdings: Audiobooks 54; DVDs 1,117; Large Print Bks 53; Bk Titles 13,463; Per Subs 40
Subject Interests: Local hist
Automation Activity & Vendor Info: (Cataloging) Follett Software; (Circulation) Follett Software; (ILL) Mel Cat
Wireless access
Mem of White Pine Library Cooperative
Open Mon & Wed 10-7, Fri 10-5

MARCELLUS

P MARCELLUS TOWNSHIP-WOOD MEMORIAL LIBRARY*, 205 E Main St, 49067. (Mail add: PO Box 49, 49067-0049), SAN 308-2520. Tel: 269-646-9654. FAX: 269-646-9603. *Librn,* Christine Nofsinger; E-mail: cnofsinger@gmail.com
Circ 15,860
Library Holdings: Bk Titles 30,000; Per Subs 108
Automation Activity & Vendor Info: (Cataloging) Follett Software; (Circulation) Follett Software
Wireless access
Partic in Southwest Michigan Library Cooperative
Open Mon, Tues & Thurs 12-7, Wed 10-7, Fri 12-5, Sat 10-2
Friends of the Library Group

MARENISCO

S MICHIGAN DEPARTMENT OF CORRECTIONS*, Ojibway Correctional Facility Library, PO Box 236, 49947. Tel: 906-787-2217. FAX: 906-787-2324. *Librn,* Thomas G Lee; E-mail: leetg@michigan.gov; *Asst Librn,* Kathy Kafczynski
Library Holdings: Bk Vols 5,000
Automation Activity & Vendor Info: (ILL) Winnebago Software Co
Open Mon-Sun 7am-8:30pm

MARION

P M ALICE CHAPIN MEMORIAL LIBRARY*, 120 E Main St, 49665. (Mail add: PO Box 549, 49665), SAN 308-2539. Tel: 231-743-2421. FAX: 231-743-2421. E-mail: marionlibrary@sbcglobal.net. *Dir,* Shelley Ann Scott; Staff 3 (Non-MLS 3)
Library Holdings: Bk Vols 22,500
Wireless access
Partic in Mid-Michigan Library League
Open Mon-Fri 10-5, Sat 10-Noon

MARLETTE

P MARLETTE DISTRICT LIBRARY*, 3116 Main St, 48453. SAN 308-2547. Tel: 989-635-2838. FAX: 989-635-8005. Web Site: www.marlettelibrary.org. *Dir,* Jessica Moore; E-mail: j.moore@vlc.lib.mi.us; Staff 3 (Non-MLS 3)
Founded 1921. Pop 5,815; Circ 48,608
Apr 2005-Mar 2006 Income $108,900. Mats Exp $19,400. Sal $46,500
Library Holdings: DVDs 200; Bk Titles 20,505; Per Subs 55; Talking Bks 650
Special Collections: Local Newspaper, microfilm; Michigan Coll
Automation Activity & Vendor Info: (Cataloging) SirsiDynix; (Circulation) SirsiDynix; (OPAC) SirsiDynix; (Serials) SirsiDynix
Database Vendor: SirsiDynix
Partic in Valley Libr Consortium; White Pine Libr Coop
Open Mon, Wed & Fri 9-5, Tues & Thurs 12-8, Sat 9-2

MARQUETTE

M MARQUETTE GENERAL HEALTH SYSTEM*, Kevin F O'Brien Health Sciences Library, East 84 Bldg, 3rd Flr, 580 W College Ave, 49855. SAN 308-2563. Tel: 906-225-3429. FAX: 906-225-3524. Web Site: www.mgh.org/library/index.html. *Libr Mgr,* Janis Lubenow; E-mail: janis.lubenow@mghs.org
Founded 1974
Library Holdings: e-journals 200; Bk Titles 2,700; Per Subs 100
Subject Interests: Allied health, Med, Nursing
Automation Activity & Vendor Info: (Cataloging) SIRSI WorkFlows; (OPAC) SirsiDynix; (Serials) SirsiDynix
Database Vendor: Cinahl, Dialog, EBSCOhost, OCLC FirstSearch, OVID Technologies, STAT!Ref (Teton Data Systems), UpToDate
Wireless access
Partic in Greater Midwest Regional Medical Libr Network; Medical Library Association (MLA); Michigan Health Sciences Libraries Association; Upper Peninsula Health Sci Libr Consort; Upper Peninsula Region of Library Cooperation, Inc
Open Mon-Fri 9-4

S MARQUETTE REGIONAL HISTORY CENTER*, John M Longyear Research Library, 145 W Spring St, 49855. SAN 308-2555. Tel: 906-226-3571. FAX: 906-226-0919. Web Site: www.marquettehistory.org. *Librn,* Rosemary Michelin; E-mail: rosemary@marquettehistory.org; Staff 1 (Non-MLS 1)
Founded 1918
Library Holdings: Bk Titles 16,000; Per Subs 45
Special Collections: Breitung-Kaufman Papers; Burt Papers; Business Records; Carroll Watson Rankin Papers; Family Records; J M Longyear Coll; Local Newspapers on Microfilm from 1870s; Military (Local Service Men); Municipal Records; Regional Genealogy Coll. Oral History
Subject Interests: Ethnology, Geol, Great Lakes, Mining, Railroads
Publications: Harlow's Wooden Man (Quarterly)
Partic in OCLC Online Computer Library Center, Inc
Open Mon-Fri 10-5, Wed 10-8, Sat 10-3
Restriction: In-house use for visitors

C NORTHERN MICHIGAN UNIVERSITY*, Lydia M Olson Library, 1401 Presque Isle, 49855. SAN 308-258X. Tel: 906-227-2117. Circulation Tel: 906-227-2260. Interlibrary Loan Service Tel: 906-227-2065. Reference Tel: 906-227-2294. FAX: 906-227-1333. TDD: 906-227-1232. E-mail: ais@nmu.edu. Reference E-mail: info@nmu.edu. Web Site: www.nmu.edu/library. *Dean,* Darlene M Walch; E-mail: dwalch@nmu.edu; *Head, Pub Serv,* Mary P Freier; Tel: 906-227-1061, E-mail: mfreier@nmu.edu; *Head, Tech Serv,* Krista Clumpner; Tel: 906-227-1205, E-mail: kclumpne@nmu.edu; *Librn,* SaraJane Tompkins; Tel: 906-227-2431, E-mail: stompkin@nmu.edu; *Coordr, Instruction,* Michael Strahan; Tel: 906-227-2463, E-mail: mstrahan@nmu.edu; *Cat,* Stephen Peters; Tel: 906-227-2123, E-mail: speters@nmu.edu; *Circ, ILL,* Kathy Godec; Tel: 906-227-2261, E-mail: kgodec@nmu.edu; *Coll Develop,* Douglas Black; Tel: 906-227-1208, E-mail: doblack@nmu.edu; *Govt Doc,* Bruce Sarjeant; Tel: 906-227-1580, E-mail: bsarjean@nmu.edu; *Libr Syst Support,* John Hambleton; Tel: 906-227-2741, E-mail: jhamblet@nmu.edu; *Ref,* Michael Burgmeier; Tel: 906-227-2187, E-mail: mburgmei@nmu.edu; *Ref,* Kevin McDonough; Tel: 906-227-2118, E-mail: kmcdonou@nmu.edu; Staff 14 (MLS 10, Non-MLS 4)
Founded 1899. Enrl 9,347; Fac 326; Highest Degree: Master
Library Holdings: AV Mats 8,251; e-books 20,372; e-journals 77; Electronic Media & Resources 4,573; Bk Vols 615,406; Per Subs 1,722
Special Collections: Holocaust Coll; Moses Coit Tyler Coll. State Document Depository; US Document Depository
Automation Activity & Vendor Info: (Acquisitions) Ex Libris Group; (Cataloging) Ex Libris Group; (Circulation) Ex Libris Group; (ILL) OCLC ILLiad; (OPAC) Ex Libris Group
Wireless access
Partic in Midwest Collaborative for Library Services (MCLS); OCLC Online Computer Library Center, Inc

P UPPER PENINSULA LIBRARY FOR THE BLIND & PHYSICALLY HANDICAPPED*, 1615 Presque Isle Ave, 49855. SAN 308-0706. Tel: 906-228-7697. Toll Free Tel: 800-562-8985. FAX: 906-228-5627. Web Site: www.uproc.lib.mi.us/uplbph/index.html. *Dir,* Suzanne Dees; E-mail: sdees@uproc.lib.mi.us; *Asst Dir,* Ruth Ruff; E-mail: rruff@uproc.lib.mi.us; *Outreach Coordr,* Dorothy Dickey; E-mail: dorothy@uproc.lib.mi.us; Staff 1 (MLS 1)
Founded 1980. Pop 1,017; Circ 32,000
Special Collections: Coping Skills Information File
Publications: Large Print Books in Upper Peninsula Libraries
Special Services for the Blind - Info on spec aids & appliances; Ref serv

P PETER WHITE PUBLIC LIBRARY, 217 N Front St, 49855. SAN 308-2601. Tel: 906-228-9510. Interlibrary Loan Service Tel: 906-226-4315. Reference Tel: 906-226-4311. Administration Tel: 906-228-7434. FAX:

906-226-1783. E-mail: pwpl@uproc.lib.mi.us. Web Site: www.pwpl.info. *Dir,* Pamela R Christensen; E-mail: pamc@uproc.lib.mi.us; *Asst Dir, Circ,* Bruce A MacDonald; Tel: 906-226-4310, E-mail: bmac@uproc.lib.mi.us; *Acq & Ref,* Cathy Seblonka; *Ch Serv,* Sarah Rehborg; *Tech Serv,* Tracy Boehm; Staff 28 (MLS 6, Non-MLS 22)
Founded 1871. Pop 36,441; Circ 278,295
Jul 2012-Jun 2013 Income $1,688,500. Mats Exp $137,950. Sal $800,000 (Prof $253,000)
Library Holdings: Audiobooks 7,959; CDs 12,610; DVDs 6,042; e-books 3,054; Large Print Bks 1,341; Microforms 1,200; Bk Vols 188,461; Per Subs 230; Videos 5,072
Special Collections: Children's Historical Book Coll; Finnish Coll; Guns, Railroads, Ships (Miller Coll); Local History Coll; Merrit Coll; Nadeau Coll; Shiras Coll; Submarines (William Nelson Coll). Municipal Document Depository
Automation Activity & Vendor Info: (Cataloging) SIRSI WorkFlows; (Circulation) SIRSI WorkFlows; (ILL) Mel Cat; (OPAC) SirsiDynix
Wireless access
Function: 24/7 Electronic res, 24/7 Online cat, Accessibility serv available based on individual needs, Adult bk club, Adult literacy prog, After school storytime, Art exhibits, Audio & video playback equip for onsite use, Audiobks via web, AV serv, Bk club(s), Bus archives, CD-ROM, Children's prog, Computer training, Computers for patron use, Copy machines, Digital talking bks, Distance learning, Doc delivery serv, Electronic databases & coll, Equip loans & repairs, Exhibits, Family literacy, Fax serv, Games & aids for the handicapped, Govt ref serv, Handicapped accessible, Holiday prog, Homebound delivery serv, Homework prog, ILL available, Jazz prog, Large print keyboards, Libr develop, Magazines, Mango lang, Microfiche/film & reading machines, Movies, Music CDs, Newsp ref libr, Online cat, Online searches, Orientations, Outside serv via phone, mail, e-mail & web, OverDrive digital audio bks, Passport agency, Photocopying/Printing, Preschool reading prog, Printer for laptops & handheld devices, Prog for adults, Prog for children & young adult, Pub access computers, Ref serv available, Referrals accepted, Scanner, Serves mentally handicapped consumers, Spoken cassettes & CDs, Spoken cassettes & DVDs, Story hour, Summer reading prog, Tax forms, Teen prog, Telephone ref, VHS videos, Video lending libr, Web-Braille, Wheelchair accessible, Workshops, Writing prog
Partic in Superiorland Library Cooperative; Upper Peninsula Region of Library Cooperation, Inc
Open Mon-Thurs 10-9, Fri 10-6, Sat 10-5, Sun (Sept-May) 1-6
Restriction: Non-resident fee
Friends of the Library Group

MARSHALL

P MARSHALL DISTRICT LIBRARY*, 124 W Green St, 49068. SAN 308-2628. Tel: 269-781-7821. FAX: 269-781-7090. Web Site: www.marshalldistrictlibrary.org. *Dir,* Laurie St Laurent; E-mail: stlaurentl@marshalldistrictlibrary.org; *Dep Dir,* Angela Semifero; E-mail: semiferoa@marshalldistrictlibrary.org; *Head, Adult Serv,* Dawn Hernandez; E-mail: hernandezd@marshalldistrictlibrary.org; *Head, Youth Serv,* Kathy Lane; Tel: 269-781-7821, Ext 16, E-mail: lanek@marshalldistrictlibrary.org; Staff 5 (MLS 5)
Founded 1912. Pop 15,401; Circ 156,845
Jul 2006-Jun 2007 Income $950,954, State $8,020, Locally Generated Income $942,934. Mats Exp $96,407, Books $77,630, AV Mat $18,777. Sal $465,248 (Prof $182,566)
Library Holdings: Bk Titles 60,315; Per Subs 140; Talking Bks 2,617; Videos 4,384
Automation Activity & Vendor Info: (Cataloging) Innovative Interfaces, Inc; (Circulation) Innovative Interfaces, Inc; (ILL) Auto-Graphics, Inc; (OPAC) Innovative Interfaces, Inc
Database Vendor: EBSCOhost, Gale Cengage Learning, Innovative Interfaces, Inc, LexisNexis, Newsbank, OCLC FirstSearch, OCLC WorldShare Interlibrary Loan, ProQuest, Wilson - Wilson Web
Wireless access
Function: Adult bk club, Bk club(s), Bks on cassette, Bks on CD, Children's prog, Computer training, Computers for patron use, Copy machines, e-mail serv, Electronic databases & coll, Free DVD rentals, ILL available, Mail & tel request accepted, Music CDs, Online cat, Online ref, Online searches, Outside serv via phone, mail, e-mail & web, Photocopying/Printing, Preschool outreach, Prog for adults, Prog for children & young adult, Pub access computers, Ref & res, Ref serv available, Scanner, Senior computer classes, Senior outreach, Spoken cassettes & CDs, Summer reading prog, Tax forms, Teen prog, Telephone ref, VHS videos, Video lending libr, Web-catalog, Wheelchair accessible, Workshops
Mem of Woodlands Library Cooperative
Partic in Midwest Collaborative for Library Services (MCLS)
Special Services for the Blind - Closed circuit TV
Open Mon-Thurs 10-8:30, Fri 10-5:30, Sat 10-3, Sun (Sept-May) 1-4
Restriction: Non-resident fee

MARTIN

P J C WHEELER PUBLIC LIBRARY*, 1576 S Main St, 49070-9728. (Mail add: PO Box 226, 49070-0226), SAN 308-2636. Tel: 269-672-7875. Web Site: www.wheelerpl.michlibrary.org. *Dir,* Alicia Kershaw
Founded 1922. Circ 15,000
Library Holdings: Bk Vols 11,290; Per Subs 23
Partic in Lakeland Library Cooperative
Open Mon 12-7, Tues, Wed & Fri 10-5, Sat 9-1
Friends of the Library Group

MAYVILLE

P MAYVILLE DISTRICT PUBLIC LIBRARY*, 6090 Fulton St, 48744. (Mail add: PO Box 440, 48744-0440), SAN 308-2652. Tel: 989-843-6522. FAX: 989-843-0078. Web Site: www.mayvillelibrary.org. *Dir,* Jill Fox; E-mail: jill@mayvillelibrary.org; *Asst Librn,* Kathy Jansen; E-mail: kathy@mayvillelibrary.org
Founded 1950. Pop 6,094; Circ 47,366
Jul 2005-Jun 2006 Income $156,369. Mats Exp $10,900, Books $9,000, Per/Ser (Incl. Access Fees) $900, AV Mat $1,000. Sal $60,600
Library Holdings: AV Mats 1,247; Bks on Deafness & Sign Lang 22; Large Print Bks 50; Bk Vols 21,000; Per Subs 65; Talking Bks 717
Automation Activity & Vendor Info: (Cataloging) Auto-Graphics, Inc; (Circulation) Auto-Graphics, Inc
Wireless access
Partic in Mich Libr Asn; White Pine Libr Coop
Open Tues 10-8, Wed-Fri 10-6, Sat 10-2
Friends of the Library Group

MCBAIN

P MCBAIN COMMUNITY LIBRARY*, 107 E Maple St, 49657-9672. Tel: 231-825-2197. FAX: 231-825-2477. Web Site: www.mcbain.org. *Coordr,* Diane Eisenga
Library Holdings: Bks on Deafness & Sign Lang 15; Bk Vols 20,000; Per Subs 40
Automation Activity & Vendor Info: (Cataloging) Auto-Graphics, Inc; (Circulation) Auto-Graphics, Inc; (OPAC) Auto-Graphics, Inc
Partic in Mid-Michigan Library League
Open Mon, Tues & Thurs (Winter) 8:30-7, Wed 8:30-6, Fri 8:30-4, Sat 9-1; Mon-Thurs (Summer) 11-6, Fri 11-4, Sat 9-1

MECOSTA

P MORTON TOWNSHIP PUBLIC LIBRARY*, 110 S James, 49332-9334. (Mail add: PO Box 246, 49332-0246), SAN 308-2660. Tel: 231-972-8583. FAX: 231-972-4332. E-mail: mortwplib@centurytel.net. Web Site: morton.michlibrary.org. *Libr Dir,* Mary Ann Lenon; Tel: 231-972-8315, Ext 203, E-mail: mortwplib@centurytel.net; *Asst Libr Dir,* Holly Jo Swincicki; Tel: 231-972-8315, Ext 204, E-mail: hsmtplibrary@centurytel.net; *Youth Serv Dir,* Juliane Schafer; Tel: 231-972-8315, Ext 209, E-mail: jlmtplibrary@centurytel.net; Staff 8 (MLS 1, MLS 1, Non-MLS 3, Non-MLS 3)
Founded 1966. Pop 6,634; Circ 63,296
Library Holdings: Bks on Deafness & Sign Lang 30; Bks on Deafness & Sign Lang 30; Large Print Bks 225; Large Print Bks 225; Bk Vols 22,137; Bk Vols 22,137; Per Subs 80; Per Subs 80; Talking Bks 880; Talking Bks 880
Automation Activity & Vendor Info: (Acquisitions) Auto-Graphics, Inc; (Cataloging) Auto-Graphics, Inc; (Circulation) Auto-Graphics, Inc
Database Vendor: Auto-Graphics, Inc
Wireless access
Function: Handicapped accessible, Homebound delivery serv, ILL available, Online cat, Preschool reading prog, Prog for adults, Prog for children & young adult, Scanner, Senior computer classes, Story hour, Summer reading prog, Tax forms, Teen prog, Wheelchair accessible
Partic in Mid-Michigan Library League
Special Services for the Deaf - Bks on deafness & sign lang
Open Tues, Thurs & Fri 10-5, Wed 10-7, Sat 10-1
Friends of the Library Group

MELVINDALE

P MELVINDALE PUBLIC LIBRARY*, 18650 Allen Rd, 48122. SAN 308-2679. Tel: 313-429-1090. Toll Free Tel: 888-672-8983. FAX: 313-388-0432. Web Site: www.melvindale.lib.mi.us. *Dir,* Theresa Kieltyka; E-mail: kieltyka@melvindale.lib.mi.us
Founded 1928. Pop 11,216; Circ 42,668
Library Holdings: Bks on Deafness & Sign Lang 15; DVDs 200; Large Print Bks 300; Bk Vols 47,000; Per Subs 85; Talking Bks 680; Videos 600
Automation Activity & Vendor Info: (Cataloging) SirsiDynix; (Circulation) SirsiDynix; (OPAC) SirsiDynix
Special Services for the Deaf - TDD equip

Special Services for the Blind - Bks on cassette; Large print bks
Open Mon-Thurs (Winter) 12-8, Sat 12-5; Mon-Thurs (Summer) 12-8, Fri 12-5

MENDON

P MENDON TOWNSHIP LIBRARY*, 314 W Main St, 49072. SAN 308-2687. Tel: 269-496-4865. FAX: 269-496-4635. *Dir,* Kim Foghino
Founded 1882. Pop 4,999; Circ 10,916
Library Holdings: Bk Vols 17,000
Special Collections: Local History, scrapbks, bks; Mich & Local History; Mich & Local History, albums
Subject Interests: Foreign lang, Genealogy
Mem of Woodlands Library Cooperative
Open Tues, Wed & Fri 10-5, Thurs Noon-7, Sat 10-2
Friends of the Library Group

MENOMINEE

P SPIES PUBLIC LIBRARY*, 940 First St, 49858-3296. SAN 308-2695. Tel: 906-863-3911. FAX: 906-863-5000. TDD: 800-649-3777. E-mail: spies@uproc.lib.mi.us. Web Site: www.uproc.lib.mi.us/spies. *Dir,* Cheryl Hoffman; Tel: 906-863-2900, E-mail: cherylh@uproc.lib.mi.us; *Cataloger, Syst Adminr,* Amber Allard; Staff 10 (MLS 1, Non-MLS 9)
Founded 1903. Pop 10,313; Circ 66,682
Jul 2005-Jun 2006 Income $490,600. Mats Exp $35,431. Sal $191,619 (Prof $44,768)
Library Holdings: AV Mats 2,248; e-books 35; Bk Vols 56,907; Per Subs 126
Automation Activity & Vendor Info: (Acquisitions) SirsiDynix; (Cataloging) SirsiDynix; (Circulation) SirsiDynix; (ILL) SirsiDynix; (OPAC) SirsiDynix; (Serials) SirsiDynix
Wireless access
Partic in Superiorland Library Cooperative; Upper Peninsula Region of Library Cooperation, Inc
Open Mon, Fri & Sat (Winter) 9-5, Tues-Thurs 9-9; Mon-Fri (Summer) 9-6, Sat 9-12
Friends of the Library Group

MERRILL

P MERRILL DISTRICT LIBRARY*, 321 W Saginaw, 48637. SAN 308-2709. Tel: 989-643-7300. FAX: 989-643-7300. E-mail: mer_ill@yahoo.com. *Dir,* Sara Kipfmiller
Circ 24,512
Library Holdings: Bk Vols 23,158; Per Subs 52
Subject Interests: Mich
Partic in White Pine Libr Coop

MIDDLEVILLE

P THORNAPPLE KELLOGG SCHOOL & COMMUNITY LIBRARY*, 3885 Bender Rd, 49333-9273. SAN 308-2717. Tel: 269-795-5434. Administration Tel: 269-795-5436. FAX: 269-795-8997. Web Site: www.tkschools.org/community/library. *Dir,* Barb Hubers; *Asst Librn,* Susan Postema
Circ 45,000
Library Holdings: Bk Vols 38,000; Per Subs 26
Automation Activity & Vendor Info: (Cataloging) Innovative Interfaces, Inc; (Circulation) Innovative Interfaces, Inc
Database Vendor: OCLC FirstSearch
Wireless access
Partic in Lakeland Library Cooperative
Open Mon, Wed & Fri (Winter) 8-4, Tues & Thurs 8-8; Tues (Summer) 2-6, Wed 10-3, Thurs 12-8
Friends of the Library Group

MIDLAND

P GRACE A DOW MEMORIAL LIBRARY*, 1710 W St Andrews Ave, 48640-2698. SAN 308-2725. Tel: 989-837-3430. Reference Tel: 989-837-3449. FAX: 989-837-3468. Web Site: www.midland-mi.org/gracedowlibrary. *Dir,* Melissa Barnard; E-mail: mbarnard@midland-mi.org; Staff 17 (MLS 16, Non-MLS 1)
Founded 1899. Pop 76,707; Circ 789,851
Jul 2012-Jun 2013 Income $3,735,060. Mats Exp $372,349, Books $186,947, Per/Ser (Incl. Access Fees) $15,188, AV Mat $50,031, Electronic Ref Mat (Incl. Access Fees) $120,183
Library Holdings: Audiobooks 9,610; CDs 8,975; DVDs 10,032; e-books 2,290; Large Print Bks 6,062; Bk Vols 214,983; Per Subs 291
Special Collections: Municipal Document Depository
Subject Interests: Local hist
Automation Activity & Vendor Info: (Acquisitions) SirsiDynix; (Cataloging) SirsiDynix; (Circulation) SirsiDynix; (OPAC) SirsiDynix
Wireless access
Publications: Library Connection (Newsletter)
Partic in Mideastern Michigan Library Cooperative
Special Services for the Blind - Aids for in-house use
Open Mon-Fri 9:30-8:30, Sat 10-5, Sun (Sept-May) 1-5
Friends of the Library Group

R MEMORIAL PRESBYTERIAN CHURCH*, Greenhoe Library-Rainbow Children's Library, 1310 Ashman St, 48640. SAN 308-2733. Tel: 989-835-6759. *Chair,* Beth Schmidt; E-mail: beth@billbeth.com; *Librn,* Marjorie Pochert; Staff 2 (MLS 1, Non-MLS 1)
Founded 1945
Jan 2010-Dec 2010 Income $1,078. Mats Exp $960, Books $600, Per/Ser (Incl. Access Fees) $160, AV Equip $200
Library Holdings: AV Mats 1,600; CDs 321; DVDs 89; Large Print Bks 167; Bk Titles 8,018; Bk Vols 7,189; Per Subs 6; Talking Bks 10; Videos 624
Special Collections: Children's Library, bks, flm, tapes
Subject Interests: Biblical studies, Church hist, Fiction

S MICHIGAN MOLECULAR INSTITUTE, Raymond F Boyer Resource Center, 1910 W St Andrews Rd, 48640. SAN 324-7139. Tel: 989-832-5555. FAX: 989-832-5560. E-mail: ResearchPartner@mmi.org. Web Site: www.mmi.org/mmi. *Dir, Libr & Info Serv,* Judy Eastland; *Interim Librn,* Molly Warren-Haycock; E-mail: warren-haycock@mmi.org; Staff 1 (MLS 1)
Founded 1971
Library Holdings: Bk Titles 4,000; Bk Vols 5,000; Per Subs 125
Subject Interests: Mat sci, Polymer sci, Polymer tech
Automation Activity & Vendor Info: (Circulation) Horizon; (ILL) OCLC
Database Vendor: EBSCOhost, OCLC FirstSearch, SirsiDynix
Function: Res libr
Partic in OCLC-LVIS; Valley Library Consortium
Open Mon, Wed & Thurs 8-4
Restriction: Access at librarian's discretion, Authorized scholars by appt, Borrowing requests are handled by ILL, By permission only, External users must contact libr, In-house use for visitors, Non-circulating coll, Open to others by appt, Staff use only

S MIDLAND COUNTY HISTORICAL SOCIETY LIBRARY*, 3417 W Main St, 48640. (Mail add: 1801 West St, Andrews Rd, 48640-2695), SAN 327-4373. Tel: 989-631-5930, Ext 1300. Web Site: www.mcfta.org. *Dir,* Gary F Skory; E-mail: Skory@mcfta.org; Staff 4 (Non-MLS 4)
Founded 1952
Library Holdings: Bk Titles 1,500; Per Subs 10
Special Collections: Area Genealogy Coll; Dow Chemical Company Archival Material, photos; Midland County Circuit Court Records. Municipal Document Depository; Oral History

M MIDMICHIGAN MEDICAL CENTER*, Health Sciences Library, 4005 Orchard Dr, 48670. SAN 325-2248. Tel: 989-839-3262. FAX: 989-631-1401. *Mgr,* Patricia Wolfgram
Library Holdings: Bk Vols 3,000; Per Subs 400
Special Collections: Health Sciences Coll
Open Mon-Fri 9-4:30

C NORTHWOOD UNIVERSITY*, Strosacker Library, 4000 Whiting Dr, 48640-2398. SAN 346-8933. Tel: 989-837-4333. Toll Free Tel: 800-837-2291. FAX: 989-832-5031. E-mail: milibrary@northwood.edu. *Dir,* Alice Parsons; Tel: 989-837-4339, E-mail: parsonsa@northwood.edu; *Ref,* Rochelle Zimmerman; Tel: 989-837-4275, E-mail: zimmerma@northwood.edu; Staff 9 (MLS 3, Non-MLS 6)
Founded 1959. Enrl 1,936; Fac 45; Highest Degree: Master
Library Holdings: AV Mats 86; Bk Titles 33,892; Bk Vols 39,671; Per Subs 334
Automation Activity & Vendor Info: (Cataloging) SirsiDynix; (Circulation) SirsiDynix; (Course Reserve) Docutek; (ILL) SirsiDynix; (OPAC) SirsiDynix
Database Vendor: EBSCOhost, Factiva.com, Gale Cengage Learning, LexisNexis, OCLC FirstSearch, ProQuest, ReferenceUSA, SirsiDynix, STAT!Ref (Teton Data Systems), Wilson - Wilson Web
Wireless access
Partic in OCLC Online Computer Library Center, Inc; Valley Libr Consortium
Open Mon-Thurs 7:30am-10:30pm, Fri 7:30-4, Sat 1-5, Sun 2-10

MILAN

S FEDERAL CORRECTIONAL INSTITUTION LIBRARY*, E Arkona Rd, 48160. (Mail add: PO Box 49999, 48160), SAN 308-2741. Tel: 734-439-1511, Ext 3241. FAX: 734-439-3608.
Library Holdings: Bk Vols 20,000; Per Subs 35
Special Collections: Bureau of Prison Program Statements & Institutions Supplements; Federal Law Books & Statutes; Reference Works
Database Vendor: LexisNexis, Westlaw
Partic in Washtenaw-Livingston Libr Network
Open Mon-Sun 7:30-4:30 & 5-8:30

P MILAN PUBLIC LIBRARY*, 151 Wabash St, 48160. SAN 308-275X. Tel: 734-439-1240. FAX: 734-439-5625. E-mail: info@milanlibrary.org. Web Site: www.milanlibrary.org. *Dir,* Susan Wess; E-mail: susan.wess@milanlibrary.org; *Asst Dir/Ref Librn,* Barbara Benton; Staff 7 (MLS 2, Non-MLS 5)
Founded 1935. Pop 17,462; Circ 79,995
Library Holdings: Large Print Bks 400; Bk Titles 33,000; Bk Vols 33,324; Per Subs 90; Videos 1,606
Subject Interests: Genealogy, Local hist
Function: Homebound delivery serv, ILL available, Photocopying/Printing, Prog for adults, Prog for children & young adult, Ref serv available, Summer reading prog, Telephone ref
Partic in OCLC Online Computer Library Center, Inc
Open Mon-Thurs 10-8, Fri 10-6, Sat 10-4
Friends of the Library Group

MILFORD

P MILFORD PUBLIC LIBRARY*, 330 Family Dr, 48381-2000. SAN 308-2768. Tel: 248-684-0845. FAX: 248-684-2923. E-mail: milfref@milfordlibrary.info. Web Site: milfordlibrary.info. *Dir,* Tina Hatch; E-mail: thatch@milfordlibrary.info; *Head, Adult Serv,* Karin Boughey; E-mail: kboughey@milfordlibrary.info; *Head, Circ,* Dawn Chlebo; E-mail: dchlebo@milfordlibrary.info; *Head, Youth Serv,* Mary Rice; Staff 20 (MLS 7, Non-MLS 13)
Founded 1929. Pop 19,512; Circ 124,457
Library Holdings: Bk Vols 45,000; Per Subs 120
Special Collections: Art Geyer Civil War Coll
Subject Interests: Local hist, Mich
Database Vendor: Gale Cengage Learning, SirsiDynix
Publications: Library Register (Newsletter)
Partic in Midwest Collaborative for Library Services (MCLS)
Open Mon-Thurs 9:30-8, Fri & Sat 9:30-5, Sun (Sept-May) 12:30-5
Friends of the Library Group

MILLINGTON

P MILLINGTON ARBELA DISTRICT LIBRARY*, 8530 Depot St, 48746. (Mail add: PO Box 306, 48746-0306), SAN 308-2776. Tel: 989-871-2003. FAX: 989-871-5594. Web Site: www.millingtonlibrary.org. *Dir,* Margaret E Olsen; *Asst Dir,* Katherine G Halloran
Founded 1937. Pop 7,678; Circ 40,000
Library Holdings: Bk Titles 27,351; Bk Vols 29,653; Per Subs 65
Automation Activity & Vendor Info: (Circulation) Auto-Graphics, Inc; (OPAC) Auto-Graphics, Inc
Open Mon & Wed 9-8, Tues & Thurs 12-8, Fri 9-6, Sat 9-5

MIO

P OSCODA COUNTY LIBRARY, 430 W Eighth St, 48647. SAN 308-2784. Tel: 989-826-3613. FAX: 989-826-5461. E-mail: ocl@m33access.com. Web Site: www.oscoda.lib.mi.us. *Dir,* Amy R Knepp; *Asst Librn,* Position Currently Open; Staff 2 (MLS 1, Non-MLS 1)
Founded 1948. Pop 9,000; Circ 41,249
Library Holdings: Bks on Deafness & Sign Lang 10; High Interest/Low Vocabulary Bk Vols 100; Bk Titles 30,000; Per Subs 70
Special Collections: County Papers 1932-Present
Automation Activity & Vendor Info: (Cataloging) Evergreen; (Circulation) Evergreen; (ILL) Evergreen
Database Vendor: Gale Cengage Learning, OCLC FirstSearch
Wireless access
Partic in Northland Library Cooperative
Open Mon-Fri 9-5:30, Sat 11-2

MOLINE

P LEIGHTON TOWNSHIP PUBLIC LIBRARY*, 4451 12th St, 49335. (Mail add: PO Drawer H, 49335-0250), SAN 346-3508. Tel: 616-877-4143. FAX: 616-877-4484. E-mail: mol@lakeland.lib.mi.us. Web Site: llmol.llcoop.org, www.lakeland.lib.mi.us. *Dir,* Martha Jackson
Library Holdings: Bk Vols 22,000; Per Subs 65
Partic in Lakeland Library Cooperative

MONROE

SR IHM LIBRARY/RESOURCE CENTER*, Congregational Library, 610 W Elm Ave, 48162-7909. SAN 308-2806. Tel: 734-240-9713. Circulation Tel: 734-240-9678. FAX: 734-240-8347. E-mail: library@ihmsisters.org. Web Site: www.ihmsisters.org. *Dir,* Sister Anne Marie Murphy; *Librn,* Carol Kelly; *Acq of New Ser/Per, Librn,* Sister Antoinette McNamara; Staff 7 (MLS 3, Non-MLS 4)
Founded 1927
Jul 2009-Jun 2010. Mats Exp $12,000, Books $3,000, Per/Ser (Incl. Access Fees) $3,600, Other Print Mats $500, AV Mat $400. Sal $20,000
Library Holdings: Audiobooks 150; CDs 350; DVDs 450; Large Print Bks 450; Bk Vols 30,000; Per Subs 100; Spec Interest Per Sub 20; Videos 2,200
Subject Interests: Art, Ecology, Fiction, Relig, Theol
Function: AV serv, Bk club(s), Bks on cassette, Bks on CD, CD-ROM, Computers for patron use, Copy machines, Free DVD rentals, Handicapped accessible, Home delivery & serv to Sr ctr & nursing homes, Learning ctr, Magnifiers for reading, Mail loans to mem, Music CDs, Online searches, Photocopying/Printing, Ref serv available, Res libr, Spoken cassettes & CDs, VHS videos, Video lending libr, Wheelchair accessible
Partic in Catholic Library Association
Special Services for the Blind - Assistive/Adapted tech devices, equip & products
Open Mon-Fri 10:30-4:30, Sat 9:30-12, Sun 1-3
Restriction: Authorized patrons, Authorized scholars by appt, Circ to mem only, External users must contact libr, Open to pub for ref & circ; with some limitations, Open to researchers by request, Private libr, Restricted pub use, Sub libr
Friends of the Library Group

J MONROE COUNTY COMMUNITY COLLEGE*, Learning Resources Center, 1555 S Raisinville Rd, 48161. SAN 308-2792. Tel: 734-384-4204. Interlibrary Loan Service Tel: 734-384-4399. Reference Tel: 734-384-4400. Administration Tel: 734-384-4244. FAX: 734-384-4160. Web Site: www.monroeccc.edu/library. *Dir,* Barbara McNamee; Tel: 734-384-4244, E-mail: bmcnamee@monroeccc.edu; *Head, Tech Serv, Ref,* Terri Kovach; Tel: 734-384-4161, E-mail: tkovach@monroeccc.edu; *Librn,* Mary Bullard; E-mail: mbullard@monroeccc.edu; *Librn,* Larry Yaek; E-mail: lyaek@monroeccc.edu; *Pub Serv Librn,* Cindy Yonovich; E-mail: cyonovich@monroeccc.edu; Staff 3 (MLS 3)
Founded 1966. Enrl 4,500; Fac 3; Highest Degree: Associate
Jul 2006-Jun 2007 Income $859,025. Mats Exp $444,575, Books $51,500, Per/Ser (Incl. Access Fees) $33,000, Micro $2,000, AV Mat $10,000, Electronic Ref Mat (Incl. Access Fees) $50,000, Presv $2,500. Sal $414,450 (Prof $242,265)
Library Holdings: AV Mats 4,944; Bk Titles 50,333; Bk Vols 56,000; Per Subs 335
Special Collections: Professional Library
Automation Activity & Vendor Info: (Acquisitions) SirsiDynix; (Cataloging) SirsiDynix; (Circulation) SirsiDynix; (ILL) OCLC; (OPAC) SirsiDynix; (Serials) SirsiDynix
Database Vendor: 3M Library Systems, Baker & Taylor, Bowker, EBSCOhost, Ex Libris Group, Facts on File, Gale Cengage Learning, Hoovers, JSTOR, OCLC FirstSearch, ProQuest, SirsiDynix, Standard & Poor's, ValueLine
Wireless access

S MONROE COUNTY HISTORICAL MUSEUM, 126 S Monroe St, 48161. SAN 327-439X. Tel: 734-240-7787. FAX: 734-240-7788. *Archivist,* Christine Kull; E-mail: chris_kull@monroemi.org; Staff 1 (Non-MLS 1)
Library Holdings: Bk Vols 600
Subject Interests: County hist, Mich hist
Function: Archival coll
Open Wed-Sat 10-1 & 1:30-5
Restriction: Access at librarian's discretion

P MONROE COUNTY LIBRARY SYSTEM, Mary K Daume Library Service Center, 840 S Roessler St, 48161. Tel: 734-241-5770. FAX: 734-241-4722. Web Site: monroe.lib.mi.us. *Dir,* Nancy Bellaire; E-mail: nancy.bellaire@monroe.lib.mi.us; Staff 23 (MLS 22, Non-MLS 1)
Jan 2013-Dec 2013 Income (Main Library and Branch(s)) $7,109,729. Mats Exp $734,948, Books $431,108, Per/Ser (Incl. Access Fees) $45,371, AV Mat $153,145, Electronic Ref Mat (Incl. Access Fees) $105,324
Library Holdings: AV Mats 24,304; e-books 7,597; Bk Vols 467,728; Per Subs 841; Videos 42,701
Special Collections: General George A Custer Coll, bks, media, microfilm
Database Vendor: Innovative Interfaces, Inc
Wireless access
Special Services for the Deaf - TDD equip
Special Services for the Blind - Large print bks
Friends of the Library Group
Branches: 16
BEDFORD BRANCH LIBRARY, 8575 Jackman Rd, Temperance, 48182, SAN 346-9387. Tel: 734-847-6747. FAX: 734-847-6591. Web Site: www.mymcls.com. *Commun Librn,* Jodi Russ
Subject Interests: Genealogy, Local hist
Special Services for the Deaf - TDD equip
Open Mon-Thurs 9-9, Fri & Sat 9-5, Sun (Sept-May) 12-5
Friends of the Library Group
BLUE BUSH, 2210 Blue Bush, 48162-9643, SAN 328-7505. Tel: 734-242-4085. *Commun Librn,* Jane Steed; *Br Tech,* Elizabeth Pifer
Founded 1986
Special Services for the Deaf - TDD equip
Open Mon, Tues & Thurs 1-5, Wed 1-8, Fri 10-5, Sat 10-2
Friends of the Library Group

CARLETON BRANCH, 1444 Kent St, Carleton, 48117. (Mail add: PO Box 267, Carleton, 48117-0267), SAN 346-8992. Tel: 734-654-2180. FAX: 734-654-8767. *Commun Librn,* David Ross; E-mail: david.ross@monroe.lib.mi.us
Special Services for the Deaf - TDD equip
Open Mon & Thurs 12-8, Tues & Wed 9-8, Fri & Sat 9-5
Friends of the Library Group

DORSCH MEMORIAL, 18 E First St, 48161-2227, SAN 346-9026. Tel: 734-241-7878. FAX: 734-241-7879. *Commun Librn,* Cindy Green
Special Services for the Deaf - TDD equip
Friends of the Library Group

DUNDEE BRANCH, 144 E Main St, Dundee, 48131-1202, SAN 346-9050. Tel: 734-529-3310. FAX: 734-529-7415. *Commun Librn,* Jennifer Grudnoski
Founded 1934
Special Services for the Deaf - TDD equip
Open Mon & Wed 9-6, Tues & Thurs 10-8, Fri 9-5, Sat 10-2
Friends of the Library Group

ELLIS LIBRARY & REFERENCE CENTER, 3700 S Custer Rd, 48161-9716, SAN 346-9085. Tel: 734-241-5277. FAX: 734-242-9037. *Libr Mgr,* Bill Reiser; *Ref Mgr,* Louis Komorowski
Special Services for the Deaf - TDD equip
Open Mon-Thurs 9-9, Fri & Sat 9-5, Sun (Sept-May) 12-5
Friends of the Library Group

ERIE BRANCH, 2065 Erie Rd, Erie, 48133-9757, SAN 346-9115. Tel: 734-848-4420. FAX: 734-848-4420. *Br Librn,* Carol Laurie
Founded 1935
Special Services for the Deaf - TDD equip
Open Mon 2-8, Tues 9-1, Wed 10-6, Thurs 2-6, Fri 1-5
Friends of the Library Group

FRENCHTOWN-DIXIE, 2881 Nadeau Rd, 48162-9334, SAN 346-914X. Tel: 734-289-1035. FAX: 734-289-3867. *Commun Librn,* Jane Steed
Special Services for the Deaf - TDD equip
Open Mon-Thurs 9-8, Fri & Sat 9-5, Sun (May-Sept) 12-5
Friends of the Library Group

IDA BRANCH, 3016 Lewis Ave, Ida, 48140. (Mail add: PO Box 56, Ida, 48140-0056), SAN 346-9174. Tel: 734-269-2191. FAX: 734-269-3315. *Commun Librn,* Suzanne Krueger
Founded 1930
Special Services for the Deaf - TDD equip
Open Mon 12-8, Tues 10-6, Wed-Fri 10-5, Sat 10-1
Friends of the Library Group

MAYBEE BRANCH, 9060 Raisin St, Maybee, 48159. (Mail add: PO Box 165, Maybee, 48159-0165), SAN 346-9239. Tel: 734-587-3680. FAX: 734-587-3680. *Br Tech,* Catherine Masson
Special Services for the Deaf - TDD equip
Open Mon 12-8, Tues 12-5, Thurs 9-1, Fri 9-5, Sat 9-2
Friends of the Library Group

L S NAVARRE BRANCH, 1135 E Second St, 48161-1920, SAN 346-9263. Tel: 734-241-5577. FAX: 734-241-5577. *Commun Librn,* Amber Reed
Special Services for the Deaf - TDD equip
Open Mon, Wed & Thurs 1-6, Tues 10-8, Fri & Sat 1-5

NEWPORT BRANCH, 8120 N Dixie Hwy, Newport, 48166. Tel: 734-586-2117. FAX: 734-586-1116. *Commun Librn,* David E Ross; E-mail: david.ross@monroe.lib.mi.us; *Br Tech,* Sue Young
Friends of the Library Group

RASEY MEMORIAL, 4349 Oak St, Luna Pier, 48157. (Mail add: PO Box 416, Luna Pier, 48157-0416), SAN 346-9204. Tel: 734-848-4572. FAX: 734-848-4572. *Br Librn,* Carol Laurie
Founded 1935
Special Services for the Deaf - TDD equip
Open Mon, Thurs & Sat 9-1, Tues 2-8, Wed 2-6, Fri 1-5
Friends of the Library Group

SOUTH ROCKWOOD BRANCH, 12776 Dixie Hwy, South Rockwood, 48179. (Mail add: PO Box 47, South Rockwood, 48179-0047), SAN 346-9352. Tel: 734-379-3333. FAX: 734-379-3333. *Commun Librn,* David E Ross; E-mail: david.ross@monroe.lib.mi.us; *Br Tech,* Alesia Testorelli
Special Services for the Deaf - TDD equip
Friends of the Library Group

SUMMERFIELD-PETERSBURG BRANCH, 60 E Center St, Petersburg, 49270. (Mail add: PO Box 567, Petersburg, 49270-0567), SAN 346-9328. Tel: 734-279-1025. FAX: 734-279-2328. *Commun Librn,* Doris Sheldon
Founded 1936
Special Services for the Deaf - TDD equip
Open Mon & Tues 10-7, Wed 12-8, Thurs 3-8, Fri 10-5, Sat 10-1
Friends of the Library Group

ROBERT A VIVIAN BRANCH, 2664 Vivian Rd, 48162-9212, SAN 346-9417. Tel: 734-241-1430. FAX: 734-241-1430. *Commun Librn,* Jane Steed; *Br Tech,* Pat Boitnott
Founded 1975
Special Services for the Deaf - TDD equip
Open Mon & Wed 12-8, Thurs 9-2, Fri 12-5
Friends of the Library Group
Bookmobiles: 1

MORENCI

P STAIR PUBLIC LIBRARY*, 228 W Main St, 49256-1421. SAN 308-2822. Tel: 517-458-6510. FAX: 517-458-3378. E-mail: stair@monroe.lib.mi.us. Web Site: www.stairlib.org.
Founded 1930. Pop 3,134; Circ 17,402
Library Holdings: Bk Vols 19,000; Per Subs 85
Automation Activity & Vendor Info: (Cataloging) Auto-Graphics, Inc; (Circulation) Auto-Graphics, Inc
Mem of Woodlands Library Cooperative
Open Mon & Wed 10-7, Tues, Thurs & Fri 1-5, Sat 9-1
Friends of the Library Group

MORLEY

P WALTON ERICKSON PUBLIC LIBRARY*, 4808 Northland Dr, 49336-9522. SAN 308-2830. Tel: 231-856-4298. FAX: 231-856-0307. *Dir,* Cory Taylor
Founded 1965. Pop 8,840; Circ 23,112
Library Holdings: Bk Titles 28,000; Per Subs 40
Partic in Mid-Michigan Library League
Open Mon & Wed 9-4:30, Tues 12:30-8, Thurs 9-8, Fri 9-12

MOUNT CLEMENS

S MACOMB COUNTY HISTORICAL SOCIETY*, The Crocker House Museum Library, 15 Union St, 48043. SAN 328-560X. Tel: 586-465-2488. Web Site: www.crockerhousemuseum.com. *Dir,* Kimberly Parr
Founded 1869
Library Holdings: Bk Titles 2,500
Subject Interests: County hist, Local hist
Restriction: Non-circulating, Open by appt only

P MOUNT CLEMENS PUBLIC LIBRARY, 150 Cass Ave, 48043. SAN 308-2873. Tel: 586-469-6200. FAX: 586-469-6668. E-mail: askmcpl@libcoop.net. Web Site: www.mtclib.org. *Dir,* Donald E Worrell, Jr; E-mail: worrelld@libcoop.net; *Asst Dir,* Deborah J Larsen; E-mail: larsend@libcoop.net; *Ch Serv,* Marjorie Kinzy; E-mail: kinzym@libcoop.net; *Pub Serv,* Kristy Taormina; Staff 20 (MLS 7, Non-MLS 13)
Founded 1865. Pop 23,937; Circ 161,000
Library Holdings: Bk Vols 124,000; Per Subs 212
Special Collections: Local History & Genealogy (Michigan Coll) bks, doc, flm, pamphlets, per. Oral History
Automation Activity & Vendor Info: (Acquisitions) SirsiDynix; (Cataloging) SirsiDynix; (Circulation) SirsiDynix; (OPAC) SirsiDynix; (Serials) SirsiDynix
Database Vendor: EBSCO Information Services, ProQuest
Publications: Library Online (Newsletter)
Partic in Suburban Library Cooperative
Open Mon-Thurs 9-9, Fri 9-5, Sat 9-5 (9-1 Summer)

M MOUNT CLEMENS REGIONAL MEDICAL CENTER*, Stuck Medical Library, 1000 Harrington Blvd, 48043. SAN 308-2865. Tel: 586-493-8047. FAX: 586-493-8739. *Mgr,* Mary Carr; E-mail: mcarr@mcrmc.org; Staff 1 (MLS 1)
Founded 1957
Library Holdings: AV Mats 300; CDs 100; e-books 2,000; e-journals 8,000; Bk Titles 3,000; Per Subs 90; Spec Interest Per Sub 90
Subject Interests: Allied health, Health bus, Med, Nursing
Automation Activity & Vendor Info: (Acquisitions) SirsiDynix; (Cataloging) SirsiDynix; (Circulation) SirsiDynix; (ILL) SirsiDynix; (OPAC) SirsiDynix; (Serials) SirsiDynix
Database Vendor: EBSCOhost, Elsevier MDL, Gale Cengage Learning, OCLC FirstSearch, OCLC WorldShare Interlibrary Loan, PubMed, SirsiDynix, WebMD
Wireless access
Function: Audio & video playback equip for onsite use, Copy machines, Doc delivery serv, Electronic databases & coll, Health sci info serv, ILL available, Online searches, Prof lending libr
Partic in Detroit Area Library Network; Docline; Michigan Health Sciences Libraries Association
Open Mon-Fri 8-4:30
Restriction: In-house use for visitors, Lending to staff only, Non-circulating coll, Open to pub for ref only, Restricted borrowing privileges, Restricted pub use, Staff & prof res

MOUNT PLEASANT

C CENTRAL MICHIGAN UNIVERSITY*, Charles V Park Library, Park 407, 48859. (Mail add: 300 E Preston, 48859), SAN 308-2881. Tel: 989-774-3500. Circulation Tel: 989-774-3114. Interlibrary Loan Service Tel: 989-774-3022. Reference Tel: 989-774-3470. Automation Services Tel:

989-774-2338. FAX: 989-774-2179. Interlibrary Loan Service FAX: 989-774-4459. Reference FAX: 989-774-1350. Automation Services FAX: 989-774-2656. Web Site: www.lib.cmich.edu. *Dean of Libr,* Thomas J Moore; E-mail: thomas.j.moore@cmich.edu; *Assoc Dean of Libr,* Katherine M Irwin; Tel: 989-774-6421, E-mail: irwin1km@cmich.edu; *Dir, Coll Develop,* Matthew I Ismail; Tel: 989-774-2143, E-mail: ismai1md@cmich.edu; *Dir, Info Serv,* Timothy Peters; Tel: 989-774-3720, E-mail: peter1t@cmich.edu; *Head, Syst,* Daniel Ferrer; E-mail: daniel.ferrer@cmich.edu; *Head, Tech Serv,* Pamela Grudzien; Tel: 989-774-6488, E-mail: pamela.grudzien@cmich.edu; *Bus Mgr,* Bradley Stambaugh; Tel: 989-774-6415, E-mail: stamb1bb@cmich.edu; *Access Serv,* Diane Thomas; Tel: 989-774-2286, E-mail: diane.k.thomas@cmich.edu; Staff 67 (MLS 33, Non-MLS 34)
Founded 1892. Enrl 29,315; Fac 1,233; Highest Degree: Doctorate
Jul 2011-Jun 2012 Income (Main Library Only) $9,059,116. Mats Exp $6,674,571, Books $598,725, Per/Ser (Incl. Access Fees) $3,142,613, Manu Arch $5,203, Micro $1,358,172, AV Mat $102,028, Electronic Ref Mat (Incl. Access Fees) $1,421,438, Presv $29,741. Sal $3,546,345 (Prof $2,215,314)
Library Holdings: CDs 18,318; DVDs 3,262; e-books 18,917; e-journals 8,443; Microforms 1,358,172; Music Scores 7,440; Bk Titles 1,512,490; Per Subs 2,973; Videos 5,156
Special Collections: State Document Depository; US Document Depository
Automation Activity & Vendor Info: (Acquisitions) Innovative Interfaces, Inc; (Cataloging) Innovative Interfaces, Inc; (Circulation) Innovative Interfaces, Inc; (Course Reserve) Innovative Interfaces, Inc; (OPAC) Innovative Interfaces, Inc; (Serials) Innovative Interfaces, Inc
Database Vendor: Innovative Interfaces, Inc
Wireless access
Function: Art exhibits, Computers for patron use, Copy machines, Distance learning, Doc delivery serv, E-Reserves, Electronic databases & coll, Exhibits, Handicapped accessible, ILL available, Music CDs, Online cat, Online ref, Online searches, Orientations, Photocopying/Printing, Pub access computers, Ref serv available, Scanner, Telephone ref, Video lending libr, Wheelchair accessible
Publications: The Off-Campus Library Services Conference Proceedings
Partic in Midwest Collaborative for Library Services (MCLS); OCLC Online Computer Library Center, Inc
Special Services for the Deaf - Assistive tech
Special Services for the Blind - Assistive/Adapted tech devices, equip & products
Open Mon-Thurs 7:50am-Midnight, Fri 7:50am-8pm, Sat 9-6, Sun Noon-Midnight
Friends of the Library Group

Departmental Libraries:

CLARKE HISTORICAL LIBRARY, 250 E Preston, 48859, SAN 323-8741. Tel: 989-774-3352. Reference Tel: 989-774-3864. FAX: 989-774-2160. E-mail: clarke@cmich.edu. Web Site: www.clarke.cmich.edu. *Dir,* Frank Boles; Tel: 989-774-3965, E-mail: frank.j.boles@cmich.edu; *Archivist,* Marian Matyn; Tel: 989-774-3990, E-mail: matyn1mj@cmich.edu; *Ref Librn,* John Fierst; Tel: 989-774-2601, E-mail: fiers1j@cmich.edu; Staff 3 (MLS 2, Non-MLS 1)
Founded 1954
Jul 2007-Jun 2008 Income $918,073. Mats Exp $55,055, Books $26,242, Per/Ser (Incl. Access Fees) $1,662, Micro $21,413, Electronic Ref Mat (Incl. Access Fees) $4,938, Presv $800. Sal $532,507 (Prof $211,288)
Library Holdings: Microforms 11,000; Bk Titles 80,000
Special Collections: Africana & Afro-American (Wilbert Wright Coll); Aladdin Manufacturing Company Records; Angling (Reed T Draper Coll); Class of 1968 Presidential Campaign Biography Coll; Former US Senator & Michigan State Supreme Court Justice Robert P Griffin Papers; Literacy (Lucile Clarke Memorial Children's Library), fiction, textbks; Maureen Hathawy Michigan Culinary Archive, cookbks (M); Michigan Hemingway Coll; Molson Children's Art Coll; Russell Kirk Papers. State Document Depository
Subject Interests: African-Am, Am hist, Children's lit, Mich, Presidents (US)
Function: Archival coll, Electronic databases & coll, Ref serv in person
Publications: Michigan Historical Review
Open Mon-Fri 8-5
Restriction: Closed stack, Internal use only, Non-circulating
Friends of the Library Group

KROMER INSTRUCTIONAL MATERIALS CENTER, 134 EHS Bldg, 48859, SAN 320-0531. Tel: 989-774-3549. *Interim Dir,* Mary Jo Davis

P CHIPPEWA RIVER DISTRICT LIBRARY*, Veterans Memorial Library, 301 S University Ave, 48858-2597. SAN 346-9476. Tel: 989-773-3242. FAX: 989-772-3280. Web Site: www.crdl.org. *Dir,* Lise Mitchell; Tel: 989-772-3488, Ext 12, E-mail: lhmitch@crdl.org; *Commun Relations Librn,* Sue Ellen Deni-Owen; Tel: 989-772-3488, Ext 27, E-mail: sdowen@crdl.org; *Syst Librn,* Monica Fox; Tel: 989-772-3488, Ext 32, E-mail: mfox@crdl.org; *Cat,* Dianne Holt; Tel: 989-772-3488, Ext 24, E-mail: dholt@crdl.org; *Coll Develop,* Alice Jenicke; Tel: 989-772-3488, Ext 20, E-mail: ajenicke@crdl.org; Staff 11 (MLS 4, Non-MLS 7)
Founded 1909. Pop 63,723; Circ 340,489
Library Holdings: Bk Titles 109,032; Bk Vols 160,918; Per Subs 300
Special Collections: Indian Culture & Heritage
Automation Activity & Vendor Info: (Acquisitions) TLC (The Library Corporation); (Cataloging) TLC (The Library Corporation); (Circulation) TLC (The Library Corporation); (OPAC) TLC (The Library Corporation); (Serials) TLC (The Library Corporation)
Database Vendor: Gale Cengage Learning, OCLC FirstSearch
Wireless access
Function: Adult bk club, Art exhibits, Audiobks via web, Bks on cassette, Bks on CD, Children's prog, Computer training, Computers for patron use, Copy machines, Electronic databases & coll, Fax serv, Free DVD rentals, ILL available, Jazz prog, Music CDs, Notary serv, Online cat, Online ref, Preschool outreach, Prog for adults, Prog for children & young adult, Pub access computers, Ref serv available, Scanner, Story hour, Summer reading prog, Tax forms, Teen prog, Telephone ref, VHS videos, Web-catalog, Wheelchair accessible
Partic in Mideastern Michigan Library Cooperative; Midwest Collaborative for Library Services (MCLS); OCLC Online Computer Library Center, Inc
Open Mon-Thurs 9-8, Fri & Sat 10-6, Sun (Sept-May) 1-5
Friends of the Library Group

Branches: 4

COE TOWNSHIP, 308 W Wright Ave, Shepherd, 48883, SAN 346-9506. Tel: 989-828-6801. FAX: 989-828-6801. *Br Mgr,* Janet Silverthorn; E-mail: jsilvert@crdl.org; Staff 1 (Non-MLS 1)
Library Holdings: Bk Titles 14,225
Open Mon & Wed 10-6, Tues & Thurs 12-8, Sat 10-4
Friends of the Library Group

FREMONT TOWNSHIP, 2833 W Blanchard Rd, Winn, 48896. (Mail add: PO Box 368, Winn, 48896-0368), SAN 346-9573. Tel: 989-866-2550. FAX: 989-866-2550. *Br Mgr,* Wes Umstead; E-mail: wumstead@crdl.org; Staff 1 (Non-MLS 1)
Library Holdings: Bk Titles 8,923
Open Mon & Thurs 12-8, Tues & Wed 3-8, Sun 12-4

FAITH JOHNSTON MEMORIAL, 4035 N Mission, Rosebush, 48878. (Mail add: PO Box 151, Rosebush, 48878-0235), SAN 325-4178. Tel: 989-433-0006. FAX: 989-433-0006. *Br Mgr,* Rebecca Bundy; E-mail: rbundy@crdl.org; Staff 1 (Non-MLS 1)
Library Holdings: Bk Titles 9,384
Open Mon & Wed 10-6, Tues & Thurs 12-8, Sun 1-5
Friends of the Library Group

ROLLAND TOWNSHIP, 324 Main St, Blanchard, 49310. (Mail add: PO Box 39, Blanchard, 49310-0039), SAN 346-9565. Tel: 989-561-2480. FAX: 989-561-2480. *Br Mgr,* Ken Newman; E-mail: knewman@crdl.org; Staff 1 (Non-MLS 1)
Library Holdings: Bk Titles 11,156
Open Mon & Wed 10-6, Thurs 2-8, Fri 1-5, Sat 10-2

MULLIKEN

P MULLIKEN DISTRICT LIBRARY*, 135 Main St, 48861. (Mail add: PO Box 246, 48861-0246), SAN 308-292X. Tel: 517-649-8611. FAX: 517-649-2207. E-mail: mulldistlib@yahoo.com. *Dir,* Bobbette Walling; E-mail: mulldistlib@yahoo.com; Staff 3 (Non-MLS 3)
Founded 1903. Pop 1,903; Circ 23,385
Library Holdings: Bk Titles 13,668; Bk Vols 15,638; Per Subs 30
Automation Activity & Vendor Info: (Cataloging) Follett Software; (Circulation) Follett Software
Mem of Woodlands Library Cooperative
Open Mon 10-6, Tues & Thurs 3-8, Fri 1-6

MUNISING

S MICHIGAN DEPARTMENT OF CORRECTIONS*, Alger Maximum Correctional Facility Library, N6141 Industrial Park Dr, 49862. SAN 371-6759. Tel: 906-387-5000, Ext 1302. FAX: 906-387-5033. *Librn,* Janice Yoak; Staff 1 (MLS 1)
Founded 1990
Library Holdings: Bk Vols 8,200
Special Collections: ABE, preGED & GED Prepatory Materials; Native American, African-American & Hispanic History
Subject Interests: Law
Automation Activity & Vendor Info: (Circulation) Follett Software
Restriction: Staff & inmates only

MUSKEGON

C BAKER COLLEGE OF MUSKEGON LIBRARY, 1903 Marquette Ave, 49442-3404. SAN 308-2970. Tel: 231-777-5330. Reference Tel: 231-777-5333, 231-777-5335. Toll Free Tel: 800-937-0337. FAX: 231-777-5334. E-mail: library-mu@baker.edu. Web Site: www.baker.edu. *Dir, Info & Tech Res,* Gail Powers-Schaub; Tel: 231-777-5331, E-mail: gail.powersschaub@baker.edu; *Ref Librn,* Elizabeth Lofgren; *Ref Librn,* Becky Ulrey; *Circ Supvr,* Isabel Rios; *Learning Res Coordr,* Ryan DeCoster; Staff 5 (MLS 4, Non-MLS 1)
Founded 1883. Enrl 4,000; Fac 270; Highest Degree: Doctorate

Library Holdings: Bk Vols 35,000; Per Subs 125
Automation Activity & Vendor Info: (Cataloging) SIRSI WorkFlows; (Circulation) SIRSI WorkFlows; (Course Reserve) SIRSI WorkFlows; (ILL) OCLC; (OPAC) SIRSI WorkFlows; (Serials) EBSCO Online
Wireless access
Partic in Midwest Collaborative for Library Services (MCLS)
Special Services for the Deaf - Accessible learning ctr; ADA equip; Assisted listening device; Assistive tech; Bks on deafness & sign lang; Closed caption videos; Coll on deaf educ; Deaf publ
Special Services for the Blind - Accessible computers; Assistive/Adapted tech devices, equip & products; Audio mat; Bks on CD; Magnifiers
Open Mon-Thurs 7:30am-9pm, Fri 7:30-6, Sat 10-4

P HACKLEY PUBLIC LIBRARY*, 316 W Webster Ave, 49440. SAN 308-2962. Tel: 231-722-7276. Reference Tel: 231-722-7276, Ext 228. Administration Tel: 231-722-7276, Ext 222. FAX: 231-726-5567. Administration FAX: 231-726-4724. E-mail: askus@hackleylibrary.org. Web Site: www.hackleylibrary.org. *Dir,* Martha Ferriby; E-mail: mferriby@hackleylibrary.org; *Asst Dir,* Mary Murphy; Tel: 231-722-7276, Ext 241, E-mail: mmurphy@hackleylibrary.org; *Ref Librn,* Stephani Gibson; E-mail: gibson@hackleylibrary.org; *Circ Mgr,* Dorothy Johnson; Tel: 231-722-7276, Ext 231, E-mail: djohnson@hackleylibrary.org; *Ref Serv, Ad, Website Mgr,* Jocelyn Shaw; Tel: 231-722-7276, Ext 272, E-mail: jshaw@hackleylibrary.org; *Tech Serv,* Mary Susan Kroes; Tel: 231-722-7276, Ext 237, E-mail: skroes@hackleylibrary.org; *Youth Serv,* Cassandra Hamilton; Tel: 231-722-7276, Ext 229, E-mail: chamilton@hackleylibrary.org. Subject Specialists: *Media,* Stephani Gibson; Staff 5.5 (MLS 5.5)
Founded 1890. Pop 40,898; Circ 170,880
Jul 2012-Jun 2013 Income $1,784,569, State $18,281, Locally Generated Income $1,766,288. Mats Exp $123,423, Books $80,658, Per/Ser (Incl. Access Fees) $9,898, Micro $4,238, AV Mat $26,394, Electronic Ref Mat (Incl. Access Fees) $2,235. Sal $934,037 (Prof $205,506)
Library Holdings: CDs 5,898; DVDs 5,478; e-books 3,009; Bk Vols 128,514; Per Subs 169
Special Collections: US Document Depository
Subject Interests: Civil War, Genealogy, Lumbering, Regional hist
Automation Activity & Vendor Info: (Cataloging) OCLC; (Circulation) Innovative Interfaces, Inc; (ILL) Innovative Interfaces, Inc; (OPAC) Innovative Interfaces, Inc; (Serials) Innovative Interfaces, Inc
Database Vendor: Baker & Taylor, Booksite, Checkpoint Systems, Inc, Gale Cengage Learning, H W Wilson, OCLC FirstSearch, OCLC WorldShare Interlibrary Loan, ProQuest, Wilson - Wilson Web
Wireless access
Publications: Community Ink (Quarterly)
Partic in Lakeland Library Cooperative; Midwest Collaborative for Library Services (MCLS)
Open Mon-Tues 12-8, Wed-Sat 10-5
Friends of the Library Group

S LAKESHORE MUSEUM CENTER ARCHIVES*, 471 W Western Ave, 49440-1040. (Mail add: Lakeshore Museum Center, 430 W Clay Ave, 49440-1002), SAN 372-8013. Tel: 231-722-0278. FAX: 231-728-4119. E-mail: info@muskegonmuseum.org. Web Site: www.muskegonmuseum.org. *Archivist,* Beryl Gabel; E-mail: beryl@lakeshoremuseum.org. Subject Specialists: *Muskegon County,* Beryl Gabel
Founded 1937
Library Holdings: Bk Titles 1,728; Bk Vols 2,230; Per Subs 10; Spec Interest Per Sub 10
Special Collections: Lumbering (Charles Yates Coll), photogs; Muskegon County History, bks, mss, photogs. Oral History
Subject Interests: Local hist
Function: Archival coll
Restriction: Open by appt only

M MERCY HEALTH PARTNERS*, Amos Health Science Library, 1500 E Sherman Blvd, 49443. SAN 329-8949. Tel: 231-672-3972. FAX: 231-672-3842. *Med Librn,* Sandra Swanson; Staff 0.7 (MLS 0.7, Non-MLS 0)
Library Holdings: e-journals 800; Bk Titles 1,628; Per Subs 115
Subject Interests: Allied health, Med, Nursing
Automation Activity & Vendor Info: (Cataloging) EOS International; (Circulation) EOS International; (ILL) OCLC; (OPAC) EOS International
Database Vendor: EBSCOhost, Elsevier, MD Consult, Natural Standard, OVID Technologies, ProQuest, PubMed, UpToDate, Wiley InterScience
Wireless access
Partic in Medical Library Association (MLA); Midwest Collaborative for Library Services (MCLS)
Restriction: Authorized patrons, Authorized scholars by appt, Badge access after hrs, Lending to staff only

S MICHIGAN DEPARTMENT OF CORRECTIONS*, Muskegon Correctional Facility Library, 2400 S Sheridan Dr, 49442. Tel: 231-773-3201, Ext 271. FAX: 231-773-3657. *Librn,* Elisia Hardiman; E-mail: hardimane@michigan.gov
Library Holdings: Bk Vols 13,000; Per Subs 20
Open Mon, Fri & Sat 7:30-4, Tues-Thurs 7:30am-9pm, Sun 12-9

P MUSKEGON AREA DISTRICT LIBRARY*, 4845 Airline Rd, Unit 5, 49444-4503. SAN 346-959X. Tel: 231-737-6248. FAX: 231-737-6307. TDD: 231-722-4103. Web Site: www.madl.org. *Dir,* Stephen Dix; E-mail: sdix@madl.org; *Asst Dir, Cent Libr Serv,* Karla Bates; *Asst Dir, Pub Serv,* Richard Schneider; *Bus Mgr,* Brenda Hall; *Youth Serv Coordr,* Michele Wittkopp; Staff 33 (MLS 9, Non-MLS 24)
Founded 2007. Pop 115,715; Circ 496,826
Jan 2012-Dec 2012 Income (Main Library and Branch(s)) $3,005,205, State $120,587, Locally Generated Income $2,459,596, Other $425,022. Mats Exp $289,341, Books $242,100, Per/Ser (Incl. Access Fees) $35,241, Micro $2,000, AV Mat $10,000. Sal $927,777
Library Holdings: Audiobooks 7,000; Large Print Bks 5,000; Bk Vols 231,582; Per Subs 554; Videos 3,000
Special Collections: Blind & Physically Handicapped Library
Automation Activity & Vendor Info: (Cataloging) Innovative Interfaces, Inc; (Circulation) Innovative Interfaces, Inc; (ILL) Innovative Interfaces, Inc; (OPAC) Innovative Interfaces, Inc
Database Vendor: Gale Cengage Learning, Newsbank, ProQuest, World Book Online
Wireless access
Special Services for the Deaf - TDD equip
Special Services for the Blind - Aids for in-house use; Audio mat; Bks & mags in Braille, on rec, tape & cassette; Bks available with recordings; Bks on CD; Braille equip; Children's Braille; Closed circuit TV; Descriptive video serv (DVS); Reader equip
Open Mon-Fri 8-5
Friends of the Library Group
Branches: 10

P BLIND & PHYSICALLY HANDICAPPED LIBRARY, 4845 Airline Rd, Unit 5, 49444. Tel: 231-737-6310. Toll Free Tel: 877-569-4801. FAX: 231-737-6307. TDD: 231-722-4103. E-mail: mclsm@llcoop.org. Web Site: www.madl.org/lbph.htm. *Librn,* Sheila Miller
Founded 1979
Partic in Lakeland Library Cooperative
Special Services for the Deaf - TDD equip
Special Services for the Blind - Bks on cassette; Descriptive video serv (DVS)

DALTON TOWNSHIP BRANCH, 3175 Fifth St, Twin Lake, 49457-9501, SAN 346-9654. Tel: 231-828-4188. FAX: 231 724-6675. E-mail: dal@llcoop.org. Web Site: www.madl.org/dalton. *Br Head,* Sue Monson
Circ 26,370
Library Holdings: AV Mats 508; Bk Vols 14,823; Per Subs 42
Open Mon & Wed 9-7, Tues, Thurs & Fri 9-5, Sat 10-1
Friends of the Library Group

EGELSTON BRANCH, 5428 E Apple Ave, 49442-3008, SAN 346-9689. Tel: 231-788-6477. FAX: 231-724-6675. TDD: 231-722-4106. E-mail: ege@llcoop.org. Web Site: www.madl.org/egelston. *Librn,* Andrew Hammond
Circ 60,563
Library Holdings: AV Mats 1,192; Bk Vols 26,596; Per Subs 77
Special Services for the Deaf - TDD equip
Open Mon & Wed 10-8, Thurs-Sat 10-5
Friends of the Library Group

FRUITPORT BRANCH, Park & Third Sts, Fruitport, 49415-0911, SAN 346-9719. Tel: 231-865-3461. FAX: 231-737-6307. TDD: 231-722-4103. E-mail: fru@llcoop.org. Web Site: www.madl.org/fruitport. *Br Head,* Rachel Church
Circ 23,878
Library Holdings: AV Mats 634; Bk Vols 14,501; Per Subs 43
Open Mon & Tues 11-7, Wed & Fri 11-5, Sat 9-12
Friends of the Library Group

NORTON SHORES JACOB O FUNKHOUSER BRANCH, 705 Seminole Rd, 49441-4797, SAN 346-9832. Tel: 231-780-8844. FAX: 231-780-5436. TDD: 231-722-4103. E-mail: nor@llcoop.org. Web Site: www.madl.org/shores. *Librn,* Mark Ames
Founded 1974. Circ 125,270
Library Holdings: AV Mats 1,987; Bk Vols 52,855; Per Subs 134
Open Mon-Wed 9:30-8, Thurs-Sat 9:30-5
Friends of the Library Group

HOLTON BRANCH, 8776 Holton Duck Lake Rd, Holton, 49425. (Mail add: PO Box 129, Holton, 49425-9616), SAN 346-9743. Tel: 231-821-0268. FAX: 231-724-6675. TDD: 231-722-4103. E-mail: hlt@llcoop.org. Web Site: www.madl.org/holton. *Librn,* Karla Bates
Circ 9,556
Library Holdings: AV Mats 499; Bk Vols 12,230; Per Subs 28
Open Mon & Wed 11-7, Fri 11-5, Sat 10-1
Friends of the Library Group

MONTAGUE BRANCH, 8778 Ferry St, Montague, 49437-1233, SAN 346-9778. Tel: 231-893-2675. FAX: 231-737-6307. TDD: 231-722-4103. E-mail: mon@llcoop.org. Web Site: www.madl.org/montague. *Br Head,* Sharron Smith
Circ 24,019
Library Holdings: AV Mats 765; Bk Vols 21,375; Per Subs 64
Special Services for the Deaf - TDD equip
Open Mon & Tues 11-8, Wed & Fri 11-5, Sat 10-1
Friends of the Library Group

MUSKEGON HEIGHTS BRANCH, 2808 Sanford St, Muskegon Heights, 49444-2010, SAN 346-9808. Tel: 231-739-6075. FAX: 231-737-6307. TDD: 231-722-4103. E-mail: muh@llcoop.org. Web Site: www.madl.org/heights. *Br Head,* Karen Pease
Circ 11,004
Library Holdings: AV Mats 404; Bk Vols 21,770; Per Subs 35
Special Services for the Deaf - TDD equip
Open Mon-Thurs 10-6, Fri & Sat 10-3

NORTH MUSKEGON WALKER BRANCH, 1522 Ruddiman Dr, North Muskegon, 49445-3038, SAN 346-9891. Tel: 231-744-6080. FAX: 231-719-8056. TDD: 231-722-4103. E-mail: nmu@llcoop.org. Web Site: www.madl.org/walker. *Librn,* Char Zoet
Circ 65,995
Library Holdings: AV Mats 1,406; Bk Vols 23,928; Per Subs 98
Special Services for the Deaf - TDD equip
Open Mon & Tues 10-8, Wed-Sat 10-5
Friends of the Library Group

RAVENNA BRANCH, 12278 Stafford, Ravenna, 49451-9410, SAN 346-9867. Tel: 231-853-6975. FAX: 231-737-6307. TDD: 231-722-4103. E-mail: rav@llcoop.org. Web Site: www.madl.org/ravenna. *Br Head,* Diane Landheer
Circ 27,389
Library Holdings: AV Mats 524; Bk Vols 17,962; Per Subs 41
Special Services for the Deaf - TDD equip
Open Mon 11-8, Tues, Wed & Fri 11-5, Sat 9-12

J MUSKEGON COMMUNITY COLLEGE*, Hendrik Meijer Library, 221 S Quarterline Rd, 49442. SAN 308-2989. Tel: 231-777-0269. Circulation Tel: 231-777-0270. Interlibrary Loan Service Tel: 231-777-0205. Reference Tel: 231-777-0326. Automation Services Tel: 231-777-0416. Toll Free Tel: 866-711-4622. FAX: 231-777-0279. TDD: 231-777-0410. Web Site: www.muskegoncc.edu/library. *Coordr, Ref Librn,* Carol Briggs-Erickson; E-mail: carol.briggs-erickson@muskegoncc.edu; *Ref Librn,* Charlotte Griffith; Tel: 231-777-0260; *Cataloger, Ref Librn,* Robert J Vanderlaan; Tel: 231-777-0267; *Adjunct Ref Librn,* Darlene DeHudy; E-mail: darlene.dehudy@muskegoncc.edu; *Adjunct Ref Librn,* Mary Ellen VanStempvoort; Tel: 231-777-0268, E-mail: vanstemm@muskegoncc.edu
Founded 1926. Enrl 5,000; Fac 105; Highest Degree: Associate
Library Holdings: CDs 211; DVDs 546; e-books 21,000; e-journals 19,000; Bk Titles 55,000; Per Subs 150; Videos 1,250
Subject Interests: Careers, Children's lit
Automation Activity & Vendor Info: (Cataloging) OCLC; (Circulation) SirsiDynix; (OPAC) SirsiDynix
Wireless access
Partic in Midwest Collaborative for Library Services (MCLS); OCLC Online Computer Library Center, Inc
Special Services for the Blind - Computer with voice synthesizer for visually impaired persons
Open Mon-Thurs (Fall & Winter) 7:30am-10pm, Fri 7:30-4:30, Sun 1-6

NASHVILLE

P PUTNAM DISTRICT LIBRARY*, 327 N Main St, 49073-9578. (Mail add: PO Box 920, 49073-0920), SAN 308-2997. Tel: 517-852-9723. FAX: 517-852-9723. Web Site: woodlands.lib.mi.us/putnam/putnam.html. *Dir,* Shauna Lea Swantek; *Asst Dir,* Emily Mater; Staff 2 (Non-MLS 2)
Founded 1923
Subject Interests: Local hist
Automation Activity & Vendor Info: (Acquisitions) Follett Software; (Cataloging) Follett Software; (Circulation) Follett Software; (ILL) Mel Cat; (OPAC) Mel Cat
Wireless access
Mem of Woodlands Library Cooperative
Open Mon & Wed 10-6, Tues 3-8, Fri 10-5, Sat 9-12

NEGAUNEE

P NEGAUNEE PUBLIC LIBRARY*, 319 W Case St, 49866. (Mail add: PO Box 548, 49866-0548), SAN 308-3012. Tel: 906-475-9400, Ext 18. FAX: 906-475-4880. Web Site: www.uplibraries.org. *Dir,* Marcia Mattfield; E-mail: mmatt@uproc.lib.mi.us
Founded 1890. Circ 34,723
Library Holdings: Bk Vols 34,000; Per Subs 80
Partic in Superiorland Library Cooperative
Open Mon 1-7, Tues-Fri 10-4

NEW BALTIMORE

P MACDONALD PUBLIC LIBRARY*, 36480 Main St, 48047-2509. SAN 308-3020. Tel: 586-725-0273. FAX: 586-725-8360. E-mail: goikea@libcoop.net. Web Site: www.libcoop.net/newbaltimore. *Dir,* Margaret A Thomas; E-mail: thomasm@libcoop.net; Staff 14 (MLS 2, Non-MLS 12)
Founded 1941. Pop 8,987
Library Holdings: CDs 450; DVDs 800; Bk Vols 42,000; Per Subs 130; Talking Bks 1,200; Videos 1,450
Automation Activity & Vendor Info: (Cataloging) SirsiDynix; (Circulation) SirsiDynix; (ILL) SirsiDynix; (OPAC) SirsiDynix; (Serials) SirsiDynix
Wireless access
Function: Home delivery & serv to Sr ctr & nursing homes, ILL available, Magnifiers for reading, Online searches, Prog for children & young adult, Ref serv available, Summer reading prog, Telephone ref, Wheelchair accessible
Publications: Books & Bytes by the Bay (Newsletter)
Partic in Suburban Library Cooperative
Open Mon-Thurs 10-8, Fri 10-5, Sat 10-4
Friends of the Library Group

NEW BUFFALO

P NEW BUFFALO TOWNSHIP PUBLIC LIBRARY*, 33 N Thompson St, 49117. SAN 308-3039. Tel: 269-469-2933. FAX: 269-469-3521. Web Site: www.nbtpl.org. *Dir,* Julie Grynwich; E-mail: jagryn711@att.net
Founded 1938
Library Holdings: Bk Vols 50,000; Per Subs 112
Subject Interests: Local hist, Mich
Automation Activity & Vendor Info: (Cataloging) Follett Software; (Circulation) Follett Software
Wireless access
Partic in Southwest Michigan Library Cooperative
Open Mon, Tues & Thurs 10-8, Wed & Fri 10-5:30, Sat 10-3
Friends of the Library Group

NEW HAVEN

P LENOX TOWNSHIP LIBRARY*, 58976 Main St, 48048-2685. SAN 308-3047. Tel: 586-749-3430. FAX: 586-749-3245. Web Site: www.libcoop.net/lenox. *Dir,* Joann E Hoffmeyer; E-mail: hoffmeyj@libcoop.net; *Syst Mgr,* Lynn Couck; E-mail: coucklm@libcoop.net; Staff 2 (MLS 1, Non-MLS 1)
Founded 1948. Pop 8,433; Circ 19,450
Library Holdings: Bk Vols 20,000; Per Subs 51
Automation Activity & Vendor Info: (Acquisitions) SirsiDynix; (Cataloging) SirsiDynix; (Circulation) SirsiDynix; (OPAC) SirsiDynix; (Serials) SirsiDynix
Wireless access
Partic in Suburban Library Cooperative
Open Mon-Thurs 10-8, Fri 10-5, Sat (Sept-May) 10-4

NEWAYGO

P NEWAYGO AREA DISTRICT LIBRARY*, 44 N State Rd, 49337-8969. SAN 308-3063. Tel: 231-652-6723. FAX: 231-652-6616. Web Site: www.newaygo.llcoop.org. *Libr Dir,* Dennis Caplis; E-mail: newdc@llcoop.org
Founded 1914. Pop 10,268
Partic in Lakeland Library Cooperative
Special Services for the Blind - Talking bks
Open Mon-Fri 10-6, Sat 10-4
Friends of the Library Group

NEWBERRY

S NEWBERRY CORRECTIONAL FACILITY LIBRARY*, 3001 Newberry Ave, 49868. SAN 377-161X. Tel: 906-293-6200. FAX: 906-293-6323. *Librn,* Janice Yoak; Staff 1 (MLS 1)
Founded 1995
Library Holdings: High Interest/Low Vocabulary Bk Vols 150; Bk Vols 7,200; Per Subs 31
Restriction: Residents only

NILES

M LAKELAND HOSPITAL-NILES*, Health Sciences Library, 31 N St Joseph Ave, 49120. Tel: 269-683-5510. Web Site: www.lakelandhealth.org. *Librn,* Nancy Johns
Library Holdings: Bk Vols 200; Per Subs 85
Restriction: Staff use only

P NILES DISTRICT LIBRARY*, 620 E Main St, 49120. SAN 308-308X. Tel: 269-683-8545. FAX: 269-683-0075. E-mail: info@nileslibrary.net. Web Site: www.nileslibrary.com. *Dir,* Nancy Studebaker; Tel: 269-683-8545, Ext 122, E-mail: director@nileslibrary.net; *Head, Adult Serv,* Kaye Janet; Tel: 269-683-8545, Ext 112; *Head, Cat & Circ,* Deb Solloway; Tel: 269-683-8545, Ext 104; *Head, Youth Serv,* Tara Hunsberger; Tel: 269-683-8545, Ext 109, E mail: youthservices@nileslibrary.net; Staff 21 (MLS 3, Non-MLS 18)
Founded 1903. Pop 25,565; Circ 135,443
Library Holdings: Bk Vols 126,764; Per Subs 250
Special Collections: Niles Newspapers, 1834 to date, microflm; Ring Lardner (Complete Works). Oral History
Automation Activity & Vendor Info: (Cataloging) Evergreen; (Circulation) Evergreen; (OPAC) Evergreen; (Serials) EBSCO Online
Database Vendor: Gale Cengage Learning, ReferenceUSA
Wireless access
Partic in Southwest Michigan Library Cooperative
Open Mon-Thurs 9-8, Fri & Sat 10-6
Friends of the Library Group

NORTH ADAMS

P NORTH ADAMS COMMUNITY MEMORIAL LIBRARY, 110 E Main St, 49262. (Mail add: PO Box 248, 49262-0248). Tel: 517-287-4426. E-mail: NorthAdamsLibrary@gmail.com. Web Site: www.northadamscml.michlibrary.org. *Dir,* Phyllis J Rickard; Staff 1 (Non-MLS 1)
Founded 1921. Pop 4,469
Library Holdings: Large Print Bks 227; Bk Vols 12,150; Per Subs 24; Talking Bks 39
Database Vendor: Auto-Graphics, Inc
Wireless access
Function: Computers for patron use, Free DVD rentals, Handicapped accessible, Preschool reading prog, Pub access computers, Scanner, Story hour, Summer reading prog, Tax forms, Wheelchair accessible
Mem of Woodlands Library Cooperative
Open Wed 12-5, Thurs & Fri 11-5, Sat 9-12
Restriction: In-house use for visitors

NORTH BRANCH

P NORTH BRANCH TOWNSHIP LIBRARY*, 3714 Huron St (M-90), 48461-8117. (Mail add: PO Box 705, 48461-0705), SAN 308-3101. Tel: 810-688-2282. FAX: 810-688-3165. Web Site: www.northbranchlibrary.org. *Dir,* Karen Lambert
Pop 9,124; Circ 38,523
Library Holdings: AV Mats 2,547; Bk Titles 30,000; Per Subs 67; Videos 1,047
Partic in Mideastern Michigan Library Cooperative
Open Mon & Fri 9-5:30, Tues-Thurs 9-8, Sat 9-2

NORTHPORT

P LEELANAU TOWNSHIP PUBLIC LIBRARY*, 119 E Nagonaba St, 49670. (Mail add: PO Box 235, 49670-0235), SAN 308-311X. Tel: 231-386-5131. FAX: 231-386-5874. E-mail: leelanautwplib@yahoo.com. Web Site: leelanautownshiplibrary.org. *Dir,* Deborah Stannard
Founded 1856. Pop 3,000; Circ 30,000
Library Holdings: AV Mats 2,000; CDs 1,800; Large Print Bks 700; Bk Titles 17,000; Bk Vols 20,000; Per Subs 46; Talking Bks 500
Special Collections: US Constitution Coll
Subject Interests: Local hist
Wireless access
Function: Handicapped accessible, ILL available, Online searches, Photocopying/Printing, Prog for adults, Prog for children & young adult, Ref serv available, Summer reading prog, Telephone ref, Wheelchair accessible
Publications: Library Report (Newsletter)
Partic in Mid-Michigan Library League
Open Tues, Thurs, Fri & Sat 9:30-5, Wed 3-8
Friends of the Library Group

NORTHVILLE

P NORTHVILLE DISTRICT LIBRARY*, 212 W Cady St, 48167-1560. SAN 308-3136. Tel: 248-349-3020. FAX: 248-349-8250. Web Site: www.northvillelibrary.org. *Dir,* Julie Herrin; E-mail: jherrin@northvillelibrary.org; Staff 13 (MLS 13)
Founded 1889. Pop 34,467; Circ 255,185
Library Holdings: Large Print Bks 800; Bk Titles 96,000; Per Subs 214
Subject Interests: Local hist
Automation Activity & Vendor Info: (Cataloging) SirsiDynix; (Circulation) SirsiDynix; (OPAC) SirsiDynix; (Serials) SirsiDynix
Wireless access
Function: Handicapped accessible, Home delivery & serv to Sr ctr & nursing homes, Homebound delivery serv, ILL available, Large print keyboards, Magnifiers for reading, Online searches, Photocopying/Printing, Prog for adults, Prog for children & young adult, Ref serv available, Summer reading prog, Wheelchair accessible
Partic in The Library Network
Open Mon-Thurs 10-9, Fri & Sat 10-5, Sun (Sept-May) 1-5
Friends of the Library Group

NOVI

S CLAYTON GROUP SERVICES, INC*, Library & Information Center, 22345 Roethel Dr, 48375-4710. SAN 308-4167. Tel: 248-344-1770. FAX: 248-344-2654. *Dir,* Bob Lieckfield; Staff 1 (MLS 1)
Founded 1954
Library Holdings: Bk Vols 10,000; Per Subs 150
Special Collections: OSHA & EPA Government Documents
Subject Interests: Air pollution, Chem, Noise pollution, Occupational safety, Pollution, Pub health, Toxicology, Waste disposal, Water pollution
Restriction: Staff use only

P NOVI PUBLIC LIBRARY*, 45245 W Ten Mile Rd, 48375. SAN 308-3152. Tel: 248-349-0720. FAX: 248-349-6520. TDD: 248-349-3853. Web Site: www.novilibrary.org. *Dir,* Julie Farkas; E-mail: jfarkas@novilibrary.org; *Asst Dir,* Mary Ellen Mulcrone; E-mail: memulcrone@novilibrary.org; *Asst Dir, Pub Serv,* Margi Karp-Opperer; *Electronic Serv Librn,* Evan Smale; Staff 33 (MLS 13, Non-MLS 20)
Founded 1960. Pop 47,579; Circ 352,814
Jul 2006-Jun 2007 Income $2,709,100. Mats Exp $330,550, Books $233,710, Per/Ser (Incl. Access Fees) $10,000, AV Mat $42,840, Electronic Ref Mat (Incl. Access Fees) $44,000
Library Holdings: AV Mats 12,581; Bk Vols 123,897; Per Subs 153
Automation Activity & Vendor Info: (Acquisitions) SirsiDynix; (Cataloging) SirsiDynix; (Circulation) SirsiDynix; (ILL) SirsiDynix; (OPAC) SirsiDynix
Database Vendor: Gale Cengage Learning, Newsbank, OCLC FirstSearch, OCLC WorldShare Interlibrary Loan, ProQuest, Wilson - Wilson Web
Wireless access
Function: Bk club(s), Copy machines, Electronic databases & coll, Home delivery & serv to Sr ctr & nursing homes, Homebound delivery serv, ILL available, Magnifiers for reading, Online ref, Prog for adults, Prog for children & young adult, Ref serv available, Senior computer classes, Spoken cassettes & CDs, Summer reading prog, Tax forms, Telephone ref, VHS videos
Partic in The Library Network
Special Services for the Deaf - Assistive tech; Bks on deafness & sign lang; Closed caption videos; High interest/low vocabulary bks; TDD equip
Special Services for the Blind - Assistive/Adapted tech devices, equip & products; Bks available with recordings; Bks on cassette; Bks on CD; Closed circuit TV magnifier; Computer with voice synthesizer for visually impaired persons; Copier with enlargement capabilities; Extensive large print coll; Home delivery serv; Low vision equip; Magnifiers
Open Mon-Thurs 10-9, Fri & Sat 10-5, Sun (Sept-May) 1-5
Friends of the Library Group

C WALSH COLLEGE*, Novi Campus Library, 41500 Gardenbrook Rd, 48375-1313. Tel: 248-679-1410. FAX: 248-349-7616. *Librn,* Kim Reeves; E-mail: kreeves@walshcollege.edu
Library Holdings: Bk Vols 100; Per Subs 427
Automation Activity & Vendor Info: (Cataloging) SirsiDynix; (Circulation) SirsiDynix; (Course Reserve) SirsiDynix; (OPAC) SirsiDynix
Open Mon-Thurs 3:30-10:30

OAK PARK

R CONGREGATION BETH SHALOM*, Rabbi Mordecai S Halpern Memorial Library, 14601 W Lincoln Rd, 48237-1391. SAN 308-3160. Tel: 248-547-7970. FAX: 248-547-0421. E-mail: cbs@congbethshalom.org. Web Site: www.congbethshalom.org/resources.html. *Exec Dir,* Steven Weiss; E-mail: execdir@congbethshalom.org
Founded 1953
Library Holdings: Bk Vols 8,000
Subject Interests: Judaica (lit or hist of Jews)
Open Wed 4-6, Sun 9-12

SR MICHIGAN JEWISH INSTITUTE LIBRARY*, 25401 Coolidge Hwy, 48237. Tel: 248-414-6900. FAX: 248-414-6907. E-mail: info@mji.edu. Web Site: www.mji.edu. *Dean,* T Hershel Gardin; Tel: 248-414-6900, Ext 101, E-mail: thgardin@mji.edu; *Librn,* Karen Robertson-Henry; Tel: 248-414-6900, Ext 105, E-mail: krhenry@mji.edu
Founded 1994. Enrl 350; Fac 45; Highest Degree: Bachelor
Library Holdings: Bk Vols 25,000; Per Subs 50
Special Collections: Art Scroll Coll; Fineberg Coll
Wireless access

P OAK PARK PUBLIC LIBRARY*, 14200 Oak Park Blvd, 48237-2089. SAN 308-3209. Tel: 248-691-7480. FAX: 248-691-7155. TDD: 248-547-8216. Web Site: ci.oak-park.mi.us/library. *Dir,* Beth Tompkins; E-mail: btompkins@ci.oak-park.mi.us; Staff 10.5 (MLS 5, Non-MLS 5.5)
Founded 1957. Pop 32,493; Circ 131,377
Library Holdings: High Interest/Low Vocabulary Bk Vols 300; Bk Vols 97,530; Per Subs 185; Spec Interest Per Sub 9
Subject Interests: Arabic lang, Judaica (lit or hist of Jews), Russian (Lang)
Automation Activity & Vendor Info: (Acquisitions) SirsiDynix; (Cataloging) SirsiDynix; (Circulation) SirsiDynix; (ILL) SirsiDynix; (OPAC) SirsiDynix; (Serials) SirsiDynix
Database Vendor: SirsiDynix
Mem of Metropolitan Library System
Special Services for the Deaf - TDD equip
Open Mon-Thurs Noon-8, Fri Noon-6
Friends of the Library Group

OKEMOS

S AUTISM SOCIETY OF MICHIGAN LIBRARY*, 2178 Commons Pkwy, 48864. SAN 374-9673. Tel: 517-882-2800. Toll Free Tel: 800-223-6722. FAX: 517-882-2816. E-mail: autism@autism-mi.org. Web Site: www.autism-mi.org. *Librn,* Anne Carpenter
Library Holdings: Bk Vols 1,000
Open Mon-Fri 8-4:30

OLIVET

C OLIVET COLLEGE LIBRARY*, Burrage Library, 333 S Main St, 49076-9730. SAN 346-9921. Tel: 269-749-7608. FAX: 269-749-7121. Web Site: www.olivetcollege.edu. *Dir,* Elaine Hoeltzel; Tel: 269-749-7582, E-mail: ehoeltzel@olivetcollege.edu; *ILL Coordr,* Gretchen Peters; Tel: 269-749-6658, E-mail: gpeters@olivetcollege.edu; *Libr Asst,* Judy Fales; Tel: 269-749-7595; Staff 3 (MLS 1, Non-MLS 2)
Founded 1844. Enrl 1,059; Fac 69; Highest Degree: Master
Library Holdings: Bk Titles 80,000; Bk Vols 90,000; Per Subs 180
Automation Activity & Vendor Info: (Acquisitions) Civica; (Cataloging) Civica; (Circulation) Civica; (ILL) OCLC; (OPAC) Civica
Database Vendor: BioOne, Civica, Gale Cengage Learning, LearningExpress, OCLC FirstSearch, Project MUSE
Wireless access
Partic in OCLC Online Computer Library Center, Inc
Open Mon-Thurs (Winter) 7:30-11, Fri 7:30-6, Sat 11-3, Sun 2-11; Mon-Fri (Summer) 8:30-4

ONTONAGON

P ONTONAGON TOWNSHIP LIBRARY*, 311 N Steel St, 49953-1398. SAN 308-3233. Tel: 906-884-4411. FAX: 906-884-2829. Web Site: www.uproc.lib.mi.us/Ontonagon. *Dir, Libr Serv,* Alainna Ikola; Staff 1 (Non-MLS 1)
Founded 1904. Pop 4,225; Circ 32,146
Library Holdings: Electronic Media & Resources 297; Large Print Bks 795; Bk Vols 38,953; Per Subs 76; Talking Bks 1,254; Videos 299
Special Collections: Michigan Local History Coll
Automation Activity & Vendor Info: (Cataloging) Follett Software; (Circulation) Follett Software; (ILL) OCLC FirstSearch
Database Vendor: OCLC FirstSearch
Function: Handicapped accessible, ILL available, Online searches, Photocopying/Printing, Summer reading prog
Partic in Susquehanna Library Cooperative
Open Mon & Wed 11-8, Tues & Fri 11-5, Sat 10-2
Branches: 1
ROCKLAND TOWNSHIP, 40 National Ave, Rockland, 49960. (Mail add: PO Box 251, Rockland, 49960-0251). Tel: 906-886-2821. FAX: 906-886-2821. E-mail: rocklib@chartermi.net. *Dir,* Kathleen Preiss; E-mail: merwin24_42@hotmail.com; Staff 2 (Non-MLS 2)
Founded 1968
Library Holdings: Bk Vols 1,000
Open Mon-Wed & Fri 2-5, Sat 12:30-3:30

ORCHARD LAKE

R SS CYRIL & METHODIUS SEMINARY*, Adam Cardinal Maida Alumni Library, 3535 Indian Trail, 48324. SAN 308-3241. Tel: 248-706-4211. Reference Tel: 248-683-0524. FAX: 248-683-0526. E-mail: library@sscms.edu. Web Site: www.sscms.edu/library/index.html. *Dir,* Caryn Noel; E-mail: cnoel@sscms.edu; *Acq Librn, Cataloger,* Judith Edwards; E-mail: jedwards@sscms.edu; Staff 2 (MLS 2)
Founded 1885. Enrl 74; Fac 18; Highest Degree: Master
Library Holdings: AV Mats 1,639; High Interest/Low Vocabulary Bk Vols 50; Bk Titles 86,214; Bk Vols 90,000; Per Subs 150
Special Collections: Polish Language Coll; Polish Language Rare Books
Subject Interests: Culture, Ethnic studies, Lang, Polish (Lang), Theol
Automation Activity & Vendor Info: (Cataloging) SirsiDynix; (Circulation) SirsiDynix; (ILL) OCLC Online; (OPAC) SirsiDynix
Wireless access
Function: ILL available
Partic in Detroit Area Consortium of Catholic Colleges; Midwest Collaborative for Library Services (MCLS); OCLC Online Computer Library Center, Inc
Restriction: In-house use for visitors

ORION

C MIDWESTERN BAPTIST COLLEGE*, B R Lakin Library, 3400 Morgan Rd, 48359-2042. SAN 308-3500. Tel: 248-334-0961. FAX: 248-334-2185. Web Site: www.midwesternbaptistcollege.net. *Dir,* Felister Millie-Koo; Staff 1 (MLS 1)
Founded 1975. Enrl 250; Fac 26; Highest Degree: Doctorate
Library Holdings: Bk Titles 25,000
Subject Interests: Educ, Hist, Relig, Shakespearean lit
Open Mon, Wed & Fri 9-3:30, Tues & Thurs 9-3:30 & 6-8:30

ORTONVILLE

P BRANDON TOWNSHIP PUBLIC LIBRARY*, 304 South St, 48462. SAN 308-325X. Tel: 248-627-1460. Reference Tel: 248-627-1461. Administration Tel: 248-627-1464. FAX: 248-627-9880. Reference FAX: 248-627-1491. Web Site: www.brandonlibrary.org. *Dir,* Rebecca Higgerson; E-mail: rhiggerson@brandonlibrary.org; *Head, Circ,* Gail Carpenter; Tel: 248-627-1472, E-mail: gcarpenter@brandonlibrary.org; *Head, Youth Serv,* Frances Hotchkiss; Tel: 248-627-1473; Staff 32 (MLS 7, Non-MLS 25)
Founded 1924. Pop 14,900; Circ 110,000
Library Holdings: CDs 514; DVDs 900; e-books 3,614; Bk Vols 67,650; Per Subs 182; Talking Bks 2,419; Videos 1,465
Special Collections: Local History, unabridged audiobooks
Subject Interests: Genealogy
Database Vendor: SirsiDynix
Wireless access
Function: Adult literacy prog, Art exhibits, Digital talking bks, Handicapped accessible, Homebound delivery serv, ILL available, Magnifiers for reading, Online searches, Photocopying/Printing, Prog for adults, Prog for children & young adult, Ref serv available, Spoken cassettes & CDs, Summer reading prog, Telephone ref, VHS videos, Wheelchair accessible
Publications: Sequels (Newsletter)
Partic in TLN
Special Services for the Blind - Assistive/Adapted tech devices, equip & products; Audio mat; Bks on cassette; Bks on CD
Open Mon-Thurs 9-9, Fri 9-6, Sat 9-3
Friends of the Library Group

OTSEGO

P OTSEGO DISTRICT PUBLIC LIBRARY*, 401 Dix St, 49078. SAN 308-3268. Tel: 269-694-9690. FAX: 269-694-9129. Web Site: www.otsegolibrary.org. *Dir,* Andrea Estelle; E-mail: aestelle@otsegolibrary.org; *Asst Dir,* Brenda Morris; E-mail: bmorris@otsegolibrary.org; Staff 12 (MLS 1, Non-MLS 11)
Founded 1844. Pop 14,952; Circ 152,812
Jan 2013-Dec 2013 Income $483,424, State $8,382, County $53,000, Locally Generated Income $375,901, Other $46,141. Mats Exp $72,523, Books $36,153, Per/Ser (Incl. Access Fees) $4,000, AV Mat $25,000. Sal $234,000
Library Holdings: AV Mats 435; CDs 2,892; DVDs 3,834; Bk Titles 40,224; Per Subs 100
Special Collections: History of Otsego, 12 volume Coll, bks & micro; Michigan Pioneer Coll
Automation Activity & Vendor Info: (Acquisitions) Auto-Graphics, Inc; (Cataloging) Auto-Graphics, Inc; (Circulation) Auto-Graphics, Inc; (OPAC) Auto-Graphics, Inc
Wireless access
Function: Archival coll, Homebound delivery serv, ILL available
Partic in Midwest Collaborative for Library Services (MCLS); Southwest Michigan Library Cooperative
Open Mon-Thurs 9-8, Fri 9-5:30, Sat 9-2:30
Restriction: 24-hr pass syst for students only
Friends of the Library Group

OVID

P OVID PUBLIC LIBRARY*, 206 N Main St, 48866. (Mail add: PO Box 105, 48866-0105), SAN 320-4847. Tel: 989-834-5800. FAX: 989-834-5113. Web Site: www.ovidlibrary.org. *Dir,* Sharlyn S Huyck; Staff 2 (Non-MLS 2)
Founded 1949. Pop 5,569; Circ 42,152
Library Holdings: Bk Vols 20,000; Per Subs 72
Automation Activity & Vendor Info: (Cataloging) Auto-Graphics, Inc; (Circulation) Auto-Graphics, Inc; (ILL) Mel Cat

Database Vendor: Auto-Graphics, Inc
Wireless access
Partic in White Pine Libr Coop
Open Mon-Wed & Fri 10-8, Sat 10-1

OWOSSO

C BAKER COLLEGE LIBRARY OF OWOSSO*, 1020 S Washington St, 48867-4400. SAN 370-0097. Tel: 989-729-3325. Toll Free Tel: 800-879-3797. FAX: 989-729-3429. E-mail: library-ow@baker.edu. Web Site: www.baker.edu. *Ref Librn,* Derrick Burton; E-mail: derrick.burton@baker.edu; Staff 3 (MLS 2, Non-MLS 1)
Founded 1984. Enrl 3,000; Highest Degree: Bachelor
Library Holdings: Bk Titles 30,000; Per Subs 200
Subject Interests: Allied health, Bus, Computers, Electronics, Eng, Fashion, Interior design, Travel
Automation Activity & Vendor Info: (Cataloging) SirsiDynix; (Circulation) SirsiDynix; (ILL) SirsiDynix
Wireless access

P SHIAWASSEE DISTRICT LIBRARY, Owosso Branch, 502 W Main St, 48867-2607. SAN 308-3306. Tel: 989-725-5134. FAX: 989-723-5444. Web Site: www.sdl.lib.mi.us. *Dir,* Steven Flayer; E-mail: steven.flayer@sdl.lib.mi.us; *Adult Serv, Asst Dir,* Margaret Ann Bentley; E-mail: margaret.bentley@sdl.lib.mi.us; *Ch,* Natalie Young; E-mail: natalie.young@sdl.lib.mi.us; Staff 7 (MLS 2, Non-MLS 5)
Founded 1910. Pop 28,742; Circ 90,815
Library Holdings: AV Mats 5,600; Bk Vols 60,387; Per Subs 158; Videos 1,149
Special Collections: Genealogy, includes surname file; James Oliver Curwood Coll, bks, ms, pictures. Oral History
Subject Interests: Local hist
Automation Activity & Vendor Info: (Circulation) Follett Software; (ILL) OCLC Online; (OPAC) Follett Software
Database Vendor: CredoReference, Gale Cengage Learning, Grolier Online, OCLC FirstSearch
Wireless access
Function: ILL available, Magnifiers for reading, Prog for children & young adult, Ref serv available, Summer reading prog, Telephone ref
Partic in Mideastern Michigan Library Cooperative
Open Mon-Thurs (Winter) 10-9, Fri & Sun 1-5, Sat 10-5; Mon-Thurs (Summer) 10-9, Fri 10-5, Sat 10-2
Restriction: Open to pub for ref & circ; with some limitations
Friends of the Library Group
Branches: 1
DURAND MEMORIAL BRANCH, 700 N Saginaw St, Durand, 48429-1245, SAN 308-0536. Tel: 989-288-3743. FAX: 989-288-3743. *Asst Dir,* Nancy Folaron; E-mail: nancy.folaron@sdl.lib.mi.us; Staff 4 (Non-MLS 4)
Founded 1954. Pop 4,532
Library Holdings: AV Mats 1,928; Bk Vols 21,000; Per Subs 69
Special Collections: City of Durand Coll
Subject Interests: Genealogy, Mich
Automation Activity & Vendor Info: (ILL) Follett Software
Database Vendor: Booksite
Open Mon-Thurs 9:30-8, Fri 9:30-6, Sat 9:30-3
Friends of the Library Group

OXFORD

P OXFORD PUBLIC LIBRARY*, 530 Pontiac Rd, 48371-4844. SAN 308-3314. Tel: 248-628-3034. FAX: 248-628-5008. Web Site: www.oxford.lib.mi.us. *Dir,* Bryan Cloutier; *Head, Adult Serv,* Pat Cebelak; *Head, Support Serv,* Nancy Wier; *Head, Youth Serv,* Shae Smith; Staff 25 (MLS 7, Non-MLS 18)
Founded 1916. Pop 16,025; Circ 95,000
Library Holdings: Bk Vols 47,000; Per Subs 120
Automation Activity & Vendor Info: (Cataloging) SirsiDynix; (Circulation) SirsiDynix; (OPAC) SirsiDynix
Database Vendor: SirsiDynix
Wireless access
Open Mon-Thurs 10-9, Fri & Sat 10-5, Sun (Sept-May) 1-5

PALMER

P RICHMOND TOWNSHIP LIBRARY*, Smith St, 49871. (Mail add: PO Box 35, 49871-0035), SAN 308-3322. Tel: 906-475-5241. FAX: 906-475-7516. E-mail: richtown@uproc.lib.mi.us. Web Site: www.uproc.lib.mi.us/rich. *Dir,* Jan St Germain; Staff 1 (MLS 1)
Founded 1975. Pop 1,095
Library Holdings: Bk Titles 5,600; Bk Vols 7,000; Per Subs 32
Special Collections: Finnish Coll
Partic in Superiorland Library Cooperative
Open Mon 12-6, Tues 11-5 & 7-9, Fri 11-5

PARADISE

P WHITEFISH TOWNSHIP COMMUNITY LIBRARY*, 7247 North M Hwy 123, 49768. (Mail add: PO Box 197, 49768-0197), SAN 376-7086. Tel: 906-492-3500. FAX: 906-492-3500. Web Site: eup.k12.mi.us. *Dir,* Cindy Bulmer; E-mail: cbulmer@eup.k12.mi.us
Founded 1975. Circ 1,470
Library Holdings: Bk Titles 8,700; Bk Vols 10,000; Per Subs 30
Automation Activity & Vendor Info: (Cataloging) SirsiDynix; (Circulation) SirsiDynix
Open Tues, Thurs & Fri 10-4, Wed 12-8, Sat 10-2

PARCHMENT

P PARCHMENT COMMUNITY LIBRARY*, 401 S Riverview Dr, 49004-1200. SAN 308-3330. Tel: 269-343-7747. FAX: 269-343-7749. Web Site: www.parchmentlibrary.org. *Dir,* Teresa L Stannard; Tel: 269-343-7747, Ext 203, E-mail: teresa@parchmentlibrary.org; Staff 12 (MLS 3, Non-MLS 9)
Founded 1963. Pop 9,969; Circ 109,180
Library Holdings: Audiobooks 1,333; CDs 1,341; DVDs 1,475; Large Print Bks 1,330; Bk Vols 46,209; Per Subs 98
Special Collections: Parchment History Coll, newsp, pictures. Oral History
Automation Activity & Vendor Info: (Cataloging) Insignia Software; (Circulation) Insignia Software; (ILL) Innovative Interfaces, Inc - Millenium; (OPAC) Insignia Software; (Serials) Insignia Software
Wireless access
Function: Adult bk club, Archival coll, Audio & video playback equip for onsite use, Audiobks via web, Bks on CD, Children's prog, Computers for patron use, Fax serv, Free DVD rentals, Handicapped accessible, Notary serv, Online cat, Photocopying/Printing, Preschool reading prog, Printer for laptops & handheld devices, Prog for adults, Prog for children & young adult, Pub access computers, Ref serv available, Scanner, Story hour, Summer reading prog, Tax forms, Teen prog, Telephone ref, Web-catalog
Partic in Southwest Michigan Library Cooperative
Open Mon-Thurs 10-8, Fri 10-6, Sat 10-4
Friends of the Library Group

PAW PAW

P PAW PAW DISTRICT LIBRARY*, 609 W Michigan Ave, 49079-1072. SAN 308-3349. Tel: 269-657-3800. FAX: 269-657-2603. E-mail: ppdl49079@yahoo.com. Web Site: www.pawpaw.lib.mi.us. *Dir,* John Mohney; Staff 2 (MLS 2)
Founded 1920. Pop 12,398; Circ 64,950
Library Holdings: Bk Vols 66,636; Per Subs 142
Special Collections: Michigan Coll
Automation Activity & Vendor Info: (Cataloging) Auto-Graphics, Inc; (Circulation) Auto-Graphics, Inc; (ILL) Auto Graphics, Inc; (OPAC) Auto Graphics, Inc; (Serials) Auto-Graphics, Inc
Partic in Mich Libr Asn; Southwest Michigan Library Cooperative
Open Mon, Tues & Thurs 9-8, Wed 12-8, Fri & Sat 9-5

PECK

P ELK TOWNSHIP LIBRARY*, 29 E Lapeer St, 48466. (Mail add: PO Box 268, 48466-0268), SAN 308-3357. Tel: 810-378-5409. FAX: 810-378-5016. E-mail: library@airadv.net. Web Site: www.elktwplibrary.org. *Dir,* Janet Dyki
Founded 1938. Pop 4,088; Circ 10,000
Apr 2008-Mar 2009 Income $50,000. Mats Exp $6,200, Books $5,400, Per/Ser (Incl. Access Fees) $800. Sal $24,000
Library Holdings: CDs 131; Large Print Bks 450; Bk Vols 10,000; Per Subs 30; Videos 100
Wireless access
Partic in White Pine Libr Coop
Open Tues & Thurs 9-12 & 1-7, Wed & Fri 9-12 & 1-5, Sat 9-1

PENTWATER

P PENTWATER TOWNSHIP LIBRARY*, 402 E Park, 49449. SAN 308-3365. Tel: 231-869-8581. FAX: 231-869-4000. Web Site: www.pentwaterlibrary.org. *Dir,* Marilyn Cluchey; E-mail: mcluchey@pentwaterlibrary.org
Circ 19,000
Library Holdings: Bk Vols 17,000; Per Subs 100
Special Collections: Michigan Coll
Automation Activity & Vendor Info: (Cataloging) Auto-Graphics, Inc; (Circulation) Auto-Graphics, Inc
Wireless access
Partic in Mid-Michigan Library League
Open Mon & Thurs 9-8:30, Tues, Wed & Fri 9-5, Sat 9-2
Friends of the Library Group

PETOSKEY

S LITTLE TRAVERSE HISTORY MUSEUM LIBRARY*, 100 Depot Ct, 49770. SAN 321-2335. Tel: 231-347-2620. FAX: 231-347-2875. E-mail: info@petoskeymuseum.org. Web Site: www.petoskeymuseum.org. *Dir,* Mary Candace Eaton; Staff 1 (Non-MLS 1)
Founded 1905
Library Holdings: Bk Vols 4,400
Special Collections: Little Traverse Bay Area; Petoskey Newspapers 1875-1979
Subject Interests: Local hist
Open Mon-Fri (May-Oct) 10-4, Sat 1-4

J NORTH CENTRAL MICHIGAN COLLEGE LIBRARY*, 1515 Howard St, 49770. SAN 308-3381. Tel: 231-348-6615. FAX: 231-348-6629. E-mail: library@ncmich.edu. Web Site: library.ncmich.edu. *Librn,* Eunice Teel; Tel: 231-348-6715, E-mail: eteel@ncmich.edu; Staff 2 (MLS 1, Non-MLS 1)
Founded 1958. Enrl 3,200; Fac 32; Highest Degree: Associate
Library Holdings: e-books 67,000; Bk Titles 36,000; Per Subs 300
Special Collections: Nuclear Documents. US Document Depository
Subject Interests: Hist, Soc sci & issues
Automation Activity & Vendor Info: (Circulation) Follett Software; (Course Reserve) Follett Software; (OPAC) Follett Software
Database Vendor: EBSCOhost, Gale Cengage Learning, LexisNexis, OCLC FirstSearch, ProQuest
Wireless access
Special Services for the Blind - Aids for in-house use

M NORTHERN MICHIGAN REGIONAL HOSPITAL*, Dean C Burns Health Sciences Library, 416 Connable Ave, 49770. SAN 308-339X. Tel: 231-487-4500. FAX: 231-487-7892. E-mail: library@northernhealth.org. Web Site: www.northernhealth.org. *Librn,* Anne Foster
Library Holdings: Per Subs 400
Subject Interests: Health sci
Open Mon-Fri 8:30-5

P PETOSKEY DISTRICT LIBRARY*, 500 E Mitchell St, 49770. SAN 308-3403. Tel: 231-758-3100. Circulation Tel: 231-758-3111. Reference Tel: 231-758-3114. Administration Tel: 231-758-3120. E-mail: library@petoskeylibrary.org. Web Site: www.petoskeylibrary.org. *Dir,* Karen L Sherrard; E-mail: director@petoskeylibrary.org; *Ch Serv,* Ronald A Fowler; Tel: 231-758-3112, E-mail: rfowler@petoskeylibrary.org; Staff 9 (MLS 1, Non-MLS 8)
Founded 1905. Pop 14,568; Circ 124,000
Library Holdings: Bk Vols 75,000; Per Subs 140
Special Collections: Great Lakes Americana (William H Ohle Coll)
Automation Activity & Vendor Info: (Cataloging) SirsiDynix; (Circulation) SirsiDynix; (OPAC) SirsiDynix; (Serials) SirsiDynix
Wireless access
Function: Adult literacy prog, Art exhibits, Audiobks via web, Bks on cassette, Bks on CD, Children's prog, Computers for patron use, Copy machines, E-Reserves, Electronic databases & coll, Family literacy, Fax serv, Games & aids for the handicapped, Handicapped accessible, Holiday prog, Home delivery & serv to Sr ctr & nursing homes, ILL available, Instruction & testing, Magnifiers for reading, Mail & tel request accepted, Music CDs, Newsp ref libr, Online cat, Online ref, Photocopying/Printing, Preschool outreach, Prog for adults, Prog for children & young adult, Provide serv for the mentally ill, Pub access computers, Ref & res, Ref serv in person, Scanner, Spoken cassettes & CDs, Spoken cassettes & DVDs, Story hour, Summer reading prog, Tax forms, Teen prog
Partic in Northland Library Cooperative
Open Mon-Thurs 10-7, Fri-Sun 12-5
Restriction: Non-resident fee
Friends of the Library Group

PIGEON

P PIGEON DISTRICT LIBRARY*, 7236 Nitz St, 48755. (Mail add: PO Box 357, 48755-0357), SAN 308-3411. Tel: 989-453-2341. FAX: 989-453-2266. E-mail: pdl@pigeondistrictlibrary.com. Web Site: www.pigeondistrictlibrary.com. *Dir,* Jeanette Bach; *Asst Dir,* Jane Himmel; Staff 8 (Non-MLS 8)
Founded 1913. Pop 9,300; Circ 59,116
Jul 2005-Jun 2006 Income $197,091. Mats Exp $20,993. Sal $98,711
Library Holdings: Bks on Deafness & Sign Lang 36; CDs 308; DVDs 289; High Interest/Low Vocabulary Bk Vols 339; Large Print Bks 1,042; Bk Vols 44,000; Per Subs 98; Talking Bks 805; Videos 3,227
Special Collections: Joann Haist Coll (Details births, deaths, marriages, and history of Pigeon businesses from 1897.); Michigan Vertical File (Newspaper clippings from area newspapers - see website for a listing of files in Michigan Vertical File); Parent Resource Center (Books and audio books on parenting)
Subject Interests: Adult lit, Local hist
Automation Activity & Vendor Info: (Circulation) SirsiDynix; (ILL) SirsiDynix
Database Vendor: OCLC FirstSearch
Wireless access
Function: Home delivery & serv to Sr ctr & nursing homes, ILL available, Magnifiers for reading, Photocopying/Printing, Prog for children & young adult, Summer reading prog, Wheelchair accessible
Partic in White Pine Libr Coop
Special Services for the Deaf - Assistive tech; Bks on deafness & sign lang; High interest/low vocabulary bks
Special Services for the Blind - Aids for in-house use; Bks on CD; Copier with enlargement capabilities; Extensive large print coll; Large print bks; Lending of low vision aids; Low vision equip; Magnifiers; Talking bks
Friends of the Library Group

PINCKNEY

P PINCKNEY COMMUNITY PUBLIC LIBRARY*, 125 Putnam St, 48169. SAN 308-342X. Tel: 734-878-3888. Administration Tel: 734-878-2952. FAX: 734-878-2907. Web Site: www.pinckneylibrary.org. *Dir,* Hope Siasoco; *Asst Dir, Youth/Young Adult Librn,* Sara Castle; Staff 9 (MLS 2, Non-MLS 7)
Founded 1952. Pop 10,548; Circ 34,675
Library Holdings: AV Mats 1,363; High Interest/Low Vocabulary Bk Vols 150; Large Print Bks 277; Bk Vols 18,820; Per Subs 55
Special Collections: Graphic Novels; Michigan/Local History (Village of Pinckney), doc, microfilms, newsp, yearbks
Automation Activity & Vendor Info: (Acquisitions) Brodart; (Cataloging) Follett Software; (Circulation) Follett Software; (OPAC) Follett Software
Function: Home delivery & serv to Sr ctr & nursing homes, Homebound delivery serv, ILL available, Photocopying/Printing, Prog for children & young adult, Summer reading prog
Partic in Mich Libr Asn; Midwest Collaborative for Library Services (MCLS); The Library Network
Open Mon, Wed & Fri 10-6, Tues & Thurs 10-8, Sat 10-2
Friends of the Library Group

PITTSFORD

P PITTSFORD PUBLIC LIBRARY, 9268 E Hudson Rd, 49271. SAN 308-3438. Tel: 517-523-2565. FAX: 517-523-2565. *Dir,* Susan Ruder; E-mail: sruder@monroe.lib.mi.us
Founded 1962. Pop 4,291; Circ 11,281
Library Holdings: Large Print Bks 400; Bk Vols 14,000; Per Subs 40; Talking Bks 64; Videos 300
Automation Activity & Vendor Info: (Cataloging) Book Systems; (Circulation) Book Systems; (OPAC) Book Systems
Mem of Woodlands Library Cooperative
Open Tues 11-7, Wed & Fri 12-5, Thurs 11-5, Sat 10-12

PLAINWELL

P CHARLES A RANSOM DISTRICT LIBRARY*, 180 S Sherwood Ave, 49080-1896. SAN 308-3446. Tel: 269-685-8024. FAX: 269-685-2266. Web Site: www.ransomlibrary.org. *Dir,* Katie Bell Moore; E-mail: kbmoore@ransomlibrary.org; *Asst Dir, Youth Serv,* Joe Gross; *Circ,* Karena Chapman; *Circ,* Julie Stout; *ILL,* Dawn Holtman; Staff 2 (MLS 1, Non-MLS 1)
Founded 1868. Pop 13,593
Library Holdings: Bk Vols 55,000; Per Subs 79
Special Collections: Burchfield Room; Sandy Stamm Archives Room
Subject Interests: Adult educ
Automation Activity & Vendor Info: (Cataloging) Follett Software; (Circulation) Follett Software
Partic in Southwest Michigan Library Cooperative
Special Services for the Blind - Reader equip
Open Mon-Thurs 10-9, Fri & Sat 10-5, Sun (Sept-May) 1-5
Friends of the Library Group

PLYMOUTH

P PLYMOUTH DISTRICT LIBRARY*, 223 S Main St, 48170-1687. SAN 308-3454. Tel: 734-453-0750. Circulation Tel: 734-453-0750, Ext 3. Reference Tel: 734-453-0750, Ext 1. Automation Services Tel: 734-453-0750, Ext 6. FAX: 734-453-0733. TDD: 734-453-6712. E-mail: info@plymouthlibrary.org. Web Site: plymouthlibrary.org. *Dir,* Carol Souchock; Tel: 734-453-0750, Ext 218, E-mail: csouchock@plymouthlibrary.org; *Teen Librn,* Barb Dinan; Tel: 734-453-0750, Ext 271, E-mail: bdinan@plymouthlibrary.org; *Bus Mgr,* Robyn Lowenstein; Tel: 734-453-0750, Ext 215; *Mgr, Network Serv,* Frank Ferguson; Tel: 734-453-0750, Ext 239, E-mail: ferguson@plymouthlibrary.org; *Adult Serv Coordr,* Holly Hibner; Tel: 734-453-0750, Ext 213; *Youth Serv Coordr,* Carol Champagne; Tel: 734-453-0750, Ext 237, E-mail: cchamp@plymouthlibrary.org; Staff 42 (MLS 15, Non-MLS 27)
Founded 1923. Pop 36,820; Circ 947,000

Library Holdings: Bk Vols 220,000; Per Subs 200
Automation Activity & Vendor Info: (Acquisitions) SirsiDynix; (Cataloging) SirsiDynix; (Circulation) SirsiDynix; (OPAC) SirsiDynix; (Serials) SirsiDynix
Partic in TLN
Open Mon-Thurs 9:30-9, Fri 9:30-6, Sat 9:30-5, Sun 12-5
Friends of the Library Group

S PLYMOUTH HISTORICAL MUSEUM ARCHIVES, 155 S Main St, 48170-1635. SAN 371-6546. Tel: 734-455-8940. FAX: 734-455-7797. E-mail: secretary@plymouthhistory.org. Web Site: www.plymouthhistory.org. *Exec Dir,* Elizabeth Kelley Kerstens; E-mail: director@plymouthhistory.org; *Archivist,* Heidi Nielsen; E-mail: archivist@plymouthhistory.org; Staff 1 (MLS 1)
Founded 1976
Library Holdings: Bk Titles 5,000; Per Subs 10
Special Collections: Civil War History (War of the Rebellion Coll), bks, rec; Local Newspapers & Census Records, microfilm; Michigan History; Petz Abraham Lincoln Coll, bks, papers, photos; Plymouth Birth/Death Records; Schrader Funeral Home Records
Publications: Plymouth's First Century - Innovators & Industry

PONTIAC

GL ADAMS-PRATT OAKLAND COUNTY LAW LIBRARY*, 1200 N Telegraph Rd, Bldg 14 E, 48341-0481. SAN 308-3519. Tel: 248-858-0012. Administration Tel: 248-452-9472. Automation Services Tel: 248-858-0011. FAX: 248-858-1536. E-mail: asklaw@oakgov.com. Web Site: www.oakgov.com/libraries/pages/default.aspx. *Dir, Libr Serv,* Laura Mancini; Staff 4 (MLS 2, Non-MLS 2)
Founded 1904
Special Collections: Michigan Legislative History, 1973 to 2002; Michigan Statutes, 1838 to date. Municipal Document Depository; State Document Depository; US Document Depository
Subject Interests: State law
Automation Activity & Vendor Info: (Acquisitions) SirsiDynix; (Cataloging) Horizon; (Circulation) SirsiDynix; (OPAC) SirsiDynix; (Serials) Horizon
Database Vendor: Westlaw
Wireless access
Partic in Detroit Area Library Network; OCLC Online Computer Library Center, Inc
Open Mon-Fri 8:30-5
Restriction: Non circulating to the pub
Friends of the Library Group

M MCLAREN OAKLAND*, Medical Library, 50 N Perry St, 48342-2217. SAN 308-3543. Tel: 248-338-5000, Ext 3155. FAX: 248-338-5025. E-mail: library@mclaren.org. *Librn,* Sheela John; E-mail: sheela.john@mclaren.org; Staff 1 (MLS 1)
Founded 1962
Library Holdings: Bk Titles 2,250; Per Subs 172
Wireless access
Partic in Metrop Detroit Med Libr Group; Michigan Health Sciences Libraries Association; MLC

S OAKLAND COUNTY JAIL LIBRARY*, 1201 N Telegraph Rd, 48341-0450. Tel: 248-858-2925. *Supvr,* Kurt Rachar; E-mail: rachark@oakgov.com

S OAKLAND COUNTY PIONEER & HISTORICAL SOCIETY, Library & Archives, 405 Cesar E Chavez Ave, 48342-1068. SAN 373-2169. Tel: 248-338-6732. FAX: 248-338-6731. E-mail: office@ocphs.org. Web Site: www.ocphs.org. *Coordr,* Leilani Ward
Founded 1874
Library Holdings: Bk Vols 3,500
Special Collections: Oral History
Subject Interests: Civil War, Local hist, Manuscripts, Oral hist
Wireless access
Function: Res performed for a fee
Publications: Oakland Gazette (Newsletter)
Open Tues-Thurs 11-4
Restriction: Non-circulating

S OAKLAND COUNTY RESEARCH LIBRARY*, 1200 N Telegraph Rd, Bldg 14 E, 48341-0453. SAN 308-3527. Tel: 248-858-0012. Administration Tel: 248-452-9472. FAX: 248-858-1536. E-mail: reslib@oakgov.com. Web Site: www.oakgov.com/libraries/pages/default.aspx. *Dir, Libr Serv,* Laura Mancini; E-mail: mancinil@oakgov.com; Staff 3 (MLS 1, Non-MLS 2)
Founded 1969
Special Collections: Census; Local Documents; Local History & Genealogy. State Document Depository; US Document Depository
Subject Interests: Bus & mgt, Census, Local govt, Personnel mgt, Planning, Sewage, Sociol, Transportation
Automation Activity & Vendor Info: (Cataloging) Horizon; (Circulation) SirsiDynix; (OPAC) Horizon; (Serials) Horizon
Wireless access
Partic in Detroit Area Library Network; The Library Network
Open Mon-Fri 8:30-5
Friends of the Library Group

P PONTIAC PUBLIC LIBRARY*, 60 E Pike St, 48342. SAN 346-9980. Tel: 248-758-3942. FAX: 248-758-3990. E-mail: pont@tln.lib.mi.us. Web Site: www.pontiac.lib.mi.us. *Dir,* Stephanie McCoy; Tel: 248-758-3940
Library Holdings: Bk Titles 80,000; Bk Vols 90,000; Per Subs 150
Subject Interests: Hist
Open Mon-Wed 9-8, Thurs & Fri 9-6, Sat 10-2
Friends of the Library Group

M SAINT JOSEPH MERCY OAKLAND HOSPITAL LIBRARY*, 44405 Woodward Ave, 48341-2985. SAN 308-3551. Tel: 248-858-3495. FAX: 248-858-6496. *Mgr,* Dana Blumenstein; Staff 2 (MLS 1, Non-MLS 1)
Library Holdings: Bk Titles 4,000; Per Subs 300
Subject Interests: Consumer health, Med, Nursing
Automation Activity & Vendor Info: (Acquisitions) EOS International; (Cataloging) EOS International; (Circulation) EOS International
Database Vendor: OVID Technologies
Partic in National Network of Libraries of Medicine; OCLC Online Computer Library Center, Inc; Regional Med Libr - Region 3
Friends of the Library Group

PORT AUSTIN

P PORT AUSTIN TOWNSHIP LIBRARY*, 114 Railroad St, 48467. SAN 308-3586. Tel: 989-738-7212. FAX: 989-738-7983. Web Site: www.portaustinlibrary.org. *Dir,* Mary Jaworski; E-mail: m.jaworski@vlc.lib.mi.us
Founded 1947. Pop 4,074; Circ 17,500
Library Holdings: Large Print Bks 150; Bk Titles 10,100; Bk Vols 10,890; Per Subs 46; Talking Bks 200
Subject Interests: Local hist
Partic in White Pine Libr Coop
Open Mon & Thurs 1-8, Tues 10-12 & 1-5, Wed 10-12 & 1-8, Fri 1-4, Sat 10-2
Friends of the Library Group

PORT HURON

C BAKER COLLEGE OF PORT HURON LIBRARY*, 3403 Lapeer Rd, 48060-2597. Tel: 810-989-2122. Toll Free Tel: 888-262-2442. FAX: 810-985-6920. E-mail: library-ph@baker.edu. Web Site: www.baker.edu. *Acad Res Coordr,* Ellen Horon; E-mail: ellen.horton@baker.edu
Library Holdings: Bk Vols 10,000; Per Subs 90
Automation Activity & Vendor Info: (Acquisitions) SirsiDynix; (Cataloging) SirsiDynix; (Circulation) SirsiDynix; (OPAC) SirsiDynix
Database Vendor: ABC-CLIO, Discovery Education, EBSCO - WebFeat, EBSCOhost, Facts on File, Gale Cengage Learning, Medline, Mergent Online, Newsbank, OCLC FirstSearch, OCLC WorldShare Interlibrary Loan, ProQuest, ScienceDirect, Wilson - Wilson Web
Wireless access

J SAINT CLAIR COUNTY COMMUNITY COLLEGE*, Learning Resources Center, 323 Erie St, 48060. (Mail add: PO Box 5015, 48061-5015), SAN 308-3608. Tel: 810-984-3881, 810-989-5640. Reference Tel: 810-989-5640, Ext 2. Toll Free Tel: 800-553-2427, Ext 5640. FAX: 810-984-2852. E-mail: lrc@sc4.edu. Web Site: www.sc4.edu/lrc. *Dean,* Cindy Rourke; E-mail: crourke@sc4.edu; *Dir,* Kathleen James; *Pub Serv,* Jane Lewandoski; *Pub Serv,* Janine Odelvak; *Pub Serv,* Larry Yaek; *Tech Serv,* Judy Wager; Staff 14 (MLS 5, Non-MLS 9)
Founded 1923. Enrl 3,033; Fac 80; Highest Degree: Associate
Library Holdings: Bk Titles 56,541; Bk Vols 61,960; Per Subs 575
Automation Activity & Vendor Info: (Acquisitions) Horizon; (Cataloging) Horizon; (Circulation) Horizon; (Course Reserve) Horizon; (ILL) Horizon; (Media Booking) Horizon; (OPAC) Horizon; (Serials) Horizon
Database Vendor: SirsiDynix
Partic in Midwest Collaborative for Library Services (MCLS); OCLC Online Computer Library Center, Inc
Open Mon-Thurs (Fall & Winter) 7:30am-9pm, Fri 7:30-4, Sat 8-4, Sun 1-5; Mon-Thurs (Spring) 7:30am-9pm, Fri 7:30-4

P SAINT CLAIR COUNTY LIBRARY SYSTEM, 210 McMorran Blvd, 48060-4098. SAN 347-0199. Tel: 810-987-7323. Toll Free Tel: 877-987-7323. FAX: 810-987-7874. Web Site: www.sccl.lib.mi.us. *Dir,* Allison Arnold; Tel: 810-987-7323, Ext 122, E-mail: aarnold@sccl.lib.mi.us; *Br Coordr,* Melba Moss; Tel: 810-987-7323, Ext

136, E-mail: mmoss@sccl.lib.mi.us; *Mkt Coordr,* Position Currently Open; *Circ & ILL,* Anne Marie Bedard; Tel: 810-987-7323, Ext 143, E-mail: abedard@sccl.lib.mi.us; *Tech Serv,* Position Currently Open; *Youth Serv,* Janet Rose; Tel: 810-987-7323, Ext 132, E-mail: jrose@sccl.lib.mi.us; Staff 11 (MLS 11)
Founded 1917. Pop 163,040; Circ 793,748
Library Holdings: Bk Vols 389,519; Per Subs 1,161
Special Collections: Michigan & the Great Lakes (W L Jenks Historical Coll), bks, maps, microfilm, ms, per, photog. Can & Prov; State Document Depository; US Document Depository
Subject Interests: Local hist
Automation Activity & Vendor Info: (Acquisitions) SirsiDynix; (Cataloging) SirsiDynix; (Circulation) SirsiDynix; (OPAC) SirsiDynix; (Serials) SirsiDynix
Database Vendor: Gale Cengage Learning, ProQuest, Standard & Poor's, TumbleBookLibrary, Westlaw, World Book Online
Wireless access
Publications: Annual Report; Library Links (Newsletter)
Partic in Midwest Collaborative for Library Services (MCLS); The Library Network
Special Services for the Deaf - TTY equip
Special Services for the Blind - Aids for in-house use; Bks on cassette; Bks on CD; Braille servs; Closed circuit TV; Computer with voice synthesizer for visually impaired persons; Descriptive video serv (DVS); Dragon Naturally Speaking software; Large print bks & talking machines; Low vision equip; Machine repair; Magnifiers; Reader equip; Talking bk & rec for the blind cat; Talking bks
Open Mon-Thurs 8:30am-9pm, Fri & Sat 8:30-5
Friends of the Library Group

Branches: 11

BURTCHVILLE TOWNSHIP, 7093 Second St, Lakeport, 48059. Tel: 810-385-8550. *Br Mgr,* Jane Fortushniak; E-mail: jfortushniak@sccl.lib.mi.us
Pop 3,500
Open Mon & Thurs 12-8, Tues, Wed, Fri & Sat 9-5
Friends of the Library Group

G LYNN CAMPBELL BRANCH, 1955 N Allen Rd, Kimball, 48074, SAN 347-0229. Tel: 810-982-9171. FAX: 810-987-9689. *Br Mgr,* Patricia Kenner; E-mail: pkenner@sccl.lib.mi.us
Founded 1962
Library Holdings: Bk Vols 12,939
Open Mon & Thurs 12-8, Tues, Wed, Fri & Sat 9-5
Friends of the Library Group

CAPAC PUBLIC, 111 N Main St, Capac, 48014, SAN 347-0253. Tel: 810-395-7000. FAX: 810-395-2863. *Br Mgr,* Nancy Godinez; E-mail: ngodinez@sccl.lib.mi.us
Founded 1919. Pop 2,000
Library Holdings: Bk Vols 18,268
Open Mon & Thurs 12-8, Tues, Wed, Fri & Sat 9-5
Friends of the Library Group

IRA TOWNSHIP, 7013 Meldrum Rd, Fair Haven, 48023, SAN 347-0318. Tel: 586-725-9081. FAX: 586-725-1256. *Br Mgr,* Gary Kupper; E-mail: gkupper@sccl.lib.mi.us
Founded 1965. Pop 5,500
Library Holdings: Bk Vols 15,613
Open Mon & Thurs 12-8, Tues, Wed, Fri & Sat 9-5
Friends of the Library Group

P LIBRARY FOR THE BLIND & PHYSICALLY HANDICAPPED, 210 McMorran Blvd, 48060, SAN 347-0164. Tel: 810-982-3600. Toll Free Tel: 800-272-8570. FAX: 810-987-7327. TDD: 810-455-0200. *Librn,* Mary Redigan
Publications: LBPH (Newsletter)
Special Services for the Deaf - TTY equip
Friends of the Library Group

LITERACY PROJECT, 210 McMorran Blvd, 48060, SAN 371-8808. Tel: 810-987-7323, Ext 156. FAX: 810-987-7327. *Pres, Literacy Project,* Sue Rutledge
Library Holdings: Bk Vols 2,000
Publications: Ready to Read
Friends of the Library Group

MARINE CITY PUBLIC, 300 S Parker Rd, Marine City, 48039, SAN 347-0342. Tel: 810-765-5233. FAX: 810-765-4376. *Br Mgr,* Lois Kaufman; E-mail: lkaufman@sccl.lib.mi.us
Founded 1889. Pop 4,500
Library Holdings: Bk Vols 21,475
Open Mon-Thurs 9-8, Fri & Sat 9-5
Friends of the Library Group

MARYSVILLE PUBLIC, 1175 Delaware, Marysville, 48040, SAN 347-0377. Tel: 810-364-9493. FAX: 810-364-7491. *Br Mgr,* Mike Mercatante; E-mail: mmercatante@sccl.lib.mi.us
Pop 8,500
Library Holdings: Bk Vols 22,972
Open Mon-Thurs 9-8, Fri & Sat 9-5
Friends of the Library Group

MEMPHIS PUBLIC, 34830 Potter St, Memphis, 48041, SAN 347-0407. Tel: 810-392-2980. FAX: 810-392-3206. *Br Mgr,* Andrew Webb; E-mail: awebb@sccl.lib.mi.us
Founded 1973
Library Holdings: Bk Vols 16,296
Open Mon & Thurs 12-8, Tues, Wed, Fri & Sat 9-5
Friends of the Library Group

SAINT CLAIR PUBLIC, 310 S Second St, Saint Clair, 48079, SAN 347-0466. Tel: 810-329-3951. FAX: 810-329-7142. *Br Mgr,* Julie Alef; E-mail: jalef@sccl.lib.mi.us
Founded 1869. Pop 5,000
Library Holdings: Bk Vols 24,643
Open Mon-Thurs 9-8, Fri & Sat 9-5
Friends of the Library Group

YALE PUBLIC, Two Jones St, Yale, 48097, SAN 347-0490. Tel: 810-387-2940. FAX: 810-387-2051. *Br Mgr,* Lori Herrington; E-mail: lherrington@sccl.lib.mi.us
Library Holdings: Bk Vols 20,311
Open Mon-Thurs 9-8, Fri & Sat 9-5
Friends of the Library Group

M SAINT CLAIR COUNTY MENTAL HEALTH SERVICE LIBRARY*, 311 Electric Ave, 48060. SAN 373-2177. Tel: 810-985-8900. FAX: 810-985-7620. Web Site: www.scccmh.org. *Librn,* Sandy Kammer; E-mail: skammer@scccmh.org
Library Holdings: Bk Vols 600; Per Subs 40

PORT SANILAC

P SANILAC DISTRICT LIBRARY*, 7130 Main St, 48469. (Mail add: PO Box 525, 48469-0525), SAN 308-3616. Tel: 810-622-8623. E-mail: sdlcircdesk@yahoo.com. Web Site: www.sanilacdistrictlibrary.lib.mi.us. *Dir,* Beverly Dear; E-mail: sanilacdistrictlibrary@yahoo.com; Staff 4 (Non-MLS 4)
Founded 1936. Pop 4,545; Circ 40,430
Library Holdings: Bk Vols 39,018
Subject Interests: Aviation, Local hist
Automation Activity & Vendor Info: (Acquisitions) Follett Software; (Circulation) Follett Software
Wireless access
Publications: BookTalk (newsletter)
Partic in White Pine Libr Coop
Open Mon, Tues, Thurs & Fri 11-5, Wed 11-9, Sat 11-2
Friends of the Library Group

PORTAGE

P PORTAGE DISTRICT LIBRARY*, 300 Library Lane, 49002. SAN 308-3624. Tel: 269-329-4544. FAX: 269-324-9222. E-mail: info@portagelibrary.info. Web Site: www.portagelibrary.info. *Dir,* Christine A Berro; Tel: 269-329-4542, Ext 700, E-mail: cberro@portagelibrary.info; *Head, Adult Serv,* Lawrence Kapture; Tel: 269-329-4542, Ext 710, E-mail: lkapture@portagelibrary.info; *Head, Youth Serv,* Christine Klein; Tel: 269-329-4542, Ext 721, E-mail: cklein@portagelibrary.info; *Bus Mgr,* Robert Foti; Tel: 269-329-4542, Ext 702, E-mail: rfoti@portagelibrary.info; *Bus Librn,* Nicolette Warisse Sosulski; Tel: 269-329-4542, Ext 714, E-mail: nsosulski@portagelibrary.info; *Circ Supvr,* Jill Austin; Tel: 269-329-4542, Ext 706, E-mail: jaustin@portagelibrary.info; *Web Coordr, Youth Serv Librn,* Laura Wright; E-mail: lwright@portagelibrary.info; *Libr Syst Adminr,* Rolfe Behrje; Tel: 269-329-4542, Ext 704, E-mail: rbehrje@portagelibrary.info. Subject Specialists: *Bus,* Nicolette Warisse Sosulski; Staff 19 (MLS 16, Non-MLS 3)
Founded 1962. Pop 49,265; Circ 357,248
Library Holdings: Bk Titles 113,077; Bk Vols 136,034; Per Subs 211
Special Collections: John Todd Coll, aerial photos; Local History (Heritage Room Coll), letters, bks, archival mat. Oral History
Automation Activity & Vendor Info: (Acquisitions) Horizon; (Cataloging) Horizon; (OPAC) Horizon; (Serials) Horizon
Database Vendor: Gale Cengage Learning, OCLC FirstSearch
Wireless access
Publications: Portage & Its Past; Women in Business & Management - A Bibliography
Partic in OCLC Online Computer Library Center, Inc; Southwest Michigan Library Cooperative
Special Services for the Deaf - Bks on deafness & sign lang; Spec interest per; Videos & decoder
Open Mon-Thurs 9-9, Fri 9-6, Sat 9-5, Sun (Sept-May) 1-5
Friends of the Library Group

PORTLAND

P PORTLAND DISTRICT LIBRARY*, 334 Kent St, 48875-1735. SAN 308-3632. Tel: 517 647-6981. FAX: 517-647-2738. Web Site: www.pdl.michlibrary.org. *Dir,* Cory E Grimminck; Staff 7 (Non-MLS 7)
Founded 1905. Pop 12,449; Circ 59,529

Library Holdings: AV Mats 3,138; Bks on Deafness & Sign Lang 10; Large Print Bks 353; Bk Vols 26,010; Per Subs 100; Talking Bks 818
Subject Interests: Genealogy, Local hist
Automation Activity & Vendor Info: (Cataloging) Follett Software; (Circulation) Follett Software; (ILL) Mel Cat
Wireless access
Function: AV serv, For res purposes, Health sci info serv, ILL available, Online searches, Photocopying/Printing, Prog for children & young adult, Ref serv available, Summer reading prog
Mem of Woodlands Library Cooperative
Open Mon-Thurs 9-8, Fri 9-5, Sat 9-2
Friends of the Library Group

POTTERVILLE

P POTTERVILLE BENTON TOWNSHIP DISTRICT LIBRARY*, 150 Library Lane, 48876. (Mail add: PO Box 158, 48876-0158), SAN 308-3640. Tel: 517-645-2989. FAX: 517-645-0268. Web Site: www.pottervillelibrary.org. *Dir,* Lu Ann Stachnik; E-mail: director@pottervillelibrary.org; *Asst Librn,* Evelyn VanFossen
Pop 4,880; Circ 19,000
Library Holdings: Bk Vols 16,000; Per Subs 30
Automation Activity & Vendor Info: (Acquisitions) Baker & Taylor; (Circulation) Auto-Graphics, Inc; (ILL) Auto-Graphics, Inc
Mem of Woodlands Library Cooperative
Open Mon, Thurs & Fri 12:30-5:30, Tues 10-6, Wed 12:30-7, Sat 10-1
Friends of the Library Group

RAY

P RAY TOWNSHIP LIBRARY*, 64255 Wolcott Rd, 48096. Tel: 586-749-7130. FAX: 586-749-6190. E-mail: raylibrary@comcast.net. Web Site: www.libcoop.net/ray. *Dir,* Suzanne Graham
Founded 1983
Library Holdings: Bk Vols 10,000; Per Subs 32
Automation Activity & Vendor Info: (Cataloging) SirsiDynix
Function: Copy machines
Partic in Suburban Library Cooperative
Open Mon 4-7, Tues 1-4 & 6-8, Wed 6-8, Thurs 9-12 & 6-8

READING

P READING COMMUNITY LIBRARY*, 104 N Main St, 49274. (Mail add: PO Box 184, 49274-0649), SAN 308-3659. Tel: 517-283-3916. FAX: 517-283-2510. E-mail: rclforfun@yahoo.com. Web Site: www.rcl.michlibrary.org. *Librn,* Liberty Burlew; Staff 2 (Non-MLS 2)
Founded 1939. Pop 4,110; Circ 10,000
Jul 2012-Jun 2013. Mats Exp $5,500, Books $4,500, Per/Ser (Incl. Access Fees) $900, AV Mat $100
Library Holdings: Audiobooks 192; CDs 180; DVDs 309; Large Print Bks 216; Bk Vols 11,674; Per Subs 36
Automation Activity & Vendor Info: (Acquisitions) Auto-Graphics, Inc; (Cataloging) Auto-Graphics, Inc; (Circulation) Auto-Graphics, Inc; (ILL) Mel Cat
Wireless access
Function: ILL available
Mem of Woodlands Library Cooperative
Open Mon 4-8, Tues 10-6, Wed & Fri 10-5, Sat 9-1
Friends of the Library Group

REDFORD

P REDFORD TOWNSHIP DISTRICT LIBRARY, 25320 W Six Mile, 48240. SAN 308-0307. Tel: 313-531-5960. FAX: 313-531-1721. E-mail: rtdl@redfordlibrary.org. Web Site: redfordlibrary.org. *Dir,* Lisa Hoenig; Tel: 313-531-6900, E-mail: lhoenig@redfordlibrary.org; *Head, Adult Serv,* Carol Deckert; E-mail: cdeckert@redfordlibrary.org; *Head, Automation,* Martin Smith; E-mail: msmith@redfordlibrary.org; *Head, Ch,* Patricia Slater; E-mail: pslater@redfordlibrary.org; *Adult Prog Coordr, Adult Ref Librn,* Linda Pride; E-mail: lpride@redfordlibrary.org; *Ch,* Karen Clinton; E-mail: kclinton@redfordlibrary.org; *Children & Teen Librn,* Kendra Wesner; E-mail: kwesner@redfordlibrary.org; *Bldg Mgr/Supvr,* Harvey DeWitt; E-mail: hdewitt@redfordlibrary.org; *Circ Supvr,* Michael Gazzarari; E-mail: mgazzarari@redfordlibrary.org; *Multimedia, Webmaster,* Brooke Somerville; E-mail: bsomerville@redfordlibrary.org; Staff 11 (MLS 7, Non-MLS 4)
Founded 1947. Pop 48,362; Circ 297,454
Library Holdings: Audiobooks 4,095; Bks on Deafness & Sign Lang 50; CDs 4,163; DVDs 7,162; e-books 16,244; Large Print Bks 2,103; Bk Vols 160,318; Per Subs 161; Videos 1,528
Automation Activity & Vendor Info: (Circulation) SIRSI WorkFlows; (ILL) Mel Cat; (OPAC) SirsiDynix
Database Vendor: Comprise Technologies Inc, EBSCOhost, Overdrive, Inc, ProQuest, SirsiDynix, TumbleBookLibrary, ValueLine
Wireless access
Partic in Mich Libr Asn; The Library Network
Special Services for the Deaf - ADA equip; Assistive tech; Closed caption videos
Special Services for the Blind - Assistive/Adapted tech devices, equip & products; Bks on cassette; Bks on CD; Copier with enlargement capabilities; Large print bks; Magnifiers; ZoomText magnification & reading software
Open Mon-Wed 10-8:30, Thurs-Sat 10-5
Restriction: Restricted access
Friends of the Library Group

REED CITY

P REED CITY PUBLIC LIBRARY*, 410 W Upton Ave, 49677-1152. SAN 308-3667. Tel: 231-832-2131. FAX: 231-832-2131. E-mail: rclib@hotmail.com. *Dir,* Tracy Logan; *Asst Dir,* Cynthia K Tyler; Staff 5 (MLS 1, Non-MLS 4)
Pop 8,508; Circ 47,874
Library Holdings: AV Mats 486; Large Print Bks 450; Bk Titles 21,000; Per Subs 58; Talking Bks 385
Special Collections: Memorial Cookbook Coll
Wireless access
Function: Copy machines, ILL available, Prog for adults, Prog for children & young adult, Ref serv available, Spoken cassettes & CDs, Summer reading prog
Partic in Mid-Michigan Library League
Open Mon & Fri 9-5, Tues & Thurs 11-8, Wed 11-5, Sat (Sept-May) 10-2

REESE

P REESE UNITY DISTRICT LIBRARY*, 2065 Gates St, 48757-9580. (Mail add: PO Box 413, 48757), SAN 376-6322. Tel: 989-868-4120. FAX: 989-868-4123. Web Site: reeseunitylibrary.org. *Dir,* Carole Brown; *Librn,* Delphine Bailey
Founded 1990. Pop 6,295; Circ 28,000
Library Holdings: Large Print Bks 325; Bk Titles 18,053; Bk Vols 19,000; Per Subs 41; Talking Bks 300
Wireless access
Partic in White Pine Libr Coop
Open Mon-Thurs 10-7, Fri 10-4, Sat 9-1
Friends of the Library Group

REMUS

P WHEATLAND TOWNSHIP LIBRARY*, 207 Michigan Ave, 49340. (Mail add: PO Box 217, 49340-0217), SAN 308-3675. Tel: 989-967-8271. FAX: 989-967-8271. *Dir,* Becky Kurtz
Pop 2,929
Library Holdings: Bk Vols 15,000; Per Subs 26; Talking Bks 342; Videos 335
Partic in Mid-Michigan Library League
Open Tues-Fri 10-5, Sat 9-12
Friends of the Library Group

REPUBLIC

P REPUBLIC-MICHIGAMME PUBLIC LIBRARY, 227 Maple St, 49879-9998. SAN 308-3683. Tel: 906-376-2239, 906-376-2277. FAX: 906-376-8299. *Dir,* Nancy Currie; E-mail: ncurrie@maresa.org
Library Holdings: Audiobooks 112; DVDs 50; Bk Titles 12,028; Per Subs 25
Wireless access
Partic in Superiorland Library Cooperative
Open Tues-Fri (Winter) 3:15-7; Tues & Thurs (Summer) 9-12, Wed 3-7

RICHMOND

P LOIS WAGNER MEMORIAL LIBRARY*, 35200 Division Rd, 48062. SAN 308-3691. Tel: 586-727-2665. FAX: 586-727-3774. E-mail: lwml@libcoop.net. Web Site: www.libcoop.net/richmond/. *Dir,* Janis M Reghi; E-mail: reghij@libcoop.net; *Syst Mgr,* Martina Murawski; E-mail: murawskm@libcoop.net; *Libr Tech,* Colleen Kelley; E-mail: kelleyc@libcoop.net
Founded 1912. Circ 58,076
Library Holdings: Bk Vols 35,636; Per Subs 44
Special Collections: Pictorial History of Richmond, photos
Automation Activity & Vendor Info: (Cataloging) SirsiDynix; (Circulation) SirsiDynix
Wireless access
Publications: Library Information Hand-outs; Newsletter (Quarterly)
Partic in Suburban Library Cooperative
Open Mon-Thurs 10-8, Fri 10-5, Sat 10-2
Friends of the Library Group

RIVER ROUGE

P WAYNE COUNTY LIBRARY*, River Rouge Branch, 221 Burke St, 48218. SAN 308-3705. Tel: 313-843-2040. FAX: 313-842-4716. Web Site: www.river-rouge.lib.mi.us/. *Dir,* Gurpreet Samra; *Youth Serv Librn,* Linda Przybylowicz
Founded 1958. Pop 10,060; Circ 14,984
Library Holdings: Bk Vols 26,179; Per Subs 75
Automation Activity & Vendor Info: (Cataloging) SirsiDynix; (Circulation) SirsiDynix; (OPAC) SirsiDynix
Open Mon-Wed 12-7, Thurs 12-6, Fri (June-Aug) 12-5, Sat (Sept-May) 12-5

RIVERDALE

P SEVILLE TOWNSHIP PUBLIC LIBRARY*, 6734 N Lumberjack Rd, 48877. (Mail add: PO Box 160, 48877-0160), SAN 308-3713. Tel: 989-833-7776. FAX: 989-833-7776. *Dir,* Cristy Omans
Founded 1941. Pop 2,948; Circ 13,222
Library Holdings: Bk Titles 11,217; Bk Vols 12,200; Per Subs 50
Wireless access
Partic in Mid-Michigan Library League
Open Mon, Tues & Fri 9-5, Wed 2-7, Sat 9-12

RIVERVIEW

P RIVERVIEW PUBLIC LIBRARY*, 14300 Sibley Rd, 48193. SAN 308-3721. Tel: 734-283-1250. FAX: 734-283-6843. Web Site: riverviewpubliclibrary.com. *Ch, Dir,* Kirk A Borger; E-mail: kborger@tln.lib.mi.us; *Librn,* Alice Gorgas; E-mail: agorgas@tln.lib.mi.us; Staff 8 (MLS 2, Non-MLS 6)
Founded 1962. Pop 13,894; Circ 61,456
Jul 2005-Jun 2006 Income $521,403, State $11,535, City $456,271, County $17,577, Locally Generated Income $36,020. Mats Exp $82,000, Books $70,000, Per/Ser (Incl. Access Fees) $12,000. Sal $179,046
Library Holdings: Bk Vols 57,201; Per Subs 120
Automation Activity & Vendor Info: (Cataloging) SirsiDynix; (Circulation) SirsiDynix; (OPAC) SirsiDynix
Database Vendor: Gale Cengage Learning, OCLC FirstSearch
Wireless access
Partic in Libr Network of Mich
Open Mon-Wed (Winter) 1-9, Thurs 10-9, Sat 12-5, Sun 1-5; Mon-Wed (Summer) 12-8, Thurs 10-8, Fri 10-5

ROCHESTER

M CRITTENTON HOSPITAL MEDICAL CENTER*, Ullmann Medical Library, 1101 W University Dr, 48307-1831. Tel: 248-652-5202. FAX: 248-652-5001. Web Site: www.crittenton.com. *Mgr,* Rosemary Rojas; Tel: 248-601-6138, E-mail: rrojas@crittenton.com
Founded 1967
Library Holdings: Bk Vols 541; Per Subs 50
Automation Activity & Vendor Info: (Cataloging) Inmagic, Inc.; (Circulation) Inmagic, Inc.
Restriction: Med staff only

C OAKLAND UNIVERSITY LIBRARY*, Kresge Library, 2200 N Squirrel Rd, 48309-4402. (Mail add: 300 Kresge Library, 48309-4484), SAN 308-3756. Tel: 248-370-4426. Interlibrary Loan Service Tel: 248-370-2132. FAX: 248-370-2474. E-mail: ref@oakland.edu. Web Site: library.oakland.edu. *Dean,* Adriene Lim; E-mail: ailim@oakland.edu; *Asst Dean,* Linda Kreger; Tel: 248-370-2488, E-mail: kreger@oakland.edu; *Dir, Med Libr,* Nancy Bulgarelli; Tel: 248-370-2481, E-mail: bulgarel@oakland.edu; *Bus Librn,* Mariela Hristova; Tel: 248-370-2464, E-mail: gunn@oakland.edu; *Digital Assets Librn,* Meghan Finch; Tel: 248-370-2457, E-mail: mmfinch@oakland.edu; *First Year Experience Librn,* Katie Greer; Tel: 248-370-2480, E-mail: greer@oakland.edu; *Health Sci, Nursing & Fac Res Support Librn,* Julia Rodriguez; Tel: 248-370-2490, E-mail: juliar@oakland.edu; *Humanities Librn,* Frank Lepkowski; E-mail: lepkowsk@oakland.edu; *Humanities Librn, Hist & Modern Lang,* Dominique Daniel; Tel: 248-370-2478, E-mail: daniel@oakland.edu; *Govt Doc, Outreach Librn,* Anne Switzer; Tel: 248-370-2475, E-mail: switzer2@oakland.edu; *Pub Serv Librn,* Daniel Ring; Tel: 248-370-2498, E-mail: ring@oakland.edu. Subject Specialists: *Health sci, Nursing,* Julia Rodriguez; *Linguistics, Modern lang,* Dominique Daniel; Staff 21 (MLS 16, Non-MLS 5)
Founded 1959. Enrl 18,920; Fac 992; Highest Degree: Doctorate
Jul 2006-Jun 2007. Mats Exp $1,868,000, Books $359,000, Per/Ser (Incl. Access Fees) $757,000, Electronic Ref Mat (Incl. Access Fees) $752,000. Sal $2,570,000 (Prof $759,000)
Library Holdings: e-books 50,000; Bk Vols 800,000; Per Subs 75,000
Special Collections: 17th-19th Century Books by Women (Hicks Coll); Bingham Historical Children's Literature Coll; China Coll; Folklore & Witchcraft (James Coll); Gaylor Coll of GLBT Literature; Lincolniana (Springer Coll); University Archives. US Document Depository
Automation Activity & Vendor Info: (Acquisitions) Ex Libris Group; (Cataloging) Ex Libris Group; (Circulation) Ex Libris Group; (Course Reserve) Ex Libris Group; (ILL) OCLC ILLiad; (OPAC) Ex Libris Group; (Serials) Ex Libris Group
Database Vendor: Dialog, Gale Cengage Learning, JSTOR, LexisNexis, OCLC FirstSearch, OVID Technologies, SerialsSolutions
Wireless access
Partic in Midwest Collaborative for Library Services (MCLS); OCLC Online Computer Library Center, Inc

P ROCHESTER HILLS PUBLIC LIBRARY, 500 Olde Towne Rd, 48307-2043. SAN 308-373X. Tel: 248-656-2900. Circulation Tel: 248-650-7174. Reference Tel: 248-650-7130. Administration Tel: 248-650-7122. FAX: 248-650-7121. TDD: 248-650-7153. Web Site: www.rhpl.org. *Dir,* Christine Lind Hage; E-mail: christine.hage@rhpl.org; *Dir, Info Tech,* Derek Brown; Tel: 248-650-7123, E-mail: derek.brown@rhpl.org; *Mgr, Outreach & Bkmobile Serv,* Deb Motley; Tel: 248-650-7152, E-mail: Deb.Motley@rhpl.org; *Adult Serv,* Rebekah Craft; Tel: 248-650-7132, Fax: 248-650-7131, E-mail: rebekah.craft@rhpl.org; *Circ,* Ginger Olson; Tel: 248-650-7162, E-mail: ginger.olson@rhpl.org; *Youth Serv,* Claire Poynter; Tel: 248-650-7142, E-mail: Claire.Poynter@rhpl.org; Staff 56 (MLS 24, Non-MLS 32)
Founded 1924. Pop 100,485; Circ 1,861,311
Jan 2015-Dec 2015 Income $5,828,400, State $1,613,900, City $2,377,000, County $260,700, Other $1,576,800. Mats Exp $700,500, Books $348,300, Per/Ser (Incl. Access Fees) $25,300, AV Mat $155,000, Electronic Ref Mat (Incl. Access Fees) $171,900. Sal $2,913,000
Library Holdings: AV Mats 64,377; Bk Vols 223,817; Per Subs 382
Special Collections: Photographic Archives. Oral History
Automation Activity & Vendor Info: (Acquisitions) Innovative Interfaces, Inc; (Cataloging) Innovative Interfaces, Inc; (Circulation) Innovative Interfaces, Inc; (OPAC) Innovative Interfaces, Inc; (Serials) Innovative Interfaces, Inc
Database Vendor: Gale Cengage Learning, Grolier Online, Overdrive, Inc, ValueLine
Wireless access
Function: Handicapped accessible, Home delivery & serv to Sr ctr & nursing homes, Homebound delivery serv, ILL available, Online searches, Photocopying/Printing, Prog for adults, Prog for children & young adult, Ref serv available, Summer reading prog
Publications: News & Views (Newsletter)
Partic in Metro Net Libr Consortium; The Library Network
Special Services for the Blind - Accessible computers; Aids for in-house use; Assistive/Adapted tech devices, equip & products; BiFolkal kits; Bks & mags in Braille, on rec, tape & cassette; Bks on flash-memory cartridges; Braille & cassettes; Braille alphabet card; Braille bks; Braille equip; Children's Braille; Closed circuit TV magnifier; Compressed speech equip; Computer access aids; Computer with voice synthesizer for visually impaired persons; Copier with enlargement capabilities; Descriptive video serv (DVS); Digital talking bk; Digital talking bk machines; Extensive large print coll; Handicapped awareness prog; Home delivery serv; Large print bks; Large print bks & talking machines; Large screen computer & software; Large type calculator; Lending of low vision aids; PC for handicapped; Screen enlargement software for people with visual disabilities; Talking bk & rec for the blind cat; Talking bk serv referral
Open Mon-Thurs 9-9, Fri & Sat 9-6, Sun (Sept-May) 1-6
Friends of the Library Group
Bookmobiles: 2

ROCHESTER HILLS

C ROCHESTER COLLEGE*, Ennis & Nancy Ham Library, 800 W Avon Rd, 48307. SAN 308-3748. Tel: 248-218-2260. Reference Tel: 248-218-2266. FAX: 248-218-2265. E-mail: library@rc.edu. Web Site: www.rc.edu/lib. *Actg Dir,* Allie Keller; Tel: 248-218-2268, E-mail: akeller@rc.edu; *Librn,* Carla Caretto; *Librn,* Vicki Dixon; *ILL,* Jeanette A MacAdam; Tel: 248-218-2263, E-mail: jmacadam@rc.edu. Subject Specialists: *Sciences,* Carla Caretto; Staff 5 (MLS 4, Non-MLS 1)
Founded 1959. Enrl 1,030; Fac 41; Highest Degree: Master
May 2009-Jun 2010. Mats Exp $86,620, Books $15,850, Per/Ser (Incl. Access Fees) $21,280, Micro $960, AV Equip $5,000, AV Mat $3,150, Electronic Ref Mat (Incl. Access Fees) $40,380. Sal $184,284 (Prof $143,300)
Library Holdings: AV Mats 2,542; Bks on Deafness & Sign Lang 14; CDs 779; DVDs 900; e-books 11,534; Electronic Media & Resources 63; Music Scores 80; Bk Vols 44,831; Per Subs 130; Talking Bks 52; Videos 811
Subject Interests: Biblical studies, Bus, Communications, Early childhood educ, Hist, Lit, Music, Psychol, Relig
Automation Activity & Vendor Info: (Acquisitions) SirsiDynix; (Cataloging) SirsiDynix; (Circulation) SirsiDynix; (Course Reserve) SirsiDynix; (ILL) OCLC; (OPAC) SirsiDynix; (Serials) SirsiDynix
Database Vendor: American Chemical Society, Cinahl, CIOS (Communication Institute for Online Scholarship), EBSCOhost, Gale Cengage Learning, H W Wilson, JSTOR, LearningExpress, LexisNexis,

OCLC FirstSearch, OCLC WorldShare Interlibrary Loan, ProQuest, SirsiDynix, Wilson - Wilson Web, WT Cox
Wireless access
Function: Video lending libr
Partic in Detroit Area Library Network; Midwest Collaborative for Library Services (MCLS)
Special Services for the Blind - Bks on CD
Open Mon, Tues & Thurs (Winter) 9am-11pm, Wed 9-6 & 8:30-11, Fri 9-6, Sat 12-5, Sun 7am-11pm; Mon-Fri (Summer) 9-6, Sat 12-5

ROGERS CITY

P PRESQUE ISLE DISTRICT LIBRARY*, 181 E Erie St, 49779-1709. SAN 308-3764. Tel: 989-734-2477. Circulation Tel: 989-734-2477, Ext 224. Interlibrary Loan Service Tel: 989-734-2477, Ext 226. Reference Tel: 989-734-2477, Ext 225. FAX: 989-734-4899. E-mail: librarian@pidl.org. Web Site: www.pidl.org. *Dir,* Michael J Grulke; Tel: 989-734-2477, Ext 222, E-mail: director@pidl.org; *Asst Dir,* Carolyn J Chrzan; Tel: 989-734-2477, Ext 223; *Children & Youth Serv Librn,* Don Dimick; *Cat Supvr,* Kay Spomer; *Circ Supvr,* Tara Talaska; Staff 12 (MLS 2, Non-MLS 10)
Founded 1945. Pop 15,600; Circ 69,297
Library Holdings: Bk Vols 64,800; Per Subs 65
Special Collections: Great Lakes Nautical Coll; Michigan Coll
Automation Activity & Vendor Info: (Acquisitions) Baker & Taylor; (Cataloging) SirsiDynix; (Circulation) SirsiDynix; (ILL) SirsiDynix; (OPAC) SirsiDynix; (Serials) EBSCO Online
Database Vendor: Bowker, H W Wilson, Medline, OCLC FirstSearch, OCLC WorldShare Interlibrary Loan, ProQuest, SirsiDynix, Wilson - Wilson Web
Wireless access
Function: Adult literacy prog, AV serv, Bk club(s), Bks on cassette, Bks on CD, CD-ROM, Children's prog, Computer training, Computers for patron use, Copy machines, Distance learning, e-mail serv, E-Reserves, Electronic databases & coll, Exhibits, Fax serv, Free DVD rentals, Games & aids for the handicapped, Handicapped accessible, Holiday prog, Home delivery & serv to Sr ctr & nursing homes, Homebound delivery serv, ILL available, Jail serv, Magnifiers for reading, Mail & tel request accepted, Online cat, Online ref, Outreach serv, Outside serv via phone, mail, e-mail & web, Photocopying/Printing, Preschool outreach, Prog for adults, Prog for children & young adult, Pub access computers, Ref serv available, Ref serv in person, Referrals accepted, Senior computer classes, Senior outreach, Serves mentally handicapped consumers, Spoken cassettes & CDs, Spoken cassettes & DVDs, Story hour, Summer reading prog, Tax forms, Teen prog, VHS videos, Video lending libr, Web-catalog, Wheelchair accessible, Workshops
Publications: November Requiem (Local historical information)
Partic in Michicard Borrowing Serv; Northland Library Cooperative
Special Services for the Deaf - ADA equip; Adult & family literacy prog; Bks on deafness & sign lang; Closed caption videos; Coll on deaf educ; High interest/low vocabulary bks; Sign lang interpreter upon request for prog
Special Services for the Blind - Accessible computers; Assistive/Adapted tech devices, equip & products; Audio mat; Bks & mags in Braille, on rec, tape & cassette; Bks available with recordings; Bks on cassette; Bks on CD; Cassettes; Computer with voice synthesizer for visually impaired persons; Copier with enlargement capabilities; Extensive large print coll; Home delivery serv; Large print & cassettes; Large print bks; Magnifiers; Recorded bks; Ref serv; Screen enlargement software for people with visual disabilities; Sound rec; Talking bks
Open Mon & Thurs 9:30-7:30, Tues, Wed & Fri 10-5:30, Sat 10-3
Friends of the Library Group
Branches: 3
GRAND LAKE BRANCH, 18132 Lake Esau Hwy, Presque Isle, 49777, SAN 321-4087. Tel: 989-595-5051. FAX: 989-595-3146. *Br Mgr,* Elizabeth Fitch
Special Services for the Blind - Computer with voice synthesizer for visually impaired persons
Open Tues & Thurs 2-7, Wed, Fri & Sat 10-4
Friends of the Library Group
ONAWAY BRANCH, 20774 State St, Onaway, 49765, SAN 321-4079. Tel: 989-733-6621. FAX: 989-733-7842. E-mail: onaway@pidl.org. *Librn,* Kathy Radzibon
Special Services for the Blind - Computer with voice synthesizer for visually impaired persons
Open Mon, Wed & Thurs 2-7, Tues & Fri 10-5, Sat 10-2:30
Friends of the Library Group
POSEN BRANCH, 6987 Turtle St, Posen, 49776, SAN 321-4095. Tel: 989-766-2233. FAX: 989-766-9977. E-mail: posen@pidl.org. *Br Mgr,* Kathy Yaklin
Open Mon 1-7, Tues-Thurs 1-5, Fri 10-2
Friends of the Library Group

ROMULUS

P ROMULUS PUBLIC LIBRARY*, 11121 Wayne Rd, 48174. SAN 308-3780. Tel: 734-942-7589. FAX: 734-941-3575. Web Site: www.romulus.lib.mi.us. *Dir,* Patty Braden
Pop 39,868; Circ 50,000
Library Holdings: Bk Vols 51,000; Per Subs 19
Special Collections: Michigan Coll
Wireless access
Function: Adult literacy prog
Partic in The Library Network
Open Mon-Thurs 10-8, Fri & Sat 12-5
Friends of the Library Group

ROSCOMMON

J KIRTLAND COMMUNITY COLLEGE LIBRARY*, 10775 N St Helen Rd, 48653. SAN 308-3799. Tel: 989-275-5000, Ext 246. FAX: 989-275-8510. E-mail: library@kirtland.edu. Web Site: www.kirtland.edu/library. *Dir,* Deb Shumaker; Tel: 989-275-5000, Ext 235, E-mail: shumaked@kirtland.edu; Staff 2 (MLS 2)
Founded 1966. Enrl 1,800; Fac 75; Highest Degree: Associate
Jul 2005-Jun 2006 Income $246,000. Mats Exp $58,000, Books $30,000, Per/Ser (Incl. Access Fees) $22,000, Micro $2,000, AV Mat $4,000. Sal $124,000 (Prof $93,000)
Library Holdings: AV Mats 1,000; Bks on Deafness & Sign Lang 12; e-books 19,000; Bk Titles 29,000; Bk Vols 31,000; Per Subs 205; Talking Bks 150
Automation Activity & Vendor Info: (Cataloging) SirsiDynix; (Circulation) SirsiDynix; (OPAC) SirsiDynix
Wireless access
Function: Archival coll, Distance learning, Handicapped accessible, Health sci info serv, ILL available, Orientations, Photocopying/Printing, Ref serv available, Spoken cassettes & CDs, Telephone ref, Wheelchair accessible
Open Mon-Thurs (Fall & Winter) 8-8, Fri 8-4:30; Mon-Fri (Summer) 8-4:30
Restriction: Open to pub for ref & circ; with some limitations

ROSE CITY

P OGEMAW DISTRICT LIBRARY, 107 W Main St, 48654. SAN 322-6484. Tel: 989-685-3300. FAX: 989-685-3647. E-mail: ogemawdistrictlibrary@hotmail.com. Web Site: www.ogemawlibrary.net. *Dir,* Jeanette Leathorn; E-mail: librarianzim@aol.com
Founded 1977. Pop 12,561; Circ 74,321
Library Holdings: Bk Titles 24,193; Bk Vols 37,817
Subject Interests: Genealogy, Local hist
Wireless access
Open Mon 10-7, Tues-Thurs 10-5, Fri & Sat 10-2
Friends of the Library Group
Branches: 2
OGEMAW EAST, 200 Washington, Prescott, 48756, SAN 325-3406. Tel: 989-873-5807. E-mail: prescottlibrary@hotmail.com. *Librn,* Sharon Arndt
Library Holdings: Bk Vols 15,000; Per Subs 20
SKIDWAY LAKE, 2129 Greenwood Rd, Prescott, 48756. (Mail add: PO Box 4520, Prescott, 48756). Tel: 989-873-5086. FAX: 989-873-4646. *Librn,* Melissa Rousseau

ROSEVILLE

P ROSEVILLE PUBLIC LIBRARY*, 29777 Gratiot Ave, 48066. SAN 308-3802. Tel: 586-445-5407. Automation Services Tel: 586-203-8725. E-mail: rsvlibrary@libcoop.net. Web Site: www.rosevillelibrary.org. *Dir,* Jacalynn Harvey; *Asst Dir,* Annamarie Lindstrom; Staff 26 (MLS 8, Non-MLS 18)
Founded 1936. Pop 48,129; Circ 235,067
Library Holdings: Bk Titles 132,171; Per Subs 301
Automation Activity & Vendor Info: (Acquisitions) SirsiDynix; (Cataloging) SirsiDynix; (Circulation) SirsiDynix; (OPAC) SirsiDynix; (Serials) SirsiDynix
Database Vendor: Gale Cengage Learning, OCLC FirstSearch
Wireless access
Function: Adult literacy prog, Handicapped accessible, Homebound delivery serv, ILL available, Magnifiers for reading, Prog for adults, Prog for children & young adult, Ref serv available, Spoken cassettes & CDs, Summer reading prog, Telephone ref, VHS videos, Wheelchair accessible
Partic in Suburban Library Cooperative
Open Mon-Thurs 9-8, Fri 9-5:30
Friends of the Library Group

ROYAL OAK

M WILLIAM BEAUMONT HOSPITAL, Medical Library, 3601 W 13 Mile Rd, 48073-6769. SAN 308-3810. Tel: 248-898-1750. Interlibrary Loan Service Tel: 248-898-1744. FAX: 248-898-1060. E-mail:

rodocdelivery@beaumont.edu. *Dir,* Janet Zimmerman; E-mail: janet.zimmerman@beaumont.edu; Staff 8 (MLS 4, Non-MLS 4)
Founded 1956
Library Holdings: e-books 325; e-journals 15,550; Bk Titles 10,000; Per Subs 30
Database Vendor: SirsiDynix
Wireless access
Restriction: Badge access after hrs, Hospital employees & physicians only

J OAKLAND COMMUNITY COLLEGE, Royal Oak Campus Library, 739 S Washington Ave, Bldg C, 48067-3898. SAN 308-3829. Tel: 248-246-2525. Interlibrary Loan Service Tel: 248-246-2527. Reference Tel: 248-246-2519. FAX: 248-246-2520. Web Site: www.oaklandcc.edu/library. *Librn, Ref,* Carol Benson; Tel: 248-246-2528, E-mail: ctbenson@oaklandcc.edu; *Ref,* Darlene Johnson-Bignotti; Tel: 248-246-2526, E-mail: dxjohnso@oaklandcc.edu; Staff 6 (MLS 3, Non-MLS 3)
Founded 1974. Enrl 6,831; Fac 63; Highest Degree: Associate
Jul 2013-Jun 2014. Mats Exp $45,323, Books $22,482, Per/Ser (Incl. Access Fees) $19,001, Other Print Mats $2,269
Library Holdings: AV Mats 904; DVDs 242; e-books 32,521; Microforms 1,103; Bk Vols 42,192; Per Subs 171; Videos 662
Special Collections: Career Coll; Children's Literature Coll; Dante Alighieri Society Coll, bks in Italian & English; ESL Coll
Automation Activity & Vendor Info: (Acquisitions) Horizon; (Cataloging) Horizon; (Circulation) Horizon; (Course Reserve) Horizon; (ILL) Horizon; (OPAC) Horizon; (Serials) Horizon
Database Vendor: ARTstor, Baker & Taylor, Bowker, Brodart, Checkpoint Systems, Inc, Cinahl, College Source, CQ Press, EBSCO Discovery Service, EBSCO Information Services, EBSCOhost, Electric Library, Elsevier, Gale Cengage Learning, H W Wilson, JSTOR, LearningExpress, LexisNexis, Medline, Micromedex, Newsbank, OCLC, OCLC FirstSearch, OCLC WorldShare Interlibrary Loan, Oxford Online, ProQuest, PubMed, ScienceDirect, SirsiDynix, Standard & Poor's, Wilson - Wilson Web
Wireless access
Partic in Detroit Area Library Network; Midwest Collaborative for Library Services (MCLS)
Special Services for the Blind - Assistive/Adapted tech devices, equip & products
Open Mon-Thurs (Fall & Winter) 8:30am-10pm, Fri 8:30-7, Sat 10-2

P ROYAL OAK PUBLIC LIBRARY*, 222 E Eleven Mile Rd, 48067-2633. (Mail add: PO Box 494, 48068-0494), SAN 308-3837. Tel: 248-246-3700. Interlibrary Loan Service Tel: 248-246-3720. Reference Tel: 248-246-3727. Administration Tel: 248-246-3711. FAX: 248-246-3701. Web Site: www.ropl.org. *Dir, Head, Youth & Teen Serv,* Mary Karshner; Tel: 248-246-3710, E-mail: mary@ropl.org; *Head, Adult Serv,* Anna Vidal; Tel: 248-246-3716, E-mail: anna@ropl.org; *Head, Support Serv,* Matthew Day; Tel: 248-246-3732, E-mail: matthew@ropl.org; *Ad,* Rosemary Mirsky; Tel: 248-246-3715, E-mail: rosemary@ropl.org; *Tech Serv, Webmaster,* Eric Hayes; Tel: 248-246-3751; Staff 12 (MLS 12)
Founded 1856. Pop 62,656; Circ 210,000
Library Holdings: AV Mats 13,931; CDs 4,441; DVDs 1,796; Large Print Bks 1,421; Bk Vols 121,011; Per Subs 250
Special Collections: Auto Repair Manuals; Royal Oak History Coll. State Document Depository; US Document Depository
Automation Activity & Vendor Info: (Cataloging) SirsiDynix; (Circulation) SirsiDynix; (OPAC) SirsiDynix; (Serials) SirsiDynix
Database Vendor: SirsiDynix
Wireless access
Publications: Leaflet (Newsletter); Pathfinder (Newsletter); Twigs (Newsletter)
Partic in The Library Network
Open Mon-Thurs 10-9, Fri & Sat 10-6
Friends of the Library Group

SAGINAW

M CMU HEALTH, Knowledge Services, (Formerly Synergy Medical Education Alliance), Covenant Houghton Bldg, 2nd Flr, 1000 Houghton Ave, Ste 2000, 48602-5398. SAN 320-8109. Tel: 989-583-6846. FAX: 989-583-6898. E-mail: library@cmich.edu. Web Site: www.synergymedical.org. *Mgr,* Tamara Sawyer; E-mail: tamara.sawyer@cmich.edu; *Tech Asst,* Sheila Allen; E-mail: sheila.allen@cmich.edu; *Ref Asst,* Bethany Figg; Staff 11 (MLS 4, Non-MLS 7)
Founded 1978
Library Holdings: Bk Titles 3,600; Bk Vols 4,500; Per Subs 150
Subject Interests: Clinical med
Automation Activity & Vendor Info: (Cataloging) EOS International; (Circulation) EOS International; (OPAC) EOS International; (Serials) EOS International
Database Vendor: Dialog, OCLC FirstSearch, OVID Technologies
Wireless access
Partic in Michigan Health Sciences Libraries Association
Open Mon-Fri 8-4:30
Branches:
SAINT MARY'S BRANCH, 800 S Washington, 2nd Flr, 48601-2551. Tel: 989-907-8204. FAX: 989-907-8616. *Librn,* Susan Keefer
Library Holdings: Bk Vols 1,000; Per Subs 36
Open Mon-Fri 8-4:30
Restriction: Open to pub for ref only

GM DEPARTMENT OF VETERANS AFFAIRS*, Aleta E Lutz VA Medical Center & Health Science Libary, 1500 Weiss St, 48602. SAN 308-3896. Tel: 989-497-2500, Ext 3302. FAX: 989-791-2224. *Mgr,* Debbie Zapolski; E-mail: debra.zapolski@va.gov
Library Holdings: Bk Vols 825; Per Subs 100
Special Collections: AV Coll
Partic in Dialog Corp; Veterans Affairs Libr Network (VALNET)
Open Mon-Fri 8-4:30

P PUBLIC LIBRARIES OF SAGINAW*, Hoyt Main Library, 505 Janes Ave, 48607. SAN 347-058X. Tel: 989-755-0904. FAX: 989-755-9829. TDD: 989-755-9831. E-mail: saginaw@saginawlibrary.org. Web Site: www.saginawlibrary.org. *Dir,* Kimberly White; *Cat, Govt Doc,* Anne Birkam; *Coll Develop,* Ruth Ann Reinert; *Ref,* Kate Tesdell; *YA Serv,* Amy Churchill; Staff 70 (MLS 16, Non-MLS 54)
Founded 1890. Pop 135,000
Library Holdings: AV Mats 23,635; Electronic Media & Resources 60; Bk Vols 411,598; Per Subs 762
Special Collections: African Heritage Coll; Genealogy, Saginaw Valley History & Michigan History (Eddy Historical & Genealogy Coll). US Document Depository
Subject Interests: Art, Genealogy, Local hist, Multicultural, Parenting, Sci tech
Automation Activity & Vendor Info: (Acquisitions) SirsiDynix; (Circulation) SirsiDynix; (OPAC) SirsiDynix
Database Vendor: OCLC FirstSearch
Partic in Mideastern Michigan Library Cooperative
Open Mon-Thurs 9-9, Fri & Sat 9-5
Friends of the Library Group
Branches: 4
BUTMAN-FISH, 1716 Hancock, 48602, SAN 347-061X. Tel: 989-799-9160. FAX: 989-799-8149. *Librn,* Paul Lutenske
Library Holdings: Bk Vols 92,754
Special Collections: African Heritage Coll; Hispanic Heritage Coll; Large Print Books
Open Mon-Thurs 9-9, Fri & Sat 9-5
Friends of the Library Group
ARCHER A CLAYTOR LIBRARY, 1410 N 12th St, 48601, SAN 347-0644. Tel: 989-753-5591. FAX: 989-753-6850. *Librn,* Stacey Ogea
Library Holdings: Bk Vols 27,799
Special Collections: African Heritage Coll; Hispanic Heritage Coll
Open Mon-Thurs 12-6
Friends of the Library Group
RUTH BRADY WICKES LIBRARY, 1713 Hess, 48601, SAN 347-0679. Tel: 989-752-3821. FAX: 989-752-8685. *Librn,* Stacey Ogea
Library Holdings: Bk Vols 43,492
Special Collections: African Heritage Coll; Hispanic Heritage Coll; Spanish Language Materials
Open Mon-Thurs 12-6
Friends of the Library Group
ZAUEL MEMORIAL LIBRARY, 3100 N Center Rd, 48603, SAN 347-0709. Tel: 989-799-2771. FAX: 989-799-1771. *Head of Libr,* Thomas H Birch; Staff 5 (MLS 3, Non-MLS 2)
Library Holdings: Bk Vols 117,102
Special Collections: African Heritage Coll; Hispanic Heritage Coll; Parenting Coll
Friends of the Library Group

S SAGINAW ART MUSEUM*, The John & Michele Bueker Research Library, 1126 N Michigan Ave, 48602-4763. SAN 308-3861. Tel: 989-754-2491. FAX: 989-754-9387. E-mail: info@saginawartmuseum.org. Web Site: www.saginawartmuseum.org/collections/library.php. *Dep Dir,* Ryan Kaltenbach
Founded 1948
Library Holdings: Bk Titles 1,500
Special Collections: Eanger Irving Couse Coll (bks, per, doc, correspondences, photog, etc)
Subject Interests: Archit, Fine arts, Graphic design, Photog
Wireless access
Open Wed-Thurs 12-8, Fri & Sat 10-5, Sun 1-5
Restriction: Not a lending libr

L SAGINAW COUNTY LAW LIBRARY*, 111 S Michigan Ave, Rm LL007, 48602. SAN 329-4218. Tel: 989-790-5533. FAX: 989-790-5248. *Librn,* Patricia Becker
Library Holdings: Bk Vols 20,000

P THOMAS TOWNSHIP LIBRARY*, 8207 Shields Dr, 48609-4814. SAN 376-7884. Tel: 989-781-3770. FAX: 989-781-3881. Web Site: www.thomastownshiplibrary.org. *Dir,* Tari L Dusek
Library Holdings: Bk Titles 68,000; Bk Vols 71,100; Per Subs 160
Automation Activity & Vendor Info: (Cataloging) Follett Software; (Circulation) Follett Software; (OPAC) Follett Software
Partic in White Pine Libr Coop
Open Mon-Thurs 10-8, Fri & Sat 10-5, Sun (Oct-April) 1-5

SAINT CHARLES

P SAINT CHARLES DISTRICT LIBRARY*, 104 W Spruce St, 48655-1238. SAN 308-3918. Tel: 989-865-9451. FAX: 989-865-6666. E-mail: s.charles@vlc.lib.mi.us. Web Site: www.stcharlesdistrictlibrary.org. *Dir,* Nannette Pretzer; Tel: 989-865-9371, E-mail: n.pretzer@vlc.lib.mi.us; Staff 7 (Non-MLS 7)
Founded 1907. Pop 7,798; Circ 30,135
Library Holdings: Bk Vols 24,202; Per Subs 99
Special Collections: Michigan Coll
Automation Activity & Vendor Info: (Acquisitions) Horizon; (Cataloging) Horizon; (Circulation) Horizon; (Course Reserve) Horizon; (ILL) Horizon; (Media Booking) Horizon; (OPAC) Horizon; (Serials) Horizon
Wireless access
Function: Accelerated reader prog, Adult bk club, After school storytime, Bks on cassette, Bks on CD, CD-ROM, Children's prog, Computers for patron use, Copy machines, Electronic databases & coll, Fax serv, Free DVD rentals, Holiday prog, ILL available, Music CDs, Photocopying/Printing, Preschool reading prog, Prog for adults, Prog for children & young adult, Pub access computers, Scanner, Story hour, Summer & winter reading prog, Tax forms, VHS videos, Web-catalog
Partic in White Pine Libr Coop
Open Mon-Thurs 10-7, Fri 10-5, Sat (Sept-May) 10-2
Restriction: Badge access after hrs
Friends of the Library Group

SAINT CLAIR SHORES

S RIGHT TO LIFE OF MICHIGAN, Macomb County Educational Resource Center, 27417 Harper, 48081. Tel: 586-774-6050. FAX: 586-774-5192. E-mail: info@rtl.org. Web Site: www.rtl.org.
Founded 1987
Library Holdings: AV Mats 339; Bk Titles 251; Videos 112
Subject Interests: Abortion, Euthanasia
Open Mon & Fri 10-4, Tues-Thurs 10-5

P SAINT CLAIR SHORES PUBLIC LIBRARY*, 22500 11 Mile Rd, 48081-1399. SAN 308 3926. Tel: 586-771-9020. FAX: 586-771-8935. TDD: 586-771-7384. Web Site: www.libcoop.net/stclairshores. *Dir,* Rosemary Orlando; E-mail: orlandor@libcoop.net; *Asst Dir, Youth Serv Coordr,* Sue A Mihalic; Tel: 586-771-9020, E-mail: mihalics@libcoop.net; *Outreach Serv Librn,* Donna Sakowski; *Youth Serv Librn,* Amy Shaughnessy; *Youth Serv Librn,* Lisa Valerio-Nowc; *Archivist,* Cynthia Bieniek; *Youth Serv,* Dale Humeston; *Ch Serv,* Dale Humeston; Staff 33 (MLS 9, Non-MLS 24)
Founded 1935. Pop 63,096; Circ 310,687
Library Holdings: Bk Vols 114,259; Per Subs 385
Special Collections: Great Lakes History; Local History, bks, photogs. Oral History
Subject Interests: Careers, Great Lakes, Mich
Automation Activity & Vendor Info: (Acquisitions) SirsiDynix; (Cataloging) SirsiDynix; (Circulation) SirsiDynix; (ILL) SirsiDynix; (OPAC) SirsiDynix; (Serials) SirsiDynix
Publications: Inside the Library (Newsletter); Muskrat Tales (Local history magazine)
Partic in Suburban Library Cooperative
Special Services for the Deaf - TDD equip
Open Mon-Thurs 9-9, Fri 9-5, Sat (Sept-May) 9-5
Friends of the Library Group

SAINT HELEN

P RICHFIELD TOWNSHIP PUBLIC LIBRARY*, 1410 Saint Helen Rd, 48656. (Mail add: PO Box 402, 48656-0402), SAN 308-3934. Tel: 989-389-7630. FAX: 989-389-4956. E-mail: library@richfieldtownship.com. Web Site: www.richfieldtpl.michlibrary.org. *Dir,* Lynn Taylor; Staff 2 (MLS 1, Non-MLS 1)
Founded 1965. Pop 4,500; Circ 16,000
Library Holdings: Bk Vols 11,000; Per Subs 52
Wireless access
Partic in Mid-Michigan Library League
Open Mon 9:30-7:30, Tues 9:30-4:30, Sat 10-1
Friends of the Library Group

SAINT IGNACE

P SAINT IGNACE PUBLIC LIBRARY*, 110 W Spruce St, 49781-1649. SAN 308-3942. Tel: 906-643-8318. FAX: 906-643-9809. Web Site: joomla.uproc.lib.mi.us/stignace. *Dir,* Skip Schmidt; E-mail: sschmidt@uproc.lib.mi.us
Pop 4,284; Circ 26,000
Library Holdings: Bk Vols 23,000; Per Subs 70
Automation Activity & Vendor Info: (Acquisitions) SirsiDynix, (Cataloging) SirsiDynix; (Circulation) SirsiDynix; (ILL) SirsiDynix
Wireless access
Open Mon, Tues & Fri 10-5, Wed & Thurs 10-7, Sat 10-3
Friends of the Library Group

SAINT JOHNS

P BRIGGS PUBLIC LIBRARY*, 108 E Railroad St, 48879-1526. SAN 308-3950. Tel: 989-224-4702. FAX: 989-224-1205. Web Site: www.briggspubliclibrary.org. *Dir,* Sara B Morrison; E-mail: smorrison@briggspubliclibrary.org; *Coordr, Ch Serv,* Marie Geller; Staff 4 (MLS 1, Non-MLS 3)
Founded 1939. Pop 18,189; Circ 129,984
Jul 2009-Jun 2010 Income $406,154. Mats Exp $36,632. Sal $205,136
Library Holdings: Audiobooks 2,039; DVDs 1,205; Large Print Bks 691; Bk Vols 34,621; Per Subs 79; Videos 1,518
Special Collections: Local Genealogy Coll; Local History Coll
Automation Activity & Vendor Info: (Cataloging) Follett Software; (Circulation) Follett Software; (OPAC) Follett Software
Wireless access
Mem of White Pine Library Cooperative
Open Mon-Thurs 9:30-8, Fri 9:30-5, Sat 9:30-1
Friends of the Library Group

SAINT JOSEPH

R FIRST CONGREGATIONAL UNITED CHURCH OF CHRIST LIBRARY*, 2001 Niles Ave, 49085-1614. SAN 308-3969. Tel: 269-983-5519. FAX: 269-983-5988. E-mail: office@fccstjoseph.org.
Founded 1854
Library Holdings: Bk Vols 3,692
Special Collections: Video Tapes for Children & Adults
Subject Interests: Biblical studies, Educ, Psychol
Open Mon-Thurs 9-4, Sun 8-12
Restriction: Congregants only

S THE HERITAGE MUSEUM & CULTURAL CENTER*, Research Library & Archives, 601 Main St, 49085. Tel: 269-983-1191. FAX: 269-983-1274. E-mail: azapal@theheritagemcc.org. Web Site: www.theheritagemcc.org. *Mus Dir,* Christina Hirn Arseneau; *Curator,* Caitlyn Perry Dial
Library Holdings: Bk Vols 1,000; Per Subs 12
Special Collections: Oral History
Subject Interests: Local hist
Wireless access
Partic in Southwest Michigan Library Cooperative
Restriction: Open by appt only

M LAKELAND HEALTH CARE*, Physician's Health Sciences Library, 1234 Napier Ave, 49085-2158. Tel: 269-982-4904. FAX: 269-982-4993. Web Site: www.lakelandhealth.org/PhysicianLibrary. *Librn,* Mike Dill; E-mail: mdill@lakelandregional.org
Library Holdings: Bk Vols 200; Per Subs 85
Wireless access
Restriction: Staff use only

P MAUD PRESTON PALENSKE MEMORIAL LIBRARY*, 500 Market St, 49085. SAN 308-3977. Tel: 269-983-7167, Reference Tel: 269-983-7167, Ext 10. Automation Services Tel: 269-983-7167, Ext 15. FAX: 269-983-5804. E-mail: sjlibrarymi@yahoo.com. Web Site: www.stjoseph.lib.mi.us. *Libr Dir,* Stephanie Masin; Staff 7 (MLS 2, Non-MLS 5)
Founded 1903. Pop 18,831; Circ 250,000
Jul 2008-Jun 2009 Income $782,890. Mats Exp $83,989, Books $55,730, Per/Ser (Incl. Access Fees) $10,510, AV Mat $14,461, Electronic Ref Mat (Incl. Access Fees) $3,288. Sal $435,293
Library Holdings: Bk Titles 94,366; Bk Vols 113,093; Per Subs 180
Subject Interests: Local hist
Automation Activity & Vendor Info: (Cataloging) TLC (The Library Corporation); (Circulation) TLC (The Library Corporation); (ILL) Mel Cat; (OPAC) TLC (The Library Corporation)
Database Vendor: ProQuest, ReferenceUSA
Wireless access
Function: Bks on cassette, Bks on CD, Chess club, Children's prog, Computers for patron use, Copy machines, Electronic databases & coll, Exhibits, Fax serv, Homebound delivery serv, ILL available, Magnifiers for reading, Mail & tel request accepted, Music CDs, Online cat,

Photocopying/Printing, Preschool outreach, Prog for adults, Prog for children & young adult, Pub access computers, Scanner, Story hour, Summer reading prog, Tax forms, Teen prog, Wheelchair accessible
Partic in Southwest Michigan Library Cooperative
Open Mon-Thurs 10-9, Fri & Sat 10-6
Friends of the Library Group

SAINT LOUIS

S MID-MICHIGAN CORRECTIONAL FACILITY LIBRARY*, 8201 N Croswell Rd, 48880. SAN 373-9139. Tel: 989-681-4361, Ext 2315. FAX: 989-681-4203.
Founded 1990
Library Holdings: Bk Titles 10,000; Bk Vols 15,000
Special Collections: Law
Restriction: Not open to pub

P SAINT LOUIS PUBLIC LIBRARY*, T A Cutler Memorial Library, 312 Michigan Ave, 48880. SAN 308-3985. Tel: 989-681-5141. FAX: 989-681-2077. E-mail: cutlerlibrary@live.com. Web Site: www.stlouismi.com/1/stlouis/library.asp. *Dir,* Jessica Little; Staff 2.6 (MLS 1, Non-MLS 1.6)
Founded 1936. Pop 10,600; Circ 27,500
Jul 2012-Jun 2013 Income $165,253, State $5,049, City $47,271, County $96,611, Locally Generated Income $15,322, Other $1,000. Mats Exp $12,197, Books $9,664, Per/Ser (Incl. Access Fees) $1,363, AV Mat $915, Electronic Ref Mat (Incl. Access Fees) $255. Sal $62,445
Library Holdings: Audiobooks 1,024; CDs 114; DVDs 785; Large Print Bks 693; Microforms 97; Music Scores 4; Bk Titles 28,314; Per Subs 47; Videos 461
Special Collections: Local History Coll (St Louis, Alma, Breckenridge & Gratiot County), bks, newsp clippings, pamplets, yearbks; Pine River Superfund Documents
Automation Activity & Vendor Info: (Cataloging) Auto-Graphics, Inc; (Circulation) Auto-Graphics, Inc; (ILL) Mel Cat; (OPAC) Auto-Graphics, Inc
Wireless access
Function: Bk club(s), Bks on cassette, Bks on CD, Computer training, Computers for patron use, Fax serv, ILL available, Music CDs, Online cat, Photocopying/Printing, Prog for children & young adult, Pub access computers, Story hour, Summer reading prog, Tax forms, Video lending libr
Partic in White Pine Libr Coop
Special Services for the Deaf - Closed caption videos; Staff with knowledge of sign lang
Special Services for the Blind - Bks on CD; Large print bks
Open Mon, Tues & Thurs 10-7, Wed & Fri 10-5, Sat (Sept-May) 10-2
Friends of the Library Group

SALINE

G MICHIGAN DEPARTMENT OF COMMUNITY HEALTH*, Center for Forensic Psychiatry Library, 8303 Platt Rd, 48176. (Mail add: PO Box 2060, Ann Arbor, 48106-2060), SAN 371-5671. Tel: 734-429-2531, Ext 4296. Administration Tel: 734-295-4296. FAX: 734-429-7951. TDD: 734-994-7012. *Dir,* Carol E Holden; Staff 1 (MLS 1)
Founded 1974
Library Holdings: Bk Titles 5,724; Bk Vols 7,104; Per Subs 75
Subject Interests: Forensic psychiat, Forensic psychol
Automation Activity & Vendor Info: (Acquisitions) Inmagic, Inc.; (Cataloging) Inmagic, Inc.; (Circulation) Inmagic, Inc.; (Serials) EBSCO Online
Database Vendor: EBSCOhost, LexisNexis, OCLC FirstSearch
Partic in Metrop Detroit Med Libr Group
Special Services for the Deaf - TDD equip
Restriction: Not open to pub

P SALINE DISTRICT LIBRARY*, 555 N Maple Rd, 48176. SAN 308-3993. Tel: 734-429-5450. FAX: 734-944-0600. Web Site: www.saline.lib.mi.us. *Dir,* Leslee Niethammer; Tel: 734-429-2313, E-mail: leslee@saline.lib.mi.us; *Asst Dir,* Marlee Horrocks; E-mail: marlee@saline.lib.mi.us; *Circ Mgr,* Sheila Little; E-mail: sheila@saline.lib.mi.us; *Youth Serv Mgr,* Paula Schaffner; E-mail: paula@saline.lib.mi.us; Staff 38 (MLS 8, Non-MLS 30)
Founded 1900. Pop 21,938
Dec 2005-Nov 2006 Income $1,489,494, State $29,932, County $46,416, Locally Generated Income $1,252,576, Other $160,570. Mats Exp $143,033, Books $83,354, Per/Ser (Incl. Access Fees) $7,951, Micro $1,120, AV Mat $30,608, Electronic Ref Mat (Incl. Access Fees) $20,000. Sal $568,039 (Prof $223,220)
Library Holdings: CDs 2,087; DVDs 1,409; Large Print Bks 621; Bk Titles 77,840; Per Subs 143; Talking Bks 4,502; Videos 4,365
Subject Interests: Local hist
Automation Activity & Vendor Info: (Cataloging) Innovative Interfaces, Inc; (Circulation) Innovative Interfaces, Inc; (OPAC) Innovative Interfaces, Inc; (Serials) Innovative Interfaces, Inc
Database Vendor: CQ Press, Facts on File, Gale Cengage Learning, Newsbank, OCLC FirstSearch, ProQuest, ReferenceUSA, ValueLine
Wireless access
Partic in The Library Network
Open Mon-Thurs 9-9, Fri & Sat 10-5, Sun 1-5
Friends of the Library Group

SANDUSKY

P SANDUSKY DISTRICT LIBRARY*, 55 E Sanilac Ave, 48471-1146. (Mail add: PO Box 271, 48471-0271), SAN 308-4000. Tel: 810-648-2644. FAX: 810-648-1904. Web Site: www.sandusky.lib.mi.us. *Dir,* Gail Ann Nartker; E-mail: gnartker@sandusky.lib.mi.us; *Asst Librn,* Jackie Graves; Staff 6 (Non-MLS 6)
Founded 1937. Pop 7,333; Circ 80,000
Library Holdings: Large Print Bks 667; Bk Titles 25,000; Bk Vols 35,000; Per Subs 100; Talking Bks 1,000
Subject Interests: Genealogy, Local hist
Automation Activity & Vendor Info: (Cataloging) Follett Software; (Circulation) Follett Software; (OPAC) Follett Software
Database Vendor: Gale Cengage Learning, OCLC FirstSearch
Partic in White Pine Libr Coop
Open Mon-Fri 9:30-7, Sat 9:30-2:30
Friends of the Library Group

SARANAC

P SARANAC PUBLIC LIBRARY*, 61 Bridge St, 48881. (Mail add: PO Box 27, 48881-0027), SAN 308-4019. Tel: 616-642-9146. FAX: 616-642-6430. E-mail: sar@llcoop.org. Web Site: saranac.llcoop.org. *Dir,* Sherri Rasmus; E-mail: sarsr@llcoop.org; *Asst Dir,* Mike Platte
Circ 18,726
Library Holdings: Bk Vols 35,000; Per Subs 100
Automation Activity & Vendor Info: (Cataloging) Innovative Interfaces, Inc; (Circulation) Innovative Interfaces, Inc; (OPAC) Innovative Interfaces, Inc
Partic in Lakeland Library Cooperative; Mich Libr Asn
Open Mon 12-7, Tues-Fri 9-5, Sat 9-1
Branches: 1
CLARKSVILLE BRANCH, 130 S Main St, Clarksville, 48815. (Mail add: PO Box 200, Clarksville, 48815-0200). Tel: 616-693-1001. FAX: 616-693-2365. E-mail: cla@llcoop.org. Web Site: www.clarksville.llcoop.org. *Librn,* Noreen Steward
Library Holdings: Bk Vols 9,652
Open Wed 12-7, Thurs & Fri 9-5, Sat 9-1

SAULT SAINTE MARIE

C LAKE SUPERIOR STATE UNIVERSITY*, Kenneth J Shouldice Library, 906 Ryan Ave, 49783. SAN 308-4051. Tel: 906-635-2815. FAX: 906-635-2193. Web Site: www.lssu.edu/library/. *Dean,* Fredrick Michels; E-mail: fmichels@LSSU.edu; *Cat Librn,* Maureen Delaney-Lehman; *Pub Serv Librn,* Ruth Neveu; *Circ Supvr,* Cris Roll; *AV,* Charles Gustafson; *ILL,* Mary June; *Pub Serv,* Beth Hronek; Staff 5 (MLS 5)
Founded 1946. Enrl 3,000; Fac 110; Highest Degree: Bachelor
Library Holdings: Bk Vols 111,429; Per Subs 811
Special Collections: Great Lakes (Marine-Laker); Michigan History (Michigan Room). US Document Depository
Automation Activity & Vendor Info: (Acquisitions) Ex Libris Group; (Cataloging) Ex Libris Group; (Circulation) Ex Libris Group; (Course Reserve) Ex Libris Group; (ILL) Ex Libris Group; (Media Booking) Ex Libris Group; (OPAC) Ex Libris Group; (Serials) Ex Libris Group
Function: ILL available
Partic in OCLC Online Computer Library Center, Inc; Sault Area Int Libr Asn; Upper Peninsula Region of Library Cooperation, Inc
Open Mon-Wed (Winter) 7:30am-Midnight, Thurs 7:30am-11pm, Fri 7:30-6, Sat 11-6, Sun 1pm-Midnight; Mon, Thurs & Fri (Summer) 8-5, Tues & Wed 8am-9pm, Sat 10-2

P SUPERIOR DISTRICT LIBRARY*, 541 Library Dr, 49783. SAN 308-4035. Tel: 906-632-9331. FAX: 906-635-0210. E-mail: bayref@baylisslibrary.org. Web Site: www.baylisslibrary.org. *Dir,* Kenneth B Miller, Jr; E-mail: kmiller@baylisslibrary.org; *Asst Dir, Ref,* Susan James; E-mail: sjames@baylisslibrary.org; *Ch,* Debbie Lehman; E-mail: debbiel@baylisslibrary.org; *Ref Serv,* Amber Clement; E-mail: aclement@baylisslibrary.org; Staff 4 (MLS 1, Non-MLS 3)
Founded 1905
Library Holdings: Bk Titles 88,000; Per Subs 145
Special Collections: History (Judge Joseph H Steere Coll), bks, ms. State Document Depository
Automation Activity & Vendor Info: (Cataloging) SirsiDynix; (Circulation) SirsiDynix; (OPAC) SirsiDynix

Wireless access
Partic in Superiorland Library Cooperative; Upper Peninsula Region of Library Cooperation, Inc
Special Services for the Blind - Accessible computers; Assistive/Adapted tech devices, equip & products; Audio mat; Bks on cassette; Bks on CD; Closed circuit TV magnifier; Club for the blind; Computer with voice synthesizer for visually impaired persons; Descriptive video serv (DVS); Extensive large print coll; Free checkout of audio mat; Internet workstation with adaptive software; Large print & cassettes; Large print bks; Large screen computer & software; PC for handicapped; Text reader; ZoomText magnification & reading software
Open Tues & Thurs 9-9, Wed & Fri 9-5:30, Sat 9-4
Friends of the Library Group
Branches: 6
BREVORT TOWNSHIP COMMUNITY, 4009 N Church St, Moran, 49760. (Mail add: PO Box 30, Moran, 49760-0030). FAX: 906-643-6525. E-mail: brevort@sault.com. *In Charge,* Bernice J Peterson
Open Mon & Wed 9-2, Tues & Thurs 3-8
Friends of the Library Group
CURTIS PUBLIC, N 9220 Portage Ave, Curtis, 49820. Tel: 906-586-9411. FAX: 906-586-6166. E-mail: curtislib@uproc.lib.mi.us. *In Charge,* Linda C Blanchard
Open Mon 11-7, Thurs & Fri 9-4:30
Friends of the Library Group
DRUMMOND ISLAND BRANCH, 29934 E Court St, Drummond Island, 49726. (Mail add: PO Box 202, Drummond Island, 49726-0202). Tel: 906-493-5243. FAX: 906-493-5924.
Open Mon, Tues & Fri 10:30-3:30, Thurs 2-7
Friends of the Library Group
ENGADINE BRANCH, W13920 Melville St, Engadine, 49827. Tel: 906-477-6313, Ext 140. FAX: 906-477-6643. *In Charge,* Janice Wagner; E-mail: jwagner@eup.k12.mi.us
Open Mon 12-4:30 & 7-10, Tues & Thurs 7-10pm, Wed & Fri 12-4:30, Sat 9-Noon
Friends of the Library Group
LES CHENEAUX COMMUNITY, 75 E Hodeck St, Cedarville, 49719. (Mail add: PO Box 99, Cedarville, 49719-0157). Tel: 906-484-3547. FAX: 906-484-3547. E-mail: lcclib@uproc.lib.mi.us. *Br Mgr,* Jane French
Open Tues, Wed & Fri 11-5, Thurs 1-8, Sat 10-3
Friends of the Library Group
PICKFORD COMMUNITY LIBRARY, 230 E Main St, Pickford, 49774. Tel: 906-647-1288. FAX: 906-647-1288. Web Site: www.baylisslibrary.org/pickford. *Mgr,* Michelle Satchell; E-mail: msatchell@uproc.lib.mi.us

SCHOOLCRAFT

P SCHOOLCRAFT COMMUNITY LIBRARY*, 330 N Centre St, 49087. SAN 371-5701. Tel: 616-679-5959. FAX: 616-679-5599. Web Site: schoolcraftlibrary.org. *Dir,* Position Currently Open; Staff 6 (MLS 2, Non-MLS 4)
Founded 1988. Pop 3,686; Circ 4,800
Mar 2005-Feb 2006 Income $140,689, State $2,919, Provincial $13,980, Locally Generated Income $113,351, Other $10,439. Mats Exp $17,752, Books $13,566, Per/Ser (Incl. Access Fees) $1,131, Other Print Mats $1,000, AV Mat $2,055
Library Holdings: AV Mats 1,235; DVDs 429; Large Print Bks 421; Bk Titles 30,425; Per Subs 25; Talking Bks 803
Automation Activity & Vendor Info: (Acquisitions) Follett Software; (Cataloging) Follett Software; (Circulation) Follett Software; (ILL) Auto-Graphics, Inc
Database Vendor: OCLC FirstSearch
Wireless access
Function: Copy machines, e-mail serv, Fax serv, Handicapped accessible, Home delivery & serv to Sr ctr & nursing homes, Homebound delivery serv, ILL available, Photocopying/Printing, Preschool outreach, Prog for children & young adult, Ref serv available, Spoken cassettes & CDs, Summer reading prog, Tax forms, Telephone ref, VCDs, VHS videos, Wheelchair accessible
Mem of Woodlands Library Cooperative
Open Mon 10-7:30, Tues & Wed 1-7:30, Thurs 10-5, Fri 1-5, Sat 10-1
Friends of the Library Group

SCOTTVILLE

J WEST SHORE COMMUNITY COLLEGE*, William M Anderson Library, 3000 N Stiles Rd, 49454. SAN 308-4078. Tel: 231-843-5529, 231-845-6211. Toll Free Tel: 800-848-9722. FAX: 231-845-2007. Web Site: www.westshore.edu/library. *Librn,* Mike Hypio; E-mail: mrhypio@westshore.edu
Founded 1967. Enrl 1,400
Library Holdings: CDs 2,000; e-books 50; Bk Titles 10,000; Bk Vols 23,000; Per Subs 150
Automation Activity & Vendor Info: (Cataloging) Book Systems; (Circulation) Book Systems
Partic in Mid-Michigan Library League
Open Mon-Thurs 8am-8:30pm, Fri 8-4:30

SEBEWAING

P SEBEWAING TOWNSHIP LIBRARY, 41 N Center St, 48759-1406. SAN 308-4086. Tel: 989-883-3520. FAX: 989-883-3520. E-mail: sebewainglibrary@att.net. Web Site: www.sebewainglibrary.org. *Dir,* Margo Bonini
Pop 4,509; Circ 26,000
Library Holdings: Bk Vols 20,000; Per Subs 50
Special Collections: Local Newspapers on Microfilm
Wireless access
Partic in White Pine Libr Coop
Open Mon & Wed 10-6, Tues & Fri 10-5, Sat 10-1

SHELBY

P SHELBY AREA DISTRICT LIBRARY*, 189 Maple St, 49455-1134. SAN 308-4094. Tel: 231-861-4565. FAX: 231-861-6868. E-mail: shelbylibrary@yahoo.com. Web Site: www.shelbylibrary.org. *Dir,* Tiffany Haight; *Asst Dir,* Quinn Maynard; Staff 1 (Non-MLS 1)
Founded 1907. Pop 11,192
Mar 2005-Feb 2006 Income $263,400. Mats Exp $27,500, Books $20,500, Per/Ser (Incl. Access Fees) $3,200, AV Mat $2,700. Sal $135,000 (Prof $25,500)
Library Holdings: CDs 35; DVDs 35; Bk Vols 35,000; Per Subs 115; Talking Bks 1,200; Videos 1,700
Automation Activity & Vendor Info: (Cataloging) Auto-Graphics, Inc; (Circulation) Auto-Graphics, Inc; (OPAC) Auto-Graphics, Inc
Partic in Mich Libr Asn; Mid-Michigan Library League
Open Mon-Thurs 9-7, Fri 9-5, Sat 9-1
Friends of the Library Group
Bookmobiles: 1. Librn, Quinn Maynard

SHELBY TOWNSHIP

P SHELBY TOWNSHIP LIBRARY*, 51680 Van Dyke, 48316-4448. SAN 308-4604. Tel: 586-739-7414. FAX: 586-726-0535. Web Site: www.libcoop.net/shelby. *Dir,* Katie Ester; Tel: 586-726-2344, E-mail: esterk@libcoop.net; *Asst Dir,* Diane Burgeson; *Adult Serv,* Susan Ferrell; *Ch Serv,* Merry Jane Benner; *Ch Serv,* Kathleen Lozen; Staff 17 (MLS 5, Non-MLS 12)
Founded 1972. Pop 65,159; Circ 261,689
Jul 2005-Jun 2006. Mats Exp $154,000
Library Holdings: AV Mats 14,056; Electronic Media & Resources 543; Large Print Bks 2,592; Bk Vols 116,327; Per Subs 262; Talking Bks 3,755
Automation Activity & Vendor Info: (Cataloging) SirsiDynix; (Circulation) SirsiDynix; (ILL) OCLC; (OPAC) SirsiDynix; (Serials) EBSCO Online
Database Vendor: SirsiDynix
Wireless access
Function: Homebound delivery serv, ILL available, Online searches, Prog for children & young adult, Serves mentally handicapped consumers, Summer reading prog, Telephone ref, Wheelchair accessible
Publications: Friends of the Shelby Township Library (Newsletter); Shelby News Worth Knowing (Newsletter)
Partic in Suburban Library Cooperative
Open Mon-Thurs 9-8, Fri & Sat 9-5
Friends of the Library Group

SIDNEY

J MONTCALM COMMUNITY COLLEGE LIBRARY*, 2800 College Dr, 48885. SAN 308-4108. Tel: 989-328-2111, Ext 261, 989-328-2111, Ext 291. Web Site: www.montcalm.edu/library.
Founded 1965. Enrl 2,000; Fac 24; Highest Degree: Associate
Library Holdings: Bk Titles 30,000; Per Subs 220
Database Vendor: Gale Cengage Learning, OCLC FirstSearch, ProQuest
Function: ILL available
Open Mon-Thurs 9-8, Fri 9-Noon

SODUS

P SODUS TOWNSHIP LIBRARY*, 3776 Naomi Rd, 49126-9783. SAN 308-4116. Tel: 269-925-0903. FAX: 269-925-1823. E-mail: sodustwplib@comcast.net. Web Site: www.sodustwplibrary.org. *Dir,* Lynn Sisson; Staff 1 (Non-MLS 1)
Founded 1939. Pop 1,932; Circ 7,200
Library Holdings: Bk Titles 15,000; Per Subs 53
Wireless access
Partic in Southwest Michigan Library Cooperative
Open Mon 2-7, Tues 10-6, Wed & Thurs 2-6, Fri 2-5, Sat 10-1
Friends of the Library Group

SOUTH HAVEN

S MICHIGAN MARITIME MUSEUM*, Marialyce Canonie Great Lakes Research Library, 91 Michigan Ave, 49090. Tel: 269-637-9156. Administration Tel: 269-637-8078. Toll Free Tel: 800-747-3810. FAX: 269-637-1594. E-mail: library@michiganmaritimemuseum.org. Web Site: www.michiganmaritimemusem.org/museum/library. *Exec Dir,* Patti Montgomery Reinert; *Educ Dir,* Katie Bleil; Staff 3 (MLS 1, Non-MLS 2)
Founded 1985
Library Holdings: Bk Vols 2,400; Per Subs 45
Subject Interests: Great Lakes maritime hist
Partic in Southwest Michigan Library Cooperative
Restriction: Open by appt only

P SOUTH HAVEN MEMORIAL LIBRARY, 314 Broadway St, 49090. SAN 308-4124. Tel: 269-637-2403. FAX: 269-639-1685. E-mail: shml@shmlibrary.org. Web Site: www.shmlibrary.org. *Dir,* Jim France; E-mail: jimfrance@shmlibrary.org; *Children & Teen Librn,* Gail Patterson; E-mail: gailpatterson@shmlibrary.org; *Bus Mgr,* Dorothy Buchler; Staff 5 (MLS 2, Non-MLS 3)
Founded 1910. Pop 9,059; Circ 51,814
Jul 2014-Jun 2015 Income $345,860. Mats Exp $371,973. Sal $191,528
Library Holdings: Bks on Deafness & Sign Lang 10; High Interest/Low Vocabulary Bk Vols 120; Bk Titles 57,000; Per Subs 120
Subject Interests: Great Lakes, Local hist
Automation Activity & Vendor Info: (Cataloging) Follett Software; (Circulation) Follett Software; (ILL) Auto-Graphics, Inc; (OPAC) Follett Software
Database Vendor: EBSCOhost
Wireless access
Partic in Southwest Michigan Library Cooperative
Special Services for the Deaf - Bks on deafness & sign lang; High interest/low vocabulary bks
Special Services for the Blind - Aids for in-house use
Open Mon-Thurs 10-8, Fri 10-6, Sat 10-4
Restriction: Open to pub for ref & circ; with some limitations
Friends of the Library Group

SOUTH LYON

P LYON TOWNSHIP PUBLIC LIBRARY*, 27005 S Milford Rd, 48178. SAN 308-3055. Tel: 248-437-8800. FAX: 248-437-4621. Web Site: www.lyon.lib.mi.us. *Dir,* Holly Teasdle; E-mail: hteasdle@lyon.lib.mi.us; *Youth Serv Librn,* Robin Linkowski; E-mail: rlinkowski@lyon.lib.mi.us; *Computer Tech,* Marj O'Donnel; E-mail: modonnel@lyon.lib.mi.us; *Genealogist,* Catherine Cottone; E-mail: ccottone@lyon.lib.mi.us; *Tech Serv,* Pam Quackenbush; E-mail: pquackenbush@lyon.lib.mi.us; Staff 2.5 (MLS 1.5, Non-MLS 1)
Founded 1956. Pop 11,041; Circ 81,634
Library Holdings: Bk Vols 50,000; Per Subs 120
Subject Interests: Genealogy
Automation Activity & Vendor Info: (Cataloging) SirsiDynix; (Circulation) SirsiDynix; (OPAC) SirsiDynix
Wireless access
Function: Adult bk club, Archival coll, Bks on CD, Children's prog, Computer training, Computers for patron use, Copy machines, e-mail serv, Fax serv, Free DVD rentals, Genealogy discussion group, Handicapped accessible, ILL available, Mus passes, Music CDs, Online searches, Photocopying/Printing, Preschool outreach, Prog for adults, Prog for children & young adult, Scanner, Senior computer classes, Story hour, Summer reading prog, Tax forms, Teen prog, VHS videos, Web-catalog, Wheelchair accessible
Open Mon-Thurs 10-8, Fri & Sat 12-5, Sun 12-4
Friends of the Library Group

P SALEM-SOUTH LYON DISTRICT LIBRARY*, 9800 Pontiac Trail, 48178-7021. SAN 308-4132. Tel: 248-437-6431. FAX: 248-437-6593. Web Site: www.ssldl.info. *Dir,* Doreen Hannon; Tel: 248-437-6431, Ext 206, E-mail: dhannon@ssldl.info; *Asst Dir/Network Adminr,* Garrett Hungerford; Tel: 248-437-6431, Ext 208, E-mail: ghungerford@ssldl.info; *Head, Adult Serv,* Jillian Essenmacher; Tel: 248-437-6431, Ext 201, E-mail: jessenmacher@ssldl.info; *Head, Youth Serv,* Caryn Bartone; Tel: 248-437-6431, Ext 204, E-mail: cbartone@ssldl.info; *Pub Relations Coordr,* Lindsay Gerhardt; Tel: 248-437-6431, Ext 209, E-mail: lgerhardt@ssldl.info; Staff 5 (MLS 5)
Founded 1939. Pop 16,954; Circ 318,433
Jul 2012-Jun 2013 Income $1,100,793. Mats Exp $165,374. Sal $639,959
Library Holdings: CDs 2,999; DVDs 1,515; Large Print Bks 1,402; Bk Vols 58,034; Per Subs 103; Talking Bks 2,342; Videos 3,662
Special Collections: South Lyon Herald from 1929, CD-ROM
Automation Activity & Vendor Info: (Acquisitions) SirsiDynix; (Cataloging) SirsiDynix; (Circulation) SirsiDynix; (ILL) SirsiDynix; (OPAC) SirsiDynix; (Serials) SirsiDynix
Wireless access
Function: Adult bk club, After school storytime, Art exhibits, Audio & video playback equip for onsite use, AV serv, Bk club(s), CD-ROM, Computer training, Copy machines, Digital talking bks, e-mail serv, Electronic databases & coll, Equip loans & repairs, Fax serv, Games & aids for the handicapped, Handicapped accessible, Homebound delivery serv, Homework prog, ILL available, Magnifiers for reading, Mail & tel request accepted, Music CDs, Online ref, Online searches, Orientations, Outside serv via phone, mail, e-mail & web, Photocopying/Printing, Preschool outreach, Prog for adults, Prog for children & young adult, Ref & res, Ref serv available, Senior computer classes, Spoken cassettes & CDs, Spoken cassettes & DVDs, Summer reading prog, Tax forms, Telephone ref, VHS videos, Video lending libr, Wheelchair accessible, Workshops
Partic in The Library Network
Special Services for the Blind - Closed circuit TV magnifier; Magnifiers; ZoomText magnification & reading software
Open Mon-Thurs 9-9, Fri & Sat 10-5
Friends of the Library Group

SOUTHFIELD

R CONGREGATION SHAAREY ZEDEK LIBRARY & AUDIO VISUAL CENTER*, 27375 Bell Rd, 48034. SAN 308-4191. Tel: 248-357-5544. FAX: 248-357-0227. E-mail: csz.info@shaareyzedek.org. Web Site: www.shaareyzedek.org. *Exec Dir,* Janet Pont; E-mail: jpont@shaareyzedek.org; *Librn,* Irene Mellin
Founded 1861
Library Holdings: Bk Titles 35,250; Bk Vols 40,250; Per Subs 12
Special Collections: Modern Hebrew lit, Holtzman Coll
Subject Interests: Holocaust, Judaica (lit or hist of Jews), Juv delinquency, Lit
Automation Activity & Vendor Info: (Cataloging) Follett Software
Open Mon & Wed 10-12, Tues & Thurs 10-3, Sun 9:30-12:30

M HELEN L DEROY MEDICAL LIBRARY*, 16001 W Nine Mile Rd, 48075. SAN 308-4272. Tel: 248-849-3294. FAX: 248-849-3201. Web Site: www.realmedicine.org/providence/library. *Dir,* Alexia Estabrook; E-mail: alexia.estabrook@stjohn.org; Staff 4 (MLS 3, Non-MLS 1)
Founded 1950
Library Holdings: e-books 10; e-journals 8,000; Bk Titles 3,500; Bk Vols 4,000; Per Subs 325
Subject Interests: Med
Automation Activity & Vendor Info: (Acquisitions) CyberTools for Libraries; (Cataloging) OCLC Connexion; (Circulation) CyberTools for Libraries; (OPAC) CyberTools for Libraries; (Serials) CyberTools for Libraries
Database Vendor: Dialog, EBSCO Information Services, OCLC WorldShare Interlibrary Loan, OVID Technologies, PubMed, RefWorks, STAT!Ref (Teton Data Systems), UpToDate
Wireless access
Open Mon-Fri 8:30-4:30

L JAFFE RAITT HEUER & WEISS, Law Library, 27777 Franklin Rd, Ste 2500, 48034-8214. SAN 372-0403. Tel: 248-351-3000, 248-727-1470. FAX: 248-351-3082. E-mail: libreq@jaffelaw.com. Web Site: www.jaffelaw.com. *Head Librn,* Sylvia Arakelian; Staff 1.25 (MLS 1, Non-MLS 0.25)
Founded 1964
Restriction: Access at librarian's discretion

C LAWRENCE TECHNOLOGICAL UNIVERSITY LIBRARY*, 21000 W Ten Mile Rd, 48075-1058. SAN 308-4256. Tel: 248-204-3000. FAX: 248-204-3005. E-mail: refdesk@ltu.edu. Web Site: library.ltu.edu. *Dir,* Gary R Cocozzoli; E-mail: gcocozzol@ltu.edu; *Head, Ref, Instrul Serv,* Gretchen Young Weiner; E-mail: gweiner@ltu.edu; *Head, Tech Serv,* Cathy Phillips; E-mail: cphillips@ltu.edu; *Access Serv Librn,* Cynthia Simpson; E-mail: csimpson@ltu.edu; *Digital Projects Librn,* Adrienne Aluzzo; Tel: 248-204-2821, E-mail: aaluzzo@ltu.edu; *Ref Librn,* Sheila Gaddie; E-mail: sgaddie@ltu.edu; *Ref Librn,* Mary Alice Power; E-mail: mpower@ltu.edu; *Ref & Instruction Librn,* Natalie Zebula; E-mail: nzebula@ltu.edu; *Coordr, Access Serv,* Cynthia Simpson; E-mail: csimpson@ltu.edu; *Circ & Tech Serv Asst,* Barbara L Jackson; E-mail: bjackson@ltu.edu; Staff 9 (MLS 7, Non-MLS 2)
Founded 1932. Enrl 4,300; Fac 713; Highest Degree: Doctorate
Library Holdings: DVDs 800; e-books 105,000; e-journals 115,000; Microforms 2,000; Bk Titles 48,000; Bk Vols 113,300; Per Subs 1,000; Videos 60
Special Collections: Architectural Materials (Albert F Kahn Coll)
Subject Interests: Archit, Eng, Mgt
Automation Activity & Vendor Info: (Acquisitions) OCLC; (Cataloging) OCLC; (Circulation) OCLC; (Course Reserve) OCLC; (ILL) OCLC; (OPAC) OCLC WorldShare Interlibrary Loan; (Serials) OCLC
Database Vendor: ACM (Association for Computing Machinery), American Psychological Association (APA), ASCE Research Library,

ebrary, EBSCOhost, Elsevier, Emerald, Faulkner Information Services, Gale Cengage Learning, H W Wilson, IEEE (Institute of Electrical & Electronics Engineers), IOP, LearningExpress, LexisNexis, Marquis Who's Who, Material ConneXion, Medline, Mergent Online, Nature Publishing Group, OCLC, OCLC ArticleFirst, OCLC CAMIO, OCLC FirstSearch, OCLC WorldShare Interlibrary Loan, OCLC Worldshare Management Services, Project MUSE, ProQuest, ReferenceUSA, RefWorks, Safari Books Online, Sage, ScienceDirect, Scopus, Springshare, LLC, Wilson - Wilson Web
Wireless access
Function: Computers for patron use, Copy machines, Distance learning, Doc delivery serv, e-mail & chat, Electronic databases & coll, Free DVD rentals, ILL available, Mail & tel request accepted, Microfiche/film & reading machines, Online cat, Outside serv via phone, mail, e-mail & web, Photocopying/Printing, Ref serv available, Telephone ref, Video lending libr
Partic in Midwest Collaborative for Library Services (MCLS); OCLC Online Computer Library Center, Inc; Southeastern Michigan League of Libraries
Open Mon-Thurs 8:30am-9:30pm, Fri 8:30-7:30, Sat 10:30-4:30

J OAKLAND COMMUNITY COLLEGE, Southfield Campus Library-Information Commons, 22322 Rutland Dr, Rm A212, 48075-4793. SAN 376-9801. Tel: 248-233-2830. Circulation Tel: 248-233-2825. Reference Tel: 248-233-2826. FAX: 248-233-2828. Web Site: www.oaklandcc.edu/library. *Fac Librn, Ref,* Stacy C Charlesbois-Nordan; E-mail: sbcharle@oaklandcc.edu; Staff 3 (MLS 1, Non-MLS 2)
Founded 1998. Enrl 4,200; Fac 8; Highest Degree: Associate
Jul 2014-Jun 2015. Mats Exp $16,000, Books $12,000, Per/Ser (Incl. Access Fees) $4,000. Sal $131,595
Library Holdings: DVDs 100; Bk Vols 3,000; Per Subs 20; Talking Bks 55
Special Collections: Browsing (Urban Fiction Specialty)
Subject Interests: African-Am studies, Allied health, Nursing
Automation Activity & Vendor Info: (Cataloging) SirsiDynix; (Circulation) SirsiDynix; (Course Reserve) SirsiDynix; (ILL) Mel Cat; (OPAC) SirsiDynix; (Serials) SirsiDynix
Database Vendor: Alexander Street Press, ARTstor, Bowker, Brodart, Cinahl, College Source, CQ Press, ebrary, EBSCO Discovery Service, EBSCO Information Services, EBSCOhost, Electric Library, Elsevier, Gale Cengage Learning, JSTOR, LearningExpress, Micromedex, Newsbank, OCLC WorldShare Interlibrary Loan, Oxford Online, ProQuest, ScienceDirect, SirsiDynix, ValueLine
Wireless access
Function: Audio & video playback equip for onsite use, Bks on CD, Computers for patron use, Copy machines, Doc delivery serv, e-mail & chat, e-mail serv, Electronic databases & coll, Handicapped accessible, Health sci info serv, ILL available, Magnifiers for reading, Online info literacy tutorials on the web & in blackboard, Online ref, Orientations, Photocopying/Printing, Pub access computers, Ref & res, Ref serv in person, Tax forms, Wheelchair accessible
Partic in Detroit Area Library Network; Midwest Collaborative for Library Services (MCLS)
Special Services for the Blind - Assistive/Adapted tech devices, equip & products; Computer with voice synthesizer for visually impaired persons; Low vision equip; Magnifiers
Open Mon-Thurs 8:30am-9:45pm, Fri & Sat 8:30-4:45

L PEPPER, HAMILTON LLP*, Law Library, 4000 Town Ctr, Ste 1800, 48075. SAN 372-042X. Tel: 248-359-7300. FAX: 248-359-7700. *Librn,* Angela Booth; Staff 1 (MLS 1)
Library Holdings: Bk Vols 12,000; Per Subs 20

L SOMMERS, SCHWARTZ, SILVER & SCHWARTZ*, Law Library, 2000 Town Ctr, Ste 900, 48075. SAN 372-0470. Tel: 248-355-0300. FAX: 248-746-4001.
Library Holdings: Bk Vols 14,000; Per Subs 250
Database Vendor: LexisNexis, Westlaw
Function: For res purposes, Res libr
Restriction: Co libr, Not a lending libr, Not open to pub, Private libr

P SOUTHFIELD PUBLIC LIBRARY*, David Stewart Memorial Library, 26300 Evergreen Rd, 48076. (Mail add: PO Box 2055, 48037-2055), SAN 308-4299. Tel: 248-796-4200. Circulation Tel: 248-796-4208. Reference Tel: 248-796-4280. FAX: 248-796-4305. Web Site: www.southfieldlibrary.org. *Dir,* Dave Ewick; Tel: 248-796-4300, E-mail: dewick@sfldlib.org; *Dep Librn,* Mary Beall; Tel: 248-796-4302, E-mail: mbeall@sfldlib.org; *Actg Adult Coordr,* Position Currently Open; *Coordr, Tech Serv,* Robin Gardella; Tel: 248-796-4340, E-mail: rgardella@sfldlib.org; Staff 37 (MLS 23, Non-MLS 14)
Founded 1960. Pop 71,000; Circ 714,326
Jul 2009-Jun 2010 Income $8,517,624, State $32,559, City $7,760,862, County $105,335, Locally Generated Income $533,422, Other $8,178. Mats Exp $487,830, Books $327,830, AV Mat $80,000, Electronic Ref Mat (Incl. Access Fees) $80,000. Sal $2,556,100
Library Holdings: Bk Vols 254,926; Per Subs 445
Special Collections: United States Census Affiliate Center
Automation Activity & Vendor Info: (Acquisitions) Innovative Interfaces, Inc; (Cataloging) Innovative Interfaces, Inc; (Circulation) Innovative Interfaces, Inc; (OPAC) Innovative Interfaces, Inc; (Serials) Innovative Interfaces, Inc
Wireless access
Publications: Newsletter (Bi-monthly)
Partic in Metronet; Midwest Collaborative for Library Services (MCLS); The Library Network
Open Mon-Thurs 9:30-9, Fri & Sat 9:30-5:30, Sun (Sept-May) 1-5
Friends of the Library Group

SOUTHGATE

P SOUTHGATE VETERANS MEMORIAL LIBRARY*, 14680 Dix-Toledo Rd, 48195. SAN 308-4310. Tel: 734-258-3002. FAX: 734-284-9477. Web Site: www.southgate.lib.mi.us. *Dir,* Joyce Farkas; E-mail: farkas@tln.lib.mi.us; *Asst Dir,* Katherine Cox; E-mail: kcox@tln.lib.mi.us; *Youth Serv Librn,* Charlyn Watch
Pop 30,771; Circ 92,159
Library Holdings: Bk Vols 77,000; Per Subs 122
Function: Prog for children & young adult, Summer reading prog
Partic in The Library Network
Open Mon-Thurs 10-9, Fri & Sat 10-5

SPARTA

P SPARTA TOWNSHIP LIBRARY*, 80 N Union St, 49345. SAN 308-4329. Tel: 616-887-9937. FAX: 616-887-0179. Web Site: www.sparta.llcoop.org. *Dir,* Lois Lovell; E-mail: spall@llcoop.org
Founded 1917. Pop 8,938; Circ 42,915
Library Holdings: Bk Vols 59,965; Per Subs 48
Subject Interests: Genealogy, Local hist
Automation Activity & Vendor Info: (Cataloging) Innovative Interfaces, Inc; (Circulation) Innovative Interfaces, Inc
Wireless access
Partic in Lakeland Library Cooperative
Open Mon & Tues 9-8, Wed & Fri 9-5, Sat 9-12
Friends of the Library Group

SPRING ARBOR

C SPRING ARBOR UNIVERSITY*, Hugh A & Edna C White Library, 106 E Main St, 49283. SAN 308-4337. Tel: 517-750-6441. Circulation Tel: 517-750-6742. Interlibrary Loan Service Tel: 517-750-6439. Toll Free Tel: 800-968-9103, Ext 1742. FAX: 517-750-2108. Web Site: www.arbor.edu/whitelibrary. *Dir,* Roy Meador; Tel: 800-968-9103, Ext 1444, E-mail: rmeador@arbor.edu, *Educ Librn,* Stephanie Davis; Tel: 800-968-9103, Ext 1435, E-mail: sdavis@arbor.edu; *Pub Serv, Ref Librn,* Karen Parsons; Tel: 800-968-9103, Ext 1436, E-mail: kparsons@arbor.edu; *Circ Supvr,* Lois Hunt; Tel: 800-968-9103, Ext 1442, E-mail: lhunt@arbor.edu; *Tech Serv,* David Burns; Tel: 800-968-9103, Ext 1443, E-mail: dburns@arbor.edu; Staff 9 (MLS 4, Non-MLS 5)
Founded 1873. Enrl 2,478; Fac 77; Highest Degree: Master
Library Holdings: Bk Vols 101,620; Per Subs 572
Partic in Cap Area Libr Network Inc; OCLC Online Computer Library Center, Inc
Open Mon-Thurs 7:45am-11pm, Fri 7:45am-9pm, Sat 10-10, Sun 5pm-11pm

SPRING LAKE

P SPRING LAKE DISTRICT LIBRARY*, 123 E Exchange St, 49456-2018. SAN 308-4353. Tel: 616-846-5770. FAX: 616-844-2129. Web Site: www.sllib.org. *Dir,* Claire Sheridan; *Asst Dir,* Barbara Anderson; Staff 3 (MLS 2, Non-MLS 1)
Pop 13,140
Library Holdings: AV Mats 3,210; Bk Vols 69,000; Per Subs 175
Automation Activity & Vendor Info: (Cataloging) Innovative Interfaces, Inc; (Circulation) Innovative Interfaces, Inc; (ILL) Innovative Interfaces, Inc; (OPAC) Innovative Interfaces, Inc; (Serials) Innovative Interfaces, Inc
Wireless access
Partic in Lakeland Library Cooperative
Open Mon-Thurs 9:30-8:30, Fri & Sat 9:30-5, Sun (Winter) 2-5
Friends of the Library Group

STANTON

P WHITE PINE LIBRARY, 106 E Walnut, 48888-9294. SAN 308-4361. Tel: 989-831-4327. FAX: 989-831-4976. E-mail: whitepinelibrary1@hotmail.com. Web Site: whitepinelibrary.org. *Dir,* Katie Arwood; *Asst Librn,* Tammy Bowen
Founded 1935. Pop 10,320; Circ 44,000

Library Holdings: Bk Vols 22,000; Per Subs 50
Subject Interests: Genealogy, Local hist
Automation Activity & Vendor Info: (Cataloging) Follett Software; (Circulation) Follett Software; (OPAC) Follett Software
Wireless access
Partic in Mid-Michigan Library League
Open Mon & Fri 9-5:30, Tues 12:30-5:30, Wed 12-7, Thurs 9-7, Sat 10-12
Friends of the Library Group

STEPHENSON

P MENOMINEE COUNTY LIBRARY*, S319 Railroad St, 49887. (Mail add: PO Box 128, 49887-0128), SAN 347-0768. Tel: 906-753-6923. FAX: 906-753-4678. E-mail: mcl@uproc.lib.mi.us. Web Site: www.uproc.lib.mi.us/menominee. *Dir,* Patricia F Cheski; E-mail: cheskip@uproc.lib.mi.us; *Outreach Coordr,* Sally Harris; E-mail: harriss@uproc.lib.mi.us; Staff 4.5 (MLS 1, Non-MLS 3.5)
Founded 1944. Pop 15,013
Library Holdings: CDs 971; DVDs 615; Large Print Bks 3,494; Bk Vols 42,997; Per Subs 86; Talking Bks 537; Videos 412
Automation Activity & Vendor Info: (Cataloging) SIRSI WorkFlows; (Circulation) SIRSI WorkFlows; (OPAC) SIRSI-iBistro
Wireless access
Function: ILL available
Partic in Superiorland Library Cooperative
Open Mon & Sat 9-1, Tues-Fri 8-5
Friends of the Library Group
Branches: 1
HERMANSVILLE BRANCH, W5480 First St, Hermansville, 49847, SAN 347-0792. Tel: 906-498-2253. *Br Coordr,* Laurie Riedy; Staff 0.4 (Non-MLS 0.4)
Open Tues & Wed 9-3, Thurs 9-1
Friends of the Library Group
Bookmobiles: 1

STERLING HEIGHTS

P STERLING HEIGHTS PUBLIC LIBRARY, 40255 Dodge Park Rd, 48313-4140. SAN 308-4388. Tel: 586-446-2665. Reference Tel: 586-446-2642. Administration Tel: 586-446-2640. FAX: 586-276-4067. E-mail: shpl@libcoop.net. Web Site: www.shpl.net. *Dir,* Tammy Turgeon; Tel: 586-446-2641, E-mail: turgeont@libcoop.net; *Supvr, Circ,* Anne Schultz; E-mail: schultza@libcoop.net; *Supvr, Pub Serv,* Karen Stine; E-mail: stinek@libcoop.net; *Supvr, Tech Serv,* Catherine Les; Tel: 586-446-2649, E-mail: lesc@libcoop.net; *Pub Relations & Prog Coordr,* Jason Groth; E-mail: grothj@libcoop.net; Staff 26 (MLS 9, Non-MLS 17)
Founded 1971. Pop 129,699; Circ 536,485
Library Holdings: AV Mats 20,230; Bk Vols 189,822; Per Subs 359
Special Collections: International Language Coll. Oral History
Subject Interests: Careers, Children's lit
Automation Activity & Vendor Info: (Acquisitions) SirsiDynix; (Cataloging) SirsiDynix; (Circulation) SirsiDynix; (ILL) SirsiDynix; (OPAC) SirsiDynix; (Serials) SirsiDynix
Database Vendor: Gale Cengage Learning, Wilson - Wilson Web
Wireless access
Function: Story hour, Study rm, Summer reading prog, Tax forms, Teen prog, Wheelchair accessible
Partic in Suburban Library Cooperative
Open Mon-Thurs 9:30-9, Fri 1-5, Sat 9:30-5
Friends of the Library Group

STEVENSVILLE

P LINCOLN TOWNSHIP PUBLIC LIBRARY*, 2099 W John Beers Rd, 49127. SAN 308-4396. Tel: 269-429-9575. FAX: 269-429-3500. Web Site: www.lincolntownshiplibrary.org. *Dir of Libr,* Dina M Reilly; Staff 6 (MLS 3, Non-MLS 3)
Founded 1959. Pop 20,720; Circ 231,285
Library Holdings: Electronic Media & Resources 57; High Interest/Low Vocabulary Bk Vols 265; Bk Vols 81,242; Per Subs 214
Special Collections: Bartz Poetry Coll; Michigan Governors (Towne Square Coll)
Subject Interests: Gardening
Automation Activity & Vendor Info: (Cataloging) SirsiDynix; (Circulation) SirsiDynix; (ILL) Auto-Graphics, Inc; (OPAC) SirsiDynix
Database Vendor: SirsiDynix
Function: After school storytime, AV serv, CD-ROM, Digital talking bks, Handicapped accessible, Home delivery & serv to Sr ctr & nursing homes, Homebound delivery serv, ILL available, Magnifiers for reading, Music CDs, Online searches, Photocopying/Printing, Prog for adults, Prog for children & young adult, Spoken cassettes & CDs, Summer reading prog, Telephone ref, VHS videos, Wheelchair accessible, Workshops
Partic in Southwest Michigan Library Cooperative
Special Services for the Deaf - TDD equip
Open Mon-Thurs 10-9, Fri & Sat 10-5
Restriction: Lending limited to county residents
Friends of the Library Group

STURGIS

P STURGIS DISTRICT LIBRARY*, 255 North St, 49091. SAN 308-440X. Tel: 269-659-7224. FAX: 269-651-4534. Web Site: www.sturgis-library.org. *Dir,* Todd Reed; Tel: 269-659-7225, E-mail: treed@sturgis-library.org; *Asst Admin,* Julie Burch; *ILL,* Aaron Morris; *Tech Serv,* Henrietta Sagar; *Youth Serv,* Barbara Rowe; E-mail: browe@sturgis-library.org; Staff 11 (MLS 1, Non-MLS 10)
Founded 2006. Pop 18,500; Circ 175,000
Library Holdings: Bk Vols 57,275; Per Subs 160
Special Collections: Genealogy, bks, microfilm; Local History, maps, bks, pictures; Michigan History
Subject Interests: Bus & mgt
Open Mon-Wed 9:30-8, Thurs & Fri 9:30-5:30, Sat 9:30-2
Friends of the Library Group

SUNFIELD

P SUNFIELD DISTRICT LIBRARY*, 112 Main St, 48890. (Mail add: PO Box 97, 48890-0097), SAN 308-4418. Tel: 517-566-8065. FAX: 517-566-8065. Web Site: www.sunfieldlibrary.michlibrary.org.
Pop 2,578; Circ 23,237
Library Holdings: Bk Vols 18,000; Per Subs 40
Special Collections: Local History (Loretta L Peabody Memorial Coll)
Mem of Woodlands Library Cooperative
Open Tues-Fri 2-8, Sat 9-1
Friends of the Library Group

SUTTONS BAY

P SUTTONS BAY BINGHAM DISTRICT LIBRARY*, 416 Front St, 49682. (Mail add: PO Box 340, 49682-0340), SAN 308-4426. Tel: 231-271-3512. FAX: 231-271-2914. E-mail: librarian@suttonsbaylibrary.org. Web Site: www.suttonsbaylibrary.org. *Dir,* Ryan Deery; Staff 3 (MLS 1, Non-MLS 2)
Pop 5,400; Circ 46,042
Library Holdings: Audiobooks 982; Bks-By-Mail 207; Bks on Deafness & Sign Lang 5; Braille Volumes 1; CDs 1,601; DVDs 934; High Interest/Low Vocabulary Bk Vols 1,861; Large Print Bks 804; Bk Vols 26,289; Per Subs 70; Videos 594
Special Collections: Adult & Children Graphic Novels Coll; Michigan Local History Coll
Wireless access
Publications: Annual Report; Newsletter
Partic in Mid-Michigan Library League
Special Services for the Deaf - Accessible learning ctr; Assistive tech; Bks on deafness & sign lang; Closed caption videos; High interest/low vocabulary bks
Special Services for the Blind - Accessible computers; Audio mat; Bks available with recordings; Bks on cassette; Bks on CD; Internet workstation with adaptive software
Open Tues & Wed 10-6, Thurs 1-7:30, Fri 10-4, Sat 10-2
Friends of the Library Group

TAYLOR

P TAYLOR COMMUNITY LIBRARY*, 12303 Pardee Rd, 48180-4219. SAN 308-4434. Tel: 734-287-4840. FAX: 734-287-4141. Web Site: www.taylor.lib.mi.us. *Dir,* Theresa Powers; E-mail: tpowers@taylor.lib.mi.us; *Adult Serv,* Jacqueline Whinihan
Pop 70,800
Library Holdings: Bk Titles 132,000; Per Subs 210
Automation Activity & Vendor Info: (Circulation) SirsiDynix
Wireless access
Open Mon-Thurs 9-8, Fri & Sat 9-5, Sun 1-5
Friends of the Library Group

J WAYNE COUNTY COMMUNITY COLLEGE*, John Dingell LRC Library, 21000 North Line Rd, 48180-4798. Tel: 734-374-3228. Administration Tel: 734-374-3524. FAX: 734-374-0240. *Coordr,* Ronghua Luo; E-mail: rluo1@wcccd.edu
Library Holdings: Bk Vols 19,500; Per Subs 85
Automation Activity & Vendor Info: (Cataloging) Horizon; (Circulation) Horizon; (OPAC) Horizon
Open Mon-Thurs 8:30am-9pm, Fri 8:30-4:30, Sat 8:30-3:30

TECUMSEH

P TECUMSEH DISTRICT LIBRARY*, 215 N Ottawa St, 49286-1564. SAN 308-4450. Tel: 517-423-2238. FAX: 517-423-5519. Web Site: www.tecumsehlibrary.org. *Dir,* S Gayle Hazelbaker; E-mail: sghazelbaker@tecumsehlibrary.org; *Ch,* Mary Beth Reasoner; E-mail: mreasoner@tecumsehlibrary.org; *Hist Coll Librn, Ref Librn,* Chuck Harpst; E-mail: charpst@tecumsehlibrary.org; *Teen Librn,* Anne Keller; E-mail:

akeller@tecumsehlibrary.org; *Circ Serv Supvr,* Sonja Downey; E-mail: sdowney@tecumsehlibrary.org; *Supvr, Tech Serv,* Gina Walmsley; E-mail: gwalmsley@tecumsehlibrary.org; Staff 6 (MLS 3, Non-MLS 3)
Founded 2003. Pop 18,100; Circ 139,000
Jul 2005-Jun 2006 Income $720,071. Mats Exp $108,900, Books $75,000, Per/Ser (Incl. Access Fees) $12,000, AV Mat $10,000, Electronic Ref Mat (Incl. Access Fees) $11,900. Sal $157,353
Library Holdings: Bk Vols 53,087; Per Subs 157
Special Collections: Tecumseh Herald Newspaper, 1850-present, micro. Oral History
Subject Interests: Civil War, Indians, Local hist
Automation Activity & Vendor Info: (Acquisitions) Auto-Graphics, Inc; (Cataloging) Auto-Graphics, Inc; (Circulation) Auto-Graphics, Inc
Wireless access
Function: Archival coll, Handicapped accessible, ILL available, Photocopying/Printing, Prog for children & young adult, Ref serv available, Summer reading prog, Telephone ref
Mem of Woodlands Library Cooperative
Partic in Midwest Collaborative for Library Services (MCLS)
Open Mon-Thurs 10-8, Fri & Sat 10-5, Sun 1-5
Friends of the Library Group

TEKONSHA

P TEKONSHA PUBLIC LIBRARY*, 230 S Church St, 49092. SAN 308-4469. Tel: 517-767-4769. FAX: 517-767-4769. Web Site: www.tekonlib.michlibrary.org. *Dir,* Sharla A Vincent
Pop 1,957; Circ 4,800
Library Holdings: Bk Vols 15,000
Mem of Woodlands Library Cooperative
Open Mon, Fri & Sat 10-5, Tues-Thurs 3-7
Friends of the Library Group

THOMPSONVILLE

P BETSIE VALLEY DISTRICT LIBRARY*, 14731 Thompson Ave, 49683. (Mail add: PO Box 185, 49683-0185). Tel: 231-378-2716. FAX: 231-378-2716. E-mail: bvdlibrary@acegroup.cc. *Librn,* Michelle Guerra
Library Holdings: Bk Vols 8,000; Per Subs 10
Partic in Mid-Michigan Library League
Open Tues & Thurs 11-5, Wed 2-7, Fri 2-6, Sat 10-2

THREE OAKS

P THREE OAKS TOWNSHIP PUBLIC LIBRARY*, Three N Elm St, 49128-1303. SAN 308-4477. Tel: 269-756-5621. FAX: 269-756-3004. Web Site: www.threeoaks.michlibrary.org. *Dir,* Erik J Nieman; *Genealogy Librn, Local Hist Librn,* Jane M Ward. Subject Specialists: *Genealogy, Local hist,* Jane M Ward; Staff 2 (Non-MLS 2)
Founded 1859
Library Holdings: Bk Vols 27,500; Per Subs 80
Automation Activity & Vendor Info: (Cataloging) Follett Software; (Circulation) Follett Software; (ILL) Auto-Graphics, Inc; (OPAC) Follett Software
Wireless access
Function: Archival coll, Handicapped accessible, Homebound delivery serv, ILL available, Photocopying/Printing, Prog for adults, Prog for children & young adult, Ref serv available, Summer reading prog, Wheelchair accessible
Partic in Southwest Michigan Library Cooperative
Open Mon, Wed & Fri 10-6, Tues & Thurs 10-8, Sat 10-4
Friends of the Library Group

THREE RIVERS

P THREE RIVERS PUBLIC LIBRARY, 920 W Michigan Ave, 49093-2137. SAN 308-4485. Tel: 269-273-8666. FAX: 269-279-9654. Web Site: www.threeriverslibrary.org. *Dir,* Melissa McPherson; E-mail: mmcpherson@threeriverslibrary.org; *Ch,* Brandi DeRuiter; *YA Librn,* Stephanie Morgan; Staff 3 (MLS 1, Non-MLS 2)
Founded 1889. Pop 14,253; Circ 84,885
Jul 2011-Jun 2012 Income $526,512, State $53,735, City $417,904, Locally Generated Income $26,005, Other $28,868. Mats Exp $526,512, Books $90,000, Per/Ser (Incl. Access Fees) $8,170, AV Mat $3,740, Electronic Ref Mat (Incl. Access Fees) $5,125. Sal $117,860 (Prof $90,000)
Library Holdings: Audiobooks 466; AV Mats 91; Bks on Deafness & Sign Lang 42; Braille Volumes 6; CDs 1,523; DVDs 988; e-books 2,987; Electronic Media & Resources 339; High Interest/Low Vocabulary Bk Vols 100; Large Print Bks 1,402; Microforms 101; Music Scores 10; Bk Titles 49,884; Per Subs 88; Videos 1,954
Subject Interests: Local hist
Automation Activity & Vendor Info: (Acquisitions) Auto-Graphics, Inc; (Cataloging) Auto-Graphics, Inc; (Circulation) Auto-Graphics, Inc; (ILL) Auto-Graphics, Inc; (OPAC) Auto-Graphics, Inc
Wireless access
Partic in Southwest Michigan Library Cooperative
Open Mon-Fri 10-9, Sat & Sun 10-5

TOPINABEE

P TOPINABEE PUBLIC LIBRARY*, 1576 Straits Hwy, 49791. (Mail add: PO Box 266, 49791-0266), SAN 308-4493. Tel: 231-238-7514. FAX: 231-238-2112. E-mail: topinab1@northland.lib.mi.us. Web Site: nlc.lib.mi.us/members/topinabe/htm. *Dir,* Patricia King
Pop 1,197; Circ 13,021
Library Holdings: Bk Vols 7,126; Per Subs 40
Wireless access
Partic in Northland Library Cooperative
Open Tues & Fri 10-5, Wed 1-5, Thurs 1-8
Friends of the Library Group

TRAVERSE CITY

L GRAND TRAVERSE COUNTY LAW LIBRARY*, Old Courthouse, 4th Flr, 328 Washington St, 49684. Tel: 231-922-4715. FAX: 231-922-4489.
Library Holdings: Bk Vols 7,000; Per Subs 10
Wireless access
Open Mon-Fri 8:30-5
Restriction: Non-circulating, Not a lending libr

MUNSON HEALTHCARE

M COMMUNITY HEALTH LIBRARY*, 550 Munson Ave, Ste 100, 49686. Tel: 231-935-9265. Toll Free Tel: 800-468-6766. FAX: 231-935-9267. Web Site: www.munsonhealthcare.org. *Coordr,* Roberta Craig. Subject Specialists: *Consumer health,* Roberta Craig; Staff 3 (MLS 2, Non-MLS 1)
Founded 2000
Library Holdings: AV Mats 500; Bk Vols 2,700; Per Subs 20
Subject Interests: Consumer health
Automation Activity & Vendor Info: (Cataloging) Follett Software; (Circulation) Follett Software; (OPAC) Follett Software; (Serials) Follett Software
Database Vendor: Cinahl, Marcive, Inc, McGraw-Hill, MD Consult, Medline, Micromedex, Natural Standard, OVID Technologies, PubMed, STAT!Ref (Teton Data Systems), UpToDate
Function: For res purposes, Games & aids for the handicapped, Handicapped accessible, Health sci info serv, Homebound delivery serv, ILL available, Magnifiers for reading, Mail loans to mem, Online searches, Outside serv via phone, mail, e-mail & web, Photocopying/Printing, Prog for adults, Prog for children & young adult, Ref serv available, Referrals accepted, Telephone ref, Wheelchair accessible, Workshops
Partic in Midwest Collaborative for Library Services (MCLS); National Network of Libraries of Medicine Greater Midwest Region
Open Mon-Thurs 8:30-12 & 12:30-5:30, Fri 8:30-12:30

M DEPARTMENT OF LIBRARY SERVICES*, 1105 Sixth St, 49684. Tel: 231-935-6170. FAX: 231-935-7124. *Mgr, Libr Serv,* Barbara Platts; Tel: 231-935-6544; Staff 7 (MLS 4, Non-MLS 3)
Library Holdings: e-books 225; e-journals 250; Bk Vols 3,500; Per Subs 200
Subject Interests: Allied health, Leadership develop, Med, Nursing
Automation Activity & Vendor Info: (Cataloging) Follett Software; (Circulation) Gateway; (OPAC) Follett Software; (Serials) Follett Software
Database Vendor: Cinahl, EBSCO Information Services, Elsevier, Marcive, Inc, MD Consult, Micromedex, Natural Standard, OVID Technologies, PubMed, STAT!Ref (Teton Data Systems), UpToDate, WebMD
Function: Archival coll, Audio & video playback equip for onsite use, Bks on CD, CD-ROM, Computer training, Computers for patron use, Copy machines, Doc delivery serv, e-mail serv, Electronic databases & coll, For res purposes, Health sci info serv, ILL available, Instruction & testing, Mail loans to mem, Online cat, Online searches, Orientations, Outreach serv, Outside serv via phone, mail, e-mail & web, Photocopying/Printing, Prof lending libr, Ref serv available, Res libr, Scanner, Telephone ref, VHS videos, Web-catalog
Open Mon-Fri 8-4:30
Restriction: Authorized personnel only, Badge access after hrs, Circulates for staff only, Med & health res only, Med staff & students, Not open to pub, Open to researchers by request, Prof mat only, Restricted access

J NORTHWESTERN MICHIGAN COLLEGE*, Mark & Helen Osterlin Library, 1701 E Front St, 49686-3061. SAN 347-1063. Tel: 231-995-1063. Circulation Tel: 231-995-1060. Reference Tel: 231-995-1540. FAX: 231-995-1056. E-mail: library@nmc.edu. Web Site: www.nmc.edu/library. *Dir,* Maggie Bacon; *Librn,* Charla Kramer; Tel: 231-995-1973, E-mail: ckramer@message.nmc.edu; *Govt Doc Librn,* Ann Swaney; Tel: 231-995-1065, E-mail: aswaney@message.nmc.edu; Staff 6 (MLS 3, Non-MLS 3)

Founded 1951. Enrl 4,000; Fac 125; Highest Degree: Associate
Library Holdings: e-books 15; Electronic Media & Resources 2,000; Bk Titles 4,950; Bk Vols 50,480; Per Subs 258
Special Collections: New York Times Index. State Document Depository; US Document Depository
Automation Activity & Vendor Info: (Cataloging) SirsiDynix; (Circulation) SirsiDynix; (Course Reserve) SirsiDynix; (OPAC) SirsiDynix; (Serials) SirsiDynix
Database Vendor: EBSCOhost, Gale Cengage Learning, LexisNexis, OCLC FirstSearch, SerialsSolutions
Function: Archival coll, Distance learning, Govt ref serv, ILL available, Learning ctr, Online searches, Photocopying/Printing, Ref serv available, Telephone ref
Partic in Mid-Michigan Library League

P PENINSULA COMMUNITY LIBRARY*, Old Mission Peninsula School, 2735 Island View Rd, 49686. SAN 308-4515. Tel: 231-223-7700. FAX: 231-223-7708. E-mail: pcl@tadl.tcnet.org. Web Site: tadl.tcnet.org/branchmemberlibs/pclib.htm. *Librn,* Victoria M Shurly
Founded 1957. Pop 5,265; Circ 39,107
Library Holdings: Bk Vols 27,000; Per Subs 110
Partic in Mid-Michigan Library League
Open Mon & Thurs (Winter) 9-9, Tues, Wed & Fri 9-5:30, Sat 9-1; Mon & Thurs (Summer) 9-9, Tues, Wed & Fri 9-3
Friends of the Library Group

P TRAVERSE AREA DISTRICT LIBRARY*, 610 Woodmere Ave, 49686. SAN 347-1128. Tel: 231-932-8500. Circulation Tel: 231-932-8504. Reference Tel: 231-932-8502. Administration Tel: 231-932-8501. FAX: 231-932-8578. TDD: 231-932-8507. E-mail: libadmin@tadl.tcnet.org. Web Site: www.tadl.org. *Dir,* Michael McGuire; Fax: 231-932-8538; *Asst Dir,* Barbara Nowinski; Staff 53 (MLS 9, Non-MLS 44)
Founded 1897. Pop 70,279; Circ 789,081
Library Holdings: Audiobooks 29,834; CDs 137,532; DVDs 102,846; Bk Vols 410,323; Per Subs 808; Videos 12,343
Subject Interests: Deaf, Genealogy, Hearing impaired, Local hist, Sheet music
Automation Activity & Vendor Info: (Acquisitions) Baker & Taylor; (Cataloging) Evergreen; (Circulation) Evergreen; (ILL) Evergreen; (OPAC) Evergreen
Database Vendor: Foundation Center
Wireless access
Function: Adult bk club, Art exhibits, Audio & video playback equip for onsite use, Bks on cassette, Bks on CD, Children's prog, Computer training, Computers for patron use, e-mail serv, E-Reserves, Exhibits, Fax serv, Free DVD rentals, Handicapped accessible, ILL available, Jazz prog, Magnifiers for reading, Mail & tel request accepted, Music CDs, Notary serv, Online cat, Online ref, Online searches, Photocopying/Printing, Prog for adults, Prog for children & young adult, Ref & res, Scanner, Story hour, Summer reading prog, Tax forms, Teen prog, VHS videos, Wheelchair accessible
Publications: TADL-Tales (Monthly newsletter)
Open Mon-Thurs 9-9, Fri & Sat 9-6, Sun 12-5
Friends of the Library Group
Branches: 3
EAST BAY BRANCH, 1989 Three Mile Rd N, 49686, SAN 347-1152. Tel: 231-922-2085. FAX: 231-922-2087. E-mail: ebb@tadl.tcnet.org. *In Charge,* Barbara Nowinski
Founded 1972
Library Holdings: Bk Vols 18,000
Special Services for the Blind - Rec of textbk mat
Open Tues & Thurs 10-8, Wed & Fri 10-6, Sat 10-3
Friends of the Library Group
KINGSLEY BRANCH, 104 S Brownson Ave, Kingsley, 49649. (Mail add: PO Box 427, Kingsley, 49649-0427), SAN 308-2172. Tel: 231-263-5484. FAX: 231-263-5526. E-mail: kpl@tadl.tcnet.org. Web Site: www.tadl.org/branchmemberlibs/kingsleylib.htm. *Librn,* Mary Fraquelli
Founded 1910. Pop 3,475; Circ 13,423
Library Holdings: Bk Vols 18,000
Partic in OCLC Online Computer Library Center, Inc
Open Tues, Wed & Fri 9-5, Thurs 10-6, Sat 10-3
Friends of the Library Group

P SUBREGIONAL LIBRARY FOR THE BLIND & PHYSICALLY HANDICAPPED, 610 Woodmere, 49686, SAN 377-7782. Tel: 231-932-8558. Toll Free Tel: 877-931-8558. FAX: 231-932-8578. E-mail: lbph@tadl.tcnet.org. *Librn,* Kathy Kelto
Founded 1972
Partic in Mid-Michigan Library League
Open Mon-Fri 9-5
Friends of the Library Group

TRENTON

P TRENTON VETERANS MEMORIAL LIBRARY*, 2790 Westfield Rd, 48183-2482. SAN 308-4523. Tel: 734-676-9777. FAX: 734-676-9895. E-mail: tren@trenton.lib.mi.us. Web Site: www.trenton.lib.mi.us. *Dir,* Francene Sanak; Staff 6 (MLS 3, Non-MLS 3)
Founded 1928. Pop 72,708; Circ 236,365
Library Holdings: Audiobooks 2,941; CDs 2,729; DVDs 3,563; Electronic Media & Resources 3; Bk Vols 99,611; Per Subs 162; Talking Bks 1,610
Automation Activity & Vendor Info: (Cataloging) SirsiDynix; (Circulation) SirsiDynix; (OPAC) SirsiDynix
Database Vendor: Overdrive, Inc, ProQuest, SirsiDynix
Wireless access
Partic in The Library Network
Open Mon-Thurs 10-9, Fri & Sat 10-6, Sun 1-5
Friends of the Library Group

TROY

L HARNESS, DICKEY & PIERCE, PLC*, Law Library, 5445 Corporate Dr, Ste 200, 48098. SAN 372-0489. Tel: 248-641-1600, Ext 1250. FAX: 248-641-0270. Web Site: www.hdp.com. *Librn,* Kristine Potter
Founded 1921
Library Holdings: Bk Vols 10,000; Per Subs 37
Restriction: Staff use only

S MERITOR, INC*, Reference Center, 2135 W Maple Rd, 48084-7186. SAN 308-4531. Tel: 248-435-1668. FAX: 248-435-1670. Web Site: www.arvinmeritor.com. *Coop Librn,* Cheryl A Barden
Founded 1960
Library Holdings: Bk Vols 2,600; Per Subs 550
Special Collections: Annual Reports 732; Conference Boards Reports (US & Canadian); Focus on the Family; ISO/Din Specs; SAE Coll; Standards ((ASTM, AWS, SAE J, ISO, DIN, Chinese, Ford, General Motors, DaimlerChrysler))
Subject Interests: Advertising, Eng, Metallurgy, Mkt
Automation Activity & Vendor Info: (Cataloging) Livelink for Libraries; (Circulation) EOS International; (Serials) EOS International
Database Vendor: DATASTAR Inc, Factiva.com

P TROY PUBLIC LIBRARY*, 510 W Big Beaver Rd, 48084-5289. SAN 347-1187. Tel: 248-524-3538. Reference Tel: 248-524-3537. Automation Services Tel: 248-524-3549. FAX: 248-524-0112. TDD: 248-740-0253. Web Site: www.troylibrary.info. *Dir,* Cathy Russ; E-mail: c.russ@troymi.gov; Staff 35 (MLS 35)
Founded 1962. Pop 80,959; Circ 1,418,442
Library Holdings: DVDs 21,657; e-books 3,719; Electronic Media & Resources 85; Bk Vols 206,198; Per Subs 656; Talking Bks 26,890
Special Collections: Frances Teasdale (Civil War Coll); International Language; Morgan - West White House Memorabilia
Automation Activity & Vendor Info: (Acquisitions) SirsiDynix; (Cataloging) SirsiDynix; (Circulation) SirsiDynix; (OPAC) SirsiDynix; (Serials) SirsiDynix
Database Vendor: Gale Cengage Learning, Newsbank, OCLC FirstSearch, OCLC WorldShare Interlibrary Loan, ProQuest, Westlaw, Wilson - Wilson Web
Wireless access
Special Services for the Deaf - TDD equip
Open Mon-Thurs 10-9, Fri & Sat 10-6, Sun 1-6
Friends of the Library Group

C WALSH COLLEGE*, Troy Campus Library, 3838 Livernois Rd, 48083-5066. (Mail add: PO Box 7006, 48007-7006), SAN 308-454X. Tel: 248-823-1228. Interlibrary Loan Service Tel: 248-823-1337. Reference Tel: 248-823-1335. FAX: 248-689-9066. E-mail: librarian@walshcollege.edu. Web Site: www.walshcollege.edu. *Libr Dir,* Nancy Brzozowski; Tel: 248-823-1254, E-mail: Brzozow@walsgcollege.edu; Staff 7 (MLS 4, Non-MLS 3)
Founded 1922. Enrl 3,842; Fac 220; Highest Degree: Doctorate
Library Holdings: e-journals 8,300; Bk Vols 30,272; Per Subs 215
Subject Interests: Acctg, Bus & mgt, Econ, Tax, Taxation (finance)
Automation Activity & Vendor Info: (Acquisitions) SirsiDynix; (Cataloging) SirsiDynix; (Circulation) SirsiDynix; (ILL) SirsiDynix; (OPAC) Docutek; (Serials) SirsiDynix
Database Vendor: Baker & Taylor, Dialog, EBSCOhost, Factiva.com, Gale Cengage Learning, JSTOR, LexisNexis, OCLC FirstSearch, OCLC WorldShare Interlibrary Loan, ProQuest, ScienceDirect, SerialsSolutions, SirsiDynix
Function: Doc delivery serv
Partic in Detroit Area Library Network; Midwest Collaborative for Library Services (MCLS); Southeastern Michigan League of Libraries
Special Services for the Blind - Assistive/Adapted tech devices, equip & products; Bks on cassette; Bks on CD; Computer with voice synthesizer for visually impaired persons; Reader equip

Open Mon-Thurs 8:30am-10:30pm, Fri 8:30-6, Sat 8-5, Sun 12-5
Restriction: Use of others with permission of librn

UBLY

P SLEEPER PUBLIC LIBRARY*, 2236 Main St, 48475-9726. SAN 308-4558. Tel: 989-658-8901. FAX: 989-658-8788. E-mail: ublylibrary@sbcglobal.net. *Dir,* Barbara Butch
Circ 8,117
Library Holdings: Bk Vols 16,495; Per Subs 95
Open Mon & Fri 10-5, Tues-Thurs 10-8, Sat 10-2
Friends of the Library Group

UNIONVILLE

P COLUMBIA TOWNSHIP LIBRARY*, 6456 Center St, 48767. SAN 308-4574. Tel: 989-674-2651. FAX: 989-674-2138. E-mail: columbiatwplibrary@gmail.com. Web Site: www.columbiatwplibrary.org. *Dir,* Kay E Montei; *Librn,* Sandra Gnagey; Staff 1.1 (MLS 0.6, Non-MLS 0.5)
Founded 1952. Pop 2,193; Circ 15,000
Library Holdings: Audiobooks 10; AV Mats 2,705; CDs 111; DVDs 1,251; Large Print Bks 280; Bk Vols 17,417; Per Subs 20
Automation Activity & Vendor Info: (Cataloging) Biblionix; (Circulation) Biblionix; (ILL) Mel Cat
Wireless access
Function: Accelerated reader prog, After school storytime, Bks on CD, Computer training, Computers for patron use, E-Reserves, Electronic databases & coll, Fax serv, Handicapped accessible, Homework prog, ILL available, Music CDs, Online cat, OverDrive digital audio bks, Photocopying/Printing, Preschool reading prog, Scanner, Senior computer classes, Spoken cassettes & DVDs, Story hour, Summer reading prog, Tax forms, VHS videos, Wheelchair accessible
Mem of White Pine Library Cooperative
Open Mon-Thurs 10-7, Sat 9-1

UNIVERSITY CENTER

J DELTA COLLEGE LIBRARY*, 1961 Delta Rd, 48710. SAN 308-4582. Tel: 989-686-9822. Circulation Tel: 989-686-9310. Interlibrary Loan Service Tel: 989-686-9013. Reference Tel: 989-686-9560. FAX: 989-686-4131. E-mail: library@delta.edu. Web Site: www.delta.edu. *Dir,* Jack G Wood; E-mail: jackwood@delta.edu; *Librn,* Mark Ewing; E-mail: meewing@delta.edu; *Librn,* Jennean Kabat; E-mail: jlkabat@delta.edu; *Librn,* Anne Wooden; E-mail: annewooden@delta.edu; Staff 10 (MLS 4, Non-MLS 6)
Founded 1961. Enrl 11,300; Highest Degree: Associate
Jul 2005-Jun 2006. Mats Exp $132,000, Books $45,000, Per/Ser (Incl. Access Fees) $51,000, Manu Arch $6,000, Micro $3,000, Electronic Ref Mat (Incl. Access Fees) $27,000
Library Holdings: Bk Titles 59,663; Per Subs 296
Special Collections: Delta College Archives; Federal. US Document Depository
Automation Activity & Vendor Info: (Acquisitions) Horizon; (Cataloging) Horizon; (Circulation) Horizon; (Course Reserve) Horizon; (ILL) Horizon; (OPAC) SirsiDynix; (Serials) SirsiDynix
Database Vendor: Gale Cengage Learning, JSTOR, Marcive, Inc, Newsbank, OCLC FirstSearch, OCLC WorldShare Interlibrary Loan, PubMed, SirsiDynix, Wilson - Wilson Web
Wireless access
Function: Art exhibits
Partic in Midwest Collaborative for Library Services (MCLS); Valley Libr Consortium
Open Mon-Thurs 7:30am-9pm, Fri 7:30-3, Sat 10-2, Sun 1-5:30

C SAGINAW VALLEY STATE UNIVERSITY*, Melvin J Zahnow Library, 7400 Bay Rd, 48710. SAN 308-4590. Tel: 989-964-4240. Reference Tel: 989-964-4242. Administration Tel: 989-964-4237. Toll Free Tel: 866-381-7878. FAX: 989-964-4383. Interlibrary Loan Service FAX: 989-964-2034. Administration FAX: 989-964-2003. E-mail: library@svsu.edu. Web Site: www.svsu.edu/library. *Dir,* Linda Farynk; Tel: 989-964-4236, E-mail: lfarynk@svsu.edu; *Head, Access Serv,* Thomas Zantow; Tel: 989-964-4238, E-mail: tzantow@svsu.edu; *Acq, Head, Coll Develop,* Jennifer Dean; Tel: 989-964-7092, E-mail: jldean@svsu.edu; *Head, Ref Serv,* Anita Dey; Tel: 989-964-7094, E-mail: adey@svsu.edu; Staff 20 (MLS 10, Non-MLS 10)
Founded 1963. Enrl 10,250; Fac 295; Highest Degree: Master
Jul 2011-Jun 2012 Income $2,179,980. Mats Exp $803,435, Books $140,000, Per/Ser (Incl. Access Fees) $820,959, Other Print Mats $59,000. Sal $1,109,115 (Prof $692,000)
Library Holdings: AV Mats 27,023; e-books 102,228; e-journals 41,794; Microforms 370,628; Bk Vols 200,451; Per Subs 105
Special Collections: Cramton Jazz Coll; Flying Melzoras Circus Coll; Ken Follett Coll; Local History Coll; University Archives
Automation Activity & Vendor Info: (Cataloging) Innovative Interfaces, Inc; (Circulation) Innovative Interfaces, Inc; (Course Reserve) Innovative Interfaces, Inc; (ILL) OCLC ILLiad; (OPAC) Innovative Interfaces, Inc; (Serials) Innovative Interfaces, Inc
Database Vendor: ABC-CLIO, ACM (Association for Computing Machinery), Alexander Street Press, American Chemical Society, American Mathematical Society, American Psychological Association (APA), Bowker, Cambridge Scientific Abstracts, Cinahl, CQ Press, CredoReference, ebrary, EBSCOhost, Elsevier, Facts on File, Gale Cengage Learning, IEEE (Institute of Electrical & Electronics Engineers), Innovative Interfaces, Inc, JSTOR, Medline, Modern Language Association, Newsbank, OCLC CAMIO, OCLC FirstSearch, OCLC WorldShare Interlibrary Loan, OVID Technologies, Oxford Online, Plunkett Research, Ltd, Project MUSE, ProQuest, PubMed, ScienceDirect, Springer-Verlag, Springshare, LLC, Westlaw, Wiley, Wilson - Wilson Web
Wireless access
Partic in Midwest Collaborative for Library Services (MCLS); OCLC Online Computer Library Center, Inc
Open Mon-Thurs 8am-11pm, Fri 8-4:30, Sat 9-5, Sun 1-9

UTICA

P UTICA PUBLIC LIBRARY*, 7530 Auburn Rd, 48317-5216. SAN 308-4612. Tel: 586-731-4141. FAX: 586-731-0769. Web Site: www.libcoop.net/utica. *Dir,* Marsha C Doege; E-mail: doegem@libcoop.net; Staff 3 (Non-MLS 3)
Founded 1933. Pop 4,750; Circ 37,000
Library Holdings: Bk Vols 20,000; Per Subs 40
Special Collections: Utica Sentinel Newspaper Coll (1876-1971), micro (1986 to present)
Automation Activity & Vendor Info: (Acquisitions) SirsiDynix; (Cataloging) SirsiDynix; (Circulation) SirsiDynix; (Serials) SirsiDynix
Wireless access
Function: Homebound delivery serv, ILL available, Photocopying/Printing, Prog for adults, Prog for children & young adult, Ref serv available, Summer reading prog, Wheelchair accessible
Mem of Mid-York Library System
Partic in Suburban Library Cooperative
Open Mon-Wed 10-8, Thurs 10-6, Fri 11-4, Sat (Sept-May) 11-2

VASSAR

P BULLARD SANFORD MEMORIAL LIBRARY*, 520 W Huron Ave, 48768. SAN 308-4620. Tel: 989-823-2171. FAX: 989-823-8573. TDD: 989-823-8822. Web Site: www.vassarlib.org. *Libr Dir,* Eric D Andreychuk; E-mail: librarian@vassarlib.org; *Dep Dir,* Rita Bouvy; Staff 6 (MLS 1, Non-MLS 5)
Founded 1906. Pop 10,000; Circ 52,000
Library Holdings: Bk Vols 45,000; Per Subs 100
Special Collections: Large Print Coll
Automation Activity & Vendor Info: (Cataloging) Auto-Graphics, Inc; (Circulation) Auto-Graphics, Inc; (OPAC) Auto-Graphics, Inc
Wireless access
Partic in White Pine Libr Coop
Special Services for the Deaf - TDD equip
Special Services for the Blind - Talking bks
Open Mon 10-8, Tues & Thurs 12-8, Wed & Fri 10-6, Sat 12-4
Friends of the Library Group
Bookmobiles: 1. Bk vols 1,500

VERMONTVILLE

P VERMONTVILLE TOWNSHIP LIBRARY*, 120 E First St, 49096. (Mail add: PO Box G, 49096-0910), SAN 308-4639. Tel: 517-726-1362. FAX: 517-726-1362. E-mail: vermontvillelibrary@yahoo.com. Web Site: www.vermontvillelibrary.com. *Dir,* Carla Rumsey; *Asst Dir,* Rita Miller; *Librn,* Kim Eldred; *Librn,* Diana Reid
Founded 1949. Pop 3,842; Circ 10,309
Library Holdings: Bk Vols 21,933
Automation Activity & Vendor Info: (Acquisitions) Follett Software; (Cataloging) Follett Software; (Circulation) Follett Software; (ILL) Follett Software; (OPAC) Follett Software; (Serials) Follett Software
Mem of Woodlands Library Cooperative
Open Tues 1-8, Wed-Fri 11-6, Sat 9-1

VERNON

P VERNON DISTRICT PUBLIC LIBRARY*, 115 E Main St, 48476. (Mail add: PO Box 416, 48476-0416), SAN 308-4647. Tel: 989-288-6486. FAX: 989-288-2422. E-mail: vernonlibrary@gmail.com. Web Site: vernon.michlibrary.org. *Dir,* Cheryl Cole
Founded 1969. Pop 4,989; Circ 12,044
Library Holdings: Audiobooks 296; Bks on Deafness & Sign Lang 20; DVDs 384; e-books 1,982; Large Print Bks 200; Bk Vols 15,895; Per Subs 12

Automation Activity & Vendor Info: (Cataloging) OCLC; (Circulation) Follett Software; (OPAC) Follett Software
Database Vendor: Overdrive, Inc
Wireless access
Partic in Mideastern Michigan Library Cooperative
Open Mon, Tues & Thurs 10-7, Wed & Fri 10-5, Sat 10-2

VESTABURG

P RICHLAND TOWNSHIP LIBRARY*, 8821 Third St, 48891. (Mail add: PO Box 220, 48891-0220), SAN 308-4655. Tel: 989-268-5044. FAX: 989-268-5629. E-mail: rtl@cmsinter.net. *Dir,* Sherma Horrocks
Founded 1912. Pop 3,764; Circ 18,334
Library Holdings: Bk Vols 12,388; Per Subs 50; Videos 1,826
Automation Activity & Vendor Info: (Cataloging) Auto-Graphics, Inc; (Circulation) Auto-Graphics, Inc
Partic in Mid-Michigan Library League
Open Mon 10-5, Tues 10-7, Wed & Fri 11-5, Thurs 1-5

VICKSBURG

P VICKSBURG DISTRICT LIBRARY, 215 S Michigan Ave, 49097. SAN 308-4663. Tel: 269-649-1648. FAX: 269-649-3666. E-mail: info@vicksburglibrary.org. Web Site: www.vicksburglibrary.org. *Dir,* John Sheridan; E-mail: jsheridan@vicksburglibrary.org; *Asst Dir/Ch,* Kristy Zeluff; E-mail: kzeluff@vicksburglibrary.org; *Teen Librn/Ref,* Andrea Smalley; E-mail: asmalley@vicksburglibrary.org; *Circ Supvr,* Beth Dowson; E-mail: bdowson@vicksburglibrary.org; Staff 4 (MLS 1, Non-MLS 3)
Founded 1902. Pop 11,350; Circ 49,100
Library Holdings: CDs 500; DVDs 2,100; Bk Vols 41,525; Per Subs 71; Talking Bks 720
Subject Interests: Local hist
Automation Activity & Vendor Info: (Circulation) Auto-Graphics, Inc; (ILL) Auto-Graphics, Inc; (OPAC) Auto-Graphics, Inc
Wireless access
Partic in Southwest Michigan Library Cooperative
Open Mon-Thurs 10-8:30, Fri & Sat 10-5, Sun 1-5

WAKEFIELD

P WAKEFIELD PUBLIC LIBRARY*, 401 Hancock St, 49968. SAN 308-4671. Tel: 906-229-5236. FAX: 906-229-5974. Web Site: www.uproc.lib.mi.us/wakefield. *Dir,* Denise Engel; E-mail: dengel@uproc.lib.mi.us
Founded 1934. Circ 23,584
Library Holdings: Bk Vols 20,000; Per Subs 30
Special Collections: Foreign Language (Italian, Polish & Finnish)
Automation Activity & Vendor Info: (Cataloging) Follett Software; (Circulation) Follett Software
Partic in Superiorland Library Cooperative
Open Mon 10-6, Tues & Thurs 12-4:30, Wed 12-6, Fri 10:30-4:30, Sat (Sept-May) 10-12
Friends of the Library Group

WALDRON

P WALDRON DISTRICT LIBRARY*, 107 N Main St, 49288-9811. (Mail add: PO Box 136, 49288-0136), SAN 376-7051. Tel: 517-286-6511. FAX: 517-286-6511. Web Site: waldrondistlib.michlibrary.org. *Dir,* Carol Newcomer
Pop 2,475
Aug 2011-Jul 2012 Income $66,257, State $1,052, Federal $834, County $6,025, Locally Generated Income $48,913, Other $9,433. Mats Exp $5,194, Books $4,979, Per/Ser (Incl. Access Fees) $100, AV Mat $115. Sal $42,337
Library Holdings: Audiobooks 183; CDs 56; DVDs 192; Bk Vols 16,656; Per Subs 4; Talking Bks 229; Videos 764
Automation Activity & Vendor Info: (Cataloging) Follett Software; (Circulation) Follett Software
Wireless access
Mem of Woodlands Library Cooperative
Open Tues-Thurs 11-7, Fri 11-4:30, Sat 9-12
Friends of the Library Group

WALLED LAKE

P WALLED LAKE CITY LIBRARY*, 1499 E West Maple Rd, 48390. SAN 308-4698. Tel: 248-624-3772. FAX: 248-624-0041. E-mail: admin@walledlakelibrary.org. Web Site: www.walledlakelibrary.org. *Dir,* Donna Rickabaugh; E-mail: donna@walledlakelibrary.org; *Asst Dir,* Bill Wines; E-mail: bill@walledlakelibrary.org; Staff 6 (MLS 2, Non-MLS 4)
Founded 1963. Pop 6,900; Circ 50,000
Library Holdings: Bk Vols 50,500; Per Subs 70
Automation Activity & Vendor Info: (Cataloging) SirsiDynix; (Circulation) SirsiDynix; (ILL) SirsiDynix; (OPAC) SIRSI-iBistro
Database Vendor: Gale Cengage Learning, LearningExpress, Newsbank, OCLC FirstSearch, World Book Online
Wireless access
Function: Adult literacy prog, Audiobks via web, Bks on CD, Computer training, Computers for patron use, Copy machines, Digital talking bks, Electronic databases & coll, Handicapped accessible, Home delivery & serv to Sr ctr & nursing homes, Homebound delivery serv, ILL available, Mail & tel request accepted, Mus passes, Music CDs, Online cat, Photocopying/Printing, Prog for adults, Prog for children & young adult, Pub access computers, Senior computer classes, Story hour, Summer reading prog, Tax forms, Telephone ref, Web-catalog
Partic in The Library Network
Open Mon, Tues & Thurs (Winter) 10-8, Wed & Sat 10-5, Sun 1-5; Mon, Tues & Thurs (Summer) 10-8, Wed & Fri 10-5
Friends of the Library Group

WALLOON LAKE

P CROOKED TREE DISTRICT LIBRARY*, Walloon Lake Library, 2203 Walloon St, 49796. (Mail add: PO Box 518, 49796-0518), SAN 376-6470. Tel: 231-535-2111. FAX: 231-535-2790. E-mail: walloon@crookedtreelibrary.com. Web Site: www.crookedtreelibrary.org. *Dir,* Karen Walker; Staff 1 (MLS 1)
Founded 1977. Pop 3,953
Automation Activity & Vendor Info: (Cataloging) SirsiDynix; (Circulation) SirsiDynix; (OPAC) SirsiDynix
Wireless access
Partic in Northland Library Cooperative
Open Mon 4-8, Tues & Wed 10-5:30, Thurs 1:30-8, Sat 10-1
Friends of the Library Group
Branches: 1
BOYNE FALLS BRANCH, 3008 Railroad St, Boyne Falls, 49713. (Mail add: PO Box 17, Boyne Falls, 49713-0017), SAN 376-8201. Tel: 231-549-2277. E-mail: bflibrary@centurytel.net. *Dir,* Karen Walker; *Br Mgr,* Judith Planck
Founded 1977
Open Mon 4-8, Tues & Wed 10-4, Thurs 1:30-8, Sat 10-1

WARREN

M HENRY FORD BI-COUNTY HOSPITAL*, Medical Library, 13355 E Ten Mile Rd, 48089. SAN 327-5272. Tel: 586-759-7345. FAX: 586-759-1490. *Dir,* Gayle Williams
Library Holdings: Bk Vols 2,500; Per Subs 200
Subject Interests: Med
Restriction: Staff use only

GENERAL MOTORS CORP
S INFORMATION RESEARCH*, GM Technical Ctr, MC 480-106-314, 30500 Mound Rd, 48090-9055, SAN 347-1365. Tel: 586-986-2000. FAX: 586-986-2009. *Libr Mgr,* Joe Scleuher; Staff 24 (MLS 22, Non-MLS 2)
Founded 1917
Library Holdings: e-journals 1,500; Bk Vols 30,000; Per Subs 200
Subject Interests: Automotive, Bus, Sci tech
Automation Activity & Vendor Info: (Acquisitions) Innovative Interfaces, Inc; (Cataloging) Innovative Interfaces, Inc; (Circulation) Innovative Interfaces, Inc
Function: Electronic databases & coll, Online cat, Online searches, Ref & res
Partic in OCLC Online Computer Library Center, Inc
Restriction: Access for corporate affiliates

M KERN HOSPITAL*, Medical Library, 21230 Dequindre Rd, 48091. SAN 371-6724. Tel: 586-427-1000. FAX: 586-759-0237. *In Charge,* Shirley Wise
Founded 1973
Library Holdings: Bk Vols 700; Per Subs 173
Subject Interests: Podiatry

J MACOMB COMMUNITY COLLEGE LIBRARIES*, South Campus, 14500 E 12 Mile Rd, J-Bldg, 48088-3896. SAN 308-4728. Tel: 586-445-7401, Ext 2. Reference Tel: 586-445-7779. FAX: 586-445-7157. Web Site: www.macomb.edu. *Dean, Libr & Learning Res,* Michael Balsamo; Tel: 586-445-7141, E-mail: balsamom@macomb.edu; *Electronic Serv Librn,* Mary Kickham-Samy; Tel: 586-445-7419, E-mail: kickham-samym@macomb.edu; *Syst Librn,* Bruce Bett; Tel: 586-445-7880, E-mail: bettb@macomb.edu; Staff 10 (MLS 5, Non-MLS 5)
Founded 1954. Enrl 5,500; Fac 900; Highest Degree: Associate
Library Holdings: AV Mats 5,281; CDs 242; DVDs 840; e-books 10,000; Bk Titles 83,734; Bk Vols 102,500; Per Subs 160
Subject Interests: Law
Automation Activity & Vendor Info: (Acquisitions) SirsiDynix; (Cataloging) SirsiDynix; (Circulation) SirsiDynix; (OPAC) SirsiDynix; (Serials) SirsiDynix

Database Vendor: ARTstor, EBSCOhost, Gale Cengage Learning, JSTOR, Newsbank, OCLC WorldShare Interlibrary Loan, ProQuest, Westlaw
Wireless access
Function: Online ref
Partic in Detroit Area Library Network; OCLC Online Computer Library Center, Inc
Open Mon-Thurs 8am-9:45pm, Fri 8-2:15, Sat 9-4:15, Sun 12-5:45
Departmental Libraries:
CENTER CAMPUS, 44575 Garfield Rd, C-Bldg, Clinton Township, 48038-1139, SAN 346-9441. Tel: 586-286-2104, Ext 2. Reference Tel: 586-286-2056. Web Site: www.macomb.edu/future-students/student-resources/library/index.html. *Coll & Res Librn,* Cassandra Spieles; Tel: 586-445-7778, E-mail: spielesc@macomb.edu; *Electronic Info Librn,* Teresa Biegun; Tel: 586-286-2233, E-mail: biegunt@macomb.edu; *Pub Serv Librn,* Steve Rybicki; Tel: 586-286-2026, E-mail: rybickis@macomb.edu; Staff 7 (MLS 4, Non-MLS 3)
Founded 1963. Enrl 15,000; Highest Degree: Associate
Library Holdings: AV Mats 4,935; CDs 187; DVDs 125; e-books 10,000; Bk Titles 60,541; Bk Vols 86,000; Per Subs 100
Automation Activity & Vendor Info: (Cataloging) Horizon; (Circulation) Horizon; (OPAC) Horizon
Database Vendor: ALLDATA Online, ARTstor, EBSCO Discovery Service, EBSCOhost, Facts on File, Gale Cengage Learning, IBISWorld, JSTOR, LexisNexis, OCLC FirstSearch, OCLC WorldShare Interlibrary Loan, ProQuest, Wilson - Wilson Web
Partic in Detroit Area Library Network; Midwest Collaborative for Library Services (MCLS)
Open Mon-Thurs 8am-9:45pm, Fri 8-2:15, Sat 9-4:15, Sun 12-5:45

M ST JOHN MACOMB HOSPITAL CENTER LIBRARY*, 11800 E 12 Mile Rd, 48093. SAN 320-3859. Tel: 586-573-5117. FAX: 586-573-5042. *In Charge,* Jennifer Randazzo; E-mail: jennifer.randazzo@stjohn.org; Staff 1 (MLS 1)
Library Holdings: Bk Titles 2,200; Bk Vols 2,500; Per Subs 180
Subject Interests: Allied health, Med, Nursing
Wireless access
Open Mon-Thurs 8-4

P WARREN PUBLIC LIBRARY*, Civic Center Library, One City Sq, Ste 100, 48093-2396. SAN 347-1454. Tel: 586-574-4564. Web Site: www.libcoop.net/warren. *Dir,* Amy Henderstein; Staff 7 (MLS 5, Non-MLS 2)
Founded 1958. Pop 138,247; Circ 603,725
Library Holdings: Bk Vols 258,623; Per Subs 525
Automation Activity & Vendor Info: (Acquisitions) SirsiDynix; (Cataloging) SirsiDynix; (Circulation) SirsiDynix; (ILL) SirsiDynix; (OPAC) SirsiDynix; (Serials) SirsiDynix
Database Vendor: Gale Cengage Learning, OCLC FirstSearch
Wireless access
Open Mon & Wed 12-8, Tues & Thurs 9-8, Fri & Sat 9-5
Friends of the Library Group
Branches: 3
MAYBELLE BURNETTE BRANCH, 22005 Van Dyke Ave, 48089, SAN 347-1489. Tel: 586-758-2115. Web Site: www.libcoop.net/warren/brances/wmb.html. *Br Mgr,* Jane Koger; Staff 3 (MLS 1, Non-MLS 2)
Library Holdings: Per Subs 90
Subject Interests: Irish
Special Services for the Blind - Closed circuit TV magnifier; Magnifiers; Reader equip
Open Mon, Tues & Thurs 12-8, Wed & Sat 9-5; Mon (Summer) 12-8, Tues-Fri 9-5
Friends of the Library Group
DOROTHY M BUSCH BRANCH, 23333 Ryan Rd, 48091, SAN 347-1519. Tel: 586-755-5750. *Br Mgr,* Position Currently Open; Staff 2 (MLS 1, Non-MLS 1)
Library Holdings: Per Subs 98
Open Mon, Fri & Sat 9-5, Tues-Thurs 12-8
Friends of the Library Group
ARTHUR J MILLER BRANCH, 5460 Arden St, Ste 303, 48092, SAN 347-1578. Tel: 586-751-5377. TDD: 586-751-5377. Web Site: www.libcoop.net/warren/branches/wam.html. *Br Mgr,* Sharon Linsday; Staff 6 (MLS 5, Non-MLS 1)
Library Holdings: Per Subs 221
Special Collections: State Document Depository; US Document Depository
Subject Interests: Bus, Sheet music
Special Services for the Deaf - TDD equip
Open Tues-Thurs 12-8, Fri & Sat 9-5
Friends of the Library Group

WASHINGTON

P ROMEO DISTRICT LIBRARY*, Graubner Library, 65821 Van Dyke, 48095. SAN 370-758X. Tel: 586-752-0603. Circulation Tel: 586-752-0603, Ext 1000. Reference Tel: 586-752-0603, Ext 1021. FAX: 586-752-8416. Web Site: www.libcoop.net/romeo. *Dir,* Kristen Valyi-Hax; E-mail: kristen@romeodistrictlibrary.org; *Head, Ch,* Michelle Yochim; E-mail: michelle@romeodistrictlibrary.org; *Head, Circ,* Maureen Swanwick; E-mail: maureen@romeodistrictlibrary.org; *Ad,* Kathy Fannon; *Ad,* Glen Sowles; *Ad,* Heather VanFleet; *Ch Serv Librn,* Bethanie Connors; *Ch,* Chuck Schacht; *Ch,* Jeanette Smith; Staff 32 (MLS 10, Non-MLS 22)
Founded 1909. Pop 17,294; Circ 329,952
Library Holdings: AV Mats 9,475; Electronic Media & Resources 420; Bk Titles 79,500; Bk Vols 83,516; Per Subs 311; Talking Bks 4,679
Automation Activity & Vendor Info: (Acquisitions) SirsiDynix; (Cataloging) SirsiDynix; (Circulation) SirsiDynix; (OPAC) SirsiDynix; (Serials) SirsiDynix
Partic in Suburban Library Cooperative
Open Mon-Thurs 9-9, Fri & Sat 9-5, Sun 1-4
Friends of the Library Group
Branches: 1
KEZAR BRANCH, 107 Church St, Romeo, 48065, SAN 308-3772. Tel: 586-752-2583. FAX: 586-336-7300. *Br Librn,* Stacie Guzzo; E-mail: stacie@romeodistrictlibrary.org; Staff 2 (MLS 1, Non-MLS 1)
Founded 1909
Database Vendor: Gale Cengage Learning
Open Tues & Thurs 11-7, Wed, Fri & Sat 9:30-5:30
Friends of the Library Group

WATERFORD

J OAKLAND COMMUNITY COLLEGE*, Highland Lakes Campus Library, Woodland Hall, 7350 Cooley Lake Rd, 48327-4187. SAN 308-4566. Tel: 248-942-3125. Reference Tel: 248-942-3126. FAX: 248-942-3132. Web Site: www.oaklandcc.edu/library. *Dept Chair, Ref,* Beth Garnsey; Tel: 248-942-3128, E-mail: bagarnse@oaklandcc.edu; *Librn,* Allison McFadden-Keesling; Tel: 248-942-3127, E-mail: acmcfadd@oaklandcc.edu; Staff 5 (MLS 2, Non-MLS 3)
Founded 1965. Enrl 6,664; Fac 56; Highest Degree: Associate
Jun 2010-Jun 2011. Mats Exp $97,782, Books $60,000, Per/Ser (Incl. Access Fees) $27,500, Other Print Mats $3,282, Micro $7,000. Sal $293,000 (Prof $165,000)
Library Holdings: AV Mats 1,133; Bks on Deafness & Sign Lang 19; e-books 16,499; Bk Titles 27,914; Bk Vols 30,713; Per Subs 236
Subject Interests: Allied health, Dental hygiene, Nursing
Automation Activity & Vendor Info: (Cataloging) SirsiDynix; (Circulation) SirsiDynix; (Course Reserve) SirsiDynix; (ILL) SirsiDynix; (OPAC) SirsiDynix; (Serials) SirsiDynix
Database Vendor: ARTstor, Bowker, EBSCO Information Services, EBSCOhost, Gale Cengage Learning, JSTOR, Micromedex, Oxford Online, ProQuest, PubMed, ScienceDirect
Wireless access
Function: Audio & video playback equip for onsite use, CD-ROM, Copy machines, Doc delivery serv, e-mail serv, Electronic databases & coll, Handicapped accessible, Health sci info serv, ILL available, Music CDs, Online ref, Orientations, Ref & res, VHS videos
Special Services for the Blind - Computer with voice synthesizer for visually impaired persons
Open Mon-Thurs 8am-10pm, Fri 8-4:30, Sat 9-3

P WATERFORD TOWNSHIP PUBLIC LIBRARY*, 5168 Civic Center Dr, 48329. SAN 347-0075. Tel: 248-674-4831. FAX: 248-674-1910. Web Site: www.waterford.lib.mi.us. *Coordr, Libr Serv, Dir,* Joan M Rogers; Tel: 248-618-7691, E-mail: jrogers@twp.waterford.mi.us; *Head, Adult & Outreach Serv,* Jean Hansen; Tel: 248-618-7682, E-mail: jhansen@tep.waterford.mi.us; *Head, Ch,* Cynthia Walker; Tel: 248-618-7684, E-mail: cwalker@twp.waterford.mi.us; *Head, Tech Serv,* Position Currently Open; *Coordr, Circ,* Michael Neal; Staff 11 (MLS 11)
Founded 1964. Pop 71,997; Circ 347,496
Jan 2011-Dec 2011 Income $2,254,548, State $34,440, County $88,696, Locally Generated Income $2,050,603, Other $42,000
Library Holdings: AV Mats 7,600; e-books 20,800; Bk Titles 123,000; Per Subs 250
Subject Interests: Careers, Mich
Automation Activity & Vendor Info: (Acquisitions) SirsiDynix; (Circulation) SirsiDynix; (ILL) SirsiDynix; (OPAC) SirsiDynix
Database Vendor: Comprise Technologies Inc, Gale Cengage Learning, ProQuest, ReferenceUSA
Wireless access
Function: Adult bk club, Art exhibits, Audiobks via web, Bk club(s), Bks on cassette, Bks on CD, Children's prog, Computer training, Computers for patron use, Copy machines, e-mail & chat, e-mail serv, Electronic databases & coll, Fax serv, Free DVD rentals, Genealogy discussion group, Handicapped accessible, Home delivery & serv to Sr ctr & nursing homes, ILL available, Large print keyboards, Literacy & newcomer serv,

Magnifiers for reading, Mail & tel request accepted, Mus passes, Music CDs, Online cat, Online ref, Online searches, Orientations, Outreach serv, Outside serv via phone, mail, e-mail & web, Photocopying/Printing, Preschool outreach, Prog for adults, Prog for children & young adult, Pub access computers, Ref serv in person, Senior outreach, Spoken cassettes & CDs, Spoken cassettes & DVDs, Story hour, Summer reading prog, Tax forms, Teen prog, Telephone ref, VHS videos, Video lending libr
Special Services for the Blind - BiFolkal kits; Bks on cassette; Bks on CD; Home delivery serv; Large print bks; Large screen computer & software; Lending of low vision aids; Low vision equip; Magnifiers; Scanner for conversion & translation of mats; Screen enlargement software for people with visual disabilities; ZoomText magnification & reading software
Open Mon-Thurs 9-9, Sat 10-5, Sun 1-5
Friends of the Library Group

WATERVLIET

P WATERVLIET DISTRICT LIBRARY*, 333 N Main St, 49098-9793. SAN 308-4760. Tel: 269-463-6382. FAX: 269-463-3117. Web Site: www.watervlietlibrary.org. *Dir,* Lois R Hartman; E-mail: lrhartman8@yahoo.com; Staff 6 (Non-MLS 6)
Founded 1923. Pop 5,235; Circ 34,439
Library Holdings: Bks on Deafness & Sign Lang 30; High Interest/Low Vocabulary Bk Vols 25; Bk Titles 23,000; Bk Vols 26,500; Per Subs 53
Special Collections: Civil War Coll
Automation Activity & Vendor Info: (Cataloging) Follett Software; (Circulation) Follett Software
Wireless access
Function: Archival coll, CD-ROM, Doc delivery serv, Handicapped accessible, ILL available, Online searches, Photocopying/Printing, Prog for children & young adult, Ref serv available, Spoken cassettes & CDs, Summer reading prog, Telephone ref, VHS videos, Wheelchair accessible
Partic in Midwest Collaborative for Library Services (MCLS); Southwest Michigan Library Cooperative
Open Mon 1-8, Tues & Fri 1-5, Wed 10-8, Thurs 10-5, Sat 10-2

WAYLAND

P HENIKA DISTRICT LIBRARY*, 149 S Main St, 49348-1208. SAN 308-4779. Tel: 269-792-2891. FAX: 269-792-0399. E-mail: way@henikalibrary.org. Web Site: www.henikalibrary.org. *Dir,* Lynn Mandaville
Founded 1899. Pop 6,921; Circ 39,363
Library Holdings: Bk Vols 37,000; Per Subs 56
Wireless access
Partic in Lakeland Library Cooperative
Open Mon & Wed 9-8, Tues, Thurs & Fri 9-6, Sat 9-3
Friends of the Library Group

WAYNE

P WAYNE PUBLIC LIBRARY*, 3737 S Wayne Rd, 48184. SAN 308-4809. Tel: 734-721-7832. FAX: 734-721-0341. Web Site: wayne.lib.mi.us. *Dir,* Paulette Medvecky; E-mail: medvecky@wayne.lib.mi.us; *Ad,* Kathleen Kozakowski; E-mail: kkozakowski@wayne.lib.mi.us; *Librn,* Carola Fisher; E-mail: cfisher@wayne.lib.mi.us; *Librn,* John O'Connell; *Youth Serv Librn,* Jody Wolak; E-mail: jwolak@wayne.lib.mi.us; Staff 9 (MLS 6, Non-MLS 3)
Founded 1927. Pop 19,051; Circ 151,080
Jul 2005-Jun 2006 Income $716,272, State $14,261, City $632,711, Federal $6,045, County $18,924, Locally Generated Income $44,331. Mats Exp $112,000, Books $74,745, Per/Ser (Incl. Access Fees) $13,000, AV Mat $14,000, Electronic Ref Mat (Incl. Access Fees) $10,255. Sal $470,380
Library Holdings: AV Mats 12,371; High Interest/Low Vocabulary Bk Vols 75; Large Print Bks 1,841; Bk Vols 95,034; Per Subs 138
Automation Activity & Vendor Info: (Acquisitions) SirsiDynix; (Cataloging) SirsiDynix; (Circulation) SirsiDynix; (OPAC) SirsiDynix; (Serials) SirsiDynix
Database Vendor: ProQuest, ReferenceUSA, SirsiDynix
Wireless access
Publications: Communique (Newsletter)
Partic in Libr Network of Mich
Special Services for the Deaf - TDD equip
Special Services for the Blind - Closed circuit TV magnifier
Open Mon-Thurs 10-9, Fri & Sat 12-5, Sun (Sept-May) 1-5
Friends of the Library Group

WEST BLOOMFIELD

R JEWISH COMMUNITY CENTER OF METROPOLITAN DETROIT*, Henry & Delia Meyers Library, 6600 W Maple Rd, 48322-3022. SAN 308-4825. Tel: 248-432-5547. FAX: 248-432-5552. Web Site: www.jccdet.org. *Librn,* Francine Menken; Tel: 248-432-5546, E-mail: fmenken@jccdet.org; Staff 1 (Non-MLS 1)
Founded 1959
Library Holdings: DVDs 100; Large Print Bks 100; Bk Vols 12,000; Per Subs 35; Talking Bks 15; Videos 50
Special Collections: American-Jewish Coll, per & newsp
Subject Interests: Judaica (lit or hist of Jews)
Automation Activity & Vendor Info: (Cataloging) Follett Software; (Circulation) Follett Software
Function: Bk club(s), Prog for adults, Prog for children & young adult
Special Services for the Blind - Magnifiers; Telesensory screen enlarger & speech synthesis interface to the OPAC
Open Mon & Tues 10-5, Wed & Thurs 10:30-5, Fri 10-12, Sun 10-1
Friends of the Library Group

R TEMPLE ISRAEL LIBRARIES & MEDIA CENTER*, 5725 Walnut Lake Rd, 48323. SAN 308-0390. Tel: 248-661-5700. FAX: 248-661-1302. E-mail: info@temple-israel.org. Web Site: www.temple-israel.org. *Dir,* Lauren Johnson; E-mail: ljohnson@temple-israel.org; *Archivist, Asst Librn,* Judy Solomon; E-mail: judy@temple-israel.org; Staff 2 (MLS 2)
Founded 1941
Library Holdings: Bk Titles 13,560; Bk Vols 16,010; Per Subs 20
Special Collections: Jewish Children's Literature Coll; Jewish Heritage Coll, video; Reform Judaism Coll
Subject Interests: Holocaust, Israel, Jewish hist, Judaism
Automation Activity & Vendor Info: (Cataloging) Follett Software; (Circulation) Follett Software

P WEST BLOOMFIELD TOWNSHIP PUBLIC LIBRARY*, 4600 Walnut Lake Rd, 48323. SAN 347-1756. Tel: 248-682-2120. Circulation Tel: 248-232-2201. Reference Tel: 248-232-2290. Administration Tel: 248-232-2329. Automation Services Tel: 248-232-2315. FAX: 248-232-2291. Administration FAX: 248-232-2333. TDD: 248-232-2292. Web Site: www.wblib.org. *Dir,* Clara Nalli Bohrer; *Br Mgr,* Steve Ketcham; Tel: 248-363-4022, Fax: 248-363-7243; *Br Mgr,* Brenda Plizga; Tel: 248-232-2293, E-mail: plizgabr@wblib.org; *Coord, Ad Serv,* Mary Killian; Tel: 248-232-2307, E-mail: killianm@wblib.org; *IT Coordr,* Robert Pesale; Tel: 248-232-2315, E-mail: pesalero@wblib.org; *Coordr, Support Serv,* Jeff Crocker; Tel: 248-232-2207, E-mail: crockerj@wblib.org; *Coordr, Youth Serv,* Penny Neef; Tel: 248-232-2252, E-mail: neefpenn@wblib.org; Staff 95 (MLS 27, Non-MLS 68)
Founded 1934. Pop 64,860; Circ 1,885,986
Apr 2006-Mar 2007 Income $60,338,564. Mats Exp $983,518. Sal $2,514,411
Library Holdings: AV Mats 39,376; Bk Vols 225,617; Per Subs 525
Automation Activity & Vendor Info: (Acquisitions) Innovative Interfaces, Inc; (Cataloging) Innovative Interfaces, Inc; (Circulation) Innovative Interfaces, Inc; (ILL) Innovative Interfaces, Inc; (OPAC) Innovative Interfaces, Inc; (Serials) Innovative Interfaces, Inc
Database Vendor: Gale Cengage Learning, Newsbank, OCLC FirstSearch, ProQuest
Wireless access
Partic in Metro Net Libr Consortium; The Library Network
Special Services for the Deaf - Assistive tech; Bks on deafness & sign lang; Closed caption videos; TTY equip
Special Services for the Blind - Audio mat; Bks on cassette; Bks on CD; Computer with voice synthesizer for visually impaired persons; Large print bks; Magnifiers; Reader equip
Open Mon-Thurs 9-9, Fri & Sat 9-6, Sun 12-8 (12-5 Summer)
Friends of the Library Group
Branches: 1
WESTACRES, 7321 Commerce Rd, 48324, SAN 347-1780. Tel: 248-363-4022. Circulation Tel: 248-232-2410. Reference Tel: 248-232-2420. FAX: 248-363-7243. *Br Mgr,* Steve Ketchan; Tel: 248-232-2401
Founded 1938
Library Holdings: Bk Titles 43,651; Per Subs 150
Open Mon-Thurs 9-9, Fri & Sat 9-6, Sun 12-8 (12-5 Summer)
Friends of the Library Group

WEST BRANCH

P WEST BRANCH PUBLIC LIBRARY*, 119 N Fourth St, 48661. SAN 308-4833. Tel: 989-345-2235. FAX: 989-345-8735. E-mail: wbranch@vlc.lib.mi.us. Web Site: westbranchlibrary.org. *Dir,* Marsha Boyd; Staff 8 (MLS 1, Non-MLS 7)
Founded 1905. Pop 9,922; Circ 50,466
Automation Activity & Vendor Info: (Acquisitions) SirsiDynix; (Cataloging) SirsiDynix; (Circulation) SirsiDynix; (Course Reserve) SirsiDynix; (ILL) SirsiDynix; (Media Booking) SirsiDynix; (OPAC) SirsiDynix; (Serials) SirsiDynix
Wireless access
Partic in Valley Library Consortium; White Pine Libr Coop
Open Mon & Wed 10-7, Tues, Thurs & Fri 10-5, Sat 10-2
Friends of the Library Group

WESTLAND

P WAYNE COUNTY REGIONAL LIBRARY FOR THE BLIND & PHYSICALLY HANDICAPPED*, 30555 Michigan Ave, 48186-5310. SAN 308-4787. Tel: 734-727-7300. Toll Free Tel: 888-968-2737. FAX: 734-727-7333. TDD: 734-727-7330. E-mail: wcrlbph@wayneregional.lib.mi.us. Web Site: wayneregional.lib.mi.us. *Dir,* Maria McCarville; Tel: 734-727-7310; *Librn,* Lynne Coles; *Librn,* Judy Danish; *Librn,* Sue Steiger
Founded 1931
Library Holdings: Bk Vols 125,000
Special Services for the Blind - Large print bks; Talking bks & player equip
Open Mon-Fri 8-4:30

P WESTLAND PUBLIC LIBRARY*, William P Faust Library, 6123 Central City Pkwy, 48185. Tel: 734-326-6123. FAX: 734-595-4612. E-mail: administration@westlandlibrary.org. Web Site: www.westland.lib.mi.us. *Dir,* Sheila Collins; E-mail: sheila.collins@westlandlibrary.org; *Head, Adult Serv,* Marilyn Kwik; E-mail: marilyn.kwik@westlandlibrary.org; *Head, Circ & Tech Serv,* Diane Mehl; E-mail: diane.mehl@westlandlibrary.org; *Ref Librn,* Tara Scott; E-mail: tara.scott@westlandlibrary.org; *Tech Serv Librn,* Susan Hanson; E-mail: susan.hanson@westlandlibrary.org; *Tech Librn/Adult Literacy Prog Coordr,* Kristy Cooper; E-mail: kristy.cooper@westlandlibrary.org; *Homebound Delivery Coordr,* Andrea Perez; E-mail: andea.perez@westlandlibrary.org; *Libr Prog, Adult Serv,* Andy Schuck; E-mail: andy.schuck@westlandlibrary.org
Open Mon-Thurs 9-9, Fri & Sat 9-5, Sun Noon-5

WHITE CLOUD

P WHITE CLOUD COMMUNITY LIBRARY*, 1038 Wilcox Ave, 49349. (Mail add: PO Box 995, 49349-0995), SAN 308-485X. Tel: 231-689-6631. FAX: 231-689-6699. E-mail: circ1@whitecloudlibrary.net. Web Site: www.whitecloudlibrary.net. *Dir,* Nancy L Harper; E-mail: director@whitecloudlibrary.net; *Asst Dir,* Jessie Long; *Circ Librn,* Patty Novak; E-mail: circ2@whitecloudlibrary.net; *Cat,* Amy Maike; E-mail: processing@whitecloudlibrary.net; *Ch Serv,* Jessica Hunt; E-mail: childrens@whitecloudlibrary.net; Staff 8 (Non-MLS 8)
Founded 1955. Pop 8,536; Circ 83,000
Jul 2011-Jun 2012 Income $383,853, State $3,766, Locally Generated Income $380,087. Mats Exp $327,684. Sal $162,215
Library Holdings: AV Mats 7,735; CDs 337; DVDs 1,823; Electronic Media & Resources 232; Large Print Bks 1,186; Bk Titles 45,250; Per Subs 142; Videos 2,123
Special Collections: Civil War-Lincoln Coll (Louis Fry); Local History (Douglass Coll), bks & photos; Local History (Martha Evans Coll); Newaygo County Genealogy & History Coll
Automation Activity & Vendor Info: (Acquisitions) Innovative Interfaces, Inc; (Cataloging) Innovative Interfaces, Inc; (Circulation) Innovative Interfaces, Inc; (ILL) Innovative Interfaces, Inc; (OPAC) Innovative Interfaces, Inc
Database Vendor: Gale Cengage Learning, Innovative Interfaces, Inc, OCLC FirstSearch
Wireless access
Function: Adult bk club, After school storytime, Archival coll, Bk club(s), Bks on cassette, Bks on CD, CD-ROM, Children's prog, Computers for patron use, Copy machines, e-mail serv, Electronic databases & coll, Exhibits, Fax serv, Free DVD rentals, Handicapped accessible, Holiday prog, ILL available, Instruction & testing, Magnifiers for reading, Mail & tel request accepted, Music CDs, Newsp ref libr, Notary serv, Online cat, Online ref, Online searches, OverDrive digital audio bks, Photocopying/Printing, Prog for adults, Prog for children & young adult, Ref serv available, Ref serv in person, Scanner, Spoken cassettes & CDs, Spoken cassettes & DVDs, Story hour, Summer reading prog, Tax forms, Teen prog, Telephone ref, VHS videos, Video lending libr, Web-catalog, Wheelchair accessible, Workshops
Publications: Library News (Newsletter)
Partic in Lakeland Library Cooperative; Midwest Collaborative for Library Services (MCLS)
Open Mon & Wed 9:30-7, Tues, Thurs & Fri 9:30-5:30, Sat 9:30-1
Friends of the Library Group

WHITE LAKE

P WHITE LAKE TOWNSHIP LIBRARY*, 7527 E Highland Rd, 48383-2938. SAN 375-376X. Tel: 248-698-4942. FAX: 248-698-2550. E-mail: reference@whitelakelibrary.org. Web Site: www.whitelakelibrary.org. *Dir,* Lawrence Ostrowski; Tel: 248-698-4942, Ext 7, E-mail: lostrowski@whitelakelibrary.org; Staff 16 (MLS 6, Non-MLS 10)
Founded 1975. Pop 29,000; Circ 153,000
Library Holdings: Bk Vols 50,000; Per Subs 85
Automation Activity & Vendor Info: (Cataloging) SirsiDynix; (Circulation) SirsiDynix
Wireless access
Function: Handicapped accessible
Publications: News & Reviews from White Lake Township Library (Newsletter)
Partic in The Library Network
Open Mon-Thurs 10-9, Fri & Sat 10-5
Friends of the Library Group

WHITE PIGEON

P WHITE PIGEON TOWNSHIP LIBRARY, 102 N Kalamazoo St, 49099-9726. (Mail add: PO Box 399, 49099-0399), SAN 308-4868. Tel: 269-483-7409. FAX: 269-483-9923. E-mail: wplibrary@monroe.lib.mi.us. *Dir,* Perri Saunders; E-mail: perri@monroe.lib.mi.us
Founded 1881. Pop 5,239; Circ 35,408
Jul 2012-Jun 2013 Income $194,200
Automation Activity & Vendor Info: (Acquisitions) Evolve; (Cataloging) Evolve; (Circulation) Evolve
Wireless access
Function: 24/7 Electronic res, 24/7 Online cat, Adult bk club, Bk club(s), Bks on CD, Children's prog, Computer training, Computers for patron use, Copy machines, eReaders, Fax serv, Free DVD rentals, Handicapped accessible, Holiday prog, Homebound delivery serv, ILL available, Laminating, Magazines, Magnifiers for reading, Mail & tel request accepted, Microfiche/film & reading machines, Notary serv, Online cat, OverDrive digital audio bks, Photocopying/Printing, Preschool outreach, Preschool reading prog, Printer for laptops & handheld devices, Prog for adults, Prog for children & young adult, Pub access computers, Ref serv in person, Scanner, Senior computer classes, Spanish lang bks, Spoken cassettes & CDs, Story hour, Summer reading prog, Tax forms, Teen prog, Telephone ref, VHS videos, Wheelchair accessible
Mem of Woodlands Library Cooperative
Open Mon, Wed & Fri 9-5, Tues & Thurs 9-7, Sat 9-1
Friends of the Library Group

WHITE PINE

P CARP LAKE TOWNSHIP LIBRARY*, 36349 Mall Circle Cr, 49971. (Mail add: PO Box 157, 49971-0157), SAN 308-4876. Tel: 906-885-5888. FAX: 906-885-5888. E-mail: library306@chartermi.net. Web Site: www.uproc.lib.mi.us/CarpLake. *Dir,* Wanda Tessmer
Founded 1954. Circ 5,702
Library Holdings: Bk Vols 10,000; Per Subs 42
Automation Activity & Vendor Info: (Cataloging) Brodart; (Circulation) Brodart; (OPAC) Brodart
Partic in Superiorland Library Cooperative
Open Tues 3-8, Wed & Thurs 10-3

WHITEHALL

P WHITE LAKE COMMUNITY LIBRARY*, 3900 White Lake Dr, 49461-9257. SAN 308-4884. Tel: 231-894-9531. FAX: 231-893-8821. E-mail: whi@llcoop.org. Web Site: www.whitelakelibrary.michlibrary.org. *Dir,* Shelley Williams; E-mail: whisw@llcoop.org; *Asst Dir,* Pam Osborn; *Circ/Customer Serv Mgr,* Susan Dreyer; Staff 6 (MLS 1, Non-MLS 5)
Founded 1880. Pop 11,811; Circ 152,513
Library Holdings: Bk Titles 35,952; Per Subs 95; Videos 2,568
Subject Interests: Local hist, Mich
Wireless access
Partic in Lakeland Library Cooperative
Open Mon-Thurs 10-8, Fri & Sat 10-5
Friends of the Library Group

WIXOM

P WIXOM PUBLIC LIBRARY*, 49015 Pontiac Trail, 48393-2567. SAN 308-4892. Tel: 248-624-2512. FAX: 248-624-0862. Web Site: www.wixomlibrary.org. *Dir,* Cindy Mack; *Support Serv Librn,* Andrea Dickson; *Ch Serv,* Jane Kahan; *Ref,* Karin Caporale; Staff 6 (MLS 5.5, Non-MLS 0.5)
Founded 1973. Pop 13,498; Circ 207,890
Jul 2012-Jun 2013 Income $740,071. Mats Exp $83,000
Special Collections: ESL Coll; Large Print Coll
Automation Activity & Vendor Info: (Circulation) SirsiDynix; (OPAC) SirsiDynix; (Serials) SirsiDynix
Database Vendor: SirsiDynix
Wireless access
Function: Adult bk club, Bk club(s), Bks on CD, Children's prog, Computers for patron use, Copy machines, Electronic databases & coll, Fax serv, Free DVD rentals, Handicapped accessible, ILL available, Magnifiers for reading, Mus passes, Music CDs, Online cat, Prog for adults, Prog for children & young adult, Pub access computers, Ref serv available, Summer reading prog, Tax forms, Telephone ref, Wheelchair accessible
Partic in TLN
Special Services for the Deaf - Bks on deafness & sign lang; TTY equip

Special Services for the Blind - Bks on cassette; Bks on CD; Copier with enlargement capabilities; Large print bks; Magnifiers; Playaways (bks on MP3); Sound rec
Open Mon-Thurs 10-8, Fri & Sat 10-5
Friends of the Library Group

WOLVERINE

P WOLVERINE COMMUNITY LIBRARY*, 5716 W Main St, 49799-9403. (Mail add: PO Box 310, 49799-9403), SAN 308-4906. Tel: 231-525-8800. FAX: 231-525-8713. E-mail: wolveri1@northland.lib.mi.us. *Dir,* Susan Warner
Founded 1950. Circ 6,620
Library Holdings: Bk Vols 16,000; Per Subs 42
Partic in Northland Library Cooperative
Open Mon-Wed & Fri 10-5, Thurs 10-8

WOODLAND

P GEORGE W SPINDLER MEMORIAL LIBRARY*, 186 N Main St, 48897-0068. Tel: 269-367-4694. Web Site: www.gwspindler.michlibrary.org. *Dir,* Kay Bursley
Library Holdings: Bk Vols 8,300
Mem of Woodlands Library Cooperative
Open Mon 3-7, Wed 12-6, Thurs 9-4, Sat 10-1

WYANDOTTE

P BACON MEMORIAL DISTRICT LIBRARY*, 45 Vinewood, 48192-5221. SAN 308-4914. Tel: 734-246-8357. FAX: 734-282-1540. Web Site: www.baconlibrary.org. *Dir,* Anita O'Brien; E-mail: aobrien@baconlibrary.org; *Head, Circ,* Jayne Johnson; *Hist Librn,* Wallace Hayden; *Ref Librn,* Laura Gramlich; *Ref Librn,* Annie Spence; *Youth Librn,* Kelly Ray; Staff 19 (MLS 5, Non-MLS 14)
Founded 1869. Pop 25,883
Library Holdings: AV Mats 8,179; CDs 2,130; DVDs 712; Large Print Bks 1,088; Bk Vols 55,917; Per Subs 198; Talking Bks 1,406; Videos 3,931
Subject Interests: Local hist, Mil hist
Automation Activity & Vendor Info: (Acquisitions) SirsiDynix; (Cataloging) SirsiDynix; (Circulation) SirsiDynix; (ILL) SirsiDynix; (OPAC) SirsiDynix; (Serials) SirsiDynix
Database Vendor: Newsbank, Overdrive, Inc, ProQuest
Wireless access
Function: Adult bk club, Archival coll, Children's prog, Computer training, Computers for patron use, Copy machines, Fax serv, Homebound delivery serv, ILL available, Notary serv, OverDrive digital audio bks, Prog for children & young adult, Ref serv available, Summer reading prog, Wheelchair accessible
Partic in The Library Network
Open Mon-Thurs 10-9, Fri & Sat 10-5
Friends of the Library Group

M HENRY FORD WYANDOTTE HOSPITAL*, Medical Library, Rehabilitation Bldg, 4th Flr, 2333 Biddle Ave, 48192-4668. Tel: 734-246-7361. FAX: 734-246-6069. E-mail: wylibrary@hfhs.org. Web Site: www.henryfordconnect.com/hfwhlibrary. *Mgr,* Sue Skoglund; E-mail: sskoglu1@hfhs.org; Staff 2 (MLS 1, Non-MLS 1)
Library Holdings: AV Mats 600; Bk Vols 2,000; Per Subs 85
Wireless access
Open Mon-Fri 7:30-4:30
Restriction: Non-circulating to the pub

S FORD-MACNICHOL HOME, WYANDOTTE MUSEUM, ARCHIVES*, 2610 Biddle Ave, 48192. SAN 321-0413. Tel: 734-324-7297. FAX: 734-324-7283. E-mail: museum@wyan.org. Web Site: www.wyandottemuseums.org.
Founded 1958
Library Holdings: Bk Titles 2,000; Per Subs 10
Special Collections: Oral History
Subject Interests: Detroit hist, Local hist, Mich hist, Wayne County hist
Open Mon-Fri 9-5

WYOMING

M METRO HEALTH HOSPITAL*, Skytron Medical Library, 5900 Byron Ctr Ave SW, 49519. (Mail add: PO Box 916, 49509). Tel: 616-252-7200. Toll Free Tel: 800-968-0051. FAX: 616-252-7265. Web Site: www.metrohealth.net. *Librn,* Mary B Loftis; E-mail: mary.loftis@metrogr.org
Founded 1942
Library Holdings: Bk Vols 2,500; Per Subs 100
Open Mon-Fri 8-4:30

YPSILANTI

C EASTERN MICHIGAN UNIVERSITY, Bruce T Halle Library, Administrative Office, Rm 200, 955 W Circle Dr, 48197. SAN 308-4949. Circulation Tel: 734-487-2562. Interlibrary Loan Service Tel: 734-487-2596. Reference Tel: 734-487-2445. Administration Tel: 734-487-2633. Interlibrary Loan Service FAX: 734-487-5399. Administration FAX: 734-484-1151. Web Site: www.emich.edu/halle. *Univ Librn,* Tara Lynn Fulton; Tel: 734-487-2573, E-mail: tara.fulton@emich.edu; *Dept Head,* Susann deVries; Tel: 734-487-2475, E-mail: sdevries@emich.edu; *Acq Librn,* Joe Badics; Tel: 734-487-2402, E-mail: joseph.badics@emich.edu; *Info Literacy Librn, Women's & Gender Studies Librn,* Suzanne Gray; Tel: 734-487-2517, E-mail: suzanne.gray@emich.edu; *Pub Serv Librn,* Keith Stanger; Tel: 734-487-2509, E-mail: keith@stanger.com; *Tech Serv Coordr,* Walter Hogan; Tel: 734-487-2399, E-mail: walter.hogan@emich.edu; *Govt Doc,* Rhonda Fowler; Tel: 734-487-2587, E-mail: rhonda.fowler@emich.edu; *Archivist,* Alexis Braun Marks; Tel: 734-487-2594, E-mail: abraunma@emich.edu; Staff 32 (MLS 26, Non-MLS 6)
Founded 1849. Enrl 23,341; Fac 688; Highest Degree: Doctorate
Jul 2012-Jun 2013. Mats Exp $3,134,156. Sal $4,593,991
Library Holdings: AV Mats 15,759; e-books 90,000; Bk Titles 695,000; Bk Vols 785,000; Per Subs 44,145
Special Collections: State Document Depository; US Document Depository
Subject Interests: Educ
Automation Activity & Vendor Info: (Acquisitions) Ex Libris Group; (Cataloging) Ex Libris Group; (Circulation) Ex Libris Group; (Course Reserve) Docutek; (ILL) OCLC ILLiad; (OPAC) Ex Libris Group; (Serials) Ex Libris Group
Database Vendor: Cambridge Scientific Abstracts, Gale Cengage Learning, OCLC FirstSearch, OVID Technologies, ProQuest
Wireless access
Publications: Numbered Bibliography Series; Study Guides
Partic in Midwest Collaborative for Library Services (MCLS); OCLC Online Computer Library Center, Inc
Open Mon-Thurs 7:30am-Midnight, Fri 7:30am-8pm, Sat 9-6, Sun Noon-Midnight
Friends of the Library Group

P YPSILANTI DISTRICT LIBRARY*, Whittaker Road Library, 5577 Whittaker Rd, 48197. Tel: 734-482-4110. FAX: 734-482-0047. Web Site: www.ypsilibrary.org. *Dir,* Jill Morey; *Asst Dir,* Lori Kunkel-Coryell; Staff 45 (MLS 18, Non-MLS 27)
Founded 1863. Pop 79,826; Circ 856,475
Dec 2007-Nov 2008 Income (Main Library and Branch(s)) $4,308,119, State $63,736, County $164,352, Locally Generated Income $3,810,111, Other $269,920. Mats Exp $682,702, Books $432,174, Per/Ser (Incl. Access Fees) $18,350, AV Mat $160,060, Electronic Ref Mat (Incl. Access Fees) $72,118. Sal $2,524,941
Library Holdings: AV Mats 39,000; e-books 4,280; Bk Vols 272,623; Per Subs 440
Special Collections: Library of Congress Veterans' History Project; Ypsilanti & Michigan History Coll
Automation Activity & Vendor Info: (Acquisitions) SirsiDynix; (Cataloging) SirsiDynix; (Circulation) SirsiDynix; (OPAC) SirsiDynix
Wireless access
Function: Adult bk club, Adult literacy prog, Art exhibits, Audiobks via web, Bk club(s), Bks on CD, Chess club, Children's prog, Computer training, Computers for patron use, Copy machines, Digital talking bks, e-mail & chat, e-mail serv, E-Reserves, Electronic databases & coll, Exhibits, Family literacy, Fax serv, Free DVD rentals, Handicapped accessible, Holiday prog, Home delivery & serv to Sr ctr & nursing homes, Homebound delivery serv, ILL available, Jazz prog, Large print keyboards, Literacy & newcomer serv, Magnifiers for reading, Mail & tel request accepted, Mus passes, Music CDs, Online cat, Online ref, Online searches, Orientations, Outreach serv, Outside serv via phone, mail, e-mail & web, Photocopying/Printing, Preschool outreach, Prog for adults, Prog for children & young adult, Pub access computers, Ref & res, Ref serv available, Ref serv in person, Referrals accepted, Senior computer classes, Senior outreach, Spoken cassettes & CDs, Spoken cassettes & DVDs, Story hour, Summer reading prog, Tax forms, Teen prog, Telephone ref, VHS videos, Video lending libr, Visual arts prog, Web-catalog, Wheelchair accessible
Publications: Latitudes (Newsletter)
Partic in The Library Network
Special Services for the Deaf - Adult & family literacy prog; Bks on deafness & sign lang; Closed caption videos; High interest/low vocabulary bks
Special Services for the Blind - Audio mat; Bks available with recordings; Bks on cassette; Bks on CD; Copier with enlargement capabilities; Digital talking bk; Extensive large print coll; Home delivery serv; Large print bks; Low vision equip; Magnifiers; Recorded bks; Ref serv; Talking bks; Talking bks & player equip

Open Mon-Thurs 9-9, Fri & Sat 10-6, Sun 1-5
Friends of the Library Group
Branches: 2
SUPERIOR TOWNSHIP, 8975 MacArthur Blvd, 48198. Tel: 734-482-3747. Automation Services Tel: 734-482-4110. FAX: 734-482-3757. Automation Services FAX: 734-482-0047. *Head, Outreach Serv,* Mary Garboden; E mail: garboden@ypsilibrary.org
WEST MICHIGAN AVENUE, 229 W Michigan Ave, 48197-5485, SAN 308-4957. Tel: 734-482-4110. FAX: 734-482-0047. *Br Mgr,* Joy Cichewicz
Open Mon-Thurs 10-9, Fri & Sat 10-6
Friends of the Library Group
Bookmobiles: 1. Head of Outreach Servs, Mary Garboden. Bk titles 3,600

ZEELAND

R FIRST CRC ZEELAND LIBRARY*, 15 S Church St, 49464. SAN 308-4965. Tel: 616-772-2866. FAX: 616-772-2620. E-mail: office@firstzeeland.org. Web Site: firstzeeland.org.
Founded 1930
Library Holdings: Bk Titles 4,500; Per Subs 15
Special Collections: Church History (Acts of Synod, 1857-present), bound
Subject Interests: Biographies, Fiction, Inspirational
Open Sun 9:30-10, 5-5:30 & 6:30-7

P HOWARD MILLER PUBLIC LIBRARY*, 14 S Church St, 49464-1728. SAN 308-499X. Tel: 616-772-0874. FAX: 616-772-3253. E-mail: zee@llcoop.org. Web Site: www.hmpl.org. *Dir,* Dennis M Martin; E-mail: zeedm@llcoop.org; Staff 15 (MLS 2, Non-MLS 13)
Founded 1969. Pop 15,325; Circ 239,000
Library Holdings: Bks on Deafness & Sign Lang 23; High Interest/Low Vocabulary Bk Vols 50; Bk Vols 67,000; Per Subs 184
Automation Activity & Vendor Info: (Cataloging) Innovative Interfaces, Inc; (Circulation) Innovative Interfaces, Inc; (ILL) Innovative Interfaces, Inc; (OPAC) Innovative Interfaces, Inc
Database Vendor: Gale Cengage Learning, Innovative Interfaces, Inc, OCLC FirstSearch
Wireless access
Publications: Children's Services (Quarterly newsletter)
Partic in Lakeland Library Cooperative
Open Mon-Thurs 9:30-8, Fri 9:30-5, Sat 9-1

M ZEELAND COMMUNITY HOSPITAL*, Medical Library, 8333 Felch St, 49464. Tel: 616-772-5775. FAX: 616-748-8748. Web Site: www.zch.org/. *In Charge,* Judith Ellis; E-mail: jellis@zch.org; Staff 1 (Non-MLS 1)
Founded 1928
Library Holdings: Bk Vols 150; Per Subs 30
Wireless access
Function: ILL available
Open Mon, Tues, Thurs & Fri 9-2
Restriction: Circulates for staff only, In-house use for visitors

MINNESOTA

Date of Statistics: FY 2013
Population, 2010 U.S. Census: 5,303,925
Population, 2012, estimated: 5,368,972
Number of Public Libraries: 141 administrative units comprising 356 buildings and 8 bookmobiles
Total Materials in Public Libraries: 17,314,104
Items Per Capita: 3.2
Total Public Library Circulation: 54,350,897
Circulation Per Capita: 10.1
Source of Income: Local: 81.7%, State: 9.6%, Federal: 0.1%, Other: 8.6%
Local Tax Support: 90% of the 2011 state-certified level of library support
Total Public Library Operating Expenditures (includes grants): $212,253,288
Operating Expenditures Per Capita: $39.50
Number of Regional Public Library Systems: 12
Number of Bookmobiles: 8
Number of Multi-type Library Systems: 7
State Aid: (12 regional public library systems) $13,570,000
Regional Library Telecommunication Aid: $2,300,000
Multitype Library Systems: (Seven multicounty multitype library systems) $1,300,000

ALBERT LEA

P ALBERT LEA PUBLIC LIBRARY*, 211 E Clark St, 56007. SAN 308-5015. Tel: 507-377-4350. FAX: 507-377-4339. Web Site: www.city.albertlea.org. *Dir,* Peggy Havener; Tel: 507-377-4355, E-mail: phavener@selco.info; *Librn,* Theresa Schmidt; *Ch Serv,* Patty Greibrok; Staff 11 (MLS 3, Non-MLS 8)
Founded 1897. Pop 32,238; Circ 417,035
Library Holdings: Bk Vols 71,000; Per Subs 300
Special Collections: Obituary Index to Local Newspaper
Database Vendor: SirsiDynix
Partic in Southeastern Libraries Cooperating
Open Mon-Thurs 9-7, Sun 1-5
Friends of the Library Group

S FREEBORN COUNTY HISTORICAL MUSEUM LIBRARY*, 1031 N Bridge Ave, 56007. SAN 308-5023. Tel. 507-373-8003. FAX: 507-552-1269. Web Site: www.smig.net/fchm. *Librn,* Linda Evenson
Founded 1968
Library Holdings: Bk Titles 600
Special Collections: Lea College 1966-72; Local Newspapers, 1860-present, microfilm; Lt Col Albert Miller Lea Coll; Morin Coll; Obituaries; Photo Coll of County; Sorenson Cartoon Coll; Spicer Coll
Subject Interests: Genealogy, Local hist
Function: For res purposes
Open Tues-Fri 10-5
Restriction: Not a lending libr

ALEXANDRIA

J ALEXANDRIA TECHNICAL COLLEGE LIBRARY*, 1601 Jefferson St, Rm 305, 56308. SAN 378-3863. Tel: 320-762-4465. Toll Free Tel: 888-234-1222. E-mail: library@alextech.edu. Web Site: www.alextech.edu. *Dir,* Sheree Cochran; E-mail: shereec@alextech.edu
Library Holdings: Bk Titles 11,000; Per Subs 125
Subject Interests: Communication arts, Interior design
Automation Activity & Vendor Info: (Cataloging) PALS; (Circulation) PALS; (Course Reserve) PALS; (ILL) PALS
Database Vendor: ALLDATA Online, EBSCOhost, Ex Libris Group, Facts on File, Faulkner Information Services, H W Wilson, Hoovers, Material ConneXion, Medline, OCLC FirstSearch, OCLC WorldShare Interlibrary Loan, ProQuest, PubMed, ReferenceUSA, Westlaw, Wilson - Wilson Web
Wireless access
Open Mon-Thurs 7:30-6, Fri 7:30-4, Sat 8-12

P DOUGLAS COUNTY LIBRARY*, 720 Fillmore St, 56308-1763. SAN 308-504X. Tel: 320-762-3014. FAX: 320-762-3036. Web Site: www.douglascountylibrary.org. *Interim Dir,* Tammy Schmidt; *Youth Librn,* Sarah Wethem; *Ref Serv,* Betty Ann Hegland; Staff 2 (MLS 2)
Founded 1878. Pop 30,000; Circ 311,000
Library Holdings: Bk Vols 60,150; Per Subs 176
Special Collections: Kensington Runestone
Wireless access
Mem of Viking Library System
Open Mon-Thurs 10-8, Fri 10-5, Sat 10-3
Friends of the Library Group
Bookmobiles: 1

ANOKA

S ANOKA COUNTY HISTORY CENTER & LIBRARY*, 2135 Third Ave N, 55303. SAN 308-5066. Tel: 763-421-0600. FAX: 763-323-0218. E-mail: achs@ac-hs.org. Web Site: www.ac-hs.org. *Exec Dir,* Todd Mahon; Tel. 763-421-0600, Ext 104
Founded 1934
Library Holdings: Bk Titles 1,020; Per Subs 20
Special Collections: Genealogical Books for Research throughout US & Foreign Countries
Subject Interests: Census records, Family hist, Local hist, Maps
Function: For res purposes
Open Tues 10-8, Wed-Fri 10-5, Sat 10-4

L ANOKA COUNTY LAW LIBRARY*, 325 E Main St, 55303. SAN 323-8563. Tel: 763-422-7487. FAX: 763-422-7453. Web Site: www.co.anoka.mn.us. *Librn,* Gene Myers; E-mail: gene.myers@co.anoka.mn.us; *Assoc Librn,* Merry Conway; Staff 2 (Non-MLS 2)
Jan 2006-Dec 2006 Income $390,000. Mats Exp $209,000, Books $185,000, Per/Ser (Incl. Access Fees) $1,500, Manu Arch $750, Other Print Mats $1,500, Micro $1,500, Electronic Ref Mat (Incl. Access Fees) $18,000, Presv $750. Sal $181,000
Library Holdings: Bk Titles 1,750; Bk Vols 42,000
Special Collections: Local Municipal Ordinances. US Document Depository
Open Mon-Fri 8-4:30

J ANOKA TECHNICAL COLLEGE*, Library Media Center, 1355 W Hwy 10, 55303. SAN 308-5058. Tel: 763-576-4820. FAX: 763-576-4821. E-mail: librarian@anokatech.edu. Web Site: www.anokatech.edu/current_students/research.
Enrl 1,800; Fac 80; Highest Degree: Associate
Subject Interests: Allied health, Nursing
Wireless access
Partic in Metronet; MnPALS
Open Mon-Thurs 7:30am-8pm, Fri 7:30-4

APPLETON

P APPLETON PUBLIC LIBRARY*, 322 W Schlieman Ave, 56208-1299. SAN 347-6855. Tel: 320-289-1681. FAX: 320-289-1681. Web Site: iii.pioneerland.lib.mn.us. *Librn,* Cindy Hendrickx; E-mail: cindyh@appleton.lib.mn.us
Pop 3,482; Circ 23,801
Library Holdings: Bk Vols 18,000; Per Subs 25

Automation Activity & Vendor Info: (Cataloging) Innovative Interfaces, Inc; (Circulation) Innovative Interfaces, Inc; (OPAC) Innovative Interfaces, Inc
Mem of Pioneerland Library System
Open Mon & Fri 10-5, Tues-Thurs 10-5 & 7-8:30, Sat 10-12

ARLINGTON

P ARLINGTON PUBLIC LIBRARY*, 321 West Main St, 55307. (Mail add: PO Box 391, 55307-0391), SAN 347-4216. Tel: 507-964-2490. FAX: 507-964-2490. E-mail: libtsa@tds.lib.mn.us. *Dir,* Kathy Homme
Library Holdings: Bk Vols 10,530
Database Vendor: SirsiDynix
Wireless access
Function: Fax serv, Home delivery & serv to Sr ctr & nursing homes, Photocopying/Printing
Mem of Traverse Des Sioux Library Cooperative
Open Mon 9-12 & 12:30-7:30, Tues & Fri 9-12 & 12:30-5:30, Wed 9-12 & 12:30-6:30, Sat 9-12
Friends of the Library Group

ATWATER

P ATWATER PUBLIC LIBRARY*, 322 Atlantic Ave W, 56209. (Mail add: PO Box 465, 56209-0465), SAN 348-0992. Tel: 320-974-3363. *Librn,* Lynda Behm; E-mail: lynda.behm@pioneerland.lib.mn.us
Founded 1956. Pop 2,358; Circ 11,188
Library Holdings: AV Mats 716; Bk Titles 14,700; Per Subs 18; Talking Bks 171
Subject Interests: Animals, Farming
Mem of Pioneerland Library System
Open Mon 10:30-6:30, Tues, Thurs & Fri 3:30-6:30, Wed 1:30-6:30

AURORA

P AURORA PUBLIC LIBRARY, 14 W Second Ave N, 55705-1314. SAN 308-5120. Tel: 218-229-2021. *Librn,* Paula J Chapman; *Asst Librn,* Bonnie Harma
Founded 1914. Pop 1,679; Circ 31,460
Library Holdings: AV Mats 2,249; Bk Vols 21,006; Per Subs 54
Wireless access
Function: Adult bk club, Bks on CD, Children's prog, Computers for patron use, Copy machines, E-Reserves, Electronic databases & coll, Free DVD rentals, Handicapped accessible, ILL available, Life-long learning prog for all ages, Magazines, Movies, Music CDs, Online cat, Outreach serv, OverDrive digital audio bks, Photocopying/Printing, Preschool outreach, Prog for adults, Prog for children & young adult, Pub access computers, Ref serv in person, Spoken cassettes & CDs, Story hour, Summer & winter reading prog, Summer reading prog, Tax forms, VHS videos, Web-catalog, Wheelchair accessible, Winter reading prog
Open Mon 10-7:30, Tues-Thurs 1-7:30, Fri 10-5
Friends of the Library Group

AUSTIN

P AUSTIN PUBLIC LIBRARY*, 323 Fourth Ave NE, 55912-3370. SAN 347-190X. Tel: 507-433-2391. FAX: 507-433-8787. TDD: 507-433-8665. E-mail: aplref@selco.info. Web Site: www.austinpubliclibrary.org. *Dir,* Ann Hokanson; Staff 4 (MLS 3, Non-MLS 1)
Founded 1904. Pop 38,890; Circ 280,069
Library Holdings: Bk Titles 89,051; Per Subs 352
Subject Interests: Local hist
Automation Activity & Vendor Info: (Cataloging) Horizon; (Circulation) Horizon; (OPAC) Horizon
Publications: Library Link; Reading Reporter
Mem of CTLS, Inc (Connecting Texas Libraries Statewide)
Special Services for the Deaf - TDD equip
Open Mon-Thurs 9-9, Fri & Sat 9-5, Sun 1-5
Friends of the Library Group

J RIVERLAND COMMUNITY COLLEGE*, Austin Campus Library, 1600 Eighth Ave NW, 55912. SAN 308-5139. Tel: 507-433-0533. FAX: 507-433-0515. E-mail: library@riverland.edu. Web Site: www.riverland.edu/library. *Librn,* Jeannie Kearney; Staff 2 (MLS 1, Non-MLS 1)
Founded 1940. Enrl 2,500
Library Holdings: Bk Vols 26,147; Per Subs 100
Automation Activity & Vendor Info: (Cataloging) OCLC; (Circulation) Ex Libris Group; (Course Reserve) Ex Libris Group; (ILL) PALS; (OPAC) Ex Libris Group
Database Vendor: EBSCOhost, OVID Technologies, ProQuest
Wireless access
Partic in Minitex Library Information Network; OCLC Online Computer Library Center, Inc
Open Mon-Fri 9-6:30, Sat 9 - 2

BABBITT

P BABBITT PUBLIC LIBRARY*, 71 South Dr, 55706-1232. SAN 308-5155. Tel: 218-827-3345. FAX: 218-827-3345. E-mail: als@arrowhead.lib.mn.us. Web Site: arrowhead.library.mn.us. *Librn,* Debby Bocnuk; *Asst Librn,* Sandy Gibson
Founded 1959. Pop 1,562; Circ 37,043
Library Holdings: Bk Vols 33,429; Per Subs 16
Special Collections: Babbitt History Coll, bulletins, clippings, pictures
Automation Activity & Vendor Info: (Cataloging) SirsiDynix; (Circulation) SirsiDynix; (OPAC) SirsiDynix
Mem of Arrowhead Library System
Open Mon 10-7, Tues & Thurs 12-7, Wed & Fri 12-5
Friends of the Library Group

BAUDETTE

P BAUDETTE PUBLIC LIBRARY*, 110 First Ave SW, 56623. (Mail add: PO Box 739, 56623-0739), SAN 308-5163. Tel: 218-634-2329. FAX: 218-634-2329. *Dir,* Roxanne Larson
Founded 1912. Pop 1,170; Circ 25,281
Library Holdings: Bk Vols 10,413; Per Subs 38
Automation Activity & Vendor Info: (Cataloging) SirsiDynix; (Circulation) SirsiDynix; (OPAC) SirsiDynix
Database Vendor: ProQuest
Mem of Arrowhead Library System
Open Mon, Tues, Thurs & Fri (Winter) 10-4, Wed 10-6:30, Sat 10-12:30; Mon, Tues & Fri (Summer) 10-4, Wed & Thurs 10-6:30

BAYPORT

P BAYPORT PUBLIC LIBRARY*, 582 N Fourth St, 55003-1111. SAN 308-5171. Tel: 651-275-4416. FAX: 651-275-4417. E-mail: books@bayportlibrary.org. Web Site: www.bayportlibrary.org. *Dir,* Kathy L MacDonald; E-mail: kmacdonald@ci.bayport.mn.us
Founded 1960. Pop 3,220; Circ 58,908
Library Holdings: Bk Vols 31,000; Per Subs 138
Special Collections: Large Print Coll; Local History Coll
Automation Activity & Vendor Info: (Cataloging) Horizon; (Circulation) Horizon; (OPAC) Horizon
Wireless access
Publications: Library Log
Partic in Metropolitan Library Service Agency
Open Mon 10-8, Tues 10-6, Wed & Thurs 12-8, Fri 10-5, Sat (Sept-May) 10-2
Friends of the Library Group

S MINNESOTA CORRECTIONAL FACILITY*, Education Library, 970 Pickett St N, Education/Library, 55003-1490. SAN 308-8103. Tel: 651-779-2700, Ext 2575. FAX: 651-351-3602. *Librn,* Deborah Garbison; Staff 1 (MLS 1)
Founded 1979
Library Holdings: High Interest/Low Vocabulary Bk Vols 100; Large Print Bks 100; Bk Titles 8,356; Bk Vols 10,313; Per Subs 53; Videos 500
Subject Interests: Law
Automation Activity & Vendor Info: (Cataloging) Follett Software; (Circulation) Follett Software; (OPAC) Follett Software; (Serials) Follett Software
Open Mon-Thurs 1-8:45, Fri 8-3

BEMIDJI

P BEMIDJI PUBLIC LIBRARY*, 509 America Ave NW, 56601. SAN 320-4529. Tel: 218-751-3963. FAX: 218-333-0523. E-mail: bemidji@krls.org. *Br Mgr,* Paul Ericsson; Staff 8 (MLS 1, Non-MLS 7)
Founded 1907. Pop 45,264; Circ 219,959
Library Holdings: Bk Titles 62,932
Subject Interests: Native Am studies
Automation Activity & Vendor Info: (Acquisitions) Innovative Interfaces, Inc; (Circulation) Innovative Interfaces, Inc; (OPAC) Innovative Interfaces, Inc
Database Vendor: EBSCOhost, ProQuest
Wireless access
Publications: Friends (Newsletter)
Mem of Kitchigami Regional Library
Special Services for the Deaf - Assisted listening device; Bks on deafness & sign lang
Special Services for the Blind - Accessible computers; Assistive/Adapted tech devices, equip & products; Extensive large print coll; Low vision equip
Open Mon-Thurs 9-7, Fri & Sat 9-5
Friends of the Library Group

C BEMIDJI STATE UNIVERSITY*, A C Clark Library, 1500 Birchmont Dr NE, No 28, 56601-2699. SAN 308-518X. Tel: 218-755-3342. Circulation Tel: 218-755-3345. Interlibrary Loan Service Tel: 218-755-2968. Toll Free

Tel: 800-860-0234. FAX: 218-755-2051. Web Site: www.bemidjistate.edu/library. *VPres,* Robert Griggs; *Acq/Ser Librn,* Tammy Bobrowsky; Tel: 218-755-4110; *Cat Librn,* Dianne Narum; Tel: 218-755-3340; *ILL Librn,* Pat Conely; Tel: 218-755-3339; *Libr Instruction, Spec Coll & Archives Librn,* William Shaman; Tel: 218-755-3349; *Circ, Syst & Distance Learning Librn,* Peter McDonnell; Tel: 218-755-2967; *Circ, Libr Tech,* Mary K Leuthard; Tel: 218-755-2956; Staff 10 (MLS 5, Non-MLS 5)
Founded 1919. Enrl 4,955; Fac 311; Highest Degree: Master
Library Holdings: Bk Titles 361,317; Bk Vols 459,421
Special Collections: US Document Depository
Subject Interests: Am Indian hist, Northern Minn hist
Database Vendor: EBSCOhost, Gale Cengage Learning, LexisNexis, Newsbank, OCLC FirstSearch, OVID Technologies, ProQuest, SerialsSolutions, Wilson - Wilson Web
Wireless access
Partic in OCLC Online Computer Library Center, Inc
Open Mon-Thurs 7:45am-11:45pm, Fri 7:45-8:45, Sat 11-4:45, Sun 1-11:45
Friends of the Library Group

JR OAK HILLS CHRISTIAN COLLEGE*, Cummings Library, 1600 Oak Hills Rd SW, 56601-8832. SAN 308-5198. Tel: 218-751-8670, Ext 1299. FAX: 218-751-8825. E-mail: it@oakhills.edu. Web Site: www.oakhills.edu. *Dir,* Keith Bush; Staff 2 (Non-MLS 2)
Founded 1946. Enrl 155; Fac 13
Library Holdings: Bk Vols 25,000; Per Subs 160
Subject Interests: Philos, Relig studies

BENSON

P BENSON PUBLIC LIBRARY*, 200 13th St N, 56215-1223. SAN 308-5201. Tel: 320-842-7981. FAX: 320-843-4948. E-mail: benson@benson.lib.mn.us. Web Site: www.bensonlibrary.com. *Actg Librn,* Cindy Hendrick
Founded 1913. Circ 53,129
Library Holdings: Bk Vols 19,000; Per Subs 50
Mem of Pioneerland Library System
Open Mon, Tues & Thurs 10-7, Wed & Fri 10-6, Sat 10-4
Friends of the Library Group

SR OUR REDEEMERS LUTHERAN CHURCH LIBRARY*, 800 Tenth St S, 56215. SAN 308-521X. Tel: 320-843-3151. *Librn,* Marlene Skold
Founded 1956
Library Holdings: Bk Vols 1,900; Videos 30
Open Mon-Sun 8-4

BIRD ISLAND

P BIRD ISLAND PUBLIC LIBRARY*, 260 S Main, 55310-1226. (Mail add: PO Box 217, 55310-0217), SAN 348-1026. Tel: 320-365-4640. FAX: 320-365-4640. *Librn,* Shirley Schulte; E-mail: shirleys@birdisland.lib.mn.us
Pop 1,320; Circ 16,414
Library Holdings: Large Print Bks 120; Bk Vols 11,400; Per Subs 23; Talking Bks 275
Automation Activity & Vendor Info: (Cataloging) Innovative Interfaces, Inc; (Circulation) Innovative Interfaces, Inc; (OPAC) Innovative Interfaces, Inc
Function: Homebound delivery serv, ILL available, Online searches, Photocopying/Printing, Prog for adults, Prog for children & young adult, Summer reading prog, Wheelchair accessible
Mem of Pioneerland Library System
Open Mon 6-8, Tues & Wed 10-5, Thurs 10-4 & 6-8, Fri 9-2

BLACKDUCK

P BLACKDUCK COMMUNITY LIBRARY*, 72 First St SE, 56630. (Mail add: PO Box 326, 56630-0119), SAN 347-772X. Tel: 218-835-6600. FAX: 218-835-6600. E-mail: blackduck@krls.org. Web Site: www.krls.org. *Librn,* Nance M Kunkel; *Asst Librn,* Paula Erickson; Staff 2 (Non-MLS 2)
Founded 1909. Pop 5,000; Circ 20,000
Library Holdings: Bks on Deafness & Sign Lang 4; Braille Volumes 1; CDs 100; DVDs 60; High Interest/Low Vocabulary Bk Vols 10; Large Print Bks 600; Bk Vols 16,500; Per Subs 35; Talking Bks 200; Videos 500
Special Collections: Hispanic Materials Coll
Automation Activity & Vendor Info: (Acquisitions) Innovative Interfaces, Inc
Database Vendor: Baker & Taylor, BWI, EBSCO Auto Repair Reference, EBSCO Information Services, EBSCOhost, Gale Cengage Learning, OCLC FirstSearch, OCLC WorldShare Interlibrary Loan, ProQuest
Wireless access
Function: ILL available
Mem of Kitchigami Regional Library
Open Tues & Fri 2-6, Wed & Sat 9-1, Thurs 3-7

BLAINE

P ANOKA COUNTY LIBRARY*, 707 County Rd 10 NE, 55434-2398. SAN 347-2027. Tel: 763-785-3695. FAX: 763-717-3262. E-mail: register@co.anoka.mn.us. Web Site: anokacountylibrary.org. *Dir,* Marlene Moulton Janssen; E-mail: Marlene.MoultonJanssen@anoka.mn.us; Staff 33 (MLS 21, Non-MLS 12)
Founded 1958. Pop 313,033; Circ 2,920,574
Jan 2007-Dec 2007 Income $7,202,711. Mats Exp $856,038. Sal $6,365,690
Library Holdings: Bk Vols 614,106; Per Subs 1,377
Automation Activity & Vendor Info: (Acquisitions) SirsiDynix; (Cataloging) SirsiDynix; (Circulation) SirsiDynix; (OPAC) SirsiDynix; (Serials) SirsiDynix
Database Vendor: SirsiDynix
Wireless access
Partic in Metropolitan Library Service Agency
Open Mon & Wed 12-8, Tues & Thurs 10-6, Fri 12-6, Sat 10-5
Friends of the Library Group
Branches: 8
CENTENNIAL, 100 Civic Heights Circle, Circle Pines, 55014-1786. (Mail add: 707 County Rd Ten NE, 55434-2398), SAN 347-2051. Tel: 763-717-3294. FAX: 763-717-3297. *Librn,* Carrie Braaten; Staff 3 (MLS 1, Non-MLS 2)
Library Holdings: Bk Vols 44,083; Per Subs 100
Open Mon-Wed 12-8, Tues & Thurs 10-6, Fri 12-6, Sat 10-5
CROOKED LAKE, 11440 Crooked Lake Blvd, Coon Rapids, 55433-3441, SAN 347-2116. Tel: 763-576-5972. FAX: 763-576-5973. *Br Librn,* Jenn Straumann; Staff 5 (MLS 1, Non-MLS 4)
Library Holdings: Bk Vols 63,226; Per Subs 137
Open Mon-Thurs 10-9, Fri & Sat 10-5:30
JOHNSVILLE, 12461 Oak Park Blvd, 55434. (Mail add: 707 County Rd 10 NE, 55434-2398), SAN 326-8039. Tel: 763-767-3853. FAX: 763-767-3878. *Librn,* Stephanie Opstad
Open Mon & Wed 12-8, Tues & Thurs 10-6, Fri 12-6, Sat 10-5
Friends of the Library Group
MISSISSIPPI, 410 Mississippi St NE, Fridley, 55432-4416. (Mail add: 707 County Rd 10 NE, 55434-2398), SAN 347-2140. Tel: 763-571-1934. FAX: 763-574-8026. *Br Mgr,* Theresa Schroeder; Staff 3 (MLS 3)
Library Holdings: Bk Vols 52,880; Per Subs 155
Open Mon & Wed 12-8, Tues & Thurs 10-6, Fri 12-6, Sat 10-5
Friends of the Library Group
NORTH CENTRAL, 17565 Central Ave NE, Ham Lake, 55304-4302, SAN 347-2175. Tel: 763-434-6542. FAX: 763-434-6542. *Librn,* Susan Webb; Staff 1 (Non-MLS 1)
Library Holdings: Bk Vols 29,549; Per Subs 70
Open Mon & Wed 12-8, Tues & Thurs-Sat 10-5:30
NORTHTOWN, 711 County Rd 10 NE, 55434-2398. (Mail add: 707 County Rd 10 NE, 55434-2398), SAN 347-2035. Tel: 763-717-3267. FAX: 763-717-3259. *Librn,* Ruth Hemingson
Open Mon & Wed 12-8, Tues & Thurs 10-6, Fri 12-6, Sat 10-5, Sun (Sept-May) 1-5
Friends of the Library Group
RUM RIVER, 4201 Sixth Ave N, Anoka, 55303. (Mail add: 707 County Rd 10 NE, 55434-2398), SAN 329-5842. Tel: 763-576-4695. FAX: 763-576-4699. *Librn,* Kim Johnson
Open Mon & Wed 12-8, Tues & Thurs 10-6, Fri 12-6, Sat 10-5
Friends of the Library Group
ST FRANCIS BRANCH, 3519 Bridge St NW, Saint Francis, 55070-9754. (Mail add: 707 County Rd 10 NE, 55434), SAN 347-2191. Tel: 763-753-2131. FAX: 763-753-0085. *Librn,* Mary Healy
Open Mon & Wed 12-8, Tues & Thurs 10-12 & 1-6, Fri 12-6, Sat (Sept-May) 10-2
Friends of the Library Group

BLOOMINGTON

L LARKIN, HOFFMAN, DALY & LINDGREN*, Law Library, 7900 Xerxes Ave S, Ste 1500, 55431. SAN 372-283X. Tel: 952-835-3800. FAX: 952-896-3333. Web Site: larkinhoffman.com. *Librn,* Marilynn Hallen; E-mail: mhallen@larkinhoffman.com
Library Holdings: Bk Vols 15,000; Per Subs 125
Database Vendor: Westlaw
Wireless access
Open Mon-Fri 8:30-5

J NORMANDALE COMMUNITY COLLEGE LIBRARY*, 9700 France Ave S, 55431. SAN 308-5252. Tel: 952-487-8290. Reference Tel: 952-487-8295. FAX: 952-487-8101. TDD: 952-487-7032. Web Site: www.normandale.edu/library. *Chair, Head, Circ, Head, Per,* Carol Johnson; Tel: 952-487-8298, E-mail: carol.johnson@normandale.edu; *Head, Acq, Head, Coll Develop, Head, Coll Serv,* Rosalie Bunge; Tel: 952-487-8296, E-mail: rosalie.bunge@normandale.edu; *Head, Automation, Head, Cat,* Adam G Marsnik; Tel: 952-487-8297, E-mail: adam.marsnik@normandale.edu; *Circ Tech, Head, ILL,* JoAnn Jucko;

E-mail: joann.hucko@normandale.edu; *Acq,* Lorna I Redding; Tel: 952-487-8292, E-mail: lorna.redding@normandale.edu; *Acq,* Kathryn Rudd; E-mail: kathryn.rudd@normandale.edu; *Cat, Libr Tech,* Jacqueline Burns; Tel: 952-487-8293, E-mail: jacqueline.burns@normandale.edu; *Circ,* Tim Albrecht; Tel: 952-487-8444, E-mail: tim.albrecht@normandale.edu; *Circ,* Susan Borgfelt; Tel: 952-487-8437, E-mail: susan.borgfelt@normandale.edu; *Circ,* Constance Navratil; E-mail: constance.navratil@normandale.edu; *Libr Tech, Per,* Kimberly Christianson; Tel: 952-487-8291, E-mail: kimberly.christianson@normandale.edu; *Ref,* Susan Milis; E-mail: susan.milis@normandale.edu; *Ref,* Tom Tollman; Tel: 952-487-8294, E-mail: tom.tollman@normandale.edu; *Technology Tech,* Mayya Rabinovich; Tel: 952-487-7092, E-mail: mayya.rabinovich@normandale.edu; Staff 14 (MLS 5, Non-MLS 9)
Founded 1968. Enrl 14,129; Fac 349; Highest Degree: Associate
Jul 2008-Jun 2009 Income $964,892. Mats Exp $347,216, Books $158,958, Per/Ser (Incl. Access Fees) $65,487, Micro $19,908, AV Mat $33,845, Electronic Ref Mat (Incl. Access Fees) $68,170, Presv $848. Sal $659,292
Library Holdings: AV Mats 12,671; Bks on Deafness & Sign Lang 27; Electronic Media & Resources 1,211; High Interest/Low Vocabulary Bk Vols 15; Large Print Bks 133; Bk Titles 89,733; Bk Vols 95,477; Per Subs 650; Talking Bks 118
Special Collections: Career & Academic Planning Center; College Success Center; Minnesota Authors Coll; Picture Books Coll; Writing Center
Subject Interests: Juv lit, Minn hist
Automation Activity & Vendor Info: (Acquisitions) Ex Libris Group; (Cataloging) Ex Libris Group; (Circulation) Ex Libris Group; (Course Reserve) Ex Libris Group; (ILL) Ex Libris Group; (OPAC) Ex Libris Group; (Serials) Ex Libris Group
Database Vendor: ABC-CLIO, Baker & Taylor, BioOne, Cambridge Scientific Abstracts, EBSCOhost, Gale Cengage Learning, LexisNexis, Newsbank, OCLC FirstSearch, OVID Technologies, ProQuest, SerialsSolutions, Wilson - Wilson Web
Wireless access
Function: AV serv, Distance learning, Doc delivery serv, Handicapped accessible, ILL available, Libr develop, Photocopying/Printing, Ref serv available, Wheelchair accessible
Publications: New Materials Added to the Normandale Library (Acquisition list)
Partic in Minitex Library Information Network; MnPALS; OCLC Online Computer Library Center, Inc
Open Mon-Thurs 7:45am-9:50pm, Fri 7:45-6, Sat 9-4:50

C NORTHWESTERN HEALTH SCIENCES UNIVERSITY*, Greenawalt Library, 2501 W 84th St, 55431-1599. SAN 308-7816. Tel: 952-885-5419. Interlibrary Loan Service Tel: 952-885-5463. FAX: 952-884-3318. Web Site: www.nwhealth.edu. *Dir, Libr Serv,* Della Shupe; Tel: 952-885-5417, E-mail: dshupe@nwhealth.edu; *Pub Serv,* Anne Mackereth; Tel: 952-885-5419, Ext 218, E-mail: amackereth@nwhealth.edu; *Ser,* Dian Larson; E-mail: dlarson@nwhealth.edu; *Tech Serv,* Ann Kempke; Tel: 952-885-5419, Ext 221, E-mail: akempke@nwhealth.edu; Staff 4 (MLS 4)
Founded 1966. Enrl 800; Fac 75; Highest Degree: Doctorate
Library Holdings: Bk Titles 15,540; Per Subs 305
Special Collections: Acupuncture & Oriental Medicine Journals & Other Materials; Chiropractic Journals & Other Materials; Complementary & Alternative Medicine Journals & Other Materials; Therapeutic Massage Coll
Automation Activity & Vendor Info: (Cataloging) TLC (The Library Corporation); (Circulation) TLC (The Library Corporation); (OPAC) TLC (The Library Corporation); (Serials) TLC (The Library Corporation)
Database Vendor: EBSCOhost, OCLC FirstSearch, OCLC WorldShare Interlibrary Loan, OVID Technologies
Wireless access
Publications: New Materials List (Monthly)
Partic in Chiropractic Libr Consortium; Health Scis Librs of Minn; Twin Cities Biomedical Consortium
Open Mon-Thurs 7:30am-11pm, Fri 7:30-7, Sat 10-6, Sun 9am-10pm

BLUE EARTH

P BLUE EARTH COMMUNITY LIBRARY*, 124 W Seventh St, 56013-1308. SAN 372-5790. Tel: 507-526-5012. FAX: 507-526-4683. TDD: 507-526-5638. E-mail: libtfb@tds.lib.mn.us. Web Site: libraries.tds.lib.mn.us/blueearth. *Dir,* Eva Gaydon; *Ch Serv,* Lena Lee; Staff 7 (MLS 1, Non-MLS 6)
Founded 1902. Pop 4,000
Library Holdings: Bk Titles 35,212; Bk Vols 38,322; Per Subs 70
Special Collections: DVD videos; Local newspapers from 1861
Subject Interests: Local hist
Automation Activity & Vendor Info: (Cataloging) PALS; (Circulation) PALS; (ILL) PALS; (OPAC) PALS
Database Vendor: Gale Cengage Learning, OCLC FirstSearch
Mem of Traverse Des Sioux Library Cooperative
Special Services for the Deaf - TDD equip
Open Mon-Thurs 10-8, Fri 8:30-5, Sat 10-1

BOVEY

P BOVEY PUBLIC LIBRARY*, 402 Second St, 55709. (Mail add: PO Box 130, 55709-0130), SAN 308-5279. Tel: 218-245-3691. FAX: 218-245-3691. *Dir,* Patrick Perry; E-mail: pperry@arrowhead.lib.mn.us
Founded 1930. Pop 858; Circ 12,574
Library Holdings: Bk Vols 20,000; Per Subs 50
Special Collections: Genealogy Coll
Automation Activity & Vendor Info: (Cataloging) SirsiDynix; (Circulation) SirsiDynix; (OPAC) SirsiDynix
Mem of Arrowhead Library System
Open Mon & Thurs 9:30-8, Tues & Wed 12-8, Fri 11-5

BRAINERD

P BRAINERD PUBLIC LIBRARY*, 416 S Fifth St, 56401. SAN 320-4537. Tel: 218-829-5574. FAX: 218-829-0055. E-mail: brainerd@krls.org. Web Site: www.krls.org.
Founded 1882. Pop 40,000; Circ 322,555
Library Holdings: Bk Vols 80,000
Special Collections: Foundation Center Cooperating Coll
Automation Activity & Vendor Info: (Acquisitions) Innovative Interfaces, Inc; (Cataloging) Innovative Interfaces, Inc; (Circulation) Innovative Interfaces, Inc; (Course Reserve) Innovative Interfaces, Inc; (ILL) Innovative Interfaces, Inc; (Media Booking) Innovative Interfaces, Inc; (OPAC) Innovative Interfaces, Inc; (Serials) Innovative Interfaces, Inc
Function: Handicapped accessible, ILL available, Photocopying/Printing, Prog for children & young adult, Summer reading prog, Telephone ref, Wheelchair accessible, Workshops
Mem of Kitchigami Regional Library
Open Mon-Thurs 9-8, Fri 9-6, Sat 9-3
Friends of the Library Group
Bookmobiles: 1

J CENTRAL LAKES COLLEGE LIBRARY*, 501 W College Dr, 56401. SAN 308-5287. Tel: 218-855-8178. Toll Free Tel: 800-933-0346, Ext 8178. FAX: 218-855-8179. Web Site: www.clcmn.edu/library. *Librn,* Larry M Kellerman; E-mail: lkellerm@clcmn.edu
Founded 1938. Enrl 3,600; Fac 130
Library Holdings: AV Mats 3,100; e-books 4,200; Bk Titles 41,000; Bk Vols 45,600; Per Subs 210
Special Collections: American Indian Coll
Subject Interests: Hist, Law enforcement, Local govt, Nursing
Automation Activity & Vendor Info: (Cataloging) Ex Libris Group; (Circulation) Ex Libris Group; (Course Reserve) Ex Libris Group; (ILL) Ex Libris Group; (OPAC) Ex Libris Group
Wireless access
Publications: Library Handbook
Partic in OCLC Online Computer Library Center, Inc
Open Mon-Thurs 8am-9pm, Fri 8-4

S CROW WING COUNTY HISTORICAL SOCIETY ARCHIVES LIBRARY*, 320 Laurel St, 56401-3523. (Mail add: PO Box 722, 56401-0722), SAN 326-0291. Tel: 218-829-3268. FAX: 218-828-4434. *Exec Dir,* Mary Lou Moudry
Founded 1983
Library Holdings: Bk Vols 300
Special Collections: Brainerd Address Directories 1901-present; Forsythe-Hoffman Diaries
Subject Interests: Local hist
Partic in Northern Lights Library Network
Open Tues-Fri (Winter) 1-4:30, Sat 10-1:30; Mon-Fri (Summer) 10-12 & 1-3:30
Restriction: Non-circulating to the pub

BRECKENRIDGE

S WILKIN COUNTY MUSEUM LIBRARY*, 704 Nebraska Ave, 56520. SAN 373-224X. Tel: 218-643-1303, 218-643-1703. *In Charge,* Ruth Poppel
Library Holdings: Bk Vols 1,000
Subject Interests: Genealogy, Local hist
Open Tues-Thurs (Summer) 1:30-4

BROOKLYN PARK

J NORTH HENNEPIN COMMUNITY COLLEGE LIBRARY*, 7411 85th Ave N, 55445-2298. SAN 308-5295. Tel: 763-424-0732. Circulation Tel: 763-424-0739. Interlibrary Loan Service Tel: 763-424-0935. Reference Tel: 763-424-0734. Administration Tel: 763-424-0738. Toll Free Tel: 800-818-0395. FAX: 763-493-3569. Web Site: www.nhcc.edu/library. *Librn,* Lisa Forslund; E-mail: lisa.forslund@nhcc.edu; *Librn,* Craig Larson; Tel: 763-424-0733, E-mail: clarson@nhcc.edu; Staff 6 (MLS 2, Non-MLS 4)
Founded 1966. Enrl 8,100; Fac 200; Highest Degree: Associate
Library Holdings: AV Mats 3,162; Bk Titles 37,178; Bk Vols 42,000

Automation Activity & Vendor Info: (Acquisitions) Ex Libris Group; (Cataloging) Ex Libris Group; (Circulation) Ex Libris Group; (Course Reserve) Ex Libris Group; (ILL) Ex Libris Group; (OPAC) Ex Libris Group
Database Vendor: EBSCOhost, Electric Library, OCLC WorldShare Interlibrary Loan, ProQuest
Wireless access
Partic in Minitex Library Information Network; OCLC Online Computer Library Center, Inc
Open Mon-Thurs 7:30am-10pm, Fri 7:30-4, Sat 8:30-4, Sun 12:30-4

BROWNS VALLEY

P BROWNS VALLEY PUBLIC LIBRARY*, 15 S Third St, 56219. (Mail add: PO Box 307, 56219-0307), SAN 320-894X. Tel: 320-695-2318. FAX: 320-695-2125. *Dir,* Bernice Piechowski; E-mail: bpiechowski@brownsvalley.lib.mn.us
Founded 1908. Pop 957; Circ 22,941
Library Holdings: AV Mats 1,275; Large Print Bks 350; Bk Vols 16,630; Per Subs 101; Talking Bks 75
Special Collections: Native American Coll
Automation Activity & Vendor Info: (Cataloging) Horizon; (Circulation) Horizon; (OPAC) Horizon
Wireless access
Mem of Viking Library System
Open Mon, Tues & Thurs 1-6, Wed & Fri 10-6, Sat 9-12

BROWNSDALE

P BROWNSDALE GRACE GILLETTE PUBLIC LIBRARY*, 103 E Main St, 55918-8817. (Mail add: PO Box 302, 55918-0302), SAN 347-1934. Tel: 507-567-9951. FAX: 507-567-2250. Web Site: brownsdale.lib.mn.us. *Librn,* Debara Smith; E-mail: dsmith@selco.info
Jan 2006-Dec 2006 Income $17,582. Mats Exp $4,150. Sal $10,000
Library Holdings: Bk Vols 9,574; Per Subs 10
Partic in Southeastern Libraries Cooperating
Open Mon, Wed & Fri 12:30-5:30, Tues 9-2, Thurs 3-8

BROWNTON

P BROWNTON PUBLIC LIBRARY*, 528 Second St N, 55312. (Mail add: PO Box 97, 55312-0097), SAN 348-1050. Tel: 320-328-5900. FAX: 320-328-5318. *Librn,* Jackie Fountain
Founded 1978. Pop 801; Circ 10,176
Library Holdings: AV Mats 45; DVDs 35; Large Print Bks 200; Bk Vols 6,295; Per Subs 21; Videos 70
Mem of Pioneerland Library System
Open Mon 3:30-7, Tues 1-5, Wed 2-5, Thurs 9-12 & 1-5, Sat 10-12

BUHL

P BUHL PUBLIC LIBRARY*, 400 Jones Ave, 55713. (Mail add: PO Box 664, 55713-0664), SAN 308-5309. Tel: 218-258-3391. FAX: 218-258-3391. Web Site: www.buhl.lib.mn.us. *Libr Dir,* April K Larson
Founded 1918. Circ 27,000
Automation Activity & Vendor Info: (Cataloging) Horizon; (Circulation) Horizon; (OPAC) Horizon
Database Vendor: EBSCOhost, Gale Cengage Learning
Open Mon-Fri 10-5
Friends of the Library Group

BURNSVILLE

M FAIRVIEW-RIDGES HOSPITAL*, Medical Staff Library, 201 E Nicollet Blvd, 55337. SAN 370-8519. Tel: 952-892-2414. FAX: 952-892-2277. Web Site: www.fairview.org. *Librn,* Janet Erdman; E-mail: jerdman2@fairview.org
Library Holdings: Bk Titles 1,200; Per Subs 75
Wireless access

CALEDONIA

P CALEDONIA PUBLIC LIBRARY*, 231 E Main St, 55921-1321. SAN 308-5317. Tel: 507-725-2671. FAX: 507-725-5258. Web Site: www.caledonia.govoffice.com. *Librn,* Marla Burns; E-mail: marla@selco.info; *Asst Librn,* Eileen Jacobson; Staff 1 (MLS 1)
Founded 1895. Pop 3,465; Circ 35,350
Library Holdings: AV Mats 550; Large Print Bks 58; Bk Titles 21,752; Per Subs 73; Talking Bks 250
Special Collections: Caledonia Argus (newspaper) 1900 - present; Caledonia Journal, 1868-1956
Open Tues & Thurs 9:30-12 & 1-5:30, Wed & Fri 1-6:30, Sat 10-12
Friends of the Library Group

CALUMET

P CALUMET PUBLIC LIBRARY*, 932 Gary St, 55716. (Mail add: PO Box 356, 55716), SAN 308-5325. Tel: 218-247-3108. FAX: 218-247-3108. *Librn,* Melanie Lefebvre
Pop 460; Circ 2,446
Library Holdings: Bk Vols 7,000; Per Subs 15
Mem of Arrowhead Library System
Open Mon 1-7, Tues & Wed 1-5, Thurs 9-5

CAMBRIDGE

J ANOKA-RAMSEY COMMUNITY COLLEGE*, Cambridge Campus Library, 300 Spirit River Dr S, 55008. SAN 377-838X. Tel: 763-433-1807. Web Site: www.anokaramsey.edu/resources/Success/Library/CambridgeLibrary.aspx. *Librn,* Bonnie Boese; E-mail: bonnie.boese@anokaramsey.edu; *Libr Tech,* Martha Muehlhauser; Tel: 763-433-1875, E-mail: martha.muehlhauser@anokaramsey.edu; Staff 1 (Non-MLS 1)
Founded 1987. Enrl 1,000; Highest Degree: Associate
Library Holdings: AV Mats 1,200; CDs 285; e-books 8,000; Bk Titles 12,200; Bk Vols 14,600; Per Subs 129; Talking Bks 35
Special Collections: State Document Depository
Subject Interests: Art, Minn hist
Database Vendor: ARTstor, Baker & Taylor, Cinahl, CountryWatch, CQ Press, EBSCOhost, Gale Cengage Learning, H W Wilson, JSTOR, OCLC WorldShare Interlibrary Loan, OVID Technologies, ProQuest
Wireless access
Partic in MnPALS
Open Mon-Thurs (Winter) 8am-9pm, Fri 8-4:30, Sat 10-2; Mon & Thurs (Summer) 9-4:30, Tues & Wed 9-7

P EAST CENTRAL REGIONAL LIBRARY*, 244 S Birch, 55008-1588. SAN 347-2353. Tel: 763-689-7390. Toll Free Tel: 888-234-1293. FAX: 763-689-7389. E-mail: ecregion@ecrlib.org. Web Site: www.ecrlib.org. *Dir,* Barbara Misselt; E-mail: bmisselt@ecrlib.org; *Asst Dir,* Nick Dimassis; E-mail: ndimassis@ecrlib.org; *ILL Librn, Ref Librn,* Bob Gray; E-mail: bgray@ecrlib.org; *Tech Serv Librn,* Marilyn McGriff; E-mail: mmcgriff@ecrlib.org; *Youth & Commun Serv Librn,* Vickie Sorn; E-mail: vsorn@ecrlib.org; *Syst Coordr,* Andy Nordin; E-mail: anordin@ecrlib.org; Staff 8 (MLS 6, Non-MLS 2)
Founded 1959. Pop 175,494; Circ 1,271,237
Jan 2009-Dec 2009 Income $2,684,629, State $522,599, County $1,905,192, Locally Generated Income $50,040, Other $206,798. Mats Exp $386,561, Books $268,573, Per/Ser (Incl. Access Fees) $22,301, Electronic Ref Mat (Incl. Access Fees) $30,741. Sal $1,867,724
Library Holdings: Bk Titles 217,676; Bk Vols 388,155; Per Subs 635
Automation Activity & Vendor Info: (Cataloging) Evergreen; (Circulation) Evergreen; (ILL) Fretwell-Downing; (OPAC) Evergreen
Wireless access
Member Libraries: East Central Regional Library; McGregor Public Library; Mora Public Library; North Branch Area Library; Pine City Public Library; Princeton Area Library; Rush City Public Library, Sandstone Public Library
Partic in Central Minnesota Libraries Exchange; Minitex Library Information Network
Friends of the Library Group
Branches: 6
AITKIN PUBLIC LIBRARY, 110 First Ave NE, Aitkin, 56431-1319, SAN 347-2388. Tel: 218-927-2339. FAX: 218-927-2339. E-mail: aimail@ecrlib.org. Web Site: www.ecrlib.org/aitkin.html. *Librn,* Mary Beth Woodrow
Pop 7,450; Circ 58,110
Library Holdings: Bk Vols 10,000; Per Subs 60
Automation Activity & Vendor Info: (Cataloging) SirsiDynix; (Circulation) SirsiDynix; (OPAC) SirsiDynix
Database Vendor: EBSCOhost, Gale Cengage Learning
Mem of East Central Regional Library
Open Mon & Wed-Fri 9:30-5:30, Tues 9:30-7:30, Sat 9:30-3:30
Friends of the Library Group
CHISAGO LAKES AREA PUBLIC LIBRARY, 11754 302nd St, Chisago City, 55013, SAN 347-2442. Tel: 651-257-2817. FAX: 651-257-2817. E-mail: chisagolakes@ecrlib.org. Web Site: www.ecrlib.org/chisagolakes.html. *Br Supvr,* Carla Lydon; Staff 4 (MLS 1, Non-MLS 3)
Pop 10,500; Circ 27,310
Library Holdings: Bk Vols 18,000; Per Subs 50
Mem of East Central Regional Library
Open Mon & Fri Noon-6, Tues Noon-8, Wed 10-6, Thurs 10-8, Sat 10-2
Friends of the Library Group
HINCKLEY PUBLIC LIBRARY, 106 First St SE, Hinckley, 55037. (Mail add: PO Box 336, Hinckley, 55037-0336), SAN 347-2418. Tel: 320-384-6351. FAX: 320-384-6351. E-mail: hinckley@ecrlib.org. Web Site: www.ecrlib.org/hinckley.html. *Librn,* Cecile M Cross-Maser; Staff 1 (Non-MLS 1)

Pop 2,602; Circ 26,413
Library Holdings: Bk Vols 10,000; Per Subs 80
Automation Activity & Vendor Info: (Cataloging) SirsiDynix; (Circulation) SirsiDynix; (OPAC) SirsiDynix
Database Vendor: Gale Cengage Learning, ProQuest, SirsiDynix
Open Tues 10:30-5, Wed 12:30-8, Thurs 12:30-5, Fri 10:30-6, Sat 9-1

MCGREGOR PUBLIC LIBRARY, Center Ave & Second St, McGregor, 55760. (Mail add: PO Box 56, McGregor, 55760), SAN 347-2477. Tel: 218-768-3305. FAX: 218-768-3305. E-mail: mcgregor@ecrlib.org. Web Site: www.ecrlib.org/mcgregor.html. *Librn,* Penny R Olson
Pop 3,250; Circ 30,153
Library Holdings: AV Mats 1,805; Bk Titles 8,511; Per Subs 20
Automation Activity & Vendor Info: (Acquisitions) SirsiDynix; (Cataloging) SirsiDynix; (Circulation) SirsiDynix; (ILL) PALS; (OPAC) SirsiDynix
Open Tues & Thurs 2-7, Wed 10-5:30, Fri 10-4:30, Sat 9-1
Friends of the Library Group

MILACA COMMUNITY LIBRARY, 235 First St E, Milaca, 56353-1122, SAN 347-2507. Tel: 320-983-3677. FAX: 320-983-3677. E-mail: mimail@ecrlib.org. Web Site: www.ecrlib.org/milaca.html. *Br Mgr,* Sharon Strack
Pop 7,587; Circ 30,568
Library Holdings: AV Mats 760; Bk Titles 9,847; Per Subs 40
Automation Activity & Vendor Info: (Cataloging) SirsiDynix; (Circulation) SirsiDynix; (OPAC) SirsiDynix
Database Vendor: EBSCOhost, Gale Cengage Learning
Mem of East Central Regional Library
Open Tues & Thurs 10-7, Wed & Fri 10-5, Sat 10-3
Friends of the Library Group

MILLE LACS COMMUNITY LIBRARY, 285 2nd Ave S, Isle, 56342-0147. (Mail add: PO Box 147, Isle, 56342), SAN 329-1510. Tel: 320-676-3929. FAX: 320-676-3929. E-mail: mlmail@ecrlib.org. Web Site: www.ecrlib.org/millelacslake.html. *Librn,* Katherine Morrow
Founded 1985. Pop 3,915; Circ 20,230
Library Holdings: Large Print Bks 400; Bk Vols 10,000; Per Subs 48
Automation Activity & Vendor Info: (Cataloging) SirsiDynix; (Circulation) SirsiDynix; (OPAC) SirsiDynix
Database Vendor: EBSCOhost, ProQuest
Mem of East Central Regional Library
Open Tues, Wed & Fri 10-5, Thurs 3-8, Sat 10-2
Friends of the Library Group

S ISANTI COUNTY HISTORICAL SOCIETY*, Reference Research Library, 33525 Flanders St NE, 55008. (Mail add: PO Box 525, 55008-0525), SAN 323-7257. Tel: 763-689-4229. FAX: 763-552-0740. E-mail: ichs@nsatel.net. Web Site: www.ichs.ws. *Bibliog Instr, Exec Dir,* Kathleen McCully; E-mail: ichsdirector@izoom.net; Staff 3 (Non-MLS 3)
Founded 1965
Library Holdings: Bk Vols 400; Per Subs 10; Spec Interest Per Sub 10
Special Collections: Swedish Immigration from Dalarna Sweden to Isanti County, bks, photogs, tapes. Oral History
Subject Interests: Swedish immigrants hist
Function: Archival coll, Bus archives, Newsp ref libr, Photocopying/Printing, Ref serv available, Res libr
Publications: Art & History Passport; Braham Minnesota, 100 Years 1899-1999; Home Folks II; Isanti County College; Isonti, Minnesota Centennial; Local Cemetery Records; Preserving a Sense of Heritage
Restriction: In-house use for visitors, Not a lending libr, Open to students, Pub use on premises

CANBY

P CANBY PUBLIC LIBRARY*, 110 Oscar Ave N, 56220-1332. SAN 308-5341. Tel: 507-223-5738. FAX: 507-223-5738. Web Site: www.canbylibrary.info. *Librn,* Kathie Behrens; Staff 2 (Non-MLS 2)
Founded 1928. Pop 2,081; Circ 51,399
Jan 2007-Dec 2007 Income $111,442, City $82,251, County $28,591, Locally Generated Income $600. Mats Exp $111,442, Books $10,000, Per/Ser (Incl. Access Fees) $1,700, Micro $30, AV Mat $2,469. Sal $58,888
Library Holdings: Bk Vols 20,000; Per Subs 81
Automation Activity & Vendor Info: (Cataloging) Innovative Interfaces, Inc; (Circulation) Innovative Interfaces, Inc; (OPAC) Innovative Interfaces, Inc
Function: Adult bk club, Audiobks via web, Bks on cassette, Bks on CD, Children's prog, Computer training, Computers for patron use, Copy machines, Fax serv, Free DVD rentals, Games & aids for the handicapped, Handicapped accessible, ILL available, Music CDs, Online cat, Online ref, Online searches, Photocopying/Printing, Prog for adults, Prog for children & young adult, Spoken cassettes & CDs, Summer reading prog, Tax forms, Teen prog, VHS videos
Mem of Pioneerland Library System
Partic in Library Information Network of Clackamas County
Open Mon, Tues, Thurs & Fri 10:30-1 & 1:30-6, Wed 12-6 & 6:30-7:30, Sat 10-3
Restriction: Non-resident fee

CANNON FALLS

P CANNON FALLS LIBRARY*, 306 W Mill St, 55009-2045. SAN 308-535X. Tel: 507-263-2804. E-mail: cfl_ill@selco.info. *Dir,* Justin C Padgett; Staff 1 (MLS 1)
Founded 1951. Pop 7,636; Circ 92,478
Library Holdings: AV Mats 4,726; Bks on Deafness & Sign Lang 29; Large Print Bks 210; Bk Titles 26,000; Per Subs 131; Talking Bks 1,067
Special Collections: Cannon Falls Beacon, microfilm, bd per; Family Search Geneological; Local Cemetery Indexes; Minnesota Census, microfilm (Goodhue County & Dakota County)
Subject Interests: Regional hist especially city, Regional hist especially county
Automation Activity & Vendor Info: (Acquisitions) SirsiDynix; (Cataloging) SirsiDynix; (Circulation) SirsiDynix; (OPAC) SirsiDynix; (Serials) SirsiDynix
Mem of Southeast Library System (SELS)
Partic in Southeastern Libraries Cooperating
Special Services for the Deaf - TTY equip
Special Services for the Blind - Reader equip
Open Mon & Fri 10-5, Tues-Thurs 12-8, Sat 9-2
Friends of the Library Group

CARLTON

P CARLTON PUBLIC LIBRARY*, 310 Chestnut Ave, 55718. (Mail add: PO Box 309, 55718-0309), SAN 308-5368. Tel: 218-384-3322. FAX: 218-384-4229. Web Site: www.cityofcarlton.com/library.htm. *Dir,* Karen Kemi; *Libr Assoc,* Carol Beckstrom; *Libr Assoc,* Sue Melin
Pop 884; Circ 5,661
Library Holdings: Large Print Bks 60; Bk Vols 7,500; Per Subs 21; Talking Bks 100; Videos 150
Mem of Arrowhead Library System
Open Tues & Thurs 11-7, Wed & Fri 11-4, Sat 9-1
Friends of the Library Group

CASS LAKE

P CASS LAKE COMMUNITY LIBRARY*, 223 Cedar, 56633. (Mail add: PO Box 836, 56633-0836), SAN 347-7789. Tel: 218-335-8865. FAX: 218-335-8865. E-mail: casslake@krls.org. Web Site: www.krls.org/cl. *Br Supvr,* Bona-Carol Enstrom
Pop 3,500; Circ 22,091
Library Holdings: Bk Vols 10,420; Per Subs 12
Automation Activity & Vendor Info: (Cataloging) Innovative Interfaces, Inc; (Circulation) Innovative Interfaces, Inc; (OPAC) Innovative Interfaces, Inc
Database Vendor: ProQuest
Mem of Kitchigami Regional Library
Open Tues 4-8, Wed & Sat 10-2, Thurs & Fri 1-5

C LEECH LAKE TRIBAL COLLEGE LIBRARY*, 6945 Littlewolf Rd NW, 56633. (Mail add: PO Box 180, 56633-0180). Tel: 218-335-4240. FAX: 218-335-4282. Web Site: www.lltc.edu. *Librn,* Melissa Pond; E-mail: melissa.pond@lltc.edu; Staff 1 (MLS 1)
Enrl 250; Fac 55; Highest Degree: Master
Library Holdings: AV Mats 250; Bk Vols 4,600; Per Subs 30
Special Collections: Native American-Ojibwe Coll. Oral History
Subject Interests: Culture, Environment, Hist, Maps, Native Am, Renewable energy
Automation Activity & Vendor Info: (Cataloging) Winnebago Software Co; (Circulation) Winnebago Software Co; (OPAC) Winnebago Software Co
Open Mon-Thurs 8-8, Fri 8-4:30
Restriction: Non-circulating to the pub

CENTER CITY

S HAZELDEN BETTY FORD FOUNDATION LIBRARY, Hazelden Library CO-4, 15251 Pleasant Valley Rd, 55012-0011. SAN 371-7372. Tel: 651-213-4093. Toll Free Tel: 800-257-7800. Web Site: www.hazelden.org/library. *Mgr,* Barbara Weiner; E-mail: bweiner@hazelden.org. Subject Specialists: *Addictions,* Barbara Weiner; Staff 1 (MLS 1)
Founded 1966
Library Holdings: AV Mats 2,500; Bk Titles 17,500; Per Subs 50
Special Collections: History of Alcoholism; Spirituality & Temperance (Hazelden Pittman Archives) manuscripts
Subject Interests: Addictions, Alcohol & drug counseling, Alcohol & drug treatment, Alcohol abuse, Alcohol addiction, Alcohol, drug & tobacco prevention, Drug abuse, Drug addiction, Drug rehab, Recovery, Self help, Spirituality, Substance abuse

Automation Activity & Vendor Info: (OPAC) Inmagic, Inc.
Wireless access
Partic in Central Minnesota Libraries Exchange; Docline; Health Scis Librs of Minn; Minitex Library Information Network

CHASKA

P CARVER COUNTY LIBRARY*, Four City Hall Plaza, 55318-1963. SAN 347-2655. Tel: 952-448-9395. FAX: 952-448-9392. Web Site: www.carverlib.org. *Dir,* Position Currently Open; *Asst Dir,* Janet Karius; E-mail: jkarius@co.carver.mn.us; Staff 5 (MLS 5)
Founded 1975
Library Holdings: Bk Vols 193,129; Per Subs 680
Automation Activity & Vendor Info: (Acquisitions) Innovative Interfaces, Inc; (Cataloging) Innovative Interfaces, Inc; (Circulation) Innovative Interfaces, Inc; (OPAC) Innovative Interfaces, Inc; (Serials) Innovative Interfaces, Inc
Database Vendor: Gale Cengage Learning
Partic in Metropolitan Library Service Agency
Open Mon-Fri 8-5
Friends of the Library Group
Branches: 5
CHANHASSEN BRANCH, 7711 Kerber Blvd, Chanhassen, 55317-9634. (Mail add: PO Box 1130, Chanhassen, 55317), SAN 347-2671. Tel: 952-227-1500. FAX: 952-227-1510. *Br Mgr,* Kathy Bognanni; E-mail: kbognanni@co.carver.mn.us
Open Mon-Thurs 10-9, Fri & Sat 10-5, Sun 1-5
Friends of the Library Group
CHASKA BRANCH, Three City Hall Plaza, 55318, SAN 347-268X. Tel: 952-448-3886. FAX: 952-279-5216. *Br Mgr,* Janet Karius
Open Mon-Thurs 10-8, Fri 10-5, Sat 10-3
Friends of the Library Group
NORWOOD YOUNG AMERICA BRANCH, 314 Elm St W, Norwood Young America, 55397, SAN 347-2779. Tel: 952-467-2665. FAX: 952-467-4219. *Br Mgr,* Heidi Hoks
Open Mon & Thurs 1-7, Tues & Fri 10-5, Wed 1-5, Sat 1-4
Friends of the Library Group
WACONIA BRANCH, 217 S Vine St, Waconia, 55387-1337, SAN 347-271X. Tel: 952-442-4714. FAX: 952-856-4242. *Br Mgr,* Heidi Hoks
Open Mon & Tues 10-8, Wed & Thurs 10-6, Fri 10-5, Sat 10-3
Friends of the Library Group
WATERTOWN BRANCH, 309 Lewis Ave, Watertown, 55388-0277, SAN 347-2744. Tel: 952-955-2939. FAX: 952-955-2939. *Br Mgr,* Heidi Hoks
Open Mon & Wed 1-8, Tues & Fri 1-5, Thurs 10-5, Sat 9-Noon
Friends of the Library Group

CHATFIELD

S CHATFIELD BRASS BAND, INC*, Music Lending Library, 81 Library Lane, 55923. (Mail add: PO Box 578, 55923-0578), SAN 326-0658. Tel: 507-867-3275. E-mail: chatband@selco.info. Web Site: www.chatfieldband.lib.mn.us. *Libr Mgr,* Teresa Cerling; E-mail: tcerling@selco.info; Staff 6 (Non-MLS 6)
Founded 1971
Library Holdings: Music Scores 75,000
Special Collections: Jan Bily Small Orchestra Coll
Wireless access
Publications: Newsletter
Mem of Southeast Library System (SELS)
Open Mon-Wed 8-12 & 1-4

P CHATFIELD PUBLIC LIBRARY*, 314 S Main St, 55923. SAN 308-5384. Tel: 507-867-3480. FAX: 507-867-3480. Web Site: www.chatfieldpubliclibrary.org. *Dir,* Monica Jean Erickson; E-mail: monica@selco.info; *Asst Librn,* Charlotte Brevig; *Ch Serv,* Kay Myhrom-Kirtz; Staff 4 (Non-MLS 4)
Founded 1911. Pop 5,436; Circ 37,934
Jan 2005-Dec 2005 Income $115,700. Mats Exp $17,661. Sal $54,700
Library Holdings: Bk Vols 19,000; Per Subs 42
Special Collections: Local History Coll
Automation Activity & Vendor Info: (Cataloging) SirsiDynix; (Circulation) SirsiDynix; (OPAC) SirsiDynix
Database Vendor: Gale Cengage Learning, ProQuest
Wireless access
Partic in Southeastern Libraries Cooperating
Open Tues & Wed 10-6:30, Thurs 10-8:30, Fri 9-5, Sat 9-2
Friends of the Library Group

CHISHOLM

P CHISHOLM PUBLIC LIBRARY*, 300 W Lake, 55719-1718. SAN 308-5392. Tel: 218-254-7913. FAX: 218-254-7952. *Libr Supvr-Popular Libr,* Mary Zaitz; E-mail: mzaitz@arrowhead.lib.mn.us
Pop 5,000; Circ 45,000
Jan 2007-Dec 2007 Income $235,300. Mats Exp $20,000. Sal $109,799
Library Holdings: Bk Vols 17,000; Per Subs 25
Automation Activity & Vendor Info: (Cataloging) SirsiDynix; (Circulation) SirsiDynix; (OPAC) SirsiDynix
Mem of Arrowhead Library System
Open Mon-Fri 8:30-5
Friends of the Library Group

S MINNESOTA DISCOVERY CENTER*, Iron Range Research Center Library, 801 SW Hwy 169, Ste 1, 55719. SAN 324-7716. Tel: 218-254-1222, 218-254-7959. Reference Tel: 218-254-1221. Toll Free Tel: 800-372-6437. FAX: 218-254-7971. E-mail: yourroots@mndiscovery.com. Web Site: mndiscoverycenter.com. *Exec VPres, Mus & Libr,* Steven D Harsin; Tel: 218-254-1220; *Librn,* Jessica Oftelie. Subject Specialists: *Genealogy, Hist,* Steven D Harsin; *Genealogy, Local hist,* Jessica Oftelie; Staff 5 (MLS 3, Non-MLS 2)
Founded 1979
Library Holdings: AV Mats 12,400; Bk Titles 7,000; Bk Vols 8,000; Spec Interest Per Sub 50
Special Collections: Butler Brothers/Hanna Mining Company Records; CCC Coll; Iron Range (manuscript records for local organizations); Iron Range City & Township Government Records; Jones & Laughlin Hill Annex Mining Records; Photograph Coll (historical photogs from the Iron Range); US Steel Photo Coll; USDA Superior National Forest Records. Municipal Document Depository; Oral History; State Document Depository
Subject Interests: Genealogy, Geol, Immigration, Labor, Local hist, Logging, Mining, Oral hist
Function: Archival coll, Copy machines, Electronic databases & coll, For res purposes, Genealogy discussion group, Handicapped accessible, ILL available, Mail & tel request accepted, Mus passes, Newsp ref libr, Online cat, Online ref, Outside serv via phone, mail, e-mail & web, Photocopying/Printing, Prog for adults, Prog for children & young adult, Ref & res, Ref serv available, Res libr, Telephone ref, Wheelchair accessible, Workshops
Publications: Entrepreneurs & Immigrants: Life on the Industrial Frontier of Northeastern Minnesota
Partic in Minitex Library Information Network
Open Tues, Wed, Sat & Sun 10-4:30, Thurs 10-9
Friends of the Library Group

CLARA CITY

P CLARA CITY PUBLIC LIBRARY*, 126 N Main St, 56222. (Mail add: PO Box 651, 56222-0651), SAN 347-688X. Tel: 320-847-3535. FAX: 320-847-3535. Web Site: www.montevideolibrary.org/clara-city-public-library. *Head Librn,* Karen Rothers; E-mail: karen.rothers@pioneerland.lib.mn.us
Library Holdings: Bk Vols 14,577; Per Subs 60
Wireless access
Mem of Pioneerland Library System
Open Mon & Wed 1-5:30 & 7-9, Tues & Thurs 1-6, Fri 1-5, Sat 9-3

CLOQUET

S CARLTON COUNTY HISTORICAL SOCIETY, 406 Cloquet Ave, 55720. SAN 328-1639. Tel: 218-879-1938. FAX: 218-879-1938. E-mail: director@carltoncountyhistory.org. Web Site: www.carltoncountyhistory.org. *Dir,* Rachael Martin; E-mail: rmartin@carltoncountyhistory.org
Founded 1949
Library Holdings: Bk Titles 450; Videos 50
Special Collections: Carlton County History Coll; The Fires of 1918 Coll, photog. Oral History
Subject Interests: Local hist
Wireless access
Open Tues-Sat 9-4
Restriction: Non-circulating to the pub

P CLOQUET PUBLIC LIBRARY*, 320 14th St, 55720-2100. SAN 308-5406. Tel: 218-879-1531. FAX: 218-879-6531. Web Site: www.cloquet.lib.mn.us. *Librn,* Mary Lukkarila; E-mail: mlukkari@arrowhead.lib.mn.us; *Ch Serv,* Lisbeth Boutang; Staff 8 (MLS 1, Non-MLS 7)
Founded 1895. Pop 11,463; Circ 144,528
Jan 2005-Dec 2005. Mats Exp $45,000, Books $39,000, AV Mat $6,000
Library Holdings: Bk Vols 54,197; Per Subs 155
Automation Activity & Vendor Info: (Acquisitions) Horizon; (Cataloging) Horizon; (Circulation) Horizon; (OPAC) Horizon
Wireless access
Function: Prog for children & young adult, Wheelchair accessible
Mem of Arrowhead Library System
Open Mon-Thurs 10-8, Fri 10-5
Friends of the Library Group

COLERAINE

P COLERAINE PUBLIC LIBRARY*, 203 Cole Ave, 55722. (Mail add: PO Box 225, 55722-0225), SAN 308-5422. Tel: 218-245-2315. FAX: 218-245-2315. E-mail: illcol@arrowhead.lib.mn.us. *Librn,* Jo Anne Mikulich; E-mail: jmikulic@arrowhead.lib.mn.us
Founded 1911. Pop 2,921; Circ 23,283
Library Holdings: Bk Titles 17,000; Per Subs 60
Special Collections: Historic Photographs of Local Area; Local History Items; Promotional Items of Local Businesses of the Past
Wireless access
Mem of Arrowhead Library System
Open Mon, Tues & Thurs 10-7 (10-6 Summer), Wed 10-8, Fri 10-4

COLLEGEVILLE

C SAINT JOHN'S UNIVERSITY*, Alcuin Library, 2835 Abbey Plaza, 56321. SAN 308-5430. Tel: 320-363-2122. Interlibrary Loan Service Tel: 320-363-3822. Reference Tel: 320-363-2125. Administration Tel: 320-363-2119. FAX: 320-363-2126. Web Site: www.csbsju.edu/library. *Dir, Libr, Media & Archives,* Kathleen Parker; Tel: 320-363-2121, E-mail: kparker@csbsju.edu; *Assoc Dir, Ref, Res & Instruction,* Jim Parsons; Tel: 320-363-5907, E-mail: jparsons@csbsju.edu; *Cat/Metadata Librn,* Janice Rod; Tel: 320-363-2617, E-mail: jrod@csbsju.edu; *Coll Develop Librn,* David Wuolu; Tel: 320-363-2128, E-mail: dwuolu@csbsju.edu; *Fine Arts Librn,* David Malone; Tel: 320-363-2127, E-mail: dmalone@csbsju.edu; *Govt & Bus Info Librn,* Amy Springer; Tel: 320-363-2601, E-mail: aspringer@csbsju.edu; *Humanities Librn,* Molly Ewing; Tel: 320-363-5513, E-mail: mewing@csbsju.edu; *Info Literacy Librn,* Sarah Gewirtz; Tel: 320-363-5802, E-mail: sgewirtz@csbsju.edu; *Sci Librn,* Jonathan Carlson; Tel: 320-363-2579, E-mail: jcarlson@csbsju.edu; *Soc Sci Librn,* Diana Symons; Tel: 320-363-5296, Fax: 320-363-5197, E-mail: dsymons@csbsju.edu; *Syst Librn,* Tess Kasling; Tel: 320-363-3280, E-mail: tkasling@csbsju.edu; *Archivist,* Peggy Roske; Tel: 320-363-2129, E-mail: proske@csbsju.edu. Subject Specialists: *Bus, Govt,* Amy Springer; *Sci,* Jonathan Carlson; *Music,* Tess Kasling; Staff 14 (MLS 11, Non-MLS 3)
Founded 1856. Enrl 2,048; Fac 159; Highest Degree: Master
Jul 2010-Jun 2011. Mats Exp $1,668,793, Books $139,229, Per/Ser (Incl. Access Fees) $340,094, Micro $18,459, AV Mat $26,304, Electronic Ref Mat (Incl. Access Fees) $56,435, Presv $6,372. Sal $692,506 (Prof $403,428)
Library Holdings: AV Mats 26,221; e-journals 2,865; Microforms 73,420; Bk Titles 351,723; Bk Vols 420,724; Per Subs 2,376
Special Collections: US Document Depository
Subject Interests: Benedictina, Bks, Liturgical design, Liturgy, Printing, Theol
Automation Activity & Vendor Info: (Acquisitions) Ex Libris Group; (Cataloging) Ex Libris Group; (Circulation) Ex Libris Group; (ILL) Ex Libris Group; (OPAC) Ex Libris Group; (Serials) Ex Libris Group
Database Vendor: ABC-CLIO, ACM (Association for Computing Machinery), Alexander Street Press, American Chemical Society, American Mathematical Society, American Physical Society, Annual Reviews, ARTstor, BioOne, Cinahl, CQ Press, CredoReference, ebrary, EBSCOhost, Elsevier, Ex Libris Group, Gale Cengage Learning, Gallup, HeinOnline, Hoovers, IOP, ISI Web of Knowledge, JSTOR, LexisNexis, McGraw-Hill, Mergent Online, Modern Language Association, Nature Publishing Group, Newsbank, OCLC, OCLC FirstSearch, OCLC WorldShare Interlibrary Loan, OVID Technologies, Project MUSE, ProQuest, ScienceDirect, Springer-Verlag, Thomson - Web of Science, ValueLine, Wiley, YBP Library Services
Wireless access
Partic in Central Minnesota Libraries Exchange; OCLC Online Computer Library Center, Inc
Open Mon-Thurs 8am-Midnight, Fri 8-5, Sat 10-10, Sun 1-Midnight
Restriction: Limited access for the pub

COLUMBIA HEIGHTS

P COLUMBIA HEIGHTS PUBLIC LIBRARY*, 820 40th Ave NE, 55421. SAN 308-5449. Tel: 763-706-3690. FAX: 763-706-3691. Web Site: www.anoka.lib.mn.us. *Dir,* Rebecca Loader; *Adult Serv,* Dana Weigman; *Ch Serv,* Marsha Tubbs; Staff 3 (MLS 1, Non-MLS 2)
Founded 1928. Pop 23,977; Circ 120,000
Library Holdings: Bk Vols 71,000; Per Subs 110
Automation Activity & Vendor Info: (Cataloging) SirsiDynix; (Circulation) SirsiDynix; (OPAC) SirsiDynix
Wireless access
Partic in Metropolitan Library Service Agency
Special Services for the Deaf - TTY equip
Open Mon-Thurs 9-8:30, Fri 9-5, Sat 10-4
Friends of the Library Group

COMFREY

P COMFREY PUBLIC LIBRARY*, 306 Brown St W, 56019-1167. SAN 308-5457. Tel: 507-877-6600. FAX: 507-877-3492. E-mail: libtbc1@tds.lib.mn.us. *Head Librn,* Michelle Kastner
Pop 1,051; Circ 14,620
Library Holdings: Bk Titles 11,000; Bk Vols 12,000; Per Subs 30
Mem of Traverse Des Sioux Library Cooperative
Open Mon (Winter) 8:30-11:30 & 12:30-3:30, Tues, Wed & Thurs 8:30-11:30 & 12:30-7, Fri 8:30-11:30 & 12:30-5, Sat 9-Noon; Tues, Wed & Fri (Summer) 4-8, Thurs 1-8, Sat 9-Noon
Friends of the Library Group

COOK

P COOK PUBLIC LIBRARY, 103 S River St, 55723. (Mail add: PO Box 126, 55723-0126), SAN 320-8958. Tel: 218-666-2210. *Dir,* Crystal Phillips; E-mail: cphillips@arrowhead.lib.mn.us
Pop 800; Circ 4,885
Library Holdings: Bk Vols 13,000
Special Collections: Fishing Coll; Hunting Coll; Outdoors Coll
Wireless access
Mem of Arrowhead Library System
Open Tues 1-4, Wed & Thurs 12-6, Fri 10-4
Friends of the Library Group

COON RAPIDS

J ANOKA-RAMSEY COMMUNITY COLLEGE*, Coon Rapids Campus Library, 11200 Mississippi Blvd NW, 55433. SAN 308-5465. Tel: 763-433-1150. Web Site: www.anokaramsey.edu/en/resources/success/library/coonrapidslibrary.aspx. *Librn,* Al Mamaril; Tel: 763-433-1552, E-mail: al.mamaril@anokaramsey.edu; *Librn,* Gina Pancerella-Willis; Tel: 763-433-1197, E-mail: gina.pancerella-willis@anokaramsey.edu; *Librn,* Barbara Sloboden; Tel: 763-433-1466; *Libr Tech,* Ruth Martin; Tel: 763-433-1384, E-mail: ruth.martin@anokaramsey.edu; Staff 4 (MLS 3, Non-MLS 1)
Founded 1965
Library Holdings: Bks on Deafness & Sign Lang 26; Electronic Media & Resources 38,000; Bk Titles 41,000; Per Subs 260
Automation Activity & Vendor Info: (Acquisitions) Baker & Taylor; (Cataloging) PALS; (Circulation) PALS; (Course Reserve) PALS; (ILL) PALS; (OPAC) PALS
Database Vendor: Baker & Taylor, Cinahl, CQ Press, EBSCOhost, Ex Libris Group, Gale Cengage Learning, JSTOR, OCLC FirstSearch, OCLC WorldShare Interlibrary Loan, ProQuest, Wilson - Wilson Web
Wireless access
Partic in Minitex Library Information Network; MnPALS
Open Mon-Thurs (Winter) 7:30am-8pm, Fri 7:30-4, Sat 9-1; Mon & Thurs (Summer) 7:30-4, Tues & Wed 7:30am-8pm

CROOKSTON

C UMC LIBRARY*, 2900 University Ave, 56716-0801. SAN 308-5481. Tel: 218-281-8399. FAX: 218-281-8080. Interlibrary Loan Service FAX: 218-281-8398. Web Site: www.crk.umn.edu/library. *Dir,* Owen Williams; *Acq, Cat, Coll Develop,* Jim Carlson; *ILL, Ser,* Krista Proulx
Founded 1966. Enrl 1,650; Fac 75
Library Holdings: AV Mats 1,544; DVDs 450; e-books 61,182; e-journals 63,497; Microforms 26,170; Bk Titles 55,303; Per Subs 600
Special Collections: Agriculture, Business, Foods, Equine Research Center, Hospitality, Minnesota Census Data, UMC Archives. State Document Depository
Automation Activity & Vendor Info: (Cataloging) Ex Libris Group; (Circulation) Ex Libris Group; (Course Reserve) Ex Libris Group; (ILL) Ex Libris Group
Database Vendor: Agricola, ebrary, EBSCO Information Services, EBSCOhost, Elsevier, Ex Libris Group, Gale Cengage Learning, Grolier Online, H W Wilson, Infotrieve, Ingenta, ISI Web of Knowledge, JSTOR, LexisNexis, Medline, OCLC, OCLC FirstSearch, OCLC WorldShare Interlibrary Loan, Project MUSE, ProQuest, PubMed, Sage, ScienceDirect, Springer-Verlag, Wiley InterScience, YBP Library Services
Wireless access
Partic in Northern Lights Library Network; OCLC Online Computer Library Center, Inc

CROSBY

P JESSIE F HALLETT MEMORIAL LIBRARY, 101 First St SE, 56441. SAN 308-549X. Tel: 218-546-8005. FAX: 218-546-7287. E-mail: hallett@hallettlibrary.com. Web Site: www.hallettlibrary.org. *Head Librn,* Peggi Beseres; E-mail: peggi@hallettlibrary.org; *Ch,* Deb Weide
Founded 1978. Pop 11,400; Circ 46,500
Library Holdings: e-books 1,800; Bk Vols 46,000, Per Subs 108
Automation Activity & Vendor Info: (ILL) Biblionix

Database Vendor: Overdrive, Inc
Wireless access
Open Mon & Wed 10-6, Tues & Thurs 10-8, Fri & Sat 10-2
Friends of the Library Group

DASSEL

P DASSEL PUBLIC LIBRARY*, 460 Third St N, 55325. (Mail add: PO Box 385, 55325-0385), SAN 348-1115. Tel: 320-275-3756. FAX: 320-275-3756. E-mail: dassel@dassel.lib.mn.us. *Head Librn,* Jeanette Stottrup
Founded 1972
Library Holdings: Bk Titles 6,837; Per Subs 25
Automation Activity & Vendor Info: (Cataloging) PALS; (Circulation) PALS; (OPAC) PALS
Mem of Pioneerland Library System
Open Mon-Wed & Fri 2-5:30, Thurs 1-7

DAWSON

P DAWSON PUBLIC LIBRARY*, 676 Pine St, 56232. SAN 347-691X. Tel: 320-769-2069. FAX: 320-769-2069. Web Site: dawsonmn.com/business_listings/034. *Head Librn,* Kathie Behrens; *Teen Librn,* Mitch Ehler
Pop 2,100; Circ 28,434
Library Holdings: Bk Vols 25,000; Per Subs 55
Publications: Article Dawson Sentinel
Mem of Pioneerland Library System
Special Services for the Blind - Reader equip
Open Mon & Thurs 10-1 & 1:30-6, Tues, Wed & Fri 10-1 & 1:30-5:30, Sat 10:30-2:30

DETROIT LAKES

S BECKER COUNTY HISTORICAL SOCIETY*, Walter D Bird Memorial Library & Archives, 714 Summit Ave, 56501. (Mail add: PO Box 622, 56502-0622), SAN 327-831X. Tel: 218-847-2938. E-mail: mail@beckercountyhistory.org. Web Site: www.beckercountyhistory.org. *Board Pres,* Carolyn Engebretson
Library Holdings: Microforms 500; Bk Vols 4,000; Spec Interest Per Sub 5
Special Collections: Minnesota Historical Photos (Becker County Coll)
Open Tues-Sat 10-4

DODGE CENTER

P DODGE CENTER PUBLIC LIBRARY, 13 First Ave NW, 55927. (Mail add: PO Box 430, 55927-0430), SAN 308-5503. Tel: 507-374-2275. FAX: 507-374-2694. *Head Librn,* Angie Fern; E-mail: DC_Dir@selco.info; *Asst Librn,* Jean Kent
Founded 1909. Pop 6,000; Circ 29,000
Jan 2013-Dec 2013. Mats Exp $7,000
Library Holdings: Bk Vols 29,000; Per Subs 15
Automation Activity & Vendor Info: (Cataloging) SirsiDynix; (Circulation) SirsiDynix; (OPAC) SirsiDynix
Partic in Southeastern Libraries Cooperating
Open Mon-Wed & Fri 10-5, Thurs 10-8, Sat 9-12
Friends of the Library Group

DULUTH

C COLLEGE OF SAINT SCHOLASTICA LIBRARY, 1200 Kenwood Ave, 55811-4199. SAN 347-2809. Tel: 218-723-6140. Interlibrary Loan Service Tel: 218-723-6178. Reference Tel: 218-723-6473. FAX: 218-723-5948. TDD: 218-422-6942. E-mail: cssill@css.edu, library@css.edu. Web Site: libguides.css.edu/csslibrary. *Dir,* Kevin W McGrew; Tel: 218-723-6198, E-mail: kmcgrew@css.edu; *Electronic Res, Head Ref Librn,* Todd A White; E-mail: twhite@css.edu; *Cat & Syst Librn,* Laura Hoelter; Tel: 218-723-6141, E-mail: lhoelter@css.edu; *Distance Educ Librn,* Julie Rustad; Tel: 218-723-6535, E-mail: jrustad@css.edu; *Info Literacy Librn,* Heidi Johnson; Tel: 218-723-6488, E-mail: hjohnso2@css.edu; *Coll Develop, Per Librn,* Brad Snelling; Tel: 218-723-6644, E-mail: bsnellin@css.edu; *Access Serv Mgr,* Karen Ostovich; E-mail: kostovic@css.edu; *Acq Spec,* Julie Walkowiak; Tel: 218-723-6649, E-mail: jwalkowi@css.edu; *ILL, Libr Spec, Ref,* Jennifer Lund; E-mail: jlund1@css.edu; Staff 9 (MLS 6, Non-MLS 3)
Founded 1912. Enrl 4,100; Fac 200; Highest Degree: Doctorate
Jul 2013-Jun 2014. Mats Exp $326,362. Sal $495,695 (Prof $361,340)
Special Collections: Children's Literature; James Franklin Louis Archives; North American Indian Studies Coll
Subject Interests: Health sci, Indians of NAm, Relig, Theol
Automation Activity & Vendor Info: (Acquisitions) PALS; (Cataloging) PALS; (Circulation) PALS; (Course Reserve) PALS; (ILL) PALS; (OPAC) PALS; (Serials) PALS
Database Vendor: Alexander Street Press, American Chemical Society, Baker & Taylor, Cinahl, CQ Press, CredoReference, Discovery Education, EBSCO Discovery Service, EBSCO Information Services, EBSCOhost, Elsevier, Ex Libris Group, Facts on File, Gale Cengage Learning, H W Wilson, JSTOR, LexisNexis, Medline, Newsbank, OCLC ArticleFirst, OCLC FirstSearch, OCLC WorldShare Interlibrary Loan, OVID Technologies, Oxford Online, Paratext, Plunkett Research, Ltd, ProQuest, PubMed, Sage, ScienceDirect, Springshare, LLC, ValueLine, Wiley, Wilson - Wilson Web
Wireless access
Function: Archival coll, Art exhibits, Computers for patron use, Copy machines, Electronic databases & coll, Games & aids for the handicapped, Handicapped accessible, ILL available, Online cat, Online info literacy tutorials on the web & in blackboard, Photocopying/Printing, Pub access computers, Ref serv in person, Tax forms, Wheelchair accessible
Publications: The Browser (Bibliographies)
Partic in Minitex Library Information Network; MnPALS; OCLC Online Computer Library Center, Inc
Open Mon-Thurs 7:45am-11pm, Fri 7:45-5, Sat 9-7, Sun Noon-11
Restriction: Borrowing requests are handled by ILL, In-house use for visitors, Open to researchers by request, Open to students, fac, staff & alumni

S DULUTH NEWS TRIBUNE LIBRARY*, 424 W First St, 55802. SAN 326-3304. Tel: 218-723-5374. FAX: 218-720-4120. Web Site: www.duluthnewstribune.com. *In Charge,* Michelle McEwen; E-mail: mmcewen@duluthnews.com
Founded 1975
Wireless access
Restriction: Staff use only

P DULUTH PUBLIC LIBRARY, 520 W Superior St, 55802. SAN 347-2922. Tel: 218-730-4200. Interlibrary Loan Service Tel: 218-730-4228. Administration Tel: 218-730-4221. Automation Services Tel: 218-730-4251. FAX: 218-730-5926. TDD: 218-730-4201. E-mail: webmail@duluthmn.gov. Web Site: www.duluthlibrary.org. *Libr Mgr,* Carla Powers; Tel: 218-730-4225, E-mail: cpowers@duluthmn.gov; *ILL Librn,* Stacy LaVres; E-mail: slavres@duluthmn.gov; *Spec Coll & Archives Librn,* Kristine Aho; Tel: 218-730-4209, E-mail: kaho@duluthmn.gov; *Bus Off Mgr,* Myra Kenner; Tel: 218-730-4223, E-mail: mkenner@duluthmn.gov; *Circ Supvr,* Jane Wester; Tel: 218-730-4242, E-mail: jwester@duluthmn.gov; *Libr Supvr, Digital & Outreach Serv,* Renee Zurn; Tel: 218-730-4240, E-mail: rzurn@duluthmn.gov; *Libr Supvr, Pub Serv,* David Ouse; Tel: 218-730-4208, E-mail: douse@duluthmn.gov; *Libr Supvr, Tech & Support Serv,* David Lull; E-mail: dlull@duluthmn.gov; *Nonfict & Ref Coordr,* Julie Levang; Tel: 218-730-4247, E-mail: jlevang@duluthmn.gov; *Youth Serv Coordr,* Susan Schumacher; Tel: 218-730-4219, E-mail: sschumacher@duluthmn.gov; *Commun Serv, Webmaster,* Nancy Eaton; Tel: 218-730-4236, E-mail: neaton@duluthmn.gov; *Govt Doc,* Roseann Agriesti; Tel: 218-730-4243, E-mail: ragriesti@duluthmn.gov; Staff 43.67 (MLS 20.21, Non-MLS 23.46)
Founded 1890. Pop 86,319; Circ 959,432
Jan 2013-Dec 2013 Income (Main Library and Branch(s)) $4,236,287, State $5,534, City $4,138,100, Other $92,653. Mats Exp $344,152, Books $261,641, AV Mat $77,121, Electronic Ref Mat (Incl. Access Fees) $5,390. Sal $2,736,525
Library Holdings: Audiobooks 8,286; CDs 6,437; DVDs 9,513; Large Print Bks 5,931; Bk Vols 427,853, Per Subs 464
Special Collections: Local History (Duluth Coll); Regional History (Great Lakes Region); Regional History (Minnesota Coll). US Document Depository
Subject Interests: Great Lakes
Automation Activity & Vendor Info: (Acquisitions) Innovative Interfaces, Inc; (Cataloging) Innovative Interfaces, Inc; (Circulation) Innovative Interfaces, Inc; (ILL) Innovative Interfaces, Inc; (OPAC) Innovative Interfaces, Inc; (Serials) Innovative Interfaces, Inc
Database Vendor: Baker & Taylor, Booksite, EBSCOhost, Foundation Center, Gale Cengage Learning, LearningExpress, Medline, Newsbank, OCLC ArticleFirst, OCLC CAMIO, OCLC FirstSearch, OCLC WorldShare Interlibrary Loan, Overdrive, Inc, ProQuest, ReferenceUSA, TumbleBookLibrary
Wireless access
Function: Adult bk club, Archival coll, Audiobks via web, Bks on CD, Children's prog, Computer training, Computers for patron use, Copy machines, e-mail & chat, E-Reserves, Electronic databases & coll, eReaders, Free DVD rentals, Genealogy discussion group, Govt ref serv, Handicapped accessible, Homebound delivery serv, ILL available, Jail serv, Life-long learning prog for all ages, Magazines, Mail & tel request accepted, Microfiche/film & reading machines, Movies, Mus passes, Music CDs, Newsp ref libr, Online cat, Online ref, Online searches, Outside serv via phone, mail, e-mail & web, OverDrive digital audio bks, Photocopying/Printing, Prog for adults, Prog for children & young adult, Pub access computers, Ref serv available, Ref serv in person, Scanner, Senior computer classes, Story hour, Summer & winter reading prog, Tax forms, Teen prog, Telephone ref, Web-catalog
Publications: How Do I Contact? (Reference guide)
Partic in Minitex Library Information Network

Special Services for the Deaf - Sign lang interpreter upon request for prog; Sorenson video relay syst; TDD equip
Special Services for the Blind - Accessible computers; Audio mat; BiFolkal kits; Bks on CD; Extensive large print coll; Internet workstation with adaptive software; Large print bks; Reader equip; Recorded bks; Sound rec
Friends of the Library Group
Branches: 2
MOUNT ROYAL, 105 Mount Royal Shopping Circle, 55803, SAN 378-1976. Tel: 218-730-4290. *Br Librn,* Julie Kapke; E-mail: jkapke@duluthmn.gov
Founded 1998
Friends of the Library Group
WEST DULUTH, 5830 Grand Ave, 55807, SAN 372-4905. Tel: 218-730-4280. *Br Librn,* Andrea Pearson; E-mail: apearson@duluthmn.gov
Founded 1991

M ESSENTIA INSTITUTE OF RURAL HEALTH, Health Sciences Library, 407 E Third St, 55805-1984. SAN 308-5635. Tel: 218-786-4396. FAX: 218-786-4249. E-mail: library@eirh.org. *Librn,* Elizabeth Sobczak; Staff 5 (MLS 2, Non-MLS 3)
Library Holdings: e-journals 5,000; Bk Vols 2,000; Per Subs 400
Subject Interests: Allied health, Med, Nursing
Wireless access
Open Mon-Fri 8-4:30

S NATURAL RESOURCES RESEARCH INSTITUTE*, Natural Resources Library, University of Minnesota-Duluth, 5013 Miller Trunk Hwy, 55811. SAN 325-190X. Tel: 218-720-4235. FAX: 218-720-4219. *Librn,* Susan Rhead Hendrickson; E-mail: shendric@nrri.umn.edu; Staff 1 (MLS 1)
Library Holdings: Bk Titles 7,000; Per Subs 250
Special Collections: Peat
Subject Interests: Ecosystems, Environ sci, Forest products, Peat
Automation Activity & Vendor Info: (Cataloging) EOS International; (ILL) OCLC; (OPAC) EOS International
Publications: Quarterly Report
Partic in OCLC Online Computer Library Center, Inc
Open Mon-Fri 8-4:30

S NORTHEAST MINNESOTA HISTORICAL CENTER*, University of Minnesota-Duluth Library, 416 Library Dr, Annex 202, 55812. SAN 308-5589. Tel: 218-726-8526. FAX: 218-726-6205. Web Site: www.d.umn.edu/lib. *Curator,* Patricia Maus; E-mail: pmaus@d.umn.edu.
Subject Specialists: *Archives, Local hist,* Patricia Maus
Founded 1977
Library Holdings: Bk Titles 6,000; Bk Vols 8,000; Per Subs 670
Special Collections: Historical Photographs. Oral History
Subject Interests: Commercial fishing on Lake Superior's N shore, Environ, Hist of NE Minn, Lumbering, Mining, Soc welfare, Transportation, Women in bus
Wireless access
Open Mon-Fri 8-12 & 1:15-4:30

R PILGRIM CONGREGATIONAL CHURCH LIBRARY*, 2310 E Fourth St, 55812. SAN 328-1159. Tel: 218-724-8503. FAX: 218-724-0848. E-mail: pilgrimdlh@msn.com.
Founded 1918
Library Holdings: Bk Titles 1,850; Bk Vols 1,900
Special Collections: Bible (Liberal Theology Coll), bks; UCC & Congregational History Coll
Open Mon-Fri 9-4

L SAINT LOUIS COUNTY LAW LIBRARY, Alan Mitchell Law Library, 100 N Fifth Ave W, Rm 15, 55802. SAN 308-5538. Tel: 218-726-2611. FAX: 218-726-2612. E-mail: lawlibrary@stlouiscountymn.gov.
Library Holdings: Bk Vols 20,000; Per Subs 15
Database Vendor: Westlaw
Wireless access
Open Mon-Fri 8-4:30

M ST LUKE'S HOSPITAL*, Hilding Medical & Health Sciences Library, 915 E First St, 55805. SAN 308-5627. Tel: 218-249-5320. FAX: 218-249-5926. Web Site: www.slhduluth.com. *Librn,* Doreen Roberts; Staff 1 (MLS 1)
Founded 1941
Library Holdings: Per Subs 230
Subject Interests: Clinical med, Nursing
Partic in Southeastern Massachusetts Consortium of Health Science Libraries
Open Mon-Fri 8-4:30

G UNITED STATES ENVIRONMENTAL PROTECTION*, Mid Continent Ecology Division, 6201 Congdon Blvd, 55804-2595. SAN 308-5554. Tel: 218-529-5000. Interlibrary Loan Service Tel: 218-529-5085. FAX: 218-529-5418. Web Site: www.epa.gov/med. *Librn,* John Bankson; E-mail: bankson.john@epa.gov; Staff 2 (MLS 1, Non-MLS 1)
Founded 1967
Library Holdings: Bk Titles 5,000; Bk Vols 12,000; Per Subs 100
Subject Interests: Effluent testing, Freshwater toxicology, Predictive toxicity model, Wetland ecology
Partic in OCLC-LVIS
Open Mon-Fri 8-4:30

C UNIVERSITY OF MINNESOTA DULUTH LIBRARY*, 416 Library Dr, 55812. SAN 347-3104. Tel: 218-726-8102. Circulation Tel: 218-726-6120. Interlibrary Loan Service Tel: 218-726-6628. Reference Tel: 218-726-8100. Administration Tel: 218-726-8130. Automation Services Tel: 218-726-8129. FAX: 218-726-8019. Interlibrary Loan Service FAX: 218-726-6205. E-mail: lib@d.umn.edu. Web Site: www.d.umn.edu/lib. *Dir,* Basil Sozansky; Tel: 218-726-6562, E-mail: bsozansk@d.umn.edu; *Asst Dir,* Elizabeth Benson Johnson; Tel; 218-726-6561, E-mail: ejohnso1@d.umn.edu; *Syst Coordr,* Darlene Morris; E-mail: dmorris@d.umn.edu; *Acq,* Anne Hovde; Tel: 218-726-7887, E-mail: ahovde@d.umn.edu; *Archivist,* Tom Ambrosi; Tel: 218-726-7681, E-mail: tambrosi@d.umn.edu; *Tech Serv-Section Head,* Shixing Wen; Tel: 218-276-8498, E-mail: swen@d.umn.edu; Staff 33 (MLS 14, Non-MLS 19)
Founded 1947. Enrl 11,184; Fac 523; Highest Degree: Doctorate
Jul 2006-Jun 2007 Income $2,815,877. Mats Exp $1,460,126, Books $237,560, Per/Ser (Incl. Access Fees) $1,131,489, AV Mat $22,627, Electronic Ref Mat (Incl. Access Fees) $43,450, Presv $25,000. Sal $1,591,074 (Prof $604,334)
Library Holdings: AV Mats 18,196; e-books 30,886; e-journals 26,272; Bk Vols 368,904; Per Subs 1,411
Special Collections: Northeast Minnesota Historical Center; Ramseyer Bible; UMD Archives; Voyager Coll. Oral History; US Document Depository
Automation Activity & Vendor Info: (Acquisitions) Ex Libris Group; (Cataloging) Ex Libris Group; (Circulation) Ex Libris Group; (Course Reserve) Ex Libris Group; (ILL) OCLC; (OPAC) Ex Libris Group; (Serials) Ex Libris Group
Database Vendor: American Chemical Society, American Mathematical Society, American Physical Society, ARTstor, BioOne, Cambridge Scientific Abstracts, CIOS (Communication Institute for Online Scholarship), CQ Press, CRC Press/Taylor & Francis Group, EBSCOhost, Elsevier, Emerald, Ex Libris Group, Gale Cengage Learning, Gallup, Greenwood Publishing Group, Grolier Online, H W Wilson, Haworth Pres Inc, IEEE (Institute of Electrical & Electronics Engineers), JSTOR, Knovel, LexisNexis, Mergent Online, Modern Language Association, Nature Publishing Group, OCLC FirstSearch, OCLC WorldShare Interlibrary Loan, Oxford Online, Project MUSE, ProQuest, RefWorks, Safari Books Online, Sage, ScienceDirect, Springer-Verlag, Thomson - Web of Science, Wiley InterScience, World Book Online
Wireless access
Publications: Newsletter
Partic in Minitex Library Information Network; OCLC Online Computer Library Center, Inc
Special Services for the Deaf - Assistive tech; Closed caption videos; High interest/low vocabulary bks; Sorenson video relay syst
Special Services for the Blind - Accessible computers; Assistive/Adapted tech devices, equip & products; Audio mat; Bks on cassette; Bks on CD; Braille equip; Cassette playback machines; Cassettes; Closed caption display syst; Computer with voice synthesizer for visually impaired persons; Copier with enlargement capabilities; Dragon Naturally Speaking software; Inspiration software; Integrated libr/media serv; Internet workstation with adaptive software; Low vision equip; Networked computers with assistive software; PC for handicapped; Reader equip; Scanner for conversion & translation of mats; Screen enlargement software for people with visual disabilities; Screen reader software; Sound rec; Text reader

EAGAN

C ARGOSY UNIVERSITY*, Twin Cities Library, 1515 Central Pkwy, 55121. Tel: 651-846-3351. Toll Free Tel: 888-844-2004. FAX: 651-994-0105. E-mail: autclibrary@argosy.edu. Web Site: library.argosy.edu/twincities. *Dir, Libr Serv,* Carl Ralston; E-mail: cralston@argosy.edu; *Librn,* Toni Canfield; *Librn,* Carol Gardener; *Librn,* Jesse Leraas
Library Holdings: e-books 20,000; Bk Titles 9,000; Per Subs 170
Database Vendor: EBSCOhost, ProQuest, Sage, ScienceDirect
Wireless access
Open Mon-Thurs 7:30am-8pm, Fri 7:30-6, Sat & Sun 10-6

P DAKOTA COUNTY LIBRARY SYSTEM*, 1340 Wescott Rd, 55123-1099. SAN 347-2205. Tel: 651-450-2900. Interlibrary Loan Service Tel: 651-450-2945. Administration Tel: 651-450-2925. FAX: 651-450-2915.

Administration FAX: 651-450-2934. Web Site: www.dakotacounty.us/library. *Dir,* Ken Behringer; Tel: 615-450-2930, E-mail: ken.behringer@co.dakota.mn.us; *Dep Dir,* Roseanne Byrne; Tel: 651-450-2931, E-mail: roseanne.byrne@co.dakota.mn.us; *Asst Dir,* Mary Johnson; Tel: 651-450-2929, E-mail: mary.johnson@co.dakota.mn.us; *Head, Ref,* Maureen Gormley; Tel: 651-450-2938, E-mail: maureen.gormley@co.dakota.mn.us; *Tech Mgr,* Mike Turbes; Tel: 651-450-2991, E-mail: mike.turbes@co.dakota.mn.us; *Admin Serv,* Paul Deaven; Tel: 651-450-2927, E-mail: paul.deaven@co.dakota.mn.us; *Adult Serv,* Rebecca Wilson; Tel: 651-450-2939, E-mail: rebecca.wilson@co.dakota.mn.us; *Tech Serv,* Ardell Bengtson; Tel: 651-450-2937, E-mail: ardell.bengston@co.dakota.mn.us; *Teen Serv,* Kalla Kalloway; Tel: 651-450-2941, E-mail: kalla.kalloway@co.dakota.mn.us; Staff 61.23 (MLS 61.23)
Founded 1959. Pop 384,233; Circ 4,456,891
Jan 2008-Dec 2008 Income $12,344,606, State $63,471, County $10,086,507, Other $2,194,628. Mats Exp $1,516,457, Books $1,101,950, AV Mat $293,263, Electronic Ref Mat (Incl. Access Fees) $121,244. Sal $8,746,653
Library Holdings: AV Mats 86,925; e-books 5,799; Bk Vols 922,306; Per Subs 1,538
Special Collections: US Document Depository
Automation Activity & Vendor Info: (Acquisitions) SirsiDynix; (Cataloging) SirsiDynix; (Circulation) SirsiDynix; (OPAC) SirsiDynix; (Serials) EBSCO Online
Database Vendor: EBSCOhost, Gale Cengage Learning, ProQuest
Function: Homebound delivery serv, ILL available, Photocopying/Printing, Prog for adults, Prog for children & young adult, Ref serv available, Summer reading prog, VHS videos
Member Libraries: South Saint Paul Public Library
Partic in Metropolitan Library Service Agency
Open Mon-Thurs 10-8:30, Fri & Sat 10-5:30, Sun 1-5
Friends of the Library Group
Branches: 9
BURNHAVEN COMMUNITY, 1101 W County Rd 42, Burnsville, 55306, SAN 347-223X. Tel: 952-891-0300. FAX: 952-435-3476. *Br Mgr,* Naomi Golv; Tel: 952-891-0306, E-mail: naomi.golv@co.dakota.mn.us
Open Mon-Thurs 10-8:30, Fri & Sat 10-5:30, Sun (Sept-May) 1-5
FARMINGTON BRANCH, 508 Third St, Farmington, 55024-1357, SAN 347-2264. Tel: 651-438-0250. FAX: 651-463-7979. *Br Mgr,* Mary Scheide; Tel: 651-438-0254, E-mail: mary.scheide@co.dakota.mn.us
Open Mon-Wed (Sept-May) Noon-8:30, Thurs-Sat 10-5:30; Mon & Tues(June-Aug) 10-8:30, Wed-Fri 10-5:30, Sat 10-2
Friends of the Library Group
GALAXIE, 14955 Galaxie Ave, Apple Valley, 55124, SAN 370-9272. Tel: 952-891-7045. FAX: 952-891-7048. *Br Mgr,* Anne Murray Robertson; Tel: 952-891-7054
Open Mon-Thurs 10-8:30, Fri & Sat 10-5:30, Sun 1-5
HERITAGE, 20085 Heritage Dr, Lakeville, 55044. Tel: 952-891-0360. *Br Mgr,* Murray Wilson; Tel: 952-891-0373, E-mail: murray.wilson@co.dakota.mn.us
Circ 558,088
Open Mon-Thurs 10-8:30, Fri & Sat 10-5:30, Sun (Sept-May) 1-5
Friends of the Library Group
INVER GLEN, 8098 Blaine Ave, Inver Grove Heights, 55076. Tel: 651-554-6840. FAX: 651-552-7522. *Br Mgr,* Jean Silverberg
Open Mon-Wed (Sept-May) 12-8:30, Thurs-Sat 10-5:30; Mon & Tues (June-Aug) 10-8:30, Wed-Fri 10-5:30, Sat 12-4
Friends of the Library Group
PLEASANT HILL, 1490 S Frontage Rd, Hastings, 55033, SAN 347-2299. Tel: 651-437-0200. FAX: 651-480-4944. *Br Mgr,* Mary Scheide; Tel: 651-438-0204, E-mail: mary.scheide@co.dakota.mn.us
Open Mon-Thurs 10-8:30, Fri & Sat 10-5:30, Sun (Sept-May) 1-5
ROBERT TRAIL, 14395 S Robert Trail, Rosemount, 55068. Tel: 651-480-1200. Circulation Tel: 651-480-1201. FAX: 651-480-1212. *Mgr,* Jamie Jurgensen; Tel: 651-480-1205, E-mail: jamie.jurgensen@co.dakota.mn.us
Open Mon-Thurs 10-8:30, Fri & Sat 10-5:30, Sun (Sept-May) 1-5
WENTWORTH, 199 E Wentworth Ave, West Saint Paul, 55118, SAN 347-2329. Tel: 651-554-6800. FAX: 651-451-1914. *Br Mgr,* Murray Wilson; E-mail: murray.wilson@co.dakota.mn.us
Open Mon-Thurs 10-8:30, Fri & Sat 10-5:30, Sun (Sept-May) 1-5
WESCOTT, 1340 Wescott Rd, 55123, SAN 347-2256. Tel: 651-450-2900. Administration Tel: 651-450-2925. FAX: 651-450-2955. Administration FAX: 651-450-2934. TDD: 651-450-2921. *Br Mgr,* Mary Wussow
Open Mon-Thurs 10-8:30, Fri & Sat 10-5:30, Sun (Sept-May) 1-5
Friends of the Library Group
Bookmobiles: 1

L THOMSON REUTERS WESTLAW*, Library Services, 610 Opperman Dr, 55123. SAN 371-7143. Tel: 651-848-2760. FAX: 651-848-2627. E-mail: eagan.libraryservices@thomsonreuters.com. *Librn,* Cynthia Schriber; E-mail: cindy.schriber@thomsonreuters.com; Staff 3 (MLS 1, Non-MLS 2)
Library Holdings: Bk Titles 6,000; Bk Vols 300,000; Per Subs 500

EAST GRAND FORKS

P EAST GRAND FORKS CAMPBELL LIBRARY*, 422 Fourth St NW, 56721. SAN 308-5651. Tel: 218-773-9121. FAX: 218-773-2645. Web Site: library.efg.mn. *Dir,* Charlotte Helgeson; E-mail: chelgeson@egf.mn
Founded 1963. Pop 8,537; Circ 80,832
Library Holdings: Bk Vols 47,000; Per Subs 77
Open Mon-Thurs 8-8, Fri 8-5, Sat 10-2, Sun 12-4:30
Friends of the Library Group

J NORTHLAND COMMUNITY & TECHNICAL COLLEGE LIBRARY*, East Grand Forks Campus, 2022 Central Ave NE, 56721. Tel: 218-793-2435. E-mail: egf.library@northlandcollege.edu. Web Site: www.northlandcollege.edu/library. *Libr Tech,* Amanda Johnson
Enrl 1,749; Fac 123
Library Holdings: Bk Titles 6,049; Bk Vols 8,040; Per Subs 123
Automation Activity & Vendor Info: (Cataloging) Ex Libris Group; (Circulation) Ex Libris Group; (OPAC) Ex Libris Group
Wireless access
Partic in Minitex Library Information Network; MnPALS; Northern Lights Library Network; OCLC Online Computer Library Center, Inc
Open Mon-Thurs 8-5, Fri 8-4
Friends of the Library Group

EDGERTON

P EDGERTON PUBLIC LIBRARY*, 811 First Ave, 56128. (Mail add: PO Box 25, 56128-0025), SAN 324-1416. Tel: 507-442-7071. FAX: 507-442-7071. Web Site: www.plumcreeklibrary.org/edgerton. *Dir,* Elberta De Jager; E-mail: edejager@plumcreeklibrary.net; *City Librn,* Lisa Brands
Founded 1950. Pop 1,189; Circ 77,539
Jan 2010-Dec 2010 Income $57,022, City $25,000, County $12,220, Locally Generated Income $6,680, Other $13,122. Mats Exp $12,170, Books $6,511, Per/Ser (Incl. Access Fees) $1,067, Other Print Mats $1,403, AV Mat $3,189. Sal $35,926
Library Holdings: Audiobooks 1,065; CDs 600; DVDs 2,235; Electronic Media & Resources 76; Bk Vols 20,883; Videos 1,000
Wireless access
Function: ILL available, Photocopying/Printing, Prog for children & young adult, Summer reading prog
Mem of Plum Creek Library System
Open Mon, Tues & Thurs-Sat 9:30-5, Wed 9:30-8

EDINA

M FAIRVIEW-SOUTHDALE HOSPITAL*, Mary Ann King Health Sciences Library, 6401 France Ave S, 55435. SAN 308-5678. Tel: 952-924-5005. FAX: 952-924-5933. *Librn,* Mary B Carlson; E-mail: mcarlso1@fairview.org
Founded 1975
Library Holdings: Bk Vols 1,000; Per Subs 100
Subject Interests: Bus, Cardiology, Nursing, Obstetrics, Orthopedics
Partic in Metronet; Midwest Health Sci Libr Network; Twin Cities Biomedical Consortium
Open Mon-Fri 7-3:30

ELBOW LAKE

P THORSON MEMORIAL LIBRARY, 117 Central Ave N, 56531. (Mail add: PO Box 1040, 56531-1040), SAN 308-5686. Tel: 218-685-6850. FAX: 218-685-6852. E-mail: library@runestone.net. Web Site: www.elbowlakepubliclibrary.org. *Dir,* Gail Hedstrom; Tel: 320-808-6394, E-mail: ghedstrom@elbowlake.lib.mn.us; *Ch Prog,* Janice Nelson; *Libr Asst,* Susan Sanford
Founded 1903. Pop 2,220; Circ 44,527
Library Holdings: Audiobooks 500; CDs 500; DVDs 3,000; Bk Vols 20,000; Per Subs 46; Videos 300
Subject Interests: Norwegian lit
Automation Activity & Vendor Info: (Cataloging) SirsiDynix; (Circulation) SirsiDynix; (ILL) SirsiDynix; (OPAC) SirsiDynix
Function: 24/7 Electronic res, 24/7 Online cat, Accelerated reader prog, Accessibility serv available based on individual needs, Adult bk club, Adult literacy prog, Archival coll, Art exhibits, Audio & video playback equip for onsite use, Bk club(s), Bks on cassette, Bks on CD, CD-ROM, Children's prog, Computer training, Computers for patron use, Copy machines, Digital talking bks, Distance learning, e-mail & chat, e-mail serv, E-Reserves, Electronic databases & coll, Fax serv, Free DVD rentals, Handicapped accessible, ILL available, Life-long learning prog for all ages, Magazines, Movies, Music CDs, Newsp ref libr, Outside serv via phone, mail, e-mail & web, Photocopying/Printing, Preschool reading prog, Prog for adults, Prog for children & young adult, Pub access computers, Serves mentally handicapped consumers, Spanish lang bks, Spoken cassettes & CDs, Spoken cassettes & DVDs, Story hour, Summer reading prog, Tax forms, Telephone ref, VCDs, VHS videos, Video lending libr, Wheelchair accessible, Winter reading prog, Workshops, Writing prog
Mem of Viking Library System

Open Mon, Wed & Fri 9-5, Tues & Thurs 12-8, Sat 9-2
Friends of the Library Group

ELMORE

P ELMORE PUBLIC LIBRARY*, 107 E Willis St, 56027. (Mail add: PO Box 56, 56027-0056), SAN 376-7159. Tel: 507-943-3150. FAX: 507-943-3434. E-mail: libtfe@tds.lib.mn.us. *Dir,* Nancy Ziegler
Library Holdings: Bk Titles 1,000
Wireless access
Mem of Traverse Des Sioux Library Cooperative
Open Mon 3-5, Tues & Fri 2-6, Wed 1-5, Thurs 3-7, Sat 9-11

ELY

P ELY PUBLIC LIBRARY*, 30 S First Ave E, 55731. SAN 308-5708. Tel: 218-365-5140. FAX: 218-365-6107. Web Site: www.elylibrary.org. *Dir,* Rachel Heinrich; E-mail: rheinric@arrowhead.lib.mn.us; Staff 3 (MLS 1, Non-MLS 2)
Founded 1922. Pop 3,883; Circ 54,791
Library Holdings: Bk Vols 35,000; Per Subs 80
Function: ILL available, Photocopying/Printing, Prog for children & young adult, Summer reading prog
Mem of Arrowhead Library System
Open Mon-Fri 10-7, Sat 8-Noon
Friends of the Library Group

J VERMILION COMMUNITY COLLEGE LIBRARY*, 1900 E Camp St, 55731. SAN 308-5716. Tel: 218-365-7226. FAX: 218-365-7218. E-mail: library@vcc.edu. Web Site: www.vcc.mnscu.edu/info_sru/library/libmain.htm. *Dir,* Sharon Evensen
Founded 1922. Enrl 670; Highest Degree: Associate
Library Holdings: Bk Vols 36,000; Per Subs 200
Special Collections: Ojibway Native American Coll
Subject Interests: Natural res
Automation Activity & Vendor Info: (Cataloging) PALS; (Circulation) PALS; (ILL) PALS; (OPAC) PALS; (Serials) PALS
Database Vendor: Gale Cengage Learning, LexisNexis
Partic in OCLC Online Computer Library Center, Inc
Open Mon-Thurs 8am-9pm, Fri 9-3, Sun 4-8

EVELETH

P EVELETH PUBLIC LIBRARY*, 614 Pierce St, 55734-1697. SAN 308-5724. Tel: 218-744-7499. FAX: 218-744-9635. Web Site: arrowhead.lib.mn.us. *Dir,* Mary Beth Kafut; E-mail: mkafut@arrowhead.lib.mn.us; Staff 1 (MLS 1)
Founded 1914. Pop 7,384; Circ 36,015
Library Holdings: Bk Vols 27,000; Per Subs 83
Automation Activity & Vendor Info: (Cataloging) SirsiDynix; (Circulation) SirsiDynix; (OPAC) SirsiDynix
Database Vendor: TLC (The Library Corporation)
Mem of Arrowhead Library System
Open Mon-Wed (Winter) 12-7, Thurs & Fri 9-5, Sat 10-2; Mon-Fri (Summer) 9-5

FAIRFAX

P FAIRFAX PUBLIC LIBRARY*, 124 SE First St, 55332. (Mail add: PO Box Q, 55332-0108), SAN 376-7728. Tel: 507-426-7269. FAX: 507-426-7269. Web Site: www.pals.msus.edu. *Asst Librn,* Jane Blumhoefer
Library Holdings: Bk Vols 6,000; Per Subs 18
Mem of Pioneerland Library System
Open Tues & Fri 9-5, Wed 1-5 & 6-8

FAIRMONT

S MARTIN COUNTY HISTORICAL SOCIETY, INC, Pioneer Museum Research Library, 304 E Blue Earth Ave, 56031. SAN 370-1557. Tel: 507-235-5178. FAX: 507-235-5179. E-mail: mch@frontiernet.net. Web Site: www.fairmont.org/mchs. *Exec Dir,* Lenny Tvedten; *Asst Admin,* Sandra Nuss; *Curator,* James Marushin; Staff 6 (MLS 3, Non-MLS 3)
Founded 1929. Pop 21,000
Special Collections: Martin County - City Directories, Family Histories, History Files, Microfilm, Obituaries, Picture Files, Plat Books, Telephone Directories, Video Library; Martin County Local Newspapers, 1874-. Oral History
Subject Interests: Civil War, County hist, Minn
Wireless access
Function: Archival coll, For res purposes, Newsp ref libr, Photocopying/Printing, Res libr
Open Mon-Fri 8:30-12 & 1-4:30
Restriction: Open to pub for ref & circ; with some limitations, Open to researchers by request, Open to students, fac & staff, Pub use on premises

P MARTIN COUNTY LIBRARY*, 110 N Park St, 56031-2822. SAN 308-5767. Tel: 507-238-4207. FAX: 507-238-4208. Web Site: www.martincountylibrarysystem.org. *Dir,* Jenny Trushenski; E-mail: jjepse@tds.lib.mn.us; *Ch,* Jennifer Tow; *Circ Librn,* Deena Frerichs; *Tech Serv Librn,* Nancy Warner; Staff 1 (MLS 1)
Founded 1943. Pop 22,000; Circ 200,000
Library Holdings: Bk Titles 100,000; Per Subs 225
Wireless access
Mem of Traverse Des Sioux Library Cooperative
Partic in OCLC Online Computer Library Center, Inc
Open Mon, Wed & Thurs 9-9, Tues 9-6, Fri & Sat 9-5
Branches: 4
SHERBURN BRANCH, 21 N Main St, Sherburn, 56171-1052, SAN 376-9917. Tel: 507-764-7611. E-mail: libtms@tds.lib.mn.us. *Br Mgr,* Becky Tish
Library Holdings: Bk Vols 8,560; Per Subs 17
Open Mon-Fri 1:30-5:30
Friends of the Library Group
TRIMONT BRANCH, 190 W Main St, Trimont, 56176, SAN 378-2018. Tel: 507-639-2571. E-mail: libtmt@tds.lib.mn.us. *Br Mgr,* Dianne Adamson
Library Holdings: Bk Vols 5,000; Per Subs 13
Open Mon & Tues 1:30-5, Wed 2:30-6, Thurs 9-12 & 1:30-5, Sat 9-12
Friends of the Library Group
TRUMAN BRANCH, 101 E Ciro St, Truman, 56088-2017. (Mail add: PO Box 97, Truman, 56088-0097), SAN 376-9925. Tel: 507-776-2717. *Br Mgr,* Theresa Ricard
Library Holdings: Bk Titles 5,000; Per Subs 12
Open Mon-Thurs 1:30-5, Fri 12-6
Friends of the Library Group
WELCOME BRANCH, 304 First St, Welcome, 56181. (Mail add: PO Box 345, Welcome, 56181-0345), SAN 376-9933. Tel: 507-728-8376. E-mail: librarym@frontiernet.net. *Br Mgr,* Mary Ann Frerichs
Library Holdings: Bk Vols 2,080
Open Mon, Wed & Fri 2-5
Friends of the Library Group

FARIBAULT

S ANTIQUE STOVE ASSOCIATION LIBRARY*, 823 Lincoln Ave SW, 55021-6636. SAN 328-090X. Tel: 507-210-4304. *Librn,* David Petricka
Founded 1985
Library Holdings: Bk Vols 2,000
Special Collections: Stove Manufacturers Catalogs 1860-1935
Restriction: Open by appt only

P BUCKHAM MEMORIAL LIBRARY*, 11 Division St E, 55021-6000. SAN 308-5775. Tel: 507-334-2089. FAX: 507-384-0503. Web Site: www.faribault.org/library. *Dir,* Delane James; *Ch Serv,* Frances Veit; *Pub Serv,* Allyn McColley; Staff 3 (MLS 3)
Founded 1897. Pop 32,000; Circ 270,000
Library Holdings: AV Mats 1,400; CDs 3,400; DVDs 1,500; Electronic Media & Resources 1,200; Large Print Bks 500; Bk Vols 85,000; Per Subs 225; Videos 3,000
Wireless access
Function: Adult bk club, Bk club(s), Computer training, Copy machines, Digital talking bks, E-Reserves, Handicapped accessible, Home delivery & serv to Sr ctr & nursing homes, Homebound delivery serv, ILL available, Prog for adults, Prog for children & young adult, Ref serv available, Summer reading prog, Tax forms, Wheelchair accessible
Partic in Southeastern Libraries Cooperating
Friends of the Library Group

P MINNESOTA BRAILLE & TALKING BOOK LIBRARY, 388 SE Sixth Ave, 55021-6340. SAN 308-5791. Tel: 507-333-4828. Toll Free Tel: 800-722-0550. FAX: 507-333-4832. E-mail: mn.btbl@state.mn.us. Web Site: www.mnbtbl.org. *Dir,* Catherine A Durivage; Tel: 507-384-6860, E-mail: catherine.durivage@statc.mn.us; *Librn,* Rene Perrance; Tel: 507-384-6870, E-mail: rene.perrance@state.mn.us; *Digital Ref Librn,* Dan Malosh; Tel: 507-384-6869, E-mail: dan.malosh@state.mn.us; Staff 8 (MLS 3, Non-MLS 5)
Founded 1933
Library Holdings: Braille Volumes 32,800; Large Print Bks 6,232; Talking Bks 322,365; Videos 257
Automation Activity & Vendor Info: (Cataloging) Keystone Systems, Inc (KLAS); (Circulation) Keystone Systems, Inc (KLAS); (OPAC) Keystone Systems, Inc (KLAS)
Function: Bks on cassette, Digital talking bks, e-mail serv, Handicapped accessible, Online cat, Web-Braille, Web-catalog
Special Services for the Blind - Assistive/Adapted tech devices, equip & products; Audio mat; Bks & mags in Braille, on rec, tape & cassette; Braille equip; Braille servs; Children's Braille; Computer with voice synthesizer for visually impaired persons; Dragon Naturally Speaking software; Home delivery serv; Internet workstation with adaptive software; Large print bks; Large screen computer & software; Local mags & bks

recorded; Mags & bk reproduction/duplication; Networked computers with assistive software; Newsletter (in large print, Braille or on cassette); Newsline for the Blind; Ref serv; Scanner for conversion & translation of mats; Screen enlargement software for people with visual disabilities; Screen reader software; Soundproof reading booth; Spanish Braille mags & bks; Talking bk & rec for the blind cat; Videos on blindness & phys handicaps; Volunteer serv; ZoomText magnification & reading software
Restriction: Authorized patrons

S MINNESOTA DEPARTMENT OF CORRECTIONS*, Minnesota Correctional Facility - Faribault-Rogers Library, 1101 Linden Lane, 55021-6400. Tel: 507-334-0753. FAX: 507-334-0880. Web Site: www.doc.state.mn.us. *Educ Dir,* Ruth Stadheim
Library Holdings: Bk Vols 1,800; Per Subs 52
Special Collections: Law Coll
Automation Activity & Vendor Info: (Cataloging) Follett Software; (Circulation) Follett Software
Open Mon-Wed & Fri 1-8:30, Thurs 1-3:30, Sat 8-12

S RICE COUNTY HISTORICAL SOCIETY, Rice County Museum of History Archives Library, 1814 Second Ave NW, 55021. SAN 327-8336. Tel: 507-332-2121. FAX: 507-332-2121. E-mail: rchs@rchistory.org. Web Site: www.rchistory.org. *Exec Dir,* Susan Garwood; E-mail: sgarwood@rchistory.org; Staff 2 (MLS 1, Non-MLS 1)
Founded 1926
Library Holdings: Bk Vols 1,400
Function: Ref & res, Ref serv available, Res performed for a fee, Web-catalog, Wheelchair accessible, Workshops
Publications: 2000 Rice County Pictorial History; Portraits & Memories of Rice County; Reprinted Rice County 1882; Rice County Families
Open Mon-Fri 9-4
Restriction: Fee for pub use, Non-circulating, Not a lending libr, Open to pub for ref only

C SOUTH CENTRAL COLLEGE LIBRARY*, Faribault Campus, 1225 SW Third St, 55021. SAN 375-4286. Tel: 507-332-5883. FAX: 507-332-5888. Web Site: www.southcentral.edu. *Librn,* Ala Garlinska; E-mail: ala.garlinska@southcentral.edu
Library Holdings: Bk Vols 4,000; Per Subs 19
Subject Interests: Carpentry
Wireless access
Open Mon-Thurs 8-8, Fri 8-4

FERGUS FALLS

P FERGUS FALLS PUBLIC LIBRARY*, 205 E Hampden, 56537-2930. SAN 308-5813. Tel: 218-739-9387. FAX: 218-736-5131. E-mail: library@fergusfalls.lib.mn.us. *Dir,* Walter J Dunlap; *Ch Serv,* Erin Smith; *Ref,* Candace Herbert; Staff 7 (MLS 3, Non-MLS 4)
Founded 1891. Pop 19,242; Circ 218,298
Jan 2007-Dec 2007 Income $638,978, City $554,570, County $84,408. Mats Exp $81,774, Books $68,187, AV Mat $13,587. Sal $409,356
Library Holdings: Bk Vols 93,924; Per Subs 195
Automation Activity & Vendor Info: (Acquisitions) SirsiDynix; (Cataloging) TLC (The Library Corporation); (Circulation) SirsiDynix; (OPAC) SirsiDynix
Database Vendor: SirsiDynix
Wireless access
Mem of Viking Library System
Partic in Northern Lights Library Network
Friends of the Library Group

R LUTHERAN BRETHREN SEMINARY*, Christiansen Memorial Library, 815 W Vernon Ave, 56537. SAN 327-7747. Tel: 218-739-1211. Administration Tel: 218-739-3375. Administration FAX: 218-739-1259. Web Site: www.lbs.edu/seminary. *Admin Librn,* Michelle Solberg; E-mail: msolberg@lbs.edu; *Info Serv Librn,* Barbara Gail Ellis; E-mail: bellis@lbs.edu; *Media Spec,* Anders Swendsrud; E-mail: aswendsrud@lbs.edu. Subject Specialists: *Res,* Michelle Solberg; *Tech,* Anders Swendsrud; Staff 3 (MLS 1, Non-MLS 2)
Founded 1902. Enrl 35; Highest Degree: Master
May 2011-Apr 2012 Income $15,500. Mats Exp $15,500, Books $6,000, Per/Ser (Incl. Access Fees) $7,500, AV Mat $400. Sal $16,000
Library Holdings: CDs 100; DVDs 20; Bk Titles 20,000; Per Subs 100; Videos 100
Subject Interests: Church hist, Missions, New Testament, Old Testament, Relig, Theol
Automation Activity & Vendor Info: (Acquisitions) Surpass; (Cataloging) Surpass; (Circulation) Surpass; (Serials) EBSCO Online
Database Vendor: EBSCOhost, ProQuest, Surpass
Wireless access
Function: Photocopying/Printing, Wheelchair accessible
Partic in Northern Lights Library Network
Open Mon-Fri 8-5
Restriction: Not a lending libr

J MINNESOTA STATE COMMUNITY & TECHNICAL COLLEGE*, Fergus Falls Campus Library, 1414 College Way, 56537-1000. SAN 308-5805. Tel: 218-736-1650. FAX: 218-736-1510. Web Site: www.minnesota.edu. *Librn,* Deb Kelman; E-mail: deb.kelman@minnesota.edu
Founded 1960. Enrl 1,208; Fac 77
Library Holdings: Bk Titles 33,000; Per Subs 102
Subject Interests: Environment
Automation Activity & Vendor Info: (Cataloging) PALS; (Circulation) PALS; (Course Reserve) PALS
Wireless access
Partic in Northern Lights Library Network; OCLC Online Computer Library Center, Inc
Open Mon-Thurs 7:45am-9pm, Fri 7:45-5

S OTTER TAIL COUNTY HISTORICAL SOCIETY*, E T Barnard Library, 1110 Lincoln Ave W, 56537. SAN 329-2789. Tel: 218-736-6038. FAX: 218-739-3075. E-mail: otchs@prtel.com. Web Site: otchs.org. *Archivist, Curator,* Kathy Evavold; *Res Serv Spec,* Vicky Anderson
Founded 1927
Library Holdings: Bk Titles 300; Per Subs 25
Special Collections: Otter Tail County Newspapers (1871-present). Oral History
Subject Interests: Educ
Publications: Otter Tail Record (Quarterly)
Open Mon-Fri 9-5
Restriction: Non-circulating to the pub

P VIKING LIBRARY SYSTEM*, 204 N Cascade St, 56537. (Mail add: PO Box 717, 56537-0717), SAN 308-583X. Tel: 218-739-5286. FAX: 218-739-5287. Web Site: www.viking.lib.mn.us. *Dir,* Peg Werner; E mail: pwerner@viking.lib.mn.us; *Pub Libr Consult,* Nancy Alsop; E-mail: nalsop@viking.lib.mn.us; Staff 11 (MLS 2, Non-MLS 9)
Founded 1975. Pop 124,698
Library Holdings: CDs 2,247; Bk Vols 13,789; Per Subs 58; Videos 4,135
Automation Activity & Vendor Info: (Acquisitions) Horizon; (Cataloging) Horizon; (Circulation) Horizon; (ILL) Horizon; (OPAC) Horizon
Database Vendor: SirsiDynix
Wireless access
Function: Online cat, Online searches, Outreach serv
Member Libraries: Browns Valley Public Library; Douglas County Library; Fergus Falls Public Library; Glenwood Public Library; Hancock Community Library; Morris Public Library; New York Mills Public Library; Pelican Rapids Public Library; Perham Area Public Library; Thorson Memorial Library; Wheaton Community Library
Partic in Northern Lights Library Network
Restriction: Not open to pub
Bookmobiles: 2

FOREST LAKE

P WASHINGTON COUNTY LIBRARY*, Hardwood Creek Branch, 19955 Forest Rd N, 55025. SAN 308-5848. Tel: 651-275-7300. Administration Tel: 651-275-8500. FAX: 651 275 7301. Administration FAX: 651-275-8509. Web Site: www.co.washington.mn.us/library. *Mgr,* Amy Worwa; Tel: 651-275-7302, E-mail: amy.worwa@co.washington.mn.us
Founded 1941. Circ 229,068
Library Holdings: Bk Vols 91,000
Automation Activity & Vendor Info: (Cataloging) SirsiDynix; (Circulation) SIRSI WorkFlows; (OPAC) SirsiDynix
Wireless access
Partic in Metropolitan Library Service Agency
Open Mon-Thurs 9:30-8, Fri & Sat 9:30-5

FOUNTAIN

S FILLMORE COUNTY HISTORY CENTER*, The Emery & Almeda Eickhoff Genealogy Library, 202 County Rd 8, 55935. SAN 373-3696. Tel: 507-268-4449. FAX: 507-268-4492. E-mail: fchc@frontier.com. Web Site: fillmorecountyhistory.wordpress.com. *Exec Dir,* Debra J Richardson
Library Holdings: Bk Vols 2,500
Subject Interests: Local hist
Open Tues-Sat 9-4

FULDA

P FULDA MEMORIAL LIBRARY*, 101 Third St NE, 56131-1106. (Mail add: PO Box 346, 56131-0346), SAN 308-5872. Tel: 507-425-3277. Web Site: www.plumcreeklibrary.org/fulda. *Dir,* Beth Cuperus; E-mail: bcuperus@plumcreeklibrary.net
Pop 1,330; Circ 19,108
Library Holdings: Bk Vols 14,890; Per Subs 60

Automation Activity & Vendor Info: (Cataloging) TLC (The Library Corporation); (Circulation) TLC (The Library Corporation); (OPAC) TLC (The Library Corporation)
Mem of Plum Creek Library System
Open Mon & Thurs 12-6, Tues, Wed & Fri 12-5, Sat 10-2
Friends of the Library Group

GAYLORD

P GAYLORD PUBLIC LIBRARY*, 428 Main Ave, 55334. (Mail add: PO Box 797, 55334-0797), SAN 347-4240. Tel: 507-237-2280. FAX: 507-237-4177. E-mail: libtsg@tds.lib.mn.us. Web Site: www.tds.lib.mn.us/gaylord. *Dir,* Wanda Messner
Library Holdings: Bk Vols 14,000; Per Subs 56
Automation Activity & Vendor Info: (Cataloging) SirsiDynix; (Circulation) SirsiDynix; (OPAC) SirsiDynix
Database Vendor: EBSCOhost
Wireless access
Mem of Traverse Des Sioux Library Cooperative
Open Mon 2:30-7:30, Tues & Thurs 2:30-6:30, Wed 9-5:30, Fri 12-4:30, Sat 9-12
Friends of the Library Group

GIBBON

P GIBBON PUBLIC LIBRARY*, 1050 Adams Ave, 55335. (Mail add: PO Box 138, 55335-0138), SAN 347-4275. Tel: 507-834-6640. FAX: 507-834-6640. E-mail: libtsb@tds.lib.mn.us. *Dir,* Kimberly J Holmquist; Staff 1.5 (Non-MLS 1.5)
Founded 1975
Library Holdings: Bk Vols 9,824; Per Subs 50
Automation Activity & Vendor Info: (Cataloging) SirsiDynix; (Circulation) SirsiDynix; (OPAC) SirsiDynix
Wireless access
Mem of Traverse Des Sioux Library Cooperative
Open Mon-Fri 10-6, Thurs 10-8, Sat 9-12
Friends of the Library Group

GILBERT

P GILBERT PUBLIC LIBRARY*, 17 N Broadway, 55741. (Mail add: PO Box 758, 55741-0758), SAN 308-5880. Tel: 218-748-2230. FAX: 218-748-2229. E-mail: illgil@arrowhead.lib.mn.us. Web Site: www.gilbert.lib.mn.us. *Dir,* Amy Hay; Staff 4 (MLS 1, Non-MLS 3)
Founded 1924. Pop 1,847; Circ 23,906
Jan 2007-Dec 2007 Income $130,425, City $113,250, Locally Generated Income $10,175, Other $7,000. Mats Exp $14,000. Sal $78,750
Library Holdings: AV Mats 40; CDs 74; DVDs 196; Bk Titles 10,800; Per Subs 59; Talking Bks 149; Videos 784
Special Collections: Careers; NE Minnesota
Automation Activity & Vendor Info: (Cataloging) Horizon; (Circulation) Horizon; (OPAC) Horizon
Database Vendor: EBSCOhost, Gale Cengage Learning, OCLC WorldShare Interlibrary Loan, ProQuest, SirsiDynix
Mem of Arrowhead Library System
Partic in Minitex Library Information Network
Open Mon-Thurs (Winter) 10:30-7:30, Fri 10:30-6, Sat 10:30-1:30; Mon-Fri (Summer) 10:30-6

GLENCOE

P GLENCOE PUBLIC LIBRARY*, 719 13th St E, 55336-1597. SAN 348-114X. Tel: 320-864-3919. FAX: 320-864-1919. Web Site: iii.pioneerland.lib.mn.us. *Librn,* Jackee Fountain; E-mail: jackeef@glencoe.lib.mn.us
Pop 5,247; Circ 39,686
Library Holdings: Bk Vols 26,000; Per Subs 102
Automation Activity & Vendor Info: (Cataloging) Innovative Interfaces, Inc; (Circulation) Innovative Interfaces, Inc; (OPAC) Innovative Interfaces, Inc
Mem of Pioneerland Library System
Open Mon & Tues 2-9, Wed 12-9, Thurs 10-9, Fri 2-5, Sat 10-3
Friends of the Library Group

GLENWOOD

P GLENWOOD PUBLIC LIBRARY*, 108 SE First Ave, 56334-1622. SAN 308-5899. Tel: 320-634-3375. FAX: 320-634-5099. Web Site: www.viking.lib.mn.us. *Dir,* Leslie Randall; E-mail: lrandall@glenwood.lib.mn.us
Founded 1907. Pop 5,002; Circ 67,943
Jan 2011-Jan 2012 Income $283,740, City $175,940, County $107,800
Library Holdings: AV Mats 440; Bks on Deafness & Sign Lang 5; CDs 1,094; DVDs 1,652; Large Print Bks 376; Music Scores 45; Bk Vols 23,777; Per Subs 61; Videos 361
Wireless access
Mem of Viking Library System
Open Mon & Wed 1-8, Tues & Thurs 10-5:30, Fri 1-5:30, Sat 10-2
Friends of the Library Group

S POPE COUNTY HISTORICAL SOCIETY, 809 S Lake Shore Dr, 56334. SAN 326-0631. Tel: 320-634-3293. E-mail: popecountymuseum@gmail.com. Web Site: popecountymuseum.wordpress.com. *Dir,* Merlin Peterson
Founded 1932
Jan 2013-Dec 2013 Income $75,000. Sal $38,435
Library Holdings: Bk Vols 1,000
Special Collections: History of Pope County, bks, bibles, ed, fiction; Newspapers (1891-present); Pope County Platt Book (from 1874); Population Census 1880-1920 (not 1890), microfilm
Subject Interests: Genealogy
Open Tues-Sat 10-5
Restriction: Open to pub for ref only

GRACEVILLE

P GRACEVILLE PUBLIC LIBRARY*, 415 Studdart Ave, 56240. (Mail add: PO Box 457, 56240-0457), SAN 347-6944. Tel: 320-748-7332. FAX: 320-748-7338. E-mail: gracevil@graceville.lib.mn.us. *Librn,* Vicki Grimli
Pop 659; Circ 16,794
Library Holdings: Bk Vols 17,371; Per Subs 15
Automation Activity & Vendor Info: (Circulation) PALS; (OPAC) PALS
Mem of Pioneerland Library System
Open Tues 11-5, Wed 2-7, Thurs 12-6, Fr 1-5, Sat 10-1
Friends of the Library Group

GRAND MARAIS

P GRAND MARAIS PUBLIC LIBRARY, 104 Second Ave W, 55604. (Mail add: PO Box 280, 55604-0280), SAN 308-5929. Tel: 218-387-1140. FAX: 218-387-1848. E-mail: gmlib@arrowhead.lib.mn.us. Web Site: www.grandmaraislibrary.org. *Dir,* Steve Harsin; *Ch Serv,* Patsy Ingebrigtsen; *Tech Serv,* Mark Luttinen; Staff 4 (MLS 1, Non-MLS 3)
Founded 1904. Pop 5,168; Circ 72,465
Library Holdings: Bk Vols 23,000; Per Subs 107
Subject Interests: Cook County, Local hist, N Eastern Minn
Automation Activity & Vendor Info: (Cataloging) SirsiDynix; (Circulation) SirsiDynix; (ILL) SirsiDynix; (OPAC) SirsiDynix
Wireless access
Function: Web-catalog
Mem of Arrowhead Library System
Open Mon, Tues, Thurs & Fri 10-5, Wed 10-8, Sat 10-2
Friends of the Library Group

GRAND MEADOW

P GRAND MEADOW PUBLIC LIBRARY*, 125 Grand Ave E, 55936. SAN 347-1969. Tel: 507-754-5859. FAX: 507-754-5859. Web Site: www.grandmeadow.lib.mn.us. *Librn,* Alicia Baugh; E-mail: abaugh@selco.info
Library Holdings: Bk Vols 14,000; Per Subs 20
Partic in Southeastern Libraries Cooperating
Open Tues & Thurs 9-6, Wed 9-5, Sat 9-1

GRAND PORTAGE

S US NATIONAL PARK SERVICE*, Grand Portage National Monument Library, 170 Mile Creek Rd, 55605. (Mail add: PO Box 426, 55605-0426), SAN 370-3134. Tel: 218-475-0123. FAX: 218-475-0174. Web Site: www.nps.gov/grpo. *In Charge,* Pam Neil
Library Holdings: Bk Vols 1,211; Per Subs 50
Subject Interests: Fur trade, Ojibwe culture
Restriction: Open by appt only, Open to pub for ref only

GRAND RAPIDS

P GRAND RAPIDS AREA LIBRARY*, 140 NE Second St, 55744-2601. SAN 308-5937. Tel: 218-326-7640. Circulation Tel: 218-326-7641. Interlibrary Loan Service Tel: 218-327-8821. Reference Tel: 218-327-8820. FAX: 218-326-7644. TDD: 218-327-7831. E-mail: illrap@arrowhead.lib.mn.us. Web Site: www.grandrapids.lib.mn.us. *Dir,* Marcia Anderson; Tel: 218-327-8826, E-mail: manderso@arrowhead.lib.mn.us; *Asst Dir,* Amy Dettmer; E-mail: adettmer@arrowhead.lib.mn.us; *Ch,* Darla Kirwin; *Ref Librn,* Will Richter; Staff 7.75 (MLS 3, Non-MLS 4.75)
Founded 1900. Pop 19,138; Circ 195,000
Jan 2006-Dec 2006 Income $745,142, City $532,360, County $125,000, Locally Generated Income $81,502, Other $6,280. Mats Exp $745,142, Books $55,750, Per/Ser (Incl. Access Fees) $8,000, Other Print Mats $2,500, Micro $150, AV Mat $3,500, Electronic Ref Mat (Incl. Access Fees) $4,500. Sal $411,142

Library Holdings: AV Mats 500; CDs 2,000; DVDs 1,215; Large Print Bks 3,650; Bk Titles 68,000; Per Subs 200; Talking Bks 1,714; Videos 1,118
Subject Interests: Judy Garland, Local authors, World War I
Automation Activity & Vendor Info: (Acquisitions) SirsiDynix; (Cataloging) OCLC CatExpress; (Circulation) SirsiDynix; (Course Reserve) SirsiDynix; (OPAC) SirsiDynix; (Serials) SirsiDynix
Database Vendor: Baker & Taylor, EBSCOhost, OCLC FirstSearch, ProQuest, SirsiDynix
Wireless access
Function: Adult bk club, Adult literacy prog, Art exhibits, AV serv, Bk club(s), Copy machines, Digital talking bks, Distance learning, e-mail serv, E-Reserves, Electronic databases & coll, Equip loans & repairs, Family literacy, Fax serv, Handicapped accessible, Homework prog, ILL available, Mail & tel request accepted, Online searches, Photocopying/Printing, Prog for adults, Prog for children & young adult, Ref & res, Spoken cassettes & CDs, Summer reading prog, Tax forms, Telephone ref, VHS videos, Wheelchair accessible
Mem of Arrowhead Library System
Special Services for the Deaf - TDD equip
Open Mon-Thurs 9-8, Fri 2-6, Sat 9-1
Friends of the Library Group

C ITASCA COMMUNITY COLLEGE LIBRARY*, 1851 E Hwy 169, 55744. SAN 308-5945. Tel: 218-322-2350. FAX: 218-327-4299. Web Site: www.itascacc.edu. *Librn,* Steven Bean; Tel: 218-327-4147
Founded 1922. Enrl 920; Fac 40
Library Holdings: Bk Titles 30,000; Per Subs 150
Automation Activity & Vendor Info: (Cataloging) Ex Libris Group; (Circulation) Ex Libris Group; (Course Reserve) Ex Libris Group; (ILL) Ex Libris Group; (OPAC) Ex Libris Group; (Serials) Ex Libris Group
Database Vendor: EBSCOhost, Gale Cengage Learning, LexisNexis, ProQuest
Wireless access
Partic in OCLC Online Computer Library Center, Inc; Project for Automated Systs
Open Mon-Thurs (Winter) 8-8, Fri 8-4:30, Sat 10-3; Mon-Fri (Summer) 8-4:30

S ITASCA COUNTY HISTORICAL SOCIETY*, Karjala Genealogy & History Research Center, 201 Pokegama Ave N, 55744. SAN 373-2258. Tel: 218-326-6431. E-mail: ichs@paulbunyan.net. Web Site: www.itascahistoricalorg. *Exec Dir,* Lilah Crowe
Library Holdings: Bk Vols 750
Subject Interests: Local hist
Wireless access

GRANITE FALLS

P GRANITE FALLS PUBLIC LIBRARY*, 155 Seventh Ave, 56241. SAN 308-5953. Tel: 320-564-3738. FAX: 320-564-4666. E-mail: granite@granitefalls.lib.mn.us. *Br Mgr,* Madelyn Bronson; Staff 2 (Non-MLS 2)
Founded 1877. Pop 5,000; Circ 26,421
Jan 2006-Dec 2006 Income $95,110
Library Holdings: Large Print Bks 1,200; Bk Vols 20,500; Per Subs 87; Talking Bks 540; Videos 725
Special Collections: Large Print Coll; Local History Coll; Native American Coll; Norway (Sons of Norway Coll)
Mem of Pioneerland Library System
Open Mon-Wed 9-6, Thurs 9-8, Fri 9-3, Sat 9-2

GROVE CITY

P GROVE CITY PUBLIC LIBRARY*, 210 Atlantic Ave W, 56243. (Mail add: PO Box 248, 56243-0248), SAN 348-1174. Tel: 320-857-2550. FAX: 320-857-2322. E-mail: grovecit@grovecity.lib.mn.us. *Head Librn,* Jeanette Stottrup; Staff 1 (Non-MLS 1)
Pop 597; Circ 6,330
Library Holdings: Bk Vols 5,618; Per Subs 39
Automation Activity & Vendor Info: (Circulation) Innovative Interfaces, Inc; (OPAC) Innovative Interfaces, Inc
Wireless access
Mem of Pioneerland Library System
Open Mon 10-5, Tues 2-6, Wed & Thurs 3-6, Fri 2-5

HANCOCK

P HANCOCK COMMUNITY LIBRARY*, 662 Sixth St, 56244-9998. SAN 308-5961. Tel: 320-392-5666. FAX: 320-392-5132. Web Site: www.viking.lib.mn.us. *Dir,* Phyllis Joos; E-mail: pjoos@hancock.lib.mn.us
Founded 1920. Pop 750; Circ 10,083
Library Holdings: Bk Titles 7,890; Per Subs 36
Special Collections: Large Print Coll
Automation Activity & Vendor Info: (Cataloging) Horizon; (Circulation) Horizon; (OPAC) Horizon
Mem of Viking Library System
Partic in Northern Lights Library Network
Open Mon, Tues & Thurs 11-6
Friends of the Library Group

HANSKA

P HANSKA COMMUNITY LIBRARY, 201 W Broadway Ave, 56041. (Mail add: PO Box 91, 56041-0082), SAN 376-7167. Tel: 507-439-6428. Web Site: cityofhanska.com/community-library, tdslib.org/hanska-community-library. *Dir,* Darlene Nelson; E-mail: dnelson@tds.lib.mn.us; *Libr Asst,* Rhonda Froehling; Staff 2 (Non-MLS 2)
Pop 450
Library Holdings: Bk Titles 6,300
Special Collections: Hanska History Coll
Automation Activity & Vendor Info: (Cataloging) SirsiDynix; (Circulation) SirsiDynix; (OPAC) SirsiDynix
Database Vendor: OCLC FirstSearch
Function: Archival coll
Mem of Traverse Des Sioux Library Cooperative
Open Mon & Tues 11-5, Wed 9-5, Thurs 2-6
Friends of the Library Group

HARMONY

P HARMONY PUBLIC LIBRARY*, 225 Third Ave SW, 55939-6635. (Mail add: PO Box 488, 55939-0488), SAN 308-597X. Tel: 507-886-8133. FAX: 507-886-1433. E-mail: har_dir@selco.info. Web Site: harmony.lib.mn.us. *Librn,* Stephanie Silvers; E-mail: ssilvers@selco.info; Staff 3 (MLS 1, Non-MLS 2)
Founded 1916. Pop 2,500; Circ 24,125
Library Holdings: Bk Vols 17,000; Per Subs 60
Special Collections: Beginning Genealogy; Local Old Photographs & History
Function: ILL available
Partic in Southeastern Libraries Cooperating
Open Mon, Wed & Fri 10-6, Tues & Thurs 2-8, Sat 10-1

HASTINGS

P PLEASANT HILL LIBRARY*, 1490 S Frontage Rd, 55033. SAN 376-9356. Tel: 651-438-0200. FAX: 651-480-4944. Web Site: www.dakotacounty.us/library. *Dir,* Ken Behringer
Library Holdings: Bk Titles 86,000; Per Subs 130
Automation Activity & Vendor Info: (Acquisitions) SirsiDynix; (Cataloging) SirsiDynix; (Circulation) SirsiDynix; (OPAC) SirsiDynix; (Serials) SirsiDynix
Database Vendor: EBSCOhost, Gale Cengage Learning, ProQuest
Wireless access
Partic in Metropolitan Library Service Agency
Open Mon-Thurs 10-8:30, Fri & Sat 10-5:30, Sun (Sept-May) 1-5
Friends of the Library Group

HECTOR

P HECTOR PUBLIC LIBRARY*, 126 S Main, 55342. (Mail add: PO Box 368, 55342-0368), SAN 376-7191. Tel: 320-848-2841. FAX: 320-848-2841. *Br Mgr, Commun Relations Librn,* Jill Schwiderski; E-mail: jills@hector.lib.mn.us; Staff 0.75 (Non-MLS 0.75)
Founded 1985. Pop 1,146; Circ 20,152
Jan 2008-Dec 2008 Income $45,381. Mats Exp $4,500. Sal $27,500
Library Holdings: AV Mats 625; Large Print Bks 277; Bk Vols 12,250; Per Subs 20
Automation Activity & Vendor Info: (Acquisitions) Baker & Taylor
Wireless access
Mem of Pioneerland Library System
Open Mon, Tues & Fri 11:30-4:30, Wed 10-12 & 1-4:30, Thurs 11:30-4:30 & 6:30-8, Sat 10-12
Friends of the Library Group

HENDERSON

P HENDERSON PUBLIC LIBRARY, 110 S Sixth St, 56044-7734. (Mail add: PO Box 404, 56044), SAN 347-4305. Tel: 507-248-3880. E-mail: libtsh@tds.lib.mn.us. *Dir,* Kathy Engel
Library Holdings: Bk Vols 9,376
Automation Activity & Vendor Info: (Acquisitions) SirsiDynix; (Cataloging) SirsiDynix; (Circulation) SirsiDynix; (Course Reserve) SirsiDynix; (Media Booking) SirsiDynix; (Serials) SirsiDynix
Wireless access
Mem of Traverse Des Sioux Library Cooperative
Friends of the Library Group

HIBBING

P HIBBING PUBLIC LIBRARY*, 2020 E Fifth Ave, 55746-1702. SAN 308-5996. Tel: 218-362-5959. FAX: 218-312-9779. TDD: 218-362-5956. E-mail: hibbingpl@arrowhead.lib.mn.us. Web Site: www.hibbing.lib.mn.us. *Dir,* Ginny Richmond; E-mail: grichmon@arrowhead.lib.mn.us; *Acq, Cat, Ref,* Position Currently Open; *Ch Serv,* April Larson; E-mail: alarson@arrowhead.lib.mn.us; Staff 3 (MLS 1, Non-MLS 2)
Founded 1908. Pop 17,017; Circ 138,822
Jan 2007-Dec 2007 Income $808,000. Mats Exp $68,000. Sal $400,000
Library Holdings: Bk Vols 80,000; Per Subs 125
Special Collections: Bob Dylan Coll
Automation Activity & Vendor Info: (Acquisitions) SirsiDynix; (Cataloging) OCLC CatExpress; (Circulation) SirsiDynix; (OPAC) SirsiDynix; (Serials) SirsiDynix
Database Vendor: EBSCOhost, Gale Cengage Learning, OCLC FirstSearch, ProQuest
Wireless access
Function: Bks on cassette, Bks on CD, Children's prog, Computers for patron use, Copy machines, Electronic databases & coll, Exhibits, Homebound delivery serv, ILL available, Music CDs, Photocopying/Printing, Pub access computers, Story hour, Summer reading prog, Tax forms
Special Services for the Deaf - TDD equip
Open Mon-Thurs 10-7, Fri 10-5
Friends of the Library Group

HOKAH

P HOKAH PUBLIC LIBRARY*, 57 Main, 55941. (Mail add: PO Box 503, 55941-0503), SAN 376-7833. Tel: 507-894-2665. FAX: 507-894-2665. *Dir,* Barbara Bissen; E-mail: barbb@selco.info
Library Holdings: CDs 600; DVDs 500; Bk Vols 20,600; Per Subs 34; Talking Bks 55; Videos 1,500
Automation Activity & Vendor Info: (Cataloging) Horizon; (Circulation) Horizon; (OPAC) Horizon
Wireless access
Partic in Southeastern Libraries Cooperating
Open Mon & Thurs 2-8, Tues 9-12 & 6-8, Fri 10-12 & 2-8, Sat (Nov-April) 10-12
Friends of the Library Group

HOYT LAKES

P HOYT LAKES PUBLIC LIBRARY*, 206 Kennedy Dr, 55750. SAN 308-6011. Tel: 218-225-2412. FAX: 218-225-2399. *Librn,* Susan Sowers
Founded 1959. Circ 36,000
Library Holdings: Bk Vols 23,000; Per Subs 62
Automation Activity & Vendor Info: (Cataloging) SirsiDynix; (Circulation) SirsiDynix; (OPAC) SirsiDynix; (Serials) SirsiDynix
Database Vendor: OCLC FirstSearch
Wireless access
Mem of Arrowhead Library System
Open Mon 10-8, Tues-Thurs 1-8, Fri 10-5, Sat (Sept-May) 10-2
Friends of the Library Group

HUTCHINSON

P HUTCHINSON PUBLIC LIBRARY*, 50 Hassan St SE, 55350-1881. SAN 348-1204. Tel: 320-587-2368. FAX: 320-587-4286. Web Site: www.hutchinson.lib.mn.us. *Librn,* Pamela Dille; E-mail: pamela.dille@pioneerland.lib.mn.us; *Ch,* Sherry Lund; Staff 4 (Non-MLS 4)
Pop 12,989; Circ 90,355
Library Holdings: Bk Vols 40,865; Per Subs 129
Automation Activity & Vendor Info: (Circulation) PALS; (OPAC) PALS
Mem of Pioneerland Library System; South Central Kansas Library System
Open Mon-Thurs 10-9, Fri & Sat 10-5
Friends of the Library Group

J RIDGEWATER COLLEGE LIBRARY*, Hutchinson Campus, Two Century Ave, 55350. SAN 378-3715. Tel: 320-234-8567. Interlibrary Loan Service Tel: 320-234-8566. Reference Tel: 320-234-8565. FAX: 320-234-8640. Web Site: www.ridgewater.edu/library/hutchinson-library/index.cfm. *Librn,* Yvonne Johnson; E-mail: yvonne.johnson@ridgewater.edu; Staff 2 (MLS 1, Non-MLS 1)
Founded 1997. Enrl 1,200; Fac 56; Highest Degree: Associate
Library Holdings: Bk Vols 11,000; Per Subs 120
Automation Activity & Vendor Info: (Cataloging) Ex Libris Group; (Circulation) Ex Libris Group; (OPAC) Ex Libris Group
Database Vendor: Gale Cengage Learning, ProQuest
Open Mon-Thurs (Fall & Spring) 8am-9pm, Fri 8-4; Mon-Thurs (Summer) 9-1

INTERNATIONAL FALLS

P INTERNATIONAL FALLS PUBLIC LIBRARY, 750 Fourth St, 56649. SAN 308-602X. Tel: 218-283-8051. FAX: 218-283-4379. Web Site: internationalfallslibrary.us. *Dir,* Diane Adams; E-mail: dadams@arrowhead.lib.mn.us; Staff 3 (MLS 1, Non-MLS 2)
Founded 1911. Pop 5,906; Circ 89,858
Library Holdings: AV Mats 1,966; Bk Titles 48,687; Per Subs 106
Special Collections: Vigilance Coll (mats to encourage citizen involvement in commun & govt)
Subject Interests: Minn hist
Automation Activity & Vendor Info: (Acquisitions) SirsiDynix; (Cataloging) SirsiDynix; (Circulation) SirsiDynix; (ILL) SirsiDynix; (OPAC) SirsiDynix; (Serials) SirsiDynix
Database Vendor: EBSCOhost, TLC (The Library Corporation)
Wireless access
Open Mon-Wed 10-8, Thurs & Fri 10-6, Sat (Winter) 10-3
Friends of the Library Group

S KOOCHICHING COUNTY HISTORICAL MUSEUM LIBRARY*, 214 Sixth Ave, 56649. SAN 326-2456. Tel: 218-283-4316. FAX: 218-283-8243. *Exec Dir,* Edgar Oerichbauer
Library Holdings: Bk Vols 1,950; Per Subs 12
Special Collections: International Lumber Co Coll, photogs & records; Mando/Boise Cascade Coll, photogs & records; Sawmill, Logging, Papermill Coll. Oral History
Open Mon-Fri 9-5

J RAINY RIVER COMMUNITY COLLEGE LIBRARY*, 1501 Hwy 71, 56649. SAN 308-6038. Tel: 218-285-7722, Ext 220. FAX: 218-285-2239. Web Site: www.rrcc.mnscu.edu. *Librn,* Stephanie Olson; Tel: 218-285-2220, E-mail: stephanie.olson@rainyriver.edu; *Tech Serv,* Diane Raboin; Tel: 218-285-2250, E-mail: diane.raboin@rainyriver.edu; Staff 1 (MLS 1)
Founded 1967. Enrl 399
Library Holdings: Bk Titles 16,500; Bk Vols 19,000; Per Subs 32; Videos 740
Publications: LRC Handbook
Partic in Dialog Corp
Open Mon-Fri 8:30-4:30

INVER GROVE HEIGHTS

J INVER HILLS COMMUNITY COLLEGE LIBRARY*, 2500 80th St E, 55076-3209. SAN 308-6046. Tel: 651-450-3625. Interlibrary Loan Service Tel: 651-450-3624. FAX: 651-450-3679. E-mail: library@inverhills.edu. Web Site: www.inverhills.edu/library. *Instr, Librn,* Brenda Besser; Tel: 651-450-3798, E-mail: bbesser@inverhills.edu; *Ref,* Julie Benolken; Tel: 651-450-8622, E-mail: jbenolk@inverhills.edu; *Ref,* Ann Schroder; Tel: 651-450-8623, E-mail: aschrod@inverhills.edu; *Tech Serv,* David Colwell; *Tech Serv,* Chad Gilman; Tel: 651-450-3876, E-mail: cgilman@inverhills.edu; Staff 4 (MLS 3, Non-MLS 1)
Founded 1970. Enrl 6,100; Fac 180; Highest Degree: Associate
Library Holdings: Bk Titles 64,000; Per Subs 200
Automation Activity & Vendor Info: (Acquisitions) Ex Libris Group; (Cataloging) Ex Libris Group; (Circulation) Ex Libris Group; (Course Reserve) Ex Libris Group; (ILL) Ex Libris Group; (OPAC) Ex Libris Group; (Serials) Ex Libris Group
Database Vendor: CredoReference, EBSCOhost, Gale Cengage Learning, JSTOR, LexisNexis, Micromedex, OCLC WorldShare Interlibrary Loan, OVID Technologies, Oxford Online, ProQuest, Westlaw
Wireless access
Partic in Minitex Library Information Network; MnPALS; OCLC Online Computer Library Center, Inc
Open Mon-Thurs 8am-9pm, Fri 8-4, Sat 9-3

IVANHOE

P IVANHOE PUBLIC LIBRARY*, 401 N Harold, 56142. (Mail add: PO Box 25, 56142-0025), SAN 376-7574. Tel: 507-694-1555. FAX: 507-694-1738. Web Site: www.plumcreeklibrary.org/ivanhoe. *Librn,* Susan Vizecky
Library Holdings: Bk Titles 10,000; Bk Vols 15,000; Per Subs 20
Mem of Plum Creek Library System
Open Mon, Wed & Fri 9-1 & 2-4, Thurs 11-3 & 4-7

JACKSON

P JACKSON COUNTY LIBRARY*, 311 Third St, 56143-1600. SAN 308-6054. Tel: 507-847-4748. FAX: 507-847-5470. E-mail: jacksoncolibrary@plumcreeklibrary.net. Web Site: www.plumcreeklibrary.org/Jackson. *Dir,* Tamera Marie Erickson; E-mail: terickson@plumcreeklibrary.net; *Asst Librn,* Pam Grussing; E-mail: pgrussing@plumcreeklibrary.net; *Asst Librn,* Dawn Skow; E-mail:

dskow@plumcreeklibrary.net; *Ch Serv,* Carrie Dose; E-mail: cdose@plumcreeklibrary.net; Staff 7 (Non-MLS 7)
Pop 11,636; Circ 109,825
Library Holdings: CDs 200; Bk Vols 22,829; Per Subs 100; Talking Bks 1,684; Videos 1,358
Automation Activity & Vendor Info: (Cataloging) TLC (The Library Corporation); (Circulation) TLC (The Library Corporation); (OPAC) TLC (The Library Corporation)
Database Vendor: Gale Cengage Learning, OCLC FirstSearch, Wilson - Wilson Web
Mem of Plum Creek Library System
Open Mon, Tues & Thurs (Winter) 10-8, Wed & Fri 10-5, Sat 10-3, Sun 1-4; Mon, Tues & Thurs (Summer) 10-8, Wed & Fri 10-5
Friends of the Library Group
Branches: 2
HERON LAKE BRANCH, 401 Ninth St, Heron Lake, 56137-1440. (Mail add: PO Box 348, Heron Lake, 56137-0348), SAN 322-6719. Tel: 507-793-2641. FAX: 507-793-2641. *Br Mgr,* Sunny Osland
Pop 1,000; Circ 9,723
Library Holdings: Bk Vols 7,521; Per Subs 22
Open Tues & Thurs 1-5:30, Wed 3-8 (1-8 Summer), Fri 1-5, Sat 10-12
LAKEFIELD BRANCH, 410 Main St, Lakefield, 56150-1201. (Mail add: PO Box 723, Lakefield, 56150-0723). Tel: 507-662-5782. FAX: 507-662-5782. *Br Mgr,* Kathy Weeks-Wegner
Library Holdings: Bk Vols 10,608; Per Subs 34
Open Mon-Wed 11-5:30, Thurs 11-7, Fri 11-5, Sat 10-1

KASSON

P KASSON PUBLIC LIBRARY*, 16 First Ave NW, 55944. SAN 308-6062. Tel: 507-634-7615. FAX: 507-634-7630. E-mail: kassonlibrary@gmail.com. Web Site: www.kasson.lib.mn.us. *Dir,* Art Tiff; E-mail: atiff@selco.info
Founded 1899. Pop 9,761; Circ 60,547
Library Holdings: AV Mats 3,301; Bk Titles 20,272
Wireless access
Partic in Southeastern Libraries Cooperating
Open Mon & Wed 10-7, Tues & Thurs 10-6, Fri 10-5
Friends of the Library Group

KEEWATIN

P KEEWATIN PUBLIC LIBRARY*, 125 W Third Ave, 55753. (Mail add: PO Box 220, 55753-0220), SAN 308-6070. Tel: 218-778-6377. FAX: 218-778-6193. *Dir,* Paula Fowler; E-mail: pfowler@arrowhead.lib.mn.us; *Librn,* Janice Kunze
Pop 1,300; Circ 11,614
Library Holdings: Bk Vols 7,390; Per Subs 20
Mem of Arrowhead Library System
Open Mon-Thurs 10-7, Fri 10-4

KENYON

P KENYON PUBLIC LIBRARY, 709 Second St, 55946-1339. SAN 308-6089. Tel: 507-789-6821. FAX: 507-789-5604. Web Site: www.kenyon.lib.mn.us. *Dir,* Michelle Otte, E-mail: motte@selco.info; Staff 3 (MLS 1, Non-MLS 2)
Founded 1907. Pop 4,500; Circ 35,000
Library Holdings: Bk Vols 15,500
Wireless access
Partic in Southeastern Libraries Cooperating
Open Mon, Wed & Fri 10-4:30, Tues & Thurs 10-6:30

KERKHOVEN

P KERKHOVEN PUBLIC LIBRARY*, 208 N Tenth, 56252. (Mail add: PO Box 508, 56252-0508), SAN 347-6952. Tel: 320-264-2141. FAX: 320-264-2141. E-mail: kerk@kerkhoven.lib.mn.us. *Br Mgr,* Faye Helms; Staff 1 (MLS 1)
Pop 740; Circ 7,787
Library Holdings: Bk Vols 4,323; Per Subs 16
Automation Activity & Vendor Info: (Circulation) PALS; (OPAC) PALS
Mem of Pioneerland Library System
Open Mon & Tues 2-5, Wed 2-7, Thurs 11-5, Fri 1-5

KINNEY

P KINNEY PUBLIC LIBRARY*, 400 Main St, 55758. (Mail add: PO Box D7, 55758), SAN 308-6097. Tel: 218-258-2232. FAX: 218-258-2232. Web Site: www.arrowhead.lib.mn.us/area-libraries/kinney. *Dir,* Katie Pastore; E-mail: kpastore@arrowhead.lib.mn.us
Pop 447; Circ 4,270
Library Holdings: Bk Vols 8,500; Per Subs 30
Mem of Arrowhead Library System
Open Mon-Thurs 3-6

LA CRESCENT

P LA CRESCENT PUBLIC LIBRARY*, 321 Main St, 55947. SAN 375-6157. Tel: 507-895-4047. FAX: 507-895-7153. Web Site: www.lacrescent.lib.mn.us. *Dir,* LaVonne M Beach; E-mail: lbeach@selco.lib.mn.us; *Asst Librn,* Judy Ready; Staff 6 (MLS 1, Non-MLS 5)
Founded 1985. Pop 7,705; Circ 69,374
Library Holdings: Audiobooks 1,709; AV Mats 35; CDs 572; DVDs 1,648; e-books 2,100; Large Print Bks 1,580; Microforms 32; Bk Vols 37,535; Per Subs 60; Videos 403
Special Collections: State Document Depository; US Document Depository
Automation Activity & Vendor Info: (Cataloging) Horizon; (Circulation) Horizon; (OPAC) Horizon
Database Vendor: EBSCOhost, Gale Cengage Learning, OCLC FirstSearch, Overdrive, Inc, ProQuest
Wireless access
Partic in Southeastern Libraries Cooperating
Special Services for the Deaf - Bks on deafness & sign lang
Special Services for the Blind - Bks on cassette
Open Mon, Tues & Fri 10-6, Wed & Thurs 10-7, Sat 10-2
Friends of the Library Group

LAKE BENTON

P LAKE BENTON PUBLIC LIBRARY*, 110 E Benton, 56149. (Mail add: PO Box 377, 56149), SAN 376-690X. Tel: 507-368-4641. *Librn,* Shanna Worth; E-mail: sworth@plumcreeklibrary.net
Library Holdings: Bk Titles 8,100; Per Subs 40
Mem of Plum Creek Library System
Open Mon, Wed & Fri 9-12 & 1-5, Sat 9-12
Friends of the Library Group

LAKE CITY

P LAKE CITY PUBLIC LIBRARY*, 201 S High St, 55041. SAN 308-6100. Tel: 651-345-4013. FAX: 651-345-5923. Web Site: www.selco.lib.mn.us/lcpl/. *Dir,* Kathleen A Durand
Founded 1904. Pop 4,505; Circ 40,174
Library Holdings: Bk Vols 42,000; Per Subs 125
Open Mon-Wed 12-8, Thurs 10-8, Fri 12-5, Sat 9-12
Friends of the Library Group

LAKE LILLIAN

P LAKE LILLIAN PUBLIC LIBRARY, 431 Lakeview St, 56253. (Mail add: PO Box 38, 56253-0038), SAN 348-1239. Tel: 320-664-4514. FAX: 320-664-4514. *Br Mgr,* Villa Lippert; E-mail: villa.lippert@pioneerland.lib.mn.us; Staff 1 (Non-MLS 1)
Pop 228; Circ 22,282
Library Holdings: Bk Vols 6,393; Per Subs 43
Wireless access
Mem of Pioneerland Library System
Open Mon & Tues 11-5, Thurs 11-7

LAKEFIELD

S JACKSON COUNTY HISTORICAL SOCIETY LIBRARY*, 307 N Hwy 86, 56150. SAN 328-820X. Tel: 507-662-5505. *Mgr,* Michael Kirchmeier
Library Holdings: Bk Titles 200
Special Collections: Cemetery & Census Records; Genealogical Publications
Subject Interests: County hist
Wireless access
Open Mon-Fri 9:30-4:30, Sat 8-12

LAMBERTON

P LAMBERTON PUBLIC LIBRARY*, 101 E Second Ave, 56152-1047. (Mail add: PO Box 505, 56152-0505), SAN 308-6127. Tel: 507-752-7220. FAX: 507-752-7220. *Dir,* Linda Elaine Werner; E-mail: lwernerlib@yahoo.com
Founded 1933. Pop 1,010; Circ 8,000
Jan 2008-Dec 2008 Income $43,296, City $32,616, County $6,781, Locally Generated Income $3,899. Mats Exp $7,642, Books $6,709, AV Mat $933. Sal $18,237
Library Holdings: Audiobooks 211; AV Mats 1,415; CDs 50; DVDs 360; Large Print Bks 218; Bk Titles 9,350; Bk Vols 9,356; Per Subs 12; Videos 1,235
Automation Activity & Vendor Info: (Acquisitions) SirsiDynix; (Cataloging) SirsiDynix; (Circulation) SirsiDynix; (ILL) SirsiDynix; (OPAC) SirsiDynix; (Serials) SirsiDynix
Wireless access
Mem of Plum Creek Library System

Open Mon-Fri 12-6
Friends of the Library Group

LANESBORO

P LANESBORO PUBLIC LIBRARY*, 202 Parkway Ave S, 55949. (Mail add: PO Box 330, 55949-0330), SAN 376-7892. Tel: 507-467-2649. FAX: 507-467-2346. Web Site: www.lanesboro.lib.mn.u. *Dir,* Tara Johnson; E-mail: tjohnson@selco.info
Library Holdings: Bk Vols 15,000; Per Subs 50
Partic in Southeastern Libraries Cooperating
Open Mon, Wed & Fri 1-6, Tues & Thurs 3-8, Sat 9-2
Friends of the Library Group

LEROY

P LE ROY PUBLIC LIBRARY*, 605 N Broadway, 55951. (Mail add: PO Box 357, 55951-0357), SAN 347-1993. Tel: 507-324-5641. FAX: 507-324-5641. Web Site: leroy.lib.mn.us, www.selco.lib.mn.us. *Dir,* Rhonda Lee Barnes
Founded 1915. Pop 1,000
Library Holdings: Bk Vols 15,000; Per Subs 29
Wireless access
Partic in Southeastern Libraries Cooperating
Open Mon-Thurs 1-8, Sat 9-1

LINO LAKES

S MINNESOTA DEPARTMENT OF CORRECTIONS*, Minnesota Correctional Facility - Lino Lakes, 7525 Fourth Ave, 55014. Tel: 651-717-6684. FAX: 651-717-6598. Web Site: www.doc.state.mn.us. *Librn,* Ria Newhouse; E-mail: rianewhouse@state.mn.us
Library Holdings: Bk Vols 9,700
Special Collections: Law Coll
Automation Activity & Vendor Info: (Cataloging) Follett Software; (Circulation) Follett Software
Open Mon-Thurs 1:35-4:15 & 6:30-8:55, Fri 1:30-4:15

LITCHFIELD

P LITCHFIELD PUBLIC LIBRARY*, 216 N Marshall Ave, 55355. (Mail add: PO Box 817, 55355-0817), SAN 320-5274. Tel: 320-693-2483. FAX: 320-693-2484. E-mail: litch@litchfield.lib.mn.us. Web Site: www.litch.com/library. *Head Librn,* Beth Cronk; E-mail: elizabethc@litchfield.lib.mn.us; Staff 3 (MLS 1, Non-MLS 2)
Founded 1904. Pop 12,000; Circ 110,000
Jan 2005-Dec 2005 Income $169,207. Mats Exp $27,920, Books $24,000, Per/Ser (Incl. Access Fees) $2,720, AV Mat $1,200. Sal $102,898
Library Holdings: AV Mats 1,754; DVDs 274; Large Print Bks 1,057; Per Subs 65; Talking Bks 692; Videos 788
Subject Interests: County hist
Automation Activity & Vendor Info: (Acquisitions) Innovative Interfaces, Inc; (Cataloging) Innovative Interfaces, Inc; (Circulation) Innovative Interfaces, Inc; (ILL) Fretwell-Downing; (OPAC) Innovative Interfaces, Inc; (Serials) Innovative Interfaces, Inc
Database Vendor: Gale Cengage Learning
Mem of Pioneerland Library System
Open Mon-Thurs 10-8, Fri & Sat 10-5
Friends of the Library Group

LITTLE FALLS

M SAINT GABRIEL'S HOSPITAL LIBRARY*, 815 SE Second St, 56345. SAN 329-9902. Tel: 320-632-5441. FAX: 320-632-1190. *Mgr,* Peggy Martin
Library Holdings: Bk Vols 100; Per Subs 10
Restriction: Med staff only

S CHARLES A WEYERHAEUSER MEMORIAL MUSEUM*, R D Musser Library, 2151 Lindbergh Dr S, 56345. (Mail add: PO Box 239, 56345-0239), SAN 326-470X. Tel: 320-632-4007. E-mail: contactstaff@morrisoncountyhistory.org. Web Site: www.morrisoncountyhistory.org. *Exec Dir,* Jan Warner; Staff 2 (Non-MLS 2)
Founded 1975
Library Holdings: Bk Vols 2,000; Per Subs 8
Special Collections: County Newspapers & Census Materials, micro; Little Falls Transcript 1892-1982, bd vols; Morrison County Record 1969-present
Subject Interests: Genealogy, Local hist
Function: Ref serv available
Open Tues-Sat 10-5
Restriction: Non-circulating to the pub

LONG LAKE

S WEST HENNEPIN COUNTY PIONEERS ASSOCIATION LIBRARY*, 1953 W Wayzata Blvd, 55356-9362. (Mail add: PO Box 332, 55356-0332), SAN 326-4416. Tel: 952-473-6557. Web Site: www.whcpa-museum.org. *Pres,* Steven Kelly
Founded 1907
Library Holdings: Bk Titles 600; Per Subs 25
Special Collections: Oral History
Subject Interests: Local hist
Publications: Newsletter (Quarterly)
Restriction: Open by appt only

LONGVILLE

P MARGARET WELCH MEMORIAL LIBRARY*, Longville Library, 5051 State Hwy 84, 56655. (Mail add: PO Box 106, 56655-0106), SAN 347-7878. Tel: 218-363-2710. FAX: 218-363-2710. E-mail: longville@krls.org. *Mgr,* Holly Somrak
Founded 1954. Pop 2,500; Circ 28,000
Library Holdings: AV Mats 500; Bk Titles 15,700; Bk Vols 16,000; Per Subs 30; Talking Bks 504
Subject Interests: Mysteries, World War II
Mem of Kitchigami Regional Library
Open Tues, Thurs & Sat 10-2, Wed & Fri 1-5
Friends of the Library Group

LUVERNE

P ROCK COUNTY COMMUNITY LIBRARY*, 201 W Main, 56156. SAN 308-6151. Tel: 507-449-5040. FAX: 507-449-5034. Web Site: www.plumcreeklibrary.org/luverne. *Dir,* Clint Wolthuizen; E-mail: clintw@plumcreeklibrary.net; *Asst Librn,* Barb Verhey; E-mail: bverhey@plumcreeklibrary.net; *Ch Serv,* Bronwyn Wenzel; E-mail: bwenzel@plumcreeklibrary.net; Staff 3 (Non-MLS 3)
Founded 1907. Pop 9,966; Circ 94,001
Jan 2007-Dec 2007 Income $263,000. Mats Exp $45,000. Sal $141,500
Library Holdings: Bk Vols 38,000; Per Subs 75
Automation Activity & Vendor Info: (Cataloging) SIRSI WorkFlows; (Circulation) SIRSI WorkFlows; (OPAC) SIRSI-iLink
Database Vendor: EBSCOhost, Gale Cengage Learning, Westlaw
Wireless access
Mem of Plum Creek Library System
Open Mon-Thurs 10-8, Fri 10-5, Sat 10-2
Friends of the Library Group

MABEL

P MABEL PUBLIC LIBRARY*, 110 E Newburg Ave, 55954. (Mail add: PO Box 118, 55954-0118), SAN 308-616X. Tel: 507-493-5336. FAX: 507-493-3336. Web Site: mabel.lib.mn.us. *Dir,* Donna Johnson; E-mail: donnaj@selco.info
Founded 1920. Pop 900; Circ 5,791
Library Holdings: Bk Titles 8,000
Wireless access
Partic in Southeastern Libraries Cooperating
Open Mon & Wed 2-7, Tues, Thurs & Fri 9-2, Sat 9-12
Friends of the Library Group

MADISON

S LAC QUI PARLE COUNTY HISTORICAL SOCIETY*, Museum Library, 250 Eighth Ave S, 56256. SAN 328-3771. Tel: 320-598-7678. *Curator,* Janet Liebl
Founded 1948
Library Holdings: Bk Vols 1,500
Function: Res libr
Open Mon-Sat (May-Oct) 9-4:30

P MADISON PUBLIC LIBRARY*, 401 Sixth Ave, 56256-1236. SAN 347-6979. Tel: 320-598-7938. E-mail: madison@madison.lib.mn.us. Web Site: www.madisonlibrary.info. *Librn,* Kathie Behrens; *Ch,* Latain Sandau
Founded 1904. Pop 1,930; Circ 37,578
Library Holdings: AV Mats 2,167; CDs 345; DVDs 867; Large Print Bks 475; Bk Vols 23,894; Per Subs 61; Talking Bks 753; Videos 1,236
Wireless access
Mem of Pioneerland Library System
Open Mon & Wed 10-1 & 1:30-5:30, Tues & Thurs 10-1 & 1:30-7:30, Fri & Sat 1:30-5:30

MANKATO

CR BETHANY LUTHERAN COLLEGE MEMORIAL LIBRARY*, 700 Luther Dr, 56001-4490. SAN 308-6194. Tel: 507-344-7000. Circulation Tel: 507-344-7349. Interlibrary Loan Service Tel: 507-344-7437. Reference Tel: 507-344-7874. Administration Tel: 507-344-7350. FAX: 507-344-7376.

E-mail: library@blc.edu. Web Site: www.blc.edu/library. *Dir, Libr Serv,* Orrin Ausen; E-mail: oausen@blc.edu; *Cat Librn,* Harris Burkhalter; Tel: 507-344-7850, E-mail: harris.burkhalter@blc.edu; *Electronic Res & Ref Librn,* Alyssa Inniger; E-mail: alyssa.inniger@blc.edu; *Libr Serv Supvr,* Colin Scharf; E-mail: colin.scharf@blc.edu; *Circ & ILL Coordr,* Ramsey Turner; E-mail: ramsy.turner@blc.edu; Staff 7 (MLS 2, Non-MLS 5)
Founded 1927. Enrl 592; Fac 48; Highest Degree: Bachelor
Jul 2012-Jun 2013 Income $124,400. Mats Exp $99,400, Books $12,000, Per/Ser (Incl. Access Fees) $18,000, Other Print Mats $10,000, AV Equip $3,000, AV Mat $7,000, Electronic Ref Mat (Incl. Access Fees) $48,900, Presv $500. Sal $185,000 (Prof $55,000)
Library Holdings: Audiobooks 68; AV Mats 5,190; CDs 2,657; DVDs 1,590; e-books 2,725; Electronic Media & Resources 25,000; Music Scores 648; Bk Titles 67,465; Bk Vols 70,469, Per Subs 174, Videos 875
Automation Activity & Vendor Info: (Acquisitions) Ex Libris Group; (Cataloging) Ex Libris Group; (Circulation) Ex Libris Group; (Course Reserve) Ex Libris Group; (ILL) Ex Libris Group; (Media Booking) Ex Libris Group; (OPAC) Ex Libris Group; (Serials) Ex Libris Group
Database Vendor: 3M Library Systems, American Psychological Association (APA), Baker & Taylor, Booklist Online, Bowker, Brodart, Cambridge Scientific Abstracts, College Source, CQ Press, CredoReference, Discovery Education, ebrary, EBSCOhost, Ex Libris Group, Facts on File, Gale Cengage Learning, JSTOR, LearningExpress, Modern Language Association, OCLC ArticleFirst, OCLC CAMIO, OCLC FirstSearch, OCLC WebJunction, OCLC WorldShare Interlibrary Loan, OneSource, Oxford Online, ProQuest, Sage, Standard & Poor's, WT Cox
Wireless access
Function: Archival coll, Audio & video playback equip for onsite use, Bks on CD, CD-ROM, Computer training, Computers for patron use, Copy machines, e-mail & chat, e-mail serv, Electronic databases & coll, Free DVD rentals, Handicapped accessible, ILL available, Instruction & testing, Learning ctr, Music CDs, Online cat, Online info literacy tutorials on the web & in blackboard, Online ref, Online searches, Orientations, Photocopying/Printing, Ref serv available, Ref serv in person, Referrals accepted, Scanner, Tax forms, VHS videos
Partic in Minitex Library Information Network; MnPALS
Open Mon-Thurs 8am-11pm, Fri 8-4:30, Sat 1-5, Sun 1-11
Restriction: Borrowing requests are handled by ILL, Non-circulating coll, Non-circulating of rare bks, Open to students, fac, staff & alumni, Photo ID required for access

P BLUE EARTH COUNTY LIBRARY SYSTEM*, 100 E Main St, 56001. SAN 347-4186. Tel: 507-304-4001. Circulation Tel: 507-304-4010. Reference Tel: 507-304-4022, 507-304-4023. Administration Tel: 507-304-4007. FAX: 507-304-4009. Web Site: www.beclibrary.org. *Dir,* Tim Hayes; E-mail: Tim.Hayes@co.blue-earth.mn.us; *Asst Dir,* Renee Schneider; Tel: 507-304-4016; Staff 2 (MLS 2)
Founded 1902. Pop 55,810; Circ 400,613
Library Holdings: Bk Titles 250,000; Bk Vols 300,000; Per Subs 520
Special Collections: Maud Hart Lovelace Coll; Minnesota Print Material
Automation Activity & Vendor Info: (Cataloging) SirsiDynix; (Circulation) SirsiDynix; (OPAC) SirsiDynix; (Serials) SirsiDynix
Database Vendor: EBSCOhost, Gale Cengage Learning, OCLC FirstSearch, ProQuest, Westlaw
Function: AV serv, Handicapped accessible, ILL available, Magnifiers for reading, Orientations, Photocopying/Printing, Prog for adults, Prog for children & young adult, Ref serv available, Spoken cassettes & CDs, VHS videos, Wheelchair accessible
Open Mon & Tues 10-8, Wed-Sat 9-5, Sun (Winter) 1-5
Friends of the Library Group
Branches: 2
LAKE CRYSTAL PUBLIC LIBRARY, 100 Robinson St, Lake Crystal, 56055, SAN 347-433X. Tel: 507-726-2726. FAX: 507-726-2265. *Br Supvr,* Lo Rae Dressler; Staff 1 (Non-MLS 1)
Founded 1919. Pop 2,085; Circ 16,465
Open Mon & Thurs 1-5:30, Tues 12-5:30, Wed 9:30-5:30, Fri 9:30-6:30, Sat 9:30-12
Friends of the Library Group
MAPLETON BRANCH, 104 First Ave, Mapleton, 56065. (Mail add: PO Box 405, Mapleton, 56065). Tel: 507-524-3513. FAX: 507-524-4536. *Br Coordr,* Bonnie Klein; Staff 1 (Non-MLS 1)
Founded 1910. Pop 1,515; Circ 5,460
Open Tues & Thurs 1-5, Wed 10-2, 1-5 & 6-8, Fri 1-5 & 6-8, Sat 10-12
Friends of the Library Group
Bookmobiles: 1

C MINNESOTA STATE UNIVERSITY, MANKATO*, Library Services, ML3097, 56001. (Mail add: PO Box 8419, 56002-8419), SAN 308-6216. Tel: 507-389-5952. Circulation Tel: 507-389-5151, 507-389-5759. Interlibrary Loan Service Tel: 507-389-5959. Reference Tel: 507-389-5958. FAX: 507-389-5155. Web Site: www.lib.mnsu.edu. *Dean,* Joan Roca; Tel: 507-389-5953; *Asst Dean,* Leslie M Peterson; Tel: 507-389-2290, E-mail: l.peterson@mnsu.edu; *Access Serv Librn,* Lynne Weber; *Cat Librn,* Jessica Schomberg; *Instrul Serv Librn, Ref Librn,* Kellian Clink; *Instrul Serv Librn, Ref Librn,* Kathy Piehl; *Media Librn,* Barbara Bergman; *Ref Librn,* Lisa Baures; *Ref Librn, Supvr, ILL,* Polly Frank; *Ref Librn, Ser,* Becky Schwartzkopf; *Electronic Res, Sci Librn,* Casey Duevel; *Archivist, Spec Coll Librn,* Daardi Sizemore; *Syst Librn,* Peg Lawrence; *Circ Mgr,* Joni Myers; *Coordr, Acq,* Victoria Peters; *Coordr, Ref (Info Serv),* Mark McCullough; *Coll Develop,* Diane Richards; *Govt Doc,* Evan Rusch; *Info Tech,* Dawn Clyne; *Info Tech,* Rosie Mock; Staff 40 (MLS 19, Non-MLS 21)
Founded 1868. Enrl 13,000; Fac 650
Library Holdings: Bk Titles 450,498; Bk Vols 827,341; Per Subs 2,195
Special Collections: Curriculum Materials Coll; Minnesota History (Center for Minnesota Studies Coll); University Archives. Oral History; State Document Depository; US Document Depository
Automation Activity & Vendor Info: (Acquisitions) Ex Libris Group; (Cataloging) Ex Libris Group; (Circulation) Ex Libris Group; (Course Reserve) Ex Libris Group; (ILL) Ex Libris Group; (Media Booking) Ex Libris Group; (OPAC) Ex Libris Group; (Serials) Ex Libris Group
Database Vendor: EBSCOhost, Gale Cengage Learning, LexisNexis, OCLC FirstSearch, OVID Technologies, ProQuest, SirsiDynix
Wireless access
Function: ILL available, Ref serv available
Publications: Quarterly Newsletter
Partic in OCLC Online Computer Library Center, Inc; South Central Minnesota Interlibrary Exchange (SMILE)
Special Services for the Blind - Reader equip
Open Mon-Thurs 7:45am-11:45pm, Fri 7:45-6, Sat 10-6, Sun 1-11:45

P TRAVERSE DES SIOUX LIBRARY COOPERATIVE*, 1400 Madison Ave, Ste 622, 56001-5488. SAN 308-6224. Tel: 507-625-6169. FAX: 507-625-4049. Web Site: tdslib.org. *Exec Dir,* Dayle Zelenka; Tel: 507-625-6169, Ext 28, E-mail: dzelen@tds.lib.mn.us; *Asst Dir,* Orrin Ausen; Tel: 507-625-6169, Ext 27, E-mail: oausen@tds.lib.mn.us; *Tech Serv Librn,* Dani Kroon; Tel: 507-625-6169, Ext 29, E-mail: dkroon@tds.lib.mn.us; *Tech Librn,* John Miller; Tel: 507-625-6169, Ext 32, E-mail: jmille@tds.lib.mn.us; *ILL Spec,* Darla Sorenson; Tel: 507-625-6169, Ext 26, E-mail: dsoren@tds.lib.mn.us; Staff 7 (MLS 7)
Founded 1975. Pop 220,000
Automation Activity & Vendor Info: (Acquisitions) SirsiDynix; (Cataloging) SirsiDynix; (Circulation) SirsiDynix; (OPAC) SirsiDynix; (Serials) SirsiDynix
Member Libraries: Arlington Public Library; Blue Earth Community Library; Comfrey Public Library; Dyckman Free Library; Elmore Public Library; Faribault County Library Service; Gaylord Public Library; Gibbon Public Library; Hanska Community Library; Henderson Public Library; Martin County Library; Muir Library; New Ulm Public Library; North Mankato Taylor Library; Saint Peter Public Library; Springfield Public Library; Waseca-Le Sueur Regional Library; Watonwan County Library; Wells Public Library; Winthrop Public Library
Open Mon-Fri 7:30-5:30

MANTORVILLE

S DODGE COUNTY HISTORICAL SOCIETY LIBRARY*, 615 N Main, 55955. (Mail add: PO Box 433, 55955-0433), SAN 373-370X. Tel: 507-635-5508. E-mail: dchs@kmtel.com. *Dir,* Idella Conwell
Library Holdings: Bk Vols 1,000
Subject Interests: Genealogy, Local hist

MARBLE

P MARBLE PUBLIC LIBRARY*, 302 Alice Ave, 55764. (Mail add: PO Box 409, 55764-0409), SAN 308-6232. Tel: 218-247-7676. FAX: 218-247-7676. *Dir,* Tanja Smith; *Asst City Librn,* Alicia Wikstrom
Pop 699
Jan 2006-Dec 2006 Income $26,411
Library Holdings: Bk Vols 17,000
Special Collections: Christian Romances & Inspirational Series; Stephen King, Dean Koontz & Danielle Steel Colls
Mem of Arrowhead Library System
Open Mon & Fri (Sept-May) 10-11:30 & 2-4:30, Tues & Thurs 3-8, Wed 1-8; Mon, Tues & Thurs (June-Aug) 1-5, Wed 3-8, Fri 10-1

MARSHALL

P MARSHALL-LYON COUNTY LIBRARY*, 301 W Lyon St, 56258. SAN 347-4488. Tel: 507-537-7003. E-mail: library@marshalllyonlibrary.org. Web Site: www.marshalllyonlibrary.org. *Libr Dir,* Position Currently Open; *Interim Dir,* Bob Boese; *Ch,* Mary Beth Sinclair; *Outreach Librn,* Paula Nemes; *Teen Serv Librn,* Lacey Louwagie; *Libr Assoc,* Linda Lange; *Libr Asst I,* Jean Gau; *Libr Asst I,* Rose Thomasson; *Libr Asst II,* Anna-Marie Pickering; *Cataloger,* Arlyss Hovland; Staff 10 (MLS 1, Non-MLS 9)
Founded 1886. Pop 21,605; Circ 205,403
Jan 2005-Dec 2005 Income (Main Library and Branch(s)) $620,343, City $391,050, County $195,524, Other $33,769. Mats Exp $67,184. Sal $444,537
Library Holdings: AV Mats 6,218; Bk Vols 81,795; Per Subs 188

Special Collections: Cake Pans
Automation Activity & Vendor Info: (Cataloging) TLC (The Library Corporation); (Circulation) TLC (The Library Corporation); (OPAC) TLC (The Library Corporation)
Database Vendor: TLC (The Library Corporation)
Mem of Plum Creek Library System
Open Mon- Thurs 9:30-7:30, Fri 9:30-5:30, Sat 10-3
Friends of the Library Group
Branches: 2
BALATON COMMUNITY, 134 Third St, Balaton, 56115-9451. (Mail add: PO Box 326, Balaton, 56115-0326), SAN 347-4518. Tel: 507-734-2034. FAX: 507-734-2316.
Open Mon & Wed 2-7, Fri 12:30-6, Sat 9:30-2
Friends of the Library Group
COTTONWOOD COMMUNITY, 86 W Main St, Cottonwood, 56229. (Mail add: PO Box 106, Cottonwood, 56229-0106), SAN 347-4542. Tel: 507-423-6488. FAX: 507-423-5368. *Librn,* Char Rekedal; Staff 1 (Non-MLS 1)
Library Holdings: AV Mats 589; Bk Vols 7,092
Open Mon 9-12 & 1-7, Wed & Fri 12-5:30

C SOUTHWEST MINNESOTA STATE UNIVERSITY LIBRARY*, McFarland Library, 1501 State St, 56258. SAN 347-4577. Tel: 507-537-7278. Interlibrary Loan Service Tel: 507-537-6127. Reference Tel: 507-537-6176. Administration Tel: 507-537-6372. FAX: 507-537-6200. Web Site: www.smsu.edu/library/. *Univ Librn,* Kathleen Ashe; Tel: 507-537-6372, E-mail: kathleen.ashe@smsu.edu; *Ref Coordr,* Maria Brandt; Tel: 507-537-6165, E-mail: maria.brandt@smsu.edu; *Cat, Syst Librn,* Kathleen Ashe; Tel: 507-537-6142, E-mail: kathleen.ashe@smsu.edu; *Circ Supvr,* Carolyn McDonald; Tel: 507-537-6143, E-mail: carolyn.mcdonald@smsu.edu; *Acq, Govt Doc,* Peggy Anderson; Tel: 507-537-6148, E-mail: peggy.andersonp@smsu.edu; *Acq, Per,* Sandy Hoffbeck; Tel: 507-537-6134, E-mail: sandy.hoffbeck@smsu.edu; *Cat,* Kristi Petersen; Tel: 507-537-6162, E-mail: Kristi.Petersen@smsu.edu; *ILL,* Connie Stensrud; Tel: 507-537-6127, E-mail: conni.stensrud@smsu.edu; Staff 9 (MLS 5, Non-MLS 4)
Founded 1967. Enrl 3,800; Fac 5; Highest Degree: Master
Library Holdings: AV Mats 5,296; e-books 8,166; Bk Vols 197,057; Per Subs 804
Special Collections: Autographs (Z L Begin Coll); Grants-Scholarship Coll; Rare Books Coll. Oral History; US Document Depository
Automation Activity & Vendor Info: (Acquisitions) PALS; (Cataloging) PALS; (Circulation) PALS; (Course Reserve) PALS; (ILL) PALS; (Media Booking) PALS; (OPAC) PALS; (Serials) PALS
Wireless access
Function: Archival coll, Handicapped accessible
Partic in Minitex Library Information Network; OCLC Online Computer Library Center, Inc

MAYNARD

P MAYNARD PUBLIC LIBRARY*, 321 Mabel Ave, 56260. (Mail add: PO Box 247, 56260-0247), SAN 347-7002. Tel: 320-367-2143. FAX: 320-367-2143. Web Site: www.maynard.lib.mn.us. *Head Librn,* Gloria Sims; E-mail: gloria.sims@pioneerland.lib.mn.us; Staff 1 (Non-MLS 1)
Pop 388; Circ 9,611
Library Holdings: Bk Vols 10,000; Per Subs 19
Automation Activity & Vendor Info: (Cataloging) Innovative Interfaces, Inc; (Circulation) Innovative Interfaces, Inc; (OPAC) Innovative Interfaces, Inc
Wireless access
Mem of Pioneerland Library System
Open Mon, Tues & Thurs 1-5:30, Wed 1-7:30

MCKINLEY

P MCKINLEY PUBLIC LIBRARY*, 5454 Grand Ave, 55741-9502. (Mail add: PO Box 2085, 55741-2085), SAN 308-6178. Tel: 218-749-5313. FAX: 218-749-5313. *Dir,* Lora Wyrick
Library Holdings: Bk Vols 11,000; Per Subs 6
Open Tues & Thurs 3-5:30

MINNEAPOLIS

S ALLINA HEALTH LIBRARY SERVICES*, 800 E 28th St, Mail Stop 14001, 55407. SAN 308-7840. Tel: 612-863-4312. FAX: 612-863-5695. E-mail: library.services@allina.com. Web Site: www.allina.com/ahs/libmedia.nsf. *Dir,* Darlene Helmer
Automation Activity & Vendor Info: (Acquisitions) EOS International; (Cataloging) EOS International; (Circulation) EOS International; (OPAC) EOS International; (Serials) EOS International
Branches:
ABBOTT NORTHWESTERN HOSPITAL, 800 E 28th St, 55407, SAN 308-6917. Tel: 612-863-4312. FAX: 612-863-5695. *Team Leader,* Jim Bulger
Founded 1943
Subject Interests: Cardiology, Neurology, Nursing, Pediatrics, Perinatology, Rehabilitation med, Spinal cord injury
Open Mon-Fri 8-4:30
Restriction: Open to pub for ref only
MERCY HOSPITAL, 4050 Coon Rapids Blvd, Coon Rapids, 55433, SAN 308-5473. Tel: 612-863-4312. *Mgr,* Jim Bulger
UNITY HOSPITAL, 550 Osborne Rd, Fridley, 55432. Tel: 612-863-4312. *Mgr,* Jim Bulger

S AMERICAN CRAFT COUNCIL LIBRARY*, 1224 Marshall St NE, Ste 200, 55413. SAN 311-5755. Tel: 612-206-3118. FAX: 612-355-2330. E-mail: library@craftcouncil.org. Web Site: www.craftcouncil.org. *Librn,* Jessica Shaykett; E-mail: jshaykett@craftcouncil.org. Subject Specialists: *Art hist, Craft hist,* Jessica Shaykett; Staff 1 (MLS 1)
Founded 1956
Library Holdings: AV Mats 230; Bk Titles 15,000; Per Subs 132
Special Collections: ACM Slide Study Coll; American Craft Council Archives; American Craft Museum Exhibition & Photograph Archives until 1990; Craft Artist Database & Files
Subject Interests: Contemporary Am crafts
Automation Activity & Vendor Info: (Cataloging) OCLC Connexion
Database Vendor: EBSCOhost, H W Wilson, OCLC FirstSearch, Wilson - Wilson Web
Wireless access
Function: Archival coll, Art exhibits, Online cat, Ref & res, Ref serv available, Ref serv in person
Publications: Research Guides on Craft Subjects
Open Mon-Fri 10-5
Restriction: Open to pub for ref only

S AMERICAN SWEDISH INSTITUTE*, Wallenberg Library & Archives, 2600 Park Ave, 55407. SAN 308-6291. Tel: 612-870-3348. FAX: 612-871-8682. E-mail: info@americanswedishinst.org. Web Site: www.asimn.org/exhibitions-collections/library-and-archives. *Chief Exec Officer, Pres,* Bruce N Karstadt; *Archivist, Librn,* Position Currently Open. Subject Specialists: *Swedish hist,* Position Currently Open; Staff 1 (MLS 1)
Founded 1929
Library Holdings: Bk Vols 17,000; Per Subs 2
Special Collections: Swedish History & Literature (Swan J Turnblad Library); Swedish Immigration History Coll (Victor Lawson Coll); Turnblad Lending Library
Subject Interests: Swedish hist
Open Wed 4-8, Fri 12-4, Sat 10-2
Restriction: Closed stack, Non-circulating

C AUGSBURG COLLEGE*, The James G Lindell Family Library, 2211 Riverside Ave, 55454. SAN 308-6305. Tel: 612-330-1604. FAX: 612-330-1436. Web Site: www.augsburg.edu/library. *Dir, Libr Serv,* Jane Ann Nelson; Tel: 612-330-1603, E-mail: nelsonj1@augsburg.edu; *Instrul Serv Librn, Ref Serv,* Boyd Koehler; *Ref & 1st Year Learning Experience Librn,* Stacy Cutinella; *Circ, Syst Librn,* Micheal Bloomberg; *Adult Serv, Ref Serv,* Mary Lee McLaughlin; *Coll Mgt,* Ron Kurpiers; *Digital Learning Libr Serv,* Chris Pegg; *Pub Serv,* William Wittenbreer; Staff 8 (MLS 8)
Founded 1869. Enrl 3,317; Fac 211; Highest Degree: Master
Library Holdings: Bk Vols 185,000; Per Subs 620
Special Collections: Meridel LeSueur Papers; Modern Scandinavian Music, rec, tapes & scores
Automation Activity & Vendor Info: (Circulation) Innovative Interfaces, Inc
Wireless access
Partic in Cooperating Libraries in Consortium; OCLC Online Computer Library Center, Inc
Open Mon-Fri 8am-Midnight, Sat 8am-7pm, Sun Noon-Midnight

S THE BAKKEN*, The Bakken Library of Electricity in Life, 3537 Zenith Ave S, 55416. SAN 326-4459. Tel: 612-926-3878. Reference Tel: 612-926-3878, Ext 227. FAX: 612-927-7265. Web Site: www.thebakken.org. *Chief Curator,* Dr Juliet Burba; Tel: 612-926-3878, Ext 217, E-mail: burba@thebakken.org; *Curator of Bks,* Rachel Howell; E-mail: howell@thebakken.org; *Curator,* Adrian Fischer; Tel: 612-926-3878, Ext 201, E-mail: fischer@thebakken.org; Staff 1 (MLS 1)
Founded 1975
Library Holdings: Bk Vols 12,000; Per Subs 10
Special Collections: Instrument Coll
Subject Interests: Hist of electricity, Hist of magnetism, Hist of med, Hist of sci
Wireless access
Function: Ref serv available, Res libr
Partic in OCLC Online Computer Library Center, Inc
Open Mon-Fri 9-5
Restriction: Not a lending libr

L BOWMAN & BROOKE, Law Library, 150 S Fifth St, Ste 3000, 55402. SAN 372-0500. Tel: 612-339-8682. FAX: 612-672-3200. Web Site: www.bowmanandbrooke.com. *Librn,* Donna Trimble; E-mail: donna.trimble@bowmanandbrooke.com
Database Vendor: LexisNexis, Westlaw
Restriction: Staff use only

L BRIGGS & MORGAN*, Law Library, 2200 IDS Ctr, 80 S Elg, 55402. SAN 372-2856. Tel: 612-977-8400. Web Site: www.briggs.com. *Librn,* Arlene Lundgren; *Librn,* Susan J Redalen; Staff 3 (MLS 2, Non-MLS 1)
Automation Activity & Vendor Info: (Cataloging) Inmagic, Inc.
Open Mon-Fri 8-5

R CENTRAL LUTHERAN CHURCH LIBRARY*, 333 12th St S, 55404. SAN 308-6348. Tel: 612-870-4416. FAX: 612-870-0417. Web Site: www.centralmpls.org. *Librn,* Elizabeth Shelver
Library Holdings: Bk Vols 3,500; Per Subs 12

M A CHANCE TO GROW*, Kretsch Brain Resource Library, 1800 Second St NE, 55418. SAN 370-3282. Tel: 612-789-1236. FAX: 612-706-5555. E-mail: actg@actg.org. Web Site: actg.org. *Dir,* Bob DeBore; *Dir,* Kathy DeBore
Library Holdings: Bk Vols 2,000
Open Mon-Fri 9-4

S DELOITTE & TOUCHE LLP*, Research Center, 50 S Sixth St, Ste 2800, 55402. SAN 308-6372. Tel: 612-397-4636. Web Site: www.deloitte.com. *Mgr,* Marsha Collins; Tel: 612-397-4000, E-mail: mcollins@deloitte.com; Staff 1 (MLS 1)
Library Holdings: Bk Vols 790; Per Subs 100
Subject Interests: Acctg, Taxation
Wireless access
Partic in Dialog Corp
Open Mon-Fri 8-5

GM DEPARTMENT OF VETERANS AFFAIRS*, Medical Center Library, One Veterans Dr, 142 D, 55417. SAN 308-6976. Tel: 612-467-4200. FAX: 612-725-2046. *Mgr,* Dorothy Sinha; E-mail: dorothy.sinha@va.gov; *Librn,* Barbara Winge; E-mail: barbara.winge@va.gov; *Patient Educ Librn,* Kathy Mackay; Tel: 612-467-4212, E-mail: kathleen.mackay@va.gov; *Libr Tech,* Michele Mackey; E-mail: michele.mackey@va.gov; Staff 3.5 (MLS 2.5, Non-MLS 1)
Library Holdings: AV Mats 375; Bk Vols 7,000; Per Subs 520; Videos 1,300
Special Collections: Medical AV Coll; Patient Education
Subject Interests: Allied health, Hospital admin, Med, Nursing
Automation Activity & Vendor Info: (Circulation) EOS International; (OPAC) EOS International
Partic in Docline
Open Mon-Fri 8-4:30
Branches:
PATIENT EDUCATION CENTER LIBRARY, One Veterans Dr, 142D1, 55417. Tel: 612-467-4212. FAX: 612-725-2046. *Librn,* Kathy McKay; E-mail: kathleen.mackay@med.va.gov; Staff 1 (MLS 1)
Founded 1978
Library Holdings: AV Mats 375; Bk Titles 500
Subject Interests: Patient health educ

S DONALDSON CO, INC*, Corporate Library, PO Box 1299, MS 301, 55440-1299. SAN 308-6399. Tel: 952-887-3019. FAX: 952-887-3555. *Coop Libr Mgr,* Julie Eskritt; E-mail: julie.eskritt@donaldson.com; *Coop Librn,* Karen Mackey; E-mail: karen.mackey@donaldson.com; Staff 2 (MLS 2)
Founded 1969
Library Holdings: AV Mats 50; Electronic Media & Resources 8; Bk Vols 3,000; Per Subs 100
Subject Interests: Bus, Eng with emphasis on filtration, Pollution control
Restriction: Co libr, Employees only, Not open to pub

L DORSEY & WHITNEY*, Information Resource Center, 50 S Sixth St, 55402. SAN 308-6402. Tel: 612-492-5522. FAX: 612-492-2868. *Dir,* Linda Will; Staff 33 (MLS 10, Non-MLS 23)
Library Holdings: Bk Vols 60,000; Per Subs 400
Restriction: Not open to pub

J DUNWOODY COLLEGE OF TECHNOLOGY*, John A Butler Learning Center, 818 Dunwoody Blvd, 55403. SAN 308-6410. Tel: 612-374-5800, Ext 2404. Web Site: www.dunwoody.edu. *Librn,* Kristina Oberstar; E-mail: koberstar@dunwoody.edu
Library Holdings: Bk Vols 10,000; Per Subs 150
Open Mon-Fri 6-6

L FAEGRE & BENSON, LLP*, Information Resources, 2200 Wells Fargo Ctr, 90 South Seventh St, 55402-3901. SAN 308-6437. Tel: 612-766-7000. Toll Free Tel: 800-328-4393. FAX: 612-766-1600. E-mail: library@faegre.com. *Dir, Info Res,* Norma Knudson; *Acq,* Sarah Jirik; *ILL,* Oona Peterson; *Law Librn,* Hagen Odenwald; *Libr Assoc,* Jane Bowden; *Mgr, Res,* Carrie Long; *Res Librn,* Bob Allen; *Res Librn,* Sheri Brenden; *Res Librn,* Jill Strand; *Tech Serv Mgr,* Jeanette Woessner; *Tech Coordr,* Amy Srypek; *Tech Spec,* Barb Minor; Staff 13 (MLS 10, Non-MLS 3)
Library Holdings: Bk Vols 31,800; Per Subs 515
Automation Activity & Vendor Info: (Acquisitions) SydneyPlus

S FEDERAL RESERVE BANK OF MINNEAPOLIS*, Research Library, 90 Hennepin Ave, 55401-2171. (Mail add: PO Box 291, 55480-0291), SAN 308-6461. Tel: 612-204-5509. *Librn,* Karen Hovermale; *Librn,* Brooke Tosi
Founded 1940
Library Holdings: Bk Vols 15,000; Per Subs 2,000
Special Collections: Federal Reserve System Publications Coll
Subject Interests: Econ, Finance, Monetary policy
Automation Activity & Vendor Info: (Acquisitions) SydneyPlus; (Cataloging) SydneyPlus; (Circulation) SydneyPlus; (ILL) OCLC; (OPAC) SydneyPlus; (Serials) SydneyPlus
Database Vendor: EBSCOhost, Factiva.com
Restriction: Open by appt only, Staff use only

L FELHABER, LARSON, FENLON & VOGT*, Law Library, 220 S Sixth St, Ste 2200, 55402-4302. SAN 372-2864. Tel: 612-339-6321. FAX: 612-338-0535. Web Site: www.felhaber.com. *Librn,* Annette C Borer; Tel: 612-373-8441, E-mail: aborer@felhaber.com
Library Holdings: Bk Vols 10,500; Per Subs 107

R FIRST BAPTIST CHURCH LIBRARY*, 1021 Hennepin Ave, 55403. SAN 308-647X. Tel: 612-332-3651. FAX: 612-332-3661. Web Site: fbcminneapolis.org. *In Charge,* Mary Krizon
Library Holdings: Bk Vols 3,000
Special Collections: Commentaries & Sermons (Dr W B Riley, founder of Northwestern Bible College)
Open Sun 9am-11am

L FREDRIKSON & BRYON, Law Library, 200 S Sixth St, Ste 4000, 55402. SAN 372-0519. Tel: 612-492-7000. FAX: 612-492-7077. Web Site: www.fredlaw.com. *Dir,* Jeanette Woessner; E-mail: jwoessner@fredlaw.com; Staff 7 (MLS 6, Non-MLS 1)
Library Holdings: Bk Vols 20,000; Per Subs 300
Wireless access

GENERAL MILLS, INC

S JAMES FORD BELL LIBRARY & INFORMATION SERVICES*, 9000 Plymouth Ave N, 55427, SAN 347-4666. Tel: 763-764-6460. Interlibrary Loan Service Tel: 763-764-2761. FAX: 763-764-3166. *Dir, Knowledge Discovery Serv,* Fred Hulting
Founded 1961
Library Holdings: Bk Titles 18,000; Bk Vols 20,000; Per Subs 750
Subject Interests: Food sci
Automation Activity & Vendor Info: (Acquisitions) Sydney; (Cataloging) Sydney; (Circulation) Sydney; (OPAC) Sydney; (Serials) Sydney
Database Vendor: Dialog, OCLC FirstSearch
Partic in Dialog Corp; Dow Jones News Retrieval; OCLC Online Computer Library Center, Inc
Publications: Foods Adlibra; Internal newsletters; Periodical Holdings List (Annual)
Open Mon-Fri 8:30-4:30
Restriction: Not open to pub

S BUSINESS INFORMATION CENTER*, One General Mills Blvd, 55426-1347, SAN 347-4631. Tel: 763-764-5461. Web Site: www.generalmills.com. *Sr Assoc,* Gail Wolfson; Staff 2 (MLS 1, Non-MLS 1)
Founded 1965
Library Holdings: Bk Vols 1,500; Per Subs 200
Subject Interests: Consumerism, Food indust
Automation Activity & Vendor Info: (Acquisitions) SydneyPlus; (Cataloging) SydneyPlus; (Circulation) SydneyPlus; (OPAC) SydneyPlus; (Serials) SydneyPlus
Database Vendor: Factiva.com
Restriction: Not open to pub

L GRAY, PLANT, MOOTY*, Law Library, 500 IDS Ctr, 80 S Eighth St, 55402. SAN 329-9678. Tel: 612-632-3000, 612-632-3122. *Librn,* Peggy Lahammer; Staff 3 (MLS 2, Non-MLS 1)
Library Holdings: Bk Titles 2,000; Per Subs 150
Subject Interests: Law
Restriction: Staff use only

GL HENNEPIN COUNTY LAW LIBRARY*, Anne W Grande Law Library, C-2451 Government Ctr, 300 S Sixth St, 55487. SAN 308-6526. Tel: 612-348-3022. Circulation Tel: 612-348-3024. Reference Tel: 612-348-2903. FAX: 612-348-4230. E-mail: ll.reference@co.hennepin.mn.us. Web Site: hclaw.co.hennepin.mn.us. *Dir,* Edward W Carroll; Tel: 612-348-8860, E-mail: edward.carroll@co.hennepin.mn.us; *Asst Dir,* Timothy Devine; Tel: 612-348-7982, E-mail: timothy.devine@co.hennepin.mn.us; Staff 7 (MLS 3, Non-MLS 4)
Founded 1883
Library Holdings: Bk Vols 108,279
Automation Activity & Vendor Info: (Cataloging) Innovative Interfaces, Inc; (Circulation) Innovative Interfaces, Inc; (OPAC) Innovative Interfaces, Inc; (Serials) Innovative Interfaces, Inc
Database Vendor: EBSCOhost, Gale Cengage Learning, HeinOnline, LexisNexis, Newsbank, OCLC WorldShare Interlibrary Loan, SerialsSolutions, Westlaw
Wireless access
Function: Audio & video playback equip for onsite use, CD-ROM, Computers for patron use, Copy machines, Electronic databases & coll, Pub access computers, Ref serv in person, Web-catalog, Wheelchair accessible
Publications: HCLL Alert (Newsletter); Library Guide
Open Mon-Fri 8-6
Restriction: Circ limited
Friends of the Library Group

M HENNEPIN COUNTY MEDICAL CENTER*, Medical Library Services, Mail Code R2, 701 Park Ave, 55415. SAN 308-6585. Tel: 612-873-2710. Reference Tel: 612-873-2714. FAX: 612-904-4248. E-mail: ms.hsl.req@hcmed.org. Web Site: www.hcmc.org/healthprofs/prof_resources.htm. *Libr Mgr,* Kathleen Warner; E-mail: kathleen.warner@hcmed.org; *Circ, ILL,* Paul Reid; E-mail: paul.reid@hcmed.org; *Ser,* Bonnie Moore; Tel: 612-873-2711, E-mail: bonnie.moore@hcmed.org; Staff 3 (MLS 1, Non-MLS 2)
Founded 1976
Jul 2012-Jun 2013. Mats Exp $450,000
Library Holdings: e-books 165; e-journals 2,000; Bk Titles 7,700; Bk Vols 8,000; Per Subs 530; Videos 144
Subject Interests: Clinical med
Automation Activity & Vendor Info: (Cataloging) CyberTools for Libraries; (Circulation) CyberTools for Libraries; (OPAC) CyberTools for Libraries; (Serials) CyberTools for Libraries
Database Vendor: EBSCOhost, OVID Technologies
Wireless access
Function: Computers for patron use, Doc delivery serv, Electronic databases & coll, Health sci info serv, Learning ctr, Online cat, Online searches, Orientations
Partic in Health Scis Librs of Minn; Minitex Library Information Network; OCLC Online Computer Library Center, Inc
Open Mon-Fri 8-5
Restriction: Med staff only, Open to staff, patients & family mem, Open to students, fac & staff, Residents only

S HISTORICAL SOCIETY OF HENNEPIN COUNTY*, Hennepin History Museum Library, 2303 Third Ave S, 55404-3599. SAN 326-5773. Tel: 612-870-1329. FAX: 612-870-1320. Web Site: www.hhmmuseum.org. *Curator,* Jack A Kabrud
Library Holdings: Bk Vols 1,300
Special Collections: Historic Photographs; Manuscripts
Publications: Hennepin History Magazine (Periodical)
Open Tues 10-2, Wed, Fri & Sat 1-5, Thurs 1-8

R HOLY TRINITY LUTHERAN CHURCH LIBRARY*, 2730 E 31st St, 55406. SAN 308-6542. Tel: 612-729-8358. FAX: 612-729-6773. E-mail: office@htlcmpls.org. Web Site: www.htlcmpls.org. *In Charge,* Janice Lehman
Founded 1963
Library Holdings: Bk Vols 4,000
Subject Interests: Holocaust
Open Mon-Fri 7-4

S JEWISH COMMUNITY RELATIONS COUNCIL*, 12 North 12th St, Ste 480, 55403-1331. SAN 327-8212. Tel: 612-338-7816. FAX: 612-349-6569. E-mail: info@minndakjcrc.org. Web Site: www.minndakjcrc.org. *Exec Dir,* Stephen Silberfarb
Library Holdings: Bk Vols 100
Open Mon-Fri 9-5

L LEONARD, STREET & DEINARD*, Law Library, 150 S Fifth St, Ste 2300, 55402. SAN 372-0527. Tel: 612-335-1616. FAX: 612-335-1657. E-mail: research.services@leonard.com. *Dir, Res Serv,* Patricia K Cummings; E-mail: pat.cummings@leonard.com; *Mgr, Res Syst,* Susan Hayles; Staff 8 (MLS 5, Non-MLS 3)
Library Holdings: Bk Vols 15,000; Per Subs 150
Open Mon-Fri 8-5

L LOCKRIDGE, GRINDAL, NAUEN PLLP*, Law Library, 100 Washington Ave S, Ste 2200, 55401. SAN 372-0497. Tel: 612-339-6900. FAX: 612-339-0981. *Librn,* Kathy Kelly; E-mail: kjkelly@locklaw.com
Database Vendor: Westlaw
Open Mon-Wed 8-5

L MACKALL, CROUNSE & MOORE*, Law Library, 1400 AT&T Tower, 901 Marquette Ave, 55402-2859. SAN 372-0535. Tel: 612-305-1687. FAX: 612-305-1414. Web Site: www.mcmlaw.com. *Librn,* Terri Gruenberg
Library Holdings: Bk Vols 11,000; Per Subs 92
Database Vendor: Westlaw
Open Mon-Fri 8-5

C MINNEAPOLIS COLLEGE OF ART & DESIGN LIBRARY*, 2501 Stevens Ave, 55404-3593. SAN 308-6674. Tel: 612-874-3791. FAX: 612-874-3704. E-mail: library@mcad.edu. Web Site: library.mcad.edu. *Libr Dir,* Amy Naughton; Tel: 612-874-3752, E-mail: amy_naughton@mcad.edu; *Tech Serv Librn,* Kay Kroeff-Streng; Tel: 612-874-3734, E-mail: kay_streng@mcad.edu; *Visual Res,* Allan Kohl; Tel: 612-874-3781, E-mail: allan_kohl@mcad.edu; Staff 5.74 (MLS 3.06, Non-MLS 2.68)
Founded 1886. Enrl 772; Fac 125; Highest Degree: Master
Library Holdings: CDs 221; DVDs 331; Bk Titles 45,760; Bk Vols 54,700; Per Subs 115; Videos 1,000
Special Collections: Artists Books; College Archives
Subject Interests: Contemporary art
Automation Activity & Vendor Info: (Cataloging) Ex Libris Group; (Circulation) Ex Libris Group; (Course Reserve) Ex Libris Group; (ILL) Ex Libris Group; (OPAC) Ex Libris Group
Database Vendor: ARTstor, EBSCO Information Services, EBSCOhost, Ex Libris Group, Gale Cengage Learning, JSTOR, OCLC WorldShare Interlibrary Loan, ProQuest
Wireless access
Publications: Accessions List
Partic in Minitex Library Information Network; MnPALS
Open Mon-Thurs 9am-10pm, Fri 9-5, Sat 12-5, Sun 12-7
Restriction: Circ limited

J MINNEAPOLIS COMMUNITY & TECHNICAL COLLEGE LIBRARY*, Wheelock Whitney Hall, 1501 Hennepin Ave, 55403. SAN 308-664X. Tel: 612-659-6290. Interlibrary Loan Service Tel: 612-659-6294. FAX: 612-659-6295. TDD: 612-659-6288. Web Site: www.minneapolis.edu/library. *Chair,* Thomas Eland; Tel: 612-659-6286; *Acq, Cat, Libr Tech,* Dawn Pepper; Tel: 612-659-6289; *Cat, Libr Tech,* John Daniels; *Circ, Libr Tech, Ref Serv,* Cori Cain; Tel: 612-659-6297; *Circ, ILL, Libr Tech,* Thulani Jwacu; Tel: 612-659-6294; *Coll Develop, Ref Serv,* Julie Setnosky; Tel: 612-659-6292; *Ref Serv, Tech Serv,* Kathleen Daniels; Tel: 612-659-6285; *Ref Serv,* Jane Jurgens; Tel: 612-659-6287; *Ref Serv, Ser,* Anne Ryan; Tel: 612-659-6291; *Tech Serv,* Virginia Heinrich; Staff 10 (MLS 6, Non-MLS 4)
Founded 1965. Enrl 10,000; Highest Degree: Associate
Library Holdings: Bk Titles 65,000; Per Subs 600
Special Collections: Alternative & Small Press Coll, bks, cd's, dvd's, periodicals, zines
Wireless access
Partic in Minitex Library Information Network; Minn Interlibr

S MINNEAPOLIS INSTITUTE OF ARTS*, Art Research & Reference Library, 2400 Third Ave S, 55404. SAN 308-6682. Tel: 612-870-3117. FAX: 612-870-3004. Web Site: www.artsmia.org. *Head Librn,* Janice Lurie; Staff 3 (MLS 3)
Founded 1915. Highest Degree: Master
Library Holdings: Bk Vols 55,000; Per Subs 120
Special Collections: Botany & Fashion (Minnich Coll); Five Hundred Years of Sporting Books (John Daniels Coll), drawings; History of Printing (Leslie Coll)
Subject Interests: Art hist, Chinese bronzes, Drawing, English silver, Furniture, Jades, Painting, Prints, Sculpture, Textiles
Automation Activity & Vendor Info: (Cataloging) Ex Libris Group; (Circulation) Ex Libris Group
Database Vendor: OCLC FirstSearch, Wilson - Wilson Web
Publications: Arts; Surrealism: Beyond the Printed Word; The Minneapolis Institute of Arts Research & Reference Library: History & Guide; Villa I Tatti
Open Tues-Fri 11:30-4:30
Restriction: Non-circulating to the pub
Friends of the Library Group

S MINNESOTA ORCHESTRA MUSIC LIBRARY*, 1111 Nicollet Mall, 55403. SAN 329-9155. FAX: 612-371-0838. E-mail: info@mnorch.org. Web Site: www.minnesotaorchestra.org. *Librn,* Paul Gunther; Tel:

612-371-5622, E-mail: pgunther@mnorch.org; *Assoc Principal Librn,* Eric Sjostrom; Tel: 612-371-5623, E-mail: esjostrom@mnorch.org; *Actg Asst Principal Librn,* Valerie Little; Tel: 612-371-5663, E-mail: vlittle@mnorch.org; Staff 3 (Non-MLS 3)
Library Holdings: CDs 2,000; e-journals 20; Bk Titles 200; Bk Vols 300; Spec Interest Per Sub 6
Special Collections: Minnesota Orchestra Archives; Orchestral & Chamber Works
Subject Interests: Orchestra performance
Restriction: Authorized scholars by appt, Circ limited, Employees & their associates, Open by appt only, Open to pub by appt only, Private libr

C NORTH CENTRAL UNIVERSITY LIBRARY*, T J Jones Library, 915 E 14th St, 55404. (Mail add: 910 Elliot Ave, 55404-1391), SAN 308-6798. Tel: 612-343-4490. FAX: 612-343-8069. Web Site: www.northcentral.edu. *Dir,* Melody Reedy; Tel: 612-343-4491, E-mail: mareedy@northcentral.edu; Staff 5 (MLS 1, Non-MLS 4)
Founded 1930. Enrl 1,135; Fac 41; Highest Degree: Bachelor
Jun 2006-May 2007 Income $319,243. Mats Exp $108,511. Sal $210,732 (Prof $50,708)
Library Holdings: Bks on Deafness & Sign Lang 302; Bk Vols 73,350; Per Subs 282; Videos 676
Special Collections: Pentecostal Studies
Automation Activity & Vendor Info: (Acquisitions) Ex Libris Group; (Cataloging) Ex Libris Group; (Circulation) Ex Libris Group; (Course Reserve) Ex Libris Group; (ILL) OCLC; (OPAC) Ex Libris Group; (Serials) Ex Libris Group
Database Vendor: EBSCOhost, Gale Cengage Learning, OCLC ArticleFirst, OCLC FirstSearch, OCLC WorldShare Interlibrary Loan
Wireless access
Function: Accelerated reader prog
Partic in Christian Library Consortium; Minitex Library Information Network; OCLC Online Computer Library Center, Inc
Open Mon-Thurs 7am-Midnight, Fri 7-7, Sat 2-6, Sun 6pm-10pm

L OPPENHEIMER WOLFF & DONNELLY LIBRARY*, 45 S Seventh St, 55402. SAN 308-7824. Tel: 612-607-7290. FAX: 612-607-7100. Web Site: www.oppenheimer.com. *Dir,* Trudi Busch; E-mail: tbusch@oppenheimer.com; Staff 2 (Non-MLS 2)
Library Holdings: Bk Vols 3,500; Per Subs 300
Subject Interests: Antitrust law, Corporate law, Corporate securities, Intellectual property, Intl bus law, Litigation, Minn law, Patents, Taxes
Partic in American Association of Law Libraries (AALL); SLA
Restriction: Staff use only

S PLANNED PARENTHOOD OF MINNESOTA & SOUTH DAKOTA*, Phyllis Cooksey Resource Center, 1200 Lagoon Ave S, 55408. SAN 327-2028. Tel: 612-823-6568. FAX: 612-825-3522. Web Site: www.ppmsd.org. *Librn,* Lisa Sharkey; *Coll Develop,* Theresa Wolner; E-mail: twolner@usinternet.com; Staff 1 (MLS 1)
Library Holdings: Bk Vols 2,000; Per Subs 75
Special Collections: Archives Coll, audio-visual
Subject Interests: Human sexuality, Reproductive health

SR SAINT LAWRENCE CATHOLIC CHURCH*, Newman Center Library, 1203 Fifth St SE, 55414. SAN 308-6771. Tel: 612-331-7941. FAX: 612-378-1771. Web Site: www.stlawrencenewman.org. *Dir,* John Behnke
Founded 1946
Library Holdings: Bk Vols 11,500; Per Subs 15
Subject Interests: Biblical, Relig studies, Scriptural works, Theol

R SAINT OLAF LUTHERAN CHURCH*, Carlsen Memorial Library, 2901 Emerson Ave N, 55411. SAN 308-6909. Tel: 612-529-7726. FAX: 612-529-4385. Web Site: www.stolaflutheran.org. *In Charge,* Dale Hulme
Founded 1963
Library Holdings: Bk Vols 1,750

S SONS OF NORWAY*, International Resource Library, 1455 W Lake St, 55408. SAN 308-6925. Tel: 612-827-3611. Toll Free Tel: 800-945-8851. FAX: 612-827-0658. Web Site: www.sonsofnorway.com. *Librn,* Colin Thompson
Founded 1962
Library Holdings: Bk Titles 1,000; Bk Vols 2,500
Special Collections: Norwegian-American Culture & Immigration (Norwegian-American Studies)
Open Mon-Thurs 7:30-5, Fri 8-Noon
Friends of the Library Group

S STAR TRIBUNE*, News Research, 425 Portland Ave, 55488. SAN 308-6690. Tel: 612-673-4375. FAX: 612-673-4459. Web Site: www.startribune.com. *Dir,* Sandra Date; Tel: 613-673-7176, E-mail: sdate@startribune.com; *Asst Dir,* Robert H Jansen; E-mail: bjansen@startribune.com; *Res,* Roberta Hovde; *Res,* Linda Scheimann
Founded 1946
Library Holdings: Bk Vols 4,000
Restriction: Not open to pub

R TEMPLE ISRAEL LIBRARY*, 2324 Emerson Ave S, 55405-2695. SAN 308-6933. Tel: 612-377-8680. FAX: 612-377-6630. *Librn,* Georgia Kalman; Tel: 612-374-0338, E-mail: gkalman@templeisrael.com; Staff 2 (MLS 1, Non-MLS 1)
Founded 1929
Library Holdings: Bk Titles 15,000; Per Subs 20
Subject Interests: Art, Childrens' bks, Fiction, Hist, Holocaust
Open Mon-Thurs 2-5, Sat & Sun 9-12

G UNITED STATES COURT OF APPEALS*, Branch Library, 1102 US Courthouse, 300 S Fourth St, Rm 1102, 55415. SAN 325-4348. Tel: 612-664-5830. FAX: 612-664-5835. E-mail: library8th@ca8.uscourts.gov. Web Site: www.1b8.uscourts.gov. *Br Librn,* Nancee Halling; E-mail: nancee_halling@ca8.uscourts.gov; *Libr Tech,* Tracey Smith; E-mail: tracey_smith@ca8.uscourts.gov; Staff 1.5 (MLS 1, Non-MLS 0.5)
Library Holdings: Bk Vols 28,000; Per Subs 25
Open Mon-Fri 8:30-5
Restriction: Limited access for the pub, Ref only to non-staff, Restricted borrowing privileges

C UNIVERSITY OF MINNESOTA LIBRARIES-TWIN CITIES*, 499 O Meredith Wilson Library, 309 19th Ave S, 55455-0414. SAN 347-5298. Tel: 612-625-9148. FAX: 612-626-9353. Web Site: www.lib.umn.edu. *Univ Librn,* Wendy Pradt Lougee; *Assoc Univ Librn, Acad Prog,* Karen Williams; *Assoc Univ Librn, Info Tech,* John Butler; *Assoc Univ Librn, Organizational Develop,* Linda DeBeau-Melting; *Assoc Univ Librn, Res & Learning,* Claire Stewart; *Coll Develop,* Charles G Spetland; Tel: 612-626-7960
Founded 1851. Enrl 65,753; Fac 2,869; Highest Degree: Doctorate
Library Holdings: Bk Vols 6,587,430; Per Subs 43,303
Special Collections: African-American Literature & Life (Givens Coll); Berman Upper Midwest Jewish Archives; British-Indian Interaction (Ames Library of South Asia); Children's Literature Research Coll; Gay, Lesbian, Bisexual & Transgender (Jean-Nickolaus Tretter Coll); History of European Expansion Prior to 1800 (James Ford Bell Library); History of Immigration from Eastern & Southeastern Europe (Immigration History Research Center); History of Information Processing (Charles Babbage Institute); History of Photomechanics (Mertle Coll); Kautz Family YMCA Archives; Literary Manuscripts Coll; Northwest Architectural Archives; Performing Arts Archives; Plants, Plant Cultivation, Landscape Architecture (Andersen Horticultural Library); Sherlock Holmes Coll; Social Welfare History Archives; Swedish Americana (Dahllof Coll); University of Minnesota Archives; Wangensteen Historical Library of Biology & Medicine. State Document Depository; UN Document Depository; US Document Depository
Automation Activity & Vendor Info: (Acquisitions) Ex Libris Group; (Cataloging) Ex Libris Group; (Circulation) Ex Libris Group; (Course Reserve) Ex Libris Group; (ILL) OCLC; (OPAC) Ex Libris Group; (Serials) Ex Libris Group
Publications: Continuum (Periodical)
Partic in Association of Research Libraries (ARL), Council of Independent Colleges (CIC); Digital Libr Fedn; OCLC Online Computer Library Center, Inc
Friends of the Library Group

Departmental Libraries:

AMES LIBRARY OF SOUTH ASIA, S-10 Wilson Library, 309 19th Ave S, 55455, SAN 347-5719. Tel: 612-624-4857. FAX: 612-626-9353. *Librn,* David Faust; E-mail: faust011@umn.edu; Staff 2 (MLS 1, Non-MLS 1)

ANDERSEN HORTICULTURAL LIBRARY, 3675 Arboretum Dr, Chaska, 55318, SAN 378-0759. Tel: 952-443-1405. FAX: 952-443-2521. *Librn,* Katherine Allen
Open Mon-Fri 8-4:30, Sat & Sun 11-4:30

ARCHITECTURE & LANDSCAPE ARCHITECTURE LIBRARY, 210 Rapson Hall, 89 Church St SE, 55455, SAN 329-756X. Tel: 612-624-6383. FAX: 612-625-5597. *Librn,* Deborah K Ultan Boudewyns. Subject Specialists: *Archit, Art, Performing arts,* Deborah K Ultan Boudewyns
Open Mon-Fri 9-4:30

CHARLES BABBAGE INSTITUTE, 211 Elmer L Andersen Library, 222 21st Ave S, 55455, SAN 371-3083. Tel: 612-624-5050. FAX: 612-625-8054. *Archivist,* Amy West

JAMES FORD BELL LIBRARY, 472 Wilson Library, 309 19th Ave S, 55455, SAN 347-5328. Tel: 612-624-1528. FAX: 612-626-9353. *Curator,* Marguerite Ragnow

JOHN R BORCHERT MAP LIBRARY, S-76 Wilson Library, 309 19th Ave S, 55455, SAN 347-6642. Tel: 612-624-4549. FAX: 612-626-9353. *Head of Libr,* Kristi Jensen

CHILDREN'S LITERATURE RESEARCH COLLECTIONS, Elmer L Andersen Library, 222 21st Ave S, Ste 113, 55455, SAN 347-6103. Tel: 612-624-4576. FAX: 612-626-0377. *Curator,* Karen Nelson Hoyle
Open Mon-Fri 8:30-4:30

EAST ASIAN, S-75 Wilson Library, 309 19th Ave S, 55455, SAN 347-657X. Tel: 612-624-9833. *Head of Libr,* Yao Chen

ENTOMOLOGY, FISHERIES & WILDLIFE, 375 Hodson Hall, 1980 Folwell Ave, Saint Paul, 55108, SAN 378-0910. Tel: 612-624-9288. FAX: 612-624-0719. *Head, Ref,* Linda Eells
Open Mon-Fri 9-12 & 1-4:30

FORESTRY, B-50 Skok Hall, 2003 Upper Buford Circle, Saint Paul, 55108, SAN 378-0953. Tel: 612-624-3222. FAX: 612-624-3733. *Asst Librn,* Philip Herold
Function: Res libr

CM HEALTH SCIENCES LIBRARIES, Diehl Hall, 505 Essex St SE, 55455, SAN 347-5352. Tel: 612-626-0998. FAX: 612-626-5822. Web Site: www.biomed.lib.umn.edu. *Interim Dir,* Janice Jaguszewski; E-mail: j-jagu@umn.edu; *Dir,* Position Currently Open; Staff 42 (MLS 13, Non-MLS 29)

IMMIGRATION HISTORY RESEARCH CENTER, Elmer L Andersen Library, 222 21st Ave S, Ste 311, 55455, SAN 378-0996. Tel: 612-625-4800. FAX: 612-626-0018. E-mail: ihrc@umn.edu. Web Site: www.ihrc.umn.edu. *Dir,* Erika Lee; Tel: 612-625-5573
Open Mon-Fri 8:30-11:30 & 12:30-4:30
Friends of the Library Group

CL LAW, 120 Law Bldg, 229 19th Ave S, 55455, SAN 378-1046. Tel: 612-625-4300. FAX: 612-625-3478. Web Site: www.law.umn.edu. *Assoc Dean, Info Tech,* Joan Howland; E-mail: howla001@umn.edu
Special Collections: The Papers of Clarence Darrow
Partic in OCLC Research Library Partnership

MATHEMATICS, 310 Vincent Hall, 206 Church St SE, 55455, SAN 347-5891. Tel: 612-624-6075. FAX: 612-624-4302. E-mail: library@math.umn.edu. Web Site: math.lib.umn.edu. *Librn,* Kristine Fowler; Staff 4 (MLS 1, Non-MLS 3)

MUSIC, 70 Ferguson Hall, 2106 S Fourth St, 55455, SAN 347-6251. Tel: 612-624-5890. FAX: 612-625-6994. *Assoc Librn,* S Timothy Maloney

SPECIAL COLLECTIONS & RARE BOOKS, Elmer L Andersen Library, 222 21st Ave S, Ste 111, 55455, SAN 347-6731. Tel: 612-626-9166. FAX: 612-625-5525. *Assoc Librn, Curator,* Timothy Johnson

CM VETERINARY MEDICAL, 450 Veterinary Science Bldg, 1971 Commonwealth Ave, Saint Paul, 55108, SAN 378-1224. Tel: 612-624-4281. FAX: 612-624-9782. *Head Librn,* Andre J Nault; Tel: 612-624-5376. Subject Specialists: *Veterinary med,* Andre J Nault

CM WANGENSTEEN HISTORICAL LIBRARY OF BIOLOGY & MEDICINE, 568 Diehl Hall, 505 Essex St SE, 55455, SAN 347-5506. Tel: 612-626-6881. FAX: 612-626-6500. *Curator,* Elaine Challacombe

REFERENCE SERVICES (WILSON LIBRARY), 309 19th Ave S, 55455, SAN 371-3156. Tel: 612-626-2227. FAX: 612-626-9353. *Coordr, Ref (Info Serv),* Mary Schoenborn; Tel: 612-626-7308

CM UNIVERSITY OF MINNESOTA MEDICAL CENTER - FAIRVIEW, LIBRARY*, 2450 Riverside Ave, 55454. SAN 308-6615. Tel: 612-273-6546. FAX: 612-273-2675. E-mail: library10@fairview.org. *Mgr, Libr Serv,* Kolleen Olsen; Tel: 612-273-6595, E-mail: kolsen6@fairview.org; *ILL, Per,* Renee Jacobson; E-mail: rjacobs2@fairview.org; Staff 3 (MLS 2, Non-MLS 1)
Library Holdings: e-journals 15,000; Bk Vols 2,500; Per Subs 350
Subject Interests: Nursing
Automation Activity & Vendor Info: (Acquisitions) EOS International; (Cataloging) EOS International; (Circulation) EOS International; (OPAC) EOS International; (Serials) EOS International
Database Vendor: EBSCOhost, Gale Cengage Learning, Micromedex, OCLC FirstSearch, OVID Technologies, ProQuest, PubMed, ScienceDirect
Wireless access
Function: Doc delivery serv, For res purposes, Health sci info serv, ILL available, Online searches, Orientations, Photocopying/Printing, Prof lending libr, Ref serv available, Res libr, Telephone ref
Partic in Docline; Minitex Library Information Network; Twin Cities Biomedical Consortium
Open Mon-Fri 8-4
Restriction: In-house use for visitors, Open to pub for ref only, Prof mat only

C WALDEN UNIVERSITY LIBRARY, 100 Washington Ave S, Ste 900, 55401. SAN 303-0857. Toll Free Tel: 855-764-4433. E-mail: library@waldenu.edu. Web Site: library.waldenu.edu. *Dir of Libr Serv,* Jennie Ver Steeg; Tel: 612-312-2379, Fax: 612-338-5092, E-mail: jennie.versteeg@waldenu.edu; *Assoc Dir,* Lisa Raymond; E-mail: lisa.raymond@waldenu.edu; *Coll Mgr,* Miki Scholl; E-mail: miki.scholl@waldenu.edu; *Mgr, Info Literacy,* Michelle Hajder; E-mail: michelle.hajder@waldenu.edu; *IT Mgr,* Heather Westerlund; E-mail: heather.westerlund@waldenu.edu; *Ref Coordr,* Erin Gabrielson; E-mail: erin.gabrielson@waldenu.edu; Staff 17 (MLS 17)
Founded 1992. Enrl 45,619; Fac 1,000; Highest Degree: Doctorate
Library Holdings: e-books 164,703; e-journals 64,136
Automation Activity & Vendor Info: (Acquisitions) SerialsSolutions; (Cataloging) SerialsSolutions; (OPAC) LibLime; (Serials) EBSCO Online
Database Vendor: Alexander Street Press, American Psychological Association (APA), Annual Reviews, Bowker, CQ Press, ebrary, EBSCO - WebFeat, EBSCOhost, Elsevier, Emerald, Gale Cengage Learning, IEEE (Institute of Electrical & Electronics Engineers), LexisNexis, LibLime, OVID Technologies, Oxford Online, Project MUSE, ProQuest, PubMed, Safari Books Online, Sage, ScienceDirect, SerialsSolutions, Thomson - Web of Science, Wiley, YBP Library Services
Function: Distance learning, Doc delivery serv, e-mail serv, Electronic databases & coll, Online info literacy tutorials on the web & in blackboard, Online ref, Ref serv available, Telephone ref
Open Mon-Fri 8am-1am, Sat & Sun Noon-1am
Restriction: Not a lending libr

L WINTHROP & WEINSTINE*, Law Library, 225 S Sixth St, Ste 3500, 55402. SAN 372-2872. Tel: 612-604-6450. FAX: 612-604-6850. Web Site: www.winthrop.com. *Dir, Res Serv,* Nancy Evans; E-mail: nevans@winthrop.com; Staff 2 (MLS 1, Non-MLS 1)
Database Vendor: Dialog, LexisNexis, Westlaw
Wireless access
Restriction: Private libr

L ZELLE, HOFMANN, VOELBEL, MASON & GETTE*, Law Library, 500 Washington Ave S, Ste 4000, 55415. SAN 372-2813. Tel: 612-336-9129. FAX: 612-336-9100. Web Site: www.zelle.com. *Librn,* Janet L Rongitsch; E-mail: jrongits@zelle.com
Library Holdings: Bk Vols 10,000; Per Subs 200
Wireless access
Open Mon-Fri 8-5

MINNEOTA

P MINNEOTA PUBLIC LIBRARY*, 103 N Jefferson St, 56264-0217. SAN 308-6992. Tel: 507-872-5473. FAX: 507-872-6144. Web Site: www.plumcreeklibrary.org/Minneota. *Librn,* Mary Buysse; E-mail: mbuysse@plumcreeklibrary.net; *Asst Librn,* Elana Nomeland; Staff 2 (Non-MLS 2)
Founded 1902. Pop 1,500; Circ 7,310
Library Holdings: Bk Titles 6,369; Per Subs 14
Function: Home delivery & serv to Sr ctr & nursing homes
Mem of Plum Creek Library System
Open Tues & Thurs 9-5, Wed 2-8, Fri 11-2, Sat 9-12
Friends of the Library Group

MINNETONKA

P HENNEPIN COUNTY LIBRARY, 12601 Ridgedale Dr, 55305-1909. SAN 347-3163. Tel: 612-543-8593. Interlibrary Loan Service Tel: 612-543-8318, 612-543-8319. Reference Tel: 612-543-5669. Administration Tel: 612-543-8518. FAX: 612-543-8600. Interlibrary Loan Service FAX: 612-543-8148. Web Site: www.hclib.org. *Dir,* Lois Langer Thompson; Tel: 612-543-8541, E-mail: lthompson@hclib.org; *Dep Dir,* Position Currently Open; *Div Mgr, Libr Serv,* Janet Mills; Tel: 612-543-8535, E-mail: jmills@hclib.org; *Div Mgr, Operations,* Nancy Palmer; Tel: 612-919-8787, E-mail: npalmer@hclib.org; *Div Mgr, Res Serv,* Position Currently Open; *Div Mgr, Syst Serv,* Ali Turner; Tel: 612-543-8516, E-mail: aturner@hclib.org; Staff 611 (MLS 179.3, Non-MLS 431.7)
Founded 1885. Pop 1,163,060; Circ 16,656,427
Jan 2012-Dec 2012 Income (Main Library and Branch(s)) $69,000,000. Mats Exp $66,648,547
Library Holdings: AV Mats 198,115; e-books 78,062; Electronic Media & Resources 36,567; Music Scores 52,497; Bk Vols 4,475,860; Per Subs 8,502
Special Collections: 19th Century American Studies Coll; Heffelfinger Aesop's & Others' Fables Coll; History of Books & Printing Coll; Hoag Mark Twain Coll; Huttner Abolition & Anti-Slavery Coll; Kittleson World War II Coll; Louis Dodge Autograph Coll; Minneapolis Athenaeum (includes Early American Exploration & Travel Coll); Minneapolis Coll including Oral History; North American Indians Coll; Picture Coll; Spencer Natural History Coll. Oral History; US Document Depository
Wireless access
Partic in Metropolitan Library Service Agency; OCLC Online Computer Library Center, Inc
Special Services for the Deaf - Accessible learning ctr; ADA equip; Assisted listening device; Assistive tech; Closed caption videos; Sign lang interpreter upon request for prog; Videos & decoder
Special Services for the Blind - Assistive/Adapted tech devices, equip & products; Audio mat; Bks on cassette; Bks on CD; Internet workstation with adaptive software; Large print & cassettes; Magnifiers; Micro-computer access & training; Reader equip
Friends of the Library Group

Branches: 41

AUGSBURG PARK, 7100 Nicollet Ave S, Richfield, 55423-3117, SAN 347-3198. Tel: 612-543-6200. FAX: 612-543-6202. *Sr Librn,* Pat Palahniuk; Tel: 612-543-6203, E-mail: ppalahniuk@hclib.org
Open Mon-Wed 9-8, Thurs-Sat 9-5, Sun 12-5
Friends of the Library Group

PIERRE BOTTINEAU, 55 Broadway St NE, Minneapolis, 55413-1811, SAN 347-4992. Tel: 612-543-6850. FAX: 612-543-6852. *Sr Librn,* Jerry Blue; Tel: 612-543-6078, E-mail: jblue@hclib.org
Open Mon & Thurs 12-8, Tues, Wed, Fri & Sat 9-5
Friends of the Library Group

BROOKDALE, 6125 Shingle Creek Pkwy, Brooklyn Center, 55430-2110, SAN 347-3228. Tel: 612-543-5600. FAX: 612-543-5602. *Sr Librn,* Susan Glenn; Tel: 612-543-5631, E-mail: sglenn@hclib.org
Open Mon-Thurs 9-9, Fri & Sat 9-5, Sun 12-5
Friends of the Library Group

BROOKLYN PARK, 8600 Zane Ave N, Brooklyn Park, 55443-1897, SAN 347-3252. Tel: 612-543-6225. FAX: 612-543-6227. *Sr Librn,* Sherry Anderson; Tel: 612-543-6228, E-mail: sanderson@hclib.org
Open Mon-Wed 9-8, Thurs-Sat 9-5, Sun 12-5
Friends of the Library Group

CHAMPLIN, 12154 Ensign Ave N, Champlin, 55316-9998, SAN 347-3287. Tel: 612-543-6250. FAX: 612-543-6252. *Sr Librn,* Molly Schaaf; Tel: 612-543-6253, E-mail: mschaaf@hclib.org
Open Mon, Wed, Fri & Sat 9-5, Tues & Thurs 12-8
Friends of the Library Group

EAST LAKE, 2727 E Lake St, Minneapolis, 55406, SAN 347-481X. Tel: 612-543-8425. FAX: 612-543-8427. *Sr Librn,* Deborah Reierson; Tel: 612-543-8428, E-mail: djreierson@hclib.org
Open Mon, Tues & Thurs 9-8, Wed, Fri & Sat 9-5, Sun 12-5
Friends of the Library Group

EDEN PRAIRIE, 565 Prairie Center Dr, Eden Prairie, 55344-5319, SAN 347-3317. Tel: 612-543-6275. FAX: 612-543-6277. *Sr Librn,* Saad Samatar; Tel: 612-543-6279, E-mail: ssamatar@hclib.org
Open Mon-Thurs 9-9, Fri & Sat 9-5, Sun 12-5
Friends of the Library Group

EDINA, 5280 Grandview Sq, Edina, 55436, SAN 347-3341. Tel: 612-543-6325. FAX: 612-543-6327. *Sr Librn,* Tracy Hvezda-Lehtola; Tel: 612-543-6330, E-mail: thvezda-lehtola@hclib.org
Open Mon-Wed 9-8, Thurs-Sat 9-5, Sun 12-5
Friends of the Library Group

EXCELSIOR, 337 Water St, Excelsior, 55331-1878, SAN 347-3376. Tel: 612-543-6350. FAX: 612-543-6352. *Sr Librn,* Peggy Bauer; Tel: 612-543-6353, E-mail: pbauer@hclib.org
Open Mon, Wed, Fri & Sat 9-5, Tues & Thurs 12-8
Friends of the Library Group

FRANKLIN, 1314 E Franklin Ave, Minneapolis, 55404-2924, SAN 347-4844. Tel: 612-543-6925. FAX: 612-543-6927. *Sr Librn,* Angela Fiero; Tel: 612-543-6928, E-mail: adfiero@hclib.org; *Literacy Coordr - Franklin Learning Ctr,* Nancy Thornbury; Tel: 612-543-6939, E-mail: nbthornbury@hclib.org
Open Mon, Fri & Sat 9-5, Tues-Thurs 9-8, Sun 12-5
Friends of the Library Group

GOLDEN VALLEY, 830 Winnetka Ave N, Golden Valley, 55427-4532, SAN 347-3406. Tel: 612-543-6375. FAX: 612-543-6377. *Sr Librn,* Mary Anderson; Tel: 612-543-6378, E-mail: manderson@hclib.org
Open Mon-Wed 9-8, Thurs-Sat 9-5, Sun 12-5
Friends of the Library Group

HOPKINS, 22 11th Ave N, Hopkins, 55343-7575, SAN 347-3430. Tel: 612-543-6400. FAX: 612-543-6402. *Sr Librn,* Lisa Bjerken; Tel: 612-543-6403, E-mail: lbjerken@hclib.org
Open Mon-Wed 9-8, Thurs-Sat 9-5, Sun 12-5
Friends of the Library Group

HOSMER, 347 E 36th St, Minneapolis, 55408-4567, SAN 347-4879. Tel: 612-543-6900. FAX: 612-543-6902. *Sr Librn,* Bethany Wagenaar; Tel: 612-543-6903, E-mail: bwagenaar@hclib.org
Open Mon-Wed 9-8, Thurs-Sat 9-5, Sun 12-5
Friends of the Library Group

LINDEN HILLS, 2900 W 43rd St, Minneapolis, 55410-1515, SAN 347-4909. Tel: 612-543-6825. FAX: 612-543-6827. *Sr Librn,* Toni Miller; Tel: 612-543-6128, E-mail: ammiller@hclib.org
Open Mon, Wed, Fri & Sat 9-5, Tues & Thurs 12-8
Friends of the Library Group

LONG LAKE, 1865 Wayzata Blvd W, Long Lake, 55356-9587, SAN 328-7335. Tel: 612-543-6425. FAX: 612-543-6427. *Sr Librn,* Nan Nystrom-Hilk; Tel: 612-543-6153, E-mail: nnystrom@hclib.org
Open Mon 12-8, Wed & Fri 9-5
Friends of the Library Group

MAPLE GROVE, 8001 Main St N, Maple Grove, 55369-4617, SAN 328-9184. Tel: 612-543-6450. FAX: 612-543-6452. *Sr Librn,* Lois Porfiri; Tel: 612-543-6477, E-mail: porfiri@hclib.org; *Sr Librn,* Kathryn Zimmerman; Tel: 612-543-6456, E-mail: kzimmerman@hclib.org
Open Mon-Thurs 9-9, Fri & Sat 9-5, Sun 12-5
Friends of the Library Group

MAPLE PLAIN, 5184 Main St E, Maple Plain, 55359-9648, SAN 347-349X. Tel: 612-543-5700. FAX: 612-543-6452. *Sr Librn,* Joyce Cobb; Tel: 612-543-6178, E-mail: jcobb@hclib.org
Open Tues 12-8, Thurs & Sat 9-5
Friends of the Library Group

MINNEAPOLIS CENTRAL, 300 Nicollet Mall, Minneapolis, 55401, SAN 347-4755. Tel: 612-543-8000. FAX: 612-543-8173. *Sr Librn,* Helen Burke; Tel: 612-543-8079, E-mail: hburke@hclib.org; *Sr Librn,* Bernie Farrell; Tel: 612-543-8030, E-mail: bfarrell@hclib.org; *Sr Librn,* Ted Hathaway; Tel: 612-543-8203, E-mail: ehathaway@hclib.org; *Sr Librn,* Constance Hill; Tel: 612-543-8124, E-mail: chill@hclib.org; *Sr Librn,* Marcelyn Sletten; Tel: 612-543-8143, E-mail: msletten@hclib.org; *Sr Librn,* Dillon Young; Tel: 612-543-8080, E-mail: dyoung@hclib.org
Special Collections: 19th Century American Studies Coll; History of Books & Printing Coll; Hoag Mark Twain Coll; Huttner Abolition & Anti-Slavery Coll; Kittleson World War II Coll; Louis Dodge Autograph Coll; Minneapolis Athenaeum (includes Early American Exploration & Travel Coll, Heffelfinger Aesop's & Others' Fables Coll, North American Indians Coll, Spencer Natural History Coll); Minneapolis Coll including Oral History; Picture Coll. Oral History; US Document Depository
Special Services for the Deaf - Accessible learning ctr
Special Services for the Blind - Assistive/Adapted tech devices, equip & products; Networked computers with assistive software
Open Mon-Thurs 9-9, Fri & Sat 9-5, Sun 12-5
Friends of the Library Group

MINNETONKA, 17524 Excelsior Blvd, 55345-1099, SAN 347-3554. Tel: 612-543-5725. FAX: 612-543-5727. *Sr Librn,* Peggy Bauer; Tel: 612-543-5728, E-mail: pbauer@hclib.org
Open Mon & Tues 12-8, Wed-Sat 9-5
Friends of the Library Group

NOKOMIS, 5100 34th Ave S, Minneapolis, 55417-1545, SAN 347-4933. Tel: 612-543-6800. FAX: 612-543-6802. *Sr Librn,* Amy McNally; Tel: 612-543-6803, E-mail: amcnally@hclib.org
Open Mon & Thurs 12-8, Tues, Wed, Fri & Sat 9-5
Friends of the Library Group

NORTH REGIONAL, 1315 Lowry Ave N, Minneapolis, 55411, SAN 347-478X. Tel: 612-543-8450. FAX: 612-543-8452. *Sr Librn,* Anna Schwindt DeGroot; Tel: 612-543-8463, E-mail: aschwindtdegroot@hclib.org
Open Mon, Tues & Thurs 9-8, Wed, Fri & Sat 9-5, Sun 12-5
Friends of the Library Group

NORTHEAST, 2200 Central Ave NE, Minneapolis, 55418-3708, SAN 347-4968. Tel: 612-543-6775. FAX: 612-543-6777. *Sr Librn,* Laurie Simenson; Tel: 612-543-6778, E-mail: llsimenson@hclib.org
Open Mon, Tues, Fri & Sat 9-5, Wed & Thurs 12-8
Friends of the Library Group

OSSEO, 415 Central Ave, Osseo, 55369-1194, SAN 347-3589. Tel: 612-543-5750. FAX: 612-543-5752. *Sr Librn,* Lois Porfiri; Tel: 612-543-6477, E-mail: lporfiri@hclib.org; *Sr Librn,* Kathryn Zimmerman; Tel: 612-543-6456, E-mail: kzimmerman@hclib.org
Open Mon 12-8, Tues & Thurs 9-5
Friends of the Library Group

OXBORO, 8801 Portland Ave S, Bloomington, 55420-2997, SAN 347-3619. Tel: 612-543-5775. FAX: 612-543-5777. *Sr Librn,* Pearl Hunt-McCain; Tel: 612-543-5778, E-mail: phuntmccain@hclib.org
Open Mon & Thurs-Sat 9-5, Tues & Wed 12-8
Friends of the Library Group

PENN LAKE, 8800 Penn Ave S, Bloomington, 55431-2022, SAN 347-3643. Tel: 612-543-5800. FAX: 612-543-5802. *Sr Librn,* Susan Woodwick; Tel: 612-543-5803, E-mail: smwoodwick@hclib.org
Open Mon-Wed 9-8, Thurs-Sat 9-5, Sun 12-5
Friends of the Library Group

PLYMOUTH, 15700 36th Ave N, Plymouth, 55446, SAN 375-6130. Tel: 612-543-5825. FAX: 612-543-5827. *Sr Librn,* Trudy Hanus; Tel: 612-543-5828, E-mail: thanus@hclib.org; *Sr Librn,* Maryann Weidt; Tel: 612-543-5860, E-mail: mweidt@hclib.org
Open Mon-Thurs 9-9, Fri & Sat 9-5, Sun 12-5
Friends of the Library Group

RIDGEDALE, 12601 Ridgedale Dr, 55305-1909. Tel: 612-543-8800. FAX: 612-543-8819. *Sr Librn,* Roberta Kemp; Tel: 612-543-8568, E-mail: rkemp@hclib.org; *Sr Librn,* Loren Taylor; Tel: 612-543-8820, E-mail: ltaylor@hclib.org; *Sr Librn, Outreach Serv,* Patrick Jones; Tel: 612-543-8859, E-mail: pjones@hclib.org
Open Mon-Thurs 9-9, Fri & Sat 9-5, Sun 12-5
Friends of the Library Group

ROCKFORD ROAD, 6401 42nd Ave N, Crystal, 55427-1499, SAN 347-3678. Tel: 612-543-5875. FAX: 612-543-5877. *Sr Librn,* Juanita Foster; Tel: 612-543-5878, E-mail: jfoster@hclib.org
Open Mon-Wed 9-8, Thurs-Sat 9-5, Sun 12-5
Friends of the Library Group

ROGERS, 21300 John Milless Dr, Rogers, 55374-9998, SAN 347-3686. Tel: 612-543-6050. FAX: 612-543-6052. *Sr Librn,* Molly Schaaf; Tel: 612-543-6253, E-mail: mschaaf@hclib.org
Open Mon & Thurs 12-8, Tues, Wed, Fri & Sat 9-5
Friends of the Library Group

ROOSEVELT, 4026 28th Ave S, Minneapolis, 55406, SAN 347-5026. Tel: 612-543-6700. FAX: 612-543-6702. *Sr Librn,* Amy McNally; Tel: 612-543-6701, E-mail: amcnally@hclib.org
Open Tues & Thurs 12-8, Sat 9-5
Friends of the Library Group

SAINT ANTHONY, 2941 Pentagon Dr NE, Saint Anthony, 55418-3209, SAN 347-3708. Tel: 612-543-6075. FAX: 612-543-6077. *Sr Librn,* Jerry Blue; Tel: 612-543-6078, E-mail: jblue@hclib.org
Open Mon & Tues 12-8, Wed-Sat 9-5
Friends of the Library Group

SAINT BONIFACIUS, 8624 Kennedy Memorial Dr, Saint Bonifacius, 55375-9998, SAN 347-3732. Tel: 612-543-6100. FAX: 612-543-6102. *Sr Librn,* Joyce Cobb; Tel: 612-543-6178, E-mail: jcobb@hclib.org
Open Mon & Wed 12-8, Sat 9-5
Friends of the Library Group

SAINT LOUIS PARK, 3240 Library Lane, Saint Louis Park, 55426-4101, SAN 347-3767. Tel: 612-543-6125. FAX: 612-543-6127. *Sr Librn,* Toni Miller; Tel: 612-543-6128, E-mail: ammiller@hclib.org
Open Mon, Tues & Thurs 9-8, Wed, Fri & Sat 9-5, Sun 12-5
Friends of the Library Group

SOUTHDALE, 7001 York Ave S, Edina, 55435-4287, SAN 347-3791. Tel: 612-543-5900. FAX: 612-543-5976. *Sr Librn,* Anita Bealer; Tel: 612-543-5971, E-mail: abealer@hclib.org; *Sr Librn,* Elizabeth Feinberg; Tel: 612-543-5990, E-mail: efeinberg@hclib.org
Open Mon-Thurs 9-9, Fri & Sat 9-5, Sun 12-5
Friends of the Library Group

SOUTHEAST, 1222 Fourth St SE, Minneapolis, 55414, SAN 347-5050. Tel: 612-543-6725. FAX: 612-543-6727. *Sr Librn,* Laurie Simenson; Tel: 612-543-6726, E-mail: llsimenson@hclib.org
Open Tues & Sat 9-5, Thurs 12-8
Friends of the Library Group

SUMNER, 611 Van White Memorial Blvd, Minneapolis, 55411-4196, SAN 347-5085. Tel: 612-543-6875. FAX: 612-543-6877. *Sr Librn,* Mary Anderson; Tel: 612-543-6878, E-mail: manderson@hclib.org
Special Collections: African American History (Gary N Sudduth Coll)
Open Mon & Thurs 12-8, Tues, Wed, Fri & Sat 9-5
Friends of the Library Group

WALKER, 2880 Hennepin Ave, Minneapolis, 55408-1957, SAN 347-5115. Tel: 612-543-8400. FAX: 612-543-8402. *Sr Librn,* Maryann Weidt; Tel: 612-543-8403, E-mail: mweidt@hclib.org
Open Mon & Wed 12-8, Tues & Thurs-Sat 9-5
Friends of the Library Group

WASHBURN, 5244 Lyndale Ave S, Minneapolis, 55419-1222, SAN 347-514X. Tel: 612-543-8375. FAX: 612-543-8377. *Sr Librn,* Ann Melrose; Tel: 612-543-8378, E-mail: amelrose@hclib.org
Open Mon, Wed, Fri & Sat 9-5, Tues & Thurs 12-8
Friends of the Library Group

WAYZATA, 620 Rice St, Wayzata, 55391-1734, SAN 347-3821. Tel: 612-543-6150. FAX: 612-543-6152. *Sr Librn,* Nan Nystrom-Hilk; Tel: 612-543-6153, E-mail: nnystrom@hclib.org
Open Mon & Wed 12-8, Tues & Thurs-Sat 9-5
Friends of the Library Group

WEBBER PARK, 4310 Webber Pkwy, Minneapolis, 55412, SAN 347-5174. Tel: 612-543-6750. FAX: 612-543-6752. *Sr Librn,* Juanita Foster; Tel: 612-543-5878, E-mail: jfoster@hclib.org
Open Tues & Thurs 12-8, Sat 9-5
Friends of the Library Group

WESTONKA, 2079 Commerce Blvd, Mound, 55364-1594, SAN 347-3856. Tel: 612-543-6175. FAX: 612-543-6184. *Sr Librn,* Joyce Cobb; Tel: 612-543-6178, E-mail: jcobb@hclib.org
Open Mon & Wed 12-8, Tues & Thurs-Sat 9-5
Friends of the Library Group

MONTEVIDEO

P MONTEVIDEO PUBLIC LIBRARY*, 224 S First St, 56265. SAN 347-6820. Tel: 320-269-6501. FAX: 320-269-8696. Web Site: www.montevideolibrary.org. *Head Librn,* David Lauritsen; E-mail: david.lauritsen@pioneerland.lib.mn.us; *Children's & Teen Serv,* Marie Pederson; E-mail: marie.pederson@pioneerland.lib.mn.us; Staff 1 (Non-MLS 1)
Founded 1879. Pop 8,000; Circ 80,000
Jan 2014-Dec 2014 Income $217,530, City $94,730, County $117,800, Locally Generated Income $5,000. Mats Exp $31,600, Books $25,000, Per/Ser (Incl. Access Fees) $3,600, AV Mat $3,000. Sal $105,600 (Prof $48,600)
Library Holdings: Audiobooks 823; AV Mats 54; Bks on Deafness & Sign Lang 10; CDs 112; DVDs 1,292; High Interest/Low Vocabulary Bk Vols 426; Large Print Bks 2,046; Microforms 325; Bk Titles 56,000; Bk Vols 57,800; Per Subs 170; Spec Interest Per Sub 20; Talking Bks 84; Videos 1,169
Special Collections: 16mm Film Coll; Spanish Language (Uruguayan Materials Coll)
Subject Interests: Film
Automation Activity & Vendor Info: (Acquisitions) Innovative Interfaces, Inc; (Cataloging) Innovative Interfaces, Inc; (Circulation) Innovative Interfaces, Inc; (ILL) Innovative Interfaces, Inc; (Media Booking) Innovative Interfaces, Inc; (OPAC) Innovative Interfaces, Inc
Database Vendor: OCLC FirstSearch
Wireless access
Mem of Pioneerland Library System
Special Services for the Blind - Closed circuit TV magnifier
Open Mon-Thurs 9-7:30, Fri 9-5, Sat 9-2

GL C A ROLLOFF LAW LIBRARY*, Chippewa County Courthouse, 11th St & Hwy 7, 56265. SAN 321-8317. Tel: 320-269-8550. FAX: 320-269-7733. *Librn,* Nancy Johnson
Founded 1951
Library Holdings: Bk Titles 6,000
Open Mon-Fri 8-4:30

MOORHEAD

C CONCORDIA COLLEGE*, Carl B Ylvisaker Library, 901 S Eighth St, 56562. SAN 308-700X. Tel: 218-299-4640. Circulation Tel: 218-299-4641. Interlibrary Loan Service Tel: 218-299-3239. Reference Tel: 218-299-4656. FAX: 218-299-4253. E-mail: library@cord.edu. Web Site: www.cord.edu/academics/library. *Dir,* Sharon Hoverson; Tel: 218-299-4642, E-mail: hoverson@cord.edu; *Head, Info Serv,* Linda Swanson; Tel: 219-299-4402, E-mail: swanson@cord.edu; *Head of Instruction,* Virginia Connell; Tel: 218-299-3237, E-mail: vconnell@cord.edu; *Access & Delivery Librn,* Amy Soma; Tel: 218-299-4937, E-mail: soma@cord.edu; *Col Archivist/Librn,* Lisa Sjoberg; Tel: 218-299-3180, E-mail: sjoberg@cord.edu; *Computer & Web Serv Librn,* Erika Rux; E-mail: rux@cord.edu; *Curric Center Librn,* Connie Jones; Tel: 218-299-3238, E-mail: cjones@cord.edu; *Spec Projects Librn,* Molly Flaspohler; Tel: 218-299-4643, E-mail: mflaspoh@cord.edu; *Circ & ILL Mgr,* Leah Anderson; E-mail: landerso@cord.edu; *Electronic Res,* Theresa Borchert; Tel: 218-299-3235, E-mail: borchert@cord.edu; Staff 20 (MLS 10, Non-MLS 10)
Founded 1891. Enrl 2,823; Fac 218; Highest Degree: Master
Library Holdings: AV Mats 25,015; e-books 12,741; Microforms 44,055; Bk Vols 333,367; Per Subs 3,425
Subject Interests: Lutheran hist, Philos, Relig studies, Scandinavian studies
Automation Activity & Vendor Info: (Acquisitions) Ex Libris Group; (Cataloging) Ex Libris Group; (Circulation) Ex Libris Group; (Course Reserve) Ex Libris Group; (ILL) Ex Libris Group; (Media Booking) Ex Libris Group; (OPAC) Ex Libris Group; (Serials) Ex Libris Group
Database Vendor: ABC-CLIO, Alexander Street Press, American Chemical Society, Annual Reviews, Blackwell, Cambridge Scientific Abstracts, Cinahl, CIOS (Communication Institute for Online Scholarship), CountryWatch, CredoReference, EBSCO Information Services, EBSCOhost, Elsevier, Emerald, Facts on File, Gale Cengage Learning, Greenwood Publishing Group, H W Wilson, JSTOR, LearningExpress, LexisNexis, Medline, Modern Language Association, Nature Publishing Group, OCLC FirstSearch, OCLC WorldShare Interlibrary Loan, OVID Technologies, Oxford Online, Project MUSE, ProQuest, PubMed, RefWorks, Sage, ScienceDirect, Wiley InterScience, Wilson - Wilson Web
Wireless access
Function: Archival coll, Audio & video playback equip for onsite use, Bks on CD, Computers for patron use, Copy machines, Doc delivery serv, e-mail & chat, E-Reserves, Electronic databases & coll, Exhibits, ILL available, Instruction & testing, Online cat, Online ref, Online searches, Orientations, Outside serv via phone, mail, e-mail & web, Photocopying/Printing, Prof lending libr, Pub access computers, Ref & res, Ref serv available, Ref serv in person, Scanner, Spoken cassettes & CDs, Spoken cassettes & DVDs, Telephone ref, VHS videos, Video lending libr, Web-catalog, Wheelchair accessible
Partic in MnPALS; Tri-College University Libraries Consortium
Special Services for the Deaf - ADA equip; Assistive tech; High interest/low vocabulary bks
Special Services for the Blind - Accessible computers; Bks on CD; Computer with voice synthesizer for visually impaired persons; Copier with enlargement capabilities; Large screen computer & software
Open Mon-Thurs 7:45am-Midnight, Fri 7:45-5, Sat 10-5, Sun Noon-Midnight
Restriction: Borrowing requests are handled by ILL, In-house use for visitors, Non-circulating coll, Non-circulating of rare bks, Open to pub for ref & circ; with some limitations, Restricted access

P LAKE AGASSIZ REGIONAL LIBRARY*, 118 S Fifth St, 56560-2756. (Mail add: PO Box 900, 56561-0900), SAN 347-7096. Tel: 218-233-3757. Toll Free Tel: 800-247-0449. FAX: 218-233-7556. Web Site: larl.org. *Regional Libr Dir,* Liz Lynch; Tel: 218-233-3757, Ext 127, E-mail: lynchl@larl.org; *Coll Develop Librn,* Jeanne Anderson; Tel: 218-233-3757, Ext 122, E-mail: andersonj@larl.org; *Automation Coordr,* Sharon Douglas; Tel: 218-233-3757, Ext 138, E-mail: douglass@larl.org; Staff 9 (MLS 9)
Founded 1961. Pop 130,981; Circ 815,385

Library Holdings: Bk Vols 332,247
Automation Activity & Vendor Info: (Acquisitions) Innovative Interfaces, Inc; (Cataloging) Innovative Interfaces, Inc; (Circulation) Innovative Interfaces, Inc; (OPAC) Innovative Interfaces, Inc
Wireless access
Open Mon-Fri 7:30-4:30
Branches: 13
ADA PUBLIC LIBRARY, 107 E Fourth Ave, Ada, 56510-1302, SAN 347-7126. Tel: 218-784-4480. FAX: 218-784-2594. E-mail: ada@larl.org. Web Site: www.larl.org/locations/ada-library. *Br Librn,* Candace Osborn
Founded 1945. Pop 3,964
Library Holdings: Bk Vols 14,000; Per Subs 52
Open Tues & Thurs 2-8, Wed & Fri 10-6, Sat 10-2
Friends of the Library Group
BAGLEY PUBLIC LIBRARY, 79 Spencer Ave SW, Bagley, 56621. (Mail add: PO Box G, Bagley, 56621-1008), SAN 328-6975. Tel: 218-694-6201. FAX: 218-694-6201. E-mail: bagley@larl.org. Web Site: www.larl.org/locations/bagley-public-library. *Br Librn,* Karen Edevold
Founded 1910. Pop 9,500; Circ 19,247
Library Holdings: Bk Vols 5,400; Per Subs 30
Open Tues & Thurs 2-8, Wed & Fri 10-6, Sat 10-2
Friends of the Library Group
BARNESVILLE PUBLIC LIBRARY, 104 N Front St, Barnesville, 56514. (Mail add: PO Box 549, Barnesville, 56514-0549), SAN 347-7150. Tel: 218-354-2301. FAX: 218-354-7064. E-mail: barnesville@larl.org. Web Site: www.larl.org/locations/barnesville-public-library. *Br Librn,* Kaia Lynd
Founded 1949. Pop 3,452
Library Holdings: Bk Vols 12,064; Per Subs 80
Open Tues & Wed 12-8, Thurs & Fri 10-6, Sat 10-2
Friends of the Library Group
BRECKENRIDGE PUBLIC LIBRARY, 205 N Seventh St, Breckenridge, 56520-1519, SAN 347-7185. Tel: 218-643-2113. FAX: 218-643-2113. E-mail: breckenridge@larl.org. Web Site: www.larl.org/locations/breckenridge-library. *Br Supvr,* Erin Thunderson
Founded 1912. Pop 6,554
Library Holdings: Bk Vols 16,653; Per Subs 61
Automation Activity & Vendor Info: (Cataloging) SirsiDynix; (Circulation) SirsiDynix; (Course Reserve) SirsiDynix; (ILL) SirsiDynix; (Media Booking) SirsiDynix; (OPAC) SirsiDynix
Open Mon & Tues 12-8, Wed 10-6, Thurs 10-8, Fri 12-6, Sat 10-2
Friends of the Library Group
CLIMAX PUBLIC LIBRARY, 104 W Broadway, Climax, 56523-2314, SAN 347-7215. Tel: 218-857-2455. FAX: 218-857-2455. E-mail: climax@larl.org. Web Site: www.larl.org/locations/climax-library. *Br Librn,* Jane Vigness
Founded 1960. Pop 787
Library Holdings: Bk Vols 5,410; Per Subs 18
Open Mon 4-8, Tues 1-6, Thurs 1-8, Fri 10-2
Friends of the Library Group
CROOKSTON PUBLIC LIBRARY, 110 N Ash St, Crookston, 56716-1702, SAN 347-724X. Tel: 218-281-4522. FAX: 218-281-4523. E-mail: crookston@larl.org. Web Site: www.larl.org/locations/crookston-library. *Hub Supvr,* Christ Voike
Founded 1903. Pop 11,000
Library Holdings: Bk Vols 56,590; Per Subs 85
Open Mon-Wed 10-8, Thurs & Fri 10-6, Sat 10-5, Sun (Winter) 1-5
Friends of the Library Group
DETROIT LAKES PUBLIC LIBRARY, 1000 Washington Ave, Detroit Lakes, 56501-3414, SAN 347-7274. Tel: 218-847-2168. FAX: 218-847-2160. E-mail: detroit@larl.org. Web Site: www.larl.org/locations/detroit-lake-library. *Hub Supvr,* Mary Haney
Founded 1908. Pop 30,000
Library Holdings: Bk Vols 32,669; Per Subs 134
Open Mon-Wed 10-9, Thurs & Fri 10-6, Sat 10-4
Friends of the Library Group
FERTILE PUBLIC LIBRARY, 101 S Mill St, Fertile, 56540. (Mail add: PO Box 418, Fertile, 56540-0418). Tel: 218-945-6137. FAX: 218-945-6137. E-mail: fertile@larl.org. Web Site: www.larl.org/locations/fertile-public-library. *Br Librn,* Rebecca Diaz
Founded 1967. Pop 803
Library Holdings: Bk Vols 6,700; Per Subs 31
Open Tues, Thurs & Fri 10-6, Wed 12-8
Friends of the Library Group
FOSSTON PUBLIC LIBRARY, 421 Foss Ave N, Fosston, 56542, SAN 347-7339. Tel: 218-435-1320. FAX: 218-435-1320. E-mail: fosston@larl.org. Web Site: www.larl.org/locations/fosston-library. *Br Librn,* Tammi Jalowiec
Founded 1918. Pop 4,530
Library Holdings: Bk Vols 13,150; Per Subs 34
Open Mon, Wed & Fri 10-6, Tues & Thurs 12-8, Sat 10-2
Friends of the Library Group
HAWLEY PUBLIC LIBRARY, 421 Hartford St, Hawley, 56549. (Mail add: PO Box 519, Hawley, 56549-0519), SAN 347-7363. Tel: 218-483-4549. FAX: 218-483-4549. E-mail: hawley@larl.org. Web Site: www.larl.org/branch/hawley.html. *Br Librn,* Verna Olson
Founded 1950. Pop 3,580
Library Holdings: Bk Vols 11,508; Per Subs 45
Open Mon & Wed 10-1 & 2-8, Thurs 2-8, Fri 2-5, Sat 10-2
MAHNOMEN PUBLIC LIBRARY, 203 S Main St, Mahnomen, 56557. (Mail add: PO Box 476, Mahnomen, 56557-0476), SAN 308-6186. Tel: 218-935-2843. FAX: 218-935-2574. E-mail: mahnomen@larl.org. Web Site: www.larl.org/locations/mahnomen-library. *Br Librn,* Lois Schaedler
Pop 5,000; Circ 10,000
Library Holdings: Bk Vols 13,000; Per Subs 24
Open Tues 1-7, Wed & Fri 10-6, Thurs 12-6, Sat 10-2
Friends of the Library Group
MCINTOSH PUBLIC LIBRARY, 115 Broadway NW, McIntosh, 56556. (Mail add: PO Box 39, McIntosh, 56556-0039), SAN 347-7398. Tel: 218-563-4555. FAX: 218-563-3042. E-mail: mcintosh@larl.org. Web Site: www.larl.org/locations/mcintosh-library. *Br Librn,* Julie Malmanger
Founded 1941. Pop 977
Library Holdings: Bk Vols 7,000; Per Subs 15
Open Mon 10-3, Tues & Thurs 5-8, Wed & Fri 12-5
MOORHEAD PUBLIC LIBRARY, 118 Fifth St S, 56560. (Mail add: PO Box 900, 56561-0900), SAN 347-7428. Tel: 218-233-7594. FAX: 218-236-7405. E-mail: moorhead@larl.org. Web Site: www.larl.org/locations/moorhead-library. *Br Librn,* Megan Krueger
Founded 1906. Pop 41,245
Library Holdings: Bk Vols 123,228; Per Subs 299
Open Mon-Thurs 10-8, Fri & Sat 10-6
Friends of the Library Group

C MINNESOTA STATE UNIVERSITY MOORHEAD*, Livingston Lord Library, 1104 Seventh Ave S, 56563. SAN 308-7018. Tel: 218-477-2922. Interlibrary Loan Service Tel: 218-477-2924. Reference Tel: 218-477-2345. FAX: 218-477-5924. Web Site: www.mnstate.edu/library. *Assoc VPres & Dean,* Brittney Goodman; Tel: 218-477-2923, E-mail: goodmanb@mnstate.edu; *Distance Learning & Web Librn,* Travis Dolence; E-mail: dolence@mnstate.edu; *Instruction/Info Lit Librn,* Belle Nelson; Tel: 218-477-5919, E-mail: nelsonb@mnstate.edu; *Spec Coll Librn,* Carol Sibley; E-mail: sibley@mnstate.edu; *Archivist,* Terry Shoptaugh; E-mail: shoptaug@mnstate.edu; *Coll Develop,* Larry Schwartz; E-mail: schwartz@mnstate.edu; *Electronic Res,* Stacy Voeller; E-mail: voeller@mnstate.edu; *Govt Doc,* William Kenz; E-mail: kenz@mnstate.edu; *ILL,* Dianne Schmidt; *Pub Serv,* Pam Werre; E-mail: werrepa@mnstate.edu; *Tech Serv,* Jean Kramer; E-mail: kramer@mnstate.edu; Staff 20 (MLS 10, Non-MLS 10)
Founded 1887. Enrl 7,600; Fac 349; Highest Degree: Master
Library Holdings: Bk Vols 570,000; Per Subs 4,000
Special Collections: State Document Depository; US Document Depository
Subject Interests: Juv, Media, Res
Automation Activity & Vendor Info: (Acquisitions) PALS; (Cataloging) PALS; (Circulation) PALS; (Course Reserve) PALS; (ILL) PALS; (Media Booking) PALS; (OPAC) PALS; (Serials) PALS
Wireless access
Function: ILL available, Online searches, Photocopying/Printing, Ref serv available, Wheelchair accessible
Partic in Minn Interlibr Teletype Exchange; OCLC Online Computer Library Center, Inc; Tri-College University Libraries Consortium
Open Mon-Thurs 7:30am-11:45pm, Fri 7:30-4:45, Sat 10-4:45, Sun 1-11:45

R TRINITY LUTHERAN CHURCH LIBRARY*, 210 S Seventh St, 56560-2794. (Mail add: PO Box 188, 56561-0188), SAN 308-7026. Tel: 218-236-1333. FAX: 218-236-8918. *Librn,* Jane Loeffler; Staff 4 (MLS 1, Non-MLS 3)
Founded 1959
Library Holdings: DVDs 110; Large Print Bks 60; Bk Titles 4,200; Spec Interest Per Sub 2; Videos 230
Subject Interests: Bible study resources, Biblical ref, Personal faith

MOOSE LAKE

S MINNESOTA DEPARTMENT OF CORRECTIONS*, Minnesota Correctional Facility - Willow River/Moose Lake, 1000 Lake Shore Dr, 55767. Tel: 218-485-5000, Ext 5202. FAX: 218-485-5113. Web Site: www.doc.state.mn.us. *Librn,* Becky Pemberton; E-mail: becky.pemberton@state.mn.us
Library Holdings: DVDs 645; Bk Vols 13,500; Per Subs 68
Automation Activity & Vendor Info: (Cataloging) Follett Software; (Circulation) Follett Software
Open Tues 8:30-11:30, 1-4 & 5:30-8:15, Wed & Fri 8:30-11:30 & 1-4, Thurs 1:15-4 & 5:30-8:15, Sat 8-12 & 1-4

P MOOSE LAKE PUBLIC LIBRARY*, 313 Elm Ave, 55767. (Mail add: PO Box 277, 55767-0277), SAN 308-7034. Tel: 218-485-4424. FAX: 218-485-4424. Web Site: www.mooselake.lib.mn.us. *Dir,* Deb Shaw; E-mail: dshaw@arrowhead.lib.mn.us; Staff 2.29 (Non-MLS 2.29)
Founded 1938. Pop 2,751; Circ 48,434
Library Holdings: Audiobooks 788; DVDs 1,597; Bk Titles 14,800; Per Subs 101
Automation Activity & Vendor Info: (Cataloging) Horizon; (Circulation) Horizon; (OPAC) Horizon
Wireless access
Open Mon & Thurs 10-8, Tues, Wed & Fri 10-5, Sat (Fall-Spring) 10-2
Friends of the Library Group

MORA

S KANABEC COUNTY HISTORICAL SOCIETY*, Kanabec History Center, 805 W Forest Ave, 55051-1466. (Mail add: PO Box 113, 55051-0113), SAN 373-2274. Tel: 320-679-1665. FAX: 320-679-1673. E-mail: center@kanabechistory.org. Web Site: www.kanabechistory.org. *Dir,* Janet L Franz; *Dir,* Sharon L Vogt
Founded 1978
Library Holdings: Bk Vols 2,800
Subject Interests: Genealogy

P MORA PUBLIC LIBRARY*, 200 W Maple Ave, 55051-1330. SAN 347-2531. Tel: 320-679-2642. E-mail: momail@ecrl.lib.mn.us. Web Site: www.ecrl.lib.mn.us. *Librn,* Wendy Prokosch
Pop 11,266; Circ 71,622
Library Holdings: Bk Vols 15,000; Per Subs 40
Automation Activity & Vendor Info: (Circulation) SirsiDynix; (OPAC) SirsiDynix
Mem of East Central Regional Library
Open Mon 12-5, Tues & Thurs 12-8, Wed & Fri 10-5, Sat 10-2
Friends of the Library Group

MORGAN

P MORGAN PUBLIC LIBRARY, 210 Vernon Ave, 56266. (Mail add: PO Box 128, 56266-0128), SAN 308-7050. Tel: 507-249-3153. FAX: 507-249-3839. E-mail: morganlibrary@redred.com. Web Site: www.plumcreeklibrary.org/morgan. *Dir, Head Librn,* Vanessa Hoffmann; *Librn,* Barb Christensen; Staff 3 (Non-MLS 3)
Founded 1939. Pop 76,053; Circ 320,061
Library Holdings: Bk Titles 13,000; Per Subs 25
Database Vendor: TLC (The Library Corporation)
Wireless access
Mem of Plum Creek Library System
Open Mon, Wed & Fri 9-5, Tues & Thurs 1-7

MORRIS

P MORRIS PUBLIC LIBRARY*, 102 E Sixth St, 56267-1211. SAN 308-7069. Tel: 320-589-1634. FAX: 320-589-8892. Web Site: www.viking.lib.mn.us. *Librn,* Rita Mulcahy; E-mail: rmulcahy@morris.lib.mn.us; Staff 4 (MLS 1, Non-MLS 3)
Pop 5,366; Circ 128,000
Library Holdings: Bk Vols 50,000; Per Subs 100
Special Collections: Local History Coll
Automation Activity & Vendor Info: (Cataloging) SirsiDynix; (Circulation) SirsiDynix; (OPAC) SirsiDynix
Wireless access
Mem of Viking Library System
Open Mon-Thurs 10-8, Fri & Sat 10-5
Friends of the Library Group

C UNIVERSITY OF MINNESOTA-MORRIS*, Rodney A Briggs Library, 600 E Fourth St, 56267. SAN 308-7077. Tel: 320-589-6175. Reference Tel: 320-589-6176. FAX: 320-589-6168. Web Site: www.morris.umn.edu/library. *Dir,* LeAnn Lindquist Dean; Tel: 320-589-6226, E-mail: deanl@morris.umn.edu; *Instruction Coordr,* Melissa Engleman; Tel: 320-589-6227, E-mail: menglema@morris.umn.edu; *Metadata Coordr,* Jayne Blodgett; Tel: 320-589-6174, E-mail: blodgetj@morris.umn.edu; *Ref Coordr,* Peter Bremer; Tel: 320-589-6173, E-mail: pbremer@morris.umn.edu; *Digital Serv,* William Straub; Tel: 320-589-6164, E-mail: wlstraub@morris.umn.edu; Staff 9 (MLS 5, Non-MLS 4)
Founded 1960. Enrl 1,872; Fac 121; Highest Degree: Bachelor
Jul 2011-Jun 2012 Income $958,890. Mats Exp $400,240, Books $60,240, Per/Ser (Incl. Access Fees) $50,000, Manu Arch $300, Electronic Ref Mat (Incl. Access Fees) $235,000. Sal $558,650 (Prof $329,167)
Library Holdings: e-books 99,810; Bk Vols 265,000; Per Subs 64,000
Special Collections: Archives; Career Center Resources; Children's Literature; Faculty Teaching & Learning Coll; Little Magazines Coll; Native American Boarding School Coll; Poetry Coll; UMM Scholarship Coll; West Central Minnesota Historical Research Coll. US Document Depository
Automation Activity & Vendor Info: (Acquisitions) Ex Libris Group; (Cataloging) Ex Libris Group; (Circulation) Ex Libris Group; (Course Reserve) Ex Libris Group; (ILL) Ex Libris Group; (OPAC) Ex Libris Group; (Serials) Ex Libris Group
Database Vendor: EBSCOhost, Gale Cengage Learning, JSTOR, LexisNexis, ProQuest, Springer-Verlag, Wiley
Wireless access
Partic in Minitex Library Information Network; Northern Lights Library Network; OCLC Online Computer Library Center, Inc
Open Mon-Thurs 8am-1am, Fri 8-6, Sat 11-7, Sun Noon-1am
Friends of the Library Group

S WEST CENTRAL MINNESOTA HISTORICAL RESEARCH CENTER, University of Minnesota, 600 E Fourth St, 56267. SAN 371-6236. Tel: 320-589-6172. Web Site: www.mrs.umn.edu/academic/history/wchrc. *Dir,* Stephen Gross; E-mail: grosssj@morris.umn.edu
Founded 1960
Library Holdings: Bk Vols 457
Special Collections: Campus Archives, Local Records & Manuscripts; Univ. Oral History; State Document Depository
Subject Interests: Local hist
Wireless access

MOUNTAIN IRON

P ARROWHEAD LIBRARY SYSTEM*, 5528 Emerald Ave, 55768-2069. SAN 308-8189. Tel: 218-741-3840. Toll Free Tel: 800-257-1442. FAX: 218-748-2171. E-mail: als@arrowhead.lib.mn.us. Web Site: www.arrowhead.lib.mn.us. *Dir,* Jim Weikum; *Bus & Finance Mgr,* Shari Fisher; *Tech Librn,* Mark Koukol; *Continuing Educ Supvr,* Rebecca Patton; *Tech Serv Supvr,* Shelley Rogers; Staff 23 (MLS 5, Non-MLS 18)
Founded 1966. Pop 311,294
Jan 2006-Dec 2006 Income $2,623,448
Library Holdings: AV Mats 7,883; Bks-By-Mail 50,952; Bks on Deafness & Sign Lang 406; Bk Vols 22,204; Per Subs 33; Talking Bks 3,030
Special Collections: AIDS; Described Videos; Native Americans
Automation Activity & Vendor Info: (Circulation) SirsiDynix; (OPAC) SirsiDynix; (Serials) SirsiDynix
Database Vendor: OCLC FirstSearch, ProQuest, SirsiDynix
Member Libraries: Babbitt Public Library; Baudette Public Library; Bovey Public Library; Calumet Public Library; Carlton Public Library; Chisholm Public Library; Cloquet Public Library; Coleraine Public Library; Ely Public Library; Eveleth Public Library; Gilbert Public Library; Grand Rapids Area Library; Hoyt Lakes Public Library; Keewatin Public Library; Kinney Public Library; Marble Public Library; Mountain Iron Public Library; Silver Bay Public Library; Virginia Public Library
Open Mon-Fri 7:30-4:30
Bookmobiles: 1

P MOUNTAIN IRON PUBLIC LIBRARY*, 5742 Mountain Ave, 55768-9636. (Mail add: PO Box 477, 55768-0477), SAN 308-7085. Tel: 218-735-8625. FAX: 218-735-8252. Web Site: www.ci.mountain-iron.mn.us. *Dir,* Sally Peterangelo; *Asst Librn,* Laurie Nieters
Pop 4,134; Circ 29,300
Library Holdings: Bk Vols 30,000; Per Subs 90
Special Collections: Local History Coll
Automation Activity & Vendor Info: (Cataloging) Horizon; (Circulation) Horizon; (OPAC) Horizon
Mem of Arrowhead Library System
Open Mon-Thurs (Winter) 12-7:30, Sat 10-2; Mon-Thurs (Summer) 12-5

MOUNTAIN LAKE

P MOUNTAIN LAKE PUBLIC LIBRARY*, 1054 Fourth Ave, 56159-1455. (Mail add: PO Box 477, 56159-0477), SAN 308-7093. Tel: 507-427-2506. FAX: 507-427-2506. Web Site: www.mountainlakepubliclibrary.org. *Librn,* Carol Lehman; E-mail: clehman@plumcreeklibrary.net
Pop 2,000; Circ 35,408
Library Holdings: Bk Vols 25,000; Per Subs 95
Special Collections: Mennonite Heritage Coll
Automation Activity & Vendor Info: (Cataloging) TLC (The Library Corporation); (Circulation) TLC (The Library Corporation); (ILL) TLC (The Library Corporation); (OPAC) TLC (The Library Corporation)
Mem of Plum Creek Library System
Open Mon & Wed-Fri 10-5:30, Tues 10-8, Sat 10-1
Friends of the Library Group

NEW BRIGHTON

R UNITED THEOLOGICAL SEMINARY OF THE TWIN CITIES, The Spencer Library, 3000 Fifth St NW, 55112-2598. SAN 308-7115. Tel: 651-255-6142. Interlibrary Loan Service Tel: 651-255-6145. Administration

Tel: 651-255-6143. FAX: 651-633-4315. E-mail: library@unitedseminary.edu. Web Site: www.unitedseminary.edu/library/spencer-library. *Dir,* Susan K Ebbers; E-mail: sebbers@unitedseminary.edu; *Assoc Dir,* Dale Dobias; *ILL, Per,* Penny Truax; Staff 3 (MLS 2, Non-MLS 1)
Founded 1962. Enrl 191; Fac 13; Highest Degree: Doctorate
Library Holdings: Bk Titles 85,106; Per Subs 189
Subject Interests: Liberation theol, Native Am, Reformed tradition, Sexuality, Theol, Women's studies in relig
Automation Activity & Vendor Info: (Acquisitions) OCLC; (Cataloging) OCLC; (Circulation) OCLC; (Course Reserve) OCLC; (ILL) OCLC WorldShare Interlibrary Loan; (OPAC) OCLC; (Serials) OCLC
Database Vendor: OCLC FirstSearch, OCLC WorldShare Interlibrary Loan, OCLC Worldshare Management Services, WT Cox, YBP Library Services
Wireless access
Partic in Minnesota Theological Library Association
Open Mon, Wed & Fri 8-5, Tues & Thurs 8am-9pm, Sat 10-2

NEW LONDON

P NEW LONDON PUBLIC LIBRARY*, 15 Ash St, 56273-9567. (Mail add: PO Box 156, 56273-0156), SAN 348-1298. Tel: 320-354-2943. *Head Librn,* Sheila Bosch
Pop 1,000; Circ 12,253
Library Holdings: Bk Vols 10,500; Per Subs 20
Automation Activity & Vendor Info: (Cataloging) Innovative Interfaces, Inc; (Circulation) Innovative Interfaces, Inc; (OPAC) Innovative Interfaces, Inc
Mem of Pioneerland Library System
Open Mon 12-5, Tues & Fri 1-5, Wed 10-2, Sat 9-12

NEW ULM

S BROWN COUNTY HISTORICAL SOCIETY*, Research Library, Two N Broadway, 56073. SAN 370-5250. Tel: 507-233-2616, 507-233-2619. FAX: 507-354-1068. E-mail: researchlibrary@browncountyhistorymnusa.org. Web Site: www.browncountyhistorymnusa.org. *Res,* Darla Gebhard
Founded 1930
Library Holdings: Bk Titles 1,000
Special Collections: Dakota War Coll; New Ulm POW Camp Coll; New Ulm Turnverein Coll; Wanda Gag Coll
Publications: News Notes (Quarterly)
Open Mon-Fri (May-Oct) 9-12 & 1-4, Sat 10-3; Tues-Fri (Nov-April) 9-12 & 1-4, Sat 10-3
Restriction: Non-circulating to the pub

C MARTIN LUTHER COLLEGE LIBRARY, 1995 Luther Ct, 56073-3965. SAN 308-7123. Tel: 507-354-8221, Ext 242. FAX: 507-233-9107. *Dir,* Linda M Kramer; Tel: 507-354-8221, Ext 296, E-mail: kramerlm@mlc-wels.edu; *Ser/Digital Librn,* Jan Nass; Tel: 507-354-8221, Ext 327; *Cat,* Grace Bases; Tel: 507-354-8221, Ext 364, E-mail: basesgm@mlc-wels.edu; *Ref,* Katherine Lotito; Tel: 507-354-8221, Ext 249 or 209, E-mail: lotitokm@mlc-wels.edu; Staff 4.5 (MLS 1, Non-MLS 3.5)
Founded 1995. Enrl 707; Fac 64; Highest Degree: Master
Jul 2010-Jun 2011 Income $260,843. Mats Exp $267,211, Books $33,157, Per/Ser (Incl. Access Fees) $38,683, AV Mat $5,321, Electronic Ref Mat (Incl. Access Fees) $23,884. Sal $166,199 (Prof $60,269)
Library Holdings: AV Mats 9,113; CDs 1,621; DVDs 757; e-books 16,418; e-journals 25,515; Electronic Media & Resources 419; Music Scores 4,363; Bk Titles 139,865; Bk Vols 164,495; Per Subs 309; Videos 3,603
Special Collections: American Civilization Coll, micro, bks
Subject Interests: Educ, Music, Relig studies
Automation Activity & Vendor Info: (Cataloging) OCLC WorldShare Interlibrary Loan; (Circulation) SirsiDynix; (OPAC) SIRSI-iBistro
Database Vendor: EBSCOhost, Gale Cengage Learning, Grolier Online, McGraw-Hill, OCLC ArticleFirst, OCLC FirstSearch, OCLC WorldShare Interlibrary Loan, OVID Technologies, Oxford Online, Project MUSE, ProQuest, SerialsSolutions, SirsiDynix
Wireless access
Function: Archival coll, Art exhibits, Audio & video playback equip for onsite use, Bks on cassette, Bks on CD, Computers for patron use, Copy machines, Electronic databases & coll, ILL available, Music CDs, Online cat, VHS videos
Partic in OCLC Online Computer Library Center, Inc
Open Mon-Thurs 7:30am-Midnight, Fri 7:30-5, Sat 11-5, Sun 2pm-Midnight
Restriction: Authorized patrons

P NEW ULM PUBLIC LIBRARY*, 17 N Broadway, 56073-1786. SAN 308-7131. Tel: 507-359-8331. Reference Tel: 507-359-8335. Administration Tel: 507-359-8332. FAX: 507-354-3255. Web Site: www.newulmlibrary.org. *Libr Dir, Webmaster,* Larry B Hlavsa; E-mail: lhlavs@tds.lib.mn.us; *Cat,* Betty Roiger; Tel: 507-359-8330, E-mail: broiger@tds.lib.mn.us; *Ch Serv,* Diane Zellmann; Tel: 507-359-8336, E-mail: dzellm@tds.lib.mn.us; *Programming Serv,* Lori Roholt; *Ref,* Linda Lindquist; E-mail: llindq@tds.lib.mn.us; Staff 12 (MLS 3, Non-MLS 9)
Founded 1937. Pop 13,610; Circ 182,272
Library Holdings: Audiobooks 4,095; Bk Vols 80,750; Per Subs 173; Videos 3,090
Special Collections: German-American Heritage Coll; New Ulm Journal Coll, 1940-present
Automation Activity & Vendor Info: (Cataloging) SirsiDynix; (Circulation) SirsiDynix; (OPAC) SirsiDynix
Wireless access
Function: Adult bk club, Bks on cassette, Bks on CD, Children's prog, Computers for patron use, Copy machines, Electronic databases & coll, Fax serv, Free DVD rentals, ILL available, Online cat, Photocopying/Printing, Prog for adults, Prog for children & young adult, Pub access computers, Ref & res, Ref serv available, Spoken cassettes & CDs, Spoken cassettes & DVDs, Story hour, Summer reading prog, Tax forms, Teen prog, Telephone ref, VHS videos, Wheelchair accessible, Workshops
Mem of Traverse Des Sioux Library Cooperative
Open Mon-Thurs (Winter) 9:30-9, Fri & Sat 9:30-5; Mon-Thurs (Summer) 9:30-8, Fri & Sat 9:30-5
Friends of the Library Group

NEW YORK MILLS

P NEW YORK MILLS PUBLIC LIBRARY*, 30 N Main Ave, 56567-4318. (Mail add: PO Box 279, 56567-0279), SAN 376-7175. Tel: 218-385-2436. FAX: 218-385-2508. *Librn,* Julie Adams
Library Holdings: Bk Vols 15,000; Per Subs 75
Automation Activity & Vendor Info: (Cataloging) SirsiDynix; (Circulation) SirsiDynix; (OPAC) SirsiDynix
Wireless access
Open Mon & Tues 10-6, Wed & Thurs 10-7, Fri 10-5, Sat 10-2
Friends of the Library Group

NORTH BRANCH

P NORTH BRANCH AREA LIBRARY*, 6355 379th St, 55056. SAN 321-9240. Tel: 651-674-8443. FAX: 651-674-8443. E-mail: nbmail@ecrlib.org. *Librn,* Susan Monroe; E-mail: smonroe@ecrlib.org; Staff 3 (Non-MLS 3)
Pop 10,427; Circ 58,030
Library Holdings: Bk Vols 20,000; Per Subs 45
Mem of East Central Regional Library
Open Mon, Wed & Fri 10-6, Tues & Thurs 12-8, Sat 10-2
Friends of the Library Group

NORTH MANKATO

P NORTH MANKATO TAYLOR LIBRARY*, 1001 Belgrade Ave, 56003. SAN 347-4399. Tel: 507-345-5120. FAX: 507-345-1861. Web Site: www.northmankato.com/library. *Dir,* Lucy Lowry; E-mail: llowry@nmlibrary.org; *Asst Dir,* Angela Kelly; E-mail: akelly@nmlibrary.org; *Asst Librn,* Kara Hanselman; *Ch Serv,* Michelle Zimmerman; E-mail: mzimmermann@nmlibrary.org; Staff 4 (MLS 1, Non-MLS 3)
Founded 1907
Library Holdings: Bk Vols 25,965; Per Subs 128
Mem of Traverse Des Sioux Library Cooperative
Open Mon-Thurs 10-8, Fri 10-6, Sat 10-4, Sun 12-4
Friends of the Library Group

J SOUTH CENTRAL COLLEGE*, North Mankato Campus Library, 1920 Lee Blvd, 56003-2504. SAN 374-7263. Tel: 507-389-7223, 507-389-7245. Interlibrary Loan Service Tel: 507-389-7251. FAX: 507-625-7534. E-mail: library@southcentral.edu. Web Site: southcentral.edu/library. *Dir of Libr Serv,* Johnna Horton; E-mail: johnna.horton@southcentral.edu; Staff 2 (MLS 1, Non-MLS 1)
Founded 1946. Highest Degree: Associate
Library Holdings: CDs 200; DVDs 100; e-books 9,000; Large Print Bks 15; Bk Vols 32,000; Per Subs 165
Automation Activity & Vendor Info: (Cataloging) Ex Libris Group; (Circulation) Ex Libris Group; (Course Reserve) Ex Libris Group; (ILL) Ex Libris Group; (Media Booking) Ex Libris Group; (OPAC) Ex Libris Group
Database Vendor: Baker & Taylor, EBSCOhost, Gale Cengage Learning, OCLC WorldShare Interlibrary Loan, ProQuest
Wireless access
Partic in Minitex Library Information Network; MnPALS
Open Mon-Thurs 7:30am-8pm, Fri 7:30-3:30

NORTH SAINT PAUL

S NORTH SAINT PAUL HISTORICAL SOCIETY*, Museum Library, 2666 E Seventh Ave, 55109. SAN 373-2282. Tel: 651-779-6402. *Curator,* Paul J Anderson; Tel: 651-777-8965, E-mail: anderson8965@msn.com
Founded 1976
Library Holdings: Bk Vols 1,000; Videos 20
Special Collections: Henry A Castle Coll; Local Authors, bks, vf. Oral History
Subject Interests: Hist of N St Paul
Open Fri 1-4, Sat 10-1
Friends of the Library Group

NORTHFIELD

C CARLETON COLLEGE*, Laurence McKinley Gould Library, One N College St, 55057-4097. SAN 347-7452. Tel: 507-222-4260. Interlibrary Loan Service Tel: 507-222-4257. Reference Tel: 507-222-4264. Administration Tel: 507-222-4261. FAX: 507-222-4087. Web Site: apps.carleton.edu/campus/library. *Librn,* Samuel Demas; Tel: 507-222-4267, E-mail: sdemas@carleton.edu; *Instrul Serv Librn, Res,* Carolyn Sanford; Tel: 507-222-4266, E-mail: csanford@carleton.edu; *Archivist,* Eric Hillemann; Tel: 507-222-4270, E-mail: ehillema@carleton.edu; *Coll Develop,* Kathy Tezla; Tel: 507-222-5447, E-mail: ktezla@carleton.edu; *Tech Serv,* Carol Eyler; Tel: 507-222-4268, E-mail: ceyler@carleton.edu; Staff 30 (MLS 13, Non-MLS 17)
Founded 1867. Enrl 1,948; Fac 195; Highest Degree: Bachelor
Jul 2007-Jun 2008 Income $4,973,344. Mats Exp $1,634,625, Books $440,871, Per/Ser (Incl. Access Fees) $790,202, Electronic Ref Mat (Incl. Access Fees) $373,896, Presv $29,656. Sal $1,204,509 (Prof $787,880)
Library Holdings: AV Mats 10,422; Bks on Deafness & Sign Lang 428; CDs 2,087; DVDs 4,646; e-books 338,679; e-journals 33,214; Electronic Media & Resources 49,949; Microforms 220,278; Bk Titles 641,350; Bk Vols 841,418; Per Subs 1,049; Videos 4,874
Special Collections: Lucas Jazz Records; Photos of Famous Authors by Famous Photographers; Thorsten Veblen's Library; Warming Orchid Books; Western Americana (Donald Beaty Bloch Coll). US Document Depository
Subject Interests: Geol, Liberal arts
Automation Activity & Vendor Info: (Acquisitions) Innovative Interfaces, Inc; (Cataloging) Innovative Interfaces, Inc; (Circulation) Innovative Interfaces, Inc; (Course Reserve) Docutek; (ILL) OCLC ILLiad; (OPAC) Innovative Interfaces, Inc; (Serials) Innovative Interfaces, Inc
Database Vendor: ABC-CLIO, Agricola, Alexander Street Press, American Chemical Society, American Mathematical Society, American Physical Society, American Psychological Association (APA), Annual Reviews, ARTstor, Atlas Systems, Baker & Taylor, BioOne, Bowker, Cambridge Scientific Abstracts, CountryWatch, CQ Press, EBSCOhost, Elsevier, Ex Libris Group, Gale Cengage Learning, Greenwood Publishing Group, H W Wilson, Haworth Pres Inc, IEEE (Institute of Electrical & Electronics Engineers), Ingenta, Innovative Interfaces, Inc, ISI Web of Knowledge, JSTOR, LexisNexis, Marcive, Inc, Medline, Modern Language Association, Nature Publishing Group, Newsbank, OCLC FirstSearch, OCLC WorldShare Interlibrary Loan, OVID Technologies, Oxford Online, Project MUSE, ProQuest, PubMed, RefWorks, Sage, ScienceDirect, Springer-Verlag, Standard & Poor's, Thomson - Web of Science, Wiley, Wilson - Wilson Web
Wireless access
Function: Copy machines, Doc delivery serv, E-Reserves, Electronic databases & coll, ILL available, Online ref, Online searches, VHS videos
Partic in OCLC Online Computer Library Center, Inc
Open Mon-Fri 8am-1am, Sat 9am-Midnight, Sun 9am-1am
Friends of the Library Group

P NORTHFIELD PUBLIC LIBRARY*, 210 Washington St, 55057. SAN 308-7158. Tel: 507-645-6606. FAX: 507-645-1820. TDD: 507-645-1823. Web Site: www.ci.northfield.mn.us/library. *Dir,* Teresa Jensen; Tel: 507-645-1801, E-mail: Teresa.Jensen@ci.northfield.mn.us; *Ref Librn,* Joan Ennis; Tel: 507-645-1802, E-mail: joan.ennis@ci.northfield.mn.us; *Ref Librn,* Jamie Stanley; E-mail: jamie.stanley@ci.northfield.mn.us; *Ref Librn II,* Debby Nitz; E-mail: debby.nitz@ci.northfield.mn.us; *Children's Prog Librn,* Kathy Ness; E-mail: kathy.ness@ci.northfield.mn.us; *Ref & Youth Serv Mgr,* Leesa Wisdorf; Tel: 507 645 1804, E mail: leesa.wisdorf@ci.northfield.mn.us; *Circ & Tech Serv Coordr,* Katherine Rush; Tel: 507-645-1800, E-mail: kathy.rush@ci.northfield.mn.us; Staff 5 (MLS 3, Non-MLS 2)
Founded 1857. Pop 26,674; Circ 355,666
Jan 2013-Dec 2013 Income $2,321,864, City $977,059, County $183,873, Locally Generated Income $1,160,932. Mats Exp $106,604. Sal $608,233
Library Holdings: AV Mats 56,894; e-books 25,092; Electronic Media & Resources 63; Bk Vols 61,005; Per Subs 224
Special Collections: Local History Coll
Automation Activity & Vendor Info: (Acquisitions) SirsiDynix; (Cataloging) SirsiDynix; (Circulation) SirsiDynix; (OPAC) SirsiDynix; (Serials) SirsiDynix
Wireless access
Function: Adult bk club, Audio & video playback equip for onsite use, Audiobks via web, Bilingual assistance for Spanish patrons, Bk club(s), Bks on cassette, Bks on CD, Computers for patron use, Copy machines, Distance learning, E-Reserves, Electronic databases & coll, Equip loans & repairs, Family literacy, Free DVD rentals, Handicapped accessible, Home delivery & serv to Sr ctr & nursing homes, Homebound delivery serv, ILL available, Magnifiers for reading, Mail & tel request accepted, Music CDs, Newsp ref libr, Notary serv, Online cat, Online ref, Orientations, Outside serv via phone, mail, e-mail & web, Photocopying/Printing, Prog for adults, Prog for children & young adult, Pub access computers, Scanner, Story hour, Summer reading prog, Tax forms, Teen prog, Telephone ref, VHS videos, Web-catalog
Partic in Southeastern Libraries Cooperating
Special Services for the Deaf - TDD equip
Open Mon-Thurs 9:30-8, Fri 9:30-5:30, Sat 9:30-5, Sun 1-5
Friends of the Library Group
Bookmobiles: 1

S NORWEGIAN-AMERICAN HISTORICAL ASSOCIATION ARCHIVES*, 1510 St Olaf Ave, 55057. SAN 327-1692. Tel: 507-786-3221. FAX: 507-786-3734. E-mail: naha@stolaf.edu. Web Site: www.naha.stolaf.edu. *Admin Dir,* Jackie Henry; *Archivist,* Gary De Krey
Founded 1925
Library Holdings: Bk Vols 8,000
Function: Res libr
Restriction: Open by appt only

SAINT OLAF COLLEGE

C HOWARD V & EDNA H HONG KIERKEGAARD LIBRARY*, 1510 Saint Olaf Ave, 55057-1097, SAN 374-7077. Tel: 507-646-3846. FAX: 507-646-3858. Web Site: www.stolaf.edu/collections/kierkegaard. *Spec Coll Librn,* Cynthia Wales Lund; E-mail: lundc@stolaf.edu; *Curator,* Gordon Marino; Tel: 507-646-3609, E-mail: marino@stolaf.edu; Staff 2 (MLS 1, Non-MLS 1)
Founded 1976
Library Holdings: Bk Vols 11,000
Automation Activity & Vendor Info: (Cataloging) Innovative Interfaces, Inc; (OPAC) Innovative Interfaces, Inc; (Serials) Innovative Interfaces, Inc
Partic in OCLC Online Computer Library Center, Inc
Publications: Soren Kierkegaard Society Newsletter
Open Mon-Fri 9-5
Restriction: Not a lending libr
Friends of the Library Group

C ROLVAAG MEMORIAL LIBRARY, HUSTAD SCIENCE LIBRARY, HALVORSON MUSIC LIBRARY, 1510 Saint Olaf Ave, 55057-1097, SAN 347-7517. Tel: 507-786-3634. Circulation Tel: 507-786-3224. Interlibrary Loan Service Tel: 507-786-3223. Reference Tel: 507-786-3452. FAX: 507-786-3734. Web Site: www.stolaf.edu/library. *Dir, Libr & Info Serv,* Roberta Lembke; Tel: 507-786-3097, E-mail: lembke@stolaf.edu; *Head, Coll Develop,* Mary Barbosa-Jerez; *Head, Res & Instruction,* Kasia Gonnerman; Tel: 507-786-3501, E-mail: gonnermk@stolaf.edu; *Cat Librn, Music,* Kathy Blough; Tel: 507-786-3794, E-mail: blough@stolaf.edu; *Music Librn,* Beth Christensen; Tel: 507-786-3362, E-mail: christeb@stolaf.edu; *Ref & Instrul Serv Librn,* Ken Johnson; Tel: 507-786-3793, E-mail: johnsonk@stolaf.edu; *Sci Librn,* Charles Priore; Tel: 507-786-3099, E-mail: priore@stolaf.edu; *Syst & Web Develop Librn,* Sarah Johnston; Tel: 507-786-3771, E-mail: johnsts@stolaf.edu; Staff 22.5 (MLS 13.5, Non-MLS 9)
Founded 1874. Enrl 3,096; Fac 278; Highest Degree: Bachelor
Special Collections: Norwegian-American Historical Association Coll, bks & per; Pre-1801 Imprints (Vault Coll), bks & per. US Document Depository
Subject Interests: Relig studies, Scandinavian hist, Scandinavian lit
Automation Activity & Vendor Info: (Acquisitions) Innovative Interfaces, Inc; (Cataloging) Innovative Interfaces, Inc; (Circulation) Innovative Interfaces, Inc; (Course Reserve) Innovative Interfaces, Inc; (ILL) OCLC ILLiad; (OPAC) Innovative Interfaces, Inc; (Serials) Innovative Interfaces, Inc
Database Vendor: ABC-CLIO, ACM (Association for Computing Machinery), Alexander Street Press, American Chemical Society, American Mathematical Society, American Psychological Association (APA), Annual Reviews, ARTstor, BioOne, Blackwell, Cambridge Scientific Abstracts, Children's Literature Comprehensive Database Company (CLCD), Cinahl, College Source, CQ Press, Dialog, EBSCO Information Services, EBSCOhost, Elsevier, Ex Libris Group, Facts on File, Gale Cengage Learning, Greenwood Publishing Group, Grolier Online, H W Wilson, Haworth Pres Inc, IEEE (Institute of Electrical & Electronics Engineers), Innovative Interfaces, Inc, ISI Web of Knowledge, JSTOR, LexisNexis, Modern Language Association, Newsbank, OCLC FirstSearch, OCLC WorldShare Interlibrary Loan, OVID Technologies, Oxford Online, ProQuest, Wilson - Wilson Web, YBP Library Services
Open Mon-Thurs 8am-2am, Fri 8am-9pm, Sat 9-9, Sun Noon-2am

OLIVIA

P OLIVIA PUBLIC LIBRARY*, 405 S Tenth St, 56277-1287. SAN 308-7166. Tel: 320-523-1738. E-mail: olivia.staff@pioneerland.lib.mn.us. Web Site: www.olivia.mn.us/library. *Head Librn,* Allison Girres; E-mail: allison.girres@pioneerland.lib.mn.us; Staff 5 (MLS 1, Non-MLS 4)
Founded 1916
Library Holdings: Bk Vols 27,198; Per Subs 25
Special Collections: Local Newspaper Depository
Automation Activity & Vendor Info: (Acquisitions) Innovative Interfaces, Inc - Millenium; (Circulation) Innovative Interfaces, Inc - Millenium; (OPAC) Innovative Interfaces, Inc - Millenium
Wireless access
Mem of Pioneerland Library System
Open Mon-Thurs 12-8, Fri 10-5, Sat 12-3

ORTONVILLE

P ORTONVILLE PUBLIC LIBRARY*, 412 Second St NW, 56278-1415. SAN 308-7182. Tel: 320-839-2494. FAX: 320-839-3784. E-mail: ortonville.staff@pioneerland.lib.mn.us. Web Site: www.bsclibraries.com. *Br Mgr,* Vicki Grimli; E-mail: vicki.grimli@pioneerland.lib.mn.us; Staff 2 (Non-MLS 2)
Founded 1915. Pop 4,126; Circ 41,336
Jan 2010-Dec 2010 Income $126,420, City $78,716, County $40,986, Locally Generated Income $6,718. Mats Exp $21,270, Books $16,227, Per/Ser (Incl. Access Fees) $1,316, AV Mat $3,727. Sal $55,016
Library Holdings: Audiobooks 422; DVDs 1,856; Bk Titles 20,011; Per Subs 65; Videos 175
Automation Activity & Vendor Info: (Acquisitions) Innovative Interfaces, Inc; (Cataloging) Innovative Interfaces, Inc; (Circulation) Innovative Interfaces, Inc; (ILL) Innovative Interfaces, Inc; (OPAC) Innovative Interfaces, Inc
Database Vendor: Baker & Taylor, Electric Library, OCLC FirstSearch, OCLC WebJunction, ProQuest
Wireless access
Function: Orientations, Photocopying/Printing, Prog for adults, Prog for children & young adult, Pub access computers, Scanner, Senior computer classes, Spoken cassettes & CDs, Story hour, Summer & winter reading prog, Summer reading prog, Tax forms, Teen prog, VHS videos, Wheelchair accessible
Mem of Pioneerland Library System
Open Mon-Thurs 11-7, Fri 12-5, Sat 10-3
Friends of the Library Group

OWATONNA

P OWATONNA PUBLIC LIBRARY, 105 N Elm Ave, 55060-2405. (Mail add: PO Box 387, 55060-0387), SAN 347-7606. Tel: 507-444-2460. FAX: 507-444-2465. E-mail: info@owatonna.info. Web Site: www.owatonna.info. *Dir,* Mary Kay Feltes; E-mail: marykay@owatonna.info; *Asst Dir,* Renee Lowery; E-mail: renee@owatonna.info; *Adult Serv, Ref,* Bonnie Krueger; E-mail: bonnie@owatonna.info; *AV, Per,* Mary Gontarek; E-mail: maryg@owatonna.info; *Ch Serv,* Darla Lager; E-mail: darla@owatonna.info; Staff 6 (MLS 5, Non-MLS 1)
Founded 1900. Pop 25,373; Circ 340,000
Library Holdings: Bk Vols 169,000
Special Collections: Genealogy Coll
Automation Activity & Vendor Info: (Cataloging) SirsiDynix; (Circulation) SirsiDynix; (ILL) SirsiDynix; (OPAC) SirsiDynix; (Serials) SirsiDynix
Database Vendor: EBSCOhost, Gale Cengage Learning, Westlaw
Wireless access
Partic in Southeastern Libraries Cooperating
Open Mon-Thurs 9-9, Fri & Sat 9-5, Sun (Oct-April) 1-5
Branches: 1
BLOOMING PRAIRIE BRANCH, 138 Highway Ave S, Blooming Prairie, 55917. (Mail add: PO Box 187, Blooming Prairie, 55917), SAN 347-7630. Tel: 507-583-7750. FAX: 507-583-4520. E-mail: bpbl@selco.info. *Br Mgr,* Nancy Vaillancourt; Staff 3 (Non-MLS 3)
Founded 1976. Pop 2,043; Circ 30,459
Library Holdings: Bk Vols 24,411
Open Mon-Wed 10-6, Thurs 10-8, Fri 10-5, Sat 10-1
Friends of the Library Group

PARK RAPIDS

P PARK RAPIDS AREA LIBRARY*, 210 W First St, 56470-8925. SAN 308-7190. Tel: 218-732-4966. FAX: 218-732-4966. E-mail: parkrapids@krls.org. Web Site: www.krls.org. *Librn,* Terry Zoller; *Ch Serv,* Becky Walpole; *YA Serv,* Karen Zwirtz
Founded 1903. Circ 105,815
Library Holdings: Bk Vols 25,000; Per Subs 90
Automation Activity & Vendor Info: (Cataloging) Innovative Interfaces, Inc; (Circulation) Innovative Interfaces, Inc; (OPAC) Innovative Interfaces, Inc
Database Vendor: Gale Cengage Learning, OCLC FirstSearch, ProQuest, TLC (The Library Corporation)
Mem of Kitchigami Regional Library
Open Mon, Tues, Thurs & Fri 10:30-5, Wed 10:30-8, Sat 10:30-3
Friends of the Library Group
Bookmobiles: 1

PELICAN RAPIDS

P PELICAN RAPIDS PUBLIC LIBRARY*, Multicultural Learning Center, 25 W Mill Ave, 56572. (Mail add: PO Box 371, 56572-0371), SAN 376-7183. Tel: 218-863-7055. FAX: 218-863-7056. Web Site: www.pelicanrapidslibrary.org. *Dir,* Annie M Wrigg; E-mail: awrigg@pelicanrapids.lib.mn.us; Staff 1 (MLS 1)
Library Holdings: Bk Vols 30,000; Per Subs 115
Automation Activity & Vendor Info: (Cataloging) Horizon; (Circulation) Horizon; (ILL) Horizon; (OPAC) Horizon
Wireless access
Mem of Viking Library System
Open Mon, Wed & Fri 10-6, Tues & Thurs 10-8, Sat 10-2
Friends of the Library Group

PERHAM

P PERHAM AREA PUBLIC LIBRARY*, 225 Second Ave NE, 56573-1819. SAN 308-7212. Tel: 218-346-4892. FAX: 218-346-4906. Web Site: www.perham.lib.mn.us. *Librn,* Susan Ann Heusser-Ladwig; E-mail: sheusser-ladwig@perham.lib.mn.us; Staff 2.875 (MLS 1, Non-MLS 1.875)
Founded 1922. Pop 5,879; Circ 64,409
Library Holdings: Audiobooks 1,447; AV Mats 4,041; Bk Vols 31,924; Per Subs 82
Automation Activity & Vendor Info: (Acquisitions) Horizon; (Cataloging) Horizon; (Circulation) Horizon; (OPAC) Horizon
Database Vendor: EBSCOhost, Gale Cengage Learning, OCLC FirstSearch, ProQuest
Wireless access
Function: Fax serv, Handicapped accessible, ILL available, Music CDs, Online cat, OverDrive digital audio bks, Photocopying/Printing, Ref serv available, Spoken cassettes & CDs, Story hour, Summer & winter reading prog, Tax forms
Mem of Viking Library System
Open Mon & Wed 10-8, Tues, Thurs & Fri 10-5, Sat 10-3
Friends of the Library Group

PINE CITY

P PINE CITY PUBLIC LIBRARY*, 300 Fifth St SE, 55063-1799. SAN 347-2566. Tel: 320-629-6403. FAX: 320-629-6403. E-mail: pcmail@ecrl.org. *Br Mgr,* Andrea Hermanson; E-mail: ahermanson@ecrlib.org
Founded 1921. Pop 8,858; Circ 51,225
Library Holdings: Bk Vols 11,000; Per Subs 50
Automation Activity & Vendor Info: (Cataloging) Evergreen; (Circulation) Evergreen; (OPAC) Evergreen
Wireless access
Mem of East Central Regional Library
Open Tues-Thurs 10-7, Fri 10-6, Sat 9-2
Friends of the Library Group

PINE ISLAND

P VAN HORN PUBLIC LIBRARY*, Pine Island Public Library, 115 SE Third St, 55963-6783. (Mail add: PO Box 38, 55963-0038), SAN 308-7239. Tel: 507-356-8558. FAX: 507-356-8599. E-mail: pipl@selco.info. Web Site: pineisland.lib.mn.us. *Dir,* Morgan Hansen; E-mail: mkhansen@selco.info; Staff 1 (MLS 1)
Pop 2,926; Circ 60,738
Library Holdings: Bk Vols 27,500; Per Subs 75
Special Collections: Oral History
Automation Activity & Vendor Info: (Cataloging) Horizon; (Circulation) Horizon; (OPAC) Horizon; (Serials) Horizon
Wireless access
Partic in Southeastern Libraries Cooperating
Open Mon & Fri 1-5, Tues & Thurs 11-7, Wed 9-5, Sat 9-12

PINE RIVER

P KITCHIGAMI REGIONAL LIBRARY*, 310 Second St N, 56474. (Mail add: PO Box 84, 56474-0084), SAN 347-7665. Tel: 218-587-2171. FAX: 218-587-4855. Web Site: www.krls.org. *Regional Dir,* Marian Ridge; E-mail: ridgem@krls.org; *Automation Librn, Dir, Tech Serv,* Alison Edgerton; E-mail: alison@krls.org
Founded 1969. Pop 150,000; Circ 825,000
Library Holdings: AV Mats 12,730; Large Print Bks 10,699; Bk Titles 146,949; Bk Vols 300,364; Per Subs 525; Talking Bks 7,307
Subject Interests: Am Indian-Chippewa (Ojibway)

Wireless access
Member Libraries: Bemidji Public Library; Blackduck Community Library; Brainerd Public Library; Cass Lake Community Library; Margaret Welch Memorial Library; Park Rapids Area Library; Pine River Public Library; Wadena City Library; Walker Public Library
Partic in Northern Lights Library Network; OCLC Online Computer Library Center, Inc
Special Services for the Deaf - Bks on deafness & sign lang; High interest/low vocabulary bks
Open Mon-Fri 8-5

P PINE RIVER PUBLIC LIBRARY, 212 Park Ave, 56474. (Mail add: PO Box 14, 56474-0014), SAN 347-7800. Tel: 218-587-4639. FAX: 218-587-3107. E-mail: pineriver@krls.org. Web Site: www.krls.org. *Br Mgr,* Muriel Erickson; E-mail: ericksonm@krls.org
Founded 1965
Library Holdings: Audiobooks 948; CDs 216; DVDs 559; Large Print Bks 1,453; Bk Vols 15,233; Per Subs 35; Videos 348
Automation Activity & Vendor Info: (Acquisitions) Innovative Interfaces, Inc; (Cataloging) Innovative Interfaces, Inc; (Circulation) Innovative Interfaces, Inc; (Course Reserve) Innovative Interfaces, Inc; (OPAC) Innovative Interfaces, Inc; (Serials) Innovative Interfaces, Inc
Database Vendor: Baker & Taylor
Wireless access
Mem of Kitchigami Regional Library
Open Mon 1-5, Tues & Thurs 10-5, Wed 12-7, Fri 10-3, Sat 10-1
Friends of the Library Group

PIPESTONE

P MEINDERS COMMUNITY LIBRARY*, 1401 Seventh St SW, 56164. SAN 376-7132. Tel: 507-825-6714. FAX: 507-562-7374. E-mail: pipestonelibrary@yahoo.com. Web Site: www.plumcreeklibrary.org/pipestone. *Libr Dir,* Stephanie Hall; E-mail: stephanie.hall@pas.K12.mn.us; Staff 6 (MLS 1, Non-MLS 5)
Founded 1904. Pop 5,000; Circ 46,720
Library Holdings: Bk Vols 27,000; Per Subs 110
Automation Activity & Vendor Info: (Cataloging) TLC (The Library Corporation); (Circulation) TLC (The Library Corporation); (OPAC) TLC (The Library Corporation)
Database Vendor: Gale Cengage Learning
Wireless access
Function: ILL available, Magnifiers for reading, Photocopying/Printing, Prog for children & young adult, Spoken cassettes & DVDs, Summer reading prog, Telephone ref, VHS videos, Wheelchair accessible
Mem of Plum Creek Library System
Open Mon-Thurs 10-8, Fri & Sat 10-5
Friends of the Library Group

S PIPESTONE COUNTY HISTORICAL SOCIETY*, Pipestone County Museum Research Library, 113 S Hiawatha, 56164. SAN 328-1175. Tel: 507-825-2563. Toll Free Tel: 866-747-3687. FAX: 507-825-2563. Toll Free FAX: 866-747-3687. E-mail: pipctymu@iw.net. Web Site: www.pipestoneminnesota.com/museum. *Exec Dir,* Susan Hoskins
Library Holdings: Bk Titles 500
Special Collections: County Newspapers Coll (1879-present); Doctors' Records Coll; Indian School Coll; Photo Coll. Oral History
Subject Interests: Genealogy, Local hist
Open Mon-Sat (Winter) 10-5; Mon-Sun (Summer) 10-5
Restriction: Non-circulating, Ref only

PLAINVIEW

P PLAINVIEW PUBLIC LIBRARY*, 345 First Ave NW, 55964-1295. SAN 308-7247. Tel: 507-534-3425. Web Site: www.selco.info/plainview. *Librn,* Kathie Sagissor
Founded 1865. Pop 7,438; Circ 73,139
Library Holdings: DVDs 600; Bk Titles 28,000; Per Subs 15
Automation Activity & Vendor Info: (Cataloging) Horizon; (Circulation) Horizon; (OPAC) Horizon
Partic in Southeastern Libraries Cooperating
Open Mon & Wed 9-8, Tues & Thurs 9-6, Fri 9-5, Sat 9-2

PLATO

S FAR EASTERN RESEARCH LIBRARY, Nine First Ave NE, 55370. (Mail add: PO Box 181, 55370-0181), SAN 324-0304. Tel: 320-238-2591, 612-926-6887. E-mail: laogan@fareasternlibrary.org. Web Site: www.fareasternlibrary.org. *Dir,* Dr Jerome Cavanaugh; *Acq of Monographs, Acq of New Ser/Per, Cat,* Jiaqing Liao; *Acq of Monographs & Journals, Acq of New Ser/Per,* Mingzhi Lin. Subject Specialists: *Chinese lang mat, Japanese lang mat, SE Asian lang mat,* Dr Jerome Cavanaugh; *Chinese art, Chinese modern hist,* Jiaqing Liao; *Japanese lang mat, Korean (Lang),* Mingzhi Lin; Staff 4 (MLS 3, Non-MLS 1)
Founded 1969
Library Holdings: AV Mats 75; CDs 120; DVDs 150; Bk Titles 49,326; Bk Vols 54,478; Per Subs 220; Videos 65
Special Collections: Chinese & Tibetan Linguistics (Feng Coll); Chinese Cultural Revolution Coll, doc, monographs, newsp; Chinese Dialect Materials Coll, bks, journals, ms; Chinese Internal Distribution Publications; Chinese Local History Studies, monographs, ser; Chinese Proverbs, Slang & Colloquialisms Coll; Song Yuan & Ming Drama (Chinese Pre-Modern Drama Coll); Studies on the City of Tianjin Coll
Subject Interests: Africa, Cent Am, Japan, Korea, Latin Am, Middle East, Mongolia, Russia, S Asia, SE Asia, Soviet studies, Tibet
Function: Ref serv available, Res libr
Publications: Far Eastern Research Library Bibliographical Aids Series (Bibliographies)

PRESTON

P PRESTON PUBLIC LIBRARY*, 101 St Paul St NW, 55965. (Mail add: PO Box 439, 55965-0439), SAN 308-7271. Tel: 507-765-4511. Web Site: preston.lib.mn.us. *Libr Dir,* Elizabeth Anderson; E-mail: bethand@selco.info
Founded 1908. Pop 3,165; Circ 31,000
Library Holdings: Audiobooks 1,900; AV Mats 4,000; Bk Vols 30,300; Per Subs 58
Automation Activity & Vendor Info: (Cataloging) SirsiDynix; (Circulation) SirsiDynix; (OPAC) SirsiDynix
Database Vendor: EBSCO Information Services, Grolier Online, ProQuest
Wireless access
Function: Art exhibits, Audiobks via web, Bks on cassette, Bks on CD, Children's prog, Computers for patron use, Copy machines, Free DVD rentals, Handicapped accessible, ILL available, Music CDs, Online cat, Online ref, Online searches, OverDrive digital audio bks, Photocopying/Printing, Prog for adults, Prog for children & young adult, Pub access computers, Scanner, Spoken cassettes & CDs, Story hour, Summer & winter reading prog, Tax forms, Teen prog, VHS videos, Wheelchair accessible
Open Mon & Fri 10-5, Tues & Thurs 2-8, Wed 10-8, Sat 10-2
Friends of the Library Group

PRINCETON

P PRINCETON AREA LIBRARY*, 100 S Fourth Ave, 55371. SAN 347-2590. Tel: 763-389-3753. FAX: 763-389-3753. E-mail: prmail@ecrlib.org. Web Site: ecrl.lib.mn.us. *Librn,* Robin B Suhsen
Founded 1959. Pop 17,000; Circ 90,000
Library Holdings: Bk Vols 30,000; Per Subs 85
Automation Activity & Vendor Info: (Cataloging) Horizon; (Circulation) Horizon; (OPAC) Horizon
Mem of East Central Regional Library
Open Mon, Wed & Fri 10:30-5, Tues & Thurs Noon-8, Sat 9-2
Friends of the Library Group

RAYMOND

P RAYMOND PUBLIC LIBRARY*, 208 Cofield St N, 56282. (Mail add: PO Box 203, 56282-0203), SAN 348-1328. Tel: 320-967-4411. Web Site: www.raymondcity.com. *Librn,* Villa Lippert
Pop 1,553; Circ 14,732
Library Holdings: Bk Vols 6,200; Per Subs 19
Automation Activity & Vendor Info: (Cataloging) Innovative Interfaces, Inc; (Circulation) Innovative Interfaces, Inc; (OPAC) Innovative Interfaces, Inc
Mem of Pioneerland Library System
Open Mon, Wed & Fri 1-6, Tues 3-8

RED WING

R FIRST LUTHERAN CHURCH, Schendel Memorial Library, 615 W Fifth St, 55066. SAN 308-728X. Tel: 651-388-9311. FAX: 651-388-1714. E-mail: office@firstlutheranrw.org. Web Site: www.firstlutheranrw.org. *Librn,* Nancy Thorson
Founded 1951
Library Holdings: Bk Titles 3,000
Subject Interests: Attitudes, Beliefs, Bible study, Children's lit, Christian life, Christianity, Devotional studies, Inspirational reading, Interpersonal relations, Recreational reading

S GOODHUE COUNTY HISTORICAL SOCIETY LIBRARY*, 1166 Oak St, 55066-2447. SAN 327-1714. Tel: 651-388-6024. FAX: 651-388-3577. E-mail: library@goodhistory.org. Web Site: www.goodhuehistory.mus.mn.us. *Exec Dir,* Dustin Heckman; *Archivist, Librn,* Diane Buganski
Library Holdings: Bk Vols 2,050
Publications: Goodhue County Historical News
Open Tues-Fri 10-5, Sat 1-5

S MINNESOTA DEPARTMENT OF CORRECTIONS*, Minnesota Correctional Facility - Red Wing, 1079 Hwy 292, 55066. Tel: 651-267-3644. FAX: 651-385-6425. Web Site: www.doc.state.mn.us. *Libr Tech,* Brad Wronski; E-mail: brad.wronski@state.mn.us
Library Holdings: AV Mats 350; Bk Vols 5,500; Per Subs 27
Special Collections: Law Coll
Automation Activity & Vendor Info: (Cataloging) Follett Software; (Circulation) Follett Software
Open Mon-Fri 7:30-4

P RED WING PUBLIC LIBRARY*, 225 East Ave, 55066-2298. SAN 308-7298. Tel: 651-385-3673. Reference Tel: 651-385-3645. FAX: 651-385-3644. E-mail: rwpl@selco.info. Web Site: www.redwing.lib.mn.us. *Interim Dir, Tech Serv,* Janet Brandt; E-mail: janetb@selco.info; *Circ Serv, Ref Serv,* Randy Decker; E-mail: rdecker@selco.info; *Youth Serv,* Laura Smith; Staff 14 (MLS 4, Non-MLS 10)
Founded 1894. Pop 18,900; Circ 183,000
Jan 2008-Dec 2008 Income $988,358. Mats Exp $127,000. Sal $630,797
Library Holdings: Audiobooks 1,722; CDs 1,385; DVDs 1,993; Large Print Bks 1,760; Bk Titles 56,810; Per Subs 307; Videos 695
Special Collections: Red Wing Area Genealogy Index; Red Wing History
Automation Activity & Vendor Info: (Acquisitions) SirsiDynix; (Cataloging) SirsiDynix; (Circulation) SirsiDynix; (ILL) SirsiDynix; (Media Booking) SirsiDynix; (OPAC) SirsiDynix; (Serials) SirsiDynix
Database Vendor: EBSCOhost, Gale Cengage Learning, OCLC FirstSearch, ProQuest, SirsiDynix
Wireless access
Function: ILL available, Photocopying/Printing, Ref serv available
Partic in Southeastern Libraries Cooperating
Special Services for the Deaf - Assistive tech; Closed caption videos; Spec interest per
Special Services for the Blind - Assistive/Adapted tech devices, equip & products; Home delivery serv; Large print bks; Large screen computer & software; Low vision equip; Magnifiers
Open Mon-Wed 10-7, Thurs & Fri 10-6, Sat 9-3
Friends of the Library Group

REDWOOD FALLS

P REDWOOD FALLS PUBLIC LIBRARY*, 509 S Lincoln St, 56283. SAN 308-7301. Tel: 507-627-8650. FAX: 507-627-5004. E-mail: rwf@plumcreeklibrary.net. Web Site: www.redwoodfallslibrary.org. *Dir, Libr Serv,* Robin Osland; E-mail: rosland@plumcreeklibrary.net; *Ch,* Jill Deinken; Staff 4 (MLS 1, Non-MLS 3)
Founded 1904. Pop 5,210; Circ 125,359
Library Holdings: Bk Titles 47,159; Per Subs 99
Publications: American Libraries; Library Journal
Mem of Plum Creek Library System
Open Mon-Thurs 10-8, Fri 10-5, Sat 10-2
Friends of the Library Group

RENVILLE

P RENVILLE CITY LIBRARY*, 221 N Main St, 56284. (Mail add: PO Box 609, 56284-0609), SAN 348-1336. Tel: 320-329-8193. E-mail: renville.staff@pioneerland.lib.mn.us. Web Site: www.renville.lib.mn.us. *Head Librn,* Allison Girres; E-mail: allison.girres@pioneerland.lib.mn.us
Pop 1,375; Circ 27,220
Library Holdings: Bk Vols 23,000; Per Subs 62
Automation Activity & Vendor Info: (Acquisitions) Innovative Interfaces, Inc - Millenium; (Cataloging) Innovative Interfaces, Inc - Millenium; (Circulation) Innovative Interfaces, Inc - Millenium; (OPAC) Innovative Interfaces, Inc - Millenium
Wireless access
Mem of Pioneerland Library System
Open Mon, Wed & Fri 12:30-5:30, Tues 10-4, Thurs 12:30-5:30 & 6-8

RICHFIELD

R OAK GROVE LUTHERAN CHURCH*, Juanita Carpenter Library, 7045 Lyndale Ave S, 55423-3099. SAN 308-731X. Tel: 612-869-4917. Web Site: www.oakgrovelutheran.org. *Librn,* Richard Jefferson; Staff 9 (MLS 1, Non-MLS 8)
Founded 1959
Library Holdings: Bk Vols 5,800
Subject Interests: Admin, Adult, Aging, Biblical studies, Educ of ch, Ethics, Family life, Fiction, Marriage, Psychol, Relig
Special Services for the Blind - Large print bks
Open Mon-Fri (Winter) 9-4; Mon-Fri (Summer) 9-3

ROBBINSDALE

M NORTH MEMORIAL HEALTH CARE*, Medical Library, 3300 Oakdale Ave N, 55422. SAN 308-681X. Tel: 763-581-4740. FAX: 763-581-4750. Web Site: www.northmemorial.com/library. *Librn,* Dawn Krist; *Libr Tech,* Lexi Bush; Staff 1 (MLS 0.5, Non-MLS 0.5)
Founded 1968
Library Holdings: AV Mats 825; Bk Titles 4,800; Per Subs 424
Subject Interests: Hospitals, Med, Nursing, Paramedical training
Automation Activity & Vendor Info: (Cataloging) EOS International; (OPAC) EOS International; (Serials) EOS International
Database Vendor: DynaMed, EBSCOhost, Lexi-Comp, MD Consult, Natural Standard, RefWorks
Wireless access
Partic in Minitex Library Information Network; National Network of Libraries of Medicine
Open Mon-Fri 7:30-5:30
Restriction: Med & nursing staff, patients & families

ROCHESTER

CR CROSSROADS COLLEGE*, G H Cachiaras Memorial Library, 920 Mayowood Rd SW, 55902. SAN 308-7344. Tel: 507-535-3330, 507-535-3331. FAX: 507-288-9046. E-mail: library@crossroadscollege.edu. Web Site: www.crossroadscollege.edu. *Dir,* James M Godsey; E-mail: jgodsey@crossroadscollege.edu; Staff 1 (MLS 1)
Founded 1913. Enrl 155; Fac 31; Highest Degree: Bachelor
Jul 2008-Jun 2009 Income $11,539, Locally Generated Income $2,039, Parent Institution $9,500. Mats Exp $19,535, Books $10,240, Per/Ser (Incl. Access Fees) $8,629, Electronic Ref Mat (Incl. Access Fees) $666. Sal $42,560
Library Holdings: AV Mats 1,345; CDs 347; DVDs 142; e-journals 204; Electronic Media & Resources 105; Microforms 2,530; Bk Titles 29,357; Bk Vols 32,106; Per Subs 269; Videos 714
Special Collections: Crossroads College Archives; G H Cachiaras Coll
Subject Interests: Biblical studies, Theol
Automation Activity & Vendor Info: (Acquisitions) Horizon; (Cataloging) Horizon; (Circulation) Horizon; (Media Booking) Horizon; (OPAC) Horizon; (Serials) Horizon
Wireless access
Partic in Southeastern Libraries Cooperating
Special Services for the Deaf - Bks on deafness & sign lang; Closed caption videos
Open Mon-Thurs 8am-10pm, Fri 8-4, Sat 10-4, Sun 6pm-9pm

S MAYO CLINIC LIBRARIES*, Sister Joseph Patient & Visitor Library, 1216 Second St SW, 55902. SAN 347-7967. Tel: 507-255-5434. FAX: 507-255-5254. *Librn,* Stephanie Wentz; Tel: 507-255-6925; Staff 3 (MLS 1, Non-MLS 2)
Founded 1921
Jan 2006-Dec 2006. Mats Exp $4,850, Books $1,350, Per/Ser (Incl. Access Fees) $2,500, AV Mat $1,000. Sal $170,000
Library Holdings: CDs 2,000; DVDs 300; Large Print Bks 200; Bk Vols 7,000; Per Subs 110; Videos 2,000
Subject Interests: Consumer health info
Automation Activity & Vendor Info: (Acquisitions) Innovative Interfaces, Inc; (Cataloging) Innovative Interfaces, Inc; (Circulation) Innovative Interfaces, Inc; (ILL) Innovative Interfaces, Inc; (Media Booking) Innovative Interfaces, Inc; (OPAC) Innovative Interfaces, Inc; (Serials) Innovative Interfaces, Inc
Database Vendor: Baker & Taylor, EBSCOhost
Wireless access
Special Services for the Blind - Talking bks; Talking bks & player equip
Open Mon-Fri 9:30-4:30, Sat & Sun 1-4:30
Restriction: Non-circulating to the pub

S MAYO FOUNDATION*, Medical School Library LRC, 200 First St SW, 55905. SAN 377-869X. Tel: 507-284-3893. FAX: 507-266-4065. Web Site: www.mayo.edu/medlib/medlib.html. *Librn,* Melissa Rethlefsen
Library Holdings: Bk Vols 50,000
Wireless access
Open Mon-Thurs 7:30am-11pm, Fri 7:30-5, Sat 10-6, Sun 11-11
Restriction: Open to students, fac & staff

S OLMSTED COUNTY HISTORICAL SOCIETY, History Center of Olmsted County Archives, 1195 W Circle Dr SW, 55902. SAN 326-114X. Tel: 507-282-9447. FAX: 507-289-5481. E-mail: info@olmstedhistory.com. Web Site: www.olmstedhistory.com. *Exec Dir,* Lisa Baldus; *Archivist,* Position Currently Open
Founded 1926
Special Collections: Funeral Home, Cemetery Records; Minnesota Census 1857-1930; Olmsted County & Rochester Coll; Olmsted County Probate & Guardianship Records; Rochester Newspapers 1859-present; Vital Records, Olmsted County & other Southeastern Minnesota Counties; World War I Draft Registrations
Subject Interests: Genealogy, Hist
Wireless access
Open Tues-Sat 9-5
Restriction: Non-circulating to the pub

S ROCHESTER POST-BULLETIN LIBRARY*, 18 First Ave SE, 55904-6118. SAN 322-9084. Tel: 507-285-7737. FAX: 507-285-7772. *In Charge,* Gretchen Meredith; Staff 2 (MLS 1, Non-MLS 1)
Founded 1965
Library Holdings: Bk Titles 150; Per Subs 30
Restriction: Staff use only

P ROCHESTER PUBLIC LIBRARY*, 101 Second St SE, 55904-3776. SAN 308-7387. Tel: 507-328-2300. Circulation Tel: 507-328-2304. Interlibrary Loan Service Tel: 507-328-2366. Reference Tel: 507-328-2309. Administration Tel: 507-328-2320. Automation Services Tel: 507-328-2363. FAX: 507-328-2384. Web Site: www.rochesterpubliclibrary.org. *Libr Dir,* Audrey Betcher; Tel: 507-328-2344, E-mail: audrey@rochester.lib.mn.us; *Head, Ch,* Heather Acerro; Tel: 507-328-2339, E-mail: hacerro@rochester.lib.mn.us; *Head, ILL,* Greg Sauve; Tel: 507-328-2368, E-mail: ill@rochester.lib.mn.us; *Head, Reader Serv,* Kimberly Edson; Tel: 507-328-2325, E-mail: kedson@rochester.lib.mn.us; *Head, Ref Serv,* Louise Moe; Tel: 507-328-2369, E-mail: louise@rochester.lib.mn.us; *Head, Tech Serv,* Keri Ostby; Tel: 507-328-2355, E-mail: kostby@rochester.lib.mn.us; *Automation Syst Mgr,* Steve Mosing; Tel: 507-328-2361, E-mail: stevem@rochester.lib.mn.us; *Circ Serv Mgr,* Andy Stehr; Tel: 507-328-2322, E-mail: astehr@rochester.lib.mn.us; *Communications Mgr,* John Hunziker; Tel: 507-328-2343, E-mail: jhunziker@rochester.lib.mn.us; *Admin Serv Coordr,* Purna Gurung; E-mail: pgurung@rochester.lib.mn.us; Staff 70.02 (MLS 16.17, Non-MLS 53.85)
Founded 1895. Pop 135,606; Circ 1,644,384
Jan 2011-Dec 2011 Income $6,270,770, State $27,530, City $4,866,394, Federal $6,780, County $868,540, Locally Generated Income $479,659, Other $21,867. Mats Exp $765,331. Sal $4,516,339
Automation Activity & Vendor Info: (Acquisitions) SirsiDynix; (Cataloging) SirsiDynix; (Circulation) SirsiDynix; (Course Reserve) SirsiDynix; (Media Booking) SirsiDynix; (OPAC) SirsiDynix; (Serials) SirsiDynix
Database Vendor: Brodart, Children's Literature Comprehensive Database Company (CLCD), EBSCO Auto Repair Reference, EBSCOhost, FKI Logistex, Foundation Center, Gale Cengage Learning, Grolier Online, Ingram Library Services, LearningExpress, OCLC ArticleFirst, OCLC CAMIO, OCLC FirstSearch, OCLC WebJunction, OCLC WorldShare Interlibrary Loan, Overdrive, Inc, ProQuest, ReferenceUSA, SirsiDynix, ValueLine, Westlaw
Wireless access
Function: Adult bk club, AV serv, Bi-weekly Writer's Group, Bilingual assistance for Spanish patrons, Bk club(s), Bks on CD, CD-ROM, Children's prog, Computer training, Computers for patron use, Copy machines, Digital talking bks, e-mail & chat, E-Reserves, Electronic databases & coll, Free DVD rentals, Handicapped accessible, Home delivery & serv to Sr ctr & nursing homes, Homebound delivery serv, Homework prog, ILL available, Magnifiers for reading, Music CDs, Online cat, Online info literacy tutorials on the web & in blackboard, Online ref, Online searches, Outreach serv, Outside serv via phone, mail, e-mail & web, OverDrive digital audio bks, Photocopying/Printing, Prog for adults, Prog for children & young adult, Pub access computers, Ref serv available, Ref serv in person, Scanner, Senior computer classes, Spoken cassettes & CDs, Spoken cassettes & DVDs, Story hour, Summer reading prog, Tax forms, Teen prog, Telephone ref, VHS videos, Wheelchair accessible
Partic in Minn Interlibr Telecommunication Exchange; OCLC Online Computer Library Center, Inc
Special Services for the Deaf - Bks on deafness & sign lang; Closed caption videos; High interest/low vocabulary bks; TDD equip
Special Services for the Blind - Assistive/Adapted tech devices, equip & products; Audio mat; Bks on cassette; Bks on CD; Braille equip; Cassette playback machines; Computer with voice synthesizer for visually impaired persons; Descriptive video serv (DVS); Digital talking bk; Home delivery serv; Large print & cassettes; Large print bks; Magnifiers; Videos on blindness & phys handicaps; ZoomText magnification & reading software
Open Mon-Thurs (Winter) 9:30-9, Fri & Sat 9:30-5:30, Sun 1:30-5:30; Mon-Thurs (Summer) 9:30-9, Fri 9:30-5:30, Sat 9:30-1:30
Friends of the Library Group
Bookmobiles: 1. Head, Reader Servs, Kimberly Edson

C UNIVERSITY CENTER ROCHESTER*, Goddard Library, 851 30 Ave SE, 55904. SAN 308-7360. Tel: 507-285-7233. FAX: 507-281-7772. E-mail: library@ucr.roch.edu. Web Site: www.roch.edu/library. *Coordr,* Diane Pollock; Tel: 507-285-7229; *Librn,* Jen Bruce; *Librn,* Mary Dennison; *Librn,* May Jesseph; *Librn,* Gwenn Neville; Staff 10 (MLS 5, Non-MLS 5)
Founded 1915. Enrl 4,300
Library Holdings: Bk Vols 110,000; Per Subs 350
Wireless access
Partic in OCLC Online Computer Library Center, Inc
Open Mon-Thurs 7:30am-10pm, Fri 7:30-4:30, Sat 9-5, Sun 1-5

ROSEMOUNT

J DAKOTA COUNTY TECHNICAL COLLEGE LIBRARY*, 1300 E 145th St, 55068. SAN 320-6831. Tel: 651-423-8366. Circulation Tel: 651-423-8654. Interlibrary Loan Service Tel: 651-423-8598. Reference Tel: 651-423-8345. Administration Tel: 651-423-8406. FAX: 651-423-8043. E-mail: library@dctc.edu. Web Site: dctclibrary.dctc.edu. *Head Librn,* Michael Kirby; *Ref & Instruction Librn,* Barbara Tuttle; Staff 2.9 (MLS 1.5, Non-MLS 1.4)
Founded 1973
Library Holdings: AV Mats 1,261; CDs 45; DVDs 278; e-books 8,388; Bk Titles 18,597; Per Subs 128
Automation Activity & Vendor Info: (Cataloging) PALS; (Circulation) PALS; (Course Reserve) PALS; (ILL) PALS; (OPAC) PALS
Database Vendor: CQ Press, ebrary, EBSCOhost, Facts on File, Gale Cengage Learning, LexisNexis, OCLC WorldShare Interlibrary Loan, ProQuest
Wireless access
Partic in MnPALS
Open Mon-Thurs (Fall & Spring) 7:30-6, Fri 7:30-3:30; Mon-Thurs (Summer) 7:30-1:30, Fri 9-1

ROSEVILLE

S MINNESOTA STATE HORTICULTURAL SOCIETY LIBRARY, 2705 Lincoln Dr, 55113-1334. SAN 328-4034. Tel: 651-643-3601. Toll Free Tel: 800-676-6747. FAX: 651-643-3638. E-mail: info@northerngardener.org. Web Site: www.northerngardener.org. *Adminr,* Rose Eggert
Founded 1866
Library Holdings: CDs 20; DVDs 130; Bk Titles 2,000
Special Collections: Historical Volumes relating to horticulture; Minnesota Horticulturist bound volumes from 1870s to present; Video tapes-topics relating to Northern horticultural
Subject Interests: Hort
Open Mon, Wed & Thurs 8-4:30, Tues 8-7, Fri 8-Noon
Restriction: Circ limited, In-house use for visitors
Friends of the Library Group

S UNISYS CORP*, Twin Cities InfoCenter, 2470 Highcrest Rd, 55113. SAN 329-0298. Tel: 651-635-7211. FAX: 651-635-7523.
Founded 1965
Library Holdings: Bk Titles 15,000; Per Subs 300
Subject Interests: Computer sci, Eng
Automation Activity & Vendor Info: (Acquisitions) SirsiDynix; (Cataloging) SirsiDynix; (Circulation) SirsiDynix; (ILL) SirsiDynix; (OPAC) SirsiDynix; (Serials) SirsiDynix
Wireless access
Open Mon-Fri 8-4:30

RUSH CITY

S MINNESOTA DEPARTMENT OF CORRECTIONS*, Minnesota Correctional Facility - Rush City, 7600 - 525th St, 55069. Tel: 320-358-0400, Ext 373. FAX: 763-689-7555. Web Site: www.doc.state.mn.us. *Librn,* Jonathan P Chapman; E-mail: jonathan.chapman@state.mn.us; *Libr Tech,* Frank Poquette; Staff 1 (MLS 1)
Founded 2000
Library Holdings: Bk Titles 15,054; Bk Vols 16,793; Per Subs 60; Videos 400
Special Collections: Minnesota Law Library
Automation Activity & Vendor Info: (Cataloging) Follett Software; (Circulation) Follett Software
Database Vendor: LexisNexis
Restriction: Staff & inmates only

P RUSH CITY PUBLIC LIBRARY*, 240 W Fourth St, 55069. (Mail add: PO Box 556, 55069-0556), SAN 347-2612. Tel: 320-358-3948. E-mail: rcmail@ecrlib.org. Web Site: ecrl.lib.mn.us. *Librn,* Heidi Cava
Pop 4,832; Circ 30,939
Library Holdings: Bk Vols 18,000; Per Subs 42
Automation Activity & Vendor Info: (Cataloging) SirsiDynix; (Circulation) SirsiDynix; (OPAC) SirsiDynix
Wireless access
Mem of East Central Regional Library
Open Tues 10-6, Wed 12-8, Thurs & Fri 12-6, Sat 9-1

RUSHFORD

P RUSHFORD PUBLIC LIBRARY*, 101 N Mill St, 55971. (Mail add: PO Box 250, 55971-0250), SAN 308-7433. Tel: 507-864-7600. FAX: 507-864-7003. Web Site: www.rushford.lib.mn.us. *Dir,* Susan Hart; E-mail: shart@selco.info; Staff 1.91 (Non-MLS 1.91)
Founded 1922. Pop 4,100; Circ 35,924
Jan 2012-Dec 2012 Income $119,562, City $85,302, County $32,000, Locally Generated Income $2,260. Mats Exp $15,541, Books $12,100,

Per/Ser (Incl. Access Fees) $1,300, AV Mat $2,980, Electronic Ref Mat (Incl. Access Fees) $341. Sal $86,775
Library Holdings: Audiobooks 2,239; CDs 678; DVDs 1,315; Large Print Bks 1,450; Bk Vols 2,104; Per Subs 23; Videos 1,025
Subject Interests: Local hist
Automation Activity & Vendor Info: (Acquisitions) SirsiDynix; (Cataloging) SirsiDynix; (Circulation) SirsiDynix; (Course Reserve) SirsiDynix; (ILL) SirsiDynix; (Media Booking) SirsiDynix; (OPAC) SirsiDynix; (Serials) SirsiDynix
Database Vendor: EBSCO Information Services, Gale Cengage Learning, Grolier Online, OCLC FirstSearch, Overdrive, Inc, ProQuest
Wireless access
Function: Online cat, Online searches, Outreach serv, Photocopying/Printing, Preschool reading prog, Prog for adults, Prog for children & young adult, Pub access computers, Scanner, Senior computer classes, Senior outreach, Story hour, Summer & winter reading prog, Tax forms, VHS videos
Partic in Southeastern Libraries Cooperating
Special Services for the Blind - Large print bks; Talking bks
Open Mon 2-7, Tues & Thurs 10-7, Wed & Fri 10-6, Sat 10-2

SAINT BONIFACIUS

CR CROWN COLLEGE, Peter Watne Memorial Library, 8700 College View Dr, 55375-9002. SAN 308-5228. Tel: 952-446-4240. Circulation Tel: 952-446-4241. Interlibrary Loan Service Tel: 952-446-4242. FAX: 952-446-4149. Web Site: www.crownlibrary.com. *Dir,* Dr Dennis Ingolfsland; E-mail: ingolfsland@crown.edu; *Tech Serv & Syst Librn,* Deanna Munson; Tel: 952-446-4415, E-mail: MunsonD@crown.edu; *ILL, Per,* Elaine Johnson; E-mail: johnsone@crown.edu; *Pub Serv,* Kathleen McBride; E-mail: McBridek@crown.edu; Staff 4 (MLS 2, Non-MLS 2)
Founded 1916. Enrl 1,300; Fac 42; Highest Degree: Master
Jul 2013-Jun 2014. Mats Exp $381,662, Books $43,317, Per/Ser (Incl. Access Fees) $36,193
Library Holdings: CDs 565; DVDs 592; e-books 130,000; e-journals 26,728; Microforms 70,000; Bk Titles 211,834; Bk Vols 219,036; Per Subs 71; Videos 50
Special Collections: Early American Newspapers; Evans Coll, micro print; Shaw/Shoemaker/Evans Early American Imprints, 1639-1819
Automation Activity & Vendor Info: (Acquisitions) OCLC WorldShare Interlibrary Loan; (Cataloging) OCLC; (Circulation) OCLC WorldShare Interlibrary Loan; (Course Reserve) OCLC WorldShare Interlibrary Loan; (ILL) OCLC WorldShare Interlibrary Loan; (OPAC) OCLC WorldShare Interlibrary Loan
Database Vendor: 3M Library Systems, American Psychological Association (APA), Cinahl, CredoReference, EBSCOhost, Gale Cengage Learning, JSTOR, OCLC ArticleFirst, OCLC FirstSearch, OCLC WorldShare Interlibrary Loan, ProQuest, Westlaw
Wireless access
Partic in Minitex Library Information Network; MnPALS; OCLC Online Computer Library Center, Inc
Special Services for the Blind - Assistive/Adapted tech devices, equip & products
Open Mon-Thurs 7:30am-Midnight, Fri 7:30-6, Sat Noon-3, Sun 6pm-10pm

SAINT CHARLES

P SAINT CHARLES PUBLIC LIBRARY*, 125 W 11th St, 55972-1141. SAN 308-7441. Tel: 507-932-3227. E-mail: scill@selco.info. Web Site: www.selco.info. *Dir,* Sharon Grossardt; Staff 0.87 (MLS 0.87)
Founded 1913. Pop 6,983; Circ 45,713
Jan 2010-Dec 2010 Income $126,454, City $94,455, County $30,880, Other $1,119. Mats Exp $16,995, Books $13,922, AV Mat $3,073. Sal $63,649
Library Holdings: AV Mats 2,519; e-books 15,191; Bk Vols 21,806; Per Subs 54
Special Collections: Photographs of Early St Charles
Automation Activity & Vendor Info: (Cataloging) Horizon; (Circulation) Horizon; (ILL) Horizon; (OPAC) SerialsSolutions; (Serials) Horizon
Wireless access
Function: Children's prog, Copy machines, Fax serv, Free DVD rentals, Handicapped accessible, ILL available, Mail & tel request accepted, Music CDs, Online cat, OverDrive digital audio bks, Photocopying/Printing, Preschool outreach, Prog for children & young adult, Pub access computers, Spoken cassettes & CDs, Summer & winter reading prog, Tax forms, VHS videos
Partic in Southeastern Libraries Cooperating
Open Mon & Fri 1-6, Tues & Thurs 1-8, Wed 10-6, Sat 10-1
Friends of the Library Group

SAINT CLOUD

GM DEPARTMENT OF VETERANS AFFAIRS MEDICAL CENTER*, Medical Library, 4801 Veterans Dr, 56303. SAN 308-745X. Tel: 320-255-6342. FAX: 320-255-6493. *Librn,* Jeanne Skaj; E-mail: jeanskaj@va.gov; Staff 1 (Non-MLS 1)
Founded 1925
Library Holdings: Bk Vols 1,500; Per Subs 205
Subject Interests: Geriatrics, Nursing, Psychiat, Psychol
Database Vendor: EBSCOhost, Micromedex, STAT!Ref (Teton Data Systems), UpToDate
Partic in Central Minnesota Libraries Exchange; Veterans Affairs Libr Network (VALNET)
Open Mon-Fri 7-4

P GREAT RIVER REGIONAL LIBRARY, 1300 W St Germain St, 56301-3667. SAN 347-8173. Tel: 320-650-2500. Circulation Tel: 320-650-2522. FAX: 320-650-2501. Web Site: www.griver.org. *Interim Dir,* Karen Pundsack; Tel: 320-650-2516, E-mail: karenp@grrl.lib.mn.us; *Assoc Dir, Coll Develop,* Jami Trenam; Tel: 320-650-2531, E-mail: jamit@grrl.lib.mn.us; *Assoc Dir, Human Res,* Sunny Hesse; Tel: 320-650-2511, E-mail: sunnyh@grrl.lib.mn.us; *Assoc Dir, Info Tech,* Jay Roos; Tel: 320-650-2534, E-mail: jayr@grrl.lib.mn.us; *Assoc Dir, Pub Relations,* Julie Henne; Tel: 320-650-2532, E-mail: julieh@grrl.lib.mn.us; *Patron Serv Supvr,* Brandi Canter; Tel: 320-650-2530, E-mail: brandic@grrl.lib.mn.us; *Patron Serv Supvr,* Stacy Lenarz; Tel: 320-650-2525, E-mail: stacyl@grrl.lib.mn.us; *Patron Serv Supvr,* Ryan McCormick; Tel: 320-650-2527, E-mail: ryanm@grrl.lib.mn.us; Staff 19 (MLS 19)
Founded 1969. Pop 467,188; Circ 3,820,661
Jan 2013-Dec 2013 Income $9,507,437. Mats Exp $947,100. Sal $6,915,000
Library Holdings: Audiobooks 29,523; CDs 39,595; DVDs 64,202; Bk Vols 797,293
Automation Activity & Vendor Info: (Cataloging) Horizon; (Circulation) Horizon; (OPAC) Horizon
Database Vendor: Baker & Taylor, EBSCOhost, Gale Cengage Learning, Newsbank, OCLC FirstSearch, ProQuest, SirsiDynix
Wireless access
Function: Adult bk club, Art exhibits, Audiobks via web, Bk club(s), Bks on cassette, Bks on CD, Children's prog, Computer training, Computers for patron use, Copy machines, Digital talking bks, Electronic databases & coll, Free DVD rentals, Handicapped accessible, Home delivery & serv to Sr ctr & nursing homes, ILL available, Large print keyboards, Magnifiers for reading, Music CDs, Online cat, OverDrive digital audio bks, Photocopying/Printing, Prog for adults, Prog for children & young adult, Pub access computers, Ref serv in person, Senior computer classes, Spoken cassettes & CDs, Spoken cassettes & DVDs, Story hour, Summer reading prog, Tax forms, Teen prog, Telephone ref, VHS videos, Web-catalog
Publications: Index of St Cloud Daily Times
Open Mon-Thurs 10-9, Fri 10-6, Sat 10-5
Friends of the Library Group
Branches: 32
ALBANY PUBLIC LIBRARY, 400 Railroad Ave, Albany, 56307. (Mail add: PO Box 687, Albany, 56307-0687), SAN 347-8203. Tel: 320-845-4843. FAX: 320-845-4843. *Br Mgr,* Lisa Pelkey
Founded 1960. Pop 12,488; Circ 82,071
Library Holdings: Audiobooks 520; AV Mats 520; CDs 619; DVDs 1,119; Bk Vols 16,043; Videos 1,119
Open Mon 12-7, Tues 12-8, Wed 10-6, Thurs 12-6, Fri 12-5, Sat 10-1
Friends of the Library Group
ANNANDALE PUBLIC LIBRARY, 30 Cedar St E, Annandale, 55302-1113. (Mail add: PO Box 207, Annandale, 55302-0207), SAN 347-8238. Tel: 320-274-8448. FAX: 320-274-8448. *Br Mgr,* Carla Asfeld
Pop 8,139; Circ 58,558
Library Holdings: Audiobooks 738; AV Mats 99; CDs 591; DVDs 1,373; Bk Vols 13,702; Per Subs 30
Open Mon 2-5, Tues 9-1 & 2-5, Wed 2-8, Fri 9-12 & 2-5, Sat 9-12
Friends of the Library Group
BECKER LIBRARY, 11500 Sherburne Ave, Becker, 55308. (Mail add: PO Box 414, Becker, 55308-0414), SAN 322-564X. Tel: 763-261-4454. FAX: 763-261-4454. *Libr Serv Coordr,* Jeannette Burkhardt
Founded 1984. Pop 10,504; Circ 83,009
Library Holdings: Audiobooks 501; AV Mats 586; CDs 384; DVDs 516; Bk Vols 16,851; Per Subs 28; Videos 516
Open Mon & Thurs 2-8, Tues 10-6, Wed & Fri 2-6, Sat 10-1
Friends of the Library Group
BIG LAKE LIBRARY, 160 Lake St N, Big Lake, 55309. (Mail add: PO Box 323, Big Lake, 55309-0323), SAN 322-6336. Tel: 763-263-6445. FAX: 763-263-6445. *Libr Serv Coordr,* Terry Pfleghaar
Founded 1984. Pop 15,115; Circ 75,355
Library Holdings: Audiobooks 967; AV Mats 960; CDs 547; DVDs 683; Bk Vols 20,230; Per Subs 41; Videos 684
Open Mon 2-7, Tues & Sat 10-1, Wed & Thurs 2-6, Fri 10-5
Friends of the Library Group

BRYANT LIBRARY, 430 Main St, Sauk Centre, 56378, SAN 308-8006. Tel: 320-352-3016. FAX: 320-352-3016. *Libr Serv Coordr,* Dawn Shay
Founded 1878. Pop 7,973; Circ 96,111
Library Holdings: Audiobooks 701; AV Mats 181; CDs 1,357; DVDs 1,865; Bk Vols 20,739; Per Subs 56
Special Collections: James Hendryx Coll; Sinclair Lewis Coll
Open Mon & Fri 12-5, Tues & Thurs 2-8, Wed 10-5, Sat 10-1
Friends of the Library Group

BUFFALO LIBRARY, 18 NW Lake Blvd, Buffalo, 55313, SAN 347-8262. Tel: 763-682-2753. FAX: 763-682-9290. *Libr Serv Coordr,* Amy Wittmann
Founded 1907. Pop 25,000; Circ 256,357
Library Holdings: Audiobooks 1,538; AV Mats 245; CDs 1,791; Bk Vols 38,333; Per Subs 96; Videos 3,604
Special Services for the Deaf - TDD equip
Open Mon-Wed 10-8, Thurs 12-8, Fri 11-5, Sat 10-2
Friends of the Library Group

COKATO LIBRARY, 175 Fourth St W, Cokato, 55321. (Mail add: PO Box 686, Cokato, 55321-0686), SAN 347-8297. Tel: 320-286-5760. FAX: 320-286-5760. *Libr Serv Coordr,* Sheila Reike
Pop 6,010; Circ 72,224
Library Holdings: Audiobooks 583; AV Mats 112; CDs 292; Bk Vols 12,386; Per Subs 45; Videos 1,082
Open Mon 2-6, Tues & Thurs 2-8, Wed 10-2, Fri 11-5, Sat 10-12
Friends of the Library Group

COLD SPRING LIBRARY, 27 Red River Rd, Cold Spring, 56320, SAN 347-8327. Tel: 320-685-8281. *Libr Serv Coordr,* Susan Watts
Pop 9,544; Circ 116,595
Library Holdings: Audiobooks 549; AV Mats 624; CDs 563; DVDs 625; Bk Vols 12,794; Per Subs 30; Videos 626
Open Mon 12-6, Tues & Thurs 2-8, Wed 10-5, Fri 11-5, Sat 10-1
Friends of the Library Group

DELANO LIBRARY, 160 Railroad Ave E, Delano, 55328. (Mail add: PO Box 677, Delano, 55328-0677), SAN 347-8351. Tel: 763-972-3467. FAX: 763-972-3467. *Libr Serv Coordr,* Carol Plocher
Pop 7,390; Circ 145,640
Library Holdings: Audiobooks 1,039; AV Mats 254; CDs 1,247; DVDs 2,731; Bk Vols 25,018; Per Subs 70; Videos 992
Open Mon 10-6, Tues 10-8, Wed & Thurs 1-8, Fri 1-6, Sat 10-1
Friends of the Library Group

EAGLE BEND LIBRARY, 127 E Main, Eagle Bend, 56446. (Mail add: PO Box 238, Eagle Bend, 56446-0238), SAN 321-9267. Tel: 218-738-4590. FAX: 218-738-4590. *Libr Serv Coordr,* Ellen Peters
Pop 4,221; Circ 24,036
Library Holdings: Audiobooks 244; AV Mats 119; CDs 315; DVDs 1,183; Bk Vols 9,450; Per Subs 40
Open Mon & Tues 10-5, Thurs 4-7, Sat 9-12
Friends of the Library Group

ELK RIVER LIBRARY, 13020 Orono Pkwy, Elk River, 55330, SAN 347-8386. Tel: 763-441-1641. FAX: 763-241-9286. *Libr Serv Coordr,* Will Hollerich
Pop 41,927; Circ 313,199
Library Holdings: Audiobooks 1,911; AV Mats 1,590; CDs 1,336; DVDs 1,266; Bk Vols 41,407; Per Subs 69; Videos 1,267
Open Mon & Wed 10-8, Tues & Thurs 12-8, Fri 10-5, Sat 9-2
Friends of the Library Group

FOLEY LIBRARY, 251 N Fourth Ave, Foley, 56329. (Mail add: PO Box 340, Foley, 56329-0340), SAN 347-8416. Tel: 320-968-6612. Web Site: www.griver.org/locations-and-hours/great-river-regional-library-foley. *Libr Serv Coordr,* Judy Weis; E-mail: judyw@grrl.lib.mn.us
Pop 9,135; Circ 68,914
Library Holdings: Audiobooks 467; AV Mats 100; CDs 590; DVDs 1,573; Bk Vols 13,757; Per Subs 41; Videos 611
Open Mon & Wed 2-8, Tues & Fri 9-12 & 1-6, Thurs 2-6, Sat 10-1
Friends of the Library Group

GREY EAGLE COMMUNITY LIBRARY, 118 State St E, Grey Eagle, 56336. (Mail add: PO Box 157, Grey Eagle, 56336-0157), SAN 375-6114. Tel: 320-285-2505. FAX: 320-285-2505. *Libr Serv Coordr,* Jennifer Shattuck
Pop 2,290; Circ 26,025
Library Holdings: Audiobooks 2,204; AV Mats 68; CDs 178; DVDs 462; Bk Vols 9,355; Per Subs 36
Open Mon 10-5, Wed 3-8, Fri 1-6, Sat 10-1
Friends of the Library Group

HOWARD LAKE LIBRARY, 617 Sixth Ave, Howard Lake, 55349-5644, SAN 347-8440. Tel: 320-543-2020. FAX: 320-543-2020. Web Site: www.howard-lake.mn.us/library/index.html. *Libr Serv Coordr,* Deb Cox-Johnson
Pop 6,255; Circ 49,844
Library Holdings: Audiobooks 477; AV Mats 139; CDs 493; DVDs 1,230; Bk Vols 9,911; Per Subs 40; Videos 1,230
Open Mon & Wed 2-8, Tues 2-6, Thurs 3-6, Fri 10-1 & 3-6, Sat 10-1
Friends of the Library Group

KIMBALL LIBRARY, Five Main St N, Kimball, 55353. (Mail add: PO Box 540, Kimball, 55353-0540), SAN 347-8475. Tel: 320-398-3915. FAX: 320-398-3915. *Libr Serv Coordr,* Carla Asfeld
Pop 4,104; Circ 30,986
Library Holdings: Audiobooks 444; AV Mats 50; CDs 345; DVDs 1,058; Bk Vols 7,886; Per Subs 27
Open Mon 10-1 & 2-7, Wed 10-1 & 3-6, Fri 3-6, Sat 9-12
Friends of the Library Group

LITTLE FALLS PUBLIC LIBRARY, 108 NE Third St, Little Falls, 56345-2708, SAN 308-6143. Tel: 320-632-9676. FAX: 320-632-1697. *Libr Serv Coordr,* Cindy Bruggenthies
Founded 1904. Pop 16,326; Circ 122,168
Library Holdings: Audiobooks 1,335; AV Mats 1,773; CDs 809; DVDs 867; Bk Vols 31,297; Per Subs 116; Videos 868
Open Mon & Wed 12-7, Tues & Thurs 10-7, Fri 12-6, Sat 12-3
Friends of the Library Group

LONG PRAIRIE LIBRARY, 42 Third St N, Ste 1, Long Prairie, 56347, SAN 347-8505. Tel: 320-732-2332. *Libr Serv Coordr,* Nancy Potter; E-mail: nancyp@grrl.lib.mn.us
Pop 10,293; Circ 59,800
Library Holdings: Audiobooks 410; AV Mats 124; CDs 577; DVDs 1,537; Bk Vols 10,308; Per Subs 60
Open Mon & Thurs 1-7, Tues 10-6, Wed & Fri 12-6, Sat 9-12
Friends of the Library Group

MYRTLE MABEE LIBRARY, 324 Washburn Ave, Belgrade, 56312. (Mail add: PO Box 388, Belgrade, 56312-0388), SAN 347-853X. Tel: 320-254-8842. *Br Mgr,* Kathie Harris
Pop 2,289; Circ 18,475
Library Holdings: Audiobooks 268; AV Mats 104; CDs 421; DVDs 738; Bk Vols 6,898; Per Subs 36
Open Mon & Wed 2-5, Thurs 10-1 & 2-5, Fri 2-5 & 6-8, Sat 9-12

MELROSE LIBRARY, 225 E First St N, Melrose, 56352-1153. (Mail add: PO Box 027, Melrose, 56352-0027), SAN 347-8564. Tel: 320-256-3885. FAX: 320-256-3885. *Libr Serv Coordr,* Janet Atkinson
Pop 6,624; Circ 93,446
Library Holdings: Audiobooks 604; AV Mats 105; CDs 1,240; DVDs 1,678; Bk Vols 11,435; Per Subs 40
Open Mon 2-8, Tues 2-5, Wed 2-7, Thurs 10-12 & 2-5, Fri 2-6, Sat 10-12
Friends of the Library Group

MONTICELLO LIBRARY, 200 W Sixth St, Monticello, 55362-8832, SAN 347-8599. Tel: 763-295-2322. FAX: 763-295-8321. *Libr Serv Coordr,* Deb Luken
Pop 13,388; Circ 236,220
Library Holdings: Audiobooks 1,221; AV Mats 335; CDs 1,957; DVDs 3,399; Bk Vols 39,594; Per Subs 69
Open Mon 10-8, Tues & Thurs 1-8, Wed 10-6, Fri 10-5, Sat 10-2
Friends of the Library Group

PAYNESVILLE LIBRARY, 119 Washburne Ave, Paynesville, 56362, SAN 308-7204. Tel: 320-243-7343. FAX: 320-243-7343. *Libr Serv Coordr,* Gretchen Vork
Founded 1908. Pop 5,989; Circ 52,670
Library Holdings: Audiobooks 569; AV Mats 114; CDs 580; DVDs 1,385; Bk Vols 12,887; Per Subs 32
Open Mon & Fri 2-8, Tues & Thurs 2-6, Wed 10-6, Sat 10-1
Friends of the Library Group

PIERZ LIBRARY, 220 Main St S, Pierz, 56364, SAN 347-8629. Tel: 320-468-6486. FAX: 320-468-6486. *Libr Serv Coordr,* Grace Heschke
Pop 7,404; Circ 20,820
Library Holdings: Audiobooks 234; AV Mats 536; CDs 112; DVDs 186; Bk Vols 7,852; Per Subs 30; Videos 187
Open Mon 1-5:30, Wed 2-7, Thurs 10-5, Fri 2-5:30, Sat 10-1
Friends of the Library Group

RICHMOND LIBRARY, 63 Hall Ave SW, Richmond, 56368-8108. (Mail add: PO Box 130, Richmond, 56368-0130), SAN 347-8653. Tel: 320-597-3739. FAX: 320-597-3739. *Libr Serv Coordr,* Susan Watts
Pop 3,009; Circ 29,374
Library Holdings: Audiobooks 254; AV Mats 179; CDs 218; DVDs 253; Bk Vols 6,258; Per Subs 32; Videos 253
Database Vendor: Gale Cengage Learning
Open Mon 2-8, Tues & Sat 10-1, Wed 11-1 & 3-6, Fri 3-6
Friends of the Library Group

AL RINGSMUTH LIBRARY, 253 N Fifth Ave, Waite Park, 56387-0395. (Mail add: PO Box 307, Waite Park, 56387-0307), SAN 347-8777. Tel: 320-253-9359. FAX: 320-253-9359. *Libr Serv Coordr,* Marilyn Patterson
Pop 15,818; Circ 138,573
Library Holdings: Audiobooks 823; AV Mats 149; CDs 794; DVDs 2,155; Bk Vols 15,640; Per Subs 38
Open Mon 12-8, Tues 10-2, Wed & Fri 2-6, Thurs 1-5, Sat 10-1
Friends of the Library Group

ROCKFORD PUBLIC LIBRARY, 8220 Cedar St, Rockford, 55373, SAN 373-904X. Tel: 763-477-4216. FAX: 763-477-4216. *Libr Serv Coordr,* Theresa Jacobs
Pop 6,932; Circ 82,877

Library Holdings: Audiobooks 859; AV Mats 920; CDs 542; DVDs 746; Bk Vols 18,657; Per Subs 56; Videos 746
Open Mon & Tues 2-8, Wed 10-6, Thurs 3-8, Fri 3-6, Sat 10-1
Friends of the Library Group

ROYALTON LIBRARY, 12 N Birch St, Royalton, 56373. (Mail add: PO Box 285, Royalton, 56373-0285), SAN 347-8688. Tel: 320-584-8151. FAX: 320-584-8151. *Libr Serv Coordr,* Linda Mueller
Pop 8,153; Circ 25,487
Library Holdings: Audiobooks 351; AV Mats 106; CDs 713; DVDs 1,154; Bk Vols 9,168; Per Subs 12
Open Mon 2-6, Wed 2-8, Thurs 10-1 & 2-6, Sat 10-1
Friends of the Library Group

SAINT CLOUD PUBLIC LIBRARY, 1300 W Saint Germain St, 56301, SAN 347-8718. Tel: 320-650-2500. FAX: 320-650-2501. *Patron Serv Supvr,* Ryan McCormick
Pop 101,506; Circ 1,075,161
Library Holdings: Audiobooks 5,626; AV Mats 1,602; CDs 14,086; DVDs 10,416; Bk Vols 271,308; Per Subs 421
Open Mon-Thurs 10-9, Fri 10-6, Sat 10-5
Friends of the Library Group

ST MICHAEL PUBLIC LIBRARY, 11800 Town Center Dr NE, Ste 100, Saint Michael, 55376-0309, SAN 373-9058. Tel: 763-497-1998. FAX: 763-497-1998. *Libr Serv Coordr,* Marla Scherber
Pop 23,689; Circ 210,000
Open Mon & Wed 10-8, Tues 10-6, Thurs 1-8, Fri 12-5, Sat 10-1
Friends of the Library Group

STAPLES PUBLIC LIBRARY, 122 Sixth St NE, Staples, 56479, SAN 308-8081. Tel: 218-894-1401. FAX: 218-894-1401. *Libr Serv Coordr,* Ellen Peters
Founded 1909. Pop 7,560; Circ 88,123
Library Holdings: Audiobooks 666; AV Mats 161; CDs 606; DVDs 2,322; Bk Vols 15,640; Per Subs 73
Open Mon & Wed 10-6, Tues & Thurs 2-8, Fri 1-5, Sat 10-1

STICKNEY CROSSING LIBRARY, 740 Clearwater Ctr, Clearwater, 55320. Tel: 320-558-6001. FAX: 320-558-6001. *Libr Serv Coordr,* Cyrene Bastien

SWANVILLE LIBRARY, 213 DeGraff St, Swanville, 56382. (Mail add: PO Box 295, Swanville, 56382-0295), SAN 347-8742. Tel: 320-547-2346. *Libr Serv Coordr,* Cindy Bruggenthies
Pop 2,791; Circ 20,295
Library Holdings: Audiobooks 415; AV Mats 175; CDs 136; DVDs 249; Bk Vols 6,349; Per Subs 26; Videos 250
Open Mon 2-5:30, Wed 1-7:30, Thurs 10-1:30 & 2-5:30, Sat 10-1

UPSALA LIBRARY, 117 Main St, Upsala, 56384. (Mail add: PO Box 158, Upsala, 56384-0158), SAN 328-8870. Tel: 320-573-4282. FAX: 320-573-4282. *Libr Serv Coordr,* Wanda Erickson
Pop 1,928; Circ 42,561
Library Holdings: Audiobooks 324; AV Mats 96; CDs 357; DVDs 1,093; Bk Vols 5,861; Per Subs 37
Open Mon 10-3, Wed & Fri 2-8, Sat 10-1
Friends of the Library Group

S MINNESOTA DEPARTMENT OF CORRECTIONS*, Minnesota Correctional Facility - St Cloud, 2305 Minnesota Blvd SE, 56304. Tel: 320-240-3071. Web Site: www.doc.state.mn.us. *Librn,* Teri Hams; E-mail: teri.hams@state.mn.us
Library Holdings: Bk Vols 12,600; Per Subs 56
Special Collections: Law Coll
Automation Activity & Vendor Info: (Cataloging) Follett Software; (Circulation) Follett Software

M SAINT CLOUD HOSPITAL*, Health Sciences Library, 1406 Sixth Ave N, 56303. SAN 327-8271. Tel: 320-251-2700, Ext 54686. FAX: 320-656-7039. E-mail: library@centracare.com. *Librn,* Susan Schleper; *Libr Asst,* Shari Gieseke
Library Holdings: Bk Vols 1,000; Per Subs 160
Wireless access
Open Mon-Fri 8-4:30
Restriction: Open to pub for ref only

C SAINT CLOUD STATE UNIVERSITY LIBRARY, James W Miller Learning Resource Center, 400 Sixth St S, 56301. (Mail add: Saint Cloud State University, 720 Fourth Ave S, 56301-4498), SAN 347-8807. Tel: 320-308-2084. Circulation Tel: 320-308-3083. Interlibrary Loan Service Tel: 320-308-2085. Reference Tel: 320-308-4755. Administration Tel: 320-308-2022. Toll Free Tel: 877-856-9786. E-mail: askref@stcloudstate.edu, lrs@stcloudstate.edu. Web Site: lrts.stcloudstate.edu/library. *Dean,* Mark Vargas; Tel: 320-308-2022, E-mail: mavargas@stcloudstate.edu; *Cat Librn,* Tina Gross; Tel: 320-308-4771, E-mail: tmgross@stcloudstate.edu; *Govt Pub Librn,* Michael Gorman; Tel: 320-308-2028, E-mail: msgorman@stcloudstate.edu; *Ser Librn,* Jo Flanders; Tel: 320-308-2064, E-mail: jlflanders@stcloudstate.edu; *Syst Librn,* M Keith Ewing; Tel: 320-308-4824, E-mail: kewing@stcloudstate.edu; *Circ,* Joe Franklin; Tel: 320-308-4675, E-mail: jpfranklin@stcloudstate.edu; *ILL,* Hannah Topp-Schefers; Tel: 320-308-2085, E-mail: hschefers@stcloudstate.edu
Founded 1869. Enrl 15,000; Fac 570; Highest Degree: Doctorate
Special Collections: Archives, Government Documents & Maps; ERIC Documents of Education, micro; Library of American Civilization; Minnesota Coll; Rare Book Coll; State Author Manuscript Coll. State Document Depository; US Document Depository
Automation Activity & Vendor Info: (Acquisitions) Ex Libris Group; (Cataloging) Ex Libris Group; (Circulation) Ex Libris Group; (Course Reserve) Ex Libris Group; (ILL) Ex Libris Group; (Media Booking) Ex Libris Group; (OPAC) Ex Libris Group; (Serials) Ex Libris Group
Partic in OCLC Online Computer Library Center, Inc

J SAINT CLOUD TECHNICAL COLLEGE LIBRARY*, 1540 Northway Dr, 56303-1240. SAN 320-6858. Tel: 320-308-5966. FAX: 320-308-5960. E-mail: library@sctcc.edu. Web Site: www.sctcc.edu/library. *Chief Info Officer,* Vi Bergquist; E-mail: vbergquist@sctcc.edu; *Librn,* Patricia Akerman; E-mail: pakerman@sctcc.edu; Staff 5 (MLS 2, Non-MLS 3)
Founded 1975. Enrl 2,800; Fac 300; Highest Degree: Associate
Library Holdings: Bk Titles 5,700
Automation Activity & Vendor Info: (Cataloging) Ex Libris Group; (Circulation) Ex Libris Group; (ILL) Ex Libris Group; (OPAC) Ex Libris Group
Database Vendor: Baker & Taylor, EBSCOhost, Facts on File, infoUSA, Newsbank, OCLC FirstSearch, OCLC WorldShare Interlibrary Loan, Project MUSE, ProQuest
Wireless access
Partic in Central Minnesota Libraries Exchange
Open Mon-Thurs 8-8, Fri (Summer) 8-4

S STEARNS HISTORY MUSEUM*, Research Center Library & Archives, 235 33rd Ave S, 56301-3752. SAN 325-4712. Tel: 320-253-8424. Toll Free Tel: 866-253-8424. FAX: 320-253-2172. E-mail: info@stearns-museum.org. Web Site: www.stearns-museum.org. *Archivist, Ref,* John W Decker; E-mail: jdecker@stearns-museum.org; *Archivist, Ref,* Sarah Warmka; E-mail: swarmka@stearns-museum.org; *Asst Archivist, Ref,* Tyler Pulkkinen; E-mail: tpulkkinen@stearns-museum.org; Staff 3 (MLS 1, Non-MLS 2)
Founded 1936
Library Holdings: CDs 45; Microforms 1,650; Bk Titles 2,260; Bk Vols 2,760; Per Subs 20; Videos 180
Special Collections: Myron Hall Photo Coll. Oral History
Subject Interests: Dairying, Genealogy, German, Granite indust, Immigration, Luxembourg settlement, Stearns County hist
Wireless access
Partic in Central Minnesota Libraries Exchange
Open Mon-Sat 10-5, Sun 12-5

SAINT JAMES

P SAINT JAMES LIBRARY*, 125 5th St S, 56081-1736. Tel: 507-375-1278. FAX: 507-375-5415. E-mail: libtwa@tds.lib.mn.us. Web Site: www.tds.sirsi.net. *Dir,* Cheryl Bjoin; Fax: 507-375-5415
Library Holdings: AV Mats 4,451; Bk Titles 47,685; Per Subs 79
Automation Activity & Vendor Info: (Cataloging) SirsiDynix; (Circulation) SirsiDynix; (ILL) SirsiDynix
Open Mon, Wed & Thurs 10-8, Tues & Fri 10-5:30, Sat 10-2

P WATONWAN COUNTY LIBRARY*, 125 Fifth St S, 56081. SAN 308-7468. Tel: 507-375-1278. FAX: 507-375-5415. E-mail: libtwa@tds.lib.mn.us. Web Site: www.co.watonwan.mn.us. *Dir,* Cheryl Bjoin; *Asst Dir,* Stacy Lienemann; *Ch & Youth Librn,* Celeste Clipperton; *Circ Coordr,* Jan Starks; *Tech Serv Coordr,* Shirley Coleman; *Extn Serv,* Megan Karau; Staff 9.45 (MLS 2, Non-MLS 7.45)
Founded 1943. Pop 11,876; Circ 128,015
Jan 2012-Dec 2012 Income (Main Library and Branch(s)) $582,607, State $14,396, County $548,878, Locally Generated Income $19,333. Mats Exp $67,496, Books $49,683, Per/Ser (Incl. Access Fees) $7,788, AV Mat $9,958, Presv $516. Sal $298,567 (Prof $99,039)
Library Holdings: Audiobooks 5,894; AV Mats 299; DVDs 3,421; Bk Vols 88,559; Per Subs 126
Subject Interests: Agr, Antique tractor repair, Tractors
Automation Activity & Vendor Info: (Acquisitions) SirsiDynix; (Cataloging) SirsiDynix; (Circulation) SirsiDynix; (ILL) SirsiDynix; (Serials) SirsiDynix
Database Vendor: EBSCO Information Services, ProQuest, SirsiDynix
Wireless access
Function: Bks on CD, Children's prog, Computer training, Computers for patron use, Copy machines, Digital talking bks, Fax serv, Free DVD rentals, Handicapped accessible, ILL available, Instruction & testing, Magnifiers for reading, Mail & tel request accepted, Music CDs, Online cat, OverDrive digital audio bks, Photocopying/Printing, Preschool outreach, Prog for adults, Prog for children & young adult, Pub access computers, Ref serv available, Spanish lang bks, Spoken cassettes & CDs, Spoken cassettes & DVDs, Story hour, Summer & winter reading prog,

Summer reading prog, Tax forms, Teen prog, Telephone ref, VHS videos, Web-catalog, Wheelchair accessible, Winter reading prog, Writing prog
Mem of Traverse Des Sioux Library Cooperative
Partic in OCLC Online Computer Library Center, Inc
Open Mon, Wed & Thurs 10-8, Tues & Fri 10-5:30, Sat 10-2
Friends of the Library Group
Branches: 4
BUTTERFIELD BRANCH, 111 Second St N, Butterfield, 56120-0237. (Mail add: PO Box L, Butterfield, 56120-0237), SAN 328-6819. Tel: 507-956-2361. E-mail: libtwb@tds.lib.mn.us. *Br Mgr,* Diane Rabe; *Circ,* Julie Lincheid; Staff 1 (Non-MLS 1)
Founded 1970. Pop 573; Circ 12,702
Library Holdings: AV Mats 1,012; Bk Vols 9,249; Per Subs 16
Automation Activity & Vendor Info: (OPAC) SirsiDynix
Function: Handicapped accessible, Health sci info serv, Holiday prog, Home delivery & serv to Sr ctr & nursing homes, Homebound delivery serv, Homework prog, ILL available, Instruction & testing, Jail serv, Jazz prog, Large print keyboards, Learning ctr, Legal assistance to inmates, Libr develop, Literacy & newcomer serv, Magnifiers for reading, Mail & tel request accepted, Mail loans to mem, Masonic res mat, Microfiche/film & reading machines, Monthly prog for perceptually impaired adults, Mus passes, Music CDs, Newsp ref libr, Notary serv, Online cat, Online info literacy tutorials on the web & in blackboard, Online ref, Online searches, Orientations, Outreach serv, Outside serv via phone, mail, e-mail & web, OverDrive digital audio bks, Passport agency, Photocopying/Printing, Preschool outreach, Preschool reading prog, Printer for laptops & handheld devices, Prof lending libr, Prog for adults, Prog for children & young adult, Provide serv for the mentally ill, Pub access computers, Story hour, Summer & winter reading prog, Tax forms
Open Mon & Wed 2-5 & 7-8:30, Tues, Thurs & Fri 2-5, Sat 9-12:30
DARFUR BRANCH, PO Box 191, Darfur, 56022-0190, SAN 328-6835. Tel: 507-877-5010. E-mail: libtwd@tds.lib.mn.us. *Dir,* Cheryl Bjoin; E-mail: cbjoin@tds.lib.mn.us
Founded 1941. Pop 138; Circ 2,999
Library Holdings: AV Mats 597; Bk Vols 2,114
Function: Bks on cassette, Bks on CD, Children's prog, Computers for patron use, Copy machines, ILL available, Music CDs, Prog for children & young adult, Spoken cassettes & CDs, Spoken cassettes & DVDs, Tax forms, Telephone ref
LEWISVILLE BRANCH, 105 Lewis St W, Lewisville, 56060. (Mail add: PO Box 314, Lewisville, 56060-0314), SAN 325-1748. Tel: 507-435-2781. FAX: 507-435-2781. E-mail: libtwl@tds.lib.mn.us. *Br Mgr,* Cheryl Lindell; Staff 1 (Non-MLS 1)
Founded 1941. Pop 249; Circ 4,430
Library Holdings: AV Mats 1,159; Bk Vols 4,664
Automation Activity & Vendor Info: (Cataloging) OCLC; (OPAC) SirsiDynix
Function: Bks on cassette, Bks on CD, Children's prog, Copy machines, Fax serv, ILL available, Music CDs, Online searches, Prog for children & young adult, Tax forms, VHS videos
Open Mon & Fri 3-6, Wed 3-7, Sat 9-12
Friends of the Library Group
MADELIA BRANCH, 23 First St NW, Madelia, 56062-1411, SAN 328-6797. Tel: 507-642-3511. FAX: 507-642-8144. E-mail: libtwm@tds.lib.mn.us. *Br Mgr,* Shari Byro; E-mail: sbyro@tds.lib.mn.us; *Libr Asst,* Glenda Arndt; *Libr Asst,* Cheryl Lindell; Staff 3 (Non-MLS 3)
Founded 1941. Pop 2,234; Circ 30,761
Library Holdings: AV Mats 2,206; Bk Vols 20,083; Per Subs 40
Function: Wheelchair accessible
Open Mon-Wed 10-5 & 7-8:30, Thurs & Fri 10-5, Sat 10-1:30
Friends of the Library Group

SAINT JOSEPH

C COLLEGE OF SAINT BENEDICT*, Clemens Library, 37 S College Ave, 56374. Tel: 320-363-5611. Interlibrary Loan Service Tel: 320-363-5604. Reference Tel: 320-363-5610. Administration Tel: 320-363-2119. FAX: 320-363-5197. Administration FAX: 320-363-2126. Web Site: www.csbsju.edu/library. *Dir, Libr, Media & Archives,* Kathleen Parker; Tel: 320-363-5195, E-mail: kparker@csbsju.edu; *Assoc Dir, Ref, Res & Instruction,* Jim Parsons; Tel: 320-363-5907, E-mail: jparsons@csbsju.edu; *Cat/Metadata Librn,* Janice Rod; Tel: 320-363-2617, E-mail: jrod@csbsju.edu; *Coll Develop Librn,* David Wuolu; Tel: 320-363-2128, E-mail: dwuolu@csbsju.edu; *Govt & Bus Info Librn,* Amy Springer; Tel: 320-363-2601, E-mail: aspringer@csbsju.edu; *Humanities Librn,* Molly Ewing; Tel: 320-363-5513, E-mail: mewing@csbsju.edu; *Info Literacy Librn,* Sarah Gewirtz; Tel: 320-363-5802, E-mail: sgewirtz@csbsju.edu; *Sci Librn,* Jonathan Carlson; Tel: 320-363-2579, E-mail: jcarlson@csbsju.edu; *Soc Sci Librn,* Diana Symons; Tel: 320-363-5296, E-mail: dsymons@csbsju.edu; *Syst Librn,* Tess Kasling; Tel: 320-363-3280, E-mail: tkasling@csbsju.edu; *Archivist,* Peggy Roske; Tel: 320-363-5019, E-mail: proske@csbsju.edu. Subject Specialists: *Bus, Govt,* Amy Springer; *Sci,* Jonathan Carlson; *Music,* Tess Kasling; Staff 14 (MLS 11, Non-MLS 3)
Founded 1913. Enrl 2,057; Fac 173; Highest Degree: Bachelor
Library Holdings: AV Mats 13,204; e-journals 2,865; Microforms 47,865; Music Scores 8,809; Bk Titles 204,209; Bk Vols 219,814; Per Subs 701
Subject Interests: Nursing, Women studies
Automation Activity & Vendor Info: (Acquisitions) Ex Libris Group; (Cataloging) Ex Libris Group; (Circulation) Ex Libris Group; (Course Reserve) Ex Libris Group; (ILL) Ex Libris Group; (OPAC) Ex Libris Group; (Serials) Ex Libris Group
Database Vendor: ABC-CLIO, ACM (Association for Computing Machinery), Alexander Street Press, American Chemical Society, American Mathematical Society, American Physical Society, Annual Reviews, ARTstor, BioOne, Cinahl, CQ Press, CredoReference, ebrary, EBSCOhost, Elsevier, Ex Libris Group, Gale Cengage Learning, Gallup, HeinOnline, Hoovers, IOP, ISI Web of Knowledge, JSTOR, LexisNexis, McGraw-Hill, Mergent Online, Modern Language Association, Nature Publishing Group, Newsbank-Readex, OCLC, OCLC FirstSearch, OCLC WorldShare Interlibrary Loan, OVID Technologies, Project MUSE, ProQuest, ScienceDirect, Springer-Verlag, Thomson - Web of Science, ValueLine, Wiley, YBP Library Services
Wireless access
Partic in Central Minnesota Libraries Exchange; OCLC Online Computer Library Center, Inc
Open Mon-Thurs 8am-Midnight, Fri 8am-10pm, Sat 10-10, Sun 10am-Midnight
Restriction: Open to students, fac & staff

SAINT LOUIS PARK

R BETH-EL SYNAGOGUE*, Max Shapiro Memorial Library, 5224 W 26th St, 55416. SAN 308-7484. Tel: 952-920-3512. FAX: 952-920-8755. *Librn,* Marcia Oleisky
Founded 1929
Library Holdings: Bk Vols 6,000; Per Subs 26
Special Collections: Music Coll

S PARK NICOLLET INSTITUTE*, Arneson Methodist Library, 3800 Park Nicollet Blvd, 55416. SAN 308-6879. Tel: 952-993-5451. FAX: 952-993-1322. E-mail: library@parknicollet.com. *Dir,* Penny Marsala; Staff 3 (MLS 3)
Founded 1952
Library Holdings: Bk Vols 6,500; Per Subs 291
Automation Activity & Vendor Info: (Cataloging) Inmagic, Inc.; (Circulation) Inmagic, Inc.
Database Vendor: EBSCOhost
Partic in Twin Cities Biomedical Consortium
Restriction: Staff use only, Use of others with permission of librn

SAINT PAUL

S AERO SYSTEMS ENGINEERING INC LIBRARY*, 358 E Fillmore Ave, 55107. SAN 308-6488. Tel: 651-220-1209. FAX: 651-227-0519. *Librn,* Glenn Payton; Staff 1 (MLS 1)
Founded 1967
Library Holdings: Bk Titles 2,800; Per Subs 150
Subject Interests: Aerospace res, Aircraft engine, Develop, Hush houses, Test cells, Testing, Wind tunnel design
Partic in Dialog Corp; Metronet; NASA Libraries Information System-NASA Galaxie
Open Mon-Fri 9-5

R BETHEL SEMINARY LIBRARY*, 3949 Bethel Dr, 55112. SAN 308-7530. Tel: 651-638-6184. Interlibrary Loan Service Tel: 651-635-8773. Reference Tel: 651-635-2337. Administration Tel: 651-638-6127. FAX: 651-638-6006. E-mail: sem-reference-desk@bethel.edu. Web Site: seminary.bethel.edu/library. *Dir,* Sandra Oslund
Founded 1871. Enrl 717; Fac 21; Highest Degree: Doctorate
Library Holdings: Bk Vols 170,000; Per Subs 518
Special Collections: 19th Century Pietism (Skarstedt Coll); Baptist General Conference History Center; Bethel University Archives; Devotional Literature (Nelson-Lundquist Coll); Klingberg Puritan Coll
Wireless access
Partic in Cooperating Libraries in Consortium; Minitex Library Information Network; Minnesota Theological Library Association

CR BETHEL UNIVERSITY LIBRARY*, 3900 Bethel Dr, 55112. SAN 308-7522. Tel: 651-638-6222. Reference Tel: 651-638-6224. FAX: 651-638-6001. Web Site: library.bethel.edu. *Dir, Univ Libr,* David Stewart; E-mail: d-stewart@bethel.edu; *Assoc Dir/Ref/Instruction Librn,* Carole Cragg; E-mail: cracar@bethel.edu; Staff 7 (MLS 7)
Founded 1871. Enrl 4,300; Fac 160; Highest Degree: Doctorate
Library Holdings: AV Mats 13,500; e-books 14,000; e-journals 21,000; Bk Titles 174,000; Per Subs 842
Subject Interests: Educ, Hist
Wireless access
Partic in Cooperating Libraries in Consortium

Open Mon-Thurs (Winter) 7:45am-Midnight, Fri 7:45-5, Sat 10-6, Sun 2-Midnight; Mon-Thurs (Summer) 10-8, Fri & Sat 10-4
Friends of the Library Group

C CONCORDIA UNIVERSITY*, Library Technology Center, 1282 Concordia Ave, 55104. (Mail add: 275 N Syndicate St, 55104), SAN 308-759X. Tel: 651-641-8278. Circulation Tel: 651-641-8237. Reference Tel: 651-641-8812. Administration Tel: 651-641-8241. FAX: 651-641-8782. E-mail: reference@csp.edu. Web Site: concordia.csp.edu/library. *Dir,* Dr Charlotte M Knoche; E-mail: knoche@csp.edu; *Ref Librn,* Tamara Buetow; E-mail: tbuetow@csp.edu; *Archives, Coordr, AV,* Amity Foster; Tel: 651-641-8240, E-mail: foster@csp.edu; *Cat, Electronic Res, Ref,* Greg Argo; Tel: 651-641-6315, E-mail: argo@csp.edu; *Circ, ILL, Ref,* Jennifer Borkenhagen; Tel: 651-641-8770, E-mail: borkenhagen@csp.edu; *Curric Coll, Juv Coll, Ser,* Martha Burkart; Tel: 651-606-6309, E-mail: mburkart@csp.edu; *Ref,* Geruth Beutow; Tel: 651-641-8244, E-mail: gbuetow@csp.edu; *Assoc Syst Adminr, Tech Serv,* Jeanine Gatzke; Tel: 651-641-8242, E-mail: gatzke@csp.edu
Founded 1893. Enrl 1,866; Fac 85; Highest Degree: Master
Library Holdings: AV Mats 3,321; Bk Vols 127,000; Per Subs 450
Special Collections: 16th-19th Century Coll (mainly German & Theological); Education (Children's Coll); Historical Textbooks; Hymnbook Coll. Oral History
Subject Interests: Educ, Hist, Music, Organizational mgt
Automation Activity & Vendor Info: (Cataloging) Innovative Interfaces, Inc; (Circulation) Innovative Interfaces, Inc; (Course Reserve) Innovative Interfaces, Inc; (ILL) Innovative Interfaces, Inc; (Media Booking) Innovative Interfaces, Inc; (OPAC) Innovative Interfaces, Inc; (Serials) EBSCO Online
Database Vendor: Amigos Library Services, Cambridge Scientific Abstracts, CQ Press, EBSCOhost, Hoovers, IBISWorld, JSTOR, LexisNexis, Newsbank, OCLC WorldShare Interlibrary Loan, Oxford Online, Project MUSE, ProQuest, Sage
Wireless access
Publications: The Reformation as Media Event: A Bibliography of 16th Century Materials
Partic in Cooperating Libraries in Consortium; OCLC Online Computer Library Center, Inc
Open Mon-Thurs (Winter) 7:45am-11pm, Fri 7:45-5, Sat 8-5, Sun 1-11; Mon-Thurs (Summer) 9-8, Fri 9-4, Sat 12-4

S DEBRA S FISH EARLY CHILDHOOD RESOURCE LIBRARY*, Ten Yorkton Ct, 55117-1065. SAN 327-2184. Tel: 651-641-3544. FAX: 651-645-0990. TDD: 651-641-0332. E-mail: library@resourcesforchildcare.org. Web Site: www.resourcesforchildcare.org. *Exec Dir,* Barbara Yates; *Librn,* Cathy Clair; E-mail: cclair@resourcesforchildcare.org.org; Staff 1 (MLS 1)
Founded 1997
Library Holdings: Bk Titles 2,700
Subject Interests: Early childhood
Special Services for the Deaf - TDD equip
Open Mon-Thurs 8:30-5 & 6-9, Fri 8:30-5
Friends of the Library Group

HAMLINE UNIVERSITY

C BUSH MEMORIAL LIBRARY*, 1536 Hewitt, 55104. SAN 347-8920. Tel: 651-523-2375. FAX: 651-523 2199. E-mail: bush_reference_email@gw.hamline.edu. Web Site: www.hamline.edu/bushlibrary/index.html. *Dir,* Diane Clayton; E-mail: dclayton@gw.hamline.edu; *Dir,* Julie Rochat; E-mail: jrochat@gw.hamline.edu; *Cat,* Deb Kerkvliet; *Circ,* Barbara Brokopp; *Ref,* Kate Borowske; *Ref,* Kimberly Feilmeyer; *Ref,* Kristofer Scheid; *Ref,* Amy Sheehan; *Ser,* Jan Griffith
Founded 1854. Enrl 2,000
Library Holdings: Bk Vols 154,000; Per Subs 1,148
Special Collections: Brass Rubbing Coll
Automation Activity & Vendor Info: (Acquisitions) Innovative Interfaces, Inc; (Cataloging) Innovative Interfaces, Inc; (Circulation) Innovative Interfaces, Inc; (Course Reserve) Innovative Interfaces, Inc; (ILL) Innovative Interfaces, Inc; (OPAC) Innovative Interfaces, Inc; (Serials) Innovative Interfaces, Inc
Database Vendor: EBSCOhost, Gale Cengage Learning
Partic in Cooperating Libraries in Consortium; OCLC Online Computer Library Center, Inc
Open Mon-Thurs 7:30am-11:45pm, Fri 7:30am-8:45pm, Sat 7:30-6:45, Sun 12-11:45

CL SCHOOL OF LAW LIBRARY*, 1536 Hewitt Ave, 55104, SAN 347-8955. Tel: 651-523-2379. Interlibrary Loan Service Tel: 651-523-2737. FAX: 651-523-2863. Web Site: lawlibrary.hamline.edu. *Head, Pub Serv, Interim Co-Dir,* Barb Kallusky; Tel: 651-523-2131, E-mail: bkallusky01@hamline.edu; *Head, Tech Serv, Interim Co-Dir,* Emily Waitz; E-mail: ewaitz01@hamline.edu; *Access & Circ Serv Librn,* Selva Palani; E-mail: spalani01@hamline.edu; *Cat Librn,* Susan J Vossberg; E-mail: svossberg01@hamline.edu; *Pub Serv Librn,* Megan Koltes; Staff 4 (MLS 4)
Founded 1972. Enrl 587; Fac 30; Highest Degree: Doctorate
Library Holdings: Bk Vols 274,195
Automation Activity & Vendor Info: (Acquisitions) Innovative Interfaces, Inc; (Cataloging) Innovative Interfaces, Inc; (Circulation) Innovative Interfaces, Inc; (Course Reserve) Innovative Interfaces, Inc; (ILL) Innovative Interfaces, Inc; (Media Booking) Innovative Interfaces, Inc; (OPAC) Innovative Interfaces, Inc; (Serials) Innovative Interfaces, Inc
Database Vendor: Bloomberg, EBSCOhost, HeinOnline, LexisNexis, Westlaw
Partic in Cooperating Libraries in Consortium; Metronet; OCLC Online Computer Library Center, Inc
Publications: Library Guide; Pathfinders
Open Mon-Thurs, Sat & Sun (Fall & Spring) 7:30am-11pm, Fri 7:30am-10pm; Mon-Fri (Summer) 8am-10pm, Sat & Sun 9-6

M HEALTHEAST ST JOSEPH'S HOSPITAL, Jerome Medical Library, 45 W Tenth St, 55102. SAN 308-7859. Tel: 651-232-3193. FAX: 651-326-8095. E-mail: stjosephslibrary@healtheast.org. *Sr Med Librn,* Karen L Brudvig; E-mail: kbrudvig@healtheast.org; Staff 1 (MLS 1)
Founded 1949
Library Holdings: Bk Vols 500; Per Subs 150
Wireless access
Partic in Health Scis Librs of Minn
Open Mon-Fri 7-3:30
Restriction: Open to pub for ref only

S JAMES J HILL REFERENCE LIBRARY*, 80 W Fourth St, 55102. SAN 308-7662. Tel: 651-265-5500. FAX: 651-265-5520. E-mail: info@jjhill.org. Web Site: www.jjhill.org. *Dir of Libr Serv,* Liz Sanborn
Founded 1921
Library Holdings: Bk Titles 34,460; Bk Vols 205,150; Per Subs 750; Spec Interest Per Sub 600
Subject Interests: Bus
Automation Activity & Vendor Info: (Acquisitions) PALS; (Cataloging) PALS; (ILL) PALS; (OPAC) PALS; (Serials) PALS
Database Vendor: EBSCOhost, Gale Cengage Learning
Wireless access
Function: Doc delivery serv, e-mail serv, Electronic databases & coll, Online cat, Res libr, Workshops
Partic in MnPALS; OCLC Online Computer Library Center, Inc
Open Mon-Thurs 10-5
Restriction: Not a lending libr, Open to pub for ref only

S LAND O'LAKES INC LIBRARY*, PO Box 64101, 55164-0101. SAN 327-7941. Tel: 651-481-2691. FAX: 651-481-2002. *Librn,* Donna Koenig; E-mail: djkoenig@landolakes.com
Library Holdings: Bk Vols 4,000; Per Subs 250
Subject Interests: Agr, Food sci

S LEAGUE OF MINNESOTA CITIES LIBRARY*, 145 University Ave W, 55103-2044. SAN 327-1943. Tel: 651-281-1200. FAX: 651-281-1299. Web Site: www.lmc.org. *Mgr, Res,* Jeanette Behr; Staff 4 (Non-MLS 4)
Founded 1913
Library Holdings: Bk Vols 100; Spec Interest Per Sub 60
Special Collections: Minnesota City Charters
Subject Interests: City hist, Govt
Function: Govt ref serv
Publications: Cities Bulletin; Handbook for Minnesota Cities; Human Resources Reference Manual; Information Memos on Municipal Topics; Minnesota Cities; Minnesota Mayors Handbook
Open Mon-Fri 8:30-4:30
Restriction: Authorized patrons

R LUTHER SEMINARY LIBRARY, 2481 Como Ave, 55108. SAN 308-7689. Tel: 651-641-3447. Web Site: www.luthersem.edu/library. *Dir,* Andrew Keck; Tel: 651-641-3592, E-mail: akeck001@luthersem.edu; *Access Serv Librn,* Karen Alexander; Tel: 651-641-3301, E-mail: kalexander001@luthersem.edu; *Acq Librn,* Trisha Burr; Tel: 651-641-3263, E-mail: tburr001@luthersem.edu; *Cat Librn,* Mary Ann Teske; Tel: 651-641-3446, E-mail: mteske@luthersem.edu; *Digital Res, Outreach & Instruction Librn,* Jennifer Bartholomew; Tel: 651-641-3458, E-mail: jbartholomew001@luthsem.edu; *Ref & Spec Coll,* Bruce E Eldevik; Tel: 651-641-3226, E-mail: beldevik@luthersem.edu; Staff 6 (MLS 6)
Founded 1869. Enrl 764; Fac 28; Highest Degree: Doctorate
Library Holdings: Microforms 46,820; Bk Vols 212,480; Per Subs 292
Special Collections: Doving Hymnal Coll; Pre-1800 Book Coll; Tanner Catechism Coll; Thrivent Reformation Research Coll
Subject Interests: Reformation
Automation Activity & Vendor Info: (OPAC) OCLC
Database Vendor: Alexander Street Press, EBSCOhost, Gale Cengage Learning, JSTOR, OCLC, OCLC Worldshare Management Services, Project MUSE, ProQuest, Sage, Springshare, LLC, YBP Library Services

Wireless access
Special Services for the Blind - Assistive/Adapted tech devices, equip & products
Open Mon-Thurs 7:45am-10pm, Fri 7:45-5, Sat 9-5, Sun 2-10

C MACALESTER COLLEGE, DeWitt Wallace Library, 1600 Grand Ave, 55105-1899. SAN 347-9013. Tel: 651-696-6346. Circulation Tel: 651-696-6610. Interlibrary Loan Service Tel: 651-696-6545. Reference Tel: 651-696-6618. FAX: 651-696-6617. Administration FAX: 651-696-6782. Web Site: www.macalester.edu/library. *Dir,* Teresa A Fishel; Tel: 651-696-6343, E-mail: fishel@macalester.edu; *Assoc Libr Dir, Access, Instruction & Res Serv,* Angi Faiks; Tel: 651-696-6208, E-mail: faiks@macalester.edu; *Asst Libr Dir, Coll & Discovery,* Katy Gabrio; Tel: 651-696-6703, E-mail: gabrio@macalester.edu; Staff 18 (MLS 12, Non-MLS 6)
Founded 1874. Enrl 1,999; Fac 147; Highest Degree: Bachelor
Library Holdings: AV Mats 11,000; e-books 5,196; Bk Titles 327,156; Bk Vols 439,568; Per Subs 2,038
Special Collections: Early Minnesota; Sinclair Lewis, bks, per, letters & ephemera
Automation Activity & Vendor Info: (Acquisitions) OCLC; (Cataloging) OCLC; (Circulation) OCLC; (Course Reserve) OCLC; (ILL) OCLC; (Media Booking) OCLC; (OPAC) OCLC; (Serials) OCLC
Database Vendor: ACM (Association for Computing Machinery), Alexander Street Press, American Chemical Society, American Mathematical Society, American Physical Society, American Psychological Association (APA), Annual Reviews, ARTstor, BioOne, Cambridge Scientific Abstracts, College Source, Coutts Information Service, CredoReference, ebrary, EBSCOhost, Ex Libris Group, Gale Cengage Learning, Ingenta, Ingram Library Services, ISI Web of Knowledge, JSTOR, LexisNexis, Medline, Modern Language Association, OCLC WorldShare Interlibrary Loan, Oxford Online, Project MUSE, PubMed, RefWorks, Sage, ScienceDirect
Wireless access
Partic in Minitex Library Information Network; OCLC Online Computer Library Center, Inc

S METROPOLITAN COUNCIL LIBRARY, 390 Robert St N, 55101. SAN 308-7697. Tel: 651-602-1412. FAX: 651-602-1496. Web Site: www.metrocouncil.org. *Libr & Info Res Coordr,* Jan Price; E-mail: jan.price@metc.state.mn.us; Staff 1 (MLS 1)
Founded 1967
Library Holdings: AV Mats 350; Bk Titles 10,000; Per Subs 150
Special Collections: Local Government Comprehensive Plans; Metropolitan Council, doc
Subject Interests: Housing, Regional planning, Transportation, Urban planning
Automation Activity & Vendor Info: (Cataloging) LibraryWorld, Inc; (OPAC) LibraryWorld, Inc
Database Vendor: Dialog, Gale Cengage Learning, OCLC FirstSearch, ProQuest
Wireless access
Publications: New Books in the Library (Online only)
Partic in Capital Area Library Consortium; Minitex Library Information Network
Open Mon-Fri 8:15-4:30
Restriction: Non-circulating to the pub

C METROPOLITAN STATE UNIVERSITY*, Library & Learning Center, 645 E Seventh St, 55106. (Mail add: 700 E Seventh St, 55106), SAN 378-3766. Tel: 651-793-1616. Reference Tel: 651-793-1614. Administration Tel: 651-793-1622. FAX: 651-793-1615. E-mail: library.services@metrostate.edu. Web Site: www.metrostate.edu/library. *Dean, Libr Serv,* David Barton; Tel: 651-793-1619, E-mail: david.barton@metrostate.edu; *Dir, Tech Serv,* Bruce Willms; Tel: 651-793-1618, E-mail: bruce.willms@metrostate.edu; *Head, Ref & Res Serv,* Michelle Filkins; Tel: 651-793-1621, E-mail: michelle.filkins@metrostate.edu; Staff 8 (MLS 8)
Founded 1992. Enrl 5,076; Fac 6; Highest Degree: Doctorate
Jul 2008-Jun 2009 Income $1,484,952. Mats Exp $415,057, Books $72,619, Per/Ser (Incl. Access Fees) $58,329, AV Equip $500, AV Mat $58,329, Electronic Ref Mat (Incl. Access Fees) $225,280. Sal $805,460 (Prof $475,932)
Library Holdings: CDs 253; DVDs 2,015; e-books 879; Bk Titles 32,144; Bk Vols 34,496; Per Subs 205; Videos 2,506
Special Collections: Minnesota Cookbook Coll; Musical Theatre Coll, CDs
Automation Activity & Vendor Info: (Acquisitions) Ex Libris Group; (Cataloging) Ex Libris Group; (Circulation) Ex Libris Group; (Course Reserve) Docutek; (ILL) PALS; (Media Booking) PALS; (OPAC) Ex Libris Group; (Serials) Ex Libris Group
Wireless access
Partic in Metronet; Minitex Library Information Network; Minnesota Library Information Network; MnPALS
Open Mon-Thurs 8am-11pm, Fri 8am-10pm Sat 8-8, Sun 12-11

GL MINNESOTA ATTORNEY GENERAL LIBRARY*, Bremer Tower, Ste 1050, 445 Minnesota St, 55101-2109. SAN 321-8325. Tel: 651-757-1050, 651-757-1055. FAX: 651-296-7000. TDD: 651-296-1410. E-mail: library.ag@ag.state.mn.us. Web Site: www.ag.state.mn.us. *Dir,* Anita Anderson; E-mail: anita.anderson@ag.state.mn.us; *Res Librn,* Karla Gedell; E-mail: karla.gedell@ag.state.mn.us; Staff 2 (MLS 2)
Library Holdings: Bk Titles 3,014; Bk Vols 20,607; Per Subs 600
Special Collections: Minnesota Attorney General Opinions Coll, micro, VF
Automation Activity & Vendor Info: (Cataloging) PALS; (ILL) PALS; (OPAC) PALS
Database Vendor: LexisNexis, Westlaw
Partic in OCLC Online Computer Library Center, Inc
Restriction: Staff use only

G MINNESOTA DEPARTMENT OF EMPLOYMENT & ECONOMIC DEVELOPMENT LIBRARY*, 1st National Bank Bldg, 332 Minnesota St, Ste E200, 55101-1351. SAN 308-7743. Tel: 651-259-7188. Toll Free Tel: 800-657-3858. FAX: 651-215-3841. E-mail: deed.library@state.mn.us. Web Site: www.deed.state.mn.us, www.libraries.state.mn.us/deed.html. *Librn,* Dru Frykberg; E-mail: dru.frykberg@state.mn.us; Staff 2 (MLS 1.5, Non-MLS 0.5)
Founded 1976
Jul 2006-Jun 2007 Income $60,000. Mats Exp $60,000, Books $8,000, Per/Ser (Incl. Access Fees) $16,000, Electronic Ref Mat (Incl. Access Fees) $36,000
Library Holdings: Bk Titles 7,700; Per Subs 100
Subject Interests: Econ develop, Intl trade, Workforce develop
Automation Activity & Vendor Info: (Acquisitions) Ex Libris Group; (Cataloging) Ex Libris Group; (Circulation) Ex Libris Group; (ILL) Ex Libris Group; (OPAC) Ex Libris Group; (Serials) Ex Libris Group
Database Vendor: Dialog, Dun & Bradstreet, EBSCOhost, Factiva.com, Kompass, Newsbank, OCLC WorldShare Interlibrary Loan, ProQuest, ReferenceUSA
Function: ILL available
Partic in Capital Area Library Consortium; Minitex Library Information Network; MnPALS; OCLC Online Computer Library Center, Inc
Open Mon-Fri 9-4

G MINNESOTA DEPARTMENT OF HEALTH*, R N Barr Library, 2079 Ellis Ave, 55114. SAN 308-6704. Tel: 651-201-5093. E-mail: health.library@state.mn.us. Web Site: www.health.state.mn.us/library/. *Mgr,* Position Currently Open
Founded 1872
Library Holdings: AV Mats 547; DVDs 253; e-journals 75; Bk Titles 300; Per Subs 73
Subject Interests: Environ health, Health planning, Health promotion, Pub health, Socio-econ aspects of health care
Automation Activity & Vendor Info: (Acquisitions) Ex Libris Group; (Cataloging) Ex Libris Group; (Circulation) Ex Libris Group; (ILL) Ex Libris Group; (Media Booking) Ex Libris Group; (OPAC) PALS; (Serials) Ex Libris Group
Database Vendor: EBSCOhost, SerialsSolutions
Partic in Capitol Area Library Consortium; Docline; Minitex Library Information Network; OCLC Online Computer Library Center, Inc
Open Mon-Fri 8-4:30

S MINNESOTA DEPARTMENT OF REVENUE LIBRARY*, 600 N Robert St, 55101. (Mail add: Mail Sta 2230, 55146), SAN 327-1846. Tel: 651-556-6134. FAX: 651-556-3103. *Librn,* Chris Anning; E-mail: chris.anning@state.mn.us; Staff 1 (Non-MLS 1)
Founded 1986
Jul 2012-Jun 2013. Mats Exp $50,000, Books $20,000, Per/Ser (Incl. Access Fees) $9,000, Other Print Mats $5,000, Electronic Ref Mat (Incl. Access Fees) $16,000. Sal $50,000
Library Holdings: Bk Titles 5,000; Bk Vols 10,000; Per Subs 100
Subject Interests: Taxation
Automation Activity & Vendor Info: (Cataloging) OCLC Connexion; (Circulation) PALS; (ILL) PALS; (OPAC) PALS
Database Vendor: Dialog, EBSCOhost, ProQuest
Partic in Capital Area Library Consortium; Metronet; Minitex Library Information Network; OCLC Online Computer Library Center, Inc
Restriction: Open by appt only

G MINNESOTA DEPARTMENT OF TRANSPORTATION LIBRARY*, 395 John Ireland Blvd, MS 155, 55155. SAN 308-7735. Tel: 651-366-3791. Toll Free Tel: 800-657-3774. FAX: 651-366-3789. TDD: 800-627-3529. E-mail: library.dot@state.mn.us. Web Site: www.dot.state.mn.us/library. *Dir,* Sheila C Hatchell; Tel: 651-366-3733, E-mail: sheila.hatchell@state.mn.us; *Contract Librn,* Anne Shelley; Tel: 651-366-3797, E-mail: anne.shelley@state.mn.us; *Electronic Res Librn,* Jim Byerly; Tel: 651-366-3739, E-mail: jim.byerly@state.mn.us; *Ref/Outreach*

Librn, Karen Neinstadt; Tel: 651-366-3796, E-mail: karen.neinstadt@state.mn.us; *Tech Serv Librn,* Qin Tang; Tel: 651-366-3784, E-mail: qin.tang@state.mn.us; *Per/Acq Tech,* Pamela M Gonzalez; Tel: 651-366-3749, E-mail: pamela.m.gonzalez@state.mn.us. Subject Specialists: *Transportation,* Jim Byerly; *Transportation,* Karen Neinstadt; Staff 5.5 (MLS 4.5, Non-MLS 1)
Founded 1957
Library Holdings: CDs 400; Electronic Media & Resources 694; Bk Titles 20,600; Bk Vols 28,000; Per Subs 300; Videos 900
Subject Interests: Civil eng, Mgt, Transportation
Automation Activity & Vendor Info: (Cataloging) OCLC; (Circulation) Ex Libris Group; (ILL) OCLC; (OPAC) Ex Libris Group
Database Vendor: Dialog, EBSCOhost, Factiva.com, OCLC FirstSearch, OCLC WorldShare Interlibrary Loan, OVID Technologies
Wireless access
Publications: Minnesota Transportation Libraries Recent Acquisitions
Partic in Capitol Area Library Consortium; Metronet; Midwest Transportation Knowledge Network (MTKN); Minitex Library Information Network; OCLC Online Computer Library Center, Inc
Open Mon-Fri 8-4:30

G MINNESOTA GEOLOGICAL SURVEY LIBRARY*, 2642 University Ave W, 55114-1032. SAN 324-766X. Tel: 612-627-4780. FAX: 612-627-4778. E-mail: mgs@umn.edu. Web Site: www.mngs.umn.edu/index.html. *Dir,* Harvey Thorleifson; E-mail: thorleif@umn.edu
Founded 1974
Library Holdings: Bk Vols 1,700; Per Subs 130
Subject Interests: Minn geology, Seasonal thermal energy storage, Underground construction, Underground space
Restriction: Non-circulating to the pub

S MINNESOTA HISTORICAL SOCIETY LIBRARY*, 345 Kellogg Blvd W, 55102-1906. SAN 347-9137. Tel: 651-259-3300. Interlibrary Loan Service Tel: 651-259-3308. FAX: 651-297-7436. E-mail: reference@mnhs.org. Web Site: www.mnhs.org/library. *Dir,* Jennifer Jones; Tel: 651-259-3246, E-mail: jennifer.jones@mnhs.org; *Coll Mgt,* Dennis Meissner; Tel: 651-259-3350, E-mail: dennis.meissner@mnhs.org; *Ref Serv,* Tracey Baker; E-mail: tracey.baker@mnhs.org; Staff 41 (MLS 10, Non-MLS 31)
Founded 1849
Library Holdings: Bk Titles 411,884; Per Subs 1,300
Special Collections: Art; Great Northern & Northern Pacific Railroad Papers; History of Native Peoples of Minnesota; Hubert H Humphrey Papers; Minnesota Newspapers, 1849-2008; Photographs; Posters; State & Local Government (Minnesota State Archives), rec; Walter Mondale Papers. Oral History; State Document Depository
Subject Interests: Genealogy, Minn hist
Automation Activity & Vendor Info: (Cataloging) PALS; (OPAC) PALS
Wireless access
Function: Archival coll, Audio & video playback equip for onsite use, Computers for patron use, Copy machines, e-mail serv, Electronic databases & coll, Exhibits, ILL available, Newsp ref libr, Online cat, Orientations, Ref & res, Res performed for a fee, Telephone ref
Partic in Capitol Area Librs Coop; OCLC Online Computer Library Center, Inc; OCLC Research Library Partnership
Open Tues Noon-8, Wed-Sat 9-4
Restriction: Non-circulating, Photo ID required for access, Registered patrons only

G MINNESOTA LEGISLATIVE REFERENCE LIBRARY*, 645 State Office Bldg, 100 Rev Dr Martin Luther King Jr Blvd, 55155-1050. SAN 308-7751. Tel: 651-296-3398. Reference Tel: 651-296-8338. FAX: 651-296-9731. E-mail: refdesk@lrl.leg.mn. Web Site: www.leg.state.mn.us/lrl/lrl.asp. *Dir,* Robbie La Fleur; Tel: 651-296-8310; *Dep Dir,* Elizabeth Lincoln; Tel: 651-296-0594, E-mail: elincoln@lrl.leg.mn; Staff 6 (MLS 6)
Founded 1969
Jul 2009-Jun 2010 Income $1,085,000. Mats Exp $74,500, Books $10,000, Per/Ser (Incl. Access Fees) $45,500, Electronic Ref Mat (Incl. Access Fees) $19,000. Sal $900,000
Library Holdings: Bk Titles 45,000; Per Subs 600
Special Collections: Bills Introduced for Ten Years; Interim Committee Reports; Minnesota Documents Coll; Minnesota Government Manual, 1887-present; Minnesota Government Publications, on fiche; Senate & House Journals, tapes, committee minutes. State Document Depository
Subject Interests: Govt
Automation Activity & Vendor Info: (Cataloging) Ex Libris Group; (Circulation) Ex Libris Group; (OPAC) Ex Libris Group
Database Vendor: Dialog, EBSCOhost, LexisNexis, Newsbank
Function: Govt ref serv, ILL available, Res libr
Publications: Just In (Monthly bulletin)
Partic in Capital Area Library Consortium; Minitex Library Information Network; OCLC Online Computer Library Center, Inc
Open Mon-Fri 8-4:30
Restriction: In-house use for visitors, Non-circulating to the pub, Open to pub for ref only, Pub use on premises, Restricted borrowing privileges

G MINNESOTA POLLUTION CONTROL AGENCY LIBRARY, 520 Lafayette Rd, 55155-4194. SAN 320-684X. Tel: 651-757-2547. FAX: 651-282-5446. Web Site: www.pca.state.mn.us. *Librn,* Kathleen Malec; E-mail: kathy.malec@state.mn.us; Staff 1 (MLS 1)
Library Holdings: Bk Vols 25,000; Per Subs 125
Special Collections: EPA Coll; MPCA Coll
Subject Interests: Air pollution, Pollution control, Solid wastes, Sustainable develop, Water pollution
Partic in OCLC Online Computer Library Center, Inc
Open Mon-Fri 8-4

GL MINNESOTA STATE LAW LIBRARY*, Minnesota Judicial Ctr, Rm G25, 25 Rev Dr Martin Luther King Jr Blvd, 55155. SAN 308-7794. Tel: 651-296-2775. FAX: 651-296-6740. Web Site: www.lawlibrary.state.mn.us. *Actg State Librn,* Judy Rehak; E-mail: judy.rehak@courts.state.mn.us; *Head, Pub Serv,* Susan Larson; *Head, Tech Serv,* Dennis Skrade; *Outreach & Develop Librn,* Daniel Lunde; Staff 14 (MLS 9.5, Non-MLS 4.5)
Founded 1849
Library Holdings: Bk Vols 260,000; Per Subs 600
Special Collections: Minnesota Legal Periodical Index; Minnesota Trial Coll; Program to Collect Prof Papers of Retired Justices of Minnesota Supreme Court
Subject Interests: Am law, Minn law
Automation Activity & Vendor Info: (Cataloging) Ex Libris Group; (Circulation) Ex Libris Group; (ILL) OCLC; (OPAC) Ex Libris Group; (Serials) Ex Libris Group
Database Vendor: LexisNexis, Westlaw
Wireless access
Partic in Capitol Area Library Consortium; Metronet; Minitex Library Information Network; OCLC Online Computer Library Center, Inc
Open Mon-Fri 8:30-5

R MOUNT ZION TEMPLE*, Bloom Library, 1300 Summit Ave, 55105. SAN 308-7808. Tel: 651-698-3881. FAX: 651-698-1263. E-mail: mountzion@mzion.org. Web Site: www.mzion.org. *Librn,* Robert A Epstein; Staff 1 (MLS 1)
Founded 1929
Library Holdings: Bks on Deafness & Sign Lang 2; CDs 244; DVDs 91; Large Print Bks 2; Bk Titles 9,900; Per Subs 6
Special Collections: Children's Coll; Jewish Feminism (Margolis Coll)
Subject Interests: Judaica
Automation Activity & Vendor Info: (Cataloging) ComPanion Corp; (Circulation) ComPanion Corp
Wireless access

C NORTHWESTERN COLLEGE*, Berntsen Library, 3003 Snelling Ave N, 55113. SAN 320-9326. Tel: 651-631-5241. Reference Tel: 651-286-7708. FAX: 651-631-5598. Web Site: nwc.edu/library. *Dir,* Ruth McGuire; *Cat Librn,* Dawn Krist; *Electronic Serv Librn,* Nathan Farley; *Ref & Instruction Librn,* Jessica Nelson; *Ser Librn,* Linda Rust; *Acq, Supvr,* Katie Hagen; *Circ Supvr,* Becky Schleicher; *ILL Supvr,* Cindy Carlson; *Weekend Per Supvr,* Greg Rosauer; *Archivist,* Dora Wagner; Staff 11 (MLS 6, Non-MLS 5)
Founded 1902. Enrl 2,300; Fac 99; Highest Degree: Master
Library Holdings: Bk Vols 123,000; Per Subs 919
Special Collections: W B Riley Coll, bks, ms, scrapbks
Automation Activity & Vendor Info: (Acquisitions) Innovative Interfaces, Inc; (Cataloging) Innovative Interfaces, Inc; (Circulation) Innovative Interfaces, Inc; (Course Reserve) Innovative Interfaces, Inc; (ILL) Innovative Interfaces, Inc; (Media Booking) Innovative Interfaces, Inc; (OPAC) Innovative Interfaces, Inc; (Serials) Innovative Interfaces, Inc
Wireless access
Partic in Cooperating Libraries in Consortium; OCLC Online Computer Library Center, Inc
Open Mon-Thurs 7:40am-11:30pm, Fri 7:40-6, Sat 10-6, Sun 3-10

S QUATREFOIL LIBRARY*, 1619 Dayton Ave, Ste 105, 55104-6206. SAN 329-1588. Tel: 651-641-0969. E-mail: quatrefoillibrary@yahoo.com. Web Site: www.qlibrary.org. *Librn,* Kathy Robbins
Founded 1986
Library Holdings: Braille Volumes 15; CDs 300; DVDs 500; Bk Vols 11,000; Per Subs 40; Videos 800
Subject Interests: Bisexual, Gay & lesbian
Automation Activity & Vendor Info: (OPAC) Follett Software
Publications: Quatrefolio (Quarterly)
Special Services for the Blind - Braille bks
Open Mon-Fri 7pm-9pm, Sat 10-5, Sun 1-5

GL RAMSEY COUNTY LAW LIBRARY*, 1815 Court House, 55102. SAN 308-7832. Tel: 651-266-8391. FAX: 651-266-8399. *Librn,* Sara Galligan; E-mail: sara.galligan@co.ramsey.mn.us; Staff 3.5 (MLS 2, Non-MLS 1.5)
Founded 1936

Special Collections: Self-Represented Litigants
Subject Interests: Minn law
Automation Activity & Vendor Info: (Serials) Inmagic, Inc.
Database Vendor: Westlaw
Wireless access
Partic in Metronet
Open Mon-Fri 8-4:30

M REGIONS HOSPITAL*, Medical Library, 640 Jackson St, 55101. SAN 308-7883. Tel: 651-254-3607. FAX: 651-254-3427. *Head Librn,* Mary Wittenbreer
Founded 1940
Library Holdings: Bk Vols 800; Per Subs 270
Automation Activity & Vendor Info: (Cataloging) EOS International
Wireless access
Partic in Twin Cities Biomedical Consortium
Open Mon-Fri 7:30-5

C SAINT CATHERINE UNIVERSITY*, Libraries, Media Services & Archives, 2004 Randolph Ave, Mail F-10, 55105-1794. SAN 347-8866. Tel: 651-690-6650. Circulation Tel: 651-690-8737. Interlibrary Loan Service Tel: 651-690-6655. Reference Tel: 651-690-6652. FAX: 651-690-8636. Web Site: library.stkate.edu. *Dir,* Randall Schroeder; *Head, Access Serv,* Jennifer Peters; *Head, Spec Coll, Univ Archivist,* Deborah Kloiber; Tel: 651-690-6599, E-mail: dwloiber@stkate.edu; *Head, Tech Serv,* Emily J Asch; Tel: 651-690-6653, E-mail: ejasch@stkate.edu; *Syst Librn,* Amy Shaw; Tel: 651-690-6423, E-mail: amshaw@stkate.edu; *Acad Media Serv Mgr,* Ann Piotrowski; Tel: 651-690-6658, E-mail: alpiotrowski@stkate.edu; *Br Mgr,* Cynthia Graham; Tel: 651-690-7780, E-mail: ckgraham@stkate.edu. Subject Specialists: *Music,* Amy Shaw; Staff 14.49 (MLS 10.87, Non-MLS 3.62)
Founded 1905. Enrl 5,328; Fac 261; Highest Degree: Doctorate
Jun 2011-May 2012. Mats Exp $867,460, Books $217,668, Per/Ser (Incl. Access Fees) $365,737, AV Equip $45,955, AV Mat $31,456, Electronic Ref Mat (Incl. Access Fees) $176,115, Presv $30,529. Sal $962,361 (Prof $781,674)
Library Holdings: AV Mats 7,218; Bks on Deafness & Sign Lang 699; CDs 2,278; DVDs 4,648; e-books 17,437; e-journals 60,316; Electronic Media & Resources 8,000; Microforms 180,946; Music Scores 6,079; Bk Titles 155,094; Bk Vols 185,537; Per Subs 312; Videos 4,648
Special Collections: Autographs & Manuscripts (Mother Antonia McHugh Coll), bks, letters; Children's Literature (Ruth Sawyer Coll), multi media; Liturgical Art (Ade Bethune Coll); Muellerleile Coll of Printing; Rare Bks (Charlotte Hill Slade Coll & Mitsch Coll), first editions & fine bindings. Oral History
Automation Activity & Vendor Info: (Acquisitions) Innovative Interfaces, Inc; (Cataloging) Innovative Interfaces, Inc; (Circulation) Innovative Interfaces, Inc; (Course Reserve) Innovative Interfaces, Inc; (ILL) OCLC ILLiad; (Media Booking) Innovative Interfaces, Inc; (OPAC) Innovative Interfaces, Inc; (Serials) Innovative Interfaces, Inc
Database Vendor: ABC-CLIO, Alexander Street Press, American Chemical Society, American Psychological Association (APA), Annual Reviews, ARTstor, BioOne, Cambridge Scientific Abstracts, Children's Literature Comprehensive Database Company (CLCD), Coutts Information Service, CQ Press, CredoReference, EBSCO Information Services, EBSCOhost, Elsevier, Emerald, Facts on File, Gale Cengage Learning, H W Wilson, infoUSA, Ingenta, Innovative Interfaces, Inc, JSTOR, LexisNexis, McGraw-Hill, Medline, Modern Language Association, Newsbank, OCLC, OCLC FirstSearch, OCLC WebJunction, OCLC WorldShare Interlibrary Loan, OVID Technologies, Oxford Communications, Project MUSE, ProQuest, PubMed, ReferenceUSA, RefWorks, Sage, ScienceDirect, SerialsSolutions, Springshare, LLC, Standard & Poor's, Thomson - Web of Science, ValueLine, Wiley, Wiley InterScience, Wilson - Wilson Web
Wireless access
Partic in Cooperating Libraries in Consortium; Metronet; Minitex Library Information Network; OCLC Online Computer Library Center, Inc
Special Services for the Deaf - ADA equip; Am sign lang & deaf culture; Bks on deafness & sign lang; Closed caption videos; Coll on deaf educ; Deaf publ; Sorenson video relay syst
Special Services for the Blind - Computer with voice synthesizer for visually impaired persons
Open Mon-Thurs 8am-11:30pm, Fri 8am-9:30pm, Sat 8-8, Sun 10am-11pm
Friends of the Library Group

Departmental Libraries:

MINNEAPOLIS CAMPUS, 601 25th Ave S, Minneapolis, 55454, SAN 308-6895. Tel: 651-690-7784. Web Site: www.stkate.edu. *Librn,* Cynthia Graham; Tel: 651-690-7780, E-mail: ckgraham@stkate.edu; *Media Serv Supvr,* Ronnie Carlson; Tel: 651-690-7792, E-mail: rcarlson@stkate.edu; *Circ,* Sue Gray; Tel: 651-690-7898; *ILL,* Monica Olmschenk; Tel: 651-690-7782. Subject Specialists: *Health sci,* Cynthia Graham; Staff 3 (MLS 2, Non-MLS 1)
Founded 1964. Highest Degree: Doctorate
Subject Interests: Allied health, Nursing, Phys therapy
Special Services for the Deaf - Captioned film dep; Spec interest per
Special Services for the Blind - Braille bks; Computer with voice synthesizer for visually impaired persons
Restriction: Open to students, fac & staff
Friends of the Library Group

J SAINT PAUL COLLEGE LIBRARY*, 235 Marshall Ave, 55102. SAN 308-7905. Tel: 651-846-1410. FAX: 651-221-1416. Web Site: www.saintpaul.edu/library. *Librn,* Ben Tri; E-mail: ben.tri@saintpaul.edu; Staff 1 (MLS 1)
Founded 1966. Enrl 3,000; Fac 170
Library Holdings: Bk Vols 32,000; Per Subs 200
Wireless access
Open Mon-Thurs 7am-8pm, Fri 7-4

P SAINT PAUL PUBLIC LIBRARY*, 90 W Fourth St, 55102-1668. SAN 347-9226. Tel: 651-266-7000. Interlibrary Loan Service Tel: 651-501-6306. Administration Tel: 651-266-7073. FAX: 651-266-7060. Interlibrary Loan Service FAX: 651-501-6307. TDD: 651-298-4184. E-mail: spplweb@ci.stpaul.mn.us. Web Site: www.sppl.org. *Dir,* Kit Hadley; Tel: 651-266-7070, E-mail: kit.hadley@ci.stpaul.mn.us; Staff 3 (MLS 3)
Special Collections: US Document Depository
Automation Activity & Vendor Info: (Acquisitions) Innovative Interfaces, Inc; (Cataloging) Innovative Interfaces, Inc; (Circulation) Innovative Interfaces, Inc; (ILL) Innovative Interfaces, Inc; (OPAC) Innovative Interfaces, Inc; (Serials) Innovative Interfaces, Inc
Database Vendor: OCLC FirstSearch
Wireless access
Function: Archival coll, AV serv, Govt ref serv, Handicapped accessible, Homebound delivery serv, ILL available, Magnifiers for reading, Newsp ref libr, Online searches, Outside serv via phone, mail, e-mail & web, Photocopying/Printing, Prog for adults, Prog for children & young adult, Ref serv available, Referrals accepted, Summer reading prog, Wheelchair accessible, Workshops
Publications: Communique (Newsletter)
Special Services for the Deaf - Accessible learning ctr
Restriction: 24-hr pass syst for students only
Friends of the Library Group

Branches: 12

ARLINGTON HILLS, 1105 Greenbrier St, 55106-2504, SAN 347-9250. Tel: 651-793-3930. FAX: 651-793-3932. E-mail: branch.arlington@ci.stpaul.mn.us.

DAYTON'S BLUFF, 645 E Seventh St, 55106, SAN 328-8005. Tel: 651-793-1699. FAX: 651-793-1697. E-mail: branch.daytonsbluff@ci.stpaul.mn.us.

HAMLINE - MIDWAY, 1558 W Minnehaha Ave, 55104-1264, SAN 347-9285. Tel: 651-642-0293. FAX: 651-642-0323. E-mail: branch.hamline@ci.stpaul.mn.us.

HAYDEN HEIGHTS, 1456 White Bear Ave, 55106-2405, SAN 347-9315. Tel: 651-793-3934. FAX: 651-793-3936. E-mail: branch.hayden-heights@ci.stpaul.mn.us.

HIGHLAND PARK, 1974 Ford Pkwy, 55116-1922, SAN 347-934X. Tel: 651-695-3700. FAX: 651-695-3701. E-mail: branch.highland@ci.stpaul.mn.us.

MERRIAM PARK, 1831 Marshall Ave, 55104-6010, SAN 347-9404. Tel: 651-642-0385. FAX: 651-642-0391. E-mail: branch.merriam@ci.stpaul.mn.us.

RICE STREET, 1011 Rice St, 55117, SAN 347-9439. Tel: 651-558-2223. FAX: 651-558-2225. E-mail: branch.ricestreet@ci.stpaul.mn.us.

RIVERVIEW, One E George St, 55107-2906, SAN 347-9463. Tel: 651-292-6626. FAX: 651-292-6575. E-mail: branch.riverview@ci.stpaul.mn.us.

RONDO COMMUNITY OUTREACH LIBRARY, 461 N Dale St, 55103. Tel: 651-266-7400. FAX: 651-266-7410. Web Site: branch.rondo@ci.stpaul.mn.us. *Br Mgr,* Charlene McKenzie; E-mail: charlene.mckenzie@ci.stpaul.mn.us
Library Holdings: CDs 5,835; DVDs 8,569; Bk Vols 77,382; Per Subs 85
Special Collections: ESL Coll; IBWT Coll; Small Business Partnership Coll
Subject Interests: African-Am culture, Hist
Open Mon-Thurs 10-9, Fri & Sat 10-5:30, Sun 1-5
Friends of the Library Group

SAINT ANTHONY PARK, 2245 Como Ave, 55108-1719, SAN 347-9498. Tel: 651-642-0411. FAX: 651-642-0358. E-mail: branch.stanthony@ci.stpaul.mn.us.

SUN RAY, 2105 Wilson Ave, 55119-4033, SAN 347-9528. Tel: 651-501-6300. FAX: 651-501-6303. E-mail: branch.sunray@ci.stpaul.mn.us.

WEST SEVENTH, 265 Oneida St, 55102. Tel: 651-298-5516. Web Site: branch.westseventh@ci.stpaul.mn.us. *Area Librn,* Pat Gerlach; E-mail: pat.gerlach@ci.stpaul.mn.us; *Br Mgr,* Lisa Hage; E-mail: lisa.hage@ci.stpaul.mn.us
Library Holdings: CDs 819; DVDs 1,380; Bk Titles 7,823; Per Subs 14; Talking Bks 304

Open Mon & Thurs 12:30-8, Tues 11:30-5:30, Wed & Fri 10-5:30
Friends of the Library Group
Bookmobiles: 1

S 3M INFORMATION RESEARCH & SOLUTIONS*, 3M Corporate Headquarters, 2701 Hudson Rd, 55144. SAN 347-9560. Tel: 651-733-1110, 651-736-5565. FAX: 651-736-6495. Web Site: www.mmm.com.
Library Holdings: Bk Titles 67,000; Bk Vols 100,000; Per Subs 1,550
Automation Activity & Vendor Info: (OPAC) Ex Libris Group; (Serials) Ex Libris Group
Publications: 3M Union List of Serials
Partic in Dialog Corp; OCLC Online Computer Library Center, Inc; Questal Orbit
Open Mon-Fri 8-5

A UNITED STATES ARMY*, Corps of Engineers Saint Paul District Technical Library, 180 Fifth St E, Ste 700, 55101-1678. SAN 347-9854. Tel: 651-290-5680. FAX: 651-290-5256. Web Site: www.mvp.usace.army.mil. *Librn,* Kevin Bokay; E-mail: kevin.bokay@us.army.mil
Founded 1972
Library Holdings: Bk Vols 4,884; Per Subs 350
Special Collections: Annual Reports of the Chief of Engineers, US Army
Subject Interests: DM construction, Eng, Environ studies, Hydrol, Water res
Wireless access
Partic in OCLC Online Computer Library Center, Inc
Open Mon-Fri 7:30-4:30

GL US COURTS LIBRARY*, Eighth Circuit Library, 512 Federal Court Bldg, 316 N Robert St, 55101. SAN 308-7964. Tel: 651-848-1320. FAX: 651-848-1325. Web Site: www.ca8.uscourts.gov. *Librn,* Andrea Wambach; E-mail: andrea_wambach@ca8.uscourts.gov; *Tech Serv,* Tracey Smith; Staff 2 (MLS 1, Non-MLS 1)
Library Holdings: Bk Vols 20,000; Per Subs 30
Automation Activity & Vendor Info: (Cataloging) SirsiDynix; (OPAC) SirsiDynix
Restriction: Staff use only

CR UNIVERSITY OF SAINT THOMAS*, O'Shaughnessy-Frey Library, 2115 Summit Ave, Mail Box 5004, 55105. SAN 308-7581. Tel: 651-962-5001. Circulation Tel: 651-962-5494. Administration Tel: 651-962-5014. FAX: 651-962-5406. Web Site: www.stthomas.edu/libraries/. *Dir of Libr,* Daniel Ross Gjelten; Tel: 651-962-5005, E-mail: drgjelten@stthomas.edu; *Assoc Dir, Digital Initiatives,* John Heintz; Tel: 651-962-5018, E-mail: jpheintz@stthomas.edu; *Assoc Dir, Pub Serv,* Diane Knights; Tel: 651-962-5026, E-mail: dkknights@stthomas.edu; *Assoc Dir, Res & Instruction,* Janice Kragness; Tel: 651-962-4645, E-mail: jlkragness@stthomas.edu; *Assoc Dir, Tech Serv,* Position Currently Open; *Coordr, Libr Serv,* Julie Kimlinger; E-mail: jakimlinger@stthomas.edu; *Univ Archivist,* Ann M Kenne; Tel: 651-962-5461, E-mail: amkenne@stthomas.edu; *ILL,* Faith E Bonitz; E-mail: febonitz@stthomas.edu. Subject Specialists: *English, Polit sci,* Daniel Ross Gjelten; *Communications,* Diane Knights; *Polit sci,* Position Currently Open; *Hist,* Ann M Kenne; Staff 28 (MLS 15, Non-MLS 13)
Founded 1885. Enrl 10,839; Fac 450; Highest Degree: Doctorate
Jul 2010-Jun 2011. Mats Exp $3,670,363, Books $350,856, Per/Ser (Incl. Access Fees) $1,282,256, Micro $29,355, AV Mat $64,694, Presv $19,210. Sal $2,117,011 (Prof $1,044,636)
Library Holdings: AV Mats 12,837; e-books 108,861; e-journals 44,256; Microforms 179,116; Bk Vols 302,788; Per Subs 45,266
Special Collections: Belloc-Chestereon Coll; Celtic Coll; French Memoir Coll; Luxembourgian Coll; University Archives; UST Research Online
Subject Interests: Bus, Educ, Lit, Psychol, Theol
Automation Activity & Vendor Info: (Acquisitions) Innovative Interfaces, Inc; (Cataloging) Innovative Interfaces, Inc; (Circulation) Innovative Interfaces, Inc; (Course Reserve) Innovative Interfaces, Inc; (ILL) OCLC ILLiad; (OPAC) Innovative Interfaces, Inc; (Serials) Innovative Interfaces, Inc
Database Vendor: ABC-CLIO, ACM (Association for Computing Machinery), Alexander Street Press, American Chemical Society, American Geophysical Union, American Mathematical Society, American Physical Society, American Psychological Association (APA), Annual Reviews, ARTstor, BioOne, Blackwell, Bloomberg, Bowker, Cambridge Scientific Abstracts, Coutts Information Service, CQ Press, CRC Press/Taylor & Francis Group, CredoReference, EBSCO Information Services, EBSCOhost, Elsevier, Emerald, Factiva.com, Facts on File, Gale Cengage Learning, H W Wilson, Haworth Pres Inc, HeinOnline, Hoovers, IBISWorld, IEEE (Institute of Electrical & Electronics Engineers), Ingenta, Innovative Interfaces, Inc, ISI Web of Knowledge, JSTOR, Kompass, LexisNexis, Luna Imaging/Insight, Newsbank, Newsbank-Readex, OCLC, OCLC FirstSearch, OCLC WorldShare Interlibrary Loan, OVID Technologies, ProQuest, PubMed, ReferenceUSA, RefWorks, ScienceDirect, SerialsSolutions, STAT!Ref (Teton Data Systems), Thomson - Web of Science, Wiley, Wilson - Wilson Web, YBP Library Services
Wireless access
Function: Archival coll, Audio & video playback equip for onsite use, Computers for patron use, Copy machines, Doc delivery serv, e-mail & chat, E-Reserves, Electronic databases & coll, Handicapped accessible, ILL available, Music CDs, Online cat, Online ref, Online searches, Orientations, Outside serv via phone, mail, e-mail & web, Printer for laptops & handheld devices, Pub access computers, Ref & res, Ref serv available, Ref serv in person, Res libr, Scanner, Spoken cassettes & DVDs, Telephone ref, VHS videos, Video lending libr, Web-catalog
Partic in Cooperating Libraries in Consortium; Minitex Library Information Network; OCLC Online Computer Library Center, Inc; TexSHARE - Texas State Library & Archives Commission
Special Services for the Deaf - Assistive tech; Bks on deafness & sign lang
Special Services for the Blind - Assistive/Adapted tech devices, equip & products; Computer with voice synthesizer for visually impaired persons
Open Mon-Thurs 7:30am-2am, Fri 7:30am-8pm, Sat 10-6, Sun Noon-2am

Departmental Libraries:

ARCHBISHOP IRELAND MEMORIAL LIBRARY, 2260 Summit Ave, Mail No IRL, 55105, SAN 377-0214. Tel: 651-962-5453. Administration Tel: 651-962-5451. FAX: 651-962-5460. Web Site: www.stthomas.edu/libraries/ireland. *Dir,* N Curtis Lemay; E-mail: nclemay@stthomas.edu; *Circ Mgr,* Conie Borchardt; E-mail: clborchardt@stthomas.edu; *Tech Serv,* Betsy J Polakowski; Tel: 651-962-5452, E-mail: ejpolakowski@stthomas.edu; Staff 5 (MLS 4, Non-MLS 1)
Founded 1894. Enrl 110; Fac 24; Highest Degree: Doctorate
Jul 2010-Jun 2011. Mats Exp $415,452, Books $38,364, Per/Ser (Incl. Access Fees) $60,192, Presv $3,144. Sal $369,620 (Prof $217,037)
Library Holdings: AV Mats 51; e-books 108,861; e-journals 44,256; Microforms 1,249; Bk Vols 109,149; Per Subs 393
Subject Interests: Theol
Database Vendor: ebrary, infoUSA, Ingram Library Services, Swets Information Services
Open Mon-Thurs 8am-10pm, Fri 8-6, Sat 10-5, Sun 1-10
Friends of the Library Group

CHARLES J KEFFER LIBRARY, 1000 LaSalle Ave, MOH 206, Minneapolis, 55403, SAN 377-0230. Tel: 651-962-4642. FAX: 651-962-4648. Web Site: www.stthomas.edu/libraries/keffer. *Assoc Dir, Res & Instruction,* Janice Kragness; Tel: 651-962-4645, E-mail: jlkragness@stthomas.edu; *Ref Librn,* Merrie Davidson; Tel: 651-962-4661, E-mail: merrie.davidson@stthomas.edu; *Ref Librn,* Laura Hansen; Tel: 651-962-4646, E-mail: laura.hansen@stthomas.edu; *Ref Librn,* Andrea Koeppe; Tel: 651-962-4647, E-mail: arhudson@stthomas.edu; *Ref Librn,* Donna Nix; Tel: 651-962-4662, E-mail: denix@stthomas.edu; *Circ,* Linnae Weinrich; Tel: 651-962-4644, E-mail: ljweinrich@stthomas.edu; *Circ,* William Zych; Tel: 651-962-4667, E-mail: wrzych@stthomas.edu. Subject Specialists: *Bus,* Janice Kragness; *Educ,* Merrie Davidson; *Bus,* Laura Hansen; *Bus,* Andrea Koeppe; *Educ,* Donna Nix; Staff 6 (MLS 4, Non-MLS 2)
Founded 1992. Highest Degree: Doctorate
Jul 2010-Jun 2011. Mats Exp $467,859, Presv $2,228. Sal $373,464 (Prof $243,938)
Library Holdings: AV Mats 135; e-books 108,861; e-journals 44,256; Microforms 835,727; Bk Vols 32,000; Per Subs 261
Subject Interests: Bus, Educ, Psychol
Database Vendor: Dun & Bradstreet, ebrary, infoUSA, Ingram Library Services, Project MUSE, ProQuest, ValueLine, Wiley InterScience
Function: e-mail & chat, E-Reserves, Electronic databases & coll, Handicapped accessible, ILL available, Online cat, Online info literacy tutorials on the web & in blackboard, Online ref, Online searches, Photocopying/Printing, Pub access computers, Ref & res, Ref serv available, Ref serv in person, Res libr, Scanner
Open Mon-Thurs 8am-10pm, Fri 8-6, Sat 10-5, Sun 1-10

CL WILLIAM MITCHELL COLLEGE OF LAW*, Warren E Burger Library, 871 Summit Ave, 55105. SAN 308-7980. Tel: 651-290-6333. Reference Tel: 651-290-6424. FAX: 651-290-6318. E-mail: reference@wmitchell.edu. Web Site: web.wmitchell.edu/library. *Assoc Dean, Info Res & Scholarly Communications,* Simon Canick; *Asst Dir, Coll Res,* Anne Poulter; Tel: 651-290-6303, E-mail: anne.poulter@wmitchell.edu; *Asst Dir, Libr Tech,* Position Currently Open; *Asst Dir, Res & Instrul Serv,* Karen Westwood; Tel: 651-290-7618, E-mail: karen.westwood@wmitchell.edu; Staff 7.75 (MLS 7.75)
Founded 1958. Highest Degree: Doctorate
Library Holdings: AV Mats 809; Electronic Media & Resources 28,851; Microforms 156,248; Bk Titles 74,599; Bk Vols 334,739
Subject Interests: Law, Taxation
Automation Activity & Vendor Info: (Acquisitions) Innovative Interfaces, Inc; (Cataloging) Innovative Interfaces, Inc; (Circulation) Innovative Interfaces, Inc; (Course Reserve) Innovative Interfaces, Inc; (OPAC) Innovative Interfaces, Inc; (Serials) Innovative Interfaces, Inc
Database Vendor: Bloomberg, Cassidy Cataloguing Services, Inc, EBSCOhost, Ex Libris Group, Fastcase, Gale Cengage Learning, Haworth

Pres Inc, HeinOnline, Innovative Interfaces, Inc, JSTOR, LexisNexis, Loislaw, Newsbank-Readex, OCLC FirstSearch, OCLC WorldShare Interlibrary Loan, Oxford Online, ProQuest, Sage, Thomson Carswell, Westlaw, Wiley InterScience, Wilson - Wilson Web
Wireless access
Partic in Minitex Library Information Network
Open Mon-Thurs 7:30am-Midnight, Fri 7:30am-10pm, Sat 9am-10pm, Sun 9am-Midnight

SAINT PETER

C GUSTAVUS ADOLPHUS COLLEGE, Folke Bernadotte Memorial Library, 800 W College Ave, 56082. SAN 348-0097. Tel: 507-933-7556. Circulation Tel: 507-933-7558. Interlibrary Loan Service Tel: 507-933-7564. Reference Tel: 507-933-7567. FAX: 507-933-6292. E-mail: folke@gustavus.edu. Web Site: www.gustavus.edu/library. *Chair/Ref Librn,* Daniel Mollner; Tel: 507-933-7569, E-mail: dmollner@gustavus.edu; *Coll Access & Ref Librn,* Julie Gilbert; Tel: 507-933-7552, E-mail: jgilber2@gustavus.edu; *Electronic Res & Ref Librn,* Anna Hulseberg; Tel: 507-933-7566, E-mail: ahulsebe@gustavus.edu; *Ref & Instruction Librn,* Barbara Fister; Tel: 507-933-7553, E-mail: fister@gustavus.edu; *Col Archivist, Ref Librn,* Jeff Jenson; Tel: 507-933-7572, E-mail: jjenson@gustavus.edu; *Ref Librn,* Michelle Twait; Tel: 507-933-7563, E-mail: mtwait@gustavus.edu; *Doc Delivery Spec,* Sonja Timmerman; E-mail: stimmer2@gustavus.edu; Staff 15 (MLS 6, Non-MLS 9)
Founded 1862. Enrl 2,443; Fac 214; Highest Degree: Bachelor
Jun 2013-May 2014 Income $1,871,211. Mats Exp $624,742. Sal $856,364 (Prof $760,456)
Library Holdings: AV Mats 19,509; CDs 5,284; DVDs 3,207; e-journals 149; Electronic Media & Resources 64; Microforms 43,075; Music Scores 5,356; Bk Vols 280,616; Per Subs 424; Videos 2,124
Special Collections: College Archives; Gene Basset Political Cartoons; Hasselquist International Studies Coll; Heitzig Coll; John Updike Coll; Lutheran Church Archives; Mettetal Record Coll; Rezmerski Science Fiction Coll; Scandinavian American Coll; Scullin Jazz Coll; Selma Lagerloff (Nils Sahlin Coll), bks, pamphlets. US Document Depository
Automation Activity & Vendor Info: (Acquisitions) Ex Libris Group; (Cataloging) OCLC; (Circulation) Ex Libris Group; (Course Reserve) Ex Libris Group; (ILL) Ex Libris Group; (OPAC) Ex Libris Group; (Serials) EBSCO Online
Database Vendor: Agricola, Alexander Street Press, American Chemical Society, American Mathematical Society, American Physical Society, Annual Reviews, ARTstor, Cambridge Scientific Abstracts, EBSCOhost, Ex Libris Group, Gale Cengage Learning, ISI Web of Knowledge, JSTOR, LexisNexis, Marcive, Inc, Modern Language Association, OCLC ArticleFirst, OCLC CAMIO, OCLC FirstSearch, OCLC WorldShare Interlibrary Loan, Oxford Online, Project MUSE, ProQuest, PubMed, Springer-Verlag, Springshare, LLC, Thomson - Web of Science, ValueLine, Wiley
Wireless access
Function: 24/7 Electronic res, 24/7 Online cat, Archival coll, Audio & video playback equip for onsite use, AV serv, Computers for patron use, Doc delivery serv, E-Reserves, Electronic databases & coll, Free DVD rentals, Handicapped accessible, ILL available, Magnifiers for reading, Microfiche/film & reading machines, Music CDs, Online cat, Online ref, Online searches, Printer for laptops & handheld devices, Pub access computers, Ref serv available, Ref serv in person, Scanner, Telephone ref, VHS videos, Video lending libr
Partic in Minitex Library Information Network; MnPALS; OCLC Online Computer Library Center, Inc
Special Services for the Blind - Magnifiers; Reader equip; Screen enlargement software for people with visual disabilities
Open Mon-Thurs 8am-1am, Fri 8-6, Sat 10-6, Sun 11am-1am
Restriction: Authorized patrons
Friends of the Library Group

S NICOLLET COUNTY HISTORICAL SOCIETY*, Treaty Site History Center Museum & Archives Library, 1851 N Minnesota Ave, 56082. SAN 325-500X. Tel: 507-934-2160. FAX: 507-934-8715. *Dir,* Position Currently Open
Library Holdings: Bk Titles 350; Bk Vols 500
Subject Interests: County hist, Genealogy, Hist, Southern Minn
Database Vendor: OCLC FirstSearch
Open Tues-Fri 10-4

P SAINT PETER PUBLIC LIBRARY*, 601 S Washington Ave, 56082. SAN 347-4429. Tel: 507-934-7420. FAX: 507-934-1204. E-mail: lib@saintpetermn.gov. Web Site: www.saintpetermn.gov/library. *Lead Librn,* Doug Wolfe; *Asst Librn, Tech Serv Librn,* Anissa Sandland; Staff 4 (MLS 1, Non-MLS 3)
Library Holdings: Bk Vols 45,000; Per Subs 183
Automation Activity & Vendor Info: (Acquisitions) SirsiDynix; (Cataloging) SirsiDynix; (Circulation) SirsiDynix; (Course Reserve) SirsiDynix; (ILL) SirsiDynix; (Media Booking) SirsiDynix; (OPAC) SirsiDynix; (Serials) SirsiDynix
Wireless access
Mem of Traverse Des Sioux Library Cooperative
Open Mon-Thurs 10-8, Fri 10-5, Sat 9-4
Friends of the Library Group

M SAINT PETER REGIONAL TREATMENT CENTER LIBRARIES*, MSH Education Dept Library, 2100 Sheppard Dr, 56082. SAN 348-0151. Tel: 507-985-2320. *In Charge,* Barbara Pelton; Staff 5 (MLS 1, Non-MLS 4)
Founded 1878
Library Holdings: CDs 500; DVDs 550; Bk Titles 12,000; Bk Vols 12,600; Per Subs 12
Subject Interests: Alcoholic dependents, Bks in gen for retarded readers, Drug dependence, Media in gen for retarded readers, Mentally ill patients
Wireless access
Partic in National Network of Libraries of Medicine; South Central Minnesota Interlibrary Exchange (SMILE)
Open Mon-Fri 8-4

R TRINITY LUTHERAN PARISH LIBRARY*, 511 S Fifth St, 56082. SAN 308-7999. Tel: 507-934-4786. FAX: 507-934-4562. E-mail: office@trinitystpeter.org. Web Site: www.trinitystpeter.org. *Librn,* Marilyn Christiansen
Founded 1959
Library Holdings: Bk Vols 4,500
Subject Interests: Bible, Christian life, Martin Luther, Psychol, Relig studies
Friends of the Library Group

SANDSTONE

P SANDSTONE PUBLIC LIBRARY*, 119 N Fourth St, 55072-0599. (Mail add: PO Box 599, 55072-0599), SAN 347-2620. Tel: 320-245-2270. E-mail: samail@ecrl.lib.mn.us. Web Site: ecrl.lib.mn.us. *Librn,* Jeanne Coffey
Pop 6,582; Circ 45,250
Library Holdings: Bk Vols 14,500; Per Subs 40
Wireless access
Mem of East Central Regional Library
Open Tues 12-8, Wed & Thurs 9-5, Fri 12-5, Sat 9-12
Friends of the Library Group

SAVAGE

P SCOTT COUNTY LIBRARY SYSTEM*, 13090 Alabama Ave S, 55378-1479. SAN 348-0305. Tel: 952-707-1760. FAX: 952-707-1775. Web Site: www.scott.lib.mn.us. *Dir,* Vanessa J Birdsey; Tel: 952-707-1761, E-mail: vbirdsey@co.scott.mn.us; *Assoc Dir,* Cynthia Purser; Tel: 952-707-1765, E-mail: cpurser@co.scott.mn.us; *Ref Coordr,* Eva Poppen; *Tech Serv Coordr,* Mary Kay Baden; *Tech Coordr,* Deborah L McKinley; E-mail: dmckinley@co.scott.mn.us; *Youth Serv Coordr,* Lisa Pollard; *Libr Assoc,* Julie Svenningsen; *ILL Tech,* Elizabeth Bonello; Staff 36.88 (MLS 7.91, Non-MLS 28.97)
Founded 1969. Pop 119,646; Circ 908,693
Jan 2007-Dec 2007 Income (Main Library and Branch(s)) $2,836,676, State $90,762, City $345,042, Federal $18,082, County $2,176,791, Locally Generated Income $169,426, Other $36,573. Mats Exp $389,915, Books $302,756, Per/Ser (Incl. Access Fees) $20,000, AV Mat $47,923, Electronic Ref Mat (Incl. Access Fees) $19,236. Sal $1,404,829 (Prof $1,061,711)
Library Holdings: AV Mats 23,832; Bk Vols 266,195; Per Subs 366; Talking Bks 5,361
Automation Activity & Vendor Info: (Cataloging) SIRSI Unicorn; (Circulation) SIRSI Unicorn; (OPAC) SIRSI-iBistro; (Serials) SIRSI Unicorn
Database Vendor: ALLDATA Online, EBSCO Information Services, Gale Cengage Learning, LearningExpress, Newsbank, OCLC FirstSearch, OCLC WorldShare Interlibrary Loan, ProQuest, ReferenceUSA, Standard & Poor's, Westlaw, World Book Online
Wireless access
Function: Audio & video playback equip for onsite use, Bk club(s), Bks on cassette, Bks on CD, Children's prog, Computers for patron use, Copy machines, Electronic databases & coll, Exhibits, Free DVD rentals, Handicapped accessible, Home delivery & serv to Sr ctr & nursing homes, Homework prog, ILL available, Jail serv, Magnifiers for reading, Mus passes, Music CDs, Newsp ref libr, Notary serv, Online cat, Online ref, Online searches, Outreach serv, Outside serv via phone, mail, e-mail & web, Photocopying/Printing, Preschool outreach, Prog for adults, Prog for children & young adult, Pub access computers, Ref & res, Ref serv in person, Spoken cassettes & CDs, Spoken cassettes & DVDs, Story hour, Summer reading prog, Tax forms, Teen prog, Telephone ref, VHS videos, Web-catalog, Wheelchair accessible
Open Mon-Fri 8-4:30
Friends of the Library Group

Branches: 7
BELLE PLAINE PUBLIC LIBRARY, 125 W Main St, Belle Plaine, 56011-1245, SAN 348-033X. Tel: 952-873-6767. FAX: 952-873-6767. E-mail: bplibrary@co.scott.mn.us. *Librn,* Georgine Gansen; E-mail: ggansen@co.scott.mn.us
Library Holdings: Bk Vols 13,409
Open Tues 10-6, Wed 2-8:30, Thurs 2-8, Fri 10-5, Sat (Sept-May) 10-2
JORDAN PUBLIC LIBRARY, 230 S Broadway, Jordan, 55352-1508, SAN 348-0364. Tel: 952-492-2500. FAX: 952-492-2500. *Librn,* Mary Kubista; E-mail: mkubista@co.scott.mn.us
Library Holdings: Bk Vols 15,677
Open Mon & Wed 2-8, Tues & Thurs 10-5:30, Sat (Winter) 10-2
NEW MARKET PUBLIC LIBRARY, 110 J Roberts Way, Elko New Market, 55054, SAN 348-0399. Tel: 952-496-8030. FAX: 952-496-8030. E-mail: nmlibrary@co.scott.mn.us. *Librn,* Beth Beuch; E-mail: bbeuch@co.scott.mn.us
Library Holdings: Bk Vols 6,156
Open Mon & Wed 1-8, Fri 10-5
NEW PRAGUE PUBLIC LIBRARY, 400 E Main St, New Prague, 56071-2429, SAN 348-0429. Tel: 952-758-2391. FAX: 952-758-2391. E-mail: nplibrary@co.scott.mn.us. *Librn,* Lori Weldon
Library Holdings: Bk Vols 21,980
Open Mon-Thurs 10-8, Sat 10-4, Sun (Winter) 1-5
PRIOR LAKE PUBLIC LIBRARY, 16210 Eagle Creek Ave SE, Prior Lake, 55372-9202, SAN 348-0453. Tel: 952-447-3375. FAX: 952-447-3375. E-mail: pllibrary@co.scott.mn.us. *Librn,* Hilary Toren
Library Holdings: Bk Vols 26,595
Open Mon-Wed 10-8, Thurs 10-5, Fri 1-5, Sat 10-4, Sun (Winter) 1-5
SAVAGE PUBLIC LIBRARY, 13090 Alabama Ave S, 55378, SAN 348-0488. Tel: 952-707-1770. FAX: 952-707-1775. E-mail: salibrary@co.scott.mn.us. *Br Mgr,* Pat Mitton; E-mail: pmitton@co.scott.mn.us
Library Holdings: Bk Vols 17,964
Open Mon-Thurs 10-8, Fri 10-5, Sat 10-4, Sun 1-5
SHAKOPEE PUBLIC LIBRARY, 235 S Lewis St, Shakopee, 55379, SAN 348-0518. Tel: 952-233-9590. FAX: 952-233-3851. *Librn,* Barbara Hegfors
Library Holdings: Bk Vols 35,925
Open Mon, Tues & Thurs 10-8, Wed 10-5, Fri 1-5, Sat 10-4, Sun (Jan-May) 1-5

SHAKOPEE

S MINNESOTA DEPARTMENT OF CORRECTIONS*, Minnesota Correctional Facility - Shakopee, 1010 W Sixth Ave, 55379-2213. Tel: 952-496-4916. FAX: 952-496-4460. Web Site: www.doc.state.mn.us. *Librn,* Andrea Smith; E-mail: andrea.a.smith@state.mn.us; Staff 1 (MLS 1)
Library Holdings: Bk Vols 9,500; Per Subs 45
Special Collections: Law Coll
Automation Activity & Vendor Info: (Cataloging) Follett Software; (Circulation) Follett Software

SHOREVIEW

P RAMSEY COUNTY LIBRARY*, 4570 N Victoria St, 55126. SAN 347-8025. Tel: 651-486-2200. FAX: 651-486-2220. Web Site: rclreads.org. *Dir,* Susan Nemitz; Tel: 651-486-2201, E-mail: snemitz@rclreads.org; Staff 160 (MLS 50, Non-MLS 110)
Founded 1951
Special Collections: Minnesota Coll
Subject Interests: State geog, State hist
Automation Activity & Vendor Info: (Acquisitions) SirsiDynix; (Cataloging) SirsiDynix; (Circulation) SirsiDynix
Wireless access
Partic in Metronet; Metropolitan Library Service Agency
Friends of the Library Group
Branches: 7
HEADQUARTERS LIBRARY, 2180 N Hamline Ave, Roseville, 55113-4241, SAN 347-8122. Tel: 651-628-6803. FAX: 651-628-6818. *Br Mgr,* Lynn Wyman
Open Mon-Thurs 10-9, Fri & Sat 10-5, Sun 12-5
Friends of the Library Group
MAPLEWOOD BRANCH, 3025 Southlawn Dr, Maplewood, 55109, SAN 347-8084. Tel: 651-704-2033. FAX: 651-704-2038. *Br Mgr,* Sandra Walsh
Open Mon-Thurs 10-9, Fri & Sat 10-5, Sun 12-5
Friends of the Library Group
MOUNDS VIEW BRANCH, 2576 County Rd 10, Mounds View, 55112-4032, SAN 370-1298. Tel: 763-717-3272. FAX: 763-717-3275. *Br Mgr,* Carrie Watts
Open Mon & Thurs 1-8, Wed, Fri & Sat 10-5
Friends of the Library Group
NEW BRIGHTON BRANCH, 400 Tenth St NW, New Brighton, 55112-6806, SAN 347-805X. Tel: 651-724-6002. *Br Mgr,* Meg Robertson; Staff 8 (MLS 2, Non-MLS 6)
Open Mon & Tues 1-8, Thurs-Sat 10-5
Friends of the Library Group
NORTH SAINT PAUL BRANCH, 2290 N First St, North Saint Paul, 55109, SAN 347-8114. Tel: 651-747-2700. FAX: 651-747-2705. *Br Mgr,* Carol Jackson
Open Mon, Wed & Sat 10-5, Tues & Thurs 1-8
Friends of the Library Group
SHOREVIEW BRANCH, 4570 N Victoria St, 55126, SAN 373-5184. Tel: 651-486-2300. FAX: 651-486-2313. *Br Mgr,* Eilenne Boder
Open Mon 10-9, Tues & Wed 1-9, Thurs-Sat 10-5, Sun 12-5
Friends of the Library Group
WHITE BEAR LAKE BRANCH, 4698 Clark Ave, White Bear Lake, 55110-3415, SAN 347-8149. Tel: 651-407-5302. FAX: 651-407-5305. *Br Mgr,* Therese Sonnek
Open Mon 10-8, Tues & Wed 1-8, Thurs, Fri & Sat 10-5
Friends of the Library Group

SILVER BAY

P SILVER BAY PUBLIC LIBRARY*, Nine Davis Dr, 55614-1318. SAN 308-8014. Tel: 218-226-4331. E-mail: illsil@arrowhead.lib.mn.us. Web Site: www.silverbay.com. *Librn,* Julie Billings
Founded 1955. Pop 2,900; Circ 44,184
Library Holdings: Bk Titles 28,000; Per Subs 20
Special Collections: Minnesota History (E W Davis Coll)
Automation Activity & Vendor Info: (Acquisitions) SirsiDynix; (Cataloging) SirsiDynix; (Serials) SirsiDynix
Mem of Arrowhead Library System
Open Mon-Thurs 10-8, Fri 10-6
Friends of the Library Group

SLAYTON

P SLAYTON PUBLIC LIBRARY, 2451 Broadway Ave, 56172. SAN 308-8022. Tel: 507-836-8778. E-mail: slaytonmnlibrary@gmail.com. Web Site: www.plumcreeklibrary.org/slayton. *Librn,* Sharyl Larson; E-mail: slarson@plumcreeklibrary.net; *Asst Librn,* Becky Hudson; E-mail: bletendre@plumcreeklibrary.net
Founded 1946. Pop 2,451; Circ 30,573
Library Holdings: Bk Vols 32,000; Per Subs 50
Special Collections: Song Books
Automation Activity & Vendor Info: (Cataloging) Koha; (Circulation) Koha; (OPAC) Koha
Wireless access
Mem of Plum Creek Library System
Open Mon & Tues 11-5, Wed & Fri 9-5, Thurs 11-7, Sat 9-1
Friends of the Library Group

SLEEPY EYE

P DYCKMAN FREE LIBRARY, 345 Main St W, 56085-1331. SAN 308-8030. Tel: 507-794-7655. E-mail: libtbd@tds.lib.mn.us. Web Site: dyckman.tdslib.org. Staff 1 (MLS 1)
Founded 1900. Pop 5,200; Circ 25,000
Jan 2014-Dec 2014 Income $135,450, Provincial $200, City $116,000, County $14,000, Locally Generated Income $5,250. Mats Exp $9,538, Books $7,500, AV Mat $1,500, Electronic Ref Mat (Incl. Access Fees) $538. Sal $93,500 (Prof $44,600)
Library Holdings: Audiobooks 962; AV Mats 659; e-books 3,070; e-journals 40; Bk Vols 21,495; Per Subs 22
Special Collections: Local History Artifacts
Automation Activity & Vendor Info: (Acquisitions) Innovative Interfaces, Inc; (Cataloging) Innovative Interfaces, Inc; (Circulation) Innovative Interfaces, Inc; (Course Reserve) Innovative Interfaces, Inc; (ILL) Innovative Interfaces, Inc; (OPAC) Innovative Interfaces, Inc
Database Vendor: EBSCOhost, Overdrive, Inc, ProQuest
Wireless access
Mem of Traverse Des Sioux Library Cooperative
Open Mon & Wed 9:30-8, Tues, Thurs & Fri 9:30-5, Sat 9:30-Noon

SOUTH SAINT PAUL

S DAKOTA COUNTY HISTORICAL SOCIETY*, Research Center, 130 Third Ave N, 55075. SAN 329-7268. Tel: 651-552-7548. FAX: 651-552-7265. E-mail: dakotahistory@co.dakota.mn.us. Web Site: www.dakotahistory.org. *Assoc Dir,* Rebecca Snyder; Staff 3 (Non-MLS 3)
Founded 1935
Library Holdings: Bk Titles 600; Per Subs 20
Special Collections: Oral History
Subject Interests: Dakota County, Hist
Publications: Census Transcription; Over the Years; Society Happenings (Newsletter)
Open Wed & Fri 9-5, Thurs 9-8, Sat 10-3

P SOUTH SAINT PAUL PUBLIC LIBRARY, 106 Third Ave N, 55075-2098. SAN 308-8057. Tel: 651-554-3240. FAX: 651-554-3241. Web Site: www.southstpaul.org/library. *Dir,* Kathy Halgren; Tel: 651-554-3242, E-mail: kathy.halgren@southstpaul.org; *Ad,* Honora Greenwood Rodriguez; Tel: 651-554-3243; *Youth Serv Librn,* Amy Commers; Tel: 651-554-3244; Staff 7.3 (MLS 3, Non-MLS 4.3)
Founded 1922. Pop 20,000; Circ 132,000
Library Holdings: AV Mats 7,300; Bk Vols 64,000; Per Subs 154
Automation Activity & Vendor Info: (Cataloging) SirsiDynix; (Circulation) SirsiDynix; (OPAC) SirsiDynix
Database Vendor: 3M Library Systems, ALLDATA Online, Baker & Taylor, EBSCOhost, Ingram Library Services, Newsbank, OCLC ArticleFirst, OCLC FirstSearch, OCLC WorldShare Interlibrary Loan, Overdrive, Inc, ProQuest, SirsiDynix
Wireless access
Function: 24/7 Electronic res, 24/7 Online cat, Adult bk club, Audiobks via web, Bks on cassette, Bks on CD, Children's prog, Computer training, Computers for patron use, Copy machines, Doc delivery serv, e-mail serv, Electronic databases & coll, Free DVD rentals, Handicapped accessible, Homebound delivery serv, ILL available, Magazines, Music CDs, Outreach serv, Preschool outreach, Prog for adults, Prog for children & young adult, Pub access computers, Ref serv in person, Spanish lang bks, Story hour, Summer & winter reading prog, Tax forms, Teen prog, Telephone ref, VHS videos
Mem of Dakota County Library System
Special Services for the Deaf - Bks on deafness & sign lang; Closed caption videos
Special Services for the Blind - Audio mat; Bks on cassette; Bks on CD; Cassettes; Home delivery serv; Large print bks
Open Mon & Thurs 9-8, Tues, Wed & Fri 9-6, Sat (Sept-May) 10-4

SPICER

P SPICER LIBRARY*, 198 Manitoba St, 56288-9629. (Mail add: PO Box 160, 56288-0160), SAN 348-1352. Tel: 320-796-5560. FAX: 320-796-3013. *Librn,* Sheila Bosch; E-mail: sheilab@spicer.lib.mn.us
Pop 1,164; Circ 19,660
Library Holdings: Bk Vols 32,000; Per Subs 37
Automation Activity & Vendor Info: (Cataloging) Innovative Interfaces, Inc; (Circulation) Innovative Interfaces, Inc; (OPAC) Innovative Interfaces, Inc
Mem of Pioneerland Library System
Open Tues 10-5, Wed 12-7, Thurs & Fri 11-5, Sat 9-1
Friends of the Library Group

SPRING VALLEY

P SPRING VALLEY PUBLIC LIBRARY*, 121 W Jefferson St, 55975-1244. SAN 308-8065. Tel: 507-346-2100. FAX: 507-346-1908. Web Site: www.selco.info/svpl. *Librn,* Dianne Sikkink
Founded 1901. Circ 46,000
Library Holdings: Bk Vols 22,000; Per Subs 35
Automation Activity & Vendor Info: (Cataloging) SirsiDynix; (Circulation) SirsiDynix; (OPAC) SirsiDynix
Mem of Indianhead Federated Library System
Partic in Southeastern Libraries Cooperating
Open Mon & Fri 10-6, Tues-Thurs 1-8, Sat 10-1

SPRINGFIELD

P SPRINGFIELD PUBLIC LIBRARY*, 120 N Cass Ave, 56087-1506. SAN 308-8073. Tel: 507-723-3510. FAX: 507-723-6422. E-mail: libtbs@tds.lib.mn.us. *Dir,* Linda Roiger; E-mail: lroige@tds.lib.mn.us
Founded 1932. Pop 2,211; Circ 38,280
Library Holdings: Bks on Deafness & Sign Lang 15; Large Print Bks 900; Bk Titles 25,000; Bk Vols 30,000; Per Subs 100; Talking Bks 625
Subject Interests: Local hist
Wireless access
Function: AV serv, Handicapped accessible, Home delivery & serv to Sr ctr & nursing homes, ILL available, Online searches, Prog for adults, Prog for children & young adult, Summer reading prog, Wheelchair accessible
Mem of Traverse Des Sioux Library Cooperative
Partic in OCLC Online Computer Library Center, Inc
Special Services for the Deaf - Bks on deafness & sign lang
Special Services for the Blind - Audio mat; Bks on cassette; Bks on CD; Braille bks; Children's Braille; Large print bks; Talking bks
Open Mon-Thurs 10-8, Fri 10-5, Sat (Sept-May) 9-Noon

STEWARTVILLE

P STEWARTVILLE PUBLIC LIBRARY*, 110 Second St SE, 55976-1306. SAN 308-809X. Tel: 507-533-4902. FAX: 507-533-4746. E-mail: stewpl@selco.info. Web Site: www.stewartvillelibrary.org. *Dir, Libr Serv,* Patricia Ann Woodward Johnson; E-mail: patj@selco.info; *Assoc Librn,* Debora Lofgren; *Assoc Librn, ILL,* Glynis Sturm; Staff 3 (Non-MLS 3)
Founded 1938. Pop 6,519
Library Holdings: Bk Titles 33,000; Per Subs 30
Special Collections: Holocaust Coll
Automation Activity & Vendor Info: (Cataloging) SirsiDynix; (Circulation) SirsiDynix; (ILL) SirsiDynix; (OPAC) SirsiDynix; (Serials) SirsiDynix
Database Vendor: Gale Cengage Learning, OCLC FirstSearch, ProQuest, SirsiDynix
Partic in Southeastern Libraries Cooperating
Open Mon 12-8, Tues 10-6, Wed 12-6, Thurs 10-8, Fri 12-5, Sat 10-1
Friends of the Library Group

STILLWATER

S MINNESOTA DEPARTMENT OF CORRECTIONS*, Minnesota Correctional Facility - Oak Park Heights, 5329 Osgood Ave N, 55082-1117. Tel: 651-779-1410. FAX: 651-779-1323. Web Site: www.doc.state.mn.us. *Librn,* Bao Diep; Tel: 651-770-1413
Library Holdings: AV Mats 1,475; Bk Vols 3,500; Per Subs 24
Special Collections: Law Coll
Automation Activity & Vendor Info: (Cataloging) Follett Software; (Circulation) Follett Software
Open Mon-Thurs 7:30-3:15

P STILLWATER PUBLIC LIBRARY*, 224 N Third St, 55082. SAN 308-8111. Tel: 651-275-4338. Circulation Tel: 651-275-4338, Ext 110. Administration Tel: 651-275-4338, Ext 117. Information Services Tel: 651-275-4338, Ext 111. FAX: 651-275-4342. E-mail: splinfo@ci.stillwater.mn.us. Web Site: www.stillwaterlibrary.org. *Dir,* Lynne Bertalmio; *Asst Dir,* Carolyn Blocher; *Ref,* Jan Brewer; *Youth Serv,* Angela Petrie; Staff 5 (MLS 5)
Founded 1897. Pop 18,000; Circ 335,000
Jan 2010-Dec 2010 Income $1,048,776, City $1,000,076, Locally Generated Income $48,700. Mats Exp $1,107,071, Books $63,000, Per/Ser (Incl. Access Fees) $7,000, AV Mat $19,050, Electronic Ref Mat (Incl. Access Fees) $4,700. Sal $653,591 (Prof $266,554)
Library Holdings: AV Mats 9,600; Bk Titles 89,491; Per Subs 224
Special Collections: St Croix Coll
Subject Interests: Local hist
Automation Activity & Vendor Info: (Acquisitions) Horizon; (Cataloging) Horizon; (Circulation) Horizon; (ILL) OCLC Online; (OPAC) Horizon
Database Vendor: EBSCOhost, Gale Cengage Learning, OCLC FirstSearch, ProQuest
Wireless access
Open Mon-Thurs 10-8, Fri & Sat 10-5
Friends of the Library Group

TAYLORS FALLS

P TAYLORS FALLS PUBLIC LIBRARY*, 473 Bench St, 55084. (Mail add: PO Box 195, 55084-0195), SAN 325-1608. Tel: 651-465-6905. *Librn,* Diane Dedon
Founded 1871. Pop 1,010; Circ 2,499
Library Holdings: Bk Titles 11,680
Special Collections: History of Taylors Falls Coll; The St Croix River Valley Coll
Wireless access
Open Wed 2-5 & 6:30-8, Sat 9:30-12:30

THIEF RIVER FALLS

J NORTHLAND COMMUNITY & TECHNICAL COLLEGE LIBRARY*, 1101 Hwy One E, 56701. SAN 308-812X. Tel: 218-681-0756, 218-681-0757. Web Site: www.northlandcollege.edu/library. *Librn,* Cynthia Jorstad; E-mail: cynthia.jorstad@northlandcollege.edu
Founded 1965. Enrl 2,131; Fac 90; Highest Degree: Associate
Library Holdings: Bk Titles 27,000; Bk Vols 30,000; Per Subs 100
Special Collections: Oral History
Automation Activity & Vendor Info: (Cataloging) Ex Libris Group; (Circulation) Ex Libris Group; (OPAC) Ex Libris Group
Database Vendor: EBSCOhost, Facts on File, Gale Cengage Learning, ProQuest
Wireless access
Partic in MnPALS
Open Mon-Thurs 7:30-7, Fri 7:30-4

P NORTHWEST REGIONAL LIBRARY*, 210 LaBree Ave N, 56701. (Mail add: PO Box 593, 56701), SAN 348-0542. Tel: 218-681-1066. FAX: 218-681-1095. Web Site: www.nwrlib.org. *Regional Dir,* Kristi Harms; E-mail: harmsk@nwrlib.org; *Tech Serv,* Tammee Bacon
Pop 49,617; Circ 304,318
Library Holdings: Bk Vols 142,668; Per Subs 400; Talking Bks 843
Special Collections: Large Print; Literacy; Toddler's
Automation Activity & Vendor Info: (Acquisitions) Innovative Interfaces, Inc; (Cataloging) Innovative Interfaces, Inc; (Circulation) Innovative

Interfaces, Inc; (ILL) Innovative Interfaces, Inc; (OPAC) Innovative Interfaces, Inc
Wireless access
Open Mon-Fri 8-5
Friends of the Library Group
Branches: 8
GODEL MEMORIAL LIBRARY, 314 E Johnson Ave, Warren, 56762-1235, SAN 348-0577. Tel: 218-745-5465. FAX: 218-745-8807. E-mail: warren@nwrlib.org. Web Site: www.nwrlib.org/godel.htm. *Librn,* Dawn Korynta
Pop 2,105; Circ 19,561
Library Holdings: Bk Vols 10,000; Per Subs 27; Talking Bks 1,086; Videos 1,283
Open Mon & Wed-Fri 10-5, Tues 12-7
GREENBUSH PUBLIC LIBRARY, 242 Main St N, Greenbush, 56726-0009. (Mail add: PO Box 9, Greenbush, 56726-4016), SAN 348-0607. Tel: 218-782-2218. FAX: 218-782-2218. E-mail: greenbush@nwrlib.org. Web Site: www.nwrlib.org/greenbush.shtm. *Librn,* Angela Peterson
Founded 1970. Pop 817; Circ 14,082
Library Holdings: Bk Vols 5,500; Per Subs 19
Automation Activity & Vendor Info: (Cataloging) Innovative Interfaces, Inc; (Circulation) Innovative Interfaces, Inc; (OPAC) Innovative Interfaces, Inc
Open Tues & Fri 10-5, Wed 11-6, Thurs 11-7, Sat 9-Noon
Friends of the Library Group
HALLOCK PUBLIC LIBRARY, 163 Third St S, Hallock, 56728, SAN 348-0631. Tel: 218-843-2401. FAX: 218-843-2401. E-mail: hallock@nwrlib.org. Web Site: www.nwrlib.org/hallock.shtml. *Librn,* Peggy Pearson
Pop 2,000; Circ 19,895
Library Holdings: Bk Vols 14,236; Per Subs 21; Talking Bks 892; Videos 2,003
Open Tues, Wed & Fri 10-5, Thurs 10-7, Sat 10-1
KARLSTAD PUBLIC LIBRARY, 104 - 1st South, Ste 4, Karlstad, 56732. Tel: 218-436-7323. E-mail: karlstad@nwrlib.org. *Librn,* Peggy Pearson
Open Wed 12:30-6:30, Sat 9-11
RED LAKE FALLS PUBLIC LIBRARY, 105 Champagne Ave, Red Lake Falls, 56750-4001. (Mail add: PO Box 115, Red Lake Falls, 56750-0115), SAN 348-0666. Tel: 218-253-2992. FAX: 218-253-2992. E-mail: redlake@nwrlib.org. Web Site: nwrlib.org/rlf.htm. *Librn,* Laura Schafer; *Librn,* Mary Casavan
Pop 2,100; Circ 20,729
Library Holdings: Bk Vols 8,600; Per Subs 25
Automation Activity & Vendor Info: (Cataloging) Innovative Interfaces, Inc; (Circulation) Innovative Interfaces, Inc; (OPAC) Innovative Interfaces, Inc
Open Mon, Tues, Thurs & Fri 10-5, Wed Noon-7
Friends of the Library Group
ROSEAU PUBLIC LIBRARY, 121 Center St E, Ste 100, Roseau, 56751, SAN 348-0690. Tel: 218-463-2825. FAX: 218-463-2825. E-mail: roseau@nwrlib.org. Web Site: www.mwrlib.org/roseau.shtml. *Librn,* Charles Erickson
Pop 2,272; Circ 25,258
Library Holdings: Bk Vols 6,000; Per Subs 20
Open Mon 9:30-3, Tues, Wed & Fri 9:30-5:30, Thurs 9:30-6, Sat 11-3
Friends of the Library Group
THIEF RIVER FALLS PUBLIC LIBRARY, 102 First St E, 56701. (Mail add: PO Box 674, 56701). Tel: 218-681-4325. FAX: 218-681-4355. E-mail: trfcirc@nwrlib.org. *Libr Mgr,* Ashia Gustafson; E-mail: gustafsona@nwrlib.org; *Ch,* Emily Savageau; E-mail: savageaue@nwrlib.org; *Librn,* Diane Drake; *Librn,* Judy Ducamp; *Librn,* Betty Langelett
Open Mon-Thurs 9-8:30, Fri 9-5, Sat 10-5
WARROAD PUBLIC LIBRARY, 202 Main Ave NE, Warroad, 56763, SAN 348-0720. Tel: 218-386-1283. FAX: 218-386-3408. E-mail: warroad@nwrlib.org. Web Site: nwrlib.org/warroad.htm. *Librn,* Barbara Larson; *Librn,* Rosie Orvis
Pop 2,187; Circ 9,189
Library Holdings: Bk Vols 15,000; Per Subs 97; Talking Bks 999; Videos 1,522
Database Vendor: EBSCOhost, ProQuest
Open Mon, Wed, Fri & Sat 10-5, Tues & Thurs 10-8, Sun 1-4
Friends of the Library Group

TOGO

S MINNESOTA DEPARTMENT OF CORRECTIONS*, Minnesota Correctional Facility-Thistledew Camp, 62741 County Rd 551, 55723. Tel: 218-376-4411. FAX: 218-376-4489. Web Site: www.doc.state.mn.us. *Educ Dir,* Don Stahl
Library Holdings: Bk Vols 2,500
Open Mon-Fri 9-2:30

TRACY

P TRACY PUBLIC LIBRARY*, 189 Third St, 56175. SAN 308-8138. Tel: 507-629-5548. FAX: 507-629-5549. Web Site: www.plumcreeklibrary.org/tracy. *Librn,* Position Currently Open
Founded 1936. Pop 2,516; Circ 18,000
Library Holdings: Bk Vols 30,000; Per Subs 46
Automation Activity & Vendor Info: (Cataloging) TLC (The Library Corporation); (Circulation) TLC (The Library Corporation); (OPAC) TLC (The Library Corporation)
Mem of Plum Creek Library System
Open Mon-Thurs 11-7, Fri & Sat 11-3

TWO HARBORS

P TWO HARBORS PUBLIC LIBRARY*, 320 Waterfront Dr, 55616-3201. SAN 308-8162. Tel: 218-834-3148. E-mail: thpl@arrowhead.lib.mn.us. Web Site: www.two-harbors.lib.mn.us. *Dir,* Michele Monson
Founded 1896. Pop 6,500; Circ 67,800
Library Holdings: Bk Vols 28,000; Per Subs 80
Wireless access
Open Mon-Thurs 11-8, Fri 11-5, Sat 11-4
Friends of the Library Group

TYLER

P TYLER PUBLIC LIBRARY*, 230 N Tyler St, 56178-1161. (Mail add: PO Box L, 56178-0461), SAN 308-8170. Tel: 507-247-5556. FAX: 507-247-5557. Web Site: www.plumcreeklibrary.org/tyler. *Dir,* Carla Skjong; E-mail: cskjong@plumcreeklibrary.net
Library Holdings: Bk Vols 6,000; Per Subs 50
Automation Activity & Vendor Info: (Cataloging) TLC (The Library Corporation); (Circulation) TLC (The Library Corporation); (OPAC) TLC (The Library Corporation)
Mem of Plum Creek Library System
Open Mon, Tues, Thurs & Fri 10-5, Wed 10-7, Sat 9-12

VICTORIA

S LOWRY NATURE CENTER LIBRARY*, Carver Park Reserve, Three Rivers Park District, 7025 Victoria Dr, 55386. SAN 308-5759. Tel: 763-694-7650. FAX: 952-472-5420. Web Site: www.threeriversparkdistrict.org. *Supvr,* Allison Neaton; E-mail: aneaton@threeriversparkdistrict.org
Founded 1969
Library Holdings: Bk Vols 800
Subject Interests: Birding, Conserv, General reading, Natural hist, Outdoor educ
Function: Ref serv available
Open Mon-Sat 9-5, Sun 12-5
Restriction: Non-circulating to the pub

VIRGINIA

J MESABI RANGE COMMUNITY & TECHNICAL COLLEGE LIBRARY, 1001 Chestnut St W, 55792. SAN 308-8197. Tel: 218-749-7712. Toll Free Tel: 800-657-3860. Web Site: www.mesabirange.edu/academics/library. *Libr Tech,* Valeria Johnson; E-mail: v.johnson@mesabirange.edu
Founded 1922. Enrl 1,200
Library Holdings: AV Mats 2,600; CDs 380; DVDs 1,300; e-books 10,000; Bk Titles 25,000; Per Subs 60; Videos 600
Database Vendor: Gale Cengage Learning, ProQuest
Wireless access
Open Mon-Thurs (Fall & Spring) 8-6, Fri 8-4; Mon-Thurs (Summer) 10-3

P VIRGINIA PUBLIC LIBRARY*, 215 Fifth Ave S, 55792-2642. SAN 308-8200. Tel: 218-748-7525. FAX: 218-748-7527. Web Site: www.virginia.lib.mn.us. *Dir,* Nancy Maxwell; E-mail: nancy@arrowhead.lib.mn.us; *Ch Serv,* Dawn Heisel; *Tech Serv,* Susan Krause; Staff 10 (MLS 2, Non-MLS 8)
Founded 1905. Pop 9,157; Circ 224,148
Library Holdings: AV Mats 4,000; Bk Vols 60,000; Per Subs 170
Automation Activity & Vendor Info: (Acquisitions) SirsiDynix; (Cataloging) SirsiDynix; (Circulation) SirsiDynix; (OPAC) SirsiDynix; (Serials) SirsiDynix
Wireless access
Mem of Arrowhead Library System
Special Services for the Deaf - TDD equip
Open Mon & Thurs 9-7, Tues, Wed & Fri 9-5
Friends of the Library Group

WABASHA

P WABASHA PUBLIC LIBRARY*, 168 Alleghany Ave, 55981-1286. SAN 308-8219. Tel: 651-565-3927. FAX: 651-565-3927. E-mail: wablib@yahoo.com. Web Site: www.selco.lib.mn.us/wabasha. *Librn,* Judith A Schierts
Founded 1868. Pop 2,812; Circ 22,505
Library Holdings: Bk Vols 20,000; Per Subs 70
Special Collections: Local History (Wabasha-A Sense of Place); Local Paper, Wabasha County Herald 1863-present, micro
Automation Activity & Vendor Info: (Cataloging) SirsiDynix; (Circulation) SirsiDynix; (OPAC) SirsiDynix
Partic in Southeastern Libraries Cooperating
Open Mon 10-7, Tues, Thurs & Fri 10-5, Wed 10-6, Sat 10-1

WABASSO

P WABASSO PUBLIC LIBRARY*, 1248 Oak St, 56293. (Mail add: PO Box 190, 56293-0190), SAN 320-8966. Tel: 507-342-5279. FAX: 507-342-2329. Web Site: www.plumcreeklibrary.org/wabasso. *Librn,* Marilyn Daub; E-mail: mdaub@plumcreeklibrary.net
Pop 1,090; Circ 24,950
Jan 2007-Dec 2007 Income $63,000. Mats Exp $14,000. Sal $28,000
Library Holdings: DVDs 500; Bk Vols 11,000; Per Subs 24; Talking Bks 600; Videos 1,400
Automation Activity & Vendor Info: (Cataloging) TLC (The Library Corporation); (Circulation) TLC (The Library Corporation); (OPAC) TLC (The Library Corporation)
Mem of Plum Creek Library System
Open Mon-Fri 10-12 & 1-6
Friends of the Library Group

WACONIA

S CARVER COUNTY HISTORICAL SOCIETY LIBRARY*, 555 W First St, 55387. SAN 325-5182. Tel: 952-442-4234. FAX: 952-442-3025. E-mail: historical@co.carver.mn.us. Web Site: www.carvercountyhistoricalsociety.org. *Dir,* Wendy Biorn; Staff 1 (Non-MLS 1)
Founded 1940
Library Holdings: Bk Titles 1,000
Special Collections: German & Swedish Language Reading Society Coll c 1860
Open Mon & Wed-Fri 10-4:30, Tues 10-8, Sat 10-3
Restriction: Non-circulating to the pub

WADENA

P WADENA CITY LIBRARY*, 304 First St SW, 56482-1460. SAN 347-7819. Tel: 218-631-2476. FAX: 218-631-2476. E-mail: wadena@krls.org. *Br Mgr,* Linda McIntosh
Pop 4,699; Circ 27,238
Library Holdings: Bk Vols 17,000; Per Subs 65
Mem of Kitchigami Regional Library
Open Tues 10-6, Wed & Fri 10-5, Thurs 10-8, Sat 10-3
Friends of the Library Group

WALKER

P WALKER PUBLIC LIBRARY*, 207 Fourth St, 56484. (Mail add: PO Box 550, 56484-0550), SAN 347-7843. Tel: 218-547-1019. FAX: 218-547-1019. E-mail: walker@krls.org. Web Site: www.krls.org. *Dir,* Carrie Musselman; Staff 2 (Non-MLS 2)
Founded 1909. Circ 46,084
Library Holdings: Bk Titles 19,746; Per Subs 33
Automation Activity & Vendor Info: (Cataloging) Innovative Interfaces, Inc; (Circulation) Innovative Interfaces, Inc; (Course Reserve) Innovative Interfaces, Inc; (OPAC) Innovative Interfaces, Inc
Mem of Kitchigami Regional Library
Open Wed 10-4, Thurs 12-6, Fri & Sat 10-2
Friends of the Library Group

WASECA

G WASECA COUNTY HISTORICAL SOCIETY LIBRARY*, Research Center, 315 Second Ave NE, 56093. SAN 326-5102. Tel: 507-835-7700. Web Site: www.historical.waseca.mn.us. *Co-Dir,* Joan Mooney; E-mail: director@historical.waseca.mn.us; *Co-Dir,* Shelia Morris; *Curator,* Pauline Fenelon; *Curator,* Vanessa Zimprich
Founded 1938
Library Holdings: Bk Titles 350; Per Subs 10
Special Collections: Business & Organization Records; Diaries; Waseca County Genealogy
Subject Interests: Archives, Family hist, Manuscripts
Wireless access
Partic in S Minnesota Interlibr Res Exchange
Open Tues-Fri 8-12 & 1-5
Restriction: Mem only
Friends of the Library Group

P WASECA-LE SUEUR REGIONAL LIBRARY*, 408 N State St, 56093. SAN 348-0755. Tel: 507-835-2910. FAX: 507-835-3700. Web Site: www.wasecalesueurlibraries.com. *Dir,* Theresa Meadows; *Acq,* Sue Nelson; Staff 4 (MLS 4)
Founded 1965. Pop 41,882; Circ 241,437
Library Holdings: Electronic Media & Resources 11,000; Bk Vols 150,000; Per Subs 460
Automation Activity & Vendor Info: (Cataloging) SirsiDynix; (Circulation) SirsiDynix; (OPAC) SirsiDynix; (Serials) SirsiDynix
Database Vendor: Gale Cengage Learning, ProQuest
Wireless access
Mem of Traverse Des Sioux Library Cooperative
Partic in OCLC Online Computer Library Center, Inc
Open Mon, Tues & Wed 9-8:30, Thurs & Fri 9-5, Sat 9-1
Branches: 8
ELYSIAN BRANCH, 196 W Main St, Elysian, 56028. (Mail add: PO Box 10, Elysian, 56028), SAN 376-2106. Tel: 507-267-4411. *Librn,* Anne Davies
Library Holdings: Bk Vols 3,000
Open Mon & Fri 1-5, Tues 9-12, Wed 12:30-5:30, Sat 10-12
JANESVILLE PUBLIC, 102 W Second, Janesville, 56048-3009. (Mail add: PO Box H, Janesville, 56048-0608), SAN 348-078X. Tel: 507-234-6605. E-mail: libtlj@tds.lib.mn.us. *Br Supvr,* Nicole Krienke
Library Holdings: Bk Vols 10,480
Open Mon 12-6, Tues 9-12 & 1-6, Thurs 2-8
Friends of the Library Group
LE CENTER PUBLIC, Ten W Tyrone St, Le Center, 56057, SAN 348-081X. Tel: 507-357-6792. E-mail: libtlc@tds.lib.mn.us. *Br Mgr,* Diane Wild
Library Holdings: Bk Vols 10,000
Open Mon & Tues 1-7, Thurs & Fri 1-5
Friends of the Library Group
LE SUEUR PUBLIC, 118 E Ferry St, Le Sueur, 56058, SAN 348-0844. Tel: 507-665-2662. *Librn,* Dianne Pinney
Library Holdings: Bk Vols 35,000
Open Mon 10-8, Tues & Thurs 1-8, Wed & Fri 10-5, Sat 10-2
MONTGOMERY PUBLIC, 104 Oak Ave SE, Montgomery, 56069, SAN 348-0879. Tel: 507-364-7615. E-mail: libtlm@tds.lib.mn.us. *Librn,* Nancy Noffke
Library Holdings: Bk Vols 15,000
Open Mon & Wed 10-5, Tues & Thurs 10-8, Sat 9-12, Sun (Sept-May) 1-4
Friends of the Library Group
NEW RICHLAND PUBLIC, 129 S Broadway Ave, New Richland, 56072. (Mail add: PO Box 385, New Richland, 56072-0385), SAN 348-0909. Tel: 507-465-3708. *Librn,* Linda Lynne
Library Holdings: Bk Vols 10,000
Open Mon, Wed & Thurs 12:30-6, Sat 9-12:30
WALDORF BRANCH, 109 Main St N, Waldorf, 56091. (Mail add: PO Box 166, Waldorf, 56091-0166), SAN 376-2130. Tel: 507-239-2248. *Librn,* Cheryl Marquardt
Library Holdings: Bk Vols 3,000
Open Tues 1-4:30, Wed 9-11:30 & 1-5, Thurs 12:30-5:30
WATERVILLE PUBLIC, 210 E Paquin St, Waterville, 56096, SAN 348-0933. Tel: 507-362-8462. *Librn,* Lynne Coleman
Library Holdings: Bk Vols 8,000
Open Mon 12:30-4:30, Tues & Thurs 3-7:30, Wed 9-11 & 12:30-5

WAYZATA

S CARGILL, INC*, Information Center, 15407 McGinty Rd W, 55391. (Mail add: PO Box 5670, Minneapolis, 55440-5670). Tel: 952-742-6498. FAX: 952-742-6062. *Asst VPres, Knowledge Mgt Coop Affairs,* Peter Sidney; E-mail: peter_sidney@cargill.com; *Dir, Bus Knowledge Serv,* Maribeth Bacig; *Dir, Sci Knowledge Serv,* Anne Rogers; *Sr Ref Librn/Sci & Tech,* Cory Nelson; *Ref Librn,* Cindy Acton; *Res Librn,* Jacob Westendorp; *IT Mgr,* Deo Sioco; *Archivist,* Bruce Bruemmer; *Assoc Archivist,* Jennifer I Johnson; *IT Coordr,* Ivan Nunez; Staff 11 (MLS 7, Non-MLS 4)
Founded 1956
Library Holdings: e-books 500; e-journals 50; Bk Vols 5,000; Per Subs 700
Subject Interests: Bus, Commodity trading, Corn wet milling, Finance, Food mkt, Food sci, Food serv, Grain storage, Intl trade, Livestock, Mgt, Oilseed proc, Salt, Transportation
Automation Activity & Vendor Info: (Cataloging) SydneyPlus; (Serials) SydneyPlus
Database Vendor: American Chemical Society, Blackwell, Bloomberg, Dialog, EBSCO Information Services, Elsevier, Factiva.com, IBISWorld, IHS, Infotrieve, Ingenta, Knovel, OCLC, ScienceDirect, Scopus, Springer-Verlag, STN International, Wiley
Wireless access

Partic in Minitex Library Information Network; OCLC Online Computer Library Center, Inc
Restriction: Employees only, Not open to pub

R GRACE LUTHERAN CHURCH LIBRARY*, 18360 Minnetonka Blvd, 55391-3295. SAN 308-8235. Tel: 952-473-2362. FAX: 952-473-3522.
Founded 1958
Jul 2008-Jun 2009. Mats Exp $500
Library Holdings: AV Mats 200; Large Print Bks 15; Bk Titles 7,400; Per Subs 10
Database Vendor: LibraryWorld, Inc
Wireless access
Open Mon-Fri 9-5, Sun 9-12

R WAYZATA COMMUNITY CHURCH LIBRARY*, 125 E Wayzata Blvd, 55391. SAN 308-8243. Tel: 952-473-8877. FAX: 952-473-2695. E-mail: welcome@wayzatacommunitychurch.org. Web Site: www.wayzatacommunitychurch.org. *In Charge,* Pat Kamrud
Library Holdings: Bk Vols 3,500; Per Subs 12

WELLS

P WELLS PUBLIC LIBRARY, 54 First St SW, 56097-1913. SAN 308-8251. Tel: 507-553-3702. FAX: 507-553-6141. E-mail: libtfl@tds.lib.mn.us. Web Site: www.cityofwells.net/index.php/library. *Dir,* Sheila Treptow; *Asst Libr Dir,* Tami Beto; Staff 3 (Non-MLS 3)
Founded 1976. Pop 5,451; Circ 39,000
Library Holdings: Audiobooks 542; CDs 339; DVDs 1,935; Large Print Bks 1,001; Bk Titles 20,000; Bk Vols 21,875; Per Subs 26
Special Collections: Faribault County Genealogy Files, cemetery listings, newsp clippings; USC Community Yearbooks, 1934-1959 & 1961 to present
Automation Activity & Vendor Info: (Cataloging) SirsiDynix; (Circulation) SirsiDynix; (OPAC) SirsiDynix
Database Vendor: EBSCOhost
Wireless access
Function: Bks on cassette, Bks on CD, Computers for patron use, Copy machines, e-mail serv, Exhibits, Fax serv, Free DVD rentals, Handicapped accessible, ILL available, Music CDs, Online cat, Online searches, Outreach serv, Photocopying/Printing, Prog for adults, Prog for children & young adult, Scanner, Summer reading prog, Tax forms, VHS videos, Wheelchair accessible
Mem of Traverse Des Sioux Library Cooperative
Open Mon & Wed 10-8, Tues, Thurs & Fri 10-5, Sat (Sept-May) 9-12

WEST CONCORD

P WEST CONCORD PUBLIC LIBRARY*, 180 E Main St, 55985. (Mail add: PO Box 468, 55985-0468), SAN 376-7140. Tel: 507-527-2031. FAX: 507-527-2031. Web Site: www.westconcord.mn.com. *Librn,* Sharon Dahms; E-mail: sdahms@selco.lib.mn.us
Library Holdings: Bk Titles 15,000; Per Subs 10
Automation Activity & Vendor Info: (Cataloging) Horizon; (Circulation) Horizon; (OPAC) Horizon
Database Vendor: Gale Cengage Learning, OCLC FirstSearch, SirsiDynix
Wireless access
Function: ILL available
Partic in Southeastern Libraries Cooperating
Open Mon & Thurs 1-7, Tues, Wed & Fri 10-5, Sat 10-Noon
Friends of the Library Group

WESTBROOK

P WESTBROOK PUBLIC LIBRARY*, 556 First Ave, 56183. (Mail add: PO Box 26, 56183-0026), SAN 376-6527. Tel: 507-274-6174. FAX: 507-274-6174. E-mail: westbrook@plumcreeklibrary.net. Web Site: www.plumcreeklibrary.org/Westbrook. *Dir,* Kari Ourada; E-mail: kourada@centurytel.net; *Asst Dir,* Kelly Beaty; E-mail: kbeaty@centurytel.net
Library Holdings: AV Mats 53; Bk Vols 11,362; Per Subs 73; Talking Bks 593; Videos 299
Automation Activity & Vendor Info: (Cataloging) TLC (The Library Corporation); (Circulation) TLC (The Library Corporation); (OPAC) TLC (The Library Corporation)
Mem of Plum Creek Library System
Partic in Connecticut Library Consortium; Libraries Online, Inc
Open Mon & Tues 10-6, Wed 1-6, Thurs & Fri 10-3, Sat 10-2

WHEATON

P WHEATON COMMUNITY LIBRARY*, 901 First Ave N, 56296. SAN 320-8974. Tel: 320-563-8487. FAX: 320-563-8815. *Dir,* Marian Nelson; E-mail: mnelson@wheaton.lib.mn.us; Staff 3 (Non-MLS 3)
Founded 1972. Pop 2,288; Circ 50,000
Jan 2007-Dec 2007 Income $100,000
Library Holdings: AV Mats 2,279; Large Print Bks 325; Bk Titles 16,670; Per Subs 60
Automation Activity & Vendor Info: (Cataloging) Horizon; (Circulation) Horizon; (OPAC) Horizon
Wireless access
Mem of Viking Library System
Partic in Minitex Library Information Network
Open Mon-Fri 10-6, Sat 9-Noon
Friends of the Library Group

WHITE BEAR LAKE

J CENTURY COLLEGE LIBRARY, 3300 N Century Ave, 55110. SAN 308-826X. Tel: 651 779-3968. Interlibrary Loan Service Tel: 651-779-3260. Reference Tel: 651-747-4004. FAX: 651-779-3963. Web Site: www.century.edu/library. *Acq Librn,* Cheryl Langevin; Tel: 651-779-3969, E-mail: cheryl.langevin@century.edu; *Electronic Res Librn,* Randi Madisen; Tel: 651-779-3292, E-mail: randi.madisen@century.edu; *Libr Instruction, Ref Librn,* Maura Smyth; Tel: 651-773-1762, E-mail: maura.smyth@century.edu; *Acq, Circ, Tech Serv,* Jane Young; Tel: 651-779-3264, E-mail: jane.young@century.edu; *ILL,* Cathy Adams; E-mail: cathy.adams@century.edu; Staff 10.5 (MLS 3.5, Non-MLS 7)
Founded 1967. Enrl 7,000; Fac 323; Highest Degree: Associate
Library Holdings: Audiobooks 500; AV Mats 14,000; e-books 132,000; Bk Titles 67,000; Per Subs 202
Special Collections: Fire/EMS/Safety Coll; Orthotics & Prosthetics (A Bennett Wilson Coll); Partial College Archives
Automation Activity & Vendor Info: (Acquisitions) Ex Libris Group; (Cataloging) Ex Libris Group; (Circulation) Ex Libris Group; (Course Reserve) Ex Libris Group; (ILL) Ex Libris Group; (OPAC) Ex Libris Group; (Serials) Ex Libris Group
Database Vendor: Alexander Street Press, ARTstor, Bowker, CQ Press, CredoReference, EBSCOhost, Facts on File, Gale Cengage Learning, JSTOR, Micromedex, OCLC WorldShare Interlibrary Loan, Paratext, ProQuest, PubMed, Springshare, LLC, YBP Library Services
Wireless access
Function: For res purposes
Partic in MnPALS; OCLC Online Computer Library Center, Inc
Special Services for the Deaf - Assistive tech
Special Services for the Blind - Assistive/Adapted tech devices, equip & products
Open Mon-Thurs 7:30am-8pm, Fri 7:30-4, Sat 9-3

WILLMAR

S KANDIYOHI COUNTY HISTORICAL SOCIETY*, Lawson Research Library, 610 NE Hwy 71, 56201. SAN 326-3045. Tel: 320-235-1881. FAX: 320-235-1881. E-mail: kandhist@msn.com. Web Site: kandimuseum.com. *Exec Dir,* Jill Wohnoutka; Staff 2 (MLS 1, Non-MLS 1)
Founded 1969
Library Holdings: Bk Titles 1,500; Bk Vols 1,700; Per Subs 100
Special Collections: Local Newspapers Coll, microfilm
Subject Interests: Archives, Local hist
Publications: Kandi Express (Quarterly)
Open Mon-Fri 9-5
Restriction: Non-circulating to the pub

P PIONEERLAND LIBRARY SYSTEM*, Wilmar Public Library, 410 Fifth St SW, 2nd Flr, 56201. (Mail add: PO Box 327, 56201-0327), SAN 348-0968. Tel: 320-235-6106. FAX: 320-214-0187. Web Site: www.pioneerland.lib.mn.us. *Exec Dir,* Mark Ranum; Tel: 320-235-6106, Ext 28, E-mail: mark.ranum@pioneerland.lib.mn.us; *Dir of Libr Operations,* Laurie Ortega; E-mail: laurie.ortega@pioneerland.lib.mn.us; *Automation Coordr,* Beth Lunn; Tel: 320-235-6106, Ext 29, E-mail: beth.lunn@pioneerland.lib.mn.us; *Syst Serv,* Jean Clark; Tel: 320-235-6106, Ext 30, E-mail: jean.clark@pioneerland.lib.mn.us; Staff 56 (MLS 6, Non-MLS 50)
Founded 1983. Pop 166,431; Circ 896,418
Library Holdings: Bk Titles 270,000; Bk Vols 675,000; Per Subs 415
Automation Activity & Vendor Info: (Cataloging) Innovative Interfaces, Inc; (Circulation) Innovative Interfaces, Inc; (ILL) Innovative Interfaces, Inc; (OPAC) Innovative Interfaces, Inc
Database Vendor: Gale Cengage Learning, ProQuest
Member Libraries: Appleton Public Library; Atwater Public Library; Benson Public Library; Bird Island Public Library; Brownton Public Library; Canby Public Library; Clara City Public Library; Cosmos Public Library; Dassel Public Library; Dawson Public Library; Fairfax Public Library; Glencoe Public Library; Graceville Public Library; Granite Falls Public Library; Grove City Public Library; Hector Public Library; Hutchinson Public Library; Kerkhoven Public Library; Lake Lillian Public Library; Litchfield Public Library; Madison Public Library; Maynard Public Library; Milan Public Library; Montevideo Public Library; New London Public Library; Olivia Public Library; Ortonville Public Library; Raymond Public Library; Renville City Library; Spicer Library; Willmar Public Library; Winsted Public Library

Partic in OCLC Online Computer Library Center, Inc
Open Mon-Fri 8-4:30

M RICE MEMORIAL HOSPITAL LIBRARY*, 301 Becker Ave SW, 56201. SAN 329-0948. Tel: 320-231-4248. FAX: 320-231-4463. *Librn,* Wendy Larson; Staff 1 (MLS 1)
Founded 1978
Library Holdings: Bk Titles 2,000; Per Subs 200
Subject Interests: Med, Nursing
Open Mon-Fri 9-5

C RIDGEWATER COLLEGE LIBRARY, 2101 15th Ave NW, 56201. SAN 308-8278. Tel: 320-222-7537. Toll Free Tel: 800-722-1151. Web Site: www.ridgewater.edu/Student-Portal/student-services/library/Pages/default.aspx. *Librn,* Carolyn B Kelleher; *Cat, Libr Tech,* Jolene Peterson; Staff 2 (MLS 1, Non-MLS 1)
Founded 1962. Enrl 3,000; Fac 80; Highest Degree: Bachelor
Jul 2013-Jun 2014. Mats Exp $73,500, Books $10,000, Per/Ser (Incl. Access Fees) $15,000, AV Equip $5,000, Electronic Ref Mat (Incl. Access Fees) $40,500, Presv $3,000. Sal $105,000 (Prof $75,000)
Library Holdings: AV Mats 798; DVDs 112; e-books 143,328; e-journals 10; Microforms 45,629; Bk Vols 32,128; Per Subs 99; Talking Bks 206; Videos 918
Special Collections: Private Library of Local Publisher (Lawson Library)
Automation Activity & Vendor Info: (Cataloging) Ex Libris Group; (Circulation) Ex Libris Group; (ILL) Ex Libris Group; (OPAC) Ex Libris Group
Database Vendor: 3M Library Systems, Baker & Taylor, Bowker, Brodart, CQ Press, CredoReference, EBSCOhost, Electric Library, Ex Libris Group, Gale Cengage Learning, H W Wilson, McGraw-Hill, Micromedex, OCLC ArticleFirst, OCLC CAMIO, OCLC FirstSearch, OCLC WorldShare Interlibrary Loan, ProQuest, PubMed, Sage, YBP Library Services
Wireless access
Partic in Minitex Library Information Network; Southwest Area Multicounty Multitype Interlibrary Exchange
Open Mon-Thurs 7:30am-9pm, Fri 7:30-4

P WILLMAR PUBLIC LIBRARY, 410 Fifth St SW, 56201-3298. SAN 372-8536. Tel: 320-235-3162. FAX: 320-235-3169. Web Site: www.willmarpubliclibrary.org. *Head Librn,* John Baken; *Ch Serv,* Kathy Torkelson; Staff 8 (MLS 2, Non-MLS 6)
Founded 1904. Pop 19,886; Circ 130,848
Library Holdings: Bk Vols 78,954; Per Subs 213
Automation Activity & Vendor Info: (Circulation) Innovative Interfaces, Inc; (OPAC) Innovative Interfaces, Inc
Wireless access
Function: Handicapped accessible, ILL available, Large print keyboards, Magnifiers for reading, Online searches, Photocopying/Printing, Prog for children & young adult, Ref serv available, Summer reading prog, VHS videos, Wheelchair accessible
Mem of Pioneerland Library System
Partic in Minitex Library Information Network
Open Mon-Thurs 9-8, Fri 9-5:30, Sat 9-4
Friends of the Library Group

WINDOM

S COTTONWOOD COUNTY HISTORICAL SOCIETY LIBRARY*, 812 Fourth Ave, 56101. SAN 326-3975. Tel: 507-831-1134. FAX: 507-831-2665. E-mail: cchs@windomnet.com. Web Site: www.mtn.org/mgs/othersoc/cottonwd.html. *Dir,* Linda Fransen; Staff 2 (Non-MLS 2)
Founded 1901
Library Holdings: Bk Vols 500; Videos 12
Special Collections: Local Newspapers, 1871-present, micro. Oral History
Wireless access
Function: Copy machines, Fax serv, Handicapped accessible, Wheelchair accessible
Publications: Cottonwood County Courthouse, 1904-2004 (Reference guide); Newsletter
Open Mon-Fri 8-4, Sat 10-4
Restriction: In-house use for visitors, Non-circulating, Pub use on premises

P WINDOM PUBLIC LIBRARY*, 904 Fourth Ave, 56101-1639. SAN 308-8294. Tel: 507-831-6131. Web Site: www.windom-mn.com/library.htm. *Librn,* Joan Hunter; E-mail: jhunter@plumcreeklibrary.net
Founded 1883. Pop 5,306; Circ 53,326
Jan 2011-Dec 2011 Income $165,871, City $150,505, County $10,874, Locally Generated Income $4,492. Mats Exp $36,065, Books $31,015, AV Mat $5,050. Sal $92,243
Library Holdings: Audiobooks 1,275; DVDs 335; Large Print Bks 400; Bk Vols 28,582; Per Subs 98; Talking Bks 1,680; Videos 540
Special Collections: Art & Architecture Print Coll; Local History Coll; Music Coll
Automation Activity & Vendor Info: (Cataloging) ByWater Solutions; (Circulation) ByWater Solutions; (OPAC) ByWater Solutions
Wireless access
Mem of Plum Creek Library System
Open Mon 10-8, Tues, Wed & Fri 10-5:30, Thurs 10-6:30, Sat 10-2
Friends of the Library Group

WINNEBAGO

P MUIR LIBRARY*, 36 Main St N, 56098-2097. (Mail add: PO Box 218, 56098-0218), SAN 308-8308. Tel: 507-893-3196. FAX: 507-893-4766. Web Site: www.libraries.tds.lib.mn.us/muir. *Librn,* Judy Tupper
Pop 1,562; Circ 29,761
Library Holdings: Bk Titles 21,000; Per Subs 76
Automation Activity & Vendor Info: (Cataloging) SirsiDynix; (Circulation) SirsiDynix; (OPAC) SirsiDynix
Wireless access
Mem of Traverse Des Sioux Library Cooperative
Open Mon 9-12, 2-5 & 7-9, Tues-Thurs 2-5 & 7-9, Fri 10-12 & 2-5, Sat 10-12
Friends of the Library Group

WINONA

C MINNESOTA STATE COLLEGE-SOUTHEAST TECHNICAL*, Learning Resource Center, 1250 Homer Rd, 55987. (Mail add: PO Box 409, 55987-0409), SAN 320-6823. Tel: 507-453-1413. FAX: 507-453-1450. Web Site: www.southeastmn.edu/library/lrc.html. *Coordr,* Stephen Zmyewski; Staff 1 (Non-MLS 1)
Library Holdings: Bk Vols 2,000; Per Subs 100
Automation Activity & Vendor Info: (Acquisitions) PALS; (Cataloging) PALS; (Circulation) PALS; (Course Reserve) PALS; (ILL) PALS; (Media Booking) PALS; (OPAC) PALS; (Serials) PALS
Database Vendor: EBSCOhost, Gale Cengage Learning, ProQuest, TLC (The Library Corporation)
Wireless access
Open Mon-Thurs 7:30-6, Fri 7:30-4

CR SAINT MARY'S UNIVERSITY OF MINNESOTA*, Fitzgerald Library, 700 Terrace Heights, No 26, 55987-1399. SAN 308-8324. Tel: 507-457-1561. Interlibrary Loan Service Tel: 507-457-1489. Reference Tel: 507-457-1562. Administration Tel: 507-457-6909. FAX: 507-457-1565. Web Site: www.smumn.edu/sitepages/pid2571.php. *Head Librn,* Mary J Moxness; E-mail: mmoxness@smumn.edu; *Archivist,* Cora Berg; Tel: 507-457-1563, E-mail: cberg@smumn.edu; *Cat,* Lori Pesik; Tel: 507-457-6665, E-mail: lpesik@smumn.edu; *ILL,* Sandy Beth; E-mail: sbeth@smumn.edu; *Per,* Lauren Leighton; Tel: 507-457-1564, E-mail: lleighto@smumn.edu; *Ref,* Ruth Ann Schwartz; Tel: 507-457-6664, E-mail: raschwar@smumn.edu; Staff 6 (MLS 5, Non-MLS 1)
Founded 1925. Enrl 1,732; Fac 148; Highest Degree: Doctorate
Jun 2005-May 2006 Income $682,456. Mats Exp $287,469, Books $99,881, Per/Ser (Incl. Access Fees) $141,825, AV Mat $10,016, Electronic Ref Mat (Incl. Access Fees) $33,453, Presv $2,294. Sal $343,875 (Prof $226,576)
Library Holdings: AV Mats 8,419; Bks on Deafness & Sign Lang 84; e-books 5,352; e-journals 13,813; Bk Titles 144,818; Bk Vols 193,870; Per Subs 588; Talking Bks 89; Videos 2,854
Automation Activity & Vendor Info: (Acquisitions) PALS; (Cataloging) PALS; (Circulation) PALS; (ILL) PALS; (OPAC) PALS; (Serials) PALS
Database Vendor: Bowker, Cambridge Scientific Abstracts, CQ Press, EBSCOhost, Elsevier, Gale Cengage Learning, JSTOR, OCLC FirstSearch, ProQuest
Partic in Minitex Library Information Network; MnPALS; OCLC Online Computer Library Center, Inc
Open Mon-Thurs 7:30am-Midnight, Fri 7:30-4:30, Sat 10-6, Sun Noon-Midnight

S WINONA COUNTY HISTORICAL SOCIETY*, Laird Lucas Memorial Library & Archives, 160 Johnson St, 55987. SAN 308-8332. Tel: 507-454-2723. FAX: 507-454-0006. E-mail: archives@hbci.com. Web Site: www.winonahistory.org. *Exec Dir,* Mark Peterson; *Archivist,* Walter Bennick; *Archivist,* Marianne Mastenbrook; Staff 3 (MLS 2, Non-MLS 1)
Founded 1935
Library Holdings: Bk Vols 4,000
Subject Interests: Genealogy, Local hist, Lumbering, Railroading, Steamboating
Automation Activity & Vendor Info: (Cataloging) Horizon; (OPAC) Horizon
Function: Archival coll
Publications: Argus: A Winona County Historical Society Newsletter (Bi-monthly)
Mem of Southeast Library System (SELS)

Open Mon-Fri 10-12 & 1-5
Restriction: Non-circulating to the pub

P WINONA PUBLIC LIBRARY, 151 W Fifth St, 55987-3170. (Mail add: PO Box 1247, 55987-7247), SAN 308-8340. Tel: 507-452-4582. Reference Tel: 507-452-4860. FAX: 507-452-5842. Web Site: www.winona.lib.mn.us. *Dir, Commun Serv,* Chad Ubl; E-mail: cubl@ci.winona.mn.us; *Circ, Coordr,* Debbie Lilla; E-mail: debbiel@selco.info; *Ad,* Samantha TerBeest; E-mail: sterbeest@selco.info; *Tech Serv Librn,* Linda Weinmann; E-mail: lindaw@selco.info; *Youth Serv Librn,* Lezlea Dahlke; E-mail: ldahlke@selco.info; Staff 5 (MLS 2, Non-MLS 3)
Founded 1899. Pop 51,386; Circ 306,122
Library Holdings: Audiobooks 739, CDs 6,670; DVDs 5,085; Large Print Bks 2,604; Bk Vols 107,353; Per Subs 120
Subject Interests: Minn mat, Winona city, Winona County
Automation Activity & Vendor Info: (Acquisitions) SirsiDynix; (Cataloging) SirsiDynix; (Circulation) SirsiDynix; (OPAC) SirsiDynix
Database Vendor: EBSCOhost, Gale Cengage Learning, OCLC FirstSearch, ProQuest, SirsiDynix
Wireless access
Partic in Minn Interlibr Teletype Exchange; OCLC Online Computer Library Center, Inc; Southeastern Libraries Cooperating
Open Mon & Wed 10-6, Tues & Thurs 10-7, Fri 10-5, Sat 9-2
Friends of the Library Group

C WINONA STATE UNIVERSITY, Darrell W Krueger Library, 175 W Mark St, 55987-5838. (Mail add: PO Box 5838, 55987-5838). Tel: 507-457-5140. Circulation Tel: 507-457-5149. Interlibrary Loan Service Tel: 507-457-5139. Reference Tel: 507-457-5146. Administration Tel: 507-457-5151. Interlibrary Loan Service FAX: 507-457-2953. Administration FAX: 507-457-5594. E-mail: refdesk@winona.edu. Web Site: www.winona.edu/library. *Dean,* Thomas Bremer; E-mail: tbremer@winona.edu; *Chair, Archives,* Russ Dennison; Tel: 507-457-5143, E-mail: rdennison@winona.edu; *Access Serv Librn,* Mark Eriksen; Tel: 507-457-5486, E-mail: meriksen@winona.edu; *Cat Librn,* Joe Jackson; Tel: 507-457-5152, E-mail: jjackson@winona.edu; *Emerging Serv & Liaison Librn,* Tammi Owens; Tel: 507-457-5150, E-mail: towens@winona.edu; *Liaison & Instruction Librn,* Carol Daul-Elhindi; Tel: 507-457-5147, E-mail: cdaulelhindi@winona.edu; *Ref Coordr,* Allison Quam; Tel: 507-457-2644, E-mail: aquam@winona.edu; *Syst, Govt Doc & Liaison Coordr,* Vernon Leighton; Tel: 507-457-5148, E-mail: vleighton@winona.edu; *Coll Mgt & Digital Initiatives,* Kendall Larson; Tel: 507-457-5367, E-mail: klarson@winona.edu; Staff 17 (MLS 9, Non MLS 8)
Founded 1860. Enrl 8,100; Fac 858; Highest Degree: Doctorate
Jul 2014-Jun 2015 Income $1,968,570. Mats Exp $904,092, Books $175,000, Per/Ser (Incl. Access Fees) $729,092. Sal $918,238 (Prof $650,190)
Library Holdings: AV Mats 4,399; CDs 1,593; DVDs 2,151; e-books 55,808; e-journals 34,393; Electronic Media & Resources 1,126; Microforms 120,000; Music Scores 1,600; Bk Titles 344,659; Bk Vols 479,521; Per Subs 700; Videos 4,399
Special Collections: Winona State University Archives. State Document Depository; US Document Depository
Automation Activity & Vendor Info: (Acquisitions) PALS; (Cataloging) PALS; (Circulation) PALS; (Course Reserve) PALS; (ILL) PALS; (OPAC) PALS; (Serials) PALS
Database Vendor: OCLC FirstSearch
Wireless access
Partic in Minitex Library Information Network; MnPALS; OCLC Online Computer Library Center, Inc
Open Mon-Thurs 7:30am-2am, Fri 7:30-6, Sat 10-6, Sun 1pm-2am

WINSTED

P WINSTED PUBLIC LIBRARY*, 180 Main Ave W, 55395. (Mail add: PO Box 175, 55395-0175), SAN 348-1387. Tel: 320-485-3909. FAX: 320-485-3909. *Librn,* Sharon Noerenberg
Pop 2,698; Circ 8,049
Library Holdings: Bk Vols 7,200; Per Subs 15
Mem of Pioneerland Library System
Partic in Minitex Library Information Network
Open Mon & Wed 2-7, Tues & Thurs 10-1, Fri 2-5, Sat 10-12

WINTHROP

P WINTHROP PUBLIC LIBRARY*, 305 N Main St, 55396-9998. SAN 347-4453. Tel: 507-647-5308. FAX: 507-647-3200. E-mail: libtsw@tds.lib.mn.us. Web Site: www.libraries.tds.lib.mn.us/winthrop. *Dir,* Mary Jane Ohland
Library Holdings: Bk Vols 7,869
Mem of Traverse Des Sioux Library Cooperative
Open Mon-Thurs 10-12 & 1-7, Fri 10-12 & 1-5, Sat 10-3
Friends of the Library Group

WOODBURY

P WASHINGTON COUNTY LIBRARY*, 8595 Central Park Pl, 55125-9453. SAN 347-3880. Tel: 651-275-8500. FAX: 651-275-8509. Web Site: www.co.washington.mn.us/library. *Dir,* Patricia M Conley; *Dep Dir, Human Res Mgr, Properties Mgr,* Joyce Schneider; *Coll Mgr,* Brian Kraft; *Pub Serv Mgr,* Joe Manion; *Tech Serv Mgr,* Jim Langmo; *Youth Serv Mgr,* Dawn LaBrosse
Founded 1967. Pop 213,085; Circ 2,201,828
Library Holdings: Bk Vols 392,613; Per Subs 1,186
Automation Activity & Vendor Info: (Acquisitions) SirsiDynix; (Cataloging) SirsiDynix; (Circulation) SirsiDynix; (OPAC) SirsiDynix; (Serials) SirsiDynix
Wireless access
Branches: 9
HARDWOOD CREEK BRANCH, 19955 Forest Rd N, Forest Lake, 55025, SAN 376-2149. Tel: 651-275-7300. Administration Tel: 651-275-8500. Administration FAX: 651-275-8509. *Mgr,* Amy Worwa; E-mail: amy.worwa@co.washington.mn.us
Pop 31,000; Circ 490,000
Library Holdings: Bk Vols 91,300
Open Mon-Thurs 9:30-8, Fri & Sat 9:30-5, Sun 1-5
NEWPORT BRANCH, 405 Seventh Ave, Newport, 55055-1410, SAN 347-3953. Tel: 651-459-9631. FAX: 651-459-9631. *Mgr,* Chad Lubbers; E-mail: chad.lubbers@co.washington.mn.us
Library Holdings: Bk Vols 3,187
Open Mon & Fri 10-2, Tues-Thurs 2-6
OAKDALE BRANCH, 1010 Heron Ave N, Oakdale, 55128, SAN 373-9104. Tel: 651-730-0504. FAX: 651-275-8591. *Assoc Mgr,* Lynne Michaels; E-mail: lynne.michaels@co.washington.mn.us
Library Holdings: Bk Vols 42,526
Open Mon 9:30-8, Tues-Thurs 12:30-8, Fri 12:30-5, Sat 9:30-5, Sun 1-5
PARK GROVE BRANCH, 7900 Hemingway Ave S, Cottage Grove, 55016-1833, SAN 347-397X. Tel: 651-459-2040. FAX: 651-275-8581. *Mgr,* Carol Warner; E-mail: carol.warner@co.washington.mn.us
Library Holdings: Bk Vols 76,623
Open Mon 9:30-8, Tues-Thurs 12:30-8, Fri 12:30-5, Sat 9:30-5, Sun 1-5
R H STAFFORD BRANCH, 8595 Central Park Pl, 55125-9613, SAN 347-4062. Tel: 651-731-1320. FAX: 651-275-8562. *Mgr,* Chad Lubbers; E-mail: chad.lubbers@co.washington.mn.us
Library Holdings: Bk Vols 119,612
Open Mon-Thurs 9:30-8, Fri & Sat 9:30-5, Sun 1-5
VALLEY BRANCH, 380 St Croix Trail S, Lakeland, 55043, SAN 347-4003. Tel: 651-436-5882. FAX: 651-436-5882. *Mgr,* Chad Lubbers; E-mail: chad.lubbers@co.washington.mn.us
Library Holdings: Bk Vols 13,609
Open Mon & Fri 10-2, Tues-Thurs 2-6
ROSALIE E WAHL BRANCH, 3479 Lake Elmo Ave N, Lake Elmo, 55042. Tel: 651-777-7415. FAX: 651-777-7416. *Assoc Mgr,* Lynne Michaels; E-mail: lynne.michaels@co.washington.mn.us
Library Holdings: Bk Vols 8,380
Open Mon & Fri 10-2, Tues-Thurs 2-6

L WASHINGTON COUNTY LAW LIBRARY, Washington County Courthouse, 14949 62nd St N, Rm 1005, Stillwater, 55082. (Mail add: PO Box 6, Stillwater, 55082-0006). Tel: 651-430-6330. FAX: 651-430-6331. E-mail: lawlibrary@co.washington.mn.us. *County Law Librn,* Pauline Atuso; Tel: 651-430-6954, *Librn,* Pat Dolan; *Asst Librn,* Phyllis Kittle; Staff 2 (MLS 1.5, Non-MLS 0.5)
Founded 1956
Library Holdings: Bk Vols 8,000
Database Vendor: Westlaw
Open Mon-Fri 8-4:30
Restriction: Open to pub for ref & circ; with some limitations
WILDWOOD BRANCH, 763 Stillwater Rd, Mahtomedi, 55115-2008, SAN 347-4038. Tel: 651-426-2042. FAX: 651-275-8541. *Mgr,* Margaret Stone; E-mail: margaret.stone@co.washington.mn.us
Library Holdings: Bk Vols 37,395
Open Mon 9:30-8, Tues-Thurs 12:30-8, Fri 12:30-5, Sat 9:30-5, Sun 1-5

WORTHINGTON

J MINNESOTA WEST COMMUNITY & TECHNICAL COLLEGE LIBRARIES*, Worthington Campus, 1450 College Way, 56187-3024. SAN 308-8383. Tel: 507-372-3462. Web Site: www.mnwest.edu. *Dir,* Kip Thorson; E-mail: kip.thorson@mnwest.edu; *Librn,* Sandi Mead; Tel: 507-372-3481, E-mail: sandi.mead@mnwest.edu; Staff 5 (MLS 4, Non-MLS 1)
Founded 1936. Enrl 1,900
Library Holdings: Bk Titles 37,000; Per Subs 200
Automation Activity & Vendor Info: (Acquisitions) Ex Libris Group; (Cataloging) Ex Libris Group; (Circulation) Ex Libris Group; (Course Reserve) Ex Libris Group; (ILL) PALS; (OPAC) Ex Libris Group
Database Vendor: CredoReference, EBSCOhost
Wireless access

Departmental Libraries:
CANBY CAMPUS, 1011 First St W, Canby, 56220. Tel: 507-223-7252. FAX: 507-223-5291. *Librn,* Position Currently Open; *Coordr,* Linda Pesch; E-mail: linda.pesch@mnwest.edu
Open Mon-Thurs 8-4
GRANITE FALLS CAMPUS, 1593 11th Ave, Granite Falls, 56241. Tel: 320-564-5056. FAX: 320-564-2318. *Libr Tech,* Julie Williams; E-mail: julie.williams@mnwest.edu
Open Mon-Thurs 8-4:30, Fri 8-Noon
JACKSON CAMPUS, 401 West St, Jackson, 56143. Tel: 507-847-3320.
PIPESTONE CAMPUS, 1314 N Hiawatha Ave, Pipestone, 56164. (Mail add: PO Box 250, Pipestone, 56164-0250). Tel: 507-825-6832. FAX: 507-825-4656. *Librn,* Position Currently Open

P NOBLES COUNTY LIBRARY*, 407 12th St, 56187. (Mail add: PO Box 1049, 56187-5049), SAN 308-8367. Tel: 507-372-5340. Toll Free Tel: 800-954-7160. FAX: 507-372-2982. Toll Free FAX: 800-954-7161. Web Site: www.nclibrary.org. *Dir,* Julie Wellnitz; E-mail: jwellnitz@plumcreeklibrary.net; *Ch Serv,* Jackie Van Horsen; E-mail: jvanhorsen@plumcreeklibrary.net; *Circ,* Myra Palmer; E-mail: mpalmer@plumcreeklibrary.net; *Ref,* Laurie Ebbers; E-mail: lebbers@plumcreeklibrary.net; Staff 6 (MLS 1, Non-MLS 5)
Founded 1947. Pop 19,920; Circ 179,663
Jan 2012-Dec 2012 Income (Main Library and Branch(s)) $423,400. Mats Exp $51,200, Books $45,000, Per/Ser (Incl. Access Fees) $6,200. Sal $254,000
Library Holdings: Bk Vols 72,124; Per Subs 100; Talking Bks 2,054; Videos 4,000
Special Collections: ESL for Spanish-Speaking Adults
Automation Activity & Vendor Info: (Cataloging) LibLime; (Circulation) LibLime; (OPAC) LibLime
Database Vendor: ProQuest
Mem of Plum Creek Library System
Open Mon & Thurs 8-8, Tues, Wed & Fri 8-5, Sat 10-1
Friends of the Library Group
Branches: 1
ADRIAN BRANCH, 214 Maine Ave, Adrian, 56110-1056. (Mail add: PO Box 39, Adrian, 56110-0039), SAN 325-1713. Tel: 507-483-2541. FAX: 507-483-2541. Web Site: www.plumcreeklibrary.org/adrian. *Librn,* Meredith Vaselaar; E-mail: mvaselaar@plumcreeklibrary.net
Pop 1,500; Circ 14,301
Library Holdings: Audiobooks 50; CDs 10; DVDs 200; Large Print Bks 50; Bk Titles 14,000; Per Subs 8; Videos 30
Open Mon 11-8, Tues & Thurs 12-5, Wed & Fri 11-5, Sat 10-1

P PLUM CREEK LIBRARY SYSTEM*, 290 S Lake St, 56187. (Mail add: PO Box 697, 56187-0697), SAN 308-8375. Tel: 507-376-5803. FAX: 507-376-9244. Web Site: www.plumcreeklibrary.org. *Admin Dir,* Mark Ranum; E-mail: mranum@plumcreeklibrary.net; Staff 2 (MLS 2)
Founded 1974. Pop 119,523
Library Holdings: Bk Vols 655,319
Special Collections: Framed Art Prints; Large Print Coll; Puppet Resources; Song Book Coll
Automation Activity & Vendor Info: (Cataloging) TLC (The Library Corporation); (Circulation) TLC (The Library Corporation); (OPAC) TLC (The Library Corporation)
Member Libraries: Edgerton Public Library; Fulda Memorial Library; Ivanhoe Public Library; Jackson County Library; Lake Benton Public Library; Lamberton Public Library; Marshall-Lyon County Library; Meinders Community Library; Minneota Public Library; Morgan Public Library; Mountain Lake Public Library; Nobles County Library; Redwood Falls Public Library; Rock County Community Library; Slayton Public Library; Tracy Public Library; Tyler Public Library; Wabasso Public Library; Westbrook Public Library; Windom Public Library
Partic in Southwest Area Multicounty Multitype Interlibrary Exchange
Open Mon-Fri 8-5
Bookmobiles: 1

ZUMBROTA

P ZUMBROTA PUBLIC LIBRARY*, 100 West Ave, 55992. SAN 308-8391. Tel: 507-732-5211. FAX: 507-732-1212. E-mail: zpl@selco.info. Web Site: www.zumbrota.info. *Dir,* James Hill
Pop 6,901
Jan 2006-Dec 2006 Income $307,108. Mats Exp $275,791, Books $28,908, Per/Ser (Incl. Access Fees) $3,769, AV Mat $17,536. Sal $137,373 (Prof $76,055)
Library Holdings: Bk Vols 31,348; Per Subs 98
Automation Activity & Vendor Info: (Acquisitions) Horizon; (Cataloging) Horizon; (Circulation) Horizon; (OPAC) Horizon; (Serials) Horizon
Wireless access
Partic in Southeastern Libraries Cooperating
Open Mon, Wed & Thurs 12-8, Tues 10-8, Fri 10-5, Sat 9-3

MISSISSIPPI

Date of Statistics: FY 2013
Population, 2010 U.S. Census: 2,967,297
Population, 2013 U.S. Census (est): 2,991,207
Population Served by Public Libraries: 2,989,396
Total Volumes in Public Libraries: 5,686,530
Volumes Per Capita: 1.90
Total Public Library Circulation: 8,033,915
Total Public Library Income (includes Grants-in-Aid): $52,758,706
Source of Income: Mainly public funds
Expenditures Per Capita: $16.36
Number of County or Multi-County (Regional) Libraries: 48
Counties Served: 82
Number of Bookmobiles in State: 2
Grants-in-Aid to Public Libraries:
Federal & State: $10,860,976

ALCORN STATE

C ALCORN STATE UNIVERSITY*, J D Boyd Library, 1000 ASU Dr, 39096-7500. SAN 308-8901. Tel: 601-877-6350. FAX: 601-877-3885. Web Site: jdboyd.alcorn.edu. *Dean, Univ Libr,* Jessie B Arnold; E-mail: jarnold@alcorn.edu; *Acq Librn,* Bobbie Fells; Tel: 601-877-6354, E-mail: bpfells@lorman.alcorn.edu; *Cat Librn,* Eva Smith; Tel: 601-877-6353, E-mail: eva@lorman.alcorn.edu; *Govt Doc Librn,* Danielle Terrell; Tel: 601-877-6358, E-mail: danielle@lorman.alcorn.edu; *Ref Librn,* Mary G Harris; Tel: 601-877-6357, E-mail: mharris@lorman.alcorn.edu; *Ser Librn,* Hazel L Bell; Tel: 601-877-6362, E-mail: hazel@lorman.alcorn.edu; *Archivist,* Blanche Sanders; Tel: 601-877-2359, E-mail: blanche@lorman.alcorn.edu; *Instrul Media,* May Yu; Tel: 601-877-6359, E-mail: mhyu@lorman.alcorn.edu; Staff 26 (MLS 9, Non-MLS 17)
Founded 1871. Enrl 3,400; Fac 193
Library Holdings: e-books 18,836; Bk Vols 287,133; Per Subs 1,046
Special Collections: Alcorn Archives. State Document Depository; US Document Depository
Subject Interests: Agr, Educ
Automation Activity & Vendor Info: (Acquisitions) Ex Libris Group; (Cataloging) Ex Libris Group; (Circulation) Ex Libris Group; (Course Reserve) Ex Libris Group; (Media Booking) Ex Libris Group; (OPAC) Ex Libris Group; (Serials) Ex Libris Group
Database Vendor: Agricola, Checkpoint Systems, Inc, EBSCOhost, Gale Cengage Learning, OCLC FirstSearch, OCLC WorldShare Interlibrary Loan, OVID Technologies, Westlaw, Wilson - Wilson Web
Wireless access
Partic in BRS; Lyrasis
Open Mon-Thurs 8-11, Fri 8-7, Sat 10-5, Sun 2-11

ASHLAND

P BENTON COUNTY LIBRARY SYSTEM*, Robert M Bond Memorial Library, 247 Court St, 38603. (Mail add: PO Box 308, 38603), SAN 376-6357. Tel: 662-224-6400. FAX: 662-224-6304. Web Site: www.benton.lib.ms.us. *Dir,* Jeannie Burton; E-mail: jburton@benton.lib.ms.us
Founded 1959. Pop 8,000
Automation Activity & Vendor Info: (Cataloging) Book Systems; (Circulation) Book Systems
Wireless access
Open Mon-Fri 8-5
Friends of the Library Group
Branches: 1
HICKORY FLAT PUBLIC LIBRARY, 1067 Spruce St, Hickory Flat, 38633. (Mail add: PO Box 309, Hickory Flat, 38633-0309), SAN 376-6268. Tel: 662-333-7663. FAX: 662-333-7663. E-mail: hickory@benton.lib.ms.us. *Librn,* Tina Burks
Founded 1959
Open Mon-Fri 9-5

BAY SAINT LOUIS

P HANCOCK COUNTY LIBRARY SYSTEM, 312 Hwy 90, 39520-3595. SAN 348-1417. Tel: 228-467-5282. Administration Tel: 228-467-6836. FAX: 228-467-5503. E-mail: hcls@hancock.lib.ms.us. Web Site: www.hancocklibraries.info. *Exec Dir,* Courtney Thomas; E-mail: cthomas@hancock.lib.ms.us; *IT Officer,* Jason Bans; E-mail: jbans@hancock.lib.ms.us; *Pub Relations & Develop Officer,* Mary Perkins; E-mail: mmperkins@hancock.lib.ms.us; Staff 33 (MLS 3, Non-MLS 30)
Founded 1934. Pop 43,929; Circ 246,446
Oct 2012-Sept 2013 Income (Main Library and Branch(s)) $2,761,948, State $208,504, City $496,070, Federal $1,337, County $1,504,319, Locally Generated Income $112,043, Other $378,019. Mats Exp $135,063, Books $87,021, Per/Ser (Incl. Access Fees) $15,187, AV Mat $19,230, Electronic Ref Mat (Incl. Access Fees) $12,540, Presv $1,085. Sal $904,682
Library Holdings: CDs 4,077; DVDs 9,609; e-books 568; Electronic Media & Resources 5; High Interest/Low Vocabulary Bk Vols 200; Large Print Bks 3,552; Microforms 133; Bk Vols 91,996; Per Subs 203
Special Collections: Mississippi-Louisiana (Mississippiana Coll)
Automation Activity & Vendor Info: (Acquisitions) SIRSI WorkFlows; (Cataloging) SIRSI WorkFlows; (Circulation) SIRSI WorkFlows; (OPAC) SirsiDynix; (Serials) SIRSI WorkFlows
Database Vendor: Baker & Taylor, EBSCOhost, LearningExpress, Newsbank, OCLC FirstSearch, Overdrive, Inc, ProQuest, SirsiDynix, Sybase, Wilson - Wilson Web
Wireless access
Function: Accelerated reader prog, Adult bk club, Bk club(s), Bks on CD, Children's prog, Computer training, Computers for patron use, Copy machines, Electronic databases & coll, Family literacy, Fax serv, Free DVD rentals, Handicapped accessible, Holiday prog, ILL available, Magnifiers for reading, Mail & tel request accepted, Microfiche/film & reading machines, Online cat, Online ref, Online searches, Photocopying/Printing, Prog for adults, Prog for children & young adult, Pub access computers, Ref serv available, Ref serv in person, Scanner, Senior computer classes, Senior outreach, Story hour, Summer reading prog, Tax forms, Teen prog, Telephone ref, Web-catalog, Wheelchair accessible
Open Mon, Tues & Thurs 9-7, Wed & Fri 9-5, Sat 9-4
Friends of the Library Group
Branches: 4
EAST HANCOCK PUBLIC LIBRARY, 4545 Shepherd Sq, Diamondhead, 39525. Tel: 228-255-6337. FAX: 228-255-6450. *Br Mgr,* Gerri McClesky; E-mail: gmcclesky@hancock.lib.ms.us; Staff 3 (Non-MLS 3)
Founded 2012. Pop 8,425; Circ 26,000
Library Holdings: CDs 426; DVDs 1,074; Large Print Bks 243; Bk Vols 9,029; Per Subs 14
Function: Art exhibits, Bks on CD, Children's prog, Computer training, Computers for patron use, Copy machines, Electronic databases & coll, Fax serv, Free DVD rentals, Handicapped accessible, ILL available, Online cat, Prog for adults, Pub access computers, Ref serv available, Story hour, Summer reading prog
Open Mon, Tues & Thurs 10-6, Wed & Sat 10-2, Fri 10-5

KILN PUBLIC LIBRARY, 17065 Hwy 603, Kiln, 39556, SAN 348-1433. Tel: 228-255-1724. FAX: 228-255-0644. *Br Mgr,* Laura Mills; E-mail: lmills@hancock.lib.ms.us; Staff 4 (Non-MLS 4)
Founded 2000. Circ 34,000
Library Holdings: CDs 952; DVDs 2,505; Large Print Bks 1,051; Bk Vols 20,198; Per Subs 18
Function: Accelerated reader prog, Adult bk club, Bk club(s), Bks on CD, Children's prog, Computers for patron use, Copy machines, Electronic databases & coll, Fax serv, Free DVD rentals, Handicapped accessible, Holiday prog, ILL available, Magnifiers for reading, Online cat, Online searches, Photocopying/Printing, Prog for adults, Prog for children & young adult, Pub access computers, Ref serv in person, Story hour, Summer reading prog, Tax forms, Teen prog, Wheelchair accessible
Open Mon, Tues & Thurs 9-6, Wed & Fri 9-5, Sat 9-4

PEARLINGTON PUBLIC LIBRARY, 6096 First St, Pearlington, 39572, SAN 378-1585. Tel: 228-533-0755. FAX: 228-533-0125. *Br Mgr,* Andrea Coote Pack; E-mail: apack@hancock.lib.ms.us; Staff 3 (Non-MLS 3)
Founded 1999. Circ 4,500
Library Holdings: CDs 382; DVDs 1,319; Large Print Bks 306; Bk Vols 7,265; Per Subs 6
Function: Accelerated reader prog, Bks on CD, Children's prog, Computers for patron use, Copy machines, Electronic databases & coll, Fax serv, Free DVD rentals, Handicapped accessible, Holiday prog, ILL available, Online cat, Online searches, Photocopying/Printing, Prog for adults, Prog for children & young adult, Pub access computers, Ref serv available, Story hour, Summer reading prog, Tax forms, Teen prog, Wheelchair accessible
Open Tues & Thurs 10-6, Wed 11-5, Fri 10-2, Sat 9-1

WAVELAND PUBLIC LIBRARY, 345 Coleman Ave, Waveland, 39576, SAN 348-1441. Tel: 228-467-9240. FAX: 228-467-1336. *Br Mgr,* Nancy Pepperman; E-mail: npepperman@hancock.lib.ms.us; Staff 3 (Non-MLS 3)
Circ 23,000
Library Holdings: CDs 511; DVDs 1,963; Large Print Bks 367; Bk Vols 11,045; Per Subs 11
Function: Accelerated reader prog, Bilingual assistance for Spanish patrons, Bks on CD, Computers for patron use, Copy machines, Electronic databases & coll, Family literacy, Fax serv, Free DVD rentals, Handicapped accessible, Holiday prog, ILL available, Mail & tel request accepted, Online cat, Online searches, Photocopying/Printing, Prog for adults, Prog for children & young adult, Pub access computers, Ref serv available, Story hour, Summer reading prog, Tax forms, Teen prog, Wheelchair accessible
Open Tues & Thurs 10-6, Wed & Sat 10-2, Fri 10-5

BELZONI

P HUMPHREYS COUNTY LIBRARY SYSTEM*, 105 S Hayden, 39038. SAN 348-1476. Tel: 662-247-3606. FAX: 662-247-3443. *Dir,* Joe Goldberg
Founded 1958. Pop 18,706; Circ 44,493
Library Holdings: Audiobooks 2,086; Bk Vols 40,433; Per Subs 84; Videos 2,399
Special Collections: Oral History
Automation Activity & Vendor Info: (Acquisitions) A-G Canada Ltd; (Cataloging) A-G Canada Ltd; (Circulation) A-G Canada Ltd
Database Vendor: Auto-Graphics, Inc
Wireless access
Partic in Dancing Rabbit Library Consortium
Open Mon-Fri 8:30-5
Branches: 1
ISOLA PUBLIC, 203 Julia St, Isola, 38754, SAN 348-1530. Tel: 662-962-3606. *Librn,* Kathleen Session

BLUE MOUNTAIN

C BLUE MOUNTAIN COLLEGE*, Guyton Library, 201 W Main St, 38610. (Mail add: PO Box 160, 38610-0160), SAN 308-8448. Tel: 662-685-4771, Ext 147. FAX: 662-685-9519. E-mail: library@bmc.edu. Web Site: www.bmc.edu/library. *Dir of Libr Serv,* Dr Derek Cash; E-mail: dcash@bmc.edu; *Coll Mgt Librn,* Vanessa Jones; Tel: 662-685-4771, Ext 142, E-mail: vjones@bmc.edu; Staff 5 (MLS 2, Non-MLS 3)
Founded 1873. Enrl 525; Fac 42; Highest Degree: Master
Library Holdings: CDs 748; DVDs 145; e-books 35,991; Music Scores 840; Bk Titles 42,879; Per Subs 110; Videos 527
Special Collections: Blue Mountain College Archives (archives, artifacts, furniture & pictures); Blue Mountain College Hist (May Gardner Black Alumnae Coll); China (Mary Raleigh Anderson); Mary Dean Hollis Historical Doll Coll
Subject Interests: Liberal arts
Automation Activity & Vendor Info: (Cataloging) Book Systems; (Circulation) Book Systems; (OPAC) Book Systems; (Serials) Book Systems
Database Vendor: EBSCOhost, Facts on File, Mergent Online, World Book Online
Wireless access
Partic in Private Academic Libraries of Mississippi (PALMS)
Open Mon-Thurs 7:45-11, Fri 7:45-4:30

BOONEVILLE

J NORTHEAST MISSISSIPPI COMMUNITY COLLEGE*, Eula Dees Memorial Library, 101 Cunningham Blvd, 38829. SAN 308-8464. Tel: 662-720-7237, 662-728-7751. Interlibrary Loan Service Tel: 662-720-7408. Toll Free Tel: 800-555-2154. FAX: 662-728-2428. Web Site: www.nemcc.edu, www2.nemcc.edu/library/webpage/eula.htm. *Dir,* Glenice Stone; E-mail: gwstone@nemcc.edu; *Librn,* Kristen Barnett; E-mail: kgbarnett@nemcc.edu; *Librn,* Laura Gilham; Tel: 662-720-7584, E-mail: lbgilham@nemcc.edu; *Librn,* Sherita Howell; Tel: 662-720-7583, E-mail: sjhowell@nemcc.edu; *Evening Librn,* Melissa Clemmer; E-mail: mbclemmer@nemcc.edu; *Libr Asst,* Susan Brackeen; Tel: 662-720-7407, E-mail: sibrackeen@nemcc.edu; Staff 6 (MLS 4, Non-MLS 2)
Founded 1948
Library Holdings: AV Mats 2,839; e-books 27,186; Microforms 63,092; Bk Vols 47,900; Per Subs 89
Subject Interests: Miss
Database Vendor: Alexander Street Press, CQ Press, CredoReference, EBSCOhost, Facts on File, Gale Cengage Learning, OCLC FirstSearch, ProQuest, SirsiDynix, Wilson - Wilson Web, World Book Online
Open Mon-Thurs (Sept-May) 7:30am-10pm, Fri 7:30-4, Sun 6:30pm-9pm; Mon-Fri (June-Aug) 8-4

BRANDON

P BRANDON PUBLIC LIBRARY*, 1475 W Government St, 39042. SAN 329-2835. Tel: 601-825-2672. FAX: 601-825-4156. E-mail: brandon@cmrls.lib.ms.us. Web Site: www.cmrls.lib.ms.us. *Br Mgr,* Linda Wolfe; E-mail: brbm@cmrls.lib.ms.us; *Ch,* Jeanni Thrasher; *Circ Supvr,* Nora Anderson; *Ref Supvr,* Rebecca J Beattie; E-mail: brref@cmrls.lib.ms.us. Subject Specialists: *Children's prog,* Jeanni Thrasher; *Circ & libr serv,* Nora Anderson; *Ref & database res,* Rebecca J Beattie; Staff 10 (Non-MLS 10)
Founded 1958. Pop 16,000; Circ 100,000
Library Holdings: Bk Vols 24,500; Per Subs 60
Subject Interests: Genealogy
Database Vendor: Baker & Taylor, ebrary, EBSCO Auto Repair Reference, EBSCO Information Services, EBSCOhost, Medline, OCLC WorldShare Interlibrary Loan, SirsiDynix, WebMD, World Book Online
Wireless access
Mem of Central Mississippi Regional Library System
Open Mon-Thurs 10-8, Fri 10-5, Sat 10-4
Friends of the Library Group

P CENTRAL MISSISSIPPI REGIONAL LIBRARY SYSTEM*, 104 Office Park Dr, 39042-2404. (Mail add: PO Box 1749, 39043-1749), SAN 329-5109. Tel: 601-825-0100. FAX: 601-825-0199. Web Site: www.cmrls.lib.ms.us. *Dir,* Kaileen Thieling; *Bus & Human Res Mgr,* Deena Moore; *Br Coordr,* Betty Currie; *Pub Relations Coordr,* Dorothy Vance; *Coordr, Tech Serv,* Tamara Jones; *Coordr, Youth Serv,* Kathy Sparkman; Staff 102 (MLS 4, Non-MLS 98)
Founded 1986. Pop 200,000; Circ 745,122
Oct 2006-Sept 2007 Income $3,414,158, State $633,315, City $92,680, County $1,478,028, Locally Generated Income $222,735, Other $975,946. Mats Exp $329,614. Sal $1,492,073 (Prof $125,217)
Library Holdings: CDs 6,778; DVDs 6,793; e-books 10; Large Print Bks 11,781; Bk Vols 294,806; Per Subs 530; Talking Bks 9,571; Videos 15,446
Automation Activity & Vendor Info: (Acquisitions) SirsiDynix; (Cataloging) SirsiDynix; (Circulation) SirsiDynix; (OPAC) SirsiDynix; (Serials) SirsiDynix
Wireless access
Member Libraries: Brandon Public Library; D'Lo Public Library; Evon A Ford Public Library; Forest Public Library; Lake Public Library; Magee Public Library; Mendenhall Public Library; Mize Public Library; Morton Public Library; Northwest Point Reservoir Library; Pearl Public Library; Pelahatchie Public Library; Polkville Public Library; Puckett Public Library; Raleigh Public Library; Sand Hill Public Library; Sebastopol Public Library
Open Mon-Thurs 9-8, Fri 9-5, Sat 11-4
Friends of the Library Group

P NORTHWEST POINT RESERVOIR LIBRARY*, 2230 Spillway Rd, 39047. SAN 377-5755. Tel: 601-992-2539. FAX: 601-992-7870. E-mail: reservoi@cmrls.lib.ms.us. *Librn,* Ann Marsh
Library Holdings: Bk Vols 15,000; Per Subs 35
Mem of Central Mississippi Regional Library System
Open Mon 11:30-5, Tues 10-8, Wed & Thurs 10-6, Fri 10-5, Sat 10-Noon
Friends of the Library Group

BROOKHAVEN

P LINCOLN-LAWRENCE-FRANKLIN REGIONAL LIBRARY*, 100 S Jackson St, 39601-3347. SAN 348-1654. Tel: 601-833-3369, 601-833-5038. FAX: 601-833-3381. Web Site: www.llf.lib.ms.us. *Dir,* Henry J Ledet; E-mail: hledet@llf.lib.ms.us; *Librn,* Rebecca Nations; E-mail: rnations@llf.lib.ms.us; *Bus Librn,* Nina Smith; E-mail: nsmith@llf.lib.ms.us; *Ch Serv,* Donna Kenney; E-mail: dkenney@llf.lib.ms.us; Staff 19 (MLS 3, Non-MLS 16)
Founded 1956. Pop 50,861
Library Holdings: AV Mats 2,659; CDs 1,149; Large Print Bks 3,581; Bk Titles 105,415; Per Subs 159; Talking Bks 1,278; Videos 2,985
Special Collections: John H Williams Photo Coll; Lincoln County History Coll; Whitworth College Digital Coll. Oral History
Automation Activity & Vendor Info: (Circulation) Follett Software; (OPAC) Follett Software
Open Mon & Wed 9-6, Tues & Thurs 9-8, Fri & Sat 9-5
Branches: 4
BUDE PUBLIC LIBRARY, 903-904 Railroad St, Bude, 39630. (Mail add: PO Box 69, Bude, 39630-0069), SAN 348-1689. Tel: 601-384-2348. FAX: 601-384-2348. *In Charge,* Kathy Zumbro; Staff 1 (Non-MLS 1)
Library Holdings: Bk Vols 5,223
Open Mon-Fri 8-5
FRANKLIN COUNTY PUBLIC LIBRARY, 38 First St, Meadville, 39653. (Mail add: PO Box 336, Meadville, 39653-0336), SAN 348-1719. Tel: 601-384-2997. FAX: 601-384-3003. *Br Librn,* Mary Childs; Staff 2 (MLS 1, Non-MLS 1)
Library Holdings: Bk Vols 22,000
Open Mon & Wed 9-5, Tues & Thurs 9-6, Fri & Sat 9-12
LAWRENCE COUNTY PUBLIC LIBRARY, 142 Courthouse Sq, Monticello, 39654-6014, SAN 348-1743. Tel: 601-587-2471. FAX: 601-587-7582. *Librn,* Dianne Jones; E-mail: djones@llf.lib.ms.us; Staff 3 (MLS 1, Non-MLS 2)
Library Holdings: Bk Vols 15,067
Open Mon-Thurs 10-6, Fri & Sat 10-5
NEW HEBRON PUBLIC LIBRARY, 209 Jones St, New Hebron, 39140-3986. (Mail add: PO Box 202, New Hebron, 39140-0202), SAN 348-176X. Tel: 601-694-2623. FAX: 601-694-2623. *In Charge,* Karen Turnage; Staff 1 (Non-MLS 1)
Open Mon & Tues 9:30-5:30, Wed 9:30-5, Thurs 9-4

CANTON

P MADISON COUNTY LIBRARY SYSTEM*, 102 Priestley St, 39046-4599. SAN 348-1808. Administration Tel: 601-859-7733. Administration FAX: 601-859-0014. E-mail: feedback@mcls.ms. Web Site: www.mcls.ms/library/about.html. *Dir,* Sandra Sanders; *Asst Dir,* Ray Myers; *Pub Serv Dir, Webmaster,* Maggie Lawson; *Bus Librn,* Monica Stanford; *Coll Develop,* Anne Ellison; Staff 13 (MLS 8, Non-MLS 5)
Pop 79,758; Circ 360,060
Library Holdings: Bk Vols 176,926; Per Subs 224; Talking Bks 5,038; Videos 7,604
Special Collections: Local Picture Coll; Madison County Historical Materials. Oral History
Subject Interests: African-Am hist, Local hist, Miss writers
Automation Activity & Vendor Info: (Acquisitions) SirsiDynix; (Cataloging) SirsiDynix; (Circulation) SirsiDynix
Publications: Newsletter (Quarterly)
Partic in OCLC Online Computer Library Center, Inc
Open Mon & Wed 9-6, Tues & Thurs 9-7, Fri & Sat 9-5
Friends of the Library Group
Branches: 5
CAMDEN PUBLIC LIBRARY, 116 Parkside Ave, Camden, 39045. Tel: 662-468-0309. FAX: 662-468-0309. *Br Mgr,* Lennie Beamon
Founded 2004. Pop 1,379
Open Mon & Wed 10-7, Tues & Thurs 9-6, Fri 12-5, Sat 9-12
Friends of the Library Group
CANTON PUBLIC LIBRARY, 102 Priestley St, 39046. Tel: 601-859-3202. FAX: 601-859-2728. *Br Mgr,* Christine Greenwood; Staff 4 (MLS 1, Non-MLS 3)
Pop 12,911; Circ 54,333
Library Holdings: Bk Vols 61,000; Per Subs 50
Open Mon & Wed 9-6, Tues & Thurs 9-7, Fri & Sat 9-5
Friends of the Library Group
FLORA PUBLIC LIBRARY, 144 Clark St, Flora, 39071. (Mail add: PO Box 356, Flora, 39071-0356), SAN 348-1832. Tel: 601-879-8835. FAX: 601-879-8835. *Br Supvr,* Presley Posey; Staff 2 (Non-MLS 2)
Pop 1,546; Circ 11,969
Library Holdings: Bk Vols 19,327; Per Subs 14
Special Collections: Local History Coll
Open Mon-Thurs 10-6, Fri 12-5, Sat 9-1
Friends of the Library Group
MADISON PUBLIC LIBRARY, 994 Madison Ave, Madison, 39110. (Mail add: PO Box 1153, Madison, 39139), SAN 348-1867. Tel: 601-856-2749. FAX: 601-856-2681. *Br Mgr,* Jody Perkins; *Ch,* Liz Turner; Staff 5 (MLS 1, Non-MLS 4)
Pop 14,692; Circ 119,887
Library Holdings: Bk Vols 42,187; Per Subs 43
Open Mon-Thurs 9-7, Fri & Sat 9-5
Friends of the Library Group
RIDGELAND PUBLIC LIBRARY, 397 Hwy 51 N, Ridgeland, 39157, SAN 348-1891. Tel: 601-856-4536. FAX: 601-856-3748. *Br Mgr,* Nan Crosby; *Ch Serv,* Stephanie Surss; *Ref Serv,* Sherry Whitten; Staff 7 (MLS 4, Non-MLS 3)
Pop 20,173; Circ 85,542
Library Holdings: Bk Vols 55,000; Per Subs 50
Open Mon-Thurs 9-7, Fri & Sat 9-5
Friends of the Library Group

CARROLLTON

P CARROLLTON NORTH-CARROLLTON PUBLIC LIBRARY*, 1102 Lexington St, 38917. (Mail add: PO Box 329, 38917-0329), SAN 376-6411. Tel: 662-237-6268. FAX: 662-237-6268. Web Site: cpls-verso.auto-graphics.com. *Dir,* Sharon Tollison; Staff 1 (Non-MLS 1)
Pop 10,517; Circ 13,491
Library Holdings: Bk Titles 18,000; Per Subs 20; Talking Bks 300
Function: Copy machines, Fax serv, Handicapped accessible, Summer reading prog, VHS videos
Open Mon-Fri 8-12 & 1-5
Friends of the Library Group

CHARLESTON

P TALLAHATCHIE COUNTY LIBRARY SYSTEM*, 102 N Walnut, 38921. (Mail add: PO Box 219, 38921-0219), SAN 348-1921. Tel: 662-647-2638. FAX: 662-647-0975. *Dir,* Vicki Wood; *Librn,* Betty Christian
Founded 1939. Pop 17,800; Circ 104,000
Library Holdings: Bk Vols 42,000
Partic in Dancing Rabbit Library Consortium
Open Mon-Wed 9-5, Fri 10-4
Branches: 1
TUTWILER BRANCH, PO Box 214, Tutwiler, 38963, SAN 348-1956. Tel: 662-345-8475. FAX: 662-345-8475. *Librn,* Roshella Cole
Library Holdings: Bk Titles 10,000
Open Mon-Wed 9-5, Fri 10-4

CLARKSDALE

P CARNEGIE PUBLIC LIBRARY*, 114 Delta Ave, 38614-4212. (Mail add: PO Box 280, 38614-0280), SAN 348-2014. Tel: 662-624-4461. FAX: 662-627-4344. Web Site: www2.youseemore.com/carnegie/default.asp. *Dir,* Sarah Ruskey; E-mail: sruskey@cplclarksdale.lib.ms.us; *Ch Serv,* Ramona Barrett; *Circ,* Janice Williams; *ILL, Ref,* Joanne Blue; *Tech Serv,* Courtney Schaffer; Staff 11 (MLS 1, Non-MLS 10)
Founded 1914. Pop 27,272; Circ 75,000
Special Collections: State Document Depository
Automation Activity & Vendor Info: (Acquisitions) TLC (The Library Corporation); (Cataloging) TLC (The Library Corporation); (Circulation) TLC (The Library Corporation); (OPAC) TLC (The Library Corporation)
Wireless access
Partic in Miss Libr Comn Interlibr Loan Network
Open Mon-Thurs 9-5:30, Fri 9-5, Sat 9-1
Friends of the Library Group

J COAHOMA COMMUNITY COLLEGE*, Dickerson-Johnson Library & Learning Resource Center, 3240 Friars Point Rd, 38614. SAN 308-8480. Tel: 662-621-4287. FAX: 662-627-9530. Web Site: www.ccc.cc.ms.us/Library/geninfo.htm. *Dir, Libr Serv,* Yvonne M Stanford; Tel: 662-621-4161, E-mail: ystanford@coahomacc.edu; *Librn, Media Spec,* Mary L Caradine; Tel: 662-621-4289, E-mail: mcaradine@coahomacc.edu
Founded 1949. Enrl 1,362
Library Holdings: Bk Vols 36,000; Per Subs 400
Special Collections: Special Black Studies Coll
Subject Interests: Child growth, Educ
Partic in Dancing Rabbit Library Consortium
Open Mon-Thurs (Winter) 8am-9pm, Fri 8-4; Mon-Fri (Summer) 8-4

CLEVELAND

P BOLIVAR COUNTY LIBRARY SYSTEM*, Robinson-Carpenter Memorial Library, 104 S Leflore Ave, 38732. SAN 348-2073. Tel: 662-843-2774. Toll Free Tel: 888-268-8076. FAX: 662-843-4701. Web Site: www.bolivar.lib.ms.us. *Interim Dir,* Linda Kern; E-mail: lkern@bolivar.lib.ms.us; *Circ Mgr,* Sharon Williamson; E-mail: swilliamson@boliver.lib.ms.us; *Adult/Ref Serv,* Tamara Blackwell; *Syst Adminr,* Melanie Williams; *Tech Serv,* Lydia Brinkley; *Youth Serv,* Bobbie Matheney; Staff 15 (MLS 2, Non-MLS 13)

Founded 1958. Pop 34,145; Circ 41,044
Oct 2010-Sept 2011 Income (Main Library and Branch(s)) $665,721, State $115,302, City $177,938, Federal $9,323, County $292,100, Other $71,058. Mats Exp $35,776, Books $30,517, Per/Ser (Incl. Access Fees) $3,000, AV Mat $2,259. Sal $328,929 (Prof $108,395)
Library Holdings: Audiobooks 819; DVDs 237; Bk Vols 56,088; Per Subs 103
Subject Interests: Genealogy, Local hist
Automation Activity & Vendor Info: (Acquisitions) Innovative Interfaces, Inc; (Cataloging) Innovative Interfaces, Inc; (Circulation) Innovative Interfaces, Inc; (ILL) Innovative Interfaces, Inc; (OPAC) Innovative Interfaces, Inc; (Serials) EBSCO Online
Database Vendor: Baker & Taylor, EBSCOhost, OCLC WorldShare Interlibrary Loan, Westlaw, World Book Online
Wireless access
Function: Accelerated reader prog, Archival coll, AV serv, Bk reviews (Group), Bks on CD, CD-ROM, Children's prog, Computers for patron use, Copy machines, E-Reserves, Electronic databases & coll, Equip loans & repairs, Exhibits, Fax serv, Free DVD rentals, Games & aids for the handicapped, Handicapped accessible, Holiday prog, ILL available, Jail serv, Mail & tel request accepted, Music CDs, Online cat, Outreach serv, Photocopying/Printing, Preschool outreach, Preschool reading prog, Prog for adults, Prog for children & young adult, Pub access computers, Ref & res, Ref serv in person, Scanner, Senior outreach, Story hour, Summer reading prog, Tax forms, Teen prog, Telephone ref, Web-catalog, Wheelchair accessible
Partic in Dancing Rabbit Library Consortium
Open Mon-Thurs 9-6, Fri 9-5, Sat 9-1
Friends of the Library Group
Branches: 7
BENOIT PUBLIC LIBRARY, 109 W Preston St, Benoit, 38725. (Mail add: PO Box 307, Benoit, 38725), SAN 372-7912. Tel: 662-742-3112. FAX: 662-742-3112. *Librn,* Nan Williamson; E-mail: nwilliamson@bolivar.lib.ms.us
Open Mon, Tues & Thurs 1-5
Friends of the Library Group
FIELD MEMORIAL LIBRARY, 132 N Peeler Ave, Shaw, 38773. (Mail add: PO Box 387, Shaw, 38773), SAN 348-2103. Tel: 662-754-4597. FAX: 662-754-4597. E-mail: shaw@bolivar.lib.ms.us. *Br Librn,* KaNesha L Collins
Database Vendor: EBSCOhost, LearningExpress, World Book Online
Open Mon-Wed 12-5
Friends of the Library Group
GUNNISON PUBLIC LIBRARY, 404 Main St, Gunnison, 38746. (Mail add: PO Box 91, Gunnison, 38746), SAN 348-2138. Tel: 662-747-2201. *Br Librn,* Martha Lawson; E-mail: mlawson@bolivar.lib.ms.us
Open Tues & Thurs 1-5
DR ROBERT T HOLLINGSWORTH PUBLIC LIBRARY, Old Hwy 61, Shelby, 38774. (Mail add: PO Box 789, Shelby, 38774), SAN 348-2197. Tel: 662-398-7748. FAX: 662-398-7748. *Librn,* Marie Shorter; E-mail: shelby@bolivar.lib.ms.us
Open Mon & Wed 10-5, Fri 12-5
Friends of the Library Group
MOUND BAYOU PUBLIC, 301 E Martin Luther King St, Mound Bayou, 38762. (Mail add: 104 S Laflor Ave, 38732). Tel: 662-741-3299. FAX: 662-741-3299. E-mail: moundbayou@bolivar.lib.ms.us. *Librn,* Jamil Jackson
Founded 2002
Open Tues & Thurs 1-5
Friends of the Library Group
THELMA RAYNER MEMORIAL LIBRARY, 201 Front St, Merigold, 38759. (Mail add: PO Box 308, Merigold, 38759), SAN 348-2227. Tel: 662-748-2105. FAX: 662-748-2105. *Br Librn,* Nora Moore; E-mail: merigold@bolivar.lib.ms.us
Open Tues & Thurs 1-5
ROSEDALE PUBLIC LIBRARY, 702 Front St, Rosedale, 38769, SAN 348-2162. Tel: 662-759-6632. FAX: 662-759-6332. *Br Librn,* Martha Lawson; E-mail: mlawson@bolivar.lib.ms.us
Open Mon & Wed 10-5, Fri 12-5

C DELTA STATE UNIVERSITY*, Roberts-LaForge Library, Laflore Circle at Fifth Ave, 38733-2599. SAN 308-8499. Tel: 662-846-4440. Circulation Tel: 662-846-4430. Interlibrary Loan Service Tel: 662-846-4448. Automation Services Tel: 662-846-4432. Information Services Tel: 662-846-4431. FAX: 662-846-4443. Interlibrary Loan Service FAX: 662-846-4435. E-mail: refdesk@deltastate.edu. Web Site: library.deltastate.edu. *Dir,* Jeff M Slagell; E-mail: jslagell@deltastate.edu; *Asst Dir,* Joi Phillips; Tel: 662-846-4447, E-mail: jjphilip@deltastate.edu; *Head, Circ,* Jane Waldrup; E-mail: jwaldrup@deltastate.edu; *Automation Librn,* Hongyan Sun; E-mail: hsun@deltastate.edu; *Electronic Serv Librn,* Stephen Patton; E-mail: spatton@deltastate.edu; *Instrul Serv Librn, Ref,* Melissa Dennis; E-mail: mdennis@deltastate.edu; *Instrul Serv Librn,* Frieda Quon; Tel: 662-846-4345, E-mail: fquon@deltastate.edu; *Archivist,* Emily Erwin Weaver; Tel: 662-846-4780, E-mail: eweaver@deltastate.edu; *Cat, Tech Serv,* Sheryl Stump; Tel: 662-846-4458, E-mail: sheryl@deltastate.edu; *Doc, Ref,* David Salinero; E-mail: dsaliner@deltastate.edu; *Ref,* Ann Ashmore; E-mail: aashmore@deltastate.edu; *Ref,* Michael Mounce; E-mail: mmounce@deltastate.edu; *Ser,* Paula Webb; Tel: 662-846-4456, E-mail: pwebb@deltastate.edu; *Tech Serv,* Rick Torgerson; Tel: 662-846-4438, E-mail: rick@deltastate.edu; Staff 25 (MLS 12, Non-MLS 13)
Founded 1925. Enrl 4,200; Fac 250; Highest Degree: Doctorate
Library Holdings: AV Mats 19,302; e-books 50,786; Bk Vols 360,286; Per Subs 17,368
Special Collections: Archives (Walter Sillers Coll); Art Coll; Mississippi Delta History; Mississippiana, mss. Oral History; State Document Depository; US Document Depository
Automation Activity & Vendor Info: (Acquisitions) SirsiDynix; (Cataloging) SirsiDynix; (Circulation) SirsiDynix; (Course Reserve) SirsiDynix; (ILL) SirsiDynix; (OPAC) SirsiDynix; (Serials) SirsiDynix
Database Vendor: EBSCOhost, Gale Cengage Learning, JSTOR, OCLC FirstSearch, Wilson - Wilson Web
Partic in Dancing Rabbit Library Consortium; Lyrasis; MAGNOLIA
Open Mon-Thurs 7:30am-10pm, Fri 7:30-4, Sat 10-5, Sun 2-10
Friends of the Library Group

CLINTON

SR MISSISSIPPI BAPTIST HISTORICAL COMMISSION LIBRARY*, 200 S Capitol St, 39058. (Mail add: PO Box 4024, 39058), SAN 327-2168. Tel: 601-925-3434. FAX: 601-925-3435. E-mail: mbhc@mc.edu. *Librn,* Heather Weeden; Staff 2 (MLS 1, Non-MLS 1)
Jan 2005-Dec 2005 Income $61,773
Library Holdings: Bk Titles 900
Subject Interests: Baptist hist
Wireless access
Publications: A History of Mississippi Baptists 1780-1970; Highlights of Mississippi Baptist History; Mississippi Baptist Convention Ministers: Current Biographies
Open Mon-Fri 8-12 & 1-4:30
Restriction: Non-circulating

C MISSISSIPPI COLLEGE, Leland Speed Library, 101 W College St, 39058. (Mail add: PO Box 4047, 39058-4047), SAN 348-2251. Tel: 601-925-3232. Reference Tel: 601-925-3916. FAX: 601-925-3435. Web Site: library.mc.edu. *Libr Dir,* Kathleen Hutchison; Tel: 601-925-3870, E-mail: khutchis@mc.edu; *Asst Dir,* Wanda Mosley; Tel: 601-925-3729, E-mail: mosley@mc.edu; *Head, Tech Serv,* Julie Thornton; Tel: 601-925-3436, E-mail: jthornto@mc.edu; *Ref & Instruction Librn,* Niki Carter; Tel: 601-925-7879, E-mail: sncarter@mc.edu; *Ref & Instruction Librn,* Michelle Finerty; Tel: 601-925-3944, E-mail: mlfinerty@mc.edu; *Ref & Instruction Librn,* Alex Goolsby; Tel: 601-925-3431, E-mail: aegoolsby@mc.edu; *Coordr, Ref (Info Serv),* Claudia Conklin; Tel: 601-925-3943, E-mail: cconklin@mc.edu; Staff 7 (Non-MLS 7)
Founded 1826. Fac 160; Highest Degree: Doctorate
Library Holdings: Bk Vols 241,620; Per Subs 770
Special Collections: Mississippi Baptist Historical Coll
Automation Activity & Vendor Info: (Acquisitions) Innovative Interfaces, Inc; (Cataloging) Innovative Interfaces, Inc; (Circulation) Innovative Interfaces, Inc; (Course Reserve) Innovative Interfaces, Inc; (ILL) Innovative Interfaces, Inc; (Media Booking) Innovative Interfaces, Inc; (OPAC) Innovative Interfaces, Inc; (Serials) Innovative Interfaces, Inc
Database Vendor: Alexander Street Press, American Chemical Society, American Psychological Association (APA), Cinahl, CredoReference, EBSCOhost, Elsevier, Gale Cengage Learning, Hoovers, IEEE (Institute of Electrical & Electronics Engineers), JSTOR, LexisNexis, Medline, Mergent Online, Modern Language Association, OCLC, OCLC WebJunction, Oxford Online, Project MUSE, Sage, ScienceDirect, Springshare, LLC
Wireless access
Function: ILL available
Partic in Lyrasis
Open Mon-Thurs 7:30am-1am, Fri 7:30am-Midnight, Sat Noon-Midnight, Sun 2pm-1am
Restriction: Pub use on premises
Departmental Libraries:
LAW LIBRARY
See Separate Entry in Jackson

COFFEEVILLE

P COFFEEVILLE PUBLIC LIBRARY*, 714 Main St, 38922-2590. SAN 324-3737. Tel: 662-675-8822. FAX: 662-675-2001. *Librn,* Patty M Bailey; *Asst Librn,* Joyce Snider
Founded 1960. Pop 1,100; Circ 6,067
Library Holdings: Bk Vols 9,040; Per Subs 45
Automation Activity & Vendor Info: (Circulation) Book Systems
Open Mon & Fri 9-12 & 1-5, Tues & Wed 1-5, Thurs 1-8
Friends of the Library Group

COLLINS

P COVINGTON COUNTY LIBRARY SYSTEM*, R E Blackwell Memorial, 403 S Fir Ave, 39428. (Mail add: PO Box 1539, 39428-1539), SAN 348-8195. Tel: 601-765-8582. FAX: 601-765-8582. Web Site: www.ccls.lib.ms.us/collins-ms. *Dir,* David Hollingsworth
Wireless access
Open Mon-Fri 8:30-5:30
Branches: 2
JANE BLAIN BREWER MEMORIAL, 102 S Fifth St, Mount Olive, 39119. (Mail add: PO Box 279, Mount Olive, 39119-0279), SAN 348-8373. Tel: 601-797-4955. FAX: 601-797-4955. E-mail: mtolive@ccls.lib.ms.us. Web Site: www.ccls.lib.ms/mount-olive-ms. *Librn,* Martha Diehl
Open Mon-Fri 12:30-5:30
Friends of the Library Group
CONNER-GRAHAM MEMORIAL, 101 Willow St, Seminary, 39479. (Mail add: PO Box 95, Seminary, 39479-0095), SAN 348-8497. Tel: 601-722-9041. FAX: 601-722-9041. Web Site: www.ccls.lib.ms.us/seminary-ms. *Librn,* Jamie Hoffman
Open Mon-Fri 8:30-5
Friends of the Library Group

COLUMBIA

P SOUTH MISSISSIPPI REGIONAL LIBRARY, Columbia Marion County Library, 900 Broad St, 39429. SAN 348-2316. Tel: 601-736-5516. FAX: 601-736-1379. Web Site: www.smrl.lib.ms.us. *Dir,* Linda Gail Bracey; E-mail: gbracey@smrl.lib.ms.us; *Br Mgr,* Jackie Miller; Tel: 601-943-5420, Fax: 601-943-5142, E-mail: jmiller@smrl.lib.ms.us; *Br Mgr,* Kendra Smith; Tel: 601-792-5845, Fax: 601-792-8159, E-mail: ksmith@smrl.lib.ms.us; *Youth Serv Librn,* Ryda Worthy; E-mail: rworthy@smrl.lib.ms.us; Staff 4 (MLS 2, Non-MLS 2)
Founded 1972. Pop 41,508
Library Holdings: Audiobooks 1,200; DVDs 4,800; e-books 600; e-journals 2; Bk Titles 31,602; Bk Vols 574,990; Per Subs 228
Automation Activity & Vendor Info: (Cataloging) Innovative Interfaces, Inc; (Circulation) Innovative Interfaces, Inc; (OPAC) Innovative Interfaces, Inc
Database Vendor: CredoReference, EBSCOhost, H W Wilson, LearningExpress
Wireless access
Open Mon-Thurs 8:30-6, Fri & Sat 8:30-3
Friends of the Library Group
Branches: 2
FRANK L LEGGETT PUBLIC LIBRARY, PO Box 310, Bassfield, 39421-0310, SAN 348-2340. Tel: 601-943-5420. FAX: 601-943-5420.
Open Mon-Fri 8:30-12 & 1-5
Friends of the Library Group
PRENTISS PUBLIC, PO Box 1315, Prentiss, 39474-1315, SAN 348-2375. Tel: 601-792-5845. FAX: 601-792-8159. *Librn,* Faye Speights
Open Mon-Thurs 8:30-5:30, Fri 8:30-5
Friends of the Library Group

COLUMBUS

P COLUMBUS-LOWNDES PUBLIC LIBRARY*, 314 N Seventh St, 39701. SAN 348-2405. Tel: 662-329-5300. FAX: 662-329-5156. Web Site: www.lowndeslibrary.org. *Interim Dir,* Erin B Stringer; Tel: 662-329-5303, E-mail: estringer@lowndes.lib.ms.us; *Youth Serv Librn,* Lindsey Miller; Tel: 662-329-5150, E-mail: lmiller@lowndes.lib.ms.us; *Bus Mgr,* Sharon Whitten; E-mail: swhitten@lowndes.lib.ms.us; *Archivist,* Mona Vance; Tel: 662-329-5304, E-mail: mvance@lowndes.lib.ms.us; *Cataloger, Circ,* Wil'Lani Turner; Tel: 662-329-5297, E-mail: wturner@lowndes.lib.ms.us; *Circ, Tech Serv,* Valencia Sherrod; Tel: 662-329-5306, E-mail: vsherrod@lowndes.lib.ms.us. Subject Specialists: *Local hist,* Mona Vance; Staff 22 (MLS 3, Non-MLS 19)
Founded 1940. Pop 60,933; Circ 108,868
Library Holdings: Bk Vols 94,995; Per Subs 151
Special Collections: Billups-Garth Archives; Eudora Welty Special Coll; Genealogy & Local History (Margaret Latimer Buckley Room), bks, pers & micro
Automation Activity & Vendor Info: (Acquisitions) SirsiDynix; (Cataloging) SirsiDynix; (Circulation) SirsiDynix; (ILL) SirsiDynix; (OPAC) SirsiDynix; (Serials) EBSCO Online
Database Vendor: Oxford Online, World Book Online
Wireless access
Partic in Mississippi Library Partnership
Special Services for the Blind - Bks on CD; Large print bks; Playaways (bks on MP3); Talking bk encyclopedia
Open Mon-Thurs 9-7, Fri 9-2, Sat 10-4
Friends of the Library Group
Branches: 3
ARTESIA PUBLIC, 323 Front St, Artesia, 39736, SAN 348-243X. Tel: 662-272-5255. FAX: 662-272-5255. *Br Librn,* Bernice Wilson; E-mail: bwilson@lowndes.lib.ms.us; Staff 5 (MLS 3, Non-MLS 2)
Automation Activity & Vendor Info: (Course Reserve) SirsiDynix
Function: Art exhibits, Bks on CD, Children's prog, Computer training, Computers for patron use, Copy machines, e-mail & chat, Exhibits, Fax serv, Free DVD rentals, Handicapped accessible, Holiday prog, ILL available, Online cat, Online ref, Photocopying/Printing, Prog for adults, Prog for children & young adult, Ref & res, Story hour, Summer reading prog, Tax forms, Teen prog, Telephone ref, Workshops
Partic in MAGNOLIA
Open Tues & Thurs 10-1 & 2-5:15
Friends of the Library Group
CALEDONIA PUBLIC, 754 Main St, Caledonia, 39740, SAN 348-2464. Tel: 662-356-6384. FAX: 662-356-6384. *Br Librn,* Christy Burks; E-mail: cburks@lowndes.lib.ms.us
Open Mon, Wed & Thurs 9:30-1 & 2-6
Friends of the Library Group
CRAWFORD PUBLIC, 320 Main St, Crawford, 39743, SAN 348-2472. Tel: 662-272-5144. FAX: 662-272-5144. *Br Librn,* Bernice Wilson; E-mail: bwilson@lowndes.lib.ms.us
Open Mon & Wed 10-1 & 2-5:15

COLUMBUS AFB

A UNITED STATES AIR FORCE*, Columbus Air Force Base Library, 37 Harris St, 39710-5102. SAN 348-2553. Tel: 662-434-2934. FAX: 662-434-6291. Web Site: www.cafb.com. *Dir,* Linda Dodson; E-mail: linda.dodson@columbus.af.mil; Staff 6 (MLS 1, Non-MLS 5)
Library Holdings: Bk Vols 17,500; Per Subs 87
Subject Interests: Aviation, Mil strategy
Open Mon-Thurs 9-7:30, Fri 9-6, Sun 1-5

CORINTH

P NORTHEAST REGIONAL LIBRARY*, 1023 Fillmore St, 38834-4199. SAN 348-2588. Tel: 662-287-7311. FAX: 662-286-8010. Web Site: www.nereg.lib.ms.us. *Dir,* William L McMullin; E-mail: william@nereg.lib.ms.us; *Asst Dir,* Catherine Kanady; E-mail: ckan@nereg.lib.ms.us; *Coll Develop,* Olivia H McIntyre; E-mail: mcintyre@nereg.lib.ms.us; Staff 24 (MLS 4, Non-MLS 20)
Founded 1951. Pop 101,564; Circ 346,035
Oct 2006-Sept 2007 Income (Main Library and Branch(s)) $869,838, State $268,999, Federal $875, County $442,827, Locally Generated Income $3,400, Other $153,647. Mats Exp $94,337, Books $75,502, AV Mat $18,835. Sal $447,352
Library Holdings: AV Mats 18,231; Electronic Media & Resources 49; Bk Vols 200,146; Per Subs 211
Special Collections: Oral History
Subject Interests: Genealogy
Automation Activity & Vendor Info: (Cataloging) OCLC CatExpress; (Circulation) SirsiDynix; (ILL) OCLC FirstSearch; (OPAC) Horizon
Database Vendor: SirsiDynix
Wireless access
Function: Adult bk club, Adult literacy prog, Art exhibits, Bks on cassette, Bks on CD, Computer training, Computers for patron use, Copy machines, Electronic databases & coll, Fax serv, Handicapped accessible, ILL available, Mail & tel request accepted, Music CDs, Online cat, Photocopying/Printing, Prog for children & young adult, Pub access computers, Ref serv available, Spoken cassettes & CDs, Spoken cassettes & DVDs, Summer reading prog, Tax forms, Telephone ref, VHS videos
Partic in Vermont Resource Sharing Network
Open Mon-Fri 8-5
Friends of the Library Group
Branches: 13
GEORGE E ALLEN LIBRARY, 500 W Church St, Booneville, 38829-3353, SAN 348-2820. Tel: 662-728-6553. FAX: 662-728-4127. *Librn,* Dee Horn; E-mail: dee@nereg.lib.ms.us
Library Holdings: Bk Vols 29,927
Special Collections: George E Allen Coll, (papers & memorabilia belonging to George E Allen)
Open Mon-Thurs 9-6, Fri 9-5, Sat 9-4
Friends of the Library Group
BELMONT PUBLIC LIBRARY, 102 S Third St, Belmont, 38827. (Mail add: PO Box 629, Belmont, 38827-0629), SAN 348-2677. Tel: 662-454-7841. FAX: 662-454-7841. *Librn,* Andrea Green; E-mail: agreen@nereg.lib.ms.us
Library Holdings: Bk Vols 13,689
Open Mon-Wed & Fri 9:30-5
Friends of the Library Group
BLUE MOUNTAIN PUBLIC LIBRARY, 110 Mill St, Blue Mountain, 38610. (Mail add: PO Box 188, Blue Mountain, 38610-0188), SAN 348-2707. Tel: 662-685-4721. FAX: 662-685-4031. E-mail:

bl@nereg.lib.ms.us. Web Site: www.nereg.lib.ms.us/bluemountian.htm. *Librn,* Sheila K Lence
Library Holdings: Bk Vols 5,473
Open Thurs 3-5, Fri & Sat 1-5

BURNSVILLE PUBLIC LIBRARY, Norman Ave, Burnsville, 38833. (Mail add: PO Box 188, Burnsville, 38833-0188), SAN 348-2731. Tel: 662-427-9258. FAX: 662-427-9258. *Librn,* Robert Forbes; E-mail: bu@nereg.lib.ms.us
Library Holdings: Bk Vols 10,006
Open Mon-Fri 10-4
Friends of the Library Group

CHALYBEATE PUBLIC LIBRARY, 2501-A Hwy 354, Walnut, 38683-9762, SAN 348-2766. Tel: 662-223-4621. *Librn,* Genette McKinney
Library Holdings: Bk Vols 4,248
Open Mon & Wed 1-4, Fri 12-4

CORINTH PUBLIC LIBRARY, 1023 Fillmore St, 38834. Tel: 662-287-2441. Administration Tel: 662-287-7311. FAX: 662-286-8010. E-mail: co@nereg.lib.ms.us. *Librn,* Brandon S Lowrey; E-mail: brandon@nereg.lib.ms.us
Founded 1951. Pop 35,000; Circ 123,856
Library Holdings: Bk Vols 68,173
Open Mon-Thurs 9-8, Fri & Sat 9-5
Friends of the Library Group

ANNE SPENCER COX LIBRARY, 303 N Third St, Baldwyn, 38824-1517, SAN 348-2642. Tel: 662-365-3305. FAX: 662-365-3305. *Librn,* Simone Chandler
Library Holdings: Bk Vols 14,926
Database Vendor: SirsiDynix
Open Mon-Thurs 10-6, Fri & Sat 9-1
Friends of the Library Group

IUKA PUBLIC LIBRARY, 204 N Main St, Iuka, 38852, SAN 348-288X. Tel: 662-423-6300. FAX: 662-423-6300. *Librn,* Gwen Spain; E-mail: gwen@nereg.lib.ms.us
Library Holdings: Bk Vols 29,478
Open Mon-Thurs 9-6, Fri 9-5, Sat 9-4
Friends of the Library Group

MARIETTA PUBLIC LIBRARY, Seven County Rd 4060, Marietta, 38856. (Mail add: PO Box 88, Marietta, 38856-0088), SAN 348-291X. Tel: 662-728-9320. *Librn,* Cindy Ramey
Library Holdings: Bk Vols 3,348
Open Mon-Fri 9-4:30

RIENZI PUBLIC LIBRARY, School St, Rienzi, 38865. (Mail add: PO Box 69, Rienzi, 38865-0069), SAN 348-2944. Tel: 662-462-5015. *Librn,* Rita Millsaps
Library Holdings: Bk Vols 6,303
Open Mon, Wed & Fri 12-5

RIPLEY PUBLIC LIBRARY, 308 N Commerce St, Ripley, 38663-1721, SAN 348-2979. Tel: 662-837-7773. FAX: 662-837-7773. *Librn,* Tommy Covington; E-mail: tippah@yahoo.com
Library Holdings: Bk Vols 21,955
Open Mon, Wed, Fri & Sat 9-5, Tues & Thurs 9-8

TISHOMINGO LIBRARY, 1292 Main St, Tishomingo, 38873. (Mail add: PO Box 128, Tishomingo, 38873-0128), SAN 348-3002. Tel: 662-438-7640. FAX: 662-438-7640. E-mail: ti@nereg.lib.ms.us. *Librn,* Beverly Parker
Library Holdings: Bk Vols 8,332
Open Mon, Wed & Fri 10-5, Sat 10-3
Friends of the Library Group

WALNUT PUBLIC LIBRARY, 102 S Main St, Walnut, 38683-9312, SAN 348-3037. Tel: 662-223-6768. FAX: 662-223-6768. *Librn,* Jamie Wall
Library Holdings: Bk Vols 7,538
Open Mon 10-5, Tues & Fri 11:30-5, Wed 11-5

DECATUR

J EAST CENTRAL COMMUNITY COLLEGE*, Mamie Ethel Burton Memorial Library, 275 E Broad St, 39327. (Mail add: PO Box 129, 39327-0129), SAN 308-8510. Tel: 601-635-2111, Ext 219, 601-635-2111, Ext 220. Toll Free Tel: 877-462-3222. FAX: 601-635-2150. Web Site: www.eccc.edu/library/burtonlibrary.htm. *Librn,* Leslie Hughes; E-mail: lhughes@eccc.edu; *Asst Librn,* Gail Wood
Founded 1977. Enrl 2,400
Library Holdings: Bk Vols 41,000; Per Subs 210
Open Mon-Thurs (Winter) 7:30am-9:30pm, Fri 7:30-3, Sun 6-8:30; Mon-Thurs (Summer) 7:30-3:30, Fri 7:30-3

ELLISVILLE

J JONES COUNTY JUNIOR COLLEGE*, T Terrell Tisdale Library, 900 S Court St, 39437. SAN 308-8529. Tel: 601-477-4055. FAX: 601-477-2600. E-mail: library@jcjc.edu. Web Site: www.jcjc.edu/library/terrelltisdalelibrary.php. *Dir,* Andrew Sharp; *Acq,* Julie Atwood; *Cat,* Gary Herring; Staff 4 (MLS 4)
Founded 1924. Enrl 5,186; Fac 275
Library Holdings: AV Mats 44,426; Bk Vols 65,000; Per Subs 160
Special Collections: Literary Criticism on William Faulkner & Eudora Welty, bks & flm; Mississippi Coll
Subject Interests: Genealogy
Automation Activity & Vendor Info: (Acquisitions) SirsiDynix; (Cataloging) SirsiDynix; (Circulation) SirsiDynix; (Course Reserve) SirsiDynix; (ILL) OCLC; (OPAC) SirsiDynix; (Serials) SirsiDynix
Wireless access
Publications: Library Handbook
Open Mon-Thurs 7am-9pm, Fri 7-3:30

FLORENCE

P FLORENCE PUBLIC LIBRARY*, 104 W Main St, 39073. (Mail add: PO Box 95, 39073-0095), SAN 376-6276. Tel: 601-845-6032. FAX: 601-845-4625. E-mail: florence@cmrls.lib.ms.us. Web Site: www.cmrls.lib.ms.us/florence.htm. *Br Mgr,* Jeanette Harper; *Ref,* Gwen Davis
Library Holdings: Bk Titles 15,000; Bk Vols 16,000; Per Subs 12
Automation Activity & Vendor Info: (Circulation) SirsiDynix; (ILL) SirsiDynix; (Media Booking) SirsiDynix; (Serials) SirsiDynix
Open Mon & Thurs 9:30-7, Tues & Wed 9:30-5, Fri 1-5, Sat 9-12
Friends of the Library Group

FOREST

P FOREST PUBLIC LIBRARY*, 210 S Raleigh St, 39074. (Mail add: PO Box 737, 39074-0737), SAN 376-6233. Tel: 601-469-1481. FAX: 601-469-5903. E-mail: forest@cmrls.lib.ms.us. Web Site: www.cmrls.lib.ms.us. *Br Mgr,* Shawna Alexander; *Ch Serv,* Paula Wells
Library Holdings: Bk Titles 27,836; Per Subs 25
Database Vendor: EBSCOhost, Gale Cengage Learning, OCLC FirstSearch, SirsiDynix, Wilson - Wilson Web
Function: Photocopying/Printing
Mem of Central Mississippi Regional Library System
Open Mon, Wed & Thurs 9-5:30, Tues 10-7, Fri 9-5, Sat 9-12
Friends of the Library Group

FULTON

J ITAWAMBA COMMUNITY COLLEGE*, Learning Resource Center, 602 W Hill St, 38843. SAN 348-324X. Tel: 662-862-8384. FAX: 662-862-8410. Web Site: www.iccms.edu. *Dir,* Dr Glenda Segars; Tel: 662-862-8383, E-mail: grsegars@iccms.edu; *Librn, Media Spec,* Jimmy J Humphries; Tel: 662-862-8381, E-mail: jjhumphries@iccms.edu; *Librn,* Holly Karr; Tel: 662-862-8378, E-mail: kmkarr@iccms.edu; Staff 2 (MLS 2)
Library Holdings: Bk Titles 50,000; Per Subs 254
Partic in Loanet; Lyrasis; Miss Interlibr Loan Syst
Open Mon-Thurs (Winter) 7:45am-9pm, Fri 7:45-4:30, Sun 4-8; Mon-Fri (Summer) 7:45-4:30

P PRATT MEMORIAL LIBRARY*, 210 Cedar St, 38843. SAN 348-8829. Tel: 662-862-4926. FAX: 662-862-2477. *Librn,* Jeffrey Martin; E-mail: icpl1@li.lib.ms.us; Staff 4 (MLS 4)
Founded 1966
Wireless access
Function: Bk reviews (Group), Bks on cassette, Bks on CD, Computer training, Computers for patron use, Copy machines, Fax serv, Free DVD rentals, Handicapped accessible, Holiday prog, ILL available, Online cat, Online ref, Online searches, Outreach serv, Photocopying/Printing, Preschool outreach, Prog for adults, Prog for children & young adult, Pub access computers, Senior computer classes, Spoken cassettes & CDs, Story hour, Summer reading prog, Tax forms, VHS videos, Web-catalog
Open Mon, Tues, Thurs & Fri 9-6, Sat 10-2
Friends of the Library Group

GAUTIER

J MISSISSIPPI GULF COAST COMMUNITY COLLEGE, Jackson County Campus Library, 2300 Hwy 90, 39553. (Mail add: PO Box 100, 39553-0100), SAN 308-8545. Tel: 228-497-7830. Interlibrary Loan Service Tel: 228-497-7825. Reference Tel: 228-497-7715, 228-497-7716. Administration Tel: 228-497-7642. Toll Free Tel: 866-735-1122. FAX: 228-497-7643. E-mail: jc.library@mgccc.edu. Web Site: www.mgccc.edu. *Asst Dean,* Dr Ladner Ann Pamela; E-mail: pamela.ladner@mgccc.edu; *Librn,* Gwendolyn Carter; E-mail: gwendolyn.carter@mgccc.edu; *Librn,* Tim Koehn; E-mail: tim.koehn@mgccc.edu; Staff 7 (MLS 4, Non-MLS 3)
Founded 1965. Enrl 3,189; Fac 185; Highest Degree: Associate
Automation Activity & Vendor Info: (Acquisitions) SirsiDynix
Wireless access
Partic in Lyrasis
Open Mon-Thurs 7:30am-8pm, Fri 7:30-3:30

GOODMAN

J HOLMES COMMUNITY COLLEGE*, McMorrough Library, Goodman Campus, 178 Hill St, 39079. (Mail add: PO Box 439, 39079), SAN 308-8553. Tel: 662-472-2312, Ext 1049. FAX: 662-472-9155. Web Site: www.holmescc.edu/library/library_goodman.aspx. *Librn,* Nell Branch; Tel: 662-472-9018, E-mail: nbranch@holmescc.edu; Staff 4 (MLS 2, Non-MLS 2)
Founded 1928. Enrl 3,805; Fac 132; Highest Degree: Associate
Jul 2005-Jun 2006. Mats Exp $124,696
Library Holdings: e-books 40,000; Bk Vols 57,875; Per Subs 64
Subject Interests: Juv, Miss, Shakespeare
Automation Activity & Vendor Info: (Acquisitions) SIRSI WorkFlows; (Cataloging) SIRSI WorkFlows; (OPAC) SIRSI-iBistro
Database Vendor: SirsiDynix
Wireless access
Partic in MAGNOLIA
Open Mon-Thurs (Fall & Spring) 7:30-5 & 6-9, Fri 7:30-3:30; Mon-Fri (Summer) 8-3:30
Restriction: In-house use for visitors

GREENVILLE

P WASHINGTON COUNTY LIBRARY SYSTEM*, William Alexander Percy Memorial Library, 341 Main St, 38701-4097. SAN 348-3274. Tel: 662-335-2331. FAX: 662-390-4758. Web Site: www.washington.lib.ms.us. *Dir,* Kay Clanton; E-mail: kclanton@washington.lib.ms.us; *Ch Serv,* Barbara Johnston; *Circ,* Valerie Moore; *ILL,* Ruth Ford; Staff 6 (MLS 1, Non-MLS 5)
Founded 1964
Library Holdings: Bk Vols 281,325; Per Subs 394
Special Collections: Greenville Writers Exhibit. Oral History
Subject Interests: Genealogy, Local hist, Miss hist
Automation Activity & Vendor Info: (Cataloging) Auto-Graphics, Inc
Partic in Dancing Rabbit Library Consortium
Open Mon-Wed 9-7, Thurs & Fri 9-6, Sat 1-5
Friends of the Library Group
Branches: 5
ARCOLA LIBRARY, 106 Martin Luther King Dr, Arcola, 38722, SAN 348-3304. Tel: 662-827-5262. Web Site: www.washington.lib.ms.us/arcola_library.htm. *Br Mgr,* Joan Haywood
Open Mon 2-6, (Winter) Tues-Fri 3-6; Mon (Summer) 1-5, Tues-Fri 2-5
AVON LIBRARY, 874 Riverside Rd, Avon, 38723, SAN 348-3339. Tel: 662-332-9346. Web Site: www.washington.lib.ms.us/avonlibrary.htm. *Br Mgr,* Joan Davis
Open Mon-Thurs 2-5
GLEN ALLAN LIBRARY, 970 E Lake Washington Rd, Glen Allan, 38744, SAN 348-3428. Tel: 662-839-4066. FAX: 662-839-4066. *Br Mgr,* Winnie Darnell
Open Mon 1-5, Tues-Fri 2-5
LELAND LIBRARY, 107 N Broad St, Leland, 38756-2797, SAN 348-3363. Tel: 601-686-7353. FAX: 601-686-7353. E-mail: leland@washington.lib.ms.us. *Br Mgr,* Fran Robinson
Open Mon-Fri 9-6
Friends of the Library Group
TORREY WOOD MEMORIAL, 302 East Ave N, Hollandale, 38748-3714, SAN 348-3398. Tel: 662 827-2335. Web Site: www.washington.lib.ms.us/hollandalelibrary.htm. *Br Mgr,* Andrea Ross
Open Mon 2-6, Tues-Fri 3-6
Bookmobiles: 1

GREENWOOD

S COTTONLANDIA MUSEUM*, R A Billups Memorial Library, 1608 Hwy 82 W, 38930. SAN 370-7555. Tel: 662-453-0925. FAX: 662-455-7556. Web Site: www.cottonlandia.org.
Founded 1974
Library Holdings: Bk Vols 800; Per Subs 10
Special Collections: Mississippi Archeology & History, bks, papers
Open Mon-Fri 9-5, Sat & Sun 2-5

P GREENWOOD-LEFLORE PUBLIC LIBRARY SYSTEM*, 405 W Washington St, 38930-4297. SAN 348-3452. Tel: 662-453-3634. Interlibrary Loan Service Tel: 662-453-3635. FAX: 662-453-0683. E-mail: info@glpls.com. Web Site: www.glpls.com. *Dir,* Jenniffer Stephenson; E-mail: jstephenson@greenwood.lib.ms.us; *Head, Tech Proc,* Mrs Causie Clay; E-mail: claycausie@greenwood.lib.ms.us; *Bus Mgr,* Wyvonne Burden; E-mail: wyvonne@greenwood.lib.ms.us; *Circ Supvr, Mgr, ILL,* Candace Hony; E-mail: candyhony@greenwood.lib.ms.us; *Acq,* Sue Lott; E-mail: sue1951@greenwood.lib.ms.us; *Acq, Tech Serv,* Linda Williams; E-mail: lindawms38930@greenwood.lib.ms.us; *Circ, Libr Asst,* Lucy Jones; E-mail: ljones@greenwood.lib.ms.us; *Circ, Libr Asst,* Tad Russell; E-mail: trussell@greenwood.lib.ms.us; *Youth Spec,* Barbara Goss; E-mail: bgoss@greenwood.lib.ms.us; *Youth Spec,* Jillian Rogers; E-mail: jrogers@greenwood.lib.ms.us. Subject Specialists: *Cataloging,* Mrs Causie Clay; *Genealogy,* Wyvonne Burden; *Hist,* Tad Russell; Staff 9.5 (MLS 3, Non-MLS 6.5)
Founded 1914. Pop 31,861; Circ 42,171
Oct 2011-Sept 2012 Income (Main Library and Branch(s)) $347,772, City $175,837, County $171,935
Library Holdings: AV Mats 727; Bk Vols 87,947; Per Subs 176
Special Collections: Genealogy (Mae Wilson McBee Coll), bk, microfilm
Subject Interests: Genealogy
Automation Activity & Vendor Info: (Cataloging) Auto-Graphics, Inc; (Circulation) Auto-Graphics, Inc; (ILL) Auto-Graphics, Inc; (OPAC) Auto-Graphics, Inc
Database Vendor: CredoReference, EBSCOhost
Wireless access
Function: Bk club(s), Bks on cassette, Bks on CD, Children's prog, Computer training, Computers for patron use, Copy machines, Distance learning, e-mail serv, Electronic databases & coll, Holiday prog, ILL available, Mail & tel request accepted, Microfiche/film & reading machines, Online cat, Outreach serv, Outside serv via phone, mail, e-mail & web, Photocopying/Printing, Preschool outreach, Prog for children & young adult, Pub access computers, Ref & res, Ref serv available, Ref serv in person, Res performed for a fee, Spoken cassettes & CDs, Story hour, Summer reading prog, Tax forms, Teen prog, Telephone ref, Wheelchair accessible
Special Services for the Blind - Bks on cassette; Bks on CD; Large print bks
Open Mon-Fri 8:30-5:30, Sat 8:30-Noon
Restriction: ID required to use computers (Ltd hrs), Open to pub for ref & circ; with some limitations
Branches: 1
JODIE WILSON BRANCH, 209 E Martin Luther King Jr Dr, 38930-6625, SAN 348-3606. Tel: 662-453-1761. *Br Mgr,* Ozella Nichols
Circ 815
Library Holdings: Bk Vols 8,377; Per Subs 14
Open Mon-Fri 9-12 & 1-5

GRENADA

J HOLMES COMMUNITY COLLEGE*, Grenada Center Library, 1180 W Monroe St, 38901. Tel: 662-226-0830. FAX: 662-227-2290. Web Site: www.holmescc.edu/library/library_grenada.aspx. *District Librn,* Joan E Tierce; Tel: 662-227-2312, E-mail: jtierce@holmescc.edu; *Librn,* Carla Ross; Tel: 662-227-2313, E-mail: cross@holmescc.edu
Library Holdings: Bk Titles 6,000; Per Subs 125
Automation Activity & Vendor Info: (Acquisitions) SirsiDynix; (Cataloging) SirsiDynix; (Circulation) SirsiDynix; (Course Reserve) SirsiDynix; (ILL) SirsiDynix; (OPAC) SirsiDynix
Database Vendor: EBSCOhost, Gale Cengage Learning, ProQuest, Wilson - Wilson Web
Open Mon-Thurs (Fall & Spring) 7:45-7, Fri 7:45-3:30; Mon-Fri (Summer) 8-12 & 1-3:30

P ELIZABETH JONES LIBRARY*, 1050 Fairfield Ave, 38901-3605. (Mail add: PO Box 130, 38902-0130), SAN 308-8561. Tel: 662-226-2072. FAX: 662-226-8747. E-mail: grenadapubliclibrary@elizabeth.lib.ms.us. Web Site: www.elizabeth.lib.ms.us. *Dir,* Crystal M Osborne; *Circ,* Sandra McCaulla; *Circ,* Stella Topps; *Tech Serv,* Pam Davis; Staff 4 (MLS 1, Non-MLS 3)
Founded 1933. Pop 23,000; Circ 87,563
Library Holdings: Bk Vols 50,000; Per Subs 80
Automation Activity & Vendor Info: (Acquisitions) Innovative Interfaces, Inc
Partic in Miss Libr Asn; Miss Libr Comn Interlibr Loan Network
Open Mon-Sat 10-5:15

GULFPORT

GL HARRISON COUNTY LAW LIBRARY*, 1801 23rd Ave, 39501. SAN 308-8588. Tel: 228-865-4068. FAX: 228-865-4067. *Librn,* Fran J Perry
Founded 1967
Library Holdings: Bk Titles 1,500; Bk Vols 24,000
Subject Interests: Miss
Partic in Westlaw
Open Mon-Fri 9-5

P HARRISON COUNTY LIBRARY SYSTEM*, 2600 24th Ave, No 6, 39501-2081. SAN 308-8596. Tel: 228-868-1383. FAX: 228-863-7433. Web Site: www.harrison.lib.ms.us. *Dir,* Robert Lipscomb; Tel: 228-868-1383, Ext 22, E-mail: r.lipscomb@harrison.lib.ms.us; *Head, Tech Serv,* Michael Webb; E-mail: m.webb@harrison.lib.ms.us; *Outreach Serv Librn,* Gen Thompson; E-mail: g.thompson@harrison.lib.ms.us; *Acq,* Linda Beasley; E-mail: l.beasley@harrison.lib.ms.us; *Cataloger,* Deanna Plummer; E-mail: d.plummer@harrison.lib.ms.us; *ILL,* Diane P McGee; E-mail: d.mcgee@harrison.lib.ms.us; *Syst Adminr,* Melissa Bratton; E-mail: m.bratton@harrison.lib.ms.us; Staff 74 (MLS 7, Non-MLS 67)
Founded 1898. Pop 195,000; Circ 768,332
Library Holdings: Bk Vols 275,560; Per Subs 608

Special Collections: Oral History
Subject Interests: Art, Careers, Genealogy, Local hist, Maps
Automation Activity & Vendor Info: (Acquisitions) Brodart; (Cataloging) SirsiDynix; (Circulation) SirsiDynix
Database Vendor: Dialog, SirsiDynix
Function: Ref serv available
Publications: Directory of Academic, High School, Public & Special Libraries in Harrison County
Friends of the Library Group
Branches: 9
BILOXI CENTRAL LIBRARY, 580 Howard Ave, Biloxi, 39530-2303, SAN 348-159X. Tel: 228-436-3095. FAX: 228-436-3097. *Br Mgr, Main Libr,* Paul Dubaz; *Head Librn,* Charlene Longino; Staff 1 (Non-MLS 1)
Founded 2007
Library Holdings: CDs 70; DVDs 200; Bk Vols 6,000
Automation Activity & Vendor Info: (Circulation) Horizon; (OPAC) Horizon
Function: Bks on CD, Children's prog, Computers for patron use, Copy machines, Electronic databases & coll, Fax serv, Holiday prog, Online cat, Pub access computers, Story hour, Summer reading prog, Tax forms
Friends of the Library Group
D'IBERVILLE PUBLIC, 10391 AutoMall Pkwy, D'Iberville, 39540, SAN 376-625X. Tel: 228-392-2279. FAX: 228-396-9573. *Head Librn,* Nancy Soder; *Ch,* Missy Lucas; E-mail: mlucas@harrison.lib.ms.us; *Head, Circ,* Linda Trent; E-mail: librown@harrison.lib.ms.us; Staff 6 (Non-MLS 6)
Founded 1978. Circ 112,096
Library Holdings: Bk Vols 25,000; Per Subs 30
Open Mon & Tues 9-8, Wed-Sat 9-5
Friends of the Library Group
GULFPORT LIBRARY, 1708 25th Ave, 39501. Tel: 228-871-7171. FAX: 228-871-7067. *Br Mgr,* Michael Alexander; Staff 17 (MLS 2, Non-MLS 15)
Founded 1916. Circ 211,535
Library Holdings: Bk Vols 85,000; Per Subs 150
Open Mon-Thurs 9-6, Fri 9-3, Sat 10-2
ORANGE GROVE PUBLIC, 12031 Mobile Ave, 39503-3175, SAN 377-0001. Tel: 228-832-6924. FAX: 228-832-6926. *Librn,* Lorianne Hawkins; Staff 6 (MLS 1, Non-MLS 5)
Founded 1975
Library Holdings: Bk Titles 22,000; Per Subs 15
Friends of the Library Group
PASS CHRISTIAN PUBLIC, War Memorial Park, 324 E Second St, Pass Christian, 39571, SAN 308-9053. Tel: 228-452-4596. FAX: 228-452-1111. *Br Mgr,* Sally James; E-mail: s.james@harrison.lib.ms.us; Staff 7 (MLS 1, Non-MLS 6)
Founded 1970
Library Holdings: Bk Titles 34,250; Per Subs 57
Special Collections: Postage Stamps
Open Mon-Fri 8:30-5, Sat 9-2
Friends of the Library Group
SAUCIER CHILDREN'S LIBRARY, 24006 First St, Saucier, 39574. Tel: 228-539-4419. *Br Mgr,* Rita Aalbertsburg; E-mail: r.aalbertsberg@harrison.lib.ms.us
Automation Activity & Vendor Info: (Circulation) Horizon
Open Mon 1-6, Tues 1-5, Thurs 11-5
MARGARET SHERRY BRANCH LIBRARY, 2141 Popps Ferry Rd, Biloxi, 39532-4251, SAN 348-1611. Tel: 228-388-1633. FAX: 228-388-0920. *Br Mgr,* Sharon Davis; *Head Librn,* Charlene Longino; Staff 3 (MLS 1, Non-MLS 2)
Founded 1983
Library Holdings: Bk Vols 23,157; Per Subs 42
Automation Activity & Vendor Info: (Circulation) Horizon; (OPAC) Horizon
Function: After school storytime, Art exhibits, Bks on cassette, Bks on CD, Children's prog, Computers for patron use, Copy machines, Electronic databases & coll, Fax serv, Handicapped accessible, Holiday prog, ILL available, Mail & tel request accepted, Music CDs, Prog for adults, Prog for children & young adult, Pub access computers, Ref & res, Story hour, Summer reading prog, Tax forms, Teen prog
Friends of the Library Group
WEST BILOXI LIBRARY, 2047 Pass Rd, Biloxi, 39531-3125, SAN 348-162X. Tel: 228-388-5696. FAX: 228-388-5652. *Br Mgr,* Deborah Lundy; *Head Librn,* Charline Longino; Tel: 228-388-1633, E-mail: c.longino@harrison.lib.ms.us; Staff 2 (MLS 2)
Founded 1968. Circ 90,593
Library Holdings: Bk Vols 35,195; Per Subs 60
Automation Activity & Vendor Info: (Circulation) Horizon; (OPAC) Horizon
Function: After school storytime, Art exhibits, Bks on cassette, Bks on CD, Children's prog, Computers for patron use, Copy machines, Doc delivery serv, Electronic databases & coll, Fax serv, Holiday prog, ILL available, Mail & tel request accepted, Music CDs, Online cat, Prog for adults, Prog for children & young adult, Pub access computers, Ref serv available, Story hour, Summer reading prog, Tax forms, VHS videos
Friends of the Library Group
WOOLMARKET LIBRARY, 8455 Woolmarket Rd, Biloxi, 39532. Tel: 228-354-9464. FAX: 228-354-9466. *Br Mgr,* Donna Posey; E-mail: d.posey@harrison.lib.ms.us; Staff 1 (Non-MLS 1)
Founded 2007. Pop 15,000
Library Holdings: CDs 75; DVDs 250; Bk Titles 4,000
Automation Activity & Vendor Info: (Circulation) Horizon; (OPAC) Horizon
Function: After school storytime, Bks on CD, Children's prog, Computers for patron use, Copy machines, Fax serv, Holiday prog, ILL available, Mail & tel request accepted, Online cat, Prog for children & young adult, Pub access computers, Story hour, Summer reading prog, Tax forms, Teen prog
Open Mon-Thurs 9-6, Fri & Sat 9-4
Restriction: Lending limited to county residents, Non-resident fee
Friends of the Library Group

M MEMORIAL HOSPITAL AT GULFPORT*, Roberta L Burman Medical Library, 4500 13th St, 39501. (Mail add: PO Box 1810, 39502-1810). Tel: 228-867-5366. FAX: 228-865-3214. *Dir,* Connie Keel; *Med Librn,* Sharon Fields
Library Holdings: Bk Titles 250
Restriction: Employees & their associates, Staff use only

J MISSISSIPPI GULF COAST COMMUNITY COLLEGE*, Jefferson Davis Campus Learning Resource Center, 2226 Switzer Rd, 39507. SAN 308-860X. Tel: 228-896-2525. FAX: 228-896-2521. Web Site: www.mgccc.edu. *Asst Dean,* Foster Flint; Tel: 228-895-2525, E-mail: foster.flint@mgccc.edu; *Sr Librn,* Charles M Clark; Tel: 228-897-3809, E-mail: charles.clark@mgccc.edu; *Librn,* Dianne Hurlbert; Tel: 228-897-3880, E-mail: dianne.hurlbert@mgccc.edu; Staff 5 (MLS 4, Non-MLS 1)
Founded 1966. Enrl 3,862; Fac 125; Highest Degree: Associate
Library Holdings: AV Mats 2,364; Bk Titles 44,208; Per Subs 225
Special Collections: McNaughton Coll
Automation Activity & Vendor Info: (Acquisitions) SirsiDynix; (Circulation) SirsiDynix; (OPAC) SirsiDynix
Database Vendor: SirsiDynix
Function: ILL available, Ref serv available
Publications: Bibliographie Materials; Orientation & Reference Guides
Partic in Lyrasis
Special Services for the Blind - Reader equip
Open Mon-Thurs 7:30am-8:30pm, Fri 7:30-3:30

HARRISVILLE

P HARRISVILLE PUBLIC LIBRARY*, 1767 Simpson Hwy 469, 39082-4005. (Mail add: PO Box 307, 39082-0307), SAN 376-6373. Tel: 601-847-1268. E-mail: harrisvi@cmrls.lib.ms.us. Web Site: www.cmrls.lib.ms.us. *Br Mgr,* Alicia Beam-Ingram
Library Holdings: Bk Titles 4,000
Open Tues 1-6, Fri 10-12 & 1-5, Sat 9-12
Friends of the Library Group

HATTIESBURG

M FORREST COUNTY GENERAL HOSPITAL*, Library Services, 6051 Hwy 49 S, 39402. (Mail add: PO Box 16389, 39404-6389), SAN 325-478X. Tel: 601-288-4260. FAX: 601-288-4214. E-mail: medicallibrary@forrestgeneral.com. *Libr Asst,* Vicky Buxton; Fax: 601-288-4209, E-mail: vbuxton@forrestgeneral.com; Staff 1 (Non-MLS 1)
Founded 1973
Library Holdings: Bk Vols 1,500; Per Subs 42
Subject Interests: Med
Wireless access
Partic in Docline; National Network of Libraries of Medicine; SEND
Restriction: Staff use only

P THE LIBRARY OF HATTIESBURG, PETAL, FORREST COUNTY*, 329 Hardy St, 39401-3496. SAN 348-3754. Tel: 601-582-4461. Reference Tel: 601-584-3163. FAX: 601-582-5338. E-mail: rooms@hpfc.lib.ms.us. Web Site: www.hpfc.lib.ms.us. *Dir,* Pamela J Pridgen; Tel: 601-584-3162, E-mail: pamela@hpfc.lib.ms.us; *Asst Dir, Pub Serv,* Donna Davis; E-mail: donna@hpfc.lib.ms.us; *Asst Dir, Ref/Automated Syst,* Sean Farrell; E-mail: sean@hpfc.lib.ms.us; *Head, Circ,* Deborah Herrington; *Tech Serv,* Lillie Peterson; E-mail: lillie@hpfc.lib.ms.us; *Youth Serv,* Shellie Zeigler-Hill; E-mail: shellie@hpfc.lib.ms.us; Staff 37 (MLS 5, Non-MLS 32)
Founded 1916. Pop 74,927; Circ 184,569
Library Holdings: Bk Vols 150,000; Per Subs 222
Special Collections: Adult New Reader's Coll. State Document Depository
Subject Interests: Genealogy, Miss
Automation Activity & Vendor Info: (Cataloging) Innovative Interfaces, Inc
Database Vendor: EBSCOhost, Gale Cengage Learning, OCLC FirstSearch, SirsiDynix, Wilson - Wilson Web
Wireless access

Publications: The Library (Newsletter)
Open Mon-Thurs 8-8, Fri & Sat 10-4
Friends of the Library Group
Branches: 1
PETAL BRANCH, 714 S Main St, Petal, 39465, SAN 348-3789. Tel: 601-584-7610. *Dir,* Pamela J Pridgen; E-mail: pamela@hpfc.lib.ms.us
Library Holdings: Bk Vols 12,748
Open Mon-Fri 9-6, Sat 9-1
Friends of the Library Group

C UNIVERSITY OF SOUTHERN MISSISSIPPI LIBRARY, Joseph Anderson Cook Library, 118 College Dr, No 5053, 39406. SAN 348-3843. Tel: 601-266-4241. Circulation Tel: 601-266-4250. Interlibrary Loan Service Tel: 601-266-4256. Reference Tel: 601-266-4249. FAX: 601-266-6033. Web Site: www.lib.usm.edu. *Dean of Libr,* John Eye; Tel: 601-266-4362, E-mail: john.eye@usm.edu; *Spec Coll Librn,* Jennifer Brannock; Tel: 601-266-4347, E-mail: jennifer.brannock@usm.edu; *Acq,* Gidget Coffman; Tel: 601-266-6176, E-mail: Gidget.L.Coffman@usm.edu; *Syst Adminr,* Ed Tisdale; Tel: 601-266-6177, E-mail: ed.tisdale@usm.edu; Staff 75 (MLS 29, Non-MLS 46)
Founded 1912. Enrl 15,030; Fac 713; Highest Degree: Doctorate
Jul 2005-Jun 2006. Mats Exp $2,772,300, Books $245,400, Per/Ser (Incl. Access Fees) $1,200,000, Micro $116,000, AV Equip $1,000, AV Mat $23,200, Electronic Ref Mat (Incl. Access Fees) $1,153,000, Presv $33,700. Sal $3,415,400 (Prof $1,359,962)
Library Holdings: AV Mats 26,502; e-books 160,853; Bk Titles 1,389,511; Bk Vols 1,658,991; Per Subs 25,748
Subject Interests: Biol, Chem, Computers, Criminal justice, Educ, Letters, Libr sci, Music, Nursing, Polymer sci, Psychol
Automation Activity & Vendor Info: (Acquisitions) SirsiDynix; (Cataloging) SirsiDynix; (Circulation) SirsiDynix; (Course Reserve) SirsiDynix; (ILL) OCLC ILLiad; (Media Booking) SirsiDynix; (OPAC) SirsiDynix; (Serials) SirsiDynix
Database Vendor: Cambridge Scientific Abstracts, Community of Science (COS), EBSCOhost, Gale Cengage Learning, ISI Web of Knowledge, JSTOR, LexisNexis, Newsbank, OCLC FirstSearch, OVID Technologies, ScienceDirect, TLC (The Library Corporation)
Wireless access
Publications: Juvenile Miscellany; Library Focus (Newsletter)
Partic in Lyrasis
Open Mon-Thurs 7am-Midnight, Fri 7am-9pm, Sat 9-9, Sun Noon-Midnight
Departmental Libraries:
GULF COAST LIBRARY
See Separate Entry in Long Beach
WILLIAM DAVID MCCAIN LIBRARY & ARCHIVES, 118 College Dr, No 5148, 39406, SAN 369-772X. Tel: 601-266-4345. FAX: 601-226-6269. *Spec Coll Librn,* Jennifer Brannock; Tel: 601-266-4347, E-mail: jennifer.brannock@usm.edu
Founded 1976
Library Holdings: Bk Vols 151,877
Special Collections: Association of American Editorial Cartoonists Coll; Association of American Railroads Coll; Children's Literature (Lena Y de Grummond Coll); Cleanth Brooks Literature Coll; Confederate Literature (Ernest A Walen Coll); Gulf, Mobile & Ohio Railroad Records Coll; Mississippiana Coll; Papers of Mississippi Governor & United States Senator Theodore C Bilbo, 1915-1947; Papers of Mississippi Governors Paul Johnson Sr & Paul Johnson Jr, 1917-1970; Papers of United States Representative William M Colmer, 1933-1973; Paul Yoder Marching Band Music Coll; Rare Book Coll; University Archives
Subject Interests: 19th-20th Century Am Lit, 19th-20th Century British, Art for children, Civil War, Drawings, Editorial cartoons, Genealogy, Hist of South, Lit for children, Literary criticism, Miss docs, Miss fiction, Miss publs
Partic in Lyrasis; OCLC Online Computer Library Center, Inc
Open Mon-Fri 8-5

C WILLIAM CAREY UNIVERSITY LIBRARIES*, Dumas L Smith/ I E Rouse Library, 498 Tuscan Ave, Box 5, 39401. SAN 348-3878. Tel: 601-318-6169. Toll Free Tel: 800-962-5991. FAX: 601-318-6171. Web Site: www.wmcarey.edu. *Dir of Libr,* Sherry Laughlin; E-mail: slaughlin@wmcarey.edu; *Cir & Acq Librn,* Reese Powell; E-mail: rpowell@wmcarey.edu; *Ref & Instruction,* Claudia Conklin; E-mail: cconklin@wmcarey.edu; *Ser Librn,* Jim Myers; E-mail: jmyers@wmcarey.edu; *Tech Serv & Syst Librn,* Patrivan Yuen; E-mail: pyuen@wmcarey.edu
Founded 1906. Enrl 2,400; Fac 96; Highest Degree: Master
Jul 2006-Jun 2007 Income $302,561. Mats Exp $326,289, Books $74,104, Per/Ser (Incl. Access Fees) $146,629, AV Mat $11,050, Electronic Ref Mat (Incl. Access Fees) $84,006, Presv $10,500
Library Holdings: AV Mats 1,220; Bk Titles 75,000; Bk Vols 94,995; Per Subs 773
Special Collections: Church Music (Clarence Dickinson Coll)
Subject Interests: Art, Bus, Educ, Music, Nursing, Relig studies
Automation Activity & Vendor Info: (Acquisitions) OCLC ILLiad; (Cataloging) OCLC ILLiad; (Circulation) OCLC ILLiad; (Course Reserve) OCLC ILLiad; (OPAC) OCLC ILLiad; (Serials) OCLC ILLiad
Database Vendor: Baker & Taylor, Checkpoint Systems, Inc, EBSCOhost, Gale Cengage Learning, Innovative Interfaces, Inc, JSTOR, OCLC FirstSearch, OCLC WorldShare Interlibrary Loan, ProQuest
Wireless access
Function: Copy machines, e-mail serv, Electronic databases & coll, Fax serv, ILL available, Ref serv available, VHS videos, Wheelchair accessible
Partic in Lyrasis
Restriction: Open to researchers by request, Open to students, fac & staff, Res pass required for non-affiliated visitors, Use of others with permission of librn
Friends of the Library Group
Departmental Libraries:
TRADITION LIBRARY, 19640 Hwy 67, Biloxi, 39532-8666, SAN 348-3932. Tel: 228-702-1890. *Regional Librn,* Peggy H Gossage; E-mail: pgossage@wmcarey.edu
Library Holdings: Bk Vols 18,000; Per Subs 100
Open Mon-Thurs 8am-10pm, Fri 8-4, Sat 10-2

HAZLEHURST

P COPIAH-JEFFERSON REGIONAL LIBRARY SYSTEM*, George W Covington Memorial Library, 223 S Extension St, 39083-3339. SAN 348-3967. Tel: 601-894-1681. FAX: 601-894-1672. Web Site: www.copjef.lib.ms.us. *Librn,* Sandra Johnson; E-mail: hazlehurst@copjef.lib.ms.us; *Asst Librn,* Eunice Corley; *Br Librn,* Elizabeth Malone; Staff 16 (Non-MLS 16)
Founded 1950. Pop 36,500; Circ 70,760
Library Holdings: Bk Vols 45,000
Special Collections: Mississippi Coll (Archives Room)
Subject Interests: African-Am hist
Automation Activity & Vendor Info: (Cataloging) Innovative Interfaces, Inc; (Circulation) Innovative Interfaces, Inc
Open Mon-Fri 9-6
Friends of the Library Group
Branches: 4
J T BIGGS JR MEMORIAL LIBRARY, 200 S Jackson St, Crystal Springs, 39059, SAN 348-4025. Tel: 601-892-3205. FAX: 601-892-2138. E-mail: cslibmgr@gmail.com. *Librn,* Gwen Gallman
Open Mon 12-5, Tues-Fri 9-5, Sat 9-Noon
Friends of the Library Group
GEORGETOWN LIBRARY, 1164 Railroad Ave, Georgetown, 39078, SAN 377-9955. Tel: 601-858-2202. FAX: 601-858-2202. E-mail: georgetownlib@copjef.lib.ms.us. *Librn,* Linda Dewitt
Open Mon & Tues 11-6, Wed & Thurs 11-5
LONGIE DALE HAMILTON MEMORIAL LIBRARY, 1012 Spring St, Wesson, 39191. (Mail add: PO Box 299, Wesson, 39191-0299), SAN 348-4084. Tel: 601-643-5725. FAX: 601-643-5725. E-mail: welibmgr@gmail.com. *Librn,* Susan Alsbury
Special Collections: Wesson Historical Artifacts & Information
Open Mon-Fri 9-11:30 & 12:30-5
Friends of the Library Group
JEFFERSON COUNTY LIBRARY, 1269 S Main St, Fayette, 39069. (Mail add: PO Box 578, Fayette, 39069-0578), SAN 348-405X. Tel: 601-786-3982. FAX: 601-786-9646. E-mail: falibmgr@gmail.com. *Librn,* Brenda Rankin
Open Mon, Wed & Fri 9-11:30 & 12:30-5, Tues & Thurs 9-11:30 & 12:30-6

M HARDY WILSON MEMORIAL HOSPITAL LIBRARY*, 233 Magnolia St, 39083-2200. (Mail add: PO Box 889, 39083-0889), SAN 308-8642. Tel: 601-894-4541, Ext 6270. FAX: 601-894-5800. *Dir,* Rachel McCardle
Library Holdings: Bk Vols 75
Open Mon-Fri 7:30-4

HERNANDO

P FIRST REGIONAL LIBRARY*, Headquarters Library, 370 W Commerce St, 38632. SAN 348-4114. Tel: 662-429-4439. FAX: 662-429-8853. Web Site: www.firstregional.org. *Dir,* Catherine Nathan; E-mail: cnathan@firstregional.org; *Asst Dir, Pub Serv,* Barbara Evans; E-mail: bevans@firstregional.org; *Asst Dir, Tech Serv,* Marty Coleman; E-mail: marty@firstregional.org; *Youth Serv Coordr,* Judy Card; E-mail: jcard@firstregional.org; *Cataloger,* Michelle Williams; E-mail: michellew@firstregional.org; Staff 149 (MLS 19, Non-MLS 130)
Founded 1950. Pop 289,167; Circ 1,306,906
Oct 2011-Sept 2012 Income (Main Library and Branch(s)) $5,421,817, City $1,424,700, Federal $20,165, County $2,470,014, Locally Generated Income $568,330, Other $938,608. Mats Exp $449,510, Books $251,931, Per/Ser (Incl. Access Fees) $77,534, Electronic Ref Mat (Incl. Access Fees) $120,045. Sal $3,490,313

Library Holdings: AV Mats 49,891; e-books 8,235; Electronic Media & Resources 44; Large Print Bks 15,561; Bk Titles 561,380; Per Subs 1,013; Talking Bks 31,967; Videos 31,206
Special Collections: Mississippi History & Literature. State Document Depository
Automation Activity & Vendor Info: (Acquisitions) SirsiDynix; (Cataloging) SirsiDynix; (Circulation) SirsiDynix; (OPAC) SirsiDynix
Database Vendor: 3M Library Systems, Backstage Library Works, Baker & Taylor, CredoReference, ebrary, EBSCO Discovery Service, EBSCOhost, LexisNexis, OCLC FirstSearch, OCLC WorldShare Interlibrary Loan, Overdrive, Inc, Oxford Online, ProQuest, SirsiDynix, Westlaw, World Book Online
Wireless access
Function: Adult bk club, After school storytime, Audiobks via web, Bilingual assistance for Spanish patrons, Bk club(s), Bks on CD, Children's prog, Computers for patron use, Copy machines, Distance learning, Electronic databases & coll, Exhibits, Fax serv, Free DVD rentals, Genealogy discussion group, Handicapped accessible, Holiday prog, Home delivery & serv to Sr ctr & nursing homes, Homework prog, ILL available, Learning ctr, Legal assistance to inmates, Mail & tel request accepted, Microfiche/film & reading machines, Music CDs, Online cat, Outreach serv, Outside serv via phone, mail, e-mail & web, OverDrive digital audio bks, Photocopying/Printing, Preschool outreach, Preschool reading prog, Printer for laptops & handheld devices, Prog for adults, Prog for children & young adult, Pub access computers, Ref serv available, Scanner, Senior computer classes, Senior outreach, Spoken cassettes & CDs, Story hour, Summer & winter reading prog, Summer reading prog, Tax forms, Teen prog, Telephone ref, Web-catalog, Wheelchair accessible, Workshops, Writing prog
Publications: What's Happening (Newsletter)
Partic in Dancing Rabbit Library Consortium; Mississippi Library Partnership
Special Services for the Blind - Assistive/Adapted tech devices, equip & products; BiFolkal kits; Bks on CD; Closed circuit TV magnifier; Computer access aids; Large print bks; Playaways (bks on MP3); Recorded bks; ZoomText magnification & reading software
Open Mon-Thurs 9:30-7, Fri 9:30-5:30, Sat 9:30-5
Friends of the Library Group
Branches: 13
BATESVILLE PUBLIC LIBRARY, 206 Hwy 51 N, Batesville, 38606, SAN 348-4149. Tel: 662-563-1038. FAX: 662-563-6640. *Librn,* Jennifer Hall; E-mail: jhall@firstregional.org; Staff 7 (MLS 1, Non-MLS 6)
Founded 1992. Pop 21,072; Circ 124,936
Friends of the Library Group
B J CHAIN PUBLIC LIBRARY, 6619 Hwy 305 N, Olive Branch, 38654, SAN 348-4173. Tel: 662-895-5900. FAX: 662-895-9171. *Br Mgr,* Suzanne Argo; E-mail: suzannea@firstregional.org; *Asst Mgr, Ref Spec,* Sherry James; E-mail: sherryj@firstregional.org; *Youth Serv Spec,* Teresa Spiers
M R DAVIS PUBLIC LIBRARY, 8554 Northwest Dr, Southaven, 38671, SAN 348-4440. Tel: 662-342-0102. FAX: 662-342-0556. *Librn,* Caroline Barnett; E-mail: cbarnett@firstregional.org; Staff 11 (MLS 1, Non-MLS 10)
Friends of the Library Group
M R DYE PUBLIC LIBRARY, 2885 Goodman Rd, Horn Lake, 38637, SAN 348-4297. Tel: 662-393-5654. FAX: 662-342-9468. *Librn,* Jesse Pool; Staff 1 (MLS 1)
Friends of the Library Group
JESSIE J EDWARDS PUBLIC LIBRARY, 610 E Central Ave, Coldwater, 38618. (Mail add: PO Box 591, Coldwater, 38618-0591), SAN 348-4203. Tel: 662-622-5573. FAX: 662-622-5846. *Br Mgr,* Tasha Jackson-Sow; E-mail: tjackson-sow@firstregional.org
Friends of the Library Group
HERNANDO PUBLIC LIBRARY, 370 W Commerce St, 38632-2130. Tel: 662-429-4439. FAX: 662-429-8625. *Br Head,* Heather Lawson; E-mail: hlawson@firstregional.org
Open Mon-Thurs 9:30-7, Fri 9:30-5:30, Sat 9:30-3
ROBERT C IRWIN PUBLIC LIBRARY, 1285 Kenny Hill Ave, Tunica, 38676, SAN 348-4327. Tel: 662-363-2162. FAX: 662-357-5929. *Br Mgr,* Ruth Harris; E-mail: rharris@firstregional.org
Friends of the Library Group
LAFAYETTE COUNTY-OXFORD PUBLIC LIBRARY, 401 Bramlett Blvd, Oxford, 38655, SAN 348-4351. Tel: 662-234-5751. FAX: 662-234-3155. Web Site: www.firstregional.org/oxford.html. *Head Librn,* Laura Beth Walker; E-mail: lbwalker@firstregional.org; *Asst Br Mgr, Ch,* Nancy Opalko; E-mail: nopalko@firstregional.org; *Ref Librn,* Corey Vinson; E-mail: cvinson@firstregional.org; Staff 6 (MLS 3, Non-MLS 3)
Pop 40,000; Circ 250,000
Open Mon-Thurs 10-8, Fri & Sat 10-5:30
Friends of the Library Group
SAM LAPIDUS MEMORIAL PUBLIC LIBRARY, 108 Missouri St, Crenshaw, 38621-5450. (Mail add: PO Box 246, Crenshaw, 38621-0246), SAN 348-4238. Tel: 662-382-7479. FAX: 662-382-7479. *Librn,* Martha Rayburn; E-mail: mrayburn@firstregional.org
Friends of the Library Group
EMILY JONES POINTER PUBLIC LIBRARY, 104 Main St, Como, 38619-0128. (Mail add: PO Box 128, Como, 38632), SAN 348-4262. Tel: 662-526-5283. FAX: 662-526-5283. *Br Mgr,* Alice Pierotti; E-mail: apierotti@firstregional.org
Friends of the Library Group
SARDIS PUBLIC LIBRARY, 101 McLaurin St, Sardis, 38666, SAN 348-4386. Tel: 662-487-2126. FAX: 662-487-2126. *Br Mgr,* Charlene Bradford; E-mail: charleneb@firstregional.org
Friends of the Library Group
SENATOBIA PUBLIC LIBRARY, 222 Ward St, Senatobia, 38668, SAN 348-4416. Tel: 662-562-6791. FAX: 662-562-0414. *Librn,* Laurie Madsen; E-mail: lmadsen@firstregional.org
Friends of the Library Group
WALLS PUBLIC LIBRARY, 7181 Delta Bluff Pkwy, Walls, 38680. (Mail add: PO Box 417, Walls, 38680-0417), SAN 378-0287. Tel: 662-781-3664. FAX: 662-781-3427. *Br Mgr,* Brian Mitchell; E-mail: bmitchel@firstregional.org
Open Mon-Thurs 10-6, Fri 10-5:30, Sat 10-2
Bookmobiles: 1. Early Childhood Servs Coordr, Victoria Penny

HOLLY SPRINGS

P MARSHALL COUNTY LIBRARY SYSTEM*, 109 E Gholson Ave, 38635. SAN 348-4475. Tel: 662-252-3823. FAX: 662-252-3066. E-mail: holly@marshall.lib.ms.us. Web Site: marshall.lib.ms.us. *Dir,* Amanda McDonald; Staff 10.5 (MLS 1.5, Non-MLS 9)
Founded 1955. Pop 38,000; Circ 20,000
Oct 2008-Sept 2009 Income $254,000, State $68,000, City $10,000, Federal $10,000, County $145,000, Locally Generated Income $15,000, Other $2,000. Mats Exp $22,800, Books $20,000, Per/Ser (Incl. Access Fees) $2,300, AV Mat $500. Sal $152,000 (Prof $51,000)
Library Holdings: Audiobooks 799; Bks on Deafness & Sign Lang 6; Braille Volumes 1; DVDs 234; Electronic Media & Resources 93; Large Print Bks 286; Microforms 60; Bk Titles 30,000; Bk Vols 38,000; Per Subs 75
Special Collections: Marshall County Historical & Genealogical Coll
Automation Activity & Vendor Info: (Cataloging) Book Systems; (Circulation) Book Systems; (OPAC) Book Systems; (Serials) EBSCO Online
Wireless access
Function: Fax serv, ILL available, Photocopying/Printing, Pub access computers, Telephone ref
Partic in MAGNOLIA
Open Mon, Wed & Fri 9-6, Tues & Thurs 9-8, Sat 8-2
Friends of the Library Group
Branches: 2
RUTH B FRENCH LIBRARY, 161 S Hwy 309, Byhalia, 38611. (Mail add: PO Box 412, Byhalia, 38611), SAN 348-4505. Tel: 662-838-4024. FAX: 662-838-6900. *Librn,* Esther Jones
Open Mon, Tues & Fri 1-5, Thurs 3-7, Sat 10-2
POTTS CAMP PUBLIC, 20 S Center St, Potts Camp, 38659. Tel: 601-333-7068. FAX: 601-333-7096. *Librn,* Patricia Westmoreland
Open Tues-Fri 12-5, Sat 9-12

C RUST COLLEGE*, Leontyne Price Library, 150 E Rust Ave, 38635. SAN 308-8669. Tel: 662-252-8000, Ext 4100. FAX: 662-252-8873. Web Site: www.rustcollege.edu. *Head Librn,* Anita W Moore; E-mail: amoore@rustcollege.edu; *AV, Ref Serv,* Freddie Jeffries; E-mail: fjeffries@rustcollege.edu; *Coll Develop,* Mattie Walker; E-mail: mwalker@rustcollege.edu; *Ref Serv, Ser, Spec Coll Librn,* Cynthia Cole; E-mail: ccole@rustcollege.edu; *Tech Serv,* Gwendolyn Jones; E-mail: gjones@rustcollege.edu; Staff 7 (MLS 2, Non-MLS 5)
Founded 1866. Enrl 1,100; Fac 56; Highest Degree: Bachelor
Library Holdings: Bk Titles 122,033; Per Subs 366
Special Collections: International Coll; Roy Wilkins Coll; United Methodist Religious Coll
Publications: Acquisition List (Quarterly); Circulation Handbook; Collection Development Handbook; Library Manual; Roy Wilkins Special Collections Book
Partic in Coop Col Libr Ctr, Inc; Lyrasis
Open Mon-Thurs 7:45am-Midnight, Fri 7:45-6, Sat 10-2, Sun 4-10

INDIANOLA

P SUNFLOWER COUNTY LIBRARY SYSTEM*, 201 Cypress Dr, 38751-2499. SAN 348-4599. Tel: 662-887-1672. Interlibrary Loan Service Tel: 662-887-2298. FAX: 662-887-1618. Web Site: www.sunflower.lib.ms.us. *Dir,* Mary Ann Stone; E-mail: mastone@sunflower.lib.ms.us; *Asst Dir,* Kay Slater; E-mail: kslater@sunflower.lib.ms.us
Founded 1938. Pop 35,129; Circ 63,129
Library Holdings: Bk Titles 58,259; Bk Vols 93,788; Per Subs 147
Partic in Dancing Rabbit Library Consortium; OCLC Online Computer Library Center, Inc

Open Mon-Fri 8:30-5
Friends of the Library Group
Branches: 4
DREW PUBLIC, 290 W Park Ave, Drew, 38737-3340, SAN 348-4629. Tel: 662-745-2237. FAX: 662-745-2237. E-mail: drew@sunflower.lib.ms.us. *Pub Serv,* Diane Shurden
Library Holdings: Bk Vols 17,000
Open Mon & Wed 12-6, Fri 10-3
INVERNESS PUBLIC, City Hall, 802 E Grand Ave, Inverness, 38753, SAN 348-4688. Tel: 662-265-6009. Reference Tel: 662-265-5179. FAX: 662-265-5502. E-mail: inverness@sunflower.lib.ms.us. *Pub Serv,* Elloise S Bell
Library Holdings: Bk Vols 10,000
Open Tues & Thurs 12-6, Fri 10-3
HENRY M SEYMOUR LIBRARY, 201 Cypress Dr, 38751, SAN 348-4718. Tel: 662-887-1672. FAX: 662-887-2641. E-mail: seymour@sunflower.lib.ms.us. *Coordr,* Nita Dill; E-mail: ndill@sunflower.lib.ms.us
Library Holdings: Bk Vols 45,588
Open Mon, Tues & Thurs 9-6, Wed 9-1, Fri 9-5, Sat 10-4
Friends of the Library Group
HORACE STANSEL MEMORIAL, 112 S Ruby St, Ruleville, 38771-3939, SAN 348-4653. Tel: 662-756-2226. FAX: 662-756-2809. E-mail: ruleville@sunflower.lib.ms.us. *Circ Asst,* Diane Shurden; Staff 1.5 (Non-MLS 1.5)
Pop 3,000
Library Holdings: Bk Vols 12,200
Function: After school storytime, Art exhibits, Bks on cassette, Bks on CD, Children's prog, Computers for patron use, Copy machines, e-mail serv, Fax serv, Handicapped accessible, Holiday prog, Online cat, Online ref, Online searches, Prog for adults, Prog for children & young adult, Pub access computers, Ref serv available, Story hour, Summer reading prog, Tax forms, Teen prog
Open Tues & Thurs 12-6, Sat 10-3
Friends of the Library Group

ITTA BENA

C MISSISSIPPI VALLEY STATE UNIVERSITY*, James Herbert White Library, 14000 Hwy 82 W, 38941. SAN 308-8685. Tel: 662-254-3494. Circulation Tel: 662-254-3501. Interlibrary Loan Service Tel: 662-254-3710. Reference Tel: 662-254-3497. FAX: 662-254-3499. Interlibrary Loan Service FAX: 662-254-6704. E-mail: ill@mvsu.edu. Web Site: www.mvsu.edu/library. *Dir,* Mantra Henderson; E-mail: mlhenderson@mvsu.edu; *Cat Librn,* Armajot Purewal; E-mail: apurewal@mvsu.edu; *Digital Media Librn, Ref Librn,* Violene Williams; *Ser Librn,* Dr Eddiemae Young; E-mail: eyoung@mvsu.edu; *ILL Mgr,* Marsha Belton; E-mail: bmarsha@mvsu.edu; Staff 10 (MLS 5, Non-MLS 5)
Founded 1950. Enrl 3,073; Highest Degree: Master
Library Holdings: e-books 35,216; c-journals 2,200; Bk Titles 118,496; Bk Vols 213,860; Per Subs 402
Special Collections: Martin Luther King Shelf; Mississippi Coll. State Document Depository
Subject Interests: Educ, Miss, Negroes
Automation Activity & Vendor Info: (Acquisitions) Ex Libris Group; (Cataloging) Ex Libris Group; (Circulation) Ex Libris Group; (Course Reserve) Docutek; (ILL) OCLC; (Media Booking) Ex Libris Group; (OPAC) Ex Libris Group; (Serials) Ex Libris Group
Database Vendor: EBSCOhost, Gale Cengage Learning, JSTOR, LexisNexis, OCLC FirstSearch, OVID Technologies
Function: Ref serv available
Publications: James Herbert White Library (Newsletter)
Partic in Dancing Rabbit Library Consortium; Lyrasis
Open Mon-Thurs 8am-10pm, Fri 8-4, Sat 10-4, Sun 2-10

JACKSON

CR BELHAVEN UNIVERSITY*, Warren A Hood Library, 1500 Peachtree St, 39202. SAN 308-8693. Tel: 601-968-5948. FAX: 601-968-5968. E-mail: libcomments@belhaven.edu. Web Site: www.belhaven.edu/library. *Dir of Libr,* Chris Cullnane; Tel: 601-968-5947, E-mail: ccullnane@belhaven.edu; *Cat Librn,* Stephanie Gault; Tel: 601-968-5949, E-mail: sgault@belhaven.edu; *Circ Librn,* Daylan Stephens; E-mail: dstephens@belhaven.edu; *Database Librn,* Tracy Harrington; E-mail: tharrington@belhaven.edu; *Mat Mgr,* Vicki Miner; Tel: 601-968-5945, E-mail: vminer@belhaven.edu; *Per,* Charles Gaudin; Tel: 601-968-5951, E-mail: cgaudin@belhaven.edu; Staff 8 (MLS 5, Non-MLS 3)
Founded 1910. Enrl 3,152; Fac 111; Highest Degree: Master
Library Holdings: CDs 623; DVDs 582; e-books 41,200; e-journals 10,000; Music Scores 327; Bk Titles 167,000; Per Subs 223
Subject Interests: Art, Music, Presbyterian records, Relig studies
Automation Activity & Vendor Info: (Cataloging) Innovative Interfaces, Inc; (Circulation) Innovative Interfaces, Inc; (ILL) OCLC; (OPAC) Innovative Interfaces, Inc
Database Vendor: EBSCOhost, OCLC WorldShare Interlibrary Loan, ProQuest
Wireless access
Partic in Lyrasis
Restriction: Private libr

M CENTRAL MISSISSIPPI MEDICAL CENTER*, Dr William M Suttle Medical Library, 1850 Chadwick Dr, 39204. SAN 327-1900. Tel: 601-376-1000, 601-376-1148. FAX: 601-376-2761. Web Site: www.centralmississippimedicalcenter.com. *Librn,* Ann Dubard
Library Holdings: Bk Titles 500; Bk Vols 1,200; Per Subs 100

P JACKSON/HINDS LIBRARY SYSTEM*, Administrative Office, 300 N State St, 39201-1705. SAN 348-4807. Administration Tel: 601-968-5825. Toll Free Tel: 800-968-5803. Administration FAX: 601-968-5817. Web Site: www.jhlibrary.com. *Exec Dir,* Carolyn McCallum; Tel: 601-968-5810, E-mail: cmccallum@jhlibrary.com
Wireless access
Open Mon-Fri 8-5
Friends of the Library Group
Branches: 15
MARGARET WALKER ALEXANDER LIBRARY, 2525 Robinson Rd, 39209-6256, SAN 348-5226. Tel: 601-354-8911. FAX: 601-354-8912. E-mail: alexander@jhlibrary.com. *Br Supvr,* Bernetta James; Staff 2 (Non-MLS 2)
Open Mon-Thurs 10-7, Fri 10-6, Sat 10-5
Friends of the Library Group
ELLA BESS AUSTIN LIBRARY, 420 W Cunningham Ave, Terry, 39170. (Mail add: PO Box 155, Terry, 39170-0155), SAN 348-5765. Tel: 601-878-5336. FAX: 601-878-0609. E-mail: terry@jhlibrary.com. *Br Supvr,* Gladys Reaux; Staff 2 (Non-MLS 2)
Open Mon-Fri 9-6, Sat 10-2
Friends of the Library Group
R G BOLDEN/ANNA BELL-MOORE LIBRARY, 1444 Wiggins Rd, 39209-4430, SAN 348-5889. Tel: 601-922-6076. FAX: 601-923-8144. E-mail: boldenmoore@jhlibrary.com. *Br Supvr,* Position Currently Open; Staff 1 (Non-MLS 1)
Open Mon-Fri 9-6, Sat 10-2
Friends of the Library Group
BEVERLEY J BROWN LIBRARY, 7395 South Siwell Rd, Byram, 39272-8741, SAN 374-4159. Tel: 601-372-0954. FAX: 601-373-7164. E-mail: byram@jhlibrary.com. *Br Supvr,* Karen Clarke; Staff 3 (Non-MLS 3)
Open Mon-Thurs 10-7, Fri 10-6, Sat 10-2
Friends of the Library Group
MEDGAR EVERS BOULEVARD LIBRARY, 4215 Medgar Evers Blvd, 39213-5210, SAN 348-5048. Tel: 601-982-2867. FAX: 601-982-2598. E-mail: evers@jhlibrary.com. *Br Supvr,* Shirley Simmons; Staff 3 (Non-MLS 3)
Open Mon-Fri 9-6, Sat 9-5
Friends of the Library Group
LOIS A FLAGG LIBRARY, 105 Williamson Ave, Edwards, 39066-0140. (Mail add: PO Box 140, Edwards, 39066 0140), SAN 328-8196. Tel: 601-852-2230. FAX: 601-852-4539. E-mail: edwards@jhlibrary.com. *Br Supvr,* Patricia Moss; Staff 1 (Non-MLS 1)
Open Mon-Thurs 9-6, Fri 10-6, Sat 10-2
Friends of the Library Group
FANNIE LOU HAMER LIBRARY, 3450 Albermarle Rd, 39213-6513, SAN 348-4831. Tel: 601-362-3012. FAX: 601-362-1505. E-mail: hamer@jhlibrary.com. *Br Supvr,* Jessica Bryant; Staff 1 (Non-MLS 1)
Open Mon-Fri 9-5
Friends of the Library Group
ANNIE THOMPSON JEFFERS LIBRARY, 111 Madison St, Bolton, 39041. (Mail add: PO Box 358, Bolton, 39041-0350), SAN 370-7911. Tel: 601-866-4247. FAX: 601-866-4653. E-mail: bolton@jhlibrary.com. *Br Supvr,* Alfenette Robinson; Staff 1 (Non-MLS 1)
Open Mon-Thurs 9-6, Fri 10-6, Sat 10-2
Friends of the Library Group
EVELYN T MAJURE LIBRARY, 217 W Main St, Utica, 39175-0340, SAN 348-582X. Tel: 601-885-8381. FAX: 601-885-2612. E-mail: utica@jhlibrary.com. *Br Supvr,* Barbara Barlow; Staff 1 (Non-MLS 1)
Open Mon-Thurs 9-6, Fri 10-6, Sat 10-2
WILLIE MORRIS BRANCH, 4912 Old Canton Rd, 39211-5404, SAN 370-7903. Tel: 601-987-8181. FAX: 601-987-8212. E-mail: morris@jhlibrary.com. *Br Supvr,* Carolyn Carter; Staff 4 (Non-MLS 4)
Open Mon-Thurs 10-7, Fri 10-6, Sat 10-5
Friends of the Library Group
QUISENBERRY LIBRARY, 605 E Northside Dr, Clinton, 39056-5121, SAN 348-498X. Tel: 601-924-5684. FAX: 601-924-1953. E-mail: quisenberry@jhlibrary.com. *Actg Br Mgr,* Nyma Blackerby; Staff 6 (Non-MLS 6)
Open Mon-Thurs 9-9, Fri 9-6, Sat 9-5
Friends of the Library Group

RAYMOND LIBRARY, 126 W Court St, Raymond, 39154. (Mail add: PO Box 14, Raymond, 39154-0014), SAN 348-5587. Tel: 601-857-8721. FAX: 601-857-4281. E-mail: raymond@jhlibrary.com. *Br Supvr,* Claudia Worthen; Staff 2 (Non-MLS 2)
Open Mon-Fri 9-6

CHARLES TISDALE LIBRARY, 807 E Northside Dr, 39206-5537, SAN 348-5374. Tel: 601-366-0021. FAX: 601-366-9364. E-mail: tisdale@jhlibrary.com. *Actg Br Supvr,* Anne Sanders; Staff 3 (Non-MLS 3)
Open Mon-Thurs 9-8, Fri 9-6, Sat 9-5
Friends of the Library Group

EUDORA WELTY LIBRARY (MAIN LIBRARY), 300 North State St, 39201-1705. Interlibrary Loan Service Tel: 601-968-5805. Toll Free Tel: 800-968-5803. FAX: 601-968-5806. *Ref Serv Mgr,* Michelle Hudson; Tel: 601-968-5803, Ext 5809; *Circ/AV Supvr,* Omeria Lewis; Tel: 601-968-5811; *Info Res Ctr Supvr,* Claudia Brooks; Tel: 601-968-5801; *Youth Serv Supvr,* Ruth Davis; Tel: 601-968-5820, Ext 5800; Staff 15 (MLS 1, Non-MLS 14)
Open Mon-Thurs 9-9, Fri 9-6, Sat 9-5, Sun 1-5
Friends of the Library Group

RICHARD WRIGHT LIBRARY, 515 W McDowell Rd, 39204-5547, SAN 348-5706. Tel: 601-372-1621. FAX: 601-372-7083. E-mail: wright@jhlibrary.com. *Br Supvr,* Debra Gilbert; Staff 4 (Non-MLS 4)
Open Mon-Thurs 9-8, Fri 9-6, Sat 9-5
Friends of the Library Group

C JACKSON STATE UNIVERSITY*, Henry Thomas Sampson Library, 1325 J R Lynch St, 39217. SAN 308-8723. Tel: 601-979-2123. FAX: 601-979-2239. Web Site: jsums.edu. *Head, Circ, Ref,* James Hampton; *Head, Ser Acq,* Bernadine Beasley; *Head, Tech Serv,* Linda Carol Lewis; E-mail: llewis@ccaix.jsums.edu; *Web Coordr,* Edgar Powell; *Media Spec,* Jama Lumumba; *Syst Programmer,* Roy Washington. Subject Specialists: *Ethnic studies, Psychol, Soc issues,* Linda Carol Lewis; Staff 35 (MLS 10, Non-MLS 25)
Founded 1877. Enrl 6,700; Fac 330; Highest Degree: Doctorate
Library Holdings: Bk Titles 625,000; Bk Vols 1,000,000; Per Subs 1,600
Special Collections: Ayers Decision Coll; Black Studies (Afro-American), bks, discs, pamphlets; Census & Demographic Information; Gibbs-Green Coll; Select Government Repository Library. Oral History; State Document Depository; US Document Depository
Subject Interests: African-Am studies, Eng, Ethnic studies, Soc issues, Urban planning
Automation Activity & Vendor Info: (Acquisitions) Innovative Interfaces, Inc; (Cataloging) Innovative Interfaces, Inc; (Circulation) Innovative Interfaces, Inc; (Course Reserve) Innovative Interfaces, Inc; (Media Booking) Innovative Interfaces, Inc; (OPAC) Innovative Interfaces, Inc; (Serials) Innovative Interfaces, Inc
Database Vendor: EBSCOhost, Gale Cengage Learning, LexisNexis, OCLC FirstSearch, ProQuest, Wilson - Wilson Web
Function: Telephone ref
Publications: Annual Report; H T Sampson Communicator; Media Highlights
Partic in Lyrasis; MAGNOLIA
Open Mon-Thurs 7:50am-Midnight, Fri 7:50-6, Sat 10-5, Sun 3-11
Restriction: Circ limited

Departmental Libraries:

INFORMATION SERVICES LIBRARY, 3825 Ridgewood Rd, 39211, SAN 308-8839. Tel: 601-432-6313. FAX: 601-432-6144. *Actg Dir,* Melissa Druckrey
Founded 1989
Library Holdings: Bk Vols 42,000; Per Subs 500
Subject Interests: Census, Demographic, Soc work
Partic in Miss Libr Asn
Open Mon-Thurs 9-8, Fri 9-5

C MILLSAPS COLLEGE*, Millsaps-Wilson Library, 1701 N State St, 39210-0001. SAN 308-8731. Tel: 601-974-1070, 601-974-1073. Interlibrary Loan Service Tel: 601-974-1090. FAX: 601-974-1082. E-mail: librarian@millsaps.edu. Web Site: library.millsaps.edu. *Col Librn,* Tom Henderson; Tel: 601-974-1075, E-mail: hendetw@millsaps.edu; *Assoc Librn, Coordr, Pub Serv,* Molly McManus; Tel: 601-974-1086, E-mail: molly.mcmanus@millsaps.edu; *Acq Librn,* Jamie Wilson; Tel: 601-974-1083, E-mail: jamie.wilson@millsaps.edu; *Cat Librn, Coordr, Cat & Acq,* Elizabeth Beck; Tel: 601-974-1076, E-mail: beckea@millsaps.edu; *Pub Serv Librn,* Ryan Roy; Tel: 601-974-1072, E-mail: royrw@millsaps.edu; *Archivist,* Debra McIntosh; Tel: 601-974-1077, E-mail: mcintdw@millsaps.edu; Staff 7.5 (MLS 5, Non-MLS 2.5)
Founded 1890. Enrl 1,015; Fac 90; Highest Degree: Master
Library Holdings: Bk Titles 144,206; Bk Vols 205,427; Per Subs 615
Special Collections: Anthropology (Munro Edmonson Coll); Ethics (Paul Ramsey Coll); Eudora Welty Coll; Medical Ethics (Harmon Smith Coll); Military History (Johnson Coll); Millsaps College Archives; Mississippi Methodist Archives; Rare Books; Theater & Performing Arts (Lehman Engel Coll)
Subject Interests: Applied ethics, Art, Lit, Relig studies
Automation Activity & Vendor Info: (Acquisitions) SirsiDynix; (Cataloging) SirsiDynix; (Circulation) SirsiDynix; (Course Reserve) SirsiDynix; (OPAC) SirsiDynix; (Serials) SirsiDynix
Database Vendor: ARTstor, Cambridge Scientific Abstracts, Dialog, EBSCOhost, Gale Cengage Learning, JSTOR, OCLC FirstSearch, OCLC WorldShare Interlibrary Loan, ProQuest, PubMed, SerialsSolutions, SirsiDynix, STN International, Wilson - Wilson Web
Wireless access
Partic in Associated Colleges of the South; Central Mississippi Library Council; Lyrasis; Private Academic Libraries of Mississippi (PALMS)
Restriction: Limited access for the pub

CL MISSISSIPPI COLLEGE*, Law Library, 151 E Griffith St, 39201-1391. (Mail add: PO Box 4008, 39201), SAN 348-2286. Tel: 601-925-7120. FAX: 601-925-7112. E-mail: law@mc.edu. Web Site: law.mc.edu/library/index.html. *Dir,* Mary Miller; E-mail: mmiller@mc.edu; *Dir, Tech Serv,* Karin DenBleyker; E-mail: dbleyker@mc.edu; *Acq Librn,* Judy Nettles; *Computer Librn, Ref Librn,* Thomas B Walter; E-mail: walter@mc.edu; *Circ Librn, Instrul Serv Librn, Res Librn,* Brian Barnes; E-mail: barnes01@mc.edu; *Acq, Supvr,* Patrice Sims; *Circ Supvr,* Gracie Crotwell; *Cat Supvr,* Ginger Dressler; *Supvr, Ser,* JoAnn Neil; Staff 5 (MLS 3, Non-MLS 2)
Founded 1975. Enrl 350; Fac 19; Highest Degree: Doctorate
Library Holdings: Bk Vols 314,000; Per Subs 3,500
Automation Activity & Vendor Info: (Acquisitions) Innovative Interfaces, Inc; (Cataloging) Innovative Interfaces, Inc; (Circulation) Innovative Interfaces, Inc; (Course Reserve) Innovative Interfaces, Inc; (Media Booking) Innovative Interfaces, Inc; (OPAC) Innovative Interfaces, Inc; (Serials) Innovative Interfaces, Inc
Database Vendor: HeinOnline, LexisNexis, Loislaw, Westlaw, Wilson - Wilson Web
Partic in Lyrasis; OCLC Online Computer Library Center, Inc
Open Mon-Thurs 7:30am-1am, Fri 7:30am-9pm, Sat 9-9, Sun 12pm-1am

G MISSISSIPPI DEPARTMENT OF ARCHIVES & HISTORY*, Archives & Records Services Division, 200 North St, 39201. (Mail add: PO Box 571, 39205), SAN 308-8790. Tel: 601-576-6876. FAX: 601-576-6964. E-mail: refdesk@mdah.state.ms.us. Web Site: www.mdah.state.ms.us. *Div Head,* Julia Marks Young; E-mail: jyoung@mdah.state.ms.us; Staff 36 (MLS 10, Non-MLS 26)
Founded 1902
Library Holdings: Bk Vols 70,233; Per Subs 300
Special Collections: County Records, micro; Federal Government Records Pertaining to Mississippi; Map Coll; Mississippi Businesses & Organizations, private papers, mss; Mississippi Coll, newspapers; Mississippi Confederate Records; newsfilm; Photograph Coll; State, Territorial & Provincial Government, archives. Oral History; State Document Depository
Subject Interests: Civil rights, Civil War, Mississippiana
Automation Activity & Vendor Info: (Cataloging) ByWater Solutions; (Circulation) ByWater Solutions; (OPAC) ByWater Solutions; (Serials) ByWater Solutions
Function: Archival coll
Publications: Guide to Official Records in the Department of Archives & History; Research in the Department of Archives & History
Open Mon 9-5, Tues-Fri 8-5, Sat 8-1
Restriction: Non-circulating to the pub

G MISSISSIPPI DEPARTMENT OF ENVIRONMENTAL QUALITY LIBRARY*, 700 N State St, 39202. (Mail add: PO Box 2279, 39225), SAN 308-8758. Tel: 601-961-5501. Administration Tel: 601-961-5528. Administration FAX: 601-961-5521. Web Site: www.deq.state.ms.us/MDEQ.nsf/page/HR_Library?OpenDocument. *Dir,* Michael Bograd; E-mail: michael_bograd@deq.state.ms.us
Founded 1850
Library Holdings: Bk Vols 48,000; Per Subs 100
Special Collections: National, State & International Government Publications; Topographic Maps; United States & State Geological Survey Publications
Subject Interests: Environ eng, Environ geol, Geohydrology, Geol, Hazardous waste mgt, Paleontology, Petroleum geol
Function: Res libr
Open Mon-Fri 1-4:30
Restriction: Access at librarian's discretion, Authorized patrons, Authorized scholars by appt, By permission only, Circulates for staff only, Employees only, External users must contact libr, In-house use for visitors, Non-circulating to the pub, Not a lending libr, Staff use only

P MISSISSIPPI LIBRARY COMMISSION, 3881 Eastwood Dr, 39211. SAN 348-5919. Tel: 601-432-4111. Circulation Tel: 601-432-4153. Interlibrary Loan Service Tel: 601-432-4127. Information Services Tel: 601-432-4492. Toll Free Tel: 800-647-7542. Reference Toll Free Tel: 877-594-5733. FAX: 601-432-4480. Circulation FAX: 601-432-4476. Information Services FAX: 601-432-4478. E-mail: mlcref@mlc.lib.ms.us, mslib@mlc.lib.ms.us. Web

Site: www.mlc.lib.ms.us. *Exec Dir,* Susan Cassagne; Tel: 601-432-4439, E-mail: susan@mlc.lib.ms.us; *Dir, Admin Serv Bur,* Jennifer Peacock; Tel: 601-432-4042, E-mail: jpeacock@mlc.lib.ms.us; *Dir, Develop Serv Bur,* Jennifer Walker; Tel: 601-432-4068, E-mail: jwalker@mlc.lib.ms.us; *Dir, Libr Serv Bur,* Tracy Carr; Tel: 601-432-4450, E-mail: tcarr@mlc.lib.ms.us; *Dir, Info Serv,* Shivon Hess; Tel: 601-432-4140, E-mail: shess@mlc.lib.ms.us; *Blind & Physically Handicapped Libr Dir,* Shellie Zeigler; Tel: 601-432-4123, E-mail: szeigler@mlc.lib.ms.us; *Coll Mgt Serv Dir,* Greg Sellers; Tel: 601-432-4133, E-mail: gsellers@mlc.lib.ms.us; *Patents Librn,* Lawrence Smith; Staff 49 (MLS 11, Non-MLS 38)
Founded 1926
Jul 2014-Jun 2015 Income $14,256,750, State $13,976,684, Federal $280,066
Special Collections: Blind & Physically Handicapped Coll; Large Print Coll; US Patent & Trademark Depository. State Document Depository; US Document Depository
Subject Interests: Libr sci, Mississippiana, Patents
Automation Activity & Vendor Info: (Acquisitions) Auto-Graphics, Inc; (Cataloging) OCLC; (Circulation) Auto-Graphics, Inc; (ILL) Auto-Graphics, Inc; (OPAC) Auto-Graphics, Inc; (Serials) Auto-Graphics, Inc
Database Vendor: Baker & Taylor, Bowker, CredoReference, EBSCOhost, Gale Cengage Learning, Keystone Systems, Inc (KLAS), LearningExpress, LexisNexis, Marquis Who's Who, Newsbank, OCLC FirstSearch, OCLC WorldShare Interlibrary Loan, Oxford Online, ProQuest, ReferenceUSA, Wilson - Wilson Web
Wireless access
Publications: Large Print New Books Catalog (Bibliographies); Mississippi State Government Publications Index (Quarterly); Public Library Statistics (Online only); Reading Light (Newsletter); The Packet (Newsletter)
Partic in MAGNOLIA
Special Services for the Deaf - Bks on deafness & sign lang
Special Services for the Blind - Accessible computers; Assistive/Adapted tech devices, equip & products; Bks & mags in Braille, on rec, tape & cassette; Braille equip; Braille servs; Cassette playback machines; Closed circuit TV; Club for the blind; Computer with voice synthesizer for visually impaired persons; Copier with enlargement capabilities; Descriptive video serv (DVS); Digital talking bk; Duplicating spec requests; Extensive large print coll; Handicapped awareness prog; Home delivery serv; Info on spec aids & appliances; Low vision equip; Machine repair; Magnifiers; Newsletter (in large print, Braille or on cassette); Production of talking bks; Reader equip; Soundproof reading booth; Spanish Braille mags & bks; Spec cats; Spec prog; Talking bk & rec for the blind cat; Talking bks; Tel Pioneers equip repair group; Volunteer serv; ZoomText magnification & reading software
Open Mon-Fri 8-5
Friends of the Library Group

P MISSISSIPPI LIBRARY COMMISSION*, Blind & Physically Handicapped Library Services, 3881 Eastwood Dr, 39211-6473. SAN 308-8766. Tel: 601-432-4116. Toll Free Tel: 800-446-0892. FAX: 601-432-4476. E-mail: lbph@mlc.lib.ms.us. Web Site: www.mlc.lib.ms.us/lbph.htm. *Blind & Physically Handicapped Libr Dir,* Shellie Zeigler; Tel: 601-432-4123, E-mail: szeigler@mlc.lib.ms.us; Staff 8 (MLS 2, Non-MLS 6)
Founded 1970
Library Holdings: Audiobooks 296; Braille Volumes 1,688; CDs 179; DVDs 114; Electronic Media & Resources 420; Per Subs 85; Talking Bks 60,035; Videos 819
Special Collections: Lobe Library Consortium Member, digital bks; Mississippiana Coll, descriptive videos; Playaway, digital bks; Print Reference Coll
Automation Activity & Vendor Info: (Acquisitions) Keystone Systems, Inc (KLAS); (Cataloging) Keystone Systems, Inc (KLAS); (Circulation) Keystone Systems, Inc (KLAS); (ILL) Keystone Systems, Inc (KLAS); (OPAC) Keystone Systems, Inc (KLAS); (Serials) Keystone Systems, Inc (KLAS)
Database Vendor: Keystone Systems, Inc (KLAS)
Wireless access
Publications: Bibliography of Locally Recorded Materials; Instruction Manual for Institutions & Libraries; Patron Handbook; Reader Newsletter (Quarterly); The Reading Light (Newsletter); User Manual
Special Services for the Blind - Accessible computers; Aids for in-house use; Assistive/Adapted tech devices, equip & products; Audio mat; Bks & mags in Braille, on rec, tape & cassette; Bks available with recordings; Bks on cassette; Bks on CD; Blind Club (monthly newsletter); Braille & cassettes; Braille alphabet card; Braille bks; Braille equip; Braille servs; Cassette playback machines; Cassettes; Children's Braille; Closed circuit TV; Closed circuit TV magnifier; Computer access aids; Computer with voice synthesizer for visually impaired persons; Copier with enlargement capabilities; Daisy reader; Descriptive video serv (DVS); Digital talking bk; Duplicating spec requests; Extensive large print coll; Handicapped awareness prog; Info on spec aids & appliances; Internet workstation with adaptive software; Large print & cassettes; Large print bks; Large screen computer & software; Local mags & bks recorded; Machine repair; Magnifiers; Mags & bk reproduction/duplication; Musical scores in Braille & large print; Newsletter (in large print, Braille or on cassette); PC for handicapped; Photo duplicator for making large print; Playaways (bks on MP3); Production of talking bks; Reader equip; Recorded bks; Ref in Braille; Ref serv; Screen enlargement software for people with visual disabilities; Screen reader software; Sound rec; Soundproof reading booth; Spanish Braille mags & bks; Spec cats; Spec prog; Talking bk & rec for the blind cat; Talking bk serv referral; Talking bks; Talking bks & player equip; Talking bks plus; Tel Pioneers equip repair group; Variable speed audiotape players; Videos on blindness & phys handicaps; Volunteer serv; Web-Braille; ZoomText magnification & reading software
Open Mon-Fri 8-5
Friends of the Library Group

S MISSISSIPPI MUSEUM OF ART*, Howorth Library, 201 E Pascagoula, 39201. SAN 327-2141. Tel: 601-960-1515. FAX: 601-960-1505. Web Site: www.msmuseumart.org. *Curator,* Elizabeth Williams; E-mail: ewilliams@msmuseumart.org; *Curator,* Carol Peaster; E-mail: cpeaster@msmuseumart.org
Library Holdings: Bk Vols 45,000
Open Mon-Fri 10-4

S MISSISSIPPI MUSEUM OF NATURAL SCIENCE LIBRARY*, 2148 Riverside Dr, 39202. SAN 308-8774. Tel: 601-354-7303. FAX: 601-354-7227. E-mail: library@mmns.state.ms.us. Web Site: www.mdwfp.com/museum. *Librn,* Mary P Stevens
Founded 1974
Library Holdings: Bk Vols 18,000; Per Subs 104
Subject Interests: Botany, Environ studies, Herpetology, Ichthyology, Invertebrates, Mammalogy, Ornithology, Paleontology
Partic in Dialog Corp; OCLC Online Computer Library Center, Inc
Open Mon-Fri 8-5

GM G V MONTGOMERY VA MEDICAL CENTER LIBRARY*, 1500 E Woodrow Wilson Dr, 39216. SAN 308-8855. Tel: 601-364-1273. FAX: 601-364-1316. *Chief Librn,* Sarah Isabelle Scruggs; Staff 1 (MLS 1)
Founded 1946
Library Holdings: Bk Titles 3,100; Per Subs 300
Automation Activity & Vendor Info: (Acquisitions) CyberTools for Libraries; (Cataloging) EOS International; (Circulation) CyberTools for Libraries; (OPAC) CyberTools for Libraries; (Serials) CyberTools for Libraries
Database Vendor: Baker & Taylor, EBSCOhost
Function: Computer training, Computers for patron use, Copy machines, Doc delivery serv, Electronic databases & coll, ILL available, Online searches, Ref serv in person, Web-catalog, Wheelchair accessible
Open Mon-Fri 8-4:30
Restriction: Authorized patrons, Badge access after hrs, Circ limited, Circulates for staff only, Hospital employees & physicians only, Med & nursing staff, patients & families

L PHELPS DUNBAR, LLP*, Law Library, 4270 Interstate 55 N, 39211-6391. (Mail add: PO Box 16114, 39236-6114), SAN 372-4662. Tel: 601-352-2300. FAX: 601-360-9777. Web Site: phelpsdunbar.com. *Librn,* Cynthia Jones; Staff 2 (MLS 2)
Library Holdings: Bk Vols 5,000; Per Subs 20
Subject Interests: Labor
Database Vendor: LexisNexis
Restriction: Staff use only

R REFORMED THEOLOGICAL SEMINARY LIBRARY*, 5422 Clinton Blvd, 39209-3099. SAN 308-8812. Tel: 601-923-1623. FAX: 601-923-1621. E-mail: library.jackson@rts.edu. Web Site: www.rts.edu/jackson. *Interim Dir,* John Crabb; *Circ,* Mac McCarty; Staff 2 (MLS 2)
Founded 1965. Enrl 285; Fac 18; Highest Degree: Doctorate
Library Holdings: Bk Vols 150,000; Per Subs 320
Special Collections: Southern Presbyterianism (Blackburn Coll)
Wireless access
Partic in Lyrasis
Open Mon-Thurs 8am-9pm, Fri 8-4, Sat 9-4

M SAINT DOMINIC-JACKSON MEMORIAL HOSPITAL*, Luther Manship Medical Library, 969 Lakeland Dr, 39216. SAN 308-8820. Tel: 601-200-6944. FAX: 601-200-8075. Web Site: www.stdom.com. *Dir,* Diane Mott; *Libr Mgr,* Pam Peeples; *Libr Spec,* Lucy Stevenson
Founded 1974
Special Services for the Blind - Cassettes
Open Mon-Thurs 8-4:30

GL STATE OF MISSISSIPPI JUDICIARY*, State Law Library of Mississippi, Carroll Gartin Justice Bldg, 450 High St, 39201. (Mail add: PO Box 1040, 39215-1040), SAN 308-8804. Tel: 601-359-3672. FAX: 601-359-2912.

Web Site: www.mssc.state.ms.us. *State Librn,* Charlie Pearce; E-mail: cpearce@mssc.state.ms.us; *Info Processing Librn,* Liz Thompson; E-mail: lthompson@mssc.state.ms.us; *Info Serv Librn,* Clara Joorfetz; E-mail: cjoorfetz@mssc.state.ms.us; Staff 4 (MLS 3, Non-MLS 1)
Founded 1838
Library Holdings: Bk Vols 225,000; Per Subs 267
Special Collections: Mississippiana. US Document Depository
Subject Interests: Fed law, State law
Automation Activity & Vendor Info: (Cataloging) Book Systems; (OPAC) Book Systems
Database Vendor: EBSCOhost, OCLC FirstSearch, Westlaw, Wilson - Wilson Web
Function: ILL available
Open Mon-Fri 8-5
Restriction: Circ limited

L WATKINS, LUDLAM, WINTER & STENNIS*, Law Library, 190 E Capital St, Ste 800, 39201. (Mail add: PO Box 427, 39205-0427), SAN 372-2899. Tel: 601-949-4792. FAX: 601-949-4804. Web Site: www.watkinsludlam.com. *Librn,* Joe Xu; E-mail: jxu@watkinsludlam.com
Library Holdings: Bk Titles 3,000; Bk Vols 14,000; Per Subs 52

R WESLEY BIBLICAL SEMINARY LIBRARY*, 787 E Northside Dr, 39206. (Mail add: PO Box 9938, 39286-0938), SAN 375-2143. Tel: 601-366-8880. FAX: 601-366-8832. Web Site: www.wbs.edu. *Dir, Libr Serv,* Position Currently Open; Staff 0.5 (MLS 0.5)
Library Holdings: Bk Vols 62,000; Per Subs 270
Subject Interests: Relig
Automation Activity & Vendor Info: (Cataloging) TLC (The Library Corporation); (Circulation) TLC (The Library Corporation); (OPAC) TLC (The Library Corporation); (Serials) TLC (The Library Corporation)
Open Mon, Tues & Thurs 8am-9pm, Wed & Fri 8-5, Sat 9-2
Restriction: Circ privileges for students & alumni only

KEESLER AFB

UNITED STATES AIR FORCE

A MCBRIDE LIBRARY*, 81 FSS/FSDL McBride Library, 512 Larcher Blvd Bldg 2222, 39534-2345, SAN 348-6036. Tel: 228-377-2181. Administration Tel: 228-377-2604. FAX: 228-435-0203. Web Site: www.keesler.af.mil. *Dir,* Rebecca Chapman; Staff 5 (MLS 1, Non-MLS 4)
Founded 1942
Library Holdings: Bk Vols 4,000; Per Subs 150
Special Collections: Air War College; Chief of Staff Professional Reading Test; McNaughton Lease Books; Professional Military Education; Transition Assistance Program; US Air Force Periodicals
Subject Interests: Bus admin, Computer eng, Computer sci, Data communications, Electronics, Hist, Math, Mil sci, Television, Weather
Automation Activity & Vendor Info: (Cataloging) Softlink America; (Circulation) Softlink America; (ILL) OCLC; (OPAC) Softlink America
Partic in OCLC Online Computer Library Center, Inc
Special Services for the Blind - Closed circuit TV magnifier
Open Mon-Thurs 10-8, Fri-Sun 12-7

AM MEDICAL CENTER LIBRARY*, 81st Medical Group/SGGMEL, 301 Fisher St, Rm 1A132, 39534-2519, SAN 348-6044. Tel: 228-376-4949. FAX: 228-377-6127. *Librn,* Mary Altman; Staff 2 (MLS 1, Non-MLS 1)
Founded 1942
Library Holdings: Bk Titles 6,200; Per Subs 350
Subject Interests: Allied health, Clinical med, Dentistry, Nursing
Automation Activity & Vendor Info: (Cataloging) EOS International; (Circulation) EOS International; (Serials) EOS International
Database Vendor: OVID Technologies
Partic in Gulf Coast Biomedical Libr Consortium; SE-Atlantic Regional Med Libr Servs

KOSCIUSKO

P MID-MISSISSIPPI REGIONAL LIBRARY SYSTEM*, 201 S Huntington St, 39090-9002. SAN 348-6095. Tel: 662-289-5151. Interlibrary Loan Service Tel: 662-289-5162. FAX: 662-289-5106. Web Site: www.mmrls.lib.ms.us. *Dir,* Richard O Greene; E-mail: director@midmissregional.lib.ms.us; *Asst Dir,* Linda Milner; E-mail: asstdirector@midmissregional.lib.ms.us; *Tech Coordr,* Carolyn B Steen; E-mail: genadmin@midmissregional.lib.ms.us; *Cat,* Doug Potter; E-mail: cataloger@midmissregional.lib.ms.us; *Ch Serv,* Lisa Ramage; E-mail: youthservices@midmissregional.lib.ms.us; Staff 7 (MLS 2, Non-MLS 5)
Founded 1957. Pop 93,429; Circ 299,534
Library Holdings: Bk Titles 160,000; Per Subs 531
Special Collections: Barrett Civil War Coll (Lexington); Hendrix Genealogy Coll (Louisville); Sanders Genealogy Coll (Attala)
Subject Interests: Educ, Genealogy
Automation Activity & Vendor Info: (Acquisitions) EOS International; (Cataloging) EOS International; (Circulation) EOS International; (OPAC) EOS International
Wireless access
Function: ILL available
Open Mon-Fri 9-6, Sat 9-5
Friends of the Library Group
Branches: 13

ATTALA COUNTY, 201 S Huntington St, 39090-9002, SAN 348-6125. Tel: 662-289-5141. FAX: 662-289-9983. E-mail: attala@midmissregional.lib.ms.us. Web Site: www.mmrls.lib.ms.us/attala.htm. *Librn,* Carolyn Pilgram; Staff 7 (Non-MLS 7)
Special Collections: Blaylock-Sanders Coll; Education (Reavis Coll); Miss History & Genealogy
Open Mon-Fri 9-6, Sat 9-5
Friends of the Library Group

CARTHAGE-LEAKE COUNTY, 114 E Franklin St, Carthage, 39051-3716, SAN 348-615X. Tel: 601-267-7821. FAX: 601-267-5530. E-mail: carthage@midmissregional.lib.ms.us. *Librn,* Mary Ellen Ellis; Staff 4 (Non-MLS 4)
Open Mon, Tues, Thurs & Fri 8-5:30, Wed & Sat 8-12
Friends of the Library Group

DUCK HILL PUBLIC, 127 N State St, Duck Hill, 38925-9287. (Mail add: PO Box 279, Duck Hill, 38925-0279), SAN 348-6184. Tel: 662-565-2391. FAX: 662-565-2391. E-mail: duckhill@midmissregional.lib.ms.us. Web Site: www.mmrls.lib.ms.us/duck_hill.htm. *Librn,* Dolores Kirk; Staff 1 (Non-MLS 1)
Open Mon, Tues & Fri 1-5, Thurs 8-12 & 1-5

DURANT PUBLIC, 15338 N Jackson St, Durant, 39063-3708, SAN 348-6214. Tel: 662-653-3451. FAX: 662-653-3108. E-mail: durant@midmissregional.lib.ms.us. Web Site: www.mmrls.lib.ms.us/durant_public_library.htm. *Librn,* Betty Hatchcock; Staff 2 (Non-MLS 2)
Open Mon-Fri 8-5

GOODMAN PUBLIC, 9792 Main St, Goodman, 39079. (Mail add: PO Box 374, Goodman, 39079-0374), SAN 348-6249. Tel: 662-472-0550. FAX: 662-472-0599. E-mail: goodman@mmrls.lib.ms.us. Web Site: www.mmrls.lib.ms.us/goodman_lib.htm. *Librn,* Jennette Moore; Staff 1 (Non-MLS 1)
Open Mon 1-5, Tues & Thurs 9-12 & 1:30-5, Fri 1-4

KILMICHAEL PUBLIC, 102 First St, Kilmichael, 39747. (Mail add: PO Box 316, Kilmichael, 39747-0316), SAN 348-6273. Tel: 662-262-7615. FAX: 662-262-7615. E-mail: kilmichael@midmissregional.lib.ms.us. Web Site: www.mmlrs.lib.ms.us/kilm.htm.
Open Mon, Tues & Fri 1-5, Thurs 8-12 & 1-5

LEXINGTON PUBLIC, 208 Tchula St, Lexington, 39095-3134, SAN 348-6303. Tel: 662-834-2571. FAX: 662-834-4578. E-mail: lexington@midmissregional.lib.ms.us. Web Site: www.mmrls.lib.ms.us/lexington_lib.htm. *Librn,* Laura Lawson; Staff 2 (Non-MLS 2)
Open Mon-Thurs 8-5:30, Fri 8-5

PICKENS PUBLIC, 309 Hwy 51, Pickens, 39146. (Mail add: PO Box 188, Pickens, 39146-0188), SAN 348-6338. Tel: 662-468-2391. FAX: 662-468-2392. E-mail: pickens@midmissregional.lib.ms.us. Web Site: www.mmrls.lib.ms.us/pickens_lib.htm. *Librn,* Saddie McDonald; Staff 1 (Non-MLS 1)
Open Mon-Wed 9-12 & 1-6, Fri 8:30-12 & 12:30-4

TCHULA PUBLIC, 105 Mercer St, Tchula, 39169-5235. (Mail add: PO Box 248, Tchula, 39169-0248), SAN 348-6362. Tel: 662-235-5235. FAX: 662-235-4925. E-mail: tchula@midmissregional.lib.ms.us. Web Site: www.mmrls.lib.ms.us/tchula_lib.htm. *Librn,* Yvonne Clark; Staff 1 (Non-MLS 1)
Open Mon, Tues & Fri 9-5, Wed 9-4

WALNUT GROVE PUBLIC, 146 Main St, Walnut Grove, 39189. (Mail add: PO Box 206, Walnut Grove, 39189-0206), SAN 348-6397. Tel: 601-253-2483. FAX: 601-253-9374. E-mail: walnutgrove@midmissregional.lib.ms.us. Web Site: www.mmrls.lib.ms.us/walnutgr_lib.htm. *Librn,* Linda Bounds; Staff 1 (Non-MLS 1)
Open Mon-Fri 8:30-12 & 1-5:30, Sat 12:30-5

WEST PUBLIC, 24843 Hwy 51, West, 39192. (Mail add: PO Box 9, West, 39192-0009), SAN 348-6427. Tel: 662-967-2510. FAX: 662-967-2510. E-mail: west@midmissregional.lib.ms.us. Web Site: www.mmrls.lib.ms.us/west_lib.htm. *Librn,* Angie Burrell; Staff 1 (Non-MLS 1)
Open Wed 12-4, Thurs & Fri 8-4

WINONA-MONTGOMERY COUNTY, 115 N Quitman St, Winona, 38967-2228, SAN 348-6451. Tel: 662-283-3443. FAX: 662-283-2642. E-mail: winona@midmissregional.lib.ms.us. Web Site: www.mmrls.lib.ms.us/winona_mont.htm. *Librn,* Virginia Weed; Staff 2 (Non-MLS 2)
Open Mon-Fri 8-5

WINSTON COUNTY, 301 W Park St, Louisville, 39339-3018, SAN 348-6486. Tel: 662-773-3212. FAX: 662-773-8434. E-mail: winston@midmissregional.lib.ms.us. Web Site:

www.mmrls.lib.ms.us/winston_co.htm. *Librn,* Beth Edwards; Staff 4 (Non-MLS 4)
Special Collections: Miss Genealogy Coll
Open Mon & Tues 8:30-6, Wed 8:30-5:30, Thurs & Sat 8:30-12, Fri 8:30-5

LAKE

P LAKE PUBLIC LIBRARY*, City Hall, 100 Front St, 39092. (Mail add: PO Box 160, 39092-0160), SAN 376-6179. Tel: 601-775-3560. E-mail: lake@cmrls.lib.ms.us. Web Site: www.cmrls.lib.ms.us. *Br Mgr,* Selena Swink
Library Holdings: Bk Titles 4,500
Subject Interests: Genealogy, Local hist
Mem of Central Mississippi Regional Library System
Special Services for the Deaf - Bks on deafness & sign lang; Closed caption videos
Special Services for the Blind - Audio mat; Bks on CD; Large print bks
Open Mon 12:30-5, Thurs 9-12 & 12:30-5
Friends of the Library Group

LAUREL

P LAUREL-JONES COUNTY LIBRARY SYSTEM, INC*, Laurel-Jones County Library, 530 Commerce St, 39440. SAN 348-6516. Tel: 601-428-4313. FAX: 601-428-0597. Web Site: www.laurel.lib.ms.us. *Dir,* Mary-Louise Breland; E-mail: marylouise.breland@laurel.lib.ms.us; *Asst Dir,* Carolyn Russell; Staff 4 (MLS 2, Non-MLS 2)
Founded 1919. Pop 62,500; Circ 184,393
Library Holdings: Bk Vols 82,050; Per Subs 85
Special Collections: Genealogy Library; Laurel Newspaper Coll, 1892-present, micro & print; Local Family Records
Subject Interests: Genealogy, Local hist
Automation Activity & Vendor Info: (Acquisitions) Baker & Taylor; (Cataloging) Innovative Interfaces, Inc; (Circulation) Innovative Interfaces, Inc; (Course Reserve) Innovative Interfaces, Inc; (ILL) OCLC FirstSearch; (OPAC) Innovative Interfaces, Inc; (Serials) EBSCO Online
Open Mon-Fri 8-6, Sat 9:30-3
Friends of the Library Group
Branches: 1
ELLISVILLE PUBLIC, 201 Poplar St, Ellisville, 39437, SAN 348-6540. Tel: 601-477-9271. FAX: 601-477-3004. *Br Librn,* Michelle Rogers; Staff 2.5 (Non-MLS 2.5)
Pop 3,500
Function: Children's prog, Computers for patron use, Copy machines, Fax serv, Free DVD rentals, Online cat, Online info literacy tutorials on the web & in blackboard, Pub access computers
Open Mon-Fri 1:15-5
Friends of the Library Group

S LAUREN ROGERS MUSEUM OF ART LIBRARY*, 565 N Fifth Ave, 39440-3410. (Mail add: PO Box 1108, 39441-1108), SAN 308-8863. Tel: 601-649-6374. FAX: 601-428-8601, 601-649-6379. Web Site: www.lrma.org/library.html. *Librn,* Brianna Barnard; *Curator,* Mandy Buchanan; Staff 2 (MLS 1, Non-MLS 1)
Founded 1923
Library Holdings: Bk Vols 10,000; Per Subs 75
Special Collections: Artists' Clipping Files; Bookplates; Local History, photog, mss; Museum Archives; Postcard Coll; Rare Books
Subject Interests: Am art, Georgian silver, Local hist, Mississippiana, Native Am basket
Function: Ref serv available
Publications: Jean Leon Gerome Ferris (1863-1930), American Painter Historian; Lauren Rogers Museum of Art Handbook of Collections; Lauren Rogers Museum of Art Handbook of the Collections, Revised Ed (Collection catalog); Lauren Rogers Museum of Art Newsletter (Quarterly); Mississippi Art Colony; Mississippi Portraiture; Recent Acquisitions, Lauren Rogers Museum of Art; Sam Gilliam: Folded & Hinged; The French Legacy; The Gibbons Silver Collection (Collection catalog)
Open Tues-Sat 10-4:45
Restriction: Non-circulating

CR SOUTHEASTERN BAPTIST COLLEGE*, A R Reddin Memorial Library, 4229 Hwy 15 N, 39440. SAN 308-8871. Tel: 601-426-6346. FAX: 601-426-6347. *Librn,* Amy Hinton; Staff 1 (MLS 1)
Founded 1955. Enrl 111; Fac 12; Highest Degree: Doctorate
Library Holdings: Bk Titles 30,000; Per Subs 45
Special Collections: Baptist Missionary Association of America Coll, doc
Open Mon & Tues 8-6, Wed & Thurs 8-2:30

LEAKESVILLE

S MISSISSIPPI DEPARTMENT OF CORRECTIONS*, South Mississippi Correctional Institution Library, Hwy 63 N, 39451. Tel: 601-394-5600, Ext 1079. FAX: 601-394-5600, Ext 1182. Web Site: www.mdoc.state.ms.us. *Librn,* Alvin Moody
Library Holdings: Bk Vols 9,000
Database Vendor: LexisNexis

LONG BEACH

P LONG BEACH PUBLIC LIBRARY*, 209 Jeff Davis Ave, 39560. SAN 308-8898. Tel: 228-863-0711. FAX: 228-863-8511. Web Site: www.longbeach.lib.ms.us. *Dir,* Jeannie Ripoll; E-mail: jripoll@cableone.net; *Ch Serv,* Renee Rayburn; Staff 4 (Non-MLS 4)
Founded 1895. Pop 17,320; Circ 115,495
Library Holdings: Bks on Deafness & Sign Lang 30; Bk Titles 20,000
Special Collections: Cook Books & Craft Coll
Automation Activity & Vendor Info: (Cataloging) Follett Software; (Circulation) Follett Software; (OPAC) Follett Software
Open Mon-Wed, Fri & Sat 9-5, Thurs 9-8
Friends of the Library Group

C UNIVERSITY OF SOUTHERN MISSISSIPPI*, Gulf Coast Library, 730 E Beach Blvd, 39560-2698. SAN 325-3422. Tel: 228-865-4510. FAX: 228-865-4544. Web Site: www.lib.usm.edu. *Dir,* Edward McCormack; Tel: 228-266-4241, E-mail: edward.mccormack@usm.edu; *Coll Develop,* Allisa Beck; Tel: 228-214-3468, E-mail: allisa.beck@usm.edu; *Pub Serv,* Elizabeth Doolittle; Tel: 228-214-3455, E-mail: elizabeth.doolittle@usm.edu; Staff 13 (MLS 5, Non-MLS 8)
Founded 1972. Enrl 2,300; Fac 111
Library Holdings: Bk Vols 60,000; Per Subs 630
Special Collections: Curriculum Materials Center; Gulf of Mexico Program; PDK Fastbacks
Subject Interests: Bus admin, Educ, Hospitality mgt, Humanities, Nursing, Psychol
Automation Activity & Vendor Info: (Circulation) SirsiDynix; (ILL) OCLC ILLiad; (Media Booking) SirsiDynix; (OPAC) SirsiDynix
Publications: USMGC Library Link
Partic in Lyrasis; MAGNOLIA
Open Mon-Thurs 8am-10pm, Fri 8-5, Sat & Sun 2-6

MACON

P NOXUBEE COUNTY LIBRARY SYSTEM*, 103 E King St, 39341-2832. SAN 308-891X. Tel: 662-726-5461. FAX: 662-726-4694. Web Site: www.noxubee.lib.ms.us. *Dir,* Shemka Conner; E-mail: sconner@noxubee.lib.ms.us
Founded 1933. Pop 12,604; Circ 21,762
Library Holdings: Bk Vols 26,925
Special Collections: Reference Classics (Harold Gibson Brown Memorial Coll)
Subject Interests: Mississippiana
Automation Activity & Vendor Info: (Acquisitions) Auto-Graphics, Inc; (Cataloging) Auto-Graphics, Inc; (Circulation) Auto-Graphics, Inc; (ILL) Auto-Graphics, Inc
Wireless access
Open Mon, Tues, Thurs & Fri 8-6
Friends of the Library Group
Branches: 2
BROOKSVILLE BRANCH, 100 W Main St, Brooksville, 39739, SAN 321-9429. Tel: 662-738-4559. *Librn,* Elsie R King; *Librn,* Emily Mancill
Open Mon-Fri 2-5
Friends of the Library Group
VISTA J DANIEL MEMORIAL, 402 Residence St, Shuqualak, 39361-9740. (Mail add: PO Box 248, Shuqualak, 39361-0248), SAN 321-9437. Tel: 662-793-9576. *Br Librn,* Eddie P Fox
Library Holdings: Bk Vols 12,000
Automation Activity & Vendor Info: (Serials) Auto-Graphics, Inc
Database Vendor: Auto-Graphics, Inc
Open Mon-Wed & Fri 2-5, Sat 9-12
Friends of the Library Group

MAGEE

P MAGEE PUBLIC LIBRARY*, Mims Williams Memorial Library, 120 First St NW, 39111. SAN 376-6195. Tel: 601-849-3747. FAX: 601-849-6609. E-mail: magee@cmrls.lib.ms.us. Web Site: www.cmrls.lib.ms.us. *Br Mgr,* Frances T Meadows; E-mail: mabm@cmrls.lib.ms.us; *Ch Serv,* Garnet Craft; *Circ,* Marge King; Staff 1 (Non-MLS 1)
Founded 1935. Pop 4,298; Circ 46,400
Library Holdings: CDs 100; DVDs 600; Large Print Bks 300; Bk Titles 23,000; Per Subs 20; Videos 150
Automation Activity & Vendor Info: (Circulation) Horizon
Database Vendor: EBSCO Auto Repair Reference, EBSCOhost, LearningExpress
Wireless access
Function: Bk club(s), Bks on cassette, Bks on CD, Children's prog, Computer training, Computers for patron use, Copy machines, Electronic databases & coll, Fax serv, Free DVD rentals, ILL available, Music CDs,

Online cat, Prog for adults, Prog for children & young adult, Pub access computers, Story hour, Summer reading prog, Tax forms, Teen prog, Telephone ref, VHS videos, Web-catalog, Wheelchair accessible
Mem of Central Mississippi Regional Library System
Open Mon, Wed & Fri 8:30-5:30, Tues & Thurs 10-7, Sat 9-1
Friends of the Library Group

MARKS

P MARKS-QUITMAN COUNTY LIBRARY, 315 E Main St, 38646. SAN 308-8928. Tel: 662-326-7141. FAX: 662-326-7369. E-mail: mqcl@marks.lib.ms.us. Web Site: www.marksquitmancountylibrary.org. *Dir,* William Bahr; E-mail: wlbahr@marks.lib.ms.us
Pop 10,500; Circ 23,202
Library Holdings: Bk Titles 13,000; Per Subs 29
Subject Interests: Agr, Genealogy, Hist, Miss
Wireless access
Partic in Dancing Rabbit Library Consortium
Open Mon-Fri 8-4

MCCOMB

P PIKE-AMITE-WALTHALL LIBRARY SYSTEM*, McComb Public Library (Headquarters), 1022 Virginia Ave, 39648. SAN 348-663X. Tel: 601-684-2661. Circulation Tel: 601-684-2661, Ext 17. Interlibrary Loan Service Tel: 601-684-2661, Ext 18. Administration Tel: 601-684-7034, Ext 10. FAX: 601-250-1213. Web Site: www.pawls.org. *Dir,* Darlene Morgan; Tel: 601-684-7034, Ext 11, E-mail: dmorgan@pawls.lib.ms.us; *Admin Librn,* Kelli Bennett; Tel: 601-684-7034, Ext 15, E-mail: kelli@pawls.lib.ms.us; *Ref & ILL Librn,* Veronica Williams; E-mail: vwilliams@pawls.lib.ms.us; *Circ Mgr,* Monica Wilkinson; E-mail: monica@pawls.lib.ms.us; *Ch Serv,* Mattie J Rials; Tel: 601-684-2661, Ext 12; *Tech Serv,* Patrick Sanders; Tel: 601-684-2661, Ext 14; Staff 13 (MLS 1, Non-MLS 12)
Founded 1964. Pop 68,796; Circ 136,780
Library Holdings: Audiobooks 2,016; AV Mats 11,298; CDs 334; DVDs 2,519; e-books 100; Electronic Media & Resources 55; Large Print Bks 3,555; Microforms 140; Bk Titles 88,234; Bk Vols 145,085; Per Subs 225; Videos 4,098
Subject Interests: Genealogy
Automation Activity & Vendor Info: (Acquisitions) SIRSI WorkFlows; (Cataloging) SIRSI WorkFlows; (Circulation) SIRSI WorkFlows; (ILL) OCLC WorldShare Interlibrary Loan; (OPAC) SIRSI WorkFlows; (Serials) SIRSI WorkFlows
Wireless access
Function: Art exhibits, Bks on cassette, Bks on CD, Children's prog, Computers for patron use, Copy machines, Electronic databases & coll, Fax serv, Free DVD rentals, ILL available, Microfiche/film & reading machines, Online cat, Online ref, Online searches, Photocopying/Printing, Preschool reading prog, Prog for children & young adult, Pub access computers, Story hour, Summer reading prog, Tax forms, Wheelchair accessible
Restriction: 24-hr pass syst for students only
Branches: 8
ALPHA CENTER, 414 McComb Ave, 39648, SAN 348-6664. Tel: 601-685-8312. E-mail: alphacen@pawls.lib.ms.us. *Librn,* Linda Brister; Staff 1 (Non-MLS 1)
Library Holdings: Bk Vols 1,933
Open Mon-Thurs 2-5, Fri 3-5
CROSBY BRANCH, Hwy 33, Crosby, 39633. (Mail add: PO Box 427, Crosby, 39633-0427), SAN 348-6699. Tel: 601-639-4633. E-mail: crosby@pawls.lib.ms.us. *Librn,* Laura Stokes; Staff 1 (Non-MLS 1)
Founded 1959
Library Holdings: Bk Vols 3,260
Open Mon-Thurs 2-5:30
GLOSTER BRANCH, 229 E Main, Gloster, 39638. (Mail add: PO Drawer 460, Gloster, 39638-0460), SAN 348-6729. Tel: 601-225-5147. FAX: 601-225-4341. E-mail: gloster229@pawls.lib.ms.us. *Librn,* Joyce H Waugh; Staff 1 (Non-MLS 1)
Founded 1959
Library Holdings: Bk Vols 10,992
Open Mon-Wed & Fri 10-5, Sat 11-1
LIBERTY BRANCH, 196 Clinic Dr, Liberty, 39654. (Mail add: PO Box 187, Liberty, 39654-0187), SAN 348-6753. Tel: 601-657-8781. FAX: 601-657-8781. E-mail: liberty@pawls.lib.ms.us. *Librn,* Cheryl Rape-Ott; Staff 1 (Non-MLS 1)
Library Holdings: Bk Vols 11,550
Open Mon-Wed & Fri 10:30-5:30, Sat 10-12
MAGNOLIA BRANCH, 230 S Cherry St, Magnolia, 39652, SAN 348-6788. Tel: 601-783-6565. E-mail: magnolia@pawls.lib.ms.us. *Librn,* Jo Ann K Jones; Staff 1 (Non-MLS 1)
Founded 1933
Library Holdings: Bk Vols 10,610
Open Mon-Wed & Fri 11-5, Thurs 1-7
OSYKA BRANCH, 568 W Railroad Ave, Osyka, 39657, SAN 348-6842. Tel: 601-542-5147. E-mail: osyka@pawls.lib.ms.us. *Mgr,* Nancy DeVoss; Staff 1 (Non-MLS 1)
Library Holdings: Bk Vols 6,164
Open Mon, Tues, Thurs & Fri 1-5
PROGRESS, 5071 Mt Herman Rd, 39648-9767. Tel: 601-542-5501. E-mail: progress@pawls.lib.ms.us. *Librn,* Alice D Overall; Staff 1 (Non-MLS 1)
Library Holdings: Bk Vols 4,873
Open Mon-Thurs 2-6
Friends of the Library Group
WALTHALL, 707 Union Rd, Tylertown, 39667, SAN 348-6931. Tel: 601-876-4348. FAX: 601-876-4348. E-mail: walthall@pawls.lib.ms.us. *Br Librn,* Alice Markey; E-mail: amarkey@pawls.lib.ms.us; Staff 3 (MLS 1, Non-MLS 2)
Founded 1933
Library Holdings: Bk Vols 18,203
Open Mon, Tues & Thurs 9-6, Wed 9-2, Fri 9-5, Sat 9-4
Friends of the Library Group

MENDENHALL

J COPIAH-LINCOLN COMMUNITY COLLEGE*, Fred & Jewett Taylor Library, 151 Colin Dr, 39111. Tel: 601-849-0116. FAX: 601-849-0160. *Dir,* Bryon Conville; E-mail: bryon.conville@colin.edu; *Evening Librn,* Donna Ainsworth; Tel: 601-849-0118, E-mail: donna.ainsworth@colin.edu; *Evening Librn,* Marcia Winningham
Library Holdings: Bk Vols 7,000; Per Subs 23
Database Vendor: CQ Press, Newsbank
Open Mon, Tues & Thurs 8am-8:30pm, Fri 8-4

P MENDENHALL PUBLIC LIBRARY*, 1630 Simpson Hwy 149, 39114. SAN 376-6187. Tel: 601-847-2181. FAX: 601-847-2188. E-mail: menden@cmrls.lib.ms.us. Web Site: www.cmrls.lib.ms.us/me.htm. *Br Mgr,* Rhoda Benton; *Ch,* Nancy Wright
Library Holdings: Bk Titles 25,000; Bk Vols 30,000; Per Subs 30
Automation Activity & Vendor Info: (Cataloging) SirsiDynix; (Circulation) SirsiDynix
Wireless access
Mem of Central Mississippi Regional Library System
Open Mon 10-7, Tues & Thurs 9:30-5, Fri 9-5, Sat 9-Noon
Friends of the Library Group

MERIDIAN

J MERIDIAN COMMUNITY COLLEGE*, L O Todd Library Resource Center, 910 Hwy 19 N, 39307. SAN 308-8944. Tel: 601-484-8760. Toll Free Tel: 800-622-8431. FAX: 601-482-3936. Web Site: www.mcc.cc.ms.us/libraryappllibraryhome.htm. *Dean,* Billy C Beal; *Bibliog Instr,* Douglas Jernigan; Tel: 601-484-8762; *Circ,* Rita McClure; Tel: 601-484-8761; *Tech Serv,* Suzanne Grafton; Tel: 601-484-8766; Staff 10 (MLS 3, Non-MLS 7)
Founded 1937. Enrl 3,800
Library Holdings: Bk Vols 12,000; Per Subs 180
Special Collections: Ulysses S Grant Presidential Coll
Subject Interests: Allied health
Database Vendor: EBSCOhost, Gale Cengage Learning, OCLC FirstSearch, Wilson - Wilson Web
Open Mon-Thurs 7:30-5, Fri 7:30-3:30, Sat 10-2

P MERIDIAN-LAUDERDALE COUNTY PUBLIC LIBRARY*, 2517 Seventh St, 39301. SAN 308-8952. Tel: 601-693-6771. FAX: 601-486-2260. E-mail: library@meridian.lib.ms.us. Web Site: www.meridian.lib.ms.us. *Dir, Libr Serv,* Position Currently Open; *Supvr, Maillibr,* Shirley Koch; Tel: 601-486-2263; *Supvr, Tech Serv,* Walt Barrett; E-mail: wbarrett@meridian.lib.ms.us; *Ch Serv,* Shay Smith; Tel: 601-693-6771, Ext 234; Staff 16 (MLS 2, Non-MLS 14)
Founded 1913. Pop 79,000; Circ 135,000
Oct 2011-Sept 2012 Income $1,209,201, State $186,792, Federal $14,523, County $917,000, Locally Generated Income $76,386, Other $14,500. Mats Exp $128,147, Books $92,177, Per/Ser (Incl. Access Fees) $130, Micro $26,000, AV Mat $5,178, Electronic Ref Mat (Incl. Access Fees) $2,500, Presv $2,162. Sal $631,286
Library Holdings: AV Mats 36,710; Bk Titles 137,915; Bk Vols 176,452; Per Subs 124; Talking Bks 1,767
Special Collections: State Document Depository
Subject Interests: Genealogy, Local hist, Meridian star, Miss
Automation Activity & Vendor Info: (Cataloging) Innovative Interfaces, Inc; (Circulation) Innovative Interfaces, Inc; (OPAC) Innovative Interfaces, Inc
Function: Bks on cassette, Bks on CD, Children's prog, Electronic databases & coll, Free DVD rentals, Homebound delivery serv, Notary serv, Outreach serv, Preschool outreach, Prog for children & young adult, Pub access computers, Ref & res, Ref serv available, Spoken cassettes & CDs, Story hour, Summer reading prog, Telephone ref

Publications: Mailibrary Catalog (Monthly)
Open Mon-Sat 9-6
Restriction: Non-resident fee
Friends of the Library Group

A NAS MERIDIAN LIBRARY*, Andrew Triplett Library, 220 Fuller Rd, 39309. SAN 348-6966. Tel: 601-679-2623. FAX: 601-679-5106. *Libr Tech,* Jeanelle Echols; Staff 1 (Non-MLS 1)
Founded 1960
Library Holdings: Bk Titles 9,893; Per Subs 54
Automation Activity & Vendor Info: (Cataloging) Follett Software; (Circulation) Follett Software
Function: Photocopying/Printing, Prog for children & young adult, Ref serv available, Summer reading prog, Wheelchair accessible
Restriction: Circ to mil employees only, Open to govt employees only

MISSISSIPPI STATE

S COBB INSTITUTE OF ARCHAELOGY LIBRARY*, Mississippi State University, Rm 206, PO Box AR, 39762. SAN 348-7024. Tel: 662-325-3826. FAX: 662-325-8690. *In Charge,* Kathleen Elliott
Founded 1975
Library Holdings: Bk Vols 1,604
Special Collections: Indians of the Southeastern United States; Middle Eastern & Biblical Archaeology; North American Archaeology; Numismatic literature

C MISSISSIPPI STATE UNIVERSITY*, Mitchell Memorial Library, 395 Hardy Rd, 39762. (Mail add: PO Box 5408, 39762-5408), SAN 348-6990. Tel: 662-325-7668. FAX: 662-325-9344. Web Site: nt.library.msstate.edu. *Dean of Libr,* Frances N Coleman, E-mail: fcoleman@library.msstate.edu; *Assoc Dean, Tech Serv,* June Schmidt; *Syst Coordr,* Stephen Conetto; Staff 26 (MLS 26)
Founded 1881. Highest Degree: Doctorate
Library Holdings: Bk Vols 2,051,615; Per Subs 18,103
Special Collections: David Bowen Coll; Delta & Pineland Company Papers; Eugene Butler; Gil Carmichael; GV (Sonny) Montgomery Coll; Hodding Carter Papers; John C Stennis Coll, correspondence, genealogy, mss, notes, papers, photogs; John Grisham; Mike Esty Coll; Mississippi Journalists; Mississippiana, bks, mss, newsp; Republican Party of Mississippi Papers; Sid Salter; Southern History & Politics, micro; State & Local History; Turner Catledge Papers. Oral History; State Document Depository; US Document Depository
Subject Interests: Agr, Energy, Eng, Forestry
Automation Activity & Vendor Info: (Circulation) SirsiDynix
Publications: Guide to Resources in Mammology; Guide to Resources in Ornithology; Guide to Resources of MSU Library in Education; Science Resources
Partic in Lyrasis
Open Mon-Thurs 7am-9:45pm, Fri 7-5:45, Sat 10-5:45
Friends of the Library Group

Departmental Libraries:

ARCHITECTURE, 121 Giles Hall, 889 Collegeview St, 39762. (Mail add: PO Box AQ, 39762), SAN 348-7059. Tel: 662-325-2204. FAX: 662-325-8872. E-mail: jhammett@library.msstate.edu. *Assoc Prof, Librn,* Susan Hall; E-mail: shall@library.msstate.edu, *Info Spec,* Kathrin Dodds; E-mail: kdodds@library.msstate.edu
Open Mon-Thurs 8am-10pm, Fri 8-5, Sat 1-5, Sun 2-10
Friends of the Library Group

JACKSON ARCHITECTURE, 509 E Capitol St, Jackson, 39201. Tel: 622-325-0679. FAX: 601-354-6481. *Libr Assoc,* Pamela Berberette; Tel: 601-354-6184, E-mail: pberberette@library.msstate.edu
Open Mon, Wed & Thurs 9:30-3, Tues 10-3:30
Friends of the Library Group

MERIDIAN CAMPUS, 1000 Hwy 19 N, Meridian, 39307. Tel: 601-484-0236. Reference Tel: 662-325-7667. FAX: 601-484-0139. Web Site: library.msstate.edu/content/templates/?a=142&z=49. *Librn,* Melanie Thomas; E-mail: mthomas@library.msstate.edu
Open Mon, Wed & Thurs 9-6, Tues 12-9, Fri 8-5
Friends of the Library Group

VETERINARY MEDICINE, 240 Wise Center Dr, 39762. (Mail add: PO Box 9825, 39762), SAN 348-7083. Tel: 662-325-1256. FAX: 662-325-1144. Web Site: library.msstate.edu/content/templates/?a=497. *Coordr,* Laurel Sammonds; Tel: 662-325-1114, E-mail: lsammonds@library.msstate.edu
Open Mon-Thurs 7am-11pm, Fri 7-5, Sat 10-6, Sun 2-10
Friends of the Library Group

MIZE

P MIZE PUBLIC LIBRARY*, R T Prince Memorial, 210 Hwy 28, 39116. (Mail add: PO Box 247, 39116-0247), SAN 376-639X. Tel: 601-733-9414. E-mail: mize@cmrls.lib.ms.us. Web Site: www.cmrls.lib.ms.us/rtprince.htm. *Br Mgr,* Joyce Stringer
Library Holdings: Bk Titles 1,100; Bk Vols 1,500
Automation Activity & Vendor Info: (Circulation) SirsiDynix
Mem of Central Mississippi Regional Library System
Open Mon-Wed 2:30-5:30

MOORHEAD

J MISSISSIPPI DELTA COMMUNITY COLLEGE, Stanny Sanders Library, 414 Hwy 3 South, 38761. (Mail add: PO Box 668, 38761-0668), SAN 308-8960. Tel: 662-246-6376. Circulation Tel: 662-246-6380. Reference Tel: 662-246-6235. Administration Tel: 662-246-6301. FAX: 662-246-8627. Administration FAX: 662-246-6321. E-mail: mdcc_library@msdelta.edu. Web Site: www.msdelta.edu. *Dir of Libr Serv,* Kristy Aust Bariola; Tel: 662-246-6378, E-mail: kbariola@msdelta.edu; *Res Librn,* Audrey H Beach; E-mail: abeach@msdelta.edu; *Media Ctr Coordr,* Johnnie Davis; Tel: 662-246-6384, E-mail: jdavis@msdelta.edu; *Cataloger,* Tasmine Brown Moore; Tel: 662-246-6377, E-mail: tjmoore@msdelta.edu; Staff 7 (MLS 2, Non-MLS 5)
Founded 1929. Enrl 2,900; Highest Degree: Associate
Library Holdings: DVDs 700; Bk Titles 55,000; Per Subs 207
Automation Activity & Vendor Info: (Cataloging) SIRSI WorkFlows; (Circulation) SirsiDynix; (ILL) OCLC FirstSearch
Database Vendor: Cinahl, Ebooks Corporation, EBSCO Information Services, EBSCOhost, Facts on File, Gale Cengage Learning, H W Wilson, OCLC ArticleFirst, OCLC FirstSearch, OCLC WorldShare Interlibrary Loan, ProQuest, SirsiDynix
Wireless access
Publications: Library Handbook
Partic in Dancing Rabbit Library Consortium
Open Mon-Wed 7:30am-9pm, Thurs 7:30-5

Departmental Libraries:

DREW LIBRARY, 153 N Main St, Drew, 38737. Tel: 662-745-6322. FAX: 662-745-0194. *Librn,* Audrey H Beach; E-mail: abeach@msdelta.edu; *Librn,* Merrie Knight; E-mail: mknight@msdelta.edu; Staff 2 (MLS 2)
Highest Degree: Associate

GHEC LIBRARY, 2900A Hwy 1 S, Greenville, 38701. Tel: 662-332-8467. FAX: 662-332-8931. *Librn,* Alice Permenter; E-mail: apermenter@msdelta.edu; *Librn,* Melody Sample Stapleton; E-mail: mstapleton@msdelta.edu; Staff 2 (MLS 1, Non-MLS 1)
Highest Degree: Associate
Automation Activity & Vendor Info: (Acquisitions) SIRSI WorkFlows; (Circulation) SIRSI WorkFlows; (Course Reserve) SIRSI WorkFlows; (ILL) SIRSI WorkFlows; (Media Booking) SIRSI WorkFlows; (OPAC) SIRSI WorkFlows; (Serials) SIRSI WorkFlows
Open Mon-Thurs 7:30am-9pm

GREENWOOD LIBRARY, 207 W Park Ave, Greenwood, 38930. Tel: 662-453-7377. FAX: 662-453-2043. *Librn,* Audrey Horn Beach; E-mail: abeach@msdelta.edu; *Librn,* Merrie Knight; E-mail: mknight@msdelta.edu; Staff 2 (MLS 2)
Highest Degree: Associate
Open Mon-Thurs 8-4

MORTON

P MORTON PUBLIC LIBRARY, 16 E Fourth Ave, 39117. SAN 376-6160. Tel: 601-732-6288. FAX: 601-732-6288. E-mail: morton@cmrls.lib.ms.us. Web Site: www.cmrls.lib.ms.us/morton.htm. *Br Mgr,* Matt Purvis
Library Holdings: Bk Titles 10,000; Per Subs 25
Automation Activity & Vendor Info: (Cataloging) SirsiDynix; (Circulation) SirsiDynix
Mem of Central Mississippi Regional Library System
Open Mon-Wed 10-5:30, Thurs 1-8, Fri 9:30-5:30
Friends of the Library Group

P POLKVILLE PUBLIC LIBRARY*, 6670 Hwy 13, 39117. SAN 376-6012. Tel: 601-537-3115. FAX: 601-537-3115. E-mail: polkvill@cmrls.lib.ms.us. Web Site: www.cmrls.lib.ms.us/polkville.html. *Br Mgr,* Michelle Easterling
Library Holdings: Bk Vols 600
Mem of Central Mississippi Regional Library System
Open Mon 3pm-7pm, Wed & Thurs 1:30-5:30
Friends of the Library Group

NATCHEZ

J COPIAH-LINCOLN COMMUNITY COLLEGE*, Willie Mae Dunn Library, 11 Colin Circle, 39120. SAN 308-8987. Tel: 601-446-1101. Administration Tel: 601-446-1107. FAX: 601-446-1297. Web Site: www.colin.edu/library/natchez.htm. *Libr Dir,* Nancy J McLemore; E-mail: nancy.mclemore@colin.edu; Staff 3 (MLS 1, Non-MLS 2)
Founded 1972. Enrl 959; Fac 25; Highest Degree: Associate
Library Holdings: AV Mats 780; e-books 11,000; Bk Vols 23,275; Per Subs 135
Automation Activity & Vendor Info: (OPAC) SirsiDynix
Open Mon-Thurs 7:30am-8pm, Fri 7:30-2:30

P NATCHEZ ADAMS WILKINSON LIBRARY SERVICE*, Judge George W Armstrong Library, 220 S Commerce St, 39120-3502. SAN 308-8979. Tel: 601-445-8862. FAX: 601-446-7795. E-mail: armstrong@naw.lib.ms.us. Web Site: www.naw.lib.ms.us. *Dir,* Susan S Cassagne; E-mail: scassagne@naw.lib.ms.us; *Asst Dir, Pub Serv,* Anne White; E-mail: awhite@naw.lib.ms.us; *Ref Librn, Youth Serv Coordr,* Marianne Raley; E-mail: mraley@naw.lib.ms.us; *Cataloger,* Chris Shirey; E-mail: cshirey@naw.lib.ms.us; Staff 11 (MLS 2, Non-MLS 9)
Founded 1883. Pop 42,000
Library Holdings: Bk Titles 92,000; Per Subs 230
Special Collections: Natchez Mississippi Coll
Subject Interests: Local hist
Automation Activity & Vendor Info: (Cataloging) Innovative Interfaces, Inc; (Circulation) Innovative Interfaces, Inc; (ILL) Auto-Graphics, Inc; (OPAC) Innovative Interfaces, Inc
Wireless access
Function: Bks on cassette, Bks on CD, Children's prog, Computers for patron use, Copy machines, Fax serv, Handicapped accessible, ILL available, Online cat, Photocopying/Printing, Preschool outreach, Prog for children & young adult, Pub access computers, Spoken cassettes & CDs, Story hour, Summer reading prog, Teen prog, Telephone ref, VHS videos, Wheelchair accessible
Open Mon-Wed & Fri 9-5, Thurs 9-6, Sat 9-1
Friends of the Library Group
Branches: 2
KEVIN POOLE VAN CLEAVE MEMORIAL LIBRARY, 141 W Park St N, Centreville, 39631, SAN 348-9515. Tel: 601-645-5771. FAX: 601-645-5771. E-mail: vancleave@naw.lib.ms.us.
Library Holdings: Bk Vols 6,890
Open Mon-Thurs 9-5, Sat 9-1
WOODVILLE PUBLIC LIBRARY, 489 Main St, Woodville, 39669, SAN 348-954X. Tel: 601-888-6712. FAX: 601-888-6885.
Library Holdings: Bk Vols 6,805
Open Tues-Fri 10-5, Sat 10-2
Friends of the Library Group

NEW ALBANY

P UNION COUNTY LIBRARY*, Jennie Stephens Smith Library, 219 King St, 38652. (Mail add: PO Box 846, 38652-0846), SAN 348-7113. Tel: 662-534-1991. FAX: 662-534-1937. *Dir,* Kay Sappington; E-mail: ksappington@union.lib.ms.us; Staff 9 (MLS 1, Non-MLS 8)
Founded 1933. Pop 26,000; Circ 43,500
Library Holdings: Bk Vols 70,000; Per Subs 75
Special Collections: Genealogy Coll
Subject Interests: Miss hist
Automation Activity & Vendor Info: (Cataloging) Follett Software; (Circulation) Follett Software; (ILL) Follett Software; (OPAC) Follett Software
Database Vendor: EBSCOhost, Gale Cengage Learning, OCLC FirstSearch, Wilson - Wilson Web
Wireless access
Open Mon, Wed & Fri 9-5:30, Tues & Thurs 9-8, Sat 9-1
Friends of the Library Group
Branches: 1
NANCE MCNEELY PUBLIC, 1177 B Springdale Ave, Myrtle, 38650. (Mail add: PO Box 225, Myrtle, 38650-0225), SAN 374-731X. Tel: 662-988-2895. FAX: 662-988-2895. *Librn,* Betty McNeely
Open Mon, Tues, Thurs & Fri 1:30-5:30, Sat 9-1
Friends of the Library Group

OAKLAND

P OAKLAND PUBLIC LIBRARY*, 324 Holly St, 38948. (Mail add: PO Box 69, 38948-0069), SAN 308-9029. Tel: 662-623-8651. FAX: 662-623-0089. *Librn,* Walter A Moores; E-mail: wmoores@yalobusha.lib.ms.us
Pop 2,000; Circ 9,000
Library Holdings: Bk Vols 10,000; Per Subs 18
Subject Interests: Local hist
Automation Activity & Vendor Info: (Cataloging) Book Systems; (Circulation) Book Systems
Partic in Miss Libr Comn Interlibr Loan Network
Open Mon, Wed & Fri 9-5
Friends of the Library Group

OCEAN SPRINGS

C UNIVERSITY OF SOUTHERN MISSISSIPPI-GULF COAST RESEARCH LABORATORY*, Gunter Library, 703 E Beach Dr, 39564. SAN 308-9037. Tel: 228-872-4213, 228-872-4253. FAX: 228-872-4264. Web Site: www.usm.edu/gcrl. *Head Librn & Assoc Prof,* Joyce M Shaw; E-mail: joyce.shaw@usm.edu; Staff 2.5 (MLS 1, Non-MLS 1.5)
Founded 1955. Enrl 54; Fac 1; Highest Degree: Doctorate
Jul 2007-Jun 2008. Mats Exp $150,000
Library Holdings: Bk Titles 7,148; Per Subs 120
Special Collections: GCRL History; GCRL Publications; Marine Biology (Expedition Reports); Marine Invertebrate Zoology Coll
Subject Interests: Botany, Ecology, Geol, Ichthyology, Marine biol, Microbiology, Toxicology
Database Vendor: EBSCOhost
Wireless access
Function: Archival coll, Bks on CD, Computers for patron use, Copy machines, Doc delivery serv, ILL available, Photocopying/Printing, Scanner
Publications: Gulf & Caribbean Research (Periodical); Master Serial List (Serials catalog)
Partic in MAGNOLIA; National Network of Libraries of Medicine Southeastern Atlantic Region
Open Mon-Thurs 8-12 & 1-6:30, Fri 8-12 & 1-5
Restriction: Borrowing privileges limited to fac & registered students, Circulates for staff only, In-house use for visitors, Non-circulating to the pub, Open to fac, students & qualified researchers, Open to pub for ref only

OXFORD

J NORTHWEST MISSISSIPPI COMMUNITY COLLEGE*, Lafayette-Yalobusha Technical Center Library, 1310 Belk Dr, 38655. SAN 370-4939. Tel: 662-238-7953. FAX: 662-236-4764. E-mail: nwcclibb@northwestms.edu. Web Site: www.northwestms.edu. *Librn,* Jeanette Stone; E-mail: jstone@northwestms.edu
Founded 1988
Library Holdings: Bk Vols 10,000; Per Subs 200
Open Mon-Thurs (Winter) 8am-9pm, Fri 8-3:30; Mon-Thurs (Summer) 8am-9pm

GL USDA-ARS*, National Sedimentation Laboratory Library, 598 McElroy Dr, 38655-2117. (Mail add: PO Box 1157, 38655-1157), SAN 373-0778. Tel: 662-232-2996. FAX: 662-232-2920. *Dir,* Dr Mathias Romkens
Library Holdings: Bk Vols 20,000; Per Subs 15
Open Mon-Fri 8-5

PARCHMAN

S MISSISSIPPI DEPARTMENT OF CORRECTIONS*, Mississippi State Penitentiary Library, PO Box 1057, 38738. Tel: 662-745-6611, Ext 3101. Web Site: www.mdoc.state.ms.us. *Librn,* Melinda Buckner; E-mail: mbuckner@mdoc.state.ms.us
Library Holdings: Bk Vols 3,000; Per Subs 100
Automation Activity & Vendor Info: (Cataloging) Follett Software; (Circulation) Follett Software
Open Mon-Sun 6:30-2:30 & 4:30-8

PASCAGOULA

P JACKSON-GEORGE REGIONAL LIBRARY SYSTEM, 3214 Pascagoula St, 39567. SAN 348-7202. Tel: 228-769-3099. Interlibrary Loan Service Tel: 228-769-3223. FAX: 228-769-3146. Web Site: www.jgrls.org. *Dir,* Lori Ward Barnes; E-mail: director@jgrls.org; *Bus Mgr,* Janet Beatty; Tel: 228-769-3092, E-mail: businessmgr@jgrls.org; *Pub Serv,* Rex Bridges; Tel: 228-769-3130, E-mail: pr@jgrls.org; Staff 85 (MLS 11, Non-MLS 74)
Founded 1940. Pop 155,000; Circ 858,072
Library Holdings: DVDs 13,293; Large Print Bks 12,176; Bk Vols 288,659; Per Subs 936; Talking Bks 19,137
Special Collections: Genealogy & Local History Coll
Automation Activity & Vendor Info: (Acquisitions) TLC (The Library Corporation); (Cataloging) TLC (The Library Corporation); (Circulation) TLC (The Library Corporation); (OPAC) TLC (The Library Corporation)
Database Vendor: EBSCOhost, TLC (The Library Corporation), Westlaw
Wireless access
Function: ILL available, Photocopying/Printing, Prog for children & young adult, Ref serv available, Summer reading prog, Wheelchair accessible
Open Mon-Thurs 9-8, Fri & Sat 9-5
Friends of the Library Group
Branches: 8
EAST CENTRAL PUBLIC LIBRARY, 21801 Slider Rd, Moss Point, 39562, SAN 348-7237. Tel: 228-588-6263. FAX: 228-588-6268. *Librn,* Helen Barlow; Fax: 228-588-0145; Staff 5 (MLS 1, Non-MLS 4)
Open Mon-Thurs 8-6, Fri & Sat 9-4
Friends of the Library Group
LUCEDALE-GEORGE COUNTY PUBLIC LIBRARY, 507 Oak St, Lucedale, 39452, SAN 348-7261. Tel: 601-947-2123. FAX: 601-766-3360. *Librn,* Rebecca Wheeler; Staff 5 (MLS 1, Non-MLS 4)
Open Mon, Tues & Thurs 9-6, Wed & Fri 9-5, Sat 9-1
Friends of the Library Group
KATHLEEN MCILWAIN-GAUTIER PUBLIC LIBRARY, 2100 Library Lane, Gautier, 39553, SAN 348-7326. Tel: 228-497-4531. FAX: 228-497-4560. *Librn,* Position Currently Open
Open Mon-Thurs 9-8, Fri & Sat 9-5
Friends of the Library Group

OCEAN SPRINGS MUNICIPAL LIBRARY, 525 Dewey Ave, Ocean Springs, 39564, SAN 348-7350. Tel: 228-875-1193. FAX: 228-875-1535. *Librn,* Jeanne Jones
Open Mon-Thurs 9-8, Fri & Sat 9-5
Friends of the Library Group

PASCAGOULA PUBLIC LIBRARY, 3214 Pascagoula St, 39567, SAN 348-7385. FAX: 228-769-3113. *Br Mgr,* Jessica Herr
Open Mon-Thurs 9-8, Fri & Sat 9-5
Friends of the Library Group

ST MARTIN PUBLIC LIBRARY, 15004 LeMoyne Blvd, Biloxi, 39532-5205, SAN 348-7415. Tel: 228-392-3250. FAX: 228-392-0522. *Br Mgr, Librn II,* Janis Zuleeg
Open Mon-Thurs 9-7, Fri & Sat 9-5
Friends of the Library Group

INA THOMPSON MOSS POINT LIBRARY, 4119 Bellview St, Moss Point, 39563, SAN 348-7296. Tel: 228-475-7462. FAX: 228-475-7484. *Br Mgr,* Jamie Elston; E-mail: mpmgr@jgrls.org; Staff 5 (MLS 1, Non-MLS 4)
Founded 1900
Library Holdings: Per Subs 102
Open Mon-Thurs 9-8, Fri & Sat 9-5
Friends of the Library Group

VANCLEAVE PUBLIC LIBRARY, 12604 Hwy 57, Vancleave, 39565, SAN 348-744X. Tel: 228-826-5857. FAX: 228-826-5893. *Br Mgr,* Dana Woods
Database Vendor: EBSCO Information Services
Open Mon-Thurs 9-7, Fri & Sat 9-5
Friends of the Library Group

G NATIONAL MARINE FISHERIES SERVICE*, Mississippi Laboratories Library, 3209 Frederick St, 39568. (Mail add: PO Mailing Drawer 1207, 39568-1207), SAN 308-9045. Tel: 228-762-4591. FAX: 228-769-9200. Web Site: www.lib.noaa.gov. *Librn,* Lagena Fantroy; E-mail: lagena.fantroy@noaa.gov; Staff 1 (MLS 1)
Founded 1950
Library Holdings: Bk Vols 4,000; Per Subs 200
Subject Interests: Marine biol, Oceanography, Seafood analysis, Seafood tech
Partic in Dialog Corp

M SINGING RIVER HOSPITAL SYSTEM*, Medical Library, 2809 Denny Ave, 39581. SAN 325-3163. Tel: 228-809-5040. FAX: 228-809-5439. *Librn,* Janice Debose; Staff 2 (MLS 1, Non-MLS 1)
Founded 1979
Library Holdings: Bk Vols 200; Per Subs 25
Special Collections: Community Health Information
Subject Interests: Allied health, Clinical med, Nursing
Open Mon-Fri 8-4:30

PEARL

S MISSISSIPPI DEPARTMENT OF CORRECTIONS*, Central Mississippi Correctional Facility Library, 3794 Hwy 468, 39288. (Mail add: PO Box 88550, 39208-8550). Tel: 601-932-2880, Ext 6343. FAX: 601-932-2880, Ext 6202. Web Site: www.mdoc.state.ms.us. *Dir,* Richard Caston; E-mail: rcaston@mdoc.state.ms.us
Library Holdings: Bk Vols 3,000
Database Vendor: LexisNexis
Open Mon-Fri 8-5

P PEARL PUBLIC LIBRARY*, 2416 Old Brandon Rd, 39208-4601. SAN 377-5739. Tel: 601-932-2562. FAX: 601-932-3535. E-mail: pearl@cmrls.lib.ms.us. *Br Mgr,* Cecelia Y Sandifer; *Circ Serv Supvr,* Scott Ash; E-mail: rccirc@cmrls.lib.ms.us; *Ref Serv Supvr,* Jennifer Vess; E-mail: rcref@cmrls.lib.ms.us; *Supvr, Youth Serv,* Mara Villa; E-mail: rcchild@cmrls.lib.ms.us; Staff 4 (MLS 1, Non-MLS 3)
Pop 25,000
Library Holdings: Bk Vols 53,000; Per Subs 120
Automation Activity & Vendor Info: (Circulation) Horizon; (OPAC) Horizon
Wireless access
Function: Accelerated reader prog, Adult bk club, After school storytime, Art exhibits, Audiobks via web, Bk club(s), Bks on cassette, Bks on CD, Children's prog, Computer training, Computers for patron use, Copy machines, e-mail serv, Electronic databases & coll, Exhibits, Fax serv, Free DVD rentals, Handicapped accessible, Holiday prog, ILL available, Music CDs, Online cat, Online ref, Online searches, Outreach serv, Photocopying/Printing, Preschool outreach, Prog for adults, Prog for children & young adult, Pub access computers, Ref serv available, Ref serv in person, Senior computer classes, Spoken cassettes & CDs, Spoken cassettes & DVDs, Story hour, Summer reading prog, Tax forms, Teen prog, Telephone ref, VHS videos, Wheelchair accessible
Mem of Central Mississippi Regional Library System
Open Mon-Thurs 9-8, Fri 9-5, Sat 10-4
Friends of the Library Group

PELAHATCHIE

P PELAHATCHIE PUBLIC LIBRARY*, 603 Hwy 80 East, 39145. SAN 376-6225. Tel: 601-854-8764. FAX: 601-854-8764. E-mail: pelahat@cmrls.lib.ms.us. *Br Mgr,* Janice Gailey
Library Holdings: Bk Titles 2,000
Mem of Central Mississippi Regional Library System
Open Mon-Thurs 10-1 & 2-5

PERKINSTON

J MISSISSIPPI GULF COAST COMMUNITY COLLEGE*, Perkinston Campus Learning Resources Center, PO Box 548, 39573-0011. SAN 348-7474. Tel: 601-928-5211, Ext 6380. FAX: 601-928-6359. Web Site: www.mgccc.edu/~library/pkinfo.htm. *Dir,* Brenda S Rivero; Tel: 601-928-6380, E-mail: brenda.rivero@mgccc.edu; *Dir, Media Serv,* Richard Marlowe; Tel: 601-928-6354, E-mail: richard.marlowe@mgccc.edu; *Librn,* Valerie Fairley; Tel: 601-528-8905, E-mail: valerie.fairley@mgccc.edu; *Librn,* Glenda Redmond; Tel: 601-928-6259, E-mail: glenda.redmond@mgccc.edu; *Librn,* Vanessa Ritchie; Tel: 601-928-6242, E-mail: vanessa.ritchie@mgccc.edu; Staff 5 (MLS 3, Non-MLS 2)
Founded 1925. Enrl 1,200; Fac 45
Library Holdings: Bk Vols 31,000; Per Subs 212
Subject Interests: Career, Faculty
Open Mon-Thurs (Winter) 7:30am-9pm, Fri 7:30-2:30; Mon-Thurs (Summer) 7:30-4:30, Fri 7:30-2:30

PHILADELPHIA

P NESHOBA COUNTY PUBLIC LIBRARY*, 230 Beacon St, 39350. SAN 308-907X. Tel: 601-656-4911. FAX: 601-656-6894. Web Site: neshobalibrary.net. *Interim Dir,* Theresa Ridout; E-mail: tridout@neshoba.lib.ms.us; *Ch Serv,* Position Currently Open; *Ref,* Patsy McWilliams; *Tech Serv,* Felix Griffin; Staff 5 (MLS 1, Non-MLS 4)
Founded 1929. Pop 29,905; Circ 40,000
Library Holdings: Bk Titles 36,000; Per Subs 30
Subject Interests: Choctaw Indians, Genealogy, Local hist
Automation Activity & Vendor Info: (Acquisitions) Auto-Graphics, Inc; (Cataloging) Auto-Graphics, Inc; (Circulation) Auto-Graphics, Inc; (Course Reserve) Auto-Graphics, Inc; (OPAC) Auto-Graphics, Inc; (Serials) Auto-Graphics, Inc
Database Vendor: EBSCOhost
Wireless access
Publications: Cemetery Records of Neshoba County; Our Links to the Past; The Red Clay Hills of Neshoba
Open Mon, Wed & Thurs 8-5, Tues 8-7, Fri 9-3

PICAYUNE

P PEARL RIVER COUNTY LIBRARY SYSTEM*, Margaret Reed Crosby Memorial Library, 900 Goodyear Blvd, 39466. SAN 348 7504. Tel: 601-798-5081. FAX: 601-798-5082. Web Site: www.pearlriver.lib.ms.us. *Syst Dir,* Carol Phares; E-mail: cphares@pearlriver.lib.ms.us; *Head, Tech Proc,* Phyllis Gage; E-mail: pgage@pearlriver.lib.ms.us; *Head, Circ,* Renee Buford; Staff 2 (MLS 2)
Founded 1926. Pop 39,700; Circ 150,000
Library Holdings: Bk Vols 90,000; Per Subs 70
Special Collections: Genealogy Family Files; Miss Municipal Assn Digitizing Project; W A Zeltner Mississippi Coll. Oral History; State Document Depository
Subject Interests: Drug abuse, Genealogy, Local hist
Automation Activity & Vendor Info: (Cataloging) SirsiDynix; (Circulation) SirsiDynix
Wireless access
Special Services for the Deaf - High interest/low vocabulary bks
Open Mon & Thurs 9-6, Tues & Fri 9-5, Sat 9-1
Friends of the Library Group
Branches: 1

POPLARVILLE PUBLIC, 202 W Beers St, Poplarville, 39470, SAN 348-7539. Tel: 601-795-8411. FAX: 601-795-8411. *Librn,* Cynthia Hornsby; E-mail: chornsby@pearlriver.lib.ms.us; *Head, Circ,* Vicky Mitchell; E-mail: vmitchell@pearlriver.lib.ms.us
Library Holdings: Bk Vols 30,000; Per Subs 20
Open Mon 9-6, Tues, Thurs & Fri 9-5, Sat 10-1
Friends of the Library Group

Bookmobiles: 1

PONTOTOC

P DIXIE REGIONAL LIBRARY SYSTEM*, 111 N Main St, 38863-2103. SAN 348-7598. Tel: 662-489-3960. FAX: 662-489-3929. E-mail: pclib@dixie.lib.ms.us. Web Site: www.dixie.lib.ms.us. *Dir,* Judy McNeece; Tel: 662-489-3961, E-mail: jmcneece@dixie.lib.ms.us; *Asst Dir,* Regina Graham; E-mail: asstdir@dixie.lib.ms.us; *Br Mgr,* Annette McGregor;

E-mail: amcgregor@dixie.lib.ms.us; *Tech Serv,* Mary A Hamilton; E-mail: drls3@dixie.lib.ms.us; Staff 3 (MLS 3)
Founded 1961. Pop 62,427; Circ 174,876
Library Holdings: Bk Vols 133,248; Per Subs 143
Subject Interests: Genealogy, Local hist
Automation Activity & Vendor Info: (Cataloging) Book Systems; (Circulation) Book Systems; (ILL) Auto-Graphics, Inc; (OPAC) Book Systems
Database Vendor: EBSCOhost, Gale Cengage Learning, OCLC FirstSearch, ProQuest, Wilson - Wilson Web
Wireless access
Function: Accelerated reader prog, Art exhibits, Children's prog, Computers for patron use, Copy machines, Electronic databases & coll, Handicapped accessible, Holiday prog, ILL available, Music CDs, Online cat, Online ref, Online searches, Outside serv via phone, mail, e-mail & web, Photocopying/Printing, Preschool outreach, Prog for adults, Prog for children & young adult, Pub access computers, Spoken cassettes & CDs, Spoken cassettes & DVDs, Story hour, Summer reading prog, Tax forms, Telephone ref, VHS videos, Wheelchair accessible
Publications: Dixie News (Quarterly)
Partic in MAGNOLIA
Special Services for the Blind - Large print & cassettes
Open Mon, Wed & Thurs 9-6, Tues 9-6:30, Fri 8-5, Sat 9-1
Friends of the Library Group
Branches: 8
CALHOUN CITY BRANCH, 113 E Burkitt St, Calhoun City, 38916. (Mail add: PO Box 646, Calhoun City, 38916), SAN 348-7652. Tel: 662-628-6331. FAX: 662-628-6331. E-mail: cclib@dixie.lib.ms.us. *Br Mgr,* Position Currently Open
Library Holdings: Bk Vols 10,645
Database Vendor: ProQuest
Function: Bks on cassette, Bks on CD, Children's prog, ILL available, Online cat, Photocopying/Printing, Pub access computers, Spoken cassettes & CDs, Story hour, Summer reading prog, Tax forms, VHS videos, Video lending libr
Open Mon 10-5, Tues 3-6, Thurs & Fri 9-5, Sat 8-12
EDMONDSON MEMORIAL, 109 Stovall St, Vardaman, 38878-0174, SAN 348-7776. Tel: 662-682-7333. FAX: 662-682-7333. E-mail: valib@dixie.lib.ms.us. *Br Mgr,* Janet Swindle
Library Holdings: Bk Vols 4,024
Database Vendor: CredoReference, LearningExpress, OCLC, ProQuest
Open Mon-Wed & Fri 10-5:30, Sat 8-Noon
HOULKA PUBLIC, 201 Walker St, Houlka, 38850-0275, SAN 348-7687. Tel: 662-568-2747. FAX: 662-568-2747. E-mail: hllib@dixie.lib.ms.us. *Br Mgr,* Martha Hinton; Staff 0.5 (Non-MLS 0.5)
Pop 1,657; Circ 4,316
Library Holdings: Bk Vols 4,923
HOUSTON CARNEGIE BRANCH, 105 W Madison St, Houston, 38851-2207, SAN 348-7717. Tel: 662-456-3381. FAX: 662-456-3381. E-mail: holib@dixie.lib.ms.us. *Br Mgr,* Lisa M Mims; Staff 1.75 (Non-MLS 1.75)
Founded 1909
Library Holdings: Bk Vols 10,000
Open Tues-Fri 10-6, Sat 10-1
Friends of the Library Group
OKOLONA CARNEGIE BRANCH, 321 Main St, Okolona, 38860. (Mail add: PO Box 126, Okolona, 38860-0126), SAN 348-7741. Tel: 662-447-2401. FAX: 662-447-2401. E-mail: oklib@dixie.lib.ms.us. *Br Mgr,* Estelle Ivy
Library Holdings: Bk Vols 15,000
Open Mon, Tues, Thurs & Fri 9-5, Sat 9-12
Friends of the Library Group
PONTOTOC COUNTY LIBRARY, 111 N Main St, 38863-2103, SAN 348-7628. Tel: 662-489-3960. FAX: 662-489-7777. E-mail: pclib@dixie.lib.ms.us. *Br Mgr,* Annette McGregor
Founded 1934. Pop 20,918
Library Holdings: Bk Vols 25,148
Special Collections: James Garrison Civil War Exhibit
Subject Interests: Local hist
Open Mon, Wed & Thurs 9-6, Tues 9-8, Fri 8-5, Sat 8-4
Friends of the Library Group
SHERMAN PUBLIC, 20 W Lamar St, Sherman, 38869. (Mail add: PO Box 181, Sherman, 38869-0181), SAN 373-1766. Tel: 662-840-2513. FAX: 662-840-2513. E-mail: shlib@dixie.lib.ms.us. *Br Mgr,* Celisa Russell
Library Holdings: Bk Vols 3,265
Open Mon-Fri 12-5
Friends of the Library Group
JESSE YANCY MEMORIAL LIBRARY, 314 N Newberger Ave, Bruce, 38915. (Mail add: PO Box 517, Bruce, 38915-0096), SAN 348-7806. Tel: 662-983-2220. FAX: 662-983-2220. E-mail: brlib@dixie.lib.ms.us. *Br Mgr,* Emily Taylor; Staff 1 (Non-MLS 1)
Founded 1959
Library Holdings: Bk Vols 20,000
Function: Fax serv, ILL available, Photocopying/Printing, Prog for adults, Prog for children & young adult, Spoken cassettes & CDs, Summer reading prog, VHS videos
Open Mon, Wed & Fri 10-5, Tues 10-6, Sat 10-2
Friends of the Library Group

POPLARVILLE

J PEARL RIVER COMMUNITY COLLEGE*, Garvin H Johnston Library, 101 Hwy 11 N, 39470. (Mail add: PO Box 5660, 39470-5660), SAN 308-9088. Tel: 601-403-1331. Reference Tel: 601-403-1332. Administration Tel: 601-403-1330. Automation Services Tel: 601-403-1337. FAX: 601-403-1135. E-mail: library@prcc.edu. Web Site: www.prcc.edu. *Dir of Libr,* Tracy H Smith; E-mail: tsmith@prcc.edu; *Pub Serv & Distance Educ Librn,* Position Currently Open; *Syst/Tech Proc Librn,* Debbie Huntington; Staff 3 (MLS 3)
Founded 1926. Enrl 3,500; Fac 175; Highest Degree: Associate
Library Holdings: DVDs 12; e-books 17,706; Bk Vols 57,407; Per Subs 326; Videos 4,174
Special Collections: Mississippi Coll
Subject Interests: Behav sci, Hist, Lit, Soc sci
Automation Activity & Vendor Info: (Cataloging) SirsiDynix; (Circulation) SirsiDynix; (Course Reserve) SirsiDynix; (OPAC) SirsiDynix; (Serials) SirsiDynix
Database Vendor: Baker & Taylor, EBSCOhost, Gale Cengage Learning, OCLC FirstSearch, OCLC WorldShare Interlibrary Loan, ProQuest, SirsiDynix, Wilson - Wilson Web
Partic in Lyrasis
Open Mon-Thurs (Winter) 7:45am-9pm, Fri 7:45-3; Mon-Wed (Summer) 7:45-6:30, Thurs 7:45-5
Departmental Libraries:
FORREST COUNTY CENTER LIBRARY, 5448 US Hwy 49 S, Hattiesburg, 39401, SAN 377-7758. Tel: 601-554-5522. FAX: 601-554-5470. *Librn,* Sarah Welch
Founded 1995
Library Holdings: Bk Vols 4,000; Per Subs 46
Subject Interests: Allied health
Open Mon-Thurs 7:30am-9pm, Fri 7:30-3
HANCOCK CENTER LIBRARY, 454 Hwy 90, Ste D, Waveland, 39756. Tel: 228-467-2761. FAX: 228-467-2763. *Coordr,* Maggie Smith
Founded 2005
Library Holdings: Bk Vols 2,000
Open Mon-Fri 8-6

PORT GIBSON

P HARRIETTE PERSON MEMORIAL LIBRARY*, 606 Main St, 39150-2330. (Mail add: PO Box 1017, 39150-1017), SAN 308-910X. Tel: 601-437-5202. FAX: 601-437-5787. *Dir,* Pamela Plummer; E-mail: pplummer@harriette.lib.ms.us
Founded 1914. Pop 11,831; Circ 28,350
Library Holdings: DVDs 196; Bk Titles 21,151; Per Subs 57; Talking Bks 689; Videos 1,981
Special Collections: Miss Coll
Automation Activity & Vendor Info: (Cataloging) Book Systems; (Circulation) Book Systems; (ILL) Auto-Graphics, Inc; (OPAC) Book Systems; (Serials) EBSCO Online
Open Mon-Fri 8:30-5, Sat 9-12
Friends of the Library Group

PUCKETT

P PUCKETT PUBLIC LIBRARY*, 118 Cemetery Rd, 39151. (Mail add: PO Box 550, 39151-0550), SAN 376-6217. Tel: 601-824-0180. E-mail: puckett@cmrls.lib.ms.us. Web Site: www.cmrls.lib.ms.us/pu.htm. *Librn,* Regina Hutson
Library Holdings: Bk Titles 6,000; Per Subs 14
Mem of Central Mississippi Regional Library System
Open Tues & Thurs 11-5, Sat 9-12
Friends of the Library Group

PURVIS

P LAMAR COUNTY LIBRARY SYSTEM*, 122 Shelby Speights Dr, 39475. (Mail add: PO Box 289, 39475). Tel: 601-794-6291. FAX: 601-794-6291. Web Site: www.lamar.lib.ms.us. *Dir,* Jeanne Williams; E-mail: jwilliams@lamarcountylibraries.org; *Mgr,* Kristin Finch; E-mail: kfinch@lamarcountylibraries.org; Staff 4 (MLS 2, Non-MLS 2)
Founded 1997. Pop 40,000
Library Holdings: AV Mats 1,485; Bks on Deafness & Sign Lang 10; Large Print Bks 1,426; Bk Vols 48,039; Per Subs 155; Talking Bks 747
Subject Interests: Genealogy, Local hist, Miss authors
Automation Activity & Vendor Info: (Cataloging) SirsiDynix; (Circulation) SirsiDynix; (ILL) OCLC; (OPAC) SirsiDynix
Wireless access

Open Mon-Fri 9-6
Friends of the Library Group
Branches: 4
LUMBERTON PUBLIC, 106 W Main Ave, Lumberton, 39455, SAN 348-8284. Tel: 601-796-4227. FAX: 601-794-4584. *Mgr,* Melinda Carli; E-mail: carli@lamarcountylibraries.org; Staff 2 (Non-MLS 2)
Founded 1922
Library Holdings: AV Mats 296; Large Print Bks 425; Bk Vols 10,711; Per Subs 18; Talking Bks 117
Subject Interests: Local hist
Partic in MAGNOLIA
Open Mon-Fri 9-6, Sat 10-2
Friends of the Library Group
OAK GROVE PUBLIC, 4958 Old Hwy 11, Hattiesburg, 39402. Tel: 601-296-1620. Reference Tel: 601-296-1704. FAX: 601-296-1620. *Br Mgr,* Robin Hosey; E-mail: rhosey@lamarcountylibraries.org; Staff 7 (MLS 2, Non-MLS 5)
Founded 2003
Library Holdings: AV Mats 133; Large Print Bks 127; Bk Vols 8,826; Per Subs 62; Talking Bks 51
Subject Interests: Genealogy, Local hist, Miss authors
Partic in MAGNOLIA
Open Mon-Fri 9-6, Sat 10-2
Friends of the Library Group
PURVIS PUBLIC, 122 Shelby Speights Dr, 39475. (Mail add: PO Box 289, 39475-0289), SAN 348-8438. Tel: 601-794-6291. FAX: 601-794-6291. *Br Mgr,* Kristin Finch; *Libr Assoc,* Brenda Foster; *Libr Assoc,* Cheryl Minchew; Staff 3 (MLS 1, Non-MLS 2)
Founded 1934
Library Holdings: AV Mats 441; Large Print Bks 519; Bk Vols 13,023; Per Subs 27; Talking Bks 185
Partic in MAGNOLIA
Open Mon-Fri 9-6
Friends of the Library Group
SUMRALL PUBLIC - L R BOYER MEMORIAL LIBRARY, 103 Poplar St, Sumrall, 39482. (Mail add: PO Box 327, Sumrall, 39482-0327), SAN 329-3335. Tel: 601-758-4711. FAX: 601-758-4711. *Br Mgr,* Bridgette Broom; E-mail: bbroom@lamarcounty.org; Staff 2 (Non-MLS 2)
Founded 1933
Library Holdings: AV Mats 379; Large Print Bks 500; Bk Vols 13,000; Per Subs 12; Talking Bks 250
Partic in MAGNOLIA
Open Mon & Wed-Fri 8-5, Tues 8-6
Friends of the Library Group

QUITMAN

P EAST MISSISSIPPI REGIONAL LIBRARY SYSTEM*, 116 Water St, 39355-2336. SAN 348-7830. Tel: 601-776-3881. FAX: 601-776-6599. Information Services E-mail: 4pea@emrl.lib.ms.us. Web Site: www.emrl.lib.ms.us. *Dir,* Kimberly Corbett; Staff 10 (MLS 2, Non-MLS 8)
Founded 1966. Pop 36,555; Circ 83,350
Oct 2006-Sept 2007 Income (Main Library and Branch(s)) $521,704, State $146,552, City $118,014, Federal $3,296, County $202,000, Locally Generated Income $51,809, Other $33. Mats Exp $36,776. Sal $283,082
Library Holdings: AV Mats 6,035; CDs 769; DVDs 483; Large Print Bks 4,628; Bk Vols 62,930; Per Subs 56; Talking Bks 2,423; Videos 2,151
Automation Activity & Vendor Info: (Cataloging) Innovative Interfaces, Inc; (Circulation) Innovative Interfaces, Inc; (ILL) Auto-Graphics, Inc; (OPAC) Innovative Interfaces, Inc
Function: Bks on cassette, Bks on CD, CD-ROM, Children's prog, Computers for patron use, Copy machines, Fax serv, Free DVD rentals, Handicapped accessible, ILL available, Music CDs, Online cat, Pub access computers, Ref serv available, Spoken cassettes & CDs, Summer reading prog, Tax forms, VHS videos, Web-catalog, Wheelchair accessible
Open Mon-Fri 8:30-5
Branches: 6
BAY SPRINGS MUNICIPAL, 2747 Hwy 15, Bay Springs, 39422. (Mail add: PO Drawer N, Bay Springs, 39422-1914), SAN 348-7865. Tel: 601-764-2291. FAX: 601-764-2291. Web Site: www.emrl.lib.ms.us/branch_bayspings.htm. *Librn,* Ramona Davis; *Librn,* Lee Anne Owens
Library Holdings: Bk Vols 10,000
Open Mon, Tues & Thurs 8-6:30, Wed 7:30-6
ENTERPRISE PUBLIC, Ritchey St, Enterprise, 39330. (Mail add: General Delivery, Enterprise, 39330), SAN 348-789X. Tel: 601-659-3564. *Librn,* Jane Evans; E-mail: jevans@emrl.lib.ms.us
Library Holdings: Bk Vols 8,250
Open Mon-Fri 12-5
PACHUTA PUBLIC, Hwy 11N, Pachuta, 39347. (Mail add: PO Box 189, Pachuta, 39347-0189). Tel: 601-776-3131. *Librn,* Sue Sexton; E-mail: ssexton@emrl.lib.ms.us
Library Holdings: Bk Vols 5,000
Open Mon-Thurs 12-5
MARY WEEMS PARKER MEMORIAL, 1016 N Pine Ave, Heidelberg, 39439. (Mail add: PO Box 252, Heidelberg, 39439-0252), SAN 348-792X. Tel: 601-787-3857. FAX: 601-787-3857. *Librn,* Margie McClellan
Library Holdings: Bk Vols 12,000
Open Mon-Fri 1-5, Sat 9-1
QUITMAN PUBLIC LIBRARY, 116 Water St, 39355. Tel: 601-776-2492. Administration Tel: 601-776-3881. FAX: 601-776-6599. *Librn,* Anissa Dyess; *Librn,* Sue Sexton; Staff 2 (Non-MLS 2)
Founded 1966. Pop 16,743; Circ 11,351
Library Holdings: DVDs 757; Bk Titles 16,089; Per Subs 40
Function: Computers for patron use, Copy machines, Free DVD rentals, ILL available, Microfiche/film & reading machines, Online cat, Online ref, Pub access computers, Spoken cassettes & CDs, Summer reading prog, VHS videos
Open Mon, Tues & Thurs 8-6:30, Wed 7:30-6
STONEWALL PUBLIC, 801 Erwin Rd, Stonewall, 39363-9610. (Mail add: PO Box 700, Stonewall, 39363-0700), SAN 348-8047. Tel: 601-659-3080. FAX: 601-659-3080. *Librn,* Vallie Molony
Library Holdings: Bk Vols 12,000
Open Mon, Tues & Thurs 1-6, Wed 12:30-5:30

RALEIGH

P RALEIGH PUBLIC LIBRARY*, Floyd J Robinson Memorial Library, 150 Main St, 39153. (Mail add: PO Box 266, 39153-0266), SAN 376-6349. Tel: 601-782-4277. FAX: 601-782-4400. E-mail: raleigh@cmrls.lib.ms.us. Web Site: www.cmrls.lib.ms.us/rl.htm. *Br Mgr,* Julie James
Library Holdings: Bk Titles 13,500; Per Subs 18
Mem of Central Mississippi Regional Library System
Open Mon, Tues & Thurs 10-6, Wed & Fri 10-5, 2nd Sat 9-12
Friends of the Library Group

RAYMOND

J HINDS COMMUNITY COLLEGE*, Raymond Campus Learning Resources/Library, 505 E Main St, 39154. (Mail add: PO Box 1100, 39154-1100), SAN 348-8101. Tel: 601-857-3255. Reference Tel: 601-857-3378. Administration Tel: 601-857-3380. FAX: 601-857-3293. Web Site: lrc.hindscc.edu. *Dean, Learning Res,* Dr Mary Beth Applin; *Librn,* Judy Hilkert; Tel: 601-857-3355, E-mail: jrhilkert@hindscc.edu; *Ref Archivist/Librn,* Adrienne McPhaul; Tel: 601-857-3411; *Pub Serv Librn,* Margaret J Stauble; Tel: 601-857-3743; *Re/Ser Librn,* James Kennedy; Tel: 601-857-3254, E-mail: jbkennedy@hindscc.edu; Staff 10 (MLS 9, Non-MLS 1)
Founded 1922. Enrl 12,164; Fac 488; Highest Degree: Associate
Library Holdings: Bk Titles 103,793; Bk Vols 173,675; Per Subs 1,180
Special Collections: Black Heritage Coll, Government (John Bell Williams Coll)
Automation Activity & Vendor Info: (Acquisitions) SirsiDynix
Publications: HLR Spotlight (Newsletter)
Partic in Lyrasis
Open Mon-Thurs (Winter) 7:45am-9pm, Fri 7:45-4; Mon-Thurs (Summer) 7:15am-8pm, Fri 7:15-3
Departmental Libraries:
JACKSON ACADEMIC & TECHNICAL CENTER LEARNING RESOURCES/LIBRARY, 3925 Sunset Dr, Jackson, 39213-5899, SAN 308-8715. Tel: 601-987-8123. FAX: 601-982-5804. E-mail: info@hindscc.edu. *Head Librn,* Jackie Quinn; E-mail: JYQuinn@hindscc.edu; Staff 2 (MLS 1, Non-MLS 1)
Highest Degree: Associate
Database Vendor: EBSCOhost, Gale Cengage Learning, OCLC FirstSearch, Wilson - Wilson Web
Function: Res libr
Open Mon-Thurs 7:30-7:30, Fri 7:30-3
NURSING/ALLIED HEALTH CENTER LIBRARY, 1750 Chadwick Dr, Jackson, 39204-3490, SAN 324-427X. Tel: 601-376-4816. FAX: 601-376-4966. Circulation E-mail: lrcnursingcirculation@hindscc.edu. *Librn,* Sybyl A Stringer
Open Mon, Tues & Thurs 7:30-7:30, Wed 7:30-4, Fri 7:30-3
RANKIN CAMPUS LEARNING RESOURCES/LIBRARY, 3805 Hwy 80 E, Pearl, 39208-4295, SAN 324-4288. Tel: 601-936-5538. FAX: 601-936-5542. *Admin Librn,* Renita Lane; E-mail: rlane@hindscc.edu
Open Mon-Thurs (Winter) 7:30-7:30, Fri 7:30-3; Mon-Thurs (Summer) 7am-7:30pm, Fri 7-3
UTICA CAMPUS LEARNING RESOURCES/LIBRARY, Hwy 18 W, Utica, 39175-9599, SAN 308-9207. Tel: 601-885-7035. *Admin Librn,* Jean Greene; Tel: 601-885-7034, E-mail: jbgreene@hindscc.edu; *Pub Serv Librn,* Esther Owens; E-mail: eowens@hindscc.edu; *Tech Serv,* Amanda Hubbard; Staff 3 (MLS 3)
Founded 1903. Enrl 751
Special Collections: Black Heritage Coll
Subject Interests: Behav sci, Educ, English lit, Soc sci
Open Mon-Thurs (Winter) 8-7:30, Fri 8-4; Mon-Fri (Summer) 8-4:30
Friends of the Library Group

VICKSBURG LEARNING RESOURCES/LIBRARY, 755 Hwy 27, Vicksburg, 39180-8699, SAN 324-4261. Tel: 601-629-6846. FAX: 601-629-6862. *Admin Librn,* Jennifer Meister; Staff 2 (MLS 1, Non-MLS 1)
Highest Degree: Associate
Automation Activity & Vendor Info: (OPAC) SirsiDynix
Open Mon-Thurs (Winter) 8-6:45, Fri 8-3; Mon-Thurs (Summer) 7:30-6, Fri 7:30-2

RICHLAND

P RICHLAND PUBLIC LIBRARY*, 370 Scarbrough St, 39218. SAN 376-6284. Tel: 601-932-1846. FAX: 601-932-1688. E-mail: richland@cmrls.lib.ms.us. Web Site: www.cmrls.lib.ms.us/ri.htm. *Librn,* Diane Mitchell; E-mail: ribm@cmrls.lib.ms.us
Founded 1986. Pop 8,000
Library Holdings: Bk Titles 20,000; Bk Vols 25,000; Per Subs 65
Open Mon & Thurs 10-8, Tues & Wed 10-6, Fri & Sat 10-5
Friends of the Library Group

RICHTON

P PINE FOREST REGIONAL LIBRARY*, 210 Front St, 39476-1510. (Mail add: PO Box 1208, 39746-1208), SAN 348-8136. Tel: 601-788-6539. Toll Free Tel: 800-437-2941. FAX: 601-788-9743. Web Site: www.pineforest.lib.ms.us. *Dir,* Charles Cox; Staff 29 (MLS 3, Non-MLS 26)
Founded 1958. Pop 70,638; Circ 184,283
Library Holdings: Bk Titles 150,000; Per Subs 2,400
Subject Interests: Local hist
Open Mon-Fri 8-5
Branches: 9
CONWAY HALL PUBLIC, 9220 Hwy 42, Petal, 39465, SAN 348-8225. Tel: 601-584-7469. FAX: 601-584-7469. E-mail: run@pineforest.lib.ms.us.
Open Tues & Thurs 9-5:30
LEAKESVILLE PUBLIC LIBRARY, 301 Lafayette Ave, Leakesville, 39451, SAN 348-825X. Tel: 601-394-2897. FAX: 601-394-2897. E-mail: lea@pineforest.lib.ms.us. *Br Mgr, Librn,* Sara Smith
Open Mon-Thurs 8:30-5:30
MCHENRY PUBLIC, 25 McHenry School Dr, McHenry, 39561, SAN 348-8314. Tel: 601-528-9465. FAX: 601-528-9465. E-mail: mch@pineforest.lib.ms.us. *Br Mgr,* Rhonda Darby; *Asst Br Mgr,* Heather Donohoe
Special Services for the Deaf - Bks on deafness & sign lang; Closed caption videos
Special Services for the Blind - Bks on cassette; Bks on CD; Copier with enlargement capabilities; Large print bks
Open Tues & Thurs 11-5, Wed 9-5
Friends of the Library Group
MCLAIN PUBLIC, 117 Church Ave, McLain, 39456. (Mail add: PO Box 65, McLain, 39456-0065), SAN 348-8349. Tel: 601-753-2364. FAX: 601-753-2364. E-mail: mcl@pineforest.lib.ms.us. *Librn,* Mable Cochran
Open Mon & Thurs 12:30-4:30, Fri 8-Noon
NEW AUGUSTA PUBLIC, 510 First St E, New Augusta, 39462, SAN 348-8403. Tel: 601-964-3774. FAX: 601-964-3774. E-mail: na@pineforest.lib.ms.us.
Open Mon, Wed & Thurs 9-5:30
WILLIAM ESTES POWELL MEMORIAL, 1502 Bolton Ave, Beaumont, 39423, SAN 348-8160. Tel: 601-784-3471. FAX: 601-784-3471. E-mail: bea@pineforest.lib.ms.us. *Librn,* Joyce Breland
Open Mon-Wed & Fri 12-5
RICHTON PUBLIC, 210 Front St, 39476. (Mail add: PO Box 1208, 39476-1208). Tel: 601-788-6539. FAX: 601-788-9743. E-mail: ric@pineforest.lib.ms.us. *Librn,* James Freeman
Open Mon-Fri 8:30-5:30
STATE LINE PUBLIC, Eight Farrier St, State Line, 39362. (Mail add: PO Box 279, State Line, 39362-0279), SAN 348-8527. Tel: 601-848-7011. FAX: 601-848-7011. E-mail: stl@pineforest.lib.ms.us. *Librn,* Opal Leverette
Open Mon 10-6, Tues & Thurs 12-6
STONE COUNTY, 242 Second St SE, Wiggins, 39577, SAN 348-8551. Tel: 601-928-4993. FAX: 601-928-4993. E-mail: wig@pineforest.lib.ms.us. *Librn,* Cynthia McDonald; *Asst Librn,* LaQuita Broadus
Open Mon-Fri 8:30-5:30
Friends of the Library Group

RIDGELAND

J HOLMES COMMUNITY COLLEGE*, Ernest J Adcock Library, Ridgeland Campus, 412 W Ridgeland Ave, 39158-1410. Tel: 601-605-3303. FAX: 601-605-3410. Web Site: www.holmescc.edu/library/library_ridgeland.aspx. *Br Librn,* Deb Sample; E-mail: dsample@holmescc.edu
Library Holdings: Bk Vols 11,000; Per Subs 175
Automation Activity & Vendor Info: (Acquisitions) SirsiDynix; (Cataloging) SirsiDynix; (Circulation) SirsiDynix; (Course Reserve) SirsiDynix; (ILL) SirsiDynix; (Serials) SirsiDynix
Database Vendor: EBSCOhost, Gale Cengage Learning, ProQuest, Wilson - Wilson Web
Open Mon-Thurs (Winter) 7:45am-8pm, Fri 7:45-3:30; Mon-Thurs (Summer) 7:45-3:30 & 5-8, Fri 7:45-3:30

ROLLING FORK

P SHARKEY-ISSAQUENA COUNTY LIBRARY*, 116 E China St, 39159. SAN 323-794X. Tel: 662-873-4076. FAX: 662-873-0614. E-mail: sicl@sicl.lib.ms.us. Web Site: www.sicl.lib.ms.us. *Librn,* Elissa Tucker
Library Holdings: Bk Vols 20,000; Per Subs 45
Automation Activity & Vendor Info: (Cataloging) TLC (The Library Corporation); (Circulation) TLC (The Library Corporation)
Wireless access
Open Mon-Thurs 9-6, Fri 9-5, Sat 10-2
Friends of the Library Group

ROSEDALE

R FIRST BAPTIST CHURCH*, Mattie D Hall Memorial Library, 407 Front St, 38769. (Mail add: PO Box 459, 38769-0459), SAN 308-9134. Tel: 662-759-6378.
Founded 1955
Library Holdings: Bk Vols 4,001
Publications: Consumer Reports; Home Missions; Ideals; Media; The Commission

SAND HILL

P SAND HILL PUBLIC LIBRARY*, 698 Pisgah Rd, 39161. SAN 376-6381. Tel: 601-829-1653. FAX: 601-829-1653. E-mail: sandhill@cmrls.lib.ms.us. Web Site: www.cmrls.lib.ms.us/sa.htm. *Librn,* Tanya Jones
Library Holdings: Bk Vols 6,650; Per Subs 10
Mem of Central Mississippi Regional Library System
Open Mon-Thurs 8:30-12 & 12:30-4

SCOOBA

J EAST MISSISSIPPI COMMUNITY COLLEGE*, Tubb-May Memorial Library, 1527 Kemper, 39358. (Mail add: PO Box 158, 39358-0158), SAN 348-8586. Tel: 662-476-5054. FAX: 662-476-5053. Web Site: www.eastms.edu. *District Librn,* Donna Ballard; E-mail: dballard@eastms.edu; Staff 3 (MLS 1, Non-MLS 2)
Founded 1927. Enrl 4,000
Jul 2005-Jun 2006 Income $118,225. Mats Exp $32,044, Books $12,363, Per/Ser (Incl. Access Fees) $14,872, AV Mat $1,103, Electronic Ref Mat (Incl. Access Fees) $3,706. Sal $73,715
Library Holdings: Bk Vols 46,000; Per Subs 200; Videos 26,000
Special Collections: Mississippi Coll
Subject Interests: Miss hist
Automation Activity & Vendor Info: (Cataloging) SirsiDynix; (Circulation) SirsiDynix; (Course Reserve) SirsiDynix; (OPAC) SirsiDynix; (Serials) SirsiDynix
Wireless access
Open Mon-Thurs 8am-9pm, Fri 8-4:30, Sun 3-9
Departmental Libraries:
GOLDEN TRIANGLE CAMPUS LIBRARY, 8731 S Frontage Rd, Mayhew, 39753. (Mail add: PO Box 100, Mayhew, 39753). Tel: 662-243-1914. FAX: 662-243-1952. *District Librn,* Donna S Ballard; E-mail: dballard@eastms.edu; *Asst Librn,* Edwina Hogue; E-mail: whogue@eastms.edu; *Libr Asst,* Rosemary Rice; E-mail: rrice@eastms.edu; Staff 2 (MLS 1, Non-MLS 1)
Enrl 5,000; Highest Degree: Associate
Database Vendor: SirsiDynix
Function: Computers for patron use, Copy machines, Distance learning, e-mail & chat, Electronic databases & coll, Handicapped accessible, ILL available, Instruction & testing, Outside serv via phone, mail, e-mail & web, Photocopying/Printing, Scanner, Wheelchair accessible
Partic in Mississippi Library Partnership
Open Mon-Thurs 7:30am-9pm, Fri 7:30-4:30

SEBASTOPOL

P SEBASTOPOL PUBLIC LIBRARY*, PO Box 173, 39359-0173. SAN 376-6209. Tel: 601-625-8826. FAX: 601-625-8826. E-mail: sebastop@cmrls.lib.ms.us. Web Site: www.cmrls.lib.ms.us/sebastopol.htm. *Librn,* Wanda Bishop
Library Holdings: Bk Titles 6,334; Bk Vols 7,500
Automation Activity & Vendor Info: (Cataloging) SirsiDynix; (Circulation) SirsiDynix
Mem of Central Mississippi Regional Library System
Open Mon & Tues 12-5, Wed & Thurs 1-6

SENATOBIA

J NORTHWEST MISSISSIPPI COMMUNITY COLLEGE*, R C Pugh Library, 4975 Hwy 51 N, 38668-1701. SAN 348-8640. Tel: 662-562-3278. Reference Tel: 662-562-3268. FAX: 662-562-3280. Web Site: www.northwestms.edu. *Dir, Libr Serv,* Margaret N Rogers; E-mail: mrogers@northwestms.edu; *Cat, Tech Serv Librn,* Crystal Giles; Tel: 662-562-3904, E-mail: cgiles@northwestms.edu; *Media Spec,* Keith Coleman; Tel: 662-562-3279, E-mail: kcoleman@northwestms.edu; *Pub Serv Librn, Ref Librn,* Maggie Moran; E-mail: mmoran@northwestms.edu; Staff 8.5 (MLS 4, Non-MLS 4.5)
Founded 1926. Enrl 7,172; Fac 122; Highest Degree: Associate
Library Holdings: AV Mats 9,711; CDs 1,733; DVDs 928; Bk Vols 85,863; Per Subs 286; Videos 4,288
Automation Activity & Vendor Info: (Cataloging) SirsiDynix; (Circulation) SirsiDynix; (OPAC) SirsiDynix; (Serials) SirsiDynix
Database Vendor: 3M Library Systems, Baker & Taylor, Cinahl, CredoReference, EBSCOhost, Gale Cengage Learning, H W Wilson, LearningExpress, Newsbank, OCLC FirstSearch, OCLC WorldShare Interlibrary Loan, ProQuest, SirsiDynix, Wilson - Wilson Web, World Book Online, WT Cox
Wireless access
Partic in Lyrasis
Open Mon-Thurs (Winter) 8am-9pm, Fri 8-3:30, Sun 2-7; Mon-Fri (Summer) 8-3

SOUTHAVEN

J NORTHWEST MISSISSIPPI COMMUNITY COLLEGE*, DeSoto Center Library, 5197 WE Ross Pkwy, 38671. SAN 308-9142. Tel: 662-280-6164. FAX: 662-280-6161. E-mail: nwcclibb@northwestms.edu. Web Site: www.northwestms.edu/learning%20resources/desoto.html. *Librn,* Jackie Dedwyler; E-mail: jdedwylder@northwestms.edu; *Librn,* W T Mayfield; E-mail: wmayfield@northwestms.edu; *Librn,* Wanda Pegues; E-mail: wpegues@northwestms.edu; *Computer Serv,* William Thompson; E-mail: wathompson@northwestms.edu
Founded 1979. Enrl 600; Fac 41
Library Holdings: Bk Vols 18,000; Per Subs 250
Open Mon-Fri (Winter) 8am-9pm, Sat 8:30-12; Mon-Thurs (Summer) 8am-9pm, Fri 8-4

STARKVILLE

P STARKVILLE-OKTIBBEHA COUNTY PUBLIC LIBRARY SYSTEM*, 326 University Dr, 39759. SAN 348-8675. Tel: 662-323-2766, 662-323-2783. FAX: 662-323-9140. E-mail: starkvillelibrary@yahoo.com. Web Site: www.starkville.lib.ms.us. *Dir,* Virginia Holtcamp; *YA Librn,* Anna Ruhs; *Ch Serv,* Laura Foxworth; *Circ,* Andrea Six; *Ser,* Shirley Richter; Staff 3 (MLS 3)
Pop 36,600; Circ 113,000
Library Holdings: Bk Vols 59,000; Per Subs 115
Special Collections: Genealogy (Katic-Prince Eskar Coll)
Automation Activity & Vendor Info: (Acquisitions) SirsiDynix; (Cataloging) SirsiDynix; (Circulation) SirsiDynix; (ILL) Auto-Graphics, Inc; (OPAC) SirsiDynix
Database Vendor: EBSCOhost, OCLC FirstSearch, Overdrive, Inc, SirsiDynix, World Book Online
Wireless access
Function: Archival coll, Audiobks via web, AV serv, Bk club(s), Bks on cassette, Bks on CD, Children's prog, Computers for patron use, Copy machines, Electronic databases & coll, Handicapped accessible, ILL available, Large print keyboards, Music CDs, Online cat, OverDrive digital audio bks, Photocopying/Printing, Prog for adults, Prog for children & young adult, Pub access computers, Story hour, Summer reading prog, Tax forms, Teen prog, VHS videos, Web-catalog
Partic in Mississippi Library Partnership
Open Mon-Thurs 9-6, Fri & Sat 9-4
Friends of the Library Group
Branches: 2
MABEN BRANCH, 831 Second Ave, Maben, 39750-9742. (Mail add: PO Box 507, Maben, 39750-0507), SAN 348-8705. Tel: 662-263-5619. FAX: 662-263-5619. *Librn,* Edwinna Hoque
Open Mon, Tues, Thurs & Fri 8-1:30 & 2-4, Sat 9-12
Friends of the Library Group
STURGIS PUBLIC LIBRARY, 2732 Hwy 12 W, Sturgis, 39769. (Mail add: PO Box 8, Sturgis, 39769), SAN 348-8764. Tel: 662-465-7493. FAX: 662-465-7493. E-mail: sturgispubliclib@yahoo.com. *Br Mgr, Librn,* Perian P Kerr; *Asst Librn,* Shelby Jean Griffin; Staff 32 (MLS 16, Non-MLS 16)
Founded 1967. Pop 300
Function: Bks on cassette, Bks on CD, Children's prog, Computers for patron use, Digital talking bks, Fax serv, Free DVD rentals, ILL available, Music CDs, Online cat, Photocopying/Printing, Story hour, Summer reading prog, Tax forms, VHS videos, Web-catalog
Partic in Mississippi Library Partnership
Special Services for the Deaf - Bks on deafness & sign lang
Special Services for the Blind - Bks on cassette; Bks on CD; Large print bks
Open Mon, Tues, Thurs & Fri 9-5

STENNIS SPACE CENTER

A UNITED STATES NAVY*, Matthew Fontaine Maury, 1002 Balch Blvd, Bldg 1003, 39522-5001. Tel: 228-688-4597. FAX: 228-688-4191. *Dir,* Dr Jack Breyer; E-mail: jack.breyer@navy.mil; *Librn,* Martha Elbers; *Librn,* Lori Brown Kerns; Tel: 228-688-4706, E-mail: lori.kerns@navy.mil; *Librn,* Beth Morgan; Tel: 228-688-4398, E-mail: mary.b.morgan@navy.mil; *Classified Libr Librn,* Jaime Ratliff; Tel: 228-688-4496, E-mail: jaime.ratliff@navy.mil; *Circ,* Jennifer Craft; E-mail: jennifer.craft@navy.mil; Staff 6 (MLS 4, Non-MLS 2)
Founded 1871
Library Holdings: e-journals 60; Bk Vols 400,000; Per Subs 250
Special Collections: Hydrographic Office Publications Coll; Oceanographic Expeditions Coll
Subject Interests: Biological, Cartography, Chem, Eng, Geol oceanog, Meteorology, Ocean eng, Photogrammetry, Phys oceanog
Function: Archival coll, Bks on CD, CD-ROM, Computers for patron use, Copy machines, Electronic databases & coll, ILL available, Online cat, Online ref, Online searches, Photocopying/Printing, Ref & res, Ref serv available, Res libr, Spoken cassettes & CDs
Publications: Accessions List
Partic in Fedlink; OCLC Online Computer Library Center, Inc
Restriction: Circ limited

STONEVILLE

C MISSISSIPPI STATE UNIVERSITY*, Delta Research & Extension Center Library, Bldg 1532, 82 Stoneville Rd, Mail Stop 9388, 38776. (Mail add: PO Box 197, 38776-0197), SAN 308-9150. Tel: 662-686-3261. FAX: 662-686-3342. Web Site: msucares.com/drec/index.html. *Librn,* Rhonda H Watson; E-mail: rhw1@msstate.edu; *Libr Assoc,* Bess Moss; Tel: 662-686-3260, E-mail: bmoss@drec.msstate.edu; Staff 1 (MLS 1)
Founded 1966
Library Holdings: Bk Vols 25,000
Subject Interests: Agr, Botany, Chem, Econ, Entomology, Math, Mechanical eng, Meteorology, Publ of all state experiment stations, Zoology
Database Vendor: EBSCOhost, LexisNexis, OCLC FirstSearch, OVID Technologies, TLC (The Library Corporation), Wilson - Wilson Web
Wireless access
Function: Res libr
Publications: Serials Catalog
Open Mon-Fri 8-4:30

SUMMIT

J SOUTHWEST MISSISSIPPI COMMUNITY COLLEGE*, Ford Library-Learning Resources Center, Lakeside Dr, 39666. (Mail add: 1036 College Dr, 39666), SAN 308-9169. Tel: 601-276-2004. FAX: 601-276-3748. Web Site: www.smcc.edu. *Dir,* Natalie McMahon; E-mail: nmcmahon@smcc.edu; *Dir, Learning Res Ctr,* Dawn Brumfield; E-mail: dqb@smcc.edu; *Librn,* Laura Riddle; E-mail: lporta@smcc.edu; Staff 2 (MLS 2)
Founded 1977. Enrl 1,816
Library Holdings: e-books 11,173, Bk Vols 38,808; Per Subs 123
Special Collections: Mississippi Coll
Open Mon-Thurs 7:30am-9pm, Fri 7:30-3:30

TAYLORSVILLE

P EVON A FORD PUBLIC LIBRARY*, 208 Spring St, 39168. (Mail add: PO Box 430, 39168-0430), SAN 376-6241. Tel: 601-785-4361. FAX: 601-785-6611. E-mail: taylorsv@cmrls.lib.ms.us. *Br Mgr,* Frances Gregg
Library Holdings: Bk Titles 13,000; Per Subs 12
Mem of Central Mississippi Regional Library System
Open Mon, Wed & Fri 8-1 & 2-5:30, Tues 8-1 & 1:30-5:30, Sat 9-Noon

TOUGALOO

C TOUGALOO COLLEGE*, L Zenobia Coleman Library, 500 W County Line Rd, 39174-9799. SAN 308-9177. Tel: 601-977-7706. Administration Tel: 601-977-7704. Information Services Tel: 601-977-7705. FAX: 601-977-7714. E-mail: libraryservices@tougaloo.edu. Web Site: www.tougaloo.edu/library. *Dir,* Dr Dorothy Burnett; *Coordr, Tech Serv,* Orthella Polk Moman; Tel: 601-977-7778; *Pub Serv,* Rosie Neal; E-mail: rneal@tougaloo.edu; *ILL,* Patricia Strong; E-mail: pstrong@tougaloo.edu; Staff 9 (MLS 3, Non-MLS 6)
Founded 1869. Enrl 907; Fac 89; Highest Degree: Bachelor
Library Holdings: Bk Titles 125,000; Bk Vols 139,000; Per Subs 389
Special Collections: African Materials (Ross Coll); Baily-Ward African American Coll (archives); Civil Rights & Liberties (Charles Horowitz Papers); Civil Rights Movement (Tracy Sugarman Print Coll of 1964),

prints; Mississippi Civil Rights Lawsuits of the 1960's, bks, papers; Music (B B King Coll), awards, pamphlets, papers, per; Radical Papers (Kudzu File). Oral History
Automation Activity & Vendor Info: (Acquisitions) Ex Libris Group; (Cataloging) Ex Libris Group; (Circulation) Ex Libris Group; (Course Reserve) Ex Libris Group; (ILL) OCLC; (Media Booking) Ex Libris Group; (OPAC) Ex Libris Group; (Serials) Ex Libris Group
Database Vendor: EBSCOhost, Gale Cengage Learning, JSTOR, Newsbank, OCLC WorldShare Interlibrary Loan, Westlaw
Function: Archival coll, ILL available, Ref serv available
Publications: A Classified Bibliography of the Special Collections in the L Zenobia Coleman Library
Partic in Central Mississippi Library Council; OCLC Online Computer Library Center, Inc
Open Mon-Fri 8am-11pm, Sat 12-4, Sun 5-11

TUPELO

J ITAWAMBA COMMUNITY COLLEGE*, Tupelo Branch Learning Resource Center, 2176 S Eason Blvd, 38804. SAN 308-9185. Tel: 662-620-5091. FAX: 662-620-5095. Web Site: www.iccms.edu. *Dir,* Dr Glenda Segars; Tel: 662-620-5090, E-mail: grsegars@iccms.edu; *Librn,* Janet Armour; Tel: 662-620-5092, E-mail: jyarmour@iccms.edu
Founded 1975. Enrl 1,400; Fac 125
Library Holdings: Bk Titles 20,000; Per Subs 225
Open Mon-Thurs 7:45am-8:45pm, Fri 7:45-4:30

P LEE COUNTY LIBRARY*, 219 N Madison St, 38804-3899. SAN 348-8799. Tel: 662-841-9027. Reference Tel: 662-841-9013. Administration Tel: 662-841-9029. FAX: 662-840-7615. E-mail: circulation@li.lib.ms.us. Web Site: www.li.lib.ms.us. *Dir,* Jan Willis; *Head, Ref,* Brian Hargett; E-mail: bhargett@li.lib.ms.us; *Bus Librn,* Elizabeth Turner; E-mail: eturner@li.lib.ms.us; *Ch Serv,* David Prather; E-mail: dprather@li.lib.ms.us; *Circ Librn,* Vickie Ross; *Genealogy Librn,* Melissa Holekamp; *Acq,* Debra Clayton; E-mail: dclayton@li.lib.ms.us; *Circ Asst,* Vicky Manning; Staff 14 (MLS 2, Non-MLS 12)
Founded 1942. Pop 100,195; Circ 34,565
Library Holdings: Bk Vols 142,369; Per Subs 279; Talking Bks 2,794
Subject Interests: Genealogy
Automation Activity & Vendor Info: (Acquisitions) TLC (The Library Corporation); (Cataloging) TLC (The Library Corporation); (Circulation) TLC (The Library Corporation); (OPAC) TLC (The Library Corporation); (Serials) TLC (The Library Corporation)
Database Vendor: TLC (The Library Corporation)
Wireless access
Special Services for the Deaf - Bks on deafness & sign lang; Closed caption videos
Special Services for the Blind - Assistive/Adapted tech devices, equip & products; Computer with voice synthesizer for visually impaired persons
Open Mon-Thurs 9-8, Fri & Sat 9-5
Friends of the Library Group
Bookmobiles: 1

M NORTH MISSISSIPPI MEDICAL CENTER*, Education Department Resource Center, 830 S Gloster St, 38801. SAN 371-0947. Tel: 662-377-4399. FAX: 662-377-7239. Web Site: www.nmhs.net. *Librn,* Loralei T McGee; E-mail: loralei.mcgee@nmhs.net; Staff 1 (Non-MLS 1)
Founded 1975
Library Holdings: AV Mats 500; Bk Titles 1,000; Per Subs 90

UNION

P KEMPER-NEWTON REGIONAL LIBRARY SYSTEM*, 101 Peachtree St, 39365-2617. SAN 348-8888. Tel: 601-774-5096. FAX: 601-774-5096. *Dir,* Barbara Gough; Tel: 601-774-9297, E-mail: bag@kemper.lib.ms.us; *Asst Dir, Bus Mgr,* Brenda Williams; Staff 11 (MLS 1, Non-MLS 10)
Founded 1969. Pop 31,685; Circ 50,312
Library Holdings: CDs 198; DVDs 30; Bk Titles 48,094; Per Subs 65
Subject Interests: Genealogy, Miss authors, Miss hist
Function: ILL available
Open Mon-Fri 8-5
Friends of the Library Group
Branches: 5
DECATUR PUBLIC, 306 Broad St, Decatur, 39327. (Mail add: PO Box 40, Decatur, 39327-0040), SAN 348-8942. Tel: 601-635-2777. *Br Librn,* Yvonne Hamm
Library Holdings: Bk Titles 7,492
Open Mon-Wed & Fri 12:30-5:30
DEKALB BRANCH, PO Box 710, DeKalb, 39328-0710, SAN 348-8977. Tel: 601-743-5981. *Br Head,* Lawson Smith
Library Holdings: Bk Titles 9,500
Special Collections: Kemper County History Coll
Open Mon & Tues 8:30-5, Wed 9:30-5, Fri 10-2
Friends of the Library Group
J ELLIOTT MCMULLAN LIBRARY, 300 W Church St, Newton, 39345-2208, SAN 348-9000. Tel: 601-683-3367. FAX: 601-683-3367. *Br Librn,* Maxine Dawkins; *Asst Librn,* Maxine Roachell
Library Holdings: Bk Titles 14,500
Special Collections: Mississippi Authors & History Coll
Open Mon-Wed (Oct-April) 9-5:30, Thurs 2-6, Fri 9-4, Sat 9-Noon
Friends of the Library Group
SCOOBA BRANCH, 1016 Kemper St, Scooba, 39358. (Mail add: PO Box 127, Scooba, 39358-0217), SAN 348-9035. Tel: 662-476-8452. *Br Librn,* Judith Howard
Library Holdings: Bk Titles 4,897
Open Mon Noon-4:30, Tues 9-1:30
Friends of the Library Group
UNION PUBLIC, 101 Peachtree, 39365-2617. Tel: 601-774-5096. FAX: 601-774-5096. *Br Librn,* Linda Hamm; *Asst Librn,* Eliana Richardson
Library Holdings: Bk Titles 14,082
Special Collections: Newton County History Coll
Open Mon-Thurs 8:30-5:30, Fri 8:30-4

UNIVERSITY

CL UNIVERSITY OF MISSISSIPPI*, Law Library, Three Grove Loop, 38677. (Mail add: PO Box 1848, 38677-1848), SAN 308-9193. Tel: 662-915-6824. Reference Tel: 662-915-6812. FAX: 662-915-7731. Web Site: library.law.olemiss.edu. *Dir,* Kris Gilliland; Tel: 662-915-6836, E-mail: gillilan@olemiss.edu; *Asst Dir,* Christopher Noe; Tel: 662-915-6850, E-mail: noe@olemiss.edu; *Cat,* Eugenia Minor; Tel: 662-915-6833, Fax: lweam@olemiss.edu; *Pub Serv,* Scott DeLeve; Tel: 662-915-6834, E-mail: sdeleve@olemiss.edu; *Pub Serv,* Macey Edmondson; Tel: 662-915-6819, E-mail: maceye@olemiss.edu; *Tech Serv,* Julianna S Davis; Tel: 662-915-6832, E-mail: uldavis@olemiss.edu; Staff 8 (MLS 8)
Founded 1854. Enrl 540; Fac 26; Highest Degree: Doctorate
Library Holdings: e-books 24,013; Bk Vols 336,487
Special Collections: State Document Depository; US Document Depository
Subject Interests: Space law, Tax law
Database Vendor: LexisNexis, Westlaw
Publications: Law Library (Newsletter)
Partic in Association of Southeastern Research Libraries; Lyrasis
Open Mon-Thurs 7am-Midnight, Fri 7am-9pm, Sat 9-6, Sun 10am-Midnight

C UNIVERSITY OF MISSISSIPPI*, John Davis Williams Library, One Library Loop, 38677. (Mail add: PO Box 1848, 38677-1848), SAN 348-906X. Tel: 662-915-5858. Interlibrary Loan Service Tel: 662-915-5867. Reference Tel: 662-915-5855. FAX: 662-915-5734. Interlibrary Loan Service FAX: 662-915-5453. TDD: 662-915-7907. Web Site: www.olemiss.edu/depts/general_library. *Adminr,* Mona Simpson; Tel: 662-915-7656, E-mail: mrsimpso@olemiss.edu; *Dean of Libr,* Julia M Rholes; Tel: 662-915-5672, E-mail: jrholes@olemiss.edu; *Asst Dean, Tech Serv,* Gail Herrera; Tel: 662-915-5674, E-mail: gherrera@olemiss.edu; *Operations Mgr,* Stanley Whitehorn; Tel: 662-915-7935, E-mail: swhithrn@olemiss.edu; *Head, Ref (Info Serv),* Ryan Johnson; Tel: 662-915-5877, E-mail: rjohnson@olemiss.edu; Staff 55 (MLS 27, Non-MLS 28)
Founded 1848. Enrl 14,497; Fac 830; Highest Degree: Doctorate
Library Holdings: Bk Vols 1,268,318; Per Subs 8,500
Special Collections: Mississippi Writers; Mississippiana; William Faulkner Coll. State Document Depository; US Document Depository
Subject Interests: Blues music, Culture, Lit, Southern culture, Southern hist
Automation Activity & Vendor Info: (Acquisitions) Innovative Interfaces, Inc; (Cataloging) Innovative Interfaces, Inc; (Circulation) Innovative Interfaces, Inc
Database Vendor: EBSCOhost, Innovative Interfaces, Inc, OCLC FirstSearch, OVID Technologies, TLC (The Library Corporation), Wilson - Wilson Web
Special Services for the Deaf - Staff with knowledge of sign lang; TDD equip
Friends of the Library Group
Departmental Libraries:
SCIENCE, 1031 Natural Products Ctr, 38677, SAN 369-7800. Tel: 662-915-7381. Interlibrary Loan Service Tel: 662-915-5668. FAX: 662-915-7549. Web Site: www.olemiss.edu/depts/general_library/files/science/index.html. *Head of Libr,* Elizabeth M Choinski; Tel: 662-915-7910, E-mail: ulemc@olemiss.edu; *ILL,* Deborah V McCain; E-mail: dmccain@olemiss.edu. Subject Specialists: *Bio, Math,* Elizabeth M Choinski; Staff 5 (MLS 4, Non-MLS 1)
Founded 1997. Highest Degree: Doctorate
Library Holdings: Bk Vols 70,000; Per Subs 450

Subject Interests: Analytical chem, Biochem, Inorganic chem, Organic chem, Pharmaceutics, Pharmacognosy-natural products, Pharmacology, Phys chem
Function: Doc delivery serv, Homebound delivery serv, ILL available, Libr develop, Photocopying/Printing, Ref serv available, Res libr, Telephone ref

VAIDEN

P VAIDEN PUBLIC LIBRARY*, PO Box 108, 39176-0108. SAN 376-6365. Tel: 662-464-7736. FAX: 662-464-7736. E-mail: vailiblp@carroll.lib.ms.us. *Librn,* Sharon Tollison
Library Holdings: Bk Titles 1,200; Bk Vols 1,500; Per Subs 13
Open Mon & Tues (Winter) 8-12 & 1-5, Thurs & Fri 12-5; Mon, Tues, Thurs & Fri (Summer) 12-5

VICKSBURG

M RIVER REGION MEDICAL CENTER LIBRARY*, 2100 Hwy 61 N, 39183. SAN 348-9094. Tel: 601-883-5943, 601-883-6020. FAX: 601-883-5139. *Librn,* Jeanne Monsour
Founded 1945
Library Holdings: Bk Vols 400; Per Subs 50
Subject Interests: Allied fields, Med, Surgery

A UNITED STATES ARMY*, Engineer Research & Development Center Library, 3909 Halls Ferry Rd, 39180-6199. SAN 308-9223. Tel: 601-634-2355. FAX: 601-634-2306. Web Site: acwc.sdp.sirsi.net/client/default. *Chief,* Denise Kitchens; Tel: 601-634-4120; Staff 7 (MLS 7)
Founded 1930
Library Holdings: e-books 39,000; e-journals 30,000; Bk Titles 225,000; Bk Vols 250,000; Per Subs 1,500
Subject Interests: Aquatic plant control, Coastal eng, Computer sci, Concrete, Dredged mat res, Environ effects, Explosive excavation, Hydraulics, Info tech, Pavements, Soil mechanics, Trafficability, Vehicle mobility, Weapons effects
Wireless access
Partic in Fedlink; OCLC Online Computer Library Center, Inc

S VICKSBURG & WARREN COUNTY HISTORICAL SOCIETY*, McCardle Library, Old Court House Museum, 1008 Cherry St, 39183. SAN 370-3045. Tel: 601-636-0741. E-mail: societyhistorica@bellsouth.net. Web Site: www.oldcourthouse.org. *Dir,* George C Bolm
Library Holdings: Bk Vols 2,000
Special Collections: J Mack Moore Photo Coll
Subject Interests: Genealogy, Hist
Open Mon-Fri 8:30-4:30

G VICKSBURG NATIONAL MILITARY PARK LIBRARY*, 3201 Clay St, 39183-3495. SAN 308-9231. Tel: 601-619-2908, 601-636-0583. FAX: 601-636-9497. Web Site: www.nps.gov/vick. *Librn,* Terrence Winschel
Library Holdings: Bk Vols 2,500
Special Collections: American Civil War Coll
Restriction: Open by appt only

P WARREN COUNTY-VICKSBURG PUBLIC LIBRARY*, 700 Veto St, 39180-3595. SAN 308-9266. Tel: 601-636-6411. FAX: 601-634-4809. Web Site: www.warren.lib.ms.us. *Dir,* Deborah Mitchell; E-mail: deb@warren.lib.ms.us; *Asst Dir,* Jennifer Smith; E-mail: jensmith@warren.lib.ms.us; *Operations Mgr,* Paula Benard; E-mail: benard@warren.lib.ms.us; *AV,* Zandra Demby-Miller; E-mail: zdemby@warren.lib.ms.us; *Cat,* Mary Ann Brennan; E-mail: mbrennan@warren.lib.ms.us; *Ch Serv,* Lottie Walker; E-mail: lbwalker@warren.lib.ms.us; *Circ,* Sandra Mayfield; E-mail: mayfield@warren.lib.ms.us; *ILL,* Denise Hogan; E-mail: whit10@warren.lib.ms.us; Staff 15 (MLS 4, Non-MLS 11)
Founded 1915. Pop 49,800; Circ 227,925
Oct 2008-Sept 2009 Income $891,584, State $135,396, Federal $15,529, County $698,782, Locally Generated Income $41,877. Mats Exp $149,240, Books $80,697, Per/Ser (Incl. Access Fees) $6,000, AV Mat $60,140, Electronic Ref Mat (Incl. Access Fees) $2,403. Sal $498,724
Library Holdings: Audiobooks 7,696; Electronic Media & Resources 41; Bk Vols 131,748; Per Subs 169; Videos 13,490
Subject Interests: Civil War, Miss, Miss river, Mystery novels
Automation Activity & Vendor Info: (Acquisitions) Innovative Interfaces, Inc; (Cataloging) Innovative Interfaces, Inc; (Circulation) Innovative Interfaces, Inc; (OPAC) Innovative Interfaces, Inc; (Serials) Innovative Interfaces, Inc
Database Vendor: EBSCOhost, Gale Cengage Learning, OCLC FirstSearch, Wilson - Wilson Web, World Book Online
Wireless access
Function: Adult bk club, AV serv, Bk club(s), Bks on cassette, Bks on CD, Children's prog, Computers for patron use, Copy machines, e-mail & chat, Electronic databases & coll, Exhibits, Free DVD rentals, Handicapped accessible, ILL available, Mail & tel request accepted, Music CDs, Newsp ref libr, Online cat, Photocopying/Printing, Preschool outreach, Prog for adults, Prog for children & young adult, Pub access computers, Ref & res, Ref serv available, Ref serv in person, Spoken cassettes & CDs, Spoken cassettes & DVDs, Story hour, Summer reading prog, Tax forms, Telephone ref, VHS videos
Publications: Newsletter
Open Mon-Thurs 9-7, Fri & Sat 9-5
Friends of the Library Group

WASHINGTON

G HISTORIC JEFFERSON COLLEGE LIBRARY*, PO Box 700, 39190. SAN 321-0421. Tel: 601-442-2901. FAX: 601-442-2902. E-mail: hjc@telepak.net. *In Charge,* Anne Gray
Founded 1979
Library Holdings: Bk Titles 1,033
Special Collections: 1840 Library Restoration
Subject Interests: Miss hist
Open Mon-Fri 9-5
Restriction: Open to pub for ref only

WATER VALLEY

P BLACKMUR MEMORIAL LIBRARY*, 608 Blackmur Dr, 38965-6070. SAN 308-9274. Tel: 662-473-2444. FAX: 662-473-2444. *Dir,* Joseph Gurner; E-mail: jgurner@blackmur.lib.ms.us; Staff 2 (Non-MLS 2)
Founded 1959. Pop 8,000; Circ 16,610
Library Holdings: High Interest/Low Vocabulary Bk Vols 200; Large Print Bks 150; Bk Titles 10,000; Bk Vols 16,351; Per Subs 39
Special Collections: Black History Coll; Mississippi History
Subject Interests: Genealogy, Local hist
Automation Activity & Vendor Info: (Cataloging) Book Systems; (Circulation) Book Systems; (OPAC) Book Systems
Partic in Dancing Rabbit Library Consortium
Open Mon & Fri 10-5, Tues & Thurs 10-6, Wed & Sat 10-1
Friends of the Library Group

WAYNESBORO

P WAYNESBORO-WAYNE COUNTY LIBRARY SYSTEM*, 1103A Mississippi Dr, 39367. SAN 348-8071. Tel: 601-735-2268. FAX: 601-735-6407. Web Site: www.wwcls.lib.ms.us. *Dir,* Patsy Brewer
Library Holdings: Bk Vols 40,000
Subject Interests: Genealogy
Open Mon-Fri 9-6, Sat 9-1
Friends of the Library Group

WESSON

J COPIAH-LINCOLN COMMUNITY COLLEGE, Evelyn W Oswalt Library, 1028 J C Redd Dr, 39191. (Mail add: PO Box 649, 39191-0649), SAN 308-9282. Tel: 601-643-8363. Web Site: www.colin.edu/librariesmain. *Dir, Libr Serv,* Kendall P Chapman; Tel: 601-643-8364, E-mail: ken.chapman@colin.edu; Staff 5 (MLS 1, Non-MLS 4)
Founded 1928. Enrl 2,033, Fac 135; Highest Degree: Associate
Jul 2013-Jun 2014 Income $256,301. Mats Exp $96,040, Books $10,000, Per/Ser (Incl. Access Fees) $2,700, Electronic Ref Mat (Incl. Access Fees) $83,340. Sal $160,261 (Prof $71,585)
Library Holdings: Bk Vols 33,819; Per Subs 26; Videos 1,293
Automation Activity & Vendor Info: (Cataloging) SirsiDynix; (Circulation) SirsiDynix; (OPAC) SirsiDynix
Database Vendor: Agricola, Cinahl, CQ Press, CredoReference, EBSCO Discovery Service, Facts on File, Gale Cengage Learning, H W Wilson, McGraw-Hill, Newsbank, OCLC FirstSearch, OCLC WorldShare Interlibrary Loan, Oxford Online, ProQuest, SirsiDynix, Wilson - Wilson Web, World Book Online
Wireless access
Partic in MAGNOLIA; Mississippi Electronic Libraries Online
Open Mon-Thurs (Fall & Spring) 7:30am-9:30pm, Fri 7:30-2; Mon-Thurs (Summer) 7:30-4:30, Fri 7:30-2

WEST POINT

P TOMBIGBEE REGIONAL LIBRARY SYSTEM*, Bryan Public Library, Headquarters, 338 Commerce, 39773-2923. SAN 348-9159. Tel: 662-494-4872. FAX: 662-494-0300. Web Site: www.tombigbee.lib.ms.us. *Dir,* Tanna Taylor; E-mail: ttaylor@tombigbee.lib.ms.us; *Ch,* Dawn Richardson; E-mail: drichardson@tombigbee.lib.ms.us; *Circ Librn,* Valerie Hargrove; E-mail: vhargrove@tombigbee.lib.ms.us; *Bus Mgr,* Evelyn Welsh; E-mail: ewelsh@tombigbee.lib.ms.us; *Cat,* Debbie Brownlee; *ILL,* Barbara Iles; E-mail: biles@tombigbee.lib.ms.us; Staff 19 (MLS 1, Non-MLS 18)
Founded 1916. Pop 79,800; Circ 133,892

Oct 2011-Sept 2012 Income (Main Library and Branch(s)) $866,339, State $232,870, City $320,725, Federal $27,507, County $256,347, Other $28,890. Mats Exp $60,365. Sal $475,043
Library Holdings: AV Mats 11,505; Bk Vols 129,556; Per Subs 157
Subject Interests: Genealogy, Local hist
Automation Activity & Vendor Info: (Cataloging) SirsiDynix; (Circulation) SirsiDynix; (ILL) OCLC; (OPAC) SirsiDynix
Database Vendor: Backstage Library Works, Baker & Taylor, EBSCOhost, Gale Cengage Learning, OCLC FirstSearch, Overdrive, Inc, ProQuest, SirsiDynix, Wilson - Wilson Web
Wireless access
Function: Accelerated reader prog, Archival coll, Art exhibits, Bk reviews (Group), Bks on cassette, Bks on CD, Children's prog, Computer training, Computers for patron use, Copy machines, e-mail & chat, Electronic databases & coll, Exhibits, Fax serv, Free DVD rentals, Genealogy discussion group, Handicapped accessible, Holiday prog, ILL available, Music CDs, Notary serv, Online cat, Orientations, OverDrive digital audio bks, Photocopying/Printing, Preschool outreach, Preschool reading prog, Prog for adults, Prog for children & young adult, Pub access computers, Spoken cassettes & CDs, Spoken cassettes & DVDs, Story hour, Summer reading prog, Tax forms, Teen prog, Wheelchair accessible
Publications: BPL-News from Friends (Newsletter)
Partic in Mississippi Library Partnership
Friends of the Library Group
Branches: 9
AMORY MUNICIPAL LIBRARY, 401 Second Ave N at Fourth St, Amory, 38821-3514, SAN 348-9183. Tel: 662-256-5261. FAX: 662-256-6321. *Librn,* Brenda Wilson; E-mail: brengcw@tombigbee.lib.ms.us; *Ch,* Carol Halbert; E-mail: chalbert@tombigbee.lib.ms.us; *Bus Mgr,* Linda Reich; *Ref Serv,* Ruby Holman; E-mail: rwillin@tombigbee.lib.ms.us; Staff 2 (Non-MLS 2)
Circ 44,333
Library Holdings: AV Mats 4,662; Bk Vols 19,894
Subject Interests: Genealogy, Local hist
Automation Activity & Vendor Info: (ILL) SirsiDynix
Function: Art exhibits, Bks on cassette, Bks on CD, Children's prog, Computers for patron use, Copy machines, Free DVD rentals, ILL available, Music CDs, Online cat, Prog for adults, Prog for children & young adult, Pub access computers, Ref & res, Spoken cassettes & CDs, Spoken cassettes & DVDs, Story hour, Summer reading prog, Tax forms, VHS videos, Wheelchair accessible
Open Mon-Wed 10-6, Thurs 10-8, Fri & Sat 9-5
Friends of the Library Group
CHOCTAW COUNTY PUBLIC LIBRARY, 511 Louisville St, Ackerman, 39735. (Mail add: PO Box 755, Ackerman, 39735-0755), SAN 348-9213. Tel: 662-285-6348. FAX: 662-285-3042. *Librn,* Ruby Bowie; E-mail: ackerman@tombigbee.lib.ms.us; *Asst Librn,* Margie Simpson Gilmer; Staff 1 (Non-MLS 1)
Circ 7,070
Library Holdings: AV Mats 781; Bk Vols 10,083
Special Collections: Genealogy & Local History (J P Coleman Coll)
Automation Activity & Vendor Info: (ILL) SirsiDynix
Open Mon, Tues & Thurs 9-6, Wed & Fri 9-Noon
Friends of the Library Group
EVANS MEMORIAL LIBRARY, 105 N Long St, Aberdeen, 39730, SAN 348-9248. Tel: 662-369-4601. FAX: 662-369-2971. *Br Librn,* Barbara Blair; E-mail: bblair@tombigbee.lib.ms.us; *Ch,* Patricia Waldrop; *Circ Librn,* Brenda Dobbs; Staff 2 (Non-MLS 2)
Circ 26,787
Library Holdings: AV Mats 1,238; Bk Vols 28,705
Special Collections: Photographs (McKnight Coll)
Subject Interests: Genealogy, Local hist
Automation Activity & Vendor Info: (Circulation) SirsiDynix; (ILL) SirsiDynix; (OPAC) SirsiDynix
Friends of the Library Group
HAMILTON PUBLIC LIBRARY, Old Hwy 45 S, Hamilton, 39746. (Mail add: PO Box 96, Hamilton, 39746-0096), SAN 348-9272. Tel: 601-343-8962. FAX: 601-343-8962. E-mail: hamilton@tombigbee.lib.ms.us. *Br Head,* Belinda Stahl
Circ 2,014
Library Holdings: AV Mats 149; Bk Vols 4,256
Automation Activity & Vendor Info: (ILL) SirsiDynix
DOROTHY J LOWE MEMORIAL PUBLIC LIBRARY, 182 Main St, Nettleton, 38858-6075, SAN 348-9337. Tel: 662-963-2011. FAX: 662-963-2014. E-mail: nettleton@tombigbee.lib.ms.us. *Librn,* Maridelle Dickerson
Circ 2,311
Library Holdings: AV Mats 144; Bk Vols 3,117
Automation Activity & Vendor Info: (ILL) SirsiDynix
Open Mon-Thurs 12-5
MATHISTON PUBLIC LIBRARY, Scott St, Mathiston, 39752-9214. (Mail add: PO Box 82, Mathiston, 39752-0082), SAN 348-9302. Tel: 662-263-4772. FAX: 662-263-4772. *Librn,* Gail Shurden; E-mail: gshurden@tombigbee.lib.ms.us
Circ 2,462
Library Holdings: AV Mats 102; Bk Vols 4,115
Automation Activity & Vendor Info: (ILL) SirsiDynix
WEBSTER COUNTY PUBLIC LIBRARY, 445 W Fox Ave, Eupora, 39744. (Mail add: PO Box 205, Eupora, 39744-0205), SAN 348-9396. Tel: 662-258-7515. FAX: 662-258-7519. *Br Librn,* Fran Smith; E-mail: fsmith@tombigbee.lib.ms.us
Circ 10,026
Library Holdings: AV Mats 1,084; Bk Vols 8,227
Subject Interests: Genealogy, Local hist
Automation Activity & Vendor Info: (ILL) SirsiDynix
Friends of the Library Group
WEIR PUBLIC LIBRARY, 123 Front St, Weir, 39772. (Mail add: PO Box 249, Weir, 39772-0249), SAN 348-9426. Tel: 662-547-6747. FAX: 662-547-6747. E-mail: weir@tombigbee.lib.ms.us. *Br Head,* Rebecca McDaniel
Circ 1,579
Library Holdings: AV Mats 262; Bk Vols 3,646
Automation Activity & Vendor Info: (ILL) SirsiDynix
WREN PUBLIC LIBRARY, 32655 Hwy 45 N, Aberdeen, 39730-9796, SAN 348-9450. Tel: 662-256-4957. FAX: 662-256-4950. *Librn,* Charlotte Wathen
Circ 2,685
Library Holdings: AV Mats 151; Bk Vols 4,693
Automation Activity & Vendor Info: (ILL) SirsiDynix
Friends of the Library Group

WHITFIELD

MISSISSIPPI STATE HOSPITAL
M MEDICAL LIBRARY*, Whitfield Rd, 39193, SAN 308-9304. Tel: 601-351-8000, Ext 4278. *Librn,* Jane Hull
Library Holdings: Bk Vols 1,000; Per Subs 25
Subject Interests: Alcoholism, Drug addiction, Psychiat
Open Mon & Wed 8-4, Fri 8-3
M PATIENT LIBRARY*, Whitfield Rd, 39193, SAN 376-0324. Tel: 601-351-8000, Ext 4278. *Librn,* Jane Hull
Library Holdings: Bk Vols 14,000
Open Mon & Wed 8-4, Fri 8-3

YAZOO CITY

P B S RICKS MEMORIAL LIBRARY*, 310 N Main St, 39194-4253. SAN 348-9574. Tel: 662-746-5557. Administration Tel: 662-746-5586. FAX: 662-746-7309. Web Site: www.yazoo.lib.ms.us. *Interim Dir,* Sherry Anderson; E-mail: sanderson@yazoo.lib.ms.us; *Dir,* Position Currently Open; *Ch,* Miranda Purvis; E-mail: mhenderson@yazoo.lib.ms.us; *Ref & ILL Librn,* Karen Dunaway; *Ref & Local Hist Librn,* John Ellzey; E-mail: johnellzey@yazoo.lib.ms.us; *Circ Mgr,* Tracy Roby; Staff 4 (MLS 4)
Founded 1838. Pop 27,886; Circ 46,500
Library Holdings: Bk Vols 42,000; Per Subs 110
Special Collections: Local History Coll. Oral History; State Document Depository
Automation Activity & Vendor Info: (Circulation) Auto-Graphics, Inc
Wireless access
Partic in Dancing Rabbit Library Consortium; Lyrasis
Open Mon-Thurs 8:30-5:30, Fri 8-5, Sat 8:30-Noon
Friends of the Library Group

MISSOURI

Date of Statistics: FY 2014
Population, 2010 U.S. Census: 5,988,927
Population Served by Public Libraries: 5,476,144
Unserved: 512,783
Total Volumes in Public Libraries: 16,795,429
Volumes Per Capita: 3.08
Total Public Library Circulation: 55,720,384
Circulation Per Capita: 10.18
Total Public Library Income: $243,692,987
Source of Income: Local 91.6%, State 1.7%, Federal 0.9%, Other 5.8%
Expenditure Per Capita: $40.69
Number of County & Multi-county: 66
Counties Served: 84
Number of Bookmobiles: 27
Grants-in-Aid:
State Aid: $3,504,001
Federal $2,212,267

ALBANY

P CARNEGIE PUBLIC LIBRARY*, 101 W Clay, 64402. SAN 308-9320. Tel: 660-726-5615. FAX: 660-726-4213. E-mail: librarian@carnegie.lib.mo.us. Web Site: carnegie.lib.mo.us. *Dir,* Cheryl A Lang; Staff 1 (MLS 1)
Founded 1906. Pop 1,937; Circ 15,117
Library Holdings: CDs 602; DVDs 233; Large Print Bks 440; Bk Titles 13,397; Bk Vols 13,780; Per Subs 25; Videos 1,343
Automation Activity & Vendor Info: (Cataloging) TLC (The Library Corporation)
Database Vendor: EBSCOhost
Wireless access
Partic in Grand Rivers Libr Conference
Open Mon & Wed 11-7, Tues, Thurs & Fri 11-5, Sat 9-12
Friends of the Library Group

ALTON

P OREGON COUNTY LIBRARY DISTRICT*, Alton Public Library, 20 Court Sq, 65606. (Mail add: PO Box 158, 65606-0158), SAN 377-1016. Tel: 417-778-6414. FAX: 417-778-6414. E-mail: altonpubliclibrary@hotmail.com. Web Site: oregoncountylibrary.lib.mo.us. *Head Librn,* Janice Richardson; Staff 1 (MLS 1)
Pop 710
Library Holdings: Bk Titles 11,775; Bk Vols 12,000; Per Subs 13
Database Vendor: EBSCOhost, Gale Cengage Learning
Open Mon-Fri 8:30-5
Branches: 4
KOSHKONONG PUBLIC, 302 Diggins St, Koshkonong, 65692, SAN 377-5542. Tel: 417-867-5472. FAX: 417-867-5472. E-mail: koshlibrary@gmail.com. *Head Librn,* Paula Miller; Staff 1 (MLS 1)
Pop 610
Library Holdings: Bk Titles 4,980; Bk Vols 5,126; Per Subs 11; Videos 100
Open Mon 10:30-4:30, Tues & Wed 10:30-5:30
MYRTLE PUBLIC, General Delivery, State Hwy V, Myrtle, 65778. Tel: 417-938-4350. FAX: 417-938-4350. *Head Librn,* Janis Campbell
Open Tues & Wed 9-5, Sat 9-1
THAYER PUBLIC, 121 N Second St, Thayer, 65791, SAN 377-2160. Tel: 417-264-3091. FAX: 417-264-3091. *Head Librn,* Grace Mainprize; Staff 1 (MLS 1)
Library Holdings: Bk Titles 20,000; Bk Vols 25,000; Per Subs 24; Talking Bks 56; Videos 78
Database Vendor: OCLC FirstSearch
Open Mon-Sat 8:30-4:30
THOMASVILLE PUBLIC LIBRARY, Rte HC3, Box 62, Birch Tree, 65438. Tel: 417-764-3603. FAX: 417-764-3603. E-mail: librarytville@yahoo.com. *Head Librn,* Joyce Cates
Open Tues & Wed 9-4, Thurs 10-4

APPLETON CITY

P APPLETON CITY PUBLIC LIBRARY*, 105 W Fourth St, 64724-1401. SAN 308-9339. Tel: 660-476-5513. FAX: 660-476-5513. E-mail: acpubliclibrary@yahoo.com. *Dir,* Virginia Gilmore; Staff 1 (Non-MLS 1)
Founded 1870. Pop 1,314; Circ 7,626
Jan 2012-Dec 2012 Income $16,465, State $650, City $15,815. Mats Exp $1,081, Books $931, Per/Ser (Incl. Access Fees) $150. Sal $12,656
Library Holdings: DVDs 460; Large Print Bks 900; Bk Titles 29,000; Per Subs 8; Talking Bks 356; Videos 612
Database Vendor: OCLC FirstSearch
Open Tues & Thurs 8-5, Sat 8-12

AVA

P DOUGLAS COUNTY PUBLIC LIBRARY*, 301 SW Third Ave, 65608. (Mail add: PO Box 277, 65608-0277), SAN 308-9355. Tel: 417-683-5633. FAX: 417-683-5633. Web Site: douglascountylibrary.lib.mo.us. *Access Serv, Librn,* Anita Dodd; E-mail: doddanita@gmail.com; Staff 2 (Non-MLS 2)
Founded 1979. Pop 13,084; Circ 39,316
Library Holdings: Bks-By-Mail 518; DVDs 212; Large Print Bks 873; Bk Vols 38,908; Per Subs 34; Talking Bks 1,141; Videos 840
Automation Activity & Vendor Info: (Cataloging) TLC (The Library Corporation); (Circulation) TLC (The Library Corporation); (OPAC) TLC (The Library Corporation)
Partic in Mo State Database
Open Mon-Fri 9-5, Sat 9-12
Friends of the Library Group

BLOOMFIELD

P BLOOMFIELD PUBLIC LIBRARY*, 200 Seneca St, 63825. (Mail add: PO Box 294, 63825-0294), SAN 308-9363. Tel: 573-568-3626. FAX: 573-568-3626. *Dir,* Linda Myers; Staff 1 (MLS 1)
Founded 1967. Pop 1,924; Circ 8,167
Library Holdings: Bk Titles 14,182; Bk Vols 14,391; Per Subs 12; Talking Bks 15; Videos 31
Special Collections: 1850 Newspaper Coll, microfilm; Stoddard County Records, bks, microfilm; War of the Rebellion
Automation Activity & Vendor Info: (Circulation) TLC (The Library Corporation)
Open Mon-Wed 10-5, Thurs 10-6, Fri 9-5, Sat 9-12

BLUE SPRINGS

S BLUE SPRINGS HISTORICAL SOCIETY*, Archives & Research Library, 101 SW 15th St, 64015. (Mail add: PO Box 762, 64013), SAN 373-2347. Tel: 816-224-8979, 816-229-1671. Web Site: www.rootsweb.com/~mobshs/. *Archivist,* Karol Witthar; E-mail: kwarchives@aol.com
Founded 1976
Special Collections: Oral History
Subject Interests: Local hist

Function: Archival coll
Restriction: Open by appt only

BOLIVAR

P POLK COUNTY LIBRARY*, 1690 W Broadway St, 65613. SAN 348-9639. Tel: 417-326-4531. FAX: 417-326-4366. *Dir,* Terri York; *Asst Dir,* Jeannie Saltkill; Staff 2 (MLS 1, Non-MLS 1)
Founded 1947. Pop 26,992
Library Holdings: CDs 873; DVDs 416; Large Print Bks 2,563; Bk Vols 50,000; Per Subs 57; Videos 2,089
Automation Activity & Vendor Info: (Cataloging) Book Systems; (Circulation) Book Systems; (ILL) OCLC; (OPAC) Book Systems
Database Vendor: EBSCOhost
Open Mon & Wed-Fri 10-6, Tues 10-9, Sat 10-1
Friends of the Library Group
Branches: 1
HUMANSVILLE BRANCH, 101 S Ohio St, Humansville, 65674. (Mail add: PO Box 201, Humansville, 65674-0201), SAN 348-9752. Tel: 417-754-2455. FAX: 417-754-2455. *Br Mgr,* Sharon Anderson
Library Holdings: CDs 42; DVDs 120; Large Print Bks 508; Bk Vols 11,600; Videos 629
Open Tues, Thurs & Fri 8:30-12:30 & 1-5, Sat 8:30-12:30
Friends of the Library Group

CR SOUTHWEST BAPTIST UNIVERSITY LIBRARIES*, Harriet K Hutchens Library, 1600 University Ave, 65613. SAN 308-9371. Tel: 417-328-1604, 417-328-1621. Toll Free Tel: 800-743-5774. FAX: 417-328-1652. Web Site: www.sbuniv.edu/library. *Dean, Univ Libr,* Dr Edward W Walton; Tel: 417-328-1619, E-mail: ewalton@sbuniv.edu; *Acq & Coll Develop Librn,* Kenette Harder; Tel: 417-328-1625, E-mail: kharder@sbuniv.edu; *Cat Librn,* Coleen Rose; Tel: 417-328-1631, E-mail: crose@sbuniv.edu; *Info Literacy Librn,* Bethany Messersmith; Tel: 417-328-1626, E-mail: bmessersmith@sbuniv.edu; *Ref Serv Librn,* Susan Kromrie; Tel: 417-328-1629, E-mail: skromrie@sbuniv.edu. Subject Specialists: *Admin, Electronic res,* Dr Edward W Walton; *Archives,* Susan Kromrie; Staff 6 (MLS 6)
Founded 1878. Enrl 3,099; Fac 130; Highest Degree: Doctorate
Library Holdings: AV Mats 11,202; CDs 892; e-books 16,325; e-journals 9,823; Electronic Media & Resources 397; Music Scores 3,090; Bk Titles 121,204; Bk Vols 177,526; Per Subs 407; Videos 2,520
Special Collections: Butler Baptist Heritage Coll; Christian Education Resource Lab; Library of American Civilization - Microbook Coll; Southern Baptist Convention Resource Lab. State Document Depository
Automation Activity & Vendor Info: (Acquisitions) Innovative Interfaces, Inc; (Cataloging) Innovative Interfaces, Inc; (Circulation) Innovative Interfaces, Inc; (Course Reserve) Innovative Interfaces, Inc; (ILL) OCLC; (Media Booking) Innovative Interfaces, Inc; (OPAC) Innovative Interfaces, Inc; (Serials) Innovative Interfaces, Inc
Database Vendor: EBSCOhost, Gale Cengage Learning, LexisNexis, OCLC FirstSearch, Wilson - Wilson Web
Function: Archival coll, Audio & video playback equip for onsite use, Doc delivery serv, ILL available, Mail loans to mem, Music CDs, Online searches, Photocopying/Printing, Ref serv available, VHS videos
Publications: Southern Baptist Periodical Index (Index to science materials)
Partic in Amigos Library Services, Inc; MOBIUS (Missouri Bibliographic Information User System)
Restriction: Open to pub for ref & circ; with some limitations, Open to students, fac & staff
Departmental Libraries:
MOUNTAIN VIEW CENTER LIBRARY, 209 W First St, Mountain View, 65548. (Mail add: PO Box 489, Mountain View, 65548). Tel: 417-934-5057. FAX: 417-934-5056. *Libr Supvr,* Mary McGalliard; E-mail: mmcgalliard@sbuniv.edu
Library Holdings: Bk Titles 10,972; Bk Vols 13,257
Automation Activity & Vendor Info: (Cataloging) Innovative Interfaces, Inc; (Circulation) Innovative Interfaces, Inc; (OPAC) Innovative Interfaces, Inc
Open Mon-Tues & Thurs 8-12 & 1-9, Wed & Fri 8-12 & 1-5
SPRINGFIELD CAMPUS LIBRARY, 4431 S Fremont, Springfield, 65804-7307, SAN 309-2372. Tel: 417-820-2103. FAX: 417-820-4847. *Librn,* Holli Henslee; E-mail: hhenslee@sbuniv.edu; Staff 3 (MLS 1, Non-MLS 2)
Founded 1909
Library Holdings: Bk Titles 3,059; Bk Vols 4,347; Per Subs 88
Special Collections: Archive Coll
Subject Interests: Nursing
Database Vendor: EBSCOhost, LexisNexis, OCLC FirstSearch
Open Mon-Thurs 8am-9pm, Fri 8-12
WISDOM LIBRARY, SBU Salem Ctr, 501 S Grand St, Salem, 65560. Tel: 573-729-7071. FAX: 573-729-6949. *Libr Supvr,* Nancy Eudy; E-mail: neudy@sbuniv.edu
Library Holdings: Bk Titles 4,256; Bk Vols 4,962
Automation Activity & Vendor Info: (Cataloging) Innovative Interfaces, Inc; (Circulation) Innovative Interfaces, Inc; (OPAC) Innovative Interfaces, Inc
Open Mon-Thurs 10-7, Fri 10-4

BONNE TERRE

P BONNE TERRE MEMORIAL LIBRARY*, Five SW Main St, 63628. SAN 308-938X. Tel: 573-358-2260. FAX: 573-358-5941. E-mail: btml@bonneterre.net. Web Site: www.bonneterrelibrary.org. *Dir,* Doris J Smither; *Ch, Circ Serv,* Tina Johnston; *Tech Serv Librn,* Loretta Polette; *Syst Coordr,* Darren Monie; *Spec Serv,* Amanda Carron; E-mail: bonneterrelibraryservices@live.com
Founded 1867. Pop 5,000; Circ 36,909
Oct 2007-Sept 2008 Income $132,480, State $4,065, City $128,415. Mats Exp $122,806, Books $10,879, Per/Ser (Incl. Access Fees) $724, AV Mat $1,013. Sal $79,471 (Prof $20,766)
Library Holdings: Audiobooks 595; CDs 117; DVDs 175; Large Print Bks 1,292; Bk Vols 23,050; Per Subs 29; Videos 1,102
Subject Interests: Local hist
Automation Activity & Vendor Info: (Cataloging) Follett Software; (Circulation) Follett Software
Wireless access
Function: After school storytime, Bk club(s), Bks on cassette, Bks on CD, Children's prog
Open Mon-Wed & Fri 10-6, Thurs 10-7, Sat 10-2
Friends of the Library Group

BOONVILLE

S FRIENDS OF HISTORIC BOONVILLE*, Archival Collection, 614 E Morgan, 65233. (Mail add: PO Box 1776, 65233), SAN 373-2312. Tel: 660-882-7977. Toll Free Tel: 888-588-1477. FAX: 660-882-9194. E-mail: fohb@sbcglobal.net. Web Site: www.friendsofhistoricboonville.org. *Dir,* Holly Peterson; Staff 1 (MLS 1)
Founded 1971
Library Holdings: Bk Titles 460; Bk Vols 530
Subject Interests: Local hist
Restriction: Open by appt only

BRANSON

P TANEYHILLS COMMUNITY LIBRARY*, 200 S Fourth St, 65616-2738. SAN 308-9401. Tel: 417-334-1418. FAX: 417-334-1629. E-mail: tanlib001@centurytel.net. *Dir,* Brother Philip Edward Endicott; Staff 1 (MLS 1)
Founded 1933
Library Holdings: Bk Titles 44,552; Bk Vols 46,732; Per Subs 50
Special Collections: DAR Genealogy Coll; Missouri Coll; Taney County & Ozark Region Coll
Automation Activity & Vendor Info: (Cataloging) Follett Software; (Circulation) Follett Software
Publications: Newsletter, semi-annual
Open Mon, Tues, Thurs & Fri 10-5, Wed 10-7, Sat 10-1
Friends of the Library Group

BRENTWOOD

P BRENTWOOD PUBLIC LIBRARY*, 8765 Eulalie Ave, 63144. SAN 308-941X. Tel: 314-963-8630. Circulation Tel: 314-963-8631. FAX: 314-962-8675. E-mail: circulation@bplmo.org. Web Site: www.brentwood.lib.mo.us. *Dir,* Vicki Woods; *Tech Serv Supvr,* Susan Holt; Tel: 314-963-8632; *Adult Serv,* Gina Gibbons; Tel: 314-963-8636; *Ch Serv,* Karen Moore; Tel: 314-963-4675, E-mail: kmoore@brentwoodmo.org; Staff 11 (MLS 4, Non-MLS 7)
Founded 1939. Pop 7,800; Circ 100,000
Jan 2009-Dec 2009 Income $500,344. Mats Exp $60,773
Library Holdings: Large Print Bks 31; Bk Titles 53,702; Bk Vols 54,238; Per Subs 81; Talking Bks 90; Videos 210
Automation Activity & Vendor Info: (Cataloging) SirsiDynix; (Circulation) SirsiDynix
Database Vendor: EBSCOhost, SirsiDynix
Wireless access
Partic in Municipal Library Consortium
Open Mon-Thurs 9-9, Fri 9-6, Sat 9-5
Friends of the Library Group

BRIDGETON

M DEPAUL HEALTH CENTER*, Medical Library, 12303 DePaul Dr, 63044-2588. SAN 326-0232. Tel: 314-344-6397. FAX: 314-344-6035. *Dir,* Lynne Klippel; Staff 1 (MLS 1)
Library Holdings: Bk Titles 540; Bk Vols 580; Per Subs 120
Subject Interests: Adult health
Open Mon-Fri 7:30-4
Restriction: Lending to staff only

BROOKFIELD

P BROOKFIELD PUBLIC LIBRARY*, 102 E Boston St, 64628. SAN 308-9428. Tel: 660-258-7439. FAX: 660-258-5626. Web Site: www.brookfield.lib.mo.us. *Dir,* Gina Smith; E-mail: gsmith@brookfield.lib.mo.us
Founded 1918. Pop 4,888; Circ 31,434
Library Holdings: Bk Vols 33,000; Per Subs 78
Subject Interests: Genealogy, Linn Co hist
Automation Activity & Vendor Info: (Cataloging) Mandarin Library Automation; (Circulation) Mandarin Library Automation
Mem of Waukesha County Federated Library System
Partic in Grand Rivers Libr Conference
Open Mon-Fri 10-6, Sat 10-4

BRUNSWICK

P BRUNSWICK PUBLIC LIBRARY*, 115 W Broadway, 65236. (Mail add: 310 W Broadway, 65236), SAN 375-0299. Tel: 660-548-1026, 660-548-3237. E-mail: brunswicklibrary@centurytel.net. *Dir,* Lynn Leimkuehler; Staff 1 (MLS 1)
Founded 1973. Pop 1,000
Library Holdings: Large Print Bks 34; Bk Titles 14,500; Bk Vols 15,000; Talking Bks 20; Videos 95
Function: Res libr
Open Mon & Fri 10-12 & 2-4, Tues & Thurs 3-5, Wed 10-12 & 2-8

BUFFALO

S DALLAS COUNTY HISTORICAL SOCIETY*, Historical & Genealogical Library, 224 Hemlock Dr, 65622-8649. SAN 373-2320. Tel: 417-345-7297. FAX: 417-345-7297. *In Charge,* Leni Howe; Staff 1 (Non-MLS 1)
Library Holdings: Bk Vols 705
Restriction: Open by appt only

P DALLAS COUNTY LIBRARY*, 219 W Main, 65622. (Mail add: PO Box 1008, 65622-1008), SAN 308-9436. Tel: 417-345-2647. FAX: 417-345-2647. Web Site: dallascountylibrary.missouri.org. *Dir,* Nancy Bradley; E-mail: sgy000@gmail.com; Staff 4 (Non-MLS 4)
Pop 16,107; Circ 99,556
Library Holdings: Audiobooks 1,225; Microforms 164; Bk Titles 26,970; Per Subs 25; Videos 2,361
Automation Activity & Vendor Info: (Cataloging) Follett Software; (Circulation) Follett Software; (ILL) OCLC FirstSearch
Database Vendor: OCLC FirstSearch
Partic in Amigos Library Services, Inc
Open Mon-Fri 8-5:30, Sat 8-12
Friends of the Library Group

BUTLER

P BUTLER PUBLIC LIBRARY*, 100 W Atkinson, 64730. SAN 308-9444. Tel: 660-679-4321. FAX: 660-679-4321. Web Site: www.butlerpubliclibrary.org. *Dir,* Linda Hunter; *Circ,* Linda Dickens; *Circ,* Pam Thompson
Founded 1926. Pop 15,000
Library Holdings: Bk Vols 33,000; Per Subs 17
Automation Activity & Vendor Info: (Cataloging) Follett Software; (Circulation) Follett Software
Open Mon-Fri 9:30-5:30, Sat 9:30-3:30
Friends of the Library Group

CALIFORNIA

P MONITEAU COUNTY LIBRARY @ WOOD PLACE*, 501 S Oak St, 65018. SAN 308-9452. Tel: 573-796-2642. FAX: 573-796-6108. E-mail: librarian@woodplacelibrary.org. Web Site: www.woodplacelibrary.org. *Dir,* Connie Walker; *Asst Dir,* Nancy Lewis
Founded 1956. Pop 10,472
Library Holdings: Bk Titles 14,000; Bk Vols 15,131; Per Subs 22; Talking Bks 382; Videos 217
Automation Activity & Vendor Info: (Acquisitions) Follett Software; (Cataloging) Follett Software; (Circulation) Follett Software; (Media Booking) Follett Software; (OPAC) Follett Software
Wireless access
Open Mon, Wed & Fri 10-5, Tues & Thurs 10-8, Sat 9-1
Friends of the Library Group

CAMDENTON

P CAMDEN COUNTY LIBRARY DISTRICT*, Camdenton Library, 89 Rodeo Rd, 65020. (Mail add: PO Box 1320, 65020-1320), SAN 377-1032. Tel: 573-346-5954. FAX: 573-346-1263. Web Site: www.ccld.us. *Dir,* Carolyn F Chittenden; E-mail: carolync@ccld.us; Staff 15 (MLS 1, Non-MLS 14)
Founded 1934. Pop 38,702; Circ 188,017
Library Holdings: Audiobooks 2,019; CDs 214; DVDs 3,536; Bk Vols 97,109; Per Subs 243; Videos 192
Automation Activity & Vendor Info: (Cataloging) Innovative Interfaces, Inc; (Circulation) Innovative Interfaces, Inc; (ILL) OCLC; (OPAC) Innovative Interfaces, Inc
Database Vendor: Amigos Library Services, Baker & Taylor, EBSCO Auto Repair Reference, EBSCOhost, Gale Cengage Learning, Medline, OCLC WorldShare Interlibrary Loan, Overdrive, Inc, ProQuest
Wireless access
Function: Bks on cassette, Bks on CD, Children's prog, Computer training, Computers for patron use, Copy machines, Doc delivery serv, Electronic databases & coll, Fax serv, Free DVD rentals, Genealogy discussion group, ILL available, Magnifiers for reading, Prog for children & young adult, Summer reading prog, Tax forms, VHS videos, Wheelchair accessible
Partic in Mo Libr Asn
Open Mon 9-8, Tues-Fri 9-6, Sat 9-5
Restriction: Open to pub for ref & circ; with some limitations
Branches: 5
CLIMAX SPRINGS BRANCH, 14157 N State Hwy 7, Climax Springs, 65324, SAN 377-4147. Tel: 573-347-2722. FAX: 573-347-2722. *Librn,* Carolee Apperson; Staff 1 (MLS 1)
Library Holdings: Bk Titles 7,280; Bk Vols 7,410; Per Subs 24; Talking Bks 50; Videos 50
Partic in Mo Libr Asn
Open Tues-Thurs 9-5, Sat 9-1
MACKS CREEK BRANCH, 90 State Rd N, Macks Creek, 65786. Tel: 573-363-5530. *Mgr, Br Serv,* Joan Evans; Staff 1 (Non-MLS 1)
Function: Children's prog, Copy machines, e-mail serv, Electronic databases & coll, Fax serv, Free DVD rentals, ILL available, Online cat, OverDrive digital audio bks, Preschool reading prog, Prog for children & young adult, Pub access computers, Story hour, Summer reading prog, Tax forms
Open Tues-Thurs 9-5, Sat 9-1
OSAGE BEACH BRANCH, 1064 Gutridge Lane, Osage Beach, 65065. Tel: 573-348-3282. FAX: 573-348-2883. *Mgr, Br Serv,* Karen Colgan; Staff 1 (Non-MLS 1)
Open Mon & Wed-Fri 10-6, Tues 10-8, Sat 9-5
STOUTLAND BRANCH, 132 Starling Ave, Stoutland, 65567. Tel: 417-286-3611. FAX: 417-286-3611. *Mgr, Br Serv,* Marie Brown; Staff 1 (Non-MLS 1)
Open Tues-Thurs 9-5, Sat 9-1
SUNRISE BEACH BRANCH, 14156 N State Hwy 5, Sunrise Beach, 65079. (Mail add: PO Box 1206, Sunrise Beach, 65079), SAN 377-2764. Tel: 573-374-6982. FAX: 573-374-6982. *Librn,* Claire Hammerschmidt; Staff 1 (MLS 1)
Library Holdings: Large Print Bks 10; Bk Titles 9,680, Bk Vols 9,830; Per Subs 38; Talking Bks 51; Videos 76
Open Tues-Fri 9-5, Sat 9-1

CANTON

P CANTON PUBLIC LIBRARY*, 403 Lewis St, 63435. SAN 308-9460. Tel: 573-288-5279. FAX: 573-288-5279. E-mail: cantonlibrarydirector@gmail.com. *Libr Dir,* L Susan Lowman; Staff 3 (Non-MLS 3)
Founded 1929. Pop 2,616; Circ 18,618
Library Holdings: Bk Titles 18,115; Bk Vols 18,448, Per Subs 13
Special Collections: Meridian Library; War of the Rebellion
Subject Interests: Adult fiction, Adult non-fiction, Juv fiction, Juv non-fiction
Open Mon-Fri 10-6, Sat 10-2

CR CULVER-STOCKTON COLLEGE*, Carl Johann Memorial Library, One College Hill, 63435. SAN 308-9479. Tel: 573-288-6321. FAX: 573-288-6615. Web Site: www.culver.edu/library. *Libr Dir,* Sharon K Upchurch; E-mail: supchurch@culver.edu; *Asst Librn,* Tammy Ellison; Tel: 573-288-6641, E-mail: tellison@culver.edu; *Archivist,* Carla Steinbeck; Tel: 573-288-6369, E-mail: csteinbeck@culver.edu; *Media Coordr,* Julie Wright; Tel: 573-288-6640, E-mail: jwright@culver.edu. Subject Specialists: *Children's lit,* Sharon K Upchurch; *Rare bks,* Carla Steinbeck; Staff 4 (MLS 1, Non-MLS 3)
Founded 1853. Enrl 855; Fac 50; Highest Degree: Bachelor
Library Holdings: e-books 6,000; Bk Vols 164,611; Per Subs 196
Special Collections: American Freedom Studies; History & Literature of Missouri & Midwest; History of Christian Church (Disciples of Christ Coll); Mark Twain Coll; Midwest Americana. Oral History
Subject Interests: Hist, Relig studies
Automation Activity & Vendor Info: (Acquisitions) Innovative Interfaces, Inc; (Cataloging) Innovative Interfaces, Inc; (Circulation) Innovative Interfaces, Inc; (Course Reserve) Innovative Interfaces, Inc; (ILL) Innovative Interfaces, Inc; (OPAC) Innovative Interfaces, Inc; (Serials) Innovative Interfaces, Inc

Database Vendor: EBSCOhost, JSTOR, LexisNexis, Newsbank, OCLC FirstSearch, OCLC WorldShare Interlibrary Loan, ProQuest, SerialsSolutions, Wilson - Wilson Web
Wireless access
Function: Art exhibits, AV serv, Homework prog, ILL available, Online searches, VHS videos
Publications: ExLibris (Newsletter)
Partic in Amigos Library Services, Inc; Missouri Research & Education Network (MOREnet); MOBIUS (Missouri Bibliographic Information User System); OCLC Online Computer Library Center, Inc
Open Mon-Thurs 8am-10:30pm, Fri 8-5, Sat 1-5, Sun 1-10:30
Friends of the Library Group

CAPE GIRARDEAU

P CAPE GIRARDEAU PUBLIC LIBRARY*, 711 N Clark St, 63701. SAN 308-9487. Tel: 573-334-5279. FAX: 573-334-8334. Web Site: www.capelibrary.org. *Dir,* Elizabeth Martin; E-mail: bmartin@capelibrary.org; Staff 4 (MLS 1, Non-MLS 3)
Founded 1922. Pop 35,590; Circ 243,507
Jul 2011-Jun 2012 Income $1,709,110, State $17,774, Federal $16,210, Locally Generated Income $1,675,126. Mats Exp $145,631, Books $89,500, Per/Ser (Incl. Access Fees) $6,800, Micro $900, AV Mat $17,463, Electronic Ref Mat (Incl. Access Fees) $23,119. Sal $569,138 (Prof $152,469)
Library Holdings: Audiobooks 4,088; CDs 2,084; DVDs 5,125; e-books 9,972; Large Print Bks 2,565; Bk Titles 86,069; Bk Vols 99,102; Per Subs 135; Videos 870
Special Collections: DAC & DAR Coll; Groves Genealogy Coll; Hirsch Foreign Language for Children; Mississippi River Valley Coll
Automation Activity & Vendor Info: (Acquisitions) SirsiDynix; (Cataloging) SirsiDynix; (Circulation) SirsiDynix; (ILL) OCLC FirstSearch; (OPAC) SirsiDynix
Database Vendor: Amigos Library Services, EBSCOhost, Facts on File, Foundation Center, Gale Cengage Learning, LearningExpress, OCLC FirstSearch, SirsiDynix, Tech Logic, WT Cox
Wireless access
Function: Adult bk club, Art exhibits, Bks on cassette, Bks on CD, Children's prog, Computer training, Computers for patron use, Copy machines, Fax serv, Free DVD rentals, Handicapped accessible, Holiday prog, Homebound delivery serv, ILL available, Magnifiers for reading, Music CDs, Notary serv, Online cat, OverDrive digital audio bks, Photocopying/Printing, Preschool outreach, Prog for adults, Prog for children & young adult, Pub access computers, Ref serv in person, Scanner, Spanish lang bks, Spoken cassettes & CDs, Story hour, Summer & winter reading prog, Summer reading prog, Tax forms, Teen prog, Telephone ref, VHS videos, Winter reading prog
Partic in Amigos Library Services, Inc
Special Services for the Blind - Volunteer serv
Open Mon-Thurs 9-9, Fri & Sat 9-5, Sun 1-5
Restriction: Non-resident fee
Friends of the Library Group

C SOUTHEAST MISSOURI STATE UNIVERSITY*, Kent Library, One University Plaza, Mail Stop 4600, 63701. SAN 308-9495. Tel: 573-651-2235. Circulation Tel: 573-651-2232. Interlibrary Loan Service Tel: 573-651-2152. Information Services Tel: 573-651-2230. FAX: 573-651-2666. Interlibrary Loan Service FAX: 573-651-2969. E-mail: circulationdesk@semo.edu. Web Site: library.semo.edu. *Dean, Acad Info Serv, Dir,* David Starrett; Tel: 573-651-2298, E-mail: dstarrett@semo.edu; *Head, Bibliog Control,* Catherine G Roeder; Tel: 573-651-2745, E-mail: croeder@semo.edu; *Head, Syst & Tech Support,* Jason Bruenderman; Tel: 573-986-6833, E-mail: jbruenderman@semo.edu; *Head, Access Serv,* Daenel Vaughn-Tucker; Tel: 573-651-2797, E-mail: dvtucker@semo.edu; *Head, Acq,* Mary Langston; Tel: 573-651-2746, E-mail: mlangston@semo.edu; Staff 16 (MLS 8, Non-MLS 8)
Founded 1873. Enrl 11,729; Fac 395; Highest Degree: Master
Library Holdings: Audiobooks 165; CDs 4,183; DVDs 4,730; e-books 7,594; e-journals 65,990; Microforms 1,227,884; Bk Titles 368,716; Bk Vols 439,445; Per Subs 1,093; Videos 6,495
Special Collections: Brodsky Coll of William Faulkner Materials; Charles Harrison Rare Books Coll; Little River Drainage District Coll; Regional History Coll. State Document Depository; US Document Depository
Automation Activity & Vendor Info: (Acquisitions) Innovative Interfaces, Inc; (Cataloging) Innovative Interfaces, Inc; (Circulation) Innovative Interfaces, Inc; (Course Reserve) Innovative Interfaces, Inc; (ILL) OCLC ILLiad; (Media Booking) Innovative Interfaces, Inc; (OPAC) Innovative Interfaces, Inc; (Serials) Innovative Interfaces, Inc
Wireless access
Partic in Amigos Library Services, Inc; MOBIUS (Missouri Bibliographic Information User System); OCLC Online Computer Library Center, Inc
Open Mon-Thurs 7:30am-Midnight, Fri 7:30-6, Sat Noon-5, Sun 1-11

S SOUTHEAST MISSOURIAN NEWSPAPER LIBRARY*, 301 Broadway, 63701-7330. (Mail add: PO Box 699, 63702-0699), SAN 329-7128. Tel: 573-335-6611, Ext 136. Toll Free Tel: 800-879-1210. Web Site: www.semissourian.com. *Librn,* Sharon K Sanders; E-mail: ssanders@semissourian.com; Staff 1 (MLS 1)
Founded 1965
Library Holdings: AV Mats 744; Bk Titles 691; Per Subs 10
Special Collections: Historical Research Notes; Newspaper Clippings (1965-present); Southeast Missourian & Bulletin-Journal Newspapers, microfilm
Open Mon-Fri 8-3:30

CARROLLTON

P CARROLLTON PUBLIC LIBRARY*, One N Folger, 64633. SAN 308-9509. Tel: 660-542-0183. FAX: 660-542-0654. E-mail: cplstaff@carrolltonlibrary.com. Web Site: www.carrolltonlibrary.com. *Dir,* Susan Lightfoot; E-mail: director@carrolltonlibrary.com; Staff 4 (MLS 1, Non-MLS 3)
Founded 1938. Pop 3,784; Circ 65,000
Library Holdings: Large Print Bks 10; Bk Titles 23,714; Bk Vols 24,119; Per Subs 58; Talking Bks 157; Videos 38
Automation Activity & Vendor Info: (Acquisitions) Baker & Taylor; (Cataloging) Evergreen; (Circulation) Evergreen; (Course Reserve) Evergreen; (ILL) Evergreen; (Media Booking) Evergreen; (OPAC) Evergreen; (Serials) Evergreen
Database Vendor: Amigos Library Services, Baker & Taylor, EBSCOhost
Wireless access
Function: Accelerated reader prog, Accessibility serv available based on individual needs, Adult bk club, Adult literacy prog, After school storytime, Alaskana res, Archival coll, Art exhibits, Audio & video playback equip for onsite use, Audiobks via web, AV serv, BA reader (adult literacy), Bi-weekly Writer's Group, Bilingual assistance for Spanish patrons, Bk club(s), Bk reviews (Group), Bks on cassette, Bks on CD, Bus archives, CD-ROM, Chess club, Children's prog, Citizenship assistance, Computer training, Computers for patron use, Copy machines, Digital talking bks, Distance learning, Doc delivery serv, e-mail & chat, e-mail serv, E-Reserves, Electronic databases & coll, Equip loans & repairs, Exhibits, Family literacy, Fax serv, For res purposes, Free DVD rentals, Games & aids for the handicapped, Genealogy discussion group, Govt ref serv, Handicapped accessible, Health sci info serv, Holiday prog, Home delivery & serv to Sr ctr & nursing homes, Homebound delivery serv, Homework prog, ILL available, Instruction & testing, Jail serv, Jazz prog, Large print keyboards, Learning ctr, Legal assistance to inmates, Libr develop, Literacy & newcomer serv, Magnifiers for reading, Mail & tel request accepted, Mail loans to mem, Masonic res mat, Microfiche/film & reading machines, Monthly prog for perceptually impaired adults, Mus passes, Music CDs, Newsp ref libr, Notary serv, Online cat, Online info literacy tutorials on the web & in blackboard, Online ref, Online searches, Orientations, Outreach serv, Outside serv via phone, mail, e-mail & web, OverDrive digital audio bks, Passport agency, Photocopying/Printing, Preschool outreach, Preschool reading prog, Printer for laptops & handheld devices, Prof lending libr, Prog for adults, Prog for children & young adult, Provide serv for the mentally ill, Pub access computers, Ref & res, Ref serv available, Ref serv in person, Referrals accepted, Res libr, Res performed for a fee, Satellite serv, Scanner, Senior computer classes, Senior outreach, Serves mentally handicapped consumers, Spanish lang bks, Specialized serv in classical studies, Spoken cassettes & CDs, Spoken cassettes & DVDs, Story hour, Summer & winter reading prog, Tax forms, Teen prog, Telephone ref, VCDs, VHS videos, Video lending libr, Visual arts prog, Web-Braille, Web-catalog, Wheelchair accessible, Words travel prog, Workshops
Partic in Grand Rivers Libr Conference
Open Mon, Tues, Thurs & Fri 9-5:30, Wed 9-8, Sat 9-1, Sun 1-5
Friends of the Library Group
Bookmobiles: 5. Dir, Sue Lightfoot

CARTHAGE

P CARTHAGE PUBLIC LIBRARY*, 612 S Garrison Ave, 64836. SAN 308-9517. Tel: 417-237-7040. FAX: 417-237-7041. E-mail: carthage@carthagelibrary.net. Web Site: carthage.lib.mo.us. *Dir,* Julie Yockey; E-mail: jyockey@carthagelibrary.net; *Dir, Youth Serv,* Debra Haynes; E-mail: dhaynes@carthagelibrary.net; Staff 11 (Non-MLS 11)
Founded 1902. Pop 12,668; Circ 88,738
Library Holdings: AV Mats 1,114; Bks on Deafness & Sign Lang 25; e-books 6,700; Large Print Bks 2,481; Bk Titles 48,879; Bk Vols 52,984; Per Subs 139; Talking Bks 1,135
Automation Activity & Vendor Info: (Cataloging) Follett Software; (Circulation) Follett Software; (ILL) OCLC Online; (OPAC) Follett Software
Database Vendor: EBSCOhost, OCLC FirstSearch
Function: AV serv, ILL available, Magnifiers for reading, Online searches, Photocopying/Printing, Prog for children & young adult, Ref serv available,

Referrals accepted, Summer reading prog, Telephone ref, Wheelchair accessible
Partic in Amigos Library Services, Inc
Special Services for the Deaf - TTY equip
Open Tues 9-8, Wed-Fri 9-6, Sat 9-4
Friends of the Library Group

CARUTHERSVILLE

P CARUTHERSVILLE PUBLIC LIBRARY*, 707 W 13th St, 63830. SAN 308-9525. Tel: 573-333-2480. FAX: 573-333-0552. *Dir,* Brenda Davis; Staff 4 (Non-MLS 4)
Founded 1922. Pop 7,958; Circ 34,616
Jul 2007-Jun 2008 Income $164,858. Mats Exp $20,093
Library Holdings: Bk Titles 24,117; Bk Vols 25,684; Per Subs 32; Talking Bks 371; Videos 718
Subject Interests: Behav sci, Educ, Genealogy, Law, Relig studies, Soc sci
Automation Activity & Vendor Info: (Cataloging) TLC (The Library Corporation); (Circulation) TLC (The Library Corporation)
Database Vendor: EBSCOhost
Open Mon 9:30-6:30, Tues-Fri 9:30-5:30, Sat 9:30-1:30

CENTER

P RALLS COUNTY LIBRARY*, 100 N Public, 63436-1000. (Mail add: PO Box 259, 63436-0259), SAN 377-2721. Tel: 573-267-3200. FAX: 573-267-3200. *Dir,* Kay Amos; Staff 2 (MLS 1, Non-MLS 1)
Founded 1992. Pop 9,626; Circ 17,231
Jan 2007-Dec 2007 Income $146,842. Mats Exp $45,412
Library Holdings: DVDs 30; Bk Titles 16,000; Bk Vols 16,400; Per Subs 61; Talking Bks 250; Videos 652
Wireless access
Open Mon-Fri 8:30-5:30

CENTERVILLE

P REYNOLDS COUNTY LIBRARY DISTRICT*, Centerville Branch, 2306 Pine St, 63633. (Mail add: PO Box 175, 63633-0175), SAN 349-8727. Tel: 573-648-2471. FAX: 573-648-2471. E-mail: centervillebranchlibrary@yahoo.com. Web Site: reynoldscountylibrarydistrict.webs.com. *Dir,* Patsy Rainwater; E-mail: reynoldscountylibrary@yahoo.com; *Br Librn,* Mary Dement; Staff 2 (Non-MLS 2)
Pop 6,689; Circ 35,952
Library Holdings: Audiobooks 344; DVDs 41; Bk Titles 8,421; Per Subs 4
Open Mon, Wed & Fri 8-4:30
Branches: 4
BUNKER BRANCH, 203 N Main St, Bunker, 63629. (Mail add: PO Box 67, Bunker, 63629-0067), SAN 349-8697. Tel: 573-689-2718. Administration Tel: 573-648-2471. FAX: 573-689-2718. E-mail: bunkerbranchlibrary@yahoo.com. *Br Librn,* Lesa Bishop; Staff 1 (Non-MLS 1)
Library Holdings: Audiobooks 245; Bk Titles 9,363; Per Subs 4; Videos 170
Database Vendor: Main Library Systems
Open Mon-Fri 8:30-4:30
ELLINGTON BRANCH, 130 S Main, Ellington, 63638. (Mail add: PO Box 485, Ellington, 63638), SAN 349-8751. Tel: 573-663-7289. FAX: 573-663-7289. E-mail: ellingtonlibrary@yahoo.com. *Br Librn,* April Amsden; Staff 1 (Non-MLS 1)
Library Holdings: Audiobooks 302; Bk Titles 10,782; Per Subs 5; Videos 194
Open Mon-Fri 8:30-5
LESTERVILLE BRANCH, 33285 Hwy 21, Lesterville, 63654, SAN 349-8875. Tel: 573-637-2532. Administration Tel: 573-648-2471. FAX: 573-637-2532. E-mail: lestervillebranchlibrary@yahoo.com. *Br Librn,* Mary Dement; Staff 1 (Non-MLS 1)
Library Holdings: Audiobooks 257; Bk Titles 7,466; Per Subs 3
Open Tues & Thurs 8-4:30, Wed 8-12
OATES BRANCH, 8490 Hwy J, Black, 63625, SAN 349-8964. Tel: 573-269-1117. Administration Tel: 573-648-2471. FAX: 573-269-1117. *Br Librn,* Megan Bishop; E-mail: oatesbranchlibrary@yahoo.com; Staff 1 (Non-MLS 1)
Library Holdings: Audiobooks 44; Bk Titles 3,079; Per Subs 2; Videos 3
Open Mon & Fri 8:30-12, Wed 1-5

CENTRALIA

P CENTRALIA PUBLIC LIBRARY*, 210 S Jefferson St, 65240. SAN 308-9533. Tel: 573-682-2036. FAX: 573-682-5556. E-mail: centraliapl@gmail.com. Web Site: www.centraliapubliclibrary.com. *Dir,* Pat Olsen; Staff 1 (Non-MLS 1)
Founded 1903. Pop 3,791; Circ 46,821
Library Holdings: Large Print Bks 24; Bk Titles 19,429; Bk Vols 19,500; Per Subs 63; Videos 290
Special Collections: Missouri Bks
Automation Activity & Vendor Info: (Cataloging) Innovative Interfaces, Inc; (Circulation) Innovative Interfaces, Inc
Database Vendor: EBSCOhost
Open Mon, Tues & Thurs 9-8, Wed, Fri & Sat 9-5
Friends of the Library Group

CHAFFEE

P CHAFFEE PUBLIC LIBRARY, 202 Wright Ave, 63740. SAN 308-9541. Tel: 573-887-3298. FAX: 573-887-3298. *Dir,* Tina Horton; *Librn,* Jennifer Nolen; Staff 1 (MLS 1)
Founded 1929. Pop 3,041; Circ 11,306
Apr 2010-Mar 2011. Mats Exp $8,500, Books $7,000, AV Mat $1,500. Sal $20,300
Library Holdings: Audiobooks 22; Bks-By-Mail 150; Bks on Deafness & Sign Lang 4; Braille Volumes 2; CDs 43; DVDs 434; Large Print Bks 17; Bk Titles 13,113; Bk Vols 16,614; Per Subs 12; Talking Bks 91; Videos 79
Automation Activity & Vendor Info: (Cataloging) Follett Software
Open Mon-Fri 10-6, Sat 10-1

CHARLESTON

P MISSISSIPPI COUNTY LIBRARY DISTRICT*, Clara Drinkwater Newnam Library, 105 E Marshall St, 63834. (Mail add: PO Box 160, 63834-0160), SAN 348-9817. Tel: 573-683-6748. FAX: 573-683-2761. E-mail: mx92000@yahoo.com. Web Site: missco.lib.mo.us. *Dir,* Stephanie R Bledsoe
Founded 1945. Pop 14,442; Circ 59,579
Library Holdings: Bks on Deafness & Sign Lang 15; Bk Vols 41,983; Per Subs 196
Special Collections: State & Local History Coll, micro, print, VF
Automation Activity & Vendor Info: (Acquisitions) TLC (The Library Corporation); (Cataloging) TLC (The Library Corporation); (Circulation) TLC (The Library Corporation)
Database Vendor: EBSCOhost, OCLC FirstSearch
Partic in Amigos Library Services, Inc
Open Mon, Tues, Thurs & Fri 8-5, Wed 8-8, Sat 8-4
Branches: 1
MITCHELL MEMORIAL, 204 E Washington St, East Prairie, 63845, SAN 348-9841. Tel: 573-649-2131. FAX: 573-649-2131. *Dir,* Stephanie Bledsoe
Open Mon 12-8, Tues-Fri 12-5, Sat 10-2

CHESTERFIELD

CM LOGAN UNIVERSITY/COLLEGE OF CHIROPRACTIC LIBRARY*, Learning Resources Center, 1851 Schoettler Rd, 63006. (Mail add: PO Box 1065, 63006-1065), SAN 308-955X. Tel: 636-227-2100. Circulation Tel: 636-227-2100, Ext 1781. Interlibrary Loan Service Tel: 636-227-2100, Ext 1760. Reference Tel: 636-227-2100, Ext 1788. Automation Services Tel: 636-227-2100, Ext 1783. Information Services Tel: 636-227-2100, Ext 1766. Toll Free Tel: 800-782-3344. FAX: 636-207-2448. E-mail: circdesk@logan.edu. Web Site: www.logan.edu. *Dir,* Chaba Hocine Tepe; E-mail: chabha.tepe@logan.edu; *Archivist, Cat Librn,* Christina Prucha; *Electronic Res Librn, Ref Librn,* Sheryl Walters; Staff 2 (MLS 2)
Founded 1960. Enrl 1,100; Fac 94; Highest Degree: Doctorate
Library Holdings: AV Mats 1,500; CDs 250; DVDs 500; Bk Titles 11,000; Bk Vols 13,000; Per Subs 240; Videos 750
Special Collections: Osseous, Human & Synthetic; State Chiropractic Association Newsletters
Subject Interests: Chiropractic, Neurology, Nutrition, Orthopedics, Radiology
Automation Activity & Vendor Info: (Acquisitions) Innovative Interfaces, Inc; (Cataloging) Innovative Interfaces, Inc; (Circulation) Innovative Interfaces, Inc; (OPAC) Innovative Interfaces, Inc; (Serials) Innovative Interfaces, Inc
Database Vendor: EBSCOhost, Elsevier, Gale Cengage Learning, Innovative Interfaces, Inc, OCLC WorldShare Interlibrary Loan, OVID Technologies, PubMed, ScienceDirect
Wireless access
Function: Ref serv available
Publications: In Touch (Bibliographies)
Partic in Chiropractic Libr Consortium; MOBIUS (Missouri Bibliographic Information User System)
Open Mon-Thurs 7am-10pm, Fri 7-5, Sat 10-5, Sun 12-5

CHILLICOTHE

P LIVINGSTON COUNTY LIBRARY*, 450 Locust St, 64601-2597. SAN 308-9568. Tel: 660-646-0547. FAX: 660-646-5504. E-mail: librarian@livingstoncountylibrary.org. Web Site: www.livingstoncountylibrary.org. *Dir,* Robin S Westphal; *Ch,* Judith Cunning Shoot; Staff 11 (MLS 2, Non-MLS 9)

Founded 1921. Pop 14,558; Circ 145,483
Jan 2007-Dec 2007 Income $556,000. Mats Exp $73,000. Sal $256,000
Library Holdings: AV Mats 2,084; e-books 6,000; Bk Titles 44,000; Bk Vols 54,000; Per Subs 100; Videos 1,000
Special Collections: Missouri History (George Somerville Coll)
Database Vendor: EBSCOhost
Wireless access
Open Mon-Thurs 9-7, Fri 9-5, Sat 9-4
Friends of the Library Group

CLAYTON

GL SAINT LOUIS COUNTY LAW LIBRARY*, Courts Bldg, Ste 536, 7900 Carondelet Ave, 63105. SAN 308-9584. Tel: 314-615-4726. *Librn,* Mary C Dahm; Staff 2 (MLS 1, Non-MLS 1)
Library Holdings: Bk Titles 30,000; Bk Vols 31,000; Per Subs 20
Open Mon-Thurs 8-6, Fri 8-5

CLEVER

P CLEVER PUBLIC LIBRARY, 210 S Clarke, 65631. (Mail add: PO Box 44, 65631). Tel: 417-743-2277. FAX: 417-743-2277. E-mail: clever@christiancountylibrary.org. *Dir,* Geri Olmstead; Tel: 417-209-7126, E-mail: golmstead@christiancountylibrary.org; *Libr Asst,* Dale Maisel; E-mail: dmaisel@christiancountylibrary.org
Founded 1949
Library Holdings: Bk Vols 9,000
Automation Activity & Vendor Info: (Cataloging) Innovative Interfaces, Inc; (Circulation) Innovative Interfaces, Inc; (ILL) OCLC; (OPAC) Innovative Interfaces, Inc
Open Tues-Fri 3-7, Sat 9-2
Friends of the Library Group

CLINTON

P HENRY COUNTY LIBRARY*, 123 E Green St, 64735-1462. SAN 308-9592. Tel: 660-885-2612. Toll Free Tel: 866-225-5425. FAX: 660-885-8953. Web Site: tacnet.missouri.org/hcl. *Dir of Libr Serv,* Elizabeth A Cashell; *Br Mgr,* Lenora Blackmore; Staff 14 (MLS 3, Non-MLS 11)
Founded 1946. Pop 19,215; Circ 147,319
Library Holdings: Large Print Bks 115; Bk Vols 80,000; Per Subs 96; Talking Bks 2,115; Videos 1,284
Subject Interests: Local hist
Automation Activity & Vendor Info: (Cataloging) Book Systems; (Circulation) Book Systems
Wireless access
Open Mon-Thurs 8am-9pm, Fri & Sat 8-5
Friends of the Library Group

COLUMBIA

P DANIEL BOONE REGIONAL LIBRARY*, Columbia Public Library-Headquarters, 100 W Broadway, 65203. (Mail add: PO Box 1267, 65205-1267), SAN 348-9876. Tel: 573-443-3161. Toll Free Tel: 800-324-4806. FAX: 573-443-3281. Administration FAX: 573-499-0191. TDD: 573-443-6027. Web Site: www.dbrl.org. *Dir,* Melissa Carr; E-mail: mcarr@dbrl.org; *Assoc Dir,* Elinor Barrett; *Adult Serv Mgr,* Patricia Miller; *Mgr, Ch & Youth Serv,* Sarah Howard; *Circ Mgr,* Patrick Finney; *Coll Develop Mgr,* Doyne McKenzie; *IT Mgr,* Mike Mullett; *Outreach Mgr,* Karen Neely; *Tech Serv Mgr,* Patricia Kopp; Staff 122 (MLS 25, Non-MLS 97)
Founded 1959. Pop 203,190; Circ 2,365,645
Library Holdings: Audiobooks 22,860; CDs 35,168; DVDs 29,691; Electronic Media & Resources 30,355; Bk Vols 421,613; Per Subs 925
Automation Activity & Vendor Info: (Acquisitions) SirsiDynix; (Cataloging) SirsiDynix; (Circulation) SirsiDynix; (OPAC) SirsiDynix
Wireless access
Function: Adult literacy prog, Art exhibits, Audiobks via web, Bks on CD, Children's prog, Computer training, Computers for patron use, Copy machines, e-mail & chat, Electronic databases & coll, Free DVD rentals, Handicapped accessible, Home delivery & serv to Sr ctr & nursing homes, Homebound delivery serv, ILL available, Mail & tel request accepted, Microfiche/film & reading machines, Music CDs, Notary serv, Online cat, Online ref, Online searches, Outreach serv, Outside serv via phone, mail, e-mail & web, OverDrive digital audio bks, Photocopying/Printing, Prog for adults, Prog for children & young adult, Pub access computers, Ref serv available, Ref serv in person, Scanner, Senior computer classes, Spoken cassettes & CDs, Spoken cassettes & DVDs, Story hour, Summer reading prog, Tax forms, Teen prog, Telephone ref, Web-catalog, Wheelchair accessible
Special Services for the Deaf - TDD equip
Open Mon-Thurs 9-9, Fri 9-6, Sat 9-5, Sun 1-5
Restriction: ID required to use computers (Ltd hrs)
Friends of the Library Group

Branches: 2
CALLAWAY COUNTY PUBLIC LIBRARY, 710 Court St, Fulton, 65251, SAN 348-9906. Tel: 573-642-7261. FAX: 573-642-4439. TDD: 573-642-0662. *Head Librn,* Greg Reeves; E-mail: greeves@dbrl.org; *Ref Librn,* Sherry McBride-Brown; *Ch Serv,* Jerilyn Hahn
Special Services for the Deaf - TDD equip
Open Mon-Thurs 9-9, Fri & Sat 9-5
Friends of the Library Group
SOUTHERN BOONE COUNTY PUBLIC LIBRARY, 109 N Main, Ashland, 65010. Tel: 573-657-7378. FAX: 573-657-0448. *Br Mgr,* Karen Neely; E-mail: kneely@dbrl.org
Founded 1999
Open Mon-Thurs 9-7, Fri & Sat 9-3
Friends of the Library Group
Bookmobiles: 2

SR CALVARY EPISCOPAL CHURCH LIBRARY*, 123 S Ninth St, 65201. SAN 326-0771. Tel: 573-449-3194. FAX: 573-442-9392. E-mail: info@calvaryonninth.org. Web Site: www.calvaryonninth.org. *Librn,* Donald Foster; Staff 1 (Non-MLS 1)
Founded 1975
Library Holdings: Bk Titles 1,500; Bk Vols 1,750; Videos 15
Subject Interests: Biblical studies, Church hist
Open Mon-Fri 9-5

C COLUMBIA COLLEGE*, J W & Lois Stafford Library, 1001 Rogers St, 65216. SAN 308-9606. Tel: 573-875-7381. Toll Free Tel: 800-231-2391, Ext 7381. FAX: 573-875-7379. E-mail: reference@ccis.edu. Web Site: library.ccis.edu. *Dir,* Janet Caruthers; Tel: 573-875-7376, E-mail: jaocaruthers@ccis.edu; *Asst Dir,* Dan Kammer; Tel: 573-875-4591, E-mail: dwkammer@ccis.edu; *Access Serv Librn,* Mary Batterson; Tel: 573-875-7373, E-mail: mebatterson@ccis.edu; *Ref Librn,* Lucia D'Agostino; Tel: 573-875-7395, E-mail: ladagostino@ccis.edu; *Syst Librn,* Nason Throgmorton; Tel: 573-875-7231, E-mail: nlthrogmorton@ccis.edu; *Tech Serv Librn,* Vandy Evermon; Tel: 573-875-7370, E-mail: vlevermon@ccis.edu; Staff 6 (MLS 6)
Founded 1851. Highest Degree: Master
Jul 2013-Jun 2014. Mats Exp $335,000, Books $45,000, Per/Ser (Incl. Access Fees) $40,000, Electronic Ref Mat (Incl. Access Fees) $250,000
Library Holdings: CDs 350; DVDs 250; e-books 200,000; Bk Vols 60,000; Per Subs 200; Videos 1,000
Subject Interests: Bus, Criminal justice, Educ, Hist, Lit
Automation Activity & Vendor Info: (Acquisitions) Innovative Interfaces, Inc - Millenium; (Cataloging) Innovative Interfaces, Inc - Millenium; (Circulation) Innovative Interfaces, Inc - Millenium; (Course Reserve) Innovative Interfaces, Inc - Millenium; (ILL) OCLC; (Media Booking) Innovative Interfaces, Inc - Millenium; (OPAC) Innovative Interfaces, Inc - Millenium; (Serials) Innovative Interfaces, Inc - Millenium
Database Vendor: Alexander Street Press, American Chemical Society, Amigos Library Services, Baker & Taylor, Bowker, Cinahl, CQ Press, CredoReference, ebrary, EBSCO Discovery Service, EBSCOhost, Gale Cengage Learning, H W Wilson, Innovative Interfaces, Inc, JSTOR, LearningExpress, LexisNexis, OCLC, Oxford Online, Project MUSE, ProQuest, Springshare, LLC, Standard & Poor's, ValueLine, Wilson - Wilson Web, YBP Library Services
Wireless access
Partic in Amigos Library Services, Inc; MOBIUS (Missouri Bibliographic Information User System); OCLC Online Computer Library Center, Inc
Open Mon-Thurs 8am-Midnight, Fri 8-8, Sat 9-5, Sun 2pm-Midnight
Restriction: Open to students, fac, staff & alumni

G COLUMBIA ENVIRONMENTAL RESEARCH CENTER LIBRARY*, US Geological Survey, 4200 New Haven Rd, 65201. SAN 308-9657. Tel: 573-876-1853. FAX: 573-876-1833. Web Site: www.cerc.usgs.gov/default.aspx. *Librn,* Julia Towns-Campbell; E-mail: jtowns@usgs.gov
Founded 1968
Library Holdings: Bk Titles 7,308; Bk Vols 9,000; Per Subs 80
Special Collections: Pesticides (Reprint Coll)
Subject Interests: Biol toxicity, Chem pesticides, Environ contaminants, Mo river, Water quality
Partic in OCLC Online Computer Library Center, Inc
Restriction: Open by appt only

GM DEPARTMENT OF VETERANS AFFAIRS, Harry S Truman Memorial Hospital Library, 800 Hospital Dr, 65201. SAN 308-9673. Tel: 573-814-6000, Ext 52704. FAX: 573-814-6516. *Head Librn,* Mark Fleetwood; *Med Librn,* Barbara Michael; E-mail: barbara.michael@va.gov; Staff 2 (MLS 2)
Founded 1972
Library Holdings: Bk Vols 2,000; Per Subs 100
Subject Interests: Allied health topics, Med
Partic in BRS; Coop Libr Agency for Syst & Servs; Dialog Corp; Mid-Mo Libr Network; Veterans Affairs Library Network (VALNET)

Special Services for the Deaf - High interest/low vocabulary bks
Open Mon-Fri 8-4:30

S NATIONAL ASSOCIATION OF ANIMAL BREEDERS LIBRARY*, 401 Bernadette Dr, 65203. (Mail add: PO Box 1033, 65205-1033), SAN 371-2532. Tel: 573-445-4406. FAX: 573-446-2279. E-mail: naab-css@naab-css.org. Web Site: www.naab-css.org. *Pres,* Gordon A Doak
Founded 1947
Library Holdings: Bk Vols 400
Open Mon-Fri 8-5

S STATE HISTORICAL SOCIETY OF MISSOURI LIBRARY, 1020 Lowry St, 65201-7298. SAN 308-9649. Tel: 573-882-1187. Interlibrary Loan Service Tel: 573-882-6029. Administration Tel: 573-882-7083. Toll Free Tel: 800-747-6366. FAX: 573-884-4950. E-mail: shsofmo@umsystem.edu. Web Site: shs.umsystem.edu. *Exec Dir,* Dr Gary R Kremer; E-mail: kremerg@umsystem.edu; *Assoc Dir,* Gerald Hirsch; Tel: 573-884-7906, E-mail: hirschg@umsystem.edu; *Asst Dir,* John Bradbury; Tel: 314-341-4874, E-mail: jfb@mst.edu; *Asst Dir,* William Fischetti; Tel: 314-516-5143, E-mail: Zelli@umsl.edu; *Asst Dir,* Frank Nickell; Tel: 573-651-2689, E-mail: fnickell@semo.edu; Staff 21 (MLS 8, Non-MLS 13)
Founded 1898
Special Collections: Church History (Bishop William F McMurry Coll); Literature (Mahan Memorial Mark Twain Coll & Eugene Field Coll); Manuscript Coll; Map Coll; Mid-Western History (J Christian Bay Coll); Missouri Newspapers (1808-present); Missouri's Literary Heritage for Children & Youth (Alice Irene Fitzgerald Coll); Photograph Coll; United States Census Coll, micro. Oral History
Subject Interests: Genealogy, Mo hist, Western hist
Wireless access
Function: Archival coll, Art exhibits, Audio & video playback equip for onsite use, Copy machines, Exhibits, ILL available, Mail & tel request accepted, Newsp ref libr, Online cat, Prog for adults, Ref serv available, Res performed for a fee
Publications: Missouri Historical Review (Quarterly); Missouri Times (Newsletter)
Open Tues-Fri 8-4:45, Sat 8-3:30
Restriction: Non-circulating
Friends of the Library Group

C STEPHENS COLLEGE, Hugh Stephens Library, 1200 E Broadway, 65215. SAN 348-9930. Tel: 573-876-7182. Reference Tel: 573-876-7181. FAX: 573-876-7264. E-mail: circulation@stephens.edu. Web Site: www.stephens.edu/student life/academic-support/hugh-stephens-library. *Dir,* Dan Kammer; E-mail: dkammer@stephens.edu; *Ref Librn,* James Walter; E-mail: jwalter@stephens.edu; *Circ Mgr,* Position Currently Open; *Access Serv,* Nina Stawski; E-mail: nstawski@stephens.edu; Staff 6 (MLS 3, Non-MLS 3)
Founded 1833. Enrl 740; Fac 76; Highest Degree: Master
Library Holdings: Bk Titles 115,000; Bk Vols 130,000
Special Collections: Educational Resources & Childrens Literature; Women's Studies Coll (Monographic)
Subject Interests: Women's studies
Automation Activity & Vendor Info: (Acquisitions) Innovative Interfaces, Inc; (Cataloging) Innovative Interfaces, Inc; (Circulation) Innovative Interfaces, Inc; (Course Reserve) Innovative Interfaces, Inc; (ILL) Innovative Interfaces, Inc; (Media Booking) Innovative Interfaces, Inc; (OPAC) Innovative Interfaces, Inc; (Serials) Innovative Interfaces, Inc
Wireless access
Publications: Annual report; Bibliographies
Partic in MOBIUS (Missouri Bibliographic Information User System); OCLC Online Computer Library Center, Inc
Open Mon-Thurs 8am-11pm, Fri 8-5, Sat 11-5, Sun 1-11

S TRIBUNE PUBLISHING CO, Columbia Daily Tribune Library, 101 N Fourth St, 65201-4416. (Mail add: PO Box 798, 65205-0798), SAN 373-4633. Tel: 573-815-1703. Information Services Tel: 573-815-1500. Toll Free Tel: 800-333-6799. FAX: 573-815-1701. Web Site: www.columbiatribune.com. *Archivist,* Mrs Cassidy Rohrer; E-mail: clrohrer@columbiatribune.com; Staff 1 (MLS 1)
Founded 1970
Special Collections: Columbia Daily Tribune 1901-present, microfilm; Columbia Daily Tribune Newspapers, hard copies
Function: Copy machines, Electronic databases & coll, For res purposes, Newsp ref libr, Online searches, Outside serv via phone, mail, e-mail & web, Photocopying/Printing, Ref serv available, Res libr, Res performed for a fee, Scanner, Telephone ref
Restriction: Circulates for staff only, Co libr, External users must contact libr, Fee for pub use, Internal use only, Lending to staff only, Limited access for the pub, Not a lending libr, Open to pub by appt only, Pub ref by request, Pub use on premises

C UNIVERSITY OF MISSOURI*, Western Historical Manuscript Collection - Columbia, 23 Ellis Library, 65201-5149. SAN 329-0115. Tel: 573-882-6028. FAX: 573-884-0345. E-mail: whmc@umsystem.edu. Web Site: www.umsystem.edu/whmc. *Assoc Dir,* David Moore; Tel: 573-882-0191; *Asst Dir, Coll,* Jennifer Lukomski; Tel: 573-882-7231, E-mail: lukomski@umsystem.edu; *Asst Dir, Ref,* William Stolz; Tel: 573-882-0188, E-mail: stolzw@umsystem.edu; Staff 17 (MLS 11, Non-MLS 6)
Founded 1943
Library Holdings: Bk Titles 18,076; Bk Vols 19,000; Per Subs 14
Special Collections: Archive of Soil Science; German Heritage Archives; Materials to Support Research & Teaching Interests of University of Missouri Faculty; Missouri Folklore-Folklife Archives; National Women & Media Coll; Oral History (Politics in Missouri Project & Missouri Ex-POWs Project); Papers of Present & Former Missourians; Records of Organizations in Missouri. Oral History
Function: For res purposes
Publications: Missouri Times (Newsletter)
Open Mon-Fri 8-4:45, Sat 8-3:30

UNIVERSITY OF MISSOURI-COLUMBIA

C ACADEMIC SUPPORT CENTER MEDIA RENTAL LIBRARY*, 505 E Stewart Rd, 65211-2040, SAN 308-9665. Tel: 573-882-3601. FAX: 573-882-6110. E-mail: asc-media-lib@missouri.edu. Web Site: asc.missouri.edu/medialib.html. *Assoc Dir,* John S Fick; Staff 3 (Non-MLS 3)
Library Holdings: AV Mats 13,500; DVDs 1,400; Videos 8,000
Open Mon-Fri 8-5
Restriction: Closed stack, Fee for pub use

C COLUMBIA MISSOURIAN NEWSPAPER LIBRARY*, School of Journalism, 315 Lee Hills Hall, 65205, SAN 329-8124. Tel: 573-882-4876. FAX: 573-882-5702. Web Site: www.missouri.edu/~jlibrwww. *Librn,* Dorothy Carner; Tel: 573-882-6591, E-mail: carnerd@missouri.edu; Staff 2 (MLS 1, Non-MLS 1)
Founded 1974. Enrl 23,000; Fac 106; Highest Degree: Doctorate
Library Holdings: Bk Vols 400
Special Collections: Newspaper Bound Volumes
Open Mon-Fri 8-5

C ELMER ELLIS LIBRARY*, 104 Ellis Library, 65201-5149, SAN 348-999X. Tel: 573-882-4701. Circulation Tel: 573-882-3362. Interlibrary Loan Service Tel: 573-882-1101. Reference Tel: 573-882-4581. FAX: 573-882-8044. E-mail: ellisref@missouri.edu. Web Site: library.missouri.edu. *Dir of Libr,* James A Cogswell; E-mail: cogswellja@missouri.edu; *Assoc Dir, Res & Info Serv,* Jeannette Pierce; E-mail: pierceja@missouri.edu; *Asst Dir, Tech Serv,* Ann Riley; Tel: 573-882-1685, E-mail: rileyac@missouri.edu; *Head, Access Serv,* June L DeWeese; Tel. 573-882-7315, E-mail: deweesej@missouri.edu; *Head, Acq,* Position Currently Open; *Head, Ref,* Position Currently Open; *Humanities Librn,* Anne Barker; Tel: 573-882-6324, E-mail: barkera@missouri.edu; *Humanities Librn,* Rachel Brekhus; Tel: 573-882-7563, E-mail: brekhusr@missouri.edu; *Humanities Librn,* Michael Muchow; Tel: 573-882-6824, E-mail: muchowm@missouri.edi; *Sci Librn,* Janice Dysart; Tel: 573-882-1828, E-mail: dysartj@missouri.edu; *Soc Sci Librn,* Wayne Barnes; Tel: 573-882-3310, E mail: barnese@missouri.edu; *Soc Sci Librn,* Gwen Gray; Tel: 573-882-9162, E-mail: grayg@missouri.edu; *Soc Sci Librn,* Paula Roper; Tel: 573 882-3326, E-mail: roperp@missouri.edu; *Coordr, Libr Instruction,* Goodie Bhullar; Tel: 573-882-9163, E-mail: bhullarp@missouri.edu; *Electronic Res,* Rhonda Whithaus; Tel: 573-882-9164, E-mail: whithausr@missouri.edu; *ILL,* Delores Fisher; Tel: 573-882-1101, E-mail: fisherd@missouri.edu; *ILL,* Tammy Green; Tel: 573-882-3224, E-mail: greenta@missouri.edu; *Ref Serv,* Cindy Cotner; Tel: 573-882-4693, E-mail: cotnerc@missouri.edu; *Univ Archivist,* Michael Holland; Tel: 573-882-4602, E-mail: hollandm@missouri.edu. Subject Specialists: *Lang arts, Lit, Sound rec,* Anne Barker; *Anthrop, Hist,* Rachel Brekhus; *Communications, Fine arts, Linguistics,* Michael Muchow; *Atmospheric sci, Biochem, Biological sci,* Janice Dysart; *Children's lit, Educ, Psychol,* Wayne Barnes; *Bus & mgt, Econ,* Gwen Gray; *African-Am studies, Educ,* Paula Roper; *Geog, S Asia,* Goodie Bhullar; Staff 211 (MLS 62, Non-MLS 149)
Founded 1839. Enrl 25,000; Fac 1,669; Highest Degree: Doctorate
Library Holdings: Bk Titles 667,119; Bk Vols 691,714; Per Subs 26,886; Talking Bks 2,451; Videos 3,119
Special Collections: American Best Sellers (Frank Luther Mott Coll); Cartoons (John Tinney McCutcheon Coll); Fourth of July Oration Coll; Philosophy (Thomas Moore Johnson Coll); Rare Book Coll; World War I & II Poster Coll. State Document Depository; UN Document Depository; US Document Depository
Automation Activity & Vendor Info: (Acquisitions) Innovative Interfaces, Inc; (Cataloging) Innovative Interfaces, Inc; (Circulation) Innovative Interfaces, Inc; (Course Reserve) Innovative Interfaces, Inc; (OPAC) Innovative Interfaces, Inc; (Serials) Innovative Interfaces, Inc
Partic in Merlin; MOBIUS (Missouri Bibliographic Information User System)

Publications: UMC Libraries (Newsletter); University of Missouri Library Series
Open Mon-Thurs 7:30am-2am, Fri 7:30am-8pm, Sat 9-8, Sun Noon-2am
Friends of the Library Group

C ENGINEERING LIBRARY & TECHNOLOGY COMMONS, W2001 Lafferre Hall, 65211, SAN 349-0025. Tel: 573-882-2379. FAX: 573-884-4499. Web Site: library.missouri.edu/engineering. *Librn,* Judy Siebert Maseles; Tel: 573-882-2715, E-mail: maselesj@missouri.edu; Staff 3 (MLS 1, Non-MLS 2)
Founded 1906. Highest Degree: Doctorate
Library Holdings: CDs 612; e-books 71,656; e-journals 500; Bk Vols 34,138; Per Subs 736
Subject Interests: Computer sci, Eng
Automation Activity & Vendor Info: (Circulation) Innovative Interfaces, Inc; (Course Reserve) Innovative Interfaces, Inc; (ILL) OCLC ILLiad; (OPAC) Innovative Interfaces, Inc
Database Vendor: ACM (Association for Computing Machinery), Agricola, American Chemical Society, American Geophysical Union, American Mathematical Society, Amigos Library Services, ASCE Research Library, Cinahl, ebrary, EBSCOhost, Elsevier, Emerald, Factiva.com, Gale Cengage Learning, IBISWorld, IEEE (Institute of Electrical & Electronics Engineers), Ingenta, Innovative Interfaces, Inc, IOP, JSTOR, Knovel, LexisNexis, Nature Publishing Group, OCLC WorldShare Interlibrary Loan, OVID Technologies, Oxford Online, ProQuest, Safari Books Online, Sage, ScienceDirect, Scopus, SerialsSolutions, Springer-Verlag, Swets Information Services, Wiley, Wiley InterScience, YBP Library Services
Partic in Merlin; MOBIUS (Missouri Bibliographic Information User System)
Open Mon-Thurs (Winter) 8am-Midnight, Fri 8-5, Sat 1-5, Sun 1-Midnight; Mon-Thurs (Summer) 8am-9pm, Fri 8-5, Sat 1-5, Sun 1-9

C FREEDOM OF INFORMATION CENTER*, 101 Reynolds Journalism Institute, 65211-0012, SAN 372-5022. Tel: 573-882-4856. FAX: 573-884-6204. Web Site: www.nfoic.org/foi-center. *Exec Dir,* Dr Charles N Davis; Tel: 573-882-5736, E-mail: daviscn@missouri.edu; Staff 3 (Non-MLS 3)
Founded 1958. Enrl 27,985; Highest Degree: Doctorate
Library Holdings: Bk Titles 239; Bk Vols 271
Function: Ref serv available
Open Mon-Fri 8-5
Restriction: Closed stack, Non-circulating

C GEOLOGICAL SCIENCES LIBRARY*, 201 Geological Sciences, 65211, SAN 349-005X. Tel: 573-882-4860. Interlibrary Loan Service Tel: 573-882-3224. FAX: 573-882-5458. Web Site: mulibraries.missouri.edu/geology. *Librn,* Stephen Stanton; E-mail: stantons@missouri.edu; Staff 3 (MLS 1, Non-MLS 2)
Library Holdings: Bk Titles 67,091; Bk Vols 68,774; Per Subs 663
Special Collections: 19th Century Federal Survey Publications; 19th Century State Geological Survey Publications
Subject Interests: Econ geol, Exploration, Geochemistry, Geophysics, Hydrol, Paleontology, Petrology, Siesmology, Solid earth geophysics, Statigraphy, Structural geol
Automation Activity & Vendor Info: (Cataloging) Innovative Interfaces, Inc; (Circulation) Innovative Interfaces, Inc
Partic in Merlin; MOBIUS (Missouri Bibliographic Information User System)
Open Mon-Thurs 8-12 & 1-9, Fri 8-12 & 1-5, Sun 2-5

CL LAW LIBRARY*, 203 Hulston Hall, 65211-4190, SAN 349-0114. Tel: 573-882-4597. Reference Tel: 573-884-6362. FAX: 573-882-9676. Web Site: www.law.missouri.edu/library. *Dir,* Randy Diamond; Tel: 573-882-2935, E-mail: diamondrj@missouri.edu; *Assoc Law Librn,* Resa Kerns; Tel: 573-882-5108, E-mail: kernsr@missouri.edu; *Assoc Law Librn,* Cindy Shearrer; Tel: 573-882-1125, E-mail: shearrerc@missouri.edu; *Sr Res Librn,* Steven Lambson; Tel: 573-882-6464, E-mail: lambsons@missouri.edu; *Access Serv,* John Dethman; Tel: 573-884-1760, E-mail: dethmanj@missouri.edu; *Tech Serv,* Needra Jackson; Tel: 573-882-9675, E-mail: jacksonn@missouri.edu; Staff 7 (MLS 7)
Founded 1872. Enrl 500; Fac 40; Highest Degree: Doctorate
Library Holdings: Bk Titles 180,000; Bk Vols 343,000; Per Subs 1,700
Special Collections: 19th Century Trials (John D Lawson Coll). US Document Depository
Automation Activity & Vendor Info: (Acquisitions) Innovative Interfaces, Inc; (Cataloging) Innovative Interfaces, Inc; (Circulation) Innovative Interfaces, Inc; (OPAC) Innovative Interfaces, Inc; (Serials) Innovative Interfaces, Inc
Database Vendor: Gale Cengage Learning, Innovative Interfaces, Inc, LexisNexis, OCLC FirstSearch, Westlaw
Partic in Merlin; MOBIUS (Missouri Bibliographic Information User System)
Publications: Law Library Guide (Library handbook)
Open Mon-Thurs 8-7:45, Fri 8-4:45, Sat 10-5:45, Sun 12-7:45
Restriction: Open to pub for ref & circ; with some limitations

CM LIBRARY FOR FAMILY & COMMUNITY MEDICINE*, M246 Medical Sciences Bldg, 65212, SAN 349-0130. Tel: 573-882-6183. FAX: 573-882-9096. *Librn,* Susan Meadows; Staff 1 (MLS 1)
Founded 1966. Highest Degree: Master
Library Holdings: Bk Vols 200; Per Subs 40
Subject Interests: Gerontology, Healthcare syst, Med ethics, Primary health care, Rural health, Soc aspects of med care
Open Mon-Fri 8-5

CM J OTTO LOTTES HEALTH SCIENCES LIBRARY*, One Hospital Dr, 65212. Tel: 573-882-0471. Circulation Tel: 573-882-4153. Administration Tel: 573-882-7033. FAX: 573-882-5574. E-mail: referencequestions@missouri.edu. Web Site: www.muhealth.org/~library. *Dir,* Deborah Ward; E-mail: warddh@missouri.edu
Database Vendor: Cinahl, DynaMed, Medline, OVID Technologies, PubMed, UpToDate

C FRANK LEE MARTIN MEMORIAL JOURNALISM LIBRARY*, 449 S Ninth St, 102 Reynolds Journalism Institute, 65211, SAN 349-0084. Tel: 573-882-7502. Administration Tel: 573-882-6591. FAX: 573-884-4963. E-mail: jlib@missouri.edu. Web Site: mulibraries.missouri.edu/journalism. *Head, Journalism Libr,* Dorothy J Carner; E-mail: carnerd@missouri.edu. Subject Specialists: *Advertising, Journalism, Pub relations,* Dorothy J Carner; Staff 4 (MLS 1, Non-MLS 3)
Founded 1908. Enrl 4,000; Fac 104; Highest Degree: Doctorate
Special Collections: Fields Photojournalism Coll; McDougall Photojournalism Coll; Pictures of the Year Photojournalism Coll; Weinberg Journalism Fiction Coll
Partic in Amigos Library Services, Inc
Restriction: Borrowing privileges limited to fac & registered students

C MATH SCIENCES LIBRARY*, 206 Math Sciences Bldg, 65211, SAN 349-0173. Tel: 573-882-7286. Interlibrary Loan Service Tel: 573-882-3224. FAX: 573-884-0058. Web Site: mulibraries.missouri.edu/math. *Libr Spec II,* John Meyer; E-mail: meyerjl@missouri.edu. Subject Specialists: *Math,* John Meyer; Staff 1 (Non-MLS 1)
Founded 1969
Library Holdings: Bk Vols 26,000; Per Subs 258
Subject Interests: Math
Database Vendor: Gale Cengage Learning
Partic in Merlin; MOBIUS (Missouri Bibliographic Information User System)
Restriction: Badge access after hrs

CM ZALK VETERINARY MEDICAL LIBRARY*, W-218 Veterinary-Medicine Bldg, 65211, SAN 349-0262. Tel: 573-882-2461. FAX: 573-882-2950. E-mail: vetlib@missouri.edu. Web Site: vetmedlibrary.missouri.edu. *Head Librn,* Trenton Boyd; E-mail: boydt@missouri.edu; *Info Spec I,* Laura Buck; E-mail: buckl@missouri.edu; Staff 1 (MLS 1)
Founded 1951. Enrl 252; Fac 100; Highest Degree: Doctorate
Library Holdings: Per Subs 290
Subject Interests: Clydesdales, Mules, Veterinary hist
Database Vendor: Medline, OVID Technologies, PubMed
Partic in Merlin
Open Mon-Thurs 7:30am-9pm, Fri 7:30-5, Sat 10-2, Sun 1-8

CONCEPTION

CR CONCEPTION ABBEY & SEMINARY LIBRARY*, 37174 State Hwy W, 64433. (Mail add: PO Box 501, 64433-0501), SAN 308-9681. Tel: 660-944-2803. FAX: 660-944-2833. Web Site: library.conception.edu. *Acq, Libr Dir,* Brother Thomas Sullivan; E-mail: thomas@conception.edu; *Automation Serv, Cat, Mgr, Per,* Christopher Brite; E-mail: cbrite@conception.edu; *Circ, Per, Purchasing,* Barbara Cowan; E-mail: bcowan@conception.edu; *ILL,* Pat Danner; E-mail: pdanner@conception.edu; Staff 6 (MLS 3, Non-MLS 3)
Founded 1873. Enrl 93; Fac 15; Highest Degree: Bachelor
Library Holdings: Bk Titles 115,000; Bk Vols 121,000; Per Subs 364; Videos 110
Special Collections: 17th-19th Century Catholic Theology Coll; American Catholic Church History Coll; Incunabula & Manuscripts
Subject Interests: Art, Medieval European hist, Philos, Relig studies, Roman Catholic relig
Database Vendor: EBSCOhost, OCLC FirstSearch
Partic in OCLC Online Computer Library Center, Inc
Open Mon-Fri 8-5

COTTLEVILLE

J ST CHARLES COMMUNITY COLLEGE, Paul & Helen Schnare Library, 4601 Mid Rivers Mall Dr, 63376. SAN 309-1090. Tel: 636-922-8000. Circulation Tel: 636-922-8434. Interlibrary Loan Service Tel: 636-922-8340. Reference Tel: 636-922-8620. Administration Tel: 636-922-8512. FAX: 636-922-8433. E-mail: refdrop@stchas.edu. Web Site: www.stchas.edu/library. *Dean, Learning Res,* Dr Stephanie Tolson; E-mail: stolson@stchas.edu; *Ref Librn,* Theresa Flett; Tel: 636-922-8587, E-mail:

tflett@stchas.edu; *Ref Librn,* Kelly Mitchell; Tel: 636-922-8798, E-mail: kmitchell@stchas.edu; *Ref Librn,* Julia Wilbers; Tel: 636-922-8450, E-mail: jwilbers@stchas.edu; *Pub Serv Mgr,* Ying Li; Tel: 636-922-8438, E-mail: yli@stchas.edu; *Tech Serv Mgr,* Jean Rose; Tel: 636-922-8439, E-mail: jrose@stchas.edu; *Cataloger,* Angela Burroughs Kelly; E-mail: abourroughskelly@stchas.edu; Staff 7 (MLS 7)
Founded 1987. Enrl 4,751; Fac 375; Highest Degree: Associate
Jul 2013-Jun 2014 Income $950,082. Mats Exp $195,748, Books $62,685, Per/Ser (Incl. Access Fees) $48,962, Other Print Mats $10,411, Micro $305, AV Mat $3,525, Electronic Ref Mat (Incl. Access Fees) $69,860. Sal $520,075 (Prof $369,820)
Library Holdings: AV Mats 7,451; e-books 30,147; Electronic Media & Resources 71; Bk Titles 55,651; Per Subs 384; Videos 2,394
Automation Activity & Vendor Info: (Acquisitions) Innovative Interfaces, Inc; (Cataloging) Innovative Interfaces, Inc; (Circulation) Innovative Interfaces, Inc; (Course Reserve) Innovative Interfaces, Inc; (ILL) OCLC; (Media Booking) Innovative Interfaces, Inc; (OPAC) Innovative Interfaces, Inc; (Serials) Innovative Interfaces, Inc
Database Vendor: ARTstor, CQ Press, EBSCOhost, Gale Cengage Learning, LexisNexis, OCLC WorldShare Interlibrary Loan
Wireless access
Function: 24/7 Online cat, Accessibility serv available based on individual needs, Adult bk club, Audio & video playback equip for onsite use, Bk reviews (Group), Computers for patron use, Copy machines, e-mail & chat, Electronic databases & coll, eReaders, Games & aids for the handicapped, ILL available, Magnifiers for reading, Music CDs, Online cat, Online info literacy tutorials on the web & in blackboard, Online ref, Orientations, Photocopying/Printing, Pub access computers, Ref serv available, Ref serv in person, Scanner, Study rm
Publications: Library Editions (Newsletter)
Partic in MOBIUS (Missouri Bibliographic Information User System); Northern Illinois Learning Resources Cooperative (NILRC); Saint Louis Regional Library Network
Special Services for the Deaf - Assistive tech
Special Services for the Blind - Text reader; ZoomText magnification & reading software
Open Mon-Thurs 7:30am-10pm, Fri 7:30-4:30, Sat (Fall & Spring) 9-2
Restriction: Restricted borrowing privileges

CRYSTAL CITY

P CRYSTAL CITY PUBLIC LIBRARY, 736 Mississippi Ave, 63019-1646. SAN 308-9711. Tel: 636-937-7166. FAX: 636-937-3193. E-mail: cclib63019@yahoo.com. Web Site: www.crystalcitymo.org/library/index.html. *Dir,* Tania Laughlin; *Asst Librn,* Kirsten Goings; *Asst Librn,* Marilyn Parr
Founded 1916. Pop 4,300; Circ 30,497
Library Holdings: AV Mats 2,000; Large Print Bks 697; Bk Titles 20,496; Bk Vols 21,447; Per Subs 48; Talking Bks 1,000
Special Collections: Genealogy Coll. Oral History
Automation Activity & Vendor Info: (Cataloging) Follett Software; (Circulation) Follett Software; (ILL) OCLC; (OPAC) Follett Software
Database Vendor: EBSCOhost, OCLC FirstSearch
Wireless access
Function: Handicapped accessible, ILL available, Photocopying/Printing, Prog for children & young adult, Summer reading prog
Partic in Saint Louis Regional Library Network
Open Mon-Thurs 10-7, Fri 12-5, Sat 10-1

DE SOTO

P DE SOTO PUBLIC LIBRARY*, 712 S Main St, 63020. SAN 308-972X. Tel: 636-586-3858. FAX: 636-586-1707. Web Site: desotopubliclibrary.lib.mo.us. *Dir,* Betty Olson; Staff 1 (MLS 1)
Founded 1935. Pop 6,500; Circ 72,000
Nov 2008-Oct 2009 Income $172,000, City $126,000, Locally Generated Income $20,000, Other $26,000. Mats Exp $18,000, Books $16,000, AV Mat $2,000. Sal $94,000 (Prof $40,000)
Library Holdings: Bks on Deafness & Sign Lang 5; CDs 1,021; DVDs 950; Large Print Bks 1,215; Microforms 132; Bk Titles 31,360; Per Subs 50; Videos 538
Special Collections: Local History (Felix Milfeld), negatives, photog. Oral History
Subject Interests: Jefferson County hist
Automation Activity & Vendor Info: (Cataloging) Follett Software; (Circulation) Follett Software
Wireless access
Publications: Quarterly newsletter
Open Mon-Fri 9-5, Sat 9-2
Friends of the Library Group

DEXTER

P KELLER PUBLIC LIBRARY*, 402 W Grant St, 63841. SAN 308-9738. Tel: 573-624-3764. FAX: 573-614-1051. E-mail: info@kellerpl.org. Web Site: www.kellerpl.org. *Dir,* Pamela Trammell; Staff 6 (MLS 1, Non-MLS 5)
Founded 1934. Pop 7,035
Library Holdings: AV Mats 1,175; Large Print Bks 250; Bk Titles 38,950; Bk Vols 39,016; Per Subs 62; Talking Bks 525; Videos 119
Subject Interests: Genealogy
Automation Activity & Vendor Info: (Acquisitions) SirsiDynix; (Cataloging) SirsiDynix; (Circulation) SirsiDynix
Open Mon-Wed & Fri 10-5, Thurs 10-6, Sat 10-2
Friends of the Library Group

DIAMOND

G US NATIONAL PARK SERVICE, George Washington Carver National Monument Library, 5646 Carver Rd, 64840-8314. SAN 370-3142. Tel: 417-325-4151. FAX: 417-325-4231. E-mail: GWCA_interpretation@nps.gov. Web Site: www.nps.gov/gwca. *In Charge,* James Heaney; E-mail: james_heaney@nps.gov; Staff 2 (Non-MLS 2)
Library Holdings: Bk Titles 6,808; Per Subs 10
Special Collections: Carver Coll, archives & artifacts; Original Carver Letters
Open Mon-Sun 9-5

EDINA

S KNOX COUNTY HISTORICAL SOCIETY LIBRARY*, 107 N Fourth, 63537-1470. (Mail add: PO Box 75, 63537-0075), SAN 373-3718. Tel: 660-397-2349. FAX: 660-397-3331. *Pres,* Brenton Karhoff; Staff 1 (Non-MLS 1)
Library Holdings: Bk Titles 1,907; Bk Vols 2,041
Restriction: Open by appt only

ELDON

P ELDON PUBLIC LIBRARY*, 308 E First St, 65026. SAN 377-1075. Tel: 573-392-6657. FAX: 573-392-4071. *Br Mgr,* Ruby Bunch; Staff 1 (MLS 1)
Library Holdings: Bk Titles 21,119; Bk Vols 23,240; Per Subs 32; Talking Bks 64; Videos 57
Automation Activity & Vendor Info: (Cataloging) SirsiDynix; (Circulation) SirsiDynix
Open Mon-Fri 9-5, Sat 9-1

FARMINGTON

P FARMINGTON PUBLIC LIBRARY*, 108 W Harrison St, 63640. SAN 308-9762. Tel: 573-756-5779. Interlibrary Loan Service Tel: 573-756-0624. Reference Tel: 573-756-0613. Administration Tel: 573-756-0600. FAX: 573-756-0614. E-mail: library@farmington-mo.gov. Web Site: www.farmington-mo.gov. *Dir,* Karen Roman; E-mail: kroman@farmington-mo.gov; Staff 9 (MLS 1, Non-MLS 8)
Founded 1916. Pop 14,981; Circ 103,694
Library Holdings: CDs 145; Large Print Bks 714; Bk Vols 41,061; Per Subs 95; Talking Bks 1,138; Videos 477
Special Collections: Local History & Genealogy Coll
Automation Activity & Vendor Info: (Cataloging) TLC (The Library Corporation); (Circulation) Follett Software
Wireless access
Publications: Farmington, Missouri (Local historical information)
Open Mon & Fri 9-5:30, Tues-Thurs 9-8, Sat 9-1

FAYETTE

CR CENTRAL METHODIST COLLEGE*, Smiley Memorial Library, 411 Central Methodist Sq, 65248. SAN 308-9770. Tel: 660-248-6271. FAX: 660-248-6226. E-mail: library@centralmethodist.edu. Web Site: www.centralmethodist.edu. *Dir, Info Serv,* Cynthia Dudenhoffer; E-mail: cmdudenh@centralmethodist.edu; *Archivist, Ref Serv,* John Finley; E-mail: jfinley@centralmethodist.edu; *Tech Serv,* Leasa Strodtman; E-mail: lstrodtm@centralmethodist.edu; Staff 7 (MLS 3, Non-MLS 4)
Founded 1857. Enrl 1,200; Highest Degree: Master
Library Holdings: Large Print Bks 109; Bk Titles 80,000; Bk Vols 99,142; Per Subs 200; Talking Bks 281; Videos 310
Special Collections: Religion (Missouri United Methodist Archives). State Document Depository
Subject Interests: Methodism
Automation Activity & Vendor Info: (Acquisitions) Innovative Interfaces, Inc; (Cataloging) Innovative Interfaces, Inc; (Circulation) Innovative Interfaces, Inc; (Course Reserve) Innovative Interfaces, Inc; (OPAC) Innovative Interfaces, Inc; (Serials) Innovative Interfaces, Inc
Partic in Amigos Library Services, Inc; MOBIUS (Missouri Bibliographic Information User System)
Open Mon-Thurs 7:30am-11pm, Fri 7:30-5, Sat 10-1, Sun 4-11

FERGUSON

P FERGUSON MUNICIPAL PUBLIC LIBRARY*, 35 N Florissant Rd, 63135. SAN 308-9800. Tel: 314-521-4820. FAX: 314-521-1275. TDD: 314-521-4828. Web Site: www.ferguson.lib.mo.us. *Dir,* Joan G Henderson; Tel: 314-521-1275; Staff 9 (MLS 2, Non-MLS 7)
Founded 1933. Pop 22,984; Circ 173,103
Library Holdings: Bk Titles 78,931; Bk Vols 79,804; Per Subs 126; Talking Bks 1,579; Videos 2,236
Subject Interests: City hist
Automation Activity & Vendor Info: (Cataloging) SirsiDynix; (Circulation) SirsiDynix; (OPAC) SirsiDynix
Database Vendor: EBSCOhost, SirsiDynix
Function: ILL available
Partic in Municipal Library Consortium
Special Services for the Deaf - TDD equip
Open Mon-Thurs 9-8:30, Fri 9-7, Sat 9-4
Friends of the Library Group

FESTUS

P FESTUS PUBLIC LIBRARY*, 222 N Mill St, 63028. SAN 308-9819. Tel: 636-937-2017. FAX: 636-937-3439. E-mail: festuspubliclibrary@yahoo.com. Web Site: www.cityoffestus.org. *Dir,* Lollie Gray
Founded 1934. Pop 11,000; Circ 30,073
Library Holdings: Bk Titles 35,000; Per Subs 52
Automation Activity & Vendor Info: (Cataloging) Follett Software; (Circulation) Follett Software; (OPAC) Follett Software
Partic in Saint Louis Regional Library Network
Open Mon-Wed 12-7, Thurs & Fri 10-5, Sat 10-3
Friends of the Library Group

FLORISSANT

CR SAINT LOUIS CHRISTIAN COLLEGE LIBRARY*, 1360 Grandview Dr, 63033. SAN 308-9843. Tel: 314-837-6777, Ext 1512. FAX: 314-837-8291. E-mail: librarian@slcconline.edu. Web Site: www.slcconline.edu/about/library. *Libr Mgr,* Matt DeWitt; Staff 1 (Non-MLS 1)
Founded 1956
Library Holdings: Bk Vols 30,000; Per Subs 91
Special Collections: Stone Campbell Movement Coll
Subject Interests: Bible, Biblical theol, Church hist, Linguistics, Restoration movement hist (19th century Am relig movement)
Partic in Saint Louis Regional Library Network
Open Mon-Thurs 8am-11pm, Fri 8-5, Sat 10-4

FORT LEONARD WOOD

UNITED STATES ARMY

A BRUCE C CLARKE LIBRARY ACADEMIC SERVICES DIVISION, Bldg 3202, 14020 MSCOE Loop, Ste 200, 65473-8928, SAN 362-8957. Tel: 573-563-4109. FAX: 573-563-4156. Web Site: www.wood.army.mil/library. *Libr Dir,* Claretta Crawford; Tel: 573-563-5608, E-mail: claretta.t.crawford.civ@mail.mil; *Supvry Librn,* Travis Ferrell; Tel: 573-563-6111, E-mail: travis.a.ferrell.civ@mail.mil; *Librn,* Kenneth Howard; Tel: 573-563-5318, E-mail: kenneth.r.howard.civ@mail.mil. Subject Specialists: *Chem, Law enforcement, Mil hist,* Claretta Crawford; Staff 8 (MLS 2, Non-MLS 6)
Founded 1935
Library Holdings: Audiobooks 539; CDs 314; DVDs 1,222; Bk Vols 53,100; Per Subs 45; Videos 949
Special Collections: Chemical Corps; Military Police; Military Unit Histories; Rare Book Room
Subject Interests: Chem, Law enforcement, Mil eng, Mil hist
Automation Activity & Vendor Info: (Acquisitions) SirsiDynix; (Cataloging) SirsiDynix; (Circulation) SirsiDynix; (Course Reserve) SirsiDynix; (ILL) SirsiDynix; (Media Booking) SirsiDynix; (OPAC) SirsiDynix; (Serials) SirsiDynix
Database Vendor: EBSCOhost, Gale Cengage Learning, ProQuest
Function: Bks on CD, CD-ROM, Computers for patron use, Copy machines, Electronic databases & coll, Free DVD rentals, ILL available, Online cat, Orientations, OverDrive digital audio bks, Photocopying/Printing, Ref serv available, Scanner
Partic in OCLC Online Computer Library Center, Inc
Open Mon-Thurs 7:15-7, Fri 7:15-5
Restriction: Mil, family mem, retirees, Civil Serv personnel NAF only, Non-circulating of rare bks

A BRUCE C CLARKE LIBRARY COMMUNITY SERVICES DIVISION*, Bldg 3202, 597 Manscen Loop, Ste 100, 65473-8928, SAN 349-0297. Tel: 573-563-4113. FAX: 573-563-4118. Web Site: www.library.wood.army.mil. *Librn,* Joyce Waybright; Staff 1 (MLS 1)
Founded 1941
Library Holdings: Bk Titles 66,012; Bk Vols 68,000; Per Subs 120
Special Collections: Children's Library
Subject Interests: Foreign lang, Mil art, Sci
Automation Activity & Vendor Info: (Acquisitions) SirsiDynix; (Cataloging) SirsiDynix; (Circulation) SirsiDynix; (ILL) SirsiDynix; (Media Booking) SirsiDynix; (OPAC) SirsiDynix; (Serials) SirsiDynix
Partic in OCLC Online Computer Library Center, Inc; United States Army Training & Doctrine Command
Open Mon-Wed 7:30-7:30, Sat & Sun 10-5

AM GENERAL LEONARD WOOD ARMY COMMUNITY HOSPITAL MEDICAL LIBRARY*, 126 Missouri Ave, 65473-5700, SAN 349-0378. Tel: 573-596-0131, Ext 69110. FAX: 573-596-5359. Web Site: glwach.lib.amedd.army.mil. *Med Librn,* Linda Janda; E-mail: linda.janda@amedd.army.mil; Staff 1 (MLS 1)
Founded 1945
Library Holdings: Bk Titles 2,792; Bk Vols 2,816; Per Subs 69
Automation Activity & Vendor Info: (Acquisitions) Ex Libris Group; (Cataloging) Ex Libris Group; (Circulation) Ex Libris Group; (Serials) Ex Libris Group
Database Vendor: Ex Libris Group
Open Mon-Fri 7:30-4
Restriction: Staff use only

FULTON

FULTON STATE HOSPITAL

M PATIENT'S LIBRARY*, 600 E Fifth St, 65251, SAN 349-0440. Tel: 573-592-2261. FAX: 573-592-3011. *Librn,* Tonya Hayes-Martin; Staff 2 (MLS 1, Non-MLS 1)
Founded 1949
Library Holdings: Bk Titles 7,120; Bk Vols 7,280; Per Subs 100
Restriction: Open by appt only

M PROFESSIONAL LIBRARY*, 600 E Fifth St, 65251, SAN 349-0416. Tel: 573-592-2261. FAX: 573-592-3011. *Librn,* Tonya Hayes-Martin; Staff 2 (MLS 1, Non-MLS 1)
Founded 1949
Library Holdings: Bk Titles 1,590; Bk Vols 1,900; Per Subs 101
Subject Interests: Med, Nursing, Psychiat, Psychol, Soc work
Open Mon-Fri 8-Noon

S MISSOURI SCHOOL FOR THE DEAF*, Grover C Farquhar Library, 505 E Fifth St, 65251-1703. SAN 373-0786. Tel: 573-592-2513. FAX: 573-592-2570. *Librn,* Virginia Johns; Staff 1 (Non-MLS 1)
Library Holdings: Bk Titles 13,963; Bk Vols 14,181; Per Subs 33
Open Mon-Fri 8-4

WESTMINSTER COLLEGE

C NATIONAL CHURCHILL MUSEUM*, 501 Westminster Ave, 65251-1299, SAN 308-9878. Tel: 573-592-5626. FAX: 573-592-5222. Web Site: www.nationalchurchillmuseum.org. *Exec Dir,* Dr Rob Havers; Tel: 573-592-5233, E-mail: rob.havers@churchillmemorial.org; *Develop Dir,* Kit Freudenberg; Tel: 573-592-5022, E-mail: kit.freudenberg@churchillmemorial.org; *Asst Dir,* Sara Winingear; Tel: 573-592-5234, E-mail: sara.winingear@churchillmemorial.org; *Archivist, Curator,* Liz Murphy; E-mail: liz.murphy@churchillmemorial.org; *Educ & Pub Prog Coordr,* Amanda Plybon; Tel: 573-592-6242, E-mail: mandy.plybon@churchillmemorial.org; Staff 6 (Non-MLS 6)
Founded 1962
Library Holdings: Bk Titles 1,196; Bk Vols 1,300
Special Collections: British-American Relations; Christopher Wren Coll; Sir Winston Churchill Coll
Partic in OCLC Online Computer Library Center, Inc
Publications: The Churchillian (Quarterly)
Restriction: Non-circulating of rare bks, Non-circulating to the pub, Not a lending libr, Open to pub by appt only, Open to pub for ref only, Open to qualified scholars, Open to researchers by request
Friends of the Library Group

C REEVES MEMORIAL LIBRARY*, 501 Westminster Ave, 65251-1299, SAN 308-9886. Tel: 573-592-5245. Circulation Tel: 573-592-5247. Reference Tel: 573-592-5246. Automation Services Tel: 573-592-5209. FAX: 573-642-6356. E-mail: Reeves.Library@westminster-mo.edu. Web Site: www.westminster-mo.edu/academics/resources/library/pages/default.aspx. *Dir of Libr Serv,* Angela Grogan; E-mail: angela.grogan@westminster-mo.edu; *Head, Pub Serv,* Kathryn Barden; E-mail: kat.barden@westminster-mo.edu; *Head, Tech Serv,* Corinne Caputo; E-mail: corrine.caputo@westminster-mo.edu; *Res Sharing Librn,* Cindy Schoolcraft; E-mail: cindy.schoolcraft@westminster-mo.edu; *Coordr, Ser & Electronic Res,* Kathy Renner; Tel: 573-592-5248, E-mail: kathy.renner@westminster-mo.edu; Staff 8 (MLS 4, Non-MLS 4)
Founded 1851. Enrl 1,141; Fac 90; Highest Degree: Bachelor
Library Holdings: AV Mats 7,311; CDs 285; DVDs 331; e-books 9,367; e-journals 27,437; Microforms 7,068; Bk Titles 83,888; Bk Vols 123,994; Per Subs 207; Videos 1,585
Automation Activity & Vendor Info: (Acquisitions) Innovative Interfaces, Inc; (Cataloging) Innovative Interfaces, Inc; (Circulation) Innovative Interfaces, Inc; (Course Reserve) Innovative Interfaces, Inc;

(ILL) OCLC; (OPAC) Innovative Interfaces, Inc; (Serials) Innovative Interfaces, Inc
Database Vendor: American Chemical Society, CQ Press, EBSCOhost, Gale Cengage Learning, H W Wilson, Innovative Interfaces, Inc, Innovative Interfaces, Inc, JSTOR, LearningExpress, LexisNexis, Newsbank, OCLC ArticleFirst, OCLC CAMIO, OCLC FirstSearch, OCLC WebJunction, OCLC WorldShare Interlibrary Loan, WT Cox
Partic in MOBIUS (Missouri Bibliographic Information User System)
Open Mon-Thurs 7:30am-12:30am, Fri 7:30-4:30, Sat Noon-6, Sun 1:30pm-12:30am

C WILLIAM WOODS UNIVERSITY*, Dulany Memorial Library, One University Ave, 65251. SAN 308-9894. Tel: 573-592-4291. Circulation Tel: 573-592-4289. Interlibrary Loan Service Tel: 573-592-1160. Reference Tel: 573-592-4279. FAX: 573-592-1159. E-mail: libref@williamwoods.edu. Web Site: www.williamwoods.edu. *Dir,* Erlene A Dudley; E-mail: edudley@williamwoods.edu; *Ref Librn,* Barb Davis; E-mail: barb.davis@williamwoods.edu; *Supvr, Access Serv,* Missy Martin; E-mail: mmartin@williamwoods.edu; *Tech Serv,* Tom Schultz; Staff 4 (MLS 4)
Founded 1870. Enrl 1,150; Fac 59; Highest Degree: Master
Library Holdings: Bk Vols 130,427; Per Subs 419
Special Collections: Education Coll; Equestrian Science Coll
Subject Interests: Equestrian studies, Interpreter training
Automation Activity & Vendor Info: (Acquisitions) Innovative Interfaces, Inc; (Cataloging) Innovative Interfaces, Inc; (Circulation) Innovative Interfaces, Inc; (Course Reserve) Innovative Interfaces, Inc; (ILL) Innovative Interfaces, Inc; (Media Booking) Innovative Interfaces, Inc; (OPAC) Innovative Interfaces, Inc; (Serials) Innovative Interfaces, Inc
Publications: Dulany Library Handbook
Partic in Amigos Library Services, Inc; MOBIUS (Missouri Bibliographic Information User System)
Special Services for the Deaf - Bks on deafness & sign lang

GAINESVILLE

P OZARK COUNTY LIBRARY, 200 Elm St, 65655. (Mail add: PO Box 518, 65655), SAN 377-2233. Tel: 417-679-4442. *Libr Board of Trustees Pres,* Kathryn Atkinson; *Ch Serv,* Jan Madden
Founded 1947. Pop 2,000
Mar 2014-Feb 2015 Income $7,500. Mats Exp $1,000
Library Holdings: Audiobooks 343; Bks on Deafness & Sign Lang 3; DVDs 1,000; Electronic Media & Resources 9; Large Print Bks 200; Bk Titles 19,260; Bk Vols 20,000; Videos 50
Automation Activity & Vendor Info: (Cataloging) JayWil Software Development, Inc; (Circulation) JayWil Software Development, Inc
Wireless access
Open Mon-Fri 9-3:30, Sat 9-12

GALENA

P STONE COUNTY LIBRARY*, 322 West State Hwy 248, 65656. (Mail add: PO Box 225, 65656-0225), SAN 308-9908. Tel: 417-357-6410. Toll Free Tel: 888-711-3100. FAX: 417-357-6695. Web Site: www.stonecountylibrary.org. *Dir,* David R Doennig; E-mail: ddoen@scl.lib.mo.us; *Cat Mgr,* Alice R Cummings; Staff 6 (MLS 1, Non-MLS 5)
Founded 1948. Pop 28,658; Circ 29,769
Jan 2009-Dec 2009 Income (Main Library and Branch(s)) $556,243, State $15,762, County $507,113, Locally Generated Income $27,517. Mats Exp $58,390. Sal $141,474
Library Holdings: AV Mats 8,235; Bk Titles 47,180; Bk Vols 55,415; Per Subs 60
Subject Interests: Genealogy, Local hist
Automation Activity & Vendor Info: (Cataloging) Innovative Interfaces, Inc; (Circulation) Innovative Interfaces, Inc; (OPAC) Innovative Interfaces, Inc
Database Vendor: EBSCOhost, Gale Cengage Learning, OCLC FirstSearch, ProQuest
Wireless access
Mem of White River Regional Library
Partic in Consortium of Ozarks Libraries
Open Mon 8-8, Tues-Fri 8-4:30, Sat 8-12
Friends of the Library Group
Branches: 1
CRANE AREA BRANCH, 111 Main St, Crane, 65633. (Mail add: PO Box 25, Crane, 65633-0025), SAN 308-9703. Tel: 417-723-8261. FAX: 417-723-8851. *Br Mgr,* Mary Bolton; *Circ,* Gary Webb; Staff 2 (Non-MLS 2)
Founded 1938
Automation Activity & Vendor Info: (Circulation) Innovative Interfaces, Inc; (OPAC) Innovative Interfaces, Inc
Database Vendor: EBSCOhost, Gale Cengage Learning, OCLC FirstSearch, ProQuest
Open Mon-Fri 9-5, Sat 9-1
Bookmobiles: 1. Librn, Fred Daugherty

GALLATIN

P DAVIESS COUNTY LIBRARY*, 306 W Grand, 64640-1132. SAN 349-0475. Tel: 660-663-3222. FAX: 660-663-3250. Web Site: daviess@dcplibrary.org, dcplibrary.org. *Dir,* Jan Johnson; E-mail: jjohnson@daviesscountylibrary.org; *Asst Librn,* Jone Perry; E-mail: jperry@daviesscountylibrary.org; Staff 1 (Non-MLS 1)
Founded 1947. Pop 8,016; Circ 77,615
Library Holdings: AV Mats 2,240; Large Print Bks 300; Bk Titles 38,561; Bk Vols 34,605; Per Subs 142; Talking Bks 1,220
Subject Interests: Amish culture, Genealogy
Automation Activity & Vendor Info: (Acquisitions) Mandarin Library Automation; (Cataloging) Mandarin Library Automation; (Circulation) Mandarin Library Automation; (ILL) OCLC; (OPAC) Mandarin Library Automation
Wireless access
Open Tues-Thurs 9-6, Fri 9-5, Sat 9-1:30
Friends of the Library Group
Branches: 1
JAMESPORT BRANCH, 101 E Main, Jamesport, 64648. (Mail add: PO Box 197, Jamesport, 64648-0197), SAN 349-0505. Tel: 660-684-6120. *Br Librn,* Pam Parton; E-mail: pparton@daviesscountylibrary.org
Library Holdings: Bk Titles 3,900; Bk Vols 4,600; Per Subs 16; Videos 44
Open Thurs & Fri 12-5, Sat 8-1

GERALD

P GERALD AREA LIBRARY*, 357 S Main St, 63037. (Mail add: PO Box 212, 63037-0212), SAN 377-2217. Tel: 573-764-7323. E-mail: gerlib@fidnet.com. *Pres,* Mary Ann Binkholder; *VPres,* Arline Skornia; Staff 1 (MLS 1)
Founded 1994
Library Holdings: Audiobooks 150; CDs 11; DVDs 35; Large Print Bks 300; Bk Titles 12,688; Bk Vols 13,192; Per Subs 42; Talking Bks 100; Videos 300
Automation Activity & Vendor Info: (Cataloging) TLC (The Library Corporation); (Circulation) TLC (The Library Corporation)
Wireless access
Open Tues, Wed & Fri 9-5, Sat 9-12

GLASGOW

P LEWIS LIBRARY OF GLASGOW*, 315 Market St, 65254-1537. SAN 308-9924. Tel: 660-338-2395. E-mail: lewislib@yahoo.com. *Dir,* Rosetta Fuemmeler; Staff 4 (MLS 2, Non-MLS 2)
Founded 1866. Pop 1,408; Circ 21,112
Library Holdings: AV Mats 410; Large Print Bks 42; Bk Titles 18,091; Bk Vols 19,712; Per Subs 62; Videos 308
Special Collections: Local Papers (dated back to 1840)
Database Vendor: OCLC FirstSearch
Open Mon & Wed 2-7, Tues, Thurs & Fri 3-7
Friends of the Library Group

HAMILTON

P HAMILTON PUBLIC LIBRARY*, 312 N Davis St, 64644. SAN 308-9932. Tel: 816-583-4832. FAX: 816-583-7501. E-mail: hamiltonpubliclibrary@gmail.com. Web Site: hamiltonpublic.lib.mo.us. *Dir,* Michelle Fagerstone; *Asst Librn,* Mary Gray; Staff 2 (MLS 1, Non-MLS 1)
Founded 1919. Pop 1,657; Circ 13,890
Library Holdings: e-books 3,485; Large Print Bks 734; Bk Vols 11,620; Per Subs 10; Talking Bks 98; Videos 263
Automation Activity & Vendor Info: (Acquisitions) Mandarin Library Automation; (Cataloging) Mandarin Library Automation; (Circulation) Mandarin Library Automation
Wireless access
Open Mon, Wed & Fri 8-5, Tues & Thurs 8-8, Sat 8-Noon

HANNIBAL

P HANNIBAL FREE PUBLIC LIBRARY*, 200 S Fifth St, 63401. SAN 308-9940. Tel: 573-221-0222. FAX: 573-221-0369. Web Site: hannibal.lib.mo.us. *Dir,* Hallie Yundt Silver; Staff 9 (MLS 2, Non-MLS 7)
Founded 1845. Pop 17,757; Circ 132,380
Library Holdings: e-books 9,842; Microforms 797; Bk Vols 92,333; Per Subs 121
Subject Interests: Hannibal hist, Mark Twain
Automation Activity & Vendor Info: (Cataloging) SirsiDynix; (Circulation) SirsiDynix; (OPAC) SirsiDynix; (Serials) SirsiDynix
Database Vendor: EBSCOhost, Gale Cengage Learning, LearningExpress, Newsbank, OCLC FirstSearch, Overdrive, Inc, ProQuest, TumbleBookLibrary
Wireless access
Publications: Story of Hannibal by the Hagoods (Local historical information)

Open Mon & Tues 10-8, Wed-Sat 10-6
Restriction: Non-resident fee, Open to pub for ref & circ; with some limitations
Friends of the Library Group

C HANNIBAL-LAGRANGE UNIVERSITY, Roland Library, 2800 Palmyra Rd, 63401-1999. SAN 308-9959. Tel: 573-221-3675, Ext 3132. Interlibrary Loan Service Tel: 573-629-3137. Administration Tel: 573-629-3130. FAX: 573-248-0294. E-mail: library@hlg.edu. Web Site: www.hlg.edu/library/index.php. *Dir,* Julie Andresen; Tel: 573-221-3675, Ext 3130, E-mail: jandrese@hlg.edu; Staff 5.5 (MLS 1, Non-MLS 4.5)
Founded 1858. Enrl 908; Fac 78; Highest Degree: Master
Jul 2012-Jun 2013 Income $354,959. Mats Exp $354,959, Books $22,237, Per/Ser (Incl. Access Fees) $35,996, AV Mat $7,031, Electronic Ref Mat (Incl. Access Fees) $36,796, Presv $1,049. Sal $182,223
Library Holdings: AV Mats 6,702; e-books 10,991; Bk Vols 110,849; Per Subs 274
Subject Interests: Archives, Baptist mat, Rare bks
Automation Activity & Vendor Info: (Cataloging) Innovative Interfaces, Inc; (Circulation) Innovative Interfaces, Inc; (Course Reserve) Innovative Interfaces, Inc; (ILL) OCLC; (Media Booking) Innovative Interfaces, Inc; (OPAC) Innovative Interfaces, Inc; (Serials) Innovative Interfaces, Inc
Database Vendor: Amigos Library Services, EBSCOhost, Gale Cengage Learning, JSTOR, LearningExpress, LexisNexis, OCLC ArticleFirst, OCLC CAMIO, OCLC FirstSearch, OCLC WorldShare Interlibrary Loan, OVID Technologies, PubMed, Safari Books Online
Wireless access
Function: 24/7 Electronic res, 24/7 Online cat, Archival coll, Audio & video playback equip for onsite use, Computers for patron use, Copy machines, Electronic databases & coll, Equip loans & repairs, eReaders, Exhibits, Handicapped accessible, ILL available, Laminating, Magazines, Mango lang, Microfiche/film & reading machines, Online cat, Online searches, Orientations, Photocopying/Printing, Ref serv available, Ref serv in person, Scanner, Study rm, Tax forms, VHS videos, Wheelchair accessible, Workshops
Partic in Amigos Library Services, Inc; Missouri Research & Education Network (MOREnet); MOBIUS (Missouri Bibliographic Information User System); OCLC Online Computer Library Center, Inc
Special Services for the Blind - Daisy reader; ZoomText magnification & reading software
Open Mon-Fri (Sept-April) 7:30am-Midnight, Sat Noon-5; Mon, Tues & Thurs (May-Aug) 8-6, Wed & Fri 8-4
Restriction: Fee for pub use, Open to students, fac & staff

S MARK TWAIN HOME FOUNDATION, Mark Twain Museum Library, 120 N Main St, 63401-3537. SAN 326-0542. Tel: 573-221-9010. FAX: 573-221-7975. Web Site: www.marktwainmuseum.org. *Exec Dir,* Henry Sweets; Tel: 573-221-9010, Ext 405, E-mail: henry.sweets@marktwainmuseum.org
Founded 1937
Library Holdings: DVDs 10; Bk Titles 3,700; Per Subs 10; Videos 40
Special Collections: Mark Twain Coll (First Editions & Works about Him)
Wireless access
Publications: The Fence Painter (Bi-monthly)
Restriction: Open by appt only

HARRISONVILLE

P CASS COUNTY PUBLIC LIBRARY*, Administration Office, 400 E Mechanic, 64701. SAN 349-0564. Tel: 816-380-4600. FAX: 816-884-2301. TDD: 816-331-8242. Web Site: www.casscolibrary.org. *Dir,* Christie Kessler; E-mail: ckessler@casscolibrary.org; *Asst Dir,* Seth Herschberger; Staff 1 (MLS 1)
Founded 1947. Pop 94,232; Circ 545,400
Library Holdings: Bk Vols 214,000; Per Subs 586
Special Collections: Cass County & Missouri, hist doc
Subject Interests: Genealogy
Automation Activity & Vendor Info: (Acquisitions) SirsiDynix; (Cataloging) SirsiDynix; (Circulation) SirsiDynix; (ILL) SirsiDynix; (OPAC) SirsiDynix; (Serials) SirsiDynix
Database Vendor: ALLDATA Online, EBSCOhost, Gale Cengage Learning, LearningExpress, OCLC FirstSearch, OCLC WorldShare Interlibrary Loan, ReferenceUSA, SirsiDynix
Wireless access
Function: Adult bk club, Archival coll, Bilingual assistance for Spanish patrons, Bks on cassette, Bks on CD, Children's prog, Citizenship assistance, Computer training, Computers for patron use, Copy machines, Doc delivery serv, Electronic databases & coll, Genealogy discussion group, Holiday prog, Music CDs, Preschool outreach, Prog for children & young adult, Senior computer classes
Publications: Annual Report; Summer Reading Kit
Partic in Kansas City Library Service Program; Mid-America Library Alliance/Kansas City Metropolitan Library & Information Network; Missouri Research & Education Network (MOREnet)
Special Services for the Deaf - TDD equip
Open Mon-Fri 8-5
Friends of the Library Group
Branches: 7
ARCHIE BRANCH, 315 S Main, Archie, 64725, SAN 349-0599. Tel: 816-293-5579. *Br Mgr,* Gail Roberts; E-mail: robertsg@casscolibrary.org
Open Mon 2-6, Tues & Wed 9-6, Thurs 2-7, Sat 9-1
Friends of the Library Group
DREXEL BRANCH, 211 E Main St, Drexel, 64742, SAN 349-0688. Tel: 816-657-4740. *Br Mgr,* Connie Allen; E-mail: allenc@casscolibrary.org
Open Mon 9-1 & 2-7, Wed & Thurs 9-1 & 2-6, Fri 2-5, Sat 9-12
Friends of the Library Group
GARDEN CITY BRANCH, 201 C Date St, Garden City, 64747-9211, SAN 349-0718. Tel: 816-862-6611. *Br Mgr,* Karen Allen; E-mail: allenk@casscolibrary.org
Open Mon & Wed 9-7, Thurs 9-6, Sat 9-3
Friends of the Library Group
GENEALOGY, 400 E Mechanic, 64701. Tel: 816-884-6285. *Br Mgr,* Jacqueline Polsgrove-Roberts; E-mail: robertsj@casscolibrary.org
Open Mon, Tues & Thurs 9-4 & 5-8, Wed 9-1 & 2-6, Fri & Sat 9-12 & 1-5
Friends of the Library Group
HARRISONVILLE BRANCH, 400 E Mechanic St, 64701, SAN 349-0742. Tel: 816-884-3483. *Br Mgr,* Diane Christensen; E-mail: christensend@casscolibrary.org; *Children's Spec,* Sara Steinmetz; E-mail: steinmetzs@casscolibrary.org
Open Mon-Thurs 9-8, Fri 9-6, Sat 9-5
Friends of the Library Group
NORTHERN RESOURCE CENTER, 164 Cedar Tree Sq, Belton, 64012, SAN 349-0629. Tel: 816-331-0049. *Br Mgr,* Teri Milbourn; E-mail: milbourt@casscolibrary.org
Open Mon-Thurs 9-8, Fri 9-6, Sat 9-5
Friends of the Library Group
PLEASANT HILL BRANCH, 1108 N Hwy No 7, Pleasant Hill, 64080, SAN 349-0807. Tel: 816-987-2231. *Br Mgr,* Marianna Decker; E-mail: deckerm@casscolibrary.org
Open Mon & Wed 9-6, Tues 12-7, Thurs 12-6, Fri 12-5, Sat 9-3
Friends of the Library Group
Bookmobiles: 1

HARTVILLE

P WRIGHT COUNTY LIBRARY*, Administrative Headquarters, 125 Court Sq, 65667-9998. (Mail add: PO Box 70, 65667-0070). Tel: 417-741-7595. FAX: 417-741-7927. E-mail: htvlib@wrightcountylibrary.org. Web Site: www.wrightcountylibrary.org. *Dir,* Judy Epperly; E-mail: jepperly@wrightcountylibrary.org; *Admin Librn,* Karen Moore; Staff 3 (MLS 1, Non-MLS 2)
Founded 1947
Library Holdings: Bk Titles 72,129; Bk Vols 73,048; Per Subs 71
Automation Activity & Vendor Info: (ILL) OCLC
Open Mon-Fri 8-12 & 12:30-4:30, Sat 8-12
Branches: 2
MOUNTAIN GROVE BRANCH, 206 Green St, Mountain Grove, 65711, SAN 349-098X. Tel: 417-926-4453. FAX: 417-926-6240. E-mail: mglib@wrightcountylibrary.org. *Librn,* Barbara Flageolle; *Librn,* Loretta Holden; *Librn,* Shannon McGowan; *Librn,* Teresa Miller; Staff 3 (MLS 3)
Library Holdings: Bk Titles 7,012; Bk Vols 7,690; Per Subs 11
Open Mon-Fri 8-11 & 12-5, Sat 8-12
Friends of the Library Group
LAURA INGALLS WILDER LIBRARY, PO Box 586, Mansfield, 65704-3245, SAN 349-0955. Tel: 417-924-8068. FAX: 417-924-3045. E-mail: manlib@wrightcountylibrary.org. *Librn,* Shandalyn Dickinson; *Librn,* Elizabeth Hull; Staff 3 (MLS 2, Non-MLS 1)
Library Holdings: Bk Titles 9,500; Bk Vols 10,000; Per Subs 16
Open Mon-Fri 8-12 & 12:30-4:30, Sat 8-12
Friends of the Library Group
Bookmobiles: 1

HAYTI

P CONRAN MEMORIAL LIBRARY*, 302 E Main St, 63851. SAN 308-9967. Tel: 573-359-0599. E-mail: conranlibrary@hotmail.com. *Dir,* Jeanie Stewart
Founded 1934. Pop 3,841
Library Holdings: AV Mats 150; Large Print Bks 300; Bk Vols 19,000; Per Subs 20; Talking Bks 100; Videos 100
Subject Interests: Town hist
Wireless access
Open Mon-Fri 12-5:30

HERMANN

S DEUTSCHHEIM STATE HISTORIC SITE LIBRARY*, 107 W Second St, 65041. SAN 372-7459. Tel: 573-486-2200. FAX: 573-486-2249. *Adminr,* Cynthia Browne
Founded 1978
Library Holdings: Bk Vols 300
Special Collections: German Immigrants & German Americans in Missouri 1785-1900
Open Mon-Sun 10-4; Thurs-Sun (Nov-March) 10-4

HIGGINSVILLE

P ROBERTSON MEMORIAL LIBRARY*, 19 W 20th St, 64037. SAN 308-9975. Tel: 660-584-2880. FAX: 660-584-8181. Web Site: www.higginsvillelibrary.org. *Dir,* Tina Myrick; Staff 2 (MLS 1, Non-MLS 1)
Founded 1928. Pop 4,723
Automation Activity & Vendor Info: (Acquisitions) Book Systems; (Cataloging) Book Systems; (Circulation) Book Systems; (OPAC) Book Systems
Database Vendor: EBSCOhost, Gale Cengage Learning
Wireless access
Open Tues, Thurs & Fri 10-5, Wed 10-7, Sat 10-2
Friends of the Library Group

HIGH RIDGE

P JEFFERSON COUNTY LIBRARY*, 5678 State Rd PP, 63049-2216. SAN 372-7505. Tel: 636-677-8689. FAX: 636-677-1769. E-mail: info@jeffersoncountylibrary.org. Web Site: www.jeffersoncountylibrary.org. *Dir,* Pamela R Klipsch; E-mail: pklipsch@jeffcolib.org; *Asst Dir, Bus Operations,* Debby Byron; E-mail: dbyron@jeffcolib.org; *Asst Dir, Libr Operations,* Karen Duree; Tel: 636-461-1914, Fax: 636-461-1915, E-mail: kduree@jeffcolib.org; *Tech Serv Mgr,* Jeane Tornatore; E-mail: jtornatore@jeffcolib.org; *Tech Mgr,* Jay Manning; E-mail: jmanning@jeffcolib.org; Staff 16 (MLS 13, Non-MLS 3)
Founded 1989. Pop 131,842; Circ 725,897
Jan 2012-Dec 2012 Income (Main Library and Branch(s)) $3,484,617. Mats Exp $2,601,279
Special Collections: State Document Depository
Subject Interests: Genealogy, Local hist, Parenting
Automation Activity & Vendor Info: (Acquisitions) SirsiDynix; (Cataloging) SirsiDynix; (Circulation) SirsiDynix; (OPAC) SirsiDynix
Database Vendor: Baker & Taylor, ebrary, EBSCOhost, ProQuest, ReferenceUSA, SirsiDynix
Wireless access
Partic in Saint Louis Regional Library Network
Special Services for the Deaf - Adult & family literacy prog; Bks on deafness & sign lang; Coll on deaf educ
Special Services for the Blind - Assistive/Adapted tech devices, equip & products; Audio mat; Bks on cassette; Bks on CD; Cassettes; Closed circuit TV; Computer with voice synthesizer for visually impaired persons; Home delivery serv; Large print bks; Large screen computer & software; Talking bks
Open Mon-Thurs 9-9, Fri 9-6, Sat 9-5
Friends of the Library Group
Branches: 3
ARNOLD BRANCH, 1701 Missouri State Rd, Arnold, 63010, SAN 372-7513. Tel: 636-296-2204. FAX: 636-296-5975. *Br Mgr,* Meredith McCarthy; E-mail: mmccarthy@jeffcolib.org; *Ch,* Amy Held; E-mail: aheld@jeffcolib.org; *Ref Librn,* Joshua Henry; E-mail: jhenry@jeffcolib.org; *Ref Librn,* Myra Hill; E-mail: mhill@jeffcolib.org; *Circ,* Marcia Shrader; E-mail: mshrader@jeffcolib.org; Staff 5.7 (MLS 4, Non-MLS 1.7)
Founded 1989. Pop 67,955; Circ 231,896
Special Collections: State Document Depository
Subject Interests: Bus
Open Mon-Thurs 9-9, Fri 9-6, Sat 9-5
Friends of the Library Group
NORTHWEST, 5680 State Rd PP, 63049, SAN 372-8064. Tel: 636-677-8186. FAX: 636-677-8243. E-mail: northwest@jeffcolib.org. *Br Mgr,* Cindy Hayes; E-mail: chayes@jeffcolib.org; *Ref Librn,* Molly Pfeiffer; E-mail: mpfeiffer@jeffcolib.org; *Ch Serv,* Molly Schmitt; E-mail: mschmitt@jeffcolib.org; *Circ,* Karen Jones; E-mail: kjones@jeffcolib.org; *Genealogy Serv,* Christine Merseal; E-mail: cmerseal@jeffcolib.org; Staff 6.05 (MLS 2.8, Non-MLS 3.25)
Founded 1989. Pop 45,694; Circ 246,588
Library Holdings: Audiobooks 3,160; CDs 2,658; DVDs 2,486; High Interest/Low Vocabulary Bk Vols 658; Large Print Bks 2,174; Microforms 2,300; Bk Vols 70,991; Videos 2,501
Subject Interests: Genealogy, Local hist
Open Mon-Thurs 9-9, Fri 9-6, Sat 9-5
Friends of the Library Group
WINDSOR, 7479 Metropolitian Blvd, Barnhart, 63012, SAN 378-2182. Tel: 636-461-1914. FAX: 636-461-1915. *Br Mgr,* Karen Duree; E-mail: kduree@jeffcolib.org; *Ref Librn,* Adam Tucker; E-mail: atucker@jeffcolib.org; *Ch Serv,* Patty Lagermann; E-mail: plagermann@jeffcolib.org; *Circ,* Debra Heckel; E-mail: dheckel@jeffcolib.org; *Ref Serv,* Elizabeth Cobb; E-mail: bcobb@jeffcolib.org; *Ref Serv,* Don Turner; E-mail: dturner@jeffcolib.org; Staff 7.4 (MLS 2, Non-MLS 5.4)
Founded 1989. Pop 18,193; Circ 145,624
Subject Interests: Parenting
Open Mon-Thurs 9-9, Fri 9-6, Sat 9-5
Friends of the Library Group

HILLSBORO

C JEFFERSON COLLEGE LIBRARY*, 1000 Viking Dr, 63050. SAN 308-9983. Tel: 636-797-3000, 636-942-3000. Circulation Tel: 636-789-3000, Ext 166. Reference Tel: 636-789-3000, Ext 160. FAX: 636-789-3954. Web Site: www.jeffco.edu/library. *Dir of Libr Serv,* Lisa Wolfe; E-mail: lwolfe@jeffco.edu; *Access Serv Librn,* Lisa Prichard; Staff 9 (MLS 3, Non-MLS 6)
Founded 1964. Enrl 2,930; Fac 88; Highest Degree: Associate
Library Holdings: Bk Titles 70,831; Bk Vols 72,415; Per Subs 130; Videos 1,000
Special Collections: Jefferson County History Center. State Document Depository; US Document Depository
Automation Activity & Vendor Info: (Circulation) Innovative Interfaces, Inc; (Course Reserve) Innovative Interfaces, Inc; (OPAC) Innovative Interfaces, Inc; (Serials) Innovative Interfaces, Inc
Database Vendor: EBSCOhost, LexisNexis, OCLC FirstSearch, Wilson - Wilson Web
Wireless access
Partic in Amigos Library Services, Inc; MOBIUS (Missouri Bibliographic Information User System); Saint Louis Regional Library Network
Open Mon-Thurs 7:30am-9pm, Fri 7:30-4, Sat 10-2

HOLLISTER

S WORLD ARCHAEOLOGICAL SOCIETY*, Information Center, 120 Lakewood Dr, 65672-9718. SAN 320-4871. Tel: 417-334-2377. Web Site: worldarchaeologicalsociety.com. *Dir,* Ron Miller; E-mail: ronwriterartist@aol.com
Founded 1971
Library Holdings: Bk Titles 7,000; Per Subs 30
Special Collections: Archaeology (Steve Miller Coll)
Subject Interests: Ancient med, Anthrop, Archaeology, Art hist, Biblical archaeol, Democracy, Hist, Mil hist, Museology, Writing
Function: Res libr
Publications: Special Publications; WAS (Newsletter)
Restriction: Open by appt only

HOUSTON

P TEXAS COUNTY LIBRARY*, 117 W Walnut St, 65483. SAN 349-1048. Tel: 417-967-2258. Toll Free Tel: 888-609-4469. FAX: 417-967-2262. E-mail: htlib@texascountylibrary.lib.mo.us. Web Site: texascountylibrary.lib.mo.us. *Dir,* Audrey Barnhart; Staff 7 (MLS 1, Non-MLS 6)
Founded 1946. Pop 22,000; Circ 140,330
Library Holdings: Bk Titles 58,720; Bk Vols 60,000; Per Subs 60; Talking Bks 729; Videos 836
Database Vendor: Innovative Interfaces, Inc
Wireless access
Partic in SW Mo Libr Network
Open Mon, Wed & Fri 9-5, Tues & Thurs 9-7, Sat 9-1
Friends of the Library Group
Branches: 3
CABOOL BRANCH, 418 Walnut Ave, Cabool, 65689, SAN 349-1072. Tel: 417-962-3722. Toll Free Tel: 888-609-4474. FAX: 417-962-3723. E-mail: cblib@texascountylibrary.lib.mo.us. Web Site: texascountylibrary.lib.mo.us/content/cabool-branch. *Librn,* Eliza Cannon; Staff 3 (MLS 1, Non-MLS 2)
Open Mon-Fri 11-5, Sat 9-1
Friends of the Library Group
LICKING BRANCH, 126 S Main St, Licking, 65542, SAN 349-1102. Tel: 573-674-2038. Toll Free Tel: 888-609-4479. FAX: 573-674-2148. E-mail: lklib@texascountylibrary.lib.mo.us. Web Site: texascountylibrary.lib.mo.us/content/licking-branch. *Librn,* Lee Ann Akins; Staff 2 (Non-MLS 2)
Open Mon & Fri 11-5, Tues-Thurs 11-6, Sat 9-1
Friends of the Library Group
SUMMERSVILLE BRANCH, On the Square, 139 Rogers Ave, Summersville, 65571, SAN 349-1137. Tel: 417-932-5261. FAX: 417-932-5261. *Librn,* Brenda Bates; Staff 1 (Non-MLS 1)
Open Mon, Wed & Fri 11-5, Tues & Thurs 11-6, Sat 9-1
Friends of the Library Group

IBERIA

P HEARTLAND REGIONAL LIBRARY SYSTEM*, Iberia Branch, 304 N St Louis St, 65486. (Mail add: PO Box 386, 65486-0386), SAN 377-1113. Tel: 573-793-6746. FAX: 573-793-6037. Web Site: heartland.lib.mo.us. *Librn,* Thea Roberts; Staff 3 (MLS 1, Non-MLS 2)
Library Holdings: Bk Titles 17,398; Bk Vols 17,991; Per Subs 20
Open Tues & Wed 1-5, Thurs 2-8, Fri 12-4, Sat 9-1

INDEPENDENCE

R COMMUNITY OF CHRIST LIBRARY*, The Temple, 201 S River, 64050. SAN 349-1919. Tel: 816-833-1000, Ext 2400. FAX: 816-521-3087. E-mail: rmeisinger@CofChrist.org. Web Site: www.cofchrist.org/library/default.asp. *Librn,* Rachel Killebrew; Tel: 816-833-1000, Ext 2399, E-mail: rkillebrew@CofChrist.org; Staff 3 (MLS 1, Non-MLS 2)
Founded 1865
Library Holdings: Audiobooks 2,000; Bk Titles 20,000; Per Subs 150; Videos 400
Special Collections: Book of Mormon, ms; Early Origins of the Mormon Church; Herald Publishing House Publications; Histories of States Related to Latter Day Saints Movement; Inspired Version of the Bible; Latter Day Saints History & Theology, archives, foreign language scriptures, Herald House Preservation, pamphlets,vault, unpublished, audios & videos; Latter Day Saints Pamphlets; Reorganized Church of Jesus Christ of Latter Day Saints, journals, papers, photog & rec
Subject Interests: Christianity, Mormon (Latter Day Saints) hist, Mormon (Latter Day Saints) theol, Peace studies
Automation Activity & Vendor Info: (Cataloging) SirsiDynix; (Circulation) SirsiDynix
Database Vendor: OCLC FirstSearch, ProQuest
Partic in Mid-America Library Alliance/Kansas City Metropolitan Library & Information Network
Open Mon-Fri 8-12 & 1:30-5
Restriction: Non-circulating

S JACKSON COUNTY HISTORICAL SOCIETY*, Archives & Research Library, 112 W Lexington Ave, Ste 103, 64050-3700. SAN 320-197X. Tel: 816-252-7454. FAX: 816-461-1510. Web Site: jchs.org/archives/archives.html. *Dir,* Position Currently Open; Staff 2 (Non-MLS 2)
Founded 1940
Library Holdings: Bk Titles 1,500; Per Subs 10
Subject Interests: Jackson County, Mo hist, Mo hist
Function: Archival coll
Publications: The Jackson County Historical Society Journal (Newsletter)
Restriction: Not a lending libr, Open by appt only, Pub use on premises

P MID-CONTINENT PUBLIC LIBRARY*, 15616 E US Hwy 24, 64050-2098. SAN 349-1161. Tel: 816-836-5200. FAX: 816-521-7253. E-mail: info@mymcpl.org. Web Site: www.mymcpl.org. *Dir,* Steven Potter; E-mail: spotter@mymcpl.org; *Asst Dir,* Susan Wray; Tel: 816-521-7220, E-mail: swray@mymcpl.org; *Dir, Human Res,* Don Bridgforth; E-mail: dbridgforth@mymcpl.org; *Acq Mgr,* Terri Clark; E-mail: tclark@mymcpl.org; *Adult Serv Mgr,* Marlene Boggs; *Automation Mgr,* Amy Caviness; E-mail: acaviness@mymcpl.org; *Cat Mgr,* Judith Listrom; *Libr Syst Mgr,* Todd Caviness; *Mgr, ILL,* Karen Gilson Wickwire; E-mail: kgilsonwickwire@mymcpl.org; *Mgr, Ref Serv,* Amy Fisher; *Mgr, Youth Serv,* Jessie Alexander-East; *Regional Mgr, North Region,* Vicky Baker; *Regional Mgr, South Region,* John Martin; *AV Coll,* Ted Derrick; *Mkt,* Jim Staley; Staff 34 (MLS 34)
Founded 1965. Pop 688,000; Circ 9,060,960
Jul 2007-Jun 2008 Income (Main Library and Branch(s)) $4,354,300. Mats Exp $9,761,152. Sal $21,819,295
Library Holdings: AV Mats 330,341; CDs 93,441; DVDs 36,329; High Interest/Low Vocabulary Bk Vols 6,965; Bk Titles 681,528; Bk Vols 3,106,319; Per Subs 8,283; Talking Bks 73,848
Special Collections: Handicapped Coll, AV, bks, puzzles, toys; Missouriana & Genealogy Coll; United States Census Coll, micro
Automation Activity & Vendor Info: (Acquisitions) SirsiDynix; (Cataloging) SirsiDynix; (Circulation) SirsiDynix; (ILL) SirsiDynix; (Media Booking) SirsiDynix; (OPAC) SirsiDynix; (Serials) SirsiDynix
Database Vendor: Baker & Taylor, EBSCOhost, Gale Cengage Learning, Newsbank, OCLC WorldShare Interlibrary Loan, ProQuest, ReferenceUSA, SirsiDynix, Westlaw, Wilson - Wilson Web
Wireless access
Function: Adult bk club, Adult literacy prog, Audiobks via web, AV serv, Bk club(s), Bks on cassette, Bks on CD, Children's prog, Computers for patron use, Copy machines, Digital talking bks, e-mail & chat, Electronic databases & coll, Family literacy, Fax serv, Free DVD rentals, Genealogy discussion group, Handicapped accessible, Homebound delivery serv, Homework prog, ILL available, Magnifiers for reading, Mail & tel request accepted, Music CDs, Online cat, Online ref, Online searches, Outside serv via phone, mail, e-mail & web, OverDrive digital audio bks, Prog for adults, Prog for children & young adult, Pub access computers, Ref serv available, Ref serv in person, Spoken cassettes & CDs, Spoken cassettes & DVDs, Story hour, Summer reading prog, Tax forms, Teen prog, Telephone ref, VHS videos, Video lending libr, Wheelchair accessible
Partic in Amigos Library Services, Inc; Mid-America Library Alliance/Kansas City Metropolitan Library & Information Network; OCLC Online Computer Library Center, Inc
Special Services for the Deaf - Bks on deafness & sign lang; High interest/low vocabulary bks; Spec interest per
Friends of the Library Group
Branches: 30
ANTIOCH BRANCH, 6060 N Chestnut Ave, Gladstone, 64119-1845, SAN 349-1196. Tel: 816-454-1306. FAX: 816-454-7111. *Br Mgr,* Rosalyn Spring; Staff 2 (MLS 1, Non-MLS 1)
Library Holdings: Bk Titles 21,221; Bk Vols 22,390; Per Subs 54; Talking Bks 81; Videos 178
Open Mon-Thurs 9-9, Fri 9-6, Sat 9-5
Friends of the Library Group
BLUE RIDGE BRANCH, 9253 Blue Ridge Blvd, Kansas City, 64138-4028, SAN 349-1765. Tel: 816-761-3382. FAX: 816-761-7074. *Br Mgr,* Geri Haile; Staff 2 (MLS 1, Non-MLS 1)
Founded 1956
Library Holdings: Bk Titles 20,195; Bk Vols 21,071; Per Subs 34; Videos 389
Open Mon-Thurs 9-9, Fri 9-6, Sat 9-5
Friends of the Library Group
BLUE SPRINGS NORTH BRANCH, 850 NW Hunter Dr, Blue Springs, 64015-7721, SAN 373-7195. Tel: 816-224-8772. FAX: 816-224-4723. *Br Mgr,* Robert Miller; Staff 3 (MLS 1, Non-MLS 2)
Library Holdings: Bk Titles 20,075; Bk Vols 21,192; Per Subs 36; Videos 370
Open Mon-Thurs 9-9, Fri 9-6, Sat 9-5
Friends of the Library Group
BLUE SPRINGS SOUTH BRANCH, 2220 South Hwy 7, Blue Springs, 64014-3957, SAN 349-1226. Tel: 816-229-3571. FAX: 816-224-2078. *Br Mgr,* Jacqueline Reed; Staff 2 (MLS 1, Non-MLS 1)
Library Holdings: Bk Titles 22,717; Bk Vols 23,081; Per Subs 40; Videos 315
Open Mon-Thurs 9-9, Fri 9-6, Sat 9-5
Friends of the Library Group
BOARDWALK BRANCH, 8656 N Ambassador Dr, Kansas City, 64154-2558, SAN 375-5681. Tel: 816-741-9011. FAX: 816-741-4793. *Br Mgr,* Christen Rhodes; Staff 3 (MLS 1, Non-MLS 2)
Library Holdings: Bk Titles 23,133; Bk Vols 23,609; Per Subs 36; Videos 387
Open Mon-Thurs 9-9, Fri 9-6, Sat 9-5
Friends of the Library Group
BUCKNER BRANCH, 19 E Jefferson St, Buckner, 64016-9713, SAN 349-1250. Tel: 816-650-3212. FAX: 816-650-6780. *Br Mgr,* Marybeth Hollenbach; Staff 3 (MLS 1, Non-MLS 2)
Library Holdings: Bk Titles 21,779; Bk Vols 22,011; Per Subs 33; Videos 341
Open Mon & Thurs 9-9, Tues, Wed & Fri 9-6, Sat 9-5
Friends of the Library Group
CAMDEN POINT BRANCH, 401 Hardesty St, Camden Point, 64018-2528, SAN 349-1285. Tel: 816-280-3384. FAX: 816-280-3384. *Br Mgr,* Phyllis Cluchey; Staff 2 (MLS 1, Non-MLS 1)
Library Holdings: Bk Titles 19,881; Bk Vols 20,177; Per Subs 29; Videos 305
Open Mon 9-9, Tues-Fri 9-6, Sat 9-5
Friends of the Library Group
CLAYCOMO BRANCH, 309 NE US Hwy 69, Claycomo, 64119-3116, SAN 373-7209. Tel: 816-455-5030. FAX: 816-455-6987. *Br Mgr,* Patricia Bogue; Staff 3 (MLS 1, Non-MLS 2)
Library Holdings: Bk Titles 20,079; Bk Vols 20,181; Per Subs 31; Videos 379
Open Mon & Thurs 9-9, Tues, Wed & Fri 9-6, Sat 9-5
Friends of the Library Group
COLBERN ROAD BRANCH, 1000 NE Colbern Rd, Lee's Summit, 64086-5811, SAN 373-7217. Tel: 816-525-9924. FAX: 816-525-3682. *Br Mgr,* Gayla Spurlock; Staff 2 (MLS 1, Non-MLS 1)
Library Holdings: Bk Titles 20,199; Bk Vols 20,409; Per Subs 31; Videos 336
Open Mon-Thurs 9-9, Fri 9-6, Sat 9-5
Friends of the Library Group
DEARBORN BRANCH, 206 Maple Leaf Ave, Dearborn, 64439-9085, SAN 349-1315. Tel: 816-450-3502. FAX: 816-450-3502. *Br Mgr,* Howard Buhl
Open Mon 9-9, Tues-Fri 9-6, Sat 9-5
EDGERTON BRANCH, 404 Frank St, Edgerton, 64444-9221, SAN 349-134X. Tel: 816-790-3569. FAX: 816-790-3569. *Br Mgr,* Tammy Parrott; Staff 2 (MLS 1, Non-MLS 1)
Library Holdings: Bk Titles 21,113; Bk Vols 21,449; Per Subs 31; Videos 309

Open Mon 9-9, Tues-Fri 9-6, Sat 9-5
Friends of the Library Group
EXCELSIOR SPRINGS BRANCH, 1460 Kearney Rd, Excelsior Springs, 64024-1746, SAN 349-1374. Tel: 816-630-6721. FAX: 816-630-5021. *Br Mgr,* Kirsten Grubbs; Staff 2 (MLS 1, Non-MLS 1)
Library Holdings: Bk Titles 21,143; Bk Vols 22,059; Per Subs 32; Videos 312
Open Mon-Thurs 9-9, Fri 9-6, Sat 9-5
Friends of the Library Group
GRAIN VALLEY BRANCH, 110 Front St, Grain Valley, 64029-9308, SAN 349-1439. Tel: 816-228-4020. FAX: 816-228-4007. *Br Mgr,* Mary Reeder; Staff 2 (MLS 1, Non-MLS 1)
Library Holdings: Bk Titles 21,481; Bk Vols 22,112; Per Subs 37
Open Mon & Thurs 9-9, Tues, Wed & Fri 9-6, Sat 9-5
Friends of the Library Group
GRANDVIEW BRANCH, 12930 Booth Lane, Grandview, 64030-2682, SAN 349-1463. Tel: 816-763-0550. FAX: 816-763-3924. *Br Mgr,* Linda Tarantino; Staff 3 (MLS 1, Non-MLS 2)
Library Holdings: Bk Titles 22,391; Bk Vols 22,911; Per Subs 27; Videos 281
Open Mon-Thurs 9-9, Fri 9-6, Sat 9-5
Friends of the Library Group
KEARNEY BRANCH, 100 S Platte-Clay Way, Kearney, 64060-7640, SAN 349-1498. Tel: 816-628-5055. FAX: 816-628-5645. *Br Mgr,* Angela Gillette; Staff 2 (MLS 1, Non-MLS 1)
Library Holdings: Bk Titles 19,761; Bk Vols 20,359; Per Subs 31
Open Mon-Thurs 9-9, Fri 9-6, Sat 9-5
Friends of the Library Group
LEE'S SUMMIT BRANCH, 150 NW Oldham Pkwy, Lee's Summit, 64081-1501, SAN 349-1528. Tel: 816-524-0567. FAX: 816-246-5342. *Br Mgr,* Beth Atwater
Open Mon-Thurs 9-9, Fri 9-6, Sat 9-5
LIBERTY BRANCH, 1000 Kent St, Liberty, 64068-2256, SAN 349-1536. Tel: 816-781-9240. FAX: 816-781-5119. *Br Mgr,* Janet Heitzman-Smith; Staff 2 (MLS 1, Non-MLS 1)
Library Holdings: Bk Titles 21,760; Bk Vols 22,549; Per Subs 39; Videos 301
Open Mon-Thurs 9-9, Fri 9-6, Sat 9-5
Friends of the Library Group
LONE JACK BRANCH, 211 N Bynum Rd, Lone Jack, 64070-9604, SAN 326-8365. Tel: 816-697-2528. FAX: 816-697-2917. *Br Mgr,* Kathy Dunson; Staff 3 (MLS 1, Non-MLS 2)
Library Holdings: Bk Titles 21,507; Bk Vols 22,410; Per Subs 30; Videos 310
Open Mon & Thurs 9-9, Tues, Wed & Fri 9-6, Sat 9-5
Friends of the Library Group
MIDWEST GENEALOGY CENTER, 3440 S Lee's Summit Rd, 64055-1923. Tel: 816-252-7228. Interlibrary Loan Service Tel: 816-521-7231. Administration Tel: 816-836-5200. FAX: 816-254-7146. Administration FAX: 816-521-7253. E-mail: ge@mymcpl.org. Web Site: www.midwestgenealogycenter.org. *Br Mgr,* Cheryl Lang; E-mail: clang@mymcpl.org; *Archivist, Ref Librn,* Nicole Pye; E-mail: npye@mymcpl.org; Staff 19 (MLS 3, Non-MLS 16)
Library Holdings: CDs 392; DVDs 32; Microforms 607,297; Bk Vols 174,000; Per Subs 500; Videos 99
Subject Interests: Genealogy, Local hist
Open Mon-Thurs 9-9, Fri 9-6, Sat 9-5, Sun 1-5
Friends of the Library Group
NORTH INDEPENDENCE BRANCH, 317 W US Hwy 24, 64050-2747, SAN 349-1552. Tel: 816-252-0950. FAX: 816-254-7114. *Br Mgr,* Position Currently Open; Staff 3 (MLS 1, Non-MLS 2)
Library Holdings: Bk Titles 19,808; Bk Vols 21,112; Per Subs 26; Videos 261
Open Mon-Thurs 9-9, Fri 9-6, Sat 9-5
Friends of the Library Group
NORTH OAK BRANCH, 8700 N Oak Trafficway, Kansas City, 64155-2437, SAN 349-1404. Tel: 816-436-4385. FAX: 816-436-1946. *Br Mgr,* Sheryl Williams; Staff 3 (MLS 1, Non-MLS 2)
Library Holdings: Bk Titles 21,136; Bk Vols 22,311; Per Subs 33
Open Mon-Thurs 9-9, Fri 9-6, Sat 9-5
Friends of the Library Group
OAK GROVE BRANCH, 2320 S Broadway, Oak Grove, 64075-9369, SAN 349-1587. Tel: 816-690-3213. FAX: 816-690-5681. *Br Mgr,* Liz Sypko; Staff 2 (MLS 1, Non-MLS 1)
Library Holdings: Bk Titles 21,088; Bk Vols 22,961; Per Subs 30; Videos 151
Open Mon & Thurs 9-9, Tues, Wed & Fri 9-6, Sat 9-5
Friends of the Library Group
PARKVILLE BRANCH, 8815 Tom Watson Pkwy, Parkville, 64152-3522, SAN 373-7225. Tel: 816-741-4721. FAX: 816-741-6215. *Br Mgr,* Kathy Bigley; Staff 2 (MLS 1, Non-MLS 1)
Library Holdings: Bk Titles 19,988; Bk Vols 21,042; Per Subs 29
Open Mon-Thurs 9-9, Fri 9-6, Sat 9-5
Friends of the Library Group
PLATTE CITY BRANCH, 2702 Prairie View Rd, Platte City, 64079-7604, SAN 349-1617. Tel: 816-858-2322. FAX: 816-858-3084. *Br Mgr,* Rachael Rafuse
Open Mon & Thurs 9-9, Tues, Wed & Fri 9-6, Sat 9-5
RAYTOWN BRANCH, 6131 Raytown Rd, Raytown, 64133-4006, SAN 349-1676. Tel: 816-353-2052. FAX: 816-353-5518. *Br Mgr,* Susan Haley; Staff 2 (MLS 1, Non-MLS 1)
Library Holdings: Bk Titles 20,712; Bk Vols 21,516; Per Subs 23
Open Mon-Thurs 9-9, Fri 9-6, Sat 9-5
Friends of the Library Group
RED BRIDGE BRANCH, 11140 Locust St, Kansas City, 64131-3628, SAN 349-1706. Tel: 816-942-1780. FAX: 816-942-2657. *Br Mgr,* Kevin Zeller; Staff 2 (MLS 1, Non-MLS 1)
Library Holdings: Bk Titles 18,889; Bk Vols 20,118; Per Subs 22
Open Mon-Thurs 9-9, Fri 9-6, Sat 9-5
Friends of the Library Group
RIVERSIDE BRANCH, 2700 NW Vivion Rd, Riverside, 64150-9432, SAN 349-1730. Tel: 816-741-6288. FAX: 816-741-8596. *Br Mgr,* Patrice Nollette; Staff 2 (MLS 1, Non-MLS 1)
Library Holdings: Bk Titles 20,514; Bk Vols 21,769; Per Subs 27
Open Mon & Thurs 9-9, Tues, Wed & Fri 9-6, Sat 9-5
Friends of the Library Group
SMITHVILLE BRANCH, 120 Richardson St, Smithville, 64089-9038, SAN 349-179X. Tel: 816-532-0116. FAX: 816-532-0145. *Br Mgr,* Cassidy Rogers; Staff 2 (MLS 1, Non-MLS 1)
Library Holdings: Audiobooks 2,767; CDs 1,869; DVDs 3,169; Bk Vols 53,682; Per Subs 28; Videos 798
Open Mon-Thurs 9-9, Fri 9-6, Sat 9-5
SOUTH INDEPENDENCE BRANCH, 13700 E 35th St, 64055-2464, SAN 349-182X. Tel: 816-461-2050. FAX: 816-461-4759. *Br Mgr,* John Jasumback; Staff 2 (MLS 1, Non-MLS 1)
Library Holdings: Bk Titles 20,818; Bk Vols 21,216; Per Subs 27
Open Mon-Thurs 9-9, Fri 9-6, Sat 9-5
Friends of the Library Group
WESTON BRANCH, 18204 Library Dr, Weston, 64098, SAN 349-1889. Tel: 816-640-2874. FAX: 816-640-2688. *Br Mgr,* Brandi Blankenship; Staff 2 (MLS 1, Non-MLS 1)
Library Holdings: Bk Titles 21,654; Bk Vols 21,938; Per Subs 36
Open Mon & Thurs 9-9, Tues, Wed & Fri 9-6, Sat 9-5
Friends of the Library Group

G HARRY S TRUMAN PRESIDENTIAL LIBRARY & MUSEUM, 500 W US Hwy 24, 64050-1798. SAN 309-0035. Tel: 816-268-8200. Reference Tel: 816-268-8272. Toll Free Tel: 800-833-1225. FAX: 816-268-8295. E-mail: truman.library@nara.gov, truman.reference@nara.gov. Web Site: www.trumanlibrary.org. *Actg Dir,* Amy L Williams; E-mail: amy.williams@nara.gov; Staff 28 (MLS 2, Non-MLS 26)
Founded 1957
Library Holdings: Bk Titles 25,000
Special Collections: Papers of Harry S Truman & Other Individuals
Automation Activity & Vendor Info: (Cataloging) OCLC
Function: Archival coll, For res purposes, Ref serv available
Open Mon-Fri 8:45-4:45
Restriction: Closed stack, Non-circulating, Photo ID required for access
Friends of the Library Group

IRONTON

P OZARK REGIONAL LIBRARY*, 402 N Main St, 63650. SAN 349-1978. Tel: 573-546-2615. FAX: 573-546-7225. *Dir,* John F Mertens; *Ref,* Dan Roberts; *Youth Serv,* Shaen L Pogue; Staff 18.6 (MLS 4, Non-MLS 14.6)
Founded 1947. Pop 61,819; Circ 128,792
Jan 2009-Dec 2009 Income $962,576, State $114,953, County $822,623, Locally Generated Income $14,500, Other $10,500. Mats Exp $151,694, Books $120,669, Per/Ser (Incl. Access Fees) $7,000, AV Equip $10,000, AV Mat $4,500, Electronic Ref Mat (Incl. Access Fees) $9,525. Sal $561,955 (Prof $188,946)
Library Holdings: Audiobooks 2,205; AV Mats 3,513; DVDs 245; Microforms 1,001; Bk Titles 91,333; Bk Vols 146,960; Per Subs 250; Videos 1,444
Special Collections: Eastern US Genealogy (Floyd Coll)
Database Vendor: OCLC FirstSearch
Open Mon & Wed-Fri 8-5, Tues 8-8, Sat 9-4
Branches: 8
ANNAPOLIS BRANCH, 204 N Allen St, Annapolis, 63620. (Mail add: PO Box 274, Annapolis, 63620-0274), SAN 349-2001. Tel: 573-598-3706. *Librn,* Charlotte Brown
Circ 4,941
Library Holdings: Bk Vols 4,409
Open Tues-Fri 2-6, Sat 10-2
BOURBON BRANCH, 575 Elm, Bourbon, 65441. (Mail add: PO Box 475, Bourbon, 65441-0475), SAN 349-2036. Tel: 573-732-5313. *Librn,* Sharon Fann
Circ 8,328

Library Holdings: Bk Vols 10,287
Open Tues, Wed & Fri 1-5:30, Sat 10-2
FREDERICKTOWN BRANCH, 115 S Main St, Fredericktown, 63645, SAN 349-2060. Tel: 573-783-2120. *Librn,* Deborah Anderson
Circ 21,635
Library Holdings: Bk Vols 17,635
Open Mon, Wed-Fri 10-5:30, Tues 10-8, Sat 10-3
IRONTON BRANCH, 402 N Main St, 63650, SAN 349-2095. Tel: 573-546-2615. *Librn,* John F Mertens
Circ 24,466
Library Holdings: Bk Vols 41,149
Open Mon & Wed-Fri 8-5, Tues 8-8, Sat 9-4
RECKLEIN MEMORIAL, 305 N Smith St, Cuba, 65453, SAN 349-2125. Tel: 573-885-3431. *Librn,* Cheryl Bach
Circ 14,292
Library Holdings: Bk Vols 11,757
Open Tues 10:30-7, Wed-Fri 10:30-5, Sat 10:30-2
SAINTE GENEVIEVE BRANCH, 21388 Hwy 32, Sainte Genevieve, 63670. (Mail add: PO Box 386, Sainte Genevieve, 63670-0386), SAN 349-215X. Tel: 573-883-3358. *Librn,* John A Jones; Staff 1 (MLS 1)
Circ 22,298
Library Holdings: Bk Vols 36,740
Open Mon, Tues & Thurs 10-8, Wed 8-8, Fri 10-6, Sat 10-4
STEELVILLE BRANCH, 210 S Fourth St, Steelville, 65565. (Mail add: PO Box 266, Steelville, 65565-0266), SAN 349-2184. Tel: 573-775-2338. *Librn,* Rosemary Kehr
Circ 18,613
Library Holdings: Bk Vols 20,574
Open Tues 10-8, Wed-Fri 12-5:30, Sat 10-4
VIBURNUM BRANCH, City Hall Missouri Ave, Viburnum, 65566. (Mail add: PO Box 33, Viburnum, 65566-0033), SAN 349-2214. Tel: 573-244-5986. *Librn,* Kathryn Snyder
Circ 1,174
Library Holdings: Bk Vols 4,409
Open Mon & Wed 2:30-4:30, Thurs 7-9, Sat 10-12
Bookmobiles: 1. Bk vols 2,700

JACKSON

P JACKSON PUBLIC LIBRARY*, 100 N Missouri St, 63755-1888. SAN 309-0051. Tel: 573-243-5150. FAX: 573-243-8292. Web Site: jackson.lib.mo.us, jacksonmo.com/places/libraries.html, jacksonpubliclibrary.lib.mo.us. *Librn,* Sally K Pierce; Staff 6 (MLS 1, Non-MLS 5)
Founded 1926. Pop 11,662; Circ 36,901
Library Holdings: Bk Titles 31,717; Bk Vols 32,390; Per Subs 106; Talking Bks 816; Videos 708
Special Collections: Missouri Coll
Subject Interests: Genealogy
Automation Activity & Vendor Info: (Cataloging) TLC (The Library Corporation); (Circulation) TLC (The Library Corporation); (Course Reserve) TLC (The Library Corporation); (ILL) TLC (The Library Corporation); (OPAC) TLC (The Library Corporation)
Database Vendor: OCLC FirstSearch
Open Mon-Thurs 10-8, Fri 10-5, Sat 10-1

P RIVERSIDE REGIONAL LIBRARY*, 1997 E Jackson Blvd, 63755-1949. (Mail add: PO Box 389, 63755-0389), SAN 349-2249. Tel: 573-243-8141. FAX: 573-243-8142. E-mail: riversideregionallibrary@gmail.com. Web Site: www.riversideregionallibrary.org. *Dir,* Nancy Howland; E-mail: librarylady98@gmail.com; Staff 23 (MLS 1, Non-MLS 22)
Founded 1955. Pop 66,199; Circ 272,808
Library Holdings: Bk Titles 147,028; Bk Vols 148,020; Per Subs 135; Talking Bks 2,080; Videos 11,446
Special Collections: Large Print
Subject Interests: Genealogy for local families
Automation Activity & Vendor Info: (Cataloging) TLC (The Library Corporation); (Circulation) TLC (The Library Corporation); (OPAC) TLC (The Library Corporation)
Database Vendor: OCLC FirstSearch
Function: ILL available
Partic in Amigos Library Services, Inc; Missouri Research & Education Network (MOREnet)
Special Services for the Blind - Closed circuit TV; Talking bks
Open Mon-Fri 9-7, Sat 9-4
Friends of the Library Group
Branches: 5
ALTENBURG BRANCH, 66 Poplar St, Altenburg, 63732. (Mail add: PO Box 32, Altenburg, 63732-0032), SAN 349-2362. Tel: 573-824-5267. FAX: 573-824-5267. *Br Librn,* Kathleen Schlimpert; Staff 1 (Non-MLS 1)
Library Holdings: Bk Titles 13,214; Bk Vols 14,110; Per Subs 10; Talking Bks 101; Videos 75
Open Tues 1-7, Wed 11-6, Thurs 1-6, Sat 8-11
Friends of the Library Group
BENTON BRANCH, 54 N Winchester, Benton, 63736. (Mail add: PO Box 108, Benton, 63736-0108), SAN 349-2303. Tel: 573-545-3581. FAX: 573-545-3581. *Br Librn,* Gwenell Streeter; Staff 1 (Non-MLS 1)
Library Holdings: Audiobooks 252; CDs 80; DVDs 350; Large Print Bks 100; Bk Titles 11,213; Bk Vols 12,191; Per Subs 10; Videos 50
Database Vendor: 3M Library Systems, TLC (The Library Corporation)
Open Mon, Tues & Fri 1-6, Wed 9-6, Sat 8-12
Friends of the Library Group
ORAN BRANCH, 120 Mountain St, Oran, 63771. (Mail add: PO Box 298, Oran, 63771-0298), SAN 328-8447. Tel: 573-262-3745. FAX: 573-262-3745. *Br Mgr,* Tiffany Whitmore; Staff 1 (Non-MLS 1)
Library Holdings: Bk Titles 9,757; Bk Vols 10,130; Per Subs 15; Talking Bks 101; Videos 119
Open Mon, Wed & Thurs 9-12 & 1-6, Sat 9-12
Friends of the Library Group
PERRYVILLE BRANCH, 800 City Park Dr, Ste A, Perryville, 63775, SAN 349-2338. Tel: 573-547-6508. FAX: 573-547-3715. *Br Librn,* Julie Sauer; Staff 4 (Non-MLS 4)
Library Holdings: Bk Titles 61,238; Bk Vols 62,010; Per Subs 15; Talking Bks 103; Videos 148
Open Mon-Fri 9-6, Sat 9-1
Friends of the Library Group
SCOTT CITY BRANCH, 2016 Main St, Scott City, 63780, SAN 349-2273. Tel: 573-264-2413. FAX: 573-264-2413. *Br Librn,* Glenda Kenkel; Staff 1 (Non-MLS 1)
Library Holdings: Bk Titles 22,197; Bk Vols 23,198; Per Subs 15; Talking Bks 116; Videos 152
Open Mon, Thurs & Fri 1-6, Tues & Wed 11-6, Sat 9-1
Friends of the Library Group

JEFFERSON CITY

GL COMMITTEE ON LEGISLATIVE RESEARCH*, Legislative Library, State Capitol Bldg, 117A, 65101. SAN 309-0086. Tel: 573-751-4633. FAX: 573-751-0130. E-mail: leg.library@lr.mo.gov. Web Site: www.moga.mo.gov/legres/legreshome.htm. *Librn,* Anne G Rottmann; Staff 3 (MLS 1, Non-MLS 2)
Founded 1943
Library Holdings: Bk Titles 5,560; Bk Vols 5,780; Per Subs 125
Special Collections: Missouri Bills, 1909 to date; Missouri House & Senate Journals, 1837 to date; Missouri Laws from Territorial days to date
Open Mon-Fri 8:30-4:30

C LINCOLN UNIVERSITY OF MISSOURI*, Inman E Page Library, 712 Lee Dr, 65101. SAN 309-006X. Tel: 573-681-5504. Interlibrary Loan Service Tel: 573-681-5513. Information Services Tel: 573-681-5512. FAX: 573-681-5511. Web Site: www.lincolnu.edu/pages/203.asp. *Univ Librn,* Jerome Offord; Tel: 573-681-5502, E-mail: offordj@lincolnu.edu; *Info Access Coordr,* Lois Marshall; Tel: 573-681-5509, E-mail: marshall@lincolnu.edu; Staff 9 (MLS 6, Non-MLS 3)
Founded 1866. Enrl 3,600; Fac 154; Highest Degree: Master
Jul 2006-Jun 2007. Mats Exp $180,485, Books $14,814, Per/Ser (Incl. Access Fees) $58,039, AV Mat $755, Electronic Ref Mat (Incl. Access Fees) $65,051
Library Holdings: AV Mats 5,488; CDs 687; Bk Titles 162,169; Bk Vols 208,229; Per Subs 240
Special Collections: Ethnic Studies Center Coll. Oral History
Automation Activity & Vendor Info: (Acquisitions) Innovative Interfaces, Inc; (Cataloging) Innovative Interfaces, Inc; (Circulation) Innovative Interfaces, Inc; (Course Reserve) Innovative Interfaces, Inc; (ILL) Innovative Interfaces, Inc; (OPAC) Innovative Interfaces, Inc; (Serials) Innovative Interfaces, Inc
Database Vendor: 3M Library Systems, Agricola, Alexander Street Press, Baker & Taylor, Cinahl, EBSCOhost, Gale Cengage Learning, H W Wilson, Ingram Library Services, Innovative Interfaces, Inc, Newsbank, OCLC ArticleFirst, OCLC FirstSearch, OCLC WorldShare Interlibrary Loan, Oxford Online, ValueLine, Westlaw
Wireless access
Publications: Bibliography of Books by & About Blacks
Partic in Amigos Library Services, Inc; MOBIUS (Missouri Bibliographic Information User System); OCLC Online Computer Library Center, Inc
Open Mon-Thurs (Fall & Spring) 7:30am-Midnight, Fri 8-5, Sat 11-8, Sun 3-Midnight; Mon-Thurs (Summer) 7:30am-9pm
Friends of the Library Group

S MISSOURI DEPARTMENT OF CORRECTIONS*, Offender Libraries, 2729 Plaza Dr, 65109-1146. (Mail add: PO Box 236, 65102-0236), SAN 349-2540. Tel: 573-522-1928. FAX: 573-751-4099. Web Site: www.doc.mo.gov. *Coordr, Libr Serv,* Kimberly Bresnahan; Tel: 573-526-6540
Subject Interests: Civil rights, Law
Function: Photocopying/Printing, Ref serv available
Restriction: Internal circ only

Branches:
ALGOA CORRECTIONAL CENTER, 8501 No More Victims Rd, 65101-4567. Tel: 573-751-3911, Ext 640. FAX: 573-751-7375. *Librn,* Julie Koenigsfeld; Staff 1 (Non-MLS 1)
BOONVILLE CORRECTIONAL CENTER, 1216 E Morgan St, Boonville, 65233-1300, SAN 349-2575. Tel: 660-882-6521, Ext 338. FAX: 660-882-3427. *Librn,* Terri Lucas; Staff 1 (Non-MLS 1)
FARMINGTON CORRECTIONAL CENTER, 1012 W Columbia St, Farmington, 63640-2902, SAN 377-1091. Tel: 573-218-7100, Ext 346. FAX: 573-218-7106. *Librn,* Patti Carl; *Librn,* Karen Stuchel
Library Holdings: Bk Vols 17,014; Per Subs 96
FULTON RECEPTION & DIAGNOSTIC CENTER, PO Box 190, Fulton, 65251-0190. Tel: 573-592-4040. FAX: 573-592-4020. *Librn,* Jane Swartz
JEFFERSON CITY CORRECTIONAL CENTER, 8200 No More Victims Rd, 65101-4539, SAN 349-263X. Tel: 573-751-3224, Ext 1142. FAX: 573-751-0355. *Librn,* Robyn Combs
MARYVILLE TREATMENT CENTER, 30227 US Hwy 136, Maryville, 64468-8353. Tel: 660-582-6542. FAX: 660-582-8071. *Librn,* Brenda Jennings
MISSOURI EASTERN CORRECTIONAL CENTER, 18701 US Hwy 66, Pacific, 63069-3525, SAN 329-9171. Tel: 636-257-3322, Ext 219. FAX: 636-257-5296. *Librn,* Renee Payton
Founded 1981
Library Holdings: Bk Titles 17,800; Bk Vols 21,000; Per Subs 60
MOBERLY CORRECTIONAL CENTER, Bus Rte 63 S, 5201 S Morley, Moberly, 65270. (Mail add: PO Box 7, Moberly, 65270-0007). Tel: 660-263-3778. FAX: 660-263-1730. *Librn,* Jennifer Cook
Founded 1963
Library Holdings: AV Mats 300; High Interest/Low Vocabulary Bk Vols 50; Large Print Bks 250; Bk Titles 8,190; Bk Vols 8,318; Per Subs 64; Spec Interest Per Sub 12
Subject Interests: Law
NORTHEAST CORRECTIONAL CENTER, 13698 Airport Rd, Bowling Green, 63334. Tel: 573-324-9975. FAX: 573-324-5028. *Librn,* Joyce Edwards; *Librn,* Tracey Harrison; Staff 2 (Non-MLS 2)
OZARK CORRECTIONAL CENTER, 929 Honor Camp Lane, Fordland, 65652-9700. Tel: 417-767-4491. FAX: 417-738-2400. *Librn,* Carolyn Baker; Staff 1 (MLS 1)
POTOSI CORRECTIONAL CENTER, 11593 State Hwy O, Mineral Point, 63660. Tel: 573-438-6000, Ext 560. FAX: 573-438-6006. *Librn,* Gwen Botkin; Staff 1 (Non-MLS 1)
SOUTH CENTRAL CORRECTIONAL CENTER, 255 W Hwy 32, Licking, 65542-9069. Tel: 573-674-4470. FAX: 573-674-4428. *Librn,* Denese Young; Staff 2 (Non-MLS 2)
SOUTHEAST CORRECTIONAL CENTER, Hwy 105, Charleston, 63834. Tel: 573-683-4409. FAX: 573-683-7022. *Librn,* Sandria Hutcheson; *Librn,* Dorothy Wright; Staff 2 (Non-MLS 2)
TIPTON CORRECTIONAL CENTER, 619 N Osage Ave, Tipton, 65081-8038. Tel: 660-433-2031, Ext 2325. FAX: 660-433-2804. *Librn,* Carol Rhoads; Staff 1 (Non-MLS 1)
WESTERN MISSOURI CORRECTIONAL CENTER, 609 E Pence Rd, Cameron, 64429-8823, SAN 372-5758. Tel: 816-632-1390, Ext 421. FAX: 816-632-7882. *Librn,* Kimberly Bresnahan; Staff 1 (Non-MLS 1)
WESTERN RECEPTION & DIAGNOSTIC CORRECTIONAL CENTER, 3401 Faraon St, Saint Joseph, 64506-5101. Tel: 816-387-2158. FAX: 816-387-2217. *Libr Serv Coordr,* Kimberly Bresnahan; E-mail: kimberly.bresnahan@doc.mo.gov; *Librn,* Janet McCart; Staff 1 (MLS 1)
WOMEN'S EASTERN RECEPTION & DIAGNOSTIC CORRECTIONAL CENTER, 1101 E Hwy 54, Vandalia, 63382-2905. (Mail add: PO Box 300, Vandalia, 63382-0300). Tel: 573-594-6686. FAX: 573-594-6789. *Librn,* Cherry Pasley; *Librn,* Janet Shaw; Staff 2 (MLS 1, Non-MLS 1)

P MISSOURI RIVER REGIONAL LIBRARY*, 214 Adams St, 65101-3244. (Mail add: PO Box 89, 65102-0089), SAN 349-2427. Tel: 573-634-2464. Interlibrary Loan Service Tel: 573-634-6064, Ext 228. Administration Tel: 573-634-6064. Toll Free Tel: 800-949-7323 (Cole & Osage counties only). Administration FAX: 573-634-7028. Web Site: www.mrrl.org. *Dir,* Helen Rigdon; Tel: 573-634-6034, Ext 234, E-mail: rigdonh@mrrl.org; *Asst Dir,* Betty Hagenhoff; Tel: 573-634-6064, Ext 249, E-mail: hagenhoffb@mrrl.org; *Asst Dir, Pub Serv,* Claudia Schoonover; Tel: 573-634-6064, Ext 245, E-mail: schoonoverc@mrrl.org; *Br Mgr,* Noelle Standard; Tel: 573-897-2951, E-mail: standardn@mrrl.org; *Mgr, Children's Dept,* Angie Bayne; Tel: 573-634-6064, Ext 253, E-mail: baynea@mrrl.org; *Circ Mgr,* Jessica Wieberg; Tel: 573-634-6064, Ext 223, E-mail: wiebergj@mrrl.org; *IT Mgr,* Richard Allison; Tel: 573-634-6064, Ext 256, E-mail: allisonr@mrrl.org; *Tech Serv Mgr,* Bryan Dunlap; Tel: 573-634-6064, Ext 232, E-mail: dunlapb@mrrl.org; *Adult Prog Coordr,* Madeline Matson; Tel: 573-634-6064, Ext 250, E-mail: matsonm@mrrl.org; *Automation Syst Coordr,* Position Currently Open; *Human Res Officer,* Elizabeth Beach; Tel: 573-634-6064, Ext 261, E-mail: beache@mrrl.org; *Lead Children's Programmer,* Eric Lyons; Tel: 573-634-6064, Ext 229, E-mail: lyonse@mrrl.org; *Pub Info,* Renee Struemph; Tel: 573-634-6064, ext 247, E-mail: struemphr@mrrl.org; Staff 56 (MLS 8, Non-MLS 48)
Founded 1994. Pop 89,832; Circ 734,181
Jan 2012-Dec 2012 Income (Main Library and Branch(s)) $3,037,721, State $41,807, County $2,900,914, Locally Generated Income $13,000, Other $82,000. Mats Exp $352,674, Books $298,500, Per/Ser (Incl. Access Fees) $23,460, Micro $5,714, Electronic Ref Mat (Incl. Access Fees) $25,000. Sal $2,137,686
Library Holdings: AV Mats 26,570; Bk Vols 190,719; Per Subs 500
Subject Interests: Local hist
Automation Activity & Vendor Info: (Acquisitions) Innovative Interfaces, Inc; (Cataloging) Innovative Interfaces, Inc; (Circulation) Innovative Interfaces, Inc; (OPAC) Innovative Interfaces, Inc; (Serials) Innovative Interfaces, Inc
Database Vendor: EBSCOhost, Gale Cengage Learning, Newsbank, OCLC FirstSearch, ProQuest, ReferenceUSA
Wireless access
Function: Audio & video playback equip for onsite use
Publications: MRRL News (Monthly newsletter)
Partic in MOBIUS (Missouri Bibliographic Information User System)
Special Services for the Deaf - Bks on deafness & sign lang; Closed caption videos
Special Services for the Blind - Assistive/Adapted tech devices, equip & products; Braille equip; Computer with voice synthesizer for visually impaired persons; Home delivery serv; Large print bks; Talking bks
Open Mon-Thurs 9-9, Fri 9-6, Sat 9-5, Sun 1-5
Branches: 1
OSAGE COUNTY, 1014D Main St, Hwy 50, Linn, 65051-9782. (Mail add: PO Box 349, Linn, 65051-0349), SAN 378-2468. Tel: 573-897-2951. FAX: 573-897-3815. *Br Mgr,* Noelle Standard; E-mail: standardn@mrrl.org; Staff 3 (Non-MLS 3)
Founded 1994
Open Tues & Thurs 10-7, Wed & Fri 10-5, Sat 9-1
Friends of the Library Group
Bookmobiles: 1

P MISSOURI STATE LIBRARY*, James C Kirkpatrick State Information Ctr, 600 W Main St, 65101. (Mail add: PO Box 387, 65102-0387), SAN 309-0094. Tel: 573-751-0586. Administration Tel: 573-522-4036. Toll Free Tel: 800-325-0131 (MO only). FAX: 573-751-3612. Reference FAX: 573-751-3615. E-mail: mostlib@sos.mo.gov. Web Site: www.sos.mo.gov/library. *State Librn,* Barbara Reading; E-mail: barbara.reading@sos.mo.gov; *Dir, Ref,* Bilal Waheedah; Tel: 573-751-2862, E-mail: waheedah.bilal@sos.mo.gov; Staff 20 (MLS 16, Non-MLS 4)
Founded 1907
Special Collections: Missouri Authors Coll; Missouriana. State Document Depository; US Document Depository
Subject Interests: State govt
Automation Activity & Vendor Info: (Cataloging) OCLC; (Circulation) Innovative Interfaces, Inc; (ILL) OCLC; (OPAC) Innovative Interfaces, Inc
Wireless access
Function: Digital talking bks, Govt ref serv, ILL available, Libr develop, Prof lending libr
Publications: Keeping Up (Online only); Show Me Express (Newsletter)
Partic in MOBIUS (Missouri Bibliographic Information User System)
Open Mon-Fri 7:30-5
Restriction: Open to govt employees only, Pub use on premises

P MISSOURI STATE LIBRARY*, Wolfner Talking Book & Braille Library, 600 W Main St, 65101-1532. (Mail add: PO Box 387, 65102-0387), SAN 309-2216. Tel: 573-751-8720. Administration Tel: 573-522-2767. Toll Free Tel: 800-392-2614. FAX: 573-526-2985. TDD: 800-347-1379. E-mail: wolfner@sos.mo.gov. Web Site: www.sos.mo.gov/wolfner. *Dir,* Dr Richard J Smith; E-mail: richard.smith@sos.mo.gov; Staff 5 (MLS 4, Non-MLS 1)
Founded 1924
Library Holdings: Braille Volumes 52,755; DVDs 106; Large Print Bks 4,711; Bk Titles 84,000; Bk Vols 405,477; Per Subs 70; Talking Bks 70,065; Videos 580
Automation Activity & Vendor Info: (Cataloging) Keystone Systems, Inc (KLAS); (Circulation) Keystone Systems, Inc (KLAS); (OPAC) Keystone Systems, Inc (KLAS); (Serials) Keystone Systems, Inc (KLAS)
Wireless access
Function: Audiobks via web, Digital talking bks, Summer reading prog, Web-Braille, Web-catalog, Winter reading prog
Publications: Wolfner Library News (Quarterly)
Special Services for the Deaf - TDD equip
Special Services for the Blind - Braille bks; Descriptive video serv (DVS); Digital talking bk; Digital talking bk machines; Web-Braille
Open Mon-Fri 8-5
Friends of the Library Group

GL MISSOURI SUPREME COURT LIBRARY*, Supreme Court Bldg, 207 W High St, 65101. SAN 309-0108. Tel: 573-751-2636. FAX: 573-751-2573. *Asst Librn,* Gail Cross Miller; E-mail: gail.miller@courts.mo.gov; *Libr Asst I,* Terry Brenner; Tel: 573-751-7331, E-mail: terry.brenner@courts.mo.gov; *Libr Asst II,* Lori Conley; Tel: 573-751-7322, E-mail: lori.conley@courts.mo.gov; *Archivist,* Joseph Fred Benson; Tel: 573-751-8752; Staff 5 (MLS 1, Non-MLS 4)

Founded 1820
Library Holdings: Bk Vols 120,000; Per Subs 180
Automation Activity & Vendor Info: (Cataloging) LibraryWorld, Inc
Database Vendor: LexisNexis, Westlaw
Wireless access
Partic in Mead Data Cent
Open Mon-Fri 8-5

JOPLIN

P JOPLIN PUBLIC LIBRARY*, 300 S Main St, 64801. SAN 309-0116. Tel: 417-623-7953. Reference Tel: 417-624-5465. FAX: 417-625-4728. E-mail: jpl@joplinpubliclibrary.org. Web Site: www.joplinpubliclibrary.org. *Dir,* Jacque Gage; *Ch,* Jeana Gockley; *Coll Develop Librn,* Linda Cannon; *Ref Librn,* Patty Crane; *Tech Serv Librn,* Phyllis Seesengood; *Teen Librn,* Cari Boatright-Rerat; *Info Tech,* Lee Cushing; Staff 29 (MLS 6, Non-MLS 23)
Founded 1902. Pop 48,109; Circ 452,992
Library Holdings: Bk Titles 93,917; Bk Vols 114,566; Per Subs 253
Special Collections: Fine & Decorative Arts (Winfred L & Elizabeth C Post Memorial Art Reference Library); Genealogy Coll
Automation Activity & Vendor Info: (Acquisitions) Innovative Interfaces, Inc; (Cataloging) Innovative Interfaces, Inc; (Circulation) Innovative Interfaces, Inc; (ILL) Innovative Interfaces, Inc; (OPAC) Innovative Interfaces, Inc; (Serials) Innovative Interfaces, Inc
Database Vendor: EBSCOhost, Facts on File, Gale Cengage Learning, LearningExpress, Newsbank, OCLC FirstSearch, ReferenceUSA, TumbleBookLibrary
Wireless access
Function: Adult bk club, Adult literacy prog, Art exhibits, Audiobks via web, Bk club(s), Bks on cassette, Bks on CD, CD-ROM, Children's prog, Computers for patron use, Copy machines, Electronic databases & coll, Fax serv, Free DVD rentals, ILL available, Instruction & testing, Magnifiers for reading, Microfiche/film & reading machines, Music CDs, Notary serv, Online cat, Online ref, Online searches, OverDrive digital audio bks, Photocopying/Printing, Preschool outreach, Preschool reading prog, Prog for adults, Prog for children & young adult, Pub access computers, Ref serv in person, Scanner, Spanish lang bks, Story hour, Summer reading prog, Teen prog, Telephone ref, VHS videos, Web-catalog
Partic in Amigos Library Services, Inc; SW Mo Libr Network
Open Mon-Thurs 9-8, Fri & Sat 9-6, Sun 1-5

C MISSOURI SOUTHERN STATE UNIVERSITY*, George A Spiva Library, 3950 E Newman Rd, 64801-1595. SAN 309-0132. Tel: 417-625-9386. Circulation Tel: 417-625-9362. Reference Tel: 417-625-9342. FAX: 417-625-9734. Web Site: www.mssu.edu/spivalib. *Libr Dir,* Wendy McGrane; *Archivist,* Charles E Nodler; *Doc Delivery,* James Capeci; *Pub Serv,* Amber Carr; *Ref Serv,* Nancy Schiavone; *Ser,* Robert Black; *Tech Serv,* Anna Beth Morgan; Staff 17 (MLS 7, Non-MLS 10)
Founded 1937. Enrl 5,593; Fac 353; Highest Degree: Master
Library Holdings: Bk Vols 228,945; Per Subs 499
Special Collections: Arrell Morgan Gibson Coll; Gene Taylor Congressional papers; Tri-State Mining Maps. State Document Depository; US Document Depository
Subject Interests: Educ, Nursing
Automation Activity & Vendor Info: (Acquisitions) Innovative Interfaces, Inc; (Cataloging) Innovative Interfaces, Inc; (Circulation) Innovative Interfaces, Inc; (Course Reserve) Innovative Interfaces, Inc; (Media Booking) Innovative Interfaces, Inc; (OPAC) Innovative Interfaces, Inc; (Serials) Innovative Interfaces, Inc
Wireless access
Publications: Southern Bookends (Newsletter)
Partic in Amigos Library Services, Inc; MOBIUS (Missouri Bibliographic Information User System)
Open Mon-Thurs 7:30am-11pm, Fri 7:30-5, Sat 9-5, Sun 1-11
Friends of the Library Group

C OZARK CHRISTIAN COLLEGE*, Seth Wilson Library, 1111 N Main, 64801-4804. SAN 309-0140. Tel: 417-626-1234, Ext 2700. FAX: 417-624-0090. E-mail: library@occ.edu. Web Site: occ.edu/campuscommunity/occ.library.aspx. *Cataloger, Co-Dir,* Mark Sloneker; Tel: 417-626-1234, Ext 2713, E-mail: msloneker@occ.edu; *Co-Dir, Ref Librn,* John Hunter; Tel: 417-626-1234, Ext 2708, E-mail: hunter.john@occ.edu; *AV Supvr,* Delberta Fluharty; Tel: 417-626-1234, Ext 2712, E-mail: fluharty.delberta@occ.edu; *Circ Supvr,* Randa Reed; E-mail: rreed@occ.edu; Staff 5 (MLS 2, Non-MLS 3)
Founded 1942. Enrl 763; Highest Degree: Bachelor
Library Holdings: Bks on Deafness & Sign Lang 50; Bk Titles 62,491; Bk Vols 71,104; Per Subs 370; Talking Bks 439; Videos 756
Special Collections: Restoration Movement (Christianity)
Subject Interests: Archaeology, Biblical studies
Automation Activity & Vendor Info: (Acquisitions) Follett Software; (Cataloging) TLC (The Library Corporation); (Circulation) TLC (The Library Corporation); (Course Reserve) TLC (The Library Corporation); (OPAC) TLC (The Library Corporation); (Serials) Inmagic, Inc.
Database Vendor: EBSCOhost
Wireless access
Function: ILL available, Photocopying/Printing, Ref serv available
Partic in Asn of Christian Librs
Open Mon 8am-9:30pm, Tues-Thurs 6:50am-9:30pm, Fri 6:50-6, Sat 9-6, Sun 2-5

S WINFRED L & ELIZABETH C POST FOUNDATION*, Post Memorial Art Reference Library, 300 Main St, 64801. SAN 325-1756. Tel: 417-782-7678. E-mail: info@postlibrary.org. Web Site: www.postlibrary.org. *Dir,* Leslie T Simpson; E-mail: lsimpson@postlibrary.org; Staff 2 (MLS 1, Non-MLS 1)
Founded 1981
Library Holdings: Bk Titles 4,000; Per Subs 30
Special Collections: Antique Furniture, Original Paintings & Sculpture Coll; Art objects; Joplin Historic Architecture; Painting Reproductions; Photograph Coll; Yi Dynasty Reproductions
Subject Interests: Archit, Costumes, Decorative art, Fine arts, Gardens
Wireless access
Function: Ref serv available
Open Mon & Thurs 9:30-7:30, Tues, Wed, Fri & Sat 9:30-5:30, Sun 1-5
Restriction: Non-circulating

KAHOKA

P NORTHEAST MISSOURI LIBRARY SERVICE*, 207 W Chestnut, 63445-1489. SAN 349-2729. Tel: 660-727-2327. FAX: 660-727-2327. TDD: 660-727-3262. Web Site: nemolibrary.lib.mo.us. *Dir,* Cathy James; Staff 13 (MLS 1, Non-MLS 12)
Founded 1961. Pop 27,991; Circ 137,000
Library Holdings: Bk Titles 117,000; Bk Vols 118,000; Per Subs 49
Special Collections: Large Print Material
Subject Interests: Genealogy
Special Services for the Deaf - TDD equip
Open Mon 9-6, Tues-Fri 8-5, Sat 9-1
Friends of the Library Group
Branches: 4
KNOX COUNTY PUBLIC, 120 S Main St, Edina, 63537-1427, SAN 349-2753. Tel: 660-397-2460. FAX: 660-397-2460. *Dir,* Cathy James; E-mail: viojam@hotmail.com; Staff 1 (Non-MLS 1)
Pop 5,615
Library Holdings: DVDs 621; Bk Titles 21,017; Bk Vols 22,136; Per Subs 33
Special Services for the Blind - Large print bks; Talking bks
Open Mon-Fri 8-12 & 12:30-5, Sat 8-12 & 12:30-4
LEWIS COUNTY BRANCH-LABELLE, 425 State St, LaBelle, 63447. (Mail add: PO Box 34, LaBelle, 63447), SAN 349-2788. Tel: 660-213-3600. FAX: 660-462-3600. *Br Mgr,* Roxanne Lewis; Staff 1 (Non-MLS 1)
Library Holdings: Bk Titles 7,892; Bk Vols 10,632; Per Subs 18
Open Mon, Wed & Fri 8-12 & 1-5, Sat 8-12
Friends of the Library Group
LEWIS COUNTY BRANCH-LAGRANGE, 114 S Main, LaGrange, 63448. (Mail add: PO Box 8, LaGrange, 63448-0008), SAN 349-2818. Tel: 573-655-2288. FAX: 573-655-2288. *Br Mgr,* Michele Adair; Staff 1 (Non-MLS 1)
Library Holdings: Bk Titles 11,191; Bk Vols 12,309; Per Subs 23
Open Mon 12-6, Tues-Fri 12-5:30, Sat 9-12
Friends of the Library Group
H E SEVER MEMORIAL, 207 W Chestnut, 63445, SAN 349-2877. Tel: 660-727-3262. FAX: 660-727-1055. E-mail: severmemoriallibrary@hotmail.com. *Br Mgr,* Brenda Brown; Staff 3 (MLS 1, Non-MLS 2)
Library Holdings: Bk Titles 53,765; Bk Vols 58,922; Per Subs 31
Special Collections: Large Print Materials; Three County (Knox, Lewis, Clark) Histories & Genealogy Coll, micro
Subject Interests: Med
Special Services for the Deaf - TDD equip
Open Mon 9-6, Tues-Fri 8-5, Sat 9-1
Friends of the Library Group

KANSAS CITY

S AMERICAN TRUCK HISTORICAL SOCIETY, Zoe James Memorial Library, 10380 N Ambassador Dr, Ste 101, 64153-1378. (Mail add: PO Box 901611, 64190-1611), SAN 370-9698. Tel: 816-891-9900. FAX: 816-891-9903. E-mail: info@aths.org. Web Site: www.aths.org. *Libr Dir,* Courtney Dery
Founded 1971
Library Holdings: Bk Titles 1,251; Bk Vols 1,398; Per Subs 52; Spec Interest Per Sub 28
Special Collections: Ernie Sternberg - Sterling Truck; PIE; White Motor Company Archives

Publications: Antique Truck Registry (4th edition); ATHS Show Time; Wheels of Time (Bi-monthly)
Open Mon-Fri 8-4:30

C AVILA UNIVERSITY*, Hooley-Bundschu Library, 11901 Wornall Rd, 64145. SAN 309-0183. Tel: 816-501-3621. FAX: 816-501-2456. Web Site: www.avila.edu. *Dir,* Kathleen Finegan; Tel: 816-501-3711, E-mail: kathleen.finegan@avila.edu; *Access Serv,* Larry Kramer; Tel: 816-501-3712, E-mail: larry.kramer@avila.edu; *Pub Serv,* Farrukh Hasan; Tel: 816-501-3620, E-mail: farrukh.hasan@avila.edu; *Tech Serv,* Dennis Goodyear; Tel: 816-501-3710, E-mail: dennis.goodyear@avila.edu; Staff 4 (MLS 4)
Founded 1916. Enrl 1,500; Fac 70; Highest Degree: Master
Library Holdings: Bk Titles 61,082; Bk Vols 70,000; Per Subs 500
Special Collections: Women Religious
Wireless access
Partic in MOBIUS (Missouri Bibliographic Information User System)
Open Mon-Thurs 8am-11pm, Fri 8-6, Sat 10-5, Sun 3-11

S BURNS & MCDONNELL ENGINEERING CO, Central Library, 9400 Ward Pkwy, 64114. SAN 309-0248. Tel: 816-822-3550. FAX: 816-822-3409. E-mail: library@burnsmcd.com. Web Site: www.burnsmcd.com. *Coop Librn,* Karen Bleier; *Coop Librn,* Gail Kammer; E-mail: gkammer@burnsmcd.com; *Coop Librn,* Lance Warren; Staff 4 (MLS 3, Non-MLS 1)
Library Holdings: Bk Vols 25,000; Per Subs 200
Automation Activity & Vendor Info: (Cataloging) EOS International; (Circulation) EOS International
Open Mon-Fri 8-5

CR CALVARY BIBLE COLLEGE & THEOLOGICAL SEMINARY*, Hilda Kroeker Library, 15800 Calvary Rd, 64147-1341. SAN 309-0264. Tel: 816-322-0110. FAX: 816-331-4474. Web Site: www.calvary.edu. *Librn,* Hannah Bitner; Tel: 816-322-0110, Ext 1205; Staff 1 (Non-MLS 1)
Founded 1932. Enrl 309; Fac 40; Highest Degree: Master
Library Holdings: AV Mats 1,338; CDs 985; DVDs 15; e-books 397; Bk Titles 49,000; Bk Vols 59,000; Per Subs 70; Videos 338
Subject Interests: Bible, Educ, Missions, Music
Automation Activity & Vendor Info: (Cataloging) SirsiDynix; (Circulation) SirsiDynix; (Course Reserve) SirsiDynix; (OPAC) SirsiDynix
Publications: Calvary Today
Partic in Kansas City Library Service Program
Open Mon, Tues & Thurs 7:45am-10pm, Wed & Fri 7:45-6, Sat 9-6
Restriction: Fee for pub use, Open to students, fac, staff & alumni
Friends of the Library Group

R CENTRAL PRESBYTERIAN CHURCH LIBRARY*, 3501 Campbell St, 64109. SAN 328-0926. Tel: 816-931-2515. FAX: 816-931-0882. Web Site: centralpreskc.org. *Librn,* Helen Gordon; Staff 1 (MLS 1)
Library Holdings: Bk Titles 5,690; Bk Vols 5,800; Per Subs 12
Subject Interests: Presbyterianism, Relig
Open Mon-Fri 9-1:30

M CHILDREN'S MERCY HOSPITAL*, Health Sciences Library, 2401 Gillham Rd, 64108. SAN 309-0272. Tel: 816-234-3800. FAX: 816-234-3125. Web Site: www.childrensmercy.com. *Librn,* Anne Palmer; Staff 3 (MLS 1, Non-MLS 2)
Founded 1914
Library Holdings: Bk Titles 6,000; Bk Vols 7,200; Per Subs 350
Special Collections: Library of History of Pediatrics (William L Bradford, MD)
Subject Interests: Pediatrics
Partic in Docline; Health Sciences Library Network of Kansas City, Inc; OCLC Online Computer Library Center, Inc
Open Mon-Fri 8:30-5

S CHURCH OF THE NAZARENE*, International Headquarters Resource Center-Sunday School Ministries Library, PO Box 843116, 64184-3116. SAN 327-0122. Tel: 816-333-7000, Ext 2287, 816-333-7000, Ext 2497. FAX: 816-333-4439.
Library Holdings: Bk Vols 6,000; Per Subs 80
Open Mon-Fri 8-4:30

GM DEPARTMENT OF VETERANS AFFAIRS MEDICAL LIBRARY*, 4801 E Linwood Blvd, 64128-2295. SAN 309-068X. Tel: 816-922-2315. FAX: 816-922-3340. *Dir,* Elizabeth Burns; E-mail: liz.burns@va.gov
Founded 1932
Library Holdings: Bk Vols 2,500; Per Subs 198
Subject Interests: Allied health, Med
Publications: Current New Acquistion Lists
Partic in Health Sciences Library Network of Kansas City, Inc; Mid-America Library Alliance/Kansas City Metropolitan Library & Information Network; Midcontinental Regional Med Libr Program
Open Mon-Fri 8-4:30
Restriction: Med staff only

C DEVRY UNIVERSITY*, James E Lovan Library, 11224 Holmes Rd, Second Flr, 64131. SAN 309-0493. Tel: 816-941-0430, Ext 5392. Information Services Tel: 816-941-0430, Ext 5220. Reference E-mail: devrylib@devry.edu. Web Site: www.kc.devry.edu. *Dir of Libr Serv,* Beth Ann Caldarello; E-mail: bcaldarello@devry.edu; Staff 7 (MLS 1, Non-MLS 6)
Founded 1931. Highest Degree: Master
Library Holdings: Bk Titles 19,000; Per Subs 53
Subject Interests: Bus, Computer sci, Electronics
Automation Activity & Vendor Info: (Acquisitions) Ex Libris Group; (Cataloging) Ex Libris Group; (Circulation) Ex Libris Group; (ILL) OCLC; (OPAC) Ex Libris Group
Database Vendor: EBSCOhost
Wireless access
Function: Computers for patron use
Partic in Mid-America Library Alliance/Kansas City Metropolitan Library & Information Network
Open Mon-Fri 9-9, Sat 9-3
Restriction: Borrowing privileges limited to fac & registered students

S FEDERAL RESERVE BANK OF KANSAS CITY*, Research Library, One Memorial Dr, 64198. SAN 309-0345. Tel: 816-881-2970. FAX: 816-881-2807. E-mail: research.library@kc.frb.org. *Librn,* Deng M Pan; Staff 5 (MLS 2, Non-MLS 3)
Library Holdings: Bk Titles 14,000; Bk Vols 15,500; Per Subs 20
Subject Interests: Agr, Econ, Finance, Statistics
Partic in OCLC Online Computer Library Center, Inc
Restriction: Open by appt only

S LINDA HALL LIBRARY*, 5109 Cherry St, 64110-2498. SAN 309-0353. Tel: 816-363-4600. Toll Free Tel: 800-662-1545. FAX: 816-926-8790. Reference FAX: 816-926-8782. E-mail: library@lindahall.org. Web Site: www.lindahall.org. *Pres,* Lisa Browar; Tel: 816-926-8781, E-mail: browarl@lindahall.org; *Dir of Develop,* Kimberly Allen; Tel: 816-926-8792, E-mail: allenk@lindahall.org; *Dir, Innovative Tech & Libr Res Mgt,* Keri Cascio; *Dir, IT,* Robert A Smith; Tel: 816-926-8716, E-mail: smithr@lindahall.org; *Dir, Libr Coll & Serv,* Mary Moeller; Tel: 816-926-8720, E-mail: moellerm@lindahall.org; *Dir, Tech Serv,* Anne Liebst; Tel: 816-926-8784, E-mail: liebsta@lindahall.org; *Dir, Digital Asset Mgt/Spec Projects,* Donna Swischer; Tel: 816-926-8718, E-mail: swisched@lindahall.org; *Librn, Hist of Sci/Spec Coll,* Bruce Bradley; Tel: 816-926-8737, E-mail: bradleyb@lindahall.org. Subject Specialists: *Hist of sci,* Lisa Browar; *Hist of sci,* Bruce Bradley; Staff 57 (MLS 17, Non-MLS 40)
Founded 1946
Library Holdings: Bk Titles 1,267,600; Per Subs 11,415; Videos 6,500
Special Collections: History of Science; NASA & DOE Reports; Sci-Tech Conference Proceedings; Soviet & European Sci-Tech Publications; Standards & Specifications; US Patent & Trademark Specifications
Subject Interests: Eng, Maps, US govt doc
Automation Activity & Vendor Info: (Acquisitions) SirsiDynix; (Cataloging) SirsiDynix; (Circulation) SirsiDynix; (OPAC) SirsiDynix; (Serials) SirsiDynix
Database Vendor: SirsiDynix
Publications: History of Science Exhibit Catalogs; Online Exhibition Catalogs
Partic in OCLC Online Computer Library Center, Inc; OCLC Research Library Partnership
Open Mon-Fri 9-5
Friends of the Library Group

S HALLMARK CARDS, INC*, Creative Resource Library, 2501 McGee, No 146, 64108. SAN 349-2907. Tel: 816-274-7470. FAX: 816-545-2239. Web Site: www.hallmark.com. *In Charge,* Mark Spencer; E-mail: mspenc3@hallmark.com; Staff 4 (MLS 2, Non-MLS 2)
Founded 1930
Library Holdings: Bk Titles 2,000; Bk Vols 22,000; Per Subs 180
Subject Interests: Design, Fine arts
Publications: Monthly Newsletter
Open Mon-Fri 9-6

Branches:

BUSINESS RESEARCH LIBRARY, 2501 McGee, No 203, 64108, SAN 349-2931. Tel: 816-274-4648. FAX: 816-274-7394. *Librn,* Isidro de la Herran; Staff 1 (MLS 1)
Founded 1980
Library Holdings: Bk Vols 2,000; Per Subs 55
Subject Interests: Retailing
Open Mon-Fri 9-5

S IRISH GENEALOGICAL FOUNDATION LIBRARY*, PO Box 7575, 64116. SAN 378-0015. Tel: 816-454-2410. FAX: 816-454-2410. Web Site: www.irishroots.com. *In Charge,* Mike O'Laughlin; E-mail: mike@irishroots.com; Staff 1 (Non-MLS 1)
Library Holdings: Bk Titles 3,890; Bk Vols 4,261
Special Collections: Journal of the American Irish Historical Society 1898-various by county in Ireland
Subject Interests: Genealogy, Heraldry, Irish hist
Restriction: Open by appt only
Friends of the Library Group

GL JACKSON COUNTY LAW LIBRARY, INC*, 1125 Grand Blvd, Ste 1050, 64106. SAN 321-8333. Tel: 816-221-2221. FAX: 816-221-6607. E-mail: info@jcll.org. Web Site: www.jcll.org. *Dir,* Jan D Medved; E-mail: jmedved@jcll.org; *Ref Librn,* Eric W Brust; *Tech Serv Librn,* Debbie S Steele; E-mail: dsteele@jcll.org; Staff 4 (MLS 2, Non-MLS 2)
Founded 1871
Library Holdings: Bk Titles 27,800; Bk Vols 46,914; Per Subs 31
Subject Interests: Fed law, Jury instructions, Legal res, Regulations, State law, Statute law
Automation Activity & Vendor Info: (Acquisitions) LibraryWorld, Inc; (Cataloging) LibraryWorld, Inc; (OPAC) LibraryWorld, Inc; (Serials) LibraryWorld, Inc
Function: Res libr
Publications: Brochure; Pathfinder
Open Mon-Fri 8:30-5
Restriction: Not a lending libr, Staff & mem only, Sub libr

C KANSAS CITY ART INSTITUTE LIBRARY, Jannes Library & Learning Center, 4538 Warwick Blvd, 64111. (Mail add: 4415 Warwick Blvd, 64111-1874), SAN 309-037X. Tel: 816-802-3390. FAX: 816-802-3338. E-mail: library@kcai.edu. Web Site: www.kcai.edu/library. *Dir,* M J Poehler; E-mail: mpoehler@kcai.edu; Staff 5 (MLS 2, Non-MLS 3)
Founded 1885. Enrl 730; Fac 115; Highest Degree: Bachelor
Library Holdings: e-books 166,025; Bk Titles 30,000; Per Subs 95; Spec Interest Per Sub 95
Special Collections: Artists books
Subject Interests: Fine arts
Automation Activity & Vendor Info: (Cataloging) Innovative Interfaces, Inc; (Circulation) Innovative Interfaces, Inc; (Course Reserve) Innovative Interfaces, Inc; (ILL) OCLC Connexion; (OPAC) Innovative Interfaces, Inc; (Serials) Innovative Interfaces, Inc
Database Vendor: ARTstor, EBSCOhost, JSTOR, Oxford Online, YBP Library Services
Wireless access
Function: Computers for patron use, Copy machines, e-mail & chat, E-Reserves, Electronic databases & coll, Online cat, Outside serv via phone, mail, e-mail & web, Photocopying/Printing, Pub access computers, Ref & res
Partic in Amigos Library Services, Inc; MOBIUS (Missouri Bibliographic Information User System)
Open Mon-Thurs 8:30am-9pm, Fri 8:30-5, Sun 2-10
Restriction: Open to pub for ref only, Open to students, fac & staff

P THE KANSAS CITY PUBLIC LIBRARY*, Central Library, 14 W Tenth St, 64105. SAN 349-2990. Tel: 816-701-3400. Circulation Tel: 816-701-3449. Interlibrary Loan Service Tel: 816-701-3463. Reference Tel: 816-701-3433. Information Services Tel: 816-701-4140. FAX: 816-701-3401. TDD: 816-701-3403. Web Site: www.kclibrary.org. *Dir, Cent Libr,* Lillie Brack; Tel: 816-701-3543, E-mail: lilliebrack@kclibrary.org; *Dir,* R Crosby Kemper, III; Tel: 816-701-3516, E-mail: crosbyk@kclibrary.org; *Dir of Develop,* Claudia Baker; Tel: 816-701-3518, E-mail: claudiabaker@kclibrary.org; *Dir, Human Res,* Pam Kannady; Tel: 816-701-3517, E-mail: pamkannady@kclibrary.org; *Dir, Pub Affairs & Communication,* Henry Fortunato; Tel: 816-701-3514, E-mail: henryfortunato@kclibrary.org; *Dir, Teen Serv,* Crystal Faris; Tel: 816-701-3513, E-mail: crystalfaris@kclibrary.org; *Dir, Youth Serv,* Helma Hawkins; Tel: 816-701-3450, E-mail: helmahawkins@kclibrary.org; *Dep Dir, Br,* Joel Jones; Tel: 816-701-3504, E-mail: joeljones@kclibrary.org; *Dep Exec Dir,* Cheptoo Kositany-Buckner; Tel: 816-701-3508, E-mail: cheptookositany@kclibrary.org; *Ref Librn, Govt Doc,* Carol Bruegging; Tel: 816-701-3653, E-mail: carolbruegging@kclibrary.org; *Chief Financial Officer,* Debbie Siragusa; Tel: 816-701-3515, E-mail: debbiesiragusa@kclibrary.org; *Mgr, Mo Valley Spec Coll,* Eli Paul; Tel: 816-701-3527, E-mail: elipaul@kclibrary.org; *Doc Delivery Supvr,* Terry Ann Anderson; Tel: 806-701-3564, E-mail: terryanderson@kclibrary.org; Staff 249 (MLS 41, Non-MLS 208)
Founded 1873. Pop 194,122; Circ 2,348,408
Library Holdings: Audiobooks 11,559; CDs 12,702; DVDs 22,972; Bk Vols 390,997; Videos 7,633
Special Collections: African American History Coll (John F Ramos); Civil War Coll; Kansas City Latino Heritage Coll; Missouri Valley History & Genealogy; Western Migration & Trails Coll. Oral History; State Document Depository; US Document Depository
Automation Activity & Vendor Info: (Circulation) SirsiDynix
Database Vendor: ALLDATA Online, Dun & Bradstreet, EBSCOhost, Gale Cengage Learning, H W Wilson, LearningExpress, LexisNexis, Newsbank, OCLC FirstSearch, ProQuest, ReferenceUSA, SirsiDynix, Standard & Poor's
Wireless access
Publications: Annual Report; Comprehensive Annual Financial Report
Partic in Kansas City Library Service Program; Mid-America Library Alliance/Kansas City Metropolitan Library & Information Network; OCLC Online Computer Library Center, Inc
Open Mon-Wed 9-9, Thurs 9-6, Fri 9-5, Sat & Sun 10-5
Friends of the Library Group
Branches: 9
LUCILE H BLUFORD BRANCH, 3050 Prospect Ave, 64128, SAN 349-3202. Tel: 816-701-3482. FAX: 816-701-3492. *Mgr,* Oliver Clark; Tel: 816-701-3582, E-mail: oliverclark@kclibrary.org
Library Holdings: Audiobooks 959; CDs 1,237; DVDs 1,431; Bk Vols 25,685; Videos 210
Open Mon-Thurs 10-8, Fri & Sat 10-5, Sun 1-5
NORTH-EAST, 6000 Wilson Rd, 64123, SAN 349-3148. Tel: 816-701-3485. FAX: 816-701-3495. *Mgr,* Claudia Visnich; Tel: 816-701-3589, E-mail: claudiavisnich@kclibrary.org
Library Holdings: Audiobooks 1,818; CDs 2,343; DVDs 2,938; Bk Vols 48,107; Videos 749
Open Mon-Thurs 9-8, Fri 9-6, Sat 10-5, Sun 1-5
PLAZA, 4801 Main St, 64112-2765, SAN 349-3172. Tel: 816-701-3481. FAX: 816-701-3491. Web Site: www.kclibrary.org/plaza. *Mgr,* Dorothy Elliott; Tel: 816-701-3581, E-mail: dorothyelliot@kclibrary.org; Staff 6.5 (MLS 6.5)
Library Holdings: Audiobooks 4,906; CDs 8,110; DVDs 8,826; Bk Vols 122,474; Videos 62
Open Mon-Fri 9-9, Sat 10-6, Sun 1-6
IRENE H RUIZ BIBLIOTECA DE LAS AMERICAS, 2017 W Pennway, 64108, SAN 349-3350. Tel: 816-701-3487. FAX: 816-701-3497. *Br Mgr,* Julie Robinson; E-mail: julierobinson@kclibrary.org
Library Holdings: Audiobooks 561; CDs 1,504; DVDs 2,922; Bk Vols 10,451; Videos 474
Open Mon-Thurs 10-8, Fri & Sat 10-5
SOUTHEAST, 6242 Swope Pkwy, 64130-4447, SAN 349-3261. Tel: 816-701-3484. FAX: 816-701-3494. *Br Mgr,* Ruth Stephens; Tel: 816-701-3584, E-mail: ruthstephens@kclibrary.org
Library Holdings: Audiobooks 1,254; CDs 1,857; DVDs 1,990; Bk Vols 43,590; Videos 243
Open Mon-Thurs 10-8, Fri & Sat 10-5, Sun 1-5
SUGAR CREEK BRANCH, 102 S Sterling, Sugar Creek, 64054. Tel: 816-701-3489. FAX: 816-701-3499. *Mgr,* Claudia Visnich; Tel: 816-701-3589, E-mail: claudiavisnich@kclibrary.org
Library Holdings: Audiobooks 577; CDs 1,229; DVDs 1,644; Bk Vols 10,356; Videos 187
Open Mon-Thurs 12-7, Fri-Sun 1-5
TRAILS WEST, 11401 E 23rd St, Independence, 64052, SAN 349-3326. Tel: 816-701-3483. FAX: 816-701-3493. *Mgr,* Ritchie Momon; Tel: 816-701-3583, E-mail: ritchiemomon@kclibrary.org
Library Holdings: Audiobooks 3,042; CDs 4,264; DVDs 5,350; Bk Vols 56,296; Videos 1,641
Open Mon-Thurs 9-8, Fri 9-5, Sat 10-5, Sun 1-5
WALDO COMMUNITY, 201 E 75th St, 64114, SAN 349-3296. Tel: 816-701-3486. FAX: 816-701-3496. *Mgr,* Alicia Ahlvers; Tel: 816-701-3586, E-mail: aliciaahlvers@kclibrary.org
Library Holdings: Audiobooks 2,034; CDs 4,919; DVDs 3,638; Bk Vols 44,868; Videos 634
Open Mon-Thurs 9-8, Fri 9-6, Sat 10-5, Sun 1-5
WESTPORT, 118 Westport Rd, 64111, SAN 349-3385. Tel: 816-701-3488. FAX: 816-701-3498. *Librn,* Mary Roberson; Tel: 816-701-3588, E-mail: maryroberson@kclibrary.org
Library Holdings: Audiobooks 2,677; CDs 4,341; DVDs 4,660; Bk Vols 36,197; Videos 2,293
Open Mon-Thurs 10-7, Fri & Sat 10-5

CM KANSAS CITY UNIVERSITY OF MEDICINE & BIOSCIENCES D'ANGELO LIBRARY*, 1750 Independence Ave, 64106-1453. SAN 309-0388. Tel: 816-654-7260. Interlibrary Loan Service Tel: 816-654-7266. Reference Tel: 816-654-7264. Automation Services Tel: 816-654-7262. Toll Free Tel: 800-234-4847. FAX: 816-654-7261. E-mail: library@kcumb.edu. Web Site: www.kcumb.edu/library. *Dir,* Marilyn J DeGeus; E-mail: mdegeus@kcumb.edu; *Digital Serv, Ref Librn,* Lori A Fitterling; E-mail: lfitterling@kcumb.edu; *Cataloger, Ser Librn,* V Lynn Mousseau; Tel: 816-654-7265, E-mail: lmousseau@kcumb.edu; *Access Serv/Ser Coordr,* Angie B Clemmer; Tel: 816-654-7263, E-mail: aclemmer@kcumb.edu; *Doc Delivery, Tech Spec,* Laurie A Sims; Tel: 816-654-7266, E-mail: lsims@kcumb.edu; Staff 7 (MLS 3, Non-MLS 4)
Founded 1916. Enrl 985; Fac 176; Highest Degree: Doctorate
Library Holdings: AV Mats 1,998; CDs 497; DVDs 521; e-books 840; e-journals 754; Electronic Media & Resources 297; Bk Titles 38,053; Bk Vols 48,221; Per Subs 607; Videos 312

Special Collections: Osteopathic History & Medicine (Osteopathic Coll), bk, flm, slides, tapes
Subject Interests: Med
Automation Activity & Vendor Info: (Acquisitions) Ex Libris Group; (Cataloging) Ex Libris Group; (Circulation) Ex Libris Group; (Course Reserve) Ex Libris Group; (ILL) Ex Libris Group; (Media Booking) Ex Libris Group; (OPAC) Ex Libris Group; (Serials) Ex Libris Group
Wireless access
Publications: KCUMB Library Guide
Partic in Amigos Library Services, Inc; Docline; Health Sciences Library Network of Kansas City, Inc; National Network of Libraries of Medicine Midcontinental Region
Open Mon-Thurs 7am-11:30pm, Fri 7-6, Sat 9-11:30, Sun Noon-11:30
Restriction: Borrowing privileges limited to fac & registered students, Borrowing requests are handled by ILL

METROPOLITAN COMMUNITY COLLEGE

J BLUE RIVER LIBRARY*, 20301 E 78 Hwy, Independence, 64057, SAN 377-8258. Tel: 816-604-6642. Interlibrary Loan Service Tel: 816-220-6650. FAX: 816-220-6751. Web Site: brlibrary.mcckc.edu. *Libr Dir,* Jared Rinck; Tel: 816-604-6740, E-mail: jared.rinck@mcckc.edu; *Libr Spec,* Amy Campbell; E-mail: amy.campbell@mcckc.edu; *Libr Spec,* Diane Martin; E-mail: diane.martin@mcckc.edu; Staff 3 (MLS 1, Non-MLS 2)
Founded 1990. Enrl 3,601; Fac 29; Highest Degree: Associate
Library Holdings: Bk Vols 14,000; Per Subs 85
Automation Activity & Vendor Info: (Circulation) Innovative Interfaces, Inc; (OPAC) Innovative Interfaces, Inc
Database Vendor: EBSCOhost, Gale Cengage Learning, JSTOR, LexisNexis, OVID Technologies, ProQuest
Partic in Kans City Mo Libr & Info Network; MOBIUS (Missouri Bibliographic Information User System)
Special Services for the Deaf - Assistive tech
Special Services for the Blind - Assistive/Adapted tech devices, equip & products
Open Mon-Thurs (Fall-Spring) 8am-9pm, Fri 8-4:30, Sat 9-1

J LONGVIEW CAMPUS LIBRARY*, 500 SW Longview Rd, Lee's Summit, 64081-2105, SAN 309-0787. Tel: 816-604-2080. Interlibrary Loan Service Tel: 816-604-2243. Reference Tel: 816-604-2268. Administration Tel: 816-604-2266. FAX: 816-604-2087. Web Site: www.mcckc.edu. *Libr Mgr,* Judy Rice; Tel: 816-604-2278, E-mail: judy.rice@mcckc.edu; *Librn,* Candice Baldwin; E-mail: candice.baldwin@mcckc.edu; *Ref Librn,* Marty Miller; Tel: 816-604-2654, E-mail: marty.miller@mcckc.edu; *ILL,* Sandy Findley; E-mail: sandy.findley@mcckc.edu; Staff 9.5 (MLS 4, Non-MLS 5.5)
Founded 1969. Enrl 8,000; Fac 86; Highest Degree: Associate
Jul 2010-Jun 2011. Mats Exp $121,000, Books $38,000, Per/Ser (Incl. Access Fees) $33,000, Electronic Ref Mat (Incl. Access Fees) $50,000. Sal $388,405 (Prof $205,160)
Library Holdings: Audiobooks 10; AV Mats 840; e-books 10,098; Microforms 4,200; Bk Titles 37,781; Bk Vols 44,411; Per Subs 158
Automation Activity & Vendor Info: (Acquisitions) Innovative Interfaces, Inc - Millenium; (Cataloging) Innovative Interfaces, Inc - Millenium; (Circulation) Innovative Interfaces, Inc - Millenium; (Course Reserve) Innovative Interfaces, Inc - Millenium; (ILL) Innovative Interfaces, Inc - Millenium; (Media Booking) Innovative Interfaces, Inc - Millenium; (OPAC) Innovative Interfaces, Inc - Millenium; (Serials) Innovative Interfaces, Inc - Millenium
Database Vendor: ABC-CLIO, CQ Press, EBSCO Information Services, EBSCOhost, Facts on File, Gale Cengage Learning, JSTOR, LexisNexis, Newsbank, OCLC FirstSearch, Oxford Online, ProQuest, Wilson - Wilson Web
Partic in Mid-America Library Alliance/Kansas City Metropolitan Library & Information Network; MOBIUS (Missouri Bibliographic Information User System)
Open Mon-Thurs (Fall-Spring) 8-8, Fri 8-4, Sat 10-2; Mon-Thurs (Summer) 8-7, Fri 8-4

J MAPLE WOODS COMMUNITY COLLEGE LIBRARY, 2601 NE Barry Rd, 64156, SAN 309-0434. Tel: 816-604-3080. Interlibrary Loan Service Tel: 816-604-3083. Reference Tel: 816-604-3042. FAX: 816-437-3082. Circulation FAX: 816-437-3400. Web Site: mwlibrary.mcckc.edu. *Dir,* Linda Carter; *Ref,* Marieta Knopf; *Ref,* Mary Northrup; *Ref,* Carol Schroeder; Staff 5.5 (MLS 3, Non-MLS 2.5)
Founded 1969. Enrl 5,000; Fac 52; Highest Degree: Associate
Jul 2013-Jun 2014. Mats Exp $53,948, Per/Ser (Incl. Access Fees) $10,608, Micro $12,686, Electronic Ref Mat (Incl. Access Fees) $30,654. Sal $280,401 (Prof $189,823)
Library Holdings: e-books 159,301; Bk Vols 32,509; Per Subs 84; Videos 375
Special Collections: Veterinary Medicine Coll, bks & per
Automation Activity & Vendor Info: (Acquisitions) Innovative Interfaces, Inc; (Circulation) Innovative Interfaces, Inc; (Course Reserve) Innovative Interfaces, Inc; (ILL) Innovative Interfaces, Inc; (OPAC) Innovative Interfaces, Inc; (Serials) Innovative Interfaces, Inc
Database Vendor: CQ Press, EBSCOhost, Facts on File, Gale Cengage Learning, JSTOR, LexisNexis, Oxford Online, ProQuest, Westlaw
Partic in Mid-America Library Alliance/Kansas City Metropolitan Library & Information Network; Missouri Research & Education Network (MOREnet); MOBIUS (Missouri Bibliographic Information User System)
Open Mon-Thurs 8-7, Fri 8-3:30

PENN VALLEY LIBRARY*, 3201 SW Trafficway, 64111-2764, SAN 309-0574. Tel: 816-604-4080. Web Site: mcckc.edu. *Dir,* Position Currently Open; *Libr Mgr,* Jackie Roberts; E-mail: jackie.roberts@mcckc.edu; *Librn,* Michael Korklan; Tel: 816-759-4090, E-mail: michael.korklan@mcckc.edu; *Tech Serv Coordr,* Ted Ostaszewski; Tel: 816-759-4095, E-mail: ted.ostaszewski@mcckc.edu; Staff 7 (MLS 7)
Founded 1969. Enrl 4,500; Fac 110
Library Holdings: e-books 6,296; Bk Vols 84,252; Per Subs 184
Automation Activity & Vendor Info: (Acquisitions) Innovative Interfaces, Inc; (Cataloging) Innovative Interfaces, Inc; (Circulation) Innovative Interfaces, Inc; (Course Reserve) Innovative Interfaces, Inc; (ILL) Innovative Interfaces, Inc; (Media Booking) Innovative Interfaces, Inc; (OPAC) Innovative Interfaces, Inc; (Serials) Innovative Interfaces, Inc
Partic in Amigos Library Services, Inc; Mid-America Library Alliance/Kansas City Metropolitan Library & Information Network; Missouri Research & Education Network (MOREnet); MOBIUS (Missouri Bibliographic Information User System)
Publications: Bookmarks; New Books List; Student Guides
Open Mon-Thurs 8-8, Fri 8-3:30

S MIDWEST RESEARCH INSTITUTE*, C J Patterson Memorial Library, 425 Volker Blvd, 64110. SAN 349-3504. Tel: 816-360-5188. FAX: 816-753-8420. *Sr Librn,* Kimberly A Carter; E-mail: kcarter@mriresearch.org; Staff 1.25 (MLS 1, Non-MLS 0.25)
Founded 1945
Library Holdings: Bk Vols 1,000; Per Subs 75
Subject Interests: Chem, Eng, Environ studies, Microbiology
Partic in Amigos Library Services, Inc; Health Sciences Library Network of Kansas City, Inc; Mid-America Library Alliance/Kansas City Metropolitan Library & Information Network
Open Mon-Fri 8-5
Restriction: Staff use only

R MIDWESTERN BAPTIST THEOLOGICAL SEMINARY LIBRARY*, 5001 N Oak Trafficway, 64118-4620. SAN 309-0477. Tel: 816-414-3729. Reference Tel: 816-414-3728. Administration Tel: 816-414-3730. Toll Free Tel: 877-414-3729. FAX: 816-414-3790. Web Site: www.mbts.edu/academics/library. *Dir,* Dr Craig Kubic; E-mail: ckubic@mbts.edu; *Dir, Tech Serv,* Susan Beyer; Tel: 816-414-3725, E-mail: sbeyer@mbt.edu; *Head, Acq,* Rusty Tryon; Tel: 816-414-3726, E-mail: rtryon@mbts.edu; *Head, Ref,* Judy Howie; E-mail: jhowie@mbts.edu.
Subject Specialists: *Humanities, Relig,* Dr Craig Kubic; *German, Humanities,* Rusty Tryon; Staff 4 (MLS 3, Non-MLS 1)
Founded 1951. Highest Degree: Doctorate
Library Holdings: AV Mats 4,196; CDs 623; DVDs 419; e-books 114,684; e-journals 223; Microforms 3,100; Music Scores 1,118; Bk Vols 102,493; Per Subs 371; Videos 865
Special Collections: Baptist Denominational Coll, Charles Haddon Spurgeon Personal Library; Rawlings Interfaith Evangelism Coll
Subject Interests: Biblical studies
Automation Activity & Vendor Info: (Acquisitions) Innovative Interfaces, Inc; (Cataloging) Innovative Interfaces, Inc; (Circulation) Innovative Interfaces, Inc; (ILL) Innovative Interfaces, Inc; (OPAC) Innovative Interfaces, Inc; (Serials) Innovative Interfaces, Inc
Database Vendor: EBSCOhost, OCLC FirstSearch, OCLC WorldShare Interlibrary Loan
Wireless access
Function: ILL available
Partic in MOBIUS (Missouri Bibliographic Information User System)
Open Mon, Tues, Thurs & Fri 7:30am-10pm, Wed 7:30-5, Sat 9-3
Restriction: Staff use only, Students only

GL MISSOURI COURT OF APPEALS LIBRARY*, Western District, 1300 Oak St, 64106-2970. SAN 309-0485. Tel: 816-889-3639. FAX: 816-889-3668. Web Site: www.courts.mo.gov. *Librn,* Janine Estrada-Lopez
Founded 1885
Library Holdings: Bk Titles 31,190; Bk Vols 32,500; Per Subs 150
Partic in Westlaw
Open Mon-Fri 8-4:30

G NATIONAL ARCHIVES & RECORDS ADMINISTRATION*, Central Plains Region, 400 W Pershing Rd, 64108. SAN 309-0515. Tel: 816-268-8000. FAX: 816-268-8038. E-mail: kansascity.archives@nara.gov. Web Site: www.archives.gov/central-plains/kansas-city. *Archival Operations,* Lori Cox-Paul
Founded 1969

Library Holdings: Bk Titles 35,112; Bk Vols 37,696; Per Subs 41
Special Collections: Archival records of Federal agencies & courts in Iowa, Kansas, Missouri & Nebraska; Federal Government Field Office Records of Federal Agencies within the states of Iowa, Kansas, Minnesota, Missouri, Nebraska, North Dakota, & South Dakota, 1850-1950; Federal Population Censuses, 1790-1930, microfilm; Records of Indian Territory, Kansas, Nebraska & Dakota Territories, 1854-89
Subject Interests: Econ, Ethnology, Frontier, Genealogy, Hist, Law, Natural res, Polit sci, Pub admin
Function: Photocopying/Printing
Open Tues-Sat 8-4
Restriction: Ref only to non-staff

S NATIONAL ASSOCIATION OF INSURANCE COMMISSIONERS*, Research Library, 1100 Walnut St, Ste 1500, 64106-2197. SAN 329-8345. Tel: 816-783-8250. FAX: 816-460-7682. E-mail: reslibinquiry@naic.org. Web Site: naic.softlinkliberty.net/liberty/libraryHome.do. *Libr Mgr,* Sandra Hollis; Tel: 816-783-8252, E-mail: shollis@naic.org; *Res & Automation Serv Librn,* Kay J Tyrrell; Tel: 816-783-8253, E-mail: ktyrrell@naic.org; Staff 3 (MLS 2, Non-MLS 1)
Subject Interests: Ins regulation
Automation Activity & Vendor Info: (Acquisitions) Softlink America; (Cataloging) Softlink America; (Circulation) Softlink America; (OPAC) Softlink America; (Serials) Softlink America
Database Vendor: Dun & Bradstreet, EBSCOhost, HeinOnline, LexisNexis, Westlaw
Function: Archival coll, Doc delivery serv, For res purposes, Ref serv available
Restriction: Open by appt only

R NAZARENE THEOLOGICAL SEMINARY*, Broadhurst Library, 1700 E Meyer Blvd, 64131. SAN 309-0531. Tel: 816-268-5471. Toll Free Tel: 800-831-3011. FAX: 816-822-9025. E-mail: library@nts.edu. Web Site: www.nts.edu. *Dir of Libr Serv,* Debra Bradshaw; Tel: 816-268-5472, E-mail: dlbradshaw@nts.edu; *Asst Librn,* Kendra Holcomb-Densmore; Tel: 816-268-5473, E-mail: kkholcomb@nts.edu; *Asst Librn,* Jennifer Steinford; Tel: 816-268-5474, E-mail: jrsteinford@nts.edu; Staff 10 (MLS 2, Non-MLS 8)
Founded 1945. Enrl 396; Fac 18; Highest Degree: Doctorate
Library Holdings: Bk Vols 140,588; Per Subs 526
Special Collections: Carl Bangs Arminianism Coll; History of the Holiness Movement; Methodistica-Wesleyana Coll
Database Vendor: Dialog, EBSCOhost, OCLC FirstSearch, ProQuest, SirsiDynix
Partic in Amigos Library Services, Inc; Dialog Corp; Kansas City Library Service Program; Mid-America Library Alliance/Kansas City Metropolitan Library & Information Network; OCLC Online Computer Library Center, Inc
Open Mon & Tues 8-8:30, Wed-Fri 8-5, Sat 12-4

S NELSON-ATKINS MUSEUM OF ART, Spencer Art Reference Library, 4525 Oak St, 64111-1873. SAN 309-054X. Tel: 816-751-1216. FAX: 816-751-0498. Web Site: www.nelson-atkins.org. *Head Librn,* Marilyn Carbonell; Tel: 816-751-1381, E-mail: mcarbonell@nelson-atkins.org; *Pub Serv Librn,* Amelia Nelson; Tel: 816-751-1215, E-mail: anelson@nelson-atkins.org; *Acq,* Jessica Zhang; Tel: 816-751-0407, E-mail: szhang@nelson-atkins.org; *Archivist,* Holly Wright; Tel: 816-751-1354, E-mail: hwright@nelson-atkins.org; *Cat, Ref,* Tracey Boswell; Tel: 816-751-1231, E-mail: tboswell@nelson-atkins.org; *Cat,* Katharine Reed; Tel: 816-751-0409, E-mail: kreed@nelson-atkins.org; *Cat,* Dawn Sanders; Tel: 816-751-0400, E-mail: dsanders@nelson-atkins.org; *ILL,* Roberta Wagener; Tel: 817-751-1287, E-mail: rwagener@nelson-atkins.org; *Ser,* Karen Harrell; Tel: 816-751-0408, E-mail: kharrell@nelson-atkins.org; *Visual Res,* Noriko Ebersole; Tel: 816-751-1214, E-mail: nebersole@nelson-atkins.org; Staff 14 (MLS 5, Non-MLS 9)
Founded 1933
Library Holdings: AV Mats 300; Microforms 100; Bk Titles 140,000; Bk Vols 200,000; Per Subs 500; Spec Interest Per Sub 45,800
Special Collections: Auction Catalogs; Decorative Arts, per; Oriental Art; Prints & Drawings (The John H Bender Library)
Subject Interests: Art hist, Asian art, Decorative art, European art
Automation Activity & Vendor Info: (Acquisitions) Ex Libris Group; (Cataloging) Ex Libris Group; (Circulation) Ex Libris Group; (Course Reserve) Ex Libris Group; (ILL) OCLC; (OPAC) Ex Libris Group; (Serials) Ex Libris Group
Database Vendor: Amigos Library Services, EBSCOhost, Ex Libris Group, JSTOR, Luna Imaging/Insight, OCLC CAMIO, OCLC FirstSearch, OCLC WorldShare Interlibrary Loan, OCLC-RLG, Oxford Online, ProQuest, YBP Library Services
Wireless access
Function: Archival coll, Ref & res
Partic in Amigos Library Services, Inc
Open Wed 10-5, Thurs & Fri 10-6, Sat & Sun 1-4
Restriction: Non-circulating

L POLSINELLI SHUGHART PC*, Law Library, 700 W 47th St, Ste 1000, 64112. SAN 323-8911. Tel: 816-753-1000. FAX: 816-753-1536. Web Site: www.polsinelli.com. *Librn,* Kelsey Roberts; E-mail: kroberts@polsinelli.com; *Librn,* Avis C Bates; *Librn,* Michelle Rogers; *Librn,* Betty Solar; Staff 4 (MLS 2, Non-MLS 2)
Library Holdings: Bk Titles 4,000; Bk Vols 15,000; Per Subs 150
Automation Activity & Vendor Info: (Acquisitions) EOS International; (Serials) EOS International
Wireless access
Restriction: Staff use only

M RESEARCH MEDICAL CENTER*, Carl R Ferris Medical Library, 2316 E Meyer Blvd, 64132-1199. SAN 309-0582. Tel: 816-276-4309. FAX: 816-276-3106. Web Site: www.hcamidwest.com. *Med Librn,* Kitty Serling; E-mail: kitty.serling@hcamidwest.com. Subject Specialists: *Consumer health, Nursing,* Kitty Serling; Staff 1 (MLS 1)
Founded 1963
Library Holdings: e-journals 2,000; Bk Titles 2,000; Per Subs 730
Subject Interests: Nursing
Database Vendor: OVID Technologies
Wireless access
Function: Archival coll, Doc delivery serv, For res purposes, Health sci info serv, ILL available, Online searches, Orientations, Photocopying/Printing, Prof lending libr, Ref serv available, Referrals accepted, Res libr, Wheelchair accessible
Partic in Health Sciences Library Network of Kansas City, Inc; Mid-America Library Alliance/Kansas City Metropolitan Library & Information Network; National Network of Libraries of Medicine Midcontinental Region
Open Mon-Fri 8-4:30
Restriction: Access for corporate affiliates, Authorized patrons, Circulates for staff only, Co libr, In-house use for visitors, Pub use on premises, Restricted borrowing privileges, Use of others with permission of librn

C ROCKHURST UNIVERSITY, Greenlease Library, 1100 Rockhurst Rd, 64110-2561. SAN 309-0590. Tel: 816-501-4142. Reference Tel: 816-501-4116. FAX: 816-501-4666. E-mail: library@rockhurst.edu. Web Site: www.rockhurst.edu/library. *Libr Dir,* Laurie Hathman; Tel: 816-501-4655, E-mail: laurie.hathman@rockhurst.edu; *Access & Learning Serv Librn,* Ellie Kohler; Tel: 816-501-4121, E-mail: ellie.kohler@rockhurst.edu; *Content Mgt & Discovery Librn,* Jennifer Peters; Tel: 816-501-4134, E-mail: jennifer.peters@rockhurst.edu; *Content Serv Librn,* Melanie Church; Tel: 816-501-4143, E-mail: melanie.church@rockhurst.edu; *Univ Archivist,* Ed Kos, PhD; Tel: 816-501-4161, E-mail: edward.kos@rockhurst.edu; *Discovery Serv Asst,* Carolyn Smith; Tel: 816-501-4131, E-mail: carolyn.smith@rockhurst.edu; Staff 7.5 (MLS 5, Non-MLS 2.5)
Founded 1917. Enrl 2,986; Fac 150; Highest Degree: Master
Special Collections: US Document Depository
Automation Activity & Vendor Info: (Acquisitions) Innovative Interfaces, Inc - Millenium; (Cataloging) Innovative Interfaces, Inc - Millenium; (Circulation) Innovative Interfaces, Inc - Millenium; (Course Reserve) Innovative Interfaces, Inc - Millenium; (ILL) OCLC; (OPAC) Innovative Interfaces, Inc - Millenium; (Serials) Innovative Interfaces, Inc - Millenium
Database Vendor: 3M Library Systems, Alexander Street Press, American Chemical Society, American Psychological Association (APA), Cambridge Scientific Abstracts, Cinahl, CQ Press, CredoReference, EBSCOhost, Gale Cengage Learning, H W Wilson, Innovative Interfaces, Inc, JSTOR, LearningExpress, LexisNexis, Newsbank, OCLC, OCLC WorldShare Interlibrary Loan, ProQuest, PubMed, Sage, SerialsSolutions, Swets Information Services, Wiley, Wilson - Wilson Web, YBP Library Services
Wireless access
Function: 24/7 Electronic res, 24/7 Online cat, Accessibility serv available based on individual needs, Archival coll, Audio & video playback equip for onsite use, Computers for patron use, Doc delivery serv, e-mail & chat, E-Reserves, Electronic databases & coll, Exhibits, Govt ref serv, Handicapped accessible, ILL available, Microfiche/film & reading machines, Music CDs, Online cat, Online info literacy tutorials on the web & in blackboard, Online ref, Online searches, Photocopying/Printing, Ref serv available, Ref serv in person, Spoken cassettes & CDs, Spoken cassettes & DVDs, Study rm, VHS videos, Web-catalog
Partic in Mid-America Library Alliance/Kansas City Metropolitan Library & Information Network; Missouri Research & Education Network (MOREnet); MOBIUS (Missouri Bibliographic Information User System)
Special Services for the Deaf - TDD equip
Open Mon-Thurs (Fall & Spring) 8am-Midnight, Fri 8-4:30, Sat Noon-4:30, Sun Noon-Midnight; Mon-Thurs (Summer) 8-8, Fri 8-4:30, Sat Noon-4:30
Restriction: In-house use for visitors, Open to students, fac, staff & alumni, Pub use on premises, Restricted pub use
Friends of the Library Group

M SAINT LUKE'S HOSPITAL*, Health Sciences Library, 4141 Mill St, 64111. SAN 309-0612. Tel: 816-531-0560. FAX: 816-531-6316. E-mail: library@saint-lukes.org. *Dir,* Karen Wiederaenders; E-mail: kwiederaenders@saint-lukes.org; *Librn,* Marie Thompson; *Ser,* Mary Webb; Staff 3 (MLS 3)
Founded 1948
Library Holdings: e-journals 4,746; Bk Titles 2,416; Bk Vols 2,611; Per Subs 21
Function: ILL available
Publications: Newsletter
Partic in Mid-America Library Alliance/Kansas City Metropolitan Library & Information Network
Open Mon-Thurs 7:30am-8pm, Fri 7:30-5, Sat 9-Noon
Restriction: Circulates for staff only

SR SAINT PAUL SCHOOL OF THEOLOGY*, Dana Dawson Library, 5123 E Truman Rd, 64127. SAN 309-0639. Web Site: www.spst.edu/library/. *Dir, Libr & Info Serv,* Logan S Wright; E-mail: lswright@spst.edu; *Ref & Instruction Librn,* John Oyler; E-mail: joyler@spst.edu; *Archivist,* Magda ("Maggi") Mueller; E-mail: maggim@spst.edu; Staff 3 (MLS 3)
Founded 1958. Enrl 187; Fac 21; Highest Degree: Doctorate
Library Holdings: Bk Titles 90,000; Bk Vols 100,000; Per Subs 550; Videos 500
Special Collections: Methodistica Coll; Wesleyana Coll
Automation Activity & Vendor Info: (Cataloging) Innovative Interfaces, Inc; (Circulation) Innovative Interfaces, Inc; (Course Reserve) Innovative Interfaces, Inc; (ILL) Innovative Interfaces, Inc; (OPAC) Innovative Interfaces, Inc; (Serials) Innovative Interfaces, Inc
Database Vendor: Innovative Interfaces, Inc
Wireless access
Partic in Amigos Library Services, Inc; MOBIUS (Missouri Bibliographic Information User System); OCLC Online Computer Library Center, Inc
Open Mon-Wed 8-8, Thurs-Fri 8-5, Sat 12-4

L SHOOK, HARDY & BACON*, Law Library, 2555 Grand Blvd, 3rd Flr, 64108-2613. SAN 309-0647. Tel: 816-474-6550. FAX: 816-421-5547. *Dir,* Lori Weiss; *Mgr,* Jeff Sewell; *Cat,* Mike McReynolds; *Electronic Res,* Janet McKinney; *Ref,* Marit Bang; *Ref,* Julie Parmenter; *Ref,* Heidi Putz; *Ref,* R Scott Russell; *Ref,* Joyce Sickel; *Ref,* Valerie Vogt; *Ref,* Eddie White; *Tech Serv,* Janet Peters
Library Holdings: Bk Vols 40,000; Per Subs 900
Partic in Health Sciences Library Network of Kansas City, Inc

L STINSON, MORRISON, HECKER LIBRARY*, 1201 Walnut St, No 2500, 64106-2149. SAN 309-0507. Tel: 816-691-2600. FAX: 816-691-3495. Web Site: www.stinson.com. *Dir,* Dale Magariel; Tel: 816-842-8600, Fax: 816-691-3496; Staff 1 (MLS 1)
Library Holdings: Bk Titles 18,076; Bk Vols 21,000; Per Subs 50
Subject Interests: Law
Partic in Westlaw
Open Mon-Fri 8:30-5

GL US COURT LIBRARY - EIGHTH CIRCUIT*, Kansas City Branch, 9440 Charles Evans Whittaker US Courthouse, 400 E Ninth St, 64106. SAN 309-0663. Tel: 816-512-5790. FAX: 816-512-5799. Administration FAX: 314-244-2676. Web Site: www.168.uscourts.gov. *Librn,* Deborah Showalter-Johnson; Staff 2 (MLS 1, Non-MLS 1)
Library Holdings: Bk Vols 40,355
Special Collections: Historic Missouri Legal Materials

C UNIVERSITY OF MISSOURI, Research Center-Kansas City, 302 Newcomb Hall, 5123 Holmes St, 64110-2499. SAN 329-2754. Tel: 816-235-1543. FAX: 816-235-5500. E-mail: shsofmo-kc@umsystem.edu. Web Site: shs.umsystem.edu/about/kansascity.shtml. *Assoc Dir,* David Boutros; Tel: 816-235-1544, E-mail: boutrosd@umkc.edu; *Ms Spec,* Peter Foley; Tel: 816-235-1549, E-mail: foleyp@umkc.edu; Staff 3.5 (MLS 2, Non-MLS 1.5)
Library Holdings: Bk Titles 1,500; Bk Vols 1,684
Special Collections: Oral History
Subject Interests: Kansas City area hist, Mo hist
Function: Archival coll
Restriction: Open evenings by appt

C UNIVERSITY OF MISSOURI-KANSAS CITY LIBRARIES*, University Libraries, 800 E 51st St, 64110. (Mail add: 5100 Rockhill Rd, 64110-2446), SAN 349-3687. Tel: 816-235-1531. Interlibrary Loan Service Tel: 816-235-1586. FAX: 816-333-5584. Interlibrary Loan Service FAX: 816-235-5531. Web Site: library.umkc.edu. *Dean, Univ Libr,* Bonnie Postlethwaite; Tel: 816-235-1531; *Dir of Advan,* Mark Mattison; Tel: 816-235-5828; *Dir, Coll & Access Mgt,* Buddy Pennington, Jr; Tel: 816-235-1548; *Dir, Music/Media Libr,* Nara Newcomer; Tel: 816-235-1679; *Dir, Pub Serv,* Cynthia Thompson; Tel: 816-235-1511; *Dir, Scholarly Communications,* Brenda Dingley; Tel: 816-235-2226; *Dir, Spec Coll,* Stuart Hinds; Tel: 816-235-1532; *Asst Dir, Adm Serv,* Jennifer Eigsti; Tel: 816-235-1533; *Head, ILL & Grad Student Serv,* Patrick Bickers; Tel: 816-235-2225; *Head, Spec Formats & Cat,* Wendy Sistrunk; Tel: 816-235-5291; *Head, Acq,* Sherry Farrell; Tel: 816-235-6461; *Head, Cat & Metadata Serv,* Kathleen Schweitzberger; Tel: 816-235-2227; *Head, Circ Serv,* Mary Anderson; Tel: 816-235-1678; *Head, Coll,* Steve Alleman; Tel: 816-235-1580; *Head, Teaching & Learning Serv,* Diane Hunter; Tel: 816-235-1537; *Dental Librn,* Marie Thompson; Tel: 816-235-2063; *Coordr, Virtual Libr,* Brent Husher; Tel: 816-235-1281. Subject Specialists: *Music,* Nara Newcomer; Staff 37 (MLS 26, Non-MLS 11)
Founded 1933. Enrl 14,256; Fac 602; Highest Degree: Doctorate
Library Holdings: AV Mats 458,549; e-books 202,156; Electronic Media & Resources 42,435; Microforms 1,459,439; Bk Vols 1,313,266
Special Collections: American Sheet Music Coll; Americana (Snyder Coll) bks, ms; English & American; English & American Literature (Baker Coll); Holocaust Studies; Midwest Center for American Music (Amy Beach & Paul Creston Coll); Sound Archives. State Document Depository; US Document Depository
Automation Activity & Vendor Info: (Acquisitions) Innovative Interfaces, Inc; (Cataloging) Innovative Interfaces, Inc; (Circulation) Innovative Interfaces, Inc; (Course Reserve) Innovative Interfaces, Inc; (ILL) Innovative Interfaces, Inc; (Media Booking) Innovative Interfaces, Inc; (OPAC) Innovative Interfaces, Inc; (Serials) Innovative Interfaces, Inc
Wireless access
Publications: UMKC Friends of the Library Bookmark (Newsletter)
Partic in Center for Research Libraries; Merlin; Mo Res Consortium of Libs; OCLC Online Computer Library Center, Inc
Open Mon-Thurs 7:30am-11pm, Fri 7:30-5, Sat 10-5, Sun 1-11
Friends of the Library Group

Departmental Libraries:

DENTAL LIBRARY, 650 E 25th St, 64108, SAN 349-3806. Tel: 816-235-2030. FAX: 816-235-6540. *Librn,* Marie Thompson; Tel: 816-235-2063, E-mail: thompsonmarie@umkc.edu; Staff 4.5 (MLS 2.5, Non-MLS 2)
Founded 1916. Enrl 500; Fac 108; Highest Degree: Doctorate
Library Holdings: AV Mats 1,406; Microforms 1,582; Bk Vols 27,573; Per Subs 360
Special Collections: History of Dentistry Coll
Partic in Health Sciences Library Network of Kansas City, Inc
Open Mon-Thurs 7:30am-9pm, Fri 7:30-6, Sat & Sun 12-5
Restriction: Authorized patrons, Borrowing privileges limited to fac & registered students, Borrowing requests are handled by ILL, Circ limited, External users must contact libr, ID required to use computers (Ltd hrs)

HEALTH SCIENCES LIBRARY, 2411 Holmes St, 64108, SAN 349-3717. Tel: 816-235-1880. FAX: 816-235-6570. *Dir,* Margaret Mullaly-Quijas; Tel: 816-235-1871; *ILL,* Jonice Rogers; Tel: 816-235-1878; Staff 4 (MLS 4)
Founded 1965. Highest Degree: Doctorate
Library Holdings: Bk Vols 79,303; Per Subs 695
Subject Interests: Clinical med, Nursing
Partic in Dialog Corp; Midcontinental Regional Med Libr Program; National Network of Libraries of Medicine; SDC Search Serv
Open Mon-Thurs 8am-10pm, Fri 8-5:30, Sat 9-5, Sun 2-10

CL UNIVERSITY OF MISSOURI-KANSAS CITY LIBRARIES*, Leon E Bloch Law Library, 500 E 52nd St, 64110. (Mail add: 5100 Rockhill Rd, 64110-2499), SAN 349-3741. Tel: 816-235-1650. FAX: 816-235-5274. Web Site: law.umkc.edu/library/. *Libr Dir,* Paul D Callister; *Assoc Dir,* Michael J Robak; *Head, Tech Serv,* Nancy Stancel; *Electronic Communications Librn,* Ayyoub Ajmi; *Acq,* Glenn G Higley; *Circ,* Nancy Morgan; *Govt Doc,* Cindi Ernst; *Instruction/Coll Develop,* Lawrence MacLachlan; *Tech,* Rick Thomas; Staff 15 (MLS 7, Non-MLS 8)
Founded 1895. Highest Degree: Doctorate
Library Holdings: Bk Vols 202,809; Per Subs 1,820
Special Collections: Urban Law Coll. US Document Depository
Subject Interests: Law
Automation Activity & Vendor Info: (Acquisitions) Innovative Interfaces, Inc - Millenium; (Cataloging) Innovative Interfaces, Inc - Millenium; (Circulation) Innovative Interfaces, Inc - Millenium; (ILL) OCLC; (OPAC) Innovative Interfaces, Inc
Database Vendor: Bloomberg, Checkpoint Systems, Inc, EBSCOhost, Gale Cengage Learning, HeinOnline, JSTOR, LexisNexis, OCLC FirstSearch, OVID Technologies, ProQuest, SerialsSolutions, Westlaw, Wilson - Wilson Web
Wireless access
Publications: Acquisitions List
Partic in Merlin; MOBIUS (Missouri Bibliographic Information User System)

CR WESTERN BAPTIST BIBLE COLLEGE MEMORIAL LIBRARY*, 2119 Tracy, 64108. SAN 309-0701. Tel: 816-842-4195. FAX: 816-842-3050. E-mail: wbbible@sbcglobal.net. *Dean,* Robert Baynham; Staff 1 (MLS 1)
Library Holdings: Bk Titles 14,601; Bk Vols 15,089; Per Subs 39; Talking Bks 67; Videos 52

Subject Interests: African-Am hist, Archaeology, Bible hist, Drama, Eng lit, European hist, Music, Philos, Psychol, Relig, Relig hist educ, Sociol, Theol, World hist
Open Mon-Fri 10-3

M WESTERN MISSOURI MENTAL HEALTH CENTER*, Charles B Wilkinson MD Memorial Library, 1000 E 24th St, 64108. SAN 309-071X. Tel: 816-512-7303. FAX: 816-512-7308. Web Site: www.dmh.missouri.gov/wmmhc. *Librn,* Arnold Lewis; Staff 1 (Non-MLS 1)
Founded 1968
Library Holdings: AV Mats 1,225; Bk Vols 2,600; Per Subs 19; Spec Interest Per Sub 30; Talking Bks 325; Videos 900
Special Collections: Charles B Wilkinson's Professional Coll
Subject Interests: Behav sci, Psychiat, Psychol, Soc sci
Automation Activity & Vendor Info: (Cataloging) Marcive, Inc; (ILL) OCLC; (Serials) EBSCO Online
Partic in Health Sciences Library Network of Kansas City, Inc; Mid-America Library Alliance/Kansas City Metropolitan Library & Information Network; OCLC Online Computer Library Center, Inc
Open Mon-Fri 9-4

KENNETT

P DUNKLIN COUNTY LIBRARY*, 209 N Main, 63857. SAN 349-3865. Tel: 573-888-2261, 573-888-3561. FAX: 573-888-6393. Web Site: dunklin-co.lib.mo.us. *Dir,* JoNell Minton; E-mail: jonell@dunklin-co.lib.mo.us; Staff 1 (MLS 1)
Founded 1947. Pop 32,000; Circ 316,825
Library Holdings: Bk Vols 180,000; Per Subs 150; Talking Bks 1,000; Videos 1,000
Special Collections: Charles H Baker Military Coll. Oral History
Subject Interests: Genealogy
Automation Activity & Vendor Info: (Acquisitions) Innovative Interfaces, Inc; (Cataloging) TLC (The Library Corporation); (Circulation) Innovative Interfaces, Inc; (ILL) OCLC
Database Vendor: Baker & Taylor, EBSCOhost
Open Mon-Sat 8:30-5:30
Friends of the Library Group

Branches: 8

ARBYRD BRANCH, 100A N Douglas Ave, Arbyrd, 63821, SAN 349-389X. Tel: 573-654-2385. *Librn,* Janice Cureton
Open Tues 10-2, Thurs 12-5

CAMPBELL BRANCH, 404 W Grand, Campbell, 63933, SAN 349-392X. Tel: 573-246-2112. *Librn,* Brenda Cummins
Library Holdings: Bk Titles 19,000
Open Mon-Sat 1-5

CARDWELL BRANCH, Main St, Cardwell, 63829. (Mail add: PO Box 305, Cardwell, 63829-0305), SAN 349-3954. Tel: 573-654-3366. *Librn,* Janice Cureton
Open Mon, Wed & Thurs 12-5, Tues 9-2, Fri 1-5

CLARKTON BRANCH, 113 S Main St, Clarkton, 63837, SAN 349-3989. Tel: 573-448-3803. *Librn,* Peggy Gilkey
Library Holdings: Bk Titles 15,000
Open Mon-Fri 1-5

HOLCOMB BRANCH, W Main St, Holcomb, 63852, SAN 349-4012. Tel: 573-792-3268. *Librn,* Marge Schubert
Library Holdings: Bk Titles 7,000
Open Mon, Wed & Fri 1-5

HORNERSVILLE BRANCH, 502 School St, Hornersville, 63855, SAN 349-4047. Tel: 573-737-2728. *Br Librn,* Glenda Scott
Library Holdings: Bk Titles 10,000
Open Mon, Wed & Fri 1-5

MALDEN BRANCH, 113 N Madison, Malden, 63863, SAN 349-4071. Tel: 573-276-3674. *Librn,* Jeanette Wright
Library Holdings: Bk Titles 32,000
Open Mon-Sat 8:30-5:30

SENATH BRANCH, 108 N Main St, Senath, 63876, SAN 349-4101. Tel: 573-738-2363. *Librn,* Lady Calahan
Library Holdings: Bk Titles 20,000
Open Mon-Fri 1-5

R FIRST BAPTIST CHURCH LIBRARY*, 300 Saint Francis St, 63857. SAN 309-0728. Tel: 573-888-4689. FAX: 573-888-4680. E-mail: fbc@fbckennett.com. Web Site: www.fbckennett.com. *Librn,* David LaGore; *Librn,* Sara LaGore; Staff 2 (Non-MLS 2)
Founded 1948
Library Holdings: Bk Vols 3,450; Per Subs 27; Videos 10
Subject Interests: Bible characters, Child missionaries, Devotions, Holidays
Open Wed 5:45pm-6:15pm, Sun 9-9:30 & 5-6

KIRKSVILLE

CM A T STILL UNIVERSITY LIBRARY*, A T Still Memorial Library, Kirksville Campus, 800 W Jefferson St, 63501. SAN 309-0736. Tel: 660-626-2345. Interlibrary Loan Service Tel: 660-626-2030. Reference Tel: 660-626-2340. FAX: 660-626-2031, 660-626-2333. Web Site: www.atsu.edu/library/index.htm. *Dir,* Jean Louise Sidwell; E-mail: jsidwell@atsu.edu; *Distance Support Librn,* Margaret Hoogland; E-mail: mhoogland@atsu.edu; *Tech Serv Librn,* Mary Sims; Tel: 660-626-2635, E-mail: msims@atsu.edu; *Pub Serv Mgr,* David Owens; Tel: 660-626-2645, E-mail: dowens@atsu.edu; *Ser/Circ Coordr, Weekend Supvr,* Carlo Caroli; Tel: 660-626-2886, E-mail: ccaroli@atsu.edu; *Acq,* Daryl Shafer; Tel: 660-626-2124, E-mail: dshafer@atsu.edu; *Pub Serv Asst/Doc Delivery & Media Serv,* Leisa Walter; Tel: 660-626-2679, E-mail: lwalter@atsu.edu; Staff 7 (MLS 4, Non-MLS 3)
Founded 1897. Enrl 3,293; Fac 165; Highest Degree: Master
Library Holdings: CDs 113; DVDs 192; e-books 5,500; e-journals 6,500; Bk Titles 25,250; Bk Vols 74,098; Per Subs 627; Videos 2,664
Subject Interests: Behav sci, Biomed sci, Dentistry, Med, Osteopathic med, Pub health admin, Soc sci
Automation Activity & Vendor Info: (Acquisitions) Innovative Interfaces, Inc; (Cataloging) Innovative Interfaces, Inc; (Circulation) Innovative Interfaces, Inc; (OPAC) Innovative Interfaces, Inc
Function: Computers for patron use
Partic in Docline; MOBIUS (Missouri Bibliographic Information User System); OCLC Online Computer Library Center, Inc
Open Mon-Fri 7am-Midnight, Sat 9am-Midnight, Sun 11am-Midnight
Restriction: Borrowing requests are handled by ILL, Open to students, fac, staff & alumni

P ADAIR COUNTY PUBLIC LIBRARY, One Library Lane, 63501. SAN 309-0752. Tel: 660-665-6038. FAX: 660-627-0028. E-mail: acpl@adairco.org. Web Site: youseemore.com/adaircpl. *Dir,* Glenda Hunt; Staff 4 (MLS 1, Non-MLS 3)
Founded 1986. Pop 25,572; Circ 207,407
Jan 2013-Dec 2013 Income $422,285, State $12,804, County $347,931, Locally Generated Income $44,507, Other $17,043. Mats Exp $73,205, Books $56,140, AV Mat $17,065. Sal $205,689
Library Holdings: Audiobooks 1,805; CDs 1,192; DVDs 2,565; e-books 21,095; Large Print Bks 1,453; Microforms 400; Bk Titles 58,014; Bk Vols 60,108; Per Subs 70
Special Collections: Adair County
Subject Interests: Mo hist
Automation Activity & Vendor Info: (Cataloging) TLC (The Library Corporation); (Circulation) TLC (The Library Corporation); (OPAC) TLC (The Library Corporation)
Database Vendor: Amigos Library Services, EBSCOhost, Gale Cengage Learning, LearningExpress, OCLC FirstSearch, Overdrive, Inc, ProQuest, TLC (The Library Corporation)
Wireless access
Partic in Grand Rivers Libr Conference
Open Tues & Wed 9-8, Thurs & Fri 9-6, Sat 12-4
Friends of the Library Group

C TRUMAN STATE UNIVERSITY*, Pickler Memorial Library, 100 E Normal, 63501-4211. SAN 309-0744. Tel: 660-785-4038. Circulation Tel: 660-785-4533. Interlibrary Loan Service Tel: 660-785-4534. Reference Tel: 660-785-4051. Interlibrary Loan Service FAX: 660-785-4536. Administration FAX: 660-785-7415. Web Site: library.truman.edu. *Dean, Libr & Mus,* Richard J Coughlin; E-mail: coughlin@truman.edu; *Head, Pub Serv,* Janet Romine; Tel: 660-785-7418, E-mail: jiromine@truman.edu; *Head, Tech Serv,* Stephen Wynn; Tel: 660-785-4535, E-mail: swynn@truman.edu; *Spec Coll & Archives Librn,* Amanda Langendoerfer; Tel: 660-785-7546, E-mail: alang@truman.edu; *Supvr, Access Serv,* Gayla McHenry; Tel: 660-785-4037, E-mail: gmchenry@truman.edu; *Media Spec,* Sharon Hackney; Tel: 660-785-7366, E-mail: shackney@truman.edu; *Per,* Daisy Rearick; Tel: 660-785-4048, E-mail: drearick@truman.edu; Staff 13 (MLS 12, Non-MLS 1)
Founded 1867. Enrl 5,615; Fac 357; Highest Degree: Master
Jul 2011-Jun 2012 Income $2,722,249. Mats Exp $1,463,500, Books $194,562, Per/Ser (Incl. Access Fees) $891,938, Manu Arch $8,767, Micro $62,359, AV Mat $45,605, Presv $16,575. Sal $1,008,564 (Prof $544,606)
Library Holdings: Audiobooks 1,618; AV Mats 52,534; CDs 6,360; DVDs 11,904; e-books 83,887; Music Scores 7,585; Bk Vols 505,210; Videos 12,864
Special Collections: Eugenics Coll (Harry Laughlin), ms; Glenn Frank Coll, ms; Lincoln (Fred & Ethel Schwengel Coll), artifacts & bks; Missouriana (Violette McClure Coll); Rare Books Coll. US Document Depository
Subject Interests: Bus, Health, Liberal arts, Sciences
Database Vendor: Innovative Interfaces, Inc, OCLC FirstSearch
Partic in Amigos Library Services, Inc; MOBIUS (Missouri Bibliographic Information User System)

Special Services for the Blind - Scanner for conversion & translation of mats
Open Mon-Thurs 7:30am-1am, Fri 7:30am-9pm, Sat 11-6, Sun 1-1

KIRKWOOD

P KIRKWOOD PUBLIC LIBRARY*, 140 E Jefferson Ave, 63122. SAN 309-0760. Tel: 314-821-5770. FAX: 314-822-3755. E-mail: infoservices@kirkwoodpubliclibrary.org. Web Site: kirkwoodpubliclibrary.org. *Dir,* Sarah Erwin; Tel: 314-821-5770, Ext 1016, E-mail: serwin@kirkwoodpubliclibrary.org; *Dir of Libr Operations,* Lisa Henry; Tel: 314-821-5770, Ext 13, E-mail: lhenry@kirkwoodpubliclibrary.org; *Dir, Prog & Youth Serv,* Lynn Bosso; Tel: 314-821-5770, Ext 1011, E-mail: lbosso@kirkwoodpubliclibrary.org; *Dir, Tech Serv,* Bonnie Petersen; Tel: 314-821-5770, Ext 1014, E-mail: bpetersen@kirkwoodpubliclibrary.org; *Circ Mgr,* Nick O'Neal; Tel: 314-821-5770, Ext 1027, E-mail: noneal@kirkwoodpubliclibrary.org; *Ref Mgr,* Pat Rohan; Tel: 314-821-5770, Ext 1025, E-mail: prohan@kirkwoodpubliclibrary.org; *Teen & Tech Coordr,* Chris Durr; Tel: 314-821-5770, Ext 1020, E-mail: cdurr@kirkwoodpubliclibrary.org; Staff 14 (MLS 5, Non-MLS 9)
Founded 1924. Pop 27,156; Circ 316,526
Library Holdings: AV Mats 18,062; Bk Vols 81,000; Per Subs 342
Special Collections: Kirkwood History Coll; Nonprofit Resources Special Coll
Automation Activity & Vendor Info: (Acquisitions) SirsiDynix; (Cataloging) SirsiDynix; (Circulation) SirsiDynix; (ILL) OCLC FirstSearch; (OPAC) SirsiDynix; (Serials) SirsiDynix
Database Vendor: EBSCOhost, Gale Cengage Learning, Newsbank, SirsiDynix
Wireless access
Function: Adult bk club, Audiobks via web, Bk club(s), Bks on CD, Chess club, Children's prog, Computer training, Computers for patron use, Copy machines, Electronic databases & coll, Fax serv, Free DVD rentals, Handicapped accessible, Home delivery & serv to Sr ctr & nursing homes, Homebound delivery serv, ILL available, Magnifiers for reading, Music CDs, Online searches, Outreach serv, OverDrive digital audio bks, Passport agency, Preschool outreach, Preschool reading prog, Prog for adults, Prog for children & young adult, Pub access computers, Ref serv available, Ref serv in person, Scanner, Senior outreach, Story hour, Summer reading prog, Tax forms, Teen prog, Telephone ref, Web-catalog, Wheelchair accessible, Writing prog
Partic in Municipal Library Consortium; Saint Louis Regional Library Network
Open Mon-Thurs 9-9, Fri & Sat 9-5, Sun 1-5
Friends of the Library Group

LA PLATA

P LA PLATA PUBLIC LIBRARY, 103 E Moore, 63549. (Mail add: 30006 Kodiak Pl, 63549), SAN 309-0779. Tel: 660-332-4945. FAX: 660-332-4945. E-mail: LaPlataLibrary@cableone.net. *Librn,* Cynthia A Moore
Founded 1939. Pop 1,486; Circ 11,105
Library Holdings: Bk Vols 15,170; Per Subs 25
Special Collections: Doc Savage Coll
Subject Interests: Genealogy, Local hist
Wireless access
Open Mon 1-6, Wed & Fri 1-5, Tues & Thurs 8-1, Sat 10-Noon

LAMAR

P BARTON COUNTY LIBRARY*, 300 W Tenth St, 64759. Tel: 417-682-5355. FAX: 417-682-3206. Web Site: www.bartoncountylibrary.com. *Dir,* Julie Potter; E-mail: jpotter@bartoncountylibrary.com; *Tech Serv Mgr,* Aimee Brunner; E-mail: abrunner@bartoncountylibrary.com; *Tech Coordr,* Kay Hicks; E-mail: khicks@bartoncountylibrary.com
Founded 1932. Pop 12,541
Automation Activity & Vendor Info: (Cataloging) TLC (The Library Corporation); (Circulation) TLC (The Library Corporation); (ILL) OCLC; (OPAC) TLC (The Library Corporation)
Database Vendor: Gale Cengage Learning, LearningExpress, Newsbank
Wireless access
Function: Accelerated reader prog, After school storytime, AV serv, Bks on cassette, Bks on CD, Children's prog, Computer training, Computers for patron use, Copy machines, Electronic databases & coll, Fax serv, Free DVD rentals, Handicapped accessible, ILL available, Magnifiers for reading, Mail & tel request accepted, Photocopying/Printing, Prog for children & young adult, Pub access computers, Ref serv in person, Scanner, Senior computer classes, Story hour, Summer reading prog, Teen prog, VHS videos, Video lending libr, Wheelchair accessible
Friends of the Library Group

LAWSON

G MISSOURI DEPARTMENT OF NATURAL RESOURCES*, Watkins Woolen Mill State Historic Site Archives, 26600 Park Rd N, 64062. SAN 327-8808. Tel: 816-580-3387. FAX: 816-580-3782. *Adminr,* Michael Beckett; E-mail: michael.beckett@dnr.mo.gov; Staff 1 (Non-MLS 1)
Founded 1964
Library Holdings: Bk Titles 690; Bk Vols 750; Per Subs 1,000
Special Collections: 19th Century Agriculture, 19th Century Woolen Textile Manufacturing; 19th Century Gristmilling; Watkins Family Letters 1820's-1940's; Watkins Mill Association Records 1959-1990
Function: Archival coll
Restriction: Open by appt only
Friends of the Library Group

LEBANON

P LEBANON-LACLEDE COUNTY LIBRARY*, 915 S Jefferson Ave, 65536-3667. SAN 349-4136. Tel: 417-532-2148. Administration Tel: 417-532-4212. FAX: 417-532-7424. E-mail: askref@lebanon-laclede.lib.mo.us. Web Site: www.lebanon-laclede.lib.mo.us. *Dir,* Cathy Dame; Staff 9 (MLS 3, Non-MLS 6)
Pop 89,281; Circ 357,389
Library Holdings: Large Print Bks 215; Bk Titles 91,864; Bk Vols 93,410; Per Subs 119; Talking Bks 338; Videos 490
Subject Interests: Genealogy, Local hist
Automation Activity & Vendor Info: (Cataloging) Innovative Interfaces, Inc; (Circulation) Innovative Interfaces, Inc
Database Vendor: EBSCOhost
Partic in Mo Libr Film Coop; SW Mo Libr Network
Open Mon-Thurs 8-8, Fri & Sat 8-5
Friends of the Library Group
Bookmobiles: 2

LEXINGTON

J WENTWORTH MILITARY ACADEMY*, Sellers-Coombs Library, 1880 Washington Ave, 64067. SAN 309-0809. Tel: 660-259-2221. FAX: 660-259-2677. Web Site: www.wma1880.org. *Librn,* Linda Tanner; Staff 2 (MLS 1, Non-MLS 1)
Founded 1884. Enrl 350
Library Holdings: Bk Titles 17,336; Bk Vols 18,000; Per Subs 35; Videos 51
Subject Interests: Mil sci
Open Mon-Fri 7:30-3:45

LIBERTY

S CLAY COUNTY ARCHIVES & HISTORICAL LIBRARY*, 210 E Franklin St, 64068-1790. (Mail add: PO Box 99, 64069-0099), SAN 323-5238. Tel: 816-781-3611. E-mail: info@claycountyarchives.org. Web Site: www.claycountyarchives.org/. *Pres,* Stuart Elliott; Staff 1 (MLS 1)
Library Holdings: Bk Titles 1,200; Bk Vols 1,340; Per Subs 15
Subject Interests: Family hist, Genealogy
Open Mon-Wed 9-4

C WILLIAM JEWELL COLLEGE*, Charles F Curry Library, 500 College Hill, 64068-1843. SAN 309-0825. Tel: 816-415-7609. Information Services Tel: 816-415-7610. FAX: 816-415-5021. Web Site: campus.jewell.edu/academics/curry/library/default.html. *Dir,* Stephanie DeClue; Tel: 816-415-7606, E-mail: declues@william.jewell.edu; *Assoc Dir, Educ Tech,* Elise Fisher; Tel: 816-415-7611, E-mail: fishere@william.jewell.edu; *Coll Mgt Librn,* Cheryl Couch-Thomas; Tel: 816-415-7613, E-mail: couch-thoma@william.jewell.edu; *Ref/Archives Librn,* Rebecca Hamlett; *Syst Librn,* Steve Bailey; *Circ Supvr,* Dee Day; *Evening Supvr,* Barbara Wright; *Acq Asst,* Dee Doll; Staff 5 (MLS 4, Non-MLS 1)
Founded 1849. Enrl 1,170; Fac 95; Highest Degree: Bachelor
Jul 2007-Jun 2008 Income $466,700. Mats Exp $355,504
Library Holdings: Bk Vols 258,352; Per Subs 613
Special Collections: Baptist History (Partee Center for Baptist Historical Studies); Children"s Literature (Lois Lenski Coll), bk, drawing; Missouri History (Missouri Coll); Puritan Literature (Charles Haddon Spurgeon Coll); Western Americana (Settle Coll), bk, photo, slides. US Document Depository
Automation Activity & Vendor Info: (Acquisitions) Innovative Interfaces, Inc; (Cataloging) Innovative Interfaces, Inc; (Circulation) Innovative Interfaces, Inc; (Course Reserve) Docutek; (ILL) Innovative Interfaces, Inc; (OPAC) Innovative Interfaces, Inc; (Serials) Innovative Interfaces, Inc
Database Vendor: EBSCOhost, Gale Cengage Learning, LexisNexis, OCLC FirstSearch, ProQuest, Wilson - Wilson Web
Wireless access
Partic in Amigos Library Services, Inc; BRS; Mid-America Library Alliance/Kansas City Metropolitan Library & Information Network;

MOBIUS (Missouri Bibliographic Information User System); OCLC Online Computer Library Center, Inc
Open Mon-Thurs 7:30am-11pm, Fri 7-5, Sat 10-5, Sun 1-11

LILBOURN

P LILBOURN MEMORIAL LIBRARY*, 210 E Lewis Ave, 63862. (Mail add: PO Box 282, 63862), SAN 309-0833. Tel: 573-688-2622. *Librn,* Betty Allred; Staff 1 (MLS 1)
Founded 1936. Pop 1,306; Circ 9,798
Library Holdings: Large Print Bks 44; Bk Titles 11,542; Bk Vols 11,781; Per Subs 10; Talking Bks 32; Videos 51
Open Tues-Fri (Winter) 1-4; Tues-Fri (Summer) 2-5

LOCKWOOD

P LOCKWOOD PUBLIC LIBRARY*, 721 Main St, 65682. (Mail add: PO Box 286, 65682-0286), SAN 309-0841. Tel: 417-232-4204. *Librn,* Leota Queen; Staff 1 (MLS 1)
Pop 1,050; Circ 14,500
Library Holdings: Bk Titles 21,070; Bk Vols 21,646; Per Subs 18; Talking Bks 130; Videos 553
Special Collections: Dade County History; Lockwood Newspapers from 1890-1980
Open Mon, Tues & Thurs 8-5, Sat 8-12

LOUISIANA

P LOUISIANA PUBLIC LIBRARY*, 121 N Third St, 63353. SAN 309-085X. Tel: 573-754-4491. FAX: 573-754-4208. *Librn,* Holly Mabry; E-mail: hollymabry4@aol.com; Staff 1 (MLS 1)
Founded 1904. Pop 3,954; Circ 17,323
Library Holdings: Bk Vols 29,000; Per Subs 30; Talking Bks 328; Videos 281
Automation Activity & Vendor Info: (Cataloging) Book Systems; (Circulation) Book Systems
Database Vendor: EBSCOhost
Open Mon & Wed-Fri 10:30-5:30, Tues 12-8, Sat 9:30-1:30
Friends of the Library Group

MACON

P MACON PUBLIC LIBRARY*, 210 N Rutherford St, 63552. SAN 309-0868. Tel: 660-385-3314. FAX: 660-385-6610. E-mail: maconlibrary@yahoo.com. Web Site: www.maconlibrary.org. *Libr Dir,* Elaine Nuhn
Founded 1912. Pop 5,680; Circ 34,538
Library Holdings: Bk Vols 33,000; Per Subs 75
Subject Interests: Genealogy, Macon County
Automation Activity & Vendor Info: (Cataloging) SirsiDynix; (Circulation) SirsiDynix
Partic in NE Mo Libr Network
Open Mon, Tues, Thurs & Fri 10-8, Wed 10-5, Sat 10-3
Friends of the Library Group

MAPLEWOOD

P MAPLEWOOD PUBLIC LIBRARY*, 7550 Lohmeyer Ave, 63143. SAN 309-0876. Tel: 314-781-7323. FAX: 314-781-2191. E-mail: maplewoodpl@yahoo.com. Web Site: www.maplewood.lib.mo.us. *Dir,* Terrence Donnelly; Staff 7 (MLS 1, Non-MLS 6)
Founded 1935. Pop 9,228; Circ 73,188
Library Holdings: AV Mats 1,509; Bk Titles 31,907; Bk Vols 38,000; Per Subs 118
Subject Interests: Local hist
Automation Activity & Vendor Info: (Cataloging) SirsiDynix; (Circulation) SirsiDynix; (ILL) SirsiDynix; (OPAC) SirsiDynix; (Serials) SirsiDynix
Database Vendor: EBSCOhost, Gale Cengage Learning, Newsbank, OCLC FirstSearch, Plunkett Research, Ltd, ReferenceUSA
Function: Homebound delivery serv, ILL available, Photocopying/Printing, Prog for children & young adult, Ref serv available, Summer reading prog, Telephone ref, Wheelchair accessible
Publications: Booked Up (Newsletter)
Open Mon-Thurs 9-9, Fri 9-7, Sat 9-5

MARBLE HILL

P BOLLINGER COUNTY LIBRARY*, 302 Conrad St, 63764. (Mail add: PO Box 919, 63764-0919), SAN 309-0884. Tel: 573-238-2713. FAX: 573-238-2879. E-mail: bollynger@yahoo.com. Web Site: www.bocolib.com, www.bollingercountylibrary.net. *Dir,* Eva M Dunn; *Asst Dir,* Joyce James
Founded 1947. Pop 12,024
Library Holdings: Bk Vols 90,000; Per Subs 50
Subject Interests: Agr, Feminism, Genealogy, Handicraft, Hist, Natural sci
Automation Activity & Vendor Info: (Cataloging) Mandarin Library Automation; (Circulation) Mandarin Library Automation
Database Vendor: EBSCOhost, Gale Cengage Learning, LearningExpress, Newsbank, OCLC FirstSearch, OCLC WebJunction, OCLC WorldShare Interlibrary Loan
Wireless access
Open Mon, Wed & Fri 9-6, Tues & Thurs 9-8, Sat 9-1

MARCELINE

P MARCELINE CARNEGIE LIBRARY*, 119 E California Ave, 64658. SAN 309-0892. Tel: 660-376-3223. FAX: 660-376-3577. E-mail: marcelinelibrary@hotmail.com. Web Site: marcelinelibrary.lib.mo.us. *Librn,* Joyce Clapp; Staff 2 (MLS 1, Non-MLS 1)
Founded 1920. Pop 2,781; Circ 7,096
Library Holdings: Bk Titles 15,000; Bk Vols 15,181; Per Subs 32; Talking Bks 50; Videos 110
Special Collections: Walt Disney Coll
Open Mon-Fri 9-5, Sat 9-12
Friends of the Library Group

MARSHALL

P MARSHALL PUBLIC LIBRARY*, 214 N Lafayette, 65340. SAN 370-6680. Tel: 660-886-3391. FAX: 660-886-2492. Web Site: www.marshallpublib.org. *Libr Dir,* Amy Crump; E-mail: crumpa@marshallpublib.org; Staff 10 (MLS 1, Non-MLS 9)
Founded 1990. Pop 12,711; Circ 83,941
Library Holdings: Bks on Deafness & Sign Lang 35; Bk Titles 37,500; Per Subs 98
Special Collections: Saline County Genealogy & Local History Coll
Automation Activity & Vendor Info: (Cataloging) SirsiDynix; (Circulation) SirsiDynix
Database Vendor: EBSCOhost, OCLC FirstSearch
Open Mon-Thurs 9-9, Fri 9-6, Sat 9-5, Sun 1-5
Friends of the Library Group

C MURRELL MEMORIAL LIBRARY*, Missouri Valley College, Tech Center Bldg, 500 E College St, 65340. SAN 309-0906. Tel: 660-831-4180, 660-831-4181. Reference Tel: 660-831-4187. Administration Tel: 660-831-4123. Information Services Tel: 660-831-4005. FAX: 660-831-4068. E-mail: library@moval.edu. Web Site: www.moval.edu/library. *Dir,* Pamela K Reeder; E-mail: reederp@moval.edu; *Librn,* Mary C Slater; E-mail: slaterm@moval.edu; *Libr Serv Coordr,* Norine Gaskill; E-mail: gaskilln@moval.edu; *Spec Events Coordr,* Brian Hampton; *Circ Serv,* Bathsheba Love; E-mail: loveb@moval.edu. Subject Specialists: *Music,* Pamela K Reeder; *Art,* Mary C Slater; *English,* Norine Gaskill; Staff 5 (MLS 2, Non-MLS 3)
Founded 1889. Enrl 1,437; Fac 59; Highest Degree: Master
Library Holdings: Audiobooks 145; AV Mats 2,481; e-books 10,857; Microforms 29,423; Bk Titles 54,597; Bk Vols 55,818; Per Subs 410; Videos 412
Special Collections: Cumberland Presbyterian Church Archives; Missouri History (John Ashford Coll)
Subject Interests: Bus, Educ, Missouriana
Automation Activity & Vendor Info: (Acquisitions) Innovative Interfaces, Inc; (Cataloging) Innovative Interfaces, Inc; (Circulation) Innovative Interfaces, Inc; (Course Reserve) Innovative Interfaces, Inc; (ILL) OCLC Connexion; (Media Booking) Innovative Interfaces, Inc; (OPAC) Innovative Interfaces, Inc; (Serials) Innovative Interfaces, Inc
Database Vendor: 3M Library Systems, ABC-CLIO, Alexander Street Press, American Psychological Association (APA), Backstage Library Works, BioOne, Cinahl, CredoReference, EBSCO Information Services, EBSCOhost, Gale Cengage Learning, Greenwood Publishing Group, Innovative Interfaces, Inc, LearningExpress, LexisNexis, Medline, Modern Language Association, Newsbank, OCLC FirstSearch, ProQuest, PubMed, Wilson - Wilson Web
Wireless access
Function: Adult bk club, Archival coll, Art exhibits, Audio & video playback equip for onsite use, Bks on CD, CD-ROM, Computer training, Computers for patron use, Copy machines, Distance learning, e-mail & chat, e-mail serv, Electronic databases & coll, Exhibits, Free DVD rentals, Handicapped accessible, Holiday prog, ILL available, Instruction & testing, Music CDs, Online cat, Online info literacy tutorials on the web & in blackboard, Online ref, Online searches, Orientations, Photocopying/Printing, Prog for adults, Ref & res, Ref serv available, Scanner, Summer reading prog, VHS videos, Wheelchair accessible
Publications: Acquisition List; Annual Report (Library statistics & report); Library Guide (Library handbook); The Educated Viking (Newsletter)
Partic in Amigos Library Services, Inc; MOBIUS (Missouri Bibliographic Information User System)
Open Mon-Thurs 7:45am-11pm, Fri 7:45-4, Sat 1-5, Sun 2-11
Restriction: Fee for pub use, In-house use for visitors, Limited access for the pub, Open to students, fac & staff, Restricted pub use

MARYVILLE

P MARYVILLE PUBLIC LIBRARY*, 509 N Main, 64468. SAN 309-0914. Tel: 660-582-5281. FAX: 660-582-2411. E-mail: admin@maryvillepubliclibrary.org. Web Site: www.maryvillepubliclibrary.lib.mo.us. *Dir,* Stephanie Patterson; *Asst Dir,* Wilma Henggeler; *YA Librn,* Jill Emerson; Staff 4 (MLS 1, Non-MLS 3)
Founded 1904. Pop 10,557; Circ 77,587
Library Holdings: Bk Vols 55,000; Per Subs 45; Talking Bks 1,114; Videos 375
Automation Activity & Vendor Info: (Cataloging) Mandarin Library Automation; (Circulation) Mandarin Library Automation
Open Mon-Fri 9-6, Sat 9-3
Friends of the Library Group

S NODAWAY COUNTY HISTORICAL SOCIETY/MARY H JACKSON RESEARCH CENTER*, 110 N Walnut St, 64468-2251. (Mail add: PO Box 324, 64468-0324), SAN 373-2363. Tel: 660-582-8176. FAX: 660-562-3377. E-mail: nodawaycountyhistoricalsociety@embarqmail.com. Web Site: www.nodawayhistorical.org. *Head, Cat,* Carolyn Fisher; *Coll Coordr,* Margaret Kelley; *Curator,* Tom Carneal
Founded 1944
Library Holdings: Bk Titles 8,900; Bk Vols 12,000
Special Collections: Oral History
Subject Interests: Genealogy, Local hist
Open Tues-Fri (Mar-Dec) 1-4

C NORTHWEST MISSOURI STATE UNIVERSITY*, B D Owens Library, 800 University Dr, 64468-6001. SAN 349-4284. Tel: 660-562-1192. Interlibrary Loan Service Tel: 660-562-1592. Reference Tel: 660-562-1193. FAX: 660-562-1049. E-mail: library@nwmissouri.edu. Web Site: www.nwmissouri.edu/library/index.html. *Dir of Libr,* Dr Leslie Galbreath; *Head, Access Serv,* Glenn Morrow; E-mail: morrow@nwmissouri.edu; *Head, Info Serv,* Frank Baudino; E-mail: baudino@nwmissouri.edu; *Info Librn,* Carolyn Johnson; E-mail: carolyn@nwmissouri.edu; *Info Librn,* Lori Mardis; E-mail: lmardis@nwmissouri.edu; *ILL Coordr,* Glenn Morrow; E-mail: morrow@nwmissouri.edu; *Coordr, Tech Serv,* Sara Duff; E-mail: sduff@nwmissouri.edu; *Automation Spec,* Hong Gyu Han; E-mail: hanwiz@nwmissouri.edu; *Ref Spec,* Pat Wyatt; E-mail: pjp@nwmissouri.edu; Staff 10 (MLS 6, Non-MLS 4)
Founded 1905. Enrl 7,076; Fac 275; Highest Degree: Master
Jul 2008-Jun 2009 Income (Main Library Only) $2,179,219. Mats Exp $736,055. Sal $913,443 (Prof $532,099)
Library Holdings: AV Mats 7,517; e-books 48,895; e-journals 25,375; Bk Titles 215,890; Bk Vols 259,651; Per Subs 459
Special Collections: Missouri History & Government (Missouriana), multi-media. State Document Depository; US Document Depository
Automation Activity & Vendor Info: (Acquisitions) Innovative Interfaces, Inc; (Cataloging) Innovative Interfaces, Inc; (Circulation) Innovative Interfaces, Inc; (Course Reserve) Innovative Interfaces, Inc; (ILL) Innovative Interfaces, Inc; (Media Booking) Innovative Interfaces, Inc; (OPAC) Innovative Interfaces, Inc; (Serials) Innovative Interfaces, Inc
Database Vendor: 3M Library Systems, ABC-CLIO, ACM (Association for Computing Machinery), Agricola, Alexander Street Press, American Chemical Society, American Psychological Association (APA), Annual Reviews, Career Guidance Foundation, College Source, CountryWatch, CQ Press, Dialog, ebrary, EBSCOhost, Facts on File, Gale Cengage Learning, H W Wilson, JSTOR, Knovel, LexisNexis, Library Automation Technologies, Inc. (LAT), Modern Language Association, Newsbank, OCLC FirstSearch, OCLC WorldShare Interlibrary Loan, Oxford Online, ProQuest, SerialsSolutions, STAT!Ref (Teton Data Systems), ValueLine, Wilson - Wilson Web, YBP Library Services
Wireless access
Partic in Amigos Library Services, Inc; MOBIUS (Missouri Bibliographic Information User System); OCLC Online Computer Library Center, Inc
Open Mon-Thurs 7:30am-Midnight, Fri 7:30-5, Sat 11-5, Sun 1-Midnight
Restriction: In-house use for visitors, Restricted pub use
Departmental Libraries:
HORACE MANN LIBRARY, Brown Hall 121, 800 University Dr, 64468, SAN 349-4314. Tel: 660-562-1271. FAX: 660-562-1992. *Librn,* Mary Shields; E-mail: mshields@nwmissouri.edu; Staff 3 (MLS 1, Non-MLS 2)
Special Collections: Elementary Curricula
Subject Interests: Children's lit
Automation Activity & Vendor Info: (Cataloging) Innovative Interfaces, Inc - Millenium; (Circulation) Innovative Interfaces, Inc - Millenium
Open Mon-Fri (Aug-May) 7:45-4

MEMPHIS

P SCOTLAND COUNTY MEMORIAL LIBRARY*, 306 W Madison, 63555. SAN 309-0922. Tel: 660-465-7042. FAX: 660-465-7334. Web Site: scotland.lib.mo.us. *Dir,* Melissa Schuster; Staff 3.2 (Non-MLS 3.2)
Founded 1958. Pop 4,843; Circ 40,165
Jan 2012-Dec 2012 Income $130,345, State $11,523, County $110,260, Other $8,562. Mats Exp $23,399, Books $17,217, Per/Ser (Incl. Access Fees) $1,182, AV Mat $5,000. Sal $62,019
Library Holdings: Audiobooks 990; CDs 797; DVDs 990; Large Print Bks 2,463; Bk Vols 31,574; Per Subs 63; Talking Bks 990; Videos 238
Subject Interests: Consumer health, Genealogy, Local hist
Automation Activity & Vendor Info: (Cataloging) Book Systems; (Circulation) Book Systems; (ILL) OCLC; (OPAC) Book Systems
Database Vendor: OCLC FirstSearch, World Book Online
Wireless access
Publications: Ella Ewing, Missouri Giantess
Partic in OCLC Online Computer Library Center, Inc
Special Services for the Blind - Bks on CD
Open Mon, Wed & Fri 9-5:30, Tues & Thurs 9-7, Sat 9-1

MEXICO

P MEXICO-AUDRAIN COUNTY LIBRARY DISTRICT*, 305 W Jackson St, 65265. SAN 349-4349. Tel: 573-581-4939. FAX: 573-581-7510. E-mail: mexicoaudrain@netscape.net. Web Site: mexico-audrain.lib.mo.us. *Dir,* Ray Hall; *Br Mgr, IT Dir,* Christal Bruner; Staff 23 (MLS 4, Non-MLS 19)
Founded 1912
Library Holdings: Bk Titles 86,000; Bk Vols 150,000; Per Subs 154
Special Collections: Audrain County Genealogy
Automation Activity & Vendor Info: (Cataloging) TLC (The Library Corporation); (Circulation) TLC (The Library Corporation)
Database Vendor: TLC (The Library Corporation)
Partic in Amigos Library Services, Inc; Missouri Research & Education Network (MOREnet)
Open Mon-Thurs 9-8, Fri 9-5:30, Sat 9-4:30
Friends of the Library Group
Branches: 4
FARBER BRANCH, 113 W Front St, Farber, 63345, SAN 349-4373. Tel: 573-249-2012. FAX: 573-249-2012. E-mail: frbrlibrary0@gmail.com. *Br Mgr,* Vernelle Hull; Staff 1 (Non-MLS 1)
Library Holdings: CDs 20; DVDs 35; Large Print Bks 200; Bk Titles 8,919; Bk Vols 9,636; Per Subs 21; Talking Bks 25; Videos 30
Database Vendor: EBSCOhost
Open Mon & Tues 1:30-5, Wed 9-12 & 1:30-5, Sat 9-12
Friends of the Library Group
ED FRENCH MEMORIAL, 204 E Second St, Laddonia, 63352, SAN 349-4403. Tel: 573-373-2393. FAX: 573-373-2393. E-mail: 2laddonialibrary@gmail.com. *Br Mgr,* Pam Mozee; Staff 1 (Non-MLS 1)
Open Tues-Fri 1-5, Sat 9-Noon
Friends of the Library Group
MARTINSBURG BRANCH, 201 E Washington St, Martinsburg, 65264, SAN 370-002X. Tel: 573-492-6254. FAX: 573-492-6254. *Br Mgr,* Paula Vomund
Open Tues-Thurs 1-5, Fri & Sat 9-Noon
Friends of the Library Group
VANDALIA BRANCH, 309 S Main St, Vandalia, 63382, SAN 349-4438. Tel: 573-594-6600. FAX: 573-594-3590. *Br Mgr,* Crystal McCurdy; Staff 3 (Non-MLS 3)
Special Collections: Vandalia History Coll
Open Mon-Fri 9-5:30, Sat 9-1
Friends of the Library Group

MILAN

P SULLIVAN COUNTY PUBLIC LIBRARY*, 109 E Second St, 63556. SAN 309-0930. Tel: 660-265-3911. FAX: 660-265-3911. E-mail: sullivanco63556@gmail.com. *Dir,* Shirley De Sha; *Asst Librn,* Jody Kimmel; Staff 5 (MLS 1, Non-MLS 4)
Founded 1972
Library Holdings: Bk Titles 21,113; Bk Vols 23,165; Per Subs 18; Talking Bks 200; Videos 150
Automation Activity & Vendor Info: (Cataloging) Book Systems; (Circulation) Book Systems; (Course Reserve) Book Systems; (ILL) Book Systems; (OPAC) Book Systems
Database Vendor: OCLC FirstSearch
Open Mon-Wed & Fri 9-5, Thurs 9-7, Sun 9-Noon
Bookmobiles: 1

MOBERLY

CR CENTRAL CHRISTIAN COLLEGE OF THE BIBLE LIBRARY*, Reese Resource Center Library, 911 E Urbandale Dr, 65270. SAN 321-1819. Tel: 660-263-3933. Administration Tel: 660-263-3900. Toll Free Tel: 888-263-3900. FAX: 660-263-3533. Administration FAX: 660-263-3936. E-mail: library@cccb.edu. Web Site: cccb.edu/academics/library. *Dir,* Patricia A Agee; E-mail: pagee@cccb.edu; Staff 2.23 (MLS 1.5, Non-MLS 0.73)
Founded 1957. Enrl 329; Fac 24; Highest Degree: Bachelor
Library Holdings: Audiobooks 50; AV Mats 9,866; Bks on Deafness & Sign Lang 24; DVDs 300; e-books 70,000; e-journals 120; Electronic

Media & Resources 3; Large Print Bks 10; Bk Titles 67,000; Bk Vols 78,000; Per Subs 202; Spec Interest Per Sub 180; Talking Bks 100; Videos 250
Special Collections: Preaching Charts of John Hall & Edsil Dale; Rosetta Stone Language Program; Walter S Coble Mission File Coll
Subject Interests: Bible, Communication, Counseling, Missions, Theol
Automation Activity & Vendor Info: (Cataloging) Follett Software; (Circulation) Follett Software; (Course Reserve) Follett Software; (ILL) OCLC FirstSearch; (OPAC) Follett Software
Database Vendor: CredoReference, ebrary, EBSCOhost
Wireless access
Function: Computers for patron use, Copy machines, e-mail & chat, Handicapped accessible, ILL available, Ref & res, Scanner, VHS videos
Partic in Amigos Library Services, Inc; Christian Library Consortium
Open Mon-Thurs (Winter) 7am-11:30pm, Fri 7-6, Sat 11-8; Mon-Fri (Summer) 8-5
Restriction: Open to pub for ref & circ; with some limitations, Open to students, fac, staff & alumni, Photo ID required for access

P LITTLE DIXIE REGIONAL LIBRARIES*, 111 N Fourth St, 65270-1577. SAN 349-4462. Tel: 660-263-4426. FAX: 660-263-4024. E-mail: sysadmin@little-dixie.lib.mo.us. Web Site: www.ldrl.org. *Dir,* Karen Hayden; E-mail: khayden@little-dixie.lib.mo.us; *Ch,* Paula Hayslip; E-mail: phayslip@little-dixie.lib.mo.us; *Adult Serv/Young Adult Librarian,* Rachael Grime; E-mail: rgrime@little-dixie.lib.mo.us; Staff 3 (MLS 1, Non-MLS 2)
Founded 1966. Pop 34,451; Circ 20,500
Jan 2012-Dec 2012 Income (Main Library and Branch(s)) $1,275,000, State $13,000, County $1,197,000, Other $47,000
Library Holdings: Audiobooks 3,772; DVDs 4,800; Large Print Bks 12,000; Microforms 1,000; Bk Titles 122,059; Bk Vols 181,343; Per Subs 214; Videos 5,480
Special Collections: Missouri Civil War Coll; Randolph County Genealogy
Automation Activity & Vendor Info: (Cataloging) Book Systems; (Circulation) Book Systems; (Media Booking) Book Systems; (OPAC) Book Systems; (Serials) Book Systems
Database Vendor: Booksite, EBSCOhost, Facts on File, Gale Cengage Learning, LearningExpress, ReferenceUSA, TumbleBookLibrary, World Book Online
Wireless access
Function: AV serv, Games & aids for the handicapped, Handicapped accessible, Home delivery & serv to Sr ctr & nursing homes, Homebound delivery serv, ILL available, Large print keyboards, Libr develop, Magnifiers for reading, Outside serv via phone, mail, e-mail & web, Photocopying/Printing, Prog for adults, Prog for children & young adult, Ref serv available, Spoken cassettes & CDs, Summer reading prog, Telephone ref, VHS videos, Wheelchair accessible, Workshops
Special Services for the Deaf - Assistive tech; TTY equip
Special Services for the Blind - Assistive/Adapted tech devices, equip & products; Computer with voice synthesizer for visually impaired persons
Open Mon, Tues & Thurs 9-8, Wed & Fri 9-6, Sat 9-4
Friends of the Library Group
Branches: 3
DULANY MEMORIAL, 101 N Main, Paris, 65275-1398, SAN 349-4551. Tel: 660-327-4707. FAX: 660-327-4094. *Librn,* Sue Mattingly; E-mail: smattingly@little-dixie.lib.mo.us
Special Collections: Monroe County Genealogy
Special Services for the Deaf - Assistive tech
Special Services for the Blind - Aids for in-house use; Assistive/Adapted tech devices, equip & products; Computer with voice synthesizer for visually impaired persons
Open Mon, Tues & Fri 12-5, Wed 9:30-5, Thurs 12-7, Sat 9-12
HUNTSVILLE BRANCH, 102 E Library St, Huntsville, 65259-1125, SAN 349-4497. Tel: 660-277-4518. FAX: 660-277-4333. *Librn,* Lora Colley; E-mail: lcolley@little-dixie.lib.mo.us
Special Services for the Deaf - Assistive tech
Special Services for the Blind - Aids for in-house use; Assistive/Adapted tech devices, equip & products; Computer with voice synthesizer for visually impaired persons
Open Mon 12-7, Tues, Thurs & Fri 12-5, Wed 9:30-5, Sat 9-12
MADISON BRANCH, 113 E Broadway, Madison, 65263, SAN 349-4527. Tel: 660-291-3695. FAX: 660-291-8695. *Librn,* Carol Kroeckel; E-mail: ckroekel@little-dixie.lib.mo.us
Special Services for the Deaf - Assistive tech
Special Services for the Blind - Aids for in-house use; Assistive/Adapted tech devices, equip & products; Computer with voice synthesizer for visually impaired persons
Open Mon, Thurs & Fri 12-5, Tues 12-7, Wed 9:30-5, Sat 9-12

J MOBERLY AREA COMMUNITY COLLEGE*, Kate Stamper Wilhite Library, Main Bldg, 2nd Flr, 101 College Ave, 65270-1304. SAN 309-0957. Tel: 660-263-4110, Ext 244. Toll Free Tel: 800-622-2070. FAX: 660-263-6448. E-mail: info@macc.edu. Web Site: www.macc.edu/~library/index.shtml. *Dir of Libr Serv,* Valerie J Darst; E-mail: valeriedarst@macc.edu; Staff 3 (MLS 1, Non-MLS 2)
Founded 1927. Enrl 2,500; Highest Degree: Associate
Library Holdings: Bk Titles 21,899; Bk Vols 22,170; Per Subs 50; Talking Bks 48; Videos 118
Special Collections: Jack Conroy American Studies Coll; Stamper Science & Technology Coll
Subject Interests: Behav sci, Hist, Natural sci, Soc sci
Automation Activity & Vendor Info: (Cataloging) Innovative Interfaces, Inc; (Circulation) Innovative Interfaces, Inc
Partic in MOBIUS (Missouri Bibliographic Information User System)
Open Mon-Thurs (Fall & Spring) 7:30am-8:30pm, Fri 7:30-4; Mon & Tues (Summer) 7:30-4 & 5:30-7:30, Wed-Fri 7:30-4

MONETT

P BARRY-LAWRENCE REGIONAL LIBRARY, 213 Sixth St, 65708-2147. SAN 349-4586. Tel: 417-235-6646. FAX: 417-235-6799. E-mail: execdir@blrlibrary.org. Web Site: tlc.library.net/bll. *Dir,* Gina Gail Milburn; *Cataloger, Coll Develop,* Rhonda Duff; E-mail: rhonda@blrlibrary.org; *Cataloger,* Joyce Frazier; E-mail: joycefrazier@blrlibrary.org; *Computer Tech, Libr Asst, Adult Serv,* Joyce K Reed; E-mail: joycek@blrlibrary.org; *Computer Tech, Libr Asst, Adult Serv,* Lee Ann Rosewicz; E-mail: leeann@blrlibrary.org; Staff 27 (MLS 1, Non-MLS 26)
Founded 1954. Pop 74,231; Circ 467,974
Jul 2013-Jun 2014 Income (Main Library and Branch(s)) $1,566,981, State $89,617, County $1,326,581, Locally Generated Income $137,430, Other $13,353. Mats Exp $150,913, Books $125,622, Per/Ser (Incl. Access Fees) $8,141, Micro $841, AV Mat $16,309. Sal $777,552 (Prof $741,331)
Library Holdings: Audiobooks 302; CDs 4,139; DVDs 14,792; Large Print Bks 9,862; Microforms 684; Bk Titles 186,246; Bk Vols 182,513; Per Subs 114; Videos 2,857
Special Collections: Local History (Missouri Coll)
Automation Activity & Vendor Info: (Cataloging) TLC (The Library Corporation); (Circulation) TLC (The Library Corporation); (OPAC) TLC (The Library Corporation)
Database Vendor: EBSCOhost, Gale Cengage Learning, Ingram Library Services, LearningExpress, OCLC FirstSearch, OCLC WebJunction, OCLC WorldShare Interlibrary Loan, Overdrive, Inc, ProQuest, TLC (The Library Corporation), WT Cox
Wireless access
Function: Adult bk club, After school storytime, Bk club(s), Bks on CD, Children's prog, Computer training, Computers for patron use, Copy machines, Electronic databases & coll, Fax serv, Free DVD rentals, Handicapped accessible, Homebound delivery serv, ILL available, Preschool reading prog, Prog for adults, Prog for children & young adult, Pub access computers, Story hour, Summer reading prog, Tax forms, Teen prog
Special Services for the Deaf - ADA equip; Bks on deafness & sign lang
Special Services for the Blind - Bks on cassette; Bks on CD; Free checkout of audio mat; Large print bks
Open Mon-Thurs 8:30-7, Fri & Sat 8:30-5:30
Friends of the Library Group
Branches: 10
AURORA BRANCH, 202 Jefferson, Aurora, 65605, SAN 349-4594. Tel: 417-678-2036. FAX: 417-678-2041. E-mail: aurora@blrlibrary.org. *Br Supvr,* Martha Pettegrew; *Libr Asst, Adult Serv,* Vickey Maples; *Libr Asst, Youth Serv,* Maria Cross; Staff 3.7 (Non-MLS 3.7)
Circ 73,965
Library Holdings: Audiobooks 31; CDs 676; DVDs 1,778; Large Print Bks 1,723; Microforms 42; Bk Titles 27,967; Bk Vols 28,773; Per Subs 14; Videos 707
Open Mon-Thurs 8:30-7, Fri & Sat 8:30-5:30
Friends of the Library Group
CASSVILLE BRANCH, 301 W 17th St, Cassville, 65625-1044. (Mail add: PO Box D, Cassville, 65625), SAN 349-4616. Tel: 417-847-2121. FAX: 417-847-4679. E-mail: cassville@blrlibrary.org. *Br Supvr,* Cheryl Williams; *Libr Asst, Adult Serv,* Amanda Ray; *Libr Asst, Youth Serv,* Verna Fry; Staff 4.4 (Non-MLS 4.4)
Circ 89,321
Library Holdings: Audiobooks 51; CDs 770; DVDs 2,196; Large Print Bks 1,359; Microforms 72; Bk Titles 31,156; Bk Vols 32,555; Per Subs 13; Videos 410
Special Collections: Barry County Genealogy
Open Mon-Thurs 8:30-6, Fri & Sat 8:30-5:30
Friends of the Library Group
EAGLE ROCK BRANCH, 27824 State Hwy 86, Eagle Rock, 65641. (Mail add: PO Box 147, Eagle Rock, 65641-0147), SAN 375-8745. Tel: 417-271-3186. FAX: 417-271-3186. E-mail: eaglerock@blrlibrary.org. *Br Supvr, Youth Serv,* Jennifer Cochran; Staff 1 (Non-MLS 1)
Circ 16,909
Library Holdings: Audiobooks 8; CDs 108; DVDs 939; Large Print Bks 303; Bk Titles 4,528; Bk Vols 4,597; Per Subs 6; Videos 32
Open Tues-Fri 9-5
Friends of the Library Group
MARIONVILLE BRANCH, 303 W Washington St, Marionville, 65705. (Mail add: PO Box 418, Marionville, 65705), SAN 349-4640. Tel: 417-463-2675. FAX: 417-463-2116. E-mail: marionville@blrlibrary.org.

Br Supvr, Youth Serv Coordr, Janea Kay Coker; *Libr Asst, Adult Serv,* Position Currently Open; *Libr Asst, Youth Serv,* Cindy Magallanes; Staff 3.2 (Non-MLS 3.2)
Circ 33,352
Library Holdings: Audiobooks 104; CDs 326; DVDs 1,220; Large Print Bks 925; Bk Titles 15,405; Bk Vols 15,657; Per Subs 12; Videos 413
Open Mon-Fri 9-5, Sat 9-1
Friends of the Library Group

MILLER BRANCH, 112 E Main St, Miller, 65707. (Mail add: PO Box 84, Miller, 65707-0084), SAN 349-4675. Tel: 417-452-3466. FAX: 417-452-3466. E-mail: miller@blrlibrary.org. *Br Supvr, Youth Serv,* Pam Glassco; Staff 0.95 (Non-MLS 0.95)
Circ 17,135
Library Holdings: Audiobooks 1; CDs 145; DVDs 933; Large Print Bks 340; Bk Titles 8,135; Bk Vols 8,310; Per Subs 7; Videos 82
Open Tues, Wed & Fri 9-5, Sat 9-1

MONETT BRANCH, 213 Sixth St, 65708, SAN 349-4705. Tel: 417-235-6646. FAX: 417-235-6799. E-mail: monett@blrlibrary.org. *Br Supvr,* Cindy Frazier; *Libr Asst, Adult Serv,* Betty Alyea; *Libr Asst, Youth Serv,* Jeanne Ann Camp; Staff 4.3 (Non-MLS 4.3)
Circ 96,049
Library Holdings: Audiobooks 33; CDs 798; DVDs 2,122; Large Print Bks 1,753; Microforms 354; Bk Titles 32,509; Bk Vols 33,877; Per Subs 22; Videos 404
Open Mon-Thurs 8:30-7, Fri & Sat 8:30-5:30
Friends of the Library Group

MOUNT VERNON BRANCH, 206 W Water, Mount Vernon, 65712, SAN 349-4764. Tel: 417-466-2921. FAX: 417-466-2936. E-mail: mtvernon@blrlibrary.org. *Br Supvr,* Cindy Rinker; *Libr Asst, Adult Serv,* Edwana Kennedy; *Libr Asst, Youth Serv,* Julie McCollum; Staff 4.2 (Non-MLS 4.2)
Circ 84,923
Library Holdings: Audiobooks 38; CDs 735; DVDs 1,728; Large Print Bks 1,443; Microforms 175; Bk Titles 27,841; Bk Vols 28,469; Per Subs 13; Videos 264
Special Collections: Lawrence County Genealogy & Historical Coll
Open Mon-Thurs 8:30-7, Fri & Sat 8:30-5:30
Friends of the Library Group

PIERCE CITY BRANCH, 101 N Walnut St, Pierce City, 65723. Tel: 417-476-5110. FAX: 417-476-5110. E-mail: lirpa12@blrlibrary.org. *Br Supvr,* Terry Canady; *Libr Asst, Youth Serv,* Carolyn Dean; Staff 1.3 (Non-MLS 1.3)
Circ 19,256
Library Holdings: Audiobooks 18; CDs 230; DVDs 1,304; Large Print Bks 761; Microforms 43; Bk Titles 14,820; Bk Vols 15,045; Per Subs 11; Videos 385
Open Tues-Fri 9-6, Sat 9-1
Friends of the Library Group

PURDY BRANCH, 403 Hwy C, Purdy, 65734. (Mail add: PO Box 246, Purdy, 65734), SAN 349-473X. Tel: 417-442-7314. FAX: 417-442-7314. E-mail: purdy@blrlibrary.org. *Br Supvr,* Melissa Jones; *Libr Asst, Youth Serv,* Connie Curbow; Staff 0.97 (Non-MLS 0.97)
Circ 13,712
Library Holdings: Audiobooks 7; CDs 103; DVDs 1,132; Large Print Bks 343; Bk Titles 6,500; Bk Vols 6,614; Per Subs 8; Videos 108
Open Mon, Wed & Fri 8:30-5

SHELL KNOB BRANCH, 24931 State Hwy 39, Shell Knob, 65747. (Mail add: PO Box 349, Shell Knob, 65747-0349), SAN 349-4756. Tel: 417-858-3618. FAX: 417-858-3618. E-mail: shellknob@blrlibrary.org. *Br Supvr,* Suzy Anglim; *Libr Asst, Youth Serv,* Angie Heuback; Staff 1.65 (Non-MLS 1.65)
Circ 23,352
Library Holdings: Audiobooks 11; CDs 248; DVDs 1,440; Large Print Bks 912; Bk Titles 12,369; Bk Vols 12,531; Per Subs 8; Videos 52
Open Tues-Fri 8:30-5:30, Sat 8:30-12:30
Friends of the Library Group

MONROE CITY

P MONROE CITY PUBLIC LIBRARY*, 109A Second St, 63456. SAN 309-0965. Tel: 573-735-2665. FAX: 573-735-4943. *Librn,* Carroll Hood; Staff 1 (Non-MLS 1)
Founded 1918. Pop 2,557; Circ 10,110
Library Holdings: Bk Titles 11,050; Bk Vols 11,561; Per Subs 35; Talking Bks 33
Subject Interests: Recreation
Automation Activity & Vendor Info: (Cataloging) Mandarin Library Automation; (Circulation) Mandarin Library Automation
Wireless access
Open Mon-Fri 11:30-5:30, Sat 10-12

MONTGOMERY CITY

P MONTGOMERY CITY PUBLIC LIBRARY*, 224 N Allen St, 63361. SAN 309-0973. Tel: 573-564-8022. FAX: 573-564-6159. *Librn,* Linda Eatherton; E-mail: mcplmo@gmail.com; Staff 2 (Non-MLS 2)
Founded 1927. Pop 2,442; Circ 53,184
Jul 2008-Jun 2009 Income $158,985. Mats Exp $17,942. Sal $60,625
Library Holdings: Audiobooks 774; Bk Vols 23,053; Per Subs 62
Automation Activity & Vendor Info: (Cataloging) Mandarin Library Automation; (Circulation) Mandarin Library Automation; (ILL) OCLC; (OPAC) Mandarin Library Automation
Partic in Amigos Library Services, Inc; Missouri Research & Education Network (MOREnet)
Open Mon 8-8, Tues & Thurs 8 6:30, Wed & Fri 8-5, Sat 9-1

MOUND CITY

P MOUND CITY PUBLIC LIBRARY*, 207 E Sixth St, 64470. (Mail add: PO Box 93, 64470), SAN 309-0981. Tel: 660-442-5700. FAX: 660-442-3149. E-mail: mclib@live.com. Web Site: www.moundcitypubliclibrary.lib.mo.us. *Libr Dir,* Carly Edwards; *Asst Dir,* Becky Poe
Founded 1908. Pop 1,358; Circ 8,400
Library Holdings: DVDs 225; Bk Titles 18,500; Bk Vols 19,450; Per Subs 31; Talking Bks 60; Videos 100
Subject Interests: Fiction
Wireless access
Open Mon & Wed-Fri 12-5, Tues 10-5, Sat 9-12
Friends of the Library Group

MOUNT VERNON

S MISSOURI VETERANS' HOME LIBRARY*, 1600 S Hickory, 65712-2045. SAN 377-1148. Tel: 417-466-7103. FAX: 417-466-4040. Web Site: www.mvc.dps.mo.gov. *Librn,* David Kloppenborg
Library Holdings: Bk Vols 600; Per Subs 10
Restriction: Not open to pub

MOUNTAIN VIEW

P MOUNTAIN VIEW PUBLIC LIBRARY*, 125 S Oak St, 65548. (Mail add: PO Box 1389, 65548-1389), SAN 309-1007. Tel: 417-934-6154. FAX: 417-934-5100. Web Site: mvpubliclibrary.webs.com. *Dir,* Beth Gilbert; E-mail: bgilbertmvpl@centurytel.net; *Asst Dir,* Katrina Wood; *Cataloger,* Hilary Connolly; Staff 2 (MLS 1, Non-MLS 1)
Founded 1950. Pop 2,450; Circ 42,500
Jul 2007-Jun 2008 Income $118,583. Sal $59,000
Library Holdings: Large Print Bks 1,000; Bk Titles 50,000; Per Subs 30; Videos 12,000
Subject Interests: Hist of Ozarks scenic river
Automation Activity & Vendor Info: (Cataloging) TLC (The Library Corporation); (Circulation) TLC (The Library Corporation); (ILL) OCLC; (OPAC) TLC (The Library Corporation)
Publications: Poems for Children; Seasons of the Ozarks
Open Mon-Wed & Fri 9-5, Thurs 9-8, Sat 8-Noon
Friends of the Library Group

NEOSHO

J CROWDER COLLEGE*, Bill & Margot Lee Library, 601 Laclede Ave, 64850. SAN 309-1015. Tel: 417-455-5610. Circulation Tel: 417-455-5606. Reference Tel: 417-455-5689. FAX: 417-451-4280. Web Site: www.crowder.edu/student-services/crowder-library/index.php. *Dir,* Mary Largent; E-mail: mlargent@crowder.edu; *Ref & Circ Librn,* Lynne Edgar; E-mail: lynneedgar@crowder.edu; *Libr Spec,* Denna Clymer; E-mail: dennaclymer@crowder.edu; Staff 1 (MLS 1)
Founded 1964. Enrl 2,102; Fac 75; Highest Degree: Associate
Library Holdings: AV Mats 4,200; DVDs 200; e-books 21,500; Bk Titles 39,500; Per Subs 170; Videos 316
Automation Activity & Vendor Info: (Acquisitions) Innovative Interfaces, Inc - Millenium; (Cataloging) Innovative Interfaces, Inc; (Circulation) Innovative Interfaces, Inc; (ILL) OCLC FirstSearch; (OPAC) Innovative Interfaces, Inc; (Serials) Innovative Interfaces, Inc
Database Vendor: 3M Library Systems, ABC-CLIO, CountryWatch, EBSCOhost, Gale Cengage Learning, Grolier Online, Innovative Interfaces, Inc, LearningExpress, Micromedex, Newsbank, OCLC ArticleFirst, OCLC FirstSearch, OCLC WorldShare Interlibrary Loan, ProQuest
Wireless access
Function: Audio & video playback equip for onsite use, Bks on cassette, Bks on CD, CD-ROM, Copy machines, Distance learning, Doc delivery serv, e-mail serv, Electronic databases & coll, Fax serv, Handicapped accessible, ILL available, Instruction & testing, Online searches, Orientations, Outside serv via phone, mail, e-mail & web, Photocopying/Printing, Ref & res, Ref serv available, Scanner, Spoken cassettes & CDs, Spoken cassettes & DVDs, Telephone ref, VHS videos

Partic in Amigos Library Services, Inc; Missouri Research & Education Network (MOREnet); MOBIUS (Missouri Bibliographic Information User System)
Open Mon-Thurs 8am-8:30pm, Fri 8-4:30, Sun 1:30-4:30
Restriction: Non-circulating coll, Open to students, fac & staff, Restricted pub use
Friends of the Library Group

P NEOSHO/NEWTON COUNTY LIBRARY*, 201 W Spring St, 64850. SAN 349-4799. Tel: 417-451-4231. FAX: 417-451-6438. Web Site: www.neosholibrary.org. *Dir,* Ginny Ray; *Syst Adminr,* Jerry Parker; *Tech Serv,* Sharon Meredith; Staff 8 (MLS 1, Non-MLS 7)
Founded 1966. Pop 55,000; Circ 180,000
Library Holdings: Bk Titles 50,000; Bk Vols 51,118; Per Subs 132; Talking Bks 618; Videos 2,891
Automation Activity & Vendor Info: (Acquisitions) SirsiDynix; (Cataloging) SirsiDynix; (Circulation) SirsiDynix; (OPAC) SirsiDynix
Database Vendor: SirsiDynix
Wireless access
Partic in OCLC Online Computer Library Center, Inc
Open Mon-Thurs 9-8, Fri 9-5:30, Sat 9-5
Friends of the Library Group
Branches: 1
SENECA BRANCH, 1216 Cherokee, Seneca, 64865. Tel: 417-776-2705. FAX: 417-776-8003. *Br Mgr,* Mitzi Thurman
Library Holdings: DVDs 250; Bk Vols 11,000; Per Subs 19; Videos 100
Open Mon & Wed-Fri 9-5, Tues 9-7, Sat 9-Noon
Friends of the Library Group

NEVADA

J COTTEY COLLEGE*, Blanche Skiff Ross Memorial Library, 225 S College St, 64772-2892. (Mail add: 1000 W Austin, 64772-2763), SAN 309-1023. Tel: 417-667-8181, Ext 2153. FAX: 417-448-1040. Web Site: www.cottey.edu/library/new/home.html. *Libr Dir,* Becky Kiel; E-mail: bkiel@cottey.edu; Staff 5 (MLS 1, Non-MLS 4)
Founded 1884. Enrl 310; Fac 35; Highest Degree: Associate
Library Holdings: CDs 641; Bk Titles 56,000; Per Subs 205
Special Collections: College Archives; Henry Moore Coll; bks, cats
Subject Interests: Gen liberal arts, Women's leadership
Automation Activity & Vendor Info: (Acquisitions) OCLC CatExpress; (Cataloging) Innovative Interfaces, Inc; (Circulation) Innovative Interfaces, Inc; (Course Reserve) Innovative Interfaces, Inc; (ILL) OCLC WorldShare Interlibrary Loan; (Media Booking) Innovative Interfaces, Inc - Millenium; (OPAC) Innovative Interfaces, Inc - Millenium; (Serials) Innovative Interfaces, Inc - Millenium
Database Vendor: Agricola, American Chemical Society, Bowker, College Source, EBSCOhost, Gale Cengage Learning, Innovative Interfaces, Inc, JSTOR, Medline, Newsbank, OCLC WorldShare Interlibrary Loan, ProQuest
Wireless access
Function: ILL available
Partic in Amigos Library Services, Inc; Missouri Research & Education Network (MOREnet); MOBIUS (Missouri Bibliographic Information User System)
Open Mon-Thurs 7:30am-11pm, Fri 7:30-6, Sat 12-6, Sun 2-11

P NEVADA PUBLIC LIBRARY*, 218 W Walnut, 64772-0931. (Mail add: 212 W Walnut St, 64772), SAN 309-1031. Tel: 417-448-2770. FAX: 417-448-2771. Web Site: www.nevadapubliclibrary.com. *Dir,* Jodi Polk; E-mail: jodipolk@gmail.com; Staff 5 (MLS 2, Non-MLS 3)
Founded 1898. Pop 8,691; Circ 80,000
Library Holdings: Bks on Deafness & Sign Lang 18; High Interest/Low Vocabulary Bk Vols 25; Large Print Bks 36; Bk Titles 40,600; Bk Vols 40,710; Per Subs 72; Spec Interest Per Sub 12; Talking Bks 698; Videos 1,115
Special Collections: State Document Depository
Database Vendor: OCLC FirstSearch
Special Services for the Deaf - TDD equip
Special Services for the Blind - Computer with voice synthesizer for visually impaired persons
Open Mon, Wed & Fri 9-5, Tues & Thurs 9-8, Sat 10-2
Friends of the Library Group

NORBORNE

P NORBORNE PUBLIC LIBRARY*, 109 E Second St, 64668. SAN 309-1066. Tel: 660-593-3514. FAX: 660-593-3514. *Librn,* Doris S Wightman
Founded 1930. Pop 931; Circ 7,844
Library Holdings: High Interest/Low Vocabulary Bk Vols 10; Large Print Bks 75; Bk Titles 1,200; Bk Vols 10,000; Per Subs 18; Talking Bks 125; Videos 103
Subject Interests: Town hist
Open Mon-Fri 8-12 & 1-5, Sat 8-12

NORTH KANSAS CITY

M NORTH KANSAS CITY HOSPITAL*, Medical Library, 2800 Clay Edwards Dr, 64116. SAN 373-2371. Tel: 816-691-1692. FAX: 816-346-7192. *Librn,* Evelyn J Vail; E-mail: evelyn.vail@nkch.org
Library Holdings: Bk Titles 6,200; Bk Vols 6,700; Per Subs 300
Subject Interests: Allied health, Nursing
Partic in Health Sciences Library Network of Kansas City, Inc
Open Mon-Fri 7:30-5

P NORTH KANSAS CITY PUBLIC LIBRARY*, 2251 Howell St, 64116. SAN 309-1082. Tel: 816-221-3360. FAX: 816-221-8298. Web Site: www.northkclibrary.org. *Dir,* Position Currently Open; *Asst Dir,* Vickie Lewis; E-mail: vickielewis@northkclibrary.org; *Bus Mgr,* Paula Kemper; E-mail: paulakemper@northkclibrary.org; *Ch Serv,* Nancy Robinson; E-mail: nancyrobinson@northkclibrary.org; Staff 10 (MLS 2, Non-MLS 8)
Founded 1939. Pop 4,859; Circ 76,994
Library Holdings: Large Print Bks 98; Bk Titles 65,000; Bk Vols 72,000; Per Subs 186; Talking Bks 1,144; Videos 2,816
Automation Activity & Vendor Info: (Acquisitions) SirsiDynix; (Cataloging) SirsiDynix; (Circulation) SirsiDynix; (ILL) SirsiDynix; (OPAC) SirsiDynix; (Serials) SirsiDynix
Database Vendor: EBSCOhost, Newsbank, SirsiDynix
Partic in Kansas City Library Service Program
Open Mon-Thurs (Winter) 7-9, Fri 7-6, Sat 9-5, Sun 1-5; Mon-Thurs (Summer) 9-9, Fri 9-6, Sat 9-5
Friends of the Library Group

OREGON

P OREGON PUBLIC LIBRARY, 103 S Washington St, 64473. (Mail add: PO Box 288, 64473-0288), SAN 309-1112. Tel: 660-446-3586. FAX: 660-446-3586. E-mail: opl-52011@hotmail.com. *Librn,* Allison Russell; Staff 2 (MLS 1, Non-MLS 1)
Founded 1938. Pop 1,500; Circ 6,741
Library Holdings: Large Print Bks 75; Bk Titles 15,161; Bk Vols 15,878; Per Subs 32; Talking Bks 138; Videos 147
Mem of South Central Library System
Open Mon & Thurs-Sat 2-5, Tues 10-5, Wed 1-7

OSCEOLA

P SAINT CLAIR COUNTY LIBRARY*, 115 Chestnut St, 64776-2502. SAN 309-1120. Tel: 417-646-2214. FAX: 417-646-8643. E-mail: stclaircountylibrary@gmail.com. Web Site: mostclair.lib.mo.us. *Dir,* Angie Jones
Founded 1948. Pop 9,862; Circ 60,885
Library Holdings: Bk Titles 34,697; Per Subs 32
Special Collections: County Historical Society
Automation Activity & Vendor Info: (Acquisitions) Book Systems; (Cataloging) Book Systems; (Circulation) Book Systems; (ILL) OCLC FirstSearch; (Media Booking) Book Systems; (OPAC) Book Systems; (Serials) Book Systems
Wireless access
Open Mon-Thurs 8am-9pm, Fri 8-5, Sat 9-2
Friends of the Library Group
Branches: 1
LOWRY CITY BRANCH, 406 Fourth St, Lowry City, 64763. Tel: 417-644-2255. FAX: 417-644-2257. *Dir,* Angie Jones
Open Tues-Thurs 1-7, Fri 9-5, Sat 9-2
Bookmobiles: 1

OZARK

P CHRISTIAN COUNTY LIBRARY*, 1005 N Fourth Ave, 65721. SAN 309-1139. Tel: 417-581-2432. FAX: 417-581-8855. E-mail: info@christiancounty.lib.mo.us. Web Site: christiancounty.lib.mo.us. *Dir,* Mabel Gaye Phillips; E-mail: mphillip@christiancounty.lib.mo.us; *Ch,* Lucinda Dailey; E-mail: ldailey@christiancounty.lib.mo.us; *Tech Serv,* Connie Powell; E-mail: cpowell@christiancounty.lib.mo.us; Staff 21 (MLS 2, Non-MLS 19)
Founded 1956. Pop 77,422; Circ 216,538
Jan 2011-Dec 2011 Income $1,005,026, State $32,927, Locally Generated Income $930,765, Other $41,334. Mats Exp $157,389, Books $91,603, Per/Ser (Incl. Access Fees) $6,328, AV Mat $23,756, Electronic Ref Mat (Incl. Access Fees) $35,552, Presv $150. Sal $451,675
Library Holdings: AV Mats 2,658; e-books 7,575; Electronic Media & Resources 82; Large Print Bks 8,200; Bk Titles 69,701; Bk Vols 75,858; Per Subs 203; Talking Bks 1,613
Special Collections: Southwest Missouri & the Ozarks. Oral History
Subject Interests: Antiques

Automation Activity & Vendor Info: (Acquisitions) Baker & Taylor; (Cataloging) Innovative Interfaces, Inc; (Circulation) Innovative Interfaces, Inc; (ILL) OCLC FirstSearch; (OPAC) Innovative Interfaces, Inc
Database Vendor: EBSCO Information Services, EBSCOhost, Facts on File, Gale Cengage Learning, infoUSA, LearningExpress, Newsbank, OCLC FirstSearch, OCLC WebJunction, ProQuest, ReferenceUSA
Wireless access
Function: Adult bk club, Archival coll, Bks on CD, Children's prog, Computers for patron use, Copy machines, Digital talking bks, Electronic databases & coll, Exhibits, Free DVD rentals, Handicapped accessible, Home delivery & serv to Sr ctr & nursing homes, ILL available, Instruction & testing, Large print keyboards, Magnifiers for reading, Mail & tel request accepted, Microfiche/film & reading machines, Online cat, Online searches, Outreach serv, OverDrive digital audio bks, Photocopying/Printing, Prog for children & young adult, Ref serv available, Ref serv in person, Res performed for a fee, Senior computer classes, Spoken cassettes & CDs, Spoken cassettes & DVDs, Story hour, Summer reading prog, Tax forms, Teen prog, VHS videos, Video lending libr, Web-catalog, Wheelchair accessible, Workshops, Writing prog
Partic in Consortium of Ozarks Libraries; Missouri Research & Education Network (MOREnet); MOBIUS (Missouri Bibliographic Information User System)
Open Mon-Thurs 8:30-8, Fri & Sat 8:30-5
Restriction: Authorized patrons, In-house use for visitors
Friends of the Library Group
Bookmobiles: 1. In Charge, Scott Villarreal. Bk vols 600

PALMYRA

P MARION COUNTY SUB-DISTRICT LIBRARY*, 212 S Main St, 63461. SAN 309-1147. Tel: 573-769-2830. FAX: 573-769-0405. E-mail: palmyralibrary@gmail.com. Web Site: marioncounty1.lib.mo.us, www.palmyralibrary.org. *Dir,* Peggy Northcraft; *Circ Mgr,* Ruth Garner; *Ch Serv,* Mary Lynne Jones; Staff 2 (MLS 1, Non-MLS 1)
Founded 1913. Pop 6,000
Library Holdings: Bk Titles 21,040; Bk Vols 22,000; Per Subs 17; Talking Bks 413; Videos 546
Special Collections: Civil War; History Local Battles; Mark Twain Coll
Subject Interests: Local hist
Automation Activity & Vendor Info: (Cataloging) ComPanion Corp; (Circulation) ComPanion Corp; (ILL) OCLC FirstSearch; (OPAC) ComPanion Corp
Database Vendor: EBSCOhost, OCLC FirstSearch
Wireless access
Publications: Local Paper Column (Weekly)
Open Mon, Wed & Fri 10-5:30, Tues & Thurs 10-6

PARK HILLS

J MINERAL AREA COLLEGE*, C H Cozean Library, 5270 Flat River Rd, 63601. (Mail add: PO Box 1000, 63601-1000), SAN 308-9835. Tel: 573-518-2141. FAX: 573-518-2162. Web Site: www.mineralarea.edu/library. *Dir,* Melissa Hopkins; Tel: 573-518-2177, E-mail: mhopkins@mineralarea.edu; *Instrul Librn, ILL Librn,* Ryan Harrington; Tel: 573-518-2236, E-mail: rkharrin@mineralarea.edu; *Libr Spec,* Rebecca Young; Tel: 573-518-2141, E-mail: rkyoung@mineralarea.edu
Founded 1969. Enrl 3,000; Fac 81; Highest Degree: Associate
Library Holdings: AV Mats 5,046; Bk Titles 29,389; Bk Vols 33,999; Per Subs 166; Videos 868
Special Collections: State Document Depository
Automation Activity & Vendor Info: (Acquisitions) Innovative Interfaces, Inc; (Cataloging) Innovative Interfaces, Inc; (Circulation) Innovative Interfaces, Inc; (Course Reserve) Innovative Interfaces, Inc; (ILL) Innovative Interfaces, Inc; (Media Booking) Innovative Interfaces, Inc; (OPAC) Innovative Interfaces, Inc; (Serials) Innovative Interfaces, Inc
Database Vendor: Innovative Interfaces, Inc
Partic in Amigos Library Services, Inc; MOBIUS (Missouri Bibliographic Information User System)
Open Mon-Thurs 7:30am-8pm, Fri 7:30-4

P PARK HILLS PUBLIC LIBRARY*, 16 S Coffman St, 63601. SAN 308-9827. Tel: 573-431-4842. FAX: 573-431-2110. *Dir,* Lisa Sisk; E-mail: parkhillspubliclibrary02@yahoo.com; *Asst Dir,* Wendy Walker; Staff 3 (MLS 1, Non-MLS 2)
Founded 1934. Pop 12,000; Circ 32,000
Library Holdings: Bk Titles 45,000; Bk Vols 46,000; Per Subs 43; Talking Bks 838; Videos 392
Subject Interests: Local hist
Automation Activity & Vendor Info: (Acquisitions) Follett Software; (Cataloging) Follett Software; (Circulation) Follett Software
Open Mon & Tues 10-7, Wed-Fri 11-5, Sat (Sept-May) 9-12
Friends of the Library Group

PARKVILLE

C PARK UNIVERSITY LIBRARY*, 8700 NW River Park Dr, 64152. SAN 309-1155. Tel: 816-584-6285. Administration Tel: 816-584-6704. Toll Free Tel: 800-270-4347. FAX: 816-741-4911. Web Site: www.park.edu/library. *Dir, Libr Syst,* Ann Schultis; E-mail: ann.schultis@park.edu; *Ref Librn,* Rebecca Cox; Tel: 816-584-6840, E-mail: rebecca.cox@park.edu; *Ref Librn,* Mary Shriner; Tel: 816-584-6464, E-mail: mary.shriner@park.edu; *Archivist,* Carolyn Elwess; Tel: 816-584-6891, E-mail: carolyn.elwess@park.edu; *Acq,* Veronica Spottswood; Tel: 816-741-2000, Ext 6284, E-mail: veronica.spottswood@park.edu; *Cat,* Betty Dusing; Tel: 816-584-6281, E-mail: betty.dusing@park.edu; *Circ,* Bobbi Shaw; E-mail: bobbi.shaw@park.edu; *ILL,* Betty Vestal; Tel: 816-584-6283, E-mail: parkill@park.edu; Staff 8 (MLS 3, Non-MLS 5)
Founded 1875. Enrl 4,777; Fac 106; Highest Degree: Master
Library Holdings: Electronic Media & Resources 53; Bk Titles 108,708; Bk Vols 153,359; Per Subs 591; Videos 1,223
Special Collections: History (Platte County Historical Society Archives); Park College & Park University History Coll. Oral History
Automation Activity & Vendor Info: (Acquisitions) SirsiDynix; (Cataloging) SirsiDynix; (Circulation) SirsiDynix; (Course Reserve) SirsiDynix; (OPAC) SirsiDynix; (Serials) SirsiDynix
Publications: Friends of the Library (Newsletter)
Partic in Kansas City Library Service Program; Mid-America Library Alliance/Kansas City Metropolitan Library & Information Network
Open Mon-Thurs (Winter) 8am-9:30pm, Fri 8-4:30, Sat 10-4, Sun 4-9:30pm; Mon-Thurs (Summer) 8-8, Fri 8-4:30, Sat 10-4, Sun 4-8
Friends of the Library Group

PINEVILLE

P MCDONALD COUNTY LIBRARY*, Pineville Library, 808 Bailey Rd, 64856. SAN 309-118X. Tel: 417-223-4489. FAX: 417-223-4011. Web Site: librarymail.org. *Dir,* Carrie Cline; E-mail: carecline@yahoo.com; Staff 9 (MLS 1, Non-MLS 8)
Founded 1949. Pop 21,681; Circ 68,539
Library Holdings: Bks on Deafness & Sign Lang 14; Bk Titles 33,000; Bk Vols 36,000; Per Subs 50; Talking Bks 1,023; Videos 3,633
Special Collections: Jesse James Coll
Automation Activity & Vendor Info: (Cataloging) Book Systems; (Circulation) Book Systems; (OPAC) Book Systems
Database Vendor: EBSCOhost, OCLC FirstSearch
Wireless access
Open Mon-Thurs 9-6, Fri 1-6, Sat 9-3
Friends of the Library Group
Branches: 2
ANNE CROXDALE MEMORIAL LIBRARY, 102 N Main St, Southwest City, 64863. Tel: 417-762-7323. FAX: 417-762-7322. *Br Mgr,* Retha Mitchell
Open Tues-Thurs 10-6, Fri 1-6, Sat 10-3
NOEL LIBRARY, 626 Johnson Dr, Noel, 64854. Tel: 417-475-3223. FAX: 417-475-3223. *Br Mgr,* Wes Ferguson
Library Holdings: DVDs 550; Bk Vols 4,000; Talking Bks 50; Videos 600
Open Tues-Thurs 11-6, Fri 1-6, Sat 9-3

POINT LOOKOUT

COLLEGE OF THE OZARKS
C BROWNELL RESEARCH CENTER LIBRARY*, Ralph Foster Museum, One Cultural Ct, 65726. (Mail add: PO Box 17, 65726-0017). Tel: 417-690-3407. FAX: 417-690-2606. *Dir,* Annette Sain; E-mail: sain@cofo.edu
Founded 1975
Library Holdings: Bk Titles 4,000; Per Subs 4
Special Collections: Artifacts & Antiques Coll
Subject Interests: Hist
Function: For res purposes
Restriction: Not a lending libr, Staff & prof res
C LYONS MEMORIAL LIBRARY*, One Opportunity Ave, 65726. (Mail add: PO Box 17, 65726-0017). Tel: 417-690-3411. FAX: 417-334-3085. Web Site: www.cofo.edu/library/default.asp. *Libr Supvr-Popular Libr,* Karla Jenkins; E-mail: kjenkins@cofo.edu; *ILL, Pub Serv, Ref Serv,* Linda Schmidt; E-mail: schmidt@cofo.edu; *Media Spec, Spec Coll,* Gwen Simmons; E-mail: simmons@cofo.edu; *Tech Serv,* Ronald D Wyly; E-mail: wyly@cofo.edu; Staff 4 (MLS 4)
Founded 1906. Enrl 1,440; Fac 83; Highest Degree: Bachelor
Library Holdings: AV Mats 3,306; Bk Vols 120,782; Per Subs 715
Special Collections: Ozarks (Ozarkiana Coll), bks, photogs, tapes, mss, letters
Automation Activity & Vendor Info: (Circulation) Innovative Interfaces, Inc; (OPAC) Innovative Interfaces, Inc
Partic in Amigos Library Services, Inc; Missouri Research & Education Network (MOREnet); OCLC Online Computer Library Center, Inc
Open Mon-Thurs 8am-10pm, Fri 8-5, Sat 1-5, Sun 2-5

POPLAR BLUFF

P POPLAR BLUFF PUBLIC LIBRARY*, 318 N Main St, 63901. SAN 349-4918. Tel: 573-686-8639. FAX: 573-785-6876. E-mail: library@poplarbluff.org. Web Site: poplarbluff.org/library. *Dir,* Sue Crites Szostak; E-mail: szostak@poplarbluff.org; *Asst Dir,* Shannon Mangrum; E-mail: shannon@poplarbluff.org; *Ch,* Erin Rigby; E-mail: erin@poplarbluff.org; *Coll Develop Spec,* Shon Griffen; E-mail: shon@poplarbluff.org
Founded 1916. Pop 25,000; Circ 180,000
Library Holdings: Bk Vols 47,000; Per Subs 105
Automation Activity & Vendor Info: (Acquisitions) TLC (The Library Corporation); (Cataloging) TLC (The Library Corporation); (Circulation) TLC (The Library Corporation); (ILL) OCLC Connexion; (OPAC) TLC (The Library Corporation)
Database Vendor: TLC (The Library Corporation)
Wireless access
Partic in Mid-America Library Alliance/Kansas City Metropolitan Library & Information Network
Open Mon-Thurs 9-7, Fri & Sat 10-5
Friends of the Library Group

S W E SEARS YOUTH CENTER*, Sollars Library, 9400 Sears Lane, 63901-9716. SAN 309-1198. Tel: 573-840-9280. FAX: 573-840-9352. *Mgr,* Rick Stewart; *Librn,* Cassie Willey
Founded 1970
Library Holdings: Bk Titles 5,000; Bk Vols 5,100; Per Subs 21
Partic in Mo Statewide ILL Network
Open Mon-Fri 8:30-4

J THREE RIVERS COMMUNITY COLLEGE LIBRARY*, Rutland Library, 2080 Three Rivers Blvd, 63901. SAN 309-1201. Tel: 573-840-9654. FAX: 573-840-9659. E-mail: arc@trcc.edu. Web Site: www.trcc.edu. *Dir,* Position Currently Open; Staff 1 (MLS 1)
Founded 1966. Enrl 3,400; Highest Degree: Associate
Library Holdings: Bk Vols 35,000; Per Subs 175; Videos 500
Special Collections: McManus Civil War Coll; Ozarks & Southeast Missouri History. State Document Depository
Automation Activity & Vendor Info: (Cataloging) OCLC Online; (Circulation) Innovative Interfaces, Inc; (ILL) OCLC Online; (OPAC) Innovative Interfaces, Inc
Database Vendor: EBSCOhost, OCLC WorldShare Interlibrary Loan, ProQuest
Partic in Amigos Library Services, Inc; MOBIUS (Missouri Bibliographic Information User System); OCLC Online Computer Library Center, Inc
Restriction: Open to pub for ref & circ; with some limitations

GM VETERANS AFFAIRS MEDICAL CENTER*, John J Pershing Library, 1500 N Westwood, 63901-3318. SAN 309-121X. Tel: 573-778-4120. FAX: 573-778-4239. *Dir,* Nancy Nelson; E-mail: nancy.nelson2@va.gov
Library Holdings: Bk Titles 1,581; Bk Vols 2,344; Per Subs 4
Partic in Midcontinental Regional Med Libr Program; Veterans Affairs Libr Network (VALNET)
Open Mon-Fri 8-4:30

PORTAGEVILLE

P NEW MADRID COUNTY LIBRARY*, 309 E Main St, 63873. SAN 309-1228. Tel: 573-379-3583. FAX: 573-379-9220. *Dir,* Susan Newman
Founded 1948. Pop 18,954; Circ 69,243
Library Holdings: Bk Vols 85,857; Per Subs 52
Subject Interests: Genealogy, Local hist
Automation Activity & Vendor Info: (Cataloging) TLC (The Library Corporation); (Circulation) Follett Software
Database Vendor: EBSCOhost
Open Mon-Sat 8-5
Branches: 3
MOREHOUSE SERVICE CENTER, 204 Beech St, Morehouse, 63868. (Mail add: 309 E Main St, 63873), SAN 377-3744. Tel: 573-379-3583. *Librn,* Judith Hankins
Library Holdings: Bk Vols 4,500
NEW MADRID MEMORIAL, 431 Mill St, New Madrid, 63869. (Mail add: 309 E Main St, 63873), SAN 321-9453. Tel: 573-748-2378. FAX: 573-748-7637. *Librn,* Rhonda Bickerstaff; *Librn,* Kathy Marchbanks
Library Holdings: Bk Titles 25,669; Per Subs 10
Open Mon-Fri 9-5, Sat 9-12
RHODES MEMORIAL, Main St, Gideon, 63848. (Mail add: 309 E Main St, 63873), SAN 308-9916. Tel: 573-379-3583. *Dir,* Susan Newman
Library Holdings: Bk Titles 12,290
Automation Activity & Vendor Info: (Circulation) Follett Software; (OPAC) Follett Software
Database Vendor: EBSCOhost
Open Mon-Fri 1-5

POTOSI

P WASHINGTON COUNTY LIBRARY, 235 E High St, 63664. SAN 309-1236. Tel: 573-438-4691. FAX: 573-438-6423. E-mail: washingtoncolibrary@hotmail.com. Web Site: www.thewashingtoncolibrary.com. *Librn,* Melissa G Mercer; *Asst Librn,* Judy Eye
Founded 1948. Pop 23,344; Circ 65,197
Library Holdings: Bk Titles 58,366; Bk Vols 66,561; Per Subs 138
Special Collections: Historical Coll, bks & micro
Automation Activity & Vendor Info: (Cataloging) Follett Software; (Circulation) Follett Software
Wireless access
Open Mon 9-8, Tues-Fri 9-5, Sat 9-1
Bookmobiles: 1

PRINCETON

P MERCER COUNTY LIBRARY*, 601 W Grant St, 64673. SAN 309-1244. Tel: 660-748-3725. FAX: 660-748-3723. TDD: 660-748-4514. E-mail: mercou@gmail.com. Web Site: www.mcl.lib.mo.us. *Dir,* Judy Cox; *Adult, Youth & Ch Librn,* Marilyn Hardy; *Circ Librn,* Billie Day; *ILL Librn,* Dixie Moore; *Tech Librn,* Rhonda Hamilton; Staff 6 (Non-MLS 6)
Founded 1926. Pop 4,610; Circ 35,475
Library Holdings: Bk Titles 19,435; Bk Vols 20,000; Per Subs 36; Talking Bks 117; Videos 538
Subject Interests: Genealogy
Automation Activity & Vendor Info: (Cataloging) Book Systems; (Circulation) Book Systems
Database Vendor: OCLC FirstSearch
Wireless access
Partic in Lyrasis; OCLC Online Computer Library Center, Inc
Open Mon-Wed & Fri 9-5, Thurs 9-8, Sat 9-12

REPUBLIC

S NATIONAL PARK SERVICE*, Mr & Mrs John K Hulston Civil War Library, Wilson's Creek National Battlefield, 6424 W Farm Rd 182, 65738-9514. SAN 321-0006. Tel: 417-732-2662. FAX: 417-732-1167. Web Site: www.nps.gov/wicr. *Mgr,* Jeffrey Patrick; E-mail: jeffrey_patrick@nps.gov; Staff 1 (Non-MLS 1)
Founded 1985
Library Holdings: Bk Vols 7,000
Subject Interests: Civil War, Mo
Function: Res libr
Restriction: Not a lending libr
Friends of the Library Group

RICHLAND

P PULASKI COUNTY LIBRARY DISTRICT*, 111 Camden St, 65556. (Mail add: PO Box 340, 65556-0340), SAN 349-4225. Tel: 573-765-3642. FAX: 573-765-5395. Web Site: www.pulaskicounty.lib.mo.us. *Dir,* Osa Kays; Staff 10 (Non-MLS 10)
Founded 1965
Library Holdings: Bk Vols 50,000; Per Subs 27
Automation Activity & Vendor Info: (Acquisitions) Innovative Interfaces, Inc; (Cataloging) Innovative Interfaces, Inc; (Circulation) Innovative Interfaces, Inc; (Course Reserve) Innovative Interfaces, Inc; (ILL) Innovative Interfaces, Inc; (Media Booking) Innovative Interfaces, Inc; (OPAC) Innovative Interfaces, Inc; (Serials) Innovative Interfaces, Inc
Database Vendor: EBSCOhost, LearningExpress, Medline
Partic in National Network of Libraries of Medicine Midcontinental Region
Open Tues 9-7, Wed & Thurs 9-6, Fri 9-5, Sat 9-1
Friends of the Library Group
Branches: 2
CROCKER BRANCH, 602 N Commercial St, Crocker, 65452. (Mail add: PO Box 854, Crocker, 65452-0854). Tel: 573-736-5592. FAX: 573-736-5427. *Br Mgr,* Stephanie Lupardus
Founded 1999
Database Vendor: Innovative Interfaces, Inc, OVID Technologies
Open Tues-Thurs 9-6, Fri 9-5, Sat 9-1
Friends of the Library Group
WAYNESVILLE BRANCH, 306 Historic 66 W, Waynesville, 65536, SAN 349-425X. Tel: 573-774-2965. FAX: 573-774-6429. *Br Mgr,* Connie Buttram
Database Vendor: Innovative Interfaces, Inc, OVID Technologies
Open Mon, Wed & Thurs 9-6, Tues 9-7, Fri 9-5, Sat 9-1
Friends of the Library Group

RICHMOND

S RAY COUNTY HISTORICAL SOCIETY & MUSEUM LIBRARY*, 901 W Royle St, 64085-1545. SAN 372-6568. Tel: 816-776-2305. E-mail: raycountymuseum@yahoo.com. *Curator,* Linda Emeley; Staff 1 (MLS 1)
Founded 1973

Library Holdings: Bk Titles 1,376; Bk Vols 1,500
Special Collections: Jesse James Coll; Russell Ogg Coll; William Burke Coll
Publications: The Looking Glass (Newsletter)
Open Wed-Sat 10-4

P RAY COUNTY LIBRARY, 215 E Lexington, 64085-1834. SAN 309-1252. Tel: 816-776-5102, 816-776-5104. FAX: 816-776-5103. E-mail: raycopublibrary@yahoo.com. Web Site: www.raycountylibrary.homestead.com. *Dir,* Steve Meyer; E-mail: raycolibrarydirector@yahoo.com; Staff 1 (Non-MLS 1)
Founded 1947. Pop 23,494; Circ 76,143
Jan 2013-Dec 2013 Income $377,974, State $12,561, Federal $24,742, County $310,137, Locally Generated Income $30,531. Mats Exp $85,779, Books $61,074, Per/Ser (Incl. Access Fees) $1,250, AV Mat $3,661, Electronic Ref Mat (Incl. Access Fees) $19,794. Sal $166,320 (Prof $52,500)
Library Holdings: Audiobooks 1,285; Large Print Bks 1,350; Microforms 161; Bk Titles 60,000; Bk Vols 62,500; Per Subs 89; Videos 2,860
Automation Activity & Vendor Info: (Cataloging) Book Systems; (Circulation) Book Systems; (ILL) OCLC WorldShare Interlibrary Loan
Wireless access
Open Mon & Wed 8:30-6, Tues & Thurs 8:30-8, Fri 8:30-5, Sat 9-12
Friends of the Library Group

RICHMOND HEIGHTS

P RICHMOND HEIGHTS MEMORIAL LIBRARY*, 8001 Dale Ave, 63117. SAN 309-1260. Tel: 314-645-6202. FAX: 314-781-3434. Web Site: rhml.lib.mo.us. *Libr Dir,* Jeanette Moore Piquet; E-mail: jpiquet@rhmlibrary.org; *Ad,* Scott Bonner; *Ch,* Elizabeth Simmons; *Info Serv Librn,* Ray Harrison; Staff 9 (MLS 4, Non-MLS 5)
Founded 1935. Pop 9,600; Circ 195,738
Library Holdings: Bk Titles 59,432; Bk Vols 61,402; Per Subs 117; Talking Bks 448; Videos 349
Automation Activity & Vendor Info: (Cataloging) SirsiDynix; (Circulation) SirsiDynix; (OPAC) SirsiDynix; (Serials) SirsiDynix
Database Vendor: EBSCOhost, Gale Cengage Learning, infoUSA, Medline, OCLC FirstSearch, ReferenceUSA, SirsiDynix
Wireless access
Function: Adult bk club, After school storytime, Art exhibits, Audiobks via web, Bk club(s), Bks on CD, Children's prog, Computer training, Computers for patron use, Copy machines, Digital talking bks, Electronic databases & coll, Exhibits, Fax serv, Free DVD rentals, Handicapped accessible, Holiday prog, ILL available, Magnifiers for reading, Mail & tel request accepted, Music CDs, Newsp ref libr, Online cat, OverDrive digital audio bks, Preschool outreach, Preschool reading prog, Prog for adults, Prog for children & young adult, Pub access computers, Ref serv available, Ref serv in person, Scanner, Senior outreach, Story hour, Summer & winter reading prog, Tax forms, Teen prog, Telephone ref, VHS videos, Video lending libr, Web-catalog, Wheelchair accessible
Partic in MLC; Saint Louis Regional Library Network
Special Services for the Blind - Aids for in-house use; Audio mat; Bks on cassette; Bks on CD; Copier with enlargement capabilities; Extensive large print coll, Large print bks; Magnifiers; Ref serv; Sound rec
Open Mon-Thurs 9-9, Fri 9-8, Sat 9-5, Sun 1-5
Friends of the Library Group

ROCK HILL

P ROCK HILL PUBLIC LIBRARY*, 9811 Manchester Rd, 63119. SAN 309-1279. Tel: 314-962-4723. FAX: 314-962-3932. Web Site: www.rockhill.lib.mo.us. *Dir,* Kelley Sallade; Staff 7 (Non-MLS 7)
Founded 1943. Pop 4,765; Circ 50,418
Apr 2011-Mar 2012 Income $278,476. Mats Exp $17,700, Books $10,000, Per/Ser (Incl. Access Fees) $2,700, AV Mat $5,000. Sal $134,731
Library Holdings: Audiobooks 400; CDs 1,020; DVDs 2,099; Bk Titles 26,898; Per Subs 70; Videos 495
Automation Activity & Vendor Info: (Cataloging) SirsiDynix; (Circulation) SirsiDynix; (ILL) OCLC Online; (OPAC) SirsiDynix; (Serials) SirsiDynix
Database Vendor: EBSCOhost, LearningExpress, Newsbank, OCLC FirstSearch, Overdrive, Inc, SirsiDynix, TumbleBookLibrary
Wireless access
Function: Handicapped accessible, ILL available, Prog for children & young adult, Ref serv available, Summer reading prog
Partic in Municipal Library Consortium; Saint Louis Regional Library Network
Open Mon-Thurs 12-8, Fri 12-5, Sat 10-2
Restriction: Open to pub for ref & circ; with some limitations

ROCK PORT

P ATCHISON COUNTY LIBRARY*, 200 S Main St, 64482-1532. SAN 349-5000. Tel: 660-744-5404. FAX: 660-744-2861. Web Site: acl.tlcdelivers.com. *Dir,* Janice S Rosenbohm; E-mail: rockport@aclibrary.net; *Librn,* Rebecca Adams; *Librn,* Karen Culjat; *Librn,* Darlene Schmidt; *Librn,* Bob Simpson; Staff 5 (MLS 1, Non-MLS 4)
Founded 1946. Pop 6,430; Circ 42,535
Library Holdings: Large Print Bks 350; Bk Vols 60,836; Per Subs 95; Talking Bks 1,555; Videos 5,067
Subject Interests: Genealogy, Local hist
Automation Activity & Vendor Info: (Cataloging) OCLC CatExpress; (Circulation) TLC (The Library Corporation); (ILL) OCLC; (OPAC) TLC (The Library Corporation)
Database Vendor: EBSCOhost
Partic in Amigos Library Services, Inc; Grand Rivers Libr Conference; Missouri Research & Education Network (MOREnet); Mo Libr Asn
Open Mon, Wed & Fri 9-5, Tues & Thurs 9-8, Sat 9-12
Branches: 2
FAIRFAX BRANCH, 118 Main St, Fairfax, 64446, SAN 349-5035. Tel: 660-686-2204. *Librn,* Amanda Agnew; Staff 1 (MLS 1)
Open Mon 9-11:30 & 12-5, Wed & Fri 12-5, Thurs 12-7
TARKIO BRANCH, 405 S 11th St, Tarkio, 64491, SAN 349-506X. Tel: 660-736-5832. *Librn,* Cheryl Freeman; Staff 1 (Non-MLS 1)
Open Mon & Fri 9-12 & 1-5, Tues 12-5, Thurs 12-5 & 6-8

ROLLA

C CURTIS LAWS WILSON LIBRARY*, 400 W 14th St, 65409-0060. SAN 309-1317. Tel: 573-341-4227. Circulation Tel: 573-341-4008. Interlibrary Loan Service Tel: 573-341-4006. Reference Tel: 573-341-4007. FAX: 573-341-4233. E-mail: library@mst.edu. Web Site: library.mst.edu. *Dir,* Tracy Primich; Tel: 573-341-4011; *Asst Dir, Tech Serv,* Maggie Trish; Tel: 573-341-4014, E-mail: trishm@mst.edu; *Head, Acq & Electronic Res,* Jennifer Bleiler; Tel: 573-341-4015, E-mail: bleilerj@mst.edu; *Head, Cat,* Mary Aycock; Tel: 573-341-7826, E-mail: aycockm@mst.edu; *Head, Circ/ILL,* Dawn Mick; Tel: 573-341-7832, E-mail: mickd@mst.edu; *Institutional Repository/Digital Coll Librn,* Roger Weaver; Tel: 573-341-4221, E-mail: weaverjr@mst.edu; *Ref Librn,* Chris Jocius; Tel: 573-341-7842, E-mail: jociusc@mst.edu; *Ref Librn,* Sherry Mahnken; Tel: 573-341-7843, E-mail: mahnkens@mst.edu; *Ref Librn,* Matthew Pickens; Tel: 573-341-7839, E-mail: mpickens@mst.edu; *Per,* Becky Merrell; Tel: 573-341-4013, E-mail: rmerrell@mst.edu; Staff 20 (MLS 8, Non-MLS 12)
Founded 1871. Enrl 7,647; Fac 492; Highest Degree: Doctorate
Library Holdings: AV Mats 4,634; CDs 946; e-books 197,674; e-journals 72,324; Microforms 67,337; Music Scores 677; Bk Vols 293,699; Per Subs 253
Special Collections: John H Dougherty Coll. US Document Depository
Subject Interests: Chem, Eng, Geol, Mat sci, Metallurgy, Mgt, Mining
Automation Activity & Vendor Info: (Acquisitions) Innovative Interfaces, Inc; (Cataloging) Innovative Interfaces, Inc; (Circulation) Innovative Interfaces, Inc; (Course Reserve) Innovative Interfaces, Inc; (OPAC) Innovative Interfaces, Inc; (Serials) Innovative Interfaces, Inc
Database Vendor: ACM (Association for Computing Machinery), American Chemical Society, Baker & Taylor, ebrary, EBSCOhost, IEEE (Institute of Electrical & Electronics Engineers), IOP, JSTOR, Knovel, LexisNexis, Medline, Mergent Online, OCLC, Project MUSE, ProQuest, Safari Books Online, ScienceDirect, Scopus, SerialsSolutions, Springer-Verlag, Wiley InterScience, YBP Library Services
Wireless access
Function: Computers for patron use, E-Reserves, Electronic databases & coll, Fax serv, Govt ref serv, Online cat, Photocopying/Printing, Pub access computers, Ref serv available, Scanner, Tax forms
Partic in Amigos Library Services, Inc; Merlin; MOBIUS (Missouri Bibliographic Information User System); OCLC Online Computer Library Center, Inc
Special Services for the Blind - Magnifiers; Reader equip; Ref serv
Open Mon-Fri 7:30am-Midnight, Sat & Sun 8am-Midnight

G MISSOURI DEPARTMENT OF NATURAL RESOURCES*, Division of Geology & Land Survey Library, 111 Fairgrounds Rd, 65401-2909. (Mail add: PO Box 250, 65401-2250), SAN 309-1287. Tel: 573-368-2100. FAX: 573-368-2111. E-mail: geology@dnr.mo.gov. *In Charge,* Patrick Mulvany; Tel: 573-368-2139, E-mail: patrick.mulvany@dnr.mo.gov; Staff 1 (MLS 1)
Founded 1853
Library Holdings: Bk Titles 57,400; Bk Vols 58,112; Per Subs 37
Special Collections: Missouri Geology (Fowler File & Ed Clark Museum), bks, artifacts, maps
Open Mon-Fri 8-5

P ROLLA FREE PUBLIC LIBRARY*, 900 Pine St, 65401. SAN 309-1295. Tel: 573-364-2604. FAX: 573-341-5768. E-mail: rollalib@fidnet.com. Web Site: rollapubliclibrary.org. *Dir,* Cheryl A Goltz; Staff 1 (MLS 1)
Founded 1938. Pop 16,000; Circ 258,000
Library Holdings: AV Mats 8,000; Bk Vols 53,000; Per Subs 121
Special Collections: Local Paper, 1860-present, micro
Subject Interests: Missouriana
Automation Activity & Vendor Info: (Cataloging) TLC (The Library Corporation); (Circulation) TLC (The Library Corporation); (ILL) OCLC; (OPAC) TLC (The Library Corporation)

Special Services for the Deaf - TDD equip
Special Services for the Blind - Bks on cassette; Braille bks
Open Mon-Thurs 9-9, Fri & Sat 9-5, Sun 1:30-5
Friends of the Library Group

C UNIVERSITY OF MISSOURI*, Western Historical Manuscript Collection - Rolla, G-3 Curtis Laws Wilson Library, MS&T, 400 W 14th St, 65409-1420. SAN 326-4548. Tel: 573-341-4874. E-mail: whmcinfo@mst.edu. Web Site: web.mst.edu/~whmcinfo. *Interim Assoc Dir,* John F Bradbury; E-mail: jfb@mst.edu; Staff 2 (Non-MLS 2)
Special Collections: State Historical Society of Missouri; Western Historical Manuscript Coll
Subject Interests: Hist, Mineral, Mining, Mo hist
Function: Archival coll
Partic in Association of Research Libraries (ARL)
Open Mon-Fri 8-5

SAINT CHARLES

C LINDENWOOD UNIVERSITY*, Margaret Legget Butler Library, 209 S Kingshighway, 63301. SAN 309-1333. Tel: 636-949-4820. Reference Tel: 636-949-4144. FAX: 636-949-4822. E-mail: library@lindenwood.edu. Web Site: www.lindenwood.edu/library. *Dean of Libr Serv,* MacDonald Elizabeth; Tel: 636-949-4396, E-mail: emacdonald@lindenwood.edu; *Asst Dean, Libr Serv,* Candance Virgil; Tel: 636-949-4194, E-mail: cvirgil@lindenwood.edu; *Head, Access Serv,* Lisa Young; Tel: 636-949-4670, E-mail: lyoung@lindenwood.edu; *Head, Tech Serv, Ref Librn,* Suzanne Gleason; Tel: 636-949-4881, E-mail: sgleason@lindenwood.edu; *Digital Librn,* Michael Anthony Fetters; Tel: 636-949-4574, E-mail: mfetters@lindenwood.edu; *Media Librn, Ref Librn,* Michael Dorlac; Tel: 636-949-4347, E-mail: mdorlac@lindenwood.edu; *Ref Librn,* Carl Hubenschmidt; Tel: 636-949-4758, E-mail: chubenschmidt@lindenwood.edu; *Circ Supvr,* Bianca Ray; Tel: 636-949-2529, E-mail: bray@lindenwood.edu; *Archivist,* Paul Huffman; Tel: 636-949-4823, E-mail: phuffman@lindenwood.edu; Staff 9 (MLS 6, Non-MLS 3)
Founded 1827. Enrl 17,000; Fac 200; Highest Degree: Master
Library Holdings: e-books 127,000; Bk Vols 130,412; Per Subs 578
Special Collections: Japanese Culture (Sakahara Coll); Mary E Ambler Archival Coll; McKissack Center for Black Children's Literature. US Document Depository
Automation Activity & Vendor Info: (Acquisitions) Innovative Interfaces, Inc; (Cataloging) Innovative Interfaces, Inc; (Circulation) Innovative Interfaces, Inc; (Course Reserve) Innovative Interfaces, Inc; (OPAC) Innovative Interfaces, Inc; (Serials) Innovative Interfaces, Inc
Database Vendor: Innovative Interfaces, Inc
Wireless access
Function: Archival coll, ILL available, Photocopying/Printing, Telephone ref
Partic in Amigos Library Services, Inc; Higher Educ Coun of St Louis; MOBIUS (Missouri Bibliographic Information User System); OCLC Online Computer Library Center, Inc; Saint Louis Regional Library Network; Statewide California Electronic Library Consortium (SCELC)
Open Mon-Thurs (Fall & Spring) 8am-Midnight, Fri 8-5, Sat 9-4, Sun 2-Midnight; Mon-Thurs (Winter & Summer) 8-8, Fri 8-5, Sat 10-3, Sun 1-5
Restriction: Open to pub for ref & circ; with some limitations

S SAINT CHARLES COUNTY HISTORICAL SOCIETY ARCHIVES*, 101 S Main St, 63301-2802. SAN 329-9295. Tel: 636-946-9828. E-mail: scchs@mail.win.org. Web Site: www.scchs.org. *Archivist,* Bill Popp
Library Holdings: Bk Titles 500
Special Collections: Circuit & Probate Court Records-St Charles County, indexes, photographs
Open Mon, Wed & Fri 10-3
Restriction: Non-circulating

S SAINT JOSEPH HEALTH CENTER*, Health Science Library, 300 First Capitol Dr, 63301. SAN 327-1595. Tel: 636-947-5109. *Coordr,* Lynn Kripple; Tel: 314-344-6397
Library Holdings: Bk Titles 400; Per Subs 80
Subject Interests: Med
Open Mon-Fri 9-2:30

SAINT JAMES

P JAMES MEMORIAL LIBRARY*, 300 W Scioto St, 65559. SAN 309-135X. Tel: 573-265-7211. FAX: 573-265-8771. E-mail: stjlibrary@centurytel.net. *Admin Librn,* Diana Jenkins; Staff 4 (MLS 1, Non-MLS 3)
Founded 1951. Pop 6,500; Circ 54,829
Jan 2008-Dec 2008 Income $98,648. Mats Exp $18,150. Sal $90,160 (Prof $31,000)
Library Holdings: CDs 240; Large Print Bks 500; Bk Titles 30,100; Bk Vols 30,640; Per Subs 58; Talking Bks 586; Videos 722
Special Collections: History of Ozarks, photog
Automation Activity & Vendor Info: (Cataloging) Follett Software; (Circulation) Follett Software
Open Mon 12-8, Tues-Fri 10-5, Sat 9-4

SAINT JOSEPH

R FIRST CHRISTIAN CHURCH LIBRARY*, 927 Faraon St, 64501. SAN 309-1392. Tel: 816-233-2556. FAX: 816-233-0247. Web Site: fccstjo.org.
Founded 1957
Library Holdings: Bk Titles 3,110; Bk Vols 3,220; Per Subs 11
Subject Interests: Biog, Children's bks, Fiction
Restriction: Not open to pub

M HEARTLAND REGIONAL MEDICAL CENTER*, Library Services, 5325 Faraon St, 64506-3398. SAN 326-4831. Tel: 816-271-6075. FAX: 816-271-6074. Web Site: www.heartland-health.com. *Librn,* Cynthia Nicks; E-mail: cindi.nicks@heartland-health.com
Library Holdings: Bk Titles 790; Per Subs 456
Subject Interests: Med, Nursing
Publications: Newsletter
Partic in Health Sci Libr Network; Kans City Mo Libr & Info Network
Open Mon-Fri 8-4:30

R HUFFMAN MEMORIAL UNITED METHODIST CHURCH LIBRARY*, 2802 Renick St, 64507-1897. SAN 309-1406. Tel: 816-233-0239. FAX: 816-233-0683. Web Site: www.huffmanumc.org. *Librn,* Cathy George; Tel: 816-232-7809; Staff 1 (Non-MLS 1)
Founded 1958
Library Holdings: Bk Titles 4,391; Bk Vols 4,562; Per Subs 10
Open Mon-Fri 9-3

C MISSOURI WESTERN STATE UNIVERSITY, Hearnes Center, 4525 Downs Dr, 64507-2294. SAN 309-1414. Tel: 816-271-4368. Circulation Tel: 816-271-4360. Interlibrary Loan Service Tel: 816-271-4572. Reference Tel: 816-271-4573. Administration Tel: 816-271-4200. Toll Free Tel: 866-866-6972. FAX: 816-271-4574. TDD: 816-271-5690. E-mail: refdesk@missouriwestern.edu. *Dir,* Julia Schneider; E-mail: schneide@missouriwestern.edu; *Asst Dir, Access Serv,* Terry Weaver; E-mail: weaver@missouriwestern.edu; *Info Serv Librn/Spec Coll,* Sarah McCumber; E-mail: mccumber@missouriwestern.edu; *Asst Cat Librn,* Jennifer Callow; E-mail: jcallow@missouriwestern.edu; *Acq of New Ser/Per, Coll Develop,* Michelle Diaz; E-mail: diaz@missouriwestern.edu; *Circ,* Lisa Hensley; E-mail: lhensley1@missouriwestern.edu; *ILL,* Rodema Gnuschke; E-mail: gnuschke@missouriwestern.edu; *Per,* Terry Weaver; E-mail: weaver@missouriwestern.edu; *Ref,* Jackie Burns; E-mail: jburns@missouriwestern.edu; *Ref,* James Mulder; E-mail: mulder@missouriwestern.edu; *Tech Serv,* Andrew McGarrell; E-mail: mcgarrel@missouriwestern.edu; Staff 15 (MLS 8, Non-MLS 7)
Founded 1915. Enrl 6,100; Fac 300; Highest Degree: Master
Jul 2011-Jun 2012. Mats Exp $489,000. Sal $765,578
Library Holdings: Bk Titles 226,000; Bk Vols 240,000; Per Subs 1,481
Special Collections: Women Writers Along the Rivers. State Document Depository
Automation Activity & Vendor Info: (Acquisitions) Innovative Interfaces, Inc; (Cataloging) Innovative Interfaces, Inc; (Circulation) Innovative Interfaces, Inc; (Course Reserve) Innovative Interfaces, Inc; (ILL) Innovative Interfaces, Inc; (OPAC) Innovative Interfaces, Inc; (Serials) Innovative Interfaces, Inc
Database Vendor: ABC-CLIO, BioOne, Dialog, ebrary, EBSCOhost, JSTOR, LexisNexis, OCLC FirstSearch, OVID Technologies, STN International, Westlaw, YBP Library Services
Wireless access
Publications: Library Link
Partic in Amigos Library Services, Inc; MOBIUS (Missouri Bibliographic Information User System)
Special Services for the Deaf - TDD equip
Special Services for the Blind - Braille equip; Reader equip; ZoomText magnification & reading software

P ROLLING HILLS CONSOLIDATED LIBRARY*, 1904 N Belt Hwy, 64506-2201. (Mail add: 1912 N Belt Hwy, 64506), SAN 349-5396. Tel: 816-232-5479. Circulation Tel: 816-232-5479, Ext 2101. Interlibrary Loan Service Tel: 816-232-5479, Ext 2201. Reference Tel: 816-232-5479, Ext 2202. Administration Tel: 816-232-5479, Ext 2402. FAX: 816-236-2133. Web Site: www.rollinghills.lib.mo.us. *Dir,* Michelle Mears; Staff 30 (MLS 4, Non-MLS 26)
Library Holdings: Bk Vols 77,235
Wireless access
Open Mon-Thurs 9-9, Fri-Sat 9-6, Sun 1-5
Friends of the Library Group

Branches: 1
SAVANNAH, 514 W Main St, Savannah, 64485-1670, SAN 349-5426. Tel: 816-324-4569. Administration Tel: 816-232-5479, Ext 2401. FAX: 816-324-3562. Administration FAX: 816-236-2133. *Dir,* Michelle Mears; Staff 3 (MLS 1, Non-MLS 2)
Founded 1963
Open Mon, Wed & Fri 9-6, Tues & Thurs 9-8, Sat 9-5, Sun 1-5
Friends of the Library Group

S ST JOSEPH MUSEUMS INC*, St Joseph Museum Library, 3406 Frederick Ave, 64506. (Mail add: PO Box 8096, 64508-8096), SAN 309-1430. Tel: 816-232-8471. Toll Free Tel: 800-530-8866. FAX: 816-232-8482. E-mail: sjm@stjosephmuseum.org. Web Site: www.stjosephmuseum.org. *Exec Dir,* Jackie Lewin; E-mail: jackie@stjosephmuseum.org; *Curator of Coll,* Sarah Elder; E-mail: sarah@stjosephmuseum.org; Staff 10 (Non-MLS 10)
Founded 1927
Library Holdings: Bk Titles 5,000; Bk Vols 5,280; Per Subs 15
Special Collections: History of St Joseph State Hospital (number two); Missouri History; Natural History; Oregon-California Trail; Pony Express; St Joseph During the Civil War; St Joseph History; Western Expansion
Function: Ref serv available
Publications: Happenings (Newsletter)
Open Mon-Fri 9-12 & 1-4
Restriction: In-house use for visitors, Non-circulating

P ST JOSEPH PUBLIC LIBRARY*, Downtown Library, 927 Felix St, 64501-2799. SAN 349-5450. Tel: 816-232-7729. Interlibrary Loan Service Tel: 816-232-3812. Reference Tel: 816-232-8151. Administration Tel: 816-232-4038. FAX. 816-279-3372. Reference FAX: 816-232-7516. TDD: 816-236-2160. Web Site: sjpl.lib.mo.us. *Dir,* Mary Beth Revels; E-mail: mrevels@gmail.com; *Br Mgr,* Carolyn Cunningham; E-mail: ccunningham@sjpl.lib.mo.us; Staff 31 (MLS 6, Non-MLS 25)
Founded 1891. Pop 65,064; Circ 389,864
Jul 2011-Jun 2012 Income (Main Library and Branch(s)) $3,102,704. Mats Exp $202,919, Books $145,985, Per/Ser (Incl. Access Fees) $15,782, Micro $2,281, AV Mat $20,567, Electronic Ref Mat (Incl. Access Fees) $18,304. Sal $1,161,609
Library Holdings: AV Mats 48,184; Bks-By-Mail 3,148; e-books 5,948; Large Print Bks 8,542; Bk Vols 242,308; Per Subs 192
Special Collections: Literature (Eugene Field Coll); Local History Coll; Medicine (Dr Wayne Toothaker Medical Library). State Document Depository; US Document Depository
Automation Activity & Vendor Info: (Acquisitions) SirsiDynix; (Cataloging) SirsiDynix; (Circulation) SirsiDynix; (ILL) OCLC WorldShare Interlibrary Loan; (OPAC) SirsiDynix
Database Vendor: Baker & Taylor, EBSCOhost, Gale Cengage Learning, LearningExpress, Marcive, Inc, Newsbank, OCLC FirstSearch, OCLC WorldShare Interlibrary Loan, Overdrive, Inc, ProQuest, SirsiDynix
Wireless access
Publications: Library Matters (Monthly newsletter)
Special Services for the Deaf - TTY equip
Open Mon-Wed 9-9, Thur, Fri & Sat 9-5
Friends of the Library Group
Branches: 3
CARNEGIE PUBLIC, 316 Massachusetts St, 64504-1449, SAN 349-5485. Tel: 816-238-0526. FAX: 816-238-9438. *Br Mgr,* Audrey Sheets; E-mail: asheets@sjpl.lib.mo.us
Founded 1902
Library Holdings: AV Mats 4,828; Bk Vols 29,295
Open Mon 1-5, Tues & Thurs 11-7, Wed, Fri & Sat 10-6
EAST HILLS LIBRARY, 502 N Woodbine Rd, 64506. Tel: 816-236-2136. FAX: 816-236-1429. *Br Mgr,* Steven Kent Olson; E-mail: solson@sjpl.lib.mo.us; *Outreach Serv Librn,* Deborah Gentry; Tel: 816-236-2107, E-mail: dgentry@sjpl.lib.mo.us; *Tech Serv,* Kim Tullis; Tel: 816-236-1423, E-mail: ktullis@sjpl.lib.mo.us
Founded 2004
Library Holdings: AV Mats 22,156; Bks-By-Mail 3,148; Bk Vols 93,035
Open Mon, Tues & Thurs 9-9, Wed, Fri & Sat 9-5
WASHINGTON PARK, 1821 N Third St, 64505-2533, SAN 349-5515. Tel: 816-232-2052. FAX: 816-236-2151. *Br Mgr,* Karen Schultz; E-mail: kschultz@sjpl.lib.mo.us
Founded 1910
Library Holdings: AV Mats 5,312; Bk Vols 30,879
Open Mon, Wed & Fri 9-5, Tues & Thurs 12-8, Sat 1-5

SAINT LOUIS

M AMERICAN ASSOCIATION OF ORTHODONTISTS, Charles R Baker Memorial Library, 401 N Lindbergh Blvd, 63141. SAN 372-6207. Tel: 314-292-6542. FAX: 314-997-1745. E-mail: library@aaortho.org. *Libr Serv Mgr,* Jackie Hittner; Staff 1.5 (MLS 1, Non-MLS 0.5)
Library Holdings: Bk Titles 2,000; Per Subs 80
Subject Interests: Dentistry, Orthodontics
Automation Activity & Vendor Info: (Cataloging) SydneyPlus; (Circulation) SydneyPlus; (OPAC) SydneyPlus; (Serials) SydneyPlus
Database Vendor: PubMed
Function: Archival coll
Open Mon-Fri 8-5
Restriction: Mem only

S ANHEUSER-BUSCH CO, INC*, Corporate Library, One Busch Pl, 63118. Tel: 314-577-2000. *Librn,* Tracy Lauer; Staff 2 (MLS 2)
Founded 1932
Library Holdings: Bk Vols 40,000; Per Subs 1,000
Subject Interests: Beer, Brewing
Automation Activity & Vendor Info: (Circulation) Softlink America; (OPAC) Softlink America; (Serials) Softlink America
Publications: New Publications; Union List of Periodicals
Partic in OCLC Online Computer Library Center, Inc

R SAUL BRODSKY JEWISH COMMUNITY LIBRARY*, 12 Millstone Campus Dr, 63146-5776. SAN 309-1732. Tel: 314-442-3720. Administration Tel: 314-442-3721. FAX: 314-432-1277. E-mail: brodsky-library@jfedstl.org. Web Site: www.brodskylibrary.org. *Libr Dir,* Barbara Raznick; E-mail: braznick@jfedstl.org; *Asst Librn,* Lorraine Landy; E-mail: llandy@jfedstl.org; *Archivist,* Diane M Everman; E-mail: deverman@jfedstl.org; Staff 4 (MLS 2, Non-MLS 2)
Founded 1983
Library Holdings: Bk Titles 22,000; Per Subs 75
Special Collections: Hebrew Literature; Holocaust; Jewish Children's Books; National & International Newspapers in English, Yiddish, Hebrew & Russian; Russian Literature
Subject Interests: Hist, Holocaust, Israel, Jewish art, Lit, Philos
Automation Activity & Vendor Info: (Cataloging) Follett Software; (Circulation) Follett Software
Open Mon, Wed & Thurs 9-5, Tues 9-8, Fri 9-4, Sun 10-2
Friends of the Library Group

L BRYAN CAVE LLP*, Law Library, One Metropolitan Sq, 211 N Broadway, Ste 3600, 63102-2750. SAN 328-3054. Tel: 314-259-2298. FAX: 314-259-2020. Web Site: www.bryancave.com. *Dir, Libr Serv,* Judy Harris; E-mail: jlharris@bryancave.com; Staff 1 (MLS 1)
Library Holdings: Bk Titles 21,815; Bk Vols 22,000; Per Subs 100
Special Collections: Annual Reports
Publications: Annual Report; Library Bulletin; Library Guide
Partic in OCLC Online Computer Library Center, Inc
Open Mon-Fri 8:30-5

SR CATHOLIC CENTRAL VEREIN OF AMERICA*, Central Bureau Library, 3835 Westminster Pl, 63108. SAN 328-3618. Tel: 314-371 1653. FAX: 314-371-0889. E-mail: centbur@sbcglobal.net. Web Site: www.socialjusticereview.org. *Dir,* Fr Edward Krause; Staff 2 (MLS 1, Non-MLS 1)
Founded 1908
Library Holdings: Bk Vols 250,000; Per Subs 20
Special Collections: German Americana Coll
Subject Interests: Hist, Philos, Theol
Publications: Social Justice Review (Bi-monthly)
Restriction: Non-circulating to the pub, Open to students

R CONCORDIA HISTORICAL INSTITUTE, 804 Seminary Pl, 63105-3014. SAN 309-1783. Tel: 314-505-7900. Reference Tel: 314-505-7935. Administration Tel: 314-505-7911. FAX: 314-505-7901. E-mail: chi@lutheranhistory.org, reference@lutheranhistory.org. Web Site: www.lutheranhistory.org. *Exec Dir,* Daniel Harmelink; E-mail: dharmelink@lutheranhistory.org; *Archivist,* Todd Zittlow; E-mail: tzittlow@lutheranhistory.org; Staff 7 (MLS 1, Non-MLS 6)
Founded 1927
Jul 2008-Jun 2009 Income $773,000, Locally Generated Income $373,000, Parent Institution $400,000. Mats Exp $5,000, Books $1,000, Manu Arch $3,500, Micro $250, AV Mat $250. Sal $326,687
Library Holdings: Bk Vols 59,000; Per Subs 180
Special Collections: Archives of the Lutheran Church-Missouri Synod, 1839-present, ms; History of Lutheranism, bks, ms; Lutheran Foreign Missions (Walter A Maier, Buenger, Graebner, Behnken & Rehwinkel Manuscript Coll); Lutheran Hour, broadcast discs; Lutheranism in America, History & Theology
Subject Interests: Lutheran churches, Lutheranism, Lutheranism in Am, Lutheranism in hist, Lutheranism in theol
Automation Activity & Vendor Info: (Cataloging) OCLC
Wireless access
Function: Archival coll
Publications: Concordia Historical Institute Quarterly; Historical Footnotes (Quarterly)
Open Mon-Fri 8:30-4
Restriction: Non-circulating
Friends of the Library Group

R CONCORDIA SEMINARY LIBRARY*, 801 Seminary Pl, 63105-3199. SAN 309-1570. Tel: 314-505-7038. Circulation Tel: 314-505-7030. Interlibrary Loan Service Tel: 314-505-7031. Reference Tel: 314-505-7032. FAX: 314-505-7046. Circulation E-mail: librarycirc@csl.edu. Interlibrary Loan Service E-mail: libraryill@csl.edu. Reference E-mail: libraryref@csl.edu. Web Site: www.csl.edu/library. *Dir of Libr Serv,* David O Berger; Tel: 314-505-7040, E-mail: bergerd@csl.edu; *Pub Serv Librn,* Eric Stancliff; Tel: 314-505-7033, E-mail: stancliffe@csl.edu; *Tech Serv Librn,* Bradley Hess; Tel: 314-505-7042, E-mail: hessb@csl.edu; *Coordr of Libr Tech,* Mark Bliese; Tel: 314-505-7036, E-mail: bliesem@csl.edu; Staff 5 (MLS 3, Non-MLS 2)
Founded 1839. Enrl 448; Fac 49; Highest Degree: Doctorate
Library Holdings: AV Mats 25,500; Bks on Deafness & Sign Lang 200; Braille Volumes 10; CDs 3,020; DVDs 417; e-journals 75; Music Scores 1,200; Bk Titles 195,450; Bk Vols 229,950; Per Subs 983; Videos 2,417
Special Collections: Hymnology & Liturgics; Lutherana Coll; Peasant's War
Subject Interests: Biblical studies, Lutheranism, Reformation
Automation Activity & Vendor Info: (Course Reserve) Blackboard Inc; (ILL) OCLC
Database Vendor: Checkpoint Systems, Inc, EBSCOhost, Gale Cengage Learning, OCLC FirstSearch, OCLC WorldShare Interlibrary Loan
Wireless access
Function: Copy machines, Distance learning, Doc delivery serv, E-Reserves, Electronic databases & coll, Exhibits, Handicapped accessible, ILL available, Magnifiers for reading, Online cat, Ref serv available, Res libr
Partic in Amigos Library Services, Inc; Saint Louis Regional Library Network
Open Mon-Thurs 7:30am-10pm, Fri 7:30-4:30, Sat 1-5, Sun 6pm-10pm
Restriction: Open to students, fac, staff & alumni, Pub use on premises

R COVENANT THEOLOGICAL SEMINARY*, Buswell Library, 12330 Conway Rd, 63141. SAN 309-1589. Tel: 314-392-4100, 314-434-4044. Interlibrary Loan Service Tel: 314-392-4104, 314-392-4105. Reference Tel: 314-392-4101, 314-392-4102. FAX: 314-392-4116, 314-434-4819. E-mail: library@covenantseminary.edu. Web Site: library.covenantseminary.edu. *Dir,* James Cotton Pakala; E-mail: jim.pakala@covenantseminary.edu; *Access Serv Librn,* Christopher Todd Goodman; Tel: 314-392-4103, E-mail: chris.goodman@covenantseminary.edu; *Assoc Librn, Pub Serv,* Steve Jamieson; E-mail: steve.jamieson@covenantseminary.edu; *Assoc Librn, Tech Serv,* Denise Marchand Pakala; E-mail: denise.pakala@covenantseminary.edu; *Ser,* Joanna DeYoung; Tel: 314-392-4108, E-mail: joanna.deyoung@covenantseminary.edu; *Tech Serv Spec,* Brady Shuman; E-mail: brady.shuman@covenantseminary.edu; Staff 8 (MLS 4, Non-MLS 4)
Founded 1956. Enrl 550; Highest Degree: Doctorate
Jul 2010-Jun 2011 Income $438,506. Mats Exp $465,795, Books $28,710, Per/Ser (Incl. Access Fees) $10,319, Micro $323, AV Mat $858, Electronic Ref Mat (Incl. Access Fees) $21,725, Presv $4,598. Sal $321,390 (Prof $261,384)
Library Holdings: AV Mats 3,584; e-journals 36,207; Microforms 1,599; Bk Vols 74,137; Per Subs 308
Special Collections: Bible & Theology Coll; Church History (Post-Reformation) Coll; Practical Theology Coll; Presbyterian Church in America Archives
Subject Interests: Counseling, Relig
Automation Activity & Vendor Info: (Acquisitions) Innovative Interfaces, Inc; (Cataloging) Innovative Interfaces, Inc; (Circulation) Innovative Interfaces, Inc; (ILL) Innovative Interfaces, Inc; (Media Booking) Innovative Interfaces, Inc; (OPAC) Innovative Interfaces, Inc; (Serials) Innovative Interfaces, Inc
Database Vendor: 3M Library Systems, Backstage Library Works, EBSCO Information Services, EBSCOhost, Facts on File, Gale Cengage Learning, H W Wilson, Innovative Interfaces, Inc, Newsbank, OCLC ArticleFirst, OCLC FirstSearch, OCLC WorldShare Interlibrary Loan, ProQuest, Sage
Wireless access
Partic in Amigos Library Services, Inc; Missouri Research & Education Network (MOREnet); MOBIUS (Missouri Bibliographic Information User System); Saint Louis Regional Library Network; Saint Louis Theological Consortium
Open Mon, Tues & Thurs 8am-10pm, Wed & Fri 8-6, Sat 10-6

GM DEPARTMENT OF VETERANS AFFAIRS*, Medical Library, 142D/JC, 915 N Grand Blvd, 63106. SAN 309-2186. Tel: 314-289-6421. FAX: 314-289-6321. *Librn,* John C Chesmelewski; E-mail: john.chesmelewski@va.gov; *Libr Tech,* Annette Brown; E-mail: annette.brown@va.gov; Staff 2 (MLS 1, Non-MLS 1)
Founded 1954
Library Holdings: e-books 78; e-journals 98; Electronic Media & Resources 10; Bk Titles 985; Per Subs 110; Videos 82
Automation Activity & Vendor Info: (Cataloging) EOS International; (Circulation) EOS International; (OPAC) EOS International
Open Mon-Fri 7:30-4

M DRUSCH PROFESSIONAL LIBRARY*, Chamberlain College of Nursing Library, 11830 Westline Industrial Dr, Ste 106, 63146. SAN 309-1600. Tel: 314-991-6213. FAX: 314-991-6284. *Clinical Libr Coordr,* Saskia Farber; *Clinical Libr Spec,* Valerie R Meyer. Subject Specialists: *Alternative med, Health sci, Pub health,* Saskia Farber; *Nursing,* Valerie R Meyer
Founded 1942. Enrl 450; Fac 15; Highest Degree: Bachelor
Jul 2012-Jun 2013 Income $170,000. Mats Exp $72,000, Books $20,000, Per/Ser (Incl. Access Fees) $33,000, AV Mat $5,000, Electronic Ref Mat (Incl. Access Fees) $14,000. Sal $90,000 (Prof $50,000)
Library Holdings: DVDs 100; e-books 6,000; e-journals 60; Bk Titles 2,900; Bk Vols 4,319; Per Subs 69
Subject Interests: Nursing
Automation Activity & Vendor Info: (Acquisitions) Baker & Taylor; (Cataloging) Ex Libris Group; (Circulation) Ex Libris Group; (OPAC) Ex Libris Group; (Serials) EBSCO Online
Database Vendor: EBSCO Information Services, Medlib, OCLC FirstSearch, OCLC WorldShare Interlibrary Loan, ProQuest, PubMed
Wireless access
Function: Computers for patron use, Copy machines, Doc delivery serv, e-mail & chat, e-mail serv, Electronic databases & coll, ILL available, Mail & tel request accepted, Mail loans to mem, Online cat, Online info literacy tutorials on the web & in blackboard, Online ref, Online searches, Orientations, Ref & res
Partic in Amigos Library Services, Inc; National Network of Libraries of Medicine; Saint Louis Regional Library Network
Open Mon-Thurs 7:30am-9pm, Fri 8-4, Sat 11-3
Restriction: Authorized personnel only, Circ privileges for students & alumni only, Employees only, Open to pub for ref only, Open to students, fac & staff

G EAST WEST GATEWAY COUNCIL OF GOVERNMENTS LIBRARY*, One Memorial Dr, Ste 1600, 63102. SAN 327-1676. Tel: 314-421-4220, Ext 201. FAX: 314-231-6120. Web Site: www.ewgateway.org/library/library.htm. *In Charge,* Karen Kunkel; Staff 1 (MLS 1)
Library Holdings: Bk Titles 5,280; Bk Vols 5,590; Per Subs 16; Talking Bks 50; Videos 50
Open Mon-Fri 8-5

SR THE EPISCOPAL DIOCESE OF MISSOURI ARCHIVES*, 1210 Locust St, 63103-2322. SAN 325-2280. Tel: 314-231-1220. FAX: 314-231-3373. Web Site: www.diocesemo.org. *Archivist,* Sue Rehkopf; E-mail: srehkopf@diocesemo.org; Staff 1 (Non-MLS 1)
Founded 1840
Library Holdings: Bk Vols 1,600
Special Collections: Diocesan Archives & Historical Coll
Subject Interests: Anglican Church, Church hist, Episcopal church
Wireless access
Restriction: Open by appt only

S FEDERAL RESERVE BANK OF SAINT LOUIS, Research Library, One Federal Reserve Bank Plaza, 63102-2005. (Mail add: 1421 Dr Martin Luther King Dr, 63106-3716), SAN 309-1643. Tel: 314-444-8552. Interlibrary Loan Service Tel: 314-444-8906. Reference Tel: 314-444-4291. FAX: 314-444-8694. E-mail: ref@stls.frb.org. Web Site: research.stlouisfed.org. *Dir,* Katrina L Stierholz; E-mail: katrina.l.stierholz@stls.frb.org; *Digital Projects Librn,* Pamela Campbell; Tel: 314-444-8907, E-mail: pamela.d.campbell@stls.frb.org; *Coordr, Digital Projects Librn,* Jane Davis; Tel: 314-444-8961, E-mail: jane.m.davis@stls.frb.org; *Ref/Data Acq Librn,* Adrienne Brennecke; Tel: 314-444-7479, E-mail: adrienne.j.brennecke@stls.frb.org; *Cat,* Anna Xiao; Tel: 314-444-8551, E-mail: xiaohong.a.xiao@stls.frb.org; *Ref Serv,* Kathy E Cosgrove; E-mail: kathy.e.cosgrove@stls.frb.org; Staff 7 (MLS 6, Non-MLS 1)
Founded 1923
Library Holdings: Bk Vols 20,000; Per Subs 350
Special Collections: Federal Reserve System Publications
Subject Interests: Banking, Econ
Automation Activity & Vendor Info: (Acquisitions) SirsiDynix; (Cataloging) SirsiDynix; (Circulation) SirsiDynix; (OPAC) SirsiDynix; (Serials) SirsiDynix
Database Vendor: Dialog, EBSCOhost, LexisNexis, SirsiDynix
Function: Res libr
Partic in Amigos Library Services, Inc; OCLC Online Computer Library Center, Inc

CR FONTBONNE UNIVERSITY*, Jack C Taylor Library, 6800 Wydown Blvd, 63105. SAN 309-1651. Tel: 314-889-1417. FAX: 314-719-8040. Web Site: www.fontbonne.edu/library. *Univ Librn,* Sharon McCaslin; Tel: 314-889-4567; *Electronic Res & Ref Librn,* Megahan Justin; Tel: 314-719-8088, E-mail: jmegahan@fontbonne.edu; *Ref & Instrul Serv Librn,* Peggy Ridlen; Tel: 314-889-4616, E-mail: pridlen@fontbonne.edu; *Ref & Learning Commons Librn,* Jane Theissen; Tel: 314-889-4570, E-mail:

jtheissen@fontbonne.edu; *Tech Serv Librn,* Julie Portman; Tel: 314-889-4569, E-mail: jportman@fontbonne.edu; Staff 10.5 (MLS 6, Non-MLS 4.5)
Founded 1923. Enrl 2,298; Fac 118; Highest Degree: Master
Jul 2011-Jun 2012. Mats Exp $223,194, Books $81,419, Per/Ser (Incl. Access Fees) $100,664, AV Mat $31,258, Presv $9,853. Sal $435,643
Library Holdings: AV Mats 5,000; CDs 828; e-books 8,691; e-journals 73,234; Bk Titles 66,739; Bk Vols 75,235; Per Subs 251; Videos 4,076
Subject Interests: Educ
Automation Activity & Vendor Info: (Acquisitions) Innovative Interfaces, Inc; (Cataloging) Innovative Interfaces, Inc; (Circulation) Innovative Interfaces, Inc; (Course Reserve) Innovative Interfaces, Inc; (ILL) Innovative Interfaces, Inc; (Media Booking) Innovative Interfaces, Inc; (OPAC) Innovative Interfaces, Inc; (Serials) Innovative Interfaces, Inc
Database Vendor: EBSCOhost, JSTOR, LexisNexis, ProQuest
Wireless access
Partic in Amigos Library Services, Inc; Missouri Research & Education Network (MOREnet); MOBIUS (Missouri Bibliographic Information User System); OCLC Online Computer Library Center, Inc
Open Mon-Fri 7:30am-11pm, Sat 9-5, Sun 1-9

L GALLOP, JOHNSON & NEUMAN LC*, Law Library, 101 S Hanley Rd, Ste 1700, 63105. SAN 374-4809. Tel: 314-615-6000. FAX: 314-615-6001. Web Site: www.gjn.com. *Librn,* Sue Dees; Staff 2 (MLS 1, Non-MLS 1)
Library Holdings: Bk Vols 9,500
Partic in Westlaw
Open Mon-Fri 8-5

CM GOLDFARB SCHOOL OF NURSING AT BARNES-JEWISH COLLEGE*, George W S & Juanita D Way Library, 4483 Duncan Ave, Mail Stop 90-30-697, 63110. SAN 349-5639. Tel: 314-362-1699, 314-454-7055. Toll Free Tel: 800-832-9009. Web Site: www.barnesjewishcollege.edu. *Dir, Libr & Info Serv,* Renee Gorrell; Tel: 314-454-8171, E-mail: rgorrell@bjc.org; Staff 3 (MLS 1, Non-MLS 2)
Founded 1984. Enrl 600; Highest Degree: Master
Library Holdings: AV Mats 500; Bk Titles 3,200; Bk Vols 14,500; Per Subs 150
Special Collections: American Nurses Association (ANA) Publications
Subject Interests: Clinical labs, Health serv admin, Holistic health, Nursing, Pain mgt, Palliative care
Database Vendor: EBSCOhost, OCLC FirstSearch, OVID Technologies, PubMed, Swets Information Services
Partic in Amigos Library Services, Inc; Library Systems Service; Mid Continental Med Libr Asn; OCLC-LVIS; Saint Louis Regional Library Network
Open Mon-Thurs 7:30am-10pm, Fri 7:30-6
Restriction: In-house use for visitors, Open to students, fac & staff

S GREENSFELDER, HEMKER & GALE, PC LIBRARY*, Ten S Broadway, Ste 2000, 63102. SAN 329-7713. Tel: 314-241-9090. FAX: 314-241-8624. Web Site: www.greensfelder.com. *Librn,* Sally Crowley; Staff 1 (Non-MLS 1)
Library Holdings: Bk Titles 11,296; Bk Vols 12,800; Per Subs 400
Open Mon-Fri 8:30-5

C HARRIS-STOWE STATE UNIVERSITY LIBRARY*, AT&T Library & Technology Resource Center, 3011 Laclede Ave, 63103. SAN 309-1708. Tel: 314-340-3621. FAX: 314-340-3630. Web Site: www.hssu.edu. *Dir,* Barbara N Noble; E-mail: NobleB@hssu.edu; *Ref & ILL Librn,* Bettye Brown; *Coordr, Spec Serv,* Linda Orzel; Staff 7 (MLS 5, Non-MLS 2)
Founded 1857. Highest Degree: Bachelor
Library Holdings: CDs 105; Bk Titles 92,385; Bk Vols 93,612; Per Subs 333; Videos 227
Special Collections: St Louis Public School Archives
Subject Interests: Educ, Ethnic studies, Urban studies
Automation Activity & Vendor Info: (Cataloging) TLC (The Library Corporation); (Circulation) TLC (The Library Corporation)
Partic in Saint Louis Regional Library Network
Open Mon-Fri 7:30-5

S HEALTH CAPITAL CONSULTANTS, LLC LIBRARY*, 1143 Olivette Executive Pkwy, 63132. SAN 377-824X. Tel: 314-994-7641. Toll Free Tel: 800-394-8258. FAX: 314-991-3435. E-mail: books@healthcapital.com. Web Site: www.healthcapital.com. *Pres,* Robert James Cimasi; Staff 3 (MLS 1, Non-MLS 2)
Founded 1993
Library Holdings: Bk Titles 3,500; Bk Vols 3,800; Per Subs 80
Special Collections: Business Valuation; Healthcare Industry (Financial, Economic & Policy Areas of Healthcare Services)
Automation Activity & Vendor Info: (Cataloging) Inmagic, Inc.; (Circulation) Inmagic, Inc.

L HUSCH BLACKWELL SANDERS LLP*, Law Library, 190 Carondelet Plaza, Ste 600, 63105. SAN 372-4751. Tel: 314-480-1500. FAX: 314-480-1505. Web Site: www.huschblackwell.com. *Librn,* Karla A Morris-Holmes; Staff 1 (Non-MLS 1)
Library Holdings: Bk Titles 9,500; Bk Vols 10,000; Per Subs 95
Open Mon-Fri 8:30-5

S JEFFERSON NATIONAL EXPANSION MEMORIAL LIBRARY*, 11 N Fourth St, 63102. SAN 309-1724. Tel: 314-655-1600. FAX: 314-655-1652. Web Site: www.nps.gov/jeff. *Librn,* Tom Dewey; Tel: 314-655-1632, E-mail: tom_dewey@partner.nps.gov
Founded 1935
Library Holdings: Bk Vols 6,150; Per Subs 60
Special Collections: Jefferson National Expansion Memorial Archives
Subject Interests: St Louis hist, Westward expansion
Function: Res libr
Open Mon-Fri 8-4:30
Restriction: Non-circulating to the pub

R KENRICK-GLENNON SEMINARY*, Charles L Souvay Memorial Library, 5200 Glennon Dr, 63119. SAN 309-1740. Tel: 314-792-6100. FAX: 314-792-6503. E-mail: souvaylibrary@kenrick.edu. Web Site: archstl.org/souvay-library, www.kenrick.edu/souvay-library. *Dir,* Mary Ann Audin; Tel: 314-792-6302, E-mail: aubin@kenrick.edu; *Tech Serv & Syst Librn,* William W Toombs; Tel: 314-792-6144, E-mail: toombs@kenrick.edu; *Acq, Ser,* Rose Lawson; Tel: 314-792-6131, E-mail: lawson@kenrick.edu; Staff 4 (MLS 3, Non-MLS 1)
Founded 1893. Enrl 77; Fac 15; Highest Degree: Master
Library Holdings: Bk Vols 80,000
Special Collections: Cuneiform Tablets; Official Catholic Directory; Pre-Vatican II Catechism Coll; Rare Book Coll; Thomas Merton Coll
Subject Interests: Archives, Canon law, Liturgics, Patristics, Roman Catholic theol, Scripture
Database Vendor: EBSCOhost, Gale Cengage Learning
Partic in MOBIUS (Missouri Bibliographic Information User System); OCLC Online Computer Library Center, Inc

L LASHLY & BAER PC*, Law Library, 714 Locust St, 63101. SAN 375-0523. Tel: 314-621-2939, Ext 1017. FAX: 314-621-6844. Web Site: www.lashlybaer.com. *In Charge,* Mimi Hubert; Staff 1 (Non-MLS 1)
Library Holdings: Bk Titles 9,600; Bk Vols 11,500; Per Subs 10
Restriction: Not open to pub

S LAUMEIER SCULPTURE PARK LIBRARY & ARCHIVE, 12580 Rott Rd, 63127. SAN 374-5708. Tel: 314-615-5280. FAX: 314-615-5283. E-mail: library@laumeier.org. Web Site: www.laumeier.org. *Dir,* Marilu Knode, *Archivist, Librn,* Joy Wright; Staff 1 (MLS 1)
Founded 1986
Library Holdings: Bk Titles 3,200; Per Subs 18
Special Collections: Contemporary Sculpture Coll
Function: Ref serv available
Restriction: Open by appt only

L LAW LIBRARY ASSOCIATION OF SAINT LOUIS*, 1300 Civil Courts Bldg, Ten N Tucker Blvd, 63101. SAN 309-1775. Tel: 314-622-4386. FAX: 314-241-0911. E-mail: rabtech@swbell.net. Web Site: tlc.library.net/lla. *Libr Dir,* Jean Moorleghen; Staff 5 (MLS 1, Non-MLS 4)
Founded 1838
Library Holdings: Bk Vols 70,000; Per Subs 120
Open Mon-Fri 8:30-6

S LEWIS, RICE & FINGERSH LAW LIBRARY*, 500 N Broadway, Ste 2000, 63102-2147. SAN 327-7437. Tel: 314-444-7600. FAX: 314-612-7681. Web Site: www.lewisrice.com. *Librn,* Helen Capdevielle; Staff 3 (MLS 1, Non-MLS 2)
Library Holdings: CDs 29; Large Print Bks 38; Bk Titles 21,117; Bk Vols 22,184; Per Subs 112; Videos 115
Publications: Monthly accessions list
Partic in LivEdgar; Westlaw
Restriction: Staff use only

M LUTHERAN MEDICAL CENTER SCHOOL OF NURSING & MEDICAL STAFF LIBRARY*, Louise Kraus-Ament Memorial Library, 3547 S Jefferson, 63118. SAN 309-1791. Tel: 314-577-5864. FAX: 314-268-6160. Web Site: www.nursingschoollmc.com/library.shtm. *Med Librn,* Jeff Spinks; E-mail: jeff.spinks@sahstl.com; Staff 2 (MLS 1, Non-MLS 1)
Library Holdings: Bk Titles 4,675; Bk Vols 5,000; Per Subs 73
Subject Interests: Nursing educ, Primary educ
Open Mon-Thurs 7:30-7:30, Fri 7:30-3:30, Sun 1-5

S MALLINCKRODT*, Pharma Info Center, 3600 N Second St, 63147-3457. SAN 309-1813. Tel: 314-654-1515. Administration Tel: 314-654-1511. FAX: 314-654-1513. Web Site: www.mallinckrodt.com. *Mgr,* Phyllis A

Fischer; E-mail: phyllis.fisher@mallinckrodt.com; Staff 7 (MLS 5, Non-MLS 2)
Founded 1867
Library Holdings: Bk Titles 10,740; Bk Vols 11,500; Per Subs 150
Special Collections: Pre-1900 German Chemistry & Pharmaceutical Monographs; Pre-1900 Pharmacopeias
Subject Interests: Chem, Pharmaceutical chem
Automation Activity & Vendor Info: (Cataloging) EOS International; (ILL) OCLC; (Serials) EOS International
Wireless access
Partic in OCLC Online Computer Library Center, Inc
Open Mon-Fri 7:30-4

C MARYVILLE UNIVERSITY LIBRARY, 650 Maryville University Dr, 63141. SAN 309-1821. Tel: 314-529-9595. Interlibrary Loan Service Tel: 314-529-9591. Administration Tel: 314-529-9491. FAX: 314-529-9941. E-mail: library@maryville.edu. Web Site: www.maryville.edu/library. *Dean,* Dr Genie V McKee; Tel: 314-529-9509, E-mail: gmckee@maryville.edu; *Asst Dean, Head, Tech Serv,* Mary Ann Mercante; Tel: 314-529-9650, E-mail: mmercante@maryville.edu; *Electronic Res, Info Literacy Librn,* Ying Lin; Tel: 314-529-6879, E-mail: ylin@maryville.edu; *Online Med Librn,* Mark Spasser; Tel: 314-529-9490, E-mail: mspasser1@maryville.edu; *Online Nursing Ref Librn,* Jacob Beard; Tel: 314-529-6528, E-mail: jbeard1@maryville.edu; *Ref Serv,* Gail Keutzer; Tel: 314-529-9494, E-mail: gkeutzer@maryville.edu. Subject Specialists: *Med,* Mark Spasser; Staff 11 (MLS 5, Non-MLS 6)
Founded 1872. Enrl 3,564; Fac 502; Highest Degree: Doctorate
Jun 2013-May 2014. Mats Exp $403,385. Sal $593,952 (Prof $304,806)
Library Holdings: AV Mats 148,111; e-books 187,193; e-journals 84,496; Microforms 29,773; Bk Vols 64,248; Per Subs 262
Special Collections: Maryville Archives; Papers of Edward S Dowling. US Document Depository
Subject Interests: Actuarial sci, Educ, Music therapy, Nursing
Automation Activity & Vendor Info: (Acquisitions) Innovative Interfaces, Inc; (Cataloging) Innovative Interfaces, Inc; (Circulation) Innovative Interfaces, Inc; (Course Reserve) Innovative Interfaces, Inc; (ILL) OCLC ILLiad; (OPAC) Innovative Interfaces, Inc; (Serials) Innovative Interfaces, Inc
Database Vendor: ABC-CLIO, Alexander Street Press, American Psychological Association (APA), Amigos Library Services, ARTstor, CQ Press, EBSCO Discovery Service, EBSCOhost, HeinOnline, JSTOR, LexisNexis, OCLC FirstSearch, OCLC WorldShare Interlibrary Loan, OVID Technologies, ProQuest, RefWorks, SBRnet (Sports Business Research Network), ScienceDirect, Springshare, LLC, UpToDate, Westlaw
Wireless access
Partic in Amigos Library Services, Inc; Docline; MOBIUS (Missouri Bibliographic Information User System); OCLC Online Computer Library Center, Inc; Saint Louis Regional Library Network
Open Mon-Thurs 7am-Midnight, Fri 7-7, Sat 11-7, Sun 11am-Midnight
Friends of the Library Group

M MISSOURI BAPTIST MEDICAL CENTER*, Medical Library, 3015 N Ballas Rd, 63131. SAN 321-6209. Tel: 314-996-5000. FAX: 314-996-5031. Web Site: www.missouribaptist.org. *Libr Serv Mgr,* Sandra Decker; Tel: 314-996-5531, E-mail: sdecker@bjc.org
Founded 1965
Library Holdings: Bk Titles 610; Bk Vols 701; Per Subs 125
Open Mon-Fri 7-5

C MISSOURI BAPTIST UNIVERSITY*, Jung-Kellogg Library, One College Park Dr, 63141-8698. SAN 309-1864. Tel: 314-434-1115. Circulation Tel: 314-392-2320. Reference Tel: 314-392-2340. FAX: 314-392-2343. Circulation E-mail: circdsk@mobap.edu. Web Site: www.mobap.edu/library. *Dir, Libr Serv,* Nitsa Hindeleh; Tel: 314-392-2319, E-mail: hindeleh@mobap.edu; *Acq,* Rebekah McKinney; Tel: 314-392-2336, E-mail: mckinneyr@mobap.edu; *Cat,* Anne Calhoun; E-mail: calhoaf@mobap.edu; *Circ,* Ling Thumin; E-mail: thuminl@mobap.edu; *Circ & ILL,* Linda Webb; *Circ/Reserves,* Linda Webb; E-mail: circdsk@mobap.edu; *Monographs Cataloger,* Elaine Trost; Tel: 314-392-2342, E-mail: trosteh@mobap.edu; *Ref Serv,* Lynne Koestner; E-mail: koestner@mobap.edu; *Ref Serv,* Fred McKinney; E-mail: mckinney@mobap.edu; Staff 11 (MLS 4, Non-MLS 7)
Founded 1968. Enrl 5,207; Fac 85; Highest Degree: Doctorate
Library Holdings: AV Mats 9,750; Bk Titles 91,200; Bk Vols 91,300; Per Subs 250; Talking Bks 10; Videos 2,178
Automation Activity & Vendor Info: (Acquisitions) Innovative Interfaces, Inc; (Cataloging) OCLC; (Circulation) Innovative Interfaces, Inc; (Course Reserve) Innovative Interfaces, Inc; (ILL) OCLC; (OPAC) Innovative Interfaces, Inc; (Serials) Innovative Interfaces, Inc
Database Vendor: Amigos Library Services, Annual Reviews, BCR: Christian Periodical Index, College Source, ebrary, EBSCO Information Services, EBSCOhost, Gale Cengage Learning, H W Wilson, LexisNexis, Newsbank, OCLC, OCLC FirstSearch, OCLC WorldShare Interlibrary Loan, Oxford Online, Wilson - Wilson Web
Wireless access
Partic in Amigos Library Services, Inc; Missouri Research & Education Network (MOREnet); MOBIUS (Missouri Bibliographic Information User System); Saint Louis Regional Library Network
Open Mon, Tues & Thurs (Winter) 7:30-9:30, Wed & Fri 7:30-5, Sat 10-2; Mon, Tues & Thurs (Summer) 8-7, Wed 8-4:30, Fri 8-12

S MISSOURI BOTANICAL GARDEN*, Peter H Raven Library, 4500 Shaw Blvd, 63110. (Mail add: 4344 Shaw Blvd, 63110), SAN 309-1872. Tel: 314-577-5155. Reference Tel: 314-577-5159. FAX: 314-577-0840. E-mail: library@mobot.org. Web Site: www.missouribotanicalgarden.org. *Dir,* Douglas L Holland; Tel: 314-577-0842, E-mail: doug.holland@mobot.org; Staff 12 (MLS 7, Non-MLS 5)
Founded 1859
Library Holdings: Bk Vols 200,000; Per Subs 800
Special Collections: Archives; Bryology (Steere Coll); Ewan Coll; Folio Coll; Post-Linnaean Rare Book Coll; Pre-Linnaean Coll; Pre-Linnean Botany (Sturtevant Coll); Rare Book Coll. Oral History
Subject Interests: Bot exploration, Botanical hist, Botany, Hort
Automation Activity & Vendor Info: (Acquisitions) Innovative Interfaces, Inc; (Cataloging) Innovative Interfaces, Inc; (Circulation) Innovative Interfaces, Inc; (OPAC) Innovative Interfaces, Inc; (Serials) Innovative Interfaces, Inc
Database Vendor: Innovative Interfaces, Inc
Publications: Accessions List (Monthly)
Partic in OCLC Online Computer Library Center, Inc
Open Mon-Fri 8:30-5

L MISSOURI COURT OF APPEALS*, Eastern District Library, One Old Post Office Sq, Rm 304, 815 Olive St, 63101. SAN 372-4131. Tel: 314-539-4300. FAX: 314-539-4324. *Librn,* Maureen Jacquot; Staff 1 (MLS 1)
Library Holdings: Bk Titles 28,618; Bk Vols 29,000; Per Subs 12
Special Collections: Regional Reports Appellate; United States Supreme Court Cases
Restriction: Staff use only

S MISSOURI HISTORY MUSEUM, Library & Research Center, 225 S Skinker Blvd, 63105. (Mail add: PO Box 11940, 63112-0040), SAN 309-1880. Tel: 314-746-4500. FAX: 314-746-4548. E-mail: library@mohistory.org. Web Site: www.mohistory.org. *Librn,* Emily Jaycox; *Cat Librn,* Debbie Schraut; *Ref & Info Serv, Web Coordr,* Jason D Stratman; *ILL,* Carol S Verble; *Presv Spec,* Randall Blomquist; Staff 6 (MLS 2, Non-MLS 4)
Founded 1866
Library Holdings: Bk Titles 77,623; Bk Vols 81,496; Per Subs 250
Special Collections: Charles Lindbergh; Lewis & Clark Expedition; Trade Catalogs
Subject Interests: Am fur trade, Family hist, Genealogy, Hist of Mo, Hist of St Louis, Sheet music, St Louis World's Fair 1904, Trade catalogs, Westward expansion
Automation Activity & Vendor Info: (Acquisitions) Innovative Interfaces, Inc - Millenium; (Cataloging) Innovative Interfaces, Inc; (Circulation) Innovative Interfaces, Inc - Millenium; (OPAC) Innovative Interfaces, Inc - Millenium; (Serials) Innovative Interfaces, Inc - Millenium
Database Vendor: EBSCOhost, JSTOR
Wireless access
Function: Archival coll
Publications: In Her Own Write
Partic in Amigos Library Services, Inc; Saint Louis Regional Library Network; Saint Louis Research Libraries Consortium (SLRLC)
Open Tues-Fri 12-5, Sat 10-5
Restriction: Non-circulating

S MISSOURI SCHOOL FOR THE BLIND LIBRARY, 3815 Magnolia Ave, 63110. SAN 372-6703. Tel: 314-776-4320, Ext 3257. FAX: 314-773-3762. Web Site: www.msb.dese.mo.gov. *Librn,* Mary Dingus; E-mail: mary.dingus@msb.dese.mo.gov; *Asst Librn,* Chris Davidson; Staff 2 (MLS 1, Non-MLS 1)
Library Holdings: Braille Volumes 10,500; DVDs 304; Large Print Bks 3,800; Bk Titles 21,400; Bk Vols 26,000; Per Subs 52; Talking Bks 10,000; Videos 350
Special Collections: Blind Education Coll
Automation Activity & Vendor Info: (Cataloging) Follett Software; (Circulation) Follett Software; (OPAC) Follett Software
Special Services for the Blind - Accessible computers; Bks & mags in Braille, on rec, tape & cassette; Bks on CD; Braille Webster's dictionary; Cassette playback machines; Children's Braille; Closed circuit TV; Daisy reader; Descriptive video serv (DVS); Digital talking bk; Extensive large print coll; Internet workstation with adaptive software; Large screen computer & software; Screen enlargement software for people with visual disabilities; Screen reader software; ZoomText magnification & reading software
Open Mon-Fri 8:15-3:45
Restriction: Open to students, fac & staff, Pub use on premises

S MONSANTO COMPANY*, Library Services, 800 N Lindbergh Blvd, 63167. SAN 309-1902. Tel: 314-694-4747. FAX: 314-694-8748. E-mail: c.c.library@monsanto.com. Web Site: www.monsanto.com. *Mgr,* Gail Hoef; Staff 9 (MLS 2, Non-MLS 7)
Founded 1961
Library Holdings: Bk Titles 40,000; Bk Vols 49,000; Per Subs 500; Talking Bks 159; Videos 289
Subject Interests: Agr, Biol, Chem
Automation Activity & Vendor Info: (Acquisitions) SirsiDynix; (Cataloging) SirsiDynix; (Circulation) SirsiDynix; (ILL) OCLC; (Serials) SirsiDynix
Wireless access
Publications: Catalogs; Indexes; In-House Alerting Services; Newsletter
Partic in OCLC Online Computer Library Center, Inc
Restriction: Not open to pub

S MUSEUM OF TRANSPORTATION*, Reference Library, 3015 Barrett Station Rd, 63122. SAN 309-1910. Tel: 314-615-8668, 314-965-8214. FAX: 314-965-0242. Web Site: www.museumoftransport.org. *Archivist,* Nick Ohlman
Founded 1944
Library Holdings: Bk Vols 8,000; Per Subs 10
Special Collections: Transportation Coll
Subject Interests: Air, Automobiles, Marine, Rail
Restriction: Open by appt only
Friends of the Library Group

S NESTLE PURINA PET CARE CO*, Library & Information Services, Checkerboard Sq 2S, 63164. SAN 309-1961. Interlibrary Loan Service Tel: 314-982-2150. FAX: 314-982-3259. Web Site: www.purina.com. *Mgr,* Justin Smith; *Coordr, Search Serv,* Geri Heberlie; Staff 4 (MLS 2, Non-MLS 2)
Founded 1929
Library Holdings: e-journals 95; Bk Titles 6,350; Per Subs 251
Subject Interests: Animal, Food proc, Human nutrition, Sanitation, Veterinary med
Automation Activity & Vendor Info: (Cataloging) EOS International; (Circulation) EOS International; (ILL) OCLC; (OPAC) EOS International; (Serials) EOS International
Database Vendor: OCLC FirstSearch
Wireless access
Partic in Amigos Library Services, Inc; Dialog Corp; OCLC Online Computer Library Center, Inc
Open Mon-Fri 8-4:30

L POLSINELLI SHUGHART PC*, Law Library, 7733 Forsyth Blvd, Ste 1200, 63105. SAN 372-4727. Tel: 314-727-7676, Ext 7151. FAX: 314-727-7166. *Librn,* Mary K Macaulay; E-mail: mmacaulay@polsinelli.com; Staff 1 (MLS 1)
Library Holdings: Bk Titles 2,880; Bk Vols 3,000; Per Subs 21
Open Mon-Fri 8:30-5

S PULITZER, INC*, Saint Louis Post-Dispatch News Research Department, 900 N Tucker Blvd, 63101. SAN 309-1953. Tel: 314-340-8270. Administration Tel: 314-340-8275. Toll Free Tel: 800-365-0820, Ext 8275. FAX: 314-340-3006. Web Site: www.stltoday.com. *Dir,* Mike Meinors. Subject Specialists: *News,* Mike Meinors; Staff 15 (MLS 3, Non-MLS 12)
Founded 1922
Library Holdings: Bk Titles 3,500
Special Collections: Housing (Pruitt-Igoe Housing Development Coll), flm; Post-Dispatch Authors Coll; Saint Louis Sun Times, microfilm; St. Louis Post-Dispatch Archives; Theater (St Louis Municipal Opera Coll), clippings
Subject Interests: Intl news, Newsp clipping files, Newsp photogs, Newsp subjects related to nat
Function: Archival coll, Res libr
Restriction: Not open to pub

M SAINT JOHN'S MERCY MEDICAL CENTER*, Thomas F Frawley Medical Center Library, Tower B, 621 S New Ballas Rd, Ste 1000, 63141. SAN 309-1988. Tel: 314-251-6340. FAX: 314-251-4299. E-mail: medlib@mercy.net. Web Site: www.stjohnsmercy.org/library. *Dir,* Jennifer P Plaat; E-mail: plaajp@stlo.mercy.net; *Asst Dir,* Kathleen Alsup; E-mail: alsuks@stlo.mercy.net; *Doc Delivery,* Judy Duffy; *Doc Delivery,* Mayris Woods
Library Holdings: e-books 110; e-journals 180; Bk Vols 10,000; Per Subs 475
Subject Interests: Clinical med, Dentistry, Nursing
Database Vendor: EBSCOhost, OVID Technologies
Partic in Dialog Corp; Docline; National Network of Libraries of Medicine; OCLC Online Computer Library Center, Inc; Philnet
Open Mon-Fri 7-5

S SAINT LOUIS ART MUSEUM*, Richardson Memorial Library, One Fine Arts Dr, Forest Park, 63110-1380. SAN 309-1996. Tel: 314-655-5252. FAX: 314-721-6172. E-mail: library@slam.org. Web Site: www.slam.org. *Head Librn,* Marianne L Cavanaugh; Tel: 314-655-5255; *Archivist,* Norma Sindelar; Tel: 314-655-5452; *Pub Serv,* Clare Vasquez; *Tech Serv,* Christopher Handy; Tel: 314-655-5456; Staff 4 (MLS 3, Non-MLS 1)
Founded 1915
Library Holdings: AV Mats 6,000; Bk Titles 83,000; Bk Vols 112,000; Per Subs 200
Special Collections: Contemporary Art Ephemera; Louisiana Purchase Exposition 1904 Records; Museum History Coll; Rare Art Books Coll
Subject Interests: Art hist
Automation Activity & Vendor Info: (Acquisitions) Innovative Interfaces, Inc; (Cataloging) Innovative Interfaces, Inc; (Circulation) Innovative Interfaces, Inc; (OPAC) Innovative Interfaces, Inc; (Serials) Innovative Interfaces, Inc
Partic in OCLC Online Computer Library Center, Inc; Saint Louis Research Libraries Consortium (SLRLC)
Open Tues-Fri 10-5
Restriction: Non-circulating to the pub

M SAINT LOUIS CHILDREN'S HOSPITAL*, Medical Library, One Children's Pl, 63110. SAN 329-3823. Tel: 314-454-2768. FAX: 314-454-2340. *Mgr, Libr Serv,* Lauren Yaeger; E-mail: yaegerl@wustl.edu; Staff 1 (Non-MLS 1)
Library Holdings: Bk Titles 1,226; Per Subs 28
Subject Interests: Med, Nursing, Pediatrics
Database Vendor: OVID Technologies
Wireless access

CM ST LOUIS COLLEGE OF PHARMACY, O J Cloughly Alumni Library, 4588 Parkview Pl, 63110. SAN 309-2003. Tel: 314-446-8361. FAX: 314-446-8360. E-mail: library@stlcop.edu. Web Site: www.stlcop.edu/library. *Dir,* Jill Nissen; Tel: 314-446-8362, E-mail: Jill.Nissen@stlcop.edu; *Cat Librn,* Shirley Moreno; Tel: 314-446-8364, E-mail: Shirley.Moreno@stlcop.edu; *Ref Librn/Archives,* Teri-Ann Wallace; Tel: 314-446-8367, E-mail: Teri-ann.Wallace@stlcop.edu; *Ser Librn,* Jill Bright; Tel: 314-446-8363, E-mail: Jill.Bright@stlcop.edu; Staff 4 (MLS 4)
Founded 1948. Enrl 1,340; Fac 100; Highest Degree: Doctorate
Library Holdings: Bk Titles 29,204; Bk Vols 54,221; Per Subs 400
Special Collections: Archives
Automation Activity & Vendor Info: (Cataloging) Innovative Interfaces, Inc; (Circulation) Innovative Interfaces, Inc; (ILL) OCLC; (OPAC) Innovative Interfaces, Inc; (Serials) Innovative Interfaces, Inc
Database Vendor: ABC-CLIO, DynaMed, EBSCO Information Services, EBSCOhost, Elsevier, Haworth Pres Inc, Innovative Interfaces, Inc, JSTOR, Lexi-Comp, LexisNexis, McGraw-Hill, Micromedex, Natural Standard, Newsbank, OCLC, OCLC ArticleFirst, OCLC FirstSearch, OCLC WorldShare Interlibrary Loan, OVID Technologies, ProQuest, PubMed, ScienceDirect, Scopus, STAT!Ref (Teton Data Systems), Wiley InterScience, Wilson - Wilson Web
Wireless access
Partic in Amigos Library Services, Inc; Missouri Research & Education Network (MOREnet), MOBIUS (Missouri Bibliographic Information User System); OCLC Online Computer Library Center, Inc, Saint Louis Regional Library Network
Open Mon-Thurs 7:30am-Midnight, Fri 7:30am-8pm, Sat 10-8, Sun Noon-Midnight
Restriction: Badge access after hrs, Circ privileges for students & alumni only

SAINT LOUIS COMMUNITY COLLEGE

J FLORISSANT VALLEY CAMPUS LIBRARY*, 3400 Pershall Rd, Ferguson, 63135-1408, SAN 349-5965. Tel: 314-513-4511. Circulation Tel: 314-513-4514. Reference Tel: 314-513-4420, 314-513-4517. FAX: 314-513-4053. Web Site: www.stlcc.edu. *Libr Serv Supvr,* Roger Thomas; Tel: 314-513-4529, E-mail: rthomas1@stlcc.edu; *Coordr, Libr Serv,* Christopher C White; Tel: 314-513-4484, E-mail: cwhite@stlcc.cc.mo.us; Staff 24 (MLS 7, Non-MLS 17)
Founded 1963. Enrl 3,639; Fac 244; Highest Degree: Associate
Library Holdings: Bk Titles 91,853; Bk Vols 102,439; Per Subs 584; Talking Bks 589; Videos 1,260
Automation Activity & Vendor Info: (Acquisitions) Innovative Interfaces, Inc; (Cataloging) Innovative Interfaces, Inc; (Circulation) Innovative Interfaces, Inc; (Course Reserve) Innovative Interfaces, Inc; (OPAC) Innovative Interfaces, Inc; (Serials) Innovative Interfaces, Inc
Database Vendor: EBSCOhost, Gale Cengage Learning, LexisNexis, OCLC FirstSearch, OVID Technologies, ProQuest
Function: Ref serv available
Partic in Amigos Library Services, Inc; MOBIUS (Missouri Bibliographic Information User System); Saint Louis Regional Library Network
Special Services for the Deaf - TDD equip

J FOREST PARK CAMPUS LIBRARY*, 5600 Oakland Ave, 63110-1316, SAN 349-599X. Tel: 314-644-9209. Circulation Tel: 314-644-9210. Reference Tel: 314-644-9214. FAX: 314-644-9240. TDD: 314-644-9969. Web Site: www.stlcc.edu. *Libr Mgr,* June S Williams; E-mail: jswilliams@stlcc.edu; *Coordr, Libr Serv,* Jean Thomas; Tel: 314-644-9206, E-mail: jthomas@stlcc.edu; *Libr Spec,* Renee Potts; Tel: 314-644-9681, E-mail: rpotts@stlcc.edu; Staff 11 (MLS 4, Non-MLS 7)
Founded 1965. Enrl 4,095; Fac 127; Highest Degree: Associate
Library Holdings: AV Mats 5,481; Bk Vols 82,766; Per Subs 624
Special Collections: Black Studies (Afro-American) bks, per
Subject Interests: Allied health, Food indust, Med, Nursing, Restaurant mgt, Tourism
Automation Activity & Vendor Info: (Circulation) Innovative Interfaces, Inc; (Course Reserve) Innovative Interfaces, Inc; (OPAC) Innovative Interfaces, Inc; (Serials) Innovative Interfaces, Inc
Database Vendor: EBSCOhost, Gale Cengage Learning, LexisNexis, OCLC FirstSearch
Partic in Missouri Research & Education Network (MOREnet); MOBIUS (Missouri Bibliographic Information User System); Saint Louis Regional Library Network
Publications: Collection Development Statement; Library Guide; Library Services for the Faculty
Special Services for the Deaf - TDD equip

J INSTRUCTIONAL RESOURCES, 5460 Highland Park Dr, 63110, SAN 349-5930. Tel: 314-644-9555. Interlibrary Loan Service Tel: 314-644-9560. Web Site: www.stlcc.edu. *Dir,* Sheila Ouellette; Tel: 314-644-9557, E-mail: souellette@stlcc.edu; *Acq, Coordr, Libr Serv,* Kimberly Linkous; Tel: 314-644-9559, E-mail: klinkous@stlcc.edu; *Libr Spec, ILL,* Bridgette Lee; E-mail: blee@stlcc.edu; Staff 12 (MLS 6, Non-MLS 6)
Founded 1962. Highest Degree: Associate
Library Holdings: AV Mats 94; DVDs 35; e-books 10,000; Bk Vols 393; Per Subs 21; Videos 1,731
Special Collections: College Archives; Video Library
Automation Activity & Vendor Info: (Acquisitions) Innovative Interfaces, Inc; (Cataloging) Innovative Interfaces, Inc; (Circulation) Innovative Interfaces, Inc; (ILL) OCLC; (Media Booking) Dymaxion; (OPAC) Innovative Interfaces, Inc; (Serials) Innovative Interfaces, Inc
Database Vendor: ABC-CLIO, ACM (Association for Computing Machinery), Alexander Street Press, American Chemical Society, Annual Reviews, ARTstor, Bowker, Cinahl, College Source, CQ Press, CredoReference, EBSCOhost, Elsevier, Facts on File, Gale Cengage Learning, H W Wilson, Ingram Library Services, Innovative Interfaces, Inc, LexisNexis, Medianet, Newsbank, OCLC WorldShare Interlibrary Loan, OVID Technologies, Paratext, Plunkett Research, Ltd, ProQuest, Sage, ScienceDirect, SerialsSolutions, Standard & Poor's, Westlaw, WT Cox
Partic in Higher Educ Coun of St Louis; Missouri Research & Education Network (MOREnet); MOBIUS (Missouri Bibliographic Information User System); Saint Louis Regional Library Network

J MERAMEC CAMPUS LIBRARY*, 11333 Big Bend Rd, 63122-5720, SAN 349-6023. Tel: 314-984-7616. Circulation Tel: 314-984-7797. Reference Tel: 314-984-7613. FAX: 314-984-7225. Web Site: www.stlcc.edu/libraries. *Sr Mgr, Campus Libr & Instrul Res,* Bonnie Sanguinet; Tel: 314-984-7624, E-mail: bsanguinet@stlcc.edu; *Supvr, Libr Serv,* Patrick Mallory; Tel: 314-984-7615, E-mail: pmallory1@stlcc.edu; Staff 8.5 (MLS 6.5, Non-MLS 2)
Founded 1963. Enrl 11,500; Fac 8; Highest Degree: Associate
Library Holdings: AV Mats 12,945; e-books 17,218; Bk Titles 113,306; Bk Vols 120,906; Per Subs 553
Automation Activity & Vendor Info: (Cataloging) Innovative Interfaces, Inc - Millenium; (Circulation) Innovative Interfaces, Inc - Millenium; (Course Reserve) Innovative Interfaces, Inc - Millenium; (OPAC) Innovative Interfaces, Inc; (Serials) Innovative Interfaces, Inc - Millenium
Database Vendor: 3M Library Systems, ABC-CLIO, ACM (Association for Computing Machinery), Alexander Street Press, ARTstor, Bowker, Cinahl, College Source, CQ Press, CredoReference, EBSCOhost, Facts on File, Gale Cengage Learning, Innovative Interfaces, Inc, LexisNexis, Medianet, Medline, Newsbank, OVID Technologies, Oxford Online, Plunkett Research, Ltd, Project MUSE, ProQuest, Sage, ScienceDirect, SerialsSolutions, Wilson - Wilson Web
Function: Audio & video playback equip for onsite use, Bks on cassette, Bks on CD, Computers for patron use, Copy machines, Doc delivery serv, e-mail & chat, Electronic databases & coll, Free DVD rentals, Games & aids for the handicapped, Handicapped accessible, ILL available, Magnifiers for reading, Music CDs, Newsp ref libr, Notary serv, Online cat, Online info literacy tutorials on the web & in blackboard, Online ref, Online searches, Orientations, Outside serv via phone, mail, e-mail & web, Photocopying/Printing, Prof lending libr, Pub access computers, Ref & res, Ref serv available, Ref serv in person, Serves mentally handicapped consumers, Spoken cassettes & CDs, Spoken cassettes & DVDs, Telephone ref, VHS videos, Web-catalog, Wheelchair accessible
Partic in Higher Educ Coun of Metrop St Louis; Missouri Research & Education Network (MOREnet); MOBIUS (Missouri Bibliographic Information User System); Saint Louis Regional Library Network
Publications: A Guide to Meramec Library; Services & Products Booklets
Special Services for the Deaf - Accessible learning ctr; ADA equip; Assisted listening device; Assistive tech; Bks on deafness & sign lang; Closed caption videos; High interest/low vocabulary bks
Special Services for the Blind - Accessible computers; Aids for in-house use; Assistive/Adapted tech devices, equip & products; Bks on cassette; Bks on CD; Braille equip; Computer with voice synthesizer for visually impaired persons; Copier with enlargement capabilities; Daisy reader; Dragon Naturally Speaking software; Integrated libr/media serv; Internet workstation with adaptive software; Networked computers with assistive software; Rec of textbk mat; Recorded bks; Scanner for conversion & translation of mats; Screen enlargement software for people with visual disabilities; Screen reader software; Soundproof reading booth; Talking bks; Talking bks & player equip
Open Mon-Thurs 7:30am-10pm, Fri 7:30-5, Sat 8-5, Sun 1-5

P SAINT LOUIS COUNTY LIBRARY, Headquarters, 1640 S Lindbergh Blvd, 63131-3598. SAN 349-6058. Tel: 314-994-3300. FAX: 314-997-7602. Web Site: www.slcl.org. *Dir, Admin Serv,* Kristen Sorth; E-mail: ksorth@slcl.org; *Asst Dir, Adult & Support Serv,* Barbara Brain; Tel: 314-994-3300, Ext 2153, E-mail: bbrain@slcl.org; *Asst Dir, Advan,* Barbara Turkington; Tel: 314-994-3300, Ext 2152, E-mail: bturkington@slcl.org; *Asst Dir, Br Serv,* Eric Button; Tel: 314-994-3300, Ext 3253, E-mail: ebutton@slcl.org; *Asst Dir, Info Tech Serv,* Gib Van Cleve; Tel: 314-994-3300, Ext 2201, E-mail: gvancleve@slcl.org; *Mgr, Acq & Coll Develop,* Kathy Wiese; Tel: 314-994-3300, Ext 2370, E-mail: kwiese@slcl.org; *Cat & Proc Mgr,* Tracy Fletcher; Tel: 314-994-3300, Ext 2350, E-mail: tfletcher@slcl.org; *Develop Mgr,* Jim Bogart; Tel: 314-994-3300, Ext 2156; *Mgr, Outreach Serv,* Colleen Hall; Tel: 314-994-3300, Ext 2330, E-mail: chall@slcl.org; *Mgr, Youth Serv,* Nicole Clawson; Tel: 314-994-3300, Ext 2230; *Ref Mgr,* Chris Pryor; Tel: 314-997-3300, Ext 2052, E-mail: cpryor@slcl.org. Subject Specialists: *Develop, Foundations,* Barbara Turkington; Staff 602 (MLS 70, Non-MLS 532)
Founded 1946. Pop 859,148; Circ 15,073,462
Jan 2013-Dec 2013. Mats Exp $7,000,645, Books $3,025,645, Per/Ser (Incl. Access Fees) $275,000, Other Print Mats $100,000, Micro $35,000, AV Mat $1,965,000, Electronic Ref Mat (Incl. Access Fees) $900,000. Sal $18,032,448 (Prof $3,981,671)
Library Holdings: Audiobooks 43,029; AV Mats 286,905; Bks on Deafness & Sign Lang 1,114; CDs 108,984; DVDs 167,016; e-books 34,297; Electronic Media & Resources 49,265; Large Print Bks 39,818; Microforms 216,825; Music Scores 728; Bk Titles 309,276; Bk Vols 1,307,245; Per Subs 4,924
Special Collections: State Document Depository; US Document Depository
Subject Interests: Asian mat, Bus, Fiction, Finance, Genealogy, Local hist, Mgt
Automation Activity & Vendor Info: (Acquisitions) Innovative Interfaces, Inc; (Cataloging) Innovative Interfaces, Inc; (Circulation) Innovative Interfaces, Inc; (ILL) Innovative Interfaces, Inc; (Media Booking) Innovative Interfaces, Inc; (OPAC) Innovative Interfaces, Inc; (Serials) Innovative Interfaces, Inc
Database Vendor: 3M Library Systems, ALLDATA Online, Dun & Bradstreet, EBSCOhost, Gale Cengage Learning, Hoovers, infoUSA, Innovative Interfaces, Inc, LearningExpress, Mergent Online, Newsbank, OCLC FirstSearch, Oxford Online, ProQuest, ReferenceUSA, Standard & Poor's, TumbleBookLibrary, ValueLine, World Book Online
Wireless access
Function: Archival coll
Publications: Co-Lib Chronicle (Newsletter); Friends (Quarterly); Guide to St Louis Catholic Archdiocesan Parish Records (Research guide)
Partic in Amigos Library Services, Inc
Special Services for the Deaf - Bks on deafness & sign lang; Closed caption videos; Spec interest per; Staff with knowledge of sign lang; TDD equip; TTY equip
Special Services for the Blind - BiFolkal kits; Bks on CD; Playaways (bks on MP3); Recorded bks; Videos on blindness & phys handicaps
Open Mon-Thurs 9-9, Fri & Sat 9-5, Sun (Sept-May) 1-5
Restriction: Open to pub for ref & circ; with some limitations
Friends of the Library Group
Branches: 20
DANIEL BOONE BRANCH, 300 Clarkson Rd, Ellisville, 63011-2222, SAN 349-6112. Tel: 314-994-3300, Ext 3100. *Br Mgr,* Amy Hanaway
Open Mon-Thurs 9-9, Fri & Sat 9-5, Sun 1-5
BRIDGETON TRAILS BRANCH, 3455 McKelvey Rd, Bridgeton, 63044-2500, SAN 349-6082. Tel: 314-994-3300, Ext 3000. *Br Mgr,* Roz Kohen
Founded 1978
Library Holdings: Bk Vols 80,000

Open Mon-Thurs 9-9, Fri & Sat 9-5
Friends of the Library Group
CLIFF CAVE BRANCH, 5430 Telegraph Rd, 63129, SAN 374-4590. Tel: 314-994-3300, Ext 3050. *Br Mgr,* Dottie Wobbe
Open Mon-Thurs 9-9, Fri & Sat 9-5, Sun 1-5
EUREKA HILLS BRANCH, 156 Eureka Towne Center Dr, Eureka, 63025-1032, SAN 323-8113. Tel: 314-994-3300, Ext 3200. *Br Mgr,* Michael Cohen; E-mail: mcohen@slcl.org
Open Mon-Thurs 9-9, Fri & Sat 9-5
FLORISSANT VALLEY BRANCH, 195 New Florissant Rd S, Florissant, 63031-6796, SAN 349-6147. Tel: 314-994-3300, Ext 3250. *Br Mgr,* Julie Mangner; E-mail: jmangner@slcl.org
Open Mon-Thurs 9-9, Fri & Sat 9-5, Sun 1-5
GRAND GLAIZE BRANCH, 1010 Meramec Station Rd, Manchester, 63021-6943, SAN 349-6171. Tel: 314-994-3300, Ext 3300. *Br Mgr,* Paul Bayless; E-mail: pbayless@slcl.org
Open Mon-Thurs 9-9, Fri & Sat 9-5
HISTORY & GENEALOGY DEPARTMENT, 1640 S Lindbergh Blvd, 63131-3598, SAN 328-476X. Tel: 314-994-3300. *Asst Mgr, Hist & Genealogy Dept,* Scott Holl
Special Collections: African-American Research (Julius K Hunter & Friends Coll); Jewish Genealogical Society of St Louis Coll; National Genealogical Society Library Coll; St Louis Genealogical Society Library Coll
Subject Interests: Genealogy, Local hist
Open Mon-Thurs 9-9, Fri & Sat 9-5, Sun 1-5
INDIAN TRAILS BRANCH, 8400 Delport Dr, 63114-5904, SAN 349-6201. Tel: 314-994-3300, Ext 3350. *Br Mgr,* Aaron Eller; E-mail: aeller@slcl.org
Open Mon-Thurs 9-9, Fri & Sat 9-5
Friends of the Library Group
JAMESTOWN BLUFFS BRANCH, 4153 N Hwy 67, Florissant, 63034-2825, SAN 377-6085. Tel: 314-994-3300, Ext 3400. *Br Mgr,* Trudy Williams
Open Mon-Thurs 9-9, Fri & Sat 9-5
LEWIS & CLARK BRANCH, 9909 Lewis-Clark Blvd, 63136-5322, SAN 349-6260. Tel: 314-994-3300, Ext 3450. *Br Mgr,* Jennifer Jung; E-mail: jjung@slcl.org
Open Mon-Thurs 9-9, Fri & Sat 9-5
MERAMEC VALLEY BRANCH, 625 New Smizer Mill Rd, Fenton, 63026-3518, SAN 328-6878. Tel: 314-994-3300, Ext 3550. *Br Mgr,* Donna Spaulding; E-mail: dspaulding@slcl.org
Open Mon-Wed 9:30-8, Thurs-Sat 9:30-5
MID-COUNTY BRANCH, 7821 Maryland Ave, 63105-3875, SAN 349-6295. Tel. 314-994-3300, Ext 3500. *Br Mgr,* Gina Sheridan; E-mail: gsheridan@slcl.org
Open Mon-Thurs 9-9, Fri & Sat 9-5
NATURAL BRIDGE BRANCH, 7606 Natural Bridge Rd, 63121-4905, SAN 349-6325. Tel: 314-994-3300, Ext 3600. *Br Mgr,* Alaina Culbertson; E-mail: aculbertson@slcl.org
Open Mon-Thurs 9-9, Fri & Sat 9-5, Sun 1-5
OAK BEND BRANCH, 842 S Holmes Ave, 63122-6507, SAN 328-6894. Tel: 314-994-3300, Ext 3650. *Br Mgr,* Keir Haug; E-mail: khaug@slcl.org
Open Mon-Thurs 9-9, Fri & Sat 9-5
PRAIRIE COMMONS BRANCH, 915 Utz Lane, Hazelwood, 63042-2739, SAN 328-6851. Tel: 314-994-3300, Ext 3700. *Br Mgr,* Rachel Nowell; E-mail: rnowell@slcl.org
Open Mon-Thurs 9-9, Fri & Sat 9-5
ROCK ROAD BRANCH, 10267 St Charles Rock Rd, Saint Ann, 63074-1812, SAN 349-635X. Tel: 314-994-3300, Ext 3750. *Br Mgr,* Connie Dee; E-mail: cdee@slcl.org
Open Mon-Thurs 9-9, Fri & Sat 9-5
SAMUEL C SACHS BRANCH, 16400 Burkhardt Pl, Chesterfield, 63017-4660. Tel: 314-994-3300, Ext 3800. *Br Mgr,* Marsha Ramey; E-mail: mramey@slcl.org
Open Mon-Thurs 9-9, Fri & Sat 9-5
TESSON FERRY BRANCH, 9920 Lin-Ferry Dr, 63123-6914, SAN 349-6384. Tel: 314-994-3300, Ext 3850. *Br Mgr,* Anne Arthur; E-mail: aarthur@slcl.org
Open Mon-Thurs 9-9, Fri & Sat 9-5, Sun 1-5
THORNHILL BRANCH, 12863 Willowyck Dr, 63146-3771, SAN 349-6414. Tel: 314-994-3300, Ext 3900. *Br Mgr,* Kathy Muller; E-mail: kmuller@slcl.org
Open Mon-Thurs 9-9, Fri & Sat 9-5, Sun 1-5
WEBER ROAD BRANCH, 4444 Weber Rd, 63123-6744, SAN 349-6449. Tel: 314-994-3300, Ext 3950. *Br Mgr,* Anna Strackeljahn; E-mail: astrackeljahn@slcl.org
Open Mon-Thurs 9-9, Fri & Sat 9-5
Bookmobiles: 7. Outreach Manager, Colleen Hall

S SAINT LOUIS MERCANTILE LIBRARY AT THE UNIVERSITY OF MISSOURI-ST LOUIS*, Thomas Jefferson Library Bldg, One University Blvd, 63121-4400. SAN 309-2054. Tel: 314-516-7240, 314-516-7247. FAX: 314-516-7241. Web Site: www.umsl.edu/mercantile. *Dir,* John Neal Hoover; Tel: 314-516-7245, E-mail: jhoover@umsl.edu; *Asst Dir,* Charles E Brown; Tel: 314-516-7243, E-mail: cebrown@umsl.edu; *Curator,* Gregg Ames; Tel: 314-516-7253, E-mail: gpames@umsl.edu; *Curator,* Bette Gorden; Tel: 314-516-7244, E-mail: bgorden@umsl.edu; Staff 7 (MLS 5, Non-MLS 2)
Founded 1846
Library Holdings: Bk Vols 250,000
Special Collections: Alchemy Coll; American Railroads 1840's - Present (John W Barriger III Coll), bks, comn rpts, monographs, mss, pamphlets, papers, photogs, speeches; Art Coll; Early Western Americana; Herman T Pott Coll; National Inland Waterways Coll, bks, mss, maps, photogs, rpts & pamphlets; St Louis History Coll, atlases, maps, newsp, photogs from the early 19th century
Publications: Annual Report
Partic in Amigos Library Services, Inc; OCLC Online Computer Library Center, Inc; Saint Louis Regional Library Network
Open Mon-Thurs 7:30am-10:30pm, Fri 7:30-5, Sat 9-5, Sun 1-9
Friends of the Library Group

S SAINT LOUIS METROPOLITAN POLICE DEPARTMENT*, Saint Louis Police Library, 315 S Tucker Blvd, 63102. SAN 325-447X. Tel: 314-444-5581. FAX: 314-444-5689. E-mail: library@slmpd.org. *Librn,* Barbara Miksicek; Staff 1 (Non-MLS 1)
Founded 1947
Jul 2008-Jun 2009 Income $67,500. Mats Exp $67,500, Books $24,000, Per/Ser (Incl. Access Fees) $29,500, Electronic Ref Mat (Incl. Access Fees) $14,000
Library Holdings: Audiobooks 50; CDs 50; DVDs 50; Bk Vols 20,000; Per Subs 120
Special Collections: Police Department Annual Reports, 1861-present
Subject Interests: Law enforcement
Automation Activity & Vendor Info: (Cataloging) TLC (The Library Corporation); (Circulation) TLC (The Library Corporation); (ILL) TLC (The Library Corporation); (OPAC) TLC (The Library Corporation); (Serials) TLC (The Library Corporation)
Database Vendor: TLC (The Library Corporation)
Publications: Directory of Law Enforcement Agencies in Metropolitan St Louis; In the Line of Duty
Partic in Saint Louis Regional Library Network
Restriction: Open by appt only

S SAINT LOUIS PSYCHIATRIC REHABILITATION CENTER*, Clients Library, 5300 Arsenal St, 63139. SAN 372-6363. Tel: 314-877-6500. *Librn,* Suzanne Jackson
Library Holdings: Bk Titles 6,000; Bk Vols 6,202; Per Subs 30
Special Services for the Deaf - Bks on deafness & sign lang; High interest/low vocabulary bks
Open Mon & Fri 8-5, Wed 8-Noon

S SAINT LOUIS PSYCHOANALYTIC INSTITUTE*, Betty Golde Smith Library, 8820 Ladue Rd, 3rd Flr, 63124-2079. SAN 309-2062. Tel: 314-361-7075. FAX: 314-361-6269. E-mail: library@stlpi.org. Web Site: www.stlpi.org/services/library/. *Librn,* Sheila Heckman; Tel: 314-361-7075, Ext 324; Staff 1 (MLS 1)
Founded 1957
Library Holdings: CDs 20; Bk Titles 4,500; Per Subs 35; Talking Bks 100; Videos 20
Subject Interests: Psychiat, Psychoanalysis, Psychol
Function: AV serv
Open Mon-Fri 8:30-3:30

P SAINT LOUIS PUBLIC LIBRARY*, Administrative Offices, 1415 Olive St, 63103-2315. SAN 349-6597. Tel: 314-539-0300. FAX: 314-241-3840. Web Site: www.slpl.org. *Exec Dir,* Waller McGuire; E-mail: wmcguire@slpl.org; *Dep Dir,* Diane Freiermuth; E-mail: dfreiermuth@slpl.org; *Assoc Dep Dir,* Kathy Leitle; E-mail: kleitle@slpl.org; *Dir, Br Serv,* Judy Bruce; E-mail: jbruce@slpl.org; *Dir, Tech Serv,* Kim Peterson; E-mail: kpeterson@slpl.org; *Dir of Tech,* David Smith; E-mail: dsmith@slpl.org; *Dir, Youth Serv,* Patty Carleton; E-mail: pcarleton@slpl.org; Staff 300 (MLS 52, Non-MLS 248)
Founded 1865. Pop 348,189; Circ 2,500,000
Library Holdings: Audiobooks 2,200; AV Mats 132,400; e-books 1,850; Electronic Media & Resources 70; Microforms 727,600; Bk Vols 3,843,627; Per Subs 6,618
Special Collections: Architecture (Steedman Coll); Black History (Julia Davis Coll); Foundation Center/Grants Coll; Genealogy Coll; NJ Werner Coll of Typography; St Louis Media Archives. State Document Depository; US Document Depository
Subject Interests: Civil War, Genealogy, Heraldry, St Louis hist
Automation Activity & Vendor Info: (Acquisitions) SirsiDynix; (Cataloging) SirsiDynix; (Circulation) SirsiDynix; (ILL) SirsiDynix; (OPAC) SirsiDynix; (Serials) SirsiDynix
Database Vendor: ALLDATA Online, ARTstor, Baker & Taylor, BWI, College Source, CQ Press, Dialog, EBSCO Information Services,

EBSCOhost, Facts on File, Foundation Center, Gale Cengage Learning, Grolier Online, H W Wilson, IHS, infoUSA, JSTOR, LearningExpress, LexisNexis, McGraw-Hill, Medianet, Mergent Online, Modern Language Association, Newsbank, OCLC FirstSearch, OCLC WorldShare Interlibrary Loan, Overdrive, Inc, ProQuest, ReferenceUSA, SirsiDynix, ValueLine, Wilson - Wilson Web, World Book Online
Wireless access
Publications: African-American Heritage of St Louis; German-American Heritage of St Louis; St Louis by the Numbers
Partic in OCLC Online Computer Library Center, Inc; Saint Louis Regional Library Network
Special Services for the Deaf - Bks on deafness & sign lang; Spec interest per; TDD equip
Special Services for the Blind - Assistive/Adapted tech devices, equip & products; Audio mat; BiFolkal kits; Bks on CD; Braille equip; Braille servs; Copier with enlargement capabilities; Large print bks; Magnifiers; Playaways (bks on MP3); Screen enlargement software for people with visual disabilities
Open Mon-Fri 8-5
Friends of the Library Group
Branches: 17
BADEN, 8448 Church Rd, 63147-1898, SAN 349-6627. Tel: 314-388-2400. FAX: 314-388-0529. *Br Mgr,* Jan Daley; Staff 4 (MLS 1, Non-MLS 3)
Library Holdings: Bk Vols 27,270
Open Mon & Sat 9-6, Tues-Thurs 12-7, Fri 11-6
BARR, 1701 S Jefferson Ave, 63104, SAN 349-6651. Tel: 314-771-7040. FAX: 314-771-9054. *Br Mgr,* Erin Guss; Staff 4 (MLS 2, Non-MLS 2)
Library Holdings: Bk Vols 28,085
Open Mon & Sat 9-6, Tues-Thurs 12-7, Fri 11-6
BUDER, 4401 Hampton Ave, 63109-2237, SAN 349-6716. Tel: 314-352-2900. FAX: 314-352-5387. *Regional Mgr,* James Moses; Staff 20 (MLS 5, Non-MLS 15)
Library Holdings: Bk Vols 86,783
Open Mon-Thurs 9-9, Fri & Sat 9-6, Sun 1-5
CABANNE, 1106 Union Blvd, 63113, SAN 349-6740. Tel: 314-367-0717. FAX: 314-367-7802. *Br Mgr,* Barbara Henderson; Staff 4 (MLS 1, Non-MLS 3)
Library Holdings: Bk Vols 35,956
Open Mon & Sat 9-6, Tues-Thurs 12-7, Fri 11-6
Friends of the Library Group
CARONDELET, 6800 Michigan Ave, 63111, SAN 349-6775. Tel: 314-752-9224. FAX: 314-752-7794. *Br Mgr,* Jennifer Halla-Sindelar; Staff 4 (MLS 1, Non-MLS 3)
Library Holdings: Bk Vols 53,840
Open Mon & Sat 9-6, Tues-Thurs 12-7, Fri 11-6
CARPENTER, 3309 S Grand Ave, 63118, SAN 349-6805. Tel: 314-772-6586. FAX: 314-772-1871. *Regional Mgr,* Cynthia E Jones; Staff 13 (MLS 3, Non-MLS 10)
Library Holdings: Bk Vols 65,726
Open Mon-Thurs 9-9, Fri & Sat 9-6, Sun 1-5
CENTRAL EXPRESS, 815 Olive St, 63101. Tel: 314-206-6755. FAX: 314-621-0215. *Librn,* Ed Witowski; Staff 2 (MLS 1, Non-MLS 1)
Open Mon-Wed & Fri 9-6, Thurs 9-9, Sat 9-5
CENTRAL LIBRARY, 1301 Olive St, 63103. Tel: 314-241-2288. FAX: 314-539-0393. TDD: 314-539-0364. *Dir, Cent Serv,* Brenda McDonald; E-mail: bmcdonald@slpl.org
Special Collections: Architecture (Steedman Coll); Foundation Center/Grants Coll; Genealogy Coll; NJ Werner Coll of Typography; Saint Louis Media Archives. Municipal Document Depository; State Document Depository; UN Document Depository
Subject Interests: Civil War, Genealogy, Heraldry' Saint Louis hist
Special Services for the Deaf - Bks on deafness & sign lang; Spec interest per; TDD equip
Special Services for the Blind - Assistive/Adapted tech devices, equip & products; Audio mat; BiFolkal kits; Bks on CD; Braille equip; Braille servs; Copier with enlargement capabilities; Large print bks; Magnifiers; Playaways (bks on MP3); Screen enlargement software for people with visual disabilities
Open Mon 10-9, Tues-Fri 10-6, Sat 9-5
CHARING CROSS, 356 N Skinker Blvd, 63130, SAN 322-5917. Tel: 314-726-2653. FAX: 314-726-6541. *Libr Tech,* Charles Lamkin; Staff 1 (Non-MLS 1)
Library Holdings: Bk Vols 3,863
Open Tues-Fri 1-6, Sat 9-12 & 1-6
COMPTON LIBRARY, 1624 Locust St, 63103. *Dir, Cent Serv,* Brenda McDonald
JULIA DAVIS BRANCH, 4415 Natural Bridge Rd, 63115, SAN 349-6864. Tel: 314-383-3021. FAX: 314-383-0251. *Regional Mgr,* Floyd Council; Staff 9 (MLS 2, Non-MLS 7)
Library Holdings: Bk Vols 71,850
Open Mon-Thurs 9-9, Fri & Sat 9-6, Sun 1-5
Friends of the Library Group
DIVOLL, 4234 N Grand Blvd, 63107, SAN 349-6929. Tel: 314-534-0313. FAX: 314-534-3353. *Br Mgr,* Scott Morris; Staff 4 (MLS 1, Non-MLS 3)
Library Holdings: Bk Vols 28,051
Open Mon & Sat 9-6, Tues-Thurs 12-7, Fri 11-6
KINGSHIGHWAY, 2260 S Vandeventer Ave, 63110, SAN 349-6988. Tel: 314-771-5450. FAX: 314-771-9877. *Br Mgr,* Joe Sedey; Staff 4 (MLS 1, Non-MLS 3)
Library Holdings: Bk Vols 41,578
Database Vendor: Baker & Taylor
Function: Adult bk club, Art exhibits, Audio & video playback equip for onsite use, Children's prog, Computers for patron use, Copy machines, Electronic databases & coll, Handicapped accessible, Homework prog, ILL available, Music CDs, Online cat, Prog for adults, Prog for children & young adult, Pub access computers, Spoken cassettes & CDs, Summer reading prog, Tax forms, Teen prog, VHS videos, Wheelchair accessible
Open Mon & Sat 9-6, Tues-Thurs 12-7, Fri 11-6
Friends of the Library Group
MACHACEK, 6424 Scanlan Ave, 63139, SAN 349-7046. Tel: 314-781-2948. FAX: 314-781-8441. *Br Mgr,* Nancy Doerhoff; Staff 4 (MLS 2, Non-MLS 2)
Library Holdings: Bk Vols 58,240
Open Mon & Sat 9-6, Tues-Thurs 12-7, Fri 11-6
SAINT LOUIS MARKETPLACE, 6548 Manchester Ave, 63139, SAN 376-9526. Tel: 314-647-0939. FAX: 314-647-1062. *Libr Tech,* Homer Hudson; Staff 2 (Non-MLS 2)
Open Tues-Thurs 11-7, Fri 11-6, Sat 9-6
SCHLAFLY, 225 N Euclid Ave, 63108, SAN 349-7011. Tel: 314-367-4120. FAX: 314-367-4814. *Regional Mgr,* Leandrea Lucas; Staff 13 (MLS 3, Non-MLS 10)
Library Holdings: Bk Vols 50,160
Open Mon-Thurs 9-9, Fri & Sat 9-6, Sun 1-5
WALNUT PARK, 5760 W Florissant Ave, 63120, SAN 349-7135. Tel: 314-383-1210. FAX: 314-383-2079. *Br Mgr,* Rodney Freeman; Staff 4 (MLS 1, Non-MLS 3)
Library Holdings: Bk Vols 36,888
Open Mon & Sat 9-6, Tues-Thurs 12-7, Fri 11-6
Bookmobiles: 3

C SAINT LOUIS UNIVERSITY*, Pius XII Memorial Library, 3650 Lindell Blvd, 63108-3302. SAN 349-7194. Tel: 314-977-3100. Circulation Tel: 314-977-3087. Interlibrary Loan Service Tel: 314-977-3104. Reference Tel: 314-977-3103. Automation Services Tel: 314-977-3112. Information Services Tel: 314-977-3580. FAX: 314-977-3108. E-mail: piusweb@slu.edu. Web Site: www.slu.edu/libraries/pius. *Dean of Libr,* David Cassens; Tel: 314-977-3095, E-mail: dcassens@slu.edu; *Asst Dean for Coll Mgt,* Jean Parker; Tel: 314-977-3098, E-mail: parkerjm@slu.edu; *Asst Dean, Libr Assessment,* Patricia Gregory, PhD; Tel: 314-977-3107, E-mail: gregorypl@slu.edu; *Asst Dean, Spec Coll,* Gregory Pass, PhD; Tel: 314-977-3196, E-mail: passga@slu.edu; *Chair, Res & Instrul Serv,* Martha Allen; Tel: 314-977-3596, E-mail: allenmh@slu.edu; *Electronic Res & Ref Librn,* Georgia Baugh; Tel: 314-977-3598, E-mail: baughga@slu.edu; *Coordr, Coll Mgt,* Jane Gillespie; Tel: 314-977-3592, E-mail: gillesj@slu.edu; *Coordr, Info Literacy,* Rebecca Hyde; Tel: 314-977-3106, E-mail: rhyde1@slu.edu; *ILL,* Shawnee Magparangalan; E-mail: levrausg@slu.edu; *Univ Archivist,* John Waide; Tel: 314-977-3091, E-mail: waide@slu.edu; Staff 58 (MLS 26, Non-MLS 32)
Founded 1818. Enrl 12,225; Fac 26; Highest Degree: Doctorate
Jul 2012-Jun 2013. Mats Exp $2,954,597. Sal $2,732,017 (Prof $2,099,732)
Library Holdings: AV Mats 70,839; DVDs 2,549; e-books 12,398; e-journals 7,043; Microforms 1,265,054; Bk Vols 1,338,279; Per Subs 7,735
Special Collections: 16th-19th Century Theology, Church History, Patristics & Jesuitica (Rare Books Coll); Medieval & Renaissance Manuscript Studies (Knights of Columbus Vatican Film Library), microfilm; University Archives & Manuscripts (Walter J Ong & Tristan da Cunha Colls). US Document Depository
Subject Interests: Medieval & Renaissance studies, Philos, Theol
Automation Activity & Vendor Info: (Acquisitions) Innovative Interfaces, Inc; (Cataloging) Innovative Interfaces, Inc; (Circulation) Innovative Interfaces, Inc; (Course Reserve) Docutek; (ILL) OCLC ILLiad; (OPAC) Innovative Interfaces, Inc; (Serials) SerialsSolutions
Database Vendor: ABC-CLIO, ACM (Association for Computing Machinery), Agricola, American Chemical Society, American Geophysical Union, American Mathematical Society, American Physical Society, Amigos Library Services, Annual Reviews, BioOne, Community of Science (COS), Coutts Information Service, CQ Press, CRC Press/Taylor & Francis Group, DynaMed, ebrary, EBSCO Discovery Service, EBSCO Information Services, EBSCOhost, Elsevier, Emerald, Fastcase, Gale Cengage Learning, HeinOnline, IBISWorld, IEEE (Institute of Electrical & Electronics Engineers), Ingenta, Ingram Library Services, Innovative Interfaces, Inc, IOP, ISI Web of Knowledge, JSTOR, LearningExpress, LexisNexis, Loislaw, Marcive, Inc, McGraw-Hill, MD Consult, Medline, Mergent

Online, Nature Publishing Group, Newsbank, Newsbank-Readex, OCLC, OCLC WorldShare Interlibrary Loan, OVID Technologies, Oxford Online, Project MUSE, ProQuest, PubMed, Safari Books Online, Sage, SBRnet (Sports Business Research Network), ScienceDirect, Scopus, SerialsSolutions, Springer-Verlag, Springshare, LLC, Standard & Poor's, STAT!Ref (Teton Data Systems), Thomson - Web of Science, Wiley, YBP Library Services
Wireless access
Function: Archival coll, Art exhibits, Audio & video playback equip for onsite use, Bks on cassette, Bks on CD, CD-ROM, Computers for patron use, Copy machines, Doc delivery serv, e-mail & chat, e-mail serv, E-Reserves, Electronic databases & coll, Exhibits, Govt ref serv, Handicapped accessible, Health sci info serv, ILL available, Music CDs, Online cat, Online info literacy tutorials on the web & in blackboard, Online ref, Online searches, Orientations, Outreach serv, Outside serv via phone, mail, e-mail & web, Photocopying/Printing, Pub access computers, Ref & res, Ref serv available, Ref serv in person, Scanner, Spoken cassettes & CDs, Spoken cassettes & DVDs, Telephone ref, VHS videos, Web-catalog, Wheelchair accessible
Publications: Library Guides/research aids; Manuscripta: A Journal for Manuscript Research; University Libraries (Monthly newsletter)
Partic in Amigos Library Services, Inc; MOBIUS (Missouri Bibliographic Information User System); OCLC Online Computer Library Center, Inc; Saint Louis Regional Library Network
Restriction: Off-site coll in storage - retrieval as requested, Photo ID required for access
Friends of the Library Group

Departmental Libraries:

CM MEDICAL CENTER LIBRARY, 1402 S Grand Blvd, 63104, SAN 349-7259. Tel: 314 977-8800. Interlibrary Loan Service Tel: 314-977-8805. Reference Tel: 314-977-8801. Administration Tel: 314-977-8803. Automation Services Tel: 314-977-8808. FAX: 314 977-5573. Web Site: www.slu.edu/libraries/hsc. *Asst VPres, Univ Libr,* Gail Staines, PhD; Tel: 314-977-3102, Fax: 314-977-3587, E-mail: gstaines@slu.edu; *Dir,* Patrick McCarthy; E-mail: mccartpg@slu.edu; *ILL,* PJ Koch; Tel: 314-977-8806, E-mail: kochpj@slu.edu; *Ref Serv,* Mary Krieger; Tel: 314-977-8810, E-mail: kriegerm@slu.edu; Staff 6 (MLS 5, Non-MLS 1)
Founded 1890. Enrl 11,977; Highest Degree: Doctorate
Jul 2010-Jun 2011. Mats Exp $1,434,763. Sal $654,538 (Prof $393,537)
Library Holdings: DVDs 241; e-books 355; Microforms 23,472; Bk Vols 152,241; Per Subs 205
Special Collections: US Document Depository
Subject Interests: Allied health, Med, Nursing, Pub health
Automation Activity & Vendor Info: (OPAC) Innovative Interfaces, Inc
Function: Computers for patron use, Copy machines, Doc delivery serv, E-Reserves, Electronic databases & coll, Health sci info serv, ILL available, Online cat, Online info literacy tutorials on the web & in blackboard, Photocopying/Printing, Ref serv in person, Wheelchair accessible
Partic in MOBIUS (Missouri Bibliographic Information User System); National Network of Libraries of Medicine; OCLC Online Computer Library Center, Inc; Saint Louis Regional Library Network
Friends of the Library Group

CL OMER POOS LAW LIBRARY, Morrissey Hall, 3700 Lindell Blvd, 63108-3478, SAN 349-7283. Tel: 314-977-3081. Interlibrary Loan Service Tel: 314 977 3991. Reference Tel: 314-977-1447. Administration Tel: 314-977-7201. FAX: 314-977-3966. Web Site: law.slu.edu/library. *Dir,* Joe Custer; Tel: 314-977-4531, E-mail: jcuster1@slu.edu; *Assoc Dir,* Richard C Amelung; Tel: 314-977-2743, E-mail: amelunrc@slu.edu; *Head, Ref,* Peggy McDermott; Tel: 314-977-2739, E-mail: mcdermmh@slu.edu; *Head, Tech Serv,* Ting James; Tel: 314-977-3356, E-mail: jamests@slu.edu; *Access Serv Librn,* Joanne C Vogel; Tel: 314-977-2758, E-mail: vogeljc@slu.edu; *Govt Doc,* Kathleen Casey; Tel: 314-977-2742, E-mail: caseyke@slu.edu; *Ref,* Erika Cohn; Tel: 314-977-2759, E-mail: ecohn2@slu.edu; *Ref,* David Kullman; Tel: 314-977-3947, E-mail: kullmand@slu.edu; *Ref,* Lynn Hartke; Tel: 314-977-2756, E-mail: hartkelk@slu.edu; Staff 10 (MLS 10)
Founded 1842. Highest Degree: Doctorate
Library Holdings: AV Mats 677; Microforms 1,392,051; Bk Titles 664,083; Per Subs 3,565
Special Collections: Early State Records, microfilm; Father Brown Labor Arbitration Coll; Missouri & Illinois Briefs; Smurfit Irish Law Coll; Sullivan Manuscript Coll; US Briefs, microcard & fiche. State Document Depository; US Document Depository
Subject Interests: Constitutional law, Ill law, Irish law, Labor law, Legal hist, Med legal, Mo law, Polish law, Urban problems
Automation Activity & Vendor Info: (Acquisitions) Innovative Interfaces, Inc; (Cataloging) OCLC Online; (Circulation) Innovative Interfaces, Inc; (Course Reserve) Innovative Interfaces, Inc; (ILL) OCLC Online; (OPAC) Innovative Interfaces, Inc; (Serials) Innovative Interfaces, Inc
Database Vendor: Amigos Library Services, Bloomberg, Cassidy Cataloguing Services, Inc, Fastcase, HeinOnline, Innovative Interfaces, Inc, LexisNexis, Loislaw, OCLC, OCLC WorldShare Interlibrary Loan, ProQuest, SerialsSolutions, Westlaw, YBP Library Services
Partic in Council of Law Librs of AJCU; Mid-America Law Library Consortium
Open Mon-Thurs 7:30am-Midnight, Fri 7:30-7, Sat 9-7, Sun 9am-Midnight
Restriction: Access for corporate affiliates
Friends of the Library Group

S SAINT LOUIS ZOO LIBRARY*, One Government Dr, 63110. SAN 328-4018. Tel: 314-781-0900. FAX: 314-646-5535. Web Site: www.stlzoo.org. *Librn,* Jill Gordon; Tel: 314-781-0900, Ext 4554, E-mail: gordon@stlzoo.org; Staff 1 (MLS 1)
Library Holdings: Bk Vols 6,000; Per Subs 100
Special Collections: St Louis Zoo History Coll
Subject Interests: Conserv, Natural hist, Zoology
Automation Activity & Vendor Info: (Cataloging) EOS International; (OPAC) EOS International
Database Vendor: Dialog
Partic in Saint Louis Regional Library Network
Open Mon-Fri 9-5

M SAINT MARY'S HEALTH CENTER*, Health Sciences Library, 6420 Clayton Rd, 63117. SAN 349-7348. Tel: 314-768-8112. FAX: 314-768-8974. *Dir,* Kathy Mullen; *Asst Librn,* Ruby O'Quinn; Staff 2 (MLS 1, Non-MLS 1)
Library Holdings: Bk Titles 800; Bk Vols 16,000; Per Subs 200
Subject Interests: Clinical med, Consumer health, Gynecology, Obstetrics
Partic in Docline
Open Mon-Fri 7:30-4:30

Branches:

NANCY SUE CLAYPOOL HEALTH INFORMATION CENTER, 6420 Clayton Rd, 63117, SAN 376-8600. Tel: 314-768-8636. FAX: 314-768-8974. *Dir,* Kathy Mullen; Staff 1 (MLS 1)
Library Holdings: Bk Titles 520; Bk Vols 700
Subject Interests: Consumer health
Open Mon-Fri 9:30-4:30

R SHAARE EMETH TEMPLE*, Rubin Library, 11645 Ladue Rd, 63141. SAN 321-5822. Tel: 314-569-0010. FAX: 314-569-0271. *Exec Dir,* Don Kriss
Founded 1960
Library Holdings: Bk Vols 15,000; Per Subs 11
Open Mon & Thurs 9-5, Tues & Wed 9-8, Fri 9-3, Sat & Sun 9-11:30

S SIGMA-ALDRICH CORP*, Research Library, 3500 Dekalb St, 63118-4100. (Mail add: PO Box 14508, 63178-4508), SAN 377-2748. Tel: 314-771-5765. FAX: 314-772-8826. Web Site. www.sigma aldrich.com.
Library Holdings: Bk Titles 4,430; Bk Vols 4,500; Per Subs 100
Open Mon-Fri 9-5

S TEAM FOUR, INC LIBRARY*, 14 N Newstead Ave, 63108. SAN 327-1374. Tel: 314-533-2200. FAX: 314-533-2203. Web Site: www.teamfourstl.com. *In Charge,* Sandy Matreci
Library Holdings: Bk Titles 1,000; Bk Vols 1,112; Per Subs 12
Special Collections: Architecture Catalogs & Books
Open Mon-Fri 8-5

R THIRD BAPTIST CHURCH LIBRARY*, 620 N Grand Blvd, 63103. SAN 309-2097. Tel: 314-533-7340, Ext 21. FAX: 314-533-7310. Web Site: www.third-baptist.org. *Media Spec,* Rea Finn
Founded 1943
Library Holdings: Bk Titles 4,000
Open Wed 5pm-7:30pm, Sun 9am-12:30pm
Restriction: Mem only

L THOMPSON COBURN LLP*, Law Library, One US Bank Plaza, 63101. SAN 372-4468. Tel: 314-552-6000. Circulation Tel: 314-552-6323. Interlibrary Loan Service Tel: 314-552-6093. Reference Tel: 314-552-6000, Ext 1483. Administration Tel: 314-552-6275. Automation Services Tel: 314-552-6382. FAX: 314-552-7000. Circulation FAX: 314-552-7323. Interlibrary Loan Service FAX: 314-552-7093. Administration FAX: 314-552-7275. Web Site: www.thompsoncoburn.com. *Dir,* Mary Kay Jung; Fax: 314-552-7275, E-mail: mkjung@thompsoncoburn.com; *Bus & Intelligence Librn,* Sabina Assar; Tel: 314-552-6424, Fax: 314-552-7472, E-mail: mfulton@thompsoncoburn.com; *Head, Pub Serv,* Shirley G Canup; Tel: 314-552-6260, Fax: 314-552-7260, E-mail: scanup@thompsoncoburn.com; *Head, Tech Serv,* Donna Barratt; Tel: 314-552-6347, Fax: 314-552-7347, E-mail: dbarratt@thompsoncoburn.com; *Computer Serv,* Jennifer Spector; Fax: 314-552-7382, E-mail: jspector@thompsoncoburn.com; Staff 7 (MLS 4, Non-MLS 3)
Library Holdings: Bk Titles 4,800; Bk Vols 26,000; Per Subs 3,600
Automation Activity & Vendor Info: (Cataloging) EOS International; (Circulation) EOS International; (ILL) OCLC; (OPAC) EOS International; (Serials) EOS International

Database Vendor: LexisNexis, OCLC FirstSearch, Westlaw
Partic in Amigos Library Services, Inc
Restriction: Not open to pub

R UNITED HEBREW CONGREGATION LIBRARY*, 13788 Conway Rd, 63141. SAN 309-2151. Tel: 314-469-0700. FAX: 314-434-7821. *Librn,* Louise Zimerman
Library Holdings: Bk Titles 3,814
Subject Interests: Hist, Jewish holidays
Wireless access
Open Mon-Thurs 9-5, Fri 9-3, Sun 9-2

A UNITED STATES ARMY*, Technical Information & Library Services, Ray Bldg, 1222 Spruce St, Rm No 4202, 63103-2833. SAN 349-7437. Tel: 314-331-8883. FAX: 314-331-8677. Web Site: www.mvs.usace.army.mil. *Tech Serv,* Phyllis Thomas; Staff 1 (Non-MLS 1)
Founded 1968
Library Holdings: Bk Titles 8,412; Bk Vols 8,510; Per Subs 688
Special Collections: River & Harbor acts, Congressional Documents, 1899-date; River Basin Studies
Subject Interests: Civil eng, Environ, Outdoor recreation, Water res
Publications: Holdings List (biannual); Library Users Guide; New Books List (quarterly)
Partic in Dialog Corp; OCLC Online Computer Library Center, Inc
Open Mon-Fri 7:30-4

GL UNITED STATES COURT OF APPEALS LIBRARY*, US Courts Library 8th Circuit, Thomas F Eagleton US Courthouse, 111 S Tenth St, Rm 22-300, 63102. SAN 309-216X. Tel: 314-244-2665. FAX: 314-244-2675. E-mail: library8th@ca8.uscourts.gov. Web Site: www.lb8.uscourts.gov. *Dir,* Ann T Fessenden; *Dep Dir,* James R Voelker; *Archivist,* Joan Voelker; Staff 10.7 (MLS 4.6, Non-MLS 6.1)
Library Holdings: Bk Vols 63,776
Subject Interests: Fed law
Automation Activity & Vendor Info: (Acquisitions) SirsiDynix; (Cataloging) SirsiDynix; (OPAC) SirsiDynix; (Serials) SirsiDynix
Database Vendor: LexisNexis, Westlaw
Partic in Fedlink
Restriction: Non-circulating to the pub

CM UNIVERSITY OF MISSOURI-COLUMBIA*, Missouri Institute of Mental Health Library, 5400 Arsenal St, 63139-1403. SAN 309-1899. Tel: 314-877-6522. FAX: 314-877-6521. Web Site: www.mimh.edu/library. *Dir,* Joseph Grailer. Subject Specialists: *Mental health,* Joseph Grailer; Staff 5 (MLS 1, Non-MLS 4)
Founded 1962
Library Holdings: Bk Titles 9,500; Bk Vols 10,000; Per Subs 260
Special Collections: Saint Louis State Hospital Archives
Subject Interests: Psychiat, Psychiat nursing, Psychol, Substance abuse
Automation Activity & Vendor Info: (Circulation) Follett Software; (OPAC) TLC (The Library Corporation)
Database Vendor: OVID Technologies
Wireless access
Partic in OCLC Online Computer Library Center, Inc; Saint Louis Regional Library Network

C UNIVERSITY OF MISSOURI-SAINT LOUIS LIBRARIES*, One University Blvd, 63121. SAN 349-7496. Tel: 314-516-5060. Interlibrary Loan Service Tel: 314-516-5066. FAX: 314-516-5853. Web Site: www.umsl.edu. *Dean of Libr,* Christopher Dames; *Assoc Dean of Libr,* Marilyn Rodgers; *Head, Tech Serv,* David Owens; *ILL,* Mary Zettwoch; Staff 47 (MLS 27, Non-MLS 20)
Founded 1963. Enrl 16,802; Fac 539; Highest Degree: Doctorate
Jul 2010-Jun 2011. Mats Exp $2,174,241. Sal $2,241,859
Library Holdings: e-books 1,190; Microforms 1,335,705; Bk Vols 1,228,382; Per Subs 3,000
Special Collections: Colonial Latin American History; Historic Rail & River Travel; Mercantile; Utopian Literature & Science Fiction; Western Americana. US Document Depository
Automation Activity & Vendor Info: (Acquisitions) Innovative Interfaces, Inc; (Cataloging) Innovative Interfaces, Inc; (Circulation) Innovative Interfaces, Inc; (Course Reserve) Innovative Interfaces, Inc; (OPAC) Innovative Interfaces, Inc; (Serials) Innovative Interfaces, Inc
Database Vendor: EBSCOhost, Gale Cengage Learning, JSTOR, LexisNexis, OCLC FirstSearch, OVID Technologies
Wireless access
Publications: Libraries' (Newsletter)
Partic in BRS; Merlin; Midwest Region Libr Network; MOBIUS (Missouri Bibliographic Information User System); OCLC Online Computer Library Center, Inc; Saint Louis Regional Library Network
Open Mon-Thurs 7:30am-10:30pm, Fri 7:30-5, Sat 9-5, Sun 1-9
Friends of the Library Group

Departmental Libraries:

WARD E BARNES LIBRARY, One University Blvd, 63121, SAN 349-7526. Tel: 314-516-5576. Circulation Tel: 314-516-5572. FAX: 314-516-6468. *Head of Libr,* Cheryle Cann; E-mail: cann@umsl.edu; Staff 5 (MLS 2, Non-MLS 3)
Highest Degree: Doctorate
Special Collections: Juvenile Literature Coll; Textbook Coll
Subject Interests: Educ, Nursing, Optometry
Open Mon-Thurs 8am-10pm, Fri 8-5, Sat 10-6, Sun 2-10
Friends of the Library Group

C WASHINGTON UNIVERSITY LIBRARIES*, John M Olin Library, One Brookings Dr, Campus Box 1061, 63130-4862. SAN 349-7550. Tel: 314-935-5400. Circulation Tel: 314-935-5420. Interlibrary Loan Service Tel: 314-935-5442. Reference Tel: 314-935-5410. FAX: 314-935-4045. Web Site: library.wustl.edu. *Univ Librn,* Jeffrey Trzeciak; E-mail: Jeffrey.Trzeciak@wustl.edu; *Assoc Univ Librn, Admin,* Virginia Toliver; E-mail: vtoliver@wustl.edu; *Assoc Univ Librn,* Trevor Dawes; *Assoc Univ Librn,* Jeff Huestis; Tel: 314-935-5951, E-mail: huestis@wustl.edu; *Assoc Univ Librn,* Gail Oltmanns; Tel: 314-935-9334, E-mail: goltmanns@wustl.edu; *Head, Access Serv,* Stephanie Atkins; Tel: 314-935-8235, E-mail: satkins@wustl.edu; *Head, Coll & Acq,* William Wibbing; Tel: 314-935-4551, E-mail: wwibbing@wustl.edu; *Head, Libr Outreach,* Rudolph Clay; *Head, Libr Syst,* Bill Fryman; *Univ Archivist,* Sonya Rooney; Staff 108 (MLS 104, Non-MLS 4)
Founded 1853. Enrl 13,210; Fac 757; Highest Degree: Doctorate
Library Holdings: AV Mats 74,196; CDs 6,146; DVDs 1,973; e-books 198,091; Bk Titles 1,723,043; Bk Vols 3,745,746; Per Subs 44,806; Videos 23,189
Special Collections: 19th Century & Modern Literature, bks, ms; American & New; Classical Archaeology & Numismatics (John M Wolfing Coll); Early History of Communications-Semantics (Philip M Arnold Coll); Ernst Krohn Musicological Coll; George N Meissner Rare Book Department; German Language & Literature (Praetorius Memorial Coll); Henry Hampton Archives; History of Architecture (Bruce Coll); History of Printing (Isador Mendle Coll); History of Russian Revolutionary Movement & the Soviet Union (Edna Gellhorn Coll); Literature Coll (Conrad Aiken, Samuel Beckett, Robert Creely, James Dickey & Ford Maddox Ford); Romance Languages & Literature (Max W Bryant Coll); York Stock Exchange Reports. US Document Depository
Subject Interests: Behav sci, Soc sci
Automation Activity & Vendor Info: (Acquisitions) Innovative Interfaces, Inc; (Cataloging) Innovative Interfaces, Inc; (Circulation) Innovative Interfaces, Inc; (Course Reserve) Innovative Interfaces, Inc; (ILL) Innovative Interfaces, Inc; (OPAC) Innovative Interfaces, Inc; (Serials) Innovative Interfaces, Inc
Wireless access
Partic in Amigos Library Services, Inc; Greater Western Library Alliance; Higher Educ Coun of Metrop St Louis; MOBIUS (Missouri Bibliographic Information User System); OCLC Online Computer Library Center, Inc; Saint Louis Regional Library Network
Open Mon-Thurs 7:30am-2am, Fri 7:30am-8pm, Sat 9am-10pm, Sun 10am-2am

Departmental Libraries:

ART & ARCHITECTURE, One Brookings Dr, Campus Box 1061, 63130-4862. Tel: 314-935-5268. E-mail: artarch@wumail.wustl.edu. Web Site: library.wustl.edu/units/artarch. *Supv Librn,* Rina Vecchiola; Tel: 314-935-7658, E-mail: rvecchio@wustl.edu; Staff 2 (MLS 2)
Library Holdings: Bk Vols 105,882; Per Subs 310
Special Collections: Bryce Coll; Eames & Young Coll; East Asian Coll (oriental art); Sorger Coll
Subject Interests: Archit, Art, Art hist, Classical archeol, Communication arts, E Asian art, Fashion design, Landscape archit, Planning design
Open Mon-Thurs 8:30am-11pm, Fri 8:30-5, Sat Noon-5, Sun 1-9

CM BERNARD BECKER MEDICAL LIBRARY, 660 S Euclid Ave, Campus Box 8132, 63110, SAN 349-7828. Tel: 314-362-7080. Circulation Tel: 314-747-0023. Interlibrary Loan Service Tel: 314-747-0029. Reference Tel: 314-362-7085. FAX: 314-454-6606. Web Site: becker.wustl.edu. *Dir,* Paul Schoening; Tel: 314-362-3119, E-mail: paul.schoening@wustl.edu; *Assoc Dir, Coll Mgt,* Marysue Schaffer; Tel: 314-362-0997, E-mail: schaffem@wustl.edu; *Assoc Dir, Health Info Res,* Deborah Thomas; Tel: 314-362-2729, E-mail: thomasde@wustl.edu; *Assoc Dir, Strategic Projects,* Betsy Kelly; Tel: 314-362-2783, E-mail: betsy.kelly@wustl.edu; *Assoc Dir, Translational Res Support,* Robert Engeszer; Tel: 314-362-4735, E-mail: engeszer@wustl.edu; *Librn,* Reka Kozak; *Librn,* Kim Lipsey; Tel: 314-362-4733, E-mail: lipseyk@wustl.edu; *Librn,* Ann Repetto; E-mail: repettoa@wustl.edu; *Cat Librn,* Anna Vani; Tel: 314-362-3481, E-mail: vania@wustl.edu; *Rare Bk Librn,* Elisabeth Brander; Tel: 314-362-4235, E-mail: brandere@wustl.edu; *Archivist,* Stephen Logsdon; Tel: 314-362-4239, E-mail: logsdons@wustl.edu; Staff 48 (MLS 15, Non-MLS 33)
Founded 1837. Enrl 1,062; Fac 831
Library Holdings: CDs 582; e-books 176; e-journals 1,612; Bk Vols 295,748; Per Subs 2,595

Special Collections: Dental Medicine (Henry J McKellops Coll); Opthalmology (Bernard Becker Coll); Otology & Deaf Education (Max A Goldstein - CID Coll); Robert E Schlueter Paracelsus Coll. Oral History
Subject Interests: Health admin, Med, Occupational therapy, Phys therapy
Partic in Saint Louis Regional Library Network
Publications: Library Guide; Special Collections Guide
Open Mon-Thurs 7:30am-12am, Fri 7:30am-10pm, Sat 9-6, Sun 11-11

GEORGE WARREN BROWN SCHOOL OF SOCIAL WORK, One Brookings Dr, Campus Box 1196, 63130-4862, SAN 349-7917. Tel: 314-935-6633. FAX: 314-935-8511. Web Site: brownschool.wustl.edu/admissions/pages/library.aspx. *Dir,* H Sylvia Toombs; Tel: 314-935-8644, E-mail: toombshs@wustl.edu; *Ref Librn,* Lori Siegel; Tel: 314-935-4064, E-mail: lsiegel@wustl.edu; Staff 3 (MLS 2, Non-MLS 1)
Enrl 500; Fac 72; Highest Degree: Doctorate
Library Holdings: DVDs 226; Bk Vols 56,966; Per Subs 494; Videos 562
Subject Interests: Alcoholism, Econ develop, Epidemiology, Family therapy, Gerontology, Mental health, Pub health, Soc develop, Soc work, Women's issues, Youth
Partic in MOBIUS (Missouri Bibliographic Information User System)
Open Mon 8:30am-Midnight, Tues-Thurs 8:30am-11pm, Fri 8:30-6, Sat 10-6, Sun Noon-Midnight

CHEMISTRY, 549 Louderman Hall, Campus Box 1134, 63130. Tel: 314-935-4818, 314-935-6591. FAX: 314-935-4778. E-mail: chem@wumail.wustl.edu. *Librn,* Dr Robert McFarland; E-mail: rmcfarland@wustl.edu; Staff 1 (MLS 1)
Library Holdings: Bk Vols 45,979; Per Subs 321
Subject Interests: Inorganic, Organic, Phys chem, Spectroscopy
Partic in CDP
Open Mon-Thurs 8:30am-9pm, Fri 8:30-5, Sat & Sun 12-5

EARTH & PLANETARY SCIENCE, One Brookings Dr, Campus Box 1061, 63130. Tel: 314-935-4817, 314-935-5406. E-mail: eps@wumail.wustl.edu. Web Site: library.wustl.edu/units/epsc. *Librn,* Clara McLeod; E-mail: cpmcleod@wustl.edu; Staff 1 (MLS 1)
Highest Degree: Doctorate
Library Holdings: Bk Vols 39,968; Per Subs 215
Special Collections: Missouri State Geological Survey; USGS Maps. US Document Depository
Subject Interests: Geochemistry, Geol, Geomorphology, Geophysics, Petrology, Planetary sci, Sedimentation, Structural geol
Open Mon-Thurs (Winter) 8:30am-9pm, Fri 8:30-5, Sun 12-3; Mon-Fri (Summer) 8:30-5

EAST ASIAN, One Brookings Dr, Campus Box 1061, 63130-4862. Tel: 314-935-5525. E-mail: ea@wumail.wustl.edu. Web Site: library.wustl.edu/units/ea. *Librn,* Tony Chang; Tel: 314-935-4816, E-mail: tchang@wustl.edu; Staff 2 (MLS 2)
Library Holdings: Bk Vols 141,191; Per Subs 272
Special Collections: Cultural Revolution of China, 1966-69 (Robert Elegant Coll)
Subject Interests: Art hist, Hist, Lang, Lit, Philos, Relig, Soc sci
Publications: A Guide to Library Resources for Japanese Studies
Open Mon-Fri 8:30am-10pm, Sat & Sun 1-6

GAYLORD MUSIC LIBRARY, 6500 Forsyth Blvd, Campus Box 1061, 63130. Tel: 314-935-5563. E-mail: music@wumail.wustl.edu. Web Site: library.wustl.edu/units/music. *Librn,* Bradley Short; Tel: 314-935-5529, E-mail: short@wustl.edu; Staff 4 (MLS 2, Non-MLS 2)
Founded 1948. Enrl 10,889; Fac 3,098; Highest Degree: Doctorate
Library Holdings: AV Mats 27,683; CDs 20,661; DVDs 528; e-journals 379; Electronic Media & Resources 10; Microforms 3,719; Music Scores 51,177; Bk Vols 62,603; Per Subs 592; Videos 613
Special Collections: American Hymnals & Tune Books; Early Music Editions (Beethoven, Mozart, 19th Century French Opera); Local Music Manuscripts; Sheet Music
Automation Activity & Vendor Info: (Course Reserve) Atlas Systems; (ILL) OCLC ILLiad
Database Vendor: EBSCOhost, Innovative Interfaces, Inc, JSTOR, OCLC FirstSearch, OCLC WorldShare Interlibrary Loan, Oxford Online, Project MUSE, ProQuest, YBP Library Services
Open Mon-Thurs 8:30am-9pm, Fri 8:30-5, Sat & Sun 1-6

KOPOLOW BUSINESS LIBRARY, One Brookings Dr, Campus Box 1133, 63130-4899, SAN 349-764X. Tel: 314-935-6963. FAX: 314-935-4970. Web Site: www.olin.wustl.edu/library. *Dir,* Ron Allen; Tel: 314-935-6739, E-mail: allenron@wustl.edu; *Sr Libr Mgr,* Lamira Martin; Tel: 314-935-4914, E-mail: martinl@wustl.edu; *Evening Mgr,* Kristen Dattoli; E-mail: kdattoli@wustl.edu; *Access Serv, Data Res Assoc,* Madjid Zeggane; E-mail: zeggane@wustl.edu; *Res Assoc,* Margie Craig; Tel: 314-935-6332, E-mail: craigm@wustl.edu; Staff 4.6 (MLS 1, Non-MLS 3.6)
Enrl 1,974; Highest Degree: Doctorate
Library Holdings: Bk Vols 15,000
Database Vendor: ebrary, EBSCOhost, Factiva.com, Gale Cengage Learning, Hoovers, IBISWorld, JSTOR, LexisNexis, OCLC, ProQuest, SerialsSolutions, Standard & Poor's, ValueLine
Function: Accessibility serv available based on individual needs, e-mail serv, E-Reserves, Electronic databases & coll, Exhibits, ILL available, Mail & tel request accepted, Online cat, Online info literacy tutorials on the web & in blackboard, Online ref, Online searches, Orientations, Outreach serv, Photocopying/Printing, Ref & res, Ref serv available, Ref serv in person, Referrals accepted, Res libr, Scanner
Publications: Recent Acquisitions
Open Mon-Thurs 8am-Midnight, Fri 8-5, Sat 12-5, Sun Noon-Midnight
Restriction: Access at librarian's discretion, Access for corporate affiliates, Borrowing requests are handled by ILL, In-house use for visitors
Friends of the Library Group

CL LAW LIBRARY, Washington Univ Sch Law, Anheuser-Busch Hall, One Brookings Dr, Campus Box 1171, 63130, SAN 349-7798. Tel: 314-935-6450. FAX: 314-935-7125. Web Site: law.wustl.edu/library. *Assoc Dean,* Phillip Berwick; Tel: 314-935-6440, E-mail: berwick@wulaw.wustl.edu; *Actg Dir,* Russell Osgood; *Dir, Pub Serv,* Dorie Bertram; Tel: 314-935-6484, E-mail: bertram@wulaw.wustl.edu; *Dir, Tech Serv,* Wei Luo; Tel: 314-935-8045, E-mail: luo@wulaw.wustl.edu; *Cat,* Frederick Chan; Tel: 314-935-6415, E-mail: fchan@wulaw.wustl.edu; *Electronic Res,* Hyla Bondareff; Tel: 314-935-6434, E-mail: bondareh@wulaw.wustl.edu; *Pub Serv,* Mark Kloempken; Tel: 314-935-7124, E-mail: kloempkm@wulaw.wustl.edu; *Ref,* Anne Cleester Taylor; Tel: 314-935-4829, E-mail: actaylor@wulaw.wustl.edu; Staff 9 (MLS 9)
Founded 1867. Enrl 800; Fac 44; Highest Degree: Doctorate
Library Holdings: Bk Titles 148,270; Bk Vols 675,776; Per Subs 6,109
Special Collections: Ashman British Coll; Neuhoff Rare Book Coll. State Document Depository; US Document Depository
Subject Interests: Chinese law, Corp law, European Union law, Intellectual property law, Intl trade law, Tax law
Database Vendor: Gale Cengage Learning, LexisNexis, OVID Technologies, Wilson - Wilson Web
Partic in Mid-America Law Library Consortium
Publications: Faculty Services Guide; Law Library Guide; New Student Orientation Guide; Research Guides; Select Acquisitions List
Open Mon-Thurs 7am-11pm, Fri 7-7, Sat 10-6, Sun Noon-12
Friends of the Library Group

PFEIFFER PHYSICS LIBRARY, One Brookings Dr, 340 Compton Lab, 63130, SAN 349-7887. Tel: 314-935-6215. FAX: 314-935-6219. Web Site: libguides.wustl.edu/physics. *Librn,* Alison Verbeck; E-mail: alison@wustl.edu; Staff 1 (MLS 1)
Library Holdings: Bk Vols 49,106; Per Subs 233
Subject Interests: Astronomy, Astrophysics, Atomic, High energy particles, Math, Nuclear physics, Physics, Quantum mechanics, Solid state physics
Open Mon-Thurs 7:30-6, Fri 7:30-5

C WEBSTER UNIVERSITY*, Emerson Library, 101 Edgar Rd, 63119. (Mail add: 470 E Lockwood Ave, 63119-3194), SAN 309-2208. Tel: 314-968-6952. Reference Tel: 314-968-6950. Toll Free Tel: 800-985-4279. FAX: 314-968-7113. Web Site: library.webster.edu. *Dean, Univ Libr,* Laura Rein; Tel: 314-968-7152, E-mail: lrein@webster.edu; *Sr Assoc Dean, Univ Libr,* Eileen Condon; Tel: 314-246-7954, E-mail: econdon@webster.edu; *Head, Instruction, Liaison & Ref Serv,* Holly Hubenschmidt; Tel: 314-968-8673, E-mail: holly@webster.edu; *Head, Access Serv,* Matt Wier; Tel: 314-246-7806, E-mail: mwier@webster.edu; *Acq Librn,* Maya Grach; Tel: 314-968-6971, E-mail: mgrach@webster.edu; *Doc Delivery,* Rick Kaeser; Tel: 314-968-5994, E-mail: docdel@webster.edu; *ILL,* Sara Fitzpatrick; Tel: 314-246-7807, E-mail: ill@webster.edu; Staff 29 (MLS 13, Non-MLS 16)
Founded 1969. Enrl 21,500; Highest Degree: Doctorate
Library Holdings: Bk Vols 242,425; Per Subs 1,500
Special Collections: Children's Literature (Hochschild Coll); Harry James Cargas Coll; Reformed Church History (James I Good Coll)
Automation Activity & Vendor Info: (Acquisitions) Innovative Interfaces, Inc; (Cataloging) Innovative Interfaces, Inc; (Circulation) Innovative Interfaces, Inc; (Course Reserve) Docutek; (OPAC) Innovative Interfaces, Inc; (Serials) Innovative Interfaces, Inc
Database Vendor: ABC-CLIO, ACM (Association for Computing Machinery), American Psychological Association (APA), Amigos Library Services, Bowker, Checkpoint Systems, Inc, Dun & Bradstreet, EBSCOhost, Innovative Interfaces, Inc, JSTOR, LexisNexis, OCLC FirstSearch, ProQuest, RefWorks, Scopus, Wilson - Wilson Web
Partic in Amigos Library Services, Inc; Higher Educ Coun of St Louis; MOBIUS (Missouri Bibliographic Information User System); OCLC Online Computer Library Center, Inc; Saint Louis Regional Library Network
Open Mon-Thurs 8am-Midnight, Fri & Sat 8-8, Sun Noon-Midnight

SAINT PETERS

P SAINT CHARLES CITY COUNTY LIBRARY DISTRICT*, 77 Boone Hills Dr, 63376-0529. (Mail add: PO Box 529, 63376-0529), SAN 349-5094. Tel: 636-441-2300. FAX: 636-441-3132. E-mail: library@stchlibrary.org. Web Site: www.youranswerplace.org. *Dir,* Jim Brown; *Dep Dir,* Betty Murr; *Adult Coll Mgr,* Lucy Lockley; *Mgr, Commun Br & Adult Programming,* Sara Nielsen; *Coordr, Children's Res & Mkt,* Margaret Preiss; *Coordr, Finance & Support Serv,* Richard Schultz; *Coordr, Human Res,* Denise Mandle; *Coordr, Info Tech,* Frank Noto; *Coordr, Planning & Develop,* Kristin Williams; Staff 35 (MLS 35)
Founded 1973. Pop 353,000; Circ 6,367,709
Jul 2009-Jun 2010 Income (Main Library and Branch(s)) $15,458,190, State $250,238, Locally Generated Income $15,207,952. Mats Exp $2,204,399, Books $846,314, Per/Ser (Incl. Access Fees) $101,059, AV Equip $10,000, AV Mat $508,281, Electronic Ref Mat (Incl. Access Fees) $738,745. Sal $7,688,371
Library Holdings: Audiobooks 36,336; CDs 27,751; DVDs 64,070; e-books 9,356; Electronic Media & Resources 186; Large Print Bks 18,001; Bk Titles 376,688; Bk Vols 839,034; Per Subs 8,507; Videos 8,828
Special Collections: Bizelli-Fleming Local History Coll; Business Coll; Non-Profit Coll; Your Healthy Answer Place
Subject Interests: Bus info, Consumer health info, Genealogy, Local hist
Database Vendor: ALLDATA Online, Baker & Taylor, Booklist Online, Bowker, BWI, CQ Press, Dun & Bradstreet, EBSCO Auto Repair Reference, EBSCO Information Services, EBSCOhost, Facts on File, Gale Cengage Learning, Grolier Online, H W Wilson, Hoovers, infoUSA, Ingram Library Services, LearningExpress, LexisNexis, Loislaw, Mergent Online, Newsbank, OCLC FirstSearch, OCLC WorldShare Interlibrary Loan, ProQuest, PubMed, Standard & Poor's, Wilson - Wilson Web, World Book Online
Wireless access
Function: Bks on CD, Children's prog, Computers for patron use, Copy machines, E-Reserves, Electronic databases & coll, Govt ref serv, Health sci info serv, ILL available, Music CDs, Online ref, Photocopying/Printing, Preschool outreach, Prog for adults, Prog for children & young adult, Ref serv available, Senior computer classes, Senior outreach, Summer reading prog, Tax forms, Teen prog, Telephone ref, Wheelchair accessible
Publications: Salary Survey of West North Central States
Partic in Amigos Library Services, Inc; Saint Louis Regional Library Network
Friends of the Library Group
Branches: 12
BOONE'S TRAIL BRANCH, Ten Fiddlecreek Plaza, New Melle, 63365. (Mail add: PO Box 277, New Melle, 63365-0277), SAN 377-676X. Tel: 636-398-6200. FAX: 636-398-6200. *Br Mgr,* Sara Nielsen; E-mail: snielsen@stchlibrary.org
Circ 58,293
Library Holdings: Bk Vols 13,000
Open Mon & Tues 12-8, Wed & Sat 9-12, Thurs 9-8
Friends of the Library Group
CORPORATE PARKWAY BRANCH, 1200 Corporate Pkwy, Wentzville, 63385-4828, SAN 349-5302. Tel: 636-327-4010, 636-332-8280. Reference Tel: 626-332-9966. Administration Tel: 636-441-2300. FAX: 636-327-0548. Administration FAX: 636-441-3132. E-mail: cpbranch@stchlibrary.org. *Br Mgr,* Diana Tucker; E-mail: dtucker@stchlibrary.org; Staff 2 (MLS 2)
Circ 491,298
Library Holdings: Bk Vols 162,341
Special Services for the Deaf - TDD equip
Open Mon-Thurs 9-9, Fri & Sat 9-6, Sat 1-5
Friends of the Library Group
DEER RUN BRANCH, 1300 N Main, O'Fallon, 63366-2013, SAN 375-6270. Tel: 636-978-3251, 636-980-1332. Reference Tel: 636-978-3261. FAX: 636-978-3209. *Br Mgr,* Tim DeGhelder; E-mail: tdeghelder@stchlibrary.org
Founded 1995. Circ 469,817
Library Holdings: Bk Vols 85,694
Special Services for the Deaf - TDD equip
Open Mon-Thurs 9-9, Fri & Sat 9-6, Sun 1-5
Friends of the Library Group
KISKER ROAD BRANCH, 1000 Kisker Rd, Saint Charles, 63304-8726, SAN 370-1115. Tel: 636-447-7323, 636-926-7323. FAX: 636-926-0869. *Br Mgr,* Position Currently Open
Circ 504,038
Library Holdings: Bk Vols 100,272
Open Mon-Thurs 9-9, Fri & Sat 9-6, Sun 1-5
Friends of the Library Group
LIBRARY EXPRESS @ DISCOVERY VILLAGE, 378 Shadow Pines Dr, Wentzville, 63385-3745. Tel: 636-332-6476. FAX: 636-332-4165. *Br Mgr,* Sara Nielsen; E-mail: snielsen@stchlibrary.org
Circ 186,410
Library Holdings: Bk Vols 15,000
Open Mon-Thurs 9-9, Fri & Sat 9-6, Sun 1-5
LIBRARY EXPRESS @ WINGHAVEN, 7435 Village Center Dr, O'Fallon, 63368-4768. Tel: 636-561-3385. FAX: 636-561-3819. *Br Mgr,* Sara Nielsen; E-mail: snielsen@stchlibrary.org
Circ 219,920
Library Holdings: Bk Vols 15,000
Open Mon-Thurs 9-9, Fri & Sat 9-6, Sun 1-5
KATHRYN LINNEMANN BRANCH, 2323 Elm St, Saint Charles, 63301, SAN 349-5159. Tel: 636-723-0232, 636-946-6294. Reference Tel: 636-946-0789. FAX: 636-947-0692. *Br Mgr,* Ann King; E-mail: aking@stchlibrary.org; Staff 7 (MLS 7)
Circ 840,000
Library Holdings: Bk Vols 193,030
Subject Interests: Local hist
Open Mon-Thurs 9-9, Fri & Sat 9-6, Sun 1-5
Friends of the Library Group
MCCLAY, 2760 McClay Rd, Saint Charles, 63303-5427, SAN 377-6786. Tel: 636-441-7577. Reference Tel: 636-441-6454. FAX: 636-441-5898. *Br Mgr,* Asia Gross; E-mail: agross@stchlibrary.org
Circ 662,524
Library Holdings: Bk Vols 94,592
Open Mon-Thurs 9-9, Fri & Sat 9-6, Sun 1-5
Friends of the Library Group
MIDDENDORF-KREDELL BRANCH, 2750 Hwy K, O'Fallon, 63368-7859, SAN 375-6289. Tel: 636-272-4999, 636-978-7926. Reference Tel: 636-978-7997. FAX: 636-978-7998. *Br Mgr,* Martha Radginski; E-mail: mradginski@stchlibrary.org
Circ 1,155,443
Library Holdings: Bk Vols 179,097
Special Collections: US Document Depository
Special Services for the Deaf - TDD equip
Open Mon-Thurs 9-9, Fri & Sat 9-6, Sun 1-5
Friends of the Library Group
NORTH COUNTY BRANCH, 1825 Commonfield Rd, Portage des Sioux, 63373. (Mail add: PO Box 190, Portage des Sioux, 63373-0190), SAN 349-5183. Tel: 636-753-3070. FAX: 636-753-3070. *Br Mgr,* Sara Nielsen; E-mail: snielsen@stchlibrary.org
Circ 19,994
Library Holdings: Bk Vols 9,410
Open Mon & Tues 12-8, Thurs 9-8, Sat 9-12
Friends of the Library Group
SOUTH COUNTY BRANCH, 198 Jackson St, Augusta, 63332-1772. (Mail add: PO Box 128, Augusta, 63332-0128), SAN 349-5272. Tel: 636-228-4855. FAX: 636-228-4855. *Br Mgr,* Sara Nielsen; E-mail: snielsen@stchlibrary.org
Circ 35,793
Library Holdings: Bk Vols 11,581
Open Mon & Tues 12-8, Thurs 9-8, Sat 9-12
Friends of the Library Group
SPENCER ROAD BRANCH, 427 Spencer Rd, 63376. (Mail add: PO Box 529, 63376-0529), SAN 349-5248. Tel: 636-441-0522, 636-447-2320. Reference Tel: 636-441-0794. FAX: 636-926-3948. *Br Mgr,* Laurie St Laurent; E-mail: lstlaurent@stchlibrary.org
Circ 743,682
Library Holdings: Bk Vols 185,200
Special Collections: Business Services
Special Services for the Deaf - TDD equip
Open Mon-Thurs 9-9, Fri & Sat 9-6, Sun 1-5
Friends of the Library Group

SALEM

P SALEM PUBLIC LIBRARY*, 102 N Jackson, 65560. SAN 309-2224. Tel: 573-729-4331. FAX: 573-729-2123. Web Site: www.salempubliclibrary.lib.mo.us. *Dir,* Glenda Wofford; E-mail: glendabrown1@gmail.com; Staff 3 (MLS 1, Non-MLS 2)
Founded 1930. Pop 4,854; Circ 40,436
Library Holdings: Bk Titles 30,763; Bk Vols 32,123; Per Subs 75; Talking Bks 742; Videos 848
Subject Interests: Genealogy
Automation Activity & Vendor Info: (Cataloging) TLC (The Library Corporation); (Circulation) TLC (The Library Corporation)
Database Vendor: OCLC FirstSearch
Open Mon-Wed & Fri 10-5, Thurs 10-7, Sat 10-1
Friends of the Library Group

SALISBURY

P DULANY MEMORIAL LIBRARY*, 501 S Broadway, 65281. SAN 309-2232. Tel: 660-388-5712. FAX: 660-388-5712. E-mail: contact@dulanylibrary.org. Web Site: dulanylibrary.org. *Dir,* Cheryl Springer; *Asst Dir,* Carolyn McNeall; *Head, Circ,* Wilma Dameron; Staff 2 (MLS 1, Non-MLS 1)
Founded 1928. Pop 1,960; Circ 19,600
Library Holdings: Large Print Bks 30; Bk Titles 14,890; Bk Vols 15,795; Per Subs 37; Talking Bks 78; Videos 230

Automation Activity & Vendor Info: (Cataloging) Mandarin Library Automation; (Circulation) Mandarin Library Automation; (OPAC) Mandarin Library Automation
Open Mon-Fri 12-5, Sat 8-1

SARCOXIE

P SARCOXIE PUBLIC LIBRARY*, 506 Center St, 64862. (Mail add: PO Box 103, 64862-0103), SAN 329-2533. Tel: 417-548-2736. FAX: 417-548-3104. Web Site: sarcoxiemo.com/library/index.htm. *Dir,* Carolina Chapman; E-mail: librarydirector@sarcoxiemo.com; Staff 3 (MLS 1, Non-MLS 2)
Founded 1960. Pop 1,470; Circ 13,591
Library Holdings: AV Mats 110; Bk Titles 13,551; Bk Vols 13,872; Per Subs 16; Talking Bks 151; Videos 389
Database Vendor: EBSCOhost, Newsbank, OCLC FirstSearch
Wireless access
Open Mon-Fri 9-6, Sat 9-1
Friends of the Library Group

SEDALIA

P BOONSLICK REGIONAL LIBRARY*, 219 W Third St, 65301-4347. SAN 349-7941. Tel: 660-827-7111. FAX: 660-827-4668. Web Site: brl.lib.mo.us. *Dir,* Linda Allcorn; E-mail: allcornl@brl.lib.mo.us; *Ref,* Debbie Mueller; Staff 12 (MLS 1, Non-MLS 11)
Founded 1953. Pop 53,068; Circ 402,333
Library Holdings: Bk Vols 200,000; Per Subs 175
Automation Activity & Vendor Info: (Acquisitions) TLC (The Library Corporation); (Cataloging) TLC (The Library Corporation); (Circulation) TLC (The Library Corporation)
Wireless access
Publications: Adult Book List, Annual Report; Bookmobile Schedules; Childrens Newsletter; Informational Brochures; Seasonal Ideas
Partic in Mid-Mo Libr Network; Mo Libr Asn
Special Services for the Deaf - TDD equip
Open Mon-Wed & Fri 9-6, Thurs 9-7, Sat 9-5
Friends of the Library Group
Branches: 4
BOONVILLE BRANCH, 618 Main St, Boonville, 65233, SAN 349-7976. Tel: 660-882-5864. FAX: 660-882-7953. *Br Supvr,* Melanie Spencer; Staff 2 (MLS 1, Non-MLS 1)
Open Mon-Fri 9-6, Sat 9-4
Friends of the Library Group
COLE CAMP BRANCH, 701 W Main St, Cole Camp, 65325, SAN 349-800X. Tel: 660-668-3887. FAX: 660-668-3852. *Br Supvr,* Patricia Beckman; E-mail: beckman_patricia@hotmail.com; Staff 1 (MLS 1)
Open Tues-Fri 1:30-6:30, Sat 9-2
Friends of the Library Group
PETTIS COUNTY, 219 W Third St, 65301, SAN 329-5834. Tel: 660-827-7323. Administration Tel: 660-827-7111. FAX: 660-827-4668. *Br Supvr,* JoEllen Williamson; Staff 2 (MLS 1, Non-MLS 1)
Open Mon-Wed & Fri 9-6, Thurs 9-7, Sat 9-5
Friends of the Library Group
WARSAW BRANCH, 102 E Jackson, Warsaw, 65355, SAN 349-8034. Tel: 660-438-5211. FAX: 660-438-9567. *Br Supvr,* Joanne Glowczewski; Staff 2 (MLS 1, Non-MLS 1)
Open Mon-Sat 9-5:30
Friends of the Library Group
Bookmobiles: 1

P SEDALIA PUBLIC LIBRARY*, 311 W Third St, 65301-4399. SAN 309-2240. Tel: 660-826-1314. FAX: 660-826-0396. Web Site: www.sedalialibrary.com. *Dir,* Pam Hunter; E-mail: phunter@sedalialibrary.com; Staff 12 (MLS 1, Non-MLS 11)
Founded 1895. Pop 20,185; Circ 120,708
Library Holdings: Bks on Deafness & Sign Lang 47; CDs 680; DVDs 1,000; e-books 6,579; Electronic Media & Resources 213; Large Print Bks 3,113; Bk Titles 80,000; Bk Vols 82,000; Per Subs 155; Videos 2,481
Subject Interests: Local hist
Automation Activity & Vendor Info: (Cataloging) OCLC CatExpress; (Circulation) SirsiDynix; (OPAC) SirsiDynix
Database Vendor: EBSCOhost, Newsbank, OCLC FirstSearch, OCLC WorldShare Interlibrary Loan, ProQuest
Wireless access
Special Services for the Deaf - Assistive tech; Bks on deafness & sign lang; Closed caption videos; Coll on deaf educ; Staff with knowledge of sign lang; TDD equip
Special Services for the Blind - Assistive/Adapted tech devices, equip & products; Audio mat; Bks on cassette; Bks on CD; Large print & cassettes; Large print bks; Low vision equip; Magnifiers; Talking bks; Videos on blindness & phys handicaps
Open Mon 9-8, Tues-Fri 9-6, Sat 9-5, Sun 1-5
Friends of the Library Group

J STATE FAIR COMMUNITY COLLEGE*, Donald C Proctor Library, 3201 W 16th St, 65301. SAN 309-2259. Tel: 660-530-5842. FAX: 660-596-7468. Web Site: www.sfccmo.edu. *Dir,* Robin Hargrave; E-mail: rhargrave@sfccmo.edu; *Evening Supvr,* Shanelle King; E-mail: sking3@sfccmo.edu; *Acq,* Shirley Bergeson; E-mail: sbergeson@sfccmo.edu; *Circ & ILL,* Linda Wheeler; E-mail: lwheeler@sfccmo.edu; Staff 4 (MLS 1, Non-MLS 3)
Founded 1969
Library Holdings: AV Mats 4,345; Bk Titles 43,617; Per Subs 277
Special Collections: Audio Visual (videotapes & cassette tape kits); Juvenile Coll; Missouri Coll; Ragtime Coll
Subject Interests: Agr, Art, Automotive, Bus educ, Nursing
Automation Activity & Vendor Info: (Cataloging) Innovative Interfaces, Inc; (Circulation) Innovative Interfaces, Inc; (ILL) OCLC; (OPAC) Innovative Interfaces, Inc; (Serials) Innovative Interfaces, Inc
Database Vendor: EBSCOhost, ProQuest
Publications: Library Handbook; Recent Acquisitions Bulletin
Partic in Amigos Library Services, Inc; MOBIUS (Missouri Bibliographic Information User System)
Open Mon-Thurs 7:30am-8:30pm, Fri 7:30-5

SHELBINA

P SHELBINA CARNEGIE PUBLIC LIBRARY*, 102 N Center, 63468. SAN 309-2267. Tel: 573-588-2271. FAX: 573-588-2271. E-mail: shelbinalibrary@gmail.com. Web Site: shelbinacarnegie.lib.mo.us. *Libr Dir,* Linda K Kropf; *Ch,* Sharon Winn; *Cataloger,* Bonnie Wood; E-mail: bonywood@yahoo.com; *Circ,* Cheryl Kendrick; *Circ,* Sharon Utz; Staff 1 (MLS 1)
Founded 1917. Pop 2,175; Circ 36,000
Library Holdings: AV Mats 827; Bk Titles 30,362; Per Subs 73; Videos 305
Special Collections: Centennial Farms Records of Shelby County; Early Census Records of Shelby County; Genealogy (Burial Records of Shelby County, History of Schools, Churches & Families in Area); Shelby County Newspapers
Open Mon, Wed-Fri 11-5:30, Sat 9-12

SHELDON

P SHELDON LIBRARY*, 216 W Main St, 64784. (Mail add: PO Box 502, 64784-0502), SAN 377-2179. Tel: 417-884-2909. *In Charge,* Darlene Sheridan
Library Holdings: Bk Titles 5,816; Bk Vols 6,000; Per Subs 17; Talking Bks 128; Videos 290
Open Tues & Thurs 1-5, Sat 9-12
Friends of the Library Group

SIKESTON

P SIKESTON PUBLIC LIBRARY*, 121 E North St, 63801. (Mail add: PO Box 1279, 63801-1279), SAN 309-2275. Tel: 573-471-4140. FAX: 573-471-6048. Web Site: www.sikeston.lib.mo.us. *Dir,* Suzanne Tangeman; E-mail: stangeman@sikeston.lib.mo.us; *Asst Dir,* Ron Eifert; E-mail: reifert@sikeston.lib.mo.us; Staff 6 (Non-MLS 6)
Founded 1938. Pop 17,100; Circ 52,000
Library Holdings: Audiobooks 735; AV Mats 1,852; Bks on Deafness & Sign Lang 13, CDs 84; DVDs 135; Large Print Bks 1,134; Microforms 363; Bk Titles 42,500; Per Subs 109; Videos 932
Automation Activity & Vendor Info: (Acquisitions) Baker & Taylor; (Cataloging) Follett Software; (Circulation) Follett Software; (ILL) OCLC FirstSearch; (OPAC) Follett Software; (Serials) EBSCO Online
Database Vendor: EBSCOhost, OCLC FirstSearch
Wireless access
Function: Adult bk club, Audiobks via web, Bk club(s), Bks on cassette, Bks on CD, Children's prog, Computers for patron use, Copy machines, e-mail serv, Exhibits, Fax serv, Free DVD rentals, Handicapped accessible, Holiday prog, ILL available, Instruction & testing, Microfiche/film & reading machines, Music CDs, Photocopying/Printing, Preschool outreach, Prog for adults, Prog for children & young adult, Pub access computers, Spanish lang bks, Story hour, Summer reading prog, Tax forms, VHS videos, Wheelchair accessible
Partic in Missouri Research & Education Network (MOREnet)
Open Mon-Thurs 10-8, Fri 10-6, Sat 10-4, Sun 1-5
Friends of the Library Group

SLATER

P SLATER PUBLIC LIBRARY*, 201 N Main, 65349. SAN 309-2291. Tel: 660-529-3100. *Librn,* Donna Haynie
Founded 1927. Pop 2,610; Circ 22,752
Library Holdings: Bk Vols 40,438
Special Collections: Dickens & Mark Twain Coll
Mem of Central Iowa Library Services
Open Mon-Fri 2-5

SPRINGFIELD

CR ASSEMBLIES OF GOD THEOLOGICAL SEMINARY*, Cordas C Burnett Library, 1435 N Glenstone Ave, 65802-2131. SAN 309-2305. Tel: 417-268-1000. Toll Free Tel: 800-467-2487. FAX: 417-268-1001. E-mail: library@agseminary.edu. Web Site: www.agts.edu/lib. *Dir, Libr Serv,* Joseph F Marics, Jr; Tel: 417-268-1060, E-mail: jmarics@agts.edu; *Asst Dir,* Rick Oliver; Tel: 417-268-1059, E-mail: roliver@agts.edu; *Coordr, Acq,* Tae Kang; Tel: 417-268-1062, E-mail: tkang@agts.edu; *Coordr, Cat,* Juliana Tilden; Tel: 417-268-1061, E-mail: jtilden@agts.edu; *Circ Serv Coordr,* Laura da Silva; Tel: 417-268-1063, E-mail: ldasilva@agts.edu; Staff 5 (MLS 2, Non-MLS 3)
Founded 1973. Enrl 409; Fac 25; Highest Degree: Doctorate
Library Holdings: AV Mats 5,538; Microforms 78,309; Bk Vols 101,093; Per Subs 303
Subject Interests: Anthrop, Biblical studies, Communication, Missions, Pentecostalism, Psychol, Theol
Automation Activity & Vendor Info: (Acquisitions) Innovative Interfaces, Inc; (Cataloging) Innovative Interfaces, Inc; (Circulation) Innovative Interfaces, Inc; (Course Reserve) Innovative Interfaces, Inc; (ILL) OCLC; (OPAC) Innovative Interfaces, Inc; (Serials) Innovative Interfaces, Inc
Database Vendor: ebrary, EBSCOhost, OCLC FirstSearch, OCLC WorldShare Interlibrary Loan, ProQuest
Wireless access
Partic in Amigos Library Services, Inc; Missouri Research & Education Network (MOREnet); MOBIUS (Missouri Bibliographic Information User System); OCLC Online Computer Library Center, Inc
Open Mon-Fri 9am-9:30pm, Sat 10-6

CR BAPTIST BIBLE COLLEGE*, G B Vick Memorial Library, 628 E Kearney St, 65803. SAN 349-8069. Tel: 417-268-6075. Administration Tel: 417-268-6074. Toll Free Tel: 800-228-5754. FAX: 417-268-6694. E-mail: info@gobbc.edu. Web Site: www.gobbc.edu/library. *Dir of Libr Serv,* Jon Jones; E-mail: jjones@gobbc.edu; *Tech Serv,* Torsten Rothman; E-mail: trothman@gobbc.edu; Staff 5 (MLS 1, Non-MLS 4)
Founded 1956. Enrl 650; Fac 35; Highest Degree: Master
Library Holdings: Bk Vols 55,923; Per Subs 332
Special Collections: Baptist History; Fellowship Authors
Subject Interests: Educ, Music, Relig studies
Automation Activity & Vendor Info: (Acquisitions) Innovative Interfaces, Inc; (Cataloging) Innovative Interfaces, Inc; (Circulation) Innovative Interfaces, Inc; (Course Reserve) Innovative Interfaces, Inc; (ILL) OCLC Online; (OPAC) Innovative Interfaces, Inc; (Serials) Innovative Interfaces, Inc
Database Vendor: EBSCOhost, Gale Cengage Learning, Newsbank, OVID Technologies, Wilson - Wilson Web
Function: AV serv, Distance learning, Doc delivery serv, For res purposes, ILL available, Online searches, Ref serv available, Telephone ref
Partic in MOBIUS (Missouri Bibliographic Information User System); OCLC Online Computer Library Center, Inc
Open Mon, Tues & Thurs 6:30am-11pm, Wed & Fri 6:30-6, Sat 8am-11pm

M COXHEALTH LIBRARIES*, North Library, Cox Medical Ctr N, 1423 N Jefferson Ave, J-200, 65802. SAN 323-5580. Tel: 417-269-3460. FAX: 417-269-3492. E-mail: library@coxhealth.com. Web Site: www.coxhealth.com/libraries. *Dean, Info Serv,* Wilma Bunch; Tel: 417-269-3460, E-mail: wilma.bunch@coxhealth.com; *Librn,* Patricia E Leembruggen; Tel: 417-269-8892, Fax: 417-269-6140, E-mail: patricia.leembruggen@coxhealth.com; *Librn,* Nicole Montgomery; Tel: 417-269-8018, E-mail: nicole.montgomery@coxhealth.com; *Librn,* Daphne Smith; Tel: 417-269-8861, E-mail: daphne.smith@coxhealth.com; Staff 7 (MLS 4, Non-MLS 3)
Library Holdings: Bk Titles 7,891; Bk Vols 8,744; Per Subs 514
Subject Interests: Health sci, Med, Nursing
Automation Activity & Vendor Info: (Acquisitions) Marcive, Inc; (Cataloging) EOS International; (OPAC) EOS International; (Serials) EOS International
Database Vendor: EBSCOhost, OCLC, OVID Technologies, PubMed
Wireless access
Function: CD-ROM, Computers for patron use, Copy machines, Electronic databases & coll, Online cat, Orientations, Web-catalog
Partic in Docline; Health Sciences Library Network of Kansas City, Inc; MCMLA; Medical Library Association (MLA); OCLC Online Computer Library Center, Inc
Open Mon-Fri 8-4:30
Restriction: Circ limited, Med & nursing staff, patients & families, Open to students, fac & staff
Branches:
DAVID MILLER MEMORIAL LIBRARY, Cox Medical Ctr S, 3801 S National Ave, 65807. Tel: 417-269-3460. FAX: 417-269-3492. E-mail: library@coxhealth.com. *Librn,* Patricia E Leembruggen; *Librn,* Nicole Montgomery; *Librn,* Daphne Smith; Staff 3 (MLS 3)
Library Holdings: Bk Titles 7,828; Per Subs 249
Subject Interests: Med, Nursing
Automation Activity & Vendor Info: (Cataloging) Marcive, Inc
Open Mon-Fri 8-4:30

CR DRURY UNIVERSITY*, F W Olin Library, 900 N Benton Ave, 65802. SAN 309-2321. Tel: 417-873-7282. Circulation Tel: 417-873-7338. Interlibrary Loan Service Tel: 417-873-7277. Reference Tel: 417-873-7337. FAX: 417-873-7432. Web Site: library.drury.edu. *Dir,* Stephen K Stoan; Tel: 417-873-7282, E-mail: sstoan@drury.edu; *Acq Mgr,* Myna Berry; Tel: 417-873-7425, E-mail: mberry@drury.edu; *Circ Mgr,* Tracy Sullivan; Tel: 417-873-7481, E-mail: tsulliva@drury.edu; *Mgr, Ser,* Whitney Miano; Tel: 417-873-7340, E-mail: wmiano@drury.edu; *Asst Circ Mgr,* Barbi Dickensheet; Tel: 417-873-7486, E-mail: bdickensheet@drury.edu; *Syst Adminr, Web Developer,* Victoria Johnson; Tel: 417-873-7348, E-mail: vjohnson@drury.edu. Subject Specialists: *Chem, Math, Physics,* Stephen K Stoan; Staff 12 (MLS 7, Non-MLS 5)
Founded 1873. Enrl 4,635; Fac 440; Highest Degree: Master
Library Holdings: AV Mats 3,706; CDs 330; DVDs 341; e-books 16,325; e-journals 590; Music Scores 527; Bk Titles 121,896; Bk Vols 176,304; Per Subs 993; Videos 3,459
Special Collections: Claude Thornhill Music Coll; John F Kennedy Memorabilia. US Document Depository
Subject Interests: Archit
Automation Activity & Vendor Info: (Acquisitions) Innovative Interfaces, Inc; (Cataloging) Innovative Interfaces, Inc; (Circulation) Innovative Interfaces, Inc; (Course Reserve) Docutek; (ILL) OCLC; (Media Booking) Innovative Interfaces, Inc; (OPAC) Innovative Interfaces, Inc; (Serials) Innovative Interfaces, Inc
Database Vendor: Cambridge Scientific Abstracts, EBSCOhost, Gale Cengage Learning, JSTOR, LexisNexis, Newsbank, OCLC FirstSearch, OCLC WorldShare Interlibrary Loan, PubMed, Westlaw, Wilson - Wilson Web
Partic in Amigos Library Services, Inc; Missouri Research & Education Network (MOREnet); MOBIUS (Missouri Bibliographic Information User System)
Open Mon-Thurs (Winter) 7:45am-Midnight, Fri 7:45-6, Sat 10-5, Sun 1-Midnight; Mon-Thurs (Summer) 8am-9pm, Fri 8-5

C EVANGEL UNIVERSITY*, Klaude Kendrick Library, 1111 N Glenstone Ave, 65802. SAN 309-233X. Tel: 417-865-2815, Ext 7268. Web Site: www.evangel.edu/library/index.asp. *Dir of Libr/Media Serv,* Dale R Jensen; E-mail: jensend@evangel.edu; *Ref Librn,* Murl Winters; *Archivist,* Shirley Shedd; *Cataloger,* Debbie Buesking; Staff 9 (MLS 3, Non-MLS 6)
Founded 1955. Enrl 2,100; Fac 100; Highest Degree: Master
May 2006-Apr 2007 Income $582,805. Mats Exp $230,200, Books $50,000, Per/Ser (Incl. Access Fees) $75,000, Micro $40,000, AV Equip $4,000, AV Mat $9,000, Electronic Ref Mat (Incl. Access Fees) $50,000, Presv $2,200. Sal $297,855 (Prof $148,748)
Library Holdings: CDs 1,250; DVDs 400; e-books 7,000; e-journals 12,000; Bk Titles 120,000; Bk Vols 130,000; Per Subs 700; Videos 500
Special Collections: Library of American Civilization, micro; O'Reilly Hospital, photog & doc; University Archives
Automation Activity & Vendor Info: (Acquisitions) Ex Libris Group; (Cataloging) Ex Libris Group; (Circulation) Ex Libris Group; (Course Reserve) Ex Libris Group; (ILL) Ex Libris Group; (Media Booking) Ex Libris Group; (OPAC) Ex Libris Group; (Serials) Ex Libris Group
Database Vendor: 3M Library Systems, Baker & Taylor, EBSCOhost, OCLC WorldShare Interlibrary Loan, ProQuest, Westlaw
Wireless access
Function: Archival coll, Computers for patron use, Copy machines, Electronic databases & coll, Fax serv, Free DVD rentals, Handicapped accessible, ILL available, Learning ctr, Music CDs, Online cat, Online ref, Photocopying/Printing, Ref & res, Ref serv in person
Partic in Amigos Library Services, Inc; BRS; Christian Libr Network; OCLC Online Computer Library Center, Inc
Open Mon-Thurs 7:30am-11:45pm, Fri 7:30-4:30, Sat 1-5, Sun 8pm-Midnight
Restriction: Borrowing privileges limited to fac & registered students, In-house use for visitors, Mem organizations only, Non-circulating coll, Non-circulating of rare bks, Non-circulating to the pub, Pub use on premises

M MERCY HEALTH, Springfield Medical Library, 1235 E Cherokee St, 65804-2263. SAN 326-4823. Tel: 417-820-2795. Interlibrary Loan Service Tel: 417-820-2070. Administration Tel: 417-820-3253. FAX: 417-820-5399. E-mail: libstaff@mercy.net. Web Site: www.mercy.net/st-johns-hospital/medical-library-services. *Dir, Libr Serv,* Holly Henderson; E-mail: holly.henderson@mercy.net; *Librn,* Jean M Lewis; E-mail: jlewis2@mercy.net; *Librn,* Shelley White; Tel: 417-820-2539, Fax: 417-820-8761, E-mail: shelley.white@mercy.net; *ILL,* LaRee LaMar; E-mail: llamar@mercy.net; Staff 4 (MLS 3, Non-MLS 1)
Founded 1940
Library Holdings: AV Mats 372; e-books 160; e-journals 4,196; Bk Titles 2,829; Per Subs 169
Subject Interests: Allied health, Healthcare mgt, Med, Nursing

Automation Activity & Vendor Info: (Cataloging) Innovative Interfaces, Inc; (Circulation) Innovative Interfaces, Inc; (OPAC) Innovative Interfaces, Inc; (Serials) Innovative Interfaces, Inc
Database Vendor: Dialog, EBSCO Information Services, EBSCOhost, Elsevier MDL, Majors, Marcive, Inc, Micromedex, OCLC WorldShare Interlibrary Loan, OVID Technologies, PubMed, UpToDate
Wireless access
Function: Health sci info serv
Partic in Docline; Health Sciences Library Network of Kansas City, Inc; National Network of Libraries of Medicine Midcontinental Region
Open Mon-Fri 8-4:30
Restriction: Open to others by appt
Branches:
VAN K SMITH COMMUNITY HEALTH LIBRARY, Mercy O'Reilly Cancer Ctr, 2055 S Fremont, 65804-2263. (Mail add: 1235 E Cherokee, 65804-2273). Tel: 417-820-2539. Toll Free Tel: 800-432-2273. FAX: 417-820-2587. *Libr Dir,* Holly Henderson; E-mail: holly.henderson@mercy.net; Staff 1 (MLS 1)
Founded 1990
Library Holdings: AV Mats 889; e-books 16; Bk Vols 2,797; Per Subs 106
Subject Interests: Consumer health
Database Vendor: Innovative Interfaces, Inc, MD Consult, OCLC FirstSearch
Open Mon-Fri 8-4:30

GL MISSOURI STATE COURT OF APPEALS*, Southern District Law Library, University Plaza, 300 Hammons Pkwy, 65806. SAN 309-2364. Tel: 417-895-6813. FAX: 417-895-6817. *Librn,* Amy Bailey; Staff 1 (Non-MLS 1)
Library Holdings: Bk Titles 17,500; Bk Vols 19,500; Per Subs 30
Open Mon-Fri 8-12 & 1-5
Restriction: Not open to pub

C MISSOURI STATE UNIVERSITY*, Duane G Meyer Library, 850 S John Q Hammons Pkwy, 65807. (Mail add: 901 S National, 65897-0001), SAN 349-8158. Tel: 417-836-4525. Circulation Tel: 417-836-4700. Interlibrary Loan Service Tel: 417-836-4540. Reference Tel: 417-836-4535. Automation Services Tel: 417-836-8777. FAX: 417-836-4764. Interlibrary Loan Service FAX: 417-836-4538. Web Site: www.library.missouristate.edu. *Dean of Libr Serv,* Thomas Peters; E-mail: thomaspeters@missouristate.edu; *Assoc Dean, Libr Serv,* Neosha A Mackey; E-mail: neoshamackey@missouristate.edu; *Head, Access Serv,* Joshua Lambert; Tel: 417-836-3183, E-mail: joshualambert@missouristate.edu; *Head, Acq & Coll Develop,* Lynn S Cline; Tel: 417-836-4658, E-mail: lynncline@missouristate.edu; *Head, Cat,* Marilyn A McCroskey; Tel: 417-836-4541, E-mail: marilynmccroskey@missouristate.edu; *Head Music Libr,* Drew Beisswenger; Tel: 417-836-5499, E-mail: drewbeisswenger@missouristate.edu; *Head, Ref & Govt Serv,* Byron Y Stewart; Tel: 417-836-4533, E-mail: byronstewart@missouristate.edu; *Head, Spec Coll,* David E Richards; Tel: 417-836-4299, E-mail: davidrichards@missouristate.edu; *Head, Syst,* David L Adams; Tel: 417-836-6211, E-mail: davidadams@missouristate.edu; Staff 65 (MLS 29, Non-MLS 36)
Founded 1907. Enrl 18,700; Fac 673; Highest Degree: Doctorate
Library Holdings: AV Mats 34,097; Bk Vols 1,738,708; Per Subs 4,200
Special Collections: African-American History of the Ozarks (Katherine Lederer Coll); Jean Arthur Rimbaud (William Jack Jones Coll); Michel Butor Coll; Ozarks Labor Union Archives; Ozarks Lesbian and Gay Archives; Robert Wallace Coll; University Archives. Oral History; State Document Depository; UN Document Depository; US Document Depository
Automation Activity & Vendor Info: (Acquisitions) Innovative Interfaces, Inc; (Cataloging) Innovative Interfaces, Inc; (Circulation) Innovative Interfaces, Inc; (Course Reserve) Innovative Interfaces, Inc; (ILL) Innovative Interfaces, Inc; (Media Booking) Innovative Interfaces, Inc; (OPAC) Innovative Interfaces, Inc; (Serials) Innovative Interfaces, Inc
Database Vendor: Dialog, EBSCOhost, Gale Cengage Learning, LexisNexis, OCLC FirstSearch, OVID Technologies, Wilson - Wilson Web
Publications: "Check It Out" (Newsletter)
Partic in Amigos Library Services, Inc; Missouri Research & Education Network (MOREnet); MOBIUS (Missouri Bibliographic Information User System)
Special Services for the Deaf - TDD equip
Open Mon-Thurs 7am-Midnight, Fri 7-6, Sat 9-6, Sun 12-Midnight
Friends of the Library Group
Departmental Libraries:
HASELTINE LIBRARY, Greenwood Laboratory School, 901 S National, Rm 3, 65897, SAN 349-8182. Tel: 417-836-8563. *Libr Assoc,* Rhonda O'Connor; E-mail: rhondaoconnor@missouristate.edu; *Media Spec,* Dea Borneman; E-mail: deaborneman@missouristate.edu; Staff 1 (MLS 1)
Library Holdings: Bk Titles 1,986; Bk Vols 2,100; Per Subs 43
Open Mon-Fri 8-5
Friends of the Library Group
MUSIC LIBRARY, Ellis Hall, Rm 209, 901 S National, 65804-0095, SAN 328-6916. Tel: 417-836-5434. *Head of Libr,* Drew Beisswenger; Tel: 417-836-5499, E-mail: drewbeisswenger@missouristate.edu; *Supvr,* Sue Reichling; E-mail: suereichling@missouristate.edu; Staff 1 (MLS 1)
Library Holdings: Bk Titles 4,886; Bk Vols 5,000; Per Subs 100
Special Collections: Missouri Music Educators Association Archives
Open Mon-Thurs 8am-10pm, Fri 8-5, Sat 12-4, Sun 1-10
Friends of the Library Group

R ST PAUL UNITED METHODIST CHURCH LIBRARY*, 413 E Walnut, 65806. SAN 309-2380. Tel: 417-866-4326. *Librn,* Virginia Gleason; Staff 1.5 (MLS 1, Non-MLS 0.5)
Founded 1964
Jan 2010-Dec 2010. Mats Exp $465, Books $350, Per/Ser (Incl. Access Fees) $90, AV Mat $25
Library Holdings: AV Mats 100; CDs 10; DVDs 10; Large Print Bks 20; Bk Titles 2,000; Spec Interest Per Sub 2; Videos 20
Special Collections: Methodism
Subject Interests: Fiction, Gen, Non-fiction
Publications: Annual Report

S SPRINGFIELD ART MUSEUM*, Reference Library, 1111 E Brookside Dr, 65807. SAN 309-2399. Tel: 417-837-5700. FAX: 417-837-5704. E-mail: artmuseum@springfieldmo.gov. Web Site: www.springfieldmo/gov/art. *Librn,* Position Currently Open
Founded 2008
Library Holdings: Bk Vols 6,623; Per Subs 65
Subject Interests: Am painting, Decorative art, European painting, Prints, Sculpture
Wireless access
Partic in SW Mo Libr Network
Open Tues-Fri 9-5
Friends of the Library Group

P SPRINGFIELD-GREENE COUNTY LIBRARY DISTRICT, 4653 S Campbell, 65810-1723. (Mail add: PO Box 760, 65801-0760), SAN 349-8212. Tel: 417-882-0714. Reference Tel: 417-883-5341. Administration Tel: 417-883-5366. FAX: 417-883-9348. Administration FAX: 417-889-2547. Web Site: thelibrary.org. *Exec Dir,* Regina Cooper; E-mail: reginac@thelibrary.org; *Assoc Dir,* Jim Schmidt; E-mail: jims@thelibrary.org; *Libr Found Dir,* Valerie Richardson; *Electronic Res Librn,* Renee Brumett; E-mail: reneeb@thelibrary.org; *Planning & Develop Librn,* Gay Wilson; E-mail: gayw@thelibrary.org; *Mgr, Coll Serv,* Lisa Sampley; E-mail: lisas@thelibrary.org; *Commun Relations Mgr,* Kathleen O'Dell; E-mail: kathleeno@thelibrary.org; *Human Res Mgr,* Lori Strawhun; E-mail: loris@thelibrary.org; *Ref Serv Mgr,* Kathi Woodward; E-mail: kathiw@thelibrary.org; *Youth Serv Coordr,* Nancee Dahms-Stinson; E-mail: nanceed@thelibrary.org; *Info Tech,* David Patillo; E-mail: davidp@thelibrary.org; Staff 177.69 (MLS 32.05, Non-MLS 145.64)
Founded 1903. Pop 275,174; Circ 341,414
Jul 2013-Jun 2014 Income (Main Library and Branch(s)) $13,107,421. Mats Exp $2,191,804. Sal $5,796,803
Library Holdings: Audiobooks 28,313; AV Mats 88,025; CDs 27,986; DVDs 50,769; e-books 8,485; Bk Titles 427,355; Per Subs 1,125
Special Collections: Burt Buhrman Music Coll; Genealogy & Missouri History; Max Hunter Folk Songs Coll; Turnbo Papers
Automation Activity & Vendor Info: (Acquisitions) Innovative Interfaces, Inc; (Cataloging) Innovative Interfaces, Inc; (Circulation) Innovative Interfaces, Inc; (ILL) Innovative Interfaces, Inc; (OPAC) Innovative Interfaces, Inc; (Serials) Innovative Interfaces, Inc
Database Vendor: EBSCO Information Services, EBSCOhost, Foundation Center, Gale Cengage Learning, Innovative Interfaces, Inc, LearningExpress, Newsbank, OCLC, OCLC FirstSearch, ProQuest, ReferenceUSA, TumbleBookLibrary, ValueLine
Wireless access
Function: Handicapped accessible, Homebound delivery serv, ILL available, Online searches, Photocopying/Printing, Prog for adults, Prog for children & young adult, Ref serv available, Summer reading prog, Wheelchair accessible
Partic in MOBIUS (Missouri Bibliographic Information User System); OCLC Online Computer Library Center, Inc
Special Services for the Deaf - Closed caption videos; TDD equip; Videos & decoder
Special Services for the Blind - Assistive/Adapted tech devices, equip & products; Newsline for the Blind; Talking bks
Friends of the Library Group
Branches: 11
ASH GROVE BRANCH, 101 E Main, Ash Grove, 65604-0248, SAN 349-8247. Tel: 417-751-2933. FAX: 417-751-2275. *Br Mgr,* Sarah Francka-Jones; E-mail: sarahf@thelibrary.org; Staff 3.7 (MLS 1, Non-MLS 2.7)
Circ 38,377
Function: Online searches, Photocopying/Printing, Prog for adults, Prog for children & young adult, Ref serv available, Summer reading prog

Open Mon-Thurs 9:30-7, Fri & Sat 9:30-6
Friends of the Library Group
BRENTWOOD, 2214 Brentwood Blvd, 65804, SAN 349-8271. Tel: 417-883-1974. FAX: 417-883-6412. *Br Mgr,* Kim Flores; Staff 17 (MLS 3, Non-MLS 14)
Founded 1970. Circ 495,651
Function: Online searches, Photocopying/Printing, Prog for adults, Prog for children & young adult, Ref serv available, Summer reading prog
Open Mon-Thurs 8:30am-9pm, Fri & Sat 8:30-6
Friends of the Library Group
FAIR GROVE BRANCH, 81 S Orchard Blvd, Fair Grove, 65648-8421. Tel: 417-759-2637. FAX: 417-759-2638. *Br Mgr,* Whitney Austin; Staff 4 (MLS 1, Non-MLS 3)
Circ 72,353
Function: Online searches, Photocopying/Printing, Prog for adults, Prog for children & young adult, Ref serv available, Summer reading prog
Open Mon-Thurs 9:30-7, Fri & Sat 9:30-6
Friends of the Library Group
THE LIBRARY CENTER, 4653 S Campbell, 65810-1723, SAN 349-8328. Tel: 417-882-0714. Reference Tel: 417-883-5341. FAX: 417-883-9348. *Br Mgr,* Jessie Alexander-East; E-mail: jessieae@thelibrary.org; Staff 48 (MLS 6.5, Non-MLS 41.5)
Circ 1,043,343
Function: ILL available, Online searches, Photocopying/Printing, Prog for adults, Prog for children & young adult, Ref serv available, Summer reading prog, Wheelchair accessible
Open Mon-Sat 8:30am-9pm, Sun 1-5
Friends of the Library Group
LIBRARY STATION, 2535 N Kansas Expressway, 65803-1114, SAN 349-8301. Tel: 417-865-1340. FAX: 417-862-6514. *Br Mgr,* Melissa Davis; E-mail: melissad@thelibrary.org; Staff 25 (MLS 5, Non-MLS 20)
Circ 565,501
Function: Online searches, Photocopying/Printing, Prog for adults, Prog for children & young adult, Ref serv available, Summer reading prog
Open Mon-Sat 8:30am-9pm, Sun 1-5
Friends of the Library Group
MIDTOWN CARNEGIE BRANCH, 397 E Central, 65802-3834. Tel: 417-862-0135. FAX: 417-866-1259. *Br Mgr,* Eva Pelkey; E-mail: evap@thelibrary.org; Staff 14 (MLS 3, Non-MLS 11)
Circ 222,532
Open Mon-Thurs 8:30-7:30, Fri 8:30-6, Sat 8:30-5
Friends of the Library Group
OUTREACH SERVICES, 4653 S Campbell, 65810-8113, SAN 376-2386. Tel: 417-883-5366. FAX: 417-889-2547. *Mgr, Outreach Serv,* Allison Eckhardt; Staff 8 (Non-MLS 8)
Circ 186,195
Function: Home delivery & serv to Sr ctr & nursing homes, Homebound delivery serv, Summer reading prog
Friends of the Library Group
PARK CENTRAL BRANCH, 128 Park Central Sq, 65806-1311. Tel: 417-831-1342. *Br Mgr,* Kristin Bennett; E-mail: kristinb@thelibrary.org
Circ 63,597
Open Mon-Fri 8:30am-9pm, Sat 9:30-9
Friends of the Library Group
REPUBLIC BRANCH, 921 N Lindsey Ave, Republic, 65738-1248, SAN 349-8360. Tel: 417-732-7284. FAX: 417-732-1256. *Br Mgr,* Erin Gray; E-mail: ering@thelibrary.org; Staff 7 (MLS 1, Non-MLS 6)
Circ 194,142
Function: Online searches, Photocopying/Printing, Prog for adults, Prog for children & young adult, Ref serv available, Summer reading prog
Open Mon-Thurs 8:30am-9pm, Fri & Sat 8:30-6
Friends of the Library Group
STRAFFORD BRANCH, 101 S State Hwy 125, Strafford, 65757-8998. Tel: 417-736-9233. *Br Mgr,* Whitney Austin; E-mail: whitneya@thelibrary.org
Circ 68,985
Open Mon-Thurs 9:30-7, Fri & Sat 9:30-6
WILLARD BRANCH, East Shopping Ctr, Willard, 65781-0517, SAN 376-2378. Tel: 417-742-4258. FAX: 417-742-4589. *Br Mgr,* Sarah Francka-Jones; E-mail: sarahf@thelibrary.org; Staff 4 (MLS 1, Non-MLS 3)
Circ 102,350
Function: Online searches, Photocopying/Printing, Prog for adults, Prog for children & young adult, Ref serv available, Summer reading prog
Open Mon-Thurs 9:30-7, Fri & Sat 9:30-6
Friends of the Library Group
Bookmobiles: 1. Outreach Services Mgr, Allison Eckhardt. Bk vols 3,800

S SPRINGFIELD NEWS-LEADER LIBRARY*, 651 Boonville, 65806. SAN 373-465X. Tel: 417-836-1215. FAX: 417-837-1381. Web Site: www.news-leader.com. *Librn,* Gale Doubledee; Staff 1 (MLS 1)
Library Holdings: Bk Titles 280; Bk Vols 300; Per Subs 50
Restriction: Not open to pub

STANBERRY

P GENTRY COUNTY LIBRARY*, 304 N Park, 64489. SAN 309-2402. Tel: 660-783-2335. FAX: 660-783-2335. Web Site: www.gentrycountylibrary.org. *Dir,* Judy Garrett; *Asst Dir,* Lana Smith; Staff 5 (MLS 2, Non-MLS 3)
Founded 1955. Pop 6,488; Circ 74,290
Library Holdings: CDs 19; Large Print Bks 37; Bk Titles 53,731; Bk Vols 54,121; Per Subs 70; Talking Bks 431; Videos 1,581
Subject Interests: Genealogy, Mo
Database Vendor: EBSCOhost
Open Tues, Thurs & Fri 8-5, Wed 8-7, Sat 9-12
Friends of the Library Group
Bookmobiles: 1

STEELE

P STEELE PUBLIC LIBRARY*, 108 E Main St, 63877-1528. SAN 309-2410. Tel: 573-695-3561. FAX: 573-695-3021. *Dir,* Myrna McKay; Staff 3 (MLS 1, Non-MLS 2)
Founded 1937. Pop 2,419; Circ 10,426
Library Holdings: Bk Titles 15,678; Bk Vols 16,323; Per Subs 22; Talking Bks 237; Videos 562
Partic in Missouri Research & Education Network (MOREnet)
Open Mon-Fri 12:30-4:30
Friends of the Library Group

SULLIVAN

P SULLIVAN PUBLIC LIBRARY*, 104 W Vine St, 63080. SAN 329-1057. Tel: 573-468-4372. FAX: 573-860-4648. Web Site: www.sullivan.lib.mo.us. *Dir,* Mark Smith; Staff 2 (MLS 1, Non-MLS 1)
Founded 1948. Pop 6,351
Library Holdings: Large Print Bks 500; Bk Titles 12,900; Bk Vols 13,000; Per Subs 50; Talking Bks 673
Automation Activity & Vendor Info: (Cataloging) OCLC; (Circulation) TLC (The Library Corporation); (ILL) OCLC; (OPAC) TLC (The Library Corporation)
Database Vendor: EBSCOhost, Gale Cengage Learning, Newsbank, TLC (The Library Corporation)
Open Mon & Fri 9-5, Tues & Thurs 9-6, Wed 9-7, Sat 9-1

SWEET SPRINGS

P SWEET SPRINGS PUBLIC LIBRARY, 217 Turner St, 65351. SAN 309-2429. Tel: 660-335-4314. E-mail: sweetspringslibrary@hotmail.com. *Librn,* Janet L Scott; *Asst Librn,* Jennie Aiken; Staff 2 (Non-MLS 2)
Founded 1939. Pop 1,596
Library Holdings: Bk Titles 13,465; Bk Vols 13,475; Per Subs 12
Special Collections: Books on Missouri Coll
Database Vendor: EBSCOhost, OCLC FirstSearch
Wireless access
Function: ILL available, Photocopying/Printing
Open Tues & Fri 12-5, Thurs 12-7, Sat 9-12
Friends of the Library Group

TIPTON

P PRICE JAMES MEMORIAL LIBRARY*, 104 E Morgan, 65081. (Mail add: PO Box 187, 65081-0187), SAN 309-2445. Tel: 660-433-5622. *Dir,* Linda Schuster; Staff 1 (MLS 1)
Pop 6,623; Circ 20,000
Library Holdings: Large Print Bks 3,000; Bk Titles 15,000; Talking Bks 203; Videos 125
Subject Interests: Classics, Fiction, Humanities, Juv, Relig studies, Sci
Automation Activity & Vendor Info: (Cataloging) Follett Software; (Circulation) Follett Software
Open Mon, Wed, Fri 10-5, Tues 4-8, Sat 9-12

TRENTON

P GRUNDY COUNTY-JEWETT NORRIS LIBRARY*, 1331 Main St, 64683. SAN 309-2453. Tel: 660-359-3577. FAX: 660-359-6220. Web Site: grundycountylibrary.org. *Dir,* Theresa Hunsaker; E-mail: theresa@grundycountylibrary.org; *Acq, Asst Dir,* Doris Baker; E-mail: doris@grundycountylibrary.org; *Librn,* Dylan Boyle; E-mail: dylan@grundycountylibrary.org; *Ch Serv,* Charity Halstead; E-mail: charity@grundycountylibrary.org
Founded 1890. Pop 10,500; Circ 36,000
Library Holdings: Bk Titles 31,252; Per Subs 53
Subject Interests: Genealogy
Automation Activity & Vendor Info: (Acquisitions) Follett Software; (Cataloging) Follett Software; (Circulation) Follett Software
Database Vendor: EBSCOhost, Gale Cengage Learning, OCLC FirstSearch, ProQuest
Wireless access

Function: Bks on cassette, Bks on CD, CD-ROM, Children's prog, Computer training, Computers for patron use, Copy machines, e-mail & chat, Fax serv, Free DVD rentals, Genealogy discussion group, Handicapped accessible, ILL available, Instruction & testing, Magnifiers for reading, Newsp ref libr, Online searches, Outreach serv, Photocopying/Printing, Preschool outreach, Printer for laptops & handheld devices, Prog for children & young adult, Provide serv for the mentally ill, Pub access computers, Referrals accepted, Scanner, Senior computer classes, Story hour, Summer reading prog, Tax forms, Teen prog, Wheelchair accessible
Open Mon 8:30-7, Tues-Fri 8:30-5, Sat 8:30-12
Friends of the Library Group

J NORTH CENTRAL MISSOURI COLLEGE LIBRARY, Geyer Hall, Second & Third Flr, 1301 Main St, 64683. SAN 309-2461. Tel: 660-359-3948, Ext 1322, 660-359-3948, Ext 1325, 660-359-3948, Ext 1335, 660-359-3948, Ext 322. FAX: 660-359-2211. Web Site: www.ncmissouri.edu. *Librn,* Beth Ann Caldarello; E-mail: bcaldarello@mail.ncmissouri.edu; Staff 4 (MLS 2, Non-MLS 2)
Founded 1967
Library Holdings: Bk Titles 21,306; Bk Vols 30,000; Per Subs 131; Videos 205
Special Collections: State Document Depository
Automation Activity & Vendor Info: (Acquisitions) Innovative Interfaces, Inc; (Cataloging) Innovative Interfaces, Inc; (Circulation) Innovative Interfaces, Inc; (OPAC) Innovative Interfaces, Inc
Wireless access
Partic in Amigos Library Services, Inc; MOBIUS (Missouri Bibliographic Information User System)
Open Mon-Wed 7:30am-9pm, Thurs 7:30-6, Fri 7:30-4:30
Restriction: Badge access after hrs, Borrowing privileges limited to anthropology fac & libr staff, Borrowing privileges limited to fac & registered students, Borrowing requests are handled by ILL, By permission only, Circ limited, Circ privileges for students & alumni only, Circ to mem only

TROY

P POWELL MEMORIAL LIBRARY*, 951 W College, 63379. SAN 309-247X. Tel: 636-528-7853. *Librn,* Sharon Hasekamp
Founded 1949. Pop 12,000; Circ 45,000
Library Holdings: AV Mats 50; Large Print Bks 100; Bk Titles 30,000; Per Subs 10; Talking Bks 250
Special Collections: Missouri Genealogical Coll. Oral History
Subject Interests: Local hist
Automation Activity & Vendor Info: (Cataloging) Follett Software; (Circulation) Follett Software; (OPAC) Follett Software
Wireless access
Open Mon & Tues 8:30-7, Wed-Fri 8:30-4, Sat 8:30-12:30
Restriction: Residents only

UNION

J EAST CENTRAL COLLEGE LIBRARY*, 1964 Prairie Dell Rd, 63084-4344. SAN 309-2488. Tel: 636-584-6560. FAX: 636-583-1897. E-mail: library@eastcentral.edu. Web Site: www.eastcentral.edu/library. *Dir, Libr Serv,* Lisa Farrell; E-mail: lmfarrell@eastcentral.edu; *Assoc Dir, Libr Serv,* Sheila Driemeyer; E-mail: sadrieme@eastcentral.edu; Staff 2 (MLS 2)
Founded 1969. Enrl 2,700; Fac 190; Highest Degree: Associate
Library Holdings: AV Mats 2,100; Bks on Deafness & Sign Lang 14; CDs 421; DVDs 1,500; e-books 10,232; Bk Vols 20,000; Per Subs 175; Talking Bks 316
Special Collections: Abraham Lincoln (John E Baker, Jr Memorial Coll); Harrison Eaton Children's Coll
Automation Activity & Vendor Info: (Cataloging) Innovative Interfaces, Inc; (Circulation) Innovative Interfaces, Inc; (Course Reserve) Innovative Interfaces, Inc; (ILL) OCLC; (OPAC) Innovative Interfaces, Inc; (Serials) Innovative Interfaces, Inc
Database Vendor: Alexander Street Press, ARTstor, CQ Press, CredoReference, EBSCOhost, Facts on File, Gale Cengage Learning, LearningExpress, Newsbank
Wireless access
Partic in Amigos Library Services, Inc; Missouri Research & Education Network (MOREnet); MOBIUS (Missouri Bibliographic Information User System); Saint Louis Regional Library Network
Open Mon-Thurs 7:30am-7:30pm, Fri 7:30-2
Friends of the Library Group

R FIRST BAPTIST CHURCH LIBRARY*, 801 E Hwy 50, 63084. SAN 309-2496. Tel: 636-583-2386. FAX: 636-583-4281. Web Site: www.fbcunion.org. *Adminr,* Kristi Neace; Staff 1 (Non-MLS 1)
Library Holdings: Bk Titles 4,200; Bk Vols 4,314; Per Subs 20
Open Mon-Thurs 9-4

P SCENIC REGIONAL LIBRARY OF FRANKLIN, GASCONADE & WARREN COUNTIES*, Union Service Center, 308 Hawthorne Dr, 63084. SAN 349-8395. Tel: 636-583-3224. Web Site: www.scenicregional.org. *Libr Dir,* Kenneth J Rohrbach; *Asst Dir,* Vivienne Beckett; *Ch,* Christy Schink; *Ref Librn,* Carolyn Scheer; *Br Coordr,* Chris Brown; Staff 28.7 (MLS 5, Non-MLS 23.7)
Founded 1959. Pop 116,117; Circ 536,742
Jan 2009-Dec 2009 Income $2,315,056. Mats Exp $452,204, Books $233,833, Per/Ser (Incl. Access Fees) $15,800, AV Mat $71,548, Electronic Ref Mat (Incl. Access Fees) $69,291. Sal $809,819 (Prof $289,550)
Library Holdings: Audiobooks 5,746; CDs 7,476; DVDs 2,675; Large Print Bks 6,595; Bk Vols 245,509; Per Subs 464; Videos 3,583
Database Vendor: ALLDATA Online, Discovery Education, Gale Cengage Learning, Newsbank, OCLC FirstSearch, OCLC WebJunction, OCLC WorldShare Interlibrary Loan, Overdrive, Inc, ProQuest, ReferenceUSA, ValueLine
Wireless access
Function: Adult bk club, Art exhibits, Audio & video playback equip for onsite use, AV serv, Copy machines, e-mail serv, Electronic databases & coll, Handicapped accessible, Health sci info serv, Home delivery & serv to Sr ctr & nursing homes, ILL available, Magnifiers for reading, Mail & tel request accepted, Mail loans to mem, Music CDs, Newsp ref libr, Online ref, Online searches, Photocopying/Printing, Preschool outreach, Prog for adults, Prog for children & young adult, Ref & res, Ref serv available, Spoken cassettes & CDs, Spoken cassettes & DVDs, Summer reading prog, Tax forms, Telephone ref, VCDs, VHS videos, Video lending libr, Wheelchair accessible
Partic in Saint Louis Regional Library Network
Open Mon, Tues, Thurs & Fri 8-6, Wed 8-8, Sat 9-3
Branches: 6
HERMANN BRANCH, 601 Market St, Hermann, 65041, SAN 349-8425. Tel: 573-486-2024. *Br Supvr,* Sheri Hausman
Circ 36,130
Library Holdings: Audiobooks 904; CDs 883; DVDs 258; Large Print Bks 888; Bk Vols 28,347; Per Subs 41; Videos 414
Special Collections: City Newspapers, micro; City Records, micro; County Census Records, micro
Database Vendor: EBSCOhost
Open Tues, Thurs & Fri 9-6, Wed 11-8, Sat 9-3
NEW HAVEN BRANCH, 901 Maupin, New Haven, 63068, SAN 349-845X. Tel: 573-237-2189. *Br Supvr,* Judy Brock
Circ 16,023
Library Holdings: Audiobooks 385; CDs 634; DVDs 180; Large Print Bks 446; Bk Vols 15,410; Per Subs 42; Videos 380
Database Vendor: infoUSA, World Book Online
Function: e-mail serv, Handicapped accessible, ILL available, Mail & tel request accepted, Online ref, Online searches, Photocopying/Printing, Ref serv available, Spoken cassettes & CDs, Spoken cassettes & DVDs, Summer reading prog, Tax forms, Telephone ref, VHS videos, Video lending libr
Open Tues, Thurs & Fri 8:30-12:30 & 1-5:30, Wed 8:30-12:30 & 1-7, Sat 8:30-1
OWENSVILLE BRANCH, 107 N First St, Owensville, 65066, SAN 349-8484. Tel: 573-437-2188. *Br Supvr,* Linda G Little
Circ 27,567
Library Holdings: Audiobooks 631; CDs 867; DVDs 211; Large Print Bks 684; Bk Vols 21,278; Per Subs 40; Videos 393
Database Vendor: infoUSA, World Book Online
Function: AV serv, Copy machines, Digital talking bks, e-mail serv, Electronic databases & coll, Handicapped accessible, ILL available, Music CDs, Online ref, Online searches, Photocopying/Printing, Ref & res, Ref serv available, Spoken cassettes & CDs, Spoken cassettes & DVDs, Summer reading prog, Tax forms, Telephone ref, VCDs, VHS videos, Video lending libr, Wheelchair accessible
Open Tues, Thurs & Fri 8:30-12:30 & 1-5:30, Wed 8:30-12:30 & 1-7, Sat 8:30-1
Friends of the Library Group
PACIFIC BRANCH, 119 W Saint Louis St, Pacific, 63069, SAN 349-8514. Tel: 636-257-2712. *Br Supvr,* Georgia Mofield
Circ 54,454
Library Holdings: Audiobooks 505; CDs 999; DVDs 318; Large Print Bks 811; Bk Vols 22,665; Per Subs 40; Videos 421
Database Vendor: infoUSA, World Book Online
Function: AV serv, Copy machines, Digital talking bks, e-mail serv, Electronic databases & coll, Handicapped accessible, ILL available, Music CDs, Online ref, Online searches, Photocopying/Printing, Prog for children & young adult, Ref & res, Ref serv available, Spoken cassettes & CDs, Spoken cassettes & DVDs, Summer reading prog, Tax forms, Telephone ref, VCDs, VHS videos, Video lending libr, Wheelchair accessible
Open Tues, Thurs & Fri 9-6, Wed 9-8, Sat 9-3
SAINT CLAIR BRANCH, 570 S Main St, Saint Clair, 63077, SAN 349-8549. Tel: 636-629-2546. *Br Supvr,* Karen Fogelbach
Circ 37,477

Library Holdings: Audiobooks 619; CDs 741; DVDs 204; Large Print Bks 756; Bk Vols 23,153; Per Subs 32; Videos 503
Database Vendor: infoUSA, World Book Online
Function: Copy machines, Digital talking bks, e-mail serv, E-Reserves, Electronic databases & coll, Handicapped accessible, ILL available, Music CDs, Online ref, Online searches, Photocopying/Printing, Prog for children & young adult, Ref & res, Ref serv available, Spoken cassettes & CDs, Spoken cassettes & DVDs, Summer reading prog, Tax forms, Telephone ref, VCDs, VHS videos, Video lending libr, Wheelchair accessible
Open Tues, Thurs & Fri 8:30-12:30 & 1-5:30, Wed 8:30-12:30 & 1-7, Sat 9-1:30

WARREN COUNTY, 912 S Hwy 47, Warrenton, 63383-2600, SAN 349-8603. Tel: 636-456-3321. *Br Supvr,* Marlys Mertens
Circ 116,705
Library Holdings: Audiobooks 1,007; CDs 1,325; DVDs 529; Large Print Bks 1,140; Bk Vols 41,413; Per Subs 43; Videos 684
Special Collections: Census records & area newspapers, micro
Database Vendor: EBSCOhost, infoUSA, World Book Online
Function: Audio & video playback equip for onsite use, AV serv, Copy machines, Digital talking bks, e-mail serv, Electronic databases & coll, Handicapped accessible, Home delivery & serv to Sr ctr & nursing homes, ILL available, Music CDs, Newsp ref libr, Online ref, Online searches, Photocopying/Printing, Prog for children & young adult, Ref & res, Ref serv available, Spoken cassettes & CDs, Spoken cassettes & DVDs, Summer reading prog, Tax forms, Telephone ref, VCDs, VHS videos, Video lending libr, Wheelchair accessible
Open Mon, Thurs & Fri 9-6, Tues & Wed 9-8, Sat 9-3

Bookmobiles: 1. Clerk, Connie Vest. Bk vols 11,236

UNIONVILLE

P PUTNAM COUNTY PUBLIC LIBRARY, 115 S 16th St, 63565-1624. SAN 309-250X. Tel: 660-947-3192. FAX: 660-947-7039. E-mail: pclib@yahoo.com. Web Site: putnamcl.lib.mo.us. *Dir,* Leatha Walsh; Staff 4 (Non-MLS 4)
Founded 1946. Pop 5,223; Circ 50,375
Jan 2011-Dec 2011 Income $124,561, State $12,053, County $98,801, Locally Generated Income $12,407, Other $1,300. Mats Exp $28,136, Books $18,040, Per/Ser (Incl. Access Fees) $1,500, AV Equip $5,796, AV Mat $2,000, Electronic Ref Mat (Incl. Access Fees) $800. Sal $49,491 (Prof $21,638)
Library Holdings: Audiobooks 687; AV Mats 8; CDs 82; DVDs 1,774; Electronic Media & Resources 16; Large Print Bks 777; Microforms 135; Bk Titles 33,998; Bk Vols 34,125; Per Subs 74; Videos 564
Subject Interests: Genealogy of Putnam County, Local hist
Automation Activity & Vendor Info: (Cataloging) Book Systems; (Circulation) Book Systems; (OPAC) Book Systems
Database Vendor: EBSCOhost, ProQuest
Wireless access
Publications: Atlas of Putnam County, 1877 & 1897
Partic in Midwest Collaborative for Library Services (MCLS); Missouri Research & Education Network (MOREnet); OCLC Online Computer Library Center, Inc
Special Services for the Blind - Aids for in-house use; Assistive/Adapted tech devices, equip & products; Audio mat; Bks on cassette; Bks on CD; Copier with enlargement capabilities; Extensive large print coll; Large print bks; Lending of low vision aids; Low vision equip; Magnifiers; Playaways (bks on MP3)
Open Mon 9-7, Tues-Fri 9-5, Sat 9-12
Friends of the Library Group

UNITY VILLAGE

R UNITY LIBRARY & ARCHIVES*, 1901 NW Blue Pkwy, 64065-0001. SAN 309-2518. Tel: 816-251-3503, 816-524-3550, Ext 2370. E-mail: librarycontact@unityonline.org. Web Site: www.unity.org/library. *Dir, Libr & Archives,* Linda M Bray; Tel: 816-524-3550, Ext 2010, E-mail: braylm@unityonline.org; *Acq, Circ,* Judy Cournyea; *Archivist,* Eric Page; Tel: 816-524-3550, Ext 2021, E-mail: archivescontact@unityonline.org; *Cataloger, ILL,* Margaret Hiltbrunn; E-mail: hiltbrunnmm@unityonline.org; Staff 2 (MLS 1, Non-MLS 1)
Founded 1942
Library Holdings: Audiobooks 730; AV Mats 2,000; CDs 1,030; DVDs 700; Bk Titles 38,500; Per Subs 160; Videos 1,684
Special Collections: Unity Archives from 1889, AV, bks, per
Subject Interests: Relig studies
Automation Activity & Vendor Info: (Cataloging) SirsiDynix; (Circulation) SirsiDynix; (Course Reserve) SirsiDynix; (ILL) SirsiDynix; (OPAC) SirsiDynix; (Serials) SirsiDynix
Database Vendor: OCLC ArticleFirst, OCLC FirstSearch, OCLC WorldShare Interlibrary Loan, SirsiDynix
Wireless access
Function: Archival coll, AV serv, Bks on CD, Copy machines, Distance learning, e-mail serv, Exhibits, For res purposes, ILL available, Online cat, Ref & res, Ref serv available, Res libr, Telephone ref, VHS videos
Partic in Kansas City Library Service Program; Mid-America Library Alliance/Kansas City Metropolitan Library & Information Network
Open Mon 7:30-7, Tues-Thurs 7:30-5
Restriction: Open to employees & special libr, Open to pub for ref & circ; with some limitations, Open to students, fac & staff

UNIVERSITY CITY

P UNIVERSITY CITY PUBLIC LIBRARY*, 6701 Delmar Blvd, 63130. SAN 309-2534. Tel: 314-727-3150. FAX: 314-727-6005. E-mail: reference@ucpl.lib.mo.us. Web Site: www.ucpl.lib.mo.us. *Dir,* Patrick Wall; E-mail: pjwall@ucpl.lib.mo.us; *Dir, Tech Serv,* Sally Master; E-mail: smaster@ucpl.lib.mo.us; *Head, Youth Serv,* Marilyn Phillips; E-mail: mphillips@ucpl.lib.mo.us; *Ref Librn,* Annie Fuller; E-mail: afuller@ucpl.lib.mo.us; *AV,* Michael Ludwig; E-mail: mludwig@ucpl.lib.mo.us; *Info Tech,* Christa Van Herreweghe; Staff 11 (MLS 8, Non-MLS 3)
Founded 1939. Pop 37,428; Circ 491,420
Jul 2008-Jun 2009 Income $1,749,927, State $32,501, City $1,466,812, Federal $30,301, Locally Generated Income $220,313. Mats Exp $247,000, Books $176,959, Per/Ser (Incl. Access Fees) $14,861, AV Mat $40,358, Electronic Ref Mat (Incl. Access Fees) $14,822. Sal $972,424 (Prof $331,401)
Library Holdings: Audiobooks 3,826; CDs 6,803; DVDs 5,718; e-books 6,850; Electronic Media & Resources 10; High Interest/Low Vocabulary Bk Vols 628; Large Print Bks 3,091; Music Scores 745; Bk Titles 186,441; Per Subs 250; Videos 3,375
Special Collections: Archive of Local History; Locally Produced Art Pottery & Artifacts, circa 1910
Automation Activity & Vendor Info: (Acquisitions) SirsiDynix; (Cataloging) SirsiDynix; (Circulation) SirsiDynix; (OPAC) SirsiDynix; (Serials) SirsiDynix
Database Vendor: Baker & Taylor, Booksite, BWI, Gale Cengage Learning, LearningExpress, Newsbank, OCLC WorldShare Interlibrary Loan, Plunkett Research, Ltd, SirsiDynix
Wireless access
Publications: Checkout (Newsletter)
Partic in Municipal Library Consortium
Open Mon-Fri 9-9, Sat 9-5, Sun 1-5
Friends of the Library Group

VALLEY PARK

P VALLEY PARK COMMUNITY LIBRARY*, 320 Benton St, 63088. SAN 309-2542. Tel: 636-225-5608. FAX: 636-825-0079. Web Site: www.valleyparklibrary.org. *Librn,* Bonnie Morris; *Asst Librn,* Pamela Kettler; Staff 2 (MLS 2)
Founded 1943. Pop 3,859; Circ 7,900
Library Holdings: Bk Titles 57; Bk Vols 89
Subject Interests: Local hist
Partic in Municipal Library Consortium
Open Mon, Wed, Fri 1-6, Tues, 10-6, Thurs 10-8, Sat 10-4

VAN BUREN

P CARTER COUNTY LIBRARY DISTRICT*, Van Buren Library, 403 Ash St, 63965. (Mail add: PO Box 309, 63965-0309), SAN 349-8638. Tel: 573-323-4315. FAX: 573-323-0188. E-mail: library_vb@yahoo.com. *Dir,* Jane Kowalski
Founded 1947. Pop 6,265; Circ 50,381
Jan 2011-Dec 2011 Income $110,000, State $3,000, County $107,000. Mats Exp $7,000. Sal $50,000 (Prof $10,000)
Library Holdings: Audiobooks 560; DVDs 354; Large Print Bks 600; Bk Titles 20,403
Special Collections: State Document Depository
Subject Interests: Children's folklore, Genealogy, Local hist
Automation Activity & Vendor Info: (Acquisitions) Autolib Library & Information Management Systems; (Cataloging) Autolib Library & Information Management Systems; (Circulation) Autolib Library & Information Management Systems
Database Vendor: Autolib Library & Information Management Systems
Wireless access
Partic in Missouri Research & Education Network (MOREnet); SE Mo Libr Network
Open Mon-Fri 9-5, Sat 9-12

Branches: 2

ELLSINORE BRANCH, PO Box 312, Ellsinore, 63937. Tel: 573-322-0015. *Librn,* Gloria Copeland; Staff 1 (Non-MLS 1)
Circ 500
Library Holdings: Bk Titles 1,200
Open Tues & Fri 9-5, Sat 9-12

GRANDIN BRANCH, PO Box 274, Grandin, 63943-0274, SAN 349-8816. Tel: 573-593-4084. *Librn,* John Grow; Staff 1 (Non-MLS 1)
Library Holdings: Bk Titles 1,000
Open Tues & Thurs 1-6

S NATIONAL PARK SERVICE*, Ozark National Scenic Riverways Reference Library, 404 Watercress Dr, 63965. (Mail add: PO Box 490, 63965-0490), SAN 309-2550. Tel: 573-323-4236. FAX: 573-323-4140. *In Charge,* Bryan Culpepper; Tel: 573-323-4236, Ext 4806; Staff 2 (Non-MLS 2)
Founded 1974
Library Holdings: Bk Titles 1,179; Bk Vols 1,211; Per Subs 14
Special Collections: Oral History
Subject Interests: Background studies associated with Riverways area, General natural, Hist data relative to Ozark area
Function: Res libr
Open Mon-Fri 8-4:30

VERSAILLES

P MORGAN COUNTY LIBRARY*, 600 N Hunter, 65084-1830. SAN 309-2569. Tel: 573-378-5319. FAX: 573-378-6166. E-mail: mocolibrary@hotmail.com. *Dir,* Nita Loganbill; Staff 4 (Non-MLS 4)
Founded 1946. Pop 22,000; Circ 87,808
Library Holdings: Bks on Deafness & Sign Lang 15; CDs 1,878; DVDs 7,147; Electronic Media & Resources 226; Bk Vols 36,500; Per Subs 89; Talking Bks 2,890; Videos 7,147
Subject Interests: Genealogy, Local hist
Automation Activity & Vendor Info: (Cataloging) Follett Software; (Circulation) Follett Software
Wireless access
Partic in Missouri Research & Education Network (MOREnet)
Open Tues-Fri 9-5:30, Sat 9-1
Friends of the Library Group

WARRENSBURG

S JOHNSON COUNTY HISTORICAL SOCIETY*, Mary Miller Smiser Heritage Library, 302 N Main St, 64093. SAN 328-0195. Tel: 660-747-6480. *Curator,* Lisa Earl; Staff 2 (MLS 1, Non-MLS 1)
Founded 1969
Library Holdings: Bk Titles 2,110; Bk Vols 2,340; Per Subs 11
Special Collections: Johnson County; Local History, Newsp. Oral History
Open Mon-Fri 1-4

P TRAILS REGIONAL LIBRARY*, 432 N Holden St, 64093. SAN 349-9170. Tel: 660-747-1699. Circulation Tel: 660-747-9177. FAX: 660-747-5774. Web Site: www.trailslibrary.org. *Dir,* Karen Hicklin; E-mail: hicklink@trailslibrary.org; *Asst Dir, Ch Serv,* Anita Love; E-mail: lovea@trailslibrary.org; *Asst Dir, Fac & Tech,* Bill Thoms; E-mail: thomsb@trailslibrary.org; *Asst Dir, Human Res & Prog,* Position Currently Open; *Head, Tech Serv,* Kathy Cox; E-mail: coxk@trailslibrary.org; *Coll Develop Spec,* Position Currently Open; Staff 41 (MLS 4, Non-MLS 37)
Founded 1957. Pop 81,482; Circ 390,653
Jul 2012-Jun 2013 Income (Main Library and Branch(s)) $2,625,275. Mats Exp $246,421, Books $143,625, Per/Ser (Incl. Access Fees) $14,027, AV Mat $26,359, Electronic Ref Mat (Incl. Access Fees) $29,848. Sal $1,743,106
Library Holdings: Audiobooks 2; CDs 4,067; DVDs 4,482; e-books 13,732; Bk Vols 141,000; Videos 3
Automation Activity & Vendor Info: (ILL) OCLC
Database Vendor: EBSCO Auto Repair Reference, EBSCOhost, Gale Cengage Learning, LearningExpress, Overdrive, Inc, World Book Online
Wireless access
Partic in Mid-America Library Alliance/Kansas City Metropolitan Library & Information Network
Friends of the Library Group
Branches: 9
CONCORDIA BRANCH, 813 S Main, Concordia, 64020, SAN 349-9200. Tel: 660-463-2277. *Br Mgr,* Debra Kirchhoff; E-mail: kirchhoffd@trailslibrary.org
Open Mon-Fri 9:30-5:30, Sat 9:30-4:30
Friends of the Library Group
CORDER BRANCH, 221 N Lafayette, Corder, 64021, SAN 349-9235. Tel: 660-394-2565. *Br Mgr,* Linda Markworth; E-mail: markworthl@trailslibrary.org
Open Mon, Wed & Fri 9-5, Sat 9-3
HOLDEN BRANCH, 207 S Main St, Holden, 64040, SAN 308-9991. Tel: 816-732-4545. *Br Mgr,* Jeannae Dickerson; E-mail: dickersonj@trailslibrary.org; Staff 1 (MLS 1)
Founded 1941. Pop 2,389; Circ 10,901
Library Holdings: CDs 51; Large Print Bks 88; Bk Titles 18,941; Bk Vols 19,802; Per Subs 35; Talking Bks 80; Videos 112
Open Mon, Wed & Fri 9-5, Tues & Thurs 9-7, Sat 9-4
Friends of the Library Group
KNOB NOSTER BRANCH, 202 N Adams, Knob Noster, 65336, SAN 349-926X. Tel: 660-563-2997. FAX: 660-563-2997. *Br Mgr,* Julie Dolph; E-mail: dolphj@trailslibrary.org
Open Mon-Fri 9:30-5:30, Sat 9:30-4:30
LEETON EXPRESS BRANCH, 500 N Main St, Leeton, 64761. Tel: 660-653-2301, Ext 125, 660-653-4731. *Br Mgr,* Cherie Tibbetts; E-mail: tibbetts@leeton.k12.mo.us
Library Holdings: AV Mats 500; Bk Vols 14,000; Per Subs 35
Automation Activity & Vendor Info: (Cataloging) Follett Software; (Circulation) Follett Software; (OPAC) Follett Software
Open Tues-Thurs 3:30-7, Sat 9-Noon
LEXINGTON BRANCH, 1008 Main St, Lexington, 64067, SAN 349-9294. Tel: 660-259-3071. FAX: 660-259-3071. *Br Mgr,* Carol Nolte; E-mail: noltec@trailslibrary.org
Open Mon-Thurs 8:30-7, Fri & Sat 8:30-5
Friends of the Library Group
ODESSA BRANCH, 204 S First, Odessa, 64076, SAN 349-9324. Tel: 816-633-4089. *Br Mgr,* Linda Washam; E-mail: washaml@trailslibrary.org
Open Mon-Thurs 9-7, Fri & Sat 9-5
Friends of the Library Group
WARRENSBURG BRANCH, 432 N Holden, 64093, SAN 349-9359. Tel: 660-747-9177. FAX: 660-747-7928. *Br Mgr,* Mary Barnhart; E-mail: barnhartm@trailslibrary.org
Open Mon-Thurs 8-7, Fri 8-5:30, Sat 8-5
Friends of the Library Group
WAVERLY BRANCH, 203 E Kelling, Waverly, 64096, SAN 349-9383. Tel: 660-493-2987. *Br Mgr,* Amy Boland; E-mail: bolanda@trailslibrary.org
Open Mon, Wed & Fri 9-5, Sat 9-3

C UNIVERSITY OF CENTRAL MISSOURI*, James C Kirkpatrick Library, 601 S Missouri, 64093. SAN 349-9111. Tel: 660-543-4140. Circulation Tel: 660-543-4283. Interlibrary Loan Service Tel: 660-543-4508. Reference Tel: 660-543-4154. FAX: 660-543-4144. Interlibrary Loan Service FAX: 660-543-8001. TDD: 660-543-4756. Web Site: library.ucmo.edu. *Dean, Libr Serv,* Mollie Dinwiddie; E-mail: dinwiddie@ucmo.edu; *Chair,* Linda Medaris; Tel: 660-543-8844, E-mail: medaris@ucmo.edu; Staff 41 (MLS 16, Non-MLS 25)
Founded 1871. Enrl 11,063; Fac 437; Highest Degree: Master
Library Holdings: Bk Titles 635,607; Bk Vols 960,813; Per Subs 783; Talking Bks 7,205; Videos 13,564
Special Collections: Civil War (Personal Narratives & Unit Histories), bks, flm; Geography (Missouri & International Speleology); Literature (Izaac Walton's Compleat Angler); Missouri Coll; Research Coll in Children's Literature. State Document Depository; US Document Depository
Automation Activity & Vendor Info: (Acquisitions) Innovative Interfaces, Inc - Millenium; (Cataloging) Innovative Interfaces, Inc - Millenium; (Circulation) Innovative Interfaces, Inc - Millenium; (Course Reserve) Innovative Interfaces, Inc - Millenium; (ILL) OCLC ILLiad; (Media Booking) Innovative Interfaces, Inc - Millenium; (OPAC) Innovative Interfaces, Inc - Millenium; (Serials) Innovative Interfaces, Inc - Millenium
Wireless access
Publications: Info One (Newsletter)
Partic in Amigos Library Services, Inc; Mid-America Library Alliance/Kansas City Metropolitan Library & Information Network; MOBIUS (Missouri Bibliographic Information User System); OCLC Online Computer Library Center, Inc
Open Mon-Thurs 7:30am-Midnight, Fri 7:30-6, Sat 10-6, Sun 1-Midnight

WARRENTON

S WARREN COUNTY HISTORICAL SOCIETY*, Museum & Historical Library, 102 W Walton St, 63383-1918. SAN 373-4668. Tel: 636-456-3820. *Mgr,* William Frick
Founded 1982
Library Holdings: Bk Vols 240
Special Collections: Central Wesleyen College
Subject Interests: Local hist

WASHINGTON

P WASHINGTON PUBLIC LIBRARY, 410 Lafayette St, 63090. SAN 309-2577. Tel: 636-390-1070. FAX: 636-239-1744. Web Site: www.washmolib.org. *Dir,* Jackie Hawes; Tel: 636-390-1071, E-mail: jhawes@ci.washington.mo.us; Staff 3 (MLS 1, Non-MLS 2)
Founded 1924. Pop 8,713; Circ 154,000
Oct 2010-Sept 2011 Income $378,981, State $7,905, Locally Generated Income $298,058, Other $73,018. Mats Exp $47,305, Books $38,611, Per/Ser (Incl. Access Fees) $4,917, AV Mat $3,777. Sal $192,450 (Prof $53,040)
Library Holdings: Audiobooks 1,630; CDs 276; DVDs 1,479; Electronic Media & Resources 13; Large Print Bks 8,082; Bk Vols 43,389; Per Subs 125

Automation Activity & Vendor Info: (Cataloging) OCLC CatExpress; (ILL) OCLC Connexion
Database Vendor: EBSCOhost, Gale Cengage Learning, LearningExpress, OCLC WebJunction, OCLC WorldShare Interlibrary Loan
Wireless access
Function: Adult bk club, Art exhibits, Bk club(s), Bks on CD, Chess club, Children's prog, Computer training, Computers for patron use, Copy machines, Electronic databases & coll, Fax serv, Free DVD rentals, Handicapped accessible, ILL available, Magnifiers for reading, Music CDs, Notary serv, Online cat, Online searches, Passport agency, Photocopying/Printing, Preschool reading prog, Printer for laptops & handheld devices, Prog for adults, Prog for children & young adult, Pub access computers, Ref serv in person, Senior computer classes, Spanish lang bks, Story hour, Summer reading prog, Tax forms, Teen prog, Video lending libr, Web-catalog, Wheelchair accessible
Partic in Amigos Library Services, Inc; Mid-America Library Alliance/Kansas City Metropolitan Library & Information Network; Missouri Evergreen; Saint Louis Regional Library Network
Open Mon-Thurs 8-8, Fri 8-6, Sat 9-5, Sun Noon-4
Restriction: ID required to use computers (Ltd hrs), Non-resident fee, Residents only
Friends of the Library Group

WEBB CITY

P WEBB CITY PUBLIC LIBRARY*, 101 S Liberty, 64870. SAN 309-2585. Tel: 417-673-4326. FAX: 417-673-5703. Web Site: www.webbcitylibrary.com. *Librn,* Sue Oliveira; Staff 3 (MLS 1, Non-MLS 2)
Founded 1913. Pop 9,822; Circ 33,628
Library Holdings: Bk Titles 27,651; Bk Vols 28,000; Per Subs 91; Talking Bks 491; Videos 452
Subject Interests: Genealogy, Local hist
Automation Activity & Vendor Info: (Cataloging) Inlex; (Circulation) Inlex
Database Vendor: SirsiDynix
Publications: The Miner (Quarterly)
Open Mon, Tues & Thurs 9-8, Wed, Fri & Sat 9-5
Friends of the Library Group

WEBSTER GROVES

P WEBSTER GROVES PUBLIC LIBRARY, 301 E Lockwood Ave, 63119-3102. SAN 309-2593. Tel: 314-961-3784. Reference Tel: 314-961-7277. FAX: 314-961-4233. E-mail: reference@wgpl.org. Web Site: www.wgpl.org. *Dir,* Tom Cooper; E-mail: tcooper@wgpl.org; *Ch Serv,* Michelle Haffer; Tel: 314-961-7262, E-mail: mhaffer@wgpl.org; Staff 10 (MLS 2, Non-MLS 8)
Founded 1928. Pop 23,230; Circ 335,776
Library Holdings: Bk Titles 68,363; Bk Vols 69,406; Per Subs 152; Talking Bks 6,529; Videos 2,900
Subject Interests: Local hist
Automation Activity & Vendor Info: (Cataloging) SirsiDynix; (Circulation) SirsiDynix
Database Vendor: EBSCO Information Services, Facts on File, Gale Cengage Learning, Newsbank, Plunkett Research, Ltd
Wireless access
Publications: Page 61 (Newsletter)
Open Mon-Thurs 9-9, Fri & Sat 9-4:30, Sun 2-5
Friends of the Library Group

WELLSVILLE

P WELLSVILLE PUBLIC LIBRARY*, 108 W Hudson St, 63384. SAN 309-2607. Tel: 573-684-6151. FAX: 573-684-6151. E-mail: wellsvillelibrary@gmail.com. Web Site: wellsvillelibrary.lib.mo.us. *Librn,* Margaret Harrelson; Staff 1 (MLS 1)
Founded 1944. Pop 1,216; Circ 4,434
Apr 2010-Mar 2011 Income $24,758. Mats Exp $2,344. Sal $14,112
Library Holdings: Audiobooks 45; DVDs 50; Bk Titles 12,716; Per Subs 2; Videos 330
Function: Adult bk club, Bks on CD, Computers for patron use, Copy machines, Fax serv, Free DVD rentals, ILL available, Photocopying/Printing, Pub access computers, Ref serv available, Summer reading prog, Tax forms, Telephone ref, VHS videos
Open Mon-Wed 12-5:30, Fri 10-5
Friends of the Library Group

WEST PLAINS

C MISSOURI STATE UNIVERSITY-WEST PLAINS*, Garnett Library, 304 W Trish Knight St, 65775. SAN 376-2300. Tel: 417-255-7945. Administration Tel: 417-255-7949. FAX: 417-255-7944. *Dir of Libr Serv,* Sylvia Kuhlmeier; E-mail: sylviakuhlmeier@missouristate.edu; *Ref/Cat Librn,* Rose Scarlet; Tel: 417-255-7948, E-mail: rosescarlet@missouristate.edu; *Asst Librn,* Neva Parrott; Tel: 417-255-7947, E-mail: nevaparrott@missouristate.edu; *Circ/Shelving Supvr,* Sophia Skinner; E-mail: sophiaskinner@missouristate.edu; Staff 4 (MLS 3, Non-MLS 1)
Founded 1963. Enrl 2,142; Fac 135; Highest Degree: Associate
Library Holdings: Bk Vols 42,000; Per Subs 155
Special Collections: Local History Audiocassette Coll
Subject Interests: Gen, Nursing, Rare bks
Automation Activity & Vendor Info: (Acquisitions) Baker & Taylor; (Cataloging) OCLC Connexion; (Circulation) Innovative Interfaces, Inc - Millenium; (Course Reserve) Innovative Interfaces, Inc - Millenium; (ILL) Innovative Interfaces, Inc - Millenium; (Media Booking) Innovative Interfaces, Inc - Millenium; (OPAC) Innovative Interfaces, Inc - Millenium; (Serials) EBSCO Online
Database Vendor: ABC-CLIO, CQ Press, Emerald, H W Wilson, Ingenta, JSTOR, McGraw-Hill, Newsbank, OCLC WorldShare Interlibrary Loan, Oxford Online, ScienceDirect, Standard & Poor's
Wireless access
Publications: Footnotes (Newsletter)
Open Mon-Thurs 8am-10pm, Fri 8-6, Sat 1-5, Sun 1-9
Friends of the Library Group

P WEST PLAINS PUBLIC LIBRARY*, 750 W Broadway, 65775-2369. SAN 309-2615. Tel: 417-256-4775. FAX: 417-256-8316. Web Site: www.westplains.net. *Libr Dir,* Sherry Russell; *Tech Serv Coordr,* Mary Oakley; *Ch Serv,* Kelli Cook; Staff 9 (Non-MLS 9)
Founded 1948. Pop 10,065; Circ 135,776
Library Holdings: Audiobooks 2,574; Large Print Bks 3,141; Bk Titles 77,908; Per Subs 117; Videos 2,568
Automation Activity & Vendor Info: (Cataloging) SirsiDynix; (Circulation) SirsiDynix; (ILL) OCLC; (OPAC) SirsiDynix
Database Vendor: Gale Cengage Learning, LearningExpress, Newsbank, OCLC FirstSearch, ProQuest
Wireless access
Special Services for the Blind - Aids for in-house use; Audio mat; Bks on cassette; Bks on CD; Cassettes; Computer access aids; Large print & cassettes; Large print bks; Large screen computer & software; Magnifiers; Reading & writing aids; Recorded bks
Open Mon-Fri 9-6, Sat 9-5
Friends of the Library Group

WHITEMAN AFB

A UNITED STATES AIR FORCE*, Whiteman Air Force Base Library FL4625, 509 FSS/FSDL, 511 Spirit Blvd, Bldg 515, 65305-5019. SAN 349-9413. Tel: 660-687-5614. FAX: 660-687-6240. *Dir,* Dennis Wilson; Staff 2 (MLS 1, Non-MLS 1)
Subject Interests: Mil, Polit sci
Automation Activity & Vendor Info: (Cataloging) SIRSI WorkFlows; (Circulation) SIRSI WorkFlows; (ILL) OCLC WorldShare Interlibrary Loan; (OPAC) SIRSI WorkFlows
Database Vendor: CountryWatch, EBSCOhost, Gale Cengage Learning, Newsbank, OCLC FirstSearch, OCLC WorldShare Interlibrary Loan, Overdrive, Inc, Safari Books Online
Wireless access
Open Mon-Fri 8:30-6, Sat 8:30-4

WINDSOR

P LENORA BLACKMORE PUBLIC LIBRARY*, 105 W Benton St, 65360. SAN 309-2623. Tel: 660-647-2298. *Dir,* Sandra Fosno; Staff 3 (MLS 2, Non-MLS 1)
Founded 1937. Pop 3,053; Circ 19,307
Library Holdings: AV Mats 183; Bk Vols 18,000; Per Subs 15
Open Mon, Wed, Thurs & Fri 11-5, Tues 11-7, Sat 11-2

MONTANA

Date of Statistics: FY 2012-2013
Population, 2010 U.S. Census: 989,415
Population, 2013 U.S. Census (est.): 1,015,165
Population Served by Public Libraries: 994,226
Counties Served: 56
Number of Public Libraries: 82
Number of Public Library Branches: 35
Number of Academic Libraries: 27
Number of Institutional Libraries: 2
Number of Special Libraries: 58
Number of School Libraries: 563
Total Volumes in Public Libraries: 4,465,788
Volumes Per Capita: 4.49
Total Public Library Circulation: 6,257,814
Total Public Library Income: $25,291,155
Income per Capita: $25.44
Source of Income: Mainly public funds
State Tax Rate: 5-Mill county tax (permissive); 7-Mill for cities & towns (permissive)
Total Public Library Expenditures: $23,931,236
Expenditures Per Capita: $24.07
Number of Bookmobiles in State: 5
Federal Grants-in-Aid to Public Libraries-Library Services and Technology Act: $1,045,540
Grants-in-State Aid to Public Libraries: $278,949

ANACONDA

P HEARST FREE LIBRARY*, 401 Main St, 59711. SAN 309-2631. Tel: 406-563-6932. FAX: 406-563-5393. Web Site: www.hearstfreelibrary.org. *Dir,* Mitch Grady; E-mail: mgrady@mtlib.org; *Asst Dir,* Colleen Fergusen; E-mail: cferg@mtlib.org; Staff 4.25 (MLS 1, Non-MLS 3.25)
Founded 1895. Pop 8,000; Circ 41,000
Jul 2008-Jun 2009 Income $515,000, State $15,000, City $250,000, Locally Generated Income $250,000. Mats Exp $60,000, Books $30,000, Per/Ser (Incl. Access Fees) $10,000, Micro $1,000, AV Equip $5,000, AV Mat $10,000, Electronic Ref Mat (Incl. Access Fees) $2,000. Sal $100,000
Library Holdings: Bk Titles 31,000; Per Subs 86
Automation Activity & Vendor Info: (Cataloging) SirsiDynix; (Circulation) SirsiDynix; (ILL) OCLC FirstSearch; (OPAC) SIRSI-iBistro
Database Vendor: EBSCO Auto Repair Reference, Gale Cengage Learning
Wireless access
Publications: Anaconda's Treasure: Hearst Free Library (Local historical information)
Open Mon, Fri & Sat 9-5, Tues-Thurs 9-8
Friends of the Library Group

ARLEE

P JOCKO VALLEY LIBRARY*, 212 Culloyah St, 59821. (Mail add: PO Box 158, 59821-0158). Tel: 406-726-3572. *Dir,* Cherie Garcelon
Library Holdings: Bk Titles 8,000
Subject Interests: Montana, Native Am
Automation Activity & Vendor Info: (Acquisitions) LibraryWorld, Inc; (Cataloging) LibraryWorld, Inc; (Circulation) LibraryWorld, Inc; (ILL) LibraryWorld, Inc
Open Mon & Wed-Fri 1-5, Tues 1-7, Sat 11-2
Bookmobiles: 1

BAKER

P FALLON COUNTY LIBRARY*, Six W Fallon Ave, 59313. (Mail add: PO Box 1037, 59313-1037), SAN 309-2666. Tel: 406-778-7160. FAX: 406-778-7116. *Dir,* Vera M Abrams; E-mail: vabrams@mtlib.org; Staff 3 (Non-MLS 3)
Founded 1922. Pop 2,837
Library Holdings: CDs 94; DVDs 14; Large Print Bks 971; Bk Titles 19,229; Bk Vols 20,117; Per Subs 38; Talking Bks 702; Videos 665
Automation Activity & Vendor Info: (Cataloging) Follett Software; (Circulation) Follett Software; (ILL) OCLC; (OPAC) Follett Software
Database Vendor: EBSCOhost, Gale Cengage Learning, OCLC FirstSearch
Function: ILL available
Mem of Sagebrush Federation
Open Mon-Thurs 9:30-7, Fri 10-5, Sat 9-1
Friends of the Library Group

BELGRADE

P BELGRADE COMMUNITY LIBRARY, 106 N Broadway, 59714. SAN 309-2674. Tel: 406-388-4346. FAX: 406-388-6586. Web Site: belgradelibrary.org. *Dir,* Gale Bacon; Staff 7 (MLS 2, Non-MLS 5)
Founded 1932. Pop 12,960; Circ 80,984
Jul 2013-Jun 2014 Income $386,776, State $18,845, City $177,588, County $132,796, Locally Generated Income $57,547. Mats Exp $36,119, Books $31,887, Per/Ser (Incl. Access Fees) $1,900, Electronic Ref Mat (Incl. Access Fees) $1,900. Sal $169,045 (Prof $117,909)
Library Holdings: Audiobooks 1,199; Bks on Deafness & Sign Lang 18; DVDs 1,554; e-books 19,046; Large Print Bks 883; Bk Titles 45,751; Per Subs 57
Automation Activity & Vendor Info: (Cataloging) SirsiDynix; (Circulation) SirsiDynix; (ILL) OCLC
Database Vendor: OCLC FirstSearch, SirsiDynix
Wireless access
Function: Alaskana res
Open Mon-Thurs 11-7, Fri & Sat 11-5
Friends of the Library Group

BELT

P BELT PUBLIC LIBRARY, 404 Millard St, 59412. (Mail add: PO Box 467, 59412-0467), SAN 309-2682. Tel: 406-277-3136. FAX: 406-277-3136. E-mail: beltlib@3rivers.net. Web Site: www.beltlibrary.org. *Libr Dir,* Gladys Rayhill; Staff 0.6 (Non-MLS 0.6)
Founded 1898. Pop 1,100; Circ 61,524
Jul 2014-Jun 2015 Income $15,325, State $525, County $13,000, Other $1,800. Mats Exp $5,000. Sal $16,000
Library Holdings: Audiobooks 80; DVDs 461; Large Print Bks 350; Bk Titles 6,351; Bk Vols 6,391; Per Subs 15
Automation Activity & Vendor Info: (Cataloging) Follett Software; (Circulation) Follett Software; (ILL) OCLC FirstSearch
Wireless access
Mem of Pathfinder Regional Library System
Special Services for the Blind - Accessible computers; Aids for in-house use; Bks on cassette; Bks on CD; Large print bks; Low vision equip; Magnifiers; ZoomText magnification & reading software
Open Mon-Fri 11-6

BIG TIMBER

P CARNEGIE PUBLIC LIBRARY*, 314 McLeod St, 59011. (Mail add: PO Box 846, 59011-0846), SAN 309-2690. Tel: 406-932-5608. E-mail: bigtlib@mtintouch.net. Web Site: www.bigtimberlibrary.org. *Dir,* Kate Lewis
Pop 3,500; Circ 29,953
Library Holdings: Bk Titles 16,000; Per Subs 60
Special Collections: County Newspapers
Automation Activity & Vendor Info: (Cataloging) SirsiDynix; (Circulation) SirsiDynix
Partic in S Cent Fedn of Libr

Open Mon-Thurs 11-9, Fri & Sat 10-4
Friends of the Library Group

BILLINGS

P BILLINGS PUBLIC LIBRARY, (Formerly Parmly Billings Library), 510 N Broadway, 59101-1196. SAN 309-2747. Tel: 406-657-8258. Reference Tel: 406-657-8290. Administration Tel: 406-657-8391. Automation Services Tel: 406-247-8531. FAX: 406-657-8293. E-mail: refdesk@ci.billings.mt.us. Web Site: ci.billings.mt.us/catalog, www.billings.lib.mt.us. *Dir,* Bill Cochran; Tel: 406-657-8292, E-mail: cochranb@ci.billings.mt.us; *Asst Dir,* Dee Ann Redman; Tel: 406-657-8295, E-mail: redmand@ci.billings.mt.us; *Syst Adminr,* Kathy Robins; E-mail: robinsk@ci.billings.mt.us; *Bus Mgr,* Mary Murphrey; E-mail: murphreym@ci.billings.mt.us; Staff 29 (MLS 9, Non-MLS 20)
Founded 1901. Pop 147,126; Circ 858,087
Jul 2012-Jun 2013 Income $3,068,898, State $14,585, City $2,084,607, County $730,975, Other $238,731. Mats Exp $375,334, Books $144,750, Per/Ser (Incl. Access Fees) $35,000, Other Print Mats $72,040, AV Mat $60,600, Electronic Ref Mat (Incl. Access Fees) $62,944. Sal $1,827,495
Library Holdings: Audiobooks 12,170; DVDs 23,242; e-books 10,669; Electronic Media & Resources 44; Bk Vols 220,359; Per Subs 144
Special Collections: Montana Room
Subject Interests: Genealogy
Automation Activity & Vendor Info: (Acquisitions) SIRSI WorkFlows; (Cataloging) SIRSI WorkFlows; (Circulation) SIRSI WorkFlows; (OPAC) SIRSI-iBistro
Database Vendor: Booksite, Cinahl, EBSCO Auto Repair Reference, EBSCO Discovery Service, EBSCO Information Services, EBSCOhost, Facts on File, Gale Cengage Learning, LexisNexis, Library Ideas, LLC, OCLC FirstSearch, Overdrive, Inc, ProQuest, SirsiDynix
Wireless access
Function: Archival coll, Home delivery & serv to Sr ctr & nursing homes, Large print keyboards, Notary serv
Publications: The Turning Page (Newsletter)
Special Services for the Deaf - Assisted listening device; Closed caption videos
Special Services for the Blind - Accessible computers; Assistive/Adapted tech devices, equip & products; Audio mat; Bks on CD; Home delivery serv; Large print bks; Large screen computer & software; Low vision equip
Open Mon-Thurs 10-9, Fri 10-6, Sat 10-5, Sun 1-5
Friends of the Library Group
Bookmobiles: 2. Senior Outreach, Kelsie Raddas

L CROWLEY FLECK PLLP LIBRARY*, 490 N 31st St, Ste 500, 59101-1267. (Mail add: PO Box 2529, 59103-2529), SAN 329-1669. Tel: 406-252-3441. FAX: 406-259-4159. Web Site: www.crowleyfleck.com. *Librn,* Diane Paszkowski; Staff 1 (MLS 1)
Library Holdings: Bk Vols 32,000
Subject Interests: Law
Database Vendor: LexisNexis, OCLC FirstSearch
Function: ILL available
Partic in OCLC Online Computer Library Center, Inc
Restriction: Not open to pub

S DOWL HKM LIBRARY, 222 N 32nd, Ste 700, 59101-1976. (Mail add: PO Box 31318, 59107-1318), SAN 327-1471. Tel: 406-656-6399. FAX: 406-656-6398. *Librn,* Kimberly Ann Neill
Library Holdings: Bk Vols 13,000
Subject Interests: Civil eng

C MONTANA STATE UNIVERSITY*, Billings Library, 1500 University Dr, 59101-0298. SAN 309-2720. Tel: 406-657-2262. Interlibrary Loan Service Tel: 406-657-1666. Reference Tel: 406-657-1662. FAX: 406-657-2037. Web Site: www.msubillings.edu/Library. *Dir,* Brent S Roberts; Tel: 406-657-1655, E-mail: broberts@msubillings.edu; *Admin Assoc,* Lynda Hoover; *Ref & Coll Develop Librn,* Jan Fandrich; Tel: 406-657-1665, E-mail: jfandrich@msubillings.edu; *Ref Librn,* Megan Thomas; Tel: 406-657-1663, E-mail: mthomas@msubillings.edu; *Instruction Coordr, Ref Librn,* Jenks TyRee; Tel: 406-657-1654, E-mail: tjenks@msubillings.edu; *Archivist, Ref Librn,* Eileen Wright; Tel: 406-657-1656, E-mail: ewright@msubillings.edu; *Tech & Access Serv Librn,* Darlene Hert; Tel: 406-657-1661, E-mail: dhert@msubillings.edu; *Cat/Acq Tech,* Jessica Torgerson Lundin; Tel: 406-657-1664, E-mail: jessica.torgerson@msubillings.edu; *Circ Tech,* Carol Jestrab; *Govt Doc & Ser Tech,* Kathy Gurney; Tel: 406-657-1659, E-mail: kgurney@msubillings.edu; *ILL Tech,* Cheryl Hoover; E-mail: choover@msubillings.edu; Staff 11 (MLS 6, Non-MLS 5)
Founded 1927. Enrl 4,000; Fac 172; Highest Degree: Master
Library Holdings: Bk Vols 338,933; Per Subs 1,713
Special Collections: Billings, Yellowstone County & Eastern Montana, ms; Montana & Western History (Dora C White Memorial Coll); Terry C Johnston Research Coll. State Document Depository; US Document Depository
Subject Interests: Bus, Educ, Health, Native Am studies, Spec educ
Automation Activity & Vendor Info: (Cataloging) SirsiDynix; (Circulation) SirsiDynix; (ILL) OCLC ILLiad; (OPAC) SirsiDynix
Database Vendor: EBSCOhost, Gale Cengage Learning, JSTOR, LexisNexis, OCLC FirstSearch, ProQuest, SerialsSolutions, SirsiDynix
Publications: Montana Foundation Directory (Bi-annually)
Partic in OCLC Online Computer Library Center, Inc
Special Services for the Blind - Assistive/Adapted tech devices, equip & products; Braille equip; Closed circuit TV; Computer with voice synthesizer for visually impaired persons; Reader equip; VisualTek equip
Open Mon-Thurs 7:30am-10pm, Fri 7:30-5, Sat 9-5, Sun Noon-10
Friends of the Library Group

S PARENTS, LET'S UNITE FOR KIDS, PLUK Parent Center, 516 N 32nd St, 59101-6003. SAN 377-4422. Tel: 406-255-0540. Toll Free Tel: 800-222-7585, 888-773-2189 (MT only). FAX: 406-255-0523. E-mail: library@pluk.org. Web Site: www.pluk.org. *Coordr,* Libby Wolfe; Tel: 888-748-9857, E-mail: libby.wolfe@pluk.org
Library Holdings: Bk Vols 5,000
Subject Interests: Disabilities, Health, Learning disabilities, Med
Partic in Billings Area Health Sciences Information Consortium (BAHSIC)
Open Mon-Fri 8-5

S RIMROCK FOUNDATION LIBRARY*, 1231 N 29th St, 59101. SAN 324-0711. Tel: 406-248-3175. Toll Free Tel: 800-227-3953, Ext 404. FAX: 406-248-3821. E-mail: comm@rimrock.org. Web Site: www.rimrock.org. *Dir,* Hugh Kilborne
Founded 1975
Library Holdings: Bk Vols 2,000
Subject Interests: Adolescent substance abuse, Adult children of alcoholics, Co-dependency, Compulsive behaviors, Eating disorders
Partic in Billings Area Health Sciences Information Consortium (BAHSIC)

C ROCKY MOUNTAIN COLLEGE*, Paul M Adams Memorial Library, 1511 Poly Dr, 59102-1796. SAN 309-2755. Tel: 406-657-1087. FAX: 406-657-1085. E-mail: ill@rocky.edu. Web Site: www.library.rocky.edu/academics/library. *Libr Dir,* Bill Kehler; Tel: 406-657-1140, E-mail: kehlerb@rocky.edu; *Asst Dir,* Bobbi Otte; Tel: 406-657-1086, E-mail: otteb@rocky.edu; *Libr Assoc,* Bethany Dopp; E-mail: bethany.dopp@rocky.edu; Staff 3.5 (MLS 2, Non-MLS 1.5)
Founded 1878. Enrl 950; Fac 63; Highest Degree: Master
Library Holdings: Audiobooks 25; AV Mats 45; CDs 381; DVDs 1,035; e-books 1,230; e-journals 60; Music Scores 1,088; Bk Titles 41,442; Bk Vols 67,701; Per Subs 375; Spec Interest Per Sub 12; Videos 250
Special Collections: College Archives; Geology Coll; Rare Books Coll
Subject Interests: Aviation, Equestrian
Automation Activity & Vendor Info: (Cataloging) OCLC Connexion; (Circulation) SIRSI WorkFlows; (Course Reserve) SIRSI WorkFlows; (ILL) OCLC; (OPAC) SIRSI Unicorn; (Serials) EBSCO Online
Database Vendor: CountryWatch, CredoReference, EBSCO Information Services, EBSCOhost, Gale Cengage Learning, Nature Publishing Group, OCLC FirstSearch, OCLC WorldShare Interlibrary Loan, Oxford Online, PubMed, ValueLine, YBP Library Services
Wireless access
Partic in Billings Area Health Sciences Information Consortium (BAHSIC); OCLC Online Computer Library Center, Inc; OMNI
Open Mon-Thurs (Winter) 7:30am-10pm, Fri 7:30-4:30, Sat 1-5, Sun 1-10; Mon-Fri (Summer) 8:30-4:30

S WESTERN ORGANIZATION OF RESOURCE COUNCILS LIBRARY*, 220 S 27th St, Ste B, 59101. SAN 371-4535. Tel: 406-252-9672. FAX: 406-252-1092. Web Site: www.worc.org. *Dir,* John Smillie
Library Holdings: Bk Titles 200; Per Subs 31

CR YELLOWSTONE BAPTIST COLLEGE*, Ida Dockery Owen Library, 1515 S Shiloh Rd, 59106. SAN 377-242X. Tel: 406-656-9950. *Librn,* Jeannie Ferriss; E-mail: jferriss@yellowstonebaptist.edu; Staff 1 (MLS 1)
Founded 1974. Enrl 52; Fac 23; Highest Degree: Bachelor
Library Holdings: Bk Vols 22,000; Per Subs 60
Special Collections: Native American Resource Center
Open Mon, Tues & Thurs 8am-10pm, Wed & Fri 8-5, Sat 9-1

BOULDER

P JEFFERSON COUNTY LIBRARY SYSTEM*, Boulder Community Library, 202 S Main St, 59632. (Mail add: PO Box 589, 59632-0589), SAN 376-6888. Tel: 406-225-3241. FAX: 406-225-3241. E-mail: bldrlib@mtlib.org. *Br Librn,* Jodi K Smiley; Staff 3 (Non-MLS 3)
Founded 1974. Pop 10,049
Library Holdings: AV Mats 1,500; Bk Vols 15,000; Per Subs 32
Special Collections: Montana Coll
Automation Activity & Vendor Info: (Cataloging) SirsiDynix; (Circulation) SirsiDynix; (ILL) OCLC; (OPAC) SirsiDynix
Database Vendor: Gale Cengage Learning

Open Mon 6:30-8:30, Tues & Thurs 10-2 & 1-5, Wed 10-12, 1-5 & 6:30-8:30, Fri & Sun 1-5
Friends of the Library Group
Branches: 2
CLANCY COMMUNITY LIBRARY, PO Box 169, Clancy, 59634-0169.
Library Holdings: AV Mats 600; Bk Vols 7,500; Per Subs 20
Friends of the Library Group
WHITEHALL COMMUNITY LIBRARY, 110 First St W, Whitehall, 59759. (Mail add: PO Box 659, Whitehall, 59759-0659), SAN 376-6462. Tel: 406-287-3763. FAX: 406-287-3763. *Librn,* Donna Worth; E-mail: dworth@mtlib.org; Staff 1 (Non-MLS 1)
Founded 1974
Library Holdings: AV Mats 2,000; High Interest/Low Vocabulary Bk Vols 200; Bk Vols 12,000; Per Subs 26
Open Mon & Sat 12-5, Tues & Thurs 3-7:30, Wed & Fri 10-12 & 1-5
Friends of the Library Group

S MONTANA DEPARTMENT OF CORRECTIONS*, Riverside Youth Correctional Facility Library, Two Riverside Rd, 59632. (Mail add: PO Box 88, 59632-0088). Tel: 406-225-4500. FAX: 406-225-4511. *Librn,* Melody Grant; Staff 1 (Non-MLS 1)
Jul 2009-Jun 2010 Income $2,500. Sal $2,700
Library Holdings: Bk Titles 4,500
Open Mon-Fri 7:45-4

BOX ELDER

J STONE CHILD COLLEGE*, Rocky Boy Public Library, 8294 Upper Box Elder Rd, 59521. SAN 375-6262. Tel: 406-395-4875. *Dir,* Helen Windyboy; *Asst Librn,* Joy Bridwell; Staff 2 (MLS 1, Non-MLS 1)
Founded 1986. Enrl 200
Library Holdings: Bk Titles 11,000; Bk Vols 12,000; Per Subs 136
Automation Activity & Vendor Info: (Acquisitions) Follett Software; (Cataloging) Follett Software; (Circulation) Follett Software; (Course Reserve) Follett Software; (ILL) Follett Software; (Media Booking) Follett Software; (OPAC) Follett Software; (Serials) Follett Software
Open Mon-Thurs 8-4:30, Fri 8-3

BOZEMAN

P BOZEMAN PUBLIC LIBRARY*, 626 E Main St, 59715. SAN 309-2798. Tel: 406-582-2400. Circulation Tel: 406-582-2407, 406-582-2408. Interlibrary Loan Service Tel: 406-582-2414. Reference Tel: 406-582-2410, 406-582-2411. Administration Tel: 406-582-2401. Automation Services Tel: 406-582-2422. Information Services Tel: 406 582-2427. FAX: 406-582-2424. TDD: 406-582-2301. Web Site: www.bozemanlibrary.org. *Dir,* Susan Gregory; E-mail: sgregory@bozeman.net; *Head, Automation, Head, Tech Serv,* Lois Dissly; *Head, Circ,* Mary Jo Stanislao; Tel: 406-582-2409; *Head, Ref & Adult Serv,* Terri Dood; Tel: 406-582-2406; Staff 23 (MLS 8.5, Non-MLS 14.5)
Founded 1891. Pop 47,805; Circ 671,501
Jul 2010-Jun 2011 Income $1,606,072, State $7,799, City $1,121,512, County $476,761. Mats Exp $155,000, Books $86,000, Per/Ser (Incl. Access Fees) $20,000, AV Mat $35,000, Electronic Ref Mat (Incl. Access Fees) $14,000. Sal $1,134,265 (Prof $375,000)
Library Holdings: Audiobooks 4,134; AV Mats 15,690; Bks on Deafness & Sign Lang 68; Braille Volumes 21; CDs 6,312; DVDs 4,317; e-books 12,707; Electronic Media & Resources 22; Large Print Bks 3,248; Bk Vols 117,365; Per Subs 246; Videos 6,396
Special Collections: Foundation Center. US Document Depository
Subject Interests: Montana hist
Automation Activity & Vendor Info: (Cataloging) SirsiDynix; (Circulation) SirsiDynix; (OPAC) SirsiDynix; (Serials) EBSCO Online
Database Vendor: 3M Library Systems, Booksite, Gale Cengage Learning, OCLC WorldShare Interlibrary Loan, ReferenceUSA, SirsiDynix, Westlaw
Wireless access
Function: Adult bk club, Archival coll, Art exhibits, Bi-weekly Writer's Group, Bks on cassette, Bks on CD, CD-ROM, Chess club, Children's prog, Computer training, Computers for patron use, Copy machines, E-Reserves, Electronic databases & coll, Exhibits, Fax serv, Free DVD rentals, Handicapped accessible, Holiday prog, Homebound delivery serv, ILL available, Jazz prog, Magnifiers for reading, Mail & tel request accepted, Mus passes, Music CDs, Notary serv, Online cat, Online searches, OverDrive digital audio bks, Photocopying/Printing, Preschool outreach, Prof lending libr, Prog for adults, Prog for children & young adult, Pub access computers, Ref & res, Scanner, Senior computer classes, Senior outreach, Spoken cassettes & CDs, Spoken cassettes & DVDs, Story hour, Summer reading prog, Teen prog, Telephone ref, VHS videos, Video lending libr, Wheelchair accessible
Publications: Check It Out (Newsletter)
Open Mon-Thurs 10-8, Fri & Sat 10-5, Sun (Sept-May) 1-5
Restriction: Non-circulating of rare bks, Non-resident fee
Friends of the Library Group

CR MONTANA BIBLE COLLEGE*, Gail Horton Library, 100 Discovery Way, 59718. SAN 377-5577. Tel: 406-556-7215. E-mail: library@montanabiblecollege.edu. Web Site: www.montanabiblecollege.edu/library. *Libr Dir,* Micah Forsythe; E-mail: micah.forsythe@montanabiblecollege.edu; *Asst Librn,* Jessica Carlson; E-mail: jessica.carlson@montanabiblecollege.edu; Staff 2 (Non-MLS 2)
Founded 1987. Enrl 99; Fac 14; Highest Degree: Bachelor
Library Holdings: e-books 6,500; Bk Titles 10,000; Per Subs 15
Wireless access
Open Mon-Thurs 8am-9pm, Fri 10-3, Sun 5-9

C MONTANA STATE UNIVERSITY LIBRARIES*, Roland R Renne Library, Centennial Mall, 59717. (Mail add: PO Box 173320, 59717-3320), SAN 349-9448. Tel: 406-994-3119. Circulation Tel: 406-994-3139. Interlibrary Loan Service Tel: 406-994-3161. Reference Tel: 406-994-3171. FAX: 406-994-2851. Web Site: www.lib.montana.edu. *Dean of Libr,* Kenning Arlitsch; Tel: 406-994-6978, E-mail: kenning.arlitsch@montana.edu; *Assoc Dean of Libr,* Brian Rossmann; Tel: 406-994-5298, E-mail: brossmann@montana.edu; *Ref Librn,* Greg Notes; Tel: 406-994-6563, E-mail: align@montana.edu; *Univ Archivist,* Kim Allen Scott; Tel: 406-994-4242, E-mail: kascott@montana.edu; Staff 20 (MLS 17, Non-MLS 3)
Founded 1893. Enrl 12,338; Fac 768; Highest Degree: Doctorate
Library Holdings: CDs 2,446; DVDs 5,540; e-journals 6,000; Music Scores 4,117; Bk Vols 712,241; Per Subs 8,757
Special Collections: Burton K Wheeler Coll; Canadian Coll; Montana History Coll; Trout Coll; Yellowstone National Park Coll, bks, mss, pictures. State Document Depository; US Document Depository
Subject Interests: Agr, Health sci, Natural sci, Sci tech
Automation Activity & Vendor Info: (Cataloging) OCLC; (Circulation) SirsiDynix; (Course Reserve) SirsiDynix; (ILL) OCLC ILLiad; (OPAC) SirsiDynix; (Serials) EBSCO Online
Wireless access
Open Mon-Thurs 7am-2am, Fri 7am-8pm, Sat 10-5, Sun 10am-2am
Friends of the Library Group

BRIDGER

P BRIDGER PUBLIC LIBRARY*, 119 W Broadway Ave, 59014. (Mail add: PO Box 428, 59014-0428), SAN 309-281X. Tel: 406-662-3598. FAX: 406-662-3598. *Libr Dir,* Krystal Zentner
Founded 1906. Pop 2,778; Circ 12,000
Library Holdings: Bk Vols 12,000
Special Collections: Bridger Times, 1909-1958
Automation Activity & Vendor Info: (Acquisitions) Follett Software
Wireless access
Function: Adult bk club, Bks on cassette, Bks on CD, Computers for patron use, Copy machines, Fax serv, Free DVD rentals, ILL available, Summer reading prog
Mem of South Cent Fedn
Open Mon 1-5, Tues 9-12 & 1-5, Wed 1-5 & 7-9
Friends of the Library Group

BROADUS

P HENRY A MALLEY MEMORIAL LIBRARY*, 101 S Lincoln, 59317. (Mail add: PO Box 345, 59317-0345), SAN 309-2828. Tel: 406-436-2812. E-mail: broaduslibrary@rangeweb.net. *Dir,* Diane Stuver; *Librn,* June Ray
Pop 1,900; Circ 17,000
Library Holdings: Bk Vols 20,000; Per Subs 35
Mem of Sagebrush Federation
Open Mon & Thurs 12-7, Tues, Wed, Fri & Sat 12-5

BROWNING

J BLACKFEET COMMUNITY COLLEGE*, Medicine Spring Library, US Hwy Two & 89, 59417. (Mail add: PO Box 819, 59417-0819), SAN 321-107X. Tel: 406-338-5441. Toll Free Tel: 800-549-7457. FAX: 406-338-5454. *Dir, Libr Serv,* Ginny Weeks; *Tech Serv,* Erin Gilham; *Tech Serv,* Mikel Kennedy; Staff 3 (MLS 1, Non-MLS 2)
Founded 1981. Enrl 350; Fac 52; Highest Degree: Associate
Library Holdings: AV Mats 100; Bks on Deafness & Sign Lang 20; Large Print Bks 50; Bk Titles 14,500; Bk Vols 15,000; Per Subs 250; Talking Bks 50
Special Collections: Blackfeet Tribal Coll
Subject Interests: Blackfeet hist, Culture, Native Am studies
Automation Activity & Vendor Info: (Cataloging) Follett Software; (Circulation) Follett Software
Database Vendor: EBSCOhost, Gale Cengage Learning, OCLC FirstSearch
Function: ILL available
Open Mon-Fri 8-4

BUTTE

P BUTTE-SILVER BOW PUBLIC LIBRARY*, 226 W Broadway, 59701. SAN 309-2836. Tel: 406-723-3361. Automation Services Tel: 406-723-2138. FAX: 406-782-1825. Web Site: www.buttepubliclibrary.info. *Dir,* Lee Miller; E-mail: lmiller@buttepubliclibrary.info; *Head, Ref,* Stef Johnson; E-mail: sjohnson@buttepubliclibrary.info; *Head, Tech Serv,* Diane Giop; E-mail: dgiop@buttepubliclibrary.info; *Ch Serv,* Nancy DeBarathy; E-mail: ndebarathy@buttepubliclibrary.info; Staff 18 (MLS 3, Non-MLS 15)
Founded 1890. Pop 34,606; Circ 92,875
Library Holdings: AV Mats 4,955; Bk Vols 96,655; Per Subs 226; Talking Bks 2,578; Videos 2,374
Subject Interests: Fishing, Local hist, Montana hist
Automation Activity & Vendor Info: (Circulation) Follett Software; (OPAC) LibLime
Database Vendor: EBSCOhost
Wireless access
Function: AV serv, Doc delivery serv, Govt ref serv, Handicapped accessible, Homebound delivery serv, ILL available, Magnifiers for reading, Newsp ref libr, Online searches, Outside serv via phone, mail, e-mail & web, Photocopying/Printing, Prog for adults, Prog for children & young adult, Ref serv available, Summer reading prog, Telephone ref, Wheelchair accessible
Open Mon, Fri & Sat 10-5, Tues-Thurs 10-8
Friends of the Library Group
Branches: 1
SOUTH BRANCH, Butte Plaza Mall, 3100 Harrison Ave, 59701. Tel: 406-723-3361, Ext 6400. *Br Mgr,* Linda Zeller
Library Holdings: CDs 40; DVDs 100; Bk Vols 300; Per Subs 8

S CLARK FORK & BLACKFOOT LLC*, Law Library, 40 E Broadway, 59701. SAN 327-1498. Tel: 406-497-2130. FAX: 406-497-2451. *Librn,* Tracy Killoy
Library Holdings: Bk Titles 1,000; Bk Vols 7,000

C MONTANA TECH LIBRARY*, 1300 W Park St, 59701-8997. SAN 309-2844. Tel: 406-496-4281. Reference Tel: 406-496-4282. FAX: 406-496-4133. Web Site: www.mtech.edu/library. *Dir,* Ann St Clair; Tel: 406-496-4284, E-mail: astclair@mtech.edu; *Head, Pub Serv,* Frances Holmes; Tel: 406-496-4222, E-mail: fholmes@mtech.edu; *Head, Tech Serv,* Connie Daugherty; Tel: 406-496-4668, E-mail: cdaugherty@mtech.edu; *Ref Librn,* Scott Juskiewicz; Tel: 406-496-4523, E-mail: sjuskiewicz@mtech.edu; *Ref Librn,* Elizabeth Ramsey; Tel: 406-496-4839, E-mail: eramsey@mtech.edu; *Ref Librn,* Debbie Todd; Tel: 406-496-4286, E-mail: dtodd@mtech.edu; *Computer Support Spec,* Marcia Lubick; Tel: 406-496-4287, E-mail: mlubick@mtech.edu. Subject Specialists: *Chem, Eng,* Scott Juskiewicz; *Letters, Prof studies, Sci,* Elizabeth Ramsey; *Liberal studies,* Debbie Todd; Staff 9 (MLS 4, Non-MLS 5)
Founded 1900. Enrl 2,363; Fac 122; Highest Degree: Master
Library Holdings: AV Mats 148; CDs 4,316; e-books 109,025; e-journals 50,690; Electronic Media & Resources 3,962; Microforms 5,302; Bk Titles 51,865; Bk Vols 75,584; Per Subs 400; Videos 148
Special Collections: US Patent & Trademark Coll. US Document Depository
Subject Interests: Environ eng, Geochemistry, Geol, Geophysics, Metallurgy, Mining, Petroleum eng
Automation Activity & Vendor Info: (Acquisitions) Ex Libris Group; (Cataloging) Ex Libris Group; (Circulation) Ex Libris Group; (Course Reserve) Ex Libris Group; (ILL) OCLC ILLiad; (OPAC) Ex Libris Group; (Serials) Ex Libris Group
Database Vendor: ACM (Association for Computing Machinery), American Chemical Society, Annual Reviews, Cambridge Scientific Abstracts, Career Guidance Foundation, College Source, Dialog, Ebooks Corporation, ebrary, EBSCOhost, Elsevier, Emerald, Gale Cengage Learning, JSTOR, Medline, Nature Publishing Group, Newsbank, OCLC FirstSearch, OCLC WorldShare Interlibrary Loan, ReferenceUSA, RefWorks, Safari Books Online, ScienceDirect, SerialsSolutions, Springer-Verlag, Wiley InterScience
Wireless access
Open Mon-Thurs 7:30am-10pm, Fri 7:30 5, Sat Noon-4, Sun 1-9
Friends of the Library Group

S NATIONAL CENTER FOR APPROPRIATE TECHNOLOGY*, Research Library, 3040 Continental Dr, 59701. (Mail add: PO Box 3838, 59702-3838), SAN 320-3921. Tel: 406-494-8643. FAX: 406-494-2905. *Dir,* Rose Sullivan; E-mail: roses@ncat.org
Founded 1978
Library Holdings: Bk Titles 7,000; Per Subs 300
Subject Interests: Biofuels, Commun develop, Greenhouses, Internet, Low cost tech, Low income housing, Micro-hydro power, Mkt, Small scale, Solar energy, Superinsulation
Restriction: Staff use only

M ST JAMES HEALTHCARE*, Medical Library, 400 S Clark St, 59701. SAN 323-6323. Tel: 406-723-2523. FAX: 406-723-2813. *Librn,* Laurel Egan
Founded 1981
Library Holdings: Bk Titles 125; Per Subs 83
Wireless access
Open Mon, Wed & Fri 8:30-12:30, Tues & Thurs 12:30-4:30

J UNIVERSITY OF MONTANA*, College of Technology Learning Center, 25 Basin Creek Rd, 59701. SAN 320-6890. Tel: 406-496-3737. FAX: 406-496-3710. *Dir,* Kathy Reick
Founded 1969
Library Holdings: Bk Vols 700; Per Subs 24
Subject Interests: Auto mechanics, Civil eng, Computers, Draft, Electronics, Nursing, Welding

CASCADE

P WEDSWORTH MEMORIAL LIBRARY, 13 Front St N, 59421. (Mail add: PO Box 526, 59421-0526), SAN 309-2852. Tel: 406-468-2848. E-mail: wedsworth.library@gmail.com. Web Site: www.cascademontana.com/wedsworth. *Dir,* Nancy Royan; Staff 1 (Non-MLS 1)
Founded 1936. Pop 900; Circ 15,288
Library Holdings: Bk Titles 5,000; Per Subs 20; Talking Bks 520
Special Collections: Cascade Historical Coll, photog; Local Newspaper, microfilm
Automation Activity & Vendor Info: (Cataloging) Follett Software; (Circulation) Follett Software; (ILL) OCLC
Database Vendor: Gale Cengage Learning
Wireless access
Open Mon (Winter) 9-1 & 2-6, Tues 9-1 & 3-5, Wed-Fri 2-5; Mon (Summer) 9-1 & 2-6, Tues-Fri 9-1
Friends of the Library Group

CHESTER

P LIBERTY COUNTY LIBRARY*, 100 E First St, 59522. (Mail add: PO Box 458, 59522-0458), SAN 309-2860. Tel: 406-759-5445. FAX: 406-759-5445. E-mail: library@ttc-cmc.net. *Dir,* Teresa Fenger
Founded 1945. Pop 2,500; Circ 16,000
Library Holdings: Bk Vols 25,000; Per Subs 51
Special Collections: Broken Mountains Genealogical Library Coll
Automation Activity & Vendor Info: (Acquisitions) Follett Software; (Cataloging) Follett Software; (Circulation) Follett Software; (Course Reserve) Follett Software; (ILL) Follett Software; (Media Booking) Follett Software; (OPAC) Follett Software
Database Vendor: OCLC FirstSearch
Mem of Pathfinder Regional Library System
Open Mon, Wed & Fri 9-5, Tues & Thurs 1-8
Friends of the Library Group

CHINOOK

P BLAINE COUNTY LIBRARY*, 94 Fourth St, 59523. (Mail add: PO Box 610, 59523-0610), SAN 349-9502. Tel: 406-357-2932. FAX: 406-357-2552. *Dir,* Valerie Frank; *Web Developer,* Heather DePriest; E-mail: amgarage@mtintouch.net
Founded 1920. Pop 6,800; Circ 25,000
Library Holdings: Bk Vols 18,000; Per Subs 39
Automation Activity & Vendor Info: (Acquisitions) SirsiDynix; (Cataloging) SirsiDynix; (Circulation) SirsiDynix; (Course Reserve) SirsiDynix; (ILL) SirsiDynix; (Media Booking) SirsiDynix; (OPAC) SirsiDynix; (Serials) SirsiDynix
Open Mon & Wed 1-6 & 7-9, Tues & Thurs 10-12 & 1-6, Fri 1-6

CHOTEAU

P CHOTEAU/TETON PUBLIC LIBRARY*, 17 N Main, 59422. (Mail add: PO Box 876, 59422-0876), SAN 309-2879. Tel: 406-466-2052. FAX: 406-466-2052. E-mail: cpl@3rivers.net. Web Site: tetonlibrarynetwork.net/choteau.htm. *Dir,* Marsha Hinch; *Asst Librn,* Bonnie Andersen
Pop 5,000; Circ 35,000
Library Holdings: Bk Titles 20,100; Per Subs 13
Subject Interests: Authors, Montana hist
Automation Activity & Vendor Info: (Cataloging) Follett Software; (Circulation) Follett Software
Wireless access
Mem of Pathfinder Regional Library System
Special Services for the Blind - Bks on cassette; Talking bks
Open Mon-Wed 12-8, Thurs 10-8, Fri 12-6
Friends of the Library Group

CIRCLE

P GEORGE MCCONE MEMORIAL COUNTY LIBRARY*, 1101 C Ave, 59215. (Mail add: PO Box 49, 59215-0049), SAN 309-2887. Tel: 406-485-2350. E-mail: mcl@midrivers.com. *Dir,* Emmie Loberg
Founded 1930. Pop 1,900
Library Holdings: Bk Vols 19,314; Per Subs 42
Subject Interests: Montana, Western states
Wireless access
Mem of Sagebrush Federation
Open Mon-Fri 12-6

COLUMBUS

P STILLWATER COUNTY LIBRARY, 27 N Fourth St, 59019. (Mail add: PO Box 266, 59019-0266), SAN 349-9561. Tel: 406-322-5009. FAX: 406-322-5009. E-mail: slibrary@mtlib.org. *Dir,* Della Haverland; *Ch,* Robert Smith; E-mail: rsmith@mtlib.org; *Tech,* Brooke Hampton; E-mail: bhampton@mtlib.org; Staff 3 (Non-MLS 3)
Founded 1928. Pop 9,117
Jul 2005-Jun 2006 Income $133,486, State $1,100, County $131,386, Locally Generated Income $1,000. Mats Exp $26,500, Books $21,000, Per/Ser (Incl. Access Fees) $3,000, Electronic Ref Mat (Incl. Access Fees) $2,500. Sal $60,000 (Prof $31,631)
Library Holdings: Audiobooks 2,151; CDs 200; DVDs 2,607; e-books 5,230; Electronic Media & Resources 5,237; Bk Titles 20,554; Per Subs 38; Videos 367
Special Collections: Montana; Stillwater County
Automation Activity & Vendor Info: (Acquisitions) SIRSI WorkFlows; (Cataloging) SIRSI WorkFlows; (Circulation) SIRSI WorkFlows; (ILL) OCLC
Database Vendor: EBSCOhost, OCLC FirstSearch, Overdrive, Inc
Wireless access
Special Services for the Blind - Bks on cassette; Bks on CD
Open Mon-Fri (Winter) 9:30-5:30, Sat 9-1; Mon-Fri (Summer) 9:30-5:30
Friends of the Library Group

CONRAD

P CONRAD PUBLIC LIBRARY*, 15 Fourth Ave SW, 59425. SAN 309-2909. Tel: 406-271-5751. FAX: 406-271-5751. *Dir,* Carolyn Donath; Staff 3 (Non-MLS 3)
Founded 1925. Pop 6,087; Circ 29,000
Library Holdings: Bks on Deafness & Sign Lang 32; Bk Titles 26,869; Per Subs 9
Special Collections: Montana Coll
Automation Activity & Vendor Info: (Acquisitions) Follett Software; (Cataloging) Follett Software; (Circulation) Follett Software; (Course Reserve) Follett Software; (ILL) Follett Software; (Media Booking) Follett Software; (OPAC) Follett Software; (Serials) Follett Software
Database Vendor: OCLC FirstSearch
Mem of Pathfinder Regional Library System
Special Services for the Blind - Talking bks
Open Mon & Wed 9-5, Tues & Thurs 11-5 & 7-9, Fri 11-5
Friends of the Library Group

CROW AGENCY

J LITTLE BIG HORN COLLEGE LIBRARY*, One Forestry Lane, 59022. (Mail add: PO Box 370, 59022-0370). Tel: 406-638-3123. Interlibrary Loan Service Tel: 406-638-3174. FAX: 406-638-3170. Web Site: lib.lbhc.edu. *Dir,* Tim Bernardis; Tel: 406-638-3113, E-mail: tim@lbhc.edu; *Asst Librn,* Edwin Springfield; Tel: 406-638-3160; *Archivist,* Jon Ille; Tel: 406-638-3182
Library Holdings: Bk Vols 22,000; Per Subs 30
Open Mon 8-6, Tues-Thurs 8-7, Fri 8-5

CUT BANK

P GLACIER COUNTY LIBRARY*, 21 First Ave SE, 59427. SAN 349-9715. Tel: 406-873-4572. FAX: 406-873-4845. E-mail: gclibrary@bresnan.net. Web Site: www.glaciercountygov.com/library. *Dir,* Jamie Greco; Staff 5 (MLS 1, Non-MLS 4)
Founded 1944. Pop 13,578; Circ 38,121
Library Holdings: Audiobooks 879; AV Mats 899; CDs 20; DVDs 192; Large Print Bks 267; Bk Vols 38,290; Per Subs 57; Videos 707
Special Collections: Lewis & Clark Coll; Montana Authors & History
Automation Activity & Vendor Info: (Cataloging) OCLC Connexion; (Circulation) SIRSI WorkFlows; (ILL) OCLC FirstSearch
Database Vendor: Gale Cengage Learning
Wireless access
Open Mon, Tues & Thurs 11-7, Wed & Fri 10-5, Sat 11-3
Friends of the Library Group
Branches: 2
BROWNING BRANCH, PO Box 550, Browning, 59417, SAN 349-974X. Tel: 406-338-7105. FAX: 406-338-5436. *Librn,* Kathy McDaniel; Staff 1 (Non-MLS 1)
Open Mon 2-8, Tues-Fri 11:30-5:30, Sat 10-2
EAST GLACIER PARK BRANCH, PO Box 234, East Glacier Park, 59434, SAN 349-9774. Tel: 406-873-4572. *Dir,* Jamie Greco
Open Wed 4-6

DARBY

P DARBY COMMUNITY PUBLIC LIBRARY*, 101 1/2 Marshall St, 59829. (Mail add: PO Box 909, 59829-0909), SAN 309-2917. Tel: 406-821-4771. FAX; 406-821-3964. E-mail: darbylibrary@cybernet1.com. Web Site: www.darbylibrary.net. *Dir,* Amy Fannin; Staff 1 (Non-MLS 1)
Founded 1921. Circ 4,300
Library Holdings: Bk Titles 7,500
Open Mon & Tues 1-6, Thurs & Fri 10-6, Sat 10-2
Friends of the Library Group

DEER LODGE

P WILLIAM K KOHRS MEMORIAL LIBRARY*, 501 Missouri Ave, 59722-1152. SAN 309-2933. Tel: 406-846-2622. FAX: 406-846-2622. E-mail: wkkohrs@yahoo.com. Web Site: www.kohrslibrary.org. *Dir,* Cindy Griefhaber; Staff 3 (Non-MLS 3)
Founded 1902. Pop 7,000; Circ 25,500
Jul 2007-Jun 2008 Income $77,000. Mats Exp $13,500. Sal $41,000
Library Holdings: AV Mats 4,200; Bk Titles 30,000; Per Subs 41
Special Collections: Newspapers (The New Northwest 1869-1885 & Silver State Post 1893-Present), bd
Automation Activity & Vendor Info: (OPAC) Follett Software
Database Vendor: EBSCO Auto Repair Reference, EBSCOhost, Gale Cengage Learning, Overdrive, Inc, ProQuest
Wireless access
Open Mon-Thurs 11-7, Fri & Sat 11-5
Friends of the Library Group

S MONTANA STATE PRISON LIBRARY*, Cottonwood Union, 600 Conley Lake Rd, 59722. SAN 309-2941. Tel: 406-846-1320, Ext 2410. FAX: 406-846-2951. *Libr Dir,* Linda Murphy; E-mail: lmurphy2@mt.gov; *Libr Tech,* George W Smith, Jr; E-mail: gsmith3@mt.gov; Staff 3 (MLS 1, Non-MLS 2)
Special Collections: Native American Indian Coll
Subject Interests: College reference works, Law

S NATIONAL PARK SERVICE*, Grant-Kohrs Ranch National Historic Site Library, 266 Warren Lane, 59722. SAN 323-8504. Tel: 406-846-2070. FAX: 406-846-3962. Web Site: www.nps.gov/grko. *Librn,* Christine Ford; Tel: 406-846-2070, Ext 242
Founded 1972
Library Holdings: Bk Titles 2,000; Per Subs 20
Special Collections: Oral History
Open Mon-Fri 8-4:30
Restriction: Limited access for the pub, Open to pub for ref & circ; with some limitations

DENTON

P DENTON PUBLIC LIBRARY*, 515 Broadway, 59430. (Mail add: PO Box 986, 59430-0986), SAN 376-7841. Tel: 406-567-2571. FAX: 406-567-2571. E-mail: dentonpl@ttc-cmc.net. *Dir,* Position Currently Open; Staff 1 (Non-MLS 1)
Pop 300
Library Holdings: Bk Titles 6,000
Mem of South Cent Fedn
Partic in Amigos Library Services, Inc
Open Mon-Fri 9-5

DILLON

S BEAVERHEAD COUNTY MUSEUM RESEARCH LIBRARY*, 15 S Montana St, 59725. (Mail add: PO Box 265, 59725-0265), SAN 321-8481. Tel: 406-683-5027. E-mail: bvhdmuseum@hotmail.com. Web Site: beaverheadcountymuseum.org. *Dir,* Lynn Giles
Founded 1947
Library Holdings: Bk Titles 250
Special Collections: Oral History
Subject Interests: SW Montana
Wireless access
Publications: Newsletter (Quarterly)
Open Mon-Fri 9-5
Restriction: Non-circulating to the pub

P DILLON CITY LIBRARY*, 121 S Idaho, 59725-2500. SAN 309-2976. Tel: 406-683-4544. Toll Free Tel: 877-683-4544. E-mail: dillon_city_library@yahoo.com. Web Site: www.mtdi.mt.lib.org. *Libr Dir,* Marie Habener; *Asst Dir,* Mary Holt; Staff 2 (Non-MLS 2)
Founded 1890. Pop 9,246; Circ 26,741
Library Holdings: Bk Titles 17,996; Per Subs 31
Automation Activity & Vendor Info: (Circulation) SirsiDynix
Database Vendor: Gale Cengage Learning, OCLC FirstSearch
Wireless access
Open Tues-Fri 11-7, Sat 11-3, Sun 12:30-4:30

C UNIVERSITY OF MONTANA WESTERN*, Lucy Carson Memorial Library & Swysgood Technology Center, 710 S Atlantic St, 59725. SAN 309-2984. Tel: 406-683-7541. Circulation Tel: 406-683-7542. Interlibrary Loan Service Tel: 406-683-7491. Reference Tel: 406-683-7492. FAX: 406-683-7493. Web Site: www.umwestern.edu/library. *Dir,* Michael Schulz; Tel: 406-683-7492, E-mail: m_schulz@umwestern.edu; *Librn,* Anne Kish; Tel: 406-683-7494, E-mail: a_kish@umwestern.edu; *Instrul Serv Librn,* Otis Anderson; Tel: 406-683-7163, E-mail: o_anderson@umwestern.edu; *Instrul Serv Librn,* William Dwyer; Tel: 406-683-7164, E-mail: b_dwyer@umwestern.edu; *Circ,* Denice Rust; E-mail: d_rust@umwestern.edu; *Tech Serv,* Barbara Van Cleave; Tel: 406-683-7491, E-mail: b_vancleave@umwestern.edu. Subject Specialists: *Automation,* William Dwyer; *Cataloging,* Barbara Van Cleave; Staff 4 (MLS 2, Non-MLS 2)
Founded 1893. Enrl 1,100; Fac 55; Highest Degree: Bachelor
Jul 2005-Jun 2006 Income $354,931. Mats Exp $118,107, Books $57,024, Per/Ser (Incl. Access Fees) $51,083, AV Equip $10,000. Sal $217,163 (Prof $93,168)
Library Holdings: Bk Titles 64,176; Bk Vols 65,658; Per Subs 358
Special Collections: Emerick Art Coll; Montana History Coll; NASA Teacher Resource Center; State Educational Media Library
Subject Interests: Educ
Automation Activity & Vendor Info: (Acquisitions) Ex Libris Group; (Cataloging) Ex Libris Group; (Circulation) Ex Libris Group; (Course Reserve) Ex Libris Group; (ILL) Ex Libris Group; (Media Booking) Ex Libris Group; (OPAC) Ex Libris Group; (Serials) Ex Libris Group
Database Vendor: Agricola, Gale Cengage Learning, JSTOR, Newsbank, OCLC FirstSearch, OCLC WorldShare Interlibrary Loan, OVID Technologies, ScienceDirect, SerialsSolutions, Wilson - Wilson Web
Publications: Unravelling the Patchwork: A Handbook for Rural School Librarians
Partic in OCLC Online Computer Library Center, Inc
Friends of the Library Group

DRUMMOND

P DRUMMOND SCHOOL & COMMUNITY LIBRARY*, 124 First St, 59832. (Mail add: PO Box 349, 59832-0349), SAN 325-2590. Tel: 406-288-3700. Web Site: drummondlibrary.org. *Dir,* Jodi Oberweiser
Pop 1,117; Circ 10,200
Library Holdings: Audiobooks 111; CDs 30; DVDs 300; e-books 9,111; Large Print Bks 250; Bk Titles 12,893; Per Subs 6; Videos 150
Special Collections: Fiction & Non-fiction; Montana Coll
Automation Activity & Vendor Info: (Cataloging) SirsiDynix; (Circulation) SirsiDynix; (OPAC) SirsiDynix
Database Vendor: EBSCOhost, OCLC FirstSearch, OCLC WebJunction, OCLC WorldShare Interlibrary Loan, SirsiDynix, WebMD, World Book Online
Wireless access
Open Mon & Thurs 1-7, Tues & Wed 1-5, Fri 11-1, Sat 2-6
Friends of the Library Group

DUTTON

P DUTTON/TETON PUBLIC LIBRARY*, 22 Main St W, 59433. SAN 309-295X. Tel: 406-476-3382. FAX: 406-476-3382. E-mail: duttonpubliclibrary@gmail.com. Web Site: www.tetonlibrarynetwork.net/Dutton.htm. *Dir,* Kelby Blanchet
Pop 1,389; Circ 4,035
Library Holdings: AV Mats 89; Bk Titles 5,000; Bk Vols 7,000
Automation Activity & Vendor Info: (Cataloging) Follett Software
Open Mon 5-8:30, Tues & Thurs 11:30-3, Wed 11:30-6, Fri 10-1:30

EKALAKA

P EKALAKA PUBLIC LIBRARY*, 115 Main St, 59324. (Mail add: PO Box 482, 59324-0482), SAN 325-0199. Tel: 406-775-6336. FAX: 406-775-6325. E-mail: ekalakalibrary@gmail.com, epl@midrivers.com. *Dir,* Janet Livingston
Founded 1976. Pop 1,160; Circ 33,000
Library Holdings: AV Mats 827; Large Print Bks 220; Bk Titles 6,900
Special Collections: Carter County History Books Coll; Local History Coll; Local Literature Coll; Montana History Coll
Automation Activity & Vendor Info: (Cataloging) Follett Software; (Circulation) Follett Software
Database Vendor: EBSCO Auto Repair Reference, OCLC FirstSearch, OCLC WorldShare Interlibrary Loan
Wireless access
Function: Computers for patron use
Open Mon-Thurs 12-5

ENNIS

P MADISON VALLEY PUBLIC LIBRARY, 210 Main St, 59729. SAN 309-300X. Tel: 406-682-7244. FAX: 406-682-7669. E-mail: ennislib@3rivers.net. *Dir,* Molly Aagard; Staff 1 (MLS 1)
Founded 1974. Pop 1,700; Circ 16,407
Library Holdings: Bk Vols 16,000; Per Subs 40
Special Collections: Western Coll
Wireless access
Open Mon-Fri 9-6, Sat 10-3
Friends of the Library Group

FAIRFIELD

P FAIRFIELD/TETON PUBLIC LIBRARY*, 14 North Fourth St, 59436. (Mail add: PO Box 324, 59436-0324), SAN 309-3018. Tel: 406-467-2477. FAX: 406-467-2477. E-mail: cottall13@yahoo.com. *Libr Dir,* Brett Allen; *Asst Librn,* Karen West
Pop 1,350; Circ 14,441
Library Holdings: Bk Vols 9,000; Per Subs 24
Automation Activity & Vendor Info: (Acquisitions) Follett Software; (Cataloging) Follett Software; (Circulation) Follett Software; (ILL) Follett Software; (Media Booking) Follett Software; (OPAC) Follett Software; (Serials) Follett Software
Mem of Pathfinder Regional Library System
Open Mon, Wed & Fri 10-2, Tues & Thurs 3:30-7
Friends of the Library Group

FORSYTH

P ROSEBUD COUNTY LIBRARY*, 201 N Ninth Ave, 59327. (Mail add: PO Box 7, 59327-0007), SAN 309-3026. Tel: 406-346-7561. FAX: 406-346-7685. *Dir,* Cheryl J Heser; *Asst Librn,* Susan Martin; *Cat Librn,* Ruth Propp; Staff 4 (Non-MLS 4)
Pop 6,092; Circ 24,605
Library Holdings: High Interest/Low Vocabulary Bk Vols 25; Bk Vols 31,350; Per Subs 50; Spec Interest Per Sub 10
Special Collections: Local newspapers from 1894-present
Subject Interests: Western hist
Automation Activity & Vendor Info: (Acquisitions) SirsiDynix; (Cataloging) SirsiDynix; (Circulation) SirsiDynix; (ILL) SirsiDynix; (OPAC) SirsiDynix; (Serials) SirsiDynix
Database Vendor: EBSCO Information Services, Gale Cengage Learning, Ingram Library Services, OCLC FirstSearch, OCLC WebJunction, OCLC WorldShare Interlibrary Loan
Wireless access
Function: Adult bk club, After school storytime, Archival coll, Art exhibits, Audio & video playback equip for onsite use, AV serv, BA reader (adult literacy), Bks on cassette, Bks on CD, CD-ROM, Children's prog, Citizenship assistance, Computer training, Computers for patron use, Copy machines, e-mail serv, Electronic databases & coll, Family literacy, Fax serv, Free DVD rentals, Genealogy discussion group, Govt ref serv, Handicapped accessible, Holiday prog, Home delivery & serv to Sr ctr & nursing homes, Homework prog, ILL available, Libr develop, Mail & tel request accepted, Music CDs, Online ref, Online searches, Orientations, Outside serv via phone, mail, e-mail & web, Photocopying/Printing, Preschool outreach, Prog for adults, Prog for children & young adult, Ref serv available, Scanner, Senior computer classes, Spoken cassettes & CDs, Spoken cassettes & DVDs, Summer reading prog, Tax forms, Telephone ref, VHS videos, Wheelchair accessible, Workshops
Mem of Sagebrush Federation
Special Services for the Deaf - Adult & family literacy prog; Bks on deafness & sign lang; Closed caption videos; High interest/low vocabulary bks; Spec interest per
Special Services for the Blind - Audio mat; Bks on cassette; Bks on CD; Cassette playback machines; Cassettes; Computer with voice synthesizer for visually impaired persons; Copier with enlargement capabilities; Extensive large print coll; HP Scan Jet with photo-finish software; Large print & cassettes; Large print bks; Reader equip; Videos on blindness & phys handicaps
Open Mon-Thurs 11-7, Fri 11-5, Sat 10-1
Friends of the Library Group
Branches: 1
BICENTENNIAL LIBRARY OF COLSTRIP, 419 Willow Ave, Colstrip, 59323. (Mail add: PO Box 1947, Colstrip, 59323-1947), SAN 373-9120. Tel: 406-748-3040. FAX: 406-748-2133. *Dir,* Mary Kay Bullard; Staff 4 (Non-MLS 4)
Founded 1976. Pop 5,689; Circ 30,158
Library Holdings: Bk Titles 21,860; Per Subs 45

Automation Activity & Vendor Info: (Circulation) SIRSI WorkFlows; (ILL) OCLC; (OPAC) OCLC WorldShare Interlibrary Loan
Special Services for the Deaf - Bks on deafness & sign lang
Open Mon, Thurs & Fri 12-5, Tues & Wed 10-5 & 7-9, Sat 9-12
Friends of the Library Group

FORT BENTON

P CHOUTEAU COUNTY LIBRARY*, 1518 Main St, 59442. (Mail add: PO Box 639, 59442-0639), SAN 349-9804. Tel: 406-622-5222. FAX: 406-622-5294. E-mail: fblibrary@mtintouch.net. Web Site: chouteaucountylibrary.googlepages.com. *Dir,* Debbie Wellman; *Asst Librn,* Lila Nansel
Founded 1915. Pop 5,900; Circ 57,000
Library Holdings: Bk Vols 47,000; Per Subs 80
Subject Interests: Chouteau County, Fort Benton, Lewis & Clark expedition, Mo river, Montana
Automation Activity & Vendor Info: (Acquisitions) Follett Software; (Cataloging) OCLC CatExpress; (Circulation) Follett Software; (Course Reserve) Follett Software; (ILL) OCLC FirstSearch; (Media Booking) Follett Software; (OPAC) Follett Software; (Serials) Follett Software
Database Vendor: EBSCO Auto Repair Reference, Gale Cengage Learning
Wireless access
Mem of Pathfinder Regional Library System
Friends of the Library Group
Branches: 2
BIG SANDY BRANCH, 230 First St N, Big Sandy, 59520. (Mail add: PO Box 1247, Big Sandy, 59520-0007), SAN 349-9839. Tel: 406-378-2161. E-mail: bsbl@ttc-cmc.net. *Librn,* Vicki Silvan
Circ 800
Special Collections: Big Sandy Mountaineer
Automation Activity & Vendor Info: (Acquisitions) Horizon; (Circulation) Horizon; (ILL) Horizon
Database Vendor: OCLC WorldShare Interlibrary Loan
Function: After school storytime, Copy machines, Handicapped accessible, Home delivery & serv to Sr ctr & nursing homes, Homebound delivery serv, ILL available, Photocopying/Printing, Preschool outreach, Prog for children & young adult, Spoken cassettes & CDs, Spoken cassettes & DVDs, Summer reading prog, Tax forms, VHS videos
Friends of the Library Group
GERALDINE BRANCH, 603 Main St, Geraldine, 59446. (Mail add: PO Box 316, Geraldine, 59446-0326), SAN 349-9863. Tel: 406-737-4331. E-mail: geraldinebranchlibrary@yahoo.com. *Librn,* Sheila Burke
Special Collections: Geraldine Review, newsp

FORT HARRISON

GM VETERANS ADMINISTRATION CENTER*, Fort Harrison, 3687 Veterans Dr, 59636. (Mail add: PO Box 196, 59636-0196), SAN 309-3034. Tel: 406-447-7366. FAX: 406-447-7992. *Chief Librn,* Gail Wilkerson; Tel: 406-814-5615, E-mail: gail.wilkerson@va.gov; *Tech Spec,* Kathryn Poelman; E-mail: kathryn.poelman@va.gov; Staff 2 (MLS 1, Non-MLS 1)
Founded 1930
Library Holdings: Bk Titles 2,000; Per Subs 50
Subject Interests: Health, Veterans
Partic in Docline; Veterans Affairs Libr Network (VALNET)
Open Mon-Fri 8-4:30

GARDINER

S YELLOWSTONE NATIONAL PARK*, Research Library & Archives, Yellowstone Heritage & Research Ctr, 200 Old Yellowstone Trail, 59030. (Mail add: PO Box 168, Yellowstone National Park, 82190), SAN 318-515X. Tel: 307-344-2264. FAX: 406-848-9958. E-mail: yell_research_library@nps.gov. Web Site: wyldweb.state.wy.us/yrl. *Librn,* Jackie Jerla; E-mail: Jackie_Jerla@contractor.nps.gov; *Librn,* Heather Thams; E-mail: heather_thams@partner.nps.gov; *Archivist,* Harold Housley; Tel: 307-344-2563, E-mail: Harold_Housley@nps.gov; Staff 2 (MLS 1, Non-MLS 1)
Founded 1933
Library Holdings: Bk Titles 10,700; Per Subs 55
Special Collections: Montana Historical Society Coll (1876-present); Yellowstone Area (Rare Bks Coll). US Document Depository
Subject Interests: Yellowstone National Park
Function: Archival coll, For res purposes
Partic in WYLDCat Members

GLASGOW

P GLASGOW CITY-COUNTY LIBRARY*, 408 Third Ave S, 59230. SAN 309-3050. Tel: 406-228-2731. FAX: 406-228-8193. *Dir,* Position Currently Open; *Actg Dir,* Karen L Anderson
Founded 1904. Pop 7,675; Circ 41,733
Jul 2011-Jun 2012 Income $190,443, State $1,113, City $31,007, Federal $3,011, County $149,030, Locally Generated Income $6,282. Mats Exp $190,443, Books $14,000, Per/Ser (Incl. Access Fees) $3,907, AV Mat $4,287. Sal $95,502 (Prof $36,480)
Library Holdings: Audiobooks 1,139; AV Mats 2,203; CDs 333; e-books 7,684; Bk Titles 43,641; Per Subs 65
Special Collections: Glasgow Courier 1895-1988
Subject Interests: Culinary, Montana genealogy
Automation Activity & Vendor Info: (Acquisitions) Follett Software; (Cataloging) OCLC CatExpress; (Circulation) Follett Software; (ILL) OCLC; (OPAC) Follett Software
Database Vendor: EBSCO Auto Repair Reference, Gale Cengage Learning
Wireless access
Mem of Golden Plains Library Federation
Open Mon-Thurs 10-7, Fri 10-5, Sat 10-3
Friends of the Library Group

GLENDIVE

J DAWSON COMMUNITY COLLEGE LIBRARY, Jane Carey Memorial Library, 300 College Dr, 59330. (Mail add: PO Box 421, 59330-0421), SAN 309-3077. Tel: 406-377-9413. Reference Tel: 406-377-9414. FAX: 406-377-8132. E-mail: info@dawson.edu. Web Site: www.dawson.edu/students/jane-carey-memorial-library. *Dir,* Todd Knispel; E-mail: knispelt@dawson.edu; Staff 2 (MLS 1, Non-MLS 1)
Founded 1940. Enrl 350; Fac 26; Highest Degree: Associate
Library Holdings: AV Mats 1,150; Bk Vols 20,468; Per Subs 160
Special Collections: State Document Depository
Subject Interests: Art, Law enforcement
Automation Activity & Vendor Info: (Acquisitions) SirsiDynix; (Cataloging) SirsiDynix; (Circulation) SirsiDynix; (Course Reserve) SirsiDynix; (ILL) OCLC; (OPAC) SirsiDynix; (Serials) SirsiDynix
Database Vendor: Agricola, CredoReference, EBSCOhost, Ex Libris Group, LexisNexis, Newsbank, OCLC FirstSearch, OCLC WorldShare Interlibrary Loan, ProQuest, SerialsSolutions, SirsiDynix
Wireless access
Partic in OCLC Online Computer Library Center, Inc
Open Mon & Fri 8-4, Tues-Thurs 8-4 & 6:30-9

P GLENDIVE PUBLIC LIBRARY*, 200 S Kendrick, 59330. SAN 349-9928. Tel: 406-377-3633. FAX: 406-377-4568. E-mail: booksrus@midrivers.com. *Dir,* Gail Nagle; E-mail: gnagle@midrivers.com; *ILL,* Dawn Kingstad
Founded 1915. Pop 9,000; Circ 45,000
Library Holdings: Bk Titles 20,000; Bk Vols 23,000; Per Subs 85
Special Collections: German-Russian Immigrations; Montana History
Automation Activity & Vendor Info: (Cataloging) SirsiDynix
Database Vendor: Gale Cengage Learning
Function: ILL available
Mem of Sagebrush Federation
Open Mon-Wed 10-7, Thurs & Fri 10-5, Sat 1-5
Friends of the Library Group
Branches: 1
RICHEY PUBLIC LIBRARY, 223 S Main St, Richey, 59259. (Mail add: PO Box 149, Richey, 59259-0149), SAN 349-9952. Tel: 406-773-5585. *Librn,* Betty Keysor
Library Holdings: Bk Vols 10,000; Per Subs 12
Function: ILL available
Open Mon, Wed & Fri 12:30-4:30

GREAT FALLS

S GREAT FALLS GENEALOGY SOCIETY LIBRARY, 301 Second Ave N, 59404. SAN 326-4025. Tel: 406-727-3922. E-mail: gfgenealogy@genlibrary.org. Web Site: gfgenealogy.org. *Pres,* Janet Thomson
Founded 1975
Library Holdings: Bk Vols 5,000; Per Subs 105
Special Collections: Local Cemeteries; Marriages, County Schools; Vital Records, Inquests
Subject Interests: Genealogy
Wireless access
Publications: Treasure State Lines (Quarterly)
Open Tues-Sat 10-4

P GREAT FALLS PUBLIC LIBRARY*, 301 Second Ave N, 59401-2593. SAN 309-3115. Tel: 406-453-0349. FAX: 406-453-0181. E-mail: questions@greatfallslibrary.org. Web Site: www.greatfallslibrary.org. *Dir,* Kathy Mora; Tel: 406-453-0349, Ext 221, E-mail: kmora@greatfallslibrary.org; *Info Serv Supvr,* Susie McIntyre; Tel: 406-453-0349, Ext 232, E-mail: smcintyre@greatfallslibrary.org; *Tech Serv Supvr,* Judy Ellinghausen; Tel: 406-453-0349, Ext 216, E-mail: jellinghausen@greatfallslibrary.org; *Children's & Youth Serv,* Nola Huey; Tel: 406-453-0349, Ext 215, E-mail: nhuey@greatfallslibrary.org; *Circ,*

Gwen Carter; Tel: 406-453-0349, Ext 213, E-mail: gcarter@greatfallslibrary.org; Staff 26 (MLS 4, Non-MLS 22)
Founded 1890. Pop 77,128; Circ 370,291
Library Holdings: Bk Titles 124,071; Bk Vols 159,769; Per Subs 354
Special Collections: City; Montana History Coll
Automation Activity & Vendor Info: (Acquisitions) SirsiDynix; (Cataloging) SirsiDynix; (Circulation) SirsiDynix; (ILL) OCLC Connexion; (OPAC) SirsiDynix
Database Vendor: EBSCO Auto Repair Reference, EBSCOhost, OCLC FirstSearch, OCLC WebJunction, OCLC WorldShare Interlibrary Loan, ProQuest, SirsiDynix
Wireless access
Function: ILL available
Open Mon, Fri & Sat (Oct-May) 10-6, Tues 10-8, Sun 1-5; Mon, Fri & Sat (June-Sept) 10-6, Tues 10-8
Friends of the Library Group
Bookmobiles: 1

S LEWIS & CLARK TRAIL HERITAGE FOUNDATION, INC*, William P Sherman Library & Archives, PO Box 3434, 59403-3434. Tel: 406-761-3950. Toll Free Tel: 888-701-3434. E-mail: library@lewisandclark.org. Web Site: www.lewisandclark.org. *Librn,* Lois Baker; *Librn,* Kathy Murray
Founded 1968
Library Holdings: Bk Vols 2,500
Open Mon-Fri 9-1

S MONTANA SCHOOL FOR THE DEAF & BLIND LIBRARY*, 3911 Central Ave, 59405-1697. SAN 320-6904. Tel: 406-771-6051. FAX: 406-771-6164. TDD: 406-771-6063. E-mail: info@msdb.mt.gov. *Librn,* Staci Bechard; Staff 1 (Non-MLS 1)
Library Holdings: Bks on Deafness & Sign Lang 300; Braille Volumes 1,000; Large Print Bks 500; Bk Vols 9,500
Automation Activity & Vendor Info: (Cataloging) SirsiDynix; (Circulation) SirsiDynix
Special Services for the Deaf - Accessible learning ctr; Captioned film dep; Described encaptioned media prog
Special Services for the Blind - Braille bks; Large print bks
Open Mon-Fri 8-4
Restriction: Not open to pub

J MONTANA STATE UNIVERSITY - GREAT FALLS COLLEGE OF TECHNOLOGY*, Weaver Library, 2100 16th Ave S, 59405. SAN 373-6784. Tel: 406-771-4398. Interlibrary Loan Service Tel: 406-771-5544. Administration Tel: 406-771-4318. FAX: 406-771-4317. E-mail: library@msugf.edu. Web Site: library.msugf.edu. *Dir, eLearning & Libr Serv,* Laura M Wight; E-mail: laura.wight@msugf.edu; Staff 4 (MLS 2, Non-MLS 2)
Founded 1976. Enrl 1,800; Fac 50; Highest Degree: Associate
Jul 2010-Jun 2011 Income $261,000, Parent Institution $231,000, Other $30,000. Sal $202,000 (Prof $100,000)
Library Holdings: AV Mats 972; e-books 22,465; e-journals 43,130; Bk Vols 8,813; Per Subs 72
Automation Activity & Vendor Info: (Acquisitions) SirsiDynix; (Cataloging) SirsiDynix; (Circulation) SirsiDynix; (Course Reserve) SirsiDynix; (ILL) OCLC ILLiad; (OPAC) SirsiDynix; (Serials) SerialsSolutions
Database Vendor: Agricola, ARTstor, Cinahl, CQ Press, CredoReference, EBSCO Information Services, EBSCOhost, Gale Cengage Learning, JSTOR, LexisNexis, Medline, Newsbank, OCLC WorldShare Interlibrary Loan, Oxford Online, ProQuest, PubMed, SerialsSolutions, SirsiDynix, Springshare, LLC, YBP Library Services
Wireless access
Function: Audio & video playback equip for onsite use, Audiobks via web, Bk club(s), Bks on cassette, Bks on CD, Computers for patron use, Copy machines, Distance learning, e-mail & chat, E-Reserves, Electronic databases & coll, Fax serv, Free DVD rentals, Handicapped accessible, Instruction & testing, Online cat, Online ref, Online searches, Orientations, Outside serv via phone, mail, e-mail & web, Photocopying/Printing, Pub access computers, Ref & res, Ref serv in person, Scanner, Telephone ref, VHS videos, Web catalog, Wheelchair accessible
Open Mon-Thurs 8am-9pm, Fri 8-5, Sun 12:30-9
Restriction: Borrowing requests are handled by ILL

S C M RUSSELL MUSEUM LIBRARY, Frederic G Renner Library, 400 13th St N, 59401. SAN 327-1552. Tel: 406-727-8787, Ext 348. FAX: 406-727-2402. Web Site: www.cmrussell.org. *Chief Curator,* Sarah Burt; Tel: 406-727-8787, Ext 312, E-mail: sburt@cmrussell.org; *Archivist,* Kathryn Marie Kramer; Tel: 406-727-8787, Ext 336, E-mail: kkramer@cmrussell.org; Staff 2 (MLS 1, Non-MLS 1)
Founded 1980
Library Holdings: Bk Titles 3,700; Bk Vols 4,000; Per Subs 15; Spec Interest Per Sub 9
Special Collections: Frederic G & Ginger K Renner Coll; J H Sharp Coll, photog; John Taliaferro Papers; Richard Flood Coll
Subject Interests: Art, Artists, Western Am art, Western US hist
Wireless access
Restriction: Non-circulating, Open by appt only

CR UNIVERSITY OF GREAT FALLS LIBRARY*, 1301 20th St S, 59405-4948. SAN 309-3085. Tel: 406-791-5315. Reference Tel: 406-791-5318. Administration Tel: 406-791-5317. FAX: 406-791-5395. E-mail: library@ugf.edu. Web Site: www.ugf.edu/library. *Dir,* David Bibb; E-mail: dbibb01@ugf.edu; *Coll Mgt Librn,* Oliver Pflug; Tel: 406-791-5311, E-mail: opflug01@ugf.edu; *Info Serv,* Susan M Lee; E-mail: slee@ugf.edu; Staff 5 (MLS 3, Non-MLS 2)
Founded 1932. Enrl 958; Highest Degree: Master
Library Holdings: AV Mats 5,988; e-books 7,746; e-journals 23,119; Microforms 21,995; Bk Vols 85,201; Per Subs 236
Special Collections: Americana (Microbook Library of American Civilization)
Subject Interests: Criminal justice, Educ, Law, Relig
Automation Activity & Vendor Info: (Acquisitions) SirsiDynix; (Cataloging) SirsiDynix; (Circulation) SirsiDynix; (Course Reserve) SirsiDynix; (ILL) OCLC FirstSearch; (OPAC) SirsiDynix; (Serials) EBSCO Online
Database Vendor: CredoReference, EBSCO Auto Repair Reference, EBSCOhost, Gale Cengage Learning, JSTOR, ProQuest, Westlaw, World Book Online
Wireless access
Function: Computers for patron use, Copy machines, Distance learning, Electronic databases & coll, Fax serv, Free DVD rentals, Handicapped accessible, ILL available, Mail & tel request accepted, Music CDs, Online cat, Online ref, Online searches, Orientations, Photocopying/Printing, Pub access computers, Scanner, VHS videos, Web-catalog
Partic in Northwest Association of Private Colleges & Universities (NAPCU); OMNI
Open Mon-Thurs (Winter) 8am-10pm, Fri 8-5, Sat 12-5, Sun 1-10; Mon-Thurs (Summer) 8-6, Fri 8-5, Sat 12-5
Restriction: Fee for pub use, Non-circulating of rare bks

HAMILTON

P BITTERROOT PUBLIC LIBRARY*, 306 State St, 59840-2759. SAN 309-3123. Tel: 406-363-1670. FAX: 406-363-1678. Web Site: www.bitterrootpubliclibrary.org. *Dir,* Trista Smith; E-mail: director@bitterrootpubliclibrary.org; *Ad,* Nansu Roddy; *Ch Serv Librn,* Sally Belvins; Staff 6 (Non-MLS 6)
Founded 1903. Pop 24,945; Circ 105,734
Jul 2005-Jun 2006 Income $354,638, State $18,043, County $10,663, Locally Generated Income $69,311, Other $256,621. Mats Exp $43,859, Books $32,657, Per/Ser (Incl. Access Fees) $4,301, AV Equip $4,816, Electronic Ref Mat (Incl. Access Fees) $2,085. Sal $169,916 (Prof $85,188)
Library Holdings: AV Mats 2,592; e-books 9,058; Electronic Media & Resources 28; Large Print Bks 1,423; Bk Titles 43,345; Bk Vols 46,907; Per Subs 74
Special Collections: Bitterroot Valley, Montana; Lewis & Clark Expedition; Ravalli County, Montana
Automation Activity & Vendor Info: (Circulation) SirsiDynix; (ILL) OCLC Online
Database Vendor: Checkpoint Systems, Inc, Gale Cengage Learning, OCLC FirstSearch, OCLC WorldShare Interlibrary Loan, SirsiDynix
Wireless access
Special Services for the Deaf - Closed caption videos
Open Mon & Thurs-Sat 12-5, Tue & Wed 10-8
Friends of the Library Group

G NIH, NATIONAL INSTITUTE OF ALLERGY & INFECTIOUS DISEASES*, Rocky Mountain Laboratories Library, 903 S Fourth St, 59840-2932. SAN 309-3131. Tel: 406-363-9212. Administration Tel: 406-363-9211. FAX: 406-363-9336. *Librn,* Martha Thayer; E-mail: mthayer@niaid.nih.gov; Staff 1.25 (MLS 1, Non-MLS 0.25)
Founded 1927
Library Holdings: Bk Titles 3,250; Bk Vols 3,500; Per Subs 11
Subject Interests: Allergy, Bacteriology, Biochem, Immunology, Med entomology, Microbiology, Parasitology, Venereal disease, Veterinary sci, Virology, Wildlife, Zoology
Automation Activity & Vendor Info: (Cataloging) OCLC; (Circulation) Innovative Interfaces, Inc; (OPAC) Innovative Interfaces, Inc; (Serials) Innovative Interfaces, Inc
Database Vendor: EBSCOhost, Innovative Interfaces, Inc, ISI Web of Knowledge, JSTOR, OCLC FirstSearch, Scopus, Thomson - Web of Science
Wireless access
Partic in Docline
Restriction: Badge access after hrs, External users must contact libr

S RAVALLI COUNTY MUSEUM*, Miles Romney Memorial Library, 205 Bedford, 59840. SAN 324-3605. Tel: 406-363-3338. FAX: 406-363-6588. E-mail: rcmuseum@cybernet1.com. Web Site: www.cybernet1.com/rcmuseum. *Dir,* Helen A Bibler
Founded 1979
Library Holdings: Bk Titles 500; Per Subs 15
Special Collections: Bitter Root Valley Historical Society Coll; Bitter Root Valley Newspapers; Museum Collections 35 Display. Oral History
Function: Res libr
Open Mon, Thurs & Fri 10-4, Sat 10-2, Sun 1-4
Restriction: Not a lending libr

HARDIN

P BIG HORN COUNTY PUBLIC LIBRARY*, 419 N Custer Ave, 59034. SAN 309-314X. FAX: 406-665-1804. Web Site: montanalibraries.org/bhc.asp. *Dir,* Eric Halverson; *Ch Serv,* Donnelle R Boyer; *Instr,* Anita Shoppe; *Pub Serv,* Ray Dale; *Pub Serv,* Donna Howe. Subject Specialists: *Adult educ,* Anita Shoppe; Staff 5 (MLS 1, Non-MLS 4)
Founded 1909. Pop 11,337; Circ 67,398
Jul 2009-Jun 2010 Income $236,000. Mats Exp $17,500, Books $10,000, Per/Ser (Incl. Access Fees) $2,500, Electronic Ref Mat (Incl. Access Fees) $5,000. Sal $90,000
Library Holdings: AV Mats 2,500; Bks on Deafness & Sign Lang 10; CDs 450; Large Print Bks 2,500; Bk Titles 29,500; Per Subs 30; Videos 1,500
Special Collections: Battle of Little Big Horn; Cheyenne Indian Culture & History; Crow Indian Culture & History
Automation Activity & Vendor Info: (Cataloging) SirsiDynix; (Circulation) SirsiDynix; (ILL) OCLC; (OPAC) SirsiDynix
Database Vendor: 3M Library Systems, Alexander Street Press, EBSCO Information Services, Gale Cengage Learning, Ingram Library Services, OCLC FirstSearch, OCLC WorldShare Interlibrary Loan, Overdrive, Inc, SirsiDynix
Wireless access
Special Services for the Blind - Audio mat; Bks on cassette
Open Mon-Thurs 10-7, Fri 10-6
Restriction: Residents only
Friends of the Library Group

HARLEM

J AANIIIH NAKODA COLLEGE LIBRARY*, Hwy 2 & 66, 59526. (Mail add: PO Box 159, 59526-0159), SAN 375-3522. Tel: 406-353-2607, Ext 311. FAX: 406-353-2898. Web Site: www.ancollege.edu. *Dir,* Eva English, Tel: 406-353-2607, E-mail: eenglish@ancollege.edu; Staff 1 (MLS 1)
Founded 1984. Enrl 176; Fac 10
Library Holdings: Bk Titles 8,000; Bk Vols 10,000; Per Subs 65
Special Collections: Oral History
Automation Activity & Vendor Info: (Acquisitions) SirsiDynix; (Cataloging) SirsiDynix; (Circulation) SirsiDynix; (Course Reserve) SirsiDynix; (ILL) SirsiDynix; (Media Booking) SirsiDynix; (OPAC) SirsiDynix; (Serials) SirsiDynix
Wireless access
Open Mon, Wed & Fri 8-5, Tues & Thurs 8-7

P HARLEM PUBLIC LIBRARY*, 37 First Ave S, 59526. (Mail add: PO Box 519, 59526-0519), SAN 349-9537. Tel: 406-353-2712. FAX: 406-353-2616. Web Site: harlemlib@live.com, www.harlempubliclibrary.com. *Dir,* Colleen Brommer; *Asst Librn,* Carly Haluszka
Pop 2,555; Circ 16,271
Jul 2010-Jun 2011 Income $85,733, State $3,000, County $82,733. Mats Exp $17,032, Books $15,644, Electronic Ref Mat (Incl. Access Fees) $1,388. Sal $51,888
Library Holdings: Audiobooks 157; DVDs 536; Large Print Bks 60; Bk Titles 13,416; Per Subs 54
Automation Activity & Vendor Info: (Acquisitions) SirsiDynix; (Cataloging) SirsiDynix; (Circulation) SirsiDynix; (Course Reserve) SirsiDynix; (ILL) SirsiDynix; (Media Booking) SirsiDynix; (OPAC) SirsiDynix; (Serials) SirsiDynix
Open Mon & Wed 12:30-5:30, Tues & Fri 9-1, Thurs 12:30-5:30 & 7-9

HARLOWTON

P HARLOWTON PUBLIC LIBRARY*, 17 S Central Ave, 59036. (Mail add: PO Box 663, 59036-0663), SAN 309-3158. Tel: 406-632-5584. *Librn,* Kathleen Schreiber
Founded 1932. Pop 2,246; Circ 16,902
Library Holdings: Bk Titles 10,000; Bk Vols 11,500; Per Subs 38
Open Mon-Thurs 9:30-1 & 2-9, Fri 9:30-1 & 2-5:30, Sun 6pm-9pm

HAVRE

P HAVRE HILL COUNTY LIBRARY*, 402 Third St, 59501. SAN 309-3174. Tel: 406-265-2123. FAX: 406-262-1091. E-mail: library@havrehill.org. Web Site: havrehilllibrary.org. *Dir,* Bonnie Williamson; *Ch Serv,* Carrie Wilson; *Circ,* Shelma Seidel; *Coll Develop,* Margaret Stallkamp; *Ref,* Francine Brady; Staff 5 (Non-MLS 5)
Founded 1983. Pop 16,663; Circ 93,215
Jul 2005-Jun 2006 Income $257,139. Mats Exp $31,000, Books $28,000, Per/Ser (Incl. Access Fees) $3,000. Sal $132,009
Library Holdings: Bks on Deafness & Sign Lang 180; Braille Volumes 15; CDs 150; DVDs 25; Large Print Bks 4,500; Bk Titles 63,937; Per Subs 137; Talking Bks 1,122; Videos 1,382
Subject Interests: Genealogy, Montana
Automation Activity & Vendor Info: (Cataloging) SirsiDynix; (Circulation) SirsiDynix
Database Vendor: EBSCOhost, OCLC FirstSearch, OCLC WorldShare Interlibrary Loan, SirsiDynix
Open Mon & Tues 10-9, Wed & Thurs 10-6, Fri 10-5, Sat 12-5
Friends of the Library Group

C MONTANA STATE UNIVERSITY-NORTHERN*, Vande Bogart Library, 300 11th St W, 59501. (Mail add: PO Box 7751, 59501-7751), SAN 309-3182. Tel: 406-265-3706. FAX: 406-265-3799. Web Site: www.msun.edu/infotech/library. *Dir,* Vicki Gist; E-mail: gist@msun.edu; *Archivist, Tech Serv,* Valerie Hickman; E-mail: hickman@msun.edu; *Circ, ILL,* William Lorett; E-mail: william.lorett@msun.edu; *Circ, Doc, Ser,* Belinda Potter; E-mail: bpotter@msun.edu; Staff 4 (MLS 1, Non-MLS 3)
Founded 1929. Enrl 1,058; Fac 98; Highest Degree: Master
Library Holdings: CDs 671; DVDs 132; e-books 216,409; e-journals 41,507; Bk Vols 133,910; Per Subs 98; Videos 11
Special Collections: Education (Educational Resources Information Center Coll), micro. State Document Depository; US Document Depository
Subject Interests: Applied tech, Educ, Nursing, Western hist
Automation Activity & Vendor Info: (Cataloging) SirsiDynix; (Circulation) SirsiDynix; (Course Reserve) SirsiDynix; (ILL) OCLC ILLiad; (OPAC) SirsiDynix; (Serials) SirsiDynix
Wireless access
Open Mon-Thurs 7:30am-10pm, Fri 7:30-5, Sun 1-10

HELENA

S ALTERNATIVE ENERGY RESOURCES ORGANIZATION LIBRARY*, 432 N Last Chance Gulch St, 59601-5014. SAN 329-4420. Tel: 406-443-7272. FAX: 406-442-9120. E-mail: aero@aeromt.org. *In Charge,* Joan DeCrosby
Library Holdings: Bk Vols 1,200; Per Subs 50
Restriction: Mem only

C CARROLL COLLEGE*, Jack & Sallie Corette Library, 1601 N Benton Ave, 59625. SAN 309-3204. Tel: 406-447-4340. Circulation Tel: 406-447-4346. Reference Tel: 406-447-4343. Administration Tel: 406-447-4344. FAX: 406-447-4525. Web Site: www.carroll.edu/library/index.cc. *Dir,* Christian Frazza; E-mail: cfrazza@carroll.edu; *Ref & Instrul Serv Librn,* Heather Navratil; E-mail: hnavratil@carroll.edu; *Circ Supvr,* Peggy Kude; E-mail: pkude@carroll.edu; *Supvr, Per,* Karla Hokit; E-mail: khokit@carroll.edu; *Tech Serv Supvr,* Cathi Burgoyne; Tel: 406-447-4342, E-mail: cburgoyn@carroll.edu; Staff 5 (MLS 2, Non-MLS 3)
Founded 1909. Enrl 1,400; Fac 100; Highest Degree: Bachelor
Jul 2005-Jun 2006 Income $493,106, Locally Generated Income $2,232, Parent Institution $490,874. Mats Exp $158,710, Books $68,710, Per/Ser (Incl. Access Fees) $80,000, Micro $3,000, AV Mat $2,000, Electronic Ref Mat (Incl. Access Fees) $5,000. Sal $278,469
Library Holdings: Bk Titles 83,425; Bk Vols 98,257; Videos 1,000
Special Collections: US Document Depository
Subject Interests: Allied health, Natural sci, State hist, Theol
Automation Activity & Vendor Info: (Acquisitions) SirsiDynix; (Cataloging) OCLC; (Circulation) SirsiDynix; (ILL) OCLC; (OPAC) SirsiDynix; (Serials) SirsiDynix
Database Vendor: American Psychological Association (APA), Annual Reviews, EBSCOhost, Gale Cengage Learning, JSTOR, LexisNexis, Micromedex, OCLC FirstSearch, OVID Technologies, Project MUSE, ProQuest, SerialsSolutions, SirsiDynix
Wireless access
Partic in National Network of Libraries of Medicine; OCLC Online Computer Library Center, Inc; OMNI
Open Mon-Thurs 8am-Midnight, Fri 8-4:30, Sat 9-5, Sun 1-Midnight

P LEWIS & CLARK LIBRARY*, 120 S Last Chance Gulch, 59601. SAN 349-9987. Tel: 406-447-1690. Circulation Tel: 406-447-1690, Ext 123. Reference Tel: 406-447-1690, Ext 100. Administration Tel: 406-447-1690, Ext 117. FAX: 406-447-1687. TDD: 406-447-1678. Web Site: www.lewisandclarklibrary.org. *Dir,* Judith E Hart; E-mail: jhart@mtlib.org; *Bus Mgr,* Patricia Sternberg; Tel: 406-447-1690, Ext 121, E-mail:

tsberg@mtlib.org; *Fiscal Officer,* Rebecca W Foster; Tel: 406-447-1690, Ext 112, E-mail: rwfoster@mtlib.org; *Adult Serv,* Suzanne Schwichtenberg; Tel: 406-447-1690, Ext 130, E-mail: suzanne@mtlib.org; *Cat,* Donald Cornish; E-mail: dcornish@mtlib.org; *Ch Serv,* Candice Morris; Tel: 406-447-1690, Ext 115, E-mail: cmorris@mtlib.org; *Circ,* Gail S Wilson; Tel: 406-447-1690, Ext 122, E-mail: gswilson@mtlib.org; *Coll Develop,* Karla Ritten; Tel: 406-447-1690, Ext 133, E-mail: kritten@mtlib.org; *Info Tech,* Matthew A Beckstrom; Tel: 406-447-1690, Ext 111, E-mail: mbeckstr@mtlib.org; *Pub Info Officer,* Patricia Spencer; Tel: 406-447-1690, Ext 124, E-mail: pspencer@mtlib.org; *Ref,* John A Heldt; Tel: 406-447-1690, Ext 136, E-mail: jheldt@mtlib.org; Staff 27.1 (MLS 6.5, Non-MLS 20.6)
Founded 1868. Pop 56,335; Circ 647,806
Library Holdings: Bk Titles 129,420; Per Subs 203
Special Collections: Local Energy Resource Center; Local Government Info Center; Local Montana History Coll. Oral History
Subject Interests: Energy resources, Govt info
Automation Activity & Vendor Info: (Acquisitions) Infor Library & Information Solutions; (Cataloging) Infor Library & Information Solutions; (Circulation) Infor Library & Information Solutions; (ILL) Infor Library & Information Solutions; (OPAC) Infor Library & Information Solutions
Database Vendor: Checkpoint Systems, Inc, EBSCOhost, Electric Library, FileMaker, Gale Cengage Learning, OCLC FirstSearch, OCLC WorldShare Interlibrary Loan, ReferenceUSA, Wilson - Wilson Web
Wireless access
Function: Adult bk club, Adult literacy prog, Art exhibits, CD-ROM, Computer training, Copy machines, Doc delivery serv, e-mail serv, Electronic databases & coll, Fax serv, Genealogy discussion group, Handicapped accessible, Homebound delivery serv, ILL available, Online ref, Online searches, Photocopying/Printing, Preschool outreach, Prog for adults, Prog for children & young adult, Ref serv available, Senior computer classes, Serves mentally handicapped consumers, Spoken cassettes & CDs, Spoken cassettes & DVDs, Summer reading prog, Tax forms, Telephone ref, VHS videos, Wheelchair accessible, Workshops
Publications: Annual Report
Partic in OCLC Online Computer Library Center, Inc
Restriction: Lending limited to county residents, Non-resident fee
Friends of the Library Group
Branches: 2
AUGUSTA BRANCH, 205 Main St, Augusta, 59410. (Mail add: PO Box 387, Augusta, 59410-0387). Tel: 406-562-3348. FAX: 406-562-3358. *Br Mgr,* Susan Geise; E-mail: sgeise@lclibrary.org
Open Mon 1-5, Tues & Wed 10-12 & 1-5, Thurs 10-12 & 1-3, Sun 3-7
LINCOLN BRANCH, 102 Ninth Ave S, Lincoln, 59639. (Mail add: PO Box 309, Lincoln, 59639-0309). Tel: 406-362-4300. FAX: 406-362-4039. *Br Mgr,* Sherri Wood; E-mail: swood@mtlib.org
Automation Activity & Vendor Info: (Course Reserve) Infor Library & Information Solutions

G MONTANA DEPARTMENT OF COMMERCE, Census & Economic Information Center, 301 S Park, 59620. (Mail add: PO Box 200505, 59620-0505), SAN 320-1996. FAX: 406-841-2731. E-mail: ceic@mt.gov. Web Site: ceic.mt.gov. *Bur Chief,* Mary Craigle; Tel: 406-841-2740, E-mail: mcraigle@mt.gov; *Sr Res Economist,* Joe Ramler; Tel: 406-841-2719, E-mail: jramler@mt.gov; Staff 5 (Non-MLS 5)
Founded 1970
Library Holdings: CDs 150; DVDs 50; Bk Titles 100; Bk Vols 250
Subject Interests: Demographics, Econ
Open Mon-Fri 8-5

S MONTANA HISTORICAL SOCIETY*, Research Center, 225 N Roberts St, 59601-4514. (Mail add: PO Box 201201, 59620-1201), SAN 309-3220. Tel: 406-444-2681. Interlibrary Loan Service Tel: 406-444-3485. Administration Tel: 406-444-4787. Toll Free Tel: 800-243-9900. FAX: 406-444-5297. E-mail: mhslibrary@mt.gov. Web Site: montanahistoricalsociety.org. *Dir,* Molly Kruckenberg; E-mail: mkruckenberg@mt.gov; *Tech Serv Librn,* Roberta Gebhardt; Tel: 406-444-4702, E-mail: rgebhardt@mt.gov; *Libr Mgr,* Brian Shovers; Tel: 406-444-7415, E-mail: bshovers@mt.gov; *Photog Archives Mgr,* Lory Morrow; Tel: 406-444-4714, E-mail: dmorrow@mt.gov; *Digital Newsp Project Coordr,* Christine Kirkham; Tel: 406-444-0203, E-mail: ckirkham@mt.gov; *Digital Newsp Project Asst,* Ashley Fejeran; Tel: 406-444-7428, E-mail: afejeran@mt.gov; *State Archivist,* Jodie Foley; Tel: 406-444-7482, E-mail: jofoley@mt.gov; *Sr Archivist,* Richard Aarstad; Tel: 406-444-6779, E-mail: raarstad@mt.gov; *Archivist, Oral Historian,* Rachel Lilley; Tel: 406-444-4774, E-mail: rlilley@mt.gov; *Archivist,* Jeff Malcomsom; Tel: 406-444-7427, E-mail: jmalcomsom@mt.gov; *Electronic Rec Archivist,* Caitlin Patterson; Tel: 406-444-4770, E-mail: cpatterson@mt.gov; *Photo Archivist,* Rebecca Kohl; Tel: 406-444-3317, E-mail: bkohl@mt.gov; *Photo Archivist,* Matthew Peek; E-mail: mpeek@mt.gov; *ILL,* Lea Solberg; E-mail: lsolberg@mt.gov; *Ref Historian,* Zoe Ann Stoltz; Tel: 406-444-1988, E-mail: zstoltz@mt.gov; *Tech Support,* Barbara Pepper-Rotness; Tel: 406-444-9526, E-mail: bapepperrotness@mt.gov. Subject Specialists: *Manuscripts,* Rachel Lilley; Staff 17.75 (MLS 15, Non-MLS 2.75)
Founded 1865
Jul 2008-Jun 2009 Income $969,984, State $872,308, Federal $12,613, Locally Generated Income $58,385, Other $26,678. Mats Exp $17,348, Books $15,848, Electronic Ref Mat (Incl. Access Fees) $1,500. Sal $843,996
Library Holdings: Bk Vols 56,000; Per Subs 385
Special Collections: 20th Century Homesteading Photos (Cameron Coll); Cattle Industry (Huffmann Coll), photog; Genealogy (Daughters of American Revolution Coll); George Armstrong Custer (Edgar I Stewart Coll); Montana Newspapers; Montana State Archives; Range Cattle Industry 1860-1945 (Teakle Coll); Yellowstone Park, Pacific Northwest & North Plains Photos (Haynes Coll). Oral History; State Document Depository
Subject Interests: Montana, Western Americana
Automation Activity & Vendor Info: (Cataloging) SirsiDynix; (Circulation) SirsiDynix; (OPAC) SirsiDynix; (Serials) SirsiDynix
Database Vendor: OCLC FirstSearch, SirsiDynix
Wireless access
Function: Govt ref serv, ILL available, Newsp ref libr, Ref serv available, Telephone ref
Publications: Montana: The Magazine of Western History (Quarterly)
Partic in OCLC Online Computer Library Center, Inc
Open Tues-Fri 9-5, Sat 9-1
Restriction: Circulates for staff only, Closed stack, In-house use for visitors, Non-circulating coll

G MONTANA LEGISLATIVE REFERENCE CENTER*, State Capitol, Rm 10, 59620. (Mail add: PO Box 201706, 59620-1706), SAN 320-2003. Tel: 406-444-3588. FAX: 406-444-2588. E-mail: leglib@mt.gov. Web Site: leg.mt.gov/. *Libr Dir,* Sonia Gavin; E-mail: sgavin@mt.gov; *Libr Tech,* Pam Weitz; E-mail: pweitz@mt.gov; Staff 2 (MLS 1, Non-MLS 1)
Founded 1975
Library Holdings: Bk Titles 7,581; Bk Vols 10,456; Per Subs 489
Special Collections: Montana Legislature Interim Study Archives
Subject Interests: Law, Legis hist, Montana constitutional, Pub admin, Pub affairs
Automation Activity & Vendor Info: (Acquisitions) Inmagic, Inc.; (Cataloging) Inmagic, Inc.; (Circulation) Inmagic, Inc.; (ILL) Inmagic, Inc.; (OPAC) Inmagic, Inc.; (Serials) Inmagic, Inc.
Database Vendor: LexisNexis, OCLC FirstSearch
Function: ILL available, Photocopying/Printing, Telephone ref
Publications: Catalog of Publications & Interim Study Final Reports (1957-1999); Sources of Information & Publications (8th ed 2000)
Partic in BRS; OCLC Western Service Center
Open Mon-Fri 8-5

S MONTANA MASONIC LIBRARY*, 425 N Park Ave, 59624. (Mail add: PO Box 1158, 59624-1158), SAN 309-3212. Tel: 406-442-7774. FAX: 406-442-1321. E-mail: mtglsec@grandlodgemontana.org. Web Site: www.grandlodgemontana.org. *Librn,* Reid L Gardiner
Founded 1866
Library Holdings: Bk Titles 1,500
Special Collections: Early Montana & Masonic History, first issue copies & original handwritten mss
Subject Interests: Freemasonry, Masonry
Function: ILL available
Friends of the Library Group

G MONTANA OFFICE OF PUBLIC INSTRUCTION*, Resource Center, 1300 11th Ave, 59601-3916. (Mail add: PO Box 202501, 59620-2501), SAN 309-3239. Tel: 406-444-2082. FAX: 406-444-3924. Web Site: www.opi.mt.gov. *Librn,* Cheri Bergeron; E-mail: cbergeron@mt.gov
Special Collections: Montana Education Archives
Subject Interests: Educ policy
Partic in OCLC Online Computer Library Center, Inc

G MONTANA STATE DEPARTMENT OF NATURAL RESOURCES & CONSERVATION*, Research & Information Center, PO Box 201601, 59620-1601. SAN 320-6912. Tel: 406-444-6603. FAX: 406-444-0533. Web Site: www.dnrc.mt.gov.
Library Holdings: Bk Titles 9,000; Per Subs 91
Special Collections: (includes Columbia, Missouri & Yellowstone River basin studies & general natural resource planning); Energy Planning & Development; Environmental Impact Statements; Montana Department of Natural Resources Publications & Water Planning
Publications: DNRC Publications List & Addendum
Restriction: Staff use only

P MONTANA STATE LIBRARY*, 1515 E Sixth Ave, 59620-1800. (Mail add: PO Box 201800, 59620-1800), SAN 350-0136. Tel: 406-444-3115. Information Services Tel: 406-444-3016. Toll Free Tel: 800-338-5087. FAX: 406-444-0266. E-mail: MSLReference@mt.gov. Web Site: msl.mt.gov. *State Librn,* Jennie Stapp; E-mail: jstapp2@mt.gov; *Dir, Statewide Libr Res,* Sarah McHugh; E-mail: samchugh@mt.gov; *Digital*

Libr Dir, Evan Hammer; *Mgr,* Kris Schmitz; Tel: 406-444-3117, E-mail: kschmitz@mt.gov; *Supvr, Libr & Info Serv,* James Kammerer; Tel: 406-444-5432, E-mail: jkammerer@mt.gov; *Supvr, Montana Talking Bk Libr Serv,* Christie O Briggs; Tel: 406-444-5399, E-mail: cbriggs@mt.gov; Staff 35 (MLS 9, Non-MLS 26)
Founded 1929
Library Holdings: Braille Volumes 129,000; CDs 339; DVDs 16; e-books 324; e-journals 46; Electronic Media & Resources 3,067; Bk Titles 42,171; Bk Vols 55,929; Per Subs 123; Talking Bks 151,576; Videos 413
Special Collections: Braille Twin Vision, combined textile & vision bks; Descriptive Videos (DV's); Geographic Information System; Library & Information Science; MT Natural Resource Index; Natural Resource Information System; Talking Book Library; Water Information System. State Document Depository
Subject Interests: Librarianship, Natural res, State govt, Water
Automation Activity & Vendor Info: (Cataloging) SirsiDynix; (Circulation) SirsiDynix; (ILL) OCLC FirstSearch; (OPAC) Keystone Systems, Inc (KLAS); (Serials) EBSCO Online
Database Vendor: BioOne, EBSCOhost, Gale Cengage Learning, infoUSA, Keystone Systems, Inc (KLAS), LexisNexis, OCLC FirstSearch, OCLC WorldShare Interlibrary Loan, PubMed, ReferenceUSA, SirsiDynix
Wireless access
Function: Govt ref serv, Homebound delivery serv, ILL available, Ref serv available, Wheelchair accessible, Workshops
Publications: Big Sky (Newsletter); Bits of Gold (Newsletter); Montana Certification Program Manual; Montana Library Directory (Online only); Montana Public Library Annual Statistics
Partic in Mountain Plains Libr Asn; Nat Libr Serv READS Prog; OCLC Online Computer Library Center, Inc; Pac NW Libr Asn
Special Services for the Deaf - Assisted listening device; Assistive tech; Staff with knowledge of sign lang; TTY equip
Special Services for the Blind - Accessible computers; Assistive/Adapted tech devices, equip & products; Audio mat; Braille alphabet card; Braille servs; Cassette playback machines; Children's Braille; Closed circuit TV; Computer with voice synthesizer for visually impaired persons; Digital talking bk; Digital talking bk machines; Duplicating spec requests; Info on spec aids & appliances; Internet workstation with adaptive software; Local mags & bks recorded; Low vision equip; Machine repair; Magnifiers; Mags & bk reproduction/duplication; Networked computers with assistive software; Newsline for the Blind; Production of talking bks; Ref serv; Screen enlargement software for people with visual disabilities; Soundproof reading booth; Spec cats; Talking bk & rec for the blind cat; Tel Pioneers equip repair group; Volunteer serv; Web-Braille
Open Mon-Fri 8-5

M ST PETER'S HOSPITAL*, Medical Library, 2475 Broadway, 59601. SAN 320-8656. Tel: 406-447-2462. FAX: 406-447-2468. E-mail: medlibrary@stpetes.org. Web Site: www.stpetes.org.
Founded 1973
Library Holdings: Bk Titles 250; Per Subs 40
Subject Interests: Med
Wireless access
Function: Doc delivery serv, Electronic databases & coll, ILL available, Mail & tel request accepted, Online searches, Photocopying/Printing, Ref serv available
Open Mon-Fri 7am-12:30pm

M SHODAIR HOSPITAL*, Medical Library, 2755 Colonial Dr, 59601-4926. (Mail add: PO Box 5539, 59604-5539), SAN 320-6920. Tel: 406-444-7500. FAX: 406-444-7536. *Librn,* Marjorie McNellis; Tel: 406-444-7518; Staff 1 (Non-MLS 1)
Founded 1979
Library Holdings: AV Mats 100; Bk Titles 1,800; Per Subs 100
Special Collections: Lay Information on Genetic Disorders
Subject Interests: Birth defects, Child psychology, Clinical genetics, Cytogenetics, Genetic counseling, Genetic disorders, Med genetics, Prenatal diagnosis
Database Vendor: EBSCOhost, Gale Cengage Learning, OCLC FirstSearch
Partic in Docline; National Network of Libraries of Medicine; OCLC Online Computer Library Center, Inc
Open Mon-Fri 8- 5

GL STATE LAW LIBRARY OF MONTANA*, 215 N Sanders, 59601-4522. (Mail add: PO Box 203004, 59620-3004). Tel: 406-444-3660. Toll Free Tel: 800-710-9827 (MT only). FAX: 406-444-3603. E-mail: mtlawlibrary@mt.gov. Web Site: www.courts.mt.gov/library. *Dir,* Position Currently Open; *Ref Librn,* Susan Lupton; Tel: 406-444-3636, E-mail: slupton@mt.gov; *Access Serv Coordr,* Rita Gibson; *Cataloger,* Laura Tretter; *Electronic Res,* Kevin Cook; *ILL,* Judith Rogers. Subject Specialists: *Legal ref,* Susan Lupton; Staff 8 (MLS 3, Non-MLS 5)
Founded 1866
Jul 2008-Jun 2009 Income $941,375. Mats Exp $425,961, Books $328,391, Electronic Ref Mat (Incl. Access Fees) $97,570. Sal $383,719
Library Holdings: Bk Titles 19,000; Bk Vols 190,000; Per Subs 550
Special Collections: State Justice Institute Depository. US Document Depository
Subject Interests: Legal hist, Legis hist
Automation Activity & Vendor Info: (Acquisitions) SirsiDynix; (Cataloging) SirsiDynix; (Circulation) SirsiDynix; (Course Reserve) SirsiDynix; (ILL) SirsiDynix; (Media Booking) SirsiDynix; (OPAC) SirsiDynix; (Serials) SirsiDynix
Database Vendor: HeinOnline, LexisNexis, Westlaw
Wireless access
Publications: A Guide to Montana Legal Research; Audio/Visual Catalogs; Historic Sketch of the State Law Library of Montana; Legal Materials for Non-lawyers; Periodicals Catalog; State Law Library Users Guide
Partic in OCLC Online Computer Library Center, Inc
Open Mon-Fri 8-5

C UNIVERSITY OF MONTANA-HELENA*, College of Technology Library, 1115 N Roberts St, 59601. SAN 373-6865. Tel: 406-444-2743. FAX: 406-444-6892. E-mail: library@umh.umt.edu. Web Site: www.umhelena.edu/library. *Dir of Libr Serv,* Janice C Bacino; E-mail: bacinoj@umhelena.edu; Staff 2 (MLS 2)
Founded 1992. Enrl 1,300; Highest Degree: Associate
Library Holdings: Audiobooks 2,400; AV Mats 200; DVDs 300; e-books 92,000; e-journals 41,600; Bk Vols 9,200; Per Subs 97; Videos 200
Subject Interests: Aviation, Computer tech, Construction, Diesel, Electronic, Fire protection, Nursing, Teaching, Technologies, Trades
Automation Activity & Vendor Info: (Cataloging) Ex Libris Group; (Circulation) Ex Libris Group; (OPAC) Ex Libris Group
Wireless access
Function: Audio & video playback equip for onsite use, Computers for patron use, Copy machines, e-mail & chat, Electronic databases & coll, Free DVD rentals, Handicapped accessible, ILL available, Online cat, Online info literacy tutorials on the web & in blackboard, Online ref, Online searches, Orientations, OverDrive digital audio bks, Photocopying/Printing, Printer for laptops & handheld devices, Ref serv in person, VHS videos, Video lending libr
Partic in Lyrasis; OCLC Online Computer Library Center, Inc
Open Mon-Thurs 8-6, Fri 8-5
Restriction: Open to pub for ref & circ; with some limitations, Open to students, fac & staff

HERON

P LAURIE HILL LIBRARY*, PO Box 128, 59844-0128. SAN 376-7701. Tel: 406-847-2520. *Dir,* Mary Williams
Library Holdings: Bk Titles 8,000; Bk Vols 9,000
Wireless access
Open Wed 3-5:30, Thurs 11-1, Sat 11-3

HOT SPRINGS

P PRESTON TOWN-COUNTY LIBRARY OF HOT SPRINGS*, 203 E Main St, 59845. (Mail add: PO Box 850, 59845-0850), SAN 309-328X. Tel: 406-741-3491. FAX: 406-741-3493. E-mail: hslibrar@hotsprgs.net. Web Site: www.hotsprgs.net/~hslibrar/. *Dir,* Kimberly Brooks
Founded 1963
Library Holdings: Bk Titles 15,000
Special Collections: Chinese-Herbal Therapy Coll; Montana & Western Coll. Oral History
Database Vendor: OCLC FirstSearch
Open Mon & Wed 10-5, Sat 10-4
Friends of the Library Group
Bookmobiles: 1

JOLIET

P JOLIET PUBLIC LIBRARY*, 211 E Front Ave, 59041. (Mail add: PO Box 213, 59041-0213), SAN 376-785X. Tel: 406-962-3013. E-mail: jolietlib@yahoo.com. *Dir,* Debbie Hronek
Founded 2004
Open Tues-Thurs 10-6, Sat 9-1
Friends of the Library Group

JORDAN

P GARFIELD COUNTY LIBRARY*, 228 E Main St, 59337. (Mail add: PO Box 69, 59337-0069), SAN 309-3298. Tel: 406-557-2297. E-mail: garflibr@midrivers.com. *Dir,* Leah LaVoie
Founded 1948. Pop 1,589; Circ 7,000
Library Holdings: Bk Titles 10,261
Automation Activity & Vendor Info: (Acquisitions) Follett Software; (Cataloging) Follett Software; (Circulation) Follett Software; (Course Reserve) Follett Software; (ILL) Follett Software; (Media Booking) Follett Software; (OPAC) Follett Software; (Serials) Follett Software
Mem of Sagebrush Federation
Open Mon-Thurs 12:30-5:30

KALISPELL

J FLATHEAD VALLEY COMMUNITY COLLEGE LIBRARY*, 777 Grandview Dr, 59901. SAN 309-331X. Tel: 406-756-3856. Administration Tel: 406-756-3853. FAX: 406-756-3854. Web Site: www.fvcc.edu/academics/student-resources/library. *Dir,* Michael J Ober; E-mail: mober@fvcc.edu; *Acq, Tech Serv,* Carrie Nelson; Tel: 406-756-3855, E-mail: cnelson@fvcc.edu; *Circ, ILL,* Sinda M Puryer; Tel: 406-756-3856, E-mail: spuryer@fvcc.edu; Staff 3 (MLS 1, Non-MLS 2)
Founded 1967. Enrl 1,988; Fac 48; Highest Degree: Associate
Jul 2008-Jun 2009 Income $158,000, Locally Generated Income $2,000, Parent Institution $156,000. Mats Exp $84,360, Books $32,000, Per/Ser (Incl. Access Fees) $17,000, AV Mat $7,000, Electronic Ref Mat (Incl. Access Fees) $15,000. Sal $140,100 (Prof $58,538)
Library Holdings: DVDs 1,109; e-books 2,700; Bk Titles 34,050; Bk Vols 39,990; Per Subs 138; Videos 1,721
Subject Interests: Allied health, Classical lit, Forestry, Indians of NAm, Montana hist, Tourism
Automation Activity & Vendor Info: (Acquisitions) SirsiDynix; (Cataloging) SirsiDynix; (Circulation) SirsiDynix; (Course Reserve) SirsiDynix; (ILL) OCLC; (Media Booking) SirsiDynix; (OPAC) SirsiDynix; (Serials) SirsiDynix
Database Vendor: Cinahl, EBSCO Information Services, Gale Cengage Learning, Grolier Online, Newsbank, OCLC FirstSearch, OCLC WorldShare Interlibrary Loan, ProQuest, SirsiDynix
Wireless access
Function: Art exhibits, Computer training, Computers for patron use, Copy machines, e-mail & chat, Electronic databases & coll, Exhibits, Fax serv, Free DVD rentals, Handicapped accessible, ILL available, Instruction & testing, Mail & tel request accepted, Online cat, Online ref, Online searches, Orientations, Outside serv via phone, mail, e-mail & web, Photocopying/Printing, Ref & res, Ref serv available, Ref serv in person, Referrals accepted, Telephone ref, VHS videos, Wheelchair accessible
Partic in OCLC Online Computer Library Center, Inc
Open Mon-Thurs 8-8, Fri 8-5

P IMAGINEIF LIBRARIES*, 247 First Ave E, 59901. SAN 350-0195. Tel: 406-758-5820. Circulation Tel: 406-758-5819. Interlibrary Loan Service Tel: 406-758-5817. Reference Tel: 406-758-5815. FAX: 406-758-5868. Web Site: imagineiflibraries.org. *Dir,* Kim Crowley; Tel: 406-758-5826, E-mail: kcrowley@imagineif.org; *Tech Coordr,* Brett Fisher; Staff 26 (MLS 4, Non-MLS 22)
Founded 1943. Pop 74,471; Circ 440,414
Library Holdings: AV Mats 8,743; e-books 3,000; Bk Vols 206,750; Per Subs 231
Special Collections: Montana Author & Subject Coll
Automation Activity & Vendor Info: (Acquisitions) SirsiDynix; (Cataloging) SirsiDynix; (Circulation) SirsiDynix; (Media Booking) SirsiDynix; (OPAC) SirsiDynix; (Serials) SirsiDynix
Database Vendor: Gale Cengage Learning
Wireless access
Function: ILL available, Photocopying/Printing, Prog for children & young adult, Ref serv available, Summer reading prog, Telephone ref
Partic in OCLC Online Computer Library Center, Inc
Open Mon-Wed 10-8, Thurs & Fri 10-6, Sat 10-5
Friends of the Library Group
Branches: 3
BIGFORK BRANCH, 525 Electric Ave, Bigfork, 59911. Tel: 406-837-6976. *Br Mgr,* Annie Lieberman
Open Tues 12-5, Wed 10-7, Thurs-Sat 12-5
Friends of the Library Group
COLUMBIA FALLS BRANCH, 130 Sixth St W, Columbia Falls, 59912, SAN 350-025X. Tel: 406-892-5919. FAX: 406-892-5919. *Br Mgr,* Deena Stacy; E-mail: dstacy@imagineiflibraries.org; Staff 4 (Non-MLS 4)
Open Mon & Thurs 10-6, Tues & Wed 10-7, Fri 12-6, Sat 12-4
Friends of the Library Group
MARION BRANCH, 205 Gopher Lane, Marion, 59925, SAN 323-8105. Tel: 406-854-2333. *Br Mgr,* Kathy Franken; Staff 1 (Non-MLS 1)
Open Tues & Thurs 3-7, Wed 3-5

M KALISPELL REGIONAL MEDICAL CENTER*, Medical Library, 310 Sunnyview Lane, 59901. SAN 309-3328. Tel: 406-752-1739. FAX: 406-752-8771. E-mail: medicallibrarian@krmc.org. Web Site: www.kalispellregional.org, www.kalispellregional.org/nwhc/employees/medical-library. *Lead Med Librn,* Heidi Sue Adams; E-mail: hadams@krmc.org; *PRN Med Librn,* Laurie Blasingame; *Med Librn,* Rachel Helbing; E-mail: rhelbing@krmc.org; Staff 2 (MLS 2)
Founded 1976
Library Holdings: e-books 50; e-journals 2,500; Bk Titles 1,000; Per Subs 160
Subject Interests: Allied health, Med, Nursing
Automation Activity & Vendor Info: (Acquisitions) SirsiDynix; (Cataloging) SirsiDynix; (Circulation) SirsiDynix; (OPAC) SirsiDynix
Function: Accessibility serv available based on individual needs, Doc delivery serv, Health sci info serv, ILL available, Online cat, Online searches, Orientations, Outreach serv, Outside serv via phone, mail, e-mail & web, Photocopying/Printing, Ref serv available, Scanner, Telephone ref
Partic in National Network of Libraries of Medicine; OCLC Online Computer Library Center, Inc
Open Mon-Fri 8-4
Restriction: Access at librarian's discretion, Access for corporate affiliates, Authorized patrons, Badge access after hrs, Circ limited, Circulates for staff only, Employees & their associates, External users must contact libr, Hospital employees & physicians only, Hospital staff & commun, Lending to staff only, Limited access for the pub, Med & nursing staff, patients & families, Med staff & students, Open to pub by appt only, Prof mat only, Serves prof staff, students & interns only, Staff & patient use, Staff & prof res, Use of others with permission of librn

LAME DEER

J CHIEF DULL KNIFE COLLEGE*, Dr John Woodenlegs Memorial Library, One College Dr, 59043. (Mail add: PO Box 98, 59043-0098), SAN 321-8120. Tel: 406-477-8293. FAX: 406-477-6575. Web Site: www.cdkc.edu. *Dir,* Joan Hantz; *Asst Librn,* Audrey Arpen; Staff 2 (MLS 1, Non-MLS 1)
Founded 1979. Enrl 405; Fac 18
Oct 2005-Sept 2006 Income $74,000. Mats Exp $13,000, Books $6,500, Per/Ser (Incl. Access Fees) $6,500. Sal $50,000
Library Holdings: High Interest/Low Vocabulary Bk Vols 4,000; Bk Titles 22,000; Bk Vols 24,000; Per Subs 119; Spec Interest Per Sub 10
Special Collections: Local History; Native American Studies
Automation Activity & Vendor Info: (Acquisitions) SirsiDynix; (Cataloging) SirsiDynix; (Circulation) SirsiDynix; (Course Reserve) SirsiDynix; (ILL) SirsiDynix; (Media Booking) SirsiDynix; (OPAC) SirsiDynix; (Serials) SirsiDynix
Database Vendor: EBSCOhost, Gale Cengage Learning
Wireless access
Open Mon-Thurs 8-6, Fri 8-4:30

LAUREL

P LAUREL PUBLIC LIBRARY*, 720 W Third St, 59044. (Mail add: PO Box 68, 59044-0068), SAN 309-3336. Tel: 406-628-4961. FAX: 406-628-4961. E-mail: laurelpl@mtlib.org. Web Site: www.laurelpubliclibrary.org. *Libr Dir,* Nancy L Schmidt; E-mail: nschmidt@mtlib.org
Founded 1916. Pop 6,255; Circ 38,462
Library Holdings: Large Print Bks 620; Bk Vols 19,700; Per Subs 25; Talking Bks 300; Videos 770
Automation Activity & Vendor Info: (Acquisitions) SirsiDynix; (Cataloging) SirsiDynix; (Circulation) SIRSI WorkFlows; (OPAC) SIRSI-iBistro
Database Vendor: EBSCO Auto Repair Reference, EBSCOhost, OCLC FirstSearch
Wireless access
Mem of South Cent Fedn
Special Services for the Deaf - ADA equip; Bks on deafness & sign lang
Special Services for the Blind - Accessible computers; Bks on cassette; Bks on CD; Braille alphabet card; Large print bks; Low vision equip; Screen reader software; ZoomText magnification & reading software
Open Mon-Thurs 9-7:30, Sat 9-3
Friends of the Library Group

LEWISTOWN

P LEWISTOWN PUBLIC LIBRARY*, 701 W Main St, 59457. SAN 309-3344. Tel: 406-538-5212. FAX: 406-538-3920. E-mail: library@lewistownlibrary.org. Web Site: lewistownlibrary.org. *Dir, Libr Serv,* KellyAnne Terry; E-mail: lpldirector@lewistownlibrary.org; *Local Hist & Ref Librn,* Nancy Watts; E-mail: nancyw@lewistownlibrary.org; *Outreach Serv Librn,* Nancy Sackett; E-mail: bkloner@lewistownlibrary.org; *Circ & ILL Mgr,* Dan Bell; E-mail: dan@lewistownlibrary.org; *Pub Serv,* Lora Poser-Brown; E-mail: lora@lewistownlibrary.org; *Youth Serv,* Nancy Bostrom; E-mail: nancyb@lewistownlibrary.org; Staff 5 (MLS 1, Non-MLS 4)
Founded 1905. Pop 11,080; Circ 88,925
Jul 2007-Jun 2008 Income $285,630, State $1,385, City $165,000, County $40,000, Locally Generated Income $79,245. Mats Exp $44,898, Books $28,187, Per/Ser (Incl. Access Fees) $1,500, Other Print Mats $1,000, AV Mat $3,000, Electronic Ref Mat (Incl. Access Fees) $10,211, Presv $1,000. Sal $182,305
Library Holdings: Bks on Deafness & Sign Lang 10; CDs 150; DVDs 30; Electronic Media & Resources 20; Large Print Bks 1,500; Bk Titles 36,000; Bk Vols 38,500; Per Subs 54; Talking Bks 1,500; Videos 250
Special Collections: Local Historic Photographs. Oral History
Subject Interests: Local hist, Montana

Automation Activity & Vendor Info: (Acquisitions) SIRSI WorkFlows; (Cataloging) SirsiDynix; (Circulation) SirsiDynix; (ILL) OCLC; (Media Booking) SIRSI WorkFlows; (OPAC) SIRSI-iBistro
Database Vendor: EBSCO Auto Repair Reference, Gale Cengage Learning, Ingram Library Services, OCLC FirstSearch, OCLC WebJunction, OCLC WorldShare Interlibrary Loan, Overdrive, Inc, ProQuest, SirsiDynix
Wireless access
Function: After school storytime, Archival coll, Audio & video playback equip for onsite use, Audiobks via web, AV serv, Bks on cassette, Bks on CD, CD-ROM, Children's prog, Computer training, Computers for patron use, Copy machines, Digital talking bks, e-mail & chat, E-Reserves, Electronic databases & coll, Free DVD rentals, Genealogy discussion group, Govt ref serv, Handicapped accessible, Home delivery & serv to Sr ctr & nursing homes, ILL available, Learning ctr, Magnifiers for reading, Mail & tel request accepted, Mail loans to mem, Music CDs, Newsp ref libr, Online cat, Online ref, Online searches, Outside serv via phone, mail, e-mail & web, OverDrive digital audio bks, Photocopying/Printing, Preschool outreach, Prog for adults, Prog for children & young adult, Provide serv for the mentally ill, Pub access computers, Ref & res, Ref serv available, Ref serv in person, Referrals accepted, Senior computer classes, Senior outreach, Serves mentally handicapped consumers, Spoken cassettes & CDs, Spoken cassettes & DVDs, Story hour, Summer reading prog, Tax forms, Teen prog, Telephone ref, VHS videos, Video lending libr, Web-catalog, Wheelchair accessible
Mem of South Cent Fedn
Special Services for the Blind - Talking bks & player equip
Open Tues-Fri 10-6, Sat 10-2
Friends of the Library Group

LIBBY

P LINCOLN COUNTY PUBLIC LIBRARIES*, 220 W Sixth St, 59923-1898. SAN 350-0403. Tel: 406-293-2778. FAX: 406-293-4235. E-mail: library@lincolncountylibraries.com. Web Site: www.lincolncountylibraries.com. *Dir,* Rick Ball; *Ad,* Jessie Pate; *Circ Librn,* Lynn Zimmerman
Founded 1920. Pop 19,000; Circ 79,401
Library Holdings: Bk Titles 45,000; Per Subs 125
Automation Activity & Vendor Info: (Acquisitions) AmLib Library Management System; (Cataloging) AmLib Library Management System; (Circulation) AmLib Library Management System; (Course Reserve) AmLib Library Management System; (ILL) AmLib Library Management System; (OPAC) AmLib Library Management System; (Serials) AmLib Library Management System
Database Vendor: EBSCO Auto Repair Reference, Gale Cengage Learning, OCLC FirstSearch
Wireless access
Publications: Library Journal
Open Mon-Fri 9:30-6, Sat 9:30-3
Friends of the Library Group
Branches: 2
EUREKA BRANCH, 318 Dewey Ave, Eureka, 59917. (Mail add: PO Box 401, Eureka, 59917-0401), SAN 350-0438. Tel: 406-296-2613. FAX: 406-296-2613. *Librn,* Esther Brandt; E-mail: ebrandt@lincolncountylibraries.com; Staff 2 (Non-MLS 2)
Library Holdings: Bk Vols 7,000; Per Subs 35
Open Tues-Fri 11-5, Sat 11-2
Friends of the Library Group
TROY BRANCH, Third & Kalispell Ave, Troy, 59935. (Mail add: PO Box 430, Troy, 59935-0430), SAN 350-0462. Tel: 406-295-4040. FAX: 406-295-4040. *Librn,* Stacy Walenter
Open Tues-Fri (Winter) 11-6, Sat 11-1; Tues & Thurs (Summer) 11-6, Wed 1-6, Sat 11-1
Friends of the Library Group

LIVINGSTON

S INTERNATIONAL FEDERATION OF FLYFISHERS, Lewis A Bell Memorial Library, 5237 US Hwy 89 S, Ste 11, 59047. SAN 374-8227. Tel: 406-222-9369. FAX: 406-222-5823. E-mail: support@fedflyfishers.org. Web Site: www.fedflyfishers.org. *Coll Coordr,* Holly Sandbo; Tel: 406-222-9369, Ext 110, E-mail: holly@fedflyfishers.org
Founded 1983
Library Holdings: AV Mats 200; Bk Titles 2,300; Bk Vols 2,500; Per Subs 15; Spec Interest Per Sub 15
Subject Interests: Fly fishing
Open Mon-Fri 8-5

P LIVINGSTON-PARK COUNTY PUBLIC LIBRARY*, 228 W Callender St, 59047-2618. SAN 309-3379. Tel: 406-222-0862. FAX: 406-222-6522. Web Site: www.livingstonpubliclibrary.org. *Dir,* Tammy Brawn; E-mail: tammy@livingstonpubliclibrary.org; Staff 6.4 (MLS 2, Non-MLS 4.4)
Founded 1901. Circ 93,600
Library Holdings: AV Mats 3,309; Bk Titles 49,771; Bk Vols 53,000; Per Subs 239
Special Collections: Fly Fishing Coll; Montana Coll
Automation Activity & Vendor Info: (Cataloging) OCLC Connexion; (Circulation) Follett Software; (ILL) OCLC WorldShare Interlibrary Loan; (OPAC) Follett Software
Database Vendor: EBSCOhost, Gale Cengage Learning
Wireless access
Function: After school storytime, Audio & video playback equip for onsite use, CD-ROM, Computer training, Copy machines, Handicapped accessible, ILL available, Mail & tel request accepted, Music CDs, Online ref, Preschool outreach, Prog for adults, Prog for children & young adult, Ref serv available, Summer reading prog, Tax forms, Telephone ref, VHS videos, Wheelchair accessible
Open Mon & Tues 12-8, Wed & Thurs 10-8, Fri 10-6, Sat 10-5
Friends of the Library Group

MALMSTROM AFB

A UNITED STATES AIR FORCE*, Arden G Hill Memorial Library Malmstrom Air Force Base FL4626, 341 SVS/SVMG, 7356 Fourth Ave N, 59402-7506. SAN 350-0497. Tel: 406-731-4638. Interlibrary Loan Service Tel: 406-731-2301. Administration Tel: 406-731-2748. FAX: 406-727-6104. Administration FAX: 406-731-3667. Web Site: www.341services.com. *Librn,* Carol Banas; E-mail: banasc83@hotmail.com; Staff 4 (MLS 1, Non-MLS 3)
Founded 1953
Library Holdings: Bk Vols 31,000; Per Subs 125
Automation Activity & Vendor Info: (Acquisitions) Softlink America; (Cataloging) Softlink America; (Circulation) Softlink America; (Course Reserve) Softlink America; (ILL) Softlink America; (Media Booking) Softlink America; (Serials) Softlink America
Wireless access
Publications: Bulletin (Monthly)
Partic in Dialog Corp; OCLC Online Computer Library Center, Inc
Open Mon-Thurs 9:30-6:45, Fri & Sat 9:30-5:45

MALTA

P GOLDEN PLAINS LIBRARY FEDERATION*, Ten S Fourth St E, 59538. (Mail add: PO Box 840, 59538-0840), SAN 309-3069. Tel: 406-654-2407. FAX: 406-654-2407. *Dir,* Janeen Brookie
Founded 1917. Pop 4,201
Library Holdings: Bk Vols 32,000
Automation Activity & Vendor Info: (Cataloging) OCLC; (Circulation) Follett Software
Member Libraries: Daniels County Free Library; Fort Peck Community College Library; Glasgow City-County Library; Opheim Community Library; Phillips County Library; Roosevelt County Library; Sheridan County Library
Open Mon & Wed 10-12, 1-5 & 7-9, Tues, Thurs & Fri 10-12 & 1-5, Sat (Sept-May) 10-2

P PHILLIPS COUNTY LIBRARY*, 10 S Fourth St E, 59538. (Mail add: PO Box 840, 59538-0840), SAN 350-0527. Tel: 406-654-2407. FAX: 406-654-2407. E-mail: philibr@itstriangle.com. *Dir,* Janeen Brookie; *Asst Librn,* Michelle Mitchell; *Asst Librn,* Halle Williamson, Staff 2 (Non MLS 2)
Founded 1917. Pop 4,100; Circ 2,800
Library Holdings: Bk Titles 24,431
Database Vendor: EBSCOhost, Gale Cengage Learning
Mem of Golden Plains Library Federation
Open Mon & Wed 10-12, 1-5 & 7-9, Tues, Thurs & Fri 10-12 & 1-5, Sat (Sept-May) 10-2
Branches: 2
DODSON BRANCH, 121 Second St E, Dodson, 59524, SAN 350-0551. *Librn,* Bonnie Marney
Open Tues 11-5
SACO BRANCH, PO Box 74, Saco, 59261, SAN 350-0586. *Librn,* Esther Brosseau
Open Tues & Sat 2-4:30

MANHATTAN

P MANHATTAN COMMUNITY LIBRARY*, 200 W Fulton Ave, 59741. SAN 309-3395. Tel: 406-284-3341, Ext 222. *Dir,* Kari Eliason; E-mail: keliason@manhattan.k12.mt.us
Pop 2,500; Circ 10,400
Library Holdings: Large Print Bks 324; Bk Titles 10,800; Bk Vols 11,200; Per Subs 36; Talking Bks 212
Automation Activity & Vendor Info: (Cataloging) Follett Software; (Circulation) Follett Software; (OPAC) Follett Software
Open Mon-Thurs 1-7, Fri 2-6, Sat 10-3

MILES CITY

P MILES CITY PUBLIC LIBRARY*, One S Tenth St, 59301-3398. SAN 309-3409. Tel: 406-234-1496. FAX: 406-234-2095. E-mail: mcpl@midrivers.com. Web Site: milescitypubliclibrary.org. *Dir,* Sonja A Woods; *Cataloger,* Michelle Cunningham; *Ch Serv,* Hannah Nash; *Hist Archivist,* Jean Nielsen; *ILL,* Gloria Archdale; Staff 5 (MLS 1, Non-MLS 4)
Founded 1902. Pop 12,000
Library Holdings: Bk Titles 47,000; Bk Vols 60,000; Per Subs 70
Subject Interests: Montana, State hist
Automation Activity & Vendor Info: (Circulation) SirsiDynix; (ILL) OCLC; (OPAC) SirsiDynix
Database Vendor: Gale Cengage Learning, OCLC FirstSearch
Function: Doc delivery serv, ILL available, Online searches, Photocopying/Printing, Prog for children & young adult, Summer reading prog, Telephone ref, Wheelchair accessible
Friends of the Library Group

J MILES COMMUNITY COLLEGE LIBRARY*, 2715 Dickinson, 59301. SAN 309-3417. Tel: 406-874-6105. Toll Free Tel: 800-541-9281. FAX: 406-874-6282. Web Site: www.milescc.edu/campusservices/library. *Librn,* Ann Rutherford; E-mail: rutherforda@milescc.edu; *Asst Librn,* Teena Friesz; E-mail: frieszt@milescc.edu; *Asst Librn,* Wendy Hudgson; E-mail: hudgsonw@milescc.edu
Library Holdings: Bk Vols 15,000; Per Subs 275
Open Mon-Thurs 8-8, Fri 8-5

S MONTANA DEPARTMENT OF CORRECTIONS*, Pine Hills Youth Correctional Facility, Four North Haynes, 59301-1058. SAN 375-314X. Tel: 406-233-2216. FAX: 406-233-2204. *Librn,* Julie Sagissor; E-mail: jsagissor@mt.gov
Library Holdings: Bk Titles 7,500
Special Collections: Native American Coll, bks & videos

MISSOULA

M THE LEARNING CENTER*, Medical Library, 500 W Broadway, 59802-4587. SAN 309-3441. Tel: 406-329-5710. FAX: 406-329-5688. E-mail: library@saintpatrick.org. Web Site: chi.saintpatrick.org. *Librn,* Dana Kopp; Tel: 406-329-5711, E-mail: dkopp@saintpatrick.org; *Libr Tech,* Lisa Autio; Tel: 406-329-5712, E-mail: lgautio@saintpatrick.org; Staff 2 (MLS 1, Non-MLS 1)
Founded 1946
Library Holdings: Audiobooks 40; AV Mats 300; CDs 100; DVDs 40; e-books 5; e-journals 125; Bk Titles 5,000; Per Subs 200
Special Collections: Consumer Health & Nursing Coll; Death, Dying & Grieving Coll; General Hospital Leadership (LEAD Coll); Medical Humanities & Ethics (Ridge Coll)
Subject Interests: Admin, Consumer health, Nursing
Automation Activity & Vendor Info: (Acquisitions) Ex Libris Group; (Cataloging) Ex Libris Group; (Circulation) Ex Libris Group; (Course Reserve) Ex Libris Group; (Media Booking) Ex Libris Group; (OPAC) Ex Libris Group; (Serials) EBSCO Online
Database Vendor: Blackwell, Cinahl, EBSCOhost, Elsevier, Gale Cengage Learning, Medline, Micromedex, OVID Technologies, ScienceDirect, UpToDate, Wiley InterScience
Partic in Consortium of Acad & Spec Libr in Mont
Open Mon-Thurs (Winter) 8-7, Fri 8-4:30; Mon-Fri (Summer) 8-4:30

P MISSOULA PUBLIC LIBRARY*, 301 E Main, 59802-4799. SAN 350-0616. Tel: 406-721-2665. FAX: 406-728-5900. E-mail: mslaplib@missoula.lib.mt.us. Web Site: www.missoulapubliclibrary.org. *Dir,* Honore Bray; E-mail: hbray@missoula.lib.mt.us; *Asst Dir,* Elizabeth Jonkel; E-mail: ejonkel@missoula.lib.mt.us; *Cat Librn,* Paulette Parpart; E-mail: parpart@missoula.lib.mt.us; *Ch,* Pam Harrington; *Ref Librn,* Cara Cadena; *Ref Librn,* Marie Doyle; *Ref Librn,* Molly Ledermann; *Ser Librn, YA Librn,* Lyndy Bartlett; *YA Librn,* Linette Greene; Staff 32 (MLS 3, Non-MLS 29)
Founded 1894. Pop 99,000; Circ 802,216
Library Holdings: Audiobooks 2,215; AV Mats 133; CDs 11,215; DVDs 7,224; e-books 2,524; Large Print Bks 3,206; Bk Titles 210,234; Bk Vols 236,714; Per Subs 571; Videos 3,242
Special Collections: Montana Hist Coll; Northwest Hist Coll, bks, docs. State Document Depository
Automation Activity & Vendor Info: (Acquisitions) SirsiDynix; (Cataloging) SirsiDynix; (Circulation) SirsiDynix
Database Vendor: Gale Cengage Learning, OCLC FirstSearch, SirsiDynix
Wireless access
Function: Handicapped accessible, Home delivery & serv to Sr ctr & nursing homes, Homebound delivery serv, ILL available, Online searches, Photocopying/Printing, Prog for adults, Prog for children & young adult, Ref serv available, Summer reading prog, Telephone ref, Wheelchair accessible
Special Services for the Deaf - Assistive tech
Open Mon-Wed 10-9, Thurs-Sat 10-6, Sun 1-5
Friends of the Library Group
Branches: 2
SEELEY LAKE COMMUNITY, 456 Airport Rd, Seeley Lake, 59868. (Mail add: PO Box 416, Seeley Lake, 59868-0416), SAN 329-5575. Tel: 406-677-8995. FAX: 406-677-2949. *Librn,* Sue Stone; *Librn,* Katrina Stout
Open Mon, Tues & Thurs 10-6, Wed 11-7, Sat (Sept-May) 9-3
Friends of the Library Group
SWAN VALLEY COMMUNITY, 6811 Hwy 83, Condon, 59826. (Mail add: PO Box 1128, Condon, 59826-1128), SAN 350-0691. Tel: 406-754-2521. E-mail: svlibrary@missoula.lib.mt.us. *Librn,* Fern Kauffman; Staff 1 (Non-MLS 1)
Founded 1988
Library Holdings: Audiobooks 30; CDs 20; DVDs 50; Large Print Bks 30; Bk Titles 5,000; Videos 300
Open Tues & Fri 11-4, Wed 11-7
Bookmobiles: 1

UNIVERSITY OF MONTANA

CL WILLIAM J JAMESON LAW LIBRARY*, 32 Campus Dr, 59812, SAN 350-073X. Tel: 406-243-2699. Web Site: www.umt.edu/law/library. *Dir,* Stacey Gordon; Tel: 406-243-6808, E-mail: stacey.gordon@umontana.edu; Staff 5 (MLS 3, Non-MLS 2)
Founded 1911. Enrl 226; Fac 17; Highest Degree: Doctorate
Library Holdings: Bk Titles 20,000; Per Subs 1,795
Special Collections: Indian Law, bks & micro
Automation Activity & Vendor Info: (Acquisitions) Ex Libris Group; (Cataloging) Ex Libris Group; (Circulation) Ex Libris Group; (Course Reserve) Ex Libris Group; (ILL) Ex Libris Group; (Media Booking) Ex Libris Group; (OPAC) Ex Libris Group; (Serials) Ex Libris Group
Partic in Westlaw
Open Mon-Thurs 7:30am-9pm, Fri 7:30-5, Sat 8:30-5, Sun 12-5

C MAUREEN & MIKE MANSFIELD LIBRARY*, 32 Campus Dr, No 9936, 59812-9936, SAN 350-0705. Tel: 406-243-6866. Circulation Tel: 406-243-6734. Interlibrary Loan Service Tel: 406-243-6736. Administration Tel: 406-243-6800. FAX: 406-243-4067. Administration FAX: 406-243-6864. TDD: 406-243-2953. E-mail: ic@mail.lib.umt.edu. Web Site: www.lib.umt.edu. *Dean of Libr,* Shali Zhang, PhD; E-mail: shali.zhang@mso.umt.edu; *Head, Access & Coll Serv,* Barry Brown; E-mail: barry.brown@umontana.edu; *Head, Admin Serv,* Kathy Hendricks; Tel: 406-243-4583, E-mail: kathy.hendricks@umontana.edu; *Head, Archives & Spec Coll,* Donna McCrea; Tel: 406-243-4403, E-mail: donna.mccrea@umontana.edu; *Head, Bibliog Mgt Serv,* Teressa Keenan; Tel: 406-243-4592, E-mail: teressa.keenan@umontana.edu; *Head, Info & Res Serv,* Kim Granath; Tel: 406-243-6017, E-mail: kim.granath@umontana.edu; *Head, Mansfield Libr at Missoula Col UM,* Samantha Hines; Tel: 406-243-7818; *Head, Tech & Syst Serv,* John Greer; Tel: 406-243-2539; *Acq & Electronic Res Librn,* Angela Dresselhaus; Tel: 406-243-4728, E-mail: angela.dresselhaus@umontana.edu; *Digital Initiatives Librn,* Wendy Walker; Tel: 406-243-6004, E-mail: wendy.walker@mso.umt.edu; *Educ, Human Sci & Psychol Librn,* Kate Zoellner; Tel: 406-243-4421; *Diversity Coordr, Ethnic Studies Librn,* Julie Edwards; Tel: 406-243-4505; *Govt Doc Librn,* Susanne Caro; Tel: 406-243-4548, E-mail: susanne.caro@umontana.edu; *Humanities Librn, Instruction Coordr,* Sue Samson; Tel: 406-243-4335; *Soc Sci Librn,* Karen Jaskar; Tel: 406-243-4558, E-mail: karen.jaskar@umontana.edu; *Media Res Coordr, Visual & Performing Arts Librn,* Tammy Ravas; Tel: 406-243-4402, E-mail: tammy.ravas@umontana.edu; *Acq Mgr,* Carol Leese; Tel: 406-243-5926; *Mgr, Circ, ILL & Copy Ctr,* Patricia DaSilva; E-mail: patricia.dasilva@umontana.edu; *Electronic Res Mgr,* Jennifer Rusk; Tel: 406-243-6731; *Undergrad Serv Coordr,* Megan Stark; Tel: 306-243-2864; *ILL Spec,* Pam Marek; Tel: 406-243-5976; *Digital Archivist,* Sam Meister; Tel: 406-243-4036, E-mail: sam.meister@mso.umt.edu. Subject Specialists: *Sci info literacy,* Barry Brown; Staff 66 (MLS 18, Non-MLS 48)
Founded 1893. Enrl 14,525; Fac 915; Highest Degree: Doctorate
Library Holdings: Audiobooks 3,039; AV Mats 73,946; CDs 15,117; DVDs 8,234; e-books 218,078; e-journals 67,156; Microforms 347,441; Music Scores 14,307; Bk Titles 785,934; Bk Vols 892,519; Per Subs 69,615; Talking Bks 3,039; Videos 15,541
Special Collections: Chaucer & His Times (Mirsilees Coll); English & American Literature (Whicker Coll); Lumber Industry & Other Montana Business; Montana Coll; Montana Politicians (Mike Mansfield, James Murray, James Gerard & Joseph Dixon Colls), ms; Natural History Coll. Oral History; US Document Depository
Automation Activity & Vendor Info: (Acquisitions) Ex Libris Group; (Cataloging) Ex Libris Group; (Circulation) Ex Libris Group; (Course Reserve) Docutek; (ILL) OCLC ILLiad; (Media Booking) Ex Libris Group; (OPAC) Ex Libris Group; (Serials) SerialsSolutions
Partic in OCLC Online Computer Library Center, Inc
Open Mon-Thurs 7am-2am, Fri 7-7, Sat 11-7, Sun 11am-2am

MOORE

P MOORE PUBLIC LIBRARY*, 403 Fergus Ave, 59464. (Mail add: PO Box 125, 59464-0125), SAN 309-3476. Tel: 406-374-2364. FAX: 406-374-2364. E-mail: moorelib2002@yahoo.com. *Access Serv, Acq, Dir,* Debbie Bauman; Staff 1 (MLS 1)
Founded 1918. Pop 212; Circ 2,739
Library Holdings: AV Mats 211; Large Print Bks 140; Bk Titles 7,621; Talking Bks 40
Function: Handicapped accessible, Home delivery & serv to Sr ctr & nursing homes, Homebound delivery serv, ILL available, Magnifiers for reading, Photocopying/Printing, Prog for children & young adult, Summer reading prog
Mem of South Cent Fedn
Open Tues-Thurs 12-5

OPHEIM

P OPHEIM COMMUNITY LIBRARY*, 100 Rock St, 59250. (Mail add: PO Box 108, 59250-0108), SAN 376-7876. Tel: 406-762-3213. FAX: 406-762-3348. *Librn,* Terry Risa; E-mail: trisa@ohsvikings.org
Library Holdings: Bk Titles 9,000; Bk Vols 10,000; Per Subs 35
Automation Activity & Vendor Info: (Acquisitions) Follett Software; (Cataloging) Follett Software; (Circulation) Follett Software; (Course Reserve) Follett Software; (ILL) Follett Software; (Media Booking) Follett Software; (OPAC) Follett Software; (Serials) Follett Software
Mem of Golden Plains Library Federation
Open Mon-Thurs 8-4, Fri 8-2:30
Friends of the Library Group

PABLO

C SALISH KOOTENAI COLLEGE*, D'Arcy McNickle Library, PO Box 70, 59855. SAN 373-6326. Tel: 406-275-4875. Interlibrary Loan Service Tel: 406-275-4874. Administration Tel: 406-275-4876. FAX: 406-275-4812. Web Site: skclibrary.skc.edu. *Dir,* Fred Noel; E-mail: fred_noel@skc.edu; *ILL,* Natalie Malaterre; Staff 5 (MLS 3, Non-MLS 2)
Founded 1979. Enrl 954; Fac 56; Highest Degree: Bachelor
Library Holdings: Bk Vols 47,000; Per Subs 200
Special Collections: Confederated Salish & Kootenai Tribal History
Subject Interests: Environ studies, Native Am studies, Nursing
Automation Activity & Vendor Info: (Acquisitions) Ex Libris Group; (Cataloging) Ex Libris Group; (Circulation) Ex Libris Group; (Course Reserve) Docutek; (ILL) OCLC; (OPAC) Ex Libris Group; (Serials) Ex Libris Group
Database Vendor: ACM (Association for Computing Machinery), EBSCO Auto Repair Reference, EBSCOhost, Gale Cengage Learning, Medline, OCLC FirstSearch, OCLC WorldShare Interlibrary Loan, ProQuest, Westlaw
Wireless access
Open Mon-Thurs 7:30-8, Fri 7:30-4:30, Sat 10-4:30

PHILIPSBURG

P PHILIPSBURG PUBLIC LIBRARY*, 102 S Sansome, 59858. (Mail add: PO Box 339, 59858-0339), SAN 321-7817. Tel: 406 859 5030. FAX: 406-859-3821. E-mail: pbl5030@blackfoot.net. *Dir,* Susan McCann
Pop 1,680; Circ 3,485
Library Holdings: AV Mats 25; Bk Vols 4,500
Open Mon 3-8, Wed & Fri 1:30-5:30

PLAINS

P PLAINS PUBLIC LIBRARY DISTRICT*, 108 W Railroad, 59859. (Mail add: PO Box 399, 59859-0339), SAN 309-3484. Tel: 406-826-3101. FAX: 406-826-3101. *Dir,* Carrie M Terrell; E-mail: cterrell@mtlib.org; Staff 3 (Non-MLS 3)
Founded 1918. Pop 3,801; Circ 30,000
Library Holdings: Bk Titles 14,000; Bk Vols 15,000; Per Subs 42
Special Collections: Montana Coll
Automation Activity & Vendor Info: (Acquisitions) SirsiDynix; (Cataloging) SirsiDynix; (Circulation) SirsiDynix; (ILL) SirsiDynix; (OPAC) SirsiDynix
Database Vendor: EBSCO Auto Repair Reference, EBSCO Information Services, Gale Cengage Learning, OCLC FirstSearch
Wireless access
Open Mon & Tues 11-6, Wed & Thurs 12-7, Sat 10-12
Friends of the Library Group

PLENTYWOOD

P SHERIDAN COUNTY LIBRARY*, 100 W Laurel Ave, 59254. SAN 309-3492. Tel: 406-765-2317. FAX: 406-765-2129. *Librn,* Sheila Lee; E-mail: slee@co.sheridan.mt.us; Staff 2 (Non-MLS 2)
Founded 1914. Pop 3,524; Circ 23,066
Jul 2005-Jun 2006 Income $112,961, State $4,031, County $106,497, Locally Generated Income $2,433. Mats Exp $26,210, Books $20,643, Per/Ser (Incl. Access Fees) $2,039, Micro $1,873, Electronic Ref Mat (Incl. Access Fees) $1,655. Sal $58,218
Library Holdings: AV Mats 1,728; Large Print Bks 816; Bk Titles 34,802; Bk Vols 36,485; Per Subs 63
Special Collections: Local Newspapers on Microfilm; Sheet Music Coll
Automation Activity & Vendor Info: (Cataloging) OCLC Connexion; (Circulation) Follett Software; (ILL) OCLC FirstSearch
Database Vendor: Gale Cengage Learning, OCLC FirstSearch, OCLC WorldShare Interlibrary Loan
Mem of Golden Plains Library Federation
Open Mon-Wed 10-8, Thurs-Sat 10-5
Friends of the Library Group

POLSON

P POLSON CITY LIBRARY*, Two First Ave E, 59860. (Mail add: PO Box 820, 59860-0820), SAN 309-3506. Tel: 406-883-8225. FAX: 406-883-8239. E-mail: polsoncl@polson.lib.mt.us. *Dir,* Marilyn M Trosper; *Asst Librn,* Allison Reed
Founded 1910. Pop 15,000; Circ 62,619
Library Holdings: Bk Vols 45,000; Per Subs 35
Automation Activity & Vendor Info: (Cataloging) SirsiDynix; (Circulation) SirsiDynix
Open Mon-Fri 11-6, Sat 11-4
Friends of the Library Group

POPLAR

J FORT PECK COMMUNITY COLLEGE LIBRARY*, Fort Peck Tribal Library, 605 Indian St, 59255. (Mail add: PO Box 398, 59255-0398), SAN 326-7032. Tel: 406-768-6340. FAX: 406-768-6301. *Dir,* Anita A Scheetz; E-mail: ascheetz@fpcc.edu; Staff 1 (Non-MLS 1)
Founded 1981. Enrl 350; Fac 20; Highest Degree: Associate
Library Holdings: Bk Titles 12,000; Per Subs 140; Spec Interest Per Sub 25
Special Collections: Fort Peck Assiniboine
Subject Interests: Native Am, Western Americana
Automation Activity & Vendor Info: (Acquisitions) Follett Software; (Cataloging) Follett Software; (Circulation) EOS International; (Course Reserve) EOS International; (ILL) OCLC FirstSearch; (Media Booking) EOS International; (OPAC) EOS International; (Serials) EOS International
Database Vendor: Discovery Education, EBSCO Auto Repair Reference, EBSCOhost, EOS International, Newsbank, OCLC FirstSearch, ProQuest, World Book Online
Wireless access
Function: ILL available
Mem of Golden Plains Library Federation
Open Mon-Thurs 8-6, Fri 8-3

RED LODGE

P RED LODGE CARNEGIE LIBRARY, Three W Eighth St, 59068. (Mail add: PO Box 1068, 59068-1068), SAN 309-3514. Tel: 406-446-1905. E-mail: rlibrary@bresnan.net. *Dir,* Jodie Moore; Staff 1.5 (MLS 1, Non-MLS 0.5)
Founded 1915. Pop 5,000; Circ 21,910
Jul 2012-Jun 2013 Income $183,922, State $2,195, City $65,128, County $110,711, Locally Generated Income $1,000, Other $4,888. Mats Exp $13,315, Books $10,073, Per/Ser (Incl. Access Fees) $860, AV Mat $1,507, Electronic Ref Mat (Incl. Access Fees) $875. Sal $81,762 (Prof $62,800)
Library Holdings: Audiobooks 823; Bks on Deafness & Sign Lang 12; DVDs 423; High Interest/Low Vocabulary Bk Vols 450; Large Print Bks 162; Bk Titles 14,252; Bk Vols 14,539; Per Subs 26; Videos 865
Automation Activity & Vendor Info: (Acquisitions) SirsiDynix; (Cataloging) SirsiDynix; (Circulation) SirsiDynix; (ILL) OCLC WorldShare Interlibrary Loan; (OPAC) SirsiDynix
Database Vendor: EBSCOhost, OCLC WorldShare Interlibrary Loan
Wireless access
Function: 24/7 Online cat, Audiobks via web, Bks on cassette, Bks on CD, Children's prog, Computers for patron use, Copy machines, e-mail & chat, e-mail serv, Electronic databases & coll, Free DVD rentals, Handicapped accessible, ILL available, Life-long learning prog for all ages, Magazines, Movies, Online cat, Online searches, Outreach serv, Outside serv via phone, mail, e-mail & web, OverDrive digital audio bks, Photocopying/Printing, Preschool outreach, Preschool reading prog, Printer for laptops & handheld devices, Prog for adults, Prog for children & young adult, Pub access computers, Ref & res, Ref serv available, Ref serv in person, Scanner, Spoken cassettes & CDs, Story hour, Summer & winter reading prog, Summer reading prog, Tax forms, Telephone ref, VHS videos, Video lending libr, Web-catalog, Wheelchair accessible, Winter reading prog
Open Tues-Fri 10-6, Sat 12-6
Friends of the Library Group

RONAN

P RONAN LIBRARY DISTRICT*, 203 Main St SW, 59864. SAN 309-3522. Tel: 406-676-3682. FAX: 406-676-3683. E-mail: ronanlibrarydistrict@gmail.com. Web Site: ronancitylibrary.org/. *Dir,* Michelle Fenger; *Tech Spec,* Dylan Carey; Staff 2 (MLS 1, Non-MLS 1)
Founded 1923. Pop 8,645; Circ 31,379
Jul 2010-Jun 2011 Income $60,407, State $3,474, City $20,876, County $11,057, Locally Generated Income $25,000
Library Holdings: Audiobooks 855; DVDs 481; Large Print Bks 664; Per Subs 7; Videos 691
Special Collections: Montana Coll
Automation Activity & Vendor Info: (Acquisitions) Follett Software; (Cataloging) Follett Software; (Circulation) Follett Software; (Course Reserve) Follett Software; (ILL) Follett Software; (OPAC) Follett Software; (Serials) Follett Software
Database Vendor: OCLC WorldShare Interlibrary Loan
Wireless access
Function: Bks on cassette, Bks on CD, Children's prog, Computers for patron use, Copy machines, Family literacy, Fax serv, Free DVD rentals, ILL available, Photocopying/Printing, Prog for adults, Prog for children & young adult, Pub access computers, Scanner, Story hour, Summer & winter reading prog, Summer reading prog, Tax forms, Telephone ref
Partic in Mont Libr Asn
Open Tues & Fri 11-6, Wed 10:30-6, Thurs 10-6, Sat 10-2
Friends of the Library Group

ROUNDUP

P ROUNDUP COMMUNITY LIBRARY*, 601 Sixth Ave W, 59072. SAN 309-3530. Tel: 406-323-1802. FAX: 406-323-1346. *Dir,* Dale R Alger; *Commun Librn,* Vera Stockert; Staff 1 (MLS 1)
Founded 1931. Pop 4,106; Circ 29,482
Library Holdings: Bk Vols 28,000; Per Subs 54
Automation Activity & Vendor Info: (Cataloging) SirsiDynix; (Circulation) SirsiDynix; (ILL) OCLC FirstSearch; (OPAC) SIRSI-iBistro
Mem of South Cent Fedn
Open Mon & Fri (Winter) 8-4, Tues & Thurs 8-8, Wed 8-5, Sat 10-2; Tues & Thurs (Summer) 4-8, Wed, Fri & Sat 10-2
Friends of the Library Group

SCOBEY

P DANIELS COUNTY FREE LIBRARY*, 203 Timmons St, 59263. (Mail add: PO Box 190, 59263-0190), SAN 309-3557. Tel: 406-487-5502. FAX: 406-487-5502. *Librn,* Marlene MacHart
Founded 1946. Pop 2,000; Circ 23,286
Library Holdings: Bk Vols 20,000; Per Subs 45
Automation Activity & Vendor Info: (Acquisitions) Follett Software; (Cataloging) Follett Software; (Circulation) Follett Software; (Course Reserve) Follett Software; (ILL) Follett Software; (Media Booking) Follett Software; (OPAC) Follett Software; (Serials) Follett Software
Mem of Golden Plains Library Federation
Open Mon-Fri 9-5, Sat (Sept-May) 1-4
Friends of the Library Group

SHELBY

P TOOLE COUNTY LIBRARY*, 229 Second Ave S, 59474. SAN 350-0764. Tel: 406-424-8345. FAX: 406-424-8346. E-mail: toolelib@yahoo.com. *Librn,* Heidi Alford
Founded 1948. Pop 5,046; Circ 19,000
Library Holdings: Bk Titles 20,000; Per Subs 30
Special Collections: Montana Indian Coll
Automation Activity & Vendor Info: (Cataloging) Follett Software; (Circulation) Follett Software
Wireless access
Mem of Pathfinder Regional Library System
Open Mon, Wed & Thurs 1-5 & 7-9, Tues 10-5 & 7-9, Fri 10-12 & 1-5, Sat 1-4
Friends of the Library Group
Branches: 1
SUNBURST BRANCH, 105 First St N, Sunburst, 59482. (Mail add: PO Box 158, Sunburst, 59482), SAN 350-0799. Tel: 406-937-6980. FAX: 406-937-6980. *Librn,* Mary Jo Aschim; E-mail: aschim@northerntel.net
Library Holdings: Bk Titles 8,000
Open Mon 12-7:30, Wed 10-5:30, Fri 10-3

SHERIDAN

P SHERIDAN PUBLIC LIBRARY*, 109 E Hamilton St, 59749. (Mail add: PO Box 107, 59749-0107), SAN 309-3565. Tel: 406-842-5770. FAX: 406-842-5770. E-mail: sheridanlibrary@gmail.com. Web Site: sheridanwired.com/index.php/community/libraries-and-museums, sites.google.com/site/sheridanlibrary. *Libr Dir,* William Talbott
Founded 1902. Pop 1,005; Circ 11,491
Library Holdings: AV Mats 24; Bk Vols 12,300; Per Subs 3
Special Collections: Montana Authors Coll
Wireless access
Open Tues 9-5, Wed 10-7, Thurs-Sat 10-5
Friends of the Library Group

SIDNEY

S MONDAK HERITAGE CENTER*, Lillian Anderson-Jensen Library, 120 Third Ave SE, 59270-0050. SAN 309-3573. Tel: 406-433-3500. FAX: 406-433-3503. E-mail: mdhc@midrivers.com. Web Site: www.mondakheritagecenter.org. *Asst Coordr,* Sandy Turner
Founded 1972
Library Holdings: Bk Titles 1,500
Subject Interests: Genealogy
Open Tues-Fri 10-4, Sat 1-4
Restriction: In-house use for visitors

P SIDNEY PUBLIC LIBRARY*, 121 Third Ave NW, 59270-4025. SAN 309-3581. Tel: 406-433-1917. FAX: 406-433-4642. Web Site: www.richland.org. *Dir,* Renee Goss; E-mail: rgoss@mtlib.org; Staff 1 (MLS 1)
Founded 1914. Pop 9,800; Circ 163,604
Library Holdings: Bk Titles 25,518; Bk Vols 25,718; Per Subs 60
Automation Activity & Vendor Info: (Cataloging) Follett Software; (Circulation) Follett Software; (OPAC) Follett Software
Mem of Sagebrush Federation
Open Mon, Fri & Sat 10-5, Tues-Thurs 11:30-7:30

STANFORD

P JUDITH BASIN COUNTY FREE LIBRARY*, 19 Third N, 59479. (Mail add: PO Box 486, 59479-0486), SAN 350-0829. Tel: 406-566-2277, Ext 123. FAX: 406-566-2211. E-mail: jbclibrary@mtintouch.net. *Dir,* Jeanne M Lillegard; *Asst Dir,* Norma Zimmer; Staff 2 (Non-MLS 2)
Founded 1946. Pop 2,329; Circ 14,125
Jul 2006-Jun 2007 Income $66,910, Federal $2,910, County $63,000, Locally Generated Income $1,000
Library Holdings: CDs 250; Large Print Bks 50; Bk Vols 21,322; Per Subs 30; Talking Bks 152
Automation Activity & Vendor Info: (Cataloging) Follett Software; (Circulation) Follett Software
Wireless access
Function: AV serv, Handicapped accessible, Homebound delivery serv, ILL available, Prog for adults, Prog for children & young adult, Wheelchair accessible
Special Services for the Blind - Audio mat; Bks on cassette; Bks on CD; Large print bks; Talking bks
Open Mon, Tues & Thurs 9:30-5:30, Wed 9:30-9, Fri 9:30-5
Branches: 1
HOBSON COMMUNITY LIBRARY, 210 Central Ave, Hobson, 59452, SAN 350-0861. Tel: 406-423-5453. Web Site: www.hobsonlibrary.org. *Librn,* Jennifer Hammontree
Library Holdings: Bk Vols 7,000
Automation Activity & Vendor Info: (Cataloging) LiBRARYSOFT; (Circulation) LiBRARYSOFT; (OPAC) LiBRARYSOFT
Open Mon & Wed 2-6, Tues & Thurs 10-6
Friends of the Library Group

STEVENSVILLE

P NORTH VALLEY PUBLIC LIBRARY*, Stevensville Library, 208 Main St, 59870. SAN 309-359X. Tel: 406-777-5061. FAX: 406-777-5061. E-mail: library@northvalleylibrary.org. Web Site: www.northvalleylibrary.org. *Dir,* Desiree Dramstad; E-mail: desireedramstad@northvalleylibrary.org; *Asst Librn,* Carrie Anderson; E-mail: carrieanderson@northvalleylibrary.org; *Asst Librn,* Amy Ling; E-mail: amysuarez@northvalleylibrary.org; *Libr Asst,* Sheryl Benskin; E-mail: sherylbenskin@northvalleylibrary.org; *Libr Asst,* Phyllis Daniels; E-mail: phyllisdaniels@northvalleylibrary.org; *Libr Asst,* Donna Larson; E-mail: donnalarson@northvalleylibrary.org; Staff 3 (MLS 1, Non-MLS 2)
Founded 1909. Pop 9,500; Circ 143,468
Jul 2009-Jun 2010 Income $143,555, State $20,677, County $118,000, Locally Generated Income $4,878. Mats Exp $24,700, Books $18,000, Per/Ser (Incl. Access Fees) $1,500, AV Mat $4,200, Electronic Ref Mat (Incl. Access Fees) $1,000. Sal $141,774 (Prof $123,978)
Special Collections: Graphic Novels; Montana Coll; Spanish Language Coll
Automation Activity & Vendor Info: (Cataloging) SIRSI WorkFlows; (Circulation) SIRSI WorkFlows; (ILL) OCLC FirstSearch; (OPAC) SIRSI-iBistro
Database Vendor: EBSCO Auto Repair Reference, EBSCO Information Services, OCLC FirstSearch, OCLC WorldShare Interlibrary Loan, Overdrive, Inc
Wireless access

Function: After school storytime, AV serv, ILL available, Music CDs, Online searches, Orientations, Photocopying/Printing, Prof lending libr, Prog for children & young adult, Ref serv available, Spoken cassettes & CDs, Summer reading prog, Telephone ref, VHS videos, Wheelchair accessible
Special Services for the Deaf - Staff with knowledge of sign lang
Special Services for the Blind - Large print bks
Open Mon, Thurs & Fri Noon-7, Tues & Wed 10-7, Sat 10-5
Friends of the Library Group

SUPERIOR

S MINERAL COUNTY MUSEUM & HISTORICAL SOCIETY LIBRARY*, 301 Second Ave E, 59872. (Mail add: PO Box 533, 59872-0533), SAN 371-7119. Tel: 406-822-3543. E-mail: mchs1976@blackfoot.net. *Librn,* Cathryn Strombo
Founded 1977
Library Holdings: Bk Titles 100; Per Subs 60
Special Collections: John Mullan & Mullan Military Road Coll; Montana Civil War Veterans Coll. Oral History
Publications: Mullan Chronicles (Quarterly)
Open Tues & Thurs 3-6
Friends of the Library Group

P MINERAL COUNTY PUBLIC LIBRARY*, 301 Second Ave E, 59872. (Mail add: PO Box 430, 59872-0430), SAN 350-0977. Tel: 406-822-3563. FAX: 406-822-3569. E-mail: mcpl@blackfoot.net. Web Site: www.mineralcountylibrary.org. *Dir,* Guna K Chaberek; Staff 5 (Non-MLS 5)
Founded 1936. Pop 3,633; Circ 28,835
Library Holdings: Bks on Deafness & Sign Lang 20; CDs 324; DVDs 70; High Interest/Low Vocabulary Bk Vols 150; Large Print Bks 186; Bk Titles 25,434; Per Subs 17; Talking Bks 560; Videos 1,064
Subject Interests: Montana hist
Automation Activity & Vendor Info: (Acquisitions) SIRSI Unicorn; (Cataloging) OCLC; (Circulation) SIRSI WorkFlows; (ILL) OCLC FirstSearch; (OPAC) SIRSI-iBistro
Database Vendor: EBSCO Auto Repair Reference, Gale Cengage Learning, OCLC FirstSearch, World Book Online
Wireless access
Function: Bks on cassette, Bks on CD, CD-ROM, Children's prog, Computers for patron use, Copy machines, e-mail serv, Electronic databases & coll, Fax serv, Free DVD rentals, Handicapped accessible, Holiday prog, ILL available, Music CDs, Online cat, Online ref, Photocopying/Printing, Pub access computers, Scanner, Summer reading prog, VHS videos, Web-catalog, Wheelchair accessible
Special Services for the Blind - Talking bks
Open Mon, Tues, Thurs & Fri 11:45-7
Friends of the Library Group

SWAN LAKE

P SWAN LAKE PUBLIC LIBRARY*, Milemarker 71 Hwy 83 S, 59911. (Mail add: PO Box 5115, 59911-5115), SAN 376-5067. Tel: 406-886-2086. FAX: 406-886-2086. E-mail: sllib@centurytel.net. *Librn,* Terry McLeod
Library Holdings: Bk Titles 9,000; Bk Vols 10,000

TERRY

P PRAIRIE COUNTY LIBRARY*, 309 Garfield Ave, 59349. (Mail add: PO Box 275, 59349-0275), SAN 309-3603. Tel: 406-635-5546. FAX: 406-635-5546. *Dir,* Rolane Christofferson; Staff 0.75 (Non-MLS 0.75)
Pop 1,179
Jul 2010-Jun 2011 Income $48,193, State $1,961, County $43,743, Other $2,489. Mats Exp $5,972, Books $4,963, AV Mat $1,009. Sal $22,340
Library Holdings: Audiobooks 439; DVDs 510; Large Print Bks 100; Bk Titles 13,120; Bk Vols 13,250
Automation Activity & Vendor Info: (Cataloging) SirsiDynix; (Circulation) SirsiDynix
Wireless access
Function: Audio & video playback equip for onsite use, Handicapped accessible, Homebound delivery serv, ILL available, Photocopying/Printing, Telephone ref, VHS videos, Wheelchair accessible
Mem of Sagebrush Federation
Open Tues 2-5 & 7-8:30, Wed-Fri 2-5

THOMPSON FALLS

P THOMPSON FALLS PUBLIC LIBRARY*, 911 Main St, 59873. (Mail add: PO Box 337, 59873-0337), SAN 309-3611. Tel: 406-827-3547. E-mail: tflibrary@blackfoot.net. Web Site: tflibrary.googlepages.com. *Dir,* Lynne Kersten
Pop 4,500; Circ 19,000
Library Holdings: Bk Titles 18,000; Per Subs 40
Automation Activity & Vendor Info: (Cataloging) SirsiDynix; (Circulation) SirsiDynix
Wireless access
Open Tues-Thurs 10-6, Fri 10-5, Sat 10-2
Friends of the Library Group

THREE FORKS

P THREE FORKS COMMUNITY LIBRARY*, 607 Main St, 59752. (Mail add: PO Box 1350, 59752-1350), SAN 309-362X. Tel: 406-285-3747. E-mail: tflibrary@hotmail.com. Web Site: www.threeforkslibrary.org. *Librn,* Debbi Kramer; Staff 3 (Non-MLS 3)
Founded 1934. Pop 4,500
Library Holdings: AV Mats 98; Bk Titles 16,800; Per Subs 25
Automation Activity & Vendor Info: (Acquisitions) SIRSI WorkFlows; (Cataloging) SIRSI WorkFlows; (Circulation) SIRSI WorkFlows; (Course Reserve) SIRSI WorkFlows; (ILL) OCLC FirstSearch; (OPAC) SIRSI WorkFlows
Database Vendor: ebrary, EBSCO Auto Repair Reference, EBSCO Information Services, EBSCOhost, OCLC, ProQuest
Wireless access
Special Services for the Blind - Audio mat; Large print & cassettes
Open Mon-Wed 10-6, Thurs & Fri 10-5, Sat 10-2
Friends of the Library Group

TOWNSEND

P BROADWATER SCHOOL & COMMUNITY LIBRARY*, 201 N Spruce, 59644. SAN 309-3638. Tel: 406-266-5060. FAX: 406-266-4962. Web Site: www.townsend.k12.mt.us. *Librn,* Angela Giono; Staff 4 (Non-MLS 4)
Founded 1995. Pop 4,000; Circ 15,949
Library Holdings: Bks on Deafness & Sign Lang 25; Bk Vols 38,000; Per Subs 59
Automation Activity & Vendor Info: (Cataloging) Follett Software; (Circulation) Follett Software
Database Vendor: Gale Cengage Learning
Open Mon-Fri 2-7, Sat 9-3
Friends of the Library Group

TWIN BRIDGES

P TWIN BRIDGES PUBLIC LIBRARY*, 206 S Main St, 59754. (Mail add: PO Box 246, 59754-0246), SAN 373-790X. Tel: 406-684-5416. FAX: 406-684-5260. E-mail: twin@3rivers.net. *Libr Dir,* Betty Humbert; *Asst Librn,* Roberta High; *Asst Librn,* Donna Wagner; Staff 3 (MLS 1, Non-MLS 2)
Founded 1897. Pop 700; Circ 5,805
Jul 2011-Jun 2012 Income $44,149, State $1,787, City $4,000, County $35,920, Other $2,442. Mats Exp $8,468, Books $5,802, Manu Arch $200, Electronic Ref Mat (Incl. Access Fees) $1,466, Presv $1,000. Sal $17,091
Library Holdings: Audiobooks 200; DVDs 350; Large Print Bks 30; Bk Vols 9,000; Per Subs 16; Videos 1,458
Subject Interests: Archives, Local hist
Automation Activity & Vendor Info: (Acquisitions) OCLC FirstSearch; (Cataloging) SirsiDynix; (Circulation) SirsiDynix; (ILL) OCLC FirstSearch
Database Vendor: EBSCO Information Services, OCLC FirstSearch
Wireless access
Special Services for the Blind - BiFolkal kits
Open Mon-Fri 10-6, Sat 10-3
Restriction: Authorized patrons
Friends of the Library Group

VALIER

P VALIER PUBLIC LIBRARY*, 400 Teton Ave, 59486. (Mail add: PO Box 247, 59486-0247), SAN 309-3646. Tel: 406-279-3366. FAX: 406-279-3368. E-mail: valpubl@3rivers.net. Web Site: valierpubliclibrary.org. *Dir,* Cathy S Brandvold
Pop 1,986; Circ 12,687
Library Holdings: Bk Vols 12,000; Per Subs 10
Automation Activity & Vendor Info: (Acquisitions) SirsiDynix; (Cataloging) SirsiDynix; (Circulation) SirsiDynix; (Course Reserve) SirsiDynix; (ILL) SirsiDynix; (Media Booking) SirsiDynix; (OPAC) SirsiDynix
Wireless access
Mem of Pathfinder Regional Library System
Open Mon 9-6, Tues 12-6, Wed 11-6, Thurs 12-5, Fri 9-5
Friends of the Library Group

VIRGINIA CITY

P THOMPSON-HICKMAN FREE COUNTY LIBRARY*, Madison County Library, 217 Idaho St, 59755. (Mail add: PO Box 128, 59755-0128), SAN 309-3654. Tel: 406-843-5346. FAX: 406-843-5347. *Dir,* Joanne C Erdall-Van De Riet
Founded 1924. Pop 4,875; Circ 14,390
Library Holdings: Bk Titles 10,208; Per Subs 27
Special Collections: Dick Pace Archives

Automation Activity & Vendor Info: (Cataloging) SirsiDynix; (Circulation) SirsiDynix
Wireless access
Open Mon-Thurs 9:30-5:30, Fri 9:30-4:30

WARM SPRINGS

S MONTANA STATE HOSPITAL LIBRARY*, 151 Blizzard Way, 59756. (Mail add: PO Box 300, 59756-0300), SAN 309-2925. Tel: 406-693-7133. FAX: 406-693-7127. *Librn,* Terry Ferguson; E-mail: teferguson@mt.gov; Staff 2 (Non-MLS 2)
Founded 1968
Jul 2007-Jun 2008 Income $7,500, State $6,000, Parent Institution $1,500
Library Holdings: CDs 54; DVDs 21; e-journals 2; Large Print Bks 76; Bk Titles 5,700; Per Subs 35; Videos 106
Subject Interests: Music, Psychol
Automation Activity & Vendor Info: (OPAC) Follett Software
Database Vendor: Gale Cengage Learning
Partic in Docline; OCLC Online Computer Library Center, Inc
Open Mon-Fri 8-4

WEST YELLOWSTONE

P WEST YELLOWSTONE PUBLIC LIBRARY*, 23 N Dunraven St, 59758. (Mail add: PO Box 370, 59758-0370), SAN 321-7825. Tel: 406-646-9017. *Dir,* Bruce McPherson
Founded 1981. Pop 1,200; Circ 6,000
Library Holdings: Bk Titles 12,500; Bk Vols 15,000; Per Subs 5
Automation Activity & Vendor Info: (Cataloging) SirsiDynix; (Circulation) SirsiDynix
Wireless access
Open Tues & Thurs 9-5, Wed & Fri 10-5, Sat 10-Noon

WHITE SULPHUR SPRINGS

P MEAGHER COUNTY CITY LIBRARY, 15 First Ave SE, 59645. (Mail add: PO Box S, 59645), SAN 309-3689. Tel: 406-547-2250. FAX: 406-547-3691. E-mail: mccl@itstriangle.com. Web Site: www.meaghercountylibrary.org. *Dir,* Jessica A Ketola; Staff 1 (Non-MLS 1)
Founded 1940. Pop 2,500; Circ 9,730
Library Holdings: Audiobooks 250; AV Mats 75; CDs 50; DVDs 300; e-books 300; High Interest/Low Vocabulary Bk Vols 100; Large Print Bks 300; Bk Titles 15,000; Bk Vols 15,500; Per Subs 15; Talking Bks 275; Videos 350
Special Collections: Meagher County History; Montana History (Historical Society); Rare Books
Automation Activity & Vendor Info: (Cataloging) SirsiDynix; (Circulation) SirsiDynix
Wireless access
Function: AV serv, Handicapped accessible, Health sci info serv, Home delivery & serv to Sr ctr & nursing homes, Homebound delivery serv, Magnifiers for reading, Newsp ref libr, Online searches, Photocopying/Printing, Prof lending libr, Prog for adults, Prog for children & young adult, Ref serv available, Spoken cassettes & CDs, Summer reading prog, Telephone ref, VHS videos, Wheelchair accessible
Special Services for the Deaf - Bks on deafness & sign lang; High interest/low vocabulary bks
Special Services for the Blind - Audio mat; Audiovision-a radio reading serv; Bks on cassette; Bks on CD; Blind Club (monthly newsletter); Copier with enlargement capabilities; Home delivery serv; HP Scan Jet with photo-finish software; Large print bks; Magnifiers; Mags & bk reproduction/duplication; Talking bks
Open Mon, Tues, Thurs & Fri 10-1 & 2-5, Wed 1-7
Friends of the Library Group

WHITEFISH

P WHITEFISH COMMUNITY LIBRARY*, Nine Spokane Ave, 59937. SAN 350-0373. Tel: 406-862-9914. FAX: 406-862-1407. Web Site: whitefishlibrary.org. *Dir,* Joey Kositzky; E-mail: joeyk@whitefishlibrary.org
Library Holdings: Bk Vols 47,000
Automation Activity & Vendor Info: (ILL) OCLC WorldShare Interlibrary Loan
Database Vendor: EBSCOhost
Wireless access
Open Mon 10-7, Tues-Thurs 10-6, Fri & Sat 12-5
Friends of the Library Group

WIBAUX

P WIBAUX PUBLIC LIBRARY*, 115 S Wibaux, 59353. (Mail add: PO Box 332, 59353-0332), SAN 309-3697. Tel: 406-796-2452. FAX: 406-796-2452. *Dir,* Jackie Quinn
Pop 1,068; Circ 7,434
Library Holdings: Bk Vols 14,595
Automation Activity & Vendor Info: (Cataloging) Follett Software; (Circulation) Follett Software
Mem of Sagebrush Federation
Open Mon, Tues, Thurs & Fri 12-5, Wed 9-8
Friends of the Library Group

WINNETT

P PETROLEUM COUNTY COMMUNITY LIBRARY*, Winnett School Library, 205 S Broadway, 59087. (Mail add: PO Box 188, 59087), SAN 309-3700. Tel: 406-429-2451. FAX: 406-429-7631. E-mail: pcclibrary@midrivers.com, winnettl@yahoo.com. Web Site: www.midrivers.com/~pcclibrary. *Dir,* Nancy Freburg; E-mail: ngf@midrivers.com; *Hist Coll Librn,* Sue McKenna. Subject Specialists: *Genealogy, Local hist,* Nancy Freburg; *Genealogy, Local hist,* Sue McKenna; Staff 4 (Non-MLS 4)
Founded 1974. Pop 565; Circ 10,214
Jul 2007-Jun 2008 Income $21,179, State $1,723, County $15,734, Locally Generated Income $3,722. Mats Exp $14,089, Books $9,650, Per/Ser (Incl. Access Fees) $1,000, AV Equip $500, AV Mat $589, Electronic Ref Mat (Incl. Access Fees) $1,850, Presv $500. Sal $27,900
Library Holdings: Audiobooks 636; AV Mats 500; Bks on Deafness & Sign Lang 28; CDs 200; DVDs 50; Electronic Media & Resources 26; Large Print Bks 68; Bk Titles 14,833; Bk Vols 15,470; Per Subs 51; Videos 1,500
Special Collections: Local History; Montana. Oral History
Automation Activity & Vendor Info: (Cataloging) Follett Software; (Circulation) Follett Software; (ILL) OCLC
Database Vendor: Gale Cengage Learning, OCLC FirstSearch
Function: Adult bk club, Audio & video playback equip for onsite use, AV serv, CD-ROM, Computer training, Copy machines, e-mail serv, Electronic databases & coll, Free DVD rentals, Handicapped accessible, Homebound delivery serv, ILL available, Libr develop, Magnifiers for reading, Mail & tel request accepted, Mail loans to mem, Music CDs, Online ref, Online searches, Photocopying/Printing, Prof lending libr, Prog for children & young adult, Ref & res, Ref serv available, Satellite serv, Spoken cassettes & CDs, Spoken cassettes & DVDs, Story hour, Telephone ref, VHS videos, Video lending libr, Wheelchair accessible
Open Mon 8-4, Tues & Thurs 8-5 & 7-9, Wed 8-4 & 7-9, Fri 8-2:40

WOLF POINT

P ROOSEVELT COUNTY LIBRARY*, 220 Second Ave S, 59201-1599. SAN 350-106X. Tel: 406-653-2411. FAX: 406-653-1365. E-mail: read@nemontel.net. *Dir,* Andrea Hayes; *ILL,* Ina Downs
Pop 10,999
Library Holdings: Bk Titles 53,394; Per Subs 96
Automation Activity & Vendor Info: (Cataloging) Follett Software; (Circulation) Follett Software
Mem of Golden Plains Library Federation
Open Mon, Wed & Fri 10-5, Tues & Thurs 10-5 & 7-9, Sat 10-1
Friends of the Library Group
Branches: 3
CULBERTSON PUBLIC, 307 Broadway Ave, Culbertson, 59218. (Mail add: PO Box 415, Culbertson, 59218-0415), SAN 350-1124. Tel: 406-787-5275. E-mail: culbertsonpubliclibrary@yahoo.com. *Dir,* Beth Hekkel
Library Holdings: Bk Titles 7,000
Open Mon, Tues & Thurs 11-5
FROID PUBLIC, 110 Main, Froid, 59226. (Mail add: PO Box 334, Froid, 59226-0334), SAN 350-1159. Tel: 406-766-2492. E-mail: 4hbranch@nemontel.net. *Librn,* Kelly Strandlund
Library Holdings: Bk Titles 7,000
Open Mon & Tues 9-12:30, Wed & Thurs 2-5:30
Friends of the Library Group
POPLAR CITY PUBLIC, 208 Third Ave W, Poplar, 59255. (Mail add: PO Box 515, Poplar, 59255-0515), SAN 350-1183. Tel: 406-768-3749. E-mail: poplar@nemontel.net. *Librn,* Jackie Hagadone
Library Holdings: Bk Titles 7,000
Open Tues 9-5, Wed 9-3, Thurs 9-1

NEBRASKA

Date of Statistics: FY 2013
Population, 2010 U.S. Census: 1,826,341
Population, 2013 U.S. Census (est.): 1,868,516
Population Served by Public Libraries: 1,531,925
Total Book Volumes in Public Libraries: 5,549,691
Total Items in Public Libraries: 9,359,462
Total Public Library Circulation: 13,217,839
Total Public Library Income: $53,930,142
Source of Income: Property Tax 94%
Grants-in-Aid to Public Libraries: $519,099
Number of County or Multi-County (Regional) Libraries: 14
Number of Bookmobiles in State: 7

AINSWORTH

P AINSWORTH PUBLIC LIBRARY*, 445 N Main St, 69210. (Mail add: PO Box 207, 69210-0207), SAN 309-3727. Tel: 402-387-2032. FAX: 402-387-0209. E-mail: aplibrary@threeriver.net. Web Site: www.ainsworthlibrary.com. *Librn,* Gail J Irwin
Founded 1911. Pop 4,031; Circ 35,000
Library Holdings: Bk Vols 25,300; Per Subs 88
Special Collections: Oral History
Automation Activity & Vendor Info: (Cataloging) Follett Software; (Circulation) Follett Software
Partic in Ill Networking
Open Mon & Fri 11-6, Tues & Thurs 11-8, Wed & Sat 1-5

ALBION

P ALBION PUBLIC LIBRARY*, 437 S Third St, 68620. SAN 309-3735. Tel: 402-395-2021. Web Site: www.albionlibrary.org. *Dir,* Colleen Verge; *Ad,* Cindy Stanczak; *Youth Serv Librn,* Susan Kruger
Founded 1900. Pop 2,500; Circ 23,394
Library Holdings: Bk Titles 18,773; Per Subs 37
Automation Activity & Vendor Info: (Cataloging) Follett Software; (Circulation) Follett Software; (OPAC) Follett Software
Open Mon, Wed & Thurs 2-9, Tues & Fri 10-12 & 2-6, Sat 10-4

ALEXANDRIA

P TUCKER MEMORIAL PUBLIC LIBRARY*, 313 Harbine St, 68303. (Mail add: PO Box 184, 68303-0184), SAN 309-3743, *Dir,* Maxine Strain; Tel: 402-749-3750
Pop 200; Circ 4,500
Library Holdings: Bk Vols 4,000
Open Sat 9-12 & 1-4

ALLEN

P SPRINGBANK TOWNSHIP LIBRARY*, 100 E Second St, 68710. (Mail add: PO Box 158, 68710-0158), SAN 309-3751, *Librn,* Peggy Terry
Pop 411; Circ 2,007
Library Holdings: Bk Vols 7,627; Per Subs 30
Open Fri 9am-11am, Sat 8-Noon

ALLIANCE

P ALLIANCE PUBLIC LIBRARY*, 1750 Sweetwater Ave, Ste 101, 69301-4438. (Mail add: PO Box D, 69301-0770), SAN 309-376X. Tel: 308-762-1387. FAX: 308-762-4148. Web Site: www.cityofalliance.net. *Dir,* Stephanie O'Connor; E-mail: soconnor@cityofalliance.net
Pop 9,869; Circ 91,000
Library Holdings: Bk Vols 47,500; Per Subs 127
Automation Activity & Vendor Info: (Cataloging) Follett Software; (Circulation) Follett Software
Mem of Panhandle Libr Syst
Open Mon-Wed 8-6, Thurs 8-8, Fri 8-5, Sat 10-2
Friends of the Library Group

GL BOX BUTTE COUNTY LAW LIBRARY*, Courthouse, 515 Box Butte Ave, Ste 302, 69301. SAN 374-9762. Tel: 308-762-5354. FAX: 308-762-7703. *In Charge,* Brian Silverman
Library Holdings: Bk Vols 10,000
Open Mon-Fri 8-5

ALMA

P HOESCH MEMORIAL PUBLIC LIBRARY, City Park W Second, 68920. (Mail add: PO Box 438, 68920-0438), SAN 309-3778. Tel: 308-928-2600. FAX: 308-928-2662. E-mail: libry@megavision.com. Web Site: www.almalibrary.com. *Librn,* Keri Anderson
Founded 1910. Pop 1,674; Circ 18,036
Library Holdings: Bk Vols 15,963; Per Subs 21
Subject Interests: Hist
Automation Activity & Vendor Info: (Cataloging) LibLime Koha; (Circulation) LibLime Koha; (OPAC) LibLime Koha
Wireless access
Open Tues-Thurs 10-8, Fri & Sat 10-5
Friends of the Library Group

ARAPAHOE

P ARAPAHOE PUBLIC LIBRARY*, 302 Nebraska Ave, 68922. (Mail add: PO Box 598, 68922-0598), SAN 309-3794. Tel: 308-962-7806. FAX: 308-962-3806. *Dir,* Cheryl Ahrens; *Asst Librn,* Benita Adams; *Asst Librn,* Sheryl Koller
Founded 1985. Pop 1,050; Circ 33,000
Library Holdings: Bk Titles 20,000; Per Subs 33
Automation Activity & Vendor Info: (Cataloging) Follett Software; (Circulation) Follett Software
Wireless access
Open Mon, Thurs & Fri 1-5, Tues 9-5, Wed 1-8, Sat 9-1
Friends of the Library Group

ARCADIA

P ARCADIA TOWNSHIP LIBRARY*, 100 S Reynolds, 68815. (Mail add: PO Box 355, 68815-0355), SAN 309-3808. Tel: 308-789-6346. FAX: 308-789-6284. E-mail: arcadialibrary@nctc.net. *Librn,* Janet Luthje
Pop 530; Circ 6,337
Library Holdings: Bk Vols 7,500; Per Subs 27
Wireless access
Open Tues, Wed & Fri 2:30-6, Thurs 4:30-8

ARLINGTON

P ARLINGTON PUBLIC LIBRARY*, 410 W Elm, 68002. (Mail add: PO Box 39, 68002-0039), SAN 309-3816. Tel: 402-478-4545. E-mail: arlingtonpubliclibrary@gmail.com. *Dir,* Kay Stork
Pop 1,117; Circ 6,809
Library Holdings: Bk Titles 7,251; Per Subs 21
Wireless access
Mem of Eastern Libr Syst
Open Mon 2-7, Tues-Fri 3-6, Sat 10-1

ARNOLD

P FINCH MEMORIAL PUBLIC LIBRARY*, 205 N Walnut, 69120. (Mail add: PO Box 247, 69120-0247), SAN 309-3824. Tel: 308-848-2219. FAX: 308-848-4729. E-mail: finlib@yahoo.com. *Librn,* Darlene Rimpley; *Asst Librn,* Marcy Lucas
Pop 1,400; Circ 8,381
Library Holdings: Bk Vols 12,500; Per Subs 28
Open Mon-Fri 1-5:30, Sat 1:30-5:30
Friends of the Library Group

ARTHUR

P ARTHUR COUNTY PUBLIC LIBRARY*, 205 Fir St, 69121. (Mail add: PO Box 146, 69121-0146), SAN 309-3832. Tel: 308-764-2219. FAX: 308-764-2216. E-mail: arthlib@yahoo.com. *Librn,* Twylia Cullinan
Founded 1939. Pop 650
Library Holdings: Bk Titles 7,258
Mem of Panhandle Libr Syst
Open Mon-Fri 2-4

ASHLAND

P ASHLAND PUBLIC LIBRARY*, 207 N 15th St, 68003-1816. SAN 309-3840. Tel: 402-944-7430. FAX: 402-944-7430. Web Site: www.ashlandpubliclibrary.com. *Dir,* Pamela Jordan; E-mail: pjordan@ashland.lib.oh.us
Founded 1904. Pop 2,276; Circ 17,713
Library Holdings: Bk Titles 12,000; Per Subs 30
Automation Activity & Vendor Info: (Cataloging) Follett Software; (Circulation) Follett Software
Open Mon-Thurs & Sat 9-12 & 1-6

ATKINSON

P ATKINSON PUBLIC LIBRARY, 210 W State St, 68713. (Mail add: PO Box 938, 68713-0938), SAN 309-3859. Tel: 402-925-2855. FAX: 402-925-2855. E-mail: atkplib@gpcom.net. Web Site: libraries.ne.gov/atkinson. *Dir,* Judy Hagan; *Asst Librn,* Terri Shearer
Founded 1927. Pop 2,127; Circ 28,592
Library Holdings: Bk Vols 21,000; Per Subs 54
Automation Activity & Vendor Info: (Cataloging) LibLime Koha; (Circulation) LibLime Koha; (OPAC) LibLime Koha
Wireless access
Open Mon & Thurs 9-5, Tues 9-6, Wed 1-6, Fri & Sat 9-3
Friends of the Library Group

AUBURN

P AUBURN MEMORIAL LIBRARY*, 1810 Courthouse Ave, 68305-2323. SAN 309-3867. Tel: 402-274-4023. FAX: 402-274-4433. E-mail: a_library@yahoo.com. Web Site: www.auburnmemoriallibrary.com. *Dir,* Sherry Black; E-mail: shblack99@yahoo.com; Staff 6 (Non-MLS 6)
Founded 1914. Pop 8,367; Circ 65,393
Library Holdings: Bk Titles 29,985; Per Subs 80
Automation Activity & Vendor Info: (Cataloging) Follett Software; (Circulation) Follett Software
Database Vendor: OCLC FirstSearch
Wireless access
Mem of Southeast Library System (SELS)
Open Mon, Tues & Thurs 10-8, Wed & Fri 10-5, Sat 10-4
Friends of the Library Group

AURORA

P ALICE M FARR LIBRARY*, 1603 L St, 68818-2132. SAN 309-3875. Tel: 402-694-2272. FAX: 402-694-2273. E-mail: afl@hamilton.net. Web Site: www.auroranebraska.com. *Dir,* Jan Thomsen; *Asst Librn,* Patricia Oswald
Pop 8,600; Circ 67,176
Library Holdings: Bk Vols 49,000; Per Subs 124
Special Collections: Hamilton County History
Automation Activity & Vendor Info: (Cataloging) OCLC CatExpress; (Circulation) Follett Software
Special Services for the Deaf - Bks on deafness & sign lang; Captioned film dep; High interest/low vocabulary bks; Spec interest per; Videos & decoder
Open Mon, Wed & Thurs 12-9, Tues 9-9, Fri 12-6, Sat 9-2
Friends of the Library Group

AXTELL

P AXTELL PUBLIC LIBRARY*, 305 N Main St, 68924. (Mail add: PO Box 65, 68924-0065). Tel: 308-743-2592. *Dir,* Janice Soderquist
Pop 696; Circ 2,500
Library Holdings: CDs 40; DVDs 50; Bk Vols 8,000; Per Subs 20; Talking Bks 75
Automation Activity & Vendor Info: (Cataloging) Follett Software; (Circulation) Follett Software
Wireless access
Mem of North Central Kansas Libraries System
Open Mon 1:30-4:30, Tues 9-11:30 & 1:30-4:30, Wed 3-7, Thurs 9am-11:30am

BANCROFT

P BANCROFT PUBLIC LIBRARY*, 103 E Poplar St, 68004. (Mail add: PO Box 67, 68004-0067), SAN 309-3891. Tel: 402-648-3350. *Chief Librn,* Ruthann Bargmann; *Asst Librn,* Lesa Bargmann; Staff 5.25 (MLS 5.25)
Founded 1974. Pop 750; Circ 5,831
Oct 2012-Sept 2013 Income $18,895, State $695, City $15,950, County $2,250. Mats Exp $3,725, Books $3,500, Per/Ser (Incl. Access Fees) $225. Sal $8,100
Library Holdings: DVDs 121; Large Print Bks 75; Bk Vols 8,400; Per Subs 20; Talking Bks 140; Videos 208
Special Collections: Cakepans; Games
Automation Activity & Vendor Info: (Cataloging) Follett Software; (Circulation) Follett Software; (OPAC) Follett Software
Wireless access
Function: Adult bk club
Open Tues 9-12 & 1-5, Wed 1-6, Thurs 4:30-7:30, Fri & Sat 9-Noon
Friends of the Library Group

S NEBRASKA STATE HISTORICAL SOCIETY, John G Neihardt Research Library, John G Neihardt State Historic Site, 306 W Elm, 68004. (Mail add: PO Box 344, 68004-0344), SAN 309-3905. Tel: 402-648-3388. Toll Free Tel: 888-777-4667. FAX: 402-648-3388. Toll Free FAX: 888-777-4667. E-mail: neihardt@gpcom.net. Web Site: www.neihardtcenter.org. *Dir,* Kinley Hadden; Staff 2 (MLS 1, Non-MLS 1)
Founded 1976
Library Holdings: Bk Titles 200; Bk Vols 300
Special Collections: Bound Nebraska History Coll; Dr John G Neihardt Coll, bks, critiques, mss. Oral History
Wireless access
Open Mon-Fri 9-5
Restriction: Non-circulating

BARTLEY

P BARTLEY PUBLIC LIBRARY*, 411 Commercial St, 69020. (Mail add: PO Box 194, 69020-0194), SAN 309-3913. Tel: 308-692-3313. *Dir,* Ronni Renee Harding
Pop 339; Circ 1,811
Library Holdings: Bk Vols 5,725; Per Subs 18
Special Collections: Oral History
Open Mon, Wed & Thurs 2:30-6, Sat 10-2:30

BASSETT

P ROCK COUNTY PUBLIC LIBRARY*, 400 State St, 68714. (Mail add: PO Box 465, 68714-0465), SAN 309-3921. Tel: 402-684-3800. FAX: 402-684-3930. E-mail: rockcolib@huntel.net. Web Site: www.huntel.net/rockcolib. *Dir,* Evelyn Ost; *Asst Dir,* Carol Yaw
Founded 1929. Pop 2,019; Circ 22,181
Library Holdings: Bk Vols 18,500; Per Subs 23
Friends of the Library Group

BATTLE CREEK

P LIED BATTLE CREEK PUBLIC LIBRARY*, 100 S Fourth St, 68715. (Mail add: PO Box D, 68715-0106), SAN 309-393X. Tel: 402-675-6934. FAX: 402-675-3911. E-mail: battlecreeklibrary@cableone.net. Web Site: www.battlecreeklibrary.org. *Dir,* Kathy Bretschneider; *Asst Dir,* Mae Toelle; Staff 1 (Non-MLS 1)
Pop 1,158; Circ 35,000
Library Holdings: CDs 170; DVDs 196; e-books 10,540; Large Print Bks 325; Bk Titles 34,810; Per Subs 48; Talking Bks 972; Videos 2,232
Special Collections: Nebraska Authors or Subjects
Automation Activity & Vendor Info: (Cataloging) Follett Software; (Circulation) Follett Software; (OPAC) Follett Software

Database Vendor: Ingram Library Services, OCLC ArticleFirst, OCLC FirstSearch, OCLC WorldShare Interlibrary Loan, Wilson - Wilson Web
Wireless access
Open Mon & Wed 1-8, Tues, Thurs & Fri 10-6, Sat 9-3

BAYARD

P BAYARD PUBLIC LIBRARY*, 509 Ave A, 69334. (Mail add: PO Box B, 69334-0676), SAN 309-3948. Tel: 308-586-1144. FAX: 308-586-1061. E-mail: bayardlibrary@yahoo.com. *Dir,* Sharon Ulbrich
Founded 1921. Pop 1,435
Library Holdings: Bk Vols 14,365; Per Subs 50
Automation Activity & Vendor Info: (Cataloging) Follett Software; (Circulation) Follett Software
Mem of Panhandle Libr Syst
Open Mon-Fri (Winter) 12:30-5:30, Sat 8:30-1:30; Mon-Sat (Summer) 8:30-1:30

BEATRICE

P BEATRICE PUBLIC LIBRARY*, 100 N 16th St, 68310-4100. SAN 309-3956. Tel: 402-223-3584. FAX: 402-223-3913. TDD: 402-223-4168. *Dir,* Laureen Riedesel; E-mail: lriedesel@beatrice.lib.ne.us; *Ch Serv,* Carolyn Baker; E-mail: cbaker@beatrice.lib.ne.us; *Info Serv, Tech Coordr,* Carolyn Bennett; E-mail: cbennett@beatrice.lib.ne.us; Staff 2 (MLS 2)
Founded 1893. Pop 12,510; Circ 149,656
Library Holdings: AV Mats 5,176; Bk Vols 94,349; Per Subs 165
Special Collections: Nebraska State Genealogical Society Coll
Automation Activity & Vendor Info: (Cataloging) SirsiDynix; (Circulation) SirsiDynix; (OPAC) SirsiDynix
Database Vendor: SirsiDynix
Mem of Southeast Library System (SELS)
Special Services for the Deaf - TDD equip
Open Mon-Thurs 9-8, Fri & Sat 9-6, Sun 2-5
Friends of the Library Group

S BEATRICE STATE DEVELOPMENTAL CENTER*, Media Resource Center, 3000 Lincoln Blvd, 68310. SAN 321-5563. Tel: 402-223-6175. FAX: 402-223-7546. *Librn,* Greg Hamm; Staff 1 (Non-MLS 1)
Founded 1981
Library Holdings: Bk Titles 10,000; Per Subs 85
Special Collections: Materials appropriate for persons with developmental disabilities
Subject Interests: Early hist of this institution
Automation Activity & Vendor Info: (Acquisitions) Follett Software; (Cataloging) Follett Software; (Circulation) Follett Software
Database Vendor: OCLC FirstSearch
Function: ILL available
Publications: Bibliography
Partic in OCLC Online Computer Library Center, Inc

J SOUTHEAST COMMUNITY COLLEGE LIBRARY*, 4771 W Scott Rd, 68310-7042. Tel: 402-228-3468. FAX: 402-228-2218. Web Site: www.southeast.edu. *Dean,* Catherine Barringer; Staff 2 (MLS 1, Non-MLS 1)
Founded 1986. Enrl 1,000
Library Holdings: Bk Titles 15,000; Per Subs 100
Automation Activity & Vendor Info: (Cataloging) Mandarin Library Automation; (Circulation) Mandarin Library Automation; (ILL) OCLC; (OPAC) Mandarin Library Automation
Database Vendor: EBSCOhost, Gale Cengage Learning, Newsbank, OCLC FirstSearch, ProQuest
Partic in OCLC Online Computer Library Center, Inc

S US NATIONAL PARK SERVICE*, Homestead National Monument of America Research Library, 8523 W State Hwy 4, 68310. SAN 370-2944. Tel: 402-223-3514. FAX: 402-228-4231. Web Site: www.nps.gov/home. *Librn,* Todd Arrington; E-mail: todd_arrington@nps.gov
Library Holdings: Bk Vols 1,700; Per Subs 15
Restriction: Open to pub for ref only

BEAVER CITY

P BEAVER CITY PUBLIC LIBRARY*, 408 Tenth St, 68926. (Mail add: PO Box 431, 68926-0431), SAN 309-3964. Tel: 308-268-4115. E-mail: bclibrary@atcjet.net. *Dir,* Rachelle Clason; *Asst Librn,* Ramona MacDondald
Founded 1922. Circ 7,000
Library Holdings: Bk Titles 10,000; Per Subs 41
Automation Activity & Vendor Info: (Cataloging) Follett Software; (Circulation) Follett Software
Database Vendor: Baker & Taylor
Open Tues & Thurs 1-7, Wed 9-12 & 1-5, Fri 1-5, Sat 9-Noon

GL FURNAS COUNTY LAW LIBRARY*, Courthouse, 912 R St, 68926. (Mail add: PO Box 373, 68926-0373), SAN 374-8294. Tel: 308-268-4025. *In Charge,* Marjory Lambert
Library Holdings: Bk Vols 1,000
Open Mon-Fri 8-4

BEEMER

P KARLEN MEMORIAL LIBRARY*, 215 Blaine St, 68716. (Mail add: PO Box 248, 68716-0248), SAN 309-3972. Tel: 402-528-3476. FAX: 402-528-3476. *Dir,* Tammy Lorenz
Founded 1923. Pop 853; Circ 14,104
Library Holdings: Bk Vols 11,847; Per Subs 40
Automation Activity & Vendor Info: (Acquisitions) Follett Software; (Cataloging) Follett Software; (Circulation) Follett Software; (OPAC) Follett Software; (Serials) Follett Software
Open Mon & Fri 9-12 & 1-5, Wed 9-12 & 1-6:30
Friends of the Library Group

BELLEVUE

P BELLEVUE PUBLIC LIBRARY*, 1003 Lincoln Rd, 68005-3199. SAN 309-3999. Tel: 402-293-3157. FAX: 402-293-3163. Web Site: www.bellevuelibrary.org. *Dir,* Guadalupe J Mier; *Asst Dir, Ref,* Beverly A Lusey; *Dir, Tech Serv,* Sandra Astleford; *Adult Serv,* Julia Dinville; *Ch Serv,* Alice Boeckman; *ILL,* Linda Ray; Staff 22 (MLS 4, Non-MLS 18)
Founded 1929. Pop 45,617; Circ 242,612
Library Holdings: Bk Titles 120,270; Per Subs 204
Special Collections: Local History Coll
Subject Interests: Local hist
Automation Activity & Vendor Info: (Acquisitions) SirsiDynix; (Cataloging) SirsiDynix; (Circulation) SirsiDynix; (ILL) SirsiDynix; (OPAC) SirsiDynix; (Serials) SirsiDynix
Database Vendor: EBSCOhost, OCLC FirstSearch, SirsiDynix, Wilson - Wilson Web
Wireless access
Function: ILL available
Publications: Bellevue Library Times (Bi-monthly)
Open Mon-Thurs 9-9, Fri & Sat 9-5, Sun 12-5
Friends of the Library Group

C BELLEVUE UNIVERSITY, Freeman-Lozier Library, 1000 Galvin Rd S, 68005. SAN 309-3980. Tel: 402-557-7314. Interlibrary Loan Service Tel: 402-557-7307. Reference Tel: 402-557-7313. Toll Free Tel: 800-756-7920. FAX: 402-557-5427. E-mail: library@bellevue.edu. Web Site: www.bellevue.edu/services/library.aspx. *Sr Dir for Libr Serv,* Robin R Bernstein; Tel: 402-557-7300, E-mail: robin.bernstein@bellevue.edu; *Asst Dir,* Christine Armstrong; Tel. 402-557-7301, E-mail: christine.armstrong@bellevue.edu; *Ref & Instruction Librn,* Matthew Colbert; Tel: 402-557-7303, E-mail: matthew.colbert@bellevue.edu; *Syst Librn,* Joel Hartung; Tel: 402-557-7317, E-mail: joel.hartung@bellevue.edu; *Tech Serv Librn,* Casey Kralik; Tel: 402-557-7309, E-mail: casey.kralik@bellevue.edu; *Circ Supvr, ILL,* D Barbara Haney; E-mail: barbara.haney@bellevue.edu; *Access Serv,* Chrystal Dawson; Tel: 402-557-7305, E-mail: chrystal.dawson@bellevue.edu; *Circ,* Jessica Omer; Tel: 402-557-7308, E-mail: jessica.omer@bellevue.edu; *Circ Asst,* Allison Schafer; E-mail: allison.schafer@bellevue.edu; *Digital Serv Spec,* Colin Kehm; Tel: 402-557-7299, E-mail: colin.kehm@bellevue.edu; *Doc Delivery,* Alice O'Connor; Tel: 402-557-7311, E-mail: allie.oconnor@bellevue.edu; *Ref,* Linda Black; Tel: 402-557-7315, E-mail: linda.black@bellevue.edu; *Ref,* Margie McCandless; Tel: 402-557-7302, E-mail: margie.mccandless@bellevue.edu; *Ref Serv,* Lorraine Patrick; Tel: 402-557-7316, E-mail: lorraine.patrick@bellevue.edu; *Ser,* Diane Osborne; Tel: 402-557-7312, E-mail: diane.osborne@bellevue.edu; *Tech Asst,* Jacob Lee; Tel: 402-557-7304, E-mail: jacob.lee@bellevue.edu; Staff 16 (MLS 6, Non-MLS 10)
Founded 1966. Enrl 7,441; Fac 272; Highest Degree: Doctorate
Jul 2013-Jun 2014. Mats Exp $478,873, Books $86,550, Per/Ser (Incl. Access Fees) $67,159, Micro $6,229, AV Mat $20,000, Electronic Ref Mat (Incl. Access Fees) $297,550, Presv $1,385. Sal $575,752 (Prof $281,360)
Library Holdings: AV Mats 6,728; e-books 177,290; e-journals 68,859; Microforms 17,444; Bk Titles 90,366; Bk Vols 120,487; Per Subs 442
Automation Activity & Vendor Info: (Acquisitions) SirsiDynix; (Cataloging) SirsiDynix; (Circulation) SirsiDynix; (ILL) OCLC; (Media Booking) SirsiDynix; (OPAC) SirsiDynix; (Serials) SirsiDynix
Database Vendor: 3M Library Systems, Alexander Street Press, American Psychological Association (APA), Baker & Taylor, Bowker, Cambridge Scientific Abstracts, Carroll Publishing, Checkpoint Systems, Inc, CQ Press, CredoReference, ebrary, EBSCOhost, Electric Library, Factiva.com, Facts on File, Faulkner Information Services, Gale Cengage Learning, H W Wilson, Hoovers, Infotrieve, infoUSA, JSTOR, LexisNexis, Medline, OCLC ArticleFirst, OCLC FirstSearch, OCLC WebJunction, OCLC WorldShare Interlibrary Loan, OneSource, Oxford Online, Plunkett Research, Ltd, ProQuest, PubMed, ReferenceUSA, ScienceDirect, SerialsSolutions, SirsiDynix, Springer-Verlag, Springshare, LLC, Standard

& Poor's, TechBooks, ValueLine, WebMD, Westlaw, Wiley InterScience, Wilson - Wilson Web
Wireless access
Publications: More Than Books (Newsletter)
Mem of Eastern Libr Syst
Partic in ICON Library Consortium; OCLC Online Computer Library Center, Inc
Open Mon-Fri 7:30am-10:30pm, Sat 8-5, Sun 10-7

BELVIDERE

S THAYER COUNTY MUSEUM*, Historical & Genealogical Library, 311 Seventh St, 68315. SAN 373-3726. Tel: 402-768-2147. *Curator,* Jacqueline J Williamson; E-mail: kjwmson@windstream.net
Subject Interests: Genealogy, Local hist
Open Sun & Wed 1-5

BENKELMAN

P DUNDY COUNTY LIBRARY*, 126 Seventh Ave E, 69021. (Mail add: PO Box 53, 69021-0053). Tel: 308-423-2333. E-mail: ducolibrary@yahoo.com. *Dir,* Nana Real
Pop 1,006; Circ 6,289
Library Holdings: AV Mats 46; Bk Vols 10,443; Talking Bks 52
Automation Activity & Vendor Info: (Cataloging) Follett Software; (Circulation) Follett Software
Wireless access
Function: ILL available
Open Mon-Fri 2-7

BENNINGTON

P BENNINGTON PUBLIC LIBRARY*, 15505 Warehouse St, 68007. (Mail add: PO Box 32, 68007-0032), SAN 309-4006. Tel: 402-238-2201. FAX: 402-238-2218. E-mail: benlib@bl.omhcoxmail.com. *Dir,* Lisa M Flaxbeard; E-mail: lisa@bl.omhcoxmail.com; *Asst Dir,* Dalene Clark; *Cat,* Karrie Ellermeier; *Circ,* Janiece Coe; *Circ, Ch,* Sally Hanson; *Patron Serv,* Debra Kois; Staff 4 (Non-MLS 4)
Founded 1948. Pop 4,692; Circ 31,652
Library Holdings: Bk Vols 24,155; Per Subs 28
Special Collections: Cake Pans
Automation Activity & Vendor Info: (Cataloging) Follett Software; (Circulation) Follett Software; (OPAC) Follett Software
Database Vendor: OCLC FirstSearch, Wilson - Wilson Web
Open Mon 2-7:30, Tues & Wed 2-6, Thurs 10-6, Sat 9-12
Friends of the Library Group

BIG SPRINGS

P BIG SPRINGS PUBLIC LIBRARY*, 400 Pine St, 69122. (Mail add: PO Box 192, 69122-0192), SAN 309-4022. Tel: 308-889-3482. *Co-Librn,* Marilyn Holdorf; *Co-Librn,* Janie Jimenez
Founded 1927. Pop 505; Circ 1,605
Library Holdings: Bk Vols 5,738; Per Subs 16
Mem of Panhandle Libr Syst
Open Mon 1:30-4:30, Thurs 1:30-6:30, Sat 9-11

BLAIR

P BLAIR PUBLIC LIBRARY*, 210 S 17th St, 68008. SAN 309-4030. Tel: 402-426-3617. E-mail: library@huntel.net. Web Site: www.blairpubliclibrary.com. *Dir,* Ruth Peterson; *Ch Serv,* Caroline True; Staff 5 (Non-MLS 5)
Founded 1915. Pop 7,500; Circ 61,620
Oct 2005-Sept 2006 Income $255,630
Library Holdings: AV Mats 1,023; CDs 50; DVDs 324; Large Print Bks 1,769; Bk Titles 35,029; Per Subs 96; Talking Bks 1,104; Videos 1,100
Automation Activity & Vendor Info: (Cataloging) Follett Software; (Circulation) Follett Software; (ILL) OCLC; (OPAC) Follett Software
Open Mon-Thurs 10-8, Fri 10-5, Sat 10-4
Friends of the Library Group

BLOOMFIELD

P BLOOMFIELD PUBLIC LIBRARY*, 121 S Broadway, 68718. (Mail add: PO Box 548, 68718-0548), SAN 309-4057. Tel: 402-373-4588. FAX: 402-373-2601. E-mail: plibrary548@yahoo.com. *Dir,* Jennifer Lauck; *Asst Dir,* Marge Stottler; Staff 1 (Non-MLS 1)
Founded 1915. Pop 1,393; Circ 8,821
Oct 2007-Sept 2008 Income $13,680, State $763, City $7,200, County $3,000, Locally Generated Income $2,717. Mats Exp $5,474, Books $4,181, Per/Ser (Incl. Access Fees) $1,293. Sal $20,365
Library Holdings: Audiobooks 30; Bks on Deafness & Sign Lang 5; Braille Volumes 1; DVDs 50; Bk Titles 500; Per Subs 35
Automation Activity & Vendor Info: (Cataloging) Follett Software; (Circulation) Follett Software; (OPAC) Follett Software
Wireless access
Mem of Pioneer Library System
Partic in Bergen County Cooperative Library System
Open Mon 12-7, Tues, Thurs & Fri 1:30-5:30, Wed 12-5:30, Sat 10-2:30
Friends of the Library Group

BLUE HILL

P BLUE HILL PUBLIC LIBRARY*, 317 W Gage St, 68930. (Mail add: PO Box 278, 68930-0278), SAN 309-4065. Tel: 402-756-2701. *Dir,* Judy Grandstaff; Staff 1 (Non-MLS 1)
Founded 1929. Pop 883; Circ 4,200
Library Holdings: Bk Vols 7,000; Per Subs 35
Automation Activity & Vendor Info: (Cataloging) Follett Software; (Circulation) Follett Software; (OPAC) Follett Software
Open Mon & Sat (Winter) 9-12, Wed & Thurs 1-6; Mon & Sat (Summer) 9-2, Wed & Thurs 1-5
Friends of the Library Group

BOYS TOWN

S FATHER FLANAGAN'S BOYS HOME*, Boys Town Library Services, 13727 Flanagan Blvd, 68010. SAN 309-4073. Tel: 402-498-3292. FAX: 402-498-3294. *Mgr,* Position Currently Open; Staff 1 (MLS 1)
Founded 1975
Library Holdings: Bk Titles 3,500; Per Subs 45
Partic in Dialog Corp; OCLC Online Computer Library Center, Inc

BRIDGEPORT

P BRIDGEPORT PUBLIC LIBRARY*, 722 Main St, 69336. (Mail add: PO Box 940, 69336-0940), SAN 309-4081. Tel: 308-262-0326. FAX: 308-262-1412. Web Site: www.cityofbport.com. *Dir,* Tammy Howitt-Covalt; *Libr Asst,* Lori Leonard
Founded 1905. Pop 1,650; Circ 15,507
Library Holdings: Bk Titles 15,000; Per Subs 41
Automation Activity & Vendor Info: (Cataloging) Follett Software; (Circulation) Follett Software
Mem of Panhandle Libr Syst
Partic in Lyrasis; Valley Library Consortium
Open Tues & Thurs 10-8, Wed & Fri 10-5, Sat 10-4
Friends of the Library Group

BROKEN BOW

P BROKEN BOW PUBLIC LIBRARY*, 626 South D St, 68822. SAN 309-4103. Tel: 308-872-2927. FAX: 308-872-2927. E-mail: bbpl@kdsi.net. Web Site: www.brokenbowlibrary.net. *Dir,* K Joan Birnie; Staff 3 (Non-MLS 3)
Founded 1885. Pop 3,491; Circ 44,718
Oct 2006-Sept 2007 Income $150,899, State $1,464, City $147,372, Locally Generated Income $2,063. Mats Exp $20,984, Books $18,966, AV Mat $1,443, Electronic Ref Mat (Incl. Access Fees) $575. Sal $104,957
Library Holdings: Audiobooks 350; CDs 157; DVDs 25; Electronic Media & Resources 21; Large Print Bks 350; Bk Vols 25,438; Per Subs 117; Talking Bks 507; Videos 375
Special Collections: DAR Holdings; Genealogy Coll; Local History Coll; Local Newspapers from 1882, bound; Nebraska History & Authors. Municipal Document Depository
Automation Activity & Vendor Info: (Cataloging) Follett Software; (Circulation) Follett Software; (ILL) OCLC FirstSearch; (OPAC) Follett Software
Database Vendor: OCLC ArticleFirst, OCLC FirstSearch, OCLC WorldShare Interlibrary Loan
Wireless access
Function: Adult bk club, Adult literacy prog, After school storytime, Audiobks via web, BA reader (adult literacy), Bk club(s), Bks on cassette, Bks on CD, CD-ROM, Children's prog, Computers for patron use, Copy machines, Distance learning, Electronic databases & coll, Family literacy, Fax serv, Free DVD rentals, Handicapped accessible, Home delivery & serv to Sr ctr & nursing homes, Homebound delivery serv, ILL available, Large print keyboards, Online cat, OverDrive digital audio bks, Photocopying/Printing, Prog for adults, Prog for children & young adult, Pub access computers, Referrals accepted, Satellite serv, Story hour, Summer reading prog, Tax forms, Teen prog, VHS videos
Mem of Southeastern Public Library System of Oklahoma
Open Mon-Thurs 10-8, Fri 10-6, Sat 10-2
Friends of the Library Group

L CUSTER COUNTY LAW LIBRARY*, Courthouse, 431 S Tenth, 68822. SAN 375-1287. Tel: 308-872-2121. FAX: 308-872-5826. *In Charge,* Amy Oxford
Founded 1910
Library Holdings: Bk Titles 1,000
Wireless access

BRUNING

P BRUNING PUBLIC LIBRARY*, 141 Main St, 68322. (Mail add: PO Box 250, 68322-0250), SAN 328-0233, *Librn,* Marie Huber
Founded 1922. Pop 332; Circ 3,000
Library Holdings: Large Print Bks 50; Bk Titles 7,000; Videos 15
Special Collections: Quilting Magazines
Open Sat 9am-11am

BRUNSWICK

P BRUNSWICK PUBLIC LIBRARY*, 303 Franklin St, 68720. (Mail add: PO Box 11, 68720-0011), SAN 377-0966. Tel: 402-842-2105. E-mail: brunslibrary@yahoo.com. *Librn,* Joan Mosat
Library Holdings: Large Print Bks 193; Bk Vols 5,650; Per Subs 27; Talking Bks 27; Videos 530
Wireless access
Open Tues 9-12 & 6-8, Thurs & Sat 9-2
Friends of the Library Group

BURWELL

P GARFIELD COUNTY LIBRARY*, 217 G St, 68823. (Mail add: PO Box 307, 68823-0307), SAN 309-412X. Tel: 308-346-4711. FAX: 308-346-4711. E-mail: gcl@nctc.net. *Librn,* Joye Lee
Pop 2,363; Circ 14,154
Library Holdings: Bk Vols 15,399; Per Subs 37
Wireless access
Open Mon & Wed (Winter) 2:30-7:30, Fri 2-5, Sat 9-12; Mon & Wed (Summer) 2-5 & 7-9, Fri 2-5, Sat 9-12
Friends of the Library Group

BYRON

P BYRON PUBLIC LIBRARY*, 119 Kansas Ave, 68325. (Mail add: PO Box 91, 68325-0091), SAN 309-4146. Tel: 402-236-8752. *Librn,* Henrietta Graucrholz; *Asst Librn,* Lois Nelson
Founded 1964. Pop 300; Circ 3,000
Oct 2011-Sept 2012 Income $4,665, City $4,615, Other $50. Mats Exp $283, Books $236, AV Equip $47. Sal $2,452
Library Holdings: Audiobooks 1; Bks-By-Mail 120; CDs 42; DVDs 33; Large Print Bks 55; Bk Vols 13,456; Videos 295
Open Wed 2-5, Sat 9-12

CALLAWAY

P NIGEL SPROUSE MEMORIAL LIBRARY*, 102 E Kimball, 68825. (Mail add: PO Box 277, 68825-0277), SAN 309-4154. Tel: 308-836-2610. FAX: 308-836-2610. *Dir,* Beverly Stivers
Pop 1,052; Circ 4,508
Library Holdings: Bk Vols 12,500
Open Mon, Wed & Fri 1-6:30, Sat 9-1

CAMBRIDGE

P BUTLER MEMORIAL LIBRARY*, 621 Penn St, 69022. (Mail add: PO Box 448, 69022-0448), SAN 309-4162. Tel: 308-697-3836. FAX: 308-697-3173. E-mail: bumemlib@swnebr.net. *Librn,* Debra Young; *Asst Librn,* Patricia Young
Founded 1951. Pop 1,107; Circ 16,246
Library Holdings: Bk Vols 16,000; Per Subs 21
Automation Activity & Vendor Info: (Cataloging) Follett Software; (Circulation) Follett Software; (OPAC) Follett Software
Open Mon, Tues & Thurs 2-9, Wed & Fri 2-5, Sat 9-12

CAMPBELL

P CAMPBELL PUBLIC LIBRARY*, 721 Broad St, 68932. (Mail add: PO Box 215, 68932-0215), SAN 377-1814. Tel: 402-756-8121. *Librn,* Jeanne Penney
Library Holdings: Bk Vols 15,000
Open Tues 9-12 & 1-4, Sat 9-Noon

CARROLL

P CARROLL PUBLIC LIBRARY*, 506 Main St, 68723. (Mail add: PO Box 215, 68723-0215), SAN 309-4197. Tel: 402-585-4586. *Dir,* Charlene Jones
Library Holdings: Bk Vols 850
Open Tues 3:30-5:30, Sat 9-11

CEDAR RAPIDS

P CEDAR RAPIDS PUBLIC LIBRARY*, 423 W Main St, 68627. (Mail add: PO Box 344, 68627-0344), SAN 309-4200. Tel: 308-358-0603. FAX: 308-358-0117. E-mail: licedrap@gpcom.net. Web Site: www.megavision.net/crpl. *Dir,* Marilyn Jo Schuele; *Asst Librn,* Mary Pat Boesch
Founded 1914. Pop 407; Circ 5,000
Library Holdings: AV Mats 650; CDs 120; Large Print Bks 100; Bk Vols 10,821; Per Subs 10; Talking Bks 395; Videos 725
Special Collections: Cedar Rapids Nebraska Newspaper Items 1901-1935
Open Wed & Fri 9-11 & 2:30-5:30, Sat 2-5 & 7-9
Friends of the Library Group

CENTRAL CITY

P CENTRAL CITY PUBLIC LIBRARY, 1604 15th Ave, 68826. SAN 309-4219. Tel: 308-946-2512. FAX: 308-946-3290. E-mail: cc.library.ne@gmail.com. Web Site: libraries.ne.gov/centralcity. *Dir,* Sara Lee; *Asst Librn,* Adele Maynard; *Youth Librn,* Judy Marco
Founded 1895. Pop 2,868; Circ 68,004
Library Holdings: Bks on Deafness & Sign Lang 17; e-books 4,079; Bk Vols 34,274; Per Subs 75
Subject Interests: Genealogy, Music
Automation Activity & Vendor Info: (Cataloging) LibLime; (Circulation) LibLime; (ILL) OCLC; (OPAC) LibLime
Wireless access
Open Mon-Thurs 10-8, Fri 10-6, Sat 10-2

CERESCO

P CERESCO COMMUNITY LIBRARY*, 425 S Second St, 68017. (Mail add: PO Box 158, 68017-0158), SAN 309-4227. Tel: 402-665-2112. FAX: 402-665-2036. E-mail: ceresco@microlnk.com. *Dir,* Wylene Twombly; Tel: 402-785-2585, E-mail: lwylene@aol.com
Founded 1976. Pop 1,001
Library Holdings: Bks-By-Mail 25; CDs 45; Bk Titles 8,480; Per Subs 12; Talking Bks 55; Videos 220
Automation Activity & Vendor Info: (Cataloging) Follett Software; (Circulation) Follett Software; (OPAC) Follett Software
Open Tues-Thurs 10-12 & 3:30-8, Sat 10-3
Friends of the Library Group

CHADRON

P CHADRON PUBLIC LIBRARY*, 507 Bordeaux, 69337. SAN 309-4235. Tel: 308-432-0531. FAX: 308-432-0534. E-mail: cpublib507@gmail.com. Web Site: www.chadronpubliclibrary.com. *Dir,* Rossella Tesch; E-mail: rtesch@chadronpubliclibrary.com; *Asst Dir,* Annette Bellu; Staff 4 (MLS 3, Non-MLS 1)
Founded 1911. Pop 5,933; Circ 73,000
Library Holdings: Bk Vols 30,000; Per Subs 82
Automation Activity & Vendor Info: (Cataloging) Follett Software; (Circulation) Follett Software; (OPAC) Follett Software
Wireless access
Publications: Annual Special Library Edition: 1989, A 100-year History
Mem of Panhandle Libr Syst
Open Mon-Thurs 10-8, Fri & Sat 12-5
Friends of the Library Group

C CHADRON STATE COLLEGE*, Reta E King Library, 300 E 12th St, 69337. SAN 309-4243. Tel: 308-432-6271. Web Site: www.csc.edu. *Dir of Libr Serv,* Milton Wolf; *Asst Dir, Pub Serv,* Shawn Hartman; *Pub Serv,* Christine Fullerton; *Pub Serv,* Glenda Gamby; *Tech Serv,* Sally Zahn; Staff 5 (MLS 5)
Founded 1911. Fac 110, Highest Degree: Master
Library Holdings: Bk Vols 215,000; Per Subs 550
Database Vendor: EBSCOhost, Gale Cengage Learning, Innovative Interfaces, Inc, OCLC FirstSearch, SerialsSolutions, Westlaw, Wilson - Wilson Web
Wireless access
Function: Adult literacy prog, After school storytime
Partic in OCLC Online Computer Library Center, Inc
Special Services for the Blind - Reader equip
Restriction: Access at librarian's discretion

S MUSEUM OF THE FUR TRADE LIBRARY*, 6321 Hwy 20, 69337. Tel: 308-432-3843. FAX: 308-432-5963. E-mail: museum@furtrade.org. Web Site: www.furtrade.org. *Dir,* Gail DeBuse-Potter
Library Holdings: Bk Vols 10,000
Function: Res libr
Restriction: Not open to pub

CHAPPELL

P CHAPPELL MEMORIAL LIBRARY & ART GALLERY*, 289 Babcock Ave, 69129. (Mail add: PO Box 248, 69129-0248), SAN 309-4251. Tel: 308-874-2626. FAX: 308-874-2626. *Librn,* Dixie Riley
Pop 1,095; Circ 7,823
Library Holdings: Bk Vols 11,170; Per Subs 15
Automation Activity & Vendor Info: (Circulation) Follett Software
Wireless access
Mem of Panhandle Libr Syst

Open Tues & Thurs 1-7, Sat 2-5
Friends of the Library Group

CHESTER

P CHESTER PUBLIC LIBRARY*, 623 Thayer Ave, 68327. (Mail add: PO Box 335, 68327-0335). Tel: 402-324-5755. *Dir,* Judy Smith
Pop 235; Circ 2,028
Library Holdings: Bk Vols 1,000
Open Mon-Fri 8:30-4:30

CLARKS

P CLARKS PUBLIC LIBRARY*, 101 W Amity, 68628. (Mail add: PO Box 223, 68628-0223), SAN 377-1830. Tel: 308-548-2864. *Librn,* Barbee Sweet
Founded 1917
Library Holdings: Bk Vols 6,500; Per Subs 23
Wireless access
Partic in NE Nebr Libr Asn
Open Mon 12:30-6, Tues-Fri 12:30-5
Friends of the Library Group

CLARKSON

P CLARKSON PUBLIC LIBRARY, 318 Pine St, 68629. SAN 309-4278. Tel: 402-892-3235. FAX: 402-892-3235. E-mail: clarksonpubliclibrary@gmail.com. Web Site: libraries.ne.gov/clarkson. *Dir,* Tricia Dusatko; *Asst Librn,* Mady Groene; *Asst Librn,* Debra Nadrchal
Pop 699; Circ 3,643
Library Holdings: Bk Vols 12,000; Per Subs 24
Special Collections: Czechoslavakian Coll
Automation Activity & Vendor Info: (Cataloging) Follett Software; (Circulation) Follett Software
Wireless access
Open Mon, Tues, Thurs & Fri 2-6, Wed 10-1 & 4-7, Sat 10-1

CLAY CENTER

P CLAY CENTER PUBLIC LIBRARY*, 117 W Edgar St, 68933. SAN 309-4286. Tel: 402-762-3861. FAX: 402-762-3861. E-mail: cclibrary@clay-center.net. Web Site: www.clay-center.net/library. *Dir,* Cheryl Green
Founded 1912. Pop 1,000; Circ 10,931
Library Holdings: Bk Titles 15,267; Per Subs 50
Automation Activity & Vendor Info: (Cataloging) Follett Software; (Circulation) Follett Software
Open Mon & Wed 3-7, Tues & Thurs 2-6, Sat 11-3
Friends of the Library Group

CLEARWATER

P CLEARWATER PUBLIC LIBRARY, 626 Main St, 68726. (Mail add: PO Box 172, 68726-0116), SAN 309-4294. Tel: 402-485-2034. FAX: 402-485-2365. E-mail: clearwaterpubliclibrary@yahoo.com. *Dir,* Marelee Thorneberry
Pop 409; Circ 3,077
Library Holdings: Bk Vols 5,271
Wireless access
Open Mon, Wed & Fri 1-6

COLUMBUS

J CENTRAL COMMUNITY COLLEGE*, Columbus Resource Center, 4500 63rd St, 68601. (Mail add: PO Box 1027, 68602-1027), SAN 309-4316. Tel: 402-562-1202. Administration Tel: 402-562-1418. Toll Free Tel: 877-222-0780 (in-state). FAX: 402-562-1227. Web Site: www.cccneb.edu. *Dir,* Dee Johnson, II; E-mail: djohnson@cccneb.edu; *Assoc Dir,* Denette Drum; Tel: 402-562-1445, E-mail: ddrum@cccneb.edu
Founded 1969. Enrl 2,000; Fac 100; Highest Degree: Associate
Library Holdings: Bk Vols 24,000; Per Subs 150
Automation Activity & Vendor Info: (Cataloging) SirsiDynix; (Circulation) SirsiDynix; (OPAC) SirsiDynix; (Serials) OCLC
Database Vendor: EBSCOhost, OCLC FirstSearch, Wilson - Wilson Web

P COLUMBUS PUBLIC LIBRARY*, 2504 14th St, 68601-4988. SAN 309-4308. Tel: 402-564-7116. FAX: 402-563-3378. *Dir,* Jill Owens; *Cat,* RoJean Lambrecht; *Ch Serv,* Brad Hruska; *Circ,* Peggy Engel; *Info Tech,* Donna Thiem; E-mail: dthiem@columbusne.us; Staff 15 (MLS 1, Non-MLS 14)
Founded 1900. Pop 33,000; Circ 197,700
Oct 2005-Sept 2006 Income $729,682, State $6,689, City $533,650, County $153,247, Locally Generated Income $14,575. Mats Exp $114,000, Books $78,200, Per/Ser (Incl. Access Fees) $4,500, AV Mat $4,500, Electronic Ref Mat (Incl. Access Fees) $8,500. Sal $504,216 (Prof $58,000)
Library Holdings: AV Mats 6,500; CDs 2,000; DVDs 1,200; Large Print Bks 2,200; Bk Titles 81,500; Bk Vols 88,880; Per Subs 170; Talking Bks 3,400; Videos 3,200
Special Collections: Play & Theatre Coll. State Document Depository
Automation Activity & Vendor Info: (Acquisitions) SirsiDynix; (Cataloging) SirsiDynix; (Circulation) SirsiDynix; (Media Booking) SirsiDynix; (OPAC) SirsiDynix; (Serials) SirsiDynix
Mem of South Central Library System
Partic in ONELibrary Consortium
Open Mon-Thurs 9:30-9, Fri 9:30-5, Sat 10-5, Sun 1:30-5
Friends of the Library Group
Bookmobiles: 1. Librn, Karen Hake

COZAD

P WILSON PUBLIC LIBRARY*, 910 Meridian, 69130-1755. SAN 309-4340. Tel: 308-784-2019. E-mail: wpublib@cozadtel.net. Web Site: www.wilsonpubliclibrary.com. *Dir,* Laurie Yocom
Pop 3,828; Circ 51,286
Library Holdings: Bk Vols 27,444; Per Subs 48
Subject Interests: Local hist
Wireless access
Open Mon-Thurs 10-7, Fri 10-5, Sat 10-1
Friends of the Library Group

CRAWFORD

P CRAWFORD PUBLIC LIBRARY*, 601 Second St, 69339. SAN 309-4367. Tel: 308-665-1780. FAX: 308-665-3932. E-mail: crawlib@yahoo.com. Web Site: www.crawfordpubliclibrary.com. *Head Librn,* Ellyn Renken; *Ch, Libr Asst,* Cleone Hoyda
Founded 1916. Circ 26,889
Library Holdings: Bk Vols 14,000; Per Subs 22
Automation Activity & Vendor Info: (Cataloging) Follett Software; (Circulation) Follett Software; (OPAC) Follett Software
Mem of Panhandle Libr Syst
Open Mon-Fri 2-7, Sat 10-2
Friends of the Library Group

CREIGHTON

P CREIGHTON PUBLIC LIBRARY*, 701 State St, 68729-4000. (Mail add: PO Box 158, 68729-0158), SAN 309-4375. Tel: 402-358-5115. FAX: 402-358-3767. E-mail: crpulib@gpcom.net. *Dir,* Lindsay Nelson; Staff 3 (Non-MLS 3)
Founded 1914. Pop 1,223; Circ 15,000
Library Holdings: Bk Titles 13,108; Per Subs 54
Special Collections: Old West Coll; Second World War Coll
Automation Activity & Vendor Info: (Cataloging) Follett Software; (Circulation) Follett Software
Special Services for the Deaf - High interest/low vocabulary bks; Spec interest per
Open Mon & Wed 1-5 & 7-9, Tues 10-5, Thurs & Fri 1-5, Sat 9-1

CRETE

P CRETE PUBLIC LIBRARY*, 305 E 13th St, 69333. (Mail add: PO Box 156, 68333-0156), SAN 309-4383. Tel: 402-826-3809. FAX: 402-826-4199. Web Site: www.crete-ne.gov/library. *Dir,* Lisa Olivigni; E-mail: lolivigni@crete-ne.gov; *Children's & YA Librn,* Laura Renker; E-mail: lrenker@crete-ne.gov; *ILL,* Vel Busboom; E-mail: vbusboom@crete-ne.gov; *Outreach Serv,* Carol Aden; E-mail: caden@crete-ne.gov
Founded 1878. Pop 5,100; Circ 39,722
Library Holdings: Bk Vols 27,548; Per Subs 55
Special Collections: Czechoslovakian Coll; Nebraska Coll
Automation Activity & Vendor Info: (Cataloging) Follett Software; (Circulation) Follett Software; (OPAC) Follett Software
Wireless access
Mem of Southeast Library System (SELS)
Open Mon, Wed, Fri & Sat 10-7:30
Friends of the Library Group

C DOANE COLLEGE*, Perkins Library, 1014 Boswell Ave, 68333-2421. SAN 309-4391. Tel: 402-826-8287. FAX: 402-826-8303. E-mail: library@doane.edu. Web Site: www.doane.edu. *Dir,* Julie Pinnell; E-mail: julie.pinnell@doane.edu; *Coll Develop Librn,* Jayne Germer; E-mail: jayne.germer@doane.edu; *Archivist, Pub Serv,* Janet Jeffries; E-mail: janet.jeffries@doane.edu; *Acq,* Janis Mitchell; E-mail: janis.mitchell@doane.edu; *Cat,* Holly Barber; E-mail: holly.barber@doane.edu; *Per,* Judy Bespalec; E-mail: judy.bespalec@doane.edu; Staff 3 (MLS 3)
Founded 1872. Enrl 1,794; Fac 104; Highest Degree: Master
Library Holdings: AV Mats 3,418; e-books 6,000; Bk Vols 96,000; Per Subs 515

Special Collections: Doane College Archives Coll; Rall Art Gallery; Rossman Historiography; United Church of Christ Coll. State Document Depository; US Document Depository
Subject Interests: Liberal arts
Automation Activity & Vendor Info: (Acquisitions) SirsiDynix; (Cataloging) OCLC; (Circulation) SirsiDynix; (Course Reserve) SirsiDynix; (ILL) OCLC; (OPAC) SirsiDynix; (Serials) EBSCO Online
Database Vendor: EBSCOhost, JSTOR, OCLC FirstSearch, Wilson - Wilson Web
Publications: Accessions List
Partic in Lyrasis; NICLC; OCLC Online Computer Library Center, Inc
Open Mon-Thurs 8am-11pm, Fri 8-5, Sat 12-4, Sun 2-11

CROFTON

P EASTERN TOWNSHIP PUBLIC LIBRARY*, 206 W Main St, 68730. (Mail add: PO Box 455, 68730-0455), SAN 377-5380. Tel: 402-388-4915. FAX: 402-388-4915. E-mail: easterntownshiplib@gpcom.net. *Dir,* Diane Limoges; Staff 1 (Non-MLS 1)
Pop 853
Library Holdings: Bk Titles 6,500; Per Subs 15; Videos 75
Database Vendor: OCLC FirstSearch, Wilson - Wilson Web
Open Mon, Tues & Thurs 1-5, Wed 9-1 & 6:30-8:30, Sat 9-11

CULBERTSON

P CULBERTSON PUBLIC LIBRARY*, 507 New York St, 69024. (Mail add: PO Box 327, 69024-0327), SAN 309-4405. Tel: 308-278-2135. *Librn,* Dana Wade; E-mail: danawade2003@yahoo.com
Founded 1908. Pop 795; Circ 2,898
Library Holdings: Bk Vols 10,430; Per Subs 22
Special Collections: Art Prints; Old Books; Old History of Hitchcock County (Otis Rogers Coll), clippings & pictures
Open Wed 1-8, Fri 9-1, Sat 1-5

CURTIS

P KLYTE BURT MEMORIAL PUBLIC LIBRARY*, 316 Center Ave, 69025. (Mail add: PO Box 29, 69025-0029), SAN 309-4413. Tel: 308-367-4148. E-mail: kbmlib@curtis-ne.com. *Dir,* Marcia Wortman; Staff 1 (Non-MLS 1)
Founded 1940. Pop 3,416; Circ 10,800
Library Holdings: Bk Titles 13,460; Per Subs 23
Wireless access
Function: Adult bk club, After school storytime, Bks on cassette, Bks on CD, Children's prog, Computers for patron use, Copy machines, e-mail & chat, Electronic databases & coll, Free DVD rentals, ILL available, Prog for children & young adult, Pub access computers, Scanner, Story hour, Summer & winter reading prog, Summer reading prog, Telephone ref, VHS videos
Open Mon, Wed, Thurs & Fri 1:30-5:30, Tues 2-7, Sat 2-5

C NEBRASKA COLLEGE OF TECHNICAL AGRICULTURE LIBRARY*, 404 E Seventh St, 69025. (Mail add: RR 3 Box 23A, 69025-0069), SAN 371-702X. Tel: 308-367-5213. FAX: 308-367-5209. Web Site: ncta.unl.edu. *Curator,* Mo Khamouna; E-mail: mkhamouna1@unl.edu; Staff 1 (Non-MLS 1)
Enrl 234; Fac 22
Library Holdings: Bk Titles 6,410; Per Subs 320
Automation Activity & Vendor Info: (Acquisitions) Follett Software; (Cataloging) Follett Software; (Circulation) Follett Software; (ILL) Follett Software; (OPAC) Follett Software; (Serials) Follett Software
Wireless access
Open Mon-Fri 8am-10pm, Sun 6pm-10pm

DAKOTA CITY

P DAKOTA CITY PUBLIC LIBRARY*, 1710 Broadway, 68731. (Mail add: PO Box 189, 68731-0189), SAN 309-4421. Tel: 402-987-3778. FAX: 402-987-3778. E-mail: dakotacitypubliclibrary@yahoo.com. *Dir,* Barbara Stansberry
Pop 1,440; Circ 5,726
Library Holdings: Bk Vols 7,835; Per Subs 20
Special Collections: Library of America Classics; War of the Rebellion Coll
Automation Activity & Vendor Info: (Cataloging) Follett Software; (Circulation) Follett Software
Wireless access
Open Mon & Thurs 1-8, Tues & Wed 1:30-5:30, Sat 9-12
Friends of the Library Group

DALTON

P DALTON PUBLIC LIBRARY*, 306 Main St, 69131. (Mail add: PO Box 353, 69131-0353), SAN 309-443X. Tel: 308-377-2413. E-mail: daltonlibrary@daltontel.net. *Librn,* Joann Evans
Pop 568; Circ 2,247
Library Holdings: Audiobooks 18; Large Print Bks 90; Bk Vols 3,000; Videos 23
Mem of Panhandle Libr Syst
Open Tues-Sat 9-Noon
Friends of the Library Group

DAVENPORT

P DAVENPORT PUBLIC LIBRARY, 109 N Maple Ave, 68335. (Mail add: PO Box 236, 68335-0236), SAN 309-4448. Tel: 402-364-2147. E-mail: davenportlib@superiorinet.net. *Librn,* Sharon Littrel
Pop 339; Circ 19,624
Library Holdings: Bk Vols 12,000; Per Subs 17
Wireless access
Open Mon-Thurs 2-5:30

DAVID CITY

P ROMAN L & VICTORIA E HRUSKA MEMORIAL PUBLIC LIBRARY*, 399 N Fifth St, 68632. Tel: 402-367-4456. Tel: 402-367-3100. FAX: 402-367-3105. E-mail: hruskalibrary@gmail.com. Web Site: www.davidcitylibrary.com. *Dir,* Kay Schmid
Founded 1891
Subject Interests: County hist
Automation Activity & Vendor Info: (Acquisitions) Brodart; (Cataloging) Follett Software; (Circulation) Follett Software; (ILL) Follett Software
Database Vendor: OCLC FirstSearch
Wireless access
Function: Adult bk club, After school storytime, Archival coll, Audiobks via web, Bks on CD, Children's prog, Computer training, Computers for patron use, Copy machines, e-mail serv, Electronic databases & coll, Exhibits, Fax serv, Free DVD rentals, Handicapped accessible, Home delivery & serv to Sr ctr & nursing homes, ILL available, Instruction & testing, Mail & tel request accepted, Microfiche/film & reading machines, Music CDs, Online cat, OverDrive digital audio bks, Photocopying/Printing, Preschool reading prog, Prog for adults, Prog for children & young adult, Pub access computers, Scanner, Senior computer classes, Senior outreach, Serves mentally handicapped consumers, Story hour, Summer & winter reading prog, Tax forms, Web-catalog, Wheelchair accessible
Open Mon-Thurs 10-7, Sat 9-1
Friends of the Library Group

DAWSON

P JOHN G SMITH MEMORIAL PUBLIC LIBRARY*, 517 Ridge St, 68337. (Mail add: 1220 Nemaha St, 68337), SAN 309-4464. Tel: 402-855-4815. *Librn,* Carol Kean
Founded 1946. Pop 1,000; Circ 71,340
Library Holdings: Bk Vols 8,500; Per Subs 5
Open Tues 1-5
Friends of the Library Group

DESHLER

P DESHLER PUBLIC LIBRARY*, 310 E Pearl St, 68340. (Mail add: PO Box 520, 68340-0520), SAN 309-4472. Tel: 402-365-4107. FAX: 402-365-4107. E-mail: depulio1@gpcom.net. *Librn,* Joyce Schmidt; *Asst Librn,* Karen Sims
Founded 1937. Pop 997; Circ 6,500
Library Holdings: AV Mats 20; Bk Vols 13,489; Per Subs 15
Function: ILL available
Mem of Southeast Library System (SELS)
Open Mon-Fri 3-5:30, Wed 7pm-9pm, Sat 9-12

DEWITT

P BURKLEY LIBRARY & RESOURCE CENTER*, 208 E Fillmore, 68341. (Mail add: PO Box 375, 68341-0375). Tel: 402-683-2145. FAX: 402-683-2145. E-mail: brc@galaxycable.net. *Dir,* Geraldine Powers
Pop 577; Circ 2,363
Library Holdings: AV Mats 419; CDs 35; Bk Vols 10,000; Per Subs 20; Talking Bks 237
Automation Activity & Vendor Info: (Cataloging) Biblionix; (Circulation) Biblionix; (OPAC) Biblionix
Open Mon & Thurs 3-6, Tues & Wed 2-6, Sat 9-12

DODGE

P JOHN ROGERS MEMORIAL PUBLIC LIBRARY*, 703 Second St, 68633. SAN 309-4502. Tel: 402-693-2512. E-mail: johnrogerslibrary@yahoo.com. Web Site: libraries.ne.gov/dodge. *Libr Dir,* Jenny Praest; *Asst Librn,* Mary Mandel
Pop 700; Circ 1,000
Library Holdings: Bk Vols 6,500; Per Subs 22
Automation Activity & Vendor Info: (Cataloging) OCLC WorldShare Interlibrary Loan; (Circulation) OCLC WorldShare Interlibrary Loan; (OPAC) OCLC WorldShare Interlibrary Loan
Wireless access
Open Tues & Wed 11:30-5, Thurs 11:30-8, Sat 9-Noon

DORCHESTER

P DORCHESTER PUBLIC LIBRARY*, Sixth & Washington, 68343. (Mail add: PO Box 268, 68343-0268), SAN 377-2489. Tel: 402-946-3891. *Librn,* Gerry Boller
Pop 614; Circ 732
Library Holdings: Bk Vols 5,875
Open Wed 3-5, Sat 9:30-11:30
Friends of the Library Group

DOUGLAS

P DOUGLAS PUBLIC LIBRARY*, Main St, 68344. (Mail add: 944 S Eighth Rd, 68344-8942), SAN 377-1873. Tel: 402-799-3175. *In Charge,* Ardys Brugman
Library Holdings: Bk Vols 4,000

ELGIN

P ELGIN PUBLIC LIBRARY*, 503 S Second St, 68636-3222. (Mail add: PO Box 240, 68636-0240), SAN 309-4529. Tel: 402-843-2460. FAX: 402-843-2460. E-mail: elgpblib@gpcom.net. *Dir,* Joyce Sullivan
Pop 649; Circ 6,796
Library Holdings: CDs 75; DVDs 60; Large Print Bks 680; Bk Titles 11,581; Per Subs 7; Talking Bks 101; Videos 184
Automation Activity & Vendor Info: (Cataloging) Biblionix; (Circulation) Biblionix; (Course Reserve) Biblionix
Wireless access
Function: Adult bk club, Bks on cassette, Bks on CD, Children's prog, Computers for patron use, Copy machines, e-mail & chat, e-mail serv, Fax serv, Free DVD rentals, Home delivery & serv to Sr ctr & nursing homes, Homebound delivery serv, ILL available, Pub access computers, Spoken cassettes & CDs, Spoken cassettes & DVDs, Story hour, Summer reading prog, VHS videos, Video lending libr, Wheelchair accessible
Open Mon 5pm-7pm, Tues, Thurs & Fri 1-5, Wed 1-7

ELM CREEK

P ELM CREEK PUBLIC LIBRARY*, 241 N Tyler St, 68836. (Mail add: PO Box 489, 68836-0489), SAN 377-189X. Tel: 308-856-4394. *Dir,* Jane Walker
Library Holdings: Bk Vols 9,000; Per Subs 16
Open Wed 8:30-11:30 & 1-5:30, Sat 8:30-11:30 & 1-6

ELMWOOD

P ELMWOOD PUBLIC LIBRARY*, 124 West D St, 68349. (Mail add: PO Box 283, 68349-0283), SAN 309-4545. Tel: 402-994-4125. FAX: 402-994-4125. E-mail: elmwoodlibrary@windstream.net. Web Site: libraries.ne.gov/elmwood, www.elmwoodnebraska.com. *Libr Dir,* Janet Sorensen
Founded 1917. Pop 600; Circ 4,636
Library Holdings: Bk Vols 11,089; Per Subs 23
Special Collections: Autographed Books (Bess Streeter Aldrich Coll)
Automation Activity & Vendor Info: (Cataloging) Follett Software; (Circulation) Follett Software
Wireless access
Open Mon 3-8, Tues & Wed 2-6, Thurs & Sat 10-2
Friends of the Library Group

ELWOOD

P ELWOOD PUBLIC LIBRARY*, 505 Ripley St, 68937. (Mail add: PO Box 327, 68937-0327), SAN 309-4553. Tel: 308-785-2035. FAX: 308-785-2035. *Dir,* Jane Hilton; E-mail: jane.hilton@hotmail.com
Pop 2,140; Circ 18,492
Library Holdings: Bk Vols 18,226; Per Subs 18
Open Mon 7pm-9:30pm, Tues, Thurs & Sat 1-5:30

EMERSON

P EMERSON PUBLIC LIBRARY*, 110 Main St, 68733. (Mail add: PO Box 160, 68733-0160), SAN 309-4561. Tel: 402-695-2449. FAX: 402-695-2449. E-mail: emlib@huntel.net. *Libr Dir,* Carol Kielty
Founded 1930. Pop 874; Circ 7,001
Library Holdings: Bk Titles 10,000; Per Subs 20
Automation Activity & Vendor Info: (Acquisitions) OCLC Online; (Cataloging) Follett Software; (Circulation) Follett Software; (OPAC) Follett Software
Wireless access
Function: Accelerated reader prog, Accessibility serv available based on individual needs, Adult bk club, Adult literacy prog, After school storytime, Alaskana res, Archival coll, Art exhibits, Audio & video playback equip for onsite use, Audiobks via web, AV serv, BA reader (adult literacy), Bi-weekly Writer's Group, Bilingual assistance for Spanish patrons, Bk club(s), Bk reviews (Group), Bks on cassette, Bks on CD, Bus archives, CD-ROM, Chess club, Citizenship assistance, Computer training, Computers for patron use, Copy machines, Digital talking bks, Distance learning, Doc delivery serv, e-mail & chat, e-mail serv, E-Reserves, Electronic databases & coll, Equip loans & repairs, Exhibits, Family literacy, Fax serv, For res purposes, Free DVD rentals, Games & aids for the handicapped, Genealogy discussion group, Govt ref serv, Handicapped accessible, Health sci info serv, Holiday prog, Home delivery & serv to Sr ctr & nursing homes, Homebound delivery serv, Homework prog, ILL available, Instruction & testing, Jail serv, Jazz prog, Large print keyboards, Learning ctr, Legal assistance to inmates, Libr develop, Literacy & newcomer serv, Magnifiers for reading, Mail & tel request accepted, Mail loans to mem, Masonic res mat, Microfiche/film & reading machines, Monthly prog for perceptually impaired adults, Mus passes, Music CDs, Newsp ref libr, Notary serv, Online cat, Online info literacy tutorials on the web & in blackboard, Online ref, Online searches, Orientations, Outreach serv, Outside serv via phone, mail, e-mail & web, OverDrive digital audio bks, Passport agency, Photocopying/Printing, Preschool outreach, Preschool reading prog, Printer for laptops & handheld devices, Prof lending libr, Prog for adults, Prog for children & young adult, Provide serv for the mentally ill, Pub access computers, Ref & res, Ref serv available, Ref serv in person, Referrals accepted, Res libr, Res performed for a fee, Satellite serv, Scanner, Senior computer classes, Senior outreach, Serves mentally handicapped consumers, Spanish lang bks, Specialized serv in classical studies, Spoken cassettes & CDs, Spoken cassettes & DVDs, Story hour, Summer & winter reading prog, Tax forms, Teen prog, Telephone ref, VCDs, VHS videos, Video lending libr, Visual arts prog, Web-Braille, Web-catalog, Wheelchair accessible, Words travel prog, Workshops
Open Mon & Fri 9-5, Wed 1-8, Thurs 4-7, Sat 9-12
Friends of the Library Group

EUSTIS

P EUSTIS PUBLIC LIBRARY*, 108 N Morton St, 69028. (Mail add: PO Box 68, 69028-0068), SAN 309-457X. Tel: 308-486-2651. *Librn,* Ramona Koch
Founded 1935. Pop 500; Circ 2,280
Library Holdings: Bk Vols 9,000
Open Wed 3-6, Thurs (Apr-Nov) 6-8, Sat 9:30-11:30

EWING

P EWING TOWNSHIP LIBRARY*, 202 E Nebraska, 68735. (Mail add: PO Box 55, 68735-0055), SAN 309-4588. *Librn,* Idella Tuttle
Founded 1927. Pop 387
Library Holdings: Audiobooks 9; DVDs 77; Large Print Bks 324; Bk Titles 5,296; Videos 131
Wireless access
Partic in Nebr Network
Open Mon 2-5, Thurs 9-12 & 3-5, Sat 9-Noon

EXETER

P EXETER PUBLIC LIBRARY, 202 S Exeter Ave, 68351. (Mail add: PO Box 96, 68351-0096), SAN 309-4596. Tel: 402-266-3031. FAX: 402-266-3061. E-mail: epublib@hotmail.com. *Dir,* Jessica Votipka; Staff 2 (Non-MLS 2)
Pop 712; Circ 5,194
Library Holdings: AV Mats 348; Bk Titles 12,160; Per Subs 10; Talking Bks 81
Automation Activity & Vendor Info: (Circulation) Follett Software
Mem of Southeast Library System (SELS)
Open Mon, Wed & Fri 8-12 & 1-5, Sat 9-12

FAIRBURY

P FAIRBURY PUBLIC LIBRARY*, 601 Seventh St, 68352. SAN 309-460X. Tel: 402-729-2843. FAX: 402-729-2880. E-mail: fairburypubliclibrary@yahoo.com, fairburyreference@yahoo.com. Web Site:

www.fairburylibrary.org. *Libr Dir,* Karen Fox; *Ch,* Jean Naiman; Staff 3 (Non-MLS 3)
Founded 1909. Pop 4,335; Circ 24,392
Library Holdings: Audiobooks 1,249; DVDs 47; Large Print Bks 2,156; Bk Vols 30,884; Per Subs 72; Videos 381
Automation Activity & Vendor Info: (Cataloging) Follett Software; (Circulation) Follett Software; (OPAC) Follett Software
Wireless access
Mem of Southeast Library System (SELS)
Open Mon, Wed & Fri 11:30-6, Tues & Thurs 11:30-8, Sat 9-12

FAIRFIELD

P FAIRFIELD PUBLIC LIBRARY, 412 North D St, 68938. (Mail add: PO Box 278, 68938-0278), SAN 309-4626. Tel: 402-726-2220. FAX: 402-726-2388. E-mail: fplibrary@hotmail.com. Web Site: libraries.ne.gov/fairfield. *Libr Dir,* Stephanie Haack
Founded 1914. Pop 367; Circ 2,699
Oct 2014-Sept 2015 Income $16,000. Sal $8,060
Library Holdings: Bk Vols 5,000; Per Subs 13
Automation Activity & Vendor Info: (Acquisitions) Book Systems; (Cataloging) Book Systems; (Circulation) Book Systems
Wireless access
Function: Accelerated reader prog, Bks on CD, Computers for patron use, Copy machines, Electronic databases & coll, Fax serv, Free DVD rentals, Homebound delivery serv, ILL available, Laminating, Magazines, Movies, Newsp ref libr, Online cat, Online searches, Outside serv via phone, mail, e-mail & web, OverDrive digital audio bks, Photocopying/Printing, Printer for laptops & handheld devices, Pub access computers, Scanner, VHS videos
Open Mon, Wed & Fri 1:35-5:25
Friends of the Library Group

FAIRMONT

P FAIRMONT PUBLIC LIBRARY*, 600 F St, 68354. (Mail add: PO Box 428, 68354-0428), SAN 309-4634. Tel: 402-268-6081. FAX: 402-268-6081. Web Site: www.ci.fairmont.ne.us/library.htm. *Dir,* Wanda Marget; E-mail: wmarget@galaxycable.net; Staff 1 (Non-MLS 1)
Founded 1916. Pop 709
Library Holdings: Bk Vols 10,966; Per Subs 57
Automation Activity & Vendor Info: (Cataloging) Follett Software; (Circulation) Follett Software; (OPAC) Follett Software
Database Vendor: OCLC FirstSearch
Open Mon (Winter) 8-12, 1-5:30 & 6:30-9, Wed 6:30pm-9pm, Fri 1-5:30, Sat 8-12; Mon (Summer) 8-12 & 1-5:30, Wed 7pm-10pm, Fri 1-5:30, Sat 8-12

FALLS CITY

P THE FALLS CITY LIBRARY & ARTS CENTER*, 1400 Stone St, 68355. SAN 309-4642. Tel: 402-245-2913. FAX: 402-245-3031. E-mail: info@fallscitylibrary.org. Web Site: www.fallscitylibrary.org. *Dir,* Hope Schawang
Pop 4,671
Library Holdings: Bk Vols 50,000; Per Subs 100
Special Collections: Local Artists Coll, paintings
Wireless access
Open Mon-Thurs 10-8, Sat 9-Noon
Friends of the Library Group

FARNAM

P FARNAM PUBLIC LIBRARY*, 313 Main St, 69029. (Mail add: PO Box 8, 69029-0008), SAN 309-4650. Tel: 308-569-2318. E-mail: farnambook@atcjet.net. *Dir,* Shirley Minges
Pop 220; Circ 3,663
Library Holdings: Bk Vols 8,500
Open Wed 8:30-11:30 & 3-5, Sat 1-5

FORT CALHOUN

S WASHINGTON COUNTY HISTORICAL ASSOCIATION*, Museum Library, 14th & Monroe Sts, 68023. (Mail add: PO Box 25, 68023-0025), SAN 326-5811. Tel: 402-468-5740. FAX: 402-468-5741. E-mail: curator@newashcohist.org. Web Site: www.newashcohist.org. *Access Serv,* Faith Norwood
Founded 1938
Special Collections: Books with Copyright Date from 1850's to 1950's & Histories Principly Midwest/Nebraska
Publications: 1876 History of Washington, with index
Restriction: Non-circulating to the pub

FRANKLIN

P FRANKLIN PUBLIC LIBRARY*, 1502 P St, 68939-1200. SAN 309-4669. Tel: 308-425-3162. FAX: 308-425-3500. E-mail: frklnlbry@gtmc.net. *Librn,* Linda Gooder
Pop 1,000; Circ 11,500
Library Holdings: Bk Titles 12,000; Per Subs 21
Automation Activity & Vendor Info: (Cataloging) Follett Software; (Circulation) Follett Software; (OPAC) Follett Software
Wireless access
Open Mon 1-8, Wed & Fri 10-5, Thurs 10-6, Sat 9-Noon
Friends of the Library Group

FREMONT

S DODGE COUNTY HISTORICAL SOCIETY*, May Museum Library, 1643 N Nye, 68025. SAN 327-2265. Tel: 402-721-4515. FAX: 402-721-8354. E-mail: maymuseum@juno.com. Web Site: www.connectfremont.org. *Dir,* Patty Manhart
Library Holdings: Bk Titles 1,000

S EASTERN NEBRASKA GENEALOGICAL SOCIETY LIBRARY*, PO Box 541, 68026-0541. SAN 370-8551. Tel: 402-721-9553. Web Site: www.connectfremont.org/club/engs.htm. *In Charge,* Claire Mares
Founded 1972
Library Holdings: Bk Vols 400; Per Subs 200
Publications: Newsletter (Quarterly); Roots & Leaves (Quarterly)
Restriction: Open by appt only

P KEENE MEMORIAL LIBRARY*, 1030 N Broad St, 68025-4199. SAN 309-4677. Tel: 402-727-2694. FAX: 402-727-2693. Web Site: www.keene.lib.ne.us. *Dir,* Janet Davenport; E-mail: janet.davenport@fremontne.gov; *Adult Serv/Circ Librn,* Barbara Bandlow; *Youth Serv Librn,* Laura England-Biggs; Staff 4 (MLS 2, Non-MLS 2)
Founded 1901. Pop 25,000; Circ 194,654
Library Holdings: Bk Titles 90,000; Per Subs 235
Special Collections: Classics (Taylor)
Automation Activity & Vendor Info: (Acquisitions) SirsiDynix; (Cataloging) SirsiDynix; (Circulation) SirsiDynix; (OPAC) SirsiDynix; (Serials) SirsiDynix
Database Vendor: OCLC FirstSearch
Wireless access
Partic in OCLC Online Computer Library Center, Inc
Open Mon-Thurs 9:30-8:30, Fri & Sat 9:30-5:30, Sun 12:30-4:30
Friends of the Library Group

CR MIDLAND UNIVERSITY, Luther Library, 900 N Clarkson, 68025. SAN 309-4685. Tel: 402-941-6250. FAX: 402-727-6223. E-mail: library@midlandu.edu. Web Site: www.midlandu.edu/landing/page/luther-library. *Dir,* Shane Perrien; E-mail: perrien@midlandu.edu; *Librn,* Annette Pardy-Maass; *Libr Asst,* Barbara Coke; E-mail: coke@midlandu.edu; Staff 4 (MLS 2, Non-MLS 2)
Founded 1883. Enrl 720; Fac 53; Highest Degree: Bachelor
Library Holdings: AV Mats 500; CDs 1,400; DVDs 500; e-books 172,000; e-journals 12,000; Bk Titles 51,000; Bk Vols 88,600; Per Subs 125; Videos 1,000
Special Collections: Biblical Literature. US Document Depository
Automation Activity & Vendor Info: (Acquisitions) OCLC WorldShare Interlibrary Loan; (Cataloging) OCLC WorldShare Interlibrary Loan; (Circulation) OCLC WorldShare Interlibrary Loan; (Course Reserve) OCLC WorldShare Interlibrary Loan; (ILL) OCLC WorldShare Interlibrary Loan; (Media Booking) OCLC WorldShare Interlibrary Loan; (OPAC) OCLC WorldShare Interlibrary Loan; (Serials) OCLC WorldShare Interlibrary Loan
Database Vendor: BioOne, ebrary, EBSCOhost, LexisNexis, OCLC FirstSearch, Wilson - Wilson Web
Wireless access
Partic in Nebr Independent Col Libr Consortium; OCLC Online Computer Library Center, Inc
Open Mon-Thurs 7:45am-11pm, Fri 7:45-4:30, Sat 1-4, Sun 3-11

FRIEND

P GILBERT PUBLIC LIBRARY*, 628 Second St, 68359-1308. SAN 309-4693. Tel: 402-947-5081. E-mail: gilbertlibrary@diodecom.net. *Dir,* Jackie Larson
Founded 1916. Circ 3,046
Library Holdings: Bk Vols 11,391; Per Subs 35
Wireless access
Mem of Southeast Library System (SELS)
Open Mon & Wed 1:30-7:30, Tues & Thurs 9-1, Sat 9-Noon

FULLERTON

P FULLERTON PUBLIC LIBRARY, 903 Broadway, 68638. (Mail add: PO Box 578, 68638-0578), SAN 309-4707. Tel: 308-536-2382. FAX: 308-536-2382. E-mail: fpl@hamilton.net. Web Site: www.libraries.ne.gov/fullerton. *Dir,* Kimberly Saum
Founded 1913. Pop 1,452; Circ 12,008
Library Holdings: Bk Vols 13,000; Per Subs 40
Automation Activity & Vendor Info: (Cataloging) Follett Software; (Circulation) Follett Software
Wireless access
Open Mon 12-5 & 7-9, Tues 10-5, Wed 2-6 & 7-9, Thurs & Fri 1-5, Sat 10-Noon
Friends of the Library Group

GENEVA

P GENEVA PUBLIC LIBRARY*, 1043 G St, 68361. SAN 309-4715. Tel: 402-759-3416. FAX: 402-759-3416. *Dir,* Donna Shearer
Pop 3,032; Circ 40,536
Library Holdings: AV Mats 2,890; Bk Titles 21,728; Per Subs 51; Talking Bks 1,023
Automation Activity & Vendor Info: (Cataloging) Follett Software; (Circulation) Follett Software; (OPAC) Follett Software
Open Mon, Wed & Thurs 2-8, Tues 10-12 & 2-8, Fri 12-8, Sat 10-2

GENOA

P GENOA PUBLIC LIBRARY*, 421 Willard Ave, 68640. (Mail add: PO Box 279, 68640-0279), SAN 309-4723. Tel: 402-993-2943. E-mail: glibry@megavision.com. Web Site: www.megavision.com/glbry. *Libr Dir,* Tammi Thiem; *Children's Activities Dir,* Kimberly Thiem
Pop 1,090; Circ 12,079
Library Holdings: Bk Vols 8,597; Per Subs 29
Automation Activity & Vendor Info: (Cataloging) Follett Software; (Circulation) Follett Software
Function: Computer training, Copy machines, Electronic databases & coll, Fax serv, Homebound delivery serv, ILL available, Magnifiers for reading, Music CDs, Photocopying/Printing, Prog for children & young adult, Summer reading prog, Tax forms, VHS videos, Wheelchair accessible
Open Mon 10-Noon, Tues 12-5 & 6-8, Wed 2-5 & 6-8, Thurs 3-5 & 6-8, Fri 3-5, Sat 9-11
Friends of the Library Group

GERING

P GERING PUBLIC LIBRARY*, 1055 P St, 69341. SAN 309-4731. Tel: 308-436-7433. FAX: 308-436-6869. E-mail: gpl@geringlibrary.org. Web Site: www.geringlibrary.org. *Dir,* Diane Downer; Tel: 308-436-6868; *Pub Serv Librn,* Stephanie Cacciavillani; *Tech Serv Librn,* Kathyrn Wasserburger; *Youth Serv Librn,* Beth Trupp; Staff 5.6 (MLS 1, Non-MLS 4.6)
Founded 1895. Pop 7,886; Circ 81,000
Library Holdings: Bk Titles 40,000; Per Subs 100
Automation Activity & Vendor Info: (Cataloging) Follett Software; (Circulation) Follett Software; (OPAC) Follett Software
Function: Adult bk club, Children's prog, Computers for patron use, Copy machines, e-mail & chat, Electronic databases & coll, Fax serv, Free DVD rentals, Homebound delivery serv, ILL available, Photocopying/Printing, Prog for children & young adult, Story hour, Summer reading prog, Tax forms, Teen prog, VHS videos
Mem of Panhandle Libr Syst
Open Mon-Thurs 10-7, Fri & Sat 10-5
Friends of the Library Group

S NATIONAL PARK SERVICE*, Scotts Bluff National Monument, Oregon Trail Museum Library, 190276 Old Oregon Trail, 69341-8504. (Mail add: PO Box 27, 69341-0027), SAN 309-474X. Tel: 308-436-9721. FAX: 308-436-7611. Web Site: www.nps.gov/scbl. *In Charge,* Valerie Newman
Library Holdings: Bk Vols 1,300
Open Mon-Sun 8-5
Restriction: In-house use for visitors

CR SUMMIT CHRISTIAN COLLEGE LIBRARY*, 2025 21st St, 69341. SAN 309-6246. Tel: 308-632-6933. FAX: 308-632-8599. *Librn,* Jennifer Powell; Staff 1 (Non-MLS 1)
Founded 1952. Enrl 50; Fac 10; Highest Degree: Bachelor
Jul 2006-Jun 2007 Income $20,000
Library Holdings: Bk Vols 20,000; Per Subs 25
Wireless access
Function: CD-ROM, Computers for patron use, Distance learning, e-mail serv, Electronic databases & coll, ILL available, Online searches, VHS videos
Restriction: Fee for pub use, Open to fac, students & qualified researchers, Photo ID required for access

GIBBON

P GIBBON PUBLIC LIBRARY*, 116 LaBarre, 68840. (Mail add: PO Box 309, 68840-0309), SAN 309-4758. Tel: 308-468-5889. FAX: 308-468-5501. E-mail: gpl@nctc.net. Web Site: libraries.ne.gov/gibbon. *Dir,* Linda Nickel; *Youth Serv Librn,* Susan Webster; *Libr Asst,* Missy Onate
Founded 1909. Pop 1,792
Library Holdings: Bk Vols 10,223; Per Subs 72
Automation Activity & Vendor Info: (Cataloging) Book Systems; (Circulation) Book Systems
Wireless access
Function: Adult bk club, After school storytime, Bks on cassette, Bks on CD, Children's prog, Computers for patron use, Copy machines, Electronic databases & coll, Fax serv, Free DVD rentals, Handicapped accessible, ILL available, Mail & tel request accepted, Photocopying/Printing, Preschool outreach, Prog for adults, Prog for children & young adult, Pub access computers, Story hour, Summer reading prog, Tax forms, Teen prog, VHS videos, Wheelchair accessible
Open Mon & Fri 2-5, Tues & Thurs 9-7, Wed 2-7, Sat 9-Noon
Friends of the Library Group

GILTNER

P GILTNER PUBLIC LIBRARY*, 4020 N Commercial Ave, 68841. (Mail add: PO Box 185, 68841-0185), SAN 377-1903. Tel: 402-849-2290.
Library Holdings: Large Print Bks 150; Bk Vols 2,500
Mem of Southeast Library System (SELS)
Open Tues 3-5, Wed 7pm-9pm

GLENVIL

P BRUMBAUGH PUBLIC LIBRARY*, 202 Fink, 68941, *Dir,* Darlene Brumbaugh; E-mail: darbrumbaugh31@hotmail.com
Pop 325
Library Holdings: Bk Vols 24,000; Talking Bks 50; Videos 200

GORDON

P GORDON CITY LIBRARY*, 101 W Fifth St, 69343. SAN 309-4766. Tel: 308-282-1198. FAX: 308-282-0417. E-mail: gorcitli@gpcom.net. Web Site: www.gordoncitylibrary.org. *Dir,* Maria Kling; *Asst Librn,* Dawn Weber
Founded 1922. Pop 1,924
Library Holdings: Bk Titles 12,067; Per Subs 82
Special Collections: Gordon Journal Coll from 1894, micro; Interpreter's Bible; Large Print Coll; Nebraska History Coll
Subject Interests: Hist, Literary criticism
Automation Activity & Vendor Info: (Cataloging) Follett Software; (Circulation) Follett Software; (OPAC) Follett Software
Mem of Panhandle Libr Syst
Open Mon-Thurs 2-8, Sat 12-6
Friends of the Library Group

GOTHENBURG

P GOTHENBURG PUBLIC LIBRARY*, 1104 Lake Ave, 69138-1903. SAN 309-4774. Tel: 308-537-2591. FAX: 308-537-3667. E-mail: gothlibrary@yahoo.com. *Dir,* Mary Koch
Founded 1915. Pop 3,480; Circ 50,000
Library Holdings: Bk Vols 27,000; Per Subs 65
Automation Activity & Vendor Info: (Cataloging) Follett Software; (Circulation) Follett Software; (OPAC) Follett Software
Open Mon-Thurs 9-8, Fri 9-5, Sat 9-12

GRAND ISLAND

J CENTRAL COMMUNITY COLLEGE, Grand Island Campus Library, 3134 W Hwy 34, 68802. (Mail add: PO Box 4903, 68802-4903), SAN 377-1741. Tel: 308-398-7395, 308-398-7396. Web Site: www.cccneb.edu. *Librn,* Linda Bowden; E-mail: lbowden@cccneb.edu; Staff 1 (MLS 1)
Highest Degree: Associate
Library Holdings: Bk Vols 8,500; Per Subs 50
Automation Activity & Vendor Info: (Cataloging) SirsiDynix; (Circulation) SirsiDynix; (OPAC) SirsiDynix
Database Vendor: EBSCOhost, OCLC ArticleFirst, OCLC FirstSearch, OCLC WorldShare Interlibrary Loan, Wilson - Wilson Web
Wireless access
Partic in OCLC Online Computer Library Center, Inc
Open Mon-Thurs 8-8, Fri 8-4; Mon-Thurs (Summer) 8-4

P GRAND ISLAND PUBLIC LIBRARY*, Edith Abbott Memorial Library, 211 N Washington St, 68801-5855. SAN 309-4782. Tel: 308-385-5333. Administration Tel: 308-385-5333, Ext 127. FAX: 308-385-5339. E-mail: refdesk@gi.lib.ne.us. Web Site: www.gi.lib.ne.us. *Dir,* Steve Fosselman; E-mail: sf@gi.lib.ne.us; *Mgr,* Patsy Arnold; Tel: 308-385-5333, Ext 153, E-mail: pa@gi.lib.ne.us; *Cat,* Gerianne Pickering; Tel: 308-385-5333, Ext

124, E-mail: gp@gi.lib.ne.us; *Ch Serv,* Merry VonSeggern; Tel: 308-385-5333, Ext 125, E-mail: mvs@gi.lib.ne.us; *Circ, Coll Develop, Ref Serv,* Kathleen Nonneman; E-mail: kn@gi.lib.ne.us; *Info Tech, Ref Serv, YA Serv,* Celine Stahlnecker; Tel: 308-385-5333, Ext 154, E-mail: cs@gi.lib.ne.us; Staff 6 (MLS 1, Non-MLS 5)
Founded 1884. Pop 48,000; Circ 385,985
Library Holdings: AV Mats 10,713; Bk Vols 123,032; Per Subs 300
Special Collections: Abbott Sisters Research Center; Genealogy (Lue R Spencer State DAR Coll & Ella Sprague Coll)
Automation Activity & Vendor Info: (Acquisitions) SirsiDynix; (Cataloging) OCLC; (Circulation) SirsiDynix; (ILL) OCLC; (OPAC) SirsiDynix; (Serials) SirsiDynix
Database Vendor: 3M Library Systems, ALLDATA Online, Baker & Taylor, EBSCOhost, Electric Library, Grolier Online, H W Wilson, Marquis Who's Who, OCLC FirstSearch, Overdrive, Inc, ProQuest, ReferenceUSA, SirsiDynix, ValueLine, Wilson - Wilson Web
Wireless access
Open Mon-Thurs 9-9, Fri & Sat 9-6, Sun 1-5
Friends of the Library Group
Bookmobiles: 1

S STUHR MUSEUM OF THE PRAIRIE PIONEER*, Research Library, 3133 W Hwy 34, 68801-7280. SAN 309-4790. Tel: 308-385-5316. FAX: 308-385-5028. E-mail: research@stuhrmuseum.org. Web Site: www.stuhrmuseum.org/research. *Curator,* Karen Keehr; E-mail: kkeehr@stuhrmuseum.org; Staff 1 (Non-MLS 1)
Founded 1967
Library Holdings: Bk Titles 10,000; Per Subs 10
Special Collections: Arthur F Bentley Coll; Judge Bayard H Paine Coll
Publications: Bartenbach Opera House; Prairie Pioneer Press; Schimmer's Sand Krog-Resort on the Platte; Sheep King; Townbuilders

GRANT

P HASTINGS MEMORIAL LIBRARY*, Grant Public Library, 505 Central Ave, 69140-3017. SAN 309-4812. Tel: 308-352-4894. FAX: 308-352-2358. E-mail: hml@gpcom.net. *Dir,* Robin Quinn
Pop 1,270; Circ 13,299
Library Holdings: Bk Vols 15,000; Per Subs 10
Open Mon-Wed 10-5:30, Thurs 2:30-5:30, Sat 9-12
Friends of the Library Group

GREELEY

P GREELEY VILLAGE PUBLIC LIBRARY*, 102 S Kildare St, 68842. (Mail add: PO Box 330, 68842-0330), SAN 309-4820. Tel: 308-428-4010. FAX: 308-428-2675. E-mail: vog@centercable.tv. *Librn,* Kim Everhart
Pop 562; Circ 2,392
Library Holdings: Large Print Bks 200; Bk Vols 3,000
Wireless access
Open Tues-Fri 9-4

GREENWOOD

P GREENWOOD PUBLIC LIBRARY*, 619 Main St, 68366. (Mail add: PO Box 29, 68366-0029), SAN 309-4839. Tel: 402-789-2301. FAX: 402-789-2323. *Dir,* Karen Frank; E-mail: kfranklibrary@hotmail.com
Pop 587; Circ 2,663
Library Holdings: Bk Titles 13,500; Per Subs 12; Talking Bks 91
Open Wed 9-12 & 1-5, Thurs & Fri 1-6, Sat 10-2
Friends of the Library Group

GRETNA

P GRETNA PUBLIC LIBRARY*, 736 South St, 68028. SAN 309-4855. Tel: 402-332-4480. FAX: 402-332-2506. E-mail: library@cityofgretna.com. Web Site: www.gretnapubliclibrary.org. *Dir,* Todd Schlechte; Staff 5 (MLS 1, Non-MLS 4)
Founded 1929. Pop 6,000; Circ 55,797
Library Holdings: Bk Titles 21,398; Bk Vols 23,677; Per Subs 99
Wireless access
Open Mon & Fri 10-6, Tues, Wed & Thurs 10-8, Sat 10-2
Friends of the Library Group

GUIDE ROCK

P AULD-DOUDNA PUBLIC LIBRARY*, 155 W Grant St, 68942. (Mail add: PO Box 126, 68942-0126), SAN 309-4863. Tel: 402-257-4015. E-mail: guiderocklib@yahoo.com. *Dir,* Barbara Sholtz
Founded 1918. Pop 245; Circ 1,559
Library Holdings: AV Mats 50; Bk Titles 10,892; Per Subs 11
Open Tues & Fri 1:30-4:30

HARRISON

P SIOUX COUNTY PUBLIC LIBRARY*, 182 W Third St, 69346. (Mail add: PO Box 31, 69346). Tel: 308-668-9431. FAX: 308-668-2443. E-mail: sioux_county_public_library@hotmail.com. *Dir,* Kristy Lotton
Pop 2,000; Circ 2,149
Library Holdings: DVDs 50; Bk Vols 11,000; Talking Bks 152; Videos 400
Automation Activity & Vendor Info: (Cataloging) Follett Software; (Circulation) Follett Software
Wireless access
Open Mon 9-12 & 1-5, Tues, Wed & Fri 1-5, Thurs 3:30-6:30, Sat 9-12
Friends of the Library Group

HARTINGTON

P HARTINGTON PUBLIC LIBRARY*, 106 S Broadway, 68739. (Mail add: PO Box 458, 68739-0458), SAN 309-4871. Tel: 402-254-6245. FAX: 402-254-6245. E-mail: citylibrary@hartel.net. Web Site: www.hartingtonpublibrary.org. *Dir,* Tami L Anderson; *Asst Librn, Ch Serv,* Carol Craig; Staff 5 (Non-MLS 5)
Founded 1914. Pop 2,000; Circ 3,600
Library Holdings: Bk Vols 20,000; Per Subs 50
Automation Activity & Vendor Info: (Cataloging) Follett Software; (Circulation) Follett Software; (OPAC) Follett Software
Open Mon-Thurs (Winter) 9-7, Fri 9-5, Sat 10-4; Mon & Wed (Summer) 9-7, Tues, Thurs & Fri 9-5, Sat 9-12
Friends of the Library Group

HARVARD

P HARVARD PUBLIC LIBRARY*, 309 N Clay Ave, 68944. (Mail add: PO Box 130, 68944-0130), SAN 309-488X. Tel: 402-772-7201. E-mail: reference@harvardpubliclibrary.org. *Librn,* Lisa Wilford
Founded 1915. Pop 998; Circ 4,416
Library Holdings: Bk Vols 6,560; Per Subs 30
Partic in Central & Western Massachusetts Automated Resource Sharing
Open Tues-Thurs 3:30-7:30, Fri & Sat 9-1

HASTINGS

S ADAMS COUNTY HISTORICAL SOCIETY ARCHIVES*, 1330 N Burlington Ave, 68902. (Mail add: PO Box 102, 68902-0102), SAN 309-4898. Tel: 402-463-5838. E-mail: achs@inebraska.com. Web Site: www.adamshistory.org. *In Charge,* Catherine Renschler; E-mail: achs@inebraska.com. Subject Specialists: *Adams County hist,* Catherine Renschler
Founded 1965
Library Holdings: Bk Vols 1,500
Special Collections: Adams County Archives; Adams County Newspapers, micro; Church Records Coll; Dust Bowl Years, oral hist; Friborg Architectural Coll, drawings; Probate Records; School Records Coll
Subject Interests: Genealogy, Local hist
Publications: Historical News (Bi-monthly)
Restriction: Non-circulating to the pub

J CENTRAL COMMUNITY COLLEGE, HASTINGS CAMPUS*, Nuckolls Library, 550 S Technical Blvd, 68902-1024. (Mail add: PO Box 1024, 68902-1024), SAN 309-4901. Tel: 402-461-2538. FAX: 402-460-2135. Web Site: www.cccneb.edu. *Managing Librn,* Sherrie Dux-Ideus; E-mail: sideus@cccneb.edu; Staff 3 (MLS 1, Non-MLS 2)
Founded 1970. Enrl 1,420; Fac 135
Library Holdings: Bk Titles 3,939; Bk Vols 4,112; Per Subs 70
Database Vendor: OCLC FirstSearch, Wilson - Wilson Web
Open Mon-Thurs (Fall & Spring) 7:30am-9pm, Fri 7:30-4; Mon-Fri (Summer) 8-4

R FIRST PRESBYTERIAN CHURCH LIBRARY, 621 N Lincoln, 68901. SAN 309-491X. Tel: 402-462-5147. FAX: 402-462-6818. Web Site: www.fpchastings.org. *Librn,* Susan Medsker-Nedderman; E-mail: sue@fpchastings.org; Staff 1 (MLS 1)
Founded 1950
Jan 2009-Dec 2009 Income $1,400. Mats Exp $1,400, Books $1,300, Per/Ser (Incl. Access Fees) $100
Library Holdings: Audiobooks 5; CDs 20; DVDs 75; Large Print Bks 125; Bk Titles 5,000; Per Subs 11
Subject Interests: Philos, Relig
Wireless access
Friends of the Library Group

C HASTINGS COLLEGE, Perkins Library, 705 E Seventh St, 68901-7620. SAN 309-4928. Tel: 402-461-7330. Circulation Tel: 402-461-7454. Interlibrary Loan Service Tel: 402-461-7701. FAX: 402-461-7480. Web Site: www.hastings.edu/library. *Coll Develop, Dir,* Susan Franklin; *Media*

Spec, Ref, Pam Bohmfalk; *Tech Serv,* Billie Cotterman; Staff 5 (MLS 3, Non-MLS 2)
Founded 1882. Enrl 1,400; Fac 80; Highest Degree: Master
Library Holdings: AV Mats 4,500; e-books 95,000; Bk Titles 105,000; Bk Vols 140,000; Per Subs 450
Special Collections: Holcomb Lewis & Clark Coll; Plains & Western History (Brown Coll)
Automation Activity & Vendor Info: (Acquisitions) OCLC; (Cataloging) OCLC; (Circulation) OCLC; (Course Reserve) OCLC; (ILL) OCLC; (Media Booking) OCLC; (OPAC) OCLC; (Serials) OCLC
Wireless access
Partic in Nebr Independent Col Libr Consortium; OCLC Online Computer Library Center, Inc
Open Mon-Thurs 7:30am-Midnight, Fri 7:30-5, Sat 12-5, Sun Noon-Midnight

S HASTINGS MUSEUM OF NATURAL & CULTURAL HISTORY LIBRARY, 1330 N Burlington Ave, 68901. (Mail add: PO Box 1286, 68902-1286), SAN 309-4936. Tel: 402-461-4629. FAX: 402-461-2379. E-mail: collections@hastingsmuseum.org. Web Site: hastingsmuseum.org. *Dir,* Rebecca Matticks; E-mail: rmatticks@hastingsmuseum.org; *Curator,* Teresa Kreutzer-Hodson
Library Holdings: Bk Vols 1,000; Per Subs 15
Special Collections: Bureau of American Ethnology Reports: Smithsonian Institution, (1880 to 1930)
Wireless access
Open Tues-Fri 9-5
Restriction: Non-circulating to the pub

P HASTINGS PUBLIC LIBRARY, 517 W Fourth St, 68901-7560. (Mail add: PO Box 849, 68902-0849), SAN 309-4944. Tel: 402-461-2346. FAX: 402-461-2359. TDD: 402-461-2357. E-mail: staff@hastings.lib.ne.us. Web Site: www.hastings.lib.ne.us. *Dir,* Amy Hafer; E-mail: amy@hastings.lib.ne.us; *Educ Librn,* Beth McCracken; E-mail: beth@hastings.lib.ne.us; *Tech & Patron Serv Librn,* Jake Rundle; E-mail: jrundle@hastings.lib.ne.us; Staff 17 (MLS 3, Non-MLS 14)
Founded 1903. Pop 32,769; Circ 259,846
Oct 2007-Sept 2008 Income $1,120,054, State $12,036, City $910,707, County $169,000, Locally Generated Income $27,361, Other $950
Library Holdings: Audiobooks 4,025; AV Mats 1,104; CDs 2,463; DVDs 1,087; Large Print Bks 7,242; Microforms 798; Bk Vols 142,632; Per Subs 157; Videos 2,115
Automation Activity & Vendor Info: (Acquisitions) SirsiDynix; (Cataloging) SirsiDynix; (Circulation) SirsiDynix; (ILL) OCLC; (OPAC) SirsiDynix; (Serials) SirsiDynix
Database Vendor: ALLDATA Online, Bowker, EBSCOhost, Facts on File, OCLC FirstSearch, ProQuest, ReferenceUSA, SirsiDynix, Wilson - Wilson Web
Wireless access
Publications: Friends News (Newsletter)
Special Services for the Deaf - Closed caption videos; Staff with knowledge of sign lang; TDD equip
Special Services for the Blind - Magnifiers
Open Mon-Thurs 9-9, Fri 9-6, Sat 9-5, Sun (Sep-May) 1-5
Friends of the Library Group
Bookmobiles: 1

S HASTINGS REGIONAL CENTER*, Medical/Client Library, 4200 W Second St, 68901-9700. (Mail add: PO Box 579, 68902-0579), SAN 350-1213. Tel: 402-462-1971, Ext 3391. FAX: 402-460-3100. *Exec Dir,* William Gibson; E-mail: william.gibson@dhhs.ne.gov; Staff 1 (Non-MLS 1)
Founded 1938
Jul 2005-Jun 2006 Income $39,993. Mats Exp $1,800, Books $650, Per/Ser (Incl. Access Fees) $1,000. Sal $38,193
Library Holdings: CDs 180; DVDs 35; High Interest/Low Vocabulary Bk Vols 150; Large Print Bks 50; Bk Titles 5,584; Per Subs 20; Talking Bks 10; Videos 650
Special Collections: Hastings Regional Center Archives; Hastings Regional Center History
Subject Interests: Adolescence, Adult, Psychiat, Psychol
Automation Activity & Vendor Info: (Cataloging) Follett Software; (Circulation) Follett Software; (OPAC) Follett Software
Function: Audio & video playback equip for onsite use, Digital talking bks, For res purposes, Handicapped accessible, ILL available, Magnifiers for reading, Music CDs, Online searches, Photocopying/Printing, Prof lending libr, Provide serv for the mentally ill, Ref serv available, Serves mentally handicapped consumers, Spoken cassettes & CDs, Spoken cassettes & DVDs, VHS videos, Wheelchair accessible
Open Mon-Sun 9-8
Restriction: Employee & client use only, Not open to pub, Open to researchers by request, Pub ref by request, Registered patrons only, Restricted access

HAY SPRINGS

P CRAVATH MEMORIAL LIBRARY*, 243 N Main, 69347. (Mail add: PO Box 309, 69347-0309). Tel: 308-638-4541. E-mail: cravath@haysprings.net. *Dir,* Marianne Hanks
Circ 3,500
Library Holdings: Bk Vols 11,747; Videos 190
Open Tues & Thurs 9-4, Sat 10-4

HAYES CENTER

P HAYES CENTER PUBLIC LIBRARY*, 402 Troth St, 69032. (Mail add: PO Box 174, 69032-0174), SAN 309-4960. Tel: 308-286-3411. E-mail: hayescenterlibrary@yahoo.com. *Librn,* Deb Lawson
Pop 231; Circ 2,010
Library Holdings: Bk Vols 6,000; Per Subs 12
Wireless access
Open Mon & Thurs 1-5

HEBRON

P HEBRON SECREST LIBRARY*, 146 N Fourth St, 68370. (Mail add: PO Box 125, 68370-0125), SAN 309-4979. Tel: 402-768-6701. FAX: 402-768-6701. E-mail: hslibrary@diodecom.net. *Dir,* Terry Olson
Founded 1921. Pop 1,565; Circ 11,309
Library Holdings: Bk Vols 11,052; Per Subs 27
Special Collections: Local Memorabilia
Subject Interests: Church hist
Automation Activity & Vendor Info: (Cataloging) Follett Software; (Circulation) Follett Software; (OPAC) Follett Software
Wireless access
Publications: Library Folder for 60th Anniversary, 1921-81
Open Mon, Wed & Fri 10-5, Tues & Thurs 12-7, Sat 10-1

HEMINGFORD

P HEMINGFORD PUBLIC LIBRARY*, 812 Box Butte, 69348. (Mail add: PO Box 6, 69348-0006), SAN 309-4987. Tel: 308-487-3454. FAX: 308-487-3835. E-mail: hpl@bbc.net. *Dir & Librn,* Deb Finley
Pop 1,023; Circ 2,058
Library Holdings: Bk Vols 10,000; Per Subs 17
Mem of Panhandle Libr Syst
Open Mon 10-12 & 2-6, Tues 1-6, Wed 1-7, Thurs & Sat 9-12

HENDERSON

SR BETHESDA MENNONITE CHURCH LIBRARY*, PO Box 130, 68371-0130. SAN 309-4995. Tel: 402-723-4562. FAX: 402-723-4567. E-mail: bethesda@mainstaycomm.net. Web Site: www.mainstaycomm.net/bethesda. *Chairperson,* Rozella Swartzendruber
Library Holdings: Bk Vols 4,500
Special Collections: Children's & Christian Literature Coll

HILDRETH

P HILDRETH PUBLIC LIBRARY*, 248 Commercial Ave, 68947. (Mail add: PO Box 112, 68947-0112), SAN 309-5002. Tel: 308-938-2471. FAX: 308-938-2545. E-mail: hpl@gtmc.net. *Librn,* Vicki Casper
Pop 370; Circ 4,286
Library Holdings: Bk Vols 8,000; Per Subs 12
Automation Activity & Vendor Info: (Cataloging) Follett Software; (Circulation) Follett Software; (OPAC) Follett Software
Open Tues-Thurs 1:30-7, Fri 1:30-5, Sat 9-12
Friends of the Library Group

HOLDREGE

P HOLDREGE AREA PUBLIC LIBRARY*, 604 East Ave, 68949. SAN 309-5029. Tel: 308-995-6556. FAX: 308-995-5732. E-mail: info@holdregelibrary.org. Web Site: www.holdregelibrary.org. *Dir,* Pamela Soreide; *Cat,* Cynthia Blum; *Ch Serv,* Cynthia Gitt; *Circ, Ref,* Linda Davey; Staff 10 (MLS 1, Non-MLS 9)
Founded 1895. Pop 9,175; Circ 131,983
Jul 2007-Jun 2008 Income $416,265, State $3,465, City $231,285, County $146,684, Other $34,831. Mats Exp $45,123, Books $32,330, Per/Ser (Incl. Access Fees) $3,759, AV Mat $6,778, Electronic Ref Mat (Incl. Access Fees) $2,210, Presv $46. Sal $282,885
Library Holdings: Audiobooks 2,135; DVDs 1,612; Large Print Bks 2,928; Bk Titles 58,773; Per Subs 90; Videos 1,096
Special Collections: State Document Depository
Automation Activity & Vendor Info: (Cataloging) Follett Software; (Circulation) Follett Software
Wireless access
Function: Audiobks via web, Bks on cassette, Bks on CD, Children's prog, Computers for patron use, Copy machines, Electronic databases & coll, Fax serv, Free DVD rentals, Handicapped accessible, Home delivery & serv to Sr ctr & nursing homes, ILL available, Magnifiers for reading,

Online cat, Outreach serv, OverDrive digital audio bks, Photocopying/Printing, Prog for adults, Prog for children & young adult, Pub access computers, Scanner, Story hour, Summer reading prog, Tax forms, Teen prog
Open Mon-Thurs 9-8, Fri & Sat 9-5
Friends of the Library Group

S NEBRASKA PRAIRIE MUSEUM*, Don O Lindgren Library, N Hwy 183, 68949. (Mail add: PO Box 164, 68949-0164), SAN 325-2256. Tel: 308-995-5015. FAX: 308-995-2241. E-mail: prairie995@gmail.com. Web Site: www.nebraskaprairie.org. *Exec Dir,* Dan Christensen; *Head, Genealogy Libr,* Sandy Slater; Staff 1 (Non-MLS 1)
Founded 1972
Library Holdings: Bk Vols 4,200
Special Collections: POW Archives. Oral History
Subject Interests: Genealogy, Local hist, Phelps County
Wireless access
Open Mon-Fri (Oct-April) 10-4, Sat & Sun 1-4; Mon-Fri (May-Sept) 9-5, Sat & Sun 1-5

HOOPER

P HOOPER PUBLIC LIBRARY*, 126 N Main, 68031. (Mail add: PO Box 45, 68031-0045), SAN 309-5037. Tel: 402-654-3833. E-mail: hooperlibr@yahoo.com. *Dir,* Karla Shafer
Pop 1,000
Library Holdings: DVDs 30; Large Print Bks 200; Bk Vols 10,169; Per Subs 35; Talking Bks 50; Videos 200
Automation Activity & Vendor Info: (Acquisitions) Follett Software; (Cataloging) Follett Software
Wireless access
Function: Adult bk club, After school storytime, Audio & video playback equip for onsite use, Copy machines, ILL available, Online searches, Prog for children & young adult, Summer reading prog, Video lending libr, Workshops
Mem of Eastern Libr Syst
Partic in Eastern Nebr Libr Asn
Open Tues, Wed & Thurs 2-7, Fri & Sat 9-1
Friends of the Library Group

HOWELLS

P HOWELLS PUBLIC LIBRARY*, 128 N Third St, 68641. (Mail add: PO Box 337, 68641-0337), SAN 309-5045. Tel: 402-986-1210. FAX: 402-986-1210. E-mail: howellspubliclibrary@yahoo.com. *Dir,* Amy Kucera; *Asst Librn,* Paula Tichota; E-mail: ptichot@esu7.org
Pop 632; Circ 927
Library Holdings: Bk Vols 9,600; Per Subs 71
Automation Activity & Vendor Info: (Cataloging) Chancery SMS; (Circulation) Chancery SMS
Wireless access
Publications: Booklist
Open Mon 2-6:30, Wed 9-2 & 4-9, Fri 2-5:30, Sat 9-Noon
Friends of the Library Group

HUMBOLDT

P BRUUN MEMORIAL PUBLIC LIBRARY*, 730 Third St, 68376. (Mail add: PO Box 368, 68376-0368), SAN 309-5053. Tel: 402-862-2914. E-mail: bmemorial@neb.rr.com. *Chief Librn,* Jorene Herr
Founded 1884. Pop 950; Circ 23,524
Library Holdings: Audiobooks 629; CDs 146; DVDs 426; Large Print Bks 335; Bk Titles 17,584; Per Subs 15; Videos 572
Special Collections: State Document Depository; UN Document Depository; US Document Depository
Automation Activity & Vendor Info: (Cataloging) Follett Software; (Circulation) Follett Software
Open Mon 2-8:30, Tues & Thurs 10-12 & 2-5:30, Wed & Fri 2-5:30, Sat 9-12
Friends of the Library Group

HUMPHREY

P HUMPHREY PUBLIC LIBRARY*, 307 Main St, 68642. (Mail add: PO Box 266, 68642-0266), SAN 309-5061. Tel: 402-923-0957. FAX: 402-923-0957. E-mail: humphreypl@hotmail.com. Web Site: www.humphreylibrary.com. *Dir,* Michele Hastreiter; *Asst Librn,* Betty Sueper
Founded 1938. Pop 740; Circ 18,763
Library Holdings: Bk Vols 15,600; Per Subs 61
Automation Activity & Vendor Info: (Circulation) Follett Software
Open Mon & Wed 1-8, Tues & Fri 9-12, Thurs 9-12 & 2-6, Sat 8-12

HYANNIS

P GRANT COUNTY LIBRARY*, Harrison & Grant St, 69350. (Mail add: PO Box 328, 69350-0328), SAN 309-507X. Tel: 308-458-2218. FAX: 308-458-2485. *Librn,* Vickie Retzlaff
Founded 1929. Pop 747; Circ 3,030
Library Holdings: Bk Vols 8,000; Per Subs 42
Automation Activity & Vendor Info: (Cataloging) Follett Software; (Circulation) Follett Software; (OPAC) Follett Software
Mem of Panhandle Libr Syst; Southwest Kansas Library System
Open Mon, Wed & Fri 9-12 & 1-5

IMPERIAL

P LIED IMPERIAL PUBLIC LIBRARY*, 703 Broadway, 69033. (Mail add: PO Box 728, 69033-0728), SAN 309-5088. Tel: 308-882-4754. E-mail: imperiallibrary@gpcom.net. Web Site: www.imperiallibrary.org. *Dir,* Beth Falla
Pop 4,000; Circ 59,026
Automation Activity & Vendor Info: (Cataloging) Follett Software; (Circulation) Follett Software; (ILL) OCLC
Wireless access
Open Mon & Wed 10-6, Tues & Thurs 10-7, Fri 10-5, Sat 10-1
Friends of the Library Group

INDIANOLA

P INDIANOLA PUBLIC LIBRARY*, 122 N Fourth St, 69034. (Mail add: PO Box 300, 69034-0300). Tel: 308-364-9259. E-mail: inpuli01@gpcom.net. *Dir,* Judith Hollers
Pop 642; Circ 700
Library Holdings: AV Mats 170; Bk Vols 6,370; Per Subs 12; Talking Bks 24
Open Tues & Thurs 1-5, Wed 4-8, Sat 9-12

KEARNEY

P KEARNEY PUBLIC LIBRARY*, 2020 First Ave, 68847. SAN 309-510X. Tel: 308-233-3282. Reference Tel: 308-233-3256. FAX: 308-233-3291. Web Site: www.kearneylib.org. *Dir,* Williams R Williams; Tel: 308-233-3280, E-mail: mwilliams@kearneygov.org; *Asst Libr Dir,* Christine Walsh; Tel: 308-233-3283, E-mail: cwalsh@kearneygov.org; *Youth Serv Coordr,* Shawna Lindner; Tel: 308-233-3284, E-mail: slindner@kearneygov.org; *Access Serv,* Mike Marchand; Tel: 308-233-3285, E-mail: mmarchand@kearneygov.org; *Ref Serv,* Rita Horst; E-mail: rhorst@kearneygov.org; Staff 26 (MLS 3, Non-MLS 23)
Founded 1890. Pop 27,431; Circ 489,078
Library Holdings: Bk Vols 109,985; Per Subs 169
Special Collections: Kearney Coll, VF
Subject Interests: Genealogy
Automation Activity & Vendor Info: (Acquisitions) SirsiDynix; (Cataloging) OCLC; (Circulation) SirsiDynix; (ILL) OCLC; (OPAC) SirsiDynix; (Serials) SirsiDynix
Database Vendor: ALLDATA Online, Bowker, CountryWatch, ebrary, OCLC FirstSearch, ProQuest, ReferenceUSA
Wireless access
Open Mon-Thurs 9-9, Fri & Sat 9-5
Friends of the Library Group
Bookmobiles: 1

C UNIVERSITY OF NEBRASKA AT KEARNEY, Calvin T Ryan Library, 2508 11th Ave, 68849-2240. Tel: 308-865-8535. Circulation Tel: 308-865-8599. Interlibrary Loan Service Tel: 308-865-8594. Reference Tel: 308-865-8586. FAX: 308-865-8722. Web Site: library.unk.edu. *Dean,* Janet Stoeger Wilke; Tel: 308-865-8546, E-mail: wilkej@unk.edu; *Head, Access Serv,* Dee Urwiller; Tel: 308-865-8597, E-mail: goedertd@unk.edu; *Assessment Librn, Coordr, User Serv,* Ronald Wirtz; Tel: 308-865-8592, E-mail: wirtzrl@unk.edu; *Curric/Nonbk Librn,* Rochelle Krueger; Tel: 308-865-8276, E-mail: kruegerr@unk.edu; *Electronic Res/Ser Librn,* Jon Ritterbush; Tel: 308-865-8585, E-mail: ritterbushjr@unk.edu; *Coordr, Instruction, Govt Doc Librn,* Julia Powell; Tel: 308-865-8542, E-mail: powelljm@unk.edu; *Web Serv Librn,* Michael Sutherland; Tel: 308-865-8544, E-mail: sutherlandmj@unk.edu; *Coordr, Coll Serv,* Susan Mueller; Tel: 308-865-8853, E-mail: muellersm@unk.edu; *Univ Archivist,* Laurinda Weisse; Tel: 308-865-8593, E-mail: weissell@unk.edu; *Diversity Spec,* Anthanett Mendoza; Tel: 308-865-8587, E-mail: mendozaac@unk.edu; *ILL/Doc Delivery Serv,* Sheryl Heidenreich; Tel: 308-865-8721, E-mail: heidenreichs@unk.edu; Staff 13 (MLS 10, Non-MLS 3)
Founded 1906. Enrl 7,052; Fac 322; Highest Degree: Master
Jul 2013-Jun 2014 Income $3,835,919, State $3,122,846, Locally Generated Income $708,580, Parent Institution $4,493. Mats Exp $1,257,958, Books $156,511, Per/Ser (Incl. Access Fees) $514,826, Micro $32,975, AV Mat $15,085, Electronic Ref Mat (Incl. Access Fees) $538,320, Presv $241. Sal $1,296,770 (Prof $823,564)

Library Holdings: AV Mats 92,926; Bks on Deafness & Sign Lang 255; CDs 2,036; DVDs 2,391; e-books 161,923; e-journals 79,831; Electronic Media & Resources 98,827; Microforms 78,271; Music Scores 3,935; Bk Titles 240,875; Bk Vols 276,235; Per Subs 569; Videos 2,181
Special Collections: State Document Depository; US Document Depository
Subject Interests: Great Plains, Nebr
Automation Activity & Vendor Info: (Acquisitions) Innovative Interfaces, Inc; (Cataloging) Innovative Interfaces, Inc; (Circulation) Innovative Interfaces, Inc; (Course Reserve) Innovative Interfaces, Inc; (ILL) OCLC ILLiad; (OPAC) Innovative Interfaces, Inc; (Serials) Innovative Interfaces, Inc
Database Vendor: ACM (Association for Computing Machinery), American Chemical Society, CQ Press, ebrary, EBSCOhost, Elsevier, Emerald, Gale Cengage Learning, JSTOR, LexisNexis, Nature Publishing Group, OCLC FirstSearch, OCLC WorldShare Interlibrary Loan, Oxford Online, Project MUSE, ProQuest, Sage, SerialsSolutions, Springer-Verlag, Springshare, LLC, Standard & Poor's, ValueLine, Wiley
Wireless access
Publications: In Brief (Newsletter)
Partic in Lyrasis; OCLC Online Computer Library Center, Inc
Open Mon-Thurs 7:30am-Midnight, Fri 7:30-5, Sat 10-5, Sun 2-Midnight

S YOUTH REHABILITATION & TREATMENT CENTER LIBRARY*, 2802 30th Ave, 68845. SAN 377-1806. Tel: 308-865-5313, Ext 287. FAX: 308-865-5323. *Libr Dir, Media Spec,* Susan Divan; Tel: 308-338-2011, Ext 287, E-mail: sue.divan@nebraska.gov
Founded 1879
Library Holdings: Bk Titles 7,000; Bk Vols 7,300; Per Subs 50; Talking Bks 40
Automation Activity & Vendor Info: (Cataloging) Follett Software; (Circulation) Follett Software; (OPAC) Follett Software
Wireless access

KIMBALL

P KIMBALL PUBLIC LIBRARY, 208 S Walnut St, 69145. SAN 309-5126. Tel: 308-235-4523. FAX: 308-235-2971. E-mail: kplib@megavision.com. Web Site: www.ci.kimball.ne.us. *Dir,* Jan Sears; Staff 3 (Non-MLS 3)
Pop 2,200; Circ 15,104
Library Holdings: Bk Vols 27,000; Per Subs 60
Special Collections: Kimball County History Coll, newsp clippings, photog. Oral History
Automation Activity & Vendor Info: (Cataloging) Follett Software; (Circulation) Follett Software
Function: Accelerated reader prog, Archival coll, Art exhibits, Audiobks via web, Bks on cassette, Bks on CD, Computers for patron use, Copy machines, Distance learning, e-mail & chat, Electronic databases & coll, Exhibits, Free DVD rentals, Genealogy discussion group, Handicapped accessible, Home delivery & serv to Sr ctr & nursing homes, Homebound delivery serv, ILL available, Music CDs, OverDrive digital audio bks, Photocopying/Printing, Scanner, Summer reading prog, VHS videos, Wheelchair accessible
Mem of Panhandle Libr Syst
Partic in Panhandle Library Access Network
Special Services for the Blind - Accessible computers; Audio mat; Bks on cassette; Bks on CD; Copier with enlargement capabilities; Digital talking bk; Home delivery serv; Large print bks; Magnifiers
Open Mon, Wed & Fri 10-5:30, Tues & Thurs 1-7, Sat 10-1
Friends of the Library Group

LA VISTA

P LA VISTA PUBLIC LIBRARY, 9110 Giles Rd, 68128. SAN 309-5134. Tel: 402-537-3900. FAX: 402-537-3902. E-mail: lvlibrary@cityoflavista.org. Web Site: www.cityoflavista.org. *Dir,* Rose Barcal; E-mail: rbarcal@cityoflavista.org; *Asst Dir,* Jodi Norton; E-mail: jnorton@cityoflavista.org; Staff 5 (MLS 3, Non-MLS 2)
Founded 1972. Pop 17,344; Circ 167,743
Library Holdings: DVDs 420; e-books 29,000; Large Print Bks 660; Bk Vols 52,000; Per Subs 85; Talking Bks 900; Videos 2,500
Special Collections: Harold "Andy" Anderson Civic Leadership Coll; Joseph J Barmettler Law Coll
Automation Activity & Vendor Info: (Cataloging) Biblionix/Apollo; (Circulation) Biblionix/Apollo; (OPAC) Biblionix/Apollo
Database Vendor: Biblionix/Apollo, EBSCO Auto Repair Reference, LearningExpress, Newsbank, Overdrive, Inc, ReferenceUSA
Wireless access
Function: Handicapped accessible, ILL available, Prog for adults, Prog for children & young adult, Summer reading prog, VHS videos
Mem of Eastern Libr Syst
Open Mon-Thurs 8am-9pm, Fri & Sat 8-5, Sun 1-5
Restriction: Circ to mem only

LAUREL

P LAUREL COMMUNITY LEARNING CENTER*, 502 Wakefield St, 68745-0248. (Mail add: PO Box 8, 68745). Tel: 402-256-3431. FAX: 402-256-9465. Web Site: www.laurel.esu1.org. *Dir,* Maggie Huetig; E-mail: mhuetig@esu1.org
Pop 870; Circ 21,000
Library Holdings: Bk Vols 18,763; Per Subs 15; Talking Bks 346
Automation Activity & Vendor Info: (Cataloging) Chancery SMS; (Circulation) Chancery SMS; (OPAC) Chancery SMS
Wireless access
Open Mon-Thurs 8-8, Fri 8-4, Sat & Sun 1-5
Friends of the Library Group

LEIGH

P LEIGH PUBLIC LIBRARY*, 156 Main St, 68643. (Mail add: PO Box 158, 06843-0158), SAN 309-5142. Tel: 402-487-2507. FAX: 402-487-2507. E-mail: leilib@frontiernet.net. *Dir,* Susan Finkral
Pop 509; Circ 4,703
Library Holdings: CDs 25; DVDs 25; Large Print Bks 30; Bk Vols 5,000; Per Subs 20; Talking Bks 50; Videos 200
Special Collections: Nebraska History/Authors Coll
Open Tues & Sat 9-11 & 2-5, Wed 2-6, Thurs 5-8

LEWELLEN

P LEWELLEN PUBLIC LIBRARY*, 208 Main St, 69147. (Mail add: PO Box 104, 69147-0104), SAN 309-5150. Tel: 308-778-5428. FAX: 308-778-5427. *Librn,* Leone Wolfe
Founded 1920. Pop 280
Library Holdings: Bk Vols 4,500
Mem of Panhandle Libr Syst
Open Tues & Fri 2-5

LEXINGTON

P LEXINGTON PUBLIC LIBRARY*, 907 N Washington, 68850. (Mail add: PO Box 778, 68850-0778), SAN 309-5169. Tel: 308-324-2151. FAX: 308-324-2140. Web Site: lexingtonlibrary.org. *Head Librn,* Kathleen Thomsen; *Asst Libr Dir,* JoAnn Grove; *Ch,* Brenda Schwartz
Pop 10,011; Circ 73,019
Library Holdings: Bk Titles 30,179; Per Subs 109
Automation Activity & Vendor Info: (Cataloging) Follett Software; (Circulation) Follett Software; (Course Reserve) Follett Software; (ILL) Follett Software; (OPAC) Follett Software
Wireless access
Open Mon-Thurs 9-9, Fri & Sat 9-5, Sun 1-5
Friends of the Library Group

LINCOLN

S AMERICAN HISTORICAL SOCIETY OF GERMANS FROM RUSSIA, Library & Archives, 631 D St, 68502-1199. SAN 328-0454. Tel: 402-474-3363. FAX: 402-474-7229. E-mail: ahsgr@ahsgr.org. Web Site: www.ahsgr.org. *Librn,* Diane Wilson; Staff 1 (MLS 1)
Founded 1968
Library Holdings: Bk Titles 5,250; Per Subs 225
Special Collections: Ancestor database; Censuses; Family histories; Surname charts
Subject Interests: Germans from Russia
Automation Activity & Vendor Info: (ILL) OCLC; (OPAC) ResourceMATE
Wireless access
Function: Archival coll, ILL available, Ref & res, Res performed for a fee
Publications: AHSGR Journal (Quarterly); AHSGR Newsletter (Quarterly)
Mem of Southeast Library System (SELS)
Open Mon-Fri 9-4, Sun 1-4
Restriction: Restricted loan policy

JM BRYANLGH COLLEGE OF THE HEALTH SCIENCES*, BryanLGH Medical Center Library, 5035 Everett St, 68506. SAN 327-2281. Tel: 402-481-3908. FAX: 402-481-3138. *Dir, Libr Serv,* Anne Heiman; E-mail: anne.heimann@bryanlgh.org; Staff 3 (MLS 2, Non-MLS 1)
Library Holdings: Bk Titles 5,000; Per Subs 300
Subject Interests: Nursing
Automation Activity & Vendor Info: (Acquisitions) Follett Software; (Cataloging) Follett Software; (Circulation) Follett Software; (Course Reserve) Follett Software
Database Vendor: EBSCOhost
Restriction: Open to pub for ref only, Open to students, fac & staff

M CATHOLIC HEALTH INITIATIVES*, Saint Elizabeth Regional Medical Center Library, 555 S 70th St, 68510. SAN 309-5290. Tel: 402-219-7306. FAX: 402-219-7335. E-mail: library@stez.org. *Coordr,* Maria Ford; Staff 1 (MLS 1)

Founded 1928
Library Holdings: Bk Vols 2,579; Per Subs 97
Special Collections: Allied Health Coll; Cultural Diversity Coll; Leadership Coll; Medical Coll; Nursing Coll
Subject Interests: Burn therapy, Family practice, Neonatal med, Obgyn, Pediatrics
Automation Activity & Vendor Info: (Cataloging) LibraryWorld, Inc; (Circulation) LibraryWorld, Inc; (OPAC) LibraryWorld, Inc; (Serials) LibraryWorld, Inc
Database Vendor: EBSCOhost
Wireless access
Publications: AV Catalog
Partic in ICON Library Consortium; National Network of Libraries of Medicine Midcontinental Region
Open Mon-Fri 8-4:30

R CHRIST UNITED METHODIST CHURCH LIBRARY*, 4530 A St, 68510. SAN 309-5185. Tel: 402-489-9618. FAX: 402-489-9675. E-mail: admin@christumclinc.org. *Librn,* Sandra Herzinger
Library Holdings: Bk Vols 4,550
Automation Activity & Vendor Info: (Cataloging) Church Related Online Software Systems (CROSS)
Wireless access
Open Mon-Fri 8-4, Sun 8-Noon

S CHRISTIAN RECORD SERVICES FOR THE BLIND*, Lending Library, 4444 S 52nd St, 68516. (Mail add: PO Box 6097, 68506-0097), SAN 327-6058. Tel: 402-488-0981. FAX: 402-488-7582. Administration FAX: 402-488-1902. E-mail: info@ChristianRecord.org. Web Site: www.ChristianRecord.org. *Librn/Asst Ed,* Richard Clark; E-mail: richard.clark@christianrecord.org
Founded 1899
Library Holdings: Bk Titles 2,243
Special Services for the Blind - Braille bks; Talking bks
Open Mon-Thurs 8-5:30

S CHURCH OF JESUS CHRIST OF LATTER-DAY SAINTS*, Family History Center, 3100 Old Cheney Rd, 68516-2775. (Mail add: PO Box 82244, 68501-2244), SAN 377-3825. Tel: 402-423-4561. *Dir,* Tina Wells; E-mail: tmwells@radiks.net
Library Holdings: Bk Vols 350
Open Tues 10-4 & 6-9, Wed 10-2 & 6-9, Thurs 6-9, Sat 10-4

S DIAGNOSTIC & EVALUATION CENTER LIBRARY*, 3220 W Van Dorn St, 68522-9278. (Mail add: PO Box 22800, 68542-2800). Tel: 402-471 3330. FAX: 402-479-6368. *Librn,* Jane Licklider
Library Holdings: Bk Vols 4,750; Per Subs 20
Open Mon-Fri 7-3:30

C KAPLAN UNIVERSITY*, Lincoln Campus Library, 1821 K St, 68508. SAN 377-158X. Tel: 402-474-5315. Toll Free Tel: 800-987-7734. Web Site: library.kaplan.edu/li. *Librn,* Kit Keller; Tel: 402-437-5315, Ext 2122, E-mail: kkeller2@kaplan.edu; Staff 1 (MLS 1)
Enrl 550; Fac 75; Highest Degree: Bachelor
Library Holdings: e-journals 3,000; Bk Vols 3,000; Per Subs 6; Videos 60
Automation Activity & Vendor Info: (Cataloging) TLC (The Library Corporation); (Circulation) TLC (The Library Corporation); (Course Reserve) TLC (The Library Corporation); (OPAC) TLC (The Library Corporation)
Database Vendor: EBSCOhost, LexisNexis, Westlaw
Wireless access
Function: ILL available, Ref serv available, Telephone ref
Special Services for the Blind - Rec of textbk mat
Open Mon-Thurs 8am-10pm, Fri 9-4, Sat 9-Noon
Restriction: Open to students, fac & staff

P LINCOLN CITY LIBRARIES*, Bennett Martin Public Library, 136 S 14th St, 68508-1899. SAN 350-1272. Tel: 402-441-8500. Circulation Tel: 402-441-8525. Interlibrary Loan Service Tel: 402-441-8537. Reference Tel: 402-441-8530. Administration Tel: 402-441-8503. FAX: 402-441-8586. TDD: 402-441-8589. E-mail: library@lincolnlibraries.org. Web Site: www.lincolnlibraries.org. *Libr Dir,* Pat Leach; Tel: 402-441-8510, E-mail: p.leach@lincolnlibraries.org; *Asst Dir,* Julee Hector; Tel: 402-441-8511, E-mail: j.hector@lincolnlibraries.org; *Automation Syst Coordr,* Rod Cummings; Tel: 402-441-8522, E-mail: r.cummings@lincolnlibraries.org; *Libr Res Coordr,* Tammy Teasley; Tel: 402-441-8575, E-mail: t.teasley@lincolnlibraries.org; *Coordr, Youth Serv,* Vicki Wood; Tel: 402-441-8565, E-mail: v.wood@lincolnlibraries.org; *Pub Serv Coordr,* Julie Beno; Tel: 402-441-8535, E-mail: j.beno@lincolnlibraries.org; Staff 107 (MLS 25, Non-MLS 82)
Founded 1877. Pop 285,407; Circ 3,293,741
Sept 2011-Aug 2012 Income (Main Library and Branch(s)) $8,512,858, State $62,860, City $6,548,703, County $658,902, Locally Generated Income $515,132, Other $727,171. Mats Exp $1,370,963, Books $813,383, Other Print Mats $273,394, Electronic Ref Mat (Incl. Access Fees) $284,186. Sal $5,770,346
Library Holdings: Audiobooks 54,000; DVDs 47,891; e-books 5,338; Electronic Media & Resources 63; Bk Vols 678,094; Per Subs 1,821
Special Collections: Nebraska Authors. State Document Depository
Automation Activity & Vendor Info: (Acquisitions) Baker & Taylor; (Cataloging) LibLime; (Circulation) LibLime; (ILL) OCLC ILLiad; (OPAC) LibLime; (Serials) EBSCO Online
Database Vendor: EBSCOhost, Gale Cengage Learning, OCLC FirstSearch
Wireless access
Function: Adult bk club, Art exhibits, Audiobks via web, BA reader (adult literacy), Bks on cassette, Bks on CD, CD-ROM, Chess club, Children's prog, Computer training, Computers for patron use, Copy machines, e-mail serv, E-Reserves, Electronic databases & coll, Exhibits, Free DVD rentals, Handicapped accessible, Homebound delivery serv, ILL available, Mail & tel request accepted, Music CDs, Online cat, Online ref, Outreach serv, OverDrive digital audio bks, Preschool outreach, Prog for adults, Prog for children & young adult, Pub access computers, Scanner, Spoken cassettes & CDs, Story hour, Summer reading prog, Tax forms, Teen prog, Telephone ref, Web-catalog, Wheelchair accessible
Partic in OCLC Online Computer Library Center, Inc
Special Services for the Blind - Assistive/Adapted tech devices, equip & products; Audio mat; Bks on CD; Closed circuit TV; Computer with voice synthesizer for visually impaired persons; Large print bks; Reader equip
Restriction: Non-resident fee
Friends of the Library Group
Branches: 7
VICTOR E ANDERSON BRANCH, 3635 Touzalin Ave, 68507-1698, SAN 350-1302. Tel: 402-441-8540. FAX: 402-441-8543. *Br Supvr,* Kim Shelley; Tel: 402-441-8542, E-mail: k.shelley@lincolnlibraries.org
Open Mon-Thurs 10-8, Fri & Sat 10-6, Sun 12-8
BETHANY BRANCH, 1810 N Cotner Blvd, 68505, SAN 350-1396. Tel: 402-441-8550. FAX: 402-441-8552. *Br Supvr,* Kim Shelley
Open Mon-Thurs 1-9, Fri & Sat 10-6
Friends of the Library Group
LOREN COREY EISELEY BRANCH, 1530 Superior St, 68521. Tel: 402-441-4250. FAX: 402-441-4253. *Br Supvr,* Sheila Jacobs
Open Mon-Thurs 10-9, Fri & Sat 10-6, Sun 1:30-5:30
CHARLES H GERE BRANCH, 2400 S 56th St, 68506-3599, SAN 350-1426. Tel: 402-441-8560. FAX: 402-441-8563. *Br Supvr,* Carol Swanson
Open Mon-Thurs 10-8, Fri & Sat 10-6, Sun 12-8
SOUTH BRANCH, 2675 South St, 68502-3099, SAN 350-1485. Tel: 402-441-8570. FAX: 402-441-8572. *Br Supvr,* Julie Beno; Tel: 402-441-8535, E-mail: j.beno@lincolnlibraries.org
Open Mon-Thurs 10-9, Fri & Sat 10-6, Sun 1:30-5:30
BESS DODSON WALT BRANCH, 6701 S 14th St, 68512. Tel: 402-441-4460. FAX: 402-441-4463. *Br Supvr,* Jodene Glaesemann
Open Mon-Thurs 10-8, Fri & Sat 10-6, Sun 12-8
DAN A WILLIAMS BRANCH, 5000 Mike Scholl St, 68524. Tel: 402-441-8580. *Br Supvr,* Sheila Jacobs; Tel: 402-441-4252, E-mail: s.jacobs@lincolnlibraries.org
Open Mon-Thurs 4-8, Fri 4-6, Sat & Sun 1-6
Bookmobiles: 1. Librn, Rebecca Hueske. Bk vols 4,500

S LINCOLN CORRECTIONAL CENTER LIBRARY*, 3216 W Van Dorn St, 68522. (Mail add: PO Box 22800, 68542-2800), SAN 377-1601. Tel: 402-471-2861, Ext 6137. FAX: 402-479-6100. *Librn,* Sandra Elton
Library Holdings: Bk Vols 10,000; Per Subs 44

S LINCOLN FAMILY MEDICINE PROGRAM LIBRARY*, 4600 Valley Rd, Ste 210, 68510-4892. SAN 377-1563. Tel: 402-483-4591. FAX: 402-483-5079. Web Site: www.lmep.com. *In Charge,* Carole Ortmeier
Library Holdings: Bk Vols 300; Per Subs 16
Partic in Lincoln Libr Group

S LINCOLN JOURNAL STAR LIBRARY*, 926 P St, 68508. (Mail add: PO Box 81689, 68501-1689), SAN 309-5223. Tel: 402-473-7297. Toll Free Tel: 800-742-7315, Ext 7297. FAX: 402-473-7291. E-mail: library@journalstar.com. Web Site: www.journalstar.com. *Librn,* Denise I Matulka; Staff 1 (MLS 1)
Founded 1954
Library Holdings: Bk Titles 2,000; Per Subs 36
Special Collections: Charles Starkweather Coll, clippings, photos, timelines; Lincoln Journal Star Microfilm, 1867-present; Lincoln Journal Star Newspaper Clippings, 1956-1996; LJS Photo Archive, 1956-present; NU Husker Coll, articles, photos, stats; Southeast Nebraska Coll, clippings, microfiche, microfilm, photos
Database Vendor: LexisNexis, Newsbank, ProQuest
Function: Archival coll, Newsp ref libr, Ref serv available
Mem of Southeast Library System (SELS)
Open Tues-Fri 9:30-1
Restriction: Co libr, Fee for pub use, Internal use only, Non-circulating

M LINCOLN REGIONAL CENTER
RESOURCE CENTER, W Prospector Pl & Folsom St, 68509. (Mail add: PO Box 94949, 68509-4949), SAN 350-154X. Tel: 402-479-5475. FAX: 402-479-5460. *Dir & Librn,* Tom Schmitz; E-mail: tom.schmitz@nebraska.gov
Library Holdings: Large Print Bks 50; Bk Titles 3,000; Per Subs 8; Spec Interest Per Sub 3
Subject Interests: Mental health, Psychiat, Psychol
Automation Activity & Vendor Info: (Acquisitions) Follett Software; (Cataloging) Follett Software; (Circulation) Follett Software; (OPAC) Follett Software
Database Vendor: OCLC FirstSearch
Function: ILL available, Ref serv available
Partic in NE Nebr Libr Asn; Nebr Institutional Asn for Librs
Mem of Southeast Library System (SELS)
Open Mon-Fri 9-12 & 1-5:30

M MADONNA REHABILITATION HOSPITAL*, Medical Library, 5401 South St, 68506-2134. SAN 327-6074. Tel: 402-489-7102. Interlibrary Loan Service Tel: 402-413-4401. FAX: 402-486-8381. Interlibrary Loan Service FAX: 402-413-4408. *In Charge,* Marcie Stoner
Library Holdings: Bk Titles 300
Wireless access
Partic in Docline
Restriction: Not open to pub

S NATIONAL PARK SERVICE*, Midwest Archeological Center Library, Federal Bldg, Rm 474, 100 Centennial Mall North, 68508. SAN 309-5231. Tel: 402-437-5392, Ext 110. FAX: 402-437-5098. Web Site: www.nps.gov/history/mwac. *Librn,* Holly Staggs
Founded 1969
Library Holdings: Bk Titles 34,369; Per Subs 46
Special Collections: Archeology Coll, ms
Subject Interests: Archaeology, Hist
Function: For res purposes, Res libr
Restriction: Authorized scholars by appt, Circulates for staff only, In-house use for visitors, Internal circ only, Lending to staff only, Not a lending libr, Prof mat only

G NDOR TRANSPORTATION RESOURCE LIBRARY*, 1500 Nebraska Hwy 2, 68502-5480. (Mail add: PO Box 94759, 68509-4759), SAN 377-1628. Tel: 402-479-4316. FAX: 402-479-3989. *Transportation Res Librn,* Mary Neben; E-mail: mary.neben@nebraska.gov; Staff 1 (Non-MLS 1)
Founded 1968
Library Holdings: CDs 365; DVDs 58; Bk Titles 19,000; Per Subs 96; Videos 415
Special Collections: Road-Related Historical Publications
Subject Interests: Hwys, Rail, Transportation
Special Services for the Blind - BiFolkal kits
Open Mon-Fri 8:30-5

S NEBRASKA DEPARTMENT OF CORRECTIONS*, Nebraska State Penitentiary Library, PO Box 2500, Sta B, 68502. SAN 377-3922. Tel: 402-471-3161, Ext 3267. Administration Tel: 402-479-5757. FAX: 402-479-5819. *Dir,* Sam Shaw
Library Holdings: Bk Vols 15,000; Per Subs 79
Subject Interests: Classics
Automation Activity & Vendor Info: (ILL) OCLC
Partic in SE Nebr Libr Asn

G NEBRASKA DEPARTMENT OF ECONOMIC DEVELOPMENT LIBRARY*, 301 Centennial Mall S, 68509. (Mail add: PO Box 94666, 68509-4666), SAN 370-6443. Tel: 402-471-3111. Toll Free Tel: 800-426-6505. FAX: 402-471-3778. Web Site: www.neded.org. *Res Coordr,* Thomas R Doering
Library Holdings: Bk Vols 2,000
Wireless access
Open Mon-Fri 8-5

G NEBRASKA DEPARTMENT OF NATURAL RESOURCES LIBRARY*, State Office Bldg, 4th Flr, 301 Centennial Mall S, 68509-4676. (Mail add: PO Box 94676, 68509-4676), SAN 377-371X. Tel: 402-471-2081. Administration Tel: 402-471-2363. FAX: 402-471-2900. Web Site: www.dnr.ne.gov. *Librn,* Maggie Hoagstrom
Library Holdings: Bk Vols 2,000; Per Subs 30
Wireless access

M NEBRASKA HEALTH CARE ASSOCIATION LIBRARY*, 3900 NW 12th St, Ste 100, 68521. SAN 375-6750. Tel: 402-435-3551. FAX: 402-475-6289. Web Site: www.nehca.org. *Dir, Libr & Info Serv,* Position Currently Open
Library Holdings: Bk Titles 900; Bk Vols 920; Per Subs 25
Open Mon-Fri 8-5

G NEBRASKA LEGISLATIVE COUNCIL*, Legislative Research Library, 1201 State Capitol Bldg, 1445 K St, 68508. SAN 328-1760. Tel: 402-471-2221. FAX: 402-479-0967. *Librn,* Mary Rasmussen; Tel: 402-471-0075; Staff 2 (Non-MLS 2)
Founded 1980
Library Holdings: Bk Titles 6,000; Per Subs 124
Subject Interests: Legis mat
Automation Activity & Vendor Info: (Acquisitions) EOS International; (Cataloging) EOS International; (Circulation) EOS International; (OPAC) EOS International; (Serials) EOS International
Database Vendor: OCLC FirstSearch, ProQuest, Wilson - Wilson Web
Publications: Acquisitions List (Monthly); Annotated Periodicals List
Partic in Dialog Corp
Restriction: Not open to pub

P NEBRASKA LIBRARY COMMISSION*, The Atrium, 1200 N St, Ste 120, 68508-2023. SAN 350-1604. Tel: 402-471-2045. Reference Tel: 402-471-4016. Toll Free Tel: 800-307-2665 (NE only). FAX: 402-471-2083. Web Site: www.nlc.state.ne.us. *Dir,* Rod Wagner; Tel: 402-471-4001, E-mail: rod.wagner@nebraska.gov; *Dir, Info Serv,* Lisa Kelly; Tel: 402-471-4015, E-mail: lisa.kelly@nebraska.gov; *Dir, Libr Develop,* Richard Miller; *Talking Bk/Braille Serv Dir,* David Oertli; *Tech & Access Serv Dir,* Devra Dragos; *Acq Librn,* Cathy Hatterman; Tel: 402-471-4034, E-mail: cathy.hatterman@nebraska.gov; *Cat Librn,* Emily Nimsakont; Tel: 402-471-4031; *Fed Doc Librn,* Lori Sailors; Tel: 402-471-7741; *Govt Info Librn,* Mary Sauers; *Online Serv Librn,* Susan Knisely; Tel: 402-471-3849; *Spec Projects Librn,* Christa Burns; Tel: 402-471-3107; *Tech & Access Serv Librn,* Allana Novotny; Tel: 402-471-6681; *Tech Innovation Librn,* Michael Sauers; Tel: 402-471-3106; *Bus Mgr,* Jerry Breazile; *Communications Coordr,* Mary Jo Ryan; Tel: 402-471-3434, E-mail: maryjo.ryan@nebraska.gov; *Planning & Data Serv Coordr,* John Felton; Tel: 402-471-3216; Staff 32 (MLS 15, Non-MLS 17)
Founded 1901. Pop 1,711,263
Jul 2006-Jun 2007 Income $5,286,376, State $3,672,148, Federal $1,501,688, Locally Generated Income $112,540. Mats Exp $77,406. Sal $2,223,920
Library Holdings: AV Mats 2,275; Bk Vols 102,735; Per Subs 716; Videos 2,191
Special Collections: State Document Depository; US Document Depository
Automation Activity & Vendor Info: (Cataloging) OCLC; (Circulation) Mandarin Library Automation; (ILL) OCLC; (Media Booking) Mandarin Library Automation; (OPAC) Mandarin Library Automation; (Serials) Mandarin Library Automation
Database Vendor: CQ Press, H W Wilson, Loislaw, OCLC FirstSearch, Overdrive, Inc, Wilson - Wilson Web
Wireless access
Publications: Interchange (Bi-monthly); Magazine in Special Format; N3-Nebraska Library Commission Network Services News (Bi-monthly); NCompass (Quarterly); NLCommunicator (Bi-monthly); What's Up Doc (Bi-monthly)
Partic in OCLC Online Computer Library Center, Inc
Special Services for the Blind - Braille bks; Talking bks
Open Mon-Fri 8-5
Branches: 1
TALKING BOOK & BRAILLE SERVICE
See Separate Entry

P NEBRASKA LIBRARY COMMISSION*, Talking Book & Braille Service, 1200 N St, Ste 120, 68508-2023. SAN 309-5258. Tel: 402-471-4038. Toll Free Tel: 800-742-7691. FAX: 402-471-2083. E-mail: nlc.tbbs@nebraska.gov. Web Site: www.nlc.nebraska.gov/tbbs. *Dir,* David L Oertli; E-mail: david.oertli@nebraska.gov
Founded 1952
Library Holdings: Braille Volumes 2,855; CDs 690; DVDs 154; Bk Titles 62,153; Bk Vols 106,958; Talking Bks 59,496; Videos 607
Special Collections: Children's Braille; Nebraska Coll (cassette bks, digital bks)
Wireless access
Publications: Interchange (Newsletter)

S NEBRASKA STATE HISTORICAL SOCIETY LIBRARY*, Division of Library-Archives, 1500 R St, 68501. (Mail add: PO Box 82554, 68501), SAN 309-5266. Tel: 402-471-4751. Toll Free Tel: 800-833-6747. FAX: 402-471-3100. E-mail: nshs.reference@nebraska.gov. Web Site: www.nebraskahistory.org. *Dir,* Mike Smith; Tel: 407-471-4745, E-mail: michael.smith@nebraska.gov; *Assoc Dir,* Andrea Faling; Tel: 402-471-4785, E-mail: andrea.faling@nebraska.gov; *Curator, Tech Serv,* Cindy S Drake; Tel: 402-471-4786, E-mail: cindy.drake@nebraska.gov; *Archivist,* Gayla Koerting; Tel: 402-471-4783, E-mail: gayla.koerting@nebraska.gov. Subject Specialists: *Genealogy, Local hist,* Cindy S Drake; Staff 7.5 (MLS 2, Non-MLS 5.5)
Founded 1878

Library Holdings: Bk Vols 80,000; Per Subs 300
Special Collections: State Document Depository
Subject Interests: Genealogy, Native Am, Nebr hist, Western hist
Automation Activity & Vendor Info: (OPAC) Mandarin Library Automation
Open Tues-Fri 10-4, Sat 8-5
Restriction: Non-circulating

GL NEBRASKA STATE LIBRARY*, 325 State Capitol, 1445 K St, 68509. (Mail add: PO Box 98931, 65809-8931), SAN 309-5274. Tel: 402-471-3189. FAX: 402-471-1011. E-mail: nsc.lawlibrary@nebraska.gov. Web Site: supremecourt.ne.gov/1082/state-library. *Dep Dir,* Marie Wiechman
Founded 1854
Library Holdings: Bk Titles 132,000
Special Collections: US Document Depository
Subject Interests: Law
Wireless access
Open Mon-Fri 8-5

R NEBRASKA UNITED METHODIST HISTORICAL CENTER ARCHIVES*, Nebraska Wesleyan University, Cochrane-Woods Library, Lower Level, 5000 Saint Paul Ave, 68504. SAN 309-5215. Tel: 402-465-2175. FAX: 402-464-6203. *Dir/Curator,* Karrie L Dvorak; E-mail: kdvorak@greatplainsumc.org; Staff 1 (Non-MLS 1)
Founded 1942
Jan 2012-Dec 2012 Income $200. Mats Exp $2,400. Sal $24,000
Library Holdings: Bk Titles 2,000
Special Collections: Nebraska Conference Minutes 1856-2012 (includes Methodist, Evangelical United Brethren & United Methodist)
Wireless access
Function: Archival coll
Open Tues & Thurs 9:30-3, Wed 10:30-3, Fri 12-3
Restriction: Closed stack

C NEBRASKA WESLEYAN UNIVERSITY*, Cochrane-Woods Library, 50th & St Paul, 68504. SAN 309-5282. Tel: 402-465-2400. Reference Tel: 402-465-2406. Administration Tel: 402-465-2401. FAX: 402-465-2189. E-mail: library@nebrwesleyan.edu. Web Site: library.nebrwesleyan.edu. *Univ Librn,* Margaret Emons; E-mail: memons@nebrwesleyan.edu; *Head, Tech & Archives, Librn,* Barbara Cornelius; *Online Serv, Pub Serv,* Dr Martha Tanner; Staff 7 (MLS 4, Non-MLS 3)
Founded 1888. Enrl 1,809; Fac 130; Highest Degree: Master
Library Holdings: Bk Vols 203,000; Per Subs 641
Special Collections: Mignon G Eberhart Coll; Publications of Faculty, bks, ms; Rare Books/College Archives
Wireless access
Publications: Newsletter
Partic in Nebr Independent Col Libr Consortium; OCLC Online Computer Library Center, Inc

S NOVARTIS CONSUMER HEALTH LIBRARY*, 10401 Hwy 6, 68517. SAN 377-1717. Tel: 402-464-6311, Ext 68915. *Librn,* Nancy Carlson
Library Holdings: Bk Vols 2,000; Per Subs 25

J SOUTHEAST COMMUNITY COLLEGE-LINCOLN CAMPUS*, LRC Library, 8800 O St, 68520. SAN 350-1663. Tel: 402-437-2585. Interlibrary Loan Service Tel: 402-437-2587. FAX: 402-437-2404. Web Site: www.southeast.edu. *Cat, Dir,* Jo Shimmin; Tel: 402-437-2586; *Ref & ILL Librn, Spec,* Pat Peterson; *Per, Spec,* Jeannette Bean; Tel: 402-437-2589; Staff 4 (MLS 2, Non-MLS 2)
Founded 1973. Highest Degree: Associate
Library Holdings: Bk Titles 13,000; Per Subs 300
Automation Activity & Vendor Info: (Cataloging) Mandarin Library Automation; (Circulation) Mandarin Library Automation; (OPAC) Mandarin Library Automation
Database Vendor: Baker & Taylor, Checkpoint Systems, Inc, CQ Press, EBSCO Auto Repair Reference, EBSCOhost, Electric Library, Facts on File, Gale Cengage Learning, infoUSA, MITINET, Inc, Newsbank, OCLC ArticleFirst, OCLC CAMIO, OCLC FirstSearch, OCLC WorldShare Interlibrary Loan, ProQuest, ReferenceUSA, Wilson - Wilson Web
Wireless access
Open Mon-Thurs 7:30am-9pm, Fri 7:30-5, Sat 7:45-Noon

R TIFERETH ISRAEL SYNAGOGUE LIBRARY*, 3219 Sheridan Blvd, 68502. SAN 309-5312. Tel: 402-423-8569. Web Site: www.tiferethisraellincoln.org. *Librn,* Brenda Ingraham
Founded 1955
Library Holdings: Bk Titles 2,500; Per Subs 20
Subject Interests: Hebrew lang, Judaica, Yiddish (Lang)

C UNION COLLEGE LIBRARY, 3800 S 48th St, 68506-4386. SAN 350-1728. Tel: 402-486-2514. FAX: 402-486-2678. Web Site: www.ucollege.edu/library. *Dir, Electronic Res/Ser Librn, Spec Coll & Archives Librn,* Sabrina Riley; E-mail: sariley@ucollege.edu; *Pub Serv,* Jeannette Wetmore; *Tech Serv,* Gillian Connors; Staff 4.5 (MLS 3, Non-MLS 1.5)
Founded 1891. Enrl 800; Fac 4; Highest Degree: Master
Jun 2006-May 2007 Income $591,167. Mats Exp $175,790. Sal $283,533 (Prof $164,959)
Library Holdings: DVDs 243; e-books 36,474; Bk Vols 161,546; Per Subs 594; Videos 715
Special Collections: College Archives; E N Dick Coll; Heritage Room
Subject Interests: Genealogy, Seventh Day Adventists
Automation Activity & Vendor Info: (Acquisitions) OCLC; (Cataloging) OCLC; (Circulation) OCLC; (Course Reserve) OCLC; (ILL) OCLC WorldShare Interlibrary Loan; (OPAC) OCLC; (Serials) OCLC
Database Vendor: Alexander Street Press, American Chemical Society, Annual Reviews, Baker & Taylor, CredoReference, Dialog, EBSCOhost, Elsevier, Gale Cengage Learning, Infotrieve, JSTOR, LexisNexis, OCLC ArticleFirst, OCLC WorldShare Interlibrary Loan, OCLC Worldshare Management Services, OVID Technologies, Oxford Online, ValueLine, Wilson - Wilson Web
Wireless access
Function: Archival coll, Computers for patron use, Copy machines, e-mail & chat, e-mail serv, Electronic databases & coll, Exhibits, ILL available, Laminating, Magazines, Mango lang, Microfiche/film & reading machines, Movies, Online cat, Prog for adults, Ref serv in person, Study rm, Telephone ref, Wheelchair accessible
Partic in Adventist Librs Info Coop; OCLC Online Computer Library Center, Inc
Open Mon-Thurs 8:30am-10:30pm, Fri 8:30-1, Sun 1-10:30
Restriction: Open to pub for ref & circ; with some limitations, Open to students, fac, staff & alumni

C UNIVERSITY OF NEBRASKA-LINCOLN*, University Libraries, 318 Love Library, 13th & R Strs, 68588. (Mail add: PO Box 884100, 68588-4100). Tel: 402-472-2526. Circulation Tel: 402-472-9568. Interlibrary Loan Service Tel: 402-472-2522. Reference Tel: 402-472-2848. Administration FAX: 402-472-5181. Web Site: libraries.unl.edu. *Dean of Libr,* Dr Nancy Busch; E-mail: nbusch2@unl.edu; *Dir, Computing Operations & Research Serv,* DeeAnn Allison; E-mail: dallison1@unl.edu; *Chair, Digital Initiatives & Spec Coll,* Katherine Walter; E-mail: kwalter1@unl.edu; *Chair, Discovery & Res Mgt,* Mary Bolin; E-mail: mbolin2@unl.edu; *Chair, Res & Instrul Serv,* Charlene Maxey-Harris; E-mail: cmaxeyharris2@unl.edu; *Spec Coll & Archives Librn,* Mary Ellen Ducey; E-mail: mducey2@unl.edu; *Fac Mgr,* Debra Pearson; E-mail: dpearson1@unl.edu; Staff 45 (MLS 45)
Founded 1869. Enrl 24,610; Fac 1,271; Highest Degree: Doctorate
Jul 2010-Jun 2011 Income (Main and Other College/University Libraries) $15,174,693. Mats Exp $6,835,352. Sal $6,595,209 (Prof $3,095,447)
Library Holdings: Bk Vols 3,121,239; Per Subs 40,660
Special Collections: Agriculture; Ethnic American Coll (Czech, Latvian, Asian American, etc); Folklore; French Revolutionary War; Great Plains History; Literature (Willa Cather, Ted Kooser, Wright Morris, Prairie Schooner, etc); Natural History & Sciences; Quilts, Quiltmakers, Quilt History; Railroads (US); Russian History; University of Nebraska-Lincoln Archvies; US Military & Wartime History. State Document Depository; UN Document Depository; US Document Depository
Automation Activity & Vendor Info: (Acquisitions) Innovative Interfaces, Inc; (Cataloging) Innovative Interfaces, Inc; (Circulation) Innovative Interfaces, Inc; (Course Reserve) Innovative Interfaces, Inc; (OPAC) Innovative Interfaces, Inc; (Serials) Innovative Interfaces, Inc
Wireless access
Partic in OCLC Online Computer Library Center, Inc
Friends of the Library Group

Departmental Libraries:

ARCHITECTURE LIBRARY, Architecture Hall, Rm 308, City Campus 0108, 68588-0108. Tel: 402-472-1208. *In Charge,* Kay Logan-Peters; E-mail: klogan-peters1@unl.edu
Library Holdings: Bk Vols 45,822; Per Subs 158
Friends of the Library Group

ENGINEERING LIBRARY, Nebraska Hall, Rm W204, City Campus 0516, 68588-0516. Tel: 402-472-3411. FAX: 402-472-0663. *Asst Prof,* Ted Naylor
Library Holdings: Bk Vols 145,543; Per Subs 250

EXTENSION CENTER, 4502 Ave I, Scottsbluff, 69361. Tel: 308-632-1230. FAX: 308-632-1365. *Librn,* Joan Giesecke; E-mail: jgiesecke@unl.edu
Library Holdings: Bk Vols 3,000
Open Mon-Fri 8-5

GEOLOGY LIBRARY, Bessey Hall, Rm 10, City Campus 0344, 68588-0344. Tel: 402-472-2653. *In Charge,* Adonna Fleming; Tel: 402-472-3628
Library Holdings: Bk Vols 56,407; Per Subs 189

MATHEMATICS LIBRARY, 14 Avery Hall, 68588-0129. Tel: 402-472-6900. E-mail: mathmail@unlnotes.unl.edu. *In Charge,* Adonna Fleming
Library Holdings: Bk Vols 33,604; Per Subs 28

MUSIC LIBRARY, Westbrook Music Bldg 30, 68588-0101. Tel: 402-472-6300. FAX: 402-472-1592. *Head of Libr,* Anita Breckbill; E-mail: abreckbill1@unl.edu
Founded 1980
Library Holdings: Bk Vols 30,661; Per Subs 44

CL MARVIN & VIRGINIA SCHMID LAW LIBRARY, 40 Fair St, 68583. (Mail add: PO Box 830902, Ross McCollum Hall, 68583-0902). Tel: 402-472-3547. Reference Tel: 402-472-3548. FAX: 402-472-8260. Web Site: www.law.unl.edu. *Dir,* Richard Leiter; Tel: 402-472-5737; *Pub Serv,* Sandy Placzek; *Ref,* Stefanie Pearlman; *Tech Serv,* Brian D Striman; Staff 5 (MLS 5)
Founded 1891. Enrl 420; Fac 28; Highest Degree: Doctorate
Library Holdings: Bk Titles 48,041; Bk Vols 199,473; Per Subs 2,858
Special Collections: Anglo-American Law Coll; Tax Law Coll
Open Mon-Fri 8am-Midnight

C Y THOMPSON LIBRARY, East Campus, 38th & Holdrege Sts, 68583-0717, SAN 350-1841. Tel: 402-472-4407. Circulation Tel: 402-472-4401. Interlibrary Loan Service Tel: 402-472-4406. FAX: 402-472-7005. *Chair, Res & Instrul Serv,* Position Currently Open
Library Holdings: Bks on Deafness & Sign Lang 21,010; Bk Vols 382,885; Per Subs 878
Subject Interests: Agr, Animal sci, Biochem, Communication disorders, Dentistry, Entomology, Food sci, Natural res, Nutrition, Plant sci, Spec educ, Textiles
Open Mon-Thurs 8am-Midnight, Fri 8-8, Sat 9-5, Sun Noon-Midnight
Friends of the Library Group

LODGEPOLE

P NANCY FAWCETT MEMORIAL LIBRARY*, 724 Oberfelder St, 69149-0318. (Mail add: PO Box 318, 69149-0318), SAN 309-5363. Tel: 308-483-5714. E-mail: nafameli@daltontel.net. *Pres,* Dixie Kripal; *Dir, Librn,* Norma Michelman
Founded 1930. Pop 368; Circ 2,330
Library Holdings: Bk Vols 6,200; Per Subs 10
Mem of Panhandle Libr Syst
Partic in Panhandle Library Access Network
Open Mon-Thurs 2:30-6:30

LOOMIS

P LOOMIS PUBLIC LIBRARY*, 301 Commercial St, 68958. (Mail add: PO Box 226, 68958-0226). Tel: 308-876-2334. FAX: 308-876-2334. E-mail: loomisvill@atcjet.net. *Dir,* Maxine Berry
Pop 375
Library Holdings: DVDs 100; Bk Vols 6,000; Talking Bks 100
Open Mon-Fri 9-5

LOUISVILLE

P LOUISVILLE PUBLIC LIBRARY*, 217 Main St, 68037. (Mail add: PO Box 39, 68037-0039), SAN 309-5371. Tel: 402-234-6265. E-mail: louisvillelibrary@gmail.com. *Librn,* Darla McDonald
Pop 1,048; Circ 5,988
Library Holdings: Bk Titles 12,000
Automation Activity & Vendor Info: (Cataloging) Biblionix; (Circulation) Biblionix; (OPAC) Biblionix
Wireless access
Open Mon 10:30-6, Wed 12-7, Fri 10-5, Sat 9-Noon

LOUP CITY

P LOUP CITY PUBLIC LIBRARY*, 800 N Eighth St, 68853. SAN 309-538X. Tel: 308-745-1589. *Librn,* Mrs Jennifer L Fowler; E-mail: loupcitylibrary@yahoo.com
Founded 1917. Pop 3,999; Circ 16,000
Library Holdings: High Interest/Low Vocabulary Bk Vols 500; Large Print Bks 200; Bk Vols 27,000; Per Subs 60; Talking Bks 100; Videos 350
Special Collections: Nebraska History Coll
Automation Activity & Vendor Info: (Cataloging) LibraryWorld, Inc; (Circulation) LibraryWorld, Inc; (OPAC) LibraryWorld, Inc
Wireless access
Open Mon, Tues, Thurs & Fri (Winter) 8-6, Wed 8-6 & 7-9, Sat 2-5; Tues (Summer) 9-1 & 2-8, Thurs & Fri 2-6, Wed 2-6 & 7-9, Sat 2-5

LYMAN

P LYMAN PUBLIC LIBRARY*, 313 Jeffers St, 69352. (Mail add: PO Box 384, 69352-0384), SAN 309-5398. Tel: 308-787-1366. FAX: 308-787-1366. *Dir,* Keitha Green; E-mail: greenkeitha@yahoo.com; *Asst Librn,* Brenda Goodro
Pop 551; Circ 3,552
Library Holdings: Bk Titles 8,000; Per Subs 20
Wireless access
Mem of Panhandle Libr Syst
Open Mon-Wed 2-5, Thurs & Sat 9-Noon

LYNCH

P LYNCH PUBLIC LIBRARY*, 423 W Hoffman, 68746. (Mail add: PO Box 385, 68746-0385), SAN 377-208X. Tel: 402-569-3491. E-mail: lynnelib@threeriver.net. *Actg Dir,* Jane Greene; E-mail: windmills3@hotmail.com
Library Holdings: Bk Vols 13,000
Open Mon & Wed 2-5, Fri 9-12

LYONS

P LYONS PUBLIC LIBRARY*, 305 Main, 68038. (Mail add: PO Box 198, 68038-0198), SAN 309-5401. Tel: 402-687-2895. FAX: 402-687-2895. E-mail: lyonslibrary@abbnebraska.com. Web Site: www.cityoflyons.net/?page_id=9. *Libr Dir,* Michael Heavrin
Pop 851
Library Holdings: CDs 38; Large Print Bks 800; Bk Titles 10,400; Per Subs 20; Talking Bks 205; Videos 483
Automation Activity & Vendor Info: (Cataloging) Biblionix; (Circulation) Biblionix; (ILL) OCLC; (OPAC) Biblionix
Mem of Eastern Libr Syst
Special Services for the Blind - Audio mat; Bks available with recordings; Bks on cassette; Bks on CD; Extensive large print coll; Home delivery serv
Open Mon & Wed 1-8, Tues & Thurs 9-12 & 4-8, Fri 5:30-8:30, Sat 9-2
Friends of the Library Group

MACY

J NEBRASKA INDIAN COMMUNITY COLLEGE*, Tribal Library, PO Box 428, 68039-0428. SAN 377-1733. Tel: 402-837-5078. FAX: 402-837-4183. *In Charge,* Mary Johnson; E-mail: mjohnson@thenicc.edu
Library Holdings: Bk Vols 3,000; Per Subs 10
Open Mon-Fri 9-5

MADISON

P MADISON PUBLIC LIBRARY*, 208 W Third St, 68748. (Mail add: PO Box 387, 68748-0387), SAN 309-5444. Tel: 402-454-3500. FAX: 402-454-3376. E-mail: madlibr@cableone.net. *Dir,* Nichole Lawless
Pop 2,425; Circ 12,000
Library Holdings: Bk Titles 19,000; Per Subs 41
Open Mon-Thurs 11:30-7, Fri 11:30-5, Sat 10-Noon

MASON CITY

P SUNSHINE TOWNSHIP LIBRARY*, Main St, 68855. (Mail add: PO Box 12, 68855-0012), SAN 309-5452, *Librn,* Joan Cox
Founded 1926. Pop 332; Circ 1,300
Library Holdings: Bk Titles 5,145
Special Collections: Central Nebraska Authors; History Books of Area Towns
Open Wed & Sat 2-5

MCCOOK

S HIGH PLAINS MUSEUM LIBRARY*, 413 Norris Ave, 69001. SAN 309-541X. Tel: 308-345-3661. *Curator,* Marilyn Hawkins
Founded 1961
Library Holdings: Bk Vols 1,000
Special Collections: Frank Lloyd Wright Coll; German Bibles & School Books; Men & Women Fashion Catalogues; Old Medical Books & Equipment. Oral History
Subject Interests: Cooking

J MCCOOK COMMUNITY COLLEGE*, Von Riesen Library, 1205 E Third St, 69001-2631. SAN 309-5428. Tel: 308-345-6303, Ext 8127. Toll Free Tel: 800-658-4348. FAX: 308-345-8193. *Dir,* Pat Bonge; E-mail: bongep@mpcc.edu; Staff 2 (MLS 2)
Founded 1926. Enrl 801; Fac 44
Library Holdings: Bk Titles 25,000; Per Subs 240
Wireless access
Partic in OCLC Online Computer Library Center, Inc
Open Mon-Thurs 7:30am-9:30pm, Fri 7:30-4, Sun 5pm-9:30pm

P MCCOOK PUBLIC LIBRARY*, 802 Norris Ave, 69001-3143. SAN 309-5436. Tel: 308-345-1906. FAX: 308-345-1461. E-mail: mlibrary@cityofmccook.com. Web Site: mccooklibrary.info. *Dir,* Patricia Hall
Pop 11,000
Library Holdings: Large Print Bks 4,000; Bk Titles 50,000; Per Subs 90
Subject Interests: Braille
Automation Activity & Vendor Info: (Cataloging) OCLC FirstSearch; (Circulation) Follett Software; (OPAC) Follett Software
Open Mon-Thurs 9-8, Fri & Sat 9-5

S NEBRASKA DEPARTMENT OF CORRECTIONAL SERVICES*, Work Ethic Camp Library, 2309 N Hwy 83, 69001. Tel: 308-345-8405, Ext 224. FAX: 308-345-8407. Web Site: www.corrections.state.ne.us. *Coordr,* Diana Hipple
Library Holdings: Bk Vols 700

MEAD

P MEAD PUBLIC LIBRARY*, 316 S Vine, 68041. (Mail add: PO Box 203, 68041-0203), SAN 309-5460. Tel: 402-624-6605. FAX: 402-624-6605. *Dir,* Vera Kuhr
Pop 595; Circ 2,800
Oct 2010-Sept 2011 Income $43,870, State $700, Provincial $21,935, City $21,000, Locally Generated Income $235. Mats Exp $1,700. Sal $105,000
Library Holdings: Audiobooks 80; CDs 30; DVDs 180; Large Print Bks 40; Bk Titles 11,000; Per Subs 20; Videos 545
Special Collections: Mead Ordnance Plant Administrative Records
Automation Activity & Vendor Info: (Cataloging) Follett Software; (Circulation) Follett Software; (OPAC) Follett Software
Wireless access
Mem of Eastern Libr Syst
Open Tues & Thurs 9-11 & 2-7, Wed 3-5, Sat 9-1
Friends of the Library Group

MEADOW GROVE

P MEADOW GROVE PUBLIC LIBRARY*, 205 Main St, 68752. (Mail add: PO Box 198, 68752-0198). Tel: 402-634-2266. FAX: 402-634-2266. *Dir,* Mardell Kohl; Staff 2 (MLS 2)
Founded 1926. Pop 332; Circ 11,614
Oct 2005-Sept 2006 Income $27,116, State $716, City $20,000, County $6,400. Mats Exp $25,740. Sal $14,347
Library Holdings: Large Print Bks 60; Bk Vols 6,877; Per Subs 27; Talking Bks 92
Automation Activity & Vendor Info: (Cataloging) Follett Software
Open Mon & Sat 9-12, Tues & Thurs 1-5:30, Wed & Fri 3-7
Friends of the Library Group

MERNA

P BRENIZER PUBLIC LIBRARY*, 430 W Center Ave, 68856. (Mail add: PO Box 8, 68856-0008), SAN 309-5487. Tel: 308-643-2268. FAX: 308-643-2268. *Dir,* Vickie Burnett; *Asst Librn,* Carol Squier
Founded 1916. Pop 1,000; Circ 9,200
Jul 2011-Jun 2012 Income $23,600, City $22,000, Other $1,600. Mats Exp $2,950, Books $2,500, Per/Ser (Incl. Access Fees) $450. Sal $6,000
Library Holdings: Audiobooks 25; CDs 100; DVDs 20; Bk Titles 17,500; Per Subs 36; Videos 300
Wireless access
Open Tues & Thurs 12:30-5, Sat 12:30-5:30

MILFORD

J SOUTHEAST COMMUNITY COLLEGE*, Stanley A Matzke Learning Resource Center, 600 State St, 68405. SAN 309-5495. Tel: 402-761-2131, Ext 8245. FAX: 402-761-2324. Web Site: www.southeast.edu. *Dir,* Janalee Petsch
Founded 1975. Enrl 1,000; Fac 82
Library Holdings: Bk Titles 23,000; Per Subs 350
Special Collections: Vocational/Technical
Automation Activity & Vendor Info: (Acquisitions) Mandarin Library Automation; (Cataloging) Mandarin Library Automation; (Circulation) Mandarin Library Automation; (Course Reserve) Mandarin Library Automation; (ILL) Mandarin Library Automation; (Media Booking) Mandarin Library Automation; (OPAC) Mandarin Library Automation; (Serials) Mandarin Library Automation
Wireless access
Open Mon-Thurs 7:30-6, Fri 7:30-4

P WEBERMEIER MEMORIAL PUBLIC LIBRARY*, 617 Second St, 68405. (Mail add: PO Box 705, 68405-0705), SAN 309-5509. Tel: 402-761-2937. FAX: 402-761-2937. E-mail: milfordlibrary@gmail.com. Web Site: www.wmlmilford.org. *Dir,* George Matzen; *Asst Librn,* Position Currently Open
Founded 1930. Pop 2,110; Circ 15,513
Library Holdings: Bk Vols 17,940; Per Subs 51
Open Mon & Thurs 12:30-5 & 7-9, Tues 12:30-5, Wed 10-5 & 7-9, Sat 10-5
Friends of the Library Group

MILLIGAN

P MILLIGAN PUBLIC LIBRARY*, 424 Main St, 68406. (Mail add: PO Box 324, 68406-0324), SAN 309-5517. Tel: 402-629-4405. *Librn,* E'Lonna Gesch
Library Holdings: AV Mats 150; Bk Vols 4,050; Videos 170
Open Mon & Wed 3-5, Sat 9-11

MINATARE

P MINATARE PUBLIC LIBRARY*, 309 Main St, 69356. (Mail add: PO Box 483, 69356-0483), SAN 309-5525. Tel: 308-783-1414. FAX: 308-783-1414. E-mail: minatarepubliclibrary@yahoo.com. *Librn,* Willadean Maurer
Pop 1,100; Circ 5,761
Library Holdings: Large Print Bks 30; Bk Vols 7,550; Talking Bks 30
Mem of Panhandle Libr Syst
Open Mon-Fri 10:30-12 & 2-4:30

MINDEN

P JENSEN MEMORIAL LIBRARY*, 443 N Kearney, 68959. (Mail add: PO Box 264, 68959-0264), SAN 309-5533. Tel: 308-832-2648. FAX: 308-832-1642. E-mail: mindenlibrary@gmail.com. Web Site: jensenmemoriallibrary.com. *Dir,* Janene Hill
Founded 1907. Pop 2,939; Circ 29,814
Library Holdings: Bk Vols 28,934; Per Subs 69; Videos 2,066
Special Collections: Genealogy Reference Coll. Oral History
Automation Activity & Vendor Info: (Cataloging) Follett Software; (Circulation) Follett Software; (OPAC) Follett Software
Open Mon-Wed 10-8, Thurs & Fri 10-5:30, Sat 10-4
Friends of the Library Group

MITCHELL

P MITCHELL PUBLIC LIBRARY*, 1449 Center Ave, 69357. SAN 309-5541. Tel: 308-623-2222. FAX: 308-623-2222. E-mail: mipl@actcom.net. *Dir,* Maryruth Reed; Staff 1 (MLS 1)
Founded 1920. Pop 1,743; Circ 20,271
Oct 2008-Sept 2009 Income $57,546. Mats Exp $10,800. Sal $38,396
Library Holdings: AV Mats 293; Microforms 1; Bk Titles 16,043; Per Subs 5
Subject Interests: Nebr hist
Automation Activity & Vendor Info: (Cataloging) Follett Software; (Circulation) Follett Software; (ILL) OCLC; (OPAC) Follett Software
Database Vendor: OCLC FirstSearch
Wireless access
Mem of Panhandle Libr Syst
Open Mon-Thurs 11-6, Fri & Sat 11-5
Friends of the Library Group

MORRILL

P MORRILL PUBLIC LIBRARY*, 119 E Webster, 69358. (Mail add: PO Box 402, 69358-0402), SAN 309-555X. Tel: 308-247-2611. FAX: 308-247-2309. E-mail: morrillpl@charter.net. Web Site: www.morrillpubliclibrary.org. *Dir,* Allison Reisig; *Libr Asst,* John Hudson; Staff 3 (Non-MLS 3)
Founded 1916. Pop 940; Circ 5,410
Library Holdings: AV Mats 87; Large Print Bks 196; Bk Vols 10,825; Per Subs 28; Talking Bks 135
Automation Activity & Vendor Info: (Cataloging) ComPanion Corp; (OPAC) ComPanion Corp
Database Vendor: EBSCOhost, H W Wilson, Medline, OCLC ArticleFirst, OCLC WorldShare Interlibrary Loan, ProQuest, Wilson - Wilson Web
Wireless access
Function: Bks on cassette, Bks on CD, Children's prog, Copy machines, Fax serv, Free DVD rentals, ILL available, Photocopying/Printing, Preschool outreach, Prog for children & young adult, Pub access computers, Ref serv in person, Scanner, Story hour, Summer reading prog, Tax forms, Teen prog, VHS videos
Mem of Panhandle Libr Syst
Special Services for the Deaf - Bks on deafness & sign lang
Special Services for the Blind - Bks on cassette; Bks on CD; Large print bks
Open Mon & Thurs 1-7, Tues, Wed & Fri 1-5:30
Friends of the Library Group

MULLEN

P HOOKER COUNTY LIBRARY*, 102 N Cleveland Ave, 69152. (Mail add: PO Box 479, 69152-0479), SAN 309-5568. Tel: 308-546-2240. FAX: 308-546-2240. *Librn,* Julie Pfeiffer; E-mail: jpfeiffer41@hotmail.com
Pop 977; Circ 16,630
Library Holdings: Bk Vols 15,000; Per Subs 22
Open Mon, Wed & Fri 3-6, Tues & Thurs 2-6, Sat 1-5

NEBRASKA CITY

P MORTON-JAMES PUBLIC LIBRARY*, 923 First Corso, 68410. SAN 309-5576. Tel: 402-873-5609. FAX: 402-873-5601. E-mail: mlibrary@neb.rr.com. Web Site: www.morton-jamespubliclibrary.com. *Dir,* Barbara E Hegr; E-mail: barbarahegr@neb.rr.com; Staff 9 (Non-MLS 9)
Founded 1896. Pop 7,228; Circ 88,889
Oct 2011-Sept 2012 Income $544,947, State $1,304, City $499,051, Other $44,592. Mats Exp $42,951, Books $30,355, Per/Ser (Incl. Access Fees) $2,200, AV Mat $10,396. Sal $267,180
Library Holdings: CDs 1,154; DVDs 2,062; e-books 27,500; Large Print Bks 2,121; Microforms 587; Bk Vols 31,907; Per Subs 72; Videos 437
Special Collections: Nebraska City & Otoe County Genealogy & History Coll
Automation Activity & Vendor Info: (Acquisitions) Biblionix; (Cataloging) OCLC CatExpress; (Circulation) Biblionix; (ILL) OCLC; (OPAC) Biblionix; (Serials) Biblionix
Database Vendor: Baker & Taylor, ebrary, EBSCOhost, H W Wilson, Newsbank, OCLC FirstSearch, OCLC WorldShare Interlibrary Loan, Overdrive, Inc, ProQuest, Wilson - Wilson Web, World Book Online
Wireless access
Function: Adult bk club, Archival coll, Art exhibits, Audiobks via web, Bi-weekly Writer's Group, Bks on CD, Children's prog, Computers for patron use, Copy machines, Electronic databases & coll, Free DVD rentals, Handicapped accessible, Holiday prog, Home delivery & serv to Sr ctr & nursing homes, ILL available, Microfiche/film & reading machines, Music CDs, Online cat, Online searches, Outside serv via phone, mail, e-mail & web, OverDrive digital audio bks, Preschool outreach, Prog for adults, Prog for children & young adult, Pub access computers, Scanner, Spanish lang bks, Summer reading prog, Tax forms, Web-catalog, Wheelchair accessible
Mem of Southeast Library System (SELS)
Open Mon-Thurs 9-6, Fri & Sat 9-5
Restriction: Borrowing requests are handled by ILL, Non-circulating coll

S NEBRASKA CENTER FOR THE EDUCATION OF CHILDREN WHO ARE BLIND OR VISUALLY IMPAIRED*, 824 Tenth Ave, 68410. (Mail add: PO Box 129, 68410), SAN 377-0982. Tel: 402-873-5513. FAX: 402-873-3463. Web Site: www.ncecbvi.org. *Actg Librn,* Karen Duffy
Library Holdings: Bk Vols 15,000; Per Subs 25

NELIGH

P NELIGH PUBLIC LIBRARY*, 710 Main St, 68756-1246. SAN 309-5584. Tel: 402-887-5140. FAX: 402-887-4530. E-mail: nelighpub@frontiernet.net. Web Site: www.nelighlibrary.com. *Dir,* Jennifer Norton; E-mail: jn@nelighlibrary.com; *Youth Serv Dir,* Anne Dexter; *Ref Librn,* Danielle Reynolds; *Asst Librn,* Jean Jones; Staff 4 (Non-MLS 4)
Founded 1905. Pop 1,599; Circ 67,149
Oct 2011-Sept 2012 Income $149,873. Mats Exp $45,000
Library Holdings: Audiobooks 683; AV Mats 635; e-books 3,000; Electronic Media & Resources 21; Bk Titles 28,000; Per Subs 73
Special Collections: Art Prints/Posters; Nebraska Coll; Wood Carving Patterns
Automation Activity & Vendor Info: (Cataloging) Follett Software; (Circulation) Follett Software; (ILL) OCLC; (OPAC) Follett Software
Database Vendor: EBSCOhost, OCLC FirstSearch
Open Mon-Thurs 10-8, Fri & Sat 10-2
Friends of the Library Group

NELSON

P NELSON PUBLIC LIBRARY*, Ten W Third St, 68961. (Mail add: PO Box 322, 68961-0322), SAN 309-5592. Tel: 402-225-7111. FAX: 402-225-7111. E-mail: nelsonlibrary@superiorinet.net. *Librn,* Mary Statz
Founded 1907. Circ 2,854
Oct 2006-Sept 2007 Income $15,500, City $13,000, Locally Generated Income $2,500. Mats Exp $1,440, Books $1,400, Micro $40. Sal $8,293 (Prof $5,715)
Library Holdings: Large Print Bks 275; Bk Vols 9,100; Per Subs 12; Talking Bks 54; Videos 300
Automation Activity & Vendor Info: (Acquisitions) Follett Software; (Cataloging) Follett Software; (Circulation) Follett Software; (ILL) OCLC WorldShare Interlibrary Loan
Database Vendor: OCLC FirstSearch, OCLC WebJunction, OCLC WorldShare Interlibrary Loan
Wireless access
Open Tues & Thurs 3:30-7:30, Wed 2-7, Sat 9-12
Friends of the Library Group

NEWMAN GROVE

P NEWMAN GROVE PUBLIC LIBRARY*, 615 Hale Ave, 68758. (Mail add: PO Box 430, 68758-0430), SAN 309-5606. Tel: 402-447-2331. FAX: 402-447-2331. E-mail: ngpl@megavision.com. Web Site: www.megavision.com/ngpl. *Dir,* Sandy Zurovski; Staff 3 (Non-MLS 3)
Founded 1923. Pop 930; Circ 9,341
Library Holdings: AV Mats 337; Large Print Bks 150; Bk Titles 13,795; Bk Vols 14,494; Per Subs 25; Talking Bks 125; Videos 283
Special Collections: Local Newspaper, micro
Automation Activity & Vendor Info: (Cataloging) Follett Software; (Circulation) Follett Software; (OPAC) Follett Software
Open Tues-Thurs 9-12 & 2-7, Fri & Sat 9-12

NIOBRARA

J NEBRASKA INDIAN COMMUNITY COLLEGE LIBRARY*, 425 Frazier Ave N, Ste 1, 68760. SAN 377-3590. Tel: 402-857-2434. FAX: 402-857-2543. Web Site: www.thenicc.edu. *In Charge,* Mary Johnson; E-mail: mjohnson@thenicc.edu
Library Holdings: Bk Vols 5,500
Open Mon-Fri 9-5

P NIOBRARA PUBLIC LIBRARY*, 25414 Park Ave, Ste 3, 68760. (Mail add: PO Box 15, 68760-0015), SAN 309-5614. Tel: 402-857-3565. FAX: 402-857-3824. E-mail: niolib2@gpcom.net. Web Site: www.niobrarane.com. *Librn,* Judy L Kopp
Pop 419
Library Holdings: CDs 15; DVDs 120; Large Print Bks 300; Bk Vols 8,500; Per Subs 25; Talking Bks 200; Videos 300
Special Collections: Niobrara Nebraska Centennial History Coll
Subject Interests: Local hist
Automation Activity & Vendor Info: (Cataloging) Follett Software; (OPAC) Follett Software
Wireless access
Special Services for the Blind - Audio mat; Bks on cassette; Bks on CD
Open Tues 9-2, Wed 12-7, Thurs 1-6, Sat 9-12

NORFOLK

P NORFOLK PUBLIC LIBRARY*, 308 Prospect Ave, 68701-4138. SAN 309-5630. Tel: 402-844-2100. Administration Tel: 402-844-2103. FAX: 402-844-2102. Web Site: www.ci.norfolk.ne.us/library. *Dir,* Jessica Chamberlain; E-mail: jchamberlain@ci.norfolk.ne.us; *Head, Tech Serv,* Sally Stahlecker; Tel: 402-844-2107, E-mail: sstahlec@ci.norfolk.ne.us; *Head, Youth Serv,* Karen Drevo; Tel: 402-844-2108, E-mail: kdrevo@ci.norfolk.ne.us; *Ref/Outreach Supvr,* Judy Hilkemann; Tel: 402-844-2104, E-mail: jhilkema@ci.norfolk.ne.us; *Circ,* Doug Collier; Tel: 402-844-2105; *ILL, Youth Serv,* Marci Retzlaff; Tel: 402-844-2109, E-mail: mretzlaf@ci.norfolk.ne.us; Staff 16 (MLS 2, Non-MLS 14)
Founded 1906. Pop 29,875
Oct 2005-Sept 2006 Income $1,084,232, State $8,061, City $1,040,270, Locally Generated Income $35,901. Mats Exp $171,034, Books $125,981, Per/Ser (Incl. Access Fees) $14,750, AV Mat $15,803, Electronic Ref Mat (Incl. Access Fees) $12,250, Presv $2,250. Sal $742,074
Library Holdings: AV Mats 2,256; e-books 5,700; Large Print Bks 3,037; Bk Titles 73,914; Per Subs 177; Talking Bks 1,429
Subject Interests: Genealogy, Nebr hist, Poetry
Automation Activity & Vendor Info: (Acquisitions) SirsiDynix; (Cataloging) SirsiDynix; (Circulation) SirsiDynix; (Course Reserve) SirsiDynix; (ILL) SirsiDynix; (Media Booking) SirsiDynix; (OPAC) SirsiDynix; (Serials) SirsiDynix
Database Vendor: 3M Library Systems, EBSCO Auto Repair Reference, Electric Library, H W Wilson, infoUSA, Ingram Library Services, LearningExpress, OCLC FirstSearch, OCLC WebJunction, OCLC WorldShare Interlibrary Loan, ProQuest, ReferenceUSA, SirsiDynix, ValueLine, WebMD, Wilson - Wilson Web
Wireless access
Partic in ONELibrary Consortium
Special Services for the Blind - Audio mat; Bks on CD; Braille bks; Cassettes; Computer with voice synthesizer for visually impaired persons; Large print bks; Low vision equip
Open Mon-Thurs 9-8, Fri & Sat 9-5, Sun 1:30-4:30

M NORFOLK REGIONAL CENTER*, Resident Library, 1700 N Victory Rd, 68701. (Mail add: PO Box 1209, 68701-1209), SAN 350-1930. Tel: 402-370-3290, 402-370-3401. FAX: 402-370-3194. *Librn,* Ellen Weed
Library Holdings: Bk Titles 3,000; Per Subs 20
Subject Interests: Educ, Recreation
Automation Activity & Vendor Info: (Cataloging) Follett Software; (Circulation) Follett Software; (ILL) Follett Software; (OPAC) Follett Software
Open Mon-Fri 12:30-4:30

J NORTHEAST COMMUNITY COLLEGE*, Library Resource Center, 801 E Benjamin Ave, 68702. (Mail add: PO Box 469, 68702-0469), SAN 309-5649. Tel: 402-844-7130. FAX: 402-844-7293. Web Site: northeast.edu/LS/index.php. *Dir, Libr Serv,* Mary Louise Irene Foster; Tel: 402-844-7131, E-mail: marylouise@northeast.edu; Staff 5 (MLS 1, Non-MLS 4)
Founded 1928. Enrl 3,200; Fac 120; Highest Degree: Associate
Library Holdings: Bk Titles 28,250; Per Subs 180

Automation Activity & Vendor Info: (Acquisitions) SirsiDynix; (Cataloging) SirsiDynix; (Circulation) SirsiDynix; (OPAC) SirsiDynix
Database Vendor: Alexander Street Press, CQ Press, EBSCO Discovery Service, EBSCOhost, Facts on File, Gale Cengage Learning, H W Wilson, OCLC FirstSearch, ProQuest, Wilson - Wilson Web
Wireless access
Open Mon-Thurs (Winter) 7:30am-9pm, Fri 7:30-5:30; Mon-Fri (Summer) 7:30-5:30

NORTH BEND

P NORTH BEND PUBLIC LIBRARY*, 140 E Eighth St, 68649. (Mail add: PO Box 279, 68649-0279), SAN 309-5657. Tel: 402-652-8356. FAX: 402-652-8356. E-mail: northbendlibrary@gpcom.net. Web Site: www.northbendlibrary.com. *Dir,* Amy Williams; *Librn,* Amy Reznicek; *Librn,* Joyce Ruzicka; *Librn,* Jan Vopalensky
Pop 1,368; Circ 14,970
Library Holdings: Audiobooks 436; DVDs 735; Electronic Media & Resources 19; Large Print Bks 125; Bk Titles 10,467; Per Subs 18
Special Collections: Cake Pans
Automation Activity & Vendor Info: (Cataloging) Follett Software; (Circulation) Follett Software; (OPAC) Follett Software
Wireless access
Partic in Eastern Nebr Libr Asn
Open Mon, Wed & Thurs 1-6:30, Tues 9-12 & 1-6:30, Fri 1-5, Sat 9-Noon
Friends of the Library Group

NORTH LOUP

P NORTH LOUP TOWNSHIP LIBRARY*, 112 South B St, 68859. (Mail add: PO Box 157, 68859-0157), SAN 309-5665. Tel: 308-496-4230. E-mail: nlpl@nctc.net. *Librn,* Corinne Hawley
Founded 1925. Pop 563; Circ 1,433
Library Holdings: Bk Vols 6,044; Per Subs 12
Special Collections: North Loup Newspapers, 1887-1942, microfilm & reader printer
Special Services for the Blind - Bks on cassette; Large print bks
Open Mon 2:30-7, Wed & Fri 2:30-4:30

NORTH PLATTE

J NORTH PLATTE COMMUNITY COLLEGE*, Learning Resource Center, 601 W State Farm Rd, 69101. SAN 309-5673. Tel: 308-535-3726. FAX: 308-535-3794. Web Site: www.mpcc.edu/mpcc_libraries.html. *Area Dir, Learning Res,* Sarah Dockray; Tel: 308-535-3727; Staff 7 (MLS 2, Non-MLS 5)
Founded 1965. Enrl 500; Fac 65
Library Holdings: Bk Vols 25,000; Per Subs 35
Automation Activity & Vendor Info: (Cataloging) Auto-Graphics, Inc; (Circulation) Auto-Graphics, Inc; (Course Reserve) Auto-Graphics, Inc; (ILL) OCLC; (OPAC) Auto-Graphics, Inc
Database Vendor: EBSCOhost, Electric Library, Gale Cengage Learning, H W Wilson, LexisNexis, ProQuest, Wilson - Wilson Web
Wireless access
Function: Computers for patron use, Free DVD rentals, Handicapped accessible, ILL available, Instruction & testing, Music CDs, Online cat, Online ref, Outside serv via phone, mail, e-mail & web, Photocopying/Printing, Pub access computers, Ref serv available, Ref serv in person, Scanner, Telephone ref, Video lending libr, Web-catalog
Open Mon-Thurs 7:30am-9:30pm, Fri 7:30-4, Sun 5-9:30

P NORTH PLATTE PUBLIC LIBRARY, 120 W Fourth St, 69101-3993. SAN 309-5681. Tel: 308-535-8036. FAX: 308-535-8296. E-mail: library@ci.north-platte.ne.us. Web Site: www.ci.north-platte.ne.us/library. *Dir,* Cecelia C Lawrence; E-mail: lawrencecc@ci.north-platte.ne.us; *Info Syst Mgr,* Sara Aden; E-mail: adensj@ci.north-platte.ne.us; *Acq, Tech Serv,* Brenda Anderson; E-mail: andersonbl@ci.north-platte.ne.us; *Ch Serv,* Mitzi Mueller; E-mail: muellermm@ci.north-platte.ne.us; *Circ,* Kaycee Anderson; E-mail: Andersonkm@ci.north-platte.ne.us; *ILL, Ref,* Sharon Lohoefener; E-mail: lohoefenersm@ci.north-platte.ne.us; *Tech Serv,* Dianne Jensen; E-mail: jensendf@ci.north-platte.ne.us; *YA Serv,* Carol Eshleman; E-mail: eshlemancy@ci.north-platte.ne.us; Staff 17 (MLS 2, Non-MLS 15)
Founded 1912. Pop 34,632; Circ 225,403
Oct 2013-Sept 2014 Income $1,118,084, State $5,300, City $1,072,574, County $40,210. Mats Exp $113,725, Books $79,000, Per/Ser (Incl. Access Fees) $5,160, AV Mat $14,000, Electronic Ref Mat (Incl. Access Fees) $15,565. Sal $640,101 (Prof $142,267)
Library Holdings: Audiobooks 4,412; CDs 2,025; DVDs 5,047; e-books 10,816; Large Print Bks 9,205; Bk Titles 102,338; Bk Vols 118,497; Per Subs 94
Special Collections: Travel Packets. Oral History
Subject Interests: Genealogy, Local hist, Nebr hist
Automation Activity & Vendor Info: (Cataloging) SirsiDynix; (Circulation) SirsiDynix; (OPAC) SirsiDynix; (Serials) SirsiDynix
Database Vendor: EBSCO Auto Repair Reference, EBSCOhost, Electric Library, OCLC FirstSearch, Wilson - Wilson Web
Wireless access
Function: 24/7 Electronic res, 24/7 Online cat, Accelerated reader prog, Accessibility serv available based on individual needs, Adult literacy prog, Archival coll, Audio & video playback equip for onsite use, Audiobks via web, Bks on CD, Children's prog, Computer training, Computers for patron use, Copy machines, e-mail & chat, Electronic databases & coll, Fax serv, Free DVD rentals, Genealogy discussion group, Handicapped accessible, Health sci info serv, ILL available, Instruction & testing, Large print keyboards, Life-long learning prog for all ages, Magazines, Magnifiers for reading, Mail & tel request accepted, Microfiche/film & reading machines, Music CDs, Newsp ref libr, Online cat, Online ref, Outreach serv, OverDrive digital audio bks, Photocopying/Printing, Preschool reading prog, Prog for adults, Prog for children & young adult, Pub access computers, Ref & res, Ref serv available, Ref serv in person, Res performed for a fee, Scanner, Senior computer classes, Serves mentally handicapped consumers, Story hour, Summer reading prog, Tax forms, Teen prog, Wheelchair accessible
Publications: Friends of the Library (Newsletter)
Partic in OCLC Online Computer Library Center, Inc
Open Mon-Thurs 9-9, Fri & Sat 9-6
Friends of the Library Group

OAKDALE

P LOIS JOHNSON MEMORIAL LIBRARY*, 406 Fifth St, 68761. (Mail add: PO Box 187, 68761-0187), SAN 309-569X. Tel: 402-776-2602. FAX: 402-776-2602. E-mail: libra@gpcom.net. *Dir,* Judy Hershberger; Staff 2 (Non-MLS 2)
Pop 350; Circ 7,273
Library Holdings: Bk Titles 4,800; Per Subs 54
Special Collections: Large Print Book Coll; Oakdale Sentinel Newspaper Back Issues, 1887-1960, microfilm
Wireless access
Open Mon 8:30-10 & 3-6, Wed 8:30-10 & 3-7, Thurs 8:30-10 & 3-5, Sat 10-2
Friends of the Library Group

OAKLAND

P OAKLAND PUBLIC LIBRARY*, 110 E Third St, 68045-1356. SAN 309-5703. Tel: 402-685-5113. FAX: 402-685-5113. E-mail: books@oakland-library.org. *Dir,* Rosa Schmidt
Pop 1,393; Circ 158,001
Library Holdings: Bk Vols 20,365; Per Subs 42
Wireless access
Open Mon & Wed 1:30-8:30, Tues & Thurs 8:30-12 & 1:30-6, Sat 8:30-Noon
Friends of the Library Group

OFFUTT AFB

A UNITED STATES AIR FORCE*, Thomas S Power Library, 55 FSS/FSDL, Bldg 73, 510 Custer Dr, 68113-2150. SAN 350-199X. Tel: 402-294-5276, 402-294-7506. Interlibrary Loan Service Tel: 402-294-5823. FAX: 402-294-7124. E-mail: 55fss.fsdl@acc.af.mil. Web Site: www.offutt55fss.com/amenities/library.html, www.offuttbaselibrary.org. *Dir,* Rebecca Sims, Tel: 402-294-5523, E-mail: rebecca.sims@us.af.mil; *Asst Dir,* Pat McCary; Tel: 402-294-5822; *IT Mgr,* Diane Panek; Tel: 402-294-5543; *ILL,* Alex Keith-Henry; *Acq,* Frankie Hannan; Staff 4.5 (MLS 2.5, Non-MLS 2)
Founded 1948
Library Holdings: Bk Vols 70,000; Per Subs 50; Talking Bks 1,500; Videos 3,500
Special Collections: Foreign Language Coll, dictionaries, foreign films, grammar, reading mat, usage; Military Professional Reading Lists (US Air Force, Air Force Weather, Navy, Army, Marines, Joint Chiefs of Staff)
Subject Interests: Computers, Foreign affairs, Mil hist, Tech, World cultures
Automation Activity & Vendor Info: (Cataloging) SirsiDynix; (Circulation) SirsiDynix; (OPAC) SirsiDynix
Database Vendor: CountryWatch, EBSCO Auto Repair Reference, Jane's, Knovel, Newsbank, OCLC FirstSearch, OCLC WorldShare Interlibrary Loan, Overdrive, Inc, ProQuest
Wireless access
Function: Audio & video playback equip for onsite use, Audiobks via web, Bk club(s), Bks on cassette, Bks on CD, Children's prog, Computers for patron use, Copy machines, Distance learning, Doc delivery serv, Electronic databases & coll, Fax serv, Free DVD rentals, Handicapped accessible, Homework prog, ILL available, Learning ctr, Mail & tel request accepted, Music CDs, Online cat, Online ref, Online searches, Orientations, Outreach serv, Outside serv via phone, mail, e-mail & web, OverDrive digital audio bks, Photocopying/Printing, Prof lending libr, Prog for adults, Prog for children & young adult, Pub access computers, Ref & res, Ref serv available, Ref serv in person, Referrals accepted, Scanner, Senior

computer classes, Spoken cassettes & CDs, Story hour, Summer reading prog, Teen prog, Telephone ref, VHS videos, Video lending libr, Web-catalog, Wheelchair accessible
Partic in Fedlink; OCLC Online Computer Library Center, Inc; OCLC-LVIS
Special Services for the Blind - Aids for in-house use; Playaways (bks on MP3); Talking bks & player equip
Open Mon-Thurs 10-7:30, Fri 10-5, Sat 10-4, Sun 12-4
Restriction: External users must contact libr, Open to researchers by request, Restricted access

OGALLALA

P GOODALL CITY LIBRARY*, 203 West A St, 69153-2544. SAN 309-5711. Tel: 308-284-4354. Administration Tel: 308-284-8467. FAX: 308-284-6390. E-mail: goodall@megavision.com. Web Site: www.goodallcitylibrary.com. *Dir,* Kendra Caskey; E-mail: kcaskey@megavision.com; *Ad,* Shelley French; E-mail: lmcelvain@megavision.com; *Ch Serv Librn,* Carolyn Lowitz; E-mail: clowitz@megavision.com; Staff 1 (MLS 1)
Founded 1913. Pop 8,800; Circ 85,713
Library Holdings: CDs 69; Large Print Bks 863; Bk Titles 35,968; Per Subs 87; Talking Bks 1,527; Videos 1,033
Special Collections: Nebraska History & Western Culture
Automation Activity & Vendor Info: (Cataloging) Follett Software; (Circulation) Follett Software; (ILL) OCLC; (OPAC) Follett Software
Database Vendor: OCLC FirstSearch
Mem of Panhandle Libr Syst
Open Mon-Thurs 9-8, Fri 9-5, Sat 10-1
Friends of the Library Group

OMAHA

M ALEGENT HEALTH BERGAN MERCY MEDICAL CENTER*, John D Hartigan Medical Library, 7500 Mercy Rd, 68124-9832. SAN 325-3228. Tel: 402-398-6092. FAX: 402-398-6923. *Librn,* Cindy Perkins; Staff 1 (MLS 1)
Founded 1975
Jul 2008-Jun 2009 Income $197,000. Mats Exp $197,000, Books $10,000, Per/Ser (Incl. Access Fees) $130,000, Other Print Mats $12,000, Electronic Ref Mat (Incl. Access Fees) $35,000. Sal $50,000
Library Holdings: e-books 3; High Interest/Low Vocabulary Bk Vols 80; Bk Titles 800; Bk Vols 824; Per Subs 187
Database Vendor: Cinahl, EBSCO Information Services, EBSCOhost, Majors
Partic in Info Consortium; Medical Library Association (MLA)
Open Mon-Fri 8-4

M BOY'S TOWN NATIONAL RESEARCH HOSPITAL*, Information Resources Center, 555 N 30th St, 68131. SAN 377-435X. Tel: 402-498-6511. FAX: 402-498-6351.
Library Holdings: Bk Vols 200
Partic in Info Consortium; Mid-Continental Regional Med Librs Asn

C CLARKSON COLLEGE LIBRARY*, 101 S 42nd St, 68131-2739. SAN 327-4764. Tel: 402-552-3387. FAX: 402-552-2899. E-mail: library@clarksoncollege.edu. Web Site: www.clarksoncollege.edu/library.htm. *Dir,* Nancy M Ralston; Tel: 402-552-2557, E-mail: ralston@clarksoncollege.edu; *Access Serv Librn,* Amy Masek; *Access Serv Librn,* Ann S Moore; *Res Librn,* Nicole Koborg; Staff 4 (MLS 4)
Highest Degree: Doctorate
Library Holdings: Bk Titles 8,000; Bk Vols 13,749; Per Subs 264
Automation Activity & Vendor Info: (Cataloging) Sydney; (Circulation) EOS International; (OPAC) EOS International
Database Vendor: EBSCOhost, OCLC FirstSearch, ProQuest, Wilson - Wilson Web
Partic in Docline; ICON Library Consortium; OCLC-LVIS
Open Mon-Thurs 8-8, Fri 8-5, Sat 9-5, Sun 1-8

CR COLLEGE OF SAINT MARY LIBRARY, 7000 Mercy Rd, 68106-2606. SAN 309-572X. Tel: 402-399-2471. Interlibrary Loan Service Tel: 402-399 2631. Reference Tel: 402-399-2468. FAX: 402-399-2686. E-mail: csmlibrary@csm.edu. Web Site: www.csm.edu/academics/library. *Dir,* Sara Williams; Tel: 402-399-2467, E-mail: swilliams@csm.edu; *ILL Librn,* Sister Judy Pat Healy; E-mail: jhealy@csm.edu; *Circ Supvr, Ref Librn,* Michael Steinbrink; E-mail: msteinbrink@csm.edu; *Archivist, Cataloger,* Danielle Kessler; Tel: 402-399-2464, E-mail: dkessler@csm.edu; Staff 4 (MLS 3, Non-MLS 1)
Founded 1923. Enrl 1,000; Fac 125; Highest Degree: Doctorate
Jul 2014-Jun 2015 Income $154,022. Mats Exp $133,649, Books $28,971, Per/Ser (Incl. Access Fees) $61,657, Electronic Ref Mat (Incl. Access Fees) $43,021. Sal $192,954 (Prof $157,343)
Library Holdings: AV Mats 1,999; e-books 15,193; Bk Vols 88,503; Per Subs 178
Subject Interests: Educ, Leadership, Nursing, Occupational therapy
Automation Activity & Vendor Info: (Acquisitions) OCLC; (Cataloging) OCLC Connexion; (Circulation) OCLC; (Course Reserve) OCLC; (ILL) OCLC; (OPAC) OCLC; (Serials) OCLC
Database Vendor: EBSCOhost, Electric Library, Elsevier, Gale Cengage Learning, LexisNexis, Medline, OCLC, OCLC ArticleFirst, OCLC CAMIO, OCLC FirstSearch, OCLC WorldShare Interlibrary Loan, OCLC Worldshare Management Services, PubMed, Westlaw, Wiley InterScience, Wilson - Wilson Web, WT Cox
Wireless access
Function: Archival coll, Copy machines, Electronic databases & coll, Fax serv, ILL available, Online cat, Orientations, Photocopying/Printing, Printer for laptops & handheld devices, Ref serv in person
Partic in Nebr Independent Col Libr Consortium; OCLC Online Computer Library Center, Inc
Open Mon-Thurs 7:30am-10pm, Fri 7:30-5, Sat 10-4, Sun 1-10
Restriction: Open to students, fac, staff & alumni, Pub use on premises

C CREIGHTON UNIVERSITY*, Reinert-Alumni Memorial Library, 2500 California Plaza, 68178-0209. SAN 350-2023. Tel: 402-280-2260. Interlibrary Loan Service Tel: 402-280-2219. Reference Tel: 402-280-2227. Administration Tel: 402-280-2706. Automation Services Tel: 402-280-3065. FAX: 402-280-2435. E-mail: askus@creighton.edu. Web Site: reinert.creighton.edu. *Dir,* Michael J LaCroix; Tel: 402-280-2217, E-mail: michaellacroix@creighton.edu; *Head, Access Serv,* Debra Sturges; Tel: 402-280-4756, E-mail: dsturges@creighton.edu; *Head, Ref (Info Serv),* Mary Nash; Tel: 402-280-2226, E-mail: mdnash@creighton.edu; *Head, Tech Serv & Electronic Res,* Rick Kerns; Tel: 402-280-2228, E-mail: rickkerns@creighton.edu; *Ref Librn/Instrul Serv,* Maoria Kirker; Tel: 402-280-2927, E-mail: mjkirker@creighton.edu; *Syst Librn,* Becky Wymer; Tel: 402-280-2220, E-mail: beckywymer@creighton.edu; *Archivist,* David Crawford; Tel: 402-280-2746, E-mail: davidecrawford@creighton.edu; *Cat,* Arnette Payne; Tel: 402-280-1806, E-mail: apayne@creighton.edu; *ILL,* Lynn Schneidermann; E-mail: lynns@creighton.edu; *Ref, Webmaster,* Christine Carmichael; Tel: 402-280-1757, E-mail: christinecarmichael@creighton.edu; *Ref Serv,* Mike Poma; Tel: 402-280-2298, E-mail: mapoma@creighton.edu. Subject Specialists: *Soc sci,* Maoria Kirker; Staff 20 (MLS 9, Non-MLS 11)
Founded 1878. Enrl 4,949; Fac 291; Highest Degree: Doctorate
Jul 2012-Jun 2013 Income (Main Library Only) $3,080,099. Mats Exp $3,130,447, Books $221,076, Per/Ser (Incl. Access Fees) $504,270, Manu Arch $15,000, Other Print Mats $86,211, Micro $32,439, AV Mat $20,443, Electronic Ref Mat (Incl. Access Fees) $382,509, Presv $4,500. Sal $1,083,372 (Prof $703,718)
Library Holdings: AV Mats 11,362; CDs 3,462; DVDs 3,037; e-books 114,380; e-journals 56,798; Electronic Media & Resources 328; Bk Titles 369,000; Bk Vols 383,000; Per Subs 420; Videos 3,865
Special Collections: Early Christian Writings, bks, micro; Fables of Aesop & La Fontaine. US Document Depository
Subject Interests: Physics, Theol
Automation Activity & Vendor Info: (Acquisitions) SirsiDynix; (Cataloging) SirsiDynix; (Circulation) SirsiDynix; (Course Reserve) Docutek; (ILL) OCLC; (OPAC) SirsiDynix; (Serials) SirsiDynix
Database Vendor: American Physical Society, American Psychological Association (APA), ARTstor, Bowker, Cambridge Scientific Abstracts, Career Guidance Foundation, Dialog, Dun & Bradstreet, ebrary, EBSCOhost, Elsevier MDL, Factiva.com, Gale Cengage Learning, H W Wilson, Haworth Pres Inc, Ingenta, ISI Web of Knowledge, JSTOR, LexisNexis, Marquis Who's Who, Nature Publishing Group, OCLC FirstSearch, OCLC WebJunction, OCLC WorldShare Interlibrary Loan, Olive Software, Inc, OVID Technologies, ProQuest, ReferenceUSA, RefWorks, Sage, ScienceDirect, SirsiDynix, Wilson - Wilson Web, YBP Library Services
Wireless access
Publications: Creighton Cornerstone (Newsletter)
Partic in OCLC Online Computer Library Center, Inc; OCLC-LVIS
Open Mon-Thurs 6:30am-2am, Fri 6:30am-11pm, Sat 9am-10pm, Sun 10am-2am
Restriction: Access for corporate affiliates, Borrowing privileges limited to anthropology fac & libr staff, Borrowing privileges limited to fac & registered students, By permission only, Circ to mem only, Circ to mil employees only, Circulates for staff only, Clients only, Closed stack, Co libr

Departmental Libraries:

CM HEALTH SCIENCES LIBRARY-LEARNING RESOURCE CENTER, 2770 Webster St, 68178-0210. (Mail add: 2500 California Plaza, 68178), SAN 350-2058. Tel: 402-280-5108. Circulation Tel: 402-280-5109. Interlibrary Loan Service Tel: 402-280-5144. Reference Tel: 402-280-5138. Administration Tel: 402-280-5135. FAX: 402-280-5134. E-mail: refdesk@creighton.edu. Web Site: hsl.creighton.edu. *Dir,* James Bothmer; Tel: 402-280-5120, E-mail: jbothmer@creighton.edu; *Dept Head,* Diana Boone; Tel: 402-280-5175, E-mail: dboone@creighton.edu; *Head, Info Serv,* Richard Jizba; Tel: 402-280-5142, E-mail: rjizba@creighton.edu; *Head, User Serv,* John Mitchell; Tel: 402-280-4127, E-mail: jmitchell@creighton.edu; *Outreach Serv Librn,*

Judi Bergjord; Tel: 402-280-5199; *Educ Coordr,* Jeanne Burke; *Ser,* Bryan Stack; Tel: 402-280-5137. Subject Specialists: *Educ,* Jeanne Burke; Staff 22 (MLS 10, Non-MLS 12)
Founded 1977. Enrl 2,200; Fac 641; Highest Degree: Doctorate
Jul 2011-Jun 2012 Income $355,211. Mats Exp $1,342,988, Books $14,576, Per/Ser (Incl. Access Fees) $1,046,000, AV Mat $23,110, Electronic Ref Mat (Incl. Access Fees) $251,302, Presv $8,000. Sal $1,005,820 (Prof $715,865)
Library Holdings: AV Mats 4,598; e-books 12,635; e-journals 4,056; Bk Titles 32,610; Per Subs 249
Special Collections: Mulitcultural Health. State Document Depository; US Document Depository
Subject Interests: Dentistry, Med, Nursing, Occupational therapy, Pharm, Phys therapy
Automation Activity & Vendor Info: (Acquisitions) SIRSI-iLink; (Cataloging) OCLC; (Circulation) SIRSI-iLink; (OPAC) SIRSI-iLink; (Serials) SerialsSolutions
Database Vendor: Annual Reviews, BioOne, Bowker, CRC Press/Taylor & Francis Group, ebrary, EBSCO - WebFeat, EBSCO Information Services, Elsevier, McGraw-Hill, MD Consult, Medline, Micromedex, Nature Publishing Group, OCLC ArticleFirst, Oxford Online, Project MUSE, RefWorks, Sage, SerialsSolutions, Springer-Verlag, STAT!Ref (Teton Data Systems), Thomson - Web of Science, UpToDate, Wiley InterScience
Function: Audio & video playback equip for onsite use, CD-ROM, Computer training, Computers for patron use, Copy machines, Distance learning, Doc delivery serv, e-mail & chat, e-mail serv, E-Reserves, Electronic databases & coll, Exhibits, Handicapped accessible, Health sci info serv, ILL available, Learning ctr, Online cat, Online searches, Orientations, Outreach serv, Outside serv via phone, mail, e-mail & web, Photocopying/Printing, Pub access computers, Ref & res, Ref serv available, Ref serv in person, Res libr, Res performed for a fee, Telephone ref, VHS videos
Partic in ICON Library Consortium; MCMLA
Publications: BicInformer (Newsletter)
Special Services for the Deaf - Accessible learning ctr
Open Mon-Thurs 7am-Midnight, Fri 7am-10pm, Sat 10-6, Sun 10am-Midnight

CL KLUTZNICK LAW LIBRARY - MCGRATH NORTH MULLIN & KRATZ LEGAL RESEARCH CENTER, School of Law, 2500 California Plaza, 68178-0340, SAN 350-2082. Tel: 402-280-2251, 402-280-2875. FAX: 402-280-2244. E-mail: lawref@lists.creighton.edu. Web Site: law.creighton.edu/current-students/law-library. *Dir,* Kay L Andrus; *Ref/Electronic Serv Librn,* Troy Johnson; *Acq, Ser,* Heather Buckwalter; *Cat, Ref,* Corinne Jacox; *Ref,* George Butterfield; Staff 12 (MLS 5, Non-MLS 7)
Founded 1904. Enrl 435; Fac 26
Library Holdings: CDs 263; DVDs 237; e-books 42,290; e-journals 2,574; Microforms 96,883; Bk Titles 48,050; Bk Vols 205,389; Videos 138
Special Collections: History of Anglo-American Law (Te Poel Coll); US Supreme Court Coll, briefs & rec. US Document Depository
Subject Interests: Jury instructions
Automation Activity & Vendor Info: (OPAC) SirsiDynix
Database Vendor: HeinOnline, LexisNexis, OCLC FirstSearch, Westlaw
Partic in Mid-America Law Library Consortium; OCLC Online Computer Library Center, Inc
Publications: Acquisitions List (Monthly)
Open Mon-Thurs 7am-Midnight, Fri 7am-8pm, Sat 9-8, Sun 10am-Midnight

GL DOUGLAS COUNTY DISTRICT COURT*, Law Library, Hall of Justice, 1701 Farnam St, 1st Flr, 68183. SAN 309-5738. Tel: 402-444-7174. FAX: 402-444-3927. *Librn,* Ann Borer; E-mail: aborer@co.douglas.ne.us; Staff 2 (MLS 1, Non-MLS 1)
Founded 1905
Library Holdings: Bk Vols 25,000; Per Subs 12
Database Vendor: LexisNexis, Westlaw
Function: Res libr
Publications: Nebraska Bankruptcy Service
Open Mon-Fri 8:30-4:30
Friends of the Library Group

S DOUGLAS COUNTY HISTORICAL SOCIETY*, Library Archives Center, 5730 N 30th St, No 11A, 68111. SAN 328-3178. Tel: 402-451-1013. FAX: 402-453-9448. E-mail: archivist@douglascohistory.org. Web Site: www.douglascohistory.org. *Exec Dir,* Kathy Aultz; *Res Librn,* Gary R Rosenberg
Library Holdings: Bk Titles 3,000; Per Subs 30
Special Collections: Company & Individual Official Archives of Douglas County: Documents to early 1800; Omaha World-Herald Newspaper Clipping Coll
Subject Interests: Local hist
Function: Photocopying/Printing, Ref serv available
Publications: History Lectures; Local Historical Works; Newsletter
Open Tues-Fri 10-4
Restriction: Non-circulating, Not a lending libr, Open to pub with supv only

S DOUGLAS COUNTY YOUTH CENTER LIBRARY*, 1301 S 41st St, 68105. SAN 377-5658. Tel: 402-444-1702, 402-444-7492. FAX: 402-444-4188.
Library Holdings: Bks on Deafness & Sign Lang 1; e-books 5; High Interest/Low Vocabulary Bk Vols 1,000; Large Print Bks 100; Bk Vols 5,000
Open Mon-Fri 7-3:30
Friends of the Library Group

SR FIRST CHRISTIAN CHURCH (DISCIPLES OF CHRIST) LIBRARY*, 6630 Dodge St, 68132-2742. SAN 328-5626. Tel: 402-558-1939. FAX: 402-558-1941. Web Site: www.firstchristian-omaha.org.
Library Holdings: Bk Vols 1,500; Per Subs 10
Open Mon-Fri 9-3, Sun 8-12

CR GRACE UNIVERSITY LIBRARY*, 823 Worthington, 68108-3642. (Mail add: 1311 S Ninth St, 68108-3629), SAN 309-5754. Tel: 402-449-2893. FAX: 402-449-2919. Web Site: www.graceuniversity.edu/libraryindex.cfm. *Dir,* Stanley Udd; E-mail: sudd@graceu.edu; Staff 2 (MLS 1, Non-MLS 1)
Founded 1943. Enrl 544; Fac 27; Highest Degree: Master
Library Holdings: e-books 18,487; Bk Titles 41,719; Bk Vols 53,894; Per Subs 233
Subject Interests: Biblical studies, Counseling, Theol
Automation Activity & Vendor Info: (Acquisitions) SirsiDynix; (Cataloging) SirsiDynix; (Circulation) SirsiDynix; (Course Reserve) SirsiDynix; (OPAC) SirsiDynix; (Serials) SirsiDynix
Database Vendor: EBSCOhost, OCLC FirstSearch
Partic in Nebr Independent Col Libr Consortium
Open Mon-Thurs 7:30am-10:30pm, Fri 8-5, Sat 10-5:30

M IMMANUEL MEDICAL CENTER*, Professional Library, 6901 N 72nd St, 68122. SAN 325-3767. Tel: 402-572-2121, 402-572-2345. FAX: 402-572-2797. Web Site: www.alegent.org. *Librn,* Joy A Winkler
Library Holdings: Bk Titles 750; Per Subs 225
Restriction: Staff use only

S JOSLYN ART MUSEUM*, Milton R & Pauline S Abrahams Library, 2200 Dodge St, 68102-1296. SAN 309-5770. Tel: 402-661-3300. FAX: 402-342-2376. Web Site: www.joslyn.org. *Head Librn,* Peter Konin
Founded 1931
Library Holdings: Bk Vols 30,000; Per Subs 50; Spec Interest Per Sub 45
Special Collections: Artists' Clipping Files; Publications of the Metropolitan Museum of Art, microfiche set; Western Americana: Frontier History of the Trans-Mississippi West, microfilm set
Subject Interests: Art, Native Am art, Western Am art
Automation Activity & Vendor Info: (Cataloging) TLC (The Library Corporation); (Circulation) TLC (The Library Corporation); (OPAC) TLC (The Library Corporation)
Partic in OCLC Online Computer Library Center, Inc; OCLC-LVIS
Open Thurs & Sat 10-1, Sun 12-4
Restriction: Not a lending libr

R KRIPKE JEWISH FEDERATION LIBRARY, 333 S 132nd St, 68154. SAN 309-5762. Tel: 402-334-6462. FAX: 402-334-6464. E-mail: jewishlibrary@jewishomaha.org. Web Site: www.jewishomaha.org/education/kripke-jewish-federation-library. *Libr Spec,* Shirly Banner; E-mail: sbanner@jewishomaha.org; Staff 6 (MLS 1, Non-MLS 5)
Founded 1945
Library Holdings: Bk Titles 40,000; Per Subs 50
Subject Interests: Archeology, Bible, Comparative relig, Holocaust, Israel, Judaica, Middle East
Automation Activity & Vendor Info: (Cataloging) Follett Software; (Circulation) Follett Software
Database Vendor: Gale Cengage Learning
Wireless access
Publications: Index to the Omaha Jewish Press
Open Mon-Thurs 9-6, Fri 9-4
Friends of the Library Group

L KUTAK ROCK LLP*, Law Library, 1650 Farnam St, 68102-2186. SAN 327-490X. Tel: 402-346-6000. FAX: 402-346-1148. Web Site: www.kutakrock.com. *Librn,* Lynn Koperski; E-mail: lynn.koperski@kutakrock.com
Library Holdings: Bk Vols 10,000; Per Subs 100
Wireless access
Restriction: Open by appt only

L LAMSON, DUGAN & MURRAY LLP*, Law Library, 10306 Regency Pkwy Dr, 68114. SAN 377-3868. Tel: 402-397-7300. FAX: 402-397-7824. Web Site: www.ldmlaw.com. *Librn,* Evelyn Owens
Library Holdings: Bk Vols 20,000; Per Subs 50
Database Vendor: LexisNexis

J METROPOLITAN COMMUNITY COLLEGE LIBRARY*, 30th & Fort Sts, 68103. (Mail add: PO Box 3777, 68103-0777), SAN 350-2112. Tel: 402-457-2368. Toll Free Tel: 800-228-9553. FAX: 402-457-2655. Web Site: www.mccneb.edu/library. *Dean,* Susan R Raftery; E-mail: sraftery@mccneb.edu; *Automation Syst Coordr,* Michael S Blanchard; Tel: 402-457-2521, E-mail: mblanchard@mccneb.edu; *Acq,* Dorothy Mittlieder; Tel: 402-457-2762, E-mail: dmittlieder@mccneb.edu; *Cat,* Diane Schram; Tel: 402-457-2761, E-mail: dschram@mccneb.edu; *ILL,* Pam Neseth; Tel: 402-457-2760, E-mail: pneseth@mccneb.edu; Staff 20 (MLS 1, Non-MLS 19)
Founded 1974. Enrl 12,000; Fac 186; Highest Degree: Associate
Library Holdings: AV Mats 7,995; Bks on Deafness & Sign Lang 649; e-books 21,547; High Interest/Low Vocabulary Bk Vols 246; Large Print Bks 18; Bk Titles 34,899; Bk Vols 44,851; Per Subs 575
Automation Activity & Vendor Info: (Acquisitions) Infor Library & Information Solutions; (Cataloging) Infor Library & Information Solutions; (Circulation) Infor Library & Information Solutions; (OPAC) Infor Library & Information Solutions; (Serials) Infor Library & Information Solutions
Database Vendor: EBSCOhost, Gale Cengage Learning, LexisNexis, OCLC FirstSearch, ProQuest, Wilson - Wilson Web
Function: Handicapped accessible, ILL available, Photocopying/Printing, Ref serv available, Telephone ref, Wheelchair accessible
Mem of Eastern Libr Syst
Special Services for the Deaf - Bks on deafness & sign lang; TDD equip
Open Mon-Fri 7:30am-10pm, Sat 7:30-4:30, Sun 1-5

Departmental Libraries:

ELKHORN VALLEY CAMPUS, 204th & W Dodge Rd, 68022. (Mail add: PO Box 3777, 68103-0777), SAN 350-2201. Tel: 402-289-1206. FAX: 402-289-1286. *Libr Supvr,* Scott Mahoney; E-mail: smahoney@mccneb.edu

FORT OMAHA CAMPUS, 30th & Fort St, 68111. (Mail add: PO Box 3777, 68103-0777), SAN 350-2147. Tel: 402-457-2306. FAX: 402-457-2859. *Libr Supvr,* Ann Wills; Tel: 402-457-2630, E-mail: awills@mccneb.edu

SOUTH OMAHA CAMPUS, Mahoney Bldg, 2909 Edward "Babe" Gomez Ave, 68107. (Mail add: PO Box 3777, 68103-0777), SAN 350-2171. Tel: 402-738-4506. FAX: 402-738-4738. *Br Mgr,* Scott Mahoney; E-mail: smahoney@mccneb.edu

S NATIONAL PARK SERVICE*, Midwest Regional Library, 601 Riverfront Dr, 68102-4226. SAN 309-5797. Tel: 402-661-3006. *Dir,* Verne Haselwood; Staff 1 (MLS 1)
Founded 1938
Library Holdings: Bk Titles 9,000
Special Collections: Early Western Travels; Pacific Railroad Surveys; Westerners Brand Book
Subject Interests: Archaeology, Botany, Ethnology, Geol, Western Americana, Zoology
Publications: National Park Service Reports on the Midwest Region
Restriction: Employees only

CM NEBRASKA METHODIST COLLEGE*, John Moritz Library, 720 N 87th St, 68114. SAN 327-4888. Tel: 402-354-7251. Interlibrary Loan Service Tel: 402-354-7248. Reference Tel: 402-354-7246. FAX: 402-354-7250. E-mail: library@methodistcollege.edu. Web Site: www.methodistcollege.edu/library. *Dir,* Beverly Sedlacek; Tel: 402-354-7249, E-mail: bev.sedlacek@methodistcollege.edu; *Libr Asst, ILL,* Tem Adair; E-mail: tem.adair@methodistcollege.edu; *Libr Asst, Tech,* Sonja Maddox; Tel: 402-354-7252, E-mail: sonja.maddox@methodistcollege.edu. Subject Specialists: *Nursing,* Beverly Sedlacek; Staff 3 (MLS 1, Non-MLS 2)
Enrl 800; Fac 100; Highest Degree: Master
Library Holdings: DVDs 100; e-books 50; e-journals 2,000; Bk Titles 4,000; Per Subs 120; Videos 150
Subject Interests: Nursing, Nursing educ
Automation Activity & Vendor Info: (Acquisitions) SirsiDynix; (Cataloging) SirsiDynix; (Circulation) SirsiDynix; (Course Reserve) SirsiDynix; (Media Booking) SirsiDynix; (OPAC) SirsiDynix; (Serials) SirsiDynix
Database Vendor: EBSCOhost, OCLC FirstSearch, OCLC WorldShare Interlibrary Loan, OVID Technologies, PubMed, ScienceDirect, SirsiDynix, STAT!Ref (Teton Data Systems), WT Cox
Wireless access
Partic in National Network of Libraries of Medicine; OCLC-LVIS
Open Mon-Thurs 8am-11pm, Fri 8-4:30, Sun 3-11

S OMAHA CORRECTIONAL CENTER LIBRARY*, 2323 East Ave J, 68111. SAN 377-4511. Tel: 402-595-3964. FAX: 402-595-2227. *Dir,* Denise Morton
Library Holdings: Bk Vols 10,600; Per Subs 29
Automation Activity & Vendor Info: (Cataloging) LiBRARYSOFT; (Circulation) LiBRARYSOFT; (ILL) OCLC; (OPAC) LiBRARYSOFT
Partic in Nebr Inst Librs
Open Mon-Sun 8-4

P OMAHA PUBLIC LIBRARY*, W Dale Clark Library, 215 S 15th St, 68102-1629. SAN 350-2295. Tel: 402-444-4800. Circulation Tel: 402-444-4809. Interlibrary Loan Service Tel: 402-444-4857. Administration Tel: 402-444-4844. FAX: 402-444-4504. TDD: 402-444-3825. E-mail: webdesk@omahapubliclibrary.org. Web Site: www.omahapubliclibrary.org. *Libr Dir,* Gary Wasdin; E-mail: gwasdin@omahalibrary.org; *Asst Dir,* Maggie Tarelli-Falcon; Tel: 402-444-4854, E-mail: mtarelli-falcon@omahapubliclibrary.org; *Bus Mgr,* Lori Wynn; Tel: 402-444-4815, E-mail: llwynn@omahalibrary.org; *Circ Mgr,* Deb Barelos; E-mail: dbarelos@omahalibrary.org; *Commun Serv Mgr,* Linda S Trout; Tel: 402-444-4838, E-mail: ltrout@omahapubliclibrary.org; *Fac Mgr,* Mary Griffin; Tel: 402-444-3470, E-mail: mgriffin@omahapubliclibrary.org; *Mkt Mgr,* Emily Getzschman; E-mail: egetzschman@omahalibrary.org; *Tech Mgr,* Patrick Esser; E-mail: pesser@omahalibrary.org; *Adult Serv Coordr,* Amy Mather; E-mail: amather@omahalibrary.org; *Staff Develop Coordr,* Terry Wingate; Tel: 402-444-4835, E-mail: twingate@omahapubliclibrary.org; *Youth Serv Coordr,* Position Currently Open; Staff 47 (MLS 41, Non-MLS 6)
Founded 1872. Pop 552,806; Circ 299,219
Library Holdings: AV Mats 86,329; CDs 17,571; Large Print Bks 16,955; Bk Titles 255,160; Bk Vols 898,395; Per Subs 2,282; Talking Bks 29,918; Videos 19,671
Special Collections: African-American History (Black Culture Coll); Local History Coll; TransMississippi Exposition Photo Coll. State Document Depository; US Document Depository
Subject Interests: Foreign lang, Genealogy, Local hist
Automation Activity & Vendor Info: (Acquisitions) SirsiDynix; (Cataloging) SirsiDynix; (Circulation) SirsiDynix; (ILL) OCLC; (OPAC) SirsiDynix; (Serials) SirsiDynix
Database Vendor: EBSCOhost, Gale Cengage Learning, OCLC FirstSearch, ProQuest, SirsiDynix, Wilson - Wilson Web
Wireless access
Function: Archival coll, AV serv, Handicapped accessible, Home delivery & serv to Sr ctr & nursing homes, Homebound delivery serv, ILL available, Online searches, Prog for adults, Prog for children & young adult, Ref serv available, Summer reading prog, Telephone ref, Wheelchair accessible
Publications: BST Bulletin (Monthly); Omaha Public Library Connection (Quarterly)
Special Services for the Deaf - TTY equip
Special Services for the Blind - Bks on cassette; Bks on CD; Braille equip; Home delivery serv; Large print & cassettes; Large print bks
Open Mon-Thurs 10-8, Fri & Sat 10-6, Sun 1-6
Friends of the Library Group

Branches: 10

MILTON R ABRAHAMS BRANCH, 5111 N 90th St, 68134, SAN 329-6032. Tel: 402-444-6284. FAX: 402-444-6590. *Br Mgr,* Susan Thornton
Founded 1988. Circ 344,719
Library Holdings: AV Mats 11,987; Bk Vols 94,628
Open Mon, Tues & Thurs 10-8, Wed, Fri & Sat 10-6, Sun 1-6
Friends of the Library Group

BENSON, 6015 Binney St, 68104, SAN 350-2325. Tel: 402-444-4846. FAX: 402-444-6595. *Br Mgr,* Steiner Rachel
Founded 1923. Circ 149,261
Library Holdings: AV Mats 6,913; Bk Vols 57,528
Open Tues & Wed 10-8, Thurs, Fri & Sat 10-6
Friends of the Library Group

WILLA CATHER BRANCH, 1905 S 44th St, 68105-2807, SAN 350-235X. Tel: 402-444-4851. FAX: 402-444-6662. *Br Mgr,* Edgington Evonne
Founded 1956. Circ 150,364
Library Holdings: AV Mats 6,133; Bk Vols 49,471
Open Tues & Thurs 10-8, Wed, Fri & Sat 10-6
Friends of the Library Group

FLORENCE, 2920 Bondesson, 68112, SAN 350-2384. Tel: 402-444-5299. FAX: 402-444-6607. *Br Mgr,* Gloria Sorensen
Founded 1923. Circ 73,585
Library Holdings: AV Mats 4,213; Bk Vols 34,517
Open Mon, Thurs & Sat 10-6, Tues & Wed 10-8
Friends of the Library Group

BESS JOHNSON ELKHORN PUBLIC LIBRARY, 2100 Reading Plaza, Elkhorn, 68022. (Mail add: PO Box 674, Elkhorn, 68022-0674), SAN 309-4537. Tel: 402-289-4367. FAX: 402-289-0420. *Br Mgr,* Wendy Anderson; E-mail: wanderson@omahalibrary.org
Pop 7,635; Circ 41,485

Library Holdings: Bk Vols 37,264; Per Subs 60
Open Mon-Thurs 10-9, Fri & Sat 10-5
MILLARD, 13214 Westwood Lane, 68144, SAN 350-2449. Tel: 402-444-4848. FAX: 402-444-6623. *Br Mgr,* Lois Imig
Founded 1952. Circ 827,517
Library Holdings: AV Mats 12,206; Bk Vols 129,033
Open Mon-Wed 10-8, Thurs-Sat 10-6, Sun 1-6
Friends of the Library Group
A V SORENSEN BRANCH, 4808 Cass St, 68132–3031, SAN 350-2503. Tel: 402-444-5274. FAX: 402-444-6592. *Br Mgr,* Lucy Lewis
Founded 1976. Circ 119,065
Library Holdings: AV Mats 5,864; Bk Vols 41,200
Open Tues & Thurs 10-8, Wed, Fri & Sat 10-6
Friends of the Library Group
SOUTH OMAHA, 2808 Q St, 68107, SAN 350-2538. Tel: 402-444-4850. FAX: 402-444-6644. *Br Mgr,* Norma Pountney; E-mail: npountney@omahalibrary.org
Founded 1904. Circ 82,860
Library Holdings: AV Mats 5,034; Bk Vols 41,865
Special Collections: ESL Materials
Open Tues & Wed 10-7, Thurs-Sat 10-6
Friends of the Library Group
W CLARKE SWANSON BRANCH, 9101 W Dodge Rd, 68114–3305, SAN 350-2562. Tel: 402-444-4852. FAX: 402-444-6651. *Br Mgr,* Rachel Steiner; Tel: 402-444-5492, E-mail: rsteiner@omahalibrary.org
Founded 1966. Circ 235,860
Library Holdings: AV Mats 9,084; Bk Vols 103,355
Special Collections: Children's Historic Literature Coll
Open Tues & Wed 10-8, Thurs-Sat 10-6
Friends of the Library Group
CHARLES B WASHINGTON BRANCH, 2868 Ames Ave, 68111–2426, SAN 350-2473. Tel: 402-444-4849. FAX: 402-444-6658. *Br Mgr,* Joanne Ferguson Cavanaugh; E-mail: jferguson@omahalibrary.org
Founded 1921. Circ 34,354
Library Holdings: AV Mats 4,222; Bk Vols 36,239
Special Collections: African-American History (Black Culture Coll)
Open Mon-Wed 10–8, Thurs-Sat 10–6
Friends of the Library Group

S OMAHA WORLD-HERALD LIBRARY*, 1314 Douglas St, Ste 700, 68102. SAN 325-0938. Tel: 402-444-1000. FAX: 402-345-0183. Web Site: www.omaha.com. *Chief Librn,* Jeanne Hauser; Tel: 402-444-1012, E-mail: jeanne.hauser@owh.com; Staff 5 (Non-MLS 5)
Founded 1900
Library Holdings: Bk Titles 150; Bk Vols 400
Restriction: Not open to pub

A UNITED STATES ARMY*, Corps of Engineers Omaha District Library, 1616 Capitol Ave, Rm 764, 68102-4909. SAN 309-5827. Tel: 402-995-2534, 402-995-2535. FAX: 402-995-2623. E-mail: cenwo.library@usace.army.mil. Web Site: www.nwd.usace.army.mil/im/library/home.asp. *Librn,* Barbara L Slater; E-mail: barbra.l.slater@usace.army.mil; Staff 1 (MLS 1)
Library Holdings: Bk Titles 8,862; Bk Vols 13,665; Per Subs 100
Special Collections: Engineering Design Memo Coll; Sediment Series Coll
Subject Interests: Eng, Law
Automation Activity & Vendor Info: (Cataloging) EOS International; (Circulation) EOS International; (ILL) OCLC; (OPAC) EOS International; (Serials) EOS International
Function: Mail & tel request accepted, Online cat, Online ref, Online searches, Scanner, Telephone ref
Partic in OCLC Online Computer Library Center, Inc
Open Mon-Fri 8-4
Restriction: Authorized personnel only, Circ limited, Co libr, Employees only, Not open to pub, Photo ID required for access

G US COURT LIBRARY - EIGHTH CIRCUIT*, Omaha Branch, 111 S 18th Plaza, Ste 4104, 68102-1322. SAN 325-4321. Tel: 402-661-7590. FAX: 402-661-7591. *Librn,* Jeri Kay Hopkins
Library Holdings: Bk Vols 15,000; Per Subs 16
Open Mon-Fri 8-4:30

C UNIVERSITY OF NEBRASKA AT OMAHA*, Dr C C & Mabel L Criss Library, 6001 Dodge St, 68182-0237. SAN 309-5835. Tel: 402-554-2640. Circulation Tel: 402-554-3206. Interlibrary Loan Service Tel: 402-554-3209. Reference Tel: 402-554-2661. Toll Free Tel: 800-858-8648, Ext 43206. FAX: 402-554-3215. Interlibrary Loan Service FAX: 402-554-3593. Web Site: library.unomaha.edu/. *Actg Dean, Libr Serv,* Audrey DeFrank; Tel: 402-554-3200, E-mail: adefrank@unomaha.edu; *Dir of Coll,* James Shaw; Tel: 402-554-2225, E-mail: jshaw@unomaha.edu; *Dir, Patron Serv,* Joyce Neujahr; Tel: 402-554-3607, E-mail: jneujahr@unomaha.edu; *Dir, Virtual Serv,* Rene Erlandson; Tel: 402-554-2144, E-mail: rerlandson@unomaha.edu; *Bus Mgr,* Sarah K Grieb; Tel: 402-554-2916, E-mail: skgrieb@unomaha.edu; *Coll Develop Librn, Spec Coll,* Robert Nash; Tel: 402-554-2884, E-mail: rnash@unomaha.edu; *Electronic Res Coordr,* John Reidelbach; Tel: 402-554-2846, E-mail: jreidelb@unomaha.edu; Staff 20 (MLS 13, Non-MLS 7)
Founded 1908. Enrl 15,300; Fac 723; Highest Degree: Doctorate
Library Holdings: Bk Vols 750,000
Special Collections: Arthur Paul Afghanistan Coll; Icarian Community Coll; Mary L Richmond - Cummings Press Coll; Nebraska Authors & History; Omaha Federal Writers Project Papers (WPA). State Document Depository; US Document Depository
Automation Activity & Vendor Info: (Acquisitions) Innovative Interfaces, Inc; (Cataloging) Innovative Interfaces, Inc; (Circulation) Innovative Interfaces, Inc; (Course Reserve) Docutek; (ILL) OCLC; (OPAC) Innovative Interfaces, Inc; (Serials) Innovative Interfaces, Inc
Database Vendor: EBSCOhost, OCLC FirstSearch
Wireless access
Function: Archival coll, Art exhibits, Audio & video playback equip for onsite use, CD-ROM, Computers for patron use, Copy machines, Distance learning, e-mail serv, E-Reserves, Electronic databases & coll, Equip loans & repairs, Exhibits, Fax serv, Govt ref serv, Handicapped accessible, ILL available, Instruction & testing, Large print keyboards, Magnifiers for reading, Music CDs, Newsp ref libr, Online cat, Online info literacy tutorials on the web & in blackboard, Online ref, Online searches, Photocopying/Printing, Pub access computers, Ref & res, Ref serv available, Ref serv in person, Res libr, Scanner, Tax forms, VHS videos, Wheelchair accessible
Partic in Dialog Corp; OCLC Online Computer Library Center, Inc
Open Mon-Thurs 7am-Midnight, Fri 7-5, Sat 9-5, Sun Noon-Midnight
Friends of the Library Group

CM UNIVERSITY OF NEBRASKA MEDICAL CENTER*, McGoogan Library of Medicine, 600 S 42nd St, 68198-6705. (Mail add: 986705 Nebraska Medical Center, 68198-6705), SAN 350-2597. Tel: 402-559-7079. Circulation Tel: 402-559-4006. Interlibrary Loan Service Tel: 402-559-7085. Reference Tel: 402-559-6221. FAX: 402-559-5498. E-mail: askus@unmc.edu. Web Site: www.unmc.edu/library/. *Dir,* Emily McElroy; E-mail: emily.mcelroy@unmc.edu; *Assoc Dir,* Mary E Helms; Tel: 402-559-7099, E-mail: mhelms@unmc.edu; *Assoc Dir,* Marie A Reidelbach; Tel: 402-559-7087, E-mail: mreidelb@unmc.edu; *Syst Coordr,* Thomas F Gensichen; Tel: 402-559-8119, E-mail: tgenisch@unmc.edu; *Adminr,* Ann E Newman; E-mail: anewman@unmc.edu; *Cat,* Helen K Yam; Tel: 402-559-7091, E-mail: hyam@unmc.edu; *Circ,* Rodney W Cope; Tel: 402-559-4006, E-mail: rcope@unmc.edu; *Coll Develop,* Rose Schinker; Tel: 402-559-5418, E-mail: rschinke@unmc.edu; *ILL,* Sara Andrews; E-mail: sandrewl@unmc.edu; *Media Spec, Ad,* Stuart K Dayton; Tel: 402-559-6334, E-mail: sdayton@unmc.edu; *Ref Serv, YA,* Roxanne Cox; Tel: 402-559-7228, E-mail: rcox@unmc.edu; *Ser,* Sheryl L William; Tel: 402-559-7098, E-mail: swilliam@unmc.edu; Staff 37 (MLS 13, Non-MLS 24)
Founded 1902. Enrl 2,044; Fac 926; Highest Degree: Doctorate
Library Holdings: Bk Titles 65,294; Bk Vols 234,011; Per Subs 1,427
Special Collections: Consumer Health Information Resource Services Coll, bks, journals; History of Medicine, bks, memorabilia; Obstetrics & Gynecology (Moon Coll); Surgery & Related Subjects (H Winnett Orr Coll & American College of Surgeons Coll), bks, memorabilia
Subject Interests: Allied health, Med
Automation Activity & Vendor Info: (Cataloging) Innovative Interfaces, Inc; (Circulation) Innovative Interfaces, Inc; (ILL) OCLC; (Media Booking) Innovative Interfaces, Inc; (OPAC) Innovative Interfaces, Inc; (Serials) Innovative Interfaces, Inc
Database Vendor: EBSCOhost, OCLC FirstSearch
Publications: Focus on Friends (Semi-annual); Point of Access (Quarterly)
Partic in National Network of Libraries of Medicine Midcontinental Region
Open Mon-Thurs 7:30am-12am, Fri 7:30am-9pm, Sat 9-5, Sun 1-Midnight
Friends of the Library Group

GM VETERANS AFFAIRS MEDICAL LIBRARY*, 4101 Woolworth Ave, 68105. SAN 309-5843. Tel: 402-346-8800, Ext 3531. FAX: 402-449-0692. *Librn,* Darrel Willoughby; E-mail: darrel.willoughby@va.gov; Staff 1 (MLS 1)
Founded 1950
Library Holdings: Bk Titles 650; Per Subs 195; Videos 600
Subject Interests: Allied health, Med
Partic in Docline; Veterans Affairs Libr Network (VALNET)
Open Mon-Fri 8-4:30

O'NEILL

P O'NEILL PUBLIC LIBRARY, 601 E Douglas, 68763. SAN 309-586X. Tel: 402-336-3110. FAX: 402-336-3268. E-mail: oneilllibrary@hotmail.com. Web Site: www.oneillpubliclibrary.com. *Dir,* Position Currently Open; *Ch,* M Menish; *Asst Librn,* Sue Tooker
Founded 1913. Pop 3,700; Circ 84,000
Library Holdings: Bk Titles 27,000; Per Subs 138

Automation Activity & Vendor Info: (Acquisitions) Follett Software; (Cataloging) Follett Software; (Circulation) Follett Software; (ILL) OCLC ILLiad; (OPAC) Follett Software
Wireless access
Partic in OCLC Online Computer Library Center, Inc
Open Mon, Tues, Fri & Sat 10:30-5:30, Wed & Thurs 10:30-9
Friends of the Library Group

ORCHARD

P ORCHARD PUBLIC LIBRARY*, 232 Windom, 68764. (Mail add: PO Box 317, 68764-0317), SAN 309-5878. Tel: 402-893-4606. FAX: 402-893-4606. E-mail: orchpl@bloomnet.com. Web Site: orchardpubliclibrary.org. *Librn,* Linda Risinger; Staff 3 (Non-MLS 3)
Founded 1902. Pop 650; Circ 6,218
Library Holdings: AV Mats 363; Bk Titles 14,103; Per Subs 35; Talking Bks 215
Special Collections: Orchard News, 1902-to-date, 1903-1983 on micro-film
Database Vendor: OCLC FirstSearch, Wilson - Wilson Web
Function: Accelerated reader prog, Audio & video playback equip for onsite use, Bks on cassette, Bks on CD, Children's prog, Computers for patron use, Copy machines, e-mail & chat, Electronic databases & coll, Fax serv, Free DVD rentals, Handicapped accessible, Homebound delivery serv, ILL available, Online cat, Photocopying/Printing, Pub access computers, Ref serv in person, Scanner, Story hour, Summer reading prog, Tax forms, VHS videos, Web-catalog, Wheelchair accessible
Open Mon & Thurs 10-3 & 7-9, Wed 7pm-9pm, Sat 10-3
Friends of the Library Group

ORD

P ORD TOWNSHIP LIBRARY*, 1718 M St, 68862. (Mail add: PO Box 206, 68862-0206), SAN 309-5886. Tel: 308-728-3012. FAX: 308-728-3126. Web Site: www.ordlibrary.org. *Dir,* Kristi Hagstrom; E-mail: director@ordlibrary.org
Pop 3,000; Circ 18,000
Library Holdings: Bk Vols 23,000; Per Subs 65
Automation Activity & Vendor Info: (Cataloging) Biblionix; (Circulation) Biblionix; (ILL) OCLC WorldShare Interlibrary Loan; (OPAC) Biblionix
Wireless access
Partic in OCLC Online Computer Library Center, Inc
Open Mon, Wed & Fri 12-5:30, Tues & Thurs 12-8, Sat 1-4, Sun 2-4

ORLEANS

P CORDELIA B PRESTON MEMORIAL LIBRARY, 510 Orleans Ave, 68966. (Mail add: PO Box 430, 68966-0430), SAN 309-5894. Tel: 308-473-3425. FAX: 308-473-3425. E-mail: olibry@frontiernet.net. Web Site: libraries.ne.gov/orleans. *Librn,* Raylene Stephens; *Asst Librn,* Myrna Lennemann
Founded 1917. Pop 523; Circ 5,592
Library Holdings: Bk Vols 10,000; Per Subs 10
Special Collections: Civil War (War of Rebellion)
Automation Activity & Vendor Info: (Cataloging) Follett Software; (Circulation) Follett Software
Wireless access
Open Mon 3-8, Tues-Thurs 3-6, Sat 9-Noon
Friends of the Library Group

OSCEOLA

P OSCEOLA PUBLIC LIBRARY, 131 N Main, 68651. (Mail add: PO Box 448, 68651-0448), SAN 309-5908. Tel: 402-747-4301. FAX: 402-747-4991. E-mail: osceolalibrary@windstream.net. Web Site: libraries.ne.gov/osceola/. *Dir,* April Stevens
Founded 1895. Pop 1,400; Circ 10,000
Library Holdings: Audiobooks 150; CDs 70; DVDs 200; Large Print Bks 800; Bk Titles 13,200; Per Subs 47; Videos 400
Automation Activity & Vendor Info: (Cataloging) Follett Software; (Circulation) Follett Software; (OPAC) Follett Software
Wireless access
Open Mon & Fri 12:30-5:30, Wed 12:30-8, Sat 10-3
Friends of the Library Group

OSHKOSH

P OSHKOSH PUBLIC LIBRARY*, 307 W First St, 69154. (Mail add: PO Box 140, 69154-0140), SAN 309-5916. Tel: 308-772-4554. FAX: 308-772-4492. E-mail: oshpublib@embarqmail.com. Web Site: www.oshkoshpubliclibrary.org/. *Dir,* Carol Kyser; *Librn,* Roma Rogers; Staff 2 (Non-MLS 2)
Founded 1943. Pop 887; Circ 12,337
Library Holdings: Bk Titles 8,524; Per Subs 42; Talking Bks 279; Videos 430
Special Collections: Cake Pan Coll
Automation Activity & Vendor Info: (Cataloging) Follett Software; (Circulation) Follett Software; (ILL) OCLC
Mem of Panhandle Libr Syst
Partic in OCLC Online Computer Library Center, Inc
Open Mon 1-7, Tues-Fri 1-5:30
Friends of the Library Group

OSMOND

P OSMOND PUBLIC LIBRARY*, 412 N State St, 68765. (Mail add: PO Box 478, 68765-0478), SAN 309-5924. Tel: 402-748-3382. FAX: 402-748-3382. E-mail: ospuli@huntel.net. *Dir,* Linda Gutz; Staff 1 (Non-MLS 1)
Founded 1937. Pop 1,419; Circ 14,500
Library Holdings: AV Mats 807; Bks on Deafness & Sign Lang 10; Large Print Bks 185; Bk Vols 14,000; Per Subs 40; Talking Bks 212
Automation Activity & Vendor Info: (Cataloging) Follett Software
Open Mon, Tues, Thurs & Fri 2-6, Wed 2-8, Sat 9-Noon
Friends of the Library Group

OVERTON

P OVERTON COMMUNITY LIBRARY*, 407 Hwy 30, 68863. (Mail add: PO Box 117, 68863-0117), SAN 309-5932. Tel: 308-987-2543. *Dir,* Nancy Purintun
Pop 660; Circ 3,238
Library Holdings: Bk Vols 6,500
Open Mon & Fri (Winter) 2-5; Mon, Wed & Fri (Summer) 2-5

OXFORD

P OXFORD MUNICIPAL LIBRARY*, 411 Ogden St, 68967. (Mail add: PO Box 156, 68967-0156), SAN 309-5940. Tel: 308-824-3381. FAX: 308-824-3381. *Librn,* Abi Bauer
Founded 1941. Pop 1,109
Library Holdings: Bk Vols 14,000; Per Subs 36
Special Collections: American Heritage, History of the United States; Bess Streeter Aldrich; Civil War; Encyclopedia of Collectibles; Lexicon Universal - World Book; Louisa May Alcott; Mari Sandoz; Mark Twain; Nebraska Authors; The Old West; Time-Life, History of World War II; Vietnam, encyclopedia; Willa Cather; Winston Churchill; World War II; Zane Gray
Open Mon & Thurs 2-8, Tues, Wed & Sat 2-5, Fri 9-11 & 2-5

PALMER

P PALMER LIBRARY*, 202 Commercial St, 68864. (Mail add: PO Box 248, 68864-0248), SAN 309-5967. Tel: 308-894-5305. FAX: 308-894-8245. *Dir,* Mary Gregoski
Library Holdings: Bk Vols 12,000; Per Subs 20
Wireless access
Open Mon-Fri 8-3:30

PALMYRA

P PALMYRA MEMORIAL LIBRARY*, 525 Illinois Pl, 68418. SAN 322-6816. Tel: 402-780-5344. FAX: 402-780-5344. *Librn,* Glenda Willnerd
Pop 510; Circ 1,725
Library Holdings: CDs 30; Bk Vols 10,315; Talking Bks 35; Videos 47
Wireless access
Open Mon-11-6, Wed 3-8, Sun 12:30-5:30

PAPILLION

CR NEBRASKA CHRISTIAN COLLEGE*, Loren T & Melva M Swedburg Library, 12550 S 114th St, 68046. SAN 309-5622. Tel: 402-935-9400. FAX: 402-935-9500. Web Site: www.nechristian.edu. *Librn,* Linda Lu Lloyd; E-mail: llloyd@nechristian.edu; Staff 1 (MLS 1)
Founded 1945
Library Holdings: Bk Vols 27,000; Per Subs 173
Special Collections: Rare Bibles
Subject Interests: Christian church, Relig studies, Restoration hist
Automation Activity & Vendor Info: (Cataloging) Mandarin Library Automation; (Circulation) Mandarin Library Automation; (OPAC) Mandarin Library Automation
Wireless access
Open Mon-Thurs 7:30am-10pm, Fri 7:30-5, Sat 10-3, Sun 2-5 & 8-10

P SUMP MEMORIAL LIBRARY*, 222 N Jefferson St, 68046. SAN 309-5975. Tel: 402-597-2040. FAX: 402-339-8019. Web Site: www.sumplibrary.info. *Dir,* Robin R Clark; E-mail: robin.r.clark@gmail.com; *Youth Serv,* Cathy McMahon; Staff 5 (Non-MLS 5)
Founded 1921. Pop 15,700
Library Holdings: DVDs 540; Bk Vols 54,619; Per Subs 169; Talking Bks 2,337; Videos 1,104

Automation Activity & Vendor Info: (Cataloging) Follett Software; (Circulation) Follett Software; (OPAC) Follett Software
Database Vendor: OCLC FirstSearch
Wireless access
Special Services for the Deaf - Closed caption videos
Special Services for the Blind - Audio mat; BiFolkal kits; Bks on cassette; Bks on CD; Copier with enlargement capabilities; Descriptive video serv (DVS); Large print bks; Reader equip; Talking bks
Open Mon-Thurs 9-9, Fri & Sat 9-5, Sun 1-5
Friends of the Library Group

PAWNEE CITY

P PAWNEE CITY PUBLIC LIBRARY*, 735 Eighth St, 68420. (Mail add: PO Box 311, 68420-0311), SAN 309-5983. Tel: 402-852-2118. FAX: 402-852-3134. Web Site: pawnee.biblionix.com. *Dir,* Lola Seitz; Staff 2 (Non-MLS 2)
Founded 2011. Pop 932; Circ 12,151
Library Holdings: Bks on Deafness & Sign Lang 5; DVDs 668; Large Print Bks 1,041; Bk Titles 12,733; Talking Bks 271; Videos 608
Special Collections: Adult Fiction Coll; Children's Fiction Coll; Harold Lloyd Coll
Automation Activity & Vendor Info: (Cataloging) Biblionix; (Circulation) Biblionix; (OPAC) Biblionix
Function: VCDs
Mem of Southeast Library System (SELS)
Open Mon-Fri 9:30-12:30 & 1:30-6, Sat 9:30-1:30
Friends of the Library Group

PAXTON

P PAXTON PUBLIC LIBRARY*, 108 N Oak St, 69155. (Mail add: PO Box 278, 69155-0278), SAN 309-5991. Tel: 308-239-4763. E-mail: paxtonlibrary@nebnet.net. *Librn,* Dianne Jay; Staff 1 (MLS 1)
Founded 1932. Pop 1,175; Circ 3,878
Library Holdings: Large Print Bks 30; Bk Vols 8,590; Per Subs 28; Talking Bks 114; Videos 82
Special Collections: Local History Coll; Nebraska Coll
Mem of Panhandle Libr Syst
Open Mon 2-6:30, Tues 9-1, Thurs 3-6:30, Sat 9-2
Friends of the Library Group

PENDER

P HOUSE MEMORIAL PUBLIC LIBRARY*, 220 Thurston Ave, 68047. (Mail add: PO Box 509, 68047-0509), SAN 309-6009. Tel: 402-385-2521. FAX: 402-385-2521. E-mail: hmlibrary@huntel.net. *Dir,* Ann Bachman; *Asst Dir,* Donna McQuistan
Pop 1,148; Circ 18,298
Library Holdings: Bk Titles 14,000; Per Subs 70
Automation Activity & Vendor Info: (Cataloging) Follett Software; (Circulation) Follett Software; (OPAC) Follett Software
Open Mon & Thurs 2-8, Tues, Wed & Fri 2-5, Sat 10-4

PERU

C PERU STATE COLLEGE LIBRARY, 600 Hoyt St, 68421. SAN 309-6017. Tel: 402-872-2311. E-mail: library@peru.edu. Web Site: www.peru.edu/library. *Libr Dir,* Veronica McAsey; E-mail: vmcasey@peru.edu; Staff 3 (MLS 1, Non-MLS 2)
Founded 1867. Enrl 1,600; Fac 47; Highest Degree: Master
Library Holdings: e-books 240,000; Bk Titles 117,969
Special Collections: Oral History
Wireless access
Partic in OCLC Online Computer Library Center, Inc
Open Mon-Thurs 7:30am-9pm, Fri 7:30-5, Sun 2-9

PETERSBURG

P PETERSBURG PUBLIC LIBRARY*, 103 S Second St, 68652. (Mail add: PO Box 60, 68652-0060), SAN 325-2582. Tel: 402-386-5755. *Librn,* Belle Esau; E-mail: lbesau@yahoo.com
Founded 1984. Pop 380; Circ 917
Library Holdings: Bk Titles 5,000; Per Subs 40
Wireless access
Open Mon, Wed & Thurs 2-5

PIERCE

P LIED PIERCE PUBLIC LIBRARY*, 207 W Court St, 68767. (Mail add: PO Box 39, 68767-0039), SAN 309-6025. Tel: 402-329-6324. FAX: 402-329-6442. E-mail: pplib@ptcnet.net. Web Site: piercepubliclibrary.org. *Dir,* Dawnn Tucker; Staff 4 (Non-MLS 4)
Founded 1911. Pop 1,779; Circ 24,000
Library Holdings: Bk Vols 23,150; Per Subs 45
Automation Activity & Vendor Info: (Circulation) Follett Software
Database Vendor: OCLC FirstSearch
Open Mon & Wed 1-5:30 & 7-9, Tues & Thurs 10-12 & 1-5:30, Fri 1-5:30, Sat 10-4
Friends of the Library Group

PILGER

P PILGER PUBLIC LIBRARY*, 120 Main St, 68768. (Mail add: PO Box 54, 68768-0054), SAN 309-6033. Tel: 402-396-3550. FAX: 402-396-3550. E-mail: pilgerlibrary@cableone.net. *Librn,* Elaine Tobias
Founded 1934. Pop 378; Circ 2,500
Library Holdings: DVDs 350; Bk Vols 7,200; Per Subs 30; Talking Bks 38; Videos 127
Automation Activity & Vendor Info: (Acquisitions) LibraryWorld, Inc
Wireless access
Open Mon & Thurs 2-6, Wed 2-7, Sat 10-12

PLAINVIEW

P PLAINVIEW CARNEGIE PUBLIC LIBRARY, 102 S Main St, 68769. (Mail add: PO Box 728, 68769-0728), SAN 309-6041. Tel: 402-582-4507. FAX: 402-582-4813. E-mail: plibrary@plvwtelco.net. Web Site: www.libraries.ne.gov/plainview. *Dir,* Donna Christiansen; *Asst Librn,* LaJean Elwood
Founded 1917. Pop 1,483; Circ 14,592
Library Holdings: Audiobooks 275; Bk Vols 15,000; Per Subs 20; Videos 600
Wireless access
Open Mon, Thurs & Fri 1-5, Tues 10-6, Wed 12-8, Sat 10-2
Friends of the Library Group

PLATTSMOUTH

P PLATTSMOUTH PUBLIC LIBRARY*, 401 Ave A, 68048. SAN 309-605X. Tel: 402-296-4154. FAX: 402-296-4712. E-mail: plattsmouthpubliclibrary@hotmail.com. *Dir,* Karen Mier; *Circ,* Evis Zamora; Staff 12 (MLS 1, Non-MLS 11)
Founded 1885. Pop 6,887; Circ 52,344
Library Holdings: Bk Vols 40,897; Per Subs 96
Special Collections: Local & Nebraska History
Subject Interests: Local genealogy
Automation Activity & Vendor Info: (OPAC) Follett Software
Database Vendor: OCLC FirstSearch, Wilson - Wilson Web
Friends of the Library Group

PLYMOUTH

P PLYMOUTH LIBRARY*, 103 N Jefferson Ave, 68424-0378. (Mail add: PO Box 378, 68424). Tel: 402-656-4335. E-mail: plymouthlibrary@diodecom.net. *Dir,* Jenny Washburn
Pop 3,681
Library Holdings: AV Mats 50; Bk Vols 6,500
Wireless access
Open Mon & Fri (Winter) 9-1, Tues & Thurs 4-7:30; Mon, Wed & Fri (Summer) 9-1, Tues 4-7
Friends of the Library Group

POLK

P POLK PUBLIC LIBRARY*, 180 N Main St, 68654. (Mail add: PO Box 49, 68654-0049), SAN 309-6068. Tel: 402-765-7266. FAX: 402-765-7266. *Librn,* Mary Jane Nyberg; *Asst Librn,* Marie Brown; Staff 0.6 (Non-MLS 0.6)
Founded 1913. Pop 322; Circ 7,838
Oct 2006-Sept 2007 Income $24,702, State $676, City $16,087, County $2,000, Locally Generated Income $5,939. Mats Exp $3,364. Sal $11,395
Library Holdings: DVDs 93; Bk Titles 7,901; Per Subs 21; Talking Bks 54; Videos 475
Subject Interests: Nebr
Wireless access
Function: Adult bk club, Children's prog, Computers for patron use, Copy machines, Handicapped accessible, Holiday prog, Homebound delivery serv, ILL available, Prog for adults, Prog for children & young adult, Pub access computers, Story hour, Summer reading prog, VHS videos, Wheelchair accessible
Open Mon 1:30-4:30, Wed 1:30-5, Thurs 4:30-8, Sat 9-2

PONCA

P PONCA CARNEGIE LIBRARY*, 203 W Second St, 68770. (Mail add: PO Box 368, 68770-0368), SAN 309-6084. Tel: 402-755-2739. E-mail: poncalib@gpcom.net. Web Site: www.poncapubliclibrary.org. *Dir,* Beth Foulks; Staff 3 (Non-MLS 3)
Founded 1913. Pop 982; Circ 1,562
Library Holdings: Bk Titles 11,235; Per Subs 30

Special Collections: Dixon County Census, 1860-1930, microfilm; Lewis & Clark Materials; Newspapers, 1884-1996, microfilm
Subject Interests: Genealogy
Automation Activity & Vendor Info: (Cataloging) Follett Software; (Circulation) Follett Software
Wireless access
Open Tues 4-9, Wed & Fri 1-6, Sat 10-4

POTTER

P POTTER PUBLIC LIBRARY*, 333 Chestnut, 69156. (Mail add: PO Box 317, 69156-0317), SAN 377-192X. Tel: 308-879-4345. *Dir,* Stacie Hermes; Staff 1 (Non-MLS 1)
Pop 750; Circ 1,520
Sept 2006-Oct 2007 Income $6,800. Mats Exp $2,000, Books $1,800, Per/Ser (Incl. Access Fees) $150, Presv $50. Sal $4,300
Library Holdings: Bk Vols 7,000; Per Subs 10
Automation Activity & Vendor Info: (Circulation) JayWil Software Development, Inc
Wireless access
Mem of Panhandle Libr Syst
Special Services for the Blind - Talking bks
Open Wed 9-12 & 1-5, Sat 9-Noon

PRIMROSE

P PRIMROSE PUBLIC LIBRARY*, 229 Commercial St, 68655. (Mail add: 445 Walnut St, 68655-0005), SAN 377-1946, *Dir,* Sue McIntyre
Pop 140
Jul 2011-Jun 2012 Income $500. Mats Exp $367, Books $362, Other Print Mats $5
Library Holdings: Large Print Bks 20; Bk Vols 1,788

RALSTON

P HOLLIS & HELEN BARIGHT PUBLIC LIBRARY*, 5555 S 77th St, 68127-2899. SAN 309-6092. Tel: 402-331-7636. FAX: 402-331-1168. Web Site: ralstonlibrary.org. *Dir,* Francine Canfield; *Ch Serv,* Dee Huff; Staff 4.5 (MLS 2.5, Non-MLS 2)
Founded 1922. Pop 6,214; Circ 83,288
Oct 2012-Sept 2013 Income $512,000. Mats Exp $66,000, Books $42,000, Per/Ser (Incl. Access Fees) $4,000, AV Mat $10,000, Electronic Ref Mat (Incl. Access Fees) $10,000. Sal $247,000
Library Holdings: Bk Titles 27,650; Bk Vols 31,000; Per Subs 87
Automation Activity & Vendor Info: (OPAC) Innovative Interfaces, Inc - Millenium
Database Vendor: OCLC FirstSearch, OCLC WorldShare Interlibrary Loan, ReferenceUSA
Wireless access
Open Mon-Thurs 1-9, Fri & Sat 10-5, Sun 1-5
Friends of the Library Group

RANDOLPH

P THE LIED RANDOLPH PUBLIC LIBRARY*, 111 N Douglas St, 68771-5510. (Mail add: PO Box 307, 68771-0307), SAN 309-6106. Tel: 402-337-0046. FAX: 402-337-0046. E-mail: librarian@rlibrary.org. Web Site: www.rlibrary.org. *Dir,* Peggy Leiting
Founded 1918. Pop 930
Library Holdings: CDs 43; DVDs 65; Large Print Bks 40; Bk Vols 16,000; Per Subs 35; Talking Bks 52; Videos 360
Special Collections: Agriculture Coll; History Coll
Automation Activity & Vendor Info: (Cataloging) Follett Software; (Circulation) Follett Software
Wireless access
Open Mon, Tues & Thurs 10-12 & 1-6, Wed 10-12 & 1-8, Sat 10-12 & 1-4
Friends of the Library Group

RAVENNA

P RAVENNA PUBLIC LIBRARY*, 121 W Seneca St, 68869-1362. SAN 309-6114. Tel: 308-452-4213. FAX: 308-452-4210. E-mail: ravennapubliclibrary@nctc.net. Web Site: 162.127.106.25/opac/rpl/index.html. *Libr Dir,* Karrie Huryta; Staff 1 (Non-MLS 1)
Founded 1918. Pop 1,300; Circ 10,672
Library Holdings: Audiobooks 560; DVDs 85; Large Print Bks 480; Bk Titles 8,400; Per Subs 38; Videos 440
Automation Activity & Vendor Info: (OPAC) Book Systems
Wireless access
Function: Fax serv, Free DVD rentals, Home delivery & serv to Sr ctr & nursing homes, Homebound delivery serv, Online cat, Photocopying/Printing, Prog for children & young adult, Pub access computers, Scanner, Spoken cassettes & CDs, Story hour, Summer reading prog, Tax forms, VHS videos, Web-catalog
Open Tues 10-8, Wed & Thurs 10-6, Fri 10-5, Sat 10-1
Friends of the Library Group

RED CLOUD

P AULD PUBLIC LIBRARY*, 537 N Webster St, 68970. SAN 309-6122. Tel: 402-746-3352. E-mail: rclibr@hotmail.com. *Dir,* Nancy Sherwood; *Asst Librn,* Terri Eberly
Founded 1917. Pop 960; Circ 9,491
Library Holdings: Audiobooks 50; Bks on Deafness & Sign Lang 2; DVDs 260; Large Print Bks 100; Bk Titles 9,000; Per Subs 31; Videos 234
Automation Activity & Vendor Info: (Cataloging) Follett Software
Wireless access
Function: Bks on CD, Copy machines, Free DVD rentals, Homebound delivery serv, VHS videos
Open Mon, Wed & Fri 12-3, Tues & Thurs 1-5, Sat 9-Noon

S THE WILLA CATHER FOUNDATION, 413 N Webster St, 68970-2466. SAN 309-6130. Tel: 402-746-2653. Toll Free Tel: 866-731-7304. FAX: 402-746-2652. E-mail: info@willacather.org. Web Site: www.willacather.org. *Exec Dir,* Ashley M Olson
Founded 1955
Library Holdings: Bk Titles 300; Bk Vols 400
Special Collections: Willa Cather Pioneer Memorial & Educational Foundation Coll
Subject Interests: Webster County, Willa Cather

S WEBSTER COUNTY HISTORICAL MUSEUM LIBRARY, 721 W Fourth Ave, 68970. (Mail add: PO Box 464, 68970-0464), SAN 377-1474. Tel: 402-746-2444. E-mail: wchmdirector@gpcom.net. *Dir,* Teresa Young
Library Holdings: Bk Vols 300

RISING CITY

P RISING CITY COMMUNITY LIBRARY*, 675 Main St, 68658-3868. (Mail add: PO Box 190, 68658-0190), SAN 309-6149, *Librn,* Diane Dunker
Founded 1963. Pop 300; Circ 3,000
Library Holdings: Audiobooks 110; Large Print Bks 350; Bk Titles 6,600; Per Subs 10; Videos 750
Special Collections: Large Print Coll; Zane Grey Series
Open Tues 7pm-8pm, Fri 2-5, Sat 9am-11am
Friends of the Library Group

RUSHVILLE

P RUSHVILLE PUBLIC LIBRARY*, 207 Sprague St, 69360. (Mail add: PO Box 389, 69360-0389), SAN 309-6157. Tel: 308-327-2740. FAX: 308-327-2740. E-mail: rpublib@gpcom.net. Web Site: rushvillelibrary.org. *Libr Dir,* Teri Whipple; *Libr Assoc,* Joann Anderson; *Libr Asst,* David Exendine; Staff 1 (Non-MLS 1)
Pop 999; Circ 8,300
Library Holdings: Bk Vols 10,000; Per Subs 17
Special Collections: Native American History & Literature Coll; Nebraska & South Dakota Authors (Local Author Coll)
Automation Activity & Vendor Info: (Acquisitions) Winnebago Software Co; (Cataloging) Winnebago Software Co; (Circulation) Winnebago Software Co; (Serials) Winnebago Software Co
Wireless access
Function: Bks on cassette, Bks on CD, Computers for patron use, Copy machines, Fax serv, ILL available, Story hour, Summer reading prog, VHS videos
Mem of Panhandle Libr Syst
Special Services for the Blind - Audio mat; Bks on cassette; Bks on CD; Large print bks
Open Mon & Sat 12-5, Tues & Thurs 12-8, Wed & Fri 10-5

S SHERIDAN COUNTY HISTORICAL SOCIETY, INC*, Benschoter Memorial Library, Hwy 20 & Nelson Ave, 69360. (Mail add: PO Box 291, Hay Springs, 69347-0291), SAN 371-6627. Tel: 308-638-7643. *Curator,* David Perkins; E-mail: dsperkins@gpcom.net; Staff 1 (Non-MLS 1)
Founded 1960
Library Holdings: Bk Titles 700
Special Collections: Camp Sheridan Nebraska 1874-1881, bks, micro, monographs
Restriction: Non-circulating to the pub

SAINT EDWARD

P SAINT EDWARD PUBLIC LIBRARY*, 302 Beaver, 68660. (Mail add: PO Box 249, 68660-0249), SAN 309-6173. Tel: 402-678-2204. FAX: 402-678-2204. E-mail: sepl@gpcom.net. *Librn,* Deanna Reardon
Pop 2,074; Circ 5,948
Library Holdings: Bk Vols 11,850; Per Subs 20
Open Tues 12-6, Wed 12-8, Thurs 9-12 & 1-6, Sat 9-Noon
Friends of the Library Group

SAINT PAUL

P SAINT PAUL LIBRARY*, 1301 Howard Ave, 68873-2021. SAN 309-6181. Tel: 308-754-5223. *Dir,* Laura Martinsen
Pop 2,094; Circ 21,011
Library Holdings: Bk Vols 40,000; Per Subs 67
Wireless access
Open Mon-Fri 8-8, Sat 10-3, Sun 1-4

SARGENT

P SARGENT TOWNSHIP LIBRARY, 504 Main St, 68874. (Mail add: PO Box 476, 68874-0476), SAN 309-6203. Tel: 308-527-4241. E-mail: sargentlibrary@nctc.net. Web Site: libraries.ne.gov/sargent. *Librn,* Gayle Mattox
Founded 1928. Pop 800; Circ 2,741
Library Holdings: Bk Vols 9,000
Database Vendor: Overdrive, Inc
Wireless access
Open Mon 9-3, Wed 1-7, Sat 9-Noon

SCHUYLER

P SCHUYLER PUBLIC LIBRARY*, 1123 A St, 68661-1929. SAN 309-6211. Tel: 402-352-2221. FAX: 402-352-5377. *Dir,* Meme Smith
Founded 1909. Pop 6,370
Library Holdings: Bk Titles 27,000; Per Subs 75
Open Mon-Thurs 10-8, Fri 10-5, Sat 10-1

SCOTIA

P SCOTIA PUBLIC LIBRARY*, PO Box 188, 68875-0188. SAN 309-622X. Tel: 308-245-3191. FAX: 308-245-3191. E-mail: scotialibrary@nctc.net. *Librn,* Pam Sweley
Pop 349; Circ 5,094
Library Holdings: Audiobooks 13; DVDs 12; Large Print Bks 68; Bk Vols 6,046
Special Collections: Pioneer
Open Mon, Wed & Fri 2-5

SCOTTSBLUFF

P LIED SCOTTSBLUFF PUBLIC LIBRARY, 1809 Third Ave, 69361-2493. SAN 309-6254. Tel: 308-630-6250. Interlibrary Loan Service Tel: 308-630-6252. FAX: 308-630-6293. E-mail: librarydirector@scottsbluff.org. Web Site: www.scottsbluff.org/departments/library. *Dir,* Abby Yellman; Tel: 308-630-6251, E-mail: ayellman@scottsbluff.org; *Adult Serv,* Jana Kehn; E-mail: jkehn@scottsbluff.org; *Ch Serv,* Debra Carlson; Tel: 308-630-6284, E-mail: dcarlson@scottsbluff.org; *ILL,* Roberta Boyd; E-mail: rboyd@scottsbluff.org; *Tech Serv,* Judith Oltmanns; Tel: 308-630-6207, E-mail: judyo@scottsbluff.org; Staff 11 (MLS 2, Non-MLS 9)
Founded 1917. Pop 14,737; Circ 146,968
Library Holdings: Bk Titles 65,666; Per Subs 105
Special Collections: DAR Coll; Rebecca Winter Genealogical Coll; Western Americana (Western History Coll). State Document Depository; US Document Depository
Automation Activity & Vendor Info: (Acquisitions) SirsiDynix; (Cataloging) SirsiDynix; (Circulation) SirsiDynix; (OPAC) SirsiDynix; (Serials) SirsiDynix
Database Vendor: OCLC FirstSearch, SirsiDynix
Wireless access
Function: 24/7 Electronic res, 24/7 Online cat, Adult bk club, After school storytime, Audiobks via web, Bk club(s), Children's prog, Computer training, Computers for patron use, Electronic databases & coll, Fax serv, Free DVD rentals, ILL available, Magazines, Mango lang, Movies, Music CDs, Notary serv, Online cat, OverDrive digital audio bks, Photocopying/Printing, Prog for adults, Prog for children & young adult, Pub access computers, Scanner, Senior computer classes, Story hour, Summer & winter reading prog, Summer reading prog, Tax forms, Teen prog
Mem of Panhandle Libr Syst
Special Services for the Deaf - Pocket talkers
Special Services for the Blind - Bks on cassette; Bks on CD; Talking bk serv referral
Open Mon-Thurs 9-7, Fri & Sat 9-6
Friends of the Library Group

M REGIONAL WEST MEDICAL CENTER LIBRARY*, 4021 Ave B, 69361. SAN 377-1458. Tel: 308-630-1368. FAX: 308-630-1721. *Librn,* Michele Parks; E-mail: parksm@rwmc.net
Library Holdings: Bk Vols 3,300; Per Subs 250
Partic in Mid-Continental Regional Med Libr Asn

J WESTERN NEBRASKA COMMUNITY COLLEGE LIBRARY*, 1601 E 27th NE, 69361-1899. SAN 309-6238. Tel: 308-635-6040. Circulation Tel: 308-635-6068. Reference Tel: 308-635-6041. FAX: 308-635-6086. E-mail: library@wncc.net. Web Site: www.wncc.net/library. *Dir,* Valetta Schneider; E-mail: vschneid@wncc.edu; *Acq,* Deb Kildow; *Pub Serv,* Andrea Gonzales; *Tech Serv,* Jill Ellis
Founded 1926. Enrl 1,398; Fac 43
Automation Activity & Vendor Info: (Cataloging) Follett Software; (Circulation) OCLC Online; (OPAC) Follett Software
Database Vendor: Baker & Taylor, Cinahl, EBSCO Information Services, EBSCOhost, Electric Library, Grolier Online, H W Wilson, LearningExpress, LexisNexis, OCLC ArticleFirst, OCLC FirstSearch, OCLC WorldShare Interlibrary Loan, ProQuest, Wilson - Wilson Web
Wireless access
Partic in OCLC Online Computer Library Center, Inc
Special Services for the Deaf - Pocket talkers
Special Services for the Blind - Braille bks; Braille equip
Open Mon-Thurs 7:30am-9pm, Fri 7:30-4, Sat 10-2
Departmental Libraries:
SIDNEY LEARNING RESOURCE CENTER, Sidney Campus, 371 College Dr, Sidney, 69162. (Mail add: 1601 E 27th St, 69361), SAN 374-5287. Tel: 308-254-7452. *In Charge,* Donna Maddox; E-mail: maddoxd@wncc.edu
Open Mon-Thurs 8am-9pm, Fri 8-4

S WESTERN NEBRASKA VETERANS HOME LIBRARY*, 1102 W 42nd St, 69361-4713. SAN 377-3779. Tel: 308-632-0300. FAX: 308-632-1384. *Librn,* Laura Singleton
Founded 1975
Library Holdings: DVDs 25; Bk Vols 1,000; Per Subs 15; Talking Bks 3

SCRIBNER

P SCRIBNER PUBLIC LIBRARY, 504 Main St, 68057. (Mail add: PO Box M, 68057), SAN 309-6262. Tel: 402-664-3540. FAX: 402-664-3540. E-mail: stories@gpcom.net. *Dir,* Jeanette Groppe; *Asst Librn,* Margaret Alt; *Asst Librn,* Dianne Cooper
Founded 1902. Pop 950; Circ 10,000
Library Holdings: Bk Titles 10,000; Per Subs 30
Wireless access
Open Mon 10-8, Tues 1-5, Thurs 1-8, Fri 10-5, Sat 9-Noon

SEWARD

C CONCORDIA UNIVERSITY*, Link Library, 800 N Columbia Ave, 68434-1595. SAN 309-6270. Tel: 402-643-7254. Interlibrary Loan Service Tel: 402-643-7255. Reference Tel: 402-643-7256. Administration Tel: 402-643-7358. Toll Free Tel: 800-535-5494. FAX: 402-643-4218. E-mail: library@cune.edu. Web Site: www.cune.edu/library. *Dir, Libr Serv,* Philip Hendrickson; E-mail: philip.hendrickson@cune.edu; *Cat Librn,* Holly Helmer; E-mail: holly.helmer@cune.edu; *Ref & Instruction Librn,* Tom Krenzke; E-mail: tom.krenzke@cune.edu; *Circ Supvr,* Kathy Rippstein; E-mail: kathy.rippstein@cune.edu; *ILL, Ser,* Lois Mannigel; E-mail: lois.mannigel@cune.edu; Staff 4.5 (MLS 3, Non-MLS 1.5)
Founded 1912. Enrl 1,932; Fac 85; Highest Degree: Master
Special Collections: Children's Literature; Curriculum
Subject Interests: Educ, Music, Relig
Automation Activity & Vendor Info: (Cataloging) OCLC; (Circulation) OCLC; (Course Reserve) OCLC; (ILL) OCLC; (Media Booking) OCLC; (OPAC) OCLC; (Serials) OCLC
Database Vendor: EBSCOhost, Gale Cengage Learning, JSTOR, LexisNexis, OCLC, OCLC FirstSearch, Oxford Online
Wireless access
Partic in OCLC Online Computer Library Center, Inc
Special Services for the Blind - Magnifiers
Open Mon-Thurs 8am-Midnight, Fri 8-5, Sat 1-5, Sun 1pm-Midnight

P SEWARD MEMORIAL LIBRARY*, 233 S Fifth St, 68434. SAN 309-6289. Tel: 402-643-3318. Web Site: www.sewardlibrary.org. *Dir,* Becky Baker; Staff 8 (Non-MLS 8)
Founded 1888. Pop 5,700; Circ 97,002
Library Holdings: Bk Vols 33,000; Per Subs 99
Special Collections: Large Print Coll; Nebraska Coll
Open Mon-Thurs (Winter) 9-8, Fri 9-5, Sat 9-3, Sun 1-4; Mon-Wed (Summer) 9-6, Thurs 9-8, Fri 9-5, Sat 9-Noon
Friends of the Library Group

SHELBY

P SHELBY COMMUNITY LIBRARY*, 650 N Walnut, 68662. (Mail add: PO Box 146, 68662-0146), SAN 377-1989. Tel: 402-527-5181. FAX: 402-527-5181. Web Site: libraries.ne.gov/shelby. *Dir,* Laura Alt; Tel: 402-527-5256; *Asst Librn,* Lynne Veburg; Tel: 402-527-5495; *Media Spec,* Sherri Nielsen; Tel: 402-669-9726
Library Holdings: Bk Vols 6,000
Wireless access
Open Mon, Tues & Thurs 9:30-12 & 12:30-4:30, Wed 12:30-4:30, Fri & Sat 9:30-1:30
Friends of the Library Group

SHELTON

P SHELTON TOWNSHIP LIBRARY, 313 C St, 68876. (Mail add: PO Box 10, 68876-0010), SAN 309-6297. Tel: 308-647-5182. E-mail: sheltonlibrary@nctc.net. Web Site: www.sheltonlibrary.com. *Dir,* Kathy Holley
Pop 1,497
Library Holdings: Bk Vols 8,500; Per Subs 33
Friends of the Library Group

SHICKLEY

P VIRGIL BIEGERT PUBLIC LIBRARY*, 214 N Market, 68436. (Mail add: PO Box 412, 68436-0412), SAN 309-6300. Tel: 402-627-3365. FAX: 402-627-3365. *Librn,* Carolyn K Schlegel
Pop 376; Circ 5,202
Jul 2005-Jun 2006. Mats Exp $5,400
Library Holdings: Large Print Bks 154; Bk Vols 15,051; Per Subs 65; Talking Bks 130; Videos 551
Automation Activity & Vendor Info: (Cataloging) Follett Software
Open Mon & Fri 9-11 & 1:30-5:30, Wed 2:30-6:30, Sat 9:30am-11:30am

SHUBERT

P SHUBERT PUBLIC LIBRARY*, 313 Main St, 68437. (Mail add: PO Box 148, 68437-0148), SAN 377-2004. Tel: 402-883-2593. *Dir,* Peggy Oliver; *Librn,* Connie Shafer
Pop 200
Library Holdings: Bk Vols 3,500; Per Subs 20
Open Tues 3-5, Sat 8-11

SIDNEY

P SIDNEY PUBLIC LIBRARY*, 1112 12th Ave, 69162. SAN 309-6319. Tel: 308-254-3110. FAX: 308-254-3710. E-mail: spl@sidneypubliclibrary.org. Web Site: www.sidneypubliclibrary.org. *Dir,* Doris Jensen; E-mail: doris@sidneypubliclibrary.org; *Bus Mgr,* Stephanie Mika; E-mail: stephanie@sidneypubliclibrary.org; *Adult Serv, ILL,* Vickie Morlock; E-mail: vickie@sidneypubliclibrary.org; *Cat, Tech Serv,* Sandy Nelson; E-mail: sandy@sidneypubliclibrary.org; *Ch Serv, YA Serv,* Eileen Nightingale; E-mail: eileen@sidneypubliclibrary.org; Staff 5 (Non-MLS 5)
Pop 9,830; Circ 100,460
Library Holdings: CDs 1,152; DVDs 646; Large Print Bks 1,801; Bk Titles 49,361; Bk Vols 49,363; Per Subs 214; Talking Bks 2,417; Videos 1,598
Special Collections: The Sidney Telegraph, 1875-, microfilm
Subject Interests: Local hist, Nebr authors
Automation Activity & Vendor Info: (Acquisitions) Follett Software; (Cataloging) OCLC CatExpress; (Circulation) Follett Software; (ILL) OCLC; (OPAC) Follett Software
Database Vendor: Gale Cengage Learning, OCLC FirstSearch, OCLC WorldShare Interlibrary Loan, Wilson - Wilson Web
Wireless access
Function: AV serv, Bks on cassette, Bks on CD, Children's prog, Computers for patron use, Copy machines, Fax serv, Handicapped accessible, ILL available, Mail & tel request accepted, Music CDs, Online cat, Photocopying/Printing, Prog for children & young adult, Ref & res, Ref serv available, Spoken cassettes & CDs, Summer reading prog, Tax forms, Telephone ref, VHS videos, Web-catalog
Mem of Panhandle Libr Syst
Open Mon-Thurs 9-7:30, Fri & Sat 9-6
Friends of the Library Group
Bookmobiles: 1. Librn, Vicky Morlock

SILVER CREEK

P TOWNSHIP LIBRARY OF SILVER CREEK*, 309 Vine St, 68663. (Mail add: PO Box 249, 68663-0249), SAN 309-6327. Tel: 308-773-2594. *Librn,* Elissia Vanek
Founded 1934. Pop 437; Circ 1,975
Jul 2010-Jun 2011 Income $10,000. Mats Exp $1,030, Books $1,000, Per/Ser (Incl. Access Fees) $30. Sal $4,500
Library Holdings: Bk Vols 6,400
Open Mon-Fri 2-5

SNYDER

P SNYDER PUBLIC LIBRARY*, 203 Ash St, 68664. (Mail add: PO Box 26, 68664-0026), SAN 309-6335. Tel: 402-568-2570. FAX: 402-568-2688. E-mail: snyder68664@yahoo.com. *Dir,* Betty Niewohner
Pop 390; Circ 9,022
Library Holdings: Bk Vols 3,489
Open Tues & Thurs 3-6, Sat 9-Noon

SOUTH SIOUX CITY

P SOUTH SIOUX CITY PUBLIC LIBRARY*, 2121 Dakota Ave, 68776-3031. SAN 309-6343. Tel: 402-494-7545. FAX: 402-494-7546. E-mail: publiclibrary@southsiouxcity.org. Web Site: www.southsiouxcity.org/library. *Libr Dir,* David Mixdorf; E-mail: dwmixdorf@southsiouxcity.org; *Asst Dir,* Dan Nieman; *Ch,* Odessa Meyer; Staff 6 (MLS 1, Non-MLS 5)
Founded 1920. Pop 12,000; Circ 35,000
Oct 2005-Sept 2006 Income $292,900, State $2,180, City $259,308, Locally Generated Income $31,412. Mats Exp $40,100, Books $36,650, Per/Ser (Incl. Access Fees) $3,000, Electronic Ref Mat (Incl. Access Fees) $450. Sal $176,652 (Prof $48,121)
Library Holdings: AV Mats 112; Bks-By-Mail 578; Bks on Deafness & Sign Lang 13; CDs 93; DVDs 179; e-books 15,179; Electronic Media & Resources 7; High Interest/Low Vocabulary Bk Vols 944; Large Print Bks 1,976; Bk Titles 36,222; Bk Vols 465; Per Subs 100; Talking Bks 658; Videos 900
Special Collections: Nebraska
Automation Activity & Vendor Info: (Acquisitions) LibLime; (Cataloging) LibLime; (Circulation) LibLime; (OPAC) LibLime; (Serials) LibLime
Wireless access
Open Mon-Thurs 9-8, Fri & Sat 9-5

SPALDING

P SPALDING PUBLIC LIBRARY*, 141 Saint Joseph St, 68665. (Mail add: PO Box 101, 68665-0101), SAN 309-6351. Tel: 308-497-2705. *Dir,* Helen Langer; Tel: 308-497-2695
Library Holdings: Bk Vols 7,000
Open Tues 9-12 & 1-5:30, Sat 9am-11:30am

SPENCER

P SPENCER TOWNSHIP LIBRARY*, 110 Main St, 68777. (Mail add: PO Box 189, 68777-0189), SAN 309-636X. Tel: 402-589-1131. E-mail: spnlib@nntc.net. *Librn,* Carol Sedivy
Pop 596; Circ 1,200
Library Holdings: Bk Vols 6,355; Per Subs 15
Open Mon, Wed & Fri 1:30-5

SPRINGFIELD

P SPRINGFIELD MEMORIAL LIBRARY*, 665 Main St, 68059. (Mail add: PO Box 40, 68059-0040), SAN 309-6378. Tel: 402-253-2797. FAX: 402-253-2797. E-mail: sml665@charter.net. *Dir,* Constance Manzer
Pop 1,526; Circ 13,694
Library Holdings: Bk Vols 17,000; Per Subs 70
Automation Activity & Vendor Info: (Acquisitions) Biblionix; (Cataloging) Biblionix; (Circulation) Biblionix; (OPAC) Biblionix
Wireless access
Open Mon & Wed 10-5, Tues & Thurs 1-8, Sat 10-3
Friends of the Library Group

SPRINGVIEW

P KEYA PAHA COUNTY LIBRARY*, 118 Main St, 68778. (Mail add: PO Box 134, 68778-0134). Tel: 402-497-2626. FAX: 402-497-2627. *Dir,* Judy Cronk; E-mail: cronk5@juno.com
Pop 1,000; Circ 2,800
Library Holdings: CDs 15; DVDs 30; Bk Vols 13,000; Talking Bks 30; Videos 270
Wireless access
Open Tues & Fri 1-5, Wed 10-2, Thurs 4-7

STANTON

P STANTON PUBLIC LIBRARY*, 1009 Jackpine St, 68779. (Mail add: PO Box 497, 68779-0497), SAN 309-6386. Tel: 402-439-2230. FAX: 402-439-2248. E-mail: spl68779@stanton.net. Web Site: www.stanton.net/library1.html. *Dir,* Carol Armbruster; *Asst Librn,* Laura Hess
Founded 1886. Pop 1,577; Circ 16,609
Library Holdings: Audiobooks 73; DVDs 1,140; Large Print Bks 247; Bk Titles 14,019; Per Subs 18; Videos 148
Automation Activity & Vendor Info: (Acquisitions) Follett Software; (Cataloging) Follett Software; (Circulation) Follett Software; (OPAC) Follett Software
Database Vendor: Bowker, EBSCOhost, Electric Library, H W Wilson, OCLC FirstSearch, OCLC WorldShare Interlibrary Loan, Overdrive, Inc
Wireless access
Open Mon 2-8, Tues-Thurs 12-6, Fri 2-5, Sat 9-Noon
Friends of the Library Group

STAPLETON

P LOGAN COUNTY PUBLIC LIBRARY*, 317 Main St, 69163. (Mail add: PO Box 8, 69163-0008), SAN 309-6394. Tel: 308-636-2343. *Libr Dir,* Kathy Hoberg; E-mail: hobergs@aol.com
Founded 1939. Pop 340; Circ 3,400
Library Holdings: Bk Titles 6,688
Open Tues 9:30-4:30, Thurs 12:30-6:30
Friends of the Library Group

STELLA

P STELLA COMMUNITY LIBRARY, 222 N Main St, 68442. (Mail add: PO Box 5, 68442-0005), SAN 321-2408. Tel: 402-883-2232. FAX: 402-883-2232. E-mail: stellalibrary@sentco.net. *Librn,* Shadow J Loveless; Tel: 402-245-8190, E-mail: theshadow2000_82@yahoo.com
Founded 1908. Pop 280
Library Holdings: Bk Vols 2,344
Wireless access
Open Wed & Sat 9-11:30

STERLING

P STERLING PUBLIC LIBRARY*, 150 Broadway St, 68443. (Mail add: PO Box 57, 68443-0057), SAN 309-6408. Tel: 402-866-2056. E-mail: skw8754@Live.com. *Librn,* Susan Wilken
Pop 510; Circ 5,759
Library Holdings: Bk Titles 9,955; Per Subs 35
Wireless access
Open Tues & Thurs 2-5, Sat 8-Noon

STRATTON

P STRATTON PUBLIC LIBRARY, 502 Bailey St, 69043. (Mail add: PO Box 182, 69043-0182), SAN 309-6416. Tel: 308-276-2463. E-mail: straplib@gpcom.net. *Dir,* Beverly Henderson
Library Holdings: Bk Vols 5,000
Open Mon 1-5, Thurs 12-5, Sat 1-4

STROMSBURG

P STROMSBURG PUBLIC LIBRARY*, 320 Central St, 68666. (Mail add: PO Box 366, 68666-0366), SAN 309-6424. Tel: 402-764-7681. FAX: 402-764-7681. E-mail: stromsburgpl@windstream.net. Web Site: libraries.ne.gov/Stromsburg, www.stromsburgnebraska.com/community-library.htm. *Dir,* Diana Johnson; *Asst Librn,* Monica Tidyman
Founded 1918. Pop 1,241; Circ 14,084
Library Holdings: Bk Vols 15,000; Per Subs 53
Automation Activity & Vendor Info: (Cataloging) Follett Software; (Circulation) Follett Software
Database Vendor: OCLC FirstSearch, Wilson - Wilson Web
Wireless access
Open Mon & Fri 1-5, Tues & Wed 1-8, Sat 10-2
Friends of the Library Group

STUART

P STUART TOWNSHIP LIBRARY*, Second & Main St, 68780. (Mail add: PO Box 207, 68780-0207), SAN 309-6432. Tel: 402-924-3242. *Dir,* Angie Olberding; E-mail: aolberding6@hotmail.com
Pop 1,102; Circ 2,123
Library Holdings: Bk Vols 4,897; Per Subs 23
Wireless access
Open Mon & Wed 2-5:30, Fri 11-5:30
Friends of the Library Group

SUPERIOR

P SUPERIOR PUBLIC LIBRARY, 449 N Kansas, 68978-1852. SAN 309-6440. Tel: 402-879-4200. E-mail: superiorlibrary@hotmail.com. *Dir,* Vicki Perrie
Founded 1901. Pop 2,010; Circ 23,200
Library Holdings: Bk Vols 24,000
Wireless access
Open Mon-Fri 1:30-5:30 & 7-9, Sat 10-12 & 1:30-5:30

SUTHERLAND

P SUTHERLAND PUBLIC LIBRARY*, 900 Second St, 69165. (Mail add: PO Box 275, 69165-0275), SAN 309-6459. Tel: 308-386-2228. E-mail: sutherlandpubliclib@gmail.com. *Librn,* Nichole Bermel
Pop 1,200
Oct 2010-Sept 2011. Mats Exp $7,000
Library Holdings: Bk Vols 18,000
Open Tues & Thurs 10-12, 2-5 & 6-8, Sat 10-12 & 1-5

SUTTON

P SUTTON MEMORIAL LIBRARY*, 201 S Saunders, 68979. (Mail add: PO Box 433, 68979-0433), SAN 309-6467. Tel: 402-773-5259. FAX: 402-773-5259. E-mail: memlibrary@telcoweb.net. *Head Librn,* Shelly A Reed; *Asst Librn,* Carole Grady
Founded 1908. Pop 1,447; Circ 15,213
Jul 2005-Jun 2006 Income $28,570, State $770, City $27,743, Other $57. Mats Exp $5,614. Sal $14,160
Library Holdings: AV Mats 671; Large Print Bks 127; Bk Vols 15,516; Per Subs 40; Talking Bks 193; Videos 636
Automation Activity & Vendor Info: (Circulation) Follett Software
Open Mon-Thurs 3-8, Fri 10-12 & 2-5, Sat 9-Noon
Friends of the Library Group

SYRACUSE

P SYRACUSE PUBLIC LIBRARY*, 480 Fifth St, 68446. (Mail add: PO Box 8, 68446-0008), SAN 309-6475. Tel: 402-269-2336. *Librn,* Sue Antes
Pop 2,000; Circ 17,917
Library Holdings: Bk Titles 24,000; Per Subs 27
Automation Activity & Vendor Info: (Acquisitions) Biblionix; (Cataloging) Biblionix; (Circulation) Biblionix; (Course Reserve) Biblionix; (Serials) Biblionix
Wireless access
Partic in Lyrasis
Friends of the Library Group

TALMAGE

P TALMAGE PUBLIC LIBRARY*, 405 Main, 68448. (Mail add: PO Box 7, 68448-0007), SAN 309-6491. Tel: 402-264-3875. E-mail: talmagepl@jagwireless.net. *Librn,* Carol Fisher
Founded 1904. Pop 268; Circ 1,564
Oct 2008-Sept 2009 Income $4,497, City $4,052, Locally Generated Income $395, Other $50. Mats Exp $107, Books $57, Other Print Mats $50. Sal $1,995
Library Holdings: Bk Vols 6,000
Wireless access
Special Services for the Deaf - Captioned film dep
Open Mon 1-5, Wed 2-5, Fri 12-3
Friends of the Library Group

TAYLOR

P TAYLOR PUBLIC LIBRARY*, 106 Williams St, 68879-0206. SAN 309-6505. Tel: 308 942-6125. *Librn,* Janice Unruh; Tel: 308-942-6213
Pop 683; Circ 2,714
Library Holdings: Bk Vols 5,300
Wireless access
Function: ILL available
Open Mon & Fri 1-5

TECUMSEH

S NEBRASKA DEPARTMENT OF CORRECTIONS*, Tecumseh State Correctional Institution Library, 2725 N Hwy 50, 68450. Tel: 402-335-5998. FAX: 402-335-5115. *Librn,* Patty Hughes
Library Holdings: Bk Vols 9,000; Per Subs 59; Talking Bks 10
Open Sun-Sat 8-8

P TECUMSEH PUBLIC LIBRARY*, 170 Branch St, 68450. SAN 309-6513. Tel: 402-335-2060. FAX: 402-335-2069. E-mail: tlibrary@neb.rr.com. *Dir,* Susie Kerner
Founded 1907. Pop 1,702; Circ 16,014
Library Holdings: Bk Titles 11,680; Per Subs 28
Automation Activity & Vendor Info: (Cataloging) Follett Software; (Circulation) Follett Software; (OPAC) Follett Software
Database Vendor: OCLC FirstSearch
Open Mon & Wed 9-5:30, Fri 12:45-5:30, Sat 9-1

TEKAMAH

S BURT COUNTY MUSEUM, INC LIBRARY, 319 N 13th St, 68061. (Mail add: PO Box 125, 68061-0125), SAN 372-6088. Tel: 402-374-1505. E-mail: burtcomuseum@abbnebraska.com, burtcomuseum@huntel.net. Web Site: sites.google.com/site/officialburtcountymuseum. *Curator,* Bonnie Newell
Founded 1967
Library Holdings: Bk Titles 625; Bk Vols 950
Special Collections: History of Burt County 1929; Story of an Old Town 1902; Tekamah Book 1904; Tekamah Cemetery Book 1984; Tekamah Centennial Book 1854-1954; The Life & Times
Subject Interests: Genealogy
Friends of the Library Group

P TEKAMAH PUBLIC LIBRARY*, 204 S 13th St, 68061-1304. SAN 309-6521. Tel: 402-374-2453. FAX: 402-374-2453. E-mail: teklibrary@abbnebraska.com. *Dir,* Joyce Grass; *Ch Serv Librn,* Terri Donnely; Staff 1 (Non-MLS 1)
Founded 1916. Pop 3,409; Circ 27,000
Library Holdings: CDs 34; DVDs 20; Large Print Bks 82; Bk Titles 15,510; Per Subs 72; Talking Bks 219; Videos 604
Automation Activity & Vendor Info: (Cataloging) Follett Software; (Circulation) Follett Software; (OPAC) Follett Software
Wireless access
Function: Bks on cassette, Bks on CD, Children's prog, Computers for patron use, Copy machines, Exhibits, Fax serv, Home delivery & serv to Sr ctr & nursing homes, Homebound delivery serv, ILL available, Music CDs, Photocopying/Printing, Prog for children & young adult, Pub access computers, Scanner, Story hour, Summer reading prog, Teen prog, Telephone ref, VHS videos
Special Services for the Blind - Bks on cassette; Bks on CD; Large print bks
Open Mon 1-8, Tues 1-5, Wed 11-8, Fri 9-5, Sat 1-3

THEDFORD

P THOMAS COUNTY LIBRARY*, 503 Main St, 69166. (Mail add: PO Box 228, 69166-0228), SAN 350-2686. Tel: 308-645-2237. E-mail: thomascolibrary@neb-sandhills.net. *Librn,* Ronda Haumann; *Asst Librn,* Rosalee Hamilton
Founded 1958. Pop 3,079; Circ 38,006
Jul 2010-Jun 2011 Income $34,029. Mats Exp $10,774, Books $9,849, Per/Ser (Incl. Access Fees) $500, AV Mat $425. Sal $16,373
Library Holdings: Bks on Deafness & Sign Lang 10; High Interest/Low Vocabulary Bk Vols 200; Large Print Bks 30; Bk Vols 21,107; Per Subs 37; Talking Bks 25
Special Collections: Indians of North America; Library of American Literature Coll; Western History (especially Nebraska)
Subject Interests: Archit, Art, Educ, Natural sci
Open Mon 7pm-9pm, Tues-Thurs 2-6, Fri 2-5
Bookmobiles: 1. Librn, Lenore Holt. Bk titles 1,000

TILDEN

P RAYMOND A WHITWER TILDEN PUBLIC LIBRARY*, 202 S Center St, 68781. (Mail add: PO Box 457, 68781-0457), SAN 309-653X. Tel: 402-368-5306. FAX: 402-368-5515. E-mail: librarian@tildenlibrary.org. Web Site: www.tildenlibrary.org. *Dir,* Cindy Simeon; E-mail: csimeon@tildenlibrary.org; *Head Librn,* Gloria Hatterman; E-mail: ghatterman@tildenlibrary.org; *Librn,* Hella Bauer; E-mail: hbauer@tildenlibrary.org; *Librn,* Jeanne Dahl; E-mail: jeanne.m.dahl@gmail.com
Founded 1922. Pop 953; Circ 22,321
Oct 2010-Sept 2011 Income $81,923, State $1,440, City $45,938, Federal $444, County $9,517, Locally Generated Income $3,400, Other $21,184. Mats Exp $12,144, Books $10,351, Per/Ser (Incl. Access Fees) $700, AV Mat $993, Electronic Ref Mat (Incl. Access Fees) $100. Sal $45,038
Library Holdings: Audiobooks 370; CDs 25; Large Print Bks 450; Bk Vols 20,354; Per Subs 51; Videos 1,233
Automation Activity & Vendor Info: (Cataloging) Follett Software; (Circulation) Follett Software; (OPAC) Follett Software
Database Vendor: Overdrive, Inc, P4 Performance Management, Inc, ProQuest
Wireless access
Function: Accessibility serv available based on individual needs, Adult bk club, Archival coll, Audio & video playback equip for onsite use, Bks on CD, Children's prog, Computers for patron use, Copy machines, Electronic databases & coll, Exhibits, Fax serv, Free DVD rentals, Handicapped accessible, Holiday prog, Home delivery & serv to Sr ctr & nursing homes, ILL available, Jazz prog, Large print keyboards, Magnifiers for reading, Microfiche/film & reading machines, Music CDs, Newsp ref libr, OverDrive digital audio bks, Photocopying/Printing, Pub access computers, Scanner, Summer reading prog, Tax forms, VHS videos, Web-catalog
Special Services for the Deaf - ADA equip
Special Services for the Blind - Bks on CD; Dragon Naturally Speaking software; ZoomText magnification & reading software
Open Mon & Thurs 10-8, Tues, Wed & Fri 10-6, Sat 10-2
Friends of the Library Group

TOBIAS

P TOBIAS PUBLIC LIBRARY*, Main St, 68453. (Mail add: PO Box 97, 68453-0097), SAN 309-6548. Tel: 402-243-2256. *Dir,* Jackie Niederklein
Library Holdings: DVDs 4; Large Print Bks 25; Bk Vols 2,000; Videos 50
Open Sat 8:30am-10:30am

TRENTON

P TRENTON PUBLIC LIBRARY*, 406 Main St, 69044. (Mail add: PO Box 307, 69044-0307), SAN 309-6556. Tel: 308-334-5413. E-mail: read2trenton@gpcom.net. Web Site: www.villageoftrenton.net/library/library.htm. *Dir,* Larry Evans; *Librn,* Nadine Dewey; Staff 2 (Non-MLS 2)
Pop 560; Circ 2,600
Oct 2009-Sept 2010 Income $14,125, City $14,025, County $100. Mats Exp $3,100, Books $3,000, Per/Ser (Incl. Access Fees) $100. Sal $5,200
Library Holdings: DVDs 238; Large Print Bks 210; Bk Vols 10,500; Per Subs 15
Automation Activity & Vendor Info: (OPAC) OpenBiblio
Database Vendor: MITINET, Inc
Wireless access
Open Wed 1-5, Thurs 2-7, Sat 9-2
Friends of the Library Group

ULYSSES

P ULYSSES TOWNSHIP LIBRARY*, 410 C St, 68669. (Mail add: PO Box 217, 68669-0217), SAN 309-6564. Tel: 402-549-2451. FAX: 402-549-2450. E-mail: ulysseslib@clarks.net. *Dir,* Jan Crocker
Founded 1914. Pop 504; Circ 3,540
Library Holdings: Bk Vols 8,000; Per Subs 22; Videos 690
Open Mon, Tues & Thurs 5-8, Wed 3-6, Sat 9-Noon
Friends of the Library Group

VALENTINE

S CHERRY COUNTY HISTORICAL SOCIETY LIBRARY*, Box 284, 69201-0284. SAN 377-4295. Tel: 402-376-2015. *Curator,* Jan Howell
Library Holdings: Bk Vols 1,500
Open Thurs-Sat 1-5

SR SAINT JOHNS EPISCOPAL CHURCH LIBRARY*, 372 N Main St, 69201. (Mail add: PO Box 261, 69201-0261), SAN 373-8205. Tel: 402-376-1723, 402-376-4929. *Librn,* Solveig Perrett
Founded 1993
Library Holdings: Bk Titles 575; Bk Vols 668
Special Collections: Episcopal Church Holdings Coll

P VALENTINE PUBLIC LIBRARY*, 324 N Main St, 69201. SAN 309-6572. Tel: 402-376-3160. FAX: 402-376-3160. E-mail: vallibrary@shwisp.net. *Dir,* Anne Quigley; Staff 3 (Non-MLS 3)
Founded 1921. Pop 5,713; Circ 35,138
Library Holdings: Bk Vols 28,383; Per Subs 46
Special Collections: Mari Sandoz American Indian Coll
Automation Activity & Vendor Info: (Acquisitions) OCLC; (Cataloging) Biblionix; (Circulation) Biblionix; (ILL) OCLC FirstSearch; (OPAC) Biblionix
Database Vendor: OCLC
Wireless access
Function: Accessibility serv available based on individual needs, Adult bk club, Art exhibits, Audiobks via web, Bk club(s), Bks on CD, Computer training, Computers for patron use, Copy machines, e-mail & chat, E-Reserves, Electronic databases & coll, Fax serv, Free DVD rentals, Handicapped accessible, Health sci info serv, Holiday prog, Home delivery & serv to Sr ctr & nursing homes, Homebound delivery serv, ILL available, Microfiche/film & reading machines, Online ref, Online searches, Outside serv via phone, mail, e-mail & web, OverDrive digital audio bks, Photocopying/Printing, Printer for laptops & handheld devices, Prog for adults, Prog for children & young adult, Pub access computers, Ref & res, Scanner, Senior outreach, Serves mentally handicapped consumers, Spoken cassettes & CDs, Spoken cassettes & DVDs, Story hour, Summer reading prog, Web-catalog, Wheelchair accessible, Workshops
Special Services for the Blind - Audio mat; Bks on cassette; Bks on CD
Restriction: Non-resident fee, Open to pub for ref & circ; with some limitations
Friends of the Library Group
Bookmobiles: 1

VALLEY

P VALLEY PUBLIC LIBRARY*, 232 N Spruce St, 68064. (Mail add: PO Box 353, 68064-0353), SAN 309-6580. Tel: 402-359-9924. FAX: 402-932-6258. *Dir,* Claire Bushong; E-mail: cbushong@valley.omhcoxmail.com; *Asst Librn,* Gail White
Founded 1902. Pop 1,788; Circ 14,000
Library Holdings: Bk Vols 12,000; Per Subs 25
Special Collections: Nebraska Authors Coll
Wireless access
Open Mon, Wed & Fri 10-5, Tues & Thurs 3-8, Sat 10-2
Friends of the Library Group

VALPARAISO

P VALPARAISO PUBLIC LIBRARY*, 300 W Second St, 68065. (Mail add: PO Box 440, 68065-0440), SAN 309-6599. Tel: 402-784-0321. FAX: 402-784-6141. E-mail: ValLibrary@WindStream.net. Web Site: libraries.ne.gov/valparaiso. *Dir,* Maria Cadwallader; *Librn,* Sue Blackman; Staff 2 (MLS 1, Non-MLS 1)
Pop 563
Library Holdings: Bk Vols 6,652
Automation Activity & Vendor Info: (Circulation) Follett Software
Wireless access
Mem of Eastern Libr Syst
Partic in Saunders County Libr Coop
Open Tues 3-8, Wed 3-8 (Summer 1-8), Thurs 1-8, Sat 9-Noon
Friends of the Library Group

VERDIGRE

P VERDIGRE PUBLIC LIBRARY*, 101 E Third St, 68783. (Mail add: PO Box 40, 68783-0040), SAN 309-6602. Tel: 402-668-2677. FAX: 402-668-2677. E-mail: vplibr2@gpcom.net. *Dir,* Deb Hamilton
Pop 519; Circ 2,000
Library Holdings: DVDs 26; Large Print Bks 450; Bk Vols 12,000; Per Subs 50; Talking Bks 150; Videos 500
Automation Activity & Vendor Info: (Acquisitions) Winnebago Software Co; (Cataloging) Winnebago Software Co
Wireless access
Open Tues & Fri 12:30-4:30, Wed & Thurs 12:30-7, Sat 10-Noon

WAHOO

P WAHOO PUBLIC LIBRARY*, 637 N Maple St, 68066 1673. SAN 309-6610. Tel: 402-443-3871. FAX: 402-443-3877. Web Site: www.wahoo.ne.us. *Libr Dir,* Denise Lawver; E-mail: denise@wahoo.ne.us; *Children's Serv Coordr,* Carrie Trutna
Founded 1923. Pop 4,100; Circ 93,000
Oct 2013-Sept 2014. Mats Exp $27,800, Books $20,000, Per/Ser (Incl. Access Fees) $3,000, AV Mat $4,800. Sal Prof $35,000
Library Holdings: Bk Vols 33,000; Per Subs 70
Automation Activity & Vendor Info: (Cataloging) Biblionix; (Circulation) Biblionix; (Course Reserve) Biblionix; (Serials) EBSCO Online
Wireless access
Partic in Saunders County Libr Coop
Open Mon-Thurs 9:30-8, Fri 9:30-5:30, Sat 9:30-1
Friends of the Library Group

WAKEFIELD

P GARDNER PUBLIC LIBRARY*, 114 W Third St, 68784. (Mail add: PO Box 150, 68784-0150), SAN 309-6629. Tel: 402-287-2334. FAX: 402-287-2334. *Dir,* Kathy Muller; E-mail: gplibrarian@gmail.com
Founded 1915. Pop 1,451
Wireless access
Special Services for the Blind - Computer with voice synthesizer for visually impaired persons; Copier with enlargement capabilities; Large print bks
Open Mon-Fri 9-11 & 2 6, Sat 9-11
Friends of the Library Group

WALLACE

P FAITH MEMORIAL LIBRARY*, 122 N Garrison Ave, 69169. (Mail add: PO Box 40, 69169). Tel: 308-387-4537. *Dir,* Debbie Andrews; E-mail: debbie@wallacehotel.net
Pop 320; Circ 952
Library Holdings: DVDs 25; Bk Vols 9,959; Talking Bks 180; Videos 955
Wireless access
Open Tues-Thurs 1-5
Friends of the Library Group

WALTHILL

P WALTHILL PUBLIC LIBRARY*, PO Box 466, 68067. SAN 309-6637. Tel: 402-846-5051. *Librn,* Nola Briggs
Pop 847
Library Holdings: Bk Vols 6,500
Open Mon-Fri 1:30-4:30

WATERLOO

P WATERLOO PUBLIC LIBRARY*, 23704 Cedar Dr, 68069. SAN 309-6645. Tel: 402-779-4171. FAX: 402-779-4369. E-mail: wpl205@aol.com. *Dir,* Linda Oyster
Pop 450; Circ 2,478
Library Holdings: Bk Vols 10,000; Per Subs 12
Wireless access
Open Mon 9:30-12 & 1-5:30, Tues 9:30-12 & 1-7, Thurs 9:30-12 & 1:30-5:30, Sat 9:30-12:30
Friends of the Library Group

WAUNETA

P WAUNETA PUBLIC LIBRARY*, 319 N Tecumseh Ave, 69045. (Mail add: Po Box 14, 69045-0014), SAN 309-6653. Tel: 308-394-5243. FAX: 308-394-5243. E-mail: wplibrary@bwtelcom.net. *Librn,* Ruth Hohl
Pop 675; Circ 5,690
Library Holdings: Bk Vols 5,700
Open Mon & Thurs 12:30-5:30

WAUSA

P LIED LINCOLN TOWNSHIP LIBRARY, 602 East Norris St, 68786. (Mail add: PO Box H, 68786-0319), SAN 309-6661. Tel: 402-586-2454. FAX: 402-586-2454. E-mail: linctnlb@gpcom.net. Web Site: lincolntownshiplibrary.com. *Dir,* Virginia E Lindquist
Pop 900; Circ 3,921
Library Holdings: Bk Vols 20,000; Per Subs 70
Automation Activity & Vendor Info: (Cataloging) Follett Software; (Circulation) Follett Software; (OPAC) Follett Software
Open Mon, Tues & Thurs 1:30-5:30, Wed 3-8, Fri 9-1

WAYNE

P WAYNE PUBLIC LIBRARY*, Robert B & Mary Y Benthack Library-Senior Ctr, 410 Pearl St, 68787. SAN 309-667X. Tel: 402-375-3135. FAX: 402-375-5772. E-mail: wpublib@cityofwayne.org. *Dir,* Lauran Lofgren; E-mail: llofgren@cityofwayne.org; *Ad,* Rita McLean; *Youth Serv Librn,* Julie Osnes; Staff 1 (MLS 1)
Founded 1902. Pop 5,583; Circ 43,719
Library Holdings: AV Mats 1,665; Bk Vols 22,600; Per Subs 90
Special Collections: Nebraska Coll, video, book on tape, art reproduction
Subject Interests: Nebr
Automation Activity & Vendor Info: (Cataloging) SirsiDynix; (Circulation) SirsiDynix; (OPAC) SirsiDynix; (Serials) SirsiDynix
Open Mon-Thurs 10-8:30, Fri 10-6, Sat 10-4, Sun (Sept-May) 2-5

C WAYNE STATE COLLEGE*, Conn Library, 1111 Main St, 68787. SAN 309-6688. Tel: 402-375-7258. Reference Tel: 402-375-7263. Administration Tel: 402-375-7257. Information Services Tel: 402-375-7570. FAX: 402-375-7538. E-mail: library@wsc.edu. Web Site: academic.wsc.edu/conn_library. *Dir,* David Graber; Tel: 402-375-7272, E-mail: dagrabe1@wsc.edu; *Head, Tech Serv,* Marilyn Quance; Tel: 402-375-7474, E-mail: maquanc1@wsc.edu; *Acq Librn, Archivist,* Marcus Schlichter; Tel: 402-375-7266, E-mail: maschli1@wsc.edu; *Distance Learning Librn,* Valerie Knight; Tel: 402-375-7443, E-mail: vaknigh1@wsc.edu; *Electronic Serv Librn,* Robert Donahue; Tel: 402-375-7568, E-mail: rodonah1@wsc.edu; *Coll Develop, Ref Librn,* Charissa Loftis; Tel: 402-375-7729, E-mail: chlofti1@wsc.edu; *Instrul Res Coordr,* Jenny Putnam; Tel: 402-375-7732, E-mail: jeputna1@wsc.edu. Subject Specialists: *Bus, Hist,* David Graber; *Physics, Psychol,* Marilyn Quance; *Journalism, Philos, Relig,* Marcus Schlichter; *Educ,* Valerie Knight; *Computer sci,* Robert Donahue; *Art, Med,* Charissa Loftis; *Curric, Educ,* Jenny Putnam; Staff 13 (MLS 6, Non-MLS 7)
Founded 1892. Enrl 2,849; Fac 187; Highest Degree: Master
Library Holdings: AV Mats 13,310; CDs 1,853; e-journals 15,295; Electronic Media & Resources 372; High Interest/Low Vocabulary Bk Vols 5,110; Large Print Bks 10; Music Scores 4,485; Bk Titles 185,067; Bk Vols 886,079; Per Subs 2,180; Videos 6,502
Special Collections: Instructional Resources; Juvenile & Young Adults; Kessler Art Coll; Musical Score Coll; Val Peterson Archives. State Document Depository; US Document Depository
Automation Activity & Vendor Info: (Acquisitions) Innovative Interfaces, Inc; (Cataloging) Innovative Interfaces, Inc; (Circulation) Innovative Interfaces, Inc; (OPAC) Innovative Interfaces, Inc; (Serials) Innovative Interfaces, Inc
Database Vendor: Cambridge Scientific Abstracts, EBSCOhost, Gale Cengage Learning, LexisNexis, OCLC FirstSearch, Wilson - Wilson Web
Wireless access
Function: Audio & video playback equip for onsite use, AV serv, BA reader (adult literacy), Digital talking bks, Distance learning, Doc delivery serv, Govt ref serv, Handicapped accessible, Homebound delivery serv, ILL available, Magnifiers for reading, Mail loans to mem, Online searches, Outside serv via phone, mail, e-mail & web, Photocopying/Printing, Prog for adults, Ref serv available, Referrals accepted, Satellite serv, Wheelchair accessible, Workshops
Publications: Children/Young Adults Materials Review; Nebraska Young Adult Authors Anthology; Northeast Nebraska Young Authors Anthology
Partic in Nebr State Col Syst; OCLC Online Computer Library Center, Inc
Special Services for the Blind - Closed circuit TV; Closed circuit TV magnifier; Magnifiers; Networked computers with assistive software
Open Mon-Thurs 7:30am-Midnight, Fri 7:30-5, Sat 1-6, Sun 3-Midnight

WEEPING WATER

P WEEPING WATER PUBLIC LIBRARY*, 206 West H St, 68463. (Mail add: PO Box 425, 68463-0425), SAN 309-6696. Tel: 402-267-3050. E-mail: weepingwaterlibrary@gmail.com. Web Site: www.weepingwaternebraska.com. *Dir,* Aimee Morlan
Founded 1914. Pop 1,100; Circ 9,741
Library Holdings: Bk Titles 15,000; Per Subs 10
Wireless access
Open Mon, Wed & Fri 10-5, Tues & Thurs 5-8, Sat 9-1

WEST POINT

P JOHN A STAHL LIBRARY*, 330 N Colfax St, 68788. SAN 309-670X. Tel: 402-372-3831. E-mail: info@wplibrary.com. Web Site: wplibrary.com. *Librn,* Mary Jo Mack; E-mail: maryjo@wplibrary.com
Circ 37,717
Library Holdings: Bk Vols 28,000; Per Subs 86
Special Collections: Leila Stahl Buffett Genealogy Center
Open Mon, Wed & Thurs 10-9, Tues, Fri & Sat 10-5:30

WESTERN

P STRUCKMAN-BAATZ PUBLIC LIBRARY*, 104 SW Ave, 68464. (Mail add: PO Box 338, 68464-0338), SAN 309-6718. Tel: 402-433-2177. FAX: 402-433-2177. *Dir,* Barbara J Schwisow
Pop 287; Circ 1,682
Library Holdings: Bk Titles 6,027; Per Subs 12
Wireless access
Open Tues-Fri 1:30-5:30, Sat 9:30-Noon

WILBER

P DVORACEK MEMORIAL LIBRARY*, 419 W Third St, 68465. (Mail add: PO Box 803, 68465-0803), SAN 309-6726. Tel: 402-821-2832. E-mail: dmlibrary@windstream.net. Web Site: www.czechlibrary.org. *Dir,* Susie Homolka; *Dir,* Nancy Vacek; Staff 2 (MLS 2)
Founded 1968. Pop 1,760; Circ 15,952
Library Holdings: Bk Titles 16,000; Per Subs 15
Special Collections: Czech Materials, bks
Automation Activity & Vendor Info: (Cataloging) Follett Software; (Circulation) Follett Software
Wireless access
Open Mon-Fri (Sept-May) 10-5, Sat 9-Noon; Mon-Fri (June-Aug) 9-5, Sat 9-Noon

WILCOX

P WILCOX PUBLIC LIBRARY*, 121 S Main St, 68982. (Mail add: PO Box 37, 68982-0037), SAN 377-4627. Tel: 308-478-5554. *Librn,* Julie Hansen
Library Holdings: Bk Vols 3,000
Wireless access
Open Mon 9-11:30, Wed 3-5, Sat 9-11

WILSONVILLE

P WILSONVILLE PUBLIC LIBRARY*, 203 Iva St, 69046. (Mail add: PO Box 100, 69046-0100), SAN 309-6734. Tel: 308-349-4367. *Librn,* Connie Holliday
Pop 100; Circ 3,729
Library Holdings: Bk Vols 6,128
Special Collections: Memorials
Partic in Library Information Network of Clackamas County
Open Mon 8:30-11:30 & 6-8, Wed 9-12 & 4-6, Sat 9-10

WINNEBAGO

J LITTLE PRIEST TRIBAL COLLEGE LIBRARY*, 601 E College Dr, 68071. (Mail add: PO Box 270, 68071). Tel: 402-878-3334. FAX: 402-878-2319. Web Site: www.littlepriest.edu/lptclibrary. *Libr Dir,* Mary Austin; E-mail: maustin@littlepriest.edu; *Circ Supvr,* Natalie Davis; Staff 1 (MLS 1)
Enrl 165; Highest Degree: Associate
Library Holdings: Audiobooks 861; AV Mats 768; CDs 88; DVDs 1,788; e-journals 1,700; Large Print Bks 831; Bk Vols 23,465; Per Subs 83
Special Collections: Native American Coll, adult & children's bks, Indian Law mats, journals, newsp, ref works, v-tapes
Automation Activity & Vendor Info: (Cataloging) TLC (The Library Corporation); (Circulation) TLC (The Library Corporation); (OPAC) TLC (The Library Corporation)
Wireless access
Function: Fax serv, ILL available, Photocopying/Printing
Partic in National Network of Libraries of Medicine
Open Mon-Fri 8:30-5

WINSIDE

P LIED WINSIDE PUBLIC LIBRARY*, 417 Main St, 68790. (Mail add: PO Box 217, 68790-0217), SAN 309-6750. Tel: 402-286-1122. *Librn,* JoAnn V Field; Staff 1 (Non-MLS 1)
Founded 1911. Pop 434; Circ 4,966
Library Holdings: AV Mats 502; Bk Titles 9,543; Per Subs 35
Wireless access
Open Mon & Wed (Winter) 1-6, Tues 3-7, Sat 9-12 & 1-4; Mon (Summer) 1-5 & 7-9, Tues 4-7, Wed 1-6, Sat 9-12 & 1-4
Friends of the Library Group

WISNER

P WISNER PUBLIC LIBRARY*, PO Box 547, 68791-9999. SAN 309-6769. Tel: 402-529-6018. FAX: 402-529-6018. E-mail: director324@hotmail.com. *Dir,* Carol Duncan
Pop 1,270; Circ 13,999
Library Holdings: Bk Vols 8,700; Per Subs 16
Automation Activity & Vendor Info: (Cataloging) Follett Software; (Circulation) Follett Software
Open Mon 9-8, Wed 9:30-7:30, Fri 9-6

WOLBACH

P WOLBACH COMMUNITY LIBRARY*, 610 Kingston St, 68882. (Mail add: PO Box 67, 68882-0067), SAN 309-6777. Tel: 308-246-5232. FAX: 308-246-5234. *Dir,* Susan Jewell
Pop 301; Circ 380
Library Holdings: Bk Vols 22,000; Per Subs 20
Open Mon-Fri 8-4

WOOD RIVER

P MALTMAN MEMORIAL PUBLIC LIBRARY*, 910 Main St, 68883. (Mail add: PO Box 10, 68883), SAN 309-6785. Tel: 308-583-2349. *Dir,* Nancy Jack; *Asst Dir,* Marian Hensley
Founded 1905. Pop 1,250; Circ 8,826
Library Holdings: Bk Titles 17,500; Per Subs 34
Open Mon 2-5, Wed & Thurs 1-5

WYMORE

P WYMORE PUBLIC LIBRARY*, 116 W F St, 68466. SAN 309-6793. Tel: 402-645-3787. FAX: 402-645-3787. E-mail: wymorelibrary@hotmail.com. *Dir,* Janet Roberts
Founded 1917. Pop 1,841; Circ 16,494
Library Holdings: Bk Vols 15,000; Per Subs 55
Wireless access
Mem of Southeast Library System (SELS)
Open Mon, Tues, Thurs & Fri 12:30-5:30, Wed 12:30-7:30, Sat 9-Noon
Friends of the Library Group

YORK

S NEBRASKA DEPARTMENT OF CORRECTIONS*, Nebraska Correctional Center for Women Library, 1107 Recharge Rd, 68467-8003. SAN 377-1334. Tel: 402-362-3317, Ext 260. Administration Tel: 402-310-1779. FAX: 402-362-3892. *Media Spec,* Kay Kronberg; E-mail: kay.kronberg@nebraska.gov; Staff 6 (Non-MLS 6)
Jul 2009-Jun 2010 Income $800. Mats Exp $800, Books $300, Per/Ser (Incl. Access Fees) $500
Library Holdings: CDs 43; High Interest/Low Vocabulary Bk Vols 75; Large Print Bks 150; Bk Titles 4,000; Per Subs 25; Spec Interest Per Sub 10
Subject Interests: African-Am culture, Law, Spanish lang mat
Mem of Southeast Library System (SELS)
Partic in Nebr Institutional Asn for Librs
Restriction: Not open to pub

C YORK COLLEGE, Levitt Library Learning Center, 1125 E Eighth St, 68467-2699. SAN 309-6807. Tel: 402-363-5703. Circulation Tel: 402-363-5708. Interlibrary Loan Service Tel: 402-363-5706. FAX: 402-363-5685. Web Site: www.york.edu/levitt/index.asp. *Dir,* Ruth Carlock; E-mail: rmcarlock@york.edu; *Asst Dir,* Ramona Ratliff; E-mail: rjratliff@york.edu; *ILL,* Leo Miller; E-mail: leo.miller@york.edu; Staff 3 (MLS 2, Non-MLS 1)
Founded 1956. Enrl 449; Fac 35; Highest Degree: Bachelor
Jul 2012-Jun 2013. Mats Exp $42,063, Books $372, Per/Ser (Incl. Access Fees) $23,072, Electronic Ref Mat (Incl. Access Fees) $18,619. Sal $104,352 (Prof $62,511)
Library Holdings: AV Mats 1,333; Bks on Deafness & Sign Lang 64; CDs 253; DVDs 42; e-books 50,770; Electronic Media & Resources 113,399; Microforms 20,177; Bk Titles 40,380; Bk Vols 59,802; Per Subs 147; Videos 2

Special Collections: Church History (Restoration Movement); Missions; Yorkana. Oral History
Automation Activity & Vendor Info: (Acquisitions) Winnebago Software Co; (Cataloging) OCLC Connexion; (Circulation) Follett Software; (ILL) OCLC WorldShare Interlibrary Loan; (OPAC) Follett Software; (Serials) Follett Software
Database Vendor: EBSCOhost, Electric Library, McGraw-Hill, OCLC FirstSearch, OCLC WorldShare Interlibrary Loan, Oxford Online, Wilson - Wilson Web
Wireless access
Partic in OCLC Online Computer Library Center, Inc
Open Mon, Tues & Thurs (Fall & Spring) 8am-9:55am & 10:30am-11pm, Wed 8am-9:55am, 10:30-6 & 7:30-11, Fri 8am-9:55am & 10:30-5, Sat 1-5, Sun 2-5:30 & 7:30-11; Mon-Fri (Summer) 8-5
Friends of the Library Group

P YORK PUBLIC LIBRARY*, Kilgore Memorial Library, 520 Nebraska Ave, 68467-3095. SAN 309-6815. Tel: 402-363-2620. FAX: 402-363-2627. Web Site: www.yorklib.org. *Dir,* Scott Childers; *Asst Dir, Youth Serv,* Judy Andrews; Staff 5 (MLS 2, Non-MLS 3)
Founded 1885. Pop 8,081; Circ 76,000
Library Holdings: AV Mats 4,383; Bk Vols 54,802; Per Subs 110
Special Collections: State Document Depository
Automation Activity & Vendor Info: (Acquisitions) SirsiDynix; (Cataloging) SirsiDynix; (Circulation) SirsiDynix; (OPAC) SirsiDynix; (Serials) SirsiDynix
Wireless access
Open Mon-Thurs 10-9, Fri & Sat 10-5, Sun 2-5
Friends of the Library Group

YUTAN

P YUTAN PUBLIC LIBRARY*, 502 Third St, 68073. (Mail add: PO Box 241, 68073-0241), SAN 309-6823. Tel: 402-625-2111. FAX: 402-625-2111. *Librn,* Nicole Irvin
Founded 1966. Pop 1,350; Circ 5,179
Library Holdings: Bk Vols 6,698
Friends of the Library Group

NEVADA

Date of Statistics: FY 2011
Population, 2010 U.S. Census: 2,700,551
Population: 2,724,634 (State Demographer, July 2011)
Population Served by Public Libraries: 2,724,634
Total Holdings in Public Libraries: 5,767,866
Holdings Per Capita: 2.12
Total Public Library Circulation (excluding bookmobiles): 19,407,575
Circulation Per Capita: 7.12
Total Public Library Operating Expenditures (including Grants-in-Aid): $79,134,645
Expenditure Per Capita: $29.12
Source of Income: Local Funds, State Grants, Federal LSTA
Number of County & Regional Libraries: County 13, District 9
Number of Bookmobiles in State: 3
State Grants-in-Aid to Public Libraries (FY 2011): $335,000

AMARGOSA VALLEY

P THE AMARGOSA VALLEY LIBRARY*, 829 E Farm Rd, HCR 69, Box 401T, 89020. SAN 320-488X. Tel: 775-372-5340. FAX: 775-372-1188. E-mail: library@amargosavalley.com. Web Site: www.amargosalibrary.com. *Libr Dir,* Jean Adams; *ILL,* Osvaldo Granados; Staff 3 (Non-MLS 3)
Founded 1977. Pop 1,400
Special Collections: US Document Depository
Subject Interests: Local hist
Automation Activity & Vendor Info: (Cataloging) Follett Software; (Circulation) Follett Software
Open Mon & Wed 10-7, Tues & Thurs 9-6, Fri 9-4
Friends of the Library Group

BEATTY

P BEATTY LIBRARY DISTRICT*, 400 N Fourth St, 89003. (Mail add: PO Box 129, 89003-0129), SAN 309-684X. Tel: 775-553-2257. FAX: 775-553-2257. E-mail: beattylibrary@sbcglobal.net. *Dir,* Sharon Jennings; E-mail: spjennin@clan.lib.nv.us; *Cat,* Dianna Smith; Staff 3 (MLS 1, Non-MLS 2)
Founded 1966. Pop 1,060; Circ 6,591
Jul 2009-Jun 2010 Income $51,809. Mats Exp $5,200
Library Holdings: AV Mats 480; DVDs 795; Large Print Bks 200; Bk Vols 17,129; Per Subs 39; Videos 828
Special Collections: Nevada Coll
Subject Interests: Local hist, Nev
Automation Activity & Vendor Info: (Serials) Innovative Interfaces, Inc
Wireless access
Function: e-mail serv, E-Reserves, Electronic databases & coll, Fax serv, Handicapped accessible, ILL available, Magnifiers for reading, Mail & tel request accepted, Music CDs, Online searches, Photocopying/Printing, Prog for adults, Prog for children & young adult, Ref serv available, Spoken cassettes & CDs, Summer reading prog, Tax forms, Telephone ref, VHS videos, Wheelchair accessible
Partic in CLAN (Cooperative Libraries Automated Network/Nevada)
Open Mon & Wed 10-4, Tues 12-7, Sat 10-Noon

BOULDER CITY

P BOULDER CITY LIBRARY*, 701 Adams Blvd, 89005-2697. SAN 309-6858. Tel: 702-293-1281. FAX: 702-293-0239. Web Site: www.bclibrary.org. *Dir,* Lynn Schofield-Dahl; E-mail: lynn@bclibrary.org; *Youth Serv Librn,* Kim Diehm; E-mail: childrens@bclibrary.org; *Adult Serv, Electronic Res, Ref,* Deanna Duffy; E-mail: ref@bclibrary.org; *Libr Tech Spec,* Samantha Evangelo; E-mail: tech@bclibrary.org; Staff 4 (MLS 4)
Founded 1933. Pop 16,000; Circ 155,000
Library Holdings: AV Mats 4,000; Large Print Bks 6,000; Bk Titles 95,000; Bk Vols 100,000; Per Subs 250; Talking Bks 4,000
Special Collections: Local History Coll
Automation Activity & Vendor Info: (Cataloging) Innovative Interfaces, Inc; (Circulation) Innovative Interfaces, Inc; (ILL) OCLC; (OPAC) Innovative Interfaces, Inc
Database Vendor: EBSCOhost, Overdrive, Inc
Wireless access
Function: Art exhibits, Audio & video playback equip for onsite use, Bi-weekly Writer's Group, Bks on CD, Children's prog, Computer training, Computers for patron use, Copy machines, Exhibits, Free DVD rentals, Handicapped accessible, ILL available, Instruction & testing, Magnifiers for reading, Microfiche/film & reading machines, Music CDs, Online cat, OverDrive digital audio bks, Photocopying/Printing, Preschool reading prog, Prog for adults, Prog for children & young adult, Pub access computers, Ref serv in person, Scanner, Senior computer classes, Spoken cassettes & CDs, Spoken cassettes & DVDs, Story hour, Summer & winter reading prog, Tax forms, Wheelchair accessible, Winter reading prog
Open Mon-Thurs 9-8:30, Fri 9-5, Sat 11-4, Sun (Winter) 1-4

S LAKE MEAD NATIONAL RECREATION AREA LIBRARY*, Alan Bible Visitor Ctr, Intersection of Hwys 93 & 166, 89005. (Mail add: 601 Nevada Hwy, 89005), SAN 309-6874. Tel: 702-293-8990. FAX: 702-293-8029. E-mail: lame_interpretation@nps.gov. Web Site: www.nps.gov/lame. *Librn,* Ann Langevin; Staff 1 (MLS 1)
Founded 1962
Jan 2005-Dec 2005. Mats Exp $1,000
Library Holdings: Bk Titles 1,650
Subject Interests: Amphibians, Archaeology, Botany, Geol, Hist, Indians, Interpretation, Nat Park Serv, Natural hist, Reptiles, Water res
Open Mon-Sun 8:30-4:30
Restriction: Open to pub for ref only

CARSON CITY

P CARSON CITY LIBRARY*, 900 N Roop St, 89701. SAN 309-6963. Tel: 775-887-2244. FAX: 775-887-2273. Web Site: www.carsoncitylibrary.org. *Dir,* Sena Loyd; Tel: 775-887-2244, Ext 1018, E-mail: sloyd@clan.lib.nv.us; Staff 20 (MLS 5, Non-MLS 15)
Founded 1966. Pop 75,000; Circ 365,900
Library Holdings: AV Mats 10,000; Bk Vols 125,000; Per Subs 327
Special Collections: Large Print Coll; Nevada Coll
Automation Activity & Vendor Info: (Cataloging) Innovative Interfaces, Inc; (Circulation) Innovative Interfaces, Inc; (ILL) OCLC; (OPAC) Innovative Interfaces, Inc; (Serials) Innovative Interfaces, Inc
Database Vendor: EBSCOhost, Gale Cengage Learning
Wireless access
Partic in CLAN (Cooperative Libraries Automated Network/Nevada)
Open Mon-Thurs 10-8, Fri & Sat 10-6
Friends of the Library Group

M CARSON-TAHOE REGIONAL MEDICAL CENTER*, Lahontan Basin Medical Library, 1600 Medical Pkwy, 89703. SAN 309-6912. Tel: 775-445-8788. FAX: 775-888-3203. E-mail: medical.library@ctrh.org. *In Charge,* Michon Mills
Founded 1972
Special Collections: Core Coll of Clinical Medicine & Nursing Materials
Subject Interests: Consumer health, Med, Nursing

Database Vendor: Cinahl, EBSCO Information Services, EBSCOhost, Electric Library, Elsevier, Elsevier MDL, MD Consult, OVID Technologies, PubMed, Springer-Verlag, UpToDate
Wireless access
Partic in Dialog Corp; Pac NW Regional Med Libr Serv
Open Mon-Fri 8-5

S NEVADA DEPARTMENT OF CORRECTIONS*, Warm Springs Correctional Center Library, PO Box 7007, 89702. Tel: 775-684-3005. FAX: 775-684-3051. *Supvr,* Gregg White; Tel: 775-684-3005, Ext 3063
Library Holdings: Bk Vols 1,500
Open Mon-Fri 8-11 & 12:30-3:30

S NEVADA LEGISLATIVE COUNSEL BUREAU*, Research Library, 401 S Carson St, 89701-4747. Tel: 775-684-6827. FAX: 775-684-6400. E-mail: library@lcb.state.nv.us. Web Site: www.leg.state.nv.us/lcb/research/library. *Chief Librn,* Nan Bowers; Staff 3 (MLS 2, Non-MLS 1)
Founded 1971
Library Holdings: Bk Titles 12,000; Bk Vols 14,500; Per Subs 250
Special Collections: Nevada Legislative History Coll. State Document Depository
Automation Activity & Vendor Info: (Acquisitions) Inmagic, Inc.; (Cataloging) Inmagic, Inc.; (OPAC) Inmagic, Inc.
Open Mon-Fri 8-5
Restriction: Non-circulating

P NEVADA STATE LIBRARY & ARCHIVES, 100 N Stewart St, 89701-4285. SAN 350-2740. Tel: 775-684-3360. Circulation Tel: 775-684-3365. Toll Free Tel: 800-922-2880 (NV only). FAX: 775-684-3330. Web Site: nsla.nv.gov. *Adminr,* Daphne DeLeon; Tel: 775-684-3315, E-mail: ddeleon@admin.nv.gov; *Head Govt Publ,* Ann Brinkmeyer; Tel: 775-684-3309, E-mail: acbrinkm@admin.nv.gov; *Cat,* Ann Sanford; Tel: 775-684-3308; Staff 39 (MLS 9, Non-MLS 30)
Founded 1859. Pop 2,000,000
Library Holdings: Bk Vols 67,350; Per Subs 150
Special Collections: Nevada Newspaper Coll (microform, retrospective); US Bureau of the Census Data Center. Oral History; State Document Depository; US Document Depository
Subject Interests: Govt affairs, Nev, Statistics
Automation Activity & Vendor Info: (Acquisitions) Innovative Interfaces, Inc; (Cataloging) Innovative Interfaces, Inc; (Circulation) Innovative Interfaces, Inc; (ILL) Innovative Interfaces, Inc; (Media Booking) Innovative Interfaces, Inc; (OPAC) Innovative Interfaces, Inc; (Serials) Innovative Interfaces, Inc
Database Vendor: EBSCOhost, Gale Cengage Learning, LexisNexis, Newsbank, OCLC FirstSearch, OCLC WebJunction, OCLC WorldShare Interlibrary Loan, Wilson - Wilson Web
Wireless access
Publications: Nevada Library Directory & Statistics; Nevada Official Publications; Nevada Records; Silver Lining (Talking Books); State Data Center Report
Partic in OCLC Online Computer Library Center, Inc; RLIN (Research Libraries Information Network)
Branches: 2
ARCHIVES & RECORDS, 100 N Stewart St, 89701. Tel: 775-684-3313. FAX: 775-684-3311. Web Site: nsla.nv.gov/Archives/Nevada_State_Archives. *Adminr,* Daphne DeLeon; *Asst Adminr, Archives & Rec,* Jeffrey Kintop; Staff 34 (MLS 10, Non-MLS 24)
Founded 1965
Library Holdings: Bk Titles 289,445
Special Collections: 1862-1875 Territorial & State Censuses, micro; Bureau of Indian Affairs, micro; Nevada History Coll
Subject Interests: Local govt, State govt
Function: Archival coll
Open Mon-Fri 10-2
Restriction: Restricted access

P REGIONAL LIBRARY FOR THE BLIND & PHYSICALLY HANDICAPPED, 100 N Stewart St, 89701-4285, SAN 309-6939. Tel: 775-684-3354. Toll Free Tel: 800-922-9334. FAX: 775-684-3355. TDD: 775-687-8338. *Librn,* Hope Williams; Staff 5 (MLS 1, Non-MLS 4)
Founded 1968. Pop 1,907,815
Library Holdings: Bk Titles 45,680; Bk Vols 77,455
Special Collections: Nevada Authors; Nevada Titles
Subject Interests: Gen fiction
Partic in CLAN (Cooperative Libraries Automated Network/Nevada); Information Nevada
Publications: Silver Lining (Newsletter)
Special Services for the Blind - Closed circuit TV
Open Mon-Fri 8-5

S NEVADA STATE MUSEUM LIBRARY*, 600 N Carson St, 89701-4004. SAN 327-4624. Tel: 775-687-4810, Ext 239, 775-687-4810, Ext 240. FAX: 775-687-4168. Web Site: www.nevadaculture.org. *Curator,* Robert Nylen
Library Holdings: Bk Vols 6,000
Subject Interests: Nev hist
Wireless access
Function: Ref serv available
Restriction: Open by appt only

GL NEVADA SUPREME COURT LIBRARY*, Supreme Court Bldg, 201 S Carson St, Ste 100, 89701-4702. SAN 309-6955. Tel: 775-684-1640. FAX: 775-684-1662. Reference FAX: 775-684-1640. TDD: 775-684-1665. E-mail: Reference@nvcourts.nv.gov. Web Site: lawlibrary.nvsupremecourt.us. *Dir,* Kathleen Harrington; Tel: 775-684-1670, E-mail: harrington@nvcourts.nv.gov; *Asst Librn, Coll Develop,* Christine Timko; *Cat,* Ann Whitney; *Doc, Ref Serv,* Paula Doty; Staff 4 (MLS 3, Non-MLS 1)
Founded 1973
Jul 2008-Jun 2009 Income $1,742,377. Mats Exp $768,769, Books $562,656, Per/Ser (Incl. Access Fees) $10,803, Micro $3,151, Electronic Ref Mat (Incl. Access Fees) $186,357, Presv $5,802. Sal Prof $400,739
Library Holdings: Bk Titles 11,625; Bk Vols 135,896; Per Subs 330
Special Collections: American & English Law. US Document Depository
Automation Activity & Vendor Info: (Cataloging) Innovative Interfaces, Inc; (OPAC) Innovative Interfaces, Inc
Database Vendor: Checkpoint Systems, Inc, HeinOnline, LexisNexis, Westlaw
Wireless access
Publications: New Titles List
Partic in CLAN (Cooperative Libraries Automated Network/Nevada)
Open Mon-Fri 8-5

J WESTERN NEVADA COMMUNITY COLLEGE*, Library & Media Services, 2201 W College Pkwy, 89703. SAN 350-2805. Tel: 775-445-3229. FAX: 775-445-3363. Web Site: library.wncc.nevada.edu. *Dir,* Ken Sullivan; Tel: 775-445-4246, E-mail: ken@wnc.edu; *Librn,* Valerie Andersen; *Librn,* Larry Calkins; *Librn,* Danna Sturm; *Libr Serv Supvr,* Kristie Gangestad; E-mail: kgangest@wnc.edu; *Circ Spec,* Eric Holcombe; *AV,* Howard Collett; *Media Serv,* Ralph Schilling; Staff 11 (MLS 4, Non-MLS 7)
Founded 1972. Enrl 5,688; Fac 90
Library Holdings: Bk Vols 40,000; Per Subs 180
Automation Activity & Vendor Info: (Acquisitions) Innovative Interfaces, Inc; (Cataloging) Innovative Interfaces, Inc; (Circulation) Innovative Interfaces, Inc; (Course Reserve) Innovative Interfaces, Inc; (ILL) Innovative Interfaces, Inc; (Media Booking) Innovative Interfaces, Inc; (OPAC) Innovative Interfaces, Inc; (Serials) Innovative Interfaces, Inc
Open Mon-Thurs 8-8, Fri 8-5, Sat 10-4
Departmental Libraries:
BECK LIBRARY & MEDIA SERVICES, 160 Campus Way, Fallon, 89406, SAN 372-8420. Tel: 775-423-5330. *Libr Support Spec,* Ron Belbin
Library Holdings: Bk Vols 7,222; Per Subs 52
Open Mon-Thurs 8:30-8, Fri 8:30-5, Sat 9-1

DYER

P FISH LAKE LIBRARY*, Hwy 264 Bluebird Lane, 89010. (Mail add: PO Box 250, 89010-0250), SAN 309-703X. Tel: 775-572-3311. FAX: 775-572-3311. *Librn,* Sheila Stover; E-mail: skstover@clan.lib.nv.us
Circ 8,900
Library Holdings: Bk Vols 6,000
Special Collections: Bilingual Coll; Nevada Local History; Spanish Coll
Automation Activity & Vendor Info: (Cataloging) Innovative Interfaces, Inc; (Circulation) Innovative Interfaces, Inc; (OPAC) Innovative Interfaces, Inc
Partic in CLAN (Cooperative Libraries Automated Network/Nevada)
Open Thurs-Sat 9-4

ELKO

P ELKO-LANDER-EUREKA COUNTY LIBRARY SYSTEM*, Elko County Library, 720 Court St, 89801. SAN 350-283X. Tel: 775-738-3066. FAX: 775-738-8262. Web Site: www.elkocountylibrary.org. *Dir,* Jeanette M Hammons; E-mail: jmhammons@clan.lib.nv.us; *Asst Dir,* Laura Oki; E-mail: ljoki@clan.lib.nv.us; *Ch,* Mary Jo King; *Ref Librn,* Patrick Dunn; E-mail: pfdunn@clan.lib.nv.us; *Supvr, Circ,* Mildred Hart; *Cataloger,* Athena Girard; Staff 37 (MLS 2, Non-MLS 35)
Founded 1922. Pop 59,000; Circ 250,000
Library Holdings: AV Mats 4,000; CDs 500; DVDs 2,000; Bk Titles 180,000; Per Subs 151; Videos 6,000
Special Collections: State Document Depository; US Document Depository
Subject Interests: Mining, Nev
Automation Activity & Vendor Info: (Cataloging) Innovative Interfaces, Inc; (Circulation) Innovative Interfaces, Inc; (ILL) Innovative Interfaces, Inc; (OPAC) Innovative Interfaces, Inc

Database Vendor: EBSCOhost, Gale Cengage Learning, LexisNexis, OCLC FirstSearch
Wireless access
Function: ILL available
Partic in CLAN (Cooperative Libraries Automated Network/Nevada)
Open Mon & Tues 9-8, Wed & Thurs 9-6, Fri & Sat 9-5
Friends of the Library Group
Branches: 10
AUSTIN BRANCH, 88 Main St, Austin, 89310. (Mail add: PO Box 121, Austin, 89310), SAN 350-2864. Tel: 775-964-2428. FAX: 775-964-2426. *Br Librn,* Sharon T Linhart
Library Holdings: Bk Vols 2,500
Special Collections: Mining; Nevada
Open Mon 1-5, Wed 2-5, Fri 9-Noon
Friends of the Library Group
BATTLE MOUNTAIN BRANCH, 625 S Broad St, Battle Mountain, 89820. (Mail add: PO Box 141, Battle Mountain, 89820-0141), SAN 350-2899. Tel: 775-635-2534. *In Charge,* Rosemary Fuller
Library Holdings: Bk Vols 5,000
Special Collections: Mining; Nevada
Database Vendor: Grolier Online
Open Mon 11-5, Tues 12-6, Wed 2-6, Thurs 4-8, Fri 2-4, Sat 12-2
BEOWAWE BRANCH, Hwy 306, Main St, HC 66, Unit 1, Box 3, Beowawe, 89821, SAN 350-2929. Tel: 775-468-2103. *In Charge,* Shirley Davidson
Library Holdings: Bk Vols 1,000
Database Vendor: Grolier Online
Open Mon 10-2:30, Thurs 1-5:30
CARLIN BRANCH, 811 Main St, Carlin, 89822. (Mail add: PO Box 1120, Carlin, 89822-1120), SAN 373-8558. Tel: 775-754-6766. FAX: 775-754-6621. *In Charge,* Tammy Cadwell
Library Holdings: Bk Vols 2,500
Database Vendor: Grolier Online
Open Mon, Tues & Fri 12-5, Wed 4-8, Thurs 10-3
Friends of the Library Group
CRESCENT VALLEY BRANCH, Cresent Valley Town Ctr, 5045 Tenabo Ave, Cresent Valley, 89821. (Mail add: PO Box 3, Cresent Valley, 89821-9701), SAN 377-757X. Tel: 775-468-0249. *In Charge,* Shirley Davidson
Library Holdings: Bk Vols 1,000
Database Vendor: Grolier Online
Open Tues & Wed 10-2:30
EUREKA BRANCH, 10190 Monroe St, Eureka, 89316. (Mail add: PO Box 293, Eureka, 89316-0293), SAN 350-2953. Tel: 775-237-5307. *In Charge,* Robin Evans
Library Holdings: Bk Vols 4,000
Database Vendor: Grolier Online
Open Mon 4-8, Tues 10-4, Wed Fri 12-5
JACKPOT BRANCH, 2301 Progressive Rd, Jackpot, 89825. (Mail add: PO Box 530, Jackpot, 89825-0530). Tel: 775-755-2356. *In Charge,* Gloria Ridge
Library Holdings: Bk Vols 20,000
Database Vendor: Grolier Online
Open Tues-Thurs 2-7, Fri 2-6, Sat 10-4
TUSCARORA BRANCH, 55 Weed St, Tuscarora, 89834, SAN 350-2988. Tel: 775-756-6597. *In Charge,* Julie Parks
Library Holdings: Bk Vols 500
Open Mon Fri 8-5
WELLS BRANCH, 208 Baker St, Wells, 89835. (Mail add: PO Box 691, Wells, 89835-0691), SAN 350-3011. Tel: 775-752-3856. *In Charge,* Jessica Boyer
Library Holdings: Bk Vols 6,000
Database Vendor: Grolier Online
WEST WENDOVER BRANCH, 590 Camper Dr, West Wendover, 89883. (Mail add: PO Box 5040, West Wendover, 89883-5040), SAN 329-059X. Tel: 775-664-2510. FAX: 775-664-2226. *In Charge,* Carla Loncar
Library Holdings: Bk Vols 5,000
Database Vendor: Grolier Online
Open Mon & Wed 12-6, Tues 1-5 & 6-8, Thurs & Fri 12-5
Bookmobiles: 1. Asst Dir, Laura Oki. Bk vols 5,000

C GREAT BASIN COLLEGE LIBRARY, Learning Resources Center, 1500 College Pkwy, 89801. SAN 309-7005. Tel: 775-753-2222. Interlibrary Loan Service Tel: 775-753-2183. Reference Tel: 775-753-2280. FAX: 775-753-2296. E-mail: gbclib@gbcnv.edu. Web Site: www.gbcnv.edu/library. *Ref Librn,* Karen Dannehl; Tel: 775-753-2300, E-mail: karen.dannehl@gbcnv.edu; *Ref Librn,* Eric Walsh; E-mail: eric.walsh@gbcnv.edu; *Govt Doc, ILL,* Christina Park; E-mail: christina.park@gbcnv.edu; Staff 5 (MLS 3, Non-MLS 2)
Founded 1967. Enrl 2,000; Fac 85; Highest Degree: Bachelor
Library Holdings: DVDs 320; e-books 50,000; Bk Titles 113,514; Bk Vols 175,889; Per Subs 53
Special Collections: American Indian; Basque; Nevada. US Document Depository
Subject Interests: Juv lit
Automation Activity & Vendor Info: (Acquisitions) Innovative Interfaces, Inc; (Circulation) Innovative Interfaces, Inc; (OPAC) Innovative Interfaces, Inc
Database Vendor: CredoReference, EBSCOhost, Gale Cengage Learning, Innovative Interfaces, Inc, Newsbank, OCLC, OCLC FirstSearch, ProQuest, YBP Library Services
Wireless access
Open Mon-Thurs 8-5:30, Fri 8-5

S NEVADA YOUTH TRAINING CENTER LIBRARY*, 100 Youth Center Rd, 89801. (Mail add: PO Box 459, 89803-5907). Tel: 775-738-5907, Ext 257. *Librn,* Position Currently Open
Library Holdings: Bk Titles 11,070; Per Subs 37
Automation Activity & Vendor Info: (Acquisitions) Follett Software; (Cataloging) Follett Software; (Circulation) Follett Software; (OPAC) Follett Software
Database Vendor: EBSCOhost, Gale Cengage Learning
Wireless access
Function: Prog for children & young adult
Restriction: Open to students, fac & staff

S NORTHEASTERN NEVADA MUSEUM LIBRARY*, 1515 Idaho St, 89801. SAN 309-6998. Tel: 775-738-3418. FAX: 775-778-9318. E-mail: archives@museumelko.org. Web Site: www.museumelko.org. *Archivist,* Toni Mendive
Founded 1968
Library Holdings: Bk Titles 2,500
Special Collections: Area Newspaper Coll (1869-present), bd, micro; Elko Coll; Jarbidge, Lamoille, Wells, Metropolis & Area Railroads Coll, Pioneer vehicles; Tuscarora Coll
Subject Interests: Anthrop, Hist, Natural hist, NE Nev hist
Publications: Northeastern Nevada Historical Society Quarterly

ELY

NEVADA DEPARTMENT OF CORRECTIONS
S ELY STATE PRISON - LAW LIBRARY*, 4569 N State Rte 490, 89301. (Mail add: PO Box 1989, 89301). Tel: 775-289-8800, Ext 2264. FAX: 775-289-1263. E-mail: pio@doc.nv.gov. Web Site: www.doc.nv.gov. *Supvr,* Position Currently Open
Library Holdings: Bk Vols 3,000
Open Mon-Fri 8-4:30
S ELY STATE PRISON LIBRARY*, 4569 N State Rte 490, 89301. (Mail add: Mountain High School, Ave C, 89301). Tel: 775-289-8800, Ext 2244. FAX: 775-289-1273. Web Site: www.doc.nv.gov. *In Charge,* Ron Schafer
Library Holdings: Bk Vols 14,000; Per Subs 10

P WHITE PINE COUNTY LIBRARY*, 950 Campton, 89301-1965. SAN 350-3046. Tel: 775-289-3737. FAX: 775-289-1555. Web Site: www.whitepinecountylibrary.com. *Dir,* Lori Romero; E-mail: lromero@clan.lib.nv.us
Founded 1961. Pop 10,600; Circ 51,680
Library Holdings: Bk Vols 35,000; Per Subs 69
Special Collections: Local History (White Pine County Historical Society), photog; Nevada Materials. Oral History
Automation Activity & Vendor Info: (Cataloging) Innovative Interfaces, Inc; (Circulation) Innovative Interfaces, Inc; (OPAC) Innovative Interfaces, Inc
Wireless access
Partic in CLAN (Cooperative Libraries Automated Network/Nevada); Information Nevada
Open Mon-Thurs 9-6, Fri 9-1, Sat 10-2
Friends of the Library Group

FALLON

P CHURCHILL COUNTY LIBRARY*, 553 S Maine St, 89406-3387. SAN 309-7021. Tel: 775-423-7581. FAX: 775-423-7766. E-mail: info@churchillcountylibrary.org. Web Site: www.churchillcountylibrary.org. *Libr Dir,* Carol Lloyd; E-mail: celloyd@clan.lib.nv.us; *Ad,* Diane F Wargo; *Ch,* Joyce Betts; *Tech Serv Librn,* Brenda Owens
Founded 1932. Pop 22,580; Circ 152,046
Library Holdings: e-journals 50; Bk Vols 90,843; Per Subs 45
Special Collections: Nevada History
Automation Activity & Vendor Info: (Cataloging) Innovative Interfaces, Inc; (Circulation) Innovative Interfaces, Inc; (OPAC) Innovative Interfaces, Inc
Wireless access
Publications: Footnotes (Newsletter)
Partic in CLAN (Cooperative Libraries Automated Network/Nevada)
Open Mon, Thurs & Fri 9-6, Tues & Wed 9-8, Sat 9-5
Friends of the Library Group

GABBS

P GABBS COMMUNITY LIBRARY*, 602 Third St, 89409. (Mail add: PO Box 206, 89409), SAN 377-3434. Tel: 775-285-2686. *Librn,* Nancy Howerton
Founded 1944. Pop 300
Library Holdings: Bks on Deafness & Sign Lang 5; High Interest/Low Vocabulary Bk Vols 75; Large Print Bks 400; Bk Titles 20,000; Bk Vols 25,000; Per Subs 15; Talking Bks 200; Videos 800
Special Collections: Nevada Coll. Oral History
Wireless access
Partic in Information Nevada
Open Tues 9-4 & 6-7:30, Wed 9-3, Thurs 9-4
Friends of the Library Group

HAWTHORNE

P MINERAL COUNTY PUBLIC LIBRARY*, 110 First St, 89415. (Mail add: PO Box 1390, 89415-1390), SAN 350-3135. Tel: 775-945-2778. FAX: 775-945-0703. *Dir,* Courtney Oberhansli; *Asst Dir,* Christina Boyles; *Circ,* Myra Drake
Founded 1955. Pop 4,000; Circ 36,000
Jul 2007-Jun 2008 Income (Main Library and Branch(s)) $195,500. Mats Exp $30,000. Sal $90,000
Library Holdings: Audiobooks 920; Large Print Bks 1,260; Bk Vols 30,600; Per Subs 20; Videos 1,720
Special Collections: State of Nevada History Coll
Automation Activity & Vendor Info: (Cataloging) Innovative Interfaces, Inc; (Circulation) Innovative Interfaces, Inc; (OPAC) Innovative Interfaces, Inc
Wireless access
Partic in CLAN (Cooperative Libraries Automated Network/Nevada)
Open Mon-Thurs (Winter) 10-7, Fri 10-6, Sat 11-4; Mon-Fri (Summer) 10-6, Sat 11-4
Friends of the Library Group
Branches: 1
MINA-LUNING LIBRARY, 908 B St, Mina, 89422. (Mail add: PO Box 143, Mina, 89422-0143), SAN 350-316X. Tel: 775-573-2505. FAX: 775-573-2505. *Br Mgr,* Carol Jean Souza
Library Holdings: Large Print Bks 340; Bk Vols 7,000; Videos 410
Special Collections: State of Nevada History Coll
Open Mon, Wed & Fri 1-5
Friends of the Library Group

HENDERSON

P HENDERSON DISTRICT PUBLIC LIBRARIES*, Paseo Verde Library, 280 S Green Valley Pkwy, 89012. Tel: 702-492-7252. FAX: 702-492-1711. Web Site: www.hdpl.org. *Exec Dir,* Angela Thornton; E-mail: athornton@hdpl.org; *Asst Dir,* Gayle Homaday; E-mail: gmhomaday@hdpl.org; *Br Mgr,* Joan Dalusung
Founded 1944. Pop 213,670; Circ 772,527
Library Holdings: Bk Vols 108,500
Automation Activity & Vendor Info: (Cataloging) Innovative Interfaces, Inc; (Circulation) Innovative Interfaces, Inc; (OPAC) Innovative Interfaces, Inc
Database Vendor: EBSCOhost
Wireless access
Open Mon-Thurs 9:30-8, Fri & Sat 9:30-5
Friends of the Library Group
Branches: 2
JAMES I GIBSON LIBRARY, 100 W Lake Mead Pkwy, 89015, SAN 309-7056. Tel: 702-565-8402. Reference Tel: 702-564-9261. FAX: 702-565-8832. *Br Mgr,* Candace Kingsley; E-mail: clkingsley@hdpl.org
Library Holdings: Bk Vols 138,500
Open Mon-Thurs 9:30-8, Fri & Sat 9:30-5
Friends of the Library Group
GREEN VALLEY LIBRARY, 2797 N Green Valley Pkwy, 89014. Tel: 702-207-4260. *Br Mgr,* Stephen Platt; E-mail: smplatt@hdpl.org
Open Tues-Thurs 9:30-8, Fri & Sat 9:30-6

C NEVADA STATE COLLEGE*, NSC Library, 1125 Nevada State Dr, 89002. Tel: 702-992-2800. FAX: 702-992-2801. E-mail: library@nsc.edu. Web Site: nsc.edu/library.asp. *Dir, Libr Serv,* Nathaniel King; E-mail: nathaniel.king@nsc.edu; Staff 1 (MLS 1)
Founded 2003. Enrl 2,000; Highest Degree: Bachelor
Jul 2005-Jun 2006. Mats Exp $200,000. Sal $61,000
Library Holdings: Bk Vols 20,000; Per Subs 83; Videos 120
Automation Activity & Vendor Info: (Cataloging) Innovative Interfaces, Inc; (Circulation) Innovative Interfaces, Inc; (Course Reserve) Innovative Interfaces, Inc; (OPAC) Innovative Interfaces, Inc
Wireless access
Open Mon-Thurs 8-8, Fri 8-5

S TITANIUM METALS CORPORATION OF AMERICA*, Henderson Technical Library, PO Box 2128, 89009. SAN 323-4371. Tel: 702-564-2544, Ext 396. FAX: 702-564-9038. *In Charge,* Sally Canada; E-mail: sally.canada@timet.com
Library Holdings: Bk Titles 20,000; Per Subs 75
Restriction: Not open to pub

INCLINE VILLAGE

C SIERRA NEVADA COLLEGE*, Prim Library, 999 Tahoe Blvd, 89450-9500. SAN 309-7064. Tel: 775-831-1314, Ext 7501, 775-881-7501. FAX: 775-832-6134. E-mail: library@sierranevada.edu. Web Site: www.sierranevada.edu. *Libr Dir,* Dr Betts Markle; Tel: 775-831-1314, Ext 7511, E-mail: emarkle@sierranevada.edu; *Libr Tech,* Sandra Delaski; E-mail: sdelaski@sierranevada.edu; Staff 2 (MLS 1, Non-MLS 1)
Founded 1969. Enrl 500; Fac 30; Highest Degree: Bachelor
Library Holdings: Bk Titles 20,000; Bk Vols 23,000; Per Subs 174
Subject Interests: Calif, Computer sci, Environ studies, Hospitality indust, Music, Nev, Nursing, Resort mgt, Sierra maps, Teacher educ, Visual arts
Automation Activity & Vendor Info: (Cataloging) Innovative Interfaces, Inc; (Circulation) Innovative Interfaces, Inc; (OPAC) Innovative Interfaces, Inc
Database Vendor: EBSCOhost, LexisNexis
Function: ILL available
Partic in CLAN (Cooperative Libraries Automated Network/Nevada); Information Nevada
Open Mon-Thurs 8am-10pm, Fri 8-5, Sat 10-4, Sun 2-10

LAS VEGAS

GL CLARK COUNTY LAW LIBRARY, 309 S Third St, Ste 400, 89155. (Mail add: PO Box 557340, 89155-7340), SAN 309-7099. Tel: 702-455-4696. FAX: 702-455-5120. E-mail: askccll@clarkcountynv.gov. Web Site: www.clarkcountynv.gov/lawlibrary. *Dir,* Karen Byrd; *Law Librn,* Shelly Newton; *Law Librn,* Summer Youngquest; Staff 7 (MLS 1, Non-MLS 6)
Founded 1923
Library Holdings: Bk Vols 84,000; Per Subs 420
Special Collections: Nevada Coll, Statutes of each state
Subject Interests: Cases, Formbks, Regulations, Statutes, Treatises
Automation Activity & Vendor Info: (Acquisitions) Follett Software; (OPAC) Follett Software
Wireless access
Publications: News & Notes
Partic in Westlaw
Open Mon-Fri 8-5, Sat 10-5
Friends of the Library Group

C COLLEGE OF SOUTHERN NEVADA*, West Charleston Campus, 6375 W Charleston Blvd, W10I, 89146. SAN 309-7188. Tel: 702-651-5716. Circulation Tel: 702-651-5723. Interlibrary Loan Service Tel: 702-651-5007. Reference Tel: 702-651-5729. FAX: 702-651-5718. Interlibrary Loan Service FAX: 702-651-5725. Reference FAX: 702-651-5003. E-mail: library@csn.edu. Web Site: www.csn.edu/library. *Dir,* Clarissa Erwin; Tel: 702-651-5863, E-mail: clarissa.erwin@csn.edu; *Digital Serv Librn,* Sarah New; Tel: 702-651-7511, E-mail: sarah.new@csn.edu; *Ref Librn,* Jeanette Jones; Tel: 702-651-5085, E-mail: jeanette.jones@csn.edu; *Ref Librn,* Christine Shore; Tel: 702-651-5069, E-mail: christine.shore@csn.edu; *Acq, Tech Serv Librn,* Lynn Best; Tel: 702-651-5527, E-mail: lynn.best@ccsn.edu; *Circ,* Corey Cohen; Tel: 702-651-5781, E-mail: coreh.cohen@csn.edu; *Ref & Instruction,* Ted Chodock; Tel: 702-651-5509, E-mail: ted.chodock@csn.edu; *ILL, Libr Tech,* Marion Martin; E-mail: marion.martin@csn.edu; *Libr Tech, Tech Serv,* Maggie Slomka; Tel: 702-651-5882, Fax: 702-651-7643, E-mail: maggie.slomka@csn.edu; Staff 27 (MLS 12, Non-MLS 15)
Founded 1972. Enrl 22,000; Highest Degree: Bachelor
Library Holdings: Bk Titles 96,704; Bk Vols 98,481; Per Subs 399
Subject Interests: Computer sci, Criminal justice, Culinary arts, Dental hygiene, Electronics, Fire sci, Gaming, Hort, Nursing, Resorts
Automation Activity & Vendor Info: (Acquisitions) Innovative Interfaces, Inc; (Circulation) Innovative Interfaces, Inc; (ILL) Innovative Interfaces, Inc; (Serials) Innovative Interfaces, Inc
Database Vendor: ABC-CLIO, Alexander Street Press, ARTstor, Cinahl, CQ Press, CredoReference, EBSCOhost, Facts on File, Gale Cengage Learning, Greenwood Publishing Group, H W Wilson, Infotrieve, Innovative Interfaces, Inc, ISI Web of Knowledge, JSTOR, LearningExpress, LexisNexis, McGraw-Hill, Medline, OCLC FirstSearch, OCLC WorldShare Interlibrary Loan, Oxford Online, ProQuest, PubMed, Safari Books Online, Sage, ScienceDirect, SerialsSolutions, Thomson - Web of Science, Westlaw, World Book Online, YBP Library Services
Wireless access
Function: Ref serv available

Departmental Libraries:

CHEYENNE CAMPUS, 3200 E Cheyenne Ave, C2A, North Las Vegas, 89030, SAN 376-8805. Tel: 702-651-4419. FAX: 702-643-4812. *Ref Librn,* Susan Gregg; Tel: 702-651-4622, E-mail: susan.gregg@csn.edu; *Ref Librn,* Jack Sawyer; Tel: 702-651-4444, E-mail: jack.sawyer@csn.edu; *Circ,* Lazara Gonzalez; Tel: 702-651-4014, E-mail: lazara.gonzalez@csn.edu

HENDERSON CAMPUS, 700 S College Dr, H1A, Henderson, 89002, SAN 321-6071. Tel: 702-651-3066. Reference Tel: 702-651-3039. FAX: 702-651-3513. *Ref Librn,* Paula Grenell; E-mail: paula.grenell@csn.edu; *Ref Librn,* Jeanette Jones; E-mail: jeanette.jones@csn.edu; *Circ,* Cleo Wilson; E-mail: cleo.wilson@csn.edu

S DESERT RESEARCH INSTITUTE*, Sulo & Aileen Maki Research Library, 755 E Flamingo Rd, 89119-7363. Tel: 702-862-5405. FAX: 702-862-5542. Web Site: www.library.dri.edu. *Dir,* Melanie Scott; Tel: 775-674-7083

Library Holdings: Bk Vols 3,000

Wireless access

Open Mon-Fri 8-5

S JFSA HOLOCAUST RESOURCE CENTER*, Sperling-Mack-Kronberg Holocaust Library, 4794 S Eastern Ave, Ste A, 89119. SAN 375-7757. Tel: 702-433-0005. E-mail: sperlinghl@aol.com. *Chair,* Edythe Katz Yarchever; *Librn,* Kim Nastaszewski; Staff 1 (Non-MLS 1)

Founded 1980

Library Holdings: Bk Titles 3,000

Friends of the Library Group

P LAS VEGAS CLARK COUNTY LIBRARY DISTRICT, 7060 W Windmill Lane, 89113. SAN 350-3194. Tel: 702-734-7323. Administration Tel: 702-507-6186. Administration FAX: 702-507-6187. Web Site: www.lvccld.org. *Exec Dir,* Dr Ronald R Heezen; *Dep Dir,* Tom Fay; Tel: 702-507-6290; Staff 91 (MLS 91)

Founded 1985. Pop 1,500,000; Circ 14,868,023

Library Holdings: Bk Vols 2,727,762; Per Subs 3,865

Special Collections: International Languages Coll; Nevada State Data Center; State Publication Distribution Center. State Document Depository; US Document Depository

Subject Interests: Gaming, Grants, Health sci, Local hist, Nev hist, Patents trademarks, SW hist

Automation Activity & Vendor Info: (Acquisitions) Innovative Interfaces, Inc; (Cataloging) Innovative Interfaces, Inc; (Circulation) Innovative Interfaces, Inc; (OPAC) Innovative Interfaces, Inc

Database Vendor: EBSCOhost

Wireless access

Function: 24/7 Electronic res, 24/7 Online cat, Accessibility serv available based on individual needs, Activity rm, Adult bk club, Adult literacy prog, After school storytime, Art exhibits, Audio & video playback equip for onsite use, Audiobks via web, BA reader (adult literacy), Bilingual assistance for Spanish patrons, Bk club(s), Bks on CD, Children's prog, Citizenship assistance, Computer training, Computers for patron use, Copy machines, Digital talking bks, e-mail & chat, e-mail serv, E-Reserves, Electronic databases & coll, eReaders, Exhibits, Family literacy, Fax serv, Free DVD rentals, Genealogy discussion group, Govt ref serv, Handicapped accessible, Health sci info serv, Holiday prog, Home delivery & serv to Sr ctr & nursing homes, Homebound delivery serv, Homework prog, ILL available, Jail serv, Jazz prog, Large print keyboards, Life-long learning prog for all ages, Literacy & newcomer serv, Magazines, Magnifiers for reading, Mail & tel request accepted, Microfiche/film & reading machines, Movies, Music CDs, Online cat, Online ref, Online searches, Orientations, OverDrive digital audio bks, Photocopying/Printing, Preschool outreach, Printer for laptops & handheld devices, Prog for adults, Prog for children & young adult, Pub access computers, Ref & res, Ref serv available, Ref serv in person, Senior computer classes, Senior outreach, Spanish lang bks, Spoken cassettes & CDs, Spoken cassettes & DVDs, Story hour, Study rm, Summer reading prog, Tax forms, Teen prog, Telephone ref, Web-catalog, Wheelchair accessible, Workshops, Writing prog

Partic in OCLC Online Computer Library Center, Inc

Branches: 27

BLUE DIAMOND LIBRARY, 14 Cottonwood Dr, Blue Diamond, 89004. (Mail add: PO Box 40, Blue Diamond, 89004-0040), SAN 350-3259. Tel: 702-875-4295. FAX: 702-875-4095. *Br Assoc,* Nina Mata; Staff 2 (Non-MLS 2)

Founded 1970. Circ 9,017

BUNKERVILLE LIBRARY, Ten W Virgin St, Bunkerville, 89007. (Mail add: PO Box 7208, Bunkerville, 89007-7208), SAN 350-3283. Tel: 702-346-5238. FAX: 702-346-5784. *Br Assoc,* Carolynn Leavitt; Staff 2 (Non-MLS 2)

Founded 1973. Circ 19,032

CENTENNIAL HILLS LIBRARY, 6711 N Buffalo Dr, 89131, SAN 325-4224. Tel: 702-507-6100. FAX: 702-507-6147. *Br Mgr,* Tammy Giesking

Founded 2009. Circ 935,867

CITY OF LAS VEGAS DETENTION FACILITY, 3100 E Stewart Ave, 89101. Tel: 702-384-4887. FAX: 702-671-3971. *Adminr,* Tom Olsen; Staff 1 (Non-MLS 1)

CLARK COUNTY DETENTION FACILITY, 330 S Casino Center Blvd, 89101, SAN 350-3453. Tel: 702-384-4887. FAX: 702-671-3971. *Librn,* Tom Olsen

Subject Interests: Circulating paperbacks, Fed law bk vols, Nev

CLARK COUNTY LIBRARY, 1401 E Flamingo Rd, 89119, SAN 350-3348. Tel: 702-507-3400. FAX: 702-507-3482. *Br Mgr,* Marie Nicholl-Lynam

Founded 1966. Circ 988,212

Special Collections: Government Documents; Southern Nevada Nonprofit Information Center

Open Mon-Thurs 10-8, Fri-Sun 10-6

ENTERPRISE LIBRARY, 25 E Shelbourne Ave, 89123, SAN 377-6565 Tel: 702-507-3760. FAX: 702-507-3779. *Br Mgr,* Salvador Avila

Founded 1996. Circ 696,976

Open Mon-Thurs 10-8, Fri-Sun 10-6

GOODSPRINGS LIBRARY, 365 W San Pedro Ave, Goodsprings, 89019. (Mail add: PO Box 667, Goodsprings, 89019), SAN 350-3372. Tel: 702-874-1366. FAX: 702-874-1335. *Br Assoc,* Jacques Alimusa

Founded 1968. Circ 14,597

INDIAN SPRINGS LIBRARY, 715 Gretta Lane, Indian Springs, 89018. (Mail add: PO Box 628, Indian Springs, 89018-0628), SAN 350-3402. Tel: 702-879-3845. FAX: 702-879-5227. *Br Assoc,* Marie Reed

Founded 1969. Circ 31,237

LAS VEGAS LIBRARY, 833 Las Vegas Blvd N, 89101, SAN 350-3437. Tel: 702-507-3500. FAX: 702-507-3540. *Br Mgr,* Theron Nisson

Founded 1973. Circ 541,046

Special Collections: Nevada Data Center; State Publication Distribution Center. State Document Depository; US Document Depository

Subject Interests: Gaming, Local hist

Open Mon-Thurs 10-8, Fri-Sun 10-6

LAUGHLIN LIBRARY, 2840S Needles Hwy, Laughlin, 89029. (Mail add: PO Box 32225, Laughlin, 89028-2225). Tel: 702-507-4070. FAX: 702-507-4067. *Br Mgr,* Karen Lassen

Founded 1987. Circ 199,493

Friends of the Library Group

MEADOWS LIBRARY, 251 W Boston Ave, 89102, SAN 378-1755. Tel: 702-474-0023. *Regional Br Serv Dir,* Mario Aguilar

Founded 1994. Circ 47,455

Subject Interests: Spanish lang

MESQUITE LIBRARY, 121 W First North St, Mesquite, 89027-4759, SAN 350-3550. Tel: 702-507-4312. Administration Tel: 702 507 4080. FAX: 702-346-5224, 702-346-5788. *Br Assoc,* Judith Sargent

Founded 1973. Circ 194,666

Library Holdings: High Interest/Low Vocabulary Bk Vols 28,000

MOAPA TOWN LIBRARY, 1340 E Hwy 168, Moapa, 89025. (Mail add: PO Box 250, Moapa, 89025-0250), SAN 374-4132. Tel. 702-864-2438. FAX: 702-864-2467. *Br Assoc,* Jan Johnson

Founded 1988. Circ 26,844

MOAPA VALLEY LIBRARY, 36 N Moapa Valley Blvd, Overton, 89040-0397. (Mail add: PO Box 397, Overton, 89040-0397), SAN 350-3461. Tel: 702-397-2690. FAX: 702-397-2698. *Br Assoc,* April Heath

Founded 1967. Circ 146,769

MOUNT CHARLESTON LIBRARY, 75 Ski Chalet Pl, HCR 38, Box 269, 89124, SAN 350-347X. Tel: 702-872-5585. FAX: 702-872-5631. *Br Assoc,* Raychel Lendis

Founded 1980. Circ 5,784

RAINBOW LIBRARY, 3150 N Buffalo Dr, 89128, SAN 325-4240. Tel: 702-507-3710. FAX: 702-507-3730. *Br Mgr,* Sufa Anderson

Founded 1985. Circ 1,024,639

Open Mon-Thurs 10-7, Fri-Sun 10-6

SAHARA WEST LIBRARY, 9600 W Sahara Ave, 89117. Tel: 702-507-3630. FAX: 702-507-3673. *Br Mgr,* Kim Clanton-Green

Founded 1992. Circ 1,025,356

Open Mon-Thurs 10-8, Fri-Sun 10-6

SANDY VALLEY LIBRARY, 650 W Quartz Ave, HCR 31 Box 377, Sandy Valley, 89019, SAN 322-5828. Tel: 702-723-5333. FAX: 702-723-1010. *Br Mgr,* Deborah Wadley

Founded 1984. Circ 39,997

SEARCHLIGHT LIBRARY, 200 Michael Wendell Way, Searchlight, 89046. (Mail add: PO Box 98, Searchlight, 89046-0098), SAN 350-3496. Tel: 702-297-1442. FAX: 702-297-1782. *Br Assoc,* Rebecca Wallace

Founded 1969. Circ 25,666

SPRING VALLEY LIBRARY, 4280 S Jones Blvd, 89103, SAN 325-4208. Tel: 702-507-3820. FAX: 702-507-3838. *Br Mgr,* Nikki Winslow

Founded 1985. Circ 961,092

Open Mon-Thurs 10-8, Fri-Sun 10-6

SUMMERLIN LIBRARY & PERFORMING ARTS CENTER, 1771 Inner Circle Dr, 89134, SAN 374-4140. Tel: 702-507-3860. FAX: 702-507-3880. *Br Mgr,* Gregory C Carr

Founded 1993. Circ 565,353

Open Mon-Thurs 10-8, Fri-Sun 10-6

SUNRISE LIBRARY, 5400 Harris Ave, 89110, SAN 350-3526. Tel: 702-507-3900. FAX: 702-507-3914. *Br Mgr,* Timothy McDonald
Founded 1987. Circ 887,167
Open Mon-Thurs 10-8, Fri-Sun 10-6

WEST CHARLESTON LIBRARY, 6301 W Charleston Blvd, 89146-1124, SAN 350-3313. Tel: 702-507-3940. FAX: 702-507-3950. *Br Mgr,* Florence Jakus
Founded 1973. Circ 739,428
Subject Interests: Health sci, Med
Open Mon-Thurs 10-8, Fri-Sun 10-6

WEST LAS VEGAS LIBRARY, 951 W Lake Mead Blvd, 89106, SAN 350-3585. Tel: 702-507-3980. FAX: 702-507-3996. *Br Mgr,* Leo Seguro
Founded 1973. Circ 349,983
Special Collections: African American Experience
Subject Interests: Local hist
Open Mon-Thurs 10-8, Fri-Sun 10-6

WHITNEY LIBRARY, 5175 E Tropicana Ave, 89122, SAN 370-9280. Tel: 702-507-4010. FAX: 702-507-4026. *Br Mgr,* Ann Lagumina
Founded 1994. Circ 866,652
Open Mon-Thurs 10-8, Fri-Sun 10-6

WINDMILL LIBRARY, 7060 W Windmill Lane, 89113. Tel: 702-507-6030. FAX: 702-507-6064. *Br Mgr,* Arthur V Cabrales
Circ 909,791
Open Mon-Thurs 10-8, Fri-Sun 10-6

S LAS VEGAS FAMILYSEARCH LIBRARY*, Family History Library, 509 S Ninth St, 89101. SAN 309-7080. Tel: 702-382-9695. FAX: 702-382-1597. E-mail: nv_lasvegas@ldsmail.net. Web Site: lasvegasfsl.org. *Dir,* R Wayne Stoker; Tel: 702-528-2348, Fax: 702-243-4228, E-mail: rws-cjs@cox.net; Staff 85 (Non-MLS 85)
Founded 1965
Library Holdings: Bk Vols 12,000
Special Collections: Local Histories (Nevada); State & County History (US & Canada)
Subject Interests: Family hist
Wireless access
Open Tues-Thurs 10-7, Fri & Sat 10-5

S NATIONAL SECURITY TECHNOLOGIES*, Nuclear Testing Archive, 755 C East Flamingo, 89119. (Mail add: PO Box 98521, M/S 400, 89193-8521), SAN 373-4684. Tel: 702-794-5106. FAX: 702-794-5107. E-mail: cic@nv.doe.gov. Web Site: www.nv.doe.gov. *Mgr,* Martha DeMarre
Founded 1981
Library Holdings: Bk Vols 420,000; Videos 102
Special Collections: Human Radiation Experiments Coll; Nuclear Testing Archive
Subject Interests: Nuclear weapons testing
Open Mon-Fri 7:30-4:30

S NEVADA POWER CO LIBRARY*, 6226 W Sahara Ave, 89151. SAN 377-2330. Tel: 702-367-5055. FAX: 702-227-2023. *Team Leader,* Ruth Hurst; E-mail: rhurst@nevp.com; *Doc,* Lufonda Cone; E-mail: lcone@nevp.com; *Doc,* Elizabeth Ramirez; E-mail: eramirez@nevp.com; *Res,* Margaret Edner; *Res,* Maria Finney; *Res,* Tiah Hunter; E-mail: thunter@nevp.com; *Res,* Mary Nellis; *Res,* Margaret Romig; *Res,* Vicki Snyder; E-mail: vsnyder@nevp.com; Staff 7 (MLS 1, Non-MLS 6)
Library Holdings: Bk Titles 3,000; Per Subs 250
Special Collections: EPRI Technical Reports; Utility Industry Standards
Database Vendor: Gale Cengage Learning, Innovative Interfaces, Inc, LexisNexis, OCLC FirstSearch
Function: Res libr
Open Mon-Fri 7:30-5

S NEVADA STATE MUSEUM*, Historical Society Library, 700 Twin Lakes Dr, 89107. Tel: 702-486-5205, Ext 240. Web Site: dmla.clan.lib.nv.us/docs/museums/lv/vegas.htm. *Curator of Ms & Libr,* Crystal Van Dee
Library Holdings: Bk Titles 2,200; Per Subs 48
Open Wed-Sat 12-4

M SUNRISE HOSPITAL & MEDICAL CENTER*, Medical Library, 3186 S Maryland Pkwy, 89109. SAN 309-7153. Tel. 702-731-8210. FAX: 702-731-8674. Web Site: www.sunrisecme.com. *Med Librn,* Amber Carter; E-mail: amber@sunrisecme.com; Staff 3 (Non-MLS 3)
Founded 1975
Library Holdings: Bk Titles 1,000; Per Subs 1,500
Special Collections: Ciba slides
Subject Interests: Clinical med
Database Vendor: EBSCOhost
Wireless access
Partic in National Network of Libraries of Medicine; National Network of Libraries of Medicine Pacific Northwest Region; Nevada Medical Library Group
Open Mon-Fri 7:30-4

G UNITED STATES DEPARTMENT OF ENERGY*, Nevada Operations Office Technical Information Resource Center, PO Box 98518, 89193-8518. SAN 309-7161. Tel: 702-295-1274. FAX: 702-295-0109. E-mail: nevada@nv.doe.gov. Web Site: www.nv.doe.gov. *In Charge,* Ron Thomas; E-mail: thomasrc@nv.doe.gov; Staff 1 (Non-MLS 1)
Founded 1969
Library Holdings: CDs 1,500; DVDs 25; Microforms 40,000; Bk Titles 8,000
Special Collections: Peaceful Uses of Nuclear Explosions
Subject Interests: Alternate energy sources, Environ restoration, Geol, Hydrol, Nuclear explosions, Radiation bioenviron effects, Radioactive waste storage, Waste mgt
Automation Activity & Vendor Info: (Acquisitions) Brodart; (Cataloging) AmLib Library Management System; (Circulation) Brodart; (ILL) AmLib Library Management System; (Media Booking) AmLib Library Management System
Database Vendor: IHS, LexisNexis, Medline, OCLC, OCLC FirstSearch, OCLC WorldShare Interlibrary Loan, PubMed
Partic in LexisNexis; OCLC Online Computer Library Center, Inc
Open Mon-Thurs 5am-3:30pm

G UNITED STATES ENVIRONMENTAL PROTECTION*, National Exposure Research Laboratory-Environmental Sciences Division Technical, 944 E Harmon Ave, POS 19, 89119-6794. (Mail add: PO Box 93478, 89193-3478), SAN 371-9073. Tel: 702-798-2218. FAX: 702-798-2622. E-mail: Library-lv@epa.gov. Web Site: www.epa.gov/nerlesd1/trc/home6.htm. *Librn,* Richard Steele; E-mail: steele.richard@epa.gov; Staff 1 (MLS 1)
Founded 1966
Library Holdings: Bk Titles 19,147; Per Subs 34
Special Collections: National Estuary Surveys
Subject Interests: Radiation effects
Automation Activity & Vendor Info: (Cataloging) OCLC Online
Database Vendor: Dialog, OCLC FirstSearch, ScienceDirect
Function: ILL available, Online searches, Orientations, Photocopying/Printing, Res libr, Telephone ref
Restriction: Access at librarian's discretion, Authorized patrons, Authorized scholars by appt, By permission only, Circulates for staff only, Restricted pub use

M UNIVERSITY MEDICAL CENTER OF SOUTHERN NEVADA*, Medical Library, 2040 W Charleston Blvd, Ste 500, 89102. SAN 309-7145. Tel: 702-383-2368. FAX: 702-383-2369. Web Site: www.umcsn.com. *Dir,* Terry Henner; Staff 2 (Non-MLS 2)
Founded 1960
Library Holdings: Bk Titles 2,000; Bk Vols 18,000; Per Subs 1,000
Subject Interests: Health sci, Med
Automation Activity & Vendor Info: (Cataloging) LibraryWorld, Inc; (Circulation) LibraryWorld, Inc; (Serials) LibraryWorld, Inc
Database Vendor: EBSCOhost
Function: For res purposes
Partic in Nev Libr Asn
Open Mon-Fri 7:30-4

C UNIVERSITY OF NEVADA, LAS VEGAS LIBRARIES*, Lied Library, 4505 Maryland Pkwy, Box 457001, 89154-7001. SAN 350-3615. Tel: 702-895-2286. Circulation Tel: 702-895-2111. Interlibrary Loan Service Tel: 702-895-2152. Reference Tel: 702-895-2100. FAX: 702-895-2287. Circulation FAX: 702-895-2281. Interlibrary Loan Service FAX: 702-895-2283. Reference FAX: 702-895-2284. TDD: 702-895-2279. Web Site: www.library.unlv.edu. *Dean, Univ Libr,* Patricia Iannuzzi; E-mail: patricia.iannuzzi@unlv.edu; *Assoc Dean,* Scott Smith; *Dir, Info Serv,* Maggie Ressel; *Dir, Res & Info Serv,* Victoria Nozero; Tel: 702-895-2285, E-mail: victoria.nozero@unlv.edu; *Dir, Spec Coll,* Peter Michel; Tel: 702-895-2243, E-mail: peter.michel@unlv.edu; *Dir, Tech Serv,* Tamara Hanken; *Dir of Tech,* Jason Vaughan; Tel: 702-895-2179, E-mail: jason.vaughn@unlv.edu; *Dir, User Serv,* Wendy Starkweather; *Head, Access Serv & Doc Delivery, ILL,* Nancy Kress; E-mail: nancy.kress@unlv.edu; *Head, Coll Mgt,* Cory Tucker; *Head, Doc Serv,* Ed Silva; *Head of Instruction,* Anne Zald; *Head, Res Serv,* Sidney Lowe; Staff 38 (MLS 34, Non-MLS 4)
Founded 1957. Enrl 24,000; Fac 1,405; Highest Degree: Doctorate
Library Holdings: AV Mats 800; CDs 900; Bk Vols 30,800; Per Subs 1,500; Talking Bks 560; Videos 300
Special Collections: Architectural Drawings (Martin Stern Coll); Gaming; Union Pacific Railroad Coll; Urban & Regional Historical Coll. State Document Depository; US Document Depository
Automation Activity & Vendor Info: (Cataloging) Innovative Interfaces, Inc; (Circulation) Innovative Interfaces, Inc; (Course Reserve) Innovative Interfaces, Inc; (ILL) Innovative Interfaces, Inc; (OPAC) Innovative Interfaces, Inc; (Serials) Innovative Interfaces, Inc
Database Vendor: EBSCOhost, Innovative Interfaces, Inc, OCLC FirstSearch, OVID Technologies

Wireless access
Function: Res libr
Publications: Communications; Ex Libris (Newsletter); TechNotes
Open Mon-Thurs 7:30am-Midnight, Fri 7:30-7, Sat 9-6, Sun 11am-Midnight
Departmental Libraries:
ARCHITECTURE STUDIES, Paul B Sogg Architecture Bldg, Box 454049, 89154-4049. Tel: 702-895-1959. FAX: 702-895-1975. Web Site: library.nevada.edu/arch. *Head of Libr,* Caroline Smith; E-mail: caroline.smith@unlv.edu; Staff 10 (MLS 2, Non-MLS 8)
Open Mon-Thurs 9-9, Fri 9-5, Sun 1-9
CURRICULUM MATERIALS, Carlson Education Bldg, Rm 101, 89154. Tel: 702-895-3593. FAX: 702-895-3528. Web Site: library.nevada.edu/cml. *Head of Libr,* Jennifer Fabbi; E-mail: jennifer.fabbi@unlv.edu; Staff 4 (MLS 1, Non-MLS 3)
Subject Interests: Children's lit
Open Mon-Thurs 8-8, Fri 8-5, Sat 9-5
MUSIC, 4505 S Maryland Pkwy, 89154-7002. Tel: 702-895-2541. Web Site: library.nevada.edu/music. *Head of Libr,* Cheryl Taranto; Tel: 702-895-2549, E-mail: cheryl.taranto@unlv.edu; Staff 1 (MLS 1)
Library Holdings: AV Mats 3,000; CDs 6,000; Music Scores 26,000; Videos 1,000
Open Mon-Thurs 9-9, Fri 9-6, Sun 1-9

CL WIENER-ROGERS LAW LIBRARY, William S Boyd School of Law, 4505 Maryland Pkwy, 89154-1080. (Mail add: PO Box 451080, 89154-1080). Tel: 702-895-2400. Reference Tel: 702-895-2420. Administration Tel: 702-895-2327. FAX: 702-895-2410. Administration FAX: 702-895-2416. Web Site: www.law.unlv.edu/library.html. *Dir,* Jeanne Frazier Price; Tel: 702-895-2404, E-mail: jeanne.price@unlv.edu; *Law Libr Operations Mgr,* Cindy Claus; *Ref Librn,* Jennifer L Gross; *Ref Librn,* Chad Schatzle; *Circ Supvr,* Beverly Galloway; *Head, Coll Develop & Instrul Serv,* Matthew Wright; *Head, Tech Serv,* Sean Saxon
Subject Specialists: *Law,* Jeanne Frazier Price
Founded 1997
Partic in Desert States Law Library Consortium
Restriction: Circ limited, Open to students, fac & staff

LOVELOCK

S NEVADA DEPARTMENT OF CORRECTIONS*, Lovelock Correctional Center Library, 1200 Prison Rd, 89419. Tel: 775-273-1300. FAX: 775-273-4277. Web Site: www.doc.nv.gov. *Supv Librn,* Bruce Harkreader
Library Holdings: Bk Vols 1,000
Open Mon-Fri 7:30-4

P PERSHING COUNTY LIBRARY*, 1125 Central, 89419. (Mail add: PO Box 781, 89419-0781), SAN 350-3674. Tel: 775-273-2216. FAX: 775-273-0421. Web Site: www.clan.lib.nv.us. *Dir,* Kathie Brinkerhoff; E-mail: kbrinker@clan.lib.nv.us; Staff 3.75 (MLS 1, Non-MLS 2.75)
Founded 1930. Pop 6,753; Circ 25,180
Jul 2010-Jun 2011 Income $225,224, State $2,568, Federal $5,000, County $215,839, Locally Generated Income $1,817. Mats Exp $30,885, Books $23,500, Per/Ser (Incl. Access Fees) $1,558, Other Print Mats $1,193, AV Mat $4,634. Sal $204,699
Library Holdings: Audiobooks 1,800; AV Mats 1,947; Bks on Deafness & Sign Lang 19; CDs 741; DVDs 634; Large Print Bks 224; Bk Titles 26,819; Bk Vols 30,355; Per Subs 50; Talking Bks 1,434; Videos 1,372
Special Collections: Art Coll; Cooking Coll; Handicrafts; History Coll; Nevada Coll
Automation Activity & Vendor Info: (Cataloging) Innovative Interfaces, Inc; (Circulation) Innovative Interfaces, Inc; (OPAC) Innovative Interfaces, Inc
Database Vendor: EBSCOhost
Partic in CLAN (Cooperative Libraries Automated Network/Nevada); OCLC Online Computer Library Center, Inc
Open Mon & Tues 9-5, Wed 9-8, Thurs 10-8, Fri 10-5
Friends of the Library Group

MINDEN

P DOUGLAS COUNTY PUBLIC LIBRARY, Minden Library, 1625 Library Lane, 89423-4420. (Mail add: PO Box 337, 89423), SAN 350-3739. Tel: 775-782-9841. Administration Tel: 775-783-6406. FAX: 775-782-5754. Administration FAX: 775-782-6766. E-mail: info@douglas.lib.nv.us. Web Site: www.douglas.lib.nv.us. *Dir,* Linda L Deacy; E-mail: ldeacy@douglas.lib.nv.us; *Circ Mgr/Librn,* Sarah Bates; E-mail: sbates@douglas.lib.nv.us; *Coll Develop Librn,* Luise Davis; E-mail: ldavis@douglas.lib.nv.us; *Youth Serv Librn,* Kathy Echavarria; E-mail: kechavarria@douglas.lib.nv.us; *Pub Serv Mgr,* Linda Wilson; Tel: 775-782-6841, E-mail: lwilson@douglas.lib.nv.us; *Tech Serv Coordr,* Karen Fitzgerald; E-mail: kfitzgerald@douglas.lib.nv.us; Staff 14.275 (MLS 5, Non-MLS 9.275)
Founded 1967. Pop 49,500; Circ 185,000
Jul 2014-Jun 2015 Income (Main Library and Branch(s)) $1,515,000, County $1,500,000, Locally Generated Income $15,000. Mats Exp $164,000, Books $105,000, Per/Ser (Incl. Access Fees) $9,000, AV Mat $30,000, Electronic Ref Mat (Incl. Access Fees) $20,000. Sal $650,000 (Prof $350,000)
Library Holdings: Bk Titles 81,000; Bk Vols 114,030; Per Subs 140; Talking Bks 835
Special Collections: Carson Valley History (Van Sickle Coll), ms, micro; Nevada Historical Society. Municipal Document Depository; Oral History
Automation Activity & Vendor Info: (Acquisitions) Innovative Interfaces, Inc; (Cataloging) Innovative Interfaces, Inc; (Circulation) Innovative Interfaces, Inc; (ILL) Innovative Interfaces, Inc; (OPAC) Innovative Interfaces, Inc; (Serials) Innovative Interfaces, Inc
Database Vendor: EBSCOhost, Gale Cengage Learning, Grolier Online, ProQuest, ReferenceUSA, Wilson - Wilson Web
Wireless access
Function: After school storytime, Audio & video playback equip for onsite use, Audiobks via web, Bks on cassette, Bks on CD, CD-ROM, Children's prog, Computer training, Computers for patron use, Copy machines, Digital talking bks, Electronic databases & coll, Equip loans & repairs, Exhibits, Free DVD rentals, Genealogy discussion group, Handicapped accessible, Home delivery & serv to Sr ctr & nursing homes, Homebound delivery serv, ILL available, Large print keyboards, Magnifiers for reading, Mail & tel request accepted, Music CDs, Online cat, Orientations, Outreach serv, Photocopying/Printing, Preschool outreach, Prog for adults, Prog for children & young adult, Pub access computers, Ref serv available, Senior computer classes, Senior outreach, Spoken cassettes & CDs, Spoken cassettes & DVDs, Story hour, Summer reading prog, Tax forms, Teen prog, Telephone ref, VHS videos, Video lending libr, Wheelchair accessible, Workshops
Publications: Douglas County's Architectural Heritage (Local historical information)
Special Services for the Deaf - Assistive tech; Bks on deafness & sign lang; High interest/low vocabulary bks; Videos & decoder
Special Services for the Blind - Assistive/Adapted tech devices, equip & products; Computer with voice synthesizer for visually impaired persons; Home delivery serv
Open Mon-Wed 10-7, Thurs & Fri 10-6, Sat 10-5
Friends of the Library Group
Branches: 1
LAKE TAHOE, 233 Warrior Way, Zephyr Cove, 89448. (Mail add: PO Box 4770, Stateline, 89449-4770), SAN 350-3763. Tel: 775-588-6411. Administration Tel: 775-782-9841. FAX: 775-588-6464. Interlibrary Loan Service FAX: 775-782-5754. *Br Head,* Sarah Bates
Pop 50,000; Circ 185,000
Library Holdings: Bk Vols 32,696
Special Collections: Lake Tahoe Heritage Coll
Function: ILL available, Photocopying/Printing, Prog for children & young adult, Summer reading prog, Telephone ref
Open Wed 11-7, Thurs-Sat 9-5

NORTH LAS VEGAS

P NORTH LAS VEGAS LIBRARY DISTRICT*, 2300 Civic Center Dr, 89030-5839. SAN 309-7196. Tel: 702-633-1070. FAX: 702-649-2576. Web Site: www.nlvld.org. *Dir,* Kathy Pennell; *Assoc Librn,* Garett Dacey; *Ch,* Patrick Hinrichs
Founded 1962. Pop 117,250
Library Holdings: Bk Vols 115,000; Per Subs 102
Special Collections: Auto Repairs Manuals; Nevada Coll
Automation Activity & Vendor Info: (Cataloging) Innovative Interfaces, Inc - Millenium; (Circulation) Innovative Interfaces, Inc - Millenium; (OPAC) Innovative Interfaces, Inc - Millenium
Open Mon-Thurs 10:30-8, Fri 9-6
Friends of the Library Group
Branches: 2
ALEXANDER LIBRARY, 1755 W Alexander Rd, 89032. Tel: 702-633-2880. FAX: 702-399-9813. *Br Mgr,* Forest Lewis; E-mail: lewisf@cityofnorthlasvegas.com; *Librn,* Shelly Alexander; E-mail: alexanders@cityofnorthlasvegas.com; *Pub Serv Librn,* Bradley Squires; E-mail: squiresb@cityofnorthlasvegas.com
Library Holdings: CDs 420; DVDs 2,500; Bk Vols 49,000; Per Subs 30; Talking Bks 300
Open Mon-Thurs 10:30-8, Sat 9-6
ALIANTE LIBRARY, 2400 Deer Springs Way, 89084. Tel: 702-839-2980. FAX: 702-839-5707. *Dir,* Kathy Pennell; *Br Mgr,* Jean Anderson
Open Mon-Thurs 10:30-8, Fri & Sat 9-6

PAHRUMP

P PAHRUMP COMMUNITY LIBRARY*, 701 E St, 89048-2164. SAN 309-720X. Tel: 775-727-5930. FAX: 775-727-6209. Web Site: www.pahrumplibrary.com. *Dir,* Susan Wonderly; *Asst Dir,* Mandy Caffeo; E-mail: asstdir@pahrumplibrary.com; *Ch Serv, YA Serv,* Brenda Gibbons; E-mail: childrens@pahrumplibrary.com; *Ref,* Lynne Ivy; E-mail: reference@pahrumplibrary.com
Pop 30,000; Circ 90,000

Library Holdings: Bk Titles 50,000; Per Subs 54
Special Collections: Nevada Coll
Automation Activity & Vendor Info: (Cataloging) Follett Software; (Circulation) Follett Software; (OPAC) Follett Software
Wireless access
Open Mon-Thurs 9-7, Fri & Sat 9-5
Friends of the Library Group

PIOCHE

P LINCOLN COUNTY LIBRARY*, 63 Main St, 89043. (Mail add: PO Box 330, 89043-0330), SAN 309-7218. Tel: 775-962-5244. FAX: 775-962-5244. *Dir,* Jo Lloyd
Pop 4,130; Circ 20,000
Library Holdings: Bk Vols 47,829; Per Subs 14
Automation Activity & Vendor Info: (Cataloging) Winnebago Software Co; (Circulation) Winnebago Software Co
Partic in CLAN (Cooperative Libraries Automated Network/Nevada); Nev Libr Asn
Open Mon, Wed & Thurs 10-3, Tues 1-6
Branches: 2
ALAMO BRANCH, 100 South First W, Alamo, 89001. (Mail add: PO Box 239, Alamo, 89001-0239). Tel: 775-725-3343. FAX: 775-725-3344. *Librn,* Vicki Higbee
Library Holdings: Bk Vols 13,000
Open Mon 1-6, Tues-Thurs 11-4
CALIENTE BRANCH, 100 Depot Ave, Caliente, 89008-0306. (Mail add: PO Box 306, Caliente, 89008-0306), SAN 324-1084. Tel: 775-726-3104. *Librn,* Carolyn Wilcox; E-mail: crwilcox@clan.lib.nv.us
Library Holdings: Bk Vols 12,000
Open Mon-Wed 10-3, Thurs 1-6
Bookmobiles: 1

RENO

S CHURCH OF JESUS CHRIST OF LATTER-DAY SAINTS*, Reno Family History Center, 4751 Neil Rd, 89502. (Mail add: 2931 Randolph Ct, 89502), SAN 370-6656. Tel: 775-826-1130. *Dir,* Loren Spencer; *Coll Develop,* LaRene Spencer
Library Holdings: CDs 250; Microforms 8,000; Bk Titles 5,000; Per Subs 2
Special Collections: Genealogy Coll
Wireless access
Open Tues-Thurs 10-9

S DESERT RESEARCH INSTITUTE, Patrick Squires Library, 2215 Raggio Pkwy, 89512-1095. SAN 309-7323. Tel: 775-674-7042. FAX: 775-674-7183. Web Site: www.dri.edu/library. *Dir, Libr Serv,* Melanie Scott; Tel: 775-674-7083, E-mail: melanie.scott@dri.edu; *Res Info Spec,* John Ford, Jr; E-mail: jford@dri.edu; Staff 2 (MLS 1, Non-MLS 1)
Founded 1977
Library Holdings: Bk Vols 13,350
Subject Interests: Atmospheric sci, Environ sci
Database Vendor: EBSCOhost, OCLC FirstSearch, ProQuest, TLC (The Library Corporation)
Wireless access
Function: For res purposes
Publications: New Books; Newsletter
Open Mon-Fri 8-5

L LIBRARY OF THE US COURTS*, 400 S Virginia St, Rm 1001, 89501. SAN 372-3410. Tel: 775-686-5776. FAX: 775-686-5779. *Librn,* Cheryl Bjerke
Library Holdings: Bk Titles 1,102; Bk Vols 22,000
Restriction: Not open to pub

C MORRISON UNIVERSITY LIBRARY*, 10315 Professional Circle, Ste 201, 89521. SAN 326-0305. Tel: 775-850-0700. FAX: 775-850-0711. Web Site: www.morrison.anthem.edu. *Dir,* Usha Mehta; E-mail: umehta@morrison.anthem.edu
Enrl 300; Fac 25
Library Holdings: Bk Titles 2,625; Bk Vols 3,035; Per Subs 40
Database Vendor: LexisNexis
Partic in Nev Libr Asn

S NEVADA DEPARTMENT OF TOURISM & CULTURAL AFFAIRS DIVISION OF MUSEUMS & HISTORY*, Research Library, 1650 N Virginia St, 89503. SAN 309-7250. Tel: 775-688-1190, Ext 227. FAX: 775-688-2917. Web Site: www.nevadaculture.org. *Librn,* Michael Maher; E-mail: mmaher@nevadaculture.org
Founded 1904
Library Holdings: Bk Titles 30,000; Per Subs 260
Special Collections: Nevada History Coll, ephemera, ms, maps, photogs. Oral History; State Document Depository; US Document Depository
Subject Interests: Communication in Nev, Gambling, Lumber, Mining, Transportation, Water, Western US
Publications: Nevada Historical Society (Quarterly)
Open Wed-Sat 12-4

M SAINT MARY'S REGIONAL MEDICAL CENTER*, Max C Fleischmann Medical Library, 235 W Sixth St, 89520-0108. SAN 309-7269. Tel: 775-770-3108. FAX: 775-770-3685. Web Site: www.saintmarysreno.com. *Librn,* Donna M Alexander; E-mail: donna.alexander@saintmarysreno.com; Staff 1 (MLS 1)
Founded 1956
Library Holdings: Bk Vols 900; Per Subs 100
Subject Interests: Allied health, Med, Nursing
Automation Activity & Vendor Info: (Acquisitions) EOS International; (Cataloging) EOS International; (Circulation) EOS International; (ILL) EOS International; (OPAC) EOS International; (Serials) EOS International
Partic in Nevada Medical Library Group; Northern California & Nevada Medical Library Group (NCNMLG); Pacific Southwest Regional Medical Library (PSRML)
Restriction: Staff use only

J TRUCKEE MEADOWS COMMUNITY COLLEGE*, Elizabeth Sturm Library, 7000 Dandini Blvd, 89512-3999. SAN 320-6947. Tel: 775-674-7600. Reference Tel: 775-674-7602. FAX: 775-673-8231. Web Site: www.tmcc.edu/library. *Dir, Libr Serv,* Michelle Noel; Tel: 775-674-7610, Fax: 775-674-8231, E-mail: mnoel@tmcc.edu; *Libr Syst Spec, Ref Librn,* John Fitzsimmons; Tel: 775-674-7609, E-mail: jfitzsimmons@tmcc.edu; *Ref Librn,* Maureen Leshendok; *Ref Librn,* Neil Siegel; Tel: 775-674-7608, E-mail: nsiegel@tmcc.edu; Staff 13 (MLS 5, Non-MLS 8)
Founded 1973. Enrl 6,210; Fac 175; Highest Degree: Associate
Jul 2005-Jun 2006 Income $1,043,946. Mats Exp $215,295, Books $136,754, Per/Ser (Incl. Access Fees) $11,877, Micro $217, AV Mat $15,908, Electronic Ref Mat (Incl. Access Fees) $49,926, Presv $613. Sal $596,382 (Prof $345,342)
Library Holdings: AV Mats 8,097; Bks on Deafness & Sign Lang 61; Braille Volumes 6; CDs 700; DVDs 1,000; e-journals 35; Music Scores 6; Bk Titles 47,560; Per Subs 105; Videos 1,000
Subject Interests: Career educ, Folklore, Health educ, Indust, Tech fields
Automation Activity & Vendor Info: (Acquisitions) Ex Libris Group; (Cataloging) Ex Libris Group; (Circulation) Ex Libris Group; (Course Reserve) Ex Libris Group; (ILL) Ex Libris Group; (OPAC) Ex Libris Group; (Serials) Ex Libris Group
Database Vendor: Agricola, ALLDATA Online, CQ Press, CredoReference, EBSCOhost, Ex Libris Group, Facts on File, Gale Cengage Learning, Ingram Library Services, JSTOR, Medline, Newsbank, ProQuest, PubMed, Sage, Westlaw
Wireless access
Special Services for the Deaf - Bks on deafness & sign lang
Special Services for the Blind - Accessible computers; Braille bks; Computer with voice synthesizer for visually impaired persons; Copier with enlargement capabilities; Networked computers with assistive software; Screen reader software; Ultimate talking dictionary
Open Mon-Thurs (Winter) 8am-9pm, Fri 8-5, Sat 10-5; Mon-Fri (Summer) 8-5
Departmental Libraries:
HI-TECH CENTER AT REDFIELD, 18600 Wedge Pkwy, Bldg B, 89511. Tel: 775-850-4049. FAX: 775-850-4030. *Libr Tech,* Ana Lidia Ferreira; E-mail: aferreira@tmcc.edu
Open Mon-Thurs 8-4:30
NELL J REDFIELD LEARNING RESOURCE CENTER, Technical Institute, 475 Edison Way, 89502-4103. Tel: 775-857-4990. FAX: 775-857-4976. *Libr Tech,* Avis Andrulli; E-mail: aandrulli@tmcc.edu
Library Holdings: Bks on Deafness & Sign Lang 25; e-journals 4,000; Bk Vols 300; Per Subs 20

C UNIVERSITY OF NEVADA-RENO*, Mathewson-IGT Knowledge Center, 1664 N Virginia St, Mailstop 0322, 89557-0322. SAN 350-3828. Tel: 775-682-5684. Circulation Tel: 775-682-5625. Interlibrary Loan Service Tel: 775-682-5636. Information Services Tel: 775-682-5657. FAX: 775-784-4529. Circulation FAX: 775-327-2181. Interlibrary Loan Service FAX: 775-784-1751. Web Site: www.knowledgecenter.unr.edu. *Dean, Libr & Teaching & Learning Tech,* Kathlin L Ray; E-mail: kray@unr.edu; *Asst Dean, Admin Serv,* Janita Jobe; Tel: 775-682-5688, E-mail: jobe@unr.edu; *Asst Dean, Coll & Knowledge Access Serv,* Steven R Harris; Tel: 775-682-5671, E-mail: stevenharris@unr.edu; *Acq,* Olivia Sullivan; Tel: 775-682-5582, Fax: 775-784-1328, E-mail: olivias@unr.edu; *Cat & Metadata,* Dana Miller; Tel: 775-682-5614, E-mail: danamiller@unr.edu; *Develop,* Millie Mitchell; Tel: 775-682-5682, E-mail: mimitchell@unr.edu; *Media & Data Serv,* Duncan Aldrich; Tel: 775-682-5669, E-mail: duncan@unr.edu; *Res Serv,* Pat Ragains; Tel: 775-682-5593, E-mail: ragains@unr.edu; *Spec Coll & Basque Libr,* Donnelyn Curtis; Tel: 775-682-5668, E-mail: dcurtis@unr.edu; *Tech Serv,* Paoshan Yue; Tel: 775-682-5599; Staff 28 (MLS 24, Non-MLS 4)
Founded 1886. Enrl 17,423; Fac 681; Highest Degree: Doctorate

Library Holdings: AV Mats 21,290; e-books 122,621; Microforms 3,771,392; Bk Vols 1,369,268; Per Subs 41,540
Special Collections: Basque Studies; Nevada & the Great Basin; Women in the West
Automation Activity & Vendor Info: (Cataloging) Innovative Interfaces, Inc; (Circulation) Innovative Interfaces, Inc; (Course Reserve) Innovative Interfaces, Inc; (ILL) Innovative Interfaces, Inc; (Media Booking) Innovative Interfaces, Inc; (OPAC) Innovative Interfaces, Inc; (Serials) Innovative Interfaces, Inc
Database Vendor: EBSCOhost, Gale Cengage Learning, LexisNexis, OCLC FirstSearch, OVID Technologies, ProQuest, Wilson - Wilson Web
Wireless access
Publications: Friends of the University Library Newsletter (Bi-annually); Knowledge Matters (Quarterly); Recently in the KC
Partic in OCLC Online Computer Library Center, Inc
Friends of the Library Group

Departmental Libraries:

DELAMARE LIBRARY, 1664 N Virginia St, MS 262, 89557-0262. Tel: 775-784-6945. FAX: 775-784-6949. *Head Librn,* Tod Colegrove; Tel: 775-682-5644, E-mail: pcolegrove@unr.edu. Subject Specialists: *Physics,* Tod Colegrove; Staff 3 (MLS 3)
Founded 1997. Highest Degree: Doctorate
Special Collections: US Geological Survey. US Document Depository
Subject Interests: Computer sci, Earth sci, Eng, Geog, Maps
Friends of the Library Group

CM SAVITT MEDICAL LIBRARY & IT DEPARTMENT, Pennington Medical Education Bldg, 1664 N Virginia St, Mail Stop 306, 89557, SAN 350-3976. Tel: 775-784-4625. FAX: 775-784-4489. Web Site: www.med.unr.edu/medlib. *Dir,* Terry Henner; E-mail: thenner@medicine.nevada.edu; *Circ Mgr,* Annie Abinanti; *Mgr, Info Sys,* Mark Sexton; *Head, Cat,* Carole Keith; *Head of Doc Delivery,* Norman Huckle; *Head, Ser,* Bonnie Ragains; Staff 9 (MLS 2, Non-MLS 7)
Founded 1978. Highest Degree: Doctorate
Library Holdings: e-books 41; e-journals 3,417; Bk Titles 13,631; Bk Vols 72,180; Per Subs 3,443
Special Collections: Nevada Medical Archives; Sons of Italy Birth Defects & Genetics Coll
Subject Interests: Audiology, Consumer health, Med, Pub health, Speech pathology
Function: Doc delivery serv, Health sci info serv, Homebound delivery serv, ILL available, Online searches, Outside serv via phone, mail, e-mail & web, Ref serv available, Referrals accepted, Telephone ref, Wheelchair accessible
Partic in National Network of Libraries of Medicine Pacific Southwest Region; Nevada Medical Library Group
Open Mon-Thurs (Winter) 7:30am-10pm, Fri 7:30-5, Sat 12-7, Sun 1-10; Mon-Thurs (Summer) 8-8, Fri 8-5, Sat & Sun 1-5

GL WASHOE COUNTY LAW LIBRARY*, 75 Court St, Rm 101, 89501. (Mail add: PO Box 30083, Courthouse, 89520-3083), SAN 309-7293. Tel: 775-328-3250. FAX: 775-328-3441. E-mail: lawlib@washoecounty.us. Web Site: www.washoecounty.us/lawlib. *Libr Dir,* Position Currently Open; *Interim Dir,* Howard Conyers; *Ref Librn,* Myndi Clive; *Tech Serv Librn,* Judy Chalmers; Staff 6 (MLS 3, Non-MLS 3)
Founded 1915
Library Holdings: Bk Titles 5,099; Bk Vols 52,755; Per Subs 315
Special Collections: General Law Library (Nevada Law, California Law Coll). US Document Depository
Automation Activity & Vendor Info: (Cataloging) SirsiDynix
Publications: Library Acquisitions Lists
Partic in Nev Educ Online Network; RLIN (Research Libraries Information Network); Westlaw
Open Mon & Fri 8-5, Tues, Wed & Thurs 8-7, Sat 10-5
Friends of the Library Group

P WASHOE COUNTY LIBRARY SYSTEM, 301 S Center St, 89501-2102. (Mail add: PO Box 2151, 89505-2151), SAN 350-4069. Interlibrary Loan Service Tel: 775-327-8333. Administration Tel: 775-327-8341. Interlibrary Loan Service FAX: 775-327-8334. Administration FAX: 775-327-8393. E-mail: library@washoecounty.us. Web Site: www.washoecountylibrary.us. *Dir,* Arnold Maurins; Tel: 775-327-8340, E-mail: amaurins@washoecounty.us; *Sr Pub Serv Librn,* Tammy Cirrincione; Tel: 775-327-8345, Fax: 775-327-8392, E-mail: tcirrincione@washoecounty.us; Staff 26 (MLS 13, Non-MLS 13)
Founded 1904. Pop 427,704
Jul 2012-Jun 2013 Income (Main Library and Branch(s)) $10,251,996, State $7,349, Federal $19,500, County $9,820,049, Locally Generated Income $176,188, Other $228,910. Mats Exp $702,543
Special Collections: State Document Depository; US Document Depository
Subject Interests: Gambling, Literacy, Nev hist
Automation Activity & Vendor Info: (Acquisitions) ByWater Solutions; (Cataloging) ByWater Solutions; (Circulation) ByWater Solutions; (OPAC) ByWater Solutions; (Serials) ByWater Solutions
Database Vendor: ABC-CLIO, Baker & Taylor, CQ Press, EBSCO Auto Repair Reference, EBSCOhost, Gale Cengage Learning, Grolier Online, LearningExpress, Newsbank, OCLC WorldShare Interlibrary Loan
Wireless access
Function: Adult bk club, Art exhibits, Audiobks via web, Bk club(s), Bks on CD, CD-ROM, Children's prog, Computer training, Computers for patron use, Copy machines, e-mail serv, Electronic databases & coll, Exhibits, Fax serv, Free DVD rentals, Govt ref serv, Handicapped accessible, Holiday prog, ILL available, Microfiche/film & reading machines, Music CDs, Online cat, Online ref, OverDrive digital audio bks, Preschool outreach, Prog for adults, Prog for children & young adult, Provide serv for the mentally ill, Pub access computers, Ref serv available, Spoken cassettes & CDs, Story hour, Summer & winter reading prog, Summer reading prog, Tax forms, Teen prog, Telephone ref, Web-catalog, Wheelchair accessible
Publications: Annual Report; Branch Monthly Calendars; Library Newsletter (Monthly); Listing of Branches (Reference guide)
Partic in Coop Libr Agency for Syst & Servs; Information Nevada
Special Services for the Deaf - High interest/low vocabulary bks; Staff with knowledge of sign lang
Special Services for the Blind - Large print bks
Friends of the Library Group

Branches: 12

DOWNTOWN RENO LIBRARY, 301 S Center St, 89501. (Mail add: PO Box 2151, 89505-2151). Tel: 775-327-8300. FAX: 775-327-8390. *Mgr,* Scottie Wallace; Tel: 775-327-8304; Staff 16 (MLS 4, Non-MLS 12)
Special Collections: State Document Depository; US Document Depository
Function: Art exhibits, Bilingual assistance for Spanish patrons, Bks on CD, Computers for patron use, Copy machines, e-mail serv, Electronic databases & coll, Exhibits, Fax serv, Free DVD rentals, ILL available, Microfiche/film & reading machines, Music CDs, Online cat, OverDrive digital audio bks, Photocopying/Printing, Pub access computers, Ref serv available, Ref serv in person, Scanner, Spanish lang bks, Story hour, Summer reading prog, Wheelchair accessible
Open Tues-Thurs 9-5, Sun 10-5
Friends of the Library Group

DUNCAN-TRANER COMMUNITY LIBRARY, 1650 Carville Dr, 89512. (Mail add: PO Box 2151, 89505-2151), SAN 374-7131. Tel: 775-333-5134. FAX: 775-333-5076. *Partnership Supvr,* Sarah Jaeck
Open Tues & Thurs 3-5:30
Friends of the Library Group

GERLACH COMMUNITY LIBRARY, 555 E Sunset Blvd, Gerlach, 89412. (Mail add: PO Box 2151, 89505-2151), SAN 371-9782. Tel: 775-557-2326. FAX: 775-557-2587. *Mgr,* Judy Conley
Library Holdings: Bk Vols 6,607
Open Mon & Wed-Fri 8-2, Tues 5:30-7:30
Friends of the Library Group

INCLINE VILLAGE LIBRARY, 845 Alder Ave, Incline Village, 89451. (Mail add: PO Box 2151, 89505-2151), SAN 350-4093. Tel: 775-832-4130. FAX: 775-832-4180. *Mgr,* Pam Rasmussen; Tel: 775-832-4132, E-mail: prasmussen@washoecounty.us
Library Holdings: Bk Vols 37,023
Special Collections: Lake Tahoe Coll
Open Tues-Sat 11-6
Friends of the Library Group

NORTH VALLEYS LIBRARY, 1075 N Hills Blvd, No 340, 89506. (Mail add: PO Box 2151, 89505-2151), SAN 350-4158. Tel: 775-972-0281. FAX: 775-972-6810. *Mgr,* Patti Day; Tel: 775-972-0271, E-mail: pday@washoecounty.us
Open Tues, Thurs & Fri 10-5, Wed 10-7, Sat 10-4
Friends of the Library Group

NORTHWEST RENO LIBRARY, 2325 Robb Dr, 89523. (Mail add: PO Box 2151, 89505), SAN 374-7123. Tel: 775-787-4100. FAX: 775-787-4127. *Managing Librn,* Kristin Reinke; Tel: 775-787-4117, E-mail: kreinke@washoecounty.us
Library Holdings: Bk Vols 94,487
Special Collections: Holocaust Education. State Document Depository; US Document Depository
Subject Interests: Nev
Open Tues & Wed 11-7, Thurs & Fri 10-6, Sat 10-5
Friends of the Library Group

SENIOR CENTER LIBRARY, 1155 E Ninth St, 89512. (Mail add: PO Box 2151, 89505-2151), SAN 350-4115. Tel: 775-328-2586. FAX: 775-785-4610. *Partnership Supvr,* Sarah Jaeck
Open Tues-Fri 9-1
Friends of the Library Group

SIERRA VIEW LIBRARY, 4001 S Virginia St, 89502. (Mail add: PO Box 2151, 89505-2151), SAN 329-6385. Tel: 775-827-3232. FAX: 775-827-8792. *Mgr,* John Crockett; Tel: 775-827-0327
Founded 1987
Open Tues-Fri 10-6, Sat 10-5
Friends of the Library Group

SOUTH VALLEYS LIBRARY, 15650A Wedge Pkwy, 89511. (Mail add: PO Box 2151, 89505-2151), SAN 373-5001. Tel: 775-851-5190. FAX: 775-851-5188. *Mgr,* Julie Ullman; Tel: 775-851-8540
Library Holdings: Bk Vols 60,072
Open Tues & Wed 11-7, Thurs & Fri 10-6, Sat 10-5
Friends of the Library Group

SPANISH SPRINGS LIBRARY, 7100A Pyramid Lake Hwy, Sparks, 89436-6669. (Mail add: PO Box 2151, 89505-2151). Tel: 775-424-1800. FAX: 775-424-1840. *Libr Mgr,* Julie Machado; Tel: 775-424-1844, E-mail: jmachado@washoecounty.us
Library Holdings: Bk Vols 69,199
Open Mon, Wed & Thurs 10-6, Tues 11-7, Sun 10-5
Friends of the Library Group

SPARKS LIBRARY, 1125 12th St, Sparks, 89431. (Mail add: PO Box 2151, 89505-2151), SAN 350-4123. Tel: 775-352-3200. FAX: 775-352-3207. *Mgr,* Corinne Dickman; Tel: 775-352-3204
Founded 1932
Special Collections: Auto Repair Manual Coll, classic-current; Rail City Coll, railroads & rails
Special Services for the Blind - Talking bks
Open Tues 11-7, Wed-Fri 10-6, Sat 10-5
Friends of the Library Group

VERDI COMMUNITY LIBRARY, 270 Bridge St, Verdi, 89439. (Mail add: PO Box 2151, 89505-2151), SAN 371-9790. Tel: 775-345-8104. FAX: 775-345-8106. *Partnership Supvr,* Sarah Jaeck
Open Wed 3-7, Sat 10-4
Friends of the Library Group

ROUND MOUNTAIN

P SMOKY VALLEY LIBRARY DISTRICT*, Round Mountain Public Library, 73 Hadley Circle, 89045. (Mail add: PO Box 1428, 89045-1428). Tel: 775-377-2215. FAX: 775-377-2699. *Dir,* Jeanne Bleecker; *Asst Dir,* Andrea Madziarek; E-mail: andream@smokeyvalleylibrarydistrict.com; Staff 6 (Non-MLS 6)
Pop 1,773; Circ 55,000
Library Holdings: CDs 500; DVDs 2,500; Large Print Bks 200; Bk Titles 35,000; Per Subs 45; Videos 2,500
Automation Activity & Vendor Info: (Cataloging) Follett Software; (Circulation) Follett Software; (Media Booking) Innovative Interfaces, Inc
Wireless access
Function: Accelerated reader prog, Bilingual assistance for Spanish patrons, Bks on cassette, Bks on CD, Children's prog, Computers for patron use, Copy machines, Distance learning, Electronic databases & coll, Exhibits, Fax serv, Free DVD rentals, Holiday prog, Homework prog, ILL available, Music CDs, Notary serv, Online cat, Online ref, Online searches, Photocopying/Printing, Summer reading prog, Tax forms, VHS videos, Video lending libr
Open Mon-Fri 8-8, Sat 10-2
Friends of the Library Group
Branches: 1
MANHATTAN BRANCH, Schoolhouse & Gold Sts, Manhattan, 89022. (Mail add: PO Box 95, Manhattan, 89022-0095). Tel: 775-487-2326. FAX: 775-377-2699. *Librn,* Tony Grimes; Staff 0.5 (Non-MLS 0.5)
Pop 120; Circ 1,500
Library Holdings: Bk Vols 5,000
Function: Fax serv, Music CDs, Online ref, Photocopying/Printing, Tax forms, VHS videos, Video lending libr, Wheelchair accessible
Open Wed, Fri & Sat 10-3, Thurs 2-7

SILVERPEAK

P SILVERPEAK LIBRARY*, Ten Montezuma St, 89047. (Mail add: PO Box 128, 89047-0128). Tel: 775-937-2215. FAX: 775-937-2215. *Dir,* Kristine MacDonald; E-mail: kemacdon@clan.lib.nv.us
Library Holdings: Bk Vols 6,000
Automation Activity & Vendor Info: (Cataloging) Innovative Interfaces, Inc; (Circulation) Innovative Interfaces, Inc; (OPAC) Innovative Interfaces, Inc
Partic in CLAN (Cooperative Libraries Automated Network/Nevada)
Open Tues 1-8, Wed 10-6, Thurs 10-4
Branches: 1
GOLDFIELD PUBLIC LIBRARY, 233 Crook St, Goldfield, 89013. (Mail add: PO Box 430, Goldfield, 89013-0430), SAN 309-7048. Tel: 775-485-3236. FAX: 775-485-3236. *Dir,* Kristine MacDonald; *Librn,* Amanda Elsea; E-mail: arelsea@clan.lib.nv.us
Founded 1976. Pop 558
Library Holdings: Bk Vols 8,000
Open Tues 1-8, Wed 10-6, Thurs 12-6

TONOPAH

S CENTRAL NEVADA MUSEUM & HISTORICAL SOCIETY*, 1900 Logan Field Rd, 89049. (Mail add: PO Box 326, 89049-0326), SAN 373-241X. Tel: 775-482-9676. FAX: 775-482-5423. E-mail: cnmuseum@citlink.net. Web Site: www.tonopahnevada.com. *Curator,* Eva La Rue; Staff 2 (Non-MLS 2)
Founded 1981
Library Holdings: Bk Titles 2,000; Videos 200
Special Collections: Central Nevada History Coll. Oral History
Function: Audio & video playback equip for onsite use, Bus archives, CD-ROM, Newsp ref libr, Photocopying/Printing, VHS videos, Wheelchair accessible
Open Tues-Sat 9-5
Restriction: Restricted access

L NYE COUNTY LAW LIBRARY*, 101 Radar Rd, 89049. (Mail add: PO Box 393, 89049), SAN 373-0794. Tel: 775-482-8103. FAX: 775-482-8198. *Librn,* Jerie Clifford; Tel: 775-482-8141
Library Holdings: Bk Vols 9,500
Partic in Westlaw
Open Mon-Fri 8-5

P TONOPAH LIBRARY DISTRICT*, 167 S Central St, 89049. (Mail add: PO Box 449, 89049-0449). Tel: 775-482-3374. FAX: 775-482-5143. E-mail: tonopahlibrary@hotmail.com. *Interim Dir,* Sandy Baldwin
Circ 14,823
Library Holdings: DVDs 300; Bk Vols 9,679; Talking Bks 2,387
Special Collections: Topographic Maps
Subject Interests: Geol, Mining
Automation Activity & Vendor Info: (Acquisitions) Innovative Interfaces, Inc; (Cataloging) Innovative Interfaces, Inc; (Circulation) Innovative Interfaces, Inc; (OPAC) Innovative Interfaces, Inc
Wireless access
Partic in CLAN (Cooperative Libraries Automated Network/Nevada)
Open Tues-Fri 1-6, Sat 11-2
Friends of the Library Group

WINNEMUCCA

P HUMBOLDT COUNTY LIBRARY*, 85 E Fifth St, 89445. SAN 350-4182. Tel: 775-623-6388. FAX: 775-623-6438. *Dir,* Sharon Allen; *Asst Dir,* LeAnn Autrey; *Ch,* Lawana Ferier
Founded 1923. Pop 16,500; Circ 160,000
Library Holdings: Bk Vols 55,000; Per Subs 171
Special Collections: Local History Coll; Nevada Coll
Partic in CLAN (Cooperative Libraries Automated Network/Nevada)
Open Mon, Thurs-Sat 9-5, Tues & Wed 9-9
Branches: 2
DENIO BRANCH, PO Box 230, Denio, 89404-0230. Tel: 775-941-0330. FAX: 775-941-0330. E-mail: deniolibrary@hotmail.com. *Librn,* Sherry Ranf
Library Holdings: Bk Vols 2,000
Open Tues & Thurs 1-5, Wed 7pm-9pm
MCDERMITT BRANCH, Hwy 95, McDermitt, 89421. (Mail add: PO Box 444, McDermitt, 89421-0444). Tel: 775-532-8014. FAX: 775-532-8018. E-mail: mcdlibrary89421@yahoo.com. *Librn,* Victoria Easterday
Library Holdings: Bk Titles 6,000
Bookmobiles: 1. Librn, Ginny Dufurrena

S NORTH CENTRAL NEVADA HISTORICAL SOCIETY*, Humboldt Museum Research Department, Maple Ave & Jungo Rd, 89446. (Mail add: PO Box 819, 89446-0819), SAN 373-2428. Tel: 775-623-2912. FAX: 775-623-5640. Web Site: www.humboldtmuseum.org. *Curator,* Pansilee Larson
Library Holdings: Bk Vols 5,000
Publications: The Humboldt Historian
Open Mon-Fri 9-4, Sat (Summer) 1-4

YERINGTON

P LYON COUNTY LIBRARY SYSTEM*, 20 Nevin Way, 89447. SAN 350-4271. Tel: 775-463-6645. FAX: 775-463-6646. Web Site: www.lyon-county.org. *Libr Mgr,* Amy Geddes; E-mail: ageddes@clan.lib.nv.us; *ILL,* Lynn Evans
Pop 26,680; Circ 101,716
Library Holdings: Bk Vols 108,000; Per Subs 65
Automation Activity & Vendor Info: (Cataloging) Innovative Interfaces, Inc; (Circulation) Innovative Interfaces, Inc; (OPAC) Innovative Interfaces, Inc
Partic in CLAN (Cooperative Libraries Automated Network/Nevada); Coop Libr Syst Region II
Open Tues & Wed 1-6, Sat 11-4
Friends of the Library Group
Branches: 4
DAYTON VALLEY BRANCH, 321 Old Dayton Valley Rd, Dayton, 89403-8902, SAN 377-0257. Tel: 775-246-6212. FAX: 775-246-6213. *Br Mgr,* Summer Bell; E-mail: sdbell@clan.lib.nv.us
Open Tues & Thurs 11-4, Wed 1-6
Friends of the Library Group

FERNLEY BRANCH, 575 Silver Lace Blvd, Fernley, 89408-8547, SAN 350-4301. Tel: 775-575-3366. FAX: 775-575-3368. *Mgr,* Jonnica McClure
Circ 19,000
Open Tues-Fri 9-6, Sat 11-4
Friends of the Library Group

SILVER-STAGE BRANCH, 3905 Hwy 50 W, Silver Springs, 89429, SAN 350-428X. Tel: 775-577-5015. FAX: 775-577-5013. *Br Mgr,* Leigh Zevenbergen
Open Wed-Fri 9-6, Sat 9-4
Friends of the Library Group

SMITH VALLEY BRANCH, 22 Day Lane, Smith, 89430-9707, SAN 377-0273. Tel: 775-465-2369. FAX: 775-465-2309. *Mgr,* Ginny Stockman
Open Tues-Fri 1-6, Sat 11-4
Friends of the Library Group

NEW HAMPSHIRE

Date of Statistics: FY 2013
Population, U.S. Census 2010: 1,316,470
Population Served by Public Libraries: 1,002,752
Total Volumes in Public Libraries: 5,841,411
Volumes Per Capita: 4.44
Total Public Library Circulation: 10,861,922
Circulation Per Capita: 8.25
Total Public Library Income (not including Grants-in-Aid): $55,529,982
Income Per Capita: $55.35
Source of Income: Mainly public funds (2/3 public, 1/3 endowment)
Total Public Library Expenditures: $55,063,080
Expenditures Per Capita: $41.83

ACWORTH

P ACWORTH SILSBY LIBRARY*, Five Lynn Hill Rd, 03601. (Mail add: PO Box 179, 03601-0179), SAN 324-3729. Tel: 603-835-2150. E-mail: acworthlibrary@myfairpoint.net. Web Site: www.acworthlibrary.org. *Adminr,* Susan Metsack; *Adminr,* Linda Thomson-Mohr
Founded 1891. Pop 1,511; Circ 3,883
Library Holdings: AV Mats 361; Bk Titles 8,000; Per Subs 13; Talking Bks 210
Subject Interests: NH hist
Publications: Library & Town (Newsletter)
Open Tues & Thurs 11:30-5:30, Sat & Sun 11:30-4:30
Friends of the Library Group

ALEXANDRIA

P HAYNES LIBRARY*, 33 Washburn Rd, 03222-6532. (Mail add: 567 Washburn Rd, 03222-6532), SAN 320-4898. Tel: 603-744-6529. *Librn,* Nancy Butler; E-mail: nancybutler77@yahoo.com; *Asst Librn,* Ruth Harrow
Founded 1885. Circ 1,218
Library Holdings: Bk Vols 7,000
Special Collections: Local History Coll
Open Mon 1:30-4:30 & 7-8

ALLENSTOWN

P ALLENSTOWN PUBLIC LIBRARY*, 59 Main St, 03275-1716. SAN 309-7358. Tel: 603-485-7651. E-mail: allenstownlib@comcast.net. *Dir,* Position Currently Open; *Children & Young Adult Supvr,* Pat Adams; *Adult Serv,* Rose Bergerone
Pop 5,000; Circ 5,784
Library Holdings: Bk Vols 12,500; Per Subs 28
Subject Interests: Historic maps, Town hist
Open Mon 1-5 & 6-8, Tues 10-12, 1-5 & 6-8, Thurs 10-12 & 1-5, Fri 12-8
Restriction: Residents only

ALSTEAD

P SHEDD-PORTER MEMORIAL LIBRARY*, Three Main St, 03602. (Mail add: PO Box 209, 03602-0209), SAN 309-7366. Tel: 603-835-6661. Web Site: sheddporter.wordpress.com. *Dir,* Shelli Huntley; E-mail: shelli.huntley@sheddporter.org; *Asst Librn,* Gaale Klein; Staff 1 (Non-MLS 1)
Founded 1910. Pop 1,463; Circ 20,000
Library Holdings: Bk Vols 33,500; Per Subs 20
Wireless access
Open Wed & Fri 11-5, Thurs 11-7, Sat 9-Noon

ALTON

P GILMAN PUBLIC LIBRARY, 100 Main St, 03809. (Mail add: PO Box 960, 03809-0960), SAN 309-7374. Tel: 603-875-2550. FAX: 603-875-2550. E-mail: gilmanlibrary@metrocast.net. Web Site: gilmanlibrary.org. *Libr Dir,* Holly Brown; *Asst Dir,* Rozalind Benoit
Founded 1951. Pop 3,800; Circ 23,426
Jan 2013-Dec 2013 Income $139,127. Mats Exp $14,530, Books $7,871, AV Mat $5,384, Electronic Ref Mat (Incl. Access Fees) $1,275. Sal $89,960
Library Holdings: CDs 1,134; DVDs 2,647; e-books 7,219; Bk Titles 18,265; Per Subs 51
Automation Activity & Vendor Info: (Acquisitions) Biblionix/Apollo; (Cataloging) Biblionix/Apollo; (Circulation) Biblionix/Apollo; (Course Reserve) Biblionix/Apollo
Database Vendor: Biblionix/Apollo
Wireless access
Open Tues & Thurs 11-7, Wed & Fri 9-5, Sat 9-1
Friends of the Library Group

AMHERST

P AMHERST TOWN LIBRARY*, 14 Main St, 03031. SAN 309-7382. Tel: 603-673-2288. FAX: 603-672-6063. E-mail: library@amherstlibrary.org. Web Site: www.amherstlibrary.org. *Dir,* Amy LaPointe; E-mail: alapointe@amherstlibrary.org; *Head, Ch,* Sarah Hydorn; E-mail: shydorn@amherstlibrary.org; *Head, Circ & Pub Servs,* Sarah Leonardi; E-mail: sleonardi@amherstlibrary.org; *Head, Ref & Adult Prog,* Ruslyn Vear; E-mail: rvear@amherstlibrary.org; Staff 21 (MLS 4, Non-MLS 17)
Founded 1891. Pop 10,000; Circ 138,107
Library Holdings: Bk Titles 55,783; Bk Vols 73,483; Per Subs 136
Automation Activity & Vendor Info: (Cataloging) SirsiDynix; (Circulation) SirsiDynix; (OPAC) SirsiDynix; (Serials) SirsiDynix
Database Vendor: EBSCOhost, Gale Cengage Learning, OCLC FirstSearch, ProQuest
Partic in GMILCS, Inc
Special Services for the Blind - Magnifiers; Screen enlargement software for people with visual disabilities; Talking bks
Open Mon-Thurs 9:30-8:30, Fri & Sat 9:30-5, Sun 1-5
Friends of the Library Group

ANDOVER

P ANDOVER PUBLIC LIBRARY*, 11 School St, 03216. (Mail add: PO Box 450, 03216), SAN 309-7390. Tel: 603-735-5333. FAX: 603-735-6975. E-mail: andoverpl@comcast.net. Web Site: www.andover.k12.nh.us. *Librn,* Priscilla Poulin
Pop 1,584; Circ 10,328
Library Holdings: Bk Vols 11,000; Per Subs 33
Wireless access
Open Mon 6:30pm-8:30pm, Wed 9-12 & 6:30-8:30, Thurs 12:30-4:30
Friends of the Library Group

ANTRIM

P JAMES A TUTTLE LIBRARY*, 45 Main St, 03440-3906. (Mail add: PO Box 235, 03440-0235), SAN 309-7412. Tel: 603-588-6786. E-mail: tuttlelib@comcast.net. Web Site: www.antrimnh.org. *Dir,* Kathryn R Chisholm; E-mail: krchisholm@yahoo.com; *Asst Dir,* Melissa Lawless; *Ch,* Maureen Reider; Staff 5 (Non-MLS 5)
Founded 1908. Pop 2,700; Circ 28,191
Library Holdings: Bk Titles 22,000
Subject Interests: Genealogy, NH hist
Automation Activity & Vendor Info: (Acquisitions) Follett Software; (Cataloging) Follett Software; (Circulation) Follett Software; (ILL) SirsiDynix; (OPAC) Follett Software
Database Vendor: OCLC FirstSearch, ProQuest
Wireless access
Function: Archival coll, Audiobks via web, Bks on cassette, Bks on CD, Children's prog, Computers for patron use, Copy machines, Digital talking bks, Electronic databases & coll, Free DVD rentals, Handicapped accessible, Holiday prog, Homebound delivery serv, ILL available, Mail & tel request accepted, Music CDs, OverDrive digital audio bks, Photocopying/Printing, Prog for adults, Prog for children & young adult, Pub access computers, Ref serv available, Spoken cassettes & CDs, Spoken cassettes & DVDs, Story hour, Summer reading prog, Tax forms, Telephone ref, VHS videos, Wheelchair accessible
Partic in New Hampshire Automated Information Systems (NHAIS)
Open Mon & Wed 2-6, Tues & Thurs 2-8, Fri 9-12, Sat 10-4
Restriction: Authorized patrons
Friends of the Library Group

ASHLAND

P ASHLAND TOWN LIBRARY*, 42 Main St, 03217. (Mail add: PO Box 660, 03217-0660), SAN 309-7420. Tel: 603-968-7928. FAX: 603-968-7928. E-mail: ashlandlibrary@roadrunner.com. Web Site: www.ashlandtownlibrary.org/. *Dir,* Sara Weinberg; *Asst Dir,* Terry Fouts
Pop 1,915; Circ 4,777
Library Holdings: Bk Titles 18,000; Per Subs 28
Automation Activity & Vendor Info: (Circulation) Follett Software
Open Mon, Tues & Thurs 1-7, Fri & Sat 10-2

ASHUELOT

P THAYER PUBLIC LIBRARY*, Three Main St, 03441-2616. (Mail add: PO Box 67, 03441-0067). Tel: 603-239-4099. E-mail: thayerlibrary@gmail.com. *Dir,* Jennifer Bellan; E-mail: jennbellan@myfairpoint.net
Pop 4,200
Library Holdings: Bk Vols 5,600; Talking Bks 50
Open Mon & Thurs 1-6

ATKINSON

P KIMBALL LIBRARY*, Five Academy Ave, 03811-2202. SAN 309-7439. Tel: 603-362-5234. FAX: 603-362-6095. E-mail: kimballpubliclibrary@hotmail.com. Web Site: www.kimballlibrary.com. *Dir,* Diane Heer; E-mail: director@kimballlibrary.com; Staff 11 (MLS 1, Non-MLS 10)
Founded 1894. Pop 7,000; Circ 93,880
Jan 2010-Dec 2010 Income $355,147. Mats Exp $48,600, Books $30,000, AV Equip $6,600, AV Mat $10,000, Electronic Ref Mat (Incl. Access Fees) $2,000
Library Holdings: Audiobooks 1,925; CDs 816; DVDs 2,241; Large Print Bks 322; Bk Vols 31,605; Per Subs 98
Special Collections: New England, audio, bks, large-print bks
Subject Interests: Local hist
Automation Activity & Vendor Info: (Circulation) Follett Software; (OPAC) Follett Software; (Serials) Follett Software
Wireless access
Partic in WinnShare Libr Coop
Open Mon-Fri 10-8, Sat 10-3
Friends of the Library Group

AUBURN

P GRIFFIN FREE PUBLIC LIBRARY*, 22 Hooksett Rd, 03032. (Mail add: PO Box 308, 03032-0308), SAN 309-7447. Tel: 603-483-5374. FAX: 603-483-0483. Web Site: griffinfree.com/. *Dir,* Ricky Sirois; E-mail: director@griffinfree.com; *Tech Serv Librn,* Deborah Dimitriadis
Pop 4,200
Library Holdings: Bk Vols 16,500; Per Subs 12
Automation Activity & Vendor Info: (Circulation) SirsiDynix
Open Tues & Fri 10-5, Wed & Thurs 12:30-8, Sat (Sept-June) 10-1
Friends of the Library Group

BARRINGTON

P BARRINGTON PUBLIC LIBRARY, 105 Ramsdell Lane, 03825. SAN 309-7463. Tel: 603-664-9715. Administration Tel: 603 664-0193. FAX: 603-664-5219. Web Site: www.barringtonlibrary.com. *Dir,* Amy Inglis; E-mail: director@barringtonlibrary.com; *Ch,* Wendy Rowe; E-mail: children@barringtonlibrary.com; *Circ Librn,* David Berube; E-mail: circulation@barringtonlibrary.com; *ILL,* Heather Dyer; E-mail: interlibraryloan@barringtonlibrary.com; Staff 5 (MLS 1, Non-MLS 4)
Founded 1795. Pop 8,576; Circ 100,000
Jan 2013-Dec 2013 Income $284,708, City $260,694, Locally Generated Income $22,349, Other $1,665. Mats Exp $26,682. Sal $162,345 (Prof $86,830)
Library Holdings: Audiobooks 9,159; Bks on Deafness & Sign Lang 30; CDs 641; DVDs 3,177; e-books 15,664; High Interest/Low Vocabulary Bk Vols 51; Large Print Bks 495; Bk Vols 42,858; Per Subs 51
Special Collections: Local Historical Society, bks & doc. Oral History
Subject Interests: Genealogy, Local area histories, Modern poetry
Automation Activity & Vendor Info: (Cataloging) Book Systems; (Circulation) Book Systems; (ILL) SirsiDynix; (OPAC) Book Systems
Database Vendor: EBSCOhost, Evanced Solutions, Inc, Overdrive, Inc, ProQuest
Wireless access
Function: ILL available, Photocopying/Printing, Telephone ref
Partic in New Hampshire Automated Information Systems (NHAIS)
Special Services for the Blind - Bks on CD
Open Mon & Fri 10-6, Tues & Thurs 10-7, Wed 10-8, Sat 10-3
Friends of the Library Group

BARTLETT

P BARTLETT PUBLIC LIBRARY*, Main St, 03812. (Mail add: PO Box 399, 03812-0399), SAN 309-7471. Tel: 603-374-2755. FAX: 603-374-2755. E-mail: bartlettpubliclibrary@roadrunner.com. Web Site: www.barlettpubliclibrary.org. *Dir,* Kathy Van Deursen; *Asst Librn,* Beth Lincoln
Library Holdings: Bk Titles 19,000; Per Subs 60
Automation Activity & Vendor Info: (Circulation) Follett Software
Open Mon & Wed 2-8, Tues & Thurs 2-5, Sat 11-3

BATH

P BATH PUBLIC LIBRARY*, Two W Bath Rd, 03740. (Mail add: PO Box 5, 03740-0005), SAN 309-748X. Tel: 603-747-3372. FAX: 603-747-3372. E-mail: bathlibrary@together.net. *Libr Dir,* Bernie Prochnik; *Asst Librn,* Kathie Bonor
Pop 893; Circ 2,900
Library Holdings: AV Mats 259; Bk Vols 13,748
Open Tues & Thurs 9-12 & 1-6, Sat 9-Noon

BEDFORD

P BEDFORD PUBLIC LIBRARY*, Three Meetinghouse Rd, 03110-5406. SAN 309-7498. Tel: 603-472-2300, 603-472-3023. FAX: 603-472-2978. Web Site: www.bedford.lib.nh.us. *Dir,* Mary Ann Senatro; E-mail: msenatro@bedford.lib.nh.us; *Asst Dir,* Miriam J Johnson; *Dir, Ch Serv,* Luci Albertson; *Head, Circ,* Caitlin Stevens; *Head, Ref Serv,* Emily Weiss; *Head, Tech Serv,* Anne Murphy; Staff 6 (MLS 5, Non-MLS 1)
Founded 1789. Pop 18,274; Circ 210,198
Jan 2006-Dec 2006 Income $897,090. Mats Exp $86,020. Sal $413,035
Library Holdings: Bk Vols 69,365; Per Subs 124
Special Collections: Sheet Music Coll. State Document Depository
Automation Activity & Vendor Info: (Acquisitions) Innovative Interfaces, Inc; (Cataloging) Innovative Interfaces, Inc; (Circulation) Innovative Interfaces, Inc; (OPAC) Innovative Interfaces, Inc; (Serials) Innovative Interfaces, Inc
Database Vendor: EBSCOhost, Gale Cengage Learning
Publications: Town Directory & Friends Newsletter
Friends of the Library Group

BELMONT

P BELMONT PUBLIC LIBRARY*, 146 Main St, 03220-0308. (Mail add: PO Box 308, 03220-0308), SAN 309-751X. Tel: 603-267-8331. FAX: 603-267-5924. E-mail: bpl@worldpath.net. Web Site: belmontpubliclibrary.org. *Dir,* Becky Albert; Staff 1 (Non-MLS 1)
Founded 1928. Pop 7,100; Circ 14,932
Library Holdings: CDs 155; DVDs 165; Electronic Media & Resources 370; High Interest/Low Vocabulary Bk Vols 335; Large Print Bks 285; Bk Titles 13,677; Bk Vols 15,178; Per Subs 53; Videos 496
Automation Activity & Vendor Info: (Cataloging) Follett Software; (Circulation) Follett Software; (OPAC) Follett Software
Function: Accelerated reader prog, Adult bk club, Adult literacy prog, After school storytime
Open Mon 12-6, Wed & Fri 10-4, Tues & Thurs 12-7, Sat 9-1

BENNINGTON

P GEP DODGE LIBRARY*, Two Main St, 03442. (Mail add: Seven School St, Unit 204, 03442), SAN 309-7528. Tel: 603-588-6585. FAX: 603-588-6585. E-mail: dodgelibrary1@comcast.net, dodgelibrary2@comcast.net. Web Site: www.dodgelibrary.com. *Dir,* Leslie MacGregor; *Asst Dir,* Melissa Searles
Founded 1906. Pop 1,183; Circ 13,618
Library Holdings: Audiobooks 973; AV Mats 1,245; CDs 453; Bk Vols 20,000; Per Subs 45; Talking Bks 839
Automation Activity & Vendor Info: (Cataloging) Follett Software; (Circulation) Follett Software
Database Vendor: EBSCOhost
Wireless access
Open Mon 9-7, Tues 9-6, Thurs 12-8, Fri 12-5, Sun 4-6
Friends of the Library Group

BERLIN

M ANDROSCOGGIN VALLEY HOSPITAL*, Medical Library, 59 Page Hill Rd, 03570. SAN 327-747X. Tel: 603-326-5833. FAX: 603-752-2501. *Librn,* Joyce LeClerc
Library Holdings: Bk Titles 200; Per Subs 85
Wireless access
Restriction: Open to staff only

P BERLIN PUBLIC LIBRARY, 270 Main St, 03570. SAN 309-7536. Tel: 603-752-5210. FAX: 603-752-8568. E-mail: librarian@berlinnh.gov. Web Site: berlinnh.gov/pages/berlinnh_library/index. *Dir,* Denise Jensen; *Ch,* Kathy Godin; Staff 4 (Non-MLS 4)
Founded 1893. Pop 9,743; Circ 31,327
Jul 2013-Jun 2014 Income $195,450. Mats Exp $19,000. Sal $54,946
Library Holdings: Audiobooks 3,868; CDs 8; DVDs 5,987; Large Print Bks 175; Bk Titles 14,733; Per Subs 462; Videos 1,119
Special Collections: French Fiction Coll
Wireless access
Partic in Central & Western Massachusetts Automated Resource Sharing; New Hampshire Automated Information Systems (NHAIS)
Open Mon, Tues, Thurs & Fri 10-6, Wed 12-7

S NEW HAMPSHIRE DEPARTMENT OF CORRECTIONS, Northern New Hampshire Correctional Facility Library, 138 E Milan Rd, 03570. Tel: 603-752-0160. FAX: 603-752-0405. Web Site: www.state.nh.us/nhdoc. *Librn,* Angela Poulin; E-mail: apoulin@nhdoc.state.nh.us
Founded 2000
Library Holdings: Bk Vols 8,250
Automation Activity & Vendor Info: (Cataloging) Follett Software; (Circulation) Follett Software
Database Vendor: LexisNexis
Open Mon-Fri 8-2:30

J WHITE MOUNTAINS COMMUNITY COLLEGE*, Fortier Library, 2020 Riverside Dr, 03570-3799. SAN 309-7552. Tel: 603-752-1113. Toll Free Tel: 800-445-4525. FAX: 603-752-6335. E-mail: berlinlibrary@ccsnh.edu. Web Site: www.wmcc.edu/services/lib. *Libr Dir,* Meagan Carr; Tel: 603-342-3086, E-mail: mcarr@ccsnh.edu; Staff 2 (MLS 1, Non-MLS 1)
Founded 1970. Enrl 1,000; Fac 50
Library Holdings: Bk Vols 17,000; Per Subs 125
Special Collections: State Document Depository
Automation Activity & Vendor Info: (Cataloging) TLC (The Library Corporation); (OPAC) TLC (The Library Corporation)
Database Vendor: ebrary, EBSCOhost, OCLC FirstSearch, ProQuest, TLC (The Library Corporation)
Wireless access
Partic in Docline; OCLC Online Computer Library Center, Inc
Open Mon-Thurs (Fall & Spring) 7am-9pm, Fri 7-7, Sat 9-2

BETHLEHEM

P BETHLEHEM PUBLIC LIBRARY, 2245 Main St, 03574. (Mail add: PO Box 250, 03574-0250), SAN 309-7560. Tel: 603-869-2409. FAX: 603-869-2410. Web Site: www.bethlehemlibrary.org. *Dir,* Laura Clerkin; E-mail: lclerkin@bethlehemlibrary.org; Staff 4 (MLS 2, Non-MLS 2)
Founded 1913. Pop 2,526; Circ 18,546
Library Holdings: DVDs 900; Bk Vols 14,800; Per Subs 57
Automation Activity & Vendor Info: (Cataloging) Book Systems; (Circulation) Book Systems; (OPAC) Book Systems
Database Vendor: EBSCOhost, OCLC WorldShare Interlibrary Loan, ProQuest
Wireless access
Function: Adult bk club, Audiobks via web, Bks on CD, Children's prog, Computers for patron use, Copy machines, E-Reserves, Electronic databases & coll, Fax serv, Free DVD rentals, Handicapped accessible, Homebound delivery serv, ILL available, Online cat, OverDrive digital audio bks, Photocopying/Printing, Printer for laptops & handheld devices, Prog for adults, Prog for children & young adult, Pub access computers, Ref serv in person, Scanner, Summer reading prog, Teen prog
Open Mon, Wed & Thurs 1-7, Tues & Fri 10-4, Sat 9-1
Friends of the Library Group

BOSCAWEN

P BOSCAWEN PUBLIC LIBRARY*, 116 N Main St, 03303-1123. SAN 350-4336. Tel: 603-753-8576. Web Site: www.boscawenlibrary.org. *Dir,* Eileen Gilbert; E-mail: boscawenpl@gmail.com; Staff 1 (Non-MLS 1)
Founded 1897. Pop 4,696; Circ 20,000
Library Holdings: Audiobooks 200; CDs 60; DVDs 500; e-books 3,000; Large Print Bks 600; Bk Titles 16,000; Bk Vols 18,000; Per Subs 30; Videos 1,500
Special Collections: Local History Coll; Town Records Coll
Wireless access
Function: Adult bk club, After school storytime, Children's prog, Computer training, Computers for patron use, Copy machines, Electronic databases & coll, ILL available, Online cat, Outside serv via phone, mail, e-mail & web, OverDrive digital audio bks, Photocopying/Printing, Preschool reading prog, Prog for adults, Prog for children & young adult, Pub access computers, Spoken cassettes & CDs, Spoken cassettes & DVDs, Story hour, Summer & winter reading prog
Open Mon 12-8, Tues-Thurs 10-6, Sat 9-1
Friends of the Library Group

BOW

P BAKER FREE LIBRARY*, 509 South St, 03304-3413. SAN 309-7579. Tel: 603-224-7113. FAX: 603-224-2063. E-mail: bowbakerfreelibrary@comcast.net. Web Site: www.bowbakerfreelibrary.org. *Dir,* Lori Fisher; *Ch,* Jennifer Ericsson; Staff 2 (MLS 1, Non-MLS 1)
Founded 1914. Pop 7,900; Circ 75,456
Jul 2007-Jun 2008 Income $377,111. Mats Exp $43,708, Books $23,258, Per/Ser (Incl. Access Fees) $5,500, AV Mat $13,500, Electronic Ref Mat (Incl. Access Fees) $1,200, Presv $250. Sal $205,958 (Prof $50,000)
Library Holdings: AV Mats 2,471; Bk Vols 34,786; Per Subs 138
Automation Activity & Vendor Info: (Cataloging) Follett Software; (Circulation) Follett Software; (OPAC) Follett Software
Wireless access
Function: Adult bk club, Art exhibits, Bks on CD, Children's prog, Electronic databases & coll, Fax serv, Homebound delivery serv, ILL available, Magnifiers for reading, Mus passes, Music CDs, Online cat, OverDrive digital audio bks, Photocopying/Printing, Prog for adults, Prog for children & young adult, Pub access computers, Summer reading prog, Teen prog
Open Mon-Thurs 10-8, Fri 10-7, Sat 9-1
Friends of the Library Group

BRADFORD

P BROWN MEMORIAL LIBRARY*, 78 W Main St, 03221-3308. (Mail add: PO Box 437, 03221-0437), SAN 309-7587. Tel: 603-938-5562. E-mail: brownml@conknet.com. *Dir,* Meg Fearnley; *Asst Librn,* Elsa Weir; Staff 3 (Non-MLS 3)
Founded 1893. Pop 1,500; Circ 11,445
Library Holdings: Bk Vols 11,000; Per Subs 15
Open Mon 10-8, Wed 10-7, Sat 10-3
Friends of the Library Group

BRENTWOOD

P MARY E BARTLETT MEMORIAL LIBRARY*, 22 Dalton Rd, 03833. SAN 309-7595. Tel: 603-642-3355. FAX: 603-642-3383. E-mail: bartlettlibrary@comcast.net. Web Site: www.brentwoodlibrary.org. *Dir,* Betsy Solon; E-mail: mebdirector@gmail.com; *Ch,* Joyce Miller; Staff 2 (Non-MLS 2)
Founded 1893. Pop 4,008; Circ 55,000
Jan 2007-Dec 2007 Income $171,219, City $155,530, Other $10,247. Mats Exp $26,814, Books $21,809, Per/Ser (Incl. Access Fees) $1,744, AV Mat $3,261. Sal $110,674
Library Holdings: Audiobooks 1,105; AV Mats 1,780; Bks on Deafness & Sign Lang 15; CDs 451; DVDs 330; Electronic Media & Resources 5; Large Print Bks 604; Bk Vols 35,401; Per Subs 75; Videos 1,264
Automation Activity & Vendor Info: (Cataloging) Follett Software; (Circulation) Follett Software; (OPAC) Follett Software
Database Vendor: Baker & Taylor, EBSCOhost, OCLC WebJunction
Wireless access
Partic in New Hampshire Automated Information Systems (NHAIS)
Open Mon 2-7, Tues-Thurs 9-5, Fri & Sat 9-1
Friends of the Library Group

BRISTOL

P MINOT-SLEEPER LIBRARY*, 35 Pleasant St, 03222-1407. SAN 309-7609. Tel: 603-744-3352. E-mail: mslibr@townofbristolnh.org. Web Site: www.townofbristolnh.org. *Dir,* Sharon Warga
Pop 3,033; Circ 12,556
Library Holdings: AV Mats 888; Bk Vols 13,195; Per Subs 53
Special Collections: Stuffed Bird Coll
Open Mon, Wed & Thurs 10-8, Fri 10-6, Sat 10-2
Friends of the Library Group

BROOKLINE

P BROOKLINE PUBLIC LIBRARY*, 16 Main St, 03033. (Mail add: PO Box 157, 03033-0157), SAN 309-7617. Tel: 603-673-3330. FAX: 603-673-0735. E-mail: library@brookline.nh.us. Web Site: www.brookline.nh.us/Library/. *Dir,* Myra Emmons; E-mail: library@brookline.nh.us; *Asst Dir,* Patricia Leonard; *Ch,* Aimee Gaudette
Pop 4,800; Circ 41,000
Library Holdings: Bk Vols 29,000; Per Subs 200
Automation Activity & Vendor Info: (Cataloging) Follett Software; (Circulation) Follett Software
Wireless access
Open Mon & Thurs 2-8, Tues 10-8, Wed & Fri 10-2, Sat (Sept-June) 10-2
Friends of the Library Group

CAMPTON

P CAMPTON PUBLIC LIBRARY*, 1110 New Hampshire, Rte 175, 03223. SAN 376-5113. Tel: 603-726-4877. FAX: 603-726-4877. E-mail: camptonpubliclibrary@gmail.com. Web Site: www.camptonlibrary.com/. *Dir,* Tara McKenzie
Library Holdings: DVDs 100; Bk Titles 13,000; Per Subs 16; Talking Bks 250; Videos 500
Automation Activity & Vendor Info: (Circulation) Follett Software
Wireless access
Open Tues, Thurs & Fri 3-9, Wed & Sat 9-4

CANAAN

P CANAAN TOWN LIBRARY*, 1173 US Rte 4, 03741. (Mail add: PO Box 368, 03741-0368), SAN 309-7633. Tel: 603-523-9650. E-mail: circulationdesk@canaanlibrary.org. Interlibrary Loan Service E-mail: ill@canaanlibrary.org. Web Site: www.canaanlibrary.org. *Libr Dir,* Amy Thurber; E-mail: athurber@canaanlibrary.org; *Asst Librn,* Lori Dacier; *Asst Librn,* Sharon Duffy; *Asst Librn,* Nancy Pike; *Asst Librn,* Pam Wotton; *ILL Librn,* Jenna McAlister; Staff 5 (Non-MLS 5)
Founded 1804. Pop 2,464; Circ 20,211
Library Holdings: Bk Vols 27,000; Per Subs 65
Automation Activity & Vendor Info: (Cataloging) Follett Software; (Circulation) Follett Software; (OPAC) Follett Software
Wireless access
Open Mon 3-9, Tues & Thurs 1-5, Wed 1-9, Fri 9-12, Sat 9-3
Friends of the Library Group

CANDIA

P SMYTH PUBLIC LIBRARY*, 55 High St, 03034. SAN 309-880X. Tel: 603-483-8245. FAX: 603-483-5217. E-mail: librarian@smythpl.org. Web Site: www.smythpl.org. *Dir,* Heidi Deacon; Staff 3 (Non-MLS 3)
Founded 1888. Pop 4,000; Circ 23,000
Jan 2006-Dec 2006 Income $124,000. Mats Exp $14,000. Sal $65,000
Library Holdings: Bk Vols 23,000; Per Subs 50
Special Collections: Local History Coll
Automation Activity & Vendor Info: (Cataloging) Follett Software; (Circulation) Follett Software; (OPAC) Follett Software
Open Mon-Wed 2-8, Thurs 10-8, Fri 5-8, Sat 10-2, Sun (Jan-March) 1-4
Friends of the Library Group

CANTERBURY

P ELKINS PUBLIC LIBRARY*, Nine Center Rd, 03224. (Mail add: PO Box 300, 03224-0300), SAN 309-7641. Tel: 603-783-4386. FAX: 603-783-4817. E-mail: sleclair@elkinspubliclibrary.org. Web Site: www.elkinspubliclibrary.org. *Dir,* Susan LeClair; E-mail: sleclair@elkinspubliclibrary.org; *Ch,* Rachel Baker; *Circ Mgr,* Debi Folsom
Founded 1927. Pop 2,037; Circ 22,330
Jan 2007-Dec 2007 Income $98,842. Mats Exp $9,500. Sal $58,100 (Prof $27,315)
Library Holdings: AV Mats 1,932; Large Print Bks 53; Bk Titles 17,698; Per Subs 28; Talking Bks 783; Videos 1,171
Special Collections: Shaker Coll
Automation Activity & Vendor Info: (Acquisitions) Baker & Taylor; (Cataloging) Baker & Taylor; (Circulation) Follett Software
Wireless access
Partic in New Hampshire Automated Information Systems (NHAIS)
Open Mon 2-8, Tues 12-6, Wed & Thurs 9-8, Sat 9-12

CARROL

P TWIN MOUNTAIN PUBLIC LIBRARY*, 92 School St, 03595. (Mail add: PO Box 149, Twin Mountain, 03595-0149), SAN 309-765X. Tel: 603-846-5818. FAX: 603-846-5712. E-mail: twinmountainpl@roadrunner.com. *Dir,* Tom McCorkill; Tel: 603-846-5818
Pop 722; Circ 900
Library Holdings: Bk Titles 6,000
Special Collections: White Mountain & Surrounding Region Material Coll (1800's), bks, pictures
Wireless access
Partic in New Hampshire Automated Information Systems (NHAIS)
Open Mon 5-8:30, Tues 9:30-1, Wed 1-5, Sat 1-4 (10-2 Summer)
Friends of the Library Group

CENTER BARNSTEAD

P OSCAR FOSS MEMORIAL LIBRARY, 111 S Barnstead Rd, 03225. (Mail add: Rte 126, PO Box 219, 03225-0219), SAN 309-7455. Tel: 603-269-3900. E-mail: ofml@metrocast.net. Web Site: www.oscarfoss.org. *Dir,* Sharon Archambault; *Youth Serv,* Christy Verville; E-mail: christy.ofml@gmail.com
Pop 3,000; Circ 8,655
Jan 2007-Dec 2007. Mats Exp $14,500
Library Holdings: Audiobooks 762; CDs 488; DVDs 606; e-books 5; Bk Vols 15,231; Per Subs 35
Automation Activity & Vendor Info: (Acquisitions) Book Systems; (Cataloging) Book Systems; (Circulation) Book Systems; (OPAC) Book Systems
Database Vendor: EBSCOhost
Wireless access
Open Mon 2-8, Tues & Wed 10-5, Thurs 5-8, Fri 2-5, Sat 9-12
Friends of the Library Group

CENTER HARBOR

P THE JAMES E NICHOLS MEMORIAL LIBRARY*, 35 Plymouth St, 03226-3341. (Mail add: PO Box 1339, 03226-1339), SAN 309-7668. Tel: 603-253-6950. FAX: 603-253-7219. E-mail: nicholsl@metrocast.net. Web Site: jnml.wordpress.com, www.metrocast.net/nicholslibrary. *Dir,* Allen Jon Kinnaman; Staff 3 (MLS 2, Non-MLS 1)
Founded 1910. Pop 1,018; Circ 13,037
Library Holdings: Audiobooks 675; CDs 228; DVDs 328; Large Print Bks 96; Bk Vols 15,850; Per Subs 33; Talking Bks 675
Automation Activity & Vendor Info: (OPAC) Follett Software
Database Vendor: EBSCOhost
Wireless access
Partic in Five Rivers Area Libr Network
Special Services for the Deaf - Closed caption videos
Special Services for the Blind - Bks available with recordings
Open Mon, Wed & Fri 10-6, Tues, Thurs & Sat 10-1

CENTER OSSIPEE

P OSSIPEE PUBLIC LIBRARY*, 74 Main St, 03814. (Mail add: PO Box 638, 03814), SAN 309-9210. Tel: 603-539-6390. FAX: 603-539-5758. E-mail: opl@worldpath.net. *Dir,* Maria Moulton; *Librn,* Polly Sheffer; *Asst Librn,* Jen Allen
Pop 4,678; Circ 31,106
Library Holdings: AV Mats 11,517; e-books 1,449; Bk Vols 30,895; Per Subs 38
Subject Interests: NH hist
Automation Activity & Vendor Info: (Acquisitions) Baker & Taylor; (Cataloging) Book Systems; (Circulation) Book Systems; (OPAC) Book Systems
Wireless access
Open Mon & Thurs 12-8, Tues & Fri 10-5, Sat 9-1
Friends of the Library Group

CENTER SANDWICH

P SAMUEL H WENTWORTH LIBRARY*, 35 Main St, 03227. SAN 309-9482. Tel: 603-284-6665. FAX: 603-284-6577. E-mail: sandwichlibrary@gmail.com. *Dir,* Glynis Miner
Pop 1,300; Circ 24,000
Library Holdings: Bk Vols 21,000; Per Subs 50
Automation Activity & Vendor Info: (Circulation) Book Systems
Wireless access
Publications: Library History
Open Mon-Thurs 12-6, Fri 10-6, Sat 10-1
Friends of the Library Group

CENTER STRAFFORD

P HILL LIBRARY*, 1151 Parker Mountain Rd, 03815. (Mail add: PO Box 130, 03815-0130), SAN 376-656X. Tel: 603-664-2800. FAX: 603-664-2800. E-mail: straflib@metrocast.net. Web Site: www.metrocast.net/~straflib. *Dir,* Kenneth Berry; *Asst Librn,* Charlotte Berry
Founded 1893. Pop 3,700
Library Holdings: Bk Titles 12,500; Per Subs 23
Automation Activity & Vendor Info: (Cataloging) Follett Software; (Circulation) Follett Software
Database Vendor: EBSCOhost
Wireless access
Open Mon 2-6, Tues 12-8, Wed & Thurs 2-8, Sat 10-2
Friends of the Library Group

CENTER TUFTONBORO

P TUFTONBORO FREE LIBRARY*, 221 Middle Rd, 03816. (Mail add: PO Box 73, 03816-0073), SAN 309-9733. Tel: 603-569-4256. FAX: 603-569-5885. E-mail: info@tuftonborolibrary.org. Web Site: www.tuftonborolibrary.org. *Co-Dir,* Lindalee M Lambert; *Co-Dir,* Christie V Sarles; Staff 2 (MLS 1, Non-MLS 1)
Founded 1839. Pop 2,500; Circ 40,000
Library Holdings: AV Mats 917; High Interest/Low Vocabulary Bk Vols 237; Large Print Bks 324; Bk Titles 20,923; Per Subs 28; Talking Bks 544
Subject Interests: Country living, Local hist, Nature
Automation Activity & Vendor Info: (Circulation) Follett Software
Database Vendor: EBSCO Information Services, EBSCOhost, Overdrive, Inc
Wireless access
Function: Adult bk club, Art exhibits, Audiobks via web, AV serv, Bk club(s), Bks on cassette, Bks on CD, Children's prog, Computers for patron use, Copy machines, Doc delivery serv, e-mail serv, E-Reserves, Electronic databases & coll, Exhibits, Fax serv, Free DVD rentals, Handicapped accessible, Holiday prog, Homebound delivery serv, ILL available, Mus passes, Music CDs, Online cat, Online searches, Orientations, Outreach serv, Outside serv via phone, mail, e-mail & web, OverDrive digital audio bks, Preschool outreach, Prog for adults, Prog for children & young adult, Pub access computers, Ref serv in person, Spoken cassettes & CDs, Spoken cassettes & DVDs, Story hour, Summer reading prog, Tax forms, Telephone ref, VHS videos, Video lending libr, Wheelchair accessible, Workshops
Partic in New Hampshire Automated Information Systems (NHAIS)
Open Tues-Fri 10-5:30, Sat 10-2
Restriction: Non-circulating coll, Non-resident fee, Open to pub for ref & circ; with some limitations
Friends of the Library Group

CHARLESTOWN

P SILSBY FREE PUBLIC LIBRARY*, 226 Main St, 03603. (Mail add: PO Box 307, 03603-0307), SAN 309-7676. Tel: 603-826-7793. FAX: 603-826-7793. E-mail: silsby@charlestown-nh.gov. Web Site: www.charlestown-nh.gov. *Librn,* Sandra Perron; *Ch,* Holly Shaw; *ILL Librn,* Lois Corcoran; Staff 2 (MLS 1, Non-MLS 1)
Founded 1896. Pop 4,950; Circ 26,000
Library Holdings: AV Mats 360; CDs 180; DVDs 399; Large Print Bks 1,078; Bk Vols 21,332; Per Subs 71; Talking Bks 263; Videos 285
Subject Interests: Local genealogical mat, Local hist
Automation Activity & Vendor Info: (Cataloging) Follett Software; (Circulation) Follett Software; (OPAC) Follett Software
Database Vendor: OCLC FirstSearch
Wireless access
Partic in Librarians of the Upper Valley Coop
Special Services for the Blind - Large print bks
Open Mon & Wed 1-7, Tues & Fri 10-5, Thurs 1-5, Sat 9-12

P UNITY FREE PUBLIC LIBRARY*, 13 Center Rd, 03603. SAN 309-9741. Tel: 603-543-3253. FAX: 603-542-9736. E-mail: unitylibrary@yahoo.com. *Dir,* Kathleen Pearson
Pop 1,300; Circ 3,086
Library Holdings: Bk Vols 4,200; Per Subs 30
Special Collections: Government Publications; Rare Book Coll; Town History
Wireless access
Open Mon 12-5, Wed 12-6, Fri 2-7, Sat 9-1
Friends of the Library Group

CHESTER

P CHESTER PUBLIC LIBRARY*, Three Chester St, Jct 121 & 102, 03036. (Mail add: PO Box 277, 03036-0277), SAN 309-7684. Tel: 603-887-3404. FAX: 603-887-2701. E-mail: chesterpubliclibrary@gmail.com. Web Site: www.chesterlibrary.com. *Dir,* Tim Sheehan; *Asst Dir,* Arrato Gavish Diane
Pop 4,621; Circ 23,000
Library Holdings: Bk Vols 45,000; Per Subs 40
Subject Interests: New England
Automation Activity & Vendor Info: (Circulation) Follett Software
Wireless access
Partic in Merry-Hill Rock Libr Coop
Open Mon & Wed 3-8, Tues & Thurs 10-8, Fri 1-5, Sat 10-2
Friends of the Library Group

CHESTERFIELD

P CHESTERFIELD PUBLIC LIBRARY, 524 Rte 63, 03443-0158. SAN 309-7706. Tel: 603-363-4621. FAX: 603-363-4958. E-mail: info@chesterfieldlibrary.org. Web Site: www.chesterfieldlibrary.org. *Dir,* Jane Anderson; E-mail: janderson@chesterfieldlibrary.org; *Asst Dir, Children & Youth Serv Librn,* Claudette Russell
Founded 1939. Pop 3,600; Circ 16,446
Jan 2011-Dec 2011 Income $130,000. Mats Exp $17,500. Sal $65,000
Library Holdings: CDs 1,677; DVDs 1,161; Large Print Bks 1,200; Bk Titles 31,655; Per Subs 35
Special Collections: Large Print
Subject Interests: Biographies, Cooking, Health, Hist, Mysteries, Natural sci, New England hist, Relig studies
Automation Activity & Vendor Info: (Cataloging) OpenAccess Software, Inc; (Circulation) OpenAccess Software, Inc; (OPAC) OpenAccess Software, Inc
Database Vendor: EBSCOhost, Newsbank
Wireless access
Function: Adult bk club, Art exhibits, Bk club(s), Bks on cassette, Bks on CD, Children's prog, Computers for patron use, Copy machines, Exhibits, Handicapped accessible, Homebound delivery serv, ILL available, OverDrive digital audio bks, Photocopying/Printing, Preschool reading prog, Prog for adults, Prog for children & young adult, Pub access computers, Ref serv in person, Spoken cassettes & CDs, Spoken cassettes & DVDs, Story hour, Summer reading prog, Teen prog, Telephone ref, VHS videos, Wheelchair accessible
Partic in New Hampshire Automated Information Systems (NHAIS); Nubanusit Library Cooperative
Special Services for the Deaf - Assistive tech
Special Services for the Blind - Audio mat; Bks on CD; Large print bks; Low vision equip; Magnifiers; Talking bks; Volunteer serv
Open Mon 10-5, Tues 1-8, Wed 1-5, Thurs 10-8, Sat 9-1
Friends of the Library Group

CHICHESTER

P CHICHESTER TOWN LIBRARY*, 161 Main St, 03258. SAN 309-7714. Tel: 603-798-5613. FAX: 603-798-5439. E-mail: clibrary@comcast.net. Web Site: www.chichesternh.org. *Librn,* Lisa Prizio
Founded 1899. Pop 2,500; Circ 15,000
Library Holdings: AV Mats 1,200; Bk Titles 12,173; Per Subs 28
Function: ILL available, Mail loans to mem, Outside serv via phone, mail, e-mail & web, Photocopying/Printing, Ref serv available, Telephone ref
Special Services for the Deaf - Bks on deafness & sign lang
Open Mon & Wed 2:30-8:30, Tues & Thurs 10-1:30, Fri 1:30-4:30, Sat 9-12
Friends of the Library Group

CHOCORUA

P CHOCORUA PUBLIC LIBRARY*, 125 Deer Hill Rd, 03817. (Mail add: PO Box 128, 03817), SAN 309-7722. Tel: 603-323-8610. E-mail: chocorualibrary@adelphia.net. *Libr Dir,* Marion Posner; *Libr Asst,* Peggy Johnson
Founded 1888. Pop 2,200; Circ 4,000
Library Holdings: Bk Vols 12,500; Per Subs 30
Wireless access
Function: Adult bk club, After school storytime, Archival coll, Art exhibits, Audio & video playback equip for onsite use, Bk reviews (Group), Bks on cassette, Bks on CD, Chess club, Children's prog, Computer training, Computers for patron use, Copy machines, Digital talking bks, e-mail & chat, e-mail serv, E-Reserves, Exhibits, Free DVD rentals, Handicapped accessible, Health sci info serv, Holiday prog, Home delivery & serv to Sr ctr & nursing homes, Homework prog, ILL available, Instruction & testing, Jail serv, Learning ctr, Libr develop, Magnifiers for reading, Mail & tel request accepted, Mail loans to mem, Music CDs, Newsp ref libr, Photocopying/Printing, Prog for adults, Prog for children & young adult, Pub access computers, Ref & res, Ref serv available, Referrals accepted, Satellite serv, Serves mentally handicapped consumers, Spoken cassettes & CDs, Spoken cassettes & DVDs, Story hour, Summer reading prog, Tax forms, Telephone ref, VHS videos, Video lending libr, Wheelchair accessible
Open Mon & Thurs 1-7, Sun 1-5

CLAREMONT

P FISKE FREE LIBRARY*, 108 Broad St, 03743-2673. SAN 309-7730. Tel: 603-542-7017. FAX: 603-542-7029. *City Librn,* Michael Grace; *Asst City Librn,* Marta Smith; E-mail: msmith@claremontnewhampshire.com; *Circ Librn,* Colin Sanborn; *Ch Serv, YA Librn,* Brenda Tripodes
Founded 1873. Pop 13,902; Circ 121,852
Library Holdings: Bk Vols 48,000; Per Subs 150
Special Collections: Local Genealogy Coll; Local History Coll
Automation Activity & Vendor Info: (Circulation) Follett Software; (OPAC) Follett Software
Wireless access
Open Mon, Tues & Thurs 9-7, Wed 9-5, Fri 11-5, Sat 9-1
Friends of the Library Group

J RIVER VALLEY COMMUNITY COLLEGE*, The Charles P Puksta Library, One College Dr, 03743. SAN 309-7749. Tel: 603-542-7744, Ext 465. FAX: 603-543-1844. E-mail: rivervalley@ccsnh.edu. Web Site: www.rivervalley.edu. *Dir,* Jim Allen; E-mail: jallen@ccsnh.edu; *Asst Librn,* Gloria Oakes; E-mail: goakes@ccsnh.edu
Founded 1969
Library Holdings: Bk Titles 13,505; Per Subs 90
Special Collections: Deaf Education; New Hampshire Local History
Subject Interests: Allied health educ, Nursing
Automation Activity & Vendor Info: (Acquisitions) TLC (The Library Corporation); (Cataloging) TLC (The Library Corporation); (Circulation) TLC (The Library Corporation); (Course Reserve) TLC (The Library Corporation); (ILL) TLC (The Library Corporation); (OPAC) TLC (The Library Corporation); (Serials) TLC (The Library Corporation)
Wireless access
Special Services for the Deaf - Bks on deafness & sign lang; Spec interest per; Staff with knowledge of sign lang
Open Mon-Thurs 8am-8:30pm, Fri 8-4:30, Sat 9-2

M VALLEY REGIONAL HOSPITAL, Medical Library, 243 Elm St, 03743. SAN 373-2436. Tel: 603-542-1839, 603-542-7771. FAX: 603-542-7830. Web Site: www.vrh.org. *Educ Adminr,* Beth Thibault; E-mail: beth.thibault@vrh.org
Library Holdings: Bk Vols 120; Per Subs 1,000
Wireless access

COLEBROOK

P COLEBROOK PUBLIC LIBRARY, 126 Main St, 03576. (Mail add: PO Box 58, 03576-0058), SAN 309-7757. Tel: 603-237-4808. FAX: 603-237-5069. Web Site: colebrookpubliclibrary.weebly.com. *Dir,* Julie Colby; *Ch,* Judy Santangelo; *Libr Asst,* Kathy Frizzell; Staff 2 (Non-MLS 2)
Founded 1928. Pop 2,744; Circ 26,350
Library Holdings: Bk Vols 18,900; Per Subs 40
Wireless access
Open Mon, Tues & Thurs 2-5:30, Wed & Fri 10-5:30, Sat 10-Noon

CONCORD

S AUDUBON SOCIETY OF NEW HAMPSHIRE*, Francis Beach White Library, 84 Silk Farm Rd, 03301-8311. SAN 323-8296. Tel: 603-224-9909. FAX: 603-226-0902. E-mail: nha@nhaudubon.org. Web Site: www.nhaudubon.org. *Libr Mgr,* Kathie Palfy; Tel: 603-224-9909, Ext 310, E-mail: kpalfy@nhaudubon.org
Founded 1972
Library Holdings: Bk Titles 3,000; Per Subs 61
Subject Interests: Ecology, Natural hist, Ornithology

P CONCORD PUBLIC LIBRARY*, 45 Green St, 03301-4294. SAN 350-4395. Tel: 603-225-8670. FAX: 603-230-3693. E-mail: library@concordnh.gov. Web Site: www.concordpubliclibrary.net. *Dir,* Position Currently Open; *Adult & Tech Serv Mgr,* Sandra Lee; Tel: 603-230-3685, E-mail: slee@ConcordNH.gov; *Children's Mgr,* Pamela Stauffacher; Tel: 603-230-3688; Staff 6 (MLS 6)
Founded 1855. Pop 42,970; Circ 310,618
Jul 2008-Jun 2009 Income (Main Library and Branch(s)) $1,700,565. Mats Exp $222,780, Books $172,160, Per/Ser (Incl. Access Fees) $16,670, Micro $2,920, AV Mat $16,340, Electronic Ref Mat (Incl. Access Fees) $10,690, Presv $4,000. Sal $981,504 (Prof $491,819)
Library Holdings: AV Mats 12,032; Bk Vols 123,744; Per Subs 356
Special Collections: Concord Historical Coll. State Document Depository
Automation Activity & Vendor Info: (Acquisitions) Innovative Interfaces, Inc - Millenium; (Cataloging) Innovative Interfaces, Inc - Millenium; (Circulation) Innovative Interfaces, Inc - Millenium; (OPAC) Innovative Interfaces, Inc - Millenium; (Serials) Innovative Interfaces, Inc - Millenium
Wireless access
Open Mon & Tues 9-8:30, Wed, Fri & Sat 9-5:30, Thurs 11-5:30
Friends of the Library Group

Branches: 1
PENACOOK BRANCH, Three Merrimack St, Penacook, 03303. (Mail add: PO Box 97, Penacook, 03303), SAN 350-4425. Tel: 603-753-4441. *Br Supvr, Ch Serv,* Pam Stauffacher; Tel: 603-225-8670
Library Holdings: Bk Vols 10,000
Open Mon 2:30-8:30, Wed 2:30-5:30, Sat 9-12
Friends of the Library Group

GL NEW HAMPSHIRE DEPARTMENT OF JUSTICE*, Office of the Attorney General Library, 33 Capitol St, 03301-6397. SAN 377-2713. Tel: 603-271-3658. FAX: 603-271-2110. Web Site: www.doj.nh.gov.
Library Holdings: Bk Vols 10,000
Database Vendor: LexisNexis, Westlaw
Restriction: Staff use only

G NEW HAMPSHIRE DIVISION OF PUBLIC HEALTH SERVICES*, Public Health Services Library, 29 Hazen Dr, 03301. Tel: 603-271-0562, 603-271-7060. Toll Free Tel: 800-852-3345, Ext 0562. FAX: 603-271-0542. Web Site: www.dhhs.nh.gov/dphs/library.htm. *Libr Assoc,* Carol Firman; E-mail: cfirman@dhhs.state.nh.us; *Libr Tech,* Joyce Verdone
Library Holdings: AV Mats 400; Bk Vols 500; Per Subs 25
Subject Interests: Diabetes, Disaster preparedness, Fitness, Nutrition, Older adults, Pub health training, Sch health, Tobacco prevention
Partic in Docline
Open Mon-Fri 8-4

M NEW HAMPSHIRE FAMILY VOICES LIBRARY*, Dept Health & Human Servs, Spec Med Servs, Thayer Bldg, 129 Pleasant St, 03301. Tel: 603-271-4525. Toll Free Tel: 800-852-3345, Ext 4525 (NH only). FAX: 603-271-4902. E-mail: nhfv@yahoo.com. Web Site: nhfv.org. *Co-Dir,* Martha-Jean Madison; *Co-Dir,* Terry Ohlson-Martin
Library Holdings: AV Mats 100; Bk Vols 1,700
Open Mon-Fri 9-5

S NEW HAMPSHIRE HISTORICAL SOCIETY LIBRARY*, 30 Park St, 03301-6384. SAN 309-7781. Tel: 603-228-6688. Reference Tel: 603-856-0641. Administration Tel: 603-856-0643. FAX: 603-224-0463. E-mail: library@nhhistory.org. Web Site: www.nhhistory.org. *Libr Dir,* Sarah Hays; E-mail: shays@nhhistory.org; Staff 3 (MLS 1, Non-MLS 2)
Founded 1823
Oct 2010-Sept 2011 Income $210,000, Locally Generated Income $10,000, Parent Institution $200,000. Mats Exp $49,000, Books $15,000, Per/Ser (Incl. Access Fees) $3,000, Manu Arch $20,000, Other Print Mats $2,000, Presv $9,000. Sal $95,000
Library Holdings: AV Mats 200,000; Microforms 400; Music Scores 300; Bk Titles 40,000; Bk Vols 50,000; Per Subs 130; Videos 200
Special Collections: New Hampshire Church Records, 1700-1900, ms vols; New Hampshire Manuscripts, 1700-1990; New Hampshire Maps, 1700-1960; New Hampshire Newspapers, 1790-1900, microfilm; New Hampshire Photographs, 1850-1990; New Hampshire Provincial Deeds, 1640-1770, micro
Subject Interests: Archit, Decorative art, Genealogy, Hist of NH, Local hist
Automation Activity & Vendor Info: (Cataloging) MINISIS Inc; (OPAC) MINISIS Inc
Database Vendor: ProQuest
Wireless access
Function: Archival coll, Exhibits, Wheelchair accessible
Special Services for the Deaf - Accessible learning ctr; ADA equip; Adult & family literacy prog; Am sign lang & deaf culture; Assisted listening device
Special Services for the Blind - Assistive/Adapted tech devices, equip & products
Open Tues-Fri 9:30-5
Restriction: Fee for pub use, Free to mem, Non-circulating, Not a lending libr

M NEW HAMPSHIRE HOSPITAL, Dorothy M Breene Memorial Library, 36 Clinton St, 03301-3861. SAN 309-779X. Tel: 603-271-5420. FAX: 603-271-5425. E-mail: breenelibrary@dhhs.state.nh.us. Web Site: www.dhhs.state.nh.us. *Librn,* Karen Goodman. Subject Specialists: *Med, Psychiat, Psychol,* Karen Goodman; Staff 1 (MLS 1)
Founded 1880
Jul 2013-Jun 2014. Mats Exp $64,353, Books $3,000, Per/Ser (Incl. Access Fees) $48,353
Library Holdings: AV Mats 700; Bk Titles 2,000; Per Subs 75
Subject Interests: Commun mental health, Geriatrics, Neurology, Nursing, Occupational therapy, Psychiat, Psychol, Recreational therapy, Soc sci, Soc work
Automation Activity & Vendor Info: (Acquisitions) EOS International; (Cataloging) EOS International; (Circulation) EOS International; (Course Reserve) EOS International; (ILL) EOS International; (Media Booking) EOS International; (OPAC) EOS International; (Serials) EOS International
Database Vendor: EBSCOhost, LibraryWorld, Inc, OVID Technologies

Partic in National Network of Libraries of Medicine New England Region
Open Mon-Thurs 8-3:30

L NEW HAMPSHIRE LAW LIBRARY*, Supreme Court Bldg, One Charles Doe Dr, 03301-6160. SAN 350-4514. Tel: 603-271-3777. FAX: 603-513-5450. E-mail: lawlibrary@courts.state.nh.us. Web Site: www.courts.state.nh.us/lawlibrary. *Dir,* Mary S Searles; E-mail: msearles@courts.state.nh.us; *Acq,* Erin Hubbard; E-mail: ehubbard@courts.state.nh.us; *Libr Asst,* Rachel Catano; Staff 3 (MLS 2, Non-MLS 1)
Founded 1819
Library Holdings: Bk Vols 100,100; Per Subs 110
Special Collections: Laws & Court Reports; New Hampshire Material. State Document Depository; US Document Depository
Automation Activity & Vendor Info: (Acquisitions) SirsiDynix; (Cataloging) SirsiDynix; (Circulation) SirsiDynix; (OPAC) SirsiDynix; (Serials) SirsiDynix
Wireless access
Function: Copy machines, Doc delivery serv, e-mail & chat, e-mail serv, Electronic databases & coll, Fax serv, ILL available, Mail & tel request accepted, Online cat, Photocopying/Printing, Pub access computers
Open Mon-Fri 8:30-4:30
Restriction: Open to pub for ref & circ; with some limitations

P NEW HAMPSHIRE STATE LIBRARY*, 20 Park St, 03301-6316. SAN 350-445X. Tel: 603-271-2392. Circulation Tel: 603-271-2541. FAX: 603-271-2205, 603-271-6826. Web Site: www.nh.gov/nhsl. *State Librn,* Michael York; Tel: 603-271-2397, E-mail: michael.york@dcr.nh.gov; *Adminr, Libr Operations,* Janet Eklund; E-mail: janet.eklund@dcr.nh.gov; *Tech Res Librn,* Bobbi Lee Slossar; Tel: 603-271-2143, E-mail: bobbilee.slossar@dcr.nh.gov; *Librn II,* Linda Kent; E-mail: linda.kent@dcr.nh.gov; *Ref Librn II,* Charles Shipman; E-mail: charles.shipman@dcr.nh.gov; *Ref Librn II,* Rebecca Troy-Horton; E-mail: rebecca.troy-horton@dcr.nh.gov; *Youth Serv Librn II,* Ann Hoey; Tel: 603-271-2865, E-mail: ann.hoey@dcr.nh.gov; *Supvr, NHAIS Serv,* Mary Russell; Tel: 603-271-2866, E-mail: mary.russell@dcr.nh.gov; *Supvr, Spec Serv,* Nancy Cristiano; Tel: 603-271-1188, E-mail: nancy.cristiano@dcr.nh.gov; *Ref/Info Serv Supvr,* Donna Gilbreth; Tel: 603-271-2060, E-mail: donna.gilbreth@dcr.nh.gov; *Tech Serv Supvr,* Linda Jayes; Tel: 603-271-2429, E-mail: linda.jayes@dcr.nh.gov; Staff 44 (MLS 15, Non-MLS 29)
Founded 1716
Library Holdings: Braille Volumes 570; Bk Vols 567,699; Per Subs 73; Talking Bks 72,683; Videos 3,888
Special Collections: Historical Children's Books; New Hampshire Authors; New Hampshire Government & History; New Hampshire Imprints; New Hampshire Maps. Oral History; State Document Depository; US Document Depository
Subject Interests: Biog, Genealogy, Info sci, Law, Libr sci, Pub admin, Soc sci
Automation Activity & Vendor Info: (Cataloging) SirsiDynix; (ILL) SirsiDynix; (OPAC) SirsiDynix
Database Vendor: EBSCOhost
Publications: Checklist of New Hampshire State Departments' Publications (Bi-ennial); Granite Bits (Irregularly); Granite State Libraries (Bi-monthly newsletter); New Hampshire Libraries (Annual directory); New Hampshire Library Statistics (Annual)
Partic in Lyrasis
Open Mon-Fri 8-4:30

P NEW HAMPSHIRE STATE LIBRARY, Talking Book Services, Gallen State Office Park, Dolloff Bldg, 117 Pleasant St, 03301-3852. SAN 309-7803. Tel: 603-271-2417, 603-271-3429. Administration Tel: 603-271-1498, 603-271-2392. Toll Free Tel: 800-491-4200 (NH only). FAX: 603-271-8370. E-mail: talking@dcr.nh.gov. Web Site: www.state.nh.us/nhsl/talkbks. *Supvr,* Marilyn Stevenson; *Libr Asst,* Joan Nelson; E-mail: joan.nelson@dcr.nh.gov; *Libr Asst II,* Jody Matisko; *Libr Tech,* Brenda Corey; Staff 1 (MLS 1)
Founded 1970
Function: Bks on cassette, Digital talking bks, Equip loans & repairs, ILL available, Mail & tel request accepted, Outreach serv, OverDrive digital audio bks, VHS videos
Publications: Granite Bits (Newsletter)
Special Services for the Blind - Braille servs; Children's Braille; Descriptive video serv (DVS); Digital talking bk; Newsletter (in large print, Braille or on cassette); Newsline for the Blind; Ref serv; Scanner for conversion & translation of mats; Screen enlargement software for people with visual disabilities; Talking bks & player equip; Tel Pioneers equip repair group; Web-Braille; ZoomText magnification & reading software
Open Mon-Fri 8-4:30
Restriction: Registered patrons only

S NEW HAMPSHIRE STATE PRISON LIBRARY, 281 N State St, 03301. (Mail add: PO Box 14, 03302-0014), SAN 309-7811. Tel: 603-271-1929. FAX: 603-271-0401. *Media Spec,* John Perkins; E-mail: john.e.perkins@nhdoc.state.nh.us
Founded 1918
Jul 2011-Jun 2012 Income $43,000. Mats Exp $43,000, Books $1,000, Per/Ser (Incl. Access Fees) $2,000, Other Print Mats $8,000, Electronic Ref Mat (Incl. Access Fees) $32,000. Sal $45,000
Library Holdings: Bks on Deafness & Sign Lang 50; Electronic Media & Resources 1; High Interest/Low Vocabulary Bk Vols 300; Large Print Bks 800; Music Scores 300; Bk Titles 12,000; Bk Vols 16,000; Per Subs 8; Videos 325
Special Collections: Law Coll; Lois Law Coll
Subject Interests: Educ, Hobby craft, Law, Penology, Recreational
Database Vendor: Loislaw
Special Services for the Deaf - Assisted listening device
Special Services for the Blind - Talking bks & player equip
Restriction: Staff & inmates only

J NHTI, CONCORD'S COMMUNITY COLLEGE*, 31 College Dr, 03301-7425. SAN 309-782X. Tel: 603-271-7186. FAX: 603-271-7189. E-mail: nhtilibrary@ccsnh.edu. Web Site: www.nhti.edu/library. *Dir, Learning Res,* Stephen P Ambra; Tel: 603-271-7185, E-mail: sambra@ccsnh.edu; *Asst Dir, Learning Res, ILL Librn,* Anne Wirkkala; Tel: 603-271-7720, E-mail: awirkkala@ccsnh.edu; *Head, Ref Serv, Ref Librn,* Sarah Hébert; Tel: 603-271-7219, E-mail: shebert@ccsnh.edu; *Ref Librn,* Christine Wanta; Tel: 603-271-7187, E-mail: cwanta@ccsnh.edu; *Circ Supvr,* Claudette Welch; E-mail: cwelch@ccsnh.edu; *Circ,* Nathan Clasby; E-mail: nclasby@ccsnh.edu; *Circ,* John Dennett; E-mail: jdennett@ccsnh.edu; *Circ,* Elisabeth Jewell; E-mail: ejewell@ccsnh.edu; *Circ,* Stephanie Weinert; E-mail: sweinert@ccsnh.edu; *Ref,* Carol Nelson; E-mail: cnelson@ccsnh.edu; *Ser,* Joyce Verdone; E-mail: jverdone@ccsnh.edu; *Ser/Archives,* Rachel Catano; E-mail: rcatano@ccsnh.edu; *Tech Serv,* Charlotte Green; E-mail: cgreen@ccsnh.edu; Staff 6 (MLS 6)
Founded 1965. Enrl 3,850; Fac 150; Highest Degree: Associate
Library Holdings: Bk Titles 60,000; Per Subs 300
Special Collections: College Archives; Houses of Concord, NH; NEARA Coll
Subject Interests: Archit, Architectural eng tech, Autism, Dental hygiene, Diagnostic ultrasound, Early childhood educ, Electronic, Emergency med care, Landscape archit, Mental health, Nursing, Radiologic tech
Automation Activity & Vendor Info: (Cataloging) TLC (The Library Corporation); (Circulation) TLC (The Library Corporation); (OPAC) TLC (The Library Corporation)
Database Vendor: ARTstor, ebrary, EBSCOhost, Gale Cengage Learning, JSTOR, LexisNexis, Medline, TLC (The Library Corporation), YBP Library Services
Wireless access
Publications: Acquisitions List; Bibliographies; Page Notes

L ORR & RENO LAW LIBRARY*, 45 S Main St, 03302. (Mail add: PO Box 3550, 03302-3550), SAN 323-7419. Tel: 603-223-9105. FAX: 603-223-9005. Web Site: www.orr-reno.com. *Librn,* Chris Dunn; E-mail: cdunn@orr-reno.com; Staff 1 (MLS 1)
Library Holdings: Bk Titles 500; Per Subs 35
Subject Interests: Bus law, Immigration, Tax law
Database Vendor: LexisNexis, Westlaw
Function: ILL available
Restriction: Staff use only

CL UNIVERSITY OF NEW HAMPSHIRE SCHOOL OF LAW*, Two White St, 03301. SAN 309-7838. Tel: 603-228-1541, Ext 1130. Circulation Tel: 603-228-1541, Ext 1131. Reference Tel: 603-228-1541, Ext 1193. Administration Tel: 603-228-1541, Ext 1129. Automation Services Tel: 603-228-1541, Ext 1135. FAX: 603-228-0388. Web Site: www.library.law.unh.edu. *Dir, Law Libr,* Sue Zago; *Cat Librn,* Matt Jenks; *Electronic Res Librn,* Tom Hemstock; *IP Librn,* Jon R Cavicchi; *Ref Librn, Pub Serv,* Kathy Fletcher; *Syst Librn,* Melanie Cornell; *Acq, Supvr,* Kathie Goodwin; *Supvr, Ser,* Ellen Phillips; Staff 12 (MLS 6, Non-MLS 6)
Founded 1973. Enrl 450; Fac 25; Highest Degree: Doctorate
Jul 2005-Jun 2006 Income $1,793,441. Mats Exp $1,001,600. Sal $504,198
Library Holdings: Bk Titles 94,706; Bk Vols 181,286; Per Subs 1,237
Special Collections: US Document Depository
Subject Interests: Electronic commerce, Intellectual property
Automation Activity & Vendor Info: (Acquisitions) Innovative Interfaces, Inc; (Cataloging) Innovative Interfaces, Inc; (Circulation) Innovative Interfaces, Inc; (Course Reserve) Innovative Interfaces, Inc; (ILL) OCLC; (OPAC) Innovative Interfaces, Inc; (Serials) Innovative Interfaces, Inc
Database Vendor: Dialog, Gale Cengage Learning, Innovative Interfaces, Inc, LexisNexis, OCLC FirstSearch, Westlaw
Wireless access
Function: ILL available
Publications: Newsletter (Bi-monthly)
Partic in Innopac; Lyrasis; New England Law Library Consortium, Inc

Special Services for the Blind - Closed circuit TV magnifier
Restriction: Access at librarian's discretion, Closed stack, Open to students, fac & staff

CONTOOCOOK

P HOPKINTON TOWN LIBRARY*, 61 Houston Dr, 03229. (Mail add: PO Box 217, 03229-0217), SAN 309-8494. Tel: 603-746-3663. FAX: 603-746-6799. E-mail: info@hopkintontownlibrary.org. Web Site: hopkintontownlibrary.org. *Dir,* Donna Dunlop; E-mail: ddunlop@hopkintontownlibrary.org; *Ch,* Leigh Maynard; *Ref Librn,* Karen Dixon; Staff 2 (MLS 2)
Founded 1870. Pop 5,617; Circ 70,195
Jan 2007-Dec 2007 Income $274,731
Database Vendor: EBSCOhost, OCLC WorldShare Interlibrary Loan, Overdrive, Inc
Wireless access
Function: Adult bk club, Art exhibits, Audiobks via web, Bks on cassette, Bks on CD, Children's prog, Citizenship assistance, Computer training, Computers for patron use, Copy machines, e-mail serv, E-Reserves, Electronic databases & coll, Exhibits, Fax serv, Handicapped accessible, Homebound delivery serv, ILL available, Mail & tel request accepted, Mus passes, Music CDs, Online cat, Online searches, Outreach serv, OverDrive digital audio bks, Photocopying/Printing, Preschool outreach, Prog for adults, Prog for children & young adult, Pub access computers, Ref serv available, Senior computer classes, Story hour, Summer reading prog, Tax forms, Teen prog, Telephone ref, VHS videos, Wheelchair accessible, Writing prog
Open Tues & Wed 10-8, Thurs 10-6, Fri 10-5, Sat 10-3; Sun (Winter) 1-5
Friends of the Library Group

CONWAY

P CONWAY PUBLIC LIBRARY, 15 Main St, 03818. (Mail add: PO Box 2100, 03818-2100), SAN 350-4662. Tel: 603-447-5552. FAX: 603-447-6921. E-mail: info@conwaypubliclibrary.org. Web Site: conwaypubliclibrary.org. *Dir,* David Smolen; E-mail: dsmolen@conwaypubliclibrary.org; *Head, Youth Serv,* Tara McKenzie; *Asst Librn,* Betty Parker; *ILL Librn,* Kate Darlington; *Tech Serv Librn,* Gail Fike; *Ch Serv,* Olga Morrill; Staff 4 (MLS 1, Non-MLS 3)
Founded 1900. Pop 10,000; Circ 83,500
Library Holdings: Bk Vols 37,000; Per Subs 95
Subject Interests: Local hist
Automation Activity & Vendor Info: (Cataloging) TLC (The Library Corporation); (Circulation) TLC (The Library Corporation); (OPAC) TLC (The Library Corporation)
Database Vendor: EBSCOhost
Wireless access
Open Mon, Tues & Thurs 10-8, Wed 10-6:30, Fri & Sat 10-5
Friends of the Library Group

CORNISH

S SAINT-GAUDENS NATIONAL HISTORIC SITE LIBRARY, National Park Service, 139 Saint-Gaudens Rd, 03745-4232. SAN 309-7846. Tel: 603-675-2175. FAX: 603-675-2701. Web Site: www.nps.gov/saga. *In Charge,* Gregory C Schwarz. Subject Specialists: *Local hist, Sculpture,* Gregory C Schwarz
Founded 1919
Library Holdings: Bk Vols 2,000
Special Collections: Cornish Art Colony Coll 1885-1935
Subject Interests: Art, Sculpture
Open Mon-Fri 9-4:30

CORNISH FLAT

P GEORGE H STOWELL FREE LIBRARY*, 24 School St, 03746. (Mail add: PO Box 360, 03746-0360), SAN 309-7854. Tel: 603-543-3644. E-mail: stowelllibrary@comcast.net. *Dir,* Brenda Freeland
Pop 1,500; Circ 3,800
Library Holdings: Bks on Deafness & Sign Lang 10; High Interest/Low Vocabulary Bk Vols 50; Bk Titles 9,750; Bk Vols 10,000; Per Subs 30
Subject Interests: Cornish hist
Wireless access
Open Mon & Fri 4-6, Wed 4-8, Sat 10-12

DALTON

P DALTON PUBLIC LIBRARY*, Town of Dalton Municipal Bldg, 756 Dalton Rd, 03598. SAN 309-7870. Tel: 603-837-2751. FAX: 603-837-2273. E-mail: daltonpubliclibrary@gmail.com, library@townofdalton.com. Web Site: www.townofdalton.com/library.html. *Librn,* Doris Mitton
Founded 1892. Pop 1,000; Circ 1,775
Jan 2012-Dec 2012. Mats Exp $1,818. Sal $8,788
Library Holdings: AV Mats 414; Bk Vols 7,000; Per Subs 17
Open Mon & Wed 2-6, Sat 10-Noon

DANBURY

P GEORGE GAMBLE LIBRARY*, 29 Rte 104, 03230-0209. (Mail add: PO Box 209, 03230-0209), SAN 309-7889. Tel: 603-768-3765. *Dir,* Linda Olmsted
Founded 1911. Pop 1,300; Circ 1,525
Jan 2010-Dec 2010. Mats Exp $1,500
Library Holdings: Audiobooks 15; AV Mats 20; CDs 17; DVDs 10; Large Print Bks 24; Bk Vols 6,238; Talking Bks 16; Videos 67
Special Services for the Blind - Audio mat
Open Wed & Sat 11-4

DANVILLE

P COLBY MEMORIAL LIBRARY*, Seven Colby Rd, 03819-5104. (Mail add: PO Box 10, 03819-0010), SAN 309-7897. Tel: 603-382-6733. FAX: 603-382-0487. E-mail: colbylibrary@comcast.net. Web Site: townofdanville.org/library.shtml. *Dir,* Dorothy Billbrough; *Circ Librn,* Pam MacLean
Founded 1892. Pop 2,200; Circ 4,000
Library Holdings: Bk Titles 20,000; Per Subs 47
Automation Activity & Vendor Info: (Cataloging) Follett Software; (Circulation) Follett Software; (OPAC) Follett Software
Partic in Merri-Hill-Rock Library Cooperative
Open Mon & Tues 12-8, Wed & Thurs 10-6, Sat 10-1
Friends of the Library Group

DEERFIELD

P PHILBRICK-JAMES LIBRARY*, Four Church St, 03037-1426. SAN 309-7919. Tel: 603-463-7187. E-mail: pjlibrary@metrocast.net. *Dir,* Evelyn F DeCota; *ILL Librn,* Melissa J Graykin; *Libr Asst,* Ann H Vennerbeck; Staff 1.75 (Non-MLS 1.75)
Founded 1880. Pop 4,280; Circ 16,623
Jan 2011-Dec 2011 Income $86,505. Mats Exp $12,500, Books $12,000, Per/Ser (Incl. Access Fees) $500. Sal $42,000
Library Holdings: Audiobooks 358; DVDs 125; Large Print Bks 225; Bk Titles 22,547; Per Subs 19
Wireless access
Function: Adult bk clubs, Art exhibits, Audiobks via web, Bks on cassette, Bks on CD, Children's prog, Computer training, Computers for patron use, Copy machines, Electronic databases & coll, Free DVD rentals, Handicapped accessible, ILL available, Mus passes, Music CDs, Online cat, OverDrive digital audio bks, Photocopying/Printing, Prog for adults, Prog for children & young adult, Pub access computers, Spoken cassettes & CDs, Story hour, Summer reading prog, Teen prog, VHS videos, Wheelchair accessible
Special Services for the Deaf - Bks on deafness & sign lang
Special Services for the Blind - Audio mat; Bks on cassette; Bks on CD; Large print bks; Reader equip; Talking bk serv referral
Open Mon & Wed 1-8, Tues & Thurs 9-5, Fri 1-5, Sat 9-Noon
Friends of the Library Group

DEERING

P DEERING PUBLIC LIBRARY*, 762 Deering Center Rd, 03244. SAN 309-7927. Tel: 603-464-5108. FAX: 603-464-3804. Web Site: www.deering.nh.us.
Founded 1926. Pop 1,875
Library Holdings: Bk Vols 5,500; Per Subs 10
Open Tues & Sat 10-12, Wed 10-12:30, Thurs 3-7
Friends of the Library Group

DERRY

P DERRY PUBLIC LIBRARY, 64 E Broadway, 03038-2412. SAN 309-7935. Tel: 603-432-6140. FAX: 603-432-6128. TDD: 603-432-6756. E-mail: derrylib@derrypl.org. Web Site: www.derrypl.org. *Libr Dir,* Cara Barlow; E-mail: carab@derrypl.org; *Asst Dir, Head, Adult Serv,* Susan Brown; E-mail: susanb@derrypl.org; *Head, Ch,* Nicole Giroux; E-mail: nicoleg@derrypl.org; *Head, Tech Serv,* Kathy Piasek; *Circ, ILL Librn,* Cathy Goldthwaite; *YA Librn,* Erin Robinson; *Communications Coordr,* Meryle Zusman; *Ref Serv, Ad,* Sherryl Bailey; Staff 10 (MLS 8, Non-MLS 2)
Founded 1905. Pop 33,223; Circ 215,294
Jul 2013-Jun 2014 Income $1,173,641, City $1,158,641, Locally Generated Income $15,000. Mats Exp $100,515, Books $50,588, Per/Ser (Incl. Access Fees) $5,906, Micro $1,107, AV Mat $16,791, Electronic Ref Mat (Incl. Access Fees) $11,011. Sal $860,658
Library Holdings: Audiobooks 2,294; CDs 5,671; DVDs 4,676; e-books 13,312; Large Print Bks 1,371; Bk Vols 90,625; Per Subs 152
Special Collections: Houses of Derry (Harriet Newell Books); Robert Frost Material; Tasha Tudor Drawings

Automation Activity & Vendor Info: (Acquisitions) Innovative Interfaces, Inc; (Cataloging) Innovative Interfaces, Inc; (Circulation) Innovative Interfaces, Inc; (ILL) Innovative Interfaces, Inc; (OPAC) Innovative Interfaces, Inc; (Serials) Innovative Interfaces, Inc
Database Vendor: 3M Library Systems, CredoReference, EBSCO Auto Repair Reference, EBSCOhost, Facts on File, LearningExpress, OCLC FirstSearch, Overdrive, Inc, ProQuest
Wireless access
Function: Adult bk club, After school storytime, Audiobks via web, Bk club(s), Bks on CD, Children's prog, Computer training, Computers for patron use, Copy machines, Electronic databases & coll, Free DVD rentals, Handicapped accessible, ILL available, Magnifiers for reading, Microfiche/film & reading machines, Mus passes, Music CDs, Online cat, Outside serv via phone, mail, e-mail & web, OverDrive digital audio bks, Photocopying/Printing, Preschool outreach, Prog for adults, Prog for children & young adult, Pub access computers, Scanner, Spoken cassettes & CDs, Summer reading prog, Tax forms
Partic in GMILCS, Inc
Special Services for the Deaf - Staff with knowledge of sign lang
Open Mon-Thurs 9:30-8:30, Fri & Sat 9:30-5
Friends of the Library Group

M PARKLAND MEDICAL CENTER*, Medical Library, One Parkland Dr, 03038. SAN 323-6889. Tel: 603-421-2318. FAX: 603-421-2060. *Med Librn,* Mimi Guessferd; E-mail: mary.guessferd@hcahealthcare.com; Staff 0.5 (MLS 0.5)
Library Holdings: Bk Titles 260; Per Subs 77
Wireless access
Function: Electronic databases & coll, Health sci info serv, ILL available
Partic in Docline
Restriction: Hospital employees & physicians only

DOVER

P DOVER PUBLIC LIBRARY*, 73 Locust St, 03820-3785. SAN 309-796X. Tel: 603-516-6050. Reference Tel: 603-516-6082. FAX: 603-516-6053. Web Site: library.dover.nh.gov. *Dir,* Cathleen C Beaudoin; E-mail: c.beaudoin@dover.nh.gov; *Ad,* Laura Horwood-Benton; E-mail: l.horwood benton@dover.nh.gov; *Ch,* Kathleen Thorner; E-mail: k.thorner@dover.nh.gov; *ILL Librn,* Sue Vincent; E-mail: s.vincent@dover.nh.gov; *Ref Librn,* Denise LaFrance; E-mail: d.lafrance@dover.nh.gov; *Ref Librn,* Carrie Tremblay; E-mail: c.tremblay@dover.nh.gov; *Tech & Syst Librn,* Peggy Thrasher; E-mail: p.thrasher@dover.nh.gov; *Cataloger,* Phuong Openo; E-mail: p.openo@dover.nh.gov; Staff 7 (MLS 6, Non-MLS 1)
Founded 1883. Pop 30,000; Circ 294,000
Jul 2013-Jun 2014 Income $1,110,582, City $1,056,082, Locally Generated Income $47,000, Other $7,500. Mats Exp $161,548, Books $125,400, Per/Ser (Incl. Access Fees) $6,000, Micro $600, AV Mat $25,548, Electronic Ref Mat (Incl. Access Fees) $4,000. Sal $633,593 (Prof $360,325)
Library Holdings: AV Mats 5,266; CDs 2,057; DVDs 1,000; Large Print Bks 1,400; Music Scores 1,557; Bk Titles 94,323; Bk Vols 104,441; Per Subs 294; Talking Bks 1,637; Videos 2,565
Special Collections: New Hampshire & New England Historical & Genealogical Materials
Subject Interests: Local hist
Automation Activity & Vendor Info: (Acquisitions) ByWater Solutions; (Cataloging) ByWater Solutions; (Circulation) ByWater Solutions; (OPAC) ByWater Solutions; (Serials) ByWater Solutions
Database Vendor: Baker & Taylor, Bowker, EBSCOhost, Gale Cengage Learning, OCLC FirstSearch, Overdrive, Inc, ProQuest, ValueLine
Wireless access
Function: Adult bk club, Archival coll, Art exhibits, Audio & video playback equip for onsite use, Audiobks via web, AV serv, Bks on CD, Children's prog, Computer training, Computers for patron use, Copy machines, e-mail serv, Electronic databases & coll, Exhibits, Fax serv, Free DVD rentals, Handicapped accessible, ILL available, Instruction & testing, Magnifiers for reading, Mail & tel request accepted, Microfiche/film & reading machines, Mus passes, Music CDs, Online cat, Online ref, Online searches, OverDrive digital audio bks, Photocopying/Printing, Preschool reading prog, Printer for laptops & handheld devices, Prog for adults, Prog for children & young adult, Pub access computers, Ref serv available, Ref serv in person, Spoken cassettes & CDs, Spoken cassettes & DVDs, Story hour, Summer reading prog, Tax forms, Teen prog, Telephone ref, VCDs, VHS videos, Wheelchair accessible, Workshops
Publications: DPL (Newsletter)
Open Mon & Tues 9-8:30, Wed-Fri 9-5:30, Sat 9-5 (Summer 9-1)
Friends of the Library Group

DUBLIN

P DUBLIN PUBLIC LIBRARY*, 1114 Main St, 03444. (Mail add: PO Box 442, 03444-0442), SAN 309-7986. Tel: 603-563-8658. FAX: 603-563-8751. E-mail: librarypublicdublin@myfairpoint.net. *Dir,* Elizabeth McIntyre; *Asst Librn,* Mary Edick
Pop 1,556; Circ 7,500
Library Holdings: Bk Vols 20,000; Per Subs 40
Open Mon, Tues & Thurs 4-8, Wed 9-12 & 4-8, Sat 9-1
Friends of the Library Group

DUNBARTON

P DUNBARTON PUBLIC LIBRARY*, 1004 School St, 03046-4816. SAN 309-8001. Tel: 603-774-3546. FAX: 603-774-5563. E-mail: dunlib@gsinet.net. Web Site: www.dunbartonlibrary.org. *Dir,* Andrea Douglas; *Librn,* Nancy C Lang; Staff 1.5 (MLS 1, Non-MLS 0.5)
Founded 1893. Pop 2,600; Circ 11,000
Library Holdings: Bk Vols 14,000; Per Subs 40
Special Collections: Dunbarton History Coll
Automation Activity & Vendor Info: (Cataloging) Follett Software; (Circulation) Follett Software; (OPAC) Follett Software
Wireless access
Open Tues & Thurs 1-8, Wed & Fri 10-4, Sat 10-2

DURHAM

P DURHAM PUBLIC LIBRARY, 49 Madbury Rd, 03824. SAN 377-5372. Tel: 603-868-6699. FAX: 603-868-9944. E-mail: durhampl@gmail.com. Web Site: www.durhampubliclibrary.org. *Dir,* Thomas Madden; E-mail: tmadden@ci.durham.nh.us; *Asst Dir,* Nancy Miner; E-mail: nminer@ci.durham.nh.us; *Children's & YA Librn,* Lisa Kleinmann; Staff 3 (MLS 1, Non-MLS 2)
Founded 1997. Pop 15,182; Circ 62,432
Jan 2014-Dec 2014 Income $402,515, City $389,575, Locally Generated Income $12,940. Mats Exp $23,618, Books $15,768, Per/Ser (Incl. Access Fees) $2,800, AV Mat $5,050. Sal $186,623
Library Holdings: Bk Vols 31,176; Per Subs 35
Automation Activity & Vendor Info: (Cataloging) Innovative Interfaces, Inc; (Circulation) Innovative Interfaces, Inc; (OPAC) Innovative Interfaces, Inc
Wireless access
Open Mon 2:30-8, Tues-Thurs 10-8, Fri & Sat 10-5
Friends of the Library Group

C UNIVERSITY OF NEW HAMPSHIRE LIBRARY*, 18 Library Way, 03824. SAN 350-4727. Tel: 603-862-1540. Circulation Tel: 603-862-1535. Reference Tel: 603-862-1544. FAX: 603-862-0247. *Interim Dean of Libr,* Dr Annie Donahue; Tel: 603-862-1506; *Asst Dean, Libr Admin,* Tracey Lauder; Tel: 603-862-3041, E-mail: tracey.lauder@unh.edu; *Head, Tech Serv,* Christina Bellinger; Tel: 603-862-0073, Fax: 603-862-0085, E-mail: cb1@cisunix.unh.edu; *Coll Develop Librn,* Jennifer Carroll; Tel: 603-862-4049, Fax: 603-862-0294, E-mail: jennifer.carroll@unh.edu; *Spec Coll Librn,* Dr William E Ross; Tel: 603-862-0346, Fax: 603-862-2956, E-mail: wer@cisunix.unh.edu; *Doc,* Linda Johnson; Tel: 603 862-2453, Fax: 603-862-3403, E-mail: linda@cisunix.unh.edu; *ILL,* Jan Salas; Tel: 603-862-1173, E-mail: jsalas@cisunix.unh.edu; *Ref,* Deborah Watson; Tel: 603-862-3800, Fax: 603-862-2637, E-mail: dewatson@cisunix.unh.edu; Staff 83 (MLS 23, Non-MLS 60)
Founded 1868. Enrl 14,766; Fac 678; Highest Degree: Doctorate
Jul 2008-Jun 2009 Income (Main and Other College/University Libraries) $15,658,611. Mats Exp $5,502,496, Books $759,175, Per/Ser (Incl. Access Fees) $3,849,060, Electronic Ref Mat (Incl. Access Fees) $822,990, Presv $71,271. Sal $4,892,198 (Prof $1,521,081)
Library Holdings: AV Mats 44,887; Bk Vols 1,804,960; Per Subs 54,691
Special Collections: Amy Beach Papers; Angling (Milne Coll); Contra Dance & Folk Music (Ralph Page Coll); Donald Hall Coll; Frost Archives; Galway Kinnell Coll; Senator McIntyre Papers; Senator Norris Cotton Papers; US Patent Document Depository. State Document Depository; UN Document Depository; US Document Depository
Automation Activity & Vendor Info: (Acquisitions) Innovative Interfaces, Inc; (Cataloging) Innovative Interfaces, Inc; (Circulation) Innovative Interfaces, Inc; (OPAC) Innovative Interfaces, Inc; (Serials) Innovative Interfaces, Inc
Database Vendor: ACM (Association for Computing Machinery), Agricola, American Chemical Society, American Psychological Association (APA), Annual Reviews, BioOne, Bowker, Cambridge Scientific Abstracts, CQ Press, CredoReference, EBSCOhost, Facts on File, Infotrieve, JSTOR, LexisNexis, Mergent Online, Modern Language Association, Newsbank, OCLC FirstSearch, OCLC WorldShare Interlibrary Loan, OCLC-RLG, OVID Technologies, Oxford Online, ProQuest, PubMed, ReferenceUSA, ScienceDirect, SerialsSolutions, Westlaw, Wiley
Wireless access
Function: Doc delivery serv

Partic in Boston Library Consortium, Inc; New Hampshire College & University Council; OCLC Online Computer Library Center, Inc
Friends of the Library Group

Departmental Libraries:

CHEMISTRY, Parsons Hall, 23 College Rd, 03824-3598, SAN 350-4816. Tel: 603-862-1083. FAX: 603-862-4278. Web Site: www.library.unh.edu/branches/chemgide.html. *Librn,* Emily LeViness Poworoznek; Tel: 603-862-4168, E-mail: el@cisunix.unh.edu; *Libr Assoc,* Robert Constantine; E-mail: rjc3@cisunix.unh.edu; Staff 2 (MLS 1, Non-MLS 1)
Library Holdings: Bk Vols 32,472; Per Subs 129
Subject Interests: Chem, Mat sci
Open Mon-Thurs 8am-10pm, Fri 8-5, Sat 1-5, Sun 2-10
Friends of the Library Group

DAVID G CLARK MEMORIAL PHYSICS LIBRARY, DeMeritt Hall, Nine Library Way, 03824-3568, SAN 350-4875. Tel: 603-862-2348. FAX: 603-862-2998. Web Site: www.library.unh.edu/branches/physlib.html. *Librn,* Emily LeViness Poworoznek; E-mail: el@cisunix.unh.edu; *Libr Assoc,* Heather Gagnon; Staff 2 (MLS 1, Non-MLS 1)
Founded 1976
Library Holdings: Bk Vols 29,654; Per Subs 161
Subject Interests: Astronomy, Physics
Partic in Northeast Research Libraries Consortium (NERL)
Open Mon-Thurs 8am-10pm, Fri 8-4:30, Sat 1-5, Sun 2-10
Friends of the Library Group

ENGINEERING, MATHEMATICS & COMPUTER SCIENCE, Kingsbury Hall, 33 Academic Way, 03824, SAN 350-4840. Tel: 603-862-1196. FAX: 603-862-4112. Web Site: www.library.unh.edu/branches/engmathcs.html. *Librn,* Emily L Poworoznek; Tel: 603-862-4168, E-mail: el@cisunix.unh.edu; *Libr Assoc,* Alan L Bryce; Tel: 603-862-1740, E-mail: abryce@cisunix.unh.edu; Staff 2 (MLS 1, Non-MLS 1)
Founded 1949
Library Holdings: Bk Vols 49,642; Per Subs 720
Subject Interests: Computer sci, Eng, Mat sci, Math, Statistics
Open Mon-Thurs 8am-11pm, Fri 8-5, Sat 1-5, Sun 2-11
Friends of the Library Group

EAST ANDOVER

P WILLIAM ADAMS BACHELDER LIBRARY, 12 Chase Hill Rd, 03231. SAN 309-801X. Tel: 603-735-5333. E-mail: wablibrary@comcast.net. *Dir,* Gail Fitzpatrick
Circ 1,960
Jan 2005-Dec 2005. Mats Exp $5,000
Library Holdings: Bk Vols 6,000; Per Subs 21
Automation Activity & Vendor Info: (Cataloging) Readerware; (Circulation) Readerware
Open Tues 9-12:30 & 6:30-8:30, Thurs 6:30-8:30, Fri 1:30-5

EAST DERRY

P TAYLOR LIBRARY*, 49 E Derry Rd, 03041. (Mail add: PO Box 110, 03041-0110), SAN 309-7943. Tel: 603-432-7186. FAX: 603-432-0985. E-mail: taylorlibrary@comcast.net. Web Site: www.taylorlibrary.org. *Librn,* Linda Merrill; *Asst Librn,* Frances Mears
Founded 1878. Pop 35,000
Library Holdings: Bk Vols 20,010; Per Subs 30
Wireless access
Open Mon & Wed 10-5, Tues & Thurs 12-8, Fri 10-3
Friends of the Library Group

EAST KINGSTON

P EAST KINGSTON PUBLIC LIBRARY*, 47 Maplevale Rd, 03827. (Mail add: PO Box 9, 03827-0009), SAN 320-8443. Tel: 603-642-8333. E-mail: info@eastkingstonlibrary.org. Web Site: www.eastkingstonlibrary.org. *Dir,* Tracy Waldron; E-mail: twaldron@eastkingstonlibrary.org; *Asst Librn,* Diane Sheckells
Pop 1,775; Circ 14,500
Library Holdings: Bk Vols 14,000; Per Subs 30
Automation Activity & Vendor Info: (Circulation) Follett Software
Open Mon 9-7, Tues & Thurs 3-7, Wed 1-7, Fri & Sat 9-1
Friends of the Library Group

EAST LEMPSTER

P MINER MEMORIAL LIBRARY*, Three 2nd NH Tpk, 03605. (Mail add: PO Box 131, 03605-0131), SAN 321-0448. Tel: 603-863-0051. FAX: 603-863-8105. E-mail: minerlibrary@gmail.com. *Dir,* Bonnietta Cilley; Tel: 603-863-6925; Staff 0.35 (MLS 0.35)
Founded 1893. Pop 1,099; Circ 2,000
Library Holdings: AV Mats 560; Bk Vols 6,000
Automation Activity & Vendor Info: (Cataloging) LibraryWorld, Inc; (OPAC) LibraryWorld, Inc
Wireless access
Function: Adult bk club, Bks on CD, Children's prog, Computers for patron use, Copy machines, Exhibits, Holiday prog, Summer reading prog
Partic in Librarians of the Upper Valley Coop
Open Mon 10-12 & 2-7, Wed 1:30-6, Sun 2-5, Sat (Summer) 10-12
Friends of the Library Group

EAST ROCHESTER

P EAST ROCHESTER PUBLIC LIBRARY*, 57 Main St, 03868. (Mail add: PO Box 6006, 03868-6006), SAN 309-9393. Tel: 603-332-8013. E-mail: erpl@metrocast.net. *Dir,* Carol Shannon; E-mail: shannonsnest@metrocast.net
Pop 2,500
Library Holdings: Bk Vols 6,000
Mem of Monroe County Library System
Open Mon, Tues & Fri 12-5
Friends of the Library Group

EFFINGHAM

P EFFINGHAM PUBLIC LIBRARY*, 30 Town House Rd, 03882. SAN 309-8036. Tel: 603-539-1537. Web Site: effingham.lib.nh.us. *Interim Dir,* Crystal Hoyt; Staff 2 (Non-MLS 2)
Founded 1893. Pop 1,273; Circ 1,500
Jan 2010-Dec 2010 Income $55,026. Mats Exp $14,100. Sal $39,926
Library Holdings: AV Mats 895; CDs 53; DVDs 114; Large Print Bks 195; Bk Titles 8,278; Bk Vols 8,735; Per Subs 8; Talking Bks 259; Videos 513
Special Collections: Local Authors Coll (Books & audio books by featured presenters at our monthly Writers' Night)
Subject Interests: Classics, Local hist, New England, Northern Indians (New England), State hist
Automation Activity & Vendor Info: (Cataloging) Follett Software; (Circulation) Follett Software; (ILL) SirsiDynix; (OPAC) Follett Software
Wireless access
Function: Handicapped accessible, ILL available, Libr develop, Online searches, Photocopying/Printing, Prog for adults, Prog for children & young adult, Summer reading prog, Telephone ref, Wheelchair accessible, Workshops
Special Services for the Deaf - Closed caption videos
Special Services for the Blind - Large print bks; Sound rec
Open Tues & Wed 1-7, Fri & Sat 1-3
Friends of the Library Group

ENFIELD

P ENFIELD FREE PUBLIC LIBRARY*, 23 Main St, 03748. (Mail add: PO Box 1030, 03748-1030), SAN 309-8044. Tel: 603-632-7145. FAX: 603-632-4055. Web Site: www.enfield.nh.us/Pages/EnfieldNH_Library/index. *Dir,* Marjorie Carr; E-mail: mcarr@enfield.nh.us; *Asst Dir,* Nancy Tiedemann
Founded 1893. Pop 4,202; Circ 37,776
Jan 2005-Dec 2005 Income $157,436. Mats Exp $33,583. Sal $91,406
Library Holdings: Bk Vols 30,884; Per Subs 45
Special Collections: Shaker Coll; Town of Enfield Historical Records
Wireless access
Open Mon, Tues & Thurs 1-8, Wed 10-6, Sat 10-2

EPPING

P HARVEY MITCHELL MEMORIAL LIBRARY*, 151 Main St, 03042. SAN 309-8052. Tel: 603-679-5944. FAX: 603-679-5884. E-mail: harvmitch@gmail.com. Web Site: www.eppinglibrary.com. *Dir,* Bradley Green; *Ch,* Tracie Wilkins; Staff 1 (MLS 1)
Pop 6,000; Circ 40,000
Jan 2011-Dec 2011 Income $163,440
Library Holdings: Bk Vols 20,000; Videos 1,000
Special Collections: New Hampshire Coll
Automation Activity & Vendor Info: (Cataloging) Follett Software; (Circulation) Follett Software
Wireless access
Open Mon-Fri 10-8, Sat 10-2
Friends of the Library Group

EPSOM

P EPSOM PUBLIC LIBRARY*, 1775 Dover Rd, 03234. SAN 309-8060. Tel: 603-736-9920. FAX: 603-736-9920. E-mail: epl@metrocast.net. Web Site: www.epsomlibrary.com. *Dir,* Nancy Claris; *Ch,* Vickie Benner
Pop 3,300
Library Holdings: Bk Vols 17,000; Per Subs 32
Automation Activity & Vendor Info: (Circulation) Follett Software
Open Mon-Thurs 10-7, Sat 9-1
Friends of the Library Group

ERROL

P ERROL PUBLIC LIBRARY, 67 Main St, 03579. (Mail add: PO Box 130, 03579-0007), SAN 309-8079. Tel: 603-482-7720. E-mail: errolbks@gmail.com. *Co-Dir,* Pat Calder; *Co-Dir,* Carol Hall
Pop 292; Circ 8,523
Library Holdings: Audiobooks 27; CDs 10; DVDs 533; Large Print Bks 236; Bk Vols 6,288; Per Subs 10
Subject Interests: Christian living, Fiction, Handicrafts, Local hist
Wireless access
Open Mon 6pm-8pm, Wed, Fri & Sat 9-1, Thurs 1-5

ETNA

P HANOVER TOWN LIBRARY*, 130 Etna Rd, 03750. (Mail add: PO Box 207, 03750-0207), SAN 309-8346. Tel: 603-643-3116. FAX: 603-643-3116. Web Site: www.hanovernh.org/etnalibrary. *Dir,* Barbara Prince; E-mail: barbara.prince@hanovernh.org; Staff 2 (Non-MLS 2)
Founded 1905. Pop 9,212
Library Holdings: Bk Titles 6,000; Per Subs 18; Talking Bks 441
Subject Interests: Local hist
Automation Activity & Vendor Info: (Circulation) Innovative Interfaces, Inc
Database Vendor: Innovative Interfaces, Inc
Open Mon & Thurs 2-7, Tues 9-2, Wed 2-6, Fri 9-4, Sat 10-12

EXETER

S AMERICAN INDEPENDENCE MUSEUM LIBRARY*, One Governors Lane, 03833. SAN 373-2843. Tel: 603-772-2622. FAX: 603-772-0861. E-mail: info@independencemuseum.org. Web Site: www.independencemuseum.org. *Dir,* Julie Hall Williams
Founded 1902
Library Holdings: Bk Titles 920; Bk Vols 950
Special Collections: 18th Century NH & US History, bks, doc, pamphlets; Original 18th & 19th Century Documents, Maps & Letters
Subject Interests: Am Revolution
Wireless access
Restriction: Open by appt only

M EXETER HOSPITAL INC*, Health Sciences Library, Five Alumni Dr, 03833-2160. SAN 377-9556. Tel: 603-580-6226. FAX: 603-580-7928. *Librn,* Gayle Tudisco; Staff 1 (MLS 1)
Library Holdings: Bk Titles 500; Per Subs 100
Subject Interests: Med, Nursing
Function: ILL available
Partic in Health Sciences Libraries of New Hampshire & Vermont; Medical Library Association (MLA); National Network of Libraries of Medicine Greater Midwest Region; North Atlantic Health Sciences Libraries, Inc
Restriction: Open to others by appt, Staff use only

P EXETER PUBLIC LIBRARY*, Four Chestnut St, 03833. SAN 309-8087. Tel: 603-772-3101, 603-772-6036. FAX: 603-772-7548. E-mail: epl@exeterpl.org. Web Site: exeterpl.org. *Dir,* Hope Godino; E-mail: dewey@exterpl.org; *Asst Dir,* Pam Darlington; *ILL Librn,* Gail Ferraro; *Teen Librn,* Jean Grout
Founded 1853. Pop 13,000; Circ 211,013
Library Holdings: Bk Vols 80,000; Per Subs 194
Special Collections: New Hampshire Coll
Automation Activity & Vendor Info: (Circulation) Follett Software
Wireless access
Open Mon-Thurs 8:30-8, Fri 8:30-5, Sat 9-5 (10-1 Summer)

FARMINGTON

P GOODWIN LIBRARY*, 422 Main St, 03835-1519. SAN 309-8095. Tel: 603-755-2944. Circulation Tel: 603-755-2944, Ext 101, 603-755-2944, Ext 103. Administration Tel: 603-755-2944, Ext 102. Automation Services Tel: 603-755-2944, Ext 105. FAX: 603-755-2944. Administration FAX: 603-755-3681. E-mail: goodwinl@worldpath.net. Web Site: www.goodwinlibrary.com. *Dir,* Shannon Smith; E-mail: Shanna@goodwinlibrary.org; *Asst Dir, Dir, Tech Serv,* Tami LaRock; E-mail: reference@goodwinlibrary.com; *Ad,* Amy Cornwell; E-mail: amy@goodwinlibrary.org; *Ch Serv,* Joyce White; E-mail: children@goodwinlibrary.com; Staff 5 (MLS 1, Non-MLS 4)
Founded 1928. Pop 6,300; Circ 21,000
Jan 2009-Dec 2009 Income $283,741, City $264,591, Locally Generated Income $19,150. Mats Exp $37,400, Books $28,000, Per/Ser (Incl. Access Fees) $2,500, AV Mat $5,500, Electronic Ref Mat (Incl. Access Fees) $900, Presv $500. Sal $108,915 (Prof $36,926)
Library Holdings: Audiobooks 4,678; DVDs 503; Electronic Media & Resources 22; Large Print Bks 286; Bk Vols 21,736; Per Subs 60; Videos 119
Special Collections: Farmington News, mid 1800-1970's, microfilm; New Hampshire History, Authors & Books; Town & Family Histories of Farmington (Museum Artifacts)
Automation Activity & Vendor Info: (Cataloging) Follett Software; (Circulation) Follett Software
Database Vendor: EBSCOhost, Overdrive, Inc
Function: Adult bk club, Adult literacy prog, Audiobks via web, Bi-weekly Writer's Group, Bk club(s), Bks on CD, CD-ROM, Children's prog, Computer training, Computers for patron use, Copy machines, Doc delivery serv, e-mail serv, Electronic databases & coll, Family literacy, For res purposes, Free DVD rentals, Handicapped accessible, Holiday prog, Homebound delivery serv, Homework prog, ILL available, Large print keyboards, Learning ctr, Literacy & newcomer serv, Mail & tel request accepted, Mus passes, Newsp ref libr, Online cat, Online ref, Online searches, Outreach serv, OverDrive digital audio bks, Photocopying/Printing, Preschool outreach, Prog for adults, Prog for children & young adult, Pub access computers, Ref & res, Ref serv available, Ref serv in person, Res libr, Scanner, Spoken cassettes & CDs, Story hour, Summer reading prog, Tax forms, Teen prog, Telephone ref, VHS videos, Video lending libr, Wheelchair accessible, Workshops, Writing prog
Special Services for the Blind - Accessible computers; Audio mat; Bks on CD; Computer access aids; Copier with enlargement capabilities; Extensive large print coll; Home delivery serv; Large print bks; Recorded bks; Ref serv; Talking bk serv referral
Open Mon & Wed 12-8, Tues & Thurs 2-5, Fri 12-5, Sat 9-2
Restriction: Non-circulating coll, Non-resident fee, Pub ref by request, Researchers by appt only
Friends of the Library Group

FITZWILLIAM

P FITZWILLIAM TOWN LIBRARY, 11 Templeton Tpk, 03447. SAN 309-8109. Tel: 603-585-6503. FAX: 603-585-6738. E-mail: info@fitzlib.org. Web Site: www.fitzlib.org. *Libr Dir,* Kate Thomas; *Asst Librn,* Donna Hill; *Libr Asst,* Jeremy VanDerKern; Staff 3 (MLS 1, Non-MLS 2)
Founded 1913. Pop 2,100; Circ 25,000
Library Holdings: Audiobooks 853; DVDs 1,584; Large Print Bks 135; Bk Vols 17,321; Per Subs 40
Automation Activity & Vendor Info: (Cataloging) ByWater Solutions; (Circulation) ByWater Solutions; (OPAC) ByWater Solutions
Database Vendor: EBSCOhost
Wireless access
Function: 24/7 Electronic res, 24/7 Online cat, Activity rm, Adult bk club, Art exhibits, Audiobks via web, Bk club(s), Children's prog, Computer training, Computers for patron use, Copy machines, e-mail & chat, E-Reserves, Electronic databases & coll, Equip loans & repairs, eReaders, Free DVD rentals, Handicapped accessible, Holiday prog, ILL available, Magazines, Magnifiers for reading, Mango lang, Movies, Online cat, Online ref, OverDrive digital audio bks, Photocopying/Printing, Preschool reading prog, Prog for adults, Prog for children & young adult, Summer reading prog, Tax forms, Teen prog, Telephone ref, Web-catalog
Open Mon 2-8, Tues & Thurs 2-6, Wed 9-12 & 2-8, Sat 9-Noon
Friends of the Library Group

FRANCESTOWN

P GEORGE HOLMES BIXBY MEMORIAL LIBRARY*, 52 Main St, 03043-3025. (Mail add: PO Box 69, 03043-0069), SAN 309-8117. Tel: 603-547-2730. FAX: 603-547-2730. E-mail: francestownlibrary@gmail.com. *Dir,* Carol Brock; *Ch,* Mary Farrell
Founded 1827. Pop 1,500; Circ 10,099
Library Holdings: Bk Titles 15,000; Per Subs 40; Talking Bks 150
Special Collections: Oral History
Wireless access
Publications: Conservation Letter; Monthly Calendar
Open Tues 1-5, Wed & Fri 10-12 & 1-5, Thurs 1-6, Sat 9-1

FRANCONIA

P ABBIE GREENLEAF LIBRARY*, 439 Main St, 03580. (Mail add: PO Box 787, 03580-0787), SAN 309-8125. Tel: 603-823-8424. FAX: 603-823-5581. E-mail: library@franconianh.org. *Dir,* Jane Cloran; *Asst Dir, ILL Librn,* Sybil Carey
Founded 1892. Pop 1,203; Circ 22,044
Library Holdings: Bk Vols 22,000; Per Subs 45
Special Collections: Franconia Coll; New Hampshire Coll
Subject Interests: NH Franconia Region
Database Vendor: EBSCOhost
Open Mon & Tues 2-6, Wed 2-7, Thurs 10-12 & 2-5, Fri 2-5, Sat 10-1
Friends of the Library Group

FRANKLIN

P FRANKLIN PUBLIC LIBRARY*, 310 Central St, 03235. SAN 309-8133. Tel: 603-934-2911. FAX: 603-934-7413. *Dir,* Robert Sargent; E-mail: rob.sargent@franklin.lib.nh.us; *Ch,* Rachel Stolworthy; *Circ, ILL,* Ruth Niven; Staff 5 (MLS 1, Non-MLS 4)

Founded 1907. Pop 8,300; Circ 57,000
Library Holdings: AV Mats 3,000; Bk Titles 24,000; Bk Vols 27,000; Per Subs 100
Special Collections: Franklin History; New Hampshire History
Automation Activity & Vendor Info: (Cataloging) Follett Software; (Circulation) Follett Software; (OPAC) Follett Software
Open Mon-Thurs 8-8, Fri & Sat 9-5

FREEDOM

P FREEDOM PUBLIC LIBRARY*, 38 Old Portland Rd, 03836. (Mail add: PO Box 159, 03836-0159), SAN 309-8141. Tel: 603-539-5176. FAX: 603-539-1098. E-mail: freedomlibrary@adelphia.net. Web Site: www.freedompubliclibrary.org. *Dir,* Elizabeth Rhymer; *Asst Librn,* Pat Parker; Staff 3 (MLS 2, Non-MLS 1)
Pop 1,400
Library Holdings: Bk Vols 14,000; Per Subs 13
Special Collections: Oral History
Subject Interests: NH
Wireless access
Open Tues & Thurs 2-7, Wed 10-2, Fri 12-5, Sat 10-1
Friends of the Library Group

FREMONT

P FREMONT PUBLIC LIBRARY*, Seven Jackie Bernier Dr, 03044. SAN 309-815X. Tel: 603-895-9543. FAX: 603-895-0549. E-mail: frelib@comcast.net. *Dir,* Bethany Brace; *Asst Librn,* Catherine Murdock; *Ch,* Lynda Miller
Founded 1894. Pop 4,000; Circ 23,000
Automation Activity & Vendor Info: (Cataloging) Follett Software; (Circulation) Follett Software; (OPAC) Follett Software
Wireless access
Open Mon 12-6, Tues & Thurs 1-8, Wed & Fri 9-5, Sat 9-2

GILFORD

P GILFORD PUBLIC LIBRARY*, 31 Potter Hill Rd, 03249-6803. SAN 309-8168. Tel: 603-524-6042. FAX: 603-524-1218. E-mail: library@gilfordlibrary.org. Web Site: www.gilfordlibrary.org. *Dir,* Katherine Dormody; E-mail: katherine@gilfordlibrary.org; *Asst Librn,* Elizabeth Tidd; *Ch,* Tracey Petrozzi; *Circ Librn,* Molly Harper; Staff 8 (MLS 2, Non-MLS 6)
Founded 1894. Pop 6,800
Library Holdings: Bk Vols 49,000; Per Subs 100
Subject Interests: NH
Automation Activity & Vendor Info: (Circulation) SirsiDynix; (OPAC) SirsiDynix
Database Vendor: EBSCOhost
Wireless access
Open Mon, Wed & Fri 9-6, Tues & Thurs 10-8, Sat 10-2
Friends of the Library Group

GILMANTON

P GILMANTON CORNER PUBLIC LIBRARY, 503 Province Rd, 03237-9205. (Mail add: PO Box 504, 03237-0504), SAN 309-8176. Tel: 603-267-6200. *Vols Librn,* Linda Hudziec
Founded 1912. Pop 3,060
Mar 2013-Feb 2014 Income $3,700. Mats Exp $2,400
Library Holdings: Audiobooks 75; Braille Volumes 2; CDs 150; DVDs 100; Large Print Bks 50; Music Scores 50; Bk Vols 8,000; Per Subs 3
Special Collections: State Document Depository
Open Mon & Thurs (May-Oct) 2-8, Tues 2-4, Wed & Fri 2-6; Mon & Wed (Nov-Apr) 3-5, Sat 10-Noon

GILMANTON IRON WORKS

P GILMANTON YEAR-ROUND LIBRARY*, 1358 NH Rte 140, 03837. Tel: 603-364-2400. E-mail: gyrla@metrocast.org. Web Site: www.gyrla.org. *Librn,* Tasha LeRoux Stetson; *Ch,* Pam Jansury; *Libr Asst,* Jean Henry; Staff 1 (Non-MLS 1)
Founded 1916. Pop 1,500
Library Holdings: Bk Titles 5,000
Open Tues & Sat 9:30-12, Wed (Summer) 4-6
Friends of the Library Group

GILSUM

P GILSUM PUBLIC LIBRARY, 650 Rte 10, 03448-7502. SAN 309-8206. Tel: 603-357-0320. FAX: 603-352-0845. E-mail: gilsumlibrary@comcast.net. *Dir,* Gail Bardwell
Founded 1892. Pop 800; Circ 4,555
Library Holdings: Bk Vols 10,800; Per Subs 23
Wireless access
Open Mon 12-4 & 6-8, Tues 6-8, Wed 12-4, Sat 10-12

GOFFSTOWN

P GOFFSTOWN PUBLIC LIBRARY, Two High St, 03045-1910. SAN 309-8214. Tel: 603-497-2102. FAX: 603-497-8437. E-mail: goflib@goffstownlibrary.com. Web Site: www.goffstownlibrary.com. *Dir,* Dianne Hathaway; E-mail: dianneh@goffstownlibrary.com; *Ch,* Patti Penick; E-mail: pattip@goffstownlibrary.com; *Adult Serv & Outreach Coordr,* Sandra Whipple; E-mail: sandyw@goffstownlibrary.com; Staff 11 (MLS 1, Non-MLS 10)
Founded 1888. Pop 18,000; Circ 105,551
Jan 2013-Dec 2013 Income $721,546. Mats Exp $43,126. Sal $409,628
Automation Activity & Vendor Info: (Acquisitions) Innovative Interfaces, Inc; (Cataloging) Innovative Interfaces, Inc; (Circulation) Innovative Interfaces, Inc; (OPAC) Innovative Interfaces, Inc; (Serials) Innovative Interfaces, Inc
Database Vendor: EBSCO Auto Repair Reference, EBSCOhost, Facts on File, Gale Cengage Learning, Newsbank, OCLC FirstSearch, OCLC WorldShare Interlibrary Loan, Overdrive, Inc
Wireless access
Function: Adult bk club, After school storytime, Bks on CD, Children's prog, Computer training, Computers for patron use, Copy machines, e-mail & chat, e-mail serv, E-Reserves, Electronic databases & coll, Free DVD rentals, Handicapped accessible, Home delivery & serv to Sr ctr & nursing homes, Homebound delivery serv, ILL available, Instruction & testing, Mail & tel request accepted, Mus passes, Music CDs, Online cat, Outreach serv, Photocopying/Printing, Prog for adults, Prog for children & young adult, Pub access computers, Senior outreach, Summer reading prog, Tax forms, Teen prog, Wheelchair accessible, Writing prog
Partic in GMILCS, Inc
Open Mon, Thurs & Fri 9-5, Tues & Wed 9-8, Sat (Winter) 9-2
Friends of the Library Group

S NEW HAMPSHIRE DEPARTMENT OF CORRECTIONS*, State Prison for Women Library, 317 Mast Rd, 03045. Tel: 603-668-6137. Web Site: www.state.nh.us/nhdoc. *Librn,* Becky Harding
Library Holdings: Bk Vols 3,000
Database Vendor: LexisNexis
Open Mon-Sun 8-8

GORHAM

P GORHAM PUBLIC LIBRARY*, 35 Railroad St, 03581. SAN 309-8222. Tel: 603-466-2525. E-mail: gorhampubliclibrary@ne.rr.com. *Dir,* Elizabeth Thompson; *Asst Librn,* Constance Landry
Founded 1895. Pop 3,600; Circ 24,856
Library Holdings: Bk Vols 30,000; Per Subs 28
Special Collections: New Hampshire Books Coll
Automation Activity & Vendor Info: (Acquisitions) Biblionix
Wireless access
Open Mon-Fri 10-6, Sat 10-Noon

GOSHEN

P OLIVE G PETTIS MEMORIAL LIBRARY, Goshen Library, 36 Mill Village Rd N, 03752. (Mail add: PO Box 57, 03752-0057), SAN 309-8230. Tel: 603-863-6921. E-mail: info@goshenlibrary.org. Web Site: www.goshenlibrary.org. *Librn,* Cynthia Reardon Phillips; Staff 2 (Non-MLS 2)
Pop 742; Circ 2,020
Apr 2013-Mar 2014 Income $24,628, City $24,128, Locally Generated Income $500. Mats Exp $2,100, Books $1,200, Per/Ser (Incl. Access Fees) $260, AV Mat $240, Electronic Ref Mat (Incl. Access Fees) $400. Sal $15,840
Library Holdings: Audiobooks 300; DVDs 200; Large Print Bks 20; Bk Vols 7,400; Per Subs 12; Spec Interest Per Sub 4
Special Collections: John Gunnison
Subject Interests: Local hist
Automation Activity & Vendor Info: (Cataloging) LibraryWorld, Inc; (Circulation) LibraryWorld, Inc
Database Vendor: Booklist Online, EBSCOhost, LibraryWorld, Inc, Newsbank, OCLC WebJunction
Wireless access
Function: Adult bk club, Audiobks via web, Bks on CD, Children's prog, Computer training, Computers for patron use, Copy machines, e-mail serv, Electronic databases & coll, Free DVD rentals, Handicapped accessible, Homebound delivery serv, Homework prog, ILL available, Mus passes, Music CDs, Online cat, Online searches, OverDrive digital audio bks, Photocopying/Printing, Preschool outreach, Preschool reading prog, Printer for laptops & handheld devices, Prog for adults, Prog for children & young adult, Pub access computers, Satellite serv, Scanner, Senior computer classes, Senior outreach, Story hour, Summer reading prog, Teen prog, Wheelchair accessible
Partic in SW Libr District
Open Tues-Thurs 2-7, Fri & Sat 10-2

Restriction: Authorized patrons, Circ to mem only, External users must contact libr, ID required to use computers (Ltd hrs), In-house use for visitors, Non-circulating of rare bks, Non-resident fee
Friends of the Library Group

GRAFTON

P GRAFTON PUBLIC LIBRARY*, 47 Library Rd, 03240. (Mail add: PO Box 313, 03240-0310), SAN 309-8249. Tel: 603-523-7865. *Librn,* Debra Clough
Pop 998; Circ 2,355
Library Holdings: Bk Vols 6,000; Per Subs 10
Open Wed 10-11:30 & 4:30-8; Sat 10-12

GRANTHAM

P DUNBAR FREE LIBRARY*, 401 Rte 10 S, 03753. (Mail add: PO Box 1580, 03753-1580), SAN 309-8257. Tel: 603-863-2172. FAX: 603-863-2172. E-mail: info@dunbarlibrary.org. Web Site: www.dunbarlibrary.org. *Dir,* Dawn Huston; *Asst Librn, ILL Librn,* B Joey Holmes; *Ch, Programming Librn,* Lisette Scott; E-mail: dflprogramming@comcast.net; Staff 3 (MLS 1, Non-MLS 2)
Founded 1901. Pop 2,985; Circ 56,000
Library Holdings: Large Print Bks 175; Bk Titles 18,076; Per Subs 69; Talking Bks 953; Videos 1,169
Automation Activity & Vendor Info: (Cataloging) Follett Software; (Circulation) Follett Software
Database Vendor: EBSCOhost, OCLC WorldShare Interlibrary Loan
Wireless access
Function: Adult bk club, Audiobks via web, Bk club(s), Bks on cassette, Bks on CD, Children's prog, Computer training, Computers for patron use, Copy machines, Electronic databases & coll, Fax serv, Free DVD rentals, Handicapped accessible, Homebound delivery serv, ILL available, Mus passes, Music CDs, Online cat, OverDrive digital audio bks, Preschool reading prog, Prog for children & young adult, Pub access computers, Ref serv available, Scanner, Spoken cassettes & CDs, Story hour, Summer reading prog, Tax forms, Telephone ref, VHS videos, Web-catalog, Wheelchair accessible
Open Mon & Wed 9-7:30, Thurs 9-5, Fri 9-12, Sat 9-2
Restriction: Non-circulating of rare bks
Friends of the Library Group

GREENFIELD

P STEPHENSON MEMORIAL LIBRARY, Greenfield Library, 761 Forest Rd, 03047-0127. (Mail add: PO Box 127, 03047-0127), SAN 309-8265. Tel: 603-547-2790. E-mail: stephensonlib@myfairpoint.net. *Libr Dir,* Julie Steenson; *Youth Serv,* Kristin Readel; Staff 1 (MLS 1)
Library Holdings: Bk Vols 15,000; Per Subs 25
Special Collections: American Anthology of Music, recs; Greenfield (Town & Local Events), photos
Publications: New Town History
Friends of the Library Group

GREENLAND

P WEEKS PUBLIC LIBRARY, 36 Post Rd, 03840-2312. (Mail add: PO Box 430, 03840-0430), SAN 309-8273. Tel: 603-436-8548. FAX: 603-427-0913. E-mail: weekspl@comcast.net. Web Site: www.weekslibrary.org. *Dir,* Denise Grimse; E-mail: dgrimsewpl@comcast.net; *Asst Dir/Ch,* Susan MacDonald; *Circ Librn,* Elaine Molleur; *ILL Librn,* Lee Atkinson; *Librn/Teen & Tween Serv,* Candace Yost; E-mail: librarianwpl@comcast.net; *Cataloger, Circ,* Meredith Hoyt; *Circ, Programming,* Margaret Mooers; Staff 2.8 (MLS 1, Non-MLS 1.8)
Founded 1897. Pop 3,549; Circ 45,950
Jan 2013-Dec 2013 Income $246,845, City $241,853, Locally Generated Income $4,992. Mats Exp $40,719, Books $20,418, Per/Ser (Incl. Access Fees) $1,675, AV Mat $12,730, Electronic Ref Mat (Incl. Access Fees) $5,896. Sal $150,816 (Prof $112,671)
Library Holdings: Audiobooks 890; CDs 681; DVDs 2,473; e-books 15,701; Electronic Media & Resources 7,219; Bk Vols 20,867; Per Subs 37
Special Collections: New Hampshire
Automation Activity & Vendor Info: (Cataloging) Book Systems; (Circulation) Book Systems; (OPAC) Book Systems
Database Vendor: EBSCOhost, Library Ideas, LLC, Overdrive, Inc
Wireless access
Function: Adult bk club, Audiobks via web, AV serv, Bks on CD, Children's prog, Computer training, Copy machines, Digital talking bks, Distance learning, E-Reserves, Electronic databases & coll, eReaders, Free DVD rentals, ILL available, Laminating, Magazines, Mango lang, Movies, Mus passes, Music CDs, Online cat, Photocopying/Printing, Prog for adults, Prog for children & young adult, Pub access computers, Scanner, Spoken cassettes & CDs, Story hour, Summer reading prog, Tax forms, Teen prog, Workshops
Publications: Book Bytes (Bi-monthly); Weeks Public Library (Monthly newsletter)
Open Mon-Thurs 10-8, Fri 10-5, Sat 9-1
Friends of the Library Group

GREENVILLE

P CHAMBERLIN FREE PUBLIC LIBRARY*, 46 Main St, 03048. (Mail add: PO Box 499, 03048-0499), SAN 309-8281. Tel: 603-878-1105. FAX: 603-878-4092. E-mail: cfpl_green@hotmail.com. Web Site: www.chamberlinlibrary.org. *Dir,* Charles Brault; E-mail: charlesbrault@hotmail.com; *ILL,* Diane Steele
Founded 1876. Pop 2,200; Circ 13,255
Library Holdings: Bk Vols 17,000; Per Subs 100
Special Collections: Cook Book Coll; Gardening Coll; Occult Coll
Automation Activity & Vendor Info: (Acquisitions) New Generation Technologies Inc. (LiBRARYSOFT); (Cataloging) New Generation Technologies Inc. (LiBRARYSOFT); (Circulation) New Generation Technologies Inc. (LiBRARYSOFT); (Course Reserve) New Generation Technologies Inc. (LiBRARYSOFT); (ILL) New Generation Technologies Inc. (LiBRARYSOFT); (OPAC) New Generation Technologies Inc. (LiBRARYSOFT); (Serials) New Generation Technologies Inc. (LiBRARYSOFT)
Open Mon & Wed 3-8, Tues & Thurs 9-8, Fri 9-5, Sat 9-1

GROVETON

P NORTHUMBERLAND PUBLIC LIBRARY*, 31 State St, 03582. Tel: 603-636-2066. FAX: 603-636-2066. E-mail: grovetonlibrary@yahoo.com. *Dir,* Gail Rossetto; E-mail: grovetonlibrary@gmail.com; *Asst Librn,* Rae Davenport
Pop 2,478; Circ 28,056
Library Holdings: Bk Vols 25,000; Per Subs 18
Open Tues-Fri 10-5, Sat 10-2

HAMPSTEAD

P HAMPSTEAD PUBLIC LIBRARY*, Nine Mary E Clark Dr, 03841. (Mail add: PO Box 190, 03841-0190), SAN 309-829X. Tel: 603-329-6411. FAX: 603-329-6036. E-mail: director@hampstead.lib.nh.us. Web Site: www.hampstead.lib.nh.us. *Dir,* Debra Hiett; *Asst Dir,* Merrily Samuels; E-mail: msamuels@hampstead.lib.nh.us; *Ad,* Janet Arden; *Youth Serv Librn,* Patty Falconer; Staff 9 (MLS 2, Non-MLS 7)
Founded 1898. Pop 8,300; Circ 55,000
Jan 2006-Dec 2006 Income $329,068, Federal $728, Locally Generated Income $307,868, Other $20,472. Mats Exp $44,689, Books $35,974, Per/Ser (Incl. Access Fees) $3,450, AV Mat $1,385, Electronic Ref Mat (Incl. Access Fees) $3,880. Sal $226,702 (Prof $80,504)
Library Holdings: AV Mats 3,328; Bk Titles 42,116; Per Subs 80
Special Collections: Civil War Coll
Automation Activity & Vendor Info: (Cataloging) Follett Software; (Circulation) Follett Software; (OPAC) Follett Software
Database Vendor: EBSCOhost
Wireless access
Partic in Merri-Hill-Rock Library Cooperative
Open Mon, Tues & Thurs 9-8, Wed 1-8, Fri 9-6, Sat 9-2
Friends of the Library Group

HAMPTON

S HAMPTON HISTORICAL SOCIETY*, Tuck Museum Library, 40 Park Ave, 03842. (Mail add: PO Box 1601, 03843), SAN 373-2444. Tel: 603-929-0781. E-mail: info@hamptonhistoricalsociety.org. Web Site: www.hamptonhistoricalsociety.org. *Dir,* Betty Moore
Founded 1925
Library Holdings: Bk Vols 500
Special Collections: Local History, Genealogy & NH Town Histories, postcards, photos of Hampton area
Subject Interests: Educ, Genealogy
Restriction: Non-circulating, Open by appt only

P LANE MEMORIAL LIBRARY*, Two Academy Ave, 03842. SAN 309-8303. Tel: 603-926-3368. FAX: 603-926-1348. E-mail: library@hampton.lib.nh.us. Web Site: www.hampton.lib.nh.us. *Dir,* Amanda Reynolds Cooper; E-mail: acooper@hampton.lib.nh.us; *Asst Dir, Head, Tech Serv,* William H Teschek; E-mail: bteschek@hampton.lib.nh.us; *Ad,* Darrell Eifert; E-mail: deifert@hampton.lib.nh.us; *Ch,* Paulina Shadowens; Tel: 603-926-4729, E-mail: pshadowens@hampton.lib.nh.us. Subject Specialists: *Genealogy,* William H Teschek; Staff 14 (MLS 4, Non-MLS 10)
Founded 1881. Pop 15,000; Circ 165,749
Library Holdings: Bk Vols 55,555; Per Subs 279; Talking Bks 4,556; Videos 3,585
Special Collections: Genealogy Coll; Local History Coll; New Hampshire Coll

Automation Activity & Vendor Info: (Cataloging) TLC (The Library Corporation); (Circulation) TLC (The Library Corporation); (OPAC) TLC (The Library Corporation)
Wireless access
Function: Adult literacy prog, Home delivery & serv to Sr ctr & nursing homes, ILL available, Photocopying/Printing, Prog for children & young adult, Ref serv available, Summer reading prog, Telephone ref, Wheelchair accessible
Open Mon-Thurs 9-8, Fri & Sat 9-5
Friends of the Library Group

HAMPTON FALLS

P HAMPTON FALLS FREE PUBLIC LIBRARY, Seven Drinkwater Rd, 03844-2116. SAN 309-8311. Tel: 603-926-3682. FAX: 603-926-0170. E-mail: hamptonfalls.library@comcast.net. Web Site: www.hamptonfallslibrary.org. *Dir,* Judith Haskell; *Youth Serv Librn,* Carol Sanborn; *Libr Asst,* Barbara Tosiano; Staff 2 (MLS 1, Non-MLS 1)
Pop 2,100; Circ 21,400
Library Holdings: Bk Vols 15,000; Per Subs 45
Automation Activity & Vendor Info: (Acquisitions) Biblionix/Apollo; (Circulation) Biblionix/Apollo
Database Vendor: Biblionix/Apollo, EBSCOhost, LearningExpress, World Book Online
Wireless access
Function: Adult bk club, After school storytime, Art exhibits, Audiobks via web, Bks on CD, Children's prog, Computers for patron use, Free DVD rentals, Handicapped accessible, Homebound delivery serv, ILL available, Magnifiers for reading, Online cat, OverDrive digital audio bks, Photocopying/Printing, Prog for adults, Prog for children & young adult, Summer reading prog
Open Tues 10-8, Wed 1-8, Thurs & Fri 10-5, Sat 10-2
Friends of the Library Group

HANCOCK

P HANCOCK TOWN LIBRARY*, 25 Main St, 03449. (Mail add: PO Box 130, 03449-0130), SAN 309-832X. Tel: 603-525-4411. E-mail: hancocklibrary@comcast.net. *Dir,* Amy Markus; *Ch,* Rennie Timm
Founded 1860. Pop 1,800; Circ 23,603
Library Holdings: Bk Titles 18,000; Per Subs 55
Subject Interests: Town hist
Automation Activity & Vendor Info: (Acquisitions) Follett Software
Database Vendor: EBSCOhost
Wireless access
Open Mon & Wed 2-6, Tues & Thurs 10-7, Sat 10-4
Friends of the Library Group

HANOVER

C DARTMOUTH COLLEGE LIBRARY*, 6025 Baker Berry Library, Rm 115, 03755-3527. SAN 350-493X. Tel: 603-646-2236. FAX: 603-646-3702. Web Site: library.dartmouth.edu. *Dean of Libr,* Jeff Horrell; *Head of Acq Serv,* Judy Maynes; *Assoc Librn,* Elizabeth Kirk; *Assoc Librn,* David Seaman; *Cat,* Cecilia Tittemore; Staff 184 (MLS 54, Non-MLS 130)
Founded 1769. Enrl 5,328; Fac 951; Highest Degree: Doctorate
Library Holdings: e-journals 40,731; Bk Vols 2,511,667; Per Subs 17,533
Wireless access
Partic in Association of Research Libraries (ARL); Coun of Libr Info Resources; Digital Libr Fedn; Lyrasis; New Eng Res Librs; OCLC Online Computer Library Center, Inc
Friends of the Library Group

Departmental Libraries:

BAKER-BERRY LIBRARY, 6025 Baker-Berry Library, 03755-3527. Tel: 603-646-2704. Interlibrary Loan Service Tel: 603-646-2596. FAX: 603-646-2167. E-mail: ris@dartmouth.edu. Web Site: www.dartmouth.edu/~library/bakerberry. *Dean of Libr, Librn of the Col,* Jeffrey Horrell; Tel: 603-646-2236, E-mail: Jeffrey.L.Horrell@Dartmouth.edu; *Head, Acq,* Judy Maynes; Tel: 603-646-2593; *Head, Cat & Metadata Serv,* Cecilia Tittemore; Tel: 603-646-2180; *Head, Digital Libr Tech,* Anthony Helm; Staff 42 (MLS 12, Non-MLS 30)
Founded 1928
Library Holdings: Bk Vols 1,695,575; Per Subs 11,366
Open Mon-Fri 8am-2am, Sat & Sun 10am-2am
Friends of the Library Group

CM BIOMEDICAL LIBRARIES (DANA BIOMEDICAL & MATTHEWS-FULLER HEALTH SCIENCES LIBRARY), Dana Biomedical Library/HB 6168, 37 Dewey Field Rd, 3rd Flr, 03755-1417, SAN 350-4964. Tel: 603-650-1658, 603-650-7658. Interlibrary Loan Service Tel: 603-646-8629. Reference Tel: 603-650-7660. Interlibrary Loan Service FAX: 603-650-1354. E-mail: biomedical.libraries.reference@dartmouth.edu. Web Site: www.dartmouth.edu/~library/biomed. *Dir,* Laura Cousineau; Tel: 603-650-1661, Fax: 603-650-1789, E-mail: laura.k.cousineau@dartmouth.edu; *Assoc Dir, Health Sci Libr,* Cindy Stewart; Tel: 603-650-4967, E-mail: cynthia.l.stewart@dartmouth.edu; *Assoc Dir, Info Res,* Peggy Sleeth; Tel: 603-650-1635, E-mail: margaret.k.sleeth@dartmouth.edu; *Mgr, Computing & Media Serv,* David Izzo; Tel: 603-650-1663, E-mail: david.j.izzo@dartmouth.edu; Staff 8 (MLS 7, Non-MLS 1)
Subject Interests: Bio, Med, Nursing

FELDBERG BUSINESS ADMINISTRATION & ENGINEERING LIBRARY, 6193 Murdough Ctr, 03755-3560, SAN 350-4999. Tel: 603-646-2191. FAX: 603-646-2384. E-mail: feldberg.reference@dartmouth.edu. Web Site: www.dartmouth.edu/~feldberg. *Head of Libr,* James R Fries; E-mail: james.r.fries@dartmouth.edu; *Ref Librn,* Anne Esler; *Ref Librn,* Richard Felver; *Ref Librn,* Janifer Holt; *Ref Librn,* Mark Mounts; *Ref Librn,* Karen Sluzenski; Staff 10 (MLS 5, Non-MLS 5)
Founded 1973. Highest Degree: Doctorate
Library Holdings: Bk Vols 115,988; Per Subs 2,673

KRESGE PHYSICAL SCIENCES LIBRARY, 6115 Fairchild Hall, 03755-3571, SAN 350-5022. Tel: 603-646-3563. FAX: 603-646-3681. E-mail: kresge.library@dartmouth.edu. Web Site: www.dartmouth.edu/~library/kresge. *Head of Libr,* Jane Quigley; *Phys Sci Librn,* Lora Leligdon; *Phys Sci Librn,* Shirley Zhao; *Libr Supvr,* Karen MacPhee; *Coll Spec,* Lisa Ladd; *Doc, Tech Spec,* Marcia Pirone; Staff 6 (MLS 3, Non-MLS 3)
Library Holdings: Bk Vols 129,634; Per Subs 1,533

PADDOCK MUSIC LIBRARY, 6245 Hopkins Ctr, 03755. Tel: 603-646-3234. Reference Tel: 603-646-3120. E-mail: Paddock.Music.Library@Dartmouth.edu. Web Site: www.dartmouth.edu/~library/paddock. *Head of Libr,* Patricia B Fisken; E-mail: patricia.fisken@dartmouth.edu; *Libr Supvr,* Joy Weale; *Libr Spec,* David Bowden; *Libr Spec,* Rachel McConnell. Subject Specialists: *Dance, Music,* Patricia B Fisken; Staff 4 (MLS 1, Non-MLS 3)
Library Holdings: CDs 29,200; DVDs 1,670; Bk Vols 75,600; Per Subs 378
Subject Interests: Dance, Music
Automation Activity & Vendor Info: (Acquisitions) Innovative Interfaces, Inc; (Cataloging) Innovative Interfaces, Inc; (Circulation) Innovative Interfaces, Inc - Millenium

RAUNER SPECIAL COLLECTIONS LIBRARY, 6065 Webster Hall, 03755-3519, SAN 378-0546. Tel: 603-646-0538. FAX: 603-646-0447. Web Site: www.dartmouth.edu/~library/rauner. *Spec Coll Librn,* Jay Satterfield; *Col Archivist,* Peter Carini; Staff 13 (MLS 3, Non-MLS 10)
Library Holdings: Bk Vols 126,797; Per Subs 489
Special Collections: American Calligraphy Coll; Bookplates; Dartmouth Archives; Don Quixote Coll; George Ticknor Library; German & English Plays (Barrett Clark Coll); Horace (Barlow Coll); New England Early Illustrated Books (1926 Memorial); New Hampshire History & Imprints Coll; Polar Regions (Stefansson Coll); Private Presses; Railroads (Chase Streeter Coll); Robert Frost Coll; Shakespeare (Hickmott Coll); Spanish Civilization (Bryant Coll); Spanish Plays; White Mountains
Open Mon-Fri 8-6
Friends of the Library Group

SANBORN ENGLISH LIBRARY, Department of English, HB 6032 Sanborn House, 03755-3525. Tel: 603-646-3993. FAX: 603-646-2159. E-mail: english.department@dartmouth.edu. *Dept Adminr,* Jeanne Briand; E-mail: jeanne.briand@dartmouth.edu; Staff 2 (Non-MLS 2)
Founded 1928. Enrl 5,700; Highest Degree: Doctorate
Library Holdings: Bk Vols 8,749; Per Subs 40
Special Collections: Poetry Chapbooks
Subject Interests: Eng lit
Restriction: Non-circulating, Not a lending libr
Friends of the Library Group

SHERMAN ART LIBRARY, Carpentar Hall, Hinman Box 6025, 03755-3570, SAN 350-5081. Tel: 603-646-2305. E-mail: sherman.library.reference@dartmouth.edu. Web Site: www.dartmouth.edu/~library/sherman. *Visual Arts Librn,* Laura Graveline; Tel: 603-646-3831, E-mail: laura.graveline@dartmouth.edu; *Visual Arts Info Spec,* Joseph Wright; Tel: 603-646-6469, E-mail: joseph.wright@dartmouth.edu
Founded 1929
Library Holdings: Bk Vols 129,298; Per Subs 642
Special Collections: Artists Books
Subject Interests: Archit, Photog

P HOWE LIBRARY*, 13 South St, 03755. SAN 309-8354. Tel: 603-643-4120. Circulation Tel: 603-640-3269. Administration Tel: 603-640-3251. Information Services Tel: 603-640-3267. FAX: 603-643-0725. E-mail: howe.library@thehowe.org. Web Site: www.howelibrary.org. *Dir,* Mary H White; E-mail: mary.h.white@thehowe.org; *Head, Adult Serv,* Mary Hardy; *Head, Tech Serv, Syst Librn,* Pam Smith; *Head, Youth Serv,* Denise Reitsma; *Circ,* Kristina Burnett; *ILL,* Peter Appleton; Staff 14 (MLS 8, Non-MLS 6)
Founded 1900. Pop 11,260; Circ 250,932
Library Holdings: Audiobooks 16,441; DVDs 4,077; e-books 8,873; Bk Vols 70,100; Per Subs 336

Automation Activity & Vendor Info: (Acquisitions) Evergreen; (Cataloging) Evergreen; (Circulation) Evergreen; (OPAC) Evergreen
Database Vendor: EBSCOhost, OCLC FirstSearch
Wireless access
Function: Adult bk club, After school storytime, Art exhibits, Audiobks via web, Bk club(s), Bks on CD, Chess club, Children's prog, Computers for patron use, Copy machines, Digital talking bks, e-mail & chat, e-mail serv, Electronic databases & coll, Exhibits, Free DVD rentals, Handicapped accessible, Home delivery & serv to Sr ctr & nursing homes, Homebound delivery serv, ILL available, Large print keyboards, Magnifiers for reading, Mail & tel request accepted, Mus passes, Music CDs, Online ref, Online searches, Outreach serv, Outside serv via phone, mail, e-mail & web, OverDrive digital audio bks, Photocopying/Printing, Prog for adults, Prog for children & young adult, Pub access computers, Ref serv available, Ref serv in person, Spoken cassettes & CDs, Spoken cassettes & DVDs, Story hour, Summer reading prog, Tax forms, Teen prog, Telephone ref, Wheelchair accessible
Special Services for the Blind - Assistive/Adapted tech devices, equip & products; Computer with voice synthesizer for visually impaired persons; Home delivery serv
Open Mon-Thurs 10-8, Fri 12-6, Sat 10-5, Sun 1-5

A UNITED STATES ARMY*, Engineer Research & Development Center Library, 72 Lyme Rd, 03755-1290. SAN 350-5111. Tel: 603-646-4779. FAX: 603-646-4712. Web Site: itl.erdc.usace.army.mil/library. *Librn,* Elizabeth Hoffmeister; Tel: 603-646-4338, E-mail: elizabeth.r.hoffmeister@erdc.usace.army.mil; *Librn,* Elisabeth Smallidge; Tel: 603-646-4238, E-mail: elisabeth.r.smallidge@erdc.usace.army.mil; Staff 3 (MLS 2, Non-MLS 1)
Founded 1952
Library Holdings: e-journals 1,500; Bk Titles 20,000; Per Subs 150
Special Collections: Cold Regions Science & Technology Bibliography
Subject Interests: Eng, Geol, Math, Meteorology, Physics
Automation Activity & Vendor Info: (Cataloging) SirsiDynix; (Circulation) SirsiDynix; (OPAC) SirsiDynix; (Serials) SirsiDynix
Wireless access
Function: Res libr
Publications: Bibliography of Cold Regions Science & Technology (Bibliographies)
Partic in OCLC Online Computer Library Center, Inc
Restriction: Internal use only, Open by appt only

HARRISVILLE

P HARRISVILLE PUBLIC LIBRARY*, Seven Canal St, 03450. (Mail add: PO Box 387, 03450-0387), SAN 309 8362. Tel: 603-827-2918, FAX: 603-827-2919. *Dir,* Susan Weaver; E-mail: sweaver@harrisville.lib.nh.us; *Ch,* Kris Finnegan
Pop 1,075; Circ 7,332
Library Holdings: AV Mats 400; DVDs 40; Bk Vols 5,500; Per Subs 18
Wireless access
Open Mon 10-1 & 6:30-8:30, Tues 3-5, Wed 2-5, Thurs 10-1, Fri 3-6:30, Sat 9-12
Friends of the Library Group

HAVERHILL

P HAVERHILL LIBRARY ASSOCIATION*, 67 Court St, 03765. (Mail add: PO Box 117, 03765-0117), SAN 309-8370. Tel: 603-989-5578. *Ad, Dir,* Nanci Myers; *Ch,* Anne Marie Ballam; Staff 3 (Non-MLS 3)
Founded 1880. Pop 350; Circ 7,850
Library Holdings: AV Mats 266; Bk Vols 15,235; Per Subs 27; Talking Bks 92; Videos 174
Special Collections: Oral History; State Document Depository
Special Services for the Blind - Large print bks
Open Mon & Wed 4-8, Tues & Sat 10-1

HEBRON

P HEBRON LIBRARY*, Eight Church Lane, 03241. (Mail add: PO Box 90, 03241-0090), SAN 309-8419. Tel: 603-744-7998. E-mail: hebronlibrary@metrocast.net. *Dir,* Robin Orr
Pop 342; Circ 3,533
Library Holdings: AV Mats 152; Bk Vols 8,000; Per Subs 14
Open Wed (Winter) 1-5, Sat 10-12; Wed (Summer) 1-6, Sat 10-1

HENNIKER

C NEW ENGLAND COLLEGE, H Raymond Danforth Library, 196 Bridge St, 03242-3298. (Mail add: 98 Bridge St, 03242-3298), SAN 350-5146. Tel: 603-428-2344. FAX: 603-428-4273. Web Site: www.nec.edu/library. *Interim Dir,* Russ Rattray; E-mail: rrattray@nec.edu; *Circ Librn,* Betsy Davis; *Distance Serv Librn,* Chelsea Hanrahan; *Ref & Instruction Librn,* Karin Heffernan; *Ref & ILL Librn,* Catherine Ryan; Staff 5 (MLS 4, Non-MLS 1)
Founded 1946. Enrl 2,000; Fac 42; Highest Degree: Doctorate
Library Holdings: Bk Vols 102,000; Per Subs 150
Special Collections: College Archives & Art Coll; New Hampshiriana; Shakespeare Coll (Adams Col)
Automation Activity & Vendor Info: (Acquisitions) SirsiDynix; (Cataloging) SirsiDynix; (Circulation) SirsiDynix; (Course Reserve) SirsiDynix; (OPAC) SirsiDynix; (Serials) SirsiDynix
Database Vendor: EBSCOhost, LexisNexis
Wireless access
Partic in GMILCS, Inc; New Hampshire College & University Council
Open Mon-Thurs 7:30am-Midnight, Fri 7:30am-8pm, Sat 10-5, Sun 10am-Midnight
Friends of the Library Group

P TUCKER FREE LIBRARY, 31 Western Ave, 03242. (Mail add: PO Box 688, 03242-0688), SAN 309-8427. Tel. 603-428-3471. FAX; 603-428-7106. E-mail: tuckerfree@comcast.net. Web Site: www.tuckerfreelibrary.org. *Dir,* Lynn Piotrowicz; E-mail: lynnpiotrowicz@tuckerfreelibrary.org; Staff 9 (MLS 1, Non-MLS 8)
Founded 1903. Pop 4,500; Circ 40,000
Library Holdings: Bk Vols 30,000; Per Subs 60
Automation Activity & Vendor Info: (Cataloging) Biblionix; (Circulation) Biblionix
Wireless access
Open Tues-Thurs 10-8, Fri-Sun 12-5
Friends of the Library Group

HILL

P HILL PUBLIC LIBRARY*, 30 Crescent St, 03243. (Mail add: PO Box 257, 03243), SAN 309-8435. Tel: 603-934-9712. FAX: 603-934-9712. E-mail: hillpubliclibrary@comcast.net. Web Site: www.hillpubliclibrary.com. *Librn,* Lynn Christopher; Staff 1 (Non-MLS 1)
Pop 1,078; Circ 5,500
Jan 2012-Dec 2012 Income $28,000
Library Holdings: Bk Titles 11,000; Videos 1,500
Wireless access
Function: Adult bk club, Audiobks via web, Bk club(s), Children's prog, Computer training, Computers for patron use, Copy machines, e-mail & chat, Free DVD rentals, Handicapped accessible, Holiday prog, ILL available, Microfiche/film & reading machines, OverDrive digital audio bks, Photocopying/Printing, Preschool reading prog, Prog for adults, Prog for children & young adult, Pub access computers, Story hour, Summer reading prog, VHS videos, Wheelchair accessible
Partic in New Hampshire Downloadable Books Consortium
Special Services for the Blind - Large print bks
Open Tues 12-8, Wed-Fri 10-6
Restriction: Circ to mem only, Free to mem, In-house use for visitors
Friends of the Library Group

HILLSBORO

P FULLER PUBLIC LIBRARY*, 29 School St, 03244. (Mail add: PO Box 43, 03244-0043), SAN 309-8443. Tel: 603-464-3595. FAX: 603-464-4572. Web Site: fullerlibrary.info. *Dir,* Robin Sweetser; E-mail: director@fullerlibrary.info
Founded 1877. Pop 6,000; Circ 35,000
Library Holdings: Bk Vols 35,090; Per Subs 62
Automation Activity & Vendor Info: (Cataloging) Follett Software; (Circulation) Follett Software
Wireless access
Open Mon & Fri 12-5, Tues & Thurs 9-8, Sat 9-1

HINSDALE

P HINSDALE PUBLIC LIBRARY*, 122 Brattleboro Rd, 03451. (Mail add: PO Box 6, 03451-0006), SAN 309-8451. Tel: 603-336-5713. E-mail: hinsdalelibrary@yahoo.com. *Dir,* Mary Major; *Asst Dir,* Ann Hartnett
Pop 4,000; Circ 6,193
Library Holdings: Bk Vols 25,000; Per Subs 15
Open Mon, Wed & Thurs 2-5 & 6:30-8, Fri 10-12 & 2-5, Sat 10-12

HOLDERNESS

P HOLDERNESS LIBRARY*, 866 US Rte 3, 03245. (Mail add: PO Box L, 03245-0712), SAN 309-846X. Tel: 603-968-7066. E-mail: holdernesslibrary@roadrunner.com. Web Site: www.holdernesslibrary.org. *Dir,* Victoria A Lang; *Asst Librn,* Kelly Schwaner; Staff 3 (Non-MLS 3)
Founded 1878. Pop 2,200; Circ 7,000
Library Holdings: Audiobooks 463; Bks on Deafness & Sign Lang 6; DVDs 1,000; Large Print Bks 93; Bk Titles 13,500; Per Subs 32; Videos 300
Special Collections: New Hampshire Special Coll, bks, pamphlets
Automation Activity & Vendor Info: (Cataloging) Follett Software; (Circulation) Follett Software; (OPAC) Follett Software
Database Vendor: EBSCOhost, Gale Cengage Learning, OCLC FirstSearch

Wireless access
Partic in MUM Coop; New Hampshire Automated Information Systems (NHAIS)
Special Services for the Deaf - Closed caption videos
Special Services for the Blind - Large print bks
Open Mon 9-6, Tues & Sat 8-12, Wed 9-8, Fri 9-5
Friends of the Library Group

HOLLIS

P HOLLIS SOCIAL LIBRARY*, Two Monument Sq, 03049. (Mail add: PO Box 659, 03049-0659), SAN 309-8478. Tel: 603-465-7721. FAX: 603-465-3507. Web Site: www.hollislibrary.org. *Dir,* Lucinda Mazza; E-mail: director@hollislibrary.org; *Ch,* Victoria Sandin; Staff 9 (MLS 2, Non-MLS 7)
Founded 1799. Pop 7,603; Circ 85,632
Jan 2005-Dec 2005 Income $243,961, City $217,022, Locally Generated Income $26,939. Mats Exp $70,267, Books $50,227, Per/Ser (Incl. Access Fees) $3,690, AV Mat $16,350. Sal $133,167
Library Holdings: AV Mats 5,279; CDs 634; DVDs 1,549; Large Print Bks 749; Bk Vols 55,000; Per Subs 75; Talking Bks 1,625; Videos 1,471
Subject Interests: Local hist
Automation Activity & Vendor Info: (Cataloging) TLC (The Library Corporation); (Circulation) TLC (The Library Corporation); (OPAC) TLC (The Library Corporation); (Serials) TLC (The Library Corporation)
Wireless access
Publications: HSL Newsletter (Monthly)
Partic in New Hampshire Automated Information Systems (NHAIS)
Open Mon-Thurs 10:30-8:30, Fri 10:30-5:30, Sat 10:30-5, Sun 1-5
Friends of the Library Group

HOOKSETT

P HOOKSETT PUBLIC LIBRARY*, 31 Mount Saint Mary's Way, 03106-1852. SAN 309-8486. Tel: 603-485-6092. FAX: 603-485-6193. Web Site: www.hooksettlibrary.org. *Dir,* Heather Rainier; E-mail: hshumway@hooksettlibrary.org; *Asst Dir/Ref Librn,* Mathew Bose; E-mail: mbose@hooksettlibrary.org; *Youth Serv Librn,* Ellen Tweedy; E-mail: etweedy@hooksettlibrary.org; *Circ Supvr,* LeeAnn Chase; E-mail: lchase@hooksettlibrary.org; Staff 8 (MLS 1, Non-MLS 7)
Founded 1909. Pop 11,000; Circ 54,000
Library Holdings: Bk Titles 43,000; Per Subs 100
Special Collections: New Hampshire Coll
Automation Activity & Vendor Info: (Cataloging) SirsiDynix; (Circulation) SirsiDynix; (OPAC) SirsiDynix
Wireless access
Partic in GMILCS, Inc
Open Mon-Wed 9-8, Thurs 11-8, Fri & Sat 9-5
Friends of the Library Group

HOPKINTON

S NEW HAMPSHIRE ANTIQUARIAN SOCIETY LIBRARY*, 300 Main St, 03229. SAN 326-0836. Tel: 603-746-3825. E-mail: nhas@tds.net. Web Site: nhantiquarian.org. *Exec Dir,* Heather Mitchell
Library Holdings: Bk Vols 14,000
Special Collections: Primitive Portraits Costume Coll
Open Thurs & Fri 9-4, Sat 9-1

HUDSON

P GEORGE H & ELLA M RODGERS MEMORIAL LIBRARY, 194 Derry Rd, 03051. SAN 309-8508. Tel: 603-886-6030. Interlibrary Loan Service Tel: 603-886-6030, Ext 4509. Reference Tel: 603-886-6030, Ext 4522. Automation Services Tel: 603-886-6030, Ext 4525. FAX: 603-816-4501. E-mail: askus@rodgerslibrary.org. Web Site: www.rodgerslibrary.org. *Dir,* Charlie Matthews; Tel: 603-886-6030, Ext 4511, E-mail: charliematthews@rodgerslibrary.org; *Tech Librn,* Kate Butler; E-mail: katebutler@rodgerslibrary.org; *Syst Adminr,* Brian Hewey; E-mail: brianhewey@rodgerslibrary.org; *Adult Serv,* Amy Friedman; E-mail: amyfriedman@rodgerslibrary.org; *Cat,* Ann Carle; Tel: 603-886-6030, Ext 4512, E-mail: anncarle@rodgerslibrary.org; *Ch Serv,* Betsey Martel; Tel: 603-886-6030, Ext 4519; *Circ,* Natalie Coolen; Tel: 603-886-6030, Ext 4516, E-mail: nataliecoolen@rodgerslibrary.org; *Teen Serv,* Danny Arsenault; E-mail: dannyarsenault@rodgerslibrary.org; Staff 7 (MLS 6, Non-MLS 1)
Founded 2009. Pop 25,000; Circ 227,746
Jul 2014-Jun 2015 Income $925,120
Library Holdings: Audiobooks 2,259; AV Mats 6,322; CDs 1,041; DVDs 2,845; Bk Titles 50,536; Bk Vols 53,528; Per Subs 130
Special Collections: Zylonis Lithuanian Heritage Coll
Subject Interests: Genealogy, Local hist
Automation Activity & Vendor Info: (Acquisitions) Evergreen; (Cataloging) Evergreen; (Circulation) Evergreen; (ILL) Evergreen; (OPAC) Evergreen; (Serials) Evergreen
Database Vendor: EBSCO Auto Repair Reference, EBSCOhost, LearningExpress, Newsbank, Overdrive, Inc, ProQuest, World Book Online
Wireless access
Function: Adult bk club, After school storytime, Archival coll, Audiobks via web, Bk club(s), Bks on CD, Children's prog, Computers for patron use, Copy machines, e-mail serv, Exhibits, Fax serv, Genealogy discussion group, Handicapped accessible, ILL available, Magnifiers for reading, Mail & tel request accepted, Mus passes, Music CDs, Notary serv, Online cat, Online searches, OverDrive digital audio bks, Photocopying/Printing, Preschool outreach, Prog for adults, Prog for children & young adult, Pub access computers, Ref & res, Senior computer classes, Story hour, Summer reading prog, Tax forms, Teen prog, Telephone ref, Video lending libr, Wheelchair accessible, Workshops
Partic in Merri-Hill-Rock Library Cooperative
Special Services for the Blind - Accessible computers; Aids for in-house use; Assistive/Adapted tech devices, equip & products; Bks on CD; Home delivery serv; Large print bks
Open Mon-Thurs 9-9, Fri 9-6, Sat 9-5
Friends of the Library Group

JACKSON

P JACKSON PUBLIC LIBRARY*, 125 Main St, 03846. (Mail add: PO Box 276, 03846-0276), SAN 309-8524. Tel: 603-383-9731. FAX: 603-383-9731. E-mail: jacksonpubliclibrary@gmail.com. Web Site: jacksonlibrarynh.org. *Dir,* Lichen J Rancourt; *Ch,* Meredith Piotrow
Founded 1879. Pop 800; Circ 12,233
Library Holdings: Bk Vols 11,000
Automation Activity & Vendor Info: (Cataloging) Follett Software; (Circulation) Follett Software; (OPAC) Follett Software
Function: Adult bk club, Copy machines, ILL available, Mail & tel request accepted, Prog for children & young adult, Spoken cassettes & CDs, Summer reading prog, VHS videos
Open Tues & Thurs 11-6, Wed 11-2, Sat 10-1
Friends of the Library Group

JAFFREY

P JAFFREY PUBLIC LIBRARY*, 38 Main St, 03452-1196. SAN 309-8532. Tel: 603-532-7301. FAX: 603-532-7301. E-mail: library@town.jaffrey.nh.us. Web Site: www.townofjaffrey.com/library. *Dir,* Emily Donnelly; E-mail: edonnelly@townofjaffrey.com; *Asst Dir, Ch,* Sheila Vanderhorst; *ILL,* Linda Gleason; E-mail: library1@town.jaffrey.nh.us; *ILL,* Marilyn Simmons; Staff 4 (MLS 2, Non-MLS 2)
Founded 1896. Pop 5,434; Circ 47,730
Library Holdings: AV Mats 1,200; Electronic Media & Resources 16; Bk Vols 30,366; Per Subs 59; Talking Bks 859
Special Collections: Amos Fortune Historical Coll; Puppet Coll
Automation Activity & Vendor Info: (Circulation) Follett Software
Database Vendor: EBSCOhost
Wireless access
Partic in Nubanusit Library Cooperative
Open Mon & Wed 10-5:30, Tues & Thurs 1-7:30, Fri 10-4:30, Sat 10-2
Friends of the Library Group

JEFFERSON

P JEFFERSON PUBLIC LIBRARY*, 737 Presidential Hwy, 03583. (Mail add: PO Box 27, 03583-0027), SAN 309-8540. Tel: 603-586-7791. E-mail: lookitup@ne.rr.com. Web Site: www.myjeffersonlibrary.com. *Libr Dir,* Joy Corkhill
Pop 802; Circ 2,544
Library Holdings: AV Mats 440; Large Print Bks 50; Bk Vols 7,000; Per Subs 12; Videos 320
Subject Interests: Town hist
Database Vendor: JayWil Software Development, Inc
Wireless access
Open Tues & Thurs 2-8, Sat 10-2
Friends of the Library Group

KEENE

C ANTIOCH UNIVERSITY NEW ENGLAND LIBRARY*, 40 Avon St, 03431-3516. SAN 309-8559. Tel: 603-283-2400. FAX: 603-357-7345. E-mail: library@antiochne.edu. Web Site: www.antiochne.edu/library. *Dir,* Marcia Leversee; *Res & Instruction Librn,* Rachel Sperling; *Libr Serv Supvr,* Abagail Jones; *ILL & Distance Libr Serv Spec, Syst Serv,* Catherine Boswell; Staff 5 (MLS 3, Non-MLS 2)
Library Holdings: Bk Vols 38,320; Per Subs 1,625
Subject Interests: Dance movement therapy, Doctoral programs in psychology, Educ, Environ studies, Experienced educators prog, Family therapy, Marriage, Organization, Psychol, Substance abuse, Waldorf educ
Automation Activity & Vendor Info: (Acquisitions) Ex Libris Group; (Cataloging) Ex Libris Group; (Circulation) Ex Libris Group; (Course

Reserve) Ex Libris Group; (ILL) Ex Libris Group; (OPAC) Ex Libris Group; (Serials) Ex Libris Group
Wireless access
Open Mon-Fri 7:30am-9pm, Sat & Sun 8-6

M CHESHIRE MEDICAL CENTER*, Medical Library, 580 Court St, 03431. SAN 309-8567. Tel: 603-354-6664. Web Site: www.cheshire-med.com. *Librn,* Jean Slepian
Founded 1956
Library Holdings: Bk Vols 700; Per Subs 160
Subject Interests: Consumer health

S HISTORICAL SOCIETY OF CHESHIRE COUNTY*, 246 Main St, 03431. (Mail add: PO Box 803, 03431-0803), SAN 323-9675. Tel: 603-352-1895. FAX: 603-352-9226. E-mail: hscc@hsccnh.org. Web Site: www.hsccnh.org. *Dir,* Alan Rumrill; Staff 1 (MLS 1)
Founded 1927
Library Holdings: CDs 130; Bk Titles 11,500; Spec Interest Per Sub 15; Videos 40
Special Collections: Cheshire County History, bks, ms, photog; New England Genealogy & Local History Coll. Oral History
Wireless access
Publications: Newsletter
Open Tues, Thurs & Fri 9-4, Wed 9-9, Sat 9-12

P KEENE PUBLIC LIBRARY*, 60 Winter St, 03431-3360. SAN 309-8575. Tel: 603-352-0157. FAX: 866-743-0446. Web Site: www.keenepubliclibrary.org. *Dir,* Nancy Vincent; E-mail: nvincent@ci.keene.nh.us; *Asst Dir, Tech Serv Librn,* Jennifer Bone; E-mail: jbone@ci.keene.nh.us, *Acq Librn,* Pat Holmes; *Adult Serv, ILL Librn,* John Johnson; E-mail: jjohnson@ci.keene.nh.us; *AV Serv Librn,* Sheila Williams; *Ch,* Gail Zachariah; E-mail: gzachariah@ci.keene.nh.us; *Circ Librn,* Susan Hansmeier; *Ser Librn,* Colleen Swider; *Coll Develop, Electronic Res,* B J Wahl; E-mail: bjwahl@ci.keene.nh.us
Founded 1857. Pop 23,000
Jul 2006-Jun 2007 Income $1,285,943. Mats Exp $136,500. Sal $946,168
Library Holdings: AV Mats 11,459; Bk Vols 116,764; Per Subs 233
Subject Interests: NH
Automation Activity & Vendor Info: (Acquisitions) Innovative Interfaces, Inc; (Cataloging) Innovative Interfaces, Inc; (Circulation) Innovative Interfaces, Inc; (ILL) Innovative Interfaces, Inc; (Media Booking) Innovative Interfaces, Inc; (OPAC) Innovative Interfaces, Inc; (Serials) Innovative Interfaces, Inc
Database Vendor: Innovative Interfaces, Inc
Open Mon-Thurs 9-9, Fri 9-6, Sat 9-5 (9-1 Summer)
Friends of the Library Group

C KEENE STATE COLLEGE*, Wallace E Mason Library, 229 Main St, 03435-3201. SAN 309-8583. Tel: 603-358-2711. Interlibrary Loan Service Tel: 603-358-2715. Reference Tel: 603-358-2710. Administration Tel: 603-358-2723. FAX: 603-358-2745. Interlibrary Loan Service FAX: 603-358-2743. Web Site: www.keene.edu/library. *Dean,* Celia Rabinowitz; *Asst Dean, Head, Pub Serv,* Kathleen Halverson; Tel: 603-358-2712, E-mail: khalvers@keene.edu; *Coll Develop Librn, Head, Access Serv,* Jennifer Ditkoff; Tel: 603-358-2725, E-mail: jditkoff@keene.edu; *Head, Libr Syst,* Kara Young; Tel: 603-358-2716, E-mail: kyoung1@keene.edu; *Head, Tech Serv,* Patrick O'Brien; Tel: 603-358-2713, E-mail: pobrien@keene.edu; *Libr Dept Fac Chair,* Peg Barrett; Tel: 603-358-2714, E-mail: pbarrett@keene.edu; *Info Literacy Librn,* Elizabeth Dolinger; Tel: 603-358-2749, E-mail: edolinger@keene.edu; *Libr Serv Supvr/Cat,* Kathryn Manning; Tel: 603-358-2726, E-mail: kmanning@keene.edu; *Libr Serv Supvr/Cat,* Cecil Maxfield; Tel: 603-358-2758, E-mail: cmaxfield@keene.edu; *Libr Serv Supvr/Circ,* Micki Harrington; Tel: 603-358-2782, E-mail: mharrington2@keene.edu; *Libr Serv Supvr/ILL,* Linda Madden; E-mail: lmadden@keene.edu; *Libr Syst Support Tech,* Charles Hornbeck; Tel: 603-358-2739, E-mail: chornbeck1@keene.edu; *Libr Syst Tech II,* Dana Clark; Tel: 603-358-2755, E-mail: dclark5@keene.edu; *Archivist,* Rodney Obien; Tel: 603-358-2717, E-mail: robien@keene.edu; Staff 19 (MLS 10, Non-MLS 9)
Founded 1909. Enrl 5,000; Fac 198; Highest Degree: Master
Jul 2008-Jun 2009 Income $2,780,000. Mats Exp $1,094,857. Sal $496,909 (Prof $698,679)
Library Holdings: AV Mats 9,000; Bk Vols 200,000; Per Subs 790
Special Collections: Cohen Center for Holocaust & Genocide Studies; College Archives; K-12 Curriculum Library; New Hampshire History Coll; Orang Asli Archives. State Document Depository
Subject Interests: Curric related mat for K-12, Educ, State hist
Automation Activity & Vendor Info: (Acquisitions) Innovative Interfaces, Inc; (Cataloging) Innovative Interfaces, Inc; (Circulation) Innovative Interfaces, Inc; (Course Reserve) Innovative Interfaces, Inc; (ILL) OCLC ILLiad; (OPAC) Innovative Interfaces, Inc; (Serials) Innovative Interfaces, Inc
Database Vendor: ARTstor, EBSCOhost, JSTOR, LexisNexis, OCLC FirstSearch, Project MUSE
Wireless access
Partic in New Hampshire Automated Information Systems (NHAIS); New Hampshire College & University Council; OCLC Online Computer Library Center, Inc; Westchester Academic Library Directors Organization (WALDO)
Special Services for the Blind - Closed circuit TV magnifier; Computer with voice synthesizer for visually impaired persons; Reader equip; ZoomText magnification & reading software
Open Mon-Thurs 8am-Midnight, Fri 8am-10pm, Sat 10-10, Sun 10am-Midnight

KENSINGTON

P KENSINGTON SOCIAL & PUBLIC LIBRARY*, 126 Amesbury Rd, 03833-5621. SAN 309-8605. Tel: 603-772-5022. FAX: 603-778-2953. E-mail: kensingtonlibrary@comcast.net. Web Site: www.kensingtonpubliclibrary.org. *Dir,* Susan Gilbert; *Ch Serv,* Lindsey Myers; Staff 4 (MLS 1, Non-MLS 3)
Pop 2,089
Library Holdings: Bk Vols 13,068; Per Subs 49
Special Collections: Antiques & Art Coll
Function: Adult bk club, Audiobks via web, Bks on cassette, Bks on CD, Children's prog, Computers for patron use, Copy machines, Electronic databases & coll, Fax serv, Free DVD rentals, Handicapped accessible, ILL available, Mus passes, Music CDs, OverDrive digital audio bks, Photocopying/Printing, Prog for adults, Prog for children & young adult, Pub access computers, Ref serv in person, Story hour, Summer reading prog, VHS videos, Wheelchair accessible
Partic in New Hampshire Automated Information Systems (NHAIS)
Open Tues & Thurs 9-8, Wed & Sat 9-1
Friends of the Library Group

KINGSTON

P KINGSTON COMMUNITY LIBRARY*, Two Library Lane, 03848. SAN 309-8613. Tel: 603-642-3521. FAX: 603-642-3135. E-mail: info@kingston-library.org. Web Site: www.kingston-library.org. *Dir,* Charlotte Arredondo; E-mail: director@kingston-library.org; *Ad,* Patricia Walker; *Youth Serv Librn,* South Harmon
Founded 1898. Circ 42,140
Library Holdings: Bk Vols 22,000; Per Subs 71
Subject Interests: Hist
Automation Activity & Vendor Info: (Cataloging) Follett Software; (Circulation) Follett Software
Database Vendor: EBSCOhost
Mem of Carroll & Madison Library System
Open Mon & Fri 10-4, Tues-Thurs 10-8, Sat 9-1

LACONIA

P LACONIA PUBLIC LIBRARY*, 695 Main St, 03246-2780. SAN 350-5170. Tel: 603-524-4775. FAX: 603-527-1277. E-mail: reflpl@metrocast.net. Web Site: www.laconialibrary.org. *Dir,* Randy Brough; E-mail: rbroughlpl@metrocast.net; *Ad,* Deann Hunter; Staff 11 (MLS 3, Non-MLS 8)
Founded 1903. Pop 17,233; Circ 129,583
Jul 2008-Jun 2009 Income (Main Library and Branch(s)) $754,880. Mats Exp $92,500, Books $64,000, Per/Ser (Incl. Access Fees) $11,700, Micro $1,800, AV Mat $11,000, Electronic Ref Mat (Incl. Access Fees) $2,000, Presv $2,000. Sal $456,385
Library Holdings: Audiobooks 1,745; AV Mats 5,776; CDs 951; DVDs 1,311; Large Print Bks 1,050; Bk Vols 48,106; Per Subs 130; Videos 1,728
Special Collections: State Document Depository
Automation Activity & Vendor Info: (Cataloging) TLC (The Library Corporation); (Circulation) TLC (The Library Corporation); (OPAC) TLC (The Library Corporation)
Database Vendor: EBSCOhost, Gale Cengage Learning, Newsbank, Overdrive, Inc, ProQuest, TLC (The Library Corporation)
Wireless access
Publications: Browsing (Newsletter)
Partic in Urban Libr Consortia
Open Mon-Thurs 9-8, Fri 9-6, Sat 9-4
Branches: 1
LAKEPORT (OSSIAN WILBUR GOSS READING ROOM), 188 Elm St, 03246, SAN 350-5200. Tel: 603-524-3808. *Librn,* Susan Laramie; Staff 1 (Non-MLS 1)
Founded 1907. Pop 17,233
Library Holdings: Bk Vols 3,283
Open Mon 11-6, Wed 1-8, Fri 9-12:30 & 1:30-5

J LAKE REGION COMMUNITY COLLEGE*, Bennett Library, 379 Belmont Rd, 03246. SAN 309-8621. Tel: 603-524-3207. FAX: 603-524-8084. E-mail: laconialibrary@ccsnh.edu. Web Site: www.lrcc.edu/library/index.html. *Dir,* Cynthia Davis; E-mail: cdavis@ccsnh.edu; Staff 2 (MLS 1, Non-MLS 1)
Founded 1968. Enrl 1,150; Fac 37; Highest Degree: Associate

Library Holdings: e-books 45,000; Bk Titles 12,500; Per Subs 90
Subject Interests: Bus, Computers, Fire sci, Nursing
Automation Activity & Vendor Info: (Cataloging) TLC (The Library Corporation); (Circulation) TLC (The Library Corporation)
Wireless access
Open Mon-Thurs 7:30am-8:30pm, Fri 7:30-4
Friends of the Library Group

LANCASTER

P WILLIAM D WEEKS MEMORIAL LIBRARY*, 128 Main St, 03584-3031. SAN 309-863X. Tel: 603-788-3352. FAX: 603-788-3203. E-mail: weekslib@ncia.net. *Dir,* Barbara R Robarts; E-mail: weekslib@ncia.net; *Youth Serv Librn,* Ronnie Zajac; Staff 1 (MLS 1)
Founded 1884. Pop 3,500; Circ 4,500
Library Holdings: AV Mats 1,400; Large Print Bks 114; Bk Vols 45,000; Per Subs 150; Talking Bks 892
Subject Interests: NH
Open Mon, Wed & Fri 1-4:30 & 7-9, Tues & Thurs 9-4:30, Sat 10-12
Friends of the Library Group

LEBANON

J LEBANON COLLEGE LIBRARY*, 15 Hanover St, 03766. Tel: 603-448-2445, Ext 110. FAX: 603-448-2491. Web Site: www.lebanoncollege.edu. *Libr Dir,* Don Watson; E-mail: dwatson@lebanoncollege.edu; Staff 0.1 (Non-MLS 0.1)
Highest Degree: Associate
Library Holdings: AV Mats 100; Bk Vols 5,500; Per Subs 15; Videos 100
Special Collections: World War II (Yamashita Coll)
Automation Activity & Vendor Info: (Acquisitions) LibraryWorld, Inc; (Cataloging) LibraryWorld, Inc; (Circulation) LibraryWorld, Inc; (OPAC) LibraryWorld, Inc
Wireless access
Function: Computers for patron use, Handicapped accessible, ILL available, Online cat, Wheelchair accessible
Restriction: Open to students, fac & staff

P LEBANON PUBLIC LIBRARY*, Nine E Park St, 03766. SAN 350-5235. Tel: 603-448-2459. E-mail: library@leblibrary.com. Web Site: www.leblibrary.com. *Dir,* Sean Fleming; E-mail: sean.fleming@leblibrary.com; *Dep Dir,* Amy Lappin; *Ref/Tech Serv Librn,* Roger Robbins; *Ref/YA,* Susanne Collins
Founded 1909. Pop 12,568; Circ 130,000
Library Holdings: AV Mats 3,841; Bk Vols 43,400; Per Subs 143
Special Collections: Local History Coll
Automation Activity & Vendor Info: (Cataloging) LibLime; (Circulation) LibLime; (OPAC) LibLime
Wireless access
Open Mon-Thurs 10-8, Fri & Sat 10-5, Sun (Sept-March) 1-5

LEE

P LEE PUBLIC LIBRARY*, Seven Mast Rd, 03824. SAN 309-8648. Tel: 603-659-2626. FAX: 603-659-2986. E-mail: leelibrary@comcast.net. Web Site: www.lee.lib.nh.us. *Dir,* Sharon Taylor; *Ch,* Scottie Robinson; *Circ Librn, ILL Librn,* Michelle Stevens
Founded 1892. Pop 4,000; Circ 57,381
Library Holdings: AV Mats 629; Bks on Deafness & Sign Lang 10; Large Print Bks 91; Bk Titles 26,060; Per Subs 79; Talking Bks 794
Automation Activity & Vendor Info: (Circulation) Follett Software
Open Mon & Wed 12-8, Tues 3-8, Thurs & Fri 10-5, Sat 10-3
Friends of the Library Group

LINCOLN

P LINCOLN PUBLIC LIBRARY*, 22 Church St, 03251. (Mail add: PO Box 98, 03251-0098), SAN 309-8656. Tel: 603-745-8159. FAX: 603-745-2037. E-mail: library@lincolnnh.org. Web Site: www.lincoln.lib.nh.us. *Dir,* Carol Riley; *Circ Librn,* Janet Peltier; *Circ Librn,* Pat Wishart
Pop 1,100; Circ 11,000
Library Holdings: Bk Vols 12,000; Per Subs 40
Subject Interests: NH
Automation Activity & Vendor Info: (Acquisitions) ComPanion Corp; (Cataloging) ComPanion Corp; (Circulation) ComPanion Corp; (OPAC) ComPanion Corp
Database Vendor: EBSCOhost, ProQuest
Wireless access
Function: Fax serv, Photocopying/Printing
Open Mon-Fri 12-8, Sat 10-2

LISBON

P LISBON PUBLIC LIBRARY*, 45 School St, 03585. SAN 309-8664. Tel: 603-838-6615. FAX: 603-838-6615. E-mail: lisbonpubliclibrary@roadrunner.com. Web Site: lisbonpubliclibrary.org. *Dir,* Karla Houston; E-mail: Karla@lisbonpubliclibrary.org; *Asst Librn,* Kerry MacNayr
Founded 1864. Pop 1,543; Circ 9,200
Library Holdings: Bk Vols 10,188; Per Subs 29
Special Collections: Local Culture & History (New Hampshire Coll)
Open Mon, Wed & Fri 11-5, Tues & Thurs 2-6, Sat 10-2

LITCHFIELD

P AARON CUTLER MEMORIAL LIBRARY*, 269 Charles Bancroft Hwy, 03052. SAN 309-8516. Tel: 603-424-4044. FAX: 603-424-4044. E-mail: cutler_library@comcast.net. *Dir,* Vicki Varick; E-mail: acml_director@comcast.net; *Adult Serv,* Alexandra Robinson; *Ch Serv,* Carrie-Anne Pace; Staff 3 (Non-MLS 3)
Founded 1821. Pop 8,500; Circ 26,730
Jan 2013-Dec 2013 Income $197,999. Mats Exp $14,960, Books $9,298, Per/Ser (Incl. Access Fees) $1,287, AV Mat $3,985, Electronic Ref Mat (Incl. Access Fees) $390. Sal $139,136 (Prof $110,405)
Library Holdings: Audiobooks 582; DVDs 910; Electronic Media & Resources 1; Bk Titles 12,529; Per Subs 48
Automation Activity & Vendor Info: (Acquisitions) ByWater Solutions; (Cataloging) ByWater Solutions; (Circulation) ByWater Solutions; (OPAC) ByWater Solutions
Database Vendor: EBSCOhost
Wireless access
Function: Adult bk club, Bks on CD, Children's prog, Computers for patron use, Electronic databases & coll, Fax serv, Free DVD rentals, ILL available, Mus passes, Online cat, OverDrive digital audio bks, Photocopying/Printing, Story hour, Summer reading prog, Tax forms
Open Tues-Thurs 10-8, Fri 10-6, Sat (Sept-June) 9-12
Friends of the Library Group

LITTLETON

P LITTLETON PUBLIC LIBRARY*, 92 Main St, 03561-1238. SAN 309-8672. Tel: 603-444-5741. FAX: 603-444-1706. E-mail: littlib@gmail.com. Web Site: www.ncia.net/library/littleton/. *Dir,* Jeanne Dickerman; *Ch,* Steffaney Smith; *ILL Librn,* Angie Marchetti; Staff 4 (Non-MLS 4)
Founded 1890. Pop 5,845; Circ 45,148
Library Holdings: Bk Vols 39,870; Per Subs 77; Talking Bks 634
Special Collections: Kilburn Stereoptic Views Coll; NH History and Genealogy Coll
Automation Activity & Vendor Info: (Cataloging) Follett Software; (Circulation) Follett Software; (OPAC) Follett Software
Function: ILL available
Partic in Five Rivers Area Libr Network
Special Services for the Blind - Closed circuit TV magnifier
Open Tues-Thurs 9-7, Fri & Sat 9-4

M LITTLETON REGIONAL HOSPITAL*, Gale Medical Library, 600 St Johnsbury Rd, 03561. SAN 377-273X. Tel: 603-444-9564. FAX: 603-444-7491. Web Site: www.littletonhospital.org. *Dir,* Anne Conner
Library Holdings: Bk Titles 400; Bk Vols 500; Per Subs 125
Special Collections: Anna Connors Patient & Family Resource Center
Wireless access
Restriction: Open to pub by appt only

J WHITE MOUNTAINS COMMUNITY COLLEGE*, Littleton Academic Center Library, 646 Union St, Ste 300, 03561. Tel: 603-444-1326. FAX: 603-444-0981. Web Site: www.wmcc.edu. *Prog Coordr,* Melanie Robbins; E-mail: mrobbins@ccsnh.edu
Library Holdings: Bk Vols 2,000; Per Subs 24
Database Vendor: EBSCOhost, OCLC FirstSearch, ProQuest
Wireless access
Function: ILL available
Open Mon-Thurs 8:30-8:30, Fri 8:30-3, Sat 9-1

LONDONDERRY

P LEACH LIBRARY, 276 Mammoth Rd, 03053. SAN 309-8680. Tel: 603-432-1132. FAX: 603-437-6610. Web Site: www.londonderrynh.org/Pages/LondonderryNH_Library/Index. *Dir,* Barbara Ostertag-Holtkamp; E-mail: bostertag-holtkamp@londonderrynh.org; Staff 15 (MLS 6, Non-MLS 9)
Founded 1880. Pop 24,567; Circ 395,847
Jul 2014-Jun 2015 Income $1,239,981
Library Holdings: Bk Vols 69,231; Per Subs 203
Special Collections: Local History Coll
Automation Activity & Vendor Info: (Cataloging) Follett Software; (Circulation) Follett Software; (OPAC) Follett Software
Database Vendor: EBSCOhost
Wireless access
Publications: Children's Room News; Leach Library News
Partic in Merri-Hill-Rock Library Cooperative; Urban Pub Libr Consortium

Open Mon-Thurs 9-8, Fri 10-2, Sat 9-5
Friends of the Library Group

LOUDON

P MAXFIELD PUBLIC LIBRARY*, Eight Rte 129, 03307. SAN 309-8699. Tel: 603-798-5153. E-mail: maxlib@comcast.ne. *Dir,* Nancy Hendy; *Tech Serv,* Barbara Sullivan
Pop 5,000; Circ 28,572
Jul 2010-Jun 2011 Income $193,753. Mats Exp $20,000. Sal $114,503
Library Holdings: Bk Vols 20,000; Per Subs 54
Automation Activity & Vendor Info: (Cataloging) Follett Software
Wireless access
Publications: Newsletter (Bi-annually)
Partic in New Hampshire Automated Information Systems (NHAIS)
Open Tues & Thurs 10-9, Wed 1-9, Sat 9-1

LYME

P CONVERSE FREE LIBRARY*, 38 Union St, 03768-9702. SAN 350-5294. Tel: 603-795-4622. FAX: 603-795-9346. E-mail: Info@lymenhlibrary.org. Web Site: lymenhlibrary.org. *Dir,* Judith G Russell
Pop 1,700; Circ 15,932
Library Holdings: Bk Vols 22,000; Per Subs 30
Automation Activity & Vendor Info: (Cataloging) Follett Software; (Circulation) Follett Software; (OPAC) Follett Software
Database Vendor: EBSCOhost
Open Mon 1-5, Tues & Thurs 10-5, Wed 10-8, Fri 10-3, Sat 9-12
Friends of the Library Group

LYNDEBOROUGH

P J A TARBELL LIBRARY*, 136 Forest Rd, 03082. (Mail add: PO Box 54, 03082-0054), SAN 376-5075. Tel: 603-654-6790. FAX: 603-654-6790. E-mail: jat@tellink.net. *Dir,* Brenda Cassidy; *Asst Librn,* Carole Thompson
Library Holdings: Bk Vols 8,800; Per Subs 29
Open Mon (Winter) 12-5 & 6-8, Wed 10-8, Fri 1-4, Sat 9-12; Mon (Summer) 12-5 & 6-8, Wed 1-8, Fri 1-4
Friends of the Library Group

MADBURY

P MADBURY PUBLIC LIBRARY*, Nine Town Hall Rd, 03823. Tel: 603-743-1400. E-mail: library@madburylibrary.org. Web Site: www.madburylibrary.org. *Dir,* Susan Sinnott; E-mail: directormpl@comcast.net; *Asst Librn,* Peggy Wolcott; E-mail: assistantmpl@comcast.net; *Ch,* Crystal Lisbon; E-mail: childrensmpl@comcast.net
Library Holdings: AV Mats 500; Bk Vols 9,000
Automation Activity & Vendor Info: (Cataloging) Follett Software; (Circulation) Follett Software; (OPAC) Follett Software; (Serials) Follett Software
Database Vendor: EBSCOhost, Newsbank
Open Mon & Wed 10-8, Thurs 10-4, Sat 10-2

MADISON

P MADISON LIBRARY*, 1895 Village Rd, 03849. (Mail add: PO Box 240, 03849-0240), SAN 309-8702. Tel: 603-367-8545. FAX: 603-367-4479. E-mail: librarian@madison.lib.nh.us. Web Site: www.madison.lib.nh.us. *Dir,* Mary Cronin; *Asst Librn,* Camilla Spence; *Asst Librn,* Sloane Jarell; Staff 3 (Non-MLS 3)
Founded 1893. Pop 2,200; Circ 16,511
Library Holdings: Bk Vols 20,000; Per Subs 40
Automation Activity & Vendor Info: (Cataloging) ByWater Solutions; (Circulation) ByWater Solutions; (OPAC) ByWater Solutions
Database Vendor: TumbleBookLibrary
Wireless access
Partic in New Hampshire Automated Information Systems (NHAIS)
Open Mon, Wed & Fri 2-5, Tues 10-5, Thurs 10-8, Sat 9-1
Friends of the Library Group

MANCHESTER

S AMERICAN-CANADIAN GENEALOGICAL SOCIETY LIBRARY*, Four Elm St, 03103-7242. (Mail add: PO Box 6478, 03108-6478), SAN 326-212X. Tel: 603-622-1554. E-mail: acgs@acgs.org. Web Site: www.acgs.org. *Pres,* Gerry Savard
Founded 1973
Library Holdings: Bk Titles 7,000; Bk Vols 8,843
Special Collections: Canadian Marriage Records; Digitized Drouin Microfilm Coll; Diocese of Moncton, microfilm; Drouin Index; IGI Files of the Family History Library of the Church of Jesus Christ of Latter Day Saints; Loiselle, microfilm & fiche; Manchester, New Hampshire Vitals; Massachusetts Vital Records; N B Records; State of New Hampshire Vitals; State of Vermont Vitals
Wireless access
Publications: American-Canadian Genealogist (Quarterly); Repertoires of the Marriages, Baptisms & Burials of Several New England & New York State Catholic Churches
Open Wed 9-9, Fri 9-6, Sat 9-5
Restriction: Circ to mem only

SR BROOKSIDE CONGREGATIONAL CHURCH LIBRARY*, 2013 Elm St, 03104. SAN 373-4706. Tel: 603-669-2807. FAX: 603-668-9041. Web Site: www.brooksidecc.org. *Librn,* Donna Moody
Library Holdings: Bk Vols 500
Open Mon-Fri 9-2

M CATHOLIC MEDICAL CENTER*, Health Sciences Library, 100 McGregor St, 03102-3770. SAN 309-8710. Tel: 603-663-6520. FAX: 603-668-5348. *Librn,* Cynthia David; Staff 3 (MLS 1, Non-MLS 2)
Founded 1978
Library Holdings: Bk Vols 3,081; Per Subs 463
Subject Interests: Cardiac, Geriatrics, Hospital mgt, Orthopedics, Psychiat
Function: Ref serv available
Partic in Greater NE Regional Med Libr Serv
Open Mon & Wed-Fri 8-5:30, Tues 8-12

S CURRIER MUSEUM OF ART, Art Reference Library & Archive, 150 Ash St, 03104. SAN 377-2446. Tel: 603-669-6144. FAX: 603-669-7194. E-mail: library@currier.org. Web Site: www.currier.org. *Librn & Archivist,* Meghan Petersen; Tel: 603-669-6144, Ext 127; Staff 1 (MLS 1)
Founded 1929
Library Holdings: Bk Vols 15,000; Per Subs 25
Subject Interests: Decorative art, European art, Photog
Open Thurs 11-4
Restriction: Non-circulating to the pub

M ELLIOT HOSPITAL*, Health Sciences Library, One Elliot Way, 03103. Tel: 603-663-2334. FAX: 603-663-3507. Web Site: www.elliothospital.org. *Libr Mgr,* Megan Long; Staff 1 (MLS 1)
Library Holdings: Bk Vols 600; Per Subs 65
Database Vendor: EBSCOhost, Elsevier, MD Consult, PubMed, STAT!Ref (Teton Data Systems), UpToDate
Function: Doc delivery serv, ILL available, Online searches, Ref serv available
Partic in Basic Health Sciences Library Network; Health Sciences Libraries of New Hampshire & Vermont
Restriction: Circulates for staff only

P MANCHESTER CITY LIBRARY*, 405 Pine St, 03104-6199. SAN 309-8737. Tel: 603-624-6550. FAX: 603-624-6559. E-mail: library@manchesternh.gov. Web Site: www.manchester.lib.nh.us, www.manchesterlibrary.org. *Dir,* Denise van Zanten; E-mail: dvanzant@manchesternh.gov; *Dep Libr Dir,* Dee Santoso; E-mail: dsantoso@manchesternh.gov; *Head, Ch,* Karyn Isleb; E-mail: kisleb@manchesternh.gov; *Head, Circ,* Claudia Mayer; E-mail: cmayer@manchesternh.gov; *Head, Info & Tech,* Steve Viggiano; E-mail: sviggiano@manchesternh.gov; *Head, Tech Serv,* David Smolen; Fax: 603-628-6018, E-mail: dsmolen@manchesternh.gov; Staff 17.5 (MLS 12, Non MLS 5.5)
Founded 1854. Pop 109,000; Circ 537,784
Jul 2011-Jun 2012 Income (Main Library and Branch(s)) $2,130,444. Sal $1,072,154 (Prof $684,306)
Library Holdings: Audiobooks 10,703; DVDs 8,414; Microforms 7,479; Bk Vols 184,713; Per Subs 182
Special Collections: ArtBook Coll; New Hampshire History. State Document Depository; US Document Depository
Automation Activity & Vendor Info: (Acquisitions) Innovative Interfaces, Inc; (Cataloging) Innovative Interfaces, Inc; (Circulation) Innovative Interfaces, Inc; (OPAC) Innovative Interfaces, Inc; (Serials) Innovative Interfaces, Inc
Database Vendor: EBSCOhost
Wireless access
Function: Adult bk club, Adult literacy prog, Archival coll, Audiobks via web, Bk club(s), Bks on CD, Children's prog, Computer training, Computers for patron use, Copy machines, Digital talking bks, Doc delivery serv, e-mail serv, Electronic databases & coll, Family literacy, Free DVD rentals, Govt ref serv, Health sci info serv, Holiday prog, Home delivery & serv to Sr ctr & nursing homes, Homebound delivery serv, ILL available, Magnifiers for reading, Microfiche/film & reading machines, Mus passes, Music CDs, Newsp ref libr, Online cat, Orientations, OverDrive digital audio bks, Photocopying/Printing, Preschool outreach, Prog for adults, Prog for children & young adult, Pub access computers, Ref & res, Spanish lang bks, Spoken cassettes & CDs, Story hour, Summer reading prog, Tax forms, Teen prog, Telephone ref, Wheelchair accessible
Publications: MCL Notes (Newsletter)
Partic in GMILCS, Inc

Open Mon, Tues & Thurs 8:30-8:30, Wed & Fri 8:30-5:30, Sat 9:30-2:30
Restriction: Access at librarian's discretion
Branches: 1
WEST COMMUNITY BRANCH LIBRARY, 76 N Main St, 03102-4084, SAN 377-029X. Tel: 603-624-6560. FAX: 603-628-6216. *Br Mgr,* Sarah Basbas
Library Holdings: Audiobooks 1,889; DVDs 2,693; Bk Vols 30,172; Per Subs 20
Special Services for the Deaf - Accessible learning ctr; ADA equip
Open Wed 12:30-8:30, Thurs & Fri 9:30-5:30

J MANCHESTER COMMUNITY COLLEGE LIBRARY, 1066 Front St, 03102. SAN 309-8761. Tel: 603-206-8150. E-mail: manchesterlibrary@ccsnh.edu. Web Site: library.mccnh.edu. *Libr Dir,* Position Currently Open; *Asst Libr Dir,* Vandana Dhakar; E-mail: vdhakar@ccsnh.edu; *Circ Supvr,* Mark McShane; E-mail: mmshane@ccsnh.edu; Staff 2 (MLS 2)
Founded 1968. Enrl 1,320; Fac 77; Highest Degree: Associate
Library Holdings: AV Mats 2,190; Bk Titles 15,800; Bk Vols 18,000; Per Subs 65
Subject Interests: Bldg tech, Nursing
Automation Activity & Vendor Info: (Cataloging) TLC (The Library Corporation); (Circulation) TLC (The Library Corporation); (Course Reserve) TLC (The Library Corporation); (ILL) OCLC WorldShare Interlibrary Loan; (OPAC) TLC (The Library Corporation)
Database Vendor: CQ Press, EBSCOhost, Gale Cengage Learning, ProQuest
Wireless access
Partic in New Hampshire Automated Information Systems (NHAIS); New Hampshire College & University Council; OCLC Online Computer Library Center, Inc; Westchester Academic Library Directors Organization (WALDO)
Open Mon-Thurs 7:30am-8pm, Fri 7:30-6, Sat 8-2

S MANCHESTER HISTORIC ASSOCIATION LIBRARY, 129 Amherst St, 03101. SAN 309-8745. Tel: 603-622-7531. E-mail: library@manchesterhistoric.org. Web Site: www.manchesterhistoric.org. *Actg Dir,* Jeffrey Barraclough; *Libr Asst,* Benjamin Baker
Founded 1896
Library Holdings: Bk Vols 3,500
Special Collections: Correspondence, notes & reports; Personal Files (F C Dumaine Coll); Photographs - 19th Century & early 20th; Textile Design, graphs & notes
Subject Interests: Amoskeag industries, Amoskeag Manufacturing Co (Textiles), Hist of Manchester
Publications: Guide to Amoskeag Manufacturing Company Collections in the Manchester Historic Association

L MCLANE, GRAF, RAULERSON & MIDDLETON PA*, Law Library, 900 Elm St, 03101. (Mail add: PO Box 326, 03105-0326), SAN 323-7133. Tel: 603-628-1428. FAX: 603-625-5650. E-mail: library@mclane.com. *Dir,* Jennifer M Finch; E-mail: jennifer.finch@mclane.com; Staff 1.2 (MLS 1.2)
Library Holdings: Bk Titles 2,250; Bk Vols 9,000; Per Subs 100
Special Collections: New Hampshire Legal, Legislative, Regulatory & Historical Information Coll
Automation Activity & Vendor Info: (Cataloging) CyberTools for Libraries; (Circulation) CyberTools for Libraries; (ILL) OCLC FirstSearch; (OPAC) CyberTools for Libraries; (Serials) CyberTools for Libraries
Database Vendor: HeinOnline, LexisNexis, Loislaw, OCLC FirstSearch, PubMed, Westlaw, Westlaw Business
Wireless access
Restriction: Employees only

S NEW HAMPSHIRE YOUTH SERVICES CENTER*, Lionel Washington Johnson Memorial Library, 1056 N River Rd, 03104. SAN 371-7283. Tel: 603-625-5471. FAX: 603-665-9381. *Librn,* Lynn N Dermott; E-mail: ldermott@dhhs.state.nh.us
Library Holdings: Bk Titles 8,000; Per Subs 85
Subject Interests: Soc issues
Automation Activity & Vendor Info: (Cataloging) Follett Software; (Circulation) Follett Software
Open Mon-Fri 8-3

C SAINT ANSELM COLLEGE*, Geisel Library, 100 Saint Anselm Dr, 03102-1310. SAN 309-8796. Tel: 603-641-7300. Interlibrary Loan Service Tel: 603-641-7303. Reference Tel: 603-641-7306. FAX: 603-641-7345. Web Site: www.anselm.edu/library. *Dir,* Getchell M Charles, Jr; *Asst Dir,* John Dillon; *Coll Develop,* Gwen Verkuilen; *ILL,* Susan Gagnon; Staff 28 (MLS 13, Non-MLS 15)
Founded 1889. Enrl 2,000; Fac 146; Highest Degree: Bachelor
Jul 2008-Jun 2009. Mats Exp $551,400, Books $183,000, Per/Ser (Incl. Access Fees) $200,000, Micro $700, AV Mat $700, Electronic Ref Mat (Incl. Access Fees) $162,000, Presv $5,000
Library Holdings: CDs 2,260; DVDs 1,690; e-journals 36,000; Electronic Media & Resources 8,800; Microforms 74,790; Bk Titles 189,900; Bk Vols 239,000; Per Subs 1,100; Videos 2,210
Special Collections: Archives of College; New England History. State Document Depository; US Document Depository
Subject Interests: Hist, New England hist, Nursing, Theol
Automation Activity & Vendor Info: (Acquisitions) Innovative Interfaces, Inc; (Cataloging) Innovative Interfaces, Inc; (Circulation) Innovative Interfaces, Inc; (Serials) Innovative Interfaces, Inc
Wireless access
Publications: Friends Forum (Newsletter); Geisel Library News (Newsletter)
Partic in Lyrasis; New Hampshire College & University Council; OCLC Online Computer Library Center, Inc
Open Mon-Thurs (Winter) 8am-Midnight, Fri 8am-11pm, Sat Noon-11, Sun 11am-Midnight; Mon-Fri (Summer) 8:30-4:30
Friends of the Library Group

L SHEEHAN PHINNEY BASS & GREEN PA LIBRARY*, 1000 Elm St, No 1800, 03105. (Mail add: PO Box 3701, 03105-3701), SAN 371-568X. Tel: 603-668-0300. FAX: 603-627-8121. Web Site: www.sheehan.com. *In Charge,* Debra Piotrowski; Staff 3 (MLS 1, Non-MLS 2)
Library Holdings: Bk Vols 10,000
Restriction: Staff use only

C SOUTHERN NEW HAMPSHIRE UNIVERSITY*, Shapiro Library, 2500 N River Rd, 03106-1045. SAN 378-486X. Tel: 603-645-9605. Reference Tel: 603-668-2161. FAX: 603-645-9685. E-mail: reference@snhu.edu. Web Site: www.snhu.edu/library.asp. *Dean, Univ Libr,* Kathy Growney; Tel: 603-668-2211, Ext 2166, E-mail: k.growney@snhu.edu; *Evening Ref Librn,* Lennie Ogden; *Evening Ref Librn,* Steve Viggiano; *Evening Ref Librn,* Pat Wilcox; *Ref Librn,* Parneet Arora; *Sunday Ref Librn,* Barbara Gannon; *Access Serv,* Christopher Cooper; Tel: 603-668-2211, Ext 2160, E-mail: c.cooper@snhu.edu; *Acq,* Paula Krampfert; *Acq,* Sharon Lally; *Cat,* Sandy Spakoski; Tel: 603-645-9605, Ext 2169, E-mail: s.spakoski@snhu.edu; *Circ & ILL,* Barbara Hickok; *Electronic Res,* Carol West; Tel: 603-645-9605, Ext 2159, E-mail: c.west@snhu.edu; *Per,* Chris Roy; *Tech Serv,* Steve Robichaud; Staff 11 (MLS 9, Non-MLS 2)
Founded 1963. Enrl 5,150; Fac 129; Highest Degree: Doctorate
Jul 2006-Jun 2007. Mats Exp $771,931, Books $253,549, Per/Ser (Incl. Access Fees) $131,162, Micro $20,416, Electronic Ref Mat (Incl. Access Fees) $366,804. Sal $576,844 (Prof $298,892)
Library Holdings: Bk Vols 94,042; Per Subs 755
Special Collections: AMEX & NYSE 10K & Annual Reports, fiche; Business History Coll, micro; Education Resource Coll; Social Science & History (Library of American Civilization), fiche. State Document Depository; US Document Depository
Subject Interests: Acctg, Behav sci, Bus, Econ, Educ, Hotels, Humanities, Indust, Soc sci, Tourism
Automation Activity & Vendor Info: (Acquisitions) SirsiDynix; (Cataloging) SirsiDynix; (Circulation) SirsiDynix; (Course Reserve) SirsiDynix; (OPAC) SirsiDynix; (Serials) SirsiDynix
Wireless access
Publications: Accession List (Monthly); Periodical List; Periodical Subject List
Partic in GMILCS, Inc; Lyrasis; New Hampshire College & University Council
Open Mon-Thurs 8am-Midnight, Fri 8-8, Sat 10-8, Sun Noon-Midnight

C UNIVERSITY OF NEW HAMPSHIRE AT MANCHESTER LIBRARY*, 400 Commercial St, 03101. SAN 320-6955. Tel: 603-641-4173. Interlibrary Loan Service Tel: 603-641-4183. FAX: 603-641-4124. E-mail: unhm.library@unh.edu. Web Site: unhm.unh.edu. *Assoc Prof, Ref & Instruction Librn,* Carolyn Gamtso; Tel: 603-641-4172, E-mail: Carolyn.Gamtso@unh.edu; *Tech Serv Librn,* Cindy Tremblay; E-mail: cindy.tremblay@unh.edu; *Libr Serv Supvr,* Ginger Borase; Staff 5 (MLS 4, Non-MLS 1)
Founded 1967. Enrl 790; Fac 40; Highest Degree: Master
Library Holdings: AV Mats 1,979; Bk Vols 32,261; Per Subs 259
Special Collections: Twentieth Century European Intellectual Thought
Subject Interests: Deafness, Early New Hampshire newspapers, Sign lang
Automation Activity & Vendor Info: (Cataloging) Innovative Interfaces, Inc; (Circulation) Innovative Interfaces, Inc; (Course Reserve) Innovative Interfaces, Inc; (ILL) Clio; (OPAC) Innovative Interfaces, Inc; (Serials) Innovative Interfaces, Inc
Database Vendor: ABC-CLIO, Agricola, Alexander Street Press, American Psychological Association (APA), BioOne, Cambridge Scientific Abstracts, CQ Press, EBSCOhost, Facts on File, Hoovers, Infotrieve, Innovative Interfaces, Inc, ISI Web of Knowledge, JSTOR, LexisNexis, Medline, Mergent Online, Modern Language Association, OCLC FirstSearch, OCLC WorldShare Interlibrary Loan, Project MUSE, PubMed, RefWorks, Safari Books Online, ScienceDirect, SerialsSolutions, Standard & Poor's, Westlaw, YBP Library Services
Wireless access
Publications: Handbook; Library Research Guides

Partic in Boston Library Consortium, Inc; New Hampshire College & University Council
Special Services for the Deaf - Accessible learning ctr; Assistive tech; Bks on deafness & sign lang; Coll on deaf educ; TTY equip
Special Services for the Blind - Braille equip
Open Mon-Thurs 8:30am-9:30pm, Fri 8:30-5, Sat & Sun 12-5

GM VETERANS AFFAIRS MEDICAL CENTER LIBRARY*, 718 Smyth Rd, No 142D, 03104-7004. SAN 309-8818. Tel: 603-624-4366, Ext 6030. Toll Free Tel: 800-892-8384. FAX: 603-626-6503. *Libr Dir,* Jona Bostwick; Staff 1 (MLS 1)
Founded 1950
Oct 2005-Sept 2006. Mats Exp $70,000
Library Holdings: e-journals 50; Bk Titles 450; Per Subs 100; Videos 250
Subject Interests: Dentistry, Med, Nursing
Function: Audio & video playback equip for onsite use, Health sci info serv, ILL available, Ref serv available, Telephone ref
Partic in Health Sciences Libraries of New Hampshire & Vermont
Open Mon-Thurs 9-2
Restriction: Circulates for staff only, Clients only, Employees & their associates, In-house use for visitors

MARLBOROUGH

P FROST FREE LIBRARY*, 28 Jaffrey Rd, 03455. (Mail add: PO Box 457, 03455-0457), SAN 309-8826. Tel: 603-876-4479. FAX: 603-876-4479. E-mail: library@frostfree.org. Web Site: www.frostfree.org. *Dir,* Kathleen Ash; E-mail: kash@frostfree.org; *Asst Librn,* Rhonda Capasco Tralli; *Asst Librn,* Jane Richards-Jones; Staff 1 (MLS 1)
Founded 1865. Pop 2,025, Circ 12,818
Library Holdings: Bk Vols 13,286; Per Subs 47
Automation Activity & Vendor Info: (Circulation) Follett Software
Wireless access
Publications: Bemis History of Marlborough (Local historical information)
Partic in New England Libr Asn; Nubanusit Library Cooperative
Open Tues & Wed 2-8, Thurs & Fri 10-5, Sat 10-1
Friends of the Library Group

MARLOW

P MARLOW TOWN LIBRARY, 12 Church St, 03456. (Mail add: PO Box 64, 03456), SAN 309-8834. Tel: 603-446-3466. FAX: 603-446-3466. E-mail: marlowtownlibrary@gmail.com. Web Site: www.marlownewhampshire.org/library.php, www.marlownh.gov. *Librn,* Jennifer Brown; *Asst Librn,* Tristan Smith
Library Holdings: Bk Vols 11,000; Per Subs 15
Automation Activity & Vendor Info: (OPAC) LibraryWorld, Inc
Database Vendor: EBSCOhost
Wireless access
Partic in Nubanusit Library Cooperative
Open Mon 10-12, 1-5 & 6-8, Wed 4-8, Sat 10-12

MASON

P MASON PUBLIC LIBRARY*, 16 Darling Hill Rd, 03048. SAN 309-8842. Tel: 603-878-3867. FAX: 603-878-6146. E-mail: masonlib@myfairpoint.net. *Dir,* Susanne V Wolpert; *Asst Librn,* Denise Ginzler
Pop 1,270; Circ 8,858
Library Holdings: AV Mats 811; Bk Vols 11,091; Per Subs 25; Videos 529
Special Collections: Video Classics Project Coll
Database Vendor: EBSCOhost
Publications: Booklist
Mem of NorthNet Library System
Open Tues 1-8, Wed 9-5, Thurs 10-8, Sat 1-4

MEREDITH

P MEREDITH PUBLIC LIBRARY*, 91 Main St, 03253. (Mail add: PO Box 808, 03253-0808), SAN 309-8850. Tel: 603-279-4303. FAX: 603-279-5352. Web Site: www.meredithlibrary.org/. *Dir,* Erin Apostolos; E-mail: erin@meredithlibrary.org; *Asst Dir,* Judy Hodges; E-mail: judy@meredithlibrary.org; *Ch,* Karen Henchey; *ILL Librn,* Cherie Gable; *Tech Serv Librn,* Christopher Leland; *YA Librn,* John Lock; Staff 7 (MLS 2, Non-MLS 5)
Founded 1882. Pop 4,636; Circ 115,201
Library Holdings: Bk Vols 35,500; Per Subs 72
Special Collections: Oral History
Automation Activity & Vendor Info: (Cataloging) Follett Software; (Circulation) Follett Software
Wireless access
Open Tues-Thurs 9-8, Fri 9-5, Sat 9-2

MERIDEN

P MERIDEN LIBRARY, 22 Bean Rd, 03770. (Mail add: PO Box 128, 03770-0128), SAN 309-8869. Tel: 603-469-3252. E-mail: meridenlibrary@comcast.net. Web Site: www.meridennhlibrary.org. *Dir,* Mary King; *Libr Asst,* Terri Crane; *Libr Asst,* Lori Estey
Founded 1797. Pop 2,364; Circ 9,668
Library Holdings: Audiobooks 248; DVDs 277; Bk Vols 9,406
Special Collections: Boyd's History (Plainfield) 4 vols; History Coll; Plainfield Oral History
Automation Activity & Vendor Info: (Serials) Evergreen
Wireless access
Open Mon & Tues 1-7, Thurs 10-7, Sat 9-Noon
Friends of the Library Group

MERRIMACK

P MERRIMACK PUBLIC LIBRARY, 470 Daniel Webster Hwy, 03054-3694. SAN 309-8885. Tel: 603-424-5021. FAX: 603-424-7312. E-mail: merrimackpl@merrimacklibrary.org. Web Site: www.merrimacklibrary.org. *Dir,* Yvette Couser; E-mail: yvette@merrimacklibrary.org; *Head, Adult Serv,* Alex Estabrook; E-mail: alex@merrimacklibrary.org; *Head, Tech Serv,* Nancy Vigezzi; Staff 31 (MLS 8, Non-MLS 23)
Founded 1892. Pop 26,577; Circ 235,361
Library Holdings: Bk Titles 73,675; Per Subs 148
Automation Activity & Vendor Info: (Acquisitions) Innovative Interfaces, Inc; (Cataloging) Innovative Interfaces, Inc; (Circulation) Innovative Interfaces, Inc; (Course Reserve) Innovative Interfaces, Inc; (ILL) Innovative Interfaces, Inc; (OPAC) Innovative Interfaces, Inc; (Serials) Innovative Interfaces, Inc
Wireless access
Publications: Library Link
Partic in GMILCS, Inc
Open Mon-Thurs 10-9, Fri 10-5, Sat 9-1, Sun 1-5
Friends of the Library Group

C THOMAS MORE COLLEGE OF LIBERAL ARTS*, Warren Memorial Library, Six Manchester St, 03054-4805. SAN 373-0816. Tel: 603-880-0425. FAX: 603-880-9280. Web Site: www.thomasmorecollege.edu. *Dir,* Dr Mary K Mumbach; *Col Librn,* Thomas W Syseskey; E-mail: tsyseskey@charter.net; Staff 2 (MLS 1, Non-MLS 1)
Founded 1978. Enrl 90; Fac 8; Highest Degree: Bachelor
Library Holdings: AV Mats 800; Bk Titles 32,000; Bk Vols 40,000; Per Subs 20
Subject Interests: Biol, Hist, Lit, Philos, Relig
Partic in New Hampshire Automated Information Systems (NHAIS)
Open Mon-Thurs (Sept-May) 10am-12, Fri & Sat 10-5, Sun 1pm-Midnight; Mon, Thurs & Sat (June-Aug) 10-5

MILAN

P DUMMER PUBLIC LIBRARY*, 63 Hill Rd, 03588-9711. Tel: 603-449-0995. E-mail: dummerpubliclibrary@gmail.com. *Dir,* Corine Bergeron; *Librn,* Katie Doherty
Library Holdings: AV Mats 500; Bk Vols 8,000; Talking Bks 50
Automation Activity & Vendor Info: (Cataloging) JayWil Software Development, Inc; (Circulation) JayWil Software Development, Inc
Wireless access
Open Mon & Thurs 3-7
Friends of the Library Group

P MILAN PUBLIC LIBRARY*, 20 Bridge St, 03588. (Mail add: PO Box 263, 03588-0263), SAN 309-8893. Tel: 603-449-7307. E-mail: gotmorebooks@gmail.com. *Dir,* Vickie Plourde
Pop 1,370; Circ 1,500
Library Holdings: AV Mats 114; Bk Vols 7,800
Subject Interests: Local hist
Wireless access
Open Mon 1:30-7:30, Tues 11-4, Thurs 1-6:30

MILFORD

P WADLEIGH MEMORIAL LIBRARY*, 49 Nashua St, 03055-3753. SAN 309-8907. Tel: 603-249-0645. FAX: 603-672-6064. E-mail: wadleigh@wadleighlibrary.org. Circulation E-mail: wmlcirc@wadleighlibrary.org. Interlibrary Loan Service E-mail: wmlill@wadleighlibrary.org. Reference E-mail: refdesk@wadleighlibrary.org. Web Site: www.wadleighlibrary.org. *Libr Dir,* Michelle Sampson; E-mail: director@wadleighlibrary.org; *Head, Circ,* Mary Ann Shea; E-mail: mshea@wadleighlibrary.org; *Ch,* Letisha Goerner; E-mail: lgoerner@wadleighlibrary.org; *Ref & Ad Serv Librn,* Kim Gabert; E-mail: kgabert@wadleighlibrary.org; *Tech Serv Librn,* Diana LeBlanc; E-mail: dleblanc@wadleighlibrary.org; *YA Serv,* Katie Spofford; E-mail: wadleighya@gmail.com; Staff 11 (MLS 4, Non-MLS 7)

Founded 1868. Pop 15,000; Circ 186,733
Jan 2005-Dec 2005 Income $592,803, City $563,099, Other $29,704. Mats Exp $84,430, Books $46,918, Per/Ser (Incl. Access Fees) $9,128, Micro $253, AV Mat $14,320, Electronic Ref Mat (Incl. Access Fees) $13,811. Sal $366,673 (Prof $150,000)
Library Holdings: CDs 1,715; e-books 900; Bk Vols 67,494; Per Subs 180; Talking Bks 1,977; Videos 3,071
Special Collections: Hutchinson Family Singers; Local History; Local Newspapers 1800-present, microfilm
Automation Activity & Vendor Info: (Acquisitions) SirsiDynix; (Cataloging) Horizon; (Circulation) Horizon; (OPAC) Horizon; (Serials) Horizon
Database Vendor: Baker & Taylor, EBSCOhost, Gale Cengage Learning, Newsbank, OCLC FirstSearch, ProQuest, ReferenceUSA, Wilson - Wilson Web
Wireless access
Function: Adult bk club, Adult literacy prog, Archival coll, BA reader (adult literacy), Bk club(s), Computer training, Copy machines, Digital talking bks, e-mail serv, Family literacy, Fax serv, Handicapped accessible, Homebound delivery serv, ILL available, Magnifiers for reading, Mail & tel request accepted, Music CDs, Online ref, Online searches, Photocopying/Printing, Prog for adults, Prog for children & young adult, Ref serv available, Senior computer classes, Spoken cassettes & CDs, Spoken cassettes & DVDs, Summer reading prog, Tax forms, Telephone ref, VHS videos, Video lending libr, Wheelchair accessible, Workshops
Partic in GMILCS, Inc; Urban Pub Libr Consortium
Open Mon-Thurs 9:30-8:30, Fri 9:30-5, Sat 9-1, Sun (Sept-May) 1-5
Friends of the Library Group

MILTON

P NUTE LIBRARY, 22 Elm St, 03851. SAN 350-5359. Tel: 603-652-7829. FAX: 603-652-4793. E-mail: nutelibrary@gmail.com. Web Site: sites.google.com/site/nutelibrary. *Librn,* Jody Gourlay; *Sch Librn,* Helen Brock; Tel: 603-652-4591, E-mail: helen.brock@sau64.org; Staff 2 (MLS 1, Non-MLS 1)
Pop 4,000; Circ 15,069
Library Holdings: Bk Vols 15,000; Per Subs 15
Special Collections: Local History Coll
Automation Activity & Vendor Info: (Cataloging) Book Systems; (Circulation) Book Systems; (OPAC) Book Systems
Function: 24/7 Online cat, Activity rm, Bks on CD, Children's prog, Computers for patron use, Electronic databases & coll, Fax serv, Free DVD rentals, Handicapped accessible, ILL available, Magazines, Online cat, Photocopying/Printing, Pub access computers
Partic in New Hampshire Automated Information Systems (NHAIS)
Open Mon, Tues & Thurs 9-5, Wed 9-7, Fri 9-2:15, Sat 9-12

MILTON MILLS

P MILTON FREE PUBLIC LIBRARY*, 13 Main St, 03852. (Mail add: PO Box 127, 03852-0127). Tel: 603-473-8535. E-mail: mfpl@metrocast.net. Web Site: www.miltonfreepubliclibrary.org. *Dir,* Betsy Baker; *Asst Librn,* Sarah Clarke; *Asst Librn,* Bess Rowden; Staff 3 (Non-MLS 3)
Founded 1916. Pop 3,940
Library Holdings: AV Mats 100; Large Print Bks 35; Bk Vols 8,500; Talking Bks 90
Wireless access
Partic in New Hampshire Automated Information Systems (NHAIS)
Open Tues-Fri 3-7, Sat 10-1
Friends of the Library Group

MONROE

P MONROE PUBLIC LIBRARY*, 19 Plains Rd, 03771. (Mail add: PO Box 67, 03771-0067), SAN 309-8915. Tel: 603-638-4736. E-mail: monroepubliclibrary@roadrunner.com. *Librn,* Jessica Sherman; *Circ,* Becky Gibson
Pop 618; Circ 17,887
Library Holdings: Bk Vols 19,000; Per Subs 40
Special Collections: State Document Depository
Wireless access
Partic in New Hampshire Automated Information Systems (NHAIS)
Open Mon & Sat 9-12, Tues 12-7:30, Thurs 2-5

MONT VERNON

P DALAND MEMORIAL LIBRARY, Five N Main St, 03057. (Mail add: PO Box 335, 03057-0335), SAN 309-8923. Tel: 603-673-7888. FAX: 603-673-7888. E-mail: dalandlibrary@comcast.net. Web Site: www.dalandlibrary.wordpress.com. *Dir,* Bonnie Angulas; *Children's Dir,* JoAnn Kitchel
Founded 1892. Pop 2,000
Library Holdings: Bk Vols 14,000; Per Subs 14
Automation Activity & Vendor Info: (Circulation) Follett Software
Open Tues & Thurs 10-5:30, Wed 12-8, Fri 2-6, Sat 10-1
Friends of the Library Group

MOULTONBOROUGH

P MOULTONBOROUGH PUBLIC LIBRARY*, Four Holland St, 03254. (Mail add: PO Box 150, 03254-0150), SAN 309-8931. Tel: 603-476-8895. Web Site: www.moultonboroughlibrary.org. *Dir,* Nancy McCue; *Asst Librn,* Jane Rice; *Ch,* Judi Knowles; *Circ Librn,* Linda Nolin; *Circ Librn,* Susan Stokes; Staff 6 (MLS 1, Non-MLS 5)
Founded 1890. Pop 4,800; Circ 61,725
Library Holdings: Bk Vols 25,000; Per Subs 75
Subject Interests: Local hist
Automation Activity & Vendor Info: (Acquisitions) Follett Software; (Cataloging) Follett Software; (Circulation) Follett Software
Database Vendor: Baker & Taylor
Wireless access
Function: Computer training, Copy machines, Fax serv, Handicapped accessible, Homebound delivery serv, ILL available, Magnifiers for reading, Music CDs, Prog for adults, Prog for children & young adult, Ref serv available, Spoken cassettes & CDs, Spoken cassettes & DVDs, Summer reading prog, Tax forms, Telephone ref, VHS videos, Wheelchair accessible
Open Mon-Thurs 10-8, Fri 10-5, Sat 10-2
Friends of the Library Group

NASHUA

C DANIEL WEBSTER COLLEGE*, Anne Bridge Baddour Library, 20 University Dr, 03063-1300. SAN 309-8966. Tel: 603-577-6559. Interlibrary Loan Service Tel: 603-577-6542. Administration Tel: 603-577-6540. Automation Services Tel: 603-577-6543. Information Services Tel: 603-577-6541. FAX: 603-577-6199. E-mail: librarian@dwc.edu. Web Site: www.web.dwc.edu. *Dir,* Francesca Denton; E-mail: denton@dwc.edu; *Mgr, Access Serv,* Marilyn Frankland; E-mail: frankland@dwc.edu; *Educ Tech Support Spec,* Judy Brophy; Tel: 603-577-6411, E-mail: brophy@dwc.edu; Staff 10 (MLS 5, Non-MLS 5)
Founded 1965. Enrl 1,200; Fac 166; Highest Degree: Master
Library Holdings: AV Mats 24; CDs 208; DVDs 615; e-books 1,207; Bk Titles 31,136; Bk Vols 34,972; Per Subs 175; Videos 1,188
Subject Interests: Aviation, Bus mgt, Computer sci, Eng, Sport mgt
Automation Activity & Vendor Info: (Acquisitions) Innovative Interfaces, Inc; (Cataloging) Innovative Interfaces, Inc; (Circulation) Innovative Interfaces, Inc; (Course Reserve) Innovative Interfaces, Inc; (ILL) Innovative Interfaces, Inc; (Media Booking) Innovative Interfaces, Inc; (OPAC) Innovative Interfaces, Inc; (Serials) Innovative Interfaces, Inc
Database Vendor: EBSCOhost, LexisNexis, OCLC FirstSearch, ProQuest, SerialsSolutions
Function: E-Reserves, Electronic databases & coll, Online info literacy tutorials on the web & in blackboard
Partic in Lyrasis; New Hampshire College & University Council; Westchester Academic Library Directors Organization (WALDO)
Open Mon-Thurs 8am-10pm, Fri 8-8, Sat 12-6, Sun 1-9

J NASHUA COMMUNITY COLLEGE, Walter R Peterson Library & Media Center, 505 Amherst St, 03063-1026. SAN 309-8974. Tel: 603-882-6923. Reference Tel: 603-578-8905. FAX: 603-882-8690. Web Site: nashuacc.edu/library.html. *Chief Libr Officer,* Position Currently Open; *Ref Librn,* Margaret Bero; Tel: 603-882-6923, Ext 1565, E-mail: mbero@ccsnh.edu; *Cataloger,* Melissa Roberts; Tel: 603-882-6923, Ext 1532, E-mail: mrroberts@ccsnh.edu; Staff 7 (MLS 2, Non-MLS 5)
Founded 1971. Enrl 2,000; Fac 45; Highest Degree: Associate
Library Holdings: DVDs 1,200; e-books 72,000; e-journals 35,000; Bk Titles 18,000; Per Subs 250
Subject Interests: Automotive, Computer, Drafting, Electronic tech, Liberal arts, Machining, Mat sci
Automation Activity & Vendor Info: (Cataloging) TLC (The Library Corporation); (Circulation) TLC (The Library Corporation); (OPAC) TLC (The Library Corporation); (Serials) TLC (The Library Corporation)
Database Vendor: Cinahl, CredoReference, ebrary, EBSCOhost, LexisNexis, Project MUSE, ProQuest
Publications: Handbook (User's guide); PR Materials; Reference Guides
Partic in Lyrasis; Westchester Academic Library Directors Organization (WALDO)
Open Mon-Thurs 8-8, Fri 8-5, Sat 9-1

P NASHUA PUBLIC LIBRARY*, Two Court St, 03060. SAN 350-5413. Tel: 603-589-4600. Circulation Tel: 603-589-4634. Interlibrary Loan Service Tel: 603-589-4635. Reference Tel: 603-589-4611. Administration Tel: 603-589-4622. Automation Services Tel: 603-589-4621. FAX: 603-594-3457. Reference FAX: 603-589-4640. TDD: 888-692-1403. E-mail: administration@nashualibrary.org. Web Site: www.nashualibrary.org. *Dir,* Jennifer Hinderer; Tel: 603-589-4620; *Asst Dir,* Jenn Hosking; Tel: 603-589-4621; *Ch Serv,* Kathy E Bolton; Tel: 603-589-4630; *Circ Librn,* Loren Rosson; Tel: 603-589-4617; *ILL Librn,*

Judy Dominici; *Outreach Librn,* Karen Egle-Gaber; *Ref Librn,* Marsha Auerbach; *Tech Librn,* Margaret Gleeson; *YA Librn,* Jennifer Jasinski; *Commun Serv,* Carol Eyman; Tel: 603-589-4610; Staff 52 (MLS 12, Non-MLS 40)
Founded 1867. Pop 90,000; Circ 692,939
Jul 2006-Jun 2007 Income $2,131,522. Mats Exp $276,338, Books $139,291, Per/Ser (Incl. Access Fees) $39,272, Micro $8,000, AV Mat $44,775, Electronic Ref Mat (Incl. Access Fees) $34,000. Sal $1,625,747
Library Holdings: AV Mats 19,608; Bks on Deafness & Sign Lang 59; Braille Volumes 16; CDs 4,816; DVDs 4,820; Electronic Media & Resources 994; Large Print Bks 4,442; Music Scores 21; Bk Vols 240,555; Per Subs 250
Special Collections: Local & State Histories (Hunt Room Coll). State Document Depository; US Document Depository
Subject Interests: Archit, Art, Music
Automation Activity & Vendor Info: (Acquisitions) SirsiDynix; (Circulation) SirsiDynix; (Media Booking) SirsiDynix; (OPAC) SirsiDynix
Database Vendor: Baker & Taylor, CountryWatch, Dun & Bradstreet, EBSCO Information Services, EBSCOhost, Facts on File, Gale Cengage Learning, Greenwood Publishing Group, Grolier Online, H W Wilson, Marcive, Inc, Mergent Online, ReferenceUSA, SirsiDynix, Standard & Poor's, ValueLine
Wireless access
Function: Adult bk club, Art exhibits, AV serv, Bk club(s), Bus archives, Chess club, Electronic databases & coll, Govt ref serv, Handicapped accessible, Health sci info serv, Home delivery & serv to Sr ctr & nursing homes, Homebound delivery serv, Homework prog, ILL available, Jazz prog, Large print keyboards, Mail & tel request accepted, Online ref, Online searches, Orientations, Photocopying/Printing, Preschool outreach, Prog for adults, Prog for children & young adult, Ref serv available, Satellite serv, Senior computer classes, Spoken cassettes & CDs, Spoken cassettes & DVDs, Summer reading prog, Telephone ref, VHS videos, Wheelchair accessible, Workshops
Publications: Nashua Experience: History in the Making, 1673-1978
Special Services for the Deaf - TTY equip
Open Mon-Fri 9-9, Sat 9-5:30, Sun 1-5
Friends of the Library Group

R PILGRIM CONGREGATIONAL CHURCH*, Goodhue Memorial Library, Four Watson St, 03064. SAN 309-8982. Tel: 603-882-1801. FAX: 603-882-1801. E-mail: nashuapilgrimucc@aol.com. Web Site: www.pilgrimchurchnashua.org. *Librn,* Virginia Hart
Library Holdings: Bk Vols 500
Subject Interests: Congregational info, Fiction

CR RIVIER UNIVERSITY*, Regina Library, 420 S Main St, 03060-5086. SAN 309-8990. Tel: 603-897-8256. FAX: 603-897-8889. E-mail: libmail@rivier.edu. Web Site: www.rivier.edu. *Dir,* Daniel Speidel; Tel: 603-897-8576; *Asst Dir, Tech Serv,* Amy DeBrower; Tel: 603-897-8671, E-mail: adebrower@rivier.edu; *Asst Dir, User Serv,* Shawna Smith; Tel: 603-897-8536, E-mail: sesmith@rivier.edu; *Acq Librn,* Amanda Cabot, Tel: 603-897-8535, E-mail: acabot@rivier.edu; *Educ Res Ctr/Ref Librn,* Shana Friedman; Tel: 603-897-8463, E-mail: sfriedman@rivier.edu; *Electronic Info Librn,* Lee Anne Hooley; Tel: 603-897-8683, E-mail: lhooley@rivier.edu; *Ref Librn,* Alan Witt; Tel: 603-897-8673, E-mail: awitt@rivier.edu; *Circ Coordr,* Pam Richardson; E-mail: prichardson@rivier.edu; *Coordr, ILL,* Holly Klump; Tel: 603-897-8255, E-mail: hklump@rivier.edu; *Archivist,* Lorraine Arsenault; Tel: 603-897-8278, E-mail: larsenault@rivier.edu; *Tech Serv,* Elaine Bean; Tel: 603-897-8672, E-mail: ebean@rivier.edu; *Circ Asst,* Pam Richardson; E-mail: prichardson@rivier.edu; *ILL Asst,* Lena Robert; Tel: 603-897-8587, E-mail: lrobert@rivier.edu; Staff 20 (MLS 9, Non-MLS 11)
Founded 1933. Enrl 1,685; Highest Degree: Master
Library Holdings: e-books 40,000; Bk Vols 90,000; Per Subs 450
Special Collections: Franco-American Literary Criticism (Rocheleau-Rouleau Coll); Patristics (Gilbert Coll)
Subject Interests: Educ, Law, Nursing
Automation Activity & Vendor Info: (Acquisitions) Innovative Interfaces, Inc; (Cataloging) Innovative Interfaces, Inc; (Circulation) Innovative Interfaces, Inc; (Course Reserve) Innovative Interfaces, Inc; (ILL) OCLC Online; (Media Booking) Innovative Interfaces, Inc; (OPAC) Innovative Interfaces, Inc; (Serials) Innovative Interfaces, Inc
Database Vendor: EBSCOhost, Gale Cengage Learning, JSTOR, LexisNexis, ProQuest, Wilson - Wilson Web
Wireless access
Function: ILL available
Partic in Lyrasis; New Hampshire College & University Council
Special Services for the Blind - Reader equip
Open Mon-Thurs 8am-Midnight, Fri 8-8, Sat 9-6, Sun 11-11

M ST JOSEPH HOSPITAL*, Health Science Library, 172 Kinsley St, 03061. SAN 377-9572. Tel: 603-595-3143. FAX: 603-595-3124. *Librn,* Cindy Sloan
Library Holdings: Bk Titles 400; Per Subs 150
Partic in Basic Health Sciences Library Network; Health Sciences Libraries of New Hampshire & Vermont; North Atlantic Health Sciences Libraries, Inc
Open Mon-Fri 8-1

NELSON

P OLIVIA RODHAM MEMORIAL LIBRARY*, Nelson Library, One Nelson Common Rd, 03457-9703. SAN 324-2862. Tel: 603-847-3214. E-mail: library@townofnelson.com. *Dir,* Kristine Finnegan; Staff 1 (Non-MLS 1)
Founded 1926. Pop 670
Library Holdings: Bk Vols 8,000; Per Subs 25
Wireless access
Partic in Nubanusit Library Cooperative
Open Mon & Sat 10-1, Tues-Thurs 3-7
Friends of the Library Group

NEW BOSTON

P WHIPPLE FREE LIBRARY*, 67 Mont Vernon Rd, 03070. (Mail add: PO Box 237, 03070-0237), SAN 309-9016. Tel: 603-487-3391. FAX: 603-487-2886. E-mail: wfl@wfl.mv.com. Web Site: www.whipplefreelibrary.org. *Dir,* Sarah Chapman; *Asst Dir,* Mary Girard; *Ch,* Barbara Ballou; *Tech Serv Librn,* Ronna LaPenn; *ILL,* Julie Steenson
Pop 5,100
Library Holdings: Bk Vols 19,500; Per Subs 72
Automation Activity & Vendor Info: (Acquisitions) Biblionix; (Cataloging) Biblionix; (Circulation) Biblionix; (OPAC) Biblionix
Wireless access
Open Mon & Wed 9:30-8:30, Thurs 2:30-6:30, Fri 9:30-5, Sat 9:30-12:30
Friends of the Library Group

NEW CASTLE

P NEW CASTLE PUBLIC LIBRARY*, 301 Wentworth Rd, 03854. (Mail add: PO Box 329, 03854-0329), SAN 309-9024. Tel: 603-431-6773. FAX: 603-431-6773. E-mail: nwcstle.library@comcast.net. *Dir,* Christine Collins
Pop 1,100; Circ 6,500
Jul 2006-Jun 2007 Income $48,000. Mats Exp $16,000. Sal $31,000
Library Holdings: Bk Vols 15,000; Per Subs 23
Special Collections: Genealogy Coll; International Mystery Coll; Local History, bks, prints
Automation Activity & Vendor Info: (Cataloging) Follett Software; (Circulation) Follett Software
Wireless access
Open Tues, Wed & Fri 12-5, Thurs 9-3, Sat 9-Noon

NEW DURHAM

P NEW DURHAM PUBLIC LIBRARY*, Two Old Bay Rd, 03855-2214. (Mail add: PO Box 206, 03855-0206), SAN 309-9032. Tel: 603-859-2201. FAX: 603-859-2201. E-mail: newdurhamlibrary@gmail.com. *Dir,* Max Wirestone; *Ch,* Cathy Allyn; *Circ Librn,* Donna Swett
Founded 1894. Pop 2,200; Circ 7,800
Library Holdings: Bk Titles 12,315; Per Subs 27
Subject Interests: Local genealogy, Local hist
Automation Activity & Vendor Info: (Cataloging) Follett Software; (Circulation) Follett Software
Open Mon-Thurs 1-7, Fri 10-5, Sat 10-2
Friends of the Library Group

NEW HAMPTON

P GORDON-NASH LIBRARY*, 69 Main St, 03256. SAN 309-9040. Tel: 603-744-8061. FAX: 603-744-6555. E-mail: gordonnash@metrocast.net. Web Site: www.gordon-nash.org. *Dir,* Cathy Nolan Vincevic; *Ch,* Melanie Benedict; *Ch,* Christine Hunewell; *Asst Librn,* Pamela Dorsett; *Asst Librn,* Michelle DuBreuil; Staff 4 (Non-MLS 4)
Founded 1895. Pop 2,135; Circ 25,517
Jan 2007-Dec 2007 Income $163,413. Mats Exp $10,935
Library Holdings: Audiobooks 938; Bk Titles 35,241; Per Subs 61; Videos 1,716
Automation Activity & Vendor Info: (Circulation) Follett Software
Partic in New Hampshire Automated Information Systems (NHAIS)
Open Tues-Thurs 10-8, Fri 10-6, Sat 10-2
Friends of the Library Group

NEW IPSWICH

P NEW IPSWICH LIBRARY*, Six Main St, 03071. (Mail add: PO Box 320, 03071-0320). Tel: 603-878-4644. E-mail: nilibrary@comcast.net. *Librn,* Anne Soini; *Asst Librn,* Ann-Marie Howard
Library Holdings: AV Mats 400; CDs 25; DVDs 125; Large Print Bks 40; Bk Vols 15,000; Per Subs 40; Videos 75

Automation Activity & Vendor Info: (Cataloging) New Generation Technologies Inc. (LiBRARYSOFT); (Circulation) New Generation Technologies Inc. (LiBRARYSOFT); (OPAC) New Generation Technologies Inc. (LiBRARYSOFT)
Wireless access
Open Mon & Wed 2-8, Tues & Fri 9-1, Sat (Sep-July) 9-12

NEW LONDON

C COLBY-SAWYER COLLEGE*, Susan Colgate Cleveland Library & Learning Center, 541 Main St, 03257-4648. SAN 309-9067. Tel: 603-526-3685. Interlibrary Loan Service Tel: 603-526-3065. Reference Tel: 603-526-3687. FAX: 603-526-3777. E-mail: library@colby-sawyer.edu. Web Site: www.colby-sawyer.edu/information/index.html. *Dir,* Kenneth Kochien; *Col Librn,* Carrie P Thomas; Tel: 603-526-3686, E-mail: cathomas@colby-sawyer.edu; *Cat, Ref Librn,* Sondra VanderPloeg; Tel: 603-526-3375, E-mail: svanderploeg@colby-sawyer.edu; *Syst Analyst,* Charles Krajewski; *Archivist,* Kelliann Bogan; Tel: 603-526-3360, E-mail: kbogan@colby-sawyer.edu; *Acq,* Nancy Langley; Tel: 603-526-3684, E-mail: nlangley@colby-sawyer.edu; *E-Res & Journals,* Nancy Kingsley; Tel: 603-526-3169, E-mail: nkingsley@colby-sawyer.edu; Staff 12 (MLS 4, Non-MLS 8)
Founded 1837. Enrl 1,000; Fac 100; Highest Degree: Bachelor
Library Holdings: AV Mats 3,000; Bk Vols 98,000; Per Subs 600
Automation Activity & Vendor Info: (Cataloging) Horizon; (Circulation) Horizon; (OPAC) Horizon
Database Vendor: EBSCOhost, Gale Cengage Learning, OVID Technologies
Wireless access
Function: Copy machines
Partic in Lyrasis; New Hampshire College & University Council; Westchester Academic Library Directors Organization (WALDO)
Open Mon-Thurs 8am-11pm, Fri 8am-9pm, Sat 10-9, Sun Noon-11pm
Friends of the Library Group

P TRACY MEMORIAL LIBRARY*, 304 Main St, 03257-7813. SAN 309-9075. Tel: 603-526-4656. FAX: 603-526-8035. Web Site: www.tracylibrary.org. *Dir,* Sandra Licks; E-mail: slicks@tracylibrary.org; *Asst Dir,* Jo-Ann Roy; E-mail: jroy@tracylibrary.org; *Head, Youth Serv,* Kathy Tracy; E-mail: ktracy@tracylibrary.org; Staff 8 (MLS 3, Non-MLS 5)
Pop 5,000; Circ 100,000
Jan 2008-Dec 2008 Income $475,280. Mats Exp $51,009, Books $26,539, Per/Ser (Incl. Access Fees) $5,172, AV Equip $828, AV Mat $18,470. Sal $331,007
Library Holdings: AV Mats 4,331; Large Print Bks 1,275; Bk Titles 30,068; Per Subs 125
Automation Activity & Vendor Info: (Circulation) Follett Software; (OPAC) Follett Software
Function: Homebound delivery serv
Partic in New Hampshire Automated Information Systems (NHAIS)
Open Tues & Thurs 9-8, Wed & Fri 9-5, Sat 9-1
Friends of the Library Group

NEWBURY

P NEWBURY PUBLIC LIBRARY*, 933 Rte 103, 03255-5803. (Mail add: PO Box 245, 03255-0245), SAN 309-9083. Tel: 603-763-5803. FAX: 603-763-5803. E-mail: newburypubliclibrary@yahoo.com. Web Site: www.newburylibrary.net. *Dir,* Rosina Johnson; *Asst Dir,* Lea McBain; *Ch,* Jane Moss; *Ref/ILL,* Shannon Storm; Staff 3 (MLS 1, Non-MLS 2)
Founded 1893
Library Holdings: Bk Titles 13,100; Per Subs 55
Automation Activity & Vendor Info: (Cataloging) Follett Software; (Circulation) Follett Software; (OPAC) Follett Software
Database Vendor: EBSCOhost
Open Mon 12-8, Tues-Thurs & Sun 12-5, Sat 10-2
Friends of the Library Group

NEWFIELDS

P PAUL MEMORIAL LIBRARY, 76 Main St, 03856-8312. SAN 309-9091. Tel: 603-778-8169. FAX: 603-772-9004. E-mail: newpl@comcast.net. Web Site: www.paulmemoriallibrary.org. *Dir,* Pamela Burch; E-mail: pamburch@comcast.net; *Ch,* Mary Duquette; *Libr Asst,* Doris Goerner; *Libr Asst,* Lee Woodworth
Founded 1893. Pop 1,670; Circ 4,375
Library Holdings: Bk Vols 11,500; Per Subs 16
Subject Interests: Newfields hist
Automation Activity & Vendor Info: (Acquisitions) LibraryWorld, Inc; (Cataloging) LibraryWorld, Inc; (Circulation) LibraryWorld, Inc; (OPAC) LibraryWorld, Inc
Database Vendor: EBSCO Information Services
Function: Adult bk club, Audiobks via web, Bks on CD, Children's prog, Computers for patron use, ILL available, Mus passes, Online searches, Photocopying/Printing, Prog for adults, Prog for children & young adult, Ref serv available, Summer reading prog, Web-catalog, Wheelchair accessible, Workshops
Open Mon & Fri 12-4, Tues & Thurs 10-5, Wed 10-7, Sat 9-1
Friends of the Library Group

NEWINGTON

P LANGDON LIBRARY*, 328 Nimble Hill Rd, 03801. SAN 309-9105. Tel: 603-436-5154. FAX: 603-436-5154. E-mail: langdonlib@comcast.net. *Dir of Libr,* Scott Campbell
Founded 1892. Pop 900; Circ 13,110
Library Holdings: Bk Titles 17,000; Per Subs 36
Special Collections: Historical Records & Photographs Coll
Automation Activity & Vendor Info: (Cataloging) Follett Software; (Circulation) Follett Software; (Course Reserve) Follett Software
Database Vendor: EBSCOhost
Wireless access
Publications: Newington Neighbor (Quarterly newsletter)
Open Tues 3-8, Wed 12-5, Thurs & Fri 10-5, Sat 10-3
Friends of the Library Group

NEWMARKET

P NEWMARKET PUBLIC LIBRARY*, One Elm St, 03857-1201. SAN 309-9113. Tel: 603-659-5311. FAX: 603-659-8849. *Dir,* Carrie Gadbois; E-mail: carrie@newmarketlibrary.org; *Ch,* Ellisa Arbogast
Pop 4,292; Circ 10,517
Library Holdings: Bk Vols 32,000; Per Subs 60
Subject Interests: Town hist
Open Mon & Wed 2-8, Tues & Fri 10-5, Thurs 10-8, Sat 10-4
Friends of the Library Group

NEWPORT

P RICHARDS FREE LIBRARY*, 58 N Main St, 03773-1597. SAN 309-9121. Tel: 603-863-3430. FAX: 603-863-3022. E-mail: rfl@newport.lib.nh.us. Web Site: www.newport.lib.nh.us. *Dir,* Andrea Thorpe; E-mail: athorpe@newport.lib.nh.us; *Asst Dir, ILL Librn,* Vicky Carl; *Youth Serv Librn,* Moriah Churchill; Staff 6 (MLS 2, Non-MLS 4)
Founded 1888. Pop 6,110
Jan 2006-Dec 2006 Income $275,000. Mats Exp $27,000. Sal $179,000
Library Holdings: CDs 100; DVDs 200; Large Print Bks 404; Bk Vols 36,102; Per Subs 60; Talking Bks 1,372; Videos 1,700
Special Collections: Kenneth Andler NH Hist Coll; Local Newspapers (Argus Champion 1878 to present), micro; Sarah Hosepha Hale Coll
Automation Activity & Vendor Info: (Cataloging) Follett Software; (Circulation) Follett Software; (OPAC) Follett Software
Database Vendor: EBSCOhost, OCLC FirstSearch
Wireless access
Function: Adult bk club, Adult literacy prog, Bk club(s), Handicapped accessible, Homebound delivery serv, ILL available, Magnifiers for reading, Prog for adults, Prog for children & young adult, Spoken cassettes & CDs, Wheelchair accessible
Open Mon 1-6, Tues & Thurs 10-8, Wed & Fri 10-6, Sat 10-2
Friends of the Library Group

NEWTON

P GALE LIBRARY*, 16 S Main St, 03858-3310. (Mail add: PO Box 208, 03858-0208), SAN 309-913X. Tel: 603-382-4691. FAX: 603-382-2528. E-mail: galelibraryreads@comcast.net. *Dir,* Theresa Caswell; *Asst Dir, Ch,* Sue Mears; *Asst Librn,* Nicole Belisle-Briggs; *Asst Librn,* Lauri Gaudet; *Asst Librn,* Elizabeth Standling; Staff 6 (Non-MLS 6)
Pop 4,000; Circ 24,000
Library Holdings: Bk Vols 26,000; Per Subs 50
Special Collections: New Hampshire Coll
Automation Activity & Vendor Info: (Cataloging) Follett Software; (Circulation) Follett Software; (OPAC) Follett Software
Database Vendor: EBSCOhost
Wireless access
Open Mon & Wed 12-8, Tues & Sat 9-1, Fri 10-6
Friends of the Library Group

NORTH CONWAY

M MEMORIAL HOSPITAL*, Health Sciences Library, 3073 White Mountain Hwy, 03860. (Mail add: PO Box 5001, 03860-5001), SAN 377-9513. Tel: 603-356-5461. FAX: 603-356-8135. Web Site: www.thememorialhospital.org. *Mgr,* Barbara Rosman; Tel: 603-356-5461, Ext 157, E-mail: brosman@memorialhospitalnh.org
Library Holdings: Bk Titles 150; Per Subs 25
Open Mon-Sun 7-7
Restriction: Non-circulating

S MOUNT WASHINGTON OBSERVATORY*, Gladys Brooks Memorial Library, 2779 Main St, 03860. (Mail add: PO Box 2310, 03860-2310), SAN 371-2370. Tel: 603-356-2137, Ext 203. FAX: 603-356-0307. Web Site: www.mountwashington.org/education/library. *Curator,* Peter Crane; E-mail: pcrane@mountwashington.org
Library Holdings: Bk Vols 3,000; Per Subs 10
Subject Interests: Meteorology, Polar regions, White Mountains
Automation Activity & Vendor Info: (Acquisitions) Follett Software; (Cataloging) Follett Software; (Circulation) Follett Software
Partic in New Hampshire Automated Information Systems (NHAIS)
Restriction: Open by appt only

P NORTH CONWAY PUBLIC LIBRARY, 2719 White Mountain Hwy, 03860. (Mail add: PO Box 409, 03860-0409), SAN 376-5083. Tel: 603-356-2961. E-mail: ncpl@myfairpoint.net. Web Site: www.northconwaylibrary.com. *Libr Dir,* Andrea Masters; *Asst Librn,* Martha Pedersen; Staff 3 (Non-MLS 3)
Founded 1887. Pop 2,000
Jan 2013-Dec 2013 Income $90,000, City $7,500, Locally Generated Income $30,000, Parent Institution $52,500. Mats Exp $8,000, Books $6,000, Per/Ser (Incl. Access Fees) $400, AV Mat $1,000
Library Holdings: CDs 400; DVDs 1,100; e-books 40; Large Print Bks 50; Bk Vols 20,000; Per Subs 18; Videos 50
Automation Activity & Vendor Info: (OPAC) Follett Software
Wireless access
Function: Adult bk club, Audiobks via web, Bks on CD, Computers for patron use, Copy machines, eReaders, Magazines, Tax forms, VHS videos
Open Mon, Tues & Fri 12-5, Wed & Thurs 12-6
Friends of the Library Group

NORTH HAMPTON

P NORTH HAMPTON PUBLIC LIBRARY, 237A Atlantic Ave, 03862-2341. SAN 309-9148. Tel: 603-964-6326. FAX: 603-964-1107. E-mail: nhpl@nhplib.org. Web Site: www.nhplib.org. *Dir,* Susan Grant; *Asst Dir, Ch & Youth Librn,* Lorreen Keating; *Adult Serv, ILL,* Elizabeth Flot; *Tech Serv,* Barbara Dewing; Staff 3 (MLS 2, Non-MLS 1)
Founded 1892. Pop 4,259; Circ 45,847
Library Holdings: AV Mats 1,070; Bks on Deafness & Sign Lang 20; Bk Vols 28,327; Per Subs 76
Automation Activity & Vendor Info: (Cataloging) Follett Software; (Circulation) Follett Software; (OPAC) Follett Software
Database Vendor: OCLC FirstSearch, ProQuest
Open Mon & Wed 10-8, Tues, Thurs & Fri 10-5, Sat 10-2
Friends of the Library Group

NORTH HAVERHILL

P PATTEN-NORTH HAVERHILL LIBRARY*, 2885 Dartmouth College Hwy, 03774-4533. (Mail add: 360 Horsemeadow Rd, 03774-4929), SAN 309-8389. Tel: 603-787-2542. E-mail: pattenlibrary@yahoo.com. *Dir,* Debi English; *Asst Librn,* Audrey Clough
Pop 4,416; Circ 7,000
Jan 2005-Dec 2005. Mats Exp $4,500
Library Holdings: Bk Vols 25,000; Per Subs 20; Talking Bks 35; Videos 75
Open Mon 2-7, Wed 2-6

NORTH STRATFORD

P STRATFORD PUBLIC LIBRARY*, 74 Main St, 03590. (Mail add: PO Box 313, 03590-0366). Tel: 603-922-9016. E-mail: library03590@gmail.com. Web Site: www.stratfordnhlibraries.com. *Librn,* Tracy Kostka
Library Holdings: DVDs 50; Bk Titles 10,000; Talking Bks 20
Wireless access
Open Mon 2-6, Tues 9-1, Wed 9-Noon, Thurs 9-12 & 1-5

NORTH WOODSTOCK

P MOOSILAUKE PUBLIC LIBRARY*, 165 Lost River Rd, 03262. (Mail add: PO Box 21, 03262), SAN 309-9156. Tel: 603-745-9971. E-mail: moosilpl@roadrunner.com. *Librn,* Wendy L Pelletier; Staff 1 (Non-MLS 1)
Founded 1896. Pop 1,200; Circ 3,299
Jan 2010-Dec 2010 Income $57,000. Mats Exp $7,500, Books $750
Library Holdings: Audiobooks 25; AV Mats 398; DVDs 50; Large Print Bks 51; Bk Vols 10,302; Per Subs 30; Talking Bks 76; Videos 450
Special Collections: White Mountains & Local History
Wireless access
Open Mon & Thurs 9-8, Fri & Sat 9-5

NORTHFIELD

P HALL MEMORIAL LIBRARY*, 18 Park St, 03276. SAN 309-9717. Tel: 603-286-8971. FAX: 603-286-2278. E-mail: hallmemo@metrocast.net. Web Site: www.hallmemoriallibrary.org. *Dir,* Jenna Moulton; *Ch,* Julie Dylingwoski; Staff 3.75 (Non-MLS 3.75)
Founded 1886. Pop 8,350; Circ 65,000
Jan 2009-Dec 2009 Income $255,400, Locally Generated Income $236,400, Other $19,000
Special Collections: 19th Century; Civil War Regiment Records; Northfield History, bks, illustrations, town rpts & tax lists
Automation Activity & Vendor Info: (Cataloging) Gateway; (Circulation) Gateway; (OPAC) Gateway; (Serials) Basch Subscriptions, Inc
Database Vendor: EBSCOhost
Wireless access
Partic in New Hampshire Automated Information Systems (NHAIS)
Open Mon & Thurs 10-8, Tues, Wed & Fri 10-6, Sat 10-2

NORTHWOOD

P CHESLEY MEMORIAL LIBRARY, Eight Mountain Ave, 03261. SAN 309-9172. Tel: 603-942-5472. FAX: 603-942-5132. E-mail: chesleydirector@gmail.com. *Libr Dir,* Donna Bunker; Staff 1 (Non-MLS 1)
Founded 1954. Pop 4,235; Circ 26,133
Library Holdings: Bk Vols 17,625; Per Subs 30
Wireless access
Open Mon-Thurs 10-7, Sat 10-1
Friends of the Library Group

NOTTINGHAM

P BLAISDELL MEMORIAL LIBRARY*, 129 Stage Rd, 03290. (Mail add: PO Box 115, 03290-0115), SAN 320-8451. Tel: 603-679-8484. FAX: 603-679-6774. E-mail: blaisdellml@comcast.net. Web Site: www.nottinghamlibrary.org. *Librn,* Rhoda Capron; *Asst Librn,* Pat Vachon
Pop 2,500; Circ 14,200
Library Holdings: Bk Vols 12,000; Per Subs 10
Open Mon 2-9, Tues & Thurs 9-5, Wed 9-9, Sat 9-1, Sun 1-4
Friends of the Library Group

ORFORD

P ORFORD SOCIAL LIBRARY*, 573 NH Rte 10, 03777. (Mail add: PO Box 189, 03777-0189), SAN 309-9202. Tel: 603-353-9756. E-mail: oslib@myfairpoint.net. *Librn,* Sandra Gunther
Founded 1792. Pop 926; Circ 1,778
Library Holdings: CDs 125; DVDs 50; Large Print Bks 50; Bk Vols 8,750; Per Subs 15; Videos 200
Open Mon & Thurs 1-8, Wed & Sat 9-1
Friends of the Library Group

ORFORDVILLE

P ORFORD FREE LIBRARY, 2539 Rte 25A, 03777. (Mail add: PO Box 186, 03777-0186), SAN 309-9199. Tel: 603-353-9166. FAX: 603-353-9166. E-mail: orfordfreelibrary@mytopsmail.com. *Librn,* Laurel Fulford
Founded 1893. Pop 926; Circ 2,211
Library Holdings: Bk Vols 7,755
Special Collections: Clothing; Old Snapshots
Wireless access
Partic in New Hampshire Automated Information Systems (NHAIS)
Open Tues & Fri 3:30-7:30, Sat 9-11:30, Sun 2-5
Friends of the Library Group

PELHAM

P PELHAM PUBLIC LIBRARY*, 24 Village Green, 03076. SAN 309-9229. Tel: 603-635-7581. FAX: 603-635-6952. E-mail: newpl@comcast.net. Web Site: www.pelhampubliclibrary.org. *Interim Dir,* Carol Roberts; E-mail: croberts@pelhamweb.com; *Ch Serv Librn,* Debra Laffond; E-mail: dlaffond@pelhamweb.com; Staff 5 (MLS 1, Non-MLS 4)
Founded 1892. Pop 12,440; Circ 83,824
Jan 2009-Dec 2009 Income $228,756. Mats Exp $34,840. Sal $194,580 (Prof $46,000)
Library Holdings: Audiobooks 520; DVDs 1,550; Large Print Bks 791; Bk Titles 27,925; Bk Vols 28,879; Per Subs 77
Automation Activity & Vendor Info: (Cataloging) Follett Software; (Circulation) Follett Software; (OPAC) Follett Software
Database Vendor: EBSCOhost, Gale Cengage Learning, LearningExpress, Newsbank, OCLC WorldShare Interlibrary Loan, Overdrive, Inc, ProQuest, Wilson - Wilson Web
Wireless access
Function: Art exhibits, Audiobks via web, Bks on CD, Children's prog, Computers for patron use, Copy machines, Doc delivery serv, Electronic databases & coll, Handicapped accessible, ILL available, Mus passes,

Online cat, OverDrive digital audio bks, Photocopying/Printing, Prog for adults, Prog for children & young adult, Pub access computers, Ref serv available, Story hour, Summer reading prog, Tax forms, Teen prog, Telephone ref, Wheelchair accessible
Open Mon, Wed & Fri 9-5, Tues 9-8, Thurs 1-8, Sat 10-2
Restriction: Non-resident fee
Friends of the Library Group

PEMBROKE

P PEMBROKE TOWN LIBRARY*, 313 Pembroke St, 03275. SAN 309-9237. Tel: 603-485-7851. FAX: 603-485-3351. E-mail: pembrokelibrary@comcast.net. Web Site: home.comcast.net/~pembrokelibrary. *Dir,* Stosse Cynthia; *Asst Dir,* Heather Tiddes; *Ch,* Marie Mehegan; Staff 3 (Non-MLS 3)
Pop 6,724; Circ 23,000
Jan 2005-Dec 2005 Income $136,465. Mats Exp $17,000
Library Holdings: Bk Vols 21,000; Per Subs 78
Automation Activity & Vendor Info: (Circulation) Follett Software
Function: Handicapped accessible, ILL available, Photocopying/Printing, Prog for adults, Prog for children & young adult, Summer reading prog
Open Mon 2-6, Tues & Thurs 10-6, Wed 10-7, Fri 12-4, Sat 10-2
Friends of the Library Group

PETERBOROUGH

S MARIPOSA MUSEUM LIBRARY*, 26 Main St, 03458. Tel: 603-924-4555. FAX: 603-924-3212. E-mail: info@mariposamuseum.org. Web Site: www.mariposamuseum.org. *Dir,* Karla Hostetler; *Adminr,* Mose Olenik
Founded 2002
Library Holdings: Bk Vols 5,000
Restriction: Open by appt only, Open to pub for ref only

S MONADNOCK CENTER FOR HISTORY & CULTURE AT PETERBOROUGH HISTORICAL SOCIETY, Morison Library & Archives, (Formerly Peterborough Historical Society Library), 19 Grove St, 03458-1422. (Mail add: PO Box 58, 03458-0058), SAN 328-1442. Tel: 603-924-3235. FAX: 603-924-3200. E-mail: info@MonadnockCenter.org. Web Site: www.MonadnockCenter.org. *Exec Dir,* Michelle M Stahl; Staff 2 (Non-MLS 2)
Founded 1902
Library Holdings: Bk Vols 800
Special Collections: Mills Records Coll (1796-1920); Peterborough 1796-1873 (Dr Albert Smith Coll); letters; Peterborough Photograph Coll (1860-present)
Subject Interests: Genealogy, Local hist
Wireless access

M MONADNOCK COMMUNITY HOSPITAL*, Thomas Eckfeldt Memorial Medical Library, 452 Old Street Rd, 03458. SAN 323-6277. Tel: 603-924-7191, Ext 1100. Web Site: www.monadnockcommunityhospital.org. *Librn,* Jean Slepian; Staff 1 (MLS 1)
Founded 1970
Library Holdings: Bk Titles 200; Per Subs 35

P PETERBOROUGH TOWN LIBRARY*, Two Concord St, 03458. SAN 309-9245. Tel: 603-924-8040. FAX: 603-924-8041. E-mail: library@townofpeterborough.us. Web Site: www.townofpeterborough.com. *Dir,* Corinne Chronopoulos; E-mail: cchronopoulos@townofpeterborough.us; *Asst Dir, Tech Librn,* Linda Tiernan Kepner; *Ch,* Lisa Bearce; *ILL, Ref Librn,* Brian Hackert; Staff 7 (MLS 4, Non-MLS 3)
Founded 1833. Pop 5,883; Circ 93,073
Library Holdings: Large Print Bks 738; Bk Vols 44,030; Per Subs 172
Special Collections: Town Histories (McGilvray Coll). State Document Depository
Subject Interests: Local hist, Original art photog, State hist, Town hist
Automation Activity & Vendor Info: (Cataloging) EOS International; (Circulation) EOS International; (OPAC) EOS International
Publications: History of the First Free Tax-Supported Library in the World-Peterborough
Partic in OCLC Online Computer Library Center, Inc
Open Mon, Wed & Fri 10-6, Tues & Thurs 10-8, Sat 10-4, Sun (Winter) 12-2
Friends of the Library Group

PIERMONT

P PIERMONT PUBLIC LIBRARY*, 130 Rte 10, 03779. (Mail add: PO Box 6, 03779-0006), SAN 309-9253. Tel: 603-272-4967. FAX: 603-272-4947. E-mail: librarian@piermontlibrary.com. *Librn,* Margaret Ladd; *ILL Librn,* Jim Meddaugh
Pop 709; Circ 12,016
Library Holdings: AV Mats 928; Bk Vols 14,039; Per Subs 16
Wireless access
Mem of Ramapo Catskill Library System
Open Mon-Thurs 3-7, Sun 1-3

PIKE

P PIKE LIBRARY*, 1585 Mount Moosilauke Hwy, 03780-5677. (Mail add: PO Box 268, 03780-0268), SAN 309-8397. Tel: 603-989-9847. *Librn,* Melissa Graves; E-mail: dolly5999@aol.com
Circ 3,000
Jan 2010-Dec 2010 Income $6,300. Mats Exp $5,100. Sal $1,200
Library Holdings: Audiobooks 50; DVDs 100; Bk Vols 5,291; Videos 200
Wireless access
Open Mon 6-8, Wed 2:30-5:30, Sat 10-12

PITTSBURG

P BREMER POND MEMORIAL LIBRARY*, One Main St, 03592. (Mail add: PO Box 98, 03592-0098), SAN 309-9261. Tel: 603-538-7032. *Librn,* Bill Stebbins; *Asst Librn,* Casey Sullivan
Pop 1,000; Circ 1,300
Library Holdings: Bk Vols 20,000; Per Subs 15
Open Mon-Fri 8-3, Wed (July & Aug) 6pm-8pm, Sat 9-1

PITTSFIELD

P JOSIAH CARPENTER LIBRARY*, 41 Main St, 03263. SAN 309-927X. Tel: 603-435-8406. E-mail: carplib@metrocast.net. Web Site: library.pittsfield-nh.com. *Asst Librn,* Millie Becker; *Asst Librn,* Carol Grainger; *Asst Librn,* Eleanor Joyce
Founded 1901. Pop 4,400
Subject Interests: Town hist
Automation Activity & Vendor Info: (Cataloging) Book Systems; (Circulation) Book Systems; (OPAC) Book Systems
Database Vendor: Baker & Taylor, EBSCOhost
Wireless access
Open Mon-Thurs 2:30-7, Fri & Sat 10-1
Friends of the Library Group

PLAINFIELD

P PHILIP READ MEMORIAL LIBRARY*, 1088 Rte 12A, 03781. SAN 309-9288. Tel: 603-675-6866. E-mail: director@plainfieldnhlibrary.org. Web Site: www.plainfieldnhlibrary.org. *Dir,* Nancy Norwalk; Staff 1 (Non-MLS 1)
Founded 1920. Pop 2,450; Circ 13,622
Jan 2010-Dec 2010 Income $63,627, City $59,608, Locally Generated Income $819, Other $3,200. Mats Exp $8,690, Books $7,517, AV Mat $1,173. Sal $32,274
Library Holdings: Audiobooks 1,103; AV Mats 1,791; Bks on Deafness & Sign Lang 10; Braille Volumes 26; Bk Titles 27,179; Per Subs 95
Special Collections: Local Author Book & Magazine Coll. Oral History
Subject Interests: Local author coll, Local hist, Oral hist tapes
Wireless access
Publications: Newsletter
Partic in Librarians of the Upper Valley Coop
Special Services for the Blind - Braille bks
Open Mon 1-9, Wed 10-9, Fri 1-5, Sat 9-12
Friends of the Library Group

PLAISTOW

P PLAISTOW PUBLIC LIBRARY*, 85 Main St, 03865. SAN 309-9296. Tel: 603-382-6011. FAX: 603-382-0202. E-mail: plaistowlibrary@comcast.net. Web Site: plaistowlibrary.com. *Dir,* Laurie Houlihan; *Ch,* Laura Magnusson; *ILL Librn,* Marjorie Knowles; *Tech Serv Librn,* Judith Meunier; Staff 9 (MLS 1, Non-MLS 8)
Founded 1897. Pop 7,800
Jan 2007-Dec 2007 Income $430,472, City $425,086, Locally Generated Income $5,386. Mats Exp $50,947. Sal $263,073
Library Holdings: Audiobooks 1,253; CDs 252; Large Print Bks 424; Bk Titles 42,659; Per Subs 71; Videos 1,400
Automation Activity & Vendor Info: (Cataloging) Follett Software; (Circulation) Follett Software; (OPAC) Follett Software
Database Vendor: EBSCOhost, Electric Library, Grolier Online, Wilson - Wilson Web
Wireless access
Open Mon-Thurs 9-7:30, Fri 9-5, Sat 9-1
Friends of the Library Group

PLYMOUTH

P BRIDGEWATER TOWN LIBRARY*, River Road Library, 955 River Rd, 03264. Tel: 603-968-7911. FAX: 603-968-3506. *Dir,* Marilyn Raymond
Pop 1,029

Library Holdings: Bk Vols 2,575
Open Tues & Wed 6-8:30

P PEASE PUBLIC LIBRARY*, One Russell St, 03264-1414. SAN 309-930X. Tel: 603-536-2616. FAX: 603-536-2369. Web Site: www.peasepubliclibrary.org/pease. *Dir,* Rebekka Mateyk; E-mail: rmateyk@peasepubliclibrary.org; *ILL Librn,* Patricia Hanscomb; *Tech Serv Librn,* Tom Merkl; *Cat/Circ,* Deborah Perloff; Staff 6 (MLS 1, Non-MLS 5)
Founded 1874. Pop 5,800; Circ 73,000
Library Holdings: Bk Vols 25,963; Per Subs 88; Talking Bks 932
Special Collections: History-Genealogy (Eva A Speare Coll)
Subject Interests: Children's lit
Automation Activity & Vendor Info: (Cataloging) Follett Software; (Circulation) Follett Software
Wireless access
Function: Adult literacy prog, Homebound delivery serv, ILL available, Photocopying/Printing, Prog for children & young adult, Ref serv available, Summer reading prog, Telephone ref, Wheelchair accessible
Partic in Statewide Libr Network
Open Mon, Tues & Wed 10-8, Thurs & Fri 10-5, Sat 10-2
Friends of the Library Group

C PLYMOUTH STATE UNIVERSITY*, Herbert H Lamson Library, 17 High St, 03264-1595. SAN 309-9318. Tel: 603-535-2258. FAX: 603-535-2445. Web Site: www.plymouth.edu/library. *Dean, Libr & Acad Support,* David Berona; Staff 8 (MLS 8)
Founded 1871. Enrl 4,300; Fac 182; Highest Degree: Doctorate
Library Holdings: Bk Vols 350,000; Per Subs 1,100
Special Collections: Brown Company Coll; McGoldrick Coll; Robert Frost Coll. State Document Depository
Automation Activity & Vendor Info: (Acquisitions) Innovative Interfaces, Inc; (Cataloging) Innovative Interfaces, Inc; (Circulation) Innovative Interfaces, Inc; (Course Reserve) Innovative Interfaces, Inc; (ILL) Infotrieve; (OPAC) Innovative Interfaces, Inc; (Serials) Innovative Interfaces, Inc
Database Vendor: OCLC FirstSearch
Wireless access
Function: Art exhibits, Copy machines, Doc delivery serv, Electronic databases & coll, ILL available
Publications: BI Publications; Bibliographies; CAI; Guide to Information Resources; Handouts; Users' Guides
Partic in Lyrasis; NHCUC; OCLC Online Computer Library Center, Inc
Open Mon-Thurs 7:30pm-11:30pm, Fri 7:30am-8pm, Sat 8:30-6, Sun 1-11:30

PORTSMOUTH

J GREAT BAY COMMUNITY COLLEGE LIBRARY, 320 Corporate Dr, 03801. SAN 309-9326. Tel: 603-427-7618. FAX: 603-559-1524. E-mail: reference@ccsnh.edu. Web Site: www.greatbay.edu/library. *Chief Libr Officer,* Rebecca Clerkin; E-mail: rclerkin@ccsnh.edu; *Electronic Res Librn,* Fran Keenan; E-mail: fkeenan@ccsnh.edu; Staff 3 (MLS 2, Non-MLS 1)
Founded 1970. Enrl 1,300; Fac 35
Library Holdings: Bk Vols 10,400; Per Subs 128
Automation Activity & Vendor Info: (Cataloging) TLC (The Library Corporation); (Circulation) TLC (The Library Corporation); (OPAC) TLC (The Library Corporation)
Database Vendor: EBSCOhost, JSTOR, ProQuest, ScienceDirect
Publications: Handbook
Open Mon-Thurs 8-7, Fri 8-4

S PORTSMOUTH ATHENAEUM*, Library-Museum-Gallery, Six-Seven Market Sq, 03821. SAN 320-2038. Tel: 603-431-2538. FAX: 603-431-7180. E-mail: athenaeum@gwi.net. Web Site: portsmouthathenaeum.org. *Dir,* Thomas Hardiman; *Librn,* Robin Silva; *Archivist,* Susan Kindstedt; Staff 4 (MLS 2, Non-MLS 2)
Founded 1817
Library Holdings: Bk Titles 40,000; Per Subs 18
Special Collections: church, institutional, business & family papers; Isles of Shoals Coll; Langdon Papers Coll; Manuscripts; NH Gazette Coll; NNH Fire & Marine Insurance Company Papers, docs; Wendell Family Papers, photographs; Wentworth-by-the Sea Hotel Coll
Subject Interests: Genealogy, Maine, Marine, Naval, New England, NH hist, Ships

P PORTSMOUTH PUBLIC LIBRARY*, 175 Parrott Ave, 03801-4452. Tel: 603-427-1540. Circulation Tel: 603-766-1700. Interlibrary Loan Service Tel: 603-766-1724. Reference Tel: 603-766-1720. FAX: 603-433-0981. E-mail: info@cityofportsmouth.com. Web Site: www.cityofportsmouth.com/library. *Dir,* Steve Butzel; E-mail: skbutzel@cityofportsmouth.com; *Ch,* Susan Laun; Tel: 603-766-1742, E-mail: sdlaun@cityofportsmouth.com; *ILL Librn,* Kate Giordano; E-mail: clgiordano@cityofportsmouth.com; *Pub Serv Librn,* Laura Horwood-Benton; *Ref Librn,* Michael Huxtable; Tel: 603-766-1722, E-mail: mjhuxtable@cityofportsmouth.com; *Tech Serv Librn,* Sarah Cornell; Staff 25 (MLS 9, Non-MLS 16)
Founded 1881. Pop 21,800; Circ 488,630
Jul 2009-Jun 2010 Income $266,008, City $146,365, Locally Generated Income $93,782, Other $25,861. Sal $932,333
Library Holdings: AV Mats 17,181; Electronic Media & Resources 58; Bk Vols 127,818; Per Subs 422
Special Collections: Municipal Document Depository; State Document Depository
Subject Interests: Local hist
Automation Activity & Vendor Info: (Acquisitions) Innovative Interfaces, Inc; (Cataloging) Innovative Interfaces, Inc; (Circulation) Innovative Interfaces, Inc, (OPAC) Innovative Interfaces, Inc; (Serials) Innovative Interfaces, Inc
Wireless access
Partic in Lyrasis; New Hampshire Automated Information Systems (NHAIS); New Hampshire Urban Pub Libr Consortium
Special Services for the Blind - ZoomText magnification & reading software
Open Mon-Thurs 9-9, Fri 9-5:30, Sat 9- 5, Sun (Sept-May) 1-5
Friends of the Library Group

M PORTSMOUTH REGIONAL HOSPITAL*, Health Science Library, 333 Borthwick Ave, 03801. SAN 377-9394. Tel: 603-433-4094. FAX: 603-433-5144. *Librn,* Eleanor Pickens; Staff 1 (MLS 1)
Founded 1987
Library Holdings: Bk Titles 80; Per Subs 140
Database Vendor: EBSCOhost
Partic in Basic Health Sciences Library Network; CinaHL; Health Sciences Libraries of New Hampshire & Vermont; North Atlantic Health Sciences Libraries, Inc
Open Mon-Fri 8-4:30

S STRAWBERY BANKE, INC*, Thayer Cumings Library & Archives, 454 Court St, 03802-4603. (Mail add: PO Box 300, 03802 0300), SAN 309-9342. Tel: 603-422-7524. FAX: 603-422-7527, 603-433-1115. Web Site: www.strawberybanke.org. *Curator,* Elizabeth Farish; Tel: 603-422-7526; Staff 1 (Non-MLS 1)
Founded 1970
Library Holdings: Bk Titles 7,000; Bk Vols 8,000; Per Subs 20
Special Collections: Manuscript Coll; Papers of Ichabod & Sarah Parker Rice Goodwin, Governor John Langdon & the Chase Family; Portsmouth Photo Coll, 1870-1970
Subject Interests: Archaeology, Archit, Art hist, Decorative art, Hort, Local hist, Presv
Publications: A Guide to the Cumings Library & Archives; Official Strawbery Banke Guide Book
Restriction: Open by appt only

S JAMES E WHALLEY MUSEUM & LIBRARY*, 351 Middle St, 03801. SAN 328-0217. Tel: 603-436-3712. Web Site: www.whalleymuseum.org. *Pres,* Mark E Furber
Founded 1962
Library Holdings: Bk Titles 3,500; Bk Vols 3,600, Per Subs 12

RANDOLPH

P RANDOLPH PUBLIC LIBRARY*, 130 Durand Rd, 03593. Tel: 603-466-5408. E-mail: rpl@ne.rr.com. *Dir,* Amy Cyr
Library Holdings: Bk Vols 6,500; Talking Bks 100; Videos 92
Wireless access
Open Mon & Sat 10-Noon, Wed & Thurs 3-8
Friends of the Library Group

RAYMOND

P DUDLEY-TUCKER LIBRARY*, Six Epping St, 03077. (Mail add: PO Box 909, 03077-0909), SAN 309-9350. Tel: 603-895-2633. FAX: 603-895-0904. E-mail: dudleytucker@comcast.net. Web Site: www.raymondnh.gov. *Dir,* Linda Hoelzel; *Asst Dir,* Patricia Currier; *Ch,* Catherine Fancher; *Ch,* Elizabeth Wynne
Founded 1894. Pop 10,000; Circ 52,000
Library Holdings: Bk Vols 26,500; Per Subs 100
Automation Activity & Vendor Info: (Cataloging) Follett Software; (Circulation) Follett Software; (OPAC) Follett Software
Database Vendor: EBSCOhost
Wireless access
Partic in Merri-Hill-Rock Library Cooperative
Open Mon & Thurs 1-8:30, Tues 10-8:30, Wed & Fri 10-5, Sat (Sept-May) 10-1
Friends of the Library Group

RICHMOND

P RICHMOND PUBLIC LIBRARY*, 19 Winchester Rd, 03470. SAN 309-9369. Tel: 603-239-6164. FAX: 603-239-7332. E-mail: richmondlibrary@wivalley.net. *Librn,* Wendy O'Brien; *Asst Librn,* Marie Juhlin
Pop 1,146; Circ 5,352
Jan 2005-Dec 2005. Mats Exp $3,500
Library Holdings: Bk Vols 15,000; Per Subs 22
Automation Activity & Vendor Info: (Cataloging) Follett Software; (Circulation) Follett Software
Open Tues 4:30-8, Wed 9-12, Thurs 4:30-7, Sat 10-2
Friends of the Library Group

RINDGE

C FRANKLIN PIERCE UNIVERSITY LIBRARY*, Frank S DiPietro Library, 40 University Dr, 03461-3114. SAN 309-9377. Tel: 603-899-4140. Reference Tel: 603-899-1149. FAX: 603-899-4375. E-mail: library@franklinpierce.edu. Web Site: library.franklinpierce.edu. *Dir, Libr Serv,* Carissa DeLizio; E-mail: delizioc@franklinpierce.edu; *Ref & Instruction Librn,* Position Currently Open; *Ref Librn,* Gladys Nielsen; *Circ Mgr,* Jill Wixom; Staff 8 (MLS 5, Non-MLS 3)
Founded 1962. Enrl 2,347; Fac 78; Highest Degree: Doctorate
Library Holdings: Bk Titles 130,000
Subject Interests: Ecology, Graphic arts, Mass communications
Automation Activity & Vendor Info: (Acquisitions) Ex Libris Group; (Cataloging) Ex Libris Group; (Circulation) Ex Libris Group; (Course Reserve) Ex Libris Group; (Media Booking) Ex Libris Group; (OPAC) Ex Libris Group; (Serials) Ex Libris Group
Database Vendor: EBSCOhost
Partic in Lyrasis; New Hampshire College & University Council
Open Sun Noon-11
Friends of the Library Group

P INGALLS MEMORIAL LIBRARY, 203 Main St, 03461. (Mail add: PO Box 224, 03461-0224), SAN 309-9385. Tel: 603-899-3303. FAX: 603-899-5797. E-mail: info@ingallslibrary.com. *Dir,* Diane Gardenour; E-mail: diane@ingallslibrary.com; *Asst Dir, ILL Librn,* Debbie Qualey; *Ch,* Georgianna Connor; *Circ Librn,* Sarah Faulkner
Founded 1894. Pop 6,130; Circ 26,485
Library Holdings: Bk Vols 29,764; Per Subs 70
Subject Interests: Humanities, NH
Automation Activity & Vendor Info: (Cataloging) ByWater Solutions; (Circulation) ByWater Solutions; (OPAC) ByWater Solutions; (Serials) ByWater Solutions
Database Vendor: ByWater Solutions
Wireless access
Partic in Nubanusit Library Cooperative
Open Mon, Wed & Fri 10-5, Tues & Thurs 2-8, Sat 9-Noon
Friends of the Library Group

ROCHESTER

M FRISBIE MEMORIAL HOSPITAL*, Medical Library, 11 Whitehall Rd, 03867. SAN 377-953X. Tel: 603-335-8419. FAX: 603-330-8946. Web Site: www.frisbiehospital.com. *Librn,* Margaret Robak
Library Holdings: Bk Titles 200; Per Subs 50
Partic in Health Sciences Libraries of New Hampshire & Vermont; Medical Library Association (MLA)
Restriction: Staff use only

P ROCHESTER PUBLIC LIBRARY*, 65 S Main St, 03867-2707. SAN 309-9407. Tel: 603-332-1428. FAX: 603-335-7582. Web Site: www.rpl.lib.nh.us. *Libr Dir,* Brian Sylvester; E-mail: brian.sylvester@rpl.lib.nh.us; *Ch Serv,* Marie Kelly; *Circ Serv,* Peggy Trout; *ILL, YA Serv,* Donna Hynes; *Ref Serv,* Elizabeth Nerbonne; *Tech Serv,* Dorinda Howard; Staff 7 (MLS 3, Non-MLS 4)
Founded 1893. Pop 29,752; Circ 276,781
Jul 2010-Jun 2011 Income $1,049,454, City $1,010,141, Locally Generated Income $33,234, Other $6,079. Sal $628,712
Special Collections: Rochester Courier
Automation Activity & Vendor Info: (Acquisitions) Innovative Interfaces, Inc; (Cataloging) OCLC Online; (Circulation) Innovative Interfaces, Inc; (ILL) OCLC Online; (OPAC) Innovative Interfaces, Inc; (Serials) Innovative Interfaces, Inc
Database Vendor: EBSCOhost
Wireless access
Partic in Urban Pub Libr Consortium
Open Mon-Thurs 9-8:30, Fri 9-5, Sat 9-4
Friends of the Library Group

ROLLINSFORD

P ROLLINSFORD PUBLIC LIBRARY*, Three Front St, Ste B-2, 03869. (Mail add: PO Box 70, 03869). Tel: 603-516-2665. E-mail: rollinsfordlibrary@comcast.net. Web Site: www.rollinsfordlibrary.org. *Dir,* Tamara Niedzolkowski
Library Holdings: CDs 200; DVDs 150; Bk Vols 10,000; Per Subs 28; Talking Bks 150
Automation Activity & Vendor Info: (Cataloging) LibraryWorld, Inc; (Circulation) LibraryWorld, Inc; (OPAC) LibraryWorld, Inc
Wireless access
Open Mon 9-7, Tues 12-8, Wed & Thurs 12-5, Sun 1-5
Friends of the Library Group

RUMNEY

P BYRON G MERRILL LIBRARY*, Ten Buffalo Rd, 03266. SAN 309-9415. Tel: 603-786-9520. E-mail: rumneylibrary@roadrunner.com. Web Site: www.rumneynh.org. *Dir,* Susan Turbyne; *Librn,* Rachel Anderson; Staff 2 (Non-MLS 2)
Founded 1906. Pop 1,466; Circ 9,416
Jan 2006-Dec 2006 Income $27,075. Mats Exp $3,994, Books $3,925, Per/Ser (Incl. Access Fees) $69. Sal Prof $15,777
Library Holdings: DVDs 458; Bk Vols 20,000; Per Subs 15
Wireless access
Open Wed 2-8, Thurs 10-12 & 2-5, Sat 10-12

RYE

P RYE PUBLIC LIBRARY*, 581 Washington Rd, 03870. SAN 309-9423. Tel: 603-964-8401. FAX: 603-964-7065. Web Site: www.ryepubliclibrary.org. *Dir,* Andrew Richmond; E-mail: arichmond@ryepubliclibrary.org; *Assoc Dir,* Tricia Quinn; E-mail: tquinn@ryepubliclibrary.org; *Head, Youth Serv,* Lisa Houde; *Ad,* Juliette Doherty; *Ad,* Shawna Healy; *Ad,* Gwen Bailey Putnam; *ILL Librn,* Pamela Woods; *Youth Serv,* Margaret Hutchins; *Youth Serv,* Brenda Nolette; Staff 9 (MLS 1, Non-MLS 8)
Founded 1911. Pop 5,182; Circ 80,000
Jan 2007-Dec 2007 Income $482,736. Mats Exp $59,490. Sal $265,750
Library Holdings: Bk Titles 43,000; Bk Vols 48,000; Per Subs 125
Subject Interests: Rye hist
Automation Activity & Vendor Info: (Cataloging) TLC (The Library Corporation); (Circulation) TLC (The Library Corporation); (OPAC) TLC (The Library Corporation)
Database Vendor: OCLC FirstSearch
Publications: Off the Shelf (Newsletter)
Special Services for the Blind - Bks on cassette
Open Mon, Wed & Fri 9-5, Tues & Thurs 9-8, Sat 9-3
Friends of the Library Group

SALEM

P KELLEY LIBRARY*, 234 Main St, 03079-3190. SAN 309-944X. Tel: 603-898-7064. FAX: 603-898-8583. E-mail: kelleylb@kelleylibrary.org. Web Site: www.kelleylibrary.org. *Dir,* Alison Baker; E-mail: abaker@kelleylibrary.org; *Asst Dir,* Michele Garneau; E-mail: mgarneau@kelleylibrary.org; *Adult Serv,* Natalie Ducharme; E-mail: nducharme@kelleylibrary.org; *Cat,* Vicki Lukas; E-mail: vlukas@kelleylibrary.org; *Ch Serv,* Coralyn Chiknas; E-mail: cchiknas@kelleylibrary.org; *Ref,* Paul Giblin; E-mail: pgiblin@kelleylibrary.org; Staff 22 (MLS 5, Non-MLS 17)
Founded 1893. Pop 29,115; Circ 290,786
Jan 2008-Dec 2008 Income $1,342,529. Mats Exp $155,084. Sal $70,000
Library Holdings: AV Mats 14,519; Large Print Bks 1,489; Bk Titles 116,949; Per Subs 312
Special Collections: Municipal Document Depository; Oral History; State Document Depository
Automation Activity & Vendor Info: (Acquisitions) Innovative Interfaces, Inc; (Cataloging) Innovative Interfaces, Inc; (Circulation) Innovative Interfaces, Inc; (ILL) Innovative Interfaces, Inc; (OPAC) Innovative Interfaces, Inc; (Serials) Innovative Interfaces, Inc
Wireless access
Partic in GMILCS, Inc
Special Services for the Blind - Bks on cassette; Bks on CD; Home delivery serv; Large print bks
Open Mon-Tues 9-7, Wed-Fri 9-9, Sat 9-2

SALISBURY

P SALISBURY FREE LIBRARY*, 641 Old Turnpike Rd, 03268. (Mail add: PO Box 284, 03268-0284), SAN 309-9458. Tel: 603-648-2278. FAX: 603-648-2278. E-mail: salisburyfreelibrary@tds.net. *Libr Dir,* Melinda Flater; Staff 1 (Non-MLS 1)
Pop 1,200; Circ 5,200
Library Holdings: AV Mats 900; Large Print Bks 65; Bk Titles 7,200
Database Vendor: EBSCO Information Services

Wireless access
Function: Handicapped accessible, ILL available, Photocopying/Printing, Prog for children & young adult, Ref serv available, Summer reading prog, Telephone ref, Wheelchair accessible
Special Services for the Blind - Magnifiers
Open Tues 11-7, Thurs 9-4, Sat 9-1
Friends of the Library Group

SANBORNTON

P SANBORNTON PUBLIC LIBRARY*, 27 Meetinghouse Hill Rd, 03269. (Mail add: PO Box 88, 03269-0088), SAN 309-9466. Tel: 603-286-8288. FAX: 603-286-9544. E-mail: spl@metrocast.net. Web Site: splnh.com. *Dir,* Marcia Haigh; *Tech Serv Librn,* Martha Bodwell; Staff 2.4 (MLS 1, Non-MLS 1.4)
Founded 1903. Pop 3,000; Circ 16,500
Library Holdings: Bks on Deafness & Sign Lang 10; Bk Vols 16,000; Per Subs 30
Subject Interests: NH
Database Vendor: ProQuest
Function: Adult bk club, Archival coll, Audiobks via web, AV serv, Bk club(s), Bks on cassette, Bks on CD, Children's prog, Computer training, Computers for patron use, e-mail serv, Exhibits, Free DVD rentals, Genealogy discussion group, Handicapped accessible, Homebound delivery serv, ILL available, Mus passes, Music CDs, Online cat, Online ref, Online searches, OverDrive digital audio bks, Photocopying/Printing, Prog for adults, Prog for children & young adult, Pub access computers, Ref & res, Ref serv available, Ref serv in person, Scanner, Spoken cassettes & CDs, Spoken cassettes & DVDs, Story hour, Summer reading prog, Telephone ref, VHS videos, Video lending libr, Visual arts prog, Web-catalog, Wheelchair accessible
Open Tues & Fri 9-5, Wed & Thurs 1-8, Sat 9-2

SANBORNVILLE

P GAFNEY LIBRARY, INC*, 14 High St, 03872. (Mail add: PO Box 517, 03872-0517), SAN 309-975X. Tel: 603-522-3401. FAX: 603-522-7123. E mail: gafney@worldpath.net. Web Site: www.gafneylibrary.org. *Dir,* Beryl Donovan; E-mail: gafney@worldpath.net; *Ch,* Diane Cassidy; Tel: 603-522-9735; Staff 4 (Non-MLS 4)
Founded 1925. Pop 6,000; Circ 15,520
Jan 2010-Dec 2010 Income $140,300. Mats Exp $11,000. Sal $75,000
Library Holdings: Bks on Deafness & Sign Lang 12; CDs 104; DVDs 507; High Interest/Low Vocabulary Bk Vols 35; Large Print Bks 243; Bk Titles 12,002; Per Subs 12; Talking Bks 364; Videos 414
Automation Activity & Vendor Info: (Circulation) Gateway
Database Vendor: Biblionix/Apollo, EBSCOhost
Wireless access
Function: Adult literacy prog, Art exhibits, Chess club, Children's prog, Computers for patron use, Copy machines, Electronic databases & coll, Fax serv, Free DVD rentals, ILL available, Mus passes, Music CDs, Notary serv, OverDrive digital audio bks, Photocopying/Printing, Story hour, Summer reading prog, Tax forms
Open Tues & Thurs 1-7:30, Wed & Fri 10-Noon, Sat 9-2
Friends of the Library Group

SANDOWN

P SANDOWN PUBLIC LIBRARY*, 305 Main St, 03873. (Mail add: PO Box 580, 03873-0580), SAN 309-9474. Tel: 603-887-3428. FAX: 603-887-0590. E-mail: sandownlibrary@comcast.net. Web Site: www.sandownlibrary.us/sandown. *Dir,* Kirsten Rundquist Corbett; *Asst Dir,* Cathy Hassard; E-mail: spl.chassard@comcast.net; *Youth Serv Dir,* Jennifer Bryant; *Asst Librn,* Julie Ball; *Circ/ILL Librn,* Susan Kehoe; Staff 10 (MLS 2, Non-MLS 8)
Founded 1892. Pop 6,000; Circ 65,000
Jan 2010-Dec 2010 Income $272,472, City $270,472, Other $2,000. Mats Exp $38,600, Books $28,000, Per/Ser (Incl. Access Fees) $2,100, AV Mat $7,500, Electronic Ref Mat (Incl. Access Fees) $1,000. Sal $164,000
Library Holdings: AV Mats 1,000; Bks on Deafness & Sign Lang 65; DVDs 750; Large Print Bks 200; Bk Titles 29,352; Bk Vols 36,000; Per Subs 67; Talking Bks 850; Videos 1,195
Special Collections: Cake Pans
Automation Activity & Vendor Info: (Circulation) Follett Software; (OPAC) Follett Software; (Serials) Follett Software
Wireless access
Function: Adult bk club, After school storytime, Audiobks via web, Bks on CD, CD-ROM, Chess club, Children's prog, Computer training, Computers for patron use, Copy machines, E-Reserves, Electronic databases & coll, Equip loans & repairs, Handicapped accessible, ILL available, Mus passes, Music CDs, Newsp ref libr, OverDrive digital audio bks, Prog for adults, Prog for children & young adult, Summer reading prog, Tax forms, VHS videos, Video lending libr, Web-catalog, Wheelchair accessible
Partic in Merri-Hill-Rock Library Cooperative
Open Mon-Thurs 9-8, Sat 9-3
Friends of the Library Group

SEABROOK

P SEABROOK LIBRARY*, 25 Liberty Lane, 03874-4506. SAN 309-9490. Tel: 603-474-2044. FAX: 603-474-1835. E-mail: ocean@sealib.org. Web Site: www.sealib.org. *Dir,* Ann Robinson; *Ch,* Lisa Michaud; *Circ/ILL Librn,* K Suzanne Weinreich; *Tech Serv Librn,* Sharon Rafferty; *Ref Serv, YA,* Susan Schatvet; Staff 10 (MLS 5, Non-MLS 5)
Pop 7,000
Open Mon, Wed & Fri 10-8, Tues & Thurs 10-6, Sat 9-1
Friends of the Library Group

SHELBURNE

P SHELBURNE PUBLIC LIBRARY*, 74 Village Rd, 03581-3209. SAN 309-9504. Tel: 603-466-2262. *Dir,* Marlene Marchand; Tel: 603-466-2089, E-mail: marchand@ncia.net; *ILL Librn,* Wendy Mayerson
Pop 385; Circ 562
Library Holdings: AV Mats 129; Bk Vols 3,505; Per Subs 10
Special Collections: Local History Coll
Open Thurs 2:30-4:30, Sat 10-11

SOMERSWORTH

P SOMERSWORTH PUBLIC LIBRARY*, 25 Main St, 03878-3198. SAN 309-9512. Tel: 603-692-4587. FAX: 603-692-9110. E-mail: library@somersworth.com. Web Site: www.somersworth.com. *Libr Dir,* Debora Longo; Staff 2 (MLS 2)
Founded 1899. Pop 11,788
Library Holdings: Bk Titles 51,000; Per Subs 65
Special Collections: Somersworth Historical Coll
Wireless access
Function: Art exhibits, Bk club(s), Bks on cassette, Bks on CD, Children's prog, Computers for patron use, Copy machines, e-mail & chat, Electronic databases & coll, Exhibits, Free DVD rentals, Handicapped accessible, Homebound delivery serv, ILL available, Mail & tel request accepted, Mus passes, OverDrive digital audio bks, Photocopying/Printing, Pub access computers, Ref & res, Ref serv in person, Story hour, Summer reading prog, Tax forms, Telephone ref, VHS videos
Open Tues-Thurs 11-7, Fri & Sat 9-5, Sat (Summer) 9-1
Restriction: Non-resident fee
Friends of the Library Group

SOUTH HAMPTON

P SOUTH HAMPTON PUBLIC LIBRARY*, 3-1 Hilldale Ave, 03827. SAN 309-9520. Tel: 603-394-7319. FAX: 603-394-7319. E-mail: southhamptonlibrary@comcast.ne. *Librn,* Carole McCarthy
Pop 844; Circ 7,440
Library Holdings: AV Mats 145; Bk Vols 7,333; Per Subs 25; Videos 21
Special Collections: Al Capp Coll; Memorial Coll; New Hampshire History
Automation Activity & Vendor Info: (Circulation) Follett Software
Open Mon 7pm-9pm, Wed & Thurs 10-5, Fri 2-6
Friends of the Library Group

SPRINGFIELD

P LIBBIE A CASS MEMORIAL LIBRARY*, 757 Main St, 03284. (Mail add: PO Box 89, 03284-0089), SAN 309-9539. Tel: 603-763-4381. FAX: 603-763-4381. E-mail: libbycass@gmail.com. *Librn,* Steve Klein
Founded 1893. Pop 970; Circ 4,300
Library Holdings: DVDs 150; Large Print Bks 120; Bk Vols 17,000; Per Subs 12; Talking Bks 500; Videos 652
Partic in Librarians of the Upper Valley Coop
Open Mon, Tues & Thurs 11-12 & 3-7, Wed & Fri 11-12 & 3-5, Sat 9-11
Friends of the Library Group

STODDARD

P DAVIS PUBLIC LIBRARY*, 1391 Rte 123 N, 03464. (Mail add: PO Box 749, 03464-0749), SAN 309-9571. Tel: 603-446-6251. E-mail: davispubliclibrary@gmail.com. *Dir,* Lauren Rettig; Staff 1 (Non-MLS 1)
Pop 1,000; Circ 3,000
Jul 2005-Jun 2006 Income $4,000, City $3,500, Locally Generated Income $500. Mats Exp $1,850, Books $1,500, Per/Ser (Incl. Access Fees) $50, AV Mat $100, Electronic Ref Mat (Incl. Access Fees) $200. Sal $3,000
Library Holdings: Large Print Bks 100; Bk Vols 5,500; Talking Bks 50; Videos 300
Function: Adult bk club, After school storytime, Family literacy, Handicapped accessible, ILL available, Preschool outreach, Prog for children & young adult, Serves mentally handicapped consumers, Spoken

cassettes & CDs, Spoken cassettes & DVDs, Summer reading prog, Tax forms, VHS videos
Open Mon & Wed 4-6, Tues 10-2, Sat 10-12

STRATHAM

P WIGGIN MEMORIAL LIBRARY*, Ten Bunker Hill Ave, 03885. SAN 309-9601. Tel: 603-772-4346. E-mail: wigginml@comcast.net. Web Site: library.strathamnh.gov. *Dir,* Lesley Kimball; E-mail: director@wigginml.org; *Asst Dir,* Patricia Ryden; E-mail: tricia@wigginml.org; *Ch, Coll Develop & Outreach,* Phyllis Danko; E-mail: phyllisd@wigginml.org; *Ch, Prog,* Jan Streelman; E-mail: missjan@wigginml.org; *ILL Librn,* Marcia MacCallum; E-mail: ill@wigginml.org
Founded 1891. Pop 7,200; Circ 90,000
Library Holdings: Bk Vols 50,000
Subject Interests: NH
Automation Activity & Vendor Info: (Circulation) ByWater Solutions
Database Vendor: Baker & Taylor, Brodart, EBSCOhost, LearningExpress, Library Ideas, LLC, World Book Online
Wireless access
Function: Adult bk club, Audio & video playback equip for onsite use, Audiobks via web, Bi-weekly Writer's Group, Bk club(s), Bks on CD, Children's prog, Computer training, Computers for patron use, Copy machines, E-Reserves, Electronic databases & coll, Free DVD rentals, Handicapped accessible, Homebound delivery serv, ILL available, Mail & tel request accepted, Mus passes, Music CDs, Online cat, Online searches, Outreach serv, OverDrive digital audio bks, Photocopying/Printing, Preschool outreach, Printer for laptops & handheld devices, Prog for adults, Prog for children & young adult, Pub access computers, Ref serv available, Story hour, Summer reading prog, Tax forms, Teen prog, Telephone ref, VHS videos, Web-catalog, Wheelchair accessible
Open Mon-Thurs 9:30-7, Fri 9:30-6, Sat 9:30-3
Friends of the Library Group

SUGAR HILL

P RICHARDSON MEMORIAL LIBRARY*, 1411 Main St, 03585. (Mail add: PO Box 622, 03585-0622), SAN 309-961X. Tel: 603-823-7001. E-mail: library@sugarhillnh.org. *Dir,* Judith Weisenberger
Pop 639; Circ 3,548
Library Holdings: AV Mats 144; Bk Vols 6,664; Per Subs 11; Videos 68
Open Mon 4-6, Tues 1-4, Thurs 10-1, Sat 9-12

SULLIVAN

P SULLIVAN PUBLIC LIBRARY*, 436 Centre St, 03445. (Mail add: PO Box 92, 03445-0092), SAN 376-7698. Tel: 603-847-3458. FAX: 603-847-9154 (Town Hall). E-mail: spl@ci.sullivan.nh.us, sullivanpubliclibrary@gmail.com. Web Site: www.ci.sullivan.nh.us/content/library/library. *Dir,* Rebecca Cole; E-mail: rcole@sullivan.lib.in.us; Staff 1 (Non-MLS 1)
Founded 1894. Pop 677
Jan 2012-Dec 2012 Income $29,273, City $26,890, Other $2,263. Mats Exp $2,421, Books $1,709, Per/Ser (Incl. Access Fees) $124, Other Print Mats $131, Electronic Ref Mat (Incl. Access Fees) $500. Sal $17,880
Library Holdings: Audiobooks 189; CDs 30; DVDs 152; Bk Vols 6,955; Per Subs 26; Videos 634
Special Collections: Local History Coll
Wireless access
Function: Adult bk club, Archival coll, Bks on cassette, Bks on CD, Children's prog, Computers for patron use, Copy machines, Electronic databases & coll, Free DVD rentals, Handicapped accessible, ILL available, Music CDs, Notary serv, OverDrive digital audio bks, Photocopying/Printing, Prog for adults, Prog for children & young adult, Pub access computers, Ref serv in person, Scanner, Serves mentally handicapped consumers, Spoken cassettes & CDs, Summer reading prog, VHS videos, Wheelchair accessible
Open Mon 1-6, Wed 6-8, Thurs 9-12 & 6-8, Sat 9-12
Friends of the Library Group

SUNAPEE

P ABBOTT LIBRARY*, 542 Rte 11, 03782. (Mail add: PO Box 314, 03782-0314), SAN 309-9636. Tel: 603-763-5513. FAX: 603-763-8765. E-mail: info@abbottlibrary.org. Web Site: www.abbottlibrary.org. *Dir,* Danko Mary; E-mail: director@abbottlibrary.org; *Asst Librn,* Sharon Montambeault; *Ch,* Joyce Martin
Founded 1926. Pop 3,500; Circ 56,000
Library Holdings: Bk Vols 36,000; Per Subs 77
Automation Activity & Vendor Info: (Cataloging) Follett Software; (Circulation) Follett Software; (OPAC) Follett Software
Open Mon & Wed 9-8, Thurs & Fri 9-6, Sat 9-1
Friends of the Library Group

SURRY

P REED FREE LIBRARY*, Eight Village Rd, 03431-8314. SAN 309-9644. Tel: 603-352-1761. E-mail: surrylibrary@webryders.net. *Librn,* Carolyn Locke; *Asst Librn,* Mary Fosher
Pop 662; Circ 2,207
Library Holdings: DVDs 32; Large Print Bks 52; Bk Vols 8,000; Videos 87
Special Collections: Oral History
Open Mon & Thurs 3-8

SUTTON MILLS

P SUTTON FREE LIBRARY*, Five Corporation Hill, 03221. (Mail add: 75 Main St, Bradford, 03221), SAN 309-9652. Tel: 603-927-4927. E-mail: suttonlibrarian@gmail.com. *Dir,* Heidi Thoma
Pop 1,086; Circ 11,369
Library Holdings: Bk Vols 9,207
Open Mon & Sat 1-4, Wed 1-4 & 6:30-8:30, Fri 2-4

SWANZEY

P MOUNT CAESAR UNION LIBRARY*, 628 Old Homestead Hwy, 03446-2312. SAN 309-9660. Tel: 603-357-0456. E-mail: mtcaesar@ne.rr.com. *Librn,* Cadigan Gregory
Founded 1885. Pop 7,000; Circ 18,354
Library Holdings: Audiobooks 520; DVDs 1,681; Bk Titles 21,157; Per Subs 17
Subject Interests: Genealogy, Local hist
Automation Activity & Vendor Info: (Circulation) ComPanion Corp
Wireless access
Publications: Newsletter
Open Mon 10-4, Tues & Thurs 10-5, Wed 2-8, Sat 10-2
Friends of the Library Group

TAMWORTH

P COOK MEMORIAL LIBRARY*, 93 Main St, 03886. SAN 309-9687. Tel: 603-323-8510. FAX: 603-323-2077. E-mail: cooklib@tamworthlibrary.org. Web Site: www.tamworthlibrary.org. *Libr Dir,* Jay Rancourt; E-mail: director@tamworthlibrary.org; *Asst Librn,* Patti Rau; *Ch,* Amy Carter; *Genealogy & Hist Librn,* Christine Clyne; Staff 2.2 (Non-MLS 2.2)
Founded 1895. Pop 2,560; Circ 34,000
Library Holdings: CDs 1,000; DVDs 2,000; Bk Titles 21,000; Per Subs 45
Special Collections: Index Card File on Vital Statistics (1777-1890); Remnants of Tamworth Social Library Coll (26 vols). Oral History
Automation Activity & Vendor Info: (Acquisitions) Baker & Taylor; (Cataloging) Follett Software; (Circulation) Follett Software; (OPAC) Follett Software
Database Vendor: Baker & Taylor, Booklist Online, EBSCO Information Services, OCLC FirstSearch
Wireless access
Function: Archival coll, Art exhibits, Bk club(s), Bks on CD, Children's prog, Computer training, Computers for patron use, Doc delivery serv, E-Reserves, Free DVD rentals, Handicapped accessible, Instruction & testing, Magnifiers for reading, Mus passes, Music CDs, Online cat, Outside serv via phone, mail, e-mail & web, OverDrive digital audio bks, Prog for adults, Prog for children & young adult, Story hour, Summer reading prog
Open Tues & Wed 10-8, Fri 10-5, Sat 10-4
Friends of the Library Group

TEMPLE

P MANSFIELD PUBLIC LIBRARY*, Five Main St, 03084. (Mail add: PO Box 210, 03084-0210), SAN 309-9695. Tel: 603-878-3100. FAX: 603-878-0654. E-mail: mansfieldlibrarynh@comcast.net. *Dir,* Katherine Fedorka; *Asst Dir,* Robin Downes
Founded 1890. Pop 1,300; Circ 8,609
Library Holdings: Bk Vols 14,407; Per Subs 48
Partic in SAILS Library Network
Open Mon & Fri 10-4, Tues & Thurs 3-8, Sat 10:30-1:30

THORNTON

P THORNTON PUBLIC LIBRARY*, 1884 NH Rte 175, 03285. SAN 309-9709. Tel: 603-726-8981. FAX: 603-726-8985. E-mail: info@thorntonpubliclibrary.org. Web Site: www.thorntonpubliclibrary.org. *Dir,* Nina Sargent; E-mail: director@thorntonpubliclibrary.org; *Libr Asst,* Susan Bigl; Staff 2 (Non-MLS 2)
Founded 1899. Pop 2,200; Circ 2,900
Library Holdings: Bk Titles 6,500; Per Subs 14
Automation Activity & Vendor Info: (Circulation) Follett Software
Database Vendor: OCLC FirstSearch, ProQuest
Wireless access

Open Mon & Wed 9-7, Tues, Thurs & Fri 9-4
Friends of the Library Group

TROY

P GAY-KIMBALL LIBRARY, 10 S Main St, 03465. (Mail add: PO Box 837, 03465-0837), SAN 309-9725. Tel: 603-242-7743. FAX: 603-242-7743. E-mail: library@troylibrary.us. Web Site: www.troylibrary.us. *Dir,* Catherine Callegari; Staff 2 (MLS 1, Non-MLS 1)
Founded 1824. Pop 2,137; Circ 19,000
Library Holdings: DVDs 1,200; Bk Vols 23,500; Per Subs 30
Special Collections: New England Coll, local area
Automation Activity & Vendor Info: (Cataloging) ByWater Solutions; (Circulation) ByWater Solutions
Database Vendor: EBSCOhost
Wireless access
Function: Adult bk club, After school storytime, Bks on CD, Computers for patron use, Copy machines, Electronic databases & coll, Free DVD rentals, ILL available, Magazines, Online cat, OverDrive digital audio bks, Photocopying/Printing, Prog for adults, Ref serv in person, Scanner, Summer reading prog, Web-catalog
Open Tues 10:30-7:30, Wed & Thurs 1:30-7:30, Sat 10-3

WAKEFIELD

P WAKEFIELD LIBRARY ASSOCIATION*, 2699 Wakefield Rd, 03872. (Mail add: PO Box 904, Sanbornville, 03872-0904), SAN 309-9768. Tel: 603-522-3032. *Librn,* Donna Lee Jackson
Founded 1895. Pop 4,800
Jan 2011-Dec 2011. Mats Exp $1,000
Library Holdings: Audiobooks 2; Large Print Bks 3; Bk Vols 5,200
Wireless access
Partic in The Alberta Library; The Regional Automation Consortium (TRAC)
Open Wed (Summer) 9-4, Sat 9-3; Wed (Winter) 1-3, Sat 10-12
Friends of the Library Group

WALPOLE

P WALPOLE TOWN LIBRARY*, Bridge Memorial Library, 48 Main St, 03608. (Mail add: PO Box 487, 03608-0487), SAN 350-5626. Tel: 603-756-9806. FAX: 603-756-3140. E-mail: walpolelibrary@comcast.net. Web Site: www.walpoletownlibrary.org/. *Dir,* Mary Farrell; *Asst Librn,* Bethany Hebert; *Asst Librn,* Fran Moses; *Asst Librn,* Carolyn Norback; Staff 4 (MLS 1, Non-MLS 3)
Founded 1795. Pop 3,594
Library Holdings: Bk Vols 25,000; Per Subs 76
Automation Activity & Vendor Info: (Cataloging) Follett Software; (Circulation) Follett Software
Partic in Nubanusit Library Cooperative
Open Mon 1:30-8, Tues & Thurs 1:30-6, Wed 10-12 & 1:30-6, Sat 8:30-1
Friends of the Library Group
Branches: 1
NORTH WALPOLE, Ten Church St, North Walpole, 03609, SAN 350-5650. Tel: 603-445-5153. FAX: 603-445 5153. E-mail: nlibrary@comcast.net. *Librn,* Rose Werden
Library Holdings: Bk Vols 6,150
Open Tues & Wed 2-4, Sat 1-4
Friends of the Library Group

WARNER

CR THE COLLEGE OF SAINT MARY MAGDALEN*, St Augustine Library, 511 Kearsarge Mountain Rd, 03278. SAN 321-7337. Tel: 603-456-2656. FAX: 603-456-2660. *Librn,* Marie Lasher; E-mail: mlasher@magdalen.edu; Staff 1 (MLS 1)
Founded 1973. Enrl 60; Fac 9; Highest Degree: Bachelor
Library Holdings: Bk Titles 21,000; Bk Vols 27,000; Per Subs 20
Subject Interests: Humanities, Theol
Automation Activity & Vendor Info: (Acquisitions) Winnebago Software Co; (ILL) OCLC FirstSearch
Wireless access
Partic in New Hampshire Automated Information Systems (NHAIS)

P PILLSBURY FREE LIBRARY*, 18 E Main St, 03278. (Mail add: PO Box 299, 03278-0299), SAN 309-9776. Tel: 603-456-2289. FAX: 603-456-3177. E-mail: info@warner.lib.nh.us. Web Site: warner.lib.nh.us. *Libr Dir, Tech Librn,* Nancy Ladd; *Asst Dir, Ch,* Susan Matott; Staff 5 (MLS 1, Non-MLS 4)
Founded 1891. Pop 3,000; Circ 36,600
Jan 2012-Dec 2012 Income $199,108, State $275, City $187,148, Locally Generated Income $11,000, Other $1,000. Mats Exp $17,000, Books $12,200, Per/Ser (Incl. Access Fees) $1,500, AV Mat $1,500, Electronic Ref Mat (Incl. Access Fees) $1,500, Presv $300. Sal $108,626 (Prof $100,000)
Library Holdings: Audiobooks 821; AV Mats 3,000; Bks on Deafness & Sign Lang 12; CDs 300; DVDs 1,700; e-books 10; Electronic Media & Resources 14; High Interest/Low Vocabulary Bk Vols 40; Large Print Bks 130; Microforms 105; Music Scores 94; Bk Titles 27,200; Bk Vols 27,300; Per Subs 70; Talking Bks 825; Videos 1,880
Special Collections: Paul Knudson Music Score Coll, sheet music; Warner Coll, print & non-print items. Oral History
Subject Interests: Town hist
Automation Activity & Vendor Info: (Circulation) ByWater Solutions; (OPAC) ByWater Solutions; (Serials) EBSCO Online
Database Vendor: EBSCOhost, ProQuest
Wireless access
Function: Adult literacy prog, Art exhibits, Audio & video playback equip for onsite use, Audiobks via web, Bks on cassette, Bks on CD, CD-ROM, Children's prog, Computer training, Computers for patron use, Copy machines, Digital talking bks, E-Reserves, Electronic databases & coll, Equip loans & repairs, Exhibits, Free DVD rentals, Handicapped accessible, Holiday prog, Homebound delivery serv, ILL available, Literacy & newcomer serv, Magnifiers for reading, Mail & tel request accepted, Microfiche/film & reading machines, Mus passes, Music CDs, Online cat, OverDrive digital audio bks, Photocopying/Printing, Preschool reading prog, Printer for laptops & handheld devices, Prog for adults, Prog for children & young adult, Pub access computers, Ref serv in person, Scanner, Spoken cassettes & CDs, Spoken cassettes & DVDs, Story hour, Summer reading prog, Tax forms, Video lending libr, Web-catalog, Wheelchair accessible
Partic in New Hampshire Automated Information Systems (NHAIS)
Special Services for the Deaf - Bks on deafness & sign lang; Closed caption videos
Special Services for the Blind - Accessible computers; Aids for in-house use; Audio mat; Bks on cassette; Bks on CD; Copier with enlargement capabilities; Digital talking bk; Home delivery serv; Large print bks; Magnifiers; Networked computers with assistive software
Open Mon & Wed 1-5, Tues & Thurs 9-12 & 1-8, Sat 9-2

WARREN

P JOSEPH PATCH LIBRARY*, 320 New Hampshire, Rte 25, 03279-9716. SAN 309-9784. Tel: 603-764-9072. E-mail: jpatchlibrary@yahoo.com. *Dir,* Veronica Mueller; *Asst Librn,* Carole Elliot
Pop 820; Circ 4,096
Jan 2011-Dec 2011 Income City $35,000. Mats Exp $8,300, Books $7,000, Per/Ser (Incl. Access Fees) $900, AV Mat $400. Sal $10,000 (Prof $8,400)
Library Holdings: Audiobooks 150; AV Mats 415; CDs 50; DVDs 200; Large Print Bks 100; Bk Titles 5,000; Per Subs 25; Videos 100
Wireless access
Function: Adult bk club, Audiobks via web, AV serv, Bk club(s), Bks on cassette, Bks on CD, CD-ROM, Children's prog, Computers for patron use, Copy machines, e-mail serv, Fax serv, Free DVD rentals, Handicapped accessible, ILL available, Mail & tel request accepted, Music CDs, OverDrive digital audio bks, Photocopying/Printing, Prog for adults, Prog for children & young adult, Pub access computers, Story hour, Summer reading prog, VHS videos, Video lending libr, Web-catalog, Wheelchair accessible
Open Mon 10-2, Tues & Wed 3-7, Sat 10-1
Restriction: Open to pub for ref & circ, with some limitations
Friends of the Library Group

WASHINGTON

P SHEDD FREE LIBRARY*, 46 N Main, 03280. (Mail add: PO Box 288, 03280-0288), SAN 309-9792. Tel: 603-495-0410. FAX: 603-495-3592. E-mail: shedd@gsinet.net. *Dir,* Jo Ellen Wright; E-mail: jwright@washingtonnh.org; *Asst Librn,* Brenda Gilliland
Founded 1869. Pop 1,100; Circ 5,514
Jan 2010-Dec 2010. Mats Exp $6,000
Library Holdings: Bk Vols 8,000; Per Subs 19
Wireless access
Open Tues 10-5, Wed (May-Oct) 10-1, Thurs 1-7, Sat 10-1
Friends of the Library Group

WATERVILLE VALLEY

P OSCEOLA LIBRARY*, Two W Branch Rd, 03215. (Mail add: PO Box 367, 03215-0367), SAN 321-1029. Tel: 603-236-4369. E-mail: wvlibrary@watervillevalley.org. *In Charge,* Maureen Fish
Founded 1888. Pop 305; Circ 1,566
Library Holdings: Audiobooks 180; Bk Vols 3,100
Special Collections: New Hampshire History Coll; Recreational Books; White Mountains Coll
Open Tues, Thurs & Sat (Winter) 3-5; Mon-Sun (Summer) 3-5

WEARE

P WEARE PUBLIC LIBRARY*, Ten Paige Memorial Lane, 03281. (Mail add: PO Box 227, 03281-0227), SAN 309-9806. Tel: 603-529-2044. FAX: 603-529-7341. E-mail: wearepl@comcast.net. *Dir,* Christine Hague; *Asst Librn,* Thelma Tracy; *Ch Serv,* Karen Metcalf; Staff 8 (Non-MLS 8)
Pop 9,000; Circ 34,974
Jan 2005-Dec 2005 Income $164,648, State $161, City $153,614, Federal $144, Other $10,729. Mats Exp $16,315, Books $14,671, AV Mat $1,644. Sal $98,356
Library Holdings: AV Mats 1,779; Bks on Deafness & Sign Lang 11; Bk Vols 19,831; Per Subs 88
Automation Activity & Vendor Info: (Cataloging) Follett Software
Function: Adult bk club, Children's prog, Computers for patron use, Copy machines, Free DVD rentals, ILL available, Mus passes, Prog for children & young adult, Tax forms, VHS videos
Open Mon & Thurs 10-8, Tues & Wed 10-6, Sat (Sept-June) 9-12
Friends of the Library Group

WEBSTER

P WEBSTER FREE PUBLIC LIBRARY*, 947 Battle St, 03303. SAN 309-9814. Tel: 603-648-2706. FAX: 603-648-2889. E-mail: websterl@tds.net. *Librn,* Cathryn Clark-Dawe
Pop 1,405; Circ 9,300
Jan 2005-Dec 2005 Income $30,000. Mats Exp $8,000. Sal $17,000
Library Holdings: Bk Vols 10,500; Per Subs 14
Automation Activity & Vendor Info: (Cataloging) Follett Software; (Circulation) Follett Software
Open Mon 1-8, Wed 9-8, Sun 12-4

WENTWORTH

P WEBSTER MEMORIAL LIBRARY*, 20 Wentworth Village Rd, 03282. (Mail add: PO Box 105, 03282-0105), SAN 309-9822. Tel: 603-764-5818. Interlibrary Loan Service E-mail: wml956@roadrunner.com. *Dir,* Nance Masterson; Staff 2 (Non-MLS 2)
Founded 1917. Pop 620; Circ 7,025
Library Holdings: AV Mats 676; Bk Vols 11,636; Per Subs 60
Open Mon 3-8, Wed 11-4, Sat 9-12

WEST STEWARTSTOWN

P DENNIS JOOS MEMORIAL LIBRARY*, 888 Washington St, 03597. (Mail add: PO Box 119, 03597-0119), SAN 309-9563. Tel: 603-246-3329. FAX: 603-246-3329. *Dir,* Donna Allen
Pop 1,004
Jan 2010-Dec 2010. Mats Exp $5,000
Library Holdings: Bk Vols 4,599
Open Mon 6-8, Tues & Thurs 2-5 (2-6 Winter)

WEST SWANZEY

P STRATTON FREE LIBRARY*, Nine Main St, 03446. (Mail add: PO Box 578, 03469-0578), SAN 309-9679. Tel: 603-352-9391. E-mail: strattonfreelibrary@ne.rr.com. *Dir,* Carol Haley; *Asst Librn,* Jennifer Gomarlo; Staff 2 (Non-MLS 2)
Founded 1885. Pop 7,200
Jan 2011-Dec 2011 Income $35,924, City $33,705, Locally Generated Income $2,219. Mats Exp $7,434. Sal Prof $17,728
Library Holdings: Audiobooks 131; e-books 5,159; Bk Vols 11,956; Per Subs 8; Videos 436
Subject Interests: Local hist
Wireless access
Partic in New Hampshire Downloadable Books Consortium
Open Tues & Thurs 2:30-8, Sat 10-3

WESTMORELAND

P WESTMORELAND PUBLIC LIBRARY*, 33 S Village Rd, 03467. SAN 309-9830. Tel: 603-399-7750. E-mail: wpl33svr@myfairpoint.net. *Dir,* Jayne Burnett
Founded 1888. Pop 1,650; Circ 5,938
Library Holdings: Bk Titles 11,000; Per Subs 10
Wireless access
Open Tues & Thurs 10-7, Sat 9-1

WHITEFIELD

P WHITEFIELD PUBLIC LIBRARY, Eight Lancaster Rd, 03598. SAN 309-9849. Tel: 603-837-2030. FAX: 603-837-3124. E-mail: whitefieldpl@myfairpoint.net. *Librn,* Sandra Holz
Founded 1893. Pop 1,724; Circ 13,680
Library Holdings: Bk Vols 12,000; Per Subs 40
Wireless access
Open Mon 9-12, Tues & Thurs 2-8, Sat 10-5

WILMOT

P WILMOT PUBLIC LIBRARY*, 11 N Wilmot Rd, 03287-4302. SAN 309-9857. Tel: 603-526-6804. FAX: 603-526-6804. E-mail: wilmotlibrary@comcast.net. Web Site: www.wilmotlibrary.org. *Dir,* Rosanna Dude
Founded 1898. Pop 1,100
Library Holdings: Bk Vols 8,000
Open Mon, Tues & Thurs 3-7, Wed 10-7, Fri 3-5, Sat 10-12
Friends of the Library Group

WILTON

P WILTON PUBLIC & GREGG FREE LIBRARY*, Seven Forest Rd, 03086. (Mail add: PO Box 420, 03086-0420), SAN 309-9865. Tel: 603-654-2581. FAX: 603-654-3674. E-mail: wiltonlibrarynh@gmail.com. Interlibrary Loan Service E-mail: ill@wiltonlibrarynh.org. Web Site: www.wiltonlibrarynh.org. *Dir,* Pat Fickett; E-mail: patf@wiltonlibrarynh.org; *Youth Serv Librn,* Allison Steele; E-mail: allisons@wiltonlibrarynh.org; *Outreach Serv, Tech Serv,* Deborah Jensen; E-mail: debj@wiltonlibrarynh.org; *IT Spec,* William Bulling; E-mail: billb@wiltonlibrarynh.org; *Circ, Libr Asst,* Joanna Stock; E-mail: jstock@wiltonlibrarynh.org. Subject Specialists: *Info tech,* William Bulling; Staff 5 (MLS 2, Non-MLS 3)
Founded 1908. Pop 3,750; Circ 28,153
Library Holdings: Audiobooks 6,881; DVDs 961; e-books 7,113; Large Print Bks 200; Bk Titles 20,733; Bk Vols 22,530; Per Subs 50; Talking Bks 425
Automation Activity & Vendor Info: (Acquisitions) Biblionix; (Cataloging) Biblionix; (Circulation) Biblionix; (OPAC) Biblionix; (Serials) Biblionix
Database Vendor: EBSCOhost
Wireless access
Open Tues-Thurs 9:30-7, Fri 1:30-5, Sat 9:30-1:30
Friends of the Library Group

WINCHESTER

P CONANT PUBLIC LIBRARY, 111 Main St, 03470. SAN 309-9873. Tel: 603-239-4331. FAX: 603-239-4331. E-mail: conant.library@comcast.net. Web Site: www.conantlibrary.org. *Dir,* Christy Menard
Founded 1892. Pop 4,223; Circ 15,746
Library Holdings: DVDs 630; Large Print Bks 228; Bk Titles 20,000; Per Subs 45
Special Collections: Keene Sentinel 1799-1999; Microfilm of Town Records 1733-1800; Winchester Star, 1895-1917
Automation Activity & Vendor Info: (Circulation) Mandarin Library Automation; (OPAC) Mandarin Library Automation
Wireless access
Open Mon, Wed & Fri 10-8, Sat 10-2

WINDHAM

P NESMITH LIBRARY*, Eight Fellows Rd, 03087. SAN 309-989X. Tel: 603-432-7154. FAX: 603-537-0097. Web Site: www.nesmithlibrary.org. *Dir,* Carl Heidenblad; E-mail: cheidenblad@nesmithlibrary.org; *Adult Serv, Asst Dir,* Diane Mayr; E-mail: dmayr@nesmithlibrary.org; *Asst Dir, ILL, Ref Serv,* Lois Freeston; *Tech Serv Librn,* Elaine Rittenhouse; *Circ Coordr,* Terrie Marietta; Staff 14 (MLS 4, Non-MLS 10)
Founded 1871. Pop 14,500; Circ 132,641
Jan 2005-Dec 2005 Income $812,870. Mats Exp $100,000, Books $64,000, Per/Ser (Incl. Access Fees) $8,000, AV Mat $19,000, Electronic Ref Mat (Incl. Access Fees) $9,000. Sal Prof $163,173
Library Holdings: AV Mats 4,844; Bks on Deafness & Sign Lang 14; Large Print Bks 750; Bk Titles 65,719; Per Subs 204; Spec Interest Per Sub 11
Special Collections: Chinese Coll; Parents/First Teachers Coll
Subject Interests: NH hist
Automation Activity & Vendor Info: (Cataloging) Follett Software; (Circulation) Follett Software; (OPAC) Follett Software
Database Vendor: Newsbank, ProQuest
Publications: Nesmith Library News (Monthly)
Partic in Lyrasis; Merri-Hill-Rock Library Cooperative
Open Mon-Thurs 9-8, Fri 9-5, Sat 9-4, Sun 1-5
Friends of the Library Group

WOLFEBORO

P WOLFEBORO PUBLIC LIBRARY, 259 S Main St, 03894. SAN 309-9903. Tel: 603-569-2428. FAX: 603-569-8180. E-mail: wolfelibdir@metrocast.net. Web Site: www.wolfeborolibrary.org. *Dir,* Cynthia L Scott; *Ch,* Barbara Widmer; *ILL Librn,* Susan Fuller; *Tech Serv Librn,* Lynne Clough; Staff 7 (MLS 1, Non-MLS 6)
Founded 1900. Pop 6,269; Circ 113,763

Jan 2013-Dec 2013 Income $478,187, City $450,400, Locally Generated Income $27,787. Mats Exp $56,771, Books $35,726, AV Mat $13,530, Electronic Ref Mat (Incl. Access Fees) $7,515. Sal $230,008
Library Holdings: CDs 3,772; DVDs 3,582; e-books 15,869; Bk Vols 43,293; Talking Bks 1,825
Automation Activity & Vendor Info: (Cataloging) Book Systems; (Circulation) Book Systems; (OPAC) Book Systems
Wireless access
Function: 24/7 Online cat, Accessibility serv available based on individual needs, Activity rm, Archival coll, Art exhibits, Audiobks via web, Bks on CD, Children's prog, Computer training, Computers for patron use, Copy machines, e-mail serv, Electronic databases & coll, eReaders, Exhibits, Free DVD rentals, Genealogy discussion group, Handicapped accessible, Holiday prog, Homebound delivery serv, ILL available, Magazines, Magnifiers for reading, Mail & tel request accepted, Movies, Mus passes, Music CDs, Online cat, OverDrive digital audio bks, Photocopying/Printing, Preschool outreach, Preschool reading prog, Printer for laptops & handheld devices, Prog for adults, Prog for children & young adult, Pub access computers, Ref serv available, Scanner, Story hour, Summer reading prog, Tax forms, Telephone ref, Web-catalog, Wheelchair accessible, Workshops
Open Mon-Thurs 9:30-8, Fri & Sat 9:30-5
Friends of the Library Group

WOODSVILLE

P WOODSVILLE FREE PUBLIC LIBRARY*, 14 School Lane, 03785. SAN 309-8400. Tel: 603-747-3483. E-mail: woodsvillelibrary@hotmail.com.
Head Librn, Dawn Langley; *Asst Librn,* Louise McGee
Pop 3,444; Circ 23,111
Library Holdings: Bk Vols 35,860; Per Subs 54
Subject Interests: Town hist
Publications: Local Paper
Open Mon, Wed & Fri 1-8

NEW JERSEY

Date of Statistics: Data Year 2013
Population, 2010 Census: 8,791,894
Population Served by Public Libraries: 8,741,619
Unserved: 50,275
Total Volumes in Public Libraries: 28,955,714
Volumes Per Capita: 3.31
Total Public Library Income: $485,717,261
Average Income Per Library: $1,728,531
Source of Income: Mainly public funds
Expenditures Per Capita: $52.65
Grants-in-Aid to Public Libraries:
Federal: $2,103,106
State Aid: $4,508,549
Number of County Libraries: 14

ABSECON

P ABSECON PUBLIC LIBRARY*, 305 New Jersey Ave, 08201. SAN 309-9911. Tel: 609-646-2228. FAX: 609-383-8992. *Dir,* Barbara Wilson; *Librn,* Leah Krafft
Founded 1937. Pop 7,000; Circ 20,429
Library Holdings: Bk Vols 25,000; Per Subs 50
Automation Activity & Vendor Info: (Cataloging) SirsiDynix; (Circulation) SirsiDynix; (OPAC) SirsiDynix
Partic in Coalition of Independent Libraries (COIL)
Open Mon & Fri 9:30-5, Tues-Thurs 9:30-8, Sat 9:30-1

ALLENDALE

P LEE MEMORIAL LIBRARY, 500 W Crescent Ave, 07401-1799. SAN 309-992X. Tel: 201-327-4338. FAX: 201-327-5838. Web Site: leememoriallibrary.org. *Dir,* Gretchen Kaser; E-mail: kaser@allendale.bccls.org; Staff 16 (MLS 2, Non-MLS 14)
Founded 1923. Pop 6,505; Circ 181,952
Jan 2010-Dec 2010 Income $647,395. Mats Exp $120,000. Sal $279,773
Library Holdings: AV Mats 8,314; Bk Vols 150,000; Per Subs 100
Wireless access
Function: 24/7 Online cat, Activity rm, Adult bk club, Adult literacy prog, After school storytime, Audiobks via web, AV serv, Bk club(s), Bk reviews (Group), Bks on CD, Children's prog, Computers for patron use, Copy machines, E-Reserves, Electronic databases & coll, Free DVD rentals, Home delivery & serv to Sr ctr & nursing homes, Homebound delivery serv, ILL available, Life-long learning prog for all ages, Magazines, Mail & tel request accepted, Mango lang, Movies, Mus passes, Music CDs, Notary serv, Online cat, Online ref, Online searches, Outreach serv, OverDrive digital audio bks, Photocopying/Printing, Preschool outreach, Preschool reading prog, Prog for adults, Prog for children & young adult, Pub access computers, Spoken cassettes & CDs, Spoken cassettes & DVDs, Story hour, Summer & winter reading prog, Summer reading prog, Tax forms, Teen prog, Telephone ref
Partic in Bergen County Cooperative Library System
Open Mon, Tues & Thurs 10-9, Wed, Fri & Sat 10-5
Friends of the Library Group

ALPHA

P W H WALTERS FREE PUBLIC LIBRARY*, 1001 East Blvd, 08865. SAN 376-0650. Tel: 908-454-1445. E-mail: alphapubliclibrary@verizon.net. Web Site: www.alphaboro.org/pages/library. *Libr Dir,* Carla Roselle
Library Holdings: Bk Titles 16,000; Per Subs 14
Wireless access
Open Mon & Wed 9-7, Thurs & Fri 9-5, Sat 9-1

ANNANDALE

S MOUNTAIN VIEW YOUTH CORRECTIONAL FACILITY LIBRARY*, Main Compound, 31 Petticoat Lane, 08801-4097. SAN 375-7463. Tel: 908-638-6191, Ext 7316. FAX: 908-638-6143. *Supvr,* Wayne VanDoren
Library Holdings: Bk Vols 5,500; Per Subs 35
Automation Activity & Vendor Info: (Cataloging) Follett Software; (Circulation) Follett Software
Restriction: Not open to pub
Branches:
MINIMUM UNIT, 31 Petticoat Lane, 08801-4097. Tel: 908-638-6191, Ext 7384. *Supvr,* Wayne VanDoren
Library Holdings: Bk Vols 1,600; Per Subs 20
Restriction: Not open to pub

ASBURY PARK

P ASBURY PARK PUBLIC LIBRARY*, 500 First Ave, 07712. SAN 309-9938. Tel: 732-774-4221. FAX: 732-988-6101. E-mail: apl-info@asburyparklibrary.org. Web Site: www.asburyparklibrary.org. *Dir,* Robert W Stewart; *Mgr, Info Sys,* Malakia Oglesay
Founded 1878. Circ 47,469
Library Holdings: Bk Titles 105,136; Bk Vols 114,399; Per Subs 406
Automation Activity & Vendor Info: (Cataloging) SirsiDynix; (Circulation) SirsiDynix; (OPAC) SirsiDynix
Database Vendor: EBSCOhost, Facts on File
Wireless access
Partic in LibraryLinkNJ, The New Jersey Library Cooperative
Open Mon-Wed 11-8, Thurs-Fri 9-5, Sat 12-5

ATCO

P WATERFORD TOWNSHIP PUBLIC LIBRARY*, 2204 Atco Ave, 08004. SAN 309-9954. Tel: 856-767-7727. FAX: 856-753-8998. E-mail: wtpl@camden.lib.nj.us. *Dir,* Eva Lynch; E-mail: elynch@camden.lib.nj.us; *Circ,* Elizabeth Diaz; *Ref,* Margaret Haggerty; Staff 9 (MLS 1, Non-MLS 8)
Founded 1964. Pop 11,000
Jan 2005-Dec 2005 Income $287,659, State $10,713, City $272,802, Locally Generated Income $4,144. Mats Exp $44,169, Books $36,499, Per/Ser (Incl. Access Fees) $3,376, AV Mat $4,294. Sal $127,950
Library Holdings: Bk Vols 25,888; Per Subs 81
Subject Interests: Parenting
Automation Activity & Vendor Info: (Circulation) Follett Software; (ILL) Auto-Graphics, Inc
Database Vendor: Baker & Taylor
Partic in The Library Network
Open Mon-Thurs 11:30-8:30, Fri 10-5, Sat 10-3
Friends of the Library Group

ATLANTIC CITY

M ATLANTIC CARE REGIONAL MEDICAL CENTER*, Health Science Library, 1925 Pacific Ave, 08401. SAN 309-9962. Tel: 609-441-8966. FAX: 609-441-2137. *Dir,* John P Doesburgh
Library Holdings: Bk Vols 2,285; Per Subs 115
Subject Interests: Med, Nursing
Open Mon-Fri 8:30-4:30

P ATLANTIC CITY FREE PUBLIC LIBRARY*, One N Tennessee Ave, 08401. SAN 350-5685. Tel: 609-345-2269. Circulation Tel: 609-345-2269, Ext 3070. Interlibrary Loan Service Tel: 609-345-2269, Ext 3046. FAX: 609-345-5570. Web Site: www.acfpl.org. *Dir,* Maureen Sherr Frank; Tel: 609-345-2269, Ext 3001, E-mail: mfrank@acfpl.org; *Asst Dir,* Robert Rynkiewicz; Tel: 609-345-2269, Ext 3024; *Head Ref Librn,* Julie Senack; Tel: 609-345-2269, Ext 3063; *Tech Serv Librn,* Constance L Swanson; Tel: 609-345-2269, Ext 3040; *Archivist,* Heather Halpin Perez; Staff 37 (MLS 9, Non-MLS 28)
Founded 1902. Pop 40,517; Circ 317,520
Library Holdings: Bk Titles 104,200; Bk Vols 135,000; Per Subs 350
Special Collections: Casino Gambling; Genealogy & Atlantic City History (Alfred M Heston Coll)
Automation Activity & Vendor Info: (Acquisitions) Innovative Interfaces, Inc - Millenium; (Cataloging) Innovative Interfaces, Inc - Millenium; (Circulation) Innovative Interfaces, Inc - Millenium
Wireless access
Publications: Atlantic City News Index; Clubs & Organizations Directory
Partic in Coalition of Independent Libraries (COIL); LibraryLinkNJ, The New Jersey Library Cooperative; OCLC Online Computer Library Center, Inc
Open Mon-Wed 9:30-8, Thurs-Sat 9:30-5, Sun 12-5

G FEDERAL AVIATION ADMINISTRATION*, William J Hughes Technical Center Library, Reference & Research Library, AJP-7200, Atlantic City International Airport, 08405. SAN 309-9970. Tel: 609-485-5124. Administration Tel: 609-485-5242. FAX: 609-485-6088. Web Site: actlibrary.tc.faa.gov. *Chief Librn,* Robert Mast; E-mail: robert.mast@faa.gov; Staff 1 (MLS 1)
Founded 1958
Library Holdings: Bk Vols 15,000
Special Collections: Technical Reports
Subject Interests: Aeronaut, Air traffic control, Airports, Aviation safety, Communications, Navigation, Radar
Automation Activity & Vendor Info: (Cataloging) EOS International; (Circulation) EOS International; (ILL) OCLC ILLiad; (OPAC) EOS International; (Serials) EOS International
Database Vendor: Dialog, EOS International, IHS, OCLC FirstSearch, OCLC WorldShare Interlibrary Loan, WT Cox
Function: ILL available, Photocopying/Printing, Res libr
Partic in OCLC Online Computer Library Center, Inc
Open Mon-Thurs 6am-4:30pm
Restriction: Closed stack, Non-circulating to the pub, Pub ref by request, Restricted borrowing privileges, Restricted pub use, Secured area only open to authorized personnel

AUDUBON

P FREE PUBLIC LIBRARY OF AUDUBON*, 239 Oakland Ave, 08106-1598. SAN 310-0006. Tel: 856-547-8686. FAX: 856-547-0277. Web Site: www.audubonlibrary.org. *Adminr,* Kathy Ostberg; Staff 7 (MLS 1, Non-MLS 6)
Pop 9,205; Circ 42,000
Library Holdings: Bk Titles 24,000; Bk Vols 28,000; Per Subs 50
Publications: Newsletter
Partic in LibraryLinkNJ, The New Jersey Library Cooperative
Open Mon-Thurs 11-8, Fri 11-6, Sat (Sept-May) 10-2

AUDUBON PARK

P AUDUBON PARK PUBLIC LIBRARY*, 20 Road C, 08106. Tel: 856-547-5236. *Librn,* Katherine Sullivan
Founded 1948
Library Holdings: Bk Vols 5,000
Mem of Camden County Library System
Open Wed & Thurs 4:30-9:30

AVALON

P AVALON FREE PUBLIC LIBRARY*, 235-32nd St, 08202-1766. SAN 378-5688. Tel: 609-967-7155. FAX: 609-967-4723. E-mail: info@avalonfreelibrary.org. Web Site: www.avalonfreelibrary.org. *Libr Dir,* Norman Gluckman
Open Mon-Thurs 9-8, Fri & Sat 9-5, Sun 11-3

AVENEL

S NEW JERSEY DEPARTMENT OF CORRECTIONS*, Adult Diagnostic & Treatment Center Library, Eight Production Way, 07001. Tel: 732-574-2250, Ext 8017. FAX: 732-382-8912. Web Site: www.doc.state.nj.us. *Educ Supvr,* Jesse Glover
Library Holdings: Bk Vols 14,000; Per Subs 25
Special Collections: Law Coll
Restriction: Not open to pub

AVON BY THE SEA

P AVON PUBLIC LIBRARY*, Garfield & Fifth Ave, 07717. SAN 310-0014. Tel: 732-502-4525. FAX: 732-775-8430. E-mail: avonlibrary@optonline.net. Web Site: www.avonbytheseanj.com. *Dir,* Sheila Watson
Founded 1916. Pop 2,163; Circ 25,174
Library Holdings: Bk Titles 21,000; Per Subs 52
Automation Activity & Vendor Info: (Cataloging) Follett Software; (Circulation) Follett Software
Wireless access
Function: ILL available
Open Mon, Wed & Thurs 12-7, Tues & Fri 1-5, Sat (Winter) 9-1; Mon-Fri (Summer) 9-1 & 6-8

BASKING RIDGE

P BERNARDS TOWNSHIP LIBRARY*, 32 S Maple Ave, 07920-1216. SAN 310-0049. Tel: 908-204-3031. FAX: 908-766-1580. Web Site: www.bernardslibrary.org. *Dir,* Ruth Lufkin; E-mail: rlufkin@bernards.org; *YA Librn,* Karen Olivari; E-mail: kolivari@bernards.org; *Supv Librn, Ch,* Ellen Stork; E-mail: estork@bernards.org; *Supv Librn, Circ,* Ann Babits; *Supv Librn, Tech Serv,* Marcia Lubansky; E-mail: mlubansky@bernards.org; *IT Mgr,* Ryan McCloskey; E-mail: rmccloskey@bernards.org; Staff 35 (MLS 9, Non-MLS 26)
Founded 1898. Pop 27,000
Library Holdings: Bk Vols 110,000; Per Subs 290
Special Collections: Local History Coll; Performing Arts Coll
Automation Activity & Vendor Info: (Cataloging) SirsiDynix; (Circulation) SirsiDynix; (OPAC) SirsiDynix
Database Vendor: SirsiDynix
Wireless access
Publications: Electronic Newsletters; History of the Library in Basking Ridge
Partic in LibraryLinkNJ, The New Jersey Library Cooperative; Morris Automated Information Network; Morris-Union Federation; Raritan Valley Fedn of Librs
Open Mon-Thurs 9:30-9, Fri 9:30-5, Sat 10-5, Sun 1-4
Friends of the Library Group

G SOMERSET COUNTY PARK COMMISSION*, Environmental Education Center Library, 190 Lord Stirling Rd, 07920. SAN 321-043X. Tel: 908-766-2489. FAX: 908-766-2687. Web Site: www.somersetcountyparks.org. *Mgr,* Catherine Schrein; Tel: 908-766-2489, Ext 324, E-mail: cschrein@scparks.org. Subject Specialists: *Environ studies,* Catherine Schrein; Staff 14 (Non-MLS 14)
Founded 1972
Library Holdings: Bk Titles 5,000; Per Subs 30
Subject Interests: Environ studies, Natural hist
Open Mon-Sun 9-5
Restriction: Restricted loan policy

BAYONNE

P FREE PUBLIC LIBRARY OF BAYONNE*, 697 Avenue C, 07002. SAN 350-5774. Tel: 201-858-6970. Interlibrary Loan Service Tel: 201-858-6160. Reference Tel: 201-858-6980. FAX: 201-437-6928. Web Site: www.bayonnelibrary.org. *Dir,* Sneh P Bains; *Head, Circ,* Susan Humenic; E-mail: shumenic@bayonnelibrary.org; *Art & Music Librn,* George Durman; E-mail: gdurman@bayonnelibrary.org; *Ref Librn,* Jeannette Torres-Hanley; E-mail: jtorres@bayonnelibrary.org; *Ref Librn,* Raymond Zaleski; E-mail: rzaleski@bayonnelibrary.org; *Ch Serv,* Paula Micalizzi; Tel: 201-858-6975, E-mail: pmicalizzi@hotmail.com; *Ref Serv,* Lisa Attanasio; E-mail: lattanasio@bayonnelibrary.org; *Tech Serv,* Pat Payette; E-mail: ppayette@bayonnelibrary.org; Staff 6 (MLS 6)
Founded 1893. Pop 63,024; Circ 190,503
Library Holdings: Audiobooks 2,777; CDs 4,964; DVDs 6,012; e-books 28,415; Large Print Bks 2,987; Bk Vols 328,527; Per Subs 129
Special Collections: Local History (New Jersey & Bayonneana). Oral History
Subject Interests: Archit, Art, Indust, Music
Automation Activity & Vendor Info: (Cataloging) SirsiDynix; (Circulation) SirsiDynix; (OPAC) SirsiDynix; (Serials) EBSCO Online
Database Vendor: EBSCOhost
Wireless access
Publications: Newsletter (Quarterly)

Partic in LibraryLinkNJ, The New Jersey Library Cooperative
Special Services for the Blind - Computer with voice synthesizer for visually impaired persons
Open Mon-Thurs 9-9, Fri & Sat 9-5
Friends of the Library Group

BEACH HAVEN

P BEACH HAVEN FREE PUBLIC LIBRARY*, 247 N Beach Ave, 08008-1865. SAN 310-0073. Tel: 609-492-7081. FAX: 609-492-1048. E-mail: bhpl@comcast.net. Web Site: www.beachhaven-nj.gov/bh_library.htm. *Dir,* Jean Frazier; *Asst Librn,* Eileen Mitchell
Founded 1924. Pop 2,400; Circ 25,924
Library Holdings: Bk Vols 25,000; Per Subs 60
Special Collections: Local History Coll; Regional History Coll
Wireless access
Partic in LibraryLinkNJ, The New Jersey Library Cooperative
Open Mon & Thurs (Winter) 12:30-8, Tues, Wed & Fri 12:30-5, Sat 10-4; Mon & Thurs (Summer) 10-4 & 6-8, Tues, Wed, Fri & Sat 10-4

BEDMINSTER

P CLARENCE DILLON PUBLIC LIBRARY, 2336 Lamington Rd, 07921. SAN 310-009X. Tel: 908-234-2325. Reference Tel: 908-234-2325, Ext 111. FAX: 908-781-9402. E-mail: ref@dillonlibrary.org. Web Site: www.clarencedillonpl.org. *Dir,* Sumner Putnam; E-mail: sputnam@dillonlibrary.org; *Asst Dir,* Marie Crenshaw; E-mail: mcrenshaw@dillonlibrary.org; *Dir, Ch Serv,* Helen Petersen; E-mail: hpetersen@dillonlibrary.org; *Tech Serv Librn,* Arthur Merchant; E-mail: amerchant@dillonlibrary.org
Pop 8,500
Special Collections: Local History (Anne O'Brien Coll)
Subject Interests: Civil War
Automation Activity & Vendor Info: (Cataloging) TLC (The Library Corporation); (Circulation) TLC (The Library Corporation)
Wireless access
Function: Homebound delivery serv
Partic in LibraryLinkNJ, The New Jersey Library Cooperative; Raritan Valley Fedn of Librs
Special Services for the Blind - Large print bks
Open Mon-Thurs 10-9, Fri & Sat 10-5 (10-3 July & Aug), Sun (Sept-May) 1-4
Friends of the Library Group

BELLEVILLE

P BELLEVILLE PUBLIC LIBRARY & INFORMATION CENTER*, 221 Washington Ave, 07109-3189. SAN 310-0103. Tel: 973-450-3434. FAX: 973-759-6731. Web Site: www.bellepl.org. *Libr Dir,* Joan Barbara Taub; E-mail: jtaub@bellepl.org; *Ch Serv,* Danielle Cesena; E-mail: dcesena@bellepl.org; *Circ,* Mia Torres; *Ref Serv,* Louise Yan; E-mail: reference@bellepl.org; *Teen Serv,* Karyn Gost; E-mail: kgost@bellepl.org; Staff 8 (MLS 3, Non-MLS 5)
Founded 1902. Pop 35,928; Circ 65,323
Library Holdings: AV Mats 5,880; Bk Titles 76,820; Bk Vols 96,447; Per Subs 156
Subject Interests: Career, City hist, State hist
Automation Activity & Vendor Info: (Cataloging) Innovative Interfaces, Inc
Database Vendor: EBSCOhost, Gale Cengage Learning
Wireless access
Partic in LibraryLinkNJ, The New Jersey Library Cooperative
Open Mon, Tues & Thurs (Winter) 9-8, Wed, Fri & Sat 9-5; Mon (Summer) 9-8, Tues-Fri 9-5
Friends of the Library Group

S 1ST CEREBRAL PALSY OF NEW JERSEY*, Dr Charles I Nadel Library, Seven Sanford Ave, 07109. SAN 375-9989. Tel: 973-751-0200. FAX: 973-751-4635. Web Site: www.cerebralpalsycenter.org. *Exec Dir,* Patrick Colligan; *Assoc Dir,* Joan Krotenberg
Library Holdings: Bk Titles 500; Per Subs 205
Subject Interests: Childrens' bks
Open Mon-Fri 8:30-4:30
Restriction: Employee & client use only

M CLARA MAASS MEDICAL CENTER*, Medical Library, One Clara Maass Dr, 07109. SAN 327-3601. Tel: 973-450-2294. FAX: 973-844-4390. Web Site: www.barnabashealth.org/hospitals/clara_maass/libraries/index.html. *Librn/Mgr,* Arlene Mangino; E-mail: amangino@barnabashealth.org; Staff 1 (MLS 1)
Library Holdings: Bk Titles 1,050; Per Subs 124
Subject Interests: Med, Nursing
Automation Activity & Vendor Info: (Cataloging) Professional Software; (Serials) Professional Software
Database Vendor: EBSCOhost, Lexi-Comp, McGraw-Hill, MD Consult, UpToDate
Wireless access
Partic in Basic Health Sciences Library Network; Cosmopolitan Biomedical Library Consortium; LibraryLinkNJ, The New Jersey Library Cooperative; National Network of Libraries of Medicine Middle Atlantic Region; New Jersey Health Sciences Library Network
Open Mon-Fri 8-4

BELMAR

P BELMAR PUBLIC LIBRARY, 517 Tenth Ave, 07719. SAN 310-012X. Tel: 732 681-0775. FAX: 732-280-1685. E-mail: library@boro.belmar.nj.us. Web Site: www.belmarlibrary.org. *Dir,* Rosemarie Korbelak; *Prog Coordr,* Margaret O'Connor; *Libr Asst,* Patricia Faugno; *Libr Asst,* Liz Griffin; *Libr Asst,* Connie Nolan; *Libr Asst,* Lorraine Walsh; Staff 3 (Non-MLS 3)
Founded 1911. Pop 5,900; Circ 12,100
Wireless access
Function: Adult bk club, Children's prog, Computers for patron use, Copy machines, Electronic databases & coll, Fax serv, Free DVD rentals, Handicapped accessible, Holiday prog, Magazines, Magnifiers for reading, Prog for adults, Prog for children & young adult, Pub access computers, Story hour, Summer reading prog, Tax forms, Wheelchair accessible
Partic in LibraryLinkNJ, The New Jersey Library Cooperative
Special Services for the Deaf - Adult & family literacy prog
Open Mon, Wed & Thurs 9-8, Tues & Fri 9-5, Sat 9-3
Friends of the Library Group

BELVIDERE

P BELVIDERE FREE PUBLIC LIBRARY*, 301 Second St, 07823-1517. SAN 310-0138. Tel: 908-475-3941. FAX: 908-475-3893. E-mail: bellib@epix.net. *Dir,* Teresa Aicher
Pop 2,771; Circ 28,277
Jan 2010-Dec 2010 Income $72,614, State $2,250, City $65,350, Locally Generated Income $1,014, Other $4,000
Library Holdings: Audiobooks 154; AV Mats 1,457; Bks on Deafness & Sign Lang 18; CDs 250; DVDs 1,478; High Interest/Low Vocabulary Bk Vols 60; Large Print Bks 278; Bk Vols 26,745; Per Subs 50; Spec Interest Per Sub 9; Videos 1,120
Special Collections: 15 Minute Reluctant Readers; Adult Basic Literacy Coll; Adult Literacy Coll; Autism Coll; Children's Mental Health; Dual Language Books Coll; Graphic Novel Coll; History of American Music; International Film Coll; International Music Coll; Japanese Culture Coll; Miniature Books; Womens History Coll; World Arts Coll
Automation Activity & Vendor Info: (Cataloging) Follett Software; (Circulation) Follett Software
Function: Accelerated reader prog, Adult literacy prog, After school storytime, Archival coll, Art exhibits, BA reader (adult literacy), Bk reviews (Group), Bks on cassette, Bks on CD, CD-ROM, Children's prog, Citizenship assistance, Computer training, Computers for patron use, Copy machines, e-mail & chat, Equip loans & repairs, Exhibits, Family literacy, Fax serv, Free DVD rentals, Games & aids for the handicapped, Govt ref serv, Handicapped accessible, Health sci info serv, Holiday prog, Home delivery & serv to Sr ctr & nursing homes, Homebound delivery serv, Homework prog, ILL available, Learning ctr, Libr develop, Literacy & newcomer serv, Magnifiers for reading, Mail & tel request accepted, Music CDs, Newsp ref libr, Online ref, Online searches, Orientations, Outreach serv, Photocopying/Printing, Preschool outreach, Prof lending libr, Prog for adults, Prog for children & young adult, Pub access computers, Ref & res, Ref serv in person, Res libr, Senior computer classes, Senior outreach, Serves mentally handicapped consumers, Spoken cassettes & CDs, Spoken cassettes & DVDs, Story hour, Summer & winter reading prog, Summer reading prog, Tax forms, Teen prog, Telephone ref, VHS videos, Video lending libr, Visual arts prog, Wheelchair accessible, Winter reading prog, Workshops
Special Services for the Deaf - Bks on deafness & sign lang; Captioned film dep
Special Services for the Blind - Accessible computers; Audio mat; Bks on cassette; Cassette playback machines; Large type calculator; Ref serv; Sound rec
Open Tues & Thurs 1-7, Wed & Fri 1-5, Sat 11-3

S WARREN COUNTY HISTORICAL SOCIETY & GENEALOGY*, Resource Room, 313 Mansfield St, 07823-1828. (Mail add: PO Box 313, 07823-0313), SAN 375-7374. Tel: 908-475-4246. *Pres,* Patricia Burnk
Library Holdings: Bk Vols 600
Open Sun 1-4

P WARREN COUNTY LIBRARY*, Two Shotwell Dr, 07823. SAN 350-5898. Tel: 908-475-6322. Interlibrary Loan Service Tel: 908-475-6327. Reference Tel: 908-475-6321. Administration Tel: 908-475-6320. Toll Free Tel: 877-475-6321. Administration FAX: 908-475-1558. Web Site:

www.warrenlib.org. *Dir,* Maureen Baker Wilkinson; Tel: 908-475-6338, E-mail: mbwilkinson@warrenlib.org; *Asst Dir,* Jill Butcher; Tel: 908-475-6252, E-mail: jillb@warrenlib.org; *Network Adminr,* Position Currently Open; *YA Librn,* Kelly Durkin; Tel: 908-475-6386, E-mail: kdurkin@warrenlib.org; *Ch Serv,* Lina Crowell; Tel: 908-475-6017, E-mail: crowell@warrenlib.org; *Homebound Serv,* Jennifer Sidie; Tel: 908-475-6246, E-mail: jsidie@warrenlib.org; *Pub Serv,* Jane Endrizzi; Tel: 908-475-6244, E-mail: jendrizzi@warrenlib.org; Staff 36 (MLS 7, Non-MLS 29)
Founded 1931. Pop 72,507; Circ 641,858
Jan 2012-Dec 2012 Income (Main Library and Branch(s)) $4,665,818, State $38,506, County $4,627,312. Mats Exp $561,995, Books $335,274, AV Mat $125,463. Sal $1,543,941
Library Holdings: Audiobooks 8,940; CDs 8,501; DVDs 24,572; e-books 5,251; Bk Titles 207,954; Bk Vols 222,895; Per Subs 302
Special Collections: Local History (Warren County Library Headquarters), bks, micro, pamphlets
Automation Activity & Vendor Info: (Cataloging) TLC (The Library Corporation); (Circulation) TLC (The Library Corporation); (OPAC) TLC (The Library Corporation); (Serials) TLC (The Library Corporation)
Wireless access
Function: Audio & video playback equip for onsite use, Bk club(s), Bks on CD, Children's prog, Computer training, Computers for patron use, Copy machines, Digital talking bks, Electronic databases & coll, Free DVD rentals, Handicapped accessible, Home delivery & serv to Sr ctr & nursing homes, Homebound delivery serv, ILL available, Magnifiers for reading, Mail & tel request accepted, Microfiche/film & reading machines, Mus passes, Music CDs, Newsp ref libr, Online cat, Online ref, Online searches, Outreach serv, OverDrive digital audio bks, Photocopying/Printing, Preschool outreach, Preschool reading prog, Printer for laptops & handheld devices, Prof lending libr, Prog for adults, Prog for children & young adult, Pub access computers, Ref serv available, Ref serv in person, Res libr, Senior computer classes, Senior outreach, Spoken cassettes & CDs, Spoken cassettes & DVDs, Story hour, Summer reading prog, Tax forms, Teen prog, Telephone ref, Wheelchair accessible, Workshops
Open Mon-Thurs 9-8:30, Fri 9-6, Sat 10-3
Friends of the Library Group
Branches: 3
FRANKLIN BRANCH, 1502 Rte 57, Washington, 07882, SAN 376-2580. Tel: 908-689-7922. FAX: 908-689-8265. *Br Mgr,* Sheri Monaco
Founded 1989
Open Mon-Thurs 9-8, Fri 9-6, Sat 10-3
Friends of the Library Group
CATHERINE DICKSON HOFMAN BRANCH, Four Lambert Rd, Blairstown, 07825, SAN 310-0227. Tel: 908-362-8335. FAX: 908-362-7775. *Br Mgr,* Marilyn Grandin
Founded 1941
Open Mon-Thurs 9-8, Fri 9-6, Sat 10-3
NORTHEAST BRANCH, 40 US Hwy 46, Hackettstown, 07840, SAN 377-7774. Tel: 908-813-3858. FAX: 908-813-3813. E-mail: nebranch@warrenlib.org. *Br Mgr,* Cindy Seelig
Founded 1993
Open Mon-Thurs 9-8, Fri 9-6, Sat 10-3
Friends of the Library Group
Bookmobiles: 1. Senior Libr Asst, Guy Collina, Bk titles 2,400

BERGENFIELD

P BERGENFIELD PUBLIC LIBRARY*, 50 W Clinton Ave, 07621-2799. SAN 310-0146. Tel: 201-387-4040. Circulation Tel: 201-387-4040, Ext 840. Interlibrary Loan Service Tel: 201-387-4040, Ext 830. Reference Tel: 201-387-4040, Ext 860. FAX: 201-387-9004. E-mail: bfldcirc@bccls.org. Web Site: www.bccls.org/bergenfield. *Dir,* Mary Riskind; Tel: 201-387-4040, Ext 829, E-mail: riskind@bccls.org; *Asst Dir,* Tina Painter; Tel: 201-387-4040, Ext 845, E-mail: painter@bccls.org; *Head, Circ,* Betty Costello; Tel: 201-387-4040, Ext 826, E-mail: costello@bccls.org; *Head, Ref,* Mary Ellen Henitz; Tel: 201-387-4040, Ext 833, E-mail: henitz@bccls.org; *Ch Serv,* Louise Moroses; Tel: 201-387-4040, Ext 896, E-mail: moroses@bccls.org; *ESL Coordr,* Rachel Lore; Tel: 201-387-4040, Ext 837, E-mail: lore@bccls.org; Staff 21.875 (MLS 5.25, Non-MLS 16.625)
Founded 1920. Pop 26,247; Circ 233,201
Jul 2005-Jun 2006 Income $1,694,009, State $32,153, City $1,610,000, Locally Generated Income $51,856. Mats Exp $134,281, Books $92,101, Per/Ser (Incl. Access Fees) $20,146, AV Mat $22,034. Sal $865,073
Library Holdings: AV Mats 10,082; Bk Vols 136,588; Per Subs 229
Special Collections: ESL Coll, New Jersey
Automation Activity & Vendor Info: (Circulation) SirsiDynix; (OPAC) SirsiDynix
Database Vendor: EBSCOhost, ProQuest, ReferenceUSA
Wireless access
Function: Adult bk club, After school storytime, Art exhibits, AV serv, Bk club(s), Copy machines, E-Reserves, Electronic databases & coll, Homebound delivery serv, ILL available, Mail & tel request accepted, Preschool outreach, Prog for adults, Prog for children & young adult, Ref & res, Spoken cassettes & CDs, Summer reading prog, Tax forms, VHS videos, Wheelchair accessible
Partic in Bergen County Cooperative Library System
Open Mon, Tues & Thurs 10-9, Wed 10-5, Fri & Sun 1-5, Sat 10-2
Friends of the Library Group

BERKELEY HEIGHTS

P BERKELEY HEIGHTS PUBLIC LIBRARY*, 290 Plainfield Ave, 07922. SAN 310-0154. Tel: 908-464-9333. FAX: 908-464-7098. E-mail: reference@bhplnj.org. Web Site: www.bhplnj.org. *Dir,* Stephanie Bakos; E-mail: sbakos@bhplnj.org; *Head, Ch,* Laura Fuhro; E-mail: lfuhro@bhplnj.org; *Head, Circ,* Magdalen Wu; E-mail: mwu@bhplnj.org; *Head, Ref,* Anne deFuria; E-mail: asdef@bhplnj.org; *Head, Tech Serv,* Virginia Lynch; E-mail: vlynch@bhplnj.org; *Ref Librn,* Ellen Zander; E-mail: ezander@bhplnj.org; *Cat,* Laurel Gould; Staff 5 (MLS 5)
Founded 1953. Pop 13,407; Circ 163,670
Jan 2006-Dec 2006 Income $1,019,898, State $13,686, City $981,212, Locally Generated Income $25,000. Mats Exp $257,500, Books $165,000, Per/Ser (Incl. Access Fees) $20,000, AV Mat $50,000, Electronic Ref Mat (Incl. Access Fees) $22,500. Sal $486,000
Library Holdings: AV Mats 3,992; DVDs 1,071; Bk Titles 70,000; Bk Vols 81,598; Per Subs 220; Talking Bks 1,696; Videos 2,354
Subject Interests: Archit, Art
Automation Activity & Vendor Info: (Acquisitions) TLC (The Library Corporation); (Cataloging) TLC (The Library Corporation); (Circulation) TLC (The Library Corporation); (OPAC) TLC (The Library Corporation)
Database Vendor: Alexander Street Press, Booklist Online, EBSCO - WebFeat, EBSCOhost, Facts on File, Grolier Online, infoUSA, Ingram Library Services, LearningExpress, ProQuest, ReferenceUSA, TLC (The Library Corporation)
Wireless access
Open Mon-Thurs 9-9, Fri & Sat 9-5, Sun 2-5
Friends of the Library Group

M RUNNELLS SPECIALIZED HOSPITAL*, Watson B Morris Medical Library, 40 Watchung Way, 07922. SAN 375-9296. Tel: 908-771-5757. FAX: 908-771-5820. *In Charge,* Monique Blackmon; E-mail: mblackmon@ucnj.org
Library Holdings: Bk Titles 250; Per Subs 37
Subject Interests: Geriatrics, Psychiat, Rehabilitation
Open Mon-Fri 8-4

BERLIN

P MARIE FLECHE MEMORIAL LIBRARY*, 49 S White Horse Pike, 08009. SAN 310-0170. Tel: 856-767-2448. FAX: 856-768-7421. E-mail: mfml@camden.lib.nj.us. *Dir,* Mary Rencic; Staff 2 (Non-MLS 2)
Founded 1957. Pop 10,000; Circ 22,470
Library Holdings: Bk Vols 26,000; Per Subs 20
Wireless access
Function: Adult bk club, Copy machines, e-mail serv, Electronic databases & coll, ILL available, Photocopying/Printing, Prog for children & young adult, Spoken cassettes & CDs, Spoken cassettes & DVDs, Summer reading prog, Tax forms, VHS videos
Mem of Camden County Library System
Open Mon-Thurs 12:30-4:30 & 7-9
Restriction: Authorized patrons, Circ to mem only, In-house use for visitors, Lending limited to county residents
Friends of the Library Group

BERNARDSVILLE

P BERNARDSVILLE PUBLIC LIBRARY*, One Anderson Hill Rd, 07924. SAN 310-0189. Tel: 908-766-0118. FAX: 908-766-2464. E-mail: librarian@bernardsvillelibrary.org. Web Site: www.bernardsvillelibrary.org. *Exec Dir,* April L Judge; *Adult Prog & Publicity Mgr,* Madelyn English; E-mail: menglish@bernardsvillelibrary.org; *Readers' Serv Manager,* Pat Kennedy-Grant; E-mail: pkennedygrant@bernardsvillelibrary.org; *Tech Serv Mgr,* Rosalie Baker; E-mail: rbaker@bernardsvillelibrary.org; *Youth Serv Mgr,* Lia Carruthers; E-mail: lcarruthers@bernardsvillelibrary.org; Staff 17 (MLS 4, Non-MLS 13)
Founded 1902. Pop 7,450; Circ 213,753
Library Holdings: AV Mats 13,412; Bks on Deafness & Sign Lang 48; Large Print Bks 428; Bk Titles 68,732; Per Subs 177
Special Collections: Family Literacy, ESL; Local History (Spinning Coll), bks, microfilm. Oral History
Automation Activity & Vendor Info: (Circulation) Innovative Interfaces, Inc
Wireless access
Publications: Bernardsville Library Times (Newsletter)
Partic in Morris-Union Federation; Raritan Valley Fedn of Librs
Special Services for the Deaf - Adult & family literacy prog; Assistive tech; Bks on deafness & sign lang; Closed caption videos; TTY equip

Special Services for the Blind - Aids for in-house use; Audio mat; Bks on cassette; Bks on CD; Home delivery serv; Low vision equip; Magnifiers; Talking bks
Open Mon, Tues & Thurs 10-9, Wed, Fri & Sat 10-5, Sun 1-5
Friends of the Library Group

BEVERLY

P BEVERLY FREE LIBRARY*, 441 Cooper St, 08010. SAN 310-0197. Tel: 609-387-1259. FAX: 609-387-1259. E-mail: beverly@bcls.lib.nj.us. *Dir,* Thomas Lowden; Staff 1 (MLS 1)
Founded 1929. Pop 10,525
Library Holdings: Bk Vols 10,830
Subject Interests: NJ
Automation Activity & Vendor Info: (Cataloging) Horizon
Mem of Burlington County Library
Open Mon & Wed 10-1, Tues & Fri 7pm-9pm, Sat 12-3

BLACKWOOD

J CAMDEN COUNTY COLLEGE LIBRARY*, Wolverton Library, College Dr, 08012. (Mail add: PO Box 200, 08012-0200), SAN 310-0200. Tel: 856-227-7200, Ext 4615. Circulation Tel: 856-227-7200, Ext 4404. Interlibrary Loan Service Tel: 856-874-6001. Reference Tel: 856-227-7200, Ext 4408. FAX: 856-374-4897. Web Site: library.camdencc.edu/. *Dir,* Position Currently Open; *Ref & Instruction Librn,* Olivia Nellums; Tel: 856-227-7200, Ext 4405, E-mail: onellums@camdencc.edu; *Coordr, Ref & Instrul Serv, Web Developer,* Miriam Mlynarski; Tel: 856-227-7200, Ext 4615, E-mail: mmlynarski@camdencc.edu; *Circ Serv, Tech Serv,* Lorraine Baggett-Heuser; Tel: 856-227-7200, Ext 4417, E-mail: lbaggett@camdencc.edu; *Coll Develop,* Patricia Fazio; Tel: 856-227-7200, Ext 4402, E-mail: pfazio@camdencc.edu; Staff 10.5 (MLS 6.5, Non-MLS 4)
Founded 1967. Enrl 16,000; Fac 900; Highest Degree: Associate
Library Holdings: Bks on Deafness & Sign Lang 250; CDs 600; e-books 42,000; e-journals 20,000; Bk Titles 70,000; Bk Vols 93,500; Per Subs 209; Videos 2,750
Subject Interests: Art, Judaica
Automation Activity & Vendor Info: (Cataloging) Innovative Interfaces, Inc; (Circulation) Innovative Interfaces, Inc; (Course Reserve) Innovative Interfaces, Inc; (ILL) L4U Library Software; (OPAC) Innovative Interfaces, Inc; (Serials) Innovative Interfaces, Inc
Database Vendor: ARTstor, CQ Press, ebrary, EBSCOhost, Elsevier, Facts on File, Gale Cengage Learning, Innovative Interfaces, Inc, JSTOR, LexisNexis, Project MUSE, ProQuest, PubMed, SerialsSolutions, Westlaw
Wireless access
Partic in LibraryLinkNJ, The New Jersey Library Cooperative; Lyrasis; OCLC Online Computer Library Center, Inc; Virtual Academic Library Environment
Restriction: In-house use for visitors
Departmental Libraries:
ROHRER E-LIBRARY, 1889 Rte 70 E, Cherry Hill, 08003. Tel: 856-874-6001, 856-874-6002. FAX: 856-874-6049. *Extn Serv,* Barbara Laynor; E-mail: blaynor@camdencc.edu; Staff 2 (MLS 1, Non-MLS 1)
Founded 2000
Library Holdings: Bk Vols 200; Per Subs 2
Function: Bk club(s), ILL available
Restriction: In-house use for visitors, Non-circulating coll, Open to students, fac & staff, Restricted pub use

BLOOMFIELD

C BLOOMFIELD COLLEGE LIBRARY*, Liberty St & Oakland Ave, 07003. SAN 310-0235. Tel: 973-748-9000, Ext 332. FAX: 973-743-3998. Web Site: www.bloomfield.edu. *Dir,* Danilo H Figueredo; Tel: 973-748-9000, Ext 337; *Head, Circ,* Annmarie Battista; *Syst Coordr,* Kate Kohli; *Acq, Per,* Stanley Porteur; Tel: 973-748-9000, Ext 335; *Cat, Ref Serv,* John Hinchcliffe; Tel: 973-748-9000, Ext 336; *ILL, Online Serv, Ref Serv,* Mark Jackson; Tel: 973-748-9000, Ext 714; *Media Spec,* Barbara Isacson; Tel: 973-748-9000, Ext 370; Staff 4 (MLS 4)
Founded 1869. Enrl 2,000; Fac 170; Highest Degree: Bachelor
Library Holdings: Bk Titles 64,000; Per Subs 400
Subject Interests: Educ, Multicultural diversity
Automation Activity & Vendor Info: (Cataloging) SirsiDynix; (Circulation) SirsiDynix; (OPAC) SirsiDynix
Wireless access
Partic in BRS; Dialog Corp; OCLC Online Computer Library Center, Inc; Virtual Academic Library Environment
Open Mon-Fri 7:30am-11pm, Sat 8-7, Sun 4-11
Departmental Libraries:
MEDIA CENTER, 80 Oakland Ave, 07003. Tel: 973-748-9000, Ext 370. FAX: 973-566-9483. Web Site: www.bloomfield.edu/mcenter. *Dir,* Barbara Isacson
Library Holdings: AV Mats 4,000
Open Mon & Fri (Winter) 8:30am-9pm, Sat 11-4; Mon-Fri (Summer) 8:30-5
Restriction: Non-circulating

P BLOOMFIELD PUBLIC LIBRARY*, 90 Broad St, 07003. SAN 310-0243. Tel: 973-566-6200. FAX: 973-566-6217. Web Site: www.bplnj.org. *Dir,* Catherine Wolverton; Tel: 973-566-6200, Ext 203; *Principal Librn,* Linda Esler; Tel: 973-566-6200, Ext 228; *Sr Librn,* Linda Pendergrass; Tel: 973-566-6200, Ext 225; *Sr Librn, Tech Serv,* Stan Ploszaj; Tel: 973-566-6200, Ext 222; *Librn,* Lisa Cohn; Tel: 973-566-6200, Ext 217; *Ch,* Emily Knorr; Tel: 973-566-6200, Ext 212; *Spec Coll Librn,* Joan Dorfman; Staff 23 (MLS 8, Non-MLS 15)
Founded 1924. Pop 48,000; Circ 201,941
Library Holdings: Bk Vols 160,000
Special Collections: Business & Labor Coll, bks, micro, per; Music Coll
Subject Interests: Labor, Local hist, Music
Automation Activity & Vendor Info: (Circulation) Infor Library & Information Solutions
Database Vendor: EBSCOhost, OCLC FirstSearch
Wireless access
Partic in OCLC Online Computer Library Center, Inc
Open Mon-Wed 10-8, Thurs & Fri 11-5, Sat 9-6
Friends of the Library Group

S CHICAGO BRIDGE & IRON CO, Lummus Technology Library, 1515 Broad St, 07003. SAN 310-0251. Tel: 973-893-2257. FAX: 973-893-2119. E-mail: cltb.library@cbi.com. *Librn,* Carol Schneider-Linn; Staff 1 (MLS 1)
Founded 1930
Library Holdings: Bk Vols 11,000; Per Subs 40
Special Collections: Crude Oil, bks & pamphlets
Subject Interests: Chem eng, Petrochemicals, Petroleum refining
Automation Activity & Vendor Info: (OPAC) Inmagic, Inc.; (Serials) Professional Software
Database Vendor: American Chemical Society, Dialog, EBSCOhost, Elsevier, Factiva.com, IHS, ScienceDirect, Springer-Verlag, STN International, Wiley InterScience
Wireless access
Partic in New Jersey Library Network
Restriction: Open to pub by appt only

BLOOMINGDALE

P BLOOMINGDALE FREE PUBLIC LIBRARY*, Municipal Bldg, 101 Hamburg Tpk, 07403-1297. SAN 310-0278. Tel: 973-838-0077. FAX: 973-838-2482. E-mail: bfpl@bloomingdalelibrary.org. Web Site: www.bloomingdalelibrary.org. *Interim Dir,* Patricia Perugino; E-mail: perugino@bloomingdalelibrary.org; *Ch,* Denise Carrozza; E-mail: carrozza@bloomingdalelibrary.org; *Prog Coordr,* Margaret Sweet; E-mail: sweet@bloomingdalelibrary.org
Founded 1926. Pop 7,610; Circ 37,369
Library Holdings: Bk Titles 26,867
Subject Interests: Bloomingdale hist
Automation Activity & Vendor Info: (Cataloging) SirsiDynix; (Circulation) SirsiDynix
Wireless access
Partic in PALS Plus, The Computer Consortium of Passaic County Libraries
Open Mon-Wed 10-8, Thurs & Fri 10-5, Sat 10-1
Friends of the Library Group

BOGOTA

P BOGOTA PUBLIC LIBRARY*, 375 Larch Ave, 07603. SAN 310-0286. Tel: 201-488-7185. FAX: 201-342-2094. E-mail: bogtcirc@bccls.org. Web Site: www.bogotapubliclibrary.org. *Dir,* Davis Jonna; E-mail: davis@bccls.org
Founded 1915. Circ 50,395
Library Holdings: Bk Vols 36,564; Per Subs 82
Automation Activity & Vendor Info: (Cataloging) SirsiDynix; (Circulation) SirsiDynix; (OPAC) SirsiDynix
Wireless access
Partic in Bergen County Cooperative Library System; NJ Regional Libr Coop, Region 2
Open Mon, Tues & Thurs 10-9, Wed & Fri 10-5, Sat (Sept-June) 10-1
Friends of the Library Group

BOONTON

P BOONTON HOLMES PUBLIC LIBRARY*, 621 Main St, 07005. SAN 310-0308. Tel: 973-334-2980. FAX: 973-334-3917. E-mail: bhpl@boontonholmeslibrary.org. Web Site: www.boontonholmeslibrary.org. *Dir,* Sam Pharo; E-mail: samopharo@gmail.com; *Local Hist & Ref Librn,* Joseph Gasparro; E-mail: joseph.gasparro@boontonholmeslibrary.org; *Youth Serv Librn,* Emily Weisenstein; E-mail:

emily.weisenstein@boontonholmeslibrary.org; Staff 4 (MLS 3, Non-MLS 1)
Founded 1893. Pop 8,400; Circ 49,000
Library Holdings: Bk Titles 32,000; Bk Vols 35,000; Per Subs 47
Special Collections: Boonton Newspaper Coll, microfiche; Boonton Photographs; Boonton Postcards; Boonton Yearbooks
Subject Interests: Local hist
Wireless access
Function: Adult bk club, Archival coll, Audiobks via web, Bi-weekly Writer's Group, Bk club(s), Bks on cassette, Bks on CD, Chess club, Children's prog, Computer training, Computers for patron use, Copy machines, e-mail & chat, Electronic databases & coll, Fax serv, Handicapped accessible, ILL available, Mus passes, Music CDs, Notary serv, Online cat, Online ref, Online searches, OverDrive digital audio bks, Photocopying/Printing, Preschool outreach, Prog for adults, Prog for children & young adult, Pub access computers, Scanner, Senior computer classes, Story hour, Summer reading prog, Tax forms, Teen prog, Telephone ref, VHS videos, Web-catalog, Wheelchair accessible
Partic in LibraryLinkNJ, The New Jersey Library Cooperative; Morris Automated Information Network
Open Mon-Thurs 10-9, Fri 10-5, Sat 10-3, Sun (Sept-June) 1-5
Friends of the Library Group

BORDENTOWN

S ALBERT C WAGNER YOUTH CORRECTIONAL FACILITY LIBRARY*, 500 Ward Ave, 08505-2928. (Mail add: PO Box 500, 08505-0500). Tel: 609-298-0500. FAX: 609-298-3639. *Librn,* Nicholas Sharkoski
Library Holdings: Bk Titles 14,300

BRADLEY BEACH

P BRADLEY BEACH PUBLIC LIBRARY*, 511 Fourth Ave, 07720. SAN 310-0367. Tel: 732-776-2995. FAX: 732-774-4591. Web Site: www.bradleybeachlibrary.org. *Dir,* Lorraine O'Dell; E-mail: director@bradleybeachlibrary.org; Staff 4 (MLS 1, Non-MLS 3)
Founded 1927. Pop 4,973; Circ 24,941
Library Holdings: AV Mats 1,648; Bk Titles 30,147; Bk Vols 37,334; Per Subs 51
Automation Activity & Vendor Info: (Acquisitions) Auto-Graphics, Inc; (Cataloging) Auto-Graphics, Inc; (Circulation) Auto-Graphics, Inc; (ILL) Auto-Graphics, Inc; (OPAC) Auto-Graphics, Inc; (Serials) Auto-Graphics, Inc
Database Vendor: EBSCOhost
Wireless access
Open Mon, Wed & Fri 9-5, Tues & Thurs 9-8, Sat 9-2
Friends of the Library Group

BRICK

M OCEAN MEDICAL CENTER*, Information Resource Center, 425 Jack Martin Blvd, 08724. SAN 329-9198. Tel: 732-836-4343. FAX: 732-206-8052. *In Charge,* Susan O'Hara; Staff 1 (Non-MLS 1)
Founded 1975
Library Holdings: Bk Titles 1,650; Bk Vols 1,800; Per Subs 170
Special Collections: Consumer Health; Nursing
Subject Interests: Med
Automation Activity & Vendor Info: (Cataloging) Ex Libris Group; (Circulation) Ex Libris Group
Database Vendor: EBSCOhost, OVID Technologies
Wireless access
Partic in NJ Regional Libr Coop
Open Mon-Fri 9-1

BRIDGETON

P BRIDGETON FREE PUBLIC LIBRARY*, 150 E Commerce St, 08302-2684. SAN 310-0375. Tel: 856-451-2620. Web Site: www.bridgetonlibrary.org. *Dir,* Gail S Robinson; Staff 2 (MLS 2)
Founded 1921. Pop 24,000; Circ 36,000
Jul 2011-Jun 2012 Income $180,000. Mats Exp $15,000
Library Holdings: Bk Titles 57,000; Bk Vols 58,000; Per Subs 45
Special Collections: American Indians (Lenni-Lenapes Coll); South Jersey History
Automation Activity & Vendor Info: (Cataloging) SirsiDynix; (Circulation) SirsiDynix; (OPAC) SirsiDynix
Wireless access
Open Mon & Fri 10-5, Tues-Thurs 10-8, Sat 10-4 (10-2 June-Aug)
Friends of the Library Group

S CUMBERLAND COUNTY JUVENILE DETENTION CENTER LIBRARY*, 135 Sunny Slope Dr, 08302. SAN 375-734X. Tel: 856-455-0717, Ext 30. FAX: 856-455-4927. *In Charge,* Susan Widjeskog
Library Holdings: Bk Vols 800; Per Subs 20
Restriction: Not open to pub

L CUMBERLAND COUNTY LAW LIBRARY*, Cumberland County Courthouse, 1st Flr, Broad & Fayette Sts, 08302. SAN 328-1515. Tel: 856-451-8000, 856-453-4530, 856-853-3539. *Librn,* Diane Frank; *Acq, Tech Serv,* Maria Buono-Gaimari
Founded 1909
Library Holdings: Bk Vols 600
Open Mon-Fri 8:30-4:30
Restriction: Non-circulating to the pub

P CUMBERLAND COUNTY LIBRARY*, 800 E Commerce St, 08302-2295. SAN 310-0383. Tel: 856-453-2210. Circulation Tel: 856-453-2210, Ext 101. Interlibrary Loan Service Tel: 856-453-2210, Ext 102. Reference Tel: 856-453-2210, Ext 106. Administration Tel: 856-453-2210, Ext 109. Automation Services Tel: 856-453-2210, Ext 111. FAX: 856-451-1940. E-mail: ref@clueslibs.org. Web Site: www.clueslibs.org. *Actg Dir,* Jean Edwards; E-mail: jeaned@clueslibs.org; *IT & Security Mgr,* Myron Estelle; E-mail: myrones@clueslibs.org; *Circ Supvr,* Margaret Allen; E-mail: margaretal@clueslibs.org; *Ref,* Tom Ayars; E-mail: tomayars@clueslibs.org; *Ref,* Donna Strickman; *Syst Coordr,* Susan D'Ottavio; E-mail: susando@clueslibs.org; *Tech Serv,* Alex Caffrey; Staff 7 (MLS 7)
Founded 1963. Pop 146,438; Circ 84,306
Library Holdings: Bk Vols 100,000; Per Subs 170
Special Collections: Adult Basic Education Materials; New Jersey Materials. State Document Depository
Automation Activity & Vendor Info: (Cataloging) SirsiDynix; (Circulation) SirsiDynix; (OPAC) SirsiDynix
Database Vendor: SirsiDynix
Member Libraries: Pennsville Public Library
Partic in Cumberland Libraries United Electronic System (CLUES); OCLC Online Computer Library Center, Inc
Special Services for the Deaf - Staff with knowledge of sign lang
Special Services for the Blind - Bks on CD
Open Mon-Wed 9-9, Thurs-Sat 9-5
Friends of the Library Group
Bookmobiles: 1. In Charge, Courtenay Reece. Bk vols 5,000

S NEW JERSEY DEPARTMENT OF CORRECTIONS*, South Woods State Prison - Facility I Library, 215 Burlington Rd S, 08302. Tel: 856-459-8145. FAX: 856-459-8125. Web Site: www.state.nj.us/corrections. *Librn,* Rosellen Muniak
Founded 1997
Library Holdings: Bk Titles 1,500; Bk Vols 1,800
Special Collections: Law Coll
Database Vendor: LexisNexis
Publications: NJ Legal Library
Restriction: Not open to pub
Branches:
SOUTH WOODS STATE PRISON - FACILITY II LIBRARY, 215 Burlington Rd S, 08302. Tel: 856-459-8249.
Library Holdings: Bk Vols 1,250
Special Collections: Law Coll
Database Vendor: Westlaw
Restriction: Not open to pub
SOUTH WOODS STATE PRISON - FACILITY III LIBRARY, 215 Burlington Rd S, 08302. Tel: 856-459-8349.
Library Holdings: Bk Vols 1,250
Special Collections: Law Coll
Database Vendor: Westlaw
Restriction: Not open to pub

BRIDGEWATER

L NORRIS, MCLAUGHLIN & MARCUS, PA*, Law Library, 721 Rte 202-206 N, 08807. (Mail add: PO Box 5933, 08807-5933), SAN 372-4824. Tel: 908-722-0700. FAX: 908-722-0755. *Librn,* Janice S Lustiger; E-mail: jslustiger@nmmlaw.com; Staff 2 (MLS 1, Non-MLS 1)
Library Holdings: Bk Vols 10,000
Restriction: Not open to pub

S SOMERSET COUNTY HISTORICAL SOCIETY*, Colonel Van Horn Library, Nine Van Veghten Dr, 08807-3259. SAN 375-507X. Tel: 908-218-1281. E-mail: schs@schsnj.com. Web Site: schsnj.org. *Librn,* George Bebbington; Staff 1 (MLS 1)
Founded 1882
Library Holdings: Bk Titles 900; Bk Vols 1,000
Special Collections: Somerset County History Coll, genealogical family rec, newsp articles, photos, unbd hist doc
Open Tues 12-3

P SOMERSET COUNTY LIBRARY SYSTEM*, One Vogt Dr, 08807-2136. (Mail add: PO Box 6700, 08807-2136), SAN 351-3661. Circulation Tel: 908-526-4016, Ext 104. Interlibrary Loan Service Tel: 908-526-4016, Ext

152. Reference Tel: 908-526-4016, Ext 105. Administration Tel: 908-526-4016, Ext 131. Automation Services Tel: 908-526-4016, Ext 120. Interlibrary Loan Service FAX: 908-526-5221. Administration FAX: 908-707-8324. Web Site: www.somerset.lib.nj.us. *Dir,* Brian Auger; Tel: 908-526-4016, Ext 129, E-mail: bauger@sclibnj.org; *Asst Dir,* W Keith McCoy; Tel: 908-526-4016, Ext 128, E-mail: kmccoy@sclibnj.org; *Head, Automation,* Wendy Clarkson; E-mail: clarkson@sclibnj.org; *Head of Mkt,* Lisa Bogart; Tel: 908-526-4016, Ext 136, E-mail: lbogart@sclibnj.org; *Head, Tech Serv,* Adele Barree; Tel: 908-526-4016, Ext 107, E-mail: abarree@sclibnj.org; *Bus Mgr,* Brian Morgan; Tel: 908-526-4016, Ext 132, E-mail: bmorgan@sclibnj.org; *Human Res Mgr,* Deanna Gray; Tel: 908-526-4016, Ext 133, E-mail: dgray@sclibnj.org; *Adult Serv,* Mun Hwa Chen; Tel: 908-526-4016, Ext 137, E-mail: mchen@sclibnj.org; *Circ Serv,* Sue Coslick; Tel: 908-526-4016, Ext 151, E-mail: scoslick@sclibnj.org; *Youth Serv,* Rebecca Crawford; Staff 206 (MLS 46, Non-MLS 160)
Founded 1930. Pop 176,402; Circ 3,104,862
Jan 2009-Dec 2009 Income (Main Library and Branch(s)) $14,921,598, State $165,559, County $13,850,133, Locally Generated Income $286,585. Mats Exp $1,825,162, Books $974,203, Per/Ser (Incl. Access Fees) $140,949, AV Mat $387,549, Electronic Ref Mat (Incl. Access Fees) $218,569. Sal $8,552,706
Library Holdings: Audiobooks 22,423; DVDs 53,292; e-books 2,048; Bk Vols 708,652
Special Collections: The New Jersey Room, bks, pamphlets, maps, micro. Oral History; State Document Depository
Automation Activity & Vendor Info: (Acquisitions) Innovative Interfaces, Inc; (Cataloging) Innovative Interfaces, Inc; (Circulation) Innovative Interfaces, Inc; (ILL) Innovative Interfaces, Inc; (Media Booking) ADLiB; (OPAC) Innovative Interfaces, Inc; (Serials) Innovative Interfaces, Inc
Database Vendor: CountryWatch, CQ Press, Dun & Bradstreet, EBSCO Auto Repair Reference, EBSCOhost, Facts on File, Gale Cengage Learning, Hoovers, Marquis Who's Who, OCLC FirstSearch, ProQuest, ValueLine, Westlaw, World Book Online
Wireless access
Function: ILL available
Partic in OCLC Online Computer Library Center, Inc
Special Services for the Blind - Accessible computers; Assistive/Adapted tech devices, equip & products; Audiovision-a radio reading serv; Bks on CD; Bks on flash-memory cartridges; Digital talking bk; Digital talking bk machines; Home delivery serv; Info on spec aids & appliances; Large print bks; Large print bks & talking machines; Low vision equip; Newsline for the Blind; Talking bk serv referral; Talking bks; Talking bks & player equip; VisualTek equip
Friends of the Library Group
Branches: 8
BRANCHBURG READING STATION, The Station House, Olive St, Neshanic Station, 08853. (Mail add: PO Box 742, Neshanic Station, 08853-0742). Tel: 908-369-5355. *Supvr,* Carolyn Della Sala
Library Holdings: AV Mats 30; Bk Vols 4,000
Open Mon & Thurs 6:30pm-8pm, Wed 1:30-5, Sat 10-12
Friends of the Library Group
HILLSBOROUGH PUBLIC, Hillsborough Municipal Complex, 379 S Branch Rd, Hillsborough, 08844, SAN 351-3696. Tel: 908-369-2200. FAX: 908-369-8242. *Dir,* Edward Hoag; E-mail: ehoag@sclibnj.org; *Head, Youth Serv,* Laura Mellor; *Circ Supvr,* Ziyan Wang; E-mail: zwang@sclibnj.org; *Adult Serv,* Cathy Briant; E-mail: cbriant@sclibnj.org; *Teen Serv,* Diane Valentine; Staff 28 (MLS 10, Non-MLS 18)
Founded 1966. Pop 42,000; Circ 450,155
Library Holdings: Bk Titles 107,000; Per Subs 200
Function: Adult bk club, Adult literacy prog, Copy machines, Electronic databases & coll, Handicapped accessible, Homework prog, ILL available, Music CDs, Online searches, Ref serv available, Tax forms
Open Mon-Thurs 9:30-9, Fri & Sat 9:30-5:30, Sun 1-5; Mon-Thurs (July & Aug) 9:30-9, Fri 9:30-5:30, Sat 9:30-2
Friends of the Library Group
MARY JACOBS MEMORIAL, 64 Washington St, Rocky Hill, 08553, SAN 351-3726. Tel: 609-924-7073. FAX: 609-924-7668. *Br Dir,* Cindy Mangel; E-mail: cmangel@sclibnj.org; *Circ Supvr,* Suzanne Ridzy; E-mail: sridzy@sclibnj.org; *Adult Serv,* Meredith Hoyer; E-mail: mhoyer@sclibnj.org; Staff 17 (MLS 4, Non-MLS 13)
Founded 1974. Pop 19,000; Circ 215,000
Library Holdings: Bk Vols 100,070; Per Subs 170
Open Mon-Thurs 9:30-9, Fri 9:30-5:30, Sat 9:30-4:30
Friends of the Library Group
NORTH PLAINFIELD LIBRARY, Six Rockview Ave, North Plainfield, 07060, SAN 351-3750. Tel: 908-755-7909. FAX: 908-755-8177. *Br Dir,* Lauren Ryan; E-mail: lryan@sclibnj.org
Pop 22,464; Circ 168,452
Library Holdings: Bk Vols 85,000; Per Subs 175
Open Mon-Thurs 9:30-9, Fri & Sat 9:30-5; Sat (July & Aug) 9:30-12:30
PEAPACK & GLADSTONE PUBLIC, School St, Peapack, 07977, SAN 310-1819. Tel: 908-234-0598. FAX: 908-719-2236. *Br Dir,* Karen Pifher; *Head, Circ,* Laura Levy; *Music, YA Serv,* Melissa John-Williams; *Ch Serv,* Jenna Galley; *Ref Serv, Ad,* Rodrick MacLennan; Staff 9 (MLS 9)
Founded 1936. Pop 2,433; Circ 31,000
Library Holdings: Large Print Bks 720,591; Bk Vols 37,000; Per Subs 70
Special Collections: Equestrian Coll
Publications: The Trumpet (Newsletter)
Open Mon-Thurs 9-9, Fri & Sat 9-5, Sun 1-5
Friends of the Library Group
WARREN TOWNSHIP BRANCH, 42 Mountain Blvd, Warren, 07059, SAN 351-3777. Tel: 908-754-5554. FAX: 908-754-2899. *Br Mgr,* Carolyn Della Sala; E-mail: cdellasa@sclibnj.org
Pop 14,260; Circ 181,500
Library Holdings: Bk Vols 100,000; Per Subs 250
Open Mon-Thurs 9:30-9, Fri 9:30-5, Sat 9:30-4
Friends of the Library Group
WASHINGTON VALLEY, Washington Valley Rd, Martinsville, 08836, SAN 310-2734. Tel: 732-356-2363. *Supvr,* Betty Beadle; *Supvr,* Marna Elliott
Founded 1950. Pop 3,400; Circ 4,533
Library Holdings: Bk Vols 4,800
Open Mon & Wed 2-4 & 7-9, Tues, Thurs & Fri 2-4, Sat 10-12
WATCHUNG PUBLIC, 12 Stirling Rd, Watchung, 07069, SAN 310-5814. Tel: 908-561-0117. FAX: 908-769-1145. *Br Dir,* Douglas Poswencyk; E-mail: dposwenc@sclibnj.org; *Circ Serv,* Elaine Stringer; *Teen Serv,* Terri Coss; *Youth Serv,* Sharon Orlando
Circ 85,715
Library Holdings: Bk Vols 36,595
Open Mon-Thurs 10-9, Fri 10-4:30, Sat 10-4
Friends of the Library Group

BRIELLE

P BRIELLE PUBLIC LIBRARY*, 610 South St, 08730-1494. SAN 310-0413. Tel: 732-528-9381. FAX: 732-223-0346. Web Site: www.briellepubliclibrary.org. *Dir,* Leslie Naughton; Staff 8 (MLS 1, Non-MLS 7)
Founded 1954. Pop 4,800; Circ 58,000
Library Holdings: Bk Vols 45,000; Per Subs 81
Subject Interests: NJ hist
Automation Activity & Vendor Info: (Acquisitions) SirsiDynix; (Cataloging) SirsiDynix; (Circulation) SirsiDynix; (OPAC) SirsiDynix
Database Vendor: EBSCOhost
Wireless access
Partic in LibraryLinkNJ, The New Jersey Library Cooperative
Open Mon, Tues & Thurs 9:30-8, Wed & Fri 12-5, Sat 10-1

BROOKSIDE

P MENDHAM TOWNSHIP LIBRARY*, One Cherry Lane, 07926. (Mail add. PO Box 500, 07926-0500), SAN 310-0421. Tel: 973-543-4018. FAX: 973-543-5472. Web Site: www.mendhamtownshiplibrary.org. *Dir,* Stephanie Cotton; E-mail: stephanie.cotton@mendhamtwplib.org; Staff 6 (MLS 1, Non-MLS 5)
Pop 4,900; Circ 60,000
Library Holdings: Bk Titles 40,000; Per Subs 70
Special Collections: Bks on Tape; Gardening Coll; Local History Coll; Mysteries Coll
Automation Activity & Vendor Info: (Cataloging) SirsiDynix; (Circulation) SirsiDynix; (OPAC) SirsiDynix
Database Vendor: EBSCOhost
Publications: Newsletter
Partic in Morris Automated Information Network
Special Services for the Blind - Bks on cassette
Open Mon-Thurs 10-8, Fri 10-6, Sat 10-3, Sun (Sept-June) 2-5
Friends of the Library Group

BROWNS MILLS

M DEBORAH HEART & LUNG CENTER*, Edith & Jack Tobin Medical Library, 200 Trenton Rd, 08015. SAN 310-043X. Tel: 609-893-6611, Ext 4397. FAX: 609-893-1566. Web Site: www.deborah.org. *Dir, Libr Serv,* Carol A Harris; Tel: 609-893-1200, Ext 4398, E-mail: harrisc@deborah.org
Founded 1971
Library Holdings: Bk Titles 2,600; Bk Vols 3,200; Per Subs 150
Subject Interests: Cardio-pulmonary diseases
Partic in Mid-Eastern Regional Med Libr Serv
Restriction: Non-circulating to the pub, Open to pub by appt only

BUENA

S NEW KUBAN EDUCATION & WELFARE ASSOCIATION*, All Cossack Museum & Library, 228 Don Rd, 08310. (Mail add: 521 Weymouth Rd, 08310), SAN 371-9286. Tel: 856-697-2255. FAX: 856-697-2255. *Librn,* Nina Sienczenko; E-mail: nkewa@comcast.net; Staff 1 (Non-MLS 1)
Founded 1953
Library Holdings: Bk Titles 5,000

Special Collections: Cossack Culture & History Coll
Subject Interests: Russian hist, Ukrainian hist
Function: Res libr
Restriction: Non-circulating, Open by appt only

BURLINGTON

S BURLINGTON COUNTY HISTORICAL SOCIETY*, Delia Biddle-Pugh Library, 457 High St, 08016-4514. SAN 310-0456. Tel: 609-386-4773. Reference Tel: 609-386-4773, Ext 2. FAX: 609-386-4828. Web Site: www.burlingtoncountyhistoricalsociety.org.
Library Holdings: Bk Vols 4,000
Special Collections: Deeds; Historic Manuscripts; James Fenimore Cooper Coll; Photographs; Vital Statistics 1795-present
Subject Interests: Genealogy, Local hist
Wireless access
Open Tues-Sat 1-5
Restriction: Non-circulating to the pub

P LIBRARY COMPANY OF BURLINGTON*, 23 W Union St, 08016. SAN 310-0464. Tel: 609-386-1273. FAX: 609-386-1273. E-mail: burlington@bcls.lib.nj.us. Web Site: www.bcls.lib.nj.us/libraries/burlington. *Dir,* Sharon Vincz
Founded 1757. Pop 20,000; Circ 30,394
Jul 2010-Jun 2011 Income $82,000. Mats Exp $6,000. Sal $61,000
Library Holdings: Audiobooks 148; Bks on Deafness & Sign Lang 8; CDs 335; DVDs 1,100; Large Print Bks 75; Bk Vols 58,770; Per Subs 54
Special Collections: Early 18th Century Vols; New Jersey History Coll
Automation Activity & Vendor Info: (Cataloging) SirsiDynix; (Circulation) SirsiDynix; (OPAC) SirsiDynix
Wireless access
Mem of Burlington County Library
Special Services for the Blind - Large print bks; Talking bks & player equip
Open Mon-Thurs 11-8, Fri 1-6, Sat 11-3
Friends of the Library Group

BUTLER

P BUTLER PUBLIC LIBRARY*, One Ace Rd, 07405. SAN 310-0480. Tel: 973-838-3262. FAX: 973-838-9436. E-mail: ContactUs@butlerlibrary.org. Web Site: www.butlerlibrary.org. *Dir,* Mary G Zaccaria
Founded 1924. Pop 7,600; Circ 37,000
Library Holdings: Bk Titles 43,000; Bk Vols 44,000; Per Subs 90
Automation Activity & Vendor Info: (Cataloging) SirsiDynix; (Circulation) SirsiDynix; (OPAC) SirsiDynix
Wireless access
Open Mon-Thurs 10-8, Fri 10-5, Sat 10-3
Friends of the Library Group

CALDWELL

C CALDWELL COLLEGE*, Jennings Library, 120 Bloomfield Ave, 07006-6195. SAN 310-0499. Tel: 973-618-3312. Interlibrary Loan Service Tel: 973-618-3564. FAX: 973-618-3360. Web Site: jenningslibrary.caldwell.edu. *Col Librn,* Peter Panos; *ILL,* Joan Reamer; Staff 14 (MLS 6, Non-MLS 8)
Founded 1939
Library Holdings: Bk Titles 110,692; Bk Vols 150,000; Per Subs 841
Special Collections: Grover Cleveland Coll of American History
Subject Interests: Archit, Art, Educ curric, Hist, Lit, Relig studies, Women's studies
Wireless access
Publications: General Information Brochure; Monthly New Acquisitions List; Newsletter
Partic in Essex County Coop Librs; LibraryLinkNJ, The New Jersey Library Cooperative; OCLC Online Computer Library Center, Inc; Virtual Academic Library Environment

P CALDWELL PUBLIC LIBRARY*, 268 Bloomfield Ave, 07006-5198. SAN 310-0502. Tel: 973 226 2837. FAX: 973-403-8606. Web Site: www.caldwellpl.org. *Dir,* Karen Kleppe-Lembo; Tel: 973-403-4649, E-mail: klembo@caldwellpl.org; *Children's Programmer,* Deborah Khost; Tel: 973-226-1636, E-mail: dkhost@caldwellpl.org; Staff 7 (MLS 1, Non-MLS 6)
Founded 1907. Pop 7,584; Circ 67,478
Library Holdings: Bk Titles 35,784; Bk Vols 37,708; Per Subs 85
Subject Interests: Local hist
Automation Activity & Vendor Info: (Circulation) SIRSI-iBistro; (OPAC) SIRSI-iBistro
Database Vendor: EBSCOhost
Wireless access
Function: ILL available
Partic in Essex County Coop Librs; PALS Plus, The Computer Consortium of Passaic County Libraries
Open Mon & Fri 9-5, Tues-Thurs 9-8, Sat (Sept-June) 9-1

CALIFON

P BUNNVALE PUBLIC LIBRARY*, Seven Bunnvale Rd, Rte 513, 07830. Tel: 908-638-8884. *In Charge,* Wendy Harding
Library Holdings: AV Mats 240; Large Print Bks 30; Bk Vols 58,427; Per Subs 50; Talking Bks 250
Automation Activity & Vendor Info: (Cataloging) SirsiDynix; (Circulation) SirsiDynix; (OPAC) SirsiDynix
Wireless access
Mem of Hunterdon County Library
Open Wed 1-8, Thurs & Fri 9-5, Sat 9-2
Friends of the Library Group

CAMDEN

S CAMDEN COUNTY HISTORICAL SOCIETY, Richard H Hineline Research Center, 1900 Park Blvd, 08103-3611. (Mail add: PO Box 378, Collingswood, 08108-0378), SAN 310-0529. Tel: 856-964-3333. E-mail: librarydirect@cchsnj.org. Web Site: www.cchsnj.org. *Exec Dir,* Jason E Allen; E-mail: execdirect@cchsnj.org
Founded 1899
Library Holdings: Bk Titles 20,000
Special Collections: Camden Courier Newspaper Coll 1882-1959, microfilm; History of Southern New Jersey (Charles Boyer Coll), author's notes, unpublished bks & ms; Legal History of Southern New Jersey (John D Morgan Coll); South New Jersey Jewish History (Tri-County Jewish Historical Society Coll). Oral History
Subject Interests: Camden County hist, County hist, Genealogy, Genealogy for S NJ & PA, Hist of Del River Valley, Quaker hist
Wireless access
Function: Res performed for a fee
Publications: Newsletter (Quarterly)
Open Wed-Fri 10-3

OUR LADY OF LOURDES
M MEDICAL CENTER LIBRARY*, 1600 Haddon Ave, 08103, SAN 350-6134. Tel: 856-757-3548. FAX: 856-757-3215. *Dir,* Susan Cleveland; Staff 1 (MLS 1)
Founded 1973
Library Holdings: Bk Titles 685; Per Subs 50
Special Collections: Hospital Archives
Subject Interests: Clinical health sci
Partic in National Network of Libraries of Medicine
Open Mon-Fri 6-2:30

M SCHOOL OF NURSING LIBRARY*, 1600 Haddon Ave, 08103, SAN 350-6169. Tel: 856-757-3722. FAX: 856-757-3767. *Librn,* Donna Soultoukis; E-mail: soultoukisd@lourdesnet.org; Staff 1 (MLS 1)
Founded 1961. Fac 14; Highest Degree: Associate
Jan 2007-Dec 2007 Income $6,500. Mats Exp $6,000, Books $4,500, Per/Ser (Incl. Access Fees) $1,500. Sal $53,000
Library Holdings: CDs 75; DVDs 50; Bk Titles 575; Bk Vols 1,900; Per Subs 35; Videos 100
Special Collections: Nursing History Coll
Subject Interests: Nursing educ
Automation Activity & Vendor Info: (Cataloging) Follett Software; (Circulation) Follett Software; (OPAC) Follett Software
Database Vendor: EBSCOhost, OVID Technologies
Partic in Basic Health Sciences Library Network; Docline; Health Sciences Library Association of New Jersey; LibraryLinkNJ, The New Jersey Library Cooperative; National Network of Libraries of Medicine South Central Region; New Jersey Health Sciences Library Network; S Jersey Regional Libr Consortium
Open Mon-Thurs 6am-11pm, Fri 6-3:30
Restriction: Students only

RUTGERS UNIVERSITY LIBRARIES
CL CAMDEN LAW LIBRARY*, 217 N Fifth St, 08102-1203, SAN 350-6223. Tel: 856-225-6172. Web Site: lawlibrary.rutgers.edu. *Dir, Law Libr & Assoc Prof of Law,* Anne Dalesandro; Tel: 856-225-8182, E-mail: dalesand@camden.rutgers.edu; *Head, Circ, Head, Digital Planning,* John Jorgensen; Tel: 856-225-6460, E-mail: jjoerg@camden.rutgers.edu; *Head, Govt Doc & Micro, Ref & Instrul Serv Librn,* A Hays Butler; Tel: 856-225-6496, E-mail: ahbutler@camden.rutgers.edu; *Head, ILL, Ref & Instrul Serv Librn,* Eric Gilson; Tel: 856-225-6462, E-mail: etg2@camden.rutgers.edu; *Head, Ref & Res Serv,* David Batista; Tel: 856-225-6469, E-mail: batista@camden.rutgers.edu; *Head, Tech Serv,* Gloria Chao; Tel: 856-225-6457, E-mail: chao@camden.rutgers.edu; *Intl Law Librn, Ref Librn,* Lucy Cox; Tel: 856-225-6464, E-mail: lcox@camden.rutgers.edu; Staff 19 (MLS 7, Non-MLS 12)
Founded 1926. Enrl 770; Fac 46; Highest Degree: Doctorate
Library Holdings: Bk Titles 94,635; Bk Vols 439,801; Per Subs 4,624

Automation Activity & Vendor Info: (Acquisitions) Innovative Interfaces, Inc; (Cataloging) Innovative Interfaces, Inc; (Circulation) Innovative Interfaces, Inc; (ILL) Innovative Interfaces, Inc; (OPAC) Innovative Interfaces, Inc; (Serials) Innovative Interfaces, Inc
Database Vendor: HeinOnline, LexisNexis, Westlaw
Partic in Association of Research Libraries (ARL); RLIN (Research Libraries Information Network)
Open Mon-Thurs 8am-Midnight, Fri 8am-10pm, Sat 9-8, Sun 10am-Midnight

C PAUL ROBESON LIBRARY, CAMDEN*, 300 N Fourth St, 08102-1404, SAN 350-6193. Tel: 856-225-2848, 856-225-6034. FAX: 856-225-6428. Web Site: www.libraries.rutgers.edu/rul/libs/robeson_lib/index.html. *Dir,* Gary A Golden; Tel: 856-225-2828, E-mail: ggolden@camden.rutgers.edu; *Bus Librn,* Theo Haynes; *Ref,* Julie Still; *Ref Serv,* Vivian Cvetkovic; *Ref Serv,* John Maxymuk; *Ref Serv,* Donna Wertheimer; *Ref,* Katie Anderson; *Ref,* Laura Spencer; *Ref,* Zara Wilkinson
Founded 1951. Highest Degree: Doctorate
Library Holdings: AV Mats 74; Bk Vols 255,804; Per Subs 1,464
Special Collections: State Document Depository; US Document Depository
Subject Interests: Grad educ, Undergrad educ
Special Services for the Blind - Assistive/Adapted tech devices, equip & products
Open Mon-Thurs 7:30am-10pm, Fri 7:30-5, Sat 9-5

G UNITED STATES COURT OF APPEALS*, James Hunter III Memorial Library, One J F Gerry Plaza, Fourth & Cooper, 08101. (Mail add: PO Box 1988, 08101), SAN 377-2055. Tel: 856-968-4859. FAX: 856-968-4871. *Br Librn,* Kristin Schroth; E-mail: kristin_schroth@ca3.uscourts.gov; Staff 1 (MLS 1)
Library Holdings: Bk Vols 10,000
Automation Activity & Vendor Info: (Cataloging) SirsiDynix
Wireless access
Open Mon-Fri 8:30-12:30 & 1:30-4:30

CAPE MAY COURT HOUSE

S CAPE MAY COUNTY HISTORICAL & GENEALOGICAL SOCIETY LIBRARY*, Alexander Memorial, 504 Rte 9 N, 08210-3090. SAN 329-8663. Tel: 609-465-3535. FAX: 609-465-4274. E-mail: genealogy@co.cape-may.nj.us. *Coordr,* Sonia Forry
Library Holdings: Bk Vols 800
Special Collections: Cape May County Family Documents & Bibles; Historic Maps (1872 Beer's Map)
Subject Interests: Family hist, Genealogy, Local hist
Function: Archival coll, Photocopying/Printing, Prog for adults, Ref serv available, Telephone ref
Publications: Cape May County Magazine of History & Genealogy (Annual report)
Open Wed-Fri 10-3:30
Restriction: Internal use only

GL CAPE MAY COUNTY LAW LIBRARY*, Cape May County Court House, Nine N Main St, 08210. (Mail add: c/o Atlantic County Law Library, 1201 Bacharach Blvd, Atlantic City, 08401), SAN 373-2878. Tel: 609 594-3429. *Law Librn,* Robert St John
Founded 1993
Library Holdings: Bk Titles 1,000; Per Subs 1
Special Collections: Casino Control Commission Hearings; NJ Legislative History
Partic in Westlaw
Open Mon-Fri 8:30-4:30
Restriction: Non-circulating

P CAPE MAY COUNTY LIBRARY*, 30 Mechanic St, 08210. (Mail add: Four Moore Rd - DN2030, 08210), SAN 350-6258. Tel: 609-463-6350. Interlibrary Loan Service Tel: 609-463-6364. Reference Tel: 609-463-6352. Information Services Tel: 609-463-6357. FAX: 609-465-3895. Web Site: www.cmclibrary.org. *Dir,* Deborah Poillon; E-mail: debp@cmclibrary.org; *ILL,* Linda Hayes; *Ref,* Lisa Brownback; *Tech Serv,* Evelyn McAnaney; Staff 61 (MLS 17, Non-MLS 44)
Founded 1925. Pop 92,250; Circ 525,000
Library Holdings: Bk Titles 180,000; Bk Vols 398,000; Per Subs 700
Automation Activity & Vendor Info: (Acquisitions) Innovative Interfaces, Inc; (Cataloging) Innovative Interfaces, Inc; (Circulation) Innovative Interfaces, Inc; (OPAC) Innovative Interfaces, Inc
Wireless access
Function: Adult bk club, Audiobks via web, Bk club(s), Bks on CD, Chess club, Children's prog, Computer training, Computers for patron use, Copy machines, Electronic databases & coll, Free DVD rentals, Handicapped accessible, Holiday prog, Home delivery & serv to Sr ctr & nursing homes, Homebound delivery serv, ILL available, Music CDs, Online cat, OverDrive digital audio bks, Photocopying/Printing, Printer for laptops & handheld devices, Prog for adults, Prog for children & young adult, Pub access computers, Ref & res, Story hour, Summer & winter reading prog, Tax forms, Wheelchair accessible
Partic in LibraryLinkNJ, The New Jersey Library Cooperative
Open Mon-Fri 8:30am-9pm, Sat 9-4:30, Sun (Oct-April) 1-5
Branches: 7
CAPE MAY CITY BRANCH, 110 Ocean St, Cape May, 08204, SAN 375-5142. Tel: 609-884-9568. *Br Mgr,* Linda Smith
Library Holdings: Bk Titles 42,000; Per Subs 32
LOWER CAPE BRANCH, 2600 Bayshore Rd, Villas, 08251, SAN 350-6290. Tel: 609-886-8999. *Librn,* Edward Carson; Staff 9 (MLS 2, Non-MLS 7)
Library Holdings: Bk Titles 50,000; Per Subs 100
Open Mon, Wed & Thurs 9-8, Tues & Fri 9-5, Sat 9-4:30
SEA ISLE CITY BRANCH, 125 John F Kennedy Blvd, Sea Isle City, 08243, SAN 350-6304. Tel: 609-263-8485.
Library Holdings: Bk Titles 15,000; Per Subs 54
Open Mon 9-1 & 1:30-9, Tues, Thurs & Fri 9-1 & 1:30-4:15, Wed 9-1 & 1:30-8, Sat 9-2
STONE HARBOR BRANCH, 9508 Second Ave, Stone Harbor, 08247, SAN 350-6312. Tel: 609-368-6809. *Br Mgr,* Geraldine Fridmann; *Libr Asst,* Tari Ryan
Library Holdings: Bk Titles 8,000; Per Subs 35
Open Mon 9-8, Tues-Fri 9-4:30, Sat 9-2
Friends of the Library Group
UPPER CAPE BRANCH, 2050 Rte 631, Petersburg, 08270, SAN 325-4267. Tel: 609-628-2607. *Librn,* Elizabeth Dusman; Staff 7 (MLS 1, Non-MLS 6)
Library Holdings: Bk Vols 45,000; Per Subs 80
Open Mon & Wed 9-8, Tues, Thurs & Fri 9-5, Sat 9-4:30
WILDWOOD CREST BRANCH, 6301 Ocean Ave, Wildwood Crest, 08260, SAN 350-6282. Tel: 609-522 0564. *Br Mgr,* Fran Tiampetti
Library Holdings: Bk Titles 15,000
WOODBINE BRANCH, 800 Monroe St, Woodbine, 08270. Tel: 609-861-2501. *Br Mgr,* Michael Conley
Bookmobiles: 1

CARLSTADT

P WILLIAM E DERMODY FREE PUBLIC LIBRARY*, 420 Hackensack St, 07072. SAN 310-060X. Tel: 201-438-8866. FAX: 201-438-2733. E-mail: carlcirc@bccls.org, carlref@bccls.org. Web Site: carlstadt.bccls.org. *Dir,* Mary Disanza; E-mail: disanza@bccls.org; *Ch,* Sara Simon; E-mail: sara.simon@bccls.org; *Ref Librn,* Margaret Rose O'Keefe; Staff 3 (MLS 3)
Founded 1936. Pop 6,127; Circ 67,170
Library Holdings: Bk Vols 31,894; Per Subs 124
Special Collections: Carlstadt Freie Press Newspaper (1873-1926 & 1936-present)
Automation Activity & Vendor Info: (Acquisitions) Baker & Taylor; (Circulation) Innovative Interfaces, Inc; (ILL) Innovative Interfaces, Inc
Database Vendor: Baker & Taylor, EBSCOhost, Gale Cengage Learning, Overdrive, Inc, ProQuest, ReferenceUSA
Wireless access
Function: Adult bk club, Bks on CD, Children's prog, Computers for patron use, Copy machines, Free DVD rentals, Literacy & newcomer serv, Music CDs, OverDrive digital audio bks, Photocopying/Printing, Preschool reading prog, Prog for adults, Prog for children & young adult, Pub access computers, Ref serv in person, Spoken cassettes & CDs, Spoken cassettes & DVDs, Story hour, Summer reading prog, Tax forms, Teen prog
Partic in Bergen County Cooperative Library System
Open Mon-Thurs 10-9, Fri 10-5, Sat (Fall-Spring) 10-2

CARNEYS POINT

J SALEM COMMUNITY COLLEGE LIBRARY*, Michael S Cettei Memorial Library, 460 Hollywood Ave, 08069. SAN 321-6233. Tel: 856-351-2681. Web Site: www.salemcc.edu/library. *Dir, Acad Info Res,* Jennifer Pierce; E-mail: jpierce@salemcc.edu; Staff 4 (MLS 1, Non-MLS 3)
Founded 1972. Enrl 1,565; Fac 28; Highest Degree: Associate
Library Holdings: Bk Titles 18,533; Bk Vols 19,000; Per Subs 28
Special Collections: State Document Depository
Subject Interests: Glassblowing
Automation Activity & Vendor Info: (Cataloging) SirsiDynix; (Circulation) SirsiDynix; (OPAC) SirsiDynix
Database Vendor: EBSCOhost, LexisNexis, ProQuest, SirsiDynix, Wilson - Wilson Web
Publications: Nursing Handbook; Student Handbook
Partic in LibraryLinkNJ, The New Jersey Library Cooperative; LOGIN (Libraries of Gloucester, Salem & Cumberland Information Network); Virtual Academic Library Environment
Open Mon-Thurs 9-9, Fri 9-5, Sat 8-12

CARTERET

P CARTERET PUBLIC LIBRARY*, 100 Cooke Ave, 07008. SAN 310-0626. Tel: 732-541-3830. FAX: 732-541-6948. Web Site: www.carteretlibrary.org. *Dir,* Sharla Emery; E-mail: semery@carteretlibrary.org; Staff 10 (MLS 2, Non-MLS 8)
Founded 1931. Pop 22,844; Circ 39,440
Library Holdings: Bk Vols 70,635; Per Subs 140
Automation Activity & Vendor Info: (Cataloging) SirsiDynix; (Circulation) SirsiDynix; (OPAC) SIRSI-iBistro
Database Vendor: EBSCOhost, Gale Cengage Learning
Wireless access
Partic in Libraries of Middlesex Automation Consortium
Open Mon-Thurs 9-8, Fri & Sat 9-5

CEDAR GROVE

P CEDAR GROVE FREE PUBLIC LIBRARY*, One Municipal Plaza, 07009. SAN 310-0642. Tel: 973-239-1447. FAX: 973-239-1275. Web Site: www.cedargrove.org/library. *Dir,* Peter Havel; E-mail: havel@palsplus.org; *Head Librn,* Usha Thampi-Lukose; E-mail: regy@palsplus.org; *Ch Serv,* Laura Florek; E-mail: florek@palsplus.org; Staff 8 (MLS 3, Non-MLS 5)
Founded 1965. Pop 12,300; Circ 84,372
Library Holdings: Bk Titles 41,500; Bk Vols 43,000; Per Subs 105
Automation Activity & Vendor Info: (Cataloging) SIRSI WorkFlows; (Circulation) SIRSI WorkFlows; (OPAC) SIRSI Unicorn
Database Vendor: Baker & Taylor, EBSCOhost, Facts on File, Overdrive, Inc, SirsiDynix
Wireless access
Function: ILL available
Partic in LibraryLinkNJ, The New Jersey Library Cooperative; PALS Plus, The Computer Consortium of Passaic County Libraries
Open Mon, Tues & Thurs 9-8, Wed & Fri 9-5, Sat (Sept-June) 9-1
Friends of the Library Group

CHATHAM

L BLUME, GOLDFADEN, BERKOWITZ, DONNELLY, FRIED & FORTE, PC*, Law Library, One Main St, 07928. SAN 371-716X. Tel: 973-635-5400, Ext 149. FAX: 973-635-9339. *Dir,* Judith T Schlissel; E-mail: jschliss@njatty.com; Staff 1 (MLS 1)
Founded 1975
Library Holdings: Bk Vols 3,000; Per Subs 58
Subject Interests: Obstetrics & gynecology, Pediatrics
Partic in New Jersey Law Librarians Association (NJLLA)
Open Mon-Thurs 8:30-4:30

P LIBRARY OF THE CHATHAMS*, 214 Main St, 07928. SAN 310-0693. Tel: 973-635-0603. FAX: 973-635-7827. Web Site: www.chatham-library.org. *Dir,* Karen Brodsky; E-mail: kbrodsky@chathamlibrary.org; *Head, Adult Serv,* Deborah R Fitzgerald; *Head, Ref,* Jay Chaterjee; *Head, Tech Serv,* Mary Kennedy; *Head, Youth Serv,* John Arthur; Staff 8 (MLS 8)
Founded 1907. Pop 18,669; Circ 196,256
Jan 2009-Dec 2009 Income $1,526,000. Mats Exp $205,000, Books $130,000, Per/Ser (Incl. Access Fees) $10,000, Micro $7,000, AV Mat $9,000, Electronic Ref Mat (Incl. Access Fees) $49,000. Sal $1,135,000
Library Holdings: AV Mats 7,000; CDs 3,000; DVDs 2,991; e-books 75; Bk Titles 95,000; Per Subs 220
Subject Interests: Consumer health, Earth sci, Health, Med, Psychol
Automation Activity & Vendor Info: (Cataloging) Innovative Interfaces, Inc; (Circulation) Innovative Interfaces, Inc; (ILL) Innovative Interfaces, Inc
Database Vendor: EBSCOhost, ProQuest
Partic in LibraryLinkNJ, The New Jersey Library Cooperative; Morris Automated Information Network; Morris-Union Federation
Open Mon-Thurs 9:30-9, Fri 9:30-6, Sat 9:30-5, Sun (Sept-May) 2-5
Friends of the Library Group

SR PRESBYTERIAN CHURCH OF CHATHAM TOWNSHIP LIBRARY*, 240 Southern Blvd, 07928. SAN 371-7178. Tel: 973-635-2340. FAX: 973-635-2447. Web Site: www.pcct-nj.org. *Librn,* Elizabeth Schweizer
Library Holdings: Bk Titles 2,800
Open Mon-Fri 8:30-5, Sun 9-Noon

CHERRY HILL

CAMDEN COUNTY COLLEGE LIBRARY
See Blackwood

P CHERRY HILL PUBLIC LIBRARY*, 1100 Kings Hwy N, 08034-1911. SAN 310-0715. Tel: 856-667-0300. Circulation Tel: 856-903-1216. Reference Tel: 856-903-1218. FAX: 856-667-9503. E-mail: info@chplnj.org. Web Site: www.chplnj.org. *Dir,* Laverne Mann; E-mail: lmann@chplnj.org; *Dir, Pub Relations & Spec Events,* Katie Hardesty; *Emerging Tech Librn, Syst Adminr,* Melissa Brisbin; *Head, Circ,* Jaclyn Harmon; *Head, Ref,* Andy Woodworth; *Head, Tech Serv,* Elizabeth Quinn; Tel: 856-903-1250, E-mail: equinn@chplnj.org; *Fac Mgr,* Greg Caponegro; *Libr Serv Mgr,* Jennie Purcell; *Automation Supvr,* Carol Puccio; Tel: 856-903-1242; *Youth Serv Supvr,* Michelle Yeager; Tel: 856-903-1232, E-mail: myeager@chplnj.org; Staff 37 (MLS 34, Non-MLS 3)
Founded 1957. Pop 70,000; Circ 541,328
Library Holdings: AV Mats 11,930; Bk Vols 156,000; Per Subs 343
Special Collections: New Jersey; Telephone Directories Coll
Subject Interests: Computers, Foreign trade, Investing, Local hist
Automation Activity & Vendor Info: (Acquisitions) SirsiDynix; (Cataloging) SirsiDynix; (Circulation) SirsiDynix; (OPAC) SirsiDynix; (Serials) SirsiDynix
Database Vendor: Baker & Taylor, Comprise Technologies Inc, EBSCOhost, Grolier Online, SirsiDynix
Wireless access
Function: Adult bk club, Art exhibits, Audio & video playback equip for onsite use, Audiobks via web, AV serv, Bk club(s), Bk reviews (Group), Bks on CD, CD-ROM, Children's prog, Computer training, Computers for patron use, Copy machines, e-mail serv, E-Reserves, Electronic databases & coll, Fax serv, Handicapped accessible, ILL available, Instruction & testing, Magnifiers for reading, Microfiche/film & reading machines, Music CDs, Newsp ref libr, Notary serv, Online cat, Online ref, Online searches, Photocopying/Printing, Preschool reading prog, Prog for adults, Prog for children & young adult, Pub access computers, Ref serv available, Ref serv in person, Scanner, Spoken cassettes & CDs, Story hour, Summer reading prog, Tax forms, Teen prog, Wheelchair accessible
Publications: Cherry Hill Area Organizations & Agencies
Partic in OCLC Online Computer Library Center, Inc
Open Mon-Thurs 9:30-9, Fri & Sat 9:30-5, Sun (Sept-May) 1-5
Restriction: 24-hr pass syst for students only
Friends of the Library Group

M KENNEDY MEMORIAL HOSPITALS-UNIVERSITY MEDICAL CENTER*, Dr Barney A Slotkin Memorial Library, 2201 Chapel Ave W, 08002-2048. SAN 320-3948. Tel: 856-488-6500, 856-488-6865. FAX: 856-488-6606. *Librn,* Francine Silverman; Staff 1 (Non-MLS 1)
Founded 1974
Library Holdings: Bk Titles 800; Per Subs 49
Subject Interests: Med, Orthopedics, Osteopathy, Psychiat
Partic in Basic Health Sciences Library Network; Health Sciences Library Association of New Jersey; SW NJ Consortium

R TEMPLE BETH SHOLOM*, Adele & Terry Uhr Memorial Library, 1901 Kresson Rd, 08003. SAN 310-1967. Tel: 856-751-6663. FAX: 856-751-2369. Web Site: www.tbsonline.org. *Librn,* Judy Brookover
Founded 1948
Library Holdings: Bk Titles 6,000; Per Subs 10; Videos 300
Wireless access
Open Mon-Thurs 9-1, Sun 10-12

R TEMPLE EMANUEL LIBRARY*, 1101 Springdale Rd, 08003. SAN 310-0723. Tel: 856-489-0035. FAX: 856-489-0032. Web Site: www.templeemanuel.org. *Librn,* Anne S Bressman; Staff 3 (MLS 2, Non-MLS 1)
Founded 1971
Library Holdings: Bk Vols 8,000
Subject Interests: Holocaust, Judaica
Database Vendor: JayWil Software Development, Inc
Wireless access
Open Mon-Fri 9-5, Sat & Sun 9-1
Friends of the Library Group

R TRINITY PRESBYTERIAN CHURCH LIBRARY*, Norman E Hjorth Memorial Library, 499 Rte 70E, 08034. SAN 310-0731. Tel: 856-428-2050. FAX: 856-795-8471. *Librn,* Barbara Cardea; Staff 2 (MLS 2)
Founded 1962
Library Holdings: AV Mats 125; Bk Titles 3,500
Special Collections: Children's Books
Subject Interests: Bible study, Christian educ
Database Vendor: EBSCOhost
Open Mon-Fri 9-4

CHESTER

P CHESTER LIBRARY*, 250 W Main St, 07930. SAN 310-074X. Tel: 908-879-7612. FAX: 908-879-8695. Web Site: chester-library.gti.net. *Dir,* Lesley Karczewski; Staff 7 (MLS 1, Non-MLS 6)
Founded 1911. Pop 8,917; Circ 15,587
Jan 2006-Dec 2006 Income $773,653, State $9,071, City $747,882, Locally Generated Income $16,700. Mats Exp $167,400, Books $126,400, Per/Ser (Incl. Access Fees) $10,000, AV Mat $25,000, Electronic Ref Mat (Incl. Access Fees) $6,000. Sal $350,002
Library Holdings: AV Mats 8,000; Bk Titles 52,419; Per Subs 100

Automation Activity & Vendor Info: (Circulation) SirsiDynix
Database Vendor: EBSCOhost, Gale Cengage Learning, Grolier Online, ProQuest, ReferenceUSA, SirsiDynix, Wilson - Wilson Web
Wireless access
Partic in Morris Automated Information Network
Open Mon-Thurs 9-9, Fri & Sat 9-5, Sun 1-5
Friends of the Library Group

CINNAMINSON

R JACK BALABAN MEMORIAL LIBRARY OF TEMPLE SINAI*, 2101 New Albany Rd, 08077-3536. SAN 310-0766. Tel: 856-829-0658. FAX: 856-829-0310. *Librn,* Shelley Sbar
Founded 1963
Library Holdings: Bk Titles 1,450
Special Collections: Encyclopaedia Judaica; Yiddish Coll
Subject Interests: Jewish authors, Jewish content
Restriction: Not open to pub

S HOEGANAES CORP LIBRARY*, 1001 Taylors Lane, 08077. SAN 310-4818. Tel: 856-829-2220, Ext 3411. FAX: 856-829-1651.
Library Holdings: Bk Vols 500; Per Subs 10
Subject Interests: Chem, Metallurgy
Open Mon-Fri 8-5
Restriction: Staff use only

CLARK

P CLARK PUBLIC LIBRARY*, 303 Westfield Ave, 07066. SAN 310-0774. Tel: 732-388-5999. FAX: 732-388-7866. Web Site: www.clarklibrary.org. *Dir,* Dawn Jenkin; E-mail: director@clarklibrary.org; *Adult Serv, Sr Ref Librn, Teen Serv,* Erin Coffey; E-mail: ecoffey@clarklibrary.org; *Cat,* Lorraine Loza; E-mail: lloza@clarklibrary.org; *Ch Serv,* Eileen Smith; *Computer Serv, Ref Librn, Sr Serv,* Jennifer Sidie; E-mail: jside@clarklibrary.org; *Circ Supvr,* Geri Reidy; E-mail: greidy@clarklibrary.org; Staff 9.8 (MLS 3.8, Non-MLS 6)
Founded 1961. Pop 14,759; Circ 110,000
Library Holdings: Bk Vols 60,000; Per Subs 190
Special Collections: Oral History
Automation Activity & Vendor Info: (Acquisitions) TLC (The Library Corporation); (Cataloging) TLC (The Library Corporation); (Circulation) TLC (The Library Corporation); (ILL) TLC (The Library Corporation); (OPAC) TLC (The Library Corporation)
Database Vendor: EBSCOhost, ProQuest
Wireless access
Function: Adult bk club, Art exhibits, Bk club(s), Chess club, Computer training, Copy machines, Digital talking bks, Handicapped accessible, Homebound delivery serv, ILL available, Music CDs, Online ref, Online searches, Photocopying/Printing, Prog for adults, Prog for children & young adult, Ref & res, Senior computer classes, Summer reading prog, Tax forms, Telephone ref
Partic in LibraryLinkNJ, The New Jersey Library Cooperative; MURAL
Open Mon, Tues & Thurs 9:30-9, Wed, Fri & Sat 9:30-5
Friends of the Library Group

CLEMENTON

P CLEMENTON MEMORIAL LIBRARY*, 195 Gibbsboro Rd, 08021. SAN 310-0790. Tel: 856-783-3233. FAX: 856-784-8794. *Librn,* Dayle Swanson; E-mail: swansond@clementon.k12.nj.us
Circ 7,278
Library Holdings: Bk Vols 8,000; Per Subs 15
Mem of Camden County Library System
Open Mon & Thurs 11-4 & 6-8, Wed 11-4:30, Sat 10-2

CLIFFSIDE PARK

P CLIFFSIDE PARK FREE PUBLIC LIBRARY*, 505 Palisade Ave, 07010. SAN 310-0804. Tel: 201-945-2867. FAX: 201-945-1016. E-mail: clpkcirc@bccls.org. Web Site: www.cliffsidepark.bccls.org. *Dir,* Camille V Steinfeld; E-mail: steinfeld@bccls.org; *Ref Librn,* Sherri Kendrick; E-mail: clpkref@bccls.org; *Cataloger,* Claudine Krystyniak; E-mail: krystyniak@bccls.org; *Ch Serv,* Brian Cazanave; *YA Serv,* Danielle Serra; E-mail: clpkref@bccls.org; Staff 14 (MLS 4, Non-MLS 10)
Founded 1913. Pop 23,000; Circ 161,745
Library Holdings: AV Mats 5,345; Bk Titles 69,354; Per Subs 121
Automation Activity & Vendor Info: (Cataloging) SirsiDynix; (Circulation) SirsiDynix; (OPAC) SirsiDynix; (Serials) Gateway
Database Vendor: EBSCOhost, Gale Cengage Learning, SirsiDynix
Wireless access
Function: Ref serv available
Partic in Bergen County Cooperative Library System
Open Mon-Thurs 10-9, Fri & Sat 10-5, Sun 1-5
Friends of the Library Group

CLIFTON

P CLIFTON PUBLIC LIBRARY*, 292 Piaget Ave, 07011. SAN 350-6347. Tel: 973-772-5500. Reference FAX: 973-478-3040. Administration FAX: 973-772-2926. Web Site: www.cliftonpl.org. *Dir,* Candice Brown; E-mail: brown@cliftonpl.org; *Sr Librn,* Justine Tomczak; E-mail: tomczak@cliftonpl.org; *Principal Librn,* Dale Bedford; E-mail: bedford@cliftonpl.org; *Principal Librn,* Patricia Vasilik; E-mail: vasilik@cliftonpl.org; *Librn,* Kathleen Grimshaw-Haven; E-mail: grimshaw@cliftonpl.org; Staff 37 (MLS 9, Non-MLS 28)
Founded 1920. Pop 78,672; Circ 303,846
Library Holdings: Bk Titles 211,224; Per Subs 295; Videos 10,624
Subject Interests: Local hist
Automation Activity & Vendor Info: (Cataloging) SirsiDynix; (Circulation) SirsiDynix; (OPAC) SirsiDynix
Database Vendor: EBSCOhost, Facts on File, Overdrive, Inc, ProQuest, ReferenceUSA
Function: Adult bk club, Art exhibits, Bk club(s), Bks on cassette, Bks on CD, Chess club, Children's prog, Computers for patron use, Copy machines, Free DVD rentals, Handicapped accessible, Home delivery & serv to Sr ctr & nursing homes, Homebound delivery serv, Homework prog, ILL available, Magnifiers for reading, Music CDs, Prog for adults, Prog for children & young adult, Pub access computers, Spoken cassettes & CDs, Spoken cassettes & DVDs, Story hour, Summer reading prog, Tax forms, Telephone ref, VHS videos, Wheelchair accessible
Partic in PALS Plus, The Computer Consortium of Passaic County Libraries
Special Services for the Deaf - Assistive tech; Bks on deafness & sign lang; TTY equip
Special Services for the Blind - Audio mat; Bks on cassette; Bks on CD; Home delivery serv; Talking bks
Open Mon-Thurs 10-8:45, Fri 10-5:45, Sat 10-4:45, Sun 1-4:45
Friends of the Library Group
Branches: 1
ALLWOOD BRANCH, 44 Lyall Rd, 07012, SAN 350-6371. Tel: 973-471-0555. FAX: 973-471-9284. *Br Mgr,* Justine Tomczak; E-mail: tomczak@cliftonpl.org; *Ch Serv,* Heather Nilsen; E-mail: nilsen@cliftonpl.org
Open Mon-Wed 10-9, Thurs & Fri 10-6, Sat 10-5

CLINTON

S CORRECTIONAL INSTITUTION FOR WOMEN*, Edna Mahan Hall Library, PO Box 4004, 08809-4004. SAN 310-0898. Tel: 908-735-7111, Ext 3641. FAX: 908-735-0108. *Dir,* Cathy Morgan; *Adminr,* William Hauck; Staff 3 (MLS 1, Non-MLS 2)
Library Holdings: Bk Vols 8,600; Per Subs 40
Special Collections: Criminal Law; Women in Prison
Restriction: Not open to pub

S HUNTERDON DEVELOPMENTAL CENTER LIBRARY*, 40 Pittstown Rd, 08809. (Mail add: PO Box 4003, 08809-4003), SAN 325-7584. Tel: 908-735-4031, Ext 1038. FAX: 908-730-1311. *Dir,* Diane Lachemayer; Tel: 908-735-4031, Ext 1147, Fax: 908-730-1359; *Librn,* Heather L Crouse; Tel: 908-735-4031, Ext 1411, E-mail: heather.crouse@dhs.state.nj.us; *Librn,* Lisa M Mabus; Tel: 908-735-4031, Ext 1028, E-mail: lisa.mabus@dhs.state.nj.us
Library Holdings: AV Mats 60, Bk Vols 5,000; Per Subs 60
Restriction: Non-circulating to the pub, Staff use only

S RED MILL MUSEUM LIBRARY*, 56 Main St, 08809. SAN 321-5970. Tel: 908-735-4101. FAX: 908-735-0914. E-mail: admin@theredmill.org. Web Site: theredmill.org. *Dir,* Eileen Morales; Tel: 908-735-4101, Ext 101, E-mail: director@theredmill.org; *Curator,* Elizabeth Cole; Tel: 908-735-4101, Ext 103, E-mail: ecole@theredmill.org
Library Holdings: Bk Titles 461; Bk Vols 475
Special Collections: Antique Textbooks; Daybooks
Subject Interests: Antiques, Local hist
Restriction: Open by appt only

CLOSTER

P CLOSTER PUBLIC LIBRARY*, 280 High St, 07624-1898. SAN 310-0901. Tel: 201-768-4197. FAX: 201-768-4220. E-mail: cltrcirc@bccls.org. Web Site: www.bccls.org/closter. *Dir, Librn,* Ruth Rando; E-mail: rando@bccls.org; *Head, Ch, Librn,* Laura Rifkin; E-mail: rifkin@bccls.org; *Head, Circ,* Deborah Leary; E-mail: dhleary@bccls.org; *Adult Serv,* Janet Fleck; E-mail: fleck@bccls.org; Staff 3 (MLS 3)
Founded 1956. Pop 8,373; Circ 164,992
Library Holdings: AV Mats 7,500; CDs 842; DVDs 1,200; Large Print Bks 500; Bk Titles 56,257; Bk Vols 58,472; Per Subs 123; Talking Bks 1,500; Videos 650
Subject Interests: Closter hist, NJ
Automation Activity & Vendor Info: (OPAC) SirsiDynix
Database Vendor: Baker & Taylor, EBSCOhost, Gale Cengage Learning, ProQuest, SirsiDynix

Wireless access
Partic in Bergen County Cooperative Library System
Open Mon-Wed 9-9, Thurs & Fri 9-5, Sat (Sept-June) 9-5
Friends of the Library Group

COLLINGSWOOD

P COLLINGSWOOD PUBLIC LIBRARY*, 771 Haddon Ave, 08108-3714. SAN 310-091X. Tel: 856-858-0649. FAX: 856-858-5016. Web Site: www.collingswoodlib.org. *Dir,* Brett Bonfield; *Circ Supvr,* F A Collings; *Ref,* Kathleen Liu
Founded 1910. Pop 14,500; Circ 70,000
Library Holdings: Bk Titles 61,000; Bk Vols 65,000; Per Subs 120
Special Collections: Southern New Jersey Coll, bks, blue prints, engravings, maps, photog, trade cat. Oral History
Automation Activity & Vendor Info: (Cataloging) Innovative Interfaces, Inc; (Circulation) Innovative Interfaces, Inc; (Media Booking) Innovative Interfaces, Inc
Database Vendor: EBSCOhost
Publications: Friends of the Library (Newsletter)
Open Mon-Fri 9:30-8:30, Sat 9:30-3:30 (9:30-1 Summer), Sun 12-4
Friends of the Library Group

CRANBURY

P CRANBURY PUBLIC LIBRARY, 23 N Main St, 08512. SAN 310-0979. Tel: 609-655-0555. FAX: 609-655-2858. E-mail: reference@cranburypubliclibrary.org. Web Site: www.cranburypubliclibrary.org. *Dir,* Marilynn Mullen; E-mail: mullen@cranburypubliclibrary.org; *Operations Adminr,* Beth Anne Kafasis; E-mail: kafasis@cranburypubliclibrary.org; *Outreach & Youth Serv Librn,* Jan Murphy; E-mail: murphy@cranburypubliclibrary.org; *Syst Adminr, Tech Librn,* Joanne Dera; E-mail: dera@cranburypubliclibrary.org; Staff 6 (MLS 3, Non-MLS 3)
Founded 1906. Pop 3,800; Circ 50,000
Library Holdings: Audiobooks 1,005; AV Mats 30; Bks on Deafness & Sign Lang 5; CDs 670; DVDs 1,440; e-books 150; Electronic Media & Resources 11; Large Print Bks 300; Microforms 1; Bk Vols 37,700; Per Subs 110
Special Collections: Cranbury Press Newspaper (1886-present), digital pdfs, microfilm; High School Coll
Subject Interests: Local hist
Automation Activity & Vendor Info: (Cataloging) Mandarin Library Automation; (Circulation) Mandarin Library Automation; (ILL) Auto-Graphics, Inc; (OPAC) Mandarin Library Automation
Database Vendor: EBSCOhost, Overdrive, Inc, ReferenceUSA, TumbleBookLibrary
Wireless access
Function: Adult bk club, Audio & video playback equip for onsite use, Audiobks via web, Bk club(s), Bks on CD, Children's prog, Computer training, Computers for patron use, Copy machines, Digital talking bks, Doc delivery serv, e-mail serv, E-Reserves, Electronic databases & coll, Fax serv, Free DVD rentals, Handicapped accessible, Home delivery & serv to Sr ctr & nursing homes, Homebound delivery serv, Homework prog, ILL available, Mail & tel request accepted, Mus passes, Music CDs, Notary serv, Online cat, Online ref, Outreach serv, Photocopying/Printing, Preschool outreach, Prog for adults, Prog for children & young adult, Pub access computers, Ref serv available, Scanner, Senior computer classes, Senior outreach, Spoken cassettes & CDs, Story hour, Summer reading prog, Tax forms, Teen prog, Telephone ref, Wheelchair accessible
Partic in LibraryLinkNJ, The New Jersey Library Cooperative; MURAL
Special Services for the Deaf - Bks on deafness & sign lang; Closed caption videos
Special Services for the Blind - Audio mat; Bks on CD; Copier with enlargement capabilities; Digital talking bk; Home delivery serv; Large print bks; Large type calculator; Playaways (bks on MP3); Recorded bks; Rental typewriters & computers; Sound rec
Open Mon-Thurs 10-9, Fri & Sat 10-5
Friends of the Library Group

CRANFORD

P CRANFORD FREE PUBLIC LIBRARY*, 224 Walnut Ave, 07016-2931. (Mail add: PO Box 400, 07016-0400), SAN 310-0987. Tel: 908-709-7272. FAX: 908-709-1658. E-mail: library@cranfordnj.org. Web Site: cranford.com/library. *Dir,* John Malar; E-mail: johnm@cranfordnj.org; *Asst Dir,* Judith Klimowicz; E-mail: jklimowicz@cranford.njpublib.org; *Sr Librn, YA Serv,* Frances Housten; E-mail: f-housten@cranfordnj.org; *Sr Librn, Syst Adminr,* Ben Stanley; *Librn,* Ronald Gorda; E-mail: rong@cranfordnj.org; Staff 11 (MLS 5, Non-MLS 6)
Founded 1908. Pop 22,578; Circ 231,877
Special Collections: Oral History
Automation Activity & Vendor Info: (Cataloging) Innovative Interfaces, Inc; (Circulation) Innovative Interfaces, Inc; (OPAC) Innovative Interfaces, Inc
Database Vendor: EBSCOhost
Wireless access
Function: Adult bk club, Archival coll, Art exhibits, Audiobks via web, Bks on cassette, Bks on CD, CD-ROM, Children's prog, Computer training, Computers for patron use, Copy machines, Digital talking bks, Electronic databases & coll, Exhibits, Fax serv, Games & aids for the handicapped, Handicapped accessible, Home delivery & serv to Sr ctr & nursing homes, Homebound delivery serv, ILL available, Magnifiers for reading, Music CDs, Newsp ref libr, Notary serv, Online cat, Photocopying/Printing, Prog for adults, Prog for children & young adult, Pub access computers, Ref serv available, Ref serv in person, Senior computer classes, Spoken cassettes & CDs, Spoken cassettes & DVDs, Story hour, Summer reading prog, Tax forms, Teen prog, Telephone ref, VHS videos, Wheelchair accessible, Workshops
Publications: Newsletter (bi-monthly)
Partic in Eastern NJ Regional Libr Coop; LibraryLinkNJ, The New Jersey Library Cooperative; Librs of Union County Consortium; MURAL
Special Services for the Deaf - High interest/low vocabulary bks
Special Services for the Blind - Home delivery serv
Open Mon-Wed 10-8, Thurs & Fri 10-5, Sat 10-4
Restriction: 24-hr pass syst for students only
Friends of the Library Group

R CRANFORD UNITED METHODIST CHURCH LIBRARY*, 201 Lincoln Ave E, 07016. SAN 310-0995. Tel: 908-276-0936.
Library Holdings: Bk Vols 3,300; Per Subs 11
Subject Interests: Children's bks, Hist, Relig studies
Restriction: Not open to pub

R FIRST PRESBYTERIAN CHURCH*, Betty Pethick Memorial Library, 11 Springfield Ave, 07016. SAN 310-1010. Tel: 908-276-8440. FAX: 908-276-2645. E-mail: office@firstprescranford.org. Web Site: www.firstprescranford.org. *Librn,* Mildred Nary
Library Holdings: Bk Vols 2,500

S CHARLES E STEVENS AMERICAN ATHEIST LIBRARY & ARCHIVES, INC*, 225 Cristiani St, 07016-3214. SAN 320-9016. Tel: 908-276-7300. FAX: 908-276-7402. E-mail: info@atheists.org. Web Site: www.atheists.org. *Pres,* David Silverman; Staff 2 (Non-MLS 2)
Founded 1968
Library Holdings: Bk Titles 20,000
Special Collections: Haldeman-Julius Publications; Ingersoll Coll; McCabe Coll; Robertson Coll
Subject Interests: Anarchism, Atheism, Church-state, Relig
Open Tues & Thurs 9-4

J UNION COUNTY COLLEGE LIBRARIES*, MacKay Library, 1033 Springfield Ave, 07016. SAN 310-1029. Tel: 908-709-7623. Reference Tel: 908-709-7620. FAX: 908-709-7589. Web Site: www.ucc.edu/about/library. *Dir, Libr & Acad Learning Ctr,* Dena Leiter; E-mail: leiter@ucc.edu; *Acq Librn,* Karen Malnati; Tel: 908-709-7027, E-mail: malnati@ucc.edu; *Instrul Serv Librn,* Susan Goodman; E-mail: susan.goodman@ucc.edu; *Ref Serv,* Josaine Royster; E-mail: royster@ucc.edu; *Tech Serv & Automation,* William Schryba; E-mail: schryba@ucc.edu. Subject Specialists: *Educ, Psychol, Sociol,* Karen Malnati; *Eng, Hist, Philos,* Susan Goodman; *Bus,* Josaine Royster; Staff 15 (MLS 8, Non-MLS 7)
Founded 1933. Enrl 11,000; Fac 205; Highest Degree: Associate
Library Holdings: DVDs 2,545; Bk Titles 84,000; Per Subs 448
Automation Activity & Vendor Info: (Acquisitions) SirsiDynix; (Cataloging) SirsiDynix; (Circulation) SirsiDynix; (Course Reserve) SirsiDynix; (ILL) SirsiDynix; (OPAC) SirsiDynix
Database Vendor: CQ Press, EBSCOhost, Facts on File, JSTOR, LexisNexis, Newsbank, ProQuest, SBRnet (Sports Business Research Network), ScienceDirect, SerialsSolutions, Springshare, LLC, Westlaw
Wireless access
Publications: Bibliographies; Handbook Guides; Newsletter
Partic in LibraryLinkNJ, The New Jersey Library Cooperative; Librs of Union County Consortium; OCLC Online Computer Library Center, Inc; Virtual Academic Library Environment

Departmental Libraries:

KELLOGG LIBRARY, 40 W Jersey St, Elizabeth, 07202-2314. Tel: 908-965-6075. *Librn,* Margaret Deng. Subject Specialists: *English as a second lang, Nursing,* Margaret Deng; Staff 2 (MLS 1, Non-MLS 1)
Highest Degree: Associate

PLAINFIELD CAMPUS, 232 E Second St, Plainfield, 07060-1308. Tel: 908-412-3545. *Librn,* Elsa Bruguier. Subject Specialists: *Allied health, Sport mgt,* Elsa Bruguier; Staff 2 (MLS 1, Non-MLS 1)
Highest Degree: Associate

CRESSKILL

P CRESSKILL PUBLIC LIBRARY, 53 Union Ave, 07626. SAN 310-1037. Tel: 201-567-3521. FAX: 201-567-5067. E-mail: cresscirc@bccls.org. Web Site: cresskill.bccls.org. *Dir,* Henrietta Browning; Tel: 201-567-5067, E-mail: browning@bccls.org; *Adult Serv,* Caitlin Hull; *Ch Serv,* Susan

Kelpin; E-mail: kelpin@bccls.org; *Libr Asst,* Kiwon Kim; E-mail: kiwon.kim@bccls.org. Subject Specialists: *Korean lang mat,* Kiwon Kim; Staff 5 (MLS 2, Non-MLS 3)
Founded 1930. Pop 8,573; Circ 148,000
Library Holdings: Bk Titles 64,776
Database Vendor: EBSCOhost, Gale Cengage Learning, ProQuest, SirsiDynix
Wireless access
Partic in Bergen County Cooperative Library System
Open Mon, Wed & Thurs 10-8, Tues & Fri 10-5, Sat 10-3
Friends of the Library Group

CROSSWICKS

P THE CROSSWICKS LIBRARY CO, Crosswicks Public Library, 483 Main St, 08515. (Mail add: PO Box 147, 08515), SAN 321-0537. Tel: 609-298-6271. FAX: 609-298-0510. E-mail: crosswicks@bcls.lib.nj.us. *Dir,* Sarah Legins; E-mail: slegins@bcls.lib.nj.us; Staff 1 (MLS 0.5, Non-MLS 0.5)
Founded 1817. Pop 8,000
Library Holdings: Bk Titles 12,346; Bk Vols 18,000
Special Collections: Oral History
Subject Interests: Antiques, Local hist, NJ hist, Quaker info
Automation Activity & Vendor Info: (Cataloging) Horizon; (Circulation) Horizon; (OPAC) Horizon
Mem of Burlington County Library
Open Mon & Thurs 9:30-7, Tues & Wed 4-8, Sat 10-2
Friends of the Library Group

DELANCO

P DELANCO PUBLIC LIBRARY*, M Joan Pearson School, 1303 Burlington Ave, 08075. SAN 310-1053. Tel: 856-461-6850. FAX: 856-461-6850. E-mail: delanco@bcls.lib.nj.us. Web Site: www.bcls.lib.nj.us. *Dir,* Katharina Radcliffe; E-mail: kradclif@bcls.lib.nj.us; *Asst Dir,* Catherine Cheyne
Founded 1865. Pop 3,361; Circ 10,732
Library Holdings: Bk Vols 45,000; Per Subs 30
Automation Activity & Vendor Info: (Cataloging) SirsiDynix; (Circulation) SirsiDynix; (OPAC) SirsiDynix
Mem of Burlington County Library
Special Services for the Deaf - Bks on deafness & sign lang; High interest/low vocabulary bks; Spec interest per
Open Mon & Fri 10-5, Tues & Thurs 2-8, Sat (Sept-June) 10-2

DEMAREST

P DEMAREST PUBLIC LIBRARY*, 90 Hardenburgh Ave, 07627-2197. SAN 310-1061. Tel: 201-768-8714. FAX: 201-767-8094. E-mail: demacirc@bccls.org. Web Site: demarest.bccls.org. *Dir,* Edna Ortega; E-mail: ortega@bccls.org; *Head, Circ,* Patty Irizarry
Founded 1965. Pop 4,950; Circ 32,494
Library Holdings: Bk Titles 26,526; Bk Vols 27,357; Per Subs 50
Automation Activity & Vendor Info: (Cataloging) SirsiDynix; (Circulation) SirsiDynix; (OPAC) SirsiDynix
Partic in Bergen County Cooperative Library System
Open Mon & Thurs 10-8, Tues, Wed & Fri 10-5, Sun 1-5

DENVILLE

P DENVILLE FREE PUBLIC LIBRARY*, 121 Diamond Spring Rd, 07834. SAN 310-107X. Tel: 973-627-6555. FAX: 973-627-1913. Web Site: www.denvillelibrary.org. *Dir,* Elizabeth L Kanouse; *Adult Serv, ILL, Ref,* Ilene Leftokwitz; *Ch Serv,* Richard Bryce; Staff 6 (MLS 6)
Founded 1921. Pop 16,635; Circ 154,438
Jan 2010-Dec 2010 Income $1,151,231, State $14,665, Locally Generated Income $1,132,866, Other $3,700. Mats Exp $69,940, Books $46,330, Per/Ser (Incl. Access Fees) $6,356, AV Mat $16,688, Electronic Ref Mat (Incl. Access Fees) $566. Sal $558,742
Library Holdings: Audiobooks 3,163; CDs 1,971; DVDs 1,898; e-books 320; Electronic Media & Resources 10; Bk Titles 41,990; Per Subs 173
Database Vendor: SirsiDynix
Wireless access
Partic in Morris Automated Information Network
Open Mon-Thurs 9:30-9, Fri & Sat 9:30-5
Friends of the Library Group

M ST CLARE'S HEALTH SERVICES*, Medical Library, 25 Pocono Rd, 07834. SAN 376-0545. Tel: 973-625-6547. FAX: 973-625-6678. *Dir,* Joan Derogatis
Library Holdings: Bk Vols 500; Per Subs 80
Wireless access
Open Mon-Fri 9-4

DEPTFORD

P JAMES H JOHNSON MEMORIAL LIBRARY, Deptford Free Public Library, 670 Ward Dr, 08096. SAN 310-1088. Tel: 856-848-9149. FAX: 856-848-1813. E-mail: webadmin@deptfordpubliclibrary.org. Web Site: www.deptfordpubliclibrary.org. *Libr Dir,* Susanne Sacchetti; E-mail: sacchettis@deptfordpubliclibrary.org; *Head, Circ,* Jean McGowen; E-mail: mcgowanj@deptfordpubliclibrary.org; *Head, Tech Serv,* Bunny Jacobsen; E-mail: jacobsenb@deptfordpubliclibrary.org; *Ch,* Susann Kaback; E-mail: kabacks@deptfordpubliclibrary.org; *Sr Libr Asst,* Ruth Stankiewicz; E-mail: stankiewiczr@deptfordpubliclibrary.org; Staff 14 (MLS 3, Non-MLS 11)
Founded 1961. Pop 30,000; Circ 200,000
Jan 2011-Dec 2011 Income $1,000,000
Library Holdings: Bk Vols 70,000; Per Subs 209
Special Collections: Deptford History Coll; Hearing Impaired
Automation Activity & Vendor Info: (Cataloging) SirsiDynix; (Circulation) SirsiDynix; (OPAC) SirsiDynix
Wireless access
Special Services for the Deaf - Bks on deafness & sign lang
Open Mon-Thurs 10-9, Fri & Sat 10-4
Friends of the Library Group

DOVER

P DOVER FREE PUBLIC LIBRARY*, 32 E Clinton St, 07801. SAN 310-1096. Tel: 973-366-0172. FAX: 973-366-0175. Web Site: www.dfpl.org. *Dir,* Rob Tambini; Staff 8 (MLS 2, Non-MLS 6)
Founded 1912. Pop 18,000; Circ 61,000
Library Holdings: Bk Titles 46,000; Bk Vols 49,000; Per Subs 90
Subject Interests: Spanish
Partic in Morris Automated Information Network
Open Mon, Tues & Thurs 9:30-9, Wed & Fri 9:30-5:30, Sat 10-5
Friends of the Library Group

M SAINT CLARE'S HEALTH SYSTEMS*, American Self-Help Clearinghouse, 375 E McFarlan St, 07801. SAN 373-4714. Tel: 973-989-1122. FAX: 973-989-1159. Web Site: www.selfhelpgroups.org. *Prog Coordr,* Edward J Madara; *Coordr, Info Serv,* Anita M Broderick; E-mail: abroderick@saintclares.org
Library Holdings: Bk Titles 350; Bk Vols 800
Publications: Self-Help Sourcebook
Open Mon-Fri 8:30-5

DUMONT

P DIXON HOMESTEAD LIBRARY, 180 Washington Ave, 07628. SAN 310-1118. Tel: 201-384-2030. FAX: 201-384-5878. E-mail: dumtcirc@bccls.org, dumtref@bccls.org. Web Site: dumont.bccls.org. *Dir,* Carolyn Blowers; E-mail: blowers@dumont.bccls.org; *Asst Dir/Ref Librn,* Kathryn McGrath; *Ch,* Anais Scott; E-mail: dumtya@bccls.org; Staff 9 (MLS 3, Non-MLS 6)
Founded 1925. Pop 17,479; Circ 134,820
Library Holdings: Bk Titles 46,801; Bk Vols 49,398; Per Subs 130
Automation Activity & Vendor Info: (Circulation) Innovative Interfaces, Inc
Wireless access
Partic in Bergen County Cooperative Library System
Open Mon-Wed 10-8, Thurs & Fri 10-5, Sat 10-2
Friends of the Library Group

DUNELLEN

P DUNELLEN PUBLIC LIBRARY*, Arnold A Schwartz Memorial Library, 100 New Market Rd, 08812. SAN 310-1134. Tel: 732-968-4585. FAX: 732-424-1370. Web Site: www.dunellenlibrary.org. *Dir,* Joan F Henry; E-mail: director@dunellenlibrary.org; *Youth Serv,* Jennifer Neely; E-mail: msjenniferdunpub@hotmail.com; Staff 1 (MLS 1)
Founded 1911. Pop 7,000; Circ 38,000
Library Holdings: Audiobooks 13,682; CDs 6,000; DVDs 2,000; e-books 21,968; Bk Vols 33,058; Per Subs 100; Videos 2,088
Special Collections: Disabilities Coll
Subject Interests: Autism
Automation Activity & Vendor Info: (Cataloging) SIRSI WorkFlows; (Circulation) SIRSI WorkFlows; (ILL) JerseyCat; (OPAC) SIRSI-iBistro
Database Vendor: EBSCOhost, ReferenceUSA
Wireless access
Function: Adult bk club
Partic in Libraries of Middlesex Automation Consortium
Special Services for the Blind - BiFolkal kits
Open Mon 10-8, Tues & Thurs 10-5, Wed 12-8, Fri 12-5, Sat 10-3
Friends of the Library Group

EAST BRUNSWICK

P EAST BRUNSWICK PUBLIC LIBRARY*, Two Jean Walling Civic Center, 08816-3599. SAN 350-6525. Tel: 732-390-6950. Interlibrary Loan Service Tel: 732-390-6785. Administration Tel: 732-390-6781. Information Services Tel: 732-390-6767. FAX: 732-390-6796. Administration FAX: 732-390-6869. Web Site: www.ebpl.org. *Dir,* MaryEllen Firestone; E-mail: mfirestone@ebpl.org; *Adult Serv,* Megan Doyle; E-mail: mdoyle@ebpl.org; *Circ,* Katherine Bowden; E-mail: kbowden@ebpl.org; *Info Serv,* Karen Parry; E-mail: kparry@ebpl.org; *Info Tech,* Dianne Hall; Tel: 732-390-6680, E-mail: dhall@ebpl.org; *Per,* Martha Hess; E-mail: mhess@ebpl.org; *Youth Serv,* Carol Phillips; Tel: 732-390-6789, E-mail: cphillips@ebpl.org; Staff 120 (MLS 20, Non-MLS 100)
Founded 1967. Pop 48,337; Circ 927,897
Jan 2006-Dec 2006 Income $4,857,718, State $58,102, City $3,513,785, Locally Generated Income $649,431, Other $636,400. Mats Exp $488,821, Books $253,749, Per/Ser (Incl. Access Fees) $28,516, Other Print Mats $293, AV Mat $108,567, Electronic Ref Mat (Incl. Access Fees) $97,696. Sal $2,534,705
Library Holdings: AV Mats 27,955; Bk Vols 135,000; Per Subs 250
Special Collections: Mystery Classics; World Language (Spanish, Korean, Hindi, Arabic, Gujarati, Russian)
Automation Activity & Vendor Info: (Acquisitions) Horizon; (Cataloging) Horizon; (Circulation) Horizon; (OPAC) Horizon
Database Vendor: EBSCOhost, Gale Cengage Learning, ProQuest
Wireless access
Function: Art exhibits, BA reader (adult literacy), CD-ROM, Handicapped accessible, Homebound delivery serv, ILL available, Music CDs, Online searches, Photocopying/Printing, Prog for children & young adult, Ref serv available, Spoken cassettes & CDs, Summer reading prog, Wheelchair accessible
Publications: The Library @ East Brunswick (Bi-monthly)
Partic in Libraries of Middlesex Automation Consortium
Special Services for the Deaf - Assistive tech; Closed caption videos; TDD equip; TTY equip
Open Mon, Tues & Thurs 9-9, Wed, Fri & Sat 9-5, Sun 1-5
Restriction: Residents only
Friends of the Library Group

R TRINITY PRESBYTERIAN CHURCH*, Media Center Library, 367 Cranberry Rd, 08816. SAN 310-1150. Tel: 732-257-6636. Web Site: www.trinity-pc.org. *Librn,* Doris Marsh
Founded 1971
Library Holdings: Bk Vols 433; Per Subs 30
Subject Interests: Family life, Presbyterian hist, Self help
Wireless access
Open Mon-Fri 9-2

EAST HANOVER

P EAST HANOVER TOWNSHIP FREE PUBLIC LIBRARY*, 415 Ridgedale Ave, 07936. SAN 310-1169. Tel: 973-428-3075. FAX: 973-428-7253. Web Site: www.easthanoverlibrary.com. *Dir,* Gayle B Carlson
Founded 1959. Pop 11,427; Circ 66,500
Library Holdings: AV Mats 8,000; Bk Vols 70,000; Per Subs 112
Database Vendor: EBSCOhost, ProQuest
Wireless access
Partic in Morris Automated Information Network
Open Mon-Thurs 9-9, Fri 9-5, Sat 10-4, Sun (Sept-June) 1-4
Friends of the Library Group

S NOVARTIS PHARMACEUTICALS*, Knowledge Center, One Health Plaza, Bldg 438, 07936-1016. SAN 310-1177. Tel: 862-778-8300, Ext 0474. FAX: 973-781-8693. Staff 16 (MLS 12, Non-MLS 4)
Founded 1984
Library Holdings: Bk Titles 10,000; Per Subs 500
Subject Interests: Biol, Med, Organic chem, Pharm, Toxicology
Database Vendor: Dialog, LexisNexis, OCLC FirstSearch, OVID Technologies, STN International
Restriction: Staff use only

EAST ORANGE

GM DEPARTMENT OF VETERANS AFFAIRS MEDICAL CENTER LIBRARY*, 385 Tremont Ave, 07018-1095. SAN 310-1207. Tel: 908-647-0180, Ext 4545, 973-676-1000, Ext 1969. FAX: 973-395-7234. *Chief Librn,* Delo James; Tel: 908-647-0180, Ext 4412, E-mail: james.delo@va.gov; *Med Librn,* Veronica Marie Valdez; Tel: 973-676-1000, Ext 1962, E-mail: veronica.valdez@va.gov; *Libr Tech,* Lisa Lowman Sheppard; E-mail: lisa.lowman@va.gov; *Libr Tech,* Kim Jaciw; E-mail: kimberly.jaciw@va.gov; Staff 4 (MLS 2, Non-MLS 2)
Founded 1955
Library Holdings: AV Mats 697; CDs 119; DVDs 12; e-books 78; e-journals 3,500; Electronic Media & Resources 18; Bk Titles 2,547; Per Subs 188; Videos 538
Subject Interests: Alcoholism, Clinical needs in med, Drug rehab, Neurology, Nursing, Psychiat, Psychol
Automation Activity & Vendor Info: (Acquisitions) LiBRARYSOFT; (Cataloging) LiBRARYSOFT; (Circulation) LiBRARYSOFT; (Serials) LiBRARYSOFT
Database Vendor: EBSCOhost, OVID Technologies, ProQuest
Function: Copy machines, Doc delivery serv, Electronic databases & coll, ILL available, Online ref, Online searches, Video lending libr
Partic in BRS; Dialog Corp
Restriction: Circulates for staff only, Med staff only

M EAST ORANGE GENERAL HOSPITAL MEDICAL LIBRARY*, 300 Central Ave, 07019. SAN 350-6584. Tel: 973-395-4112. FAX: 973-266-8435. *Librn,* Eleanor Silverman; E-mail: esilverman18@hotmail.com; Staff 1 (MLS 1)
Library Holdings: Bk Titles 350; Per Subs 60
Subject Interests: Allied health, Med, Nursing
Function: Doc delivery serv, For res purposes, ILL available, Photocopying/Printing, Wheelchair accessible
Partic in Basic Health Sciences Library Network; New Jersey Health Sciences Library Network; Regional Med Libr Network
Open Tues & Thurs 12-4
Restriction: Staff use only

P EAST ORANGE PUBLIC LIBRARY*, 21 S Arlington Ave, 07018-3892. SAN 350-6649. Tel: 973-266-5600. Circulation Tel: 973-266-5501. Reference Tel: 973-266-7049. Administration Tel: 973-266-5607. FAX: 973-674-1991. E-mail: feedback@eopl.org. Web Site: www.eopl.org. *Dir,* Carolyn Ryan Reed; Fax: 973-675-6128, E-mail: crreed@eopl.org; *Asst Dir,* Pamela V Holmes; *ILL, Sr Librn, YA Serv,* Nathalia Bermudez; *Acq, Cat, Tech Serv,* Jenny Tong; *Ch Serv,* Christal Blue; *Ref,* Robin Starkey; Staff 73 (MLS 13, Non-MLS 60)
Founded 1900. Pop 69,824; Circ 336,362
Library Holdings: AV Mats 13,922; Bk Titles 256,713; Bk Vols 405,165; Per Subs 634
Special Collections: New Jerseyana. State Document Depository; US Document Depository
Subject Interests: Ethnic studies
Database Vendor: EBSCOhost, Gale Cengage Learning, Innovative Interfaces, Inc
Partic in LibraryLinkNJ, The New Jersey Library Cooperative
Special Services for the Deaf - High interest/low vocabulary bks; Staff with knowledge of sign lang
Open Mon-Thurs 9-9, Fri 10-6, Sat 9-5
Friends of the Library Group
Branches: 3
AMPERE, 39 Ampere Plaza, 07017, SAN 350-6673. Tel: 973-266-7047, 973-266-7048. FAX: 973-674-1991. *Librn,* Nancy Tinney
Library Holdings: Bk Vols 31,250
Open Mon-Fri 1:30-5:30
ELMWOOD, 317 S Clinton St, 07018, SAN 350-6703. Tel: 973-266-7050. *Librn,* Nancy Tinney
Library Holdings: Bk Vols 24,500
Open Tues, Thurs & Fri 1:30-5:30
FRANKLIN, 192 Dodd St, 07017, SAN 350-6738. Tel: 973-266-7053. FAX: 973-674-1991. *Librn,* Nancy Tinney
Library Holdings: Bk Vols 16,000
Open Mon & Wed 1:30-5:30

EAST RUTHERFORD

P EAST RUTHERFORD MEMORIAL LIBRARY*, 143 Boiling Springs Ave, 07073. SAN 310-1215. Tel: 201-939-3930. FAX: 201-939-1231. E-mail: erutcirc@bccls.org. Web Site: www.eastrutherford.bccls.org. *Dir,* Kenneth French; E-mail: french@bccls.org; Staff 1 (MLS 1)
Pop 8,785; Circ 39,945
Library Holdings: Bk Vols 30,000; Per Subs 74
Automation Activity & Vendor Info: (Acquisitions) SirsiDynix; (Circulation) SirsiDynix; (OPAC) SirsiDynix
Database Vendor: EBSCOhost
Wireless access
Partic in Bergen County Cooperative Library System
Open Mon-Thurs 10-8, Fri 12-5, Sat (Sept-May) 1-4

EATONTOWN

P EATONTOWN LIBRARY*, 33 Broad St, 07724-1594. SAN 310-124X. Tel: 732-389-2665. FAX: 732-389-7665. Web Site: www.eatontown.lib.nj.us/. *Dir,* Amy Garibay; E-mail: agaribay@monmouthcountylib.org; *Cat,* Kathleen Accorsi; *Sr Libr Asst,* Claire Murphy
Founded 1902. Pop 14,000; Circ 43,000

Library Holdings: AV Mats 2,000; Bk Vols 25,000; Per Subs 43
Automation Activity & Vendor Info: (Cataloging) SirsiDynix; (Circulation) SirsiDynix
Wireless access
Function: Photocopying/Printing, Prog for children & young adult, Spoken cassettes & CDs, Summer reading prog, Telephone ref, VHS videos
Mem of Monmouth County Library
Open Mon & Wed 10-5 & 7-9, Tues & Thurs 2-5, Fri 10-5, Sat 10-1
Friends of the Library Group

EDGEWATER

P EDGEWATER FREE PUBLIC LIBRARY*, 49 Hudson Ave, 07020. SAN 310 1258. Tel: 201-224-6144. FAX: 201-886-3395. Web Site: www.edgewaterlibrary.org. *Dir,* Linda Corona; Staff 12 (MLS 2, Non-MLS 10)
Founded 1910. Pop 11,513; Circ 81,437
Library Holdings: AV Mats 3,410; CDs 514; DVDs 1,587; e-books 420; Large Print Bks 246; Bk Vols 24,538; Per Subs 87
Special Collections: Edgewater Works Progress Administration Papers, Photos (Edgewater Library Historical Coll). Municipal Document Depository
Automation Activity & Vendor Info: (Circulation) SirsiDynix; (ILL) Auto-Graphics, Inc; (OPAC) SirsiDynix
Database Vendor: EBSCOhost, Gale Cengage Learning, ProQuest, World Book Online
Wireless access
Function: Outreach serv
Partic in Bergen County Cooperative Library System
Open Mon-Wed 10-9, Thurs & Fri 10-6, Sat 10-5
Friends of the Library Group

EDISON

P EDISON TOWNSHIP FREE PUBLIC LIBRARY*, 340 Plainfield Ave, 08817. SAN 350-6762. Tel: 732-287-2298. Circulation Tel: 732-287-2298, Ext 221. Reference Tel: 732-287-2298, Ext 226, 732-287-2298, Ext 227. FAX: 732-819-9134. TDD: 732-777-7813. Web Site: www.lmxac.org/edisonlib. *Dir,* Judith Mansbach; *Asst Dir,* Evan T Davis; Tel: 732-548-3045, Fax: 732-549-5171; Staff 80 (MLS 17, Non-MLS 63)
Founded 1928. Pop 100,000; Circ 529,386
Library Holdings: AV Mats 14,065; CDs 1,984; DVDs 4,379; Bk Vols 280,866; Per Subs 146; Talking Bks 5,761; Videos 1,025
Subject Interests: Local hist
Automation Activity & Vendor Info: (Acquisitions) SIRSI-DRA; (Cataloging) SIRSI-DRA; (Circulation) SIRSI-DRA; (Course Reserve) SIRSI-DRA; (ILL) SIRSI-DRA; (OPAC) SIRSI-DRA; (Serials) SIRSI-DRA
Database Vendor: 3M Library Systems, Baker & Taylor, EBSCOhost
Wireless access
Function: Adult bk club, Bk club(s), Bks on cassette, Bks on CD, Children's prog, Citizenship assistance, Computers for patron use, Copy machines, e-mail & chat, E-Reserves, Electronic databases & coll, Exhibits, Fax serv, Handicapped accessible, Home delivery & serv to Sr ctr & nursing homes, Homebound delivery serv, ILL available, Music CDs, Online cat, Outreach serv, Photocopying/Printing, Prog for adults, Prog for children & young adult, Ref & res, Ref serv in person, Spoken cassettes & CDs, Spoken cassettes & DVDs, Story hour, Summer reading prog, Tax forms, Teen prog, Telephone ref, VHS videos, Video lending libr, Wheelchair accessible
Publications: Library Letter (Newsletter)
Partic in Libraries of Middlesex Automation Consortium; LibraryLinkNJ, The New Jersey Library Cooperative
Special Services for the Deaf - TTY equip
Open Mon-Wed 9:30-9, Thurs & Fri 9:30-5, Sat 10-4
Friends of the Library Group
Branches: 2
CLARA BARTON BRANCH, 141 Hoover Ave, 08837, SAN 350-6797. Tel: 732-738-0096. FAX: 732-738-8325. *Br Mgr,* Margaret Vellucci; Staff 5.5 (MLS 1.5, Non-MLS 4)
Library Holdings: AV Mats 1,814; CDs 305; DVDs 173; Bk Vols 56,923; Per Subs 99; Talking Bks 428; Videos 558
Function: Fax serv, Handicapped accessible, ILL available, Music CDs, Online cat, Photocopying/Printing, Pub access computers, Ref & res, Ref serv in person, Spoken cassettes & CDs, Spoken cassettes & DVDs, Story hour, Summer reading prog, Tax forms, Telephone ref, VHS videos, Video lending libr, Wheelchair accessible
Publications: The Library Letter (Newsletter)
Open Mon & Thurs 12:30-8, Tues 9-5, Fri & Sat 9:30-5
Friends of the Library Group
NORTH EDISON BRANCH, 777 Grove Ave, 08820, SAN 350-6827. Tel: 732-548-3045. FAX: 732-549-5171. *Asst Dir, Br Mgr,* Evan T Davis; E-mail: edavis@lmxac.org; *Ref Librn,* Christine Yang; *Coordr, Ch Serv,* Carolyn N Cullum; E-mail: cncullum@lmxac.org; *Ref Serv, Ad,* Cathy Denner; E-mail: cdenner@lmxac.org; Staff 8 (MLS 6, Non-MLS 2)
Founded 1971. Pop 99,523; Circ 257,377
Library Holdings: CDs 815; DVDs 1,902; Bk Vols 100,529; Per Subs 146; Talking Bks 2,194; Videos 451
Function: Prog for adults, Prog for children & young adult, Spoken cassettes & CDs, Story hour, Summer reading prog, Tax forms, Teen prog, VHS videos, Wheelchair accessible
Publications: The Library Letter (Newsletter)
Open Mon-Thurs 9:30-9, Fri 9:30-5, Sat 10-4
Friends of the Library Group
Bookmobiles: 1. Librn, Sharon Giniger. Bk vols 10,278

M JFK MEDICAL CENTER*, Medical Library, 65 James St, 08818-3059. SAN 320-6971. Tel: 732-321-7181. FAX: 732-744-5639. *Dir,* Lana Strazhnik
Founded 1976
Library Holdings: Bk Titles 3,000; Per Subs 250
Subject Interests: Family practice, Rehabilitation
Wireless access
Publications: Library News; Library Update (Acquisition list)
Partic in Med Resources Consortium of Cent NJ
Restriction: Open to pub by appt only

L LEVINSON/AXELROD LIBRARY*, Levinson Plaza, Two Lincoln Hwy, 08818. (Mail add: PO Box 2095, 08818-2095), SAN 375-7323. Tel: 732-494-2727. FAX: 732-494-2712. E-mail: levinson@njlawyers.com. Web Site: www.njlawyers.com. Staff 1 (MLS 1)
Library Holdings: Bk Vols 10,000; Per Subs 23
Database Vendor: Westlaw
Partic in LibraryLinkNJ, The New Jersey Library Cooperative
Restriction: Staff use only

J MIDDLESEX COUNTY COLLEGE LIBRARY, 2600 Woodbridge Ave, 08818. SAN 310-1282. Tel: 732-906-2561. Reference Tel: 732-906-4253. FAX: 732-906-4159. E-mail: refmcclibrary@gmail.com. Web Site: www2.middlesexcc.edu/academics/library.html. *Dir,* Mark Thompson; Tel: 732-906-4252, E-mail: mthompson@middlesexcc.edu; *Tech Serv Librn,* Charles Dolan; Tel: 732-906-4254, E-mail: cdolan@middlesexcc.edu
Founded 1966. Enrl 13,000; Fac 190; Highest Degree: Associate
Library Holdings: e-books 2,500; High Interest/Low Vocabulary Bk Vols 430; Bk Titles 75,909; Bk Vols 86,547; Per Subs 134; Talking Bks 27
Subject Interests: Nursing, Paralegal
Database Vendor: SirsiDynix
Wireless access
Publications: Fact Sheets; Research Guides
Partic in Libraries of Middlesex Automation Consortium; LibraryLinkNJ, The New Jersey Library Cooperative; Lyrasis; OCLC Online Computer Library Center, Inc; Virtual Academic Library Environment
Open Mon-Thurs 7:45am-10pm, Fri 7:45-5, Sat 9-4, Sun 12-5

ELIZABETH

P ELIZABETH PUBLIC LIBRARY*, 11 S Broad St, 07202. SAN 350-6851. Tel: 908 351 6060. FAX: 908-354-5845. Web Site: www.elizpl.org. *Dir,* Dorothy M Key; *Asst Dir,* Monica Eppinger; Staff 15 (MLS 15)
Founded 1908. Pop 125,000; Circ 182,689
Library Holdings: Bk Vols 38,000; Per Subs 150
Special Collections: Elizabethtown Room Coll. US Document Depository
Automation Activity & Vendor Info: (Cataloging) SirsiDynix; (Circulation) SirsiDynix; (ILL) SirsiDynix; (OPAC) SirsiDynix; (Serials) SirsiDynix
Wireless access
Partic in LibraryLinkNJ, The New Jersey Library Cooperative; LUCC; MURAL
Special Services for the Blind - Accessible computers; Computer access aids; Computer with voice synthesizer for visually impaired persons; Large screen computer & software; Screen enlargement software for people with visual disabilities
Open Mon-Fri 9-9, Sat 9-5
Branches: 3
ELIZABETH PORT, 102-110 Third St, 07206-1717. Tel: 908-289-9032. FAX: 908-289-5663. *Br Serv Mgr,* Robert Barbanell; Tel: 908-353-4820
Library Holdings: Bk Vols 9,000; Per Subs 16
Open Mon & Wed 12-8, Tues, Thurs-Sat 9-5
ELMORA, 740 W Grand St, 07202. Tel: 908-353-4820. FAX: 908-353-6877. *Br Serv Mgr,* Robert Barbanell
Library Holdings: Bk Vols 12,000; Per Subs 16
Open Mon & Wed 9-9, Tues & Thurs-Sat 9-5
LACORTE, 408 Palmer St, 07202, SAN 377-5895. Tel: 908-824-4298. FAX: 908-820-4764. *Br Serv Mgr,* Robert Barbanell; Tel: 908-353-4820
Library Holdings: Bk Vols 8,500; Per Subs 16
Open Mon, Wed & Fri 9-5, Tues & Thurs 11:45-8

M TRINITAS HOSPITAL*, Medical Library, 225 Williamson St, 07207. SAN 310-1355. Tel: 908-994-5371. FAX: 908-994-5099. Web Site: www.trinitashospital.org. *Dir,* Elisabeth Marrapodi; Tel: 908-994-5488; *Tech Serv,* Ritza Alexandre
Founded 1930
Library Holdings: Bk Vols 1,020; Per Subs 90
Subject Interests: Med, Nursing
Database Vendor: EBSCOhost
Wireless access
Partic in Basic Health Sciences Library Network; Health Sciences Library Association of New Jersey; National Network of Libraries of Medicine South Central Region; New Jersey Health Sciences Library Network; New Jersey Library Network
Restriction: Open to pub by appt only

UNION COUNTY COLLEGE
See Cranford

GL UNION COUNTY LAW LIBRARY*, Union County Courthouse Annex, Rm 407, 07207. SAN 310-138X. Tel: 908-659-4625. Web Site: judiciary.state.nj.us. *Librn,* Nicholas Tomich; Staff 1 (MLS 1)

ELMER

S ELMER LIBRARY*, 120 S Main St, 08318. SAN 375-7382. Tel: 856-358-2014. FAX: 856-358-2014. *Librn,* Linda Fritz
Library Holdings: Bk Titles 11,000
Automation Activity & Vendor Info: (Cataloging) Follett Software; (Circulation) Follett Software
Open Mon-Thurs 10-2 & 6:30-8:30, Fri 10-2, Sat 10-Noon
Friends of the Library Group

ELMWOOD PARK

P ELMWOOD PARK PUBLIC LIBRARY*, 210 Lee St, 07407. SAN 310-1401. Tel: 201-796-8888. Interlibrary Loan Service Tel: 201-796-2497. Reference Tel: 201-796-2443. FAX: 201-703-1425. E-mail: elpkcirc@bccls.org. Web Site: www.bccls.org/elmwoodpark. *Dir,* Bobbie Cretano; Tel: 201-796-2449; *Head, Circ,* Andrew Marrone; Tel: 201-796-2584; *ILL,* Carole Skeen; *Ref Serv, Ad,* Jennifer Lazidis; Staff 22 (MLS 5, Non-MLS 17)
Founded 1953. Pop 18,925; Circ 104,000
Library Holdings: CDs 1,450; DVDs 875; Large Print Bks 1,250; Bk Titles 59,000; Bk Vols 68,000; Per Subs 75; Talking Bks 1,950; Videos 1,750
Automation Activity & Vendor Info: (OPAC) SirsiDynix
Database Vendor: EBSCOhost, Gale Cengage Learning, OVID Technologies, SirsiDynix
Function: ILL available
Open Mon, Fri & Sat 10-5, Tues-Thurs 10-8, Sun 1-5
Friends of the Library Group

EMERSON

P EMERSON PUBLIC LIBRARY*, 20 Palisade Ave, 07630. SAN 310-141X. Tel: 201-261-5604. FAX: 201-262-7999. E-mail: emercirc@bccls.org. Web Site: www.bccls.org/emerson. *Dir,* Camille Valentino; E-mail: valentino@bccls.org; Staff 2 (MLS 1, Non-MLS 1)
Founded 1958. Pop 7,200; Circ 32,000
Library Holdings: AV Mats 2,400; Bk Vols 30,000; Per Subs 55; Talking Bks 735
Automation Activity & Vendor Info: (Circulation) SirsiDynix; (OPAC) SirsiDynix
Database Vendor: EBSCOhost, Gale Cengage Learning, ProQuest, SirsiDynix
Open Mon, Tues & Thurs 10-9, Wed, Fri & Sat 10-5
Friends of the Library Group

ENGLEWOOD

M ENGLEWOOD HOSPITAL & MEDICAL CENTER*, Dr Walter Phillips Health Sciences Library, 350 Engle St, 07631. SAN 310-1436. Tel: 201-894-3000, 201-894-3070. Information Services Tel: 201-894-3145. FAX: 201-894-9049. Web Site: www.englewoodhospital.com. *Coordr,* Lia Sabbagh; Tel: 201-894-3069, E-mail: lia.sabbagh@ehmc.com; Staff 1 (MLS 1)
Founded 1943
Library Holdings: Bk Titles 3,000; Per Subs 250
Subject Interests: Commun health, Consumer health, Internal med, Ophthalmology, Otolaryngology, Patient educ, Psychiat, Surgery
Wireless access
Partic in Bergen Passaic Health Sciences Library Consortium; Docline; Health Sci Libr Asn of NJ; LibraryLinkNJ, The New Jersey Library Cooperative; Medical Library Association (MLA)
Open Mon-Fri 8:30-4:30

P ENGLEWOOD PUBLIC LIBRARY*, 31 Engle St, 07631. SAN 310-1444. Tel: 201-568-2215. FAX: 201-568-6895. Web Site: www.englewoodlibrary.org. *Dir,* Catherine Wolverton; Tel: 201-568-2215, Ext 222, E-mail: wolverton@bccls.org; *Head, Ch,* Donna-Lynne Cooper; Tel: 201-568-2215, Ext 243; *Head, Ref & Adult Serv,* Charlene Taylor; *Head, Literacy,* Grace Colaneri; *Head, Tech Serv,* Jay Wolf; *Ch,* Susan Oechukwu; *Ref Librn,* Lynn Kaminski; *Sr Librn,* Monica Sanchez; *Circ Supvr,* Paul Shaver; *Sr Libr Asst,* Sheila Frisch; *Sr Libr Asst,* Matthia Gonzales; *Sr Libr Asst,* Arnie Tobias; Staff 20 (MLS 10, Non-MLS 10)
Founded 1901. Pop 26,203; Circ 249,784
Library Holdings: Bk Titles 112,276; Bk Vols 124,470; Per Subs 255
Subject Interests: African-Am studies, Careers, Jazz, Judaica, Local hist
Automation Activity & Vendor Info: (Circulation) SirsiDynix
Database Vendor: EBSCOhost, Gale Cengage Learning, ProQuest, SirsiDynix
Wireless access
Publications: Newsletter (Quarterly)
Open Mon-Thurs 9-9, Fri & Sat 9-5, Sun 1-5
Friends of the Library Group

ENGLEWOOD CLIFFS

CR SAINT PETER'S UNIVERSITY*, Englewood Cliffs Campus Library, Hudson Terrace, 07632. Tel: 201-761-7488. FAX: 201-568-6614. Web Site: www.saintpeters.edu/library. *Librn,* Mark Graceffo; E-mail: mgraceffo@saintpeters.edu; *Asst Librn,* Ann Marie Ziadie; Tel: 201-761-6459, E-mail: aziadie@saintpeters.edu; Staff 12 (MLS 8, Non-MLS 4)
Founded 1973
Library Holdings: Bk Vols 300,000; Per Subs 134
Subject Interests: Nursing
Automation Activity & Vendor Info: (Cataloging) Ex Libris Group; (Circulation) Ex Libris Group; (Course Reserve) Ex Libris Group; (ILL) Ex Libris Group; (OPAC) Ex Libris Group
Database Vendor: EBSCOhost, ProQuest
Wireless access
Partic in LibraryLinkNJ, The New Jersey Library Cooperative
Open Mon-Thurs 8am-Midnight, Fri 8am-9pm, Sat 9-6, Sun Noon-Midnight

S UNILEVER BESTFOODS INFORMATION CENTER*, 800 Sylvan Ave, 07632-3201. SAN 310-1460. Tel: 201-894-7568. FAX: 201-871-8265. *Sr Info Spec,* Karla Cicciari; E-mail: karla.cicciari@unilever.com; *Tech Serv,* Lisa Schwartz; E-mail: lisa.schwartz@unilever.com; Staff 2 (MLS 1, Non-MLS 1)
Founded 1942
Library Holdings: Bk Vols 10,000; Per Subs 250
Subject Interests: Food indust, Food sci, Nutrition
Function: Bus archives, Doc delivery serv, Online searches, Res libr
Restriction: Co libr

EWING

C THE COLLEGE OF NEW JERSEY LIBRARY*, 2000 Pennington Rd, 08628-0718. (Mail add: PO Box 7718, 08628-0718), SAN 310-5520. Tel: 609-771-2311, 609-771-2332. Interlibrary Loan Service Tel: 609-771-2028. Reference Tel: 609-771-2417. FAX: 609-637-5177. Web Site: www.tcnj.edu/~library. *Dean of Libr,* Taras Pavlovsky; *Asst Dean,* Marlena Frackowski; *Asst Dir, Pub Serv,* Maureen Gorman; *Librn,* Dr Terrence Epperson; *Librn,* Marc Meola; *Librn,* Valerie Tucci; *Cat Librn,* Yuji Tosaka; *Music & Media Librn,* Dr Linda Dempf; *Syst Librn,* Yongming Wang; *Head, Cat,* Cathy Weng; *Head, ILL, Head, Ref,* Patricia A Beaber; Tel: 609-771-2405; *Electronic Res,* Jia Mi. Subject Specialists: *Humanities,* Marc Meola; *Eng, Phys sci,* Valerie Tucci; Staff 17 (MLS 16, Non-MLS 1)
Founded 1855. Enrl 7,000; Fac 350; Highest Degree: Master
Library Holdings: Bk Vols 580,200; Per Subs 1,485
Special Collections: History of American Education, Historical Textbooks & Historical Children's Books; History of New Jersey. State Document Depository
Automation Activity & Vendor Info: (Acquisitions) Ex Libris Group; (Cataloging) Ex Libris Group; (Circulation) Ex Libris Group; (Course Reserve) Ex Libris Group; (ILL) Ex Libris Group; (OPAC) Ex Libris Group; (Serials) SerialsSolutions
Database Vendor: EBSCOhost, JSTOR, Newsbank, ProQuest, PubMed, ReferenceUSA, ScienceDirect, Westlaw, Wilson - Wilson Web
Wireless access
Partic in LibraryLinkNJ, The New Jersey Library Cooperative; Lyrasis; OCLC Online Computer Library Center, Inc; Virtual Academic Library Environment
Open Mon-Thurs 7:45am-Midnight, Fri 7:45am-8pm, Sat 10-7, Sun 11-11

FAIR HAVEN

P FAIR HAVEN LIBRARY*, 748 River Rd, 07704. SAN 310-1495. Tel: 732-747-5031, Ext 220. FAX: 732-747-6962. E-mail: fairhavenlibrary@monmouthcountylib.org. Web Site: www.fairhaven.lib.nj.us. *Dir,* Donna Powers
Founded 1933. Pop 6,000; Circ 51,000
Library Holdings: Bk Vols 25,000
Automation Activity & Vendor Info: (Cataloging) SirsiDynix; (Circulation) SirsiDynix; (OPAC) SirsiDynix
Mem of Monmouth County Library
Open Mon-Wed & Fri 9-5, Thurs 1-8, Sat (Sept-May) 10-1

FAIR LAWN

P MAURICE M PINE FREE PUBLIC LIBRARY*, 10-01 Fair Lawn Ave, 07410. SAN 310-1533. Tel: 201-796-3400. FAX: 201-794-6344. Web Site: www.fairlawnlibrary.org. *Dir,* Timothy H Murphy; E-mail: murphy@bccls.org; *Asst Dir,* Penelope Kaplan; E-mail: kaplan@bccls.org; *Ch Serv,* Kate Nafz; *Circ,* Alice Weisser; *Ref,* Leslie Kruegel; *Tech Serv,* Nancy Fezell; Staff 8 (MLS 8)
Founded 1933. Pop 32,229; Circ 392,894
Jan 2006-Dec 2006 Income $2,222,745, State $38,756, City $2,113,989, Other $70,000. Mats Exp $160,000, Books $114,000, Per/Ser (Incl. Access Fees) $10,000, AV Mat $36,000. Sal $1,390,419
Library Holdings: Bk Vols 179,205; Per Subs 204
Automation Activity & Vendor Info: (Cataloging) SirsiDynix; (Circulation) SirsiDynix; (OPAC) SirsiDynix
Database Vendor: EBSCOhost, Gale Cengage Learning, ProQuest
Wireless access
Open Mon-Wed 10-9, Thurs 10-6, Fri 10-5, Sat 9-5, Sun 1-5
Friends of the Library Group

FAIRFIELD

P FAIRFIELD PUBLIC LIBRARY*, Anthony Pio Costa Memorial Library, 261 Hollywood Ave, 07004. SAN 310-155X. Tel: 973-227-3575. FAX: 973-227-7305. E-mail: ffpl@ffpl.org. Web Site: www.ffpl.org. *Sr Libr Asst,* Frank Arcuri; Staff 9 (MLS 2, Non-MLS 7)
Founded 1962. Pop 7,800; Circ 55,000
Jan 2007-Dec 2007 Income $993,621, State $7,314, City $956,307, Locally Generated Income $30,000
Library Holdings: AV Mats 5,000; Bk Vols 61,000; Per Subs 130; Talking Bks 650
Database Vendor: EBSCOhost, Gale Cengage Learning, Hoovers, Newsbank, ProQuest, World Book Online
Wireless access
Function: Adult bk club, Bk club(s), Bks on cassette, Bks on CD, CD-ROM, Children's prog, Computers for patron use, Copy machines, Electronic databases & coll, Free DVD rentals, Handicapped accessible, Holiday prog, ILL available, Mail & tel request accepted, Music CDs, Notary serv, Online cat, Online ref, Prog for adults, Prog for children & young adult, Pub access computers, Ref serv in person, Story hour, Summer reading prog, Tax forms, Teen prog, Telephone ref, Web-catalog, Wheelchair accessible
Publications: Newsletter
Partic in PALS Plus, The Computer Consortium of Passaic County Libraries; ReBL
Open Mon & Thurs 9-9, Tues & Wed 9-8, Fri 9-5, Sat (Fall-Spring) 10-4
Friends of the Library Group

FAIRVIEW

P FAIRVIEW FREE PUBLIC LIBRARY*, 213 Anderson Ave, 07022. SAN 310-1568. Tel: 201-943-6244. FAX: 201-943-5289. Web Site: fairview.bccls.org. *Dir,* Claudine Pascale; E-mail: pascale@bccls.org
Founded 1944. Pop 13,855; Circ 46,000
Library Holdings: DVDs 2,000; e-books 4,000; Large Print Bks 300; Bk Titles 17,500; Bk Vols 21,700; Per Subs 75
Automation Activity & Vendor Info: (Acquisitions) Innovative Interfaces, Inc; (Cataloging) Innovative Interfaces, Inc; (Circulation) Innovative Interfaces, Inc; (OPAC) Innovative Interfaces, Inc
Database Vendor: EBSCOhost, Gale Cengage Learning, ProQuest
Wireless access
Partic in Bergen County Cooperative Library System
Open Mon-Fri 11-8, Sat 9:30-3:30 (10-2 July-Aug)

FANWOOD

P FANWOOD MEMORIAL LIBRARY, Five Forest Rd, 07023. SAN 310-1576. Tel: 908-322-6400. FAX: 908-322-5590. E-mail: library@fanwoodlibrary.org. Web Site: www.fanwoodlibrary.org. *Dir,* Dan Weiss; E-mail: dweiss@fanwoodlibrary.org; *Ch Serv,* Susan Staub; *Circ,* Gloria Rusnak; *ILL, YA Serv,* Annie Mackenzie; Staff 2 (MLS 2)
Founded 1903. Pop 7,300; Circ 49,000
Library Holdings: AV Mats 800; Bk Titles 30,000; Bk Vols 39,000; Per Subs 75; Talking Bks 250
Special Collections: Local History Coll
Automation Activity & Vendor Info: (Acquisitions) TLC (The Library Corporation); (Cataloging) TLC (The Library Corporation); (Circulation) TLC (The Library Corporation); (OPAC) TLC (The Library Corporation)
Wireless access
Partic in LibraryLinkNJ, The New Jersey Library Cooperative
Open Mon & Thurs 9:30-8, Tues 1-8, Wed & Fri 9:30-5, Sat 9:30-4, Sun 1-4
Friends of the Library Group

FAR HILLS

S UNITED STATES GOLF ASSOCIATION MUSEUM & ARCHIVES, Golf House, 77 Liberty Corner Rd, 07931-2570. (Mail add: PO Box 708, 07931), SAN 310-1584. Tel: 908-234-2300, 908-781-1107. FAX: 908-234-0242. E-mail: museum@usga.org. Web Site: www.usga.org. *Librn,* Nancy Stulack; Staff 2 (Non-MLS 2)
Founded 1936
Library Holdings: Bk Titles 15,000; Bk Vols 50,000; Per Subs 100
Special Collections: Bobby Jones Coll; Golf Architecture Archive; Pamela Fox Emory Oral History Coll. Oral History
Subject Interests: Golf
Wireless access
Function: Ref serv available, Res libr, Wheelchair accessible
Open Mon-Fri 9-5
Restriction: Non-circulating, Not a lending libr

FARMINGDALE

S ALLAIRE VILLAGE INC*, Research Library, 4265 Atlantic Ave, 07727. (Mail add: PO Box 220, 07727). Tel: 732-919-3500. FAX: 732-938-3302. E-mail: info@allairevillage.org. Web Site: www.allairevillage.org. Staff 1 (MLS 1)
Founded 1958
Library Holdings: AV Mats 25; Electronic Media & Resources 10; Bk Titles 500
Special Collections: Historic Allaire Village Coll, bus rec, ledgers, letters, photos; Howell Iron Works Company Coll, bus rec; James P Allaire Coll, ledgers, letters, photos
Subject Interests: 19th Century, Local hist
Function: Res libr
Publications: The Village Star (Newsletter)
Restriction: Open by appt only

FLANDERS

P MOUNT OLIVE PUBLIC LIBRARY*, 202 Flanders-Drakestown Rd, 07836. SAN 310-0448. Tel: 973-691-8686. FAX: 973-691-8542. Web Site: www.mopl.org. *Dir,* Scott Dagan; E-mail: director@mopl.org; *Ch Serv, YA Serv,* Audra Osorio; E-mail: audra.osorio@mopl.org; *Electronic Res,* Timothy Gilbert; E-mail: tim@mopl.org; *Ref Serv,* Cynthia LaPenna; Staff 25 (MLS 8, Non-MLS 17)
Founded 1974. Pop 25,540, Circ 240,000
Library Holdings: Bk Vols 72,000; Per Subs 138
Special Collections: Heritage Coll; Mount Olive History Coll; New Jersey History Coll
Automation Activity & Vendor Info: (Circulation) SirsiDynix; (ILL) SirsiDynix; (OPAC) SirsiDynix
Database Vendor: EBSCOhost, ProQuest, ReferenceUSA, SirsiDynix
Wireless access
Partic in NJ Libr Asn
Special Services for the Deaf - Assisted listening device; Assistive tech; Closed caption videos; TTY equip
Special Services for the Blind - Bks on cassette; Bks on CD; Closed circuit TV magnifier; Copier with enlargement capabilities; Home delivery serv; Large print bks; Large type calculator; Low vision equip; Magnifiers; PC for handicapped; Reader equip; Scanner for conversion & translation of mats; ZoomText magnification & reading software
Open Mon-Thurs 9-9, Fri 9-5, Sat 9-4, Sun 12-4
Friends of the Library Group

FLEMINGTON

P FLEMINGTON FREE PUBLIC LIBRARY*, 118 Main St, 08822. SAN 310-1606. Tel: 908-782-5733. FAX: 908-782-3875. E-mail: flemingtonlibrary@gmail.com. Web Site: www.flemingtonpubliclibrary.org. *Dir,* Shawn Armington; *Tech Serv,* Linda Hahn
Founded 1899. Pop 4,344; Circ 35,838
Library Holdings: Bk Vols 40,000; Per Subs 50
Subject Interests: Humanities

S HUNTERDON COUNTY HISTORICAL SOCIETY*, Hiram E Deats Memorial Library, 114 Main St, 08822. SAN 325-9307. Tel: 908-782-1091. E-mail: hunterdonhistory@embarqmail.com. Web Site: hunterdonhistory.org. *Librn,* Terry A McNealy; Staff 1 (MLS 1)
Founded 1885
Library Holdings: Bk Vols 7,000
Subject Interests: Genealogy, Local hist
Function: Res libr
Open Thurs 12-4, Sat 10-4
Restriction: Non-circulating

L HUNTERDON COUNTY LAW LIBRARY*, 65 Park Ave, 08822. SAN 325-7606. Tel: 908-237-5936. FAX: 908-237-5937. *Librn,* Phyllis Pason
Library Holdings: Bk Vols 500
Wireless access
Open Mon-Wed & Fri 8:30-1:30 & 2:30-4:30
Restriction: Non-circulating to the pub

P HUNTERDON COUNTY LIBRARY*, 314 State Rte 12, 08822. SAN 310-1614. Tel: 908-788-1444. Circulation Tel: 908-788-1437. Reference Tel: 908-788-1434. FAX: 908-806-4862. Reference FAX: 908-806-5179. E-mail: reference@hclibrary.us. Web Site: www.hclibrary.us. *Dir,* Mark Titus; *Ref, Tech Serv,* Kristin Momberg; *Youth Serv,* Adrienne Gardner; Staff 59 (MLS 21, Non-MLS 38)
Founded 1928. Pop 112,726; Circ 1,226,223
Library Holdings: AV Mats 46,816; Bk Titles 222,208; Bk Vols 384,939; Per Subs 591
Special Collections: New Jersey (Jerseyana)
Automation Activity & Vendor Info: (Acquisitions) Innovative Interfaces, Inc; (Cataloging) Innovative Interfaces, Inc; (Circulation) Innovative Interfaces, Inc
Database Vendor: EBSCOhost, ProQuest
Wireless access
Function: Adult bk club, Art exhibits, Computers for patron use, Electronic databases & coll, Large print keyboards, Online cat, OverDrive digital audio bks, Prog for adults, Prog for children & young adult
Publications: HCL Duck (Newsletter); HCL Scoop (Bi-monthly)
Member Libraries: Bunnvale Public Library; Frenchtown Public Library; High Bridge Public Library; Holland Free Public Library; Readington Township Library; Tewksbury Township Public Library; Three Bridges Public Library
Open Mon, Fri & Sat 9-5, Tues & Thurs 9-9, Sun (Sept-June) 1-5
Friends of the Library Group
Branches: 2
NORTH COUNTY, 65 Halstead St, Clinton, 08809. Tel: 908-730-6262. Reference Tel: 908-730-6135. FAX: 908-730-6467.
Library Holdings: Bk Vols 98,950
Open Mon, Fri & Sat 9-5, Tues-Thurs 9-9
Friends of the Library Group
SOUTH COUNTY, 1108-A Old York Rd, Ringoes, 08851. Tel: 908-782-3564. FAX: 908-782-0846. *Asst Libr Dir,* Jennifer Winberry; Tel: 908-788-1444
Library Holdings: Bk Vols 19,000
Open Mon & Thurs-Sat 9-5, Tues & Wed 9-9
Friends of the Library Group
Bookmobiles: 1

M HUNTERDON MEDICAL CENTER LIBRARY*, 2100 Wescott Dr, 08822. SAN 310-1622. Tel: 908-788-6100, Ext 2579. FAX: 908-788-2537. *Librn,* Karen Wenk; E-mail: wenk.karen@hunterdonhealthcare.org
Founded 1954
Library Holdings: Bk Vols 1,000; Per Subs 15
Partic in Health Sci Libr Asn of NJ; Med Resources Consortium of Cent NJ
Open Mon-Fri 8-4:30

FLORHAM PARK

L DAY PITNEY LLP*, Information Resource Center, 200 Campus Dr, 07932. (Mail add: PO Box 1945, Morristown, 07962-1945), SAN 310-3153. Tel: 973-966-6300. FAX: 973-966-1015. Web Site: www.daypitney.com. *Info Res Mgr,* Salvatore Cardinale; Staff 4 (MLS 2, Non-MLS 2)
Founded 1902
Library Holdings: Bk Titles 7,000; Bk Vols 38,000; Per Subs 150
Subject Interests: General law, NJ law
Automation Activity & Vendor Info: (Acquisitions) EOS International; (Cataloging) EOS International; (OPAC) EOS International; (Serials) EOS International
Database Vendor: Dialog, LexisNexis, Westlaw
Restriction: Staff use only

L DRINKER BIDDLE & REATH*, Law Library, 500 Campus Dr, 07932. SAN 310-3587. Tel: 973-360-1100. FAX: 973-360-9831. Web Site: www.dbr.com. *Librn,* Relly Jacobs
Library Holdings: Bk Vols 20,000; Per Subs 40
Partic in Westlaw
Restriction: Staff use only

P FLORHAM PARK PUBLIC LIBRARY*, 107 Ridgedale Ave, 07932. SAN 310-1665. Tel: 973-377-2694. FAX: 973-377-2085. Web Site: www.florhamparklib.org. *Dir,* Joan Hipp; *Children's/Ref Librn,* Judy Leane; Staff 1.75 (MLS 1.75)
Founded 1965. Pop 11,000; Circ 92,893
Jan 2010-Dec 2010 Income $889,354, State $3,362, City $863,746, Locally Generated Income $10,919, Other $11,327. Mats Exp $91,515, Books $66,424, Per/Ser (Incl. Access Fees) $8,786, AV Mat $10,407, Electronic Ref Mat (Incl. Access Fees) $5,898. Sal $367,768 (Prof $132,900)
Library Holdings: AV Mats 4,677; CDs 1,554; DVDs 1,400; e-books 321; Bk Vols 49,270; Per Subs 150
Subject Interests: Art
Automation Activity & Vendor Info: (Cataloging) Innovative Interfaces, Inc; (Circulation) Innovative Interfaces, Inc; (ILL) Innovative Interfaces, Inc; (OPAC) Innovative Interfaces, Inc
Database Vendor: Baker & Taylor, Booksite, Checkpoint Systems, Inc, EBSCOhost, Facts on File, Gale Cengage Learning, LearningExpress, Overdrive, Inc, ProQuest, ReferenceUSA
Wireless access
Function: ILL available, Photocopying/Printing, Telephone ref
Publications: Newsletter (Bi-monthly)
Partic in Morris Automated Information Network
Open Mon-Thurs 9:30-9, Fri 9:30-5, Sat 10-4, Sun 1-4
Friends of the Library Group

FORT LEE

P FREE PUBLIC LIBRARY OF THE BOROUGH OF FORT LEE*, 320 Main St, 07024. SAN 310-1673. Tel: 201-592-3614. Reference Tel: 201-592-3629. FAX: 201-585-0375. E-mail: ftlecirc@bccls.org. Web Site: www.bccls.org/fortlee. *Dir,* Rita Altomara; E-mail: altomara@bccls.org; *Adult Serv, Web Serv,* Nick Taylor; *Ch Serv,* Sarah Pardi; Tel: 201-592-3620; *Computer Serv, Ref Serv,* Wei Guan; *Tech Serv,* Carole Watson; *YA Serv,* Julia Strohmeyer; Staff 7 (MLS 7)
Founded 1930. Pop 38,000; Circ 252,682
Jan 2012-Dec 2012 Income $2,260,398, State $32,864, City $2,183,850, Other $43,684. Mats Exp $577,212, Books $139,584, Per/Ser (Incl. Access Fees) $16,200, AV Equip $1,000, AV Mat $30,492, Electronic Ref Mat (Incl. Access Fees) $9,876. Sal $1,231,000 (Prof $357,425)
Library Holdings: AV Mats 1,135; Bk Vols 5,743; Per Subs 310; Talking Bks 2,813
Special Collections: Books in Japanese & Korean; Silent Film Photos
Subject Interests: Feminism
Automation Activity & Vendor Info: (Acquisitions) Baker & Taylor; (Cataloging) Baker & Taylor; (Circulation) Innovative Interfaces, Inc; (OPAC) Innovative Interfaces, Inc
Database Vendor: SirsiDynix
Wireless access
Publications: Library Looking Glass (Newsletter)
Partic in Bergen County Cooperative Library System
Open Mon-Thurs 9:30-9, Fri & Sat 9:30-5, Sun 1-5
Friends of the Library Group

FRANKLIN LAKES

S BECTON, DICKINSON & CO*, Information Resource Center, One Becton Dr, 07417-1884. SAN 310-4893. Tel: 201-847-7230. FAX: 201-847-5377. *Dir,* Faina Menzul
Library Holdings: Bk Vols 8,000; Per Subs 300
Subject Interests: Eng, Law, Med, Plastics
Automation Activity & Vendor Info: (Cataloging) SirsiDynix; (Circulation) SirsiDynix
Restriction: Staff use only

P FRANKLIN LAKES FREE PUBLIC LIBRARY*, 470 DeKorte Dr, 07417. SAN 310-1681. Tel: 201-891-2224. FAX: 201-891-5102. Web Site: www.franklinlakeslibrary.org. *Dir,* Gerry McMahon; E-mail: mcmahon@bccls.org; *Asst Dir,* Linda Hagedorn; E-mail: hagedorn@bccls.org; *Adult Serv,* Jennifer Hendricks; E-mail: jennifer.hendricks@bccls.org; *AV Coll,* Ken Lew; E-mail: lew@bccls.org; *Ch Serv,* Sarah Tobias; E-mail: sara.tobias@bccls.org; *YA Serv,* Donna Kurdock; E-mail: donna.kurdock@bccls.org; Staff 25 (MLS 6, Non-MLS 19)
Founded 1968. Pop 10,422
Library Holdings: Bk Vols 80,000; Per Subs 255
Automation Activity & Vendor Info: (Cataloging) Innovative Interfaces, Inc; (Circulation) Innovative Interfaces, Inc; (OPAC) Innovative Interfaces, Inc

Database Vendor: EBSCOhost, Facts on File, Gale Cengage Learning, Library Ideas, LLC, Overdrive, Inc, ProQuest, ReferenceUSA, TumbleBookLibrary, World Book Online
Wireless access
Function: Art exhibits, Bk club(s), Bks on cassette, Bks on CD, Children's prog, Computer training, Computers for patron use, Copy machines, Digital talking bks, Electronic databases & coll, Free DVD rentals, Handicapped accessible, Holiday prog, Homework prog, ILL available, Online cat, OverDrive digital audio bks, Prog for adults, Prog for children & young adult, Summer reading prog, Tax forms, Teen prog, Web-catalog, Workshops
Partic in Bergen County Cooperative Library System; LibraryLinkNJ, The New Jersey Library Cooperative
Open Mon-Thurs 10-9, Fri 10-6, Sat 10-5, Sun (Sept-June) 1-5
Friends of the Library Group

FRANKLINVILLE

P FRANKLIN TOWNSHIP PUBLIC LIBRARY, 1584 Coles Mill Rd, 08322. SAN 350-8625. Tel: 856-694-2833. FAX: 856-694-1708. E-mail: ftpl@yahoo.com. *Dir,* Denise Saia; Staff 2 (MLS 2)
Founded 1966. Pop 16,820
Library Holdings: Bk Titles 88,588; Per Subs 103
Automation Activity & Vendor Info: (Circulation) SirsiDynix; (OPAC) SirsiDynix
Database Vendor: OCLC FirstSearch
Wireless access
Partic in LOGIN (Libraries of Gloucester, Salem & Cumberland Information Network)
Open Mon-Thurs 10-8, Fri 10-5, Sat 10-3

FREEHOLD

M CENTRASTATE HEALTHCARE SYSTEM LIBRARY*, 901 W Main St, 07728. SAN 375-5088. Tel: 732-431-2000. *Librn,* Robin Siegel; E-mail: rsiegel@centrastate.com; Staff 1 (MLS 1)
Library Holdings: Bk Vols 1,500; Per Subs 125
Partic in Basic Health Sciences Library Network; Docline; Health Sciences Library Association of New Jersey; LibraryLinkNJ, The New Jersey Library Cooperative; Monmouth-Ocean Biomedical Information Consortium; OCLC Online Computer Library Center, Inc
Open Mon-Fri 8-4

P FREEHOLD PUBLIC LIBRARY*, 28 1/2 E Main St, 07728-2202. SAN 310-1703. Tel: 732-462-5135. FAX: 732-577-9598. E-mail: fplib@freeholdpubliclibrary.org. Web Site: freeholdpubliclibrary.org. *Dir,* Barbara Greenberg; E-mail: bglib@yahoo.com; Staff 7 (MLS 1, Non-MLS 6)
Founded 1903. Pop 10,742; Circ 29,914
Library Holdings: Bk Vols 23,506; Per Subs 78
Special Collections: Books on Compact Discs; DVDs; Large Print Books
Subject Interests: Local hist
Automation Activity & Vendor Info: (Circulation) Mandarin Library Automation; (ILL) Mandarin Library Automation; (OPAC) Mandarin Library Automation
Wireless access
Publications: Freehold Public Library Blog; Newsletter (Online only); Patron Brochure (Monthly newsletter)
Partic in LibraryLinkNJ, The New Jersey Library Cooperative
Open Mon, Wed & Thurs 9-5 & 7-9, Tues & Fri 9-5, Sat 9-1
Friends of the Library Group

S MONMOUTH COUNTY HISTORICAL ASSOCIATION LIBRARY & ARCHIVES, 70 Court St, 07728. SAN 310-172X. Tel: 732-462-1466. FAX: 732-462-8346. E-mail: library@monmouthhistory.org. Web Site: www.monmouthhistory.org. *Archivist, Librn,* Laura M Poll; *Libr Asst,* Deb Carmody; E-mail: dcarmody@monmouthhistory.org; *Libr Asst,* Sally Weiner; E-mail: sweiner@monmouthhistory.org; Staff 1 (MLS 1)
Founded 1898
Special Collections: A&M Karagheusian Coll; Allaire Family Papers (Howell Iron Works); Battle of Monmouth Coll; Hartshorne Family Papers; John C Mills Maritime Coll; North American Phalanx Records; Pach Brothers Studio Coll; Philip Freneau Papers
Wireless access
Function: Archival coll
Publications: Collections Book; Diary of Sarah Tabitha Reid, 1868-1873; Micah Williams: Portrait Artist; Steamboats in Monmouth County: A Gazetteer
Partic in LibraryLinkNJ, The New Jersey Library Cooperative; NJ Libr Asn
Special Services for the Blind - Magnifiers
Open Wed-Sat 10-4
Restriction: Non-circulating to the pub

FRENCHTOWN

P FRENCHTOWN PUBLIC LIBRARY*, 29 Second St, 08825. SAN 310-1746. Tel: 908-996-4788. *Librn,* Sara Heil
Circ 21,514
Library Holdings: Audiobooks 100; CDs 100; DVDs 2,000; Large Print Bks 50; Bk Vols 16,000; Per Subs 30; Videos 100
Automation Activity & Vendor Info: (Cataloging) SirsiDynix; (Circulation) SirsiDynix; (OPAC) SirsiDynix
Wireless access
Mem of Hunterdon County Library
Open Mon & Fri 9:30-12:30, Tues & Wed 3-5 & 7-9

GALLOWAY

C RICHARD STOCKTON COLLEGE OF NEW JERSEY LIBRARY*, 101 Vera King Farris Dr, 08205-9441. SAN 310-4362. Tel: 609-652-4343. Circulation Tel: 609-652-4346. Reference Tel: 609-652-4266. FAX: 609-652-4964. E-mail: librarian@stockton.edu. Web Site: library.stockton.edu. *Dir,* David Pinto; E-mail: david.pinto@stockton.edu; *Assoc Dir, Pub Serv,* Gus Stamatopoulos; E-mail: gus.stamatopoulos@stockton.edu; *Assoc Dir, Tech Serv,* William Bearden; E-mail: bill.bearden@stockton.edu; Staff 9 (MLS 8, Non-MLS 1)
Founded 1971. Enrl 8,000; Fac 269; Highest Degree: Doctorate
Jul 2010-Jun 2011. Mats Exp $972,200
Library Holdings: Audiobooks 663; CDs 883; e-books 4,476; e-journals 41,000; Bk Vols 261,023; Per Subs 490; Videos 12,637
Special Collections: Cape May Jazz Festival Archives; Holocaust & Genocide Studies; John Henry "Pop" Lloyd Archives; New Jersey Pine Barrens; Southern New Jersey (William W Leap Coll). Oral History; State Document Depository; US Document Depository
Automation Activity & Vendor Info: (Acquisitions) SirsiDynix; (Cataloging) SirsiDynix; (Circulation) SirsiDynix; (OPAC) SirsiDynix; (Serials) SirsiDynix
Database Vendor: SirsiDynix
Wireless access
Partic in Lyrasis; Virtual Academic Library Environment; Westchester Academic Library Directors Organization (WALDO)
Open Mon-Thurs (Winter) 8am-Midnight, Fri 8-5, Sat 10-8, Sun Noon-Midnight; Mon-Thurs (Summer) 8am-10pm

GARFIELD

P GARFIELD PUBLIC LIBRARY*, 500 Midland Ave, 07026. SAN 310-1754. Tel: 973-478-3800. FAX: 973-478-7162. Web Site: www.bccls.org/garfield. *Dir,* Mary Jo Jennings; *Ch,* Patricia Gelinski; *Ref Librn,* Catherine Dodwell; Staff 13 (MLS 3, Non-MLS 10)
Founded 1923. Pop 29,786; Circ 71,406
Library Holdings: Bk Titles 75,000; Bk Vols 85,000, Per Subs 147
Special Collections: Black History-Literature (Black History), bks; Persian Art
Open Mon & Tues 9:30-8, Wed 9:30-9, Thurs & Fri 9:30-6, Sat 9:30-5

GARWOOD

P GARWOOD FREE PUBLIC LIBRARY*, 411 Third Ave, 07027. SAN 310-1789. Tel: 908-789-1670. FAX: 908-317-8146. Web Site: www.youseemore.com/garwood. *Dir,* Carol A Lombardo; Staff 4 (MLS 1, Non-MLS 3)
Founded 1933. Pop 4,210; Circ 11,500
Library Holdings: Bk Vols 28,000; Per Subs 35
Special Collections: New Jersey Coll
Automation Activity & Vendor Info: (Cataloging) TLC (The Library Corporation); (Circulation) TLC (The Library Corporation)
Partic in LibraryLinkNJ, The New Jersey Library Cooperative
Open Mon-Thurs 9-8, Fri 9-4:30, Sat 9-1

GIBBSBORO

P GIBBSBORO PUBLIC LIBRARY*, Borough Hall, 49 Kirkwood Rd, 08026. Tel: 856-435-3656. E-mail: gibbsborolibrary@comcast.net. Web Site: www.gibbsborotownhall.com. *Dir,* Jodie Favat
Library Holdings: DVDs 200; Bk Vols 5,000; Per Subs 35
Wireless access
Mem of Camden County Library System
Open Mon & Wed 10-4, Tues & Thurs 10-4 & 6-8, Sat 9-12

GILLETTE

P LONG HILL TOWNSHIP PUBLIC LIBRARY*, 917 Valley Rd, 07933. SAN 310-5210. Tel: 908-647-2088. FAX: 908-647-2098. Web Site: www.longhilllibrary.org. *Dir,* Mary Martin; E-mail: director@longhilllibrary.org; *Ref & ILL Librn,* Mary Grace Luderitz; E-mail: marygrace.luderitz@longhilllibrary.org; *Ch Serv,* Vicky Kulikowsky; *Circ,* Clarissa Wagner; E-mail: clarissa.wagner@longhilllibrary.org; Staff 10 (MLS 4, Non-MLS 6)

Founded 1957. Pop 9,500; Circ 105,000
Library Holdings: Bk Titles 47,000; Bk Vols 55,000; Per Subs 110
Special Collections: Cooking Coll; Gardening Coll; Large Print Coll; Parenting Coll
Automation Activity & Vendor Info: (Cataloging) SirsiDynix; (Circulation) SirsiDynix; (OPAC) SirsiDynix
Database Vendor: EBSCOhost, Gale Cengage Learning, ProQuest
Publications: newsletter
Partic in Morris Automated Information Network
Open Mon-Thurs 10-9, Fri & Sat 10-5, Sun (Sept-June) 1-5
Friends of the Library Group

GLASSBORO

C ROWAN UNIVERSITY LIBRARY*, Keith & Shirley Campbell Library, 201 Mullica Hill Rd, 08029. SAN 350-7572. Tel: 856-256-4800. Circulation Tel: 856-256-4802. Interlibrary Loan Service Tel: 856-256-4803. Reference Tel: 856-256-4801. Administration Tel: 856-256-4984. FAX: 856-256-4924. Web Site: www.lib.rowan.edu. *Dean of Libr,* Bruce Alan Whitham; Tel: 856-256-4981, E-mail: whitham@rowan.edu; Staff 40 (MLS 17, Non-MLS 23)
Founded 1923. Enrl 9,762; Fac 630; Highest Degree: Doctorate
Library Holdings: AV Mats 48,554; CDs 1,683; DVDs 764; e-books 2,000; Bk Vols 420,231; Per Subs 11,154; Videos 5,666
Special Collections: United States, New Jersey & Delaware Valley History (Stewart Coll), bks, deeds, genealogical mat, mss, papers. State Document Depository; US Document Depository
Subject Interests: Educ, Eng
Automation Activity & Vendor Info: (Acquisitions) Ex Libris Group; (Cataloging) Ex Libris Group; (Circulation) Ex Libris Group; (Course Reserve) Ex Libris Group; (ILL) Ex Libris Group; (Media Booking) Ex Libris Group; (OPAC) Ex Libris Group; (Serials) Ex Libris Group
Database Vendor: ABC-CLIO, ACM (Association for Computing Machinery), American Chemical Society, American Psychological Association (APA), Annual Reviews, Bowker, CQ Press, CredoReference, Dialog, EBSCOhost, Elsevier, Emerald, Factiva.com, Facts on File, Gale Cengage Learning, H W Wilson, IEEE (Institute of Electrical & Electronics Engineers), JSTOR, LexisNexis, Modern Language Association, Newsbank, OCLC WorldShare Interlibrary Loan, OVID Technologies, ProQuest, PubMed, ReferenceUSA, RefWorks, ScienceDirect, SerialsSolutions, STAT!Ref (Teton Data Systems), Wilson - Wilson Web, YBP Library Services
Partic in LibraryLinkNJ, The New Jersey Library Cooperative; Lyrasis; Pennsylvania Academic Library Consortium, Inc (PALCI); Tri-State College Library Cooperative; Virtual Academic Library Environment
Open Mon-Thurs 8am-Midnight, Fri 8am-9pm, Sat 9-5, Sun Noon-10pm
Friends of the Library Group

Departmental Libraries:

WILSON MUSIC LIBRARY, Main Campus, Rte 322, 08028, SAN 350-7602. Tel: 856-256-4500, Ext 3542, 856-256-4799. FAX: 856-256-4644. *Librn,* Marjorie Morris; Fax: 856-256-4924, E-mail: morrism@rowan.edu; *Cat,* Robert Lipartito; E-mail: lipartito@rowan.edu; Staff 3 (MLS 2, Non-MLS 1)
Founded 1969. Fac 17; Highest Degree: Master
Library Holdings: AV Mats 4,000; CDs 4,000; DVDs 500; Music Scores 25,000; Talking Bks 10
Special Collections: Musical Scores; Reference Books; Sound & Video Recordings
Partic in Virtual Academic Library Environment
Open Mon-Thurs 9-9, Fri 9-7, Sun (Sept-May) 1-6
Restriction: Circ limited
Friends of the Library Group

GLEN RIDGE

P GLEN RIDGE FREE PUBLIC LIBRARY, 240 Ridgewood Ave, 07028. SAN 310-1843. Tel: 973-748-5482. FAX: 973-748-9350. E-mail: glrgcirc@bccls.org. Web Site: www.glenridgelibrary.org. *Dir,* Jennifer Breuer; *Asst Dir/Ref Librn,* Helen Beckert; *Principal Libr Asst/Tech Serv & Circ,* Dawn Petretti; *Principal Libr Asst/Youth serv,* Sydney Young; Staff 10.17 (MLS 2.17, Non-MLS 8)
Founded 1912. Pop 7,527; Circ 116,628
Jan 2013-Dec 2013 Income $601,484, State $3,298, City $598,186. Mats Exp $82,025, Books $63,000, Per/Ser (Incl. Access Fees) $5,500, AV Mat $13,525. Sal $190,242 (Prof $145,687)
Library Holdings: Audiobooks 861; CDs 1,795; DVDs 2,553; Electronic Media & Resources 5; Bk Titles 46,676; Per Subs 155
Special Collections: Glen Ridge Historical Coll & Archive
Subject Interests: Local hist
Automation Activity & Vendor Info: (Acquisitions) Baker & Taylor; (ILL) JerseyCat
Database Vendor: EBSCOhost, Gale Cengage Learning, ProQuest
Wireless access
Function: 24/7 Electronic res, 24/7 Online cat, Archival coll, Bks on CD, Children's prog, Computer training, Computers for patron use, Copy machines, Digital talking bks, e-mail serv, Electronic databases & coll, eReaders, Exhibits, Fax serv, Free DVD rentals, Handicapped accessible, Homebound delivery serv, ILL available, Laminating, Magazines, Mail & tel request accepted, Mango lang, Microfiche/film & reading machines, Mus passes, Music CDs, Notary serv, Online cat, Orientations, Outside serv via phone, mail, e-mail & web, OverDrive digital audio bks, Photocopying/Printing, Preschool reading prog, Printer for laptops & handheld devices, Prog for adults, Prog for children & young adult, Pub access computers, Ref & res, Ref serv available, Ref serv in person, Scanner, Story hour, Summer reading prog, Tax forms, Teen prog, Telephone ref, Web-catalog, Wheelchair accessible, Workshops
Publications: Brochures for Library Programs; Event Flyers; Monthly Calendar; Monthly newsletter via Constant Contact
Partic in Bergen County Cooperative Library System; LibraryLinkNJ, The New Jersey Library Cooperative; ReBL
Special Services for the Blind - Home delivery serv
Open Mon & Wed 12-8, Tues 9-8, Thurs, Fri & Sat 9-5
Friends of the Library Group

GLEN ROCK

P GLEN ROCK PUBLIC LIBRARY*, 315 Rock Rd, 07452-1795. SAN 310-1851. Tel: 201-670-3970. Reference Tel: 201-670-3991. FAX: 201-445-0872. E-mail: glrkcirc@bccls.org. Web Site: glenrock.bccls.org. *Dir,* Betsy Wald; *Head, Circ & Adult Serv,* Alex Tretiak; *Cat Librn,* Susan Pescoe; *Ch,* Trisha Fishelman; E-mail: fishelman@bccls.org; *Teen/Tech Librnb,* Jennifer Lemke; Staff 25 (MLS 6, Non-MLS 19)
Founded 1922. Pop 11,500; Circ 201,000
Jan 2008-Dec 2008 Income $916,787, State $11,787, City $890,000, Locally Generated Income $15,000. Mats Exp $102,230, Books $72,000, Per/Ser (Incl. Access Fees) $5,230, AV Mat $25,000. Sal $582,400 (Prof $204,577)
Library Holdings: DVDs 563; Large Print Bks 1,000; Bk Titles 80,000; Bk Vols 84,750; Per Subs 100; Talking Bks 3,313; Videos 1,830
Automation Activity & Vendor Info: (Cataloging) Innovative Interfaces, Inc; (Circulation) Innovative Interfaces, Inc; (OPAC) Innovative Interfaces, Inc
Wireless access
Function: Adult bk club, Adult literacy prog, After school storytime, Art exhibits, Audiobks via web, AV serv, Bks on cassette, Bks on CD, CD-ROM, Children's prog, Computers for patron use, Copy machines, Digital talking bks, E-Reserves, Electronic databases & coll, Free DVD rentals, Handicapped accessible, ILL available, Instruction & testing, Magnifiers for reading, Music CDs, Online cat, Online searches, Photocopying/Printing, Prog for adults, Prog for children & young adult, Ref serv available, Spoken cassettes & CDs, Spoken cassettes & DVDs, Summer reading prog, Tax forms, Teen prog, Telephone ref, VCDs, VHS videos, Web-catalog, Wheelchair accessible
Partic in Bergen County Cooperative Library System
Open Mon, Wed & Thurs 9-9, Tues & Fri 9-5:30, Sat 9-5, Sun (Sept-June) 1-5
Friends of the Library Group

GLOUCESTER CITY

P GLOUCESTER CITY LIBRARY*, 50 N Railroad Ave, 08030. SAN 310-186X. Tel: 856-456-4181. FAX: 856-456-6724. E-mail: gc@gcpl.us. Web Site: www.gloucestercitylibrary.org. *Dir,* Elizabeth J Egan; *Ref,* Erica Cathers; *Ref,* Deena Worrell; Staff 4 (MLS 4)
Founded 1925. Pop 11,500; Circ 50,000
Library Holdings: Bk Titles 55,000; Per Subs 75
Automation Activity & Vendor Info: (Cataloging) Innovative Interfaces, Inc; (Circulation) Innovative Interfaces, Inc; (OPAC) Innovative Interfaces, Inc
Database Vendor: EBSCOhost, Gale Cengage Learning
Partic in LibraryLinkNJ, The New Jersey Library Cooperative
Open Mon 12-9, Tues-Thurs 9-9, Fri 9-5, Sat 10-1

GREENWICH

S CUMBERLAND COUNTY HISTORICAL SOCIETY LIBRARY*, The Warren Lummis Genealogical & Historical Library, 981 Great St, 08323. (Mail add: PO Box 16, 08323), SAN 375-8427. Tel: 856-455-4055, 856-455-8580. Web Site: www.cchistsoc.org/lummis. *Dir,* Warren Adams; *Asst Dir,* Mona Morgan Perry; *Librn,* Constance C Schuchard
Library Holdings: Bk Vols 1,000
Subject Interests: Genealogy
Function: Res libr
Open Wed 10-4, Sat & Sun 1-4
Restriction: Non-circulating

HACKENSACK

S BERGEN COUNTY HISTORICAL SOCIETY LIBRARY & ARCHIVES, 355 Main St, Rm 124, 07601. (Mail add: PO Box 55, River Edge, 07661-0055), SAN 377-3981. Tel: 201-343-9492. E-mail:

thebchslibrary@gmail.com. Web Site: www.bergencountyhistory.org/Pages/librarycollections.html. *Chair,* Lucille Bertram
Founded 1902
Library Holdings: Bk Titles 2,500; Bk Vols 3,000
Special Collections: Genealogy Coll; Manuscripts Coll; Map Coll; Photographs & Slides
Subject Interests: Colonial hist, Revolutionary war
Wireless access

GL BERGEN COUNTY LAW LIBRARY*, Bergen County Justice Center, Ten Main St, 1st Flr, 07601. SAN 310-1894. Tel: 201-527-2274. FAX: 201-371-1121. *Librn,* Henry Gozdz
Library Holdings: Bk Vols 36,000; Per Subs 10
Database Vendor: LexisNexis
Open Mon-Fri 8:30-4:20
Restriction: Non-circulating to the pub

C FAIRLEIGH DICKINSON UNIVERSITY*, Business Research Library-New Jersey Room, Dickinson Hall, 140 University Plaza Dr, 07601. Tel: 201-692-2608. FAX: 201-692-7048. Web Site: www.fdu.edu. *Head of Libr,* Maria Kocylowsky; E-mail: marialk@fdu.edu; *Librn,* Michele Nestory; E-mail: michele1@fdu.edu
Library Holdings: Bk Vols 17,000
Database Vendor: EBSCOhost, Gale Cengage Learning, ProQuest, Wilson - Wilson Web
Wireless access
Open Mon-Thurs 8:30-8:30, Fri 8:30-4:30, Sat 11-5

M HACKENSACK UNIVERSITY MEDICAL CENTER*, Medical Library, 30 Prospect Ave, 07601. SAN 310-1916. Tel: 201-996-2326. FAX: 201-996-2467. *Dir,* Barbara S Reich; E-mail: breich@humed.com; Staff 6 (MLS 3, Non-MLS 3)
Library Holdings: Bk Titles 3,500; Per Subs 312
Subject Interests: Hist
Partic in Basic Health Sciences Library Network; Bergen Passaic Health Sciences Library Consortium; LibraryLinkNJ, The New Jersey Library Cooperative; National Network of Libraries of Medicine; New Jersey Health Sciences Library Network; New Jersey Library Network
Open Mon-Thurs 8am-9pm, Fri 8-6

P JOHNSON FREE PUBLIC LIBRARY*, 274 Main St, 07601-5797. SAN 350-7637. Tel: 201-343-4169. Reference Tel: 201-343-4781. FAX: 201-343-1395. E-mail: hackref@bccls.org. Web Site: hackensack.bccls.org. *Dir,* Sharon Castanteen; *Asst Dir,* Barb Schuit; *Head, Ch,* Marilyn Olson; *Head, Circ,* Beverley Wyche; *Head, Govt Doc,* Sunil D Mehta; *Head, Per,* Isaac Annan; *Head, Ref,* Debbie Bock; *Head, Tech Serv,* Michael Ferrante; *Head, YA,* Keri Adams; Staff 11 (MLS 11)
Founded 1901. Pop 42,677; Circ 188,539
Library Holdings: Bk Vols 159,660; Per Subs 302
Special Collections: New Jersey History Coll, bks, microfilm, per, pictures; Spanish Language Coll. State Document Depository; US Document Depository
Automation Activity & Vendor Info: (Cataloging) Innovative Interfaces, Inc; (Circulation) Innovative Interfaces, Inc; (ILL) JerseyCat; (OPAC) Innovative Interfaces, Inc
Database Vendor: EBSCO Information Services, Grolier Online, Newsbank, ProQuest, ReferenceUSA
Wireless access
Partic in Bergen County Cooperative Library System
Open Mon-Thurs 9-9, Fri & Sat 9-5

S NORTH JERSEY MEDIA GROUP LIBRARY*, Editorial Information Services, 150 River St, 07601. SAN 375-748X. Tel: 201-646-4000. FAX: 201-646-4737. E-mail: library@northjersey.com. *Mgr,* Paul Wilder; *Librn,* Donna Blair; E-mail: blair@northjersey.com; *Librn,* Leonard Iannaccone; E-mail: iannaccone@northjersey.com; *Librn,* Anna Leypunskaya; E-mail: leypunskaya@northjersey.com; *Librn,* David Mammone; E-mail: mammone@northjersey.com; Staff 8 (MLS 2, Non-MLS 6)
Library Holdings: Bk Titles 5,000; Per Subs 150
Special Collections: The Record Clippings from 1960-1986; The Record Photo Coll
Database Vendor: Dialog, Gale Cengage Learning, LexisNexis, ProQuest
Function: Newsp ref libr
Partic in LibraryLinkNJ, The New Jersey Library Cooperative
Open Mon, Wed & Fri 7-10, Tues & Thurs 7-6, Sun 2-10
Restriction: Not open to pub

HACKETTSTOWN

C CENTENARY COLLEGE*, Taylor Memorial Library, 400 Jefferson St, 07840. SAN 310-1932. Tel: 908-852-1400, Ext 2345. FAX: 908-850-9528. Web Site: faculty.centenarycollege.edu/library. *Dir,* Nancy Madacsi; *Asst Dir,* Jane Endrizzi; *Acq,* Krystyna Pikowski; *Tech Serv,* Maryanne Fegan; Staff 8 (MLS 3, Non-MLS 5)
Founded 1867. Enrl 2,551; Fac 51
Jul 2010-Jun 2011. Mats Exp $90,000
Library Holdings: DVDs 800; Bk Titles 69,300; Bk Vols 73,000; Per Subs 75
Special Collections: Centenary College Historical Coll
Subject Interests: Liberal arts
Automation Activity & Vendor Info: (Cataloging) ByWater Solutions; (Circulation) ByWater Solutions; (Course Reserve) ByWater Solutions; (OPAC) ByWater Solutions; (Serials) ByWater Solutions
Publications: Acquisitions List; Bibliographies; Guides; Handbook for the Taylor Memorial LRC
Partic in LibraryLinkNJ, The New Jersey Library Cooperative; OCLC Online Computer Library Center, Inc; Virtual Academic Library Environment
Open Mon-Thurs 8am-10:45pm, Fri 8-4:30, Sat 9-2, Sun 1-9:30

P HACKETTSTOWN FREE PUBLIC LIBRARY*, 110 Church St, 07840. SAN 310-1940. Tel: 908-852-4936. FAX: 908-852-7850. E-mail: info@hackettstownlibrary.org. Web Site: www.hackettstownlibrary.org. *Dir,* Patricia Sherman; Staff 4.5 (MLS 1.5, Non-MLS 3)
Founded 1913. Pop 8,984; Circ 35,000
Library Holdings: AV Mats 4,156; CDs 525; DVDs 2,026; Bk Titles 32,000; Per Subs 60
Subject Interests: Local hist
Automation Activity & Vendor Info: (Circulation) Auto-Graphics, Inc; (OPAC) Auto-Graphics, Inc
Wireless access
Partic in New Jersey Library Network
Open Mon-Thurs 10-9, Fri 10-5, Sat 9-12
Friends of the Library Group

M HACKETTSTOWN REGIONAL MEDICAL CENTER*, Dr Eddy Palmer Medical Library, 651 Willow Grove St, 07840. SAN 373-2479. Tel: 908-850-7743. FAX: 908-850-6815. Web Site: www.hrmcnj.org. *Librn,* Julie-Ann Schilling; Tel: 908-850-6918
Library Holdings: Bk Vols 500; Per Subs 24
Open Mon-Fri 8-3

HADDON HEIGHTS

P HADDON HEIGHTS PUBLIC LIBRARY*, 608 Station Ave, 08035-1907. (Mail add: PO Box 240, 08035-0240), SAN 310-1959. Tel: 856-547-7132. FAX: 856-547-2867. Web Site: www.haddonheightslibrary.com. *Dir,* Christopher S Walter; *Ch Serv, Tech Serv,* Kathleen Bernardi; *ILL,* Theresa Crisostimo
Founded 1902. Pop 7,500; Circ 42,000
Library Holdings: Bk Titles 53,000; Bk Vols 54,000; Per Subs 97
Special Collections: Local History Coll; Theatrical Plays
Automation Activity & Vendor Info: (Cataloging) Innovative Interfaces, Inc; (Circulation) Innovative Interfaces, Inc; (OPAC) Innovative Interfaces, Inc
Wireless access
Open Mon-Fri 10-5 & 6:30-9, Sat 10-2
Friends of the Library Group

HADDONFIELD

S ARCHER & GREINER LIBRARY, One Centennial Sq, 08033-24544. SAN 325-7681. Tel: 856-795-2121. FAX: 856-795-0574. *Librn,* Elizabeth Olson; E-mail: lolson@archerlaw.com; Staff 2 (MLS 1, Non-MLS 1)
Library Holdings: Bk Vols 12,000
Subject Interests: Law
Restriction: Not open to pub

P HADDONFIELD PUBLIC LIBRARY*, 60 Haddon Ave, 08033-2422. SAN 310-1975. Tel: 856-429-1304. FAX: 856-429-3760. Web Site: www.haddonfieldlibrary.org. *Dir,* Susan Briant; E-mail: sbriant@haddonfieldlibrary.org; *Head, Circ,* Claire Stairiker; E-mail: cstair@haddonfieldlibrary.org; *Ch Serv,* Dorothy Peppard; E-mail: dpeppa@haddonfieldlibrary.org; *Ref Serv,* Jo-Ann Pure; E-mail: jkp@haddonfieldlibrary.org; *Tech Serv,* Anne Frontino; E-mail: auf@haddonfieldlibrary.org; Staff 12 (MLS 4, Non-MLS 8)
Founded 1803. Pop 11,659; Circ 129,843
Library Holdings: Bk Titles 74,825; Bk Vols 77,801; Per Subs 153
Special Collections: Oral History
Subject Interests: Local hist
Automation Activity & Vendor Info: (Cataloging) Innovative Interfaces, Inc; (Circulation) Innovative Interfaces, Inc; (OPAC) Innovative Interfaces, Inc
Database Vendor: EBSCOhost, Gale Cengage Learning, Newsbank, ProQuest
Wireless access

Function: ILL available, Prog for children & young adult, Summer reading prog
Partic in LibraryLinkNJ, The New Jersey Library Cooperative; Lyrasis
Open Mon-Fri 10-9, Sat 10-5, Sun 1-5
Friends of the Library Group

S HISTORICAL SOCIETY OF HADDONFIELD LIBRARY*, Research, 343 King's Hwy E, 08033. SAN 325-7703. Tel: 856-429-7375. E-mail: hadhistlib@gmail.com. Web Site: www.haddonfieldhistory.org. *Librn,* Katherine Mansfield Tassini. Subject Specialists: *Local hist,* Katherine Mansfield Tassini; Staff 1 (MLS 1)
Founded 1914
Library Holdings: Bk Titles 500; Bk Vols 750
Special Collections: Family Papers, incl Gill, Hinchman, Hopkins, Rowand, Rhoads, Tatem-Moore-Brigham & Cuthbert-Ogden
Subject Interests: Local hist
Function: Archival coll
Open Tues & Thurs 9:30-Noon, Sun (first of the month) 1-3
Restriction: Non-circulating to the pub

HALEDON

P HALEDON FREE PUBLIC LIBRARY*, 510 Bellmont Ave, 07508-1396. SAN 310-1991. Tel: 973-790-3808. E-mail: haledonstaff@palsplus.org. Web Site: www.haledonboronj.com/index.php/cable/library. *Interim Dir,* Claire Houghton-Kiel; Staff 6 (Non-MLS 6)
Founded 1958. Pop 8,252; Circ 14,000
Library Holdings: AV Mats 2,100; CDs 806; DVDs 1,093; Bk Titles 15,976; Per Subs 52
Automation Activity & Vendor Info: (Cataloging) SIRSI WorkFlows; (Circulation) SIRSI WorkFlows; (ILL) Auto-Graphics, Inc
Database Vendor: EBSCOhost
Function: Audio & video playback equip for onsite use, ILL available, Photocopying/Printing, Summer reading prog, Telephone ref
Partic in PALS Plus, The Computer Consortium of Passaic County Libraries
Open Mon, Tues & Fri 9-5, Wed 9-6, Thurs 12-8, Sat (Sept-June) 10-2

HAMILTON

P HAMILTON TOWNSHIP PUBLIC LIBRARY*, One Justice Samuel A Alito, Jr Way, 08619. SAN 351-4862. Tel: 609-581-4060. FAX: 609-581-4067. Web Site: www.hamiltonnjpl.org. *Dir,* George Conwell; E-mail: GConwell@HamiltonNJ.com; *Ch,* Liz Maggio; *Ch,* Elaine Pollak; *Ref Librn,* Scott Chianese; *Ref Librn,* Mary Lopez; *Ref Librn,* Ingrid McNamara; *Ref Librn,* Yanping Wu; *Teen Serv Librn,* Kathleen Breitenbach; *Tech Serv,* Brenda Eberst; Staff 8 (MLS 8)
Founded 1923. Pop 92,000; Circ 410,236
Library Holdings: AV Mats 13,317; Large Print Bks 3,810; Bk Titles 216,959; Bk Vols 270,214; Per Subs 440; Talking Bks 3,843
Subject Interests: Local hist
Automation Activity & Vendor Info: (Acquisitions) SirsiDynix; (Cataloging) SirsiDynix; (Circulation) SirsiDynix; (OPAC) SirsiDynix
Database Vendor: OCLC FirstSearch
Function: ILL available
Partic in LibraryLinkNJ, The New Jersey Library Cooperative; OCLC Online Computer Library Center, Inc
Special Services for the Deaf - Bks on deafness & sign lang; High interest/low vocabulary bks; Staff with knowledge of sign lang; TTY equip
Open Mon-Thurs 9-8:30, Fri & Sat 9-5
Friends of the Library Group

HARRINGTON PARK

P HARRINGTON PARK PUBLIC LIBRARY*, Ten Herring St, 07640. SAN 310-2017. Tel: 201-768-5675. FAX: 201-768-7495. Web Site: www.bccls.org. *Librn,* Judith Heldman; E-mail: heldman@bccls.org
Founded 1964. Pop 5,000; Circ 25,251
Library Holdings: Bk Vols 33,000; Per Subs 100
Automation Activity & Vendor Info: (Cataloging) SirsiDynix; (Circulation) SirsiDynix; (OPAC) SirsiDynix
Open Mon, Wed & Thurs (Winter) 10-9, Tues & Fri 12-5, Sat 10-1, Sun 1-4; Mon, Wed & Thurs (Summer) 10-9, Tues & Fri 12-5
Friends of the Library Group

HARRISON

P HARRISON PUBLIC LIBRARY, 415 Harrison Ave, 07029. SAN 310-2025. Tel: 973-483-2366. FAX: 973-483-1052. E-mail: library@townofharrison.com. Web Site: www.harrisonpubliclibrary.org. *Actg Dir,* Nelba Mejias; E-mail: nmejias@townofharrison.com; Staff 1 (Non-MLS 1)
Founded 1911. Pop 16,700; Circ 110,000
Library Holdings: Bk Vols 48,500; Per Subs 50
Automation Activity & Vendor Info: (Cataloging) TLC (The Library Corporation); (Circulation) TLC (The Library Corporation); (OPAC) TLC (The Library Corporation); (Serials) EBSCO Online
Wireless access
Partic in LibraryLinkNJ, The New Jersey Library Cooperative; New Jersey Library Network
Open Mon, Tues & Thurs 10-7, Fri 11:30-6, Sat 10-1

HASBROUCK HEIGHTS

P FREE PUBLIC LIBRARY OF HASBROUCK HEIGHTS*, 320 Boulevard, 07604. SAN 310-2033. Tel: 201-288-0484, 201-288-0488. FAX: 201-288-5467. Web Site: hasbrouckheights.bccls.org. *Dir,* Mimi Hui; E-mail: hui@bccls.org; *Head, Circ,* Ivette Pujadas; E-mail: ivette.pujadas@bccls.org; *Head, Ref,* Melissa Singlevich; E-mail: singlevich@bccls.org; *Ch,* Marie Joyce; Tel: 201-288-8911, E-mail: marie.joyce@bccls.org; *Ref Librn,* Deepti Dutta; Tel: 201-288-6653, E-mail: deepti.dutta@bccls.org; *Teen Librn,* Claire Santoro; E-mail: claire.santoro@bccls.org; Staff 4 (MLS 4)
Founded 1916. Pop 11,842; Circ 121,887
Library Holdings: DVDs 4,282; Large Print Bks 122; Bk Titles 58,643; Bk Vols 58,845; Per Subs 95
Special Collections: Oral History
Subject Interests: Local hist
Wireless access
Publications: Hasbrouck Heights: A History
Partic in Bergen County Cooperative Library System
Open Mon-Thurs (Winter) 10-9, Fri & Sat 10-5; Mon-Thurs (Summer) 10-9, Fri 10-5
Friends of the Library Group

HAWORTH

P HAWORTH MUNICIPAL LIBRARY*, 300 Haworth Ave, 07641. SAN 310-2041. Tel: 201-384-1020. FAX: 201-385-7750. E-mail: hawhcirc@bccls.org. Web Site: www.haworth.bccls.org. *Dir,* Elizabeth Rosenberg; E-mail: rosenberg@bccls.org
Circ 38,000
Library Holdings: Bk Vols 28,146; Per Subs 75
Special Collections: Local History Coll
Automation Activity & Vendor Info: (Cataloging) SirsiDynix; (Circulation) SirsiDynix; (OPAC) SirsiDynix
Wireless access
Partic in Bergen County Cooperative Library System
Open Mon & Wed 10-9, Tues, Thurs & Fri 10-5, Sat 10-1
Friends of the Library Group

HAWTHORNE

P LOUIS BAY 2ND LIBRARY*, 345 Lafayette Ave, 07506-2599. SAN 310-205X. Tel: 973-427-5745. FAX: 973-427-5269. Web Site: hawthorne.bccls.org. *Actg Dir, Head, Ref,* Kathleen Lehmann; Tel: 973-427-5745, Ext 17; *Head, Ch,* Wendy Hollis; Tel: 973-427-5745, Ext 21; *Head, Circ,* Marilyn Rees; Tel: 973-427-5745, Ext 16; *Head, Tech Serv,* Amy Fletcher; Tel: 973-427-5745, Ext 18; Staff 30 (MLS 3, Non-MLS 27)
Founded 1913. Pop 18,000; Circ 175,804
Library Holdings: Bks on Deafness & Sign Lang 115; High Interest/Low Vocabulary Bk Vols 250; Bk Vols 76,223; Per Subs 194; Spec Interest Per Sub 15
Special Collections: Deafness & Sign Language; Hawthorne & Passaic County Local History
Subject Interests: Cinema, Hist, Literacy, Quilting, Video
Automation Activity & Vendor Info: (Cataloging) SirsiDynix; (Circulation) SirsiDynix; (OPAC) SirsiDynix
Database Vendor: EBSCOhost, Gale Cengage Learning, ProQuest, SirsiDynix
Wireless access
Function: ILL available
Open Mon-Thurs 9-9, Fri 9-5:30, Sat 10-5
Friends of the Library Group

HIGH BRIDGE

P HIGH BRIDGE PUBLIC LIBRARY*, 71 Main St, 08829. SAN 310-2068. Tel: 908-638-8231. E-mail: library71@comcast.net. Web Site: www.highbridge.org/library.html. *Librn,* Theresa Steets
Founded 1914. Pop 3,770; Circ 10,304
Library Holdings: Bk Vols 8,500; Per Subs 52
Automation Activity & Vendor Info: (Cataloging) Innovative Interfaces, Inc; (Circulation) Innovative Interfaces, Inc; (OPAC) Innovative Interfaces, Inc
Wireless access
Mem of Hunterdon County Library
Open Mon & Wed 10-12 & 3-8, Fri 10-12 & 3-7, Sat 10-2
Friends of the Library Group

HIGHLAND PARK

P HIGHLAND PARK PUBLIC LIBRARY*, 31 N Fifth Ave, 08904. SAN 310-2076. Tel: 732-572-2750. FAX: 732-819-9046. Web Site: www.hpplnj.org. *Dir,* Jane Stanley; *Coord, Ad Serv,* Sherry Johnson; *Ch Serv,* Frances Lee; Staff 7 (MLS 3, Non-MLS 4)
Founded 1922. Pop 13,396; Circ 182,000
Library Holdings: Bk Vols 60,000; Per Subs 170
Wireless access
Publications: flyers
Open Mon, Tues & Thurs 10-9, Wed & Fri 10-5
Friends of the Library Group

HIGHLANDS

G NOAA, NATIONAL MARINE FISHERIES SERVICE*, Lionel A Walford Library, Northeast Fisheries Science Ctr, 74 Magruder Rd, 07732. SAN 310-2084. Tel: 732-872-3034, 732-872-3035. FAX: 732-872-3088. Web Site: www.sh.nmfs.gov. *Librn,* Claire Steimle; E-mail: claire.steimle@noaa.gov
Library Holdings: Bk Titles 5,000; Per Subs 72
Special Collections: NJ Sea Grant Coll
Subject Interests: Chem, Environ studies, Marine biol, Oceanography
Partic in Fedlink; OCLC-LVIS
Restriction: Open by appt only

HILLSDALE

P HILLSDALE FREE PUBLIC LIBRARY*, 509 Hillsdale Ave, 07642. SAN 310-2106. Tel: 201-358-5072. FAX: 201-358-5074. E-mail: hldlcirc@bccls.org. Web Site: www.bccls.org/hillsdale. *Dir,* David J Franz; E-mail: franz@bccls.org; *Librn,* Laura Leonard; E-mail: leonard@bccls.org; Staff 4 (MLS 2, Non-MLS 2)
Founded 1935. Pop 10,222; Circ 92,000
Library Holdings: Bk Vols 60,000; Per Subs 120
Automation Activity & Vendor Info: (Cataloging) SirsiDynix; (Circulation) SirsiDynix; (OPAC) SirsiDynix
Database Vendor: EBSCOhost, Gale Cengage Learning, ProQuest
Partic in Bergen County Cooperative Library System
Open Mon, Tues & Thurs 10-9, Wed 10-6, Fri & Sat 10-5, Sun 1-4
Friends of the Library Group

HILLSIDE

P HILLSIDE PUBLIC LIBRARY*, John F Kennedy Plaza, Hillside & Liberty Aves, 07205-1893. SAN 310-2122. Tel: 973-923-4413. Web Site: www.hillsidepl.org. *Dir,* Miriam Bein; E-mail: mbein@hillsidepl.org; *Head, Circ,* Michele Mitchell; *Head, Youth Serv,* Stephanie Nesmith; Staff 12 (MLS 1, Non-MLS 11)
Founded 1947. Pop 21,200; Circ 46,372
Library Holdings: Audiobooks 333; AV Mats 3,105; CDs 428; DVDs 1,093; Large Print Bks 536, Bk Titles 94,000; Bk Vols 98,000; Per Subs 109; Videos 645
Special Collections: Ethel Smith African-American Coll; Hillside Local Newspapers Digitized from 1924
Automation Activity & Vendor Info: (Cataloging) TLC (The Library Corporation); (Circulation) TLC (The Library Corporation); (ILL) JerseyCat; (OPAC) TLC (The Library Corporation)
Database Vendor: TLC (The Library Corporation)
Wireless access
Function: Adult literacy prog, After school storytime, Bilingual assistance for Spanish patrons, Bk club(s), Bk reviews (Group), Bks on CD, Chess club, Children's prog, Fax serv, Handicapped accessible, ILL available, Magnifiers for reading, Notary serv, Online cat, Online searches, Outside serv via phone, mail, e-mail & web, Photocopying/Printing, Prog for adults, Prog for children & young adult, Ref serv available, Spoken cassettes & CDs, Story hour, Summer reading prog, Tax forms, VHS videos
Publications: Info To Go (Newsletter)
Mem of Nassau Library System
Partic in LibraryLinkNJ, The New Jersey Library Cooperative
Special Services for the Blind - Bks on CD; Computer with voice synthesizer for visually impaired persons
Open Mon, Wed & Thurs 10-8, Tues & Fri 10-6, Sat (Fall-Spring) 10-4:30

HOBOKEN

P HOBOKEN PUBLIC LIBRARY*, 500 Park Ave, 07030. SAN 310-2157. Tel: 201-420-2346. Circulation Tel: 201-420-2280. Reference Tel: 201-420-2347. FAX: 201-420-2299. Circulation E-mail: hobkcirc@bccls.org. Reference E-mail: hobkref@bccls.org. Web Site: hoboken.bccls.org. *Dir,* Lina Podles; E-mail: podles@bccls.org; *Adult Serv,* Rosary Van Ingen; *Ch Serv,* Lois Gross; Staff 19 (MLS 4, Non-MLS 15)
Founded 1890. Pop 50,050; Circ 214,000
Library Holdings: Bk Vols 74,500; Per Subs 166
Special Collections: Hoboken History Coll
Automation Activity & Vendor Info: (Cataloging) SirsiDynix; (Circulation) SirsiDynix; (ILL) SirsiDynix; (OPAC) SirsiDynix
Wireless access
Function: ILL available
Partic in Bergen County Cooperative Library System; LibraryLinkNJ, The New Jersey Library Cooperative
Open Mon-Fri 9-8, Sat 10-5, Sun 11-2
Friends of the Library Group

C STEVENS INSTITUTE OF TECHNOLOGY*, Samuel C Williams Library, Castle Point on Hudson, 07030. SAN 310-2165. Tel: 201-216-5200. Circulation Tel: 201-216-5327. Interlibrary Loan Service Tel; 201-216-5420. Administration Tel: 201-216-5205. Information Services Tel: 201 216-8109. FAX: 201-216-8319, Web Site: www.lib.stevens.edu. *Actg Dir,* Ourida Oubraham; Tel: 201-216-5411, E-mail:ooubraha@stevens.edu; *Asst Admin,* Nydia Cruz; *Info Serv Librn,* Valerie Forrestal; Tel: 201-216-5361, E-mail: vforrest@stevens.edu; *Info Serv Librn,* Linda Scanlon; *Asst Curator,* Doris Oliver; Tel: 201-216-5415; *Circ,* John Cruz; Tel: 201-216-5334; *ILL,* Leah Kaufman; *ILL,* Carol Perkins; *Tech Serv,* Scott Smith; Tel: 201-216-5419; Staff 6 (MLS 4, Non-MLS 2)
Founded 1870. Enrl 3,200; Fac 200; Highest Degree: Doctorate
Library Holdings: e-books 3,500; e-journals 30,000; Bk Titles 64,105; Bk Vols 79,950; Per Subs 120
Special Collections: Art (Leonardo da Vinci Coll), bks, drawings, micro; History (Stevens Family Archives), bks, micro; Industrial Management (Frederick Winslow Taylor Coll), bks, micro
Subject Interests: Applied sci, Eng, Natural sci
Automation Activity & Vendor Info: (Cataloging) SirsiDynix; (Circulation) SirsiDynix; (ILL) OCLC; (OPAC) SirsiDynix; (Serials) SirsiDynix
Database Vendor: ACM (Association for Computing Machinery), American Chemical Society, American Mathematical Society, Annual Reviews, ASCE Research Library, Bowker, CISTI Source, EBSCOhost, Elsevier, FileMaker, Gale Cengage Learning, H W Wilson, IEEE (Institute of Electrical & Electronics Engineers), Infotrieve, infoUSA, IOP, JSTOR, Knovel, LexisNexis, McGraw-Hill, Nature Publishing Group, OCLC ArticleFirst, OCLC FirstSearch, OCLC WorldShare Interlibrary Loan, ProQuest, PubMed, ReferenceUSA, Safari Books Online, ScienceDirect, SerialsSolutions, SirsiDynix, Springer-Verlag, Wiley
Wireless access
Partic in Metropolitan New York Library Council; OCLC Online Computer Library Center, Inc; Virtual Academic Library Environment
Open Mon-Thurs 8am Midnight, Fri 8am-9pm, Sat 10-5, Sun Noon-Midnight
Restriction: In-house use for visitors
Friends of the Library Group

HO-HO-KUS

P WORTH PINKHAM MEMORIAL LIBRARY*, Ho-Ho-Kus Public Library, 91 Warren Ave, 07423. SAN 310-2130. Tel: 201-445-8078. E-mail: hohocirc@bccls.org. Web Site: www.bccls.org. *Dir,* Sandy Witkowski
Founded 1938. Pop 4,358; Circ 21,609
Library Holdings: Bk Vols 27,000; Per Subs 60
Partic in Dialog Corp; New Jersey Academic Library Network
Open Mon, Wed & Fri 10-5, Tues & Thurs 1-5 & 7-9, Sat (Sept-June) 10 1

HOPEWELL

P HOPEWELL PUBLIC LIBRARY*, 13 E Broad St, 08525. SAN 310-2203. Tel: 609-466-1625. FAX: 609-466-1996. E-mail: hpl@redlibrary.org. Web Site: www.redlibrary.org. *Dir,* Anne Zeman; *Adult Serv Coordr,* Eleanor Rock; *Children's Coordr,* Lorraine Shiarappa; *ILL Coordr,* Elaine Lesnever; *Info Tech,* Arnold Lesnever; Staff 5 (Non-MLS 5)
Founded 1914. Circ 17,500
Library Holdings: AV Mats 40; Bks on Deafness & Sign Lang 20; Large Print Bks 200; Bk Titles 15,000; Per Subs 53; Talking Bks 400
Special Collections: Local Newspaper Coll (1881-present), microfilm
Wireless access
Partic in LibraryLinkNJ, The New Jersey Library Cooperative
Open Mon & Wed 10-8, Tues & Thurs 12-8, Fri 12-5, Sat 10-3
Friends of the Library Group

IRVINGTON

P IRVINGTON PUBLIC LIBRARY*, Civic Sq, 07111-2498. SAN 350-7785. Tel: 973-372-6400. FAX: 973-372-6860. E-mail: ipl@irvingtonpubliclibrary.org. Web Site: www.irvingtonpubliclibrary.org. *Dir,* Joan Whittaker; E-mail: joan.whittaker@irvingtonpubliclibrary.org; Staff 31 (MLS 7, Non-MLS 24)
Founded 1914. Pop 61,018; Circ 73,242
Library Holdings: Large Print Bks 500; Bk Vols 200,000; Per Subs 150; Talking Bks 500

Special Collections: Adult Literacy; Audio Books; Large Print; Local History & Photographs. US Document Depository
Automation Activity & Vendor Info: (Cataloging) SirsiDynix; (Circulation) SirsiDynix; (OPAC) SirsiDynix
Wireless access
Open Mon, Tues & Thurs 9-9, Wed & Fri 9-5:30, Sat 9-5
Friends of the Library Group

ISELIN

S BASF CATALYSTS TECHNICAL INFORMATION CENTER*, 25 Middlesex-Essex Tpk, 08830. SAN 310-1274. Tel: 732-205-5269, 732-205-5271. FAX: 732-205-6900. *Mgr,* Maurica Fedors; E-mail: maurica.fedors@basf.com; *Sr Info Spec,* Arda Agulian; E-mail: arda.agulian@basf.com; Staff 3 (MLS 3)
Library Holdings: Bk Titles 4,000; Per Subs 50
Special Collections: Catalysts
Subject Interests: Catalysis, Indust applications
Wireless access
Restriction: Employees only, External users must contact libr

JAMESBURG

P JAMESBURG PUBLIC LIBRARY, 229 Gatzmer Ave, 08831. SAN 310-222X. Tel: 732-521-0440. FAX: 732-521-6136. Web Site: www.jamesburglibrary.org. *Dir,* Evalina Erbe; E-mail: eserbe@lmxac.org; Staff 1 (MLS 1)
Founded 1882. Pop 6,000; Circ 25,000
Library Holdings: CDs 800; DVDs 1,500; e-books 1,600; Bk Vols 20,000; Per Subs 62; Talking Bks 6,675
Wireless access
Partic in Libraries of Middlesex Automation Consortium; LibraryLinkNJ, The New Jersey Library Cooperative
Open Mon, Wed & Thurs 10-8:30, Tues & Fri 10-5, Sat 10-3, Sun (Sept-June) 12-4
Friends of the Library Group

JERSEY CITY

S AFRO-AMERICAN HISTORICAL SOCIETY MUSEUM LIBRARY*, c/o Greenville Library, 1841 Kennedy Blvd, 07305. Tel: 201-547-5262. FAX: 201-547-5392. *Dir,* Neal E Brunson
Library Holdings: Bk Vols 1,500
Special Collections: Genealogy Coll; Rare Book Coll
Function: Res libr
Open Mon-Sat 10-5
Restriction: Non-circulating

GL HUDSON COUNTY LAW LIBRARY*, Hudson County Admin Bldg, 595 Newark Ave, 07306. SAN 310-2246. Tel: 201-795-6629. FAX: 201-795-6603. *Librn,* Theresa Banks
Library Holdings: Bk Vols 19,000
Database Vendor: LexisNexis
Wireless access
Open Mon-Fri 8:30-4
Restriction: Non-circulating to the pub

P JERSEY CITY FREE PUBLIC LIBRARY*, 472 Jersey Ave, 07302-3499. SAN 350-7874. Tel: 201-547-4500. Circulation Tel: 201-547-4526. Reference Tel: 201-547-4501, 201-547-4502. Administration Tel: 201-547-4508. Automation Services Tel: 201-547-4294, 201-547-5881. Information Services Tel: 201-547-4579. FAX: 201-547-4584. Circulation FAX: 201-521-1742. Administration FAX: 201-547-5917. Information Services FAX: 201-547-4349. Web Site: www.jclibrary.org. *Dir,* Priscilla Gardner; Tel: 201-547-4788, E-mail: pgardner@jclibrary.org; *Asst Dir,* Sonia Araujo; Tel: 201-547-4549, Fax: 201-547-5936, E-mail: saraujo@jclibrary.org; *Asst Dir, Commun Outreach,* Position Currently Open; *Principal Librn,* John Butler; E-mail: jbutler@jclibrary.org; *Supv Librn,* Hussein Odeh; Tel: 201-547-4304, Fax: 201-946-7379, E-mail: hodeh@jclibrary.org; *Br Mgr, Biblioteca Criolla,* Patricia Vega; Tel: 201-547-4541, Fax: 201-547-5889, E-mail: pvega@jclibrary.org; *Doc,* Sharron Tucker; Tel: 201-547-4517, E-mail: stucker@jclibrary.org. Subject Specialists: *Fed docs,* Sharron Tucker; Staff 88 (MLS 23, Non-MLS 65)
Founded 1889. Pop 356,143; Circ 291,519
Jul 2010-Jun 2011 Income $7,508,866, State $113,913, City $7,394,953. Mats Exp $470,000, Books $300,000, Per/Ser (Incl. Access Fees) $50,000, Other Print Mats $68,000, Micro $32,000, AV Mat $20,000. Sal $4,140,966
Library Holdings: CDs 3,100; DVDs 16,410; Large Print Bks 5,851; Bk Titles 289,382; Bk Vols 539,645; Per Subs 839
Special Collections: New Jersey Coll; Spanish coll. US Document Depository
Automation Activity & Vendor Info: (Acquisitions) SirsiDynix; (Cataloging) SirsiDynix; (Circulation) SirsiDynix; (OPAC) SirsiDynix
Database Vendor: EBSCO Information Services, EBSCOhost, Gale Cengage Learning, Medline, PubMed, ReferenceUSA, SirsiDynix
Wireless access
Partic in OCLC Online Computer Library Center, Inc
Special Services for the Deaf - Staff with knowledge of sign lang
Special Services for the Blind - Reader equip
Open Mon 9-8, Tues-Thurs 9-6, Fri & Sat 9-5
Branches: 10
GLENN D CUNNINGHAM BRANCH LIBRARY & COMMUNITY CENTER, 275 Martin Luther King Jr Dr, 07305, SAN 350-7939. Tel: 201-547-4555. FAX: 201-547-5880. *Br Mgr,* Mary Quinn; E-mail: mquinn@jclibrary.org
Special Services for the Blind - Networked computers with assistive software; Screen reader software
Open Mon, Tues & Thurs 10-6, Wed 12-8, Fri 9-5
FIVE CORNERS, 678 Newark Ave, 07306, SAN 350-7963. Tel: 201-547-4543. FAX: 201-656-1517. *Br Mgr,* Susan Stewart; Tel: 201-547-4548, E-mail: sstewart@jclibrary.org
Open Mon 12-8, Tues-Thurs 10-6, Fri 9-5
GREENVILLE, 1841 Kennedy Blvd, 07305, SAN 350-7998. Tel: 201-547-4553. FAX: 201-433-1708. *Br Mgr,* Kenneth Uko; E-mail: kuko@jclibrary.org
Open Mon, Wed & Thurs 10-6, Tues 12-8, Fri 9-5
THE HEIGHTS, 14 Zabriskie St, 07307, SAN 350-8021. Tel: 201-547-4556. FAX: 201-876-0092. *Br Mgr,* Liz Cartaina; E-mail: lcartaina@jclibrary.org
Open Mon-Wed 10-6, Thurs 12-8, Fri 9-5
LAFAYETTE, 307 Pacific Ave, 07304, SAN 350-8056. Tel: 201-547-5017. FAX: 201-547-5878. *Br Mgr,* Vanessa Benekin; E-mail: vbenekin@jclibrary.org
Open Mon-Fri 9-5
MARION, 1017 West Side Ave, 07306, SAN 350-8080. Tel: 201-547-4552. FAX: 201-547-5888. *Br Mgr,* Jean Carter; E-mail: jcarter@jclibrary.org
Open Mon-Fri 9-5
MILLER, 489 Bergen Ave, 07304, SAN 350-8110. Tel: 201-547-4551. FAX: 201-434-1469. *Br Mgr,* Renee Moody; E-mail: rmoody@jclibrary.org
Open Mon & Tues 10-6, Wed Noon-8, Thurs 10-6, Fri & Sat 9-5
PAVONIA, 326 Eighth St, 07302, SAN 350-8145. Tel: 201-547-4808. FAX: 201-547-5222. *Br Mgr,* Patricia Mehnert; E-mail: pmehnert@jclibrary.org
Open Mon 12-8, Tues-Thurs 10-6, Fri 9-5
WATTERS MEDIA ARTS DEPARTMENT, 678 Newark Ave, 07306, SAN 329-5737. Tel: 201-547-4546. *Br Mgr,* Susan Stewart; Fax: 201-656-1517, E-mail: sstewart@jclibrary.org
Open Mon 12-8, Tues-Thurs 10-6, Fri 9-5
WEST BERGEN, 476 West Side Ave, 07304, SAN 350-817X. Tel: 201-547-4554. FAX: 201-547-5887. *Br Mgr,* Florence Cherico; E-mail: fcherico@jclibrary.org
Open Mon-Fri 9-5
Bookmobiles: 1. Asst Dir, Sonia Araujo

M JERSEY CITY MEDICAL CENTER LIBRARY*, 355 Grand St, 07302. SAN 373-2495. Tel: 201-915-2009. FAX: 201-915-2911. *Librn,* Brenda Shaw
Library Holdings: Bk Vols 800; Per Subs 180
Function: Res libr
Open Mon-Thurs 9-7, Fri 9-5
Restriction: Non-circulating, Open to pub upon request

C NEW JERSEY CITY UNIVERSITY*, Congressman Frank J Guarini Library, 2039 Kennedy Blvd, 07305-1597. SAN 310-2254. Tel: 201-200-3030. Interlibrary Loan Service Tel: 201-200-2183. Reference Tel: 201-200-3033. FAX: 201-200-2330, 201-200-2331. *Interim Dir,* Frederick Smith; Tel: 201-200-3474, E-mail: fsmith@njcu.edu; Staff 14 (MLS 13, Non-MLS 1)
Founded 1927. Enrl 10,000; Fac 240; Highest Degree: Master
Jul 2010-Jun 2011. Mats Exp $503,910, Books $123,692, Per/Ser (Incl. Access Fees) $50,355, Micro $9,842, AV Mat $13,566, Electronic Ref Mat (Incl. Access Fees) $306,455. Sal $2,583,499
Library Holdings: DVDs 3,526; e-books 3,750; e-journals 39,499; Electronic Media & Resources 152; Microforms 1,802,659; Bk Titles 2,854; Bk Vols 296,183; Per Subs 33,011; Videos 4,391
Special Collections: Anthropology (Human Relations Area Files), fiche; Eric Coll. State Document Depository; US Document Depository
Subject Interests: African-Am studies, Art, Biol, Bus admin, Caribbean studies, Chem, Computer sci, Criminal justice, Econ, Educ, English, English as a second lang, Fire sci, Geog, Geoscience, Health sci, Hist, Latin Am studies, Latino studies, Media arts, Music, Nursing, Philos, Physics, Polit sci, Psychol, Relig, Security, Sociol
Automation Activity & Vendor Info: (Acquisitions) SirsiDynix
Database Vendor: EBSCOhost, Facts on File, Gale Cengage Learning, Knovel, LearningExpress, LexisNexis, ProQuest, STN International
Wireless access

Partic in LibraryLinkNJ, The New Jersey Library Cooperative; Lyrasis; OCLC Online Computer Library Center, Inc; Virtual Academic Library Environment; Westchester Academic Library Directors Organization (WALDO)
Special Services for the Blind - Magnifiers; Open bk software on pub access PC; Screen reader software
Open Mon-Thurs (Winter) 7:30am-10pm, Fri 7:30-5, Sat 9-5, Sun 11-5; Mon-Thurs (Summer) 7:30am-10pm, Sun 11-5

CR SAINT PETER'S UNIVERSITY*, Theresa & Edward O'Toole Library, 99 Glenwood Ave, 07306. SAN 350-820X. Tel: 201-761-6453. Reference Tel: 201-761-6461. Administration Tel: 201-761-6454. FAX: 201-761-6451. Web Site: saintpeters.edu/library. *Dir,* David Hardgrove; E-mail: dhardgrove@saintpeters.edu; *Assoc Librn, Head, Pub Serv,* Tom Kenny; Tel: 201-761-6464, E-mail: tkenny@saintpeters.edu; *Assoc Librn,* Ilona MacNamara; Tel: 201-761-6463, E-mail: imacnamera@saintpeters.edu; *Col Archivist,* Mary Kinahan-Ockay; Tel: 201-761-6462, E-mail: mkinahan@saintpeters.edu; Staff 9 (MLS 9)
Founded 1872. Enrl 3,512; Fac 114; Highest Degree: Doctorate
Library Holdings: Bk Titles 180,419; Bk Vols 229,315; Per Subs 750
Special Collections: Religion, History (including local), Literature, Art, Science & Technology, Early Cinema, with Imprint Dates from the 15th to 16th Centuries
Subject Interests: Biol, Nursing, Philos, Theol
Automation Activity & Vendor Info: (Acquisitions) SirsiDynix; (Cataloging) SirsiDynix; (Circulation) SirsiDynix; (Course Reserve) SirsiDynix; (OPAC) SirsiDynix; (Serials) SirsiDynix
Database Vendor: EBSCOhost, Factiva.com, Gale Cengage Learning, LexisNexis, OCLC FirstSearch, OVID Technologies, ProQuest
Wireless access
Partic in Metropolitan New York Library Council; Virtual Academic Library Environment
Special Services for the Blind - Reader equip
Open Mon-Thurs 8am-2am, Fri 8am-9pm, Sat 9-6, Sun Noon-2am; Mon-Thurs (Summer) 8am-10pm
Friends of the Library Group

S SOCIETY OF NAVAL ARCHITECTS & MARINE ENGINEERS LIBRARY*, 601 Pavonia Ave, 07306. SAN 375-0744. Tel: 201-798-4800. FAX: 201-798-4975. Web Site: www.sname.org. *Dir, Tech Serv,* Alex Landsburg; Tel: 202-548-8932, E-mail: alandsburg@csc.com; Staff 1 (Non-MLS 1)
Library Holdings: Bk Titles 1,500; Bk Vols 2,500; Per Subs 50
Special Collections: SNAME publications
Function: Ref serv available
Restriction: Open by appt only

KEARNY

P KEARNY PUBLIC LIBRARY, 318 Kearny Ave, 07032. SAN 310-2270. Tel: 201-998-2666. FAX: 201-998-1141. E-mail: admin@kearnylibrary.org. Web Site: www.kearnylibrary.org. *Dir,* Josh Humphrey; *Sr Ch,* Joanne Friedman
Founded 1906. Pop 40,513
Library Holdings: Bk Vols 70,000; Per Subs 120
Subject Interests: Local hist
Automation Activity & Vendor Info: (Acquisitions) Innovative Interfaces, Inc; (Cataloging) Innovative Interfaces, Inc; (Circulation) Innovative Interfaces, Inc; (OPAC) Innovative Interfaces, Inc
Wireless access
Partic in LibraryLinkNJ, The New Jersey Library Cooperative
Open Mon, Tues, Thurs & Fri 9:30-6, Wed 9:30-8, Sat (Sept-June) 9-1
Friends of the Library Group
Branches: 1
KEARNY BRANCH, 759 Kearny Ave, 07032, SAN 376-2513. Tel: 201-955-7988. *Dir,* Josh Humphrey; *Br Mgr,* Kerry Kosick
Library Holdings: Bk Titles 5,200; Per Subs 15
Open Mon-Fri 1-5
Friends of the Library Group

KENILWORTH

P KENILWORTH PUBLIC LIBRARY*, 548 Blvd, 07033. SAN 310-2297. Tel: 908-276-2451. FAX: 908-276-7897. Web Site: www.kenilworthlibrary.org. *Dir,* Dale Spindel; E-mail: dale@lmxac.org; Staff 2 (MLS 1, Non-MLS 1)
Founded 1934. Pop 7,700
Library Holdings: Audiobooks 1,000; CDs 1,500; DVDs 2,100; Large Print Bks 1,800; Bk Vols 30,000; Per Subs 67
Automation Activity & Vendor Info: (Cataloging) SirsiDynix; (Circulation) SirsiDynix; (OPAC) SirsiDynix
Database Vendor: EBSCOhost
Wireless access
Function: Adult bk club, Art exhibits, Audiobks via web, Bks on CD, Children's prog, Computers for patron use, Copy machines, Digital talking bks, E-Reserves, Electronic databases & coll, Free DVD rentals, Handicapped accessible, Holiday prog, ILL available, Music CDs, Online cat, Online searches, OverDrive digital audio bks, Prog for adults, Prog for children & young adult, Pub access computers, Ref serv in person, Story hour, Summer & winter reading prog, Tax forms, Telephone ref, Web-catalog, Wheelchair accessible, Workshops
Partic in Libraries of Middlesex Automation Consortium; LibraryLinkNJ, The New Jersey Library Cooperative
Open Mon, Tues & Thurs 10-9, Wed 10-6, Fri 10-5, Sat (Sept-June) 10-2
Friends of the Library Group

KEYPORT

P KEYPORT FREE PUBLIC LIBRARY*, 109 Broad St, 07735. SAN 310-2327. Tel: 732-264-0543. FAX: 732-264-0875. Web Site: www.keyportlibrary.org. *Dir,* Jackie LaPolla; E-mail: dr_syn2001@yahoo.com; *Asst Librn,* Judy Revere
Founded 1914. Pop 7,500; Circ 22,000
Library Holdings: Bk Vols 49,000; Per Subs 80
Special Collections: War of the Rebellion: A Compilation of the Official Records of the Union & Confederate Armies
Wireless access
Partic in LibraryLinkNJ, The New Jersey Library Cooperative
Open Mon & Thurs 10-5, Tues & Fri 1-9, Wed 10-9, Sat 9-1

KINNELON

P KINNELON PUBLIC LIBRARY*, 132 Kinnelon Rd, 07405-2393. SAN 310-2335. Tel: 973-838-1321. FAX: 973-838-0741. Web Site: www.kinnelonlibrary.org. *Dir,* Sam Pharo; *Head, Circ,* Tanya Lenkow; E-mail: lenkow@main.morris.org; *Adult Serv,* Anne Mandanayake; *Cat,* Nancy Zaccagnino; E-mail: zaccagnino@main.morris.org; *Ch Serv,* Galina Adair; *Circ,* Mary Cobell; E-mail: cobell@main.morris.org; *ILL,* Tina Hitchings; E-mail: hitchings@main.morris.org; Staff 15 (MLS 3, Non-MLS 12)
Founded 1962. Pop 10,200; Circ 102,000
Jan 2011-Dec 2011 Income $825,000. Mats Exp $55,000. Sal $580,000
Library Holdings: CDs 1,143; DVDs 4,500; Bk Vols 65,308; Per Subs 130; Talking Bks 4,322; Videos 3,000
Automation Activity & Vendor Info: (Cataloging) SirsiDynix; (Circulation) SirsiDynix; (OPAC) SirsiDynix
Database Vendor: SirsiDynix
Wireless access
Function: Handicapped accessible, Homebound delivery serv, ILL available, Online searches, Outside serv via phone, mail, e-mail & web, Photocopying/Printing, Prog for adults, Prog for children & young adult, Ref serv available, Summer reading prog, Telephone ref, Wheelchair accessible
Publications: Bookmarks (Newsletter); Kinnelon Service Directory
Partic in Morris Automated Information Network
Open Mon 10-6, Tues-Thurs 10-8, Fri 10-5, Sat 10-4, Sun 12-4
Friends of the Library Group

LAKEWOOD

CR GEORGIAN COURT UNIVERSITY, S Mary Joseph Cunningham Library, 900 Lakewood Ave, 08701-2697. SAN 310-2351. Tel: 732-987-2419. Reference Tel: 732-987-2422. Administration Tel: 732 987 2421. FAX: 732-987-2017. Web Site: www.georgian.edu/library/index.html. *Dir,* Frances Young Scott; Tel: 732-987-2425, Fax: 732-987-2060, E-mail: scottf@georigian.edu; *Librn,* Mary Basso; Tel: 732 987-2427, E-mail: basso@georgian.edu; *Librn,* Barbara Herbert; Tel: 732-987-2428, E-mail: herbert@georgian.edu; *Librn,* Jaimie Donnelly; Tel: 732-987-2435, E-mail: donnellyja@georgian.edu; *Librn,* Jeff Donnelly; E-mail: donnellyj@georgian.edu; *Archivist/Librn,* Sister Barbara Williams; Tel: 732-987-2441, E-mail: williamssb@georgian.edu. Subject Specialists: *Archit, Art,* Frances Young Scott; *Humanities,* Mary Basso; *Behav sci, Bus,* Barbara Herbert; *Soc sci, Tech,* Jaimie Donnelly; *Exercise sci, Health,* Jeff Donnelly; *Nursing, Sci,* Sister Barbara Williams; Staff 18 (MLS 6, Non-MLS 12)
Founded 1908. Enrl 2,257; Fac 228; Highest Degree: Master
Jul 2014-Jun 2015. Mats Exp $477,010, Books $81,500, Per/Ser (Incl. Access Fees) $224,204, AV Mat $10,800, Electronic Ref Mat (Incl. Access Fees) $160,386, Presv $120
Library Holdings: AV Mats 5,848; CDs 874; DVDs 840; e-books 550; e-journals 53,274; Large Print Bks 15; Bk Titles 112,418; Bk Vols 160,582; Per Subs 400; Videos 1,779
Special Collections: Georgian Court University Archives; Georgian Court University Special Coll; Instructional Material Center; Thomas Merton Coll (NASA Resource Center)
Subject Interests: Educ
Automation Activity & Vendor Info: (Acquisitions) OCLC; (Cataloging) OCLC; (Circulation) OCLC; (Course Reserve) OCLC; (ILL) OCLC WorldShare Interlibrary Loan; (OPAC) OCLC; (Serials) OCLC
Database Vendor: Baker & Taylor, EBSCOhost, Elsevier, Gale Cengage Learning, Hoovers, JSTOR, LexisNexis, Marquis Who's Who, OCLC

WorldShare Interlibrary Loan, OCLC Worldshare Management Services, OVID Technologies, ProQuest, PubMed, Sage, ScienceDirect, SerialsSolutions, Standard & Poor's, STN International, ValueLine, Wilson - Wilson Web
Wireless access
Partic in LibraryLinkNJ, The New Jersey Library Cooperative; Lyrasis; New Jersey Library Network; OCLC Online Computer Library Center, Inc; Virtual Academic Library Environment; Westchester Academic Library Directors Organization (WALDO)
Open Mon-Thurs 8am-11pm, Fri 8-6, Sat 10-5, Sun 2-10
Restriction: Open to pub for ref & circ; with some limitations, Open to students, fac & staff

S WORTHINGTON BIOCHEMICAL CORP LIBRARY*, 730 Vassar Ave, 08701. SAN 375-7455. Tel: 732-942-1660. Toll Free Tel: 800-445-9603. FAX: 732-942-9270. *Librn,* Nancy Worthington; E-mail: nancyw@worthington-biochem.com
Library Holdings: Bk Titles 100; Per Subs 10
Restriction: Staff use only

LAMBERTVILLE

P LAMBERTVILLE FREE PUBLIC LIBRARY*, Six Lilly St, 08530. SAN 310-2378. Tel: 609-397-0275. FAX: 609-397-1784. E-mail: lfpl@lambertvillelibrary.org. Web Site: www.lambertvillelibrary.org. *Dir,* Harold Dunn; *Ch Serv,* Jennifer E Sirak; Staff 10 (MLS 1, Non-MLS 9)
Founded 1881. Pop 3,868; Circ 34,000
Jan 2013-Dec 2013 Income $256,800, State $1,800, City $246,000, Locally Generated Income $9,000. Mats Exp $32,900, Books $22,000, Per/Ser (Incl. Access Fees) $3,400, AV Equip $500, AV Mat $7,000. Sal $92,000
Library Holdings: Audiobooks 945; AV Mats 2,451; CDs 373; DVDs 370; e-books 52; Large Print Bks 194; Bk Vols 20,534; Per Subs 78; Videos 2,412
Special Collections: Lambertville Beacon Coll (1860-2005), microfilm; Michael Lewis Art Coll; Roger S Bowen Theater Coll
Subject Interests: Regional hist
Automation Activity & Vendor Info: (Cataloging) Surpass; (Circulation) Surpass; (OPAC) Surpass; (Serials) Surpass
Wireless access
Function: Art exhibits, Bi-weekly Writer's Group, Bks on CD, Copy machines, Free DVD rentals, Handicapped accessible, Music CDs, Online cat, Photocopying/Printing, Prog for adults, Pub access computers, Scanner, Story hour, Summer reading prog, Teen prog, Web-catalog
Open Mon, Tues, Thurs & Fri 10-9, Wed 1-9, Sat 1-5
Friends of the Library Group

LAWRENCEVILLE

S CUH2A INC LIBRARY*, 1000 Lenox Dr, 08648-2312. (Mail add: CN-5380, Princeton, 08543-5380), SAN 375-4634. Tel: 609-791-7247. FAX: 609-791-7719. *Info Res,* Michael Greenberg; Staff 1 (MLS 1)
Library Holdings: Bk Titles 600; Bk Vols 800; Per Subs 137
Subject Interests: Archit, Eng
Partic in LibraryLinkNJ, The New Jersey Library Cooperative
Restriction: Access at librarian's discretion

P MERCER COUNTY LIBRARY SYSTEM*, 2751 Brunswick Pike, 08648-4132. SAN 351-4536. Tel: 609-882-9246. Interlibrary Loan Service Tel: 609-883-0245. Reference Tel: 609-989-6922. FAX: 609-538-9238. Web Site: www.mcl.org. *Dir,* Ellen Brown; *Supv Libr Dir,* Laurence McNamara; Tel: 609-989-6915, E-mail: lmcnamar@mcl.org; *Chief Financial Officer,* Richard J Cavallo; Tel: 609-989-6918, E-mail: rcavallo@mcl.org; *Head, Circ Serv,* Patricia L Foy; *Syst Adminr,* Melissa Hasbrouck; Tel: 609-882-2134, E-mail: mhasbrou@mcl.org; *ILL,* Debbie Evernham; *Youth Serv,* Laura Gruninger; Tel: 609-989-6921, E-mail: lgruning@mcl.org; Staff 58 (MLS 18, Non-MLS 40)
Founded 1929. Pop 130,000; Circ 1,480,000
Library Holdings: Bk Titles 359,468; Per Subs 357
Special Collections: New Jersey History; Spanish & Chinese Coll
Database Vendor: EBSCOhost, SirsiDynix
Function: Res libr
Partic in OCLC Online Computer Library Center, Inc
Open Mon-Thurs 9:30-9, Fri & Sat 9:30-5, Sun (Sept-May) 12:30-5
Friends of the Library Group
Branches: 9
EWING BRANCH, 61 Scotch Rd, Ewing, 08628, SAN 351-4595. Tel: 609-882-3130. FAX: 609-538-0212. *Br Mgr,* Jackie Huff; E-mail: jhuff@mcl.org
Library Holdings: Bk Vols 103,401
Open Mon-Thurs 9-9, Fri 9-5, Sat 9:30-5, Sun (Sept-May) 12:30-5
Friends of the Library Group
HICKORY CORNER BRANCH, 138 Hickory Corner Rd, East Windsor, 08520, SAN 351-4560. Tel: 609-448-1330. FAX: 609-490-0189. *Br Mgr,* Jennifer Worringer; E-mail: jworring@mcl.org; Staff 8 (MLS 3, Non-MLS 5)
Library Holdings: Bk Vols 46,554
Open Mon-Thurs 9:30-9, Fri & Sat 9:30-5, Sun (Sept-May) 12:30-5
Friends of the Library Group
HIGHTSTOWN MEMORIAL, 114 Franklin St, Hightstown, 08520, SAN 351-4625. Tel: 609-448-1474. FAX: 609-490-0279. *Br Mgr,* Linda Cholewiek; E-mail: lcholewi@mcl.org; Staff 5 (MLS 2, Non-MLS 3)
Library Holdings: Bk Vols 29,916
Open Mon-Thurs 9:30-9, Fri & Sat 9:30-5
Friends of the Library Group
HOLLOWBROOK COMMUNITY CENTER, 320 Hollowbrook Dr, Trenton, 08638, SAN 328-8021. Tel: 609-883-5914. FAX: 609-883-3511. *Br Supvr,* Elka Frankel; E-mail: efrankel@mcl.org
Library Holdings: Bk Vols 11,832
Open Mon-Fri 9-5
HOPEWELL BRANCH, 245 Pennington-Titusville Rd, Pennington, 08534, SAN 351-4633. Tel: 609-737-2610. FAX: 609-737-7419. *Br Mgr,* Andrea Merrick; E-mail: amerrick@mcl.org
Library Holdings: Bk Vols 59,103
Open Mon-Thurs 9:30-9, Fri & Sat 9:30-5
Friends of the Library Group
LAWRENCE HEADQUARTERS, 2751 Brunswick Pike, 08648, SAN 351-465X. Tel: 609-989-6920. FAX: 609-538-9238. *Dir,* Ellen Brown
Circ 2,046,910
Library Holdings: Bk Vols 144,891
Open Mon-Thurs 9:30-9, Fri & Sat 9:30-5, Sun (Sept-May) 12:30-5
Friends of the Library Group
ROBBINSVILLE BRANCH, 42 Allentown-Robbinsville Rd, Robbinsville, 08691, SAN 351-4714. Tel: 609-259-2150. FAX: 609-259-1411. *Br Mgr,* Ann Marie Ehrenberg
Library Holdings: Bk Vols 33,752
Open Mon-Thurs 9:30-9, Fri & Sat 9:30-5
Friends of the Library Group
TWIN RIVERS BRANCH, 276 Abbington Dr, East Windsor, 08520, SAN 351-4684. Tel: 609-443-1880. FAX: 609-490-0186. *Br Mgr,* Rebecca Sloan; E-mail: rsloan@mcl.org
Library Holdings: Bk Vols 50,119
Open Mon-Thurs 9:30-9, Fri & Sat 9:30-5
Friends of the Library Group
WEST WINDSOR, 333 N Post Rd, Princeton Junction, 08550, SAN 351-4749. Tel: 609-799-0462. FAX: 609-936-9511. *Br Mgr,* Rina Banarjee
Library Holdings: Bk Vols 82,079
Open Mon-Thurs 9:30-9, Fri & Sat 9:30-5, Sun (Sept-May) 12:30-5
Friends of the Library Group

C RIDER UNIVERSITY*, Franklin F Moore Library, 2083 Lawrenceville Rd, 08648-3099. SAN 310-2394. Tel: 609-896-5111. Circulation Tel: 609-896-5000, Ext 5113. Interlibrary Loan Service Tel: 609-896-5118. Reference Tel: 609-896-5115. FAX: 609-896-8029. Web Site: library.rider.edu. *Dean of Libr,* F William Chickering; E-mail: wchickering@rider.edu; *Librn,* Robert Congleton; E-mail: rcongleton@rider.edu; *Instrul Serv Librn,* Ma Lei Hseih; Tel: 609-896-5241, E-mail: hseih@rider.edu; *Instrul Serv Librn,* Robert Lackie; Tel: 609-895-5626, E-mail: rlackie@rider.edu; *Acq,* Coleen Carr; *Acq,* Doris O'Donovan; *Cat,* Frank Gao; *Cat,* Marilyn Quinn; Tel: 609-895-5727, E-mail: quinnma@rider.edu; *Cat,* Carl Rizzo; *Circ,* Mary Ellen Eckman; *Circ,* Diane Hunter; *Doc Delivery, Per,* Marianne Lenihan; Staff 12 (MLS 12)
Founded 1865. Enrl 5,000; Fac 250; Highest Degree: Master
Library Holdings: Bk Titles 473,370; Bk Vols 1,545,034; Per Subs 2,300
Special Collections: Delaware Valley Newspapers (from Colonial Times to present); Dispatches of United States Envoys in Britain & France During Civil War Period, micro; Early Shorthand Works (Kendrick C Hill Coll), per; Historical Shorthand Materials (Leslie Coll); Typewriting History (Alan Lloyd Coll). State Document Depository; US Document Depository
Automation Activity & Vendor Info: (Acquisitions) Ex Libris Group; (Cataloging) Ex Libris Group; (Circulation) Ex Libris Group; (OPAC) Ex Libris Group; (Serials) Ex Libris Group
Wireless access
Partic in Dialog Corp; Dow Jones News Retrieval; NJ Regional Libr Coop; OCLC Online Computer Library Center, Inc; Tri-State College Library Cooperative
Open Mon-Thurs 8:30am-Midnight, Fri 8:30am-10pm, Sat 10-7, Sun Noon-11
Departmental Libraries:
KATHARINE HOUK TALBOTT LIBRARY, Westminster Choir College, 101 Walnut Lane, Princeton, 08540-3899, SAN 351-3181. Tel: 609-921-7100, Ext 8237. Interlibrary Loan Service Tel: 609-921-7100, Ext 8337. Reference Tel: 609-921-7100, Ext 8304. Administration Tel: 609-921-7100, Ext 8304. FAX: 609-497-0243. E-mail: library@rider.edu. Web Site: www.rider.edu/talbott. *Chair,* Mi-Hye Chyun; E-mail: chyun@rider.edu; *Bibliog Control Librn,* Jane Nowakowski; Tel: 609-921-7100, Ext 8305, E-mail: nowakows@rider.edu; *Instruction, Ref & Ser Librn,* Robert Terrio; Tel: 609-921-7100, Ext 8296, E-mail: rterrio@rider.edu; *Media Librn,* Kenneth Kauffman; Tel: 609-921-7100,

Ext 8338, E-mail: kkauffman@rider.edu; *Spec Coll Librn,* Amy Kimura; Tel: 609-921-7100, Ext 8375, E-mail: akimura@rider.edu; *Acq Asst,* Kylee Caldwell; Tel: 609-921-7100, Ext 8336, E-mail: carmink@rider.edu; *Cat Asst,* Frank Ferko; Tel: 609-921-7100, Ext 8297, E-mail: fferko@rider.edu; *Circ,* Rena Blakeslee; Tel: 609-921-7100, Ext 8335, E-mail: blakesle@rider.edu; *Circ,* William Vallandigham; Tel: 609-921-7100, Ext 8359, E-mail: wvallandigh@rider.edu; *Circ & ILL,* Nancy Deffeyes; E-mail: ndeffeyes@rider.edu; *Performance Coll,* Devin Mariman; Tel: 609-921-7100, Ext 8298, E-mail: dmariman@rider.edu; *Tech Asst,* Sue Nelson; Tel: 609-921-7100, Ext 8339, E-mail: snelson@rider.edu; Staff 4 (MLS 4)
Founded 1926. Enrl 500; Highest Degree: Master
Library Holdings: AV Mats 35,000; CDs 20,800; DVDs 700; e-journals 45,000; Music Scores 40,000; Bk Vols 80,000; Per Subs 150; Spec Interest Per Sub 150; Videos 400
Special Collections: Adams Coll of Dupre, memorabilia; Carl F Mueller Coll; Carl Weinrich Coll; Choral Octavo Reference File; DeWitt Wasson Research Coll; Hymnology (Erik Routley Coll); Leopold Stokowski Coll; Nathaniel Burt Coll; Organ Historical Society Archives; Robert Shaw Coll, marked scores; Tams-Witmark Coll; Tiplady Coll; Warren Marten Coll, compositions; Winfred Douglas & Walter Williams Coll, choral & liturgical music
Subject Interests: Music
Automation Activity & Vendor Info: (Acquisitions) Ex Libris Group; (Cataloging) Ex Libris Group; (Circulation) Ex Libris Group; (Course Reserve) Ex Libris Group; (ILL) OCLC; (OPAC) Ex Libris Group; (Serials) Ex Libris Group
Database Vendor: Alexander Street Press, ARTstor, EBSCO Discovery Service, JSTOR, OCLC, OCLC WorldShare Interlibrary Loan, Oxford Online, Project MUSE, ProQuest
Function: Audio & video playback equip for onsite use, Computers for patron use, Electronic databases & coll, ILL available, Online cat, Online info literacy tutorials on the web & in blackboard, Online ref, Online searches, Ref & res, Ref serv available, Ref serv in person
Partic in Lyrasis; OCLC Online Computer Library Center, Inc
Open Mon-Thurs 8:30am-10pm, Fri 8:30-5, Sat 10-5, Sun 3-10
Restriction: Borrowing privileges limited to fac & registered students, Borrowing requests are handled by ILL, In-house use for visitors, Open to fac, students & qualified researchers, Open to students, fac, staff & alumni
Friends of the Library Group

LEONIA

P LEONIA PUBLIC LIBRARY*, 227 Fort Lee Rd, 07605. SAN 310-2408. Tel: 201-592-5770. Reference Tel: 201-592-5773. FAX: 201-592-5775. E-mail: leoncirc@bccls.org. Web Site: leonia.bccls.org. *Dir,* Deborah Bigelow; Tel: 201-592-5776, E-mail: bigelow@bccls.org; *Asst Dir,* Gina Webb-Metz; Tel: 201-592-5774, E-mail: webb-metz@bccls.org; *IT Mgr,* Catherine Sandak; *Ch Serv,* Elizabeth Bender; Tel: 201-592-5777, E-mail: bender@bccls.org. Subject Specialists: *Tech,* Catherine Sandak; Staff 4 (MLS 4)
Founded 1923. Pop 8,900; Circ 105,140
Library Holdings: Bk Titles 48,000; Bk Vols 49,000; Per Subs 100
Special Collections: Local History Coll
Automation Activity & Vendor Info: (Cataloging) SirsiDynix; (Circulation) SirsiDynix; (OPAC) SirsiDynix
Database Vendor: EBSCOhost, Gale Cengage Learning, ProQuest
Partic in Bergen County Cooperative Library System; LibraryLinkNJ, The New Jersey Library Cooperative
Open Mon, Wed & Thurs 10-9, Tues, Fri & Sat 10-5, Sun 1-5
Friends of the Library Group

LINCOLN PARK

P LINCOLN PARK PUBLIC LIBRARY*, 12 Boonton Tpk, 07035. SAN 310-2416. Tel: 973-694-8283. FAX: 973-694-5515. Web Site: www.lincolnparklibrary.org. *Dir,* Stephanie Iberer; E-mail: stephanie.iberer@lincolnparklibrary.org
Founded 1922. Pop 11,400; Circ 68,200
Library Holdings: Bk Vols 54,000; Per Subs 100
Special Collections: New Jersey Coll
Automation Activity & Vendor Info: (Acquisitions) Innovative Interfaces, Inc; (Cataloging) Innovative Interfaces, Inc; (Circulation) Innovative Interfaces, Inc; (OPAC) Innovative Interfaces, Inc; (Serials) Innovative Interfaces, Inc
Wireless access
Partic in Morris Automated Information Network
Open Mon-Thurs (Sept-June) 10-9, Fri 10-5, Sat 9:30-4, Sun 12-4; Mon-Thurs (Jul & Aug) 10-9, Fri 10-5, Sat 10-2
Friends of the Library Group

LINCROFT

J BROOKDALE COMMUNITY COLLEGE*, Bankier Library, 765 Newman Springs Rd, 07738-1597. SAN 310-2424. Tel: 732-224-2706. FAX: 732-224-2982. Web Site: brookdalecc.edu/library. *Chair,* Shay Delcurla; Tel: 732-224-2438; *Exec Dir,* David Murray; Tel: 732-224-2217; Staff 11 (MLS 11)
Founded 1969. Enrl 15,000; Fac 251; Highest Degree: Associate
Jul 2009-Jun 2010. Mats Exp $293,515, Books $130,873, Per/Ser (Incl. Access Fees) $60,451, AV Mat $8,984, Electronic Ref Mat (Incl. Access Fees) $91,587, Presv $1,620. Sal $1,345,370 (Prof $680,851)
Library Holdings: Audiobooks 453; CDs 448; DVDs 1,262; e-books 4,027; Bk Titles 60,874; Bk Vols 80,592; Per Subs 425; Videos 7,381
Automation Activity & Vendor Info: (Acquisitions) Innovative Interfaces, Inc; (Cataloging) Innovative Interfaces, Inc; (Circulation) Innovative Interfaces, Inc; (Course Reserve) Innovative Interfaces, Inc; (ILL) Innovative Interfaces, Inc; (Media Booking) Innovative Interfaces, Inc; (OPAC) Innovative Interfaces, Inc; (Serials) Innovative Interfaces, Inc
Wireless access
Partic in LibraryLinkNJ, The New Jersey Library Cooperative; Lyrasis; OCLC Online Computer Library Center, Inc; Virtual Academic Library Environment

LINDEN

S INFINEUM USALP*, Infineum Information Center, 1900 E Linden Ave, 07036-1111. (Mail add: PO Box 536, 07036-0536), SAN 375-9172. Tel: 908-474-2351. FAX: 908-474-2020. Web Site: www.infineum.com. *Librn,* Julie Kale; Staff 1 (MLS 1)
Founded 1920
Library Holdings: Bk Vols 8,500; Per Subs 20
Subject Interests: Chem
Restriction: Not open to pub

P LINDEN FREE PUBLIC LIBRARY*, 31 E Henry St, 07036. SAN 350-8323. Tel: 908-298-3830. FAX: 908-486-2636. Web Site: www.lindenpl.org. *Dir,* Dennis Patrick Purves, Jr; E-mail: dpurves@lindenpl.org; *Librn,* James Fabiano; *Cat Mgr,* Sharon Albert; *Acq,* Jeffrey Wayne; *Ch Serv,* Karen Gray; *ILL,* John Medallis; *Per, Ref,* Elizabeth Piskorik; Staff 24 (MLS 5, Non-MLS 19)
Founded 1925. Pop 39,000; Circ 143,539
Library Holdings: Bk Titles 87,645; Bk Vols 88,935; Per Subs 185
Special Collections: Local History Coll
Automation Activity & Vendor Info: (Cataloging) SirsiDynix; (Circulation) SirsiDynix; (OPAC) SirsiDynix
Wireless access
Publications: Library Lineup
Partic in LibraryLinkNJ, The New Jersey Library Cooperative
Open Mon-Thurs 9-9, Fri 10-5, Sat 9-5
Friends of the Library Group

LINDENWOLD

P LINDENWOLD PUBLIC LIBRARY*, 310 E Linden Ave, 08021. SAN 310-2467. Tel: 856-784-5602. FAX: 856-566-1413. E-mail: library@lindenwold.net. Web Site: www.lindenwoldnj.gov. *Libr Supvr-Popular Libr,* Brenda Roach
Pop 18,000
Library Holdings: Bks on Deafness & Sign Lang 16; DVDs 1,800; Large Print Bks 209; Bk Titles 14,244; Bk Vols 15,281; Per Subs 37
Automation Activity & Vendor Info: (Cataloging) Follett Software; (Circulation) Follett Software; (Serials) EBSCO Online
Wireless access
Mem of Camden County Library System
Open Tues 9-8, Wed & Fri 9-5, Thurs 12-8, Sat 9-3
Friends of the Library Group

LINWOOD

P LINWOOD PUBLIC LIBRARY*, 301 Davis Ave, 08221. SAN 310-2475. Tel: 609-926-7991. FAX: 609-927-6147. E-mail: linwoodlibrary@linwoodlibrary.com. Web Site: linwoodlibrary.com/. *Dir,* Maria Moss; *Asst Dir,* Mary Ann Branciforti
Founded 1926. Pop 6,144; Circ 31,190
Library Holdings: Bk Vols 35,000; Per Subs 77
Special Collections: New Jersey Coll
Automation Activity & Vendor Info: (Cataloging) Follett Software; (Circulation) Follett Software; (OPAC) Follett Software
Wireless access
Partic in Coalition of Independent Libraries (COIL); NJ Regional Libr Coop
Open Mon-Thurs 10-8, Fri 10-5, Sat 10-4, Sun 11-3
Friends of the Library Group

LITTLE FALLS

P LITTLE FALLS PUBLIC LIBRARY, Eight Warren St, 07424. SAN 310-2483. Tel: 973-256-2784. FAX: 973-256-6312. Web Site: www.littlefallslibrary.org. *Dir,* Christine Miller; E-mail: pelchat-miller@littlefallslibrary.org; *Info & Tech Serv Librn,* Kristin Blumberg; E-mail: blumberg@littlefallslibrary.org; *Children's & Prog Serv Spec,* Linda Belen; E-mail: belen@littlefallslibrary.org; Staff 2 (MLS 2)
Founded 1906. Circ 47,000
Jan 2013-Dec 2013 Income $606,809, State $6,323, City $591,432, Locally Generated Income $9,054. Mats Exp $51,200, Books $28,000, Per/Ser (Incl. Access Fees) $6,700, AV Mat $6,800, Electronic Ref Mat (Incl. Access Fees) $9,700. Sal $287,000 (Prof $127,700)
Library Holdings: Audiobooks 518; CDs 1,300; DVDs 817; Large Print Bks 336; Bk Titles 48,000; Per Subs 82
Subject Interests: NJ
Automation Activity & Vendor Info: (Acquisitions) SirsiDynix; (Cataloging) SirsiDynix; (Circulation) SirsiDynix; (OPAC) SirsiDynix
Database Vendor: EBSCOhost, Gale Cengage Learning, ProQuest, TumbleBookLibrary
Wireless access
Function: Pub access computers, Ref serv in person, Story hour, Summer reading prog
Partic in PALS Plus, The Computer Consortium of Passaic County Libraries
Open Mon-Thurs (Winter) 10-9, Fri 10-5, Sat 10-3; Mon-Thurs (Summer) 10-9, Fri 10-5

LITTLE FERRY

P LITTLE FERRY FREE PUBLIC LIBRARY, 239 Liberty St, 07643. SAN 310-2491. Tel: 201-641-3721. FAX: 201-641-1957. Web Site: littleferry.bccls.org. *Dir,* Richard Mariconda; E-mail: mariconda@littleferry.bccls.org
Founded 1929. Pop 10,626; Circ 54,000
Library Holdings: Bk Titles 29,000; Bk Vols 30,000; Per Subs 70
Special Collections: United States Cinema History Coll
Wireless access
Special Services for the Blind - Large print bks; Talking bks
Open Mon & Tues 10-8, Wed, Thurs & Fri 10-5:30, Sat (Sept-June) 10-3
Friends of the Library Group

LITTLE SILVER

P LITTLE SILVER PUBLIC LIBRARY*, 484 Prospect Ave, 07739. SAN 310-2505. Tel: 732-747-9649. Web Site: www.littlesilver.lib.nj.us. *Dir,* Susan M Edwards; *Asst Librn,* Anita O'Brien; Staff 4 (MLS 1, Non-MLS 3)
Founded 1926. Pop 6,200; Circ 31,000
Library Holdings: Bk Titles 27,000; Bk Vols 27,500; Per Subs 50
Automation Activity & Vendor Info: (Cataloging) SirsiDynix; (Circulation) SirsiDynix; (OPAC) SirsiDynix
Wireless access
Partic in LibraryLinkNJ, The New Jersey Library Cooperative
Open Mon & Thurs 10-8:30, Tues 9-5:30, Wed 10-5:30, Fri 10-6, Sat 10-1
Friends of the Library Group

LIVINGSTON

P RUTH L ROCKWOOD MEMORIAL LIBRARY*, Livingston Public Library, Ten Robert Harp Dr, 07039. SAN 310-2513. Tel: 973-992-4600. FAX: 973-994-2346. TDD: 973-992-4654. Web Site: www.bccls.org/livingston. *Dir,* Judith Kron; E-mail: kron@bccls.org; *Asst Dir,* Amy Hyfler; *Head, Ref,* Arlene Boland; *Ch Serv,* Linda Simpfendorfer; *Tech Serv,* Susan Muntz; Staff 46 (MLS 14, Non-MLS 32)
Founded 1911. Pop 27,391; Circ 365,974
Library Holdings: Bk Titles 219,524; Per Subs 557
Special Collections: Bibliography of Dr Lyndon A Peer; Large Print Coll; New Jerseyana. Oral History
Subject Interests: Art, Holocaust
Automation Activity & Vendor Info: (Cataloging) SirsiDynix; (Circulation) SirsiDynix; (OPAC) SirsiDynix
Function: Bi-weekly Writer's Group, Monthly prog for perceptually impaired adults
Publications: Annual Report; Archival Holdings for the Township of Livingston; Footnotes (Monthly Newsletter); Livingston Local Business Directory
Special Services for the Deaf - TDD equip
Open Mon-Thurs 10-9, Fri 10-6, Sat 10-5, Sun 1-5
Friends of the Library Group

M ST BARNABAS MEDICAL CENTER*, Health Sciences Library, 94 Old Short Hills Rd, 07039. SAN 320-3964. Tel: 973-322-5050. FAX: 973-322-5279. *Dir,* Patricia Reusing; E-mail: preusing@sbhcs.com; Staff 2 (MLS 2)
Library Holdings: Bk Titles 3,000; Per Subs 325
Subject Interests: Med, Plastic surgery, Surgery
Database Vendor: OVID Technologies
Wireless access
Partic in Health Sciences Library Association of New Jersey
Open Mon-Fri 8-6

LODI

C FELICIAN COLLEGE LIBRARY*, 262 S Main St, 07644-2198. SAN 310-253X. Tel: 201-559-6071. FAX: 201-559-6148. E-mail: library@felician.edu. Web Site: www.felician.edu/library. *Assoc Prof, Dir of Libr Serv,* Paul Glassman; E-mail: glassmanp@felician.edu; *Asst Prof, Info Literacy & Outreach Librn,* Cara Berg; Tel: 201-559-6133, E-mail: scottoc@felician.edu; *Asst Prof, Pub Serv Librn,* Gerard Shea; Tel: 201-559-3514, Fax: 201-559-3328, E-mail: sheag@felician.edu; *Instr, Pub Serv Librn,* Elisabeth Gatlin; Tel: 201-559-6125, E-mail: gatline@felician.edu. Subject Specialists: *Art, Eng, Music,* Paul Glassman; *Health mgt, Nat sci, Nursing,* Cara Berg; *Bus, Mgt sci, Teacher educ,* Gerard Shea; *Hist, Soc sci,* Elisabeth Gatlin; Staff 11 (MLS 4, Non-MLS 7)
Founded 1942. Enrl 1,953; Fac 152; Highest Degree: Doctorate
Jul 2012-Jun 2013 Income $682,049. Mats Exp $682,049, Books $36,924, Per/Ser (Incl. Access Fees) $11,111, AV Mat $563, Electronic Ref Mat (Incl. Access Fees) $106,602, Presv $2,158. Sal $404,199 (Prof $354,955)
Library Holdings: CDs 1,465; DVDs 110; e-books 102,011; e-journals 26,689; Microforms 89,191; Bk Titles 183,766; Bk Vols 78,766; Per Subs 364; Videos 101
Special Collections: Children's Books; Poetry (Ammons Coll); Storytelling & Folklore (Helen Robinette Coll)
Subject Interests: Arts, Bus, Educ, Nursing
Automation Activity & Vendor Info: (Cataloging) SirsiDynix; (Circulation) SirsiDynix; (Course Reserve) SirsiDynix; (ILL) JerseyCat; (OPAC) SirsiDynix
Database Vendor: ACM (Association for Computing Machinery), Alexander Street Press, American Chemical Society, CredoReference, ebrary, EBSCOhost, Facts on File, Gale Cengage Learning, H W Wilson, Hoovers, JSTOR, LexisNexis, Modern Language Association, Newsbank-Readex, OCLC WorldShare Interlibrary Loan, Oxford Online, ProQuest, PubMed, ReferenceUSA, ScienceDirect, SirsiDynix, TDNet, Thomson - Web of Science, Wiley InterScience, Wilson - Wilson Web
Wireless access
Publications: Faculty Guide (Library handbook); Library Handbook; Library Updates (Online only)
Partic in LibraryLinkNJ, The New Jersey Library Cooperative; Lyrasis; OCLC Online Computer Library Center, Inc; Virtual Academic Library Environment
Special Services for the Blind - Computer with voice synthesizer for visually impaired persons
Open Mon-Thurs 8:45am-Midnight, Fri 8:45-4:45, Sat 10-4, Sun Noon-Midnight

P LODI MEMORIAL LIBRARY*, One Memorial Dr, 07644-1692. SAN 310-2548. Tel: 973-365-4044. Circulation Tel: 973-365-4044, Ext 4. Reference Tel: 973-365-4044, Ext 5. Administration Tel: 973-365-4044, Ext 7. FAX: 973-365-0172. E-mail: lodilibrary@bccls.org. Web Site: lodi.bccls.org. *Dir,* Barbara Hauck-Mah; Staff 3 (MLS 3)
Founded 1924. Pop 24,136; Circ 56,138
Jan 2012-Dec 2012 Income $1,023,956, State $10,681, City $685,508, Locally Generated Income $10,097, Other $280,576. Mats Exp $51,252, Books $33,820, Per/Ser (Incl. Access Fees) $4,423, AV Mat $11,009, Electronic Ref Mat (Incl. Access Fees) $2,000. Sal $456,974
Library Holdings: Audiobooks 1,402; Bks on Deafness & Sign Lang 45; CDs 1,176; DVDs 2,873; e-books 2,591; Bk Vols 60,155; Per Subs 1,540; Videos 2,260
Automation Activity & Vendor Info: (Cataloging) Innovative Interfaces, Inc; (Circulation) Innovative Interfaces, Inc; (OPAC) Innovative Interfaces, Inc
Database Vendor: EBSCOhost, ProQuest, SirsiDynix
Wireless access
Function: Children's prog
Partic in Bergen County Cooperative Library System
Open Mon, Tues & Thurs 12:30-8, Wed, Fri & Sat 9:30-5
Friends of the Library Group

LONG BRANCH

P LONG BRANCH FREE PUBLIC LIBRARY*, 328 Broadway, 07740. SAN 310-2564. Tel: 732-222-3900. FAX: 732-222-3799. Web Site: www.lmxac.org/longbranch. *Dir,* Ingrid Bruck; E-mail: ibruck@lmxac.org; *Br Mgr, Ch Mgr,* Linda Wurzel; E-mail: lwurzel@lmxac.org; *Mgr, Ad Serv,* Tonya Badillo; E-mail: tbadillo@lmxac.org; *Circ Mgr,* Barbara Williams; E-mail: bwilliam@lmxac.org; *Mgr, Tech Serv,* Francine Marks; E-mail: fmarks@lmxac.org; *Adult Serv,* Janet Birckhead; E-mail: jbirckhe@lmxac.org; *Literacy & Diversity,* Tonya Badillo; E-mail: tbadillo@lmxac.org; *Outreach & Publicity,* Kathryn Angelo; E-mail:

kangelo@lmxac.org. Subject Specialists: *Local hist*, Janet Birckhead; Staff 10 (MLS 4, Non-MLS 6)
Founded 1916. Pop 31,340; Circ 169,880
Jan 2012-Dec 2012 Income $1,641,140, State $26,000, City $1,575,140, Locally Generated Income $40,000. Mats Exp $152,500, Books $82,000, Per/Ser (Incl. Access Fees) $7,000, AV Equip $20,000, AV Mat $21,000, Electronic Ref Mat (Incl. Access Fees) $21,000, Presv $1,500. Sal $923,115 (Prof $296,146)
Library Holdings: Audiobooks 8,111; AV Mats 15,314; CDs 4,812; DVDs 10,857; e-books 6,702; Large Print Bks 2,547; Bk Titles 90,061; Per Subs 126
Special Collections: Audio Books; ESL Coll; Local Newspaper, micro; Long Branch Historical Coll; Spanish & Portuguese Coll
Automation Activity & Vendor Info: (Acquisitions) Baker & Taylor; (Cataloging) SIRSI-iBistro; (Circulation) SirsiDynix; (Course Reserve) JerseyCat; (ILL) JerseyCat; (OPAC) SIRSI-iBistro; (Serials) EBSCO Online
Database Vendor: EBSCOhost
Wireless access
Function: Adult bk club, Adult literacy prog, After school storytime, Art exhibits, Audiobks via web, AV serv, BA reader (adult literacy), Bilingual assistance for Spanish patrons, Bk club(s), Bks on CD, Chess club, Children's prog, Computer training, Computers for patron use, Copy machines, E-Reserves, Electronic databases & coll, Fax serv, Free DVD rentals, Handicapped accessible, Holiday prog, Home delivery & serv to Sr ctr & nursing homes, Homework prog, ILL available, Instruction & testing, Notary serv, Online cat, Photocopying/Printing, Preschool outreach, Prog for adults, Prog for children & young adult, Pub access computers, Senior outreach, Serves mentally handicapped consumers, Story hour, Summer reading prog, Tax forms, Telephone ref, VHS videos, Web-catalog, Wheelchair accessible, Workshops
Partic in Libraries of Middlesex Automation Consortium; LibraryLinkNJ, The New Jersey Library Cooperative
Open Mon-Thurs 10-8, Fri & Sat 12-5
Friends of the Library Group
Branches: 1
ELBERON BRANCH, 168 Lincoln Ave, Elberon, 07740, SAN 310-1312. Tel: 732-870-1776. *Br Mgr*, Linda Wurzel; E-mail: lwurzel@lmxac.org; Staff 1 (Non-MLS 1)
Library Holdings: Bk Vols 9,884
Open Mon 1-4, Tues 9-1, Wed 4-7, Fri 10-2 & 3-5, Sat 10-1
Friends of the Library Group

M MONMOUTH MEDICAL CENTER, Altschul Medical Library, 300 Second Ave, 07740. SAN 310-2572. Tel: 732-923-6645. FAX: 732-222-3742. E-mail: mmcmedicallibrary@barnabashealth.org. Web Site: www.barnabashealth.org/education/mmced/medlib/index.html. *Dir*, Frederic C Pachman; E-mail: fpachman@barnabashealth.org; Staff 1 (MLS 1)
Founded 1973
Library Holdings: Bk Titles 3,500; Bk Vols 4,000; Per Subs 20
Subject Interests: Med, Nursing, Pediatrics
Database Vendor: EBSCO Information Services, EBSCOhost, OVID Technologies, UpToDate
Wireless access
Publications: Newsletter (Quarterly)
Partic in LibraryLinkNJ, The New Jersey Library Cooperative; Nat Libr of Med/Docline; National Network of Libraries of Medicine Middle Atlantic Region

LONG VALLEY

P WASHINGTON TOWNSHIP FREE PUBLIC LIBRARY*, 37 E Springtown Rd, 07853. SAN 310-2580. Tel: 908-876-3596. FAX: 908-876-3541. Web Site: www.wtpl.org. *Dir*, Jacqueline Zuzzi; E-mail: jacqueline.zuzzi@wtpl.org; Staff 13.7 (MLS 4.2, Non-MLS 9.5)
Founded 1968. Pop 18,544; Circ 168,209
Library Holdings: Audiobooks 4,157; AV Mats 10,580; CDs 2,239; DVDs 4,184; Bk Vols 70,210; Per Subs 161
Automation Activity & Vendor Info: (Acquisitions) SIRSI-DRA; (Cataloging) SIRSI-DRA; (Circulation) SIRSI-DRA; (ILL) SIRSI-DRA; (OPAC) SIRSI-DRA
Database Vendor: EBSCOhost, ProQuest, SirsiDynix
Wireless access
Function: Art exhibits, Bk club(s), CD-ROM, Computer training, Copy machines, Electronic databases & coll, Handicapped accessible, ILL available, Music CDs, Online ref, Online searches, Photocopying/Printing, Prog for adults, Prog for children & young adult, Ref serv available, Spoken cassettes & CDs, Summer reading prog, Tax forms, Telephone ref, VHS videos
Partic in Morris Automated Information Network
Open Mon-Thurs 10-9, Fri & Sat 10-5, Sun 1-5
Friends of the Library Group

S WASHINGTON TOWNSHIP HISTORICAL SOCIETY LIBRARY*, Six Fairview Ave, 07853-3172. (Mail add: PO Box 189, 07853-0189), SAN 373-2509. Tel: 908-876-9696. E-mail: info@wthsnj.org. Web Site: www.wthsnj.org. *Chairperson*, Shelley Heretyk; *Pres*, Betsy Guzenski
Library Holdings: Bk Vols 300
Special Collections: Local Cemetery Listings; Local Church Records; New Jersey History by Henry Charlton Beck; Original Newspaper Articles; Schooley's Mountain Springs Coll
Subject Interests: Genealogy, Local hist
Open Sun 2-4

LYNDHURST

P LYNDHURST FREE PUBLIC LIBRARY*, 355 Valley Brook Ave, 07071. SAN 310-2599. Tel: 201-804-2478. FAX: 201-939-7677. E-mail: lyndcirc@bccls.org. Web Site: lyndhurst.bccls.org. *Dir*, Donna M Romeo; Tel: 201-804-2486, E-mail: romeo@bccls.org; *Dept Head, Ref Librn*, Thomas Hilton; *Ch Serv, Librn*, Maryellen Kulzy; E-mail: lyndchild@bccls.org; *Adminr*, Sandra Valvano; *Circ*, Diane McDonald; E-mail: lyndcirc@bccls.org; *Tech Serv*, Elizabeth Hughes; E-mail: lyndtech@bccls.org; Staff 11 (MLS 4, Non-MLS 7)
Founded 1914. Pop 19,400; Circ 51,000
Library Holdings: Bk Titles 56,000; Bk Vols 65,000; Per Subs 114
Special Collections: Local History Coll, slides tapes; New Jerseyana Col, bks, photog, a-tapes, slides
Automation Activity & Vendor Info: (Cataloging) SirsiDynix; (Circulation) SirsiDynix
Database Vendor: EBSCOhost, Gale Cengage Learning, ProQuest, SirsiDynix
Wireless access
Open Mon 11-8, Tues & Fri 9-5, Wed & Thurs 9-8, Sat 9-1

LYONS

DEPARTMENT OF VETERANS AFFAIRS
GM LYONS CAMPUS MEDICAL LIBRARY*, 151 Knollcroft Rd, 07939, SAN 350-8501. Tel: 908-647-0180, Ext 4545, 973-676-1000. FAX: 908-604-5837. *Librn*, Veronica Lisa; *ILL*, Kim Jaciw
Founded 1931
Library Holdings: Bk Titles 4,200; Per Subs 350
Special Collections: Patient Health Education
Subject Interests: Med, Nursing, Psychiat, Psychol
Partic in BRS
Restriction: Staff use only
GM LYONS CAMPUS PATIENT'S LIBRARY*, 151 Knollcroft Rd, 07939, SAN 350-8536. Tel: 908-647-0180, Ext 6121, 973-676-1000. FAX: 908-604-5837. *Libr Tech*, Kris Reinmann

MADISON

C DREW UNIVERSITY LIBRARY, 36 Madison Ave, 07940. SAN 310-2602. Tel: 973-408-3125. Circulation Tel: 973-408-3486. Interlibrary Loan Service Tel: 973-408-3478. Reference Tel: 973-408-3588. Administration Tel: 973-408-3471, 973-408-3661. FAX: 973-408-3770. E-mail: drewlib@drew.edu. Web Site: www.drew.edu/depts/library.aspx. *Interim Dean of Libr*, Dr Linda E Connors; Tel: 973-408-3322, E-mail: lconnors@drew.edu; *Head, Circ*, Johanna Edge; Tel: 973-408-3875, E-mail: jedge@drew.edu; *Head, ILL*, Kathy Juliano; E-mail: kjuliano@drew.edu; *Head, Ref*, Jody Caldwell; Tel: 973-408-3481, E-mail: jcaldwell@drew.edu; *Head, Spec Coll & Archives, Methodist Librn*, Christopher J Anderson, PhD; Tel: 973-408-3910, E-mail: cjanders@drew.edu; *Syst Librn*, Guy Dobson; Tel: 973-408-3207, E-mail: gdobson@drew.edu; *Theological Librn*, Jesse Mann; Tel: 973-408-3472, E-mail: jmann@drew.edu; *Conservator*, Massato Okinaka; Tel: 973-408-3476, E-mail: mokinaka@drew.edu; *Govt Doc*, Beth Patterson, PhD; Tel: 973-408-3480, E-mail: epatters@drew.edu. Subject Specialists: *Libr tech*, Guy Dobson; *Theol*, Jesse Mann; *Conserv*, Massato Okinaka; Staff 19 (MLS 12, Non-MLS 7)
Founded 1867. Enrl 2,274; Fac 193; Highest Degree: Doctorate
Library Holdings: AV Mats 6,459; e-books 13,708; Microforms 517,242; Bk Vols 642,729; Per Subs 72,381
Special Collections: 19th Century Pamphlets Coll; Carl Michalson Coll; Creamer Hymnology Coll; Dornan Coll (Russian Samizdat Archive); Drew University Archives; George D Kelsey Coll; Georges Simenon Coll; Haberly Book Arts Coll; Koehler Coll (Reformation Church Hist); Letters of John Wesley & the Wesley Family; Maser & Prinster Prayer Book Coll; McClintock Rare Book Coll; Political & Graphic Satire (Chesler Coll); Political Journalism (Bela Kornitzer Coll); Society of Biblical Literature Archives; Theology Coll, bks, ms; United Nations Coll, bks, doc; Will Herberg Coll; Willa Cather Coll; World Methodism, archives, doc, journals, ms, papers, per, publs, rec. State Document Depository; US Document Depository
Subject Interests: Biblical studies, Liberal arts, Liturgics, Methodism, Relig hist, Theol

Automation Activity & Vendor Info: (Acquisitions) SIRSI WorkFlows; (Cataloging) SIRSI WorkFlows; (Circulation) SIRSI WorkFlows; (ILL) OCLC; (OPAC) SirsiDynix
Database Vendor: Dialog, EBSCOhost, Gale Cengage Learning, JSTOR, LexisNexis, OCLC FirstSearch, OVID Technologies, ProQuest, Sage, ScienceDirect, SirsiDynix
Wireless access
Function: Microfiche/film & reading machines, Photocopying/Printing, Pub access computers, Ref serv available, Scanner, Telephone ref
Publications: Visions (Newsletter)
Partic in ISI; LibraryLinkNJ, The New Jersey Library Cooperative; Lyrasis; Oberlin Group; Virtual Academic Library Environment
Open Mon-Thurs 8:30am-11pm, Fri 8:30-7, Sat 9:30-7, Sun 1-11
Friends of the Library Group

C FAIRLEIGH DICKINSON UNIVERSITY, Florham Campus Library, 285 Madison Ave, M-LAO-03, 07940. SAN 350-8595. Tel: 973-443-8515. Interlibrary Loan Service Tel: 973-443-8530. Reference Tel: 973-443-8516. Administration Tel: 973-443-8682. FAX: 973-443-8525. Web Site: library.fdu.edu/florham. *Assoc Univ Librn, Dir, Pub Serv,* Gary Schmidt; Tel: 973-443-8533, E-mail: gschmidt@fdu.edu; *Assoc Univ Librn, Tech Serv,* Mary Marks; Tel: 973-443-8520, E-mail: marks@fdu.edu; *Head, Access Serv,* Mary Donnelly; E-mail: maryd@fdu.edu; *Electronic Res Librn,* Robert Wolf; *Instrul Serv Librn, Ref,* Dr Denise Marshall; Tel: 973-443-8627, E-mail: denimars@fdu.edu; *Tech Serv & Digital Projects Librn,* Brigid Burke; Tel: 973-443-8514, E-mail: bburke@fdu.edu; *Syst Librn,* Youbo Wang; E-mail: ywang@fdu.edu; *ILL Coordr,* Tracy Dante; E-mail: tldante@fdu.edu; *Coll Develop, Ref,* Eleanor Friedl; E-mail: friedl@fdu.edu; *Ref,* Robert Richlan; E-mail: richlan@fdu.edu; Staff 15 (MLS 7, Non-MLS 8)
Founded 1958. Enrl 2,800; Fac 130; Highest Degree: Master
Library Holdings: Audiobooks 8; CDs 250; DVDs 1,676; e-books 119,770; e-journals 1,175; Electronic Media & Resources 134; Microforms 19,000; Bk Titles 134,506; Bk Vols 148,205; Per Subs 191
Special Collections: Black Fiction Coll; Douglas Kahn Photo & Film History Coll; Lloyd Haberly Book Arts Coll
Automation Activity & Vendor Info: (Acquisitions) Ex Libris Group; (Cataloging) Ex Libris Group; (Circulation) Ex Libris Group; (Course Reserve) Ex Libris Group; (ILL) OCLC; (OPAC) Ex Libris Group; (Serials) Ex Libris Group
Database Vendor: ACM (Association for Computing Machinery), Alexander Street Press, American Chemical Society, Annual Reviews, Cinahl, CountryWatch, CredoReference, ebrary, EBSCOhost, Elsevier, Ex Libris Group, Facts on File, Gale Cengage Learning, Greenwood Publishing Group, Hoovers, Infotrieve, infoUSA, JSTOR, LexisNexis, Mergent Online, Modern Language Association, Nature Publishing Group, OCLC, Plunkett Research, Ltd, ProQuest, PubMed, ReferenceUSA, Sage, ScienceDirect, SerialsSolutions, Springshare, LLC, World Book Online, YBP Library Services
Wireless access
Function: Archival coll, Art exhibits, Audio & video playback equip for onsite use, Audiobks via web, CD-ROM, Computer training, Computers for patron use, Copy machines, Distance learning, Doc delivery serv, e-mail & chat, Electronic databases & coll, Exhibits, Fax serv, Free DVD rentals, Handicapped accessible, ILL available, Notary serv, Online cat, Online ref, Online searches, Orientations, Outside serv via phone, mail, e-mail & web, Ref & res, Ref serv available, Ref serv in person, Res libr, Scanner, Telephone ref, VHS videos, Video lending libr, Web-catalog, Workshops
Partic in OCLC Online Computer Library Center, Inc; Westchester Academic Library Directors Organization (WALDO)
Open Mon-Thurs 8:30am-11pm, Fri 8:30am-5pm, Sat 10am-6pm, Sun 2pm-10pm
Friends of the Library Group

P MADISON PUBLIC LIBRARY, 39 Keep St, 07940. SAN 310-2610. Tel: 973-377-0722. FAX: 973-377-3142. Web Site: madisonnjlibrary.org. *Dir,* Nancy S Adamczyk; E-mail: nancy.adamczyk@mainlib.org; *Supvr, Ch Serv,* Emily Weisenstein; E-mail: emily.weisenstein@mainlib.org; *Adult Serv & Tech Serv/ILL,* Adrienne Tawil; E-mail: adrienne.tawil@mainlib.org; *Circ, ILL,* Ralph Graham; E-mail: ralph.graham@mainlib.org; Staff 19.23 (MLS 6.06, Non-MLS 13.17)
Founded 1900. Pop 15,845; Circ 226,417
Library Holdings: AV Mats 13,956; Bk Vols 132,197; Per Subs 213
Special Collections: Golden Hind Press Publications; Madison History
Subject Interests: Am lit, British lit
Automation Activity & Vendor Info: (Cataloging) Innovative Interfaces, Inc; (Circulation) Innovative Interfaces, Inc; (ILL) Innovative Interfaces, Inc; (OPAC) Innovative Interfaces, Inc
Database Vendor: EBSCOhost, Facts on File, Overdrive, Inc, ProQuest
Wireless access
Function: Adult bk club, Archival coll, Art exhibits, Bks on CD, Children's prog, Copy machines, Electronic databases & coll, Free DVD rentals, Handicapped accessible, ILL available, Microfiche/film & reading machines, Mus passes, Music CDs, Online cat, Online ref, OverDrive digital audio bks, Preschool reading prog, Prog for adults, Prog for children & young adult, Pub access computers, Ref & res, Ref serv available, Story hour, Tax forms, Telephone ref, Wheelchair accessible
Publications: Newsletter (Bi-monthly)
Partic in Morris Automated Information Network; Morris-Union Federation
Open Mon-Wed 10-9, Thurs & Fri 10-6, Sat 10-5, Sun (Fall-Spring) 2-5
Restriction: Authorized patrons
Friends of the Library Group

S MUSEUM OF EARLY TRADES & CRAFTS LIBRARY*, Nine Main Street, 07940. SAN 377-483X. Tel: 973-377-2982, Ext 10. FAX: 973-377-7358. E-mail: info@metc.org. Web Site: www.metc.org. *Dir,* Vivian James; Tel: 973-377-2982, Ext 11; *Curator,* Siobhan Fitpatirck; Tel: 973-377-2982, Ext 13, E-mail: curator@metc.org
Library Holdings: Bk Vols 600
Subject Interests: Craft, Early Am hist, Tools
Open Tues-Sat (Winter) 10-4, Sun 12-5; Tues-Sat (Summer) 10-4
Restriction: Not a lending libr

R UNITED METHODIST CHURCH*, General Commission on Archives & History Library, 36 Madison Ave, 07940. SAN 312-8997. Tel: 973-408-3590. FAX: 973-408-3836. Web Site: www.drew.edu/library/methodist, www.gcah.org. *Dir,* Christopher J Anderson, PhD; E-mail: cjanders@drew.edu. Subject Specialists: *Liturgics,* Christopher J Anderson, PhD
Founded 1968
Library Holdings: Bk Titles 40,000; Bk Vols 50,000; Per Subs 600
Special Collections: Methodist/EUB/Holiness Hymnals; Missions Periodicals
Subject Interests: United Methodist Church
Automation Activity & Vendor Info: (Acquisitions) SirsiDynix; (Cataloging) SirsiDynix; (Circulation) SirsiDynix; (OPAC) SirsiDynix; (Serials) SirsiDynix
Wireless access
Open Mon-Fri 9-5
Friends of the Library Group

MAHWAH

P MAHWAH PUBLIC LIBRARY*, 100 Ridge Rd, 07430. SAN 310-2645. Tel: 201-529-7323. FAX: 201-529-9027. E-mail: mahwcirc@bccls.org. Web Site: www.mahwahlibrary.org. *Dir,* Kurt Hadeler; Staff 34 (MLS 7, Non-MLS 27)
Founded 1912. Pop 24,062; Circ 176,000
Library Holdings: AV Mats 12,126; Large Print Bks 1,082; Bk Titles 80,114; Bk Vols 85,330; Per Subs 268
Subject Interests: Theatre
Database Vendor: Gale Cengage Learning, ProQuest, SirsiDynix
Publications: Brochures; Flyers; Monthly Calendar; Monthly Newsletter
Partic in Bergen County Cooperative Library System; LibraryLinkNJ, The New Jersey Library Cooperative
Open Mon-Thurs 10-9, Fri & Sat 10-5, Sun 1-5

C RAMAPO COLLEGE OF NEW JERSEY*, George T Potter Library, 505 Ramapo Valley Rd, 07430-1623. SAN 310-2661. Tel: 201-684-7575. Interlibrary Loan Service Tel: 201-684-7579. Reference Tel: 201-684-7574. Administration Tel: 201-684-7569. Administration FAX: 201-684-7628. Web Site: library.ramapo.edu/. *Col Librn, Dean,* Elizabeth J Siecke; E-mail: esiecke@ramapo.edu; *Access Serv,* Irene Kuchta; Tel: 201-684-7577, E-mail: ikuchta@ramapo.edu; *Access Serv,* Madel Tisi; Tel: 201-684-7510, E-mail: mtisi@ramapo.edu; *Coll Develop,* Elaine Risch; Tel: 201-684-7570, E-mail: erisch@ramapo.edu; *Pub Serv,* Christina Connor; Tel: 201-684 -7584, E-mail: cconnor@ramapo.edu; *Pub Serv,* Leigh Cregan Keller; Tel: 201-684-7316, E-mail: lkeller1@ramapo.edu; *Pub Serv,* Shirley Knight; Tel: 201-684-7315, E-mail: sknight@ramapo.edu; *Pub Serv,* Susan Kurzmann; Tel: 201-684-7199, E-mail: skurzman@ramapo.edu; *Tech Serv,* Marcia Sexton; Tel: 201-684-6749, E-mail: msexton@ramapo.edu; Staff 27 (MLS 9, Non-MLS 18)
Founded 1968. Enrl 5,631; Fac 170; Highest Degree: Master
Jul 2006-Jun 2007 Income $2,099,933. Mats Exp $679,165, Books $236,000, Per/Ser (Incl. Access Fees) $140,659, Other Print Mats $69,154, Micro $15,866, Electronic Ref Mat (Incl. Access Fees) $217,486. Sal $1,338,509
Library Holdings: Bk Titles 155,038; Bk Vols 178,737; Per Subs 976
Special Collections: State Document Depository
Automation Activity & Vendor Info: (Acquisitions) LibLime; (Cataloging) OCLC; (Circulation) LibLime; (Course Reserve) LibLime; (ILL) OCLC; (OPAC) LibLime
Database Vendor: EBSCOhost, Gale Cengage Learning, JSTOR, LexisNexis, OCLC FirstSearch, OVID Technologies, ProQuest, ScienceDirect, TLC (The Library Corporation), Westlaw, Wilson - Wilson Web
Wireless access
Partic in LibraryLinkNJ, The New Jersey Library Cooperative; NJ Col & Univ Libr Coun; Virtual Academic Library Environment

MANAHAWKIN

M SOUTHERN OCEAN MEDICAL CENTER*, Health Sciences Library, 1140 Rte 72 W, 08050. Tel: 609-597-6011. FAX: 609-978-8920. Web Site: www.soch.org. *Coordr,* Joanne Zipfel
Library Holdings: Bk Vols 500; Per Subs 70
Database Vendor: EBSCOhost
Wireless access
Restriction: Open to students, fac & staff

MANALAPAN

P MONMOUTH COUNTY LIBRARY*, 125 Symmes Dr, 07726. SAN 350-7181. Tel: 732-431-7220. FAX: 732 308 2955. TDD: 732-845-0064 Web Site: www.monmouthcountylib.org. *Interim Dir,* Judith Tolchin; *Dir,* Position Currently Open; *Cat, Head, Tech Serv,* Pam Sawall; *Chief Librn Br Serv,* Pat Whitehead; *Ch Serv Librn,* Pat Findra; *Info Tech, Mem Serv Librn,* Heidi Amici; *Pub Relations Librn,* Coleen Berry; Staff 50 (MLS 50)
Founded 1922. Pop 390,000; Circ 3,500,000
Jan 2010-Dec 2010 Income (Main Library and Branch(s)) $16,514,000, State $65,000, County $16,100,000, Locally Generated Income $349,000. Mats Exp $3,693,400, Books $2,650,000, AV Mat $625,000, Electronic Ref Mat (Incl. Access Fees) $207,000
Library Holdings: Bk Titles 1,537,227
Special Collections: New Jersey History
Wireless access
Publications: Children's Newsletter; Monthly Calendar; Municipal Government (Newsletter)
Member Libraries: Eatontown Library; Fair Haven Library; Manasquan Public Library; Monmouth Beach Library; Neptune City Library; Oceanic Free Library; Tinton Falls Public Library; Union Beach Memorial Library
Partic in LibraryLinkNJ, The New Jersey Library Cooperative; OCLC Online Computer Library Center, Inc
Special Services for the Deaf - Assisted listening device; Bks on deafness & sign lang; Sign lang interpreter upon request for prog; TTY equip
Special Services for the Blind - Closed circuit TV magnifier
Open Mon-Thurs 9-9, Fri & Sat 9-5, Sun (Sept-June) 1-5
Friends of the Library Group
Branches: 12
ALLENTOWN BRANCH, 16 S Main St, Allentown, 08501, SAN 350-7211. Tel: 609-259-7565. FAX: 609-259-9620. *Librn,* Nancy Stein
Library Holdings: Bk Vols 20,350
Open Mon & Wed 10-5, Tues & Thurs 10-9, Fri 2-5, Sat 10-3
ATLANTIC HIGHLANDS BRANCH, 100 First Ave, Atlantic Highlands, 07716, SAN 309-9997. Tel: 732-291-1956. *Br Mgr,* Jane Reynolds
Founded 1926. Pop 4,895; Circ 34,440
Library Holdings: Bk Vols 20,000; Per Subs 50
Automation Activity & Vendor Info: (Cataloging) SirsiDynix, (Circulation) SirsiDynix; (OPAC) SirsiDynix
Function: Adult bk club, After school storytime, Bk club(s), Chess club, Electronic databases & coll, ILL available, Online ref, Online searches, Prog for adults, Prog for children & young adult, Spoken cassettes & CDs, Spoken cassettes & DVDs, Summer reading prog, Tax forms, VHS videos, Video lending libr
Open Mon & Tues 9-4, Wed 9-6, Thurs 1-9, Fri 1-5, Sat 9-5 (July-Aug 9-1)
Friends of the Library Group
COLTS NECK BRANCH, One Winthrop Dr, Colts Neck, 07722, SAN 350-722X. Tel: 732-431-5656. FAX: 732-462-0327. *Librn,* Matthew Ragucci
Library Holdings: Bk Vols 28,450
Open Mon, Wed & Sat 9-5, Tues & Thurs 1-9, Fri 1-5
EASTERN, 1001 Rte 35, Shrewsbury, 07702, SAN 350-7246. Tel: 732-683-8980. Toll Free Tel: 866-941-8188. FAX: 732-219-0140. *Librn,* Janet Kranis
Library Holdings: Bk Vols 145,000
Special Collections: US Document Depository
Subject Interests: Art, Educ, Law, Music
Open Mon-Thurs 9-9, Fri & Sat 9-5, Sun 1-5 (Sept-May)
HAZLET BRANCH, 251 Middle Rd, Hazlet, 07730, SAN 350-7270. Tel: 732-264-7164. FAX: 732-739-1556. *Librn,* Beth Henderson
Library Holdings: Bk Vols 54,000
Open Mon & Wed 1-9, Tues, Thurs & Sat 9-5, Fri 1-5, Sat (Summer) 9-1
HOLMDEL BRANCH, Four Crawfords Corner Rd, Holmdel, 07733, SAN 350-7300. Tel: 732-946-4118. FAX: 732-946-2980. *Librn,* Karen Nealis
Library Holdings: Bk Vols 38,000
Special Collections: Township History Coll
Open Mon & Wed 1-9, Tues, Thurs & Sat 9-5, Fri 1-5, Sat (Summer) 9-1
HOWELL BRANCH, 318 Old Tavern Rd, Howell, 07731, SAN 350-7335. Tel: 732-938-2300. FAX: 732-938-4739. *Librn,* Dianne Rieth
Library Holdings: Bk Vols 46,000
Special Collections: Township History Coll
Open Mon & Wed 10-9, Tues & Thurs 9-9, Fri 1-5, Sat 9-5
MARLBORO BRANCH, One Library Ct, Marlboro, 07746-1102, SAN 350-7394. Tel: 732-536-9406. FAX: 732-536-4708. *Librn,* Robyn Miller
Library Holdings: Bk Vols 100,000
Subject Interests: Local hist
Open Mon, Tues & Thurs 9-9, Wed 9-6, Fri 1-5, Sat 9-5 (9-1 Summer)
OCEAN TOWNSHIP, 701 Deal Rd, Ocean, 07712, SAN 350-7459. Tel: 732-531-5092. FAX: 732-531-5262. *Librn,* Beth Miller
Library Holdings: Bk Vols 64,000
Subject Interests: Local hist
Open Mon 10-9, Tues, Wed & Thurs 9-9, Fri 1-5, Sat 9-5 (9-1 Summer)
OCEANPORT BRANCH, Monmouth Blvd & Myrtle Ave, Oceanport, 07757, SAN 350-7424. Tel: 732-229-2626. FAX: 732-571-0661. *Br Mgr,* Michele Bordeaux
Library Holdings: Bk Vols 20,350
WALL TOWNSHIP, 2700 Allaire Rd, Wall, 07719, SAN 350-7483. Tel: 732-449-8877. FAX: 732-449-1732. *Librn,* Janet Trotter
Library Holdings: Bk Vols 104,000
Special Collections: Local Hist Coll
Open Mon 10-9, Tues-Thurs 9-9, Fri 1-5, Sat 9-5 (9-1 Summer)
WEST LONG BRANCH, 95 Poplar Ave, West Long Branch, 07764, SAN 310-5938. Tel: 732-222-5993. FAX: 732-229-5138. *Br Mgr,* Rachael Scalise
Library Holdings: Bk Vols 35,000; Per Subs 125
Special Collections: Monmouth County NJ History Coll
Open Mon & Thurs 10-9, Tues & Sat 9-5, Wed 9-9, Fri 1-5, Sat (Summer) 9-1

MANASQUAN

P MANASQUAN PUBLIC LIBRARY*, 55 Broad St, 08736. SAN 310-2688. Tel: 732-223-1503. FAX: 732-292-0336. E-mail: mqcirc@monmouthcountylib.org. Web Site: www.monmouthcountylib.org. *Dir,* Carol C Mennie; E-mail: mqcirc@monmouthcountylib.org
Founded 1915. Pop 5,500; Circ 36,000
Library Holdings: Bk Titles 32,000; Per Subs 50
Wireless access
Mem of Monmouth County Library
Open Mon, Tues & Thurs 10-5 & 7-9, Fri 10-5, Sat 9:30-12:30

MANVILLE

P MANVILLE PUBLIC LIBRARY*, 100 S Tenth Ave, 08835. SAN 310-2696. Tel: 908-722-9722. FAX: 908-722-0631. *Dir,* Ed Smith; E-mail: edsmith@sclibnj.org; *Ch,* Ruth Bielanski; E-mail: ruthb@lmxac.org; *Circ Serv,* Karen Holland-Kuehl; Staff 8 (MLS 1, Non-MLS 7)
Founded 1960. Pop 10,541; Circ 28,000
Jan 2010-Dec 2010 Income $367,469. Mats Exp $60,000, Books $32,000, Per/Ser (Incl. Access Fees) $3,000, Electronic Ref Mat (Incl. Access Fees) $16,000. Sal $225,269
Library Holdings: CDs 325; DVDs 840; Bk Titles 50,000; Bk Vols 53,533; Per Subs 90; Videos 1,243
Subject Interests: Coal
Automation Activity & Vendor Info: (Cataloging) SirsiDynix; (Circulation) SirsiDynix; (ILL) JerseyCat
Wireless access
Publications: Monthly Calendar; Newsletter (Quarterly)
Partic in Libraries of Middlesex Automation Consortium; Raritan Valley Fedn of Libs
Open Mon-Thurs 10-8, Fri & Sat 10-5:30
Friends of the Library Group

MAPLEWOOD

P MAPLEWOOD MEMORIAL LIBRARY*, 51 Baker St, 07040-2618. SAN 350-8684. Tel: 973-762-1622. Circulation Tel: 973-762-1622, Ext 5000. Interlibrary Loan Service Tel: 973-762-1622, Ext 5022. Reference Tel: 973-762-1622, Ext 5011. Administration Tel: 973-762-1671. Information Services Tel: 973-762-1622, Ext 5002. FAX: 973-762-0762. Web Site: www.maplewoodlibrary.org. *Dir,* Sarah Lester; E-mail: slester@maplewoodlibrary.org; *Ch Serv,* Jane Folger; Staff 10 (MLS 9, Non-MLS 1)
Founded 1913. Pop 23,868; Circ 221,148
Jan 2005-Dec 2005 Income (Main Library and Branch(s)) $1,530,552, State $29,139, City $1,407,413, Locally Generated Income $94,000. Mats Exp $171,301, Books $102,613, Per/Ser (Incl. Access Fees) $16,732, AV Mat $15,136, Electronic Ref Mat (Incl. Access Fees) $36,820. Sal $1,329,013
Library Holdings: Bk Titles 92,415; Bk Vols 131,795; Per Subs 180
Special Collections: Local History (Durand Room Coll), bks, clippings, photog, especially Asher B Durand, 1796-1886 & James A Ricalton, 1844-1929
Automation Activity & Vendor Info: (Acquisitions) Innovative Interfaces, Inc; (Cataloging) Innovative Interfaces, Inc; (Circulation) Innovative Interfaces, Inc; (ILL) Auto-Graphics, Inc; (OPAC) Innovative Interfaces, Inc

Database Vendor: EBSCOhost, Gale Cengage Learning, ProQuest
Publications: Maplewood Library News (co-published with Friends) (Newsletter)
Partic in LibraryLinkNJ, The New Jersey Library Cooperative; ReBL
Open Mon, Wed & Thurs 10-9, Tues 10-6, Fri & Sat 10-5
Friends of the Library Group
Branches: 1
HILTON, 1688 Springfield Ave, 07040-2923, SAN 350-8714. Tel: 973-762-1688. Circulation Tel: 973-762-1688, Ext 5100. *Br Mgr,* Ina Rimpau; E-mail: irimpau@maplewoodlibrary.org; *Ch,* Jenny Burkholder
Founded 1882
Library Holdings: Bk Titles 23,000; Bk Vols 27,000
Open Mon & Wed (Sept-June) 10-5, Tues & Thurs 12-8, Sat (Sept-June) 10-1
Friends of the Library Group

SR MORROW MEMORIAL UNITED METHODIST CHURCH, Library & Media Center, 600 Ridgewood Rd, 07040-2161. SAN 326-2359. Tel: 973-763-7676. FAX: 973-763-6798. E-mail: opendoors@morrowchurch.org. Web Site: www.morrowchurch.org. *Communications Spec,* Paige Chant; Tel: 973-763-7676, Ext 11; Staff 3 (MLS 1, Non-MLS 2)
Pop 861
Library Holdings: Bk Titles 800; Bk Vols 1,000
Subject Interests: Archives, Art, Church hist, Fiction, Hist
Restriction: Mem only

MARGATE CITY

P MARGATE CITY PUBLIC LIBRARY*, 8100 Atlantic Ave, 08402. SAN 310-2726. Tel: 609-822-4700. FAX: 609-823-0064. Web Site: www.margatelibrary.org. *Dir,* James J Cahill, Jr; Staff 6 (MLS 2, Non-MLS 4)
Founded 1972. Pop 9,200
Library Holdings: Bk Titles 36,593; Per Subs 120
Automation Activity & Vendor Info: (Cataloging) Innovative Interfaces, Inc - Millenium; (Circulation) Innovative Interfaces, Inc - Millenium
Database Vendor: Baker & Taylor, EBSCOhost, Facts on File, Gale Cengage Learning, Grolier Online, SirsiDynix
Wireless access
Function: Bks on CD, Computers for patron use, Copy machines, Digital talking bks, Electronic databases & coll, Online searches, Prog for adults, Prog for children & young adult, Ref serv available, Senior computer classes, Tax forms, Wheelchair accessible
Partic in Coalition of Independent Libraries (COIL); LibraryLinkNJ, The New Jersey Library Cooperative
Open Mon, Tues & Thurs 9:30-8, Wed, Fri & Sat 9:30-5, Sun 10-2
Friends of the Library Group

MATAWAN

S MADISON TOWNSHIP HISTORICAL SOCIETY*, Thomas Warne Historical Museum & Library, 4216 Rte 516, 07747. SAN 325-7746. Tel: 732-566-2108. FAX: 732-566-6943.
Founded 1964
Library Holdings: Bk Vols 1,300
Special Collections: 19th Century Tools; Handcrafts; Local History & Genealogy; Newspaper Coll, Early 1800s; Old School, bks, related items; Photograph Coll, Early 19th Century, vf ref
Function: Res libr
Publications: At the Headwaters of Cheesequake Creek (Local history book); From Groaning Board Cooks; Images of America Old Bridge
Open Fri 12-4, Sat & Sun 12-6
Restriction: Not a lending libr

P MATAWAN-ABERDEEN PUBLIC LIBRARY, 165 Main St, 07747. SAN 310-2742. Tel: 732-583-9100. E-mail: info@matawanaberdeenlibrary.com. Web Site: www.lmxac.org/mata/index.html. *Dir,* Kimberly Paone; E-mail: kpaone@lmxac.org; *Head, Adult Serv,* Jill Stafford; *Head, Circ,* Laura Beyer; Staff 24 (MLS 7, Non-MLS 17)
Founded 1903. Pop 27,020; Circ 92,462
Automation Activity & Vendor Info: (Circulation) SirsiDynix
Database Vendor: EBSCOhost, Newsbank, ProQuest
Wireless access
Function: 24/7 Electronic res, 24/7 Online cat, Activity rm, Adult bk club, After school storytime, Archival coll, Art exhibits, Bk club(s), Bks on CD, Children's prog, Computer training, Computers for patron use, Copy machines, Digital talking bks, E-Reserves, Electronic databases & coll, Free DVD rentals, Genealogy discussion group, Handicapped accessible, Holiday prog, ILL available, Magazines, Mail & tel request accepted, Mango lang, Movies, Mus passes, Music CDs, Newsp ref libr, Online cat, Online ref, Online searches, Outreach serv, OverDrive digital audio bks, Photocopying/Printing, Preschool outreach, Preschool reading prog, Prog for adults, Prog for children & young adult, Provide serv for the mentally ill, Pub access computers, Ref serv available, Scanner, Senior computer classes, Senior outreach, Serves mentally handicapped consumers, Spanish lang bks, Story hour, Summer & winter reading prog, Summer reading prog, Tax forms, Teen prog, Telephone ref, Web-catalog, Wheelchair accessible, Winter reading prog, Workshops
Partic in Libraries of Middlesex Automation Consortium
Open Mon & Thurs 9-9, Tues, Wed & Fri 9-6, Sat 9-5 (9-12:30 Summer), Sun 12-5
Restriction: Non-resident fee
Friends of the Library Group

MAYS LANDING

J ATLANTIC CAPE COMMUNITY COLLEGE*, William Spangler Library, 5100 Black Horse Pike, 08330. SAN 310-2750. Tel: 609-343-4952. Circulation Tel: 609-343-4951. Reference Tel: 609-343-5665. Web Site: www.atlantic.edu/library. *Dir,* Grant Wilinski; E-mail: wilinski@atlantic.edu; *Ref Serv,* Leslie Murtha; *Ref Serv,* Ellen Parker; E-mail: eparker@atlantic.edu; Staff 2 (MLS 2)
Founded 1966
Library Holdings: e-books 5,000; Bk Vols 81,000; Per Subs 300
Special Collections: Southern New Jersey History
Automation Activity & Vendor Info: (Cataloging) SirsiDynix; (Circulation) SirsiDynix; (OPAC) SirsiDynix
Wireless access
Partic in LibraryLinkNJ, The New Jersey Library Cooperative; Med Libr & Info Consortium; OCLC Online Computer Library Center, Inc; Virtual Academic Library Environment
Open Mon-Thurs 8am-10pm, Fri 8-4:30, Sat 11-4

P ATLANTIC COUNTY LIBRARY SYSTEM*, 40 Farragut Ave, 08330-1750. SAN 310-4346. Tel: 609-625-2776. Administration Tel: 609-646-8699. FAX: 609-625-8143. Web Site: www.atlanticlibrary.org. *Dir,* Karen L George; *Asst Libr Dir,* Edwina Wilinski; *Libr Serv Mgr,* Gair Helfrich; *Commun Relations,* Beverly Bird; *Fiscal Officer,* Brian Tomlinson; *ILL,* Clare Bebbington; *Ref,* Regina Bell; Staff 24 (MLS 24)
Founded 1926. Pop 181,307; Circ 897,590
Library Holdings: Bk Titles 248,143; Bk Vols 486,854
Special Collections: Afro-America Coll; Jerseyana; Music Coll. State Document Depository
Automation Activity & Vendor Info: (Acquisitions) SirsiDynix; (Cataloging) SirsiDynix; (Circulation) SirsiDynix; (OPAC) SirsiDynix; (Serials) SirsiDynix
Wireless access
Publications: Wavelength (Newsletter)
Partic in LibraryLinkNJ, The New Jersey Library Cooperative
Open Mon-Thurs 9-9, Fri & Sat 9-5
Friends of the Library Group
Branches: 10
BRIGANTINE BRANCH, 201 15th St S, Brigantine, 08203, SAN 321-8198. Tel: 609-266-0110. Administration Tel: 609-266-5243. FAX: 609-266-0040. *Librn,* Elizabeth Bliss
Founded 1983
Open Mon, Tues, Fri & Sat 9-5, Wed & Thurs 9-8
Friends of the Library Group
EGG HARBOR CITY BRANCH, 134 Philadelphia Ave, Egg Harbor City, 08215. Tel: 609-804-1063. FAX: 609-804-1082. *Librn,* Maura Monte
Open Mon, Wed, Fri & Sat 9-5, Tues & Thurs 12-8
EGG HARBOR TOWNSHIP BRANCH, One Swift Dr, Egg Harbor Township, 08234, SAN 320-9962. Tel: 609-927-8664. Administration Tel: 609-927-8671. FAX: 609-927-4683. *Librn,* Jean MacPherson
Open Mon-Thurs 9-8, Fri & Sat 9-5
Friends of the Library Group
GALLOWAY BRANCH, 306 E Jimmie Leeds Rd, Galloway, 08205, SAN 328-6754. Tel: 609-652-2352. FAX: 609-652-3613. *Librn,* Patricia Morrow
Founded 1970
Library Holdings: Bk Titles 8,000; Bk Vols 15,000
Open Mon-Thurs 9-8, Fri & Sat 9-5
Friends of the Library Group
HAMMONTON BRANCH, 451 Egg Harbor Rd, Hammonton, 08037, SAN 320-3603. Tel: 609-561-2264. FAX: 609-561-1816. *Librn,* Catherine Ostrum
Founded 1928
Library Holdings: Bk Vols 1,000
Open Mon-Thurs 10-8, Fri & Sat 9-5
Friends of the Library Group
LONGPORT BRANCH, 2305 Atlantic Ave, Longport, 08403, SAN 373-1901. Tel: 609-487-0272. FAX: 609-487-9521. *Librn,* Kathy Gindin
Founded 1990
Open Mon & Thurs 9-6, Wed 9-8, Fri & Sat 9-5
Friends of the Library Group
MAYS LANDING BRANCH, 40 Farragut Ave, 08330, SAN 321-818X. Tel: 609-625-2776. FAX: 609-625-8143. *Librn,* Donna Cameron
Founded 1926
Open Mon-Thurs 9-9, Fri & Sat 9-5
Friends of the Library Group

PLEASANTVILLE BRANCH, 33 Martin L King Jr Ave, Pleasantville, 08232, SAN 322-6018. Tel: 609-641-1778. FAX: 609-641-0771. *Librn,* Pamela Saunders
Founded 1955
Open Mon-Thurs 9-8, Fri & Sat 9-5
Friends of the Library Group
SOMERS POINT BRANCH, 801 Shore Rd, Somers Point, 08244, SAN 310-5040. Tel: 609-927-7113. FAX: 609-926-3062. *Librn,* Mary Jane Bolden
Founded 1906
Open Mon-Thurs 9-8, Fri & Sat 9-5
Friends of the Library Group
VENTNOR BRANCH, 6500 Atlantic Ave, Ventnor, 08406, SAN 320-3611. Tel: 609-823-4614. FAX: 609-823-2639. *Librn,* Ellen Eisen
Founded 1951
Open Mon-Thurs 9-8, Fri & Sat 9-5
Friends of the Library Group
Bookmobiles: 1

MAYWOOD

P MAYWOOD PUBLIC LIBRARY*, 459 Maywood Ave, 07607-1909. SAN 310-2777. Tel: 201-845-2915. FAX: 201-845-7387. E-mail: maywcirc@bccls.org. Web Site: maywood.bccls.org. *Assoc Dean, Tech & Learning Res, Dir,* Kulsum Quadri; E-mail: quadri@bccls.org
Founded 1951. Pop 9,523; Circ 84,000
Jan 2011-Dec 2011 Income $455,000. Mats Exp $80,268. Sal $271,023
Library Holdings: Bk Titles 61,140; Bk Vols 61,300; Per Subs 81
Automation Activity & Vendor Info: (Cataloging) SirsiDynix; (Circulation) SirsiDynix
Database Vendor: SirsiDynix
Wireless access
Open Mon-Wed 10-8, Thurs & Fri 10-5:30, Sat 10-4:30, Sun 1:30-4:30
Friends of the Library Group

MCGUIRE AFB

A UNITED STATES AIR FORCE*, John McGuire Air Force Base Library, 2603 Tuskegee Airmen Ave, 08641-5016. SAN 350-8560. Tel: 609-754-2079. Reference Tel: 609-754-5159. FAX: 609-754-5108. Web Site: www.mcguirelibrary.com. *Librn,* Mimi Cirillo; Staff 7 (MLS 2, Non-MLS 5)
Library Holdings: Bk Vols 72,000; Per Subs 230
Special Collections: Air Force History Coll
Subject Interests: Aviation, Mil hist, Quality mgt
Database Vendor: Gale Cengage Learning, OCLC FirstSearch, ProQuest
Wireless access
Function: Fax serv, ILL available
Open Mon-Thurs 10-8, Fri & Sun 12-5, Sat 10-5

MENDHAM

CR ASSUMPTION COLLEGE FOR SISTERS LIBRARY*, Mallinckrodt Convent, 350 Bernardsville Rd, 07945. SAN 310-2793. Tel: 973-543-6528, Ext 234. FAX: 973-543-1738. E-mail: acslibrary@acs350.org. *Dir,* Sister Theresa Bower; Staff 1 (MLS 1)
Founded 1961. Enrl 50; Fac 21; Highest Degree: Associate
Library Holdings: AV Mats 1,548; CDs 162; DVDs 166; Bk Titles 27,892; Bk Vols 28,300; Per Subs 91; Videos 868
Subject Interests: Philos, Theol
Automation Activity & Vendor Info: (Acquisitions) Follett Software; (Cataloging) Follett Software; (Circulation) Follett Software; (Course Reserve) Follett Software; (ILL) Follett Software; (Media Booking) Follett Software; (OPAC) Follett Software; (Serials) Follett Software
Database Vendor: EBSCOhost
Wireless access
Function: For res purposes, ILL available, Photocopying/Printing, Ref serv available
Publications: New Books Listing (Monthly)
Partic in LibraryLinkNJ, The New Jersey Library Cooperative; Virtual Academic Library Environment
Restriction: By permission only, Employees & their associates, Open by appt only, Open to fac, students & qualified researchers, Open to pub for ref & circ; with some limitations

P MENDHAM BOROUGH LIBRARY*, Ten Hilltop Rd, 07945. SAN 321-4931. Tel: 973-543-4152. FAX: 973-543-9096. Web Site: www.mendhamboroughlibrary.org. *Dir,* Janice Perrier; Staff 5 (MLS 1, Non-MLS 4)
Founded 1912. Pop 5,000
Library Holdings: AV Mats 1,000; DVDs 500; Large Print Bks 200; Bk Titles 25,000; Per Subs 100; Talking Bks 100; Videos 2,000
Special Collections: Books on Tape; Gardening Coll; Local History Coll; Mysteries Coll
Automation Activity & Vendor Info: (Cataloging) SirsiDynix; (Circulation) SirsiDynix; (OPAC) SirsiDynix
Database Vendor: EBSCOhost, ProQuest
Wireless access
Publications: Legacy Through the Lens; Library Notes (Newsletter); Mendham Poets
Partic in Morris Automated Information Network
Open Mon & Wed 9-8, Tues & Thurs 10-8, Fri 9-5, Sat 10-4
Friends of the Library Group

MERCHANTVILLE

P MERCHANTVILLE PUBLIC LIBRARY*, 130 S Centre St, 08109-2201. SAN 310-2823. Tel: 856-665-3128. FAX: 856-665-4296. Web Site: www.camdencountylibrary.org/merchantville. *Librn,* Eve Brown; Staff 1 (MLS 1)
Library Holdings: Bk Titles 4,500; Per Subs 60
Special Collections: Children's Materials; Local History
Automation Activity & Vendor Info: (Cataloging) Innovative Interfaces, Inc; (Circulation) Innovative Interfaces, Inc; (OPAC) Innovative Interfaces, Inc
Wireless access
Open Mon & Wed 2-9, Tues & Thurs 2-5, Sat 10:30-4
Friends of the Library Group

METUCHEN

P METUCHEN PUBLIC LIBRARY*, 480 Middlesex Ave, 08840. SAN 310-2831. Tel: 732-632-8526. FAX: 732-632-8535. Web Site: www.lmxac.org, www.metuchennj.org/library. *Dir,* Melody B Kokola; E-mail: mkokola@lmxac.org; *YA Librn,* Katherine Liss; *Adult Serv,* John McBride; *Ch Serv,* Glynis Brookens; *Ref,* Hsi Hsi Chung; Staff 4.5 (MLS 4.5)
Founded 1870. Pop 13,292; Circ 108,813
Jan 2009-Dec 2009 Income $863,740, State $13,021, City $816,043, Locally Generated Income $34,676. Mats Exp $90,519, Books $61,315, Per/Ser (Incl. Access Fees) $10,451, AV Mat $9,441, Electronic Ref Mat (Incl. Access Fees) $7,896. Sal $363,170
Library Holdings: Audiobooks 551; CDs 103; DVDs 1,355; Large Print Bks 1,200; Bk Vols 68,685; Per Subs 160; Videos 100
Special Collections: Chinese Language Coll; Large Print Coll. Oral History
Subject Interests: Genealogy, Literacy, Mystery
Automation Activity & Vendor Info: (Cataloging) SirsiDynix; (Circulation) SirsiDynix; (ILL) SirsiDynix; (OPAC) SirsiDynix
Database Vendor: EBSCOhost, Facts on File, ProQuest, ReferenceUSA, ValueLine
Wireless access
Function: Adult bk club, Art exhibits, Bks on CD, Children's prog, Computers for patron use, Copy machines, Exhibits, Handicapped accessible, Homebound delivery serv, Mail & tel request accepted, Mus passes, Music CDs, Online cat, Preschool outreach, Prog for adults, Prog for children & young adult, Pub access computers, Story hour, Summer reading prog, Teen prog, Telephone ref, Wheelchair accessible
Partic in Libraries of Middlesex Automation Consortium; LibraryLinkNJ, The New Jersey Library Cooperative
Special Services for the Deaf - Bks on deafness & sign lang; Deaf publ
Special Services for the Blind - Bks on CD; Info on spec aids & appliances; Large print bks; Magnifiers; Playaways (bks on MP3); Ref serv
Open Mon-Thurs (Winter) 10-9, Fri & Sat 10-5, Sun 1-5; Mon-Thurs (Summer) 10-9, Fri 10-5, Sat 10-1
Friends of the Library Group

MIDDLESEX

P MIDDLESEX PUBLIC LIBRARY*, 1300 Mountain Ave, 08846. SAN 310-284X. Tel: 732-356-6602. FAX: 732-356-8420. E-mail: info@middlesexlibrarynj.org. Web Site: www.middlesexlibrarynj.org. *Dir,* May Lein Ho; *Ch Serv,* Chrissy George; *Ref Serv,* Maryann Greczek; Staff 4 (MLS 4)
Founded 1963. Pop 13,717; Circ 74,282
Jan 2005-Dec 2005 Income $370,000. Sal $247,296
Library Holdings: Bks on Deafness & Sign Lang 12; Large Print Bks 350; Bk Titles 63,000; Per Subs 147
Database Vendor: TLC (The Library Corporation)
Partic in Libraries of Middlesex Automation Consortium
Open Mon & Wed 10-9, Tues & Thurs 1-9, Fri 10-5, Sat 10-2, Sun 1-5
Friends of the Library Group

MIDDLETOWN

P MIDDLETOWN TOWNSHIP PUBLIC LIBRARY*, 55 New Monmouth Rd, 07748. SAN 350-8749. Tel: 732-671-3700. Reference Tel: 732-671-3700, Ext 320, 732-671-3700, Ext 321. Administration Tel: 732-671-3703, Ext 311. FAX: 732-671-5839. Web Site: mtpl.org. *Libr Dir,* Susan O'Neal; Tel: 732-671-3700, Ext 315, E-mail: soneal@mtpl.org;

Head, Borrower Serv, Megan Wianecki; Tel: 732-671-3700, Ext 310, E-mail: mwianecki@mtpl.org; *Head, Ch,* Danielle Kootman; Tel: 732-671-3700, Ext 323, E-mail: dkootman@mtpl.org; *Head, Tech Serv, Ref,* Doreen Kallfisch; Tel: 732-671-3700, Ext 330, E-mail: dkallfisch@mtpl.org; *Adult Prog,* Alyssa Rosen; Tel: 732-671-3700, Ext 353, E-mail: arosen@mtpl.org; *ILL,* Pam Curchin; Tel: 732-671-3700, Ext 324, E-mail: pcurchin@mtpl.org; *Teen Serv,* Ellie Stobo; Tel: 732-671-3700, Ext 358, E-mail: pcurchin@mtpl.org; Staff 39.5 (MLS 13.5, Non-MLS 26)
Founded 1921. Pop 67,479
Jan 2010-Dec 2010 Income $3,985,097. Mats Exp $594,000. Sal $2,804,000
Library Holdings: Audiobooks 4,930; AV Mats 7,265; CDs 8,391; DVDs 17,687; e-books 6,302; Large Print Bks 2,890; Bk Titles 112,000; Bk Vols 225,000; Per Subs 200; Videos 6,000
Subject Interests: NJ mat
Automation Activity & Vendor Info: (Acquisitions) LibLime; (Cataloging) LibLime; (Circulation) LibLime; (ILL) LibLime; (OPAC) LibLime; (Serials) LibLime
Database Vendor: ABC-CLIO, Baker & Taylor, BWI, Comprise Technologies Inc, EBSCOhost, Facts on File, Gale Cengage Learning, LearningExpress, LexisNexis, Medline, Newsbank, OCLC FirstSearch, OCLC WorldShare Interlibrary Loan, Overdrive, Inc, ProQuest, ReferenceUSA, SirsiDynix, Wilson - Wilson Web
Wireless access
Function: Adult bk club, Art exhibits, Audiobks via web, Bk club(s), Bks on cassette, Bks on CD, CD-ROM, Children's prog, Computer training, Computers for patron use, Copy machines, e-mail serv, Electronic databases & coll, Exhibits, Free DVD rentals, Handicapped accessible, Holiday prog, ILL available, Magnifiers for reading, Music CDs, OverDrive digital audio bks, Photocopying/Printing, Prog for adults, Prog for children & young adult, Pub access computers, Ref & res, Senior computer classes, Spoken cassettes & DVDs, Story hour, Summer reading prog, Tax forms, Teen prog, Telephone ref, VHS videos, Video lending libr, Wheelchair accessible, Workshops
Open Mon-Thurs 9-9, Fri & Sat 9-5, Sun (Sept-June) 1-5
Restriction: Circ to mem only, Non-resident fee
Friends of the Library Group
Branches: 3
BAYSHORE, 180 Main St, Port Monmouth, 07758. (Mail add: 55 New Monmouth Rd, 07748), SAN 350-8773. Tel: 732-787-1568. *Br Mgr,* Carla Burdick
Library Holdings: Bk Vols 16,000
Open Mon & Wed 1-5 & 6-8, Tues & Thurs 1-5, Fri 9-12 & 1-5
Friends of the Library Group
LINCROFT BRANCH, 730 Newman Springs Rd, Lincroft, 07738. (Mail add: 55 New Mountain Rd, 07748), SAN 350-8803. Tel: 732-747-1140. *Br Mgr,* Eileen McGrath
Library Holdings: Bk Vols 17,000
Open Mon & Wed 1-5 & 6-8, Tues & Thurs 1-5, Fri 9-12 & 1-5
Friends of the Library Group
NAVESINK BRANCH, 149 Monmouth Ave, Navesink, 07752. (Mail add: 55 New Monmouth Rd, 07748), SAN 350-8838. Tel: 732-291-1120. *Br Mgr,* Grace Moschberger
Library Holdings: Bk Vols 16,500
Open Mon & Wed 1-5 & 6-8, Tues & Thurs 1-5, Fri 9-12 & 1-5
Friends of the Library Group

S MONMOUTH COUNTY PARK SYSTEM*, Elvin McDonald Horticultural Library, 352 Red Hill Rd, 07748. (Mail add: 805 Newman Springs Rd, Lincroft, 07738), SAN 323-6021. Tel: 732-671-6050. FAX: 732-671-6905.
Founded 1979
Library Holdings: Bk Titles 5,500; Per Subs 30; Videos 50
Subject Interests: Hort
Partic in LibraryLinkNJ, The New Jersey Library Cooperative

MIDLAND PARK

P MIDLAND PARK MEMORIAL LIBRARY, 250 Godwin Ave, 07432. SAN 310-2858. Tel: 201-444-2390. FAX: 201-444-2813. E-mail: mipkcirc@bccls.org. Web Site: www.midlandpark.bccls.org. *Ch,* Emily Myhren; Staff 5 (MLS 2, Non-MLS 3)
Founded 1937. Pop 7,047
Library Holdings: Bk Vols 55,000; Per Subs 110
Wireless access
Partic in Bergen County Cooperative Library System
Open Mon, Tues & Thurs 10-9, Wed, Fri & Sat 10-5
Friends of the Library Group

MILFORD

P HOLLAND FREE PUBLIC LIBRARY*, 129 Spring Mills Rd, 08848. SAN 310-2866. Tel: 908-995-4767. FAX: 908-995-4767. Web Site: www.hollandlibrary.org. *Dir,* Donna Longcor
Founded 1965. Pop 9,600; Circ 54,339
Library Holdings: Bk Vols 22,000; Per Subs 67
Special Collections: Large Print Coll
Automation Activity & Vendor Info: (Cataloging) Innovative Interfaces, Inc; (Circulation) Innovative Interfaces, Inc; (OPAC) Re:discovery Software, Inc
Wireless access
Publications: Library Links
Mem of Hunterdon County Library
Open Mon, Tues, Thurs & Fri 9-12 & 3-8, Sat 10-1
Friends of the Library Group

P MILFORD PUBLIC LIBRARY*, 40 Frenchtown Rd, 08848. (Mail add: PO Box F, 08848), SAN 310-2874. Tel: 908-995-4072. E-mail: library4072@verizon.net. Web Site: www.milfordnjlibrary.org. *Librn,* Jennifer Locke
Founded 1954. Pop 1,200; Circ 6,000
Library Holdings: Audiobooks 56; CDs 102; DVDs 325; Bk Vols 16,300; Per Subs 15
Wireless access
Function: Children's prog, Computers for patron use, Copy machines, Free DVD rentals, ILL available, Music CDs, Story hour
Open Mon 12-7, Tues 11-5, Wed 12-8, Thurs 11-8, Fri 10-1 & 5-8, Sat 10-1

MILLBURN

P MILLBURN FREE PUBLIC LIBRARY*, 200 Glen Ave, 07041. SAN 310-2912. Tel: 973-376-1006. FAX: 973-376-0104. Web Site: www.millburn.lib.nj.us. *Dir,* William Swinson; Tel: 973-376-1006, Ext 26, E-mail: bswinson@millburn.lib.nj.us; *Circ,* Diane Bratton; Tel: 973-376-1006, Ext 28, E-mail: diane@millburn.lib.nj.us; *Info Serv,* Susan Pober; Tel: 973-376-1006, Ext 17, E-mail: susan@millburn.lib.nj.us; *Tech Serv,* Luisa Porcella; Tel: 973-376-1006, Ext 21, E-mail: luisa@millburn.lib.nj.us; Staff 37 (MLS 13, Non-MLS 24)
Founded 1938. Pop 19,765; Circ 392,945
Library Holdings: Bk Titles 94,000; Bk Vols 110,000; Per Subs 150; Talking Bks 4,561
Automation Activity & Vendor Info: (Cataloging) SirsiDynix; (Circulation) SirsiDynix; (ILL) SirsiDynix; (OPAC) SirsiDynix
Database Vendor: EBSCOhost, Gale Cengage Learning, ProQuest, SirsiDynix
Wireless access
Open Mon-Thurs 9:30-8:45, Fri & Sat 9:30-5:15, Sun 1-4:45
Friends of the Library Group

MILLTOWN

P MILLTOWN PUBLIC LIBRARY*, 20 W Church St, 08850. SAN 310-2920. Tel: 732-247-2270. FAX: 732-745-9493. Web Site: www.lmxac.org/milltown. *Dir,* Bonnie Sterling; Staff 1 (MLS 1)
Founded 1896. Pop 7,000; Circ 53,000
Library Holdings: Bk Vols 45,000; Per Subs 70
Subject Interests: Local hist
Automation Activity & Vendor Info: (Cataloging) SirsiDynix; (Circulation) SirsiDynix; (ILL) SirsiDynix; (OPAC) SirsiDynix; (Serials) SirsiDynix
Wireless access
Open Mon, Tues & Thurs 10-9, Wed & Fri 10-5, Sat 10-3
Friends of the Library Group

MILLVILLE

P MILLVILLE PUBLIC LIBRARY, 210 Buck St, 08332. SAN 310-2939. Tel: 856-825-7087. FAX: 856-327-8572. Web Site: www.clueslibs.org. *Dir,* Susan D'Ottavio; E-mail: susando@millvillepubliclibrary.org
Founded 1864. Pop 28,600; Circ 64,000
Jul 2010-Jun 2011 Income $719,800, City $684,800, Other $35,000. Mats Exp $42,000. Sal $400,000
Library Holdings: Bk Titles 56,000; Per Subs 80
Special Collections: New Jersey Coll
Automation Activity & Vendor Info: (Cataloging) SirsiDynix; (Circulation) SirsiDynix; (OPAC) SirsiDynix
Wireless access
Partic in Cumberland Libraries United Electronic System (CLUES); LibraryLinkNJ, The New Jersey Library Cooperative
Open Mon-Thurs 10-8, Fri 10-5, Sat 10-4
Friends of the Library Group

S MUSEUM OF AMERICAN GLASS, Research Library, Wheaton Arts & Cultural Ctr, 1501 Glasstown Rd, 08332. SAN 370-3002. Tel: 856-825-6800, Ext 141. FAX: 856-825-2410. E-mail: museum@wheatonarts.org. Web Site: www.wheatonarts.org. *Dir, Exhibitions & Coll,* Kristin Qualls; *Curatorial Asst,* Dianne Wood
Library Holdings: Bk Vols 2,800
Special Collections: Charles B Gardner Coll; Glass Related Coll; Historical Documents & Photos

Subject Interests: Antiques
Restriction: Open by appt only

MONMOUTH BEACH

P MONMOUTH BEACH LIBRARY*, 18 Willow Ave, 07750. SAN 310-2947. Tel: 732-229-1187. Web Site: www.monmouthbeachlib.org. *Dir,* Judith Bakos; Staff 1 (MLS 1)
Pop 3,595; Circ 38,763
Library Holdings: AV Mats 1,000; Bk Vols 45,000; Per Subs 33
Special Collections: New Jersey Coll
Automation Activity & Vendor Info: (Cataloging) SirsiDynix; (Circulation) SirsiDynix
Wireless access
Mem of Monmouth County Library
Open Mon, Tues & Thurs 1-5 & 7-9, Wed & Fri 1-5, Sat 9-1
Friends of the Library Group

MONMOUTH JUNCTION

P SOUTH BRUNSWICK PUBLIC LIBRARY, 110 Kingston Lane, 08852. SAN 310-2955. Tel: 732-329-4000, Ext 7290. Reference Tel: 732-329-4000, Ext 7286. Administration Tel: 732-329-4000, Ext 7281. FAX: 732-329-0573. Web Site: www.sbpl.info. *Libr Dir,* Christopher Carbone; Tel: 732-329-4000, Ext 7287, E-mail: ccarbone@sbpl.info; *Head, Borrower Serv,* Judy Pietrobono; Tel: 732-329-4000, Ext 7295; *Head, Children's Dept,* Matt Kirschner; Tel: 732-329-4000, Ext 7285; *Head, Circ,* Judy Pietrobono; *Outreach Serv Librn,* Barbara Battles; Tel: 732-329-4000, Ext 7637; *Tech Librn,* Randy Marsola; Tel: 732-329-4000, Ext 7636; *Ref,* Mary Donne; Tel: 732-329-4000, Ext 7638; *Tech Serv,* Hai-Chin Chung; Tel: 732-329-4000, Ext 7284; *YA Serv,* Saleena Davidson; Tel: 732-329-4000, Ext 7634; Staff 12 (MLS 12)
Founded 1967. Pop 42,000; Circ 511,000
Library Holdings: AV Mats 11,681; Bk Vols 137,045; Per Subs 263; Spec Interest Per Sub 10
Subject Interests: Chinese, Local hist
Automation Activity & Vendor Info: (Acquisitions) SIRSI Unicorn; (Cataloging) SIRSI Unicorn; (Circulation) SIRSI Unicorn; (OPAC) SIRSI-iBistro
Database Vendor: EBSCOhost, Gale Cengage Learning
Wireless access
Publications: Calendar of Events; Compass Newsletter
Partic in Libraries of Middlesex Automation Consortium
Open Mon-Thurs 10-9, Fri 12-6, Sat 10-5, Sun 1-5
Friends of the Library Group
Bookmobiles: 1

MONROE TOWNSHIP

P MONROE TOWNSHIP PUBLIC LIBRARY*, Four Municipal Plaza, 08831-1900. SAN 375-5061. Tel: 732-521-5000. FAX: 732-521-4766. Web Site: www.monroetwplibrary.org. *Dir,* Irene Goldberg; Tel: 732-521-5000, Ext 107, E-mail: igoldberg@monroetwplibrary.org; *Asst Dir,* Leah Wagner; Tel: 732-521-5000, Ext 108, E-mail: lwagner@monroetwplibrary.org; *Head, Circ,* MaryAnn Reiner; Tel: 732-521-5000, Ext 101, E-mail: mreiner@monroetwplibrary.org; *Ch,* Lynnette Fucci; Tel: 732-521-5000, Ext 125; *Virtual Br Mgr,* Karen Klapperstuck; Tel: 732-521-5000, Ext 105; *Ref,* Susan Grotyohann; Tel: 732-521-5000, Ext 153, E-mail: sgrot@monroetwplibrary.org; *Ref,* Tyler Rousseau; Tel: 732-521-5000, Ext 123; *Ref,* Monica Teixeira; E-mail: mteixeira@monroetwplibrary.org; Staff 24 (MLS 8, Non-MLS 16)
Founded 1989. Pop 39,132; Circ 485,603
Jan 2011-Dec 2011 Income $3,295,887. Mats Exp $346,000, Books $300,000, Electronic Ref Mat (Incl. Access Fees) $46,000. Sal $1,839,290
Library Holdings: AV Mats 14,000; Large Print Bks 2,300; Bk Titles 90,700; Bk Vols 104,000; Per Subs 150
Special Collections: Holocaust (Henry Ricklis Memorial Coll), AV, bks
Automation Activity & Vendor Info: (Circulation) SirsiDynix
Wireless access
Partic in Libraries of Middlesex Automation Consortium
Special Services for the Deaf - Bks on deafness & sign lang; High interest/low vocabulary bks; Staff with knowledge of sign lang; TTY equip
Special Services for the Blind - Closed circuit TV magnifier; Large screen computer & software; Reader equip
Open Mon-Thurs 9:30-9, Fri 9:30-5, Sat 10-5, Sun 1-5
Friends of the Library Group
Bookmobiles: 1. Bk vols 2,000

MONTCLAIR

M HACKENSACKUMC MOUNTAINSIDE*, Health Sciences Library, One Bay Ave, 07042-4898. SAN 350-8986. Tel: 973-429-6240. FAX: 973-680-7850. Web Site: www.mountainsidenow.com. *Librn,* Narmin Kurzum; E-mail: narmin.kurzum@mountainsidehosp.com; Staff 2 (MLS 1, Non-MLS 1)
Library Holdings: Bk Titles 2,000; Per Subs 75
Subject Interests: Med, Nursing
Automation Activity & Vendor Info: (Acquisitions) Softlink America; (Cataloging) Softlink America; (Circulation) Softlink America; (Course Reserve) Softlink America; (ILL) Softlink America; (Media Booking) Softlink America; (OPAC) Softlink America; (Serials) Softlink America
Database Vendor: EBSCOhost, MD Consult, Medline, Micromedex, OVID Technologies, TDNet, UpToDate
Wireless access
Partic in Basic Health Sciences Library Network; LibraryLinkNJ, The New Jersey Library Cooperative; New Jersey Health Sciences Library Network
Open Mon-Fri 8-5

P MONTCLAIR FREE PUBLIC LIBRARY*, 50 S Fullerton Ave, 07042. SAN 350-8927. Tel: 973-744-0500, Ext 2226. FAX: 973-744-5268. Web Site: www.montlib.com. *Dir,* David Hinkley; *Fac Serv, Spec Projects,* Caroline Brown; *Ref Serv, Res Serv,* William T Fischer; *Youth Serv,* Maria LaBadia. Subject Specialists: *Local hist,* William T Fischer; Staff 49 (MLS 18, Non-MLS 31)
Founded 1893. Pop 38,977; Circ 312,676
Jan 2007-Dec 2007 Income (Main Library and Branch(s)) $4,064,962, State $50,184, City $3,848,749, Other $166,029. Mats Exp $397,274, Books $283,229, Per/Ser (Incl. Access Fees) $18,147, AV Mat $35,980, Electronic Ref Mat (Incl. Access Fees) $59,918. Sal $2,202,175
Library Holdings: Audiobooks 4,272; AV Mats 11,508; CDs 3,590; Bk Vols 169,730; Per Subs 277
Special Collections: Art & Music, bks, mss, repro & rec; College & Career; Delahinty Irish; Folk Arts; Howard Vogt Music; Montclair History, pictures & micro; Newberry & Caldecott
Automation Activity & Vendor Info: (Cataloging) Infor Library & Information Solutions; (Circulation) Infor Library & Information Solutions; (OPAC) Infor Library & Information Solutions
Wireless access
Function: Large print keyboards, Wheelchair accessible
Partic in Bergen County Cooperative Library System; LibraryLinkNJ, The New Jersey Library Cooperative
Special Services for the Deaf - Bks on deafness & sign lang; Closed caption videos; TTY equip
Special Services for the Blind - Braille equip; Talking bks
Open Mon-Thurs (Sept-June) 10-9, Fri & Sat 10-5, Sun 1-5; Mon-Thurs (Summer) 10-9, Fri 10-5, Sat & Sun 1-5
Friends of the Library Group
Branches: 1
BELLEVUE, 185 Bellevue Ave, Upper Montclair, 07043, SAN 350-8951. Tel: 973-744-2468. FAX: 973-744-3712. *Br Mgr,* Mary Lou Skillin
Founded 1914
Open Mon-Wed 1-6, Thurs 1-9, Fri & Sat 1-5
Friends of the Library Group

C MONTCLAIR STATE UNIVERSITY, Harry A Sprague Library, One Normal Ave, 07043-1699. SAN 310-5628. Tel: 973-655-4301. Circulation Tel: 973-655-4288. Interlibrary Loan Service Tel: 973-655-7143. Reference Tel: 973-655-4291. FAX: 973-655-7780. Web Site: www.montclair.edu/library. *Dean,* Dr Judith Lin Hunt; E-mail: huntjl@mail.montclair.edu; *Assoc Dean, Tech Serv,* Mary Mallery; Tel: 973-655-7150, E-mail: mallerym@mail.montclair.edu; *Head, Access Serv Dept, Syst Librn,* Denise O'Shea; Tel: 973-655-2098, E-mail: osheod@mail.montclair.edu; *Head, Cat, Metadata & Archival Serv,* Kathleen Hughes; Tel: 973-655-7077, E-mail: hughesk@mail.montclair.edu; *Head, Coll Develop & Acq Develop,* Suxiao Hu; Tel: 973-655-7151, E-mail: hus@mail.montclair.edu; *Head, Multimedia Res Dept,* Chung Lone; Tel: 973-655-7153, E-mail: lonec@mail.montclair.edu; *Head, Per,* Eduardo Gil; Tel: 973-655-5286, E-mail: gile@mail.montclair.edu; *Cat Librn,* Mei Ling Chow; Tel: 973-655-4422, E-mail: chowm@mail.montclair.edu; *Archivist, Cat Librn,* Paul Martinez; Tel: 973-655-3465, E-mail: martinezp@mail.montclair.edu; *Electronic Res Librn,* Steven Shapiro; Tel: 973-655-4428, E-mail: shapiros@mail.montclair.edu; *Govt Doc & Data Librn,* Darren L Sweeper; Tel: 973-655-7145, E-mail: sweeperd@mail.montclair.edu; *Online & Outreach Serv Librn,* Catherine Baird; Tel: 973-655-7144, E-mail: bairdc@mail.montclair.edu; *Ref Librn,* Laura Levy; Tel: 973-655-7148, E-mail: levyl@mail.montclair.edu; *Ref Librn,* Carol Nurse; Tel: 973-655-7667, E-mail: nursec@mail.montclair.edu; *ILL, Ref Librn,* Kevin Prendergast; E-mail: prendergask@mail.montclair.edu; Staff 21 (MLS 17, Non-MLS 4)
Founded 1908. Enrl 20,000; Fac 650; Highest Degree: Doctorate
Jul 2013-Jun 2014 Income $5,449,750. Mats Exp $1,461,099, Books $209,758, Per/Ser (Incl. Access Fees) $1,128,532, Manu Arch $1,000, AV Mat $32,451, Electronic Ref Mat (Incl. Access Fees) $85,653, Presv $3,705. Sal $2,874,120 (Prof $1,349,686)
Library Holdings: CDs 6,236; DVDs 5,358; e-books 25,840; e-journals 1,840; Electronic Media & Resources 232,825; Microforms 1,280,283; Music Scores 11,741; Bk Titles 443,328; Bk Vols 515,583; Per Subs 2,605; Videos 14,463
Special Collections: US Document Depository
Subject Interests: Communications, Modern poetry, Music, Philos, Speech, Teacher educ

Automation Activity & Vendor Info: (Acquisitions) OCLC; (Cataloging) OCLC; (Circulation) OCLC; (Course Reserve) OCLC; (ILL) OCLC WorldShare Interlibrary Loan; (OPAC) OCLC; (Serials) OCLC
Database Vendor: ACM (Association for Computing Machinery), Agricola, Alexander Street Press, Annual Reviews, ARTstor, BioOne, Cinahl, CredoReference, ebrary, EBSCO Discovery Service, EBSCOhost, Elsevier, Emerald, Hoovers, Ingenta, ISI Web of Knowledge, JSTOR, Knovel, LexisNexis, Marquis Who's Who, Medline, Mergent Online, Modern Language Association, OCLC, OCLC WorldShare Interlibrary Loan, OCLC Worldshare Management Services, Oxford Online, Project MUSE, ProQuest, PubMed, ReferenceUSA, Sage, ScienceDirect, SerialsSolutions, SirsiDynix, Springer-Verlag, Thomson - Web of Science, ValueLine, Westlaw
Wireless access
Function: Archival coll, Audio & video playback equip for onsite use, Copy machines, E-Reserves, Electronic databases & coll, Govt ref serv, Handicapped accessible, ILL available, Music CDs, Online cat, VHS videos, Wheelchair accessible
Partic in OCLC Online Computer Library Center, Inc; Virtual Academic Library Environment
Special Services for the Deaf - Bks on deafness & sign lang; Closed caption videos
Open Mon-Fri & Sun 12-12, Sat 9-5

R UNION CONGREGATIONAL CHURCH*, Schneidewind Library, 176 Cooper Ave, 07043. SAN 310-5636. Tel: 973-744-7424. FAX: 973-744-1364. E-mail: infoucc@unioncong.org. Web Site: www.unioncong.org. *Actg Librn,* Ann Ayre
Founded 1958
Library Holdings: Bk Vols 3,000
Subject Interests: Art, Biblical hist, Christian educ, Current affairs, Ecology, Mental health, Philos, Relig hist, Relig symbolism, Soc ethics, Theol
Wireless access
Open Mon-Fri 8-4
Restriction: Circ limited

MONTVALE

P MONTVALE FREE PUBLIC LIBRARY*, 12 Mercedes Dr, Ste 100, 07645. SAN 310-298X. Tel: 201-391-5090. FAX: 201-307-5647. E-mail: movlcirc@bccls.org. Web Site: montvale.bccls.org. *Dir,* Susan J Ruttenber; *Librn,* George R Galuschak; Staff 2 (MLS 2)
Founded 1975. Pop 7,844
Library Holdings: Bk Vols 75,180; Per Subs 134
Wireless access
Partic in Bergen County Cooperative Library System
Open Mon-Thurs 10-9, Fri & Sat 11-5, Sun 1-4
Friends of the Library Group

MONTVILLE

P MONTVILLE TOWNSHIP PUBLIC LIBRARY*, 90 Horseneck Rd, 07045-9626. SAN 310-3005. Tel: 973-402-0900. FAX: 973-402-0592. Web Site: www.montvillelib.org. *Dir,* Patricia K Anderson; *Ch Serv,* Ann Job; *ILL,* Sandy Calderone; *Prog Coordr, Ref Serv,* Ron Rizio; *Ref,* Elaine Reise; Staff 18 (MLS 8, Non-MLS 10)
Founded 1921. Pop 20,389; Circ 200,000
Jan 2007-Dec 2007 Income $1,700,000. Mats Exp $175,000, Books $155,000, AV Mat $20,000. Sal $695,433
Library Holdings: Bk Vols 95,000; Per Subs 150
Automation Activity & Vendor Info: (Cataloging) SirsiDynix; (Circulation) SirsiDynix; (ILL) JerseyCat; (OPAC) SirsiDynix
Database Vendor: SirsiDynix
Wireless access
Partic in Morris Automated Information Network; New Jersey Library Network
Open Mon, Tues & Thurs 10-9, Wed 1-9, Fri & Sat 10-5, Sun 1-5

MOORESTOWN

S HISTORICAL SOCIETY OF MOORESTOWN LIBRARY*, 12 High St, 08057. (Mail add: PO Box 477, 08057-0477), SAN 372-6762. Tel: 856-235-0353. E-mail: moorestownhistory@verizon.net. Web Site: www.moorestown.com/history. *Librn,* Stephanie Herz
Founded 1969
Library Holdings: Bk Titles 500; Bk Vols 550
Special Collections: Historic Buildings-House Index; Moorestown History & Genealogy. Oral History
Subject Interests: Manuscripts, Maps
Function: Photocopying/Printing
Open Tues 1-4
Restriction: Non-circulating

S LOCKHEED MARTIN*, Mission Systems & Sensors Engineering Library, 199 Borton Landing Rd, 08057-0927. (Mail add: PO Box 1027, 08057-1027), SAN 310-303X. Tel: 609-326-4750. FAX: 609-326-5301. *Librn,* Elisa Valenzuela; E-mail: elisa.valenzuela@lmco.com
Founded 1953
Library Holdings: Bk Titles 30,000; Per Subs 75
Subject Interests: Associated electronics, Bus sci, Computer sci, Electronics, Eng, Math, Mil strategy, Physics, Radar electronics
Automation Activity & Vendor Info: (Cataloging) EOS International; (Circulation) EOS International; (OPAC) EOS International
Wireless access
Partic in Dialog Corp; Interlibrary Users Association
Restriction: Staff use only

P MOORESTOWN PUBLIC LIBRARY*, 111 W Second St, 08057-2481. SAN 310-3021. Tel: 856-234-0333. FAX: 856-778-9536. E-mail: reference@moorestown.lib.nj.us. Web Site: www.moorestown.lib.nj.us. *Dir,* Joseph E Galbraith; *Sr Ref Librn,* Joanne parra; *Supvr, Circ,* Ann M DiBlasio; *Ch Serv,* Jennifer Dunne; *Ref Serv, Ad,* Maria Esche; *Teen Serv Librn,* Robin Guenther; Staff 18 (MLS 6, Non-MLS 12)
Founded 1853. Pop 20,000; Circ 180,470
Jan 2005-Dec 2005 Income $1,687,958, State $19,413, City $1,479,986, Locally Generated Income $58,744. Mats Exp $127,411, Books $102,038, Per/Ser (Incl. Access Fees) $11,413, Micro $4,000, AV Mat $5,670, Electronic Ref Mat (Incl. Access Fees) $4,290. Sal $821,740 (Prof $394,740)
Library Holdings: AV Mats 9,207; Bk Titles 119,297; Bk Vols 141,665; Per Subs 228
Automation Activity & Vendor Info: (Acquisitions) Innovative Interfaces, Inc; (Cataloging) Innovative Interfaces, Inc; (Circulation) Innovative Interfaces, Inc; (OPAC) Innovative Interfaces, Inc
Database Vendor: EBSCOhost, Factiva.com, Gale Cengage Learning, Newsbank, ProQuest, ReferenceUSA, Wilson - Wilson Web
Wireless access
Partic in LibraryLinkNJ, The New Jersey Library Cooperative
Open Mon-Thurs 9-9, Fri & Sat 9-5, Sun 1-5
Friends of the Library Group

MORGANVILLE

S NEW JERSEY SCOUT MUSEUM LIBRARY, 705 Ginesi Dr, 2nd Flr, 07751. Tel: 732-862-1282. FAX: 732-536-2850. Web Site: www.njscoutmuseum.org. *Librn,* Frederic C Pachman, V; *Curator,* Steven Buckley; E-mail: curator@njsm.com; Staff 2 (MLS 1, Non-MLS 1)
Founded 2004
Subject Interests: Boys Scouts of Am, Girls Scouts of Am, Order of the Arrow
Function: Archival coll, Photocopying/Printing, Ref & res
Publications: New Jersey Scout Museum Newsletter
Restriction: Authorized scholars by appt

MORRIS PLAINS

GM GREYSTONE PARK PSYCHIATRIC HOSPITAL, Health Science Library, 59 Koch Ave, 07950. SAN 310-1886. Tel: 973-538-1800, Ext 5262. *Actg Librn,* Stephanie Hendry; E-mail: stephanie.hendry@dhs.state.nj.us; Staff 1 (MLS 1)
Founded 1930
Library Holdings: Bks on Deafness & Sign Lang 13; DVDs 85; Bk Titles 1,930; Bk Vols 1,960; Per Subs 66; Spec Interest Per Sub 66; Videos 240
Subject Interests: Med, Nursing, Psychiat, Psychiat rehabilitation, Psychol
Automation Activity & Vendor Info: (Cataloging) Professional Software; (OPAC) Professional Software
Database Vendor: EBSCOhost
Function: ILL available
Partic in Basic Health Sciences Library Network; Docline; LibraryLinkNJ, The New Jersey Library Cooperative; New Jersey Health Sciences Library Network
Restriction: Open to others by appt, Open to staff only

P MORRIS PLAINS LIBRARY*, 77 Glenbrook Rd, 07950. SAN 310-3048. Tel: 973-538-2599. FAX: 973-538-8974. *Dir,* Camille Garretson; E-mail: camille.garretson@mainlib.org; Staff 1 (Non-MLS 1)
Founded 1881. Pop 5,700; Circ 32,947
Library Holdings: Large Print Bks 650; Bk Titles 22,576; Bk Vols 22,857; Per Subs 34
Wireless access
Open Tues & Thurs 10-7, Wed & Fri 10-5, Sat 10-2

S OLI SYSTEMS, INC LIBRARY*, 108 American Rd, 07950. SAN 375-846X. Tel: 973-539-4996. FAX: 973-539-5922. E-mail: olisys@worldnet.att.net. Web Site: www.olisystems.com. *Pres,* Marshall Rafal; Tel: 973-539-4996, Ext 21, E-mail: marshall.rafal@olisystems.com; *VPres,* Jane Rafal; *Librn, Per,* Peiming Wang; *Asst Librn,* Margaret Lencka
Founded 1990

Library Holdings: Bk Titles 1,000; Per Subs 40; Spec Interest Per Sub 20
Subject Interests: Chem, Computers, Eng
Restriction: Staff use only

MORRISTOWN

C COLLEGE OF SAINT ELIZABETH*, Mahoney Library, Two Convent Rd, 07960-6989. SAN 310-0936. Tel: 973-290-4237. Interlibrary Loan Service Tel: 973-290-4240. Reference Tel: 973-290-4248. FAX: 973-290-4226. Web Site: www.cse.edu. *Dir,* Amira Unver; Tel: 973-290-4233, E-mail: aunver@cse.edu; *Head, Info Serv,* Mina Ghajar; E-mail: mghajar@cse.edu; *Head, Ser Acq, Per,* Mark Ferguson; E-mail: mferguson@cse.edu; *Head, Tech Serv,* Bruce Marthaler; Tel: 973-290-4228, E-mail: bmarthaler@cse.edu; *Electronic Res Librn,* Amy Schleigh-Hayes; E-mail: aschleigh@cse.edu; *Evening/Weekend Librn,* Victoria Wollny; E-mail: vwollny@cse.edu; *ILL,* Robert Waks; Tel: 973-290-4240, E-mail: rwaks@cse.edu; *Ref,* Renita Krasnodebski; E-mail: rkrasnodebski@cse.edu; Staff 12 (MLS 8, Non-MLS 4)
Founded 1899. Highest Degree: Doctorate
Library Holdings: Bk Titles 108,000; Bk Vols 112,000; Per Subs 609
Special Collections: Atlases (Phillips Coll); History of Chemistry (Florence E Wall Coll); World War I (Henry C & Ann Fox Wolfe Coll), literary first & signed editions
Subject Interests: Econ, Educ, Lit, Nursing, Nutrition, Psychol, Theol
Automation Activity & Vendor Info: (Acquisitions) Ex Libris Group; (Cataloging) Ex Libris Group; (Circulation) Ex Libris Group; (Course Reserve) Ex Libris Group; (OPAC) Ex Libris Group; (Serials) Ex Libris Group
Database Vendor: ARTstor, Baker & Taylor, Dialog, EBSCOhost, Gale Cengage Learning, LexisNexis, OCLC FirstSearch, OVID Technologies, ProQuest, Wilson - Wilson Web
Wireless access
Partic in OCLC Online Computer Library Center, Inc; Virtual Academic Library Environment
Open Mon-Thurs 8:30am-9pm, Fri 8:30-5, Sat 10:30-5:30, Sun 2-6
Restriction: Authorized patrons, Authorized scholars by appt, Borrowing requests are handled by ILL, In-house use for visitors, Non-circulating of rare bks, Non-circulating to the pub

S IRISH-AMERICAN CULTURAL INSTITUTE LIBRARY*, One Lackawanna Pl, 07960. SAN 376-1592. Tel: 973-605-1991. FAX: 973-605-8875. E-mail: info@iaci-usa.org. Web Site: www.iaci-usa.org. *In Charge,* Carol Bucks
Library Holdings: Bk Titles 4,000; Bk Vols 4,500
Subject Interests: Culture, Irish, Irish hist, Politics, Sociol
Function: Res libr
Restriction: Non-circulating to the pub, Open by appt only

S MACCULLOCH HALL HISTORICAL MUSEUM ARCHIVES*, 45 Macculloch Ave, 07960. SAN 373-2525. Tel: 973-538-2404. FAX: 973-538-9428. E-mail: info@maccullochhall.org. Web Site: www.maccullochhall.org. *Curator,* Ryan Hyman; Staff 4 (Non-MLS 4)
Library Holdings: Bk Titles 1,500
Function: Res libr
Restriction: Open by appt only

L MCELROY, DEUTSCH, MULVANEY & CARPENTER, LLP*, Law Library, 1300 Mt Kemble Ave, 07962. Tel: 973-425-8810. FAX: 973-425-0161. Web Site: www.mdmc-law.com. *Dir,* Mary Ellen Kaas
Library Holdings: Bk Vols 10,000
Restriction: Not open to pub
Branches:
LAW LIBRARY, Three Gateway Ctr, 100 Mulberry St, Newark, 07102, SAN 372-4794. Tel: 973-622-7711, Ext 2065. FAX: 973-622-5314. *Librn,* Lucy Faris; *Librn,* Carrie Hayler
Library Holdings: Bk Vols 13,000
Restriction: Not open to pub

S MORRIS COUNTY HISTORICAL SOCIETY, 68 Morris Ave, 07960-4212. SAN 327-6333. Tel: 973-267-3465. FAX: 973-267-8773. E-mail: MCHSAcornHall@gmail.com. Web Site: www.acornhall.org. *Dir,* Amy E Curry; E-mail: directorMCHS@gmail.com; Staff 0.5 (MLS 0.5)
Library Holdings: DVDs 1; Bk Vols 2,700; Spec Interest Per Sub 5
Subject Interests: 19th Century life, 19th Century lit, 19th Century works of fiction & non-fiction, Morris County (NJ) hist
Restriction: Fee for pub use, Mem only, Not a lending libr, Open to pub with supv only, Open to researchers by request

GL MORRIS COUNTY LAW LIBRARY*, Court House, Eight Ann St, 07963-0900. (Mail add: PO Box 910, 07963-0910), SAN 310-3110. Tel: 973-656-3917. FAX: 973-656-3949. *Librn,* Peter DeLucia
Founded 1970
Library Holdings: Bk Vols 1,000
Function: Res libr
Open Mon-Fri 8-5

P THE MORRISTOWN & MORRIS TOWNSHIP LIBRARY, One Miller Rd, 07960. SAN 310-3099. Tel: 973-538-6161. FAX: 973-267-4064. Web Site: www.jfpl.org, www.morristownmorristwplibrary.info. *Dir,* Maria Norton; E-mail: maria.norton@mainlib.org; *Asst Dir,* Chad Leinaweaver; *Ch Serv,* Arlene Sprague; *Circ,* Ruth Bensley; *Per,* Tim Lynch; *Ref,* Mary Lynn Becza; *Tech Serv,* Jim Collins; Staff 1 (MLS 1)
Founded 1917. Pop 40,000; Circ 270,000
Library Holdings: Bk Vols 181,300; Per Subs 541
Special Collections: Manuscript Coll; Printing Coll; Topography, American History Coll. Oral History
Subject Interests: Arts, Astronomy, Genealogy, Local NJ hist, Rare children's bks
Wireless access
Publications: Early Printing in Morristown; In Lights & Shadows: Morristown in three centuries; Men from Morris County New Jersey who served in the American Revolution; Morris Township; New Jersey; New Jersey: A Glimpse into the past; Ordinary Days
Partic in Morris Automated Information Network
Open Mon-Thurs 9-9, Fri 9-6, Sat 9:30-5 (10-2 Jul & Aug), Sun 1-5
Friends of the Library Group
Branches: 1
NORTH JERSEY HISTORY & GENEALOGY CENTER, One Miller Rd, 07960. Tel: 973-538-3473. FAX: 973-267-4064. *Dir,* Maria S Norton; E-mail: maria.norton@mainlib.org; *Dept Head,* Christine Jochem; E-mail: christine.jochem@mainlib.org. Subject Specialists: *NJ hist,* Christine Jochem; Staff 5 (MLS 5)
Library Holdings: AV Mats 33,483; Electronic Media & Resources 12; Bk Vols 59,376; Per Subs 350
Special Collections: A B Frost Coll; Archival Colls, church, club, govt, local bus, orgn & sch recs, deeds, family & personal papers, hist presv res mat; Eastern US Genealogical Resources; Homer Davenport Coll; John DePol Coll; New Jersey Historical Material; Thomas Nast Coll
Function: Ref & res
Open Mon-Thurs 9-9, Fri 9-6, Sat 9:30-5 (10-2 July & Aug), Sun 1-5
Restriction: Non-circulating coll
Friends of the Library Group
Bookmobiles: 1

R MORRISTOWN JEWISH CENTER*, Beit Yisrael Library, 177 Speedwell Ave, 07960-3891. SAN 310-3137. Tel: 973-538-9292, 973-538-9293. FAX: 973-538-3229. *Head of Libr,* Barbra Kavadies
Founded 1967
Library Holdings: Bk Titles 7,500
Subject Interests: Art, Biographies, Hist, Holocaust, Israel, Judaica, Lang, Relig studies
Partic in NJ NW Regional Libr Coop
Restriction: Mem only
Friends of the Library Group

M MORRISTOWN MEMORIAL HOSPITAL MEDICAL LIBRARY*, Shinn-Lathrope Health Sciences Library, 100 Madison Ave, 07962. SAN 320-3972. Tel: 973-971-8926. FAX: 973-290-7045. E-mail: library.mmh@atlantichealth.org. Web Site: library.ahsys.org. *Mgr,* Mary K Joyce; Staff 3 (MLS 2, Non-MLS 1)
Founded 1952
Library Holdings: Bk Titles 5,000; Per Subs 270
Special Collections: Consumer Health
Subject Interests: Dentistry, Med, Nursing
Automation Activity & Vendor Info: (Cataloging) Softlink America; (Circulation) Softlink America
Wireless access
Partic in Basic Health Sciences Library Network; Health Sci Libr Asn of NJ; LibraryLinkNJ, The New Jersey Library Cooperative
Open Mon-Fri 7-5

S NATIONAL PARK SERVICE*, Morristown National Historical Park Library, 30 Washington Pl, 07960-4299. SAN 310-3145. Tel: 973-539-2313, Ext 204. FAX: 973-451-9212. Web Site: www.nps.gov/morr. *Curator,* Jude Pfister; E-mail: jude_pfister@nps.gov; Staff 1 (Non-MLS 1)
Founded 1933
Jul 2005-Jun 2006. Mats Exp $1,200, Books $1,000, Presv $200
Library Holdings: Bk Titles 16,000; Bk Vols 45,000; Per Subs 83
Special Collections: Ford Papers, ms; Hessian Document Coll; Lloyd W Smith Coll; Park Coll, ms; Washington Association of New Jersey Records
Subject Interests: 18th Century Am life, 18th Century culture, Am Revolutionary War, European cultural political hist 15th-20th century, George Washington
Publications: A Guide to the Manuscript Collection of Morristown National Historical Park; Guide to Hessian Documents of the American Revolution 1776-1783; Morristown National Historical Park Library Brochure; Orderly Books of the American Revolution in the Morristown National Historical Park Library

Open Mon-Thurs 1-4
Restriction: Non-circulating, Open by appt only
Friends of the Library Group

S PASSAIC RIVER COALITION*, Environmental Library, 330 Speedwell Ave, 07960. SAN 329-0409. Tel: 973-532-9830. FAX: 973-889-9172. E-mail: prcwater@aol.com. Web Site: www.passaicriver.org. *Acq, Adminr,* Ella F Filippone
Founded 1971
Library Holdings: Bk Vols 3,500; Per Subs 40

L PORZIO, BROMBERG & NEWMAN LIBRARY*, 100 Southgate Pkwy, 07962-1997. SAN 372-4360. Tel: 973-538-4006. FAX: 973-538-5146. Web Site: www.pbnlaw.com. *Librn,* Janice Schouten; Tel: 973-889-4368, E-mail: jmschouten@pbnlaw.com; Staff 1 (MLS 1)
Library Holdings: Bk Vols 10,000; Per Subs 75
Open Mon-Fri 9-5
Restriction: Staff use only

C RABBINICAL COLLEGE OF AMERICA*, Hoffman Memorial Library, 226 Sussex Ave, 07960-3600. (Mail add: PO Box 1996, 07962-1996), SAN 375-8478. Tel: 973-267-9404. FAX: 973-267-5208. E-mail: info@rca.edu.
Library Holdings: Bk Vols 17,000; Per Subs 50
Special Collections: Judaica Coll, cassettes
Subject Interests: Hebrew, Talmud

L RIKER, DANZIG, SCHERER, HYLAND & PERRETTI*, Law Library, Headquarters Plaza, One Speedwell Ave, 07962. SAN 372-476X. Tel: 973-538-0800. FAX: 973-538-1984. *Dir of Libr Serv,* Karen Brunner; E-mail: kbrunner@riker.com; *Res Librn,* Anne Shulman
Library Holdings: Bk Vols 5,000
Restriction: Staff use only

MOUNT ARLINGTON

P MOUNT ARLINGTON PUBLIC LIBRARY*, 333 Howard Blvd, 07856-1196. SAN 310-317X. Tel: 973-398-1516. FAX: 973-398-0171. Web Site: www.gti.net/mountarlington. *Dir,* Tina Mayer; Staff 1 (Non-MLS 1)
Founded 1968. Pop 5,050; Circ 19,845
Library Holdings: Bk Vols 25,000; Per Subs 50
Automation Activity & Vendor Info: (Acquisitions) Innovative Interfaces, Inc; (Cataloging) Innovative Interfaces, Inc; (Circulation) Innovative Interfaces, Inc; (OPAC) Innovative Interfaces, Inc; (Serials) Innovative Interfaces, Inc
Wireless access
Partic in Morris Automated Information Network
Open Mon-Thurs 12-8, Fri 12-4, Sat 9-3

MOUNT HOLLY

P MOUNT HOLLY PUBLIC LIBRARY*, 307 High St, 08060. SAN 310-3196. Tel: 609-267-7111. Web Site: www.mtholly.bcls.lib.nj.us. *Dir,* Michael Eck; Staff 8 (MLS 2, Non-MLS 6)
Founded 1765. Pop 12,713; Circ 28,000
Library Holdings: Bk Titles 5,000; Per Subs 10
Special Collections: Burlington County Lyceum; Genealogical Papers (Nathan Dunn Coll), rare bks & archives; Historical Materials (Bridgeton Coll); Indians of North America Coll (William Slaughter Coll), bks & rec; King George III 1765 Charter; Local History (Shinn Coll), bks, letters, photo, personal papers; Robert Mills' Architectural Plans for Burlington Jail and Treatise on Prison Reform
Subject Interests: Children's bks, County hist, Humanities, Local hist
Automation Activity & Vendor Info: (Cataloging) SirsiDynix; (Circulation) SirsiDynix; (OPAC) SirsiDynix
Wireless access
Mem of Burlington County Library
Partic in Burlington Libraries Information Consortium
Open Mon & Tues 10-7, Wed-Fri 10-6, Sat (Sept-June) 10-2
Friends of the Library Group

M VIRTUA MEMORIAL HOSPITAL OF BURLINGTON COUNTY*, L B Reagan Health Sciences Library, 175 Madison Ave, 08060. SAN 310-320X. Tel: 609-267-0700, Ext 43021. FAX: 609-267-8073. *Health Sci Librn,* Maura Sostack; E-mail: msostack@virtua.org
Founded 1958
Library Holdings: Bk Vols 300; Per Subs 80
Subject Interests: Allied health, Clinical med, Nursing
Database Vendor: EBSCO Information Services, EBSCOhost, Elsevier, MD Consult, Medline, OVID Technologies, PubMed, TDNet, UpToDate
Wireless access
Partic in Basic Health Sciences Library Network; LibraryLinkNJ, The New Jersey Library Cooperative
Restriction: Hospital employees & physicians only

MOUNT LAUREL

L CAPEHART & SCATCHARD, PA LIBRARY*, 8000 Midlantic Dr, Ste 300 S, 08054. SAN 323-6498. Tel: 856-234-6800, Ext 2151. FAX: 856-235-2786. Web Site: www.capehart.com. *Librn,* Francine Viden
Library Holdings: Bk Titles 367; Bk Vols 8,600; Per Subs 32
Wireless access
Open Mon-Fri 8:30-4

P MOUNT LAUREL LIBRARY, 100 Walt Whitman Ave, 08054. SAN 310-3218. Tel: 856-234-7319. FAX: 856-234-6916. Web Site: www.mtlaurel.lib.nj.us. *Dir,* Kathy Schalk-Greene; Tel: 856-234-7319, Ext 304, E-mail: kathy@mtlaurel.lib.nj.us; *Head, Adult Serv,* Joan Serpico; E-mail: jserpico@mtlaurel.lib.nj.us; *Head, Circ,* Angelika Kuntz; E-mail: angel@mtlaurel.lib.nj.us; *Head, Youth Serv,* Samantha Marker; E-mail: smarker@mtlaurel.lib.nj.us; *Syst Coordr,* Becky Boydston; E-mail: becky@mtlaurel.lib.nj.us; Staff 28 (MLS 10, Non-MLS 18)
Founded 1970. Pop 42,000; Circ 821,244
Jan 2014-Dec 2014 Income $2,256,703, State $18,371, City $2,127,632, Locally Generated Income $110,700. Mats Exp $290,000, Books $129,500, Per/Ser (Incl. Access Fees) $11,500, AV Mat $130,000, Electronic Ref Mat (Incl. Access Fees) $19,000. Sal $986,500 (Prof $50,082)
Library Holdings: AV Mats 60,086; Bk Vols 93,232; Per Subs 251
Automation Activity & Vendor Info: (Acquisitions) SirsiDynix; (Cataloging) SirsiDynix; (Circulation) SirsiDynix; (ILL) SirsiDynix; (OPAC) SirsiDynix; (Serials) SirsiDynix
Database Vendor: SirsiDynix
Wireless access
Publications: Newsletter
Partic in LibraryLinkNJ, The New Jersey Library Cooperative
Open Mon-Thurs 9:30-9, Fri 9:30-7, Sat 9:30-5, Sun 12-5
Friends of the Library Group

MOUNTAIN LAKES

P MOUNTAIN LAKES FREE PUBLIC LIBRARY*, Nine Elm Rd, 07046-1316. SAN 310-3226. Tel: 973-334-5095. FAX: 973-299-1622. Web Site: www.mtnlakes.org/library. *Dir,* Margaret J Bulfer; E-mail: peggy.bulfer@main.lib.org
Founded 1914. Pop 4,256; Circ 61,413
Library Holdings: Bk Vols 42,000; Per Subs 35
Automation Activity & Vendor Info: (Cataloging) SirsiDynix; (Circulation) SirsiDynix; (OPAC) SirsiDynix
Database Vendor: EBSCOhost, ProQuest
Partic in Morris Automated Information Network
Open Mon & Wed 9-9, Tues, Thurs & Fri 9-5, Sat 9-2
Friends of the Library Group

MOUNTAINSIDE

M CHILDREN'S SPECIALIZED HOSPITAL*, Medical Library & Family Resource Center, 150 New Providence Rd, 07092. SAN 375-6955. Tel: 908-233-3720, Ext 5227. FAX: 908-301-5569. Web Site: www.childrens-specialized.org. *Med Librn,* Lyudmila Lungin; E-mail: llungin@childrens-specialized.org; Staff 2 (MLS 1, MLS 1)
Library Holdings: DVDs 15; e-books 110; e-journals 40; Bk Titles 2,000; Per Subs 80; Videos 60
Subject Interests: Autism, Pediatric neurology, Pediatrics orthopedics, Rehabilitation
Automation Activity & Vendor Info: (Cataloging) LibraryWorld, Inc; (Circulation) LibraryWorld, Inc; (Course Reserve) EBSCO Online; (OPAC) LibraryWorld, Inc; (Serials) LibraryWorld, Inc
Database Vendor: EBSCO Information Services, EBSCOhost, McGraw-Hill, MD Consult
Partic in Basic Health Sciences Library Network; Cosmopolitan Biomedical Library Consortium; New Jersey Health Sciences Library Network
Open Mon & Tues 9-4, Wed-Fri 9-3

P MOUNTAINSIDE PUBLIC LIBRARY*, Constitution Plaza, 07092. SAN 310-3234. Tel: 908-233-0115. FAX: 908-232-7311. E-mail: info@mountainsidelibrary.org. Web Site: www.mountainsidelibrary.org. *Dir,* Lynn Favreau; E-mail: favreau@mountainsidelibrary.org; Staff 9.5 (MLS 2.5, Non-MLS 7)
Founded 1934. Pop 6,657; Circ 75,902
Jan 2008-Dec 2008 Income $681,596, State $6,695, City $644,036, Other $30,865. Mats Exp $118,758, Books $80,082, Per/Ser (Incl. Access Fees) $9,500, AV Mat $15,390, Electronic Ref Mat (Incl. Access Fees) $13,786. Sal $276,850 (Prof $134,768)
Library Holdings: CDs 2,000; DVDs 2,440; Bk Titles 55,833; Bk Vols 58,276; Per Subs 50; Talking Bks 1,210
Automation Activity & Vendor Info: (Cataloging) SirsiDynix; (Circulation) SirsiDynix; (ILL) JerseyCat; (OPAC) SirsiDynix
Database Vendor: Baker & Taylor, CountryWatch, EBSCOhost, Facts on File, Grolier Online, ProQuest, PubMed, SirsiDynix
Wireless access

Function: Computers for patron use, Copy machines, Electronic databases & coll, Fax serv, ILL available, Magnifiers for reading, Music CDs, Notary serv, Prog for adults, Prog for children & young adult, Ref serv in person, Scanner, Story hour, Summer reading prog, Tax forms, Teen prog, Wheelchair accessible
Publications: Annual Report; e-Newsletter (Monthly); Friends' Newsletter (Annual)
Partic in LibraryLinkNJ, The New Jersey Library Cooperative; MURAL
Special Services for the Deaf - Closed caption videos
Special Services for the Blind - Bks on CD; Large print bks; Magnifiers; ZoomText magnification & reading software
Open Mon-Thurs 10-9, Fri 10-5, Sat (Sept-June) 10-5
Friends of the Library Group

MULLICA HILL

S EDUCATIONAL INFORMATION & RESOURCE CENTER*, 107 Gilbreth Pkwy, Ste 200, 08062. SAN 375-3409. Tel: 856-582-7000. FAX: 856-582-4206. Web Site: www.eirc.org. *Mgr, Libr Serv,* Julie Kratchman; Tel: 856-582-7000, Ext 148, E-mail: julie.kratchman@doe.state.nj.us. Subject Specialists: *Spec educ,* Julie Kratchman; Staff 6 (Non-MLS 6)
Founded 1969
Jul 2006-Jun 2007. Mats Exp AV Mat $6,000
Library Holdings: Bks on Deafness & Sign Lang 25; Bk Titles 10,000; Spec Interest Per Sub 30
Subject Interests: Spec educ
Wireless access
Function: For res purposes, Games & aids for the handicapped, Handicapped accessible, Online searches, Photocopying/Printing, Prof lending libr, Prog for adults, Ref serv available, Res libr, Telephone ref, Wheelchair accessible, Workshops
Partic in LibraryLinkNJ, The New Jersey Library Cooperative
Open Mon, Wed & Fri 9-5, Tues & Thurs 9-8
Restriction: Open to pub for ref & circ; with some limitations

P GLOUCESTER COUNTY LIBRARY SYSTEM, Mullica Hill Branch, 389 Wolfert Station Rd, 08062. SAN 321-0820. Tel: 856-223-6000. Circulation Tel: 856-223-6060. Interlibrary Loan Service Tel: 856-223-6044. Reference Tel: 856-223-6050. FAX: 856-223-6039. E-mail: reference@gcls.org. Web Site: www.gcls.org. *Dir,* Anne Wodnick; Tel: 856-223-6010, E-mail: awodnick@gcls.org; *Head, Ref & Digital Serv,* Ralph Bingham; Tel: 856-223-6045, E-mail: rbingham@gcls.org; *Head, Info Tech,* Karen Shiles; Tel: 856-223-6019, E-mail: karen@gcls.org; *Head, Pub Serv,* Brenda Muhlbaier; Tel: 856-223-6041, E-mail: bmuhlbaier@gcls.org; *Head, Tech Serv,* Linda Gentile; Tel: 856-223-6013, E-mail: lgentile@gcls.org; Staff 69 (MLS 9, Non-MLS 60)
Founded 1976. Pop 84,380; Circ 504,118
Automation Activity & Vendor Info: (Acquisitions) SirsiDynix; (Cataloging) SirsiDynix; (Circulation) SirsiDynix; (OPAC) SirsiDynix; (Serials) SirsiDynix
Database Vendor: Baker & Taylor, EBSCO Discovery Service, EBSCOhost, Evanced Solutions, Inc, Facts on File, Gale Cengage Learning, Newsbank, SerialsSolutions
Wireless access
Function: Homebound delivery serv
Partic in LibraryLinkNJ, The New Jersey Library Cooperative; LOGIN (Libraries of Gloucester, Salem & Cumberland Information Network)
Special Services for the Deaf - Assistive tech; Closed caption videos; TDD equip
Special Services for the Blind - Audio mat; Large print bks; Talking bks
Open Mon-Thurs 10-9, Fri 10-5, Sat 10-5 (10-2 June-Labor Day), Sun (Sept-May) 1-5
Friends of the Library Group
Branches: 5
GLASSBORO BRANCH, Two Center St, Glassboro, 08028-1995, SAN 350-7513. Tel: 856-881-0001, 856-881-5571. FAX: 856-881-9338. *Br Mgr,* Bryan Bonfiglio; E-mail: bbonfiglio@gcls.org; *Youth Serv Librn,* Darby Malvey; E-mail: dmalvey@gcls.org; Staff 8.5 (MLS 2, Non-MLS 6.5)
Founded 1956
Open Mon-Thurs 10-9, Fri 10-5, Sat 10-2
GREENWICH TOWNSHIP BRANCH, 411 Swedesboro Rd, Gibbstown, 08027, SAN 310-1800. Tel: 856-423-0684. FAX: 856-423-1201. *Br Mgr,* Patricia Collins; E-mail: pcollins@gcls.org; Staff 5 (MLS 1, Non-MLS 4)
Pop 5,333; Circ 36,436
Open Mon-Thurs 10-9, Fri 10-5, Sat 10-2
LOGAN TOWNSHIP BRANCH, 498 Beckett Rd, Logan Township, 08085, SAN 376-9313. Tel: 856-241-0202. FAX: 856-241-0491. *Br Mgr,* Carolyn Oldt; Staff 5.5 (MLS 1, Non-MLS 4.5)
Founded 1979
Open Mon-Thurs 10-9, Fri 10-5, Sat 10-2
NEWFIELD PUBLIC, 115 Catawba Ave, Newfield, 08344-9511, SAN 310-3617. Tel: 856-697-0415. FAX: 856-697-1544. E-mail: newfieldlibrary@hotmail.com. *Mgr,* Carol Baughman; E-mail: cbaughman@gcls.org; Staff 3 (Non-MLS 3)
Founded 1876
Library Holdings: Bk Titles 22,379; Bk Vols 23,207; Per Subs 24
Open Mon-Thurs 10-7, Fri 10-5, Sat 10-1
SWEDESBORO BRANCH, 1442 Kings Hwy, Swedesboro, 08085, SAN 310-527X. Tel: 856-467-0111. FAX: 856-241-0594. *Br Mgr,* Marge Dombrosky; E-mail: mdombrosky@gcls.org
Pop 2,000; Circ 18,592
Subject Interests: Local hist
Open Mon-Thurs 10-8, Fri 10-5, Sat 10-2

NEPTUNE

M JERSEY SHORE UNIVERSITY MEDICAL CENTER*, Booker Health Sciences Library, 1945 Rte 33, 07754-0397. SAN 310-3269. Tel: 732-776-4265. FAX: 732-776-4530. E-mail: jsumclibrary@meridianhealth.com. *Coordr,* Catherine Mary Boss; Tel: 732-776-4266, E-mail: cboss@meridianhealth.com; *Syst Coordr,* Chunwei Ma; E-mail: cma@meridianhealth.com; *Ref,* Darlene Robertelli; E-mail: drobertelli@meridianhealth.com; Staff 3 (MLS 2, Non-MLS 1)
Library Holdings: AV Mats 1,000; Bk Vols 5,300; Per Subs 325
Special Collections: ANA Publications; NLN Publications
Subject Interests: Consumer health, Med, Nursing
Automation Activity & Vendor Info: (Acquisitions) Ex Libris Group; (Cataloging) Ex Libris Group; (Circulation) Ex Libris Group; (OPAC) Ex Libris Group; (Serials) Ex Libris Group
Database Vendor: Cinahl, EBSCOhost, Medline, OVID Technologies, PubMed, RefWorks, UpToDate
Wireless access
Publications: Journal Holdings List; Library Brochure
Partic in Basic Health Sciences Library Network; National Network of Libraries of Medicine; New Jersey Health Sciences Library Network
Open Mon-Fri 9-5

P NEPTUNE PUBLIC LIBRARY, 25 Neptune Blvd, 07753-1125. SAN 310-3277. Tel: 732-775-8241. FAX: 732-774-1132. E-mail: info@neptunepubliclibrary.org. Web Site: www.neptunepubliclibrary.org. *Dir,* Marian R Bauman; E-mail: mbauman@neptunepubliclibrary.org; *Asst Dir,* John Bonney; E-mail: jbonney@neptunepubliclibrary.org; *Sr Librn,* Sandra Michlich; E-mail: smichlich@neptunepubliclibrary.org; *Syst Adminr,* Krista Horan; E-mail: khoran@neptunepubliclibrary.org; *Youth Serv,* Cheryl Otten; E-mail: cherylotten@yahoo.com; Staff 11 (MLS 5, Non-MLS 6)
Founded 1924. Pop 27,935; Circ 150,000
Library Holdings: Bk Vols 75,000; Per Subs 104
Special Collections: Neptune Archive (Local History). Municipal Document Depository
Automation Activity & Vendor Info: (Cataloging) SirsiDynix; (Circulation) SirsiDynix; (OPAC) SirsiDynix
Database Vendor: EBSCOhost
Wireless access
Partic in LibraryLinkNJ, The New Jersey Library Cooperative
Special Services for the Blind - Bks on CD
Open Mon, Wed, Fri & Sat 9-5, Tues & Thurs 12-8; Sat (Summer) 9-1
Friends of the Library Group

NEPTUNE CITY

P NEPTUNE CITY LIBRARY*, 106 W Sylvania Ave, 07753. Tel: 732-988-8866. Web Site: www.neptunecity.lib.nj.us. *Dir,* Patty Scott
Library Holdings: AV Mats 100; DVDs 850; Large Print Bks 150; Bk Vols 13,000; Videos 250
Automation Activity & Vendor Info: (Cataloging) SirsiDynix; (Circulation) SirsiDynix; (OPAC) SirsiDynix
Wireless access
Mem of Monmouth County Library
Open Mon & Tues 10-8, Wed & Thurs 1-8, Fri & Sat 10-1
Friends of the Library Group

NEW BRUNSWICK

S JEWISH HISTORICAL SOCIETY OF CENTRAL JERSEY LIBRARY*, 222 Livingston Ave, 08901. SAN 376-0529. Tel: 732-249-4894. FAX: 732-745-7448. E-mail: info.jhscj@gmail.com. Web Site: www.jewishgen.org/jhscj. *Librn & Archivist,* Deborah Cohn; Staff 1 (MLS 1)
Founded 1977
Library Holdings: Bk Vols 807
Special Collections: NJ Jewish Organization Documents. Oral History
Subject Interests: Genealogy, Jewish hist
Function: Archival coll, For res purposes, Res libr
Publications: Newsletter (Quarterly)
Open Mon-Fri 9-1
Restriction: Not a lending libr

S JOHNSON & JOHNSON*, Corporate Communications Library, One Johnson & Johnson Plaza, 08933. SAN 375-6947. Tel: 732-524-3690. FAX: 732-524-3564. *Mgr,* Position Currently Open
Library Holdings: Bk Vols 400; Per Subs 50
Open Mon-Fri 9-5
Restriction: Not open to pub

S MIDDLESEX COUNTY CULTURAL & HERITAGE COMMISSION*, Resource & Reference Library, 703 Jersey Ave, 08901. SAN 375-6998. Tel: 732-745-4489. FAX: 732-745-4524. TDD: 732-745-3888. E-mail: culturalandheritage@co.middlesex.nj.us. Web Site: co.middlesex.nj.us/culturalheritage. *Exec Dir,* Anna Aschkenes; Staff 17 (Non-MLS 17)
Founded 1995
Library Holdings: Bk Titles 2,000
Subject Interests: Archaeology, Archit, Art educ, Folklife, Fundraising, Historic sites, Local hist, NJ hist, Nonprofit mgt
Function: Handicapped accessible
Special Services for the Deaf - TTY equip
Open Mon-Fri 8:30-4:15
Restriction: Open to pub for ref & circ; with some limitations

GL MIDDLESEX COUNTY LAW LIBRARY*, 56 Patterson St, 08901. SAN 310-3293. Tel: 732-519-3452. FAX: 732-519-3454. *Dir,* Betty Agin
Library Holdings: Bk Vols 5,000
Open Mon-Fri 8:30-4
Restriction: Non-circulating to the pub

P NEW BRUNSWICK FREE PUBLIC LIBRARY*, 60 Livingston Ave, 08901-2597. SAN 310-3315. Tel: 732-745-5108. Reference Tel: 732-745-5108, Ext 20. Administration Tel: 732-745-5108, Ext 14. FAX: 732-846-0226. E-mail: nbfpl@lmxac.org. Web Site: www.nbfpl.org. *Dir,* Robert Belvin; Tel: 732-745-5721, E-mail: bbelvin@lmxac.org; *Principal Librn,* Linda Crittenden; *Youth Serv Coordr,* Camille Thompson; Tel: 732-745-5108, Ext 32; *Ch Serv,* Darby DeCicco; Tel: 732-745-5108, Ext 15; *Ref Serv,* Hsien-min Chen; *Tech Serv,* Iren Ruschak; E-mail: iren@lmxac.org; *YA Serv,* Rosy Henderson; Tel: 732-745-5108, Ext 22; Staff 8 (MLS 8)
Founded 1883. Pop 48,500; Circ 84,000
Jan 2008-Dec 2008 Income $1,660,925, State $57,925, City $1,560,000, Locally Generated Income $33,000, Other $10,000. Mats Exp $125,000, Books $85,500, Per/Ser (Incl. Access Fees) $16,000, AV Mat $16,200, Electronic Ref Mat (Incl. Access Fees) $7,300. Sal $1,010,000
Library Holdings: Bk Vols 80,000; Per Subs 254
Special Collections: State Document Depository
Subject Interests: Hungarian, Local hist
Automation Activity & Vendor Info: (Circulation) SirsiDynix; (OPAC) SirsiDynix
Database Vendor: EBSCOhost
Wireless access
Partic in Libraries of Middlesex Automation Consortium
Open Mon-Thurs 10-9, Fri & Sat 10-5, Sun 1-5
Friends of the Library Group

R NEW BRUNSWICK THEOLOGICAL SEMINARY, Gardner A Sage Library, 21 Seminary Pl, 08901-1159. SAN 310-3331. Tel: 732-247-5243. Reference Tel: 732-247-5241, Ext 202. FAX: 732-249-5412. E-mail: sage@nbts.edu. Web Site: www.nbts.edu/newsite/sage.cfm. *Dir,* Christopher Brennan; Tel: 732-246-5604, E-mail: cbrennan@nbts.edu; *Ref & Access Serv Librn,* Bethany O'Shea; E-mail: boshea@nbts.edu; *Tech Serv Librn,* Ondrea Murphy; Tel: 732-247-5241, Ext 201, E-mail: omurphy@nbts.edu; *Acq/Ser Asst,* Wanlin Chang Tsaur; Tel: 732-247-5241, Ext 203, E-mail: wtsaur@nbts.edu; Staff 4 (MLS 3, Non-MLS 1)
Founded 1784. Highest Degree: Doctorate
Library Holdings: AV Mats 269; Bk Vols 155,000; Per Subs 231
Special Collections: Archives of Reformed Church in America; Leiby Coll
Subject Interests: Biblical studies, Classics, Dutch church hist, Theol disciplines
Automation Activity & Vendor Info: (Acquisitions) TLC (The Library Corporation); (Cataloging) TLC (The Library Corporation); (Circulation) TLC (The Library Corporation); (Course Reserve) TLC (The Library Corporation); (ILL) OCLC FirstSearch; (OPAC) TLC (The Library Corporation)
Database Vendor: EBSCOhost, OCLC WorldShare Interlibrary Loan
Wireless access
Function: Ref serv available
Partic in NY Area Theol Libr Asn; Southeastern Pennsylvania Theological Library Association; Virtual Academic Library Environment
Open Mon-Thurs 11-11, Fri 10-6, Sat 2-8
Restriction: Open to fac, students & qualified researchers

C RUTGERS UNIVERSITY LIBRARIES*, 169 College Ave, 08901-1163. SAN 350-9850. Tel: 848-932-7505. Interlibrary Loan Service Tel: 848-932-6005. FAX: 732-932-7637. Web Site: www.libraries.rutgers.edu. *Univ Librn, VPres for Info Serv,* Marianne Gaunt; *Assoc Univ Librn, Digital Libr,* Grace Agnew; Tel: 848-932-5925, E-mail: gagnew@rulmail.rutgers.edu; *Assoc Univ Librn, Planning & Organizational Res,* Jeanne Boyle; *Assoc Univ Librn, Res & Instrul Serv,* Melissa Just; Tel: 848-932-6112, E-mail: melissa.just@rutgers.edu; *Actg Assoc Univ Librn, Coll Develop,* Thomas Izbicki; Tel: 732-932-7129, Ext 125, E-mail: tizbicki@rulmail.rutgers.edu; *Dir, Admin Serv,* Lila Daum Fredenburg; E-mail: lilafred@rulmail.rutgers.edu; *Copyright & Licensing Librn,* Janice Pilch; E-mail: janice.pilch@rutgers.edu; Staff 300 (MLS 87, Non-MLS 213)
Founded 1766. Enrl 50,016; Fac 2,661; Highest Degree: Doctorate
Special Collections: State Document Depository; UN Document Depository; US Document Depository
Automation Activity & Vendor Info: (Acquisitions) SirsiDynix; (Cataloging) SirsiDynix; (Circulation) SirsiDynix; (Course Reserve) SirsiDynix; (Media Booking) SirsiDynix; (OPAC) SirsiDynix; (Serials) SirsiDynix
Database Vendor: Agricola, Alexander Street Press, Cambridge Scientific Abstracts, EBSCOhost, Factiva.com, Gale Cengage Learning, Grolier Online, Haworth Pres Inc, JSTOR, LexisNexis, Newsbank, OCLC FirstSearch, OCLC WorldShare Interlibrary Loan, OVID Technologies, ProQuest, PubMed, ScienceDirect, SerialsSolutions, SirsiDynix
Publications: Annual Report; Collection Guides; Instructional & Informational Material; Journal of the Rutgers University Libraries; Report (Newsletter)
Partic in Association of Research Libraries (ARL); Northeast Research Libraries Consortium (NERL); OCLC Online Computer Library Center, Inc; OCLC Research Library Partnership; Pennsylvania Academic Library Consortium, Inc (PALCI); Virtual Academic Library Environment
Open Mon-Fri 8:30-5

Departmental Libraries:

ARCHIBALD STEVENS ALEXANDER LIBRARY, 169 College Ave, 08901-1163, SAN 350-9885. Tel: 848-932-7851. Reference Tel: 848-932-7509. Administration Tel: 848-932-7129. FAX: 848-932-1101. Web Site: www.libraries.rutgers.edu/alexander.
Special Collections: Government Publications Coll. State Document Depository; UN Document Depository; US Document Depository
Subject Interests: Humanities, Soc sci
Special Services for the Blind - Assistive/Adapted tech devices, equip & products
Open Mon-Thurs 8am-1am, Fri 8am-9pm, Sat 10-6, Sun Noon-1am

ART LIBRARY, Voorhees Hall, 71 Hamilton St, 08901-1248, SAN 350-9974. Tel: 848-932-7739. FAX: 732-932-6743. Web Site: www.libraries.rutgers.edu/art. *Art Librn, Res & Instrul Serv,* Megan Lotts; Staff 4 (MLS 2, Non-MLS 2)
Library Holdings: Bk Vols 100,000; Per Subs 89
Special Collections: American & Russian Art & Architecture Coll
Subject Interests: Archit hist, Art, Visual arts
Open Mon-Thurs (Winter) 8:30am-10pm, Fri 8:30-5, Sat 10-5; Mon-Fri (Summer) 9-5
Restriction: Non-circulating

CENTER OF ALCOHOL STUDIES, Brinkley & Adele Smithers Hall, 607 Allison Rd, Piscataway, 08854-8001, SAN 350-994X. Tel: 732-445-4442. FAX: 732-445-5944. Web Site: alcoholstudies.rutgers.edu/library/index.html. *Dir, Info Serv,* Judit Ward; Tel: 732-445-3527
Special Collections: Alcohol History (Temperance & Prohibition Materials); Alcohol Research (McCarthy Memorial Coll), docs; Connor Alcohol Research Reference Files, survey instruments
Subject Interests: Alcohol drug abuse
Partic in NJ State Libr Network
Open Mon-Fri (Winter) 9-5; Mon-Fri (Summer) 8:30-4:30
Friends of the Library Group

STEPHEN & LUCY CHANG SCIENCE LIBRARY, Walter E Foran Hall, 59 Dudley Rd, 08901-8520. Tel: 848-932-0305. FAX: 732-932-0311. Web Site: www.libraries.rutgers.edu/chang. *Libr Supvr,* Nita Mukherjee
Library Holdings: Bk Vols 12,995; Per Subs 131
Subject Interests: Agr, Animal sci, Aquaculture, Bioeng, Fisheries, Food sci, Plant sci
Special Services for the Blind - Assistive/Adapted tech devices, equip & products
Open Mon-Thurs 8:30am-10pm, Fri 8:30-5, Sat 1-5, Sun 1-10

JOHN COTTON DANA LIBRARY
See Separate Entry in Newark

MABEL SMITH DOUGLASS LIBRARY, Eight Chapel Dr, 08901-8527, SAN 351-0123. Tel: 848-932-9411. Reference Tel: 848-932-5020. Administration Tel: 848-932-5063. FAX: 732-353-1133. Web Site: www.libraries.rutgers.edu/douglass. *Instruction & Outreach Librn,* Eileen Stec; Tel: 848-932-5009; *Music & Performing Arts Librn,* Jonathan Sauceda; Tel: 848-932-9023; *Women's & Gender Studies Librn,* Kayo Denda; Tel: 848-932-5023
Special Collections: Elizabeth Cady Stanton Papers; Gerritsen Coll, bks & per. State Document Depository; UN Document Depository
Subject Interests: Performing arts, Undergrad educ, Women's studies

Special Services for the Blind - Assistive/Adapted tech devices, equip & products
Open Mon-Thurs (Winter) 8am-11pm, Fri 8am-9pm, Sat 10-6, Sun Noon-11pm; Mon-Thurs (Summer) 8-8, Fri 8-5

EAST ASIAN LIBRARY, Alexander Library, 169 College Ave, 08901-1163, SAN 329-3491. Tel: 848-932-7129. FAX: 732-932-1101. Web Site: www.libraries.rutgers.edu/east_asian. *Librn,* Tao Yang
Library Holdings: Bk Vols 125,903; Per Subs 460
Special Collections: Chinese History, Literature, Religion & Philosophy Coll; Chinese Medicine (Professor Kuang-chung Ho Coll), bks & journals
Subject Interests: Chinese, Japanese, Korean lang mat
Open Mon-Sun 8am-9pm

INSTITUTE OF JAZZ STUDIES
See Separate Entry in Newark

CM ROBERT WOOD JOHNSON LIBRARY OF THE HEALTH SCIENCES, One Robert Wood Johnson Pl, 08903. (Mail add: PO Box 19, 08903), SAN 320-3980. Tel: 732-235-7610. FAX: 732-235-7826. *Campus Libr Dir,* Kerry O'Rourke; Tel: 732-235-7606, E-mail: orourke@rulmail.rutgers.edu; *Computer Syst Librn,* Fengzhi Fan; Tel: 732-235-7605, E-mail: fanfe@rulmail.rutgers.edu; *Info & Educ Librn,* Robert Cupryk; Tel: 732-235-7261, E-mail: cupryk@ca.rutgers.edu; *Info & Educ Librn,* Pamela Hargwood; E-mail: hargwood@rulmail.rutgers.edu; *Info & Educ Librn,* Yingting Zhang; Tel: 732-235-7604, E-mail: yzhang@ca.rutgers.edu

KILMER LIBRARY, 75 Ave E, Piscataway, 08854-8040, SAN 351-2134. Circulation Tel: 848-445-3613. Reference Tel: 848-445-3614. FAX: 732-445-3472. Web Site: www.libraries.rutgers.edu/kilmer. *Libr Supvr,* Barry Lipinsky; *Libr Supvr,* Paul Young
Founded 1969
Library Holdings: AV Mats 736; Bk Vols 143,985; Per Subs 237
Subject Interests: Bus, Career res, Undergrad educ
Special Services for the Blind - Assistive/Adapted tech devices, equip & products
Open Mon-Thurs 8am-2am, Fri 8am-Midnight, Sat 10am-Midnight, Sun Noon-2am

BLANCHE & IRVING LAURIE MUSIC LIBRARY, Eight Chapel Dr, 08901-8527, SAN 351-0255. Tel: 848-932-9023. Reference Tel: 732-932-9783, Ext 35. FAX: 732-932-6777. Web Site: www.libraries.rutgers.edu/performing_arts. *Music & Performing Arts Librn,* Jonathan Sauceda
Library Holdings: AV Mats 25,000; DVDs 250; Music Scores 66,000; Bk Vols 56,692; Per Subs 234; Videos 1,500
Subject Interests: Music
Special Services for the Blind - Assistive/Adapted tech devices, equip & products
Open Mon-Thurs 8:30am-11pm, Fri-Sun 9-9

CM LIBRARY OF SCIENCE & MEDICINE, 165 Bevier Rd, Piscataway, 08854-8009, SAN 351-2169. Tel: 848-445-3854. Reference Tel: 848-445-2895. Administration Tel: 848-445-3551. FAX: 732-445-5703. Web Site: www.libraries.rutgers.edu/lsm. *Agr & Environ Sci Librn,* Martin Kesselman; Tel: 848-445-3571; *Behav Sci Librn,* Laura Mullen; Tel: 848-445-3663; *Biological Sci Librn,* Helen Hoffman; Tel: 848-445-3581; *Chem & Physics Librn,* Laura Palumbo; Tel: 848-445-3558; *Eng Res Librn,* Xian Connie Wu; Tel: 848-445-3489; *Govt Pub Librn,* Ellen Calhoun; Tel: 848-445-3562; *Med & Pharmaceutical Sci Librn,* Shakeh Jackie Mardikian; Tel: 848-445-3563
Founded 1970
Library Holdings: AV Mats 22,442; Bk Vols 290,413; Per Subs 2,493
Special Collections: Patent & Trademark Resource Center. State Document Depository; US Document Depository
Subject Interests: Behav sci, Biological sci, Earth sci, Eng, Pharm sci
Partic in Center for Research Libraries; LibraryLinkNJ, The New Jersey Library Cooperative; Lyrasis
Special Services for the Blind - Assistive/Adapted tech devices, equip & products
Open Mon-Thurs & Sun 8am-Midnight, Fri 10-6, Sat Noon-Midnight

MATHEMATICAL SCIENCES LIBRARY, Hill Ctr for Mathematical Sciences, 110 Frelinghuysen Rd, Piscataway, 08854-8019, SAN 351-0212. Tel: 848-445-3735. FAX: 732-445-3064. Web Site: www.libraries.rutgers.edu/math. *Librn,* Mei Ling Lo; Staff 1 (MLS 1)
Library Holdings: Bk Vols 44,661; Per Subs 534
Special Collections: Technical Reports
Subject Interests: Computer sci, Math, Statistics
Open Mon-Thurs (Winter) 8:30am-10pm, Fri 8:30-5, Sat 1-5, Sun Noon-10pm; Mon-Fri (Summer) 9-5

MEDIA CENTER-DOUGLASS LIBRARY, Eight Chapel Dr, 08901. Tel: 848-932-9783. FAX: 732-932-6777. Web Site: www.libraries.rutgers.edu/media. *Libr Supvr,* Jan Reinhart; Staff 9 (MLS 4, Non-MLS 5)
Library Holdings: AV Mats 13,962; Bk Vols 365
Open Mon-Thurs 8am-11pm, Fri 8:30am-9pm, Sat 10-6, Sun Noon-11

PHYSICS LIBRARY, Serin Physics Laboratory, 136 Frelinghuysen Rd, Piscataway, 08854-8019, SAN 351-0301. Tel: 848-445-5891. FAX: 732-445-4964. Web Site: www.libraries.rutgers.edu/physics. *Librn,* Mohammad Mansouri
Library Holdings: Bk Vols 17,490; Per Subs 146
Special Collections: Preprint Coll
Subject Interests: Astronomy, Physics
Special Services for the Blind - Assistive/Adapted tech devices, equip & products
Open Mon-Thurs 9-8, Fri 9-5, Sat & Sun 1-5

PAUL ROBESON LIBRARY
See Separate Entry in Camden

SCHOOL OF MANAGEMENT & LABOR RELATIONS, SMLR Labor Educ Ctr, 50 Labor Center Way, 08901-8553, SAN 351-8553. Tel: 848-932-9513. FAX: 732-932-4699. Web Site: smlr.rutgers.edu/carey-library. *Libr Dir,* Julie Moscinski; Tel: 848-932-9608, E-mail: jmoscinski@smlr.rutgers.edu
Library Holdings: AV Mats 278; Bk Vols 6,155; Per Subs 402
Special Collections: New Jersey Public Sector Collective Bargaining Contracts
Subject Interests: Human resources, Indust relations, Labor
Special Services for the Deaf - Assistive tech
Special Services for the Blind - Assistive/Adapted tech devices, equip & products
Open Mon-Thurs 10-8, Fri & Sat 10-2

CM GEORGE F SMITH LIBRARY OF THE HEALTH SCIENCES, 30 12th Ave, Newark, 07101, SAN 310-3412. Tel: 973-972-4580. FAX: 973-972-7474. *Assoc VPres, Scholarly Info, Univ Librn,* Judith Cohn; Tel: 973-972-0560, E-mail: cohn@ca.rutgers.edu; *Assoc Dir,* Roberta Bronson Fitzpatrick; Tel: 973-972-5498, E-mail: fitzparb@rulmail.rutgers.edu; *Asst Dir, Admin & Spec Projects,* Anthony Mayo; Tel: 973-972-5317, E-mail: mayoal@rulmail.rutgers.edu; *Head, Coll Develop & E-Res Mgt,* Elizabeth Sosnowska; Tel: 973 972 4360, E-mail: sosnowsk@rulmail.rutgers.edu; *Managing Librn,* Yu-Hung Lin; Tel: 973-972-7556, E-mail: liny4@rulmail.rutgers.edu; *Managing Librn,* Yini Zhu; Tel: 973-972-9551, E-mail: zhuy2@ca.rutgers.edu; *Info & Educ Librn,* Margaret Dreker; Tel: 973-972-9549, E-mail: drekerma@rulmail.rutgers.edu; *Info & Educ Librn,* Stephen Modica; Tel: 973-972-9550, E-mail: modicasf@rulmail.rutgers.edu; *Info & Educ Librn,* Rory Phalen; Tel: 973-972-9543, E-mail: phalenra@rulmail.rutgers.edu; *Info & Educ Librn,* Marie Konyne Saimbert; Tel: 973-972-9546, E-mail: saimbemk@rulmail.rutgers.edu; *Spec Coll Librn,* Robert Vietrogoski; Tel: 973-972-7830, E-mail: vietrora@rulmail.rutgers.edu

SPECIAL COLLECTIONS & UNIVERSITY ARCHIVES, 169 College Ave, 08901-1163, SAN 323-5696. Tel: 848-932-7006. Reference Tel: 848 932-6159. Administration Tel: 848-932-6156. FAX: 732-932-7012. Web Site: www.libraries.rutgers.edu/rul/libs/scua/scua.shtml. *Head, Spec Coll & Univ Archives,* Ronald L Becker; Tel: 848-932-6155, E-mail: rbecker@rulmail.rutgers.edu; *Head, Exhibitions Prog Curator/William E Griffis Coll,* Dr Fernanda H Perrone; Tel: 848-932-6154, E-mail: hperrone@rulmail.rutgers.edu; *Head, Presv,* Timothy Corlis; Tel: 848-932-6147, E-mail: tcorlis@yahoo.com; *Head, Pub Serv, NJ Regional Studies Librn,* Christine A Lutz; Tel: 848-932-6148, E-mail: christie.lutz@rutgers.edu; *Rare Bk Librn,* Michael Joseph; Tel: 848-932-6153, E-mail: mjoseph@rulmail.rutgers.edu; *Ref Librn,* Catherine Sauceda; E-mail: catherine.rominger@rutgers.edu; *Spec Coll & Digital Projects Metadata Librn,* Melissa DeFino; Tel: 848-445-5881, Fax: 732-445-5888, E-mail: defino@rulmail.rutgers.edu; *Univ Archivist,* Thomas Frusciano; Tel: 848-932-6149, E-mail: fruscian@rulmail.rutgers.edu; *Assoc Univ Archivist,* Erika Gorder; Tel: 848-932-6150, E-mail: gorder@rulmail.rutgers.edu; *Archivist,* Catherine Carey; Tel: 848-932-6158, E-mail: cccarey25@rulmail.rutgers.edu; *Digital Archivist,* Caryn Radick; Tel: 848-932-6152, E-mail: cradick@rulmail.rutgers.edu; *Ms Curator,* Albert C King; E-mail: acking@rulmail.rutgers.edu; *Ref Curator,* David Kuzma; Tel: 848-932-6151, E-mail: kuzmadav@rulmail.rutgers.edu; *Rare Bk Cataloger,* Silvana Notarmaso; Tel: 848-932-6157, E-mail: silvanan@rulmail.rutgers.edu; Staff 12 (MLS 11, Non-MLS 1)
Founded 1946. Enrl 70,000; Fac 6; Highest Degree: Doctorate
Library Holdings: AV Mats 41,164; Bk Vols 153,033; Per Subs 1,872
Special Collections: British & American Literature (18th & 19th centuries); Diaries; Dictionaries; History of Business & Labor; Manuscript Colls; Rare Book Coll (17th & 18th Century British & American Writers); Sinclair New Jersey Coll; University Archives; Westerners in Japan; William Elliot Griffis Coll. Oral History
Subject Interests: Archives, Manuscripts, New Jerseyana, Rare bks
Function: Archival coll
Publications: Bibliographies; Collection Guides; Exhibition Catalogs
Special Services for the Blind - Assistive/Adapted tech devices, equip & products
Open Mon-Fri 9-5, Sat 1-5
Restriction: Non-circulating

M SAINT PETER'S UNIVERSITY HOSPITAL LIBRARY, 254 Easton Ave, 08903. SAN 310-3358. Tel: 732-745-8545. Reference Tel: 732-745-8508. FAX: 732-937-6091. E-mail: mlibrary@saintpetersuh.com. Web Site: www.saintpetershcs.com/medicallibrary. *Mgr,* Jeannine Creazzo; Staff 2 (MLS 2)
Founded 1907
Library Holdings: Bk Vols 25,000; Per Subs 450
Special Collections: Consumer Health Coll; Cultural Competency Coll; History of Medicine; Leadership Development Coll
Subject Interests: Gynecology, Med, Nursing, Obstetrics, Pediatrics
Wireless access
Partic in BSHL; Health Sci Libr Asn of NJ
Open Mon-Fri 9-4

NEW GRETNA

P BASS RIVER COMMUNITY LIBRARY*, Bass River Elementary School, 11 N Maple Ave, 08224. (Mail add: PO Box 256, 08224). Tel: 609-296-6942. FAX: 609-296-4953. Web Site: www.bassriver-nj.org/community-library.html.
Library Holdings: AV Mats 45; Bk Vols 10,600; Per Subs 15
Automation Activity & Vendor Info: (Cataloging) ComPanion Corp; (Circulation) ComPanion Corp
Mem of Burlington County Library
Open Tues & Thurs 1-2, Wed & Fri 6pm-9pm

NEW MILFORD

P NEW MILFORD PUBLIC LIBRARY*, 200 Dahlia Ave, 07646-1812. SAN 310-3374. Tel: 201-262-1221. FAX: 201-262-5639. *Dir,* Terri McColl; E-mail: mccoll@bccls.org; *Asst Dir, Ch Serv,* Mary Koob; E-mail: koob@bccls.org; *Head, Circ,* Yolanda Di Napoli; *Ref Librn,* Jean Castle McLaughlin; E-mail: nmilref@bccls.org; *Adult Serv, Ref,* Brian Leddy; E-mail: nmilref@bccls.org; *Adult Serv,* Jo Anne Martin; E-mail: nmilref@bccls.org; *Youth Serv,* Joanne Drolshagen; Staff 12 (MLS 5, Non-MLS 7)
Founded 1936. Pop 16,425; Circ 88,879
Jan 2005-Dec 2005 Income $613,135, State $16,742, City $581,393, Locally Generated Income $15,000. Mats Exp $63,300, Books $44,000, Per/Ser (Incl. Access Fees) $4,800, AV Mat $14,500. Sal $436,415
Library Holdings: CDs 1,092; DVDs 2,255; Large Print Bks 579; Bk Vols 54,441; Per Subs 105; Talking Bks 1,042; Videos 2,182
Subject Interests: Consumer info, Cooking
Automation Activity & Vendor Info: (Cataloging) Surpass; (Circulation) SirsiDynix; (ILL) SirsiDynix; (OPAC) SirsiDynix
Database Vendor: Baker & Taylor, EBSCOhost, Gale Cengage Learning, ProQuest, SirsiDynix
Wireless access
Partic in Bergen County Cooperative Library System; Bibliomation Inc
Open Mon & Tues 10-9, Wed 10-8, Thurs 10-6, Fri 1-5
Friends of the Library Group

NEW PROVIDENCE

S MCNEIL & FOSTER LIBRARY, Reference Library, 630 Central Ave, 07974. SAN 330-0366. Tel: 908-219-0278. FAX: 908-219-0192. *Librn,* Elizabeth M Button; Staff 2 (Non-MLS 2)
Founded 1985
Apr 2013-Mar 2014 Income $45,000. Mats Exp $3,000, Books $3,000
Library Holdings: CDs 35; DVDs 30; Bk Titles 17,000; Per Subs 250; Videos 200
Automation Activity & Vendor Info: (Acquisitions) Brodart
Database Vendor: LexisNexis, Library Systems & Services (LSSI)
Wireless access
Partic in OCLC Online Computer Library Center, Inc
Restriction: Staff use only

S NEW PROVIDENCE HISTORICAL SOCIETY LIBRARY*, c/o Memorial Library, 377 Elkwood Ave, 07974. SAN 323-4673. Tel: 908-665-1034. *Pres,* John Bale
Founded 1966
Library Holdings: Bk Vols 200
Special Collections: Oral History
Subject Interests: Local hist
Open Tues 10-12, Thurs 10-12 & 2-5

P NEW PROVIDENCE MEMORIAL LIBRARY*, 377 Elkwood Ave, 07974-1837. SAN 310-3382. Tel: 908-665-0311. FAX: 908-665-2319. E-mail: npmlref@yahoo.com. Web Site: www.newprovidencelibrary.org. *Libr Dir,* Colleen Byrne; E-mail: cbyrne@newprovidencelibrary.org; *Head, Cat,* Becky Sawyer; *Head, Ref,* Lisa Florio; *Ch Serv,* Christopher O'Hara; Staff 14 (MLS 4, Non-MLS 10)
Founded 1921. Pop 11,900; Circ 109,206
Jan 2005-Dec 2005 Income $690,000. Mats Exp $70,000. Sal $370,000
Library Holdings: Bk Titles 75,000; Bk Vols 80,000; Per Subs 120
Automation Activity & Vendor Info: (Cataloging) TLC (The Library Corporation); (Circulation) TLC (The Library Corporation); (OPAC) TLC (The Library Corporation)
Database Vendor: EBSCOhost, Gale Cengage Learning
Wireless access
Partic in LibraryLinkNJ, The New Jersey Library Cooperative; LUCC; Morris-Union Federation; MURAL
Open Mon-Thurs 9-9, Fri & Sat 9-5:30, Sun (Sept-May) 1-5
Friends of the Library Group

NEW VERNON

P KEMMERER LIBRARY HARDING TOWNSHIP*, 19 Blue Mill Rd, 07976. (Mail add: PO Box 283, 07976-0283). Tel: 973-267-2665. E-mail: desk@hardinglibrary.org. Web Site: www.hardinglibrary.org. *Dir,* Position Currently Open; *Ch,* Jennifer Carlin; *Circ,* Carolyn Antonaccio; *Circ,* Elyse Makowsky
Pop 3,400
Library Holdings: High Interest/Low Vocabulary Bk Vols 3,000; Bk Vols 7,000
Wireless access
Partic in Morris Automated Information Network
Open Mon-Wed & Fri 10-5, Thurs 10-7, Sat 10-2
Friends of the Library Group

NEWARK

M COLUMBUS HOSPITAL*, Medical Library, 495 N 13th St, 07107. SAN 376-0553. Tel: 973-268-1400, Ext 2074. FAX: 973-268-1542. *Librn,* Eleanor Silverman; E-mail: esilverman18@hotmail.com
Library Holdings: Bk Vols 400; Per Subs 25
Open Tues 9:30-1:30

J ESSEX COUNTY COLLEGE LIBRARY*, 303 University Ave, 07102. SAN 351-0395. Tel: 973-877-3238. Circulation Tel: 973-877-3028. Reference Tel: 973-877-3241. Administration Tel: 973-877-3233. FAX: 973-877-1887. Web Site: www.essex.edu/library. *Dir,* Gwendolyn C Slaton; E-mail: slaton@essex.edu; *Ref Librn,* Dr Stephen Keister; Tel: 973-877-3286, E-mail: keister@essex.edu; *Circ,* Rita Willis; E-mail: rwillis@essex.edu; *Ref,* Leola Taylor-Bandele; E-mail: ltaylor@essex.edu. Subject Specialists: *Educ, Law,* Gwendolyn C Slaton; *Eng, Math, Tech,* Dr Stephen Keister; *Art, Hist, Humanities,* Rita Willis; *Biol, Chem,* Leola Taylor-Bandele; Staff 8 (MLS 4, Non-MLS 4)
Founded 1968. Enrl 12,500; Fac 150; Highest Degree: Associate
Library Holdings: AV Mats 4,909; High Interest/Low Vocabulary Bk Vols 1,146; Bk Titles 104,234; Bk Vols 114,543; Per Subs 500
Subject Interests: Nursing
Automation Activity & Vendor Info: (Acquisitions) Innovative Interfaces, Inc; (Cataloging) Innovative Interfaces, Inc; (Circulation) Innovative Interfaces, Inc; (Course Reserve) Innovative Interfaces, Inc; (ILL) Innovative Interfaces, Inc; (OPAC) Innovative Interfaces, Inc; (Serials) Innovative Interfaces, Inc
Database Vendor: EBSCOhost, Gale Cengage Learning, Innovative Interfaces, Inc, OCLC FirstSearch, OVID Technologies, ProQuest, ReferenceUSA, Westlaw, Wilson - Wilson Web
Wireless access
Function: Audio & video playback equip for onsite use, Copy machines, Electronic databases & coll, Handicapped accessible, ILL available, Magnifiers for reading, Mail & tel request accepted, Online searches, Orientations, Photocopying/Printing, Ref & res, Ref serv available, Telephone ref, VHS videos, Wheelchair accessible
Publications: Subject Bibliographies
Partic in Eastern NJ Regional Libr Coop; LibraryLinkNJ, The New Jersey Library Cooperative; ReBL; Virtual Academic Library Environment
Open Mon-Thurs 8:30am-9pm, Fri 8-5, Sat 8-3
Restriction: Open to pub for ref & circ; with some limitations, Open to students

Departmental Libraries:

BRANCH CAMPUS, 730 Bloomfield Ave, West Caldwell, 07007, SAN 370-0259. Tel: 973-877-1883. FAX: 973-877-6635. *Librn,* Anelia Chatterjee; E-mail: achatter@essex.edu; Staff 2 (MLS 1, Non-MLS 1)
Highest Degree: Associate
Library Holdings: Bk Vols 16,000; Per Subs 90
Open Mon-Thurs 8am-9pm, Fri 8-5, Sat 8-3

L GIBBONS PC*, Law Library, One Gateway Center, 07102. SAN 371-5272. Tel: 973-596-4500. FAX: 973-639-6368. Web Site: www.gibbonslaw.com.
Library Holdings: Bk Titles 3,000; Bk Vols 10,000
Partic in LibraryLinkNJ, The New Jersey Library Cooperative
Restriction: Private libr

L MCCARTER & ENGLISH*, Law Library, Four Gateway Ctr, 100 Mulberry St, 07102-4056. SAN 310-3447. Tel: 973-622-4444, Ext 4080. FAX: 973-624-7070. Web Site: www.mccarter.com. *Dir,* Position Currently Open
Library Holdings: Bk Vols 29,000; Per Subs 200
Automation Activity & Vendor Info: (Cataloging) SydneyPlus; (Circulation) SydneyPlus; (ILL) SydneyPlus; (OPAC) SydneyPlus; (Serials) SydneyPlus
Wireless access
Restriction: Staff use only

S NEW JERSEY HISTORICAL SOCIETY LIBRARY, 52 Park Pl, 07102-4302. SAN 310-348X. Tel: 973-596-8500. FAX: 973-596-6957. TDD: 800-852-7899. E-mail: library@jerseyhistory.org. Web Site: www.jerseyhistory.org. *Res Spec,* Dr James Amemasor; Tel: 973-596-8500, Ext 249, E-mail: jamesmasor@jerseyhistory.org; Staff 4 (MLS 1, Non-MLS 3)
Founded 1845
Library Holdings: Bk Vols 65,000; Per Subs 100
Special Collections: Early New Jersey Imprints; Ephemera; Historical Newspapers; Manuscripts; Maps; Photographic Prints & Negatives; Rare Books. Oral History
Subject Interests: Am hist, NJ
Database Vendor: OCLC FirstSearch
Function: Archival coll, ILL available, Photocopying/Printing, Prog for adults, Prog for children & young adult, Ref serv available, Referrals accepted, Res libr, Telephone ref, Wheelchair accessible
Publications: New Jersey History
Partic in New Jersey Library Network; OCLC Online Computer Library Center, Inc
Special Services for the Deaf - Staff with knowledge of sign lang; TTY equip
Open Wed-Sat 12-5
Restriction: Closed stack, Non-circulating to the pub, Not a lending libr, Open to pub for ref only

C NEW JERSEY INSTITUTE OF TECHNOLOGY, Robert W Van Houten Library, University Heights, 07102-1982. SAN 310-3498. Tel: 973-596-3206. Interlibrary Loan Service Tel: 973-596-3204. Reference Tel: 973-596-3210. Administration Tel: 973-596-3207. FAX: 973-643-5601. Web Site: www.library.njit.edu. *Univ Librn,* Richard T Sweeney; E-mail: richard.sweeney@njit.edu; *Asst Univ Librn,* Ann Hoang; *Dir, Ref & Libr Info Serv,* Davida Scharf; *Dir, Circ & ILL,* Doreen Mettle; Staff 12 (MLS 11, Non-MLS 1)
Founded 1881. Enrl 9,000; Fac 361; Highest Degree: Doctorate
Library Holdings: Bk Vols 150,000; Per Subs 20,000
Special Collections: Electronic Theses & Dissertation; Weston History of Science & Technology Coll
Subject Interests: Archit, Computer sci, Eng, Sci
Automation Activity & Vendor Info: (Acquisitions) Ex Libris Group; (Cataloging) Ex Libris Group; (Circulation) Ex Libris Group; (OPAC) Ex Libris Group; (Serials) Ex Libris Group
Wireless access
Partic in OCLC Online Computer Library Center, Inc; Virtual Academic Library Environment
Open Mon-Thurs 7:30am-11:45pm, Fri 7:30am-7:45pm, Sat 10-5:45, Sun 12-8:45

Departmental Libraries:

BARBARA & LEONARD LITTMAN ARCHITECTURE LIBRARY, 456 Weston Hall, 323 King Blvd, 07102-1982. Tel: 973-596-3083. FAX: 973-643-5601. Web Site: www.library.njit.edu/archlib. *Dir,* Maya Gervits; E-mail: maya.gervits@njit.edu; Staff 2 (MLS 1, Non-MLS 1)
Founded 1975. Enrl 750; Fac 80; Highest Degree: Doctorate
Library Holdings: Bk Vols 20,000; Per Subs 100
Open Mon-Thurs 8am-8:15pm, Fri 8-5:45, Sat 12-5:45, Sun 1-6:45

L NEW JERSEY OFFICE OF THE PUBLIC DEFENDER*, Newark Branch, 31 Clinton St, 10th Flr, 07102. (Mail add: PO Box 46004, 07101), SAN 373-0840. Tel: 973-877-1200. FAX: 973-877-1239. *Librn,* David Bloustein; Tel: 973-877-1264; Staff 1 (MLS 1)
Library Holdings: Bk Vols 7,500
Subject Interests: Law, Treatises
Partic in LibraryLinkNJ, The New Jersey Library Cooperative
Restriction: Not open to pub, Staff use only

M NEWARK BETH ISRAEL MEDICAL CENTER*, Dr Victor Parsonnet Memorial Library, 201 Lyons Ave, 07112. SAN 310-3501. Tel: 973-926-7441. FAX: 973-923-4280. *Asst Librn,* Laverne Davis
Founded 1900
Library Holdings: Bk Titles 2,000; Per Subs 150
Special Collections: Antique (Classic) Medical Books; Dr Aaron Parsonnet Coll, bks
Partic in Basic Health Sciences Library Network; Health Sci Libr Asn of NJ; LibraryLinkNJ, The New Jersey Library Cooperative; New Jersey Library Network
Open Mon-Fri 9-5
Restriction: Non-circulating to the pub

S NEWARK MUSEUM LIBRARY*, 49 Washington St, 07102-3176. SAN 310-3536. Tel: 973-596-6625. FAX: 973-642-0459. E-mail: library@newarkmuseum.org. *Librn,* William A Peniston; E-mail: wpeniston@newarkmuseum.org; Staff 1 (MLS 1)
Founded 1925
Jan 2011-Dec 2011 Income $88,000. Mats Exp $11,000, Books $5,000, Per/Ser (Incl. Access Fees) $5,000, Presv $1,000. Sal $77,000 (Prof $65,000)
Library Holdings: Bk Titles 40,000; Bk Vols 50,000; Per Subs 100
Special Collections: History of the Newark Museum (Dana Coll); Tibet Coll
Subject Interests: African art, Am art, Asian art, Decorative art, Natural sci, Numismatics
Partic in LibraryLinkNJ, The New Jersey Library Cooperative
Restriction: Open by appt only

P NEWARK PUBLIC LIBRARY*, Five Washington St, 07101. (Mail add: PO Box 630, 07101-0630), SAN 351-045X. Tel: 973-733-7784, 973-733-7800. Circulation Tel: 973-733-7791. Interlibrary Loan Service Tel: 973-733-7767. Reference Tel: 973-733-7779, 973-733-7820. Administration Tel: 973-733-7758, 973-733-7780. Automation Services Tel: 973-733-7796. FAX: 973-733-5648. Administration FAX: 973-733-5919. Web Site: www.npl.org. *Dir,* Wilma J Grey; E-mail: wgrey@npl.org; *Asst Dir, Develop,* George Williams; Tel: 973-733-7793, Fax: 973-733-8539, E-mail: gwilliams@npl.org; *Asst Dir, Finance & Develop,* Joseph Casale; Tel: 973-733-7841, E-mail: jcasale@npl.org; *Asst Dir, Human Res, Security & Phys Plant,* Gerald Fitzhugh; Tel: 973-733-7748, E-mail: gfitzhugh@npl.org; *Principal Librn, ILL,* Dale Colston; Tel: 973-733-7768, E-mail: dcolston@npl.org; *Supv Librn,* James Capuano; E-mail: jcapuano@npl.org; *Supv Librn, Access Serv,* Donald Lewis; Tel: 973-733-7842, Fax: 973-733-5759, E-mail: dlewis@npl.org; *Supv Librn, Cat,* Penelope Jabido; Tel: 973-733-7737, E-mail: pjabido@npl.org; *Supv Librn, Eastern Region,* Paula Baratta; Tel: 973-733-7760, E-mail: pbaratta@npl.org; *Supv Librn, Multilingual Serv,* Ingrid Betancourt; Tel: 973-733-3637, E-mail: ibetancourt@npl.org; *Supv Librn, NJ Info Ctr,* George Hawley, PhD; Tel: 973-733-7775, E-mail: ghawley@npl.org; *Supv Librn, Ref,* Leslie Kahn; E-mail: lkahn@npl.org; *Supv Librn, Staff Develop, Outreach & Admin Initiatives,* Paul D Pattwell; Tel: 973-733-7735, E-mail: ppattwell@npl.org; *Supv Librn, Support Serv,* Maureen Ritter; Tel: 973-733-7794, E-mail: mritter@npl.org; *Supv Librn, Western Region,* Deloris Moses; Tel: 973-733-7751, E-mail: dmoses@npl.org; *Controller,* Position Currently Open. Subject Specialists: *Hist, Soc sci,* James Capuano; *Cultural diversity,* Ingrid Betancourt; *Newark hist, NJ hist,* George Hawley, PhD; Staff 37 (MLS 34, Non-MLS 3)
Founded 1888. Pop 277,140; Circ 297,207
Jan 2011-Dec 2011 Income (Main Library and Branch(s)) $13,700,799, State $301,057, City $10,906,410, Federal $1,809,377, Locally Generated Income $809,795, Other $683,955. Mats Exp $638,377, Books $454,084, Other Print Mats $800, Micro $26,000, AV Mat $38,878, Electronic Ref Mat (Incl. Access Fees) $146,320. Sal $6,430,042
Library Holdings: AV Mats 26,351; Bks on Deafness & Sign Lang 1,208; CDs 11,092; DVDs 14,221; Electronic Media & Resources 8,211; High Interest/Low Vocabulary Bk Vols 347; Large Print Bks 1,838; Music Scores 15,879; Bk Titles 720,264; Bk Vols 1,736,140; Per Subs 1,295; Talking Bks 1,297; Videos 8,760
Special Collections: Allen Fine Prints from Puerto Rico; Art (Pictures, Prints & Popular Sheet Music); Artists Books; Autographs; Bookplates; Bruce Rogers Books & Files; Childrens Books 18th, 19th & Early 20th Century (Wilbur Macy Stone Coll); Christmas Cards; Fine Printing (R C Jenkins Coll); Historic Greeting Cards; Historic Posters; Illustrated Books; Incunabula; Japanese Ehon Coll; John Tasker Howard Music Archive; McEwen Christmas Coll; Medieval Manuscripts; New Jersey Rare Books; Newark Evening News Morgue; Original Fine Prints; Postcard Sets; Puerto Rican Reference Coll; Rabin & Kreuger Archives; Shopping Bags; The Jenkinson Coll; US Patent Coll; William Macy Stone Childrens Book Coll. Municipal Document Depository; State Document Depository; US Document Depository
Subject Interests: Art, Bus, Music, Patents
Automation Activity & Vendor Info: (Acquisitions) Innovative Interfaces, Inc; (Cataloging) Innovative Interfaces, Inc; (Circulation) Innovative Interfaces, Inc; (ILL) Innovative Interfaces, Inc; (OPAC) Innovative Interfaces, Inc; (Serials) Innovative Interfaces, Inc
Database Vendor: ABC-CLIO, Baker & Taylor, BWI, CQ Press, Dialog, EBSCOhost, Facts on File, Gale Cengage Learning, Hoovers, LearningExpress, OCLC WebJunction, OCLC WorldShare Interlibrary Loan, ProQuest, ReferenceUSA, Wilson - Wilson Web, World Book Online
Wireless access
Function: Adult literacy prog, Archival coll, Art exhibits, Bilingual assistance for Spanish patrons, Bks on CD, Bus archives, CD-ROM, Children's prog, Citizenship assistance, Computer training, Computers for patron use, Copy machines, e-mail serv, E-Reserves, Electronic databases

& coll, Family literacy, Free DVD rentals, Games & aids for the handicapped, Govt ref serv, Handicapped accessible, Health sci info serv, Holiday prog, Homework prog, ILL available, Instruction & testing, Learning ctr, Libr develop, Magnifiers for reading, Mail & tel request accepted, Music CDs, Newsp ref libr, Online ref, Online searches, Orientations, Outside serv via phone, mail, e-mail & web, Preschool outreach, Prog for adults, Prog for children & young adult, Ref & res, Ref serv available, Referrals accepted, Res libr, Scanner, Senior computer classes, Serves mentally handicapped consumers, Spoken cassettes & CDs, Spoken cassettes & DVDs, Summer reading prog, Tax forms, Telephone ref, VHS videos, Video lending libr, Wheelchair accessible, Workshops
Publications: A History of Fine Printing: A Special Collection in the Newark Public Library (Research guide); Black America on Stage. The Newark Public Library. 1993 (Research guide); Exposition Retrospective DeLorenzo Homar (Research guide); Hidden Treasures: Japanese Art From the Newark Public Library. The Newark Public Library. 1991 (Research guide); Homar: An Exhibition in Appreciation of Lorenzo Homar & His Graphic Works 1954-1994. Newark Public Library, 1994 (Research guide); Lasting Impressions: Greater Newark's Jewish Legacy (Research guide); Second Century (Newsletter); The Graphic Proof (Research guide); The Magic World of the Illustrated Book (College Journal) (Research guide); The Richard C Jenkinson Collection of Books: Chosen to Show the Work of the Best Printers Vol 1 (1925) & 2 (1929); Merrymount Presse (Research guide); The Story of Saga (Research guide)
Partic in Dialog Corp; LibraryLinkNJ, The New Jersey Library Cooperative; Wilsonline
Special Services for the Deaf - Adult & family literacy prog; Assistive tech; Bks on deafness & sign lang; Deaf publ; High interest/low vocabulary bks; Interpreter on staff; Sign lang interpreter upon request for prog; Staff with knowledge of sign lang; Video & TTY relay via computer
Special Services for the Blind - Computer with voice synthesizer for visually impaired persons; Large print bks; Large screen computer & software; PC for handicapped; Ref serv; Spec prog; Talking bks
Open Mon, Tues, Thurs, Fri & Sat 9-5:30, Wed 9-8:30
Restriction: Non-resident fee
Friends of the Library Group
Branches: 8
BRANCH BROOK, 235 Clifton Ave, 07104. Tel: 973-733-7760. *Br Mgr,* Juanita Egoavil; E-mail: jegoavil@npl.org; Staff 6 (MLS 2, Non-MLS 4)
Circ 14,931
Library Holdings: Bk Titles 25,000; Per Subs 40
Open Mon, Tues, Thurs & Fri 9:30-5:30, Wed 1-8:30
Friends of the Library Group
CLINTON, 739 Bergen St, 07108, SAN 351-0514. Tel: 973-733-7754, 973-733-7757. FAX: 973-733-7757. *Br Mgr,* Paul Volpe; E-mail: pvolpe@npl.org; *Adult Ref Librn,* Vinell Spied; E-mail: vspied@npl.org; Staff 5 (MLS 2, Non-MLS 3)
Pop 18,693
Library Holdings: Bk Vols 39,896; Per Subs 40
Function: Children's prog, Computers for patron use, Copy machines, Electronic databases & coll, Holiday prog, Online cat, Online ref, Preschool outreach, Prog for children & young adult, Pub access computers, Ref serv available, Story hour, Tax forms, Telephone ref
Open Mon, Tues, Thurs & Fri 9:30-5:30, Wed 1-8
NORTH END, 722 Summer Ave, 07104, SAN 351-0549. Tel: 973-733-7766. FAX: 973-733-7835. *Supv Librn-in-Charge, Eastern Region,* Paula Baratta; Staff 5 (MLS 1, Non-MLS 4)
Library Holdings: Bk Vols 31,185; Per Subs 69
Function: Handicapped accessible, Homebound delivery serv, ILL available, Large print keyboards, Photocopying/Printing, Prog for adults, Prog for children & young adult, Ref serv available, Summer reading prog, Telephone ref
Open Mon, Tues, Thurs & Fri 9:30-5:30, Wed 1-8
ROSEVILLE, 99 N Fifth St, 07107, SAN 351-0573. Tel: 973-733-7770. *Br Mgr,* Mable Williams; E-mail: mwilliams@npl.org; Staff 3 (MLS 1, Non-MLS 2)
Library Holdings: Bk Vols 19,057; Per Subs 63
Function: ILL available, Large print keyboards, Photocopying/Printing, Prog for children & young adult, Ref serv available, Summer reading prog, Telephone ref
Open Mon, Tues, Thurs & Fri 9:30-5:30, Wed 1-8
SPRINGFIELD, 50 Hayes St, 07103, SAN 351-0603. Tel: 973-733-7736. *Br Mgr,* Clara Wilson; E-mail: cwilson@npl.org; Staff 5 (Non MLS 5)
Library Holdings: Bk Vols 33,866; Per Subs 70
Function: Handicapped accessible, ILL available, Large print keyboards, Photocopying/Printing, Prog for adults, Prog for children & young adult, Ref serv available, Summer reading prog, Telephone ref, Wheelchair accessible
Open Mon, Tues, Thurs & Fri 9:30-5:30, Wed 1-8
VAILSBURG, 75 Alexander St, 07106, SAN 351-0638. Tel: 973-733-7755. *Br Mgr,* Ina Rimpau; E-mail: irimpau@npl.org; *Ch,* Adam Schmidt; E-mail: aschmidt@npl.org; Staff 5 (MLS 2, Non-MLS 3)
Library Holdings: Bk Vols 33,866; Per Subs 66
Function: Handicapped accessible, Homebound delivery serv, ILL available, Large print keyboards, Photocopying/Printing, Prog for adults, Prog for children & young adult, Ref serv available, Summer reading prog, Telephone ref
Open Mon, Tues, Thurs & Fri 9:30-5:30, Wed 1-8
VAN BUREN, 140 Van Buren St, 07105, SAN 351-0662. Tel: 973-733-7750. FAX: 973-733-3897. *Br Mgr,* Valerie Gores; E-mail: vgores@npl.org; Staff 5 (MLS 1, Non-MLS 4)
Library Holdings: Bk Vols 37,474; Per Subs 30
Function: Handicapped accessible, ILL available, Large print keyboards, Prog for children & young adult, Ref serv available, Summer reading prog, Telephone ref, Wheelchair accessible
Open Mon, Tues, Thurs & Fri 9:30-5:30, Wed 1-8
WEEQUAHIC, 355 Osborne Terrace, 07112, SAN 351-0697. Tel: 973-733-7751. FAX: 973-733-7802. *Ch,* Shileen Shaw; E-mail: sshaw@npl.org; *Br Mgr,* Deloris Moses; E-mail: dmoses@npl.org; Staff 4 (MLS 2, Non-MLS 2)
Library Holdings: Bk Vols 27,552; Per Subs 57
Function: Handicapped accessible, ILL available, Large print keyboards, Photocopying/Printing, Prog for adults, Prog for children & young adult, Ref serv available, Summer reading prog, Telephone ref, Wheelchair accessible
Open Mon, Tues, Thurs & Fri 9:30-5:30, Wed 1-8

S NORTHERN STATE PRISON LIBRARY*, 168 Frontage Rd, 07114-3794. (Mail add: PO Box 2300, 07114-0300), SAN 371-5574. Tel: 973-465-0068, Ext 4521. FAX: 973-578-4393. *Librn,* Gail Gillespie; Staff 1 (MLS 1)
Founded 1987
Library Holdings: Bks on Deafness & Sign Lang 3; Bk Titles 4,000; Bk Vols 4,200; Per Subs 1
Partic in LibraryLinkNJ, The New Jersey Library Cooperative
Special Services for the Blind - Talking bks
Open Mon, Tues & Fri 8-10, 1-3 & 5:30-7, Wed & Thurs 8-10 & 1-3

L PRUDENTIAL FINANCIAL*, Prudential Insurance Law Library, Four Plaza, 751 Broad St, 07102-3714. SAN 351-0751. Tel: 973-802-9255. FAX: 973-802-2298. E-mail: refdesk@prudential.com. Web Site: www.prudential.com. *Dir, Libr Serv,* Johanna C Bizub; Tel: 973-367-3175, E-mail: jbizub@prudential.com; *Asst Librn, Ref,* Magali Velez; Tel: 973-802-6811, E-mail: magali.velez@prudential.com; *Asst Librn, Tech Serv,* Sarah Connell; Tel: 973-802-6804, E-mail: sarah.connell@prudential.com; Staff 5 (MLS 2, Non-MLS 3)
Library Holdings: Bk Titles 1,000; Bk Vols 7,500; Per Subs 100
Subject Interests: Ins, Law, Real estate, Securities
Database Vendor: LexisNexis, Westlaw
Restriction: Staff use only

S PUBLIC SERVICE ENTERPRISE GROUP*, Library Services, 80 Park Plaza, Mailcode P3C, 07101. SAN 310-3552. Tel: 973-430-5633, 973-430-7000. FAX: 973-802-1054. E-mail: library@pseg.com. *Mgr,* Judith A Price; Tel: 973-430-7332, Ext 5633; Staff 16 (MLS 10, Non-MLS 6)
Founded 1911
Library Holdings: Per Subs 60
Subject Interests: Distribution, Electric power, Environ, Natural gas, Nuclear energy, Safety
Automation Activity & Vendor Info: (Acquisitions) Livelink for Libraries; (Cataloging) Livelink for Libraries; (Circulation) Livelink for Libraries; (OPAC) Livelink for Libraries
Database Vendor: Bloomberg, Dialog, Dun & Bradstreet, Factiva.com, Factset, IHS, Westlaw, Westlaw Business
Partic in LibraryLinkNJ, The New Jersey Library Cooperative; Lyrasis; OCLC Online Computer Library Center, Inc
Restriction: Staff use only

RUTGERS UNIVERSITY LIBRARIES
C JOHN COTTON DANA LIBRARY*, 185 University Ave, 07102, SAN 351-0786. Tel: 973-353-5222. Circulation Tel: 973-353-5161. Interlibrary Loan Service Tel: 973-353-5902. Reference Tel: 973-353-5901. FAX: 973-353-5257. Web Site: www.libraries.rutgers.edu/dana. *Dir,* Jeanne Boyle; *Head, Pub Serv,* Natalie Borisovets; *Bus Librn, Head, Tech Serv,* Ka-Neng Au; Staff 37 (MLS 10, Non-MLS 27)
Founded 1927. Enrl 10,000; Fac 500; Highest Degree: Doctorate
Library Holdings: AV Mats 39,207; Bk Vols 346,393; Per Subs 3,223
Special Collections: State Document Depository; US Document Depository
Subject Interests: Bus, Nursing
Automation Activity & Vendor Info: (Circulation) SirsiDynix
Partic in Association of Research Libraries (ARL); BRS; Dialog Corp; Metropolitan New York Library Council; OCLC Research Library Partnership; RLIN (Research Libraries Information Network); SDC
Publications: Library Guide Series, Library News Release
Open Mon-Thurs 8am-10pm, Fri 8-5, Sat 10-6
CL DON M GOTTFREDSON LIBRARY OF CRIMINAL JUSTICE*, 123 Washington St, Ste 350, 07102-3094, SAN 327-9499. Tel: 973-353-3118. FAX: 973-353-1275. Web Site: www.libraries.rutgers.edu/rul/libs/crim_just/crim_just.shtml. *Librn,* Phyllis Schultze; E-mail: pschultz@andromeda.rutgers.edu; Staff 1 (MLS 1)

Function: ILL available
Partic in Association of Research Libraries (ARL)
Publications: Acquisitions List (Bi-monthly)
Open Mon-Thurs 9am-10pm, Fri 9-5, Sat & Sun 12-5
Friends of the Library Group

C INSTITUTE OF JAZZ STUDIES*, John Cotton Dana Library, 185 University Ave, 4th Flr, 07102, SAN 351-0808. Tel: 973-353-5595. FAX: 973-353-5944. Web Site: newarkwww.rutgers.edu/ijs, www.libraries.rutgers.edu/rul/libs/jazz/jazz.shtml. *Dir,* Dan Morgenstern; *Assoc Dir,* Edward Berger
Founded 1952
Library Holdings: CDs 100,000; Bk Vols 10,000; Per Subs 150
Special Collections: Jazz Archive Coll; Memorabilia; Realia. Oral History
Subject Interests: Jazz
Publications: Annual Review of Jazz Studies; Studies in Jazz
Open Mon-Fri 9-4:30
Restriction: Non-circulating

CL RUTGERS UNIVERSITY LIBRARY FOR THE CENTER FOR LAW & JUSTICE*, 123 Washington St, 07102-3094. SAN 351-0816. Tel: 973-353-3121. Circulation Tel: 973-353-5677. Reference Tel: 973-353-5676. FAX: 973-353-1356. Web Site: law-library.rutgers.edu. *Dep Dir,* Paul Axel-Lute; Tel: 973-353-3151; *Head, Tech Serv,* Marjorie E Crawford; Tel: 973-353-3144; *Head, User Serv,* Lee Sims; Tel: 973-353-3036, E-mail: lsims@kinoy.rutgers.edu; *Ref & Tech Librn,* Caroline Young; Tel: 973-353-3146; *Digital Serv,* Wei Fang; Tel: 973-353-3061; *Govt Doc,* Susan Lyons; Tel: 973-353-3092; *Ref Serv,* Dennis Kim-Prieto; Tel: 973-353-3037; Staff 18 (MLS 9, Non-MLS 9)
Library Holdings: Bk Vols 381,000
Special Collections: Law Library of US Supreme Court Justice Bradley. State Document Depository; US Document Depository
Automation Activity & Vendor Info: (Acquisitions) Innovative Interfaces, Inc; (Cataloging) Innovative Interfaces, Inc; (Circulation) Innovative Interfaces, Inc; (OPAC) Innovative Interfaces, Inc; (Serials) Innovative Interfaces, Inc
Database Vendor: Gale Cengage Learning, HeinOnline, LexisNexis, OCLC WorldShare Interlibrary Loan, Westlaw
Wireless access
Partic in OCLC Online Computer Library Center, Inc
Friends of the Library Group

L ST JOHN & WAYNE*, Law Library, One Riverfront Plaza, 1037 Raymond Blvd, 16th Fl, 07102. SAN 323-8334. Tel: 973-491-3300. FAX: 973-491-3555. Web Site: www.stjohnlaw.com. *Librn,* Diamond Bona; Staff 1 (MLS 1)
Founded 1971
Library Holdings: Bk Vols 8,000
Database Vendor: LexisNexis, Westlaw
Restriction: Staff use only

CL SETON HALL UNIVERSITY SCHOOL OF LAW*, Peter W Rodino Jr Law Library, One Newark Ctr, 07102. SAN 310-3579. Circulation Tel: 973-642-8720. Reference Tel: 973-642-8861. Administration Tel: 973-642-8766. Administration FAX: 973-642-8748. Web Site: law.shu.edu. *Dir,* Charles A Sullivan; *Dep Dir,* Barbara Mol; Tel: 973-642-8765; *Archivist, Govt Doc Librn, ILL & Ser,* Dianne Oster; Tel: 973-642-8195; *Ref Librn,* Maja Basioli; *Ref/Acq,* Brittany Persson; Tel: 973-642-8767, *Tech & Digital Serv Librn,* Kristina Anderson; Tel: 973-642-8764; Staff 12 (MLS 5, Non-MLS 7)
Founded 1950. Enrl 1,064; Fac 65; Highest Degree: Doctorate
Jul 2012-Jun 2013. Mats Exp $1,132,761
Library Holdings: AV Mats 200; Bk Vols 459,904; Per Subs 3,367
Special Collections: Rodino Archives. State Document Depository; US Document Depository
Subject Interests: Health law, Health policy
Automation Activity & Vendor Info: (Acquisitions) Innovative Interfaces, Inc; (Cataloging) Innovative Interfaces, Inc; (Circulation) Innovative Interfaces, Inc; (ILL) OCLC; (OPAC) Innovative Interfaces, Inc; (Serials) Innovative Interfaces, Inc
Database Vendor: LexisNexis, Westlaw
Partic in Lyrasis
Open Mon-Fri 8-6, Sat 9-5, Sun 12-7
Restriction: Restricted access

GL UNITED STATES ATTORNEY'S OFFICE LIBRARY*, 970 Broad St, Rm 700, 07102. SAN 310-3595. Tel: 973-645-2700. FAX: 973-297-2007. *Librn,* Sam Li; Staff 4 (MLS 2, Non-MLS 2)
Library Holdings: Bk Vols 6,000
Restriction: Not open to pub
Branches:
NORTH BRANCH, 970 Broad St, Ste 700, 07102, SAN 321-4982. Tel: 973-645-2709. *Law Librn,* Sam Li
Library Holdings: Bk Vols 4,000
Database Vendor: EBSCOhost
Open Mon-Fri 9-5:30
Restriction: Not open to pub
TRENTON BRANCH, 402 E State St, Trenton, 08608, SAN 321-4990. Tel: 973-645-2709. *Law Librn,* Sam Li
Library Holdings: Bk Vols 5,216
Database Vendor: EBSCOhost
Restriction: Not open to pub

GL UNITED STATES COURT OF APPEALS, United States Court Library, King Courthouse, Rm 5007, 50 Walnut St, 07102. (Mail add: PO Box 1068, 07101-1068), SAN 325-7762. Tel: 973-645-3034. *Librn,* Andrea Battel; Staff 1 (MLS 1)
Library Holdings: Bk Vols 18,000; Spec Interest Per Sub 15
Subject Interests: Law
Automation Activity & Vendor Info: (Acquisitions) SirsiDynix; (Cataloging) OCLC; (Circulation) SirsiDynix; (OPAC) SirsiDynix; (Serials) SirsiDynix
Open Mon-Fri 8:30-4:30
Restriction: Circulates for staff only

NEWFIELD

S UNEXPECTED WILDLIFE REFUGE LIBRARY*, 110 Unexpected Rd, 08344. (Mail add: PO Box 765, 08344-0765), SAN 371-4551. Tel: 856-697-3541. E-mail: info@unexpectedwildliferefuge.org. Web Site: www.animalplace.org/uwr/uwr_frame.html. *Dir,* Sarah Summerville
Library Holdings: Bk Titles 800
Subject Interests: Environ studies, Ethic studies

NEWTON

J SUSSEX COUNTY COMMUNITY COLLEGE LIBRARY*, One College Hill Rd, 07860. SAN 375-7439. Tel: 973-300-2162. Interlibrary Loan Service Tel: 973-300-2294. Reference Tel: 973-300-2292. Administration Tel: 973-300-2161. FAX: 973-300-2276. E-mail: library@sussex.edu. Web Site: sussex.edu/academics/library. *Dir,* Stephanie Cooper; E-mail: scooper@sussex.edu; *Ref Serv,* Angela Camack; Tel: 973-300-2164, E-mail: acamack@sussex.edu; Staff 3 (MLS 3)
Founded 1989. Enrl 4,008; Fac 51; Highest Degree: Associate
Library Holdings: Bks on Deafness & Sign Lang 51; CDs 35; DVDs 22; Electronic Media & Resources 16; High Interest/Low Vocabulary Bk Vols 48; Bk Titles 36,000; Per Subs 175; Spec Interest Per Sub 145; Videos 100
Subject Interests: Juv, Law
Automation Activity & Vendor Info: (Acquisitions) SirsiDynix; (Cataloging) SirsiDynix; (Circulation) SirsiDynix; (Course Reserve) SirsiDynix; (ILL) OCLC; (OPAC) SirsiDynix
Database Vendor: CredoReference, EBSCOhost, Facts on File, Gale Cengage Learning, H W Wilson, JSTOR, Medline, Newsbank, OCLC WorldShare Interlibrary Loan, Oxford Online, ProQuest, Wilson - Wilson Web
Wireless access
Function: Archival coll, Audio & video playback equip for onsite use, Computers for patron use, Copy machines, Electronic databases & coll, Handicapped accessible, ILL available, Magnifiers for reading, Online cat, Orientations, Outside serv via phone, mail, e-mail & web, Photocopying/Printing, Wheelchair accessible
Partic in LibraryLinkNJ, The New Jersey Library Cooperative; Lyrasis; Virtual Academic Library Environment
Special Services for the Deaf - Bks on deafness & sign lang; Staff with knowledge of sign lang
Special Services for the Blind - Assistive/Adapted tech devices, equip & products; Bks on CD
Open Mon-Thurs 8:30-8, Fri 8:30-4:30, Sat 9-12
Restriction: Non-circulating to the pub, Open to students, fac & staff

S SUSSEX COUNTY HISTORICAL SOCIETY LIBRARY*, 82 Main St, 07860-2046. (Mail add: PO Box 913, 07860), SAN 328-1868. Tel: 973-383-6010. FAX: 973-383-6010. E-mail: sussexcountyhs@gmail.com. Web Site: www.sussexcountyhistory.org. *In Charge,* Myra Snook; Staff 0.4 (Non-MLS 0.4)
Library Holdings: Bk Titles 1,200
Wireless access
Function: Ref & res, Ref serv available, Res libr
Restriction: Mem only, Non-circulating

L SUSSEX COUNTY LAW LIBRARY*, 4347 High St, 07860. SAN 327-9456. Tel: 973-579-0702. FAX: 973-579-0679. *Head Librn,* Joe Tuttle
Library Holdings: Bk Titles 9,000
Open Mon-Fri 8:30-4:30
Friends of the Library Group

P SUSSEX COUNTY LIBRARY SYSTEM*, 125 Morris Tpk, 07860-0076. SAN 351-0905. Tel: 973-948-3660. FAX: 973-948-2071. E-mail: sussexref@sussexcountylibrary.org. Web Site: www.sussexcountylibrary.org.

Dir, Stan Pollakoff; E-mail: pollakoff@sussexcountylibrary.org; *Head, Tech Serv,* Tim Thacker; E-mail: timtcat@sussexcountylibrary.org; *Br Coordr, Extn Serv,* Ellen Callanan; *Syst Coordr,* Kim Grohs; Staff 62 (MLS 9, Non-MLS 53)
Founded 1942. Pop 119,416; Circ 616,201
Library Holdings: Bk Titles 146,307; Per Subs 450
Special Collections: Delaware Water Gap National Recreation Area (Tocks Island Regional Advisory Council Library); Sussex County History Coll. State Document Depository; US Document Depository
Automation Activity & Vendor Info: (Circulation) Horizon
Database Vendor: SirsiDynix
Wireless access
Partic in LibraryLinkNJ, The New Jersey Library Cooperative
Open Mon-Thurs 8:30-8:30, Fri 8:30-5, Sat 9-5
Branches: 5
E LOUISE CHILDS MEMORIAL, 21 Sparta Rd, Stanhope, 07874, SAN 351-1022. Tel: 973-770-1000. FAX: 973-770-0094. *Librn,* Regina Bohn
Open Mon, Wed & Fri 9-5, Tues & Thurs 9-8:30, Sat 9-1
DENNIS MEMORIAL, 101 Main St, 07860, SAN 351-0964. Tel: 973-383-4810. FAX: 973-383-1322. *Librn,* Position Currently Open
Open Mon 9-8:30, Tues-Fri 9-5, Sat 9-1
FRANKLIN BRANCH, 103 Main St, Franklin, 07416-1517, SAN 351-0999. Tel: 973-827-6555. FAX: 973-827-9422. *Librn,* Mary Grace Zaccaria; Staff 1 (MLS 1)
Open Mon, Wed & Fri 9-5, Tues & Thurs 9-8:30, Sat 9-1
DOROTHY E HENRY MEMORIAL, 66 Rte 94, Vernon, 07462, SAN 351-1081. Tel: 973-827-8095. FAX: 973-827-8664. *Br Librn,* Jacqueline Oregero
Open Mon & Wed-Sat 9-5, Tues 12-8
Friends of the Library Group
SUSSEX-WANTAGE, 69 Rte 639, Wantage, 07461, SAN 351-1057. Tel: 973-875-3940. FAX: 973-875-1336. *Chief Librn,* Position Currently Open; Staff 1 (MLS 1)
Open Mon & Wed 9-8:30, Tues & Thurs-Sat 9-5
Friends of the Library Group

NORTH ARLINGTON

P NORTH ARLINGTON FREE PUBLIC LIBRARY*, 210 Ridge Rd, 07031. SAN 310-3633. Tel: 201-955-5640. FAX: 201-991-7850. Web Site: www.bccls.org/northarlington. *Dir,* Stephanie Burke; *Ref,* Kate Landis; Staff 6 (MLS 3, Non-MLS 3)
Founded 1939. Pop 15,000; Circ 70,000
Library Holdings: Bk Titles 90,000; Bk Vols 95,000; Per Subs 60; Talking Bks 700
Special Collections: New Jerseyana
Automation Activity & Vendor Info: (Cataloging) OCLC; (Circulation) SirsiDynix; (OPAC) SirsiDynix
Wireless access
Partic in Bergen County Cooperative Library System
Open Mon, Tues & Thurs 9:30-8:30, Wed & Fri 9:30-5:30, Sat 10-1
Friends of the Library Group

NORTH BERGEN

P NORTH BERGEN FREE PUBLIC LIBRARY*, 8411 Bergenline Ave, 07047-5097. SAN 351-1111. Tel: 201-869-4715. FAX: 201-868-0968. E-mail: nbercirc@bccls.org. Web Site: www.nbpl.org. *Dir,* Sai Rao; E-mail: srao@nbpl.org; Staff 26 (MLS 6, Non-MLS 20)
Founded 1936. Pop 58,092; Circ 101,000
Library Holdings: Bk Titles 161,000; Bk Vols 166,000; Per Subs 226
Special Collections: Foreign Language Coll; Large Print Coll; Literature Coll; New Jerseyiana
Automation Activity & Vendor Info: (Cataloging) SirsiDynix; (Circulation) SirsiDynix; (OPAC) SirsiDynix
Partic in Bergen County Cooperative Library System; LibraryLinkNJ, The New Jersey Library Cooperative
Open Mon-Thurs (Winter) 9-8, Fri & Sat 9-5; Mon & Thurs (Summer) 9-8, Tues, Wed & Fri 9-5

NORTH BRUNSWICK

C DEVRY UNIVERSITY LIBRARY*, Robert M Bocchino Library, 630 US Hwy One, 08902. Tel: 732-729-3840. FAX: 732-729-3969. Web Site: www.nj.devry.edu/library.html. *Libr Dir,* Joseph Louderback; E-mail: jlouderback@devry.edu; Staff 1 (MLS 1)
Highest Degree: Master
Automation Activity & Vendor Info: (Cataloging) Ex Libris Group
Database Vendor: EBSCOhost, LexisNexis, ProQuest
Wireless access
Partic in Illinois Library & Information Network; LibraryLinkNJ, The New Jersey Library Cooperative; Lyrasis
Open Mon-Thurs 8:30-8:30, Fri 8:30-6:30, Sat 9-3

S MIDDLESEX COUNTY ADULT CORRECTION CENTER LIBRARY*, Rte 130, Apple Orchard Lane, 08902. (Mail add: PO Box 266, New Brunswick, 08903-0266). Tel: 732-297-3636, Ext 6224. *Dir,* Catherine Albair
Library Holdings: Bk Vols 25,000
Open Mon-Fri 8:30-4:30
Restriction: Internal circ only

P NORTH BRUNSWICK FREE PUBLIC LIBRARY, 880 Hermann Rd, 08902. SAN 310-3668. Tel: 732-246-3545. FAX: 732-246-1341. E-mail: refdesk@northbrunswicklibrary.org. Web Site: www.northbrunswicklibrary.org. *Dir,* Cheryl McBride; E-mail: cmcbride@northbrunswicklibrary.org; *Ch,* Bari Coslow; E-mail: bcoslow@northbrunswicklibrary.org; *IT Librn,* Barbara Elieff; *YA Librn,* Zoltan Braz; *Ref,* Radha Dhanyamraju; *Ref,* Jean Ruch; Staff 17 (MLS 6, Non-MLS 11)
Founded 1966. Pop 40,000; Circ 257,000
Library Holdings: Bk Vols 100,000; Per Subs 240
Special Collections: Chinese Language Coll; Gujarati Language Coll; Hindi Language Coll; Spanish Language Coll; Telugu Language Coll; Urdu Language Coll
Automation Activity & Vendor Info: (Acquisitions) SirsiDynix; (Circulation) SIRSI-iBistro; (OPAC) SirsiDynix
Database Vendor: EBSCOhost, Gale Cengage Learning, ProQuest
Wireless access
Function: Adult bk club, Bks on CD, Computer training, Copy machines, Fax serv, Free DVD rentals, Handicapped accessible, Homebound delivery serv, Mail & tel request accepted, Music CDs, OverDrive digital audio bks, Photocopying/Printing, Prog for adults, Prog for children & young adult, Pub access computers, Scanner, Telephone ref
Partic in Libraries of Middlesex Automation Consortium
Open Mon-Thurs 10-9, Fri & Sat 10-5, Sun 12-5
Friends of the Library Group

NORTH HALEDON

P NORTH HALEDON FREE PUBLIC LIBRARY*, 129 Overlook Ave, 07508-2533. SAN 310-3676. Tel: 973-427-6213. FAX: 973-427-1826. Web Site: www.northhaledonlibrary.org. *Dir,* Susan Serico; Staff 1 (MLS 1)
Founded 1929. Pop 7,920; Circ 66,972
Jan 2010-Dec 2010 Income $614,690. Mats Exp $66,144, Books $39,304, Per/Ser (Incl. Access Fees) $3,351, AV Mat $21,305, Electronic Ref Mat (Incl. Access Fees) $2,184. Sal $228,959
Library Holdings: AV Mats 1,210; CDs 2,178; DVDs 2,673; e-books 1,526; Bk Vols 26,341; Per Subs 71
Automation Activity & Vendor Info: (Cataloging) SirsiDynix; (Circulation) SirsiDynix; (OPAC) SirsiDynix
Wireless access
Partic in LibraryLinkNJ, The New Jersey Library Cooperative; PALS Plus, The Computer Consortium of Passaic County Libraries
Open Mon-Thurs 9-9, Fri & Sat 9-5
Friends of the Library Group

NORTHFIELD

P OTTO BRUYNS PUBLIC LIBRARY OF NORTHFIELD*, 241 W Mill Rd, 08225. SAN 310-3684. Tel: 609-646-4476. FAX: 609-484-9006. *Dir,* Margaret Derascavage; Staff 1 (Non-MLS 1)
Founded 1926. Pop 7,875; Circ 37,082
Library Holdings: Bk Vols 29,000; Per Subs 76
Special Collections: History of Northfield, monographs
Automation Activity & Vendor Info: (Cataloging) Follett Software; (Circulation) Follett Software; (OPAC) Follett Software
Wireless access
Partic in Coalition of Independent Libraries (COIL)
Open Mon-Thurs 10-8, Fri & Sat 10-5
Friends of the Library Group

NORWOOD

P NORWOOD PUBLIC LIBRARY*, 198 Summit St, 07648-1835. SAN 310-3722. Tel: 201-768-9555. FAX: 201-767-2176. E-mail: nowdcirc@bccls.org. Web Site: nplnj.org. *Dir,* Riti Grover; E-mail: riti.grover@bccls.org; *Ch Serv,* Laura Surniak
Founded 1938. Pop 4,600; Circ 14,035
Jan 2005-Dec 2005 Income $337,100. Mats Exp $28,100. Sal $162,500
Library Holdings: Bk Titles 37,000; Per Subs 65
Automation Activity & Vendor Info: (Cataloging) Innovative Interfaces, Inc; (Circulation) Innovative Interfaces, Inc; (OPAC) Innovative Interfaces, Inc
Database Vendor: EBSCOhost, Gale Cengage Learning, ProQuest
Wireless access
Mem of Delaware County Library System
Partic in Bergen County Cooperative Library System
Special Services for the Blind - Magnifiers

Open Mon & Wed 10-9, Tues, Thurs & Fri 10-6, Sat 9-1
Friends of the Library Group

NUTLEY

S HOFFMANN-LA ROCHE, INC*, Scientific Information Management, 340 Kingsland St, Bldg 76/3, 07110-1199. SAN 351-1200. Tel: 973-235-2060. FAX: 973-235-5477. *Mgr,* Marian Koob; E-mail: marian.koob@roche.com; *Info Spec,* Sandra J DiGiacomo; Tel: 973-935-3092, Fax: 973-235-4632, E-mail: sandra.digiacomo@roche.com; Staff 2 (MLS 1, Non-MLS 1)
Founded 1930
Library Holdings: e-books 758; e-journals 7,931; Bk Titles 3,200; Per Subs 4
Subject Interests: Medicinal chem, Pharmacology
Automation Activity & Vendor Info: (OPAC) Cuadra Associates, Inc; (Serials) Cuadra Associates, Inc
Database Vendor: American Chemical Society, DATASTAR Inc, ISI Web of Knowledge, Medline, MicroPatent, ProQuest, PubMed, STN International
Wireless access
Function: Copy machines, Doc delivery serv, Electronic databases & coll, Photocopying/Printing, Ref & res
Restriction: Access for corporate affiliates, Co libr, Employees only

P NUTLEY FREE PUBLIC LIBRARY*, 93 Booth Dr, 07110-2782. SAN 310-3749. Tel: 973-667-0405. Reference FAX: 973-667-0408. Administration FAX: 973-667-4673. E-mail: library@nutleynj.org. Web Site: nutley.bccls.org. *Dir,* Sarah Lester; *Supv Librn, Circ,* Jeanne Sylvester; *Supv Librn, Ref & Tech Serv,* Kiran B Patel; *Ch & Youth Librn,* Megan Ibararran; *Ref Librn/Bus Liaison,* Michael Maziekien; *Libr Assoc,* Nicholas Van Dorn; Staff 11 (MLS 6, Non-MLS 5)
Founded 1913. Pop 27,362; Circ 141,737
Library Holdings: CDs 2,951; DVDs 2,821; Bk Vols 86,208; Per Subs 215; Talking Bks 2,793
Special Collections: Harry W Chenoweth Interviews; Nutley Sun & Nutley Journal (online access & micro)
Subject Interests: Local hist
Automation Activity & Vendor Info: (Cataloging) SIRSI Unicorn; (Circulation) SIRSI WorkFlows; (ILL) SIRSI Unicorn; (OPAC) SIRSI Unicorn
Database Vendor: Baker & Taylor, EBSCOhost, Electric Library, H W Wilson, ProQuest, ReferenceUSA, Westlaw, Wilson - Wilson Web
Wireless access
Function: Adult bk club, Art exhibits, Audio & video playback equip for onsite use, Audiobks via web, Bilingual assistance for Spanish patrons, Bk club(s), Bks on CD, CD-ROM, Chess club, Children's prog, Computer training, Computers for patron use, Copy machines, E-Reserves, Electronic databases & coll, Handicapped accessible, Holiday prog, Homebound delivery serv, ILL available, Literacy & newcomer serv, Magnifiers for reading, Mail & tel request accepted, Mus passes, Music CDs, Online cat, Online ref, Online searches, Outreach serv, Preschool outreach, Prog for adults, Prog for children & young adult, Pub access computers, Ref serv available, Senior outreach, Story hour, Summer reading prog, Tax forms, Teen prog, Telephone ref, Web-catalog, Wheelchair accessible, Writing prog
Partic in Bergen County Cooperative Library System; LibraryLinkNJ, The New Jersey Library Cooperative
Special Services for the Blind - Audio mat; Large print bks
Open Mon, Tues & Thurs 9-9, Wed, Fri & Sat 9-5
Friends of the Library Group

OAK RIDGE

P JEFFERSON TOWNSHIP PUBLIC LIBRARY*, 1031 Weldon Rd, 07438. SAN 320-2046. Tel: 973-208-6244. FAX: 973-697-7051. Web Site: www.jeffersonlibrary.net. *Dir,* Seth Stephens; *Asst Dir,* Sandy Cale; Staff 8 (MLS 1, Non-MLS 7)
Founded 1960. Pop 20,000
Library Holdings: Bk Titles 52,000; Per Subs 97
Automation Activity & Vendor Info: (Cataloging) SirsiDynix; (Circulation) SirsiDynix; (OPAC) SirsiDynix
Wireless access
Publications: Violet's Porch (Newsletter)
Partic in Morris Automated Information Network
Open Mon-Fri 9:30-9, Sat 9-6, Sun 1-5
Friends of the Library Group

OAKLAND

P OAKLAND PUBLIC LIBRARY*, Two Municipal Plaza, 07436. SAN 310-3773. Tel: 201-337-3742. FAX: 201-337-0261. E-mail: oaklcirc@bccls.org. Web Site: oakland.bccls.org. *Dir,* Abby Sanner; E-mail: sanner@bccls.org; *Cat, Ref,* Rose Marie Kollar; *Ch Serv,* Debbie Pfeuffer; *Circ,* Carol Quirk; Staff 16 (MLS 3, Non-MLS 13)
Founded 1910. Pop 11,997; Circ 95,029
Library Holdings: Bk Vols 60,500; Per Subs 180
Automation Activity & Vendor Info: (Cataloging) SirsiDynix; (Circulation) SirsiDynix; (OPAC) SirsiDynix
Partic in Bergen County Cooperative Library System
Special Services for the Blind - Magnifiers
Open Mon, Tues & Thurs 10-9, Wed, Fri & Sat 10-5
Friends of the Library Group

OAKLYN

P OAKLYN MEMORIAL LIBRARY*, 602 Newton Ave, 08107. SAN 310-3803. Tel: 856-858-8226. E-mail: oaklynmemlibrary@gmail.com. *Dir,* Andrea Cline; *Libr Asst,* Pat Koch; *Libr Asst,* Janet Larson; *Libr Asst,* Monica Rottler
Founded 1927. Pop 5,000; Circ 15,789
Library Holdings: Bk Titles 20,000; Bk Vols 25,000; Per Subs 38
Special Collections: Local History Coll; Popular Fiction Coll
Database Vendor: EBSCOhost
Wireless access
Mem of Camden County Library System
Open Mon, Tues & Thurs (Winter) 10-2 & 3-7, Wed, Fri & Sat 10-2; Mon, Tues & Thurs (Summer) 10-2 & 4-8
Friends of the Library Group

OCEAN

S OCEAN TOWNSHIP HISTORICAL MUSEUM LIBRARY*, 703 Deal Rd, 07712. (Mail add: PO Box 516, Oakhurst, 07755), SAN 377-5011. Tel: 732-531-2136. Web Site: www.oceanmuseum.org. *Pres,* Brenda Wityk
Library Holdings: Bk Vols 250
Special Collections: Oral History
Wireless access
Open Tues & Wed 1-4, Thurs 1-4 & 7-9

S PREVENTION FIRST*, Prevention & Education Resource Center, 1405 State Hwy 35N, 07712. SAN 377-533X. Tel: 732-663-1800. FAX: 732-663-1698. E-mail: info@preventionfirst.net. Web Site: www.preventionfirst.net. *Info Spec,* Denise Stevens
Library Holdings: Bk Titles 450
Partic in LibraryLinkNJ, The New Jersey Library Cooperative
Special Services for the Deaf - TDD equip
Restriction: Not open to pub

OCEAN CITY

P OCEAN CITY FREE PUBLIC LIBRARY*, 1735 Simpson Ave, Ste 4, 08226. SAN 310-382X. Tel: 609-399-2434. Circulation Tel: 609-399-2434, Ext 5221. Interlibrary Loan Service Tel: 609-399-2434, Ext 5228. Reference Tel: 609-399-2434, Ext 5231. Administration Tel: 609-399-2434, Ext 5233. Information Services Tel: 609-399-2434, Ext 5240. FAX: 609-398-0751. Web Site: www.oceancitylibrary.org. *Dir,* Position Currently Open; *Head, Circ,* Maria Farrell; E-mail: maria@oceancitylibrary.org; *Youth Serv Librn,* Sara Bruesehoff; Tel: 609-399-2434, Ext 5235, E-mail: sara@oceancitylibrary.org; *Acq,* Kathryn Brown; Tel: 609-399-2434, Ext 5223, E-mail: kathryn@oceancitylibrary.org; *Ch Serv,* Leslie Clarke; Tel: 609-399-2434, Ext 5241, E-mail: leslie@oceancitylibrary.org; *IT Serv,* John Ruban; E-mail: john@oceancitylibrary.org; *Ref Serv, Ad,* Kevin Bligh; Tel: 609-399-2434, Ext 5226, E-mail: kevin@oceancitylibrary.org; Staff 33 (MLS 7, Non-MLS 26)
Pop 15,378; Circ 437,214
Library Holdings: Bk Vols 90,000; Per Subs 250
Subject Interests: Local hist
Automation Activity & Vendor Info: (Cataloging) Innovative Interfaces, Inc; (Circulation) Innovative Interfaces, Inc; (ILL) Innovative Interfaces, Inc; (OPAC) Innovative Interfaces, Inc
Database Vendor: EBSCOhost, Gale Cengage Learning, Infotrieve, Newsbank, ProQuest, Westlaw
Wireless access
Function: Adult bk club, Adult literacy prog, After school storytime, Archival coll, Art exhibits, Audio & video playback equip for onsite use, Audiobks via web, Bi-weekly Writer's Group, Bk club(s), Bks on CD, Bus archives, Chess club, Children's prog, Citizenship assistance, Computer training, Computers for patron use, Copy machines, Digital talking bks, Doc delivery serv, e-mail & chat, E-Reserves, Electronic databases & coll, Exhibits, Fax serv, Handicapped accessible, ILL available, Magnifiers for reading, Music CDs, Newsp ref libr, Online cat, OverDrive digital audio bks, Photocopying/Printing, Prog for adults, Prog for children & young adult, Pub access computers, Ref & res, Ref serv in person, Scanner, Senior computer classes, Story hour, Summer reading prog, Tax forms, Teen prog, Telephone ref
Partic in Coalition of Independent Libraries (COIL); LibraryLinkNJ, The New Jersey Library Cooperative
Open Mon-Fri 9-9, Sat 9-5, Sun 1-5
Friends of the Library Group

S OCEAN CITY HISTORICAL MUSEUM*, Research Library, 1735 Simpson Ave, 08226. SAN 373-2533. Tel: 609-399-1801. FAX: 609-399-0544. Web Site: www.ocnjmuseum.org. *Dir,* Jeff McGranahan
Founded 1964
Library Holdings: Bk Vols 500; Per Subs 10
Subject Interests: Local hist
Function: Res libr
Open Tues, Wed & Fri 10-4, Thurs 10-7, Sat 11-2

OCEAN GROVE

S HISTORICAL SOCIETY OF OCEAN GROVE*, Museums, Archives & Library, 50 Pitman Ave, 07756. (Mail add: PO Box 446, 07756-0446), SAN 329-2991. Tel: 732-774-1869. FAX: 732-774-1685. E-mail: info@oceangrovehistory.org. Web Site: www.oceangrovehistory.org. *Librn,* Harriet Russomano; Staff 2 (MLS 1, Non-MLS 1)
Founded 1970
Library Holdings: Bk Vols 250
Subject Interests: Local hist, Victorian-era hist
Publications: Bibliographies; Newsletters

OLD BRIDGE

P OLD BRIDGE PUBLIC LIBRARY*, One Old Bridge Plaza, 08857-2498. SAN 351-1235. Tel: 732-607-7921, 732-721-5600, Ext 5010. Interlibrary Loan Service Tel: 732-721-5600, Ext 5020. Reference Tel: 732-721-5600, Ext 5033. Administration Tel: 732-721-5600, Ext 5016. FAX: 732-679-0556. Web Site: www.oldbridgelibrary.org. *Dir,* Sarah Hansen; Tel: 732-721-5600, Ext 5042, E-mail: shansen@oldbridgelibrary.org; *Adult Serv, Info Serv,* C L Quillen; E-mail: clquillen@oldbridgelibrary.org; *Circ,* Felisha McEachern; Tel: 732-721-5600, Ext 5012, E-mail: fmceachern@oldbridgelibrary.org; *ILL,* Linda Francini; Tel: 732-721-5600, Ext 5034, E-mail: linfran@oldbridgelibrary.org; *Electronic Res,* Maggie Awadalla; Tel: 732-721-5600, Ext 5039, E-mail: mawadalla@oldbridgelibrary.org; *Tech Serv,* Gail M Sankner; E-mail: gsankner@oldbirdgelibrary.org; Staff 15 (MLS 15)
Founded 1970. Pop 60,456; Circ 345,000
Library Holdings: AV Mats 10,208; Bk Titles 131,717; Bk Vols 169,843; Per Subs 538; Talking Bks 6,900
Special Collections: Gujanati, ESL & ABR
Automation Activity & Vendor Info: (Circulation) SirsiDynix; (ILL) SirsiDynix; (OPAC) SirsiDynix
Database Vendor: EBSCOhost, Gale Cengage Learning
Wireless access
Publications: Bookends (Newsletter)
Partic in Libraries of Middlesex Automation Consortium
Special Services for the Blind - Braille bks
Open Mon-Fri 9:30-9, Sat 9:30-5, Sun (Sept-June) 12:30-5
Friends of the Library Group
Branches: 1
LAURENCE HARBOR BRANCH, 277 Shoreland Circle, Laurence Harbor, 08879, SAN 351-126X. Tel: 732-566-2227. FAX: 732-583-8829. *Br Mgr,* Amy Trombetta
Open Mon, Wed & Sat 9:30-5, Tues & Thurs 1-8

OLD TAPPAN

P OLD TAPPAN FREE PUBLIC LIBRARY*, 56 Russell Ave, 07675. SAN 310-3854. Tel: 201-664-3499. FAX: 201-664-5999. E-mail: otpncirc@bccls.org. Web Site: www.bccls.org/oldtappan. *Dir,* Susan Meeske
Founded 1943. Pop 4,300; Circ 25,400
Library Holdings: Bk Vols 34,000; Per Subs 50
Automation Activity & Vendor Info: (Cataloging) SirsiDynix; (Circulation) SirsiDynix; (OPAC) SirsiDynix
Wireless access
Special Services for the Blind - Magnifiers
Open Mon, Tues & Thurs (Winter) 9-9, Wed & Fri 9-5, Sat 10-2, Sun 1-4; Mon, Wed & Fri (Summer) 9-4, Tues & Thurs 9-9, Sat 9-1

OLDWICK

P TEWKSBURY TOWNSHIP PUBLIC LIBRARY*, 31 Main St, 08858. (Mail add: PO Box 49, 08858-0049), SAN 310-3862. Tel: 908-439-3761. FAX: 908-439-2326. *Libr Mgr,* Carole Scott
Circ 23,677
Library Holdings: Bk Vols 18,000; Per Subs 67
Special Collections: Art Coll
Subject Interests: Art, Gardening, Hist
Automation Activity & Vendor Info: (Cataloging) SirsiDynix; (Circulation) SirsiDynix; (ILL) SirsiDynix; (OPAC) SirsiDynix
Database Vendor: SirsiDynix
Mem of Hunterdon County Library
Open Tues, Wed & Fri 9-5, Thurs 9-8, Sat 9-3
Friends of the Library Group

ORADELL

S BURNS & ROE ENTERPRISES, INC*, Technical Library, 800 Kinderkamack Rd, 07649. SAN 310-3870. Tel: 201-986-4224. FAX: 201-986-4418. *Librn,* Pat Bernstein; E-mail: pbernstein@roe.com
Founded 1961
Library Holdings: Bk Vols 1,500
Subject Interests: Archit, Eng
Restriction: Staff use only

P ORADELL FREE PUBLIC LIBRARY, 375 Kinderkamack Rd, 07649-2122. SAN 310-3889. Tel: 201-262-2613. FAX: 201-262-9112. Web Site: www.oradell.bccls.org. *Dir,* John J Trause; E-mail: trause@oradell.bccls.org; *Info Serv Librn,* Linda R Pabian; E-mail: linda.pabian@oradell.bccls.org; *Youth Serv Librn,* Robin Rockman; E-mail: robin.rockman@oradell.bccls.org; *Circ Mgr,* Donna Z Sweatlock; E-mail: Donna.sweatlock@oradell.bccls.org; Staff 23 (MLS 3, Non-MLS 20)
Founded 1913. Pop 8,128; Circ 105,663
Library Holdings: AV Mats 7,916; Bk Vols 57,373; Per Subs 81
Special Collections: Books Illustrated by Charles Livingston Bull. Oral History
Subject Interests: Bks, Local hist, Paper
Automation Activity & Vendor Info: (Acquisitions) Baker & Taylor; (ILL) JerseyCat
Database Vendor: EBSCOhost, Gale Cengage Learning, ProQuest, ReferenceUSA
Wireless access
Function: 24/7 Online cat, Adult bk club, Archival coll, Art exhibits, Bk club(s), Bks on CD, Children's prog, Computer training, Copy machines, e-mail serv, E-Reserves, Electronic databases & coll, eReaders, ILL available, Magazines, Music CDs, OverDrive digital audio bks, Prog for adults, Prog for children & young adult, Pub access computers, Ref serv available, Spoken cassettes & CDs, Spoken cassettes & DVDs, Story hour, Summer reading prog, Tax forms, Teen prog, Telephone ref
Publications: The Bookmark (Newsletter)
Partic in Bergen County Cooperative Library System; LibraryLinkNJ, The New Jersey Library Cooperative
Special Services for the Blind - Large print bks; Ref serv; Telesensory screen enlarger
Open Mon-Wed 10-9, Thurs-Sat 10-5
Friends of the Library Group

ORANGE

P ORANGE PUBLIC LIBRARY*, 348 Main St, 07050-2794. SAN 310-3897. Tel: 973-673-0153, Ext 10. Reference Tel: 973-673-0153, Ext 18. Administration Tel: 973-673-0153, Ext 11. FAX: 973-673-1847. Web Site: www.orangepl.org. *Actg Dir,* Alice McMillan; E-mail: amcmillan@orangepl.org; *Ch Serv,* Deborah Ferraro; Tel: 973-673-0153, Ext 15, E-mail: dferraro@orangepl.org; Staff 4 (MLS 4)
Founded 1884. Pop 32,868; Circ 98,781
Library Holdings: AV Mats 10,537; Bk Titles 133,000; Bk Vols 201,000; Per Subs 75
Special Collections: Black Literature & History; Orangeana
Database Vendor: EBSCOhost
Wireless access
Partic in NJ State Libr Network; OCLC Online Computer Library Center, Inc; PALS Plus, The Computer Consortium of Passaic County Libraries
Open Mon 9-8, Tues & Thurs 9-6, Wed & Fri 9-7, Sat (Sept-May) 9-5
Friends of the Library Group

OXFORD

P OXFORD PUBLIC LIBRARY*, 42 Washington Ave, 07863-3037. SAN 376-0480. Tel: 908-453-2625. *Dir,* Jean Docker
Founded 1921. Pop 2,307
Library Holdings: Bk Vols 2,500
Open Tues & Thurs 2-7

S WARREN COUNTY CULTURAL & HERITAGE COMMISSION LIBRARY*, Shippen Manor, Eight Belvidere Ave, 07863. SAN 376-0626. Tel: 908-453-4381. FAX: 908-453-4981. E-mail: wcchc@nac.net. Web Site: www.wcchc.org. *Curator,* Andrew Drysdale
Library Holdings: Bk Titles 400
Special Collections: Warren County History, docs, maps
Open Sun 1-4

PALISADES PARK

P PALISADES PARK FREE PUBLIC LIBRARY*, 257 Second St, 07650. SAN 310-3935. Tel: 201-585-4150. FAX: 201-585-2151. E-mail: palpcirc@bccls.org. Web Site: palisadespark.bccls.org. *Dir,* Susan Kumar; Staff 8 (MLS 1, Non-MLS 7)
Founded 1922. Pop 19,000
Library Holdings: Bk Titles 52,875; Bk Vols 54,114; Per Subs 50
Subject Interests: Korean (Lang)

Database Vendor: EBSCOhost, Gale Cengage Learning, ProQuest, SirsiDynix
Wireless access
Function: Adult literacy prog, ILL available, Prog for children & young adult, Summer reading prog
Partic in Bergen County Cooperative Library System
Open Mon-Thurs 10:30-9, Fri 10:30-5, Sat 10:30-4:30

PARAMUS

S ARMENIAN MISSIONARY ASSOCIATION OF AMERICA LIBRARY*, 31 W Century Rd, 07652. Tel: 201-265-2607. FAX: 201-265-6015. E-mail: amaa@amaa.org. Web Site: www.amaa.org. *Dir,* Levon Filian
Founded 1918
Library Holdings: Bk Titles 20,000; Per Subs 16
Open Mon-Fri 8:30-4:30
Restriction: Non-circulating

J BERGEN COMMUNITY COLLEGE*, Sidney Silverman Library & Learning Resource Center, 400 Paramus Rd, 07652-1595. SAN 310-3943. Tel: 201-447-7131. Circulation Tel: 201-447-7970. Interlibrary Loan Service Tel: 201-447-7982. Reference Tel: 201-447-7436. Administration Tel: 201-447-7130. FAX: 201-493-8167. E-mail: libraryweb@bergen.edu. Web Site: www.bergen.edu/library. *Dean, Libr Serv,* Patricia Denholm; E-mail: pdenholm@bergen.edu; *Asst Dir, Syst & Tech,* Rong Wang; Tel: 201-612-5563, E-mail: rwang@bergen.edu; *Head, Access Serv,* Joan Dalrymple; Tel: 201-612-5236, E-mail: jdalrymple@bergen.edu; *Ser Librn,* Joan G Cohen; Tel: 201-447-7984, E-mail: jcohen@bergen.edu; *Ref,* Kate McGivern; Tel: 201-447-7980, E-mail: kmcgivern@bergen.edu; *Ref,* Annemarie Roscello; E-mail: aroscello@bergen.edu; *Ref,* Lynn Schott; Tel: 201-447-8889, E-mail: lschott@bergen.edu; *Ref,* Edith Sirianni; E-mail: esirianni@bergen.edu; *Ref,* Barbara Walcott; Tel: 201-447-5243, E-mail: bwalcott@bergen.edu; *Ref,* Paula Williams; Tel: 201-612-5299, E-mail: pwilliams@bergen.edu; Staff 30 (MLS 12, Non-MLS 18)
Founded 1965. Enrl 17,000; Fac 300; Highest Degree: Associate
Automation Activity & Vendor Info: (Acquisitions) Innovative Interfaces, Inc; (Cataloging) Innovative Interfaces, Inc; (Circulation) Innovative Interfaces, Inc; (Course Reserve) Innovative Interfaces, Inc; (ILL) Innovative Interfaces, Inc; (OPAC) Innovative Interfaces, Inc; (Serials) Innovative Interfaces, Inc
Database Vendor: EBSCOhost, Gale Cengage Learning, LexisNexis, ProQuest
Wireless access
Partic in Bergen Passaic Health Sciences Library Consortium; LibraryLinkNJ, The New Jersey Library Cooperative; Lyrasis; Virtual Academic Library Environment
Open Mon-Fri 7:45am-10:30pm, Sat 9-4:30, Sun 12-5
Friends of the Library Group

M BERGEN REGIONAL MEDICAL CENTER LIBRARY*, 230 E Ridgewood Ave, 07652. SAN 310-3951. Tel: 201-967-4065. *Librn,* Jan B Hudgens
Founded 1952
Library Holdings: Bk Titles 2,500; Per Subs 70
Subject Interests: Clinical med, Psychiat
Partic in NY & NJ Regional Med Libr
Restriction: Staff use only

P PARAMUS PUBLIC LIBRARY*, E 116 Century Rd, 07652-4398. SAN 351-1324. Tel: 201-599-1300. Circulation Tel: 201-599-1302. Reference Tel: 201-599-1305. FAX: 201-599-0059. E-mail: paracirc@bccls.org. Reference E-mail: pararef@bccls.org. Web Site: www.bccls.org/paramus. *Dir,* Leonard LoPinto; *Br Coordr,* Cathy Eng; *Ch Serv,* Sharon Kalman; *Circ,* Valerie Danhart; *Coll Develop,* Hanna Blatt; *Media Serv, Per, Ref,* Dorothy Fleishman; Staff 40 (MLS 9, Non-MLS 31)
Founded 1954. Pop 26,474; Circ 340,177
Library Holdings: Bk Vols 103,781; Per Subs 338
Special Collections: Korean, Chinese, Japanese (Foreign Language Books & Media Coll)
Automation Activity & Vendor Info: (Acquisitions) Baker & Taylor; (Cataloging) Baker & Taylor; (Circulation) SirsiDynix; (ILL) Auto-Graphics, Inc; (OPAC) SirsiDynix
Database Vendor: EBSCOhost, Gale Cengage Learning, ProQuest, ReferenceUSA, SirsiDynix
Wireless access
Partic in LibraryLinkNJ, The New Jersey Library Cooperative
Open Mon-Thurs 9:30-9, Fri & Sat 9:30-5, Sun 1-5
Friends of the Library Group
Branches: 1
CHARLES E REID BRANCH, W 239 Midland Ave, 07652, SAN 351-1359. Tel: 201-444-4911. *Supvr,* Catherine Eng
Open Mon 10-9, Tues-Fri 10-6
Friends of the Library Group

PARK RIDGE

P PARK RIDGE PUBLIC LIBRARY, 51 Park Ave, 07656. SAN 310-3978. Tel: 201-391-5151. FAX: 201-391-2739. E-mail: pkrdcirc@bccls.org. Web Site: parkridge.bccls.org. *Dir,* Christina Doto; Staff 9 (MLS 1, Non-MLS 8)
Pop 8,645; Circ 115,509
Library Holdings: Audiobooks 1,332; CDs 3,386; DVDs 10,404; e-books 8,703; e-journals 100; Large Print Bks 2; Bk Titles 55,589; Per Subs 45
Automation Activity & Vendor Info: (Circulation) Innovative Interfaces, Inc
Database Vendor: Booklist Online, Booksite, EBSCOhost, Gale Cengage Learning, Grolier Online, Overdrive, Inc, ProQuest, ReferenceUSA, World Book Online
Wireless access
Function: 24/7 Electronic res, 24/7 Online cat, Adult bk club, Adult literacy prog, Art exhibits, Audiobks via web, Bks on CD, Children's prog, Computers for patron use, Copy machines, Electronic databases & coll, eReaders, Free DVD rentals, ILL available, Magazines, Music CDs, Notary serv, OverDrive digital audio bks, Prog for adults, Story hour, Summer reading prog, Web-catalog, Wheelchair accessible
Partic in Bergen County Cooperative Library System
Open Mon-Thurs 9:30-8, Fri 9:30-5, Sat 9:30-3, Sun 12-4

PARLIN

P SAYREVILLE PUBLIC LIBRARY*, 1050 Washington Rd, 08859. SAN 310-3994. Tel: 732-727-0212. FAX: 732-553-0775. Web Site: www.sayrevillelibrary.org. *Dir,* Susan Kaplan; E-mail: skaplan@lmxac.org; *Ch,* Leah Kloc; E-mail: lkloc@lmxac.org; Staff 6 (MLS 6)
Founded 1931. Pop 41,000; Circ 176,000
Library Holdings: AV Mats 5,339; Large Print Bks 1,250; Bk Titles 100,000; Per Subs 196; Talking Bks 1,355
Special Collections: Municipal Document Depository
Automation Activity & Vendor Info: (Cataloging) SirsiDynix; (Circulation) SirsiDynix; (ILL) Auto-Graphics, Inc; (OPAC) SirsiDynix
Database Vendor: EBSCOhost, Newsbank, ProQuest, Westlaw
Function: Homebound delivery serv, ILL available, Online searches, Photocopying/Printing, Prog for children & young adult, Ref serv available, Summer reading prog, Telephone ref, Wheelchair accessible
Partic in Libraries of Middlesex Automation Consortium
Special Services for the Blind - Audio mat; Bks on cassette; Bks on CD; Large print bks; Talking bks; Videos on blindness & phys handicaps
Open Mon-Thurs 9:30-7:45, Fri & Sat 9:30-5, Sun 1-4:45
Friends of the Library Group

PARSIPPANY

P PARSIPPANY-TROY HILLS FREE PUBLIC LIBRARY*, 449 Halsey Rd, 07054. SAN 351-1448. Tel: 973-887-5150. Circulation Tel: 973-887-8907, Ext 201. Administration Tel: 973-887-8907, Ext 219. Information Services Tel: 973-887-8907, Ext 209. FAX: 973-887-0062. Web Site: www.parsippanylibrary.org. *Dir,* Jayne Beline; *Head, Customer & Info Serv,* Korin Rosenkrans; *Head, Tech Serv,* Bill Harrison; *Customer Serv Supvr,* Loretto Bapiran; Staff 86 (MLS 16, Non-MLS 70)
Founded 1968. Pop 50,000; Circ 450,000
Jan 2006-Dec 2006 Income (Main Library and Branch(s)) $3,100,000, State $52,450, City $2,881,154, Other $166,396. Mats Exp $382,000, Books $270,000, Per/Ser (Incl. Access Fees) $35,000, AV Mat $60,000, Electronic Ref Mat (Incl. Access Fees) $17,000. Sal $1,175,524
Library Holdings: Bk Vols 210,000; Per Subs 210
Automation Activity & Vendor Info: (Acquisitions) SirsiDynix; (Cataloging) SirsiDynix; (Circulation) SirsiDynix; (OPAC) SirsiDynix
Database Vendor: SirsiDynix
Wireless access
Function: AV serv, Handicapped accessible, ILL available, Online searches, Photocopying/Printing, Prog for adults, Prog for children & young adult, Ref serv available, Summer reading prog, Telephone ref, Wheelchair accessible, Workshops
Partic in Morris Automated Information Network
Open Mon-Thurs 9-9, Fri & Sat 9-5, Sun (Oct-June) 1-5
Friends of the Library Group
Branches: 2
LAKE HIAWATHA BRANCH, 68 Nokomis Ave, Lake Hiawatha, 07034, SAN 351-1472. Tel: 973-335-0952. FAX: 973-335-8610. *Br Coordr,* Aida Courtney; *Head, Ch,* Margaret Clark
Friends of the Library Group
MOUNT TABOR BRANCH, 31 Trinity Park, Mount Tabor, 07878, SAN 351-1502. Tel: 973-627-9508. *Br Coordr,* Debra Insetta; *Ch,* Karen O'Malley
Friends of the Library Group

PASSAIC

P PASSAIC PUBLIC LIBRARY, Julius Forstmann Library, 195 Gregory Ave, 07055. SAN 351-1561. Tel: 973-779-0474. FAX: 973-779-0889. E-mail: circ@passaicpubliclibrary.org. Web Site: www.passaicpubliclibrary.org. *Exec Dir,* Mario Gonzalez; E-mail: mgonzalez@passaicpubliclibrary.org; *Head, Ref & Ch,* Mabel Ajala; E-mail: ajala@passaicpubliclibrary.org; *Head, Circ & Tech Serv,* Dawn Rodriguez; *Ref Librn,* Ricardo Pino; E-mail: pino@passaicpubliclibrary.org; Staff 18 (MLS 7, Non-MLS 11)
Founded 1887. Pop 70,000; Circ 210,363
Jul 2014-Jun 2015 Income (Main Library and Branch(s)) $1,203,938, State $30,572, City $1,173,366
Library Holdings: Audiobooks 1,098; AV Mats 5; CDs 1,142; DVDs 6,270; Bk Vols 107,712; Per Subs 70; Videos 956
Special Collections: Local History (Passaic Coll), bks, clippings, photog
Subject Interests: Art, Cooking, Jewish studies, Literacy, Local hist
Automation Activity & Vendor Info: (Cataloging) SirsiDynix; (Circulation) SirsiDynix; (ILL) PALS; (OPAC) SirsiDynix
Database Vendor: SirsiDynix
Wireless access
Function: 24/7 Online cat, Adult bk club, Art exhibits, Audiobks via web, Bilingual assistance for Spanish patrons, Bk club(s), Bks on CD, Children's prog, Computers for patron use, Copy machines, Electronic databases & coll, Exhibits, Fax serv, Free DVD rentals, Handicapped accessible, Home delivery & serv to Sr ctr & nursing homes, Homebound delivery serv, ILL available, Magazines, Mail & tel request accepted, Movies, Music CDs, Outreach serv, Outside serv via phone, mail, e-mail & web, OverDrive digital audio bks, Photocopying/Printing, Preschool reading prog, Prog for adults, Prog for children & young adult, Pub access computers, Ref & res, Ref serv available, Ref serv in person, Res performed for a fee, Spanish lang bks, Story hour, Summer reading prog, Tax forms, Teen prog, Telephone ref, VHS videos, Video lending libr, Wheelchair accessible
Partic in LibraryLinkNJ, The New Jersey Library Cooperative; PALS Plus, The Computer Consortium of Passaic County Libraries
Open Mon-Thurs 9-9, Fri 9-6, Sat 9-5, Sun 1-5
Branches: 1
REID MEMORIAL BRANCH, 80 Third St, 07055. (Mail add: 195 Gregory Ave, 07055), SAN 351-1626. Tel: 973-777-6044. *Br Mgr,* Ricardo Pino; E-mail: pino@passaicpubliclibrary.org; Staff 2 (MLS 1, Non-MLS 1)
Founded 1903. Pop 70,000
Library Holdings: Bk Vols 26,900; Per Subs 28
Special Collections: Spanish Language Books
Database Vendor: SirsiDynix
Open Mon-Fri 1-5
Bookmobiles: 1

PATERSON

J PASSAIC COUNTY COMMUNITY COLLEGE*, Library & Learning Resources Center, One College Blvd, 07505. SAN 310-4028. Tel: 973-684-5896. Circulation Tel: 973-684-5877. Interlibrary Loan Service Tel: 973-684-6918. Reference Tel: 973-684-5888. FAX: 973-684-6675. Web Site: www.pccc.edu/libray. *Asst Dean,* Gregory Fallon; E-mail: gfallon@pccc.edu; *Head Librn,* Mibong La; Tel: 973-684-5885, E-mail: mla@pccc.edu; *Ref Serv,* Yaro Furtak; Tel: 973-684-5696, E-mail: yfurtak@pccc.edu; *Ref Serv,* Ruth Hamman; Tel: 973-684-5880, E-mail: rhamann@pccc.edu; Staff 8 (MLS 5, Non-MLS 3)
Founded 1971. Enrl 7,000; Highest Degree: Associate
Library Holdings: AV Mats 1,500; CDs 500; Bk Titles 53,000; Bk Vols 54,064; Per Subs 230; Videos 1,200
Special Collections: Passaic County Poetry Center
Automation Activity & Vendor Info: (Cataloging) SirsiDynix; (Circulation) SirsiDynix; (Course Reserve) SirsiDynix; (ILL) SirsiDynix; (OPAC) SirsiDynix
Database Vendor: EBSCOhost, Gale Cengage Learning, LexisNexis, OCLC WorldShare Interlibrary Loan, SirsiDynix, Wilson - Wilson Web
Publications: LRC Handbook
Partic in LibraryLinkNJ, The New Jersey Library Cooperative; OCLC, Inc through Palinet; PALS Plus, The Computer Consortium of Passaic County Libraries; Virtual Academic Library Environment
Open Mon-Thurs 8am-10pm, Fri 8-8, Sat 8-3

S PASSAIC COUNTY HISTORICAL SOCIETY*, Elizabeth A Beam Memorial Historical Research Library, Lambert Castle, Three Valley Rd, 07503-2932. SAN 310-4036. Tel: 973-247-0085. FAX: 973-881-9434. Web Site: www.lambertcastle.org. *In Charge,* Dorothy Becker
Founded 1926
Library Holdings: Bk Titles 10,000
Special Collections: Derrom Family Coll; Haines Family Coll; Hewitt Coll; Hobart Family Coll; Industrial History (Society for Establishing Useful Manufactures Papers), mss; Manuscript Coll; New Jersey (John Reid Photo Coll), photos; Pamphlet Coll; Passaic General Hospital Coll; Paterson Orphans Asylum Records; Wright Aeronautical Coll
Function: Archival coll, Photocopying/Printing, Res libr
Publications: Castle Genie (Newsletter); The Historic County (Newsletter)
Open Wed-Fri 1-4
Restriction: Non-circulating

L PASSAIC VICINAGE LAW LIBRARY*, 77 Hamilton St, 2nd Flr, 07505-2096. SAN 310-4044. Tel: 973-247-8013. Web Site: www.judiciary.state.nj.us. *Librn,* Position Currently Open
Founded 1930
Library Holdings: Bk Vols 57,220
Restriction: Not open to pub

P PATERSON FREE PUBLIC LIBRARY, Danforth Memorial Library, 250 Broadway, 07501. SAN 351-1685. Tel: 973-321-1223. Circulation Tel: 973-321-1223, Ext 2319. Reference Tel: 973-321-1223, Ext 2295. Administration Tel: 973-321-1215. FAX: 973-321-1205. Web Site: www.patersonpl.org. *Dir,* Cynthia Czesak; E-mail: czesak@patersonpl.org; *Asst Dir,* Mary Wilson; Tel: 973-321-1223, Ext 2294, E-mail: wilson@patersonpl.org; *Adult Serv, Circ,* Shonn Burton; E-mail: burton@patersonpl.org; *Ch Serv,* Gwendolyn Ndubuisi; Tel: 973-321-1223, Ext 2299, E-mail: ndubuisi@patersonpl.org; *Ref Serv,* Kevin Mak; E-mail: mak@patersonpl.org; *Tech Serv,* Luz Posada; Tel: 973-321-1223, Ext 2320, E-mail: posada@patersonpl.org; Staff 10 (MLS 10)
Founded 1885. Pop 146,199; Circ 189,721
Jul 2012-Jun 2013 Income $4,175,157, State $64,015, City $3,848,025, Other $65,621. Mats Exp $301,616, Books $210,294, Per/Ser (Incl. Access Fees) $12,980, AV Mat $49,134, Electronic Ref Mat (Incl. Access Fees) $29,208. Sal $1,156,762 (Prof $581,071)
Library Holdings: CDs 3,234; DVDs 11,175; e-books 10,483; Electronic Media & Resources 9; Bk Vols 155,905; Per Subs 198; Talking Bks 405
Special Collections: African American Coll; Local History Coll; Spanish Language Coll; Western Coll
Subject Interests: Genealogy, Local hist
Automation Activity & Vendor Info: (Acquisitions) Baker & Taylor; (Cataloging) SIRSI WorkFlows; (Circulation) SIRSI WorkFlows; (ILL) JerseyCat; (OPAC) SIRSI-iBistro
Database Vendor: Baker & Taylor, Evanced Solutions, Inc, LearningExpress, World Book Online
Wireless access
Function: Family literacy
Partic in LibraryLinkNJ, The New Jersey Library Cooperative; PALS Plus, The Computer Consortium of Passaic County Libraries
Open Mon-Thurs 9-8, Fri & Sat 9-5, Sun (Oct-May) 1-5
Friends of the Library Group
Branches: 3
NORTHSIDE BRANCH, 60 Temple St, Rm 3, 07522, SAN 351-174X. Tel: 973-321-1309. *Supv Libr Asst,* Marilda Malave; E-mail: malave@patersonpl.org
Library Holdings: Bk Vols 4,612
Friends of the Library Group
SOUTH PATERSON, 930 Main St, 07503, SAN 351-1863. Tel: 973-357-3020. *Supv Libr Asst,* Noel Cardona
Library Holdings: Bk Vols 31,471
Special Collections: Arabic/Islamic Coll
Friends of the Library Group
TOTOWA BRANCH, 405 Union Ave, 07502, SAN 351-1898. Tel: 973-942-7198. *Supv Libr Asst,* Susan Johnson
Library Holdings: Bk Vols 29,516
Friends of the Library Group

M SAINT JOSEPH'S REGIONAL MEDICAL CENTER*, Health Sciences Library, 703 Main St, 07503. SAN 320-5835. Tel: 973-754-3590. FAX: 973-754-3593. E-mail: library@sjhmc.org. Web Site: www.stjosephshealth.org. *Dir,* Patricia May; E-mail: mayp@sjhmc.org; *Med Librn,* Eleanor Silverman; *Med Librn,* Madeleine Taylor; *Libr Asst,* Brian Tervo
Founded 1932
Library Holdings: Bk Vols 5,000; Per Subs 280
Open Mon, Wed & Fri 8:30-5, Tues & Thurs 8:30-8

PAULSBORO

P GILL MEMORIAL LIBRARY*, 145 E Broad St, 08066. SAN 310-4079. Tel: 856-423-5155. FAX: 856-423-9162. Web Site: www.gillmemoriallibrary.org. *Dir,* Violet Jean Valentin; E-mail: violet@gillmemoriallibrary.org; *Asst Librn,* Curtis G Banks; E-mail: curtis@gillmemoriallibrary.org; Staff 3 (Non-MLS 3)
Founded 1951. Pop 6,500
Library Holdings: Bk Titles 20,730; Per Subs 52
Special Collections: Database of Local High School Graduates, Marriages, Birth & Deaths; Microfilm of Local Newspapers; New Jersey Archives; New Jersey Museum Room with Local History
Automation Activity & Vendor Info: (Cataloging) SirsiDynix; (Circulation) SirsiDynix; (ILL) SirsiDynix
Function: ILL available

Partic in LOGIN (Libraries of Gloucester, Salem & Cumberland Information Network)
Open Mon & Wed 12-7, Tues & Thurs 12-8, Sat (Fall-Spring) 10-3

PEMBERTON

J BURLINGTON COUNTY COLLEGE LIBRARY*, 601 Pemberton-Browns Mills Rd, 08068. SAN 310-4095. Circulation Tel: 609-894-9311, Ext 1482. Reference Tel: 609-894-9311, Ext 1306. FAX: 609-894-4189. E-mail: library@bcc.edu. Web Site: www.bcc.edu. *Libr Serv Coordr,* Martin Michelle; E-mail: mmartin@bcc.edu; *Info Spec,* Tian Lanzhen; Staff 4 (MLS 4)
Founded 1969. Enrl 7,797; Fac 68; Highest Degree: Associate
Library Holdings: AV Mats 4,500; Bks on Deafness & Sign Lang 145; High Interest/Low Vocabulary Bk Vols 250; Bk Titles 87,000; Bk Vols 92,000; Per Subs 340; Talking Bks 500
Special Collections: Cinema Coll; Geneology & Local History (Pinelands Coll)
Automation Activity & Vendor Info: (Acquisitions) Horizon; (Cataloging) Horizon; (Circulation) Horizon; (Course Reserve) Horizon; (ILL) Horizon; (Media Booking) Horizon; (OPAC) Horizon; (Serials) Horizon
Database Vendor: OCLC FirstSearch
Wireless access
Partic in NJ Union List of Serials; OCLC Online Computer Library Center, Inc; S Jersey Regional Libr Network; Virtual Academic Library Environment
Open Mon-Thurs 8am-9pm, Fri 8-7, Sat & Sun 12-5

PENNINGTON

P PENNINGTON PUBLIC LIBRARY*, 30 N Main St, 08534. SAN 310-4109. Tel: 609-737-0404. FAX: 609-737-2948. Web Site: www.penningtonlibrary.org. *Dir,* Kim Ha; Staff 2.5 (MLS 1, Non-MLS 1.5)
Founded 1875. Pop 3,035; Circ 41,590
Library Holdings: Audiobooks 773; DVDs 1,594; Bk Vols 20,353; Per Subs 34
Special Collections: Pennington Newspaper, 1897-present
Automation Activity & Vendor Info: (Cataloging) Auto-Graphics, Inc; (Circulation) Auto-Graphics, Inc; (OPAC) Auto-Graphics, Inc
Database Vendor: EBSCOhost
Wireless access
Function: Adult bk club, Audiobks via web, Bk club(s), Bks on CD, Children's prog, Computers for patron use, Copy machines, Electronic databases & coll, Free DVD rentals, Holiday prog, ILL available, Online cat, Online searches, Prog for adults, Prog for children & young adult, Senior outreach, Story hour, Summer reading prog, Tax forms, Teen prog, Web-catalog, Workshops
Open Mon-Thurs 10-8, Fri 10-5, Sat 10-2
Friends of the Library Group

PENNSAUKEN

P PENNSAUKEN FREE PUBLIC LIBRARY*, Rogers Library, 5605 Crescent Blvd, 08110. SAN 310-4141. Tel: 856-665-5959. FAX: 856-486-0142. Web Site: www.pennsaukenlibrary.org. *Dir,* John Patane; E-mail: patanejohn@yahoo.com. Subject Specialists: *Bus, Mgt, Pub relations,* John Patane; Staff 21 (MLS 5, Non-MLS 16)
Founded 1959. Pop 37,500; Circ 194,000
Jan 2012-Dec 2012 Income $964,030. Mats Exp $77,500, Books $53,000, Per/Ser (Incl. Access Fees) $5,500, AV Mat $19,000
Library Holdings: Bk Titles 72,300; Per Subs 75
Special Collections: Municipal Document Depository
Subject Interests: Local hist
Automation Activity & Vendor Info: (Acquisitions) Innovative Interfaces, Inc; (Cataloging) Innovative Interfaces, Inc; (Circulation) Innovative Interfaces, Inc; (OPAC) Innovative Interfaces, Inc; (Serials) Innovative Interfaces, Inc
Database Vendor: EBSCOhost, Gale Cengage Learning, Innovative Interfaces, Inc, Newsbank, TLC (The Library Corporation)
Wireless access
Partic in LibraryLinkNJ, The New Jersey Library Cooperative; New Jersey Library Network
Special Services for the Deaf - Bks on deafness & sign lang
Special Services for the Blind - Extensive large print coll; Magnifiers; Reader equip; Ref serv; Spec prog; Talking bks
Open Mon-Thurs 10-9, Fri & Sat 10-6, Sun 1-5
Friends of the Library Group

PENNSVILLE

P PENNSVILLE PUBLIC LIBRARY, 190 S Broadway, 08070. SAN 310-415X. Tel: 856-678-5473. FAX: 856-678-8121. E-mail: pennsville@pennsvillelibrary.org. *Coll Develop,* Deborah Ecret; Staff 2 (Non-MLS 2)
Founded 1937. Pop 13,400; Circ 30,259
Library Holdings: AV Mats 350; Bk Titles 29,237; Bk Vols 32,172; Per Subs 32
Subject Interests: NJ
Automation Activity & Vendor Info: (Circulation) SIRSI WorkFlows; (OPAC) Follett Software
Database Vendor: EBSCOhost
Wireless access
Mem of Cumberland County Library
Partic in S Jersey Regional Libr Consortium
Open Mon, Tues & Thurs 10-7, Fri 10-4, Sat 10-2
Friends of the Library Group

PERTH AMBOY

P PERTH AMBOY FREE PUBLIC LIBRARY*, 196 Jefferson St, 08861. SAN 351-2010. Tel: 732-826-2600. FAX: 732-324-8079. Web Site: www.ci.perthamboy.nj.us, www.lmxac.org. *Dir,* Patricia Gandy; E-mail: patricia@lmxac.org; *Libr Asst,* Herschel Chomsky; E-mail: herschel@lmxac.org; Staff 10 (MLS 3, Non-MLS 7)
Founded 1903. Pop 51,000
Library Holdings: Bk Vols 176,236; Per Subs 444
Special Collections: Perth Amboy Historical Documents; Perth Amboy Newspaper, microfilm
Subject Interests: Local hist, Spanish (Lang)
Wireless access
Function: Archival coll, Home delivery & serv to Sr ctr & nursing homes, Homebound delivery serv, ILL available, Newsp ref libr, Prog for children & young adult, Summer reading prog
Partic in Libraries of Middlesex Automation Consortium
Open Mon, Tues & Thurs 9:30-8, Wed & Fri 9:30-5, Sat 10-4
Friends of the Library Group

M RARITAN BAY MEDICAL CENTER, Health Science Library, 530 New Brunswick Ave, 08861. SAN 310-4176. Tel: 732 324-5087. FAX: 732-324-4676. *Libr Asst,* Zinaida Kolker; E-mail: zkolker@rbmc.org; Staff 1 (Non-MLS 1)
Library Holdings: Bk Vols 450; Per Subs 123
Subject Interests: Med, Nursing
Partic in Basic Health Sciences Library Network; National Network of Libraries of Medicine; New Jersey Health Sciences Library Network; New Jersey Library Network
Restriction: Staff use only

PHILLIPSBURG

S MALLINCKRODT BAKER, INC*, The Library Center, 1904 J T Baker Way, 08865. SAN 310-4184. Tel: 908-859-2151, Ext 9418. FAX: 908-859-9454. *In Charge,* Susan Kurasz
Founded 1945
Library Holdings: Bk Vols 5,000; Per Subs 100
Subject Interests: Analytical chem, Biochem
Restriction: Staff use only

P PHILLIPSBURG FREE PUBLIC LIBRARY, 200 Broubalow Way, 08865. SAN 310-4192. Tel. 908-454-3712. Toll Free Tel: 800-452-9182. FAX: 908-859-4667. Web Site: www.pburglib.org. *Dir,* Ann DeRenzis; E-mail: director@pburglib.org; *Ad,* Deb Messling; *Ch,* Louise Delly; E-mail: ldeilyy@pburglib.org; Staff 18 (MLS 6, Non-MLS 12)
Founded 1923. Pop 14,950; Circ 111,828
Library Holdings: Audiobooks 1,650; CDs 949; DVDs 1,595; Bk Vols 93,002; Per Subs 165; Videos 985
Special Collections: ERIC repts on microfiche. State Document Depository; US Document Depository
Subject Interests: Educ
Automation Activity & Vendor Info: (Cataloging) Innovative Interfaces, Inc; (Circulation) Innovative Interfaces, Inc; (ILL) Best-Seller, Inc; (OPAC) Innovative Interfaces, Inc
Database Vendor: EBSCOhost, Newsbank, OCLC WebJunction, ProQuest
Wireless access
Partic in LibraryLinkNJ, The New Jersey Library Cooperative
Special Services for the Blind - Talking bk & rec for the blind cat; Talking bks
Open Mon-Thurs 9:30-9, Fri & Sat 9:30-5
Friends of the Library Group

M WARREN HOSPITAL*, Medical Library, 185 Roseberry St, 08865. SAN 325-7274. Tel: 908-859-6700, Ext 2012. FAX: 908-213-6698. *Librn,* June Roberts; E-mail: juneroberts@warrenhospital.org; Staff 1 (MLS 1)
Library Holdings: Bk Titles 500; Per Subs 35
Subject Interests: Med
Database Vendor: Elsevier
Restriction: Open by appt only

PICATINNY ARSENAL

A UNITED STATES ARMY, RDECOM-ARDEC*, Technical Research Center, Bldg 59, Phipps Rd, AMSRD-AAR-EMK, 07806-5000. SAN 350-6460. Tel: 973-724-4712. Reference Tel: 973-724-3757. Administration Tel: 973-724-5898. FAX: 973-724-3044. *Chief Librn,* Suseela Chandrasekar; *Automation Librn, Ref Librn,* Elizabeth Reisman; Tel: 973-724-5350, E-mail: elizabeth.reisman@us.army.mil; *Doc Librn, Ref Serv Librn,* Position Currently Open; *Acq, Info Tech, ILL,* Mimi Ng; Tel: 973-724-4750, E-mail: mimi.l.ng@us.army.mil. Subject Specialists: *Chem,* Suseela Chandrasekar; *Eng,* Elizabeth Reisman; Staff 3 (MLS 2, Non-MLS 1)
Founded 1929
Library Holdings: e-books 600; Bk Titles 34,173; Bk Vols 36,631; Per Subs 50
Special Collections: Frankford Arsenal Archives, PA; Picatinny Arsenal Archives, NJ
Subject Interests: Ammunition, Armament, Explosives, Plastics, Propellants, Pyrotechnics, Weapons
Automation Activity & Vendor Info: (Cataloging) SirsiDynix; (Circulation) SirsiDynix; (ILL) OCLC; (OPAC) SirsiDynix; (Serials) OCLC
Function: Archival coll, ILL available, Ref serv available
Partic in NW Libr Network
Restriction: Circ limited, Open to others by appt

PILESGROVE

P SALEM COUNTY LIBRARY COMMISSION*, 900 Rte 45, Bldg 3, 08098. Tel: 856-769-1082. FAX: 856-769-2018. E-mail: salemcountylibrary@salemcountynj.gov. *Coordr,* Margaret Masserini; *Outreach Serv Librn,* Rebecca Mueller; *Principal Libr Asst,* Tara Groves; Staff 3 (Non-MLS 3)
Founded 1981. Pop 65,000; Circ 25,000
Jan 2011-Dec 2011 Income $92,000. Mats Exp $10,000, Books $8,000, AV Mat $2,000. Sal $70,000
Library Holdings: Bks on Deafness & Sign Lang 12; High Interest/Low Vocabulary Bk Vols 500; Large Print Bks 10,000; Bk Vols 20,000; Talking Bks 2,000
Wireless access
Function: Games & aids for the handicapped, Handicapped accessible, Home delivery & serv to Sr ctr & nursing homes, Homebound delivery serv, Magnifiers for reading, Prog for children & young adult, Summer reading prog, Wheelchair accessible
Partic in LibraryLinkNJ, The New Jersey Library Cooperative
Special Services for the Blind - Audio mat; Cassette playback machines; Extensive large print coll; Home delivery serv; Large print bks; Lending of low vision aids; Magnifiers
Open Mon-Fri 10-5
Friends of the Library Group
Bookmobiles: 1. Coordr, M Masserini. Bk titles 15,000

PISCATAWAY

P PISCATAWAY TOWNSHIP FREE PUBLIC LIBRARY, John F Kennedy Memorial Library, 500 Hoes Lane, 08854. SAN 351-207X. Tel: 732-463-1633. Administration Tel: 732-463-3911. FAX: 732-463-9022. Web Site: www.piscatawaylibrary.org. *Dir, Libr Serv,* James Keehbler; E-mail: jkeehbler@piscatawaylibrary.org; *Head, User Serv,* Kate Vasilik; E-mail: kvasilik@piscatawaylibrary.org; *Br Mgr, Outreach Librn,* Allen McGinley; E-mail: amcginley@piscatawaylibrary.org; *Adult Serv,* Mary Piekarski; E-mail: mpiekars@piscatawaylibrary.org; *Ch Serv,* Patricia Simmonds; E-mail: simmonds@piscatawaylibrary.org; *Tech Serv,* Jack Xi; E-mail: jackxi@piscatawaylibrary.org; Staff 31 (MLS 13, Non-MLS 18)
Founded 1961. Pop 56,000; Circ 350,000
Library Holdings: Bk Vols 156,261; Per Subs 308
Special Collections: Piscataway Local History Coll, bks, ms, maps, newsp, oral hist tapes. Oral History
Subject Interests: Chinese lang, Local hist
Automation Activity & Vendor Info: (Acquisitions) SIRSI-DRA; (Cataloging) SirsiDynix; (Circulation) SirsiDynix; (Course Reserve) SirsiDynix; (OPAC) SirsiDynix; (Serials) SirsiDynix
Database Vendor: EBSCO Information Services, Facts on File, Gale Cengage Learning, SirsiDynix
Wireless access
Publications: News & Events Newsletter (Bi-monthly)
Partic in Libraries of Middlesex Automation Consortium; LibraryLinkNJ, The New Jersey Library Cooperative
Special Services for the Deaf - TTY equip
Open Mon-Thurs 10-9, Fri & Sat 10-5, Sun (Sept-June) 1-5
Friends of the Library Group
Branches: 1
JOHANNA W WESTERGARD LIBRARY, 20 Murray Ave, 08854, SAN 351-210X. Tel: 732-752-1166. FAX: 732-752-1951. *Dir,* James Keehleer
Special Collections: Gujrati Coll; Parenting Coll, bks, mag, newsp & videos; Spanish Coll
Open Mon, Tues & Thurs 10-9, Wed, Fri & Sat 10-5
Friends of the Library Group
Bookmobiles: 1

PITMAN

P MCCOWAN MEMORIAL LIBRARY*, 15 Pitman Ave, 08071. SAN 310-4265. Tel: 856-589-1656. FAX: 856-582-4982. E-mail: library@mccowan-pitman.org. Web Site: www.mccowan-pitman.org. *Dir,* Sharon Furgason; E-mail: sharon.furgason@mccowan-pitman.org; *Children's Prog Coordr,* Patti Forte; *Circ,* Dolores Novin; *ILL,* Margaret Ware; Staff 9 (MLS 1, Non-MLS 8)
Founded 1919. Pop 9,011; Circ 75,052
Library Holdings: Bk Titles 41,950; Bk Vols 43,770; Per Subs 76
Automation Activity & Vendor Info: (Acquisitions) SIRSI WorkFlows; (Cataloging) SIRSI Unicorn; (Circulation) SIRSI Unicorn; (Course Reserve) SIRSI WorkFlows; (OPAC) SirsiDynix; (Serials) EBSCO Online
Wireless access
Partic in LibraryLinkNJ, The New Jersey Library Cooperative
Open Mon-Thurs 10-9, Fri 10-6, Sat 10-2
Friends of the Library Group

PLAINFIELD

M MUHLENBERG REGIONAL MEDICAL CENTER*, E Gordon Glass MD Memorial Library, Park Ave & Randolph Rd, 07061. SAN 310-429X. Tel: 908-668-2005. FAX: 908-753-3723. Web Site: www.solaris.org. *Librn,* Lana Strazhnik; Staff 1 (MLS 1)
Founded 1963
Library Holdings: Bk Titles 4,300; Bk Vols 4,500; Per Subs 127
Subject Interests: Consumer health, Med, Nursing
Automation Activity & Vendor Info: (Cataloging) Inmagic, Inc.; (Circulation) Inmagic, Inc.
Wireless access
Partic in Docline
Restriction: Staff use only

P PLAINFIELD PUBLIC LIBRARY, 800 Park Ave, 07060-2594. SAN 310-4303. Tel: 908-757-1111. Circulation Tel: 908-757-1111, Ext 111. Reference Tel: 908-757-1111, Ext 112. Administration Tel: 908-757-2305. FAX: 908-754-0063. Web Site: www.plainfieldlibrary.info. *Dir,* Joseph Hugh Da Rold; E-mail: joseph.darold@plfdpl.info; *Actg Head, Ch, Asst Dir,* Mary Ellen Rogan; Tel: 908-757-1111, Ext 132, E-mail: me.rogan@plfdpl.info; *Head, Pub Serv,* Tina Marie Doody; Tel: 908-757-1111, Ext 139, E-mail: tina.doody@plfdpl.info; *Chief Tech Officer, Fac Mgr,* Peter Rajcevic; Tel: 908-757-1111, Ext 130, E-mail: peter.rajcevic@plfdpl.info; *Circ Mgr,* Vicky Terrones; Tel: 908-757-1111, Ext 116, E-mail: vicky.terrones@plfdpl.info; *Adult Literacy Coordr,* Scott Kuchinsky; Tel: 908-757-1111, Ext 120, E-mail: scott.kuchinsky@plfdpl.info; *ESL Coordr,* Stella Segura; Tel: 908-757-1111, Ext 121, E-mail: luz.segura@plfdpl.info; *Archivist/Head of Local Hist,* Sarah Hull; Tel: 908-757-1111, Ext 136, E-mail: sarah.hull@plfdpl.info; Staff 38 (MLS 15, Non-MLS 23)
Founded 1881. Pop 49,808; Circ 104,650
Library Holdings: Bk Titles 136,062; Bk Vols 190,060; Per Subs 275
Special Collections: Oral History
Subject Interests: 19th Century per, Civil War, Early Am hist, Genealogy, Local hist, NJ hist, Union County hist
Automation Activity & Vendor Info: (Acquisitions) SirsiDynix; (Circulation) SirsiDynix; (OPAC) SirsiDynix
Database Vendor: Baker & Taylor, EBSCOhost, Gale Cengage Learning, LearningExpress, Library Ideas, LLC, OCLC WorldShare Interlibrary Loan, ProQuest, ReferenceUSA, SirsiDynix, World Book Online
Wireless access
Function: 24/7 Electronic res, 24/7 Online cat, Adult literacy prog, Archival coll, Art exhibits, Audiobks via web, Bilingual assistance for Spanish patrons, Bks on CD, Children's prog, Citizenship assistance, Computer training, Computers for patron use, Copy machines, E-Reserves, Electronic databases & coll, Exhibits, Fax serv, Genealogy discussion group, Handicapped accessible, ILL available, Magazines, Mail & tel request accepted, Microfiche/film & reading machines, Movies, Newsp ref libr, Notary serv, Online searches, OverDrive digital audio bks, Photocopying/Printing, Printer for laptops & handheld devices, Prog for adults, Prog for children & young adult, Pub access computers, Ref serv available, Res performed for a fee, Scanner, Senior computer classes, Spanish lang bks, Story hour, Study rm, Summer reading prog, Tax forms, Telephone ref, Wheelchair accessible
Partic in Libraries of Middlesex Automation Consortium; MURAL
Open Mon-Thurs 9-9, Fri & Sat 9-5; Mon-Wed (Summer) 9-9, Thurs & Fri 9-5, Sat 9-1
Restriction: Researchers by appt only
Friends of the Library Group

UNION COUNTY COLLEGE
See Cranford

PLAINSBORO

P PLAINSBORO FREE PUBLIC LIBRARY*, Nine Van Doren St, 08536. SAN 326-3924. Tel: 609-275-2899. Circulation Tel: 609-275-2897. Reference Tel: 609-275-2898. FAX: 609-799-5883. E-mail: plibrary@lmxac.org. Web Site: www.lmxac.org/plainsboro. *Dir,* Carol Quick; *Access Serv/Syst Adminr,* Adam Pober; *Commun Serv Librn,* Sharon Mitchell; *Adult/Art Prog,* Donna Senopoulos; *Ch Serv,* Julie Donaldson; *Circ,* Neera Kothary; *Ref,* Maryann Bartholomew; *Tech Serv,* Kyung Kim; Staff 18.52 (MLS 6.21, Non-MLS 12.31)
Founded 1964. Pop 22,999; Circ 397,159
Library Holdings: Bk Vols 113,083; Per Subs 150
Special Collections: Chinese Cultural Exchange; Gujrati Coll; Hindi Coll; JFK Coll; Large Print Coll
Automation Activity & Vendor Info: (Cataloging) TLC (The Library Corporation); (Circulation) TLC (The Library Corporation); (ILL) TLC (The Library Corporation); (OPAC) TLC (The Library Corporation)
Database Vendor: EBSCOhost
Wireless access
Publications: Annual Report Newsletter; Plainsboro Community Directory
Partic in Libraries of Middlesex Automation Consortium; LibraryLinkNJ, The New Jersey Library Cooperative; OCLC Online Computer Library Center, Inc
Open Mon-Thurs 10-8:30, Fri-Sun 10-5
Friends of the Library Group

M PRINCETON HEALTHCARE SYSTEM*, Medical Library & Business Center, One Plainsboro Rd, 08536. SAN 326-2405. Tel: 609-853-6799. FAX: 609-853-6798. Web Site: www.princetonhcs.org/library. Staff 1 (MLS 1)
Founded 1953
Library Holdings: Bk Titles 2,800; Bk Vols 3,000; Per Subs 200
Subject Interests: Allied health, Med, Nursing, Psychiat, Surgery
Database Vendor: American Psychological Association (APA), Cinahl, EBSCOhost, Gale Cengage Learning, McGraw-Hill, Medline, OVID Technologies, PubMed, UpToDate, WebMD, World Book Online
Wireless access
Publications: AV Catalogue; Guide to the Library; Serial Holdings
Partic in Health Sci Libr Asn of NJ; Medcore; Medical Library Association (MLA)
Special Services for the Deaf - Interpreter on staff
Special Services for the Blind - Assistive/Adapted tech devices, equip & products; Audio mat; Bks & mags in Braille, on rec, tape & cassette; Bks on cassette; Braille bks
Open Mon 9-8, Tues-Fri 9-5
Friends of the Library Group

POMONA

M BACHARACH INSTITUTE FOR REHABILITATION*, Medical-Clinical Staff Library, 61 W Jim Leeds Rd, 08240. (Mail add: PO Box 723, 08240-0723). SAN 373-2541. Tel: 609-652-7000. Web Site: www.bacharach.org. *Dir, Libr Serv,* Mary Choromanski
Library Holdings: Bk Vols 50; Per Subs 20
Wireless access
Open Mon-Fri 9-5
Restriction: Staff & patient use

POMPTON LAKES

P POMPTON LAKES PUBLIC LIBRARY*, Emanuel Einstein Memorial Library, 333 Wanaque Ave, 07442. SAN 310-4370. Tel: 973-835-0482. FAX: 973-835-4767. Web Site: www.pomptonlakeslibrary.org. *Dir,* Michael Drazek; E-mail: mdrazek@pomptonlakeslibrary.org; *Youth Serv Librn,* Ashley Monochello; E-mail: monochello@pomptonlakeslibrary.org; *Circ & Ref,* Linda Brophy; E-mail: brophy@pomptonlakeslibrary.org; Staff 13 (MLS 1, Non-MLS 12)
Founded 1912. Pop 11,059; Circ 66,389
Jan 2010-Dec 2010 Income $493,088. Mats Exp $57,453. Sal $257,457
Library Holdings: AV Mats 1,372; Bk Vols 41,210; Per Subs 60
Special Collections: Albert Payson Terhune Coll; New Jersey History (Van Orden Coll)
Automation Activity & Vendor Info: (Cataloging) SirsiDynix; (Circulation) SirsiDynix; (OPAC) SirsiDynix
Database Vendor: EBSCOhost, SirsiDynix
Wireless access
Function: Handicapped accessible, Homebound delivery serv, ILL available, Magnifiers for reading, Online searches, Photocopying/Printing, Prog for children & young adult, Summer reading prog, Telephone ref
Open Mon-Thurs 10-9, Fri & Sat 10-5

POMPTON PLAINS

M CHILTON MEMORIAL HOSPITAL*, Medical Library, 97 West Pkwy, 07444. SAN 325-9404. Tel: 973-831-5058. FAX: 973-831-5041. *Librn,* Eleanor Silverman; Staff 1 (MLS 1)
Library Holdings: Bk Vols 1,200
Open Thurs 9-1

P PEQUANNOCK TOWNSHIP PUBLIC LIBRARY*, 477 Newark Pompton Tpk, 07444. SAN 351-2223. Tel: 973-835-7460. FAX: 973-835-1928. Web Site: www.pequannocklibrary.org. *Dir,* Rosemary Garwood; *Asst Dir,* Maureen Bartolucci; *Acq,* Julie Reeves; *Ref,* Diane Alimena; Staff 20 (MLS 4, Non-MLS 16)
Founded 1962. Pop 14,000; Circ 147,617
Jan 2005-Dec 2005 Income $909,927, State $17,013, Locally Generated Income $892,914. Mats Exp $118,040, Books $98,100, Per/Ser (Incl. Access Fees) $8,050, Other Print Mats $2,590, AV Mat $9,300. Sal $700,358 (Prof $189,748)
Library Holdings: AV Mats 8,598; Large Print Bks 1,388; Bk Vols 85,305; Per Subs 200; Talking Bks 3,542
Special Collections: Landsberger Holocaust Coll
Subject Interests: Local hist
Automation Activity & Vendor Info: (Circulation) SirsiDynix
Wireless access
Publications: Quarterly Program Brochure
Partic in Morris Automated Information Network
Open Mon-Thurs 9-9, Fri 9-5:30, Sat 10-4 (10-2 Summer)
Friends of the Library Group

PRINCETON

S EDUCATIONAL TESTING SERVICE, Carl Campbell Brigham Library & Test Collection, Landgraf Hall, Mail Stop 07-J, 660 Rosedale Rd, 08541. SAN 310-4419. Tel: 609-734-5667. E-mail: LibraryStaff@ets.org. *Dir, Knowledge Serv,* Karen McQuillen; Tel: 609-734-5664, E-mail: kmcquillen@ets.org; *Knowledge Serv Analyst,* Angela Pagliaro; Tel: 609-734-1981, E-mail: apagliaro@ets.org; *Knowledge Serv Consult,* Kelly Bergman; Tel: 609-734-1576, E-mail: kbergman@ets.org; Staff 4 (MLS 3, Non-MLS 1)
Founded 1961
Library Holdings: Bk Vols 18,000; Per Subs 250
Special Collections: ETS Online Research Library, database; Test Coll, database
Subject Interests: Artificial intelligence, Behav sci, Cognitive sci, Educ, Expert systs, Internet, Measurements, Psychol, Soc sci, Statistics
Automation Activity & Vendor Info: (Cataloging) SydneyPlus; (Circulation) SydneyPlus; (ILL) OCLC WorldShare Interlibrary Loan; (OPAC) SydneyPlus; (Serials) SydneyPlus
Database Vendor: ACM (Association for Computing Machinery), Alexander Street Press, College Source, CredoReference, Dialog, Dun & Bradstreet, EBSCO Discovery Service, EBSCOhost, Facts on File, IEEE (Institute of Electrical & Electronics Engineers), ISI Web of Knowledge, JSTOR, OCLC FirstSearch, OCLC WorldShare Interlibrary Loan, ProQuest, ReferenceUSA, Thomson - Web of Science, Wilson - Wilson Web, World Book Online
Wireless access
Partic in LibraryLinkNJ, The New Jersey Library Cooperative; OCLC Online Computer Library Center, Inc
Restriction: Borrowing requests are handled by ILL, External users must contact libr, Staff use only

S HISTORICAL SOCIETY OF PRINCETON*, Museum & Research Library, 158 Nassau St, 08542. SAN 310-4443. Tel: 609-921-6748. FAX: 609-921-6939. Web Site: www.princetonhistory.org. *Res,* Stephanie Schwartz; E-mail: research@princetonhistory.org; Staff 3 (Non-MLS 3)
Founded 1938
Library Holdings: Bk Titles 1,500
Subject Interests: Local hist, Princeton hist
Publications: Guide to Manuscripts; Princeton History Journal
Restriction: Closed stack, Non-circulating

S INSTITUTE FOR ADVANCED STUDY LIBRARIES*, Einstein Dr, 08540. SAN 310-4451. Tel: 609-734-8181, 609-734-8276. Interlibrary Loan Service Tel: 609-734-8371. FAX: 609-924-8399, 609-951-4515. E-mail: hslib@ias.edu, mnlib@ias.edu. Web Site: library.ias.edu. *Librn,* Momota Ganguli; E-mail: mg@ias.edu; *Librn,* Marcia Tucker; E-mail: tucker@ias.edu; *Acq Librn,* Kirstie Venanzi; Tel: 609-734-8374, E-mail: kvenanzi@ias.edu; *Tech Serv Librn,* Dana Van Meter; Tel: 609-734-8376, E-mail: vanmeter@ias.edu; *Archivist,* Christine Di Bella; Tel: 609-734-8375, E-mail: archives@ias.edu; *ILL,* Karen Downing; E-mail: kd@ias.edu. Subject Specialists: *Math,* Momota Ganguli; Staff 12 (MLS 6, Non-MLS 6)
Founded 1940
Library Holdings: Bk Vols 130,000; Per Subs 1,100
Special Collections: History of Science (Rosenwald Coll)

Subject Interests: Art, Classical archaeol, Classical studies, Hist, Math, Natural sci, Soc sci
Automation Activity & Vendor Info: (Acquisitions) SirsiDynix; (Cataloging) SirsiDynix; (OPAC) SirsiDynix; (Serials) SirsiDynix
Database Vendor: EBSCOhost, JSTOR, SirsiDynix
Wireless access
Function: Archival coll, Res libr
Partic in OCLC Research Library Partnership
Restriction: External users must contact libr, Limited access for the pub, Not open to pub

S INSTITUTE FOR DEFENSE ANALYSIS LIBRARY*, 805 Bunn Dr, 08540. SAN 310-446X. Tel: 609-924-4600. FAX: 609-924-3061. *Mgr,* Barbara Hamilton; Staff 2 (MLS 1, Non-MLS 1)
Founded 1959
Library Holdings: Bk Vols 15,000; Per Subs 300
Subject Interests: Computer sci, Electrical eng, Linguistics, Math
Automation Activity & Vendor Info: (Acquisitions) Sydney; (Cataloging) Sydney; (Circulation) Sydney; (OPAC) Sydney; (Serials) Sydney
Database Vendor: Dialog, EBSCOhost
Publications: Acquisitions List (Bi-annually); Journals List; Print Catalog of Book Holdings; Staff Publications List
Restriction: Staff use only

S ROBERT WOOD JOHNSON FOUNDATION*, Information Center, Rte 1 & College Rd E, 08543. (Mail add: PO Box 2316, 08543-2316), SAN 310-4478. Tel: 609-627-5895. FAX: 609-627-6421. Web Site: www.rwjf.org. *Librn,* MaryBeth Kren; E-mail: mkren@rwjf.org; Staff 1 (Non-MLS 1)
Founded 1972
Library Holdings: Bk Titles 6,500; Per Subs 100
Subject Interests: Access to healthcare, Addiction prevention, Health disparities, Med policy, Nursing, Obesity, Philanthropy, Primary health care, Pub health issues, Substance abuse issues, Tobacco, Vulnerable pop
Partic in Consortium of Foundation Libraries; Health Sci Libr Asn of NJ
Restriction: Employees only

S LEARNING ALLY*, Library & Member Services Departments, 20 Roszel Rd, 08540. SAN 312-0228. Tel: 609-452-0606. Toll Free Tel: 800-221-4792, 800-772-3248. FAX: 609-520-7990, 609-987-8116. E-mail: custserv@LearningAlly.org, PrincetonStudio@LearningAlly.org. Web Site: www.LearningAlly.org. *Coll Develop Librn,* Kristin Longmuir; Staff 17 (MLS 5, Non-MLS 12)
Founded 1948
Library Holdings: Talking Bks 63,000
Special Collections: Digital Talking Books Coll
Subject Interests: Lit
Automation Activity & Vendor Info: (Cataloging) Cuadra Associates, Inc
Function: Audiobks via web, Bks on CD, Digital talking bks, Online cat, Spoken cassettes & CDs, Summer reading prog, Web-catalog
Publications: Catalog (Online only)
Partic in Lyrasis; OCLC Online Computer Library Center, Inc
Special Services for the Blind - Talking bks
Open Mon-Thurs 9-7:30, Fri 9-1:30pm
Restriction: Circ to mem only

S MATHEMATICA POLICY RESEARCH, INC LIBRARY*, 600 Alexander Park, 08543. SAN 376-0537. Tel: 609-275-2334. FAX: 609-799-1654. Web Site: www.mathematica-mpr.com. *Librn,* Jan Watterworth; E-mail: jwatterworth@mathematica-mpr.com; *ILL,* Nicole Schatten; E-mail: nschatten@mathematica-mpr.com; Staff 3 (MLS 1, Non-MLS 2)
Library Holdings: Bk Vols 60,000; Per Subs 350
Subject Interests: Soc policy
Automation Activity & Vendor Info: (Cataloging) Inmagic, Inc.
Restriction: Staff use only

G NATIONAL OCEANIC & ATMOSPHERIC ADMINISTRATION*, Geophysical Fluid Dynamics Laboratory Library, Forrestal Campus, US Rte 1, 201 Forrestal Rd, 08542. SAN 310-4524. Tel: 609-452-6500. FAX: 609-987-5063. Web Site: www.gfdl.noaa.gov. *Librn,* Gail Haller
Founded 1968
Library Holdings: Bk Titles 8,000; Bk Vols 10,000; Per Subs 130
Subject Interests: Applied math, Meteorology, Oceanography
Partic in OCLC Online Computer Library Center, Inc

P PRINCETON PUBLIC LIBRARY, 65 Witherspoon St, 08542. SAN 310-4540. Tel: 609-924-9529. Administration Tel: 609-924-8822. FAX: 609-924-6109. Administration FAX: 609-924-7937. Web Site: www.princetonlibrary.org. *Exec Dir,* Leslie Burger; Tel: 609-924-8822, Ext 253, E-mail: lburger@princetonlibrary.org; *Develop Dir,* Janet Simon; E-mail: jsimon@princetonlibrary.org; *Dir, Mkt & Communications,* Tim Quinn; E-mail: tquinn@princetonlibrary.org; *Dept Head, Access Serv,* Janice Painter; E-mail: jpainter@princetonlibrary.org; *Dept Head, Adult Serv,* Erica Bess; E-mail: ebess@princetonlibrary.org; *Dept Head, Lending Serv,* Sonja Vloeberghs; E-mail: svloeberghs@princetonlibrary.org; *Youth Serv Dept Head,* Susan Conlon; *Coll Develop Librn - Adult,* Andre Levie; *Coll Develop Librn - Youth Serv,* Katie Bruce; E-mail: kbruce@princetonlibrary.org; *Pub Prog Librn,* Janie Hermann; Staff 58 (MLS 18, Non-MLS 40)
Founded 1909. Pop 28,572; Circ 611,400
Jan 2013-Dec 2013 Income $5,794,334, State $16,424, City $3,983,619, Locally Generated Income $1,198,553, Other $595,738. Mats Exp $383,278, Books $192,298, Per/Ser (Incl. Access Fees) $29,418, Other Print Mats $32,024, AV Mat $29,726, Electronic Ref Mat (Incl. Access Fees) $99,812. Sal $3,449,060 (Prof $50,765)
Library Holdings: Audiobooks 6,426; AV Mats 8,000; CDs 6,852; DVDs 14,299; e-books 40,868; e-journals 50; Electronic Media & Resources 27; High Interest/Low Vocabulary Bk Vols 250; Large Print Bks 1,000; Microforms 500; Bk Titles 163,830; Bk Vols 218,953; Per Subs 300
Special Collections: African Genealogy (Paul Robeson Coll); Princeton History Coll
Subject Interests: Bus, Consumer health
Automation Activity & Vendor Info: (Acquisitions) Innovative Interfaces, Inc; (Cataloging) Innovative Interfaces, Inc; (Circulation) Innovative Interfaces, Inc; (ILL) OCLC; (OPAC) Innovative Interfaces, Inc
Database Vendor: Baker & Taylor, BiblioCommons, Booklist Online, Comprise Technologies Inc, EBSCOhost, Factiva.com, Gale Cengage Learning, Hoovers, infoUSA, Ingram Library Services, Innovative Interfaces, Inc, JSTOR, OCLC FirstSearch, Overdrive, Inc, ProQuest, ReferenceUSA, SerialsSolutions, Standard & Poor's, TumbleBookLibrary, WT Cox
Wireless access
Publications: Connections (Newsletter)
Partic in LibraryLinkNJ, The New Jersey Library Cooperative
Open Mon-Fri 9-9, Sat 9-6, Sun 1-6
Friends of the Library Group

R PRINCETON THEOLOGICAL SEMINARY*, Speer Library, Mercer St & Library Pl, 08542. (Mail add: PO Box 111, 08542-0111), SAN 310-4559. Tel: 609-497-7940. FAX: 609-497-1826. Web Site: www.ptsem.edu/library/. *Dir,* Stephen D Crocco; Tel: 609-497-7930, E-mail: stephen.crocco@ptsem.edu; *Assoc Librn,* Julie Eng Dawson; *Coll Develop,* Donald M Vorp; *Curator, Spec Coll,* Clifford Anderson; *Ref,* Katherine Skrebutenas
Founded 1812. Highest Degree: Doctorate
Library Holdings: Microforms 500,000; Bk Vols 533,707; Per Subs 2,000
Special Collections: Baptist Controversy; Early American Theological Pamphlets (Sprague Coll); Hymnology (Benson Coll); Puritan Literature, bks, pamphlets
Subject Interests: Theol
Automation Activity & Vendor Info: (Acquisitions) Ex Libris Group; (Cataloging) Ex Libris Group; (Circulation) Ex Libris Group; (OPAC) Ex Libris Group; (Serials) Ex Libris Group
Wireless access
Partic in OCLC Online Computer Library Center, Inc
Open Mon-Thurs 8am-11pm, Fri 8-5, Sat 9-5, Sun 3-11

C PRINCETON UNIVERSITY*, Firestone Library, One Washington Rd, 08544-2098. SAN 351-2282. Tel: 609-258-1470. Circulation Tel: 609-258-3202. Interlibrary Loan Service Tel: 609-258-3272. Reference Tel: 609-258-5964. FAX: 609-258-0441. E-mail: firestone@princeton.edu. Web Site: libweb.princeton.edu. *Univ Librn,* Karen Trainer; Tel: 609-258-3170, E-mail: ktrainer@princeton.edu; *Dep Univ Librn, Syst Coordr,* Marvin F Bielawski; Tel: 609-258-3190, E-mail: marvinb@princeton.edu; *Assoc Univ Librn, Rare Bks & Spec Coll,* Ben Primer; Tel: 609-258-3184, E-mail: primer@princeton.edu; *Assoc Univ Librn, Res & Instrul Serv,* Keith Gresham; *Assoc Univ Librn, Tech Serv,* Richard Schulz; Tel: 609-258-5297, E-mail: rjschulz@princeton.edu; *Asst Univ Librn, Rare Bks & Spec Coll, Curator, Rare Bks,* Stephen Ferguson; Tel: 609-258-3165, E-mail: ferguson@princeton.edu; *Sr Ref Librn,* Mary George; Tel: 609-258-3254, E-mail: mwgeorge@princeton.edu; *Cat, Tech Serv,* Donald Thornbury; Tel: 609-258-3177, E-mail: doncat@princeton.edu; Staff 112 (MLS 103, Non-MLS 9)
Enrl 6,340; Fac 716; Highest Degree: Doctorate
Library Holdings: Bk Vols 5,315,332; Per Subs 37,629
Special Collections: Aeronautics Coll; Ainsworth, Barrie, the Brontes, Bulwer-Lytton, Collins, Mrs Craik, Dickens, Disraeli, Dogson, George Eliot, Mrs Gaskell, Hardy, Hughes, Kingsley, Lever, Reade, Stevenson, Thackeray, Trollope (Parrish Coll of Victorian Novelists); American Historical Manuscripts; American Woodcut Illustrated Books Coll; Americana Coll; Arts; Chateaubriand Coll; Chess Coll; Civil Rights Coll; Coins; Emblem Books; Emily Dickinson Coll; English Restoration Drama; European Historical Manuscripts; European Legal Documents (11th to 19th Century); Fishing & Angling; Graphic; Halliburton, Handel, Hemingway, Horace, Leigh Hunt, Laurence Hutton, Otto H Kahn, George Kennan, Kierkegaard, Ivy Lee, C G Leland, Lilienthal, George McAneny, Thomas Mann, E L Masters, Harold R Medina, Montaigne, W V Moody, O'Neill, Coventry Patmore, H L Piozzi, Pound, Rabelais, Rowlandson, Richard

Rush, Ruskin, Schweitzer, William Seymour, Shellabarger, H Alexander Smith, Samuel Southard, Adlai Stevenson, Julian Street, Symons, Tarkington, Allen Tate, Ridgeley Torrence, Carl Van Doren, Henry Van Dyke, Vergil, Viele-Griffin, Woodrow Wilson; History of Women; Horace Coll; Incunabula; Individual Collections: Louis Adamic, Elmer Adler, American Civil Liberties Union, Audubon, Bernard Baruch, Beardsley, Beauharnais (Administration of Italy & War Claims, Archives of Prince Eugene De Beauharnais), Blake, Boker, Boudinot Family, Aaron Burr Sr, M S Burt, F A R De Chateaubriand, William Cowper, J G Cozzens, Cruishank, John Davidson, Allan Dulles, J F Duells, Jonathan Edwards, Faulkner, F S Fitzgerald, Forrestal, Goethe,; Islamic Manuscripts; John Foster Dulles Project; Latin America (Spanish & English Language Documents, 16th to 19th Century); Manuscripts & Maps Coll; Medieval & Renaissance Manuscripts; Middle East Manuscripts; Montaigne Coll; Mormon History; Mountaineering; New Jersey History & Imprints; Papyrus Manuscripts; Pliny-Fisk Library of Economics & Finance; Publishers & Publishing (Doubleday, Harper, Holt, John Day, Scribner), papers; Rowlandson Coll; Sporting Books Coll; Story Magazine; Theater Coll; United Nations; Vergil Coll; Western Americana Coll. UN Document Depository; US Document Depository

Subject Interests: Ancient hist, Behav sci, China, Classics hist, Econ, Hist, Humanities, Intl law, Japan, Lit, Music, Natural sci, Near East, Relations, Soc sci

Publications: The Princeton University Library Chronicle

Partic in Association of Research Libraries (ARL); LibraryLinkNJ, The New Jersey Library Cooperative; RLIN (Research Libraries Information Network); Virtual Academic Library Environment

Open Mon-Fri 8am-11:45pm, Sat & Sun 9am-11:45pm

Friends of the Library Group

Departmental Libraries:

DEPARTMENT OF RARE BOOKS & SPECIAL COLLECTIONS, One Washington Rd, 08544. Tel: 609-258-3184. FAX: 609-258-2324. E-mail: rbsc@princeton.edu. Web Site: www.princeton.edu/~rbsc. *Curator,* Mark Farrell; *Head, Tech Serv,* Don Thornbury; *Cat,* Scott Carlisle

Library Holdings: Bk Vols 200,000

Open Mon-Fri 9-4:45 (8:45-4:15 Summer)

EAST ASIAN LIBRARY & THE GEST COLLECTION, 33 Frist Campus Ctr, Rm 317, 08544-. Tel: 609-258-3182. FAX: 609-258-4573. E-mail: gest@princeton.edu. Web Site: eastasianlib.princeton.edu. *Actg Dir,* Martin Heijdra; Tel: 609-258-5336, E-mail: mheijdra@princeton.edu; *Head, Tech Serv,* Iping Wei; Tel: 609-258-3259; Staff 7 (MLS 6, Non-MLS 1)

Founded 1937

Library Holdings: Bk Vols 784,000; Per Subs 36,000

Special Collections: Gest Coll of String-bound Chinese Books, most printed prior to 18th century

Partic in East Coast Consortium of East Asian Libraries; OCLC Online Computer Library Center, Inc

Open Mon-Fri (Winter) 9am-11pm, Sat 10-5, Sun 2-11; Mon-Fri (Summer) 8:30-4:30

ENGINEERING, 35 Olden St, 08544. (Mail add: Friend Center, 08544). Tel: 609-258-3200. FAX: 609-258-7366. E-mail: englib@princeton.edu. *Librn,* Andrea Baruzzi; Tel: 609-258-6567; *Circ,* Barbara Chamberlain; Staff 2 (MLS 2)

Founded 1963. Enrl 1,600; Highest Degree: Doctorate

Library Holdings: Bk Vols 600,000

Automation Activity & Vendor Info: (Acquisitions) Ex Libris Group; (Cataloging) Ex Libris Group; (Circulation) Ex Libris Group; (ILL) OCLC ILLiad; (Serials) Ex Libris Group

Open Mon-Thurs 8:30am-2am, Fri 8:30am-9pm, Sat 9-9, Sun 1pm-2am

HAROLD P FURTH LIBRARY, James Forrestal Campus, C-Site, Rm A108, 08543-0451. (Mail add: PO Box 451, 08543-0451). Tel: 609-243-3565. FAX: 609-243-2299. E-mail: ppllib@princeton.edu. Web Site: www.pppl.gov/library. *Head Librn,* Adriana Popesu; E-mail: popescua@princeton.edu. Subject Specialists: *Eng, Physics,* Adriana Popesu; Staff 2 (MLS 1, Non-MLS 1)

Founded 1951. Highest Degree: Doctorate

Library Holdings: Bk Titles 7,000; Bk Vols 18,010; Per Subs 60

Subject Interests: Fusion energy, Plasma physics, Thermonuclear fusion

Automation Activity & Vendor Info: (Acquisitions) Ex Libris Group; (Cataloging) Ex Libris Group; (Circulation) Ex Libris Group; (OPAC) Ex Libris Group; (Serials) Ex Libris Group

Function: For res purposes

Open Mon-Fri 10-4

Restriction: External users must contact libr, Photo ID required for access

INDUSTRIAL RELATIONS, Firestone Library, Social Science Reference Ctr, One Washington Rd, 08544. Tel: 609-258-4043. FAX: 609-258-2907. E-mail: firestone@princeton.edu. Web Site: www.princeton.edu. *Librn,* Phebe Dickson

Library Holdings: Bk Vols 8,900

Subject Interests: Labor mgt relations, Labor relations, Personnel admin, Soc security, Unemployment ins

Open Mon-Fri (Winter) 10-5; Mon-Fri (Summer) 10-4:30

MARQUAND LIBRARY OF ART & ARCHAEOLOGY, McCormick Hall, 08544-0001. (Mail add: One Washington Rd, 08544), SAN 351-2371. Tel: 609-258-3783. FAX: 609-258-7650. E-mail: marquand@princeton.edu. Web Site: marquand.princeton.edu. *Librn,* Sandra Brooke; Tel: 609-258-5860, E-mail: sbrooke@princeton.edu; *Asst Librn,* Rebecca Friedman; Tel: 609-258-3163, E-mail: rfriedma@princeton.edu; Staff 5 (MLS 2, Non-MLS 3)

Founded 1908

Library Holdings: Bk Vols 500,000

Subject Interests: Archaeology, Archit, Art, Gardens, Landscaping, Photog, Rare bks

Automation Activity & Vendor Info: (Acquisitions) Ex Libris Group; (Cataloging) Ex Libris Group; (Circulation) Ex Libris Group; (OPAC) Ex Libris Group

Open Mon-Fri (Fall-Spring) 8:30am-11:45pm, Sat 10am-10:45pm, Sun 12-11:45; Mon-Thurs (Summer) 8:30am-8:45pm, Fri 8:30am-5:45pm, Sat & Sun 12-5:45

Restriction: Restricted access

MENDEL MUSIC LIBRARY, Woolworth Center for Musical Studies, 08544. Tel: 609-258-3230. FAX: 609-258-6793. E-mail: muslib@princeton.edu. Web Site: library.princeton.edu/libraries/music/index.php. *Librn,* Darwin Scott; Tel: 609-258-4251, E-mail: dfscott@princeton.edu; Staff 1 (MLS 1)

Founded 1997

Library Holdings: Bk Vols 65,000

Special Collections: Old Nassau Coll (1859-1989)

Open Mon-Thurs 8:30am-Midnight, Fri 8:30-8, Sat 10-6, Sun Noon-Midnight

SEELEY G MUDD MANUSCRIPT LIBRARY, 65 Olden St, 08544. Tel: 609-258-6345. FAX: 609-258-3385. E-mail: mudd@princeton.edu. Web Site: www.princeton.edu/~mudd. *Curator, Univ Archivist,* Daniel Linke; Staff 5 (MLS 1, Non-MLS 4)

Special Collections: Manuscripts Coll; University Archives

Subject Interests: 20th Century Am, Foreign policy, Intl develop, Journalism, Law

Function: Archival coll

Open Mon-Fri 9-4:45

Restriction: Closed stack, Non-circulating

POLITICS & LAW COLLECTIONS, Firestone Library, A-17-J-1, One Washington Rd, 08544. Tel: 609-258-3209, 609-258-3701. Reference Tel: 609-258-3178. *Law Librn,* David Hollander; *Politics Librn,* Jeremy Darrington; *Law & Politics Coll Mgr,* Carol Houghton

Library Holdings: Bk Vols 20,067

Database Vendor: LexisNexis

SCHOOL OF ARCHITECTURE LIBRARY, Architecture Bldg, 2nd Flr, S-204, One Washington Rd, 08544. Tel: 609-258-3256. Web Site: www.princeton.edu. *Librn,* Hannah Bennet; Staff 4 (MLS 1, Non-MLS 3)

Founded 1967. Enrl 120; Fac 16

Library Holdings: Bk Vols 32,000; Per Subs 300

Subject Interests: Architectural hist, Landscape archit, Urban design

Open Mon-Fri 9am-11:45pm, Sat 10am-11:45pm, Sun 1-11:45

Restriction: Non-circulating

DONALD E STOKES LIBRARY - PUBLIC & INTERNATIONAL AFFAIRS & POPULATION RESEARCH, Wallace Hall, 08544. Tel: 609-258-5455. FAX: 609-258-6844. E-mail: piaprlib@princeton.edu. Web Site: stokeslib.princeton.edu/main.htm. *Head of Libr,* Nancy Pressman Levy; Tel: 609-258-4782, E-mail: pressman@princeton.edu; *Population Res Librn,* Joann Donatiello; Tel: 609-258-1377, E-mail: jdonatie@princeton.edu; *Asst Population Res Librn,* Elana Broch; Tel: 609-258-5517, E-mail: ebroch@princeton.edu; Staff 8 (MLS 3, Non-MLS 5)

Library Holdings: Bk Vols 55,000; Per Subs 500

Special Collections: Ansley J Coale Population Research Coll

Subject Interests: Census, Statistics

Open Mon-Thurs (Winter) 8:30am-Midnight, Fri 8:30am-10pm, Sat 10-9, Sun Noon-Midnight; Mon-Thurs (Summer) 8:30-8, Fri 8:30-4:30, Sat & Sun 1-5

S SIEMENS CORPORATE RESEARCH, INC*, Research Library, 755 College Rd E, 08540. SAN 375-6440. Tel: 609-734-6506. FAX: 609-734-6565. *Librn,* Ruth Weitzenfeld; Staff 2 (MLS 2)

Library Holdings: Bk Titles 12,000; Per Subs 20

Subject Interests: Computer sci

Automation Activity & Vendor Info: (Cataloging) EOS International; (Circulation) EOS International; (OPAC) EOS International; (Serials) EOS International

Database Vendor: Dialog

Restriction: Not open to pub

S TOBACCO MERCHANTS ASSOCIATION OF THE UNITED STATES*, Howard S Cullman Library, 231 Clarksville Rd, 08543. (Mail add: PO Box 8019, 08543-8019), SAN 312-0929. Tel: 609-275-4900. FAX: 609-275-8379. Web Site: www.tma.org. *In Charge,* Darryl Jason; E-mail: darryl@tma.org; Staff 2 (Non-MLS 2)

Founded 1915

Library Holdings: Bk Vols 300; Per Subs 100
Special Collections: Tobacco & Products (Trademark & Brand Files), electronic
Wireless access
Publications: Newsletters
Partic in LibraryLinkNJ, The New Jersey Library Cooperative
Restriction: Staff & mem only

RAHWAY

S EAST JERSEY STATE PRISON LIBRARY*, Lock Bag R, Woodbridge Ave, 07065. SAN 375-8451. Tel: 732-396-2695. FAX: 732-499-5023. *Librn,* Rick Liss
Library Holdings: Bk Vols 10,000
Restriction: Not open to pub
Branches:
LAW, Lock Bag R, Woodbridge Ave, 07065. Tel: 732-499-5010. *Supvr,* Liss Robert
Library Holdings: Bk Vols 20,000
Restriction: Not open to pub

M ROBERT WOOD JOHNSON UNIVERSITY HOSPITAL RAHWAY*, Health Sciences Library, 865 Stone St, 07065. Tel: 732-381-4200. Web Site: www.rwjuhr.com. *Librn,* Andrew Gerber; E-mail: agerber@rwjuhr.com; Staff 1 (MLS 1)
Library Holdings: Bk Vols 500; Per Subs 40
Automation Activity & Vendor Info: (Cataloging) LibraryWorld, Inc; (Circulation) LibraryWorld, Inc; (OPAC) LibraryWorld, Inc; (Serials) LibraryWorld, Inc
Database Vendor: EBSCOhost, MD Consult, OVID Technologies, PubMed
Wireless access
Partic in Basic Health Sciences Library Network; New Jersey Health Sciences Library Network

P RAHWAY PUBLIC LIBRARY*, Two City Hall Plaza, 07065. SAN 310-4648. Tel: 732-340-1551. FAX: 732-340-0393. E-mail: info@rahwaylibrary.org. Web Site: www.rahwaylibrary.org. *Dir,* Gail Miller; Staff 8 (MLS 3, Non-MLS 5)
Founded 1858. Pop 25,760; Circ 125,341
Library Holdings: Bk Titles 75,000; Bk Vols 90,000; Per Subs 175
Subject Interests: Local hist, NJ
Automation Activity & Vendor Info: (Cataloging) TLC (The Library Corporation); (Circulation) TLC (The Library Corporation)
Wireless access
Publications: Annual Report
Partic in LibraryLinkNJ, The New Jersey Library Cooperative
Open Mon, Wed & Thurs 9-8, Tues, Fri & Sat 9-5

RAMSEY

P RAMSEY FREE PUBLIC LIBRARY*, 30 Wyckoff Ave, 07446. SAN 310-4656. Tel: 201-327-1445. FAX: 201-327-3687. Web Site: www.ramseylibrary.org. *Dir,* Wendy B Bloom; E-mail: bloom@bccls.org; *Asst Dir,* Kathy Elwell; *Ref,* Ellen Smith; *Youth Serv,* Zambrano Margarita; Staff 4 (MLS 4)
Founded 1921. Pop 16,000; Circ 205,000
Library Holdings: Bk Vols 113,000; Per Subs 175
Special Collections: Sidoroff Language Learning Coll
Subject Interests: NJ hist, Spanish
Automation Activity & Vendor Info: (Cataloging) SirsiDynix; (Circulation) SirsiDynix; (OPAC) SirsiDynix
Database Vendor: EBSCOhost, ProQuest
Wireless access
Publications: Ramsey Reader (Newsletter)
Partic in Bergen County Cooperative Library System; LibraryLinkNJ, The New Jersey Library Cooperative
Open Mon-Thurs 9-9, Fri 9-5, Sat 10-5, Sun 12-4
Friends of the Library Group

RANDOLPH

J COUNTY COLLEGE OF MORRIS*, Sherman H Masten Learning Resource Center, 214 Center Grove Rd, 07869-2086. SAN 310-4672. Circulation Tel: 973-328-5300. Interlibrary Loan Service Tel: 973-328-5307. Reference Tel: 973-328-5296. Administration Tel: 973-328-5282. Administration FAX: 973-328-3035. Web Site: www.ccm.edu/library. *Dir,* John M Cohn; E-mail: jcohn@ccm.edu; *Assoc Dir,* Mark Tolleson; Tel: 973-328-5311, E-mail: mtolleson@ccm.edu; *Ref Librn,* Becky Hodd; E-mail: rhodd@ccm.edu; *Ref Librn,* Jane Kingsland; E-mail: jkingsland@ccm.edu; *Bibliog Instruction Coordr,* Lynee Richel; E-mail: lrichel@ccm.edu; *Ref Serv Coordr,* Geetali Basu; E-mail: gbasu@ccm.edu; *Coordr, Tech Serv,* Regina Cannizzaro; E-mail: rcannizzaro@ccm.edu; *Distance Learning Serv,* Sheri Ventura; E-mail: sventura@ccm.edu; Staff 13 (MLS 8, Non-MLS 5)
Founded 1968. Enrl 8,500; Fac 466; Highest Degree: Associate
Jul 2009-Jun 2010 Income $2,029,206
Library Holdings: Bk Titles 55,000
Special Collections: US Document Depository
Automation Activity & Vendor Info: (Acquisitions) Innovative Interfaces, Inc; (Cataloging) Innovative Interfaces, Inc; (Circulation) Innovative Interfaces, Inc; (Course Reserve) Innovative Interfaces, Inc; (ILL) Innovative Interfaces, Inc; (OPAC) Innovative Interfaces, Inc; (Serials) Innovative Interfaces, Inc
Database Vendor: American Psychological Association (APA), ARTstor, Cinahl, Dun & Bradstreet, EBSCOhost, Elsevier, Gale Cengage Learning, Infotrieve, JSTOR, LexisNexis, Marcive, Inc, McGraw-Hill, OCLC FirstSearch, ProQuest, ReferenceUSA, SerialsSolutions, Westlaw
Wireless access
Publications: Bibliographies; Function-specific guides; In-house Catalogs
Partic in LibraryLinkNJ, The New Jersey Library Cooperative; Lyrasis; OCLC Online Computer Library Center, Inc; Virtual Academic Library Environment

P RANDOLPH TOWNSHIP FREE PUBLIC LIBRARY*, 28 Calais Rd, 07869. SAN 310-4664. Tel: 973-895-3556. FAX: 973-895-4946. Web Site: www.randolphnj.org/library. *Dir,* Anita S Freeman; E-mail: anita.freeman@mainlib.org; *Asst Dir,* Robert Tambini; E-mail: rob.tambini@mainlib.org; *Ch Serv,* Lore Reinhart; E-mail: lore.reinhart@mainlib.org; Staff 4.1 (MLS 4.1)
Founded 1964. Pop 26,000; Circ 272,000
Jan 2013-Dec 2013 Income $1,195,525. Mats Exp $284,284, Books $139,000, Per/Ser (Incl. Access Fees) $9,000, Other Print Mats $10,000, AV Mat $60,000. Sal $665,000
Library Holdings: Audiobooks 3,510; CDs 5,000; DVDs 7,990; Large Print Bks 1,020; Bk Titles 115,000; Per Subs 130
Automation Activity & Vendor Info: (Circulation) Innovative Interfaces, Inc; (OPAC) Innovative Interfaces, Inc
Wireless access
Function: Adult bk club, After school storytime, Audiobks via web, Bk club(s), Bks on CD, CD-ROM, Children's prog, Computer training, Computers for patron use, Copy machines, Free DVD rentals, Handicapped accessible, ILL available, Music CDs, Notary serv, Photocopying/Printing, Preschool reading prog, Prog for adults, Prog for children & young adult, Pub access computers, Scanner, Story hour, Summer reading prog
Partic in LibraryLinkNJ, The New Jersey Library Cooperative; Morris Automated Information Network
Open Mon-Thurs (Winter) 9-9, Fri & Sat 9-5, Sun 12-4; Mon-Thurs (Summer) 9-9, Fri 9-5
Friends of the Library Group

RARITAN

S JOHNSON & JOHNSON PHARMACEUTICAL RESEARCH & DEVELOPMENT*, Hartman Library, 1003 US Hwy 202 P, 08869-0602. (Mail add: Box 300, 08869-0602), SAN 310-4699. Tel: 908-704-4919, 908-704-8998. FAX: 908-707-9860. *Dir, Libr Serv,* Donna Wahl; *Supvr,* Kathleen Amberg; Staff 6 (MLS 2, Non-MLS 4)
Founded 1944
Library Holdings: Bk Vols 8,000; Per Subs 480
Subject Interests: Biol, Chem, Med
Automation Activity & Vendor Info: (Cataloging) SirsiDynix; (Circulation) SirsiDynix; (OPAC) SirsiDynix
Database Vendor: SirsiDynix
Function: Archival coll, Doc delivery serv
Partic in Dialog Corp; Medical Library Association (MLA); SDC Info Servs; SLA
Restriction: Open by appt only

P RARITAN PUBLIC LIBRARY*, 54 E Somerset St, 08869. SAN 310-4702. Tel: 908-725-0413. FAX: 908-725-1832. E-mail: RaritanL@yahoo.com. Web Site: www.raritanlibrary.org. *Dir,* Mary Jane Paese; *Asst Dir,* Brendon Meany
Founded 1961. Pop 5,798; Circ 39,000
Library Holdings: Bk Vols 39,000; Per Subs 100
Special Collections: Basilone Congressional Record, Tribute & Citation; Basilone History Coll; Frelinghuysen Portraits Coll
Automation Activity & Vendor Info: (Acquisitions) Follett Software; (Cataloging) Follett Software; (Circulation) Follett Software; (Serials) Follett Software
Publications: Raritan Library News
Partic in NW Regional Libr Coop; Raritan Valley Fedn of Librs
Open Mon, Wed & Thurs 10-8, Tues 10-6, Fri 10-5, Sat 10-3
Friends of the Library Group

RED BANK

M MERIDIAN HEALTH, RIVERVIEW MEDICAL CENTER*, John B Movelle, MD Medical Library, One Riverview Plaza, 07701. SAN 310-4729. Tel: 732-530-2275. FAX: 732-530-2394. E-mail:

rmclibrary@meridianhealth.com. *Coordr, Libr Serv,* Position Currently Open; Staff 0.5 (MLS 0.5)
Founded 1968
Library Holdings: e-books 700; e-journals 550; Bk Titles 1,100; Spec Interest Per Sub 75
Subject Interests: Clinical med, Consumer health educ, Nursing
Automation Activity & Vendor Info: (Acquisitions) Ex Libris Group; (Cataloging) Ex Libris Group; (Circulation) Ex Libris Group; (OPAC) Ex Libris Group
Database Vendor: Cinahl, EBSCOhost, Elsevier, LexisNexis, MD Consult, Natural Standard, OVID Technologies, ScienceDirect, UpToDate
Wireless access
Function: Computers for patron use, Copy machines, Electronic databases & coll, Fax serv, Health sci info serv, ILL available, Online cat, Photocopying/Printing, Pub access computers, Ref serv available, Telephone ref, Web-catalog, Wheelchair accessible
Partic in Basic Health Sciences Library Network; NJ Regional Libr Coop
Open Mon-Fri 9-5
Restriction: Badge access after hrs, Borrowing privileges limited to fac & registered students, Non-circulating to the pub, Open to pub for ref only

P RED BANK PUBLIC LIBRARY*, Eisner Memorial Library, 84 W Front St, 07701. SAN 310-4710. Tel: 732-842-0690. FAX: 732-842-4191. Web Site: www.lmxac.org/redbank. *Dir,* Virginia Papandrea; Staff 3 (MLS 3)
Founded 1878. Pop 10,636; Circ 62,928
Library Holdings: Bk Vols 42,500; Per Subs 108
Subject Interests: NJ hist
Automation Activity & Vendor Info: (Cataloging) SirsiDynix; (Circulation) SirsiDynix; (ILL) OCLC; (OPAC) SirsiDynix
Database Vendor: ProQuest
Wireless access
Partic in Libraries of Middlesex Automation Consortium; LibraryLinkNJ, The New Jersey Library Cooperative
Open Mon, Wed & Thurs 10-9, Tues, Fri & Sat 10-5
Friends of the Library Group

RIDGEFIELD

P RIDGEFIELD PUBLIC LIBRARY*, 527 Morse Ave, 07657. SAN 310-4745. Tel: 201-941-0192. FAX: 201-941-9354. E-mail: rfldcirc@bccls.org. Web Site: ridgefield.bccls.org. *Dir,* Jane Forte; E-mail: forte@bccls.org; *Asst Dir/Ref Librn,* Yilin Sheng; E-mail: sheng@bccls.org; Staff 6 (MLS 2, Non-MLS 4)
Founded 1930. Pop 10,081; Circ 69,082
Library Holdings: Bk Vols 61,000; Per Subs 200
Special Collections: Ridgefield History Coll
Automation Activity & Vendor Info: (Cataloging) SirsiDynix; (Circulation) SirsiDynix; (ILL) SirsiDynix; (OPAC) SirsiDynix
Database Vendor: SirsiDynix
Wireless access
Open Mon 11-8, Tues & Wed 10-8, Thurs 10-5, Fri 12-5, Sat 10-2; Mon & Tues (Summer) 9:30-8, Wed, 10-8, Thurs & Fri 10-5
Friends of the Library Group

RIDGEFIELD PARK

P RIDGEFIELD PARK FREE PUBLIC LIBRARY*, 107 Cedar St, 07660. SAN 310-4753. Tel: 201-641-0689. FAX: 201-440-1058. E-mail: rfpkcirc@bccls.org. Web Site: www.ridgefieldpark.org. *Dir,* Eileen Mackesy-Karpoff; E-mail: karpoff@bccls.org; *Head, Ch,* Laura Riley; E-mail: reilly@bccls.org; *Ref/YA,* Omar Khan; Staff 4 (MLS 2, Non-MLS 2)
Founded 1890. Pop 12,854; Circ 69,561
Jan 2011-Dec 2011 Income $689,000, State $6,000, City $653,000, Locally Generated Income $30,000. Mats Exp $66,000, Books $40,000, Per/Ser (Incl. Access Fees) $3,000, AV Mat $20,000, Electronic Ref Mat (Incl. Access Fees) $3,000. Sal $318,000 (Prof $70,000)
Library Holdings: Bk Vols 62,395; Per Subs 95
Automation Activity & Vendor Info: (Cataloging) SirsiDynix; (Circulation) SirsiDynix; (ILL) SirsiDynix; (OPAC) SirsiDynix
Wireless access
Function: Adult bk club, Adult literacy prog, After school storytime, Archival coll, Audiobks via web, Bk club(s), Bks on CD, CD-ROM, Children's prog, Computer training, Computers for patron use, Copy machines, Digital talking bks, E-Reserves, Electronic databases & coll, Exhibits, Fax serv, Free DVD rentals, Handicapped accessible, Homebound delivery serv, ILL available, Magnifiers for reading, Mus passes, Music CDs, OverDrive digital audio bks, Photocopying/Printing, Preschool outreach, Prog for adults, Prog for children & young adult, Pub access computers, Ref serv available, Story hour, Summer & winter reading prog, Summer reading prog, Tax forms, Teen prog, Web-catalog
Open Mon-Thurs 9:30-9, Fri 9:30-5:30, Sat 9:30-2:30
Friends of the Library Group

RIDGEWOOD

P RIDGEWOOD PUBLIC LIBRARY*, 125 N Maple Ave, 07450-3288. SAN 351-336X. Tel: 201-670-5600. FAX: 201-670-0293. Web Site: www.ridgewoodlibrary.org. *Dir,* Nancy K Greene; *Mgr, Info Tech,* Michael Schinn; *Admin Librn,* Christine Yurgelonis; *Local Hist Librn,* Peggy Norris; *Supvr, Ad Serv,* Eileen Colyer; *Supvr, Ch Serv,* Lois Brodie; *Supvr, Ch Serv,* Roberta Carswell; *YA Serv,* Gina Mitgang; Staff 11 (MLS 11)
Founded 1923. Pop 27,000; Circ 502,000
Library Holdings: AV Mats 20,031; Bk Vols 148,000
Subject Interests: English as a second lang, Local hist
Wireless access
Publications: Annual Report
Partic in Bergen County Cooperative Library System
Open Mon-Thurs 9-9, Fri 9-6, Sat 9-5, Sun 1-5
Friends of the Library Group

M VALLEY HOSPITAL*, Medical Library, 223 N Van Dien Ave, 07450. SAN 322-9122. Tel: 201-447-8285. FAX: 201-447-8602. Web Site: www.valleyhealth.com. *Librn,* Claudia Allocco; E-mail: callocc@valleyhealth.com; Staff 2 (MLS 1, Non-MLS 1)
Library Holdings: Bk Vols 2,000; Per Subs 100
Subject Interests: Consumer health
Database Vendor: EBSCOhost
Open Mon-Fri 7-3:30

RINGWOOD

P RINGWOOD PUBLIC LIBRARY*, 30 Cannici Dr, 07456. SAN 310-477X. Tel: 973-962-6256. FAX: 973-962-7799. E-mail: ringwoodpl@hotmail.com. Web Site: www.ringwoodlibrary.org. *Dir,* Andrea R Cahoon; E-mail: cahoon@ringwoodlibrary.org; *Adult Serv,* Mary L Kane; E-mail: kane@ringwoodlibrary.org; *Ch Serv,* Ann Marie Solch; E-mail: solch@ringwoodlibrary.org; Staff 10 (MLS 3, Non-MLS 7)
Founded 1960. Pop 12,623; Circ 97,934
Jan 2012-Dec 2012 Income $750,768, State $5,412, City $679,582, Locally Generated Income $24,442, Other $41,332. Mats Exp $51,630, Books $36,609, Per/Ser (Incl. Access Fees) $3,816, AV Mat $4,241, Electronic Ref Mat (Incl. Access Fees) $6,964. Sal $539,566
Library Holdings: Audiobooks 13,192; AV Mats 11,042; e-books 6,230; Electronic Media & Resources 7; Bk Vols 65,122; Per Subs 94
Special Collections: Local Minutes of Public Agencies Coll; Official Repository for EPA Superfund Documents for Ringwood Mines Site; Oral History of Camp Midvale Coll; Oral History of Upper Ringwood Coll; Ringwood History Coll, bks, clippings, microfiche, pamphlets
Automation Activity & Vendor Info: (Cataloging) SIRSI WorkFlows; (Circulation) SIRSI WorkFlows; (OPAC) SIRSI-iBistro
Database Vendor: Baker & Taylor, EBSCOhost, Electric Library, Gale Cengage Learning, Hoovers, LearningExpress, ProQuest, ReferenceUSA, SirsiDynix
Wireless access
Function: Adult bk club, Adult literacy prog, Art exhibits, Audiobks via web, Bk club(s), Bks on cassette, Bks on CD, Chess club, Children's prog, Computer training, Computers for patron use, Copy machines, E-Reserves, Electronic databases & coll, Exhibits, Fax serv, Free DVD rentals, Handicapped accessible, Holiday prog, Homework prog, ILL available, Large print keyboards, Mus passes, Music CDs, Notary serv, Online cat, Orientations, OverDrive digital audio bks, Photocopying/Printing, Prog for adults, Prog for children & young adult, Pub access computers, Ref & res, Ref serv available, Ref serv in person, Scanner, Spoken cassettes & CDs, Story hour, Summer reading prog, Tax forms, Teen prog, Telephone ref, VHS videos, Wheelchair accessible, Writing prog
Partic in LibraryLinkNJ, The New Jersey Library Cooperative; PALS Plus, The Computer Consortium of Passaic County Libraries
Open Mon-Thurs 10-9, Fri 10-5, Sat 10-4
Friends of the Library Group

RIVER EDGE

L PECKAR & ABRAMSON*, Law Library, 70 Grand Ave, 07661. SAN 372-4298. Tel: 201-343-3434. FAX: 201-343-6306. Web Site: www.pecklaw.com. *Librn,* David H Sloves
Library Holdings: Bk Vols 5,000; Per Subs 50
Partic in New Jersey Library Network
Open Mon-Fri 9-5

P RIVER EDGE FREE PUBLIC LIBRARY*, 685 Elm Ave, 07661. SAN 310-4788. Tel: 201-261-1663. FAX: 201-986-0214. E-mail: rivecirc@bccls.org. Web Site: riveredge.bccls.org. *Dir,* Daragh O'Connor; *Youth Serv Librn,* Maryanne Guiliano; *Adult Serv,* Jennifer Kelemen; *Ref,* Margaret Churley; Staff 4 (MLS 4)
Founded 1953. Pop 10,946; Circ 148,000
Library Holdings: AV Mats 3,398; Bk Titles 70,000; Bk Vols 75,000; Per Subs 120; Talking Bks 685
Special Collections: Korean Coll

Automation Activity & Vendor Info: (Cataloging) SirsiDynix; (Circulation) SirsiDynix; (OPAC) SirsiDynix
Wireless access
Partic in Bergen County Cooperative Library System
Open Mon, Tues & Thurs 10-9, Wed, Fri & Sat 10-5
Friends of the Library Group

RIVER VALE

P RIVER VALE FREE PUBLIC LIBRARY*, 412 Rivervale Rd, 07675. SAN 310-4796. Tel: 201-391-2323. FAX: 201-391-6599. Web Site: www.bccls.org/rivervale. *Dir,* Ann McCarthy; E-mail: mccarthy@bccls.org; *Head, Ch,* Mary Anne Ketabchi; *Ref Librn,* Diane Sweatlock; *Ref/YA,* Dale Friedman; Staff 4 (MLS 3, Non-MLS 1)
Founded 1964. Pop 9,449; Circ 114,982
Library Holdings: Bk Vols 52,100; Per Subs 125
Automation Activity & Vendor Info: (Cataloging) SirsiDynix; (Circulation) SirsiDynix; (OPAC) SirsiDynix; (Serials) SirsiDynix
Database Vendor: SirsiDynix
Wireless access
Partic in LibraryLinkNJ, The New Jersey Library Cooperative
Open Mon-Thurs 10-9, Fri & Sat 10-5, Sun 1-5
Friends of the Library Group

RIVERDALE

P RIVERDALE PUBLIC LIBRARY*, 93 Newark Pompton Tpk, 07457. SAN 376-057X. Tel: 973-835-5044. FAX: 973-835-2175. Web Site: www.riverdalepubliclibrary.org. *Dir,* Carol Heinz; *Ch Serv,* Lara Cohen; Staff 9 (MLS 2, Non-MLS 7)
Founded 2002. Pop 3,559; Circ 35,239
Library Holdings: CDs 77; DVDs 1,000; Large Print Bks 600; Bk Vols 26,279; Per Subs 62; Talking Bks 3,107; Videos 2,625
Automation Activity & Vendor Info: (Cataloging) Innovative Interfaces, Inc; (Circulation) Innovative Interfaces, Inc; (OPAC) Innovative Interfaces, Inc
Wireless access
Partic in Morris Automated Information Network
Open Mon, Wed & Thurs 10-8, Tues & Fri 10-5, Sat (Summer 10-2) 10-4
Friends of the Library Group

RIVERSIDE

P RIVERSIDE PUBLIC LIBRARY ASSOCIATION, INC*, Ten Zurbrugg Way, 08075. SAN 310-480X. Tel: 856-461-6922. E-mail: riverside@bcls.lib.nj.us. *Dir,* Jean Bowker; E-mail: jbowker@bcls.lib.nj.us
Founded 1922. Pop 8,079; Circ 41,611
Library Holdings: Audiobooks 36; CDs 258; DVDs 2,244; Bk Vols 33,615; Per Subs 32
Automation Activity & Vendor Info: (Cataloging) Horizon; (Circulation) Horizon; (OPAC) Horizon
Wireless access
Open Mon & Thurs 12-5 & 6:30-8:30, Tues 12-5, Wed 10-5, Sat 10-2

ROCHELLE PARK

P ROCHELLE PARK LIBRARY*, 151 W Passaic St, 07662. Tel: 201-587-7730, Ext 8. FAX: 201-587-9855. E-mail: info@rplibrary.org. *Dir,* Nicole Williams
Library Holdings: CDs 150; DVDs 2,000; Large Print Bks 200; Bk Vols 14,000; Per Subs 75; Talking Bks 175
Automation Activity & Vendor Info: (Cataloging) SirsiDynix; (Circulation) SirsiDynix; (OPAC) SirsiDynix
Open Mon-Thurs 9-8:30, Fri 9-4, Sat 10-3

ROCKAWAY

P ROCKAWAY BOROUGH FREE PUBLIC LIBRARY*, 82 E Main St, 07866. SAN 371-5388. Tel: 973-627-5709. FAX: 973-627-5796. Web Site: rockboro.gti.net. *Dir,* Edna Puleo; *Ch Serv,* Jennifer Boyle; *ILL,* Marilyn Senesicy; Staff 9 (MLS 1, Non-MLS 8)
Founded 1914. Pop 6,500
Library Holdings: Bk Titles 30,000; Bk Vols 35,000; Per Subs 80
Subject Interests: Local hist, Nat hist, NJ hist, State hist
Automation Activity & Vendor Info: (Circulation) SirsiDynix; (ILL) SirsiDynix; (OPAC) SirsiDynix
Publications: Rockaway Borough Library Newsletter
Partic in Morris Automated Information Network
Special Services for the Blind - Magnifiers
Open Mon & Wed 12-8, Tues, Thurs & Fri 10-6, Sat 10-2
Friends of the Library Group

P ROCKAWAY TOWNSHIP FREE PUBLIC LIBRARY, 61 Mount Hope Rd, 07866. SAN 351-3424. Tel: 973-627-2344. FAX: 973-627-7658. E-mail: rockawaytwplibrary@rtlibrary.org. Web Site: www.rtlibrary.org. *Dir,* Scott Davan; *Head, Ref/IT,* Pierre Rosen; *Head, Youth Serv,* Darlene Steinhart
Founded 1966. Pop 25,000
Library Holdings: AV Mats 8,160; CDs 2,325; DVDs 4,040; Bk Vols 112,000
Automation Activity & Vendor Info: (Circulation) Innovative Interfaces, Inc; (ILL) Auto-Graphics, Inc; (OPAC) Innovative Interfaces, Inc
Database Vendor: Innovative Interfaces, Inc
Wireless access
Partic in Morris Automated Information Network; OCLC Online Computer Library Center, Inc
Open Mon-Wed & Fri 9-8, Thurs & Sat 9-5, Sun 1-4
Friends of the Library Group
Branches: 1
HIBERNIA BRANCH, 419 Green Pond Rd, Hibernia, 07842. (Mail add: 61 Mount Hope Rd, 07866), SAN 351-3459. Tel: 973-627-6872.
Library Holdings: Bk Vols 7,500
Open Mon 9:30-5:30, Wed 1-9
Friends of the Library Group

ROEBLING

P FLORENCE TOWNSHIP PUBLIC LIBRARY*, 1350 Hornberger Ave, 08554. SAN 310-4842. Tel: 609-499-0143. FAX: 609-499-0551. E-mail: florence@bcls.lib.nj.us. Web Site: www.bcls.lib.nj.us. *Librn,* LaVonna Lawrence
Circ 12,000
Library Holdings: Bk Vols 26,000; Per Subs 78
Automation Activity & Vendor Info: (Acquisitions) Horizon; (Cataloging) Horizon; (Circulation) Horizon
Wireless access
Mem of Burlington County Library
Open Mon-Thurs 11-8, Fri 11-4, Sat 10-2

ROSELAND

L CONNELL FOLEY LAW LIBRARY, 85 Livingston Ave, 07068. Tel: 973-535-0500. Interlibrary Loan Service Tel: 973-535-0500, Ext 2438. FAX: 973-535-9217. Web Site: www.connellfoley.com. *Dir,* Tae J Yoo; E-mail: tyoo@connellfoley.com; Staff 2 (MLS 1, Non-MLS 1)
Founded 1936
Library Holdings: Bk Vols 22,000
Subject Interests: Banking, Corporate, Estates, NJ law, Tax, Trusts
Database Vendor: Bloomberg, CISTI Source, Elsevier, Infotrieve, LexisNexis, Main Library Systems, McGraw-Hill, Westlaw, Westlaw Business, Wiley
Wireless access
Partic in LibraryLinkNJ, The New Jersey Library Cooperative
Open Mon-Fri 9-5
Restriction: Private libr, Restricted access

L LOWENSTEIN SANDLER PC LIBRARY*, 65 Livingston Ave, 07068. SAN 376-0707. Tel: 973-597-2500. FAX: 973-597-2400. E-mail: lawlibrary@lowenstein.com. *Dir, Knowledge & Res Serv,* Kathlyn Schweyer; Tel: 973-422-2942, Fax: 973-597-6123, E-mail: kschweyer@lowenstein.com; *Sr Res Serv Librn,* Katherine Taggart; Tel: 973-422-6442, Fax: 973-422-6443, E-mail: ktaggart@lowenstein.com; *Res Serv Librn,* Natasha Grant; E-mail: ngrant@lowenstein.com
Library Holdings: Bk Vols 25,000
Restriction: Not open to pub

L LUM, DANZIS, DRASCO & POSITAN*, Law Library, 103 Eisenhower Pkwy, 07068-1049. SAN 310-3439. Tel: 973-403-9000. FAX: 973-403-9021.
Founded 1869
Library Holdings: Bk Vols 19,500
Subject Interests: Banking, Corporate, Estates, Securities, Tax, Trusts
Partic in Dialog Corp; Westlaw
Restriction: Staff use only

P ROSELAND FREE PUBLIC LIBRARY*, 20 Roseland Ave, 07068-1235. SAN 310-4850. Tel: 973-226-8636. FAX: 973-226-6429. E-mail: rosecirc@bccls.org. Web Site: www.bccls.org. *Dir,* Christopher Lee; E-mail: lee@bccls.org; *Ch,* Martha Current; E-mail: martha.current@bccls.org; *Ref Serv Librn,* Reina Jacobowitz; E-mail: reina.jacobowitz@bccls.org; *Admin Serv,* Donna Eastman; E-mail: donna.eastman@bccls.org; Staff 22 (MLS 4, Non-MLS 18)
Founded 1961. Pop 5,300; Circ 88,000
Library Holdings: Bk Titles 63,000; Bk Vols 65,000; Per Subs 80
Automation Activity & Vendor Info: (Cataloging) SIRSI WorkFlows; (Circulation) SIRSI WorkFlows; (OPAC) SIRSI Unicorn
Database Vendor: EBSCOhost, ProQuest
Wireless access
Partic in Bergen County Cooperative Library System
Special Services for the Blind - Aids for in-house use; Bks on CD; Large print bks; Low vision equip

Open Mon-Thurs 9-9, Fri 9-5, Sat 10-3
Friends of the Library Group

ROSELLE

P ROSELLE FREE PUBLIC LIBRARY*, 104 W Fourth Ave, 07203. SAN 310-4869. Tel: 908-245-5809. FAX: 908-298-8881. Administration FAX: 908-245-2116. E-mail: roselle@lmxac.org. Web Site: www.lmxac.org/roselle. *Interim Dir,* Jeanne Ryan; E-mail: jmryan@lmxac.org; *Acq,* Mark Hunter; *Ch Serv,* Marita Parham; E-mail: mparham@lmxac.org; Staff 3.2 (MLS 2.2, Non-MLS 1)
Founded 1917. Pop 21,274; Circ 65,000
Jul 2010-Jun 2011 Income $651,000, State $9,858, City $602,000, Locally Generated Income $39,142. Mats Exp $98,080, Books $76,000, Per/Ser (Incl. Access Fees) $7,680, AV Mat $14,400. Sal $405,000
Library Holdings: AV Mats 3,400; Bk Titles 52,000; Bk Vols 57,000; Per Subs 122
Automation Activity & Vendor Info: (Cataloging) SirsiDynix; (Circulation) SirsiDynix; (ILL) Auto-Graphics, Inc; (OPAC) SirsiDynix
Wireless access
Function: Adult bk club, AV serv, Bilingual assistance for Spanish patrons, Children's prog, Computers for patron use, Copy machines, Electronic databases & coll, Fax serv, Handicapped accessible, ILL available, Music CDs, Notary serv, Online cat, Passport agency, Spoken cassettes & CDs, Summer reading prog, Tax forms, Teen prog, Web-catalog
Publications: Facts About the Library (Library handbook)
Partic in Libraries of Middlesex Automation Consortium; LibraryLinkNJ, The New Jersey Library Cooperative
Open Mon-Wed & Fri 9-8, Thurs 9-6, Sat 10-4
Friends of the Library Group

ROSELLE PARK

P ROSELLE PARK VETERANS MEMORIAL LIBRARY*, 404 Chestnut St, 07204-1506. SAN 310-4877. Tel: 908-245-2456. FAX: 908-245-9204. E-mail: rpvm.library@gmail.com. Web Site: www.roselleparklibrary.org. *Dir,* Susan Calantone; E-mail: calanton@lmxac.org; *Children's/Ref Librn,* Elana Tsomaeva; E-mail: etsomaeva@lmxac.org; *Circ Supvr,* Deborah Heiss; E-mail: dheiss@lmxac.org; *Tech Serv,* Kit Rubino; E-mail: krubino@lmxac.org; Staff 4 (MLS 2, Non-MLS 2)
Founded 1930. Pop 13,281; Circ 41,843
Library Holdings: Bk Titles 50,600; Bk Vols 55,000; Per Subs 80
Special Collections: Decorating (Weissman Coll); Jones Memorial Science Coll
Database Vendor: EBSCOhost
Wireless access
Partic in Libraries of Middlesex Automation Consortium; LUCC; Mandarin
Open Mon, Tues & Thurs 10-8, Wed & Fri 10-5, Sat 10-2; Mon & Thurs (Summer) 10-8, Tues & Wed 10-5, Fri 10-4
Friends of the Library Group

RUMSON

P OCEANIC FREE LIBRARY*, 109 Avenue of Two Rivers, 07760. SAN 310-4885. Tel: 732-842-2692. FAX: 732-842-5713. Web Site: www.oceaniclibrary.org. *Dir,* Nanette Reis
Founded 1920. Pop 7,137; Circ 29,777
Library Holdings: Bk Vols 23,500; Per Subs 12
Special Collections: Opera Libretti, autographed bks
Automation Activity & Vendor Info: (Cataloging) SirsiDynix; (Circulation) SirsiDynix; (OPAC) SirsiDynix
Wireless access
Mem of Monmouth County Library
Open Mon & Thurs 1-7, Tues, Wed & Fri 10-5, Sat 10-4 (9-12 July & Aug)
Friends of the Library Group

RUNNEMEDE

P RUNNEMEDE FREE PUBLIC LIBRARY*, Broadway & Black Horse Pike, 08078. (Mail add: PO Box 119, 08078-0119), SAN 320-491X. Tel: 856-939-4688. FAX: 856-939-6371. E-mail: runnemedelibrary@comcast.net. Web Site: www.runnemedepubliclibrary.com. *Dir,* Kathleen Ann Vasinda; *Asst Librn,* Faith E Cook; *Asst Librn,* Katherine Lewis; *Asst Librn,* Robin Petrongolo; Staff 1 (Non-MLS 1)
Founded 1975. Pop 8,533; Circ 10,583
Library Holdings: Bk Titles 25,000; Per Subs 1
Automation Activity & Vendor Info: (Acquisitions) Follett Software; (Cataloging) Follett Software; (Circulation) Follett Software
Wireless access
Open Mon & Fri 10-5, Tues 12-6, Wed & Thurs 10-8:30, Sat 10-4
Friends of the Library Group

RUTHERFORD

P RUTHERFORD PUBLIC LIBRARY*, 150 Park Ave, 07070. SAN 310-4907. Tel: 201-939-8600. Reference Tel: 201-939-8600, Ext 7. FAX: 201-939-4108. E-mail: ruthcirc@bccls.org. Web Site: www.rutherfordlibrary.org. *Dir,* Judah Hamer; E-mail: hamer@bccls.org; *Asst Dir,* Margaret Mellett; E-mail: mellett@bccls.org; *Head, Circ,* Ellen Carter; *Ch Serv Librn,* Jane Tarantino; *Ref Librn,* Rhoda Portugal; Staff 17 (MLS 4, Non-MLS 13)
Founded 1893. Pop 18,000; Circ 160,000
Library Holdings: Bk Vols 80,000; Per Subs 120
Special Collections: William Carlos Williams Coll
Automation Activity & Vendor Info: (Cataloging) Innovative Interfaces, Inc; (Circulation) Innovative Interfaces, Inc; (OPAC) Innovative Interfaces, Inc
Database Vendor: EBSCOhost, Gale Cengage Learning, ProQuest
Wireless access
Function: Adult bk club, Bks on CD, Computers for patron use, Copy machines, Fax serv, Handicapped accessible, Microfiche/film & reading machines, Music CDs, Scanner, Spanish lang bks, Story hour, Tax forms
Partic in Bergen County Cooperative Library System
Special Services for the Blind - Braille bks
Open Mon-Wed 10-8, Thurs & Fri 10-6, Sat 10-4
Friends of the Library Group

SADDLE BROOK

S FAST PULSE TECHNOLOGY, INC LIBRARY*, 220 Midland Ave, 07663. SAN 323-4584. Tel: 973-478-5757. FAX: 973-478-6115. Web Site: www.lasermetrics.com. *Pres,* Robert Goldstein
Library Holdings: Bk Vols 1,100; Per Subs 12
Restriction: Staff use only

P SADDLE BROOK FREE PUBLIC LIBRARY*, 340 Mayhill St, 07663. SAN 310-4915. Tel: 201-843-3287. FAX: 201-843-5512. Web Site: www.bccls.org/saddlebrook. *Dir,* Alma J Henderson; E-mail: henderson@bccls.org; Staff 3 (MLS 3)
Founded 1944. Pop 13,100
Library Holdings: Bk Vols 68,000; Per Subs 85
Automation Activity & Vendor Info: (Cataloging) SirsiDynix; (Circulation) SirsiDynix; (OPAC) SirsiDynix
Database Vendor: Gale Cengage Learning
Wireless access
Open Mon-Thurs 10-9, Fri 10-5, Sat 10-3

SALEM

S SALEM COUNTY HISTORICAL SOCIETY*, Josephine Jaquett Memorial Library, 79-83 Market St, 08079. SAN 310-4923. Tel: 856-935-5004. FAX: 856-935-0728. E-mail: info@salemcountyhistoricalsociety.com. Web Site: www.salemcountyhistoricalsociety.com. *Ref Librn,* Beverly Carr Stanley
Founded 1884
Library Holdings: Bk Vols 1,000; Per Subs 10
Special Collections: Family Bibles Coll; Unrecorded Deed Coll
Subject Interests: Genealogy, Hist
Wireless access
Publications: Newsletter (Quarterly)
Open Tues-Sat 12-4

P SALEM FREE PUBLIC LIBRARY, 112 W Broadway, 08079-1302. SAN 310-4931. Tel: 856-935-0526. FAX: 856-935-5110. Web Site: www.mysalemlibrary.org. *Dir,* Jeff Dilks; *Libr Supvr,* C Odessa Nokes; Staff 1 (MLS 1)
Founded 1804. Pop 6,883; Circ 12,861
Library Holdings: Bk Titles 25,000; Per Subs 62
Special Collections: Local History (Granville S Thomas Coll), bks, pamphlets; PSEG Salem Nuclear Generating Station
Wireless access
Partic in LibraryLinkNJ, The New Jersey Library Cooperative; LOGIN (Libraries of Gloucester, Salem & Cumberland Information Network)
Open Mon, Tues, Thurs & Fri 10-1 & 2-6, Wed 10-1 & 2-5:30, Sat 10-1
Friends of the Library Group

SCOTCH PLAINS

P SCOTCH PLAINS PUBLIC LIBRARY*, 1927 Bartle Ave, 07076-1212. SAN 310-494X. Tel: 908-322-5007. FAX: 908-322-0490. E-mail: info@scotlib.org. Web Site: www.scotlib.org. *Dir,* Meg Kolaya; E-mail: mkolaya@scotlib.org; *Head, Adult Serv,* Pamela Brooks; E-mail: pbrooks@scotlib.org; *Head, Ch,* Michelle Willis; E-mail: mwillis@scotlib.org; *Head, Circ Serv,* Mimi Sengupta; E-mail: msengupta@scotlib.org; *Head, Tech Serv,* Linda Rosario; Fax: lindar@scotlib.org; *Ref Librn,* Maribeth Fisher; *Ref Librn,* Robin Stayvas; Staff 5.2 (MLS 5.2)
Founded 1888. Pop 22,700

Library Holdings: Bks on Deafness & Sign Lang 40; Bk Titles 67,853; Bk Vols 74,865; Per Subs 196
Special Collections: New Jersey Local & State History Coll
Automation Activity & Vendor Info: (Cataloging) TLC (The Library Corporation); (Circulation) TLC (The Library Corporation); (ILL) JerseyCat; (OPAC) TLC (The Library Corporation)
Database Vendor: Baker & Taylor, EBSCOhost, Gale Cengage Learning, Ingram Library Services
Wireless access
Function: Adult bk club, Bks on CD, Chess club, Children's prog, Computers for patron use, Copy machines, Electronic databases & coll, Exhibits, Handicapped accessible, Homebound delivery serv, ILL available, Magnifiers for reading, Mus passes, Music CDs, Online cat, Online ref, Passport agency, Photocopying/Printing, Prog for adults, Prog for children & young adult, Pub access computers, Story hour, Summer reading prog, Tax forms, Teen prog, Wheelchair accessible
Partic in LibraryLinkNJ, The New Jersey Library Cooperative; Librs of Union County Consortium
Open Mon & Thurs 9-9, Tues, Fri & Sat 9-5, Wed 8-5, Sun 12-4
Friends of the Library Group

SEA GIRT

L NEW JERSEY STATE POLICE TRAINING BUREAU LIBRARY*, Training Bureau, 08750. SAN 375-8419. Tel: 732-449-5200, Ext 5215. FAX: 732-449-8763. *Mgr,* Linda DuBois
Library Holdings: Bk Titles 20,000
Partic in LibraryLinkNJ, The New Jersey Library Cooperative
Restriction: Not open to pub

P SEA GIRT LIBRARY*, Railroad Station at the Plaza, 08750. (Mail add: PO Box 414, 08750-0414). Tel: 732-449-1099. FAX: 732-449-4138. Web Site: www.seagirtboro.com/library.html. *Dir,* Lynn Kroll
Founded 1992
Library Holdings: AV Mats 250; Bk Vols 10,000; Per Subs 20; Talking Bks 150
Wireless access
Open Mon 6pm-8pm, Tues-Thurs 1-5, Sat 10-Noon

SECAUCUS

P SECAUCUS PUBLIC LIBRARY*, 1379 Patterson Plank Rd, 07094. SAN 310-4974. Tel: 201-330-2083. FAX: 201-330-1741, 201-617-1695. E-mail: secacirc@bccls.org. Web Site: secaucus.bccls.org. *Dir,* Jen May; Staff 2 (MLS 2)
Founded 1957. Pop 13,500; Circ 87,367
Library Holdings: Bk Vols 57,500; Per Subs 82
Special Collections: Oral History
Subject Interests: Arts, Sci
Automation Activity & Vendor Info: (Cataloging) SirsiDynix; (Circulation) SirsiDynix; (OPAC) SirsiDynix
Open Mon-Fri (Winter) 9-9, Sat 9-4, Sun 12-4; Mon-Fri (Summer) 9-9, Sat & Sun 12-4
Friends of the Library Group

SEWELL

J GLOUCESTER COUNTY COLLEGE LIBRARY*, 1400 Tanyard Rd, 08080. SAN 310-4982. Tel: 856-468-5000, Ext 2250. Interlibrary Loan Service Tel: 856-415-2251. FAX: 856-464-1695. Web Site: www.gccnj.edu. *Dir,* Jane Lopes-Crocker; *ILL,* Patricia Hirsekorn; *Per,* Anna Kehnast; Staff 4 (MLS 4)
Founded 1968. Enrl 3,351; Fac 93
Library Holdings: Bk Vols 55,000; Per Subs 78
Subject Interests: Art, Nursing
Automation Activity & Vendor Info: (Cataloging) SirsiDynix; (Circulation) SirsiDynix; (OPAC) SirsiDynix
Partic in LibraryLinkNJ, The New Jersey Library Cooperative; Virtual Academic Library Environment
Open Mon-Thurs 8am-9pm, Fri 8-5, Sat 10-4

P MARGARET E HEGGAN FREE PUBLIC LIBRARY OF THE TOWNSHIP OF WASHINGTON, 606 Delsea Dr, 08080. SAN 310-5555. Tel: 856-589-3334. FAX: 856-582-2042. Web Site: www.hegganlibrary.org. *Dir,* Sheila Mikkelson; E-mail: smikkelson@hegganlibrary.org; *Head, Ref,* Debra Rosner; E-mail: drosner@hegganlibrary.org; *Syst Librn,* Sergio Ragno; E-mail: sragno@hegganlibrary.org; *Youth Serv Librn,* Sarah Kramer; E-mail: skramer@hegganlibrary.org. Subject Specialists: *Soc & behav sci,* Sarah Kramer; Staff 4 (MLS 4)
Founded 1965. Pop 48,500; Circ 223,973
Jan 2013-Dec 2013 Income $1,582,222, State $21,247, City $1,512,881, Locally Generated Income $48,067. Mats Exp $229,462, Books $142,882, Per/Ser (Incl. Access Fees) $6,713, AV Mat $25,874, Electronic Ref Mat (Incl. Access Fees) $53,993. Sal $674,122 (Prof $303,000)
Library Holdings: Audiobooks 3,512; CDs 8,615; DVDs 6,057; Bk Vols 89,380; Per Subs 152
Subject Interests: NJ
Automation Activity & Vendor Info: (Cataloging) SIRSI WorkFlows; (Circulation) SIRSI WorkFlows; (ILL) JerseyCat
Database Vendor: EBSCOhost, Facts on File, infoUSA, LearningExpress, Marquis Who's Who, Newsbank, Overdrive, Inc, ReferenceUSA, World Book Online
Wireless access
Partic in LibraryLinkNJ, The New Jersey Library Cooperative
Open Mon-Thurs 10-9, Fri & Sat 10-5, Sun 12-5
Friends of the Library Group

SHORT HILLS

S CHRISTOPHER & DANA REEVE FOUNDATION*, Christopher & Dana Reeve Paralysis Resource Center Library, 636 Morris Tpk, Ste 3A, 07078. Tel: 973-467-8270. Interlibrary Loan Service Tel: 973-467-8270, Ext 7204. Toll Free Tel: 800-539-7309. FAX: 973-467-9845. Web Site: www.paralysis.org. *Sr Dir,* Sheila Fitzgibbon; E-mail: sfitzgibbon@christopherreeve.org; *Dir, Operations,* Angela Cantillon; Tel: 973-467-8270, Ext 7214, E-mail: acantillon@christopherreeve.org; Staff 2 (MLS 2)
Founded 2002
Library Holdings: Bk Titles 3,265; Per Subs 40; Videos 825
Subject Interests: Paralysis
Automation Activity & Vendor Info: (Cataloging) TLC (The Library Corporation); (Circulation) TLC (The Library Corporation); (ILL) OCLC; (OPAC) TLC (The Library Corporation); (Serials) TLC (The Library Corporation)
Function: ILL available, Wheelchair accessible
Publications: Paralysis Resource Guide (Consumer guide)
Open Mon-Fri 9-5

SOMERS POINT

S ATLANTIC COUNTY HISTORICAL SOCIETY LIBRARY, 907 Shore Rd, 08244. (Mail add: PO Box 301, 08244), SAN 310-5032. Tel: 609-927-5218. FAX: 609-927-5218. E-mail: achsinfo@comcast.net. Web Site: www.atlanticcountyhistoricalsocietynj.org. *Librn,* Carol Raph
Founded 1913
Library Holdings: Bk Vols 8,000
Special Collections: Atlantic County Coll, glass plate negatives, lantern slides, maps, photog; Atlantic County, diaries, deeds, genealogy, letters, ms; Family Bible; New Jersey History & Genealogy, rare & out of print bks
Subject Interests: Genealogy, Local hist
Wireless access
Publications: Annual Year Book; Quarterly Newsletter
Open Wed-Sat 10-3:30

SOMERSET

P FRANKLIN TOWNSHIP FREE PUBLIC LIBRARY*, 485 DeMott Lane, 08873. SAN 351-3572. Tel: 732-873-8700. FAX: 732-873-0746. Web Site: www.franklintwp.org. *Dir, Libr Serv,* January Adams; *Syst Librn,* Michael Ferrante; *YA Librn,* Jessica Rhodes; *Adult Serv,* Ann Smith; *Circ,* Megan Ingegno; *Youth Serv,* Anne Lemay; Staff 15 (MLS 7, Non-MLS 8)
Founded 1957. Pop 60,200; Circ 290,878
Library Holdings: Bk Titles 155,231; Bk Vols 178,859
Subject Interests: African-Am, Collectibles, Local hist, Pets
Automation Activity & Vendor Info: (Acquisitions) SirsiDynix; (Cataloging) SirsiDynix; (Circulation) SirsiDynix; (ILL) SirsiDynix; (OPAC) SirsiDynix; (Serials) SirsiDynix
Database Vendor: EBSCOhost, Facts on File, Grolier Online, ProQuest
Wireless access
Partic in LibraryLinkNJ, The New Jersey Library Cooperative
Special Services for the Blind - Reader equip
Open Mon-Thurs (Sept-June) 10-9, Fri & Sat 10-5, Sun 1-4; Mon-Thurs (July & Aug) 10-9, Fri 10-5, Sat 10-2, Sun 1-4
Branches: 1
FRANKLIN PARK BRANCH, 3391 Rte 27 S, Ste 101, Franklin Park, 08823. Tel: 732-873-8700, option 5. FAX: 732-297-3391. *Br Mgr,* Amanda Decker
Library Holdings: Bk Titles 8,102
Open Mon-Wed & Fri 10-5, Thurs 2-9, Sat 10-2

SOMERVILLE

J RARITAN VALLEY COMMUNITY COLLEGE*, Evelyn S Field Library, 118 Lamington Rd, Branchburg, 08876. (Mail add: PO Box 3300, 08876-3300), SAN 310-5083. Tel: 908-218-8865. Circulation Tel: 908-526-1200, Ext 8423. Reference Tel: 908-526-1200, Ext 8350. Administration Tel: 908-526-1200, Ext 8351. FAX: 908-526-2985. Web Site: library.raritanval.edu. *Dir,* Birthe Nebeker; E-mail: bnebeker@raritanval.edu; *Instrul Serv Librn,* Megan Dempsey; Tel:

908-526-1200, Ext 8412, E-mail: mdempsey@raritanval.edu; *Acq, Cat,* Robert Egan; Tel: 908-526-1200, Ext 8300, E-mail: regan@raritanval.edu; *Circ, Ser,* Julie Maginn; Tel: 908-526-1200, Ext 8303, E-mail: jmaginn@raritanval.edu; Staff 11 (MLS 4, Non-MLS 7)
Founded 1968. Enrl 6,117; Fac 108; Highest Degree: Associate
Jul 2008-Jun 2009. Mats Exp $241,100, Books $106,000, Per/Ser (Incl. Access Fees) $56,100, AV Mat $6,000, Electronic Ref Mat (Incl. Access Fees) $73,000
Library Holdings: Audiobooks 306; DVDs 1,369; e-books 10,243; Microforms 56; Bk Titles 80,530; Bk Vols 79,850; Per Subs 202; Videos 350
Automation Activity & Vendor Info: (Acquisitions) Innovative Interfaces, Inc; (Cataloging) Innovative Interfaces, Inc; (Circulation) Innovative Interfaces, Inc; (Course Reserve) Innovative Interfaces, Inc; (OPAC) Innovative Interfaces, Inc; (Serials) Innovative Interfaces, Inc
Database Vendor: ACM (Association for Computing Machinery), ARTstor, Bowker, CQ Press, CredoReference, ebrary, EBSCOhost, Facts on File, Gale Cengage Learning, H W Wilson, Innovative Interfaces, Inc, JSTOR, LexisNexis, McGraw-Hill, OCLC FirstSearch, OCLC WorldShare Interlibrary Loan, ProQuest, Safari Books Online, ScienceDirect, SerialsSolutions, Wilson - Wilson Web
Wireless access
Partic in NJ State Libr Network; OCLC Online Computer Library Center, Inc; Virtual Academic Library Environment
Open Mon-Thurs 8am-9pm, Fri 8-5, Sat 9-5

GL SOMERSET COUNTY LAW LIBRARY*, 20 N Bridge St, 08876. (Mail add: PO Box 3000, 08876-1262), SAN 321-9747. Tel: 908-231-7612. FAX: 908-253-8590. *Dir,* Phyllis Pason; Staff 1 (MLS 1)
Library Holdings: Bk Vols 20,000
Subject Interests: Fed law, State law
Database Vendor: LexisNexis
Wireless access
Open Mon-Fri 9-5
Restriction: Open to pub for ref only

P SOMERVILLE LIBRARY*, 35 West End Ave, 08876. SAN 310-5091. Tel: 908-725-1336. Reference Tel: 908-725-1336, Ext 12. FAX: 908-231-0608. Web Site: www.somervillenj.org. *Dir,* Melissa A Banks; *Head, Circ,* Oscar Vargas; *Ch,* Nancy Lepionka; *Ref Librn,* James Sommerville; *Adult Prog Coordr,* Kara Wilson; *Outreach Coordr, Young Adult Serv Coordr,* Carlyn Hudson
Founded 1871. Pop 12,423; Circ 66,000
Jan 2011-Dec 2011 Income $1,216,218, State $15,166, City $530,441, Federal $1,000, Locally Generated Income $669,611. Mats Exp $46,500, Books $27,000, Per/Ser (Incl. Access Fees) $7,500, AV Mat $8,000, Electronic Ref Mat (Incl. Access Fees) $4,000. Sal $303,092 (Prof $180,000)
Library Holdings: AV Mats 5,000; Bks on Deafness & Sign Lang 20; High Interest/Low Vocabulary Bk Vols 200; Bk Titles 53,457; Bk Vols 58,640; Per Subs 120; Talking Bks 1,010; Videos 2,600
Special Collections: New Jersey Archives Holdings; Paul Robeson-iana; Somerville & Somerset County, New Jersey Genealogical Material. Oral History
Subject Interests: City hist, Local hist, NJ, Somerset County hist
Automation Activity & Vendor Info: (Cataloging) SIRSI WorkFlows; (Circulation) SIRSI WorkFlows; (ILL) OCLC WorldShare Interlibrary Loan; (OPAC) SIRSI-iBistro
Database Vendor: Booksite, EBSCOhost, Facts on File, Gale Cengage Learning, Infomart, Overdrive, Inc, ProQuest
Function: Bks on cassette, Bks on CD, CD-ROM, Chess club, Children's prog, Computer training, Computers for patron use, Copy machines, Digital talking bks, e-mail serv, Electronic databases & coll, Family literacy, Free DVD rentals, Holiday prog, ILL available, Magnifiers for reading, Mail & tel request accepted, Music CDs, Notary serv, Online cat, Outside serv via phone, mail, e-mail & web, OverDrive digital audio bks, Photocopying/Printing, Preschool outreach, Prog for adults, Prog for children & young adult, Senior outreach, Spoken cassettes & CDs, Spoken cassettes & DVDs, Summer reading prog, Tax forms, Teen prog, Telephone ref
Partic in Libraries of Middlesex Automation Consortium
Open Mon-Thurs 10-8, Fri & Sat 10-5:30
Restriction: Non-resident fee
Friends of the Library Group

SOUTH AMBOY

P SADIE POPE DOWDELL LIBRARY OF SOUTH AMBOY, 100 Harold G Hoffman Plaza, 08879. SAN 310-5105. Tel: 732-721-6060. FAX: 732-721-1054. E-mail: comments@dowdell.org. Web Site: www.dowdell.org. *Dir,* Elaine R Gaber; E-mail: egaber@dowdell.org; *Head, Tech Serv,* Janet Simeone; *Head, Tech,* Michael Elson; *Circ Serv,* Robin Ball; *Circ Serv,* Barbara Bringman; *Circ Serv,* Nancy Charmello; *Circ Serv,* Jessica Festini; *Youth Serv - Coll Develop,* Marilyn Cipollari; *Youth Serv - Prog,* Laura Golia; Staff 10 (MLS 1, Non-MLS 9)
Founded 1914. Pop 7,900; Circ 65,326
Jan 2014-Dec 2014 Income $319,142, State $3,670, City $300,472, Locally Generated Income $15,000. Sal $200,000
Library Holdings: Bk Vols 69,239; Per Subs 100
Special Collections: New Jersey History Coll; Railroads Coll; South Amboy History Coll
Automation Activity & Vendor Info: (Cataloging) SirsiDynix; (Circulation) SIRSI-iBistro; (ILL) Auto-Graphics, Inc; (OPAC) SIRSI WorkFlows
Database Vendor: EBSCOhost, Ingram Library Services
Wireless access
Function: Adult bk club, Adult literacy prog, After school storytime, Archival coll, Art exhibits, Audio & video playback equip for onsite use, Audiobks via web, Bilingual assistance for Spanish patrons, Bk club(s), Bks on CD, Bus archives, CD-ROM, Children's prog, Citizenship assistance, Computer training, Computers for patron use, Copy machines, Digital talking bks, Distance learning, Doc delivery serv, e-mail serv, E-Reserves, Electronic databases & coll, eReaders, Exhibits, Family literacy, Fax serv, For res purposes, Free DVD rentals, Govt ref serv, Handicapped accessible, Holiday prog, Home delivery & serv to Sr ctr & nursing homes, Homebound delivery serv, Homework prog, ILL available, Learning ctr, Libr develop, Life-long learning prog for all ages, Literacy & newcomer serv, Magazines, Mail & tel request accepted, Mail loans to mem, Movies, Music CDs, Newsp ref libr, Notary serv, Online cat, Online info literacy tutorials on the web & in blackboard, Online ref, Online searches, Orientations, Outreach serv, Outside serv via phone, mail, e-mail & web, OverDrive digital audio bks, Photocopying/Printing, Preschool outreach, Preschool reading prog, Prog for adults, Prog for children & young adult, Pub access computers, Ref & res, Ref serv available, Ref serv in person, Referrals accepted, Scanner, Senior computer classes, Senior outreach, Spanish lang bks, Story hour, Study rm, Summer & winter reading prog, Summer reading prog, Tax forms, Teen prog, Telephone ref, Web-catalog, Wheelchair accessible, Workshops
Publications: Annual Report; History of Dowdell Library; Magazines & Newspapers (Index to periodicals); South Amboy Archives (Archives guide)
Partic in LibraryLinkNJ, The New Jersey Library Cooperative
Special Services for the Blind - Talking bks
Open Mon, Tues & Thurs 10-8, Wed & Fri 10-5, Sat (Sept-May) 12-4
Restriction: Authorized patrons, ID required to use computers (Ltd hrs), Non-resident fee
Friends of the Library Group

SOUTH ORANGE

R MONSIGNOR JAMES C TURRO SEMINARY LIBRARY*, Seton Hall University, 400 S Orange Ave, 07079. SAN 310-1045. Tel: 973-761-9198, 973-761-9336, 973-761-9584. FAX: 973-275-2074. Web Site: www.shu.edu/academics/theology/seminary-library.cfm. *Dir,* Fr Lawrence Porter; *Librn,* Sister Concetta Russo; *Librn,* Stella Wilkins; Staff 3 (MLS 1, Non-MLS 2)
Founded 1858. Enrl 223; Fac 38
Library Holdings: CDs 493; DVDs 165; Microforms 1,827; Bk Vols 65,290; Per Subs 382; Videos 645
Subject Interests: Biblical, Catechism, Christian ethics, Church hist, Church ministries, Liturgy, Philos, Theol
Automation Activity & Vendor Info: (Cataloging) Ex Libris Group; (Circulation) Ex Libris Group; (ILL) Auto-Graphics, Inc; (OPAC) Ex Libris Group
Database Vendor: EBSCOhost
Wireless access
Open Mon-Wed 9am-10pm, Thurs & Fri 9-5, Sat 10-4

C SETON HALL UNIVERSITY LIBRARIES, Walsh Library, Walsh Libary Bldg, 400 S Orange Ave, 07079. Tel: 973-761-9005. Circulation Tel: 973-761-9443. Interlibrary Loan Service Tel: 973-761-9441. Information Services Tel: 973-761-9437. FAX: 973-761-9432. Interlibrary Loan Service FAX: 973-761-9715. Web Site: www.shu.edu/academics/libraries. *Dean, Univ Libr,* John Buschman; E-mail: john.buschman@shu.edu; *Asst Dean, Info Tech, Res Acq & Description,* Elizabeth Leonard; Tel: 973-761-9445, E-mail: elizabeth.leonard@shu.edu; *Asst Dean, Learning & Outreach Serv,* Dr Naomi Gold; Tel: 973-761-2058, E-mail: naomi.gold@shu.edu; *Acq Librn,* Sulekha Kalyan; Tel: 973-761-9438, E-mail: sulekha.kalyan@shu.edu; *Bus Librn,* Richard Stern; Tel: 973-275-2046, E-mail: richard.stern@shu.edu; *Cat Librn,* Martha M Loesch; Tel: 973-761-9296, E-mail: martha.loesch@shu.edu; *Instruction Librn,* Beth Bloom; Tel: 973-275-2035, E-mail: beth.bloom@shu.edu; *Ref Librn,* Anthony E Lee; Tel: 973-761-9440, E-mail: anthony.lee@shu.edu; *Coordr, Cat,* Marta J Deyrup; Tel: 973-275-2223, E-mail: marta.deyrup@shu.edu; *Instr,* Lisa DeLuca; Tel: 973-761-7959, E-mail: lisa.deluca@shu.edu.
Subject Specialists: *Bus,* Richard Stern; *Educ,* Martha M Loesch; *Art, Health, Med sci, Music,* Beth Bloom; *African-Am studies, Catholic studies, Educ opportunities, English, Psychol,* Anthony E Lee; *Classical studies, Modern lang,* Marta J Deyrup; *Soc sci,* Lisa DeLuca; Staff 41 (MLS 16, Non-MLS 25)

Founded 1856. Enrl 9,800; Fac 430; Highest Degree: Doctorate
Jul 2012-Jun 2013 Income (Main and Other College/University Libraries) $4,308,000. Mats Exp $1,711,604, Books $377,912, Per/Ser (Incl. Access Fees) $429,320, AV Mat $4,966, Electronic Ref Mat (Incl. Access Fees) $899,406. Sal $2,119,000 (Prof $1,155,650)
Library Holdings: AV Mats 4,172; e-books 194,992; e-journals 25,000; Microforms 27,454; Bk Vols 425,880
Special Collections: American Civil War & Abraham Lincoln Coll; Brendan Byrne Coll; Irish Literature & History (McManus Coll); Oesterriecher Coll (Judeo-Christian Studies); Peter Rodino Coll; Richard Hughes Coll; Seton Hall Univ & Newark Archdiocesan Archives. State Document Depository; UN Document Depository; US Document Depository
Automation Activity & Vendor Info: (Acquisitions) Ex Libris Group; (Cataloging) Ex Libris Group; (Circulation) Ex Libris Group; (Course Reserve) Ex Libris Group; (ILL) OCLC ILLiad; (OPAC) Ex Libris Group; (Serials) Ex Libris Group
Database Vendor: 3M Library Systems, ABC-CLIO, American Chemical Society, ARTstor, Baker & Taylor, Blackwell, Bowker, Cambridge Scientific Abstracts, Cinahl, CQ Press, CredoReference, Dialog, ebrary, EBSCOhost, Elsevier, Facts on File, Gale Cengage Learning, IBISWorld, IEEE (Institute of Electrical & Electronics Engineers), JSTOR, LexisNexis, McGraw-Hill, Mergent Online, Modern Language Association, Newsbank, OCLC FirstSearch, OCLC WorldShare Interlibrary Loan, OVID Technologies, Oxford Online, ProQuest, ReferenceUSA, ScienceDirect, SerialsSolutions, Springer-Verlag, Standard & Poor's, STN International, ValueLine, Westlaw, Wiley, YBP Library Services
Wireless access
Function: Archival coll, Art exhibits, Computers for patron use, Copy machines, Doc delivery serv, Electronic databases & coll, Govt ref serv, ILL available, Microfiche/film & reading machines, Music CDs, Online cat, Online ref, Orientations, Photocopying/Printing, Pub access computers, Ref & res, Ref serv available, Ref serv in person, Scanner
Partic in LibraryLinkNJ, The New Jersey Library Cooperative; Pennsylvania Academic Library Consortium, Inc (PALCI); Virtual Academic Library Environment
Special Services for the Blind - Assistive/Adapted tech devices, equip & products
Restriction: Open to pub for ref only, Open to students, fac & staff, Photo ID required for access

P SOUTH ORANGE PUBLIC LIBRARY, 65 Scotland Rd, 07079. SAN 310-5121. Tel: 973-762-0230. FAX: 973-762-1469. E-mail: librarian@sopl.org. Web Site: www.sopl.org. *Dir,* Melissa Kopecky; E-mail: mkopecky@sopl.org; *Head, Communications & Coll,* Michael Pucci; E-mail: mpucci@sopl.org; *Head, Ref & Libr Serv,* Lindita Cani; E-mail: lcani@sopl.org; Staff 5 (MLS 5)
Founded 1864. Pop 16,964
Library Holdings: Audiobooks 3,160; AV Mats 6,528; DVDs 3,010; Electronic Media & Resources 18; High Interest/Low Vocabulary Bk Vols 20; Large Print Bks 1,035; Bk Vols 96,128; Per Subs 140
Special Collections: Local History Coll
Automation Activity & Vendor Info: (Acquisitions) Baker & Taylor; (Cataloging) TLC (The Library Corporation); (Circulation) TLC (The Library Corporation); (ILL) Auto-Graphics, Inc; (OPAC) TLC (The Library Corporation)
Database Vendor: EBSCOhost, Gale Cengage Learning, ReferenceUSA, TLC (The Library Corporation), TumbleBookLibrary, Wilson - Wilson Web
Wireless access
Partic in LibraryLinkNJ, The New Jersey Library Cooperative
Special Services for the Blind - Accessible computers; Assistive/Adapted tech devices, equip & products; Audio mat; Bks on cassette; Bks on CD; Computer with voice synthesizer for visually impaired persons; Copier with enlargement capabilities; Internet workstation with adaptive software; Low vision equip; Scanner for conversion & translation of mats; Screen enlargement software for people with visual disabilities; ZoomText magnification & reading software
Open Mon, Tues & Thurs 9-9, Wed & Fri 10-6, Sat 9-5, Sun 1-5
Friends of the Library Group

R TEMPLE SHAREY TEFILO-ISRAEL*, Abelson Echikson Ehrenkrantz Memorial Library, 432 Scotland Rd, 07079. SAN 325-948X. Tel: 973-763-4116. FAX: 973-763-3941.
Library Holdings: Bk Vols 200
Partic in Asn of Jewish Librs
Open Mon-Thurs 9-5, Fri 9-4

SOUTH PLAINFIELD

P SOUTH PLAINFIELD FREE PUBLIC LIBRARY*, 2484 Plainfield Ave, 07080. SAN 310-5156. Tel: 908-754-7885. FAX: 908-753-3846. Web Site: www.southplainfield.lib.nj.us. *Dir,* Sundra L Randolph; E-mail: sunnierandolph@yahoo.com; Staff 5 (MLS 5)
Founded 1935. Pop 21,810; Circ 188,513
Jan 2008-Dec 2008 Income $11,310,610, State $22,117, City $11,288,493. Mats Exp $181,257, Books $88,795, Per/Ser (Incl. Access Fees) $10,162, Micro $12,230, AV Mat $37,633, Electronic Ref Mat (Incl. Access Fees) $32,437. Sal $549,972
Library Holdings: AV Mats 6,345; CDs 1,460; DVDs 3,479; Large Print Bks 387; Bk Titles 66,017; Bk Vols 75,552; Per Subs 208
Subject Interests: Chinese lang, Graphic novels, Spanish lang, Vietnamese
Automation Activity & Vendor Info: (Cataloging) Innovative Interfaces, Inc; (Circulation) Innovative Interfaces, Inc; (ILL) Innovative Interfaces, Inc; (OPAC) Innovative Interfaces, Inc
Database Vendor: Baker & Taylor, BWI, EBSCOhost, Facts on File, Gale Cengage Learning, infoUSA, Ingram Library Services, Overdrive, Inc, ProQuest, ReferenceUSA, TLC (The Library Corporation)
Wireless access
Function: Audiobks via web, Bks on cassette, Bks on CD, CD-ROM, Children's prog, Computer training, Computers for patron use, Copy machines, e-mail serv, Electronic databases & coll, Exhibits, Fax serv, Free DVD rentals, Handicapped accessible, Holiday prog, Home delivery & serv to Sr ctr & nursing homes, ILL available, Magnifiers for reading, Mail & tel request accepted, Music CDs, Notary serv, OverDrive digital audio bks, Photocopying/Printing, Prog for adults, Prog for children & young adult, Pub access computers, Ref serv in person, Story hour, Summer reading prog, Tax forms, Telephone ref, VHS videos, Web-catalog, Wheelchair accessible
Open Mon, Wed & Thurs 10-9, Tues & Fri 10-6, Sat 9-5
Friends of the Library Group

SOUTH RIVER

P SOUTH RIVER PUBLIC LIBRARY*, 55 Appleby Ave, 08882-2499. SAN 310-5164. Tel: 732-254-2488. FAX: 732-254-4116. E-mail: srpl@southriverlibrary.org. Web Site: www.southriverlibrary.org. *Dir,* Andrea Londensky; E-mail: andrea@southriverlibrary.org; *Ch Serv Librn,* Dawn Bladzinski; E-mail: dawn@southriverlibrary.org; Staff 6 (MLS 2, Non-MLS 4)
Founded 1920. Pop 15,322; Circ 60,690
Library Holdings: Bk Titles 42,000; Bk Vols 46,000; Per Subs 75
Special Collections: ABR (Literacy Coll); Hungarian, Polish, Portuguese, Russian Coll; Job Opportunities; Large Print Books; Parenting
Automation Activity & Vendor Info: (Acquisitions) SirsiDynix; (Cataloging) SirsiDynix; (Circulation) SirsiDynix
Database Vendor: TLC (The Library Corporation)
Wireless access
Publications: Newsletter
Partic in Libraries of Middlesex Automation Consortium
Open Mon-Thurs 10-9, Fri 10-5, Sat 10-3

SPARTA

P SPARTA PUBLIC LIBRARY*, 22 Woodport Rd, 07871. SAN 310-5172. Tel: 973-729-3101. FAX: 973-729-1755. Web Site: www.spartalibrary.com. *Dir,* Carol Boutilier; *Asst Dir,* Diane Lapsley; *Ch Serv,* Peggy Lami; *Syst Adminr,* David Costa; Staff 15 (MLS 2, Non-MLS 13)
Founded 1841. Circ 450,000
Library Holdings: Bk Vols 68,111; Per Subs 200
Automation Activity & Vendor Info: (Cataloging) Innovative Interfaces, Inc; (Circulation) Innovative Interfaces, Inc; (ILL) Auto-Graphics, Inc; (OPAC) Innovative Interfaces, Inc
Database Vendor: EBSCOhost, Gale Cengage Learning, infoUSA, Library Ideas, LLC, LibraryInsight, Overdrive, Inc, TumbleBookLibrary
Wireless access
Partic in New Jersey Library Network
Open Mon, Wed & Thurs 9-9, Tues 9-6, Fri 9-5, Sat 9-3, Sun 1-5

SPOTSWOOD

P SPOTSWOOD PUBLIC LIBRARY, 548 Main St, 08884. SAN 310-5180. Tel: 732-251-1515. FAX: 732-251-8151. E-mail: spl@spotslibrary.org. Web Site: www.spotslibrary.org. *Dir,* C L Quillen
Founded 1965. Pop 8,140; Circ 45,500
Library Holdings: Bk Vols 30,485; Per Subs 35
Automation Activity & Vendor Info: (Cataloging) SirsiDynix; (Circulation) SirsiDynix; (ILL) SirsiDynix; (OPAC) SirsiDynix
Database Vendor: SirsiDynix
Wireless access
Function: ILL available
Partic in Libraries of Middlesex Automation Consortium
Open Mon, Wed & Thurs 10-7:30, Tues & Fri 10-5, Sat 10-2
Friends of the Library Group

SPRING LAKE

P SPRING LAKE PUBLIC LIBRARY*, 1501 Third Ave, 07762. SAN 310-5199. Tel: 732-449-6654. E-mail: info@springlakelibrary.org. Web Site: springlakelibrary.org. *Dir,* Kateri Quinn
Founded 1920. Circ 28,000

Library Holdings: Bk Vols 30,000; Per Subs 50
Special Collections: Large Print Coll
Automation Activity & Vendor Info: (Acquisitions) Follett Software; (Cataloging) Follett Software; (Circulation) Follett Software; (ILL) Follett Software; (OPAC) Follett Software; (Serials) Follett Software
Database Vendor: EBSCOhost
Partic in LibraryLinkNJ, The New Jersey Library Cooperative
Open Mon & Wed 10-5 & 7-9, Tues & Fri 10-5, Sat 10-1 (10-12 Summer)

SPRINGFIELD

P SPRINGFIELD FREE PUBLIC LIBRARY*, 66 Mountain Ave, 07081-1786. SAN 310-5202. Tel: 973-376-4930. FAX: 973-376-1334. Administration FAX: 973-912-4304. E-mail: questions@springfieldpubliclibrary.com. Web Site: www.sfplnj.org, www.springfieldpubliclibrary.com. *Dir,* Position Currently Open; *Interim Dir,* Anne Roman; *Head, Adult Serv,* Susan Tegge; E-mail: stegge@sfplnj.org; *Head, Tech Serv,* Beata Barrasso; Tel: 973-376-4930, Ext 225, E-mail: bbarrasso@springfieldpubliclibrary.com; *Head, Youth Serv,* Deborah Sandford; Tel: 973-376-4930, Ext 232; Staff 27 (MLS 7, Non-MLS 20)
Founded 1932. Pop 15,817; Circ 127,206
Jan 2010-Dec 2010 Income $1,839,031, City $1,010,208, Locally Generated Income $828,823
Library Holdings: Audiobooks 3,209; AV Mats 9,015; Bk Titles 87,019; Bk Vols 97,109; Per Subs 290
Special Collections: Local History (Sarah Bailey Coll); Local History Artifacts (Donald B Palmer Museum)
Automation Activity & Vendor Info: (Acquisitions) TLC (The Library Corporation); (Cataloging) TLC (The Library Corporation); (Circulation) TLC (The Library Corporation); (ILL) Auto-Graphics, Inc; (OPAC) TLC (The Library Corporation)
Database Vendor: EBSCOhost, Gale Cengage Learning, Wilson - Wilson Web
Wireless access
Function: Art exhibits, Audiobks via web, AV serv, Bk reviews (Group), Bks on cassette, Bks on CD, Children's prog, Computer training, Computers for patron use, Copy machines, e-mail & chat, Exhibits, Homebound delivery serv, ILL available, Magnifiers for reading, Mail & tel request accepted, Music CDs, Notary serv, Online cat, Online ref, Online searches, OverDrive digital audio bks, Prog for adults, Prog for children & young adult, Pub access computers, Ref serv available, Referrals accepted, Story hour, Summer reading prog, Tax forms, Telephone ref, VHS videos, Wheelchair accessible, Writing prog
Partic in LibraryLinkNJ, The New Jersey Library Cooperative
Open Mon, Wed & Thurs 10-9, Tues, Fri & Sat 10-5, Sun 1-5
Friends of the Library Group

STANHOPE

S CANAL SOCIETY OF NEW JERSEY*, Museum & Library, Waterloo Village, 07874. (Mail add: PO Box 737, Morristown, 07963-0737), SAN 375-2607. Tel: 908-722-9556. FAX: 908-722-9556. E-mail: nj-cnal@googlegroups.com. Web Site: www.canalsocietynj.org. *Pres,* Brian Morrell; Tel: 973-691-7448
Founded 1969
Library Holdings: Bk Vols 400
Restriction: Non-circulating, Open by appt only

STRATFORD

P STRATFORD FREE PUBLIC LIBRARY*, 303 Union Ave, 08084. SAN 310-5229. Tel: 856-783-0602. FAX: 856-435-8757. Web Site: www.stratfordnj.org/library.htm. *Dir,* Joann Gershman; Staff 1 (Non-MLS 1)
Founded 1923. Pop 7,500; Circ 30,000
Library Holdings: Bk Vols 38,000; Per Subs 25
Automation Activity & Vendor Info: (Cataloging) Winnebago Software Co; (Circulation) Winnebago Software Co
Wireless access
Open Mon 12-5 & 7-9, Tues & Thurs 12-9, Wed & Fri 12-4, Sat 12-3
Friends of the Library Group

M UNIVERSITY OF MEDICINE & DENTISTRY OF NEW JERSEY*, Health Science Library, Academic Ctr, One Medical Center Dr, 08084. SAN 320-6998. Tel: 856-566-6800. FAX: 856-566-6380. Web Site: libraries.umdnj.edu/stlibweb, www.umdnj.edu/stlibweb. *Dir,* Jan Skica; E-mail: skica@umdnj.edu; *ILL,* Elaine Mayweather; *Pub Serv,* Jenny Pierce; *Ser,* David Kaczorowski; Staff 5 (MLS 5)
Founded 1970
Library Holdings: Bk Vols 30,000; Per Subs 35
Special Collections: History of Osteopathy
Subject Interests: Clinical med, Nursing
Automation Activity & Vendor Info: (Acquisitions) Ex Libris Group; (Cataloging) Ex Libris Group; (Circulation) Ex Libris Group; (OPAC) Ex Libris Group; (Serials) Ex Libris Group
Wireless access
Publications: The Library File (quarterly newsletter)
Open Mon-Thurs 8am-11pm, Fri 8-6, Sat 9-5, Sun 1-8

SUCCASUNNA

P ROXBURY TOWNSHIP PUBLIC LIBRARY*, 103 Main St, 07876. SAN 310-5237. Tel: 973-584-2400. FAX: 973-584-5484. E-mail: comments@roxburylibrary.org. Web Site: www.roxburylibrary.org. *Dir,* William Porter
Founded 1960. Pop 23,924; Circ 188,251
Library Holdings: Bk Vols 70,482; Per Subs 217
Special Collections: Children's Historical Fiction (Mary Wolfe Thompson Coll); Historical Reference (New Jersey)
Automation Activity & Vendor Info: (Circulation) SirsiDynix
Wireless access
Partic in Morris Automated Information Network
Open Mon-Thurs 9:30-9, Fri 9:30-5, Sat 9:30-3, Sun 2-5
Friends of the Library Group

SUMMIT

M OVERLOOK HOSPITAL*, Health Sciences Library, 99 Beauvoir Ave, 07902-0220. SAN 370-1891. Tel: 908-522-2119. FAX: 908-522-2274. *Mgr,* Patricia Regenberg; Staff 2 (MLS 1, Non-MLS 1)
Library Holdings: Bk Titles 6,000; Per Subs 325
Subject Interests: Consumer health, Med
Database Vendor: EBSCOhost, OVID Technologies
Partic in Basic Health Sciences Library Network; New Jersey Health Sciences Library Network
Open Mon-Thurs 8-5:30, Fri 8-5

P SUMMIT FREE PUBLIC LIBRARY*, 75 Maple St, 07901-9984. SAN 310-5261. Tel: 908-273-0350. FAX: 908-273-0031. Web Site: www.summitlibrary.org. *Dir,* Susan Permahos; *Asst Dir,* Alexandria Arnold; *Head, Ref,* Abagail Dreyer; *Head, Children's & Young Adult Serv,* Ann-Marie Aymer; *Circ Mgr,* Diane Hull; *Adult Prog,* Robin Carroll-Mann; Tel: 908-277-9452
Founded 1874. Pop 21,131; Circ 285,687
Jan 2011-Dec 2011 Income $2,679,705, State $21,428, City $2,442,069, Locally Generated Income $74,264. Mats Exp $363,751, Books $238,160, Per/Ser (Incl. Access Fees) $17,455, Other Print Mats $3,200, AV Mat $65,624, Electronic Ref Mat (Incl. Access Fees) $39,312. Sal $1,418,700
Library Holdings: Audiobooks 5,651; Bk Vols 107,560; Per Subs 469; Videos 1,000
Automation Activity & Vendor Info: (Cataloging) SirsiDynix; (Circulation) SirsiDynix; (OPAC) SirsiDynix
Database Vendor: 3M Library Systems
Wireless access
Function: Adult bk club, Art exhibits, Bks on cassette, Bks on CD, Bus archives, Children's prog, Computer training, Computers for patron use, Copy machines, Handicapped accessible, ILL available, Music CDs, Online cat, Photocopying/Printing, Prog for adults, Prog for children & young adult, Pub access computers, Tax forms, Teen prog, Telephone ref, VHS videos, Wheelchair accessible
Partic in LibraryLinkNJ, The New Jersey Library Cooperative; Morris-Union Federation; New Jersey Library Network
Open Mon-Wed 9-9, Thurs-Sat 9-5, Sun 1-5

TEANECK

C FAIRLEIGH DICKINSON UNIVERSITY*, Frank Giovatto Library, 980 Library Circle, 07666. SAN 351-3785. Tel: 201-692-2279. Reference Tel: 201-692-2100. Administration Tel: 201-692-2278. FAX: 201-692-9815. Web Site: view.fdu.edu/?id=1840. *Assoc Univ Librn, Dir, Pub Serv,* Kathleen Stein-Smith; Tel: 201-692-2276, E-mail: kathleen_stein-smith@fdu.edu; *Assoc Univ Librn,* Maria kocylowsky; Tel: 201-692-2608, E-mail: maria_l_kocylowsy@fdu.edu; *Librn, Outreach Coordr,* Michelle Nestroy; E-mail: michele_lempert@fdu.edu; *Archivist, Res & Instruction Librn,* Richard Goerner; Tel: 201-692-2598, E-mail: richard_goerner@fdu.edu; *Res & Instruction Librn,* Patricia Murray; Tel: 201-692-2285, E-mail: patricia_murray@fdu.edu; Staff 11 (MLS 9, Non-MLS 2)
Founded 1954. Enrl 5,032; Fac 365; Highest Degree: Doctorate
Library Holdings: Audiobooks 8; CDs 405; DVDs 547; e-books 40,137; e-journals 684; Electronic Media & Resources 82; Microforms 103,000; Bk Titles 169,764; Bk Vols 260,500; Per Subs 900; Videos 547
Special Collections: Lincoln, Mf Coll Presidential Papers. State Document Depository; US Document Depository
Automation Activity & Vendor Info: (Acquisitions) Ex Libris Group; (Cataloging) Ex Libris Group; (Circulation) Ex Libris Group; (Course Reserve) Ex Libris Group; (ILL) OCLC; (OPAC) Ex Libris Group; (Serials) Ex Libris Group
Database Vendor: ACM (Association for Computing Machinery), American Chemical Society, Annual Reviews, Cambridge Scientific

Abstracts, CountryWatch, CredoReference, Dialog, ebrary, EBSCOhost, Elsevier, Ex Libris Group, Facts on File, Gale Cengage Learning, JSTOR, LexisNexis, Mergent Online, Modern Language Association, OCLC FirstSearch, OCLC WorldShare Interlibrary Loan, ProQuest, ReferenceUSA, ScienceDirect, SerialsSolutions, Westlaw
Wireless access
Partic in LibraryLinkNJ, The New Jersey Library Cooperative; Lyrasis; Metropolitan New York Library Council; OCLC Online Computer Library Center, Inc; Virtual Academic Library Environment
Open Mon-Thurs 8:30am-11pm, Fri 8:30-5, Sat 11-5, Sun 2-10
Friends of the Library Group

M HOLY NAME MEDICAL CENTER*, Medical Staff Library, 718 Teaneck Rd, 07666. SAN 310-5288. Tel: 201-530-7919. FAX: 201-833-3006. Web Site: www.holynamelibrary.org. *Managing Librn,* Keydi Boss O'Hagan; Tel: 201-833-3395, E-mail: k-ohagan@mail.holyname.org; Staff 2 (MLS 1, Non-MLS 1)
Founded 1925
Library Holdings: Bk Titles 5,000; Per Subs 123
Subject Interests: Med, Nursing
Database Vendor: EBSCOhost, OVID Technologies
Partic in Bergen Passaic Health Sciences Library Consortium; Health Sciences Library Association of New Jersey; Medical Library Association (MLA); National Network of Libraries of Medicine; New Jersey Library Network
Open Mon-Fri 8-5:30

P TEANECK PUBLIC LIBRARY*, 840 Teaneck Rd, 07666. SAN 310-5296. Tel: 201-837-4171. FAX: 201-837-0410. E-mail: teancirc@bccls.org. Web Site: www.teaneck.org. *Dir,* Michael McCue; *Ch Serv,* Amy Sears; *Circ,* Cathe Quirke; *Ref,* Weilee Liu; E-mail: liu@bccls.org; *Tech Serv,* Carol Anderson; Staff 26 (MLS 7, Non-MLS 19)
Founded 1922. Pop 39,800; Circ 625,200
Jan 2010-Dec 2010 Income $2,792,000, City $2,710,000, Locally Generated Income $82,000. Mats Exp $294,500, Books $174,000, Per/Ser (Incl. Access Fees) $16,000, Manu Arch $500, Other Print Mats $500, Micro $1,500, AV Mat $97,000, Electronic Ref Mat (Incl. Access Fees) $4,000, Presv $1,000
Library Holdings: CDs 7,900; DVDs 12,500; Large Print Bks 975; Bk Vols 126,565; Per Subs 375; Talking Bks 3,300
Special Collections: Oral History
Subject Interests: African-Am studies, Judaica
Automation Activity & Vendor Info: (Cataloging) SirsiDynix; (Circulation) SirsiDynix; (OPAC) SirsiDynix
Database Vendor: SirsiDynix
Wireless access
Partic in Bergen County Cooperative Library System
Open Mon-Thurs 9-9, Fri 9-6, Sat 9-5, Sun 12:30-5:30
Friends of the Library Group

TENAFLY

SR JEWISH COMMUNITY CENTER ON THE PALISADES*, Judaica Library, 411 E Clinton Ave, 07670. SAN 310-1452. Tel: 201-569-7900, Ext 234. FAX: 201-569-7448. Web Site: www.jcconthepalisades.org. *Dir,* Debra Turitz; *Librn,* Freida Harris
Library Holdings: Bk Vols 3,900; Per Subs 10
Open Mon-Thurs 6am-10pm, Fri 6-5, Sun 8-5
Restriction: Mem only

P TENAFLY PUBLIC LIBRARY, 100 Riveredge Rd, 07670-1962. SAN 310-5318. Tel: 201-568-8680. Administration Tel: 201-568-7809. FAX: 201-568-5475. Web Site: tenafly.bccls.org. *Dir,* Gina Webb-Metz; E-mail: webb-metz@tenafly.bccls.org; *Head, Pub Serv,* Daniel Lane; E-mail: daniel.lane@tenafly.bccls.org; *Ch,* Latricia Markle; E-mail: markle@tenafly.bccls.org; *Coll Develop/Tech Serv Librn,* Rafat Ispahany; E-mail: rafat.ispahany@tenafly.bccls.org; Staff 5 (MLS 5)
Founded 1920. Pop 14,488; Circ 230,000
Jan 2014-Dec 2014 Income $1,400,400, State $6,400, City $1,394,000. Mats Exp $115,300, Books $80,000, Per/Ser (Incl. Access Fees) $5,300, AV Mat $30,000. Sal $747,000
Library Holdings: AV Mats 5,091; Bk Titles 75,411; Bk Vols 84,000; Per Subs 140
Automation Activity & Vendor Info: (Circulation) Innovative Interfaces, Inc; (ILL) JerseyCat; (OPAC) Innovative Interfaces, Inc
Wireless access
Partic in Bergen County Cooperative Library System; LibraryLinkNJ, The New Jersey Library Cooperative
Special Services for the Blind - VisualTek equip
Open Mon, Tues & Thurs 10-9, Wed, Fri & Sat 10-5, Sun (Sept-May) 12-4
Friends of the Library Group

TETERBORO

S AVIATION HALL OF FAME & MUSEUM LIBRARY OF NEW JERSEY*, Teterboro Airport, 400 Fred Wehran Dr, 07608. SAN 375-7285. Tel: 201-288-6344. FAX: 201-288-5666. E-mail: njahof@verizon.net. Web Site: www.njahof.org. *Sr Librn,* August H Zoll; E-mail: azoll@verizon.net. Subject Specialists: *Aviation, Wright aeronautical,* August H Zoll
Library Holdings: Bk Titles 3,000
Special Collections: Aviation Scrapbooks, 1860-1990 (Bill Rhode Coll); Curtiss-Wright Aircraft Engines (Wright Aeronautical Coll)
Automation Activity & Vendor Info: (Cataloging) Follett Software; (Circulation) Follett Software
Function: Res libr
Restriction: Open to pub by appt only

THREE BRIDGES

P THREE BRIDGES PUBLIC LIBRARY*, 449 Main St, 08887. (Mail add: PO Box 465, 08887-0465). Tel: 908-782-2908. FAX: 908-782-2908. *Librn,* Theresa Stoveken; Staff 2 (MLS 2)
Library Holdings: AV Mats 350; Large Print Bks 42; Bk Vols 15,973; Per Subs 30; Talking Bks 150
Automation Activity & Vendor Info: (Cataloging) Innovative Interfaces, Inc; (Circulation) Innovative Interfaces, Inc; (OPAC) Innovative Interfaces, Inc
Wireless access
Mem of Hunterdon County Library
Open Mon, Thurs & Fri 9:30-5:30, Wed 12-8, Sat (Sept-July) 9-12
Friends of the Library Group

TINTON FALLS

P TINTON FALLS PUBLIC LIBRARY*, 664 Tinton Ave, 07724. SAN 310-5342. Tel: 732-542-3110. FAX: 732-542-6755. E-mail: tflibrary@monmouthcountylib.org. *Dir,* Ellen O'Brien
Founded 1961. Pop 16,500; Circ 57,700
Library Holdings: AV Mats 2,337; CDs 645; DVDs 190; Electronic Media & Resources 41; Large Print Bks 110; Bk Vols 37,780; Per Subs 19; Talking Bks 696; Videos 2,702
Automation Activity & Vendor Info: (Cataloging) SirsiDynix; (Circulation) SirsiDynix
Wireless access
Publications: Snippets (Newsletter)
Mem of Monmouth County Library
Open Mon-Wed 9:30-9, Thurs 9:30-7, Fri 9:30-4, Sat 10-2
Friends of the Library Group

TOMS RIVER

M COMMUNITY MEDICAL CENTER, Medical Library, 99 Hwy 37 W, 08755. SAN 375-6912. Tel: 732-557-8117. FAX: 732-557-2762. *Dir,* Reina Reisler; E-mail: rreisler@barnabashealth.org
Subject Interests: Med
Partic in Basic Health Sciences Library Network

J OCEAN COUNTY COLLEGE LIBRARY*, College Dr, 08754. (Mail add: PO Box 2001, 08754-2001), SAN 310-5350. Tel: 732-255-0392. Interlibrary Loan Service Tel: 732-255-0400, Ext 2489. Reference Tel: 732-255-0400, Ext 2287. FAX: 732-255-0421. Web Site: lib.ocean.edu. *Interim Dir,* Erin Cartwright; *Assoc Prof, Ref Librn,* Torris Andersen; Tel: 732-255-0400, Ext 2250, E-mail: tandersen@ocean.edu; *Instr, Ref Librn,* Caitlyn Cook; Tel: 732-255-0400, Ext 2163, E-mail: ccook@ocean.edu; *Asst Prof, Ref Librn,* Catherine Pontoriero; Tel: 732-255-0400, Ext 2254, E-mail: cpontoriero@ocean.edu; *Automation Serv, Instr, Ref Librn,* Gary Schmidt; Tel: 732-255-0400, Ext 2248, E-mail: gschmidt@ocean.edu; *Assoc Prof, Tech Serv Librn,* Position Currently Open; *ILL, Mgr, Circ Serv,* James Cowen. Subject Specialists: *Govt doc,* Caitlyn Cook; Staff 13 (MLS 5, Non-MLS 8)
Founded 1966. Enrl 9,900; Fac 227; Highest Degree: Associate
Library Holdings: Bk Titles 77,000
Special Collections: State Document Depository; US Document Depository
Subject Interests: Undergrad studies
Automation Activity & Vendor Info: (Acquisitions) SirsiDynix; (Cataloging) SirsiDynix; (Circulation) SirsiDynix; (Course Reserve) SirsiDynix; (ILL) JerseyCat; (OPAC) SirsiDynix; (Serials) SirsiDynix
Wireless access
Function: Govt ref serv, ILL available, Magnifiers for reading, Wheelchair accessible
Partic in LibraryLinkNJ, The New Jersey Library Cooperative; Lyrasis; OCLC Online Computer Library Center, Inc; Virtual Academic Library Environment
Special Services for the Blind - Assistive/Adapted tech devices, equip & products
Open Mon-Fri (Winter) 8am-10pm, Sat 9-5; Mon-Thurs (Summer) 8am-10pm, Fri 8-4

S OCEAN COUNTY HISTORICAL SOCIETY*, Richard Lee Strickler Research Center, 26 Hadley Ave, 08753. SAN 371-6252. Tel: 732-341-1880. FAX: 732-341-4372. E-mail: oceancounty.history@verizon.net. Web Site: www.oceancountyhistory.org.
Founded 1980
Library Holdings: AV Mats 50; Bk Titles 8,000; Bk Vols 8,500; Per Subs 45
Subject Interests: County genealogy, County hist
Open Tues & Wed 1-4
Restriction: Non-circulating

P OCEAN COUNTY LIBRARY, 101 Washington St, 08753. SAN 351-3998. Tel: 732-349-6200. Administration FAX: 732-473-1356. Information Services FAX: 732-349-0478. Web Site: www.theoceancountylibrary.org. *Dir,* Susan Quinn; E-mail: squinn@theoceancountylibrary.org; *Asst Dir, Operations,* Sara Hansen; Tel: 732-914-5412, E-mail: shansen@theoceancountylibrary.org; *Asst Dir, Pub Serv,* Valerie Bell; Tel: 732-914-5404, E-mail: vbell@theoceancountylibrary.org; *Chief Librn, Hq,* Position Currently Open; *Chief of Br Serv,* Rita Oakes; E-mail: roakes@theoceancountylibrary.org; *Chief, Admin,* Position Currently Open; Staff 520 (MLS 116, Non-MLS 404)
Founded 1925. Pop 575,397; Circ 4,514,037
Jan 2013-Dec 2013 Income (Main Library and Branch(s)) $34,653,221. Mats Exp $3,293,279, Books $1,745,224, Per/Ser (Incl. Access Fees) $167,008, AV Mat $806,202, Electronic Ref Mat (Incl. Access Fees) $574,845. Sal $17,077,791
Library Holdings: Audiobooks 39,724; AV Mats 138,912; e-books 26,370; Bk Vols 1,060,651; Per Subs 2,701
Special Collections: Local History (New Jersey Coll). State Document Depository
Automation Activity & Vendor Info: (Acquisitions) Innovative Interfaces, Inc; (Cataloging) Innovative Interfaces, Inc; (Circulation) Innovative Interfaces, Inc; (ILL) OCLC FirstSearch; (OPAC) Innovative Interfaces, Inc; (Serials) Innovative Interfaces, Inc
Database Vendor: OCLC FirstSearch
Wireless access
Function: Adult bk club, After school storytime, Audiobks via web, Bilingual assistance for Spanish patrons, Bk club(s), Bks on cassette, Bks on CD, Children's prog, Citizenship assistance, Computer training, Computers for patron use, Copy machines, Doc delivery serv, E-Reserves, Electronic databases & coll, Exhibits, Family literacy, Fax serv, Free DVD rentals, Handicapped accessible, Home delivery & serv to Sr ctr & nursing homes, Homebound delivery serv, ILL available, Music CDs, Online cat, OverDrive digital audio bks, Preschool outreach, Preschool reading prog, Prog for adults, Prog for children & young adult, Pub access computers, Ref & res, Ref serv available, Scanner, Senior computer classes, Senior outreach, Serves mentally handicapped consumers, Spanish lang bks, Spoken cassettes & CDs, Spoken cassettes & DVDs, Story hour, Summer reading prog, Teen prog, Telephone ref, Web-catalog, Wheelchair accessible
Publications: Clubs & Organizations of Ocean County, Connect Newsletter; Immigration Resource Directory; Ocean County Resource Directory; Small Business Handbook
Partic in LibraryLinkNJ, The New Jersey Library Cooperative; New Jersey Library Network; OCLC Online Computer Library Center, Inc
Special Services for the Deaf - Staff with knowledge of sign lang; TTY equip
Special Services for the Blind - Computer with voice synthesizer for visually impaired persons
Open Mon-Thurs 9-9, Fri & Sat 9-5, Sun (Sept-May) 1-5
Restriction: Co libr, Non-resident fee
Friends of the Library Group

Branches: 20

BARNEGAT BRANCH, 112 Burr St, Barnegat, 08005, SAN 351-4005. Tel: 609-698-3331. FAX: 609-698-9592. *Br Mgr,* Givane Hayes; E-mail: ghayes@theoceancountylibrary.org
Open Mon, Fri & Sat 10-5, Tues-Thurs 10-9
Friends of the Library Group

BAY HEAD READING CENTER, 136 Meadow Ave, Bay Head, 08742-5080, SAN 371-4713. Tel: 732-892-0662. FAX: 732-892-0647. *Circ Supvr,* Virginia Berkman; E-mail: vberkman@theoceancountylibrary.org
Open Mon & Wed 1-5, Tues & Sat 10-1, Thurs 1-5 & 7-9

BEACHWOOD BRANCH, 126 Beachwood Blvd, Beachwood, 08722-2810, SAN 351-4021. Tel: 732-244-4573. FAX: 732-736-1025. *Br Mgr,* Natalie Niziolek; E-mail: nniziolek@theoceancountylibrary.org
Open Mon 1-9, Tues & Fri 1-5, Wed & Thurs 10-5, Sat 10-1
Friends of the Library Group

BERKELEY BRANCH, 30 Station Rd, Bayville, 08721-2198, SAN 351-403X. Tel: 732-269-2144. FAX: 732-237-2955. *Br Mgr,* Erin DeLucia; E-mail: edelucia@theoceancountylibrary.org
Open Mon-Thurs 9-9, Fri & Sat 9-5
Friends of the Library Group

BRICK BRANCH, 301 Chambers Bridge Rd, Brick, 08723-2803, SAN 351-4056. Tel: 732-477-4513. FAX: 732-920-9314. *Br Mgr,* Susan Gardiner
Open Mon-Thurs 9-9, Fri & Sat 9-5
Friends of the Library Group

ISLAND HEIGHTS BRANCH, 121 Central Ave, Island Heights, 08732, SAN 351-4080. Tel: 732-270-6266. FAX: 732-270-0308. *Br Mgr,* Amanda Spino; E-mail: aspino@theoceancountylibrary.org
Open Mon 1-9, Tues & Thurs 10-5, Wed & Sat 10-1, Fri 1-5
Friends of the Library Group

JACKSON BRANCH, Two Jackson Dr, Jackson, 08527-3601, SAN 351-4145. Tel: 732-928-4400. FAX: 732-833-0615. *Br Mgr,* Pamela Dong
Open Mon-Thurs 9-9, Fri & Sat 9-5
Friends of the Library Group

LACEY BRANCH, Ten E Lacey Rd, Forked River, 08731-3626, SAN 351-4110. Tel: 609-693-8566. FAX: 609-971-8973. *Br Mgr,* Nancy Voitko; E-mail: nvoitko@theoceancountylibrary.org
Open Mon-Thurs 9-9, Fri & Sat 9-5
Friends of the Library Group

LAKEWOOD BRANCH, 301 Lexington Ave, Lakewood, 08701, SAN 310-236X. Tel: 732-363-1435. FAX: 732-363-1438. *Br Mgr,* Cathi Sheridan; E-mail: csheridan@theoceancountylibrary.org
Open Mon-Thurs 9-9, Fri & Sat 9-5, Sun (Sept-May) 1-5
Friends of the Library Group

LITTLE EGG HARBOR BRANCH, 290 Mathistown Rd, Little Egg Harbor, 08087, SAN 376-8317. Tel: 609-294-1197. FAX: 609-294-1302. *Br Mgr,* Kelly-Ann Pennell; E-mail: kpennell@theoceancountylibrary.org
Open Mon, Fri & Sat 10-5, Tues-Thurs 10-9
Friends of the Library Group

LONG BEACH ISLAND BRANCH, 217 S Central Ave, Surf City, 08008-4800, SAN 351-417X. Tel: 609-494-2480. FAX: 609-494-7850. *Br Mgr,* Linda Feaster; E-mail: lfeaster@theoceancountylibrary.org
Open Mon & Wed 9-9, Tues & Thurs-Sat 9-5
Friends of the Library Group

MANCHESTER BRANCH, 21 Colonial Dr, Lakehurst, 08733-3801, SAN 370-4475. Tel: 732-657-7600. FAX: 732-323-9246. *Br Mgr,* Suzanne Scro; E-mail: sscro@theoceancountylibrary.org
Open Mon-Thurs 9-9, Fri & Sat 9-5
Friends of the Library Group

PLUMSTED BRANCH, 119 Evergreen Rd, New Egypt, 08533, SAN 351-420X. Tel: 609-758-7888. FAX: 609-758-6997. *Br Mgr,* Rachael Lavoie-Dohn; E-mail: rdohn@theoceancountylibrary.org
Open Mon & Wed 1-9, Thurs 1-5, Tues & Fri 10-5, Sat 10-1
Friends of the Library Group

POINT PLEASANT BEACH BRANCH, 710 McLean Ave, Point Pleasant Beach, 08742-2522, SAN 370-4483. Tel: 732-892-4575. FAX: 732-701-1941. *Br Mgr,* Shazia Zaman; E-mail: szaman@theoceancountylibrary.org
Open Mon, Wed & Thurs 10-5, Tues 1-9, Fri 1-5, Sat 10-1
Friends of the Library Group

POINT PLEASANT BRANCH, 834 Beaver Dam Rd, Point Pleasant, 08742-3853. Tel: 732-295-1555. FAX: 732-714-1578. *Br Mgr,* Melissa Freeman; E-mail: mfreeman@theoceancountylibrary.org
Open Mon, Wed & Thurs 10-9, Tues, Fri & Sat 10-5
Friends of the Library Group

STAFFORD BRANCH, 129 N Main St, Manahawkin, 08050-2933, SAN 351-4250. Tel: 609-597-3381. FAX: 609-978-0770. *Br Mgr,* Christine Rodas; E-mail: crodas@theoceancountylibrary.org
Open Mon, Wed & Thurs 9-9, Tues, Fri & Sat 9-5, Sun (Sept-May) 1-5
Friends of the Library Group

TUCKERTON BRANCH, 380 Bay Ave, Tuckerton, 08087-2557, SAN 351-4269. Tel: 609-296-1470. FAX: 609-296-6487. *Br Mgr,* Toni Smirniw; E-mail: tsmirniw@theoceancountylibrary.org
Open Mon 1-9, Tues & Thurs 10-5, Wed & Fri 1-5, Sat 10-1
Friends of the Library Group

UPPER SHORES BRANCH, 112 Jersey City Ave, Lavallette, 08735, SAN 376-8325. Tel: 732-793-3996. FAX: 732-793-4942. *Br Mgr,* June Schneider; E-mail: jschneider@theoceancountylibrary.org
Open Mon, Thurs & Fri 10-5, Tues & Wed 10-9, Sat 10-1
Friends of the Library Group

WARETOWN BRANCH, 112 Main St, Waretown, 08758-9252, SAN 351-4277. Tel: 609-693-5133. FAX: 609-242-8784. *Br Mgr,* Erin DeLucia; E-mail: edelucia@theoceancountylibrary.org
Open Mon 1-9, Tues & Thurs 10-5, Wed & Fri 1-5, Sat 10-1
Friends of the Library Group

WHITING READING CENTER, Whiting Commons Shopping Ctr, Rte 530, Whiting, 08759. Tel: 732-849-0391. FAX: 732-849-0283. *Mgr,* Lou Nemphos; E-mail: lnemphos@theoceancountylibrary.org
Open Mon 9-7, Tues & Thurs 9-5, Wed, Fri & Sat 9-1

L OCEAN VICINAGE LAW LIBRARY*, Ocean County Courthouse, Rm 103, 118 Washington St, 08753. SAN 325-9110. Tel: 732-506-5026.
Library Holdings: Bk Vols 1,000

Wireless access
Open Mon-Fri 8:30-4:30

TOTOWA

P DWIGHT D EISENHOWER PUBLIC LIBRARY*, 537 Totowa Rd, 07512-1699. SAN 310-5377. Tel: 973-790-3265, Ext 11. FAX: 973-790-0306. Web Site: www.palsplus.org/ddepl. *Dir,* Anne Krautheim; *Ch Serv,* Annemarie Shapiola; Staff 10 (MLS 2, Non-MLS 8)
Founded 1957. Pop 9,892; Circ 29,654
Library Holdings: Bk Titles 44,158; Bk Vols 46,647; Per Subs 250
Special Collections: Library of America (60 vol set)
Subject Interests: Lit
Automation Activity & Vendor Info: (Cataloging) SirsiDynix; (Circulation) SirsiDynix; (OPAC) SirsiDynix
Partic in LibraryLinkNJ, The New Jersey Library Cooperative; PALS Plus, The Computer Consortium of Passaic County Libraries
Special Services for the Deaf - Bks on deafness & sign lang; Staff with knowledge of sign lang
Open Mon-Thurs 10-8, Fri 10-6, Sat 10-3

TRENTON

M CAPITAL HEALTH REGIONAL MEDICAL CENTER*, Health Sciences Library, 750 Brunswick Ave, 08638. SAN 310-5407. Tel: 609-394-6065. FAX: 609-278-1882. E-mail: fuldlibrary@capitalhealth.org. Web Site: www.capitalhealth.org/library. *Dir,* Erica Moncrief; *Librn,* Jennifer Kral; Staff 2 (MLS 1, Non-MLS 1)
Library Holdings: Bk Titles 3,500; Per Subs 150
Special Collections: Hist of Hospital & Nursing School
Subject Interests: Allied health, Med, Neuroscience, Nursing, Psychol
Database Vendor: OVID Technologies
Wireless access
Partic in Basic Health Sciences Library Network; New Jersey Health Sciences Library Network
Open Mon-Fri 7:30-5
Restriction: Open to students, fac & staff

M CAPITAL HEALTH SYSTEM AT MERCER*, Health Sciences Library, 446 Bellevue Ave, 08618. SAN 310-5423. Tel: 609-394-4125. FAX: 609-394-4131. Web Site: www.capitalhealth.org. *Dir,* Erica Moncrief; *Asst Librn,* Ritu Sharma; Tel: 609-394-4282; Staff 2 (MLS 2)
Founded 1947
Library Holdings: Bk Titles 3,000; Per Subs 150
Special Collections: 19th Century Medical Books
Wireless access
Partic in Basic Health Sciences Library Network; New Jersey Health Sciences Library Network
Open Mon-Fri 7:30-5
Restriction: Open to students, fac & staff

S CONGOLEUM CORP*, Technical Research Library, 861 Sloan Ave, 08619. (Mail add: PO Box 3127, 08619), SAN 310-5385. Tel: 609-584-3264. FAX: 609-584-3305. *In Charge,* Bob Dempsey
Founded 1920
Library Holdings: Bk Vols 1,000; Per Subs 38
Subject Interests: Chem, Coatings, Eng, Floor coverings, Paper, Patents, Physics, Plastics, Polymer chem, Tech ref
Restriction: Staff use only

S MERCER COUNTY CORRECTION CENTER LIBRARY*, PO Box 8068, 08650-0068. SAN 375-7013. Tel: 609-989-6901, Ext 2282. FAX: 609-397-4589. *Coordr,* Linda Rogers; E-mail: lrogers@mercercounty.org
Library Holdings: Bk Titles 4,000
Restriction: Not open to pub

G NEW JERSEY DEPARTMENT OF ENVIRONMENTAL PROTECTION, Environmental Research Library, 432 E State St, 1st Flr, 08608. (Mail add: Mail Code 432-01, PO Box 420, 08625-0420), SAN 325-9323. Tel: 609-984-2249. Administration Tel: 609-633-2151. FAX: 609-292-3298. Web Site: www.state.nj.us/dep/dsr/irc. *Librn I,* Dorothy Alibrando; E-mail: dorothy.alibrando@dep.state.nj.us; *Librn III,* Tonia Wu, E-mail: tonia.wu@dep.state.nj.us. Subject Specialists: *Air pollution, Soil pollution, Water pollution,* Dorothy Alibrando; *Ill,* Tonia Wu; Staff 2 (MLS 2)
Founded 1987
Library Holdings: Bk Vols 7,500; Per Subs 60
Special Collections: IARC Monographs; NJDEP documents; US EPA documents; USGS documents; WHO Environmental Health Criteria
Automation Activity & Vendor Info: (Acquisitions) SirsiDynix; (Cataloging) OCLC Connexion; (Circulation) SirsiDynix; (ILL) OCLC FirstSearch
Function: Govt ref serv
Partic in LibraryLinkNJ, The New Jersey Library Cooperative
Restriction: Open to pub by appt only

G NEW JERSEY DEPARTMENT OF LABOR LIBRARY*, John Fitch Plaza, 5th Flr, 08611. (Mail add: PO Box 943, 08625-0943), SAN 310-544X. Tel: 609-292-2035. FAX: 609-984-5456. *Librn I,* Hing Choi Fung; E-mail: hing-choi.fung@dol.state.nj.us; *Librn III,* Donald Carrlo; Staff 2 (MLS 1, Non-MLS 1)
Founded 1966
Library Holdings: Bk Vols 7,802; Per Subs 189
Subject Interests: Census, Disability ins, Econ, Employment, Labor, Labor law practices, Labor market info, Training, Unemployment ins, Vocational rehabilitation
Automation Activity & Vendor Info: (Cataloging) Follett Software; (Circulation) Follett Software
Function: Ref serv available
Partic in LibraryLinkNJ, The New Jersey Library Cooperative
Open Mon-Fri 8:30-4:30
Restriction: Non-circulating

GL NEW JERSEY DEPARTMENT OF LAW & PUBLIC SAFETY, Attorney General's Library, 25 Market St, West Wing, 6th Flr, 08625. (Mail add: PO Box 115, 08625-0115), SAN 310-5490. Tel: 609-292-4958. FAX: 609-633-6555. E-mail: oag.library@lps.state.nj.us. *Librn I,* Tamar Pritchard; Tel: 973-648-4849, Fax: 973-648-7445; *Acq,* Magda Maslowska; *Ref,* Jenny Healey; *Ref/Tech Serv,* Susan Moss; Staff 5 (MLS 4, Non-MLS 1)
Library Holdings: Bk Vols 50,000; Per Subs 50
Special Collections: Legal Memoranda Coll; New Jersey Legislative Material Coll
Subject Interests: Criminology, NJ law, Regulatory law
Automation Activity & Vendor Info: (Cataloging) Horizon; (Circulation) Horizon; (ILL) OCLC; (OPAC) Horizon; (Serials) Horizon
Database Vendor: EBSCOhost, HeinOnline, LexisNexis, OCLC, OCLC FirstSearch, ProQuest, PubMed
Wireless access
Function: Govt ref serv
Partic in Lyrasis
Restriction: Authorized personnel only

S NEW JERSEY DEPARTMENT OF TRANSPORTATION*, Research Library, 1035 Parkway Ave, 08618-2309. (Mail add: PO Box 600, 08625-0600). Tel: 609-530-5289. FAX: 609-530-2052. E-mail: library@dot.state.nj.us. Web Site: www.state.nj.us/transportation/refdata/library. *Librn,* Carol Paszamant; E-mail: carol.paszamant@dot.state.nj.us; *Assoc Librn,* Laurie Strow; Staff 2 (MLS 2)
Founded 1962
Library Holdings: AV Mats 170; CDs 180; DVDs 40; Electronic Media & Resources 100; Bk Titles 8,000; Per Subs 30; Videos 150
Special Collections: AASHTO Publications; Federal Highway Administration Publications; NJDOT Publications; Transportation Research Board Publications
Automation Activity & Vendor Info: (Acquisitions) Horizon; (Cataloging) Horizon; (Circulation) Horizon; (ILL) OCLC; (OPAC) Horizon
Database Vendor: Dialog, OCLC FirstSearch
Publications: Selected Recent Acquisitions (Acquisition list)
Partic in Eastern Transportation Knowledge Network (ETKN); LibraryLinkNJ, The New Jersey Library Cooperative
Restriction: In-house use for visitors, Open to pub by appt only

G NEW JERSEY STATE LEAGUE OF MUNICIPALITIES*, Bureau of Municipal Information, 222 W State St, 08608. SAN 323-4266. Tel: 609-695-3481. FAX: 609-695-5156. Web Site: www.njslom.org. *In Charge,* Taran Samhammer; E-mail: tsamhammer@njslom.com
Library Holdings: e-books 15,000
Special Collections: Ordinances
Restriction: Not open to pub

P NEW JERSEY STATE LIBRARY, 185 W State St, 08618. (Mail add: PO Box 520, 08625-0520), SAN 351-4773. Tel: 609-278-2640. Circulation Tel: 609-278-2640, Ext 104. Interlibrary Loan Service Tel: 609-278-2640, Ext 171. Reference Tel: 609-278-2640, Ext 103. FAX: 609-278-2652. Information Services FAX: 609-278-2647. TDD: 877-882-5593. E-mail: refdesk@njstatelib.org. Web Site: www.njstatelib.org. *State Librn,* Mary Chute; Tel: 609-278-2640, Ext 101, E-mail: mchute@njstatelib.org; *Dep State Librn, Innovation & Outreach,* Peggy Cadigan; Tel: 609-278-2640, Ext 113, E-mail: pcadigan@njstatelib.org; *Dep State Librn, Libr Support Serv,* Victoria Rosch; Tel: 609-278-2640, Ext 157, Fax: 609-278-2650, E-mail: vrosch@njstatelib.org; *Dep State Librn, Lifelong Learning,* Kathleen Moeller-Peiffer; Tel: 609-278-2640, Ext 152, E-mail: kpeiffer@njstatelib.org; *Dep State Librn, NJSL Talking Bk & Braille Ctr,* Adam Sczcepaniak; Tel: 609-406-7179, Ext 801, Fax: 609-406-7181, E-mail: asczcepaniak@njstatelib.org; *Dep State Librn, State Libr Info Ctr,* Colleen Daze; Tel: 609-278-2640, Ext 118, Fax: 609-278-2645, E-mail: cdaze@njstatelib.org; *Dir, Info Tech,* Michael Rasimowicz; Tel:

609-278-2640, Ext 199, Fax: 609-278-2650, E-mail: mrasimowicz@njstatelib.org; *Dir, Mkt & Strategic Partnerships,* Tiffany McClary; Tel: 609-278-2640, Ext 122, E-mail: tmcclary@njstatelib.org; *Assoc Dir, Libr Support Serv,* Michele Stricker; Tel: 609-278-2640, Ext 164, E-mail: mstricker@njstatelib.org; *Asst Dir, SLIC,* Margaret Nizolek; Tel: 609-278-2640, Ext 148, E-mail: mnizolek@njstatelib.org; *Data Coordr, Libr Support Serv,* Bob Keith; Tel: 609-278-2640, Ext 192, E-mail: rkeith@njstatelib.org; *Adult, Urban & Diversity Spec, Lifelong Learning,* Mimi Lee; Tel: 609-278-2640, Ext 191, E-mail: mlee@njstatelib.org; *Chief Financial Officer,* Sheri L Shafer; Tel: 609-278-2640, Ext 137, Fax: 609-278-2649, E-mail: sshafer@njstatelib.org; *Pub Relations & News Media Contact,* Gary Cooper; Tel: 609-278-2640, Ext 108, E-mail: gcooper@njstatelib.org; *Youth Serv Spec, Lifelong Learning,* Sharon Rawlins; Tel: 609-278-2640, Ext 116, E-mail: srawlins@njstatelib.org; *Youth Serv Spec, Talking Bk & Braille Ctr,* Elizabeth Burns; Tel: 609-406-7179, Ext 804, E-mail: eburns@njstatelib.org; Staff 94 (MLS 41, Non-MLS 53)
Founded 1796
Jul 2013-Jun 2014 Income (Main Library and Branch(s)) $18,446,000. Mats Exp $992,000, Books $543,000, Per/Ser (Incl. Access Fees) $215,000, Electronic Ref Mat (Incl. Access Fees) $234,000
Library Holdings: Audiobooks 166,469; Audiobooks 144,423; AV Mats 574; Bks-By-Mail 3,121; Bks-By-Mail 2,150; Braille Volumes 43,715; Braille Volumes 40,629; e-books 32,226; Electronic Media & Resources 1,043; Electronic Media & Resources 84,397; Large Print Bks 3,170; Large Print Bks 3,121; Bk Titles 396,321; Bk Vols 531,278; Per Subs 690; Talking Bks 342,453; Talking Bks 345,383
Special Collections: Foundations Coll; Genealogy Coll; Jerseyana; Law Coll. State Document Depository; US Document Depository
Subject Interests: Educ, Genealogy, Grantsmanship, Law, Libr sci, Mgt, Pub health, Soc sci, State govt, State hist
Automation Activity & Vendor Info: (Acquisitions) SirsiDynix; (Cataloging) SirsiDynix; (Circulation) SirsiDynix; (OPAC) SirsiDynix; (Serials) SirsiDynix
Database Vendor: BioOne, Bowker, Career Guidance Foundation, Carroll Publishing, CQ Press, Dialog, EBSCOhost, Foundation Center, Gale Cengage Learning, Hoovers, LearningExpress, LexisNexis, Newsbank, OVID Technologies, ProQuest, ReferenceUSA, SirsiDynix, Wilson - Wilson Web
Wireless access
Function: Computers for patron use, Copy machines, Digital talking bks, Electronic databases & coll, Govt ref serv, Handicapped accessible, Home delivery & serv to Sr ctr & nursing homes, Homebound delivery serv, ILL available, Notary serv, Online ref, Online searches, Outside serv via phone, mail, e-mail & web, Pub access computers, Ref serv available, Ref serv in person, Res libr, Tax forms, Wheelchair accessible
Publications: Analyses of New Jersey Public Library Statistics; Checklist of Official New Jersey Publications; New Books Lists; New Jersey Library Laws; New Jersey Public Library Statistics; NJSL Direct Newsletter (Online only); Shipping List of NJ Documents; Special Bibliographies; TBBC's Insights (Quarterly); The Link Newsletter (Monthly bulletin)
Partic in LibraryLinkNJ, The New Jersey Library Cooperative; Lyrasis; New Jersey Library Network; Virtual Academic Library Environment
Special Services for the Blind - Assistive/Adapted tech devices, equip & products; Audio mat; Audiovision-a radio reading serv; Bks on flash-memory cartridges; Braille alphabet card; Braille bks; Cassette playback machines; Cassettes; Children's Braille; Digital talking bk; Digital talking bk machines; Handicapped awareness prog; Large print bks; Large screen computer & software; Lending of low vision aids; Local mags & bks recorded; Newsletter (in large print, Braille or on cassette); Newsline for the Blind; PC for handicapped; Radio reading serv; Talking bks; Talking bks & player equip
Open Mon-Fri 8:30-5
Friends of the Library Group
Branches: 1

P TALKING BOOK & BRAILLE CENTER, 2300 Stuyvesant Ave, 08618. (Mail add: PO Box 501, 08625-0501), SAN 329-0131. Tel: 609-406-7179. Toll Free Tel: 800-792-8322. FAX: 609-406-7181. TDD: 877-882-5593. E-mail: tbbc@njstatelib.org. Web Site: njsltbbc.org. *Dep State Librn, NJSL Talking Bk & Braille Ctr,* Adam Szczepaniak, Jr; Tel: 604-406-7179, Ext 801, E-mail: aszczepaniak@njstatelib.org; *Asst Dir,* Maria Baratta; Tel: 609-406-7179, Ext 803, E-mail: mbaratta@njstatelib.org; *CUL Adminr,* Gary Zonderwyk; Tel: 609-406-7179, Ext 825, E-mail: gzonderwyk@njstatelib.org; *Supvr, Machine Lending,* Andy O'Rahilly; Tel: 609-406-7179, Ext 819, E-mail: aorahilly@njstatelib.org; *Adult Serv & Outreach Coordr,* Mary Kearns-Kaplan; Tel: 609-406-7179, Ext 834, E-mail: mkaplan@njstatelib.org; *Assistive Tech Coordr,* Christian Riehl; Tel: 609-406-7179, Ext 821, E-mail: criehl@njstatelib.org; *Youth Serv Consult,* Elizabeth Burns; Tel: 609-406-7179, Ext 804, E-mail: eburns@njstatelib.org; *Develop,* Linda Cerce; Tel: 609-406-7179, Ext 835; *Media Prod,* Mary Crain; Tel: 609-406-7179, Ext 809, E-mail: mcrain@njstatelib.org; Staff 6 (MLS 4, Non-MLS 2)
Founded 1968
Library Holdings: AV Mats 1,523; Braille Volumes 32,422; High Interest/Low Vocabulary Bk Vols 13; Bk Titles 73,202; Bk Vols 762,612; Per Subs 90; Talking Bks 45,387; Videos 876
Partic in LibraryLinkNJ, The New Jersey Library Cooperative
Publications: Insights (Newsletter); Rap Sheet (Newsletter)
Special Services for the Deaf - TDD equip; TTY equip
Special Services for the Blind - Braille bks; Talking bks
Open Mon-Fri 8:30-4
Restriction: Residents only
Friends of the Library Group

S NEW JERSEY STATE MUSEUM, 205 West State St, 08625. (Mail add: PO Box 530, 08625-0530), SAN 323-5122. Tel: 609-984-3844. FAX: 609-292-7636. Web Site: www.newjerseystatemuseum.org. *Curator of Fine Art,* Margaret O'Reilly, E-mail: margaret.oreilly@sos.state.nj.us. Subject Specialists: *Am fine art,* Margaret O'Reilly
Library Holdings: Bk Vols 4,000
Subject Interests: Fine arts
Restriction: Staff use only

L NEW JERSEY STATE PRISON*, Law Library, PO Box 861, 08625. SAN 310-5539. Tel: 609-292-9700, Ext 4285. FAX: 609-777-1885. *Dir of Educ,* Diane Patrick
Founded 1900
Library Holdings: Bk Vols 2,000
Subject Interests: Fiction, Law, Non-fiction, Philos, Psychol

M SAINT FRANCIS MEDICAL CENTER*, Medical Library, 601 Hamilton Ave, 08629-1986. SAN 310-5504. Tel: 609-599-5068. FAX: 609-599-5773. Web Site: www.stfrancismedical.com/educationprog/med_library.htm. *Dir,* Donna Barlow; E-mail: dbarlow@che-east.org; Staff 1 (MLS 1)
Founded 1930
Library Holdings: Bk Vols 8,000; Per Subs 300
Subject Interests: Allied health, Health serv admin, Med, Nursing
Database Vendor: EBSCOhost, OVID Technologies
Publications: Journal Holdings List; Library Bulletin
Open Mon-Fri 7:30-4

G STATE OF NEW JERSEY - DEPARTMENT OF BANKING & INSURANCE LIBRARY*, Roebling Building Library, 20 W State St, 08608-1206. (Mail add: PO Box 325, 08625-0325), SAN 371-7887. Tel: 609-777-0558, Ext 50274. FAX: 609-633-8213. *Librn,* Christine Severino; E-mail: christine.severino@dobi.state.nj.us
Library Holdings: Bk Titles 200; Bk Vols 600; Per Subs 98
Special Collections: New Jersey Department of Banking & Insurance Coll; New Jersey Law
Publications: Checklist of Publications
Restriction: Open by appt only

P TRENTON FREE PUBLIC LIBRARY*, 120 Academy St, 08608-1302. SAN 351-4293. Tel: 609-392-7188. FAX: 609-396-7655. Web Site: www.trentonlib.org. *Dir,* Kimberly Matthews; E-mail: kmatthews@trentonlib.org; *Head, Ref,* Cathy Stout; E-mail: cstout@trenton.lib.nj.us; *Hist Coll Librn,* Wendy Nardi; E-mail: wendynardi@hotmail.com; *Ch Serv,* Anais Scott; E-mail: ascott@trentonlib.org; *Per,* Cathy Stout; E-mail: cstout@trenton.lib.nj.us; *YA Serv,* Tyler Rousseau; E-mail: tyler.rousseau@gmail.com; Staff 36 (MLS 13, Non-MLS 23)
Founded 1750. Pop 85,403; Circ 196,949
Jul 2010-Jun 2011 Income $4,009,000. Mats Exp $288,000. Sal $2,080,000
Library Holdings: Bk Titles 300,000; Bk Vols 375,000; Per Subs 770
Special Collections: Art & Music, bks, CDs, prints, recs, scores; Trentoniana Coll, bks, pamphlets, photogs, docs. State Document Depository; US Document Depository
Automation Activity & Vendor Info: (Acquisitions) TLC (The Library Corporation); (Cataloging) TLC (The Library Corporation); (Circulation) TLC (The Library Corporation); (Course Reserve) TLC (The Library Corporation); (ILL) TLC (The Library Corporation); (Media Booking) TLC (The Library Corporation); (OPAC) TLC (The Library Corporation); (Serials) TLC (The Library Corporation)
Database Vendor: SirsiDynix
Publications: Acquisitions List (Monthly); Union List of Serials
Special Services for the Deaf - Adult & family literacy prog; Bks on deafness & sign lang; Closed caption videos; High interest/low vocabulary bks
Open Mon-Thurs 9-8, Fri & Sat 9-5
Friends of the Library Group

GL US COURTS LIBRARY*, 402 E State St, Rm 301, 08608. SAN 377-3647. Tel: 609-989-2345. FAX: 609-989-0485. Web Site: www.uscourts.gov. *Librn,* Tom Fasching
Library Holdings: Bk Titles 7,000; Bk Vols 9,000
Automation Activity & Vendor Info: (Cataloging) SirsiDynix
Open Mon-Fri 8:30-4:30

TURNERSVILLE

M KENNEDY MEMORIAL HOSPITALS-UNIVERSITY MEDICAL CENTER*, Paul Barsky Memorial Library, 435 Hurffville-Cross Keys Rd, 08012. SAN 326-1239. Tel: 856-582-2675. FAX: 856-582-3190. Web Site: www.kennedyhealth.org. *Mgr,* Elaine Mayweather; E-mail: e.mayweather@kennedyhealth.org; Staff 1 (Non-MLS 1)
Library Holdings: Bk Vols 200; Per Subs 50
Partic in Basic Health Sciences Library Network; Health Sciences Library Association of New Jersey; SW NJ Consortium
Restriction: Staff use only

UNION

C KEAN UNIVERSITY*, Nancy Thompson Library, 1000 Morris Ave, 07083. SAN 310-558X. Tel: 908-737-4600. FAX: 908-737-4620. Web Site: library.kean.edu. *Interim Univ Librn,* Kimberly Fraone; E-mail: kfraone@kean.edu; *Librn,* Craig Anderson; *Librn,* Linda Cifelli; *Librn,* Janette Gonzalez; *Librn,* Shirley Horbatt; *Librn,* Eleanor McKnight; *Librn,* Marquan Mutazz; *Librn,* Chrisler Pitts; Staff 9 (MLS 9)
Founded 1914. Enrl 15,100; Fac 400; Highest Degree: Doctorate
Library Holdings: Bk Titles 315,000; Bk Vols 379,905; Per Subs 34,000
Special Collections: History (New Jerseyana), bks, pamphlets
Subject Interests: Allied health, Computer sci, Econ, Educ, English, Occupational therapy
Automation Activity & Vendor Info: (Acquisitions) Ex Libris Group; (Cataloging) Ex Libris Group; (Circulation) Ex Libris Group; (Course Reserve) Ex Libris Group; (OPAC) Ex Libris Group; (Serials) Ex Libris Group
Wireless access
Function: e-mail & chat, E-Reserves, Electronic databases & coll, Exhibits, Handicapped accessible, ILL available, Online cat, Online info literacy tutorials on the web & in blackboard, Online ref, Photocopying/Printing, Ref serv in person, Web-catalog
Partic in LibraryLinkNJ, The New Jersey Library Cooperative; Lyrasis; OCLC Online Computer Library Center, Inc; Virtual Academic Library Environment; Westchester Academic Library Directors Organization (WALDO)
Open Mon-Thurs (Fall & Spring) 8am-2am, Fri 8-5, Sat 9-5, Sun 1-10; Mon-Thurs (Summer) 8am-2am

P UNION TOWNSHIP PUBLIC LIBRARY*, 1980 Morris Ave, 07083-3578. SAN 351-5079. Tel: 908-851-5450. Reference Tel: 908-851-5452. FAX: 908-851-4671. Web Site: www.youseemore.com/unionpl. *Dir,* Laurie D Sansone; Tel: 908-851-5453; Staff 42 (MLS 7, Non-MLS 35)
Founded 1927. Pop 50,400; Circ 248,865
Jan 2011-Dec 2011 Income (Main Library and Branch(s)) $2,502,279, State $25,529, City $2,441,454, Locally Generated Income $35,296. Mats Exp $227,667, Books $160,000, Per/Ser (Incl. Access Fees) $12,000, AV Mat $15,317, Electronic Ref Mat (Incl. Access Fees) $40,000, Presv $350. Sal $1,209,427
Library Holdings: Bk Titles 120,000; Bk Vols 225,570; Per Subs 238
Automation Activity & Vendor Info: (Acquisitions) TLC (The Library Corporation); (Cataloging) TLC (The Library Corporation); (Circulation) TLC (The Library Corporation); (OPAC) TLC (The Library Corporation); (Serials) TLC (The Library Corporation)
Wireless access
Partic in NJ State Libr Network
Open Mon-Thurs (Winter) 10-9, Fri & Sat 9-5; Mon-Thurs (Summer) 10-9, Fri 9-5
Branches: 1
VAUX HALL BRANCH, 123 Hilton Ave, Vaux Hall, 07088, SAN 351-5133. Tel: 908-851-5451. FAX: 908-810-7072. *Dir,* Laurie Sansone; Staff 1 (MLS 1)
Library Holdings: Bk Vols 24,000
Open Mon 1-8, Tues & Thurs 10:30-5:30, Wed 10-8, Sat 10-5

UNION BEACH

P UNION BEACH MEMORIAL LIBRARY*, 810 Union Ave, 07735. SAN 310-5601. Tel: 732-264-3792. *Mgr,* Evelyn Bauer; Staff 3 (MLS 3)
Library Holdings: Bk Titles 31,000
Automation Activity & Vendor Info: (Cataloging) Innovative Interfaces, Inc; (Circulation) Innovative Interfaces, Inc
Database Vendor: EBSCOhost
Mem of Monmouth County Library
Open Mon-Fri 2-6, Sat 9-1

UNION CITY

P UNION CITY PUBLIC LIBRARY*, 324 43rd St, 07087-5008. SAN 351-5168. Tel: 201-866-7500. FAX: 201-866-0962. Web Site: uclibrary.org. *Dir,* Rita Mann; E-mail: ritamann10@hotmail.com; Staff 1 (MLS 1)
Founded 1905. Pop 67,088
Library Holdings: Bk Titles 29,815; Bk Vols 42,128; Per Subs 163
Subject Interests: English lit, Film, Spanish lang
Automation Activity & Vendor Info: (Acquisitions) Follett Software; (Cataloging) Follett Software; (Circulation) Follett Software; (OPAC) Follett Software; (Serials) Follett Software
Database Vendor: EBSCOhost, Gale Cengage Learning
Wireless access
Open Mon, Wed & Fri 10-6, Tues & Thurs 10-8:30, Sat 10-5
Branches: 1
SUMMIT BRANCH, 1800 Summit Ave, 07087-4320, SAN 351-5192. Tel: 201-866-7503. FAX: 201-348-2635. *Librn,* Rita Roque; Staff 3 (Non-MLS 3)
Founded 2004. Pop 67,088
Library Holdings: Bk Titles 21,017; Bk Vols 31,806; Per Subs 72
Open Mon & Wed 12:30-8:30, Tues, Thurs & Fri 10-6, Sun 10-3
Friends of the Library Group

UPPER SADDLE RIVER

S AMERICAN INSTITUTE OF FOOD DISTRIBUTION INC*, Information & Research Center, 10 Mountainview Rd, Ste F125, 07458. SAN 374-891X. Tel: 201-791-5570, Ext 25. FAX: 201-791-5222. E-mail: food1@foodinstitute.com. Web Site: www.foodinstitute.com. *Librn,* Joan Kastrinsky
Library Holdings: Bk Titles 150; Per Subs 10
Open Mon-Fri 8:30-4:30
Restriction: Staff use only

P UPPER SADDLE RIVER PUBLIC LIBRARY*, 245 Lake St, 07458. SAN 310-5644. Tel: 201-327-2583. FAX: 201-327-3966. E-mail: usdrcirc@bccls.org. Web Site: www.uppersaddleriverlibrary.org. *Dir,* Barbara Newmark-Kruger
Founded 1959. Pop 7,700; Circ 120,000
Library Holdings: Bk Titles 69,625; Per Subs 355
Automation Activity & Vendor Info: (Circulation) SirsiDynix; (OPAC) SirsiDynix
Wireless access
Publications: Business & Residents Local Directory
Friends of the Library Group

VERONA

P VERONA PUBLIC LIBRARY*, 17 Gould St, 07044-1928. SAN 310-5679. Tel: 973-857-4848. FAX: 973-857-4851. Web Site: www.veronalibrary.org. *Dir,* James A Thomas; E-mail: jthomas@veronanj.org; *Ch Serv,* Cheryl Ashley; *Ref & Info Serv,* Catherine Adair Williams; E-mail: cawilliams@veronanj.org; *Tech Serv,* William Trafton; E-mail: wtrafton@veronanj.org; Staff 9 (MLS 4, Non-MLS 5)
Founded 1912. Pop 13,553; Circ 90,000
Library Holdings: Bk Titles 55,000; Bk Vols 60,000; Per Subs 175
Special Collections: Landsberger Holocaust Coll; Unico Italian Heritage Coll
Automation Activity & Vendor Info: (Cataloging) Auto-Graphics, Inc; (Circulation) Auto-Graphics, Inc; (ILL) JerseyCat; (OPAC) Auto-Graphics, Inc
Database Vendor: EBSCOhost, Gale Cengage Learning, Oxford Online
Wireless access
Open Mon, Tues & Thurs 9-9, Wed, Fri & Sat 9-5, Sun 2-5
Friends of the Library Group

VINCENTOWN

P SALLY STRETCH KEEN MEMORIAL LIBRARY*, 94 Main St, 08088. SAN 310-5687. Tel: 609-859-3598. Web Site: www.vincentown.lib.nj.us. *Dir,* Marsha Jones; E-mail: mjones@vincentown.lib.nj.us; *Librn,* Judy Poinsett
Founded 1923. Pop 10,000
Library Holdings: Bk Vols 40,000; Per Subs 20
Subject Interests: Civil War
Wireless access
Mem of Burlington County Library
Partic in LibraryLinkNJ, The New Jersey Library Cooperative
Open Mon & Wed 10-5, Tues & Thurs 10-7, Sat 10-2

VINELAND

R BETH ISRAEL SYNAGOGUE*, Beth Israel Community Library, 1015 E Park Ave, 08360. SAN 310-5695. Tel: 856-691-0852. FAX: 856-692-1957. *Cat, Tech Serv,* Mary Snidley; *Circ,* Position Currently Open
Founded 1926
Library Holdings: Bk Titles 7,050; Bk Vols 7,585; Per Subs 23
Special Collections: Hitler Period (Holocaust Literature)
Subject Interests: Judaica
Wireless access
Partic in Cumberland Libraries United Electronic System (CLUES)
Friends of the Library Group

J CUMBERLAND COUNTY COLLEGE LIBRARY*, 3322 College Dr, 08360. (Mail add: PO Box 1500, 08362-1500), SAN 310-5709. Tel: 856-691-8600, Ext 261. FAX: 856-691-1969. Web Site: www.cccnj.edu. *Head, Libr Serv,* Patti Schmid; E-mail: pschmid@cccnj.edu; *Librn,* Valerie Gouse; E-mail: vgouse@cccnj.edu; *Librn,* Mary Thorstensen; E-mail: mthorstensen@cccnj.edu; Staff 3.5 (MLS 3.5)
Founded 1966. Enrl 3,144; Fac 50; Highest Degree: Associate
Library Holdings: Bk Titles 33,000; Bk Vols 38,000; Per Subs 50
Special Collections: Jerseyanna
Subject Interests: Holistic health, Law, Mythology, Nursing
Automation Activity & Vendor Info: (Cataloging) SirsiDynix; (Circulation) SirsiDynix; (OPAC) SirsiDynix
Database Vendor: Baker & Taylor, Bowker, Brodart, EBSCOhost, Foundation Center, Gale Cengage Learning, Greenwood Publishing Group, H W Wilson, LearningExpress, Marquis Who's Who, McGraw-Hill, Modern Language Association, OCLC, Oxford Online, ProQuest, ReferenceUSA, Sage, SirsiDynix, Springshare, LLC, Westlaw, Wiley, Wilson - Wilson Web
Wireless access
Function: Electronic databases & coll, Handicapped accessible, Notary serv, Online cat, Online info literacy tutorials on the web & in blackboard, Orientations, Photocopying/Printing, Pub access computers, Ref & res, Ref serv in person, Scanner, Wheelchair accessible
Publications: Student Handbook
Partic in LibraryLinkNJ, The New Jersey Library Cooperative; OCLC Online Computer Library Center, Inc; Virtual Academic Library Environment
Restriction: Circ limited, In-house use for visitors, Non-resident fee, Open to pub for ref & circ; with some limitations

M VINELAND DEVELOPMENTAL CENTER HOSPITAL LIBRARY*, 1676 E Landis Ave, 08360. SAN 376-060X. Tel: 856-696-6200. *Librn,* Karen Levy; Tel: 856-794-5730
Library Holdings: Bk Titles 950; Per Subs 36
Partic in LibraryLinkNJ, The New Jersey Library Cooperative
Open Mon-Fri 7-3

S VINELAND HISTORICAL & ANTIQUARIAN SOCIETY LIBRARY*, 108 S Seventh St, 08360-4607. (Mail add: PO Box 35, 08362-0035), SAN 325-8998. Tel: 856-691-1111. E-mail: vinelandhistory@gmail.com. Web Site: www.vinelandhistory.org. *Adminr, Curator,* Patricia Martinelli; Staff 1 (Non-MLS 1)
Founded 1864
Library Holdings: Bk Vols 8,000
Special Collections: Autographs 1750-1900
Subject Interests: Genealogy, Hist
Wireless access
Restriction: 24-hr pass syst for students only, Badge access after hrs, Borrowing privileges limited to anthropology fac & libr staff, Borrowing privileges limited to fac & registered students, Borrowing requests are handled by ILL, Circ limited, Circ privileges for students & alumni only, Circ to mem only, Circ to mil employees only, Clients only, Closed stack, Co libr, Congregants only, Employee & client use only, Employees & their associates, Employees only

P VINELAND PUBLIC LIBRARY*, 1058 E Landis Ave, 08360. SAN 310-5717. Tel: 856-794-4244. FAX: 856-691-0366. Web Site: www.vinelandlibrary.org. *Dir,* Gloria Urban; *Ch Serv,* Helen Cowan; *Ref,* Holly Rogerson
Founded 1901. Pop 57,500; Circ 254,000
Library Holdings: Bk Titles 100,000; Per Subs 161
Automation Activity & Vendor Info: (Cataloging) SirsiDynix
Wireless access
Partic in Cumberland Libraries United Electronic System (CLUES); LibraryLinkNJ, The New Jersey Library Cooperative
Open Mon-Thurs 9-9, Fri & Sat 11-4, Sun (Oct-March) 1-5
Friends of the Library Group

VOORHEES

P CAMDEN COUNTY LIBRARY SYSTEM*, 203 Laurel Rd, 08043. SAN 351-5222. Tel: 856-772-1636. Circulation Tel: 856-772-1636, Ext 3355. Interlibrary Loan Service Tel: 856-772-1636, Ext 3316. Reference Tel: 856-772-1636, Ext 3311. FAX: 856-772-6105. Reference FAX: 856-772-6128. E-mail: ref@camden.lib.nj.us. Web Site: www.camdencountylibrary.org. *Dir,* Linda Devlin; *Assoc Dir,* Deborah Dennis; Tel: 856-772-1636, Ext 3344; *Br Mgr,* William Brahms; Tel: 856-772-1636, Ext 3308, E-mail: wbrahm@camden.lib.nj.us; *Adult Serv,* Position Currently Open; *Ch Serv,* David Eckert; Tel: 856-772-1636, Ext 3360, E-mail: decker@camden.lib.nj.us; *Circ,* Chris Entwisle; Tel: 856-772-1636, Ext 3309, E-mail: centwi@camden.lib.nj.us; *Info Tech,* Janice Masud-Paul; Tel: 856-772-1636, Ext 3336, E-mail: janicem@camden.lib.nj.us; *Tech Serv,* Lisa Derfler; Tel: 856-772-1636, Ext 3333, E-mail: lisa@camden.lib.nj.us; Staff 225 (MLS 46, Non-MLS 179)
Founded 1922. Pop 250,000; Circ 1,129,592
Jan 2006-Dec 2006. Mats Exp $789,450, Books $362,900, Per/Ser (Incl. Access Fees) $97,700, AV Mat $214,850, Electronic Ref Mat (Incl. Access Fees) $112,500, Presv $1,500. Sal $4,760,000
Library Holdings: AV Mats 35,065; Electronic Media & Resources 93; Bk Titles 177,726; Bk Vols 430,060; Per Subs 895
Subject Interests: NJ
Automation Activity & Vendor Info: (Acquisitions) Innovative Interfaces, Inc; (Cataloging) Innovative Interfaces, Inc; (Circulation) Innovative Interfaces, Inc; (ILL) Innovative Interfaces, Inc; (OPAC) Innovative Interfaces, Inc; (Serials) Innovative Interfaces, Inc
Database Vendor: EBSCOhost, Gale Cengage Learning, LexisNexis, Newsbank, OCLC WorldShare Interlibrary Loan, ReferenceUSA, Westlaw, Wilson - Wilson Web
Wireless access
Member Libraries: Audubon Park Public Library; Berlin Township Library; Clementon Memorial Library; Gibbsboro Public Library; Lindenwold Public Library; Marie Fleche Memorial Library; Mount Ephraim Public Library; Oaklyn Memorial Library; Somerdale Public Library; Woodlynne Public Library
Partic in LibraryLinkNJ, The New Jersey Library Cooperative; Lyrasis; National Network of Libraries of Medicine Middle Atlantic Region; New Jersey Library Network; OCLC Online Computer Library Center, Inc
Special Services for the Deaf - Assisted listening device; Closed caption videos; TTY equip
Special Services for the Blind - Large print bks; ZoomText magnification & reading software
Open Mon-Fri 10-9, Sat 10-6, Sun (Sept-May) 1-5
Friends of the Library Group
Branches: 6
RILETTA L CREAM FERRY AVENUE BRANCH, 852 Ferry Ave, Camden, 08104. Tel: 856-342 9789. FAX: 856-342-9791. Web Site: www.camden.lib.nj.us/ferry/default.htm. *Br Mgr,* Jerome Szpila
GLOUCESTER TOWNSHIP-BLACKWOOD ROTARY LIBRARY, 15 S Black Horse Pike, Blackwood, 08012, SAN 351-5257. Tel: 856-228-0022. FAX: 856-228-9085. E-mail: glouce@camden.lib.nj.us, glouce@camdencountylibrary.org. *Br Mgr,* Anne Ackroyd; Staff 3 (MLS 3)
Pop 76,519
Library Holdings: Bk Vols 55,130; Per Subs 50
Open Mon-Thurs 10-9, Fri & Sat 10-5
ANTHONY P INFANTI BELLMAWR BRANCH LIBRARY, 35 E Browning Rd, Bellmawr, 08031, SAN 378-1542. Tel: 856-931-1400. FAX: 856-931-5338. E-mail: bellmawr@camden.lib.nj.us. Web Site: www.bellmawr.camden.lib.nj.us. *Br Mgr,* Debbie Stefano; Staff 3 (MLS 3)
Pop 27,939
Library Holdings: Bk Vols 35,000; Per Subs 96
Open Mon-Thurs 10-9, Fri & Sat 10-5
Friends of the Library Group
MERCHANTVILLE PUBLIC LIBRARY, 130 S Centre St, Merchantville, 08109, Tel: 856-665-3128. FAX: 856-665-4296. E-mail: merchant@camden.lib.nj.us. Web Site: www.camden.lib.nj.us/merchantville/. *Mgr,* Eve Brown; Staff 1 (MLS 1)
Pop 7,780
Library Holdings: Bk Vols 14,125
Open Mon & Wed 2 9, Tues & Thurs 2-5, Sat 10:30-4
WILLIAM G ROHRER MEMORIAL LIBRARY - HADDON TOWNSHIP, 15 MacArthur Blvd, Westmont, 08108, SAN 351-5281. Tel: 856-854-2752. FAX: 856-854-8825. Web Site: www.camdencountylibrary.org/haddon-township-branch. *Br Mgr,* Jennifer Druce; E-mail: jdruce@camdencountylibrary.org; Staff 3 (MLS 3)
Pop 57,064
Library Holdings: Bk Vols 57,064; Per Subs 100
Open Mon-Thurs 10-9, Fri & Sat 10-5
Friends of the Library Group
SOUTH COUNTY REGIONAL BRANCH, 35 Coopers Folly Rd, Atco, 08004, SAN 351-5311. Tel: 856-753-2537. FAX: 856-753-7289. Web Site: southco.camden.lib.nj.us/. *Br Mgr,* Nancy Bennett; Tel: 856-753-2537, Ext 4404; Staff 6 (MLS 5, Non-MLS 1)
Pop 64,086
Library Holdings: Bk Vols 77,217; Per Subs 150
Open Mon-Fri 10-9, Sat 10-6, Sun (Sept-May) 1-5

M VIRTUA HEALTH SYSTEM, VOORHEES DIVISION*, Staff Medical Library, 100 Bowman Dr, Medical Library, Garden Level Rm GD550, 08043. SAN 351-5346. Tel: 856-247-3207. FAX: 856-247-3222. Web Site: www.virtua.org. *Med Librn,* Maura Sostack; E-mail: msostack@virtua.org; Staff 1 (MLS 1)
Founded 1976
Library Holdings: e-books 55; Bk Titles 200; Per Subs 100
Subject Interests: Hospital admin, Med, Nursing, Patient educ
Database Vendor: EBSCO Information Services, EBSCOhost, Elsevier, Lexi-Comp, MD Consult, Medline, OVID Technologies, PubMed, TDNet, UpToDate

Wireless access
Partic in Basic Health Sciences Library Network; LibraryLinkNJ, The New Jersey Library Cooperative; SW NJ Consortium

WALDWICK

P WALDWICK PUBLIC LIBRARY*, 19 E Prospect St, 07463-2099. SAN 310-5733. Tel: 201-652-5104. FAX: 201-652-6233. Web Site: waldwick.bccls.org. *Dir,* Lori-Ann Quinn; E-mail: quinn@bcels.org; Staff 2 (MLS 2)
Founded 1954. Pop 9,622; Circ 120,809
Library Holdings: Bk Titles 43,000; Bk Vols 55,347; Per Subs 92
Special Collections: Italian-American. Oral History
Subject Interests: Local hist
Database Vendor: EBSCOhost, Gale Cengage Learning, ProQuest
Wireless access
Open Mon-Thurs 10-9, Fri-Sat 10-5
Friends of the Library Group

WALL

S NEW JERSEY NATURAL GAS CO LIBRARY*, 1415 Wyckoff Rd, 07719. SAN 375-6939. Tel: 732-938-1000. FAX: 732-938-2134. Web Site: www.njliving.com. *Mgr,* Patricia Kendall
Library Holdings: Bk Vols 200
Partic in LibraryLinkNJ, The New Jersey Library Cooperative
Restriction: Not open to pub

WALLINGTON

P JOHN F KENNEDY MEMORIAL LIBRARY*, 92 Hathaway St, 07057. SAN 310-5741. Tel: 973-471-1692. FAX: 973-471-1387. E-mail: wallcirc@bccls.org. Web Site: www.bccls.org/wallington. *Dir,* Marianne R Willms; E-mail: marewillms@hotmail.com; *Libr Assoc/Tech Serv,* Susanna Cocker; *Libr Asst, Youth Serv,* Melissa Pagani; Staff 6 (MLS 1, Non-MLS 5)
Pop 11,500; Circ 37,000
Library Holdings: Bk Titles 40,000; Per Subs 105
Special Collections: Polish Language Material
Automation Activity & Vendor Info: (Cataloging) Spydus; (Circulation) SirsiDynix; (ILL) Livelink for Libraries; (OPAC) SirsiDynix
Database Vendor: Gale Cengage Learning, ProQuest
Open Mon 10-6, Tues 10-8, Wed & Thurs 12-8, Fri 10-5, Sat 10-4

WANAQUE

P WANAQUE PUBLIC LIBRARY*, 616 Ringwood Ave, 07465. SAN 310-575X. Tel: 973-839-4434. FAX: 973-839-8904. Web Site: www.wanaquelibrary.org. *Dir,* Gillian Buonanno; Tel: 973-839-4434, Ext 101, E-mail: buonanno@wanaquelibrary.org; *Sr Librn, Ch Serv,* Betty Waldron; *Ch Serv,* Donna O'Hanlon; Tel: 973-839-4434, Ext 103, E-mail: ohanlon@wanaque.org; *Circ,* Lori Bailey; Tel: 973-839-4434, Ext 104, E-mail: bailey@wanaque.org; Staff 7 (MLS 1, Non-MLS 6)
Founded 1968. Pop 14,256; Circ 25,155
Library Holdings: Bk Vols 31,412; Per Subs 83
Automation Activity & Vendor Info: (Acquisitions) SirsiDynix; (Cataloging) SirsiDynix; (Circulation) SirsiDynix; (OPAC) SirsiDynix
Database Vendor: EBSCOhost, SirsiDynix
Wireless access
Function: ILL available
Partic in LibraryLinkNJ, The New Jersey Library Cooperative; PALS Plus, The Computer Consortium of Passaic County Libraries
Open Mon & Fri 9-5, Tues-Thurs 9-8, Sat (Sept-May) 10-3

WASHINGTON

J WARREN COUNTY COMMUNITY COLLEGE LIBRARY, 475 Rte 57 W, 07882-4343. SAN 371-9170. Tel: 908-835-2336. *Dir, Libr Serv,* Lisa Stoll; Tel: 908-835-2337, E-mail: lstoll@warren.edu; Staff 1 (MLS 1)
Founded 1984. Enrl 1,440; Fac 40; Highest Degree: Associate
Library Holdings: Audiobooks 4; AV Mats 1,054; CDs 36; e-books 132,000; Electronic Media & Resources 55; High Interest/Low Vocabulary Bk Vols 65; Bk Titles 13,754; Per Subs 5; Videos 850
Special Collections: Juvenile Coll; WCCC Archives
Subject Interests: Humanities, Law, Nursing
Automation Activity & Vendor Info: (Acquisitions) LibLime Koha; (Cataloging) LibLime Koha; (Circulation) LibLime Koha; (ILL) OCLC WorldShare Interlibrary Loan; (OPAC) LibLime Koha; (Serials) LibLime Koha
Database Vendor: Alexander Street Press, EBSCOhost, Gale Cengage Learning, ProQuest
Wireless access
Function: AV serv, Distance learning, Doc delivery serv, Handicapped accessible, ILL available, Photocopying/Printing, Ref serv available, Telephone ref, Wheelchair accessible
Partic in Virtual Academic Library Environment
Special Services for the Deaf - Closed caption videos
Special Services for the Blind - Computer with voice synthesizer for visually impaired persons; ZoomText magnification & reading software
Open Mon-Thurs 8am-9pm, Fri 8-5, Sat 9-1
Restriction: Open to pub for ref & circ; with some limitations, Open to students, fac & staff

P WASHINGTON PUBLIC LIBRARY*, 20 W Carlton Ave, 07882. SAN 310-5792. Tel: 908-689-0201. FAX: 908-835-0803. Web Site: www.washboropl.org. *Dir,* Position Currently Open; Staff 1 (MLS 1)
Founded 1927. Pop 6,712; Circ 23,000
Jan 2010-Dec 2010 Income $238,734, State $3,760, City $234,974. Mats Exp $19,700, Books $13,808, Per/Ser (Incl. Access Fees) $3,442, Micro $519, AV Mat $1,456, Electronic Ref Mat (Incl. Access Fees) $475. Sal $180,920 (Prof $74,000)
Library Holdings: Bks on Deafness & Sign Lang 25; CDs 801; DVDs 237; Electronic Media & Resources 7; High Interest/Low Vocabulary Bk Vols 400; Large Print Bks 750; Bk Vols 49,988; Per Subs 111; Videos 1,762
Special Collections: Star Gazette Newspaper Archive
Subject Interests: Local hist
Automation Activity & Vendor Info: (Cataloging) Follett Software; (Circulation) Follett Software; (ILL) Auto-Graphics, Inc; (OPAC) Follett Software
Database Vendor: EBSCOhost
Wireless access
Special Services for the Blind - Assistive/Adapted tech devices, equip & products
Open Mon & Thurs 12:30-8, Tues & Wed 10-6, Sat 10-2

WASHINGTON TOWNSHIP

P TOWNSHIP OF WASHINGTON PUBLIC LIBRARY*, 144 Woodfield Rd, 07676. SAN 310-6047. Tel: 201-664-4586. FAX: 201-664-7331. E-mail: washcirc@bccls.org. Web Site: washingtontwp.bccls.org. *Dir,* Juliette Sobon; *Head, Ch,* Maria Halzack; *Head, Circ,* Janet Baker; Staff 1 (MLS 1)
Founded 1963. Pop 9,245; Circ 77,100
Library Holdings: Bk Titles 38,770; Bk Vols 41,238; Per Subs 100
Special Collections: Careers; Large Print Bks
Subject Interests: Cooking, Japanese culture, Mysteries, Travel
Database Vendor: EBSCOhost
Wireless access
Open Mon, Tues & Thurs 10-8, Wed & Fri 10-5, Sat 10-3
Friends of the Library Group

WAYNE

S INTERNATIONAL SPECIALTY PRODUCTS*, Technical Information Services Library, 1361 Alps Rd, 07470. SAN 310-5830. Tel: 973-628-4000, Ext 3899. FAX: 973-628-3404. Web Site: www.ispcorp.com. *Librn,* Cecilia Garcia; Staff 1 (MLS 1)
Founded 1972
Library Holdings: Bk Titles 950; Per Subs 50
Subject Interests: Acetylene chem, Bldg mat, Organic chem
Partic in BRS; Dialog Corp
Restriction: Staff use only

SR PACKANACK COMMUNITY CHURCH LIBRARY*, 120 Lake Dr E, 07470. SAN 328-3739. Tel: 973-694-0608. FAX: 973-694-7161.
Library Holdings: Bk Titles 2,200
Subject Interests: Ethics, Psychol, Relig
Restriction: Open by appt only

S URS GREINER WOODWARD-CLYDE CONSULTANTS LIBRARY*, 201 Willowbrook Blvd, 07470-0290. SAN 326-1859. Tel: 973-785-0700, Ext 281, 973-812-3100. FAX: 973-785-0023. Toll Free FAX: 877-565-8519. *In Charge,* Liz Stundon
Library Holdings: Bk Titles 9,000; Bk Vols 14,000; Per Subs 120
Special Collections: Contains reports, maps and govt surveys on geological, chemical, metallurgical and environment and climatology related subjects. Special Collections
Subject Interests: Architectural eng tech, Civil eng, Climatology, Environ studies, Geol, Metallurgy
Restriction: Staff use only

P WAYNE PUBLIC LIBRARY*, 461 Valley Rd, 07470. SAN 351-5494. Tel: 973-694-4272. Circulation Tel: 973-694-4272, Ext 5210. Interlibrary Loan Service Tel: 973-694-4272, Ext 5406. Reference Tel: 973-694-4272, Ext 5401. FAX: 973-692-0637. E-mail: wplcomments@waynepubliclibrary.org. Web Site: www.waynepubliclibrary.org. *Dir,* Jody C Treadway; Tel: 973-694-4272, Ext 5101, E-mail: treadwayj@waynepubliclibrary.org; *Asst Dir,* Doreen Shoba; Tel: 973-694-4272, Ext 5102, E-mail: shobad@waynepubliclibrary.org; Staff 14 (MLS 11, Non-MLS 3)
Founded 1922. Pop 54,717; Circ 525,295

Jan 2012-Dec 2012 Income (Main Library and Branch(s)) $3,504,521. Mats Exp $3,504,521, Books $152,575, Per/Ser (Incl. Access Fees) $24,000, Micro $22,000, AV Mat $22,000, Electronic Ref Mat (Incl. Access Fees) $45,000. Sal $1,603,140 (Prof $770,518)
Library Holdings: Bk Titles 202,239; Bk Vols 229,851; Per Subs 288
Special Collections: Business Reference; New Jersey History (Lockett Coll). State Document Depository
Subject Interests: Bus ref, NJ docs
Automation Activity & Vendor Info: (Cataloging) SirsiDynix; (Circulation) SirsiDynix; (ILL) SirsiDynix; (OPAC) SirsiDynix
Database Vendor: EBSCOhost, Gale Cengage Learning, Overdrive, Inc, ProQuest, ReferenceUSA
Wireless access
Publications: Insights (Newsletter)
Partic in PALS Plus, The Computer Consortium of Passaic County Libraries
Open Mon-Thurs 9-9, Fri 9-5:30, Sat 10-5, Sun (Sept-May) 1-5
Friends of the Library Group
Branches: 1
PREAKNESS, Wayne Civic Ctr, 1006 Hamburg Tpk, 07470, SAN 351-5559. Tel: 973-694-7110. FAX: 973-694-8415. *Librn,* Wendy Sandford; Staff 3 (MLS 1, Non-MLS 2)
Library Holdings: Bk Titles 34,209; Bk Vols 36,495; Per Subs 45
Open Mon 1-8, Tues-Fri 10-5:30
Friends of the Library Group

C WILLIAM PATERSON UNIVERSITY, David & Lorraine Cheng Library, 300 Pompton Rd, 07470. SAN 310-5865. Tel: 973-720-2541. Circulation Tel: 973-720-3180. Interlibrary Loan Service Tel: 973-720-2567. Reference Tel: 973-720-2116. FAX: 973-720-3171. E-mail: refdesk@wpunj.edu. Web Site: www.wpunj.edu/library. *Dean,* Paul Glassman; Tel: 973-720-2113, E-mail: glassmanp@wpunj.edu; *Asst Dir, Access & Info Systems,* Nancy Weiner; Tel: 973-720-2161, E-mail: weinern@wpunj.edu; *Asst Dir, Libr & Info Syst,* Kurt Wagner; Tel: 973-720-2285, E-mail: wagnerk@wpunj.edu; *Asst Dir, Res Mgt,* Pamela Theus; Tel: 973-720-2160, E-mail: theusp@wpunj.edu; *Head, Circ,* Victoria Wagner; Tel: 973-720-3190, E-mail: wagnerv@wpunj.edu; *Head, Per,* Judy Matthew; Tel: 973-720-2346, E-mail: matthewj@wpunj.edu; *Head, Ref,* Bill Duffy; Tel: 973-720-3191, E-mail: duffyb@wpunj.edu; *Cat Librn,* Mark Sandford; Tel: 973-720-2437, E-mail: sandfordm1@wpunj.edu; *Ref Librn,* Anthony Joachim; Tel: 973-720-3665, E-mail: joachima@wpunj.edu; *Ref Librn & Co-Coordr of User Educ,* Cara Berg; Tel: 973-720-3189, E-mail: bergc1@wpunj.edu; *Ref, Spec Coll Librn,* Robert Wolk; Tel: 973-720-2289, E-mail: wolkr@wpunj.edu; *Database Mgr,* Deborah Pluss; Tel: 973-720-3143, E-mail: plussd@wpunj.edu; *Electronic Res, Ref,* Richard Kearney; Tel: 973-720-2165, E-mail: kearneyr@wpunj.edu; *Govt Doc, Ref,* Susan Sabatino; Tel: 973-720-3127, E-mail: sabatinos@wpunj.edu; *Info Tech,* Ray Schwartz; Tel: 973-720-3192, E-mail: schwartzr2@wpunj.edu; *Ref,* Jane Bambrick; Tel: 973-720-2290, E-mail: bambrickj@wpunj.edu; *Ref Serv, Ch,* Yvonne Roux; Tel: 973-720-3184, E-mail: rouxy@wpunj.edu; Staff 20 (MLS 18, Non-MLS 2)
Founded 1924. Enrl 11,400; Fac 400; Highest Degree: Doctorate
Jul 2013-Jun 2014 Income $1,307,784. Mats Exp $1,320,700, Books $198,836, Per/Ser (Incl. Access Fees) $644,000, Electronic Ref Mat (Incl. Access Fees) $317,000
Library Holdings: AV Mats 23,287; Bk Titles 282,852; Bk Vols 323,420
Special Collections: First & Limited Editions of 19th & 20th Century American & British Authors; New Jerseyiana; Personal Papers of William Paterson (1745-1806). State Document Depository
Subject Interests: Bus, Educ, Law, Psychol
Automation Activity & Vendor Info: (Acquisitions) Ex Libris Group; (Cataloging) Ex Libris Group; (Circulation) Ex Libris Group; (Media Booking) Ex Libris Group; (OPAC) Ex Libris Group; (Serials) Ex Libris Group
Database Vendor: Cambridge Scientific Abstracts, EBSCOhost, Gale Cengage Learning, JSTOR, LexisNexis, OCLC FirstSearch, OVID Technologies, ProQuest, Wilson - Wilson Web
Wireless access
Publications: Bibliographic Series; Information Series; Instruction Bulletins; Newsletter
Partic in LibraryLinkNJ, The New Jersey Library Cooperative; Lyrasis; OCLC Online Computer Library Center, Inc; Virtual Academic Library Environment
Open Mon-Thurs 8am-Midnight, Fri 8am-10pm, Sat 8-8, Sun Noon-Midnight
Friends of the Library Group

WEEHAWKEN

P WEEHAWKEN FREE PUBLIC LIBRARY*, Multimedia Center, 49 Hauxhurst Ave, Ste 1, 07086. SAN 310-5873. Tel: 201-863-7823. FAX: 201-863-7958. E-mail: weehcirc@bccls.org. Web Site: www.bccls.org. *Dir,* Phillip R Greco
Founded 1942. Pop 12,715; Circ 22,116
Library Holdings: Bk Vols 22,179; Per Subs 37
Open Mon & Wed 9-9, Tues, Thurs & Fri 9-6, Sat (Sept-June) 9-5

WENONAH

P WENONAH FREE PUBLIC LIBRARY*, 101 E Mantua Ave, 08090-1950. SAN 310-5881. Tel: 856-468-6323. E-mail: wenonahlibrary@hotmail.com. *Dir,* Anne Zuber
Pop 2,278; Circ 18,000
Library Holdings: Bk Vols 15,777; Per Subs 15
Automation Activity & Vendor Info: (Acquisitions) SirsiDynix; (Cataloging) SirsiDynix; (Circulation) SirsiDynix; (Course Reserve) SirsiDynix; (ILL) SirsiDynix; (Media Booking) SirsiDynix; (OPAC) SirsiDynix; (Serials) SirsiDynix
Wireless access
Partic in LibraryLinkNJ, The New Jersey Library Cooperative; LOGIN (Libraries of Gloucester, Salem & Cumberland Information Network)
Open Mon, Tues & Thurs 3-9, Wed 9-9, Fri 1-5, Sat 10-2

WEST BERLIN

P BERLIN TOWNSHIP LIBRARY*, John J McPeak Library, 201 Veteran's Ave, 08091. SAN 310-589X. Tel: 856-767-0439. FAX: 856-753-6729. Web Site: www.berlintwp.com. *Librn,* Mary Holt
Founded 1965. Pop 8,000; Circ 8,000
Library Holdings: Bk Vols 75,471; Talking Bks 227
Mem of Camden County Library System
Open Mon & Wed 1-8:30, Tues & Thurs 9-11 & 1-8:30, Fri 1-4, Sat 10-2

WEST CALDWELL

P WEST CALDWELL PUBLIC LIBRARY*, 30 Clinton Rd, 07006. SAN 310-5903. Tel: 973-226-5441. FAX: 973-228 7572. Web Site: www.bccls.org/westcaldwell. *Dir,* Position Currently Open; *Libr Mgr,* Karen Kelly; *Head, Ref,* Ethan Galvan; Staff 14.5 (MLS 7.5, Non-MLS 7)
Founded 1915. Pop 11,000; Circ 141,792
Jan 2005-Dec 2005 Income $981,000. Mats Exp $120,000. Sal $555,000
Library Holdings: Bk Titles 40,000; Bk Vols 49,747; Per Subs 205
Automation Activity & Vendor Info: (Cataloging) SirsiDynix; (Circulation) SirsiDynix
Database Vendor: SirsiDynix
Function: Home delivery & serv to Sr ctr & nursing homes, Homebound delivery serv, ILL available, Magnifiers for reading, Online searches, Prog for children & young adult, Ref serv available, Summer reading prog, Telephone ref, Wheelchair accessible
Partic in Bergen County Cooperative Library System; LibraryLinkNJ, The New Jersey Library Cooperative; New Jersey Library Network
Open Mon-Thurs 9-8, Fri 9-6, Sat 9-5 (9-1 Summer)
Friends of the Library Group

WEST DEPTFORD

P WEST DEPTFORD PUBLIC LIBRARY*, 420 Crown Point Rd, 08086-9598. SAN 310-5326. Tel: 856-845-5593. FAX: 856-848-3689. E-mail: admin@westdeptford.lib.nj.us. Web Site: www.westdeptford.lib.nj.us. *Dir,* Marie Downes; *Ref,* Cheryl Rheiner; *Tech Serv,* Johanne Courtade; *YA Serv,* Carol Murphy; Staff 16 (MLS 4, Non-MLS 12)
Founded 1965. Pop 19,964; Circ 121,704
Jan 2007-Dec 2007 Income $1,102,799. Mats Exp $1,065,628. Sal $531,935 (Prof $228,000)
Library Holdings: Audiobooks 824; CDs 1,569; DVDs 3,932; Electronic Media & Resources 9; Bk Titles 79,261; Bk Vols 86,639; Per Subs 227
Special Collections: South Jersey Environmental Information Center Coll; United Nations Environment Programme Coll
Subject Interests: Environ, Health, Nutrition
Automation Activity & Vendor Info: (Circulation) SirsiDynix
Function: Bks on CD, Children's prog, Computer training, Computers for patron use, Copy machines, Electronic databases & coll, Handicapped accessible, ILL available, Music CDs, Notary serv, Online cat, OverDrive digital audio bks, Preschool outreach, Prog for adults, Prog for children & young adult, Pub access computers, Senior computer classes, Spoken cassettes & CDs, Spoken cassettes & DVDs, Story hour, Summer reading prog, Tax forms, Teen prog, Telephone ref, Wheelchair accessible
Publications: Check It Out (Newsletter)
Partic in LibraryLinkNJ, The New Jersey Library Cooperative; LOGIN (Libraries of Gloucester, Salem & Cumberland Information Network)
Special Services for the Deaf - Sign lang interpreter upon request for prog
Special Services for the Blind - Accessible computers; Bks on cassette; Bks on CD; Large print bks; Magnifiers
Open Mon-Thurs 10-9, Fri 10-5, Sat 10-3, Sun 1-5
Friends of the Library Group

WEST LONG BRANCH

S ARCHAEOLOGICAL SOCIETY OF NEW JERSEY LIBRARY*, Department of History & Anthropology, Monmouth University, 07764-1898. SAN 374-910X. Tel: 732-263-5699. Web Site: www.asnj.org. *Actg Librn,* Richard Veit; E-mail: rveit@monmouth.edu
Library Holdings: Bk Titles 1,000; Per Subs 15
Wireless access
Function: Res libr
Restriction: Non-circulating, Open by appt only

C MONMOUTH UNIVERSITY*, Guggenheim Memorial Library, 400 Cedar Ave, 07764. SAN 310-592X. Tel: 732-571-3450. Reference Tel: 732-571-3438. FAX: 732-263-5124. Web Site: library.monmouth.edu. *Dean,* Dr Ravindra Sharma; *Asst Admin,* Jane Calvo; *Head, Circ,* Allison Sheilds; Tel: 732-571-3450, Ext 4413; *Head, Tech Serv,* Aurora S Ioanid; Tel: 732-571-3450, Ext 5364; *Ref Librn,* Rachel M Gardner; Tel: 732-571-3450, Ext 7560; *ILL, Syst Librn,* Linda Silverstein; Tel: 732-571-3450, Ext 7521; *Govt Doc,* Susan Bucks; Tel: 732-263-5591; *Ref Serv,* George Germek; Tel: 732-571-3450, Ext 4403; Staff 10 (MLS 10)
Founded 1933. Enrl 6,000; Fac 188; Highest Degree: Master
Library Holdings: Bk Titles 23,500; Bk Vols 26,000; Per Subs 2,200
Special Collections: Lewis Mumford Coll; New Jersey History Coll. State Document Depository; US Document Depository
Automation Activity & Vendor Info: (Acquisitions) Innovative Interfaces, Inc; (Cataloging) Innovative Interfaces, Inc; (Circulation) Innovative Interfaces, Inc; (OPAC) Innovative Interfaces, Inc; (Serials) Innovative Interfaces, Inc
Database Vendor: OCLC FirstSearch
Wireless access
Partic in LibraryLinkNJ, The New Jersey Library Cooperative; Lyrasis; NJ Union List of Serials; OCLC Online Computer Library Center, Inc; Virtual Academic Library Environment
Open Mon-Thurs 8am-Midnight, Fri 8-6, Sat 9-5
Friends of the Library Group

WEST MILFORD

P WEST MILFORD TOWNSHIP LIBRARY*, 1490 Union Valley Rd, 07480. SAN 310-5946. Tel: 973-728-2820. Reference Tel: 973-728-2822. Administration Tel: 973-728-2824. FAX: 973-728-2106. E-mail: wmtl@wmtl.org. Web Site: www.wmtl.org. *Dir,* Deborah Maynard; *Head, Ch, Libr Assoc,* Theresa McArthur; Tel: 973-728-2823, E-mail: mcarthur@wmtl.org; *Head, Ref,* Joanne Grady; Tel: 973-728-2885, E-mail: grady@wmtl.org; *Librn,* Elaine Bindler; E-mail: bindler@wmtl.org; *Ref Librn,* Bruce Gilliard; E-mail: gilliard@wmtl.org; *Circ Supvr,* Elizabeth Frey; Tel: 973-728-2891, E-mail: frey@wmtl.org; *Ref & Teen Serv,* Elyse Schear; E-mail: schear@wmtl.org; Staff 6 (MLS 4.5, Non-MLS 1.5)
Founded 1954. Pop 25,850; Circ 143,280
Library Holdings: Audiobooks 2,773; CDs 14; DVDs 2,429; e-books 544; Electronic Media & Resources 12; Bk Titles 44,275; Per Subs 100
Automation Activity & Vendor Info: (Cataloging) SIRSI WorkFlows; (Circulation) SIRSI WorkFlows; (ILL) JerseyCat; (OPAC) SIRSI-iBistro
Database Vendor: CountryWatch, EBSCOhost, Facts on File, Gale Cengage Learning, Overdrive, Inc, Oxford Online, ProQuest, ReferenceUSA
Wireless access
Partic in PALS Plus, The Computer Consortium of Passaic County Libraries
Open Mon-Fri 10-8, Sat 9-5, Sun 12-4
Friends of the Library Group

WEST NEW YORK

P WEST NEW YORK PUBLIC LIBRARY, 425 60th St, 07093-2211. SAN 310-5954. Tel: 201-295-5135. Reference Tel: 201-295-5137. FAX: 201-662-1473. E-mail: wnypubliclibrary@gmail.com. Web Site: www.wnypl.org. *Dir,* Weiliang Lai; *Cat, Tech Serv,* Nina Rhodes; *Ref,* Estela Longo-Salvador; Staff 3 (MLS 3)
Founded 1916. Pop 49,708
Jan 2010-Dec 2010 Income $831,386, State $10,889, City $820,497. Mats Exp $76,000, Books $66,000, Per/Ser (Incl. Access Fees) $4,000, Other Print Mats $1,000, AV Mat $5,000. Sal $456,063 (Prof $150,000)
Library Holdings: AV Mats 1,650; CDs 310; DVDs 400; Large Print Bks 300; Bk Titles 61,000; Bk Vols 62,200; Per Subs 120; Talking Bks 190
Subject Interests: Family literacy, Jerseyana, Local hist, Parenting, Spanish
Automation Activity & Vendor Info: (Acquisitions) Innovative Interfaces, Inc; (Cataloging) Innovative Interfaces, Inc; (Circulation) Innovative Interfaces, Inc; (OPAC) Innovative Interfaces, Inc; (Serials) Innovative Interfaces, Inc
Database Vendor: EBSCOhost, ProQuest
Wireless access
Partic in LibraryLinkNJ, The New Jersey Library Cooperative
Open Mon, Tues & Thurs 9-8, Wed, Fri & Sat 9-5
Friends of the Library Group

WEST ORANGE

M KESSLER FOUNDATION MEDICAL LIBRARY*, 1199 Pleasant Valley Way, 07052-1499. SAN 375-7358. Tel: 973-324-3523. FAX: 973-243-6835. *Tech Serv,* Marita F Delmonico; Staff 2 (MLS 1, Non-MLS 1)
Founded 1948
Library Holdings: Bk Titles 1,300; Per Subs 68
Automation Activity & Vendor Info: (Acquisitions) LibraryWorld, Inc; (Cataloging) LibraryWorld, Inc; (Circulation) LibraryWorld, Inc; (OPAC) LibraryWorld, Inc; (Serials) LibraryWorld, Inc
Database Vendor: EBSCOhost, OVID Technologies
Function: For res purposes
Partic in Basic Health Sciences Library Network
Open Mon-Fri 8-4
Restriction: Internal circ only

L LAW LIBRARY OF WOLFF & SAMSON*, One Boland Dr, 07052. SAN 372-414X. Tel: 973-530-2146. FAX: 973-530-2346. *Librn,* Rosemary Walton; E-mail: rwalton@wolffsamson.com
Library Holdings: Bk Vols 12,000
Wireless access
Partic in LibraryLinkNJ, The New Jersey Library Cooperative
Open Mon-Fri 9-4:30

P WEST ORANGE FREE PUBLIC LIBRARY*, 46 Mount Pleasant Ave, 07052-4903. SAN 351-5583. Tel: 973-736-0198. Reference Tel: 973-736-0196. FAX: 973-736-1655. Web Site: www.wopl.org. *Dir,* Renee Riczker; E-mail: rriczker@westorangelibrary.org; *Head, Coll Serv,* Catherine LaBelle; E-mail: clabelle@westorangelibrary.org; *Head, Ref Serv,* Mary-Jean Gurzenda; *Head, Youth Serv,* Faith Boyle; E-mail: fboyle@westorangelibrary.org; *Circ Librn,* Debra Sarr; E-mail: dsarr@westorangelibrary.org; *Ref Librn,* Svetlana Peker; E-mail: lpeker@westorangelibrary.org; *Youth Serv Librn,* John Arthur; E-mail: jarthur@westorangelibrary.org; Staff 7 (MLS 7)
Founded 1948. Pop 46,207; Circ 364,000
Jan 2013-Dec 2013 Income $2,334,671
Library Holdings: Audiobooks 12,918; CDs 1,993; DVDs 6,741; e-books 4,563; Large Print Bks 692; Bk Vols 143,000; Per Subs 192
Automation Activity & Vendor Info: (Acquisitions) Innovative Interfaces, Inc; (Cataloging) Innovative Interfaces, Inc; (Circulation) Innovative Interfaces, Inc; (ILL) Auto-Graphics, Inc; (OPAC) Innovative Interfaces, Inc; (Serials) Innovative Interfaces, Inc
Database Vendor: Baker & Taylor, EBSCOhost, Facts on File, Grolier Online, LearningExpress, Mergent Online, Newsbank, ProQuest, ReferenceUSA, TLC (The Library Corporation)
Wireless access
Function: Adult bk club, After school storytime, Audiobks via web, Bk club(s), Bks on CD, Children's prog, Computer training, Computers for patron use, Copy machines, E-Reserves, Electronic databases & coll, Free DVD rentals, Homebound delivery serv, ILL available, Magnifiers for reading, Microfiche/film & reading machines, Music CDs, Online cat, Online ref, OverDrive digital audio bks, Preschool reading prog, Prog for adults, Prog for children & young adult, Pub access computers, Ref serv available, Spoken cassettes & CDs, Story hour, Summer reading prog, Tax forms, Teen prog, Telephone ref, Web-catalog
Partic in LibraryLinkNJ, The New Jersey Library Cooperative
Open Mon, Wed & Thurs 10-9, Tues & Fri 10-5:30, Sat 9-5, Sun (Winter) 1-5

WEST PATERSON

P ALFRED H BAUMANN FREE PUBLIC LIBRARY*, Seven Brophy Lane, 07424-2733. SAN 310-5989. Tel: 973-345-8120. FAX: 973-345-8196. Web Site: www.wpatlibrary.org. *Dir,* Robert E Lindsley; Staff 1 (MLS 1)
Founded 1962. Pop 11,400; Circ 30,834
Library Holdings: Bk Titles 37,000; Bk Vols 43,000; Per Subs 95
Automation Activity & Vendor Info: (Cataloging) SirsiDynix; (Circulation) SirsiDynix; (OPAC) SirsiDynix
Wireless access
Partic in PALS Plus, The Computer Consortium of Passaic County Libraries
Open Mon-Thurs 10-9, Fri 10-5, Sat 10-3, Sun (Oct-May) 12-3

WEST TRENTON

S ANN KLEIN FORENSIC CENTER*, Thomas A Hall Sr Library, Stuyvesant Ave, 08628. (Mail add: PO Box 7717, 08628-0717). Tel: 609-633-0884. FAX: 609-633-2817. *In Charge,* Dorothea Okwei; Staff 4 (MLS 1, Non-MLS 3)
Library Holdings: DVDs 50; Bk Titles 2,190; Bk Vols 2,245; Per Subs 31; Videos 200
Function: Provide serv for the mentally ill

Partic in LibraryLinkNJ, The New Jersey Library Cooperative
Open Mon-Fri 9-3:15

WEST WINDSOR

J MERCER COUNTY COMMUNITY COLLEGE LIBRARY, West Windsor Campus, 1200 Old Trenton Rd, 08550. SAN 351-4471. Tel: 609-570-3554, 609-570-3560. Circulation Tel: 609-570-3561. Interlibrary Loan Service Tel: 609-570-3550. FAX: 609-570-3845. E-mail: library@mccc.edu. Web Site: www.mccc.edu/student_library.shtml. *Dir, Libr Serv,* Pamela A Price; Tel: 609-570-3562, E-mail: pricep@mccc.edu; *Ref Librn,* Martin Crabtree; Tel: 609-570-3545, E-mail: crabtrem@mccc.edu; *Libr Assoc/Circ,* Lavanya Srinath; Tel: 609-570-3558, E-mail: srinathl@mccc.edu; *Libr Assoc/Copy Cataloger,* Position Currently Open; *Ref Spec,* Daniel Calandro; E-mail: calandrd@mccc.edu; *Libr Tech,* Mary McBride; Tel: 609-570-3179, E-mail: mcbridem@mccc.edu; *Acq,* Position Currently Open; *Cat,* Position Currently Open; Staff 9 (MLS 6, Non-MLS 3)
Founded 1947. Enrl 6,500; Fac 145; Highest Degree: Associate
Library Holdings: Bk Titles 54,559; Bk Vols 69,063; Per Subs 605
Special Collections: Mortuary Science Coll, disks & v-tapes
Subject Interests: Gen acad libr res
Automation Activity & Vendor Info: (Acquisitions) SirsiDynix; (Cataloging) SirsiDynix; (Circulation) SirsiDynix; (Course Reserve) SirsiDynix; (ILL) SirsiDynix; (Media Booking) SirsiDynix; (OPAC) SirsiDynix; (Serials) SirsiDynix
Database Vendor: EBSCOhost, Factiva.com, Gale Cengage Learning, JSTOR, LexisNexis, OCLC WorldShare Interlibrary Loan, ProQuest, ReferenceUSA, Westlaw, Wilson - Wilson Web
Wireless access
Publications: Library Pathfinders (Annual); Library Student Workers Handbook (Library handbook); Periodicals Directory (Union list of periodicals)
Partic in LibraryLinkNJ, The New Jersey Library Cooperative; Lyrasis; Virtual Academic Library Environment
Special Services for the Deaf - Assisted listening device; Assistive tech; Closed caption videos
Special Services for the Blind - Assistive/Adapted tech devices, equip & products
Open Mon-Thurs 8:30am-9pm, Fri 8:30-5, Sat 12-4

Departmental Libraries:

JAMES KERNEY CAMPUS, N Broad & Academy Sts, Trenton, 08690, SAN 351-4501. Tel: 609-570-3179. FAX: 609-394-8167. *Libr Tech,* Mary McBride; E-mail: mcbridem@mccc.edu; Staff 1 (Non-MLS 1)
Founded 1975. Enrl 2,000; Fac 22; Highest Degree: Associate
Library Holdings: Bk Titles 5,800; Per Subs 63
Special Collections: African Art Books; Literacy
Subject Interests: Gen acad, High sch level res
Open Mon-Thurs 9-8, Fri 9-5, Sat 9-12
Restriction: Open to students, fac & staff, Pub use on premises

WESTAMPTON

P BURLINGTON COUNTY LIBRARY*, Five Pioneer Blvd, 08060. SAN 350-9281. Tel: 609-267-9660. FAX: 609-267-4091. TDD: 609-267-2978. E-mail: referenc@bcls.lib.nj.us. Web Site: www.bcls.lib.nj.us. *Actg Dir,* Ranjna Das; Tel: 609-267-9660, Ext 3021, E-mail: rdas@bcls.lib.nj.us; *Asst Dir, Ref & Adult Serv,* Margaret Delaney; Tel: 609-267-9660, Ext 3074, E mail: mdelaney@bcls.lib.nj.us; *Head, Tech Serv, ILL Coordr,* Vicky Kolo; Tel: 609-267-9660, Ext 3020, E-mail: vkolo@bcls.lib.nj.us; *Circ Coordr,* Kim Gould; Tel: 609-267-9660, Ext 3037, E-mail: kgould@bcls.lib.nj.us; *Youth Serv Coordr,* Carole McKiernan; Tel: 609-267-9660, Ext 3068, E-mail: cmckiern@bcls.lib.nj.us; Staff 150 (MLS 45, Non-MLS 105)
Founded 1921. Pop 352,917; Circ 2,184,598
Jan 2011-Dec 2011 Income (Main Library and Branch(s)) $12,511,530, State $133,427, County $11,921,181, Other $456,922. Mats Exp $1,000,572, Books $643,578, Per/Ser (Incl. Access Fees) $70,058, AV Mat $170,784, Electronic Ref Mat (Incl. Access Fees) $116,152. Sal $5,629,587
Library Holdings: AV Mats 96,381; e-books 5,012; Large Print Bks 21,756; Bk Vols 756,007; Per Subs 863; Videos 64,849
Special Collections: Local Newspapers from 1835, bd & microfilm. State Document Depository
Subject Interests: Genealogy, Local hist
Automation Activity & Vendor Info: (Acquisitions) Horizon; (Cataloging) Horizon; (Circulation) Horizon; (ILL) OCLC; (OPAC) Horizon; (Serials) Horizon
Database Vendor: EBSCO Auto Repair Reference, EBSCO Information Services, EBSCOhost, Facts on File, Foundation Center, Gale Cengage Learning, infoUSA, LearningExpress, Library Automation Technologies, Inc. (LAT), Overdrive, Inc, ProQuest, ReferenceUSA, SirsiDynix, ValueLine
Wireless access
Function: Adult bk club, Adult literacy prog, Art exhibits, Audiobks via web, AV serv, Bk club(s), Bks on cassette, Bks on CD, CD-ROM, Chess club, Children's prog, Citizenship assistance, Computer training, Computers for patron use, Copy machines, Digital talking bks, Doc delivery serv, e-mail serv, E-Reserves, Electronic databases & coll, Exhibits, Family literacy, Fax serv, Free DVD rentals, Games & aids for the handicapped, Genealogy discussion group, Govt ref serv, Handicapped accessible, Holiday prog, Home delivery & serv to Sr ctr & nursing homes, Homebound delivery serv, Homework prog, ILL available, Literacy & newcomer serv, Magnifiers for reading, Mail & tel request accepted, Mail loans to mem, Mus passes, Music CDs, Notary serv, Online cat, Online ref, Online searches, Outreach serv, Outside serv via phone, mail, e-mail & web, OverDrive digital audio bks, Passport agency, Photocopying/Printing, Preschool outreach, Prog for adults, Prog for children & young adult, Pub access computers, Ref & res, Ref serv available, Ref serv in person, Res libr, Res performed for a fee, Scanner, Senior computer classes, Senior outreach, Spoken cassettes & CDs, Spoken cassettes & DVDs, Story hour, Summer reading prog, Tax forms, Teen prog, Telephone ref, VHS videos, Web-catalog, Wheelchair accessible, Workshops
Member Libraries: Bass River Community Library; Beverly Free Library; Delanco Public Library; Florence Township Public Library; Library Company of Burlington; Mount Holly Public Library; Sally Stretch Keen Memorial Library; The Crosswicks Library Co
Partic in Burlington Libraries Information Consortium; Lyrasis
Special Services for the Deaf - Assisted listening device; Assistive tech; Bks on deafness & sign lang; Closed caption videos; TTY equip
Special Services for the Blind - Assistive/Adapted tech devices, equip & products; Audio mat; Bks on cassette; Bks on CD; Cassettes; Copier with enlargement capabilities; Descriptive video serv (DVS); Extensive large print coll; Home delivery serv; Large print & cassettes; Large print bks; Low vision equip; Magnifiers; Playaways (bks on MP3); Sound rec
Open Mon 9-9, Tues-Fri 10-9, Sat 9-5, Sun 1-5
Friends of the Library Group

Branches: 7

BORDENTOWN BRANCH, 18 E Union St, Bordentown, 08505, SAN 350-9311. Tel: 609-298-0622. E-mail: bt@bcls.lib.nj.us. *Br Mgr,* Suzi Freedman; E-mail: sfreedma@bcls.lib.nj.us; Staff 14 (MLS 4, Non-MLS 10)
Library Holdings: Large Print Bks 756; Bk Vols 44,000; Per Subs 95
Special Collections: Bordentown Military Institute Yearbooks; Bordentown Regional High School Yearbooks; Bordentown Register (May 25, 1855+ on microfilm); New Jersey-Bordentown Coll
Open Mon-Thurs (Winter) 10-8:30, Fri & Sat 10-5; Mon-Thurs (Summer) 10-8:30, Fri 10-5
Friends of the Library Group

CINNAMINSON BRANCH, 1619 Riverton Rd, Cinnaminson, 08077, SAN 350-9346. Tel: 856-829-9340. FAX: 856-829-2243. E-mail: cb@bcls.lib.nj.us. *Br Mgr,* Eileen Rauth; E-mail: erauth@bcls.lib.nj.us; *Ad,* Christina Chichester; E-mail: cchiches@bcls.lib.nj.us; *Ad,* Scott Homan; E-mail: shoman@bcls.lib.nj.us; *Youth Serv Supvr,* Elaine Hollowell; E-mail: ehollowe@bcls.lib.nj.us
Library Holdings: Bk Vols 82,537
Open Mon-Thurs 10-8:30, Fri & Sat 10-5
Friends of the Library Group

EVESHAM BRANCH, Evesham Municipal Complex, 984 Tuckerton Rd, Marlton, 08053, SAN 350-9370. Tel: 856-983-1444. FAX: 856-983-4939. E-mail: ev@bcls.lib.nj.us. *Br Mgr, Ref Librn,* Susan Szymanik; E-mail: sszymani@bcls.lib.nj.us; *Ref Librn,* Carol Lipinski; E-mail: clipinsk@bcls.lib.nj.us; *Ref Librn,* Katheryn Woodworth; E-mail: kwoodwor@bcls.lib.nj.us; *Ch Serv,* Laurie Bowden; E-mail: lbowden@bcls.lib.nj.us; *Ch Serv,* Holly Hoskins; E-mail: hhoskins@bcls.lib.nj.us; Staff 19 (MLS 5, Non-MLS 14)
Library Holdings: Bk Vols 100,000
Open Mon-Thurs 10-8:30, Fri 10-5, Sat (Sept-June) 10-5, Sun (Sept-June) 1-5
Friends of the Library Group

MAPLE SHADE BRANCH, 200 Stiles Ave, Maple Shade, 08052. Tel: 856-779-9767. FAX: 856-779-0033. E-mail: ma@bcls.lib.nj.us. *Br Mgr,* Position Currently Open; *Ref Librn,* Concetta Verderame; E-mail: cverdera@bcls.lib.nj.us; Staff 12 (MLS 2, Non-MLS 10)
Pop 20,000
Library Holdings: Audiobooks 1,000; DVDs 3,000; Bk Vols 53,000; Per Subs 85
Open Mon-Thurs 10-8:30, Fri & Sat 10-5

PEMBERTON COMMUNITY LIBRARY, 16 Broadway, Browns Mills, 08015, SAN 328-9281. Tel: 609-893-8262. FAX: 609-893-7547. E-mail: p@bcls.lib.nj.us. Web Site: www.bcls.lib.nj.us/libraries/pemberton. *Br Mgr,* Nancy Breece; E-mail: nbreece@bcls.lib.nj.us; *Ch Serv,* Theresa Preziosa; E-mail: tprezios@bcls.lib.nj.us; *Ref Serv, Ad,* Surinder Kaur; E-mail: skaur@bcls.lib.nj.us; *Ref Serv, Ad,* Sharon Siciliano; E-mail: ssicilia@bcls.lib.nj.us; Staff 15 (MLS 4, Non-MLS 11)
Founded 1906. Pop 32,000; Circ 141,000
Library Holdings: Bk Vols 61,000
Special Collections: Foreign Language Coll; Literacy Coll
Function: Adult bk club, Art exhibits, Audiobks via web, Bks on cassette, Bks on CD, CD-ROM, Children's prog, Computer training, Computers for patron use, Copy machines, E-Reserves, Electronic databases & coll, Free DVD rentals, Handicapped accessible, Holiday

prog, Homebound delivery serv, ILL available, Magnifiers for reading, Mail & tel request accepted, Music CDs, Notary serv, Online cat, Online ref, Online searches, Outreach serv, OverDrive digital audio bks, Photocopying/Printing, Preschool outreach, Prog for adults, Prog for children & young adult, Pub access computers, Ref serv available, Scanner, Spoken cassettes & CDs, Spoken cassettes & DVDs, Story hour, Summer reading prog, Tax forms, Telephone ref, VHS videos, Wheelchair accessible
Special Services for the Deaf - Adult & family literacy prog; Closed caption videos
Special Services for the Blind - Audio mat; Bks available with recordings; Bks on cassette; Bks on CD; Large print bks; Large type calculator; Low vision equip; Magnifiers; Playaways (bks on MP3)
Open Mon-Thurs (Winter) 10-8:30, Fri & Sat 10-5, Sun 1-5; Mon-Thurs (Summer) 10-8:30, Fri 10-5
Friends of the Library Group

PINELANDS, 39 Allen Ave, Medford, 08055, SAN 350-9400. Tel: 609-654-6113. FAX: 609-953-2142. E-mail: mf@bcls.lib.nj.us. *Br Mgr,* Wei-Jie Cui; E-mail: wcui@bcls.lib.nj.us; Staff 8 (MLS 4, Non-MLS 4)
Library Holdings: Bk Vols 72,000; Per Subs 75
Special Collections: NJ Coll; Pinelands Coastal Coll
Open Mon-Thurs 10-8:30, Fri & Sat 10-5
Friends of the Library Group

RIVERTON FREE BRANCH, 306 Main St, Riverton, 08077, SAN 310-4826. Tel: 856-829-2476. Web Site: www.rivertonlibrary.burlco.org. *Br Mgr,* Michael Robinson; E-mail: mrobinso@bcls.lib.nj.us; *Asst Librn,* Jean Markovitz
Founded 1899. Circ 48,079
Library Holdings: AV Mats 1,500; Bk Vols 24,000; Per Subs 40
Open Mon-Thurs 9-5 & 6:30-8:30, Fri 9-12, Sat 9-4, Sun 1-5
Friends of the Library Group

Bookmobiles: 1. Bkmobile Coordr, Paula Manzella. Bk titles 5,189

WESTFIELD

P WESTFIELD MEMORIAL LIBRARY*, 550 E Broad St, 07090. SAN 310-6012. Tel: 908-789-4090. FAX: 908-789-0921. Web Site: www.wmlnj.org. *Dir,* Philip Israel; *Asst Dir,* Kathy Muhm; *Adult Serv, Ref,* Jennifer Schulze; *Tech Serv,* Darla Wagner; Staff 19 (MLS 7, Non-MLS 12)
Founded 1872. Pop 30,291; Circ 350,000
Jan 2010-Dec 2010 Income $2,800,000. Mats Exp $320,000. Sal $1,300,000
Library Holdings: Bk Titles 159,318; Bk Vols 195,509; Per Subs 202
Special Collections: Oral History
Subject Interests: Local hist
Automation Activity & Vendor Info: (Circulation) SirsiDynix; (OPAC) SirsiDynix
Database Vendor: EBSCOhost, Gale Cengage Learning, ProQuest
Wireless access
Publications: Take Note (Newsletter)
Partic in LibraryLinkNJ, The New Jersey Library Cooperative
Open Mon-Thurs 9:30-9, Fri & Sat 9:30-5, Sun 1-5
Friends of the Library Group

WESTMONT

S THE PATENT BOARD RESEARCH LIBRARY*, 222 Haddon Ave, 3rd Flr, 08108. (Mail add: One N La Salle, 5th Flr, Chicago, 60602), SAN 325-7568. Tel: 856-671-6800. Administration Tel: 312-205-7000. FAX: 856-671-6801. Administration FAX: 312-205-7001. E-mail: info@patentboard.com. Web Site: www.patentboard.com. *Managing Dir,* Jude Reter; *Sr Assoc, Data Coll,* Denise Forner
Library Holdings: Bk Vols 1,000
Subject Interests: Patents
Restriction: Staff use only

WESTVILLE

P WESTVILLE PUBLIC LIBRARY*, 1035 Broadway, 08093. SAN 310-6020. Tel: 856-456-0357. FAX: 856-742-8190. E-mail: westvillelibrary@comcast.net. Web Site: www.westvillelibrary.com. *Dir,* Gwen Carotenuto; *Librn,* Mary Ward
Founded 1924. Pop 4,500
Library Holdings: Bk Titles 22,000; Per Subs 54
Automation Activity & Vendor Info: (Cataloging) SirsiDynix; (Circulation) SirsiDynix
Wireless access
Partic in LOGIN (Libraries of Gloucester, Salem & Cumberland Information Network)
Open Tues & Thurs 10-8, Wed 10-5, Fri 10-2, Sat 1-4

WESTWOOD

P WESTWOOD FREE PUBLIC LIBRARY*, 49 Park Ave, 07675. SAN 310-6055. Tel: 201-664-0583. FAX: 201-664-6088. E-mail: westwood@bccls.org. Web Site: www.bccls.org/westwood. *Dir,* Martha Urbiel; E-mail: urbiel@bccls.org; *Head, Circ,* Kathy Carvalho; *Head, Tech Serv,* Joyce Creaden; *Ch,* Janet Dunn; *Ref Librn,* Susan Sampietro; *Bus Mgr,* Karen Carratura; Staff 13 (MLS 3, Non-MLS 10)
Founded 1919. Pop 10,999; Circ 127,000
Library Holdings: Bk Titles 51,000; Bk Vols 53,086; Per Subs 90
Special Collections: Literacy Program Coll
Automation Activity & Vendor Info: (Acquisitions) SirsiDynix; (Cataloging) SirsiDynix; (Circulation) SirsiDynix; (ILL) SirsiDynix
Database Vendor: SirsiDynix
Wireless access
Partic in Bergen County Cooperative Library System
Open Mon, Tues & Thurs 10-9, Wed & Fri 10-5, Sat (Sept-June) 10-4, Sun (Oct-May) 1-5
Friends of the Library Group

WHARTON

P WHARTON PUBLIC LIBRARY*, 15 S Main St, 07885. SAN 310-6063. Tel: 973-361-1333. Web Site: www.whartonlibrary.org. *Dir,* Position Currently Open; Staff 5 (MLS 1, Non-MLS 4)
Founded 1891. Pop 6,298; Circ 38,856
Library Holdings: Audiobooks 180; CDs 115; DVDs 480; Large Print Bks 88; Bk Vols 24,000; Per Subs 59; Talking Bks 354; Videos 100
Special Collections: Municipal Document Depository; Oral History
Database Vendor: SirsiDynix
Wireless access
Partic in LibraryLinkNJ, The New Jersey Library Cooperative; Morris Automated Information Network
Open Mon-Thurs 10-8, Fri 10-5, Sat (Sept-May) 9-1
Friends of the Library Group

WHIPPANY

S CONVERSE CONSULTANTS EAST LIBRARY*, Rte 10 W, Ste 10, 07981. SAN 310-0510. Tel: 973-428-0934. FAX: 973-428-0713. E-mail: whippany@converseconsultants.com. Web Site: www.converseconsultants.com. *Librn,* Judy Gonzalez
Library Holdings: Bk Vols 2,000; Per Subs 20
Subject Interests: Eng, Environ, Geotechnical

S JEWISH HISTORICAL SOCIETY OF METROWEST LIBRARY*, 901 Rte 10 E, 07981-1156. SAN 375-3123. Tel: 973-929-2994, 973-929-2995. FAX: 973-428-8327. Web Site: www.jhsmw.org. *Archivist,* Jill Hershorin; E-mail: jhershorin@jhsmw.org
Founded 1990
Library Holdings: AV Mats 100; Bk Titles 120; Per Subs 10
Special Collections: Late 19th Century to Present. Oral History
Subject Interests: Ethnic hist, Judaica
Wireless access
Function: Res libr
Publications: Newsletter; Technical Leaflets
Restriction: Access at librarian's discretion

P MORRIS COUNTY LIBRARY, 30 E Hanover Ave, 07981. SAN 310-6098. Tel: 973-285-6930. Interlibrary Loan Service Tel: 973-285-6961. Reference Tel: 973-285-6969. Administration Tel: 973-285-6934. Automation Services Tel: 973-631-5353. Information Services Tel: 973-285-6970. Interlibrary Loan Service FAX: 973-285-6965. Reference FAX: 973-285-6962. Administration FAX: 973-285-6959. Web Site: www.mclib.info. *Dir, Libr Serv,* Lynne Olver; E-mail: LOlver@co.morris.nj.us; *Head, Ch,* Princess Thomas; Tel: 973-285-6980, E-mail: PThomas@co.morris.nj.us; *Head, Circ,* Mary Sanders; E-mail: MSanders@co.morris.nj.us; *Head, Media Serv,* Ellen Stringer; Tel: 973-285-6979, E-mail: EStringer@co.morris.nj.us; *Head, Reader Serv,* Mark Anderson; E-mail: MAnderson@co.morris.nj.us; *Head, Ref Serv,* Darren O'Neill; E-mail: DOneill@co.morris.nj.us; *Head, Tech Serv,* Vidya Manohar; Tel: 973-285-6955, Fax: 973-285-6960, E-mail: VManohar@co.morris.nj.us; Staff 64 (MLS 24, Non-MLS 40)
Founded 1922. Pop 492,276; Circ 519,796
Jan 2013-Dec 2013 Income $3,657,342. Mats Exp $322,625, Books $160,894, Per/Ser (Incl. Access Fees) $59,028, AV Mat $27,623, Electronic Ref Mat (Incl. Access Fees) $73,359. Sal $3,070,460
Library Holdings: Audiobooks 5,935; AV Mats 39,726; Bks on Deafness & Sign Lang 307; CDs 21,598; DVDs 15,681; e-books 5,864; e-journals 50; Large Print Bks 7,210; Microforms 110; Music Scores 2,494; Bk Vols 250,108; Per Subs 860
Special Collections: Local Newspaper 1900-Present; Morris Authors; New Adult Readers; New Jersey History; Sheet Music. State Document Depository
Subject Interests: Bus, Law, Local hist, Music

Automation Activity & Vendor Info: (Acquisitions) Innovative Interfaces, Inc; (Cataloging) Innovative Interfaces, Inc; (Circulation) Innovative Interfaces, Inc; (ILL) OCLC; (OPAC) Innovative Interfaces, Inc; (Serials) EBSCO Online
Database Vendor: Baker & Taylor, Booksite, BWI, CountryWatch, EBSCOhost, Facts on File, H W Wilson, Ingram Library Services, JSTOR, LexisNexis, Marquis Who's Who, Mergent Online, Newsbank, OCLC WorldShare Interlibrary Loan, OCLC-RLG, Overdrive, Inc, Oxford Online, ProQuest, ReferenceUSA, Standard & Poor's, ValueLine, Westlaw, Wilson - Wilson Web, YBP Library Services
Wireless access
Function: Art exhibits, Audiobks via web, Children's prog, Computer training, Computers for patron use, Copy machines, Digital talking bks, Distance learning, Electronic databases & coll, Home delivery & serv to Sr ctr & nursing homes, ILL available, Magnifiers for reading, Microfiche/film & reading machines, Mus passes, Notary serv, Online ref, Preschool reading prog, Ref & res, Scanner, Summer reading prog, Tax forms, Web-catalog
Partic in LibraryLinkNJ, The New Jersey Library Cooperative; Morris Automated Information Network; OCLC Online Computer Library Center, Inc
Special Services for the Deaf - Assisted listening device; Bks on deafness & sign lang; Captioned film dep; Closed caption videos; Coll on deaf educ; Deaf publ; High interest/low vocabulary bks; Pocket talkers; TDD equip; TTY equip
Special Services for the Blind - Accessible computers; Bks available with recordings; Bks on cassette; Bks on CD; Large print bks; Magnifiers; PC for handicapped; Talking bks; ZoomText magnification & reading software
Open Mon-Thurs 9-9, Fri & Sat 9-5, Sun (Sept-April) 1-5
Restriction: Non-circulating of rare bks

P WHIPPANONG LIBRARY*, 1000 Rte 10, 07981. SAN 310-6101. Tel: 973-428-2460. FAX: 973-515-3771. Web Site: www.whippanong.org. *Dir,* Sulekha Das; Staff 9 (MLS 2, Non-MLS 7)
Founded 1957. Pop 12,898; Circ 72,508
Jan 2011-Dec 2011 Income $464,416
Library Holdings: Audiobooks 2,527; CDs 508; DVDs 2,216; e-books 770; Bk Titles 36,821; Bk Vols 42,813; Per Subs 80
Automation Activity & Vendor Info: (Cataloging) Innovative Interfaces, Inc; (Circulation) Innovative Interfaces, Inc; (ILL) Innovative Interfaces, Inc; (OPAC) Innovative Interfaces, Inc; (Serials) Innovative Interfaces, Inc
Wireless access
Partic in Morris Info Network
Open Mon, Tues & Thurs 9-8, Wed 9-5, Fri 9-2, Sat 9-1
Friends of the Library Group

WHITEHOUSE STATION

P READINGTON TOWNSHIP LIBRARY*, 255 Main St, 08889. (Mail add: PO Box 87, 08889-0087). Tel: 908-534-4421. FAX: 908-534-4421. E-mail: rtlibrary@hotmail.com. Web Site: www.hclibrary.us. *Librn,* Karen Konn
Library Holdings: AV Mats 1,000; Large Print Bks 125; Bk Vols 18,000; Per Subs 46; Talking Bks 150
Subject Interests: Local hist
Automation Activity & Vendor Info: (Cataloging) Innovative Interfaces, Inc; (Circulation) Innovative Interfaces, Inc; (OPAC) Innovative Interfaces, Inc
Wireless access
Mem of Hunterdon County Library
Open Mon, Wed & Fri 9-5, Tues & Thurs 12-8, Sat (Sept-July) 9-12
Friends of the Library Group

WILLIAMSTOWN

P FREE PUBLIC LIBRARY OF MONROE TOWNSHIP, 713 Marsha Ave, 08094. SAN 310-6128. Tel: 856-629-1212. Circulation Tel: 856-629-1212, Ext 210. Reference Tel: 856-629-1212, Ext 206. Administration Tel: 856-629-1212, Ext 203. FAX: 856-875-0191. Administration FAX: 856-629-5967. E-mail: info@MonroeTPL.org. Web Site: www.monroetpl.Org. *Dir,* Manuel Paredes; E-mail: MParedes@MonroeTPL.Org; *Ad, Ref Librn,* Martha Oxley; E-mail: MOxley@MonroeTPL.Org; *Cat Librn,* Lynn Harpool; E-mail: LHarpool@MonroeTPL.Org; *Ch,* Jennifer E Schillig; E-mail: JSchillig@MonroeTPL.Org; *Teen & Quarter Life Adult Librn,* DaVonne Armstrong; E-mail: DArmstrong@MonroeTPL.Org; Staff 13 (MLS 6, Non-MLS 7)
Founded 1969. Pop 40,274; Circ 121,400
Library Holdings: Bk Titles 71,000; Bk Vols 74,000; Per Subs 147; Talking Bks 2,500
Special Collections: Cinema Coll
Automation Activity & Vendor Info: (Cataloging) SirsiDynix; (Circulation) SirsiDynix; (OPAC) SirsiDynix
Wireless access
Publications: Library Lines (Monthly newsletter)
Partic in LibraryLinkNJ, The New Jersey Library Cooperative; LOGIN (Libraries of Gloucester, Salem & Cumberland Information Network)
Special Services for the Deaf - ADA equip
Special Services for the Blind - Accessible computers
Open Mon-Thurs 11-9, Fri 12-5, Sat 10-3
Friends of the Library Group

WILLINGBORO

P WILLINGBORO PUBLIC LIBRARY*, Willingboro Town Ctr, 220 Willingboro Pkwy, 08046. SAN 310-6152. Tel: 609-877-0476, 609-877-6668. FAX: 609-835-1699. E-mail: wipl@willingboro.org. Web Site: www.willingboro.org. *Dir,* Christine H King; Fax: 609-877-7941, E-mail: cking@willingboro.org; *Asst Libr Dir,* Christine M Hill; E-mail: cmhill@willingboro.org; *Head, Circ,* Dee Skwara; E-mail: dskwara@willingboro.org; *Head, Ref Serv,* Dr Susan Hacker; *Head, Youth Serv,* Sandra Cronce; E-mail: scronce@willingboro.org; *Syst Adminr,* Walt Smith; E-mail: wsmith@willingboro.org; Staff 19 (MLS 7, Non-MLS 12)
Founded 1960. Pop 33,008; Circ 104,000
Library Holdings: Bk Titles 75,566; Bk Vols 82,014; Per Subs 200
Special Collections: African American History Coll; Local History Coll
Automation Activity & Vendor Info: (Acquisitions) Horizon; (Cataloging) TLC (The Library Corporation); (Circulation) Horizon; (ILL) Horizon; (OPAC) Horizon
Database Vendor: EBSCOhost, Gale Cengage Learning, SirsiDynix
Wireless access
Function: Homebound delivery serv, ILL available, Magnifiers for reading, Online ref, Photocopying/Printing, Prog for adults, Prog for children & young adult, Spoken cassettes & CDs, Spoken cassettes & DVDs, Summer reading prog, Tax forms, Telephone ref, Wheelchair accessible
Partic in LibraryLinkNJ, The New Jersey Library Cooperative
Open Mon-Thurs 10-9, Sat 9-5
Friends of the Library Group

WOODBRIDGE

L GREENBAUM, ROWE, SMITH & DAVIS LLP*, Law Library, 99 Wood Ave S, 07095. SAN 323-6684. Tel: 732-549-5600. FAX: 732-549-1881. Web Site: www.greenbaumlaw.com. *Dir,* Leigh DeProspo; *Asst Librn,* Kathy Bruno; *Law Librn,* Carolyn Amon; Staff 3 (Non-MLS 3)
Library Holdings: Bk Vols 9,000
Wireless access
Partic in LibraryLinkNJ, The New Jersey Library Cooperative; New Jersey Law Librarians Association (NJLLA)
Open Mon-Fri 9-6

L WILENTZ, GOLDMAN & SPITZER*, Law Library, 90 Woodbridge Center Dr, 07095. SAN 372-4646. Tel: 732-855-6177. FAX: 732-726-6525. Web Site: www.wilentz.com. *Dir,* Shari Nisenson; E-mail: snisenson@wilentz.com; *Ref,* Laura J Vinci; Tel: 732-855-6140, Fax: 732-726-6503, E-mail: lvinci@wilentz.com; Staff 3 (MLS 1, Non-MLS 2)
Founded 1919
Library Holdings: Bk Vols 20,000

P WOODBRIDGE PUBLIC LIBRARY*, George Frederick Plaza, 07095. SAN 351-5648. Tel. 732-634-4450. Web Site: www.woodbridgelibrary.org. *Asst Libr Dir,* Patricia Anderson; E-mail: panderson@woodbrigelibrary.org; *Dir,* Position Currently Open; *Main Libr Supvr,* Linda Cooper; *Automation Sys Supvr,* Jerry Holtz; *Tech Serv Supvr,* Lynne Merz; *Adult Serv,* Jean Retkwa; *Ch Serv,* Nancy O'Grady; *YA Serv,* Natalie McGrath
Founded 1964. Pop 99,585
Special Collections: State Document Depository; US Document Depository
Subject Interests: Educ, Law
Automation Activity & Vendor Info: (Acquisitions) SirsiDynix; (Cataloging) SirsiDynix; (Circulation) SirsiDynix; (ILL) Baker & Taylor; (OPAC) SirsiDynix; (Serials) SirsiDynix
Database Vendor: Baker & Taylor, Bowker, Career Guidance Foundation, CountryWatch, Dialog, Dun & Bradstreet, EBSCOhost, Facts on File, Gale Cengage Learning, Greenwood Publishing Group, Grolier Online, H W Wilson, LearningExpress, Newsbank, ProQuest, Standard & Poor's, Westlaw, Wilson - Wilson Web
Wireless access
Function: Adult bk club, BA reader (adult literacy), Bks on cassette, Bks on CD, Bus archives, CD-ROM, Children's prog, Computer training, Computers for patron use, Copy machines, Electronic databases & coll, Govt ref serv, Handicapped accessible, Homebound delivery serv, ILL available, Music CDs, Online ref, Photocopying/Printing, Prog for children & young adult, Ref serv available, Telephone ref
Partic in OCLC Online Computer Library Center, Inc
Special Services for the Blind - Talking bks
Friends of the Library Group

WOODBURY

S GLOUCESTER COUNTY HISTORICAL SOCIETY LIBRARY*, 17 Hunter St, 08096-4605. SAN 310-6187. Tel: 856-845-4771. FAX: 856-845-0131. E-mail: gchs@net-gate.com. Web Site: www.rootsweb.ancestry.com/~njgchs. *Coordr,* Barbara Price
Founded 1903
Library Holdings: Microforms 3,200; Bk Titles 10,000; Per Subs 12
Special Collections: Genealogical Coll, doc, mss, typescripts, vital statistics; History of Gloucester County (Gloucester County Documents 1686-1900); Local Newspapers (Howell Family Coll), microfilm; South Jersey Church, local records; US Navy in Early 19th Century (Richard Somers Coll), doc
Subject Interests: Genealogy of the Del Valley-South Jersey area, Hist
Function: Res libr
Publications: Bulletin of the Gloucester County Historical Society (Quarterly)
Open Mon, Wed, Thurs & Fri 1-4, Tues 1-4 & 6-9:30
Restriction: Non-circulating

L GLOUCESTER COUNTY LAW LIBRARY*, 70 Hunter St, 08096. Tel: 856-686-7449. *Librn,* Diane Frank
Open Mon-Fri 8:30-4:30
Restriction: Non-circulating to the pub

M UNDERWOOD MEMORIAL HOSPITAL*, Medical Library, 509 N Broad St, 08096. SAN 320-7005. Tel: 856-845-0100, Ext 2901. FAX: 856-848-5752. Web Site: www.umhospital.org. *Librn,* Laurie Neblock; E-mail: neblockl@umhospital.org; Staff 1 (MLS 1)
Founded 1965
Library Holdings: Bk Titles 200; Per Subs 75
Database Vendor: EBSCOhost
Function: ILL available
Partic in Basic Health Sciences Library Network; Health Sciences Library Association of New Jersey
Restriction: Not open to pub

P WOODBURY PUBLIC LIBRARY*, 33 Delaware St, 08096. SAN 310-6209. Tel: 856-845-2611. E-mail: woodburylibrary@gmail.com. Web Site: www.woodburylibrary.org. *Dir,* Jean Wipf; *Head, Ch,* Mary Johnson; *Head, Circ,* Florence Meyer; *Syst Coordr,* Laurie Cranston
Founded 1790. Pop 10,350; Circ 80,000
Library Holdings: AV Mats 5,200; Bk Vols 57,000; Per Subs 75
Automation Activity & Vendor Info: (Acquisitions) SirsiDynix; (Cataloging) SirsiDynix; (Circulation) SirsiDynix
Database Vendor: EBSCOhost
Wireless access
Open Mon-Thurs 10:30-5 & 7-9, Fri 10:30-5, Sat (Sept-June) 10:30-3:30
Friends of the Library Group

WOODLAND PARK

J BERKELEY COLLEGE*, Walter A Brower Library, 44 Rifle Camp Rd, 07424. SAN 325-5573. Tel: 973-278-5400. FAX: 973-278-9141. E-mail: library@berkeleycollege.edu. Web Site: www.berkeleycollege.edu/library. *Dir of Libr Serv,* Marlene Doty; *Assoc Dir, Libr Serv,* Leslin Charles; E-mail: lhc@berkeleycollege.edu; Staff 3 (MLS 3)
Founded 1931. Enrl 640; Fac 25
Library Holdings: Bk Vols 5,400; Per Subs 91
Subject Interests: Bus mgt, Computers, Fashion, Humanities, Liberal arts, Mkt
Automation Activity & Vendor Info: (Cataloging) TLC (The Library Corporation); (Circulation) TLC (The Library Corporation); (OPAC) TLC (The Library Corporation)
Database Vendor: TLC (The Library Corporation)
Partic in OCLC Online Computer Library Center, Inc
Open Mon-Thurs 8am-9:30pm, Fri 8-4, Sat 9-4
Departmental Libraries:
MIDDLESEX CAMPUS, 430 Rahway Ave, Woodbridge, 07095, SAN 370-6966. Tel: 732-750-1800, Ext 2200. FAX: 732-726-9286. *Dir,* Bonnie Lafazan
Library Holdings: Bk Titles 4,500; Bk Vols 5,000; Per Subs 70
Subject Interests: Computer sci, Fashion, Legal
Open Mon-Thurs 8am-9pm, Fri 9-2
PARAMUS CAMPUS, 64 E Midland Ave, Paramus, 07652-3367, SAN 370-6958. Tel: 201-967-9667, Ext 1764. FAX: 201-265-6446. Web Site: berkeleycollege.edu/library. *Dir,* Maria Deptula; Staff 2 (MLS 1.5, Non-MLS 0.5)
Fac 2; Highest Degree: Bachelor
Library Holdings: DVDs 368; e-books 75,000; Electronic Media & Resources 17,500; Bk Titles 4,961; Bk Vols 5,205; Per Subs 48
Subject Interests: Interior design
Automation Activity & Vendor Info: (Acquisitions) TLC (The Library Corporation); (Cataloging) OCLC Connexion; (Circulation) TLC (The Library Corporation); (Course Reserve) TLC (The Library Corporation); (ILL) OCLC FirstSearch; (OPAC) TLC (The Library Corporation)
Database Vendor: Alexander Street Press, Baker & Taylor, College Source, CountryWatch, CQ Press, CredoReference, ebrary, EBSCOhost, Facts on File, Gale Cengage Learning, IBISWorld, LexisNexis, Material ConneXion, Mergent Online, Plunkett Research, Ltd, ProQuest, ReferenceUSA, TDNet, Westlaw
Open Mon-Thurs 8am-9pm, Fri 8-4, Sat 9-2
Restriction: Authorized patrons

WOOD-RIDGE

P WOOD-RIDGE MEMORIAL LIBRARY*, 231 Hackensack St, 07075. SAN 310-6179. Tel: 201-438-2455. FAX: 201-438-8399. E-mail: wrdgcirc@bccls.org. *Dir,* Christine Hartigan; Staff 2 (MLS 2)
Founded 1931. Pop 8,000; Circ 50,000
Library Holdings: Bk Vols 39,926; Per Subs 95
Special Collections: Local History Coll, (Wood-Ridge)
Automation Activity & Vendor Info: (Cataloging) SirsiDynix; (Circulation) SirsiDynix; (OPAC) SirsiDynix
Wireless access
Partic in Bergen County Cooperative Library System; LibraryLinkNJ, The New Jersey Library Cooperative
Open Mon-Thurs 10-9, Fri 10-5, Sat 10-3
Friends of the Library Group

WOODSTOWN

P WOODSTOWN-PILESGROVE PUBLIC LIBRARY*, 14 School Lane, 08098-1331. SAN 310-6217. Tel: 856-769-0098. Web Site: www.wplibrary.net. *Librn,* Ruth T Fritz; Staff 1 (MLS 1)
Founded 1810. Pop 13,000; Circ 22,575
Library Holdings: Audiobooks 200; DVDs 85; Bk Vols 50,000; Per Subs 35
Special Collections: New Jersey Historical Books
Wireless access
Function: Story hour
Partic in S Jersey Regional Libr Network
Open Mon-Thurs 11-1, 2:30-4:30 & 7-9 (11-1 & 7-9 Summer), Fri 11-1, Sat 10-12, Sun 1:30-3:30
Restriction: ID required to use computers (Ltd hrs)

WRIGHTSTOWN

S MID STATE CORRECTIONAL FACILITY LIBRARY*, Range Rd, 08562. (Mail add: PO Box 866, 08562-0866), SAN 375-7048. Tel: 609-723-4221, Ext 8432. FAX: 609-723-0235. *In Charge,* Emma Pervall
Library Holdings: Bk Vols 4,700; Per Subs 20
Special Collections: Law Library
Open Mon-Thurs 8:30-10:45 & 12:30-3:15, Fri 8:30-10:45 & 12:30-2:45

WYCKOFF

P WYCKOFF PUBLIC LIBRARY*, 200 Woodland Ave, 07481. SAN 310-6225. Tel: 201-891-4866. FAX: 201-891-3892. Web Site: www.wyckofflibrary.org. *Dir,* Mary Witherell; *Ad,* Marilyn Force; E-mail: force@bccls.org; *Ch,* Denise Marchetti; *Ref Librn,* Roberta Knauer; *Ref Librn,* Katie Nellen; *Teen Librn/Ref,* Barbara Weber; *Circ Supvr,* Susan Lazzari; Staff 21.5 (MLS 4.5, Non-MLS 17)
Founded 1921. Pop 16,508; Circ 259,376
Jan 2008-Dec 2008 Income $1,560,018, State $17,712, City $1,532,306, Locally Generated Income $10,000. Mats Exp $177,000, Books $110,000, Per/Ser (Incl. Access Fees) $10,000, AV Mat $42,000, Electronic Ref Mat (Incl. Access Fees) $15,000. Sal $516,054 (Prof $227,242)
Library Holdings: AV Mats 13,502; Bk Vols 67,952; Per Subs 95
Subject Interests: Local hist
Automation Activity & Vendor Info: (Circulation) SIRSI WorkFlows
Wireless access
Partic in Bergen County Cooperative Library System
Friends of the Library Group

YARDVILLE

S GARDEN STATE YOUTH CORRECTIONAL FACILITY LIBRARY*, PO Box 11401, 08620-1401. SAN 375-7471. Tel: 609-298-6300, Ext 2574. FAX: 609-298-8682. *Librn,* Vera Morris
Library Holdings: Bk Vols 16,000; Per Subs 48
Restriction: Not open to pub

NEW MEXICO

Date of Statistics: FY 2012-2013
Population, 2010 U.S. Census: 2,059,179
Population Served by Public Libraries: 1,660,528
Unserved: 398,651
Total Volumes in Public Libraries: 4,960,159
Volumes Per Capita: 2.41 (state population); 2.99 (served population)
Total Public Library Circulation: 12,396,210
Circulation Per Capita: 6.02 (state population); 7.47 (served population)
Total Public Library Income: $45,638,083
Source of Income: Public funds: municipal 75.7%, county 12.99%, tribal 2.39%, state 3.55%, federal 0.91%, other 4.33%
Expenditures Per Capita: $21.43 (state population); $26.57 (served population)
Grants-in-Aid to Public Libraries: $638,500
Number of Bookmobiles in State: 3

ABIQUIU

SR GHOST RANCH CONFERENCE CENTER LIBRARY*, HC 77, Box 11, 87510-9601. SAN 310-6233. Tel: 505-685-4333. Toll Free Tel: 877-804-4678. FAX: 505-685-4519. Web Site: www.ghostranch.org. *Librn,* Carol Merrill; E-mail: carolm@ghostranch.org; Staff 2 (MLS 1, Non-MLS 1)
Founded 1955
Library Holdings: AV Mats 100; Bk Titles 17,000; Per Subs 30
Special Collections: Southwest Coll
Subject Interests: Archaeology, Art, Geol, Relig
Automation Activity & Vendor Info: (Cataloging) TLC (The Library Corporation)
Database Vendor: OCLC WorldShare Interlibrary Loan
Wireless access
Restriction: Not open to pub
Friends of the Library Group

P PUEBLO DE ABIQUIU LIBRARY & CULTURAL CENTER, Abiquiu Public Library, Bldg 29, County Rd 187, 87510-0838. (Mail add: PO Box 838, 87510). Tel: 505-685-4884. FAX: 505-685-0754. E-mail: abiquiupl@gmail.com. *Librn,* Tara Valdez
Library Holdings: Bk Vols 12,000
Automation Activity & Vendor Info: (Cataloging) Follett Software; (Circulation) Follett Software
Database Vendor: EBSCOhost, Gale Cengage Learning
Wireless access
Open Thurs-Sun 1-6

ALAMOGORDO

P ALAMOGORDO PUBLIC LIBRARY*, 920 Oregon Ave, 88310. SAN 310-6241. Tel: 575-439-4140. Reference Tel: 575-439-4148. FAX: 575-439-4108. E-mail: COAlibrary@ci.alamogordo.nm.us. Web Site: ci.alamogordo.nm.us/coa/communityservices/library.htm. *Youth Serv Librn,* Ami Jones; E-mail: ajones@ci.alamogordo.nm.us; *ILL Spec,* Annie Tyrrell; *Homebound & Vols Coordr,* Becky Miller; E-mail: bmiller@ci.alamogordo.nm.us; Staff 4 (MLS 1, Non-MLS 3)
Founded 1899. Pop 62,298; Circ 265,585
Jul 2005-Jun 2006 Income $773,000. Mats Exp $143,000. Sal $316,700
Library Holdings: Audiobooks 2,819; AV Mats 11,123; Bk Titles 94,477; Per Subs 210
Special Collections: Eugene M Rhodes Coll, bks & mss; Mother Goose Editions (Lillian Maddox Coll). Oral History
Subject Interests: Lit, SW hist
Automation Activity & Vendor Info: (Acquisitions) TLC (The Library Corporation); (Cataloging) TLC (The Library Corporation); (Circulation) TLC (The Library Corporation); (OPAC) TLC (The Library Corporation)
Database Vendor: LearningExpress, OCLC FirstSearch, ProQuest, TLC (The Library Corporation)
Wireless access
Partic in OCLC Online Computer Library Center, Inc
Special Services for the Blind - Screen reader software
Open Mon-Thurs 10-8, Fri 10-5, Sat 11-5
Friends of the Library Group

S NEW MEXICO SCHOOL FOR THE BLIND & VISUALLY IMPAIRED LIBRARY*, 1900 N White Sands Blvd, 88310. SAN 320-2062. Tel: 575-437-3505. Toll Free Tel: 800-437-3505. FAX: 575-439-4454. Web Site: www.nmsbvi.k12.nm.us. *Librn,* June Cady; Tel: 575-437-3505, Ext 4510; Staff 1 (Non-MLS 1)
Founded 1903
Library Holdings: Audiobooks 4,000; Braille Volumes 4,000; CDs 427; Large Print Bks 1,500; Bk Vols 12,000; Per Subs 12; Talking Bks 900; Videos 400
Special Collections: Blindness, Teaching Blind or Visually Impaired Children & Multi-Handicapped (Professional Coll); Braille, Print Braille & Large Print Recreational Reading Titles & Textbooks & Instructional Materials (Depository Coll)
Subject Interests: Gen K-12 fiction, Gen K-12 nonfiction
Automation Activity & Vendor Info: (Cataloging) Keystone Systems, Inc (KLAS); (Circulation) Keystone Systems, Inc (KLAS); (OPAC) Keystone Systems, Inc (KLAS)
Database Vendor: Gale Cengage Learning
Special Services for the Blind - Assistive/Adapted tech devices, equip & products; Audio mat; Bks & mags in Braille, on rec, tape & cassette; Bks on CD; Children's Braille; Descriptive video serv (DVS); Large print bks, Magnifiers; Talking bks
Open Mon-Thurs 8-5, Fri 8-Noon

J NEW MEXICO STATE UNIVERSITY AT ALAMOGORDO, David H Townsend Library, 2400 N Scenic Dr, 88310. SAN 310-625X. Tel: 575-439-3650. FAX: 575-439-3657. E-mail: library@nmsu.edu. Web Site: nmsua.edu/library. *Dir, Libr Serv,* Dr Sharon Jenkins; Tel: 575-439-3806, E-mail: djenkins@nmsu.edu; *Libr Spec,* Lyn Johnson; Tel: 575-439-3653, E-mail: lyn@nmsu.edu; Staff 5 (MLS 1, Non-MLS 4)
Founded 1975. Enrl 2,000; Highest Degree: Associate
Library Holdings: AV Mats 1,948; e-books 15,351; Bk Vols 45,000; Per Subs 110
Special Collections: State Document Depository
Subject Interests: Allied health, Art, NMex, Nursing
Automation Activity & Vendor Info: (Acquisitions) Ex Libris Group; (Cataloging) Ex Libris Group; (Circulation) Ex Libris Group; (Course Reserve) Ex Libris Group; (ILL) Ex Libris Group; (OPAC) Ex Libris Group; (Serials) Ex Libris Group
Wireless access
Partic in OCLC Online Computer Library Center, Inc

ALBUQUERQUE

P ALBUQUERQUE-BERNALILLO COUNTY LIBRARY SYSTEM*, 501 Copper Ave NW, 87102. SAN 351-5915. Interlibrary Loan Service Tel: 505-768-5147. Administration Tel: 505-768-5100. Information Services Tel: 505-768-5141. FAX: 505-768-5191. Web Site: www.cabq.gov/library. *Dir,*

Dean P Smith; Tel: 505-768-5122, E-mail: dpsmith@cabq.gov; *Asst Dir,* Cindy C Burns; E-mail: cburns@cabq.gov; *Asst Dir,* Linda Morgan Davis; Tel: 505-768-5152, E-mail: ldavis@cabq.gov; *Asst Dir,* Jacqueline Lauren Fernandez; Tel: 505-768-5113, E-mail: jlfernandez@cabq.gov; Staff 140 (MLS 43, Non-MLS 97)
Founded 1901. Pop 639,921; Circ 4,578,070
Jul 2010-Jun 2011 Income (Main Library and Branch(s)) $11,237,518, State $51,887, City $9,578,053, Federal $48,620, County $1,558,958. Mats Exp $1,678,093, Books $923,784, Other Print Mats $202,688, AV Mat $202,688, Electronic Ref Mat (Incl. Access Fees) $348,933. Sal $6,798,613
Library Holdings: Audiobooks 43,544; e-books 2,962; Bk Vols 1,282,378
Automation Activity & Vendor Info: (Acquisitions) Innovative Interfaces, Inc; (Cataloging) Innovative Interfaces, Inc; (Circulation) Innovative Interfaces, Inc; (OPAC) Innovative Interfaces, Inc; (Serials) Innovative Interfaces, Inc
Wireless access
Partic in OCLC Online Computer Library Center, Inc
Open Mon & Thurs-Sat 10-6, Tues & Wed 10-7
Friends of the Library Group
Branches: 16
CHERRY HILLS, 6901 Barstow NE, 87111. Tel: 505-857-8321. FAX: 505-857-8323. *Mgr,* Leigh Turner; E-mail: mlturner@cabq.gov
Open Mon & Tues 10-8, Wed-Sat 10-6, Sun 1-5
Friends of the Library Group
EAST MOUNTAIN, One Old Tijeras Rd, Tijeras, 87059. (Mail add: PO Box 1570, Tijeras, 87059-1570), SAN 374-7115. Tel: 505-281-8508. FAX: 505-281-8510. E-mail: eastmountain@cabq.gov. Web Site: abclibrary.org/eastmountain. *Br Mgr,* Deborah Hayba
Open Tues, Wed, Fri & Sat 10-6, Thurs 11-7
Friends of the Library Group
ERNA FERGUSSON BRANCH, 3700 San Mateo NE, 87110, SAN 351-6008. Tel: 505-888-8100. FAX: 505-888-8109. *Mgr,* Position Currently Open
Open Mon-Thurs 10-8, Fri & Sat 10-6, Sun 1-5
Friends of the Library Group
TONY HILLERMAN BRANCH, 8205 Apache Ave NE, 87110, SAN 351-6067. Tel: 505-291-6264. FAX: 505-291-6275. *Mgr,* Linda Kennedy; E-mail: lkennedy@cabq.gov
Open Tues & Wed 10-8, Thurs-Sat 10-6
Friends of the Library Group
LOMAS-TRAMWAY, 908 Eastridge NE, 87123, SAN 329-689X. Tel: 505-291-6295. FAX: 505-291-6299. *Mgr,* Mary Hunt
Open Tues & Wed 10-8, Thurs-Sat 10-6
Friends of the Library Group
LOS GRIEGOS, 1000 Griegos Rd NW, 87107, SAN 351-6032. Tel: 505-761-4020. FAX: 505-761-4014. E-mail: losgriegos@cabq.gov. *Site Supvr,* Gail Gerstner-Miller; E-mail: ggerstnermiller@cabq.gov
Open Tues, Fri & Sat 10-6, Wed & Thurs 11-7
ALAMOSA/ROBERT L MURPHY MEMORIAL LIBRARY, 6900 Gonzales Rd SW, 87105, SAN 351-5974. Tel: 505-836-0684. FAX: 505-876-8779. *Br Mgr,* Sue Heitz; E-mail: sheitz@cabq.gov
Open Mon-Fri 10-6
Friends of the Library Group
NORTH VALLEY, 7704 Second St NW, 87107, SAN 374-7107. Tel: 505-897-8823. FAX: 505-897-8825.
Founded 1994
Open Tues, Wed, Fri & Sat 10-6, Thurs 11-7
Friends of the Library Group
ERNIE PYLE BRANCH, 900 Girard Blvd SE, 87106, SAN 351-6091. Tel: 505-256-2065. FAX: 505-256-2069. E-mail: erniepyle@cabq.gov. *Br Mgr,* Lynne Fothergill; E-mail: lfothergill@cabq.gov
Open Tues & Thurs-Sat 10-6, Wed 11-7
Friends of the Library Group
SAN PEDRO BRANCH, 5600 Trumbull Ave SE, 87108, SAN 351-6121. Tel: 505-256-2067. FAX: 505-256-2064. E-mail: sanpedro@cabq.gov. *Br Mgr,* Lynne Fothergill; E-mail: lfothergill@cabq.gov
Open Tues, Fri & Sat 10-6, Wed & Thurs 11-7
Friends of the Library Group
SOUTH BROADWAY, 1025 Broadway Blvd SE, 87102, SAN 373-9309. Tel: 505-764-1742. FAX: 505-764-1783. E-mail: southbroadway@cabq.gov. *Area Mgr,* Lindsey Miller-Escarfuller; E-mail: miller-escarfuller@cabq.gov
Open Tues-Sat 10-6
Friends of the Library Group
SOUTH VALLEY, 3904 Isleta Blvd SW, 87105, SAN 329-6938. Tel: 505-877-5170. FAX: 505-877-6639. *Mgr,* Mel Ribas; E-mail: mribas@cabq.gov
Open Tues, Wed, Fri & Sat 10-1, Thurs 11-7
Friends of the Library Group
SPECIAL COLLECTIONS, 423 Central Ave NE, 87102, SAN 351-6156. Tel: 505-848-1376. FAX: 505-764-1574. E-mail: specialcollections@cabq.gov. Web Site: abclibrary.org/specialcollections. *Mgr,* Eileen O'Connell; E-mail: eoconnell@cabq.gov; Staff 3.5 (MLS 1, Non-MLS 2.5)
Library Holdings: AV Mats 12,000; Bk Vols 32,000; Spec Interest Per Sub 300
Special Collections: Archival Coll Relating to the History & Development of the City of Albuquerque, including the Ernie Pyle Coll; History of Books & Printing, part of the Center for the Book; New Mexicana & Local, Albuquerque, History
Function: Archival coll, Art exhibits, Audio & video playback equip for onsite use, Computer training, Computers for patron use, Copy machines, e-mail serv, Exhibits, Fax serv, Handicapped accessible, Life-long learning prog for all ages, Mail & tel request accepted, Online cat, Online ref, Online searches, Orientations, Photocopying/Printing, Prog for adults, Pub access computers, Ref & res, Ref serv available, Study rm, Telephone ref, Wheelchair accessible, Workshops
Open Tues, Wed, Fri & Sat 10-6, Thurs 11-7
Restriction: Internal use only, Non-circulating, Open to pub for ref & circ; with some limitations
Friends of the Library Group
JUAN TABO BRANCH, 3407 Juan Tabo Blvd NE, 87111, SAN 351-6164. Tel: 505-291-6260. FAX: 505-291-6225. E-mail: juantabo@cabq.gov. *Br Mgr,* Brita Sauer; E-mail: besauer@cabq.gov
Open Tues & Wed 10-8, Thurs-Sat 10-6
Friends of the Library Group
TAYLOR RANCH, 5700 Bogart NW, 87120, SAN 329-6911. Tel: 505-897-8816. FAX: 505-897-8813. E-mail: taylorranch@cabq.gov. *Area Mgr,* Tanya Shelton-Council; E-mail: tshelton-council@cabq.gov
Open Mon-Thurs 10-8, Fri & Sat 10-6, Sun 1-5
Friends of the Library Group
WESTGATE, 1300 Delgado Dr SW, 87121. Tel: 505-833-6984. FAX: 505-833-6989. *Mgr,* Sue Heitz; E-mail: sheitz@cabq.gov
Open Mon-Fri 10-6
Friends of the Library Group
Bookmobiles: 1

S THE ALBUQUERQUE MUSEUM OF ART & HISTORY*, Reference Library, 2000 Mountain Rd NW, 87104. SAN 320-8664. Tel: 505-243-7255. FAX: 505-764-6546. Web Site: www.cabq.gov/museum. *Asst Dir,* Cyndy Garcia
Founded 1967
Library Holdings: Bk Vols 12,000; Per Subs 23
Subject Interests: Hist, Middle Rio Grande valley, SW art
Restriction: Open by appt only

J CENTRAL NEW MEXICO COMMUNITY COLLEGE LIBRARIES*, 525 Buena Vista SE, 87106-4023. Tel: 505-224-3292. Circulation Tel: 505-224-3274. Reference Tel: 505-224-3285. FAX: 505-224-3321. Web Site: www.cnm.edu/library. *Dir of Libr,* Poppy Johnson-Renvall; Tel: 505-224-4000, Ext 51984, E-mail: pjohnsonrenvall@cnm.edu; *Circ Supvr, Libr Mgr,* Olivia Baca; Tel: 505-224-3278, E-mail: obaca9@cnm.edu; *ILL Coordr, Ref Librn,* Renee Goodvin; Tel: 505-224-4000, Ext 52550, E-mail: rgoodvin@cnm.edu; *Ref/Syst Librn,* Yuqing Zhou; Tel: 505-224-4000, Ext 52540, E-mail: yzhou@cnm.edu; *Admin Coordr,* Pat Willems; Tel: 505-224-3295, E-mail: pwillems1@cnm.edu; *Circ Spec,* Gloria Williams; Tel: 505-224-4000, Ext 51480, E-mail: gwilliams42@cnm.edu; *Ref Spec,* Soyeon Gallo; Tel: 505-224-4000, Ext 52558, E-mail: spark14@cnm.edu; *Ref Spec,* Wynn Harris; Tel: 505-224-4000, Ext 51498, E-mail: wharris@cnm.edu; *Ser Tech,* Leda Rizzo; Tel: 505-224-4000, Ext 52538; Staff 9 (MLS 4, Non-MLS 5)
Founded 1965. Enrl 17,000; Fac 700
Library Holdings: Bk Titles 59,508; Per Subs 584
Subject Interests: Air conditioning, Alternative energy, Auto repair, Carpentry, Creativity, Culinary arts, Electronics, Hospitality, Laser optics, Law enforcement, Plumbing, Robotics, Sheet metal, Tourism, Use of tools, Welding
Automation Activity & Vendor Info: (Cataloging) TLC (The Library Corporation); (Circulation) TLC (The Library Corporation); (OPAC) TLC (The Library Corporation)
Database Vendor: EBSCOhost, Gale Cengage Learning, OCLC FirstSearch, ProQuest
Partic in New Mexico Consortium of Academic Libraries; New Mexico Consortium of Biomedical & Hospital Libraries
Open Mon-Thurs 7:30am-9pm, Fri 7:30-5, Sat 9-5
Departmental Libraries:
MONTOYA CAMPUS LIBRARY, J Bldg, Rm 123, 4700 Morris NE, 87111, SAN 320-9598. Circulation Tel: 505-224-5721. Reference Tel: 505-224-5730. FAX: 505-224-5727. *Dir of Libr,* Poppy Johnson-Renvall; Tel: 505-224-4000, Ext 51984, E-mail: pjohnsonrenvall@cnm.edu; *Libr Mgr,* Bridget O'Leary-Storer; Tel: 505-224-4000, Ext 52548, E-mail: boleary@cnm.edu; *Ref Librn,* Michael Germroth; Tel: 505-224-4000, Ext 52549, E-mail: mgermroth@cmn.edu; *Ref Spec,* Daniel Hay; Tel: 505-224-4000, Ext 52547, E-mail: dhay@cnm.edu; *Ref Spec,* Allyson James-Vigil; Tel: 505-224-4000, Ext 51342, E-mail: allyson@cnm.edu. Subject Specialists: *Bus,* Allyson James-Vigil; Staff 5 (MLS 1, Non-MLS 4)
Founded 1981. Enrl 8,000; Highest Degree: Associate
Subject Interests: Laser optics

Function: For res purposes
Open Mon-Thurs 8-8, Fri 8-5, Sat 9-5
RIO RANCHO CAMPUS LIBRARY, 2601 Campus Blvd NE, Rm 112, Rio Rancho, 87144. Tel: 505-224-4953. E-mail: reference@cnm.edu. *Ref Spec,* Martha Castillo; E-mail: mcastillo114@cnm.edu; Staff 1.5 (MLS 1.5)
Founded 2010. Enrl 1,550; Fac 50; Highest Degree: Associate
Library Holdings: AV Mats 66; High Interest/Low Vocabulary Bk Vols 22; Bk Titles 633; Per Subs 17
Subject Interests: Nursing
Database Vendor: ARTstor, Booklist Online, CQ Press, CredoReference, Facts on File, JSTOR, Safari Books Online
Function: Audio & video playback equip for onsite use, CD-ROM, Computers for patron use, Copy machines, Doc delivery serv, e-mail serv, Electronic databases & coll, Free DVD rentals, Handicapped accessible, ILL available, Mail & tel request accepted, Online cat, Online info literacy tutorials on the web & in blackboard, Online ref, Online searches, Photocopying/Printing, Pub access computers, Ref & res, Ref serv available, Ref serv in person, Scanner, Tax forms, Telephone ref, VHS videos, Video lending libr, Web-catalog, Wheelchair accessible
Partic in LIBROS Consortium
Open Mon-Thurs 9-6, Fri 8-5
Restriction: Fee for pub use, ID required to use computers (Ltd hrs), Open to pub for ref & circ; with some limitations
SOUTH VALLEY CAMPUS LIBRARY, 5816 Isleta SW, Rm SV 106, 87105. Tel: 505-224-5016. FAX: 505-224-5074. *Ref Spec,* Florinda Garcia; E-mail: florinda@cnm.edu
Library Holdings: AV Mats 203; e-journals 7; Electronic Media & Resources 16; Bk Vols 286; Per Subs 22
Automation Activity & Vendor Info: (Cataloging) Innovative Interfaces, Inc; (Circulation) Innovative Interfaces, Inc; (OPAC) Innovative Interfaces, Inc
Open Mon-Fri 8-5
WESTSIDE CAMPUS LIBRARY, WS, Rm 205, 10549 Universe Blvd NW, 87114. Tel: 505-224-5423. E-mail: reference@cnm.edu. Web Site: www.cnm.edu/depts/libraries. *Ref Librn/Copyright Coordr,* Mary Bates-Ulibarri; Tel: 505-224-4000, Ext 52552, E-mail: ulimb@cnm.edu; *Ref Spec,* Amy Baker; Tel: 505-224-4000, Ext 52551, E-mail: aupah1@cnm.edu; *Ref Spec,* Cathy Lezek; Tel: 505-224-4000, Ext 52553, E-mail: clezek@cnm.edu
Library Holdings: AV Mats 150; DVDs 12; Bk Titles 338; Bk Vols 356; Per Subs 19; Videos 138
Automation Activity & Vendor Info: (Cataloging) Innovative Interfaces, Inc; (Circulation) Innovative Interfaces, Inc; (OPAC) Innovative Interfaces, Inc
Open Mon-Thurs 8-8, Fri 8-5

SR CENTRAL UNITED METHODIST CHURCH LIBRARY*, 201 University Blvd NE, 87106-4596. SAN 371-8476. Tel: 505-243-7834. FAX: 505-242-6986. E-mail: info@centraltolife.org. Web Site: centraltolife.org. *Librn,* Rex Allender
Library Holdings: Large Print Bks 10; Bk Vols 3,000
Special Collections: Bible, AV, bks; Methodist History, AV, bks
Publications: Acquisitions List; Bibliographies; Guides
Open Mon-Fri 9-4:30, Sun 9-Noon

R CONGREGATION B'NAI ISRAEL*, Isidore & Rose Bloch Memorial Library, 4401 Indian School Rd NE, 87110-3914. SAN 310-6322. Tel: 505-266-0155. FAX: 505-268-6136. E-mail: bnaiisrael.library@aol.com. Web Site: bnaiisrael-nm.org. *Librn,* L Freedman; *Asst Librn,* J Pushkar
Library Holdings: Braille Volumes 1; CDs 640; DVDs 101; Music Scores 9; Bk Titles 2,280; Per Subs 1; Videos 340
Special Collections: American Jewish Music (Milken Archive); Judaica; Marilyn Bromberg-Marilyn Reinman Children's Coll; Norman Schwartz Memorial Music Coll
Open Mon 3-5, Thurs & Sun 9:30-Noon

R FIRST PRESBYTERIAN CHURCH LIBRARY*, 215 Locust NE, 87102. SAN 310-6349. Tel: 505-764-2900. FAX: 505-764-2940. Web Site: www.firstpresabq.org. *Dir, Christian Educ,* Elizabeth Whiteley
Founded 1955
Jul 2009-Jun 2010. Mats Exp $1,000
Library Holdings: Bk Titles 6,000; Bk Vols 7,183; Per Subs 40
Special Collections: Local History & Culture Coll; Southwest Interest Coll
Subject Interests: Biblical studies, Fiction, Personal help, Relig, Soc issues, Theol
Open Mon-Fri 8:30-5, Sun 8:45-2
Friends of the Library Group

S HISPANIC CULTURE FOUNDATION RESOURCE LIBRARY*, 1701 Fourth St SW, 87102. SAN 370-6516. Tel: 505-246-2261, Ext 165. FAX: 505-724-4778. Web Site: www.nhccnm.org. *Librn,* Mayte Villa
Founded 1986
Library Holdings: Bk Titles 12,500; Per Subs 400
Wireless access
Publications: El Puente (Newsletter); Flow of the River: Corre el Rio (also video); New Mexico Directory of Hispanic Culture
Open Tues-Sat 10-5

S LOVELACE RESPIRATORY RESEARCH INSTITUTE*, Sam White Library, 2425 Ridgecrest Dr SE, 87108-5127. SAN 310-6810. Tel: 505-348-9117. FAX: 505-348-4978. E-mail: libreq@lrri.org. Web Site: www.lrri.org. *Librn,* Robin Henry; Tel: 505-348-9178, E-mail: rhenry@lrri.org; Staff 1.5 (MLS 1.5)
Founded 1974
Library Holdings: Bk Titles 10,000; Bk Vols 25,000; Per Subs 75
Subject Interests: Aerosol physics, Fossil fuels effluents, Radiation effects, Respiratory syst, Toxicology, Veterinary med
Function: ILL available, Res libr
Restriction: Employees only

S MAXWELL MUSEUM OF ANTHROPOLOGY*, Clark Field Library & Archives, University of New Mexico, 87131. SAN 377-3280. Tel: 505-277-4405, 505-277-8675. Web Site: www.unm.edu/~maxwell/clark-field.html. *Dir,* Alan Shalette; E-mail: alshal@unm.edu
Founded 1972
Library Holdings: Bk Titles 12,000; Per Subs 35
Function: Res libr
Open Mon-Fri 9-5
Restriction: Borrowing privileges limited to anthropology fac & libr staff

S MENAUL HISTORICAL LIBRARY OF THE SOUTHWEST, 301 Menaul Blvd NE, 87107. SAN 371-2249. Tel: 505-343-7480. E-mail: archives@menaulhistoricallibrary.org. Web Site: www.menaulhistoricallibrary.org. *Adminr,* Nona Browne
Founded 1974
Jan 2010-Dec 2010 Income $16,000. Mats Exp $9,000
Library Holdings: Bk Vols 3,700; Per Subs 11; Spec Interest Per Sub 20
Special Collections: Presbyterian Church History - New Mexico, Arizona & Utah, artifacts, bks, doc. Oral History
Subject Interests: Native Am, Presbyterian churches, Presbyterian hist
Function: Res libr
Open Tues-Fri 10-4
Restriction: Non-circulating

L MILLER STRATVERT PA*, Law Library, 500 Marquette Ave NW, Ste 100, 87102-5326. SAN 372-4387. Tel: 505-842-1950. FAX: 505-243-4408. Web Site: www.mstlaw.com. *Librn,* Position Currently Open; Staff 1 (MLS 1)
Founded 1978
Library Holdings: Bk Vols 1,000; Per Subs 20

L MODRALL, SPERLING, ROEHL, HARRIS & SISK*, Law Library, PO Box 2168, 87103. SAN 372-4255. Tel: 505-848-1800. FAX: 505-848-9710. Web Site: www.modrall.com. *Librn,* Miriam Greenwood
Library Holdings: Bk Vols 10,000; Per Subs 40
Restriction: Staff use only

GM NEW MEXICO VA HEALTH CARE SYSTEM*, General & Medical Library (142D), 1501 San Pedro SE, 87108. SAN 310-6489. Tel: 505-256-2786. FAX: 505-256-2870. *Dir, Libr Serv,* Bette Jean Ingui; Staff 3 (MLS 2, Non-MLS 1)
Founded 1932
Library Holdings: Bk Vols 2,202; Per Subs 250
Subject Interests: General med, Geriatrics, Gerontology, Nursing, Psychiat, Psychol, Surgery
Automation Activity & Vendor Info: (Acquisitions) Inmagic, Inc.; (Cataloging) Inmagic, Inc.; (Circulation) Inmagic, Inc.; (OPAC) Inmagic, Inc.; (Serials) Inmagic, Inc.
Partic in N Mex Consortium of Biomedical & Hospital Libr; National Network of Libraries of Medicine; Veterans Affairs Libr Network (VALNET)
Special Services for the Deaf - Closed caption videos
Special Services for the Blind - Talking bks & player equip
Restriction: Not open to pub

M PRESBYTERIAN HOSPITAL*, Robert Shafer Memorial Library, PO Box 26666, 87125-6666. SAN 310-6411. Tel: 505-841-1516. FAX: 505-841-1067.
Founded 1962
Library Holdings: Bk Titles 900; Per Subs 120
Subject Interests: Med
Open Mon-Fri 8-4:30
Friends of the Library Group

R SAINT JOHN'S EPISCOPAL CATHEDRAL*, Kadey Memorial Library, 318 Silver SW, 87102. SAN 310-642X. Tel: 505-247-1581. FAX: 505-247-3377.
Founded 1975
Library Holdings: Bk Titles 1,000
Subject Interests: Biblical lit, Devotional, Devotional psychol, Liturgy, Philos, Relig studies, Theol
Restriction: Not open to pub

SR SAINT PAUL'S UNITED METHODIST CHURCH LIBRARY*, 9500 Constitution Ave NE, 87112. SAN 371-1218. Tel: 505-298-5596. FAX: 505-275-8066.
Library Holdings: Bk Vols 200
Open Mon-Thurs 8:30-4:30, Fri 8:30-Noon

R SANDIA BAPTIST CHURCH*, Media Library, 9429 Constitution NE, 87112. SAN 325-0814. Tel: 505-292-2713, 505-292-2717. FAX: 505-296-3009. Web Site: www.sandiabaptist.org. *Librn,* Mike Edwards
Founded 1958
Library Holdings: Bk Vols 7,100
Open Mon-Fri 8:30-4:30

M SANDIA MEDICAL LIBRARY*, 601 Martin Luther King Ave NE, 87102-3670. SAN 325-9153. Tel: 505-727-8291. FAX: 505-727-8121. *Librn,* Marian Frear; Staff 1 (MLS 1)
Library Holdings: Bk Titles 400; Per Subs 11
Partic in Docline; New Mexico Consortium of Biomedical & Hospital Libraries
Open Mon-Fri 8-Noon

S SANDIA NATIONAL LABORATORIES*, Technical Library, PO Box 5800, MS 0899, 87185-0899. SAN 310-6438. Tel: 505-845-8287. FAX: 505-844-3143. Web Site: www.sandia.gov/resources/emp-ret/library/index.html. *Mgr, Tech Libr Operations,* Donald Guy; Staff 6 (MLS 6)
Founded 1948
Library Holdings: Bk Titles 70,000
Subject Interests: Aerodynamics, Electronics, Energy res, Explosives, Nuclear safety, Nuclear waste mgt, Nuclear weapons, Ordinance, Security
Automation Activity & Vendor Info: (Cataloging) SirsiDynix; (Circulation) SirsiDynix; (OPAC) SirsiDynix
Partic in Horizon Users Group
Restriction: Staff use only

S SOUTHWEST RESEARCH & INFORMATION CENTER LIBRARY*, 105 Stanford SE, 87106-3537. (Mail add: PO Box 4524, 87106-4524), SAN 326-0089. Tel: 505-262-1862. FAX: 505-262-1864. Web Site: www.sric.org. *Librn,* Don Hancock; E-mail: sricdon@earthlink.net; Staff 1 (Non-MLS 1)
Founded 1971
Library Holdings: Bk Titles 10,000; Per Subs 450
Function: Photocopying/Printing, Ref serv available
Open Mon-Fri 9-5
Restriction: Open to pub for ref only

J SOUTHWESTERN INDIAN POLYTECHNIC INSTITUTE LIBRARIES*, 9169 Coors Rd NW, 87184. SAN 310-6454. Tel: 505-346-2352. FAX: 505-346-7713. Web Site: www.sipi.bia.edu/library.
Library Holdings: Bk Vols 30,000; Per Subs 150
Special Collections: Indian Coll, mat, tech bks
Subject Interests: Acctg electronics, Eng tech, Food tech, Mkt, Natural res, Secretarial
Automation Activity & Vendor Info: (Cataloging) Follett Software; (Circulation) Follett Software

L SUTIN, THAYER & BROWNE*, Law Library, Two Park Square Bldg, 10th Flr, 6565 Americas Pkwy NE, 87110. SAN 372-4379. Tel: 505-883-2500. FAX: 505-888-6565. Web Site: www.sutinfirm.com. *Info & Res Mgr,* Richard P McGoey; Staff 1 (Non-MLS 1)
Library Holdings: Bk Vols 10,000; Per Subs 100
Wireless access

S TELEPHONE MUSEUM OF NEW MEXICO LIBRARY*, 110 Fourth St NW, 87102. (Mail add: PO Box 1892, 87103). Tel: 505-842-2937. FAX: 505-332-4088. Web Site: nmculture.org. *Dir,* Gigi Galassini; *Librn,* G L Dybwad; Tel: 505-296-9047, E-mail: gldybwad@comcast.net; *Librn,* Delores Nebola; Staff 2 (Non-MLS 2)
Founded 1995
Library Holdings: Bk Titles 2,600; Bk Vols 3,600
Subject Interests: Telephone, Telephony
Wireless access
Restriction: Not a lending libr, Open by appt only

L UNITED STATES COURTS LIBRARY*, 333 Lomas Blvd NW, Ste 360, 87102. SAN 372-428X. Tel: 505-348-2135. FAX: 505-348-2795. *Librn,* Gregory L Townsend; E-mail: gregory_townsend@ca10.uscourts.gov; *Tech Serv,* Greg Surratt
Library Holdings: Bk Vols 19,000; Per Subs 50
Open Mon-Fri 8-12 & 1-5

C UNIVERSITY OF NEW MEXICO-UNIVERSITY LIBRARIES*, Zimmerman Library, 1900 Roma NE, 87131-0001. (Mail add: One University of New Mexico, MSC 05-3020, 87131-0001), SAN 351-6210. Interlibrary Loan Service Tel: 505-277-5617. Reference Tel: 505-277-9100. Administration Tel: 505-277-4241. Administration FAX: 505-277-7196. TDD: 505-277-4866. Web Site: elibrary.unm.edu. *Interim Dean,* Michael Kelly; E-mail: mtk@unm.edu; *Dean, Univ Libr,* Position Currently Open; *Dep Dean,* Frances C Wilkinson; E-mail: fwilkins@unm.edu; *Asst Dean,* Nancy Dennis; Tel: 505-277-2585, E-mail: ndennis@unm.edu; *Asst Dean,* Mike Kelly; Tel: 505-277-6451, E-mail: mtk@unm.edu; Staff 152 (MLS 36, Non-MLS 116)
Founded 1892. Enrl 31,795; Fac 2,963; Highest Degree: Doctorate
Special Collections: 19th & 20th Century Oaxaca, Mexico Pamphlets & Regional History; 19th Century Latin American Travel Narratives; Indian Affairs (Glenn Leonidas Emmons & Michael Steck Coll), papers; Indians (Doris Duke Foundation Coll AIM Archives); John Donald Robb Archive of Southwestern Music, a-tapes; Land Records (Maxwell Land Grant Co, US Soil Conservation Service Reports); Latin American Agrarian History, Agricultural Economics & Rural Sociology (T Lynn Smith Coll); Literary Manuscripts (Erna Fergusson Papers, Frank Waters Papers, Papers of Regional Hispanic Writers); New Mexicana; Papers of Public Figures (Thomas B Catron, Albert Bacon Fall, Miguel Antonio Otero, US Senators: Dennis Chavez, Pete V Domenici, Joseph M Montoya, Harrison H Schmitt, Congressman Manuel J Lujan); Photocopies Spanish, Mexican & New Mexican Archives; Pioneers Foundation Coll (Anglos); Popular Culture (Day Science Fiction Periodicals & Dime Novels); Puppetry (McPharlin Coll), bks, realia; Regional Historical Manuscripts: Business Records (Bell Ranch-Red River Valley Co, Charles Ilfeld Mercantile Co, First National Bank of Santa Fe); Regional Historical Photographs (William Henry Cobb, Charles Fletcher Lummis & Henry Schmidt Colls); Southwestern Americana; Southwestern Historical Architectural Documents (John Gaw Meem Coll); US Patent Dept. Oral History; State Document Depository; US Document Depository
Subject Interests: Hist of photog, Ibero-Am mat, SW archit
Automation Activity & Vendor Info: (Acquisitions) Innovative Interfaces, Inc; (Cataloging) Innovative Interfaces, Inc; (Circulation) Innovative Interfaces, Inc; (Course Reserve) Docutek; (OPAC) Innovative Interfaces, Inc; (Serials) Innovative Interfaces, Inc
Database Vendor: EBSCOhost, Innovative Interfaces, Inc, LexisNexis, OCLC FirstSearch, ProQuest, Wilson - Wilson Web
Wireless access
Function: Archival coll, For res purposes, Govt ref serv, Handicapped accessible, Homebound delivery serv, ILL available, Newsp ref libr, Online searches, Photocopying/Printing, Ref serv available, Res libr, Wheelchair accessible
Publications: Developments at University Libraries (Newsletter)
Special Services for the Deaf - Bks on deafness & sign lang; Spec interest per; TTY equip
Special Services for the Blind - Braille servs; Braille Webster's dictionary; Compressed speech equip; Reader equip; Telesensory screen enlarger & speech synthesis interface to the OPAC; VisualTek equip; World Bk Encyclopedia on cassette
Restriction: Open to students, fac & staff, Pub use on premises

Departmental Libraries:

BUREAU OF BUSINESS & ECONOMIC RESEARCH DATA BANK, 1919 Las Lomas NE, 87106. (Mail add: MSC06 3510, One University of New Mexico, 87131-0001), SAN 310-6330. Tel: 505-277-3038. Reference Tel: 505-277-6626. FAX: 505-277-2773. E-mail: dbinfo@unm.edu. Web Site: bber.unm.edu/bber_data.html. *Sr Prog Mgr,* Suzan Reagan-Kershner; E-mail: sreagan@unm.edu; *Info Spec,* Lawrence Compton; Tel: 505-277-2142, E-mail: lcompton@unm.edu. Subject Specialists: *Demographics, Econ, Statistics,* Suzan Reagan-Kershner; *Demographics, Econ, Statistics,* Lawrence Compton; Staff 2 (MLS 1, Non-MLS 1)
Founded 1967
Library Holdings: CDs 800; Bk Vols 14,000; Per Subs 45
Special Collections: New Mexico Social Statistics; New Mexico Statistics (New Mexico State & Local Government Agency Publications); New Mexico's Economy; US Census Reports
Subject Interests: Census, Demographics, Econ
Automation Activity & Vendor Info: (Cataloging) Innovative Interfaces, Inc - Millenium; (OPAC) Innovative Interfaces, Inc - Millenium
Database Vendor: Innovative Interfaces, Inc
Function: For res purposes
Partic in LIBROS Consortium
Publications: New Mexico Business-Current Economic Report (Monthly)

Open Mon, Wed & Fri 8-12 & 1-5, Tues & Thurs 8-Noon
Restriction: Open to pub for ref only

CENTENNIAL SCIENCE & ENGINEERING LIBRARY, 211 Terrace St NE, 87131-0001. (Mail add: MSC05 3020, One University of New Mexico, 87131-0001). FAX: 505-277-0702. E-mail: cselref@unm.edu. *Assoc Dean, Fac & Access Serv,* Nancy Dennis; Tel: 505-277-2585, E-mail: ndennis@unm.edu
Special Collections: Map Room; United States Patents
Friends of the Library Group

FINE ARTS & DESIGN LIBRARY, George Pearl Hall, 4th Flr, 87131. E-mail: falref@unm.edu. Web Site: elibrary.unm.edu/falref. *Mgr, Libr Operations,* Susan Hessney-Moore; Tel: 505-277-5443, E-mail: smoore3@unm.edu
Founded 1963. Highest Degree: Doctorate
Library Holdings: e-books 68,845, Bk Vols 230,000; Per Subs 250
Special Collections: Oral History; State Document Depository; US Document Depository
Subject Interests: Latin American, SW
Open Mon-Thurs 8am-10pm, Fri 8-6, Sat 10-6, Sun 12-8

CM HEALTH SCIENCES LIBRARY & INFORMATICS CENTER, MSC09-5100, One University of New Mexico, 87131-0001. Tel: 505-272-2311. Interlibrary Loan Service Tel: 505-272-8052. Administration Tel: 505-272-0634. FAX: 505-272-5350. Administration FAX: 505-272-8254. E-mail: reflib@salud.unm.edu. Web Site: hslic.unm.edu/. *Dir,* Holly Shipp Buchanan; E-mail: hbuchanant@salud.unm.edu; *Head, Ref,* Richard Carr; Staff 68 (MLS 11, Non-MLS 57)
Founded 1963. Enrl 1,860; Fac 935; Highest Degree: Doctorate
Library Holdings: Bk Titles 42,241; Bk Vols 45,814; Per Subs 1,924
Special Collections: Indian Health Services Research; Southwest & New Mexico Medicine, media; UNM Health Sciences Center Archives; World Health Organization Publications. Oral History
Subject Interests: Allied health, Med, Med hist, Native Am health, Nursing, Pharm, Pub health
Automation Activity & Vendor Info: (Acquisitions) Innovative Interfaces, Inc; (Cataloging) Innovative Interfaces, Inc; (Circulation) Innovative Interfaces, Inc; (Course Reserve) Innovative Interfaces, Inc; (ILL) OCLC; (OPAC) Innovative Interfaces, Inc; (Serials) Innovative Interfaces, Inc
Partic in Greater Western Library Alliance; National Network of Libraries of Medicine South Central Region; New England Law Library Consortium, Inc; New Mexico Consortium of Academic Libraries; OCLC Online Computer Library Center, Inc; South Central Academic Medical Libraries Consortium
Publications: Selected Bibliographies

CL LAW LIBRARY, 1117 Stanford Dr NE, 87131-1441, SAN 351-627X. Tel: 505-277-6236. FAX: 505-277-0068. Web Site: lawschool.unm.edu/lawlib/index.php. *Dir,* Carol Parker; E-mail: cparker@unm.edu; *Assoc Dir,* Michelle Rigual; E-mail: mrigual@unm.edu; *Law Librn,* Barbara Lah; *Law Librn,* Sherri Thomas; *Assoc Librn,* Eileen Cohen
Founded 1948. Enrl 320; Fac 30; Highest Degree: Doctorate
Library Holdings: Bk Titles 97,771; Bk Vols 412,694; Per Subs 3,168
Special Collections: Alternative Dispute Resolution; American Indian Law Coll; Land Grant Law Coll; Mexican Law Coll. US Document Depository
Automation Activity & Vendor Info: (Acquisitions) Innovative Interfaces, Inc; (Cataloging) Innovative Interfaces, Inc; (Circulation) Innovative Interfaces, Inc; (Course Reserve) Innovative Interfaces, Inc; (OPAC) Innovative Interfaces, Inc; (Serials) Innovative Interfaces, Inc
Open Mon-Thurs 8am-11pm, Fri 8-6, Sat 9-6, Sun Noon-11

WILLIAM J PARISH MEMORIAL BUSINESS & ECONOMICS LIBRARY, One University of New Mexico, MSC05 3020, 87131-1496. Tel: 505-277-5912. FAX: 505-277-9813. Web Site: library.unm.edu/about/libraries/pml.php. *Dir of Outreach,* Susan C Awe; E-mail: sawe@unm.edu; Staff 10 (MLS 4, Non-MLS 6)
Founded 1989. Enrl 24,000; Highest Degree: Doctorate
Library Holdings: e-books 8,000; Bk Vols 185,000; Per Subs 5,000
Subject Interests: Econ, Mgt
Function: E-Reserves, Electronic databases & coll, ILL available, Online cat, Online ref, Orientations, Pub access computers, Ref & res, Ref serv available, Tax forms
Special Services for the Deaf - ADA equip; TTY equip
Open Mon-Thurs 8am-9pm, Fri 8-6, Sun Noon-9

TAOS CAMPUS, 115 Civic Plaza Dr, Taos, 87571. (Mail add: 1157 County Rd 110, Ranchos de Taos, 87557). Tel: 575-737-6242. FAX: 575-737-6292. E-mail: unmtlib@unm.edu. Web Site: taos.unm.edu/library. *Libr Dir,* Kathleen Knoth; Tel: 575-737-6243, E-mail: kathk@unm.edu; *Asst Librn,* Ana Pacheco; E-mail: apache02@unm.edu; *Info Spec I,* Enrico Trujillo; E-mail: enrico@unm.edu; Staff 2.5 (MLS 1, Non-MLS 1.5)
Founded 1995. Enrl 1,700; Highest Degree: Associate
Library Holdings: AV Mats 720; Bk Vols 5,200; Per Subs 24
Automation Activity & Vendor Info: (Cataloging) Innovative Interfaces, Inc; (Circulation) Innovative Interfaces, Inc - Millenium; (ILL) OCLC WorldShare Interlibrary Loan
Database Vendor: College Source, EBSCOhost, Foundation Center, Gale Cengage Learning, Ingram Library Services, Innovative Interfaces, Inc, LearningExpress, LexisNexis, Newsbank, OCLC FirstSearch, OCLC WorldShare Interlibrary Loan, ProQuest, WT Cox
Function: Audio & video playback equip for onsite use, Computer training, Computers for patron use, Copy machines, Doc delivery serv, e-mail serv, Electronic databases & coll, Exhibits, For res purposes, Free DVD rentals, ILL available, Instruction & testing, Libr develop, Music CDs, Online cat, Online searches, Orientations, Outreach serv, Prog for adults, Prog for children & young adult, Ref & res, Ref serv in person, Scanner, Spoken cassettes & CDs, Spoken cassettes & DVDs, VHS videos, Wheelchair accessible, Workshops
Partic in New Mexico Consortium of Academic Libraries
Open Mon-Thurs 8-8, Fri 8-5, Sat 10-4, Sun 12-5

VALENCIA CAMPUS, 280 La Entrada, Los Lunas, 87031. Tel: 505-925-8990. FAX: 505-925-8994. Web Site: www.unm.edu/~unmvclib. *Dir,* Dr Barbara Lovato; Tel: 505-925-8991, E-mail: bllovato@unm.edu; *Info Spec,* Lisa Pate; Tel: 505-925-8992, E-mail: lpate@unm.edu; *Pub Serv,* Leann Weller; Tel: 505-925-8993, E-mail: lweller1@unm.edu; Staff 2 (MLS 2)
Enrl 2,500; Highest Degree: Associate
Library Holdings: AV Mats 2,900; Bk Vols 43,500; Per Subs 150
Open Mon-Thurs 8am-8:30pm, Fri 10:30-5

ANGEL FIRE

P THE SHUTER LIBRARY OF ANGEL FIRE*, 11 S Angel Fire Rd, 87110. (Mail add: PO Box 298, 87110-0298). Tel: 575-377-6755. FAX: 575-377-3990. E-mail: info@shuterlibrary.net. Web Site: www.shuterlibrary.net. *Librn,* Diane Martinez
Library Holdings: AV Mats 900; Bk Vols 11,063
Automation Activity & Vendor Info: (Cataloging) Follett Software; (Circulation) Follett Software
Wireless access
Open Tues 10-7, Wed-Fri 10-6, Sat 10-3
Friends of the Library Group

ARTESIA

S ARTESIA HISTORICAL MUSEUM & ART CENTER, Research Facility, 505 W Richardson Ave, 88210. SAN 373-4773. Tel: 575-748-2390. FAX: 575-748-7345 (Attn: Museum). Web Site: www.artesianm.gov. *Mgr,* Nancy Dunn; E-mail: ndunn@artesianm.gov
Founded 1970
Library Holdings: Bk Vols 500
Special Collections: City of Artesia Archives
Subject Interests: Genealogy, Local hist
Wireless access
Function: Res libr
Open Tues-Fri 9-12 & 1-5, Sat 1-5

P ARTESIA PUBLIC LIBRARY*, 306 W Richardson Ave, 88210-2499. SAN 310 6500. Tel: 575-746-4252. FAX: 575-746-3075. Web Site: www.pvtnetworks.net/~apublib. *Librn,* Pamela Castle; *Acq,* Omar Acosta; *ILL,* Peggy Swafford; *Youth Serv,* Geraldine Dosalua; Staff 8 (MLS 2, Non-MLS 6)
Founded 1902. Pop 11,000
Library Holdings: Bk Titles 60,000; Per Subs 160
Special Collections: Dr Glenn E Stone (Southwest Coll); Leah Kennedy (Southwest Coll)
Automation Activity & Vendor Info: (Cataloging) Follett Software; (Circulation) Follett Software
Wireless access
Function: Homebound delivery serv, ILL available, Photocopying/Printing, Prog for children & young adult, Spoken cassettes & CDs, Summer reading prog, Video lending libr
Open Mon 1-6, Tues-Thurs 10-7, Fri & Sat 9-6

AZTEC

P AZTEC PUBLIC LIBRARY*, 319 S Ash, 87410. SAN 310-6519. Tel: 505-334-7658. FAX: 505-334-7659. Web Site: www.azteclibrary.org. *Dir,* Sabrina Hood; Staff 3 (Non-MLS 3)
Founded 1908
Library Holdings: Bk Vols 26,600; Per Subs 61
Special Collections: Audio/Video Coll (Adult & Juvenile); Local History; Southwest Coll; UFO'S
Subject Interests: Ancient astronomy, Aztec ruins, Chaco Canyon, Mesa Verde areas
Automation Activity & Vendor Info: (Acquisitions) SirsiDynix; (Cataloging) SirsiDynix; (Circulation) SirsiDynix
Wireless access

Open Mon-Thurs 9-8, Fri 9-6
Friends of the Library Group

G NATIONAL PARK SERVICE*, Aztec Ruins National Monument Library, 84 County Rd 2900, 87410. SAN 329-0697. Tel: 505-334-6174, Ext 232. FAX: 505-334-6372. TDD: 505-334-6174, Ext 30. Web Site: www.nps.gov/azru. *In Charge,* Tracey Bodnar
Founded 1923
Library Holdings: Bk Titles 700
Subject Interests: Archaeology
Function: For res purposes
Open Mon-Sun 8-5

BAYARD

P BAYARD PUBLIC LIBRARY*, 1112 Central Ave, 88023. Tel: 575-537-6244. FAX: 575-537-6246. Web Site: www.bayardpubliclibrary.org.
Library Holdings: Bk Vols 10,000; Talking Bks 150
Open Mon-Fri 8:30-5:30, Sat 10:30-5

BELEN

P BELEN PUBLIC LIBRARY, 333 Becker Ave, 87002. SAN 310-6527. Tel: 505-864-7522. Web Site: www.belen-nm.gov/library.htm. *Interim Dir, Pub Serv Librn,* Stephanie Wallace; Tel: 505-966-2606, E-mail: stephanie.wallace@belen-nm.gov; *Electronic & Ad,* Position Currently Open; *Youth Serv Librn/Tech II,* Catherine Biancardi; Tel: 505-966-2608, E-mail: catherine.biancardi@belen-nm.gov; *Circ Mgr,* Diana A Phillips; Tel: 505-966-2607, E-mail: diana.phillips@belen-nm.gov; *Yout Serv Asst,* Susan Checchio; Tel: 505-966-2603, E-mail: susan.checchio@belen-nm.gov; Staff 7 (MLS 3.5, MLS 3.5)
Founded 1966. Pop 21,778; Circ 62,567
Library Holdings: Bk Vols 41,605; Bk Vols 41,605; Per Subs 47; Per Subs 47
Subject Interests: Local hist, SW
Automation Activity & Vendor Info: (Circulation) TLC (The Library Corporation); (OPAC) TLC (The Library Corporation)
Database Vendor: ProQuest, ProQuest, TLC (The Library Corporation), TLC (The Library Corporation)
Wireless access
Function: Adult bk club, Art exhibits, Bilingual assistance for Spanish patrons, Bks on cassette, Bks on CD, Chess club, Computers for patron use, Copy machines, Digital talking bks, Electronic databases & coll, Free DVD rentals, Handicapped accessible, ILL available, Online cat, Photocopying/Printing, Prog for children & young adult, Ref serv available, Story hour, VHS videos, Wheelchair accessible
Open Mon-Fri 10-5, Thurs 6pm-8pm, Sat 10-2
Friends of the Library Group

BERNALILLO

P SANTA ANA PUEBLO COMMUNITY LIBRARY*, Two Dove Rd, 87004. Tel: 505-867-1623. FAX: 505-771-3849. *Dir,* Melverna Lujan
Pop 727
Library Holdings: AV Mats 200; Bk Vols 6,116; Per Subs 12
Database Vendor: Gale Cengage Learning
Open Mon-Thurs (Winter) 9:30-6, Fri 8-4:30; Mon-Fri (Summer) 8-4:30

P TOWN OF BERNALILLO*, Martha Liebert Public Library, 124 Calle Malinche, 87004. (Mail add: PO Box 638, Bernalillo, 87004-0638), SAN 310-6535. Tel: 505-867-1440. FAX: 505-867-8040. Web Site: www.townofbernalillo.org/depts/library.htm. *Dir,* Kathy Banks; E-mail: kbanks@townofbernalillo.org; *Libr Asst,* Amanda Morales
Founded 1965. Pop 9,000
Library Holdings: Bk Vols 23,000; Per Subs 8
Special Collections: Historical Coll of Southwest
Wireless access
Partic in NMex Libr Asn
Open Mon-Thurs 9:30-6, Fri 9:30-5, Sat 9-1
Friends of the Library Group

BLOOMFIELD

P BLOOMFIELD PUBLIC LIBRARY*, 333 S First St, 87413-3559. SAN 375-5207. Tel: 505-632-8315. FAX: 505-632-0876. E-mail: staff@bplnm.org. Web Site: www.bplnm.org. *Librn,* Jeannette Lassell; E-mail: jeannette@bplnm.org; Staff 1 (MLS 1)
Founded 1990. Pop 7,304; Circ 22,007
Library Holdings: AV Mats 300; Bk Vols 20,000; Per Subs 30; Videos 56
Automation Activity & Vendor Info: (Cataloging) SirsiDynix; (Circulation) SirsiDynix
Special Services for the Deaf - Bks on deafness & sign lang; High interest/low vocabulary bks
Special Services for the Blind - Talking bks
Open Mon-Thurs 10-8, Fri 10-5, Sat 9-1
Friends of the Library Group

S SAN JUAN COUNTY ARCHAEOLOGICAL RESEARCH CENTER & LIBRARY AT SALMON RUINS*, Salmon Ruins Museum, 6131 US Hwy 64, 87413. (Mail add: PO Box 125, 87413-0125), SAN 326-2480. Tel: 505-632-2013. Interlibrary Loan Service Tel: 505-566-3692. FAX: 505-632-8633. E-mail: sreducation@sisna.com. Web Site: www.salmonruins.com. *Exec Dir,* Larry L Baker. Subject Specialists: *Anthrop, Archeology, Presv,* Larry L Baker
Founded 1973
Library Holdings: DVDs 10; e-books 100; Bk Titles 6,000; Per Subs 200; Spec Interest Per Sub 170; Videos 20
Special Collections: Hadlock, Rothrock & Rodgers Coll (Local Documentation of Rock Art Sites, Symbolism, Interpretation), photog, slides; Salmon Ruins Coll (Salmon Ruin Excavation & Preservation Records), photog, slides & research documentation; San Juan County Historical File (Local Information Related to Genealogy, Homesteading, Photos, Archaeological Sites, Newspaper Articles); Snyder Coll (Civilian Conservation Corps); Turbull Coll (San Juan Episcopal Mission Records); Wynhoff Coll (Native Plant Identification & Botanic Examples). Oral History
Subject Interests: Anthrop, Archaeology, Local hist, NMex, SW
Publications: San Juan County Museum Association (Documents)
Open Mon-Fri 8-5
Restriction: Circ to mem only, Restricted borrowing privileges, Secured area only open to authorized personnel

BOSQUE FARMS

P BOSQUE FARMS PUBLIC LIBRARY*, 1455 W Bosque Loop, 87068. SAN 373-8167. Tel: 505-869-2227. FAX: 505-869-3342. E-mail: bfpublib@yahoo.com. *Dir,* Sophita Kyhnsen
Founded 1985. Pop 3,931; Circ 25,311
Library Holdings: Bk Titles 25,000
Automation Activity & Vendor Info: (Cataloging) Follett Software; (Circulation) Follett Software; (OPAC) Follett Software
Open Mon-Thurs 10-5, Sat 10-2
Friends of the Library Group

CANNON AFB

A UNITED STATES AIR FORCE*, Cannon Air Force Base Library FL4855, 27 SVS/SVMG, 107 Trident Ave, Bldg 75, 88103-5211. SAN 351-6393. Tel: 505-784-2786. FAX: 505-784-6929. *Mgr,* Melissa Haraughty; E-mail: melissa.haraughty@cannon.af.mil; Staff 5 (MLS 2, Non-MLS 3)
Library Holdings: Bk Vols 35,000; Per Subs 160
Automation Activity & Vendor Info: (Acquisitions) SirsiDynix; (Cataloging) SirsiDynix; (Circulation) SirsiDynix; (Serials) SirsiDynix
Wireless access
Open Mon-Thurs 9:30-7:30, Fri & Sat 9:30-5

CAPITAN

P CAPITAN PUBLIC LIBRARY*, 101 E Second St, 88316. (Mail add: PO Box 1169, 88316-1169). Tel: 575-354-3035. FAX: 575-354-3223. E-mail: capitanlibrary@gmail.com. Web Site: www.capitanlibrary.org. *Board Pres,* George Hinch; *Dir,* Pat Garrett; *Cataloger,* Barbara Stewart
Founded 1996. Pop 2,000; Circ 10,000
Automation Activity & Vendor Info: (Cataloging) Biblionix; (Circulation) Biblionix
Database Vendor: Gale Cengage Learning
Wireless access
Function: Adult bk club, After school storytime, Art exhibits, Bks on cassette, Bks on CD, Children's prog, Computers for patron use, Copy machines, Fax serv, Handicapped accessible, ILL available, Online cat, Online searches, Photocopying/Printing, Preschool outreach, Prog for adults, Prog for children & young adult, Pub access computers, Ref & res, Referrals accepted, Summer reading prog, Tax forms, VCDs, VHS videos
Open Tues-Thurs 10-6, Fri & Sat 10-2
Friends of the Library Group

CAPULIN

G US NATIONAL PARK SERVICE*, Capulin Volcano National Monument Library, 46 Volcano Rd, 88414. (Mail add: PO Box 40, Des Moines, 88418). Tel: 575-278-2201, Ext 231. FAX: 575-278-2211. Web Site: www.nps.gov/cavo. *In Charge,* Lynn Cartnel
Library Holdings: Bk Titles 1,455; Bk Vols 1,500
Open Mon-Sun 8-4:30

CARLSBAD

M CARLSBAD MEDICAL CENTER*, Medical Staff Library, 2430 W Pierce St, 88220. SAN 321-8821. Tel: 575-887-4100. *Coordr,* Alma Martinez; Tel: 575-887-4100, Ext 4485
Library Holdings: Bk Titles 2,500; Per Subs 30
Restriction: Med staff only

P CARLSBAD PUBLIC LIBRARY*, 101 S Halagueno St, 88220. SAN 310-6543. Tel: 575-885-6776. FAX: 575-887-7706. E-mail: cplinfo@cityofcarlsbadnm.com. Web Site: www.cityofcarlsbadnm.com/library.cfm. *Dir,* Cassandra Arnold; E-mail: caarnold@cityofcarlsbadnm.com; *Asst Dir,* Sybil Walterscheid; E-mail: siwalterscheid@cityofcarlsbadnm.com; *Cat Librn,* Julie Pearson; E-mail: jlpearson@cityofcarlsbadnm.com; *Tech Serv Librn,* Samantha Villa; E-mail: srvilla@cityofcarlsbadnm.com; *Youth Serv Librn,* Beth Nieman; E-mail: banieman@cityofcarlsbadnm.com; Staff 12 (MLS 5, Non-MLS 7)
Founded 1897. Pop 35,000; Circ 119,000
Library Holdings: Bk Titles 78,000; Per Subs 200
Special Collections: Family History; New Mexico History; Waste Isolation Pilot Project
Subject Interests: Family hist, Local hist
Automation Activity & Vendor Info: (Cataloging) Biblionix; (Circulation) Biblionix; (OPAC) Biblionix
Wireless access
Publications: Friends of the Library Newletter (Quarterly)
Open Mon-Thurs 9-8, Fri & Sat 9-6
Friends of the Library Group

J NEW MEXICO STATE UNIVERSITY AT CARLSBAD*, Library & Media Center, 1500 University Dr, 88220. SAN 310-6551. Tel: 575-234-9330. E-mail: carlsbad_library@nmsu.edu. Web Site: carlsbad.nmsu.edu/departments/library. *Libr Dir,* Akilah S Nosakhere; E-mail: anosa7@nmsu.edu; Staff 1 (MLS 1)
Highest Degree: Associate
Library Holdings: Bk Titles 20,000; Per Subs 100
Open Mon-Thurs 8-8, Fri 8-5

S TFE (TECHNICAL FIELD ENGINEERS), WIPP Technical Library, 4021 National Parks Hwy, 88220. (Mail add: PO Box 2078, 88221-5608), SAN 323-7605. Tel: 575-234-7618. FAX: 575-234-7076. *Mgr,* Michael Fox; Tel: 575-234-3207; *Rec Analyst,* Ruthie Goff; E-mail: Ruthie.Goff@wipp.ws; Staff 1 (Non-MLS 1)
Library Holdings: Bk Vols 1,821; Per Subs 20
Subject Interests: Waste mgt
Database Vendor: IHS
Restriction: Not open to pub

CHAMA

P ELEANOR DAGGETT PUBLIC LIBRARY*, 299 W Fourth St, 87520-0786. (Mail add: PO Box 795, 87520-0795), SAN 310-6578. Tel: 575-756-2184. FAX: 575-756-2412. *Librn,* Lee Walters; Tel: 575-756-2184, Ext 225; Staff 1 (Non-MLS 1)
Founded 1973. Pop 3,000; Circ 16,500
Library Holdings: Bk Vols 10,000; Per Subs 27
Special Collections: Southwest Coll
Wireless access
Function: Adult bk club, Audio & video playback equip for onsite use, Bks on cassette, Bks on CD, Children's prog, Copy machines, Electronic databases & coll, Free DVD rentals, Handicapped accessible, ILL available, Photocopying/Printing, Preschool outreach, Spoken cassettes & CDs, Spoken cassettes & DVDs, Story hour, Summer reading prog, Tax forms, VHS videos, Wheelchair accessible
Partic in NMex Info Systs
Open Mon-Fri 8-12 & 1-5

CIMARRON

P NEW MEXICO STATE LIBRARY*, Rural Bookmobile Northeast, 356-D E Ninth St, 87714. (Mail add: PO Box 97, 87714-0097), SAN 310-6586. Tel: 575-376-2474. FAX: 575-376-2433. *Librn,* Charri Richards; *Libr Tech,* Leroy Chavez; *Libr Tech,* Laura Gonzales; Staff 3 (MLS 1, Non-MLS 2)
Founded 1957. Circ 61,000
Library Holdings: Bk Vols 22,000
Special Collections: Southwest Coll
Wireless access
Partic in OCLC Online Computer Library Center, Inc
Open Mon-Fri 8-12 & 1-5
Bookmobiles: 1

S PHILMONT MUSEUM & SETON MEMORIAL LIBRARY*, Philmont Scout Ranch, 17 Deer Run Rd, 87714. SAN 310-6594. Tel: 575-376-2281, Ext 1256. FAX: 575-376-2602. *Dir,* Seth I McFarland; E-mail: smcfarla@netbsa.org; *Librn,* Robin Taylor; Tel: 575-376-1136, E-mail: rtaylor@netbsa.org
Library Holdings: Bk Vols 7,500; Per Subs 12
Special Collections: Artifacts & Jewelry (Indian Coll); Natural History (Boy Scout Coll)
Subject Interests: SW hist
Open Mon-Fri 8-5

CLAYTON

P CLAYTON PUBLIC LIBRARY*, Albert W Thompson Memorial Library, 17 Chestnut St, 88415. SAN 310-6608. Tel: 575-374-9423. FAX: 575-374-9423. E-mail: claytonlibrary@yahoo.com. *Librn,* Lacie Cook; *Asst Librn,* Malcolm Callis; Staff 1 (MLS 1)
Founded 1920. Pop 4,500; Circ 13,000
Library Holdings: Bk Titles 15,000; Bk Vols 17,000; Per Subs 10
Special Collections: New Mexico & Southwest, bks, filmstrips
Partic in NMex Info Systs
Open Mon-Fri 10-5:30, Sat 10-5

CLOUDCROFT

P MICHAEL NIVISON PUBLIC LIBRARY*, 90 Swallow Pl, 88317. (Mail add: PO Box 515, 88317-0515). Tel: 575-682-1111. FAX: 575-682-1111. E-mail: library@nmex.com. Web Site: users.apo.nmsu.edu/~jb/library. *Dir,* Joyce Komraus
Library Holdings: AV Mats 24; CDs 50; DVDs 100; Bk Vols 13,600; Talking Bks 1,000
Automation Activity & Vendor Info: (Cataloging) Follett Software; (Circulation) Follett Software
Wireless access
Open Mon & Sat 10-3, Tues 12-5, Thurs 10-6, Fri 10-5
Friends of the Library Group

CLOVIS

P CLOVIS-CARVER PUBLIC LIBRARY, 701 N Main, 88101. SAN 310-6616. Tel: 505-769-7840. FAX: 505-769-7842. E-mail: library@cityofclovis.org. Web Site: www.cityofclovis.org/library. *Libr Dir,* Margaret Hinchee; E-mail: mhinchee@cityofclovis.org; *Ref Serv Librn,* Terri Gleaton; E-mail: tgleaton@cityofclovis.org; *Circ Supvr,* Scott Jones; E-mail: sjones@cityofclovis.org; *Coord, Ad Serv, ILL,* Sarah Lewis; E-mail: slewis@cityofclovis.org; *Ref,* Mary Mattimoie; E-mail: mmattimoe@cityofclovis.org; *Youth Serv,* Krissie Carter; E-mail: kcarter@cityofclovis.org; Staff 14 (Non MLS 14)
Founded 1949. Pop 37,000; Circ 171,029
Jul 2013-Jun 2014 Income $883,254, State $12,797, City $809,735, Locally Generated Income $60,722. Mats Exp $92,276, Books $69,635, Per/Ser (Incl. Access Fees) $4,122, AV Mat $3,965, Electronic Ref Mat (Incl. Access Fees) $14,554
Library Holdings: AV Mats 5,848; e-books 3,529; Large Print Bks 3,122; Bk Vols 124,125; Per Subs 155
Special Collections: New Mexico Documents. State Document Depository
Subject Interests: SW
Automation Activity & Vendor Info: (Cataloging) Innovative Interfaces, Inc; (Circulation) Innovative Interfaces, Inc; (OPAC) Innovative Interfaces, Inc
Database Vendor: OCLC FirstSearch
Wireless access
Partic in NMex Info Systs; OCLC Online Computer Library Center, Inc
Special Services for the Deaf - TDD equip
Special Services for the Blind - Talking bks
Open Mon-Thurs 9-9, Fri & Sat 9-5
Friends of the Library Group

J CLOVIS COMMUNITY COLLEGE LIBRARY*, 417 Schepps Blvd, 88101. SAN 310-6624. Tel: 575-769-4080. FAX: 575-769-4190. E-mail: ccclib@clovis.edu. Web Site: www.clovis.edu. *Dir,* Dr Deborah Anderson; *Acq,* Position Currently Open; *Circ,* Karen Jones; *Media Spec,* Rex Regnier; *Ref,* Kelly Gray; Staff 2 (MLS 2)
Founded 1969. Enrl 4,000; Fac 60; Highest Degree: Associate
Library Holdings: Bks on Deafness & Sign Lang 200; DVDs 300; Bk Titles 45,000; Bk Vols 70,000; Per Subs 300; Videos 1,700
Special Collections: Rare Books (Some Autographed); Southwest Coll
Subject Interests: SW Am
Automation Activity & Vendor Info: (Acquisitions) Innovative Interfaces, Inc; (Cataloging) Innovative Interfaces, Inc; (Circulation) Innovative Interfaces, Inc; (OPAC) Innovative Interfaces, Inc; (Serials) Innovative Interfaces, Inc
Publications: Bibliographies
Partic in Leann
Open Mon-Thurs 8-8, Fri 8-4:30

COCHITI

P COCHITI PUEBLO COMMUNITY LIBRARY*, 245 Cochiti St, 87072. (Mail add: PO Box 70, 87072-0070), SAN 321-7515. Tel: 505-465-3118. FAX: 505-465-2203. *Dir,* Nellie Pacheco
Founded 1977
Library Holdings: Bk Titles 3,600; Per Subs 20
Special Collections: Cochiti History; Cochiti Pueblo Past & Present, photogs
Open Mon-Fri 8-8
Friends of the Library Group

COCHITI LAKE

P COCHITI LAKE PUBLIC LIBRARY*, 6515 Hoochaneetsa Blvd, 87083. SAN 375-4359. Tel: 505-465-2561. FAX: 505-465-3009. E-mail: library@cochitilake.org. Web Site: www.cochitilake.org/library. *Dir,* Mary Badarak
Library Holdings: Bk Vols 9,800
Special Collections: Southwest Coll
Subject Interests: Arizona, Colorado, NMex, Tex, Utah
Automation Activity & Vendor Info: (Cataloging) Follett Software
Open Mon & Tues 11-5, Wed & Thurs 2-7, Fri 2-6, Sat 10-1
Friends of the Library Group

COLUMBUS

P COLUMBUS VILLAGE PUBLIC LIBRARY*, 222 W Broadway Ave, 88029. (Mail add: PO Box 270, 88029-0270). Tel: 575-531-2612. E-mail: columbusvillagelibrary@yahoo.com. *Dir,* Linda Werner; *Librn,* Maggie Calderon
Library Holdings: Bk Vols 12,000; Per Subs 25; Talking Bks 60
Open Mon-Fri 9-1 & 4-7, Sat 9-1

CORRALES

P CORRALES COMMUNITY LIBRARY*, 84 W La Entrada, 87048. (Mail add: PO Box 1868, 87048-1868), SAN 310-6632. Tel: 505-897-0733. FAX: 505-897-0596. E-mail: info@corraleslibrary.org. Web Site: www.corraleslibrary.org. *Dir,* Carla Spencer
Founded 1957. Pop 7,500
Library Holdings: Bk Vols 36,000; Per Subs 70
Special Collections: Southwest Coll
Automation Activity & Vendor Info: (Acquisitions) BiblioMondo; (Cataloging) BiblioMondo; (Circulation) BiblioMondo
Wireless access
Open Mon & Fri 10-5, Tues & Thurs 1-9, Wed 10-7, Sat 10-1
Friends of the Library Group

CROWNPOINT

J DINE COLLEGE*, Crownpoint Campus Library, One College Dr, 87313. (Mail add: PO Box 57, 87313). Tel: 505-786-7391. FAX: 505-786-5240. Web Site: library.dinecollege.edu. *Circ Tech,* Derek- H Begay
Library Holdings: AV Mats 300; Bk Titles 4,000; Talking Bks 100
Automation Activity & Vendor Info: (Acquisitions) Ex Libris Group; (Cataloging) Ex Libris Group; (Circulation) Ex Libris Group; (OPAC) Ex Libris Group
Database Vendor: OCLC FirstSearch
Open Mon-Thurs 10-9, Fri 8-5

CUBA

P CUBA PUBLIC LIBRARY*, 13 E Cordova Ave, 87013. (Mail add: PO Box 426, 87013-0426), SAN 321-4680. Tel: 505-289-3100. Administration Tel: 505-289-3758. FAX: 575-289-9187. Administration FAX: 575-289-3769. E-mail: cubalib2001@yahoo.com. *Dir, Libr Serv Mgr,* Barbara Trujillo
Founded 1962. Pop 13,960
Library Holdings: Bk Titles 23,400; Per Subs 51
Special Collections: Southwest Coll
Automation Activity & Vendor Info: (Acquisitions) Follett Software; (Circulation) Follett Software
Database Vendor: Baker & Taylor
Function: Outside serv via phone, mail, e-mail & web, Prog for children & young adult, Ref serv available, Summer reading prog, Telephone ref, VHS videos, Video lending libr, Wheelchair accessible, Workshops
Open Mon-Fri 8-5
Restriction: Circ to mem only, Open to pub for ref & circ; with some limitations, Open to pub with supv only, Open to students, fac & staff, Photo ID required for access, Pub use on premises, Restricted loan policy, Use of others with permission of librn
Friends of the Library Group
Bookmobiles: 1

DATIL

P BALDWIN CABIN PUBLIC LIBRARY*, Cibola National Forest, Forest Rd 100, 87821. (Mail add: PO Box 255, 87821-0255). Tel: 575-772-5230. Administration Tel: 575-299-3491, 575-772-5730. *Dir,* Linn Kennedy
Founded 1999. Pop 1,200; Circ 2,900
Library Holdings: AV Mats 400; Bks on Deafness & Sign Lang 3; CDs 40; DVDs 70; Large Print Bks 85; Bk Titles 11,000; Talking Bks 200
Special Collections: Cibola National Forest Coll; Southwest Coll
Function: Children's prog, Holiday prog, Prog for adults
Open Wed & Sat 10-2
Friends of the Library Group

DEMING

P MARSHALL MEMORIAL LIBRARY*, 110 S Diamond St, 88030-3698. SAN 310-6640. Tel: 505-546-9202. FAX: 505-546-9649. E-mail: demingpl@cityofdeming.org. *Dir,* Pat Turner; *Circ,* Jeannie Keeler; *Ref,* Amparo Torres; *YA Serv,* Angela Wilds; Staff 5 (Non-MLS 5)
Founded 1917. Pop 18,000; Circ 184,880
Library Holdings: Bk Vols 68,133; Per Subs 100
Special Collections: Southwest Coll
Subject Interests: SW US fiction
Automation Activity & Vendor Info: (Cataloging) TLC (The Library Corporation); (Circulation) TLC (The Library Corporation)
Database Vendor: Gale Cengage Learning, OCLC FirstSearch
Wireless access
Function: ILL available
Publications: Information Brochure
Open Mon, Wed & Fri 9-6, Tues & Thurs 9-8, Sat 9-1
Friends of the Library Group

DEXTER

P DEXTER PUBLIC LIBRARY*, 115 E Second, 88230. (Mail add: PO Box 249, 88230). Tel: 575-734-5482. FAX: 575-734-6605.
Library Holdings: Bk Vols 12,000
Wireless access
Open Mon-Fri 8-12:30 & 1-4:30

DIXON

P EMBUDO VALLEY PUBLIC LIBRARY*, 217 Hwy 75, 87527. (Mail add: PO Box 310, 87527-0310). Tel: 505-579-9181. FAX: 505-579-9128. E-mail: evl@cybermesa.com. Web Site: www.embudovalleylibrary.org. *Exec Dir,* Felicity Fonseca; *Dir, Libr & Info Mgt,* Position Currently Open; *Librn,* Sandy Funk; *Librn,* Einar Kvaran; Staff 3 (Non-MLS 3)
Founded 1992. Pop 1,428; Circ 10,996
Library Holdings: AV Mats 2,655; Bk Vols 12,779; Per Subs 45
Automation Activity & Vendor Info: (Acquisitions) Book Systems; (Cataloging) Book Systems; (Circulation) Book Systems; (ILL) OCLC ILLiad; (OPAC) Book Systems
Wireless access
Function: Art exhibits, Audiobks via web, AV serv, Bk reviews (Group), Bks on cassette, Bks on CD, CD-ROM, Chess club, Children's prog, Computer training, Computers for patron use, Copy machines, Digital talking bks, Distance learning, e-mail & chat, e-mail serv, E-Reserves, Electronic databases & coll, Exhibits, Family literacy, Fax serv, For res purposes, Free DVD rentals, Games & aids for the handicapped, Handicapped accessible, Health sci info serv, Homework prog, ILL available, Instruction & testing, Learning ctr, Literacy & newcomer serv, Mail & tel request accepted, Music CDs, Newsp ref libr, Notary serv, Online cat, Online searches, Outreach serv, Outside serv via phone, mail, e-mail & web, OverDrive digital audio bks, Photocopying/Printing, Preschool outreach, Preschool reading prog, Printer for laptops & handheld devices, Prog for adults, Prog for children & young adult, Pub access computers, Ref & res, Ref serv available, Ref serv in person, Referrals accepted, Res libr, Scanner, Senior computer classes, Senior outreach, Serves mentally handicapped consumers, Spanish lang bks, Spoken cassettes & CDs, Spoken cassettes & DVDs, Story hour, Summer & winter reading prog, Summer reading prog, Tax forms, Teen prog, Telephone ref, VHS videos, Video lending libr, Visual arts prog, Web-catalog, Wheelchair accessible, Winter reading prog, Workshops
Open Mon-Fri 11-6, Sat 11-5

EAGLE NEST

P EAGLE NEST PUBLIC LIBRARY*, 74 N Tomboy Dr, 87718. (Mail add: PO Box 168, 87718-0168). Tel: 505-377-0657. FAX: 505-377-2487. E-mail: eaglenestlibrary@yahoo.com. *Dir,* Luann Lorence
Pop 278; Circ 2,355
Library Holdings: AV Mats 675; Bk Vols 6,000; Talking Bks 150
Database Vendor: JayWil Software Development, Inc
Open Mon-Fri 9:30-5

EDGEWOOD

P EDGEWOOD COMMUNITY LIBRARY*, 95 Hwy 344 N, 87015. (Mail add: PO Box 1134, 87015-1134), SAN 375-5029. Tel: 505-281-0138. FAX: 505-286-9107. E-mail: ecl_cat@yahoo.com. Web Site: www.edgewoodlibrary.com. *Librn,* Andrea Corvin; *Asst Librn,* Barbara Hambek
Founded 1991. Pop 2,700; Circ 21,372
Library Holdings: DVDs 340; Bk Titles 18,106
Automation Activity & Vendor Info: (Cataloging) Biblionix; (Circulation) Biblionix
Wireless access
Open Mon-Thurs 10-6, Fri 10-5, Sat 10-3
Friends of the Library Group

EL RITO

P EL RITO PUBLIC LIBRARY*, 182 Placitas Rd, 87530. (Mail add: PO Box 5, 87530-0005). Tel: 575-581-4608. FAX: 575-581-9591. E-mail: elritopubliclibrary@yahoo.com. Web Site: www.elritolibrary.org. *Dir,* Christine Trujillo; *Librn,* Thomas Fortson; *Librn,* Marcela Barrionuevo
Founded 1986
Jul 2005-Jun 2006 Income $64,000, County $8,000, Locally Generated Income $30,000, Other $26,000
Library Holdings: CDs 100; Bk Vols 16,000; Per Subs 15; Videos 500
Automation Activity & Vendor Info: (Cataloging) Follett Software; (Circulation) Follett Software; (Course Reserve) Follett Software
Database Vendor: EBSCOhost, Gale Cengage Learning
Open Tues-Thurs (Winter) 10-5, Sat 11-5; Tues-Thurs (Summer) 11-6

ELIDA

P ELIDA PUBLIC LIBRARY*, Ruth McCowen Public Library, 703 Clark St, 88116. Tel: 505-274-6465.
Founded 1945. Pop 500; Circ 3,500
Library Holdings: Bk Titles 8,000
Open Thurs 1:30-4

ESPANOLA

P ESPANOLA PUBLIC LIBRARY*, 313 N Paseo de Onate, 87532. SAN 310-6659. Tel: 505-747-6087. Circulation Tel: 505-747-6089. FAX: 505-753-5543. Web Site: www.cityofespanola.org/library.html. *Libr Dir,* Sherry Aragon; Staff 6 (Non-MLS 6)
Founded 1969. Pop 14,000; Circ 40,707
Jul 2009-Jun 2010 Income $267,735, City $248,735, County $10,000, Other $9,000. Sal $150,904
Library Holdings: AV Mats 900; Bk Vols 43,000; Per Subs 102
Special Collections: Southwest Coll; Spanish Language Coll
Automation Activity & Vendor Info: (Cataloging) TLC (The Library Corporation); (Circulation) TLC (The Library Corporation); (ILL) TLC (The Library Corporation); (OPAC) TLC (The Library Corporation); (Serials) TLC (The Library Corporation)
Partic in NMex Info Systs
Open Mon 9-6, Tues-Thurs 9-7, Fri 9-5, Sat 9-4
Friends of the Library Group

J NORTHERN NEW MEXICO COLLEGE*, Learning Resource Center, 921 Paseo de Onate, 87532. SAN 310-7108. Tel: 505-747-2100. Circulation Tel: 505-747-2243. FAX: 505-747-2245. Web Site: www.nnmc.edu. *Dir,* Isabel Rodarte; Tel: 505-747-2241, E-mail: irodarte@nnmc.edu; Staff 1 (MLS 1)
Founded 1973. Enrl 1,100
Library Holdings: Microforms 5,000; Bk Titles 40,000; Per Subs 150
Special Collections: Local History
Automation Activity & Vendor Info: (Cataloging) OCLC; (Circulation) Innovative Interfaces, Inc; (ILL) OCLC; (OPAC) Innovative Interfaces, Inc; (Serials) EBSCO Online
Database Vendor: OCLC FirstSearch
Partic in New Mexico Consortium of Academic Libraries
Open Mon-Thurs 8am-9pm, Fri 8-5, Sat & Sun 12-5

P SANTA CLARA PUEBLO COMMUNITY LIBRARY*, PO Box 580, 87532-0580. SAN 310-6667. Tel: 505-753-7326. Web Site: www.santaclarapueblo.org/library. *Dir,* Teresa Naranjo; *Asst Librn,* Wanda Dozier
Circ 6,984
Library Holdings: Bk Titles 7,000; Bk Vols 8,535; Per Subs 60
Special Collections: Southwest Indian Special Coll
Subject Interests: Native Am
Partic in New Mexico Libr Asn Round Table
Open Mon-Thurs 8-4:30 & 6-8, Fri 8-4:30

ESTANCIA

P ESTANCIA PUBLIC LIBRARY*, 601 S Tenth St, 87016. (Mail add: PO Box 166, 87016-0166), SAN 373-837X. Tel: 505-384-9655. FAX: 505-384-3023. E-mail: estanciapblib@townofestancia.com. Web Site: www.townofestancia.com/index.php?page=library. *Head Librn,* Angela Creamer; *Asst Librn,* Jaime Kruz; Staff 2 (Non-MLS 2)
Pop 1,500; Circ 2,200
Library Holdings: Bk Vols 10,500; Per Subs 20
Special Collections: New Mexico & the Southwest (Southwest Coll)
Automation Activity & Vendor Info: (Cataloging) Follett Software
Wireless access
Open Mon & Thurs 10-6, Fri 10-5, Sat 12-5

EUNICE

P EUNICE PUBLIC LIBRARY*, 1003 Ave N, 88231. (Mail add: PO Box 1629, 88231-1629), SAN 310-6675. Tel: 575-394-2336, 575-394-2338. FAX: 575-394-0970. E-mail: eunplib@valornet.com. Web Site: elinlib.org. *Dir,* Tara G Parker; E-mail: tparker@elinlib.org; *Ch,* Kim Smith; Staff 4 (Non-MLS 4)
Founded 1957. Pop 2,922; Circ 13,524
Jul 2012-Jun 2013 Income $253,301, State $5,672, City $230,450, Federal $1,796, County $10,000, Locally Generated Income $2,315, Other $3,068. Mats Exp $16,448, Books $12,667, Per/Ser (Incl. Access Fees) $654, AV Mat $2,127, Electronic Ref Mat (Incl. Access Fees) $1,000. Sal $95,957 (Prof $43,000)
Library Holdings: Audiobooks 732; AV Mats 944; DVDs 460; Electronic Media & Resources 202; Bk Titles 24,717; Per Subs 38; Videos 406
Special Collections: Christian Books (Family Coll)
Subject Interests: Livestock, NMex, Oil field, SW
Automation Activity & Vendor Info: (Acquisitions) SIRSI Unicorn; (Cataloging) OCLC CatExpress; (Circulation) SIRSI WorkFlows; (OPAC) SIRSI WorkFlows
Database Vendor: EBSCO Auto Repair Reference, Gale Cengage Learning, OCLC FirstSearch
Wireless access
Function: Bks on cassette, Bks on CD, Children's prog, Computers for patron use, Copy machines, Fax serv, Free DVD rentals, Homebound delivery serv, ILL available, Notary serv, Online cat, Online searches, Res libr, Story hour, Summer reading prog, Tax forms, Telephone ref, VHS videos, Video lending libr, Web-catalog
Partic in Estacado Library Information Network; NMex Libr Asn; OCLC Online Computer Library Center, Inc
Special Services for the Deaf - ADA equip; Bks on deafness & sign lang
Special Services for the Blind - Large print bks; Recorded bks; Sound rec; Talking bks
Open Mon-Thurs 8-5:30, Fri 8-5, Sat 8-1

FARMINGTON

P FARMINGTON PUBLIC LIBRARY, 2101 Farmington Ave, 87401. SAN 310-6683. Tel: 505-599-1270. Reference Tel: 505-599-1272. FAX: 505-599-1257. Web Site: www.infoway.org. *Dep Dir,* Mary Lee Smith; Tel: 505-566-2205, E-mail: mlsmith@infoway.org; *Admin Dir,* Karen McPheeters; Tel: 505-599-1275, E-mail: kmcpheet@infoway.org; *Tech Serv Supvr,* Sharon BlueEyes; Tel: 505-599-1274, E-mail: sblueeyes@infoway.org; *Adult Serv Coordr,* Kathleen Browning; Tel: 505-566-2210, E-mail: kabrowning@infoway.org; *Youth Serv Coordr,* Flo Trujillo, Tel: 505-599-1261, E-mail: ftrujill@infoway.org; Staff 19 (MLS 5, Non-MLS 14)
Founded 1921. Pop 115,169; Circ 457,171
Library Holdings: Audiobooks 6,485; CDs 14,661; DVDs 8,366; e-books 6,559; Electronic Media & Resources 100; Bk Titles 170,340; Per Subs 512
Special Collections: Southwest Coll. State Document Depository; UN Document Depository; US Document Depository
Subject Interests: SW
Automation Activity & Vendor Info: (Acquisitions) SirsiDynix; (Cataloging) SirsiDynix; (Circulation) SirsiDynix; (OPAC) SirsiDynix; (Serials) SirsiDynix
Database Vendor: 3M Library Systems, ABC-CLIO, Amigos Library Services, Career Guidance Foundation, CQ Press, EBSCO Auto Repair Reference, EBSCOhost, Evanced Solutions, Inc, Facts on File, Gale Cengage Learning, infoUSA, Ingram Library Services, LearningExpress, OCLC FirstSearch, OCLC WorldShare Interlibrary Loan, Overdrive, Inc, ProQuest, ReferenceUSA, SirsiDynix, World Book Online
Wireless access
Open Mon-Thurs 9-9, Fri 9-5, Sat 10-5, Sun 1-5; Mon-Thurs (Summer) 9-7
Friends of the Library Group
Branches: 1
SHIPROCK BRANCH LIBRARY, US Hwy 491 E, (side of Shiprock Boys & Girls Club Bldg), Shiprock, 87420. (Mail add: 2101 Farmington Ave, 87401), SAN 377-0311. Tel: 505-368-3804. FAX: 505-599-1257. E-mail: shiprockbranch@infoway.org. *Br Mgr,* Glonette King

Library Holdings: Bk Vols 5,007; Per Subs 48
Open Mon-Fri 2-6

J SAN JUAN COLLEGE LIBRARY*, 4601 College Blvd, 87402. SAN 310-6691. Tel: 505-566-3249. FAX: 505-566-3381. Web Site: www.sanjuancollege.edu/lib. *Dir, Libr Serv,* Christopher Schipper; Tel: 505-566-3449, E-mail: schipperc@sanjuancollege.edu; *Ref Librn,* Danielle Burbank; *Ref Librn,* Joseph Owen; Tel: 505-566-3256, E-mail: owenj@sanjuancollege.edu; *Acq,* Cindy Williams; Tel: 505-566-3248, E-mail: williamsc@sanjuancollege.edu; Staff 9 (MLS 4, Non-MLS 5)
Founded 1964. Enrl 5,000; Fac 110; Highest Degree: Associate
Jul 2012-Jun 2013 Income $688,312. Mats Exp $317,852. Sal $317,460
Library Holdings: Bk Vols 77,678; Per Subs 304
Special Collections: San Juan County Law Coll; Southwestern Americana, bks, maps, rpts; Tom Carter Petroleum Geological Coll. State Document Depository
Automation Activity & Vendor Info: (Cataloging) Ex Libris Group; (Circulation) Ex Libris Group; (OPAC) Ex Libris Group
Database Vendor: Gale Cengage Learning, Newsbank, ProQuest
Wireless access
Publications: Information Brochures
Partic in New Mexico Consortium of Academic Libraries; New Mexico Libr Asn Round Table; OCLC Online Computer Library Center, Inc

FORT SUMNER

P FORT SUMNER PUBLIC LIBRARY*, 235 W Sumner Ave, 88119. (Mail add: PO Drawer D, 88119), SAN 310-6713. Tel: 505-355-2832. FAX: 505-355-7732. E-mail: fspl@plateautel.net. Web Site: www.fortsumner.net. *Dir,* Karla Hunt; *Ch,* Heather Davenport; E-mail: ftsumnerpl@plateautel.net; *Circ, Ref,* Bonnie Lilly
Pop 2,016
Library Holdings: Audiobooks 377; Bks on Deafness & Sign Lang 42; CDs 15; DVDs 208; Large Print Bks 481; Bk Vols 19,012; Per Subs 26; Talking Bks 407; Videos 475
Automation Activity & Vendor Info: (Acquisitions) Book Systems; (Cataloging) Book Systems; (Circulation) Book Systems; (ILL) OCLC ILLiad; (OPAC) Book Systems
Wireless access
Open Mon & Fri 10-5
Friends of the Library Group

GALLUP

P OCTAVIA FELLIN PUBLIC LIBRARY, 115 W Hill Ave, 87301. SAN 351-6423. Tel: 505-863-1291. Administration Tel: 505-863-1291, Ext 14019. FAX: 505-722-5090. E-mail: libref@ci.gallup.nm.gov. Web Site: galluplibrary.org. *Dir,* Mary Ellen Pellington; E-mail: mpellington@gallupnm.gov; *Libr Supvr,* Betty Martin; E-mail: bmartin@gallupnm.gov; *Mgr, Info Tech,* Adrian Vickers; E-mail: avickers@gallupnm.gov; *Mgr, Youth Serv,* Jenny Thurman; Tel: 505-726-6120, Fax: 505-863-9350, E-mail: jthurman@gallupnm.gov; Staff 5 (MLS 3, Non-MLS 2)
Founded 1928
Library Holdings: AV Mats 3,000; CDs 12,000; DVDs 1,671; Large Print Bks 1,452; Bk Vols 160,000; Per Subs 150
Special Collections: Southwest Coll. Oral History; State Document Depository
Subject Interests: Art, Local hist
Automation Activity & Vendor Info: (Acquisitions) TLC (The Library Corporation); (Cataloging) TLC (The Library Corporation); (Circulation) TLC (The Library Corporation); (OPAC) TLC (The Library Corporation); (Serials) TLC (The Library Corporation)
Wireless access
Publications: Community Resource Directory: An Information & Reference Service, 1978
Partic in NMex Info Systs
Open Mon-Thurs 9-8, Fri 10-6, Sat 9-6
Branches: 1
CHILDREN'S BRANCH, 200 W Aztec Ave, 87301. (Mail add: 115 W Hill Ave, 87301). Tel: 505-726-6120. FAX: 505-863-9350. *Mgr, Youth Serv,* Eckart Cory; Staff 5 (MLS 3, Non-MLS 2)
Founded 1947. Pop 72,000; Circ 300,000
Automation Activity & Vendor Info: (Acquisitions) TLC (The Library Corporation); (Cataloging) TLC (The Library Corporation); (Circulation) TLC (The Library Corporation); (Course Reserve) TLC (The Library Corporation); (ILL) TLC (The Library Corporation); (Media Booking) TLC (The Library Corporation); (Serials) TLC (The Library Corporation)
Database Vendor: ProQuest, ReferenceUSA
Open Tues-Thurs 10-7, Fri 10-6, Sat 9-6

C UNIVERSITY OF NEW MEXICO*, Zollinger Library, 200 College Rd, 87301. SAN 310-6721. Tel: 505-863-7531. Administration Tel: 505-863-7608. FAX: 505-863-7624. Web Site: www.gallup.unm.edu/academicdepts/library. *Dept Chair,* Carol D Frick; E-mail: cfrick@gallup.unm.edu; *Cat Mgr,* Rachel Hewett-Beah; Tel: 505-863-7552, E-mail: rhbeah@gallup.unm.edu; *Br Operations Coordr,* Betty Baker; Tel: 505-863-7656, E-mail: bjbaker@gallup.unm.edu; Staff 7 (MLS 2, Non-MLS 5)
Founded 1970. Enrl 1,600
Library Holdings: Bk Titles 35,000; Bk Vols 40,000; Per Subs 300
Subject Interests: Educ K-12, Health careers
Function: Copy machines, Electronic databases & coll, Handicapped accessible, Orientations, Ref serv available, VHS videos, Wheelchair accessible
Open Mon-Thurs 8am-9pm, Fri & Sat 9-4

GRANTS

P MOTHER WHITESIDE MEMORIAL LIBRARY*, 525 W High St, 87020-2526. SAN 310-673X. Tel: 505-287-4793. FAX: 505-285-6024. E-mail: library@7cities.net. Web Site: www.youseemore.com/whiteside. *Librn,* Jae Luree King; Staff 2 (MLS 1, Non-MLS 1)
Founded 1949. Pop 23,794
Library Holdings: Bk Vols 23,500; Per Subs 39
Subject Interests: Local hist, SW
Automation Activity & Vendor Info: (Cataloging) TLC (The Library Corporation); (Circulation) TLC (The Library Corporation)
Open Tues-Fri 9-6, Sat 9-3:30

S NEW MEXICO CORRECTIONS DEPARTMENT*, Western New Mexico Correctional Facility Library, Lobo Canyon, PO Drawer 250, 87020. SAN 375-4731. Tel: 505-876-8300. FAX: 505-876-8200. *Librn,* Position Currently Open; Staff 1 (Non-MLS 1)
Founded 1975
Library Holdings: Bk Titles 6,000; Per Subs 12
Automation Activity & Vendor Info: (Acquisitions) Follett Software; (Cataloging) Follett Software; (Circulation) Follett Software
Special Services for the Deaf - Bks on deafness & sign lang; High interest/low vocabulary bks
Restriction: Not open to pub

J NEW MEXICO STATE UNIVERSITY AT GRANTS*, Library, 1500 N Third St, 87020. SAN 310-6748. Tel: 505-287-6639. FAX: 505-287-6676. Web Site: grants.nmsu.edu/library. *Dir,* Cecilia D Stafford; E-mail: stafford@nmsu.edu; Staff 3 (MLS 1, Non-MLS 2)
Founded 1968. Enrl 654; Fac 50; Highest Degree: Associate
Library Holdings: Bk Vols 32,000; Per Subs 35
Special Collections: New Mexico History Coll
Automation Activity & Vendor Info: (Acquisitions) Ex Libris Group; (Cataloging) Ex Libris Group; (Circulation) Ex Libris Group; (OPAC) Ex Libris Group
Database Vendor: Amigos Library Services, CQ Press, EBSCOhost, Ex Libris Group, Gale Cengage Learning, LexisNexis, Newsbank
Wireless access
Function: Online cat, Orientations, Photocopying/Printing, Pub access computers, Ref & res, Ref serv available, Scanner, Tax forms, Telephone ref, Web-catalog
Partic in New Mexico Consortium of Academic Libraries
Open Mon-Thurs 8-8, Fri 8-5, Sat 10-2

HATCH

P HATCH PUBLIC LIBRARY*, 530 E Hall, 87937. (Mail add: PO Box 289, 87937-0289), SAN 310-6756. Tel: 575-267-5132. *Librn,* Rita Sue Medina
Founded 1946. Circ 16,006
Library Holdings: Bk Vols 10,000; Per Subs 5
Open Mon-Thurs 9-11:30 & 1-5:30, Sat 10-2:30

HILLSBORO

P HILLSBORO COMMUNITY LIBRARY*, 158 Elenora St, 88042. (Mail add: PO Box 205, 88042). Tel: 575-895-3349. FAX: 575-895-3349. E-mail: hbolib@gmail.com. Web Site: www.hillsborocommunitylibrary.com. *Pres,* John Cornell
Pop 400; Circ 1,300
Jan 2013-Dec 2013 Income $5,950, County $1,500, Locally Generated Income $4,450. Mats Exp $1,837, Books $1,743, Per/Ser (Incl. Access Fees) $94
Library Holdings: Audiobooks 110; CDs 65; DVDs 521; High Interest/Low Vocabulary Bk Vols 695; Large Print Bks 211; Bk Vols 4,659; Per Subs 2; Videos 839
Automation Activity & Vendor Info: (Cataloging) JayWil Software Development, Inc; (Circulation) JayWil Software Development, Inc; (ILL) OCLC ILLiad; (OPAC) JayWil Software Development, Inc
Wireless access
Function: Digital talking bks, Fax serv, Free DVD rentals, ILL available, Online cat, Photocopying/Printing, Pub access computers, Scanner, Spanish lang bks, VHS videos, Wheelchair accessible
Open Tues & Thurs 3:30-5:30, Wed 1-4, Fri 10-1, Sat 10-2

Restriction: Residents only
Friends of the Library Group

HOBBS

P HOBBS PUBLIC LIBRARY, 509 N Shipp, 88240. SAN 310-6772. Tel: 575-397-9328. FAX: 575-397-1508. E-mail: reference@hobbspubliclibrary.org. Web Site: hobbspubliclibrary.org. *Libr Dir,* Sandy Farrell; E-mail: sfarrell@elinlib.org; *Access Serv Librn/YA, Digital & Electronic Serv,* Tonya Allen; E-mail: tallen@elinlib.org; *Ch/Children's Serv,* Helen VanKleeck; E-mail: hvankleeck@elinlib.org; *Circ Librn/ILL,* Sharon L Wise; E-mail: swise@elinlib.org; *Ref Librn/Coll Develop,* Robert Hamilton; E-mail: rhamilton@elinlib.org; *Tech Serv Librn,* Denise Staab; E-mail: dstaab@elinlib.org; *Libr Spec,* Jacqueline Peeples; E-mail: jpeeples@elinlib.org; Staff 16 (MLS 2, Non-MLS 14)
Founded 1939. Pop 35,000; Circ 104,522
Jul 2013-Jun 2014 Income $1,084,986, State $16,463, City $1,068,523. Mats Exp $135,925, Books $75,358, Per/Ser (Incl. Access Fees) $10,798, Other Print Mats $7,084, Micro $3,013, AV Equip $1,000, AV Mat $15,248, Electronic Ref Mat (Incl. Access Fees) $23,424
Library Holdings: Audiobooks 255; CDs 5,161; DVDs 3,966; e-books 501; e-journals 42; Electronic Media & Resources 15; High Interest/Low Vocabulary Bk Vols 115; Large Print Bks 4,425; Microforms 676; Bk Vols 134,620; Per Subs 86; Spec Interest Per Sub 3; Videos 1,170
Subject Interests: Petroleum, Spanish lang, SW
Automation Activity & Vendor Info: (Cataloging) SirsiDynix; (Circulation) SirsiDynix; (OPAC) SirsiDynix; (Serials) SirsiDynix
Database Vendor: Baker & Taylor, Booklist Online, EBSCOhost, Gale Cengage Learning, OCLC, OCLC FirstSearch, Overdrive, Inc, ProQuest, SirsiDynix, TumbleBookLibrary, World Book Online, World Trade Press
Wireless access
Function: Activity rm, After school storytime, Art exhibits, Bks on CD, Children's prog, Computers for patron use, Copy machines, Electronic databases & coll, eReaders, Exhibits, Free DVD rentals, Handicapped accessible, ILL available, Magazines, Mango lang, Microfiche/film & reading machines, Movies, Music CDs, Online cat, Online ref, OverDrive digital audio bks, Photocopying/Printing, Preschool reading prog, Prog for children & young adult, Pub access computers, Spanish lang bks, Story hour, Study rm, Summer reading prog, Tax forms, Teen prog
Partic in Estacado Library Information Network; OCLC Online Computer Library Center, Inc
Special Services for the Blind - Audio mat; Large print bks
Open Mon-Wed 10-8, Thurs-Sat 10-5
Friends of the Library Group

J NEW MEXICO JUNIOR COLLEGE*, Pannell Library, One Thunderbird Circle, 88240. SAN 310-6780. Tel: 575-492-2870. FAX: 575-492-2883. E-mail: library@nmjc.edu. Web Site: www.nmjc.edu/library. *Dir, Libr Serv,* Mary Tuytschaevers; E-mail: mtuytschaevers@nmjc.edu; *Libr Tech,* Gail Drennan; E-mail: gdrennan@nmjc.edu; *Libr Tech,* Vicky Gann; E-mail: vslack@nmjc.edu; *Libr Tech,* Patricia Sanderson; E-mail: psanderson@nmjc.edu; *Libr Tech,* Cheri West; E-mail: cwest@nmjc.edu; Staff 2 (MLS 2)
Founded 1965. Enrl 3,200; Fac 175; Highest Degree: Associate
Jul 2008-Jun 2009 Income $37,500, State $32,000, Locally Generated Income $5,500. Mats Exp $211,750. Sal $288,039 (Prof $111,175)
Library Holdings: Bk Vols 88,000; Per Subs 343
Special Collections: Waste Isolation Pilot Plant Depository. Oral History; US Document Depository
Subject Interests: Automotive, Humanities, Nursing, Paralegal, Petroleum
Automation Activity & Vendor Info: (Cataloging) SirsiDynix; (Circulation) SirsiDynix; (Course Reserve) SirsiDynix; (OPAC) SirsiDynix; (Serials) SirsiDynix
Database Vendor: EBSCOhost, Gale Cengage Learning, JSTOR, LexisNexis, OCLC FirstSearch, OCLC WorldShare Interlibrary Loan, ProQuest, Westlaw
Function: Audio & video playback equip for onsite use, CD-ROM, Govt ref serv, Homebound delivery serv, ILL available, Large print keyboards, Magnifiers for reading, Online searches, Photocopying/Printing, VHS videos, Wheelchair accessible
Partic in Estacado Library Information Network
Open Mon-Thurs (Winter) 7:30am-9pm, Fri 7:30-5, Sat & Sun 10-2; Mon-Thurs (Summer) 7:30-7, Fri 7:30-5

C UNIVERSITY OF THE SOUTHWEST*, Scarborough Memorial Library, 6610 Lovington Hwy, T-30, 88240. SAN 310-6764. Tel: 575-392-6565, Ext 2141. FAX: 575-392-6006. Web Site: www.usw.edu. *Dir,* John McCance; Tel: 575-492-2141, E-mail: jmccance@usw.edu; *Cat,* Cyndi Garrison; E-mail: cgarrison@cusw.edu; Staff 1 (MLS 1)
Founded 1962. Enrl 600; Fac 22; Highest Degree: Master
Library Holdings: Bk Vols 54,292; Per Subs 200; Videos 1,583
Special Collections: Hatton W Sumners Coll; New Mexico Textbook Adoption Center; Southwest Heritage Room (Thelma A Webber Coll); Southwestern History & Art Literature
Subject Interests: Folklore, Free market econ, Lit, SW hist
Automation Activity & Vendor Info: (Cataloging) SirsiDynix; (Circulation) SirsiDynix; (Course Reserve) SirsiDynix; (OPAC) SirsiDynix
Database Vendor: OCLC FirstSearch, ProQuest
Partic in New Mexico Consortium of Academic Libraries
Open Mon-Thurs 8am-9pm, Fri 8-5, Sat 12-4, Sun (Fall & Spring) 1-5

HOLLOMAN AFB

A UNITED STATES AIR FORCE*, Ahrens Memorial Library, FL 4801, 596 Fourth St, Bldg 224, 88330-8038. SAN 351-6482. Tel: 575-572-3939. FAX: 575-572-5340. *Dir,* Marie Ludwig; Tel: 575-572-3501, E-mail: marie.ludwig@holloman.af.mil; Staff 7 (MLS 1, Non-MLS 6)
Library Holdings: e-books 7,000; Bk Titles 45,000; Per Subs 60
Special Collections: Military Studies, Foreign Relations & Management
Subject Interests: Aerospace, Foreign relations, Mil studies
Automation Activity & Vendor Info: (Cataloging) SirsiDynix; (Circulation) SirsiDynix; (ILL) OCLC; (OPAC) SirsiDynix; (Serials) SirsiDynix
Database Vendor: Gale Cengage Learning, OCLC FirstSearch
Wireless access
Partic in OCLC Online Computer Library Center, Inc
Open Mon-Thurs 11-7, Fri & Sat 12-4

ISLETA

P PUEBLO OF ISLETA LIBRARY*, Tribal Rd 67, Bldg 295A, 87022. (Mail add: PO Box 597, 87022-0597). Tel: 505-869-8119. FAX: 505-869-7690. *Dir,* Maxine Zuni; E-mail: mzuni1876@msn.com; Staff 4 (Non-MLS 4)
Founded 1995. Pop 4,500
Library Holdings: CDs 250; Large Print Bks 90; Bk Vols 16,000; Per Subs 80; Talking Bks 350
Automation Activity & Vendor Info: (Cataloging) Follett Software; (Circulation) Follett Software
Function: Handicapped accessible, ILL available, Music CDs, Prog for children & young adult, Summer reading prog, Wheelchair accessible
Open Mon-Thurs 8-8, Fri 8-4:30
Friends of the Library Group

JAL

P WOOLWORTH COMMUNITY LIBRARY*, 100 E Utah Ave, 88252. (Mail add: PO Box 1249, 88252-1249), SAN 310-6802. Tel: 505-395-3268. FAX: 505-395-2138. Web Site: www.woolworth.org. *Dir,* Joyce Pittam; E-mail: jpittam@elinlib.org; *Librn,* Kesi Marquez; *Librn,* Beth Speed
Founded 1978. Pop 1,576; Circ 26,996
Library Holdings: Bk Vols 42,000
Subject Interests: Local hist, Spanish lang, SW hist
Open Mon-Thurs 7:30-6, Fri 7:30-4, Sat 12-4

JEMEZ PUEBLO

P JEMEZ PUEBLO COMMUNITY LIBRARY*, 20 Mission Rd, 87024. (Mail add: PO Box 650, 87024-0650). Tel: 575-834-9171. FAX: 575-834-9173. *Librn,* Tamara Sandia
Library Holdings: AV Mats 2,200; Bk Vols 15,023; Per Subs 100; Talking Bks 100
Automation Activity & Vendor Info: (Cataloging) Follett Software; (Circulation) Follett Software; (OPAC) Follett Software
Open Mon-Fri 8-12 & 1-5

JEMEZ SPRINGS

P JEMEZ SPRINGS PUBLIC LIBRARY*, 30 Jemez Plaza, 87025. (Mail add: PO Box 479, 87025-0479), SAN 320-4936. Tel: 505-829-9155. FAX: 505-829-3339. E-mail: librarian@JemezSprings.org. Web Site: www.jemezsprings.org. *Dir,* Judith Isaacs; *Asst Librn,* Janet Phillips; Staff 2 (Non-MLS 2)
Pop 1,700; Circ 2,200
Library Holdings: Bk Titles 9,500; Per Subs 22
Open Tues-Thurs 9-4, Fri & Sat 9-1
Friends of the Library Group

KIRTLAND AFB

A UNITED STATES AIR FORCE*, Phillips Site Technical Library FL2809, AFRL/RVIL, 3550 Aberdeen Ave SE Bldg 570, 87117-5776. SAN 351-6571. Tel: 505-846-4767. FAX: 505-846-4790. *Contractor Librn, Mgr,* Maryhelen Jones; *Admin Senior Librn,* Becky Smith; E-mail: becky.smith@kirtland.af.mil; *Contractor Librn,* Elizabeth Luebchow; *Contractor Librn,* Lisa Meassick; Staff 4 (MLS 4)
Founded 1947
Library Holdings: Bk Vols 50,000; Per Subs 800
Subject Interests: Eng with applications in directed energy & space vehicles

Automation Activity & Vendor Info: (Acquisitions) SirsiDynix; (Cataloging) SirsiDynix; (Circulation) SirsiDynix; (Course Reserve) SirsiDynix
Open Mon-Fri 7:30-4

LA JOYA

P RIO ABAJO COMMUNITY LIBRARY, 28 Calle de Centros Sur, 87028. Tel: 505-861-8289. E-mail: raclibrary@hotmail.com. Web Site: raclibrary.info. *Librn,* Martha Carangelo; *Asst Librn,* Donna Hernandez Uda Clark
Founded 1999. Circ 2,100
Jul 2013-Jun 2014 Income $4,500, State $1,000, County $2,000, Locally Generated Income $1,500. Mats Exp $1,700, Books $1,000, Other Print Mats $700
Library Holdings: Audiobooks 50; CDs 50; DVDs 50; Large Print Bks 100; Bk Titles 5,000; Bk Vols 6,000; Per Subs 10; Talking Bks 100; Videos 50
Open Tues-Thurs 12-5:30, Fri 9-1

LAGUNA

P LAGUNA PUBLIC LIBRARY, 29 Rodeo Dr, 87026. (Mail add: PO Box 194, 87026-0194). Tel: 505-552-6280. FAX: 505-552-9388. E-mail: library@lagunapueblo-nsn.gov. Web Site: lagunalibrary.com. *Dir,* Janice Kowemy; E-mail: jkowemy@lagunapueblo-nsn.gov; Staff 1 (MLS 1)
Founded 1974. Pop 4,500
Library Holdings: Audiobooks 192; DVDs 845; e-books 75; Large Print Bks 150; Bk Titles 9,653; Per Subs 33
Automation Activity & Vendor Info: (Cataloging) Insignia Software; (Circulation) Insignia Software; (OPAC) Insignia Software
Wireless access
Open Mon-Fri 8-6:30, Sat 9-2; Mon-Fri (Winter) 8-5:30

LAS CRUCES

P THOMAS BRANIGAN MEMORIAL LIBRARY*, 200 E Picacho Ave, 88001-3499. SAN 310-6837. Tel: 575-528-4000. Interlibrary Loan Service Tel: 575-528-4024. Reference Tel: 575-528-4005. FAX: 575-528-4030. TDD: 575-528-4008. Web Site: library.las-cruces.org. *Adminr,* Lynette Schurdevin; E-mail: lschurdevin@las-cruces.org; *Adult Progs & Promotions Mgr,* Mark Pendleton; Tel: 575-528-4001, E-mail: mpendleton@las-cruces.org; *Tech Serv & Syst Mgr,* Bonnie Hobbs; Tel: 575-528-4043, E-mail: bhobbs@las-cruces.org; *Youth Serv Mgr,* Catherine Christmann; Tel: 575-528-4085, E-mail: cchristmann@las-cruces.org; *Libr Supvr,* Renee Payne; Tel: 575-528-4017, E-mail: rpayne@las-cruces.org; Staff 39 (MLS 11, Non-MLS 28)
Founded 1935. Pop 120,001; Circ 577,657
Jul 2012-Jun 2013 Income $2,086,394, State $58,440, City $1,957,954, County $30,000, Other $40,000. Mats Exp $339,667, Books $251,245, AV Mat $60,650, Electronic Ref Mat (Incl. Access Fees) $27,772. Sal $999,345
Library Holdings: Audiobooks 8,544; AV Mats 12,149; Bks-By-Mail 13,928; Bks on Deafness & Sign Lang 50; e-books 3,600; Bk Vols 142,957; Per Subs 262
Special Collections: New Mexico & Southwestern History (Helen P Caffey Coll)
Subject Interests: Archit, Art, Hist
Automation Activity & Vendor Info: (Acquisitions) Innovative Interfaces, Inc; (Cataloging) Innovative Interfaces, Inc; (Circulation) Innovative Interfaces, Inc; (Course Reserve) Innovative Interfaces, Inc; (ILL) Innovative Interfaces, Inc; (Media Booking) Innovative Interfaces, Inc; (OPAC) Innovative Interfaces, Inc; (Serials) Innovative Interfaces, Inc
Database Vendor: EBSCOhost, Gale Cengage Learning, Newsbank, OCLC FirstSearch
Wireless access
Function: Adult bk club, After school storytime, Art exhibits, Audiobks via web, Bks on CD, Children's prog, Computer training, Computers for patron use, Copy machines, Digital talking bks, Electronic databases & coll, Exhibits, Fax serv, Free DVD rentals, Genealogy discussion group, Handicapped accessible, Home delivery & serv to Sr ctr & nursing homes, Homebound delivery serv, ILL available, Magnifiers for reading, Microfiche/film & reading machines, Notary serv, Online cat, Online searches, Outreach serv, Photocopying/Printing, Preschool outreach, Prog for adults, Prog for children & young adult, Pub access computers, Ref serv available, Senior computer classes, Senior outreach, Serves mentally handicapped consumers, Spanish lang bks, Spoken cassettes & CDs, Story hour, Summer & winter reading prog, Tax forms, Teen prog, Telephone ref, Web-catalog, Wheelchair accessible
Partic in OCLC Online Computer Library Center, Inc
Special Services for the Deaf - TTY equip
Special Services for the Blind - Accessible computers; BiFolkal kits; Bks available with recordings; Bks on CD; Large print bks; Playaways (bks on MP3); Reader equip
Open Mon-Thurs 9-8, Fri 8-6, Sat 10-6, Sun 1-5
Friends of the Library Group

J DONA ANA COMMUNITY COLLEGE LIBRARY*, Central Campus, 3400 S Espina, Rm 260, 88003. Tel: 575-527-7555. Toll Free Tel: 800-903-7503. FAX: 575-527-7636. E-mail: dacclib@lib.nmsu.edu. Web Site: dabcc-www.nmsu.edu/library. *Libr Tech,* Becky Ponce; E-mail: reponce@nmsu.edu; *Coll Develop Librn,* Dean Thompson; Tel: 575-528-7064, E-mail: dthompsn@nmsu.edu; *Instrul Librn,* Yubao Li; Tel: 575-527-7556, E-mail: ybli@nmsu.edu; *AV Tech Equip Mgr,* Rodner Santos; E-mail: rosantos@nmsu.edu; *Cataloger,* Kathleen DeBoy; E-mail: kdeboy@nmsu.edu
Enrl 5,828
Library Holdings: e-books 29,000; e-journals 15; Bk Titles 18,000; Per Subs 180
Automation Activity & Vendor Info: (Cataloging) Ex Libris Group; (Circulation) Ex Libris Group; (OPAC) Ex Libris Group; (Serials) Ex Libris Group
Database Vendor: EBSCOhost, SerialsSolutions
Open Mon-Thurs 8am-9pm, Fri 8-5, Sat 10-2

Departmental Libraries:

EAST MESA CAMPUS, 2800 N Sonoma Ranch Blvd, 88011. Tel: 575-528-7260. FAX: 575-528-7422. *Div Dean,* Tammy Welch; Tel: 575-527-7675, E-mail: welchta@nmsu.edu; *Instrul Librn,* Sara Finch; *Virtual Librn,* Kendrick Keeton; *Libr Mgr,* Vita Montana
Open Mon-Fri 8-5, Sat 10-2

S INSTITUTE OF HISTORICAL SURVEY FOUNDATION LIBRARY*, 3035 S Main, 88005-3756. (Mail add: PO Box 36, Mesilla Park, 88047-0036), SAN 377-8223. Tel: 575-525-3035. FAX: 575-525-0106. E-mail: ihsf@zianet.com. *Dir,* Dr Evan Davies; *Librn,* Anne Morgan; E-mail: anmorgan@zianet.com; Staff 2 (MLS 1, Non-MLS 1)
Founded 1970
Library Holdings: Bk Titles 40,000; Bk Vols 45,000
Special Collections: Oral History
Subject Interests: Art, Geog, Hist, Philos, Photog, Relig
Function: Ref serv available, Referrals accepted, Res libr, Telephone ref
Open Mon-Fri 8-4

G NASA*, White Sands Test Facility Technical Library, 12600 NASA Rd, 88012. (Mail add: PO Box 20, 88004-0020), SAN 328-0969. Tel: 575-524-5683. Web Site: www.nasa.gov/centers/wstf/home/index.html. *Mgr,* Moira Romansky; Staff 2 (MLS 1, Non-MLS 1)
Library Holdings: Bk Titles 2,000
Partic in Dialog Corp; OCLC Online Computer Library Center, Inc

S NEW MEXICO CORRECTIONS DEPARTMENT*, Southern New Mexico Correctional Facility Library, 1983 Joe R Silva Blvd, 88004. (Mail add: PO Box 639, 88004-0639). Tel: 575-523-3200. FAX: 575-523-3337. *Librn,* Debra Barnes
Library Holdings: Bk Vols 10,500; Per Subs 40
Automation Activity & Vendor Info: (Cataloging) Winnebago Software Co; (Circulation) Winnebago Software Co
Restriction: Not open to pub

C NEW MEXICO STATE UNIVERSITY LIBRARY*, 2911 McFie Circle, 88003. (Mail add: PO Box 30006, MSC 3475, 88003-8006), SAN 351-6636. Tel: 575-646-1508. Circulation Tel: 575-646-6910. Interlibrary Loan Service Tel: 575-646-4737. Reference Tel: 575-646-5792. Toll Free Tel: 866-835-9826. FAX: 575-646-6940. Interlibrary Loan Service FAX: 575-646-4335. Web Site: lib.nmsu.edu. *Dean,* Dr Elizabeth A Titus; *Assoc Dean,* Norice Lee; *Head, Access Serv,* Susan Beck; Tel: 575-646-5091; *Head, Archives & Spec Coll,* Dr Laurence Creider; Tel: 575-646-4756; *Head, Ref & Res Serv,* Cynthia Pierard; Tel: 575-646-7010; *Head, Syst,* Carol Boyse; Tel: 575-646-6421; *Head, Tech Serv,* Ellen Bosman; Tel: 575-646-1723; Staff 34 (MLS 23, Non-MLS 11)
Founded 1888. Fac 629; Highest Degree: Doctorate
Jul 2011-Jun 2012 Income $6,402,237, State $6,127,275, Other $274,962. Mats Exp $2,920,162, Books $97,311, Per/Ser (Incl. Access Fees) $2,677,613, Manu Arch $11,802, Micro $12,850, AV Mat $8,878, Electronic Ref Mat (Incl. Access Fees) $85,334, Presv $26,374. Sal $1,805,017 (Prof $2,786,882)
Library Holdings: AV Mats 17,059; e-books 16,183; e-journals 95,127; Microforms 1,490,144; Music Scores 8,248; Bk Vols 1,830,030; Per Subs 2,620
Special Collections: Pete V Domenici Archives (Political Papers); Rio Grande Historical Coll; University Archives. Oral History; State Document Depository; US Document Depository
Automation Activity & Vendor Info: (Acquisitions) Ex Libris Group; (Cataloging) Ex Libris Group; (Circulation) Ex Libris Group; (Course Reserve) Docutek; (ILL) OCLC ILLiad; (OPAC) Ex Libris Group; (Serials) Ex Libris Group
Wireless access
Publications: New Mexico State University Library (Newsletter)
Partic in Amigos Library Services, Inc

Special Services for the Deaf - TDD equip
Open Mon-Thurs 7:30am-Midnight, Fri 7:30am-8pm, Sat 9-6, Sun 10am-Midnight

R SAINT PAUL'S UNITED METHODIST CHURCH*, Ralph Johnson Memorial Library, 225 W Griggs Ave, 88005-2608. SAN 328-1272. Tel: 575-526-6689. FAX: 575-524-7660. Web Site: www.stpaulslascruces.com. *Adminr,* Mark Ewing; Tel: 575-526-6689, Ext 1002
Founded 1961
Library Holdings: Bk Vols 6,017
Publications: History of Church
Open Mon-Thurs 8-5, Fri 8-4, Sun 8-12

R UNIVERSITY UNITED METHODIST CHURCH LIBRARY*, 2000 S Locust St, 88001. SAN 325-2833. Tel: 575-522-8220.
Founded 1967
Library Holdings: Bk Titles 4,195; Per Subs 2; Spec Interest Per Sub 2
Restriction: Not open to pub

LAS VEGAS

P CARNEGIE PUBLIC LIBRARY*, 500 National Ave, 87701. SAN 310-6853. Tel: 505-426-3304. Web Site: www.ci.las-vegas.nm.us. *Mgr,* Pasha Martinez
Founded 1904. Circ 84,557
Library Holdings: Bk Vols 61,000; Per Subs 80
Special Collections: Local history; Southwest Coll
Subject Interests: SW
Automation Activity & Vendor Info: (Cataloging) Follett Software; (Circulation) Follett Software
Wireless access
Partic in OCLC Online Computer Library Center, Inc
Open Mon-Fri 8-5, Sat 8-2
Friends of the Library Group

GM NEW MEXICO BEHAVIORAL HEALTH INSTITUTE AT LAS VEGAS*, Medical Library, 3695 Hot Springs Blvd, 87701. SAN 310-6861. Tel: 505-454-2108. FAX: 505-454-2136. *Librn,* Victor Sandoval; E-mail: victor.sandoval@state.nm.us
Founded 1970
Library Holdings: Bk Titles 7,000
Special Collections: Psychiatry; Psychology; Social Work
Subject Interests: Gen med, Nursing
Partic in National Network of Libraries of Medicine South Central Region
Restriction: Not open to pub

C NEW MEXICO HIGHLANDS UNIVERSITY, Thomas C Donnelly Library, Ninth & National Ave, 87701. SAN 310-687X. Tel: 505-454-3401. Circulation Tel: 505-454-3403. Interlibrary Loan Service Tel: 505-454-3337, 505-454-3481. Administration Tel: 505-454-3332. Automation Services Tel: 505-454-3255, 505-454-3330. Information Services Tel: 505-454-3139. FAX: 505-454-0026. TDD: 505-454-3303. Web Site: www.nmhu.edu. *Dir, Libr & Info Serv,* Ruben F Aragon; E-mail: rubenaragon@nmhu.edu; *Head, Archives & Cat Div/Librn,* Lynn Gates; *Head, Coll & Instruction Div/Librn,* Leslie Broughton; Tel: 505-454-3408, E-mail: lbroughton@nmhu.edu; *Head, External Prog & ILL Div/Librn,* Cheryl Zebrowski; E-mail: czebrowski@nmhu.edu; *Head, Govt Doc & Per Div/Librn,* Josephine Sena-Gutierrez; Tel: 505-454-3411, E-mail: jsenag@nmhu.edu; *Head, Pub Serv Div/Librn,* April Kent; E-mail: ajkent@nmhu.edu; *Libr Assoc/Acq Section,* Beatrice Ulibarri; Tel: 505-454-3336, E-mail: ulibarrib@nmhu.edu; *Libr Assoc/ILL Section,* Joseph Odermatt; E-mail: joeodermatt@nmhu.edu; Staff 17.25 (MLS 6, Non-MLS 11.25)
Founded 1893. Enrl 3,208; Fac 115; Highest Degree: Master
Library Holdings: AV Mats 2,148; CDs 291; e-books 42,605; Microforms 169,296; Bk Vols 164,828; Per Subs 700
Special Collections: Fort Union Archives, mss; Government Documents Coll; Southwest History (Arrott Coll). State Document Depository; US Document Depository
Automation Activity & Vendor Info: (Acquisitions) Innovative Interfaces, Inc; (Cataloging) Innovative Interfaces, Inc; (Circulation) Innovative Interfaces, Inc; (Course Reserve) Innovative Interfaces, Inc; (ILL) OCLC; (OPAC) Innovative Interfaces, Inc; (Serials) Innovative Interfaces, Inc
Database Vendor: Innovative Interfaces, Inc
Wireless access
Partic in New Mexico Consortium of Academic Libraries
Open Mon-Thurs 7:30am-10pm, Fri 7:30-5, Sat 1-5, Sun 1-10

LORDSBURG

P LORDSBURG-HIDALGO LIBRARY*, 208 E Third St, 88045. SAN 310-6888. Tel: 575-542-9646. FAX: 575-542-9646. E-mail: oldbkbuilding@yahoo.com. *Dir,* Marlene Siepel; *Ch Serv,* Rita Morris
Founded 1919. Pop 5,000; Circ 20,645
Library Holdings: Bk Vols 23,000; Per Subs 60
Special Services for the Deaf - Bks on deafness & sign lang
Open Mon-Fri 10-12 & 1-6
Friends of the Library Group

LOS ALAMOS

SR FIRST UNITED METHODIST CHURCH LIBRARY*, 715 Diamond Dr, 87544. SAN 373-479X. Tel: 505-662-6277.
Library Holdings: Bk Vols 1,100
Subject Interests: Theol
Wireless access
Open Mon-Fri 8-5, Sun 8-Noon

SR IMMACULATE HEART OF MARY PARISH LIBRARY*, 3700 Canyon Rd, 87544. SAN 310-690X. Tel: 505-662-6193. FAX: 505-662-5191.
Founded 1961
Library Holdings: Bk Titles 5,000; Per Subs 20
Subject Interests: Family, Marriage, Philos, Psychol, Relig, Relig educ, Socio-econ concerns, Theol
Open Mon-Fri 8-5, Sun 9-Noon

P LOS ALAMOS COUNTY LIBRARY SYSTEM*, 2400 Central Ave, 87544. SAN 370-4602. Tel: 505-662-8240. Circulation Tel: 505-662-8250. Interlibrary Loan Service Tel: 505-662-8255. Reference Tel: 505-662-8253. Automation Services Tel: 505-662-8260. FAX: 505-662-8245. Reference FAX: 505-662-8246. TDD: 505-662-8256. Web Site: www.losalamos.nm.us/library/pages.default.aspx. *Libr Mgr,* Charlie Kalogeros-Chattan; Tel: 505-662-8242, E-mail: charlie.kalogeros@lacnm.us; *Asst Libr Mgr,* Bernadine Goldman; Tel: 505-662-8254; *Electronic Serv Mgr,* Gwen Kalavaza; *Circ Supvr,* Katherine Garduno; *Ref Serv,* Veronica Encinas; *Tech Serv,* Doris Logan; Staff 27.5 (MLS 7, Non-MLS 20.5)
Founded 1943. Pop 17,950; Circ 411,356
Jul 2010-Jun 2011 Income $2,335,570. Mats Exp $267,753. Sal $1,352,639
Library Holdings: Audiobooks 4,854; AV Mats 17,936; e-books 5,132; Bk Vols 146,705; Per Subs 415
Special Collections: Southwest Americana Regional Coll bk, video
Automation Activity & Vendor Info: (Acquisitions) SirsiDynix; (Cataloging) SirsiDynix; (Circulation) SirsiDynix; (ILL) SirsiDynix; (OPAC) SirsiDynix; (Serials) SirsiDynix
Wireless access
Function: Art exhibits, Audio & video playback equip for onsite use, Audiobks via web, Bks on CD, Children's prog, Computers for patron use, Copy machines, Digital talking bks, E-Reserves, Electronic databases & coll, Exhibits, Fax serv, Free DVD rentals, Games & aids for the handicapped, Govt ref serv, Handicapped accessible, Home delivery & serv to Sr ctr & nursing homes, Homework prog, ILL available, Literacy & newcomer serv, Magnifiers for reading, Music CDs, Online cat, Outreach serv, Photocopying/Printing, Preschool outreach, Prof lending libr, Prog for adults, Prog for children & young adult, Pub access computers, Ref serv in person, Story hour, Summer reading prog, Tax forms, Teen prog, Telephone ref, Web-catalog, Wheelchair accessible
Special Services for the Deaf - TDD equip; TTY equip
Special Services for the Blind - Large print bks; Magnifiers
Open Mon-Thurs 10-9, Fri 10-6, Sat 10-5, Sun 12-5
Friends of the Library Group

S LOS ALAMOS HISTORICAL SOCIETY*, Museum Archives, 1000 Central Ave, 87544. (Mail add: PO Box 43, 87544-0043), SAN 325-903X. Tel: 505-662-6272. E-mail: archives@losalamoshistory.org. Web Site: www.losalamoshistory.org. *Exec Dir,* Heather McClenahan; *Archivist,* Rebecca Collinsworth
Founded 1976
Library Holdings: Bk Vols 4,500; Per Subs 100
Special Collections: Laura Gilpin Photographs Coll; T H Parkhurst Photographs Coll. Oral History
Subject Interests: Atomic energy, Nuclear energy
Wireless access
Function: Archival coll
Restriction: Closed stack, Non-circulating, Open by appt only

S LOS ALAMOS NATIONAL LABORATORY*, Research Library, MS-P362, PO Box 1663, 87544-7113. SAN 351-6695. Tel: 505-667-4448. Reference Tel: 505-667-5809. FAX: 505-665-6452. E-mail: library@lanl.gov. Web Site: library.lanl.gov. *Dir,* Miriam Blake
Founded 1943
Library Holdings: Bk Vols 131,500; Per Subs 6,710
Special Collections: AEC period publications; Electronic Reports; LANL Technical Reports
Wireless access
Open Mon-Fri 9-4:30

R UNITED CHURCH OF LOS ALAMOS LIBRARY*, 2525 Canyon Rd, 87544. SAN 310-6926. Tel: 505-662-2971. FAX: 505-662-5927. Web Site: www.losalamos.org/unchla. *Librn,* Jan Sinclair
Founded 1966
Library Holdings: Bk Vols 3,500; Per Subs 10
Subject Interests: Family life, Health, Psychol, Relig
Open Mon-Fri 8:30-4:30, Sun 9-Noon

C UNIVERSITY OF NEW MEXICO*, Los Alamos Campus Library, 4000 University Dr, 87544. SAN 326-1476. Tel: 505-662-0343. FAX: 505-662-0344. E-mail: ulalib@unm.edu. Web Site: losalamos.unm.edu/library. *Dir,* Dennis Davies-Wilson; E-mail: davies@unm.edu; Staff 3 (MLS 2, Non-MLS 1)
Library Holdings: Bk Titles 21,500; Per Subs 86
Special Collections: Southwest Coll
Subject Interests: Art
Automation Activity & Vendor Info: (Cataloging) Innovative Interfaces, Inc; (Circulation) Innovative Interfaces, Inc; (Course Reserve) Innovative Interfaces, Inc; (ILL) OCLC Connexion; (OPAC) Innovative Interfaces, Inc
Database Vendor: EBSCOhost, Gale Cengage Learning, Innovative Interfaces, Inc, LexisNexis, OCLC FirstSearch, OCLC WorldShare Interlibrary Loan, ProQuest, ReferenceUSA
Wireless access
Function: Art exhibits, Electronic databases & coll, Exhibits, Handicapped accessible, ILL available, Music CDs, Online cat, Online searches, Orientations, Photocopying/Printing, Pub access computers, Ref & res, Ref serv in person, Wheelchair accessible
Partic in LIBROS Consortium; OCLC Online Computer Library Center, Inc
Open Mon-Thurs 8-6, Fri 8-1

LOS LUNAS

P LOS LUNAS PUBLIC LIBRARY*, 460 Main St NE, 87031. (Mail add: PO Box 1209, 87031-1209), SAN 310-6934. Tel: 505-839-3850. FAX: 505-352-3582. Web Site: www.loslunasnm.gov. *Dir,* Cynthia J Shetter; E-mail: shetterc@loslunasnm.gov; *Asst Dir,* Tom Simmons; *Youth Serv,* Judi Y Riley-Bensley; Staff 6 (Non-MLS 6)
Founded 1959. Pop 11,500; Circ 36,000
Library Holdings: Bk Vols 28,000
Open Mon 12-5, Tues 10-7, Wed & Fri 9-5, Thurs 9-7, Sat 9-4
Restriction: Open to pub for ref & circ; with some limitations

LOVINGTON

P LOVINGTON PUBLIC LIBRARY*, 115 S Main St, 88260-4246. SAN 310-6950. Tel: 575-396-3144. FAX: 575-396-7189. Web Site: lovingtonpubliclibrary.org. *Dir,* Tueredia McBride; *Librn,* Debbie Mitchell; *Youth Serv,* Ezie Venzor; *Libr Tech,* Nancy Arreola
Founded 1931. Pop 11,000; Circ 96,105
Library Holdings: DVDs 1,100; e-books 75; Bk Vols 51,000; Per Subs 41
Subject Interests: Genealogy
Automation Activity & Vendor Info: (Cataloging) SirsiDynix; (Circulation) SirsiDynix; (ILL) SirsiDynix; (OPAC) SirsiDynix
Database Vendor: EBSCOhost, Gale Cengage Learning, OCLC FirstSearch
Wireless access
Special Services for the Deaf - Bks on deafness & sign lang; Closed caption videos
Special Services for the Blind - Cassettes; Copier with enlargement capabilities; Home delivery serv; Large print & cassettes; Large print bks; Magnifiers; ZoomText magnification & reading software
Open Mon-Fri 9:30-6
Friends of the Library Group

MAGDALENA

P MAGDALENA PUBLIC LIBRARY*, 108 N Main St, 87825. (Mail add: PO Box 145, 87825-0145). Tel: 575-854-2361. E-mail: mpl@gilanet.com. Web Site: www.magdalenapubliclibrary.org. *Dir,* Jennifer Kent
Library Holdings: Audiobooks 200; AV Mats 200; DVDs 900; e-books 2,000; Large Print Bks 300; Bk Vols 26,000; Talking Bks 200; Videos 900
Automation Activity & Vendor Info: (Acquisitions) Book Systems; (Cataloging) Book Systems; (Circulation) Book Systems; (Course Reserve) Book Systems; (ILL) Book Systems; (OPAC) Book Systems
Database Vendor: Overdrive, Inc
Wireless access
Open Tues, Thurs & Fri 10-6, Wed 10-8, Sat 10-4
Friends of the Library Group

MESCALERO

P MESCALERO COMMUNITY LIBRARY*, 148 Cottonwood Dr, 88340. (Mail add: PO Box 227, 88340). Tel: 505-464-5010. FAX: 505-464-5011. E-mail: mescalero_library@yahoo.com. *Dir,* Lillian Chavez
Oct 2010-Sept 2011 Income $101,051, State $10,098, Locally Generated Income $90,953. Mats Exp $22,950, Books $8,700, Per/Ser (Incl. Access Fees) $1,250, Other Print Mats $4,500, AV Equip $5,000, AV Mat $3,500. Sal $75,000 (Prof $48,000)
Library Holdings: Audiobooks 75; AV Mats 420; CDs 185; DVDs 235; Bk Titles 7,500; Bk Vols 3,500; Per Subs 24
Automation Activity & Vendor Info: (Acquisitions) Insignia Software; (Cataloging) Insignia Software; (Circulation) Insignia Software; (ILL) Insignia Software; (OPAC) Insignia Software
Database Vendor: 3M Library Systems, Brodart, BWI, EBSCO - WebFeat, Grolier Online, LexisNexis
Wireless access
Open Mon-Thurs 8am-8:30pm, Fri 8-4:30

MORIARTY

P MORIARTY COMMUNITY LIBRARY*, 202 S Broadway, 87035. (Mail add: PO Box 3588, 87035-3588). Tel: 505-832-2513. FAX: 505-609-8362. E-mail: moriartylibrary@gmail.com. Web Site: www.cityofmoriarty.org/index.php?page=community-library. *Libr Mgr,* Cyndi Waite; *Asst Librn,* Kyla Dennisson; *Asst Librn,* Kevin Pohl; Staff 4 (Non-MLS 4)
Library Holdings: Bk Vols 20,000; Per Subs 12
Automation Activity & Vendor Info: (Cataloging) Biblionix; (Circulation) Biblionix; (Course Reserve) Biblionix
Wireless access
Open Mon-Thurs 9-7, Fri 9-5, Sat 9-3
Friends of the Library Group

MOUNTAINAIR

P MOUNTAINAIR PUBLIC LIBRARY*, 109 Roosevelt Ave, 87036. (Mail add: PO Box 100, 87036-0100). Tel: 505-847-9676. *Dir,* Evelyn Walker; E-mail: ewalker97@mindspring.com
Library Holdings: AV Mats 30; Bk Vols 8,000; Per Subs 10; Talking Bks 50
Automation Activity & Vendor Info: (Cataloging) Follett Software; (Circulation) Follett Software
Wireless access
Open Tues 9-2, Wed & Sat 9-1, Thurs 9-12, Fri 10-4

G NATIONAL PARK SERVICE*, Salinas Pueblo Missions Research Library, Corner of Broadway & Ripley, PO Box 517, 87036-0517. SAN 374-5538. Tel: 505-847-2585. FAX: 505-847-2441. *Adminr,* Loretta Moseley; E-mail: loretta_moseley@nps.gov; *Chief, Res Mgt,* Phil Wilson; E-mail: phil_wilson@nps.gov; Staff 1 (Non-MLS 1)
Founded 1930
Library Holdings: Bk Titles 1,700
Special Collections: Archaeology; Southwest Prehistory & History. Oral History
Open Mon-Fri 8-4

NAGEEZI

G USDI NATIONAL PARK SERVICE*, Chaco Culture National, PO Box 220, 87037-0220. SAN 323-9691. Tel: 505-786-7014. FAX: 505-786-7061. Web Site: www.nps.gov/chcu. *Chief of Interpretation,* Russ Bodnar
Library Holdings: Bk Titles 5,000
Special Collections: Oral History
Open Mon-Fri 8-5

PORTALES

C EASTERN NEW MEXICO UNIVERSITY*, Golden Library, 1300 S Ave K, Sta 32, 88130-7402. (Mail add: Sta 32, 88130), SAN 351-675X. Tel: 575-562-2624. Circulation Tel: 575-562-2634. Interlibrary Loan Service Tel: 575-562-2643. Reference Tel: 575-562-2638. Toll Free Tel: 800-450-7279. FAX: 575-562-2647. Web Site: www.enmu.edu/academics/library/index.shtml. *Dir,* Melveta Walker; Tel: 575-562-2626, E-mail: melveta.walker@enmu.edu; *ILL/Distance Educ Librn,* Michele Wood; Tel: 575-562-2644, E-mail: michele.wood@enmu.edu; *Media Librn,* Richard Baysinger; Tel: 575-562-2602, E-mail: richard.baysinger@enmu.edu; *Ser Librn,* Susan Asplund; Tel: 575-562-2629, E-mail: susan.asplund@enmu.edu; *Spec Coll Librn,* Gene Bundy; Tel: 575-562-2636, E-mail: gene.bundy@enmu.edu; *Syst Coordr,* Lilah Gainey; Tel: 575-562-2640, E-mail: lilah.gainey@enmu.edu; *Cat,* Heather Christensen; Tel: 575-562-2300, E-mail: heather.christensen@enmu.edu; *Govt Doc,* David Falkowski; Tel: 575-562-2788, E-mail: david.falkowski@enmu.edu; Staff 9 (MLS 8, Non-MLS 1)
Founded 1934. Enrl 5,000; Fac 173; Highest Degree: Master

Library Holdings: AV Mats 17,095; e-books 11,000; Bk Titles 270,935; Bk Vols 346,290; Per Subs 27,000; Talking Bks 540
Special Collections: Harold Runnels Coll; NMex; Textbook Review Center; Williamson Science Fiction Coll. Oral History; State Document Depository; US Document Depository
Subject Interests: Educ, Fine arts, Liberal arts
Automation Activity & Vendor Info: (Acquisitions) Innovative Interfaces, Inc; (Cataloging) Innovative Interfaces, Inc; (Circulation) Innovative Interfaces, Inc; (Course Reserve) Innovative Interfaces, Inc; (ILL) OCLC; (OPAC) Innovative Interfaces, Inc; (Serials) Innovative Interfaces, Inc
Database Vendor: EBSCOhost, Gale Cengage Learning, OCLC FirstSearch, ProQuest, Westlaw
Wireless access
Partic in Llano Estacado Info Access Network (LEIAN); New Mexico Consortium of Academic Libraries
Open Mon-Thurs 7:30am-Midnight, Fri 7:30am-8pm, Sat 10-7, Sun Noon-Midnight

P PORTALES PUBLIC LIBRARY*, 218 S Ave B, 88130. SAN 310-6985. Tel: 505-356-3940. FAX: 505-356-3964. E-mail: ppl@yucca.net. Web Site: www.portalesnm.org/library. *Dir,* Denise Burnett; *Asst Librn, Ch,* Tawna Luscombe; *YA Librn,* Olivia Usher; *Cataloger,* Vickie Shumate; Staff 7 (MLS 1, Non-MLS 6)
Founded 1934. Pop 15,695; Circ 68,639
Library Holdings: Bk Vols 40,000; Per Subs 85
Subject Interests: Genealogy
Wireless access
Open Mon-Wed 10-6, Thurs 10-7, Fri 10-5, Sat 10-2
Friends of the Library Group

RATON

P ARTHUR JOHNSON MEMORIAL LIBRARY*, 244 Cook Ave, 87740. SAN 310-6993. Tel: 575-445-9711. FAX: 575-445-8336. E-mail: library@cityofraton.com. Web Site: www.ratonnm.gov/community/raton-library. *Libr Dir,* Thayla Wright
Founded 1912. Pop 6,584; Circ 26,765
Library Holdings: Bk Vols 48,000; Per Subs 111
Special Collections: Southwest & Local History, audio, CD, file mat, pictures, tapes, video. Oral History; State Document Depository
Partic in NMex Info Systs; OCLC Online Computer Library Center, Inc
Open Mon 1-6, Tues-Sat 10-6, Thurs 10-9
Friends of the Library Group

RED RIVER

P RED RIVER PUBLIC LIBRARY*, 702 E Main St, 87558. (Mail add: PO Box 1020, 87558-1020). Tel: 505-754-6564. FAX: 505-754-6564. E-mail: rrlib@newmex.com. Web Site: redrivernewmexico.com/libweb. *Librn,* Kerry Shepherd
Library Holdings: Audiobooks 1,183; AV Mats 2,609; Bk Vols 13,119; Per Subs 11; Videos 1,416
Special Collections: Southwest Coll
Automation Activity & Vendor Info: (Acquisitions) Biblionix; (Cataloging) Biblionix; (Circulation) Biblionix; (OPAC) Biblionix
Wireless access
Open Mon, Tues & Fri 10-12:30 & 1:30-4:30, Thurs 6pm-9pm, Sat 10-12 & 1-5

RIO RANCHO

P RIO RANCHO PUBLIC LIBRARY*, 755 Loma Colorado Dr NE, 87124. (Mail add: PO Box 15670, 87174-0670), SAN 321-7671. Tel: 505-891-5013. Circulation Tel: 505-891-5013, Ext 3081. Reference Tel: 505-896-8819. Administration Tel: 505-896-8818. FAX: 502-892-4782. Web Site: www.ci.rio-rancho.nm.us/library.htm. *Dir,* William Cicola; Tel: 505-896-8817; *Tech Serv,* Geri Hutchins; *Youth Serv,* Stephanie Zaslav; E-mail: szaslav@ci.rio-rancho.nm.us; Staff 14 (MLS 10, Non-MLS 4)
Founded 1974. Pop 68,000; Circ 502,024
Jul 2005-Jun 2006 Income $1,943,245. Mats Exp $434,634. Sal $681,768
Library Holdings: Bk Vols 149,891; Per Subs 111
Special Collections: Southwest Coll
Automation Activity & Vendor Info: (Acquisitions) Innovative Interfaces, Inc; (Cataloging) OCLC Online; (Circulation) Innovative Interfaces, Inc; (ILL) OCLC Online; (OPAC) Innovative Interfaces, Inc; (Serials) Innovative Interfaces, Inc
Database Vendor: EBSCOhost, Gale Cengage Learning, ProQuest
Function: After school storytime, CD-ROM, Handicapped accessible, Homebound delivery serv, ILL available, Learning ctr, Music CDs, Online searches, Photocopying/Printing, Prog for adults, Prog for children & young adult, Ref serv available, Satellite serv, Spoken cassettes & CDs, Summer reading prog, Telephone ref, VHS videos, Wheelchair accessible, Workshops
Publications: Booklist (Periodical)
Special Services for the Deaf - Bks on deafness & sign lang
Special Services for the Blind - VisualTek equip
Open Mon-Thurs 10-8, Fri & Sat 10-5
Friends of the Library Group
Branches: 1
ESTER BONE MEMORIAL LIBRARY, 950 Pinetree Rd SE, 87124-7615. Tel: 505-891-5012. FAX: 505-891-1396. *Br Mgr,* Robert Nankin; Tel: 505-891-5225, E-mail: rnankin@ci.rio-rancho.nm.us

ROSWELL

J EASTERN NEW MEXICO UNIVERSITY - ROSWELL*, Learning Resource Center, 52 University Blvd, 88203. (Mail add: PO Box 6000, 88202-6000), SAN 310-7027. Tel: 575-624-7282. FAX: 575-624-7479. Web Site: www.roswell.enmu.edu. *Dir,* Rollah Aston; E-mail: rollah.aston@roswell.enmu.edu; Staff 5 (MLS 1, Non-MLS 4)
Founded 1959. Enrl 4,000; Fac 150
Library Holdings: Bk Vols 45,000; Per Subs 50
Special Collections: Child Development Center; Nursing History Coll. Oral History
Automation Activity & Vendor Info: (Acquisitions) Innovative Interfaces, Inc; (Cataloging) Innovative Interfaces, Inc; (Circulation) Innovative Interfaces, Inc; (OPAC) Innovative Interfaces, Inc
Open Mon-Thurs 7:30am-9:30pm, Fri 8-12, Sat 9-4, Sun 2-5

J NEW MEXICO MILITARY INSTITUTE*, Paul Horgan Library-Toles Learning Center, Toles Learning Center, 101 W College Blvd, 88201-5173. SAN 310-7051. Tel: 575-624-8380. Circulation Tel: 575-624-8385. Interlibrary Loan Service Tel: 575-624-8394. FAX: 575-624-8390. Web Site: www.nmmi.edu/library. *Dir,* Jerry Klopfer; Tel: 575-624-8381; *Dep Libr Dir,* June Frosch; Tel: 575-624-8384; *Assoc Librn,* Joan Jump; Tel: 575-624-8387; *Asst Librn,* Desi Aguilar; Staff 6 (MLS 2, Non-MLS 4)
Founded 1902. Enrl 919; Fac 78; Highest Degree: Associate
Jul 2011-Jun 2012. Mats Exp $77,100, Books $36,000, Per/Ser (Incl. Access Fees) $7,300, Micro $3,600, AV Mat $7,000, Electronic Ref Mat (Incl. Access Fees) $22,000, Presv $1,200
Library Holdings: Bk Titles 50,000; Bk Vols 70,000; Per Subs 128
Special Collections: Henry David Thoreau Coll; Paul Horgan Writings
Subject Interests: Hist, Humanities, Mil hist (US), Napoleonic era, Natural sci, SW hist
Automation Activity & Vendor Info: (Acquisitions) Innovative Interfaces, Inc; (Cataloging) Innovative Interfaces, Inc; (Circulation) Innovative Interfaces, Inc; (Course Reserve) Innovative Interfaces, Inc; (ILL) OCLC; (OPAC) Innovative Interfaces, Inc; (Serials) Innovative Interfaces, Inc
Database Vendor: Alexander Street Press, Amigos Library Services, EBSCOhost, Gale Cengage Learning, Newsbank, OCLC FirstSearch, Oxford Online, ProQuest, Wilson - Wilson Web
Wireless access
Partic in New Mexico Consortium of Academic Libraries
Open Mon-Fri 7:15-4:30

S ROSWELL MUSEUM & ART CENTER LIBRARY*, 100 W 11th St, 88201. SAN 310-7078. Tel: 575-624-6744, Ext 25. FAX: 575-624-6765. Web Site: www.roswellmuseum.org. *Dir,* Laurie Rufe; *Librn,* Candace Jordan Russell; E-mail: jordan@roswellmuseum.org; Staff 1 (Non-MLS 1)
Jul 2009-Jun 2010. Mats Exp $3,500
Library Holdings: DVDs 60; Bk Vols 6,000; Per Subs 22; Videos 437
Special Collections: Fritz Scholder Archives; Howard Cook Archives; New Mexico Artists Files; Peter Hurd Archives; Robert H Goddard Archives & Coll; Roswell Artist-in-Residence Files; Roswell Museum & Art Center Archives
Subject Interests: Artists
Automation Activity & Vendor Info: (Cataloging) Inmagic, Inc.
Function: For res purposes
Open Mon-Fri 1-5
Restriction: Not a lending libr

P ROSWELL PUBLIC LIBRARY*, 301 N Pennsylvania Ave, 88201. SAN 310-7086. Tel: 575-622-7101. FAX: 575-622-7107. Web Site: www.roswellpubliclibrary.org. *Dir,* Betty Long; *Adult Serv,* Scott May; *AV, YA Serv,* Nancy Schummer; *Ch Serv,* DeAnne Dekle; *Circ,* Robert Briggs; *ILL, Per,* Rosemarie Klopfer; Staff 6 (MLS 4, Non-MLS 2)
Founded 1906. Pop 61,382; Circ 302,542
Jul 2008-Jun 2009 Income $1,525,401, State $93,255, City $1,432,146. Mats Exp $244,519, Books $192,942, Per/Ser (Incl. Access Fees) $6,625, Other Print Mats $427, Micro $1,200, AV Mat $26,443, Electronic Ref Mat (Incl. Access Fees) $16,882. Sal $896,101
Library Holdings: Audiobooks 3,366; AV Mats 5,722; Bks on Deafness & Sign Lang 72; CDs 3,699; DVDs 1,155; e-books 5; Large Print Bks 5,410; Bk Titles 156,821; Bk Vols 164,018; Per Subs 178; Talking Bks 2,966; Videos 1,032
Special Collections: Southwest Coll. State Document Depository
Subject Interests: Genealogy
Automation Activity & Vendor Info: (Cataloging) SirsiDynix; (Circulation) SirsiDynix; (OPAC) SirsiDynix

Database Vendor: EBSCOhost, LearningExpress, OCLC FirstSearch, ProQuest
Wireless access
Special Services for the Blind - Audio mat; Cassette playback machines; Cassettes; Home delivery serv; Large print bks; Reader equip; Talking bks
Open Mon & Tues 9-9, Wed-Sat 9-6, Sun 2-6
Friends of the Library Group

G UNITED STATES BUREAU OF LAND MANAGEMENT*, Roswell Field Office Library, 2909 W Second St, 88201-2019. SAN 310-7000. Tel: 575-627-0272. *Admin Librn,* Robin Whitebear
Library Holdings: Bk Vols 2,000
Open Mon-Fri 7:45-4:30

RUIDOSO

P RUIDOSO PUBLIC LIBRARY*, 107 Kansas City Rd, 88345. SAN 310-7094. Tel: 505-258-3704. FAX: 505-258-4619. E-mail: library@ruidoso-nm.gov. Web Site: www.youseemore.com/ruidosopl. *Dir,* Corey Bard; *Supvr, Ch Serv,* Cheryl Volosin; *Tech Serv,* Marie Slaten; Staff 6 (MLS 1, Non-MLS 5)
Founded 1950. Pop 20,000; Circ 38,000
Jul 2011-Jun 2012 Income $473,700, State $6,900, City $446,800, County $15,000, Locally Generated Income $5,000. Mats Exp $39,192, Books $32,000, Per/Ser (Incl. Access Fees) $4,000, AV Mat $2,500. Sal $254,864 (Prof $65,000)
Library Holdings: Bk Vols 40,000; Per Subs 171
Automation Activity & Vendor Info: (Cataloging) TLC (The Library Corporation); (Circulation) TLC (The Library Corporation); (ILL) OCLC; (OPAC) TLC (The Library Corporation); (Serials) EBSCO Online
Database Vendor: Gale Cengage Learning
Publications: @yourlibrary (Newsletter)
Open Mon-Thurs 9-6, Fri 9-4, Sat 10-2
Friends of the Library Group

SAN FELIPE PUEBLO

P PUEBLO OF SAN FELIPE COMMUNITY LIBRARY*, 24 Black Mesa Rd, 87001. Tel: 505-771-9970.
Library Holdings: Bk Vols 1,500
Open Mon-Fri 8-5

SAN LORENZO

S PINHOLE RESOURCE LIBRARY*, Star Rte 15, 88041. (Mail add: PO Box 1355, 88041), SAN 326-288X. Tel: 505-536-9942. E-mail: pinhole@gilanet.com. Web Site: www.pinholeresource.com. *Dir,* Eric Renner
Library Holdings: Bk Titles 400
Publications: Bibliography of Pinhole Optics; Bibliography of Pinhole Photography; Pinhole Journal
Partic in Soc for Photog Educ

SAN YSIDRO

P ZIA ENRICHMENT LIBRARY*, 162B Zia Blvd, 87053-6002. Tel: 505-867-3304, Ext 239. FAX: 505-867-3308. *Dir,* Joyce Medina
Pop 646; Circ 1,500
Library Holdings: AV Mats 100; Bk Vols 8,589; Per Subs 12
Automation Activity & Vendor Info: (Cataloging) Follett Software; (Circulation) Follett Software
Wireless access
Open Mon-Fri 8-8

SANTA FE

R CHURCH OF THE HOLY FAITH, EPISCOPAL*, Parish Library, 311 E Palace Ave, 87501. SAN 310-7124. Tel: 505-982-4447. E-mail: dawn@holyfaithchurchsf.org, library@holyfaithchurchsf.org. Web Site: holyfaithchurchsf.org. *Librn,* Wendy Hitt; Tel: 505-982-4447, Ext 113
Founded 1949
Library Holdings: Bk Titles 5,000; Per Subs 6
Subject Interests: Altar, Arts, Biblical studies, Biog, Church hist, Comparative faiths, Healing, Missions, Music, Personal relig, Symbolism, Theol
Publications: Monthly Parish Magazine; Weekly Bulletin
Open Tues-Fri 9:30-4:30
Friends of the Library Group

C INSTITUTE OF AMERICAN INDIAN & ALASKA NATIVE CULTURE & ARTS DEVELOPMENT LIBRARY*, Institute of American Indian Arts Library, 83 Avan Nu Po Rd, 87508. SAN 310-7167. Tel: 505-424-5715. FAX: 505-424-3131. Web Site: www.iaia.edu/academics/library. *Dir,* Valerie Nye; Tel: 505-424-2397, E-mail: vnye@iaia.edu; *Librn,* Jennifer James; E-mail: jjames@iaia.edu; *Cat Librn,* Pam Donegan; E-mail: pdonegan@iaia.edu; *Archivist,* Ryan Flahive; E-mail: rflahive@iaia.edu; *Libr Spec,* Grace Nuvayestewa; E-mail: gnuvayestewa@iaia.edu; Staff 5 (MLS 4, Non-MLS 1)
Founded 1962. Enrl 343; Highest Degree: Bachelor
Library Holdings: CDs 700; DVDs 900; Bk Vols 39,000; Per Subs 150
Special Collections: History of the Institute (IAIA Archives); Lee & Stewart Udall Special Coll; Lloyd Kiva New Special Coll; National Anthropological Archive Photographs (Smithsonian Photo Coll of Native American People & Places); Native American Music Coll, cassettes & rec; TC Cannon Special Coll; Visual Resources Coll
Subject Interests: Art, Native Am
Automation Activity & Vendor Info: (Cataloging) Innovative Interfaces, Inc - Millenium; (Circulation) Innovative Interfaces, Inc - Millenium; (Serials) Innovative Interfaces, Inc - Millenium
Database Vendor: ARTstor, EBSCOhost, Gale Cengage Learning, JSTOR, Project MUSE, ProQuest
Wireless access
Function: Archival coll, Electronic databases & coll, For res purposes, Handicapped accessible, Online cat
Partic in American Indian Higher Education Consortium; New Mexico Consortium of Academic Libraries
Open Mon-Thurs 8am-9pm, Fri 8-5, Sun 12-9
Restriction: Open to students, fac & staff, Pub use on premises

G LEGISLATIVE COUNCIL SERVICE LIBRARY*, 411 State Capitol, 87501. SAN 310-7183. Tel: 505-986-4600. FAX: 505-986-4680. *Sr Legis Librn,* Tracey Kimball; E-mail: tracey.kimball@nmlegis.gov; *Librn,* Laurie Canepa; E-mail: laurie.canepa@nmlegis.gov; Staff 2 (MLS 2)
Founded 1951
Library Holdings: Bk Titles 2,800; Bk Vols 4,000; Per Subs 25
Special Collections: Legislative Reports. State Document Depository
Subject Interests: Govt, Pub finance, Taxation
Wireless access
Open Mon-Fri 8-5

L MONTGOMERY & ANDREWS*, Law Library, 325 Paseo de Peralta, 87501. SAN 372-4271. Tel: 505-982-3873. FAX: 505-982-4289. *Librn,* Bertha Sandoval
Library Holdings: Bk Vols 15,000
Subject Interests: Commercial law

S MUSEUM OF INTERNATIONAL FOLK ART*, Bartlett Library, 706 Camino Lejo, 87505. (Mail add: PO Box 2087, 87504-2087), SAN 351-6903. Tel: 505-476-1200, 505-476-1210. FAX: 505-476-1300. E-mail: internationalfolkart@gmail.com. Web Site: www.internationalfolkart.org. *Librn & Archivist,* Caroline Dechert; E-mail: caroline.dechert@state.nm.us; Staff 1 (MLS 1)
Founded 1953
Library Holdings: Bk Titles 13,000; Per Subs 307
Special Collections: Oral History
Subject Interests: Conserv, Craft, Folk art, Mus studies, Outsider art, Spanish colonial art, Textiles
Function: Ref serv available, Res libr
Partic in OCLC Online Computer Library Center, Inc
Restriction: Non-circulating, Open by appt only

MUSEUM OF NEW MEXICO

S PALACE OF THE GOVERNORS-FRAY ANGELICO CHAVEZ HISTORY LIBRARY, 120 Washington Ave, 87501. (Mail add: PO Box 2087, 87504), SAN 351-6814. Tel: 505-476-5090. E-mail: historylibrary@state.nm.us. Web Site: www.palaceofthegovernors.org. *Librn,* Patricia Hewitt; *Curator,* Tomas Jaehn; E-mail: tjaehn@mnm.state.nm.us; Staff 2 (Non-MLS 2)
Founded 1885
Library Holdings: Bk Vols 50,000; Per Subs 45
Special Collections: New Mexico, maps & ms, newsp, rare bks; Southwest (Photo Archives), prints. Oral History
Subject Interests: NMex, SW, Western Americana
Database Vendor: EBSCOhost, OVID Technologies
Function: Ref serv available
Publications: El Palacio
Open Tues-Fri 1-5
Restriction: Open to pub for ref only

S MUSEUM OF FINE ARTS LIBRARY*, 107 W Palace Ave, 87501. (Mail add: PO Box 2087, 87504-2087), SAN 351-6873. Tel: 505-476-5061. FAX: 505-476-5076. Web Site: www.mfasantafe.org. *Librn,* Rebecca Potance; E-mail: rebecca.potance@state.nm.us
Founded 1917
Library Holdings: Bk Titles 7,500; Per Subs 35
Special Collections: Artist Biographies; Exchange Exhibition, cats; New Mexican & Southwestern Art Coll
Restriction: Open by appt only

S MUSEUM OF INDIAN ARTS & CULTURE-LABORATORY OF ANTHROPOLOGY LIBRARY, 708 Camino Lejo, 87505. (Mail add: PO Box 2087, 87504-2087), SAN 351-6849. Tel: 505-476-1264. FAX:

505-476-1330. E-mail: LOA.Library@State.NM.US. Web Site: www.indianartsandculture.org. *Libr Dir,* Allison Colborne; E-mail: allison.colborne@state.nm.us; Staff 1 (MLS 1)
Founded 1929
Library Holdings: Bk Vols 39,300; Per Subs 70
Special Collections: LOA Library Rare Books Coll; Mesoamerican Archaeology & Ethnohistory Coll (Sylvanus G Morley Library)
Subject Interests: Indians of Cent Am, Indians of Mexico, SW anthrop, SW archaeol, SW hist, SW Indian arts, SW Indian mat culture
Automation Activity & Vendor Info: (OPAC) ByWater Solutions
Database Vendor: Gale Cengage Learning, JSTOR, OCLC FirstSearch
Function: ILL available, Ref serv available
Publications: List of Serials Holdings
Open Mon-Fri 10-12 & 1-5
Restriction: In-house use for visitors, Open to pub for ref only

S PALACE OF THE GOVERNORS PHOTO ARCHIVES*, 120 Washington Ave, 87501. (Mail add: PO Box 2087, 87504-2087), SAN 351-6938. Tel: 505-476-5092. FAX: 505-476-5053, 505-476-5104. E-mail: photos@mnm.state.nm.us. Web Site: palaceofthegovernors.org/photoarchives.html.
Founded 1960
Library Holdings: Bk Titles 3,000
Special Collections: Photograph Coll 1850-present
Subject Interests: Agr, Anthrop, Archaeology, Australia, China, Ethnology, Hist of NMex, India, Indians, Japan, Latin Am, Middle East, Mining, New Zealand, Philippines, Railroads
Publications: Collection Guides; Photog Catalogs; Reprint Series
Open Mon-Fri 1-5
Restriction: Not a lending libr

S NEW MEXICO CORRECTIONS DEPARTMENT*, Education Bureau, 4337 State Rd 14, 87508. (Mail add: PO Box 27116, 87505), SAN 310-723X. Tel: 505-827-8503, 505-841-4282. FAX: 505-827-8548. Web Site: corrections.state.nm.us. *Bur Chief,* Johannes Hedrich; Staff 1 (MLS 1)
Library Holdings: Bk Vols 115,000; Per Subs 210
Special Collections: Arizona Legal Access Model
Subject Interests: Corrections, Law
Special Services for the Deaf - Captioned film dep; High interest/low vocabulary bks
Restriction: Staff & inmates only

S NEW MEXICO SCHOOL FOR THE DEAF LIBRARY*, 1060 Cerrillos Rd, 87505. SAN 310-7191. Tel: 505-476-6379, 505-476-6383. FAX: 505-476-6376. Web Site: www.nmsd.k12.nm.us. *Coordr, Libr Serv,* Position Currently Open
Library Holdings: Bk Vols 16,000; Per Subs 40
Subject Interests: Deaf culture, Deaf educ, Deafness, Sign lang
Wireless access
Function: After school storytime, CD-ROM, Distance learning, Photocopying/Printing
Restriction: Open to students, fac & staff

P NEW MEXICO STATE LIBRARY*, 1209 Camino Carlos Rey, 87507-5166. SAN 351-6962. Tel: 505-476-9700. Toll Free Tel: 800-477-4401. FAX: 505-476-9701. Web Site: www.nmstatelibrary.org. *Interim State Librn,* Michael Delello; E-mail: michael.delello@state.nm.us; *Dep State Librn,* Joy Poole; Tel: 505-476-9712, E-mail: joy.poole@state.nm.us; Staff 22 (MLS 22)
Founded 1929. Pop 1,819,046
Library Holdings: Bk Vols 200,000; Per Subs 2,000
Special Collections: State Document Depository; US Document Depository
Subject Interests: Govt, Pub policy
Automation Activity & Vendor Info: (Circulation) SirsiDynix
Publications: Annual Report; Annual Statistical Reports; Hitchhiker; Library Directory
Partic in OCLC Online Computer Library Center, Inc
Open Mon-Fri 10-5
Branches: 1

P LIBRARY FOR THE BLIND & PHYSICALLY HANDICAPPED, 1209 Camino Carlos Rey, 87507-5166, SAN 310-7213. Tel: 505-476-9770. Toll Free Tel: 800-456-5515. FAX: 505-476-9776. E-mail: sl.lbph@state.nm.us. *Regional Librn,* John Mugford; Tel: 505-476-9772, E-mail: john.mugford@state.nm.us; *Outreach Serv, Reader Serv,* Amy Boggess; Tel: 505-476-9760, E-mail: amy.boggess@state.nm.us; Staff 6 (MLS 1.5, Non-MLS 4.5)
Founded 1967
Library Holdings: Bk Titles 72,000; Bk Vols 150,000; Talking Bks 72,000; Videos 150
Subject Interests: NMex
Automation Activity & Vendor Info: (Cataloging) Keystone Systems, Inc (KLAS); (Circulation) Keystone Systems, Inc (KLAS); (OPAC) Keystone Systems, Inc (KLAS)
Function: Bks on cassette, Digital talking bks
Publications: New Mexico State Library News of the Library for the Blind & Physically Handicapped (Newsletter)
Special Services for the Blind - Braille bks
Open Mon-Fri 9-4
Friends of the Library Group
Bookmobiles: 3

S GEORGIA O'KEEFFE MUSEUM*, Michael S Engl Family Foundation Research Center Library, 217 Johnson St, 87501. Tel: 505-946-1011. FAX: 505-946-1093. E-mail: library@okeeffemuseum.org. Web Site: www.okeeffemuseum.org/the-research-center/library-info.aspx. *Asst Dir, Librn,* Eumie Imm-Stroukoff; E-mail: eumie@okeeffemuseum.org; *Archives & Digital Coll Librn,* Elizabeth Ehrnst; *Asst Librn,* Fran Martone; Staff 2.75 (MLS 2, Non-MLS 0.75)
Founded 2001
Library Holdings: Electronic Media & Resources 8,895; Bk Titles 10,162; Per Subs 30
Special Collections: Alfred Stieglitz Coll; American Modernism; Georgia O'Keeffe Coll; Georgia O'Keeffe Foundation Archive; Maria Chabot Archive; William Innes Homer Coll
Automation Activity & Vendor Info: (Acquisitions) Ex Libris Group; (Cataloging) Ex Libris Group; (OPAC) Ex Libris Group; (Serials) Ex Libris Group
Database Vendor: OCLC FirstSearch, Wilson - Wilson Web
Wireless access
Function: Res libr
Partic in Amigos Library Services, Inc
Restriction: By permission only

P PUEBLO OF POJOAQUE PUBLIC LIBRARY*, 37 Camino del Rincon, Ste 2, 87506-9810. Tel: 505-455-7511. FAX: 505-455-0501. *Dir,* Jill Conner; *Circ,* Doris Vigil; *Tech Serv,* Vanessa Montoya; Staff 3 (MLS 1, Non-MLS 2)
Library Holdings: AV Mats 1,500; Bk Vols 15,000; Per Subs 20
Special Collections: Southwest Coll
Open Mon-Thurs 9-7, Fri 9-5, Sat 10-3

C SAINT JOHN'S COLLEGE*, Meem Library, 1160 Camino Cruz Blanca, 87505. SAN 310-7248. Tel: 505-984-6042. Reference Tel: 505-984-6044. FAX: 505-984-6004. Web Site: www.stjohnscollege.edu. *Dir,* Jennifer Sprague; Tel: 505-984-6041, E-mail: jsprague@sjcsf.edu; *Archivist, Tech Serv,* Heather McClure; Tel: 505-984-6045, E-mail: hmcclure@sjcsf.edu; *Acq, Ser,* Chris Quinn; Tel: 505-984-6043, E-mail: cquinn@sjcsf.edu; *Circ, ILL,* Laura Cooley; E-mail: lcooley@sjcsf.edu; Staff 4 (MLS 3, Non-MLS 1)
Founded 1964. Enrl 355; Fac 70; Highest Degree: Master
Library Holdings: Bk Titles 35,000; Bk Vols 70,000; Per Subs 120
Special Collections: Hunt Coll; Music (Grumman, Holzman, Schmidt & White)
Subject Interests: Classics, Music, Philos
Automation Activity & Vendor Info: (Cataloging) SirsiDynix; (Circulation) SirsiDynix; (OPAC) SirsiDynix
Database Vendor: OCLC FirstSearch
Function: ILL available
Partic in New Mexico Consortium of Academic Libraries; OCLC Online Computer Library Center, Inc

M ST VINCENT HOSPITAL LIBRARY*, 455 St Michael's Dr, 87505. SAN 375-1929. Tel: 505-820-5218. FAX: 505-989-6478. *Librn,* Albert Robinson; E-mail: albert.robinson@stvin.org
Library Holdings: Bk Vols 2,000; Per Subs 210
Open Mon-Fri 8-2

J SANTA FE COMMUNITY COLLEGE LIBRARY*, 6401 Richards Ave, 87508-4887. Tel: 505-428-1352. FAX: 505-428-1288. Web Site: www.sfcc.edu/library. *Libr Dir,* Peg Johnson; Tel: 505-428-1506, E-mail: peg.johnson@sfcc.edu; *Circ Librn,* Briana Fiandt; Tel: 505-428-1830, E-mail: briana.fiandt@sfcc.edu; *Ref & Instruction Librn,* Deana Brown; Tel: 505-428-1213, E-mail: deana.brown@sfcc.edu; *Tech Serv Librn,* Harriet Meiklejohn; Tel: 505-428-1287, E-mail: harriet.meiklejohn@sfcc.edu; Staff 3 (MLS 3)
Founded 1983. Enrl 2,900; Highest Degree: Associate
Library Holdings: Audiobooks 150; CDs 430; DVDs 1,700; e-journals 30,000; Bk Vols 60,000; Per Subs 200
Automation Activity & Vendor Info: (Cataloging) Innovative Interfaces, Inc; (Circulation) Innovative Interfaces, Inc; (OPAC) Innovative Interfaces, Inc
Database Vendor: Amigos Library Services, ARTstor, Baker & Taylor, CredoReference, EBSCOhost, Gale Cengage Learning, JSTOR, Newsbank, WT Cox
Wireless access
Open Mon-Thurs 8-8, Fri 8-5, Sat 10-4

S SANTA FE INSTITUTE LIBRARY*, 1399 Hyde Park Rd, 87501. SAN 375-359X. Tel: 505-946-2707. Reference Tel: 505-946-2708. FAX: 505-982-0565. E-mail: mba@santafe.edu. Web Site: www.santafe.edu. *Librn,* Margaret Alexander; Staff 2 (MLS 1, Non-MLS 1)
Founded 1984
Library Holdings: e-journals 400; Bk Vols 10,000; Per Subs 30
Special Collections: Garrett Birkhoff Coll; Stanislav Ulum Coll
Automation Activity & Vendor Info: (Circulation) Innovative Interfaces, Inc; (OPAC) Innovative Interfaces, Inc
Partic in OCLC Online Computer Library Center, Inc
Open Mon-Fri 8:30-5
Restriction: Non-circulating to the pub

P SANTA FE PUBLIC LIBRARY, 145 Washington Ave, 87501. SAN 351-7020. Tel: 505-955-6780. Circulation Tel: 505-955-6785. Interlibrary Loan Service Tel: 505-955-6720. Reference Tel: 505-955-6781. Administration Tel: 505-955-6789. FAX: 505-955-6676. TDD: 505-955-6715. E-mail: library@santafenm.gov. Web Site: www.santafelibrary.org. *Dir of Libr,* Patricia C Hodapp; Tel: 505-955-6788, E-mail: pchodapp@santafenm.gov; *Dir, Tech Serv,* Margaret G Baca; Tel: 505-955-6786, E-mail: mgbaca@santafenm.gov; Staff 21.5 (MLS 18.5, Non-MLS 3)
Founded 1896. Pop 67,947; Circ 677,356
Jul 2013-Jun 2014 Income (Main Library and Branch(s)) $3,618,896, State $74,378, City $3,427,218, County $25,000, Locally Generated Income $92,300. Mats Exp $502,106, Books $349,314, Per/Ser (Incl. Access Fees) $30,967, Micro $6,000, AV Mat $58,925, Electronic Ref Mat (Incl. Access Fees) $56,900. Sal $1,410,903
Library Holdings: Audiobooks 6,971; Bks on Deafness & Sign Lang 176; CDs 6,181; DVDs 15,682; e-books 798; Electronic Media & Resources 5,173; Large Print Bks 4,030; Microforms 108; Music Scores 293; Bk Titles 175,198; Bk Vols 281,255; Per Subs 626
Special Collections: New Mexico & Santa Fe (Southwest Coll)
Subject Interests: Santa Fe, New Mexico & bordering
Automation Activity & Vendor Info: (Acquisitions) Innovative Interfaces, Inc; (Cataloging) Innovative Interfaces, Inc; (Circulation) Innovative Interfaces, Inc; (ILL) OCLC Connexion; (OPAC) Innovative Interfaces, Inc
Database Vendor: Amigos Library Services, Baker & Taylor, Gale Cengage Learning, Innovative Interfaces, Inc, Newsbank, OCLC, OCLC WorldShare Interlibrary Loan, Overdrive, Inc
Wireless access
Function: 24/7 Online cat, Accessibility serv available based on individual needs, Art exhibits, AV serv, Bilingual assistance for Spanish patrons, Bks on CD, Children's prog, Computers for patron use, Copy machines, e-mail & chat, Electronic databases & coll, Exhibits, Fax serv, Free DVD rentals, Handicapped accessible, ILL available, Magazines, Magnifiers for reading, Mango lang, Microfiche/film & reading machines, Music CDs, Newsp ref libr, Online cat, Online searches, Orientations, Outreach serv, Photocopying/Printing, Preschool outreach, Prog for adults, Prog for children & young adult, Pub access computers, Ref serv available, Spanish lang bks, Spoken cassettes & CDs, Spoken cassettes & DVDs, Story hour, Summer reading prog, Tax forms, Teen prog, Video lending libr, Web-catalog, Wheelchair accessible, Workshops
Partic in OCLC Online Computer Library Center, Inc
Special Services for the Deaf - Bks on deafness & sign lang; Closed caption videos; Sign lang interpreter upon request for prog
Special Services for the Blind - Audio mat; Bks on cassette; Bks on CD; Copier with enlargement capabilities; Extensive large print coll; Free checkout of audio mat; Large print bks; Large screen computer & software; Magnifiers; PC for handicapped; Recorded bks; Text reader
Open Mon-Thurs 10-8, Fri & Sat 10-6, Sun 1-5
Friends of the Library Group
Branches: 2
OLIVER LA FARGE BRANCH LIBRARY, 1730 Llano St, 87505-5460, SAN 351-7101. Tel: 505-955-4860. Circulation Tel: 505-955-4865. Reference Tel: 505-955-4862. FAX: 505-955-4861. *Libr Mgr,* Kathryn Spangle; Tel: 505-955-4868
Founded 1978
Function: After school storytime, Art exhibits, AV serv, Bk club(s), Bks on CD, Children's prog, Computers for patron use, Copy machines, Electronic databases & coll, Fax serv, Free DVD rentals, Handicapped accessible, ILL available, Magazines, Magnifiers for reading, Mango lang, Music CDs, Online cat, Orientations, Outreach serv, Photocopying/Printing, Preschool reading prog, Prog for adults, Prog for children & young adult, Pub access computers, Ref serv available, Spanish lang bks, Story hour, Summer reading prog, Tax forms, Teen prog, Telephone ref, VHS videos, Video lending libr, Web-catalog, Wheelchair accessible
Special Services for the Deaf - Bks on deafness & sign lang; Closed caption videos; Sign lang interpreter upon request for prog
Special Services for the Blind - Audio mat; Bks on cassette; Bks on CD; Cassette playback machines; Large print bks; Large screen computer & software; Text reader
Open Mon-Wed 10-8, Thurs-Sat 10-6
Friends of the Library Group
SOUTHSIDE BRANCH LIBRARY, 6599 Jaguar Dr, 85707. Tel: 505-955-2810. Circulation Tel: 505-955-2808. Reference Tel: 505-955-2820. FAX: 505-955-2811. *Libr Mgr,* Patricia Seavey; Tel: 505-955-2822, E-mail: paseavey@ci.santa-fe.nm.us
Function: After school storytime, Art exhibits, Bks on CD, Children's prog, Computer training, Computers for patron use, Copy machines, Electronic databases & coll, Fax serv, Free DVD rentals, Handicapped accessible, ILL available, Magazines, Magnifiers for reading, Mango lang, Music CDs, Online cat, Orientations, Outreach serv, Photocopying/Printing, Preschool reading prog, Prog for adults, Prog for children & young adult, Pub access computers, Ref serv available, Spanish lang bks, Story hour, Study rm, Summer reading prog, Tax forms, Teen prog, Telephone ref, Video lending libr, Web-catalog, Wheelchair accessible
Special Services for the Deaf - Bks on deafness & sign lang; Closed caption videos; Sign lang interpreter upon request for prog
Special Services for the Blind - Audio mat; Bks on cassette; Bks on CD; Cassette playback machines; Large print bks; Large screen computer & software; Text reader
Open Mon-Thurs 10:30-8, Fri & Sat 10:30-6, Sun 1-5
Friends of the Library Group

C SANTA FE UNIVERSITY OF ART & DESIGN*, Fogelson Library, 1600 St Michael's Dr, 87505-7634. SAN 310-7132. Tel: 505-473-6569. Reference Tel: 505-473-6594. FAX: 505-473-6593. E-mail: reference@santafeuniversity.edu. Web Site: library.santafeuniversity.edu. *Dir of Libr,* Valerie Nye; Tel: 505-473-6575, E-mail: valerie.nye@santafeuniversity.edu; *Head, Circ,* Laura Smith; E-mail: laura.smith@santafeuniversity.edu; *Librn,* Margaret VanDyk; E-mail: margaret.vandyk@santafeuniversity.edu; Staff 5.5 (MLS 2, Non-MLS 3.5)
Founded 1874. Enrl 600; Fac 50; Highest Degree: Master
Library Holdings: AV Mats 18,800; CDs 1,900; DVDs 1,200; Electronic Media & Resources 85; Music Scores 1,500; Bk Titles 199,500; Bk Vols 221,783; Per Subs 100; Videos 1,500
Special Collections: Chase Art History Library; LP Records (33 1/3) Coll; Photography (Newhall Library); Southwest & New Mexico History Coll
Subject Interests: Educ, Fine arts, Moving image arts, Performing arts
Automation Activity & Vendor Info: (Cataloging) SirsiDynix; (Circulation) SirsiDynix; (Course Reserve) SirsiDynix; (ILL) OCLC ILLiad; (OPAC) SirsiDynix
Database Vendor: Amigos Library Services, ARTstor, Baker & Taylor, BioOne, Cambridge Scientific Abstracts, Cinahl, ebrary, EBSCOhost, Gale Cengage Learning, H W Wilson, JSTOR, Newsbank, OCLC ArticleFirst, OCLC FirstSearch, OCLC WorldShare Interlibrary Loan, PubMed, SirsiDynix
Wireless access
Function: Archival coll, Audio & video playback equip for onsite use, Computers for patron use, Copy machines, Distance learning, Electronic databases & coll, Free DVD rentals, ILL available, Music CDs, Online cat, Online info literacy tutorials on the web & in blackboard, Online ref, Orientations, Photocopying/Printing, Pub access computers, Ref & res, Ref serv available, Res libr, Telephone ref, VHS videos, Web-catalog, Workshops
Partic in New Mexico Consortium of Academic Libraries
Open Mon-Wed 8am-11pm, Thurs 8am-9pm, Fri 8-5, Sat 10-5, Sun 1-9
Restriction: Circ limited, Fee for pub use, In-house use for visitors, Limited access for the pub, Non-circulating coll, Non-circulating of rare bks, Open to pub for ref & circ; with some limitations, Open to students, fac, staff & alumni, Restricted borrowing privileges, Restricted pub use
Friends of the Library Group

S SCHOOL FOR ADVANCED RESEARCH LIBRARY*, Catherine McElvain Library, 660 Garcia St, 87505. (Mail add: PO Box 2188, 87504-2188), SAN 310-7256. Tel: 505-954-7234. FAX: 505-954-7214. E-mail: library@sarsf.org. Web Site: www.sarweb.org/home/library.htm. *Librn,* Laura J Holt; E-mail: lholt@sarsf.org; Staff 1 (MLS 1)
Founded 1960
Library Holdings: Bk Titles 8,000; Per Subs 52
Special Collections: Institutional, Indian Arts Fund & Associated Individuals Archive
Subject Interests: Anthrop, Hist of anthrop, Theory & methodology
Automation Activity & Vendor Info: (Cataloging) LibLime; (Circulation) LibLime
Wireless access
Function: Res libr
Open Mon-Fri 10-12 & 1-5

C SOUTHWESTERN COLLEGE*, Quimby Memorial Library, 3960 San Felipe Rd, 87507. SAN 375-3166. Tel: 505-467-6825. Toll Free Tel: 877-471-5756, Ext 6825. FAX: 505-467-6826. E-mail: library@swc.edu. Web Site: www.swc.edu. *Libr Dir,* Leslie Clarissa Monsalve-Jones; *Libr Asst,* Jacque Major; E-mail: libassistant@swc.edu; Staff 1 (Non-MLS 1)
Founded 1963. Enrl 180; Fac 18; Highest Degree: Master

Sept 2009-Aug 2010. Mats Exp $15,000, Books $4,000, Per/Ser (Incl. Access Fees) $1,000, AV Mat $4,000, Electronic Ref Mat (Incl. Access Fees) $5,000, Presv $1,000
Library Holdings: AV Mats 258; Bk Titles 18,000; Per Subs 12
Subject Interests: Applied psychol, Art therapy, Comparative relig, Counseling, Experimental educ, Grief therapy, Metaphysics
Automation Activity & Vendor Info: (Acquisitions) Follett Software; (Cataloging) Follett Software; (Circulation) Follett Software; (Course Reserve) EBSCO Online; (OPAC) Follett Software
Database Vendor: American Psychological Association (APA), EBSCOhost, Gale Cengage Learning, OCLC FirstSearch, OCLC WorldShare Interlibrary Loan
Wireless access
Function: AV serv, Res libr
Partic in New Mexico Consortium of Academic Libraries
Open Mon-Thurs 8:30-6, Fri 8:30-4, Sat 10-5

GL SUPREME COURT LAW LIBRARY, (Formerly New Mexico Supreme Court), 237 Don Gaspar, 87501. (Mail add: PO Drawer L, 87504-0318), SAN 310-7221. Tel: 505-827-4850. FAX: 505-827-4852. E-mail: libref@nmcourts.gov. Web Site: www.supremecourtlawlibrary.org. *Sr Law Librn,* Michael Poulson; Staff 8 (MLS 4, Non-MLS 4)
Founded 1853
Library Holdings: Bk Titles 60,133; Bk Vols 175,000
Special Collections: US Document Depository
Subject Interests: Anglo-Am law, Pre-1850 Mexican Law
Automation Activity & Vendor Info: (Cataloging) EOS International; (Circulation) EOS International; (ILL) OCLC WorldShare Interlibrary Loan; (OPAC) EOS International
Wireless access
Function: 24/7 Online cat, Archival coll, Computers for patron use, Copy machines, Doc delivery serv, e-mail serv, Electronic databases & coll, ILL available, Jail serv, Mail & tel request accepted, Microfiche/film & reading machines, Online cat, Outside serv via phone, mail, e-mail & web, Pub access computers
Partic in Amigos Library Services, Inc
Open Mon-Fri 8-5
Restriction: Badge access after hrs, Non-circulating of rare bks, Open to pub for ref & circ; with some limitations

P VISTA GRANDE PUBLIC LIBRARY, 14 Avenida Torreon, 87508-9199. (Mail add: Seven Avenida Vista Grande, B7-192, 87508). Tel: 505-466-7323. FAX: 505-466-3889. E-mail: read@vglibrary.org. Web Site: www.vglibrary.org. *Dir,* Julia Kelso; *Libr Asst,* Tracey Mitchell; Staff 1.3 (Non-MLS 1.3)
Founded 2001. Pop 5,799; Circ 28,000
Library Holdings: AV Mats 2,500; Bk Vols 36,000; Per Subs 58
Automation Activity & Vendor Info: (Cataloging) Biblionix/Apollo; (Circulation) Biblionix/Apollo; (OPAC) Follett Software
Wireless access
Function: Adult bk club, Adult literacy prog, After school storytime, Bk club(s), Bks on cassette, Bks on CD, Chess club, Children's prog, Computers for patron use, Copy machines, Electronic databases & coll, Free DVD rentals, Games & aids for the handicapped, Handicapped accessible, Holiday prog, Homework prog, ILL available, Large print keyboards, Magnifiers for reading, Music CDs, Online cat, Online ref, Online searches, Photocopying/Printing, Preschool outreach, Prog for adults, Prog for children & young adult, Spoken cassettes & CDs, Summer reading prog, Tax forms, VHS videos, Video lending libr, Web-catalog, Wheelchair accessible, Workshops
Open Tues-Fri 12-6, Sat 10-4

S WHEELWRIGHT MUSEUM OF THE AMERICAN INDIAN*, Mary Cabot Wheelwright Research Library, 704 Camino Lejo, 87505. (Mail add: PO Box 5153, Sante Fe, 87502-5153), SAN 310-7264. Tel: 505-982-4636. FAX: 505-989-7386. E-mail: info@wheelwright.org. Web Site: www.wheelwright.org. *Dir,* Jonathan Batkin; *Curator,* Cheri Falkenstein-Doyle
Founded 1937
Library Holdings: Bk Vols 4,000
Subject Interests: Culture of Navajo Indians, Indians of NAm
Open Mon-Sat 10-5, Sun 1-5

SANTA ROSA

P MOISE MEMORIAL LIBRARY*, 208 S Fifth St, 88435-2329. SAN 310-7272. Tel: 575-472-3101. FAX: 575-472-4101. E-mail: moiselibrary@plateautel.net. *Dir,* Joan Chavez
Founded 1932. Pop 2,469; Circ 29,144
Library Holdings: Audiobooks 589; CDs 69; DVDs 388; Bk Vols 16,054; Per Subs 43; Videos 665
Special Collections: Municipal. Oral History
Wireless access
Special Services for the Deaf - Spec interest per
Open Mon-Fri 10-6, Sat 9-12

SANTO DOMINGO PUEBLO

P SANTO DOMINGO PUBLIC LIBRARY*, PO Box 160, 87052-0160. Tel: 505-465-2214, Ext 226. FAX: 505-465-2688. E-mail: kewalib@yahoo.com. *Librn,* Cynthia Crespin
Library Holdings: Bk Vols 2,778; Per Subs 27
Automation Activity & Vendor Info: (Cataloging) Follett Software; (Circulation) Follett Software; (OPAC) Follett Software
Function: AV serv, Children's prog, Computer training, Computers for patron use, e-mail serv, Handicapped accessible, Online ref, Prog for children & young adult, Satellite serv, Summer reading prog, Wheelchair accessible
Open Mon-Fri 8-5
Restriction: Circ limited, Open evenings by appt, Open to employees & special libr, Open to pub upon request, Open to students, Pub use on premises, Use of others with permission of librn

SHIPROCK

J DINE COLLEGE*, Senator John D Pinto Library, Hwy 64 & N 570, 87420. (Mail add: PO Box 580, 87240-0580). Tel: 505-368-3542. FAX: 505-368-3519, 505-368-3539. Web Site: library.dinecollege.edu. *Libr Mgr,* Annie Lewis; Tel: 505-368-3643; Staff 4 (Non-MLS 4)
Enrl 450; Highest Degree: Associate
Library Holdings: e-books 11,000; Bk Vols 25,000; Per Subs 35
Special Collections: American Indian Culture with Special Navajo Coll
Subject Interests: Geol of western US
Automation Activity & Vendor Info: (Acquisitions) Ex Libris Group; (Cataloging) Ex Libris Group; (Circulation) Ex Libris Group; (OPAC) Ex Libris Group
Wireless access
Open Mon-Thurs 8-9, Fri 8-4

SILVER CITY

C WESTERN NEW MEXICO UNIVERSITY*, J Cloyd Miller Library, 1000 W College Ave, 88061. (Mail add: PO Box 680, 88062-0680), SAN 310-7310. Tel: 575-538-6176. FAX: 505-538-6178. Web Site: voyager.wnmu.edu. *Univ Librn,* Gilda Ortego; Staff 20 (MLS 4, Non-MLS 16)
Founded 1893. Enrl 3,000; Fac 118; Highest Degree: Master
Library Holdings: Bks on Deafness & Sign Lang 88; Bk Titles 140,000; Bk Vols 140,250; Per Subs 950
Special Collections: Education (ERIC), fiche; Empire Zinc Strike Early 1950s ((Juan Chacon & Jack Cargill Coll); History (Library of American Civilization, Indian Claims Commission, Contemporary Newspapers of the North American Indian & Western Americana History), fiche & film; Local Newspapers from 1886; Music (Musicache Coll), fiche. State Document Depository; US Document Depository
Subject Interests: Culture, Hist, SW
Automation Activity & Vendor Info: (Acquisitions) Ex Libris Group; (Cataloging) Ex Libris Group; (Circulation) Ex Libris Group; (Course Reserve) Ex Libris Group; (ILL) Ex Libris Group; (Media Booking) Ex Libris Group; (OPAC) Ex Libris Group; (Serials) Ex Libris Group
Wireless access
Partic in OCLC Online Computer Library Center, Inc
Open Mon-Thurs 8am-9pm, Fri 8-5, Sun 12-8

SOCORRO

C NEW MEXICO INSTITUTE OF MINING & TECHNOLOGY*, Skeen Library, 801 Leroy Pl, 87801. SAN 310-7337. Tel: 575-835-5614. Interlibrary Loan Service Tel: 575-835-5173. Information Services Tel: 575-835-5201. FAX: 575-835-5754. Web Site: www.nmt.edu/~nmtlib. *Dir,* Lisa Beinhoff; Tel: 575-835-5030, Fax: 575-835-6666, E-mail: lbeinhoff@admin.nmt.edu; *Head, ILL,* Jonathan Zimmerman; E-mail: jzimmerman@admin.nmt.edu; Staff 9 (MLS 1, Non-MLS 8)
Founded 1895. Enrl 2,000; Fac 128; Highest Degree: Doctorate
Library Holdings: DVDs 1,224; e-books 111,000; Bk Titles 242,289; Bk Vols 483,038; Per Subs 2,429
Special Collections: Congressional Papers of Joseph Skeen; Theses & Dissertations; US Bureau of Mines Publications; US Geological Survey Publications, microfiche, print. State Document Depository; US Document Depository
Subject Interests: Applied math, Astrophysics, Biol, Computer sci, Electrical eng, Environ eng, Environ sci, Geol, Petroleum eng, Physics
Automation Activity & Vendor Info: (Acquisitions) Innovative Interfaces, Inc; (Cataloging) Innovative Interfaces, Inc; (Circulation) Innovative Interfaces, Inc; (ILL) OCLC ILLiad; (OPAC) Innovative Interfaces, Inc
Database Vendor: ACM (Association for Computing Machinery), Agricola, American Geophysical Union, American Mathematical Society, American Physical Society, Amigos Library Services, Baker & Taylor, Cambridge Scientific Abstracts, Cinahl, ebrary, EBSCO Information Services, EBSCOhost, Elsevier, H W Wilson, IEEE (Institute of Electrical & Electronics Engineers), Innovative Interfaces, Inc, IOP, ISI Web of

Knowledge, JSTOR, LexisNexis, Marcive, Inc, Medline, OCLC ArticleFirst, OCLC FirstSearch, OCLC WorldShare Interlibrary Loan, ProQuest, ScienceDirect, Thomson - Web of Science, Wiley, YBP Library Services
Wireless access
Function: Copy machines, Free DVD rentals, Govt ref serv, Wheelchair accessible
Partic in Amigos Library Services, Inc; New Mexico Consortium of Academic Libraries; Statewide California Electronic Library Consortium (SCELC)
Open Mon-Thurs (Winter) 8am-Midnight, Fri 8-5, Sat 12-7, Sun Noon-Midnight; Mon-Thurs (Summer) 8am-10pm, Fri 8-5, Sat 12-6, Sun 12-10

P SOCORRO PUBLIC LIBRARY*, 401 Park St, 87801-4544. SAN 310-7345. Tel: 505-835-1114. FAX: 505-835-1182. E-mail: library@adobelibrary.org. Web Site: www.adobelibrary.org. *Dir,* Paula Mertz; *Adult Serv,* Donald Padilla; E-mail: spladult@adobelibrary.org; *Youth Serv,* Jeanne Griffith; Staff 8 (MLS 2, Non-MLS 6)
Founded 1924. Pop 18,000; Circ 78,064
Library Holdings: Bk Titles 50,000; Per Subs 100
Subject Interests: Adult basic reading, Local hist, SW hist
Function: Doc delivery serv
Publications: Friends of the Socorro Public Library (Newsletter)
Partic in NMex Info Systs
Open Mon-Thurs 9-7, Fri & Sat 9-5
Friends of the Library Group

SPRINGER

P FRED MACARON LIBRARY*, 600 Colbert, 87747. (Mail add: PO Box 726, 87747-0726), SAN 310-7353. Tel: 575-483-2848. FAX: 575-483-2471. *Librn,* Norma Vigil
Circ 7,453
Library Holdings: Bk Vols 20,000; Per Subs 20
Wireless access
Open Tues-Sat 10-6

SUNLAND PARK

P SUNLAND PARK COMMUNITY LIBRARY*, 984 McNutt Rd, 88063-9039. Tel: 505-874-0873. FAX: 505-589-1222. *Dir,* Luz E Vargas
Library Holdings: AV Mats 50; Bk Vols 12,500; Per Subs 32
Automation Activity & Vendor Info: (Circulation) Innovative Interfaces, Inc; (OPAC) Innovative Interfaces, Inc
Open Mon & Thurs 10-8, Tues & Wed 10-6, Fri 9-5, Sat 10-2

SUNSPOT

S NATIONAL SOLAR OBSERVATORY*, Technical Library, One Loop Dr, 88349. SAN 310-7361. Tel: 575-434-7024. FAX: 575-434-7029. E-mail: library@nso.edu. Web Site: www.nso.edu/library. *Librn,* John Cornett
Founded 1953
Library Holdings: Bk Titles 3,900; Bk Vols 4,500; Per Subs 60
Special Collections: Publications of National Solar Observatory & Other Foreign & US Observatories; Solar Spectral Atlases
Subject Interests: Astronomy, Computer sci, Optics, Solar physics
Partic in OCLC Online Computer Library Center, Inc
Restriction: Not open to pub

TAOS

P TAOS PUBLIC LIBRARY*, 402 Camino de La Placita, 87571. SAN 310-7388. Tel: 575-758-3063. Circulation Tel: 575-737-2591. Interlibrary Loan Service Tel: 575-737-2592. Reference Tel: 575-737-2590. FAX: 575-737-2586. Web Site: www.taoslibrary.org. *Dir,* George Jaramillo; Tel: 575-737-2587; Staff 10 (MLS 1, Non-MLS 9)
Founded 1923. Pop 30,000
Library Holdings: Audiobooks 1,364; CDs 687; DVDs 1,952; Large Print Bks 1,074; Bk Titles 69,029; Bk Vols 73,702; Per Subs 110; Videos 2,384
Special Collections: D H Lawrence Coll; Frank Waters Coll; Scottish Clan MacLeod Coll; Taos-Specific Coll. Oral History; State Document Depository
Subject Interests: Fine arts, Indigenous people, SW
Automation Activity & Vendor Info: (Cataloging) TLC (The Library Corporation); (Circulation) TLC (The Library Corporation); (OPAC) TLC (The Library Corporation)
Database Vendor: Gale Cengage Learning, Newsbank, OCLC WorldShare Interlibrary Loan
Wireless access
Publications: Newsletter (Quarterly)
Partic in NMex Libr Asn
Special Services for the Blind - Magnifiers
Open Mon-Fri 10-6, Sat 10-5
Friends of the Library Group

TATUM

P TATUM COMMUNITY LIBRARY*, 323 E Broadway, 88267. (Mail add: PO Box 156, 88267-0156), SAN 310-7396. Tel: 505-398-4822. FAX: 505-398-4823. *Librn,* Carol Glover
Founded 1964. Pop 779; Circ 4,299
Jul 2008-Jun 2009 Income $13,000, State $11,000, City $2,000
Library Holdings: Audiobooks 377; CDs 92; DVDs 36; e-books 1,080; Large Print Bks 720; Bk Titles 7,000; Per Subs 32; Videos 274
Open Mon-Fri 9-6

TRUCHAS

P TRUCHAS COMMUNITY LIBRARY*, 60 County Rd 75, 87578. (Mail add: PO Box 330, 87578-0330). Tel: 505-689-2683. FAX: 505-689-1155. E-mail: truchas@cybermesa.com. *Dir of Libr,* Julie C Trujillo; *Librn,* Virginia Padilla
Pop 1,200
Library Holdings: AV Mats 42; CDs 275; DVDs 150; Large Print Bks 150; Bk Vols 6,274; Per Subs 26; Talking Bks 25; Videos 150
Automation Activity & Vendor Info: (ILL) LAC Group
Function: ILL available
Open Mon & Wed 2-7, Tues & Thurs 1-7, Fri 2-6

TRUTH OR CONSEQUENCES

P TRUTH OR CONSEQUENCES PUBLIC LIBRARY, 325 Library Lane, 87901-2375. SAN 310-7418. Tel: 505-894-3027. FAX: 505-894-2068. E-mail: torclibrary@torcnm.org. Web Site: www.torcnm.org/library.html. *Dir,* Pat O'Hanlon
Founded 1933. Pop 7,200; Circ 58,000
Library Holdings: Bk Titles 55,000; Per Subs 75
Subject Interests: SW
Partic in NMex Info Systs; OCLC Online Computer Library Center, Inc
Open Mon-Fri 9-7, Sat 9-Noon
Friends of the Library Group
Branches: 1
DOWNTOWN, 401 N Foch St, 87901. Tel: 505-894-7821. *Dir,* Pat O'Hanlon; *Asst Dir,* Denise Beard
Library Holdings: Bk Vols 3,500
Open Mon-Fri 9-12
Friends of the Library Group

TUCUMCARI

P NEW MEXICO STATE LIBRARY*, Rural Bookmobile East, 423 W Nobles, 88401. (Mail add: PO Box 1163, 88401-1163), SAN 310-7426. Tel: 575-461-1206. FAX: 575-461-1824. Web Site: www.stlib.state.nm.us. *Dir,* Paula White; *Librn,* Reyes Gonzales; *Librn,* Aleta Smith
Founded 1961. Pop 28,000
Library Holdings: Bk Titles 15,000; Per Subs 15
Open Mon-Fri 9-5

P TUCUMCARI PUBLIC LIBRARY*, 602 S Second, 88401-2899. SAN 310-7434. Tel: 505-461-0295. FAX: 505-461-0297. E-mail: library@cityoftucumcari.com. *Librn,* Maryann Molinas
Founded 1927. Pop 10,155; Circ 65,876
Library Holdings: Bk Vols 35,000; Per Subs 62
Open Mon 9:30-7, Tues-Fri 9:30-5:30, Sat 9-1

VAUGHN

P VAUGHN PUBLIC LIBRARY*, Yucca St, 88353. Tel: 575-584-2580. *Librn,* Diana Gallegos
Pop 539
Library Holdings: Bk Vols 12,000
Open Mon, Wed & Fri 4:30-8:30

VIRDEN

P VIRDEN PUBLIC LIBRARY, 209 Church St, 88045. Tel: 575-358-2544. FAX: 575-358-2544. E-mail: virdenpubliclibrary@gmail.com. *Dir,* Charlene Jones
Pop 142
Library Holdings: AV Mats 100; Bk Titles 7,000
Wireless access
Open Wed 8-5, Fri 10-12
Friends of the Library Group

WHITE SANDS MISSILE RANGE

A UNITED STATES ARMY*, Consolidated Library, Bldg 465, Rm 113, 88002-5039. SAN 351-711X. Tel: 505-678-1556, 575-678-5820. FAX: 575-678-2270. *Supvry Librn,* Mac Odom; E-mail: mac.odom@us.army.mil; *Doc Librn,* Kathleen Hogan; Tel: 575-678-1774, E-mail: kathlenn.b.hogan@us.army.mil; Staff 4 (MLS 2, Non-MLS 2)
Founded 1950

Library Holdings: Audiobooks 300; AV Mats 500; Bks on Deafness & Sign Lang 12; CDs 360; DVDs 175; e-books 700; e-journals 300; High Interest/Low Vocabulary Bk Vols 50; Large Print Bks 100; Microforms 1,000; Bk Titles 52,300; Bk Vols 55,400; Per Subs 45; Spec Interest Per Sub 12; Talking Bks 300; Videos 100
Special Collections: Military Science Coll; Southwest Coll; Technical Documents Coll
Subject Interests: SW region, US Mil
Automation Activity & Vendor Info: (Cataloging) EOS International; (Circulation) EOS International; (Course Reserve) EOS International; (Media Booking) EOS International; (OPAC) EOS International
Database Vendor: OCLC FirstSearch
Wireless access
Function: Archival coll, Bks on cassette, Bks on CD, Computers for patron use, Copy machines, Digital talking bks, e-mail & chat, e-mail serv, Electronic databases & coll, Exhibits, Govt ref serv, Holiday prog, ILL available, Mail & tel request accepted, Online cat, Online ref, Online searches, Outside serv via phone, mail, e-mail & web, Photocopying/Printing, Pub access computers, Ref & res, Ref serv available, Ref serv in person, Referrals accepted, Spoken cassettes & CDs, Spoken cassettes & DVDs, Tax forms, Telephone ref, Wheelchair accessible
Partic in OCLC Online Computer Library Center, Inc
Restriction: Authorized patrons, Govt use only, Mil, family mem, retirees, Civil Serv personnel NAF only, Not open to pub, Open to mil & govt employees only, Photo ID required for access

ZUNI

P ZUNI PUBLIC LIBRARY*, 27 E Chavez Circle, 87327. (Mail add: PO Box 339, 87327-0339). Tel: 505-782-4575. FAX: 505-782-7210. *Dir,* Cordelia Hooee
Library Holdings: AV Mats 3,760; Bk Vols 11,863
Automation Activity & Vendor Info: (Cataloging) Follett Software; (Circulation) Follett Software
Open Mon-Fri 9-6

NEW YORK

Date of Statistics: FY 2013-2014
Population, 2010 U.S. Census: 19,378,102
Population Served by Public Libraries: 19,378,102
Total Materials in Public Libraries: 136,399,248
Materials Per Capita: 7.04
Total Volumes in Public Libraries: 69,510,247
Volumes Per Capita: 3.59
Total Public Library Circulation: 154,348,192
Circulation Per Capita: 7.97
Total Public Library Income (including Capital & Grant-in-Aid): $1,281,083,574
Source of Income: Mainly public funds
Expenditure Per Capita: $63.39
Grants-in-Aid to Public Libraries:
Federal (Library Services & Technology Act): $2,335,879
State Aid: $70,096,494
Formula for Apportionment Intent: Formation of Library System to serve given area
Operation: Payment on basis of population, service, and square mileage (includes fixed annual grant)
State Library's Share from Federal Sources: $5,296,939
Number of County or Multi-county (Regional) Libraries: 23
Counties Served: 62
Number of Bookmobiles in State: 7

ADAMS

P ADAMS FREE LIBRARY*, Two N Main St, 13605. (Mail add: PO Box 58, 13605-0058), SAN 376-3102. Tel: 315-232-2265. FAX: 315-232-2265. Web Site: www.adamsfreelibrary.org. *Dir,* Cheryl Clark; Staff 1 (Non-MLS 1)
Founded 1902. Pop 1,624; Circ 8,026
Library Holdings: Bk Titles 9,568; Per Subs 45; Talking Bks 145
Automation Activity & Vendor Info: (Cataloging) SirsiDynix; (Circulation) SirsiDynix; (OPAC) SirsiDynix; (Serials) SirsiDynix
Mem of North Country Library System
Open Mon-Thurs 1-7, Fri 10-12 & 1-7, Sat 10-Noon

ADAMS CENTER

P ADAMS CENTER FREE LIBRARY*, 18267 State Rte 177, 13606. SAN 310-7442. Tel: 315-583-5501. FAX: 315-583-6247. Web Site: www.adamscenterfreelibrary.org. *Librn,* Penny Sayres-McGrath
Library Holdings: Bk Vols 9,000
Automation Activity & Vendor Info: (Cataloging) SirsiDynix; (Circulation) SirsiDynix; (OPAC) SirsiDynix; (Serials) SirsiDynix
Wireless access
Mem of North Country Library System
Open Mon 2-7, Wed & Fri 2-6, Thurs 9-Noon, Sat 10-2

ADDISON

P ADDISON PUBLIC LIBRARY*, Six South St, 14801. SAN 310-7450. Tel: 607-359-3888. FAX: 607-359-3611. Web Site: www.stls.org/addison. *Dir,* Karen Parsons; E-mail: parsonsk@stls.org
Founded 1893. Pop 2,734; Circ 19,077
Library Holdings: Bk Vols 16,500; Per Subs 30
Automation Activity & Vendor Info: (Cataloging) SirsiDynix; (Circulation) SirsiDynix; (OPAC) SirsiDynix; (Serials) SirsiDynix
Wireless access
Mem of Southern Tier Library System
Open Mon & Wed 2-8, Thurs 10-6, Fri 2-7

AFTON

P AFTON FREE LIBRARY*, 105A Main St, 13730. (Mail add: PO Box 48, 13730-0048), SAN 310-7469. Tel: 607-639-1212. FAX: 607-639-1557. Web Site: libraries.4cls.org/afton/index.html. *Libr Mgr,* Ramona Bogart
Founded 1933. Pop 2,977; Circ 12,597
Library Holdings: AV Mats 154; Bk Vols 15,118; Per Subs 47
Automation Activity & Vendor Info: (Cataloging) SirsiDynix; (Circulation) SirsiDynix; (OPAC) SirsiDynix
Mem of Four County Library System
Open Mon & Tues 12-5, Thurs 12-8, Fri 9-5, Sat 9-1

AKRON

P NEWSTEAD PUBLIC LIBRARY*, Akron Library, 33 Main St, 14001-1020. SAN 310-7477. Tel: 716-542-2327. FAX: 716-542-3703. Web Site: www.buffalolib.org/libraries/newstead/index.asp. *Dir,* Kristine Sutton; E-mail: suttonk@buffalolib.org; Staff 3 (MLS 1, Non-MLS 2)
Founded 1942. Pop 7,440; Circ 32,507
Library Holdings: Bk Titles 17,000; Per Subs 99
Automation Activity & Vendor Info: (Acquisitions) SirsiDynix
Wireless access
Mem of Buffalo & Erie County Public Library System
Open Mon & Wed 1-8, Tues, Fri & Sat 10-5
Friends of the Library Group

ALBANY

C ALBANY COLLEGE OF PHARMACY & HEALTH SCIENCES*, George & Leona Lewis Library, 106 New Scotland Ave, 12208. SAN 324-7503. Tel: 518-694-7270. FAX: 518-694-7300. E-mail: library@acphs.edu. Web Site: library.acphs.edu. *Dir, Libr Serv,* Susan L Iwanowicz; Tel: 518-694-7217, E-mail: susan.iwanowicz@acphs.edu; *Asst Dir,* Gwendolyn P H Weldy; Tel: 518-694-7274, E-mail: gwen.weldy@acphs.edu; *Ref & Educ Librn,* Kimberly Mitchell; Tel: 518-694-7124, E-mail: kimberly.mitchell@acphs.edu; *Ref & Educ Librn,* Lisa Shaffer; Tel: 518-694-7342, E-mail: lisa.shaffer@acphs.edu; Staff 4 (MLS 2, Non-MLS 2)
Founded 1960. Enrl 1,148; Fac 83; Highest Degree: Doctorate
Subject Interests: Pharm
Automation Activity & Vendor Info: (Cataloging) SirsiDynix; (Circulation) SirsiDynix; (Course Reserve) SirsiDynix; (OPAC) SirsiDynix
Database Vendor: Micromedex
Wireless access
Partic in Cap District Libr Coun for Ref & Res Resources; National Network of Libraries of Medicine; New York State Higher Education Initiative

S ALBANY INSTITUTE OF HISTORY & ART*, 125 Washington Ave, 12210-2296. SAN 310-7493. Tel: 518-463-4478. FAX: 518-463-5506. E-mail: library@albanyinstitute.org. Web Site: albanyinstitute.org. *Chief Curator, Dep Dir, Coll,* Tammis Groft; E-mail: grofttk@albanyinstitute.org. Subject Specialists: *Archives, Manuscripts,* Tammis Groft; Staff 1 (MLS 1)
Founded 1791
Library Holdings: Bk Vols 14,000; Per Subs 50
Special Collections: Albany imprints, almanacs, maps, photographs, manuscripts, broadsides, archives, architectural drawings, ephemera, scrapbooks; Albany Social, Political & Business History, 18th & 19th Centuries, maps, mss, photog; American Painters & Sculptors, mss, photog; Broadsides (including DeWitt Clinton Coll of 18th & Early 19th Century); Dutch in The Upper Hudson Valley, 17th & 18th Centuries, maps, mss; Political Broadsides
Subject Interests: Art, Hist, Local hist, Upper Hudson valleys
Automation Activity & Vendor Info: (OPAC) Follett Software

Database Vendor: EBSCOhost
Partic in Capital District Library Council
Open Thurs 1-4:30

CL ALBANY LAW SCHOOL*, Schaffer Law Library, 80 New Scotland Ave, 12208. SAN 310-7507. Tel: 518-445-2340. Circulation Tel: 518-445-2390. Interlibrary Loan Service Tel: 518-445-2338. FAX: 518-472-5842. Web Site: www.albanylaw.edu. *Dir,* Robert T Begg; Tel: 518-445-2336, E-mail: rbegg@albanylaw.edu; *Asst Dir,* Robert Emery; *Head, Tech Serv,* Colleen Smith; *Computer Librn,* Colleen Ostiguy; *AV,* Robert Eaton; *Circ, ILL, Pub Serv,* Mary Wood; *Doc,* Leslie Cunningham; *Tech Serv,* Rebecca Murphy; Staff 17 (MLS 8, Non-MLS 9)
Founded 1851. Enrl 659; Fac 51; Highest Degree: Doctorate
Library Holdings: Microforms 1,800,000; Bk Titles 90,000; Bk Vols 291,000; Per Subs 950
Special Collections: State Document Depository; US Document Depository
Automation Activity & Vendor Info: (Cataloging) OCLC Online; (Circulation) SirsiDynix; (Course Reserve) SirsiDynix; (ILL) OCLC Online; (OPAC) SirsiDynix; (Serials) SirsiDynix
Database Vendor: HeinOnline, LexisNexis, SirsiDynix, Westlaw
Wireless access
Partic in Cap District Libr Coun for Ref & Res Resources; New England Law Library Consortium, Inc; OCLC Online Computer Library Center, Inc
Open Mon-Thurs 8am-Midnight, Fri 8am-10pm, Sat 9-9, Sun 10am-Midnight

CM ALBANY MEDICAL COLLEGE*, Schaffer Library of Health Sciences, 47 New Scotland Ave, MC 63, 12208. SAN 351-7985. Tel: 518-262-5530. Interlibrary Loan Service Tel: 518-262-5538. Reference Tel: 518-262-5532. Administration Tel: 518-262-5586. FAX: 518-262-5820. E-mail: library@mail.amc.edu. Web Site: www.amc.edu/academic/schaffer/index.html. *Assoc Dean, Dir, Info Tech,* Enid Geyer; E-mail: geyere@mail.amc.edu; *Asst Dir,* Elizabeth Irish; Tel: 518-262-4980, E-mail: irishe@mail.amc.edu; *Access Serv,* Debra Wellspeak; Tel: 518-262-6460, E-mail: wellspd@mail.amc.edu; *Coll Develop,* Gail Botta; Tel: 518-262-5971, E-mail: bottag@mail.amc.edu; *Doc Delivery,* Ann Marie L'Hommebieu; Tel: 518-262-5569, E-mail: l'hommea@mail.amc.edu; *Ref Serv,* Sue Lahey; Tel: 518-262-5531, E-mail: laheys@mail.amc.edu; *Ser,* Cynthia Koman; Tel: 518-262-6058, E-mail: komanc@mail.amc.edu. Subject Specialists: *Educ,* Sue Lahey; *Educ,* Cynthia Koman; Staff 35 (MLS 9, Non-MLS 26)
Founded 1928. Enrl 1,490; Fac 417; Highest Degree: Doctorate
Library Holdings: Bk Titles 42,368; Bk Vols 148,664; Per Subs 3,810
Special Collections: Archives of Albany Medical College
Subject Interests: Med sci
Automation Activity & Vendor Info: (Cataloging) SirsiDynix; (Circulation) SirsiDynix; (Course Reserve) SirsiDynix; (OPAC) SirsiDynix; (Serials) SirsiDynix
Database Vendor: EBSCOhost, OVID Technologies, ProQuest
Publications: Fact Sheets
Partic in Cap District Libr Coun for Ref & Res Resources; National Network of Libraries of Medicine; OCLC Online Computer Library Center, Inc
Open Mon-Thurs 8am-Midnight, Fri 8am-9pm, Sat 10-10, Sun 12-12

P ALBANY PUBLIC LIBRARY*, 161 Washington Ave, 12210. SAN 351-7209. Tel: 518-427-4300. Interlibrary Loan Service Tel: 578-427-4323. Reference Tel: 518-427-4303. FAX: 518-449-3386. Interlibrary Loan Service E-mail: aplweb@albanypubliclibrary.org. Web Site: www.albanypubliclibrary.org. *Exec Dir,* Position Currently Open; *Asst Libr Dir,* Melanie Metzger; *ILL Librn,* Christopher Sagaas; *Local Hist Librn,* Ellen Gamache; Tel: 518-427-4327; *Pub Info Officer,* Stephanie Simon; Staff 61 (MLS 24, Non-MLS 37)
Founded 1833. Pop 95,000; Circ 991,442
Library Holdings: AV Mats 40,873; Large Print Bks 1,692; Bk Vols 190,432; Per Subs 720
Special Collections: Local History (Pruyn Coll), bks, pamphlets, clippings, newspr, photog. Oral History
Automation Activity & Vendor Info: (Acquisitions) Horizon; (Cataloging) Horizon; (Circulation) Horizon; (ILL) Horizon; (OPAC) Horizon; (Serials) Horizon
Database Vendor: Dialog, EBSCOhost, TLC (The Library Corporation)
Wireless access
Partic in OCLC Online Computer Library Center, Inc
Special Services for the Blind - Micro-computer access & training; Reader equip
Open Mon-Wed 9-9, Thurs & Fri 10-6, Sat 10-5, Sun 1-5
Friends of the Library Group
Branches: 6
ARBOR HILL/WEST HILL BRANCH, 148 Henry Johnson Blvd, 12210. *Librn,* Will Takach
Open Mon & Wed 12-8, Tues 10-6, Thurs & Fri 12-6, Sat 1-5
JOHN J BACH BRANCH, 455 New Scotland Ave, 12208, SAN 351-7322. Tel: 518-482-2154. E-mail: aplb1@albanypubliclibrary.org. *Br Mgr,* Mary Coon; Tel: 518-482-7911, Ext 226
Open Mon & Wed 12-8, Tues 10-6, Thurs & Fri 12-6, Sat 1-5
DELAWARE, 331 Delaware Ave, 12209, SAN 351-7268. Tel: 518-463-0254. E-mail: apld1@albanypubliclibrary.org. *Br Mgr,* Patrice Hollman; E-mail: hollmanp@albanypubliclibrary.org; *Br Librn,* Stephanie Preston; E-mail: prestons@albanypubliclibrary.org
Mem of Upper Hudson Library System
Open Mon & Wed 12-8, Tues 10-6, Thurs & Fri 12-6, Sat (Winter) 1-5
JOHN HOWE LIBRARY, 105 Schuyler St, 12202, SAN 351-7292. Tel: 518-472-9485. FAX: 518-472-9406. *Br Mgr,* Ethel LaPier; Tel: 518-482-7911, Ext 20, E-mail: lapiere@uhls.lib.ny.us
Open Mon & Wed-Fri (Winter) 12:30-5:30, Tues 12-8, Sat 9-5; Mon & Wed-Fri (Summer) 12:30-5:30, Tues 12:30-8
NORTH ALBANY BRANCH, 616 N Pearl St, 12204. Tel: 518-463-1581. *Br Supvr,* Ethel LaPier; Tel: 518-482-7911, Ext 20, E-mail: lapiere@uhls.lib.ny.us
Open Mon & Wed 12-8, Tues, Thurs & Fri 10-6, Sat (Winter) 9-5
PINE HILLS, 517 Western Ave, 12203, SAN 351-7357. Tel: 518-482-7911. FAX: 518-482-7916. *Br Mgr,* Mary Coon; Tel: 518-482-7911, Ext 226
Open Mon & Wed (Winter) 12-8, Tues 10-6, Thurs & Fri 12-6, Sat 9-5; Mon & Wed (Summer) 12-8, Tues 10-6, Thurs & Fri 12-6
Bookmobiles: 1. Outreach, Patrice Hollman. Bk titles 3,000

J BRYANT & STRATTON COLLEGE LIBRARY*, 1259 Central Ave, 12205. SAN 310-7485. Tel: 518-437-1802. FAX: 518-437-1048. Web Site: www.bryantstratton.edu. *Librn,* Mark Lasek; E-mail: mlasek@bryantstratton.edu; Staff 1 (MLS 1)
Founded 1988. Enrl 610; Fac 45; Highest Degree: Associate
Library Holdings: Bk Titles 4,700; Bk Vols 4,900; Per Subs 52
Subject Interests: Bus, Data proc, Econ, Law, Med asst, Mgt, Mkt, Off procedures, Travel
Automation Activity & Vendor Info: (Acquisitions) Follett Software; (Cataloging) Follett Software; (Circulation) Follett Software; (Course Reserve) Follett Software; (ILL) Follett Software; (OPAC) Follett Software; (Serials) Follett Software
Database Vendor: EBSCOhost, Gale Cengage Learning, Westlaw
Wireless access
Partic in Cap District Libr Coun for Ref & Res Resources
Open Mon-Thurs 8am-9:30pm, Fri 8-Noon

S CENTER FOR THE STUDY OF AGING LIBRARY*, 196 Shaker Rd, 12211-2028. SAN 328-1612. Tel: 518-465-6927. Web Site: www.centerforthestudyofaging.org. *Exec Dir,* Sara Harris; E-mail: sharri3@nycap.rr.com
Library Holdings: Bk Titles 4,500; Per Subs 20
Subject Interests: Aging, Health, Housing, Mental health, Nutrition, Psychiat, Psychol
Publications: Annotated Bibliographics Lists; Environment & Aging; Physical Activity, Aging & Sports (Vols I-IV); Safe Therapeutic Exercise for the Frail Elderly: An Introduction; Senior Citizen School Volunteer Program; Who? Me? Exercise? Safe Exercise for People Over 50
Restriction: Open by appt only

C COLLEGE OF SAINT ROSE*, Neil Hellman Library, 392-396 Western Ave, 12203. SAN 310-7515. Tel: 518-454-5180. Interlibrary Loan Service Tel: 518-454-2155. Reference Tel: 518-454-5181. FAX: 518-454-2897. E-mail: refdesk@mail.strose.edu. Web Site: library.strose.edu. *Dir,* Peter Koonz; E-mail: koonzp@mail.strose.edu; *Dir, Curric Libr,* Marisa Gitto; Tel: 518-337-4986, E-mail: gittom@mail.strose.edu; *Archivist, Spec Coll Librn,* Maria Kessler McShane; Tel: 518-454-5190, E-mail: kesslerm@mail.strose.edu; *Cat, Tech Serv,* Carl Cording; Tel: 518-458-5382, E-mail: cordingc@mail.strose.edu; *Circ, ILL, Ref,* Kate Moss; Tel: 518-454-2154, E-mail: mossk@mail.strose.edu; *Curric Libr Cataloger,* Mary Lindner; Tel: 518-337-4693, E-mail: lindnerm@strose.edu; *Electronic Res,* Peter Osterhoudt; Tel: 518-454-2026, E-mail: osterhop@mail.strose.edu; *Ref, Ser,* Steve Black; Tel: 518-458-5494, E-mail: blacks@mail.strose.edu. Subject Specialists: *Children's lit,* Marisa Gitto; Staff 17 (MLS 7, Non-MLS 10)
Founded 1920. Enrl 3,145; Fac 172; Highest Degree: Master
Library Holdings: Bk Vols 202,000; Per Subs 925
Special Collections: College Archives; Curriculum Library
Subject Interests: Educ
Automation Activity & Vendor Info: (Acquisitions) Ex Libris Group; (Cataloging) Ex Libris Group; (Circulation) Ex Libris Group; (Course Reserve) Ex Libris Group; (ILL) Ex Libris Group; (OPAC) Ex Libris Group; (Serials) Ex Libris Group
Database Vendor: Dialog, EBSCOhost, Gale Cengage Learning, LexisNexis, OCLC FirstSearch, OVID Technologies
Publications: Guide to the Neil Hellman Library
Partic in Capital District Library Council; OCLC Online Computer Library Center, Inc

G EMPIRE STATE DEVELOPMENT LIBRARY*, 12245. SAN 310-7639. Tel: 518-292-5235. FAX: 518-292-5810. E-mail: esdlibrary@esd.ny.gov. *Mgr, Info Serv,* Victoria Larson; E-mail: vlarson@esd.ny.gov; Staff 2 (MLS 1, Non-MLS 1)
Founded 1944
Library Holdings: AV Mats 40; CDs 75; DVDs 30; Bk Vols 2,500; Per Subs 70; Videos 12
Subject Interests: Bus, Econ develop, Intl trade
Automation Activity & Vendor Info: (Cataloging) Inmagic, Inc.; (ILL) OCLC; (Serials) Inmagic, Inc.
Database Vendor: Dun & Bradstreet, EBSCOhost, Factiva.com, Gale Cengage Learning, Hoovers, LexisNexis, OCLC WorldShare Interlibrary Loan, ReferenceUSA
Function: ILL available
Partic in Cap District Libr Coun for Ref & Res Resources; New York State Interlibrary Loan Network (NYSILL)
Open Mon-Fri 9-5:30

S FIRST UNITARIAN UNIVERSALIST SOCIETY OF ALBANY*, Charles R Joy Library, 405 Washington Ave, 12206. SAN 323-5459. Tel: 518-463-7135. FAX: 518-463-1429. E-mail: joylibrary@albanyuu.org. Web Site: www.fuusalbany.org/joylibrary.pdf. *Chairperson,* Sally Knapp; *Co-Chair,* Arnold Patashnick
Library Holdings: Bk Titles 1,345
Special Collections: First Unitarian Society of Albany Archives
Subject Interests: Bible, Family, Philos, Soc ethics, Theol, Unitarian Universalism, Women's issues, World relig
Wireless access
Open Mon-Fri 9-4, Sun 9-12

J ITT TECHNICAL INSTITUTE*, Learning Resource Center, 13 Airline Dr, 12205-1003. Tel: 518-452-9300, Ext 116. Toll Free Tel: 800-489-1191, Ext 116. FAX: 518-452-9393. E-mail: emonfred@itt-tech.edu. Web Site: www.itt-tech.edu. *Libr Serv Dir,* Edward Monfred; E-mail: emonfred@itt-tech.edu. Subject Specialists: *Cataloging, Internet literacy,* Edward Monfred; Staff 1 (MLS 1)
Founded 1998. Enrl 400; Fac 22; Highest Degree: Associate
Library Holdings: Bk Vols 710; Spec Interest Per Sub 9
Subject Interests: Computer aided design, Electronic, Info tech
Automation Activity & Vendor Info: (OPAC) LibraryWorld, Inc
Database Vendor: CRC Press/Taylor & Francis Group, ebrary, EBSCOhost, Gale Cengage Learning, LexisNexis, LibraryWorld, Inc, McGraw-Hill, OCLC WorldShare Interlibrary Loan, Oxford Online, ProQuest, ReferenceUSA, Sage
Wireless access
Function: Online cat
Restriction: Visitors must make appt to use bks in the libr

J MARIA COLLEGE OF ALBANY LIBRARY*, 700 New Scotland Ave, 12208. SAN 310-7574. Tel: 518-438-3111, Ext 215. FAX: 518-453-1366. Web Site: www.mariacollege.edu. *Dir,* Sister Rose Hobbs; Fax: 518-453-1366, E-mail: roseh@mariacollege.edu; Staff 3 (MLS 1, Non-MLS 2)
Founded 1958. Enrl 700
Library Holdings: Bk Vols 61,000; Per Subs 225
Subject Interests: Allied health, Early childhood
Database Vendor: EBSCOhost, Westlaw, Wilson - Wilson Web
Wireless access
Partic in Capital District Library Council
Open Mon-Thurs 8:30-9, Fri 8:30-4, Sat & Sun 9-5

L MCNAMEE, LOCHNER, TITUS & WILLIAMS, PC*, Law Library, 677 Broadway, 12207. (Mail add: PO Box 459, 12201-0459), SAN 372-4638. Tel: 518-447-3200. FAX: 518-426-4260. E-mail: mltw@mltw.com. Web Site: www.mltw.com. *In Charge,* Maggie Wiard; Staff 1 (MLS 1)
Library Holdings: Bk Vols 12,000
Restriction: Staff use only

M MEMORIAL HOSPITAL*, Health Sciences Library, 600 Northern Blvd, 12204. SAN 310-7582. Tel: 518-471-3264. FAX: 518-447-3559. *Librn,* Joanna Erwin; E-mail: snyderm@nehealth.com; Staff 3 (MLS 1, Non-MLS 2)
Founded 1960
Library Holdings: Bk Titles 3,200; Bk Vols 3,500; Per Subs 100
Subject Interests: Med, Nursing
Database Vendor: EBSCOhost, Medline, PubMed
Wireless access
Open Mon, Wed & Thurs 8-7, Tues & Fri 8-4, Sun 12-5

GL NEW YORK STATE COURT OF APPEALS LIBRARY*, 20 Eagle St, 12207-1905. SAN 310-7604. Tel: 518-455-7770. Web Site: www.courts.state.ny.us. *Librn,* Elizabeth F Murray
Founded 1870
Library Holdings: Bk Titles 1,200; Bk Vols 80,000; Per Subs 100
Subject Interests: Law
Database Vendor: Gale Cengage Learning, HeinOnline, LexisNexis, Westlaw
Wireless access
Partic in Westlaw
Restriction: Staff use only

S NEW YORK STATE DEPARTMENT OF CORRECTIONAL SERVICES*, Division of Library Services, State Campus, Bldg 2, Library Services, 1220 Washington Ave, 12226-2050. SAN 323-9772. Tel: 518-485-7109. FAX: 518-402-1742. *Supv Librn & Law Libr Coordr,* Barbara Ost; E-mail: barbara.ost@doccs.state.ny.us; *Sr Librn,* Linda Klimchak; E-mail: linda.klimchak@doccs.state.ny.us
Restriction: Not open to pub

GM NEW YORK STATE DEPARTMENT OF HEALTH*, Herbert W Dickerman Library, Wadsworth Center-NYS Department of Health, Empire State Plaza, 12201. (Mail add: PO Box 509, 12201-0509), SAN 310-7655. Tel: 518-474-6172. FAX: 518-474-3933. E-mail: dohlib@health.state.ny.us. Web Site: dickerman.wadsworth.org. *Sr Librn,* Lucy Wrightington; Staff 3 (MLS 2, Non-MLS 1)
Founded 1914
Library Holdings: e-journals 10,000; Bk Vols 40,000; Per Subs 1,100
Subject Interests: Clinical labs, Environ health, Epidemiology, Health policy, Infectious diseases, Molecular biol, Molecular genetics, Pub health, Radiol health, Toxicology, Veterinary med
Automation Activity & Vendor Info: (OPAC) Innovative Interfaces, Inc; (Serials) Innovative Interfaces, Inc
Database Vendor: OVID Technologies
Wireless access
Partic in OCLC Online Computer Library Center, Inc
Restriction: Not open to pub

GL NEW YORK STATE DEPARTMENT OF LAW LIBRARY*, The Capitol, 12224. SAN 351-7381. Tel: 518-474-3840. FAX: 518-473-1822. Web Site: albany.library@oag.state.ny.us. *Assoc Librn, Ref,* Patricia L Partello; E-mail: patricia.partello@oag.state.ny.us; *Sr Librn, Acq,* Catherine M Callahan; E-mail: catherine.callahan@oag.state.ny.us; *Sr Librn/Cat,* Patrick Weklar; E-mail: patrick.weklar@oag.state.ny.us; *Sr Librn, Coll Mgt, SIRSI Adminr,* Barbara A Ost; E-mail: barbara.ost@oag.state.ny.us; *Sr Librn, NYC Libr,* Franette Sheinwald; Tel: 212-416-8012, Fax: 212-416-6130, E-mail: fran.sheinwald@oag.state.ny.us; Staff 14 (MLS 6, Non-MLS 8)
Founded 1944
Library Holdings: Bk Vols 125,000; Per Subs 201
Special Collections: New York State Law Department Records & Briefs
Automation Activity & Vendor Info: (Acquisitions) SirsiDynix; (Cataloging) SirsiDynix; (OPAC) SirsiDynix; (Serials) SirsiDynix
Database Vendor: LexisNexis, Westlaw
Publications: Check It Out (Newsletter)
Partic in OCLC Online Computer Library Center, Inc
Restriction: Employees only

G NEW YORK STATE LEGISLATIVE LIBRARY*, State Capitol, Rm 337, 12224-0345. SAN 372-431X. Tel: 518-455-2468. FAX: 518-426-6901. *Librn,* Kate Balassie; *Librn,* Ellen Breslin; *Librn,* James Gilberto; Staff 11 (MLS 5, Non-MLS 6)
Library Holdings: Bk Vols 100,000, Per Subs 100
Special Collections: History of New York Laws; Legislative Reports; New York State Agency Reports
Subject Interests: Law, Legislation
Automation Activity & Vendor Info: (Cataloging) EOS International
Database Vendor: LexisNexis, Westlaw
Partic in Dialog Corp; Westlaw
Open Mon-Fri 9-5

P NEW YORK STATE LIBRARY*, State Education Department, Cultural Education Center, 222 Madison Ave, Empire State Plaza, 12230. SAN 351-756X. Tel: 518-474-5961. Circulation Tel: 518-473-7895. Interlibrary Loan Service Tel: 518-474-5383. Reference Tel: 518-474-5355. Administration Tel: 518-473-1189, 518-474-5930. FAX: 518-474-5786. Administration FAX: 518-486-6880. E-mail: circ@mail.nysed.gov, nyslweb@mail.nysed.gov. Web Site: www.nysl.nysed.gov. *State Librn,* Bernard Margolis; E-mail: bmargolis@mail.nysed.gov; *Res Libr Dir,* Loretta Ebert; Staff 582 (MLS 32, Non-MLS 550)
Founded 1818
Library Holdings: Bk Vols 2,500,000; Per Subs 13,796
Special Collections: Broadsides; Cartographic Coll; Dutch Colonial Records; New York State Documents; New York State Historical Newspapers; New York State History Manuscripts; New York State Political & Social History; Shaker Coll. State Document Depository; US Document Depository
Automation Activity & Vendor Info: (Acquisitions) SirsiDynix; (Cataloging) SirsiDynix; (Circulation) SirsiDynix; (ILL) SirsiDynix; (OPAC) SirsiDynix; (Serials) SirsiDynix

Database Vendor: Dialog, EBSCOhost, Gale Cengage Learning, LexisNexis, OCLC FirstSearch, ProQuest, SirsiDynix
Wireless access
Function: Archival coll, CD-ROM, Doc delivery serv, For res purposes, Govt ref serv, Handicapped accessible, Health sci info serv, Homebound delivery serv, ILL available, Libr develop, Newsp ref libr, Online searches, Orientations, Outside serv via phone, mail, e-mail & web, Photocopying/Printing, Ref serv available, Res libr, Spoken cassettes & CDs, Telephone ref
Partic in Association of Research Libraries (ARL); OCLC Online Computer Library Center, Inc; OCLC Research Library Partnership
Special Services for the Blind - Assistive/Adapted tech devices, equip & products
Open Mon-Sat 9:30-5
Restriction: Closed stack
Friends of the Library Group
Branches: 1
TALKING BOOK & BRAILLE LIBRARY
See Separate Entry

P NEW YORK STATE LIBRARY*, Talking Book & Braille Library, Cultural Education Ctr, 222 Madison Ave, 12230-0001. SAN 310-7744. Tel: 518-474-5935. Toll Free Tel: 800-342-3688. FAX: 518-486-2142. E-mail: tbbl@mail.nysed.gov. Web Site: www.nysl.nysed.gov/tbbl. *Dir,* Sharon Phillips; E-mail: sphillip@mail.ny.sed.gov; Staff 5 (MLS 5)
Founded 1896. Pop 14,700; Circ 500,000
Library Holdings: Bk Titles 68,000; Bk Vols 780,000
Automation Activity & Vendor Info: (Acquisitions) Keystone Systems, Inc (KLAS); (Cataloging) Keystone Systems, Inc (KLAS); (Circulation) Keystone Systems, Inc (KLAS); (Course Reserve) Keystone Systems, Inc (KLAS); (ILL) Keystone Systems, Inc (KLAS); (Media Booking) Keystone Systems, Inc (KLAS); (OPAC) Keystone Systems, Inc (KLAS); (Serials) Keystone Systems, Inc (KLAS)
Wireless access
Publications: Bibliographies; Newsletters
Special Services for the Blind - Braille bks; PC for handicapped; Reader equip; Talking bks
Open Mon-Fri 9-4:30

G NEW YORK STATE OFFICE OF THE STATE COMPTROLLER LIBRARY*, OSC Library, 110 State St, 14th Flr, 14EB02, 12236. SAN 310-7612. Tel: 518-473-4206. FAX: 518-473-1900. E-mail: osclibrary@osc.state.ny.us. *Librn,* Rosemary A Del Vecchio; Tel: 518-473-5960, E-mail: rdelvecchio@osc.state.ny.us; Staff 4 (MLS 2, Non-MLS 2)
Library Holdings: CDs 40; Bk Vols 8,000; Per Subs 150
Subject Interests: Govt, Law, Municipal
Database Vendor: LexisNexis, Westlaw
Wireless access
Open Mon-Fri 8-4:30

GL NEW YORK SUPREME COURT APPELLATE DIVISION*, Third Department Library, Justice Bldg, Empire State Plaza, 12223. SAN 310-7752. Tel: 518-471-4777. FAX: 518-471-4750. Web Site: www.nycourts.gov/ad3.
Library Holdings: Bk Vols 22,500
Database Vendor: LexisNexis, Westlaw
Restriction: Staff use only

S NYS SMALL BUSINESS DEVELOPMENT CENTER RESEARCH NETWORK*, 22 Corporate Woods Blvd, 3rd Flr, 12211. SAN 377-5763. Tel: 518-641-0650. Administration Tel: 518-443-5398. FAX: 518-443-5275. E-mail: sbdcrn@nyssbdc.org. Web Site: www.nyssbdc.org. *Dir,* Darrin Conroy; *Res,* Josee Fonseca; *Res,* Roger Green; *Res,* Alexis Mokler; *Web Coordr,* Amelia Birdsall; Staff 5 (MLS 5)
Founded 1991
Library Holdings: Bk Titles 1,100; Per Subs 35
Special Collections: SBA Publications; SBDC/ASBDC Publications; US EPA/NYS DEC Publications. State Document Depository
Subject Interests: Bus
Database Vendor: Dialog, LexisNexis, ProQuest
Function: For res purposes
Partic in Dialog Corp
Restriction: Open by appt only

C THE SAGE COLLEGES*, Albany Campus Library, 140 New Scotland Ave, 12208. SAN 310-7787. Tel: 518-292-1721. Interlibrary Loan Service Tel: 518-292-1742. Reference Tel: 518-292-1945. FAX: 518-292-1904. E-mail: libref@sage.edu. Web Site: www.sage.edu. *Dir,* Kingsley W Greene; Tel: 518-244-2346, Fax: 518-244-2400, E-mail: greenk@sage.edu; *Access Serv Librn,* Lisa Brainard; Tel: 518-292-1959, E-mail: brainl@sage.edu; *Info Literacy Librn,* Amy Pass; Tel: 518-292-1701, E-mail: passa@sage.edu; *Syst Librn,* Christopher White; Tel: 518-244-4521, E-mail: whitec2@sage.edu; *Web Librn,* Kelly MacWatters; Tel: 518-292-1784, E-mail: macwak@sage.edu; *Archivist, Tech Serv,* Terrance Wasielewski; Tel: 518-244-2435, E-mail: wasiet@sage.edu; Staff 9 (MLS 4, Non-MLS 5)
Founded 1957. Enrl 1,000; Fac 150; Highest Degree: Doctorate
Library Holdings: AV Mats 25,722; e-books 10,000; e-journals 50,000; Microforms 1,251; Bk Titles 58,850; Bk Vols 62,714; Per Subs 119
Subject Interests: Graphic arts, Legal studies, Mgt
Automation Activity & Vendor Info: (Acquisitions) SirsiDynix; (Cataloging) OCLC Online; (Circulation) SirsiDynix; (Course Reserve) SirsiDynix; (ILL) OCLC ILLiad; (OPAC) SirsiDynix; (Serials) SirsiDynix
Database Vendor: ARTstor, Bowker, College Source, CredoReference, EBSCOhost, Elsevier, Gale Cengage Learning, JSTOR, LexisNexis, Medline, OCLC FirstSearch, OCLC WorldShare Interlibrary Loan, OVID Technologies, ProQuest, PubMed, Safari Books Online, ScienceDirect, Westlaw, Wilson - Wilson Web
Wireless access
Partic in Cap District Libr Coun for Ref & Res Resources; OCLC Online Computer Library Center, Inc; Westchester Academic Library Directors Organization (WALDO)

C UNIVERSITY AT ALBANY, STATE UNIVERSITY OF NEW YORK*, University Libraries, 1400 Washington Ave, 12222-0001. SAN 351-7896. Tel: 518-442-3568. Circulation Tel: 518-442-3600. Interlibrary Loan Service Tel: 518-442-3613. Reference Tel: 518-442-3558. FAX: 518-442-3088. Web Site: library.albany.edu. *Dean, Libr Dir,* Dr Mary Frances Casserly; E-mail: mcasserly@albany.edu; *Assoc Dir, Coll Develop,* Mary Van Ullen; Tel: 518-442-3559, E-mail: mvanullen@albany.edu; *Assoc Dir, Pub Serv,* Mary Jane Brustman; Tel: 518-442-3540, E-mail: mbrustman@albany.edu; *Assoc Dir, Tech Serv & Syst,* Heather Miller; Tel: 518-442-3631, E-mail: hmiller@albany.edu; *Asst Dir, Finance/Admin,* Peter Recore-Migirditch; Tel: 518-442-3563, Fax: 518-442-3663, E-mail: prm@albany.edu; *Head, Circ,* Kabel Stanwicks; Tel: 518-442-3578, E-mail: kstanwicks@albany.edu; *Head, Spec Coll & Archives,* Brian Keough; Tel: 518-437-3931, E-mail: bkeough@albany.edu; Staff 60.1 (MLS 32.5, Non-MLS 27.6)
Founded 1844. Enrl 17,578; Fac 1,000; Highest Degree: Doctorate
Library Holdings: AV Mats 13,178; CDs 1,915; DVDs 3,256; e-books 24,760; e-journals 38,372; Microforms 2,938,467; Bk Vols 2,223,325; Per Subs 4,199; Talking Bks 953; Videos 5,088
Special Collections: Archives for Public Affairs & Policy; Children's Historical Literature Coll; Death Penalty Archives; German Intellectual Emigre Coll. State Document Depository; US Document Depository
Subject Interests: Criminal justice, Educ, Soc sci
Automation Activity & Vendor Info: (Acquisitions) Ex Libris Group; (Cataloging) Ex Libris Group; (Circulation) Ex Libris Group; (Course Reserve) Atlas Systems; (ILL) OCLC ILLiad; (OPAC) Ex Libris Group; (Serials) Ex Libris Group
Database Vendor: ABC-CLIO, ACM (Association for Computing Machinery), Agricola, Alexander Street Press, American Chemical Society, American Mathematical Society, American Physical Society, American Psychological Association (APA), Annual Reviews, BioOne, Bowker, Cambridge Scientific Abstracts, CIOS (Communication Institute for Online Scholarship), CountryWatch, CQ Press, Dialog, Dun & Bradstreet, EBSCOhost, Elsevier, Emerald, Gale Cengage Learning, GalleryWatch, H W Wilson, IEEE (Institute of Electrical & Electronics Engineers), JSTOR, LexisNexis, Luna Imaging/Insight, Mergent Online, Nature Publishing Group, OCLC FirstSearch, OCLC WorldShare Interlibrary Loan, OVID Technologies, Oxford Online, Project MUSE, ProQuest, PubMed, ReferenceUSA, Repere, Safari Books Online, Sage, ScienceDirect, Scopus, SerialsSolutions, Standard & Poor's, ValueLine, Westlaw, Wiley InterScience, Wilson - Wilson Web
Wireless access
Partic in Association of Research Libraries (ARL); Capital District Library Council; New York State Interlibrary Loan Network (NYSILL); OCLC Online Computer Library Center, Inc
Departmental Libraries:
THOMAS E DEWEY GRADUATE LIBRARY, 135 Western Ave, 12222, SAN 370-3320. Tel: 518-442-3696. Circulation Tel: 518-442-3693. Reference Tel: 518-442-3691. FAX: 518-442-3474. E-mail: dewref@albany.edu. Web Site: library.albany.edu/dewey. *Head of Libr,* Deborah Bernnard; Tel: 518-442-3699, E-mail: dbernnard@albany.edu; Staff 4 (MLS 3, Non-MLS 1)
Subject Interests: Criminal justice, Info sci, Libr sci, Pub admin, Soc welfare
SCIENCE LIBRARY, 1400 Washington Ave, 12222. Tel: 518-437-3948. Reference Tel: 518-437-3945. FAX: 518-437-3952. Web Site: library.albany.edu/science. *Head, Circ,* Kabel Stanwicks; Tel: 518-442-3578, E-mail: kstanwicks@albany.edu; *Digital Initiatives Librn,* Lorre Smith; E-mail: lsmith@albany.edu; *Outreach & Instruction Librn, Ref Librn,* Irina Holden; E-mail: iholden@albany.edu; *Bibliographer, Ref Librn,* Sue Kaczor; E-mail: skaczor@albany.edu; *Bibliographer, Ref Librn,* Michael Knee; E-mail: mknee@albany.edu; Staff 5 (MLS 4, Non-MLS 1)
Founded 1999
Open Mon-Thurs 8am-11pm, Fri 8-6, Sat 9-5, Sun 11-11

P UPPER HUDSON LIBRARY SYSTEM*, 28 Essex St, 12206. SAN 310-7817. Tel: 518-437-9880. FAX: 518-437-9884. E-mail: uhls@uhls.lib.ny.us. Web Site: www.uhls.org/uhls. *Exec Dir,* Timothy Burke; Tel: 518-437-9880, Ext 222, E-mail: tim.burke@uhls.lib.ny.us; *Adult Serv, Info Serv, Outreach Serv Librn,* Jo-Ann Benedetti; Tel: 518-437-9880, Ext 225, E-mail: jo-ann@uhls.lib.ny.us; *Syst Adminr,* Rawdon Cheng; Tel: 518-437-9880, Ext 233, E-mail: rawdon@uhls.lib.ny.us; *Automation Serv,* Joseph Thornton; Tel: 518-437-9880, Ext 230, E-mail: jthornton@uhls.lib.ny.us; *Youth & Family Serv,* Mary Fellows; Tel: 518-437-9880, Ext 228, E-mail: mary@uhls.lib.ny.us; Staff 10 (MLS 5, Non-MLS 5)
Founded 1960. Pop 447,103
Jan 2008-Dec 2008 Income $1,908,740, State $1,397,500, Federal $51,671, Other $229,273. Mats Exp $80,152, Books $18,294, AV Mat $25,913, Electronic Ref Mat (Incl. Access Fees) $35,945. Sal $649,263 (Prof $313,276)
Library Holdings: AV Mats 7,565; CDs 2,249; DVDs 1,123; e-books 557; Large Print Bks 1,894; Bk Vols 9,261; Per Subs 15; Videos 2,303
Automation Activity & Vendor Info: (Acquisitions) SirsiDynix; (Cataloging) SirsiDynix; (Circulation) SirsiDynix; (OPAC) SirsiDynix; (Serials) SirsiDynix
Database Vendor: SirsiDynix
Wireless access
Publications: The Latest Edition (Newsletter)
Member Libraries: Albany Public Library; Altamont Free Library; Arvilla E Diver Memorial Library; Berlin Free Town Library; Berne Public Library; Brunswick Community Library; Castleton Public Library; Cheney Library; Cohoes Public Library; East Greenbush Community Library; Grafton Community Library; Guilderland Public Library; Menands Public Library; Nassau Free Library; North Greenbush Public Library; Petersburgh Public Library; Poestenkill Public Library; RCS Community Library; Rensselaer Public Library; Rensselaerville Library; Sand Lake Town Library; Stephentown Memorial Library; The William K Sanford Town Library; Troy Public Library; Valley Falls Free Library; Voorheesville Public Library; Watervliet Public Library; Westerlo Public Library
Partic in Cap District Libr Coun for Ref & Res Resources; NY Libr Asn
Special Services for the Deaf - TTY equip
Special Services for the Blind - Bks on CD; Large print bks; Talking bks
Open Mon-Fri 8:30-5

GM VA HEALTHCARE NETWORK - UPSTATE NEW YORK*, Samuel S Stratton VA Medical Center, 113 Holland Ave, 142D, 12208. SAN 310-7825. Tel: 518-626-6219. FAX: 518-626-5557. Web Site: www1.va.gov/visns/visn02/albany.html. *Mgr,* Halyna L Korhun; Staff 2 (MLS 2)
Founded 1951
Library Holdings: Bk Titles 2,500; Per Subs 275
Subject Interests: Allied health, Med, Patient educ
Publications: AV List; Journal Holdings List; New Media List; Patient Pamphlet List
Partic in Basic Health Sciences Library Network; Capital District Library Council; Docline; Veterans Affairs Libr Network (VALNET)
Open Mon-Fri 8-4

S VAN RENSSELEAR - RANKIN FAMILY HISTORIC CHERRY HILL MUSEUM & LIBRARY*, 523 1/2 S Pearl St, 12202. SAN 327-7461. Tel: 518-434-4791. FAX: 518-434-4806. E-mail: info@historiccherryhill.org. Web Site: www.historiccherryhill.org. *Dir,* Liselle LaFrance; *Curator,* Deborah Emmons-Andarawis; *Ms Spec,* Mary Doehla
Library Holdings: Bk Vols 5,000
Open Tues-Sat 10-4

ALBERTSON

S NATIONAL BUSINESS & DISABILITY COUNCIL*, 201 I U Willetts Rd, 11507-1599. SAN 310-7833. Tel: 516-465-1519. FAX: 516-465-3730. E-mail: info@business-disability.com. Web Site: www.nbdc.com. *Dir,* Lana Smart; *Info Serv,* Laura Francis
Founded 1961
Library Holdings: Bk Vols 2,500; Per Subs 250
Subject Interests: Adjustment, Independent living for disabled personnel, Vocational rehabilitation, Work evaluation
Partic in BRS; Dialog Corp; Long Island Library Resources Council
Open Mon-Fri 8:30-4:30

P SHELTER ROCK PUBLIC LIBRARY, 165 Searingtown Rd, 11507. SAN 310-7841. Tel: 516-248-7343. Reference FAX: 516-248-4897. Administration FAX: 516-248-7968. TDD: 516-248-2367. E-mail: shelterrock@srpl.org. Web Site: www.nassaulibrary.org/shelter. *Dir,* Andrea Meluskey; *Asst Libr Dir,* MaryAnn Tweedy; *Head, Ad Ref Serv,* Ellen Miller; *Head, Ch,* Susan Nolan; *YA Serv,* Cathy Loechner; Staff 11 (MLS 11)
Founded 1962. Pop 27,188; Circ 276,000
Automation Activity & Vendor Info: (Circulation) Innovative Interfaces, Inc
Wireless access
Publications: The Scene (Monthly)
Mem of Nassau Library System
Special Services for the Deaf - TDD equip; TTY equip
Special Services for the Blind - Talking bks
Open Mon, Tues & Thurs 10-9, Wed 11-9, Fri 10-6, Sat 9-5, Sun 1-5

ALBION

S NEW YORK STATE DEPARTMENT OF CORRECTIONAL SERVICES*, Albion Correctional Facility General Library, 3595 State School Rd, 14411. SAN 327-1129. Tel: 585-589-5511, Ext 4600. *Sr Librn,* Eugene S Veress; Staff 1.5 (MLS 1, Non-MLS 0.5)
Apr 2005-Mar 2006 Income $25,702, State $15,000, Other $10,702. Mats Exp $25,702, Books $15,000, Per/Ser (Incl. Access Fees) $5,000
Library Holdings: AV Mats 409; Bk Titles 11,052; Per Subs 42
Automation Activity & Vendor Info: (Cataloging) Follett Software; (Circulation) Follett Software
Wireless access
Partic in Nioga Libr Syst
Open Mon & Thurs 1-9, Tues, Wed & Fri 8-4

S ORLEANS CORRECTIONAL FACILITY LIBRARY*, 3531 Gaines Basin Rd, 14411. SAN 327-2478. Tel: 585-589-6820, Ext 4600. FAX: 585-589-6820, Ext 3199. *Sr Librn,* Douglas Bauer; Staff 1 (MLS 1)
Library Holdings: Bk Vols 14,000; Per Subs 80
Automation Activity & Vendor Info: (Cataloging) Follett Software; (Circulation) Follett Software; (OPAC) Follett Software
Wireless access
Open Mon-Fri 9-5

P SWAN LIBRARY*, Four N Main St, 14411. SAN 310-785X. Tel: 585-589-4246. FAX: 585-589-2473. Web Site: swanlibrary.org. *Coll Develop, Dir,* Susan Rudnicky; *Ch Serv,* Michelle Watt; *Ref,* Cheryle Mowatt
Founded 1899. Pop 15,000; Circ 41,335
Library Holdings: Bk Vols 43,464; Per Subs 131; Talking Bks 900; Videos 1,200
Special Collections: Lillian Achilles Doll Coll; Local History, bks, pamphlets, photogs; Rare Books; Stuart Flintham Egg Coll; William G Curtis Civil War Library
Subject Interests: Genealogy
Automation Activity & Vendor Info: (Cataloging) SIRSI WorkFlows; (Circulation) SIRSI WorkFlows; (ILL) SIRSI WorkFlows; (OPAC) SIRSI WorkFlows; (Serials) SIRSI WorkFlows
Wireless access
Publications: Annual Report Brochure; Books & Money; History of Swan Library; Hours & Services, Welcome to Swan Library; Swan Library News
Mem of Nioga Library System
Partic in Western New York Library Resources Council
Open Mon-Thurs 11-8, Fri 11-5
Friends of the Library Group

ALDEN

P ALDEN-EWELL FREE LIBRARY*, 13280 Broadway, 14004. SAN 310-7868. Tel: 716-937-7082. FAX: 716-937-7082. Web Site: www.buffalolib.org/libraries/alden/index.asp. *Dir,* Jane H Burke, *Asst Librn,* Jamie Craft
Founded 1913. Pop 10,000; Circ 50,000
Library Holdings: Bk Vols 17,000; Per Subs 52
Database Vendor: EBSCOhost, Gale Cengage Learning
Function: Photocopying/Printing
Mem of Buffalo & Erie County Public Library System
Open Mon (Winter) 1-5 & 7-9, Tues & Thurs 9-12, 1-5 & 7-9, Sat 1-4; Mon & Wed (Summer) 11-4, Tues & Thurs 1-8, Fri 11-2

S WENDE CORRECTIONAL FACILITY LIBRARY*, 3040 Wende Rd, 14004. (Mail add: PO Box 1187, 14004-1187), SAN 327-2346. Tel: 716-937-4000. FAX: 716-937-4000, Ext 4399. *Librn,* Position Currently Open
Library Holdings: Bk Vols 12,000; Per Subs 50
Open Mon-Fri 8-4

ALEXANDRIA BAY

P MACSHERRY LIBRARY*, 112 Walton St, 13607. SAN 310-7876. Tel: 315-482-2241. FAX: 315-482-2241. Web Site: www.macsherrylibrary.org. *Librn,* Ceil Cunningham; *Asst Librn,* Siow Lee Anderson; *Asst Librn,* Luann Elizabeth; *Asst Librn,* Cindy Hutchinson; Staff 4 (Non-MLS 4)
Founded 1896. Pop 1,088; Circ 23,744
Library Holdings: AV Mats 1,133; Bk Titles 16,445; Per Subs 47
Automation Activity & Vendor Info: (Acquisitions) Baker & Taylor; (Cataloging) SIRSI WorkFlows; (Circulation) SIRSI WorkFlows; (ILL) SIRSI WorkFlows; (OPAC) SIRSI Unicorn

Wireless access
Mem of North Country Library System
Open Mon-Thurs 9-5 & 7-9, Fri & Sat 9-5
Friends of the Library Group

ALFRED

ALFRED UNIVERSITY

C HERRICK MEMORIAL LIBRARY*, One Saxon Dr, 14802, SAN 351-8043. Tel: 607-871-2184. FAX: 607-871-2299. Web Site: herrick.alfred.edu. *Dir,* Steve Crandall; Tel: 607-871-2987, E-mail: fcrandall@alfred.edu; *Instrul Librn,* Brian Sullivan; Tel: 607-871-2268, E-mail: sullivan@alfred.edu; *Access Serv, Archivist,* Laurie McFadden; Tel: 607-871-2385, E-mail: fmcfadden@alfred.edu; *Info Syst,* Ellen Bahr; Tel: 607-871-2976, E-mail: bahr@alfred.edu; Staff 11 (MLS 4, Non-MLS 7)
Founded 1857. Enrl 2,228; Fac 175; Highest Degree: Doctorate
Jul 2007-Jun 2008 Income $848,833. Mats Exp $218,000, Books $35,000, Per/Ser (Incl. Access Fees) $79,000, AV Mat $2,000, Electronic Ref Mat (Incl. Access Fees) $100,000, Presv $2,000. Sal $397,425 (Prof $239,182)
Library Holdings: AV Mats 1,100; e-books 27,000; e-journals 28,000; Bk Titles 127,500; Bk Vols 150,000; Per Subs 550
Special Collections: British Literature & History (Openhym Coll); William Dean Howells (Howells-Frechette Coll)
Subject Interests: Behav sci, Soc sci
Automation Activity & Vendor Info: (Cataloging) Ex Libris Group; (Circulation) Ex Libris Group; (Course Reserve) Docutek; (OPAC) Ex Libris Group; (Serials) Ex Libris Group
Database Vendor: 3M Library Systems, ABC-CLIO, American Chemical Society, American Mathematical Society, American Psychological Association (APA), Annual Reviews, Cambridge Scientific Abstracts, CountryWatch, ebrary, EBSCOhost, Emerald, Ex Libris Group, Gale Cengage Learning, H W Wilson, Hoovers, JSTOR, LexisNexis, Marquis Who's Who, Modern Language Association, Newsbank, OCLC FirstSearch, OCLC WorldShare Interlibrary Loan, OVID Technologies, Oxford Online, Project MUSE, ProQuest, PubMed, SerialsSolutions, TLC (The Library Corporation), ValueLine, Wilson - Wilson Web
Partic in OCLC Online Computer Library Center, Inc; S Cent Libr Res Coun; South Central Regional Library Council; Westchester Academic Library Directors Organization (WALDO)
Publications: Research Guides
Special Services for the Blind - Assistive/Adapted tech devices, equip & products
Restriction: In-house use for visitors

C SCHOLES LIBRARY OF CERAMICS*, New York State College of Ceramics at Alfred University, Two Pine St, 14802-1297, SAN 351-8078. Circulation Tel: 607-871-2492. Interlibrary Loan Service Tel: 607-871-2947. Reference Tel: 607-871-2951. Administration Tel: 607-871-2494. Administration FAX: 607-871-2349. Web Site: scholes.alfred.edu. *Dean of Libr, Libr Dir,* Carla Conrad Johnson; E-mail: ccjohnson@alfred.edu; *Info Syst Librn,* Mark A Smith; Tel: 607-871-2942, E-mail: msmith@alfred.edu; *Pub Serv Librn,* Beverly J Crowell; Tel: 607-871-2950, E-mail: crowellb@alfred.edu; *Sci/Eng Librn,* Patricia C LaCourse; Tel: 607-871-2943, E-mail: lacourpc@alfred.edu; *Asst Librn,* Fang Wan; *Archivist,* Elizabeth Gulacsy; Tel: 607-871-2948, E-mail: gulacsy@alfred.edu; *Visual Res Curator,* John Hosford. Subject Specialists: *Info syst,* Mark A Smith; *Eng,* Patricia C LaCourse; *Emerging tech, Eng,* Fang Wan; *Archives, Art,* Elizabeth Gulacsy; Staff 5 (MLS 5)
Founded 1947. Enrl 761; Fac 61; Highest Degree: Doctorate
Library Holdings: AV Mats 166,873; Bk Titles 87,459; Bk Vols 104,271; Per Subs 699
Special Collections: Charles Fergus Binns Papers; NCECA Archives; NYS College of Ceramics Archives
Subject Interests: Art, Biomed res, Ceramic art, Ceramic eng, Ceramic hist, Design, Electronic art media, Eng, Glass, Glass art, Glass sci, Mat sci, Photog, Sculpture
Automation Activity & Vendor Info: (Cataloging) Ex Libris Group; (Circulation) Ex Libris Group; (Course Reserve) Docutek; (ILL) OCLC; (OPAC) Ex Libris Group; (Serials) Ex Libris Group
Database Vendor: Dialog, Gale Cengage Learning, JSTOR, LexisNexis, Newsbank, OCLC FirstSearch, ProQuest, TLC (The Library Corporation), Wilson - Wilson Web
Function: Archival coll, AV serv, Doc delivery serv, ILL available, Ref serv available, Res libr
Partic in Nylink; OCLC
Publications: Annual Statistics (Library statistics & report)
Special Services for the Blind - Assistive/Adapted tech devices, equip & products
Open Mon-Thurs 8am-Midnight, Fri 8-8, Sat 10-6, Sun Noon-Midnight
Restriction: Open to students, fac & staff, Pub use on premises, Restricted borrowing privileges

C STATE UNIVERSITY OF NEW YORK, COLLEGE OF TECHNOLOGY*, Walter C Hinkle Memorial Library, Upper Colleg Dr, 14802. SAN 351-8108. Tel: 607-587-4313. FAX: 607-587-4351. Web Site: web.alfredstate.edu/library. *Dir,* David G Haggstrom; E-mail: haggstdg@alfredstate.edu; *Ref Librn,* Barbara Greil; E-mail: greilbj@alfredstate.edu; *Info Serv, Ref Serv,* Jane Vavala; E-mail: vavalaja@alfredstate.edu; *Tech Serv,* Joseph Petrick; E-mail: petricja@alfredstate.edu; Staff 9 (MLS 5, Non-MLS 4)
Founded 1911. Enrl 3,000; Fac 170; Highest Degree: Bachelor
Jul 2006-Jun 2007 Income $452,044. Mats Exp $122,908, Books $36,010, Per/Ser (Incl. Access Fees) $31,928, Micro $265, AV Mat $6,493, Electronic Ref Mat (Incl. Access Fees) $45,632, Presv $2,580. Sal $339,193 (Prof $229,599)
Library Holdings: Bk Titles 45,862; Bk Vols 64,125; Per Subs 293; Videos 2,805
Special Collections: Western New York State Historical Coll, bks, maps, artifacts
Subject Interests: Agr, Allied health, Eng, Vocational
Automation Activity & Vendor Info: (Circulation) Ex Libris Group
Database Vendor: CredoReference, EBSCOhost, Gale Cengage Learning, H W Wilson, LexisNexis, Newsbank, OCLC FirstSearch, OCLC WorldShare Interlibrary Loan, ProQuest, SerialsSolutions
Wireless access
Function: ILL available
Partic in South Central Regional Library Council
Open Mon-Thurs 8am-11pm, Fri 8-5, Sat 1-7, Sun 1-11

ALLEGANY

P ALLEGANY PUBLIC LIBRARY*, 90 W Main St, 14706-1204. SAN 310-7884. Tel: 716-373-1056. FAX: 716-373-1056. E-mail: alleycat33@adelphia.net. Web Site: www.geocities.com/allegany_public_library. *Dir,* Nathan Austin
Founded 1965. Pop 2,078
Library Holdings: Bk Titles 20,950; Per Subs 30
Special Collections: Freedom Shrine
Wireless access
Mem of Chautauqua-Cattaraugus Library System
Partic in OCLC Online Computer Library Center, Inc
Open Mon-Wed 10-8, Thurs & Fri 11-5, Sat 10-1

ALMOND

P TWENTIETH CENTURY CLUB LIBRARY, Main St, 14804. (Mail add: PO Box D, 14804-0504), SAN 310-7892. Tel: 607-276-6311. FAX: 607-276-6311. Web Site: www.almondlibrary.org. *Dir,* Sandra Robinson; E-mail: robinsons@stls.org; *Assoc Librn,* Cecily Hardy
Circ 9,530
Library Holdings: Bk Vols 14,500; Per Subs 22
Special Collections: Children's Coll
Subject Interests: Local hist, Quilting
Automation Activity & Vendor Info: (Cataloging) SirsiDynix; (Circulation) SirsiDynix; (Media Booking) SirsiDynix
Wireless access
Mem of Southern Tier Library System
Open Mon, Wed & Sat 9:30-1, Tues & Thurs 1-7
Friends of the Library Group

ALTAMONT

P ALTAMONT FREE LIBRARY*, 105 Park St, 12009. (Mail add: PO Box 662, 12009-0662), SAN 310-7906. Tel: 518-861-7239. FAX: 518-861-7239. Web Site: www.altamontfreelibrary.org. *Librn,* Judith Wines; E-mail: judithwines@altamontfreelibrary.org; Staff 6 (MLS 1, Non-MLS 5)
Founded 1916. Pop 1,737; Circ 22,665
Jan 2005-Dec 2005 Income $81,347, State $1,500, City $66,700, County $1,247, Locally Generated Income $8,900, Other $3,000. Mats Exp $3,820, Books $1,000, Per/Ser (Incl. Access Fees) $700, AV Equip $800, Electronic Ref Mat (Incl. Access Fees) $1,320. Sal $45,000 (Prof $33,075)
Library Holdings: High Interest/Low Vocabulary Bk Vols 60; Bk Titles 10,900; Bk Vols 12,871; Per Subs 50
Automation Activity & Vendor Info: (Circulation) SirsiDynix; (ILL) SirsiDynix; (OPAC) SirsiDynix
Database Vendor: SirsiDynix
Function: Homebound delivery serv, ILL available, Online searches, Photocopying/Printing, Prog for adults, Prog for children & young adult, Ref serv available, Summer reading prog, Telephone ref
Mem of Upper Hudson Library System
Open Mon & Wed 10-8, Tues, Thurs & Fri 10-5, Sat 9-12
Friends of the Library Group

ALTONA

P ALTONA READING CENTER*, 3124 Miner Farm Rd, 12910. (Mail add: PO Box 79, 12910-0079). Tel: 518-236-7621, Ext 109. FAX: 518-236-7621. Web Site: www.cefls.org/altona.htm. *Dir,* Ellen Montgomery
Library Holdings: Bk Vols 9,000
Mem of Clinton-Essex-Franklin Library System
Open Mon-Fri 8-4

S NEW YORK STATE DEPARTMENT OF CORRECTIONS & COMMUNITY SUPERVISION, Altona Correctional Facility Library, 555 Devils Den Rd, 12910. SAN 328-0144. Tel: 518-236-7841, Ext 4560. *Sr Librn,* Carl Paulson; E-mail: carl.paulson@doccs.ny.gov; Staff 1 (MLS 1)
Apr 2014-Mar 2015 Income $4,600
Library Holdings: High Interest/Low Vocabulary Bk Vols 50; Bk Titles 5,000; Per Subs 18
Automation Activity & Vendor Info: (Acquisitions) Follett Software
Mem of Clinton-Essex-Franklin Library System
Restriction: Staff & inmates only

AMAGANSETT

P AMAGANSETT FREE LIBRARY*, 215 Main St, 11930. (Mail add: PO Box 2550, 11930), SAN 310-7922. Tel: 631-267-3810. FAX: 631-267-0087. E-mail: amaglib@suffolk.lib.ny.us. Web Site: www.suffolk.lib.ny.us/libraries/amag. *Dir,* Cynthia Young; *Ch, YA Librn,* Kelly Harris
Pop 3,000; Circ 20,000
Library Holdings: Bk Vols 38,500; Per Subs 55
Automation Activity & Vendor Info: (Cataloging) Follett Software; (Circulation) Follett Software; (OPAC) Follett Software; (Serials) Follett Software
Mem of Suffolk Cooperative Library System
Open Mon-Wed 9-5, Thurs 10-8, Fri & Sat 10-5, Sun 1-4

AMENIA

P AMENIA FREE LIBRARY*, 3309 Rte 343, 12501-5543. (Mail add: PO Box 27, 12501-0027), SAN 310-7930. Tel: 845-373-8273. FAX: 845-373-8273. E-mail: amenialib@netscape.net. Web Site: amenia.lib.ny.us. *Dir,* Miriam Devine
Founded 1938
Library Holdings: Bk Titles 8,500; Per Subs 15
Mem of Mid-Hudson Library System
Open Mon & Fri 10-5, Tues & Thurs 1-6, Wed 10-7, Sat 9-2

AMHERST

P AMHERST PUBLIC LIBRARY*, Main Library at Audubon, 350 John James Audubon Pkwy, 14228. SAN 354-4117. Tel: 716-688-4919, 716-689-4922. FAX: 716-689-6116. E-mail: aud@buffalolib.org. Web Site: www.buffalo.org/libraries/audubon. *Dir,* Roseanne Butler-Smith
Founded 1842. Pop 116,510; Circ 1,414,518
Library Holdings: Bk Vols 333,672
Special Collections: Library Limelight Television Show, v-tapes
Open Mon-Thurs 10-9, Fri & Sat 10-5, Sun 1-5
Friends of the Library Group
Branches: 3
CLEARFIELD, 770 Hopkins Rd, Williamsville, 14221, SAN 354-4141. Tel: 716-688-4955. FAX: 716-688-0281. E-mail: cfd@buffalolib.org. *Dir,* Roseanne Butler-Smith
Open Mon & Fri 10-9, Tues, Thurs & Sat 10-5, Wed 1-9
Friends of the Library Group
EGGERTSVILLE-SNYDER BRANCH, 4622 Main St, Synder, 14226, SAN 354-4176. Tel: 716-839-0700. FAX: 716-839-4277. E-mail: egg@buffalolib.org. *Dir,* Roseanne Butler-Smith
Circ 222,685
Open Mon & Wed Noon-8, Tues, Thurs & Fri 10-5:30, Sat 10-8
Friends of the Library Group
WILLIAMSVILLE, 5571 Main St, 14221, SAN 354-4206. Tel: 716-632-6176. FAX: 716-634-2927. E-mail: wil@buffalolib.org. *Br Mgr,* Sandra Stabell
Library Holdings: AV Mats 6,620
Open Mon & Fri 10-5, Tues 12-8, Wed 10-2, Thurs 4-8, Sat (Sept-May) 10-2
Friends of the Library Group

C DAEMEN COLLEGE LIBRARY*, Research & Information Commons, 4380 Main St, 14226-3592. SAN 351-8167. Tel: 716-839-8243. FAX: 716-839-8475. Web Site: www.daemen.edu/library. *Dir,* Frank Carey; E-mail: fcarey@daemen.edu; *Asst Dir, Circ, ILL,* Kara McGuire; *Head, Ref & Instruction,* Andrea Sullivan; E-mail: asulliv1@daemen.edu; *Ref & Instruction Librn,* Vanessa Paniccia; E-mail: vpanicci@daemen.edu; *Tech Serv Librn,* Randolph Chojecki; E-mail: rchojeck@daemen.edu; Staff 5 (MLS 5)
Founded 1948. Enrl 2,224; Fac 400; Highest Degree: Doctorate
Jun 2007-May 2008 Income $749,632, State $6,748, Parent Institution $742,884. Mats Exp $361,484, Books $61,344, Per/Ser (Incl. Access Fees) $181,138, AV Mat $3,277, Electronic Ref Mat (Incl. Access Fees) $107,734, Presv $7,991. Sal $274,738
Library Holdings: AV Mats 5,763; CDs 9; DVDs 329; e-books 37,846; e-journals 24,371; Microforms 28,055; Bk Titles 84,626; Bk Vols 97,575; Per Subs 589; Videos 1,730
Subject Interests: Humanities, Liberal arts, Nursing, Phys therapy
Automation Activity & Vendor Info: (Cataloging) Innovative Interfaces, Inc; (Circulation) Innovative Interfaces, Inc; (Course Reserve) Innovative Interfaces, Inc; (ILL) OCLC; (OPAC) Innovative Interfaces, Inc; (Serials) Innovative Interfaces, Inc
Database Vendor: ABC-CLIO, Checkpoint Systems, Inc, Cinahl, Dialog, ebrary, EBSCO Information Services, EBSCOhost, Gale Cengage Learning, JSTOR, LexisNexis, OCLC WorldShare Interlibrary Loan, Project MUSE, ProQuest, PubMed, SerialsSolutions, Wilson - Wilson Web
Wireless access
Partic in OCLC Online Computer Library Center, Inc; Western New York Library Resources Council
Open Mon-Thurs 8am-Midnight, Fri 8am-9pm, Sat 10-6, Sun 1pm-Midnight
Friends of the Library Group

SR TEMPLE BETH TZEDEK*, Klein-Amdur Library, 621 Getzville Rd, 14226. SAN 327-4632. Tel: 716-838-3232. FAX: 716-835-6154. *Librn,* Craig Posmantur; Staff 2 (MLS 1, Non-MLS 1)
Library Holdings: Audiobooks 75; AV Mats 247; Braille Volumes 21; CDs 116; Large Print Bks 22; Music Scores 175; Bk Vols 9,000; Per Subs 13
Wireless access
Function: Audio & video playback equip for onsite use
Open Tues 3-6, Thurs 2:30-4:30, Sun 9-Noon

AMITYVILLE

P AMITYVILLE PUBLIC LIBRARY*, Oak & John Sts, 11701. SAN 310-7949. Tel: 631-264-0567. FAX: 631-264-2006. Web Site: www.amityvillepubliclibrary.org. *Dir,* Nora Schual; *Head, Ch,* Celine Lieffrig; *Electronic & Ad,* Ann Hofbauer; *Coll Develop,* Susan Benard Handler; *Tech Serv,* Joan Traugott; *YA Serv,* Linda Ferraro; Staff 7.5 (MLS 7.5)
Founded 1906. Pop 25,476; Circ 211,050
Jul 2005-Jun 2006 Income $2,135,702. Mats Exp $255,657, Books $159,972, Per/Ser (Incl. Access Fees) $17,500, AV Mat $59,294, Electronic Ref Mat (Incl. Access Fees) $18,500. Sal $993,227 (Prof $385,424)
Library Holdings: Bk Titles 101,000, Bk Vols 112,000; Per Subs 255
Automation Activity & Vendor Info: (Cataloging) Innovative Interfaces, Inc; (Circulation) Innovative Interfaces, Inc; (Course Reserve) Innovative Interfaces, Inc; (ILL) Innovative Interfaces, Inc; (Media Booking) Innovative Interfaces, Inc - Millenium; (OPAC) Innovative Interfaces, Inc
Database Vendor: Innovative Interfaces, Inc, LearningExpress, TumbleBookLibrary
Wireless access
Publications: Library Browser (Quarterly newsletter)
Mem of Suffolk Cooperative Library System
Open Mon-Thurs 9:30-9, Fri 9:30-6, Sat 9:30-5, Sun 1-5

AMSTERDAM

P AMSTERDAM FREE LIBRARY*, 28 Church St, 12010. SAN 310-7973. Tel: 518-842-1080. FAX: 518-842-1169. Web Site: www.amsterdamfreelibrary.com. *Librn,* Jane Getty; Staff 13 (MLS 1, Non-MLS 12)
Founded 1891. Pop 20,714; Circ 60,485
Library Holdings: Bk Vols 49,500; Per Subs 400
Special Collections: Memorabilia (Kirk Douglas Coll)
Subject Interests: Job info, Local hist, Spanish lang
Automation Activity & Vendor Info: (Cataloging) Innovative Interfaces, Inc; (Circulation) Innovative Interfaces, Inc; (OPAC) Innovative Interfaces, Inc; (Serials) Innovative Interfaces, Inc
Publications: Friends of the Library Newsletter (Quarterly)
Mem of Mohawk Valley Library System
Open Mon & Thurs 10-8, Tues, Wed & Fri 10-5:30, Sat 10-4
Friends of the Library Group

S WALTER ELWOOD MUSEUM LIBRARY*, 100 Church St, 12010-2228. SAN 329-1863. Tel: 518-843-5151. FAX: 518-843-6098. E-mail: info@walterelwoodmuseum.org. Web Site: www.walterelwoodmuseum.org. *Dir,* Ann Peconie; Staff 3 (MLS 1, Non-MLS 2)
Founded 1939
Library Holdings: Bk Titles 2,000
Special Collections: Bibles & Other Religious Tracts; Mohawk Valley & New York State; Natural History, old school bks

Function: Archival coll, Exhibits, For res purposes, Prog for adults, Prog for children & young adult, Ref serv available, Ref serv in person, Res performed for a fee, Summer reading prog, Winter reading prog, Workshops
Open Tues-Fri 10-3, Sat 10-2
Restriction: Authorized patrons, Authorized personnel only, Authorized scholars by appt, By permission only, Circ to mem only, Free to mem, Non-circulating of rare bks, Open to pub for ref only, Pub ref by request, Use of others with permission of librn

P FORT HUNTER FREE LIBRARY*, 167 Fort Hunter Rd, 12010. SAN 311-2128. Tel: 518-829-7248. FAX: 518-829-7248. Web Site: www.mvls.info/lhg/forthunter/index.html. *Dir,* Tina Shave; E-mail: tshave@sals.edu
Library Holdings: Bk Titles 11,000; Per Subs 12
Automation Activity & Vendor Info: (Circulation) Innovative Interfaces, Inc; (OPAC) Innovative Interfaces, Inc
Wireless access
Mem of Mohawk Valley Library System
Open Mon & Wed 3-8, Tues, Thurs & Fri 9:30-2:30

ANDES

P ANDES PUBLIC LIBRARY*, 242 Main St, 13731. (Mail add: PO Box 116, 13731-0016), SAN 310-799X. Tel: 845-676-3333. FAX: 845-676-3333. *Librn,* Valerie Brown
Founded 1922. Pop 372; Circ 1,200
Library Holdings: Bk Vols 5,600; Per Subs 14
Wireless access
Mem of Four County Library System
Open Mon & Tues 1-6, Wed 11-4, Thurs 5-8, Fri 1-5, Sat 10-12
Friends of the Library Group

ANDOVER

P ANDOVER FREE LIBRARY*, 40 Main St, 14806. (Mail add: PO Box 745, 14806-0745), SAN 310-8007. Tel: 607-478-8442. FAX: 607-478-5056. *Dir,* Linda Adams; E-mail: adamsl@stls.org; *Ch Serv,* Katie Johnson; E-mail: frostk@stls.org
Founded 1912. Circ 11,673
Jan 2010-Dec 2010 Income $35,000. Mats Exp $10,300, Books $9,000, AV Mat $1,300. Sal $11,200
Library Holdings: Bks on Deafness & Sign Lang 6; CDs 94; Large Print Bks 425; Bk Titles 6,700; Bk Vols 7,000; Per Subs 15; Spec Interest Per Sub 3
Automation Activity & Vendor Info: (Cataloging) SIRSI WorkFlows; (Circulation) SIRSI WorkFlows; (OPAC) SIRSI WorkFlows
Wireless access
Mem of Southern Tier Library System
Open Tues & Thurs 11-7, Wed 9:30-1:30
Friends of the Library Group

ANGELICA

P ANGELICA FREE LIBRARY*, 55 W Main St, 14709. (Mail add: PO Box 660, 14709-0660), SAN 310-8015. Tel: 585-466-7860. *Librn,* Doris Feldbauer
Founded 1900. Pop 1,000
Library Holdings: CDs 10; Large Print Bks 400; Bk Vols 15,200; Per Subs 58; Talking Bks 40; Videos 50
Mem of Southern Tier Library System
Special Services for the Blind - Talking bks
Open Tues 12-5 & 7-9, Thurs 10-5 & 7-9, Sat 9:30-1:30

ANGOLA

P ANGOLA PUBLIC LIBRARY*, 34 N Main St, 14006. SAN 310-8023. Tel: 716-549-1271. FAX: 716-549-3954. Web Site: www.buffalolib.org/libraries/angola. *Dir,* Mary Truby
Founded 1924. Pop 2,693; Circ 55,626
Library Holdings: Bk Vols 20,337; Per Subs 45
Mem of Buffalo & Erie County Public Library System
Open Mon 12-8, Tues 12-6, Wed 5-8, Thurs 2-8, Fri 10-8, Sat 12-5
Friends of the Library Group

ANNANDALE-ON-HUDSON

C BARD COLLEGE*, Stevenson Library, One Library Rd, 12504. (Mail add: PO Box 5000, 12504-5000), SAN 310-8031. Tel: 845-758-6822. Circulation Tel: 845-758-7359. Interlibrary Loan Service Tel: 845-758-7502. Reference Tel: 845-758-7281. FAX: 845-758-5801. Interlibrary Loan Service FAX: 845-758-5701. Web Site: www.bard.edu/library. *Dir of Libr,* Jeffrey Katz; E-mail: katz@bard.edu; *Cat, Syst Librn,* Bonnie S Sgarro; Tel: 845-758-7619, E-mail: sgarro@bard.edu; *Archivist,* Helene Tieger; Tel: 845-758-7396, E-mail: tieger@bard.edu; *Coll Develop, Ref Serv,* Jane Dougall; Tel: 845-758-7620, E-mail: dougall@bard.edu; *Info Tech,* Elizabeth Cawley; Tel: 845-758-7064, E-mail: cawley@bard.edu; *ILL,* Jane Hryshko; Tel: 845-758-7502, E-mail: hryshko@bard.edu; Staff 19 (MLS 8, Non-MLS 11)
Founded 1860. Enrl 1,100; Fac 140; Highest Degree: Master
Library Holdings: e-journals 22,000; Bk Titles 165,065; Bk Vols 280,000; Per Subs 1,000
Special Collections: Bardiana, publications by Bard faculty & alumnae; Hannah Arendt & Heinrich Bluecher Coll; Hudson Valley History
Database Vendor: ARTstor, EBSCOhost, Innovative Interfaces, Inc, JSTOR, LexisNexis, OCLC FirstSearch, OVID Technologies, Project MUSE, ProQuest, Wilson - Wilson Web
Wireless access
Partic in Southeastern New York Library Resources Council
Open Mon-Thurs 8:30am-1am, Fri 8:30am-10pm, Sat 10-10, Sun 10am-1am
Restriction: Circ limited, Non-circulating to the pub
Departmental Libraries:
CENTER FOR CURATORIAL STUDIES, PO Box 5000, 12504-5000. Tel: 845-758-7567. FAX: 845-758-2442. E-mail: ccslib@bard.edu. Web Site: www.bard.edu/ccs/library. *Dir, Libr & Archives,* Ann Butler; Tel: 845-758-7566, E-mail: butler@bard.edu; *Assoc Librn,* Bronwen Bitetti; Tel: 845-752-2395, E-mail: bbitetti@bard.edu; Staff 2 (MLS 2)
Founded 1990
Library Holdings: Bk Vols 25,000; Per Subs 60
Special Collections: Curating in the 20th & 21st Century Archives
Open Mon & Tues (Fall & Spring) 9:30-8, Wed & Thurs 9:30-7, Fri 9:30-5, Sat 1-5, Sun 1-7; Mon-Fri (Summer) 10-5
Restriction: Non-circulating, Open to fac, students & qualified researchers
LEVY ECONOMICS INSTITUTE LIBRARY, Blithewood Ave, 12504. Tel: 845-758-7729. FAX: 845-758-1149. *Librn,* Willis C Walker; E-mail: wwalker@levy.org. Subject Specialists: *Bus, Econ, Finance,* Willis C Walker; Staff 1 (MLS 1)
Founded 1987
Library Holdings: Bk Vols 12,000; Per Subs 70
Database Vendor: Blackwell, CQ Press, EBSCOhost, JSTOR, LexisNexis, Medline, OCLC FirstSearch, OCLC WorldShare Interlibrary Loan, Project MUSE, ProQuest, ScienceDirect
Function: Archival coll, Handicapped accessible, Online cat, Wheelchair accessible
Restriction: Closed stack, Open by appt only, Open to fac, students & qualified researchers

ANTWERP

P CROSBY PUBLIC LIBRARY*, 59 Main St, 13608-4157. SAN 310-804X. Tel: 315-659-8564. FAX: 315-659-8564. Web Site: www.crosbylibrary.org/. *Dir,* Charee Cook
Founded 1917. Pop 1,856; Circ 4,148
Library Holdings: Bk Titles 6,595; Per Subs 33
Wireless access
Mem of North Country Library System
Partic in OCLC Online Computer Library Center, Inc
Open Mon & Fri 1-6, Wed 2-8, Thurs 6:30-8, Sat 10-2

ARCADE

P ARCADE FREE LIBRARY*, 365 W Main St, 14009. SAN 310-8058. Tel: 585-492-1297. FAX: 585-492-3305. Web Site: www.arcade.pls-net.org. *Dir,* Sue Reding; E-mail: sreding@pls-net.org; *Ch Serv,* Sara Bowen; Staff 6 (MLS 1, Non-MLS 5)
Founded 1912. Pop 4,100; Circ 55,623
Library Holdings: Bk Titles 25,950; Bk Vols 27,100; Per Subs 75
Special Collections: Lone Ranger Coll
Wireless access
Mem of Pioneer Library System
Open Mon, Tues & Thurs Noon-8, Wed 9-1, Fri 9-5, Sat 10-2
Friends of the Library Group

ARDSLEY

P ARDSLEY PUBLIC LIBRARY*, Nine American Legion Dr, 10502. SAN 310-8066. Tel: 914-693-6636. FAX: 914-693-6837. Web Site: www.ardsleylibrary.org. *Dir,* Angela Z Groth; E-mail: agroth@wlsmail.org; Staff 8 (MLS 2, Non-MLS 6)
Founded 1972. Pop 4,272; Circ 139,374
Library Holdings: DVDs 1,000; Large Print Bks 350; Bk Vols 50,000; Per Subs 70; Talking Bks 1,700; Videos 1,000
Subject Interests: Best sellers, Computers, Cooking, Local hist, Parenting, Travel
Automation Activity & Vendor Info: (Cataloging) SirsiDynix; (Circulation) SirsiDynix
Database Vendor: ReferenceUSA
Wireless access
Publications: The Bookmark (Newsletter)
Mem of Westchester Library System

Open Mon-Wed, Fri & Sat 10-5:30, Thurs 1-8
Friends of the Library Group

ARGYLE

P ARGYLE FREE LIBRARY*, 21 Sheridan St, 12809. (Mail add: PO Box 238, 12809-0238), SAN 310-8082. Tel: 518-638-8911. FAX: 518-638-8911.
Founded 1920. Pop 3,688; Circ 14,861
Library Holdings: AV Mats 556; Bk Vols 11,000; Per Subs 16
Wireless access
Mem of Southern Adirondack Library System
Open Mon 1-5, Tues & Thurs 1-5 & 7-9, Wed 11-5, Sat 10-1
Friends of the Library Group

ARMONK

P NORTH CASTLE PUBLIC LIBRARY*, 19 Whippoorwill Rd E, 10504. SAN 310-8104. Tel: 914-273-3887. FAX: 914-273-5572. Web Site: www.northcastlelibrary.org. *Dir,* Cristina M Ansnes; E-mail: cansnes@wlsmail.org; *Br Coordr,* Teresa Conde; *Ch Serv,* Teresa Chang; *Ch Serv,* Maureen Petry; *Circ,* Terry Gallagher; *Ref,* Edie Martimucci; *Ref Serv,* Alice Osgood; *YA Serv,* Mary Johnson; Staff 6 (MLS 6)
Founded 1938. Pop 10,849; Circ 196,731
Jan 2005-Dec 2005 Income $1,285,340. Mats Exp $149,283. Sal $932,721 (Prof $358,605)
Library Holdings: AV Mats 12,041; Bk Titles 71,256; Per Subs 157
Automation Activity & Vendor Info: (Acquisitions) SirsiDynix; (Cataloging) SirsiDynix; (Circulation) SirsiDynix; (Course Reserve) SirsiDynix; (ILL) SirsiDynix; (Media Booking) SirsiDynix; (OPAC) SirsiDynix; (Serials) SirsiDynix
Mem of Westchester Library System
Open Mon-Wed 10-8, Thurs & Fri 10-5:30, Sat 10-4, Sun 12-4
Friends of the Library Group
Branches: 1
NORTH WHITE PLAINS BRANCH, Ten Clove Rd, North White Plains, 10603. Tel: 914-948-6359. FAX: 914-948-6359. *Dir,* Cristina M Ansnes
Library Holdings: Bk Vols 25,000
Automation Activity & Vendor Info: (Cataloging) SirsiDynix; (Circulation) SirsiDynix; (OPAC) SirsiDynix
Open Mon & Wed 10-6, Tues & Thurs 2-8, Fri 10-1, Sat 10-4

ASHVILLE

P ASHVILLE FREE LIBRARY*, 2200 N Maple St, 14710-9679. (Mail add: PO Box 379, 14710-0379), SAN 310-8112. Tel: 716-763-9906. FAX: 716-763-9906. E-mail: ashvillelib@stny.rr.com. Web Site: www.cclslib.org/Ashville. *Librn,* Tabetha Butler
Founded 1914. Pop 2,400; Circ 11,733
Library Holdings: Bk Titles 9,800; Per Subs 33
Special Collections: New York State, bks, pamphlets
Subject Interests: Local hist
Automation Activity & Vendor Info: (Cataloging) SirsiDynix; (Circulation) SirsiDynix; (OPAC) SirsiDynix; (Serials) SirsiDynix
Wireless access
Function: Bks on cassette, Bks on CD, Computer training, ILL available
Mem of Chautauqua-Cattaraugus Library System
Open Mon-Fri 9:30-4:30 & 6:30-8:30, Sat 10-1

ATHENS

P D R EVARTS LIBRARY*, 80 Second St, 12015. SAN 310-8120. Tel: 518-945-1417. FAX: 518-945-1725. E-mail: d.r.evartslibrary@gmail.com. Web Site: drevartslibrary.org. *Dir,* Bonnie Snyder
Founded 1907. Pop 3,700; Circ 7,322
Library Holdings: AV Mats 512; Bk Vols 12,997; Per Subs 23
Automation Activity & Vendor Info: (Cataloging) Innovative Interfaces, Inc; (Circulation) Innovative Interfaces, Inc; (OPAC) Innovative Interfaces, Inc
Wireless access
Mem of Mid-Hudson Library System
Open Mon 3-8, Tues & Thurs 1-6, Wed 1-8, Fri & Sat 10-2
Friends of the Library Group

ATLANTA

P E J COTTRELL MEMORIAL LIBRARY*, 30 Main St, 14808-0192. SAN 310-8139. Tel: 585-534-5030. FAX: 585-534-9316. Web Site: www.stls.org. *Dir,* Brenda Yeoman; E-mail: yeomanb@stls.org
Circ 3,568
Library Holdings: Bk Vols 9,672; Per Subs 10
Automation Activity & Vendor Info: (Cataloging) SirsiDynix; (Circulation) SirsiDynix; (OPAC) SirsiDynix
Wireless access
Mem of Southern Tier Library System
Open Mon & Tues 10-12, 1-5 & 6-8, Thurs & Fri 10-12 & 1-5, Sat 10-12

ATTICA

P STEVENS MEMORIAL COMMUNITY LIBRARY*, 146 Main St, 14011-1243. SAN 310-8147. Tel: 585-591-2733. FAX: 585-591-3855. Web Site: www.attica.pls-net.org. *Dir,* Nancy O Burns; *Asst Dir,* Barbara Helak; Staff 5 (MLS 1, Non-MLS 4)
Founded 1893. Pop 12,500
Library Holdings: Bk Titles 29,770; Per Subs 35
Special Collections: Attica Prison Riot Coll (1971)
Subject Interests: Civil War, Local hist, NY hist, Railroading, World War II
Automation Activity & Vendor Info: (Acquisitions) SirsiDynix; (Cataloging) SirsiDynix; (Circulation) SirsiDynix; (Course Reserve) SirsiDynix; (ILL) SirsiDynix; (Media Booking) SirsiDynix; (OPAC) SirsiDynix; (Serials) SirsiDynix
Wireless access
Mem of Pioneer Library System
Special Services for the Blind - ZoomText magnification & reading software
Open Mon-Thurs Noon-8, Fri 12-5, Sat 10-2
Friends of the Library Group

S WYOMING CORRECTIONAL FACILITY GENERAL LIBRARY*, PO Box 501, 14011. SAN 327-2516. Tel: 585-591-1010, Ext 4600. FAX: 585-591-1010. *Librn,* Brian Martin
Library Holdings: Bk Vols 15,000; Per Subs 70
Automation Activity & Vendor Info: (Cataloging) Follett Software; (Circulation) Follett Software; (OPAC) Follett Software; (Serials) Follett Software
Wireless access
Open Mon-Fri 8am-8:30pm, Sat & Sun 8am-11am

AU SABLE FORKS

P AU SABLE FORKS FREE LIBRARY*, Nine Church Lane, 12912-4400. (Mail add: PO Box 179, 12912-0179), SAN 310-8155. Tel: 518-647-5596. FAX: 518-647-5753. E-mail: afbooks@charter.net. Web Site: www.ausableforksfreelibrary.com. *Dir,* Susanna O Carey; *Asst Dir,* Agnes Bombard; Staff 2 (Non-MLS 2)
Founded 1962. Pop 2,100; Circ 22,000
Library Holdings: Bk Titles 20,000; Bk Vols 22,000; Per Subs 25
Special Collections: The Adirondack Coll
Automation Activity & Vendor Info: (Cataloging) Horizon; (Circulation) Horizon; (OPAC) Horizon; (Serials) Horizon
Wireless access
Function: ILL available
Mem of Clinton-Essex-Franklin Library System
Open Tues 10:30-4:30, Wed 10:30-6:30, Thurs & Fri 12:30-4:30, Sat 9-1

AUBURN

S AUBURN CORRECTIONAL FACILITY LIBRARY*, 135 State St, 13024-9000. SAN 328-5065. Tel: 315-253-8401, Ext 4650. FAX: 315-253-8401, Ext 2099. *Librn,* Andrea Abbott; Staff 1 (MLS 1)
Apr 2006-Mar 2007. Mats Exp $15,000, Books $8,000, Per/Ser (Incl. Access Fees) $6,000, AV Mat $1,000. Sal $50,000
Library Holdings: AV Mats 1,700, High Interest/Low Vocabulary Bk Vols 500; Large Print Bks 50; Bk Titles 14,000; Per Subs 35
Special Collections: Spanish Language
Subject Interests: Law
Automation Activity & Vendor Info: (Acquisitions) Brodart; (Cataloging) Brodart; (Circulation) Brodart; (OPAC) Brodart
Database Vendor: EBSCOhost
Wireless access
Mem of Finger Lakes Library System
Open Mon-Fri 1-9, Sat & Sun 1-4

J CAYUGA COUNTY COMMUNITY COLLEGE*, Bourke Memorial Library, 197 Franklin St, 13021. SAN 310-8171. Tel: 315-294-8596. Interlibrary Loan Service Tel: 315-294-8590. Reference Tel: 315-294-8599. FAX: 315-255-2050. Web Site: www.cayuga-cc.edu/library. *Interim Dir, Libr Serv,* Margaret Devereaux; E-mail: deverema@cayuga-cc.edu; *Librn,* Judith Campanella; E-mail: campanella@cayuga-cc.edu; *Circ,* Rosanne Bourke; E-mail: bourker@cayuga-cc.edu; *Tech Serv,* Sara E Davenport; E-mail: davenport@cayuga-cc.edu; Staff 9 (MLS 5, Non-MLS 4)
Founded 1953. Enrl 2,568; Fac 246; Highest Degree: Associate
Library Holdings: CDs 1,265; Bk Titles 78,922; Bk Vols 81,774; Per Subs 250; Talking Bks 112; Videos 2,537
Special Collections: College Archives; Local History
Automation Activity & Vendor Info: (Cataloging) OCLC Connexion; (Circulation) Ex Libris Group; (ILL) OCLC ILLiad; (OPAC) Ex Libris Group; (Serials) Ex Libris Group
Wireless access
Function: Wheelchair accessible

Partic in Nylink; OCLC Online Computer Library Center, Inc; South Central Regional Library Council
Special Services for the Blind - Computer with voice synthesizer for visually impaired persons
Open Mon-Thurs 8am-8:30pm, Fri 8-4:30, Sun 12:30-7
Restriction: 24-hr pass syst for students only

G CAYUGA COUNTY HISTORIAN'S OFFICE*, Research Library, Historic Old Post Off Bldg, 157 Genesee St, 13021-3490. SAN 371-5469. Tel: 315-253-1300. E-mail: historian@cayugacounty.us. Web Site: co.cayuga.ny.us/history/index. *County Historian,* Sheila Tucker
Founded 1969
Library Holdings: Bk Titles 3,000; Per Subs 20
Special Collections: African-Am census 1800-1870;; Local Churches coll; Newspapers 1811-2006; US Park Systems Network to Freedom Underground Railroad Repository, photog coll, local map coll, hist homes survey. Oral History; US Document Depository
Subject Interests: Local hist archives
Function: Res libr
Open Mon, Tues, Thurs & Fri (Winter) 9-5; Mon, Tues, Thurs & Fri (Summer) 8-4
Restriction: Not a lending libr

S CAYUGA MUSEUM LIBRARY*, 203 Genesee St, 13021. SAN 310-818X. Tel: 315-253-8051. FAX: 315-253-9829. E-mail: cayugamuseum@verizon.net. Web Site: cayugamuseum.org. *Dir,* Eileen McHugh; *Curator,* Kirsten Wise; Staff 4 (Non-MLS 4)
Founded 1936
Special Collections: Archival Coll of Local Hist; Auburn Theological Seminary; Case Research Laboratory Coll, sound motion pictures; Native American (Clark Coll)
Subject Interests: Cayuga County hist, Iroquois, Sound flm
Restriction: Non-circulating to the pub, Open by appt only

GL NEW YORK SUPREME COURT*, Seventh District Law Library, Cayuga County Court House, 152 Genesee St, 13021. SAN 310-8201. Tel: 315-255-4310. FAX: 315-255-4322. *In Charge,* Jill Fandrich; E-mail: jfandric@courts.state.ny.us; Staff 1 (Non-MLS 1)
Library Holdings: Bk Vols 7,500; Per Subs 5
Database Vendor: LexisNexis, Westlaw
Wireless access
Open Mon-Fri 9-2

S THE SEWARD HOUSE MUSEUM*, 33 South St, 13021-3929. SAN 310-8198. Tel: 315-252-1283. FAX: 315-253-3351. E-mail: info@sewardhouse.org. Web Site: www.sewardhouse.org. *Exec Dir,* Billye Chabot; E-mail: director@sewardhouse.org
Founded 1955
Library Holdings: Bk Vols 1,000
Subject Interests: Alaska, Civil War, Genealogy, Local hist
Wireless access
Open Tues-Sat 10-4

P SEYMOUR PUBLIC LIBRARY DISTRICT*, 176-178 Genesee St, 13021. SAN 310-821X. Tel: 315-252-2571. FAX: 315-252-7985. Web Site: www.seymourlibrary.org. *Dir,* Lisa Carr; E-mail: lcarr@seymourlibrary.org; *Librn,* Mary Lovell; E-mail: mlovell@seymourlibrary.org; *Commun Serv Coordr,* Stith Barbara; E-mail: bstith@seymourlibrary.org; *Ch Serv,* Danette Davis; E-mail: ddavis@seymourlibrary.org; *Computer Tech,* Donald Crowley; E-mail: dcrowley@seymourlibrary.org; *Computer Tech,* Josh Rogalski; E-mail: jrogalski@seymourlibrary.org. Subject Specialists: *Genealogy, Local hist,* Mary Lovell; Staff 30 (MLS 5, Non-MLS 25)
Founded 1876. Pop 36,008; Circ 165,200
Library Holdings: Bk Titles 105,430; Per Subs 359
Special Collections: Auburn Imprints; Auburn Prison; Harriet Tubman Coll, bks, newsp
Automation Activity & Vendor Info: (Circulation) Innovative Interfaces, Inc
Wireless access
Mem of Finger Lakes Library System
Partic in OCLC Online Computer Library Center, Inc
Open Mon-Wed 10-9, Thurs & Fri 10-6, Sat 10-4
Friends of the Library Group

AURORA

P AURORA FREE LIBRARY*, 370 Main St, 13026. (Mail add: PO Box 85, 13026-0085), SAN 376-303X. Tel: 315-364-8074. FAX: 315-364-8074. E-mail: aurorali@rochester.rr.com. Web Site: www.flls.org/auroralib. *Librn,* Sandy Groth; *Asst Librn,* Susan MacCormick
Pop 637
Library Holdings: Bk Vols 7,000
Automation Activity & Vendor Info: (Cataloging) Innovative Interfaces, Inc; (Circulation) Innovative Interfaces, Inc; (ILL) Innovative Interfaces, Inc; (OPAC) Innovative Interfaces, Inc; (Serials) Innovative Interfaces, Inc
Wireless access
Mem of Finger Lakes Library System
Open Mon, Wed & Fri 3-8, Sat 10-3

C WELLS COLLEGE*, Louis Jefferson Long Library, 170 Main St, 13026-0500. SAN 310-8228. Tel: 315-364-3351. FAX: 315-364-3412. E-mail: library@wells.edu. Web Site: www.wells.edu/library/li1.htm. *Libr Dir,* Muriel K Godbout; Tel: 315 364-3356, E-mail: mgodbout@wells.edu; *Art Coll Coordr,* Helen Bergamo; E-mail: hbergamo@wells.edu; *Coordr, Pub Serv & Outreach,* Molly Brown; Tel: 315 364-3354, E-mail: molly.brown@wells.edu; *Coordr, Tech Serv, Syst,* Julie Kabelac; Tel: 315 364-3357, E-mail: jkabelac@wells.edu; *Acq, ILL,* Kim Nolan; Tel: 315 364-3355, E-mail: knolan@wells.edu; *Circ,* Elsie Torres; E-mail: etorres@wells.edu; Staff 6 (MLS 4, Non-MLS 2)
Founded 1868. Enrl 535; Fac 60; Highest Degree: Bachelor
Library Holdings: Bk Vols 186,000; Per Subs 316
Special Collections: Chemistry-Physics; Economics (Weld Coll); Fine Arts (Morgan Coll); History (Lowe Coll); Philosophy (Lowenberg Coll); Pierce W Gaines Americana Coll; Wells Fargo Express Co, CA 1825-80, mss, personal papers
Automation Activity & Vendor Info: (Acquisitions) EOS International; (Cataloging) EOS International; (Circulation) EOS International; (Course Reserve) EOS International; (ILL) EOS International; (OPAC) EOS International; (Serials) EOS International
Database Vendor: EBSCOhost, LexisNexis, OCLC FirstSearch, ProQuest, Wilson - Wilson Web
Wireless access
Function: Archival coll, Computers for patron use, Copy machines, Doc delivery serv, e-mail serv, E-Reserves, Electronic databases & coll, Exhibits, ILL available, Instruction & testing, Literacy & newcomer serv, Newsp ref libr, Online cat, Online ref, Online searches, Outreach serv, Photocopying/Printing, Ref & res, Ref serv available, Ref serv in person, Video lending libr, Workshops
Partic in OCLC Online Computer Library Center, Inc; South Central Regional Library Council
Open Mon-Thurs (Winter) 8:15am-12am, Fri 8:15-6, Sat 1-6, Sun 11am-12am; Mon-Fri (Summer) 8:15-4:30

AVERILL PARK

P SAND LAKE TOWN LIBRARY*, 8428 Miller Hill Rd, 12018. Tel: 518-674-5050. FAX: 518-674-5050. E-mail: info@sandlaketownlibrary.org. Web Site: www.sandlaketownlibrary.org. *Dir,* Melinda Fowler
Founded 1987. Pop 7,900; Circ 56,600
Library Holdings: AV Mats 3,400; Bk Vols 32,000; Per Subs 51
Subject Interests: Adult literacy, Local hist, Parenting
Wireless access
Function: Wheelchair accessible
Mem of Upper Hudson Library System
Open Mon-Thurs 11-8, Fri 11-6, Sat 11-4, Sun (Oct-May) 1-4
Friends of the Library Group

AVOCA

P AVOCA FREE LIBRARY*, 18 N Main St, 14809-0519. (Mail add: PO Box S, 14809-0519), SAN 376-3056. Tel: 607-566-9279. FAX: 607-566-9279. E-mail: avocalib@linkny.com. Web Site: www.stls.org/avoca. *Dir,* Sandy Seager
Library Holdings: Audiobooks 55; CDs 130; DVDs 285; Large Print Bks 150; Bk Vols 18,000; Per Subs 53; Videos 1,802
Mem of Southern Tier Library System
Open Mon & Fri 5-8, Tues 9-12 & 5-8, Thurs 2-8, Sat 9-2

AVON

P AVON FREE LIBRARY*, 143 Genesee St, 14414. SAN 310-8244. Tel: 585-226-8461. FAX: 585-226-6615. Web Site: www.avon.pls-net.org. *Dir,* Jeanna Ruter
Pop 6,185; Circ 43,416
Library Holdings: Bk Titles 30,850; Bk Vols 32,000; Per Subs 60
Automation Activity & Vendor Info: (Acquisitions) SirsiDynix; (Cataloging) SirsiDynix; (Circulation) SirsiDynix; (OPAC) SirsiDynix
Wireless access
Mem of Pioneer Library System
Open Mon-Thurs 2-8:30, Fri 10-5, Sat 10-1

BABYLON

P BABYLON PUBLIC LIBRARY*, 24 S Carll Ave, 11702. SAN 310-8260. Tel: 631-669-1624. FAX: 631-669-7826. TDD: 631-422-0548. E-mail: babllib@suffolk.lib.ny.us. Web Site: www.suffolk.lib.ny.us/libraries/babl. *Dir,* Marina Sullivan; *Adult Serv,* Victoria Lever; *Ch Serv,* Ann Burke; *YA Serv,* Lori Ludlow; Staff 39 (MLS 12, Non-MLS 27)

Founded 1895. Pop 11,572; Circ 158,239
Library Holdings: Bk Vols 65,626; Per Subs 4,157
Special Collections: Large Print; Long Island History; Parenting
Subject Interests: Babylon hist
Automation Activity & Vendor Info: (Acquisitions) Innovative Interfaces, Inc; (Cataloging) Innovative Interfaces, Inc; (Circulation) Innovative Interfaces, Inc; (ILL) Innovative Interfaces, Inc; (OPAC) Innovative Interfaces, Inc; (Serials) Innovative Interfaces, Inc
Wireless access
Publications: Small Talk (Newsletter); The Anchor (Newsletter)
Mem of Suffolk Cooperative Library System
Partic in Partnership of Automated Librs in Suffolk
Special Services for the Deaf - TTY equip
Special Services for the Blind - Closed circuit TV; ZoomText magnification & reading software
Open Mon-Thurs 9:30-9, Fri & Sat 9:30-5, Sun (Sept-June) 1-5
Friends of the Library Group

BAINBRIDGE

P BAINBRIDGE FREE LIBRARY*, 13 N Main, 13733. SAN 310-8279. Tel: 607-967-5305. FAX: 607-967-5305. *Dir,* Beverly Fox
Founded 1908. Pop 3,331; Circ 9,048
Library Holdings: Bk Vols 15,510; Per Subs 24
Wireless access
Mem of Four County Library System
Open Mon & Thurs 1-5 & 6-9, Tues 9-12 & 1-6, Sat 9-12

BALDWIN

P BALDWIN PUBLIC LIBRARY*, 2385 Grand Ave, 11510-3289. SAN 310-8287. Tel: 516-223-6228. FAX: 516 623-7991. E-mail: director_ba@nassaulibrary.org. Web Site: www.nassaulibrary.org/baldwin. *Dir,* H Maria Sysak; *Asst Dir,* Catherine Overton; *Head, Circ,* Diane Lass; *Head, YA,* Jill Holleufer; *Adult Serv, Coll Develop, Ref,* Marianne Kobbe; *Cat, Per,* Edward Daly; *Ch Serv,* Wendy Rathjens; *Media Spec,* Gail Baselice; Staff 19.5 (MLS 18, Non-MLS 1.5)
Founded 1922. Pop 32,396; Circ 209,303
Jul 2007-Jun 2008 Income $3,225,178, State $26,043, Locally Generated Income $3,194,815, Other $4,320. Sal $2,280,174 (Prof $619,168)
Library Holdings: AV Mats 13,662; e-books 3,509; Large Print Bks 15,000; Bk Vols 155,339; Per Subs 2,700
Special Collections: Baldwin History; Long Island Coll
Automation Activity & Vendor Info: (Circulation) Innovative Interfaces, Inc; (OPAC) Innovative Interfaces, Inc
Database Vendor: EBSCOhost, Gale Cengage Learning, OCLC FirstSearch, ProQuest, Wilson - Wilson Web
Wireless access
Publications: Piper (Newsletter)
Mem of Indianhead Federated Library System; Nassau Library System
Partic in Long Island Library Resources Council; The Library Network
Special Services for the Deaf - Assistive tech
Special Services for the Blind - Magnifiers
Open Mon-Fri (Winter) 9-9, Sat 9-5, Sun 1-5; Mon-Thurs (Summer) 9-9, Fri 9-5, Sat 9-1

BALDWINSVILLE

P BALDWINSVILLE PUBLIC LIBRARY*, 33 E Genesee St, 13027-2575. SAN 310-8295. Tel: 315-635-5631. FAX: 315-635-6760. E-mail: info@bville.lib.ny.us. Web Site: www.bville.lib.ny.us. *Dir,* Marilyn R Laubacher; E-mail: marilynl@bville.lib.ny.us; *Adult Prog Librn,* Julia Schult; E-mail: julias@bville.lib.ny.us; *YA Librn,* Valerie Chism; E-mail: valc@bville.lib.ny.us; *Tech Coordr,* Nancy J Howe; *Ch Serv,* Corrinne Needham; E-mail: corrinnen@bville.lib.ny.us; *Ref Serv, Ad,* Margaret A Van Patten; E-mail: megv@bville.lib.ny.us; Staff 10 (MLS 10)
Founded 1948. Pop 32,300; Circ 432,305
Jan 2011-Dec 2011 Income $1,505,433, State $45,768, Federal $97,510, Locally Generated Income $1,299,532, Other $62,623. Mats Exp $230,598, Books $112,282, Per/Ser (Incl. Access Fees) $11,833, AV Equip $4,394, AV Mat $50,969, Electronic Ref Mat (Incl. Access Fees) $50,972, Presv $158. Sal $765,485 (Prof $421,831)
Library Holdings: AV Mats 6,134; DVDs 9,210; e-books 3,502; Electronic Media & Resources 159; Bk Vols 107,627; Per Subs 258
Special Collections: Newspaper Coll (1846-present), micro
Subject Interests: Local hist
Automation Activity & Vendor Info: (Cataloging) Innovative Interfaces, Inc; (Circulation) Innovative Interfaces, Inc; (OPAC) Innovative Interfaces, Inc
Database Vendor: ALLDATA Online, Baker & Taylor, Booksite, Bowker, CredoReference, Dun & Bradstreet, EBSCOhost, Facts on File, Gale Cengage Learning, Grolier Online, H W Wilson, Hoovers, LearningExpress, Library Ideas, LLC, LibraryInsight, Newsbank, OCLC FirstSearch, OCLC WorldShare Interlibrary Loan, Overdrive, Inc, ProQuest, ReferenceUSA, TumbleBookLibrary, ValueLine
Wireless access
Function: Adult bk club, Adult literacy prog, Art exhibits, Audio & video playback equip for onsite use, Audiobks via web, Bi-weekly Writer's Group, Bk club(s), Bks on cassette, Bks on CD, Children's prog, Computer training, Computers for patron use, Copy machines, Digital talking bks, e-mail & chat, E-Reserves, Electronic databases & coll, Exhibits, Fax serv, Free DVD rentals, Genealogy discussion group, Handicapped accessible, Health sci info serv, Holiday prog, Home delivery & serv to Sr ctr & nursing homes, ILL available, Large print keyboards, Magnifiers for reading, Mail & tel request accepted, Microfiche/film & reading machines, Music CDs, Notary serv, Online cat, Online ref, Online searches, Orientations, Outreach serv, Outside serv via phone, mail, e-mail & web, OverDrive digital audio bks, Photocopying/Printing, Preschool outreach, Preschool reading prog, Printer for laptops & handheld devices, Prog for adults, Prog for children & young adult, Pub access computers, Ref serv available, Ref serv in person, Scanner, Senior computer classes, Senior outreach, Spoken cassettes & CDs, Spoken cassettes & DVDs, Story hour, Summer reading prog, Tax forms, Teen prog, Telephone ref, Video lending libr, Web-catalog, Wheelchair accessible, Workshops, Writing prog
Publications: "We're Here to Serve You" (Library handbook); Activities Calendar (Monthly); Annual report
Mem of Onondaga County Public Library
Special Services for the Deaf - Assisted listening device; Bks on deafness & sign lang; Sign lang interpreter upon request for prog
Special Services for the Blind - Accessible computers; Aids for in-house use; Audio mat; Bks available with recordings; Bks on CD; Large print bks; Large print bks & talking machines; Large screen computer & software; Low vision equip; Playaways (bks on MP3); Rec & flexible discs; Recorded bks; Ref serv; Screen enlargement software for people with visual disabilities; Sound rec; Talking bk serv referral; Talking bks & player equip; VisualTek equip
Open Mon-Thurs 9-9, Fri 9-5, Sat 10-4, Sun 1-5
Friends of the Library Group

BALLSTON SPA

P BALLSTON SPA PUBLIC LIBRARY*, 21 Milton Ave, 12020. SAN 310-8309. Tel: 518-885-5022. E-mail: bal-director@sals.edu. Web Site: ballston.sals.edu. *Dir,* Andrea Simmons; *Asst Librn,* Helen King; Staff 7 (MLS 2, Non-MLS 5)
Founded 1893. Pop 4,937; Circ 81,565
Library Holdings: Bk Vols 45,000; Per Subs 73
Special Collections: Literacy Center; Parenting Center; Saratoga County (Bruce M Manzer Coll), bks, per
Function: Art exhibits, Audio & video playback equip for onsite use, Computers for patron use, ILL available, Meeting rooms, Prog for children & young adult, Tax forms
Mem of Southern Adirondack Library System
Open Tues-Fri (Winter) 10-7, Sat 10-5; Mon & Fri (Summer) 10-5, Tues-Thurs 10-7, Sat 10-1
Friends of the Library Group

BARKER

P BARKER FREE LIBRARY*, 8706 Main St, 14012. (Mail add: PO Box 261, 14012-0261), SAN 310-8317. Tel: 716-795-3344. FAX: 716-795-3344. Web Site: www.nioga.org/libraries/bar.html. *Dir,* Lisa Thomson; E-mail: lthom@nioga.org; Staff 3 (MLS 1, Non-MLS 2)
Founded 1935. Pop 2,655; Circ 12,159
Library Holdings: High Interest/Low Vocabulary Bk Vols 34; Bk Vols 15,300; Per Subs 15
Subject Interests: Adult literacy, GED programs, Local hist
Automation Activity & Vendor Info: (Acquisitions) SirsiDynix; (Cataloging) SirsiDynix; (Circulation) SirsiDynix; (Course Reserve) SirsiDynix; (ILL) SirsiDynix; (Media Booking) SirsiDynix; (OPAC) SirsiDynix; (Serials) SirsiDynix
Wireless access
Mem of Nioga Library System
Special Services for the Blind - Bks on cassette
Open Mon & Fri 10-5, Tues & Thurs 10-8, Sat 10-1
Friends of the Library Group

BARNEVELD

P BARNEVELD FREE LIBRARY*, 118 Boon St, 13304. (Mail add: PO Box 306, 13304-0306), SAN 310-8325. Tel: 315-896-2096. Web Site: www.midyork.org/Barneveld. *Librn,* Greta Madore; E-mail: gmadore@midyork.org
Founded 1874. Pop 2,499; Circ 7,556
Library Holdings: Bk Vols 9,500; Per Subs 26
Wireless access
Mem of Mid-York Library System
Open Mon (Fall-Winter) 10-12 & 7-9, Tues 1:30-5, Wed 10-12 & 3-5, Thurs 1:30-6, Fri 7pm-9pm, Sat 8am-10pm; Mon (Summer) 10-12 & 7-9, Tues 1:30-5, Wed 3-5, Thurs 1:30-6, Fri 7pm-9pm

BARRYTOWN

R UNIFICATION THEOLOGICAL SEMINARY LIBRARY*, 14 Seminary Dr, 12507. Tel: 845-752-3000, Ext 232. FAX: 845-752-3021. Web Site: www.uts.edu/library.html. *Dir,* Dr Keisuke Noda
Founded 1975
Library Holdings: AV Mats 350; Bk Titles 60,000; Per Subs 70
Subject Interests: Relig
Database Vendor: EBSCOhost

BATAVIA

J GENESEE COMMUNITY COLLEGE*, Alfred C O'Connell Library, One College Rd, 14020-9704. SAN 310-8333. Tel: 585-343-0055, Ext 6350. Circulation Tel: 585-345-6834. Reference Tel: 585-343-0055, Ext 6419. FAX: 585-345-6933. Web Site: www.genesee.edu/library. *Dir of Libr Serv,* Nina T Warren; Tel: 585-343-0055, Ext 6256, E-mail: ntwarren@genesee.edu; *Assoc Prof/Instrul Serv Librn,* Nicki Lerczak; Tel: 585-343-0055, Ext 6418, E-mail: njlerczak@genesee.edu; *Assoc Prof/Librn/Coll Develop & LMS Adminr,* Cindy A Francis; Tel: 585-343-0055, Ext 6126, E-mail: cafrancis@genesee.edu; *Instr, Ref Serv Librn,* Cindy S Hagelberger; Tel: 585-343-0055, Ext 6231, E-mail: cshagelberger@genesee.edu; *Instr, Syst/Electronic Serv Librn,* Michelle Eichelberger; Tel: 585-343-0055, Ext 6458, E-mail: maeichelberger@genesee.edu; Staff 8 (MLS 5, Non-MLS 3)
Founded 1966. Enrl 7,030; Fac 72
Library Holdings: Audiobooks 386; CDs 1,728; DVDs 565; e-books 3,000; Bk Titles 72,000; Bk Vols 86,000; Per Subs 186; Videos 1,959
Automation Activity & Vendor Info: (Cataloging) Ex Libris Group; (Circulation) Ex Libris Group; (ILL) OCLC ILLiad; (OPAC) Ex Libris Group
Database Vendor: Cinahl, CredoReference, EBSCOhost, Gale Cengage Learning, JSTOR, OCLC FirstSearch, OCLC WorldShare Interlibrary Loan, ProQuest, SerialsSolutions, Westlaw
Wireless access
Function: Archival coll, Art exhibits, Audio & video playback equip for onsite use, Bks on CD, Computers for patron use, Copy machines, Distance learning, Doc delivery serv, e-mail & chat, Electronic databases & coll, Exhibits, ILL available, Microfiche/film & reading machines, Music CDs, Online ref, Online searches, Photocopying/Printing, Preschool outreach, Preschool reading prog, Ref & res, Ref serv available, Ref serv in person, Scanner, Web-catalog, Wheelchair accessible
Partic in Western New York Library Resources Council
Special Services for the Blind - VisualTek equip
Open Mon-Thurs (Fall & Spring) 7:30am-9:30pm, Fri 7:30-4:30, Sat 11-4, Sun Noon-6; Mon-Fri (Summer) 8:30-4:30

S GENESEE COUNTY HISTORY DEPARTMENT*, Research Library, Three W Main St, 14020-2021. SAN 326-2626. Tel: 585-344-2550, Ext 2613. FAX: 585-344-8558. E-mail: history@co.genesee.ny.us. Web Site: www.co.genesee.ny.us. *Hist Coll Librn,* Susan Conklin; Staff 2 (Non-MLS 2)
Founded 1941
Jan 2008-Dec 2008 Income $127,350. Sal $85,000
Library Holdings: Bk Titles 3,000
Special Collections: County Coll; GenealogyColl, bks & files; Local History Coll, bks & files
Wireless access
Open Mon-Fri 9-12 & 1-4:30
Restriction: Non-circulating
Friends of the Library Group

P RICHMOND MEMORIAL LIBRARY, 19 Ross St, 14020. SAN 310-8341. Tel: 585-343-9550. FAX: 585-344-4651. Web Site: www.batavialibrary.org. *Dir,* Robert Conrad; E-mail: rconrad@nioga.org; *Ch Serv Librn,* Vinise Bobrov; *Adult Serv, Commun Librn,* Leslie DeLooze; *Media Serv Librn,* Rita McCormack; *Ref & Tech Librn,* Kathleen Facer; *Teen Serv Librn,* Paula Haven; *Coordr, Serv to the Aged in Genesee County,* Cathie Plaisted; *Ch Serv,* Vinise Campanella; *ILL,* Jill Crocker; Staff 12 (MLS 6, Non-MLS 6)
Founded 1889. Pop 19,244; Circ 276,533
Library Holdings: Bk Titles 105,000; Per Subs 171
Subject Interests: Genealogy, Local hist
Automation Activity & Vendor Info: (Cataloging) SirsiDynix; (Circulation) SirsiDynix; (OPAC) SirsiDynix
Database Vendor: Newsbank
Wireless access
Mem of Nioga Library System
Open Mon-Thurs 9-9, Fri & Sat 9-5
Friends of the Library Group

M UNITED MEMORIAL MEDICAL CENTER*, Medical Library, 127 North St, 14020-1697. SAN 326-5374. Tel: 585-344-5273. FAX: 585-344-7461. *Librn,* Karen Lamson; Staff 2 (MLS 1, Non-MLS 1)
Founded 1958
Library Holdings: e-books 63; e-journals 418; Electronic Media & Resources 2; Bk Titles 475; Bk Vols 525; Per Subs 2
Partic in Library Consortium of Health Institutions in Buffalo; National Network of Libraries of Medicine; Western New York Library Resources Council
Open Mon-Fri 9-3
Restriction: Circulates for staff only, In-house use for visitors, Not open to pub

BATH

GM DEPARTMENT OF VETERANS AFFAIRS*, Library Section, 76 Veterans Ave, 14810. SAN 310-8384. Tel: 607-664-4000, 607-664-4813. FAX: 607-664-4814. *Libr Mgr,* Sandy Baxter; *Libr Tech,* Susan Hauryski; E-mail: susan.hauryski@eva.gov; Staff 2 (MLS 1, Non-MLS 1)
Library Holdings: Bk Vols 1,200; Per Subs 97
Subject Interests: Med, Nursing
Automation Activity & Vendor Info: (Cataloging) Follett Software; (Circulation) Follett Software; (OPAC) Follett Software
Database Vendor: OVID Technologies
Partic in Veterans Affairs Libr Network (VALNET)
Open Mon-Fri 8-4:30

P DORMANN LIBRARY*, 101 W Morris St, 14810. SAN 310-8368. Tel: 607-776-4613. FAX: 607-776-6693. Web Site: www.dormannlibrary.org. *Dir,* Carol Berry
Founded 1869. Pop 11,819; Circ 63,607
Library Holdings: Bk Vols 35,000; Per Subs 65
Special Collections: Local History
Automation Activity & Vendor Info: (Cataloging) SirsiDynix; (Circulation) SirsiDynix; (OPAC) SirsiDynix
Wireless access
Mem of Southern Tier Library System
Open Mon-Thurs 10-8, Fri 10-6, Sat 10-2
Friends of the Library Group

GL NEW YORK SUPREME COURT*, Seventh Judicial District Law Library, Three E Pulteney Sq, 14810. SAN 310-8376. Tel: 607-664-2099. FAX: 607-776-7715. *Librn,* Kristine Gilbert
Library Holdings: Bk Vols 7,500
Subject Interests: Agr, Bankruptcy, NYS statutes
Database Vendor: LexisNexis, Westlaw
Open Mon-Fri 9-5

BAYSIDE

J QUEENSBOROUGH COMMUNITY COLLEGE, CITY UNIVERSITY OF NEW YORK*, Kurt R Schmeller Library, 222-05 56th Ave, 11364-1497. SAN 310-8414. Tel: 718-631-6227. Interlibrary Loan Service Tel: 718-281-5067. Reference Tel: 718-631-6241. FAX: 718-281-5012. Interlibrary Loan Service FAX: 718-281-5118. Web Site: qcc.libguides.com/libraryhome. *Chief Librn,* Jeanne Galvin; Tel: 718-631-6220, E-mail: jgalvin@qcc.cuny.edu; *Dep Chief Librn/Fac Outreach Librn,* Devin McKay; Tel: 718-281-5032, E-mail: dmckay@qcc.cuny.edu; *Head, Ref & Ser,* Barbara Bonous-Smit; Tel: 718-281-5010, E-mail: bbonoussmit@qcc.cuny.edu; *Electronic Res/Web Librn,* William Blick; Tel: 718-281-5778, E-mail: wblick@qcc.cuny.edu; *Emerging Tech Librn,* Jean Amaral; Tel: 718-631-5795, E-mail: jamaral@qcc.cuny.edu; *Reserves & Syst Librn,* Peijun Jeffrey Jia; Tel: 718-281-5594, E-mail: jjia@qcc.cuny.edu; *Coordr, Libr Pub Relations,* Sandra Marcus; Tel: 718-281-5072, E-mail: smarcus@qcc.cuny.edu; *Coordr, Pub Serv & Info Literacy,* Susan Sciammarella; Tel: 718-631-6601, E-mail: ssciammarella@qcc.cuny.edu; *Col Archivist, Coordr, Circ,* Constance Williams; Tel: 718-631-6567, E-mail: cwilliams@qcc.cuny.edu; *Acq, Coordr, Tech Serv,* Sheila Beck; Tel: 718-631-5711, E-mail: sbeck@qcc.cuny.edu; *Cataloger,* Jung Cho; Tel: 718-631-6218, E-mail: jcho@qcc.cuny.edu; *Cat, Ref,* Mi-Seon Kim; Tel: 718-631-5721, E-mail: mkim@qcc.cuny.edu; *ILL, Ref & Instruction,* Neera Mohess; E-mail: nmohees@qcc.cuny.edu; *Sr Col Lab Tech,* Lawrence Chan; Tel: 718-281-5595, E-mail: lchan@qcc.cuny.edu; *Sr Col Lab Tech/Media Serv,* Ramon Perez; Tel: 718-281-5407, E-mail: rperez@qcc.cuny.edu; *Col Lab Tech,* Danny Li; Tel: 718-631-6672, E-mail: dli@qcc.cuny.edu; Staff 29.5 (MLS 15.5, Non-MLS 14)
Founded 1960. Enrl 11,760; Fac 530; Highest Degree: Associate
Library Holdings: AV Mats 8,912; e-books 97,066; e-journals 59,766; Microforms 3,500; Bk Titles 132,751; Bk Vols 152,800; Per Subs 90
Wireless access
Publications: APA, MLA, Chicago Citation Style Handbooks; Glossary of Library Terms; Guide to the Library of Congress Classification System; How to Guides; Library Scene (Newsletter); Periodical Directory; Primary vs. Secondary Sources; Student Library Handbook; Student Self-Guided Library Orientation Tour; Subject Guides
Partic in Metropolitan New York Library Council
Open Mon-Thurs 8am-8:45pm, Fri 8-4:45, Sat 10-3:45
Friends of the Library Group

BAYVILLE

P BAYVILLE FREE LIBRARY*, 34 School St, 11709. SAN 310-8422. Tel: 516-628-2765. FAX: 516-628-2738. E-mail: bayvlib@optonline.net. Web Site: www.bayvillefreelibrary.org/. *Dir,* Richard Rapecis
Circ 71,351
Library Holdings: Bk Vols 55,872; Per Subs 70
Automation Activity & Vendor Info: (Circulation) Follett Software
Wireless access
Publications: Bayville Bookmark
Mem of Nassau Library System
Open Mon-Thurs (Winter) 10-9, Fri & Sat 10-5, Sun 1-5; Mon-Thurs (Summer) 10-9, Fri 10-5, Sat 10-1

BEACON

S FISHKILL CORRECTIONAL FACILITY LIBRARY*, Bldg 13, 12508. (Mail add: PO Box 307, 12508-0307), SAN 310-8430. Tel: 845-831-4800, Ext 4600. FAX: 845-831-3199. *Librn,* Cheryl Bennin; E-mail: Cheryl.Bennin@doccs.ny.gov
Library Holdings: Bk Vols 15,000; Per Subs 40; Videos 450
Subject Interests: African-Am studies, Criminology
Automation Activity & Vendor Info: (Cataloging) Follett Software; (Circulation) Follett Software; (OPAC) Follett Software
Restriction: Staff & inmates only

P HOWLAND PUBLIC LIBRARY*, 313 Main St, 12508. SAN 310-8449. Tel: 845-831-1134. FAX: 845-831-1165. E-mail: howlandlibrary@hotmail.com. Web Site: beaconlibrary.org. *Dir,* Phyllis Keaton; *Ch Serv,* Ginny Figlia; *Ref,* Peter McGivney
Founded 1872. Pop 24,000; Circ 55,800
Library Holdings: Bk Titles 40,088; Per Subs 123
Special Collections: Chinese Coll, bks, rec; Handicapped Coll, bks, kits, VF; Spanish Language (Libros Coll), bks, rec
Subject Interests: Ethnic studies, Local hist
Automation Activity & Vendor Info: (Circulation) Innovative Interfaces, Inc - Millenium
Wireless access
Mem of Mid-Hudson Library System
Open Mon, Wed & Fri 9:30-5:30, Tues & Thurs 9:30-8, Sat 10-4, Sun 12-4
Friends of the Library Group

BEAR MOUNTAIN

S BEAR MOUNTAIN TRAILSIDE MUSEUMS LIBRARY*, Bear Mountain State Park, 10911-0427. SAN 371-2095. Tel: 845-786-2701. FAX: 845-786-0496. *Dir,* Edwin Mcgowan
Library Holdings: Bk Vols 500
Wireless access
Open Mon-Fri 8:30-4:30
Restriction: Staff use only

BEAVER FALLS

P BEAVER FALLS LIBRARY*, 9607 Lewis St, 13305. (Mail add: PO Box 75, 13305-0075), SAN 310-8473. Tel: 315-346-6216. FAX: 315-346-6216. *Dir,* Carol Jackson
Founded 1920. Pop 738; Circ 9,818
Library Holdings: Bk Vols 4,000; Per Subs 20
Wireless access
Mem of North Country Library System
Open Mon 10:30-4 & 5:30-8, Thurs 10-5, Fri 3-8

BEDFORD

P BEDFORD FREE LIBRARY*, On the Village Green, 10506. (Mail add: PO Box 375, 10506-0375), SAN 310-8481. Tel: 914-234-3570. FAX: 914-234-0546. Web Site: www.bedfordfreelibrary.org. *Dir,* Ann Cloonan; E-mail: acloonan@wlsmail.org; *Ch,* Shodie Alcorn; *YA Librn,* Julie Rockefeller
Founded 1903. Pop 6,000; Circ 45,000
Library Holdings: Bk Titles 30,000; Bk Vols 35,000; Per Subs 38
Subject Interests: Biog, Local hist
Automation Activity & Vendor Info: (Acquisitions) SirsiDynix; (Cataloging) SirsiDynix; (Circulation) SirsiDynix; (Course Reserve) SirsiDynix; (ILL) SirsiDynix; (Media Booking) SirsiDynix; (OPAC) SirsiDynix; (Serials) SirsiDynix
Wireless access
Mem of Westchester Library System
Open Mon 10-7, Tues-Fri 10-6, Sat 10-2
Friends of the Library Group

BEDFORD HILLS

P BEDFORD HILLS FREE LIBRARY*, 26 Main St, 10507-1832. SAN 310-849X. Tel: 914-666-6472. FAX: 914-666-6473. Web Site: www.bedfordny.com. *Dir,* Rhoda M Gushue; *Asst Dir,* Eileen Baer
Founded 1915. Pop 6,123; Circ 70,143
Library Holdings: Bk Vols 41,517; Per Subs 99
Automation Activity & Vendor Info: (Acquisitions) SirsiDynix; (Cataloging) SirsiDynix; (Circulation) SirsiDynix; (OPAC) SirsiDynix; (Serials) SirsiDynix
Wireless access
Mem of Westchester Library System
Open Mon-Wed 1-8, Thurs & Fri 10-5:30, Sat 10-1

S NEW YORK DEPARTMENT OF CORRECTIONAL SERVICES*, Bedford Hills Correctional Facility Library, 247 Harris Rd, 10507-2499. SAN 327-1218. Tel: 914-241-3100, Ext 4540. FAX: 914-241-3100. *Sr Librn,* Anthony Litwinowicz; Staff 1 (MLS 1)
Apr 2008-Mar 2009. Mats Exp $18,000
Library Holdings: DVDs 274; Bk Vols 12,600; Per Subs 40
Automation Activity & Vendor Info: (Cataloging) Follett Software; (Circulation) Follett Software
Open Mon & Wed 1-9, Tues, Thurs & Fri 8-4
Restriction: Staff & inmates only

BELFAST

P BELFAST PUBLIC LIBRARY*, 75 S Main St, 14711-8605. (Mail add: PO Box 455, 14711-0455), SAN 310-8503. Tel: 585-365-2072. FAX: 585-365-2072. E-mail: belfast@stls.org. Web Site: www.stls.org/belfast. *Dir,* Cynthia Dutton
Pop 2,154; Circ 12,500
Library Holdings: Bk Vols 10,277; Per Subs 30
Wireless access
Mem of Southern Tier Library System
Open Mon & Sat 10-1, Tues-Thurs 3-8

BELLEVILLE

P BELLEVILLE PUBLIC LIBRARY*, Philomathean Free Library, 8086 County Rd 75, 13611. (Mail add: PO Box 27, 13611-0027), SAN 310-8511. Tel: 315-846-5103. FAX: 315-846-5103. *Librn,* Linda Strader
Founded 1904. Pop 200; Circ 7,375
Library Holdings: Bk Vols 3,000
Automation Activity & Vendor Info: (Cataloging) SirsiDynix; (OPAC) SirsiDynix
Wireless access
Mem of North Country Library System
Open Mon (Winter) 4-8, Wed & Fri 9-11 & 3-6; Mon (Summer) 3-8, Wed 1-6, Fri 2-6
Friends of the Library Group

BELLMORE

P BELLMORE MEMORIAL LIBRARY*, 2288 Bedford Ave, 11710. SAN 310-852X. Tel: 516-785-2990. FAX: 516-783-8550. Web Site: www.nassaulibrary.org/bellmore. *Dir,* Maureen Garvey; *Adult Serv,* P Paris; *Ch Serv,* D DeGrassi; *Tech Serv,* C Schuler; *YA Serv,* P Gleiberman; Staff 8 (MLS 8)
Founded 1948. Pop 12,900
Library Holdings: AV Mats 14,585; Bk Vols 102,000; Per Subs 295
Automation Activity & Vendor Info: (Acquisitions) SirsiDynix; (Circulation) SirsiDynix; (OPAC) SirsiDynix
Wireless access
Publications: Bellmore Memorial Library (Newsletter)
Mem of Nassau Library System
Special Services for the Deaf - Assistive tech; Closed caption videos; TTY equip
Special Services for the Blind - Assistive/Adapted tech devices, equip & products; Computer with voice synthesizer for visually impaired persons
Open Mon-Thurs 9:30-9, Fri 9:30-5:30, Sat 9:30-5 (9:30-1:30 Summer), Sun 1-5

BELLPORT

P SOUTH COUNTRY LIBRARY*, 22 Station Rd, 11713. SAN 310-8538. Tel: 631-286-0818. FAX: 631-286-4873. E-mail: sctylib@sctylib.org. Web Site: sctylib.org. *Dir,* Mary Haines; *Ch Serv,* Kristina Sembler; *ILL,* Annie Rowland; *Ref,* Judy Kerstetter; *YA Serv,* Andrea Graham; Staff 50 (MLS 9, Non-MLS 41)
Founded 1921. Pop 26,400; Circ 345,000
Library Holdings: AV Mats 26,373; Bk Titles 105,956; Per Subs 2,984
Subject Interests: Art, Boating, Gardening, Hispanic, Local hist, Mysteries
Database Vendor: Innovative Interfaces, Inc
Wireless access
Publications: Newsletter (Bi-monthly)

Mem of Suffolk Cooperative Library System
Friends of the Library Group

P SUFFOLK COOPERATIVE LIBRARY SYSTEM*, 627 N Sunrise Service Rd, 11713. (Mail add: PO Box 9000, 11713-9000), SAN 351-837X. Tel: 631-286-1600. FAX: 631-286-1647. TDD: 631-286-4546. Web Site: www.suffolklibrarysystem.org. *Dir,* Kevin Verbesey; E-mail: kverbesey@suffolk.lib.ny.us; *Bus Mgr,* Roger Reyes; *Mem Serv Coordr,* Diane Eidelman; *Outreach Prog,* Valerie Lewis; *Tech Serv,* Ruth Westfall; *YA Serv,* Barbara Moon; Staff 61 (MLS 16, Non-MLS 45)
Founded 1961. Pop 1,419,369; Circ 15,678,881
Library Holdings: AV Mats 8,179; Bks on Deafness & Sign Lang 56; e-books 8,412; Bk Vols 143,232; Per Subs 47,201
Special Collections: Adult New Readers (literacy); Auto & Home Appliance Repair Manuals; County Coll; Disability Reference Coll; Last Copy Center; Multi-Language Coll; Talking Books. State Document Depository; US Document Depository
Automation Activity & Vendor Info: (Acquisitions) Innovative Interfaces, Inc; (Cataloging) Innovative Interfaces, Inc; (Circulation) Innovative Interfaces, Inc; (ILL) Innovative Interfaces, Inc; (OPAC) Innovative Interfaces, Inc; (Serials) Innovative Interfaces, Inc
Database Vendor: EBSCOhost, Gale Cengage Learning, ProQuest, SerialsSolutions, Wilson - Wilson Web
Member Libraries: Amagansett Free Library; Amityville Public Library; Babylon Public Library; Baiting Hollow Free Library; Bay Shore-Brightwaters Public Library; Bayport-Blue Point Public Library; Brookhaven Free Library; Center Moriches Free Public Library; Central Islip Public Library; Cold Spring Harbor Library; Commack Public Library; Comsewogue Public Library; Connetquot Public Library; Copiague Memorial Public Library; Cutchogue-New Suffolk Free Library; Deer Park Public Library; East Hampton Library; East Islip Public Library; Elwood Public Library; Emma S Clark Memorial Library; Fishers Island Library; Floyd Memorial Library; Half Hollow Hills Community Library; Hampton Bays Public Library; Harborfields Public Library; Hauppauge Public Library; Huntington Public Library; Islip Public Library; John Jermain Memorial Library; Lindenhurst Memorial Library; Longwood Public Library; Mastics-Moriches-Shirley Community Library; Mattituck-Laurel Library; Middle Country Public Library; Montauk Library; North Babylon Public Library; North Shore Public Library; Northport-East Northport Public Library; Patchogue-Medford Library; Port Jefferson Free Library; Quogue Library; Riverhead Free Library; Rogers Memorial Library; Sachem Public Library; Sayville Library; Shelter Island Public Library; Smithtown Library; South Country Library; South Huntington Public Library; Southold Free Library; The Hampton Library; West Babylon Public Library; West Islip Public Library; Westhampton Free Library; Wyandanch Public Library
Special Services for the Deaf - Bks on deafness & sign lang; Closed caption videos; Deaf publ; Spec interest per; TDD equip; TTY equip
Special Services for the Blind - Aids for in-house use; Assistive/Adapted tech devices, equip & products; Audio mat; BiFolkal kits; Bks & mags in Braille, on rec, tape & cassette; Braille equip; Cassette playback machines; Children's Braille; Closed circuit TV; Computer with voice synthesizer for visually impaired persons; Handicapped awareness prog; Home delivery serv; Info on spec aids & appliances; Internet workstation with adaptive software; Large print bks & talking machines; Large screen computer & software; Local mags & bks recorded; Low vision equip; Machine repair; Magnifiers; Micro-computer access & training; Networked computers with assistive software; Newsletter (in large print, Braille or on cassette); Reader equip; Rec & flexible discs; Ref serv; Scanner for conversion & translation of mats; Screen reader software; Spec cats; Talking bks & player equip; Talking calculator; Talking machines; Tel Pioneers equip repair group; Videos on blindness & phys handicaps; Volunteer serv; ZoomText magnification & reading software
Branches: 1

P LONG ISLAND TALKING BOOK LIBRARY, 627 N Sunrise Service Rd, 11713. (Mail add: PO Box 9000, 11713-9000), SAN 351-840X. Tel: 631-286-1600. Toll Free Tel: 866-833-1122 (Nassau/Suffolk Counties only). FAX: 631-286-1647. TDD: 631-286-4546. E-mail: lbph@suffolk.lib.ny.us. Web Site: www.litbl.org. *Librn,* Valerie Lewis; E-mail: vlewis@suffolk.lib.ny.us; Staff 1 (MLS 1)
Founded 1972
Special Collections: Blindness & Other Disabilities Reference Materials; Inkprint Signed English Books; Print-Braille Books for Children
Publications: Fast Forward Newsletter (large print & cassette)
Special Services for the Deaf - TDD equip; TTY equip
Special Services for the Blind - Assistive/Adapted tech devices, equip & products; Braille equip; Computer with voice synthesizer for visually impaired persons; Reader equip; Talking bks; Volunteer serv
Open Mon-Fri 9-5

BELMONT

S ALLEGANY COUNTY HISTORICAL MUSEUM LIBRARY*, Seven Courthouse, Court St, 14813-1089. SAN 310-8546. Tel: 585-268-9293. FAX: 585-268-9446. E-mail: historian@alleganyco.com. *Historian,* Craig Braack
Founded 1972
Library Holdings: Bk Titles 1,000
Special Collections: Philip Church Records
Subject Interests: 19th Century Allegany County genealogical records, 20th Century Allegany County genealogical records, Land records
Restriction: Open to pub by appt only

P BELMONT LITERARY & HISTORICAL SOCIETY FREE LIBRARY*, Two Willets Ave, 14813. SAN 310-8554. Tel: 585-268-5308. FAX: 585-268-5308. Web Site: www.stls.org/belmont. *Dir,* Carrie Jefferds; E-mail: jefferdsc@stls.org; Staff 2 (Non-MLS 2)
Founded 1885. Pop 2,245; Circ 25,000
Library Holdings: Bk Titles 16,000; Per Subs 35
Special Collections: Local Newspaper Coll
Automation Activity & Vendor Info: (Acquisitions) SIRSI WorkFlows; (Cataloging) SIRSI WorkFlows; (Circulation) SIRSI WorkFlows; (Course Reserve) SIRSI WorkFlows; (ILL) SIRSI WorkFlows; (Media Booking) SIRSI WorkFlows; (OPAC) SIRSI WorkFlows; (Serials) SIRSI WorkFlows
Wireless access
Mem of Southern Tier Library System
Open Tues & Fri 1-5 & 7-9, Thurs 9-1, Sat 1-5

BEMUS POINT

P BEMUS POINT PUBLIC LIBRARY*, 13 Main St, 14712. (Mail add: PO Box 428, 14712-0428), SAN 310-8562. Tel: 716-386-2274. FAX: 716-386-2176. E-mail: bemuslibrary@stny.rr.com. *Dir,* Mary Jane Stahley
Founded 1908. Pop 444; Circ 28,279
Library Holdings: Bk Vols 13,882
Subject Interests: Local hist
Wireless access
Mem of Chautauqua-Cattaraugus Library System
Open Mon, Wed & Fri 10-12 & 1-5, Tues & Thurs 10-12, 1-5 & 7-9, Sat 10-2
Friends of the Library Group

BERGEN

P BYRON-BERGEN PUBLIC LIBRARY*, 13 S Lake Ave, 14416-9420. (Mail add: PO Box 430, 14416-0430), SAN 370-6435. Tel: 585-494-1120. FAX: 585-494-2339. Web Site: www.nioga.org/bgn.html. *Dir,* Nancy Bailey; E-mail: nbailey@nioga.org; Staff 3 (Non-MLS 3)
Founded 1962. Pop 5,000; Circ 25,000
Library Holdings: Bk Titles 9,000; Bk Vols 10,000; Per Subs 47
Subject Interests: Local hist
Automation Activity & Vendor Info: (Cataloging) SirsiDynix; (Circulation) SirsiDynix; (OPAC) SirsiDynix
Wireless access
Mem of Nioga Library System
Special Services for the Deaf - Bks on deafness & sign lang
Open Tues 10-12 & 2-8, Wed 1-8, Thurs 2-8, Fri 10-5, Sat 9-1
Friends of the Library Group

BERKSHIRE

P BERKSHIRE FREE LIBRARY, 12519 State Rte 38, 13736. (Mail add: PO Box 151, 13736-0151), SAN 310-8570. Tel: 607-657-4418. FAX: 607-657-4418. E-mail: bfl@htva.net. Web Site: www.flls.org/memberpages/berkshir.htm. *Dir,* LuAnn Whirl; Staff 2 (Non-MLS 2)
Founded 1926. Pop 2,536; Circ 7,717
Jan 2013-Dec 2013 Income $20,653, State $1,682, City $7,500, County $8,971, Other $2,500. Sal $13,160
Library Holdings: Audiobooks 94; DVDs 254; e-books 50; Bk Titles 6,181; Per Subs 18; Videos 454
Automation Activity & Vendor Info: (Acquisitions) Innovative Interfaces, Inc; (Cataloging) Innovative Interfaces, Inc; (Circulation) Innovative Interfaces, Inc; (Course Reserve) Innovative Interfaces, Inc; (ILL) OCLC WorldShare Interlibrary Loan; (Media Booking) Innovative Interfaces, Inc; (OPAC) Innovative Interfaces, Inc; (Serials) Innovative Interfaces, Inc
Database Vendor: Booklist Online, EBSCO Auto Repair Reference, EBSCOhost, Facts on File, Grolier Online, LearningExpress, OCLC FirstSearch, OCLC WorldShare Interlibrary Loan, ProQuest, Sage
Wireless access
Function: Handicapped accessible, ILL available, Online searches, Photocopying/Printing, Ref serv available, Summer reading prog, Wheelchair accessible
Mem of Finger Lakes Library System
Open Tues 12-5, Wed & Fri 1:30-7, Thurs 1-5, Sat 9-2

BERLIN

P BERLIN FREE TOWN LIBRARY*, Whitehouse Memorial Bldg, 47 Main St, 12022. (Mail add: PO Box 466, 12022-0466), SAN 310-8589. Tel: 518-658-2231. FAX: 518-658-9565. Web Site: www.bftl.org. *Dir,* Sharon Vogel; E-mail: director@bftl.org
Founded 1895. Pop 1,929; Circ 19,616
Library Holdings: Bks on Deafness & Sign Lang 10; Bk Titles 10,233; Bk Vols 11,000; Per Subs 10
Subject Interests: Civil War, Hist
Automation Activity & Vendor Info: (Acquisitions) Horizon; (Cataloging) Horizon; (Circulation) Horizon; (Course Reserve) Horizon; (ILL) Horizon; (Media Booking) Horizon; (OPAC) Horizon; (Serials) Horizon
Wireless access
Mem of Upper Hudson Library System
Open Mon & Sat 10-1, Tues & Thurs 2-5 & 7-9, Wed & Fri 2-5

BERNE

P BERNE PUBLIC LIBRARY, 1763 Helderberg Trail, 12023. (Mail add: PO Box 209, 12023-0209), SAN 310-8597. Tel: 518-872-1246. FAX: 518-872-9024. Web Site: www.bernepubliclibrary.org. *Libr Mgr,* Judith Petrosillo; E-mail: director@bernepubliclibrary.org; *Libr Asst, Youth Serv,* Kathleen Stempel; E-mail: Kathy@bernepubliclibrary.org; Staff 0.7 (Non-MLS 0.7)
Founded 1962. Pop 2,794; Circ 13,105
Jan 2014-Dec 2014 Income $37,610, State $1,100, City $34,290, Federal $100, Locally Generated Income $1,720. Mats Exp $6,155, Books $4,130, Per/Ser (Incl. Access Fees) $275, AV Mat $1,100, Electronic Ref Mat (Incl. Access Fees) $450. Sal $21,750
Library Holdings: Audiobooks 161; CDs 169; DVDs 1,218; e-books 30; High Interest/Low Vocabulary Bk Vols 15; Large Print Bks 105; Bk Titles 12,750; Per Subs 28
Automation Activity & Vendor Info: (Circulation) SirsiDynix
Database Vendor: OCLC WorldShare Interlibrary Loan
Wireless access
Function: Adult bk club, Bks on CD, Computer training, Computers for patron use, Copy machines, Fax serv, Handicapped accessible, ILL available, Music CDs, Online cat, Outreach serv, OverDrive digital audio bks, Photocopying/Printing, Preschool outreach, Preschool reading prog, Prog for adults, Prog for children & young adult, Scanner, Story hour, Summer reading prog, Tax forms, Video lending libr, Wheelchair accessible
Mem of Upper Hudson Library System
Open Mon & Wed 4-8, Tues 10-8, Thurs 2-8, Sat 10-2
Friends of the Library Group

BETHPAGE

P BETHPAGE PUBLIC LIBRARY*, 47 Powell Ave, 11714-3197. SAN 310-8600. Tel: 516-931-3907. FAX: 516-931-3926. Web Site: www.nassaulibrary.org/bethpage. *Dir,* Lois Lovisolo; *Head, Ref,* Janet Steiniger; *Ch Serv,* Linda Schnall; *Tech Serv,* Phyllis Feigenbaum; Staff 16 (MLS 6.5, Non-MLS 9.5)
Founded 1927. Pop 19,498; Circ 219,569
Library Holdings: AV Mats 11,698; Bk Vols 186,026; Per Subs 309
Special Collections: Italian Genealogy Society
Database Vendor: ALLDATA Online, Gale Cengage Learning, ProQuest, ReferenceUSA
Wireless access
Publications: Newsletter (Bi-monthly)
Mem of Nassau Library System
Partic in Long Island Library Resources Council
Open Mon-Fri (Sept-June) 9:30-9, Sat 9:30-5; Mon-Fri (July-Aug) 9:30-1; Sun (Oct-April) 12-4
Friends of the Library Group

C BRIARCLIFFE COLLEGE LIBRARY*, 1055 Stewart Ave, 11714. SAN 371-8190. Tel: 516-918-3628. FAX: 516-470-6020. Web Site: www.briarcliffe.edu. *Dir, Libr Serv,* Andrew Gibson; *Librn,* Elizabeth Trapasso; E-mail: ETrapasso@bcl.edu; Staff 3 (MLS 1, Non-MLS 2)
Founded 1966. Enrl 1,243; Fac 44; Highest Degree: Bachelor
Library Holdings: e-books 4,500; Bk Titles 13,000; Per Subs 160
Subject Interests: Acctg, Bus, Computers, Criminal justice, Graphic design, Photog
Automation Activity & Vendor Info: (Cataloging) TLC (The Library Corporation); (Circulation) TLC (The Library Corporation); (Course Reserve) TLC (The Library Corporation); (ILL) TLC (The Library Corporation); (Media Booking) TLC (The Library Corporation); (OPAC) TLC (The Library Corporation); (Serials) TLC (The Library Corporation)
Database Vendor: Hoovers, LexisNexis, ProQuest, Westlaw
Wireless access
Function: Workshops
Publications: A/V's in Briarcliffe College Library (Audio-visual catalog)
Partic in Long Island Library Resources Council
Open Mon-Thurs 8am-10pm, Fri 8-3, Sat 9-4
Departmental Libraries:
PATCHOGUE CAMPUS, 225 W Main St, Patchogue, 11772, SAN 371-8328. Tel: 631-654-5300, 631-730-2006. FAX: 631-654-5082. Web Site: bcl.edu. *Libr Dir,* Andrew Gibson; E-mail: AGibson@bcl.edu; Staff 3 (MLS 1, Non-MLS 2)
Highest Degree: Bachelor
Library Holdings: DVDs 154; Bk Vols 12,428; Per Subs 90
Automation Activity & Vendor Info: (Cataloging) TLC (The Library Corporation); (Circulation) TLC (The Library Corporation)
Database Vendor: CQ Press, LexisNexis, ProQuest, Westlaw
Open Mon-Thurs 8am-10pm, Fri 9-4, Sat 9-2

BINGHAMTON

S BROOME COUNTY HISTORICAL SOCIETY LIBRARY*, Local History Center, Broome County Public Library, 185 Court St, 13901. SAN 310-8643. Tel: 607-778-3572. FAX: 607-778-6429. E-mail: bcpl_localhistory@yahoo.com. Web Site: www.bclibrary.info/history.htm. *Dir,* Lisa Wise; *County Historian,* Gerry Smith; Staff 1 (Non-MLS 1)
Founded 1919
Library Holdings: CDs 250; Bk Vols 7,500; Per Subs 12
Special Collections: Civil War (Mattoon Coll), mss; Daniel S Dickinson, mss; Photographic Coll; Stillson Coll; Uriah Gregory Coll; Whitney Family, papers & mss; William Bingham, mss; William L Ford Coll, 1850-1870
Subject Interests: Archit, Broome County culture, Decorative art, Genealogy, Hist, Histories of NY, New England, Pa, William Bingham
Automation Activity & Vendor Info: (Cataloging) SirsiDynix; (OPAC) SirsiDynix
Wireless access
Open Mon-Thurs 10-8, Fri & Sat 10-4

P BROOME COUNTY PUBLIC LIBRARY*, 185 Court St, 13901-3503. SAN 351-8493. Tel: 607-778-6400. Circulation Tel: 607-778-6410. Reference Tel: 607-778-6451. FAX: 607-778-6429. E-mail: bcpl@bclibrary.info. Web Site: www.bclibrary.info. *Dir,* Lisa Wise; Tel: 607-778-6407, E-mail: lwise@co.broome.ny.us; *Head, Ref,* Sherry Kowalski; Tel: 607-778-6423, E-mail: skowalski@co.broome.ny.us; *Circ Supvr,* Stephen Steflik; *Computer Serv,* Patrick Smith; Tel: 607-343-8244; *ILL,* Patricia Barrett; Tel: 607-778-3571; *Youth Serv,* Sarah Reid; Tel: 607-778-6456; Staff 35 (MLS 5, Non-MLS 30)
Founded 1902. Pop 200,600; Circ 515,943
Library Holdings: Bk Vols 196,207
Special Collections: State Document Depository
Subject Interests: Local hist
Automation Activity & Vendor Info: (Acquisitions) SirsiDynix; (Cataloging) SIRSI WorkFlows; (Circulation) SirsiDynix; (ILL) OCLC; (OPAC) SirsiDynix; (Serials) SirsiDynix
Database Vendor: EBSCOhost, Foundation Center, OCLC WorldShare Interlibrary Loan, ProQuest, ReferenceUSA
Wireless access
Publications: Bibliographies; Calendar of Events
Mem of Four County Library System
Partic in OCLC Online Computer Library Center, Inc; South Central Regional Library Council
Special Services for the Deaf - Adult & family literacy prog; Bks on deafness & sign lang; Sorenson video relay syst
Special Services for the Blind - Bks on CD
Open Mon-Thurs 9-8, Fri & Sat 9-5
Friends of the Library Group

P FENTON FREE LIBRARY*, 1062 Chenango St, 13901-1736. SAN 310-8651. Tel: 607-724-8649. *Dir,* Pam Klesse
Founded 1936. Pop 7,040; Circ 74,948
Library Holdings: Bk Vols 17,769
Wireless access
Publications: Dictionary Guide to Services Offered at the Moody Memorial Library; What's New (Newsletter)
Mem of Four County Library System
Open Mon-Thurs 1-8, Fri & Sat 10-4

GL NYS SUPREME COURT LIBRARY - BINGHAMTON*, Broome County Courthouse, Rm 107, 92 Court St, 13901-3301. SAN 310-8716. Tel: 607-778-2119. FAX: 212-457-2958. E-mail: binglawlib@courts.state.ny.us. Web Site: www.nycourts.gov/6jd/countymaps/law/brmlaw/brmlaw.html. *Dir,* Judy A Lauer; E-mail: jlauer@courts.state.ny.us; Staff 3 (MLS 1, Non-MLS 2)
Founded 1859
Library Holdings: Bk Titles 7,500; Bk Vols 60,000; Per Subs 270
Subject Interests: Bankruptcy, Criminal, Criminal practice & procedure, Domestic relations, NY Fed case law, NYS & Fed statutory law

Automation Activity & Vendor Info: (Acquisitions) SirsiDynix; (Cataloging) SirsiDynix; (Circulation) SirsiDynix; (ILL) OCLC; (OPAC) SirsiDynix; (Serials) SirsiDynix
Database Vendor: LexisNexis, SirsiDynix, Westlaw
Wireless access
Partic in South Central Regional Library Council
Open Mon-Fri 9-5

M OUR LADY OF LOURDES MEMORIAL HOSPITAL LIBRARY*, Lourdes Library, 169 Riverside Dr, 13905. SAN 373-5990. Tel: 607-798-5290. FAX: 607-798-5989. Web Site: www.lourdes.com. *Librn,* Susan Bretscher; E-mail: sbretscher@lourdes.com; Staff 2 (MLS 1, Non-MLS 1)
Library Holdings: AV Mats 100; Bk Titles 1,500; Per Subs 35
Automation Activity & Vendor Info: (Cataloging) CyberTools for Libraries; (Circulation) CyberTools for Libraries; (OPAC) CyberTools for Libraries; (Serials) CyberTools for Libraries
Database Vendor: EBSCOhost, OVID Technologies, PubMed, STAT!Ref (Teton Data Systems)
Wireless access
Partic in Basic Health Sciences Library Network; National Network of Libraries of Medicine South Central Region; OCLC-LVIS
Open Mon-Fri 8-4:30

C STATE UNIVERSITY OF NEW YORK AT BINGHAMTON*, University Libraries, Vestal Pkwy E, 13902. (Mail add: PO Box 6012, 13902-6012), SAN 351-8671. Circulation Tel: 607-777-2194. Interlibrary Loan Service Tel: 607-777-4985. Reference Tel: 607-777-2345. Administration Tel: 607-777-4841. FAX: 607-777-4848. Interlibrary Loan Service FAX: 607-777-4347. Web Site: library.lib.binghamton.edu. *Dean of Libr,* John M Meador, Jr; Tel: 607-777-2346, E-mail: jmeador@binghamton.edu; Staff 79 (MLS 24, Non-MLS 55)
Founded 1946. Enrl 14,746; Fac 680; Highest Degree: Doctorate
Jul 2011-Jun 2012 Income (Main and Other College/University Libraries) $10,151,979, State $9,640,208. Mats Exp $5,303,072, Books $926,076, Per/Ser (Incl. Access Fees) $4,040,367, Presv $81,359. Sal $4,333,592
Library Holdings: AV Mats 126,483; CDs 6,714; DVDs 2,942; e-books 958,614; e-journals 58,514; Microforms 1,877,590; Music Scores 22,520; Bk Titles 2,139,710; Bk Vols 2,457,872; Videos 2,042
Special Collections: Civil War Coll; Edwin A & Marion Clayton Link Coll; Frances R Conole Archive of Recorded Sound; Max Reinhardt Archives & Library; Vera Beaudin Saeedpour Kurdish Library & Museum Coll; William J Haggerty Coll of French Colonial History; Yi-t'ung Wang Coll & East Asian Coll. State Document Depository; US Document Depository
Automation Activity & Vendor Info: (Acquisitions) Ex Libris Group; (Cataloging) Ex Libris Group; (Circulation) Ex Libris Group; (Course Reserve) Blackboard Inc; (ILL) OCLC ILLiad; (OPAC) Ex Libris Group; (Serials) Ex Libris Group
Database Vendor: ABC-CLIO, ACM (Association for Computing Machinery), Agricola, Alexander Street Press, American Chemical Society, American Mathematical Society, American Psychological Association (APA), Annual Reviews, ARTstor, Baker & Taylor, BioOne, Bowker, Cambridge Scientific Abstracts, Community of Science (COS), Coutts Information Service, CQ Press, Dialog, Dun & Bradstreet, EBSCO - WebFeat, EBSCO Information Services, EBSCOhost, Elsevier, Elsevier MDL, Emerald, Ex Libris Group, Factiva.com, Facts on File, H W Wilson, IEEE (Institute of Electrical & Electronics Engineers), Innovative Interfaces, Inc, IOP, ISI Web of Knowledge, JSTOR, LexisNexis, Marcive, Inc, Modern Language Association, Nature Publishing Group, Newsbank, OCLC FirstSearch, OCLC WorldShare Interlibrary Loan, OCLC-RLG, OVID Technologies, P4 Performance Management, Inc, ProQuest, PubMed, Safari Books Online, ScienceDirect, SerialsSolutions, Standard & Poor's, STN International, Swets Information Services, TLC (The Library Corporation), Wilson - Wilson Web, YBP Library Services
Wireless access
Partic in Center for Research Libraries; Coalition for Networked Information (CNI); Information Delivery Services Project (IDS); Inter-University Consortium for Political & Social Research (ICPSR); Lyrasis; Northeast Research Libraries Consortium (NERL); Scholarly Publ & Acad Resources Coalition; South Central Regional Library Council; SUNYConnect; Westchester Academic Library Directors Organization (WALDO)
Special Services for the Blind - Premier adaptive tech software; Reader equip; ZoomText magnification & reading software

Departmental Libraries:

LIBRARY ANNEX AT CONKLIN, 400 Corporate Pkwy, Conklin, 13748. Tel: 607-775-8364. FAX: 607-775-8339. *Asst Dir, Access Serv,* Ronnie Goldberg; Tel: 607-777-2325, E-mail: rgoldber@binghamton.edu

SCIENCE LIBRARY, Vestal Pkwy E, 13902, SAN 351-8760. Tel: 607-777-2166. FAX: 607-777-2274. *Dir, Pub Serv,* Jill Dixon; Tel: 607-777-3510, Fax: 607-777-4848, E-mail: jdixon@binghamton.edu

UNIVERSITY DOWNTOWN CENTER LIBRARY INFORMATION COMMONS & SERVICES, 67 Washington St, 13902-6000. Tel: 607-777-9225. FAX: 607-777-9136. *Coordr, Info Commons,* David Vose; Tel: 607-777-9275, E-mail: dvose@binghamton.edu

J SUNY BROOME COMMUNITY COLLEGE, Cecil C Tyrrell Library, 907 Front St, 13905-1328. (Mail add: PO Box 1017, 13902-1017), SAN 310-8635. Tel: 607-778-5020. Interlibrary Loan Service Tel: 607-778-5376. Reference Tel: 607-778-5043. Administration Tel: 607-778-5045, 607-778-5201. FAX: 607-778-5108. Interlibrary Loan Service FAX: 607-778-5552. E-mail: reference1@sunybroome.edu. Web Site: www.sunybroome.edu/library. *Dir, LRC/LAD,* Robin Petrus; E-mail: petrusre@sunybroome.edu; *Librn,* Deborah Spanfelner; Tel: 607-778-5239, E-mail: spanfelnerdl@sunybroome.edu; *Electronic Res Librn,* Sue Sliven; Tel: 607-778-5701, E-mail: slivansj@sunybroome.edu; *Ref Librn,* Karen Pitcher; Tel: 607-778-5468, E-mail: pitcherkl@sunybroome.edu; *Syst Librn,* Amanda Hollister; Tel: 607-778-5609, E-mail: hollisteraj@sunybroome.edu. Subject Specialists: *Eng,* Robin Petrus; *Liberal arts,* Deborah Spanfelner; *Bus, Fine arts, Music,* Sue Sliven; *Health sci,* Karen Pitcher; *Bio, Chem, Sports,* Amanda Hollister; Staff 6 (MLS 6)
Founded 1947. Enrl 5,700; Fac 141; Highest Degree: Associate
Library Holdings: CDs 560; DVDs 800; e-books 70,676; Bk Vols 58,000; Per Subs 174; Talking Bks 268; Videos 2,847
Special Collections: Community College Education
Subject Interests: Eng, Health sci, Liberal arts, Tech
Automation Activity & Vendor Info: (Cataloging) Ex Libris Group; (Circulation) Ex Libris Group; (Course Reserve) Ex Libris Group; (ILL) Ex Libris Group; (OPAC) Ex Libris Group
Database Vendor: Cinahl, EBSCOhost, Elsevier MDL, Gale Cengage Learning, OCLC WorldShare Interlibrary Loan, ScienceDirect
Wireless access
Function: 24/7 Electronic res, 24/7 Online cat, Accessibility serv available based on individual needs, Chess club, Computers for patron use, Copy machines, E-Reserves, Electronic databases & coll
Partic in South Central Regional Library Council; Westchester Academic Library Directors Organization (WALDO)
Special Services for the Deaf - Assistive tech; Closed caption videos; Sign lang interpreter upon request for prog; Video & TTY relay via computer
Open Mon-Thurs 7:30am-10pm, Fri 7:30-5, Sat 1-5, Sun 3-7
Restriction: Co libr, ID required to use computers (Ltd hrs), Open to pub for ref & circ; with some limitations, Open to students, fac & staff

SR UNITARIAN UNIVERSALIST CONGREGATION*, Margaret Jackson Memorial Library, 183 Riverside Dr, 13905. SAN 310-8724. Tel: 607-729-1641. FAX: 607-729-1899. E-mail: office@uubinghamton.org. Web Site: www.uubinghamton.org. *Chairperson,* Janet Landow
Founded 1891
Library Holdings: Bk Vols 3,000
Special Collections: 19th Century Universalism & Unitarianism; Church Archives; Unitarian Universalist Sermons
Subject Interests: Philos, Sociol, Theol
Open Sun 9-12

BLACK RIVER

P SALLY PLOOF HUNTER MEMORIAL LIBRARY*, 101 Public Works Dr, 13612. SAN 310-8732. Tel: 315-773-5163. FAX: 315-775-1224. Web Site: www.sallyploofhunterlibrary.org. *Libr Mgr,* Sandra Lamb
Founded 1915. Pop 1,349; Circ 23,247
Library Holdings: Bk Titles 6,100; Bk Vols 6,700
Automation Activity & Vendor Info: (Circulation) SirsiDynix
Wireless access
Mem of North Country Library System
Open Mon & Fri 1-5, Tues & Thurs 10-12 & 2-8, Wed 1-8, Sat 10-3

BLAUVELT

P BLAUVELT FREE LIBRARY*, 541 Western Hwy, 10913. SAN 310-8740. Tel: 845-359-2811. FAX: 845-398-0017. E-mail: blv@rcls.org. Web Site: www.rcls.org/blv. *Dir,* Mary E Behringer; *Ch Serv, YA Serv,* Marybeth Darnobid; *ILL,* Irene Schutz; *Ref Serv,* Tonie Ann D'Angelo; *Tech Serv,* Susan Kessell; Staff 13 (MLS 4, Non-MLS 9)
Founded 1909. Pop 5,207; Circ 62,381
Library Holdings: Bk Titles 63,000; Per Subs 417; Talking Bks 1,023
Special Collections: Area History; Blauvelt Family History; Genealogy (Blauvelt); Local History (Budke Coll)
Automation Activity & Vendor Info: (Cataloging) Horizon; (Circulation) Horizon; (OPAC) Horizon; (Serials) Horizon
Wireless access
Mem of Ramapo Catskill Library System
Open Mon-Thurs 10-9, Fri 10-5, Sat 11-5, Sun 1-5
Friends of the Library Group

C DOMINICAN COLLEGE LIBRARY*, 480 Western Hwy, 10913-2000. SAN 310-8759. Tel: 845-848-7505. FAX: 845-359-2525. Web Site: www.dc.edu. *Dir,* John Barrie; *Cat, Electronic Res,* Amy Haase-Thomas; *Per,* Virginia Dunne; *Pub Serv,* Sam Heye; *Tech Serv,* Maureen O'Keeffe; Staff 5 (MLS 5)
Founded 1957. Enrl 1,214; Fac 78; Highest Degree: Bachelor
Library Holdings: e-books 35,000; e-journals 22,000; Bk Vols 100,000; Per Subs 400
Automation Activity & Vendor Info: (Cataloging) SirsiDynix; (Circulation) SirsiDynix; (OPAC) SirsiDynix
Database Vendor: EBSCOhost, Gale Cengage Learning, OCLC FirstSearch, ProQuest, Wilson - Wilson Web
Wireless access
Partic in Southeastern New York Library Resources Council
Open Mon-Thurs 8am-10pm, Fri 8-7, Sat & Sun 12-7

BLISS

P EAGLE FREE LIBRARY*, 3413 School St, 14024. SAN 310-8767. Tel: 585-322-7701. FAX: 585-322-7701. *Dir,* Linda Lavery; E-mail: llavery@pls-net.org
Pop 1,211; Circ 8,375
Library Holdings: Bk Vols 10,000
Automation Activity & Vendor Info: (Cataloging) SirsiDynix; (Circulation) SirsiDynix; (OPAC) SirsiDynix
Wireless access
Mem of Pioneer Library System
Open Mon 3-6, Wed 9-12 & 6-9, Thurs 1-5, Fri 4-7, Sat 9:30-1:30

BLOOMFIELD

P ALLENS HILL FREE LIBRARY*, 3818 County Rd 40, 14469. SAN 311-3191. Tel: 585-229-5636. FAX: 585-229-5636. E-mail: AllenshillLibraryDirector@owwl.org. *Mgr,* Beth Gladding
Founded 1883. Pop 311; Circ 5,933
Library Holdings: Audiobooks 376; e-books 5; Electronic Media & Resources 26; Bk Titles 7,921; Per Subs 45; Videos 759
Wireless access
Mem of Pioneer Library System
Open Tues 2-5:30, Wed 6-8, Fri 2:30-8, Sat 1-4, Sun (Oct-April) 12-3

P BLOOMFIELD PUBLIC LIBRARY*, Nine Church St, 14469. (Mail add: PO Box 158, East Bloomfield, 14443-0158), SAN 311-1385. Tel: 585-657-6264. FAX: 585-657-6038. E-mail: bloomfieldlibrary@owwl.org. Web Site: bloomfieldpubliclibrary.wordpress.com. *Dir,* Laurie Newell; Staff 3 (Non-MLS 3)
Founded 1968. Pop 3,361
Jan 2005-Dec 2005 Income $162,390, State $5,357, City $139,464, Federal $215, County $5,795, Locally Generated Income $10,983, Other $576. Mats Exp $22,987, Books $16,141, Per/Ser (Incl. Access Fees) $2,376, AV Mat $4,470. Sal $75,463
Library Holdings: Bk Vols 19,184; Per Subs 50; Talking Bks 740; Videos 1,191
Automation Activity & Vendor Info: (Circulation) SirsiDynix; (OPAC) SirsiDynix
Database Vendor: EBSCOhost, Gale Cengage Learning, LearningExpress, OCLC WorldShare Interlibrary Loan
Wireless access
Function: Handicapped accessible, ILL available, Photocopying/Printing, Prog for adults, Prog for children & young adult, Ref serv available, Serves mentally handicapped consumers, Summer reading prog, Telephone ref, Wheelchair accessible
Open Mon, Wed & Thurs 2:30-8:30, Tues 10-12 & 2:30-8:30, Fri 2:30-6:30, Sat 10-2
Friends of the Library Group

BLUE MOUNTAIN LAKE

S ADIRONDACK MUSEUM LIBRARY*, Rte 28N & 30, 12812. SAN 310-8783. Tel: 518-352-7311. FAX: 518-352-7653. Web Site: www.adkmuseum.org. *Librn,* Jerold Pepper; E-mail: jpepper@adkmuseum.org
Founded 1956
Library Holdings: Bk Titles 10,000; Per Subs 95
Special Collections: Adirondack Park Agency Coll; Association for the Protection of the Adirondacks Archives; Augustus D Shephard Architectural Plans & Drawings; Emporium Co Forestry Coll; McIntyre Iron Co Papers; Photographs Coll; W H H Adirondack Murray Papers
Subject Interests: Art, Conserv, Early 20th Centuries, Ecology, Econ life, Emphasis on 19th centuries, Lumbering, Parks, Recreation, Soc
Partic in Northern New York Library Network
Open Mon-Fri 9-5

BLUE POINT

P BAYPORT-BLUE POINT PUBLIC LIBRARY*, 203 Blue Point Ave, 11715-1217. SAN 310-8791. Tel: 631-363-6133. FAX: 631-363-6133. E-mail: bprtlib@suffolk.lib.ny.us. Web Site: bprt.suffolk.lib.ny.us/. *Dir,* Position Currently Open; *Head, Ref,* Jocelyn McIntee; *Head, YA,* Kate Riley; *Ch Serv,* Elizabeth Walsh; Staff 9 (MLS 8, Non-MLS 1)
Founded 1938. Pop 13,355; Circ 172,471
Library Holdings: Bk Vols 110,412; Per Subs 378
Subject Interests: Local hist
Automation Activity & Vendor Info: (Acquisitions) Innovative Interfaces, Inc; (Cataloging) Innovative Interfaces, Inc; (Circulation) Innovative Interfaces, Inc; (OPAC) Innovative Interfaces, Inc
Database Vendor: Innovative Interfaces, Inc
Wireless access
Publications: Newsletter (bi-monthly)
Mem of Suffolk Cooperative Library System
Open Mon-Fri 10-9, Sat 10-5, Sun (Sept-June) 1-5
Friends of the Library Group

BOHEMIA

P CONNETQUOT PUBLIC LIBRARY, 760 Ocean Ave, 11716. SAN 310-8805. Tel: 631-567-5079. FAX: 631-567-5137. Web Site: www.connetquotlibrary.org. *Dir,* Kimberly DeCristofaro; E-mail: kdecrist@suffolk.lib.ny.us; *Asst Dir,* Jason Ladick; E-mail: jrladick@connetquotlibrary.org; Staff 58.5 (MLS 23, Non-MLS 35.5)
Founded 1974. Pop 40,162; Circ 384,223
Jul 2012-Jun 2013 Income $5,511,159. Mats Exp $5,898,790. Sal $2,991,056
Library Holdings: Bk Vols 253,558; Per Subs 457
Automation Activity & Vendor Info: (Acquisitions) SirsiDynix; (Cataloging) SirsiDynix; (Circulation) SirsiDynix; (OPAC) SirsiDynix; (Serials) SirsiDynix
Database Vendor: Baker & Taylor, EBSCOhost, Overdrive, Inc, ReferenceUSA, SirsiDynix, World Book Online
Wireless access
Publications: Newsletter (Quarterly)
Mem of Suffolk Cooperative Library System
Open Mon-Fri 9-9, Sat 9-5, Sun (Oct-May) 1-5

BOLIVAR

P BOLIVAR FREE LIBRARY*, 390 Main St, 14715-0512. SAN 310-8813. Tel: 585-928-2015. FAX: 585-928-2015. E-mail: bolivar_1898@yahoo.com. Web Site: www.bolivarfreelibrary.com. *Libr Dir,* Frances Dean; E-mail: deanf@stls.org; *Asst Dir,* Sue Griggs
Founded 1898. Pop 1,200; Circ 15,000
Library Holdings: Bk Vols 10,000
Special Collections: 19th Century New York & Pennsylvania Oilfield Histories; Local Newspaper, 1892-1965
Subject Interests: Contemporary, Fiction, Mystery, Romances
Wireless access
Mem of Southern Tier Library System
Special Services for the Blind - Bks on cassette; Bks on CD; Large print & cassettes
Open Mon, Wed & Thurs 6pm-8pm, Tues 12:30-4:30, Fri 9:30-4:30, Sat 12:30-3:30
Friends of the Library Group
Bookmobiles: 1

BOLTON LANDING

P BOLTON FREE LIBRARY*, 4922 Lakeshore Dr, 12814. (Mail add: PO Box 389, 12814-0389). Tel: 518-644-2233. FAX: 518-644-2233. Web Site: www.boltonfreelibrary.blogspot.com. *Dir,* Megan W Baker; E-mail: mbaker@sals.edu; Staff 1 (Non-MLS 1)
Founded 1906. Pop 2,100; Circ 55,000
Dec 2005-Nov 2006 Income $64,050, Provincial $1,600, City $30,000, County $4,700, Other $27,750. Mats Exp $11,000, Books $8,500, Per/Ser (Incl. Access Fees) $1,000, AV Mat $1,500. Sal $27,500 (Prof $25,000)
Library Holdings: AV Mats 2,550; Bk Titles 19,000; Per Subs 35
Special Collections: Adirondack Books (Roden Coll); Art Books (David Smith Coll)
Automation Activity & Vendor Info: (Cataloging) Innovative Interfaces, Inc; (Circulation) Innovative Interfaces, Inc; (OPAC) Innovative Interfaces, Inc; (Serials) Innovative Interfaces, Inc
Wireless access
Function: Adult bk club, Audiobks via web, AV serv, Bk club(s), Bks on cassette, Bks on CD, Children's prog, Computer training, Computers for patron use, Copy machines, E-Reserves, Electronic databases & coll, Fax serv, Free DVD rentals, Handicapped accessible, Home delivery & serv to Sr ctr & nursing homes, Homebound delivery serv, ILL available, Magnifiers for reading, Mail & tel request accepted, Mail loans to mem, Online cat, Online info literacy tutorials on the web & in blackboard, Online ref, Online searches, Outside serv via phone, mail, e-mail & web,

Photocopying/Printing, Preschool outreach, Prog for adults, Prog for children & young adult, Ref & res, Ref serv available, Spoken cassettes & CDs, Spoken cassettes & DVDs, Summer reading prog, Tax forms, Telephone ref, VHS videos, Video lending libr, Web-catalog, Wheelchair accessible, Workshops
Mem of Southern Adirondack Library System; Southern Adirondack Library System
Open Tues, Wed & Fri 10-6, Thurs 10-8, Sat 10-4
Friends of the Library Group

BOONVILLE

P ERWIN LIBRARY & INSTITUTE*, 104 Schuyler St, 13309. SAN 310-883X. Tel: 315-942-4834. FAX: 315-942-5629. E-mail: boonville@midyork.org. *Co-Dir,* LeeAnn Riley; *Co-Dir,* Donna Ripp; E-mail: dripp@midyork.org
Founded 1885. Pop 5,000; Circ 31,541
Library Holdings: Bk Titles 16,431; Per Subs 59
Special Collections: Edmund Wilson Children's Books; Edmund Wilson Puppet Coll; Walter D Edmond's Film & Book Coll
Automation Activity & Vendor Info: (Cataloging) SirsiDynix; (Circulation) SirsiDynix; (OPAC) SirsiDynix
Wireless access
Mem of Mid-York Library System
Open Mon & Fri 10-5 & 7-9, Tues & Thurs 10-5, Sat 10-1

BOSTON

P BOSTON FREE LIBRARY*, 9475 Boston State Rd, 14025-9768. (Mail add: PO Box 200, 14025-0200), SAN 310-8848. Tel: 716-941-3516. FAX: 716-941-0941. Web Site: www.buffalolib.org/. *Librn,* Laura McLeod
Pop 7,000; Circ 28,000
Library Holdings: Bk Vols 18,000; Per Subs 50
Mem of Buffalo & Erie County Public Library System
Open Mon 11-5 & 6:30-8:30, Tues & Thurs 1-5 & 6:30-8:30, Wed & Sat 10-1, Fri 1-5

BOVINA CENTER

P BOVINA LIBRARY ASSOCIATION, 33 Maple Ave, 13740. (Mail add: PO Box 38, 13740-0038), SAN 310-8856. Tel: 607-832-4884. FAX: 607-832-4884. E-mail: bovinalib@delhitel.net. Web Site: www.bovinalibrary.org/bovina. *Libr Dir,* Mary Pelletier
Founded 1918. Pop 550; Circ 3,938
Library Holdings: Bk Vols 8,000; Per Subs 50
Wireless access
Mem of Four County Library System
Open Tues & Thurs (Winter) 10:30-3, Wed 1-8, Sat 9-1; Tues (Summer) 3:30-8:30, Wed 1-8, Thurs 10:30-3, Sat 9-1

BRANCHPORT

P MODESTE BEDIENT MEMORIAL LIBRARY*, Branchport Library, 3699 State Rte 54A, 14418. SAN 310-8864. Tel: 315-595-2899. FAX: 315-595-2899. Web Site: www.branchportlibrary.org. *Dir,* Karen McKerlie; E-mail: mckerliek@stls.org
Founded 1913. Pop 3,908; Circ 7,353
Library Holdings: DVDs 300; Large Print Bks 800; Bk Vols 9,366
Automation Activity & Vendor Info: (Cataloging) SirsiDynix; (Circulation) SirsiDynix; (OPAC) SirsiDynix; (Serials) SirsiDynix
Wireless access
Mem of Southern Tier Library System
Open Tues 2-8, Wed 1-8, Fri 10-6, Sat 9-1

BRANT LAKE

P HORICON FREE PUBLIC LIBRARY*, 6604 State Rte 8, 12815. (Mail add: PO Box 185, 12815-0185), SAN 376-3153. Tel: 518-494-4189. FAX: 518-494-3852. *Dir,* Linda Hoyt
Library Holdings: Bk Vols 11,568; Per Subs 27
Special Collections: Adirondacks
Wireless access
Mem of Southern Adirondack Library System
Open Mon & Thurs 2-8, Tues 12-5, Sat 10-1
Friends of the Library Group

BRENTWOOD

P BRENTWOOD PUBLIC LIBRARY*, 34 Second Ave, 11717. SAN 310-8872. Tel: 631-273-7883. FAX: 631-273-7896. TDD: 631-273-9831. E-mail: brenref@suffolk.lib.ny.us. Web Site: brentwood.suffolk.lib.ny.us. *Dir,* Thomas A Tarantowicz; Staff 23 (MLS 23)
Founded 1937. Pop 70,000
Library Holdings: Large Print Bks 3,504; Bk Titles 279,778; Per Subs 553
Special Collections: Brentwood History (Verne Dyson Historical Coll), bks, mss, photogs
Automation Activity & Vendor Info: (Acquisitions) Innovative Interfaces, Inc; (Cataloging) Innovative Interfaces, Inc; (Circulation) Innovative Interfaces, Inc; (OPAC) Innovative Interfaces, Inc
Wireless access
Publications: Newsletter
Special Services for the Deaf - High interest/low vocabulary bks; TTY equip
Open Mon-Fri 9-9, Sat 9-5, Sun 12-4

J SUFFOLK COUNTY COMMUNITY COLLEGE*, Grant Campus Library, 1001 Crooked Hill Rd, 11717. SAN 351-8825. Tel: 631-851-6740. Interlibrary Loan Service Tel: 516-434-6504. FAX: 631-851-6509. Web Site: www.sunysuffolk.edu/Web/West/Library. *Head of Libr,* Dr David J Quinn; E-mail: quinnd@sunysuffolk.edu; *Circ, ILL, Reader Serv,* Joyce Gabriele; *AV,* Kevin Peterman; *Per,* Francis Parrella; *Reader Serv, Ref,* Gerald Reminick; Staff 6 (MLS 6)
Founded 1974. Enrl 7,100; Fac 125
Library Holdings: Bk Titles 47,000; Per Subs 300
Publications: Faculty handbook, newsletter, student handbook
Partic in New York State Interlibrary Loan Network (NYSILL)

BREWSTER

P BREWSTER PUBLIC LIBRARY*, 79 Main St, 10509. SAN 310-8899. Tel: 845-279-6421. FAX: 845-279-0043. E-mail: brewsterlibrary@yahoo.com. Web Site: www.brewsterlibrary.org. *Dir,* Maria Steinberg; *Ch Serv,* Lynn Lamont; Staff 6 (MLS 1, Non-MLS 5)
Founded 1896. Pop 17,000; Circ 58,000
Library Holdings: Bk Vols 29,000; Per Subs 100
Special Collections: Oral History
Wireless access
Mem of Mid-Hudson Library System
Open Mon & Wed 9-7, Tues & Thurs 1-7, Fri 9-4, Sat 10-2

BRIARCLIFF MANOR

P BRIARCLIFF MANOR PUBLIC LIBRARY*, One Library Rd, 10510. SAN 310-8910. Tel: 914-941-7072. FAX: 914-941-7091. Web Site: www.briarcliffmanorlibrary.org. *Dir,* Geraldine Mahoney; Tel: 914-733-3610, E-mail: gmahoney@wlsmail.org; *Ch, Teen Librn,* Amy Kaplan; Tel: 914-733-3612, E-mail: abgkaplan@gmail.com; *Ref Librn,* Shelley Glick; E-mail: sglick@wlsmail.org
Founded 1959. Pop 7,622; Circ 96,000
Library Holdings: AV Mats 2,500; Large Print Bks 550; Bk Titles 31,000; Per Subs 72; Talking Bks 700
Subject Interests: Art
Automation Activity & Vendor Info: (Cataloging) SirsiDynix; (Circulation) SirsiDynix; (OPAC) SirsiDynix; (Serials) SirsiDynix
Wireless access
Function: AV serv, ILL available, Photocopying/Printing, Prog for adults, Prog for children & young adult, Ref serv available, Summer reading prog, Telephone ref, Workshops
Mem of Westchester Library System
Open Mon (Winter) 10-6, Tues & Thurs 10-8, Wed, Fri & Sat 10-5; Mon (Summer) 10-6, Tues & Thurs 10-9, Wed & Fri 10-5, Sat 10-3
Friends of the Library Group

BRIDGEHAMPTON

P THE HAMPTON LIBRARY*, 2478 Main St, 11932. (Mail add: PO Box 3025, 11932-3025), SAN 310-8945. Tel: 631-537-0015. FAX: 631-537-7229. E-mail: bridlib@suffolk.lib.ny.us. Web Site: www.hamptonlibrary.org. *Libr Dir,* Position Currently Open; *Head, Ch,* Emily Herrick; E-mail: hljuv@suffolk.lib.ny.us; *Head, Circ,* Christine King; *Ref/YA,* Marcia Mitrowski; E-mail: hlya@suffolk.lib.ny.us; *Tech Serv,* Judith Iwanickyj; Staff 8 (MLS 2, Non-MLS 6)
Founded 1877. Pop 1,866; Circ 58,452
Library Holdings: AV Mats 4,431; Electronic Media & Resources 67; Bk Vols 33,671; Per Subs 71; Talking Bks 1,609
Special Collections: Long Island Coll
Automation Activity & Vendor Info: (Acquisitions) Innovative Interfaces, Inc - Millenium; (Cataloging) PALS; (Circulation) PALS; (Course Reserve) Innovative Interfaces, Inc; (ILL) PALS; (OPAC) PALS
Wireless access
Function: Audio & video playback equip for onsite use, Audiobks via web, Bk club(s), Bk reviews (Group), Bks on CD, Children's prog, Computer training, Copy machines, Digital talking bks, e-mail serv, E-Reserves, Fax serv, Free DVD rentals, Holiday prog, Homebound delivery serv, ILL available, Music CDs, Online ref, OverDrive digital audio bks, Prog for adults, Prog for children & young adult, Pub access computers, Scanner, Story hour, Summer reading prog, Tax forms, Teen prog
Mem of Suffolk Cooperative Library System

Open Mon-Thurs 9:30-7, Fri & Sat 9:30-5, Sun 1-5
Friends of the Library Group

BRIDGEWATER

P BRIDGEWATER FREE LIBRARY*, 404 Pritchard Ave, 13313. (Mail add: PO Box 372, 13313-0372), SAN 310-8953. Tel: 315-822-6475. E-mail: bridgewater@midyork.org. *Mgr,* Janet Tilbe
Pop 940; Circ 5,600
Library Holdings: Bk Vols 2,100
Wireless access
Mem of Mid-York Library System
Open Tues & Thurs 10-12, 1-3 & 6-8:30, Wed 10-12 & 1-3, Sat 9-12

BRIGHTWATERS

P BAY SHORE-BRIGHTWATERS PUBLIC LIBRARY*, One S Country Rd, 11718-1517. SAN 310-8961. Tel: 631-665-4350. Information Services Tel: 631-665-0100. FAX: 631-665-4958. E-mail: bsbwlib@suffolk.lib.ny.us. Web Site: bayshore.suffolk.lib.ny.us. *Dir,* Eileen J Kavanagh; *Asst Dir,* Rodney Marve; *Adult Serv,* Colleen Smisek; *Ch Serv,* Linda J Clark; Staff 10 (MLS 10)
Founded 1901. Pop 32,263; Circ 205,374
Jul 2005-Jun 2006 Income $2,447,834. Mats Exp $249,682. Sal $1,303,291
Library Holdings: Bk Titles 128,178; Bk Vols 139,252; Per Subs 620
Special Collections: Long Island, ESL Coll
Subject Interests: Compact discs, Music scores
Automation Activity & Vendor Info: (Acquisitions) TLC (The Library Corporation); (Cataloging) TLC (The Library Corporation); (Circulation) TLC (The Library Corporation); (Course Reserve) TLC (The Library Corporation); (ILL) TLC (The Library Corporation); (Media Booking) TLC (The Library Corporation); (OPAC) TLC (The Library Corporation); (Serials) TLC (The Library Corporation)
Mem of Suffolk Cooperative Library System
Special Services for the Blind - Bks on cassette
Open Mon, Tues & Thurs 10-9, Wed 1-9, Fri 10-6, Sat 10-5, Sun (Oct-May) 1-5
Friends of the Library Group

BROCKPORT

P SEYMOUR LIBRARY*, 161 East Ave, 14420-1987. SAN 310-8996. Tel: 585-637-1050. FAX: 585-637-1051. Web Site: www.seymourlibraryweb.org. *Dir,* Position Currently Open; *Circ Supvr, Interim Dir,* Patty Good; *Ch,* Kathleen Phillips; *Teen Serv Coordr,* Christine Daily; Staff 13 (MLS 1, Non-MLS 12)
Founded 1936. Pop 19,788
Jan 2005-Dec 2005 Income $435,669
Library Holdings: AV Mats 8,877; Bk Titles 65,371; Per Subs 100
Special Collections: Books on the Erie Canal
Automation Activity & Vendor Info: (Circulation) CARL.Solution (TLC); (OPAC) CARL.Solution (TLC)
Wireless access
Function: Archival coll, AV serv, For res purposes, Games & aids for the handicapped, Govt ref serv, Handicapped accessible, ILL available, Newsp ref libr, Photocopying/Printing, Prog for children & young adult, Ref serv available, Serves mentally handicapped consumers, Summer reading prog, Wheelchair accessible
Mem of Monroe County Library System
Open Mon-Wed 10-9, Thurs & Fri 10-6, Sat 10-3
Friends of the Library Group

C STATE UNIVERSITY OF NEW YORK COLLEGE AT BROCKPORT*, Drake Memorial Library, 350 New Campus Dr, 14420-2997. SAN 351-885X. Tel: 585-395-2140. Circulation Tel: 585-395-2277. Interlibrary Loan Service Tel: 585-395-2727. Reference Tel: 585-395-2760. Automation Services Tel: 585-395-2508. Information Services Tel: 585-395-5667. FAX: 585-395-5651. Web Site: www.brockport.edu/library/. *Dir,* Mary Jo Orzech; E-mail: morzech@brockport.edu; *Head, Integrated Pub Serv,* Pamela O'Sullivan; Tel: 585-395-5688, E-mail: posulliv@brockport.edu; *Head, Libr Tech,* Robert Cushman; Tel: 585-395-2032, E-mail: rcushman@brockport.edu; *Head, Tech Serv,* Jennifer Smathers; Tel: 585-395-2151, E-mail: jsmather@brockport.edu; *Librn,* Debra Ames; Tel: 585-395-2142, E-mail: dames@brockport.edu; *Emerging Tech Librn,* Logan Rath; Tel: 585-395-2568, E-mail: lrath@brockport.edu; *Info Literacy, Instrul Serv Librn, Res Serv,* Jennifer Little; Tel: 585-395-2482, E-mail: jlittle@brockport.edu; *MetroCenter Librn,* Linda Hacker; Tel: 585-395-2770, E-mail: lhacker@brockport.edu; *Ser Librn,* Susan Perry; Tel: 585-395-5811, E-mail: sperry@brockport.edu; *Syst Librn,* Patricia Maxwell; Tel: 585-395-2578, E-mail: pmaxwell@brockport.edu; *Archivist,* Mary Jo Gigliotti; Tel: 585-395-5834, E-mail: mgigliot@brockport.edu; *Govt Doc, Ref Serv,* Lori Lampert; Tel: 585-395-5191, E-mail: llampert@brockport.edu; *ILL,* Kim Myers; E-mail: kmyers@brockport.edu; *Ref Serv,* Charles Cowling; E-mail: ccowling@brockport.edu; *Ref Serv,* Gregory Toth; Tel: 585-395-2450, E-mail: gtoth@brockport.edu; Staff 15 (MLS 15)
Founded 1835. Enrl 8,492; Fac 301; Highest Degree: Master
Library Holdings: e-books 3,690; e-journals 14,822; Bk Vols 642,650; Per Subs 1,910; Videos 7,678
Special Collections: State Document Depository
Subject Interests: Dance, Educ, English lit, Hist
Automation Activity & Vendor Info: (Acquisitions) Ex Libris Group; (Cataloging) Ex Libris Group; (Circulation) Ex Libris Group; (Course Reserve) Ex Libris Group; (OPAC) Ex Libris Group; (Serials) SerialsSolutions
Wireless access
Partic in OCLC Online Computer Library Center, Inc; Rochester Regional Library Council
Open Mon-Thurs 7:45am-1:45am, Fri 7:45-7:45, Sat 10-5, Sun 11am-1:45am

BROCTON

P AHIRA HALL MEMORIAL LIBRARY*, 37 W Main, 14716-9747. (Mail add: PO Box Q, 14716-0676), SAN 310-9003. Tel: 716-792-9418. FAX: 716-792-7334. E-mail: ahiralib@yahoo.com. Web Site: www.cclslib.org/brocton. *Dir,* Ruth Dorogi
Founded 1903. Circ 23,600
Library Holdings: Bk Vols 15,000; Per Subs 30
Mem of Chautauqua-Cattaraugus Library System
Open Mon-Thurs 1-5 & 7-9, Fri & Sat 1-5

BRONX

M ALBERT EINSTEIN COLLEGE OF MEDICINE*, D Samuel Gottesman Library, 1300 Morris Park Ave, 10461. SAN 351-8884. Tel: 718-430-3108. Circulation Tel: 718-430-3111. Interlibrary Loan Service Tel: 718-430-3122. Reference Tel: 718-430-3104. FAX: 718-430-8795. Web Site: library.einstein.yu.edu. *Dir,* Judie Malamud; E-mail: judie.malamud@einstein.yu.edu; *Asst Dir,* Florence Schreibstein; Tel: 718-430-3110; *Archivist, Head, Ref,* Aurelia Minuti; *Cat,* Karen Laul; Tel: 718-430-3114; *Info Tech,* Nancy Glassman; *Info Tech,* Phil Shen; E-mail: phil.shen@einstein.yu.edu; *Pub Serv,* Racheline Habousha; Tel: 718-430-3115; Staff 25 (MLS 9, Non-MLS 16)
Founded 1955. Enrl 1,100; Fac 1,500; Highest Degree: Doctorate
Library Holdings: e-books 6,500; e-journals 7,000; Bk Vols 120,038
Subject Interests: Behav sci, Med, Psychol
Automation Activity & Vendor Info: (Acquisitions) Innovative Interfaces, Inc; (Cataloging) Innovative Interfaces, Inc; (Circulation) Innovative Interfaces, Inc; (Course Reserve) Innovative Interfaces, Inc; (OPAC) Innovative Interfaces, Inc; (Serials) Innovative Interfaces, Inc
Database Vendor: 3M Library Systems, American Chemical Society, American Physical Society, American Psychological Association (APA), Annual Reviews, Blackwell, Community of Science (COS), DynaMed, Electric Library, Elsevier, Foundation Center, Innovative Interfaces, Inc, ISI Web of Knowledge, Knovel, Lexi-Comp, LexisNexis, Majors, McGraw-Hill, MD Consult, Medline, Nature Publishing Group, OCLC FirstSearch, OVID Technologies, Oxford Online, PubMed, RefWorks, Sage, ScienceDirect, Scopus, SerialsSolutions, Springer-Verlag, Thomson - Web of Science, UpToDate, Wiley InterScience
Wireless access
Partic in National Network of Libraries of Medicine Greater Midwest Region; OCLC Online Computer Library Center, Inc
Restriction: By permission only

J BRONX COMMUNITY COLLEGE LIBRARY & LEARNING CENTER*, 106 Meister Hall, 2115 University Ave, 10453. SAN 310-902X. Tel: 718-289-5439, 718-289-5548. Reference Tel: 718-289-5974. Information Services Tel: 718-289-5441. FAX: 718-289-6063. Web Site: www.bcc.cuny.edu/lilbrary/. *Chief Librn,* Teresa McManus; E-mail: teresa.mcmanus@bcc.cuny.edu; *Dep Librn,* Julie Skurdenis; E-mail: julie.skurdenis@bcc.cuny.edu; *Coll Mgt Librn,* Tom Riker; E-mail: thomas.riker@bcc.cuny.edu; *ILL,* Geraldine Hebert; Tel: 718-289-5947, E-mail: geraldine.hebert@bcc.cuny.edu; *Media Spec,* LaRoi Lawton; Tel: 718-289-5348, Fax: 718-289-6471, E-mail: laroi.lawton@bcc.cuny.edu; *Coordr, Pub Serv,* Mark Padnos; Tel: 718-289-5440, E-mail: mark.padnos@bcc.cuny.edu; Staff 10 (MLS 10)
Founded 1958. Enrl 8,000; Fac 200; Highest Degree: Associate
Library Holdings: AV Mats 3,684; e-books 600; Bk Vols 106,761; Per Subs 355
Automation Activity & Vendor Info: (Acquisitions) Ex Libris Group; (Cataloging) Ex Libris Group; (Circulation) Ex Libris Group; (Course Reserve) Ex Libris Group; (ILL) Ex Libris Group; (Media Booking) Ex Libris Group; (OPAC) Ex Libris Group; (Serials) Ex Libris Group
Database Vendor: EBSCOhost, LexisNexis
Partic in Metropolitan New York Library Council; Nylink; OCLC Online Computer Library Center, Inc
Open Mon-Thurs 9-9, Fri 9-5, Sat 10-5, Sun Noon-5

S BRONX COUNTY HISTORICAL SOCIETY, Research Library & Archives, 3309 Bainbridge Ave, 10467. SAN 310-9127. Tel: 718-881-8900. FAX: 718-881-4827. E-mail: librarian@bronxhistoricalsociety.org. Web Site: www.bronxhistoricalsociety.org. *Exec Dir,* Dr Gary Hermalyn; *Librn,* Laura Tosi
Founded 1955
Library Holdings: AV Mats 825; Bk Titles 15,000; Per Subs 150
Special Collections: Birds of the Bronx; Bronx Congressmen Records, Bronx Chamber of Commerce Records; Bronx Cookbooks; Bronx County Archives (Chamber of Commerce Records); Bronx Home News 1907-1948, micro; Edgar Allan Poe Coll; Local Newspaper (all current); Maps & Atlases (1000); Photograph Coll (45,000 images). Oral History
Subject Interests: Bronx hist, Communities, Life
Publications: Annotated Primary Resources; Bicentennial of the United States Constitution Commemorative Issue; Bronx Cookbooks; Edgar Allan Poe at Fordham Teachers Guide & Workbook; Edgar Allen Poe: A Short Biography; Elected Public Officials of the Bronx Since 1898; Genealogy of the Bronx: An Annotated Guide to Sources of Information; History in Asphalt: The Origin of Bronx Street & Place Names; History of the Morris Park Racecourse & the Morris Family; Landmarks of the Bronx; Legacy of the Revolution: The Valentine-Varian House; Morris High School & the Creation of the New York City Public High School System; Poems of Edgar Allan Poe at Fordham; Presidents of the United States; The Beautiful Bronx, 1920-1950; The Birth of The Bronx, 1609-1900; The Bronx County Historical Society Journal; The Bronx in Print: An Annotated Catalogue of Books & Pamphlets About the Bronx; The Bronx in the Frontier Era; The Bronx in the Innocent Years, 1890-1925; The Bronx It Was Only Yesterday, 1935-1965; The Bronx Triangle: A Portrait of Norwood; The Study & Writing of History
Restriction: Open by appt only
Friends of the Library Group

M CALVARY HOSPITAL*, Medical Library, 1740 Eastchester Rd, 10461. SAN 351-9066. Tel: 718-518-2229. FAX: 718-518-2686. *Med Librn,* Irina Pulatova; E-mail: ipulatova@calvaryhospital.org; Staff 2 (MLS 1, Non-MLS 1)
Founded 1966
Jan 2008-Dec 2008. Mats Exp $29,000. Sal $58,000
Library Holdings: Bk Titles 1,393; Bk Vols 1,485; Per Subs 110
Special Collections: Patient & Family Education Coll
Subject Interests: Cancer, Med, Nursing, Nutrition, Oncology, Palliative care
Automation Activity & Vendor Info: (Cataloging) Marcive, Inc; (Serials) Basch Subscriptions, Inc
Database Vendor: Cinahl, OVID Technologies, UpToDate
Wireless access
Partic in Basic Health Sciences Library Network; Docline; Health Info Librs of Westchester (HILOW); Metropolitan New York Library Council; National Network of Libraries of Medicine; Nylink
Restriction: Not open to pub

C COLLEGE OF MOUNT SAINT VINCENT*, Elizabeth Seton Library, 6301 Riverdale Ave, 10471-1093. SAN 310-9054. Tel: 718-405-3395. FAX: 718-601-2091. Web Site: www.mountsaintvincent.edu/library2/index.htm. *Dir,* Sebastian Derry; *Cat,* Lina Ip; *Ref,* Sister Helen Wade
Founded 1910. Highest Degree: Master
Library Holdings: Bk Vols 125,000; Per Subs 800
Subject Interests: Biol, Communications, Irish hist, Lit, Nursing
Automation Activity & Vendor Info: (Cataloging) LibLime; (Circulation) LibLime; (OPAC) LibLime
Database Vendor: Alexander Street Press, American Psychological Association (APA), BioOne, Cambridge Scientific Abstracts, Cinahl, CQ Press, EBSCOhost, Gale Cengage Learning, JSTOR, Modern Language Association, OVID Technologies, ProQuest, SerialsSolutions
Wireless access
Publications: Discover Resources Bulletins; Library Guides; Library Lines
Partic in OCLC Online Computer Library Center, Inc; Westchester Academic Library Directors Organization (WALDO)
Open Mon-Thurs 8:30am-11pm, Fri 8:30-4:30, Sat 10-5, Sun 2-10

GM DEPARTMENT OF VETERANS AFFAIRS*, James J Peters VA Medical Center Library, 130 W Kingsbridge Rd, 10468. SAN 310-9194. Tel: 718-584-9000, Ext 6924. FAX: 718-741-4608. *Chief Librn,* Judy Steever; Tel: 718-741-4229; *ILL,* Edward Wallace; Staff 2 (MLS 1, Non-MLS 1)
Library Holdings: AV Mats 854; Bk Titles 2,700; Per Subs 100
Subject Interests: Cancer, Clinical, Dietetics, Nuclear med, Rehabilitation, Spinal cord injury
Partic in Metropolitan New York Library Council
Open Mon-Fri 8-4:30

C FORDHAM UNIVERSITY LIBRARIES*, Walsh Library, 441 E Fordham Rd, 10458-5151. SAN 351-9120. Tel: 718-817-3570. Circulation Tel: 718-817-5109. Interlibrary Loan Service Tel: 718-817-3585. Reference Tel: 718-817-3581. FAX: 718-817-3582. Web Site: www.library.fordham.edu. *Dir of Libr,* Linda LoSchiavo; E-mail: loschiavo@fordham.edu; *Asst Dir, Tech Serv,* Michael Wares; *Head, Acq,* Betty Garity; *Head, Cat,* John Williams; *Head, Circ,* John D'Angelo; *Head, ILL,* Charlotte Labbe; *Head, Info Tech,* Michael Considine; *Head, Ref,* Position Currently Open; *Head, Ser & Electronic Res,* Kira Haimovsky; *Head, Spec Coll & Archives,* Patrice Kane; *Conserv Librn, Presv Librn,* Vivian Shen; *Ref Librn,* Peter Patten; *Ref Librn,* Nancy Stout; *Mgr, User Serv,* Renato Frison; *Bibliog Instr,* Jane Suda; *Govt Doc,* Tom Giangreco; *ILL,* Charlotte Labbe; *Network Serv,* Evgheni Sandhu; *Reserves,* William Milite; *Sci,* Peter Mix; *Tech Support,* John Hurley; Staff 44 (MLS 44)
Founded 1841. Enrl 12,592; Fac 667; Highest Degree: Doctorate
Jul 2012-Jun 2013 Income $11,750,585. Mats Exp $4,253,289, Books $900,000, Per/Ser (Incl. Access Fees) $431,290, Micro $4,564, AV Mat $108,765, Electronic Ref Mat (Incl. Access Fees) $2,769,517, Presv $39,153. Sal $5,958,060 (Prof $2,215,253)
Library Holdings: CDs 11,750; e-books 355,000; e-journals 25,750; Bk Vols 2,200,000; Per Subs 2,300; Videos 313,000
Special Collections: 9/11 Coll; American Revolution & Early Federal Americana (Charles Allen Munn Coll); Arts & Architecture (Gambosville Coll); Crimes & Criminals (McGarry Coll); Detective & Mystery Fiction (Maurer Mystery Coll); French Revolution (Joseph Givernaud Coll); Gaelic (McGuire-McLees Coll); Hudson River Coll; The Jesuits (Jesuitica Coll); Vatican (Barberini Coll), microfilm; William Cobbett Coll. US Document Depository
Subject Interests: Behav sci, Bus admin, Educ, Humanities, Natural sci, Soc
Automation Activity & Vendor Info: (Acquisitions) SirsiDynix; (Cataloging) SirsiDynix; (Circulation) SirsiDynix; (Course Reserve) SirsiDynix; (ILL) OCLC; (OPAC) SirsiDynix; (Serials) SirsiDynix
Wireless access
Publications: Fordham University Library Handbook; Inside Fordham Libraries (Newsletter)
Partic in Metropolitan New York Library Council; OCLC Online Computer Library Center, Inc; Westchester Academic Library Directors Organization (WALDO)
Restriction: Open to students, fac & staff

J HOSTOS COMMUNITY COLLEGE LIBRARY*, 475 Grand Concourse, A-207, 10451. SAN 310-9097. Tel: 718-518-4222. Interlibrary Loan Service Tel: 718-518-4214. Reference Tel: 718-518-4215. Administration Tel: 718-518-4203. FAX: 718-518-4206. Web Site: www.hostos.cuny.edu/library/. *Interim Chief Librn,* Madeline Ford; Tel: 718-518-4221; *Head, Access Serv,* Rhonda Johnson; Tel: 718-518-4214, E-mail: rhjohnson@hostos.cuny.edu; *Head, Ref,* Jose Diaz; Tel: 718-518-4212, E-mail: jdiaz@hostos.cuny.edu; *Coordr, Instrul Serv, Info Literacy Librn,* Dr Miriam Laskin; Tel: 718-518-4207, E-mail: mlaskin@hostos.cuny.edu; *IT Librn, Ref Serv,* Kate Lyons; Tel: 718-518-4213; *Evening/Weekend Supvr,* Emma Kent-Traore; Tel: 718 518-4224, E-mail: ktraore@hostos.cuny.edu; *Acq, Ser,* Jennifer Tang; Tel: 718-518-4298, E-mail: jtang@hostos.cuny.edu; *Instruction & Archives,* William Casari; Tel: 718-518-4220, E-mail: wcasari@hostos.cuny.edu. Subject Specialists: *Allied health,* Madeline Ford; *Polit sci,* Rhonda Johnson; *Caribbean studies, Latin Am studies, Spanish lit,* Jose Diaz; *Eng, Lit, Writing,* Dr Miriam Laskin; *Bus, Computer sci, Info tech,* Kate Lyons; *Educ, Film, Lit,* Jennifer Tang; *Archival mgt, Communications, Hist,* William Casari; Staff 13 (MLS 8, Non-MLS 5)
Founded 1968. Enrl 4,500; Fac 160; Highest Degree: Associate
Library Holdings: Bk Vols 65,000; Per Subs 330
Special Collections: Allied Health; Black & Latino Studies; College Archives; Hostos Digital Coll; Spanish American Literature
Subject Interests: Bilingual educ, Caribbean studies, Ethnic studies, Latin Am studies, Latino art, music & women writers, Spanish lit
Automation Activity & Vendor Info: (Acquisitions) Ex Libris Group; (Cataloging) Ex Libris Group; (Circulation) Ex Libris Group; (Course Reserve) Docutek; (OPAC) Ex Libris Group; (Serials) Ex Libris Group
Database Vendor: Alexander Street Press, American Chemical Society, American Psychological Association (APA), Cambridge Scientific Abstracts, Cinahl, CQ Press, EBSCOhost, Facts on File, Gale Cengage Learning, H W Wilson, JSTOR, LearningExpress, LexisNexis, OCLC FirstSearch, OCLC WorldShare Interlibrary Loan, ProQuest, RefWorks, Wiley, Wilson - Wilson Web
Wireless access
Function: Archival coll, Health sci info serv, ILL available, Photocopying/Printing, VCDs, VHS videos, Workshops
Publications: Escriba! (College journal); Liaison Update (Current awareness service); Newsletter (Bi-annually); Recent Acquisitions (Acquisition list)
Partic in Metropolitan New York Library Council; OCLC Online Computer Library Center, Inc
Special Services for the Deaf - ADA equip; Assistive tech
Special Services for the Blind - Assistive/Adapted tech devices, equip & products; ZoomText magnification & reading software

S HUNTINGTON FREE LIBRARY*, Nine Westchester Sq, 10461-3513. SAN 310-9135. Tel: 718-829-7770. FAX: 718-829-4875. *Librn,* Catherine McChesney; Staff 4 (MLS 1, Non-MLS 3)
Founded 1892
Library Holdings: Bk Vols 1,000; Per Subs 20
Special Collections: Bronx History; Turn of Century-Genealogy
Wireless access
Restriction: Open by appt only

C LEHMAN COLLEGE, CITY UNIVERSITY OF NEW YORK*, Leonard Lief Library, 250 Bedford Park Blvd W, 10468-1589. SAN 310-9089. Tel: 718-960-8577. Circulation Tel: 718-960-8576. Interlibrary Loan Service Tel: 718-960-7762. Reference Tel: 718-960-8580. FAX: 718-960-8952. Web Site: www.lehman.cuny.edu/library/. *Chief Librn,* Kenneth Schlessinger; Tel: 718-960-7776, E-mail: kenneth.schlessinger@lehman.cuny.edu; *Head, Access Serv,* Adelaide Soto; Tel: 718-960-7773, E-mail: Adelaide.soto@lehman.cuny.edu; *Head, Coll Develop,* Jessica Hernandez; Tel: 718-960-8582, E-mail: jessica.hernandez@lehman.cuny.edu; *Head, Per,* Edwin Wallace; E-mail: edwin.wallace@lehman.cuny.edu; *Head, Ref,* Susan Voge; Tel: 718-960-7765, E-mail: susan.voge@lehman.cuny.edu; *Cat, Head, Tech Serv,* Ka-Chuen Gee; Tel: 718-960-8428, E-mail: kcgee@lehman.cuny.edu; *Tech Coordr,* Raymond Diaz; Tel: 718-960-7772, E-mail: raymond.diaz@lehman.cuny.edu; *Bibliog Instr,* Robert Farrell; Tel: 718-960-7761, E-mail: robert.farrell@lehman.cuny.edu; *Info Tech,* Wayne Halliday; Tel: 718-960-7768, Fax: 718-960-7127, E-mail: wayne.halliday@lehman.cuny.edu; *ILL,* Eugene Laper; Fax: 718-960-8090, E-mail: gene.laper@lehman.cuny.edu; *Spec Coll & Archives Librn,* Dr Janet Butler Munch; Tel: 718-960-8603, E-mail: janet.munch@lehman.cuny.edu. Subject Specialists: *Journalism, Speech comm, Theatre,* Kenneth Schlessinger; *Arts, Music,* Adelaide Soto; *Educ,* Jessica Hernandez, *Health sci,* Susan Voge; *Asian lang & culture,* Ka-Chuen Gee; *Lit, Lit,* Raymond Diaz; *Lit,* Robert Farrell; *Hist,* Dr Janet Butler Munch; Staff 47 (MLS 10, Non-MLS 37)
Founded 1968. Enrl 9,074; Fac 667; Highest Degree: Master
Library Holdings: Bk Titles 384,482; Bk Vols 577,314; Per Subs 1,826
Special Collections: Basic Liberal Arts Coll; Bronx History; Bronz Institute Archives (Oral History Coll); City; Spanish Civil War (Ponce de Leon Coll). Oral History; State Document Depository; US Document Depository
Subject Interests: Botanical sci, Educ, Ethnic studies
Automation Activity & Vendor Info: (Acquisitions) Ex Libris Group; (Cataloging) Ex Libris Group; (Circulation) Ex Libris Group; (ILL) OCLC; (OPAC) Ex Libris Group; (Serials) Ex Libris Group
Database Vendor: Cambridge Scientific Abstracts, Dialog, EBSCOhost, Gale Cengage Learning, JSTOR, LexisNexis, OCLC FirstSearch, OCLC WorldShare Interlibrary Loan, OVID Technologies, ProQuest, SerialsSolutions, Westlaw, Wilson - Wilson Web
Wireless access
Function: Doc delivery serv
Partic in Dialog Corp; Metropolitan New York Library Council; Westlaw
Special Services for the Deaf - Assistive tech
Special Services for the Blind - Assistive/Adapted tech devices, equip & products
Open Mon-Thurs 9am-10pm, Fri 9-5, Sat 10-6, Sun 12-6
Restriction: In-house use for visitors, Open to students, fac & staff
Friends of the Library Group

M LINCOLN MEDICAL CENTER*, Health Sciences Library, 234 E 149th St, 10451. SAN 327-4659. Tel: 718-579-5745. FAX: 718-579-5170. *Dir,* Inna Lipnitskaya
Founded 1971
Library Holdings: Bk Titles 2,000; Bk Vols 13,000; Per Subs 200
Subject Interests: Health sci
Automation Activity & Vendor Info: (Cataloging) Professional Software; (Circulation) Professional Software; (OPAC) Professional Software
Database Vendor: OVID Technologies
Partic in Brooklyn-Queens-Staten Island-Manhattan-Bronx Health Sciences Librarians; Metropolitan New York Library Council
Restriction: Staff use only

S THE LUESTHER T MERTZ LIBRARY, The New York Botanical Garden, 2900 Southern Blvd, 10458-5126. SAN 310-9143. Tel: 718-817-8728. Circulation Tel: 718-817-8560. Interlibrary Loan Service Tel: 718-817-8874. Reference Tel: 718-817-8604. FAX: 718-817-8956. E-mail: libref@nybg.org. Web Site: library.nybg.org. *Dir,* Susan Fraser; Tel: 718-817-8879, E-mail: sfraser@nybg.org; *Head, Conserv & Presv,* Olga Marder; Tel: 718-817-8746, E-mail: omarder@nybg.org; *Archives, Head, Info Serv, ILL,* Stephen Sinon; E-mail: ssinon@nybg.org; *Syst Librn,* Position Currently Open; *Acq, Coll Develop Mgr,* Don Wheeler; Tel: 718-817-8752, E-mail: dwheeler@nybg.org; *Exhibitions Coordr, Ref,* Mia D'Avanza; Tel: 718-817-8729, E-mail: md'avanza@nybg.org; *Circ, Ref,* Marie Long; E-mail: mlong@nybg.org. Subject Specialists: *Archives,* Susan Fraser; *Conserv,* Olga Marder; Staff 12 (MLS 12)
Founded 1899
Library Holdings: e-journals 2,500; Microforms 1,200; Bk Vols 565,000; Per Subs 1,600
Special Collections: Botanical Art Coll; Collector Field Notes; Darwiniana (Charles F Cox Coll), archives, artifacts, ms; Lord & Burnham Coll; NYBG Archives; Scientific Reprints; Seed & Nursery Catalogs. Oral History
Subject Interests: Botany, Hort, Landscape design, Landscape hist, Plant sci
Automation Activity & Vendor Info: (Acquisitions) Innovative Interfaces, Inc; (Cataloging) Innovative Interfaces, Inc; (Circulation) Innovative Interfaces, Inc; (OPAC) Innovative Interfaces, Inc; (Serials) Innovative Interfaces, Inc
Database Vendor: ISI Web of Knowledge, OCLC FirstSearch, Thomson - Web of Science
Wireless access
Function: Archival coll, Art exhibits, Copy machines, e-mail serv, Exhibits, ILL available, Online cat, Online ref, Online searches, Photocopying/Printing, Ref & res, Ref serv in person, Referrals accepted, Res performed for a fee, Scanner, Web-catalog
Publications: A Reader's Guide to the LuEsther T Mertz Library; Architectural Photo Reproductions: A Manual for Identification & Care; Darwin's Garden: an Evolutionary Adventure; Emily Dickinson's Garden: The Poetry of Flowers; European Pleasure Gardens: Rare Books & Prints of Historic Design from the Elizabeth K Reilley Collection; Glasshouses: The Architecture of Light & Air; Kiku: The Art of the Japanese Chrysanthemum; Monet's Garden; Plants & Gardens Portrayed: Rare & Illustrated Books from the LuEsther T Mertz Library; The Renaissance Herbal
Partic in Docline; Metropolitan New York Library Council; Nat Libr of Med Regional Med Libr Prog; OCLC Online Computer Library Center, Inc
Open Tues-Thurs (Winter) 12-6, Fri & Sat 12-5; Mon-Fri (Summer) 12-5
Restriction: Closed stack, Open to pub for ref & circ; with some limitations

C MONROE COLLEGE*, Thomas P Schnitzler Library, 2468 Jerome Ave, 10468. Tel: 718-933-6700. Circulation Tel: 718-933-6700, Ext 333. Reference Tel: 718-933-6700, Ext 334. FAX: 718-584-4242. E-mail: skaba@monroecollege.edu. Web Site: www.monroecoll.edu. *Libr Dir,* Angela Lauretano; E-mail: alauretano@monroecollege.edu; *Asst Dir,* Jeanette Madera; Tel: 718-933-6700, Ext 8342, E-mail: jmadera@monroecollege.edu; *Chief Librn,* Kristine Paulus; Tel: 718-933-6700, Ext 8349, E-mail: kpaulus@monroecollege.edu; Staff 6 (MLS 4, Non-MLS 2)
Enrl 5,200; Highest Degree: Master
Library Holdings: Bk Titles 92,000; Bk Vols 1,000,000; Per Subs 350
Automation Activity & Vendor Info: (Cataloging) Ex Libris Group; (Circulation) Ex Libris Group; (OPAC) Ex Libris Group
Partic in Westchester Academic Library Directors Organization (WALDO)
Open Mon-Thurs 7:30am-8:30pm, Fri 9-7, Sat 9-4

M MONTEFIORE HOSPITAL-NORTH DIVISION*, Medical Library, 600 E 233rd St, Rm B-11, 10466. SAN 351-9392. Tel: 718-920-9869. FAX: 718-920-9407. *Supvr,* Sheigla Smalling; *Librn,* Subiatu Deen; E-mail: sdeen@montefiore.org
Founded 1958
Library Holdings: Bk Vols 1,000
Partic in Metropolitan New York Library Council
Open Mon-Fri 8-4

M MONTEFIORE MEDICAL CENTER*, Tishman Learning Center Health Sciences Library, 111 E 210th St, 10467. SAN 351-9457. Tel: 718-920-4666. FAX: 718-920-4658. E-mail: medlib@montefiore.org. *Dir,* Sheigla Smalling; E-mail: ssmallin@montefiore.org; *Assoc Dir,* Marie Irma Elias; E-mail: melias@montefiore.org; *Circ,* Heather Barnabas; Staff 6 (MLS 2, Non-MLS 4)
Founded 1926
Jan 2007-Dec 2007 Income $894,780. Mats Exp $437,264, Books $41,090, Per/Ser (Incl. Access Fees) $186,004, Electronic Ref Mat (Incl. Access Fees) $210,170. Sal $324,413 (Prof $138,000)
Library Holdings: e-books 250; e-journals 4,000; Bk Titles 10,000; Bk Vols 15,000; Per Subs 500
Special Collections: Archives Materials
Subject Interests: Internal med
Automation Activity & Vendor Info: (Cataloging) OCLC; (Circulation) Innovative Interfaces, Inc; (Course Reserve) Innovative Interfaces, Inc; (Media Booking) Innovative Interfaces, Inc; (OPAC) Innovative Interfaces, Inc; (Serials) Innovative Interfaces, Inc
Database Vendor: Cinahl, Elsevier, MD Consult, UpToDate
Wireless access
Partic in Docline; RML
Restriction: Employees & their associates

M SAINT BARNABAS HOSPITAL*, Medical Library, Third Ave & 83rd St, 10457-2594. SAN 351-9511. Tel: 718-960-6113. FAX: 718-960-3050. Web Site: www.stbarnabashospital.org. *Dir, Libr Serv,* Deborah Bonelli
Library Holdings: Per Subs 282
Publications: Quarterly Newsletter
Partic in BRS; Docline; National Network of Libraries of Medicine
Open Mon-Fri 8-4

C STATE UNIVERSITY OF NEW YORK MARITIME COLLEGE*, Stephen B Luce Library, Six Pennyfield Ave, Fort Schuyler, 10465. SAN 310-9186. Tel: 718-409-7231. Reference Tel: 718-409-7230. FAX: 718-409-7256. E-mail: library@sunymaritime.edu. Web Site: www.sunymaritime.edu/library. *Chief Librn,* Position Currently Open; *Head, Tech Serv,* Joseph Williams; Tel: 718-409-7229, E-mail: jwilliams@sunymaritime.edu; *Cat,* Somer Browning; Tel: 718-409-7232, E-mail: sbrowning@sunymaritime.edu; *Reader Serv,* S Fazal; E-mail: sfazal@sunymaritime.edu; Staff 8 (MLS 6, Non-MLS 2)
Founded 1946. Enrl 1,100; Highest Degree: Master
Library Holdings: AV Mats 1,934; Bk Titles 72,120; Bk Vols 84,929; Spec Interest Per Sub 200
Special Collections: Marine Casualty Reports; Maritime History; Maritime Research, Technical Reports. US Document Depository
Subject Interests: Marine eng, Merchant marine, Nautical sci, Naval archit, Navigation, Shipping, Ships, Transportation mgt
Automation Activity & Vendor Info: (Cataloging) Ex Libris Group; (Circulation) Ex Libris Group; (OPAC) Ex Libris Group; (Serials) Ex Libris Group
Database Vendor: EBSCOhost, Elsevier, Gale Cengage Learning, OCLC FirstSearch, ProQuest, ScienceDirect
Wireless access
Function: Photocopying/Printing, Ref serv available, Telephone ref
Publications: New Accessions (Accession list)
Partic in Metropolitan New York Library Council; Nylink
Open Mon-Thurs (Winter) 8am-10pm, Fri 8-4:30, Sat 10-5, Sun 4-9; Mon-Fri (Summer) 8:30-12 & 1-4:30
Friends of the Library Group

S WILDLIFE CONSERVATION SOCIETY LIBRARY*, 2300 Southern Blvd, 10460. SAN 310-916X. Tel: 718-220-6874. E-mail: library@wcs.org. Web Site: ielc.libguides.com/wcs. *Dir,* Kerry Prendergast; E-mail: kprendergast@wcs.org; *Librn & Archivist,* Madeleine Thompson; Staff 2 (MLS 2)
Founded 1899
Library Holdings: e-journals 800; Bk Titles 8,000; Bk Vols 10,000; Per Subs 170
Special Collections: WCS Archives
Subject Interests: Wildlife conserv, Zoo biol
Automation Activity & Vendor Info: (Cataloging) Innovative Interfaces, Inc - Millenium; (Circulation) Innovative Interfaces, Inc - Millenium; (ILL) OCLC FirstSearch; (OPAC) Innovative Interfaces, Inc - Millenium; (Serials) Innovative Interfaces, Inc - Millenium
Database Vendor: EBSCOhost, ISI Web of Knowledge, OCLC WorldShare Interlibrary Loan, Springer-Verlag, Wiley InterScience
Wireless access
Function: Archival coll, ILL available
Publications: Guide to the Archives of the New York Zoological Society
Partic in Metropolitan New York Library Council; OCLC Online Computer Library Center, Inc
Restriction: Borrowing requests are handled by ILL, Open to researchers by request

BRONXVILLE

P BRONXVILLE PUBLIC LIBRARY*, 201 Pondfield Rd, 10708. SAN 310-9208. Tel: 914-337-7680. FAX: 914-337-0332. E-mail: bronxvillelibrary@gmail.com. Web Site: www.bronxvillelibrary.org. *Dir,* Gabriella Radujko; E-mail: bronxvilledirector@wlsmail.org; *Head, Ref Serv,* Patricia Root; *Head, Youth Serv,* Erin Schirota; *Ref Librn,* Tessymol John; *Ref Librn,* Christine Utchel; Staff 10 (MLS 5, Non-MLS 5)
Founded 1906. Pop 6,543; Circ 164,106
Library Holdings: AV Mats 12,199; Bk Titles 65,633; Per Subs 128
Special Collections: Bronxville History Coll
Automation Activity & Vendor Info: (Acquisitions) SirsiDynix; (Circulation) SirsiDynix; (ILL) SirsiDynix
Database Vendor: EBSCOhost, SirsiDynix
Wireless access
Publications: Friends of the Bronxville Library (Newsletter)
Mem of Westchester Library System
Open Mon, Wed & Fri (Winter) 9:30-5:30, Tues & Thurs 1-9, Sat 9:30-5, Sun 1-5; Mon, Wed & Fri (Summer) 9:30-5:30, Tues 1-9, Thurs 1-5:30, Sat 9:30-1
Friends of the Library Group

C CONCORDIA COLLEGE*, Scheele Memorial Library, 171 White Plains Rd, 10708. SAN 310-9216. Tel: 914-337-9300, Ext 2202. FAX: 914-395-4893. Web Site: www.concordia-ny.edu/academics/library. *Libr Dir,* William Perrenod; E-mail: William.Perrenod@concordia-ny.edu; *Ref Librn,* Geoff Danisher; *Acq,* Rebecca Fitzgerald; *Archivist,* Brigitte Conkling; *ILL, Reserves,* Travis Basso; *Ser,* MaryBeth Wlodarczyk; *Tech Serv,* Nevine Haider; Staff 8 (MLS 4, Non-MLS 4)
Founded 1881. Enrl 575; Fac 45; Highest Degree: Bachelor
Library Holdings: Bk Vols 73,847; Per Subs 424
Special Collections: Library of American Civilization, ultrafiche; Library of English Literature Part I, ultrafiche
Subject Interests: Bus, Relig, Teacher educ
Automation Activity & Vendor Info: (Cataloging) LibLime; (Circulation) LibLime; (OPAC) LibLime
Wireless access
Publications: Acquisitions List (Monthly)
Partic in Minitex Library Information Network; Nylink; Tri-College University Libraries Consortium; Westchester Academic Library Directors Organization (WALDO)
Open Mon-Thurs 8am-Midnight, Fri 8-5, Sat 1-5, Sun 2-12

C SARAH LAWRENCE COLLEGE*, Esther Raushenbush Library, One Mead Way, 10708. SAN 351-9570. Tel: 914-395-2474. Interlibrary Loan Service Tel: 914-395-2479. Reference Tel: 914-395-2225. Administration Tel: 914-395-2472. FAX: 914-395-2473. Web Site: library.slc.edu/index.html. *Actg Dir, Head, Tech Serv,* Bobbie Smolow; Tel: 914-395-2476, E-mail: bsmolow@sarahlawrence.edu; *Asst Dir, Res & Instrul Tech Serv,* Gary Ploski; Tel: 914-395-2475, E-mail: gploski@sarahlawrence.edu; *Syst Adminr,* David Nicholls; Tel: 914-395-2478, E-mail: nicholls@sarahlawrence.edu; *Head, ILL/Access Serv Librn,* Geoffrey Danisher; E-mail: gdanishe@sarahlawrence.edu; *Govt Doc Coordr, Head, Access Serv,* Janet Alexander; Tel: 914-395-2432, E-mail: alexand@sarahlawrence.edu; *Music Librn,* Charlotte Price; Tel: 914-395-2375, E-mail: ceprice@sarahlawrence.edu; *Ref Librn,* Gina Levitan; E-mail: glevitan@sarahlawrence.edu; *Ref Librn,* Carl Reglar; E-mail: creglar@sarahlawrence.edu
Founded 1926. Enrl 1,574; Fac 219; Highest Degree: Master
Library Holdings: Bk Vols 300,000; Per Subs 831
Special Collections: Bessie Schoenberg Dance Coll; Sarah Lawrence College Faculty Coll. US Document Depository
Subject Interests: Art, Human genetics, Music, Psychol, Women's hist
Automation Activity & Vendor Info: (Acquisitions) LibLime; (Cataloging) LibLime; (Circulation) LibLime; (Course Reserve) LibLime; (ILL) OCLC FirstSearch; (OPAC) LibLime; (Serials) LibLime
Database Vendor: EBSCOhost, JSTOR, LexisNexis, OCLC FirstSearch, OCLC WorldShare Interlibrary Loan, ProQuest
Wireless access
Partic in Metropolitan New York Library Council; OCLC Online Computer Library Center, Inc; Westchester Academic Library Directors Organization (WALDO)
Open Mon-Thurs 8:30am-1am, Fri 8:30am-Midnight, Sat 11am-Midnight, Sun 11am-1am; Mon-Fri (Summer) 9-4:30
Friends of the Library Group

Departmental Libraries:

WILLIAM SCHUMAN MUSIC LIBRARY, One Mead Way, 10708. Tel: 914-395-2375. FAX: 914-395-2507. *Music Librn,* Barbara R Walzer; E-mail: bwalzer@slc.edu; Staff 1 (MLS 1)
Enrl 2,000; Highest Degree: Bachelor
Library Holdings: CDs 5,720; Music Scores 8,246; Bk Titles 4,555; Bk Vols 6,050
Open Mon-Fri 9-5

BROOKHAVEN

P BROOKHAVEN FREE LIBRARY*, 273 Beaver Dam Rd, 11719. SAN 310-9232. Tel: 631-286-1923. FAX: 631-286-0120. E-mail: broolib@suffolk.lib.ny.us. Web Site: www.brooklib.org. *Dir,* Kathleen Scheibel; E-mail: kschiebe@suffolk.lib.ny.us; *Ch Serv,* Deb Domingos; *Circ,* Kelli Edwards; *Tech Serv,* Laura Palermo; Staff 12 (MLS 1, Non-MLS 11)
Founded 1912. Pop 26,400
Library Holdings: Bk Vols 30,239; Per Subs 130
Special Collections: Long Island History; Nautical (Bolt Coll)
Automation Activity & Vendor Info: (Cataloging) Innovative Interfaces, Inc; (Circulation) Innovative Interfaces, Inc; (ILL) Innovative Interfaces, Inc; (OPAC) Innovative Interfaces, Inc
Database Vendor: Dialog, Gale Cengage Learning, ProQuest, Wilson - Wilson Web
Wireless access
Function: CD-ROM, Homebound delivery serv, Music CDs, Online searches, Photocopying/Printing, Prog for adults, Prog for children & young adult, Ref serv available, Spoken cassettes & CDs, Summer reading prog, VHS videos
Publications: Brookhaven Free Library News (Newsletter)

Mem of Suffolk Cooperative Library System
Friends of the Library Group

BROOKLYN

S AMERICAN FOLK ART MUSEUM*, Shirley K Schlafer Library, 55 Washington St, Ste 325, 11201. SAN 311-905X. Tel: 718-249-2096. FAX: 718-249-2097. E-mail: library@folkartmuseum.org.
Founded 1961
Library Holdings: Bk Titles 11,000; Per Subs 180
Subject Interests: Self taught artists
Wireless access
Restriction: Open by appt only

C BORICUA COLLEGE*, Special Collections Library, 186 N Sixth St, 11211. SAN 375-2348. Tel: 718-782-2200. FAX: 718-782-2050. Web Site: www.boricuacollege.edu. *Dir,* Liza Rivera; E-mail: lrivera@boricuacollege.edu
Special Collections: Special Puerto Rico Coll
Automation Activity & Vendor Info: (Cataloging) JayWil Software Development, Inc
Database Vendor: EBSCOhost
Wireless access
Open Mon, Tues, Thurs & Fri 10:30-6:30, Wed 11-7

M BROOKDALE UNIVERSITY HOSPITAL & MEDICAL CENTER*, Marie Smith Schwartz Medical Library, One Brookdale Plaza, 11212. SAN 328-5642. Tel: 718-240-5312. FAX: 718-240-5030. E-mail: medicallibrary@brookdale.edu. Web Site: www.brookdale.edu. *Dir,* Timothy O'Mara; E-mail: tomara@bhmcny.org; Staff 2 (MLS 1, Non-MLS 1)
Library Holdings: Bk Titles 2,000; Per Subs 336
Subject Interests: Med, Nursing
Automation Activity & Vendor Info: (Cataloging) Professional Software; (Circulation) Professional Software; (OPAC) Professional Software; (Serials) Professional Software
Database Vendor: Gale Cengage Learning, Micromedex, OVID Technologies, PubMed, STAT!Ref (Teton Data Systems), UpToDate
Wireless access
Partic in Basic Health Sciences Library Network; Brooklyn-Queens-Staten Island-Manhattan-Bronx Health Sciences Librarians; Health Science Library Information Consortium
Restriction: Staff use only

L BROOKLYN BAR ASSOCIATION FOUNDATION INC LIBRARY*, 123 Remsen St, 2nd flr, 11201-4212. SAN 310-9283. Tel: 718-624-0868. FAX: 718-797-1713. *Exec Dir,* Avery Eli Okin
Founded 1872
Library Holdings: Bk Vols 4,000
Subject Interests: Law related govt publications
Database Vendor: Westlaw
Wireless access
Open Mon-Fri 9-5

S BROOKLYN BOTANIC GARDEN LIBRARY*, 1000 Washington Ave, 11225. SAN 310-9291. Tel. 718-623-7302. Reference Tel: 718-623-7270. FAX: 718-857-2430. E-mail: library@bbg.org. Web Site: www.bbg.org/library. *Head Librn,* Kathy Crosby; Tel: 718-623-7303; Staff 5 (MLS 1, Non-MLS 4)
Founded 1911
Library Holdings: Bk Titles 30,000; Bk Vols 55,000; Per Subs 553
Special Collections: Botanical Art; Glass Plate Negatives; Lantern Slides
Subject Interests: Botany, Ecology, Garden design, Hort, Landscaping, Systematics
Automation Activity & Vendor Info: (Cataloging) Sydney; (Circulation) Sydney; (OPAC) Sydney; (Serials) Sydney
Database Vendor: EBSCO Information Services, JSTOR, OCLC FirstSearch, OVID Technologies
Wireless access
Function: ILL available, Res libr
Partic in Metropolitan New York Library Council; OCLC Online Computer Library Center, Inc

S BROOKLYN CHILDREN'S MUSEUM*, Children's Resource Library, 145 Brooklyn Ave, 11213. SAN 351-9635. Tel: 718-735-4400, Ext 144. FAX: 718-773-4975. Web Site: www.brooklynkids.org. *Dir of Educ,* Kayla Dubb
Founded 1899
Library Holdings: Bk Vols 5,000; Per Subs 50
Special Collections: Brooklyn Children's Museum Archives, 1899-photog, clippings; Leon Kofod Ethnographic Slide Coll
Subject Interests: Anthrop, Hist, Mus educ, Natural sci
Partic in Metropolitan New York Library Council

C BROOKLYN COLLEGE LIBRARY*, 2900 Bedford Ave, 11210-2889. SAN 351-9694. Tel: 718-951-5336. Circulation Tel: 718-951-5335. Interlibrary Loan Service Tel: 718-951-4414. Reference Tel: 718-951-5628. Administration Tel: 718-951-5342. FAX: 718-951-4540. Reference FAX: 718-951-5603. Administration FAX: 718-951-4799. E-mail: ill@brooklyn.cuny.edu, refdesk@brooklyn.cuny.edu. Web Site: ait.brooklyn.cuny.edu, library.brooklyn.cuny.edu. *IT Dir, Syst Coordr,* Dr Howard Spivak; E-mail: howards@brooklyn.cuny.edu; *Chief Librn, Info Tech,* Stephanie Walker; E-mail: swalker@brooklyn.cuny.edu; *Librn,* Helen Georgas; E-mail: hgeorgas@brooklyn.cuny.edu; *Librn,* Alycia Sellie; E-mail: asellie@brooklyn.cuny.edu; *Assoc Librn, Access Serv & Res,* Miriam Deutch; Tel: 718-951-5221, E-mail: miriam@brooklyn.cuny.edu; *Assoc Librn, Coll Mgt,* Susan Vaughn; Tel: 718-951-5348, E-mail: svaughn@brooklyn.cuny.edu; *Assoc Librn, Info Serv,* Mariana Regalado; E-mail: regalado@brooklyn.cuny.edu; *Assoc Librn, Tech Serv,* Judith Wild; Tel: 718-951-5426, E-mail: jwild@brooklyn.cuny.edu; *Media Coordr,* James Liu; Tel: 718-951-4868, E-mail: jliu@brooklyn.cuny.edu; *Media Spec,* Harold Wilson; E-mail: hwilson@brooklyn.cuny.edu; *Archivist,* Marianne LaBatto; Tel: 718-951-5346, E-mail: marianne@brooklyn.cuny.edu; *Bibliog Serv,* Jill Cirasella; E-mail: cirasella@brooklyn.cuny.edu; *Conservator,* Slava Polishchuk; E-mail: slavap@brooklyn.cuny.edu; *Electronic Res,* Beth Evans; E-mail: bevans@brooklyn.cuny.edu; *Govt Doc, Per,* Jane Cramer; Tel: 718-951-5332, E-mail: janec@brooklyn.cuny.edu; *Info Serv,* Neil Dazet; Tel: 718-758-8241, E-mail: ndazet@brooklyn.cuny.edu; *Info Serv,* William Gargan; Tel: 718-951-5341, E-mail: bgargan@brooklyn.cuny.edu; *Info Serv,* Emma Lee Yu; E-mail: eyu@brooklyn.cuny.edu; *Info Tech,* Nicholas Irons; Tel: 718-951-4634, E-mail: nirons@brooklyn.cuny.edu; *Instrul Designer,* Carlos Cruz; Tel: 718-951-4667, E-mail: carlosa@brooklyn.cuny.edu; *Music,* Marguerite Iskenderian; Tel: 718-951-5347, E-mail: iskendir@brooklyn.cuny.edu; *Music,* Honora Raphael; Tel: 718-951-5845, E-mail: honorar@brooklyn.cuny.edu; *Network Serv,* Alex Rudshteyn; E-mail: alex@brooklyn.cuny.edu; *Ser,* Sally Bowdoin; Tel: 718-951-5339, E-mail: sbowdoin@brooklyn.cuny.edu. Subject Specialists: *Classics, Hist, Philos,* Helen Georgas; *Film, Performing arts, Radio,* Alycia Sellie; *Art,* Miriam Deutch; *Anthrop,* Mariana Regalado; *Computer sci, Math, Physics,* Jill Cirasella; *Conserv,* Slava Polishchuk; *Africana, Latino hist, Puerto Rican studies,* Beth Evans; *Law,* Jane Cramer; *Biol, Chem, Health,* Neil Dazet; *Classics, English, Modern lang,* William Gargan; *Training,* Nicholas Irons; *Children's lit,* Honora Raphael; Staff 88 (MLS 20, Non-MLS 68)
Founded 1930. Enrl 15,000; Fac 952; Highest Degree: Master
Library Holdings: AV Mats 22,431; e-books 45,000; Bk Vols 1,449,388; Per Subs 44,470
Special Collections: Academic Freedom Coll; Alan Dershowitz Coll; Brooklyn College Archives; Colonial Ethiopian & Somalian History Coll; Hank Kaplan Boxing Coll; William Alfred Coll. Oral History; State Document Depository; US Document Depository
Automation Activity & Vendor Info: (Acquisitions) Ex Libris Group; (Cataloging) Ex Libris Group; (Circulation) Ex Libris Group; (ILL) OCLC WorldShare Interlibrary Loan; (OPAC) Ex Libris Group; (Serials) Ex Libris Group
Database Vendor: Cambridge Scientific Abstracts, EBSCOhost, Gale Cengage Learning, JSTOR, LexisNexis, OCLC FirstSearch, OCLC WorldShare Interlibrary Loan, ProQuest, PubMed, ScienceDirect, SerialsSolutions, Wilson - Wilson Web
Wireless access
Function: AV serv, Distance learning, Doc delivery serv, For res purposes, Govt ref serv, Handicapped accessible, ILL available, Large print keyboards, Photocopying/Printing, Ref serv available, Referrals accepted
Publications: Access (Newsletter)
Partic in Academic Libraries of Brooklyn; Metropolitan New York Library Council; OCLC Online Computer Library Center, Inc
Special Services for the Deaf - Assistive tech
Special Services for the Blind - Assistive/Adapted tech devices, equip & products; Computer with voice synthesizer for visually impaired persons
Restriction: Open to students, fac & staff
Friends of the Library Group

Departmental Libraries:

WALTER W GERBOTH MUSIC LIBRARY, 2900 Bedford Ave, 11210-2889, SAN 351-9724. Tel: 718-951-5844. *Librn,* Honora Raphael; Tel: 718-951-5845, E-mail: honorar@brooklyn.cuny.edu
Library Holdings: CDs 10,000; Music Scores 30,000; Videos 500
Open Mon-Thurs 9-9, Fri 9-5, Sat & Sun 10-6
Friends of the Library Group

S BROOKLYN HISTORICAL SOCIETY OTHMER LIBRARY*, 128 Pierrepont St, 11201-2711. SAN 310-9402. Tel: 718-222-4111. FAX: 718-222-3794. Web Site: www.brooklynhistory.org/library/ask.html. *Dir, Libr & Archives,* Chela Scott Weber; E-mail: csweber@brooklynhistory.org; *Spec Coll Librn,* Position Currently Open; *Photo Archivist,* Julie May; Staff 3 (MLS 3)
Founded 1863
Library Holdings: Bk Vols 150,000
Special Collections: 19th Century Paintings & Prints Coll; Archives & Manuscripts; Brooklyn, Long Island & New York City History Coll;

Decorative Arts; Family History Coll; Genealogy Coll; Historic Photographs & Postcards; Historical Brooklyn & Long Island Atlases; Newspaper Clipping Index
Wireless access
Partic in Metropolitan New York Library Council
Open Wed-Fri 1-5

M BROOKLYN HOSPITAL CENTER*, Medical Library, 121 DeKalb Ave, 3rd Flr, 11201. SAN 310-9313. Tel: 718-250-6943, 718-250-6944. FAX: 718-250-6428. *Libr Mgr,* Laurel Wellington
Founded 1928
Library Holdings: Bk Titles 1,500; Bk Vols 3,300; Per Subs 100
Database Vendor: OVID Technologies, UpToDate
Wireless access
Partic in Docline
Restriction: Not open to pub

CL BROOKLYN LAW SCHOOL LIBRARY, 250 Joralemon St, 11201. SAN 310-9321. Tel: 718-780-7973. Reference Tel: 718-780-7567. Administration Tel: 718-780-7979. Information Services Tel: 718-780-7974. FAX: 718-780-0369. Web Site: www.brooklaw.edu/library. *Libr Dir & Assoc Prof of Law,* Janet Sinder; Tel: 718-780-7975, E-mail: janet.sinder@brooklaw.edu; *Assoc Law Librn,* Linda Holmes; Tel: 718-780-7974, E-mail: linda.holmes@brooklaw.edu; *Cat Librn,* Judy Baptiste-Joseph; Tel: 718-780-0670, E-mail: judy.joseph@brooklaw.edu; *Coll Develop & Acq Librn,* Gilda Chiu; Tel: 718-780-7976, E-mail: gilda.chiu@brooklaw.edu; *Intl Law Librn, Ref,* Jean Davis; Tel: 718-780-7534, E-mail: jean.davis@brooklaw.edu; *Govt Doc, Ref Librn,* Rosemary Campagna; Tel: 718-780-7580, E-mail: rosemary.campagna@brooklaw.edu; *Ref Librn,* Kathleen Darvil; Tel: 718-780-7544, E-mail: kathleen.darvil@brooklaw.edu; *Ref Librn,* Harold O'Grady; Tel: 718-780-7981, E-mail: harold.ogrady@brooklaw.edu; *Ref Librn,* Loreen Peritz; Tel: 718-780-7538, E-mail: loreen.peritz@brooklaw.edu; *Info Tech, Syst Librn,* Hainan Yu; Tel: 718-780-7910, E-mail: hainan.yu@brooklaw.edu; *Cat & E-Res Mgr,* Jeff Gabel; Tel: 718-780-7978, E-mail: jeff.gabel@brooklaw.edu; Staff 22 (MLS 11, Non-MLS 11)
Founded 1901. Enrl 1,510; Fac 65; Highest Degree: Doctorate
Subject Interests: Am law, Comparative law, Foreign law, Intl law
Database Vendor: Bloomberg, Dialog, EBSCOhost, Gale Cengage Learning, HeinOnline, JSTOR, LexisNexis, OCLC FirstSearch, OCLC WorldShare Interlibrary Loan, Project MUSE, ProQuest, SerialsSolutions, Thomson - Web of Science, Westlaw, Wilson - Wilson Web
Wireless access
Function: Res libr
Publications: Brooklyn Law School Library Guide (Library handbook)
Partic in Metropolitan New York Library Council; New England Law Library Consortium, Inc; OCLC Online Computer Library Center, Inc
Open Mon-Fri 8am-Midnight, Sat 9am-10pm, Sun 9am-Midnight

BROOKLYN MUSEUM

S LIBRARIES & ARCHIVES*, 200 Eastern Pkwy, 11238, SAN 351-9759. Tel: 718-501-6307. FAX: 718-501-6125. E-mail: library@brooklynmuseum.org. Web Site: www.brooklynmuseum.org. *Principal Librn,* Deirdre E Lawrence; Staff 8 (MLS 4, Non-MLS 4)
Founded 1823
Library Holdings: Bk Vols 250,000; Per Subs 2,000
Special Collections: Artists' Books; Artists' Files; Costume & Fashion Sketches (1900-1950); Documentary Photographs; Museum Archives; Rare Books
Subject Interests: Anthrop, Archaeology, Art, Art of the Americas, Arts of Africa, Asian art, Costumes, Decorative art, Drawings, Egyptology, Islamic art, Museology, Painting, Photog, Prints, Sculpture, Textiles
Automation Activity & Vendor Info: (Acquisitions) Innovative Interfaces, Inc - Millenium; (Cataloging) Innovative Interfaces, Inc - Millenium; (Circulation) Innovative Interfaces, Inc - Millenium; (OPAC) Innovative Interfaces, Inc - Millenium; (Serials) Innovative Interfaces, Inc - Millenium
Database Vendor: ARTstor, JSTOR, OVID Technologies
Partic in OCLC Research Library Partnership; RLIN (Research Libraries Information Network)
Open Wed-Fri 10-4:30
Restriction: Open to pub for ref only

S WILBOUR LIBRARY OF EGYPTOLOGY*, 200 Eastern Pkwy, 11238, SAN 351-9783. Tel: 718-501-6219. FAX: 718-501-6125. E-mail: library@brooklynmuseum.org. Web Site: www.brooklynmuseum.org. *Chief Curator,* Kevin Stayton; Staff 3 (MLS 1, Non-MLS 2)
Founded 1934
Library Holdings: Bk Titles 50,000
Special Collections: Egyptology (Seyffarth Coll), mss, rare bks
Subject Interests: Archaeology, Art, Geog, Geol, Nubiology, Philology, Relig, Travel
Automation Activity & Vendor Info: (Acquisitions) Innovative Interfaces, Inc; (OPAC) Innovative Interfaces, Inc; (Serials) Innovative Interfaces, Inc
Database Vendor: ARTstor, JSTOR, OVID Technologies, Oxford Online
Partic in New York Art Resources Consortium (NYARC); OCLC Research Library Partnership; RLIN (Research Libraries Information Network)
Open Wed-Fri 11-4:30

P BROOKLYN PUBLIC LIBRARY*, Grand Army Plaza, 11238. SAN 351-9813. Tel: 718-230-2100. Interlibrary Loan Service Tel: 718-230-2187. Information Services Tel: 718-230-2299. FAX: 718-398-3947. Interlibrary Loan Service FAX: 718-230-6717. Reference FAX: 718-230-2061. Web Site: www.bklynlibrary.org. *Pres & Chief Exec Officer,* Linda E Johnson; *Dir & Chief Librn,* Position Currently Open; *Dir, Human Res,* Lawrence Jennings; E-mail: ljennings@bklynlibrary.org; *Dir, Coll Develop,* Charlene Rue; E-mail: crue@bklynlibrary.org; *Dir, Govt & Commun Affairs,* Steven Schechter; E-mail: sschechter@bklynlibrary.org; *Dir, Neighborhood Libr,* Sheila Schofer; *Dep Dir, Neighborhood Serv,* Mary Graham; E-mail: mgraham@bklynlibrary.org
Founded 1897. Pop 2,465,326; Circ 19,579,270
Jan 2013-Dec 2013 Income $113,291,775, State $9,941,267, City $85,704,523, Federal $2,114,323, Locally Generated Income $4,177,106, Other $11,354,556. Mats Exp $6,208,015, Books $3,939,697, Per/Ser (Incl. Access Fees) $209,151, AV Equip $194,561, AV Mat $746,882, Electronic Ref Mat (Incl. Access Fees) $1,117,724. Sal $50,879,676
Library Holdings: Bk Vols 3,729,803
Special Collections: Brooklyn Coll
Automation Activity & Vendor Info: (OPAC) Infor Library & Information Solutions
Wireless access
Open Mon-Thurs 9-9, Fri & Sat 10-6, Sun 1-5
Friends of the Library Group
Branches: 60

ARLINGTON, 203 Arlington Ave, 11207, SAN 351-9872. Tel: 718-277-6105. FAX: 718-277-6177.
Library Holdings: Bk Vols 77,436
Open Mon, Tues, Thurs & Fri 10-6, Wed 10-8

BAY RIDGE, 7223 Ridge Blvd, 11209, SAN 351-9902. Tel: 718-748-5709. FAX: 718-748-7095.
Library Holdings: Bk Vols 101,792
Open Mon, Wed & Fri 10-6, Tues & Thurs 1-8, Sat 10-5
Friends of the Library Group

BEDFORD, 496 Franklin Ave, 11238, SAN 351-9937. Tel: 718-623-0012. FAX: 718-638-4271.
Library Holdings: Bk Vols 61,947
Open Tues, Thurs & Fri 10-6, Wed 10-8, Sat 10-5
Friends of the Library Group

BOROUGH PARK, 1265 43rd St, 11219, SAN 351-9961. Tel: 718-437-4085. FAX: 718-437-3021.
Library Holdings: Bk Vols 119,384
Open Mon, Wed & Fri 10-6, Tues & Thurs 1-8

BRIGHTON BEACH, 16 Brighton First Rd, 11235, SAN 351-9996. Tel: 718-946-2917. FAX: 718-946-6176.
Library Holdings: Bk Vols 88,438
Open Tues & Thurs 1-8, Wed & Fri 10-6, Sat 10-5
Friends of the Library Group

BROOKLYN HEIGHTS, 280 Cadman Plaza W, 11201, SAN 352-0021. Tel: 718-623-7100. FAX: 718-222-5681.
Library Holdings: Bk Vols 100,726
Open Mon-Fri 8-1, Sat 9-1
Friends of the Library Group

BROWER PARK, 725 Saint Marks Ave, 11216, SAN 352-0056. Tel: 718-773-7208. FAX: 718-773-7838.
Library Holdings: Bk Vols 52,783
Open Mon, Tues, Thurs & Fri 10-6, Wed 1-8
Friends of the Library Group

BROWNSVILLE, 61 Glenmore Ave, 11212, SAN 352-0080. Tel: 718-498-9721. FAX: 718-498-4071.
Library Holdings: Bk Vols 45,221
Open Mon & Wed-Fri 10-6, Tues 1-8

BUSHWICK, 340 Bushwick Ave, 11206, SAN 352-0110. Tel: 718-602-1348. FAX: 718-602-1352.
Library Holdings: Bk Vols 81,708
Open Mon-Wed & Fri 10-6, Thurs 1-8

BUSINESS, 280 Cadman Plaza W, 11201, SAN 352-0145. Tel: 718-623-7100. FAX: 718-222-5651. *Chief,* Kerwin Pilgram; Staff 12 (MLS 12)
Founded 1943
Library Holdings: Bk Vols 139,276; Spec Interest Per Sub 1,200
Special Collections: US Document Depository
Open Mon, Wed & Fri 9-6, Tues 1-8, Thurs 1-6, Sat 10-5

CANARSIE, 1580 Rockaway Pkwy, 11236, SAN 352-017X. Tel: 718-257-6547. FAX: 718-257-6557.
Library Holdings: Bk Vols 71,750
Open Mon, Tues, Thurs & Fri 10-6, Wed 1-8

CARROLL GARDENS, 396 Clinton St, 11231, SAN 352-020X. Tel: 718-596-6972. FAX: 718-596-0370.
Library Holdings: Bk Vols 79,802
Open Mon, Thurs & Fri 10-6, Tues & Wed 1-8, Sat 10-5
Friends of the Library Group

CLARENDON, 2035 Nostrand Ave, 11210, SAN 352-0234. Tel: 718-421-1159. FAX: 718-421-1244.
Library Holdings: Bk Vols 59,443
Open Mon & Wed-Fri 10-6, Tues 1-8

CLINTON HILL, 380 Washington Ave, 11238, SAN 352-0269. Tel: 718-398-8713. FAX: 718-398-8715.
Library Holdings: Bk Vols 63,734
Open Mon, Tues, Thurs & Fri 10-6, Wed 1-8, Sat 10-5
Friends of the Library Group

CONEY ISLAND, 1901 Mermaid Ave, 11224, SAN 352-0293. Tel: 718-265-3220. FAX: 718-265-5026.
Library Holdings: Bk Vols 56,933
Open Mon, Tues, Thurs & Fri 10-6, Wed 1-8

CORTELYOU, 1305 Cortelyou Rd, 11226, SAN 352-0315. Tel: 718-693-7763. FAX: 718-693-7874.
Library Holdings: Bk Vols 95,150
Open Mon, Tues, Thurs & Fri 10-6, Wed 1-8, Sat 10-5

CROWN HEIGHTS, 560 New York Ave, 11225, SAN 352-0323. Tel: 718-773-1180. FAX: 718-773-0144.
Library Holdings: Bk Vols 85,101
Open Mon & Wed-Fri 10-6, Tues 1-8, Sat 10-5

CYPRESS HILLS, 1197 Sutter Ave, 11208, SAN 352-0358. Tel: 718-277-6004. FAX: 718-277-6009.
Library Holdings: Bk Vols 77,432
Open Tues 1-8, Wed-Fri 10-6, Sat 10-5

DEKALB BRANCH, 790 Bushwick Ave, 11221, SAN 352-0382. Tel: 718-455-3898. FAX: 718-455-4071.
Library Holdings: Bk Vols 85,086
Open Mon, Tues, Thurs & Fri 10-6, Wed 1-8, Sat 10-5

DYKER, 8202 13th Ave, 11228, SAN 352-0412. Tel: 718-748-6261. FAX: 718-748-6370.
Library Holdings: Bk Vols 53,934
Open Mon, Wed & Fri 10-6, Tues & Thurs 1-8, Sat 10-5

EAST FLATBUSH, 9612 Church Ave, 11212, SAN 352-0447. Tel: 718-922-0931. FAX: 718-922-2394.
Library Holdings: Bk Vols 67,251
Open Tues 1-8, Wed-Fri 1-6, Sat 10-5

EASTERN PARKWAY, 1044 Eastern Pkwy, 11213, SAN 352-0471. Tel: 718-953-4225. FAX: 718-953-3970
Library Holdings: Bk Vols 76,606
Open Tues 1-8, Wed-Fri 10-6, Sat 10-5

FLATBUSH, 22 Linden Blvd, 11226, SAN 352-0501. Tel: 718-856-0813. FAX: 718-856-0899.
Library Holdings: Bk Vols 69,920
Open Tues 1-8, Wed-Fri 10-6, Sat 10-5

FLATLANDS, 2065 Flatbush Ave, 11234, SAN 352-0536. Tel: 718-253-4409. FAX: 718-253-5018.
Library Holdings: Bk Vols 83,574
Open Tues & Thurs 1-8, Wed & Fri 10-6, Sat 10-5
Friends of the Library Group

FORT HAMILTON, 9424 Fourth Ave, 11209, SAN 352-0560. Tel: 718-748-6919. FAX: 718-748-7335.
Library Holdings: Bk Vols 58,579
Open Mon, Wed & Fri 10-6, Tues & Thurs 1-8, Sat 10-5

GERRITSEN BEACH, 2808 Gerritsen Ave, 11229. Tel: 718-368-1435. FAX: 718-368-1506.
Library Holdings: Bk Vols 66,432
Open Mon & Wed-Fri 10-6, Tues 1-8

GRAVESEND, 303 Ave X, 11223, SAN 352-0625. Tel: 718-382-5792. FAX: 718-382-5926.
Founded 1962. Circ 335,659
Library Holdings: Bk Vols 73,500
Open Mon, Wed & Fri 10-6, Tues & Thurs 1-8

GREENPOINT, 107 Norman Ave, 11222, SAN 352-065X. Tel: 718-349-8504. FAX: 718-349-8790.
Library Holdings: Bk Vols 78,100
Open Mon, Tues & Fri 10-6, Wed & Thurs 1-8, Sat 10-5
Friends of the Library Group

HIGHLAWN, 1664 W 13th St, 11223, SAN 352-0684. Tel: 718-234-7208. FAX: 718-234-7238.
Library Holdings: Bk Vols 72,309
Open Tues & Fri 10-6, Wed & Thurs 1-8, Sat 10-5

HOMECREST, 2525 Coney Island Ave, 11223, SAN 352-0714. Tel: 718-382-5924. FAX: 718-382-5955.
Library Holdings: Bk Vols 76,315
Open Mon, Wed & Fri 10-6, Tues & Thurs 1-8

JAMAICA BAY, 9727 Seaview Ave, 11236, SAN 352-0749. Tel: 718-241-3571. FAX: 718-241-1981.
Library Holdings: Bk Vols 62,253
Open Tues, Thurs & Fri 10-6, Wed 1-8, Sat 10-5

KENSINGTON, 4207 18th Ave, 11218, SAN 352-0773. Tel: 718-436-0545.
Library Holdings: Bk Vols 72,000
Open Mon, Wed & Fri 10-6, Tues & Thurs 1-8, Sat 10-5
Friends of the Library Group

KINGS BAY, 3650 Nostrand Ave, 11229, SAN 352-0803. Tel: 718-368-1709. FAX: 718-368-1410.
Library Holdings: Bk Vols 120,335
Open Mon, Tues & Fri 10-6, Wed & Thurs 1-8, Sat 10-5

KINGS HIGHWAY, 2115 Ocean Ave, 11229, SAN 352-0811. Tel: 718-375-3037.
Library Holdings: Bk Vols 132,760
Open Mon & Fri 10-6, Tues-Thurs 10-8, Sat 10-5, Sun 1-5
Friends of the Library Group

LEONARD, 81 Devoe St, 11211, SAN 352-0838. Tel: 718-486-3365. FAX: 718-486-3370.
Library Holdings: Bk Vols 65,000
Open Mon & Wed-Fri 10-6, Tues 1-8, Sat 10-5

MACON, 361 Lewis Ave, 11233, SAN 352-0897. Tel: 718-573-5606. FAX: 718-573-5817.
Library Holdings: Bk Vols 56,003
Open Mon & Wed-Fri 10-6, Tues 1-8, Sat 10-5
Friends of the Library Group

MAPLETON, 1702 60th St, 11204, SAN 352-0927. Tel: 718-256-2117. FAX: 718-256-1487.
Library Holdings: Bk Vols 11,000
Open Mon, Wed & Fri 10-6, Tues & Thurs 1-8, Sat 10-5

MARCY, 617 DeKalb Ave, 11216, SAN 352-0951. Tel: 718-935-0032. FAX: 718-935-0045.
Library Holdings: Bk Vols 64,430
Open Tues 1-8, Wed-Fri 10-6, Sat 10-5

MCKINLEY PARK, 6802 Fort Hamilton Pkwy, 11219, SAN 352-0862. Tel: 718-748-8001. FAX: 718-748-7746.
Library Holdings: Bk Vols 87,500
Open Mon, Tues & Fri 10-6, Wed & Thurs 1-8, Sat 10-5
Friends of the Library Group

MIDWOOD, 975 E 16th St, 11230, SAN 352-0986. Tel: 718-252-0967. FAX: 718-252-1263.
Library Holdings: Bk Vols 99,781
Open Mon, Wed & Fri 10-6, Tues & Thurs 1-8

MILL BASIN, 2385 Ralph Ave, 11234, SAN 352-101X. Tel: 718-241-3973. FAX: 718-241-1957.
Library Holdings: Bk Vols 68,000
Open Tues, Thurs & Fri 10-6, Wed 1-8, Sat 10-5

NEW LOTS, 665 New Lots Ave, 11207, SAN 352-1044. Tel: 718-649-0311. FAX: 718-649-0719.
Library Holdings: Bk Vols 83,003
Open Mon, Tues, Thurs & Fri 10-6, Wed 1-8, Sat 10-5
Friends of the Library Group

NEW UTRECHT, 1743 86th St, 11214, SAN 352-1079. Tel: 718-236-4086. FAX: 718-234-7702.
Library Holdings: Bk Vols 87,742
Open Mon & Fri 10-6, Tues-Thurs 1-8, Sat 10-5
Friends of the Library Group

PACIFIC, 25 Fourth Ave, 11217, SAN 352-1109. Tel: 718-638-1531. FAX: 718-638-1580.
Library Holdings: Bk Vols 62,000
Open Tues, Thurs & Fri 10-6, Wed 1-8, Sat 10-5

PAERDEGAT, 850 E 59th St, 11234, SAN 352-1133. Tel: 718-241-3994. FAX: 718-241-1335.
Library Holdings: Bk Vols 65,563
Open Mon, Tues, Thurs & Fri 10-6, Wed 1-8

PARK SLOPE, 431 Sixth Ave, 11215, SAN 352-1168. Tel: 718-832-1853. FAX: 718-832-9024.
Library Holdings: Bk Vols 79,981
Open Mon, Wed & Fri 10-6, Tues & Thurs 1-8, Sat 10-5
Friends of the Library Group

RED HOOK, Seven Wolcott St, 11231, SAN 352-1192. Tel: 718-935-0203. FAX: 718-935-0160.
Library Holdings: Bk Vols 61,010
Open Mon & Wed-Fri 10-6, Tues 1-8

RUGBY, 1000 Utica Ave, 11203, SAN 352-1222. Tel: 718-566-0054. FAX: 718-566-0059.
Library Holdings: Bk Vols 68,906
Open Mon & Wed-Fri 10-6, Tues 1-8
Friends of the Library Group

RYDER, 5902 23rd Ave, 11204, SAN 352-1257. Tel: 718-331-2962. FAX: 718-331-3445. *Neighborhood Libr Supvr*, Liana Alaverdova; E-mail: l.alaverdova@brooklynpubliclibrary.org; Staff 8 (MLS 3, Non-MLS 5)
Founded 1970
Function: Adult bk club
Open Mon, Wed & Fri 10-6, Tues & Thurs 1-8

SARATOGA, Eight Thomas S Boyland St, @ Macon St, 11233, SAN 352-1281. Tel: 718-573-5224. FAX: 718-573-5402. *Br Mgr,* Monica D Williams; E-mail: mwilliams@bklynlibrary.org
Library Holdings: Bk Vols 87,346
Open Tues 1-8, Wed-Fri 10-6, Sat 10-5
SERVICES FOR OLDER ADULTS, 1743 86th St, 11214, SAN 352-1273. Tel: 718-236-1760. E-mail: seniors@brooklynpubliclibrary.org.
Open Mon-Fri 9-5
SHEEPSHEAD BAY, 2636 E 14th St, 11235, SAN 352-1311. Tel: 718-368-1815. FAX: 718-368-1872.
Library Holdings: Bk Vols 83,780
Open Tues & Fri 10-6, Wed & Thurs 1-8, Sat 10-5
SPRING CREEK, 12143 Flatlands Ave, 11207, SAN 352-1346. Tel: 718-257-6571. FAX: 718-257-6588.
Library Holdings: Bk Vols 66,988
Open Mon, Tues, Thurs & Fri 10-6, Wed 1-8
STONE AVENUE, 581 Mother Gaston Blvd, 11212, SAN 352-1370. Tel: 718-485-8347. FAX: 718-342-0748.
Founded 1914
Library Holdings: Bk Vols 100,000
Open Tues, Wed & Fri 10-6, Thurs 1-8, Sat 10-5
Friends of the Library Group
SUNSET PARK, 5108 Fourth Ave, 11220, SAN 352-1400. Tel: 718-567-2806. FAX: 718-567-2810.
Library Holdings: Bk Vols 98,200
Open Mon, Wed & Fri 10-6, Tues & Thurs 1-8, Sat 10-5
Friends of the Library Group
ULMER PARK, 2602 Bath Ave, 11214, SAN 352-1435. Tel: 718-265-3443. FAX: 718-265-5115.
Library Holdings: Bk Vols 72,000
Open Mon, Wed & Fri 10-6, Tues & Thurs 1-8, Sat 10-5
WASHINGTON IRVING BRANCH, 360 Irving Ave, 11237, SAN 352-1494. Tel: 718-628-8378. FAX: 718-628-8439.
Library Holdings: Bk Vols 60,700
Open Mon-Wed & Fri 10-6, Thurs 1-8
WALT WHITMAN BRANCH, 93 Saint Edwards St, 11205, SAN 352-146X. Tel: 718-935-0244. FAX: 718-935-0284.
Library Holdings: Bk Vols 52,341
Open Mon, Tues, Thurs & Fri 10-6, Wed 1-8
Friends of the Library Group
WILLIAMSBURGH, 240 Division Ave, 11211, SAN 352-1524. Tel: 718-302-3485. FAX: 718-387-6972.
Library Holdings: Bk Vols 119,489
Open Mon & Wed-Fri 10-6, Tues 1-8
WINDSOR TERRACE, 160 E Fifth St, 11218, SAN 352-1559. Tel: 718-686-9707. FAX: 718-686-0162.
Library Holdings: Bk Vols 57,787
Open Mon, Tues, Thurs & Fri 10-6, Wed 1-8, Sat 10-5
Friends of the Library Group
Bookmobiles: 4

M CONEY ISLAND HOSPITAL*, Harold Fink Memorial Library, 2601 Ocean Pkwy, 11235. SAN 352-1583. Tel: 718-616-3000, 718-616-4158. FAX: 718-616-4178. *Dir,* Laraine Tursi; E-mail: tursil@nychhc.org; Staff 1 (MLS 1)
Library Holdings: Bk Titles 3,000; Per Subs 96
Subject Interests: Gynecology, Med, Med hospital admin, Nursing, Obstetrics, Pediatrics, Pharm, Podiatry, Surgery
Publications: Journal Holdings; Library News
Partic in Basic Health Sciences Library Network; Brooklyn-Queens-Staten Island-Manhattan-Bronx Health Sciences Librarians; Metropolitan New York Library Council; National Network of Libraries of Medicine South Central Region
Restriction: Staff use only

GM DEPARTMENT OF VETERANS AFFAIRS*, Medical Center Library Service, 800 Poly Pl, 11209. SAN 310-9534. Tel: 718-836-6600, Ext 3559. FAX: 718-630-3573. *Chief Librn,* Francine Tidona; E-mail: fran.tidona@med.va.gov; Staff 4 (MLS 2, Non-MLS 2)
Library Holdings: e-journals 3,500; Bk Vols 5,000; Per Subs 50
Subject Interests: Allied health, Health admin, Med, Nursing, Patient educ, Psychol, Surgery
Automation Activity & Vendor Info: (Cataloging) EOS International
Database Vendor: PubMed
Open Mon-Fri 8-4:30

S INSTITUTE OF DESIGN & CONSTRUCTION, Vito P Battista Library, 141 Willoughby St, 11201. Tel: 718-855-3661. FAX: 718-852-5889. Web Site: www.idc.edu. *Dir,* Robert Wagner; E-mail: rwagner@idc.edu; Staff 1 (MLS 1)
Founded 2003. Highest Degree: Associate
Library Holdings: Bk Vols 1,850
Subject Interests: Archit, Archit tech, Architectural hist, Bldg construction
Automation Activity & Vendor Info: (Cataloging) Mandarin Library Automation; (OPAC) Mandarin Library Automation
Wireless access
Function: Computers for patron use, Copy machines, Electronic databases & coll, Online cat, Online searches, Orientations, Photocopying/Printing, Ref serv in person
Partic in Metropolitan New York Library Council
Restriction: Clients only

J KINGSBOROUGH COMMUNITY COLLEGE*, Robert J Kibbee Library, 2001 Oriental Blvd, 11235. SAN 310-9372. Tel: 718-368-5632. Circulation Tel: 718-368-5442. Interlibrary Loan Service Tel: 718-368-6548. FAX: 718-368-5482. Interlibrary Loan Service FAX: 718-368-5481. Web Site: www.kbcc.cuny.edu/kcclibrary. *Actg Chief Librn, Ref Serv,* Josephine Murphy; Tel: 718-368-5584, E-mail: jmurphy@kbcc.cuny.edu; *Electronic Serv Librn,* Elizabeth Tompkins; Tel: 718-368-6541, E-mail: ethompkins@kbcc.cuny.edu; *Acq,* Cecilia Salber; Tel: 718-368-5430, E-mail: csalber@kbcc.cuny.edu; *Bibliog Instr, Electronic Res,* Reabeka King; Tel: 718-368-5429, E-mail: rking@kbcc.cuny.edu; *Cat, Per, Tech Serv,* Roberta A Pike; Tel: 718-368-5639, E-mail: rpike@kbcc.cuny.edu; *ILL, Reader Serv,* Jay Bernstein; Tel: 718-368-6548, E-mail: jbernstein@kbcc.cuny.edu; *Reader Serv,* Allan Mirwis; Tel: 718-368-5971, E-mail: amirwis@kbcc.cuny.edu; Staff 10 (MLS 9, Non-MLS 1)
Founded 1964. Enrl 14,400; Fac 293; Highest Degree: Associate
Library Holdings: e-books 45,229; e-journals 32,510; Bk Vols 168,541; Per Subs 437
Special Collections: Coney Island Chamber of Commerce Coll; Kingsborough Community College Administrative Reports, College Catalogs, Yearbooks; Kingsborough Historical Society Coll, bks, memorabilia, music, newsp & photogs; Manhattan Beach (Herman Field Coll), photogs
Subject Interests: Broadcasting tech, Fisheries & marine tech, Judaica, Nursing, Puppetry, Travel & tourism
Automation Activity & Vendor Info: (Acquisitions) Ex Libris Group; (Cataloging) Ex Libris Group; (Circulation) Ex Libris Group; (Course Reserve) Ex Libris Group; (OPAC) Ex Libris Group; (Serials) Ex Libris Group
Wireless access
Publications: Bibliographic Instruction Sheets; Faculty Library Handbook; Guide to Kingsborough Community College Library; Using CUNY PLUS & Finding Books in CUNY PLUS
Partic in Metropolitan New York Library Council; Nylink
Open Mon-Thurs 8am-11pm, Fri 8-5, Sat & Sun 10-3

M KINGSBROOK JEWISH MEDICAL CENTER*, Medical Library, 585 Schenectady Ave, 11203. SAN 310-9399. Tel: 718-604-5689. Interlibrary Loan Service Tel: 718-604-5690. FAX: 718-604-5539. Web Site: www.kingsbrook.org. *Dir, Med Libr,* Liva Zigelbaum; E-mail: lzigelbaum@kingsbrook.org; Staff 3 (MLS 2, Non-MLS 1)
Founded 1925
Library Holdings: Bk Titles 2,000
Subject Interests: Internal med, Orthopedics, Phys med, Rehabilitation
Automation Activity & Vendor Info: (Cataloging) Professional Software; (Circulation) Professional Software; (OPAC) Professional Software; (Serials) Professional Software
Database Vendor: MD Consult
Wireless access
Partic in Basic Health Sciences Library Network; Brooklyn-Queens-Staten Island-Manhattan-Bronx Health Sciences Librarians; Metropolitan New York Library Council
Restriction: Not open to pub

S THE KURDISH LIBRARY*, 144 Underhill Ave, 11238. (Mail add: 345 Park Pl, 11238), SAN 329-2096. Tel: 718-783-7930. E-mail: kurdishlib@aol.com. Web Site: kurdishlibrarymuseum.com. *Dir,* Vera Beaudin Saeedpour
Founded 1986
Library Holdings: Bk Titles 2,500; Bk Vols 1,500
Special Collections: Archibald Roosevelt Jr, pamphlets, newspapers from Mahabad Republic, 1946; Dana Adams Schmidt Photographic Coll on Iraqi Kurdistan 1965; Kurd & US Foreign Policy Coll. Oral History
Function: Res libr
Publications: Kurdish Life (Quarterly); The International Journal of Kurdish Studies (Bi-annually)

S LESBIAN HERSTORY ARCHIVES*, Lesbian Herstory Educational Foundation Inc, 484 14th St, 11215-5702. SAN 325-9250. Tel: 718-768-3953. FAX: 718-768-4663. E-mail: lesbianherstoryarchives@gmail.com. Web Site: lesbianherstoryarchives.org. *Coordr,* Deborah Edel
Founded 1974
Jan 2010-Dec 2010 Income $74,214. Mats Exp $1,719, Books $119, Per/Ser (Incl. Access Fees) $100, AV Equip $500, Presv $1,000
Library Holdings: Audiobooks 10; CDs 1,000; DVDs 1,000; Bk Titles 15,000; Per Subs 100; Spec Interest Per Sub 20; Videos 1,000
Special Collections: Oral History

Subject Interests: Lesbian culture & hist
Wireless access
Restriction: Non-circulating to the pub, Open by appt only
Friends of the Library Group

C LONG ISLAND UNIVERSITY*, Brooklyn Library, One University Plaza, 11201-9926. SAN 352-1737. Tel: 718-488-1081. Circulation Tel: 718-488-1338. Reference Tel: 718-780-4513. FAX: 718-780-4057. Web Site: www.brooklyn.liu.edu/cwis/bklyn/library/home.htm. *Dean, Univ Libr,* Dr Donald Ungarelli; E-mail: donald.ungarelli@liu.edu; *Head, Cat,* Patricia Keogh; E-mail: patricia.keogh@liu.edu; *Head, Ref Serv,* Paul Tremblay; E-mail: paul.tremblay@liu.edu; *Acq Librn,* Julia Block; E-mail: julia.block@liu.edu; *Acq Librn,* Charles Guarria; E-mail: charles.guarria@liu.edu; *Cat Librn,* Diana Mitrano; E-mail: diana.mitrano@liu.edu; *Electronic Serv Librn,* Martin Zimmerman; E-mail: martin.zimmerman@liu.edu; *Ref Librn,* Elizabeth Crenshaw; E-mail: elizabeth.crenshaw@liu.edu; *Ref Librn,* Suzie Remilien; E-mail: suzie.remilien@liu.edu; *Ref & Instruction Librn,* Emily Drabinski; E-mail: emily.drabinski@liu.edu; *Ref & Instruction Librn,* Edward Keane; E-mail: edward.keane@liu.edu; *Coordr, User Serv,* Peter Salber; Tel: 718-780-4180, E-mail: peter.salber@liu.edu
Founded 1927. Highest Degree: Doctorate
Library Holdings: AV Mats 9,610; Bk Titles 175,981; Bk Vols 273,917; Per Subs 1,412
Special Collections: 19th & 20th Century Black Social & Economic Documents (Eato Aid Society Coll, William Hamilton Relief Society Coll & New York African Society for Mutual Relief Coll); Urban Architecture & City Planning (Robert Weinberg Coll), bks, correspondence, drawings, papers, artists' bks
Subject Interests: Archives, Artists bks
Automation Activity & Vendor Info: (Acquisitions) SirsiDynix; (Cataloging) SirsiDynix; (Circulation) SirsiDynix; (OPAC) SirsiDynix; (Serials) SirsiDynix
Database Vendor: Gale Cengage Learning, OCLC FirstSearch, SirsiDynix
Function: Archival coll, AV serv, ILL available, Large print keyboards, Magnifiers for reading, Online searches, Photocopying/Printing
Publications: Library Leaves (Newsletter)
Partic in Academic Libraries of Brooklyn; Dialog Corp; Metropolitan New York Library Council; OCLC Online Computer Library Center, Inc; Westchester Academic Library Directors Organization (WALDO)
Restriction: Open to fac, students & qualified researchers

M LUTHERAN MEDICAL CENTER*, Health Sciences Library, 150 55th St, 11220. SAN 310-9410. Tel: 718-630-7200. FAX: 718-630-8918. E-mail: library@lmcmc.com. Web Site: www.lmclibrary.com. *Dir,* Irina Meyman; Staff 1 (MLS 1)
Founded 1893
Library Holdings: Bk Titles 6,250; Per Subs 232
Subject Interests: Dentistry, Family practice, Internal med, Nursing, Obstetrics & gynecology, Pathology, Pediatrics, Radiology, Surgery
Automation Activity & Vendor Info: (Cataloging) LibraryWorld, Inc; (Circulation) LibraryWorld, Inc; (OPAC) LibraryWorld, Inc
Database Vendor: Medline, OVID Technologies, UpToDate
Wireless access
Partic in Basic Health Sciences Library Network; Brooklyn-Queens-Staten Island-Manhattan-Bronx Health Sciences Librarians
Open Mon-Fri 8-8, Sat 9-5, Sun 9-1

M MAIMONIDES MEDICAL CENTER*, George A Degenshein MD Memorial Library, Administration, 4802 Tenth Ave, Fifth Fl, 11219. SAN 310-9429. Tel: 718-283-7406. FAX: 718-283-7063. E-mail: library@maimonidesmed.org. *Dir,* Lydia Friedman; *Asst Librn,* Richard Patrimonia; Staff 5 (MLS 1, Non-MLS 4)
Founded 1952
Library Holdings: AV Mats 7,186; e-journals 1,000; Bk Titles 5,575; Per Subs 304
Special Collections: Judaica Coll
Subject Interests: Dentistry, Med, Nursing
Database Vendor: EBSCOhost
Wireless access
Function: AV serv, For res purposes, ILL available, Photocopying/Printing, Prof lending libr, Ref serv available, Res libr, Wheelchair accessible
Partic in Basic Health Sciences Library Network; Brooklyn-Queens-Staten Island-Manhattan-Bronx Health Sciences Librarians; Docline; Metropolitan New York Library Council
Open Mon-Thurs 7am-9pm, Fri 7-7, Sat-Sun 1-5
Restriction: Lending to staff only, Use of others with permission of librn

C MEDGAR EVERS COLLEGE*, Charles Evans Inniss Memorial Library, 1650 Bedford Ave, 11225-2010. SAN 310-9437. Tel: 718-270-4873. Interlibrary Loan Service Tel: 718-270-4997. Reference Tel: 718-270-4802. Administration Tel: 718-270-4880. Automation Services Tel: 718-270-4867. FAX: 718-270-5182. Web Site: www.mec.cuny.edu/library. *Chief Librn,* Danesh Yazdani; Tel: 718-270-4883, E-mail: yazdani@mec.cuny.edu; *Dep Chief Librn, Head, Ref Serv,* Vanrea Thomas; Tel: 718-270-4885; *Access & Prog Dir,* Alexei Oulanov; Tel: 718-270-4834, E-mail: aoulanov@mec.cuny.edu; *Acq,* Ching Chang; Tel: 718-270-4865, Fax: 718-270-4908, E-mail: chingchang@mec.cuny.edu; *Archivist,* William Daly; Tel: 718-270-4881, E-mail: william@mec.cuny.edu; *Info Literacy,* Karl Madden; Tel: 718-270-4874, E-mail: kmadden@mec.cuny.edu; *ILL,* Carl Andrews; *Ser Librn,* Karen Mason; Tel: 718-270-4875, E-mail: kmason@mec.cuny.edu. Subject Specialists: *Libr & info sci,* Danesh Yazdani; *Lit, Philos,* Vanrea Thomas; *Computer info syst, Econ, Finance,* Alexei Oulanov; *Acctg, Bus admin,* Ching Chang; *Africana studies, Caribbean studies,* William Daly; *Mass communications, Music, Sociol,* Karl Madden; *Biol, Math, Phys sci,* Carl Andrews; *Women's studies,* Karen Mason; Staff 18 (MLS 12, Non-MLS 6)
Founded 1970. Enrl 3,389; Fac 355; Highest Degree: Bachelor
Library Holdings: Bk Titles 98,345; Bk Vols 116,793; Per Subs 450
Special Collections: African American History & Literature (Dorothy Porter Coll); American Civilization; American Culture Series (PCMI Coll), ultrafiche; American Fiction Series; American Periodicals Series; Black History & Culture (Arthur A Schomburg Coll Series I), microfilm; Library of American Civilization Coll, microfiche; National Black Writers Conference Coll; Southern Africa Coll
Subject Interests: African-Am studies, Caribbean studies, Lit, Women's studies
Database Vendor: EBSCOhost, Gale Cengage Learning, JSTOR, LexisNexis, OCLC FirstSearch, OVID Technologies, Wilson - Wilson Web
Wireless access
Publications: Acquisitions List; Library Handbook; Library Newsletter
Partic in Academic Libraries of Brooklyn; Metropolitan New York Library Council; Nylink
Special Services for the Blind - Computer with voice synthesizer for visually impaired persons
Open Mon-Thurs 8:30am-Midnight, Fri & Sat 10am-11pm, Sun Noon-11pm
Friends of the Library Group

S NEW YORK AQUARIUM*, Aquarium for Wildlife Conservation, Osborn Laboratories of Marine Science Library, W Eighth St & Surf Ave, 11224. SAN 310-9461. Tel: 718-265-3406, 718-265-3437. FAX: 718-265-3420. Web Site: www.wcs.org. *Dir,* Jon Dohlin; E-mail: jdohlin@wcs.org; *Librn,* Paul Loiselle; E-mail: ploiselle@wcs.org
Founded 1967
Library Holdings: Bk Titles 3,500; Bk Vols 4,600; Per Subs 56
Subject Interests: Marine biol
Publications: Wildlife Conservation
Restriction: Open to others by appt, Staff use only

J NEW YORK CITY TECHNICAL COLLEGE*, Ursula C Schwerin Library, 300 Jay St, 11201. SAN 352-1885. Circulation Tel: 718-260-5470, 718-260-5482. Interlibrary Loan Service Tel: 718-260-5484. Reference Tel: 718-260-5485. FAX: 718-260-5631. Interlibrary Loan Service FAX: 718-260-5467. Web Site: library.citytech.cuny.edu. *Chief Librn,* Maura Smale; Staff 12 (MLS 12)
Founded 1946. Enrl 8,606; Fac 265
Library Holdings: AV Mats 5,500; Bk Titles 132,000; Bk Vols 186,000; Per Subs 600
Special Collections: College Archives; Hotel & Restaurant Management (Menu File)
Subject Interests: Dental hygiene, Eng tech, Hotel mgt, Ophthalmic dispensing, Radiologic tech, Restaurant mgt
Automation Activity & Vendor Info: (Cataloging) Ex Libris Group
Publications: Library Notes
Partic in Academic Libraries of Brooklyn; Metropolitan New York Library Council; OCLC Online Computer Library Center, Inc

M NEW YORK METHODIST HOSPITAL*, Health Sciences Library, 506 Sixth St, 11215. SAN 352-1796. Tel: 718-780-5197. Web Site: nymlibrary.nyp.org/hslibrary. *Librn,* Dorothy Schwartz; Staff 3 (MLS 1, Non-MLS 2)
Library Holdings: AV Mats 100; e-books 60; e-journals 70; Bk Titles 3,000; Per Subs 120
Special Collections: History of Methodist Hospital; Methodist Hospital Annual Reports
Subject Interests: Med, Nursing, Surgery
Database Vendor: DynaMed, McGraw-Hill, OVID Technologies, PubMed, STAT!Ref (Teton Data Systems), Swets Information Services, UpToDate
Wireless access
Partic in Brooklyn-Queens-Staten Island-Manhattan-Bronx Health Sciences Librarians; Nat Libr of Med Regional Med Libr Prog; New York State Interlibrary Loan Network (NYSILL)
Restriction: Staff use only

GL NEW YORK STATE SUPREME COURT*, Appellate Division Second Department Library, 45 Monroe Pl, 11201. SAN 310-9267. Tel: 718-722-6356. FAX: 718-722-6302. Web Site:

www.courts.state.ny.us/courts/ad2. *Dir,* Bruce Bosso; E-mail: bbosso@courts.state.ny.us; Staff 2 (MLS 1, Non-MLS 1)
Library Holdings: Bk Vols 35,000
Special Collections: Law Coll
Automation Activity & Vendor Info: (Acquisitions) EOS International; (Cataloging) EOS International; (Circulation) EOS International; (Serials) EOS International
Database Vendor: LexisNexis, Westlaw
Wireless access
Restriction: Not open to pub

GL NEW YORK STATE SUPREME COURT LIBRARY, BROOKLYN*, Supreme Court Bldg, Rm 349, 360 Adams St, 11201-3782. SAN 310-9488. Tel: 347-296-1144. FAX: 718-643-2412. *Head Librn,* Paul Henrich; E-mail: phenrich@courts.state.ny.us; *Sr Librn,* Jacqueline Cantwell; *Sr Librn,* Brenda E Pantell; *Librn,* Anton Mateika
Founded 1850
Library Holdings: Bk Vols 250,000
Special Collections: Records & Briefs of the Four Appellate Courts, the Court of Appeals of the State of New York
Subject Interests: Criminal law
Database Vendor: LexisNexis, Westlaw
Wireless access
Open Mon-Fri 9-6

C POLYTECHNIC INSTITUTE OF NYU*, Bern Dibner Library of Science & Technology, Five MetroTech Ctr, 11201-3840. SAN 352-1915. Tel: 718-260-3530. Interlibrary Loan Service Tel: 718-260-3943. Administration Tel: 718-260-3109. FAX: 718-260-3756. E-mail: blibrary@poly.edu. Web Site: www.poly.edu/library. *Dir,* Jana Stevens Richman; Staff 9 (MLS 3, Non-MLS 6)
Founded 1854. Highest Degree: Doctorate
Library Holdings: Bk Titles 144,805; Bk Vols 185,261
Special Collections: History of Science & Technology; Paint & Surface Coatings (Mathiello Memorial Coll)
Subject Interests: Computer sci, Eng, Environ studies
Automation Activity & Vendor Info: (Cataloging) OCLC; (ILL) OCLC
Partic in Academic Libraries of Brooklyn; Long Island Library Resources Council; Metropolitan New York Library Council; OCLC Online Computer Library Center, Inc
Open Mon-Fri 9am-11pm, Sat & Sun 10-9
Friends of the Library Group

C PRATT INSTITUTE LIBRARIES*, 200 Willoughby Ave, 11205-3897. SAN 352-194X. Tel: 718-399-4223. Circulation Tel: 718-636-3420. Interlibrary Loan Service Tel: 718-230-6841. Information Services Tel: 718-636-3704. FAX: 718-399-4401. Interlibrary Loan Service FAX: 718-399-4220. E-mail: libref@pratt.edu. Web Site: library.pratt.edu. *Dir,* Russell Abell; E-mail: rabell@pratt.edu; *Dir, Visual & Multimedia Serv,* Chris Arabadjis; Tel: 718-399-4356, E-mail: carabadj@pratt.edu; *Head, Tech Serv,* John Maier; Tel: 718-636-3659, E-mail: jmaier1@pratt.edu; *Coordr, Info Serv,* Jean Hines; Tel: 212-647-7547, E-mail: jhines@pratt.edu; *Visual Res Curator,* Johanna Bauman; Tel: 718-636-3716, E-mail: jbauma91@pratt.edu; Staff 20 (MLS 17, Non-MLS 3)
Founded 1887. Enrl 4,500; Highest Degree: Master
Library Holdings: AV Mats 5,969; Bk Vols 212,934; Per Subs 800
Subject Interests: Archt, Art, Design, Libr sci
Automation Activity & Vendor Info: (Acquisitions) Innovative Interfaces, Inc - Millenium; (Cataloging) Innovative Interfaces, Inc - Millenium; (Circulation) Innovative Interfaces, Inc - Millenium; (Course Reserve) Innovative Interfaces, Inc - Millenium; (ILL) OCLC; (OPAC) Innovative Interfaces, Inc - Millenium; (Serials) Innovative Interfaces, Inc - Millenium
Database Vendor: ARTstor, Emerald, JSTOR, Material ConneXion, OCLC FirstSearch, Project MUSE, ProQuest, ScienceDirect, Scopus, Wilson - Wilson Web
Wireless access
Function: Art exhibits, Audio & video playback equip for onsite use, AV serv, Computers for patron use, Copy machines, e-mail & chat, E-Reserves, Electronic databases & coll, Equip loans & repairs, Exhibits, Free DVD rentals, Handicapped accessible, ILL available, Online cat, Orientations, Photocopying/Printing, Ref & res, Scanner, VHS videos, Video lending libr, Visual arts prog, Web-catalog, Wheelchair accessible
Partic in Academic Libraries of Brooklyn; Metropolitan New York Library Council; OCLC Online Computer Library Center, Inc
Open Mon-Thurs 8:30am-11pm, Fri 8:30-6, Sat 1-6, Sun 2-9
Restriction: Authorized patrons, Authorized scholars by appt
Friends of the Library Group

Departmental Libraries:

PRATT MANHATTAN LIBRARY, 144 W 14th St, New York, 10011-7301, SAN 373-501X. Tel: 212-647-7539. FAX: 646-336-8797. *Coordr, Info Serv,* Jean Hines; E-mail: jhines@pratt.edu; Staff 1 (MLS 1)
Library Holdings: Bk Vols 14,000; Per Subs 273
Open Mon-Thurs 10-10, Fri-Sun 10-6
Restriction: Authorized patrons, Authorized scholars by appt

C ST FRANCIS COLLEGE LIBRARY*, 180 Remsen St, 11201. SAN 352-1974. Tel: 718-489-5307. Circulation Tel: 718-489-5205. FAX: 718-489-3402. E-mail: library@sfc.edu. Web Site: www.library.sfc.edu. *Dir, Libr Serv,* Dr James P Smith; Tel: 718-489-5306, Fax: 718-489-3401, E-mail: jsmith@sfc.edu; *Asst Dir,* Mona Wasserman; Tel: 718-489-5305, E-mail: mwasserman@sfc.ed; *Tech Serv,* Miyo Davis; Tel: 718-489-5206, E-mail: miyo.davis@stfranciscollege.edu; Staff 18 (MLS 8, Non-MLS 10)
Founded 1884. Enrl 2,499; Fac 121; Highest Degree: Master
Library Holdings: Bk Titles 125,999; Per Subs 573
Special Collections: Curriculum Library
Subject Interests: Behav sci, Econ, Educ, English lit, Health mgt, Philos, Relig, Sci, Soc sci
Automation Activity & Vendor Info: (Acquisitions) Ex Libris Group; (Cataloging) Ex Libris Group; (Circulation) Ex Libris Group; (Course Reserve) Ex Libris Group; (OPAC) Ex Libris Group; (Serials) Ex Libris Group
Database Vendor: ABC-CLIO, Blackwell, Bowker, Cinahl, CQ Press, Dialog, ebrary, EBSCOhost, Elsevier, Facts on File, H W Wilson, JSTOR, LexisNexis, OCLC WorldShare Interlibrary Loan, OVID Technologies, Wilson - Wilson Web
Wireless access
Function: ILL available
Partic in Academic Libraries of Brooklyn; Metropolitan New York Library Council; OCLC Online Computer Library Center, Inc; Westchester Academic Library Directors Organization (WALDO)
Restriction: In-house use for visitors

C SAINT JOSEPH'S COLLEGE*, McEntegart Hall Library, 222 Clinton Ave, 11205-3697. SAN 352-2032. Circulation Tel: 718-940-5878. Reference Tel: 718-940-5880. FAX: 718-636-7250. E-mail: bklibrary@sjcny.edu. Web Site: www.sjcny.edu/library. *Dir,* William Meng; Tel: 718-940-5884, E-mail: wmeng@sjcny.edu; *Evening Librn, Weekend Librn,* Robert Lasner; E-mail: rlasner@sjcny.edu; *Ref/Instruction/Archival Librn,* Mayumi Miyaoka; *Ref/Instruction/Info Commons Librn,* Nicole Gitau; Tel: 718-940-5879; *Acq, Instruction & Ref Serv,* Lauren Kehoe; Tel: 718-940-5877, E-mail: lkehoe@sjcny.edu; Staff 9 (MLS 5, Non-MLS 4)
Founded 1916. Enrl 4,000; Fac 180; Highest Degree: Master
Library Holdings: AV Mats 1,000; Bks on Deafness & Sign Lang 60; Bk Titles 100,000; Bk Vols 110,500; Per Subs 235
Special Collections: Local New York History
Subject Interests: Acctg, Child study, Commun health, Educ, Health admin, Liberal arts, Nursing
Automation Activity & Vendor Info: (Acquisitions) Ex Libris Group; (Cataloging) Ex Libris Group; (Circulation) Ex Libris Group; (Course Reserve) Docutek; (ILL) OCLC; (OPAC) Ex Libris Group; (Serials) EBSCO Online
Database Vendor: ABC-CLIO, Alexander Street Press, ARTstor, EBSCOhost, ProQuest, Wilson - Wilson Web
Wireless access
Function: Handicapped accessible, ILL available, Online searches, Ref serv available, Wheelchair accessible
Publications: Library News; New Acquisitions Quarterly; Periodical Holdings - 2002-2003
Partic in Academic Libraries of Brooklyn; Metropolitan New York Library Council; Midwest Collaborative for Library Services (MCLS); OCLC Online Computer Library Center, Inc; Westchester Academic Library Directors Organization (WALDO)
Special Services for the Deaf - Bks on deafness & sign lang
Restriction: Open to fac, students & qualified researchers, Use of others with permission of librn

C STATE UNIVERSITY OF NEW YORK*, Brooklyn Educational Opportunity Center, 111 Livingston St, Ste 306, 11201. SAN 310-950X. Tel: 718-802-3300, 718-802-3314. FAX: 718-802-3332. *Librn,* Joyce Bavlinka; E-mail: bavlinkaj@beoc.cuny.edu
Founded 1968
Library Holdings: Bk Vols 10,500; Per Subs 25
Subject Interests: African-Am hist
Publications: BEOC Voice (Newsletter)
Open Mon-Thurs 10-7, Fri 9-5, Sat 9-1

CM STATE UNIVERSITY OF NEW YORK DOWNSTATE MEDICAL CENTER*, Medical Research Library of Brooklyn, 395 Lenox Rd, 11203. (Mail add: 450 Clarkson Ave, PO Box 14, 11203), SAN 322-855X. Tel: 718-270-7400. Circulation Tel: 718-270-7401. Reference Tel: 718-270-7405. FAX: 718-270-7413, 718-270-7468. Web Site: library.downstate.edu. *Dean, Acad Info Access, Dir of Libr,* Richard M Winant; E-mail: richard.winant@downstate.edu; *Adminr,* Donald Lemke; Tel: 718-270-7410, E-mail: donald.lemke@downstate.edu; *Asst Dir, Educ Serv & Dir EBM Inst,* Andrea Markinson; *Asst Dir, Res Mgt Serv,* Mohamed Hussain; Tel: 718-270-7450; *Head, Tech Serv,* Violet Price; *Archivist,* Jack Termine; *Bibliog Instr, Online Serv, Ref,* Mary Doherty;

ILL, Ross Ljungquist; *Web Coordr*, Christopher Stewart; Staff 38 (MLS 10, Non-MLS 28)
Founded 1860. Enrl 1,963; Fac 306; Highest Degree: Doctorate
Library Holdings: Bks on Deafness & Sign Lang 12; e-books 85; e-journals 2,523; Bk Vols 52,967; Per Subs 2,452
Special Collections: The History of Medicine in the County of Kings. US Document Depository
Subject Interests: Allied health, Clinical health sci, Med, Nursing
Automation Activity & Vendor Info: (Acquisitions) Ex Libris Group; (Cataloging) Ex Libris Group; (Circulation) Ex Libris Group; (ILL) Ex Libris Group; (OPAC) Ex Libris Group; (Serials) Ex Libris Group
Database Vendor: EBSCOhost, Gale Cengage Learning, LexisNexis, OCLC FirstSearch
Function: Telephone ref
Publications: Library News (Newsletter)
Partic in Brooklyn-Queens-Staten Island-Manhattan-Bronx Health Sciences Librarians; Metrop Regional Res & Ref Librs; OCLC Online Computer Library Center, Inc
Restriction: Not open to pub

A UNITED STATES ARMY*, Post Library Fort Hamilton, 404 Pershing Loop, Fort Hamilton, 11252-5100. SAN 352-2091. Tel: 718-630-4875. FAX: 718-630-4038. *Libr Mgr*, Wallace Grant; Tel: 718-630-4040, E-mail: wallace.grant@us.army.mil; *Actg Librn*, Rimattee Daneshwar; E-mail: rimattee.daneshwar@us.army.mil
Founded 1942
Library Holdings: Bk Vols 22,000; Per Subs 40
Special Collections: Black History Coll; New York State & New York City Coll
Subject Interests: Mil hist, Sci, Tactics
Wireless access
Function: ILL available
Open Tues-Fri 11-6, Sat 10-5
Restriction: Circ limited, Circ to mil employees only

M WOODHULL MEDICAL & MENTAL HEALTH CENTER*, Health Sciences Library, 760 Broadway, Rm 3A160, 11206. SAN 352-1702. Tel: 718-963-8275, 718-963-8397. FAX: 718-963-8888. *Librn*, Maria N Perez; E-mail: perezm@woodhullhc.nychhc.org
Founded 1982
Library Holdings: Bk Titles 1,300; Bk Vols 2,400; Per Subs 185
Subject Interests: Allied health, Health serv admin, Med, Nursing
Automation Activity & Vendor Info: (ILL) OCLC
Wireless access
Partic in Basic Health Sciences Library Network; Brooklyn-Queens-Staten Island-Manhattan-Bronx Health Sciences Librarians; Medical Library Association (MLA); Metropolitan New York Library Council; NY NJ MLA
Open Mon-Fri 8:30-8

S WORLD JEWISH GENEALOGY ORGANIZATION LIBRARY*, Mechon Yochsin, 1605 48th St, 11204. SAN 326-095X. Tel: 718-435-7878. FAX: 718-633-7050.
Founded 1985
Library Holdings: Bk Vols 25,000
Special Collections: Jewish Genealogy Coll, Rabbinical Families from Origin to Present Day
Subject Interests: Genealogy, Hist
Function: Res libr
Restriction: Open by appt only

M WYCKOFF HEIGHTS MEDICAL CENTER*, Medical Library, 374 Stockholm St, 11237. SAN 329-8000. Tel: 718-963-7198. Interlibrary Loan Service Tel: 718-963-7197. FAX: 718-497-7649. Web Site: www.wyckoffhospital.org. *Dir*, Lyudmila Bunyatova; E-mail: lbunyatova@wyckoffhospital.org; Staff 2 (MLS 1, Non-MLS 1)
Founded 1965
Library Holdings: e-journals 300; Bk Titles 1,500; Per Subs 70
Subject Interests: Dentistry, Hist of med, Internal med, Nursing, Obstetrics & gynecology, Pediatrics, Plastic surgery, Podiatry, Surgery
Automation Activity & Vendor Info: (Cataloging) Professional Software; (Circulation) Professional Software
Database Vendor: Elsevier, OVID Technologies, ScienceDirect, STAT!Ref (Teton Data Systems), UpToDate
Wireless access
Partic in Basic Health Sciences Library Network; Brooklyn-Queens-Staten Island-Manhattan-Bronx Health Sciences Librarians; Docline; Metropolitan New York Library Council
Restriction: Open to hospital affiliates only
Friends of the Library Group

BROOKVILLE

C LONG ISLAND UNIVERSITY POST*, B Davis Schwartz Memorial Library, 720 Northern Blvd, 11548. SAN 311-2756. Tel: 516-299-2307. Circulation Tel: 516-299-2303. Interlibrary Loan Service Tel: 516-299-2898. Reference Tel: 516-299-2305. FAX: 516-299-4169. Interlibrary Loan Service FAX: 516-299-2270. Reference FAX: 516-299-4170. E-mail: post-ref@liu.edu. Web Site: www2.liu.edu/cwis/cwp/library/libhome.htm. *Dean, Univ Libr*, Valeda Frances Dent; Staff 54 (MLS 28, Non-MLS 26)
Founded 1955. Enrl 7,305; Fac 355; Highest Degree: Doctorate
Library Holdings: AV Mats 4,507; e-books 78,762; e-journals 65,477; Microforms 408,818; Bk Vols 442,919; Per Subs 341; Spec Interest Per Sub 572
Special Collections: American Juvenile Coll; Architectural Library of H T Lindeberg; Archival Letters of Henry James'to His Publisher William Heineman; Archive of Architectural Plans of LIU/Post; Archive of Circus & Buffalo Bill Materials; Archive of George Bernard Shaw Theatre Programs; Archive of Joan & John Digby; Archive of Joan Harrison: Ray Johnson: A Bad Archive; Archive of Joseph Cameron Cross Theatrical Coll; Archive of Letters from The Winthrop Palmer Coll: French & Irish Literature; Archive of LIU/Post – (Main Campus Archives & Ephemera); Archive of LIU/Post's "WCWP" Radio Station; Archive of Maps from the Nassau County Research Library; Archive of Original Movie Poster Research Coll; Archive of Samuel Becket: Theatrical Programs; Archive of Shogo Myaida; Archive of Southampton Campus; Archive of the Cedar Swamp Historical Asn Coll; Archive of the Long Island Book Collectors; Archive of the Long Island Museum Asn; Archive of the Theodore Roosevelt Asn Coll; Archive of Tilles Center Theatrical Programs; Archive of William E Hutton II/Joan Chapin Families; Archives of American Theatrical Programs; Archives of the Metropolitan New York College Career Planning Officer's Asn; Art Archives of William Randolph Hearst; Beat Generation Coll of Karl Otto Patel; Cedar Swamp Historical Society; Dorothy Dayton Sorzano Theatre Coll; Eugene & Carlotta O'Neill Library; Franklin B Lord Hunting & Fishing Coll; Henry James Coll, bks, archives; Illuminated Manuscript Facsimiles; Joan Hoerger Fern Place Elementary School "Letters to Authors Project"; LIU/Post Campus Authors; Rare Book Coll; Saidie Scudder Archival Coll of Pre-Publication Illustrations; Theodore Roosevelt Asn Coll; Underhill Quaker Coll; Winthrop Palmer Coll: French & Irish Literature. US Document Depository
Subject Interests: Libr & info sci
Automation Activity & Vendor Info: (Acquisitions) Innovative Interfaces, Inc - Millenium; (Cataloging) Innovative Interfaces, Inc - Millenium; (Circulation) Innovative Interfaces, Inc - Millenium; (Course Reserve) Innovative Interfaces, Inc - Millenium; (ILL) OCLC ILLiad; (OPAC) Innovative Interfaces, Inc - Millenium; (Serials) Innovative Interfaces, Inc - Millenium
Database Vendor: ABC-CLIO, ACM (Association for Computing Machinery), Agricola, Alexander Street Press, American Chemical Society, American Mathematical Society, American Psychological Association (APA), Annual Reviews, ARTstor, Blackwell, Bowker, Cambridge Scientific Abstracts, Children's Literature Comprehensive Database Company (CLCD), Cinahl, ebrary, EBSCO Information Services, EBSCOhost, Elsevier, Gale Cengage Learning, Hoovers, Ingenta, Innovative Interfaces, Inc, JSTOR, LexisNexis, Medline, Mergent Online, Modern Language Association, Nature Publishing Group, OVID Technologies, Oxford Online, Project MUSE, ProQuest, PubMed, RefWorks, Sage, ScienceDirect, Scopus, Springer-Verlag, Springshare, LLC, Standard & Poor's, ValueLine, Westlaw, Wiley, Wiley InterScience
Wireless access
Function: Archival coll, Art exhibits, Computers for patron use, Copy machines, e-mail & chat, e-mail serv, E-Reserves, Electronic databases & coll, Exhibits, ILL available, Instruction & testing, Mail & tel request accepted, Microfiche/film & reading machines, Music CDs, Online cat, Online ref, Online searches, Orientations, Photocopying/Printing, Ref & res, Ref serv available, Ref serv in person, Referrals accepted, VHS videos, Wheelchair accessible
Publications: Post Library Association Report
Partic in Long Island Library Resources Council
Restriction: Authorized patrons, Borrowing requests are handled by ILL
Friends of the Library Group

BROWNVILLE

P BROWNVILLE-GLEN PARK LIBRARY*, 216 Brown Blvd, 13615. (Mail add: PO Box 510, 13615-0510), SAN 310-9550. Tel: 315-788-7889. FAX: 315-786-1178. *Dir*, Candace Wilde
Pop 1,600; Circ 7,951
Library Holdings: Bk Vols 5,219; Per Subs 30
Special Collections: Local Historical materials
Mem of North Country Library System
Open Tues, Wed 10-5, Fri 1-8, Sat 10-2

BUFFALO

S ALBRIGHT-KNOX ART GALLERY*, G Robert Strauss Jr Memorial Library, 1285 Elmwood Ave, 14222-1096. SAN 310-9577. Tel: 716-270-8240. FAX: 716-882-6213. E-mail: artref@albrightknox.org. Web Site: akat.albrightknox.org, www.albrightknox.org. *Tech Serv Librn*, John C Burnett; *Cataloger*, Gabriela Zoller; Staff 2 (MLS 2)

Founded 1905
Library Holdings: AV Mats 100; Bk Titles 50,000; Per Subs 100
Subject Interests: Artists bks, Contemporary art, Illustrated bks, Modern art, Rare bks
Automation Activity & Vendor Info: (Acquisitions) Ex Libris Group; (Cataloging) Ex Libris Group; (Circulation) Ex Libris Group; (ILL) OCLC WorldShare Interlibrary Loan; (OPAC) Ex Libris Group; (Serials) Ex Libris Group
Database Vendor: OCLC FirstSearch, Oxford Online
Wireless access
Function: Archival coll, Res libr
Publications: A Guide to the Archives of the Albright-Knox Art Gallery (Archives guide)
Partic in Western New York Library Resources Council
Open Fri 3-5
Restriction: Circulates for staff only, Researchers by appt only, Restricted access

J BRYANT & STRATTON BUSINESS COLLEGE*, Library Learning Center, 465 Main St, Ste 400, 14203. SAN 310-9607. Tel: 716-884-9120, Ext 261. FAX: 716-884-0091. Web Site: www.bryantstratton.edu. *Syst Dir of Libr,* Bennett Guy; *Librn,* Christopher Dale; *Librn,* Amy Joyce; Staff 11 (MLS 2, Non-MLS 9)
Founded 1867. Enrl 650
Library Holdings: Bk Titles 3,702; Bk Vols 3,900; Per Subs 130
Special Collections: Bryant & Stratton historical materials
Subject Interests: Acctg, Criminal justice, Info tech, Med admin
Automation Activity & Vendor Info: (Cataloging) Follett Software; (Circulation) Follett Software; (OPAC) Follett Software; (Serials) EBSCO Online
Database Vendor: Dialog, Gale Cengage Learning, OCLC FirstSearch
Wireless access
Function: Res libr
Publications: Echo (Newsletter)
Partic in Western New York Library Resources Council
Open Mon-Thurs 9-9, Fri & Sat 9-1

P BUFFALO & ERIE COUNTY PUBLIC LIBRARY SYSTEM*, One Lafayette Sq, 14203-1887. SAN 352-2180. Tel: 716-858-8900. FAX: 716-858-6211. Web Site: www.buffalolib.org. *Dir,* Mary Jean Jakubowski; *Dep Dir-Chief Financial Officer,* Kenneth H Stone; E-mail: stonek@buffalolib.org; *Dep Dir-Chief Operating Officer,* Carol Batt; E-mail: battc@buffalolib.org; *Asst Dep Dir-Human Res/Labor Relations Officer,* Jeannine Doyle; E-mail: DoyleJ@buffalolib.org; *Asst Dep Dir-Human Res/Workforce Develop Officer,* Doreen M Woods; E-mail: woodsd@buffalolib.org; Staff 74 (MLS 58, Non-MLS 16)
Founded 1836. Pop 919,040; Circ 8,097,152
Jan 2010-Dec 2010 Income (Main Library and Branch(s)) $29,871,090, State $2,255,553, Federal $46,103, County $26,155,534, Locally Generated Income $949,390, Other $464,510. Mats Exp $1,417,007, Books $831,680, Per/Ser (Incl. Access Fees) $301,615, AV Mat $283,712. Sal $6,423,489 (Prof $2,671,438)
Library Holdings: CDs 77,243; DVDs 61,090; e-books 4,727; Electronic Media & Resources 4,306; Bk Vols 1,401,318; Per Subs 1,339
Special Collections: Foundations; Genealogy Coll; Local History Coll; Maps; Mark Twain Coll; Niagara Falls Prints; Patents; Sheet Music; World War I & II Posters. State Document Depository; US Document Depository
Subject Interests: Art, Bus, Foundations, Genealogy, Hist, Lit, Local hist, Maps, Music, Natural sci, Patents, Sheet music
Automation Activity & Vendor Info: (Acquisitions) SirsiDynix; (Cataloging) SirsiDynix; (Circulation) SirsiDynix; (OPAC) SirsiDynix; (Serials) SirsiDynix
Wireless access
Publications: Annual Report of Director; Horizons, newsletter of the Buffalo & Erie County Public Library
Member Libraries: Alden-Ewell Free Library; Angola Public Library; Aurora Town Public Library; Boston Free Library; Cheektowaga Public Library; City of Tonawanda Public Library; Clarence Public Library; Collins Public Library; Eden Library; Elma Public Library; Grand Island Memorial Library; Hamburg Public Library; Hulbert Public Library of the Town of Concord; Lackawanna Public Library; Lancaster Public Library; Marilla Free Library; Newstead Public Library; Orchard Park Public Library; Town of North Collins Public Library; Town of Tonawanda Public Library; West Seneca Public Library
Partic in Nylink; OCLC Online Computer Library Center, Inc; Western New York Library Resources Council
Special Services for the Blind - Computer with voice synthesizer for visually impaired persons; Descriptive video serv (DVS); Dragon Naturally Speaking software; Magnifiers; Radio reading serv; Reader equip; Talking bks; ZoomText magnification & reading software
Branches: 10
CRANE, 633 Elmwood, 14222-1801, SAN 352-2245. Tel: 716-883-6651. FAX: 716-883-6651. E-mail: cra@buffalolib.org. *Librn,* Mary Schiffhauer; E-mail: schiffhauerm@buffalolib.org
Circ 148,524
Library Holdings: CDs 3,441; DVDs 4,066; Bk Vols 17,679
Friends of the Library Group
DUDLEY, 2010 S Park, 14220-1894, SAN 352-227X. Tel: 716-823-1854. FAX: 716-823-1854. E-mail: dud@buffalolib.org. *Librn,* Suzanne Colligan; E-mail: colligans@buffalolib.org
Circ 121,764
Library Holdings: CDs 3,344; DVDs 4,816; Bk Vols 18,078
Friends of the Library Group
EAST CLINTON, 1929 Clinton, 14206-3214, SAN 352-230X. Tel: 716-823-5626. FAX: 716-823-5626. E-mail: ecl@buffalolib.org. *Br Mgr,* Susan Carson; E-mail: carsons@buffalolib.org
Circ 62,239
Library Holdings: CDs 1,618; DVDs 3,642; Bk Vols 11,574
Friends of the Library Group
EAST DELAVAN, 1187 E Delavan, 14215-3801, SAN 352-2334. Tel: 716-896-4433. FAX: 716-896-4433. E-mail: edl@buffalolib.org. *Librn,* Gwen Collier; E-mail: collierg@buffalolib.org
Circ 71,503
Library Holdings: CDs 1,460; DVDs 3,752; Bk Vols 12,966
Friends of the Library Group
ERIE COUNTY CORRECTIONAL FACILITY, 11581 Walden Ave, Alden, 14004-0300, SAN 352-2318. Tel: 716-858-7159. FAX: 716-858-7162. *Institutional Serv Mgr,* Daniel Caufield; *Adminr, Br & Commun Connections,* Position Currently Open
Circ 145,208
ERIE COUNTY HOLDING CENTER, 40 Delaware Ave, 14202-3999, SAN 352-2342. *Mgr,* Daniel Caufield; *Adminr, Br & Commun Connections,* Position Currently Open
Circ 44,386
FRANK E MERRIWEATHER JR LIBRARY, 1324 Jefferson Ave, 14208, SAN 352-2636. Tel: 716-883-4418. FAX: 716-883-4418. E-mail: mrw@buffalolib.org. *Librn,* Sandra Bush
Circ 104,137
Library Holdings: CDs 2,384; DVDs 4,281; Bk Vols 30,040
Special Collections: Black History Reference
Friends of the Library Group
NIAGARA, 280 Porter, 14201-1030, SAN 352-2601. Tel: 716-882-1537. FAX: 716-882-1537. E-mail: nia@buffalolib.org. *Librn,* Kathryn Galvin; E-mail: galvink@buffalolib.org
Circ 83,014
Library Holdings: CDs 2,348; DVDs 4,274; Bk Vols 17,016
Subject Interests: Spanish lang
Friends of the Library Group
NORTH PARK, 975 Hertel Ave, 14216, SAN 352-2660. Tel: 716-875-3748. FAX: 716-875-3748. E-mail: npk@buffalolib.org. *Mgr,* Sean Goodrich; E-mail: goodrichs@buffalolib.org
Circ 77,486
Library Holdings: CDs 1,771; DVDs 2,065; Bk Vols 8,820
Friends of the Library Group
RIVERSIDE, 820 Tonawanda, 14207-1448, SAN 352-2725. Tel: 716-875-0562. FAX: 716-875-0562. E-mail: riv@buffalolib.org. *Librn,* Brian Hoth; E-mail: hothb@buffalolib.org
Circ 89,534
Library Holdings: CDs 1,905; DVDs 4,375; Bk Vols 16,818
Friends of the Library Group

M BUFFALO GENERAL HEALTH SYSTEM*, A H Aaron Health Sciences Library, 100 High St, 14203. SAN 352-2784. Tel: 716-859-2878. FAX: 716-859-1527. Web Site: library.kaleidahealth.org. *Dir of Libr,* Diane Schwartz; E-mail: dschwartz@kaleidahealth.org
Founded 1920
Library Holdings: Bk Vols 22,145; Per Subs 350
Subject Interests: Allied health, Hospital admin, Med, Nursing
Wireless access
Partic in Library Consortium of Health Institutions in Buffalo; Western New York Library Resources Council
Open Mon-Fri 8:30-4:30

S BUFFALO HISTORY MUSEUM RESEARCH LIBRARY, One Museum Court, 14216-3199. SAN 310-9615. Tel: 716-873-9644. FAX: 716-873-8754. E-mail: library@buffalohistory.org. Web Site: www.buffalohistory.org/Learn/Research-Library.aspx. *Dir, Libr & Archives,* Cynthia M Van Ness; *Asst Librn,* Amy Miller; *Libr Tech,* Shane Stephenson. Subject Specialists: *Genealogy, Local hist,* Cynthia M Van Ness; *Cataloging,* Amy Miller; Staff 1.8 (MLS 1.5, Non-MLS 0.3)
Founded 1862
Library Holdings: Microforms 6,500; Bk Vols 25,000; Per Subs 200
Special Collections: Iconographic Coll, bulk 1870-1980, images; Manuscripts Coll; War of 1812 Coll, bks, govt doc, ms, sermons; Western New York Newspaper Coll
Subject Interests: Local hist
Automation Activity & Vendor Info: (Cataloging) OCLC Connexion; (OPAC) LibraryWorld, Inc
Database Vendor: OCLC FirstSearch, OCLC WorldShare Interlibrary Loan

Wireless access
Function: Archival coll, Mail & tel request accepted, Online cat, Online ref, Photocopying/Printing, Telephone ref
Partic in OCLC Online Computer Library Center, Inc; Western New York Library Resources Council
Open Wed-Sat 1-5
Restriction: Not a lending libr, Pub use on premises

S BUFFALO MUSEUM OF SCIENCE*, Research Library, 1020 Humboldt Pkwy, 14211. SAN 310-964X. Tel: 716-896-5200. FAX: 716-897-6723. E-mail: library@sciencebuff.org. Web Site: www.sciencebuff.org. *Asst Coll Mgr,* Kacey Page; Staff 1 (MLS 1)
Founded 1861
Library Holdings: Bk Titles 15,000; Bk Vols 45,000; Per Subs 500
Special Collections: Oriental Art & Archaelogy (Elizabeth W Hamlin Coll); Tifft Farm Oral History Coll
Subject Interests: Anthrop, Astronomy, Botany, Far Eastern archaeol, Far Eastern art, Geol, Invertebrate zool, Mineralogy, Mycology, Near Eastern archaeol, Near Eastern art, Paleontology, Vertebrate zool
Automation Activity & Vendor Info: (Cataloging) Follett Software
Wireless access
Publications: Milestones of Science
Partic in Nylink; Western New York Library Resources Council
Open Thurs 9-5

S BUFFALO NEWS LIBRARY*, One News Plaza, 14203. (Mail add: PO Box 100, 14240-0100), SAN 310-9631. Tel: 716-849-4401. FAX: 716-856-5150. E-mail: library@buffnews.com. Web Site: www.buffalonews.com. *Libr Dir,* David Valenzuela; Staff 3 (MLS 2, Non-MLS 1)
Founded 1920
Library Holdings: Bk Titles 500; Bk Vols 2,000
Subject Interests: Local hist
Wireless access
Function: For res purposes, Newsp ref libr, Telephone ref
Restriction: Access at librarian's discretion, Co libr, Internal circ only, Not a lending libr, Open by appt only, Pub ref by request

S BURCHFIELD PENNEY ART CENTER*, Charles E Burchfield Archive & Library, Buffalo State College, 1300 Elmwood Ave, 14222. SAN 375-2321. Tel: 716-878-3216, 716-878-3244. FAX: 716-878-6003. E-mail: burchfld@buffalostate.edu. Web Site: www.burchfieldpenney.org. *Archives Mgr, Curator,* Tullis Johnson; *Archivist,* Heather Gring; E-mail: gringha@buffalostate.edu; *Curator,* Nancy Weekly; E-mail: weeklyns@buffalostate.edu; Staff 3 (MLS 1, Non-MLS 2)
Founded 1966
Library Holdings: Bk Vols 3,500
Special Collections: Art Institute of Buffalo; Artpark Archive; Buffalo Society of Artists Archive; Charles Cary Rumsey Archive; Charles E Burchfield Archive; Frank K M Rehn Galleries Archive; Hollis Frampton Archive; Martha Visser't Hooft Archive; Milton Rogovin Archive; Patteran Society Archive; Paul Sharits Archive; Virgina Cuthbert/Philip Eliot Archive; Western New York Art Archives. Oral History
Function: Archival coll, Art exhibits, Res libr
Restriction: Non-circulating coll, Non-circulating of rare bks, Not a lending libr, Open by appt only

C CANISIUS COLLEGE*, Andrew L Bouwhuis Library, 2001 Main St, 14208-1098. SAN 310-9674. Tel: 716-888-2900. FAX: 716-888-8420. Web Site: library.canisius.edu. *Libr Dir,* Kristine E Kasbohm; E-mail: kasbohmk@canisius.edu; *Assoc Libr Dir,* Barbara Boehnke; E-mail: boehnkeb@canisius.edu; Staff 10 (MLS 10)
Founded 1870. Enrl 4,294; Fac 233; Highest Degree: Master
Library Holdings: AV Mats 12,324; e-books 25,921; e-journals 52,129; Bk Titles 258,779; Bk Vols 313,916; Per Subs 295
Special Collections: Jesuitica Coll
Subject Interests: Philos, Relig
Wireless access
Partic in Connect NY; Westchester Academic Library Directors Organization (WALDO); Western New York Library Resources Council

S COLLECTOR CAR APPRAISERS ASSOCIATION LIBRARY*, 24 Myrtle Ave, 14204. SAN 322-757X. Tel: 716-855-1931. E-mail: jts1944@gmail.com. *Librn,* Mary Ann Sandoro
Library Holdings: Bk Titles 2,400; Bk Vols 3,000; Per Subs 125
Subject Interests: Autos, Bikes, Motorcycles
Restriction: Open by appt only

C D'YOUVILLE COLLEGE*, Montante Family Library, 320 Porter Ave, 14201-1084. SAN 310-9690. Tel: 716-829-7618. Reference Tel: 716-829-7747. FAX: 716-829-7770. E-mail: refdesk@dyc.edu. Web Site: library.dyc.edu. *Dir,* Rand Bellavia; Tel: 716-829-7616, E-mail: bellavia@dyc.edu; *Head, Ref,* Debra Lucas; Tel: 716-829-7764, E-mail: lucasd@dyc.edu; *Syst Librn,* Ted Sherman; E-mail: shermant@dyc.edu; *Acq,* John McClester; Tel: 716-829-8129, E-mail: mcclestj@dyc.edu; *Archivist,* Sister Mary Kathleen Duggan; *Cat,* Rosemarie Spyra; Tel: 716-829-8106, E-mail: spyrar@dyc.edu; *Per,* Jill Church; Tel: 716-829-8107, E-mail: churchj@dyc.edu; Staff 9 (MLS 9)
Founded 1908. Enrl 2,400; Fac 95; Highest Degree: Doctorate
Library Holdings: AV Mats 4,000; Bk Titles 100,000; Per Subs 650
Special Collections: Education Coll (Curriculum Library)
Subject Interests: Educ, Nursing, Occupational therapy, Phys therapy
Automation Activity & Vendor Info: (Acquisitions) Horizon; (Cataloging) Horizon; (Circulation) Horizon; (Course Reserve) Horizon; (ILL) Horizon; (OPAC) Horizon; (Serials) Horizon
Database Vendor: EBSCOhost, Gale Cengage Learning, JSTOR, LexisNexis, OVID Technologies, ProQuest, Wilson - Wilson Web
Wireless access
Publications: Guides; Newsletter; Periodicals List; What's New (Quarterly)
Partic in OCLC Online Computer Library Center, Inc; Western New York Library Resources Council
Special Services for the Blind - Reader equip
Open Mon-Thurs 8am-11pm, Fri 8am-9pm, Sat 10-6, Sun Noon-11

J ERIE COMMUNITY COLLEGE-CITY CAMPUS*, Library Resource Center, 121 Ellicott St, 14203. SAN 320-0558. Tel: 716-851-1074. FAX: 716-270-5987. E-mail: library@ecc.edu. Web Site: www.ecc.edu. *Chair,* Christine Dehoff; Tel: 716-851-1076, E-mail: dehoff@ecc.edu; *Bibliog Instr,* Rose Janish; *Cat,* Kathleen McGriff-Powers; Staff 5 (MLS 5)
Founded 1971
Library Holdings: Bk Vols 26,000; Per Subs 210
Automation Activity & Vendor Info: (Cataloging) Ex Libris Group; (Circulation) Ex Libris Group; (ILL) OCLC; (OPAC) Ex Libris Group
Database Vendor: EBSCOhost, Gale Cengage Learning, LexisNexis, OCLC FirstSearch
Wireless access
Partic in OCLC Online Computer Library Center, Inc; Western New York Library Resources Council
Open Mon-Thurs 8am-8:45pm, Fri 8-4, Sat 9-3

M ERIE COUNTY MEDICAL CENTER*, W Yerby Jones Memorial Library, 462 Grider St, 14215. SAN 310-9720. Tel: 716-898-3939. FAX: 716-898-3291. E-mail: library@ecmc.edu. Web Site: www.ecmc.edu. Staff 2 (MLS 2)
Founded 1921
Library Holdings: DVDs 200; e-books 150; e-journals 2,700; Bk Titles 2,400; Bk Vols 2,500; Per Subs 185; Videos 50
Subject Interests: Burns, Kidney transplant, Med, Nursing, Surgery, Trauma
Automation Activity & Vendor Info: (Acquisitions) SirsiDynix; (Cataloging) SirsiDynix; (Circulation) SirsiDynix; (OPAC) SirsiDynix; (Serials) SirsiDynix
Database Vendor: EBSCOhost, Gale Cengage Learning, Majors, Marcive, Inc, McGraw-Hill, Micromedex, Natural Standard, OCLC FirstSearch, OCLC WorldShare Interlibrary Loan, OVID Technologies, PubMed, SerialsSolutions, SirsiDynix, STAT!Ref (Teton Data Systems), Swets Information Services, UpToDate
Wireless access
Partic in Library Consortium of Health Institutions in Buffalo; OCLC Online Computer Library Center, Inc; Western New York Library Resources Council
Restriction: Staff use only

S HAUPTMAN-WOODWARD MEDICAL RESEARCH INSTITUTE*, Biophysics & Biochemistry Library, 700 Ellicott St, 14203. SAN 329-2681. Tel: 716-898-8614. FAX: 716-898-8660. Web Site: www.hwi.buffalo.edu. *Librn,* Vivian Cody; E-mail: cody@hwi.buffalo.edu
Library Holdings: Bk Titles 2,000
Subject Interests: Crystallography, Endocrinology
Restriction: Staff use only

L HISCOCK & BARCLAY LLP, Law Library, 1100 M&T Ctr, Three Fountain Plaza, 14203. SAN 372-4603. Tel: 716-856-5400. FAX: 716-846-1222. Web Site: www.hblaw.com. *Dir, Info Res,* Elaine Knecht; Staff 2 (MLS 2)
Wireless access
Restriction: Employees only

L HODGSON RUSS LLP*, Law Library, 140 pearl St, Ste 100, 14202-4040. SAN 372-4158. Tel: 716-848-1282, 716-856-4000. FAX: 716-849-0349. Web Site: www.hodgsonruss.com. *Head Librn,* Joan T Taulbee; E-mail: jtaulbee@hodgsonruss.com
Library Holdings: Bk Vols 15,000
Automation Activity & Vendor Info: (Cataloging) EOS International; (Circulation) EOS International; (OPAC) EOS International
Database Vendor: LexisNexis, Westlaw
Wireless access
Open Mon-Fri 8:30-5

C MEDAILLE COLLEGE LIBRARY*, 18 Agassiz Circle, 14214. SAN 310-9771. Tel: 716-880-2283. FAX: 716-884-9638. Web Site: www.medaille.edu/library. *Dir,* Pamela Jones; E-mail: pjones@medaille.edu; *Libr Serv Coordr,* Thomas Orrange; E-mail: thomas.m.orrange@medaille.edu; *Ref & Instruction Librn,* Deborah Ceppaglia; E-mail: dceppaglia@medaille.edu; *Info Literacy,* Andrew Yeager; E-mail: ayeager@medaille.edu; *Info Spec,* Samantha Purpora; Staff 3 (MLS 3)
Founded 1937. Enrl 2,500; Fac 80; Highest Degree: Master
Library Holdings: DVDs 250; e-books 20,000; Bk Titles 55,000; Bk Vols 57,000; Per Subs 320
Special Collections: Elementary Education (Donna Phillips Coll); Rare Books on Buffalo History; Veterinary Technology
Subject Interests: Bus mgt systs, Children's lit, Educ, Media, Psychol, Veterinary sci
Automation Activity & Vendor Info: (Cataloging) Innovative Interfaces, Inc - Millenium; (Circulation) Innovative Interfaces, Inc - Millenium; (OPAC) Innovative Interfaces, Inc - Millenium
Database Vendor: EBSCOhost, Gale Cengage Learning, ProQuest
Wireless access
Partic in Western New York Library Resources Council
Open Mon-Thurs 7:30am-10:30pm, Fri 7:30-7, Sat 10-5, Sun 1-7

S MULTIDISCIPLINARY CENTER FOR EARTHQUAKE ENGINEERING RESEARCH*, MCEER Information Service, State University of New York at Buffalo, 304 Capen Hall, 14260. SAN 370-7059. Tel: 716-645-3377. FAX: 716-645-3399. E-mail: mceeris@buffalo.edu. Web Site: mceer.buffalo.edu/infoservice. *Dir,* Sofia A Tangalos; Staff 5 (MLS 2, Non-MLS 3)
Founded 1986
Library Holdings: Bk Titles 30,000; Bk Vols 44,000; Per Subs 80
Special Collections: Earthquake Engineering & Natural Hazards Mitigation, bks, CD-ROMs, conference proceedings, journals, slides, videos
Subject Interests: Earthquake eng, Earthquakes, Natural hazards & disaster mitigation & related topics
Wireless access
Function: Doc delivery serv, Ref serv available
Partic in OCLC Online Computer Library Center, Inc; Western New York Library Resources Council

GL NEW YORK SUPREME COURT*, Eighth Judicial District Library, 77 W Eagle St, 14202. SAN 310-981X. Tel: 716-845-9400. FAX: 716-852-3454. E-mail: sclbuff@courts.state.ny.us. Web Site: www.courts.ny.us/8jd/nyssclawlib/nysscbuff.htm. *Dir,* James R Sahlem; *Librn,* Angela Patti; Staff 7 (MLS 2, Non-MLS 5)
Founded 1863
Library Holdings: Bk Titles 6,500; Bk Vols 350,000; Per Subs 226
Special Collections: Court of Appeals Records & Briefs; Law Reports (Old English & Canadian Reports Coll); New York Nominatives; NYCRR Backfile
Subject Interests: Law
Database Vendor: LexisNexis
Wireless access
Partic in LRS; OCLC Online Computer Library Center, Inc
Open Mon-Fri 8:30-5

L PHILLIPS, LYTLE LLP LIBRARY*, 3400 HSBC Ctr, 14203. SAN 310-9836. Tel: 716-847-5470. Reference Tel: 716-847-5471. FAX: 716-852-6100. *In Charge,* Kristine Westphal
Library Holdings: Bk Titles 25,000; Per Subs 120
Subject Interests: Law, Legislation
Database Vendor: LexisNexis, Westlaw
Partic in Westlaw
Restriction: Staff use only

GM ROSWELL PARK CANCER INSTITUTE*, Mirand Library, Elm & Carlton Sts, 14263. SAN 310-9844. Tel: 716-845-5966. FAX: 716-845-8699. E-mail: ill.library@roswellpark.org. Web Site: www.roswellpark.org. *Dir,* Dr Nancy A Cunningham; Staff 5 (MLS 4, Non-MLS 1)
Founded 1898
Library Holdings: Bk Vols 92,000; Per Subs 1,200
Subject Interests: Chem, Genetics, Molecular biol, Oncology, Pharmacology
Automation Activity & Vendor Info: (Cataloging) SirsiDynix; (Circulation) SirsiDynix; (OPAC) SirsiDynix; (Serials) SirsiDynix
Wireless access
Function: Copy machines, Doc delivery serv, Electronic databases & coll, ILL available, Online cat
Partic in Docline; National Network of Libraries of Medicine; New York State Higher Education Initiative; OCLC Online Computer Library Center, Inc; Western New York Library Resources Council
Restriction: Open to fac, students & qualified researchers, Pub use on premises, Restricted borrowing privileges, Restricted loan policy

S SAINT MARY'S SCHOOL FOR THE DEAF*, Library Information Center, 2253 Main St, 14214. SAN 310-9852. Tel: 716-834-7200, Ext 152. FAX: 716-837-2080. Web Site: www.smsdk12.org. *Librn,* Sheila Thoman
Founded 1964
Library Holdings: Bk Titles 25,000; Per Subs 75
Subject Interests: Audiology, Deaf, Deaf culture, Deaf studies, Sign lang, Spec educ with emphasis on deafness
Automation Activity & Vendor Info: (Acquisitions) Follett Software; (Cataloging) Follett Software; (Circulation) Follett Software; (Course Reserve) Follett Software; (ILL) Follett Software; (Media Booking) Follett Software; (Serials) Follett Software
Database Vendor: EBSCOhost, ProQuest
Wireless access
Partic in Western New York Library Resources Council
Open Mon-Thurs 8:20-3

M SISTERS OF CHARITY HOSPITAL MEDICAL LIBRARY*, 2157 Main St, 14214. SAN 310-9860. Tel: 716-862-1256. FAX: 716-862-1883. Web Site: www.chsbuffalo.org. *Librn,* Janelle Toner; Staff 2 (MLS 1, Non-MLS 1)
Founded 1948
Library Holdings: Bk Titles 125; Bk Vols 300
Special Collections: Spiritual Care
Open Mon-Fri 8-4

C STATE UNIVERSITY OF NEW YORK COLLEGE AT BUFFALO*, E H Butler Library, 1300 Elmwood Ave, 14222-1095. SAN 310-9879. Tel: 716-878-6314. Circulation Tel: 716-878-6303. Interlibrary Loan Service Tel: 716-878-6310. Reference Tel: 716-878-6300. FAX: 716-878-3134. Interlibrary Loan Service FAX: 716-878-3163. E-mail: library@buffalostate.edu. Web Site: library.buffalostate.edu. *Assoc VPres, Libr & Instrul Tech,* Maryruth F Glogowski; E-mail: glogowmf@buffalostate.edu; *Assoc Dir, Info Commons,* Maureen A Lindstrom; Tel: 716-878-6236, E-mail: lindstma@buffalostate.edu; *Assoc Dir, Tech Serv,* Gail M Marinaccio; Tel: 716-878-6311, Fax: 716-878-4316, E-mail: marinagm@buffalostate.edu; *Archives & Spec Coll Librn,* Daniel DiLandro; Tel: 716-878-6304, E-mail: dilandm@buffalostate.edu; *ILL Librn, Syst,* Marc Dewey Bayer; Fax: 716-878-6335, E-mail: bayermd@buffalostate.edu. Subject Specialists: *Hist,* Daniel DiLandro; Staff 43 (MLS 19, Non-MLS 24)
Founded 1910. Enrl 9,413; Fac 425; Highest Degree: Master
Library Holdings: AV Mats 9,868; CDs 2,144; DVDs 7,609; e-books 124,095; Microforms 409,107; Bk Titles 472,458; Bk Vols 670,330; Per Subs 61,171
Special Collections: Children's Author Lois Lenski Coll, bks, illustrations; Courier Express Coll; Creative Education (Creative Studies Coll), bks, microfilm; Elementary & Secondary Curriculum Coll; Francis E Fronczak Coll Inventory, cats; Historical Children's Books (Hertha Ganey Coll); Historical Textbooks (Kempke-Root Coll); Isaac Klein Papers; Jazz (William H Talmadge Coll); Lester Glassner Coll; Local Polish Community (Fronczak Coll); Lois Lenski Children's Coll; Selig Adler Jewish Archives; Tom Fontana Coll
Subject Interests: African, African-Am, Applied arts, Criminal justice, Educ, Exceptional children educ, Fine arts, Local hist
Automation Activity & Vendor Info: (Acquisitions) Ex Libris Group; (Cataloging) Ex Libris Group; (Circulation) Ex Libris Group; (Course Reserve) Ex Libris Group; (ILL) OCLC ILLiad; (OPAC) Ex Libris Group; (Serials) SerialsSolutions
Database Vendor: ProQuest
Wireless access
Function: Archival coll, Art exhibits, Audio & video playback equip for onsite use, AV serv, Computer training, Computers for patron use, Copy machines, Distance learning, Doc delivery serv, Electronic databases & coll, Equip loans & repairs, Games & aids for the handicapped, Handicapped accessible, Health sci info serv, ILL available, Learning ctr, Magnifiers for reading, Mail & tel request accepted, Music CDs, Online cat, Online ref, Online searches, Photocopying/Printing, Ref serv available, Scanner, VHS videos, Video lending libr, Wheelchair accessible, Workshops
Partic in OCLC Online Computer Library Center, Inc; Westchester Academic Library Directors Organization (WALDO); Western New York Library Resources Council
Special Services for the Deaf - Assistive tech; Bks on deafness & sign lang; Coll on deaf educ; High interest/low vocabulary bks
Special Services for the Blind - Assistive/Adapted tech devices, equip & products; Audio mat; Computer with voice synthesizer for visually impaired persons; Duplicating spec requests; Micro-computer access & training; Networked computers with assistive software; Reader equip; Ref serv; Screen enlargement software for people with visual disabilities; Talking bks; Telesensory screen enlarger & speech synthesis interface to the OPAC; ZoomText magnification & reading software
Restriction: Open to pub for ref & circ; with some limitations, Open to students, fac & staff
Friends of the Library Group

R TEMPLE BETH ZION*, Aaron & Bertha Broder Center for Jewish Education, 700 Sweet Home Rd, 14226. SAN 352-3292. Tel: 716-836-6565. FAX: 716-831-1126. E-mail: education@tbz.org. Web Site: tbz.org. *Dir,* Susan Goldberg Schwartz; Tel: 716-836-6565, Ext 131
Founded 1915
Library Holdings: Bk Vols 20,000; Per Subs 22
Special Collections: Children's Judaica
Subject Interests: Judaica
Wireless access
Publications: American Jewish Odyssey, Annotated Bibliography of the Jewish Experience in America; Jewish Children's Literature, Annotated Bibliography of Books on Judaism & Jewish History; Lest We Forget, A Selected Annotated List of Books on the Holocaust

JR TROCAIRE COLLEGE LIBRARY*, Rachel R Savarino Library, 360 Choate Ave, 14220-2094. SAN 310-9887. Tel: 716-827-2434. Administration Tel: 716-827-2436. Automation Services Tel: 716-827-2447. FAX: 716-828-6102. E-mail: libraryhelp@trocaire.edu. Web Site: library.trocaire.edu. *Dir,* Judith K Schwartz; E-mail: schwartzj@trocaire.edu. Subject Specialists: *Allied health,* Judith K Schwartz; Staff 4.5 (MLS 4.5)
Founded 1958. Enrl 1,006; Fac 3; Highest Degree: Bachelor
Library Holdings: CDs 18; DVDs 422; e-books 998; e-journals 3; Electronic Media & Resources 37; Bk Titles 13,350; Bk Vols 14,200; Per Subs 85; Videos 37
Subject Interests: Allied health, Computer network, Hospitality, Liberal arts, Nursing
Automation Activity & Vendor Info: (Acquisitions) ComPanion Corp; (Cataloging) ComPanion Corp; (Circulation) ComPanion Corp; (OPAC) ComPanion Corp; (Serials) SerialsSolutions
Database Vendor: Bowker, CredoReference, EBSCOhost, Gale Cengage Learning, OCLC FirstSearch, OCLC WorldShare Interlibrary Loan, ProQuest, SerialsSolutions, Springshare, LLC
Wireless access
Function: Archival coll, Computers for patron use, Distance learning, E-Reserves, Electronic databases & coll, ILL available, Online searches, Orientations, Ref & res
Partic in Western New York Library Resources Council
Open Mon-Thurs 8-8, Fri 8-4, Sat 9-2
Restriction: Fee for pub use, Open to students, fac, staff & alumni

A UNITED STATES ARMY*, Corps of Engineers Buffalo District Technical Library, 1776 Niagara St, 14201-3199. SAN 352-3357. Tel: 716-879-4178. FAX: 716-879-6468. Web Site: www.lrb.usace.army.mil. *Librn,* Eric N Kolber; E-mail: eric.n.kolber@usace.army.mil
Founded 1976
Library Holdings: Bk Titles 15,000; Per Subs 70
Special Collections: Aerial Photography; Government Documents; Great Lakes Research; Microcomputer Software Bank; Nuclear Waste Disposal; Radioactive Waste Isolation
Subject Interests: Chem, Construction, Econ, Eng, Environ studies, Geol, Hydrol, Water res develop
Automation Activity & Vendor Info: (Cataloging) OCLC; (ILL) OCLC
Database Vendor: Dialog
Publications: Buffalo District Technical Library
Partic in Dialog Corp; OCLC Online Computer Library Center, Inc; Western New York Library Resources Council
Open Mon-Fri 8-4:30

C UNIVERSITY AT BUFFALO LIBRARIES-STATE UNIVERSITY OF NEW YORK*, University Libraries, 433 Capen Hall, 14260-1625. SAN 352-2903. Tel: 716-645-2965. Circulation Tel: 716-645-1312. Interlibrary Loan Service Tel: 716-645-2812. Reference Tel: 716-645-2820. Information Services Tel: 716-645-7744. FAX: 716-645-3844. E-mail: library@buffalo.edu. Web Site: library.buffalo.edu. *Vice Provost for Libr,* H Austin Booth; E-mail: habooth@buffalo.edu; Staff 160 (MLS 102, Non-MLS 58)
Founded 1922. Enrl 28,192; Fac 90; Highest Degree: Doctorate
Jul 2008-Jun 2009 Income (Main and Other College/University Libraries) $21,000,000. Mats Exp $8,600,000, Electronic Ref Mat (Incl. Access Fees) $6,300,000
Library Holdings: e-books 725,000; e-journals 48,400; Microforms 6,100,000; Bk Vols 3,852,074; Per Subs 80,431
Special Collections: Archives (University Archives & Manuscripts Coll); Frank Lloyd Wright/Darwin Martin House Coll; George Kelley Paperback & Pulp Fiction Coll; History of Medicine Coll; James Joyce Coll; Love Canal Coll; Poetry Coll-First Editions & Manuscripts Coll (Robert Graves, Robert Duncan,William Carlos Williams, Dylan Thomas); Polish Coll; Rare Books Coll (19th & 20th Century). Can & Prov; State Document Depository; UN Document Depository; US Document Depository
Automation Activity & Vendor Info: (Acquisitions) Ex Libris Group; (Cataloging) Ex Libris Group; (Circulation) Ex Libris Group; (Course Reserve) Ex Libris Group; (ILL) OCLC ILLiad; (OPAC) Ex Libris Group; (Serials) Ex Libris Group
Database Vendor: 3M Library Systems, ACM (Association for Computing Machinery), Alexander Street Press, American Chemical Society, American Physical Society, American Psychological Association (APA), ARTstor, Baker & Taylor, Blackwell, Bowker, Cambridge Scientific Abstracts, Cinahl, CIOS (Communication Institute for Online Scholarship), Community of Science (COS), Coutts Information Service, CQ Press, CRC Press/Taylor & Francis Group, Dun & Bradstreet, Ebooks Corporation, EBSCO Information Services, EBSCOhost, Elsevier, Emerald, Ex Libris Group, Factiva.com, Facts on File, Foundation Center, Gale Cengage Learning, Gallup, Greenwood Publishing Group, H W Wilson, Haworth Pres Inc, HeinOnline, Hoovers, IBISWorld, IEEE (Institute of Electrical & Electronics Engineers), infoUSA, Ingenta, ISI Web of Knowledge, Jane's, JSTOR, Knovel, LexisNexis, Marcive, Inc, McGraw-Hill, Medlib, Medline, Modern Language Association, Nature Publishing Group, Newsbank-Readex, OCLC FirstSearch, OCLC WorldShare Interlibrary Loan, OVID Technologies, Oxford Communications, Oxford Online, Project MUSE, ProQuest, PubMed, Quicklaw, ReferenceUSA, Safari Books Online, Sage, ScienceDirect, Scopus, SerialsSolutions, Springer-Verlag, Standard & Poor's, Swets Information Services, Thomson - Web of Science, Thomson Carswell, ValueLine, WebMD, Westlaw, Wiley, Wiley InterScience, Wilson - Wilson Web, YBP Library Services
Wireless access
Publications: ACCESS (Newsletter); Progress Report (Annual report)
Partic in Association of Research Libraries (ARL); Center for Research Libraries; National Network of Libraries of Medicine; Nylink; OCLC Online Computer Library Center, Inc; Western New York Library Resources Council
Friends of the Library Group

Departmental Libraries:

ARCHITECTURE & PLANNING, 303 Abbott Hall, 3435 Main St, 14214-3087, SAN 352-2938. Tel: 716-829-3505. FAX: 716-829-2780. E-mail: library@buffalo.edu. *Assoc Librn,* Rose Orcutt; E-mail: rmorcutt@buffalo.edu; Staff 1 (MLS 1)
Fac 1
Library Holdings: Bk Vols 40,000
Special Collections: Rudy Bruner Award for Urban Excellence Archives
Friends of the Library Group

CM HEALTH SCIENCES LIBRARY, Abbott Hall, 3435 Main St, Bldg 28, 14214-3002, SAN 352-2997. Tel: 716-829-3900. Circulation Tel: 716-829-5682. Interlibrary Loan Service Tel: 716-829-5758. Reference Tel: 716-829-5683. FAX: 716-829-2211. E-mail: askhsl@buffalo.edu. Web Site: library.buffalo.edu/hsl. *Dir, Health Sci Libr,* Dr Gary D Byrd; Tel: 716-829-5720, E-mail: gdbyrd@buffalo.edu; *Assoc Dir, Health Sci Libr,* Amy Lyons; Tel: 716-829-5719, E-mail: alyons@buffalo.edu; *Head, Multimedia Coll & Serv,* Lori Widzinski; Tel: 716-829-5744, E-mail: widz@buffalo.edu; *Assoc Librn,* Dr Diane Rein; Tel: 716-829-5749, E-mail: drein@buffalo.edu; *Outreach Librn,* Ophelia Morey; Tel: 716-829-5748, E-mail: otmorey@buffalo.edu; *Ref Librn/Health Sci Liaison,* Nell Aronoff; Tel: 716-829-5735, E-mail: naronoff@buffalo.edu; *Ref Librn/Health Sci Liaison,* Deborah Chiarella; Tel: 716-829-5753; *Ref Librn/Health Sci Liaison,* Sharon Murphy; Tel: 716-829-5750, E-mail: hslscm@buffalo.edu; *Ref Librn/Health Sci Liaison,* Elizabeth M Stellrecht; Tel: 716-829-5734, E-mail: thomann4@buffalo.edu; *Ref Librn/Health Sci Liaison,* Michelle Zafron; Tel: 716-829-5746, E-mail: mlzafron@buffalo.edu; *Web Coordr,* Pamela Rose; Tel: 716-829-5722, E-mail: pmrose@buffalo.edu; *Curator,* Linda Lohr; Tel: 716-829-5737, E-mail: lalohr@buffalo.edu; *Circ,* Evelyn Hufford; Tel: 716-829-5727, E-mail: hufford@buffalo.edu; *Coll Mgt,* Amanda Start; Tel: 716-829-5736, E-mail: start@buffalo.edu. Subject Specialists: *Bioinformatics,* Dr Diane Rein; *Med,* Nell Aronoff; *Pharm,* Deborah Chiarella; *Nursing,* Sharon Murphy; *Dentistry,* Elizabeth M Stellrecht; *Health related professions, Pub health,* Michelle Zafron; *Hist of med,* Linda Lohr; Staff 18.7 (MLS 12.7, Non-MLS 6)
Founded 1846. Enrl 27,500; Highest Degree: Doctorate
Library Holdings: e-journals 825; Bk Vols 358,880; Per Subs 453
Special Collections: History of Medicine Coll; Media Resources Center
Subject Interests: Dentistry, Health related professions, Med, Nursing, Pharm
Automation Activity & Vendor Info: (Acquisitions) Ex Libris Group; (Cataloging) Ex Libris Group; (Circulation) Ex Libris Group; (Course Reserve) Ex Libris Group; (ILL) OCLC ILLiad; (Media Booking) Ex Libris Group; (OPAC) Ex Libris Group; (Serials) Ex Libris Group
Partic in Library Consortium of Health Institutions in Buffalo; New England Law Library Consortium, Inc; State Univ of NY at Buffalo
Publications: Library Guide
Friends of the Library Group

LOCKWOOD MEMORIAL LIBRARY, 228 Lockwood Library, North Campus, 14260-2200, SAN 352-3055. Tel: 716-645-2814. Circulation Tel: 716-645-2815. Interlibrary Loan Service Tel: 716-645-2812. Reference Tel: 716-645-2820. Administration Tel: 716-645-7744. FAX: 716-645-3859. *Dir, Pub Serv, Arts & Sci Libr,* Margaret Wells; E-mail:

mwells@buffalo.edu; *Asst Dir of Libr for Access Serv & Chief Financial Officer,* Karen Senglaup; Tel: 716-645-5951, E-mail: lolkds@buffalo.edu
Special Collections: East Asian Coll; Government Documents; Graphic Novel Coll; International Leisure Reading Coll; Juvenile Coll; Polish Room. State Document Depository; US Document Depository
MUSIC, 112 Baird Hall, 14260-4750, SAN 352-311X. Tel: 716-645-2923. Reference Tel: 716-645-2924. FAX: 716-645-3906. E-mail: musique@buffalo.edu. Web Site: library.buffalo.edu/music. *Assoc Librn,* John Bewley; Staff 4 (MLS 3, Non-MLS 1)
Library Holdings: CDs 18,300; DVDs 650; Microforms 8,000; Music Scores 93,600; Bk Vols 41,800; Videos 1,000
Special Collections: Archive of the Center of the Creative & Performing Arts, 1964-1980; Buffalo Musicians' Association Records, 1889-2002; Irene Haupt Photographs of Musicians in Buffalo, ca. 1978-1999; J. Warren Perry Coll of Photographs; Jan Williams Images Coll; Morton Feldman Photographs, 1939-1987; Music Librarianship Archive; North American New Music Festival Archive

CL CHARLES B SEARS LAW LIBRARY, 217 John Lord O'Brian Hall, 14260-1110. (Mail add: 211 O'Brian Hall, 14260), SAN 352-2962. Tel: 716-645-2041. Circulation Tel: 716-645-6765. Interlibrary Loan Service Tel: 716-645-2347. Reference Tel: 716-645-2047. FAX: 716-645-3860. E-mail: asklaw@buffalo.edu. Web Site: law.lib.buffalo.edu. *Dir, Law Libr, Vice Dean, Legal Info Serv,* Elizabeth Adelman; Tel: 716-645-2089, E-mail: eadelman@buffalo.edu; *Assoc Dir & Head M Robert Koren AV Ctr,* Terrence McCormack; Tel: 716-645-2831, E-mail: cormack@buffalo.edu; *Head, Access Serv,* John Mondo; E-mail: jamondo@buffalo.edu; *Head, Cat,* Ellen McGrath; Tel: 716-645-2254, E-mail: emcgrath@buffalo.edu; *Head, Coll Mgt,* Theodora Belniak; Tel: 716-645-8504, E-mail: tbelniak@buffalo.edu; *Head, Info Serv,* Marcia Zubrow; Tel: 716-645-2160, E-mail: llmarcia@buffalo.edu; *Archives Librn, Fac Serv, Ref,* Christine George; Tel: 716-645-6690, E-mail: cgeorge3@buffalo.edu; *Foreign & Intl Law Librn,* Nina Cascio; Tel: 716-645-2633, E-mail: ncascio@buffalo.edu; *Ref Librn,* Joseph Gerken; Tel: 716-645-6769, E-mail: gerken@buffalo.edu; *Student Serv Librn,* Brian Detweiler; Tel: 716-645-2384, E-mail: briandet@buffalo.edu; *Day Circ Mgr,* Melissa Bednarz; Tel: 716-645-2301, E-mail: mmt@buffalo.edu; *Evening & Weekend Circ Mgr,* Paul Ziolkowski; E-mail: pjz5@buffalo.edu; *Cataloger,* Nancy Babb; E-mail: babb@buffalo.edu; *Instrul Support Tech,* Anne Marie Swartz; Tel: 716-645-7949, E-mail: amswartz@buffalo.edu; *Passport Serv, Student Serv, Circ,* Peggy Lyons; Tel: 716-645-0395, E-mail: peglyons@buffalo.edu. Subject Specialists: *Foreign law, Intl law,* Nina Cascio; Staff 16 (MLS 14, Non-MLS 2)
Founded 1887. Enrl 720; Fac 60; Highest Degree: Doctorate
Library Holdings: Microforms 285,936; Bk Vols 296,539; Per Subs 7,207
Special Collections: John Lord O'Brian Coll, bks, papers
Database Vendor: Bloomberg, ebrary, Fastcase, HeinOnline, LexisNexis, Loislaw, Oxford Online, ProQuest, Westlaw
Function: Passport agency
Partic in New England Law Library Consortium, Inc; Western New York Library Resources Council
Open Mon-Thurs 7:30am-11pm, Fri 7:30-5, Sat 9-5, Sun 10am-11pm
OSCAR A SILVERMAN LIBRARY, University at Buffalo, 116 Capen Hall, 14260-1672, SAN 352-3233. Tel: 716-645-2944. Reference Tel: 716-645-2820. FAX: 716-645-3714. *Dir, Pub Serv, Arts & Sci Libr,* Margaret Wells; Tel: 716-645-7744, E-mail: mwells@buffalo.edu; *Asst Dir of Libr for Access Serv & Chief Financial Officer,* Karen Senglaup; Tel: 716-645-5951, E-mail: lolkds@buffalo.edu
Special Collections: Map Coll; Multimedia Center; Science & Engineering Information Center
Subject Interests: Bio, Chem, Computer sci, Eng, Geol, Math, Phys geog, Physics

S UNIVERSITY OF BUFFALO RESEARCH INSTITUTE ON ADDICTIONS*, Research Library, 1021 Main St, 14203-1016. SAN 320-2070. Tel: 716-887-2511. FAX: 716-887-2490. *Librn,* Ann Mina Sawusch; Staff 1 (Non-MLS 1)
Founded 1974
Library Holdings: Bk Vols 8,000; Per Subs 100
Subject Interests: Alcohol abuse, Drug abuse, Gambling
Wireless access
Partic in Library Consortium of Health Institutions in Buffalo; Western New York Library Resources Council
Restriction: Open to pub by appt only

JR VILLA MARIA COLLEGE LIBRARY*, 240 Pine Ridge Rd, 14225-3999. SAN 310-9917. Tel: 716-896-0700. FAX: 716-896-0705. Web Site: www.villa.edu/library/index.html. *Dir,* Sister Anna Falbo; Tel: 716-961-1862, E-mail: smanna@catholic.org; *Info Spec,* Terasa Gipson; Tel: 716-961-1863, E-mail: gipsont@villa.edu; *Media Serv,* Barbara Wetzel; Tel: 716-961-1864, E-mail: wetzel@villa.edu; Staff 4 (MLS 3, Non-MLS 1)
Founded 1961. Enrl 500; Fac 50; Highest Degree: Bachelor
Library Holdings: AV Mats 5,000; Bk Vols 32,000; Per Subs 150
Subject Interests: Art, Children's lit, Early childhood, Graphics, Interior design, Poland, Relig studies
Automation Activity & Vendor Info: (Cataloging) Follett Software; (Circulation) Follett Software; (OPAC) Follett Software
Database Vendor: EBSCOhost, Gale Cengage Learning, ProQuest, Wilson - Wilson Web
Wireless access
Partic in Western New York Library Resources Council

M THE WOMEN & CHILDREN'S HOSPITAL OF BUFFALO*, Emily Foster Health Sciences Library, 118 Hodge Ave, 14222. SAN 310-9682. Tel: 716-878-7304. Administration Tel: 716-878-1182. FAX: 716-878-1987. E-mail: choblib@kaleidahealth.org. Web Site: library.kaleidahealth.org. *Coordr,* Elaine C Mosher; E-mail: emosher@kaleidahealth.org; Staff 1 (MLS 1)
Founded 1912
Library Holdings: e-journals 400; Bk Titles 2,000; Bk Vols 10,000; Per Subs 80
Subject Interests: Consumer health, Gynecology, Obstetrics, Pediatrics
Automation Activity & Vendor Info: (OPAC) SirsiDynix
Wireless access
Partic in National Network of Libraries of Medicine
Open Mon-Fri 8:30-4:30
Restriction: Authorized patrons

BURNT HILLS

P TOWN OF BALLSTON COMMUNITY LIBRARY*, Burnt Hills-Ballston Lake, Two Lawmar Lane, 12027. SAN 310-9933. Tel: 518-399-8174. FAX: 518-399-1687. E-mail: bur-director@sals.edu. Web Site: burnthills.sals.edu. *Dir,* Karen DeAngelo; *Ch,* Rebecca Darling; Staff 2 (MLS 2)
Founded 1952. Pop 8,200; Circ 184,850
Library Holdings: AV Mats 8,919; Bk Vols 58,805
Special Collections: Town of Ballston History, software
Subject Interests: Local hist
Automation Activity & Vendor Info: (Acquisitions) Innovative Interfaces, Inc; (Cataloging) Innovative Interfaces, Inc; (Circulation) Innovative Interfaces, Inc; (ILL) Innovative Interfaces, Inc; (OPAC) Innovative Interfaces, Inc
Database Vendor: ACM (Association for Computing Machinery), American Chemical Society, American Mathematical Society, Amigos Library Services, Annual Reviews, Baker & Taylor, BioOne, Cambridge Scientific Abstracts, CountryWatch, CQ Press, EBSCOhost, Facts on File, Gale Cengage Learning, H W Wilson, JSTOR, LexisNexis, Marcive, Inc, OCLC FirstSearch, OCLC WorldShare Interlibrary Loan, Oxford Online, ProQuest, RefWorks, ScienceDirect, SirsiDynix, Springer-Verlag, TDNet, ValueLine, Wiley, Wilson - Wilson Web
Wireless access
Function: Adult bk club, Art exhibits, Computer training, Copy machines, Fax serv, ILL available, Preschool outreach, Prog for adults, Prog for children & young adult, Spoken cassettes & CDs, Tax forms, VHS videos
Publications: Annual Report
Mem of Southern Adirondack Library System
Partic in Capital District Library Council
Open Mon-Thurs 10-8, Fri & Sat 10-2
Friends of the Library Group

CAIRO

P CAIRO PUBLIC LIBRARY*, 512 Main St, 12413-3007. (Mail add: PO Box 720, 12413-0720), SAN 310-995X. Tel: 518-622-9864. FAX: 518-622-9874. E-mail: cairolibrary@mhcable.com. Web Site: www.cairo.lib.ny.us. *Librn,* Debra Kamecke; Staff 3 (MLS 1, Non-MLS 2)
Founded 1963. Pop 7,000; Circ 60,000
Library Holdings: Bk Vols 20,000; Per Subs 32
Subject Interests: Local hist
Automation Activity & Vendor Info: (Cataloging) Innovative Interfaces, Inc; (Circulation) Innovative Interfaces, Inc; (OPAC) Innovative Interfaces, Inc; (Serials) Innovative Interfaces, Inc
Wireless access
Mem of Mid-Hudson Library System
Open Mon 10-8, Tues & Wed 10-5, Thurs 2-8, Fri & Sat 10-2
Friends of the Library Group

CALEDONIA

P CALEDONIA LIBRARY*, 3108 Main St, 14423. SAN 310-9968. Tel: 585-538-4512. FAX: 585-538-4978. Web Site: www.pls-net.org. *Dir,* Renate Goff
Pop 4,030; Circ 24,000
Library Holdings: Bk Vols 18,000
Automation Activity & Vendor Info: (Cataloging) SirsiDynix; (Circulation) SirsiDynix; (OPAC) SirsiDynix; (Serials) SirsiDynix
Wireless access
Mem of Pioneer Library System

Partic in Southeastern Libraries Cooperating
Open Mon & Thurs 2-5:30 & 7-9, Tues 9-1 & 2-5:30, Fri 2-5:30, Sat 9-1

CALLICOON

P WESTERN SULLIVAN PUBLIC LIBRARY*, Delaware Free Branch, 45 Lower Main St, 12723. (Mail add: PO Box 245, 12723-0245), SAN 310-9976. Tel: 845-887-4040. FAX: 845-887-8957. E-mail: del@rcls.org. *Br Mgr,* Roades Jennifer
Founded 1951. Circ 12,492
Library Holdings: Bk Vols 15,206
Special Collections: Sullivan County Democrat Coll, microfilm
Subject Interests: Local hist, Mysteries
Wireless access
Mem of Ramapo Catskill Library System
Special Services for the Blind - Bks on cassette; Bks on CD; Home delivery serv; Large print bks; Radio reading serv
Open Mon & Wed-Fri 10-5, Tues 5-8, Sat 1-4

CALVERTON

P BAITING HOLLOW FREE LIBRARY*, Four Warner Dr, 11933. SAN 310-9984. Tel: 631-727-8765. *Librn,* Charlotte Jacques
Founded 1903. Pop 475; Circ 1,392
Library Holdings: Bk Vols 4,800
Subject Interests: Long Island hist
Mem of Suffolk Cooperative Library System

CAMBRIDGE

P CAMBRIDGE PUBLIC LIBRARY*, 21 W Main St, 12816. SAN 311 0001. Tel: 518-677-2443. FAX: 518-677-2443. Web Site: www.cambridge.sals.edu. *Dir,* Judy B Center; E-mail: jcenter@sals.edu; *Asst Librn,* Julie Wetherby
Pop 1,925; Circ 42,665
Library Holdings: Bk Vols 18,000; Per Subs 45
Automation Activity & Vendor Info: (Circulation) Innovative Interfaces, Inc
Wireless access
Mem of Southern Adirondack Library System
Open Mon, Wed & Fri 6:30pm-9pm, Tues & Thurs 1-5, Sat 10-5
Friends of the Library Group

CAMDEN

P CAMDEN PUBLIC LIBRARY*, 57 Second St, 13316. SAN 311-001X. Tel: 315-245-1980. FAX: 315-245-1980. *Dir,* Linda Frenzel; Staff 4 (Non-MLS 4)
Founded 1890. Pop 2,667; Circ 45,000
Library Holdings: Bk Titles 20,000; Per Subs 46
Special Collections: News (Camden Advance Journal Coll)
Automation Activity & Vendor Info: (Acquisitions) SirsiDynix; (Cataloging) SirsiDynix; (Circulation) SirsiDynix; (Course Reserve) SirsiDynix; (ILL) SirsiDynix; (Media Booking) SirsiDynix; (OPAC) SirsiDynix; (Serials) SirsiDynix
Wireless access
Publications: Queen Central News
Mem of Mid-York Library System
Open Tues-Thurs 2-8, Fri 10-5, Sat 10-4

CAMILLUS

P MAXWELL MEMORIAL LIBRARY*, 14 Genesee St, 13031. SAN 311-0036. Tel: 315-672-3661. FAX: 315-672-5514. Web Site: maxwellmemoriallibrary.org. *Dir,* Kathryn Benson; Staff 1 (MLS 1)
Founded 1918. Pop 18,146; Circ 83,270
Library Holdings: Bk Vols 26,000; Per Subs 85
Automation Activity & Vendor Info: (Cataloging) Innovative Interfaces, Inc; (Circulation) Innovative Interfaces, Inc; (OPAC) Innovative Interfaces, Inc; (Serials) Innovative Interfaces, Inc
Wireless access
Mem of Onondaga County Public Library
Open Mon-Wed 10-8, Thurs & Fri 10-5, Sat 10-3
Friends of the Library Group

CAMPBELL HALL

P MOFFAT LIBRARY OF WASHINGTONVILLE, Bldg 2, Ste 2, 3348 Rt 208, 10916. SAN 312-6331. Tel: 845-496-5483. FAX: 845-496-6854. E-mail: moffat@rcls.org. Web Site: www.moffatlibrary.org. *Dir,* Carol McCrossen; E-mail: cmccrossen@rcls.org; *Head, Ref & Adult Serv,* Matt Thorenz; E-mail: mthorenz@rcls.org; *Head, Youth Serv,* Anna Gordon; E-mail: agordon@rcls.org. Subject Specialists: *Local hist,* Matt Thorenz; *Local hist,* Anna Gordon; Staff 8 (MLS 3, Non-MLS 5)
Founded 1887. Pop 24,000; Circ 129,000
Library Holdings: Audiobooks 977; AV Mats 129; CDs 1,454; DVDs 3,171; e-books 4,819; Electronic Media & Resources 35; Large Print Bks 1,100; Bk Titles 35,148; Bk Vols 36,005; Per Subs 95
Special Collections: Local History Coll
Wireless access
Function: 24/7 Electronic res, 24/7 Online cat, Adult bk club, After school storytime, Archival coll, Audiobks via web, Bk club(s), Bks on CD, Children's prog, Computer training, Computers for patron use, Copy machines, E-Reserves, Electronic databases & coll, Fax serv, Free DVD rentals, Home delivery & serv to Sr ctr & nursing homes, Homebound delivery serv, ILL available, Magazines, Magnifiers for reading, Mail & tel request accepted, Mango lang, Mus passes, Music CDs, Notary serv, Online cat, OverDrive digital audio bks, Photocopying/Printing, Preschool reading prog, Prog for adults, Prog for children & young adult, Pub access computers, Ref & res, Ref serv available, Ref serv in person, Scanner, Story hour, Summer reading prog, Tax forms, Teen prog, Telephone ref
Mem of Ramapo Catskill Library System
Open Mon-Thurs 10-8, Fri 10-6, Sat 10-5, Sun 12-5
Friends of the Library Group

CANAJOHARIE

S BEECH-NUT NUTRITION CORP LIBRARY*, 102 Church St, 13317. SAN 311-0044. Tel: 518-673-3251. FAX: 518-673-3259. *Dir,* Robert Harvey; E-mail: rharvey@herousa.com
Library Holdings: Bk Vols 900; Per Subs 40
Subject Interests: Bacteriology, Chem, Food tech, Infant feeding, Nutrition
Restriction: Staff use only

P CANAJOHARIE LIBRARY & ART GALLERY*, Two Erie Blvd, 13317. SAN 311-0052. Tel: 518-673-2314. FAX: 518-673-5243. Web Site: www.clag.org. *Dir,* Eric Trahan
Founded 1914. Pop 6,196; Circ 40,000
Library Holdings: Bk Vols 33,696; Per Subs 86
Special Collections: American Art Originals, Colonial Times to Present; Art (Gilbert Stuart, Georgia O'Keefe, Winslow Homer)
Subject Interests: Archit, Art, Local indust hist
Automation Activity & Vendor Info: (Acquisitions) Innovative Interfaces, Inc; (Circulation) Innovative Interfaces, Inc; (OPAC) Innovative Interfaces, Inc
Database Vendor: ProQuest, ReferenceUSA
Wireless access
Publications: Fire (History of Local Volunteer Fire Department); Masterpieces of American Art; The Permanent Collection; Walking Tour of Canajoharie
Mem of Mohawk Valley Library System
Open Mon-Thurs 10-7, Fri 10-5, Sat & Sun 12:30-5
Friends of the Library Group

CANANDAIGUA

P BRISTOL LIBRARY*, 6750 County Rd 32, 14424. SAN 310-897X. Tel: 585-229-5862. FAX: 585-229-2787. Web Site: www.bristollibrary.wordpress.com. *Dir,* Judy Schewe
Pop 1,802; Circ 5,700
Library Holdings: Bk Vols 8,000; Per Subs 35
Automation Activity & Vendor Info: (Cataloging) SirsiDynix; (Circulation) SirsiDynix; (OPAC) SirsiDynix; (Serials) SirsiDynix
Wireless access
Mem of Pioneer Library System
Open Mon, Wed & Thurs 3:30-8:30, Tues 10-12 & 3:30-8:30, Fri 3:30-6, Sat 10-2

J FINGER LAKES COMMUNITY COLLEGE*, Charles J Meder Library, 4355 Lakeshore Dr, 14424-8395. SAN 311-0060. Tel: 585-394-3500, Ext 7371. FAX: 585-394-8708. Web Site: library.flcc.edu. *Dir,* Frank Queener; *Circ,* Karen Clement; *Ref Librn,* Wally Babcock; *Ref Librn,* Charlotte Cooper; *Ref Librn,* Sharon Malecki; *Ref Librn,* Sarah Moon
Founded 1968. Enrl 4,723; Fac 95
Library Holdings: Bk Titles 51,692; Bk Vols 76,660; Per Subs 365
Special Collections: Canandaigua Lake Pure Waters Association Archives
Subject Interests: Environ conserv, Hort, Nursing, Paralegal, Tourism, Travel
Automation Activity & Vendor Info: (Cataloging) Ex Libris Group; (Circulation) Ex Libris Group; (OPAC) Ex Libris Group; (Serials) Ex Libris Group
Database Vendor: EBSCOhost, JSTOR, LexisNexis, OCLC FirstSearch, ProQuest, ScienceDirect, Westlaw
Wireless access
Publications: Periodicals Guide
Partic in Nylink; OCLC Online Computer Library Center, Inc; Rochester Regional Library Council
Special Services for the Deaf - Captioned film dep

Special Services for the Blind - Cassette playback machines; Integrated libr/media serv; Textbks on audio-cassettes
Open Mon-Thurs 7:45am-10pm, Fri 8-4, Sat 9-4, Sun 2-8

S ONTARIO COUNTY HISTORICAL SOCIETY LIBRARY*, 55 N Main St, 14424. SAN 311-0079. Tel: 585-394-4975. FAX: 585-394-9351. Web Site: www.ochs.org. *Dir,* Edward Varno; E-mail: director@ochs.org; *Curator,* Wilma Townsend; E-mail: curator@ochs.org; Staff 3 (Non-MLS 3)
Founded 1902
Library Holdings: Bk Titles 8,000
Special Collections: Civil War Library of Major Charles Richardson NY126 Vol; Local Imprints Coll; Manchester Subscription Library ca 1800; Western New York Land Sales (Oliver Phelps Coll), mss
Subject Interests: Ont county hist
Publications: An Illustrated History of the LISK Manufacturing Co; Backyards to Big Leagues; Early Canandaigua Architecture; Evolution of Seneca Point; Forgotten Stories of the Finger Lakes
Restriction: Non-circulating to the pub

P PIONEER LIBRARY SYSTEM*, 2557 State Rte 21, 14424. SAN 312-1593. Tel: 585-394-8260. FAX: 585-394-1935. E-mail: info@pls-net.org. Web Site: www.pls-net.org. *Exec Dir,* Position Currently Open; *Asst Dir,* Betsy Morris; E-mail: bmorris@pls-net.org; *Pub & Outreach Serv Librn,* Ellen Reynolds; *Syst Librn,* Roma Matott; E-mail: rmatott@pls-net.org; *Training Coordr,* Lindsay Stratton; E-mail: lstratton@pls-net.org; Staff 12 (MLS 5, Non-MLS 7)
Founded 1990. Pop 301,741
Library Holdings: Bk Vols 2,845
Automation Activity & Vendor Info: (Cataloging) Evergreen; (Circulation) Evergreen; (OPAC) Evergreen
Database Vendor: Overdrive, Inc
Wireless access
Publications: Directories; Pioneer Pathfinder (Newsletter)
Member Libraries: Allens Hill Free Library; Arcade Free Library; Avon Free Library; Bell Memorial Library; Bloomfield Public Library; Bristol Library; Caledonia Library; Clifton Springs Library; Clyde-Savannah Public Library; Cordelia A Greene Library; Eagle Free Library; Geneva Public Library; Gorham Free Library; Honeoye Public Library; Lima Public Library; Livonia Public Library; Lyons Public Library; Macedon Public Library; Marion Public Library; Mount Morris Library; Naples Library; Perry Public Library; Phelps Community Memorial Library; Pike Library; Red Creek Free Library; Red Jacket Community Library; Rose Free Library; Stevens Memorial Community Library; Town of Gainesville Public Library; Victor Free Library; Wadsworth Library; Walworth-Seely Public Library; Wolcott Civic Free Library; Wood Library Association; Wyoming Free Circulating Library
Partic in OCLC Online Computer Library Center, Inc; Rochester Regional Library Council

GM VETERANS ADMINISTRATION MEDICAL CENTER*, Medical Library, 400 Fort Hill Ave, 14424. SAN 311-0087. Tel: 585-393-7995. FAX: 585-393-8356. *Librn,* Sandy Baxter; E-mail: sandy.baxter@med.va.gov; Staff 2 (Non-MLS 2)
Oct 2005-Sept 2006 Income $89,000. Mats Exp $89,000
Library Holdings: Bk Titles 6,400
Subject Interests: Aging, Alcohol drug abuse, Med, Nursing, Psychiat, Psychol
Automation Activity & Vendor Info: (Cataloging) Follett Software; (Circulation) Follett Software; (ILL) OCLC; (Serials) EBSCO Online
Publications: Medical Library Newsletter
Partic in Rochester Regional Library Council; Veterans Affairs Libr Network (VALNET)
Open Mon-Fri 8-4:30

P WOOD LIBRARY ASSOCIATION*, 134 N Main St, 14424-1295. SAN 311-0095. Tel: 585-394-1381. FAX: 585-919-0247. E-mail: woodlibrary@owwl.org. Web Site: www.woodlibrary.org. *Exec Dir,* Jenny Goodemote; Tel: 585-394-1381, Ext 306, E-mail: jgoodemote@pls-net.org; *Ad, Asst Dir,* Ron Kirsop; Tel: 585-394-1381, Ext 307, E-mail: rkirsop@pls-net.org; *Ch Serv Librn,* Mary Ferris; Tel: 585-394-1381, Ext 304, E-mail: mferris@pls-net.org; *Teen & Ref Serv Librn,* Kelley Blue; Tel: 585-394-1381, Ext 302, E-mail: kblue@pls-net.org; *ILL Coordr,* Cyndi Fordham; Tel: 585-394-1381, Ext 313, E-mail: cfordham@pls-net.org; Staff 20 (MLS 4, Non-MLS 16)
Founded 1857. Pop 23,796; Circ 247,349
Library Holdings: Bk Titles 72,013; Per Subs 141
Database Vendor: EBSCOhost, LearningExpress, OCLC WorldShare Interlibrary Loan
Wireless access
Publications: Annual Report & Annual Plan of Service
Mem of Pioneer Library System
Open Mon-Thurs 10-9, Fri & Sat 10-5, Sun 12-4
Friends of the Library Group

CANASERAGA

P ESSENTIAL CLUB FREE LIBRARY*, 11 Pratt St, 14822. Tel: 607-545-6443. FAX: 607-545-6443. E-mail: canaseraga@stls.org. Web Site: www.stls.org/canaseraga. *Dir,* Kathie Sleight
Founded 1897
Library Holdings: Audiobooks 200; AV Mats 500; Large Print Bks 200; Bk Vols 10,000
Automation Activity & Vendor Info: (Cataloging) SirsiDynix; (Circulation) SirsiDynix; (OPAC) SirsiDynix
Function: Adult literacy prog, Homebound delivery serv, Prog for children & young adult, Summer reading prog
Mem of Southern Tier Library System
Special Services for the Blind - Large print bks; Talking bks; Videos on blindness & phys handicaps
Open Mon & Wed 10-12:30, 1-5 & 7-9, Sat 10-1

CANASTOTA

P CANASTOTA PUBLIC LIBRARY*, 102 W Center St, 13032. SAN 311-0117. Tel: 315-697-7030. FAX: 315-697-8653. E-mail: canastota@midyork.org. Web Site: www.canastotalibrary.org. *Dir,* Elizabeth Metzger; E-mail: lmetzger@midyork.org; Staff 2 (MLS 1, Non-MLS 1)
Founded 1896. Pop 9,352; Circ 80,469
Library Holdings: Audiobooks 1,051; CDs 200; DVDs 1,300; Bk Titles 40,408; Per Subs 150
Special Collections: Children's Books for Parents (Dorothy Canfield Fisher Award Coll)
Automation Activity & Vendor Info: (Acquisitions) Baker & Taylor; (Circulation) SirsiDynix; (ILL) OCLC WorldShare Interlibrary Loan
Database Vendor: Baker & Taylor, ProQuest, SirsiDynix
Wireless access
Function: Handicapped accessible, ILL available, Photocopying/Printing, Prog for adults, Prog for children & young adult, Ref serv available, Summer reading prog, Telephone ref, Wheelchair accessible, Workshops
Mem of Mid-York Library System
Open Mon-Thurs 9-8:30, Fri 9-5, Sat 10-4, Sun 12:30-4:30
Friends of the Library Group

CANDOR

P CANDOR FREE LIBRARY*, Two Bank St, 13743-1510. (Mail add: PO Box 104, 13743-0104), SAN 311-0125. Tel: 607-659-7258. FAX: 607-659-7500. E-mail: candorli@twcny.rr.com. Web Site: www.flls.org/candor. *Librn,* Fran Howe
Founded 1931. Pop 869; Circ 17,529
Library Holdings: Bk Vols 18,440; Per Subs 29
Subject Interests: Adult fiction, Hist, Mystery, Sci fict, Western
Automation Activity & Vendor Info: (Cataloging) SirsiDynix; (Circulation) SirsiDynix
Wireless access
Mem of Finger Lakes Library System
Open Mon, Wed & Fri 2-5, Tues & Thurs 10-12, 2-5 & 6-8, Sat 10-12 & 2-4
Friends of the Library Group

CANISTEO

P WIMODAUGHSIAN FREE LIBRARY*, 19 W Main St, 14823-1005. SAN 311-0133. Tel: 607-698-4445. FAX: 607-698-4445. E-mail: canisteo@stls.org. *Dir,* Kim Lindsay
Founded 1898. Pop 3,600; Circ 25,714
Library Holdings: Bk Vols 16,226; Per Subs 40
Special Collections: Bethesda Health & Wellness Coll; History (Steuben County Coll), bk, doc, clippings, pamphlets
Subject Interests: Gardening, Railroad hist
Automation Activity & Vendor Info: (Cataloging) SIRSI WorkFlows; (Circulation) SIRSI WorkFlows; (OPAC) SIRSI WorkFlows; (Serials) SIRSI WorkFlows
Wireless access
Function: Homebound delivery serv, Photocopying/Printing
Mem of Southern Tier Library System
Open Mon, Wed & Fri 12-6, Tues & Thurs 1-8, Sat 9-12
Friends of the Library Group

CANTON

P CANTON FREE LIBRARY, Eight Park St, 13617. (Mail add: PO Box 150, 13617-0150), SAN 311-0141. Tel: 315-386-3712. FAX: 315-386-4131. E-mail: canlib@ncls.org. Web Site: www.cantonfreelibrary.org. *Dir,* Emily Owen; *YA Spec,* Krista Briggs; *Youth Serv Spec,* Valerie White
Founded 1896. Pop 10,995; Circ 53,794
Library Holdings: Bk Titles 49,913; Per Subs 139
Special Collections: Adirondacks (Menard); Frederic Remington's Paintings; Hazel Tyrell's Bird Carvings; Tyrell Handcarved Birds Coll

Subject Interests: Genealogy, Local hist
Automation Activity & Vendor Info: (Circulation) SirsiDynix
Database Vendor: OCLC FirstSearch, SirsiDynix
Wireless access
Function: Telephone ref
Publications: At Your Library (Newsletter)
Mem of North Country Library System
Open Mon & Wed 9:30-8, Tues, Thurs & Fri 9:30-5
Friends of the Library Group
Branches: 2
MORLEY BRANCH, 7230 County Rte 27, 13617, SAN 321-138X. Tel: 315-379-0066. E-mail: morlib@ncls.org. Web Site: www.cantonfreelibrary.org/morley/index.htm. *Libr Mgr,* Agnes Hoey
Library Holdings: Bk Vols 3,248; Per Subs 18
Open Mon 5pm-7:30pm, Tues 1-3:30, Thurs 1:30-5:30
Friends of the Library Group
RENSSELAER FALLS BRANCH, 212 Rensselaer St, Rensselaer Falls, 13680. Tel: 315-344-7406. FAX: 315-344-7406. E-mail: reflib@ncls.org. Web Site: www.cantonfreelibrary.org/falls/index.htm. *Libr Mgr,* Agnes Hoey
Function: Meeting rooms, Photocopying/Printing
Special Services for the Blind - Braille bks; Large print bks
Open Mon 1-3:30, Tues 5pm-7:30pm, Wed 1:30-5:30
Friends of the Library Group

S SAINT LAWRENCE COUNTY HISTORICAL ASSOCIATION ARCHIVES, Three E Main St, 13617-1416. (Mail add: PO Box 8, 13617-0008), SAN 311-015X. Tel: 315-386-8133. E-mail: info@slcha.org. Web Site: www.slcha.org. *Archivist,* Jean Marie Martello; E-mail: archives@slcha.org; *Coll,* Sue Longshore; Staff 2 (Non-MLS 2)
Founded 1947
Library Holdings: Bk Titles 2,000
Special Collections: Silas Wright (Governor Silas Wright & Family Coll), bks, doc, letters & transcripts
Subject Interests: County hist, Genealogy, Northern NY hist, St Lawrence County hist
Wireless access
Publications: The Quarterly
Partic in Northern New York Library Network
Open Tues-Thurs & Sat 12-4, Fri 12-8
Restriction: Non-circulating to the pub

L ST LAWRENCE SUPREME COURT*, Law Library, 48 Court St, 13617. Tel: 315-379-2279. FAX: 315-379-2424. *Librn,* Tammy Lomaki
Library Holdings: Bk Vols 13,600
Subject Interests: Legal ref
Database Vendor: LexisNexis
Wireless access
Open Mon-Fri (Sept-June) 9-5; Mon-Fri (July & Aug) 8-4

C ST LAWRENCE UNIVERSITY*, Owen D Young Library, 23 Romoda Dr, 13617. SAN 311-0168. Tel: 315-229-5451. Interlibrary Loan Service Tel: 315-229-5485. Reference Tel: 315-229-5477. FAX: 315-229-5729. Web Site: www.stlawu.edu/library. *Actg Univ Librn, Assoc Librn, Syst Librn,* Michael G Alzo; Tel: 315-229-5424, Fax: 315-229-7446, E-mail: malzo@stlawu.edu; *Access Serv Librn,* Rhonda Courtney; Tel: 315-229-5479, E-mail: rcourtney@stlawu.edu; *Maps Librn,* Carol Cady; Tel: 315-229-5824, Fax: 315-229-7291, E-mail: ccady@stlawu.edu; *Sci Librn,* Eric R Williams-Bergen; Tel: 315-229-5405, E-mail: ewilliamsbergen@stlawu.edu; *Archivist, Spec Coll Librn,* Mark C McMurray; Tel: 315-229-5476, E-mail: mcm@stlawu.edu; *Acq, Coll Develop,* Michelle Gillie; Tel: 315-229-5834, Fax: 315-229-7447, E-mail: mgillie@stlawu.edu; *Acq, Coll Develop, Doc,* Robin Hutchinson; Tel: 315-229-5331, E-mail: rhutchinson@stlawu.edu; *Electronic Res,* Paul A Doty; Tel: 315-229-5483, E-mail: pdoty@stlawu.edu. Subject Specialists: *Maps,* Carol Cady; Staff 10 (MLS 10)
Founded 1856. Enrl 2,200; Highest Degree: Master
Library Holdings: Electronic Media & Resources 126; Microforms 598,500; Bk Vols 594,300; Per Subs 5,300
Special Collections: David Parish & Family, letters, papers; Edwin Arlington Robinson Coll; Frederic Remington Coll, bks, letters, prints; Irving Bacheller Coll; Nathaniel Hawthorne (Milburn Coll), bks, letters; Northern New York History, bks, doc, letters, maps; Owen D Young Papers; Poetry (Benet Coll); Rabbi Dr Seymour Siegel Coll, bks, writings; Robert Frost Coll. US Document Depository
Wireless access
Publications: Bulletin of the Friends of Owen D Young Library; Odyssey: A Newsletter of the SLU Libraries
Partic in Northern New York Library Network; OCLC Online Computer Library Center, Inc
Friends of the Library Group

Departmental Libraries:
LAUNDERS SCIENCE LIBRARY, Park St, 13617. Tel: 315-229-5400. FAX: 315-229-7291. *Maps Librn,* Carol Cady; Tel: 315-229-5824, E-mail: ccady@stlawu.edu; *Sci Librn,* Eric Williams-Bergen; Tel: 315-229-5405, E-mail: ewilliamsbergen@stlawu.edu. Subject Specialists: *Maps,* Carol Cady; Staff 2 (MLS 1, Non-MLS 1)

C STATE UNIVERSITY OF NEW YORK COLLEGE OF TECHNOLOGY*, Southworth Library, 34 Cornell Dr, 13617-1098. SAN 311-0176. Tel: 315-386-7228. FAX: 315-386-7931. Web Site: www.canton.edu/library. *Dir of Libr Serv,* Michelle Currier; Tel: 315-386-7055; *Asst Librn,* Jennifer Whittaker; Tel: 315-386-7057; *Bldg Mgr/Supvr,* Molly MacNeill; *Instrul Support Assoc, Tech Serv,* Jessica Spooner; Tel: 315-386-7054; *Customer Serv Spec,* Loreen Murphy; Staff 4.5 (MLS 1.5, Non-MLS 3)
Founded 1948. Enrl 2,987; Fac 176; Highest Degree: Bachelor
Jul 2009-Jun 2010 Income $474,735. Mats Exp $127,072, Books $23,380, Per/Ser (Incl. Access Fees) $18,799, Micro $621, AV Equip $2,408, AV Mat $2,490, Electronic Ref Mat (Incl. Access Fees) $79,374. Sal $273,411 (Prof $229,072)
Library Holdings: e-books 273; Microforms 3,822; Bk Titles 47,791; Bk Vols 55,703; Per Subs 141; Videos 987
Automation Activity & Vendor Info: (Acquisitions) Ex Libris Group; (Cataloging) Ex Libris Group; (Circulation) Ex Libris Group; (Course Reserve) Ex Libris Group; (ILL) OCLC; (OPAC) Ex Libris Group; (Serials) Ex Libris Group
Database Vendor: ARTstor, College Source, CredoReference, ebrary, EBSCOhost, Elsevier, Faulkner Information Services, Greenwood Publishing Group, Grolier Online, JSTOR, Newsbank, OCLC FirstSearch, ProQuest, Sage, ScienceDirect, Westlaw
Wireless access
Partic in Associated Colleges of the Saint Lawrence Valley; Northern New York Library Network; SUNYConnect
Open Mon-Thurs 8am-Midnight, Fri 8-4:30, Sat 1-5, Sun 2-10

CAPE VINCENT

P CAPE VINCENT COMMUNITY LIBRARY*, 157 N Real St, 13618. (Mail add: PO Box 283, 13618-0283), SAN 311-0184. Tel: 315-654-2132. FAX: 315-654-2132. Web Site: www.nc3r.org/capevincent/. *Libr Dir,* Linda Voorhees
Pop 600; Circ 16,026
Library Holdings: Bk Vols 11,000; Per Subs 32
Automation Activity & Vendor Info: (Cataloging) SIRSI WorkFlows; (Circulation) SIRSI WorkFlows; (Course Reserve) SIRSI WorkFlows; (ILL) SIRSI WorkFlows; (OPAC) SIRSI WorkFlows; (Serials) SIRSI WorkFlows
Wireless access
Mem of North Country Library System
Open Tues & Thurs 9-8, Wed 9-5, Fri & Sat 9-1
Friends of the Library Group

CARMEL

P REED MEMORIAL LIBRARY*, 1733 Rte 6, 10512. SAN 311-0206. Tel: 845-225-2439. FAX: 845-225-1436. Web Site: reed.carmel.lib.ny.us. *Dir,* Jeanne Buck
Founded 1914. Pop 8,150; Circ 50,000
Library Holdings: Bk Vols 20,000; Per Subs 75
Wireless access
Mem of Mid Hudson Library System
Open Mon, Wed & Fri 10-5, Tues & Thurs 10-8, Sat 10-3

CARTHAGE

P CARTHAGE FREE LIBRARY*, 412 Budd St, 13619. SAN 352-3381. Tel: 315-493-2620. FAX: 315-493-2620. E-mail: carlib@ncls.org. *Dir,* Linda McCullough; Staff 1 (MLS 1)
Founded 1910. Pop 5,936; Circ 30,999
Library Holdings: Bk Vols 17,000; Per Subs 40
Special Collections: Local History (New York State History Coll), mss, monographs
Automation Activity & Vendor Info: (Cataloging) SirsiDynix; (Circulation) SirsiDynix; (OPAC) SirsiDynix; (Serials) SirsiDynix
Wireless access
Mem of North Country Library System
Partic in Northern New York Library Network
Open Mon-Wed 12-8, Thurs 10-8, Fri 10-6, Sat 12-4

CASTILE

S CORDELIA A GREENE LIBRARY*, 11 S Main St, 14427. (Mail add: PO Box 208, 14427-0208), SAN 311-0214. Tel: 585-493-5466. FAX: 585-493-5782. E-mail: castilelibrary@owwl.org. Web Site: www.castile.pls-net.org. *Dir,* Erin Robinson; E-mail: erobinson@pls-net.org; Staff 2 (Non-MLS 2)
Founded 1897

Jan 2005-Dec 2005 Income $63,000, State $5,000, Locally Generated Income $48,000, Other $10,000. Mats Exp $15,700, Books $12,000, Per/Ser (Incl. Access Fees) $1,500, AV Equip $1,000, AV Mat $1,200. Sal $23,000 (Prof $17,500)
Library Holdings: Audiobooks 300; Bks on Deafness & Sign Lang 10; CDs 270; DVDs 260; High Interest/Low Vocabulary Bk Vols 200; Large Print Bks 20; Bk Vols 15,000; Per Subs 70; Videos 240
Special Collections: Dr Cordelia A Greene Coll; Frances Willard Coll
Subject Interests: Local hist
Automation Activity & Vendor Info: (Cataloging) SirsiDynix; (Circulation) SirsiDynix; (OPAC) SirsiDynix
Wireless access
Function: Ref serv available
Mem of Pioneer Library System
Open Mon & Tues 3-9, Wed & Thurs 11-7, Sat 10-2
Friends of the Library Group

CASTLETON-ON-HUDSON

P CASTLETON PUBLIC LIBRARY*, 85 S Main St, 12033. SAN 373-8353. Tel: 518-732-0879. FAX: 518-732-0835. Web Site: www.castletonpubliclibrary.org. *Dir,* Amy Peker; E-mail: director@castletonpubliclibrary.org; Staff 1 (MLS 1)
Library Holdings: Bk Titles 12,000; Bk Vols 13,000; Per Subs 19
Special Collections: Castleton-on-Hudson, bks & photogs
Wireless access
Mem of Upper Hudson Library System
Special Services for the Deaf - Bks on deafness & sign lang; Closed caption videos; High interest/low vocabulary bks
Special Services for the Blind - Audio mat; Bks available with recordings; Bks on cassette; Bks on CD
Open Mon-Wed 12-8, Thurs & Fri 10-6, Sat 10-4
Friends of the Library Group

CATO

P STEWART B LANG MEMORIAL LIBRARY, 2577 E Main St, 13033. (Mail add: PO Box 58, 13033), SAN 311-0249. Tel: 315-626-2101. FAX: 315-626-3249. E-mail: slangmem@twcny.rr.com. Web Site: www.langlibrary.org. *Librn,* Elizabeth Messina
Founded 1927. Circ 2,700
Jan 2014-Dec 2014 Income $70,000, Locally Generated Income $50,000, Other $20,000. Mats Exp $10,800, Books $9,000, Per/Ser (Incl. Access Fees) $1,000, AV Mat $800. Sal $40,000 (Prof $23,000)
Library Holdings: AV Mats 570; Bk Titles 12,000; Bk Vols 12,200; Per Subs 37; Talking Bks 238
Subject Interests: Cayuga County hist
Automation Activity & Vendor Info: (Circulation) Innovative Interfaces, Inc
Wireless access
Publications: Booklist
Mem of Finger Lakes Library System
Open Mon & Wed 1-6, Tues & Thurs 9:30-8:30, Fri 1-5, Sat 11-3

CATSKILL

P CATSKILL PUBLIC LIBRARY*, One Franklin St, 12414-1407. SAN 352-3470. Tel: 518-943-4230. FAX: 518-943-1439. Web Site: catskillpubliclibrary.org. *Dir,* Susan Ray; E-mail: cpldirector@mhcable.com; *Mgr,* Sam Alvarez; Staff 3 (MLS 3)
Founded 1893. Pop 12,608; Circ 42,015
Special Collections: Daily Mail, microfilm; Hudson River Steamboats (Saunders Coll)
Automation Activity & Vendor Info: (Acquisitions) Innovative Interfaces, Inc; (Cataloging) Innovative Interfaces, Inc; (Circulation) Innovative Interfaces, Inc; (OPAC) Innovative Interfaces, Inc
Wireless access
Mem of Mid-Hudson Library System
Open Mon & Wed 12-8; Tues 10-8, Thurs & Fri 10-5, Sat 10-2
Branches: 1
PALENVILLE BRANCH, 3335 Rte 23A, Palenville, 12463, SAN 352-3500. Tel: 518-678-3357. FAX: 518-678-9251. E-mail: palenvillelibrary@hvc.rr.com. *Br Librn,* Sam Alvarez
Open Tues & Thurs 12-7, Fri 10-5, Sat 10-1

L NEW YORK STATE SUPREME COURT LIBRARY*, Emory A Chase Memorial Law Library, Greene County Courthouse, 80 Woodland Ave, 12414. SAN 311-0257. Tel: 518-943-3130. FAX: 518-943-7763. *Librn,* Angelina Knott; E-mail: aknott@courts.state.ny.us
Founded 1908
Library Holdings: Bk Vols 14,000
Special Collections: Van Orden Survey Coll
Subject Interests: NY State law
Wireless access
Partic in South Central Regional Library Council; Southeastern New York Library Resources Council
Open Mon-Fri 9-5

CATTARAUGUS

P CATTARAUGUS FREE LIBRARY*, 21 Main St, 14719. SAN 311-0265. Tel: 716-257-9500. FAX: 716-257-9500. E-mail: cattfl@yahoo.com. Web Site: www.cclslib.org/catt. *Dir,* Kathy Parent; Staff 2 (Non-MLS 2)
Founded 1926. Circ 21,238
Library Holdings: Bk Vols 12,384; Per Subs 16
Mem of Chautauqua-Cattaraugus Library System
Open Mon 2-5, Tues 9-12 & 2-8, Thurs 1:30-5:30, Fri 2-8, Sat 10-2

CAZENOVIA

C CAZENOVIA COLLEGE*, Daniel W Terry Witherill Library, Lincklaen St, 13035. SAN 311-0273. Tel: 315-655-7132. Circulation Tel: 315-655-7204. Reference Tel: 315-655-7282. FAX: 315-655-8675. Web Site: www.cazenovia.edu. *Dir, Libr Serv,* Stanley J Kozaczka; *ILL, Ref Serv,* Judy Azzoto; E-mail: jazzoto@cazenovia.edu; *ILL, Ref Serv,* Lauren Michel; E-mail: ldmichel@cazenovia.edu; Staff 13 (MLS 4, Non-MLS 9)
Founded 1824. Enrl 825; Highest Degree: Bachelor
Library Holdings: Bk Titles 63,000; Bk Vols 73,000; Per Subs 430; Videos 2,177
Subject Interests: Women's studies
Automation Activity & Vendor Info: (Acquisitions) Innovative Interfaces, Inc; (Cataloging) Innovative Interfaces, Inc; (Circulation) Innovative Interfaces, Inc; (ILL) Innovative Interfaces, Inc; (OPAC) Innovative Interfaces, Inc; (Serials) Innovative Interfaces, Inc
Database Vendor: Cambridge Scientific Abstracts, EBSCOhost, JSTOR, LexisNexis, OCLC FirstSearch, OCLC WorldShare Interlibrary Loan, ProQuest, Wilson - Wilson Web
Wireless access
Function: ILL available
Publications: Acquisition Lists; Annual Report
Partic in Central New York Library Resources Council; Connect NY; OCLC Online Computer Library Center, Inc
Open Mon-Thurs 8am-12am, Fri 8-5, Sat 12-5, Sun 2-10

P CAZENOVIA PUBLIC LIBRARY*, 100 Albany St, 13035. SAN 311-0281. Tel: 315-655-9322. E-mail: cazenovia@midyork.org. Web Site: www.midyork.org/cazenovia. *Libr Dir,* Elizabeth Kennedy; *Asst Librn,* Mary Herbert; Staff 8.5 (MLS 1.5, Non-MLS 7)
Founded 1886. Pop 6,500; Circ 167,000
Jan 2006-Dec 2006 Income $326,016, State $2,030, Federal $989, County $13,395, Locally Generated Income $273,042, Other $36,560. Mats Exp $35,539, Books $24,209, Per/Ser (Incl. Access Fees) $1,845, AV Mat $9,485
Library Holdings: AV Mats 6,927; Bk Titles 46,199; Bk Vols 53,143; Per Subs 75
Subject Interests: Local hist
Automation Activity & Vendor Info: (Cataloging) SirsiDynix; (Circulation) SirsiDynix; (OPAC) SirsiDynix
Wireless access
Function: Adult bk club, Archival coll, Art exhibits, Bk club(s), Bks on cassette, Bks on CD, Children's prog, Copy machines, Family literacy, ILL available, Music CDs, Preschool outreach, Prog for adults, Prog for children & young adult, Ref serv available, Senior outreach, Story hour, Summer reading prog, Tax forms, VHS videos
Mem of Mid-York Library System
Open Mon-Fri 9-9, Sat 10-5
Friends of the Library Group

S NEW YORK STATE DIVISION FOR HISTORIC PRESERVATION, Lorenzo State Historic Site, 17 Rippleton Rd, 13035. SAN 311-029X. Tel: 315-655-3200. FAX: 315-655-4304. Web Site: www.lorenzony.org. *Mgr,* Barbara Bartlett
Founded 1968
Library Holdings: Bk Vols 4,000
Special Collections: Cazenovia Newspapers, 1800-1960, microfilm; Cazenovia, New York & Vicinity (Land Company Material from Amsterdam, Municipal Archives), microfilm; Childs, Fairchild & Stebbins Family Papers (Helen Kennard Coll); Ledyard, Hubbard, Burr & Allied Family Papers & Photographs; Personal & Land Accounts of John Lincklaen & Successors (Lorenzo Library Coll), bks, doc, microfilm; Store Records & Correspondence (Samuel S Forman Papers), doc, microfilm
Subject Interests: Allied families, Doc hist of Cazenovia, Holland Land Co, Lincklaen-Ledyard, Third great Western Turnpike
Restriction: Open by appt only

CENTER MORICHES

P CENTER MORICHES FREE PUBLIC LIBRARY*, 235 Main St, 11934. SAN 311-0303. Tel: 631-878-0940. FAX: 631-878-5218. Web Site: www.centermorichesllibrary.org. *Dir,* Nan Peel; E-mail: npeel@suffolk.lib.ny.us; Staff 21 (MLS 6, Non-MLS 15)
Founded 1920. Circ 222,529
Library Holdings: e-journals 5; Bk Vols 98,057; Per Subs 184
Special Collections: Local History (LI Coll) bks, records & tapes. Oral History
Automation Activity & Vendor Info: (Cataloging) Innovative Interfaces, Inc; (Circulation) Innovative Interfaces, Inc; (OPAC) Innovative Interfaces, Inc
Wireless access
Publications: Index to Moriches Bay Tide 1955 to date (local newspaper); Index to the Center Moriches Record; The Library (Newsletter)
Mem of Suffolk Cooperative Library System
Open Mon 9:30-6, Tues-Fri 9:30-8:30, Sat 9:30-5, Sun (Sept-May) 1-5
Friends of the Library Group

CENTEREACH

P MIDDLE COUNTRY PUBLIC LIBRARY*, 101 Eastwood Blvd, 11720. SAN 352-3535. Tel: 631-585-9393. FAX: 631-585-5035. Web Site: www.mcpl.lib.ny.us. *Dir,* Sophia Serlis-McPhillips; Tel: 631-585-9393, Ext 200; Staff 41.3 (MLS 40, Non-MLS 1.3)
Founded 1960. Pop 62,562; Circ 1,250,840
Jul 2010-Jun 2011 Income (Main Library and Branch(s)) $13,635,331. Sal $6,544,473 (Prof $3,065,840)
Library Holdings: AV Mats 90,393; CDs 19,243; DVDs 56,102; e-books 5,740; Electronic Media & Resources 121; Large Print Bks 4,546; Microforms 4,722; Bk Vols 334,255; Per Subs 104,112; Videos 7,921
Special Collections: Business & Finance Coll; Career Information Center Services & Coll; Catastrophe Readiness Clearinghouse; Children's Braille Coll; Children's Foreign Language Coll; Civil Service Manuals; Dual Vision & Sign Language Coll; Employment Coll; Family Education Professional Materials, Large Print Books, Adult Reader Coll (High Interest/Low Vocabulary); Health & Medical Coll; Heritage Coll; Large Print Coll; Law Coll; Local History Coll; Long Island Literary Fiction; Miller Business Coll; Multilanguage Coll; Museum Corner; Not-for-profit Coll; Parents Center; Parents Coll; Read Coll; Serials on Microfilm; Suffolk Education Clearinghouse; Tax Services Coll; Telephone Directories; Test Books; WISE Center (World of Information for Seniors & the Elderly)
Automation Activity & Vendor Info: (Acquisitions) Innovative Interfaces, Inc; (Circulation) Innovative Interfaces, Inc; (Serials) Innovative Interfaces, Inc
Database Vendor: 3M Library Systems, ALLDATA Online, Baker & Taylor, CQ Press, Dun & Bradstreet, EBSCO - WebFeat, EBSCO Auto Repair Reference, EBSCOhost, Facts on File, Foundation Center, Gale Cengage Learning, H W Wilson, Hoovers, infoUSA, Innovative Interfaces, Inc, LexisNexis, Medline, OCLC FirstSearch, Overdrive, Inc, OVID Technologies, Oxford Online, ProQuest, ReferenceUSA, SBRnet (Sports Business Research Network), Standard & Poor's, Westlaw, Wilson - Wilson Web, World Book Online
Wireless access
Function: Adult bk club, Adult literacy prog, Archival coll, Audiobks via web, BA reader (adult literacy), Bilingual assistance for Spanish patrons, Bk club(s), Bk reviews (Group), Bks on cassette, Bks on CD, CD-ROM, Chess club, Children's prog, Citizenship assistance, Computer training, Computers for patron use, Copy machines, Electronic databases & coll, Exhibits, Fax serv, Free DVD rentals, Handicapped accessible, Homebound delivery serv, ILL available, Large print keyboards, Music CDs, Notary serv, Online cat, Online ref, Online searches, OverDrive digital audio bks, Photocopying/Printing, Prog for adults, Prog for children & young adult, Pub access computers, Ref & res, Senior outreach, Summer reading prog, Tax forms, Teen prog, VHS videos, Web-catalog, Wheelchair accessible, Writing prog
Publications: Exploring Careers in Business (Bibliographies); Exploring Careers in Construction and the Trades (Bibliographies); Exploring Careers in Education & Human Services (Bibliographies); Exploring Careers in Healthcare Services (Bibliographies); Hamlet of Selden (Documents); Italian-American Bibliography (Bibliographies); Just Getting Started (Bibliographies); Long Island Bibliography; MCPL Newsletter; MCPL Program Catalog; Menu for Mealtime (Bibliographies); Miller Center in the News (Documents); Networking Resources for Women (Bibliographies); On the Go: A List of Local Places to Visit & Activities to do with Preschool Children (Bibliographies); Parenting & Early Childhood Services (Documents); Reaching the Teen Market (Reference guide); Reflections on 1788: Long Island & the Constitution (Documents); Resources to Grow Your Business (Bibliographies); Resume Books for Individuals Without College Degrees (Bibliographies); The Countdown to College (Reference guide); Toys to Go (Index to educational materials)
Mem of Suffolk Cooperative Library System
Special Services for the Deaf - Assisted listening device; Bks on deafness & sign lang; Closed caption videos; Sign lang interpreter upon request for prog
Special Services for the Blind - Accessible computers; Audio mat; BiFolkal kits; Bks & mags in Braille, on rec, tape & cassette; Bks on cassette; Bks on CD; Cassettes; Home delivery serv; Large print & cassettes; Large print bks; Magnifiers; Suffolk Family Educ Clearinghouse; Talking bks; Talking bks & player equip; Text reader; ZoomText magnification & reading software
Open Mon-Fri 9:30-9, Sat 9:30-5, Sun (Sept-May) 1-5
Friends of the Library Group
Branches: 1
SELDEN BRANCH, 575 Middle Country Rd, Selden, 11784, SAN 352-356X. Tel: 631-585-9393. FAX: 631-732-5002.
Automation Activity & Vendor Info: (Cataloging) Innovative Interfaces, Inc
Open Mon-Thurs 9:30-9, Fri & Sat 9:30-5, Sun 1-5
Friends of the Library Group

CENTERPORT

S SUFFOLK COUNTY VANDERBILT MUSEUM LIBRARY*, 180 Little Neck Rd, 17721. (Mail add: PO Box 0605, 11721-0605), SAN 373-7381. Tel: 631-854-5508, 631-854-5551. FAX: 631-854-5594. Web Site: www.vanderbiltmuseum.org. *Curator,* Stephanie Gress; E-mail: smgcurator@yahoo.com
Founded 1950
Special Collections: W K Vanderbilt II Coll, bks, photo albums & scrapbks

CENTRAL ISLIP

P CENTRAL ISLIP PUBLIC LIBRARY*, 33 Hawthorne Ave, 11722. SAN 311-0311. Tel: 631-234-9333. FAX: 631-234-9386. Web Site: www.suffolk.lib.ny.us/libraries/cisp/. *Dir,* Paul Facchiano; *Ch Serv,* Lili-Ane Niemczura; Staff 34 (MLS 9, Non-MLS 25)
Founded 1952. Pop 32,611; Circ 116,284
Library Holdings: Electronic Media & Resources 1; Bk Vols 116,000; Per Subs 269
Automation Activity & Vendor Info: (Cataloging) Innovative Interfaces, Inc; (Circulation) Innovative Interfaces, Inc; (OPAC) Innovative Interfaces, Inc
Wireless access
Mem of Suffolk Cooperative Library System
Open Mon-Fri (Winter) 10-9, Sat 10-5, Sun 1-5; Mon-Thurs (Summer) 10-9, Fri 10-5, Sat 10-5
Friends of the Library Group

L TENTH JUDICIAL DISTRICT SUPREME COURT LAW LIBRARY*, Cohalan Supreme Court Library, 400 Carleton Ave, 11722-9079. SAN 373-9295. Tel: 631-853-7530. FAX: 631-853-7533. *Librn,* John Hadler; E-mail: jhandler@courts.state.ny.us
Wireless access

C TOURO COLLEGE*, Jacob D Fuchsberg Law Center Library, 225 Eastview Dr, 11722-4539. SAN 326-7334. Tel: 631-761-7000, 631-761-7150. FAX: 631-761-7159. Web Site: www.tourolaw.edu. *Dir,* April Schwartz; E-mail: aschwartz@tourolaw.edu; *Assoc Dir,* Beth Mobley; *Head, Circ,* Marge Hudson; Tel: 631-761-7158; *Head, Tech Serv,* Beth Chamberlain; *Acq,* Allison Escoto; Tel: 631-761-7163; *Ref,* Christine Morton; *Ref,* Roy Sturgeon; *Ref,* Leslie Wong; Staff 18 (MLS 9, Non-MLS 9)
Enrl 650; Fac 35
Library Holdings: Bk Titles 56,000; Bk Vols 415,000; Per Subs 1,300
Special Collections: Foreign & International Law; Jewish Law. State Document Depository; US Document Depository
Automation Activity & Vendor Info: (Acquisitions) Innovative Interfaces, Inc; (Cataloging) Innovative Interfaces, Inc; (Circulation) Innovative Interfaces, Inc; (OPAC) Innovative Interfaces, Inc; (Serials) Innovative Interfaces, Inc
Database Vendor: LexisNexis, Westlaw
Wireless access
Partic in Law Library Microform Consortium (LLMC); Long Island Library Resources Council; OCLC Online Computer Library Center, Inc
Restriction: Not open to pub
Friends of the Library Group

CENTRAL SQUARE

P CENTRAL SQUARE LIBRARY*, 637 S Main St, 13036. (Mail add: PO Box 513, 13036-0513), SAN 311-032X. Tel: 315-668-6104. FAX: 315-668-6104. E-mail: csqlib@ncls.org. Web Site: www.centralsquarelibrary.org. *Dir,* Cindy Partrick; *Libr Asst,* Maureen Roffo; *Libr Asst,* Cindy Williams
Pop 1,646; Circ 15,019

Library Holdings: Bk Vols 28,000
Wireless access
Function: Adult bk club, Bks on CD, Computers for patron use, Copy machines, Digital talking bks, Fax serv, Free DVD rentals, Handicapped accessible, ILL available, Music CDs, Online cat, Online searches, Photocopying/Printing, Pub access computers, Scanner, Tax forms, VHS videos
Mem of North Country Library System
Open Mon, Wed & Fri 11-7, Tues, Thurs & Sat (Sept-June) 10-1
Friends of the Library Group

CENTRAL VALLEY

P WOODBURY PUBLIC LIBRARY*, Ida Cornell Branch, 23 Smith Clove Rd, 10917. (Mail add: PO Box 38, 10917-0038), SAN 373-7047. Tel: 845-928-2114. FAX: 845-928-8867. *Dir,* Jennifer Bradshaw
Wireless access
Open Mon, Thurs & Fri 10-6, Tues & Wed 10-9, Sat 11-3

CHAMPLAIN

P CHAMPLAIN MEMORIAL LIBRARY*, 148 Elm St, 12919-5317. (Mail add: PO Box 279, 12919-0297), SAN 311-0354. Tel: 518-298-8620. FAX: 518-298-8620. *Dir,* Alison M Mandeville; Staff 1 (Non-MLS 1)
Founded 1925. Pop 1,273; Circ 12,291
Library Holdings: Bk Vols 9,500
Database Vendor: Baker & Taylor
Wireless access
Mem of Clinton-Essex-Franklin Library System
Open Tues-Thurs 1-7, Sat 10-1

CHAPPAQUA

P CHAPPAQUA PUBLIC LIBRARY*, 195 S Greeley Ave, 10514. SAN 311-0362. Tel: 914-238-4779. FAX: 914-238-3597. E-mail: chappaweb@westchesterlibraries.org. Web Site: www.chappaqualibrary.org. *Dir,* Pamela Thornton; Tel: 914-238-4779, Ext 108, E-mail: thornton@wlsmail.org; *Asst Libr Dir, Head, Ref Serv,* Martha Alcott; E-mail: malcott@wlsmail.org; *Head, Ch,* Miriam Budin; E-mail: miriam@chappaqualibrary.org; *Head, Circ,* Marjorie Perlin; Tel: 914-238-4779, Ext 101, E-mail: chacirc@chappaqualibrary.org; *Head, Tech Serv,* Deb Donaldson; Tel: 917-238-4779, Ext 107, E-mail: ddonaldson@wlsmail.org; *Head, Teen Serv,* Position Currently Open; *Ch,* Teresa Bueti; *Ch,* Mercy Garland; *Ch,* Kelly-Ann Pajer; *Ref Librn,* Vicki Fuqua; *Ref Librn,* Alan Houston; *Ref Librn,* Daphne L Jackson; E-mail: dljax@optonline.net; *Ref Librn,* Cathy Paulsen; *Ref Librn,* Rebecca Rogan; *AV Coordr, Ref Librn,* Christine Trzcinski; Tel: 914-238-4779, Ext 115; Staff 32.71 (MLS 8.54, Non-MLS 24.17)
Founded 1922. Pop 16,074; Circ 453,398
Jul 2010-Jun 2011 Income $2,761,724, State $4,000, Locally Generated Income $2,699,724, Other $58,000. Mats Exp $184,578, Books $103,000, Per/Ser (Incl. Access Fees) $16,525, AV Mat $45,338, Electronic Ref Mat (Incl. Access Fees) $19,715. Sal $1,599,452 (Prof $712,794)
Library Holdings: AV Mats 21,270; e-books 2,032; Bk Vols 126,951; Per Subs 271
Special Collections: State Document Depository
Subject Interests: Local hist
Automation Activity & Vendor Info: (Cataloging) SirsiDynix; (Circulation) SirsiDynix; (ILL) SirsiDynix; (OPAC) SirsiDynix
Database Vendor: EBSCOhost, Gale Cengage Learning, JSTOR, LearningExpress, ProQuest, SirsiDynix
Wireless access
Publications: Annual Report; Community Organizations; Program Calendar (Bi-monthly); Welcome (Brochure)
Mem of Westchester Library System
Partic in Westlynx
Open Mon-Thurs 9-8, Fri 9-6, Sat 9-5, Sun 1-5
Friends of the Library Group

CHATEAUGAY

P CHATEAUGAY MEMORIAL LIBRARY, Four John St, 12920. (Mail add: PO Box 10, 12920-0010), SAN 311-0370. Tel: 518-497-0400. FAX: 518-497-0400. E-mail: chatlib@gmail.com. Web Site: www.cefls.org/chateaugay.htm. *Dir,* Melissa Erhardt
Founded 1946. Pop 3,204; Circ 9,497
Library Holdings: Bk Titles 7,145; Bk Vols 7,544; Per Subs 15
Special Collections: American Indian Coll; North Country History; Wilder, Laura Ingalls & Almonzo Coll
Subject Interests: Adirondacks
Automation Activity & Vendor Info: (Cataloging) Horizon; (Circulation) Horizon; (OPAC) Horizon
Wireless access
Function: Ref serv available
Mem of Clinton-Essex-Franklin Library System
Special Services for the Deaf - Closed caption videos
Special Services for the Blind - Audio mat; Bks on CD
Open Mon & Wed 9-6, Tues 9-1, Sat 12:30-3:30

CHATHAM

P CHATHAM PUBLIC LIBRARY*, 11 Woodbridge Ave, 12037-1399. SAN 311-0389. Tel: 518-392-3666. FAX: 518-392-1546. E-mail: chathampubliclibrary@chatham.k12.ny.us. Web Site: chatham.lib.ny.us. *Dir,* Luisa Sabine-Kildiss
Founded 1884. Pop 8,841; Circ 84,986
Library Holdings: Bk Vols 64,163; Per Subs 60
Subject Interests: Local hist
Automation Activity & Vendor Info: (Cataloging) Inmagic, Inc.; (Circulation) Innovative Interfaces, Inc; (OPAC) Innovative Interfaces, Inc
Mem of Mid-Hudson Library System
Open Mon & Wed 10-8, Tues & Fri 10-5, Thurs 11-5, Sat 10-3
Friends of the Library Group
Branches: 1
CANAAN BRANCH, 1647 County Rte 5, Canaan, 12029-3017, SAN 325-3430. Tel: 518-781-3392. E-mail: canaanlibrary@taconic.net. *In Charge,* Joanne Hanson
Open Wed & Fri 1-4
Friends of the Library Group

CHAUMONT

P LYME FREE LIBRARY*, 12165 Main St, 13622-9603. SAN 311-0397. Tel: 315-649-5454. FAX: 315-649-2911. E-mail: chalib@ncls.org. Web Site: www.lymefreelibrary.org. *Librn,* Patti Hughes
Founded 1923. Pop 1,695
Library Holdings: Bk Vols 16,000; Per Subs 17
Special Collections: Viet Nam (John La Comb Coll)
Automation Activity & Vendor Info: (Acquisitions) SIRSI WorkFlows; (Cataloging) SIRSI WorkFlows; (Circulation) SIRSI WorkFlows; (Course Reserve) SIRSI WorkFlows; (ILL) SIRSI WorkFlows; (OPAC) SIRSI WorkFlows; (Serials) SIRSI WorkFlows
Wireless access
Mem of North Country Library System
Open Mon & Sat 10-4, Tues & Fri 10-8, Wed 10-6
Friends of the Library Group

CHAUTAUQUA

P SMITH MEMORIAL LIBRARY*, Chautauqua Institution Library, 21 Miller Ave, 14722. (Mail add: PO Box 1093, 14722), SAN 311-0400. Tel: 716-357-6296. FAX: 716-357-3657. Web Site: www.smithlibrary.org. *Dir,* Lynn Kinnear; E-mail: lkinnear@ciweb.org; Staff 4 (MLS 1, Non-MLS 3)
Founded 1907. Pop 2,000; Circ 40,310
Library Holdings: AV Mats 4,803; Large Print Bks 1,082; Bk Titles 31,032; Per Subs 112
Automation Activity & Vendor Info: (Cataloging) SirsiDynix; (Circulation) SirsiDynix; (OPAC) SirsiDynix
Wireless access
Mem of Chautauqua-Cattaraugus Library System
Open Mon (Sept-June) 12-7, Wed & Fri 10-5, Sat 10-3, Sun Noon-3; Mon-Fri (July & Aug) 9-4, Sat 9-3, Sun Noon-3
Friends of the Library Group

CHAZY

P CHAZY PUBLIC LIBRARY, 1329 Fiske Rd, 12921. (Mail add: PO Box 88, 12921-0088), SAN 311-0419. Tel: 518-846-7676. FAX: 518-846-7676. Web Site: www.chazypubliclibrary.org. *Dir,* Frances F Fairchild; E-mail: director@chazypubliclibrary.org; Staff 1 (Non-MLS 1)
Founded 1901. Pop 3,067; Circ 3,380
Jul 2012-Jun 2013 Income $48,498. Mats Exp $2,875, Books $2,775, Electronic Ref Mat (Incl. Access Fees) $100
Library Holdings: Audiobooks 196; AV Mats 4,857; CDs 83; Bk Titles 6,787; Per Subs 19; Videos 161
Special Collections: Adirondack Coll/Local
Automation Activity & Vendor Info: (Cataloging) Horizon; (Circulation) Horizon; (OPAC) Horizon
Wireless access
Function: Activity rm, Art exhibits, Bks on CD, Children's prog, Computers for patron use, Copy machines, Fax serv, Free DVD rentals, Handicapped accessible, ILL available, Magazines, Mus passes, Music CDs, Online cat, Photocopying/Printing, Preschool outreach, Printer for laptops & handheld devices, Pub access computers, Scanner, Story hour, Study rm, Summer reading prog, Tax forms, Wheelchair accessible
Mem of Clinton-Essex-Franklin Library System
Open Tues & Thurs 12:30-8, Wed 10-5, Sat 9-12
Friends of the Library Group

S WILLIAM H MINER AGRICULTURAL RESEARCH INSTITUTE*, James A FitzPatrick Library, 596 Ridge Rd, 12921. (Mail add: PO Box 100, 12921-0100), SAN 326-4386. Tel: 518-846-7121, Ext 149. FAX:

518-846-7774. E-mail: library@whminer.com. Web Site: www.whminer.org. *Dir,* Amy T Bedard; Staff 1 (MLS 1)
Founded 1956
Library Holdings: Bk Titles 5,655; Per Subs 80
Subject Interests: Agr, Ecology, Environment
Database Vendor: OPALS (Open-source Automated Library System)
Wireless access
Partic in Northern New York Library Network

CHEEKTOWAGA

P CHEEKTOWAGA PUBLIC LIBRARY*, Julia Boyer-Reinstein Library, 1030 Losson Rd, 14227. SAN 376-8694. Tel: 716-668-4991. FAX: 716-668-4806. *Dir,* Salvatore Bordonaro; Staff 21.5 (MLS 6, Non-MLS 15.5)
Founded 1938. Pop 94,019; Circ 586,259
Jan 2009-Dec 2009 Income $1,296,679, State $26,169, County $1,192,873, Other $77,637. Mats Exp $255,112. Sal $596,154
Library Holdings: Bk Vols 158,643; Per Subs 499
Special Collections: Local History (Anna M Reinstein Special Local History Reference Coll)
Automation Activity & Vendor Info: (Circulation) SirsiDynix
Wireless access
Mem of Buffalo & Erie County Public Library System
Open Mon, Tues & Thurs 10-9, Wed 1-9, Fri & Sat 10-5, Sun (Winter) 1-5
Branches: 1
REINSTEIN MEMORIAL, 2580 Harlem Rd, 14225, SAN 328-9915. Tel: 716-892-8089. FAX: 716-892-3370. *Br Mgr,* Christine Bazan
Library Holdings: Bk Vols 57,801; Per Subs 224
Open Mon & Thurs 1-9, Tues & Sat 10-5, Wed 10-9, Sun (Winter) 1-5

M SISTERS OF CHARITY HOSPITAL*, Medical Staff Library, 2605 Harlem Rd, 14225. SAN 320-3999. Tel: 716-891-2400, 716-891-2500. FAX: 716-891-2616. *Librn,* Janelle Toner; Tel: 716-633-0705, E-mail: jtoner@wnylrc.org; Staff 2 (MLS 1, Non-MLS 1)
Founded 1960
Library Holdings: Bk Titles 1,053
Partic in Kentucky Medical Library Association; National Network of Libraries of Medicine Greater Midwest Region

CHERRY VALLEY

P CHERRY VALLEY MEMORIAL LIBRARY*, 61 Main St, 13320. (Mail add: PO Box 25, 13320-0025), SAN 311-0443. Tel: 607-264-8214. FAX: 607-264-8214. E-mail: cv.ill@4cls.org. Web Site: libraries.4cls.org/cherryvalley. *Dir, Mgr,* Claire Ottman; Staff 1 (Non-MLS 1)
Founded 1907. Pop 1,266; Circ 7,485
Jan 2010-Dec 2010 Income $36,188, Locally Generated Income $8,980, Other $27,208. Mats Exp $5,314, Books $2,307, Per/Ser (Incl. Access Fees) $200, Electronic Ref Mat (Incl. Access Fees) $2,807. Sal $15,729
Library Holdings: CDs 39; DVDs 17; High Interest/Low Vocabulary Bk Vols 23; Large Print Bks 20; Bk Vols 6,641; Per Subs 12
Wireless access
Function: Bks on CD, Copy machines, e-mail & chat, Fax serv, Free DVD rentals, ILL available, Mail & tel request accepted, Online cat, OverDrive digital audio bks, Photocopying/Printing, Pub access computers, Story hour, Summer reading prog, Tax forms
Mem of Four County Library System
Open Mon & Thurs 9-12, 2-5 & 6:30-8:30, Sat 9-1
Restriction: Open to pub for ref & circ; with some limitations

CHESTER

P CHESTER PUBLIC LIBRARY*, 1784 Kings Hwy, 10918. SAN 311-046X. Tel: 845-469-4252. FAX: 845-469-7583. E-mail: chsref@rcls.org. Web Site: www.rcls.org/chs. *Dir,* Position Currently Open; *Interim Dir,* Maureen Jagos; E-mail: mjagos@rcls.org; Staff 9 (MLS 1, Non-MLS 8)
Pop 12,140; Circ 100,000
Library Holdings: Bk Vols 55,000; Per Subs 120
Subject Interests: Cookery, Local hist
Automation Activity & Vendor Info: (Cataloging) SirsiDynix; (Circulation) SirsiDynix; (OPAC) SirsiDynix
Wireless access
Open Mon-Thurs 10-8, Fri 10-4, Sat 9-4, Sun 12-4
Friends of the Library Group

CHESTERTOWN

P TOWN OF CHESTER PUBLIC LIBRARY*, 6307 State Rte 9, 12817. (Mail add: PO Box 451, 12817-0451). Tel: 518-494-5384. FAX: 518-491-5171. E-mail: library@chesterlibrary.org. Web Site: www.chesterlib.adirondack.ny.us. *Dir,* Alma Alvarez; *Asst Dir,* Wendy Joy Hayes
Library Holdings: AV Mats 2,600; Bk Titles 16,600; Per Subs 900
Automation Activity & Vendor Info: (Cataloging) Innovative Interfaces, Inc; (Circulation) Innovative Interfaces, Inc; (OPAC) Innovative Interfaces, Inc
Wireless access
Mem of Southern Adirondack Library System
Open Wed (Winter) 9-8, Thurs 1-6, Fri 9-6, Sat 9-1; Mon (Summer) 9-1, Wed 9-8, Thurs 1-6, Fri 9-6, Sat 9-1

CHITTENANGO

P SULLIVAN FREE LIBRARY*, Chittenango Public Library, 101 Falls Blvd, 13037-1699. (Mail add: PO Box 310, 13037-0310), SAN 352-3748. Tel: 315-687-6331. FAX: 315-687-6512. E-mail: chittenango@midyork.org. Web Site: www.sullivanfreelibrary.org. *Dir,* Karen Traynor
Founded 1947. Pop 14,622; Circ 75,213
Library Holdings: Bk Titles 56,000; Per Subs 42
Wireless access
Mem of Mid-York Library System
Open Mon 10-8, Fri 12-6, Sat 10-4, Sun Noon-4
Friends of the Library Group
Branches: 1
BRIDGEPORT BRANCH, North Rd, Bridgeport, 13030. (Mail add: PO Box 337, Bridgeport, 13030-0337), SAN 352-3772. Tel: 315-633-2253. FAX: 315-633-2945. E-mail: bridgeport@midyork.org. *Librn,* Karen Traynor
Open Mon-Wed 12-8, Thurs 10-8, Fri 12-6, Sat 10-2
Friends of the Library Group

CHURCHVILLE

P NEWMAN RIGA LIBRARY*, One Village Park, 14428. SAN 311-0486. Tel: 585-293-2009. FAX: 585 293-0932. Web Site: www.rochester.lib.ny.us/riga/. *Dir,* Donna L Haire; E-mail: dhaire@mcls.rochester.lib.ny.us; Staff 1 (MLS 1)
Founded 1921. Pop 5,000; Circ 28,000
Jan 2005-Dec 2005 Income $134,000. Mats Exp $134,000
Library Holdings: Bk Vols 18,000; Per Subs 20
Automation Activity & Vendor Info: (Cataloging) CARL.Solution (TLC); (Circulation) CARL.Solution (TLC); (OPAC) CARL.Solution (TLC)
Mem of Monroe County Library System
Open Mon, Wed & Fri 11-5, Tues & Thurs 11-9, Sat 1-5

CINCINNATUS

P KELLOGG FREE LIBRARY*, 5681 Telephone Rd Exten, 13040. (Mail add: PO Box 150, 13040-0150), SAN 311-0508. Tel: 607-863-4300. FAX: 607-863-3430. *Dir,* Suzanne Vetter; *Ch Serv,* Patricia Eaton
Founded 1930. Pop 1,051; Circ 25,968
Library Holdings: AV Mats 800; Bk Titles 13,779; Bk Vols 16,943; Per Subs 75
Automation Activity & Vendor Info: (Cataloging) Innovative Interfaces, Inc; (Circulation) Innovative Interfaces, Inc; (OPAC) Innovative Interfaces, Inc
Wireless access
Mem of Finger Lakes Library System
Open Tues & Thurs 1-8, Wed & Fri 1-5, Sat 9-1

CLARENCE

P CLARENCE PUBLIC LIBRARY*, Three Town Pl, 14031. SAN 311-0524. Tel: 716-741-2650. FAX: 716-741-1243. Web Site: www.buffalolib.org. *Dir,* Monica Mooney; *Librn,* David Fairlie
Founded 1933. Circ 301,000
Library Holdings: Bk Vols 64,000
Automation Activity & Vendor Info: (Cataloging) SirsiDynix; (Circulation) SirsiDynix; (OPAC) SirsiDynix
Wireless access
Mem of Buffalo & Erie County Public Library System
Open Mon, Tues & Thurs 10-9, Wed 10-6, Fri & Sat 10-5
Friends of the Library Group

CLAVERACK

P CLAVERACK FREE LIBRARY*, 629 Rte 23B, 12513. (Mail add: PO Box 417, 12513-0417), SAN 311-0532. Tel: 518-851-7120. FAX: 518-851-7120. *Dir,* Sally Alderdice; E-mail: sladice@yahoo.com
Circ 29,000
Library Holdings: Bk Vols 27,000; Per Subs 50
Automation Activity & Vendor Info: (Cataloging) Innovative Interfaces, Inc; (Circulation) Innovative Interfaces, Inc; (OPAC) Innovative Interfaces, Inc
Wireless access
Mem of Mid-Hudson Library System
Open Mon & Wed 1-8, Tues & Sat 10-2, Fri 10-5

CLAYTON

S ANTIQUE BOAT MUSEUM*, Lou Smith Library, 750 Mary St, 13624. SAN 327-6473. Tel: 315-686-4104. Reference Tel: 315-686-4104, Ext 233. FAX: 315-686-2775. Web Site: www.abm.org. *Curator,* Jessica Phinney; E-mail: jphinney@abm.org; Staff 1 (Non-MLS 1)
Founded 1983
Library Holdings: Bk Titles 1,500; Bk Vols 1,600; Per Subs 33; Spec Interest Per Sub 25
Special Collections: 1000 Islands History; Fresh Water Nautical Coll, boats, mechanical artifacts, charts, maps, boat plans, photos, boat & engine catalogs & manuals; Freshwater Pleasure Boating History; Local Boat Builders. Oral History
Function: Outside serv via phone, mail, e-mail & web, Photocopying/Printing, Res libr
Publications: Gazette & Gazette Annual (Museum News to Membership)
Restriction: Non-circulating to the pub, Open by appt only

P HAWN MEMORIAL LIBRARY, 220 John St, 13624-1107. SAN 311-0540. Tel: 315-686-3762. Interlibrary Loan Service Tel: 315-782-5540. FAX: 315-686-6028. E-mail: clalib@ncls.org. Web Site: www.hawnmemoriallibrary.org. *Dir,* Kristy Perry; Staff 1 (Non-MLS 1)
Founded 1904. Pop 4,225; Circ 36,120
Library Holdings: Audiobooks 690; e-books 1,669; Bk Vols 16,008; Per Subs 29; Videos 756
Subject Interests: Local hist
Automation Activity & Vendor Info: (Acquisitions) SirsiDynix; (Cataloging) SirsiDynix; (Circulation) SirsiDynix; (Course Reserve) SirsiDynix; (ILL) SirsiDynix; (Media Booking) SirsiDynix; (OPAC) SirsiDynix; (Serials) SirsiDynix
Database Vendor: EBSCOhost, Gale Cengage Learning
Wireless access
Mem of North Country Library System
Open Mon, Wed & Fri 9-5, Tues & Thurs 9-7, Sat 9-2
Friends of the Library Group

CLAYVILLE

P CLAYVILLE LIBRARY ASSOCIATION*, 2265 Oneida St, 13322. (Mail add: PO Box 282, 13322-0282), SAN 376-3021. Tel: 315-839-5893. FAX: 315-839-5070. E-mail: clayville@midyork.org. Web Site: www.clayvillelibrary.org. *Dir,* Allison Fiegl
Library Holdings: Bk Vols 2,800; Per Subs 20
Automation Activity & Vendor Info: (Cataloging) SirsiDynix; (Circulation) SirsiDynix; (OPAC) SirsiDynix
Wireless access
Mem of Mid-York Library System
Open Mon-Fri 1-6
Friends of the Library Group

CLIFTON PARK

P CLIFTON PARK-HALFMOON PUBLIC LIBRARY*, 475 Moe Rd, 12065-3808. SAN 311-0567. Tel: 518-371-8622. FAX: 518-371-3799. Web Site: www.cphlibrary.org. *Dir,* Alexandra Gutelius; Staff 29 (MLS 10, Non-MLS 19)
Founded 1969. Pop 49,900; Circ 771,252
Library Holdings: AV Mats 25,000; Bk Vols 160,000; Per Subs 264
Special Collections: Job, Business & Finance Information; Local History (Howard I Becker Memorial Coll)
Automation Activity & Vendor Info: (Acquisitions) Innovative Interfaces, Inc; (Cataloging) Innovative Interfaces, Inc; (Circulation) Innovative Interfaces, Inc; (OPAC) Innovative Interfaces, Inc
Wireless access
Publications: Annual Report; Newsletter (Quarterly)
Mem of Southern Adirondack Library System
Open Mon-Thurs 9-9, Fri 9-6, Sat 9-5, Sun 12-5
Friends of the Library Group

S RYAN-BIGGS ASSOCIATES PC LIBRARY*, 257 Ushers Rd, 12065. SAN 329-4226. Tel: 518-406-5506. FAX: 518-406-5514. Web Site: www.ryanbiggs.com. *Librn,* Position Currently Open
Library Holdings: Bk Titles 1,723; Per Subs 44
Restriction: Not open to pub

CLIFTON SPRINGS

P CLIFTON SPRINGS LIBRARY*, Four Railroad Ave, 14432. SAN 311-0583. Tel: 315-462-7371. FAX: 315-462-2131. E-mail: CliftonLibrary@Owwl.org. *Dir,* Position Currently Open
Founded 1895. Pop 2,500; Circ 40,830
Library Holdings: Audiobooks 800; DVDs 1,400; Bk Vols 20,000; Per Subs 55
Automation Activity & Vendor Info: (Cataloging) SirsiDynix; (Circulation) SirsiDynix; (OPAC) SirsiDynix
Wireless access
Function: Fax serv, Meeting rooms, Telephone ref
Mem of Pioneer Library System
Open Mon, Wed & Fri 10-5, Tues & Thurs 12-8, Sat 10-1
Friends of the Library Group

CLINTON

C HAMILTON COLLEGE*, Burke Library, 198 College Hill Rd, 13323-1299. SAN 352-3802. Tel: 315-859-4475. Circulation Tel: 315-859-4479. Interlibrary Loan Service Tel: 315-859-4484. Reference Tel: 315-859-4735. FAX: 315-859-4578. E-mail: askref@hamilton.edu. Web Site: www.hamilton.edu/library. *Dir,* Dr David Smallen; Tel: 315-859-4489, E-mail: dsmallen@hamilton.edu; *Dir, Tech Serv,* Connie Roberts; Tel: 315-859-4490; *Dir, Info Syst,* Ken Herold; Tel: 315-859-4487; *Dir, Jazz Archives,* Monk Rowe; Tel: 315-859-4071; *Acq/Ser Librn,* Barbara Swetman; Tel: 315-859-4470; *Cat Librn,* Jean Williams; Tel: 315-859-4383; *Cat/Metadata Librn,* Lisa McFall; Tel: 315-859-4788, E-mail: lmcfall@hamilton.edu; *Ref Librn,* Glynis Asu; Tel: 315-859-4482; *Ref Librn,* Reid Larson; Tel: 315-859-4480; *Ref Librn,* Lynn Mayo; Tel: 315-859-4746; *Ref Librn,* Kristin Strohmeyer; Tel: 315-859-4481; *Info Syst Spec,* Peter MacDonald; Tel: 315-859-4493; *Archivist,* Katherine Collett; Tel: 315-859-4471; Staff 18 (MLS 11, Non-MLS 7)
Founded 1812. Enrl 1,821; Fac 208; Highest Degree: Bachelor
Jul 2011-Jun 2012 Income (Main and Other College/University Libraries) $3,219,593. Mats Exp $1,531,241, Books $243,600, Per/Ser (Incl. Access Fees) $860,591, AV Mat $17,730, Electronic Ref Mat (Incl. Access Fees) $366,090, Presv $43,225. Sal $1,231,826 (Prof $708,623)
Library Holdings: Bk Vols 615,000; Per Subs 1,900
Special Collections: Adirondacks; Almanacs; Book Arts; Civil War Regimental Histories; Communal Societies; Cruickshankiana; Ezra Pound Coll, bk, ms; Hamiltoniana (Hamilton & Alumni Coll), bks, ms; Kirklandiana, bk, ms; Lesser Antilles (Beinecke Coll), bk, ms; Munsell Coll; Provencal; Utica (NY) Imprints; Women (McIntosh Coll). Oral History
Subject Interests: Civil War, Contemporary poetry, Feminism, Govt, Hist, Relig studies
Automation Activity & Vendor Info: (Acquisitions) Ex Libris Group; (Cataloging) Ex Libris Group; (Circulation) Ex Libris Group; (Course Reserve) Ex Libris Group; (ILL) Ex Libris Group; (OPAC) Ex Libris Group; (Serials) Ex Libris Group
Database Vendor: Backstage Library Works, Cambridge Scientific Abstracts, Dialog, EBSCOhost, Gale Cengage Learning, JSTOR, LexisNexis, Newsbank, OCLC FirstSearch, OCLC WorldShare Interlibrary Loan, ProQuest, ScienceDirect, SerialsSolutions
Publications: American Communal Societies (Quarterly)
Partic in Central New York Library Resources Council; New York State Higher Education Initiative; OCLC Online Computer Library Center, Inc

Departmental Libraries:

MEDIA, Christian Johnson Bldg, 198 College Hill Rd, 13323-1299. Tel: 315-859-4923. *Media Spec,* Linda Brennan

MUSIC, McEwen Hall, 198 College Hill Rd, 13323-1299. Tel: 315-859-4349. *Coordr,* Joan Clair
Library Holdings: Music Scores 12,482

P KIRKLAND TOWN LIBRARY, 55 1/2 College St, 13323. SAN 311-0605. Tel: 315-853-2038. FAX: 315-853-1785. E-mail: clinton@midyork.org. Web Site: www.kirklandtownlibrary.org. *Dir,* Anne Debraggio; Staff 6.5 (MLS 2, Non-MLS 4.5)
Founded 1901. Pop 10,300; Circ 123,000
Library Holdings: AV Mats 3,000; CDs 1,600; DVDs 1,300; Large Print Bks 1,400; Bk Titles 24,000; Bk Vols 24,500; Per Subs 126; Talking Bks 1,700; Videos 200
Subject Interests: NY hist
Automation Activity & Vendor Info: (Circulation) SirsiDynix; (OPAC) SirsiDynix
Wireless access
Function: Adult bk club, After school storytime, Art exhibits, Bks on CD, Computer training, Computers for patron use, Copy machines, e-mail serv, E-Reserves, Electronic databases & coll, Fax serv, Free DVD rentals, Handicapped accessible, Holiday prog, Home delivery & serv to Sr ctr & nursing homes, Homebound delivery serv, ILL available, Music CDs, Online cat, OverDrive digital audio bks, Photocopying/Printing, Prog for adults, Prog for children & young adult, Ref serv available, Spoken cassettes & DVDs, Summer reading prog, Tax forms, Teen prog, VHS videos, Wheelchair accessible
Mem of Mid-York Library System
Open Mon-Thurs 10-9, Fri 10-6, Sat 10-2
Friends of the Library Group

CLYDE

P CLYDE-SAVANNAH PUBLIC LIBRARY*, 204 Glasgow St, 14433. SAN 311-0613. Tel: 315-923-7767. FAX: 315-923-9315. E-mail: clydelibrary@owwl.org. Web Site: www.clyde.pls-net.org. *Dir,* Susan Ayers; E-mail: sayers@pls-net.org; Staff 1 (Non-MLS 1)
Founded 1931. Pop 6,500; Circ 104,521
Jan 2008-Dec 2008 Income $2,228,264, City $186,764, County $7,800, Locally Generated Income $35,700. Mats Exp $58,820, Books $39,120, Per/Ser (Incl. Access Fees) $1,000, AV Mat $18,700. Sal $86,450 (Prof $39,000)
Library Holdings: AV Mats 7,640; CDs 1,640; DVDs 5,000; Large Print Bks 480; Bk Vols 37,564; Per Subs 49; Videos 1,000
Special Collections: Genealogy (local families only)
Automation Activity & Vendor Info: (Cataloging) SirsiDynix; (Circulation) SirsiDynix; (OPAC) SirsiDynix
Wireless access
Mem of Pioneer Library System
Open Mon & Wed 1-8, Tues & Thurs 10-6, Fri 1-6, Sat 10-1
Friends of the Library Group

CLYMER

P CLYMER-FRENCH CREEK FREE LIBRARY*, 564 Clymer-Sherman Rd, 14724. (Mail add: PO Box 68, 14724-0068), SAN 311-0621. Tel: 716-355-8823. FAX: 716-355-8824. E-mail: cfcplibrary@stny.rr.com. Web Site: www.cclslib.org/clymer/clymer.html. *Librn,* Pauleen Cochran
Circ 8,745
Library Holdings: Bk Titles 13,919; Per Subs 27
Mem of Chautauqua-Cattaraugus Library System
Open Mon 1-5, Wed 1-7, Fri 11-5, Sat 10-2

COBLESKILL

P COMMUNITY LIBRARY*, 110 Union St, 12043-3830. (Mail add: PO Box 219, 12043-0219), SAN 311-063X. Tel: 518-234-7897. FAX: 518-234-1163. E-mail: coblib@mvls.info. Web Site: www.comlibrary.org. *Dir,* Devon Hedges
Founded 1921. Pop 11,000; Circ 35,000
Library Holdings: Bk Vols 24,000; Per Subs 43
Special Collections: JFK Assassination Research
Subject Interests: Genealogy, Local hist
Automation Activity & Vendor Info: (Cataloging) Innovative Interfaces, Inc; (Circulation) Innovative Interfaces, Inc; (OPAC) Innovative Interfaces, Inc
Wireless access
Function: Bk club(s), Children's prog, ILL available, Meeting rooms, Music CDs, Newsp ref libr, Video lending libr
Open Tues & Thurs 10:30-8, Wed & Fri 10:30-6, Sat 10-1
Friends of the Library Group

C STATE UNIVERSITY OF NEW YORK COLLEGE OF AGRICULTURE & TECHNOLOGY*, Van Wagenen Library, 142 Schenectady Ave, 12043. SAN 311-0648. Tel: 518-234-5841. FAX: 518-255-5843. E-mail: library@cobleskill.edu. Web Site: www.cobleskill.edu/library. *Dean,* Elizabeth Orgeron; *Bibliog Instr, Coordr of Ref Serv,* Francine Apollo; Tel: 518-255-5858; *Acq & Cat,* April Davies; Tel: 518-255 5887; *Circ & ILL,* Katherine Brent; Tel: 518-255-5851; *Ser & Syst,* Peter Barvoets; Tel: 518-255-5894; Staff 5.5 (MLS 5.5)
Founded 1920. Enrl 2,440; Fac 141; Highest Degree: Bachelor
Library Holdings: Bk Vols 65,000; Per Subs 200
Special Collections: County History; Historical Material Related to Agriculture & Food Service
Subject Interests: Agr, Culinary arts, Early childhood educ
Automation Activity & Vendor Info: (Acquisitions) Ex Libris Group; (Cataloging) OCLC; (Circulation) Ex Libris Group; (Course Reserve) Ex Libris Group; (ILL) OCLC ILLiad; (OPAC) Ex Libris Group; (Serials) Ex Libris Group
Database Vendor: ACM (Association for Computing Machinery), Agricola, American Psychological Association (APA), BioOne, EBSCOhost, Gale Cengage Learning, JSTOR, LexisNexis, OCLC ArticleFirst, OCLC FirstSearch, OCLC WorldShare Interlibrary Loan, Project MUSE, ProQuest, PubMed, ScienceDirect, SerialsSolutions, Springer-Verlag
Wireless access
Publications: Library Link (Newsletter)
Partic in Capital District Library Council; New York State Higher Education Initiative; SUNYConnect
Open Mon-Thurs 7am-10pm, Fri 7-5, Sat 10-4, Sun (Sept-May) 2-10

COHOCTON

P COHOCTON PUBLIC LIBRARY*, 15 S Main St, 14826. (Mail add: PO Box 105, 14826-0105). Tel: 585-384-5170. FAX: 585-384-9044. E-mail: cohocton@stls.org. Web Site: www.stls.org/cohocton. *Dir,* Hope Decker
Founded 1977
Library Holdings: AV Mats 1,000; Large Print Bks 200; Bk Vols 10,000
Automation Activity & Vendor Info: (Cataloging) SirsiDynix; (Circulation) SirsiDynix; (OPAC) SirsiDynix
Mem of Southern Tier Library System
Open Tues & Thurs 10-12, 1-5 & 6-8, Sat 10-12 & 1-5

COHOES

P COHOES PUBLIC LIBRARY*, 169 Mohawk St, 12047. SAN 311-0656. Tel: 518-235-2570. FAX: 518-237-4195. Web Site: www.cohoespubliclibrary.com. *Dir,* Matthew Graff; Staff 4 (MLS 1, Non-MLS 3)
Founded 1969. Pop 16,000; Circ 49,484
Library Holdings: Bk Vols 32,000; Per Subs 70
Special Collections: Cohoes School Yearbooks; Local Authors
Automation Activity & Vendor Info: (Cataloging) Horizon; (Circulation) Horizon; (Media Booking) Horizon
Wireless access
Mem of Upper Hudson Library System
Open Mon & Wed 10-8, Tues, Thurs & Fri 10-5, Sat 10-4
Friends of the Library Group

COLD SPRING

P JULIA L BUTTERFIELD MEMORIAL LIBRARY*, Ten Morris Ave, 10516. SAN 311-0664. Tel: 845-265-3040. FAX: 845-265-4852. E-mail: butterfd@gmail.com. Web Site: www.butterfieldlibrary.org. *Dir,* Gillian Thorpe
Pop 2,583; Circ 17,300
Library Holdings: Bk Vols 32,381
Subject Interests: Local hist
Automation Activity & Vendor Info: (Acquisitions) Innovative Interfaces, Inc; (Cataloging) Innovative Interfaces, Inc; (Circulation) Innovative Interfaces, Inc; (Course Reserve) Innovative Interfaces, Inc; (ILL) Innovative Interfaces, Inc; (Media Booking) Innovative Interfaces, Inc; (OPAC) Innovative Interfaces, Inc; (Serials) Innovative Interfaces, Inc
Wireless access
Mem of Mid-Hudson Library System
Open Mon & Wed 10-8, Tues, Thurs & Fri 10-5, Sat 10-5, Sun 12-3
Friends of the Library Group

S PUTNAM COUNTY HISTORICAL SOCIETY & FOUNDRY SCHOOL MUSEUM LIBRARY*, Research Facilities, 63 Chestnut St, 10516. SAN 311-0672. Tel: 845-265-4010. FAX: 845-265-2884. E-mail: office@pchs-fsm.org. Web Site: www.pchs-fsm.org. *Exec Dir,* Mindy Krazmien; *Curator,* Trudie Grace
Founded 1906. Enrl 725; Fac 4; Highest Degree: Doctorate
Library Holdings: Bk Vols 3,000
Special Collections: Genealogy (Haida Davenport & Nelson Warren Coll), scrapbooks; Local Newspapers 1867-1913, microfilm
Subject Interests: Local hist
Wireless access
Function: Res libr
Open Wed 11-5

COLD SPRING HARBOR

S COLD SPRING HARBOR LABORATORY*, Library & Archives, One Bungtown Rd, 11724-2203. SAN 311-0680. Tel: 516-367-6872. Interlibrary Loan Service Tel: 516-367-8352. FAX: 516-367-6843. Web Site: library.cshl.edu. *Dir,* Ludmila Pollock; E-mail: pollock@cshl.edu; Staff 9 (MLS 5, Non-MLS 4)
Founded 1890
Library Holdings: e-journals 600; Bk Titles 21,000; Per Subs 100
Special Collections: Historical Genetics-Eugenics Coll; History of Cold Spring Harbor Science
Subject Interests: Biochem, Bioinformatics, Cancer res, Cell biol, Genetics, Molecular biol, Neurobiol, Plant genetics, Virology
Automation Activity & Vendor Info: (Cataloging) SirsiDynix; (OPAC) SirsiDynix
Database Vendor: OVID Technologies
Wireless access
Publications: Bibliographies; Newsletter
Partic in Long Island Library Resources Council; Medical & Scientific Libraries of Long Island; MLC; OCLC Online Computer Library Center, Inc
Restriction: Open by appt only

P COLD SPRING HARBOR LIBRARY, 95 Harbor Rd, 11724. SAN 311-0699. Tel: 631-692-6820. FAX: 631-692-6827. E-mail: cshrlib@cshlibrary.org. Web Site: www.cshlibrary.org. *Ch Serv, Interim Dir,* Diane Scinta; E-mail: dscinta@cshlibrary.org; *Info Serv,* Ellen Drucker-Albert; E-mail: edrucker@cshlibrary.org; Staff 29 (MLS 17, Non-MLS 12)
Founded 1886. Pop 8,349; Circ 120,000

Library Holdings: CDs 2,374; DVDs 6,376; e-books 1,664; Electronic Media & Resources 27,110; Large Print Bks 671; Bk Titles 67,415; Per Subs 256; Talking Bks 2,547
Special Collections: Environmental Center
Subject Interests: Local hist
Automation Activity & Vendor Info: (Acquisitions) Innovative Interfaces, Inc; (Cataloging) Innovative Interfaces, Inc; (Circulation) Innovative Interfaces, Inc; (ILL) Innovative Interfaces, Inc; (OPAC) Innovative Interfaces, Inc; (Serials) Innovative Interfaces, Inc
Database Vendor: Baker & Taylor, EBSCO Auto Repair Reference, EBSCOhost, Facts on File, Gale Cengage Learning, Grolier Online, H W Wilson, Innovative Interfaces, Inc, Oxford Online, ProQuest, World Book Online
Wireless access
Mem of Suffolk Cooperative Library System
Open Mon-Thurs 9:30-9, Fri & Sat 9:30-5, Sun (Sept-June) 1-5
Restriction: Residents only
Friends of the Library Group

S COLD SPRING HARBOR WHALING MUSEUM LIBRARY*, 301 Main St, 11724. (Mail add: PO Box 25, 11724-0025), SAN 327-6511. Tel: 631-367-3418. FAX: 631-692-7037. Web Site: www.cshwhalingmuseum.org. *Interim Exec Dir,* Nomi Dayan; Tel: 631-637-3418, Ext 17, E-mail: ndayan@cshwhalingmuseum.org
Library Holdings: Bk Vols 1,200
Special Collections: Whale Coll; Whale Conservation Coll
Subject Interests: Local hist, Maritime hist
Open Mon-Sun 11-5

COLLINS

S COLLINS CORRECTIONAL FACILITY LIBRARY*, PO Box 490, 14034-0490. SAN 327-2419. Tel: 716-532-4588. *Librn,* David Collins
Library Holdings: AV Mats 353; High Interest/Low Vocabulary Bk Vols 376; Large Print Bks 250; Bk Vols 23,932; Per Subs 66
Automation Activity & Vendor Info: (Cataloging) Follett Software; (Circulation) Follett Software
Function: Accelerated reader prog, Words travel prog, Writing prog

P COLLINS PUBLIC LIBRARY*, 2341 Main St, 14034-9799. (Mail add: PO Box 470, 14034-0470), SAN 311-0729. Tel: 716-532-5129. FAX: 716-532-6210. Web Site: www.buffalolib.org/libraries/collins/index.asp. *Librn,* Karen D McClure; E-mail: mcclurek@buffalolib.org; Staff 7 (MLS 1, Non-MLS 6)
Pop 8,307; Circ 63,409
Library Holdings: AV Mats 3,500; Bk Vols 22,000; Per Subs 120
Automation Activity & Vendor Info: (Cataloging) SirsiDynix; (Circulation) SirsiDynix; (OPAC) SirsiDynix
Wireless access
Function: Handicapped accessible, Photocopying/Printing, Prog for children & young adult, Summer reading prog
Mem of Buffalo & Erie County Public Library System
Open Mon, Wed & Thurs 2-8, Tues 10-2:30 & 6-8, Fri 11-5:30, Sat 10-2
Friends of the Library Group

COLTON

P COLTON HEPBURN LIBRARY*, 84 Main St, 13625. (Mail add: PO Box 7, 13625-0007), SAN 311-0737. Tel: 315-262-2310. FAX: 315-262-2182. Web Site: www.coltonhepburnlibrary.org. *Librn,* Dennis Eickhoff
Pop 1,453; Circ 19,378
Library Holdings: Bk Vols 17,373
Special Collections: Genealogy Department
Automation Activity & Vendor Info: (Serials) SIRSI-iBistro
Wireless access
Mem of North Country Library System
Open Mon & Wed 1-5 & 7-9, Thurs 1-5, Fri 9-12, Sat 9-12 & 1-4
Friends of the Library Group

COMMACK

P COMMACK PUBLIC LIBRARY*, 18 Hauppauge Rd, 11725-4498. SAN 311-0745. Tel: 631-499-0888. FAX: 631-499-0591. E-mail: cmmklib@suffolk.lib.ny.us. Web Site: www.commackpubliclibrary.org. *Dir,* Laurie Pastore; E-mail: lpastore@suffolk.lib.ny.us; *Asst Dir,* Liz Caldararo; Staff 25 (MLS 9, Non-MLS 16)
Founded 1969. Pop 15,346
Library Holdings: Audiobooks 11,101; AV Mats 5,873; e-books 4,881; Bk Vols 120,719; Per Subs 472
Automation Activity & Vendor Info: (Acquisitions) Innovative Interfaces, Inc; (Cataloging) Innovative Interfaces, Inc; (Circulation) Innovative Interfaces, Inc; (Course Reserve) Innovative Interfaces, Inc; (ILL) Innovative Interfaces, Inc; (OPAC) Innovative Interfaces, Inc
Wireless access
Publications: Colophon (Newsletter); CPL Blog (Online only); Internet Gazette (Newsletter); Teen Central Blog (Online only)
Mem of Suffolk Cooperative Library System
Open Mon-Thurs 9-9, Fri 9-6 Sat 9-5, Sun 1-5
Friends of the Library Group

SR PRESBYTERY OF LONG ISLAND*, Resource Center, 42 Hauppauge Rd, 11725. SAN 327-6538. Tel: 631-499-7171. FAX: 631-499-7063. *Librn,* Marie Zupka-Ludder
Library Holdings: Bk Vols 2,000; Per Subs 50
Open Mon-Fri (Winter) 9-5; Mon-Fri (Summer) 9-4

COMSTOCK

S GREAT MEADOW CORRECTIONAL FACILITY LIBRARY*, 11739 State Rte 22, 12821. (Mail add: PO Box 51, 12821), SAN 311-0761. Tel: 518-639-5516, Ext 4601. FAX: 518-639-5516, Ext 2099. *Librn,* Heather Larrow; Staff 1 (MLS 1)
Founded 1971
Library Holdings: High Interest/Low Vocabulary Bk Vols 300; Bk Titles 11,000; Bk Vols 11,895; Per Subs 50
Subject Interests: African-Am studies, Spanish lang
Automation Activity & Vendor Info: (Circulation) Follett Software
Database Vendor: EBSCOhost
Mem of Southern Adirondack Library System

S WASHINGTON CORRECTIONAL FACILITY LIBRARY*, PO Box 180, 12821-0180. SAN 327-2494. Tel: 518-639-4486. FAX: 518-639-3299. *Librn,* D Cartmell
Library Holdings: Bk Vols 10,000
Wireless access
Mem of Southern Adirondack Library System

CONSTABLEVILLE

P CONSTABLEVILLE VILLAGE LIBRARY*, 3158 Main St, 13325. (Mail add: PO Box 376, 13325-0376), SAN 311-077X. Tel: 315-397-2801. FAX: 315-397-2801. Web Site: www.cvillelibrary.org. *Libr Mgr,* Dorothy Valenti
Circ 5,985
Library Holdings: Bk Vols 4,100; Per Subs 26
Wireless access
Mem of North Country Library System
Open Mon & Wed 9-11 & 3-5, Tues 9-11, Thurs 6pm-8pm, Fri 3-5
Friends of the Library Group

COOPERSTOWN

M MARY IMOGENE BASSETT HOSPITAL*, Bassett Learning Commons & Mackenzie Medical Library, One Atwell Rd, 13326. SAN 311-0788. Tel: 607-547-3115. FAX: 607-547-3006. E-mail: medical.library@bassett.org. Web Site: www.bassett.org. *Mgr,* Laura Dixon; E-mail: laura.dixon@bassett.org; Staff 2 (MLS 2)
Founded 1936
Library Holdings: Bk Titles 4,500
Subject Interests: Clinical med
Automation Activity & Vendor Info: (Cataloging) CyberTools for Libraries; (Circulation) CyberTools for Libraries; (OPAC) CyberTools for Libraries
Database Vendor: EBSCOhost, Elsevier, MD Consult, Micromedex, OVID Technologies, ScienceDirect, UpToDate
Wireless access
Function: Computer training, Copy machines, Doc delivery serv, Electronic databases & coll, Health sci info serv, ILL available, Online searches, Orientations, Res libr, Scanner
Partic in New York State Interlibrary Loan Network (NYSILL)
Open Mon-Fri 8-4:30

S NATIONAL BASEBALL HALL OF FAME & MUSEUM, INC*, Library & Archives, 25 Main St, 13326-0590. SAN 311-080X. Tel: 607-547-0330. FAX: 607-547-4094. E-mail: research@baseballhall.org. Web Site: baseballhall.org. *Dir,* Jim Gates; E-mail: jgates@baseballhall.org; *Ref,* Tim Wiles; E-mail: twiles@baseballhall.org; Staff 4 (MLS 3, Non-MLS 1)
Founded 1939
Library Holdings: AV Mats 12,000; Bk Titles 30,000; Bk Vols 35,000; Per Subs 150
Special Collections: American League & National League Performance Statistics; Archives; Box Scores (1876-present); Schedules. Oral History
Subject Interests: Baseball, Econ, Sociol of baseball, Sports hist
Automation Activity & Vendor Info: (Acquisitions) Innovative Interfaces, Inc - Millenium; (Cataloging) Innovative Interfaces, Inc - Millenium
Database Vendor: ProQuest
Wireless access
Publications: Hall of Fame Yearbook; Memories & Dreams
Open Wed-Fri (Winter) 9-5; Mon-Fri (Summer) 9-5
Restriction: Fee for pub use, Free to mem, Non-circulating coll

S NEW YORK STATE HISTORICAL ASSOCIATION*, Research Library, 5798 State Hwy 80, 13326. (Mail add: PO Box 800, 13326-0800), SAN 311-0818. Tel: 607-547-1470. FAX: 607-547-1405. E-mail: library@nysha.org. Web Site: www.nysha.org/library. *Assoc Dir, Tech Serv,* Susan E B Deer; E-mail: s.deer@nysha.org; *Head Librn,* Wayne Wright; Tel: 607-547-1474, E-mail: w.wright@nysha.org; *Spec Coll Librn,* Evan Rallis; Tel: 607-547-1473, E-mail: e.rallis@nysha.org; *Reader Serv,* JoAnn Van Vranken; E-mail: j.vanvranken@nysha.org; Staff 6 (MLS 3, Non-MLS 3)
Founded 1899
Library Holdings: Bk Vols 89,000; Per Subs 320
Special Collections: New York State & Local History Coll, mss
Subject Interests: Am cultural hist, Am social, Decorative art, Mus studies, N Am Indian art, NY genealogy, NY hist
Automation Activity & Vendor Info: (Cataloging) Innovative Interfaces, Inc; (OPAC) Innovative Interfaces, Inc; (Serials) Innovative Interfaces, Inc
Wireless access
Function: Archival coll, Computers for patron use, Copy machines, Exhibits, ILL available, Ref & res, Res performed for a fee, Workshops
Partic in South Central Regional Library Council
Open Mon-Fri 10-5, Sat 1-5
Restriction: Authorized scholars by appt, Borrowing privileges limited to fac & registered students, Borrowing requests are handled by ILL, Circulates for staff only, Fee for pub use, Internal circ only, Lending to staff only, Non-circulating of rare bks, Non-circulating to the pub
Friends of the Library Group

P VILLAGE LIBRARY OF COOPERSTOWN*, 22 Main St, 13326-1331. SAN 311-0826. Tel: 607-547-8344. Interlibrary Loan Service Tel: 607-723-8236. FAX: 607-547-5487. Web Site: www.villagelibraryofcooperstown.org. *Dir,* David Kent; E-mail: co.david@4cls.org; Staff 4 (MLS 1, Non-MLS 3)
Pop 4,000; Circ 38,000
Library Holdings: CDs 50; DVDs 220; Large Print Bks 1,200; Bk Vols 22,000; Per Subs 30; Talking Bks 800; Videos 30
Automation Activity & Vendor Info: (Cataloging) SIRSI-iBistro; (Circulation) SIRSI-iBistro; (OPAC) SIRSI-iBistro
Wireless access
Mem of Four County Library System
Open Mon & Wed 9-8, Tues, Thurs & Fri 9-5, Sat 10-2
Friends of the Library Group

COPIAGUE

P COPIAGUE MEMORIAL PUBLIC LIBRARY, 50 Deauville Blvd, 11726-4103. SAN 311-0834. Tel: 631-691-1111. FAX: 631-691-5098. E-mail: information@copiaguelibrary.org. Web Site: www.copiaguelibrary.org. *Dir,* Ken Miller; Staff 50 (MLS 7, Non-MLS 43)
Founded 1961. Pop 25,758; Circ 332,121
Library Holdings: AV Mats 23,799; Large Print Bks 1,587; Bk Titles 70,962; Bk Vols 78,099; Per Subs 257
Database Vendor: Innovative Interfaces, Inc
Wireless access
Publications: Newsletter (Bi-monthly)
Mem of Suffolk Cooperative Library System
Open Mon-Fri 10-9, Sat 9:30-5:30, Sun 1-5
Friends of the Library Group

CORAM

S US GEOLOGICAL SURVEY WATER RESOURCES DIVISION*, New York Sub-District Library, Bldg 4 2045 Rte 112, 11727. SAN 370-2731. Tel: 631-736-0783. FAX: 631-736-4283. *In Charge,* Simonette Rivera
Library Holdings: Bk Vols 7,000
Subject Interests: Climatology, Geochemistry, Geol
Wireless access
Restriction: Open by appt only

CORFU

P CORFU FREE LIBRARY*, Seven Maple Ave, 14036. (Mail add: PO Box 419, 14036-0419), SAN 311-0850. Tel: 585-599-3321. FAX: 585-599-3321. E-mail: corfulibrary@nioga.org. Web Site: www.corfufreelibrary.org. *Dir,* Diana Reding; *Ch Serv,* Darlene Markle; Staff 2 (Non-MLS 2)
Founded 1920. Pop 755; Circ 14,451
Library Holdings: Bk Vols 75,000; Per Subs 25
Automation Activity & Vendor Info: (Cataloging) SirsiDynix; (Circulation) SirsiDynix; (OPAC) SirsiDynix
Wireless access
Function: ILL available
Mem of Nioga Library System
Open Mon & Wed 10-2, Tues, Thurs & Fri 2-8
Friends of the Library Group

CORINTH

P CORINTH FREE LIBRARY*, 89 Main St, 12822. SAN 311-0869. Tel: 518-654-6913. FAX: 518-654-6913. Web Site: corinth.sals.edu. *Librn,* Rebecca Fasulo; E-mail: rfasulo@sals.edu
Founded 1926. Pop 5,985; Circ 20,799
Jan 2006-Dec 2006 Income $82,656. Mats Exp $79,376. Sal $55,511
Library Holdings: AV Mats 800; Bk Vols 18,000; Per Subs 16
Automation Activity & Vendor Info: (Cataloging) Innovative Interfaces, Inc; (Circulation) Innovative Interfaces, Inc; (OPAC) Innovative Interfaces, Inc
Wireless access
Mem of Southern Adirondack Library System
Open Mon, Tues & Thurs (Sept-June) 11-5 & 7-8:30, Fri 9:30-4, Sat 10-4; Mon, Tues & Thurs (July & Aug) 9-3:30 & 7-8:30, Fri 9-4, Sat 9-1
Friends of the Library Group

CORNING

J CORNING COMMUNITY COLLEGE, Arthur A Houghton Jr Library, One Academic Dr, 14830. SAN 311-0885. Tel: 607-962-9251. FAX: 607-962-9466. E-mail: library@corning-cc.edu. Web Site: https://www.corning-cc.edu/library. *Assoc Dean, Learning Res,* Sarah Weisman; E-mail: sweisma1@corning-cc.edu; *Access Serv & Syst,* Amy Dibble; E-mail: adibble1@corning-cc.edu; *Acq,* Eileen Goltry; E-mail: goltry@corning-cc.edu; *Cat,* Rosanne Darcangelo; E-mail: darcanrm@corning-cc.edu; *Instruction & Outreach,* Erin Wilburn; E-mail: ewilburn@corning-cc.edu; *ILL,* Dawn Dobson; E-mail: dobsonde@corning-cc.edu; *Per,* Nancy Larrabee; E-mail: larrabee@corning-cc.edu; Staff 7 (MLS 3, Non-MLS 4)
Founded 1957. Enrl 3,200; Fac 150; Highest Degree: Associate
Library Holdings: Bk Vols 30,000
Automation Activity & Vendor Info: (Cataloging) Ex Libris Group; (Circulation) Ex Libris Group; (ILL) OCLC ILLiad; (OPAC) Ex Libris Group; (Serials) Ex Libris Group
Wireless access
Open Mon-Thurs 7:30-8, Fri 7:30-4, Sun 4-8

S CORNING MUSEUM OF GLASS*, Juliette K & Leonard S Rakow Research Library, Five Museum Way, 14830. SAN 311-0907. Tel: 607-974-8649. FAX: 607-974-8677. E-mail: rakow@cmog.org. Web Site: www.cmog.org/library. *Chief Librn,* James Galbraith; Staff 17.5 (MLS 8.5, Non-MLS 9)
Founded 1950
Jan 2007-Dec 2007. Mats Exp $209,000
Library Holdings: AV Mats 230,000; DVDs 1,400; Electronic Media & Resources 12; Microforms 20,000; Bk Titles 50,000; Bk Vols 55,000; Per Subs 1,000; Videos 1,500
Special Collections: Antiquarian & Rare Books Coll; Auction Catalog Coll; Design Drawings & Art on Paper; Emphera Coll; Film, Video & DVD Coll; Microform Coll; Personal & Corporate Archives; Slide Coll; Trade Catalog Coll
Subject Interests: Archaeology, Glass art, Glassware, Hist of glass, Manufacturing of glass before 1930
Automation Activity & Vendor Info: (Acquisitions) Ex Libris Group; (Cataloging) Ex Libris Group; (Circulation) Ex Libris Group; (ILL) OCLC; (OPAC) Ex Libris Group; (Serials) Ex Libris Group
Database Vendor: ARTstor, Cambridge Scientific Abstracts, EBSCOhost, H W Wilson, JSTOR, OCLC FirstSearch, OCLC WorldShare Interlibrary Loan, Oxford Online
Wireless access
Partic in Nylink; OCLC Online Computer Library Center, Inc; South Central Regional Library Council
Open Mon-Fri 9-5, Sun 12-5

P SOUTHEAST STEUBEN COUNTY LIBRARY*, 300 Civic Center Plaza, Ste 101, 14830. SAN 311-0915. Tel: 607-936-3713. Circulation Tel: 607-936-3713, Ext 501. Reference Tel: 607-936-3713, Ext 502. Administration Tel: 607-936-3713, Ext 205. FAX: 607-936-1714. Web Site: www.stls.org/corning. *Dir,* Pauline Emery; E-mail: emeryp@stls.org; *Asst Dir,* Jennifer Russell; Tel: 607-936-3713, Ext 208, E-mail: russellj@stls.org; *Ch Serv,* Sue McConnell; Tel: 607-936-3713, Ext 503, E-mail: mcconnell@stls.org; Staff 17 (MLS 3, Non-MLS 14)
Founded 2000. Pop 34,141; Circ 150,203
Library Holdings: Bk Vols 118,438; Per Subs 125
Special Collections: Caldecott & Newbery Winners & Honors Coll; Foreign, Independent & Classic Films Coll; Foundation Center Coll
Subject Interests: Glass, Literacy, Local hist
Automation Activity & Vendor Info: (Acquisitions) SirsiDynix; (Cataloging) SirsiDynix; (Circulation) SirsiDynix
Database Vendor: LearningExpress
Wireless access
Mem of Southern Tier Library System
Open Mon, Wed & Fri 10-6, Tues & Thurs 10-8, Sat 10-4, Sun 11-5
Friends of the Library Group

CORNWALL

P CORNWALL PUBLIC LIBRARY*, 395 Hudson St, 12518-1552. SAN 352-4108. Tel: 845-534-8282. FAX: 845-534-3827. E-mail: cor@rcls.org. Web Site: www.cornwallpubliclibrary.org. *Dir,* Karen LaRocca-Fels; E-mail: kfels@rcls.org; Staff 3 (MLS 3)
Pop 14,289; Circ 112,000
Library Holdings: Bk Vols 35,500; Per Subs 165
Special Collections: Biography & Literature (Local Authors Coll); Local History; The Cornwall Local, microfilm & CD
Automation Activity & Vendor Info: (Cataloging) Horizon; (Circulation) Horizon; (OPAC) Horizon
Wireless access
Function: Homebound delivery serv
Publications: Friends of the Cornwall Public Library (Newsletter); Library Newsletter
Mem of Ramapo Catskill Library System
Open Mon-Thurs 10-8, Fri 10-6, Sat 10-4, Sun 1-4
Friends of the Library Group

CORTLAND

S CORTLAND COUNTY HISTORICAL SOCIETY*, Kellogg Memorial Research Library, 25 Homer Ave, 13045. SAN 311-094X. Tel: 607-756-6071. *Dir,* Mindy Leisenring
Founded 1925
Library Holdings: Bk Titles 4,000
Special Collections: Genealogy & History of Cortland County, ms, archives
Open Tues-Sat 1-5

P CORTLAND FREE LIBRARY*, 32 Church St, 13045. SAN 311-0958. Tel: 607-753-1042. FAX: 607-758-7329. Web Site: www.flls.org/cortlandlib. *Dir,* Kay Zaharis; Staff 12 (MLS 2, Non-MLS 10)
Founded 1886. Pop 28,906; Circ 101,786
Jan 2012-Dec 2012 Income $253,600, City $150,000, Locally Generated Income $10,600, Other $86,000. Mats Exp $127,250, Books $40,000, Per/Ser (Incl. Access Fees) $13,950, AV Equip $1,400, AV Mat $7,000, Presv $1,000. Sal $230,000 (Prof $121,050)
Library Holdings: Audiobooks 1,400; CDs 210; DVDs 1,200; Large Print Bks 1,400; Bk Titles 68,152; Bk Vols 73,344; Per Subs 167; Videos 135
Subject Interests: Local hist
Automation Activity & Vendor Info: (Acquisitions) Innovative Interfaces, Inc; (Cataloging) Baker & Taylor; (Circulation) Innovative Interfaces, Inc; (ILL) Innovative Interfaces, Inc; (Serials) Innovative Interfaces, Inc
Database Vendor: EBSCO Auto Repair Reference, EBSCO Information Services, EBSCOhost, Gale Cengage Learning, Grolier Online, H W Wilson, infoUSA, LearningExpress, LexisNexis, Medline, Mergent Online, Newsbank, OCLC FirstSearch, OCLC WorldShare Interlibrary Loan, Overdrive, Inc, ProQuest, ReferenceUSA, Sage, TumbleBookLibrary, Westlaw
Wireless access
Function: Audiobks via web, Bk club(s), Bks on cassette, Bks on CD, Children's prog, Computer training, Computers for patron use, Copy machines, E-Reserves, Electronic databases & coll, Exhibits, Free DVD rentals, Handicapped accessible, Health sci info serv, Homebound delivery serv, Homework prog, ILL available, Instruction & testing, Literacy & newcomer serv, Magnifiers for reading, Music CDs, Online cat, Online ref, Online searches, OverDrive digital audio bks, Photocopying/Printing, Preschool outreach, Prog for children & young adult, Pub access computers, Ref serv in person, Senior computer classes, Spoken cassettes & CDs, Spoken cassettes & DVDs, Story hour, Summer & winter reading prog, Tax forms, Teen prog, VHS videos, Video lending libr
Publications: Cortland Free Library News (Newsletter)
Mem of Finger Lakes Library System
Open Mon-Thurs 9:30-8, Fri 9:30-5:30, Sat 9:30-4:30
Restriction: Authorized patrons

C SUNY CORTLAND*, Memorial Library, 81 Prospect Terrace, 13045. (Mail add: PO Box 2000, 13045), SAN 352-4221. Tel: 607-753-2525. Circulation Tel: 607-753-2500. Interlibrary Loan Service Tel: 607-753-2928. Reference Tel: 607-753-2590. Administration Tel: 607-753-2221. FAX: 607-753-5669. Circulation FAX: 607-753-5599. E-mail: library@cortland.edu. Web Site: library.cortland.edu. *Dir,* Gail Wood; *Bibliographer, Instrul Serv Librn,* Daniel Harms; *Automation Syst Coordr,* Dave Ritchie; *Coordr, Bibliog Serv,* Jennifer Kronenbitter; *Coordr, ILL, Per & Stack Maintenance,* Anita Kuiken; *Coordr, Ref & Instrul Serv,* Lorraine Melita; *Bibliographer,* Gretchen Herrmann; *Bibliographer, Cataloger,* Ellen McCabe; *Instr, Info & Computer Literacy,* Mark Connell; *Instr, Info & Computer Literacy,* Gretchen Douglas. Subject Specialists: *Kinesiology, Phys educ, Recreation,* Daniel Harms; *Health,* Anita Kuiken; *Educ,* Lorraine Melita; *Soc sci,* Gretchen Herrmann; *Arts, Humanities,* Ellen McCabe; Staff 20.7 (MLS 11.7, Non-MLS 9)
Founded 1868. Enrl 7,358; Fac 578; Highest Degree: Master
Library Holdings: Electronic Media & Resources 3,717; Microforms 844,212; Bk Titles 321,163; Bk Vols 420,869; Per Subs 526
Subject Interests: Educ, Health educ, Phys educ, Recreation
Automation Activity & Vendor Info: (Acquisitions) Ex Libris Group; (Cataloging) Ex Libris Group; (Circulation) Ex Libris Group; (Course Reserve) Ex Libris Group; (OPAC) Ex Libris Group
Wireless access
Function: Pub access computers
Publications: Bibliographies; Dragons Bookshelf (Newsletter); Research Guides
Partic in OCLC Online Computer Library Center, Inc; South Central Regional Library Council
Special Services for the Deaf - Assistive tech
Special Services for the Blind - Assistive/Adapted tech devices, equip & products
Open Mon-Thurs 7:30am-1am, Fri 7:30-7, Sat 10-6, Sun Noon-1am
Restriction: Vols & interns use only
Friends of the Library Group
Departmental Libraries:
ART SLIDE, Dowd Fine Arts Ctr, 13045, SAN 352-4256. Tel: 607-753-5519. *Curator,* Lisa Joyce
Special Collections: Rousey Arts in Sports Coll
Open Mon & Wed 8-5, Tues & Thurs 8-2
PERFORMING ARTS, Dowd Fine Arts Ctr, 13045, SAN 352-4310. Tel: 607-756-1200. Web Site: www.cortland.edu. *In Charge,* Karen Zimmerman; E-mail: zimmermank@cortland.edu
Open Mon-Fri 8-4

COXSACKIE

S COXSACKIE CORRECTIONAL FACILITY LIBRARY*, Rte 9W, 12051-0200. (Mail add: PO Box 200, 12051-0200), SAN 327-1323. Tel: 518-731-2781, Ext 4602. FAX: 518-731-2099. *Sr Librn,* Stephen M Almasi; E-mail: smalmasi@earthlink.net; Staff 1 (MLS 1)
Founded 1935
Library Holdings: Audiobooks 100; High Interest/Low Vocabulary Bk Vols 150; Bk Titles 4,000; Per Subs 65
Automation Activity & Vendor Info: (Cataloging) Follett Software; (Circulation) Follett Software
Function: ILL available
Open Mon & Tues 12:30-8:45, Wed-Fri 7:20-2:20

S GREENE CORRECTIONAL FACILITY*, General Library, Plank Rd, 12051. (Mail add: PO Box 8, 12051-0008), SAN 327-2532. Tel: 518-731-2741, Ext 4600. FAX: 518-741-2099. *Sr Librn,* R Torian
Library Holdings: Bk Titles 15,000; Per Subs 70
Automation Activity & Vendor Info: (Cataloging) Follett Software; (Circulation) Follett Software
Open Mon 8-4, Tues & Thurs 11-7, Wed & Fri 8am-9pm, Sat 12-7

S GREENE COUNTY HISTORICAL SOCIETY*, Vedder Research Library, 90 County Rd 42, 12051-3022. SAN 311-0990. Tel: 518-731-1033, 518-731-6822. E-mail: vedderlibrary@yahoo.com. Web Site: www.vedderlibrary.org. *Librn,* Steve Pec; *Cataloger,* Clesson S Bush
Library Holdings: Bk Vols 10,000; Per Subs 20; Spec Interest Per Sub 20
Special Collections: County Maps; County Newspapers from 1792; Family Papers; Genealogy Coll; Greene County Surrogate Court Records; Postcards; Scrapbooks
Subject Interests: Catskills, Greene County, Mid-Hudson valley
Publications: Quarterly journal - indexed each five years
Open Tues & Wed 10-4

P HEERMANCE MEMORIAL LIBRARY*, One Ely St, 12051. SAN 311-1008. Tel: 518-731-8084. FAX: 518-731-8264. Web Site: www.hml.lib.ny.us. *Dir,* Linda Deubert; E-mail: director@hml.lib.ny.us; Staff 2 (Non-MLS 2)
Founded 1908. Pop 6,196; Circ 35,765
Jan 2008-Dec 2008 Income $205,968. Mats Exp $19,900. Sal $111,325
Library Holdings: DVDs 600; Large Print Bks 500; Bk Vols 16,967; Talking Bks 528
Subject Interests: Local hist
Automation Activity & Vendor Info: (Cataloging) Innovative Interfaces, Inc; (Circulation) Innovative Interfaces, Inc; (OPAC) Innovative Interfaces, Inc; (Serials) Innovative Interfaces, Inc
Wireless access
Function: Adult bk club, Bk club(s), Handicapped accessible, Home delivery & serv to Sr ctr & nursing homes, Homebound delivery serv, Homework prog, ILL available, Music CDs, Online searches, Prog for adults, Prog for children & young adult, Ref serv available, Wheelchair accessible
Mem of Mid-Hudson Library System
Open Mon 3-6, Tues & Thurs 10-6, Wed 10-8, Fri 10-5, Sat 10-3
Friends of the Library Group

CRAGSMOOR

P CRAGSMOOR FREE LIBRARY*, 355 Cragsmoor Rd, 12420. (Mail add: PO Box 410, 12420-0410), SAN 311-1016. Tel: 845-647-4611. FAX: 845-647-4611. Web Site: www.rcls.org/crg. *Dir,* Hattie Grifo; E-mail: hgrifo@rcls.org
Founded 1913. Pop 750; Circ 5,655
Library Holdings: Audiobooks 108; CDs 160; DVDs 815; Bk Vols 10,751; Per Subs 46; Videos 300
Special Collections: Local History Coll, including art colony (1880s-1930s)
Automation Activity & Vendor Info: (Cataloging) Horizon; (Circulation) Horizon; (OPAC) Horizon
Wireless access
Publications: Art Show Catalogs; Cragsmoor: A Historical Sketch
Mem of Ramapo Catskill Library System
Open Tues 9:30-6, Thurs 11-7:30, Fri 3:30-5:30, Sat 9:30-4:30

CRANBERRY LAKE

P CLIFTON COMMUNITY LIBRARY*, Cranberry Lake Library, 7171 Rte 3, 12927. SAN 311-1024. Tel: 315-848-3256. FAX: 315-848-3554. *Librn,* Andrea S Arquette
Founded 1975. Pop 1,005; Circ 6,675
Library Holdings: Audiobooks 125; AV Mats 298; CDs 117; DVDs 150; Large Print Bks 150; Bk Vols 7,994; Per Subs 30; Talking Bks 160; Videos 227
Special Collections: Adirondack Memorial Coll
Subject Interests: Adirondack, Local hist
Wireless access
Function: Adult bk club, Bks on cassette, Bks on CD, Computers for patron use, Copy machines, Fax serv, ILL available, Music CDs, Photocopying/Printing, Satellite serv, VHS videos
Mem of North Country Library System
Open Mon & Wed 10-3 & 6-9, Fri & Sat 10-3
Restriction: Non-circulating of rare bks
Friends of the Library Group

CROGHAN

P CROGHAN FREE LIBRARY*, 9794 State Rte 812, 13327. (Mail add: PO Box 8, 13327-0008), SAN 311-1032. Tel: 315-346-6521. FAX: 315-346-6521. E-mail: crolib@ncls.org. Web Site: croghanfreelibrary.org. *Dir,* Joan Kampnich
Circ 8,694
Library Holdings: Bk Vols 12,000; Per Subs 40
Wireless access
Mem of North Country Library System
Open Mon 12-5, Wed & Fri 12-8

CROTON-ON-HUDSON

P CROTON FREE LIBRARY, 171 Cleveland Dr, 10520. SAN 311-1040. Tel: 914-271-6612. Interlibrary Loan Service Tel: 914-862-1027. Administration Tel: 914-862-1023. FAX: 914-271-0931. Web Site: www.crotonfreelibrary.org. *Dir,* Mary C Donnery; E-mail: mdonnery@wlsmail.org; *Asst Dir,* Jesse G Bourdon, Tel. 914-862-1024, E-mail: jbourdon@wlsmail.org; *Circ,* John Brosnan; *Tech Serv,* Lori Phillips; *Youth Serv,* Lauren E Dorien; Tel: 914-862-1025, E-mail: ldorien@wlsmail.org; Staff 36 (MLS 8, Non-MLS 28)
Founded 1937. Pop 8,665; Circ 170,000
Jul 2008-Jun 2009 Income $938,000, Locally Generated Income $862,000, Other $76,000. Mats Exp $131,000, Books $55,000, Per/Ser (Incl. Access Fees) $20,000, AV Mat $15,000, Electronic Ref Mat (Incl. Access Fees) $41,000. Sal $440,000 (Prof $220,000)
Library Holdings: AV Mats 6,622; DVDs 4,454; Bk Vols 75,771; Per Subs 166
Special Collections: Railroad Coll
Automation Activity & Vendor Info: (Acquisitions) SirsiDynix; (Circulation) SirsiDynix; (OPAC) SIRSI-iBistro
Database Vendor: SirsiDynix
Wireless access
Mem of Westchester Library System
Open Mon 1-9, Tues & Thurs 10-9, Wed & Fri 10-5:30, Sat 10-5 (10-1 Summer), Sun 1-5
Friends of the Library Group

CROWN POINT

P HAMMOND LIBRARY OF CROWN POINT NY*, 2732 Main St, 12928. (Mail add: PO Box 245, 12928-0245), SAN 311-1075. Tel: 518-597-3616. FAX: 518-597-3166. E-mail: hammondlibrary@nycap.rr.com. Web Site: www.hammondlibrary.org. *Dir,* Wendy L Terbeek; Staff 1 (Non-MLS 1)
Founded 1899. Pop 2,000; Circ 10,901
Library Holdings: CDs 48; DVDs 160; Electronic Media & Resources 1; Large Print Bks 437; Bk Titles 7,500; Per Subs 25; Talking Bks 346; Videos 1,105
Wireless access
Mem of Clinton-Essex-Franklin Library System
Special Services for the Blind - Audio mat; Bks on cassette; Bks on CD
Open Wed 10-6, Thurs 12-8, Fri 10-4, Sat 10-1

CUBA

P CUBA CIRCULATING LIBRARY*, 39 E Main St, 14727. SAN 311-1083. Tel: 585-968-1668. FAX: 585-968-3004. E-mail: cuba@stls.org. Web Site: www.cubalibrary.org. *Dir,* Cynthia Dutton; E-mail: duttonc@stls.org; Staff 2 (Non-MLS 2)
Founded 1872. Pop 4,672; Circ 48,475
Jan 2009-Dec 2009 Income $167,450, State $7,492, City $141,000, Federal $1,753, Locally Generated Income $16,005, Other $1,200. Mats Exp $19,700, Books $11,000, Per/Ser (Incl. Access Fees) $1,700, AV Mat $7,000. Sal $102,509 (Prof $65,961)
Library Holdings: AV Mats 2,791; Bks on Deafness & Sign Lang 30; CDs 250; High Interest/Low Vocabulary Bk Vols 100; Large Print Bks 300; Bk Vols 18,202; Per Subs 48
Subject Interests: Allegany County, Cuba hist, Genealogy
Automation Activity & Vendor Info: (Acquisitions) SirsiDynix; (Cataloging) SirsiDynix; (Circulation) SirsiDynix; (ILL) SirsiDynix; (OPAC) SirsiDynix
Wireless access
Mem of Southern Tier Library System
Open Mon-Thurs 9:30-8:30, Sat 9:30-3:30
Friends of the Library Group

CUTCHOGUE

P CUTCHOGUE-NEW SUFFOLK FREE LIBRARY*, 27550 Main Rd, 11935. (Mail add: PO Box 935, 11935-0935), SAN 311-1091. Tel: 631-734-6360. FAX: 631-734-7010. E-mail: cutclib@cnsfl.org. Web Site: www.cutchoguelibrary.org. *Dir,* Alison O'Reilly; *Supvr, Network Serv, Tech Serv Adminr,* Wendy Reeve; Staff 14 (MLS 4, Non-MLS 10)
Founded 1841. Pop 3,392; Circ 117,004
Jan 2005-Dec 2005 Income $1,006,559. Mats Exp $912,271. Sal $676,631
Library Holdings: AV Mats 13,660; Bk Vols 33,161; Per Subs 223
Subject Interests: Local hist
Automation Activity & Vendor Info: (Cataloging) Innovative Interfaces, Inc; (Circulation) Innovative Interfaces, Inc; (ILL) Innovative Interfaces, Inc, (OPAC) Innovative Interfaces, Inc
Wireless access
Function: Adult bk club, Archival coll, ILL available, Magnifiers for reading, Photocopying/Printing, Prog for adults, Prog for children & young adult, Ref serv available, Senior computer classes, Spoken cassettes & CDs, Summer reading prog, VHS videos
Mem of Suffolk Cooperative Library System
Open Mon-Fri 9:30-8, Sat 9:30-5, Sun (Nov-Mar) 1-5
Restriction: Open to pub for ref & circ; with some limitations
Friends of the Library Group

DANNEMORA

S CLINTON CORRECTIONAL FACILITY LIBRARY*, PO Box 2000, 12929-2000. SAN 328-7955. Tel: 518-492-2511. FAX: 518-492-2099. *Librn,* Kristen Rynkowski
Library Holdings: Bk Vols 8,000; Per Subs 60

P DANNEMORA FREE LIBRARY*, Village Community Ctr, 40 Emmons St, 12929. (Mail add: PO Box 730, 12929-0730), SAN 352-4345. Tel: 518-492-7005. FAX: 518-492-7005. E-mail: dannemoralibrary@yahoo.com. Web Site: www.dannemorafreelibrary.org. *Dir,* Laura Pritchard; Staff 1 (Non-MLS 1)
Founded 1940. Pop 2,006; Circ 22,943
Library Holdings: Audiobooks 414; AV Mats 194; e-books 2,600; Large Print Bks 80; Bk Vols 6,486; Per Subs 22
Automation Activity & Vendor Info: (Cataloging) Horizon; (Circulation) Horizon; (OPAC) Horizon
Function: ILL available
Mem of Clinton-Essex-Franklin Library System
Open Mon, Wed & Fri 11-4, Tues 2-8

DANSVILLE

P DANSVILLE PUBLIC LIBRARY*, Shepard Memorial Library, 200 Main St, 14437. SAN 311-1105. Tel: 585-335-6720. FAX: 585-335-6133. E-mail: director@dansville.lib.ny.us. Web Site: www.dansvillelibrary.org. *Dir,* Teresa A Dearing; Staff 1 (MLS 1)
Founded 1872. Pop 10,145; Circ 67,407
Jan 2012-Dec 2012 Income $376,804, State $2,836, Federal $136, County $11,300, Locally Generated Income $336,902, Other $25,630. Mats Exp $44,287, Books $32,884, Per/Ser (Incl. Access Fees) $4,500, Other Print

Mats $4,052, Micro $100, AV Mat $2,500, Electronic Ref Mat (Incl. Access Fees) $101, Presv $150. Sal $193,892 (Prof $65,750)
Library Holdings: CDs 1,396; DVDs 1,071; e-books 166; Microforms 1,465; Bk Vols 29,911; Per Subs 130; Talking Bks 50; Videos 25
Subject Interests: Local hist
Automation Activity & Vendor Info: (Circulation) Evergreen
Database Vendor: EBSCOhost, Gale Cengage Learning, Grolier Online, OCLC WorldShare Interlibrary Loan, ProQuest
Wireless access
Function: Audiobks via web, Bks on cassette, Bks on CD, Children's prog, Computers for patron use, Copy machines, E-Reserves, Electronic databases & coll, Exhibits, Handicapped accessible, Homebound delivery serv, ILL available, Mail & tel request accepted, Online cat, Orientations, OverDrive digital audio bks, Photocopying/Printing, Prog for adults, Prog for children & young adult, Pub access computers, Scanner, Spoken cassettes & CDs, Spoken cassettes & DVDs, Story hour, Summer reading prog, Tax forms, Teen prog, VHS videos, Web-catalog, Wheelchair accessible, Workshops
Mem of Pioneer Library System
Open Mon-Fri 10-8:30, Sat 12-4
Friends of the Library Group

DEER PARK

P DEER PARK PUBLIC LIBRARY*, 44 Lake Ave, 11729-6047. SAN 311-113X. Tel: 631-586-3000. FAX: 631-586-3006. E-mail: mail@deerparklibrary.org. Web Site: www.deerparklibrary.org. *Dir,* Gail Pepa; *Asst Dir,* Lisa Shumicky; *Ch Serv,* Kathy Greer
Founded 1964. Pop 26,000; Circ 200,000
Library Holdings: e-journals 10,470; Bk Vols 132,177; Per Subs 272
Automation Activity & Vendor Info: (Cataloging) Innovative Interfaces, Inc; (Circulation) Innovative Interfaces, Inc; (OPAC) Innovative Interfaces, Inc
Wireless access
Publications: Newsletter
Mem of Suffolk Cooperative Library System
Open Mon-Thurs 9-9, Fri 9-6, Sat 9-5, Sun (Sept-May) 12-4

DELEVAN

P DELEVAN-YORKSHIRE PUBLIC LIBRARY*, 28 School St, 14042. (Mail add: PO Box 185, 14042-0185), SAN 311-1148. Tel: 716-492-1961. FAX: 716-492-3398. E-mail: delyorkpublib@yahoo.com. Web Site: www.clslib.org/delevan. *Librn,* Gwen Bixby; E-mail: gbixby@pioneercsd.org; Staff 4 (MLS 1, Non-MLS 3)
Circ 19,336
Library Holdings: Bk Vols 19,000; Per Subs 40
Automation Activity & Vendor Info: (Cataloging) SirsiDynix; (Circulation) SirsiDynix; (OPAC) SirsiDynix
Wireless access
Mem of Chautauqua-Cattaraugus Library System
Open Mon & Wed 1-8, Tues 9-12 & 2-8, Thurs 9-8, Fri 1-6, Sat 9-1
Friends of the Library Group

DELHI

P CANNON FREE LIBRARY*, 40 Elm St, 13753. SAN 311-1156. Tel: 607-746-2662. FAX: 607-746-2662. *Dir,* Stacey Tromblee; Staff 1 (MLS 1)
Founded 1918. Pop 4,629; Circ 47,519
Jan 2011-Dec 2011. Mats Exp $9,600, Books $9,000, AV Mat $600
Library Holdings: CDs 497; DVDs 406; e-books 307; Large Print Bks 411; Bk Titles 21,645; Bk Vols 30,000; Per Subs 70
Special Collections: Delaware County Hist Coll
Automation Activity & Vendor Info: (Cataloging) SirsiDynix; (Circulation) SirsiDynix; (OPAC) SirsiDynix
Wireless access
Mem of Four County Library System
Open Tues & Thurs 10-8, Wed & Fri 10-5, Sat (Nov-Apr) 10-1

GL DELAWARE COUNTY SUPREME COURT LAW LIBRARY*, Three Court St, 13753-9990. SAN 311-1164. Tel: 607-746-3959. FAX: 607-746-8198. Web Site: www.courts.state.ny.us. *Librn,* Laurie Burpoe
Founded 1880
Library Holdings: Bk Vols 8,500
Open Mon-Thurs 9-1

C STATE UNIVERSITY OF NEW YORK COLLEGE OF TECHNOLOGY*, Louis & Mildred Resnick Library, Bush Hall, Two Main St, 13753. SAN 311-1172. Tel: 607-746-4635. FAX: 607-746-4327. E-mail: library@delhi.edu. Web Site: www.delhi.edu/library. *Dir,* Pamela J Peters; *Librn,* Steve G Dixon; Tel: 607-746-4642, E-mail: dixonsg@delhi.edu; *Electronic Res & Instruction Librn,* Amanda Mitchell; *Instruction & Ref Librn,* Megan Welsh; *Mgr, Access Serv,* Anna Reed; *Acq Mgr,* Bradley Post; Staff 7 (MLS 4, Non-MLS 3)
Founded 1915. Enrl 3,000; Fac 139; Highest Degree: Bachelor
Library Holdings: Bk Titles 50,000; Bk Vols 60,000; Per Subs 265
Special Collections: College Archives (yearbooks, photographs, student newspapers & other college publications)
Subject Interests: Culinary, Golf, Nursing, Turf mgt, Veterinary sci
Automation Activity & Vendor Info: (Acquisitions) Ex Libris Group; (Cataloging) Ex Libris Group; (Circulation) Ex Libris Group; (Course Reserve) Ex Libris Group; (ILL) Ex Libris Group; (OPAC) Ex Libris Group
Database Vendor: EBSCOhost, Elsevier, Gale Cengage Learning, OCLC FirstSearch, OCLC WorldShare Interlibrary Loan, ScienceDirect
Wireless access
Function: ILL available
Publications: Library Instruction Materials; Library Rules & Regulations; Pathfinders; Staff Handbooks; Student Handbook
Partic in OCLC Online Computer Library Center, Inc; SUNYConnect
Open Mon-Thurs 7:30am-Midnight, Fri 7:30-5, Sat 12-5, Sun 2-Midnight

DELMAR

P BETHLEHEM PUBLIC LIBRARY*, 451 Delaware Ave, 12054-3042. SAN 311-1180. Tel: 518-439-9314. Interlibrary Loan Service Tel: 518-439-9314, Ext 3013. Information Services Tel: 518-439-9314, Ext 3009. FAX: 518-478-0901. Interlibrary Loan Service FAX: 518-478-9265. Web Site: bethlehempubliclibrary.org. *Dir,* Geoffrey Kirkpatrick; E-mail: director@bethlehempubliclibrary.org; Staff 16 (MLS 16)
Founded 1913. Pop 25,965; Circ 627,987
Jul 2009-Jun 2010 Income $3,829,629, State $22,646, Locally Generated Income $339,000, Other $3,467,983. Mats Exp $367,500, Books $192,000, Per/Ser (Incl. Access Fees) $18,000, AV Equip $38,000, AV Mat $98,000, Electronic Ref Mat (Incl. Access Fees) $20,000, Presv $1,500. Sal $2,109,353
Library Holdings: Bk Titles 124,848; Per Subs 289
Special Collections: Local History & Genealogy Book Coll
Automation Activity & Vendor Info: (Circulation) SirsiDynix; (ILL) OCLC
Wireless access
Publications: Footnotes (Newsletter)
Partic in Cap District Libr Coun for Ref & Res Resources
Open Mon-Fri 9-9, Sat 10-5, Sun 12-5
Friends of the Library Group

DEPAUVILLE

P DEPAUVILLE FREE LIBRARY*, 32333 County Rte 179, 13632. (Mail add: PO Box 239, 13632-0239), SAN 311-1199. Tel: 315-686-3299. FAX: 315-686-3299. *Librn,* Connie Haver; E-mail: havercl@hotmail.com
Pop 2,499
Library Holdings: Bk Vols 2,500
Mem of North Country Library System
Open Mon & Wed 2-8, Tues & Thurs 11:30-6

DEPOSIT

P DEPOSIT FREE LIBRARY*, 159 Front St, 13754. SAN 311-1202. Tel: 607-467-2577. FAX: 607-467-1466. E-mail: depositlibrary@gmail.com. Web Site: depositfreelibrary.org. *Dir,* Audrey Babcock; E-mail: de.audrey@4cls.org
Pop 4,427; Circ 17,522
Library Holdings: Bk Titles 13,750; Per Subs 47
Automation Activity & Vendor Info: (Cataloging) SirsiDynix; (Circulation) SirsiDynix; (OPAC) SirsiDynix
Mem of Four County Library System
Open Tues-Thurs 12-8, Fri & Sat 9-3

DERUYTER

P DERUYTER FREE LIBRARY*, 735 Utica St, 13052-9613. (Mail add: PO Box 399, 13052-0399), SAN 325-1543. Tel: 315-852-6262. FAX: 315-852-6262. E-mail: deruyter@midyork.org. Web Site: www.deruyterfreelibrary.org, www.midyork.org/deruyter. *Dir,* Amy Curtis; E-mail: acurtis@midyork.org
Pop 1,458; Circ 25,000
Library Holdings: Bk Titles 19,500; Per Subs 30
Automation Activity & Vendor Info: (Cataloging) SirsiDynix; (Circulation) SirsiDynix; (OPAC) SirsiDynix
Wireless access
Mem of Mid-York Library System
Open Mon 9-5, Tues 9-7, Thurs 9-5 & 7-9, Sat 10-12
Friends of the Library Group

DEWITT

P DEWITT COMMUNITY LIBRARY, 3649 Erie Blvd E, 13214. SAN 311-1229. Tel: 315-446-3578. FAX: 315-446-1955. E-mail: dreference@onlib.org. Web Site: www.dewlib.org. *Exec Dir,* Wendy Scott; E-mail: wscott@onlib.org; *Asst Dir, Patron Serv,* Marc Wildman; *Ch,*

Jennifer Burke; *Media Spec, Ref Serv,* Linda Wozniak; Staff 9 (MLS 6, Non-MLS 3)
Founded 1962. Pop 15,546; Circ 34,418
Library Holdings: Audiobooks 6,094; AV Mats 12,602; DVDs 6,508; Electronic Media & Resources 124; Bk Titles 60,582; Per Subs 60
Automation Activity & Vendor Info: (Cataloging) Innovative Interfaces, Inc; (Circulation) Innovative Interfaces, Inc; (OPAC) Innovative Interfaces, Inc
Wireless access
Function: Adult bk club, Bks on cassette, Bks on CD, Children's prog, Computer training, Computers for patron use, Copy machines, Digital talking bks, E-Reserves, Electronic databases & coll, Free DVD rentals, Handicapped accessible, ILL available, Large print keyboards, Music CDs, Notary serv, Online cat, Online ref, Outreach serv, Outside serv via phone, mail, e-mail & web, OverDrive digital audio bks, Prog for adults, Prog for children & young adult, Pub access computers, Ref serv available, Senior outreach, Story hour, Summer reading prog, Tax forms
Publications: Dewitt Community Library (Newsletter)
Mem of Onondaga County Public Library
Open Mon-Thurs 10-9, Fri & Sat 10-5, Sun 1-5
Friends of the Library Group

DEXTER

P DEXTER FREE LIBRARY*, 120 E Kirby St, 13634. (Mail add: P O Box 544, 13634-0544), SAN 311-1237. Tel: 315-639-6785. FAX: 315-639-6785. E-mail: dexlib@ncls.org. Web Site: www.dexterfreelibrary.org. *Dir,* Jennifer Thomas
Founded 1924. Pop 1,120; Circ 5,750
Library Holdings: Bk Vols 6,395; Per Subs 30
Automation Activity & Vendor Info: (Cataloging) SirsiDynix; (Circulation) SirsiDynix; (OPAC) SirsiDynix
Wireless access
Function: After school storytime, Meeting rooms, Photocopying/Printing
Mem of North Country Library System
Open Tues & Thurs 12-5 & 6-8, Wed 10-12 & 1-5
Friends of the Library Group

DIAMOND POINT

P HILLVIEW FREE LIBRARY*, 3717 Lake Shore Dr, 12824. Tel: 518-668-3012. FAX: 518-668-3012. Web Site: adirondackminute.com/hillview-free-library. *Dir,* Dr Jane O'Connell
Founded 1899
Jul 2005-Jun 2006. Mats Exp $5,000, Books $4,500, AV Mat $500
Library Holdings: AV Mats 150; Large Print Bks 30; Bk Vols 15,000; Per Subs 15
Special Collections: Adirondack Coll. UN Document Depository; US Document Depository
Wireless access
Mem of Southern Adirondack Library System
Open Wed & Thurs (Winter) 10-3, Sat 10-1; Mon (Summer) 10-6, Tues & Fri 10-3, Wed 10-3 & 6-9, Sat 10-Noon

DIX HILLS

S DIX HILLS JEWISH CENTER LIBRARY*, 555 Vanderbilt Pkwy, 11746. SAN 323-6137. Tel: 631 499 6644. FAX: 631 499-6092. E-mail: office@dhjc.org. Web Site: www.dhjc.org. *Coordr,* Hasson Jackie; E-mail: jackibernr@aol.com
Library Holdings: Bk Vols 1,000; Per Subs 16
Open Wed 5:30-8:30, Sun 9:30-12:30
Restriction: Mem only

C FIVE TOWNS COLLEGE LIBRARY*, 305 N Service Rd, 11746. SAN 311-4899. Tel: 631-656-2138. FAX: 631-656-2171. Web Site: www.ftc.edu. *Dir, Info Literacy, Libr Dir,* John Vansteen; Tel: 631-656-3187; *Librn,* Karen Flanagan; *Librn,* Robbi Schweigert; Staff 12 (MLS 6, Non-MLS 6)
Founded 1972. Enrl 1,050; Fac 154; Highest Degree: Doctorate
Library Holdings: AV Mats 12,000; Bks on Deafness & Sign Lang 10; e-books 30,000; Music Scores 600; Bk Titles 25,000; Bk Vols 35,000; Per Subs 500; Spec Interest Per Sub 500
Special Collections: Archival Sheet Music; Popular/Classic Songbooks
Subject Interests: Educ, Film, Music, Music bus, Theatre, Video
Automation Activity & Vendor Info: (Acquisitions) EOS International; (Cataloging) EOS International; (Circulation) EOS International; (OPAC) EOS International
Database Vendor: CQ Press, EBSCOhost, Gale Cengage Learning, ProQuest, Wilson - Wilson Web
Wireless access
Function: Ref serv available, Referrals accepted
Publications: Accession List; List of Sheet Music Archives; Newsletter
Partic in Long Island Library Resources Council
Open Mon-Thurs 8:30am-10pm, Fri 8:30-7, Sat & Sun 10-6
Restriction: Borrowing privileges limited to fac & registered students

P HALF HOLLOW HILLS COMMUNITY LIBRARY*, 55 Vanderbilt Pkwy, 11746. SAN 352-440X. Tel: 631-421-4530. FAX: 631-421-0730. E-mail: hhhllib@suffolk.lib.ny.us. Web Site: hhhlibrary.org. *Dir,* Michele Lauer-Bader; E-mail: mlauerba@suffolk.lib.ny.us; *Asst Dir,* Alicja Feitzinger; Staff 36 (MLS 30, Non-MLS 6)
Founded 1959. Pop 43,745; Circ 465,405
Library Holdings: AV Mats 32,577; CDs 7,002; DVDs 5,666; Bk Vols 340,640; Videos 10,750
Subject Interests: Econ, Relig studies
Automation Activity & Vendor Info: (Acquisitions) Innovative Interfaces, Inc; (Cataloging) Innovative Interfaces, Inc; (Circulation) Innovative Interfaces, Inc; (ILL) Innovative Interfaces, Inc; (OPAC) Innovative Interfaces, Inc; (Serials) Innovative Interfaces, Inc
Database Vendor: EBSCOhost, Gale Cengage Learning, Grolier Online, OCLC FirstSearch, ProQuest, ReferenceUSA
Wireless access
Publications: Business Link Newsletter (Periodical); The First R (Newsletter)
Mem of Suffolk Cooperative Library System
Partic in Long Island Library Resources Council
Branches: 1
MELVILLE BRANCH, 510 Sweet Hollow Rd, Melville, 11747, SAN 352-4434. Tel: 631-421-4535. FAX: 631-421-3715. Web Site: hhhl.suffolk.lib.ny.us. *Br Head,* Charlene Muhr; E-mail: cmuhr@suffolk.lib.ny.us
Open Mon-Thurs 10-9, Fri & Sat 10-5

DOBBS FERRY

P DOBBS FERRY PUBLIC LIBRARY, 55 Main St, 10522. SAN 311-1253. Tel: 914-693-6614. FAX: 914-693-4671. E-mail: dobref@wlsmail.org. Web Site: www.dobbsferrylibrary.org. *Libr Dir,* Jeffrey Ault; Tel: 914-231-3051, E-mail: jault@wlsmail.org; *Adult Ref Librn, Head, Circ,* Edward Canora; Tel: 914-231-3055, E-mail: ecanora@wlsmail.org; *Adult Ref Librn,* Sara Rodgers; Tel: 914-231-3057, E-mail: srodgers@wlsmail.org; *Ch,* Cheryl Matthews; Tel: 914-693-6615, E-mail: cmatthews@wlsmail.org; *Youth Serv Librn,* Anne Quick; E-mail: aquick@wlsmail.org
Founded 1899. Pop 10,622; Circ 111,522
Jun 2012-May 2013 Income $774,334, State $2,695, City $754,923, Other $16,716. Mats Exp $88,627, Books $37,981, AV Mat $9,926, Electronic Ref Mat (Incl. Access Fees) $40,720. Sal $466,572 (Prof $337,043)
Library Holdings: Audiobooks 3,710; CDs 1,980; DVDs 2,890; e-books 42,320; Large Print Bks 625; Bk Vols 41,037; Per Subs 70; Videos 50
Automation Activity & Vendor Info: (Acquisitions) SirsiDynix; (Cataloging) SirsiDynix; (Circulation) SirsiDynix; (ILL) SirsiDynix; (Serials) SirsiDynix
Database Vendor: SirsiDynix
Wireless access
Function: Homebound delivery serv
Mem of Westchester Library System
Open Mon & Wed 10-8, Tues & Thurs 10-6, Fri & Sat 10-5, Sun (Oct-Apr) 1-5
Friends of the Library Group

C MERCY COLLEGE LIBRARIES*, 555 Broadway, 10522. SAN 311-1261. Tel: 914-674-7256. Interlibrary Loan Service Tel: 914-674-7580. Reference Tel: 914-674-7257. Administration Tel: 914-674-7260. Automation Services Tel: 914-674-7259. FAX: 914-674-7581. Administration FAX: 914-674-7494. E-mail: libref@mercy.edu. Web Site: www.mercy.edu/library. *Dir,* Judith Liebman; E-mail: jliebman@mercy.edu; *Head, Automation, Head, Tech Serv,* Nina Lee; Tel: 914-674-7263, E-mail: nlee@mercy.edu; *Bibliog Instr, Webmaster,* Susan Gaskin-Noel; Tel: 914-674-7672, E-mail: sgaskinnoel@mercy.edu; *Bibliog Instr,* Kristine Wycisk; Tel: 914-674-7293, E-mail: kwcisk@mercy.edu; *Coll Develop,* Donald Ray; Tel: 914-674-7429, E-mail: dray@mercy.edu; *ILL,* Gilda Gonzalez; Tel: 914-674-7580, E-mail: gmgonzalez@mercy.edu; *Media Spec,* Mustafa Sakarya; Tel: 914-674-7799, E-mail: msakarya@mercy.edu; Staff 15 (MLS 15)
Founded 1950. Enrl 9,028; Fac 180; Highest Degree: Doctorate
Library Holdings: Bk Vols 134,483; Per Subs 369
Special Collections: Eric doc. US Document Depository
Automation Activity & Vendor Info: (Acquisitions) Ex Libris Group; (Cataloging) Ex Libris Group; (Circulation) Ex Libris Group; (OPAC) Ex Libris Group; (Serials) Ex Libris Group
Database Vendor: JSTOR, OCLC FirstSearch, ProQuest, Wilson - Wilson Web
Wireless access
Partic in Metropolitan New York Library Council; Westchester Academic Library Directors Organization (WALDO)
Open Mon-Thurs 8am-10pm, Fri 8:30am-10pm, Sat 8:30-8, Sun 2:30-6:30
Departmental Libraries:
BRONX CAMPUS, 1200 Waters Pl, Bronx, 10461, SAN 310-9100. Tel: 718-678-8850. Circulation Tel: 718-678-8856. Circulation FAX: 718-678-8668. E-mail: libbx@mercy.edu. *Librn,* Michele Lee; Tel: 718-678-8394, E-mail: mlee@mercy.edu; *Asst Librn,* Vladimir

Strizhevsky; Tel: 718-678-8392, E-mail: vstrizhevsky@mercy.edu; Staff 2 (MLS 2)
Library Holdings: Bk Vols 29,714
Open Mon-Thurs 8:30am-10pm, Fri 8:30-8, Sat 8:30-4, Sun 8:30-3

MANHATTAN CAMPUS, 66 W 35th St, New York, 10001. Tel: 212-615-3364. FAX: 212-967-6330. *Librn,* Michele Lee; E-mail: mlee@mercy.edu; *Asst Librn,* Position Currently Open; Staff 4 (MLS 4) Fac 3
Library Holdings: Bk Vols 6,186
Open Mon-Thurs 9-9, Fri 9-5, Sat 10-5

WHITE PLAINS CAMPUS, 277 Martine Ave & S Broadway, White Plains, 10601, SAN 312-6862. Tel: 914-948-3666. FAX: 914-686-1858. E-mail: libwp@mercy.edu. *Librn,* Srivalli Rao; Tel: 914-948-3666, Ext 3329, E-mail: srao@mercy.edu; Staff 1 (MLS 1)
Library Holdings: Bk Vols 16,101
Special Collections: US & New York State Law Coll
Open Mon-Thurs 8:30am-9pm, Fri & Sat 8:30-4
Restriction: Restricted borrowing privileges

YORKTOWN CAMPUS, 2651 Strang Blvd, Yorktown Heights, 10598, SAN 312-7214. Tel: 914-245-6100. FAX: 914-962-1042. E-mail: libyktn@mercy.edu. *Librn,* Agnes Cameron; Tel: 914-245-6100, Ext 2222, E-mail: acameron@mercy.edu; Staff 1 (MLS 1)
Library Holdings: Bk Vols 41,710
Special Collections: US Document Depository
Open Mon & Thurs 12-9, Tues & Wed 8:30am-9pm

DOLGEVILLE

P DOLGEVILLE-MANHEIM PUBLIC LIBRARY*, 24 N Main St, 13329. SAN 311-1288. Tel: 315-429-3421. FAX: 315-429-3421. *Dir,* Kathy Provorse; Staff 1 (Non-MLS 1)
Founded 1890. Pop 3,527; Circ 21,937
Library Holdings: Bk Vols 12,000; Per Subs 12
Wireless access
Mem of Mid-York Library System
Special Services for the Blind - Talking bks
Open Mon-Fri 12-6

DRYDEN

P SOUTHWORTH LIBRARY ASSOCIATION*, 24 W Main St, 13053. (Mail add: PO Box 45, 13053-0045), SAN 311-1318. Tel: 607-844-4782. FAX: 607-844-5310. E-mail: southworth@twcny.rr.com. Web Site: southworthlibrary.org. *Dir,* Diane Pamel
Founded 1884. Pop 12,156; Circ 32,000
Library Holdings: Bk Titles 25,000; Per Subs 45
Special Collections: Rare Books (John Dryden Coll)
Subject Interests: Local hist, Rare bks
Automation Activity & Vendor Info: (Cataloging) Innovative Interfaces, Inc; (Circulation) Innovative Interfaces, Inc; (OPAC) Innovative Interfaces, Inc; (Serials) Innovative Interfaces, Inc
Wireless access
Mem of Finger Lakes Library System
Open Mon-Wed 1:30-7:30, Thurs 11-5:30, Fri 11-7, Sat 10-2
Friends of the Library Group

J TOMPKINS CORTLAND COMMUNITY COLLEGE*, Gerald A Barry Memorial Library, 170 North St, 13053-8504. (Mail add: PO Box 139, 13503-0139), SAN 311-1326. Tel: 607-844-8222. Circulation Tel: 607-844-8222, Ext 4361. Reference Tel: 607-844-8222, Ext 4363. Administration Tel: 607-844-8222, Ext 4354. Toll Free Tel: 888-567-8211, Ext 4363. FAX: 607-844-6540. E-mail: tc3library@tc3.edu. Web Site: www.tc3.edu/library. *Libr Dir,* Gregg Kiehl; E-mail: grjk@tc3.edu; *Librn,* Karla Block; *Acq Librn,* Susanna Vant Sant; *Instrul Serv Librn,* Barbara Kobritz; Tel: 607-844-8222, Ext 4362; *Libr Serv Librn,* Margaret Anderson; *Circ Serv Coordr,* Lucy Yang; Tel: 607-844-8222, Ext 4361, E-mail: lyw@tc3.edu; Staff 9 (MLS 5, Non-MLS 4)
Founded 1968. Enrl 3,000; Fac 75; Highest Degree: Associate
Library Holdings: Bk Titles 43,015; Bk Vols 51,709; Per Subs 350
Special Collections: State Document Depository
Subject Interests: Allied health, Bus computing, Nursing
Automation Activity & Vendor Info: (Acquisitions) Ex Libris Group; (Cataloging) Ex Libris Group; (Circulation) Ex Libris Group; (Course Reserve) Ex Libris Group
Database Vendor: Gale Cengage Learning, OCLC FirstSearch, ProQuest
Partic in Nylink; OCLC Online Computer Library Center, Inc; South Central Regional Library Council
Special Services for the Deaf - Assistive tech
Special Services for the Blind - Assistive/Adapted tech devices, equip & products; Reader equip; Scanner for conversion & translation of mats
Open Mon-Thurs 8am-9pm, Fri 8-4, Sun 1-5

DUNDEE

P DUNDEE LIBRARY, 32 Water St, 14837. SAN 311-1334. Tel: 607-243-5938. FAX: 607-243-7733. E-mail: dundee@stls.org. Web Site: www.stls.org/dundee. *Dir,* Segrid Dombroski; *Youth Serv,* Rachel Knapton; Staff 4 (MLS 2, Non-MLS 2)
Founded 1908. Pop 6,524; Circ 55,000
Library Holdings: Bks on Deafness & Sign Lang 20; DVDs 1,000; High Interest/Low Vocabulary Bk Vols 200; Large Print Bks 1,500; Bk Vols 25,000; Per Subs 38; Videos 1,000
Special Collections: Monroe Railroad Coll
Subject Interests: Local hist, Trains
Automation Activity & Vendor Info: (Cataloging) SirsiDynix; (Circulation) SirsiDynix; (OPAC) SirsiDynix
Wireless access
Function: ILL available, Photocopying/Printing, Ref serv available, Telephone ref
Mem of Southern Tier Library System
Special Services for the Blind - Bks available with recordings
Open Mon-Wed 1-6, Thurs & Fri 10-6, Sat 10-2

DUNKIRK

P DUNKIRK FREE LIBRARY*, 536 Central Ave, 14048. SAN 311-1342. Tel: 716-366-2511. FAX: 716-366-2525. E-mail: dkklib@yahoo.com. Web Site: www.cclslib.org/dunkirk. *Dir,* Mary Jane Covley-Walker; Staff 1 (MLS 1)
Founded 1904. Pop 15,310; Circ 136,208
Library Holdings: Bks on Deafness & Sign Lang 30; Braille Volumes 4; Bk Titles 41,770; Bk Vols 49,000; Per Subs 54
Function: Handicapped accessible
Mem of Chautauqua-Cattaraugus Library System
Special Services for the Blind - Braille servs
Open Mon-Thurs (Sept-June) 10-7, Fri & Sat 10-5; Mon (July & Aug) 9-7, Tues-Thurs 9-6, Fri 9-5

EARLVILLE

P EARLVILLE FREE LIBRARY*, Six N Main St, 13332. (Mail add: PO Box 120, 13332-0120), SAN 311-1350. Tel: 315-691-5931. FAX: 315-691-5931. E-mail: earlville@midyork.org. Web Site: www.midyork.org/earlville. *Dir,* Shari Taylor
Founded 1927. Pop 980; Circ 33,360
Library Holdings: Bk Vols 23,318; Per Subs 30
Special Collections: New York Indian Heroes (Ologan Coll); Wood Artifacts (Conger Coll)
Wireless access
Mem of Mid-York Library System
Open Mon-Wed 1-8, Thurs & Fri 10-5, Sat 10-1:30
Friends of the Library Group

EAST AURORA

P AURORA TOWN PUBLIC LIBRARY*, East Aurora Library, 550 Main St, 14052. SAN 351-8280. Tel: 716-652-4440. FAX: 716-655-5875. E-mail: eau@buffalolib.org. Web Site: www.buffalolib.org/libraries/eastaurora/. *Dir,* Lee Ainsworth-Mahaney; *Ch Serv,* Julia Gelsomino
Library Holdings: AV Mats 8,145; Bk Vols 46,957
Subject Interests: Roycroft Craft Movement
Automation Activity & Vendor Info: (Cataloging) SirsiDynix; (Circulation) SirsiDynix; (OPAC) SirsiDynix; (Serials) SirsiDynix
Wireless access
Mem of Buffalo & Erie County Public Library System
Partic in Western New York Library Resources Council
Open Mon & Thurs (Winter) 1-8, Tues 10-8, Wed 1-6, Fri 10-6, Sat 10-3; Mon & Thurs (Summer) 1-8, Tues 10-8, Wed & Fri 10-6
Friends of the Library Group

R CHRIST THE KING SEMINARY LIBRARY*, 711 Knox Rd, 14052. (Mail add: PO Box 607, 14052-0607), SAN 311-1369. Tel: 716-652-8959. FAX: 716-652-8903. *Cat, Dir, Online Serv,* Teresa Lubienecki; Tel: 716-655-7098; *Acq,* Mary Beth Morse; *Circ, ILL,* Sister Jane Brady; Staff 4 (MLS 3, Non-MLS 1)
Founded 1951. Enrl 96; Fac 11; Highest Degree: Master
Library Holdings: AV Mats 1,380; Bk Vols 176,000; Per Subs 437
Special Collections: Early French Canadian & Niagara Frontier History (Msgr James Bray Coll)
Subject Interests: Philos, Relig, Theol
Automation Activity & Vendor Info: (Cataloging) ComPanion Corp; (Circulation) ComPanion Corp
Partic in OCLC Online Computer Library Center, Inc; Western New York Library Resources Council

EAST ELMHURST

S NEW YORK CITY CORRECTIONAL INSTITUTION FOR MEN LIBRARY*, Law Library, 10-10 Hazen St, 11370. SAN 352-4523. Tel: 718-546-7359. FAX: 718-546-7357. *Dir,* Karen Powell
Library Holdings: Bk Vols 5,000
Restriction: Staff use only

EAST GREENBUSH

P EAST GREENBUSH COMMUNITY LIBRARY*, Ten Community Way, 12061. SAN 352-4469. Tel: 518-477-7476. FAX: 518-477-6692. Web Site: www.eastgreenbushlibrary.org. *Dir,* Evelyn Neale; E-mail: director@eastgreenbushlibrary.org; *Head, Adult Serv,* Lois Papp; E-mail: pappl@eastgreenbushlibrary.org; *Head, Ch,* Molly Chatt; *Head, Tech Serv,* Susan Dague; Staff 42 (MLS 17, Non-MLS 25)
Founded 1948. Pop 15,560; Circ 318,300
Library Holdings: AV Mats 25,000; Braille Volumes 25; e-books 7,000; Bk Vols 96,000; Per Subs 200; Talking Bks 4,000; Videos 4,800
Automation Activity & Vendor Info: (Cataloging) Horizon; (Circulation) Horizon; (ILL) OCLC; (OPAC) Horizon; (Serials) Horizon
Database Vendor: Gale Cengage Learning
Wireless access
Function: Art exhibits, BA reader (adult literacy), Handicapped accessible, Homebound delivery serv, ILL available, Music CDs, Online searches, Photocopying/Printing, Prog for adults, Prog for children & young adult, Spoken cassettes & CDs, Summer reading prog, VHS videos, Wheelchair accessible
Publications: Greenbush Bookmark (Newsletter)
Mem of Upper Hudson Library System
Open Mon-Thurs 9-9, Fri 9-6, Sat 10-5, Sun 1-5
Friends of the Library Group

EAST HAMPTON

P EAST HAMPTON LIBRARY*, 159 Main St, 11937. SAN 311-1415. Tel: 631-324-0222. FAX: 631-329-5947. E-mail: info@easthamptonlibrary.org. Web Site: www.easthamptonlibrary.org. *Dir,* Dennis Fabiszak; Tel: 631-324-0222, Ext 7, E-mail: dennis@easthamptonlibrary.org; Staff 28 (MLS 10, Non-MLS 18)
Founded 1897. Pop 13,545; Circ 158,000
Library Holdings: Bks on Deafness & Sign Lang 10; High Interest/Low Vocabulary Bk Vols 100; Bk Titles 59,000; Bk Vols 63,719; Per Subs 96
Special Collections: Long Island History, Biography & Genealogy (Pennypacker Coll), bks, microflm, memorabilia; Thomas Moran Biographical Art Coll. Oral History
Automation Activity & Vendor Info: (Cataloging) Innovative Interfaces, Inc - Millenium; (Circulation) Innovative Interfaces, Inc - Millenium; (ILL) Innovative Interfaces, Inc - Millenium; (OPAC) Innovative Interfaces, Inc - Millenium
Database Vendor: EBSCO Information Services, EBSCOhost
Wireless access
Function: Adult bk club, Adult literacy prog, Archival coll, Audiobks via web, Bilingual assistance for Spanish patrons, Bk club(s), Bks on cassette, Bks on CD, CD-ROM, Children's prog, Computer training, Computers for patron use, Copy machines, Digital talking bks, e-mail & chat, e-mail serv, E-Reserves, Electronic databases & coll, Free DVD rentals, Handicapped accessible, Homebound delivery serv, ILL available, Literacy & newcomer serv, Mail & tel request accepted, Music CDs, Newsp ref libr, Online cat, Online ref, Online searches, OverDrive digital audio bks, Photocopying/Printing, Prog for adults, Prog for children & young adult, Pub access computers, Ref & res, Ref serv available, Ref serv in person, Scanner, Senior computer classes, Spoken cassettes & CDs, Story hour, Summer reading prog, Tax forms, Teen prog, Telephone ref, VHS videos, Web-catalog, Wheelchair accessible, Workshops, Writing prog
Mem of Suffolk Cooperative Library System
Open Mon-Thurs 10-7, Fri & Sat 10-5, Sun 1-5

EAST ISLIP

P EAST ISLIP PUBLIC LIBRARY*, 381 E Main St, 11730-2896. SAN 311-1423. Tel: 631-581-9200. FAX: 631-581-2245. E-mail: eipl@suffolk.lib.ny.us. Web Site: www.eipl.org. *Dir,* Guy P Edwards; Tel: 631-581-9200, Ext 7, E-mail: edwardsg@suffolk.lib.ny.us; *Head, Adult Serv,* Jo-Ann Carhart; *Head, Ch,* Andrea Kielbasa; *Head, Circ,* Pamela Fitzsimons; *Head, Tech Serv,* Deborah Russin; *YA Librn,* Kassia Worst; Staff 33 (MLS 11, Non-MLS 22)
Founded 1960. Pop 25,796; Circ 222,286
Library Holdings: AV Mats 44,783; Bk Vols 169,754; Per Subs 494
Special Collections: Art Originals Coll; Francis Hopkinson Smith Coll; Lighthouses Coll; Local History Coll. US Document Depository
Automation Activity & Vendor Info: (Circulation) Innovative Interfaces, Inc; (ILL) Innovative Interfaces, Inc; (OPAC) Innovative Interfaces, Inc
Database Vendor: Gale Cengage Learning
Wireless access
Function: Ref serv available
Publications: East of Islip (Local History); Librafax; Little Librafax
Mem of Suffolk Cooperative Library System
Partic in Partnership of Automated Librs in Suffolk
Special Services for the Blind - Low vision equip
Open Mon-Thurs 9-9, Fri & Sat 9-5, Sun 1-5

EAST MEADOW

P EAST MEADOW PUBLIC LIBRARY*, 1886 Front St, 11554-1705. SAN 311-1431. Tel: 516-794-2570. FAX: 516-794-1272. Administration FAX: 516-794-8536. TDD: 516-794-2949. E-mail: contactus@eastmeadow.info. Web Site: www.eastmeadow.info. *Dir,* Carol Probeyahn; *Asst Dir,* Rocco Cassano; *Ch Serv,* Gail Goldfarb; *Circ Serv,* Christina Hirsch; *Media Serv,* Karen Shaw Widman; *Reader Serv,* Marcia Blackman; *Ref Serv,* Susan Newson; *YA Serv,* Paula DeVito; Staff 67 (MLS 21, Non-MLS 46)
Founded 1955. Pop 52,102; Circ 457,504
Library Holdings: DVDs 12,304; e-books 17,704; Bk Vols 255,900; Per Subs 784
Special Collections: Literary Criticism; Long Island History
Subject Interests: Behav sci, Civil serv, Relig studies, Repair manuals, Repair per, Soc sci
Automation Activity & Vendor Info: (Acquisitions) Innovative Interfaces, Inc; (Cataloging) Innovative Interfaces, Inc; (Circulation) Innovative Interfaces, Inc; (ILL) Innovative Interfaces, Inc; (OPAC) Innovative Interfaces, Inc
Database Vendor: ALLDATA Online, Baker & Taylor, College Source, Comprise Technologies Inc, CountryWatch, Dialog, Dun & Bradstreet, EBSCO Auto Repair Reference, EBSCOhost, Electric Library, Gale Cengage Learning, Grolier Online, infoUSA, LearningExpress, LexisNexis, Mergent Online, OCLC FirstSearch, OCLC WorldShare Interlibrary Loan, Overdrive, Inc, ProQuest, ReferenceUSA, Surpass
Wireless access
Function: Adult bk club, Art exhibits, Audiobks via web, AV serv, Bk club(s), Bks on CD, Chess club, Children's prog, Computer training, Computers for patron use, Copy machines, Digital talking bks, Electronic databases & coll, Exhibits, Fax serv, Free DVD rentals, Handicapped accessible, Homebound delivery serv, ILL available, Magnifiers for reading, Microfiche/film & reading machines, Mus passes, Music CDs, Newsp ref libr, Notary serv, Online cat, Online ref, OverDrive digital audio bks, Prog for adults, Prog for children & young adult, Scanner, Senior computer classes, Story hour, Summer reading prog, Tax forms, Telephone ref, Web-catalog
Publications: East Meadow: Past & Present (Local historical information); Who's Who in East Meadow (Annual)
Mem of Nassau Library System
Partic in Long Island Library Resources Council
Special Services for the Deaf - Assisted listening device; Described encaptioned media prog; TTY equip
Special Services for the Blind - Closed circuit TV magnifier; Large print bks; Recorded bks; Talking bks
Open Mon, Tues, Thurs & Fri 9-9, Wed 11-9, Sat 9-5, Sun (Winter) 1-5
Friends of the Library Group

M NASSAU UNIVERSITY MEDICAL CENTER*, Peter Addiego Health Sciences Library, 2201 Hempstead Tpk, 11554. SAN 311-144X. Tel: 516-572-8742. Interlibrary Loan Service Tel: 516-572-8741. Administration Tel: 516-572-8745. FAX: 516-572-5788. Web Site: www.numc.edu/hsl.asp. *Dir,* William F Casey; Staff 1 (MLS 1)
Library Holdings: Bk Titles 8,500; Per Subs 600
Subject Interests: Health sci, Radiology
Automation Activity & Vendor Info: (Acquisitions) SirsiDynix; (Cataloging) SirsiDynix; (Circulation) SirsiDynix; (OPAC) SirsiDynix; (Serials) SirsiDynix
Database Vendor: EBSCOhost, OCLC FirstSearch, OVID Technologies, PubMed, Westlaw
Partic in Basic Health Sciences Library Network; Long Island Library Resources Council; Medical & Scientific Libraries of Long Island
Open Mon-Fri 9-9
Restriction: Authorized patrons, Circ limited, Circulates for staff only, Hospital staff & commun, Internal circ only, Lending to staff only, Limited access for the pub

EAST NORTHPORT

P ELWOOD PUBLIC LIBRARY*, 1929 Jericho Tpk, 11731. SAN 378-410X. Tel: 631-499-3722. FAX: 631-499-0057. E-mail: elwdlib@suffolk.lib.ny.us. Web Site: elwood.suffolk.lib.ny.us, www.elwoodlibrary.org. *Dir,* Susan Goldberg; *Adult Serv,* Position Currently Open; *Ch Serv,* Jessica Toner; *Circ,* Michele Orlando; *Programming,* Andrew Story; *Tech Serv,* Eileen Murphy
Founded 2002
Library Holdings: AV Mats 9,092; Bk Vols 18,078; Per Subs 110
Automation Activity & Vendor Info: (Acquisitions) Innovative Interfaces, Inc; (Cataloging) Innovative Interfaces, Inc; (Circulation) Innovative

Interfaces, Inc; (ILL) Innovative Interfaces, Inc; (OPAC) Innovative Interfaces, Inc
Wireless access
Mem of Suffolk Cooperative Library System
Open Mon-Thurs 10-9, Fri & Sat 10-5, Sun (Oct-May) 1-5
Friends of the Library Group

EAST ROCHESTER

P EAST ROCHESTER PUBLIC LIBRARY*, 111 W Elm St, 14445. SAN 311-1466. Tel: 585-586-8302. Web Site: www.libraryweb.org/erochester. *Librn,* Meredith Fraser
Pop 6,932; Circ 85,000
Library Holdings: Bk Vols 47,799; Per Subs 60
Automation Activity & Vendor Info: (Acquisitions) TLC (The Library Corporation); (Cataloging) TLC (The Library Corporation); (Circulation) TLC (The Library Corporation); (Course Reserve) TLC (The Library Corporation); (ILL) TLC (The Library Corporation); (Media Booking) TLC (The Library Corporation); (OPAC) TLC (The Library Corporation); (Serials) TLC (The Library Corporation)
Wireless access
Open Mon-Thurs 9:30-8, Fri 9:30-5, Sat 10-2
Friends of the Library Group

EAST ROCKAWAY

P EAST ROCKAWAY PUBLIC LIBRARY*, 477 Atlantic Ave, 11518. SAN 311-1474. Tel: 516-599-1664. FAX: 516-596-0154. E-mail: eastrockpl@yahoo.com. Web Site: www.nassaulibrary.org/eastrock. *Dir,* Ellen Rockmuller; *Ref Librn,* Heather Meagher; *Ch Serv,* Betty Charvat; *Ref,* Mary Thorpe. Subject Specialists: *Media,* Heather Meagher; Staff 4 (MLS 4)
Founded 1903. Pop 12,714; Circ 105,091
Library Holdings: Bk Vols 63,900; Per Subs 95
Automation Activity & Vendor Info: (Circulation) Innovative Interfaces, Inc; (OPAC) Innovative Interfaces, Inc
Wireless access
Mem of Nassau Library System
Open Mon, Tues & Thurs 10-9, Wed, Fri & Sat 10-5
Friends of the Library Group

EAST SYRACUSE

P EAST SYRACUSE FREE LIBRARY*, 4990 James St, 13057. SAN 311-1490. Tel: 315-437-4841. FAX: 315-437-5982. Web Site: www.eastsyracusefreelibrary.org. *Dir,* Laurie Rachetta; E-mail: lrachetta@onlib.org; Staff 11 (Non-MLS 11)
Founded 1924. Pop 21,000; Circ 72,326
Jan 2005-Dec 2005 Income $249,150. Mats Exp $67,700. Sal $31,375
Library Holdings: Large Print Bks 1,173; Bk Titles 29,500; Bk Vols 30,000; Per Subs 138
Subject Interests: Local hist
Automation Activity & Vendor Info: (Cataloging) Innovative Interfaces, Inc; (Circulation) Innovative Interfaces, Inc; (OPAC) Innovative Interfaces, Inc
Database Vendor: EBSCOhost, OCLC FirstSearch, SirsiDynix
Wireless access
Function: Handicapped accessible, ILL available, Photocopying/Printing, Prog for children & young adult, Ref serv available, Summer reading prog, Telephone ref, Wheelchair accessible
Mem of Onondaga County Public Library
Special Services for the Deaf - Closed caption videos
Open Mon-Thurs 10-8, Fri 10-6, Sat 10-2

EAST WILLISTON

P EAST WILLISTON PUBLIC LIBRARY*, Two Prospect St, 11596. SAN 311-1504. Tel: 516-741-1213. FAX: 516-746-3130. E-mail: ewpl@ewlibrary.org. Web Site: www.ewlibrary.org, www.nassaulibrary.org/eastwill. *Dir,* Susan Quinn; Staff 3 (Non-MLS 3)
Founded 1937. Pop 2,515; Circ 20,000
Library Holdings: Bk Vols 18,000; Per Subs 26
Subject Interests: Local hist
Automation Activity & Vendor Info: (Cataloging) Innovative Interfaces, Inc; (Circulation) Innovative Interfaces, Inc; (OPAC) Innovative Interfaces, Inc
Database Vendor: EBSCOhost
Wireless access
Publications: East Williston Library; East Williston Public Library Online: Monthly Website Update; East Williston Reports; Williston Times Weekly Column
Mem of Nassau Library System
Open Mon-Fri 11-7:30, Sat 10:30-1

EASTCHESTER

S EASTCHESTER HISTORICAL SOCIETY*, Angelo & Harriet Bianchi Library, 390 California Rd, 10709. (Mail add: PO Box 37, 10709-0037), SAN 327-9588. Tel: 914-793-1900. *Curator of Coll,* Saul Radin
Library Holdings: Bk Vols 6,010; Per Subs 15
Special Collections: Nineteenth Century Juvenile Literature Coll
Restriction: Open by appt only

P EASTCHESTER PUBLIC LIBRARY, 11 Oakridge Pl, 10709-2012. SAN 311-1512. Tel: 914-793-5055. FAX: 914-793-7862. Web Site: www.eastchesterlibrary.org. *Dir,* Tracy Wright; Tel: 912-721-8100, E-mail: twright@wlsmail.org; *Head, Adult Serv,* Dulce M Juarbe; Tel: 914-721-8102; *Head, Ch,* Teresa Chang; Tel: 914-721-8105; *Ch,* Position Currently Open; Staff 19 (MLS 5, Non-MLS 14)
Founded 1947. Pop 18,537; Circ 245,110
Library Holdings: Bk Vols 93,853; Per Subs 200
Subject Interests: Archit, Art, Motion picture hist, Music, Mystery novels, Travel
Automation Activity & Vendor Info: (Cataloging) SirsiDynix; (Circulation) SirsiDynix; (OPAC) SirsiDynix
Database Vendor: Dialog, EBSCOhost, Gale Cengage Learning, SirsiDynix
Wireless access
Function: Ref serv available
Mem of Westchester Library System
Open Mon & Wed 9-9, Tues & Thurs-Sat 9-5, Sun 1-5
Friends of the Library Group

EDEN

P EDEN LIBRARY*, 2901 E Church St, 14057. SAN 311-1520. Tel: 716-992-4028. Interlibrary Loan Service Tel: 716-858-7126. FAX: 716-992-4340. E-mail: edn@buffalolib.org. Web Site: www.buffalolib.org/libraries/eden/index.asp. *Dir,* Joyce M Maguda; Staff 0.8 (MLS 0.8)
Founded 1911. Pop 7,688; Circ 75,797
Library Holdings: AV Mats 5,663; Electronic Media & Resources 56; Bk Vols 24,267; Per Subs 51
Special Collections: Eden High School Yearbooks, 1938-present
Wireless access
Function: Adult bk club, Audiobks via web, Bks on CD, Children's prog, Computers for patron use, Copy machines, E-Reserves, Electronic databases & coll, Free DVD rentals, Games & aids for the handicapped, Handicapped accessible, Holiday prog, ILL available, Magnifiers for reading, Music CDs, Online cat, Prog for adults, Prog for children & young adult, Pub access computers, Scanner, Spoken cassettes & CDs, Story hour, Summer reading prog, Tax forms, Teen prog, Web-catalog, Wheelchair accessible
Mem of Buffalo & Erie County Public Library System
Open Mon, Wed & Thurs (Winter) 2-8, Tues & Fri 10:30-5, Sat 10-2; Mon, Wed & Thurs (Summer) 1-8, Tues & Fri 10-5
Friends of the Library Group

EDMESTON

S EDMESTON FREE LIBRARY & MUSEUM*, Six West St, 13335. (Mail add: PO Box 167, 13335), SAN 311-1539. Tel: 607-965-8208. FAX: 607-965-8208. *Dir, Libr Mgr,* Dorothy Blackman
Jan 2011-Dec 2011 Income $19,157. Mats Exp $3,125, Books $3,000, Electronic Ref Mat (Incl. Access Fees) $125. Sal $12,024
Library Holdings: Bks on Deafness & Sign Lang 3; High Interest/Low Vocabulary Bk Vols 175; Large Print Bks 200; Bk Vols 18,000
Mem of Four County Library System
Open Tues 1-7, Wed & Thurs 1-6, Sat 9-1

EDWARDS

P HEPBURN LIBRARY OF EDWARDS*, 205 Main St, 13635. (Mail add: PO Box 9, 13635-0009), SAN 311-1547. Tel: 315-562-3521. FAX: 315-562-2600. Web Site: www.herd.org/edwards/library. *Librn,* Elaine Archer; E-mail: earcher@tds.net
Circ 11,669
Library Holdings: Bk Vols 8,962; Per Subs 28
Wireless access
Function: Fax serv, Notary serv, Photocopying/Printing, Prog for children & young adult, Scanner
Mem of North Country Library System
Open Mon & Tues 12-5 & 6:30-8, Wed & Fri 9-12, Thurs 12-4
Friends of the Library Group

ELBRIDGE

P ELBRIDGE FREE LIBRARY*, 241 E Main St, 13060. SAN 311-1555. Tel: 315-689-7111. FAX: 315-689-9448. Web Site: www.elbridgefreelibrary.org. *Dir,* Karen P White
Founded 1922. Pop 1,098; Circ 28,500
Library Holdings: Bk Vols 22,000; Per Subs 75
Special Collections: Local Newspaper (Advocate)
Automation Activity & Vendor Info: (Cataloging) Innovative Interfaces, Inc; (Circulation) Innovative Interfaces, Inc; (OPAC) Innovative Interfaces, Inc
Wireless access
Mem of Onondaga County Public Library
Open Mon 1:30-8, Tues, Thurs & Fri 1:30-6, Wed 9-8, Sat 12-4

ELDRED

P SUNSHINE HALL FREE LIBRARY*, 14 Proctor Rd, 12732-5207. (Mail add: PO Box 157, 12732-0157), SAN 311-1563. Tel: 845-557-6258. FAX: 845-557-0578. Web Site: www.rcls.org/eld. *Dir,* Patty Kennedy
Founded 1916. Circ 14,158
Library Holdings: Bk Vols 20,000; Per Subs 20
Automation Activity & Vendor Info: (Cataloging) Horizon; (Circulation) Horizon; (ILL) Horizon; (OPAC) Horizon
Wireless access
Mem of Ramapo Catskill Library System
Open Tues, Wed & Fri 12-4:30, Thurs 12-6, Sat 10-3
Friends of the Library Group

ELIZABETHTOWN

P ELIZABETHTOWN LIBRARY ASSOCIATION*, 8256 River St, 12932. (Mail add: PO Box 7, 12932-0007), SAN 311-1571. Tel: 518-873-2670. FAX: 518-873-2670. E-mail: elizabethtownlibrary@charter.net. *Dir,* Donna Norton; Staff 3 (Non-MLS 3)
Founded 1884. Pop 1,497
Library Holdings: Audiobooks 225; Large Print Bks 280; Bk Vols 6,438
Automation Activity & Vendor Info: (Cataloging) Horizon; (Circulation) Horizon; (OPAC) Horizon
Wireless access
Function: ILL available, Photocopying/Printing, Preschool outreach, Prog for children & young adult, Spoken cassettes & CDs, Spoken cassettes & DVDs, Summer reading prog, VHS videos
Mem of Clinton-Essex-Franklin Library System
Open Mon & Wed 11-6, Fri 11-4, Sat 9-3

S ESSEX COUNTY HISTORICAL SOCIETY*, Brewster Library, 7590 Court St, 12932. (Mail add: PO Box 428, 12932 0428), SAN 311-158X. Tel: 518-873-6466. FAX: 518-873-6466. E-mail: echs@adkhistorycenter.org. Web Site: www.adkhistorycenter.org. *Dir, Historian,* Margaret Gibbs; E-mail: mgibbs@adkhistorycenter.org; *Asst Dir,* Jenifer Kuba; Staff 5 (Non-MLS 5)
Founded 1956
Library Holdings: Bk Titles 1,693; Bk Vols 8,143; Per Subs 75
Special Collections: Essex County Cemetery Records, cards, mss; Essex County Place Names, cards; Genealogical Family Files; History of Essex County Towns (Smith Archive), mss, pamphlets, transcripts; Newspaper Articles, cards; North County Index, cards, local bks; North County Pamphlets; Photograph File
Function: Res libr
Publications: Index to a History of Westport, Essex County, NY
Restriction: Non-circulating, Open by appt only

ELLENBURG CENTER

P ELLENBURG CENTER LIBRARY*, 15 Brandy Brook Rd, 12934. (Mail add: PO Box 22, 12934-0022). Tel: 518-594-7489. E-mail: bll2453@twcny.rr.com. Web Site: www.cefls.org/ellenburgcenter.htm. *Dir,* Barbara Leonard
Library Holdings: AV Mats 25; Bk Vols 2,500; Talking Bks 25
Mem of Clinton-Essex-Franklin Library System
Open Tues 6pm-8pm, Sat 9-1
Friends of the Library Group

ELLENBURG DEPOT

P ELLENBURG SARAH A MUNSIL FREE LIBRARY*, 5139 Rte 11, 12935. (Mail add: PO Box 22, 12935-0022). Tel: 518-594-7314. E-mail: esamfl@gmail.com. *Dir,* Michele C Phillips
Founded 1948. Pop 1,800
Library Holdings: AV Mats 25; Bk Vols 2,462
Wireless access
Mem of Clinton-Essex-Franklin Library System
Open Thurs & Fri 12-8, Sat 9-1

ELLENVILLE

P ELLENVILLE PUBLIC LIBRARY & MUSEUM*, 40 Center St, 12428-1396. SAN 311-1598. Tel: 845-647-5530. FAX: 845-647-3554. E-mail: epl@rcls.org. Web Site: www.rcls.org/epl. *Dir,* Pamela Stocking; *Ch Serv,* Susan Mangan; Staff 4 (MLS 2, Non-MLS 2)
Founded 1893. Pop 12,563; Circ 92,973
Library Holdings: AV Mats 3,399; Bk Vols 49,436; Per Subs 90
Subject Interests: Local hist
Publications: Napanoch; Remembering Clayton's; Sampler of Old Houses
Mem of Ramapo Catskill Library System
Open Mon-Wed 9:30-8, Thurs & Fri 9:30-6, Sat 9:30-3

ELLICOTTVILLE

P ELLICOTTVILLE MEMORIAL LIBRARY, 6499 Maples Rd, 14731. (Mail add: PO Box 1226, 14731-1226), SAN 311-1601. Tel: 716-699-2842. FAX: 716-699-5597. E-mail: ellicottvillelibrary@roadrunner.com. Web Site: www.evml.org. *Dir,* Laura Flanagan; Staff 1.41 (Non-MLS 1.41)
Founded 1961. Pop 3,462; Circ 24,101
Jan 2014-Dec 2014 Income (Main Library Only) $90,305, City $60,000, Locally Generated Income $22,205, Other $8,100. Mats Exp $5,640, Books $4,540, AV Mat $400, Electronic Ref Mat (Incl. Access Fees) $700. Sal $37,440 (Prof $45,850)
Library Holdings: Audiobooks 473; DVDs 1,449; e-books 7,256; e-journals 67; Large Print Bks 201; Microforms 41; Bk Vols 12,814; Per Subs 32; Videos 487
Automation Activity & Vendor Info: (Acquisitions) SirsiDynix; (Cataloging) SirsiDynix; (Circulation) SirsiDynix
Wireless access
Function: 24/7 Electronic res, 24/7 Online cat, Activity rm, Adult bk club, Art exhibits, Audiobks via web, Bk club(s), Bks on CD, Computer training, Computers for patron use, Copy machines, Electronic databases & coll, eReaders, Free DVD rentals, Handicapped accessible, Homebound delivery serv, ILL available, Magazines, Mail & tel request accepted, Microfiche/film & reading machines, Movies, Online cat, Online ref, Outside serv via phone, mail, e-mail & web, OverDrive digital audio bks, Photocopying/Printing, Preschool reading prog, Printer for laptops & handheld devices, Prog for adults, Prog for children & young adult, Pub access computers, Ref serv in person, Scanner, Senior computer classes, Spoken cassettes & CDs, Spoken cassettes & DVDs, Story hour, Summer & winter reading prog, Summer reading prog, Tax forms, Web-catalog, Wheelchair accessible, Workshops, Writing prog
Mem of Chautauqua-Cattaraugus Library System
Open Mon & Thurs-Sat 10-5, Tues & Wed 10-8

ELLINGTON

P FARMAN FREE LIBRARY*, 760 Thornten Rd, 14732. (Mail add: PO Box 26, 14732-0026), SAN 311-161X. Tel: 716-287-2945. FAX: 716-287-3694. E-mail: farmanfreelib@stny.rr.com. Web Site: www.cclslib.org/ellington. *Dir,* Lynn Grundstrom
Pop 1,632; Circ 14,388
Library Holdings: Bk Vols 14,000; Per Subs 25
Automation Activity & Vendor Info: (Cataloging) SirsiDynix; (Circulation) SirsiDynix; (OPAC) SirsiDynix
Wireless access
Mem of Chautauqua-Cattaraugus Library System
Open Mon & Wed (Winter) 2-6, Tues 10-6, Thurs 2-7, Sat 9-12; Mon & Wed (Summer) 10-1 & 2-7, Tues & Thurs 10-12, Sat 10-12

ELLISBURG

P ELLISBURG FREE LIBRARY*, 12117 State Rte 193, 13636. SAN 311-1628. Tel: 315-846-5087. FAX: 315-846-5087. E-mail: elllib@ncls.org. *Dir,* Sheila Bettinger
Library Holdings: Bk Vols 4,900; Per Subs 32
Mem of North Country Library System
Open Mon & Thurs (Winter) 6pm-9pm, Wed & Sat 9-12; Tues & Fri (Summer) 6pm-9pm, Wed & Sat 9-12

ELMA

P ELMA PUBLIC LIBRARY*, 1860 Bowen Rd, 14059. SAN 311-1636. Tel: 716-652-2719. FAX: 716-652-0381. E-mail: elm@buffalolib.org. *Dir,* Karen Korpanty; *Ch Serv,* Kathleen Kimble; Staff 2 (MLS 2)
Founded 1941. Pop 11,304; Circ 139,040
Library Holdings: AV Mats 7,000; Bk Vols 31,000; Per Subs 182
Automation Activity & Vendor Info: (Cataloging) SirsiDynix; (Circulation) SirsiDynix; (OPAC) SirsiDynix
Wireless access
Open Mon, Wed & Fri (Winter) 1-9, Tues 10-6, Fri 10-9, Sat 10-4; Mon & Wed (Summer) 1-9, Thurs 10-6, Fri 10-9
Friends of the Library Group

ELMHURST

M ELMHURST HOSPITAL CENTER*, Health Sciences Library, 79-01 Broadway, D3-52A, 11373. SAN 311-1644. Tel: 718-334-2040. FAX: 718-334-5690. E-mail: ehc-library@nychhc.org. *Dir,* Ramer Sheryl; *Asst Dir,* Barbara Gugliuzza; Staff 1 (MLS 1)
Founded 1965
Library Holdings: e-journals 750; Bk Vols 7,500; Per Subs 200
Subject Interests: Basic sci, Educ, Med
Automation Activity & Vendor Info: (Cataloging) CyberTools for Libraries; (Circulation) CyberTools for Libraries
Database Vendor: EBSCOhost, SerialsSolutions
Open Mon-Fri 9am-10pm, Sat 9-5, Sun 12-5
Restriction: Staff use only

ELMIRA

S CHEMUNG COUNTY HISTORICAL SOCIETY, INC*, Mrs Arthur W Booth Library, 415 E Water St, 14901, SAN 326-2154. Tel: 607-734-4167. Reference Tel: 607-734-4167, Ext 207. FAX: 607-734-1565. E-mail: archivist@chemungvalleymuseum.org. Web Site: www.chemungvalleymuseum.org. *Archivist,* Rachel Dworkin; Staff 1 (Non-MLS 1)
Founded 1956
Library Holdings: Bk Titles 4,500
Special Collections: Elmira History Coll; Elmira Prison Camp Coll; Hal Roach Coll; Mark Twain Coll; Peary Arctic Exploration Coll. Oral History
Subject Interests: Genealogy, Local hist, Mil hist
Automation Activity & Vendor Info: (Cataloging) SirsiDynix
Function: Archival coll
Mem of Southern Tier Library System
Open Mon-Fri 1-5
Restriction: Non-circulating

P CHEMUNG COUNTY LIBRARY DISTRICT*, Steele Memorial Library, 101 E Church St, 14901-2799. SAN 311-1725. Tel: 607-733-9173. Interlibrary Loan Service Tel: 607-733-8603. Reference Tel: 607-733-9175. Administration Tel: 607-733-8607. FAX: 607-733-9176. Web Site: www.ccld.lib.ny.us. *Dir,* Ronald Shaw; Tel: 607-733-8611; *Ref Librn,* Owen Frank; E-mail: franko@stls.org; *Ref Librn,* Julie Mullen; E-mail: mullenj@stls.org; *Ref Librn,* Connie Ogilvie; E-mail: ogilviec@stls.org; *Ref Librn,* Phyllis Rogan; E-mail: roganp@stls.org; *Br Coordr,* Eleanore Shepson; E-mail: shepsonl@stls.org; *Youth Serv,* Caroline Poppendeck; Tel: 607-733-8604; *Admin Serv,* Joan Santulli; E-mail: santullij@stls.org; *Circ,* Cola Thayer; Staff 8 (MLS 8)
Founded 1893. Pop 91,070; Circ 387,790
Library Holdings: AV Mats 28,659; Electronic Media & Resources 540; Bk Vols 319,707; Per Subs 335
Special Collections: Oral History
Subject Interests: Art, Census, Genealogy
Automation Activity & Vendor Info: (Cataloging) SirsiDynix; (Circulation) SirsiDynix; (OPAC) SirsiDynix
Wireless access
Publications: Newsletter
Mem of Southern Tier Library System
Partic in South Central Regional Library Council
Open Mon-Thurs (Winter) 9-9, Fri & Sat 9-5, Sun 1-5; Mon-Thurs (Summer) 9-9, Fri 9-5
Friends of the Library Group
Branches: 4
BIG FLATS LIBRARY, 78 Canal St, Big Flats, 14814, SAN 378-1305. Tel: 607-562-3300. *Br Supvr,* Brian Harris; E-mail: harrisb@stls.org
Open Mon, Wed & Thurs 10-5:30, Tues 10-8, Fri 10-5, Sat 9-5
HORSEHEADS FREE LIBRARY, 405 S Main St, Horseheads, 14845, SAN 311-3299. Tel: 607-739-4581. FAX: 607-739-4592. *Head Librn,* Chris Corter; E-mail: corterc@stls.org; Staff 1 (MLS 1)
Founded 1944. Pop 27,535; Circ 123,594
Open Mon & Tues 9-9, Wed 12-9, Thurs & Fri 9-5:30, Sat 9-5
Friends of the Library Group
VAN ETTEN LIBRARY, 83 Main St, Van Etten, 14889, SAN 374-812X. Tel: 607-589-4755. *In Charge,* Bonnie Mallen
Open Mon & Wed 1-5, Fri 1-6
Friends of the Library Group
WEST ELMIRA LIBRARY, 1231 W Water St, 14905-1996, SAN 378-1364. Tel: 607-733-0541. *Br Mgr,* Dianne Patchett
Open Mon 12-8, Tues-Fri 9-5, Sat (Winter) 9-5
Friends of the Library Group
Bookmobiles: 1

C ELMIRA COLLEGE, Gannett-Tripp Library, One Park Pl, 14901. SAN 311-1679. Tel: 607-735-1862. Interlibrary Loan Service Tel: 607-735-1868. FAX: 607-735-1158. E-mail: gtl@elmira.edu. Web Site: www.elmira.edu/academics/Academic_Resources/Library/index.html. *Dean of Libr, Libr Dir,* Elizabeth Wavle-Brown; Tel: 607-735-1865, Fax: 607-735-1165, E-mail: ewavlebrown@elmira.edu; *Accreditation & Info Literacy Librn,* Martha Smith; Tel: 607-735-1866, E-mail: msmith@elmira.edu; *Info Serv Librn,* Margaret Kappanadze; Tel: 607-735-1867, E-mail: mkappanadze@elmira.edu; *Tech Serv & Archives Librn,* Mark Woodhouse; Tel: 607-735-1869, E-mail: mwoodhouse@elmira.edu. Subject Specialists: *Mark Twain,* Mark Woodhouse; Staff 10 (MLS 5, Non-MLS 5)
Founded 1855. Enrl 1,200; Highest Degree: Master
Library Holdings: Bk Vols 300,000; Per Subs 350
Special Collections: American & English Rare Books (Lande); American Literature (Mark Twain Archives), artifacts, bks, letters on microfilm, mixed media, ms, photog; American Music (Charles Tomlinson Griffes: papers, ms & bks); Elmira College Regional History (Elmira College Archives), bks, photog; New York State Local History (Julia Boyer Reinstein Coll); New York State Women's History (New York Federation of Women's Clubs), bks, papers; Women's Education. State Document Depository; US Document Depository
Automation Activity & Vendor Info: (Cataloging) Inmagic, Inc.; (Circulation) Innovative Interfaces, Inc; (Course Reserve) Innovative Interfaces, Inc; (ILL) Innovative Interfaces, Inc; (OPAC) Innovative Interfaces, Inc; (Serials) Innovative Interfaces, Inc
Wireless access
Partic in OCLC-LVIS; South Central Regional Library Council
Open Mon-Thurs 7:45am-1am, Fri 7:45am-9pm, Sat 10-9, Sun 10am-1am

S NATIONAL SOARING MUSEUM*, Joseph C Lincoln Memorial Library & Ralph S Barnaby Archives, Harris Hill, 51 Soaring Hill Dr, 14903-9204. SAN 373-4838. Tel: 607-734-3128. FAX: 607-732-6745. E-mail: nsm@soaringmuseum.org. Web Site: www.soaringmuseum.org. *Res,* William Gallagher; E-mail: billg@soaringmuseum.org; Staff 1 (Non-MLS 1)
Founded 1969
Library Holdings: Bk Titles 1,500; Bk Vols 2,500; Per Subs 20
Special Collections: Elmira Area Soaring Corp & Harris Hill Soaring Corp Archives; Paul A Schweizer Coll; Ralph S Barnaby Aviation Library, Archive & Artifact Coll; Soaring Society of America Archives
Wireless access
Function: For res purposes
Publications: NSM Historical Journal (Newsletter); NSM News (Research guide)
Restriction: Open by appt only

S NEW YORK STATE DEPARTMENT OF CORRECTIONAL SERVICES*, Elmira Correctional Facility Library, 1879 Davis St, 14901-1042. (Mail add: PO Box 500, 14902-0500), SAN 321-0014. Tel: 607-734-3901. *Librn,* Greg Harris; Staff 3 (MLS 1, Non-MLS 2)
Founded 1860
Library Holdings: High Interest/Low Vocabulary Bk Vols 200; Large Print Bks 300; Bk Titles 9,500; Bk Vols 11,000; Per Subs 90
Special Collections: Vocational Guidance Coll. Oral History
Subject Interests: African-Am, Fiction, Gen fiction
Automation Activity & Vendor Info: (Cataloging) Follett Software; (Circulation) Follett Software; (OPAC) Follett Software
Wireless access
Publications: Summary: A Penitentiary Periodical Newsletter
Open Mon-Sun 10-5

M ARNOT OGDEN MEDICAL CENTER*, Wey Memorial Library, 600 Roe Ave, 14905-1676. SAN 311-1660. Tel: 607-737-4100, 607-737-4101. FAX: 607-737-4207. *Librn,* David Lester; E-mail: dlester@aomc.org
Founded 1934
Library Holdings: Bk Titles 4,000; Bk Vols 5,000; Per Subs 310
Subject Interests: Allied health, Med, Nursing
Partic in National Network of Libraries of Medicine New England Region
Open Mon-Fri 8-8, Sat 9-4

GL CHARLES B SWARTWOOD SUPREME COURT LIBRARY*, Hazelett Bldg, 1st Flr, 203-205 Lake St, 14901. (Mail add: PO Box 588, 14902-0588), SAN 311-1733. Tel: 607-873-9444. FAX: 212-401-9101. E-mail: elmlawlib@courts.state.ny.us. Web Site: www.nycourts.gov/LIBRARY/6jd/Chemung. *Law Librn,* Position Currently Open
Founded 1895
Library Holdings: Bk Titles 15,000; Per Subs 125
Subject Interests: NY Fed law, NY State
Automation Activity & Vendor Info: (Acquisitions) Horizon; (Cataloging) Horizon; (Circulation) Horizon
Partic in OCLC Online Computer Library Center, Inc; South Central Regional Library Council

ELMONT

P ELMONT PUBLIC LIBRARY*, 700 Hempstead Tpk, 11003-1896. SAN 352-4582. Tel: 516-354-5280. FAX: 516-354-3276. Web Site: www.elmontlibrary.org. *Dir,* Maggie Gough; E-mail: mgough@elmontlibrary.org; *Head, Ref,* Pat Magee; *Ch Serv,* Kathy Guidal;

Circ, Sharon Roberts; *YA Serv,* Mara Marin; *Tech Serv,* Connie Thorpe; Staff 8 (MLS 8)
Founded 1939. Pop 49,000; Circ 241,041
Library Holdings: Audiobooks 17,122; Electronic Media & Resources 508; Bk Vols 208,774; Per Subs 306
Special Collections: Oral History
Subject Interests: Local hist
Automation Activity & Vendor Info: (Cataloging) Innovative Interfaces, Inc; (Circulation) Innovative Interfaces, Inc; (OPAC) Innovative Interfaces, Inc
Wireless access
Mem of Nassau Library System
Open Mon-Thurs 9:30-9, Fri 9:30-6, Sat 9:30-5, Sun 12-5
Branches: 2
ALDEN MANOR, 799 Elmont Rd, 11003, SAN 352-4612. Tel: 516-285-8000. FAX: 516-285-1219. *Br Mgr,* Nancy Nowak; E-mail: nnowak@elmontlibrary.org
Open Mon-Wed & Fri 10-5:30, Sat 9:30-5
STEWART MANOR BRANCH, 100 Covert Ave, Stewart Manor, 11530, SAN 352-4647. Tel: 516-354-8026. FAX: 516-358-1962. *Br Mgr,* Barbara Alston; E-mail: balston@elmontlibrary.org
Open Mon-Wed & Fri 10-5:30, Sat 9:30-5

ELMSFORD

P GREENBURGH PUBLIC LIBRARY, 300 Tarrytown Rd, 10523. SAN 311-175X. Tel: 914-721-8200. Circulation Tel: 914-721-8204. Reference Tel: 914-721-8225. Administration Tel: 914-721-8223. FAX: 914-721-8201. Web Site: www.greenburghlibrary.org. *Exec Dir,* John Sexton; E-mail: director@greenburghlibrary.org; *Asst Dir,* Jenay Engstrom; Tel: 914-721-8220, E-mail: jengstrom@greenburghlibrary.org; *Web Coordr, YA Librn,* Andrew Farber; E-mail: afarber@greenburghlibrary.org; *Ch Serv,* Gail Fell; E-mail: gfell@greenburghlibrary.org; *Ch Serv,* Sandra Hile; E-mail: shile@greenburghlibrary.org; *Ch Serv,* Joanna Rooney; E-mail: jrooney@greenburghlibrary.org; *Info Serv,* Nancy McCrory; Tel: 914-721-8232, E-mail: nmccrory@greenburghlibrary.org; Staff 35 (MLS 15, Non-MLS 20)
Founded 1962. Pop 42,000; Circ 561,646
Jan 2013-Dec 2013 Income $3,280,895. Mats Exp $171,202. Sal $1,487,919
Library Holdings: AV Mats 41,551; CDs 16,002; DVDs 15,392; e-books 50,622; Bk Titles 120,773; Per Subs 124
Subject Interests: Local hist
Automation Activity & Vendor Info: (Acquisitions) SirsiDynix; (Circulation) SirsiDynix; (OPAC) SirsiDynix
Database Vendor: EBSCOhost, Gale Cengage Learning, SirsiDynix
Wireless access
Publications: Calendar of Events (Monthly)
Mem of Westchester Library System
Partic in Westlynx
Open Mon & Thurs-Sat 10-5:30, Tues & Wed 10-9, Sun 1-5
Friends of the Library Group

S WESTCHESTER COUNTY HISTORICAL SOCIETY LIBRARY*, 2199 Saw Mill River Rd, 10523. SAN 312-584X. Tel: 914-592-4323. FAX: 914-592-4338. E-mail: info@westchesterhistory.com. Web Site: westchesterhistory.com. *Librn,* Diana D Deichert; E-mail: diana@westchesterhistory.com; Staff 1 (MLS 1)
Founded 1874
Library Holdings: Bk Titles 10,000
Special Collections: Westchester County Historical Materials, Almhouse rec, bks, doc, files, ledgers, maps, photog
Subject Interests: Genealogy, Westchester County hist
Publications: The Westchester Historian
Open Tues & Wed 9-4

ENDICOTT

P GEORGE F JOHNSON MEMORIAL LIBRARY*, 1001 Park St, 13760. SAN 311-1784. Tel: 607-757-5350. FAX: 607-757-2491. E-mail: en.web@4cls.org. Web Site: www.gfjlibrary.org. *Dir,* Edward Andrew Dunscombe; Tel: 607-757-2415, E-mail: en.ed@4cls.org; *Libr Asst,* Susan Schiff; E-mail: en.susan@4cls.org; *Libr Asst,* Donna Shofkom; E-mail: en.donnas@4cls.org; *Ref Librn, YA Serv,* Cathy Seary; E-mail: en.cathy@4cls.org; *Youth Serv Librn,* Brooke Butler; E-mail: en.brooke@4cls.org; *Youth Serv Librn,* Margaret Cooper; E-mail: en.margaret@4cls.org; *Youth Serv Librn,* Suzanne Johnson; E-mail: en.suzanne@4cls.org; *Youth Serv Librn,* Erin Singleton; E-mail: en.erin@4cls.org; *Circ Mgr,* Nancy Seitz; E-mail: en.nancy@4cls.org; *ILL,* Janet Krisko; E-mail: en.ill@4cls.org; Staff 23 (MLS 6, Non-MLS 17)
Founded 1915. Pop 13,571; Circ 196,266
Jun 2009-May 2010 Income $1,046,775, State $72,435, Locally Generated Income $921,113, Other $53,227. Mats Exp $998,475, Books $99,315, Per/Ser (Incl. Access Fees) $12,737, AV Mat $25,655, Electronic Ref Mat (Incl. Access Fees) $950. Sal $463,818 (Prof $252,000)
Library Holdings: Audiobooks 2,040; AV Mats 9,273; CDs 2,853; DVDs 3,026; High Interest/Low Vocabulary Bk Vols 100; Large Print Bks 1,107; Bk Vols 92,703; Per Subs 173; Talking Bks 2,040; Videos 4,380
Special Collections: Local Historical Photographs
Automation Activity & Vendor Info: (Circulation) SirsiDynix; (OPAC) SirsiDynix
Database Vendor: Gale Cengage Learning, OCLC FirstSearch, SirsiDynix
Wireless access
Function: Art exhibits, Audio & video playback equip for onsite use, Bk club(s), Bk reviews (Group), Bks on cassette, Bks on CD, CD-ROM, Children's prog, Computer training, Computers for patron use, Copy machines, Digital talking bks, E-Reserves, Electronic databases & coll, Exhibits, Fax serv, Free DVD rentals, Handicapped accessible, ILL available, Music CDs, Online cat, Online searches, Photocopying/Printing, Prog for adults, Prog for children & young adult, Pub access computers, Ref serv available, Spoken cassettes & CDs, Story hour, Summer reading prog, Tax forms, Teen prog, Telephone ref, VHS videos, Web-catalog, Wheelchair accessible
Publications: Curious George F News (Newsletter)
Mem of Four County Library System
Partic in S Cent Libr Res Coun
Open Mon-Thurs 9-9, Fri 9-5, Sat (Sept-May) 9-5
Restriction: 24-hr pass syst for students only, Non-resident fee
Friends of the Library Group

ESSEX

P BELDON NOBLE MEMORIAL LIBRARY*, 2759 Essex Rd, 12936. (Mail add: PO Box 339, 12936-0339), SAN 311-1806. Tel: 518-963-8079. FAX: 518-963-8079. E-mail: bnoblelib1899@willex.com. Web Site: www.cefls.org/essex.htm. *Libr Dir,* Karen East
Founded 1899
Library Holdings: Bk Vols 5,000; Per Subs 24
Subject Interests: Art
Wireless access
Mem of Clinton-Essex-Franklin Library System
Open Mon & Fri (Winter) 2-4, Wed 1-5, Sat 10-5; Mon, Tues, Thurs & Fri (Summer) 2-4, Wed 1-5, Sat 10-5

EVANS MILLS

P EVANS MILLS PUBLIC LIBRARY*, 8706 Noble St, 13637. SAN 311-1814. Tel: 315-629-4483. FAX: 315-629-5198. Web Site: www.evansmillspubliclibrary.org. *Dir,* Helen Tooley
Founded 1956. Circ 7,880
Library Holdings: Bk Vols 4,132; Per Subs 22; Talking Bks 48; Videos 21
Wireless access
Mem of North Country Library System
Open Mon & Tues 1-5 & 7-8:30, Wed 3-8, Thurs 1-5, Sat 9-Noon
Friends of the Library Group

FAIR HAVEN

P FAIR HAVEN PUBLIC LIBRARY*, 14426 Richmond Ave, 13064. (Mail add: PO Box 602, 13064-0602), SAN 320-4952. Tel: 315-947-5851. FAX: 315-947-5851. E-mail: fairhave@twcny.rr.com. Web Site: www.fairhavenlibrary.org. *Dir,* Linda L Clum
Founded 1976. Pop 900
Library Holdings: Bk Titles 10,348; Bk Vols 11,915; Per Subs 11
Subject Interests: Ecology, Environ conserv, Local hist, Sailing, Water sports
Automation Activity & Vendor Info: (Cataloging) Innovative Interfaces, Inc; (Circulation) Innovative Interfaces, Inc; (OPAC) Innovative Interfaces, Inc
Wireless access
Mem of Finger Lakes Library System
Open Mon, Wed & Fri 2-5, Tues & Thurs 2-5 & 6:30-8:30, Sat 9-Noon

FAIRPORT

P FAIRPORT PUBLIC LIBRARY*, One Fairport Village Landing, 14450. SAN 311-1822. Tel: 585-223-9091. FAX: 585-223-3998. Web Site: www.fairportlibrary.org. *Dir,* Betsy Gilbert; *Asst Dir, Ref Serv,* Linda Macholz; *Asst Dir, Tech Serv & Automation,* Tori Reilly; *Adult Serv,* Brenda Deever; *Adult Serv, AV,* Hema Parthasarathi; *Adult Serv, Programming,* Margaret Pilaroscia; *Adult Serv,* Holly Wolf; *Ch Serv,* Robin Benoit; *Ch Serv,* Amy Joslyn; *Tech Serv,* Kristin Gallagher; *Teen Serv,* Stephanie Squicciarini; Staff 33.5 (MLS 10, Non-MLS 23.5)
Founded 1906. Pop 40,055; Circ 825,737
Jul 2008-Jun 2009 Income $2,237,648, Locally Generated Income $2,101,692, Other $135,956. Mats Exp $276,592, Books $185,619, AV Mat $60,822, Electronic Ref Mat (Incl. Access Fees) $30,151. Sal $1,189,995 (Prof $572,267)
Library Holdings: AV Mats 24,094; Electronic Media & Resources 34; Microforms 1,858; Bk Vols 99,661; Per Subs 324

Automation Activity & Vendor Info: (Cataloging) TLC (The Library Corporation); (Circulation) TLC (The Library Corporation); (OPAC) TLC (The Library Corporation)
Wireless access
Function: Adult bk club, AV serv, Bk club(s), Bks on cassette, Bks on CD, Children's prog, Computer training, Computers for patron use, Copy machines, e-mail & chat, Electronic databases & coll, Free DVD rentals, Handicapped accessible, Holiday prog, ILL available, Mail & tel request accepted, Mus passes, Music CDs, Online cat, Online ref, OverDrive digital audio bks, Photocopying/Printing, Preschool outreach, Prog for adults, Prog for children & young adult, Pub access computers, Ref & res, Ref serv in person, Spoken cassettes & CDs, Spoken cassettes & DVDs, Story hour, Summer reading prog, Tax forms, Teen prog, Telephone ref, VHS videos, Wheelchair accessible, Workshops
Mem of Monroe County Library System
Open Mon-Thurs 9-9, Fri 9-6, Sat 9-5, Sun (Oct-April) 2-5
Restriction: Non-resident fee
Friends of the Library Group

FALCONER

P FALCONER PUBLIC LIBRARY*, 101 W Main St, 14733. SAN 311-1830. Tel: 716-665-3504. FAX: 716-665-9203. Web Site: www.cclslib.org/falconer. *Librn,* Sue Seamans
Founded 1921. Pop 2,735; Circ 101,000
Library Holdings: Audiobooks 1,800; Bks on Deafness & Sign Lang 47; Large Print Bks 1,500; Bk Vols 20,000; Per Subs 106
Automation Activity & Vendor Info: (Cataloging) SirsiDynix; (Circulation) SirsiDynix; (OPAC) SirsiDynix
Mem of Chautauqua-Cattaraugus Library System
Special Services for the Blind - Braille bks; Talking bks
Open Mon-Wed 9-5 & 6:30-8:30, Thurs & Fri 9-5, Sat 9-3

FALLSBURG

S SULLIVAN CORRECTIONAL FACILITY LIBRARY*, 325 Riverside Dr, 12733. (Mail add: PO Box 116, 12733-0116), SAN 327-3245. Tel: 845-434-2080. FAX: 845-434-2080. *Librn,* Charles Gramlich
Library Holdings: Bk Titles 10,000; Per Subs 100; Talking Bks 120; Videos 180
Automation Activity & Vendor Info: (Circulation) Follett Software
Wireless access
Open Mon, Wed & Fri 8-4, Tues & Thurs 12-8

FAR ROCKAWAY

M PENINSULA HOSPITAL CENTER*, Medical Library, 51-15 Beach Channel Dr, 11691-1074. SAN 311-1849. Tel: 718-734-2887. FAX: 718-734-2234. *Dir,* Milena Nenova; Staff 1 (MLS 1)
Founded 1970
Library Holdings: AV Mats 1,375; e-journals 145; Large Print Bks 100; Bk Titles 1,000; Per Subs 19; Spec Interest Per Sub 19
Subject Interests: Cardiology, Dentistry, Family practice, Nursing, Orthopedics, Podiatry, Surgery
Database Vendor: EBSCOhost, OVID Technologies
Partic in Basic Health Sciences Library Network; Brooklyn-Queens-Staten Island-Manhattan-Bronx Health Sciences Librarians; Medical & Scientific Libraries of Long Island; Metropolitan New York Library Council
Friends of the Library Group

M SAINT JOHN'S EPISCOPAL HOSPITAL-SOUTH SHORE DIVISION*, Medical Library, 327 Beach 19th St, 11691. SAN 311-1857. Tel: 718-869-7699. FAX: 718-869-8528. Web Site: www.ehs.org. *Dir,* Kalpana Desai; E-mail: kdesai@ehs.org; *Asst Librn,* Curtis Carson
Library Holdings: Bk Vols 3,000; Per Subs 180
Subject Interests: Gynecology, Med, Nursing, Obstetrics, Psychiat
Partic in Basic Health Sciences Library Network; Brooklyn-Queens-Staten Island-Manhattan-Bronx Health Sciences Librarians; Medical & Scientific Libraries of Long Island; Metropolitan New York Library Council

FARMINGDALE

P FARMINGDALE PUBLIC LIBRARY*, 116 Merritts Rd, 11735. SAN 311-1881. Tel: 516-249-9090. FAX: 516-694-9697. E-mail: fdaleref@nassaulibrary.org. Web Site: www.farmingdalelibrary.org. *Dir,* Debbie Podolski; *Head, Circ,* Valerie Miller; Tel: 516-249-9090, Ext 218; *Head, Ref,* Stuart Schaeffer; Tel: 516-249-9090, Ext 203, E-mail: fdaleref@nassaulibrary.org; *Head, Youth Serv,* Christa Lucareli; Tel: 516-249-9090, Ext 226; Staff 65 (MLS 19, Non-MLS 46)
Founded 1923. Pop 40,000; Circ 401,262
Library Holdings: Bk Vols 226,430; Per Subs 381
Subject Interests: Local hist
Automation Activity & Vendor Info: (Cataloging) Innovative Interfaces, Inc; (Circulation) Innovative Interfaces, Inc; (Course Reserve) Innovative Interfaces, Inc; (OPAC) Innovative Interfaces, Inc
Publications: Community Directory; Inside Your Library
Mem of Nassau Library System
Open Mon, Tues & Thurs 9-9, Wed 10-9, Fri 9-6, Sat 9-5, Sun 1-5
Friends of the Library Group

C FARMINGDALE STATE COLLEGE OF NEW YORK*, Thomas D Greenley Library, 2350 Broadhollow Rd, 11735-1021. SAN 311-1903. Tel: 631-420-2040. Circulation Tel: 631-420-2183. Reference Tel: 631-420-2184. FAX: 631-420-2473. Web Site: www.farmingdale.edu/library/. *Dir,* Michael G Knauth; *Acq,* Karen Gelles; *Cat, Tech Serv,* Carol Greenholz; *Circ,* George Lo Presti; *Per,* Azadeh Mirzadeh; *Ref,* Karen Gelles; *Ref,* James Macinick; Staff 18 (MLS 7, Non-MLS 11)
Founded 1912. Enrl 4,200; Fac 250; Highest Degree: Bachelor
Library Holdings: Bk Titles 125,000; Per Subs 800
Special Collections: US Document Depository
Subject Interests: Am lit, Aviation, Biol, Bus, Communication, Dental health, Eng, English lit, Hort, Med lab tech, Nursing, Psychol
Automation Activity & Vendor Info: (Acquisitions) Ex Libris Group; (Cataloging) Ex Libris Group; (Circulation) Ex Libris Group; (Course Reserve) Ex Libris Group; (ILL) OCLC; (OPAC) Ex Libris Group; (Serials) Ex Libris Group
Database Vendor: EBSCOhost, Gale Cengage Learning, LexisNexis, OCLC FirstSearch, ProQuest
Wireless access
Publications: Bibliographies; Newsletter; Research Guide
Partic in OCLC Online Computer Library Center, Inc
Open Mon-Thurs 8am-9pm, Fri 8-5, Sat 9-5

FAYETTEVILLE

P FAYETTEVILLE FREE LIBRARY*, 300 Orchard St, 13066-1386. SAN 311-1911. Tel: 315-637-6374. FAX: 315-637-2306. E-mail: fayfree@gmail.com. Web Site: www.fayettevillefreelibrary.org. *Exec Dir,* Susan L Considine; Staff 8 (MLS 5, Non-MLS 3)
Founded 1906. Pop 10,250
Library Holdings: AV Mats 4,568; Bks on Deafness & Sign Lang 100; High Interest/Low Vocabulary Bk Vols 100; Large Print Bks 500; Bk Vols 44,820; Per Subs 115
Special Collections: American Popular Sheet Music Coll; Local History Coll (Titles from 1860)
Subject Interests: 19th Century women's hist
Automation Activity & Vendor Info: (Cataloging) Innovative Interfaces, Inc; (Circulation) Innovative Interfaces, Inc; (OPAC) Innovative Interfaces, Inc
Wireless access
Mem of Onondaga County Public Library
Partic in OCLC Online Computer Library Center, Inc
Special Services for the Blind - Text reader
Open Mon-Thurs 9-9, Fri & Sat 10-5, Sun 1-5
Friends of the Library Group

FILLMORE

P WIDE AWAKE CLUB LIBRARY*, 46 W Main St, 14735-8706. (Mail add: PO Box 199, 14735-0199), SAN 311-1938. Tel: 585-567-8301. FAX: 585-567-8301. E-mail: fillmore@stls.org. Web Site: www.fillmorelibrary.com. *Libr Dir,* Roxanne Baker; E-mail: bakerr@stls.org; *Libr Mgr,* Joan Elizabeth Tavernier; E-mail: tavernierj@stls.org
Founded 1897. Pop 5,179; Circ 21,139
Library Holdings: Bks on Deafness & Sign Lang 10; High Interest/Low Vocabulary Bk Vols 500; Bk Vols 14,000; Per Subs 23
Subject Interests: Hist
Automation Activity & Vendor Info: (Cataloging) SIRSI-iBistro; (Circulation) SIRSI-iBistro; (ILL) SIRSI-iBistro; (OPAC) SIRSI-iBistro
Wireless access
Function: Adult literacy prog, Homebound delivery serv, ILL available, Online searches, Photocopying/Printing, Prog for adults, Prog for children & young adult, Summer reading prog
Mem of Southern Tier Library System
Special Services for the Deaf - TTY equip
Special Services for the Blind - Talking bks
Open Mon, Wed & Fri 9-5, Tues & Thurs 9-7, Sat 9-12

FINDLEY LAKE

P ALEXANDER FINDLEY COMMUNITY LIBRARY*, 2883 North Rd, 14736. (Mail add: PO Box 74, 14736). Tel: 716-769-6568. FAX: 716-769-7207. E-mail: findleylibrary@stny.rr.com. Web Site: www.cclslib.org/findley/findley.html. *Mgr,* Kristine Gleason
Founded 2000
Library Holdings: AV Mats 293; DVDs 673; Bk Vols 12,034; Per Subs 27; Talking Bks 35
Automation Activity & Vendor Info: (Cataloging) SirsiDynix; (Circulation) SirsiDynix; (OPAC) SirsiDynix; (Serials) SirsiDynix
Wireless access

Mem of Chautauqua-Cattaraugus Library System
Open Mon 9-2, Tues & Thurs 1-7, Sat 9-12
Friends of the Library Group

FISHERS ISLAND

P FISHERS ISLAND LIBRARY*, 988 Oriental Ave, 06390. (Mail add: PO Box 366, 06390-0366), SAN 311-1946. Tel: 631-788-7362. FAX: 631-788-7362. *Librn,* Ann Banks
Founded 1904. Circ 7,966
Library Holdings: Audiobooks 50; DVDs 30; Bk Vols 24,611; Per Subs 12; Videos 575
Wireless access
Mem of Suffolk Cooperative Library System
Open Mon & Fri (Sept-June) 1-5, Wed 1-6, Sat 9-12; Mon, Tues, Thurs & Fri (July-Aug) 9-12 & 1:30-5, Wed & Sat 9-12

FISHKILL

P BLODGETT MEMORIAL LIBRARY*, 37 Broad St, 12524-1836. SAN 311-1954. Tel: 845-896-9215. FAX: 845-896-9243. E-mail: blodmem@optonline.net. Web Site: blodgett.fishkill.lib.ny.us. *Dir, Libr Serv,* Julie Spann; Staff 2 (MLS 2)
Founded 1934. Pop 15,506; Circ 80,749
Library Holdings: Bk Vols 50,000
Subject Interests: Local hist
Automation Activity & Vendor Info: (Cataloging) Innovative Interfaces, Inc - Millenium; (Circulation) Innovative Interfaces, Inc - Millenium; (OPAC) Innovative Interfaces, Inc - Millenium
Wireless access
Mem of Mid-Hudson Library System
Open Mon, Tues & Thurs 10-8, Wed 12-8, Fri 12-6, Sat 10-4, Sun 1-4

S FISHKILL HISTORICAL SOCIETY*, Van Wyck Homestead Museum Library, 504 Rte 9, 12524-2248. (Mail add: PO Box 133, 12524-0133), SAN 328-3623. Tel: 845-896-9560. E-mail: vanwyckhomestead@aol.com. *Actg Div Chief, Archives Dir, Ref Mgr,* Roy E Jorgensen; E-mail: royjorg@aol.com; *Acq Librn,* Mary Ann Ryan; E-mail: makr25@aol.com
Founded 1962
Library Holdings: CDs 12; DVDs 3; Bk Titles 875; Per Subs 2; Videos 7
Special Collections: Family Genealogies; Papers of Harold Totten
Subject Interests: Dutchess County, Fishkill, Genealogy, Hudson Valley, NY State
Function: Photocopying/Printing
Open Sat & Sun (June-Oct) 9-12 & 1-5
Restriction: Circ limited

FLEISCHMANNS

P SKENE MEMORIAL LIBRARY*, 1017 Main St, 12430. (Mail add: PO Box 189, 12430-0189), SAN 311-1962. Tel: 845-254-4581. FAX: 845-254-4581. E-mail: librarian@skenelib.org. Web Site: www.skenelib.org. *Dir,* Linda Rodgers; *Computer Serv, Network Serv,* Fred Herzog
Founded 1901. Pop 434; Circ 13,532
Library Holdings: Bk Vols 17,000
Wireless access
Mem of Four County Library System
Open Tues-Fri (Winter) 2-6, Sat 10-2, Mon-Fri (Summer) 10-4, Sat 10-1

FLORAL PARK

P FLORAL PARK PUBLIC LIBRARY*, 17 Caroline Pl, 11001. SAN 311-1970. Tel: 516-326-6330. FAX: 516-437-6959. Web Site: www.nassaulibrary.org/fpark/. *Dir,* Tracey Simon; *Ch Serv Librn,* Jeannette Newman; *Ref,* Edwina Van Dam; *YA Serv,* Jane Zuckerman
Founded 1923
Jun 2008-May 2009 Income $1,392,635, State $4,802, Locally Generated Income $1,387,833. Mats Exp $194,249, Books $151,529, AV Mat $27,227, Electronic Ref Mat (Incl. Access Fees) $15,493. Sal $738,713
Library Holdings: AV Mats 5,446; Bk Titles 89,451; Per Subs 172
Subject Interests: Gardening, Local hist
Automation Activity & Vendor Info: (Circulation) Innovative Interfaces, Inc; (OPAC) Innovative Interfaces, Inc
Wireless access
Publications: Monthly Calendar of Events; Newsletter
Mem of Nassau Library System
Open Mon, Tues & Thurs 10-9, Wed & Fri 10-6, Sat 9-5, Sun 1-5
Friends of the Library Group

FLORIDA

P FLORIDA PUBLIC LIBRARY*, Four Cohen Circle, 10921-1514. SAN 311-1989. Tel: 845-651-7659. FAX: 845-651-7689. E-mail: fpl@rcls.org. Web Site: rcls.org/fpl. *Dir,* Madelyn Folino
Founded 1958. Pop 4,724; Circ 7,621
Library Holdings: Bk Vols 5,000
Automation Activity & Vendor Info: (Circulation) Horizon; (OPAC) Horizon
Wireless access
Mem of Ramapo Catskill Library System
Open Mon-Thurs 10-8, Fri & Sat 10-5, Sun 12-5

FLUSHING

M FLUSHING HOSPITAL MEDICAL CENTER*, Medical Library, 45th Ave at Parsons Blvd, 11355. SAN 311-2020. Tel: 718-670-5653. FAX: 718-670-3089. *Dir,* Robin L Dornbaum; E-mail: rdornbau.flushing@jhmc.org; Staff 1.5 (MLS 1, Non-MLS 0.5)
Founded 1942
Library Holdings: e-books 30; e-journals 230; Bk Vols 5,124
Subject Interests: Gynecology, Internal med, Obstetrics, Pediatrics, Surgery
Automation Activity & Vendor Info: (Cataloging) Professional Software
Database Vendor: OVID Technologies
Wireless access
Partic in Brooklyn-Queens-Staten Island-Manhattan-Bronx Health Sciences Librarians
Open Mon-Fri 9-5

QUEENS COLLEGE

C AARON COPLAND SCHOOL OF MUSIC LIBRARY*, 65-30 Kissena Blvd, 11367. Tel: 718-997-3900. FAX: 718-997-3928. Web Site: qcpages.qc.cuny.edu/Library/music_library. *Assoc Prof, Head Music Libr,* Dr Jennifer Oates; Staff 4 (MLS 1, Non-MLS 3)
Highest Degree: Master
Library Holdings: CDs 20,000; DVDs 125; e-journals 100; Music Scores 40,000; Bk Vols 35,000; Per Subs 225; Videos 175
Partic in CUNYPLUS
Open Mon-Thurs (Fall) 10-6:45, Fri 10-4:45; Mon-Thurs (Summer) 10-4:45

C BENJAMIN S ROSENTHAL LIBRARY*, 65-30 Kissena Blvd, 11367-0904, SAN 311-2039. Tel: 718-997-3700. Reference Tel: 718-997-3701. FAX: 718-997-3753. Web Site: www.qc.edu/Library. *Chief Librn,* Robert Shaddy; *Assoc Librn,* Shoshana Kaufmann; *Syst Coordr,* A Ben Chitty; *Acq, Govt Doc,* Nancy Macomber; *Access Serv, ILL,* Evelyn Silverman; *Coll Develop,* Richard Wall; *Instrul Serv Librn,* Alexandra De Luise; *Instrul Serv Librn, Ref Serv,* Subash Gandhi; E-mail: subasg.gandhi@qc.cuny.edu; *Ref,* Manuel Sanudo; *Web Coordr,* Rolf Swensen; Staff 53 (MLS 22, Non-MLS 31)
Founded 1937. Enrl 15,686; Fac 1,103; Highest Degree: Master
Library Holdings: e-books 5,000; Bk Titles 515,000; Bk Vols 780,500; Per Subs 5,820
Special Collections: Louis Armstrong Archives, mss, personal papers, photographs, rec, scrapbks & tapes; Theater & Film Coll (through 1960), posters, programs, scrapbks, scripts, stills. US Document Depository
Automation Activity & Vendor Info: (Acquisitions) Ex Libris Group; (Cataloging) Ex Libris Group; (Circulation) Ex Libris Group; (Course Reserve) Docutek; (ILL) OCLC; (OPAC) Ex Libris Group; (Serials) Ex Libris Group
Partic in Metropolitan New York Library Council; Nylink; OCLC Online Computer Library Center, Inc
Publications: PageDown (Newsletter)
Special Services for the Blind - Assistive/Adapted tech devices, equip & products
Open Mon-Thurs 9am-10pm, Fri 9-5, Sat & Sun 12-6
Friends of the Library Group

C VAUGHN COLLEGE LIBRARY*, 8601 23rd Ave, 11369. SAN 311-1407. Tel: 718-429-6600, Ext 184. FAX: 718-478-7066. Web Site: www.vaughn.edu. *Dir,* JoAnn Jayne; E-mail: joann.jayne@vaughn.edu; *Asst Dir,* Xigang Zhou; E-mail: xigang.zhou@vaughn.edu; Staff 3 (MLS 2, Non-MLS 1)
Founded 1932. Enrl 1,462; Fac 93
Library Holdings: Audiobooks 166; AV Mats 3,500; e-books 44,000; e-journals 12,000; Bk Titles 41,000; Per Subs 1,058
Special Collections: Aircraft Maintenance Manuals; NACA & Other Annual Reports, bd vols; NASA Reports; SAE Reports
Subject Interests: Aeronaut, Avionics, Electronics, Mgt
Automation Activity & Vendor Info: (Cataloging) Follett Software; (Circulation) Follett Software; (ILL) OCLC; (OPAC) Follett Software
Database Vendor: OCLC FirstSearch
Wireless access
Publications: Library handbook
Partic in Metropolitan New York Library Council
Open Mon & Tues 7:30am-11pm, Wed & Thurs 7:30am-9pm, Fri 7:30-6, Sat 8-5, Sun 12-5

FLY CREEK

S BASSETT HEALTHCARE, New York Center for Agricultural Medicine & Health Library, 6160 State Hwy 28, 13337. (Mail add: One Atwell Rd, Cooperstown, 13326), SAN 374-4965. Tel: 607-547-6023, Ext 2207. Toll Free Tel: 800-343-7527, Ext 2207. FAX: 607-547-6087. Web Site: www.necenter.org, www.nycamh.org. *Res Librn,* Deborah Dalton; E-mail: deborah.dalton@bassett.org; Staff 1 (MLS 1)
Founded 1989
Library Holdings: Bk Titles 2,000; Per Subs 40
Special Collections: Agricultural Health & Safety Coll
Subject Interests: Occupational health
Automation Activity & Vendor Info: (ILL) OCLC
Database Vendor: OCLC FirstSearch, PubMed
Partic in South Central Regional Library Council
Restriction: Open by appt only

FONDA

P FROTHINGHAM FREE LIBRARY*, 28 W Main St, 12068. (Mail add: PO Box 746, 12068-0746), SAN 311-2071. Tel: 518-853-3016. FAX: 518-853-3016. *Dir,* Kirschman Sherri; E-mail: skirschman@mvls.info
Founded 1942. Pop 6,559; Circ 18,074
Library Holdings: Large Print Bks 479; Bk Vols 16,697; Per Subs 14
Wireless access
Mem of Mohawk Valley Library System
Open Mon-Wed 11-7, Fri 12-7, Sat 9-1

G MONTGOMERY COUNTY DEPARTMENT OF HISTORY & ARCHIVES*, Research Library, Nine Park St, 12068. (Mail add: Old Courthouse, PO Box 1500, 12068-1500), SAN 325-5336. Tel: 518-853-8186. FAX: 518-853-8392. Web Site: www.co.montgomery.ny.us/historian. *County Historian,* Kelly Yacobucci Farquhar; E-mail: kfarquhar@co.montgomery.ny.us; Staff 2 (Non-MLS 2)
Founded 1934
Library Holdings: Bk Titles 8,500
Special Collections: Archival Records (early 1700-present); Extensive Genealogical & Historical Coll
Subject Interests: Genealogy, Local hist
Function: Archival coll, For res purposes, Photocopying/Printing, Res libr
Publications: Catalogue of Historical & Genealogical Materials (Collection catalog)
Open Mon-Fri (Sept-June) 8:30-4; Mon-Fri (July & Aug) 9-4
Restriction: Not a lending libr
Friends of the Library Group

FOREST HILLS

C BRAMSON ORT COLLEGE*, Library-Learning Resource Center, 69-30 Austin St, 11375. SAN 311-6522. Tel: 718-261-5800. FAX: 718-301-1976. Web Site: www.bramsonort.edu. *Head Librn,* Rivka Burkos; E-mail: rburkos@bramsonort.edu; Staff 2 (MLS 1, Non-MLS 1)
Founded 1977. Enrl 350
Library Holdings: AV Mats 200; e-journals 10; Bk Titles 25,000; Per Subs 180; Talking Bks 25
Special Collections: Judaica
Subject Interests: Bus admin, Computer prog, Electronics, English as a second lang, Jewish studies
Database Vendor: EBSCOhost
Wireless access
Partic in Metropolitan New York Library Council; Nylink
Open Mon-Thurs 9-9, Fri 9-3 (9-4 Summer), Sun 9-5

S FORT HILLS HOSPITAL*, Health Sciences Library, 102-01 66 Rd, 11375. SAN 373-1200. Tel: 718-830-4000. FAX: 718-830-4344. *Dir,* Paula Green; E-mail: pgreen@nshs.edu
Library Holdings: Bk Vols 1,500; Per Subs 160
Database Vendor: OVID Technologies, STAT!Ref (Teton Data Systems), UpToDate
Wireless access
Partic in Basic Health Sciences Library Network; Brooklyn-Queens-Staten Island-Manhattan-Bronx Health Sciences Librarians
Open Mon-Fri 8-4

FORT DRUM

A UNITED STATES ARMY*, Robert C McEwen Library, 4300 Camp Hale Rd, 13602-5284. SAN 354-3579. Tel: 315-772-6005. Circulation Tel: 315-772-9099. Interlibrary Loan Service Tel: 315-772-8503. Administration Tel: 315-772-4734. FAX: 315-772-8529. *Chief Librn,* Allen R Goudie; Tel: 315-772-4502; *Ref,* Wendy A Newell; Staff 9 (MLS 3, Non-MLS 6)
Founded 1941
Library Holdings: Audiobooks 6,011; AV Mats 5,000; Bk Vols 60,000; Per Subs 100
Subject Interests: Job hunting, Self defense
Automation Activity & Vendor Info: (Acquisitions) Innovative Interfaces, Inc; (Cataloging) Innovative Interfaces, Inc; (Circulation) Innovative Interfaces, Inc; (OPAC) Innovative Interfaces, Inc; (Serials) Innovative Interfaces, Inc
Wireless access
Function: Govt ref serv, Handicapped accessible, ILL available, Prog for children & young adult, Summer reading prog, Wheelchair accessible
Partic in Fedlink
Open Mon-Thurs 9-9, Fri 9-6, Sat & Sun 10-6
Restriction: Open to fac, students & qualified researchers

FORT EDWARD

P FORT EDWARD FREE LIBRARY*, 23 East St, 12828. SAN 311-211X. Tel: 518-747-6743. FAX: 518-747-6743. *Dir,* Victoria Plude; E-mail: vplude@sals.edu
Founded 1914. Pop 3,561; Circ 6,396
Library Holdings: Bk Vols 14,000; Per Subs 30
Mem of Southern Adirondack Library System
Open Mon-Wed (Winter) 1-5 & 6-8, Thurs & Fri 1-5, Sat 9-12; Mon-Wed (Summer) 1-5 & 6-8, Thurs 1-5, Fri 10-5

FORT PLAIN

P FORT PLAIN FREE LIBRARY*, 19 Willett St, 13339-1130. SAN 311-2136. Tel: 518-993-4646. FAX: 518-993-2455. E-mail: fpfl@sals.edu. Web Site: www.fortplainfreelibrary.org. *Dir,* Whitney Hubbard; E-mail: whubbard@mvls.info; Staff 1.8 (MLS 0.8, Non-MLS 1)
Founded 1894. Circ 27,327
Library Holdings: Bk Vols 20,965; Per Subs 41
Subject Interests: Local hist
Automation Activity & Vendor Info: (Circulation) Innovative Interfaces, Inc; (OPAC) Innovative Interfaces, Inc; (Serials) Innovative Interfaces, Inc
Database Vendor: ReferenceUSA
Wireless access
Mem of Mohawk Valley Library System
Open Mon, Wed & Fri 10-5, Tues & Thurs 10-8:30, Sat 9-12

FRANKFORT

P FRANKFORT FREE LIBRARY, 123 S Frankfort St, 13340. SAN 311-2144. Tel: 315-894-9611. FAX: 315-894-9611. E-mail: frankfort@midyork.org. Web Site: midyorklib.org/frankfort. *Dir,* Marietta Phillips
Pop 7,200; Circ 15,281
Library Holdings: Bk Vols 10,000; Per Subs 21
Automation Activity & Vendor Info: (Cataloging) SirsiDynix; (Circulation) SirsiDynix; (OPAC) SirsiDynix
Wireless access
Mem of Mid-York Library System
Open Mon & Wed 2-8, Tues & Thurs 11-8, Fri 3-7, Sat (Sept-May) 11-2

FRANKLIN

P FRANKLIN FREE LIBRARY, 334 Main St, 13775. (Mail add: PO Box 947, 13775-0947), SAN 311-2152. Tel: 607-829-2941. FAX: 607-829-5017. E-mail: fr.ill@4cls.org. Web Site: www.franklinfreelibrary.org. *Dir & Librn,* Carrie Fishner; Staff 1 (MLS 1)
Founded 1827. Pop 2,440; Circ 8,000
Library Holdings: Bk Vols 10,000; Per Subs 35
Special Collections: 200 Historic Scrapbooks (indexed); Civil War Coll; Local Newspapers on Microfilm 1857-1952; Town & Village Board Meetings 1792 -
Automation Activity & Vendor Info: (OPAC) SirsiDynix
Wireless access
Function: 24/7 Online cat, Adult bk club, After school storytime, Audiobks via web, Bks on CD, Children's prog, Computers for patron use, Copy machines, Fax serv
Mem of Four County Library System
Open Tues 9-12, 1-5 & 7-9, Wed & Sat 10-2, Thurs 9-12 & 1-5
Friends of the Library Group

FRANKLIN SQUARE

P FRANKLIN SQUARE PUBLIC LIBRARY*, 19 Lincoln Rd, 11010. SAN 311-2160. Tel: 516-488-3444. FAX: 516-354-3368. Web Site: www.franklinsquarepl.org. *Dir,* Lisa Paulo; E-mail: lpaulo@franklinsquarepl.org; *Asst Dir,* Margaret A Smith; *Acq,* Lori Seveneant; *Adult Ref,* Grace Palmisano; *Adult Serv, YA Serv,* Mary LaRosa; *Ch Serv,* Diane Gregory; *Ch Serv,* Faye Lieberman; *Circ,* Sandra Montenora; *Ref,* Karin Briller; *Tech Serv,* Renee Abbananto. Subject Specialists: *Commun serv,* Margaret A Smith; Staff 8 (MLS 8)
Founded 1938. Pop 29,000; Circ 205,003
Library Holdings: Bk Vols 106,000; Per Subs 200

Automation Activity & Vendor Info: (Cataloging) Innovative Interfaces, Inc - Millenium; (Circulation) Innovative Interfaces, Inc - Millenium; (OPAC) Innovative Interfaces, Inc - Millenium
Wireless access
Publications: Community Directory; Newsletter
Mem of Nassau Library System
Open Mon-Thurs 10-9, Fri 10-6, Sat 10-5

FRANKLINVILLE

P BLOUNT LIBRARY, INC*, Five N Main St, 14737. SAN 311-2179. Tel: 716-676-5715. FAX: 716-676-5715. E-mail: franklinville@hotmail.com. Web Site: www.cclslib.org/fran/fran.html. *Dir,* Barbara Scalise; *Asst Dir,* Deborah A McGrath; Staff 2 (Non-MLS 2)
Founded 1899. Pop 4,817; Circ 13,503
Jan 2005-Dec 2005 Income $42,150, State $7,753, City $22,400, Federal $100, Locally Generated Income $543, Other $11,354. Mats Exp $9,357, Books $9,043, AV Mat $314. Sal $16,466
Library Holdings: Bk Vols 19,325
Subject Interests: Local hist
Wireless access
Mem of Chautauqua-Cattaraugus Library System
Open Mon 3-9, Tues 9-5, Wed 2:30-5:30 & 7-9, Thurs 9-5:30, Sat 9-12:30
Friends of the Library Group

FREDONIA

P DARWIN R BARKER LIBRARY*, Seven Day St, 14063. SAN 311-2187. Tel: 716-672-8051. FAX: 716-679-3547. E-mail: barker@netsync.net. Web Site: www.barkerlibrary.org. *Dir,* Joy Harper; *Asst Librn,* Juanita Ball
Pop 11,101; Circ 110,000
Library Holdings: Bk Vols 57,000; Per Subs 100
Automation Activity & Vendor Info: (Cataloging) SirsiDynix; (Circulation) Follett Software; (OPAC) Follett Software
Wireless access
Mem of Chautauqua-Cattaraugus Library System
Open Mon-Thurs 9-9, Fri & Sat 9-5
Friends of the Library Group

C STATE UNIVERSITY OF NEW YORK AT FREDONIA*, Daniel A Reed Library, 280 Central Ave, 14063. SAN 311-2195. Tel: 716-673-3181. Circulation Tel: 716-673-3184. Interlibrary Loan Service Tel: 716-673-3180. Reference Tel: 716-672-1234, 716-673-3222. Automation Services Tel: 716-673-4837. Information Services Tel: 716-673-3195. FAX: 716-673-3185. Web Site: www.fredonia.edu/library. *Dir, Libr Serv,* Randy Gadikian; E-mail: randolph.gadikian@fredonia.edu; *Head, Circ,* Susan Wilkes; Tel: 716-673-3191, E-mail: susan.wilkes@fredonia.edu; *Head, Instrul Serv, Head, Ref,* Marianne Eimer; E-mail: marianne.eimer@fredonia.edu; *Head, Tech Serv,* Vince Courtney; Tel: 716-673-3182, E-mail: vincent.courtney@fredonia.edu; *Music Librn,* Kevin Michki; Tel: 716-673-3117, E-mail: kevin.michki@fredonia.edu; *Syst Adminr,* Kathleen Sacco; E-mail: kathleen.sacco@fredonia.edu; *Archivist,* Jeremy Linden; E-mail: jeremy.linden@fredonia.edu; *ILL,* Janet Ferry; Tel: 716-673-3194, E-mail: janet.ferry@fredonia.edu. Subject Specialists: *Music,* Kevin Michki; *Local hist,* Jeremy Linden; Staff 11 (MLS 9, Non-MLS 2)
Founded 1826. Enrl 5,200; Fac 300; Highest Degree: Master
Library Holdings: AV Mats 28,700; Bks on Deafness & Sign Lang 121; Braille Volumes 4; CDs 5,072; DVDs 406; e-books 1,988; e-journals 40,000; Electronic Media & Resources 447; Music Scores 33,548; Bk Vols 389,320; Per Subs 260; Videos 1,601
Special Collections: Chautauqua & Cattaraugus Counties' History Coll, bks, mss, micro; Holland Land Company Coll; Seneca/Iroquois History Coll, bks, mss, micro; Sigurd Rascher Coll; Stephan Zweig Coll, bks, mss, micro; West Valley Project Coll. State Document Depository
Automation Activity & Vendor Info: (Acquisitions) Ex Libris Group; (Cataloging) Ex Libris Group; (Circulation) Ex Libris Group; (Course Reserve) Ex Libris Group; (OPAC) Ex Libris Group; (Serials) Ex Libris Group
Database Vendor: Alexander Street Press, American Chemical Society, American Mathematical Society, American Psychological Association (APA), Annual Reviews, ARTstor, BioOne, Cambridge Scientific Abstracts, Cinahl, CIOS (Communication Institute for Online Scholarship), CQ Press, Dialog, EBSCOhost, Elsevier, Facts on File, Gale Cengage Learning, Hoovers, JSTOR, LexisNexis, Mergent Online, OCLC ArticleFirst, OCLC FirstSearch, OCLC WorldShare Interlibrary Loan, Oxford Online, PubMed, ScienceDirect, SerialsSolutions, Springer-Verlag, Standard & Poor's, STN International, ValueLine
Wireless access
Function: Audio & video playback equip for onsite use, Copy machines, E-Reserves, Electronic databases & coll, Handicapped accessible, Music CDs, Online ref, Online searches
Publications: Annual Report
Partic in New York Online Virtual Electronic Library (NOVEL); Nylink; SUNYConnect; Western New York Library Resources Council
Open Mon-Thurs 7:30am-1am, Fri 7:30am-8pm, Sat Noon-8, Sun 9am-1am
Friends of the Library Group

FREEPORT

P FREEPORT MEMORIAL LIBRARY*, 144 W Merrick Rd & S Ocean Ave, 11520. SAN 311-2209. Tel: 516-379-3274. FAX: 516-868-9741. E-mail: frreference@freeportlibrary.info. Web Site: freeportlibrary.info. *Dir,* Ken Bellafiore; E-mail: kbellafiore@freeportlibrary.info; Staff 15 (MLS 15)
Founded 1884. Pop 40,976; Circ 254,785
Library Holdings: AV Mats 26,902; CDs 4,197; Bk Vols 223,806; Per Subs 416
Special Collections: Long Island history; Vocational & careers
Subject Interests: Careers, Ethnic studies, Investment lit
Automation Activity & Vendor Info: (Cataloging) Innovative Interfaces, Inc; (Circulation) Innovative Interfaces, Inc; (ILL) Innovative Interfaces, Inc; (OPAC) Innovative Interfaces, Inc
Wireless access
Function: AV serv, Res libr
Publications: Freeport Memorial Library Newsletter
Mem of Nassau Library System
Special Services for the Deaf - Assisted listening device; High interest/low vocabulary bks; TDD equip; TTY equip
Special Services for the Blind - Audio mat; Bks on cassette; Bks on CD; Children's Braille; Home delivery serv; Large print bks; Talking bks; ZoomText magnification & reading software
Open Mon, Tues, Thurs & Fri (Fall & Spring) 9-9, Wed 10-9, Sat 9-5, Sun 1-5; Mon, Tues, Thurs & Fri (Summer) 9-9, Wed 10-9, Sat 9-1
Friends of the Library Group

FREWSBURG

P MYERS MEMORIAL LIBRARY*, 26 Ivory St, 14738 9517. (Mail add: PO Box 559, 14738-0559), SAN 311-2217. Tel: 716-569-5515. FAX: 716-569-2605. E-mail: myerslib@yahoo.com. Web Site: www.cclslib.org/frewsburg. *Dir,* Diane Crandall; Staff 1 (Non-MLS 1)
Founded 1923. Pop 3,500; Circ 30,000
Jan 2005-Dec 2005 Income $52,000, Locally Generated Income $14,000, Other $38,000. Mats Exp $9,200, Books $6,000, Per/Ser (Incl. Access Fees) $1,000, AV Mat $1,000, Electronic Ref Mat (Incl. Access Fees) $1,200
Library Holdings: Bks on Deafness & Sign Lang 10; CDs 75; DVDs 50; High Interest/Low Vocabulary Bk Vols 104; Large Print Bks 250; Bk Vols 18,000; Per Subs 50; Talking Bks 400; Videos 450
Special Collections: History (Robert H Jackson Coll), bks, letters; J J Myers Coll, bks
Wireless access
Function: Photocopying/Printing
Mem of Chautauqua Cattaraugus Library System
Open Mon & Wed (Winter) 2-8, Thurs 10-5, Fri 2-5, Sat 10-12; Mon & Wed (Summer) 2-8, Tues 10-8, Thurs 10-5, Fri 2-5, Sat 10-12

FRIENDSHIP

P FRIENDSHIP FREE LIBRARY*, 40 W Main St, 14739-8701. (Mail add: PO Box 37, 14739-0037), SAN 311-2225. Tel: 585-973-7724. FAX: 585-973-7724. *Dir,* Patricia Sawyer; E-mail: sawyerp@stls.com
Founded 1898. Circ 7,518
Library Holdings: DVDs 200; Large Print Bks 800; Bk Titles 13,000; Per Subs 15; Talking Bks 100; Videos 1,000
Automation Activity & Vendor Info: (Cataloging) SirsiDynix; (Circulation) SirsiDynix; (OPAC) SirsiDynix
Wireless access
Publications: Newsletter (annual)
Mem of Southern Tier Library System
Open Mon & Thurs 12:30-6, Wed 9-12 & 5-9, Fri 3-6, Sat 10-2

FULTON

J CAYUGA COMMUNITY COLLEGE*, Fulton Campus Library, 806 W Broadway, 13069. Tel: 315-294-9019. FAX: 315-592-5055. Web Site: www.cayuga-cc.edu/library. *Librn,* Judy Campanella; E-mail: campanella@cayuga-cc.edu; *Librn,* Kathy Sippling; E-mail: siplingk@cayuga-cc.edu; Staff 3 (MLS 2, Non-MLS 1)
Highest Degree: Associate
Automation Activity & Vendor Info: (Cataloging) Ex Libris Group; (Circulation) Ex Libris Group; (Course Reserve) Ex Libris Group; (OPAC) Ex Libris Group; (Serials) Ex Libris Group
Open Mon-Thurs 8am-8:30pm, Fri 8-4:30, Sun 12:30-4

P FULTON PUBLIC LIBRARY*, 160 S First St, 13069. SAN 311-2233. Tel: 315-592-5159. FAX: 315-592-4504. Web Site: www.fultonpubliclibrary.info. *Dir,* Betty Maute; Staff 7 (MLS 1, Non-MLS 6)
Founded 1895. Pop 11,855; Circ 61,148

Jan 2010-Dec 2010 Income $294,751, State $4,008, City $180,000, County $5,344, Locally Generated Income $31,000, Other $4,399. Mats Exp $32,100, Books $25,000, Per/Ser (Incl. Access Fees) $2,000, Other Print Mats $1,500, AV Mat $3,250, Electronic Ref Mat (Incl. Access Fees) $350. Sal $162,656 (Prof $40,250)
Library Holdings: AV Mats 3,100; CDs 500; DVDs 350; Electronic Media & Resources 105; Large Print Bks 650; Bk Vols 41,765; Per Subs 101; Videos 650
Subject Interests: Local hist
Automation Activity & Vendor Info: (Acquisitions) SirsiDynix; (Circulation) SirsiDynix; (OPAC) SirsiDynix
Wireless access
Function: Archival coll, Bi-weekly Writer's Group, Copy machines, Digital talking bks, E-Reserves, Electronic databases & coll, Fax serv, Handicapped accessible, ILL available, Magnifiers for reading, Mail & tel request accepted, Music CDs, Photocopying/Printing, Prog for adults, Prog for children & young adult, Ref serv available, Satellite serv, Spoken cassettes & CDs, Spoken cassettes & DVDs, Summer reading prog, Tax forms, Telephone ref, VHS videos, Wheelchair accessible, Workshops
Mem of North Country Library System
Open Mon, Fri & Sat 9-5, Tues-Thurs 9-7

GALWAY

P GALWAY PUBLIC LIBRARY*, 5264 Sacandaga Rd, 12074-2341. (Mail add: PO Box 207, 12074-0207). Tel: 518-882-6385. FAX: 518-882-6385. E-mail: gal-director@sals.edu. Web Site: www.galwaypubliclibrary.org. *Libr Dir,* Michol Tuttle; E-mail: director@galwaypubliclibrary.org; Staff 5 (MLS 1, Non-MLS 4)
Founded 1997. Pop 6,754
Library Holdings: AV Mats 1,500; Bk Vols 25,000; Per Subs 15
Automation Activity & Vendor Info: (Cataloging) Innovative Interfaces, Inc; (Circulation) Innovative Interfaces, Inc; (OPAC) Innovative Interfaces, Inc
Wireless access
Mem of Southern Adirondack Library System
Open Mon 12-6, Tues 10-6, Wed & Thurs 2-8, Fri 2-6, Sat 10-3
Friends of the Library Group

GARDEN CITY

C ADELPHI UNIVERSITY, Swirbul Library, One South Ave, 11530. (Mail add: PO Box 701, 11530-0701), SAN 352-4701. Tel: 516-877-3549. Circulation Tel: 516-877-3570. Interlibrary Loan Service Tel: 516-877-3571. Reference Tel: 516-877-3574. Administration Tel: 516-877-3520. Information Services Tel: 516-877-3340. Interlibrary Loan Service FAX: 516-877-3672. Reference FAX: 516-877-3674. Administration FAX: 516-877-3673. Web Site: libraries.adelphi.edu. *Dean, Univ Libr,* Charles W Simpson; E-mail: simpson@adelphi.edu; *Assoc Dean, Libr for Pub & Admin Serv,* Ann Minutella; Tel: 516-877-3518, E-mail: minutell@adelphi.edu; *Assoc Dean, Libr for Tech & Automated Serv,* Cynthia Clark; Tel: 516-877-3531, E-mail: cclark@adelphi.edu; *Acq Librn,* Kimberly Abrams; Tel: 516-877-3525, E-mail: kabrams@adelphi.edu; *Cat Librn,* Linda Weinberg; Tel: 516-877-3526, E-mail: lweinberg@adelphi.edu; *Coll Develop & Mgt Librn,* Debbi Smith; Tel: 516-877-3522, E-mail: smith8@adelphi.edu; *Curric Mat Librn, Ref Librn,* Amrita Madray; Tel: 516-877-3579, E-mail: madray@adelphi.edu; *Ref Librn,* Aditi Bandyopadhyay; Tel: 516-877-4166, E-mail: bandyopa@adelphi.edu; *Ref Librn,* Gary Cantrell; Tel: 516-877-3562, E-mail: cantrell@adelphi.edu; *Ref Librn,* Gloria Roberson; Tel: 516-877-3578, E-mail: roberson@adelphi.edu; *Ref & Info Literacy Librn,* Eloise Bellard; Tel: 516-877-3584, E-mail: bellard@adelphi.edu; *Ref/Electronic Res Librn,* Lois O'Neill; Tel: 516-877-3581, E-mail: oneill@adelphi.edu; *Asst Archivist, Spec Coll Librn,* Jessica Wagner; Tel: 516-877-3818, E-mail: jwagner@adelphi.edu; *Coordr of Ref Serv,* Victor Oliva; Tel: 516-877-3587, E-mail: oliva@adelphi.edu; *Univ Archivist,* Eugene T Neely; Tel: 516-877-3543, Fax: 516-877-3675, E-mail: neely@adelphi.edu. Subject Specialists: *Intl studies, Lang, Philos,* Kimberly Abrams; *Nursing,* Linda Weinberg; *Bus, Info sci, Libr sci,* Debbi Smith; *Educ,* Amrita Madray; *Computer sci, Math, Sci,* Aditi Bandyopadhyay; *Communications, Dance, Music,* Gary Cantrell; *Anthrop,* Gloria Roberson; *Criminal justice, Soc work, Sociol,* Eloise Bellard; *Communication sci & disorder, Health studies, Nursing,* Lois O'Neill; *English,* Jessica Wagner; *Hist, Polit sci,* Victor Oliva; Staff 62.5 (MLS 30, Non-MLS 32.5)
Founded 1896. Enrl 6,897; Fac 1,003; Highest Degree: Doctorate
Sept 2012-Aug 2013 Income $6,672,826, State $10,200, Parent Institution $6,622,222, Other $40,404. Mats Exp $2,436,508, Books $467,984, Per/Ser (Incl. Access Fees) $839,676, Manu Arch $6,073, Other Print Mats $133,063, Micro $14,483, AV Equip $28,634, AV Mat $21,832, Electronic Ref Mat (Incl. Access Fees) $904,751, Presv $20,012. Sal $2,929,727 (Prof $2,029,120)
Library Holdings: AV Mats 35,276; Bks on Deafness & Sign Lang 268; CDs 2,289; DVDs 6,361; e-books 127,938; e-journals 80,600; Electronic Media & Resources 252; Large Print Bks 134; Microforms 789,749; Music Scores 7,053; Bk Vols 609,568; Per Subs 929; Videos 2,912
Special Collections: Adelphi Authors Coll; Adelphiana; Americana Coll; Andres Coll; Blake Coll; Blodgett Coll; Children's Illustrated Literature Coll; Cobbett Coll; Cuala Press Coll; Dakin Coll; DePol Coll; Expatriate Coll; Hauptmann Coll; Hone Coll; Kraus-Boelte Early Childhood Education Coll; Loening Coll; Long Island Coll; McMillan Coll; Modern Chapbook Coll; Morley Coll; New York City Coll; New York State Coll; Ormont Literary Coll; Ormont Psychology Coll; Ornstein Coll; Panama Canal Coll; Rare Book Coll; Small Press Coll; Spanish Civil War Coll; St Denis Coll; Stoelzer Coll; Whitman Coll; Woodruff Coll. US Document Depository
Subject Interests: Children's lit, Lit, Panama Canal, Performing arts, Political cartoons, Spanish Civil War
Automation Activity & Vendor Info: (Acquisitions) Innovative Interfaces, Inc; (Cataloging) Innovative Interfaces, Inc; (Circulation) Innovative Interfaces, Inc; (Course Reserve) Innovative Interfaces, Inc; (ILL) OCLC ILLiad; (OPAC) Innovative Interfaces, Inc; (Serials) Innovative Interfaces, Inc
Database Vendor: ABC-CLIO, ACM (Association for Computing Machinery), Agricola, Alexander Street Press, American Chemical Society, American Mathematical Society, American Physical Society, American Psychological Association (APA), Annual Reviews, ARTstor, Blackwell, Bowker, Cambridge Scientific Abstracts, CQ Press, Dialog, Dun & Bradstreet, ebrary, EBSCO Information Services, EBSCOhost, Elsevier, Emerald, Facts on File, Gale Cengage Learning, Haworth Pres Inc, Hoovers, IEEE (Institute of Electrical & Electronics Engineers), Ingenta, Innovative Interfaces, Inc, JSTOR, LexisNexis, Medline, Mergent Online, Nature Publishing Group, OCLC FirstSearch, OCLC WorldShare Interlibrary Loan, OVID Technologies, Oxford Online, Project MUSE, ProQuest, PubMed, RefWorks, Sage, ScienceDirect, Scopus, SerialsSolutions, Springer-Verlag, Standard & Poor's, Swets Information Services, Wiley, Wiley InterScience, YBP Library Services
Wireless access
Publications: Guides & Catalogs to Special Collections
Partic in Connect NY; Long Island Library Resources Council; Metropolitan New York Library Council; OCLC Online Computer Library Center, Inc; Southeastern New York Library Resources Council; Westchester Academic Library Directors Organization (WALDO)
Special Services for the Deaf - ADA equip; Am sign lang & deaf culture; Assistive tech; Bks on deafness & sign lang; Closed caption videos; Coll on deaf educ; Deaf publ; Spec interest per; Staff with knowledge of sign lang; TTY equip; Videos & decoder
Special Services for the Blind - Accessible computers; Assistive/Adapted tech devices, equip & products; Closed circuit TV; Computer with voice synthesizer for visually impaired persons; Copier with enlargement capabilities; IBM screen reader; Large print bks; Magnifiers; PC for handicapped; Scanner for conversion & translation of mats; Screen enlargement software for people with visual disabilities; Screen reader software; Text reader; ZoomText magnification & reading software
Open Mon-Thurs 8am-Midnight, Fri & Sat 8-8, Sun 10am-Midnight
Friends of the Library Group

P GARDEN CITY PUBLIC LIBRARY*, 60 Seventh St, 11530-2891. SAN 311-2276. Tel: 516-742-8405. FAX: 516-742-2675. Web Site: www.gardencitypl.org, www.nassaulibrary.org/gardenc/. *Dir,* Carolyn Voegler; *Ch Serv,* Donna Furey; *Ch Serv,* Laura Giunta; *Ch Serv,* Barbara Grace; *Circ,* Jeanette Nicoletti; *Computer Serv,* Joseph Agolia; *Ref Serv,* Martin Bowe; *Ref Serv,* Laura Flanagan; *Ref Serv,* Ann Garnett; *Tech Serv,* Nancy Sherwood; *YA Serv,* Marge Kelly; Staff 12 (MLS 12)
Founded 1952. Pop 21,672; Circ 336,923
Jun 2009-May 2010 Income $3,617,612. Mats Exp $332,666. Sal $2,393,498
Library Holdings: Bk Vols 143,613; Per Subs 440
Special Collections: Garden City Archives; Long Island History
Automation Activity & Vendor Info: (Circulation) Innovative Interfaces, Inc; (OPAC) Innovative Interfaces, Inc
Database Vendor: EBSCOhost, Facts on File, Gale Cengage Learning, Grolier Online, LearningExpress, OCLC FirstSearch, ProQuest, ReferenceUSA, Standard & Poor's
Wireless access
Function: Archival coll, Art exhibits, Bks on CD, CD-ROM, Children's prog, Copy machines, Exhibits, Free DVD rentals, Handicapped accessible, Homebound delivery serv, ILL available, Mus passes, Music CDs, Notary serv, Online cat, OverDrive digital audio bks, Photocopying/Printing, Prog for adults, Prog for children & young adult, Pub access computers, Ref serv available, Story hour, Summer reading prog, Tax forms, Telephone ref, Wheelchair accessible
Publications: Newsletter
Special Services for the Deaf - Assistive tech
Open Mon & Wed 9:30-9, Tues, Fri & Sat 9:30-5, Thurs 1-9, Sun (Mid Oct-Mid May) 1-5
Friends of the Library Group

SR GEORGE MERCER JR SCHOOL OF THEOLOGY*, Mercer Theological Library, 65 Fourth St, 11530. SAN 311-2284. Tel: 516-248-4800, Ext 39. FAX: 516-248-4883. Web Site: www.mercerschool.org, www.youseemore.com/gmercer. *Librn & Archivist,* Charles Lee Egleston; E-mail: cegleston@dioceseli.org; Staff 1 (MLS 1)
Founded 1955. Enrl 20; Fac 1
Library Holdings: DVDs 40; Bk Titles 36,000; Per Subs 70; Videos 50
Subject Interests: Church hist, Relig educ, Theol
Automation Activity & Vendor Info: (Cataloging) CARL.Solution (TLC); (Circulation) CARL.Solution (TLC); (OPAC) CARL.Solution (TLC)
Wireless access
Function: Archival coll, Art exhibits, CD-ROM, ILL available
Open Mon-Fri 9-4:30
Restriction: Access at librarian's discretion

L MEYER, SUOZZI, ENGLISH & KLEIN*, Law Library, 990 Stewart Ave, Ste 300, 11530. (Mail add: PO Box 9194, 11530), SAN 372-4344. Tel: 516-741-6565. FAX: 516-741-6706. *In Charge,* Linda Doell
Library Holdings: Bk Vols 10,000
Restriction: Not open to pub

J NASSAU COMMUNITY COLLEGE*, A Holly Patterson Library, One Education Dr, 11530-6793. SAN 311-2306. Tel: 516-572-7400. Interlibrary Loan Service Tel: 516-572-7845. FAX: 516-572-7846. Web Site: library.ncc.edu. *Chair,* Nancy Williamson; Tel: 516-572-7400, Ext 4206; *Instrul Serv Librn,* John Day; *Automation Syst Coordr,* Sonel Emin; *Acq,* Sharon Russin; *Cat,* Lisa A Errico; *Cat,* Katrina Frazier; *Circ,* Richard Erben; *Doc, Ref,* Charles Owusu; *ILL, Ref,* David Crugnola; *Media Spec,* Ken Bellafiore; *Media Spec,* Richard Delbango; *Media Spec,* Gerald Leibowitz; *Per,* Rosanne Humes; *Ref,* Donna Seidl; *Ref,* Marsha Spiegelman; *Ref,* Bellinda Wise; *Ref Serv,* Linda Gorman; Staff 18 (MLS 14, Non-MLS 4)
Founded 1959. Enrl 20,000; Fac 700
Library Holdings: Bk Titles 161,000; Bk Vols 179,000; Per Subs 400
Special Collections: Dozenal Society; G Wilson Knight Interdisciplinary Society
Subject Interests: Fashion, Long Island hist
Publications: From the Stacks; Library Newsletter
Partic in Long Island Library Resources Council
Special Services for the Blind - Computer with voice synthesizer for visually impaired persons; VisualTek equip

GARDINER

P GARDINER LIBRARY*, 133 Farmer's Tpk, 12525-5517. (Mail add: PO Box 223, 12525-0223), SAN 376-3145. Tel: 845-255-1255. FAX: 845-255-1265. E-mail: gar@rcls.org. Web Site: www.gardinerlibrary.org. *Dir,* Nell Boucher
Library Holdings: Bk Titles 13,500; Per Subs 40
Automation Activity & Vendor Info: (Cataloging) Horizon; (Circulation) Horizon; (Course Reserve) Horizon; (ILL) Horizon; (OPAC) Horizon; (Serials) Horizon
Wireless access
Mem of Ramapo Catskill Library System
Open Mon-Thurs 10-8, Fri 10-6, Sat 11-4, Sun 12-4
Friends of the Library Group

GARNERVILLE

P HAVERSTRAW KINGS DAUGHTERS PUBLIC LIBRARY*, Ten W Ramapo Rd, 10923. SAN 352-5244. Tel: 845-786-3800. FAX: 845-786-3791. E-mail: information@hkdpl.org. Web Site: www.hkdpl.org. *Dir,* Claudia Depkin; *Asst Dir,* Donna Sopalsky; E-mail: dsopalsk@rcls.org; *Head, Adult Serv,* Naomi Goldberg Honor; E-mail: nhonor@rcls.org; *Head, Youth Serv,* Tara Morris; E-mail: tmorris@rcls.org; Staff 38.7 (MLS 12.7, Non-MLS 26)
Founded 1895. Pop 32,540; Circ 336,745
Jul 2011-Jun 2012 Income (Main Library and Branch(s)) $4,813,458, Locally Generated Income $4,674,162, Other $8,156. Mats Exp $425,299, Books $199,007, Per/Ser (Incl. Access Fees) $13,000, Micro $4,000, AV Mat $81,973, Electronic Ref Mat (Incl. Access Fees) $16,000. Sal $1,267,322 (Prof $971,768)
Library Holdings: Audiobooks 2,996; CDs 5,100; DVDs 11,853; Large Print Bks 1,840; Bk Vols 112,441; Per Subs 136; Videos 2,487
Special Collections: Local History Coll (focus on Haverstraw & the Hudson Valley); Spanish Language Material
Automation Activity & Vendor Info: (Cataloging) SirsiDynix; (Circulation) SirsiDynix; (ILL) SirsiDynix; (OPAC) SirsiDynix
Wireless access
Function: Adult bk club, Adult literacy prog, After school storytime, Art exhibits, Bilingual assistance for Spanish patrons, Bks on CD, CD-ROM, Children's prog, Computer training, Computers for patron use, Copy machines, Distance learning, E-Reserves, Electronic databases & coll, Exhibits, Fax serv, Free DVD rentals, Handicapped accessible, Homebound delivery serv, ILL available, Mail & tel request accepted, Mus passes, Music CDs, Notary serv, Online cat, Outreach serv, OverDrive digital audio bks, Photocopying/Printing, Preschool outreach, Prof lending libr, Prog for adults, Prog for children & young adult, Pub access computers, Ref & res, Ref serv available, Scanner, Senior computer classes, Story hour, Summer reading prog, Tax forms, Teen prog, Telephone ref, VHS videos, Video lending libr, Wheelchair accessible, Workshops
Mem of Ramapo Catskill Library System
Special Services for the Deaf - Bks on deafness & sign lang; TTY equip
Special Services for the Blind - Bks on cassette; Bks on CD; Talking bks
Open Mon-Thurs 10-9, Fri 10-5:30, Sat 10-5, Sun 1-5
Branches: 1
VILLAGE BRANCH, 85 Main St, Haverstraw, 10927, SAN 352-521X. Tel: 845-429-3445. FAX: 845-429-7313. *Br Mgr,* Charlotte Van Hein; Staff 19 (MLS 19)
Founded 1895. Pop 28,942; Circ 219,368
Special Collections: Haverstraw Bay Photo Archives; North Rockland History Coll
Subject Interests: Career, Local hist, Spanish (Lang)
Automation Activity & Vendor Info: (Circulation) Horizon; (ILL) Horizon; (OPAC) Horizon
Publications: Bibliographies (Reference guide); Bookmarks (Consumer guide); Computer Orientation Booklet (Consumer guide)
Special Services for the Deaf - Bks on deafness & sign lang; Video & TTY relay via computer
Special Services for the Blind - Bks on CD; Magnifiers
Open Mon 12-8, Tues-Thurs 10-6, Fri 10-5:30, Sat 10-5

GARRISON

S ALICE CURTIS DESMOND & HAMILTON FISH LIBRARY*, 472 Rte 403, 10524. (Mail add: PO Box 265, 10524). Tel: 845-424-3020. FAX: 845-424-4061. E-mail: dfl@highlands.com. Web Site: desmondfishlibrary.org. *Dir,* Carol H Donick; E-mail: donick@highlands.com
Founded 1977. Pop 6,900; Circ 61,994
Jan 2007-Dec 2007 Income $523,438, State $2,131, City $20,000. Mats Exp $32,100, Books $22,149, Per/Ser (Incl. Access Fees) $2,000, AV Mat $7,620, Electronic Ref Mat (Incl. Access Fees) $331. Sal $254,357 (Prof $67,586)
Library Holdings: AV Mats 7,195; Bk Vols 29,568; Per Subs 80; Talking Bks 2,394
Special Collections: Hudson River School Art Reference Coll, slides
Automation Activity & Vendor Info: (Circulation) Innovative Interfaces, Inc; (OPAC) Innovative Interfaces, Inc
Wireless access
Mem of Mid-Hudson Library System
Open Mon, Wed & Fri 10-5, Tues & Thurs 2-9, Sat 10-1
Friends of the Library Group

R FRANCISCAN FRIARS OF THE ATONEMENT LIBRARY*, Graymoor Rte 9, 10524-0300. (Mail add: PO Box 300, 10524-0300), SAN 352-4795. Tel: 845-424-3671. FAX: 845-424-2162. Web Site: www.atonementfriars.org. *Dir,* Jim Gardner
Founded 1960
Library Holdings: Per Subs 88
Special Collections: History of the Atonement Friars (Paul Watson Research Center), bks, doc
Subject Interests: Anglicanism, English reformation, N Am ecumenical hist, N Am ecumenical theol, Spirituality
Publications: Ecumenical Trends
Open Mon-Fri 8-5

S THE HASTINGS CENTER*, Robert S Morison Memorial Library, 21 Malcolm Gordon Dr, 10524-5555. SAN 326-1530. Tel: 845-424-4040, Ext 256. FAX: 845-424-4545. E-mail: mail@thehastingscenter.org. Web Site: www.thehastingscenter.org. Staff 1 (MLS 1)
Founded 1969
Library Holdings: Bk Titles 8,000; Per Subs 220
Subject Interests: Bioethics, Environ med, Med, Med ethics
Database Vendor: LexisNexis, OCLC FirstSearch, PubMed, Wilson - Wilson Web
Publications: Hastings Center Report; Hastings Center Studies in Ethics; IRB: A Review of Ethics & Human Resources
Partic in Southeastern New York Library Resources Council
Restriction: Open to others by appt, Staff use only

GENESEO

C STATE UNIVERSITY OF NEW YORK COLLEGE*, Milne Library, SUNY Geneseo, One College Circle, 14454-1498. SAN 352-4825. Interlibrary Loan Service Tel: 585-245-5589. Reference Tel: 585-245-5595. Administration Tel: 585-245-5591. Interlibrary Loan Service FAX: 585-245-5003. Administration FAX: 585-245-5769. Web Site: library.geneseo.edu. *Dir,* Edwin Rivenburgh; E-mail: edr@geneseo.edu; *Assoc Libr Dir,* Cyril Oberlander; E-mail: cyril@geneseo.edu; *Head,*

Teacher Educ Res Ctr, Barbara Clarke; Tel: 585-245-5592, E-mail: clarke@geneseo.edu; *Coll Develop Librn,* Kate Pitcher; Tel: 585-245-5064, E-mail: pitcher@geneseo.edu; *Cat,* Joan Cottone; *Circ, ILL,* Sonja Landes; *Govt Doc,* Tom Ottaviano; *Ser,* Diane Johnson; Staff 30 (MLS 18, Non-MLS 12)
Founded 1871. Enrl 5,308; Fac 329; Highest Degree: Master
Library Holdings: e-books 7,930; Bk Vols 637,100; Per Subs 828
Special Collections: Aldous Huxley Coll; American Architecture (Carl F Schmidt Coll), mss, bd; Children's Literature (Juvenile & Young Adult Coll); Regional History (Genesee Valley Historical Coll) bk, mss; State University of New York College at Geneseo Archives, mss, bk; Wadsworth Family (Wadsworth Homestead Papers, 1800-1950), mss. State Document Depository; US Document Depository
Subject Interests: Educ, Music
Automation Activity & Vendor Info: (Course Reserve) Ex Libris Group; (ILL) OCLC ILLiad; (OPAC) Ex Libris Group; (Serials) Ex Libris Group
Wireless access
Publications: Guide to the College Libraries (Newsletter); Serials Holdings List
Partic in OCLC Online Computer Library Center, Inc; Rochester Regional Library Council
Open Mon-Thurs 7:30am-1am, Fri 7:30am-9pm, Sat 10-9, Sun 10am-1am
Friends of the Library Group

P WADSWORTH LIBRARY*, 24 Center St, 14454. SAN 311-2349. Tel: 585-243-0440. FAX: 585-243-0429. E-mail: wadsworth@pls-net.org. Web Site: www.wadsworth.pls-net.org. *Dir,* Anna H Grace; *Ch Serv,* Sarah Matthews; Staff 5 (MLS 2, Non-MLS 3)
Founded 1842. Pop 10,730; Circ 56,672
Jul 2009-Jun 2010 Income $261,307, State $13,043, Locally Generated Income $237,264, Other $11,000. Mats Exp $59,788, Books $41,413, Per/Ser (Incl. Access Fees) $3,430, AV Mat $14,945. Sal $189,000 (Prof $76,981)
Library Holdings: AV Mats 429; Electronic Media & Resources 19; Bk Vols 25,879; Per Subs 82
Special Collections: Law Library; Local History
Subject Interests: Parenting
Automation Activity & Vendor Info: (Acquisitions) SirsiDynix; (Cataloging) SirsiDynix; (Circulation) SirsiDynix; (ILL) SirsiDynix; (OPAC) SirsiDynix; (Serials) SirsiDynix
Database Vendor: Booksite, BWI, WT Cox
Wireless access
Function: Adult bk club, Bk reviews (Group), Bks on cassette, Bks on CD, CD-ROM, Children's prog, Computers for patron use, Copy machines, e-mail serv, Electronic databases & coll, Free DVD rentals, Games & aids for the handicapped, Handicapped accessible, Holiday prog, Home delivery & serv to Sr ctr & nursing homes, Homebound delivery serv, ILL available, Large print keyboards, Literacy & newcomer serv, Magnifiers for reading, Mail & tel request accepted, Online cat, Online searches, Orientations, Outreach serv, Photocopying/Printing, Preschool outreach, Prog for adults, Prog for children & young adult, Pub access computers, Ref serv available, Referrals accepted, Story hour, Summer reading prog, Tax forms, Teen prog, Telephone ref, VHS videos, Web-catalog, Wheelchair accessible, Workshops
Mem of Pioneer Library System
Special Services for the Deaf - ADA equip; Spec interest per
Special Services for the Blind - Bks available with recordings; Bks on cassette; Bks on CD; Computer access aids; Copier with enlargement capabilities; Home delivery serv; Info on spec aids & appliances; Large screen computer & software; Lending of low vision aids; ZoomText magnification & reading software
Open Mon-Thurs 10-8:30, Fri 1:30-6, Sat 10-3
Friends of the Library Group

GENEVA

P GENEVA PUBLIC LIBRARY*, 244 Main St, 14456-2370. SAN 311-2365. Tel: 315-789-5303. FAX: 315-789-9835. Web Site: genevapubliclibrary.net. *Dir,* Beth Horn; E-mail: GenevaLibraryDirector@owwl.org; Staff 20 (MLS 4, Non-MLS 16)
Founded 1905. Pop 17,500; Circ 160,000
Library Holdings: AV Mats 5,400; Bk Vols 77,500; Per Subs 137
Subject Interests: Local hist
Automation Activity & Vendor Info: (Circulation) SirsiDynix
Wireless access
Mem of Pioneer Library System
Open Mon & Tues 9-8, Wed & Thurs 9-7, Fri 9-6, Sat 9-2
Friends of the Library Group

C HOBART & WILLIAM SMITH COLLEGES*, Warren Hunting Smith Library, 334 Pulteney St, 14456. SAN 311-2381. Tel: 315-781-3550. Reference Tel: 315-781-3552. FAX: 315-781-3560. E-mail: library@hws.edu. Web Site: library.hws.edu. *Head Librn,* Vincent Boisselle; Tel: 315-781-3549; *Head, Pub Serv,* Joseph J Chmura; *Head, Tech Serv,* Sara Greenleaf; Staff 21.5 (MLS 7.5, Non-MLS 14)
Founded 1824. Enrl 2,282; Fac 187; Highest Degree: Bachelor
Library Holdings: AV Mats 13,610; e-books 81,050; e-journals 45,883; Microforms 47,701; Bk Vols 402,358; Per Subs 721
Special Collections: Adaline Glasheen Coll; Alexander Campbell Coll; Arch Merrill Coll; David Bates Douglass Coll; E E Griffith Coll; George M B Hawley Coll; Leo Srole Coll
Subject Interests: Behav sci, English lit, Feminism, Hist, Local hist, Soc sci
Automation Activity & Vendor Info: (Acquisitions) Ex Libris Group; (Cataloging) Ex Libris Group; (Circulation) Ex Libris Group; (Course Reserve) Ex Libris Group; (ILL) OCLC ILLiad; (OPAC) Ex Libris Group; (Serials) Ex Libris Group
Database Vendor: Alexander Street Press, American Chemical Society, ARTstor, CredoReference, ebrary, EBSCOhost, Gale Cengage Learning, JSTOR, LexisNexis, Newsbank-Readex, OCLC WorldShare Interlibrary Loan, Project MUSE, ProQuest, ScienceDirect, SerialsSolutions
Wireless access
Partic in Connect NY; Information Delivery Services Project (IDS); OCLC Online Computer Library Center, Inc; Rochester Regional Library Council
Open Mon-Thurs 8am-1am, Fri 8am-11pm, Sat 9am-11pm, Sun 9am-1am

GERMANTOWN

P GERMANTOWN LIBRARY*, 31 Palatine Park Rd, 12526-5309. SAN 376-5830. Tel: 518-537-5800. FAX: 518-537-5928. E-mail: germantownlibrary@valstar.net. Web Site: www.germantownlibrary.org. *Dir,* Lynn Place
Founded 1948. Pop 2,010
Library Holdings: Bk Titles 18,000; Per Subs 45
Subject Interests: Gardening, Local hist
Automation Activity & Vendor Info: (Acquisitions) Innovative Interfaces, Inc; (Cataloging) Innovative Interfaces, Inc; (Circulation) Innovative Interfaces, Inc; (Course Reserve) Innovative Interfaces, Inc; (ILL) Innovative Interfaces, Inc; (Media Booking) Innovative Interfaces, Inc; (OPAC) Innovative Interfaces, Inc; (Serials) Innovative Interfaces, Inc
Wireless access
Function: ILL available, Photocopying/Printing
Mem of Mid-Hudson Library System
Special Services for the Blind - Audio mat; Large print bks; Talking bks
Open Tues 9-7:30, Wed 9-12, Thurs 5-8, Fri 9-5, Sat 9-2
Friends of the Library Group

GILBERTSVILLE

P GILBERTSVILLE FREE LIBRARY*, 17 Commercial St, 13776-0332. (Mail add: PO Box 332, 13776-0332), SAN 311-239X. Tel: 607-783-2832. FAX: 607-783-2832. E-mail: gi.ill@4cls.org. Web Site: www.gilbertsvillefreelibrary.org. *Dir,* Susan Rowe
Founded 1889. Pop 388
Library Holdings: Bk Titles 8,000; Per Subs 30
Subject Interests: Local hist
Wireless access
Mem of Four County Library System
Open Mon 3:15-5:15, Tues & Fri 10-12 & 3:15-5:15, Wed 10-12, 3:15-5:15 & 6:30-8, Sat 9-1
Friends of the Library Group

GLEN COVE

P GLEN COVE PUBLIC LIBRARY*, Four Glen Cove Ave, 11542-2885. SAN 311-242X. Tel: 516-676-2130. FAX: 516-676-2788. Administration FAX: 516-676-2094. E-mail: glencove@glencovelibrary.org. Web Site: www.glencovelibrary.org. *Dir,* Antonia Petrash; *Adult Serv,* Amy Gretchyn; *Automation Syst Coordr, Tech Serv,* Alexander Bellos; *Ch Serv,* Mary Beth Coco; *Ref,* Joanna Filippone; Staff 35 (MLS 13, Non-MLS 22)
Founded 1894. Pop 26,622; Circ 142,178
Jul 2009-Jun 2010 Income $2,578,500, Locally Generated Income $2,460,500, Other $42,000. Mats Exp $221,500, Books $100,000, Per/Ser (Incl. Access Fees) $47,000, AV Mat $33,500, Electronic Ref Mat (Incl. Access Fees) $40,000, Presv $1,000. Sal $1,312,000 (Prof $761,000)
Library Holdings: AV Mats 9,437; Bk Vols 136,226; Per Subs 250
Special Collections: Long Island & Glen Cove History Coll
Automation Activity & Vendor Info: (Acquisitions) Innovative Interfaces, Inc - Millenium; (Cataloging) Innovative Interfaces, Inc - Millenium; (Circulation) Innovative Interfaces, Inc - Millenium; (OPAC) Innovative Interfaces, Inc
Database Vendor: ALLDATA Online, CountryWatch, EBSCOhost, Facts on File, Gale Cengage Learning, Greenwood Publishing Group, Innovative Interfaces, Inc, OCLC FirstSearch, OCLC WorldShare Interlibrary Loan, ProQuest, World Book Online
Wireless access
Function: Archival coll, Art exhibits, AV serv, Bi-weekly Writer's Group, CD-ROM, Handicapped accessible, Home delivery & serv to Sr ctr & nursing homes, Homebound delivery serv, ILL available, Magnifiers for reading, Music CDs, Newsp ref libr, Online searches, Orientations, Photocopying/Printing, Prog for adults, Prog for children & young adult,

Ref serv available, Spoken cassettes & CDs, Summer reading prog, Telephone ref, VCDs, VHS videos, Wheelchair accessible, Workshops
Publications: Newsletter (Bi-monthly)
Mem of Nassau Library System
Special Services for the Deaf - Assisted listening device; Bks on deafness & sign lang; Sign lang interpreter upon request for prog
Special Services for the Blind - Bks on cassette; Bks on CD
Open Mon-Thurs (Oct-May) 9-9, Fri & Sat 9-5, Sun 1-5
Restriction: Open to pub for ref & circ; with some limitations, Pub use on premises
Friends of the Library Group

S HOLOCAUST MEMORIAL & TOLERANCE CENTER OF NASSAU COUNTY*, Louis Posner Memorial Library, Welwyn Preserve, 100 Crescent Beach Rd, 11542. SAN 377-2071. Tel: 516-571-8040, Ext 102, 516-571-8040, Ext 104. FAX: 516-571-8041. E-mail: info@holocaust-nassau.org. Web Site: www.holocaust-nassau.org. *Sr Dir,* Beth Lilach; Tel: 516-571-8040, Ext 105, E-mail: bethlilach@holocaust-nassau.org; *Dir of Develop,* Judy Vladimir; Tel: 516-571-8040, Ext 119, E-mail: judyvladimir@holocaust-nassau.org; Staff 6 (MLS 6)
Founded 1994
Jan 2006-Dec 2006 Income $10,000. Mats Exp $4,200, Books $3,000, AV Equip $300, AV Mat $400, Electronic Ref Mat (Incl. Access Fees) $500
Library Holdings: Bk Titles 6,000; Videos 300
Special Collections: Holocaust Curricula & Graphics. Oral History
Subject Interests: Holocaust
Automation Activity & Vendor Info: (Acquisitions) Follett Software; (Cataloging) Follett Software; (Circulation) Follett Software; (Course Reserve) Follett Software; (ILL) Follett Software; (Media Booking) Follett Software; (OPAC) Follett Software; (Serials) Follett Software
Function: Ref serv available
Restriction: Circ limited, Open by appt only

C WEBB INSTITUTE*, Livingston Library, 298 Crescent Beach Rd, 11542-1398. SAN 311-2446. Tel: 516-671-0439. FAX: 516-674-9838. Web Site: www.webb-institute.edu. *Dir,* Patricia M Prescott; E-mail: pprescot@webb-institute.edu; Staff 1 (MLS 1)
Founded 1932. Enrl 83; Fac 14; Highest Degree: Master
Library Holdings: Bk Titles 45,000; Per Subs 255
Special Collections: Marine Engineering; Marine History; Naval Architecture
Automation Activity & Vendor Info: (Acquisitions) Ex Libris Group; (Cataloging) Ex Libris Group; (Circulation) Ex Libris Group; (Course Reserve) Ex Libris Group; (ILL) Ex Libris Group; (OPAC) Ex Libris Group; (Serials) Ex Libris Group
Wireless access
Publications: Acquisitions List
Partic in Long Island Library Resources Council; OCLC Online Computer Library Center, Inc
Restriction: Open to pub by appt only

GLEN HEAD

P GOLD COAST PUBLIC LIBRARY*, 50 Railroad Ave, 11545. SAN 378-4517. Tel: 516-759-8300. FAX: 516-759-8308. E-mail: goldcoast1@optonline.net. Web Site. www.goldcoastlibrary.org. *Dir,* Genellen McGrath; *Adult Ref Librn,* Christopher Schnupp; *Adult Ref Librn,* Susan Zaremba; *Ch,* Jeffrey Vasconi; Staff 4 (MLS 4)
Founded 2005. Pop 10,974; Circ 79,489
Jan 2008-Dec 2008 Income $1,208,350
Library Holdings: AV Mats 1,406; Bk Vols 10,100; Per Subs 50
Automation Activity & Vendor Info: (Cataloging) Innovative Interfaces, Inc; (Circulation) Innovative Interfaces, Inc; (OPAC) Innovative Interfaces, Inc
Database Vendor: EBSCO Information Services, Gale Cengage Learning, Overdrive, Inc, ProQuest, ReferenceUSA
Wireless access
Mem of Nassau Library System
Open Mon, Tues & Thurs 10-9, Fri & Sat 10-6, Sun (Sept-May) 12-5
Friends of the Library Group

GLENS FALLS

P CRANDALL PUBLIC LIBRARY*, 251 Glen St, 12801-3593. SAN 311-2470. Tel: 518-792-6508. Circulation Tel: 518-792-6508, Ext 2. Reference Tel: 518-792-6508, Ext 3. FAX: 518-792-5251. E-mail: info@crandalllibrary.org. Web Site: www.crandalllibrary.org. *Dir,* Kathleen Naftaly; E-mail: naftaly@crandalllibrary.com; *Dir of Develop,* Lynn Shanks; *Head, Adult Serv,* Andrea Herman; *Head, Ch,* Pamela Frazier; *Head, Circ,* Sue Laing; *Teen Librn,* Frieda Toth; Staff 23 (MLS 13, Non-MLS 10)
Founded 1892. Pop 53,621; Circ 769,530
Jan 2009-Dec 2009 Income $4,025,395, Locally Generated Income $3,041,429, Other $983,966. Mats Exp $307,750. Sal $1,721,762
Library Holdings: AV Mats 33,333; Bk Vols 168,160; Per Subs 332
Special Collections: Americana; consumer Health Information; Family Focus Center Coll; Folklife & Local History of Northern New York Adirondacks & Upper Hudson Valley, bks, clippings, genealogy, mss, photogs & serials
Automation Activity & Vendor Info: (Acquisitions) Innovative Interfaces, Inc; (Cataloging) Innovative Interfaces, Inc; (Circulation) Innovative Interfaces, Inc; (OPAC) Innovative Interfaces, Inc
Database Vendor: Baker & Taylor, EBSCOhost, Gale Cengage Learning, OCLC WorldShare Interlibrary Loan
Wireless access
Publications: Annual Report; Budget Flyer; Film Flyer; Folklife Center Program Booklets; Fundraising Brochures
Mem of Southern Adirondack Library System
Open Mon-Thurs 9-9, Fri 9-6, Sat 9-5, Sun (Sept-June) 1-5
Friends of the Library Group

S GLENS FALLS-QUEENSBURY HISTORICAL ASSOCIATION*, Chapman Historical Museum Library, 348 Glen St, 12801. SAN 327-7178. Tel: 518-793-2826. FAX: 518-793-2831. E-mail: contactus@chapmanmuseum.org. Web Site: www.chapmanmuseum.org. *Exec Dir,* Timothy Weidner; *Curator,* Jillian Mulder
Founded 1967
Library Holdings: Bk Vols 30,000
Special Collections: Seneca Ray Stoddard Coll (1864-1917), photos; Ephemera and manuscript collections; family papers, lettters; business letters
Subject Interests: Genealogy, Local hist
Wireless access
Open Tues & Thurs 1-4
Restriction: Closed stack

S HYDE COLLECTION LIBRARY*, 161 Warren St, 12801. SAN 311-2489. Tel: 518-792-1761. FAX: 518-792-9197. Web Site: www.hydecollection.org. *Exec Dir,* Charles Allan Guerin; *Chief Curator,* Erin Coe; E-mail: ecoe@hydecollection.org
Founded 1963
Library Holdings: Bk Vols 1,080
Subject Interests: Art, Classics, First edition, Hist, Rare bks, Relig
Wireless access
Function: Res libr
Restriction: Open by appt only

GLOVERSVILLE

P GLOVERSVILLE PUBLIC LIBRARY*, 58 E Fulton St, 12078. SAN 311-2519. Tel: 518-725-2819. FAX: 518-773-0292. E-mail: gpl@sals.edu. Web Site: www.gloversvillelibrary.org. *Dir,* Barbara Madonna; *Head, Ch,* Sherry Gennett; Staff 10 (MLS 2, Non-MLS 8)
Founded 1880. Pop 15,413; Circ 51,621
Library Holdings: AV Mats 4,000; Bk Vols 44,844; Per Subs 109
Subject Interests: Local hist
Automation Activity & Vendor Info: (Cataloging) Innovative Interfaces, Inc; (Circulation) Innovative Interfaces, Inc; (OPAC) Innovative Interfaces, Inc; (Serials) Innovative Interfaces, Inc
Wireless access
Publications: Friends of the Library (Newsletter)
Mem of Mohawk Valley Library System
Open Tues & Wed 10-7, Thurs & Fri 10-6, Sat 10-4
Friends of the Library Group

R KNESSETH ISRAEL SYNAGOGUE LIBRARY*, 34 E Fulton St, 12078. SAN 311-2527. Tel: 518-725-0649. FAX: 518-725-0640. *In Charge,* Debbie Finkle; E-mail: kisdeb@gmail.com
Founded 1975
Library Holdings: Bk Titles 685; Per Subs 4
Subject Interests: Judaica
Restriction: Staff use only

GORHAM

P GORHAM FREE LIBRARY*, 2664 Main St, 14461. (Mail add: PO Box 211, 14461-0211), SAN 311-2535. Tel: 585-526-6655. FAX: 585-526-6995. Web Site: www.gorham.pls-net.org. *Dir,* Diane Hovey; E-mail: dhovey@pls-net.org
Founded 1913. Pop 6,507; Circ 18,661
Library Holdings: Bk Vols 18,000; Per Subs 40
Automation Activity & Vendor Info: (Cataloging) SirsiDynix; (Circulation) SirsiDynix; (OPAC) SirsiDynix
Wireless access
Mem of Pioneer Library System
Open Mon & Wed 9-5, Tues & Thurs 2-8, Fri 2-6, Sat 9-12

GOSHEN

P GOSHEN PUBLIC LIBRARY & HISTORICAL SOCIETY*, 203 Main St, 10924. SAN 311-2551. Tel: 845-294-6606. FAX: 845-294-7158. Web Site: www.goshenpubliclibrary.org. *Actg Dir,* Matthew Gomm; *Head, Youth Serv,* Dave Phillips; Staff 8 (MLS 6, Non-MLS 2)
Founded 1894. Pop 16,784; Circ 141,535
Jul 2005-Jun 2006 Income $1,029,396, State $22,970, County $6,204, Locally Generated Income $997,922, Other $2,500. Mats Exp $81,525, Books $37,960, Per/Ser (Incl. Access Fees) $9,000, AV Mat $30,065, Electronic Ref Mat (Incl. Access Fees) $4,500. Sal $532,822
Library Holdings: AV Mats 218; Large Print Bks 1,455; Bk Vols 41,768; Per Subs 103; Talking Bks 2,374; Videos 3,927
Subject Interests: Local hist
Automation Activity & Vendor Info: (Cataloging) SirsiDynix; (Circulation) SirsiDynix; (ILL) SirsiDynix; (OPAC) SirsiDynix; (Serials) SirsiDynix
Wireless access
Function: Adult bk club, Computer training, Copy machines, E-Reserves, Electronic databases & coll, Fax serv, Homebound delivery serv, ILL available, Mail & tel request accepted, Music CDs, Prog for adults, Prog for children & young adult, Summer reading prog, Tax forms, Telephone ref, VHS videos
Publications: A Guide to the Manuscript Collection of the Goshen Library & Historical Society; History of the Goshen Public Library
Mem of Ramapo Catskill Library System
Open Mon-Tues 9-8, Fri 10-5, Sat 9-5, Sun 1-5
Friends of the Library Group

S HARNESS RACING MUSEUM & HALL OF FAME, Peter D Haughton Memorial Library, 240 Main St, 10924-2157. SAN 311-256X. Tel: 845-294-6330. FAX: 845-294-3463. E-mail: library@harnessmuseum.com. Web Site: www.harnessmuseum.com. *Dir,* Janet Terhune; *Mgr, Info & Libr Serv,* Paul Wilder; Staff 1 (MLS 1)
Founded 1951
Library Holdings: AV Mats 2,500; Bk Titles 523; Bk Vols 1,600; Per Subs 12
Special Collections: Currier & Ives Travelling Exhibit; History & collections of standard bred horse & harness racing
Subject Interests: Art of the Am trotting horse breed, Harness racing, Hist of the Am trotting horse breed
Restriction: By permission only, Mem only
Friends of the Library Group

L NYS SUPREME COURT*, Law Library of Orange County, Orange County Govt Ctr, 255-275 Main St, 10924. SAN 311-2578. Tel: 845-291-3138. FAX: 845-291-2595. *Librn,* Suparna Barua; Staff 1 (MLS 1)
Library Holdings: Bk Titles 350; Bk Vols 24,000; Per Subs 10
Database Vendor: LexisNexis
Function: For res purposes
Open Mon-Fri 9-1 & 2-5
Restriction: Not a lending libr

GOUVERNEUR

S GOUVERNEUR CORRECTIONAL FACILITY*, General Library, Scott Settlement Rd, 13642. Tel: 315-287-7351, Ext 4600. FAX: 315-287-7351, Ext 3299. *Librn,* Lynne H Matott
Library Holdings: Bk Vols 20,000
Automation Activity & Vendor Info: (Cataloging) Follett Software; (Circulation) Follett Software; (OPAC) Follett Software

S READING ROOM ASSOCIATION OF GOUVERNEUR*, 60 Church St, 13642. SAN 311-2594. Tel: 315-287-0191. FAX: 315-287-0191. E-mail: goulib@ncls.org. Web Site: www.gouverneurlibrary.org. *Dir,* Charlotte Garofalo; Staff 1 (Non-MLS 1)
Founded 1885
Library Holdings: AV Mats 663; Bk Titles 16,484; Per Subs 34; Talking Bks 738
Automation Activity & Vendor Info: (Circulation) SirsiDynix
Wireless access
Function: Photocopying/Printing
Mem of North Country Library System
Open Mon, Tues & Thurs 12-8, Wed 9-5, Fri 12-5, Sat 10-12
Friends of the Library Group

GOWANDA

P GOWANDA FREE LIBRARY, 56 W Main St, 14070-1390. SAN 311-2608. Tel: 716-532-3451. FAX: 716-532-3415. E-mail: gfl@roadrunner.com. Web Site: www.cclslib.org/gowanda. *Mgr,* Cathy Lynn Walsh
Founded 1900. Pop 2,842; Circ 20,212
Library Holdings: DVDs 170; Bk Titles 24,770; Per Subs 36; Talking Bks 832; Videos 1,083
Special Collections: Indian Book Coll
Automation Activity & Vendor Info: (Circulation) SirsiDynix; (OPAC) SirsiDynix
Wireless access
Mem of Chautauqua-Cattaraugus Library System
Open Mon, Tues, Thurs & Fri 12:30-6:30, Sat 10-2

S NEW YORK STATE DEPARTMENT OF CORRECTIONAL SERVICES*, Gowanda Correctional Facility Library, PO Box 350, 14070-0350. Tel: 716-532-0177, Ext 4550. FAX: 716-532-0177. *Sr Librn,* Corinne Leone
Library Holdings: Audiobooks 1,200; AV Mats 1,000; DVDs 200; High Interest/Low Vocabulary Bk Vols 200; Large Print Bks 200; Bk Vols 25,500; Per Subs 96
Automation Activity & Vendor Info: (Cataloging) Follett Software; (Circulation) Follett Software; (Serials) EBSCO Online
Open Mon, Fri & Sat 8-3:30, Tues & Thurs 8-7, Wed 8-3:30 & 5:30-9, Sun 9-11 & 12:30-2

GRAFTON

P GRAFTON COMMUNITY LIBRARY*, 2455 NY Rte 2, 12082. (Mail add: PO Box H, 12082), SAN 311-2616. Tel: 518-279-0580. FAX: 518-279-0580. Web Site: www.graftoncommunitylibrary.org. *Dir,* Christian Collins; E-mail: director@graftoncommunitylibrary.org; *Libr Asst,* Amy Hart; Staff 2 (Non-MLS 2)
Founded 1946. Pop 1,989; Circ 14,935
Library Holdings: Bk Vols 11,918
Automation Activity & Vendor Info: (Cataloging) Horizon; (Circulation) Horizon; (OPAC) Horizon; (Serials) Horizon
Wireless access
Mem of Upper Hudson Library System
Open Mon, Tues, Thurs & Fri 3-7, Wed & Sat 10-1

GRAHAMSVILLE

P DANIEL PIERCE LIBRARY*, 328 Main St, 12740-5412. (Mail add: PO Box 268, 12740-0268), SAN 311-2624. Tel: 845-985-7233. FAX: 845-985-0135. E-mail: dpl@rcls.org. Web Site: www.danielpiercelibrary.org. *Dir,* Joann Gallagher
Founded 1898. Pop 2,800; Circ 7,441
Library Holdings: AV Mats 6,772; Electronic Media & Resources 78,041; Bk Vols 30,057; Per Subs 90
Automation Activity & Vendor Info: (Cataloging) Horizon; (Circulation) Horizon; (OPAC) Horizon
Mem of Ramapo Catskill Library System
Open Tues & Thurs 11-9, Wed & Fri 11-5, Sat 9-5
Friends of the Library Group

GRAND ISLAND

P GRAND ISLAND MEMORIAL LIBRARY*, 1715 Bedell Rd, 14072. SAN 311-2632. Tel: 716-773-7124. FAX: 716-774-1146. Web Site: www.buffalolib.org. *Dir,* Lynn Alan Konovitz
Pop 18,621; Circ 164,331
Jan 2010-Dec 2010 Income $497,602, State $4,977, County $460,440, Locally Generated Income $1,646. Mats Exp $78,958, Books $36,966, AV Mat $24,271, Electronic Ref Mat (Incl. Access Fees) $17,721. Sal $240,687 (Prof $116,194)
Library Holdings: AV Mats 11,372; Bk Titles 42,358; Bk Vols 49,416; Per Subs 114; Talking Bks 5,209
Automation Activity & Vendor Info: (Acquisitions) Baker & Taylor; (Circulation) SirsiDynix
Wireless access
Mem of Buffalo & Erie County Public Library System
Open Mon 10-9, Tues, Wed, Fri & Sat 10-5, Thurs 1-9
Friends of the Library Group

GRANVILLE

P PEMBER LIBRARY & MUSEUM OF NATURAL HISTORY*, 33 W Main St, 12832. SAN 311-2667. Tel: 518-642-2525. FAX: 518-642-2525. Web Site: pember.sals.edu. *Dir,* Ardyce Bresett; E-mail: abresett@sals.edu; Staff 4 (MLS 1, Non-MLS 3)
Founded 1909. Pop 2,644; Circ 38,140
Library Holdings: AV Mats 2,931; DVDs 300; Electronic Media & Resources 231; Bk Vols 19,045; Per Subs 85; Talking Bks 1,439; Videos 1,043
Subject Interests: Local hist
Automation Activity & Vendor Info: (Cataloging) Innovative Interfaces, Inc; (Circulation) Innovative Interfaces, Inc; (OPAC) Innovative Interfaces, Inc; (Serials) Innovative Interfaces, Inc
Wireless access
Function: Adult bk club, Archival coll, Audiobks via web, Bks on cassette, Bks on CD, Children's prog, Computers for patron use, Copy machines, Electronic databases & coll, Free DVD rentals, Handicapped accessible, ILL available, Online cat, Online ref, Online searches,

OverDrive digital audio bks, Photocopying/Printing, Ref serv available, VHS videos, Web-catalog
Mem of Southern Adirondack Library System
Special Services for the Blind - Large print bks; Talking bks
Open Tues 9-5, Wed & Thurs 1-8, Fri 12-5, Sat 10-3
Friends of the Library Group

GREAT NECK

P GREAT NECK LIBRARY, 159 Bayview Ave, 11023-1938. SAN 352-4884. Tel: 516-466-8055. FAX: 516-829-8297. Administration FAX: 516-487-6069. Web Site: www.greatnecklibrary.org. *Interim Dir,* Laura Weir; Tel: 516-466-8055, Ext 200, E-mail: lweir@greatnecklibrary.org; *Head, Ch,* Deidre Goode; E-mail: dgoode@greatnecklibrary.org; *Head, Circ,* Janet Fine; E-mail: jfine@greatnecklibrary.org; *Head, Ref (Info Serv),* Margery Chodosch; E-mail: mchodosch@greatnecklibrary.org; Staff 159 (MLS 46, Non-MLS 113)
Founded 1889. Pop 43,426; Circ 647,767
Jan 2009-Dec 2009 Income (Main Library and Branch(s)) $8,072,500, Federal $21,100, County $12,200, Locally Generated Income $7,824,000, Other $215,200. Mats Exp $772,000, Books $405,000, Per/Ser (Incl. Access Fees) $58,200, Manu Arch $3,000, Other Print Mats $24,000, Micro $12,500, AV Equip $1,000, AV Mat $113,400, Electronic Ref Mat (Incl. Access Fees) $152,900, Presv $2,000. Sal $4,627,300 (Prof $2,045,800)
Library Holdings: Bk Titles 197,442; Bk Vols 394,036; Per Subs 996
Subject Interests: Archit, Art, Behav sci, Soc sci
Automation Activity & Vendor Info: (Acquisitions) Innovative Interfaces, Inc; (Circulation) Innovative Interfaces, Inc; (OPAC) Innovative Interfaces, Inc
Database Vendor: EBSCOhost, Gale Cengage Learning, OCLC FirstSearch
Publications: Bimonthly Newsletter
Mem of Nassau Library System
Special Services for the Deaf - Assistive tech; TTY equip
Special Services for the Blind - Closed circuit TV magnifier; Vantage closed circuit TV magnifier
Open Mon, Tues, Thurs & Fri 9-9, Wed 10-9, Sat 9-6, Sun (Sept-June) 1-5
Branches: 3
LAKEVILLE, 475 Great Neck Rd, 11021, SAN 352-4914. Tel: 516-466-8055, Ext 231. FAX: 516-466-7863. *Br Mgr,* Ruth Klement; Staff 8 (MLS 2, Non-MLS 6)
Library Holdings: Bk Vols 24,300; Per Subs 30
Open Mon, Tues, Thurs & Fri 9-6, Sat 10-6, Wed 12-8
PARKVILLE, Ten Campbell St, New Hyde Park, 11040, SAN 352-4949. Tel: 516-466-8055, Ext 234. FAX: 516-437-1929. *Br Mgr,* Jayne Alexander; Tel: 516-466-8055, Ext 235; Staff 10 (MLS 3, Non-MLS 7)
Open Mon & Fri 9-6, Tues & Thurs 9-9, Wed & Sat 10-6, Sun 1-5
STATION, 40-B Great Neck Rd, 11021, SAN 352-4973. Tel: 516-466-8055, Ext 232. FAX: 516-466-4917. *Br Mgr,* Kathleen Cotter; Tel: 516-466-8055, Ext 233; Staff 10 (MLS 2, Non-MLS 8)
Open Mon & Thurs 9-9, Tues & Fri 9-6, Wed & Sat 10-6,

GREECE

P GREECE PUBLIC LIBRARY*, Two Vince Tofany Blvd, 14612. SAN 353-9946. Tel: 585-225-8951. FAX: 585-225-2777. E-mail: grwebmst@libraryweb.org. Web Site: www.greecelibrary.org. *Dir,* Bernadette Foster; *Admin Senior Librn,* Clare Maloney; *Adult Serv,* Diane Desimon; *Adult Serv,* Ann Patterson; *Ch Serv,* Catherine Henderson; Staff 7 (MLS 7)
Founded 1958. Pop 94,141; Circ 672,463
Library Holdings: Bk Vols 97,394
Wireless access
Mem of Monroe County Library System
Open Mon-Thurs 9-9, Fri & Sat 9-5
Friends of the Library Group
Branches: 1
BARNARD CROSSING, 2780 Dewey Ave, Rochester, 14616, SAN 353-9954. Tel: 585-663-3357. FAX: 585-663-5587. *Br Mgr,* Katherine Allen Patterson; Staff 6 (MLS 1, Non-MLS 5)
Circ 100,000
Library Holdings: Bk Vols 12,856
Open Mon & Tues 1-8, Wed-Fri 10-5, Sat 10-2 (Sept-May)
Friends of the Library Group

GREENE

P MOORE MEMORIAL LIBRARY*, 59 Genesee St, 13778-1298. SAN 311-2691. Tel: 607-656-9349. FAX: 607-656-9349. Web Site: www.4cls.org/greene/greene.html. *Librn,* Mary King; E-mail: gr.mary@4cls.org; Staff 1 (Non-MLS 1)
Founded 1902. Pop 5,729; Circ 64,736
Library Holdings: Bk Vols 34,778; Per Subs 44
Special Collections: Cemetery Records; Chenango American 1855-present
Automation Activity & Vendor Info: (Acquisitions) SirsiDynix; (Cataloging) SirsiDynix; (Circulation) SirsiDynix; (ILL) SirsiDynix; (Media Booking) SirsiDynix; (OPAC) SirsiDynix; (Serials) SirsiDynix
Database Vendor: SirsiDynix
Wireless access
Mem of Four County Library System
Open Mon-Thurs 9:30-8, Fri 9:30-5, Sat 9:30-3:30
Friends of the Library Group

GREENLAWN

P HARBORFIELDS PUBLIC LIBRARY*, 31 Broadway, 11740-1382. SAN 311-2705. Tel: 631-757-4200. FAX: 631-757-7216. Administration FAX: 631-757-4266. E-mail: harblib@suffolk.lib.ny.us. Web Site: harb.suffolk.lib.ny.us. *Libr Dir,* Carol Albano; E-mail: calbano@suffolk.lib.ny.us; *Asst Dir,* Ryan Athanas; E-mail: rathanas@suffolk.lib.ny.us; *Head, Adult Serv,* Carol Bloomgarden; E-mail: cbloomga@suffolk.lib.ny.us; *Head, Ch,* Patty Moisan; E-mail: pmoisan@suffolk.lib.ny.us; *Head, Circ,* Donna Wickers; E-mail: dwickers@suffolk.lib.ny.us; *Head, Ref,* Deborah Cunningham; E-mail: dcunning@suffolk.lib.ny.us; *Head, Tech Serv,* Leona Ceglia; E-mail: lceglia@suffolk.lib.ny.us; *Ref/Outreach Coordr,* Susan Mathews; *Ref Serv, YA,* Susan Holden; E-mail: sholden@suffolk.lib.ny.us; Staff 15 (MLS 14, Non-MLS 1)
Founded 1970. Pop 18,396; Circ 297,626
Library Holdings: Bk Vols 101,628; Per Subs 1,138
Subject Interests: Career, Consumer info, Health, Parenting, Teacher, Travel
Automation Activity & Vendor Info: (Acquisitions) Innovative Interfaces, Inc; (Cataloging) Innovative Interfaces, Inc; (Circulation) Innovative Interfaces, Inc; (Course Reserve) Innovative Interfaces, Inc; (ILL) Innovative Interfaces, Inc; (OPAC) Innovative Interfaces, Inc; (Serials) Innovative Interfaces, Inc
Wireless access
Publications: Monthly newsletter
Mem of Suffolk Cooperative Library System
Partic in Partnership of Automated Librs in Suffolk
Special Services for the Blind - Descriptive video serv (DVS)
Open Mon-Thurs 9-9, Fri 10-9, Sat 9-5, Sun 1-5
Friends of the Library Group

GREENPORT

M EASTERN LONG ISLAND HOSPITAL*, Medical Library, 201 Manor Pl, 11944. SAN 377-3701. Tel: 631-477-1000, Ext 5273. FAX: 631-477-1670. Web Site: www.elih.org. *Coordr,* Courtney Meringer
Library Holdings: Bk Vols 80; Per Subs 10
Wireless access
Open Mon-Fri 8-4

P FLOYD MEMORIAL LIBRARY, 539 First St, 11944-1399. SAN 311-273X. Tel: 631-477-0660. FAX: 631-477-2647. E-mail: flydlib@suffolk.lib.ny.us. Web Site: floydmemoriallibrary.org. *Dir,* Lisa Richland; E-mail: lisarichland@gmail.com; *Asst Dir,* Priscilla Johnson; E-mail: pjohnson@suffolk.lib.ny.us; *Head, Ch,* Joseph Cortale; E-mail: jcortale@suffolk.lib.ny.us; *Head, Circ,* Jeane Payne; *YA Librn,* Tracey Moloney; E-mail: tmoloney45@gmail.com; *Tech Coordr,* Barbara Schott; E-mail: bschott@suffolk.lib.ny.us; Staff 9 (MLS 4, Non-MLS 5)
Founded 1904. Pop 5,300; Circ 99,000
Jan 2014-Dec 2014 Income $991,772, State $1,541, Locally Generated Income $971,931, Other $18,300. Mats Exp $991,772, Books $28,000, Per/Ser (Incl. Access Fees) $7,500, AV Mat $15,750, Electronic Ref Mat (Incl. Access Fees) $7,500. Sal $510,770 (Prof $288,885)
Library Holdings: Audiobooks 1,800; CDs 1,000; DVDs 4,200; e-books 4,670; Electronic Media & Resources 131; Large Print Bks 5,700; Bk Titles 38,760; Bk Vols 39,000; Per Subs 140; Videos 50
Special Collections: Historic Preservation; Shakespeare Coll
Subject Interests: English as a second lang, Literacy, Local hist, Sailing
Automation Activity & Vendor Info: (Cataloging) Innovative Interfaces, Inc - Millenium; (Circulation) Innovative Interfaces, Inc - Millenium; (ILL) Innovative Interfaces, Inc - Millenium; (OPAC) Innovative Interfaces, Inc - Millenium
Database Vendor: ABC-CLIO, Booklist Online, CredoReference, EBSCO Auto Repair Reference, EBSCO Information Services, EBSCOhost, Evanced Solutions, Inc, Gale Cengage Learning, Hoovers, Innovative Interfaces, Inc, LearningExpress, Medline, Overdrive, Inc, ProQuest, ReferenceUSA, Wilson - Wilson Web, WT Cox
Wireless access
Function: Adult bk club, Adult literacy prog, Archival coll, Art exhibits, Audiobks via web, AV serv, Bilingual assistance for Spanish patrons, Bk club(s), Bks on cassette, Bks on CD, CD-ROM, Chess club, Children's prog, Citizenship assistance, Computer training, Computers for patron use, Copy machines, Digital talking bks, e-mail & chat, E-Reserves, Electronic databases & coll, Exhibits, Fax serv, Free DVD rentals, Handicapped accessible, Holiday prog, Home delivery & serv to Sr ctr & nursing homes,

Homebound delivery serv, Homework prog, ILL available, Literacy & newcomer serv, Magnifiers for reading, Mus passes, Music CDs, Newsp ref libr, Online cat, Online ref, Online searches, Outreach serv, OverDrive digital audio bks, Photocopying/Printing, Preschool outreach, Prog for adults, Prog for children & young adult, Pub access computers, Ref & res, Ref serv in person, Scanner, Senior outreach, Spoken cassettes & CDs, Spoken cassettes & DVDs, Story hour, Summer reading prog, Tax forms, Teen prog, Telephone ref, Wheelchair accessible
Publications: Newsletter
Mem of Suffolk Cooperative Library System
Partic in Partnership of Automated Librs in Suffolk
Special Services for the Blind - Assistive/Adapted tech devices, equip & products; Audio mat
Open Mon-Fri 9:30-8, Sat 9:30-5, Sun 1-5
Friends of the Library Group

S PARAPSYCHOLOGY FOUNDATION INC*, Eileen J Garrett Library, 308 Front St, 11944. (Mail add: PO Box 1562, New York, 10021-0043), SAN 311-9866. Tel: 212-628-1550, 631-477-2560. FAX: 212-628-1559. Web Site: www.parapsychology.org. *Exec Dir,* Lisette Coly; E-mail: lisettecoly@parapsychology.org
Founded 1951
Library Holdings: Bk Titles 10,000; Per Subs 100
Special Collections: Audio-Visual Archive
Subject Interests: Parapsychol
Publications: Guide to Sources of Information on Parapsychology (revised annually); International Conference Proceedings; International Journal of Parapsychology; Pamphet Series; Scholarly Monograph Series
Restriction: Open to pub by appt only

GREENVILLE

P GREENVILLE PUBLIC LIBRARY*, North St, Rte 32, 12083. (Mail add: PO Box 8, 11177 Rte 32, 12083-0008), SAN 311-2764. Tel: 518-966-8205. FAX: 518-966-4822. Web Site: www.greenville.lib.ny.us. *Dir,* Barbara Flach; E-mail: bflach@francomm.com; Staff 4 (Non-MLS 4)
Founded 1928. Pop 3,316; Circ 79,675
Jan 2010-Dec 2010 Income $169,576, State $1,000, County $2,438, Locally Generated Income $140,643, Other $25,495. Mats Exp $25,470, Books $21,642, Other Print Mats $3,778, Electronic Ref Mat (Incl. Access Fees) $50. Sal $96,691
Library Holdings: Audiobooks 1,953; AV Mats 2,054; e-books 224; Bk Vols 24,941; Per Subs 57
Automation Activity & Vendor Info: (Cataloging) Innovative Interfaces, Inc - Millenium; (Circulation) Innovative Interfaces, Inc - Millenium; (OPAC) Innovative Interfaces, Inc - Millenium
Wireless access
Mem of Mid-Hudson Library System
Partic in Ocean State Libraries
Open Mon & Wed 9-5, Tues & Thurs 9-6, Fri 12-5, Sat 9-1
Friends of the Library Group

GREENWICH

P EASTON LIBRARY*, 1074 State Rte 40, 12834. SAN 312-1844. Tel: 518-692-2253. FAX: 518-692-2253. Web Site: easton.sals.edu. *Dir,* Helen C Brownell; E-mail: hbrownell@sals.edu
Founded 1879. Circ 12,274
Jan 2006-Dec 2006 Income $42,832, State $1,000, Locally Generated Income $21,500, Other $20,332. Mats Exp $5,105, Books $3,074, AV Mat $2,031. Sal $13,640
Library Holdings: AV Mats 5,055; Electronic Media & Resources 43; Bk Vols 14,834; Per Subs 25
Subject Interests: Local hist
Automation Activity & Vendor Info: (Acquisitions) Innovative Interfaces, Inc; (Cataloging) Innovative Interfaces, Inc; (Circulation) Innovative Interfaces, Inc; (OPAC) Innovative Interfaces, Inc
Database Vendor: SirsiDynix
Wireless access
Mem of Southern Adirondack Library System
Open Mon, Tues & Thurs 6:30-9, Wed 9:30-12 & 1-5, Sat 10-4
Friends of the Library Group

P GREENWICH FREE LIBRARY*, 148 Main St, 12834. SAN 311-2772. Tel: 518-692-7157. FAX: 518-692-7152. E-mail: grn-director@sals.edu. Web Site: greenwich-library.org. *Dir,* Becky Wright-Sedam
Founded 1902. Pop 4,942; Circ 40,517
Library Holdings: Bk Vols 38,417; Per Subs 39
Automation Activity & Vendor Info: (Acquisitions) Innovative Interfaces, Inc; (Cataloging) Innovative Interfaces, Inc; (Circulation) Innovative Interfaces, Inc; (Course Reserve) Innovative Interfaces, Inc; (ILL) Innovative Interfaces, Inc; (Media Booking) Innovative Interfaces, Inc; (OPAC) Innovative Interfaces, Inc; (Serials) Innovative Interfaces, Inc
Wireless access
Function: Archival coll, Art exhibits, Audiobks via web, Bks on CD, Children's prog, Computer training, Computers for patron use, Copy machines, E-Reserves, Electronic databases & coll, Exhibits, Family literacy, Fax serv, Free DVD rentals, Handicapped accessible, ILL available, Magnifiers for reading, Microfiche/film & reading machines, Music CDs, Online cat, Online searches, OverDrive digital audio bks, Photocopying/Printing, Preschool reading prog, Prog for adults, Prog for children & young adult, Pub access computers, Scanner, Senior computer classes, Story hour, Summer reading prog, Tax forms, Teen prog, Telephone ref, Web-catalog, Wheelchair accessible, Workshops
Mem of Southern Adirondack Library System
Partic in OCLC Online Computer Library Center, Inc
Open Tues, Wed & Thurs 10-8, Fri 10-5, Sat 10-1
Friends of the Library Group

GREENWOOD

S GREENWOOD READING CENTER*, Main St, 14839. (Mail add: PO Box 835, 14839), SAN 328-9877. Tel: 607-225-4654. *Dir,* Betty Jean Hink; E-mail: hinkb@stls.org
Library Holdings: Bk Vols 5,000
Function: Homebound delivery serv
Mem of Southern Tier Library System
Open Mon 3-5, Tues 6-8, Wed & Thurs 10-4:30, Fri 2-4

GREENWOOD LAKE

P GREENWOOD LAKE PUBLIC LIBRARY*, 79 Waterstone Rd, 10925-2146. (Mail add: PO Box 1139, 10925-1139), SAN 311-2780. Tel: 845-477-8377. FAX: 845-477-8397. Administration FAX: 845-477-2053. E-mail: glpl@gwllibrary.org. Web Site: www.gwllibrary.org. *Dir,* Joan Carvajal; E-mail: joan@gwllibrary.org
Founded 1932. Pop 6,565; Circ 81,977
Library Holdings: AV Mats 3,172; Bk Titles 30,460; Bk Vols 32,460; Per Subs 140; Talking Bks 2,881
Subject Interests: Local hist
Wireless access
Function: ILL available
Mem of Ramapo Catskill Library System
Open Mon & Fri 9-5, Tues & Wed 9-9, Sat 10-4, Sun 11-3
Friends of the Library Group

GROTON

P GROTON PUBLIC LIBRARY*, 112 E Cortland St, 13073. SAN 311-2799. Tel: 607-898-5055. FAX: 607-898-5055. Web Site: www.flls.org/groton. *Dir,* Sara L Knobel; E-mail: director@grotonpubliclibrary.org; Staff 1 (Non-MLS 1)
Founded 1896. Pop 5,843; Circ 35,000
Automation Activity & Vendor Info: (Acquisitions) Innovative Interfaces, Inc; (Cataloging) Innovative Interfaces, Inc; (Circulation) Innovative Interfaces, Inc; (Course Reserve) Innovative Interfaces, Inc; (ILL) Innovative Interfaces, Inc; (Media Booking) Innovative Interfaces, Inc; (OPAC) Innovative Interfaces, Inc; (Serials) Innovative Interfaces, Inc
Wireless access
Mem of Finger Lakes Library System
Special Services for the Blind - Bks on cassette; Bks on CD; Large print bks
Open Mon-Thurs 2-9, Fri 10-7, Sat 10-2

GUILDERLAND

P GUILDERLAND PUBLIC LIBRARY, 2228 Western Ave, 12084-9701. SAN 310-754X. Tel: 518-456-2400. FAX: 518-456-0923. E-mail: info@guilpl.org. Web Site: www.guilpl.org. *Dir,* Tim Wiles; Tel: 518-456-2400, Ext 113; *Asst Dir,* Margaret Garrett; Tel: 518-456-2400, Ext 111, E-mail: ad@guilpl.org; *Head, Cir & Coll Serv,* Lisa Pitkin; Tel: 518-456-2400, Ext 118; *Head, Info Tech,* Sean Silvernail; Tel: 518-456-2400, Ext 199; *Head, Prog & Pub Serv,* Natalie McDonough; Tel: 518-456-2400, Ext 122; *ILL,* Maria Buhl; Tel: 518-456-2400, Ext 142; *Pub Info Officer,* Mark Curiale; Tel: 518-456-2400, Ext 112, E-mail: pio@guilpl.org; Staff 48 (MLS 18, Non-MLS 30)
Founded 1957. Pop 35,000; Circ 489,622
Library Holdings: Bk Vols 185,132; Per Subs 270
Special Collections: Altamont Enterprise microfilm, 1892 current
Automation Activity & Vendor Info: (Acquisitions) Horizon; (Cataloging) Horizon; (Circulation) Horizon; (OPAC) Horizon; (Serials) Horizon
Wireless access
Function: 24/7 Online cat, Activity rm, Adult bk club, Adult literacy prog, After school storytime, Art exhibits, Audio & video playback equip for onsite use, Audiobks via web, Bk club(s), Bks on CD, Bus archives, CD-ROM, Children's prog, Citizenship assistance, Computer training, Computers for patron use, Copy machines, Digital talking bks, e-mail & chat, e-mail serv, E-Reserves, Electronic databases & coll, eReaders, Exhibits, Family literacy, Fax serv, Free DVD rentals, Genealogy

discussion group, Govt ref serv, Handicapped accessible, Health sci info serv, Holiday prog, Home delivery & serv to Sr ctr & nursing homes, Homebound delivery serv, ILL available, Jazz prog, Life-long learning prog for all ages, Literacy & newcomer serv, Magazines, Magnifiers for reading, Mail & tel request accepted, Mango lang, Movies, Mus passes, Music CDs, Newsp ref libr, Notary serv, Online cat, Online ref, Online searches, Outreach serv, OverDrive digital audio bks, Photocopying/Printing, Preschool reading prog, Prog for adults, Prog for children & young adult, Pub access computers, Ref & res, Ref serv available, Ref serv in person, Senior outreach, Serves mentally handicapped consumers, Spanish lang bks, Spoken cassettes & CDs, Spoken cassettes & DVDs, Story hour, Study rm, Summer & winter reading prog, Summer reading prog, Tax forms, Teen prog, Telephone ref, Video lending libr, Web-catalog, Wheelchair accessible, Winter reading prog, Workshops
Publications: eNews; Guilderland Public Library News (Quarterly newsletter)
Mem of Upper Hudson Library System
Partic in Capital District Library Council; OCLC Online Computer Library Center, Inc
Open Mon-Fri 10-9, Sat 10-5, Sun (Sept-June) 1-5
Friends of the Library Group

HAMBURG

P HAMBURG PUBLIC LIBRARY*, 102 Buffalo St, 14075-5097. SAN 352-5066. Tel: 716-649-4415. Administration Tel: 716-649-4836. FAX: 716-649-4160. E-mail: ham@buffalolib.org. Web Site: www.buffalolib.org/. *Dir,* John Edson; E-mail: edsonj@buffalolib.org; *Asst Librn,* Rick Moesch; Staff 7 (MLS 4, Non-MLS 3)
Founded 1897. Pop 56,259; Circ 430,007
Library Holdings: AV Mats 5,474; Bk Vols 53,979; Per Subs 193
Subject Interests: Antiques, Art
Automation Activity & Vendor Info: (Acquisitions) SirsiDynix; (Circulation) SirsiDynix; (OPAC) SirsiDynix; (Serials) SirsiDynix
Wireless access
Function: Handicapped accessible, ILL available, Magnifiers for reading, Photocopying/Printing, Prog for children & young adult, Ref serv available, Serves mentally handicapped consumers, Summer reading prog, Telephone ref, Wheelchair accessible
Mem of Buffalo & Erie County Public Library System
Special Services for the Blind - Bks on cassette; Bks on CD; Large print bks; Radio reading serv; Talking bks; VisualTek equip; ZoomText magnification & reading software
Open Mon, Tues & Thurs 1-9, Wed & Sat 9-5, Fri 10-9, Sun 1-5
Friends of the Library Group
Branches: 1
LAKE SHORE, 4857 Lake Shore Rd, 14075, SAN 352-5120. Tel: 716-627-3017. FAX: 716-627-6505. E-mail: lsh@buffalolib.org. *Br Mgr,* Bridgette Heintz; Staff 3 (Non-MLS 3)
Pop 56,259; Circ 113,920
Library Holdings: AV Mats 3,250; Bk Vols 32,176; Per Subs 127
Function: Handicapped accessible, ILL available, Photocopying/Printing, Prog for children & young adult, Ref serv available, Telephone ref, Wheelchair accessible
Special Services for the Blind - Bks on cassette; Bks on CD; Copier with enlargement capabilities; Large print bks; Radio reading serv; Talking bks; ZoomText magnification & reading software
Open Mon 2-8, Tues 12-8, Thurs 10-6, Fri 1-5, Sat 11-5
Friends of the Library Group

C HILBERT COLLEGE*, McGrath Library, 5200 S Park Ave, 14075. SAN 311-2829. Tel: 716-649-7900, Ext 361. FAX: 716-648-6530. Web Site: www.hilbert.edu/academics/mcgrath-library. *Libr Dir,* Wil Prout; Tel: 716-649-7900, Ext 238, E-mail: wprout@hilbert.edu; *Asst Libr Dir & Info Literacy Coordr,* Katie Donahue; Tel: 716-649-7900, Ext 245, E-mail: kdonahue@hilbert.edu; *Electronic Res & Syst Librn,* Charles Chiesi; Tel: 716-649-7900, Ext 239, E-mail: chiesi@hilbert.edu; *Coord of Libr Communications/Humanities Librn,* Kathryn Maragliano; Tel: 716-649-7900, Ext 237, E-mail: kmaragliano@hilbert.edu; *Pub Serv & Libr Instruction Coordr,* Colleen Dippold; Tel: 716-649-7900, Ext 315, E-mail: cdippold@hilbert.edu; *Tech Serv Coordr,* Elizabeth Curry; Tel: 716-649-7900, Ext 246, E-mail: ecurry@hilbert.edu; *Archivist,* Sister Joanette Rutkowski; Staff 8 (MLS 7, Non-MLS 1)
Founded 1955. Enrl 940; Fac 97; Highest Degree: Bachelor
Jun 2006-May 2007 Income $473,719. Mats Exp $246,355, Books $58,520, Per/Ser (Incl. Access Fees) $58,615, Manu Arch $450, AV Mat $3,115, Electronic Ref Mat (Incl. Access Fees) $76,452. Sal $234,870
Library Holdings: AV Mats 480; Bk Titles 33,212; Bk Vols 36,311; Per Subs 337; Talking Bks 102; Videos 400
Subject Interests: Self help
Automation Activity & Vendor Info: (Cataloging) TLC (The Library Corporation); (Circulation) TLC (The Library Corporation); (OPAC) TLC (The Library Corporation)
Database Vendor: EBSCOhost, Gale Cengage Learning, LexisNexis, OCLC FirstSearch, OVID Technologies, ProQuest
Wireless access
Publications: Acquisitions List; Periodical Holdings Catalog; Student Information Sheets; Video Catalog
Partic in Western New York Library Resources Council
Open Mon-Thurs 8am-10pm, Fri 8-8, Sat 12-5, Sun 12-6
Friends of the Library Group

HAMILTON

C COLGATE UNIVERSITY*, Everett Needham Case Library, 13 Oak Dr, 13346-1398. SAN 311-2845. Tel: 315-228-7300. Interlibrary Loan Service Tel: 315-228-7597. FAX: 315-228-7934. Web Site: exlibris.colgate.edu. *Univ Librn,* Joanne Schneider; E-mail: jschneider@colgate.edu; *Head, Borrower Serv,* Franklin Gavett; E-mail: fgavett@colgate.edu; *Head, Cat,* Ann Kebabian; E-mail: akebabian@colgate.edu; *Head, Coll Develop,* Emily Hutton-hughes; E-mail: ehutton@colgate.edu; *Head, Govt Doc,* Mary Jane Walsh; E-mail: mwalsh@colgate.edu; *Spec Coll Librn,* Carl Peterson; E-mail: cpeterson@colgate.edu; *Syst Librn,* Cynthia Harper; E-mail: charper@colgate.edu; *Sci,* Deborah Huerta; E-mail: dhuerta@colgate.edu; Staff 34 (MLS 14, Non-MLS 20)
Founded 1819. Enrl 2,758; Fac 245; Highest Degree: Master
Library Holdings: AV Mats 16,184; e-journals 29,114; Bk Vols 721,189; Per Subs 1,698
Special Collections: 17th Century British Religious & Political Tracts; 19th-20th Century American & British Literature; George Bernard Shaw Coll; Gertrude Stein Coll; James Joyce Coll; John Masefield Coll; Joseph Conrad Coll; Photography (Edward Stone Coll); Private Press & Fine Printing, incunabula; T S Eliot Coll; University Archives; World War I & II Posters. State Document Depository; UN Document Depository; US Document Depository
Automation Activity & Vendor Info: (Acquisitions) Innovative Interfaces, Inc; (Cataloging) Innovative Interfaces, Inc; (Circulation) Innovative Interfaces, Inc; (Course Reserve) Innovative Interfaces, Inc; (ILL) Innovative Interfaces, Inc; (OPAC) Innovative Interfaces, Inc; (Serials) SerialsSolutions
Wireless access
Function: Doc delivery serv, For res purposes, Ref serv available
Partic in Central New York Library Resources Council; Connect NY; OCLC Online Computer Library Center, Inc
Open Mon-Thurs 8am-2am, Fri 8am-10pm, Sat 10-10, Sun 10-2
Restriction: Access at librarian's discretion
Departmental Libraries:
GEORGE R COOLEY SCIENCE LIBRARY, 13 Oak Dr, 13346-1338. Tel: 315-228-7312. *Sci Librn,* Peter Tagtmeyer; Tel: 315-228-7402; Staff 2 (MLS 1, Non-MLS 1)
Founded 1979. Highest Degree: Master
Library Holdings: Bk Vols 46,000; Per Subs 1,000
Automation Activity & Vendor Info: (Cataloging) Innovative Interfaces, Inc; (Circulation) Innovative Interfaces, Inc; (ILL) Innovative Interfaces, Inc; (OPAC) Innovative Interfaces, Inc; (Serials) Innovative Interfaces, Inc
Open Mon-Thurs 8am-Midnight, Fri 8am-10pm, Sat 10-10, Sun Noon-Midnight

P HAMILTON PUBLIC LIBRARY*, 13 Broad St, 13346. SAN 311-2853. Tel: 315-824-3060. FAX: 315-824-8420. E-mail: hamilton@midyork.org. Web Site: www.midyork.org/hamilton. *Dir,* Barbara Coger; *Asst Dir,* Sandra Crumb
Founded 1903. Pop 3,845; Circ 83,257
Library Holdings: Bk Vols 40,472; Per Subs 50
Special Collections: Biographical Review of Madison County; History of Chenango & Madison Counties, 1784-1880 (James H Smith Coll); Madison County Cemetery Records (Genealogical Records Committee of the James Madison Chapter of the Daughters of the American Revolution, 1801-1900)
Subject Interests: Archit, Cookery, Gardening, Hist, Natural sci
Automation Activity & Vendor Info: (Acquisitions) SirsiDynix; (Cataloging) SirsiDynix; (Circulation) SirsiDynix; (Course Reserve) SirsiDynix; (ILL) SirsiDynix; (Media Booking) SirsiDynix; (OPAC) SirsiDynix; (Serials) SirsiDynix
Wireless access
Open Mon-Fri 11-8, Sat 10-1
Friends of the Library Group

HAMLIN

P HAMLIN PUBLIC LIBRARY*, 422 Clarkson Hamlin TL Rd, 14464. Tel: 585-964-2320. FAX: 585-964-2374. E-mail: hamlin@libraryweb.org. Web Site: www.libraweb.org/hamlin. *Dir,* Katherine Hughes-Dennett; *Ch & Youth Librn,* Adrienne Kirby; Staff 1.25 (MLS 1.25)
Founded 2000. Pop 9,050; Circ 72,126
Library Holdings: AV Mats 4,924; Bk Vols 22,701
Automation Activity & Vendor Info: (Cataloging) CARL.Solution (TLC); (Circulation) CARL.Solution (TLC); (Course Reserve) CARL.Solution

(TLC); (ILL) CARL.Solution (TLC); (OPAC) CARL.Solution (TLC); (Serials) CARL.Solution (TLC)
Database Vendor: Overdrive, Inc
Wireless access
Function: Adult bk club, Audiobks via web, Bks on CD, Children's prog, Computers for patron use, Copy machines, Digital talking bks, E-Reserves, Electronic databases & coll, Fax serv, Free DVD rentals, Handicapped accessible, ILL available, Mail & tel request accepted, Music CDs, Online cat, Online searches, Outside serv via phone, mail, e-mail & web, Photocopying/Printing, Preschool outreach, Prog for adults, Prog for children & young adult, Pub access computers, Ref serv available, Scanner, Story hour, Summer & winter reading prog, Tax forms, Web-catalog, Wheelchair accessible
Mem of Monroe County Library System
Open Mon & Wed 10-6, Tues & Thurs 12-8, Fri 10-4, Sat 12-4
Friends of the Library Group

HAMMOND

P HAMMOND FREE LIBRARY*, 17 N Main St, 13646. SAN 311-2861. Tel: 315-324-5139. FAX: 315-324-6008. Web Site: www.hammondfreelibrary.org. *Dir,* Sherrie Moquin; Staff 0.6 (Non-MLS 0.6)
Founded 1922. Pop 1,207; Circ 7,944
Library Holdings: Bk Vols 3,409
Wireless access
Mem of North Country Library System
Open Mon & Wed 12:30-5, Tues 5-8, Thurs 12-5, Sat 9-12

HAMMONDSPORT

S GLENN H CURTISS MUSEUM OF LOCAL HISTORY*, Minor Swarthout Memorial Library, 8419 State Rte 54, 14840-0326. SAN 326-0356. Tel: 607-569-2160. FAX: 607-569-2040. E-mail: info@glennhcurtissmuseum.org. Web Site: www.glennhcurtissmuseum.org. *Dir,* Trafford Doherty; *Admin Coordr,* Jean Doherty; *Curator,* Rick Leisenring; E-mail: curator@glennhcurtissmuseum.org; Staff 6 (Non-MLS 6)
Founded 1992
Library Holdings: Bk Titles 4,000
Special Collections: Oral History
Subject Interests: Aviation, Local hist
Function: Res libr
Restriction: Open by appt only

P FRED & HARRIETT TAYLOR MEMORIAL LIBRARY*, 21 William St, 14840. (Mail add: PO Box 395, 14840-0395), SAN 311-287X. Tel: 607-569-2045. FAX: 607-569-3340. Web Site: www.stls.org/hammondsport. *Dir,* Marsha Watson; *Circ Mgr,* Marilyn Conklin
Founded 1876. Pop 2,807; Circ 27,798
Library Holdings: AV Mats 3,155; Bk Vols 26,000; Per Subs 25
Special Collections: Aircraft Coll, bks & pictures
Subject Interests: Local hist
Automation Activity & Vendor Info: (Acquisitions) SirsiDynix; (Cataloging) SirsiDynix; (Circulation) SirsiDynix; (Course Reserve) SirsiDynix; (ILL) SirsiDynix; (Media Booking) SirsiDynix; (OPAC) SirsiDynix; (Serials) SirsiDynix
Wireless access
Mem of Southern Tier Library System
Special Services for the Deaf - TTY equip
Open Mon & Wed 10-8, Tues & Thurs 2-8, Fri 10-5, Sat 10-2

HAMPTON BAYS

P HAMPTON BAYS PUBLIC LIBRARY*, 52 Ponquogue Ave, 11946-0207. SAN 311-2888. Tel: 631-728-6241. FAX: 631-728-0166. E-mail: hbaylib@suffolk.lib.ny.us. Web Site: hbay.suffolk.lib.ny.us. *Dir,* Susan LaVista; Staff 38 (MLS 13, Non-MLS 25)
Founded 1960. Pop 11,992; Circ 117,755
Jan 2007-Dec 2007 Income $1,610,708, Locally Generated Income $1,299,660, Other $311,048. Mats Exp $167,696, Books $80,983, Per/Ser (Incl. Access Fees) $12,091, AV Equip $16,194, AV Mat $36,273, Electronic Ref Mat (Incl. Access Fees) $22,155. Sal $907,129 (Prof $370,000)
Library Holdings: AV Mats 7,236; Bk Vols 65,029; Per Subs 6,334
Special Collections: Long Island History
Subject Interests: Archit, Art
Automation Activity & Vendor Info: (Cataloging) Innovative Interfaces, Inc; (Circulation) Innovative Interfaces, Inc; (ILL) Innovative Interfaces, Inc; (OPAC) Innovative Interfaces, Inc
Mem of Suffolk Cooperative Library System
Open Mon-Thurs 10-9, Fri & Sat 10-5, Sun 1-5
Friends of the Library Group

HANCOCK

P LOUISE ADELIA READ MEMORIAL LIBRARY*, 104 Read St, 13783. SAN 311-2896. Tel: 607-637-2519. FAX: 607-637-3377. E-mail: ha.ill@4cls.org. *Dir,* Joann Haberli
Founded 1955. Pop 4,100; Circ 20,000
Library Holdings: Bk Vols 17,000; Per Subs 50
Automation Activity & Vendor Info: (Cataloging) SIRSI WorkFlows; (Circulation) SIRSI WorkFlows; (OPAC) SIRSI WorkFlows; (Serials) SIRSI WorkFlows
Wireless access
Mem of Four County Library System
Open Tues & Thurs 11-4 & 6:30-9, Wed & Fri 11-4, Sat 2-4

HANNIBAL

P HANNIBAL FREE LIBRARY*, 162 Oswego St, 13074. SAN 311-2918. Tel: 315-564-5471. FAX: 315-564-5471. Web Site: www.hannibalfreelibrary.org. *Dir,* Shelly Stanton; *Dir, Children's Prog,* Tina Trumble
Pop 4,027; Circ 12,000
Library Holdings: Bk Vols 8,100; Per Subs 14
Automation Activity & Vendor Info: (Cataloging) SirsiDynix; (Circulation) SirsiDynix; (OPAC) SirsiDynix; (Serials) SirsiDynix
Wireless access
Mem of North Country Library System
Open Mon, Wed & Fri 10-4:30, Tues & Thurs 10-8, Sat 9-3
Friends of the Library Group

HARRISON

P HARRISON PUBLIC LIBRARY*, Bruce Ave, 10528. SAN 352-5155. Tel: 914-835-0324. FAX: 914-835-1564. Web Site: www.harrisonpl.org. *Dir,* Galina Chernykh; *Adult/Ref Serv, AV,* Carole Meehan; *Cat, Tech Serv,* Jennie Yang; *Ch Serv,* Margaret LoRusso; *Circ,* Donna Laygues
Founded 1905. Pop 24,154; Circ 238,731
Jan 2011-Dec 2011 Income (Main Library and Branch(s)) $2,213,529. Mats Exp $120,000, Books $100,000, AV Mat $20,000
Library Holdings: Bk Vols 122,857
Special Collections: Spanish & Japanese Language Coll
Automation Activity & Vendor Info: (Cataloging) SirsiDynix; (Circulation) SirsiDynix; (OPAC) SirsiDynix
Wireless access
Friends of the Library Group
Branches: 1
WEST HARRISON BRANCH, Two E Madison St, West Harrison, 10604, SAN 352-518X. Tel: 914-948-2092. FAX: 914-948-4350. Web Site: www.westchesterlibraries.org. *Ch Serv,* Liz Karkoff
Special Collections: Italian Language Coll
Friends of the Library Group

M SAINT VINCENT'S HOSPITAL & MEDICAL CENTER OF NEW YORK-WESTCHESTER*, Medical Library, 275 North St, 10528. SAN 327-5094. Tel: 914-967-6500. FAX: 914-925-5158. *In Charge,* Barbara Pinella; Tel: 914-967-6500, Ext 5310
Library Holdings: Bk Vols 3,500; Per Subs 50
Wireless access
Restriction: Med staff only

HARRISVILLE

P HARRISVILLE FREE LIBRARY*, 8209 Main St, 13648. SAN 311-2934. Tel: 315-543-2577. FAX: 315-543-2577. Web Site: www.harrisvillefreelibrary.org. *Librn,* Nicole Spencer
Pop 703; Circ 10,565
Library Holdings: Bk Vols 5,662; Per Subs 29
Mem of North Country Library System
Open Tues 10-5:30, Wed 12-5, Thurs 3-8:30, Sat 10-2
Friends of the Library Group

HARTWICK

P KINNEY MEMORIAL LIBRARY*, 3140 County Hwy 11, 13348-3007. (Mail add: PO Box 176, 13348-0176), SAN 311-2950. Tel: 607-293-6600. FAX: 607-293-6600. E-mail: kinymlib@stny.rr.com. Web Site: www.hartwickny.org. *Dir, Libr Serv,* Jane Voorhees
Founded 1961. Pop 3,255; Circ 12,976
Library Holdings: Bk Vols 21,433; Per Subs 20
Special Collections: Historical Artifacts, Books & Photos
Subject Interests: Genealogy
Automation Activity & Vendor Info: (Acquisitions) SirsiDynix; (Cataloging) SirsiDynix; (Circulation) SirsiDynix; (Course Reserve) SirsiDynix; (ILL) SirsiDynix; (Media Booking) SirsiDynix; (OPAC) SirsiDynix; (Serials) SirsiDynix
Wireless access
Mem of Four County Library System

Open Mon 9-1 & 7-9, Wed 12-4 & 7-9, Fri & Sat 1-5
Friends of the Library Group

HASTINGS-ON-HUDSON

P HASTINGS-ON-HUDSON PUBLIC LIBRARY*, Seven Maple Ave, 10706. SAN 311-2969. Tel: 914-478-3307. FAX: 914-478-4813. E-mail: has@westchesterlibraries.org. Web Site: www.hastingslibrary.org/. *Dir,* Susan Feir; *Adult Serv,* Michael McCoy; *Ch Serv,* Joan Vaillancourt
Founded 1913. Pop 7,750; Circ 140,000
Library Holdings: AV Mats 15,000; Bk Titles 55,000; Per Subs 125
Automation Activity & Vendor Info: (Cataloging) SirsiDynix; (Circulation) SirsiDynix; (OPAC) SirsiDynix
Wireless access
Mem of Westchester Library System
Open Mon, Tues & Thurs (Winter) 9:30-8:30, Wed, Fri & Sat 9:30-5, Sun 1-5; Mon, Tues & Thurs (Summer) 9:30-8:30, Wed 9:30-5, Fri & Sat 9:30-2
Friends of the Library Group

HAUPPAUGE

C ADELPHI UNIVERSITY, Hauppauge Center Library, 55 Kennedy Dr, 11788-4001. Tel: 516-237-8611. FAX: 516-237-8613. *Librn,* James Cassidy; E-mail: cassidy4@adelphi.edu; *Asst Librn,* Vivian Bailey; Tel: 516-237-8610, E-mail: vbailey@adelphi.edu; Staff 1 (MLS 1)
Fac 2
Library Holdings: Bk Vols 4,000; Per Subs 5
Wireless access
Open Mon-Thurs 3-9, Fri 9-2, Sat 9-1

P HAUPPAUGE PUBLIC LIBRARY*, 601 Veterans Memorial Hwy, 11788. SAN 378-407X. Tel: 631-979-1600. FAX: 631-979-4018. E-mail: hauplib@suffolk.lib.ny.us. Web Site: www.hauppaugelibrary.org. *Dir,* Matthew Bollerman
Library Holdings: AV Mats 20,069; Bk Vols 40,981; Per Subs 164
Automation Activity & Vendor Info: (Acquisitions) Innovative Interfaces, Inc; (Cataloging) Innovative Interfaces, Inc; (OPAC) Innovative Interfaces, Inc
Database Vendor: ReferenceUSA
Wireless access
Publications: Hauppauge Library (Newsletter)
Mem of Suffolk Cooperative Library System
Open Mon-Fri 9:30-9, Sat 9:30-5, Sun 1-9
Friends of the Library Group

HECTOR

P ELIZABETH B PERT LIBRARY*, Valois-Logan-Hector Fire House, Rte 414, 14841. (Mail add: PO Box 82, 14841-0082), SAN 352-4078. Tel: 607-546-2605. *Dir,* Donna Wickham; Staff 1 (Non-MLS 1)
Function: Homebound delivery serv
Mem of Southern Tier Library System
Open Tues 4-8, Thurs 3-5, Sat 10-12

HEMPSTEAD

P HEMPSTEAD PUBLIC LIBRARY*, 115 Nichols Ct, 11550-3199. SAN 311-2993. Tel: 516-481-6990. FAX: 516-481-6719. Reference E-mail: ReferenceDesk@HempsteadLibrary.info. Web Site: www.hempsteadlibrary.info. *Dir,* Irene A Duszkiewicz; *Adult Learning Ctr Spec,* Caren Cramer; *Adult Serv,* Grace DiMaria; *AV, Ref,* Erica Lang; *Ch Serv,* Anne Miltenberg; *Tech Serv,* Andrea Smernoff. Subject Specialists: *Literacy,* Caren Cramer; *Foreign lang,* Grace DiMaria; Staff 36 (MLS 16, Non-MLS 20)
Founded 1889. Pop 56,554; Circ 265,268
Library Holdings: Bk Vols 212,368; Per Subs 331
Special Collections: Adult Multi-Media; Black Studies Coll; Early American Textbooks; Foreign Language Coll for Adults & Children; Hispanic Studies Coll; Job & Education Information Center; LI Photography Coll; Literacy Materials; Long Island Coll; Walt Whitman Coll
Subject Interests: Ethnic studies, Hist
Automation Activity & Vendor Info: (Cataloging) Innovative Interfaces, Inc - Millenium; (Circulation) Innovative Interfaces, Inc - Millenium; (OPAC) Innovative Interfaces, Inc - Millenium; (Serials) Innovative Interfaces, Inc - Millenium
Database Vendor: Dialog, EBSCOhost, Gale Cengage Learning, Innovative Interfaces, Inc, OCLC FirstSearch
Wireless access
Publications: ALC Resources Bibliography; Black Studies Bibliography; Community Directory; Foreign Language Bibliography; Hispanic Studies Bibliography; Newsletter
Mem of Nassau Library System
Partic in Dialog Corp; Libraries Online, Inc; Long Island Library Resources Council; Vutext
Open Mon-Thurs 10-9, Fri 10-6, Sat (Sept-June) 9-5, Sun (Sept-May) 1-5

C HOFSTRA UNIVERSITY*, Joan & Donald E Axinn Library, 123 Hofstra University, 11549. SAN 352-5279. Circulation Tel: 516-463-5952. Interlibrary Loan Service Tel: 516-463-5946. Reference Tel: 516-463-5962. Administration Tel: 516-463-5940. Circulation FAX: 516-463-4309. Interlibrary Loan Service FAX: 516-463-4835. Reference FAX: 516-463-7485. Administration FAX: 516-463-6387. Web Site: www.hofstra.edu/library. *Dean of Libr & Info Serv,* Dr Daniel Rubey; E-mail: daniel.r.rubey@hofstra.edu; *Chair, Ref Serv & Coll Develop,* Georgina Martorella; Tel: 516-463-4980, E-mail: georgina.martorella@hofstra.edu; *Chair, Tech Serv, Sr Asst Dean, Libr Syst,* Howard Graves; Tel: 516-463-6429, Fax: 516-463-6438, E-mail: howard.e.graves@hofstra.edu; *Asst Dean, Spec Coll & Univ Archivist,* Geri Solomon; Tel: 516-463-6407, Fax: 516-463-6442, E-mail: geri.e.solomon@hofstra.edu; *Head, Access Serv, Interim Dir, Film & Media Libr,* Sarah McCleskey; Tel: 516-463-5076, E-mail: sarah.e.mccleskey@hofstra.edu; *Asst Dir, Spec Coll,* Bronwyn Hannon; *Cat Librn,* Melanie Freese; *Mgr, Off of the Dean of Libr & Info Serv,* Carol Sasso; Tel: 516-463-5943, E-mail: carol.a.sasso@hofstra.edu; *Curator, Spec Coll,* Michael O'Connor. Subject Specialists: *Archives, Manuscripts, Rare bks,* Geri Solomon; Staff 94 (MLS 36, Non-MLS 58)
Founded 1935. Enrl 12,068; Fac 1,180; Highest Degree: Doctorate
Sept 2009-Aug 2010 Income $9,273,122. Mats Exp $2,178,524, Books $332,191, Per/Ser (Incl. Access Fees) $1,125,157, Manu Arch $6,303, AV Mat $24,082, Electronic Ref Mat (Incl. Access Fees) $673,144, Presv $17,647. Sal $4,424,687 (Prof $2,269,823)
Library Holdings: DVDs 2,702; e-books 47,155; e-journals 52,264; Microforms 3,479,678; Bk Titles 555,740; Bk Vols 1,070,821; Per Subs 7,717; Videos 5,776
Special Collections: Authors Coll of Late 19th & Early 20th Century; Coll of Books About Books, Early Printed Books; Harry Wachtel Coll; Henry Kroul Coll of Nazi Culture & Propoganda; History of Hofstra Univ; Long Island Develop Coll; Nila Banton Smith Reading Coll; Physicians for Social Responsibility of Nassau County Coll; Private Press Coll; Spinzia Coll of Long Island Estates History; Utopian Communities; Weingrow Coll of Avant-Garde Art & Literature. State Document Depository; US Document Depository
Automation Activity & Vendor Info: (Acquisitions) Innovative Interfaces, Inc; (Cataloging) Innovative Interfaces, Inc; (Circulation) Innovative Interfaces, Inc; (Course Reserve) Docutek; (ILL) OCLC ILLiad; (Serials) Innovative Interfaces, Inc
Database Vendor: EBSCOhost, LexisNexis, ProQuest, ScienceDirect, Wilson - Wilson Web
Wireless access
Partic in Long Island Library Resources Council; Lyrasis; OCLC Online Computer Library Center, Inc; Westchester Academic Library Directors Organization (WALDO)
Special Services for the Blind - Reader equip; ZoomText magnification & reading software

Departmental Libraries:

SPECIAL COLLECTIONS/LONG ISLAND STUDIES INSTITUTE, 032 Axinn Library, 123 Hofstra University, 11549-1230. Tel: 516-463-6404, 516 463-6411. FAX: 516-463-6442. E-mail: lisi@hofstra.edu. Web Site: www.hofstra.edu/libraries. *Asst Dean,* Geri Solomon; *Curator,* Michael O'Connor; *Acq,* Bronwyn Hannon; Staff 3 (MLS 1, Non-MLS 2)
Founded 1935
Special Collections: Long Island Studies; Rare Books & Manuscripts Coll; University Archives
Open Mon-Fri 9-4:45
Restriction: Closed stack

CL HOFSTRA UNIVERSITY LAW LIBRARY*, Barbara & Maurice A Deane Law Library, 122 Hofstra University, 11549-1220. Tel: 516-463-5898. Reference Tel: 516-463-5908. Administration Tel: 516-463-5900. FAX: 516-463-5129. Web Site: law.hofstra.edu/library. *Dir, Law Libr & Assoc Prof of Law,* Michelle M Wu; *Admin Officer,* Dianne Kaplan; Staff 11 (MLS 10, Non-MLS 1)
Library Holdings: Bk Titles 145,766; Bk Vols 550,765
Database Vendor: SirsiDynix
Wireless access
Partic in Long Island Library Resources Council
Open Mon-Thurs 8am-Midnight, Fri 8am-9pm

S HELEN KELLER SERVICES FOR THE BLIND*, Braille Library, One Helen Keller Way, 11550. SAN 327-5116. Tel: 516-485-1234, Ext 241. FAX: 516-538-6785. Web Site: www.helenkeller.org. *Dir,* Karen Barrett; Tel: 516-485-1234, Ext 246
Library Holdings: Bk Titles 10,000
Restriction: Not open to pub

HENDERSON

P HENDERSON FREE LIBRARY*, 8939 New York State Rte 178, 13650. SAN 311-3019. Tel: 315-938-7169. FAX: 315-938-7038. E-mail: henlib@ncls.org. *Dir,* Mary Bidwell; *Libr Asst,* Nicole Briggs; Staff 1 (Non-MLS 1)
Founded 1951. Pop 1,377; Circ 11,600
Library Holdings: Bk Vols 12,343; Per Subs 52
Special Collections: State Document Depository
Automation Activity & Vendor Info: (Acquisitions) SIRSI WorkFlows
Wireless access
Function: Bk club(s), Bks on cassette, Bks on CD, Children's prog, Computers for patron use, Copy machines, e-mail serv, E-Reserves, Electronic databases & coll, Fax serv, Free DVD rentals, Handicapped accessible, ILL available, Mail & tel request accepted, Music CDs, Online cat, Photocopying/Printing, Preschool outreach, Scanner, Story hour, Summer reading prog, VHS videos
Mem of North Country Library System
Open Mon & Wed (Winter) 11-6, Tues & Thurs 9-Noon, Sat 9-1; Mon & Wed (Summer) 1-8, Tues & Thurs 9-Noon, Sat 9-1

HERKIMER

P FRANK J BASLOE LIBRARY OF HERKIMER NEW YORK*, 245 N Main St, 13350-1918. SAN 311-3027. Tel: 315-866-1733. FAX: 315-866-1733. E-mail: herkimer@midyork.org. Web Site: www.midyork.org/herkimer. *Dir,* Lesley Paul
Founded 1895. Pop 7,945; Circ 101,422
Library Holdings: AV Mats 2,517; Bk Vols 40,250; Per Subs 94
Special Collections: NYS Coll. State Document Depository
Subject Interests: Genealogy
Automation Activity & Vendor Info: (Cataloging) SirsiDynix; (Circulation) SirsiDynix; (OPAC) SirsiDynix; (Serials) SirsiDynix
Wireless access
Mem of Mid-York Library System
Open Mon-Wed 9-8, Thurs & Fri 9-5, Sat 9-3
Friends of the Library Group

J HERKIMER COUNTY COMMUNITY COLLEGE LIBRARY*, 100 Reservoir Rd, 13350. SAN 311-3035. Tel: 315-866-0300, Ext 8270. Circulation Tel: 315-866-0300, Ext 8272. Reference Tel: 315-866-0300, Ext 8394. Toll Free Tel: 888-464-4222 (NY State only). FAX: 315-866-1806. E-mail: library@herkimer.edu. Web Site: www.herkimer.edu/library. *Distance Learning Serv, Info Literacy,* Susan Bissonnette; *Pub Serv,* Mary Mullin; *Tech Serv,* Valerie Prescott; Staff 4 (MLS 4)
Founded 1967. Enrl 2,600; Fac 90; Highest Degree: Associate
Library Holdings: High Interest/Low Vocabulary Bk Vols 150; Bk Titles 69,000; Per Subs 218
Subject Interests: Art, Behav sci, Criminal justice, Educ, Law, Soc sci, Tourism
Automation Activity & Vendor Info: (Cataloging) Ex Libris Group; (Circulation) Ex Libris Group; (OPAC) Ex Libris Group; (Serials) Ex Libris Group
Database Vendor: EBSCOhost, Gale Cengage Learning, OCLC FirstSearch
Wireless access
Publications: Faculty library handbook; Library handbook; Monthly acquisitions list; Periodicals holdings list
Partic in Central New York Library Resources Council; Nylink
Open Mon-Thurs 8am-9pm, Fri 8-4, Sun 4-9

S HERKIMER COUNTY HISTORICAL SOCIETY LIBRARY, Eckler Bldg, 406 N Main St, 13350. (Mail add: 400 N Main St, 13350), SAN 311-3043. Tel: 315-866-6413. E-mail: herkimerhistory@yahoo.com. Web Site: www.rootsweb.com/~nyhchs. *Dir,* Susan R Perkins
Founded 1896
Library Holdings: Bk Vols 4,000
Special Collections: Herkimer County, New York Artifacts
Subject Interests: County hist
Publications: Local Genealogy; Local History
Open Mon-Fri 10-4, Sat (July & Aug) 10-3
Restriction: Not a lending libr

GL HERKIMER COUNTY LAW LIBRARY*, 301 N Washington St, Ste 5511, 13350-1299. SAN 311-3051. Tel: 315-867-1172. FAX: 315-866-7991. *Head of Libr,* Lisa M Liskiewicz; E-mail: lliskiew@courts.state.ny.us
Founded 1941
Library Holdings: Bk Titles 500; Bk Vols 14,000
Special Collections: Legal Reference Coll

HERMON

P HEPBURN LIBRARY OF HERMON*, 105 Main St, 13652-3100. (Mail add: PO Box A, 13652-0400), SAN 311-306X. Tel: 315-347-2285. FAX: 315-347-5058. E-mail: herlib@ncls.org. Web Site: www.hermonhepburnlibrary.org/. *Dir,* Veronica Newvine
Pop 1,080; Circ 25,333
Library Holdings: Bk Vols 14,000; Per Subs 41
Automation Activity & Vendor Info: (Cataloging) SirsiDynix; (Circulation) SirsiDynix; (OPAC) SirsiDynix
Wireless access
Mem of North Country Library System
Open Mon 1-5 & 7-9, Tues, Thurs & Fri 9-1, Wed 9-3 & 7-9, Sat 10-2

HEUVELTON

P HEUVELTON FREE LIBRARY, 57 State St, 13654. (Mail add: PO Box 346, 13654-0346), SAN 311-3078. Tel: 315-344-6550. FAX: 315-344-6550. E-mail: heulib@ncls.org. Web Site: www.heuveltonfreelibrary.org. *Dir,* Stella Todd
Founded 1912. Pop 804; Circ 17,947
Library Holdings: Bk Titles 4,729; Bk Vols 5,183; Per Subs 58
Automation Activity & Vendor Info: (Cataloging) SIRSI WorkFlows; (Circulation) SIRSI WorkFlows; (ILL) SIRSI WorkFlows
Database Vendor: Brodart
Wireless access
Mem of North Country Library System
Open Mon (Winter) 6pm-9pm, Tues 1-5, Wed 11-2 & 6-9, Fri 1-5 & 7-9, Sat 2-5; Mon (Summer) 6pm-9pm, Tues 1-5, Wed 11-2 & 6-9, Thurs 1-5, Fri 1-5 & 7-9

HEWLETT

P HEWLETT-WOODMERE PUBLIC LIBRARY*, 1125 Broadway, 11557-0903. (Mail add: PO Box 1100, 11557), SAN 311-3086. Tel: 516-374-1967. FAX: 516-569-1229. Administration FAX: 516-569-3158. Web Site: www.hwpl.org. *Dir,* William Ferro; *Asst Dir,* Tracey Simon; *AV,* Leslee Levy; *Circ,* Phyllis Costanzo; *Youth Serv,* Diane Mason; Staff 15 (MLS 15)
Founded 1947. Pop 20,265; Circ 306,197
Library Holdings: AV Mats 46,271; Bk Vols 204,106; Per Subs 429
Special Collections: Art Coll, bks, flm, slides; Music Coll, bks, cassettes, recs, scores, song indexes, tapes
Subject Interests: Art, Music
Automation Activity & Vendor Info: (Acquisitions) Innovative Interfaces, Inc; (Circulation) Innovative Interfaces, Inc; (OPAC) Innovative Interfaces, Inc
Wireless access
Function: Art exhibits, Audio & video playback equip for onsite use
Publications: Index to Art Reproductions in Books; Music & Art Catalogs; Overleaf (Newsletter); Overleaf, Jr (Newsletter)
Mem of Nassau Library System
Partic in Long Island Library Resources Council
Open Mon-Thurs 9-9, Fri 9-6, Sat 9-5, Sun 12:30-5
Friends of the Library Group

HICKSVILLE

P HICKSVILLE PUBLIC LIBRARY*, 169 Jerusalem Ave, 11801. SAN 311-3108. Tel: 516-931-1417. FAX: 516-822-5672. E-mail: hilmail@nassaulibrary.org. Web Site: www.nassaulibrary.org/hicksv. *Dir,* Carol Ahrens; *Asst Dir,* Elizabeth Goldfrank; *Librn,* James Janis; Staff 10 (MLS 10)
Founded 1926. Pop 39,330; Circ 260,000
Library Holdings: Bk Vols 240,100; Per Subs 584
Special Collections: Oral History
Subject Interests: Local hist
Database Vendor: SirsiDynix
Mem of Nassau Library System
Partic in Long Island Library Resources Council
Special Services for the Deaf - TDD equip
Open Mon-Thurs 9-9, Fri-Sat 9-5 & Sun 1-5

HIGHLAND

P HIGHLAND PUBLIC LIBRARY, 30 Church St, 12528. SAN 311-3124. Tel: 845-691-2275. FAX: 845-691-6302. Web Site: www.highlandlibrary.org. *Dir,* Julie Kelsall-Dempsey; E-mail: jkelsall@highlandlibrary.org; *Asst Dir, Ch,* Holly Sgro; Staff 8 (MLS 2, Non-MLS 6)
Founded 1915. Pop 11,075; Circ 45,810
Library Holdings: Bk Titles 32,865; Per Subs 51
Automation Activity & Vendor Info: (Acquisitions) Innovative Interfaces, Inc
Wireless access
Publications: Highland Public Library Events

Mem of Mid-Hudson Library System
Open Mon & Fri 10-5, Wed 10-8, Tues & Thurs 1-8, Sat 10-4
Branches: 1
CLINTONDALE BRANCH, Crescent at Maple, Clintondale, 12515. (Mail add: PO Box 481, Clintondale, 12515), SAN 372-560X. Tel: 845-883-5015. *Mgr,* Arlene McMahon
Automation Activity & Vendor Info: (Cataloging) Innovative Interfaces, Inc; (Circulation) Innovative Interfaces, Inc
Open Tues 10-12, Wed & Thurs 4-7

HIGHLAND FALLS

P HIGHLAND FALLS LIBRARY*, 298 Main St, 10928. SAN 352-5392. Tel: 845-446-3113. FAX: 845-446-1109. E-mail: hfl@rcls.org. Web Site: rcls.org/hfl. *Dir,* Suzanne Brahm; E-mail: sbrahm@rcls.org; Staff 1 (Non-MLS 1)
Founded 1884. Pop 5,600; Circ 28,091
Jan 2005-Dec 2005 Income $208,810, State $2,003, City $177,709, County $3,098, Locally Generated Income $26,000. Mats Exp $200,900, Books $14,458, Per/Ser (Incl. Access Fees) $2,600, AV Equip $2,325, AV Mat $4,419, Electronic Ref Mat (Incl. Access Fees) $6,000. Sal $107,332
Library Holdings: CDs 1,130; DVDs 500; Electronic Media & Resources 49,000; Bk Vols 27,855; Per Subs 40; Videos 1,000
Special Collections: Hudson River; West Point
Subject Interests: Local authors, Local hist
Automation Activity & Vendor Info: (Acquisitions) SirsiDynix; (Cataloging) SirsiDynix; (Circulation) SirsiDynix; (Course Reserve) SirsiDynix; (ILL) SirsiDynix; (Media Booking) SirsiDynix; (OPAC) SirsiDynix; (Serials) SirsiDynix
Wireless access
Mem of Ramapo Catskill Library System
Open Mon, Wed, Thurs & Fri 10-5, Tues 10-7, Sat 10-2
Friends of the Library Group

HIGHLAND MILLS

P WOODBURY PUBLIC LIBRARY*, Rushmore Memorial Branch, 16 County Rte 105, 10930-9802. SAN 311-3140. Tel: 845-928-6162. Administration Tel: 845-928-7837. FAX: 845-928-3079. E-mail: wpl@rcls.org. Web Site: www.rcls.org/wpl. *Dir,* Jennifer Bradshaw; E-mail: jbradshaw@rcls.org; *Asst Dir,* Martha LaVallee; Staff 2 (MLS 1, Non-MLS 1)
Founded 1923. Pop 9,460
Library Holdings: Bk Vols 43,991, Per Subs 120
Special Collections: Historical Coll-Town of Woodbury
Automation Activity & Vendor Info: (Cataloging) Horizon; (Circulation) Horizon; (OPAC) Horizon
Wireless access
Mem of Ramapo Catskill Library System
Partic in Bibliomation Inc
Open Mon & Thurs 10-9, Tues, Wed & Fri 10-6, Sat & Sun 11-3
Friends of the Library Group

HILLSDALE

P ROELIFF JANSEN COMMUNITY LIBRARY ASSOCIATION, INC*, 9091 Rte 22, 12529. (Mail add: PO Box 669, 12529-0669), SAN 311-3159. Tel: 518-325-4101. FAX: 518-325-4105. E-mail: rjcl9091@gmail.com. Web Site: roejanlibrary.org. *Dir,* Carol Briggs
Founded 1913. Pop 6,535; Circ 36,378
Jan 2011-Dec 2011 Income $223,404, State $3,260, County $5,614, Locally Generated Income $57,750, Other $156,780. Mats Exp $18,413, Books $12,679, Other Print Mats $4,705, Electronic Ref Mat (Incl. Access Fees) $1,029. Sal $84,665
Library Holdings: Audiobooks 1,942; CDs 706; DVDs 2,221; Bk Titles 16,793; Per Subs 42
Wireless access
Mem of Mid-Hudson Library System
Open Mon-Wed & Fri 10-5, Thurs 10-8, Sat 10-4, Sun 1-4
Friends of the Library Group

HILTON

P PARMA PUBLIC LIBRARY, Seven West Ave, 14468-1214. SAN 311-3167. Tel: 585-392-8350. FAX: 585-392-9870. Web Site: www.parmapubliclibrary.org. *Dir,* Rebecca Tantillo; Staff 13 (MLS 3, Non-MLS 10)
Founded 1885. Pop 15,633; Circ 140,267
Subject Interests: Local hist
Automation Activity & Vendor Info: (Acquisitions) CARL.Solution (TLC); (Cataloging) CARL.Solution (TLC); (Circulation) CARL.Solution (TLC); (OPAC) CARL.Solution (TLC)
Wireless access
Function: 24/7 Online cat, Adult bk club, After school storytime, Art exhibits, Audiobks via web, Bk club(s), Bks on CD, Children's prog, Computer training, Computers for patron use, Copy machines, e-mail & chat, Electronic databases & coll, Family literacy, Fax serv, Free DVD rentals, Handicapped accessible, Holiday prog, Homebound delivery serv, Magazines, Magnifiers for reading, Mail & tel request accepted, Movies, Mus passes, Music CDs, Online cat, Outreach serv, Outside serv via phone, mail, e-mail & web, OverDrive digital audio bks, Photocopying/Printing, Preschool outreach, Prog for adults, Prog for children & young adult, Pub access computers, Ref & res, Ref serv available, Ref serv in person, Scanner, Senior outreach, Serves mentally handicapped consumers, Story hour, Summer reading prog, Tax forms, Teen prog, Telephone ref, Web-catalog, Wheelchair accessible, Writing prog
Mem of Monroe County Library System
Open Mon-Thurs 10-9, Fri 10-6, Sat 10-4
Friends of the Library Group

HOGANSBURG

S AKWESASNE CULTURAL CENTER LIBRARY*, 321 State Rte 37, 13655. SAN 311-3175. Tel: 518-358-2240. FAX: 518-358-2649. E-mail: info@akwesasneculturalcenter.org. Web Site: www.akwesasneculturalcenter.org/library. *Librn,* Valerie Garrow
Library Holdings: Bk Titles 28,000; Per Subs 51
Special Collections: American Indian Coll
Automation Activity & Vendor Info: (Cataloging) Horizon; (Circulation) Horizon; (OPAC) Horizon
Wireless access
Function: Photocopying/Printing, Services for persons with disabilities
Mem of Clinton-Essex-Franklin Library System
Partic in Northern New York Library Network
Open Mon, Tues, Thurs & Fri 9-5, Wed 11-7, Sat 11-3

HOLBROOK

P SACHEM PUBLIC LIBRARY*, 150 Holbrook Rd, 11741. SAN 311-3183. Tel: 631-588-5024. FAX: 631-588-5064. E-mail: administration@sachemlibrary.org. Web Site: sachemlibrary.org. *Dir,* Judith M Willner; Fax: 631-588-3475; *Asst Dir,* Carol A Brand; *Head, Ch,* Linda Overton; *Head, Commun Serv,* Lauren Gilbert; *Head, Electronic Serv,* Alan Schelp; *Head, Ref,* Lynne Kennedy; *Head, Tech Serv,* E Renee Capitanio; *Head, Teen Serv,* Susan Tychnowicz; *Librn,* Linda Bova; *Circ Serv Coordr,* Virginia Pfeifer. Subject Specialists: *Local hist,* Linda Bova; Staff 33.5 (MLS 28, Non-MLS 5.5)
Founded 1961. Pop 83,196; Circ 982,561
Jul 2010-Jun 2011 Income $9,085,522. Mats Exp $3,872,931, Books $3,563,837, Per/Ser (Incl. Access Fees) $60,311, Micro $4,459, AV Mat $183,802, Electronic Ref Mat (Incl. Access Fees) $60,522. Sal $3,957,901 (Prof $2,695,926)
Library Holdings: AV Mats 55,619; Electronic Media & Resources 7,861; Bk Vols 266,519; Per Subs 572
Special Collections: Senior Coll; SEPTA; Virtual Reference Coll
Subject Interests: Genealogy, Local hist
Automation Activity & Vendor Info: (Acquisitions) Innovative Interfaces, Inc; (Cataloging) Innovative Interfaces, Inc; (Circulation) Innovative Interfaces, Inc; (ILL) Innovative Interfaces, Inc; (OPAC) Innovative Interfaces, Inc; (Serials) Innovative Interfaces, Inc
Database Vendor: Dialog, EBSCOhost, Gale Cengage Learning, OCLC FirstSearch, TLC (The Library Corporation), Wilson - Wilson Web
Wireless access
Publications: Guide to Nifty World Wide Web Sites; Local Directory; Newsletter; Periodicals List
Mem of Suffolk Cooperative Library System
Special Services for the Blind - Bks on cassette; Closed circuit TV magnifier; Extensive large print coll
Friends of the Library Group

HOLLAND PATENT

P HOLLAND PATENT FREE LIBRARY*, 9580 Main St, 13354-3819. (Mail add: PO Box 187, 13354-0187), SAN 311-3205. Tel: 315-865-5034. FAX: 315-865-5034. Web Site: www.midyorklib.org/hollandpatent. *Dir,* Cindy McVoy
Founded 1916. Circ 26,565
Library Holdings: Bk Vols 14,756; Per Subs 30
Wireless access
Mem of Mid-York Library System
Open Mon & Tues (Winter) 5-8, Wed & Thurs 2-6, Fri & Sat 10-1; Mon & Tues (Summer) 4-8, Wed & Thurs 2-6, Fri 10-2
Friends of the Library Group

HOLLEY

P COMMUNITY FREE LIBRARY*, 86 Public Sq, 14470. SAN 311-3213. Tel: 585-638-6987. FAX: 585-638-7436. Web Site: www.nioga.org/holley/. *Dir,* Sandra Shaw; E-mail: sshaw@nioga.org
Pop 9,621; Circ 36,920
Library Holdings: Bk Vols 27,000; Per Subs 50
Subject Interests: Local hist

Automation Activity & Vendor Info: (Cataloging) SirsiDynix; (Circulation) SirsiDynix; (OPAC) SirsiDynix
Wireless access
Mem of Nioga Library System
Open Mon, Wed & Fri 10-1 & 4-8, Tues & Thurs 10-5

HOMER

P PHILLIPS FREE LIBRARY*, 37 S Main St, 13077-1323. (Mail add: PO Box 7, 13077-0007), SAN 311-3221. Tel: 607-749-4616. FAX: 607-749-4616. E-mail: circ@phillipsfreelibrary.org. Web Site: www.phillipsfreelibrary.org. *Dir,* Priscilla Berggren-Thomas; Staff 2 (MLS 1, Non-MLS 1)
Founded 1902. Pop 12,500; Circ 45,000
Library Holdings: DVDs 340; Bk Vols 20,000; Per Subs 36; Talking Bks 630; Videos 210
Automation Activity & Vendor Info: (Circulation) Innovative Interfaces, Inc; (OPAC) Innovative Interfaces, Inc
Wireless access
Mem of Finger Lakes Library System
Open Mon 10-6, Tues & Thurs 2-8, Wed 10-8, Fri 2-6, Sat 10-2
Friends of the Library Group

HONEOYE

P HONEOYE PUBLIC LIBRARY*, 8708 Main St, 14471. (Mail add: PO Box 70, 14471-0070), SAN 311-323X. Tel: 585-229-5020. FAX: 585-229-5881. Web Site: www.honeoye.pls-net.org. *Dir,* Wendy M Krause; E-mail: wkrause@pls-net.org
Circ 32,200
Library Holdings: Bk Vols 16,000; Per Subs 23
Automation Activity & Vendor Info: (Cataloging) SIRSI-DRA; (Circulation) SIRSI-DRA; (OPAC) SIRSI-DRA
Wireless access
Mem of Pioneer Library System
Open Mon & Thurs 2:30-8:30, Tues 10-8:30, Sat 10-1

HONEOYE FALLS

P TOWN OF MENDON PUBLIC LIBRARY*, 15 Monroe St, 14472. SAN 311-3248. Tel: 585-624-6067. FAX: 585-624-4255. *Dir,* Lory Gunther; Staff 1 (MLS 1)
Pop 8,370; Circ 96,000
Library Holdings: Bk Vols 36,000; Per Subs 38
Mem of Monroe County Library System
Open Mon-Thurs 10-9, Fri 10-5, Sat 1-4
Friends of the Library Group

HOOSICK FALLS

P CHENEY LIBRARY*, 77 Classic St, 12090-1326. (Mail add: PO Box 177, 12090-0177), SAN 311-3256. Tel: 518-686-9401. FAX: 518-686-9401. Web Site: www.cheneylibrary.org. *Dir,* Carol Gaillard
Founded 1926. Circ 23,576
Library Holdings: Bk Vols 14,262; Per Subs 25
Automation Activity & Vendor Info: (Cataloging) SirsiDynix; (Circulation) SirsiDynix; (OPAC) SirsiDynix
Wireless access
Mem of Upper Hudson Library System
Open Mon, Wed & Thurs 1-8, Tues 10-5, Fri 11-4, Sat 8-1
Friends of the Library Group

HOPEWELL JUNCTION

P BEEKMAN LIBRARY*, 11 Town Center Blvd, 12533. (Mail add: PO Box 697, Poughquag, 12570-0697), SAN 376-3013. Tel: 845-724-3414. FAX: 845-724-3941. Web Site: www.beekmanlibrary.org. *Dir,* Carol Rodriguez; Staff 7.25 (MLS 1, Non-MLS 6.25)
Founded 1965. Pop 13,655; Circ 68,477
Jan 2006-Dec 2006 Income $303,175, State $3,550, County $4,625, Locally Generated Income $295,000. Mats Exp $5,100, Per/Ser (Incl. Access Fees) $1,300, AV Mat $3,800. Sal $123,112 (Prof $50,000)
Library Holdings: AV Mats 2,977; Bk Titles 20,443; Per Subs 91; Talking Bks 565
Subject Interests: Irish, Local hist
Automation Activity & Vendor Info: (Cataloging) Innovative Interfaces, Inc - Millenium; (OPAC) Innovative Interfaces, Inc
Database Vendor: EBSCOhost, Gale Cengage Learning, ProQuest
Mem of Mid-Hudson Library System
Open Mon & Wed 3-8, Tues 10-6, Thurs 10-8, Fri & Sat 10-4
Friends of the Library Group

P EAST FISHKILL PUBLIC LIBRARY DISTRICT*, 348 Rte 376, 12533-6075. SAN 312-6269. Tel: 845-221-9943. FAX: 845-226-1404. Web Site: www.eastfishkilllibrary.org. *Dir,* Gloria Goverman; *Ad,* Cindy Dubinski; Tel: 845-221-9943, Ext 225; *Youth Serv Librn,* Cathy Nuding; Tel: 845-221-9943, Ext 233; *Circ Supvr,* Catherine Swierat; Tel: 845-221-9943, Ext 228; *Tech Serv Supvr,* Kristie Simco; Tel: 845-221-9943, Ext 222; Staff 12.6 (MLS 3.7, Non-MLS 8.9)
Founded 1938. Pop 25,589; Circ 238,674
Jan 2011-Dec 2011 Income $792,000, Locally Generated Income $747,743. Mats Exp $86,000. Sal $397,000 (Prof $182,641)
Library Holdings: Audiobooks 1,901; DVDs 3,779; Bk Titles 63,000; Per Subs 134
Automation Activity & Vendor Info: (Acquisitions) Innovative Interfaces, Inc; (Cataloging) Innovative Interfaces, Inc; (Circulation) Innovative Interfaces, Inc; (OPAC) Innovative Interfaces, Inc
Wireless access
Mem of Mid-Hudson Library System
Open Mon-Thurs 10-8, Fri 10-6, Sat 10-5
Friends of the Library Group

HOPKINTON

P HOPKINTON TOWN LIBRARY*, Seven Church St, 12965. Tel: 315-328-4113. FAX: 315-328-4113. Web Site: www.hopkintonnylibrary.org. *Dir,* Brenda Nicholson
Jan 2005-Dec 2005 Income $5,700
Wireless access
Mem of North Country Library System
Open Mon 10-12 & 4-7, Wed 10-12 & 3-6, Thurs 3-6, Fri 10-1

HORNELL

P HORNELL PUBLIC LIBRARY*, 64 Genesee St, 14843-1651. SAN 311-3280. Tel: 607-324-1210. FAX: 607-324-2570. Web Site: www.stls.org. *Dir,* Alice Marie Taychert; E-mail: taycherta@stls.org; Staff 2 (MLS 2)
Founded 1868. Pop 9,019; Circ 58,646
Apr 2007-Mar 2008 Income $317,143, City $120,000. Mats Exp $390,846, AV Mat $55,663
Library Holdings: Audiobooks 958; AV Mats 1,691; Bk Vols 42,525; Per Subs 99; Spec Interest Per Sub 1,718
Special Collections: Erie Railroad
Subject Interests: Civil War, Local hist, Railroads
Automation Activity & Vendor Info: (Acquisitions) SirsiDynix; (Circulation) SirsiDynix; (ILL) SirsiDynix; (OPAC) SirsiDynix
Database Vendor: EBSCOhost, Gale Cengage Learning, OCLC FirstSearch, SirsiDynix
Wireless access
Mem of Southern Tier Library System
Special Services for the Blind - Home delivery serv
Open Mon-Thurs 10-8, Fri 10-5, Sat 10-2

P HOWARD PUBLIC LIBRARY*, 3607 County Rte 70A, 14843. SAN 310-8236. Tel: 607-566-2412. FAX: 607-566-3679. Web Site: www.stls.org/howard. *Dir,* Lorrine Nelson; E-mail: nelsonl@stls.org
Founded 1911. Pop 1,331; Circ 16,000
Jan 2005-Dec 2005 Income $47,144. Mats Exp $9,710. Sal $17,082
Library Holdings: AV Mats 1,190; DVDs 172; Bk Titles 10,154; Bk Vols 11,000; Per Subs 28; Talking Bks 154; Videos 618
Automation Activity & Vendor Info: (Cataloging) SirsiDynix; (Circulation) SirsiDynix; (OPAC) SirsiDynix; (Serials) SirsiDynix
Wireless access
Mem of Southern Tier Library System
Open Mon, Tues & Thurs 2-8, Sat 9-1

HOUGHTON

C HOUGHTON COLLEGE*, Willard J Houghton Library, One Willard Ave, 14744. SAN 352-5457. Tel: 585-567-9242. Interlibrary Loan Service Tel: 585-567-9256. Reference Tel: 585-567-9241. FAX: 585-567-9248. E-mail: circulation@houghton.edu. Web Site: www.houghton.edu/library. *Libr Dir,* David Stevick; E-mail: david.stevick@houghton.edu; *Cataloger, Ref Librn,* Betty Bunt; Tel: 585-567-9252, E-mail: betty.bunt@houghton.edu; *Tech Librn,* Glen Avery; Tel: 585-567-9615, E-mail: glen.avery@houghton.edu; *Ref & Instruction Coordr,* Bradley Wilber; Tel: 585-567-9607, E-mail: bradley.wilber@houghton.edu. Subject Specialists: *Music,* Bradley Wilber; Staff 9 (MLS 4, Non-MLS 5)
Founded 1883. Enrl 1,000; Highest Degree: Master
Library Holdings: AV Mats 47,000; CDs 9,800; DVDs 6,000; e-books 21,000; e-journals 47,000; Bk Vols 226,650; Per Subs 400
Special Collections: John & Charles Wesley & Methodism Coll
Subject Interests: Biblical studies, Intercultural studies, Music, Relig, Theol
Automation Activity & Vendor Info: (Acquisitions) SirsiDynix; (Cataloging) SirsiDynix; (Circulation) SirsiDynix; (Course Reserve) SirsiDynix; (ILL) SirsiDynix; (Media Booking) SirsiDynix; (OPAC) SirsiDynix; (Serials) SirsiDynix
Database Vendor: ABC-CLIO, Agricola, American Chemical Society, American Psychological Association (APA), BioOne, CountryWatch, CredoReference, ebrary, EBSCOhost, H W Wilson, JSTOR, OCLC, OCLC FirstSearch, OCLC WorldShare Interlibrary Loan, ProQuest, SirsiDynix

Wireless access
Function: ILL available
Partic in South Central Regional Library Council; Westchester Academic Library Directors Organization (WALDO)
Open Mon-Thurs 7:45am-11:00pm, Fri 7:45-7:00, Sat 9am-10pm

HOWES CAVE

S IROQUOIS INDIAN MUSEUM LIBRARY*, 324 Caverns Rd, 12092. (Mail add: PO Box 7, 12092-0007), SAN 376-2025. Tel: 518-296-8949. FAX: 518-296-8955. E-mail: info@iroquoismuseum.org. Web Site: www.iroquoismuseum.org. *Dir,* Erynne Ansel-McCabe; *Curator,* Stephanie Shultes
Founded 1980
Library Holdings: Bk Vols 1,200
Subject Interests: Iroquois, Local hist, Native Am
Wireless access
Open Tues-Sat (April-Dec) 10-5, Sun 12-5

HUDSON

J COLUMBIA-GREENE COMMUNITY COLLEGE LIBRARY*, 4400 Rte 23, 12534. SAN 311-3310. Tel: 518-828-4181, Ext 3286. FAX: 518-828-4396. Web Site: www.sunycgcc.edu/library. *Chairperson, Librn,* Geralynn Demarest; Tel: 518-828-4181, Ext 3290, E-mail: demarest@sunycgcc.edu; *Acq,* Tina Santiago; Tel: 518-828-4181, Ext 3284, E-mail: santiago@sunycgcc.edu; *AV,* Carl Nabozny; Tel: 518-828-4181, Ext 3294, E-mail: nabozny@sunycgcc.edu; *Circ, Ref,* Jean Anderson; Tel: 518-828-4181, Ext 3287, E-mail: jean.anderson@sunycgcc.edu; *ILL,* Lynn Erceg; Tel: 518-828-4181, Ext 3289, E-mail: erceg@sunycgcc.edu; Staff 6 (MLS 2, Non-MLS 4)
Founded 1969. Enrl 1,500; Fac 49; Highest Degree: Associate
Sept 2008-Aug 2009 Income $616,345. Mats Exp $187,321, Books $68,921, Per/Ser (Incl. Access Fees) $22,500, Micro $36,000, AV Equip $3,050, AV Mat $8,850, Electronic Ref Mat (Incl. Access Fees) $48,000. Sal $276,556 (Prof $100,556)
Library Holdings: Bk Titles 60,644; Bk Vols 63,817; Per Subs 130
Special Collections: Ettelt Children's Coll; Map Coll
Automation Activity & Vendor Info: (Circulation) Ex Libris Group
Database Vendor: ARTstor, Dialog, Elsevier, Gale Cengage Learning, JSTOR, LexisNexis, OCLC FirstSearch, TLC (The Library Corporation)
Partic in Southeastern New York Library Resources Council
Open Mon-Thurs 8am-9pm, Fri 8-4:30, Sat & Sun (Fall & Spring) 1-5

M COLUMBIA MEMORIAL HOSPITAL*, Medical Library, Columbia Memorial Hospital, 71 Prospect Ave, 12534. SAN 311-3329. Tel: 518-697-3230, 518-828-7601. FAX: 518-822-2178. *Dir,* Dr Norman Chapin; E-mail: nchapin@cmh-net.com
Library Holdings: Bk Vols 150; Per Subs 17
Subject Interests: Med, Nursing
Partic in NY & NJ Regional Med Libr; Southeastern New York Library Resources Council

P HUDSON AREA LIBRARY*, 400 State St, 12534. SAN 311-3337. Tel: 518-828-1792. FAX: 518-822-0567. E-mail: hudsonarealibrary@gmail.com. Web Site: www.hudson.lib.ny.us. *Libr Dir,* Emily Chameides
Founded 1959
Subject Interests: Local hist
Wireless access
Mem of Mid-Hudson Library System
Open Tues & Wed 9-8, Thurs & Fri 9-5, Sat 10-3
Friends of the Library Group

S NEW YORK STATE DEPARTMENT OF CORRECTIONAL SERVICES*, Hudson Correctional Facility Library, 50 E Court St, 12534-2429. (Mail add: PO Box 576, 12534-0576), SAN 327-1579. Tel: 518-828-4311, Ext 4600. FAX: 518-828-4311, Ext 2099. *Librn,* Judith A Doyle
Library Holdings: Bk Titles 9,000; Per Subs 55
Automation Activity & Vendor Info: (Cataloging) Follett Software; (Circulation) Follett Software
Open Mon & Wed-Fri 8:30-3:30, Tues 12-8

HUDSON FALLS

P HUDSON FALLS FREE LIBRARY*, 220 Main St, 12839. SAN 311-3345. Tel: 518-747-6406. FAX: 518-747-6406. Web Site: hudsonfalls.sals.edu. *Dir,* Marie L Gandron; E-mail: mgandron@sals.edu; Staff 6 (MLS 1, Non-MLS 5)
Founded 1910. Pop 13,436; Circ 34,551
Jan 2007-Dec 2007 Income $126,570, State $3,674, Provincial $24,650, City $19,000, Locally Generated Income $13,920, Other $28,714. Mats Exp $18,346, Books $13,100, Per/Ser (Incl. Access Fees) $1,485, AV Mat $3,761. Sal $58,093 (Prof $31,000)
Library Holdings: Audiobooks 3,311; AV Mats 1,228; Bks on Deafness & Sign Lang 15; CDs 250; DVDs 320; e-books 1,461; Large Print Bks 500; Bk Titles 32,000; Bk Vols 32,192; Per Subs 45; Talking Bks 850; Videos 200
Subject Interests: Fiction, Local hist
Automation Activity & Vendor Info: (Acquisitions) SirsiDynix; (Cataloging) SirsiDynix; (Circulation) SirsiDynix; (ILL) SirsiDynix; (Media Booking) SirsiDynix; (OPAC) SirsiDynix; (Serials) SirsiDynix
Publications: Newsletters (Monthly)
Mem of Southern Adirondack Library System
Open Mon, Tues & Thurs 1:30-5 & 6:30-8:30, Wed & Fri 10-12:30 & 1:30-5, Sat 10-4:30

HUNTER

P HUNTER PUBLIC LIBRARY*, 7965 Main St, 12442. (Mail add: PO Box 376, 12442-0376), SAN 311-3353. Tel: 518-263-4655. FAX: 518-263-4655. E-mail: hunter@francomm.com. Web Site: www.midhudson.org/hunterlib/ny/us. *Librn,* June Bain
Pop 3,719; Circ 12,175
Library Holdings: Bk Titles 13,000; Per Subs 27
Wireless access
Mem of Mid-Hudson Library System
Special Services for the Blind - Talking bks
Open Wed (Winter) 9:30-4 & 5:30-8, Thurs-Sat 9:30-4; Mon, Tues & Thurs-Sat (Summer) 10-4:30, Wed 9:30-4 & 5:30-8

HUNTINGTON

S HUNTINGTON HISTORICAL SOCIETY LIBRARY*, Research Center Library, 209 Main St, 11743. SAN 311-337X. Tel: 631-427-7045. FAX: 631-427-7056. Web Site: www.huntingtonhistoricalsociety.org. *Archivist,* Karen Martin; Tel: 631-427-7045, Ext 406; Staff 1 (Non-MLS 1)
Founded 1903
Library Holdings: Bk Titles 5,000; Per Subs 19
Special Collections: Long Island Genealogy (Nellie Ritch Scudder Coll), bks, bus recs, church recs, family papers, ms, photog, recs; New York State Census (Kings, Queens, Nassau & Suffolk Counties, 1915-1925), microfilm; US Federal Census (Suffolk County, 1790-1920), microfilm. Oral History
Subject Interests: Am decorative arts, Genealogies of Huntington, Local hist of town, Long Island, Long Island families
Restriction: Open by appt only

M HUNTINGTON HOSPITAL*, Medical Library, 270 Park Ave, 11743. SAN 311-3388. Tel: 631-351-2000, 631-351-2283. FAX: 631-351-2586. *Dir,* Susan Simpson; E-mail: ssimpson@hunthosp.org
Founded 1961
Library Holdings: e-books 400; e-journals 5,000; Bk Vols 200; Per Subs 15
Database Vendor: Medline
Wireless access
Open Mon-Fri 8-4

P HUNTINGTON PUBLIC LIBRARY*, 338 Main St, 11743. SAN 352-5481. Tel: 631-427-5165. FAX: 631-421-7131. Web Site: hpl.suffolk.lib.ny.us. *Dir,* Susan Hagedorn; E-mail: susan_hagedorn@huntlib.org; *Asst Dir,* Kristine Casper; E-mail: kristine_casper@huntlib.org; *Head, Customer Serv,* John Mulhern; *Head, Ref & Adult Serv,* Teresa Schwind; *Head, Tech Serv,* Tom Cohn; *Head, Youth Serv,* Laura Giuliani; Staff 17 (MLS 17)
Founded 1875. Pop 34,000; Circ 408,181
Library Holdings: Bk Titles 184,391; Per Subs 610
Special Collections: Heckscher Art Museum Coll; Long Island History; Walt Whitman Coll
Automation Activity & Vendor Info: (Circulation) Innovative Interfaces, Inc
Wireless access
Publications: Newsletter (Bi-monthly)
Mem of Suffolk Cooperative Library System
Open Mon-Fri 9-9, Sat 9-5, Sun (Sept-June) 1-5
Friends of the Library Group
Branches: 1
HUNTINGTON STATION BRANCH, 1335 New York Ave, Huntington Station, 11746, SAN 352-5511. Tel: 631-421-5053. FAX: 631-421-3488. E-mail: station@thehuntingtonlibrary.org. *Br Mgr,* Mary Kelly
Open Mon-Thurs 9-8, Fri & Sat 9-5, Sun 1-5
Friends of the Library Group

R SEMINARY OF THE IMMACULATE CONCEPTION LIBRARY*, 440 W Neck Rd, 11743. SAN 373-1189. Tel: 631-423-0483, Ext 141. FAX: 631-423-2346. Web Site: www.icseminary.edu. *Dir,* Elyse Hayes; E-mail: ehayes@icseminary.edu; Staff 2 (MLS 1, Non-MLS 1)
Library Holdings: Bk Vols 46,277; Per Subs 368
Subject Interests: Church hist, Scripture, Theol
Automation Activity & Vendor Info: (Acquisitions) LibLime; (Cataloging) LibLime; (Circulation) LibLime; (OPAC) LibLime

Database Vendor: EBSCOhost
Wireless access
Partic in Long Island Library Resources Council
Restriction: Open by appt only

HUNTINGTON STATION

P SOUTH HUNTINGTON PUBLIC LIBRARY*, 145 Pidgeon Hill Rd, 11746. SAN 311-3426. Tel: 631-549-4411. FAX: 631-549-1266. Web Site: shpl.info. *Dir,* Joseph Latini; *Asst Dir,* Janet Scherer; *Head, Ref, ILL,* Carol Leach; *AV, Head, Tech Serv,* Howard Spiegelglass; *Head, Youth Serv,* Mildred Bernstein; *Outreach Serv Librn,* Stanley Kalemaris; *Ref Librn,* Martha Kahn; *Syst Adminr,* Scott Senig; *Ch Serv,* Elizabeth Ghee; *Ch Serv,* Sally Nikolis; *Reader Serv,* Debra Cernieux; Staff 17 (MLS 17)
Founded 1961. Pop 37,045
Jul 2005-Jun 2006 Income $5,236,426, Locally Generated Income $5,105,876, Other $130,550. Mats Exp $505,021, Books $307,621, Per/Ser (Incl. Access Fees) $20,000, Micro $13,500, AV Equip $30,000, AV Mat $93,900, Electronic Ref Mat (Incl. Access Fees) $40,000. Sal $2,113,507 (Prof $1,096,574)
Library Holdings: AV Mats 22,611; Bk Vols 252,642; Per Subs 300
Subject Interests: Educ
Automation Activity & Vendor Info: (Acquisitions) Innovative Interfaces, Inc; (Cataloging) Innovative Interfaces, Inc; (Circulation) Innovative Interfaces, Inc; (ILL) Innovative Interfaces, Inc; (OPAC) Innovative Interfaces, Inc
Wireless access
Publications: Newsletter
Mem of Suffolk Cooperative Library System
Friends of the Library Group

S WALT WHITMAN BIRTHPLACE ASSOCIATION*, Research Library, 246 Old Walt Whitman Rd, 11746-4148. SAN 311-3434. Tel: 631-427-5240. FAX: 631-427-5247. Web Site: www.waltwhitman.org. *Dir,* Cynthia Shor; E-mail: director@waltwhitman.org
Founded 1949
Library Holdings: Bk Vols 380
Special Collections: Foreign Language Translations; Walt Whitman Coll, biog, studies, hist, editions of poetry, collected writings
Wireless access
Open Wed-Fri (Winter) 1-4, Sat & Sun 11-4; Mon-Fri (Summer) 11-4, Sat & Sun 11-5
Friends of the Library Group

HURLEY

P HURLEY LIBRARY DISTRICT*, 44 Main St, 12443-5106. (Mail add: PO Box 660, 12443), SAN 311-3442. Tel: 845-338-2092. FAX: 845-338-2092. E-mail: hurleylibrary@hvc.rr.com. Web Site: hurley.lib.ny.us. *Dir,* Tracey Pause; E-mail: hurleydirector@hvc.rr.com; Staff 5 (MLS 1, Non-MLS 4)
Founded 1958. Pop 3,561; Circ 12,933
Library Holdings: AV Mats 500; Bk Vols 13,000; Per Subs 19
Subject Interests: Local hist
Automation Activity & Vendor Info: (Acquisitions) Innovative Interfaces, Inc; (Cataloging) Innovative Interfaces, Inc; (Circulation) Innovative Interfaces, Inc
Wireless access
Mem of Mid-Hudson Library System
Open Mon 10-1:30, Tues & Thurs 1-7:30, Wed 10-5, Sat 10-3

HYDE PARK

C CULINARY INSTITUTE OF AMERICA*, Conrad N Hilton Library, 1946 Campus Dr, 12538-1499. SAN 311-3450. Tel: 845-451-1747. Reference Tel: 845-451-1322. FAX: 845-451-1092. E-mail: library@culinary.edu. Web Site: www.ciachef.edu. *Dir,* Eileen De Vries; *Info Serv,* Christine Crawford-Oppenheimer; *Tech Serv,* Michelle Sprague; Staff 7 (MLS 3, Non-MLS 4)
Founded 1973. Enrl 2,300; Fac 132; Highest Degree: Bachelor
Library Holdings: AV Mats 4,304; Bk Titles 59,906; Bk Vols 82,607; Per Subs 280
Special Collections: Menus
Subject Interests: Cookery, Culinary arts, Liberal arts, Rare bks, Restaurant mgt, Spirits, Wines
Automation Activity & Vendor Info: (Acquisitions) Innovative Interfaces, Inc; (Cataloging) Innovative Interfaces, Inc; (Circulation) Innovative Interfaces, Inc; (Course Reserve) Innovative Interfaces, Inc; (OPAC) Innovative Interfaces, Inc; (Serials) Innovative Interfaces, Inc
Database Vendor: Gale Cengage Learning, OCLC FirstSearch, ProQuest
Wireless access
Partic in Southeastern New York Library Resources Council

P HYDE PARK FREE LIBRARY*, Two Main St, 12538. Tel: 845-229-7791. FAX: 845-229-6521. E-mail: hpfllibrarian@yahoo.com. Web Site: www.hydeparklibrary.org. *Dir,* D Gregory Callahan; *Ch Serv,* Janet Battistoni
Founded 1927
Library Holdings: AV Mats 834; Bk Vols 30,692; Per Subs 56; Talking Bks 834
Automation Activity & Vendor Info: (Cataloging) Innovative Interfaces, Inc; (Circulation) Innovative Interfaces, Inc; (ILL) Innovative Interfaces, Inc; (OPAC) Innovative Interfaces, Inc; (Serials) Innovative Interfaces, Inc
Database Vendor: EBSCOhost, Gale Cengage Learning, ProQuest
Mem of Mid-Hudson Library System
Open Mon & Tues 9-8, Wed 12-5, Thurs 12-8, Fri 1-6, Sat 9-4, Sun 11-3

G NATIONAL ARCHIVES & RECORDS ADMINISTRATION*, Franklin D Roosevelt Presidential Library, 4079 Albany Post Rd, 12538. SAN 311-3469. Tel: 845-486-7770. Reference Tel: 845-486-1142. Toll Free Tel: 800-337-8474. FAX: 845-486-1147. E-mail: roosevelt.library@nara.gov. Web Site: www.fdrlibrary.marist.edu. *Dir,* Lynn A Bassanese; Tel: 845-486-7741, E-mail: lynn.bassanese@nara.gov; *Curator,* Herman Eberhardt; *Supvry Archivist,* Robert Clark
Founded 1941
Library Holdings: Bk Titles 32,000; Bk Vols 47,000; Per Subs 12
Special Collections: Early Juveniles Coll; Franklin D Roosevelt & Foreign Affairs, 1935-39 (seventeen volumes); Historical Materials in the Franklin D Roosevelt Library; Hudson River Valley History Coll; The Era of Franklin D Roosevelt: A Selected Bibliography of Periodicals, Essays & Dissertation Literature, 1945-1971; US Naval Hist Coll
Subject Interests: Eleanor Roosevelt, Franklin Roosevelt, Hudson River Valley hist, NY Colonial hist, Politics from 1913-1945, US Naval hist
Partic in Southeastern New York Library Resources Council
Open Mon-Fri 8:45-5

ILION

P ILION FREE PUBLIC LIBRARY*, 78 West St, 13357-1797. SAN 311-3485. Tel: 315-894-5028. FAX: 315-894-9980. E-mail: ilion@midyork.org. Web Site: www.midyork.org/ilion. *Ch Serv, Dir,* Thomasine Z Jennings; Staff 7 (MLS 1, Non-MLS 6)
Founded 1893. Pop 8,610; Circ 75,000
Library Holdings: Bk Titles 53,000; Per Subs 98
Special Collections: Ilion, New York (Seamans Coll), photog, slides. Oral History
Automation Activity & Vendor Info: (Cataloging) SirsiDynix; (Circulation) SirsiDynix; (OPAC) SirsiDynix
Wireless access
Mem of Mid-York Library System
Open Mon, Tues & Thurs 10-8, Wed & Fri 10-6, Sat 10-1
Friends of the Library Group

INDIAN LAKE

P TOWN OF INDIAN LAKE PUBLIC LIBRARY*, 113 Pelon Rd, 12842. (Mail add: PO Box 778, 12842-0778), SAN 311-3493. Tel: 518-648-5444. FAX: 518-648-6227. Web Site: indianlake.sals.edu. *Dir,* Nancy Berkowitz
Pop 1,410; Circ 28,407
Library Holdings: Bk Vols 24,000; Per Subs 55
Wireless access
Mem of Southern Adirondack Library System
Open Mon & Fri 12-4 & 7-9, Tues 11-3, Wed 1-4 & 7-9, Sat 10-1
Friends of the Library Group

INLET

P TOWN OF INLET PUBLIC LIBRARY*, 168 State Rte 28, 13360. Tel: 315-357-6494. FAX: 315-357-6494. Web Site: www.sals.edu/inlet.shtml. *Dir,* Lynn Durkin; Staff 2 (Non-MLS 2)
Library Holdings: AV Mats 969; Bk Titles 8,101; Per Subs 30; Talking Bks 446
Wireless access
Mem of Southern Adirondack Library System
Open Mon-Fri 8:30-4:30

INTERLAKEN

P INTERLAKEN PUBLIC LIBRARY*, 8390 Main St, 14847. (Mail add: PO Box 317, 14847-0317), SAN 311-3507. Tel: 607-532-4341. FAX: 607-532-4341. E-mail: iinterla@rochester.rr.com. *Librn,* Pat Moore
Founded 1902. Pop 2,200; Circ 11,000
Library Holdings: Bk Vols 11,000; Per Subs 50
Subject Interests: Hist of the town of Interlaken, Seneca County
Mem of Finger Lakes Library System
Open Mon 9-12 & 7-8:30, Tues & Thurs 1-5 & 7-8:30, Wed & Sat 9-12

IRVINGTON

P IRVINGTON PUBLIC LIBRARY*, Guiteau Foundation Library, 12 S Astor St, 10533. SAN 311-3523. Tel: 914-591-7840. FAX: 914-591-0347. E-mail: irvref@wlsmail.org. Web Site: www.irvingtonlibrary.org. *Dir,*

Pamela Strachan; *Asst Dir,* Pamela Bernstein; *Ch Serv,* Irene Glickman; Staff 6 (MLS 3, Non-MLS 3)
Founded 1866. Pop 6,631; Circ 105,846
Library Holdings: AV Mats 6,226; e-books 767; Bk Vols 57,068; Per Subs 120; Videos 1,525
Subject Interests: Local hist
Automation Activity & Vendor Info: (Circulation) SirsiDynix; (OPAC) SirsiDynix
Database Vendor: EBSCOhost
Wireless access
Mem of Westchester Library System
Partic in LibraryLinkNJ, The New Jersey Library Cooperative
Open Mon, Wed, Fri & Sat 10-5, Tues & Thurs 10-9
Friends of the Library Group

ISLAND PARK

P ISLAND PARK PUBLIC LIBRARY*, 176 Long Beach Rd, 11558. SAN 311-3531. Tel: 516-432-0122. FAX: 516-889-3584. Web Site: www.islandparklibrary.org. *Dir,* Michelle Young; Staff 10 (MLS 4, Non-MLS 6)
Founded 1938. Pop 8,857; Circ 43,466
Library Holdings: Bk Vols 70,000; Per Subs 60
Automation Activity & Vendor Info: (Acquisitions) Innovative Interfaces, Inc - Millenium; (Cataloging) Innovative Interfaces, Inc - Millenium; (Circulation) Innovative Interfaces, Inc - Millenium; (OPAC) Innovative Interfaces, Inc - Millenium
Database Vendor: Gale Cengage Learning, Grolier Online, LearningExpress
Wireless access
Mem of Nassau Library System
Open Mon-Thurs 10-9, Fri & Sat 10-5

ISLAND TREES

P ISLAND TREES PUBLIC LIBRARY*, 38 Farmedge Rd, 11756-5200. SAN 311-4201. Tel: 516-731-2211. FAX: 516-731-2395, 516-731-3798. E-mail: islandtreespubliclibrary@yahoo.com. Web Site: www.islandtreespubliclibrary.org. *Dir,* Jessica Koenig; *Ref Librn,* Anne Bauman
Founded 1967. Pop 16,000; Circ 62,304
Library Holdings: Bk Titles 42,646; Per Subs 113
Automation Activity & Vendor Info: (Cataloging) Innovative Interfaces, Inc; (Circulation) Innovative Interfaces, Inc; (OPAC) Innovative Interfaces, Inc
Database Vendor: EBSCOhost, Electric Library, ProQuest
Wireless access
Publications: Island Trees Newsletter (Quarterly)
Mem of Nassau Library System
Open Mon-Thurs 10-9, Fri & Sat 10-5

ISLIP

P ISLIP PUBLIC LIBRARY*, 71 Monell Ave, 11751-3999. SAN 311-354X. Tel: 631-581-5933. FAX: 631-277-8429. E-mail: reference@isliplibrary.org. Web Site: www.isliplibrary.org. *Dir,* Mary Schubart; E-mail: mary@isliplibrary.org; *Ch Serv,* Michele Ferrari; *Ch Serv,* Jane Hoffman; *Patron/Ref Serv,* Laurie Farr-Kindler; *Ref,* Laurie Aitken; *Ref,* Mark Irish; Staff 21 (MLS 21)
Founded 1924. Pop 19,475; Circ 248,375
Jul 2005-Jun 2006 Income $2,876,729, State $5,391, Locally Generated Income $2,728,517. Mats Exp $320,868, Books $177,966. Sal $1,257,298
Library Holdings: AV Mats 12,655; Large Print Bks 913; Bk Vols 169,543; Per Subs 1,389
Special Collections: Local History Coll
Automation Activity & Vendor Info: (Cataloging) Innovative Interfaces, Inc; (Circulation) Innovative Interfaces, Inc; (Course Reserve) Innovative Interfaces, Inc; (ILL) Innovative Interfaces, Inc; (OPAC) Innovative Interfaces, Inc
Database Vendor: Innovative Interfaces, Inc
Wireless access
Publications: The Mariner (Newsletter)
Mem of Suffolk Cooperative Library System
Special Services for the Deaf - Assistive tech
Special Services for the Blind - Closed circuit TV magnifier
Open Mon-Thurs 9-9, Fri & Sat 9-5, Sun (Sept-May) 1-5

ITHACA

M CAYUGA MEDICAL CENTER AT ITHACA, Robert Broad Medical Library, 101 Dates Dr, 14850. SAN 327-6953. Tel: 607-274-4407. FAX: 607-274-4214. *Librn,* Deborah Main; E-mail: DMain@cayugamed.org
Library Holdings: Bk Vols 250; Per Subs 30
Wireless access
Partic in South Central Regional Library Council
Open Mon-Fri 11-2

C CORNELL UNIVERSITY LIBRARY, 201 Olin Library, 14853-5301. SAN 352-5546. Tel: 607-255-3393. Circulation Tel: 607-255-4245. Interlibrary Loan Service Tel: 607-255-9564. Reference Tel: 607-255-4144. FAX: 607-255-6788. Circulation FAX: 607-254-8602. Interlibrary Loan Service FAX: 607-255-9091. Reference FAX: 607-255-3609. E-mail: libadmin@cornell.edu. Web Site: www.library.cornell.edu. *Univ Librn,* Anne R Kenney; E-mail: ark3@cornell.edu; *Assoc Univ Librn,* Ezra Delaney; E-mail: ezra.delaney@cornell.edu; *Assoc Univ Librn,* Xin Li; Tel: 607-255-7026, E-mail: xl49@cornell.edu; *Assoc Univ Librn,* Oya Rieger; Tel: 607-254-5160, E-mail: oyr1@cornell.edu; *Assoc Univ Librn,* Kornelia Tancheva; E-mail: kt18@cornell.edu; *Chief Tech Strategist,* Dean Krafft; Tel: 607-255-9214, E-mail: dean.krafft@cornell.edu; Staff 412 (MLS 126, Non-MLS 286)
Founded 1868. Enrl 22,636; Fac 3,156; Highest Degree: Doctorate
Jul 2013-Jun 2014. Mats Exp $19,423,584. Sal $23,639,397
Library Holdings: e-books 1,114,389; e-journals 110,000; Bk Vols 8,025,037
Special Collections: UN Document Depository; US Document Depository
Wireless access
Partic in New England Law Library Consortium, Inc; OCLC Online Computer Library Center, Inc; S Cent Libr Res Coun
Friends of the Library Group

Departmental Libraries:

ADELSON LIBRARY, LABORATORY OF ORNITHOLOGY, 159 Sapsucker Woods Rd, 14850-1999, SAN 352-6003. Tel: 607-254-2165. Toll Free Tel: 800-254-2473. FAX: 607-254-2111. E-mail: adelson_lib@cornell.edu. Web Site: www.birds.cornell.edu/Adelson. *Coordr,* Marc Devokaitis; Staff 1 (Non-MLS 1)
Founded 2004
Library Holdings: Bk Vols 13,000; Per Subs 150
Special Collections: Books Illustrated by Louis A Fuertes; Falconry
Subject Interests: Ornithology
Automation Activity & Vendor Info: (Cataloging) Ex Libris Group
Function: Res libr
Open Mon-Fri 10-12 & 1-4

JOHN HENRIK CLARKE AFRICANA LIBRARY, 310 Triphammer Rd, 14850, SAN 352-5821. Tel: 607-255-3822. FAX: 607-255-2493. E-mail: afrlib@cornell.edu. Web Site: www.library.cornell.edu/africana. *Head of Libr,* Eric Kofi Acree; Tel: 607-255-5229, E-mail: ea18@cornell.edu; Staff 3 (MLS 1, Non-MLS 2)
Founded 1969
Library Holdings: CDs 50; DVDs 425; Bk Vols 22,000; Per Subs 75; Videos 1,000
Open Mon-Thurs 9am-11pm, Fri 9-5, Sat 1-5, Sun 4-11

SIDNEY COX LIBRARY OF MUSIC & DANCE, Lincoln Hall, 14853-4101, SAN 352-5724. Tel: 607-255-4011. FAX: 607-254-2877. E-mail: musicref@cornell.edu. Web Site: www.library.cornell.edu/music. *Librn,* Bonna Boettcher; Tel: 607-255-7126, E-mail: bjb57@cornell.edu; Staff 6 (MLS 2, Non MLS 4)
Library Holdings: AV Mats 70,700; Microforms 8,600; Bk Vols 148,250; Per Subs 400
Special Collections: 18th Century Chamber Music; 18th-21st Century American Music Coll; 19th Century Opera; A Scarlatti Operas; Archive of Field Recordings; Early 16th Century Music Coll
Subject Interests: Dance, Music

DIVISION OF RARE & MANUSCRIPT COLLECTIONS, 2B Carl A Kroch Library, 14853, SAN 377-810X. Tel: 607-255-3530. FAX: 607-255-9524. Web Site: rmc.library.cornell.edu. *Asst Dir, Curator,* Katherine Reagan; *Univ Archivist,* Elaine Engst; E-mail: ee11@cornell.edu
Library Holdings: Bk Vols 433,858
Special Collections: 18th & 19th Century French History; American History; Anglo-American Literature; Dante; Food History; G B Shaw Coll; History of Science; Icelandic Literature & Culture; Native American History; Petrarch; Sexuality; Theater; Witchcraft; Wordsworth
Open Mon-Fri 9-5
Restriction: Non-circulating
Friends of the Library Group

ENGINEERING, Virtual Library, Carpenter Hall, 14853-2201, SAN 352-5872. Tel: 607-254-6261. E-mail: engref@cornell.edu. Web Site: engineering.library.cornell.edu/. *Dir,* Rockey Steven; E-mail: swr1@cornell.edu; *Earth Sci & Eng Outreach Librn,* Jeremy Cusker; E-mail: jpc27@cornell.edu; *Eng Librn,* Jill Powell; E-mail: jhp1@cornell.edu; Staff 4 (MLS 4)
Founded 1957
Jun 2011-Jul 2012. Mats Exp $1,174,485
Library Holdings: e-books 38,612; Bk Vols 25,000; Per Subs 730
Virtual Library; print items housed in other libraries on campus

FINE ARTS, 235 Sibley Dome, 14853-6701, SAN 352-5902. Tel: 607-255-3710. FAX: 607-255-6718. E-mail: fineartscirc@cornell.edu. Web Site: library.cornell.edu/finearts. *Dir,* Martha Walker; E-mail: maw6@cornell.edu
Library Holdings: Bk Vols 122,000

Subject Interests: Art & archit, Art hist, City planning, Landscape archit, Regional planning
Open Mon-Thurs 8am-11pm, Fri 8-6, Sat 8-5, Sun 1-11

CM FLOWER-SPRECHER VETERINARY LIBRARY, S2 160 Veterinary Education Ctr, 14853-6401, SAN 352-602X. Tel: 607-253-3510. Interlibrary Loan Service Tel: 607-253-3508. Reference Tel: 607-253-3499. FAX: 607-253-3080. E-mail: vetref@cornell.edu. Web Site: www.vet.cornell.edu/library. *Dir,* Dr Erla P Heyns; Tel: 607-253-3515, E-mail: eph8@cornell.edu; Staff 7 (MLS 3, Non-MLS 4)
Founded 1897. Enrl 321; Fac 172; Highest Degree: Doctorate
Library Holdings: Bk Vols 101,000; Per Subs 800
Subject Interests: Human med, Immunology, Microbiology, Parasitology, Pharmacology, Physiology, Veterinary med
Automation Activity & Vendor Info: (Acquisitions) Ex Libris Group; (Cataloging) Ex Libris Group; (Circulation) Ex Libris Group; (Course Reserve) Ex Libris Group; (ILL) Innovative Interfaces, Inc; (OPAC) Ex Libris Group; (Serials) Ex Libris Group
Publications: Newsletter (Quarterly)
Friends of the Library Group

HOSPITALITY, LABOR & MANAGEMENT LIBRARY, Ives Hall, Garden Ave, 14853-3901, SAN 352-5961. Tel: 607-255-2277. Reference Tel: 607-254-5370. FAX: 607-255-9641. E-mail: ilrlib@cornell.edu. Web Site: www.ilr.cornell.edu/library. *Dir,* Curtis Lyons; E-mail: lyons@cornell.edu
Founded 1945. Enrl 1,003; Fac 53
Library Holdings: Bk Vols 232,734
Friends of the Library Group

CL LAW SCHOOL, Myron Taylor Hall, 524 College Ave, 14853-4901, SAN 352-5996. Tel: 607-255-7236. Interlibrary Loan Service Tel: 607-255-5750. Reference Tel: 607-255-9577. FAX: 607-255-1357. E-mail: lawlib@cornell.edu. Web Site: library.lawschool.cornell.edu. ; Staff 10 (MLS 8, Non-MLS 2)
Founded 1887. Enrl 646; Fac 46; Highest Degree: Doctorate
Jul 2005-Jun 2006 Income $3,045,548. Mats Exp $1,441,746, Per/Ser (Incl. Access Fees) $1,210,226, Other Print Mats $93,128, Electronic Ref Mat (Incl. Access Fees) $115,796, Presv $22,596. Sal $1,441,746 (Prof $704,860)
Library Holdings: DVDs 50; e-books 588; e-journals 500; Bk Titles 216,264; Bk Vols 700,000; Per Subs 5,000; Videos 225
Special Collections: 19th Century Trials; Bennett Coll of Statutory Materials; Donovan Coll of Nuremberg Trials. US Document Depository
Subject Interests: Foreign law, Intl law, Law, Rare bks
Partic in OCLC Research Library Partnership; RLIN (Research Libraries Information Network)
Publications: InSITE (Bi-monthly); The Primary Source (Newsletter)
Open Mon-Thurs 8-8, Fri 8-5, Sat 12-5, Sun 12-8

FRANK A LEE LIBRARY, NEW YORK STATE AGRICULTURAL EXPERIMENT STATION, Jordan Hall, 630 W North St, Geneva, 14456, SAN 311-2357. Tel: 315-787-2214. FAX: 315-787-2276. E-mail: leelibrary@cornell.edu. Web Site: leelibrary.cornell.edu. *Librn,* Michael Cook; Tel: 607-255-7959, E-mail: mnc2@cornell.edu; *Coordr,* Michael Fordon; E-mail: mpf8@cornell.edu; Staff 1.1 (MLS 0.1, Non-MLS 1)
Founded 1882
Library Holdings: Bk Vols 30,000; Spec Interest Per Sub 100
Special Collections: Wine, Wine Making & Grape Growing
Subject Interests: Enology, Entomology, Food sci, Hort, Plant pathology, Seed tech, Viticulture
Publications: New in the Library (Monthly)
Open Mon-Thurs 8-12 & 1-5, Fri 8-12 & 1-4

LIBRARY ANNEX, Palm Rd, 14853. Tel: 607-253-3431. FAX: 607-253-4280. E-mail: libannex@cornell.edu. Web Site: www.library.cornell.edu/annex. *Admin Supvr,* Cammie Wyckoff; Tel: 607-253-3514, E-mail: cjh8@cornell.edu
Library Holdings: Bk Vols 3,000,000
Open Mon-Fri 9-4

ALBERT R MANN LIBRARY, Mann Library, 237 Mann Dr, 14853-4301, SAN 378-3987. Tel: 607-255-5406. Circulation Tel: 607-255-3296. Interlibrary Loan Service Tel: 607-255-7754. Administration Tel: 607-255-2285. FAX: 607-255-0850. Administration FAX: 607-255-0318. E-mail: mann-ref@cornell.edu. Web Site: www.mannlib.cornell.edu. *Dir,* Mary Ochs; E-mail: mao4@cornell.edu; Staff 53 (MLS 19, Non-MLS 34)
Library Holdings: Bk Vols 300,000; Per Subs 3,700
Special Collections: Beekeeping (Everett Franklin Phillips Coll); James E Rice Poultry Library; Lace & Lacemaking (Elizabeth C Kackenmeister Coll); Language of Flowers. US Document Depository
Subject Interests: Agr, Biological sci, Educ, Human ecology, Nutrition, Psychol
Publications: Catalogs & Indexes
Open Mon-Thurs 8-Midnight, Fri 8-6, Sat 11-5, Sun Noon-Midnight

MATHEMATICS, 420 Malott Hall, 14853-4201, SAN 352-5694. Tel: 607-255-5076. FAX: 607-254-5023. E-mail: mathlib@cornell.edu. Web Site: mathematics.library.cornell.edu/. *Dir,* Steven W Rockey; Tel: 607-255-5268, E-mail: swr1@cornell.edu; *Pub Serv Mgr,* Natalie Sheridan; Tel: 607-254-3568, E-mail: nas20@cornell.edu; Staff 3 (MLS 2, Non-MLS 1)
Founded 1865
Jul 2010-Jun 2011. Mats Exp $270,000
Library Holdings: e-books 15,000; Bk Vols 82,537; Per Subs 730
Special Collections: Chemistry, Physics (high use chemistry & physics volumes)
Subject Interests: Math, Statistics
Automation Activity & Vendor Info: (Acquisitions) Ex Libris Group; (Cataloging) Ex Libris Group; (Circulation) Ex Libris Group
Open Mon-Thurs 8am-11pm, Fri 8-5, Sat Noon-5, Sun 1-11

OLIN, KROCH, URIS LIBRARIES, 201 Olin Library, 14853, SAN 352-5562. Tel: 607-255-8199. Circulation Tel: 607-255-3537 (Uris). E-mail: okuref@cornell.edu. Web Site: asia.library.cornell.edu, www.library.cornell.edu/olinuris, www.rmc.library.cornell.edu. *Univ Librn,* Anne R Kenney; E-mail: libadmin@cornell.edu
Subject Interests: Asian studies, Humanities, Soc sci
Friends of the Library Group

PHYSICAL SCIENCES LIBRARY, Virtual Library, 283 Clark Hall, 14853, SAN 352-5759. Tel: 607-255-4016. FAX: 607-255-5288. E-mail: pslref@cornell.edu. Web Site: physicalsciences.library.cornell.edu. *Chem Librn, Coordr,* Leah Solla; Tel: 607-793-6217, E-mail: leah.colla@cornell.edu; *Physics & Astronomy Librn,* Dianne Dietrich; E-mail: dd388@cornell.edu; *Outreach Coordr & Coll Spec,* Jill Wilson; Tel: 607-255-1577. Subject Specialists: *Chem, Mat sci, Sci & tech studies,* Leah Solla; *Applied & eng physics, Astronomy, Physics,* Dianne Dietrich; Staff 4 (MLS 3, Non-MLS 1)
Jul 2011-Jun 2012. Mats Exp $1,094,280
Library Holdings: e-books 2,538; Bk Vols 20,000; Per Subs 400
Virtual Library, print items housed in other libraries on campus

CM THE SAMUEL J WOOD LIBRARY & THE C V STARR BIOMEDICAL INFORMATION CENTER, 1300 York Ave, C115, Box 67, New York, 10065-4896, SAN 311-7111. Tel: 212-746-6050. Interlibrary Loan Service Tel: 212-746-6051. Administration Tel: 212-746-6068. Information Services Tel: 212-746-6055. FAX: 212-746-6494. Administration FAX: 212-746-8375. Information Services FAX: 212-746-8364. E-mail: infodesk@med.cornell.edu. Web Site: library.med.cornell.edu/. *Dir,* Colleen Cuddy; E-mail: czc2003@med.cornell.edu; *Assoc Dir, Res Digital Serv,* Paul Albert; E-mail: paa2013@med.cornell.edu; *Assoc Dir, Res Mgt,* Mark E Funk; *Assoc Dir, User Support Res & Edu,* Diana Delgado; E-mail: did2005@med.cornell.edu; *Head, Archives,* Lisa Mix; E-mail: lim2026@med.cornell.edu; *Clinical Librn,* Helen-Ann Brown-Epstein; *Consumer Health Librn,* Rhonda Allard; E-mail: rha2002@med.cornell.edu; *Res Serv Librn,* Drew Wright; E-mail: drw2004@med.cornell.edu; *Admin Mgr,* Anny Khoubesserian; E-mail: arevod@med.cornell.edu; *Archivist,* Elizabeth Shepard; E-mail: ems2001@med.cornell.edu; *Circ,* Loretta Merlo; *Computer Serv,* Octavio Morales; Staff 40 (MLS 10, Non-MLS 30)
Founded 1899. Enrl 725; Fac 3,479; Highest Degree: Doctorate
Library Holdings: e-journals 5,713; Bk Titles 72,055; Bk Vols 190,672; Per Subs 321
Subject Interests: Biomed, Nursing, Psychiat
Automation Activity & Vendor Info: (Acquisitions) Innovative Interfaces, Inc; (Cataloging) Innovative Interfaces, Inc; (Circulation) Innovative Interfaces, Inc; (OPAC) Innovative Interfaces, Inc; (Serials) Innovative Interfaces, Inc
Function: Health sci info serv, ILL available, Online searches, Photocopying/Printing, Ref serv available
Partic in Center for Research Libraries; Metropolitan New York Library Council; National Network of Libraries of Medicine Middle Atlantic Region
Restriction: Open to students, fac & staff, Private libr

S DURLAND ALTERNATIVES LIBRARY, Anne Carry Durland Memorial Library, Cornell University, 127 Anabel Taylor Hall, Rm 127, 14853-1001. SAN 352-5589. Tel: 607-255-6486. FAX: 607-255-9985. E-mail: alt-lib@cornell.edu. Web Site: www.alternativeslibrary.org. *Dir,* Ryan Clover-Owens; E-mail: ryan@alternativeslibrary.org; *Asst Dir,* Gary Fine; E-mail: gmf5@cornell.edu; Staff 3 (MLS 1, Non-MLS 2)
Founded 1973
Library Holdings: Audiobooks 150; CDs 1,200; DVDs 800; Bk Vols 8,000; Per Subs 300; Videos 1,200
Special Collections: African Cinema & Literature; Native American Archives-Contemporary Culture
Subject Interests: Culture, Ecology, Human rights, Politics, Psychol, Sexuality
Automation Activity & Vendor Info: (Cataloging) Innovative Interfaces, Inc; (Circulation) Innovative Interfaces, Inc; (ILL) Innovative Interfaces, Inc; (OPAC) Innovative Interfaces, Inc; (Serials) Innovative Interfaces, Inc
Wireless access
Open Mon-Thurs 11-8, Fri 11-6, Sat 11-5, Sun 7pm-11pm

P FINGER LAKES LIBRARY SYSTEM*, 119 E Green St, 14850. SAN 311-3566. Tel: 607-273-4074. Toll Free Tel: 800-909-3557. FAX: 607-273-3618. Web Site: www.flls.org. *Exec Dir,* Amy Starr Zuch; *Adult Serv, Outreach Serv Librn,* Marisa Iacobucci; E-mail: marisa@flls.org; *Automation Syst Coordr,* Rex Helwig; E-mail: rhelwig@flls.org; *Ch Serv,* Annette Birdsall; E-mail: annette@flls.org; *ILL, Ref,* Linda Beins; E-mail: lbeins@flls.org; *Tech Serv,* Robert McLaughlin; E-mail: robertm@flls.org; Staff 21 (MLS 6, Non-MLS 15)
Founded 1958. Pop 312,189
Library Holdings: Bk Titles 79,025; Bk Vols 89,079; Per Subs 52
Automation Activity & Vendor Info: (Cataloging) Innovative Interfaces, Inc; (Circulation) Innovative Interfaces, Inc; (ILL) Innovative Interfaces, Inc; (OPAC) Innovative Interfaces, Inc
Database Vendor: EBSCOhost, Gale Cengage Learning
Publications: Directory (Annual); Newsletter (Quarterly)
Member Libraries: Auburn Correctional Facility Library; Aurora Free Library; Berkshire Free Library; Candor Free Library; Coburn Free Library; Cortland Free Library; Edith B Ford Memorial Library; Fair Haven Public Library; George P & Susan Platt Cady Library; Groton Public Library; Hazard Library Association; Interlaken Public Library; Kellogg Free Library; Lamont Memorial Free Library; Lodi Whittier Library; Newfield Public Library; Peck Memorial Library; Phillips Free Library; Port Byron Library; Powers Library; Seneca Falls Library; Seymour Public Library District; Southworth Library Association; Spencer Library; Springport Free Library; Stewart B Lang Memorial Library; Tappan-Spaulding Memorial Library; Tompkins County Public Library; Ulysses Philomathic Library; Waterloo Library & Historical Society; Weedsport Library
Partic in OCLC Online Computer Library Center, Inc; South Central Regional Library Council
Special Services for the Deaf - TDD equip
Special Services for the Blind - Bks on cassette; Large print bks
Open Mon-Fri 9-4:30

S THE HISTORY CENTER IN TOMPKINS COUNTY*, Library & Archive, 401 E State St, Ste 100, 14850. SAN 321-0839. Tel: 607-273-8284. FAX: 607-273-6107. Web Site: www.thehistorycenter.net. *Dir,* Jean Currie; E-mail: director@TheHistoryCenter.net; Staff 1 (Non-MLS 1)
Founded 1935
Library Holdings: Bk Titles 4,000
Special Collections: Local History (Ithaca Imprints), photos
Subject Interests: Genealogy, Tompkins County hist
Wireless access
Partic in South Central Regional Library Council
Open Tues, Thurs & Sat 11-5

C ITHACA COLLEGE LIBRARY, 953 Danby Rd, 14850-7060. SAN 311-3574. Tel: 607-274-3206. Interlibrary Loan Service Tel: 607-274-3891. Reference Tel: 607-274-3890. Administration Tel: 607-274-3182. Automation Services Tel: 607-274-3553. FAX: 607-274-1539. E-mail: libweb@ithaca.edu. Web Site: www.ithaca.edu/library. *Dir, Tech Serv, Electronic Serv,* Karin Wikoff; Tel: 607-274-1364, E-mail: kwikoff@ithaca.edu; *Col Librn,* Lisabeth Chabot; Tel: 607-274-3821, Fax: 607-274-1211, E-mail: lchabot@ithaca.edu; *Electronic Res Librn,* Calida Barboza; Tel: 607-274-1892, E-mail: cbarboza@ithaca.edu; *Web Serv Librn,* Ron Gilmour; *Mgr, Access Serv,* Ben Hogben; Tel: 607-274-1689, E-mail: bhogben@ithaca.edu; *Mgr, Libr Media Serv,* Kelly Merritt; Tel: 607-274-3880, E-mail: kmerritt@ithaca.edu; *Libr Tech Spec,* Dan Taylor; E-mail: dtaylor@ithaca.edu; *Acq,* Pam Ameigh; E-mail: pameigh@ithaca.edu; *Archivist,* Bridget Bower; Tel: 607-274-3096, E-mail: bbower@ithaca.edu; *ILL,* Sarah Shank; E-mail: sshank@ithaca.edu; *Music,* Kristina Shanton; E-mail: kshanton@ithaca.edu; Staff 33 (MLS 14, Non-MLS 19)
Founded 1892. Enrl 6,600; Fac 450; Highest Degree: Master
Jun 2013-May 2014 Income $3,742,290, State $10,000, Locally Generated Income $3,732,290. Mats Exp $1,545,990, Books $267,890, Per/Ser (Incl. Access Fees) $293,000, Manu Arch $2,400, Other Print Mats $12,700, Micro $1,000, AV Mat $79,000, Electronic Ref Mat (Incl. Access Fees) $875,000, Presv $15,000. Sal $1,438,995 (Prof $847,300)
Library Holdings: AV Mats 34,627; e-books 120,000; e-journals 37,555; Microforms 42,000; Music Scores 6,000; Bk Titles 285,600; Bk Vols 304,003; Per Subs 35,122
Special Collections: College Oral History Project; Digitized Historical Issues of the Ithacan Newspaper; Ithaca College Digitized Photographs (C Hadley Smith Coll); Twilight Zone (Rod Serling Coll). Oral History
Automation Activity & Vendor Info: (Acquisitions) Ex Libris Group; (Cataloging) Ex Libris Group; (Circulation) Ex Libris Group; (Course Reserve) Ex Libris Group; (ILL) Ex Libris Group; (OPAC) Ex Libris Group; (Serials) Ex Libris Group
Database Vendor: Agricola, Alexander Street Press, American Chemical Society, American Mathematical Society, American Psychological Association (APA), Annual Reviews, ARTstor, Atlas Systems, Bowker, Cinahl, CQ Press, Dialog, ebrary, EBSCOhost, Elsevier, Ex Libris Group, Facts on File, Gale Cengage Learning, H W Wilson, JSTOR, LexisNexis, Medline, Modern Language Association, Nature Publishing Group, Newsbank, OCLC, OCLC FirstSearch, OCLC WorldShare Interlibrary Loan, Olive Software, Inc, Oxford Online, Project MUSE, ProQuest, PubMed, Sage, SBRnet (Sports Business Research Network), ScienceDirect, SerialsSolutions, Standard & Poor's, ValueLine, Wilson - Wilson Web, YBP Library Services
Wireless access
Function: Archival coll, Doc delivery serv, Handicapped accessible, ILL available, Magnifiers for reading, Music CDs, Online searches, Orientations, Outside serv via phone, mail, e-mail & web, Photocopying/Printing, Ref serv available, Spoken cassettes & CDs, Telephone ref, VHS videos, Wheelchair accessible, Workshops
Partic in OCLC Online Computer Library Center, Inc; South Central Regional Library Council
Restriction: Open to pub for ref & circ; with some limitations

S PALEONTOLOGICAL RESEARCH INSTITUTION LIBRARY*, 1259 Trumansburg Rd, 14850. SAN 311-3582. Tel: 607-273-6623, Ext 20. FAX: 607-273-6620. Web Site: www.priweb.org. *Dir,* Dr Warren Allmon; E-mail: wda1@cornell.edu. Subject Specialists: *Earth sci, Paleontology,* Dr Warren Allmon
Founded 1932
Library Holdings: Bk Titles 60,000; Bk Vols 60,145; Per Subs 75
Subject Interests: Geol, Natural hist, Paleontology (invertebrate), Taxonomy
Wireless access
Publications: Library Serials List
Partic in South Central Regional Library Council
Open Mon-Fri 9-5

S SOUTH AMERICAN EXPLORERS LIBRARY*, 126 Indian Creek Rd, 14850. SAN 370-7016. Tel: 607-277-0488. FAX: 607-277-6122. *Dir,* Don Montague
Founded 1977
Library Holdings: Bk Titles 3,500; Per Subs 27
Open Mon-Fri 9-5

P TOMPKINS COUNTY PUBLIC LIBRARY*, 101 E Green St, 14850-5613. SAN 311-3590. Tel: 607-272-4557. Reference Tel: 607-272-4556. FAX: 607-272-8111. E-mail: reference@tcpl.org. Web Site: www.tcpl.org. *Dir,* Susan Currie; Tel: 607-272-4557, Ext 234, E-mail: scurrie@tcpl.org; *Asst Dir,* Rosemarie Rice; Tel: 607-272-4557, Ext 233, E-mail: rrice@tcpl.org; *Head, Adult Serv,* Amy Humber; Tel: 607-272-4557, Ext 247, E-mail: shumber@tcpl.org; *Head, Youth Serv,* Bonnie Wojonowski; Tel: 607-272-4557, Ext 271, E-mail: bwojnowski@tcpl.org; Staff 17 (MLS 13, Non-MLS 4)
Founded 1864. Pop 96,501; Circ 878,646
Library Holdings: Bk Vols 257,663; Per Subs 334
Special Collections: Central Book Aid Coll (Finger Lakes Library System)
Automation Activity & Vendor Info: (Acquisitions) Innovative Interfaces, Inc; (Cataloging) Innovative Interfaces, Inc; (Circulation) Innovative Interfaces, Inc; (OPAC) Innovative Interfaces, Inc
Database Vendor: 3M Library Systems, Baker & Taylor, Booksite
Wireless access
Publications: The Library Connection
Mem of Finger Lakes Library System
Partic in South Central Regional Library Council
Open Mon-Thurs 10-8:15, Fri & Sat 10-5, Sun (Sept-May) 1-5
Friends of the Library Group

JAMAICA

M JAMAICA HOSPITAL MEDICAL CENTER*, Medical Library, 8900 Van Wyck Expressway, 11418-2832. SAN 311-3639. Tel: 718-206-8450. Administration Tel: 718-206-8451. FAX: 718-206-8460. *Dir,* Carol Cave-Davis; E-mail: cdavis@jhmc.org; Staff 2 (MLS 1, Non-MLS 1)
Founded 1963
Library Holdings: Bk Titles 2,000; Per Subs 175
Automation Activity & Vendor Info: (Cataloging) Rasco; (Circulation) Professional Software; (ILL) Professional Software; (OPAC) Professional Software; (Serials) Professional Software
Database Vendor: Elsevier, Gale Cengage Learning, McGraw-Hill, Micromedex, OVID Technologies, PubMed, ScienceDirect, STAT!Ref (Teton Data Systems), UpToDate
Wireless access
Function: Computers for patron use, Copy machines, Doc delivery serv, Electronic databases & coll, ILL available, Ref serv available
Partic in Asn of Mental Health Librn (AMHL); Basic Health Sciences Library Network; Brooklyn-Queens-Staten Island-Manhattan-Bronx Health Sciences Librarians; National Network of Libraries of Medicine
Open Mon-Fri 8:30-5
Restriction: Hospital employees & physicians only, Med staff & students, Vols & interns use only

M MOUNT SINAI SERVICES-QUEENS HOSPITAL CENTER AFFILIATION, Health Sciences Library, 82-68 164th St, 11432. SAN 325-1500. Tel: 718-883-4021. FAX: 718-883-6125. *Dir,* Deborah Goss; E-mail: gossd@nychhc.org; *Asst Dir,* Virginia Gilea; Staff 3 (MLS 2, Non-MLS 1)
Founded 1960
Library Holdings: e-journals 270; Bk Vols 18,000; Per Subs 300
Database Vendor: OCLC FirstSearch
Wireless access
Partic in Brooklyn-Queens-Staten Island-Manhattan-Bronx Health Sciences Librarians; Metropolitan New York Library Council; MLC; National Network of Libraries of Medicine
Restriction: Staff use only

GL QUEENS COUNTY SUPREME COURT LIBRARY, General Court House, 88-11 Sutphin Blvd, 11435. SAN 311-3655. Tel: 718-298-1206. FAX: 718-298-1189. E-mail: law_library_queens@nycourts.gov. Web Site: www.nycourts.gov/library/queens. *Sr Law Librn,* Kellie Adams; *Sr Law Librn,* Denise Naya; Staff 3 (MLS 2, Non-MLS 1)
Founded 1911
Library Holdings: Bk Titles 10,000; Bk Vols 125,000; Per Subs 100
Subject Interests: State law
Automation Activity & Vendor Info: (Acquisitions) SirsiDynix; (Cataloging) SirsiDynix; (Circulation) SirsiDynix; (Course Reserve) SirsiDynix; (ILL) SirsiDynix; (Media Booking) SirsiDynix; (OPAC) SirsiDynix; (Serials) SirsiDynix
Database Vendor: LexisNexis, Westlaw
Wireless access
Partic in NY State Libr; OCLC Online Computer Library Center, Inc
Restriction: Non-circulating to the pub

Branches:

KEW GARDENS BRANCH, 125-01 Queens Blvd, 7th Flr, Kew Gardens, 11415, SAN 321-4214. Tel: 718-298-1327. FAX: 718-520-4661. *Dir,* Andrew Tschinkel
Library Holdings: Bk Vols 25,000
Subject Interests: Criminal law of NY

P QUEENS LIBRARY*, Central Library, 89-11 Merrick Blvd, 11432. SAN 352-6054. Reference Tel: 718-990-0728. Administration Tel: 718-990-0794. TDD: 718-990-0809. Web Site: www.queenslibrary.org. *Interim Pres & Chief Exec Officer,* Bridget Quinn-Carey; *Chief Human Res Officer,* Angelica M Huynh; *Coll Develop Coordr,* Hong Yao; E-mail: hyao@queenslibrary.org; Staff 1165 (MLS 416, Non-MLS 749)
Founded 1896. Pop 2,273,000; Circ 17,500,000
Jul 2012-Jun 2013 Income (Main Library and Branch(s)) $128,147,000, State $9,228,000, City $88,860,000, Federal $5,144,000, Other $24,915,000. Mats Exp $4,061,000. Sal $79,497,000
Library Holdings: Bks-By-Mail 13,460; CDs 178,230; DVDs 295,000; Bk Titles 1,081,536; Bk Vols 5,677,050; Per Subs 8,032; Videos 100,894
Special Collections: Long Island History. State Document Depository; US Document Depository
Subject Interests: Behav sci, Costumes, Ethnic studies, Soc sci
Automation Activity & Vendor Info: (Cataloging) Innovative Interfaces, Inc; (Circulation) Innovative Interfaces, Inc; (ILL) OCLC; (OPAC) Innovative Interfaces, Inc; (Serials) Innovative Interfaces, Inc
Wireless access
Publications: Library Matters
Partic in Dialog Corp; Dranet; Metropolitan New York Library Council; OCLC Online Computer Library Center, Inc; Vutext
Special Services for the Deaf - Bks on deafness & sign lang; High interest/low vocabulary bks; Spec interest per; TTY equip
Special Services for the Blind - Reader equip; Volunteer serv
Open Mon-Fri 10-9, Sat 10-5:30, Sun 12-5
Friends of the Library Group

Branches: 64

THE ARCHIVES AT QUEENS LIBRARY, 89-11 Merrick Blvd, 11432. Tel: 718-990-0770. FAX: 718-658-8312. *Mgr,* Judith Todman; Staff 6 (MLS 4, Non-MLS 2)
Library Holdings: Bk Vols 28,000; Per Subs 78
Special Collections: Long Island History & Culture, maps, newspaper & photogs
Open Mon 9-9, Tues 1-7, Wed-Sat 9-7, Sun 12-5

ARVERNE COMMUNITY LIBRARY, 312 Beach 54th St, Arverne, 11692, SAN 352-6119. Tel: 718-634-4784. FAX: 718-318-2757. *Br Mgr,* Nicole Gordon
Library Holdings: CDs 1,600; Bk Vols 45,087
Open Mon, Thurs & Fri 11-7, Tues 2-7, Wed 1-7
Friends of the Library Group

ASTORIA COMMUNITY LIBRARY, 14-01 Astoria Blvd, Long Island City, 11102, SAN 352-6143. Tel: 718-278-2220.
Library Holdings: CDs 1,332; Bk Vols 37,229; Videos 3,128
Open Mon, Thurs & Fri 11-7, Tues 2-7, Wed 1-7

AUBURNDALE COMMUNITY LIBRARY, 25-55 Francis Lewis Blvd, Flushing, 11358, SAN 352-6178. Tel: 718-352-2027. *Commun Libr Mgr,* Johanna Fu; E-mail: jfu@queenslibrary.org
Library Holdings: CDs 1,600; Bk Vols 80,900; Videos 4,170
Open Mon, Thurs & Fri 11-7, Tues 2-7, Wed 1-7

BAISLEY PARK COMMUNITY LIBRARY, 117-11 Sutphin Blvd, 11436, SAN 352-6208. Tel: 718-529-1590. *Commun Libr Mgr,* Bella Barclay
Library Holdings: CDs 1,087; Bk Vols 42,250; Videos 1,520

BAY TERRACE COMMUNITY LIBRARY, 18-36 Bell Blvd, Bayside, 11360, SAN 352-6240. Tel: 718-423-7004. FAX: 718-746-1794. *Commun Libr Mgr,* Eve Hammer
Library Holdings: CDs 1,343; Bk Vols 56,939; Videos 1,298
Open Mon, Thurs & Fri 11-7, Tues 2-7, Wed 1-7

BAYSIDE COMMUNITY LIBRARY, 214-20 Northern Blvd, Bayside, 11361, SAN 352-6232. Tel: 718-229-1834. FAX: 718-225-8547. *Commun Libr Mgr,* Jean Lee
Library Holdings: Audiobooks 430; CDs 3,760; DVDs 22,823; Bk Vols 122,699
Open Mon 9-8, Tues 2-7, Wed-Fri 11-7, Sat 10-5:30

BELLEROSE COMMUNITY LIBRARY, 250-06 Hillside Ave, Bellerose, 11426, SAN 352-6267. Tel: 718-831-8644. *Commun Libr Mgr,* Michelle Chan
Library Holdings: CDs 2,130; Bk Vols 82,926; Videos 169

BRIARWOOD COMMUNITY LIBRARY, 85-12 Main St, Briarwood, 11435, SAN 352-6291. Tel: 718-658-1680. *Commun Libr Mgr,* Arene Chang
Library Holdings: CDs 6,043; DVDs 6,050; Bk Vols 68,922
Open Mon, Thurs & Fri 11-7, Tues 2-7, Wed 1-7

BROAD CHANNEL COMMUNITY LIBRARY, 16-26 Cross Bay Blvd, Broad Channel, 11693, SAN 372-0268. Tel: 718-318-4943. *Commun Libr Mgr,* Carol Scheper
Library Holdings: Audiobooks 200; CDs 848; DVDs 1,200; Large Print Bks 100; Bk Vols 21,743; Per Subs 70
Open Mon, Thurs & Fri 11-7, Tues 2-7, Wed 1-7

BROADWAY COMMUNITY LIBRARY, 40-20 Broadway, Long Island City, 11103, SAN 352-6321. Tel: 718-721-2462. *Commun Libr Mgr,* Logan Ragsdale
Library Holdings: CDs 2,577; Bk Vols 107,648; Videos 2,218
Open Mon 9-8, Tues 2-7, Wed-Fri 11-7, Sat 10-5:30

CAMBRIA HEIGHTS COMMUNITY LIBRARY, 218-13 Linden Blvd, Cambria Heights, 11411, SAN 352-6356. Tel: 718-528-3535. *Commun Libr Mgr,* Denise Corcoran
Library Holdings: CDs 804; DVDs 1,425; Bk Vols 44,661
Open Mon 9-8, Tues 2-7, Wed-Fri 11-7, Sat 10-5:30
Friends of the Library Group

CORONA COMMUNITY LIBRARY, 38-23 104th St, Corona, 11368, SAN 352-6380. Tel: 718-426-2844. *Commun Libr Mgr,* Vilma Daza
Library Holdings: CDs 379; Bk Vols 22,980; Videos 607
Open Mon, Thurs & Fri 11-7, Tues 2-7, Wed 1-7

COURT SQUARE COMMUNITY LIBRARY, 25-01 Jackson Ave, Long Island City, 11101, SAN 370-0895. Tel: 718-937-2790. *Commun Libr Mgr,* Alison McKenna-Miller
Library Holdings: Audiobooks 124; Braille Volumes 1; CDs 2,232; Bk Vols 21,098
Open Mon, Thurs & Fri 11-7, Tues & Wed 1-7

DOUGLASTON-LITTLE NECK COMMUNITY LIBRARY, 249-01 Northern Blvd, Little Neck, 11363, SAN 352-6410. Tel: 718-225-8414. FAX: 718-631-8829. *Commun Libr Mgr,* Ron Wan
Library Holdings: CDs 1,917; Bk Vols 52,250; Videos 1,120
Open Mon, Thurs & Fri 11-7, Tues 2-7, Wed 1-7

EAST ELMHURST COMMUNITY LIBRARY, 95-06 Astoria Blvd, East Elmhurst, 11369, SAN 352-6445. Tel: 718-424-2619. FAX: 718-651-7045. *Commun Libr Mgr,* Johnnie O Dent
Library Holdings: CDs 2,981; Bk Vols 51,576; Videos 1,162
Open Mon, Thurs & Fri 11-7, Tues 2-7, Wed 1-7
Friends of the Library Group

EAST FLUSHING COMMUNITY LIBRARY, 196-36 Northern Blvd, Flushing, 11358, SAN 352-650X. Tel: 718-357-6643. *Commun Libr Mgr,* Florence Leung; Staff 7 (MLS 3, Non-MLS 4)
Library Holdings: CDs 1,400; Bk Vols 55,821; Videos 500
Open Mon, Thurs & Fri 11-7, Tues 2-7, Wed 1-7

ELMHURST COMMUNITY LIBRARY, 86-01 Broadway, Elmhurst, 11373, SAN 352-647X. Tel: 718-271-1020. FAX: 718-699-8069. *Commun Libr Mgr,* Yasha Hu
Library Holdings: CDs 3,440; Bk Vols 134,851; Videos 2,202
Open Mon 9-8, Tues 2-7, Wed-Fri 11-7, Sat 10-5:30
Friends of the Library Group

FAR ROCKAWAY COMMUNITY LIBRARY, 1637 Central Ave, Far Rockaway, 11691, SAN 352-6534. Tel: 718-327-2549. FAX: 718-337-4184. *Commun Libr Mgr,* Sharon Anderson
Library Holdings: CDs 1,157; Bk Vols 71,525; Videos 1,944
Open Mon 9-8, Tues 2-7, Wed-Fri 11-7, Sat 10-5:30

FLUSHING LIBRARY, 41-17 Main St, Flushing, 11355, SAN 352-6569. Tel: 718-661-1200. FAX: 718-661-1290. *Dir,* Donna Ciampa-Lauria; Tel: 718-661-1219
Library Holdings: CDs 9,259; Bk Vols 346,320; Videos 7,024
Open Mon, Wed & Thurs 9-9, Tues 1-9, Fri & Sat 9-7, Sun 12-5
Friends of the Library Group

FOREST HILLS COMMUNITY LIBRARY, 108-19 71st Ave, Forest Hills, 11375, SAN 352-6593. Tel: 718-268-7934. FAX: 718-268-1614. *Commun Libr Mgr,* Hwai-Min Chen-Wood
Library Holdings: CDs 2,642; Bk Vols 111,790; Videos 1,180
Open Mon 9-8, Tues 2-7, Wed-Fri 11-7, Sat 10-5:30

FRESH MEADOWS COMMUNITY LIBRARY, 193-20 Horace Harding Expressway, Fresh Meadows, 11365, SAN 352-6623. Tel: 718-454-7272. FAX: 718-454-5820. *Commun Libr Mgr,* Julia Hua
Library Holdings: CDs 2,200; DVDs 7,000; Bk Vols 155,003
Open Mon 9-8, Tues 2-7, Wed-Fri 11-7, Sat 10-5:30

GLEN OAKS COMMUNITY LIBRARY, 256-04 Union Tpk, Glen Oaks, 11004, SAN 352-6658. Tel: 718-831-8636. FAX: 718-831-8635. *Commun Libr Mgr,* Youshin Berger
Library Holdings: CDs 1,200; Bk Vols 63,797; Videos 2,500
Open Mon, Thurs & Fri 11-7, Tues 2-7, Wed 1-7

GLENDALE COMMUNITY LIBRARY, 78-60 73rd Pl, Glendale, 11385, SAN 352-6682. Tel: 718-821-4980. FAX: 718-821-7160. *Commun Libr Mgr,* Ann-Marie R Josephs
Library Holdings: CDs 1,297; Bk Vols 52,321; Videos 1,051
Open Mon, Thurs & Fri 11-7, Tues 2-7, Wed 1-7

HILLCREST COMMUNITY LIBRARY, 187-05 Union Tpk, Flushing, 11366, SAN 352-6704. Tel: 718-454-2786.
Library Holdings: CDs 2,298; Bk Vols 79,212; Videos 1,682
Open Mon 9-8, Tues 2-7, Wed-Fri 11-7, Sat 10-5:30

HOLLIS COMMUNITY LIBRARY, 202-05 Hillside Ave, Hollis, 11423, SAN 352-6712. Tel: 718-465-7355. FAX: 718-264-3248. *Commun Libr Mgr,* Abdullah Zahid
Library Holdings: CDs 1,718; Bk Vols 67,655; Videos 1,919
Open Mon, Thurs & Fri 11-7, Tues 2-7, Wed 1-7

HOWARD BEACH COMMUNITY LIBRARY, 92-06 156th Ave, Howard Beach, 11414, SAN 352-6747. Tel: 718-641-7086. *Commun Libr Mgr,* Elizabeth Garcia
Library Holdings: CDs 1,273; Bk Vols 60,280; Videos 1,335
Open Mon, Thurs & Fri 11-7, Tues 2-7, Wed 1-7

LANGSTON HUGHES COMMUNITY LIBRARY, 100-01 Northern Blvd, Corona, 11368, SAN 329-6458. Tel: 718-651-1100. FAX: 718-651-6258. *Exec Dir,* Andrew Jackson
Founded 1969
Library Holdings: CDs 1,091; Bk Vols 39,786; Videos 3,591
Open Mon 9-8, Tues 2-7, Wed-Fri 11-7, Sat 10-5:30
Friends of the Library Group

INFORMATION SERVICES, 89-11 Merrick Blvd, 11432. Tel: 718-990-0700. Circulation Tel: 718-990-0771. Reference Tel: 718-990-0714. FAX: 718-658-8342. *Mgr,* Zelantha A Phillip
Founded 1896. Pop 2,200,000; Circ 23,000,000
Library Holdings: Per Subs 1,350
Special Collections: State Document Depository

JACKSON HEIGHTS COMMUNITY LIBRARY, 35-51 81st St, Jackson Heights, 11372, SAN 352-6771. Tel: 718-899-2500. FAX: 718-899-7003. *Commun Libr Mgr,* Weiqing Dai; Staff 17 (MLS 8, Non-MLS 9)
Library Holdings: CDs 28,385; Bk Vols 176,367; Videos 2,204
Open Mon 9-8, Tues 2-7, Wed-Fri 11-7, Sat 10-5:30
Friends of the Library Group

KEW GARDENS HILLS COMMUNITY LIBRARY, 71-34 Main St, Flushing, 11367, SAN 352-7581. Tel: 718-261-6654. *Commun Libr Mgr,* Susan Wetjen
Library Holdings: CDs 3,000; DVDs 5,000; Bk Vols 101,480
Open Mon, Thurs & Fri 11-7, Tues 2-7, Wed 1-7
Friends of the Library Group

LAURELTON COMMUNITY LIBRARY, 134-26 225th St, Laurelton, 11413, SAN 352-6801. Tel: 718-528-2822. FAX: 718-723-6837. *Commun Libr Mgr,* Dave Wang; Staff 9 (MLS 4, Non-MLS 5)
Library Holdings: CDs 1,383; DVDs 2,500; Bk Vols 60,361; Videos 60
Open Mon & Wed-Fri 11-7, Tues 2-7

LEFFERTS COMMUNITY LIBRARY, 103-34 Lefferts Blvd, Richmond Hill, 11419, SAN 352-6836. Tel: 718-843-5950. *Commun Libr Mgr,* David Booker
Library Holdings: CDs 2,425; Bk Vols 65,000; Videos 4,500
Open Mon 9-8, Tues 2-7, Wed-Fri 11-7, Sat 10-5:30

LEFRAK CITY COMMUNITY LIBRARY, 98-30 57th Ave, Corona, 11368, SAN 352-6860. Tel: 718-592-7677. *Commun Libr Mgr,* Position Currently Open
Library Holdings: CDs 1,800; Bk Vols 65,000; Videos 150
Open Mon, Thurs & Fri 11-7, Tues 2-7, Wed 1-7

LONG ISLAND CITY COMMUNITY LIBRARY, 37-44 21 St, Long Island City, 11101. Tel: 718-752-3700. *Commun Libr Mgr,* Tienya Smith; Staff 9 (MLS 4, Non-MLS 5)
Library Holdings: CDs 2,272; DVDs 4,543; Bk Vols 50,388
Open Mon 9-8, Tues 2-7, Wed-Fri 11-7, Sat 10-5:30

MASPETH COMMUNITY LIBRARY, 69-70 Grand Ave, Maspeth, 11378, SAN 352-6925. Tel: 718-639-5228. *Commun Libr Mgr,* Usha Pinto
Library Holdings: CDs 1,446; Bk Vols 71,033; Videos 2,066
Open Mon & Wed-Fri 11-7, Tues 2-7

MCGOLDRICK COMMUNITY LIBRARY, 155-06 Roosevelt Ave, Flushing, 11354, SAN 352-6895. Tel: 718-461-1616. *Commun Libr Mgr,* Susan Xie; Staff 9 (MLS 3, Non-MLS 6)
Library Holdings: CDs 6,581; DVDs 7,000; Bk Vols 87,833
Open Mon & Wed-Fri 11-7, Tues 2-7

MIDDLE VILLAGE COMMUNITY LIBRARY, 72-31 Metropolitan Ave, Middle Village, 11379, SAN 352-695X. Tel: 718-326-1390. *Commun Libr Mgr,* Steven Nobel; Staff 4 (MLS 2, Non-MLS 2)
Library Holdings: CDs 1,149; Bk Vols 54,197
Open Mon, Thurs & Fri 11-7, Tues 2-7, Wed 1-7

MITCHELL-LINDEN COMMUNITY LIBRARY, 31-32 Union St, Flushing, 11354, SAN 352-6984. Tel: 718-539-2330. *Commun Libr Mgr,* Farzaneh Momeni
Library Holdings: CDs 1,838; Bk Vols 65,809; Videos 2,060
Open Mon & Wed-Fri 11-7, Tues 2-7

NORTH FOREST PARK COMMUNITY LIBRARY, 98-27 Metropolitan Ave, Forest Hills, 11375, SAN 352-700X. Tel: 718-261-5512. *Commun Libr Mgr,* Frances Tobin
Library Holdings: CDs 968; Bk Vols 61,356; Videos 1,011
Open Mon, Thurs & Fri 11-7, Tues 2-7, Wed 1-7
Friends of the Library Group

NORTH HILLS COMMUNITY LIBRARY, 57-04 Marathon Pkwy, Little Neck, 11362, SAN 352-7018. Tel: 718-225-3550. *Commun Libr Mgr,* Yang Zeng; Staff 5 (MLS 3, Non-MLS 2)
Library Holdings: CDs 1,450; Bk Vols 46,300; Videos 3,750
Open Mon, Thurs & Fri 11-7, Tues 2-7, Wed 1-7

OZONE PARK COMMUNITY LIBRARY, 92-24 Rockaway Blvd, Ozone Park, 11417, SAN 352-7042. Tel: 718-845-3127. FAX: 718-848-1082. *Commun Libr Mgr,* Leslie Dann
Library Holdings: CDs 1,143; Bk Vols 71,525; Videos 1,509
Open Mon & Wed-Fri 11-7, Tues 2-7

PENINSULA COMMUNITY LIBRARY, 92-25 Rockaway Beach Blvd, Rockaway Beach, 11693, SAN 352-7077. Tel: 718-990-8502. *Commun Libr Mgr,* Matthew Allison
Library Holdings: Bk Vols 60,417; Per Subs 1,451; Videos 1,353
Open Mon 9-8, Tues 2-7, Wed-Fri 11-7, Sat 10-5:30

POMONOK COMMUNITY LIBRARY, 158-21 Jewel Ave, Flushing, 11365, SAN 352-7107. Tel: 718-591-4343. *Commun Libr Mgr,* Sharon Banks
Library Holdings: Audiobooks 75; CDs 1,194; DVDs 2,500; Large Print Bks 300; Bk Vols 52,159
Open Mon, Thurs & Fri 11-7, Tues 2-7, Wed 1-7
Friends of the Library Group

POPPENHUSEN COMMUNITY LIBRARY, 121-23 14th Ave, College Point, 11356, SAN 352-7131. Tel: 718-359-1102. FAX: 718 353-8894. *Commun Libr Mgr,* Basanda Rakhminova
Library Holdings: CDs 1,500; Bk Vols 56,150; Videos 2,350
Open Mon & Wed-Fri 11-7, Tues 2-7

QUEENS LIBRARY FOR TEENS, 2002 Cornaga Ave, Far Rockaway, 11691. Tel: 718-471-2573. *Br Mgr,* Brandon Jeffries
Open Mon-Fri 2:30-6
Friends of the Library Group

QUEENS VILLAGE COMMUNITY LIBRARY, 94-11 217th St, Queens Village, 11428, SAN 352-7190. Tel: 718-776-6800. FAX: 718-479-4609. *Commun Libr Mgr,* Julia Hua
Library Holdings: CDs 6,956; DVDs 7,000; Bk Vols 97,102
Open Mon, Thurs & Fri 11-7, Tues 2-7, Wed 1-7

QUEENSBORO HILL COMMUNITY LIBRARY, 60-05 Main St, Flushing, 11355, SAN 352-714X. Tel: 718-359-8332. *Commun Libr Mgr,* Ai-Hua Chen
Library Holdings: CDs 880; Bk Vols 29,700; Videos 2,860
Open Mon, Thurs & Fri 11-7, Tues 2-7, Wed 1-7

REGO PARK COMMUNITY LIBRARY, 91-41 63rd Dr, Rego Park, 11374, SAN 352-7255. Tel: 718-459-5140. *Commun Libr Mgr,* Joseph Grosso
Library Holdings: CDs 1,091; Bk Vols 79,786; Videos 3,591
Open Mon, Thurs & Fri 11-7, Tues 2-7, Wed 1-7

RICHMOND HILL COMMUNITY LIBRARY, 118-14 Hillside Ave, Richmond Hill, 11418, SAN 352-728X. Tel: 718-849-7150. FAX: 718-849-4717. *Commun Libr Mgr,* Rebecca Alibatya
Library Holdings: CDs 2,116; Bk Vols 75,862; Videos 2,055
Open Mon & Wed-Fri 11-7, Tues 2-7
Friends of the Library Group

RIDGEWOOD COMMUNITY LIBRARY, 20-12 Madison St, Ridgewood, 11385, SAN 352-731X. Tel: 718-821-4770. FAX: 718-628-6263. *Commun Libr Mgr,* Vesna Simonovic
Library Holdings: CDs 1,788; Bk Vols 77,069; Videos 1,317
Open Mon 9-8, Tues 2-7, Wed-Fri 11-7, Sat 10-5:30
Friends of the Library Group

ROCHDALE VILLAGE COMMUNITY LIBRARY, 169-09 137th Ave, 11434, SAN 352-7344. Tel: 718-723-4440. *Commun Libr Mgr,* Position Currently Open
Library Holdings: CDs 1,288; Bk Vols 43,823; Videos 1,392
Open Mon 9-8, Tues 2-7, Wed-Fri 11-7, Sat 10-5:30
Friends of the Library Group

ROSEDALE COMMUNITY LIBRARY, 144-20 243rd St, Rosedale, 11422, SAN 352-7379. Tel: 718-528-8490. *Commun Libr Mgr,* Elizabeth Patricia Eshun; Staff 3 (MLS 3)
Library Holdings: CDs 1,070; Bk Vols 42,581; Videos 2,500

SAINT ALBANS COMMUNITY LIBRARY, 191-05 Linden Blvd, Saint Albans, 11412, SAN 352-7409. Tel: 718-528-8196. *Commun Libr Mgr,* Michael Brice
Library Holdings: CDs 1,174; Bk Vols 43,029; Videos 910
Open Mon & Wed-Fri 11-7, Tues 2-7
Friends of the Library Group

SEASIDE COMMUNITY LIBRARY, 116-15 Rockaway Beach Blvd, Rockaway Park, 11694, SAN 352-7425. Tel: 718-634-1876. FAX: 718-634-8711. *Commun Libr Mgr,* Kacper Jarecki
Library Holdings: CDs 1,411; Bk Vols 61,087; Videos 1,409
Open Mon & Wed-Fri 11-7, Tues 2-7
Friends of the Library Group

SOUTH HOLLIS COMMUNITY LIBRARY, 204-01 Hollis Ave, South Hollis, 11412, SAN 352-7433. Tel: 718-465-6779. *Commun Libr Mgr,* Position Currently Open
Library Holdings: CDs 1,385; Bk Vols 43,675; Videos 1,410
Open Mon, Thurs & Fri 11-7, Tues 2-7, Wed 1-7

SOUTH JAMAICA COMMUNITY LIBRARY, 108-41 Guy Brewer Blvd, 11433, SAN 352-7468. Tel: 718-739-4088. *Commun Libr Mgr,* Jasmin Amely
Library Holdings: CDs 550; Bk Vols 42,403; Videos 875
Open Mon, Thurs & Fri 11-7, Tues 2-7, Wed 1-7

SOUTH OZONE PARK COMMUNITY LIBRARY, 128-16 Rockaway Blvd, South Ozone Park, 11420, SAN 352-7492. Tel: 718-529-1660. *Commun Libr Mgr,* Mildred Rivera-Said
Library Holdings: CDs 1,289; Bk Vols 63,446; Videos 1,434
Open Mon, Thurs & Fri 11-7, Tues 2-7, Wed 1-7

STEINWAY COMMUNITY LIBRARY, 21-45 31st St, Long Island City, 11105, SAN 352-7522. Tel: 718-728-1965. FAX: 718-956-3575. *Commun Libr Mgr,* Laurel Hicklin
Library Holdings: CDs 2,105; Bk Vols 75,952; Videos 1,706
Open Mon 9-8, Tues 2-7, Wed-Fri 11-7, Sat 10-5:30
Friends of the Library Group

SUNNYSIDE COMMUNITY LIBRARY, 43-06 Greenpoint Ave, Long Island City, 11104, SAN 352-7557. Tel: 718-784-3033. *Commun Libr Mgr,* Anne Bagnall
Library Holdings: CDs 3,000; Bk Vols 80,892; Videos 6,000
Open Mon 9-8, Tues 2-7, Wed-Fri 11-7, Sat 10-5:30

WHITESTONE COMMUNITY LIBRARY, 151-10 14th Rd, Whitestone, 11357, SAN 352-7611. Tel: 718-767-8010. FAX: 718-357-3086. *Commun Libr Mgr,* Nonyem Illobachie
Library Holdings: CDs 1,196; Bk Vols 59,131; Videos 1,160
Open Mon & Wed-Fri 11-7, Tues 2-7

WINDSOR PARK COMMUNITY LIBRARY, 79-50 Bell Blvd, Bayside, 11364, SAN 352-7646. Tel: 718-468-8300. FAX: 718-264-0376. *Commun Libr Mgr,* Julia Tan; Staff 7 (MLS 3, Non-MLS 4)
Library Holdings: CDs 2,200; DVDs 3,200; Bk Vols 58,260
Open Mon, Thurs & Fri 11-7, Tues 2-7, Wed 1-7

WOODHAVEN COMMUNITY LIBRARY, 85-41 Forest Pkwy, Woodhaven, 11421, SAN 352-7662. Tel: 718-849-1010. *Commun Libr Mgr,* Jiang Liu
Library Holdings: CDs 1,307; Bk Vols 53,685; Videos 1,054
Open Mon & Wed-Fri 11-7, Tues 2-7
Friends of the Library Group

WOODSIDE COMMUNITY LIBRARY, 54-22 Skillman Ave, Woodside, 11377, SAN 352-7670. Tel: 718-429-4700. *Commun Libr Mgr,* Jingru Pei
Library Holdings: Audiobooks 50; CDs 1,000; DVDs 1,200; Large Print Bks 600; Bk Vols 100,000; Per Subs 120
Open Mon, Thurs & Fri 11-7, Tues 2-7, Wed 1-7

Bookmobiles: 1. In Charge, Madlyn Schneider. Bk titles 3,000

R ST PAUL OF THE CROSS PROVINCE*, Passionist Monastery Library, 86-45 Edgerton Blvd, 11432-0024. SAN 311-3620. Tel: 718-739-6502. FAX: 718-657-0543. Web Site: icmonastery.org. *In Charge,* Peter Grace; E-mail: pgrace@gmail.com; Staff 3 (MLS 1, Non-MLS 2)
Founded 1930
Library Holdings: AV Mats 700; DVDs 100; Bk Titles 40,000; Per Subs 27; Videos 500
Special Collections: Italian Encyclopedia; Patrologiae; Spanish Encyclopedia
Subject Interests: Hist of US, NY City, Philos, Preaching, Scripture liturgy, Spirituality, Theol
Restriction: Not open to pub

C YORK COLLEGE LIBRARY*, 94-20 Guy R Brewer Blvd, 11451. SAN 311-3671. Tel: 718-262-2034. Circulation Tel: 718-262-2033. Interlibrary Loan Service Tel: 718-262-2302. Administration Tel: 718-262-2021, 718-262-2026. FAX: 718-262-2027, 718-262-2997. E-mail: reference@york.cuny.edu. Web Site: www.york.cuny.edu/library. *Head, Archives, Circ & Reserve,* Robert Machalow; Tel: 718-262-2018, E-mail: rmachalow@york.cuny.edu; *Head, Cat,* Sandra Urban; Tel: 718-262-2022, E-mail: surban@york.cuny.edu; *Coordr, Electronic Res, Head, ILL, Webmaster,* Anamika Dasgupta; E-mail: adasgupta@york.cuny.edu; *Head, Info Literacy,* Scott Sheidlower; Tel: 718-262-2017, E-mail: ssheidlower@york.cuny.edu; *Head, Ref Serv,* Di Su; Tel: 718-262-2031, E-mail: disu@york.cuny.edu; *Head, Ser, Sci Librn,* Daniel E Cleary; Tel: 718-262-2037, E-mail: dcleary@york.cuny.edu; *Head, Tech Serv,* John A Drobnicki; Tel: 718-262-2025, E-mail: jdrobnicki@york.cuny.edu; *Chief Librn,* Njoki-Wa- Kinyatti; E-mail: nkinyatti@york.cuny.edu; *Mgr, Circ & Reserves,* Grace Avila; Tel: 718-262-2072, E-mail: gavila@york.cuny.edu; *Media Spec,* Christina Miller; Tel: 718-262-2475, E-mail: cmiller@york.cuny.edu; Staff 21 (MLS 12, Non-MLS 9)
Founded 1967. Enrl 7,236; Fac 210; Highest Degree: Master
Jul 2009-Jun 2010. Mats Exp $530,418, Books $191,251, Per/Ser (Incl. Access Fees) $330,921. Sal $1,207,143 (Prof $861,976)
Library Holdings: CDs 500; DVDs 50; e-books 121,781; e-journals 57,227; Microforms 148,700; Bk Titles 303,379; Bk Vols 343,336; Per Subs 417; Videos 1,828
Special Collections: American History & Literature (Library of American Civilization), ultrafiche; Books in Hebrew & Yiddish (Bassin Coll); Papers of the NAACP, film; Papers of the United Negro College Fund, fiche; Special American & Foreign Newspaper Coll, film
Subject Interests: Health, Humanities, Sci, Soc sci
Automation Activity & Vendor Info: (Acquisitions) Ex Libris Group; (Cataloging) Ex Libris Group; (Circulation) Ex Libris Group; (Course Reserve) Ex Libris Group; (ILL) OCLC; (OPAC) Ex Libris Group; (Serials) Ex Libris Group
Wireless access
Publications: Password (Newsletter)
Partic in Metropolitan New York Library Council; New York State Higher Education Initiative
Special Services for the Blind - Dragon Naturally Speaking software; Large screen computer & software; Scanner for conversion & translation of mats; Screen enlargement software for people with visual disabilities

JAMESTOWN

P CHAUTAUQUA-CATTARAUGUS LIBRARY SYSTEM, 106 W Fifth St, 14701. SAN 311-368X. Tel: 716-484-7135. FAX: 716-483-6880. Web Site: www.cclslib.org. *Exec Dir,* Tina Scott; Tel: 716-484-7135, Ext 246, Fax: 716-487-1148, E-mail: tscott@cclslib.org; *Managing Dir,* Eli Guinnee; Tel: 716-484-7135, Ext 228, Fax: 716-484-1205; *Digital Serv Librn,* Megan Disbro; Tel: 716-484-7135, Ext 251, E-mail: mdisbro@cclslib.org; *Tech Serv Librn,* Chris Spink; Tel: 716-484-7135, Ext 248, E-mail: cspink@cclslib.org; *ILL, Outreach Coordr,* Patricia Johnson; Tel: 716-484-7135, Ext 243, E-mail: pjohnson@cclslib.org; *Youth Serv Consult,* Valle Blair; Tel: 716-484-7135, Ext 230, E-mail: vblair@cclslib.org; Staff 19.3 (MLS 5.7, Non-MLS 13.6)
Founded 1960. Pop 223,705; Circ 314,913
Jan 2006-Dec 2006 Income $1,671,916, State $1,278,962, Federal $65,914, County $193,824, Other $133,216. Mats Exp $217,320, Books $150,400, Per/Ser (Incl. Access Fees) $2,240, AV Mat $35,500, Electronic Ref Mat (Incl. Access Fees) $29,180
Library Holdings: AV Mats 23,630; Bk Vols 148,135; Per Subs 16
Automation Activity & Vendor Info: (Acquisitions) SirsiDynix; (Cataloging) SirsiDynix; (Circulation) SirsiDynix; (OPAC) SirsiDynix
Wireless access
Function: Children's prog, Computer training, Doc delivery serv, e-mail serv, E-Reserves, Electronic databases & coll, Equip loans & repairs, Free DVD rentals, Handicapped accessible, Magnifiers for reading, Preschool outreach, Prof lending libr, Serves mentally handicapped consumers, Summer reading prog, VHS videos, Video lending libr, Workshops
Publications: Newsletter
Member Libraries: Ahira Hall Memorial Library; Alexander Findley Community Library; Allegany Public Library; Anderson-Lee Library; Ashville Free Library; Bemus Point Public Library; Blount Library, Inc; Cattaraugus Free Library; Clymer-French Creek Free Library; Darwin R Barker Library; Delevan-Yorkshire Public Library; Dunkirk Free Library; Ellicottville Memorial Library; Falconer Public Library; Farman Free Library; Fluvanna Free Library; Gowanda Free Library; Hazeltine Public Library; James Prendergast Library; Kennedy Free Library; King Memorial Library; Lakewood Memorial Library; Mary E Seymour Memorial Free Library; Mayville Library; Memorial Library of Little Valley; Minerva Free Library; Myers Memorial Library; Olean Public Library; Patterson Library; Portville Free Library; Randolph Free Library; Ripley Free Library; Salamanca Public Library; Seneca Nation Library; Sinclairville Free Library; Smith Memorial Library
Partic in Western New York Library Resources Council
Bookmobiles: 1

S FENTON HISTORY CENTER-LIBRARY*, 67 Washington St, 14701-6697. SAN 311-3698. Tel: 716-664-6256. FAX: 716-483-7524. E-mail: information@fentonhistorycenter.org. Web Site: www.fentonhistorycenter.org. *Dir,* Joni Blackman; *Archivist,* Karen Livsey; Staff 2 (MLS 1, Non-MLS 1)
Founded 1964
Library Holdings: Bk Titles 5,400; Per Subs 27
Special Collections: Census Reports Coll; Genealogy File, card file; Local History (Manuscript Coll); Local Newspapers, incl Deaths & Marriages
Subject Interests: Civil War period, Genealogy, Local hist, Reuben E Fenton
Wireless access
Open Mon 10-9, Tues-Sat 10-4

P FLUVANNA FREE LIBRARY*, 3532 Fluvanna Ave Ext, 14701. SAN 311-2063. Tel: 716-487-1773. FAX: 716-487-2311. E-mail: flulib@stny.rr.com. Web Site: www.cclslib.org/fluvanna. *Librn,* Christine Anderson
Founded 1914. Pop 3,150; Circ 20,000
Subject Interests: Local genealogy
Wireless access
Mem of Chautauqua-Cattaraugus Library System
Open Mon & Fri 10-8, Tues-Thurs 10-6, Sat 10-2

P HAZELTINE PUBLIC LIBRARY*, 891 Busti-Sugar Grove Rd, 14701-9510. SAN 310-9941. Tel: 716-487-1281. FAX: 716-487-0760. E-mail: hazeltinelibrary@stny.rr.com. Web Site: www.cclslib.org/busti.html. *Head Librn,* Tracy Hewitt
Founded 1924. Pop 4,502; Circ 18,758
Library Holdings: AV Mats 959; Large Print Bks 105; Bk Titles 15,515; Bk Vols 17,000; Per Subs 72
Subject Interests: Antiques
Automation Activity & Vendor Info: (Cataloging) SirsiDynix; (Circulation) SirsiDynix; (ILL) SirsiDynix; (OPAC) SirsiDynix; (Serials) SirsiDynix
Wireless access
Mem of Chautauqua-Cattaraugus Library System
Open Mon, Wed & Fri 1-5 & 6:30-8:30, Tues & Thurs 9-5, Sat 9-1

J JAMESTOWN COMMUNITY COLLEGE*, Hultquist Library, 525 Falconer St, 14702-0020. SAN 311-3701. Circulation Tel: 716-338-1008. Reference Tel: 716-338-1139. Web Site: www.sunyjcc.edu/library/hultquist. *Dir of Libr,* Dr Linda F Larkin; Tel: 716-338-1125, E-mail: LindaLarkin@mail.sunyjcc.edu; Staff 5 (MLS 2, Non-MLS 3)
Founded 1950. Enrl 3,660; Fac 70; Highest Degree: Associate
Sept 2005-Aug 2006. Mats Exp $156,500, Books $70,000, Per/Ser (Incl. Access Fees) $50,000, Micro $3,000, AV Equip $3,000, AV Mat $10,000, Electronic Ref Mat (Incl. Access Fees) $20,000, Presv $500. Sal $450,000 (Prof $180,000)
Library Holdings: AV Mats 4,762; e-books 2,000; Bk Titles 60,000; Bk Vols 66,500; Per Subs 220; Talking Bks 100
Special Collections: Scandinavian Studies
Subject Interests: Criminal justice, Nursing
Automation Activity & Vendor Info: (Cataloging) Ex Libris Group; (Circulation) Ex Libris Group; (Course Reserve) Ex Libris Group; (OPAC) Ex Libris Group; (Serials) EBSCO Online
Wireless access
Publications: Acquisitions List; Bibliographies; Newsletter; STV Alert (Monthly); TV Alert (Monthly)
Partic in OCLC Online Computer Library Center, Inc; Western New York Library Resources Council
Open Mon-Thurs 8-8, Fri 8-4, Sun 1-4

Departmental Libraries:

CATTARAUGUS COUNTY, 260 N Union St, Olean, 14760, SAN 329-3521. Tel: 716-372-1661. FAX: 716-376-7032. *Librn,* Mary Jermann; Tel: 716-376-7594; *Libr Tech,* Joan Haug; Staff 2 (MLS 1, Non-MLS 1)
Enrl 900; Fac 20; Highest Degree: Associate
Library Holdings: AV Mats 1,000; Bk Titles 20,000; Per Subs 160
Subject Interests: Criminal justice, Nursing
Function: ILL available, Ref serv available
Partic in Western New York Library Resources Council
Publications: Acquisition Lists
Open Mon-Thurs (Winter) 8-8, Fri 8-4, Sat 9-12; Mon-Thurs (Summer) 8:30-6

P JAMES PRENDERGAST LIBRARY, 509 Cherry St, 14701. SAN 311-371X. Tel: 716-484-7135. E-mail: prendergastlibrary@yahoo.com. Web Site: www.prendergastlibrary.org. *Exec Dir,* Tina Scott; E-mail: tscott@cclslib.org; Staff 20.5 (MLS 7.8, Non-MLS 12.7)
Founded 1880. Pop 31,146; Circ 528,241
Jan 2013-Dec 2013 Income $1,206,647, State $82,469, City $365,000, Federal $100, County $15,150, Locally Generated Income $495,885, Other $248,043. Mats Exp $150,823, Books $110,988, Per/Ser (Incl. Access Fees) $7,500, Micro $3,000, AV Mat $10,500, Electronic Ref Mat (Incl. Access Fees) $4,595. Sal $545,535 (Prof $259,185)
Library Holdings: AV Mats 8,673; Bk Vols 372,559; Per Subs 358
Special Collections: Art Gallery
Automation Activity & Vendor Info: (Acquisitions) SirsiDynix; (Cataloging) SirsiDynix; (Circulation) SirsiDynix; (OPAC) SirsiDynix
Database Vendor: Baker & Taylor, Brodart, Foundation Center, Gale Cengage Learning, Overdrive, Inc, SirsiDynix, TumbleBookLibrary
Wireless access
Function: Adult literacy prog, Art exhibits, AV serv, Bks on cassette, Bks on CD, Children's prog, Computer training, Computers for patron use, Copy machines, Digital talking bks, Electronic databases & coll, Family literacy, Fax serv, Handicapped accessible, ILL available, Instruction & testing, Large print keyboards, Mail & tel request accepted, Outside serv via phone, mail, e-mail & web, Preschool outreach, Prog for adults, Prog for children & young adult, Ref serv available, Spoken cassettes & CDs, Spoken cassettes & DVDs, Tax forms, Telephone ref, VHS videos, Video lending libr, Wheelchair accessible
Publications: Catalog of the Paintings of the James Prendergast Library
Mem of Chautauqua-Cattaraugus Library System
Open Mon-Fri 9-8:30, Sat 9-5, Sun 1-5
Friends of the Library Group

M WOMEN'S CHRISTIAN ASSOCIATION HEALTHCARE SYSTEM*, Health Sciences Library, 207 Foote Ave, 14701-9975. (Mail add: PO Box 840, 14702), SAN 375-3204. Tel: 716-664-8124. FAX: 716-484-1089. E-mail: library@wcahospital.org. *Asst Librn,* Bonnie Engberg; *Tech Serv,* Mary Franklin
Library Holdings: Bk Titles 1,040; Bk Vols 1,050; Per Subs 90
Database Vendor: Medline, OCLC FirstSearch, PubMed
Wireless access
Partic in Western New York Library Resources Council
Open Mon-Fri 9-3

JASPER

P JASPER FREE LIBRARY*, 3807 Preacher St, 14855. (Mail add: PO Box 53, 14855-0053), SAN 311-3728. Tel: 607-792-3494. FAX: 607-792-3494. Web Site: www.stls.org/steuben_county/jasper.htm. *Dir,* Debbie Stephens; E-mail: stephensd@stls.org
Library Holdings: Bk Vols 4,000; Per Subs 25
Mem of Southern Tier Library System
Open Mon 6:30pm-9pm, Tues & Thurs 9-12:30 & 1-4:30, Sat 8:30-12

JEFFERSONVILLE

P WESTERN SULLIVAN PUBLIC LIBRARY*, Jeffersonville Branch, 19 Center St, 12748. (Mail add: PO Box 594, 12748 0594), SAN 376-6950. Tel: 845-482-4350. FAX: 845-482-3092. E-mail: jef@rcls.org. Web Site: www.wsplonline.org. *Dir,* Susan M Scott; *Asst Dir,* Audra Everett; *Br Mgr,* Jennifer Rhoades; Staff 4 (MLS 1, Non-MLS 3)
Library Holdings: AV Mats 6,850; Electronic Media & Resources 78,041; Bk Vols 60,447; Per Subs 383
Automation Activity & Vendor Info: (Cataloging) Horizon; (Circulation) Horizon; (OPAC) Horizon; (Serials) Horizon
Wireless access
Open Tues & Wed 10-8, Thurs & Fri 10-5, Sat 10-2

JERICHO

P JERICHO PUBLIC LIBRARY, One Merry Lane, 11753. SAN 311-3736. Tel: 516-935-6790. FAX: 516-433-9581. E-mail: info@jericholibrary.org. Web Site: www.jericholibrary.org. *Dir,* Barbara Kessler; *Head, Ch,* Barbara Barrett; *Head, Circ,* Joan Gleason; *Head, Ref (Info Serv),* Deborah Neuman; *Head, T S Proc Serv,* Jean Murphy; *Tech Serv,* Carlos Munozospina; Staff 40.32 (MLS 11.91, Non-MLS 28.41)
Founded 1964. Pop 17,348; Circ 341,968
Jul 2012-Jun 2013 Income $4,746,900. Mats Exp $370,194, Books $194,860, Per/Ser (Incl. Access Fees) $26,782, AV Mat $78,495, Electronic Ref Mat (Incl. Access Fees) $70,057. Sal $2,478,454 (Prof $1,159,602)
Library Holdings: Audiobooks 4,746; AV Mats 22,562; CDs 9,589; DVDs 12,973; e-books 23,608; Large Print Bks 1,585; Bk Vols 130,911; Per Subs 350
Special Collections: Local History Coll, multi-media. Oral History
Automation Activity & Vendor Info: (Acquisitions) Baker & Taylor; (Circulation) Innovative Interfaces, Inc; (OPAC) Innovative Interfaces, Inc
Database Vendor: ABC-CLIO, ALLDATA Online, Baker & Taylor, CountryWatch, CredoReference, EBSCO Information Services, Facts on File, Gale Cengage Learning, LearningExpress, LexisNexis, McGraw-Hill, Natural Standard, OCLC FirstSearch, Overdrive, Inc, Oxford Online, ProQuest, ReferenceUSA, TumbleBookLibrary, ValueLine, World Book Online
Wireless access
Publications: Newsletter (Bi-monthly)

Mem of Nassau Library System
Open Mon, Tues & Thurs 9-9, Wed 10-9, Fri 9-6, Sat 9-5, Sun 12-5

JOHNSON CITY

M UNITED HEALTH SERVICES*, Wilson Regional Medical Center Library, 33-57 Harrison St, 13790. SAN 311-3744. Tel: 607-763-6030. FAX: 607-763-5992. E-mail: medical_library@uhs.org. *Mgr,* Terry Clift; E-mail: terry_clift@uhs.org; *Librn,* Marie DeFeo; E-mail: marie_defeo@uhs.org; Staff 2 (MLS 1, Non-MLS 1)
Founded 1935
Library Holdings: Bk Vols 6,700; Per Subs 388
Subject Interests: Healthcare admin, Med, Nursing
Partic in South Central Regional Library Council
Restriction: Open to pub for ref only

P YOUR HOME PUBLIC LIBRARY*, Johnson City Library, 107 Main St, 13790. SAN 311-3752. Tel: 607-797-4816. FAX: 607-798-8895. E-mail: jc.lib@4cls.org. Web Site: www.yhpl.org. *Interim Dir,* Maryse Quinn; Staff 8 (MLS 3, Non-MLS 5)
Founded 1917. Pop 16,578; Circ 93,609
Library Holdings: Bk Titles 46,414; Bk Vols 54,000; Per Subs 54
Automation Activity & Vendor Info: (Acquisitions) SirsiDynix; (Circulation) SirsiDynix; (OPAC) SirsiDynix
Wireless access
Mem of Four County Library System
Open Mon-Thurs 9-8:30, Fri & Sat 9-5
Friends of the Library Group

JOHNSTOWN

J FULTON-MONTGOMERY COMMUNITY COLLEGE*, Evans Library, 2805 State Hwy 67, 12095-3790. SAN 311-3760. Tel: 518-762-4651, Ext 5610. Interlibrary Loan Service Tel: 518-762-4651, Ext 5603. Reference Tel: 518-762-4651, Ext 5611. FAX: 518-762-3834. E-mail: libinfo@fmcc.suny.edu. Web Site: fmcc.suny.edu/library. *Dir,* Mary Donohue; E-mail: mdonohue@fmcc.suny.edu; *Pub Serv/Instruction Librn,* Michael V Daly; Tel: 518-762-4651, Ext 5602, E-mail: michael.daly@fmcc.edu; *Syst/Electronic Serv Librn,* Daniel Towne; Tel: 518-762-4651, Ext 5601, E-mail: daniel.towne@fmcc.edu; Staff 3 (MLS 3)
Founded 1964. Enrl 1,900; Fac 157
Library Holdings: Bk Vols 35,000; Per Subs 150
Subject Interests: Applied sci, Regional hist
Automation Activity & Vendor Info: (Cataloging) MultiLIS; (Circulation) MultiLIS; (Course Reserve) MultiLIS; (OPAC) MultiLIS
Database Vendor: EBSCOhost, Gale Cengage Learning, OCLC FirstSearch, ProQuest
Publications: Handbook
Partic in OCLC Online Computer Library Center, Inc

P JOHNSTOWN PUBLIC LIBRARY*, 38 S Market St, 12095. SAN 311-3779. Tel: 518-762-8317. FAX: 518-762-9776. *Dir,* Barbara L Germain; E-mail: bgermain@sals.edu
Founded 1901. Pop 9,058; Circ 67,491
Library Holdings: Bk Vols 35,000; Per Subs 100
Subject Interests: Genealogy, NY local hist
Automation Activity & Vendor Info: (Cataloging) SIRSI-DRA; (Circulation) SIRSI-DRA; (Course Reserve) SIRSI-DRA; (ILL) SIRSI-DRA; (OPAC) SIRSI-DRA
Wireless access
Publications: Friends of the Library Newsletter (Quarterly)
Mem of Mohawk Valley Library System
Open Mon & Thurs (Sept-May) 1-8, Tues & Wed 10-8, Fri 10-5, Sat 10-1, Sun 1-4; Mon-Wed (Summer) 10-8, Thurs Noon-8, Fri 10-5
Friends of the Library Group

JORDAN

P JORDAN BRAMLEY LIBRARY*, 15 Mechanic St, 13080. (Mail add: PO Box 923, 13080-0923), SAN 311-3787. Tel: 315-689-3296. FAX: 315-689-1231. E-mail: jordanlibrary@yahoo.com. *Dir,* Linda Byrnes; Staff 6 (Non-MLS 6)
Circ 25,000
Library Holdings: Bk Vols 28,000; Per Subs 30
Wireless access
Mem of Onondaga County Public Library
Open Mon 10-12 & 2-8, Tues-Thurs 10-12 & 2-7, Fri & Sat 10-2
Friends of the Library Group
Bookmobiles: 1

JORDANVILLE

CR HOLY TRINITY ORTHODOX SEMINARY LIBRARY*, 1407 Robinson Rd, 13361-0036. (Mail add: PO Box 36, 13361-0036), SAN 311-3795. Tel: 315-858-3116. Administration Tel: 315-858-0945. FAX: 315-858-0945. E-mail: library@hts.edu. Web Site: www.hts.edu. *Dir, Libr Serv,* Vladimir Tsurikov; E-mail: vtsurikov@hts.edu; *Librn,* Michael Perekrestov; *Libr Mgr,* Andrei Lyubimov; *Cataloger,* Michael Herrick; Staff 4 (MLS 2, Non-MLS 2)
Founded 1948. Enrl 35; Fac 15; Highest Degree: Bachelor
Library Holdings: Bk Vols 45,000; Per Subs 75
Subject Interests: Byzantine studies, Church hist, Russian (Lang), Russian lit, Russian orthodox theology, Sacred art
Automation Activity & Vendor Info: (Cataloging) Softlink America; (Circulation) Softlink America; (ILL) OCLC; (OPAC) Softlink America; (Serials) Softlink America
Wireless access
Open Mon-Fri 2-4
Restriction: Authorized patrons, Authorized scholars by appt, Borrowing privileges limited to fac & registered students, Open to researchers by request, Restricted pub use

P JORDANVILLE PUBLIC LIBRARY*, 189 Main St, 13361-2729. (Mail add: PO Box 44, 13361-0044), SAN 311-3809. Tel: 315-858-2874. FAX: 315-858-2874. E-mail: jordanville@midyork.org. Web Site: midyorklib.org/jordanville. *Dir,* Jacque Empey; E-mail: jempey@midyork.org; *Asst Dir,* Nina Pietrafesa; Staff 2 (Non-MLS 2)
Founded 1908. Circ 9,612
Library Holdings: Bk Vols 4,068; Per Subs 17
Special Collections: Roosevelt Robinson NY State Coll
Wireless access
Publications: Historical Booklet
Mem of Mid-York Library System
Open Mon 3-8, Tues & Wed 1-6, Thurs 1-8, Sat 10-2
Friends of the Library Group

KATONAH

P KATONAH VILLAGE LIBRARY*, 26 Bedford Rd, 10536-2121. SAN 311-3833. Tel: 914-232-3508. FAX: 914-232-0415. E-mail: katref@wlsmail.org. Web Site: www.katonahlibrary.org. *Dir,* Van Kozelka; *Actg Dir, Head, Tech Serv,* Virginia Fetscher; *Head, Ad Ref Serv, YA Serv,* Patricia Humphreys; *Ch Serv,* Stephanie Mandella; Tel: 914-232-1233, E-mail: smandella@wlsmail.org; Staff 10 (MLS 4, Non-MLS 6)
Founded 1880. Pop 7,003; Circ 137,000
Library Holdings: Bks on Deafness & Sign Lang 10; High Interest/Low Vocabulary Bk Vols 30; Large Print Bks 200; Bk Titles 50,000; Bk Vols 69,000; Per Subs 196; Spec Interest Per Sub 25; Talking Bks 300
Subject Interests: Art, Fishing, Lit, Poetry
Automation Activity & Vendor Info: (Cataloging) SirsiDynix; (Circulation) SirsiDynix; (Serials) EBSCO Online
Wireless access
Mem of Westchester Library System
Open Mon & Wed 10-8, Tues & Thurs 10-6, Fri 10-5:30, Sat 10-5
Friends of the Library Group

S NEW YORK STATE OFFICE OF PARKS, RECREATION & HISTORIC PRESERVATION, John Jay Homestead State Historic Site Library, 400 Rte 22, 10536. (Mail add: PO Box 832, 10536-0832), SAN 311-3817. Tel: 914-232-5651. FAX: 914-232-8085. Web Site: www.nysparks.com. *Curator,* Allan Weinreb; Staff 1 (Non-MLS 1)
Founded 1958
Library Holdings: Bk Titles 4,000
Special Collections: Papers of Ancestors & Descendants of John Jay, 1686-1953
Subject Interests: Abolitionism, Hist, Polit sci, Relig, Slavery
Restriction: Open by appt only
Friends of the Library Group

KEENE

P KEENE PUBLIC LIBRARY*, Main St, 12942. (Mail add: PO Box 206, 12942-0206), SAN 311-3841. Tel: 518-576-2200. FAX: 518-576-2200. *Dir,* Marcy LeClair
Pop 920; Circ 9,044
Library Holdings: Bk Vols 10,000; Per Subs 20
Wireless access
Mem of Clinton-Essex-Franklin Library System
Open Mon (Winter) 9-5 & 6-8, Wed 9-5, Sat 9-1; Mon & Wed (Summer) 9-5

KEENE VALLEY

P KEENE VALLEY LIBRARY ASSOCIATION*, 1796 Rte 73, 12943. (Mail add: PO Box 86, 12943-0086), SAN 311-385X. Tel: 518-576-4335. FAX: 518-576-4693. E-mail: library@kvvi.net. Web Site: keenevalleylibrary.org. *Dir,* Karen Glass; *Archivist,* Patricia Galeski; Staff 2 (MLS 2)
Founded 1888. Pop 450; Circ 13,000
Library Holdings: Bk Titles 17,000; Per Subs 30
Special Collections: Fishing (Pickard Coll); Local History (Loomis Room Coll); Mountain (Alpine Coll)

Subject Interests: Art, Mountaineering
Automation Activity & Vendor Info: (Acquisitions) SirsiDynix; (Cataloging) SirsiDynix; (Circulation) SirsiDynix; (ILL) SirsiDynix; (OPAC) SirsiDynix
Wireless access
Mem of Clinton-Essex-Franklin Library System
Open Tues & Thurs (Winter) 9-12, 1-5 & 6-8, Sat 10-12 & 1-4; Mon, Wed, Fri & Sat (Summer) 10-5, Tues & Thurs 9-5 & 6-8

KEESEVILLE

P KEESEVILLE FREE LIBRARY*, 1721 Front St, 12944. SAN 311-3868. Tel: 518-834-9054. FAX: 518-834-9054. E-mail: kesvlib@yahoo.com. Web Site: www.cefls.org/keeseville.htm. *Dir,* Mary Anne Goff
Founded 1935. Pop 2,000; Circ 17,000
Library Holdings: Bk Titles 8,000; Per Subs 30
Automation Activity & Vendor Info: (Acquisitions) Horizon; (Cataloging) Horizon; (Circulation) Horizon; (Course Reserve) Horizon; (ILL) Horizon; (Media Booking) Horizon; (OPAC) Horizon; (Serials) Horizon
Wireless access
Mem of Clinton-Essex-Franklin Library System
Open Mon (Winter) 1-7, Tues & Wed 10-12 & 1-5, Fri 1-5, Sat 9-3; Mon (Summer) 10-12 & 1-7, Tues & Thurs 11-5, Wed & Fri 10-12 & 1-5

KENMORE

P TOWN OF TONAWANDA PUBLIC LIBRARY*, Kenmore Branch, 160 Delaware Rd, 14217. SAN 352-7824. Tel: 716-873-2842. FAX: 716-873-8416. E-mail: knm@buffalolib.org. Web Site: www.buffalolib.org. *Dir,* Dorinda Darden
Founded 1925. Pop 82,000; Circ 967,880
Library Holdings: Bk Vols 111,441
Special Collections: Newspapers, micro
Automation Activity & Vendor Info: (Acquisitions) SirsiDynix; (Cataloging) SirsiDynix; (Circulation) SirsiDynix; (ILL) SirsiDynix; (OPAC) SirsiDynix; (Serials) SirsiDynix
Wireless access
Mem of Buffalo & Erie County Public Library System
Open Mon 10-6, Tues-Thurs 10-9, Fri & Sat 10-5, Sun (Sept-May) 12-5
Friends of the Library Group
Branches: 1
KENILWORTH, 318 Montrose Ave, Buffalo, 14223, SAN 352-7913. Tel: 716-834-7657. FAX: 716-834-4695. *Dir,* Kate Weeks
Library Holdings: Bk Vols 22,500
Open Mon, Tues & Thurs 10-6, Fri 1-9, Sat (May-Sept) 10-6

KENNEDY

P KENNEDY FREE LIBRARY*, Church St, 14747. (Mail add: PO Box 8, 14747-0008), SAN 311-3876. Tel: 716-267-4265. FAX: 716-267-2049. Web Site: www.cclslib.org/kennedy. *Librn,* Linda Bish
Pop 2,639; Circ 9,383
Library Holdings: Bk Vols 10,000; Per Subs 33
Automation Activity & Vendor Info: (Cataloging) SirsiDynix; (OPAC) SirsiDynix
Wireless access
Mem of Chautauqua-Cattaraugus Library System
Open Mon & Thurs 3-8, Tues & Wed 10-4, Sat 10-1
Friends of the Library Group

KENT LAKES

P KENT PUBLIC LIBRARY*, 17 Sybil's Crossing, 10512. SAN 311-0192. Tel: 845-225-8585. FAX: 845-225-8549. E-mail: library@kentlibrary.org. Web Site: www.kentlibrary.org. *Dir,* Frank Reef; *Asst Dir,* Katie Ventura
Circ 100,000
Library Holdings: AV Mats 4,000; Bk Vols 36,000; Per Subs 70
Automation Activity & Vendor Info: (Acquisitions) Innovative Interfaces, Inc; (Cataloging) Innovative Interfaces, Inc; (Circulation) Innovative Interfaces, Inc; (OPAC) Innovative Interfaces, Inc
Database Vendor: EBSCOhost, Newsbank, ProQuest
Wireless access
Mem of Mid-Hudson Library System
Open Mon- Wed 10-8, Thurs & Fri 10-5, Sat 10-3
Friends of the Library Group

KEUKA PARK

C KEUKA COLLEGE*, Lightner Library, 141 Central Ave, 14478-0038. SAN 311-3884. Tel: 315-279-5224, 315-279-5632. FAX: 315-279-5334. E-mail: library@keuka.edu, refhelp@keuka.edu. Web Site: www.keuka.edu/lightner. *Dir,* Linda Park; Tel: 315-279-5208, E-mail: lpark@keuka.edu; *Librn,* Kim Fenton; Tel: 315-279-5411, E-mail: kfenton@keuka.edu; *Ref Librn,* Melodye Campbell; Tel: 315-279-5219, E-mail: mcampbel@kekua.edu; *Ref Librn,* Sharon Tyler; E-mail: styler@keuka.edu; *Tech Spec Librn,* Hilda Mannato; E-mail: hmannato@keuka.edu; *Circ Supvr,* Carol Sackett; E-mail: csackett@keuka.edu; *Acq,* Terrill Dinehart; E-mail: tdinehar@keuka.edu; Staff 7 (MLS 4, Non-MLS 3)
Founded 1923. Enrl 940; Fac 62; Highest Degree: Master
Jul 2006-Jun 2007 Income $460,685. Mats Exp $170,000
Library Holdings: AV Mats 2,600; Bks on Deafness & Sign Lang 3,000; Bk Vols 80,000; Per Subs 175
Subject Interests: Behav sci, Biol, Criminal justice, Local hist, Nursing, Occupational therapy, Psychol, Secondary educ, Sign lang, Soc sci
Automation Activity & Vendor Info: (Acquisitions) Innovative Interfaces, Inc; (Cataloging) Innovative Interfaces, Inc; (Circulation) Innovative Interfaces, Inc; (ILL) Innovative Interfaces, Inc; (OPAC) Innovative Interfaces, Inc; (Serials) Innovative Interfaces, Inc
Database Vendor: ABC-CLIO, American Psychological Association (APA), Annual Reviews, BioOne, CQ Press, CredoReference, EBSCO Information Services, EBSCOhost, Gale Cengage Learning, H W Wilson, LexisNexis, Mergent Online, Newsbank, OCLC FirstSearch, OCLC WorldShare Interlibrary Loan, OVID Technologies, ProQuest, Standard & Poor's
Wireless access
Publications: Journal Holdings List; Keuka Library Handbook
Partic in OCLC Online Computer Library Center, Inc; South Central Regional Library Council
Open Mon-Fri 7:30am-11pm, Sat 8-6, Sun Noon-11
Friends of the Library Group

KINDERHOOK

S COLUMBIA COUNTY HISTORICAL SOCIETY LIBRARY, Columbia County Museum, Five Albany Ave, 12106. (Mail add: PO Box 311, 12106), SAN 311-3892. Tel: 518-758-9265. FAX: 518-758-2499. E-mail: cchs@cchsny.org. Web Site: www.cchsny.org. *Dir & Curator,* Diane Shewchuk
Founded 1916
Library Holdings: Bk Vols 3,000
Special Collections: Family History & Genealogies Coll; New York Colonial History Coll; Photog Coll; Town History Material Coll
Subject Interests: County, Genealogy, Regional hist
Wireless access
Open Thurs & Fri 10-4, Sat & Sun 12-4

P KINDERHOOK MEMORIAL LIBRARY*, 18 Hudson St, 12106-2003. (Mail add: PO Box 293, 12106-0293), SAN 311-3906. Tel: 518-758-6192. E-mail: info@kinderhooklibrary.org. Web Site: www.oklibrary.org. *Exec Dir,* Julie Johnson; E-mail: julie.johnson@kinderhooklibrary.org; Staff 3 (MLS 1, Non-MLS 2)
Founded 1928. Pop 4,400; Circ 32,000
Library Holdings: Bk Titles 20,200
Special Collections: Columbia County & Kinderhook; Gardening; Handicrafts
Automation Activity & Vendor Info: (Cataloging) Innovative Interfaces, Inc; (Circulation) Innovative Interfaces, Inc; (ILL) Innovative Interfaces, Inc; (OPAC) Innovative Interfaces, Inc
Wireless access
Function: ILL available
Mem of Mid Hudson Library System
Open Tues-Thurs 10-8, Fri 10-5, Sat 10-4, Sun 1-3

KINGS POINT

C UNITED STATES MERCHANT MARINE ACADEMY, Schuyler Otis Bland Memorial Library, 300 Steamboat Rd, 11024-1699. SAN 311-3922. Tel: 516-726-5747. Circulation Tel: 516-726-5751. Interlibrary Loan Service Tel: 516-726-5748. FAX: 516-726-5616. E-mail: libraryedata@usmma.edu. Web Site: www.usmma.edu. *Dir,* Dr George J Billy; E-mail: billyg@usmma.edu; *Acq,* Laura Cody; Tel: 516-726-5603, E-mail: codyl@usmma.edu; *Cat,* Kathleen Widder; Tel: 516-726-5750, E-mail: widderk@usmma.edu; *Per,* Imma Palmieri; Tel: 516-726-5746, E-mail: palmierii@usmma.edu; *Reader Serv,* Donald Gill; E-mail: gilld@usmma.edu; *Ref,* Christine Wang; E-mail: wangc@usmma.edu; *Ref,* Teresa Wilkins; E-mail: wilkinst@usmma.edu; *Tech Serv,* Marilyn Stern; Tel: 516-726-5749, E-mail: sternm@usmma.edu; Staff 4 (MLS 4)
Founded 1942. Enrl 900; Fac 80; Highest Degree: Master
Library Holdings: Audiobooks 315; CDs 967; DVDs 360; Bk Titles 175,000; Bk Vols 184,000; Per Subs 850; Videos 260
Special Collections: Marad Technical Report Coll; Nuclear Ship Savannah Coll. US Document Depository
Subject Interests: Merchant marine
Automation Activity & Vendor Info: (Cataloging) SirsiDynix; (Circulation) SirsiDynix; (Course Reserve) SirsiDynix; (OPAC) SirsiDynix; (Serials) SirsiDynix
Wireless access
Publications: Acquisitions List; Bibliography Series; Library Handbook; Newsletter; Periodicals Holdings List

Partic in Long Island Library Resources Council; OCLC Online Computer Library Center, Inc; Westchester Academic Library Directors Organization (WALDO)
Open Mon-Fri 8am-11pm, Sat & Sun 2-11

KINGSTON

M THE KINGSTON HOSPITAL MEDICAL LIBRARY*, 396 Broadway, 12401. SAN 311-3965. Tel: 845-334-2786. FAX: 845-338-0527. E-mail: library@kingstonhospital.org. Web Site: www.senylrc.org/remoteaccess/kingstonhosp.htm. *Librn,* Margaret Cirillo; Staff 1 (MLS 1)
Founded 1956
Library Holdings: Bk Titles 1,378; Per Subs 138
Subject Interests: Hospital admin, Med, Nursing, Surgery
Automation Activity & Vendor Info: (Cataloging) Mandarin Library Automation
Database Vendor: OVID Technologies
Wireless access
Function: Health sci info serv
Partic in Basic Health Sciences Library Network; Greater NE Regional Med Libr Program; Health Info Librs of Westchester (HILOW); National Network of Libraries of Medicine; Southeastern New York Library Resources Council
Restriction: Staff use only

P KINGSTON LIBRARY*, 55 Franklin St, 12401. SAN 311-3957. Tel: 845-331-0507. Reference Tel: 845-331-0988. Administration Tel: 845-339-4260. FAX: 845-331-7981. E-mail: kingstonlibrary@hvc.rr.com. Web Site: www.kingstonlibrary.org. *Dir,* Margie Menard; *Ch Serv,* Stephanie Morgan; *Circ,* L J Cormier; *Tech Serv,* Mary Lou Decker; Staff 4 (MLS 2, Non-MLS 2)
Founded 1899. Pop 23,456; Circ 84,000
Jan 2006-Dec 2006 Income $554,990, State $7,271, City $425,148, County $12,571, Locally Generated Income $30,000, Other $80,000. Mats Exp $33,640, Books $18,414, Per/Ser (Incl. Access Fees) $5,000, Other Print Mats $1,000, AV Mat $7,726, Electronic Ref Mat (Incl. Access Fees) $1,500. Sal $330,414 (Prof $92,000)
Library Holdings: AV Mats 6,587; Bk Titles 78,249; Bk Vols 95,447; Per Subs 100
Special Collections: Local Newspapers 1820-Present, micro
Automation Activity & Vendor Info: (Cataloging) Innovative Interfaces, Inc; (Circulation) Innovative Interfaces, Inc; (OPAC) Innovative Interfaces, Inc
Database Vendor: EBSCOhost, Gale Cengage Learning, OCLC FirstSearch
Mem of Mid-Hudson Library System
Partic in Southeastern New York Library Resources Council
Open Mon & Thurs 10-6, Tues & Wed 10-8, Fri 10-5, Sat 10-4
Friends of the Library Group

G NEW YORK STATE OFFICE OF PARKS RECREATION & HISTORIC PRESERVATION*, Senate House State Historic Site, 312 Fair St, 12401-3836. (Mail add: 296 Fair St, 12401-3836), SAN 311-3973. Tel: 845-338-2786. FAX: 845-334-8173. *In Charge,* Deana Preston
Founded 1927
Library Holdings: Bk Titles 700; Bk Vols 1,200
Special Collections: DeWitt Family Correspondence, mss; Ulster County Coll, doc; Van Gaasbeek Family Papers, mss; Vanderlyn Correspondence, mss
Subject Interests: NY from 17th through mid-20th centuries
Wireless access
Restriction: Open by appt only

GL NEW YORK STATE SUPREME COURT*, Third Judicial District Law Library, 285 Wall St, 12401. SAN 311-3981. Tel: 845-340-3053. FAX: 845-340-3773. *Librn,* Michael Birzenieks
Library Holdings: Bk Vols 17,000
Database Vendor: LexisNexis, Loislaw, Westlaw
Wireless access
Open Mon-Fri 9-5

P TOWN OF ULSTER PUBLIC LIBRARY*, 860 Ulster Ave, 12401. SAN 312-5726. Tel: 845-338-7881. FAX: 845-338-7884. Web Site: www.ulster.lib.ny.us. *Dir,* Tracy Priest; E-mail: director@townofulsterlibrary.org; Staff 7 (MLS 1, Non-MLS 6)
Founded 1962
Library Holdings: Bk Titles 43,000; Bk Vols 44,000; Per Subs 57
Subject Interests: Local hist
Automation Activity & Vendor Info: (Cataloging) Innovative Interfaces, Inc; (Circulation) Innovative Interfaces, Inc; (OPAC) Innovative Interfaces, Inc
Wireless access
Publications: Quarterly newsletter
Mem of Mid-Hudson Library System
Open Mon, Wed & Fri 10-5, Tues & Thurs 12-8, Sat 10-3
Friends of the Library Group

G ULSTER COUNTY PLANNING BOARD LIBRARY*, County Office Bldg, 244 Fair St, 12402. SAN 327-6996. Tel: 845-340-3340. FAX: 845-340-3429. E-mail: planning@co.ulster.ny.us. Web Site: www.co.ulster.ny.us/planning. *Dir,* Dennis Doyle
Library Holdings: Bk Vols 120
Wireless access
Open Mon-Fri 9-5
Restriction: Open to pub for ref only

LA FARGEVILLE

P ORLEANS PUBLIC LIBRARY*, Sunrise Ave, 13656. (Mail add: PO Box 139, 13656-0139), SAN 311-399X. Tel: 315-658-2703. FAX: 315-658-2513. E-mail: laflib@ncls.org. *Librn,* Kelly Orvis
Founded 1942. Circ 9,200
Library Holdings: Bk Vols 7,000; Per Subs 12
Wireless access
Mem of North Country Library System
Open Mon, Wed & Fri 9-12 & 1-5, Tues 6-8, Sat 10-12

LACKAWANNA

P LACKAWANNA PUBLIC LIBRARY*, 560 Ridge Rd, 14218. SAN 311-4007. Tel: 716-823-0630. FAX: 716-827-1997. *Dir, Pub Libr Serv,* Jennifer Johnston
Founded 1922. Pop 19,064; Circ 63,294
Library Holdings: AV Mats 4,982; Bk Vols 30,153; Per Subs 62
Subject Interests: Local hist
Wireless access
Mem of Buffalo & Erie County Public Library System
Special Services for the Blind - Talking bks
Open Mon & Wed 1-8, Tues & Thurs 10-8, Sat 10-4
Friends of the Library Group

LAFAYETTE

P LAFAYETTE PUBLIC LIBRARY*, Rte 11 N, 13084. SAN 311-4015. Tel: 315-677-3782. FAX: 315-677-0211. E-mail: lafayettelibrary13084@yahoo.com. *Dir,* Scott Kushner; Staff 1 (MLS 1)
Pop 5,105; Circ 52,320
Library Holdings: Bk Vols 22,524; Per Subs 80
Automation Activity & Vendor Info: (Cataloging) Innovative Interfaces, Inc; (Circulation) Innovative Interfaces, Inc; (OPAC) Innovative Interfaces, Inc
Wireless access
Open Mon & Tues 10-8, Wed & Fri 10-5, Thurs 12-8, Sat 10-2

LAKE GEORGE

P CALDWELL-LAKE GEORGE LIBRARY*, 336 Canada St, 12845-1118. SAN 325-5824. Tel: 518-668-2528. FAX: 518-668-2528. Web Site: caldwell-lakegeorgelibrary.weebly.com. *Dir, Librn,* Marie Ellsworth; *Asst Librn,* Ellen White; Staff 2 (Non-MLS 2)
Founded 1906. Pop 3,578
Library Holdings: Bk Vols 17,000; Per Subs 35
Automation Activity & Vendor Info: (Cataloging) Innovative Interfaces, Inc; (Circulation) Innovative Interfaces, Inc; (ILL) Innovative Interfaces, Inc; (OPAC) Innovative Interfaces, Inc; (Serials) Innovative Interfaces, Inc
Wireless access
Mem of Southern Adirondack Library System
Open Mon & Wed 10-8, Tues, Thurs & Fri 10-5

LAKE LUZERNE

P HADLEY-LUZERNE PUBLIC LIBRARY*, 19 Main St, 12846. (Mail add: PO Box 400, 12846-0400), SAN 311-4058. Tel: 518-696-3423. FAX: 518-696-4263. E-mail: luzweb@sals.edu. Web Site: hadluz.sals.edu. *Dir,* Cynthia Hedger; E-mail: chedger@sals.edu; Staff 5 (Non-MLS 5)
Founded 1969. Pop 4,444; Circ 23,725
Library Holdings: High Interest/Low Vocabulary Bk Vols 200; Bk Vols 17,487; Per Subs 24; Spec Interest Per Sub 24
Automation Activity & Vendor Info: (Acquisitions) Innovative Interfaces, Inc; (Cataloging) Innovative Interfaces, Inc; (Circulation) Innovative Interfaces, Inc; (ILL) Innovative Interfaces, Inc
Database Vendor: Baker & Taylor, Brodart, Ingram Library Services
Wireless access
Mem of Southern Adirondack Library System
Partic in Capital District Library Council
Special Services for the Blind - Bks on cassette; Videos on blindness & phys handicaps
Open Wed & Fri 9-4, Tues & Thurs 9-7, Sat 9-2

LAKE PLACID

P LAKE PLACID PUBLIC LIBRARY, 2471 Main St, 12946. SAN 311-4074. Tel: 518-523-3200. FAX: 518-523-3200. E-mail: librarian@lakeplacidlibrary.org. Web Site: www.lakeplacidlibrary.org. *Dir,* Bambi Pedu; *Asst Librn,* Linda Blair
Pop 5,000; Circ 28,884
Library Holdings: Bk Vols 24,000; Per Subs 30
Special Collections: Adirondack, Olympic Coll; Lake Placid Club Archives
Subject Interests: Local hist
Automation Activity & Vendor Info: (Cataloging) Horizon; (Circulation) Horizon; (OPAC) Horizon
Wireless access
Mem of Clinton-Essex-Franklin Library System
Open Mon, Wed & Fri 10-5:30, Tues & Thurs 10-7, Sat 10-4

LAKEWOOD

P LAKEWOOD MEMORIAL LIBRARY*, 12 W Summit St, 14750. SAN 311-4120. Tel: 716-763-6234. FAX: 716-763-3624. E-mail: lakewoodlibrary@stny.rr.com. Web Site: cclslib.org/lakewood. *Libr Dir,* Mary Miller; Staff 1 (MLS 1)
Founded 1960. Pop 7,760; Circ 32,640
Jan 2010-Dec 2010 Income $149,434. Mats Exp $17,147. Sal $92,159 (Prof $36,286)
Library Holdings: Bk Vols 29,886; Per Subs 43
Subject Interests: Local hist
Automation Activity & Vendor Info: (Cataloging) SirsiDynix; (Circulation) SirsiDynix; (OPAC) SirsiDynix
Wireless access
Function: Adult bk club, Art exhibits, Audiobks via web, Bk club(s), Bks on CD, Children's prog, Computers for patron use, Copy machines, E-Reserves, Electronic databases & coll, Exhibits, Fax serv, Free DVD rentals, Handicapped accessible, ILL available, Mail & tel request accepted, Online cat, OverDrive digital audio bks, Photocopying/Printing, Preschool outreach, Printer for laptops & handheld devices, Prog for adults, Prog for children & young adult, Pub access computers, Ref & res, Spoken cassettes & CDs, Story hour, Summer reading prog, Tax forms, Telephone ref, Wheelchair accessible
Mem of Chautauqua-Cattaraugus Library System
Partic in New York Online Virtual Electronic Library (NOVEL)
Open Mon, Wed & Fri 9:30-3, Tues & Thurs 9:30-7, Sat 9:30-1

LANCASTER

S ECOLOGY & ENVIRONMENT INC, LIBRARY*, 368 Pleasantview Dr, 14086-1316. SAN 310-9704. Tel: 716-684-8060. FAX: 716-684-0844. *Librn,* John Hood
Founded 1971
Library Holdings: Bk Vols 8,000; Per Subs 12
Subject Interests: Environ sci, Hazardous mat mgt
Automation Activity & Vendor Info: (Cataloging) Book Systems; (Circulation) Book Systems; (OPAC) Book Systems
Function: ILL available
Partic in OCLC Online Computer Library Center, Inc
Restriction: Co libr, Staff use only

P LANCASTER PUBLIC LIBRARY*, 5466 Broadway, 14086. SAN 352-8006. Tel: 716-683-1120. FAX: 716-686-0749. E-mail: LNC@buffalolib.org. *Dir,* James Stelzle; Tel: 716-683-1197; *Ch Serv,* Gwen Cassidy
Founded 1895. Circ 200,000
Library Holdings: Bk Vols 77,901
Special Collections: Local History; Parenting Resource Center
Wireless access
Mem of Buffalo & Erie County Public Library System
Partic in Lyrasis
Open Mon 10-6, Tues-Thurs 10-9, Fri & Sat 10-5, Sun (Sept-May) 1-5
Friends of the Library Group

LANSING

P LANSING COMMUNITY LIBRARY*, 27 Auburn Rd, 14882. Tel: 607-533-4939. FAX: 607-533-7196. E-mail: info@lansinglibrary.org. Web Site: www.lansinglibrary.org. *In Charge,* Barb Holbert
Founded 2001
Library Holdings: Bk Titles 12,000
Automation Activity & Vendor Info: (Cataloging) Innovative Interfaces, Inc; (Circulation) Innovative Interfaces, Inc
Wireless access
Open Mon 3-8, Tues 9-12 & 6-8, Wed 9-12 & 3-8, Thurs 6-8, Fri 9-12, Sat 9-1

LARCHMONT

P LARCHMONT PUBLIC LIBRARY*, 121 Larchmont Ave, 10538. SAN 311-4139. Tel: 914-834-2281. Web Site: www.larchmontlibrary.org. *Libr Dir,* Laura Eckley; E-mail: leckley@wlsmail.org; *Asst Libr Dir,* June Hesler; E-mail: jhesler@wlsmail.org; *Ch Serv,* Rebecca Eller Teglas; E-mail: rteglas@wlsmail.org; *Ch Serv,* Marca McClenon Grant; E-mail: mmclenon@wlsmail.org; *Ref,* Frank Connelly; E-mail: fconnelly@wlsmail.org; *Ref,* William Hegarty; E-mail: whegarty@wlsmail.org; *Youth Serv,* Paul Doherty; E-mail: pdoherty@wlsmail.org; Staff 19.8 (MLS 6.6, Non-MLS 13.2)
Founded 1926. Pop 17,626; Circ 380,926
Jun 2011-May 2012 Income $2,025,307, State $4,519, City $1,941,928, Locally Generated Income $78,860. Mats Exp $147,865. Sal $944,576 (Prof $425,059)
Library Holdings: Audiobooks 7,478; DVDs 6,484; Large Print Bks 1,583; Bk Titles 92,422; Per Subs 142
Subject Interests: Local hist
Automation Activity & Vendor Info: (Acquisitions) SirsiDynix; (Cataloging) SirsiDynix; (Circulation) SirsiDynix; (ILL) SirsiDynix; (OPAC) SirsiDynix
Database Vendor: EBSCOhost, Gale Cengage Learning, ProQuest
Wireless access
Function: Adult bk club, Art exhibits, Audiobks via web, Bk club(s), Bks on CD, Children's prog, Computer training, Computers for patron use, Copy machines, Digital talking bks, e-mail serv, E-Reserves, Electronic databases & coll, Free DVD rentals, Handicapped accessible, ILL available, Music CDs, Online cat, Online ref, Online searches, OverDrive digital audio bks, Prog for adults, Prog for children & young adult, Pub access computers, Ref & res, Ref serv available, Spoken cassettes & DVDs, Story hour, Summer reading prog, Tax forms, Telephone ref, VHS videos, Wheelchair accessible
Publications: Friends of Larchmont Public Library (Newsletter)
Mem of Westchester Library System
Special Services for the Blind - Assistive/Adapted tech devices, equip & products
Open Mon & Thurs 9-9, Tues & Wed 9-6, Fri & Sat 9-5, Sun (Sept-May) 12-5
Friends of the Library Group

LAWRENCE

P PENINSULA PUBLIC LIBRARY*, 280 Central Ave, 11559. SAN 311-4155. Tel: 516-239-3262. FAX: 516-239-8425. E-mail: pplmail@peninsulapublic.org. Web Site: www.nassaulibrary.org/peninsula. *Dir,* Karen Porcella; *YA Librn,* Rhonda Todtman; *Prog Coordr,* Gloria Pomerantz; *Ch Serv,* Priscilla Kesten; *Ch Serv,* Carolynn Matulewicz; *Circ,* Doreen Thorp; *ILL,* Carol Franzese; *Readers' Advisory,* Mary Harrow; *Ref,* James Tiberg; *YA Serv,* Filomena Perrella; Staff 24 (MLS 10, Non-MLS 14)
Founded 1951. Pop 33,988; Circ 305,559
Library Holdings: Bk Titles 100,000; Bk Vols 120,000; Per Subs 12,000
Special Collections: Judaica Coll
Automation Activity & Vendor Info: (Circulation) Innovative Interfaces, Inc - Millenium; (OPAC) Innovative Interfaces, Inc - Millenium
Wireless access
Publications: Peninsula Public Library Newsletter (Quarterly)
Mem of Nassau Library System
Open Mon-Thurs (Winter) 9-9, Fri 9-6, Sat 9-5, Sun 12-5; Mon-Thurs (Summer) 9-9, Fri 9-6, Sat & Sun 9-1

LEROY

S LEROY HISTORICAL SOCIETY LIBRARY*, 23 E Main St, 14482-1210. (Mail add: PO Box 176, 14482-0176), SAN 327-7011. Tel: 585-768-7433. FAX: 585-768-7579. *Dir,* Lynne Belluscio; E-mail: jellodirector@frontiernet.net
Founded 1940
Library Holdings: Bk Vols 4,000
Special Collections: Ingham University Archives; Lampson Papers
Subject Interests: Genealogy
Open Mon-Sat 10-4, Sun 1-4

P WOODWARD MEMORIAL LIBRARY*, Seven Wolcott St, 14482. SAN 311-4198. Tel: 585-768-8300. FAX: 585-768-4768. E-mail: wmlib@nioga.org. Web Site: www.woodwardmemoriallibrary.org. *Dir,* Sue Border; E-mail: sbord@nioga.org; *Children's & YA Librn,* Elisabeth Halverson; Staff 3 (MLS 3)
Library Holdings: Bk Vols 50,159; Per Subs 97
Special Collections: Literature (Woodward Coll)
Automation Activity & Vendor Info: (Cataloging) SirsiDynix; (Circulation) SirsiDynix; (OPAC) SirsiDynix; (Serials) SirsiDynix
Wireless access
Mem of Nioga Library System
Open Mon-Thurs (Winter) 9-8:30, Fri 9-5, Sat 10-4; Mon-Thurs (Summer) 10-8:30, Fri 10-5

LEVITTOWN

P LEVITTOWN PUBLIC LIBRARY*, One Bluegrass Lane, 11756-1292. SAN 311-421X. Tel: 516-731-5728. FAX: 516-735-3168. Administration FAX: 516-520-5745. TDD: 516-579-8585. E-mail: levtown@nassaulibrary.org. Web Site: www.nassaulibrary.org/levtown. *Dir,* Celeste Watman; *Head, Ref,* Helene Hertzlinger; *Automation Syst Coordr,* Marie Andreski; *Ch Serv,* Geraldine Farmer-Morrison; *Circ,* Michele Miemis; *Spec Coll & Archives Librn, Tech Serv,* Ann Glorioso; *YA Serv,* Joan Galante; Staff 57 (MLS 17, Non-MLS 40)
Founded 1950. Pop 47,552; Circ 419,013
Library Holdings: CDs 17,502; e-books 429; Electronic Media & Resources 24,948; Bk Vols 243,014; Per Subs 660; Videos 10,031
Special Collections: Oral History
Subject Interests: Local hist, Natural sci
Automation Activity & Vendor Info: (Acquisitions) Innovative Interfaces, Inc; (Cataloging) Innovative Interfaces, Inc; (Circulation) Innovative Interfaces, Inc; (Course Reserve) Innovative Interfaces, Inc; (ILL) Innovative Interfaces, Inc; (Media Booking) Innovative Interfaces, Inc; (OPAC) Innovative Interfaces, Inc; (Serials) Innovative Interfaces, Inc
Wireless access
Publications: Directory of Community Organizations; Going On: Calendar of Events
Mem of Nassau Library System
Special Services for the Deaf - TDD equip; TTY equip
Open Mon-Fri 9-9, Sat 9-5, Sun 1-5
Friends of the Library Group

LEWISTON

P LEWISTON PUBLIC LIBRARY*, 305 S Eighth St, 14092. SAN 311-4228. Tel: 716-754-4720. FAX: 716-754-7386. Web Site: www.lewistonpubliclibrary.org. *Dir,* Jill C Palermo; Staff 1 (MLS 1)
Founded 1902. Pop 13,458; Circ 109,988
Jan 2010-Dec 2010 Income $418,632, State $3,847, City $379,000, Federal $270, County $19,601, Locally Generated Income $1,667, Other $14,247. Mats Exp $50,500, Books $25,000, Per/Ser (Incl. Access Fees) $10,000, AV Mat $15,500. Sal $208,000 (Prof $42,000)
Library Holdings: Audiobooks 1,301; CDs 2,394; DVDs 1,945; Large Print Bks 1,712; Bk Titles 65,212; Per Subs 91; Videos 539
Special Collections: Early Lewiston Houses (Bjorne Klaussen Coll), original acrylic & oil paintings; Old Village History. Oral History
Automation Activity & Vendor Info: (Circulation) SIRSI WorkFlows; (OPAC) SIRSI WorkFlows
Wireless access
Function: Children's prog, Computer training, ILL available, Online cat, Pub access computers, Ref serv available
Publications: Lewiston - A Self-Guided Tour
Mem of Nioga Library System
Open Mon & Tues 10-8, Wed & Thurs 10-5, Fri 12-5, Sat 10-3
Friends of the Library Group

LIBERTY

P LIBERTY PUBLIC LIBRARY*, 189 N Main St, 12754-1828. Tel: 845-292-6070. FAX: 845-292-5609. Web Site: www.rcls.org/lib. *Dir,* Marjorie Linko; E-mail: mlinko@rcls.org; Staff 1 (MLS 1)
Founded 1894. Pop 10,483
Library Holdings: AV Mats 787; Bk Titles 23,965; Per Subs 79; Talking Bks 771
Automation Activity & Vendor Info: (Cataloging) Horizon; (Circulation) Horizon; (ILL) Horizon; (OPAC) Horizon; (Serials) Horizon
Wireless access
Mem of Ramapo Catskill Library System
Open Mon, Wed & Fri 11-5, Tues & Thurs 11-8, Sat 10-4

LIMA

P LIMA PUBLIC LIBRARY*, 1872 Genesee St, 14485. (Mail add: PO Box 58A, 14485-0858), SAN 311-4244. Tel: 585-582-1311. FAX: 585-582-1701. Web Site: www.lima.pls-net.org/. *Dir,* Catharine Allen; Staff 2 (Non-MLS 2)
Founded 1910. Pop 4,541
Library Holdings: Bk Vols 29,000
Special Collections: Local History, articles, bks, pamphlets
Automation Activity & Vendor Info: (Acquisitions) SIRSI WorkFlows; (Cataloging) SIRSI WorkFlows; (Circulation) SIRSI WorkFlows; (Course Reserve) SIRSI WorkFlows; (ILL) SIRSI WorkFlows; (Media Booking) SIRSI WorkFlows; (OPAC) SIRSI WorkFlows; (Serials) SIRSI WorkFlows
Wireless access
Mem of Pioneer Library System
Open Mon, Tues & Thurs 1-8:30, Wed 10-12 & 1-5, Fri 1-5, Sat 10-12
Friends of the Library Group

LINDENHURST

P LINDENHURST MEMORIAL LIBRARY*, One Lee Ave, 11757-5399. SAN 311-4252. Tel: 631-957-7755. FAX: 631-957-7114. Reference FAX: 631-957-0993. E-mail: lindlib@suffolk.lib.ny.us. Web Site: lml.suffolk.lib.ny.us. *Dir,* Peter Ward; *Computer Serv Librn,* Craig Pullen; E-mail: craigatlib@gmail.com; *Webmaster Librn,* Pamela Wells; E-mail: pamatlib@gmail.com; *AV,* Peter Muhr; *Cat, Coll Develop, Ref,* Eileen Feynman; *Ch Serv,* Lisa Smith; *Circ,* Paula Bornstein; *Pub Serv,* Patricia Leary; *YA Serv,* Amanda Lotito; Staff 13 (MLS 13)
Founded 1946. Pop 42,597; Circ 408,896
Library Holdings: AV Mats 28,795; CDs 5,239; DVDs 16,939; Bk Vols 231,058; Per Subs 520
Special Collections: History of Lindenhurst
Automation Activity & Vendor Info: (Acquisitions) Innovative Interfaces, Inc; (Cataloging) Innovative Interfaces, Inc; (Circulation) Innovative Interfaces, Inc; (OPAC) Innovative Interfaces, Inc; (Serials) Innovative Interfaces, Inc
Database Vendor: Baker & Taylor, Gale Cengage Learning, Grolier Online, LearningExpress, ReferenceUSA, World Book Online
Wireless access
Publications: Newsletter
Mem of Suffolk Cooperative Library System
Partic in Partnership of Automated Librs in Suffolk
Special Services for the Deaf - Bks on deafness & sign lang
Open Mon-Thurs 9-9, Fri 9-6, Sat 9-5, Sun 1-5

LISBON

P HEPBURN LIBRARY OF LISBON*, 6899 County Rte 10, 13658-4242. (Mail add: PO Box 86, 13658-0086), SAN 311-4260. Tel: 315-393-0111. FAX: 315-393-0111. E-mail: lislib@ncls.org. Web Site: www.hepburnlibraryoflisbon.com. *Dir,* Michelle A McLagan
Founded 1920. Pop 3,746; Circ 14,841
Library Holdings: Bk Vols 12,646; Per Subs 43
Special Collections: Local History; News Scrapbooks; Yearbooks of Local High School
Wireless access
Mem of North Country Library System
Open Mon, Tues & Thurs 3-8, Wed 9-1, Fri 9-3

LISLE

P LISLE FREE LIBRARY, 8998 Main St, 13797. (Mail add: PO Box 305, 13797-0305), SAN 311-4279. Tel: 607-692-3115. FAX: 607-692-3115. E-mail: li.ill@4cls.org. Web Site: www.4cls.org/webpages/members/lisle/index.html. *Dir,* Deborah Sturdevant
Founded 1922. Pop 2,707
Jan 2008-Dec 2008. Mats Exp $12,217
Library Holdings: Bk Vols 12,000; Per Subs 34
Wireless access
Mem of Four County Library System
Open Mon 1:30-5, Tues, Wed & Fri 1:30-8, Sat 9-12:30

LITTLE FALLS

P LITTLE FALLS PUBLIC LIBRARY*, Ten Waverly Pl, 13365. SAN 311-4287. Tel: 315-823-1542. FAX: 315-823-2995. E-mail: LittleFalls@midyork.org. *Dir,* Phillips Marietta
Founded 1911. Pop 5,929; Circ 88,572
Library Holdings: Bk Titles 25,285; Per Subs 75
Wireless access
Open Mon-Thurs 10-8, Fri & Sat 10-5

LITTLE GENESEE

P GENESEE PUBLIC LIBRARY*, 8351 Main St, 14754-9701. (Mail add: PO Box 10, 14754-0010), SAN 311-4295. Tel: 585-928-1915. FAX: 585-928-1915. E-mail: gelib@hotmail.com. *Librn,* Carolyn Sherman
Circ 1,787
Library Holdings: Bk Vols 5,000
Special Collections: Criminal Law; Game Hunters; Local History, atlases, bks, surveys, maps; Town Cookbook
Wireless access
Mem of Southern Tier Library System
Open Mon & Thurs (Winter) 9-5, Sat 12-4; Mon (Summer) 12-8, Thurs 9-5, Sat 12-4
Friends of the Library Group

LITTLE VALLEY

P MEMORIAL LIBRARY OF LITTLE VALLEY, 110 Rock City St, 14755. SAN 311-4309. Tel: 716-938-6301. FAX: 716-938-6301. E-mail: memliblv@atlanticbb.net. Web Site: www.cclslib.org/little_valley. *Dir,* Gretchen Taft; Staff 1 (Non-MLS 1)
Founded 1923. Pop 1,830; Circ 12,750

Library Holdings: Bk Vols 18,000; Per Subs 42
Subject Interests: Local hist
Database Vendor: SirsiDynix
Wireless access
Function: BA reader (adult literacy), Handicapped accessible, Homebound delivery serv, Music CDs, Photocopying/Printing, Preschool outreach, Pub access computers, Serves mentally handicapped consumers, Spoken cassettes & CDs, Spoken cassettes & DVDs, VCDs, VHS videos, Video lending libr, Wheelchair accessible, Workshops
Mem of Chautauqua-Cattaraugus Library System
Open Mon & Tues 10-4:30 & 6-8, Thurs 10-6, Fri 10-4:30, Sat (Sept-June) 10-12
Friends of the Library Group

LIVERPOOL

P LIVERPOOL PUBLIC LIBRARY*, 310 Tulip St, 13088-4997. SAN 311-4317. Tel: 315-457-0310. Interlibrary Loan Service Tel: 315-435-1800. FAX: 315-453-7867. E-mail: info@lpl.org. Web Site: www.lpl.org. *Dir,* Dan W Golden; *Outreach Serv Librn,* Susan Estes; *Bus Mgr,* Dorothy Morgan; *Commun Relations Coordr,* Diane Towlson; *Info Serv Coordr,* Regina Fredericks; E-mail: gf@lpl.org; *Youth Serv Coordr,* Linda Meyer; E-mail: lmeyer@lpl.org; *Circ Serv,* Alison Post; Staff 20 (MLS 16, Non-MLS 4)
Founded 1893. Pop 55,000; Circ 507,395
Library Holdings: AV Mats 21,470; Bk Vols 103,145; Per Subs 340
Special Collections: Local History Video Coll
Subject Interests: Local hist
Automation Activity & Vendor Info: (Cataloging) Innovative Interfaces, Inc; (Circulation) Innovative Interfaces, Inc; (Course Reserve) Innovative Interfaces, Inc; (ILL) Innovative Interfaces, Inc; (Media Booking) Innovative Interfaces, Inc; (OPAC) Innovative Interfaces, Inc; (Serials) Innovative Interfaces, Inc
Database Vendor: ALLDATA Online, EBSCOhost, Gale Cengage Learning, Grolier Online, LearningExpress, ProQuest, ReferenceUSA
Wireless access
Mem of Onondaga County Public Library
Open Mon-Thurs 9-9, Fri 9-6, Sat 10-5, Sun Noon-5
Friends of the Library Group

LIVINGSTON

P LIVINGSTON FREE LIBRARY*, Old Post Rd, 12541. (Mail add: PO Box 105, 12541-0105), SAN 311-4325. Tel: 518-851-2270. FAX: 518-851-2270. E-mail: livingstonlibrary105@gmail.com. Web Site: livingston.lib.ny.us. *Librn,* Susan Critchell
Founded 1906. Circ 1,460
Library Holdings: Bk Vols 2,900; Per Subs 15
Automation Activity & Vendor Info: (Cataloging) Innovative Interfaces, Inc; (Circulation) Innovative Interfaces, Inc; (OPAC) Innovative Interfaces, Inc
Wireless access
Mem of Mid-Hudson Library System
Open Mon 3-7, Wed 11-7, Sat 9-3

LIVINGSTON MANOR

P LIVINGSTON MANOR FREE LIBRARY*, 92 Main St, 12758-5113. SAN 311-4333. Tel: 845-439-5440. FAX: 845 439-3141. E-mail: liv@rcls.org. Web Site: www.rcls.org/liv. *Dir,* Peggy Johansen
Founded 1938. Pop 3,645; Circ 18,321
Library Holdings: Bk Vols 12,087; Per Subs 138
Automation Activity & Vendor Info: (Cataloging) Horizon; (Circulation) Horizon; (OPAC) Horizon
Wireless access
Mem of Ramapo Catskill Library System
Open Mon 11-7, Tues & Thurs 1-5, Wed 10-5, Fri 11-6, Sat 10-1

LIVONIA

P LIVONIA PUBLIC LIBRARY*, Two Washington St, 14487-9738. (Mail add: PO Box 107, 14487-0107), SAN 311-4341. Tel: 585-346-3450. FAX: 585-346-5911. Web Site: www.livonialibrary.org. *Mgr,* Frank Sykes; E-mail: fsykes@pls-net.org; Staff 4 (MLS 1, Non-MLS 3)
Founded 1917. Pop 7,286; Circ 72,175
Library Holdings: AV Mats 2,251; Bk Vols 20,086; Per Subs 91; Talking Bks 1,671; Videos 1,235
Special Collections: Livonia Hist Coll
Subject Interests: Local hist
Automation Activity & Vendor Info: (Circulation) SirsiDynix; (ILL) SirsiDynix; (OPAC) SirsiDynix
Wireless access
Mem of Pioneer Library System
Partic in The Library Network
Open Mon-Wed 1-8:30, Thurs & Fri 10-8:30, Sat 10-3
Friends of the Library Group

LOCH SHELDRAKE

J SULLIVAN COUNTY COMMUNITY COLLEGE, Hermann Memorial Library, 112 College Rd, 12759-5108. SAN 311-435X. Tel: 845-434-5750, Ext 4389. E-mail: library@sunysullivan.edu. Web Site: www.sullivan.suny.edu/library. *Libr Dir,* Evangela Q Oates; Tel: 845-434-5750, Ext 4208, E-mail: eoates@sunysullivan.edu; *Access Serv Librn,* Position Currently Open; *Pub Serv Librn,* Richard Arnold; Tel: 845-434-5750, Ext 4227, E-mail: rarnold@sunysullivan.edu; *Ref Librn,* John Klingner; E-mail: jklingner@sunysullivan.edu; *Circ,* Position Currently Open; Staff 3 (MLS 2, Non-MLS 1)
Founded 1964. Enrl 1,200; Fac 60; Highest Degree: Associate
Library Holdings: e-books 20,000; Microforms 5,000; Bk Vols 68,000; Per Subs 110; Videos 15
Subject Interests: Culinary arts, Graphic arts
Automation Activity & Vendor Info: (Cataloging) Ex Libris Group; (Circulation) Ex Libris Group; (Course Reserve) Ex Libris Group; (ILL) OCLC ILLiad; (OPAC) Ex Libris Group
Wireless access
Function: Accelerated reader prog
Publications: Newsletter; Subject Bibliographies
Partic in Southeastern New York Library Resources Council; SUNYConnect
Open Mon-Thurs 8:30-8:30, Fri 8:30-5, Sun 12-5

LOCKPORT

P LOCKPORT PUBLIC LIBRARY, 23 East Ave, 14094. (Mail add: PO Box 475, 14095-0475), SAN 311-4376. Tel: 716-433-5935. FAX: 716-439-0198. E-mail: locref@nioga.org. Web Site: www.lockportlibrary.org. *Dir,* Beverly J Federspiel; E-mail: federspiel@nioga.org; Staff 15 (MLS 6, Non-MLS 9)
Founded 1897. Pop 37,071; Circ 419,917
Library Holdings: AV Mats 25,082; e-journals 5; Bk Vols 150,645; Per Subs 184
Special Collections: Freemasonry & Anti-Masonic, bks, micro
Automation Activity & Vendor Info: (Cataloging) SIRSI WorkFlows; (Circulation) SIRSI WorkFlows; (Course Reserve) SIRSI WorkFlows; (OPAC) SIRSI WorkFlows
Wireless access
Mem of Nioga Library System
Open Mon-Thurs 10-9, Fri & Sat 10-5
Friends of the Library Group

S NIAGARA COUNTY GENEALOGICAL SOCIETY LIBRARY*, 215 Niagara St, 14094-2605. SAN 326-131X. Tel: 716-433-1033. Web Site: www.niagaragenealogy.org. *Librn,* Celeste Crawford; Staff 1 (MLS 1)
Jan 2011-Dec 2011 Income $6,000. Mats Exp $1,150, Books $400, Per/Ser (Incl. Access Fees) $400, Electronic Ref Mat (Incl. Access Fees) $350
Library Holdings: Bk Vols 1,400; Per Subs 10
Special Collections: Skinner Family Genealogies
Subject Interests: Genealogy, Local hist
Wireless access
Function: Res libr
Publications: Newsletter (Quarterly)
Open Thurs-Sat 1-5
Restriction: Non-circulating to the pub

P NIOGA LIBRARY SYSTEM*, 6575 Wheeler Rd, 14094. SAN 311-4384. Tel: 716-434-6167. FAX: 716-434 8231. Web Site: www.nioga.org. *Exec Dir,* Thomas C Bindeman; Tel: 716-434-6167, Ext 24; *Outreach Serv Librn,* Jennifer Morris; *Syst Coordr,* Justin Genter; Tel: 716-434-6167, Ext 11, E-mail: jgent@nioga.org; *Cat,* Margaret Stein; Tel: 716-434-6167, Ext 18
Founded 1959. Pop 322,662
Database Vendor: EBSCOhost, SirsiDynix
Wireless access
Publications: Nioga News; Reach Out
Member Libraries: Barker Free Library; Byron-Bergen Public Library; Community Free Library; Corfu Free Library; Gillam-Grant Community Center Library; Haxton Memorial Library; Lee-Whedon Memorial Library; Lewiston Public Library; Lockport Public Library; Middleport Free Library; Newfane Free Library; Niagara Falls Public Library; North Tonawanda Public Library; Pavilion Public Library; Ransomville Free Library; Richmond Memorial Library; Sanborn-Pekin Free Library; Swan Library; Wilson Free Library; Woodward Memorial Library; Yates Community Library; Youngstown Free Library
Partic in OCLC Online Computer Library Center, Inc; Western New York Library Resources Council

LOCUST VALLEY

P LOCUST VALLEY LIBRARY*, 170 Buckram Rd, 11560-1999. SAN 311-4392. Tel: 516-671-1837. FAX: 516-676-8164. E-mail: info@locustvalleylibrary.org. Web Site: www.locustvalleylibrary.org. *Dir,*

Janis A Schoen; E-mail: jschoen@locustvalleylibrary.org; *Asst Dir,* Kathy Ray; *Head, Ch,* Kristine Piana; *Ref,* Jennifer Santo; *Ref Serv, Ad, Ref Serv, YA,* Leslie Armstrong; Staff 6 (MLS 6)
Founded 1910. Pop 7,040; Circ 104,000
Library Holdings: Bk Vols 71,061; Per Subs 136
Special Collections: Parenting (Carol Tilliston Holmboe Coll)
Subject Interests: Local hist
Automation Activity & Vendor Info: (Acquisitions) Innovative Interfaces, Inc - Millenium; (Cataloging) Innovative Interfaces, Inc - Millenium; (Circulation) Innovative Interfaces, Inc - Millenium; (Course Reserve) Innovative Interfaces, Inc - Millenium; (ILL) Innovative Interfaces, Inc - Millenium; (Media Booking) Innovative Interfaces, Inc - Millenium; (OPAC) Innovative Interfaces, Inc - Millenium; (Serials) Innovative Interfaces, Inc - Millenium
Database Vendor: ReferenceUSA
Wireless access
Publications: Library Letter (Newsletter)
Mem of Nassau Library System
Open Mon-Thurs & Sat 9:15-9, Sun 1-5
Friends of the Library Group

LODI

P LODI WHITTIER LIBRARY*, 2155 E Seneca St, 14860. (Mail add: PO Box 208, 14860), SAN 311-4406. Tel: 607-582-6218. FAX: 607-582-6218. E-mail: lodilibr@rochester.rr.com. Web Site: www.ffls.org/memberpages/lodi.htm. *Dir,* Mary-Catherine French
Circ 3,035
Library Holdings: Bk Vols 10,000; Per Subs 24
Automation Activity & Vendor Info: (Circulation) Innovative Interfaces, Inc; (OPAC) Innovative Interfaces, Inc
Wireless access
Mem of Finger Lakes Library System
Open Mon & Thurs 1-6, Tues & Sat 9-Noon, Wed 4-8

LONG BEACH

M LONG BEACH MEDICAL CENTER*, Medical Library, 455 E Bay Dr, 11561. SAN 374-9223. Tel: 516-897-1012. FAX: 516-897-1077. Web Site: www.lbmc.org. *Librn,* Ruth Lebowitz; E-mail: rlebowitz@lbmc.org
Library Holdings: Bk Titles 400
Database Vendor: Medline
Restriction: Open to pub upon request

P LONG BEACH PUBLIC LIBRARY*, 111 W Park Ave, 11561-3326. SAN 352-8065. Tel: 516-432-7201. Administration Tel: 516-432-7258. FAX: 516-889-4641. Administration FAX: 516-432-1477. E-mail: lblibrary@yahoo.com. Web Site: www.longbeachlibrary.org. *Dir,* George Trepp; E-mail: georgetrepp@yahoo.com; *Asst Dir,* Michael Simon; Tel: 516-432-7201, E-mail: ms1947@aol.com; *Head, Youth Serv,* Jennifer Firth; E-mail: youthservices@netscape.net; *Ref Librn,* Faye H Heft; *Tech Serv Librn,* Lenora Ashford; *Tech Librn,* Philip Boccia; *Youth Serv Librn,* Jennifer Pohl; *Youth Serv Librn,* Tanya Suarez; *Adult Serv,* Mary Aileen Buss; *Adult Serv,* Eileen Pollis; *AV,* Michael Simon; *ILL,* Radika Boodram; *Senior Citizen Outreach,* Joan Yonish; *Youth Serv,* Margaret Capobianco. Subject Specialists: *Foreign lang,* Eileen Pollis; Staff 16 (MLS 12, Non-MLS 4)
Founded 1928. Pop 38,655; Circ 327,654
Jul 2012-Jun 2013 Income (Main Library and Branch(s)) $3,366,868. Mats Exp $313,784, Books $171,320, Per/Ser (Incl. Access Fees) $16,772, Micro $494, AV Mat $89,845, Electronic Ref Mat (Incl. Access Fees) $35,353. Sal $1,747,535 (Prof $767,876)
Library Holdings: Audiobooks 2,298; AV Mats 38,264; CDs 13,611; DVDs 8,179; Microforms 56,604; Bk Titles 134,334; Bk Vols 172,410; Per Subs 160; Videos 3,374
Special Collections: Congressman Allard K Lowenstein Memorabilia Coll; Foreign Language (Spanish, Russian); Long Beach Historical Coll, bks, clippings, prints; Long Beach Photographs
Subject Interests: Holocaust, Local hist
Automation Activity & Vendor Info: (Acquisitions) Innovative Interfaces, Inc; (Cataloging) Innovative Interfaces, Inc; (Circulation) Innovative Interfaces, Inc; (OPAC) Innovative Interfaces, Inc
Database Vendor: ALLDATA Online, Comprise Technologies Inc, CredoReference, Dialog, EBSCOhost, Gale Cengage Learning, Grolier Online, LearningExpress, Natural Standard, OCLC FirstSearch, Overdrive, Inc, ProQuest, ReferenceUSA, TumbleBookLibrary
Wireless access
Function: Fax serv
Publications: Channels Long Beach Public Library (Monthly newsletter); Senior Citizen Directory
Special Services for the Deaf - ADA equip; Adult & family literacy prog; Assisted listening device; Assistive tech; Bks on deafness & sign lang; Closed caption videos; Described encaptioned media prog; Lecture on deaf culture; Sign lang interpreter upon request for prog; Staff with knowledge of sign lang
Special Services for the Blind - Bks & mags in Braille, on rec, tape & cassette
Open Mon, Wed & Thurs 9-9, Tues 11-9, Fri 9-6, Sat 9-5, Sun (Sept-June) 1-5
Friends of the Library Group
Branches: 2
POINT LOOKOUT BRANCH, 26B Lido Blvd, Point Lookout, 11569, SAN 352-809X. Tel: 516-432-3409. *In Charge,* Ingrid Stillwagon
Founded 1967. Pop 1,553; Circ 16,237
Library Holdings: Audiobooks 1,578; DVDs 1,807; Bk Titles 8,627; Per Subs 11
Open Mon 4-8, Tues & Thurs 1-5, Fri & Sat 10-2
WEST END, 810 W Beech St, 11561, SAN 352-812X. Tel: 516-432-2704. *In Charge,* Patricia Witzki
Founded 1968
Library Holdings: AV Mats 1,730; Bk Vols 7,075
Function: Family literacy
Open Tues & Wed 1-5, Thurs 4-8, Fri & Sat 10-2
Restriction: Mil, family mem, retirees, Civil Serv personnel NAF only
Friends of the Library Group

R TEMPLE EMANU-EL*, Sonabend Family Library, 455 Neptune Blvd, 11561. SAN 311-4414. Tel: 516-431-4060. FAX: 516-897-7465. Web Site: www.temple-emanu-el.org. *In Charge,* Bennett Hermann
Founded 1960
Library Holdings: Bk Titles 6,000
Subject Interests: Current events, Judaica, Relig studies
Wireless access
Restriction: Not open to pub

LONG ISLAND CITY

J FIORELLO H LAGUARDIA COMMUNITY COLLEGE LIBRARY, Library Media Resources Center, 31-10 Thomson Ave, 11101. SAN 311-4422. Tel: 718-482-5421. Circulation Tel: 718-482-5426. Reference Tel: 718-482-5425. FAX: 718-482-5444, 718-609-2011. Web Site: libraries.cuny.edu/lib-lg.htm, www.lagcc.cuny.edu/library. *Chief Librn,* Jane Devine; E-mail: jane@lagcc.cuny.edu; *Dep Chief Librn,* Scott White; Tel: 718-482-5430, E-mail: swhite@lagcc.cuny.edu; *Access Serv Librn,* Chris McHale; Tel: 718-482-5441, E-mail: cmchale@lagcc.cuny.edu; *Coll Develop Librn,* Louise Fluk; Tel: 718-482-5424, E-mail: fluk@lagcc.cuny.edu; *Instruction Librn,* Hong Cheng; Tel: 718-482-6019, E-mail: hcheng@lagcc.cuny.edu; *Instruction Librn,* Charles Keyes; Tel: 718-482-6018, E-mail: ckeyes@lagcc.cuny.edu; *Ref/Soc Media Librn,* Silvia Lu; E-mail: alu@lagcc.cuny.edu; *Web Serv Librn,* Steven Ovadia; Tel: 718-482-6022, E-mail: sovadia@lagcc.cuny.edu; *Coordr, Libr Instruction,* Galina Letnikova; Tel: 718-482-5476, E-mail: gletnikova@lagcc.cuny.edu; *Ref Coordr,* Alexandra Rojas; Tel: 718-482-6020, E-mail: arojas@lagcc.cuny.edu; *Archivist,* Marie Spina; Tel: 718-482-5434, E-mail: mspina@lagcc.cuny.edu; *Electronic Res,* Catherine Stern; Tel: 718-482-6021, E-mail: cstern@lagcc.cuny.edu; *ILL,* Clementine Lewis; Tel: 718-482-5428, E-mail: clement@lagcc.cuny.edu; *Tech Serv,* Francine Egger-Sider; Tel: 718-482-5423, E-mail: fegger@lagcc.cuny.edu; Staff 19 (MLS 16, Non-MLS 3)
Founded 1973. Enrl 15,080; Fac 19; Highest Degree: Associate
Jul 2013-Jun 2014 Income $2,170,739
Library Holdings: AV Mats 3,080; CDs 1,511; DVDs 589; Bk Titles 117,330; Bk Vols 135,583; Per Subs 525
Subject Interests: Nursing, Nutrition, Occupational therapy, Veterinary med
Automation Activity & Vendor Info: (Acquisitions) Ex Libris Group
Database Vendor: Alexander Street Press, American Chemical Society, American Mathematical Society, ARTstor, Cambridge Scientific Abstracts, Career Guidance Foundation, College Source, Community of Science (COS), CredoReference, EBSCOhost, Facts on File, H W Wilson, JSTOR, LearningExpress, LexisNexis, OCLC WorldShare Interlibrary Loan, Project MUSE, ProQuest, PubMed, RefWorks, Sage, SerialsSolutions, Westlaw, Wiley InterScience, Wilson - Wilson Web, World Book Online
Function: ILL available
Publications: Library Notes (Newsletter); Periodical list
Partic in OCLC Online Computer Library Center, Inc
Restriction: Authorized patrons

LONG LAKE

P LONG LAKE LIBRARY*, 1195 Main St, 12847. Tel: 518-624-3825. FAX: 518-624-2172. Web Site: www.sals.edu/longlake.shtml. *Dir,* Emily Farr
Library Holdings: Bk Titles 13,000
Automation Activity & Vendor Info: (Cataloging) Innovative Interfaces, Inc; (Circulation) Innovative Interfaces, Inc; (OPAC) Innovative Interfaces, Inc
Wireless access
Mem of Southern Adirondack Library System
Open Tues (Winter) 1-5, Wed & Sat 9-1, Thurs 3-7, Fri 9-5; Mon (Summer) 11-4, Tues & Fri 9-5, Wed & Sat 9-1, Thurs 11-7

LOUDONVILLE

P THE WILLIAM K SANFORD TOWN LIBRARY, Town of Colonie Library, 629 Albany Shaker Rd, 12211-1196. SAN 311-4449. Tel: 518-458-9274. Reference Tel: 518-810-0314. Administration Tel: 518-810-0311. FAX: 518-438-0988. E-mail: info@colonielibrary.org. Web Site: www.colonie.org/library. *Dir,* Richard J Naylor; *Coll Develop, Outreach Serv Librn,* Joseph Nash; *Acq, Tech Serv,* Peggy Mello; *Circ,* Debbie LaRose; *Circ,* Cindy Seim; *Info Tech,* Nicole Persaud; *ILL,* Anne Stutzman; *YA Serv,* Anne-Marie Heldorfer; *Youth Serv,* David Cole; Staff 14 (MLS 8, Non-MLS 6)
Founded 1963. Pop 79,258; Circ 734,789
Jan 2014-Dec 2014 Income $2,602,709, State $22,000, City $2,480,709, Locally Generated Income $100,000. Mats Exp $274,300, Books $220,000, Per/Ser (Incl. Access Fees) $10,000, AV Mat $32,000, Electronic Ref Mat (Incl. Access Fees) $12,300. Sal $1,432,000 (Prof $481,295)
Library Holdings: Audiobooks 3,781; AV Mats 19,261; Large Print Bks 4,686; Bk Vols 188,652; Per Subs 250; Videos 11,433
Special Collections: Basic Education & English as a Second Language Coll; Business & Finance Coll; Job Education Coll; Large Print; Local History; National & Local Telephone Books; NYS Job Bank Outlet; Parent/Teacher
Automation Activity & Vendor Info: (Cataloging) Horizon; (Circulation) Horizon; (OPAC) Horizon
Database Vendor: EBSCOhost, FileMaker, Gale Cengage Learning, Grolier Online, Ingram Library Services, OCLC, Overdrive, Inc, ProQuest
Wireless access
Function: 24/7 Online cat, Activity rm, Adult bk club, Adult literacy prog, After school storytime, Art exhibits, Audio & video playback equip for onsite use, Audiobks via web, Bilingual assistance for Spanish patrons, Bk club(s), Bk reviews (Group), Bks on cassette, Bks on CD, Bus archives, Chess club, Children's prog, Citizenship assistance, Computer training, Computers for patron use, Copy machines, Digital talking bks, e-mail serv, E-Reserves, Electronic databases & coll, Exhibits, Fax serv, Free DVD rentals, Handicapped accessible, Holiday prog, ILL available, Magazines, Magnifiers for reading, Mail & tel request accepted, Mango lang, Microfiche/film & reading machines, Movies, Mus passes, Music CDs, Notary serv, Online cat, Online ref, Online searches, Orientations, Outside serv via phone, mail, e-mail & web, OverDrive digital audio bks, Photocopying/Printing, Preschool outreach, Preschool reading prog, Prog for adults, Prog for children & young adult, Pub access computers, Ref & res, Ref serv available, Ref serv in person, Scanner, Senior computer classes, Spoken cassettes & CDs, Spoken cassettes & DVDs, Story hour, Summer & winter reading prog, Summer reading prog, Tax forms, Teen prog, Telephone ref, VHS videos, Video lending libr, Web-catalog, Wheelchair accessible, Winter reading prog, Workshops
Publications: Annual Report; Bibliographies; Calendar (Monthly); Preschool Directory; Town of Colonie Dept Directory
Mem of Upper Hudson Library System
Open Mon-Thurs 9-8, Fri 9-6, Sat 9-5, Sun 1-5
Restriction: Closed stack
Friends of the Library Group

C SIENA COLLEGE, J Spencer & Patricia Standish Library, 515 Loudon Rd, 12211-1462. SAN 311-4457. Tel: 518-783-6717. Interlibrary Loan Service Tel: 518-783-2518. Reference Tel: 518-783-2988. Administration Tel: 518-783-2545. FAX: 518-783-2570. Interlibrary Loan Service FAX: 518-783-2958. E-mail: reference@siena.edu. Web Site: www.siena.edu/library. *Dir,* Loretta Ebert; E-mail: Lebert@siena.edu; *Head, Cat & Metadata Serv,* Jennifer Fairall; Tel: 518-783-2591, E-mail: jfairall@siena.edu; *Ref Serv, Website Mgr,* Kelly MacWatters; Tel: 518-783-2588, E-mail: kmacwatters@siena.edu; *Coordr, Instruction,* Catherine Crohan; Tel: 518-782-6731, E-mail: crohan@siena.edu; *Archivist,* Julian Davies; Tel: 518-782-6703, Fax: 518-786-5097, E-mail: davies@siena.edu; *Coll Develop,* William Kanalley; Tel: 518-783-2522, E-mail: kanalley@siena.edu; *Curator of Fine Art,* Sara Boivin; Tel: 518-782-6704, E-mail: sboivin@siena.edu; *ILL,* Patricia Markley; Tel: 518-783-4196, E-mail: markley@siena.edu; *Media Serv,* Sean Conley; Tel: 518-783-2539, E-mail: sconley@siena.edu; *Ser,* Alison Larsen; Tel: 518-782-6765, E-mail: alarsen@siena.edu; Staff 11.5 (MLS 10.5, Non-MLS 1)
Founded 1937. Enrl 3,069; Fac 273; Highest Degree: Master
Jun 2012-May 2013 Income $1,737,135, State $6,041, Parent Institution $1,721,960, Other $9,134. Mats Exp $1,737,135, Books $201,359, Per/Ser (Incl. Access Fees) $247,902, Manu Arch $609, Micro $829, AV Equip $5,580, AV Mat $10,073, Electronic Ref Mat (Incl. Access Fees) $215,976, Presv $19,368. Sal $892,920
Library Holdings: AV Mats 6,223; CDs 2,035; DVDs 2,401; e-books 18,401; e-journals 29,627; Electronic Media & Resources 98; Microforms 26,655; Music Scores 67; Bk Titles 247,712; Bk Vols 321,764; Per Subs 275; Videos 1,792
Special Collections: Franciscana Coll; Medieval & Early Modern Studies Coll; T E Lawrence Coll
Subject Interests: Mil hist, Multicultural studies, Relig studies
Automation Activity & Vendor Info: (Acquisitions) Innovative Interfaces, Inc; (Cataloging) Innovative Interfaces, Inc; (Circulation) Innovative Interfaces, Inc; (Course Reserve) Docutek; (ILL) OCLC ILLiad; (OPAC) Innovative Interfaces, Inc; (Serials) Innovative Interfaces, Inc
Database Vendor: ABC-CLIO, Agricola, Alexander Street Press, American Chemical Society, American Psychological Association (APA), Annual Reviews, ARTstor, Backstage Library Works, BioOne, Bowker, Cambridge Scientific Abstracts, CountryWatch, Coutts Information Service, CQ Press, Dialog, EBSCOhost, Elsevier, Emerald, Facts on File, Gale Cengage Learning, Greenwood Publishing Group, H W Wilson, Innovative Interfaces, Inc, Innovative Interfaces, Inc, JSTOR, LexisNexis, Marquis Who's Who, Medline, Modern Language Association, Nature Publishing Group, OCLC, Project MUSE, ProQuest, PubMed, ReferenceUSA, ScienceDirect, Scopus, SerialsSolutions, Springer-Verlag, Springshare, LLC, Standard & Poor's, STN International, Wiley, Wiley InterScience, Wilson - Wilson Web
Wireless access
Function: Archival coll, Art exhibits, Audio & video playback equip for onsite use, AV serv, Computers for patron use, Copy machines, E-Reserves, Electronic databases & coll, Exhibits, Handicapped accessible, ILL available, Instruction & testing, Microfiche/film & reading machines, Online searches, Photocopying/Printing, Ref & res, Scanner, VHS videos, Video lending libr, Wheelchair accessible
Partic in Cap District Libr Coun for Ref & Res Resources; Connect NY; Libraries Interested in Theology across New York (LITANY); Lyrasis; New York State Higher Education Initiative
Special Services for the Blind - Assistive/Adapted tech devices, equip & products; Braille equip
Open Mon-Thurs 7:45am-1am, Fri 7:45-6, Sat 10-6, Sun 10am-1am
Restriction: Authorized patrons, Circ privileges for students & alumni only, ID required to use computers (Ltd hrs), In-house use for visitors, Non-circulating of rare bks, Restricted borrowing privileges

LOWVILLE

M LEWIS COUNTY GENERAL HOSPITAL & RESIDENTIAL HEALTH CARE FACILITY, Medical Library, 7785 N State St, 13367. Tel: 315-376-5610. FAX: 315-376-5848. *Circuit Librn,* Brenna Tuite
Library Holdings: Bk Titles 300; Bk Vols 500; Per Subs 50
Subject Interests: Med, Nursing
Wireless access
Partic in Northern New York Library Network
Open Mon-Fri 8-4

L LEWIS COUNTY LAW LIBRARY*, 7660 State St, 2nd Flr, 13367. Tel: 315-376-5317, 315-376-5383. FAX: 315-376-4145. *Law Librn,* Ann Marie Hill; E-mail: amhill@courts.state.ny.us
Library Holdings: Bk Vols 6,000
Subject Interests: Legal ref
Database Vendor: LexisNexis
Wireless access
Open Mon-Fri 8:30-4:30

P LOWVILLE FREE LIBRARY*, 5387 Dayan St, 13367. SAN 311-4465. Tel: 315-376-2131. FAX: 315-376-2131. E-mail: lowlib@ncls.org. Web Site: www.nc3r.org/lowlibrary. *Dir,* Dawn Myers; E-mail: myersd@northnet.org
Founded 1903. Pop 4,548; Circ 33,502
Library Holdings: AV Mats 1,389; Bk Titles 17,344; Per Subs 19
Special Collections: State Document Depository
Subject Interests: Genealogy, Local hist
Wireless access
Mem of North Country Library System
Friends of the Library Group

LYNBROOK

P LYNBROOK PUBLIC LIBRARY, 56 Eldert St, 11563. SAN 311-4473. Tel: 516-599-8630. FAX: 516-596-1312. E-mail: lpl@lynbrooklibrary.org. Web Site: lynbrooklibrary.org. *Dir,* Robyn Gilloon; E-mail: lpldirector@lynbrooklibrary.org; *Asst Dir, Head, Ref,* Kathy Buchsbaum; E-mail: Kbuchsbaum@lynbrooklibrary.org; Staff 24 (MLS 6, Non-MLS 18)
Founded 1929. Pop 19,427; Circ 123,679
Library Holdings: Bk Vols 83,673
Automation Activity & Vendor Info: (Cataloging) Innovative Interfaces, Inc; (Circulation) Innovative Interfaces, Inc; (OPAC) Innovative Interfaces, Inc
Wireless access
Publications: Newsletter (Quarterly)
Mem of Nassau Library System
Special Services for the Blind - Closed circuit TV magnifier
Open Mon, Wed & Thurs 10-9, Tues 1-9, Fri 10-5, Sat (Sept-June) 10-5 (9-1 July & Aug)
Friends of the Library Group

R TEMPLE AM ECHAD*, Malcolm Eisman Memorial Library, One Saperstein Plaza, 11563. SAN 311-4481. Tel: 516-593-4004. FAX: 516-593-2739. *Co-Chair,* Carole Schrager; *Librn,* Bryna Pasoff
Jul 2011-Jun 2012. Mats Exp $5,500. Sal $27,000
Library Holdings: Bk Vols 5,000; Per Subs 12
Special Collections: Holocaust
Subject Interests: Jewish bks
Open Mon-Fri 10-6

LYNDONVILLE

P YATES COMMUNITY LIBRARY*, 15 N Main St, 14098. (Mail add: PO Box 485, 14098-0485). Tel: 585-765-9041. FAX: 585-765-9527. Web Site: www.nioga.org/lyn.html, www.yateslibrary.org. *Dir,* Emily Cebula; E-mail: ecebula@nioga.org
Founded 1949. Pop 2,371; Circ 16,371
Library Holdings: Bk Vols 16,500; Per Subs 30
Special Collections: Lyndonville Enterprise Newspaper 1906-1962, micro
Automation Activity & Vendor Info: (Cataloging) SirsiDynix; (Circulation) SirsiDynix; (OPAC) SirsiDynix
Wireless access
Mem of Nioga Library System
Open Mon, Tues & Thurs 10-8, Fri 10-5, Sat 10-2

LYONS

P LYONS PUBLIC LIBRARY*, 67 Canal St, 14489. SAN 311-4503. Tel: 315-946-9262. FAX: 315-946-3320. Web Site: www.lyons.pls-net.org. *Libr Dir,* Theresa Streb
Founded 1956. Pop 6,934; Circ 40,000
Library Holdings: Bk Vols 25,589; Per Subs 60
Subject Interests: Fiction, Law, Local hist
Automation Activity & Vendor Info: (Circulation) SirsiDynix; (OPAC) SirsiDynix
Wireless access
Mem of Pioneer Library System
Open Mon & Wed 10-5 & 7-9, Tues & Thurs 12-9, Fri 10-5, Sat 9-1
Friends of the Library Group

S WAYNE COUNTY HISTORICAL SOCIETY MUSEUM LIBRARY*, 21 Butternut St, 14489. SAN 328-3666. Tel: 315-946-4943. FAX: 315-946-0069. Web Site: www.waynehistory.org. *Exec Dir,* Larry Ann Evans; E-mail: laevans@waynehistory.org
Founded 1949
Library Holdings: Bk Titles 3,119
Wireless access
Open Tues-Fri 10-4, Sat (June-Aug) 10-4

LYONS FALLS

P LYONS FALLS FREE LIBRARY*, 3918 High St, 13368. SAN 311-4511. Tel: 315-348-6180. FAX: 315-348-6180. E-mail: lyflib@ncls.org. Web Site: www.lyonsfallslibrary.org. *Librn,* Carolyn LeVan
Founded 1923. Pop 755; Circ 9,495
Library Holdings: Bk Vols 7,500; Per Subs 12
Subject Interests: Educ, Environ studies, Indust
Automation Activity & Vendor Info: (OPAC) SirsiDynix
Wireless access
Mem of North Country Library System
Open Tues & Wed 3-7, Thurs & Fri 1-5, Sat 8-12
Friends of the Library Group

MACEDON

P MACEDON PUBLIC LIBRARY*, 30 Main St, 14502-9101. SAN 311-452X. Tel: 315-986-5932. FAX: 315-986-2952. E-mail: macedon@pls-net.org. Web Site: www.macedon.pls-net.org. *Dir,* Darlene Virkler; Staff 11 (Non-MLS 11)
Circ 60,000
Library Holdings: Bk Vols 35,000; Per Subs 30
Special Collections: Bullis Family Library Coll
Automation Activity & Vendor Info: (Cataloging) SirsiDynix
Wireless access
Mem of Pioneer Library System
Open Mon-Thurs 10-8, Fri 10-5, Sat 10-3, Sun 1-4
Friends of the Library Group

MACHIAS

G CATTARAUGUS COUNTY MUSEUM & RESEARCH LIBRARY*, 9824 Rte 16, 14101. (Mail add: PO Box 352, 14101-0352), SAN 326-2030. Tel: 716-353-8200. Web Site: www.co.cattaraugus.ny.us. *Historian,* Sharon Fellows; Staff 2 (Non-MLS 2)
Founded 1914
Library Holdings: Bk Titles 1,000; Bk Vols 1,200
Special Collections: New York State & Federal Census Records; World War II Oral History. Oral History
Subject Interests: Local hist
Open Tues-Fri 9-4

P KING MEMORIAL LIBRARY*, 9538 Rte 16, 14101. (Mail add: PO Box 509, 14101), SAN 311-4554. Tel: 716-353-9915. FAX: 716-353-4774. *Dir,* Ann Parker; E-mail: anna242parker@netscape.net
Founded 1941. Pop 2,442; Circ 10,918
Library Holdings: Bk Vols 10,185
Automation Activity & Vendor Info: (Cataloging) SirsiDynix; (Circulation) SirsiDynix; (OPAC) SirsiDynix; (Serials) SirsiDynix
Wireless access
Mem of Chautauqua-Cattaraugus Library System
Open Mon 12-5 & 6:30-8:30, Tues 10-7:30, Wed 12-5 & 5:30-7:30, Thurs 9-12 & 2-8:30, Fri 9:30-5:30, Sat 9-1:30

MADRID

P HEPBURN LIBRARY OF MADRID*, 11 Church St, 13660. (Mail add: PO Box 40, 13660-0040), SAN 311-4562. Tel: 315-322-5673. FAX: 315-322-5673. E-mail: madlib@ncls.org. *Dir,* Kathy Paige
Founded 1917. Pop 1,852; Circ 10,587
Library Holdings: Bk Vols 8,086; Per Subs 56
Automation Activity & Vendor Info: (Cataloging) SirsiDynix; (Circulation) SirsiDynix; (OPAC) SirsiDynix
Wireless access
Mem of North Country Library System
Open Mon 2-7, Tues & Thurs 2-5, Wed 3-8, Fri 9-12, Sat 10-1

MAHOPAC

P MAHOPAC PUBLIC LIBRARY*, 668 Rte 6, 10541. SAN 311-4570. Tel: 845-628-2009. FAX: 845-628-0672. E-mail: library@mahopaclibrary.org. Web Site: www.mahopaclibrary.org. *Dir,* Position Currently Open; Staff 26 (MLS 10, Non-MLS 16)
Founded 1952. Pop 26,485; Circ 308,925
Library Holdings: AV Mats 13,201; Electronic Media & Resources 4,384; Bk Vols 110,844; Per Subs 263
Special Collections: Autism Resource Center; Foundation Center; Health Info Center; Job & Education Info Center; Land Use Center; Local History Coll; Parenting Coll; Putnam County Reference Center
Automation Activity & Vendor Info: (Cataloging) Innovative Interfaces, Inc; (Circulation) Innovative Interfaces, Inc; (ILL) Innovative Interfaces, Inc; (OPAC) Innovative Interfaces, Inc
Wireless access
Publications: Calendar (Monthly); e-Newsletter (Monthly); Newsletter (Quarterly)
Mem of Mid-Hudson Library System
Partic in Southeastern New York Library Resources Council
Special Services for the Deaf - TDD equip
Special Services for the Blind - Ednalite Hi-Vision scope; Talking bks
Open Mon-Thurs (Sept-June) 9:30-9, Fri & Sat 9:30-5, Sun 1-5; Mon-Thurs (July & Aug) 9:30-9, Fri 9:30-5, Sat 9:30-3
Friends of the Library Group

MALONE

S BARE HILL CORRECTIONAL FACILITY LIBRARY*, 181 Brand Rd, 12953. Tel: 518-483-8411. FAX: 518-483-8411, Ext 2099. *Librn,* Gwen Egan
Library Holdings: Bk Vols 15,000; Per Subs 78
Automation Activity & Vendor Info: (Cataloging) Follett Software; (Circulation) Follett Software; (OPAC) Follett Software
Open Mon-Wed 1-9, Thurs & Fri 9-9, Sat 1-6

S FRANKLIN CORRECTIONAL FACILITY*, 62 Bare Hill Rd, 12953. (Mail add: PO Box 10, 12953-0010). Tel: 518-483-6040. FAX: 518-483-6040, Ext 2099. *Sr Librn,* Gretchen Holzhauer
Library Holdings: Bk Vols 3,500
Automation Activity & Vendor Info: (Cataloging) Follett Software; (Circulation) Follett Software
Wireless access
Open Mon-Fri 10-5

P WEAD LIBRARY*, 64 Elm St, 12953-1594. SAN 311-4589. Tel: 518-483-5251. FAX: 581-483-5255. E-mail: vnplib@nnyln.net. *Dir,* Susan Wool; Staff 2 (MLS 2)
Founded 1881. Pop 20,220; Circ 72,892
Library Holdings: Audiobooks 1,005; DVDs 110; Bk Vols 46,209; Per Subs 105
Special Collections: State Document Depository
Subject Interests: Genealogy, State hist
Automation Activity & Vendor Info: (Cataloging) SirsiDynix; (Circulation) SirsiDynix; (ILL) SirsiDynix; (OPAC) SirsiDynix

Database Vendor: College Source, EBSCO Information Services, Gale Cengage Learning, LearningExpress, Newsbank, OCLC FirstSearch, ProQuest, ReferenceUSA, TLC (The Library Corporation), Wilson - Wilson Web
Wireless access
Function: Bks on CD, Handicapped accessible, ILL available, Online cat, Pub access computers, Story hour, Tax forms
Mem of Clinton-Essex-Franklin Library System
Partic in Northern New York Library Network
Special Services for the Deaf - Bks on deafness & sign lang
Special Services for the Blind - Audio mat; Bks on cassette; Bks on CD; Large print bks; Magnifiers; Talking bk serv referral
Open Mon-Fri 10-8, Sat 10-3

MALVERNE

P MALVERNE PUBLIC LIBRARY, 61 Saint Thomas Pl, 11565. SAN 311-4597. Tel: 516-599-0750. FAX: 516-599-3320. E-mail: director@malvernelibrary.org. Web Site: www.malvernelibrary.org. *Libr Dir,* Maryann Ferro; *Ch,* Marie Drucker; *Teen Librn,* Jody Ruggiero; Tel: 516-599-0750, Ext 3, E-mail: jruggiero@nassaulibrary.info; Staff 12 (MLS 4, Non-MLS 8)
Founded 1928. Pop 9,054; Circ 78,000
Library Holdings: Bk Vols 55,000; Per Subs 107
Automation Activity & Vendor Info: (Acquisitions) Innovative Interfaces, Inc - Millenium; (Cataloging) Innovative Interfaces, Inc - Millenium; (Circulation) Innovative Interfaces, Inc - Millenium; (OPAC) Innovative Interfaces, Inc - Millenium
Database Vendor: ReferenceUSA
Wireless access
Mem of Nassau Library System
Open Mon, Wed & Thurs 9:30-9, Tues & Fri 9:30-5, Sat (Sept-June) 9:30-5
Friends of the Library Group

MAMARONECK

P MAMARONECK PUBLIC LIBRARY DISTRICT*, 136 Prospect Ave, 10543. SAN 311-4600. Tel: 914-698-1250. FAX: 914-381-3088. Web Site: www.mamaronecklibrary.org. *Dir,* Susan Riley; *Ch Serv,* Marcia Hupp; *Ch Serv,* Ellen McTyre; *YA Serv,* Hilary Hertzoff; *Ref,* Lori Friedli; *Ref,* Marianne Pei; Staff 27 (MLS 6, Non-MLS 21)
Founded 1922. Pop 18,752; Circ 204,278
Library Holdings: AV Mats 6,320; Bk Vols 94,494; Per Subs 30
Automation Activity & Vendor Info: (Cataloging) SirsiDynix; (Circulation) SirsiDynix; (OPAC) SirsiDynix
Wireless access
Mem of Westchester Library System
Open Mon & Wed 10-8, Tues & Thurs 10-6, Fri & Sat 10-5, Sun 1-4:30
Friends of the Library Group

MANHASSET

P MANHASSET PUBLIC LIBRARY*, 30 Onderdonk Ave, 11030. SAN 311-4619. Tel: 516-627-2300. Circulation Tel: 516 627-2300, Ext 101. Interlibrary Loan Service Tel: 516 627-2300, Ext 105. Reference Tel: 516 627-2300, Ext 201. Administration Tel: 516 365-2300, Ext 348. Information Services Tel: 516 627-2300, Ext 110. FAX: 516-627-4339. Administration FAX: 516-365-3466. Web Site: manhassetlibrary.org. *Head, Ch,* Cheryl Kallberg; Tel: 516 627 2300, Ext 305, E-mail: ckallberg@manhassetlibrary.org; *Head, Ref Serv,* Ann Marie Moore; Tel: 516 627-2300, Ext 205, E-mail: amoore@manhassetlibrary.org; *Head, Tech Serv,* Carolyn Ayers; Tel: 516 627-2300, Ext 320, E-mail: cayers@manhassetlibrary.org; *Head, YA,* Sharon Rappaport; Tel: 516 627-2300, Ext 209, E-mail: srappaport@manhassetlibrary.org; *Media Serv,* Anne May; Tel: 516 627-2300, Ext 207, E-mail: amay@manhassetlibrary.org
Founded 1945. Pop 15,961; Circ 188,457
Jul 2010-Jun 2011 Income $3,431,594, Locally Generated Income $3,523,005, Other $91,411. Mats Exp $239,560, Books $116,000, Per/Ser (Incl. Access Fees) $17,600, Other Print Mats $500, Micro $7,600, AV Equip $1,100, AV Mat $56,600, Electronic Ref Mat (Incl. Access Fees) $41,500. Sal $1,847,134 (Prof $955,211)
Library Holdings: Audiobooks 3,995; AV Mats 18,603; CDs 4,694; DVDs 8,968; Large Print Bks 1,692; Microforms 3,930; Bk Vols 116,094; Per Subs 309; Videos 2,971
Special Collections: Benedetto/Rainone Puppet Coll; Books for the Bibliophile; Career Center; Frances Hodgson Burnett Archival Coll; Long Island Coll; Manhasset Authors (local oral archives); New York Coll; Poetry for Children (Kelly Miscall Coll). Oral History
Automation Activity & Vendor Info: (Cataloging) Innovative Interfaces, Inc; (Circulation) Innovative Interfaces, Inc; (ILL) OCLC; (OPAC) Innovative Interfaces, Inc
Wireless access
Publications: Quarterly Newsletter
Mem of Nassau Library System
Special Services for the Blind - Closed circuit TV
Open Mon, Wed & Thurs 9-9, Tues 11-9, Fri 9-5:30, Sat 9-5 (9-1 Summer), Sun 1-5
Friends of the Library Group

M NORTH SHORE UNIVERSITY HOSPITAL*, Daniel Carroll Payson Medical Library, 300 Community Dr, 11030. SAN 311-4627. Tel: 516-562-4324. FAX: 516-562-2865. Web Site: www.nslijhs.com. *Dir,* Debra Eisenberg; Staff 7 (MLS 4, Non-MLS 3)
Founded 1954
Library Holdings: Bk Titles 2,000; Per Subs 500
Subject Interests: Clinical med, Hist of med, Laboratory med, Nursing
Automation Activity & Vendor Info: (Cataloging) SirsiDynix; (Circulation) SirsiDynix; (OPAC) SirsiDynix
Database Vendor: OVID Technologies, PubMed, UpToDate
Wireless access
Open Mon-Fri 8-6

MANLIUS

P MANLIUS LIBRARY*, One Arkie Albanese Ave, 13104. SAN 311-4635. Tel: 315-682-6400. FAX: 315-682-4490. E-mail: manliuslibrary@yahoo.com. Web Site: www.manliuslibrary.org. *Dir,* Patricia W Infantine; E-mail: pwinfant@onlib.org; *Asst Dir,* David D'Ambrosio; *Tech Coordr,* Patricia M Ruggeri; E-mail: pmiru@ocpl.lib.ny.us; *Ref,* Helen Vecchio; Staff 20 (MLS 9, Non-MLS 11)
Founded 1915. Pop 14,000; Circ 323,123
Library Holdings: AV Mats 11,300; Bks on Deafness & Sign Lang 42; Large Print Bks 800; Bk Titles 40,000; Bk Vols 47,022; Per Subs 146
Automation Activity & Vendor Info: (Circulation) Innovative Interfaces, Inc; (OPAC) Innovative Interfaces, Inc
Database Vendor: EBSCOhost, Gale Cengage Learning
Wireless access
Mem of Onondaga County Public Library
Partic in Central New York Library Resources Council
Open Mon-Thurs 10-9, Fri & Sat 10-5, Sun 1-5

MANNSVILLE

P MANNSVILLE FREE LIBRARY*, PO Box 156, 13661. SAN 311-4643. Tel: 315-465-4049. Web Site: www.nc3r.org/mannsv/_library. *Dir,* Mary Snyder
Circ 6,595
Library Holdings: Bk Vols 6,123; Per Subs 31
Wireless access
Mem of North Country Library System
Open Tues 3-8, Wed 2-5, Thurs 1-5, Fri 9-12
Friends of the Library Group

MARATHON

P PECK MEMORIAL LIBRARY*, 24 Main St, 13803. (Mail add: PO Box 325, 13803-0325), SAN 311-466X. Tel: 607-849-6135. FAX: 607-849-3799. *Dir,* Mary Frank
Founded 1895. Pop 1,063; Circ 16,516
Library Holdings: Bk Vols 16,000; Per Subs 26
Automation Activity & Vendor Info: (Cataloging) Innovative Interfaces, Inc; (Circulation) Innovative Interfaces, Inc, (OPAC) Innovative Interfaces, Inc
Wireless access
Function: Adult bk club, Art exhibits, Audiobks via web, Bks on cassette, Bks on CD, CD-ROM, Children's prog, Computer training, Computers for patron use, e-mail serv, Electronic databases & coll, Fax serv, Free DVD rentals, ILL available, Photocopying/Printing, Preschool outreach, Pub access computers, Scanner, Tax forms, VHS videos
Mem of Finger Lakes Library System
Open Mon & Fri 2-5, Tues 9-12 & 2-8, Wed & Thurs 2-8, Sat (Sept-June) 9-Noon
Friends of the Library Group

MARCELLUS

P MARCELLUS FREE LIBRARY*, Two Slocombe St, 13108. SAN 311-4678. Tel: 315-673-3221. FAX: 315-673-0148. E-mail: marcellus@onlib.org. Web Site: www.library.marcellusny.com. *Dir,* Carol A Johnson; Staff 5 (MLS 1, Non-MLS 4)
Founded 1913. Pop 6,319; Circ 68,000
Jan 2005-Dec 2005 Income $488,172, $168,848, State $4,598, Provincial $9,000, City $27,500, Locally Generated Income $40,000, Other $87,750. Mats Exp $66,560, $131,858, Books $30,070, Per/Ser (Incl. Access Fees) $2,131, Micro $200, Electronic Ref Mat (Incl. Access Fees) $82. Sal $68,000 (Prof $36,000)
Library Holdings: Bk Titles 22,101; Per Subs 60; Talking Bks 1,200; Videos 1,700
Special Collections: Chorale Music (Marcellus Chorale Coll), sheets

Automation Activity & Vendor Info: (Circulation) Innovative Interfaces, Inc; (OPAC) Innovative Interfaces, Inc
Wireless access
Function: AV serv, Handicapped accessible, ILL available, Photocopying/Printing, Prog for children & young adult, Summer reading prog, Telephone ref, Wheelchair accessible
Mem of Onondaga County Public Library
Open Mon-Thurs 9-8:30, Fri 9-5, Sat 10-2, Sun 2-4
Friends of the Library Group

MARGARETVILLE

P FAIRVIEW PUBLIC LIBRARY*, 43 Walnut St, 12455. (Mail add: PO Box 609, 12455-0609), SAN 310-8090. Tel: 845-586-3791. FAX: 845-586-3791. E-mail: fairviewpubliclibrary@yahoo.com. *Dir,* Diana Cope
Pop 4,015; Circ 12,808
Library Holdings: Bk Vols 10,000; Per Subs 10
Mem of Four County Library System
Open Mon, Tues & Fri 12:30-5, Wed 12:30-7, Thurs 11-5, Sat 10-2:30

MARILLA

P MARILLA FREE LIBRARY*, 11637 Bullis Rd, 14102-9727. SAN 311-4686. Tel: 716-652-7449. FAX: 716-652-7449. Web Site: www.buffalolib.org. *Dir,* Joyce Kaupa
Pop 4,864; Circ 24,878
Library Holdings: Bk Vols 14,533; Per Subs 35
Automation Activity & Vendor Info: (Cataloging) SirsiDynix; (Circulation) SirsiDynix; (OPAC) SirsiDynix
Wireless access
Mem of Buffalo & Erie County Public Library System
Open Mon, Wed & Fri 10-3, Tues & Thurs 10-8
Friends of the Library Group

MARION

P MARION PUBLIC LIBRARY*, 4036 Maple Ave, 14505. (Mail add: PO Box 30, 14505-0030), SAN 311-4694. Tel: 315-926-4933. FAX: 315-926-7038. Web Site: marionnypubliclibrary.blogspot.com. *Dir,* Tracy Whitney; E-mail: marionlibrarydirector@owwl.org; *Asst Librn,* Adrienne VanHorn
Founded 1910. Circ 46,615
Library Holdings: Bk Vols 17,000; Per Subs 30
Automation Activity & Vendor Info: (Acquisitions) SirsiDynix; (Cataloging) SirsiDynix; (Circulation) SirsiDynix; (ILL) SirsiDynix
Wireless access
Mem of Pioneer Library System
Open Mon & Wed 10-8, Tues, Thurs & Fri 2-6, Sat 9-Noon
Friends of the Library Group

MARLBORO

P MARLBORO FREE LIBRARY*, 1251 Rte 9W, 12542-5411. (Mail add: PO Box 780, 12542-0780), SAN 311-4708. Tel: 845-236-7272. FAX: 845-236-7635. E-mail: staff@marlborolibrary.org. Web Site: www.marlborolibrary.org. *Dir,* James B Cosgrove; Staff 3 (MLS 2, Non-MLS 1)
Founded 1911. Pop 11,634
Library Holdings: Bk Titles 38,466; Per Subs 210
Special Collections: Frederick W Goudy Coll. Oral History
Subject Interests: Local hist
Automation Activity & Vendor Info: (Circulation) Innovative Interfaces, Inc; (OPAC) Innovative Interfaces, Inc
Database Vendor: EBSCOhost, OCLC FirstSearch, ProQuest
Wireless access
Publications: The Inside Story (Newsletter)
Mem of Mid-Hudson Library System
Open Mon-Thurs 9:30-8:30, Fri 9:30-5, Sat 11-5, Sun (Sept-June) 1-5
Friends of the Library Group

MARTINSBURG

P WILLIAM H BUSH MEMORIAL LIBRARY*, 5605 Whitaker Rd, 13404. (Mail add: PO Box 141, 13404-0141), SAN 311-4716. Tel: 315-376-7490. FAX: 315-376-3096. E-mail: marlib@ncls.org. *Librn,* Karen R Dening
Founded 1913. Pop 350; Circ 8,393
Library Holdings: Bk Vols 15,660; Per Subs 56
Special Collections: Local Scrapbooks & Diaries
Subject Interests: Hist
Wireless access
Mem of North Country Library System
Open Mon & Wed 10-12, Fri 2-5 & 7-9

MASSAPEQUA

P PLAINEDGE PUBLIC LIBRARY*, 1060 Hicksville Rd, 11758. SAN 311-4759. Tel: 516-735-4133. FAX: 516-735-4192. E-mail: pplained@nassau.cv.net. Web Site: www.nassaulibrary.org/plnedge. *Dir,* Marilyn Kappenberg; E-mail: directorpel@nassaulibrary.org; *Asst Dir,* Judith Nilsen; *Ch Serv,* Peggy Gorman; Staff 14 (MLS 14)
Founded 1963. Pop 22,097; Circ 200,111
Library Holdings: Audiobooks 868; AV Mats 6,000; Bks on Deafness & Sign Lang 230; CDs 4,332; DVDs 4,532; Large Print Bks 600; Bk Titles 135,200; Per Subs 215; Talking Bks 4,000; Videos 500
Automation Activity & Vendor Info: (Acquisitions) Baker & Taylor; (Circulation) Innovative Interfaces, Inc; (OPAC) Innovative Interfaces, Inc; (Serials) EBSCO Online
Database Vendor: EBSCOhost, Gale Cengage Learning, OCLC FirstSearch, SirsiDynix
Wireless access
Function: ILL available, Photocopying/Printing, Ref serv available
Publications: Newsletter (Monthly)
Mem of Nassau Library System
Special Services for the Blind - Large screen computer & software; Magnifiers; Screen enlargement software for people with visual disabilities
Open Mon-Fri 9-9, Sat 9-5, Sun 1-5

MASSAPEQUA PARK

P MASSAPEQUA PUBLIC LIBRARY*, Bar Harbour Bldg, 40 Harbor Lane, 11762. SAN 352-8189. Tel: 516-799-0770. FAX: 516-541-2648. E-mail: bhlibrary@massapequalibrary.org. Web Site: www.massapequalibrary.org. *Dir,* Janis A Schoen; E-mail: jaschoen@massapequalibrary.org; *Asst Dir,* Maris Job; E-mail: mjob@massapequalibrary.org; *Adult Ref Librn,* Lisa Quinn; E-mail: lquinn@massapequalibrary.org; *Tech Coordr,* Carol Santillo; E-mail: csantillo@massapequalibrary.org; *Ch Serv,* Connie Smith; E-mail: csmith@massapequalibrary.org; *Circ,* Maryetta Garrone; E-mail: mgarrone@massapequalibrary.org; *YA Serv,* Peter Cirona; E-mail: pcirona@massapequalibrary.org; Staff 18 (MLS 18)
Founded 1952. Pop 48,931; Circ 446,292
Jul 2005-Jun 2006 Income (Main Library and Branch(s)) $4,670,835, State $25,966, Locally Generated Income $4,521,735, Other $123,134. Mats Exp $520,450, Books $375,000, Per/Ser (Incl. Access Fees) $24,500, Other Print Mats $7,350, Micro $15,000, AV Mat $56,600, Electronic Ref Mat (Incl. Access Fees) $42,000. Sal $2,351,895 (Prof $838,361)
Library Holdings: AV Mats 14,599; Bk Vols 189,442; Per Subs 590
Automation Activity & Vendor Info: (Cataloging) Innovative Interfaces, Inc; (Circulation) Innovative Interfaces, Inc; (ILL) Innovative Interfaces, Inc; (OPAC) Innovative Interfaces, Inc; (Serials) Innovative Interfaces, Inc
Database Vendor: Innovative Interfaces, Inc
Wireless access
Function: Adult bk club, Computer training, Handicapped accessible, Prog for adults, Prog for children & young adult, Summer reading prog
Publications: Monthly Calendar; Newsletter (Quarterly)
Mem of Nassau Library System
Open Mon-Thurs 9-9, Fri 9-6, Sat 9-5, Sun (Sept-June) 12-4
Branches: 1
CENTRAL AVENUE, 523 Central Ave, Massapequa, 11758, SAN 352-8154. Tel: 516-798-4607. FAX: 516-798-2804. E-mail: calibrary@massapequalibrary.org. *Adult Ref Librn,* Maris Job; E-mail: mjob@massapequalibrary.org; *Ch Serv,* Germaine Booth; E-mail: gbooth@massapequalibrary.org; *Circ,* Mary Dougherty; E-mail: mdougherty@massapequalibrary.org
Open Mon-Thurs 9-9, Fri 9-6, Sat 9-5, Sun (Sept-June) 1-5

MASSENA

M MASSENA MEMORIAL HOSPITAL LIBRARY*, One Hospital Dr, 13662. SAN 328-428X. Tel: 315-764-1711. FAX: 315-769-4780. *In Charge,* Laurie Schneller; E-mail: lschneller@massenahospital.org
Library Holdings: Bk Vols 306
Restriction: Staff use only

P MASSENA PUBLIC LIBRARY*, Warren Memorial Library, 41 Glenn St, 13662. SAN 311-4767. Tel: 315-769-9914. FAX: 315-769-5978. E-mail: maslib@ncls.org. Web Site: www.massenapubliclibrary.org. *Dir,* Elaine Dunne-Thayer; *Adult Serv,* Debbie Fuehring; *Youth Serv,* Kimberly Holmes; Staff 3 (MLS 2, Non-MLS 1)
Founded 1897. Pop 13,100; Circ 95,800
Library Holdings: Bk Vols 68,000; Per Subs 156; Talking Bks 800
Automation Activity & Vendor Info: (Circulation) SirsiDynix; (OPAC) SirsiDynix
Wireless access
Publications: Books & Beyond (Bimonthly library activities)
Mem of North Country Library System
Partic in Northern New York Library Network
Open Mon, Fri & Sat 9:30-5, Tues-Thurs 9-8:30
Friends of the Library Group

MATTITUCK

P MATTITUCK-LAUREL LIBRARY*, 13900 Main Rd, 11952. (Mail add: PO Box 1437, 11952-0991), SAN 311-4775. Tel: 631-298-4134. FAX: 631-298-4764. Web Site: www.mattlibrary.org. *Dir,* Kay Zegel; Staff 4 (MLS 4)
Pop 5,093; Circ 110,291
Library Holdings: Bk Vols 54,000; Per Subs 300
Automation Activity & Vendor Info: (Acquisitions) Innovative Interfaces, Inc; (Cataloging) Innovative Interfaces, Inc; (Circulation) Innovative Interfaces, Inc; (OPAC) Innovative Interfaces, Inc
Mem of Suffolk Cooperative Library System
Open Mon-Fri 10-8, Sat 10-5, Sun 1-4
Friends of the Library Group

MATTYDALE

P SALINA FREE LIBRARY*, 100 Belmont St, 13211. SAN 311-4783. Tel: 315-454-4524. FAX: 315-454-3466. E-mail: info@salinalibrary.org. Web Site: www.salinalibrary.org. *Dir,* Jeannine Chubon; E-mail: jchubon@salinalibrary.org; Staff 12 (MLS 2, Non-MLS 10)
Founded 1942. Pop 11,616; Circ 99,812
Library Holdings: Bk Vols 34,000
Automation Activity & Vendor Info: (Circulation) Innovative Interfaces, Inc; (OPAC) Innovative Interfaces, Inc
Wireless access
Function: Adult bk club, Art exhibits, Audiobks via web, Bks on CD, Children's prog, Computer training, Computers for patron use, Copy machines, e-mail & chat, Electronic databases & coll, Free DVD rentals, Genealogy discussion group, Holiday prog, ILL available, Magnifiers for reading, Music CDs, Online cat, OverDrive digital audio bks, Photocopying/Printing, Prog for adults, Prog for children & young adult, Summer reading prog, Tax forms
Mem of Onondaga County Public Library
Open Mon-Thurs 10-8, Fri 1-5, Sat 10-4
Friends of the Library Group

MAYBROOK

P GEORGE C BULLIS MEMORIAL LIBRARY*, 101 Main St, 12543. Tel: 845-427-2914. FAX: 845-427-2881. E-mail: gcblibrary@hvc.rr.com. *Libr Dir,* Gregory Syrianos
Library Holdings: AV Mats 700; Bk Vols 20,000; Per Subs 20; Talking Bks 50
Open Mon, Wed & Fri 9-4:30, Tues & Thurs 10-5, Sat 10-1

MAYVILLE

P MAYVILLE LIBRARY*, 92 S Erie St, 14757. SAN 311-4791. Tel: 716-753-7362. FAX: 716-753-7360. E-mail: mayvillelibrary@gmail.com. Web Site: www.mayvillelibrary.com. *Dir,* Melissa Bartok
Pop 4,666; Circ 21,000
Library Holdings: Bk Vols 19,466; Per Subs 42
Wireless access
Mem of Chautauqua-Cattaraugus Library System
Open Mon 12-8, Tues & Thurs 10-8, Wed 1-6, Fri 12-6, Sat 10-2

MCGRAW

P LAMONT MEMORIAL FREE LIBRARY, Five Main St, 13101. (Mail add: PO Box 559, 13101-0559), SAN 311-4546. Tel: 607-836-6767. FAX: 607-836-8866. E-mail: lmemoria@twcny.rr.com. *Dir,* Heather M Cobb; Staff 2 (Non-MLS 2)
Founded 1906. Pop 1,053
Automation Activity & Vendor Info: (Cataloging) Innovative Interfaces, Inc
Wireless access
Function: Children's prog, Computers for patron use, Copy machines, Fax serv, Free DVD rentals, ILL available, Magazines, Pub access computers, Summer reading prog
Mem of Finger Lakes Library System
Open Mon & Tues 2-8, Thurs 10-12 & 2-8, Fri 10-12 & 2-5, Sat 10-1

MECHANICVILLE

P MECHANICVILLE DISTRICT PUBLIC LIBRARY*, 190 N Main St, 12118. SAN 311-4805. Tel: 518-664-4646. FAX: 518-664-8641. Web Site: www.mechanicville.sals.edu. *Dir,* Laura Fisher; Staff 8 (MLS 1, Non-MLS 7)
Founded 1966. Pop 8,437; Circ 72,895
Library Holdings: AV Mats 1,449; Bk Vols 25,570; Per Subs 51; Talking Bks 1,430
Special Collections: Coach Wiegel Sports Coll; Ellsworth Coll; Local World War & Korean War Veterans Picture Coll
Subject Interests: Local hist
Automation Activity & Vendor Info: (Cataloging) SirsiDynix
Mem of Southern Adirondack Library System
Open Mon & Wed 11-8, Tues, Thurs & Fri 11-5, Sat (Winter) 11-3

MEDINA

P LEE-WHEDON MEMORIAL LIBRARY*, 620 West Ave, 14103. SAN 311-4813. Tel: 585-798-3430. FAX: 585-798-4398. E-mail: info@medinalibrary.org. Web Site: www.leewhedon.org. *Dir,* Catherine Cooper; *Asst Dir,* Kristine Mostyn
Founded 1928. Pop 11,720; Circ 102,000
Library Holdings: Bk Titles 51,534; Bk Vols 59,998; Per Subs 134
Automation Activity & Vendor Info: (Cataloging) SIRSI WorkFlows; (Circulation) SIRSI WorkFlows
Wireless access
Function: Handicapped accessible, ILL available, Prog for children & young adult, Summer reading prog, Telephone ref, Wheelchair accessible
Mem of Nioga Library System
Open Mon-Thurs 10-8, Fri & Sat 10-5
Restriction: Open to pub for ref & circ; with some limitations
Friends of the Library Group

M MEDINA MEMORIAL HOSPITAL*, Medical Library, 200 Ohio St, 14103. SAN 375-8206. Tel: 585-798-8148. Web Site: www.medinamemorial.org. *Adminr,* Tammy Prichard
Library Holdings: Bk Titles 500; Per Subs 24
Restriction: Staff use only

MELVILLE

S BUCK CONSULTANTS LLC*, Research & Information Library, 155 Pinetown Rd, Ste 200N, 11747-3245. SAN 325-7649. Tel: 516-391-8505. FAX: 516-391-8599. Web Site: www.buckconsultants.com. *Dir,* Teresa Wilkins; Staff 2 (MLS 2)
Founded 1973
Library Holdings: e-books 33; e-journals 15; Bk Titles 500; Per Subs 30; Spec Interest Per Sub 15
Subject Interests: Employee benefits
Automation Activity & Vendor Info: (Acquisitions) Inmagic, Inc.; (Cataloging) Inmagic, Inc.; (Circulation) Inmagic, Inc.; (OPAC) Inmagic, Inc.; (Serials) EBSCO Online
Database Vendor: Dialog, Ingenta, LexisNexis
Wireless access
Function: Electronic databases & coll, ILL available, Online cat, Online searches, Ref & res
Open Mon-Fri 9-5
Restriction: Open to employees & special libr

S NEWSDAY, INC LIBRARY*, 235 Pinelawn Rd, 11747-4250. SAN 311-2314. Tel: 631-843-2333. FAX: 631-843-2065. Web Site: www.newsday.com. *Mgr,* Dorothy Levin; E-mail: dorothy.levin@newsday.com; Staff 22 (MLS 6, Non-MLS 16)
Founded 1940
Library Holdings: Bk Titles 10,000; Per Subs 20
Special Collections: Newsday Clipping & Photo File, 1940-to present
Database Vendor: Dialog, Factiva.com, LexisNexis
Wireless access
Restriction: Not open to pub, Staff use only, Use of others with permission of librn

MENANDS

P MENANDS PUBLIC LIBRARY*, Four N Lyons Ave, 12204. SAN 311-4880. Tel: 518-463-4035. FAX: 518-449-3863. Web Site: www.menandslibrary.org. *Dir,* Leonard J Zapala; E-mail: zapalal@uhls.lib.ny.us; *Ch Serv,* Lisa Neuman; Staff 1 (MLS 1)
Founded 1923. Pop 4,500
Library Holdings: Bk Vols 9,300; Per Subs 43
Automation Activity & Vendor Info: (Cataloging) SirsiDynix; (OPAC) SirsiDynix
Wireless access
Mem of Upper Hudson Library System
Open Mon & Wed 12:30-8:30, Tues & Thurs 5:30-8:30, Fri 12:30-4, Sat 10-1

MERRICK

P MERRICK LIBRARY*, 2279 Merrick Ave, 11566-4398. SAN 311-4902. Tel: 516-377-6112. Circulation Tel: 516-277-6112, Ext 100. Interlibrary Loan Service Tel: 516-377-6112, Ext 112. Administration Tel: 516-377-6112, Ext 118. FAX: 516-377-1108. E-mail: merricklibrary@merricklibrary.org. Web Site: www.merricklibrary.org. *Dir,* Ellen Firer; Fax: 516-377-5197, E-mail: ellenfirer@merricklibrary.org; *Head, Ref,* Diane Bondi; Tel: 516-377-6112, Ext 102, E-mail: dianebondi@merricklibrary.org; *Ch,* Susan Goodwin; *Ref Librn,* Marisa Crowley; *Ref Librn,* Kristine Dugan; *Ref Librn,* Vivian Ho; *Ref Librn,* Carol Ann Tack; *Teen Librn,* Larissa Simonovski; *Ch Serv,* Laurie

Fensterstock; *Ch Serv,* Bonnie Markel; Tel: 516-277-6112, Ext 115, E-mail: bonniemarkel@merricklibrary.org; *Ref Serv,* Robert Ludemann
Founded 1891. Pop 19,040; Circ 259,000
Subject Interests: Local hist
Automation Activity & Vendor Info: (ILL) OCLC
Database Vendor: Baker & Taylor, EBSCOhost, Gale Cengage Learning, Grolier Online, LexisNexis, OCLC FirstSearch, ProQuest, ReferenceUSA
Wireless access
Function: Homebound delivery serv
Publications: Children's Newsletter; Library Newsletter (Quarterly)
Mem of Nassau Library System
Partic in Long Island Library Resources Council
Friends of the Library Group

MEXICO

P MEXICO PUBLIC LIBRARY*, 3269 Main St, 13114. (Mail add: PO Box 479, 13114-0479), SAN 311-4910. Tel: 315-963-3012. FAX: 315-963-7317. E-mail: mexlib@ncls.org. Web Site: www.mexicopubliclibrary.org. *Dir,* Dorothy Dineen
Library Holdings: Bk Titles 8,880; Per Subs 26
Automation Activity & Vendor Info: (Circulation) SIRSI WorkFlows; (OPAC) SIRSI WorkFlows
Wireless access
Mem of North Country Library System
Open Mon & Wed 10:30-5 & 6-8, Tues, Thurs & Fri 10:30-5, Sat 9-12
Friends of the Library Group

MIDDLE ISLAND

P LONGWOOD PUBLIC LIBRARY*, 800 Middle Country Rd, 11953. SAN 311-4929. Tel: 631-924-6400. FAX: 631-924-7538. Web Site: longwood.suffolk.lib.ny.us. *Dir,* David Clemens; E-mail: dclemens@suffolk.lib.ny.us; *Asst Dir,* Suzanne Johnson; *Ch Serv,* Dianne Roberts; Staff 26.5 (MLS 26.5)
Founded 1953. Pop 57,739; Circ 856,562
Jul 2008-Jun 2009 Income $5,596,991. Mats Exp $648,224. Sal $3,668,140
Library Holdings: Bk Titles 256,886; Per Subs 449
Special Collections: Thomas R Bayles Historical Coll
Automation Activity & Vendor Info: (Acquisitions) Innovative Interfaces, Inc; (Cataloging) Innovative Interfaces, Inc; (Circulation) Innovative Interfaces, Inc; (Course Reserve) Innovative Interfaces, Inc; (ILL) Innovative Interfaces, Inc; (Media Booking) Innovative Interfaces, Inc; (OPAC) Innovative Interfaces, Inc; (Serials) Innovative Interfaces, Inc
Wireless access
Publications: Newsletter
Mem of Suffolk Cooperative Library System
Open Mon-Fri 9:30-9, Sat 9:30-5, Sun (Summer) 1-5
Friends of the Library Group

MIDDLEBURGH

P MIDDLEBURGH LIBRARY ASSOCIATION*, 323 Main St, 12122. (Mail add: PO Box 670, 12122), SAN 311-4937. Tel: 518-827-5142. FAX: 518-827-5148. E-mail: mid@sals.edu. Web Site: www.middleburghlibrary.blogspot.com. *Librn,* Terry Pavoldi; Staff 3 (MLS 1, Non-MLS 2)
Pop 2,980; Circ 24,404
Library Holdings: Bk Titles 16,000; Per Subs 55
Special Collections: Genealogy (Frances B Spencer Coll)
Automation Activity & Vendor Info: (Circulation) Innovative Interfaces, Inc; (OPAC) Innovative Interfaces, Inc
Wireless access
Mem of Mohawk Valley Library System
Open Mon 1:30-8:30, Tues 10-5 & 6:30-8:30, Wed 10-4, Thurs 10-4 & 6:30-8:30, Sat 9-2
Friends of the Library Group

MIDDLEPORT

P MIDDLEPORT FREE LIBRARY*, Nine Vernon St, 14105. SAN 311-4953. Tel: 716-735-3281. FAX: 716-735-3281. *Libr Dir,* Rosemary Bernard; Staff 1 (Non-MLS 1)
Founded 1930. Pop 1,995; Circ 32,000
Library Holdings: Bk Titles 21,000; Bk Vols 23,000; Per Subs 55
Special Collections: Local History (Middleport Coll), bks, pamphlets
Automation Activity & Vendor Info: (Cataloging) Horizon
Wireless access
Mem of Nioga Library System
Open Mon 1-5 & 7-8:30, Tues & Thurs 11-5 & 7-8:30, Wed 1-6, Sat 11-4
Friends of the Library Group

MIDDLESEX

P MIDDLESEX READING CENTER*, 1216 Rte 245, 14507. SAN 352-3896. Tel: 585-554-6945. Web Site: www.stls.org/middlesex. *Dir,* Sabra Dunton; E-mail: duntons@stls.org
Library Holdings: Bk Titles 5,000
Wireless access
Function: Handicapped accessible, Homebound delivery serv
Mem of Southern Tier Library System
Special Services for the Blind - Bks on cassette; Bks on CD; Large print bks
Open Mon & Wed 4-7, Sat 10-2

MIDDLETOWN

P MIDDLETOWN THRALL LIBRARY*, 11-19 Depot St, 10940. SAN 311-5003. Tel: 845-341-5454. FAX: 845-341-5480. Web Site: www.thrall.org. *Dir,* Kevin Gallagher; *Coll Develop,* Mary Susan Flannery-Climes; Staff 29 (MLS 9, Non-MLS 20)
Founded 1901. Circ 280,566
Jan 2008-Dec 2008 Income $2,793,816. Mats Exp $428,900
Library Holdings: Bk Titles 151,000; Bk Vols 174,600; Per Subs 654
Special Collections: Orange County History Coll. US Document Depository
Automation Activity & Vendor Info: (Acquisitions) SirsiDynix; (Cataloging) SirsiDynix; (Circulation) SirsiDynix; (Course Reserve) SirsiDynix; (ILL) SirsiDynix; (Media Booking) SirsiDynix; (OPAC) SirsiDynix; (Serials) SirsiDynix
Publications: Newsletter
Mem of Ramapo Catskill Library System
Partic in Southeastern New York Library Resources Council
Open Mon-Thurs 9-8, Fri 9-6, Sat 10-5, Sun 1-5
Friends of the Library Group

J ORANGE COUNTY COMMUNITY COLLEGE LIBRARY*, 115 South St, 10940. SAN 311-4996. Tel: 845-341-4855. Interlibrary Loan Service Tel: 845-341-4254. Reference Tel: 845-341-4620. FAX: 845-341-4424. E-mail: lrc@sunyorange.edu. Web Site: www.sunyorange.edu/lrc. *Dir,* Susan Parry; Tel: 845-341-4251, Fax: 845-341-4250, E-mail: susan.parry@sunyorange.edu; *Librn,* Joseph R Barber; Tel: 845-562-4542; *Cat/Syst Librn,* Katherine Jezik; Tel: 845-341-4256, E-mail: katie.jezik@sunyorange.edu; *Ref Librn,* Deborah Canzano; E-mail: deborah.canzano@sunyorange.edu; *Circ, Ref Librn,* Amy Hillick; E-mail: amy.hillick@sunyorange.edu; *Coll Develop,* Mary Ann Van Benschoten; Tel: 845-341-4258, E-mail: maryann.vanbenschoten@sunyorange.edu; *Electronic Serv,* Andrew Heiz; Tel: 845-341-4253, E-mail: andrew.heiz@sunyorange.edu; Staff 23 (MLS 7, Non-MLS 16)
Founded 1950. Enrl 6,922; Fac 149; Highest Degree: Associate
Sept 2010-Aug 2011 Income (Main and Other College/University Libraries) $335,203. Mats Exp $218,465, Books $79,621, Per/Ser (Incl. Access Fees) $29,000, AV Mat $1,000, Electronic Ref Mat (Incl. Access Fees) $52,500, Presv $2,500. Sal $797,715
Library Holdings: Bk Vols 112,309; Per Subs 125
Special Collections: Orange County History & Heritage
Automation Activity & Vendor Info: (Acquisitions) Ex Libris Group; (Cataloging) OCLC CatExpress; (Circulation) Ex Libris Group; (Course Reserve) Ex Libris Group; (ILL) OCLC Online; (OPAC) Ex Libris Group
Database Vendor: ABC-CLIO, American Psychological Association (APA), Baker & Taylor, Cinahl, CountryWatch, CQ Press, EBSCOhost, Elsevier, Gale Cengage Learning, H W Wilson, JSTOR, OCLC FirstSearch, OCLC WorldShare Interlibrary Loan, ProQuest, ScienceDirect
Wireless access
Partic in OCLC Online Computer Library Center, Inc; Southeastern New York Library Resources Council
Open Mon-Fri (Fall & Spring) 8am-9pm, Sat 9-3; Mon & Thurs (Summer) 9-7, Tues & Wed 9-9, Fri 9-5

Departmental Libraries:

NEWBURGH CAMPUS, One Washington Ctr, Newburgh, 12550. Tel: 845-562-4542. *Ref Librn,* Deborah Canzano; Staff 2 (MLS 1.5, Non-MLS 0.5)
Highest Degree: Associate

P RAMAPO CATSKILL LIBRARY SYSTEM*, 619 Rte 17M, 10940-4395. SAN 352-8219. Tel: 845-343-1131. FAX: 845-343-1205. Web Site: www.rcls.org. *Exec Dir,* Robert Hubsher; Tel: 845-343-1131, Ext 242; *ILL/Tech Serv Librn,* Linda J Hendon; Tel: 845-343-1131, Ext 237, E-mail: linda@rcls.org; *ANSER Mgr & Network Adminr,* Anthony Castaldo; Tel: 845-343-1131, Ext 228, E-mail: tony@rcls.org; *Fiscal Officer,* Brenda Adams; Tel: 845-343-1131, Ext 223, E-mail: brenda@rcls.org; *Pub Serv Consult & Outreach Coordr,* Leslie S W Riley; Tel: 845-343-1131, Ext 239, E-mail: lriley@rcls.org; *Electronic Res Consult,* Jerry Kuntz; Tel: 845-343-1131, Ext 246, E-mail: jkuntz@rcls.org; *Youth Serv Consult,* Randall Enos; Tel: 845-343-1131, Ext 240, E-mail: renos@rcls.org; Staff 25 (MLS 5, Non-MLS 20)
Founded 1959

Library Holdings: Bk Vols 2,500; Per Subs 100
Subject Interests: Electronic databases, Personnel mgt, Prof libr sci mgt
Automation Activity & Vendor Info: (Acquisitions) Horizon; (Cataloging) Horizon; (Circulation) Horizon; (ILL) Horizon; (OPAC) Horizon
Database Vendor: EBSCOhost, Gale Cengage Learning
Publications: RCLS Weekly Memo (Newsletter); Trustee FYI (Newsletter)
Member Libraries: Albert Wisner Public Library; Blauvelt Free Library; Cornwall Public Library; Cragsmoor Free Library; Daniel Pierce Library; Dennis P McHugh Piermont Public Library; Ellenville Public Library & Museum; Ethelbert B Crawford Public Library; Fallsburg Library Inc; Finkelstein Memorial Library; Florida Public Library; Gardiner Library; Goshen Public Library & Historical Society; Greenwood Lake Public Library; Haverstraw Kings Daughters Public Library; Highland Falls Library; Josephine-Louise Public Library; Liberty Public Library; Livingston Manor Free Library; Mamakating Library District; Middletown Thrall Library; Moffat Library of Washingtonville; Monroe Free Library; Montgomery Free Library; Nanuet Public Library; New City Library; Newburgh Free Library; Orangeburg Library; Palisades Free Library; Pearl River Public Library; Piermont Public Library; Port Jervis Free Library; Roscoe Free Library; Rose Memorial Library; Shawangunk Correctional Facility Library; Sloatsburg Public Library; Suffern Free Library; Sunshine Hall Free Library; Tappan Library; The Nyack Library; Tomkins Cove Public Library; Tuxedo Park Library; Valley Cottage Free Library; Wallkill Public Library; West Nyack Free Library; Western Sullivan Public Library; Woodbury Public Library
Open Mon-Fri 8am-9pm, Sat & Sun 9-5

MIDDLEVILLE

P MIDDLEVILLE FREE LIBRARY*, One S Main St, 13406. (Mail add: PO Box 155, 13406-0155), SAN 311-5011. Tel: 315-891-3655. FAX: 315-891-3655. E-mail: middleville@midyork.org. Web Site: www.midyork.org/middleville. *Managing Librn,* Sandra Zaffarano
Founded 1915. Pop 550; Circ 8,000
Library Holdings: Bk Vols 10,500; Per Subs 12
Wireless access
Mem of Mid-York Library System
Open Mon & Wed 4-8, Tues, Thurs & Fri 10-12 & 2-6, Sat 10-12

MILFORD

P MILFORD FREE LIBRARY*, S Main St, 13807. (Mail add: PO Box 118, 13807), SAN 311-502X. Tel: 607-286-9076. FAX: 607-286-3461. E-mail: mflibr@yahoo.com. Web Site: www.4cls.org. *Dir,* Barbara Campbell
Founded 1923. Circ 8,900
Library Holdings: Bk Vols 8,000; Per Subs 30
Subject Interests: Local hist
Wireless access
Mem of Four County Library System
Open Mon & Thurs 6pm-9pm, Tues & Fri 1-6, Sat 10-2

MILLBROOK

S CARY INSTITUTE OF ECOSYSTEM STUDIES LIBRARY*, Plant Science Bldg, 2801 Sharon Turnpike, 12545. (Mail add: PO Box AB, 12545-0129), SAN 311-5046. Tel: 845-677-7600. FAX: 845-677-5976. Web Site: www.ecostudies.org/library.html. *Mgr, Info Serv,* Amy C Schuler; Tel: 845-677-7600, Ext 164, E-mail: schulera@caryinstitute.org; Staff 1 (MLS 1)
Founded 1985
Library Holdings: Bk Titles 9,100; Per Subs 175
Special Collections: Institutional Archives; Maps; Staff Reprints; Theses; Vertical File
Subject Interests: Ecology, Nutrient cycling, Plant-animal interactions
Automation Activity & Vendor Info: (Cataloging) LibLime; (Circulation) LibLime; (ILL) OCLC; (OPAC) LibLime; (Serials) LibLime
Database Vendor: BioOne, EBSCOhost, JSTOR, OCLC FirstSearch, Thomson - Web of Science
Wireless access
Function: Res libr
Partic in Southeastern New York Library Resources Council
Restriction: Open by appt only

P MILLBROOK FREE LIBRARY, Three Friendly Lane, 12545. (Mail add: PO Box 286, 12545-0286), SAN 311-5038. Tel: 845-677-3611. FAX: 845-677-5127. Web Site: millbrooklibrary.org. *Dir,* Stephanie Harrison; E-mail: director@millbrooklibrary.org; *Youth Serv,* Joan Frenzel; E-mail: youthservices@millbrooklibrary.org; Staff 2 (MLS 1, Non-MLS 1)
Founded 1901. Pop 4,741; Circ 57,167
Library Holdings: AV Mats 6,240; Bk Titles 50,084; Per Subs 78
Wireless access
Function: 24/7 Electronic res, 24/7 Online cat, Adult bk club, Adult literacy prog, Art exhibits, Audio & video playback equip for onsite use, Audiobks via web, Bks on cassette, Bks on CD, Children's prog, Computer training, Computers for patron use, Copy machines, Digital talking bks, Electronic databases & coll, Exhibits, Family literacy, Free DVD rentals, Genealogy discussion group, Handicapped accessible, Health sci info serv, Holiday prog, Homebound delivery serv, ILL available, Literacy & newcomer serv, Magazines, Magnifiers for reading, Music CDs, Online cat, Online ref, Online searches, Outreach serv, Photocopying/Printing, Preschool outreach, Prog for adults, Prog for children & young adult, Pub access computers, Ref serv available, Senior computer classes, Spoken cassettes & CDs, Spoken cassettes & DVDs, Story hour, Summer reading prog, Tax forms, Teen prog, Telephone ref, VHS videos, Visual arts prog, Web-catalog, Wheelchair accessible, Workshops
Mem of Mid-Hudson Library System
Open Mon & Fri 12-6, Tues & Thurs 10-6, Wed 12-8, Sat 10-4
Restriction: Registered patrons only
Friends of the Library Group

MILLERTON

P NORTHEAST-MILLERTON LIBRARY*, 75 Main St, 12546-5172. (Mail add: PO Box 786, 12546-0786), SAN 311-5054. Tel: 518-789-3340. FAX: 518-789-6802. E-mail: info@nemillertonlibrary.org. Web Site: www.nemillertonlibrary.org. *Dir,* Rhiannon Leo; Staff 1 (MLS 1)
Founded 1927. Pop 3,032; Circ 28,826
Library Holdings: DVDs 1,279; Bk Titles 22,000; Per Subs 30; Talking Bks 2,200
Automation Activity & Vendor Info: (Acquisitions) Innovative Interfaces, Inc; (Cataloging) Innovative Interfaces, Inc; (Circulation) Innovative Interfaces, Inc; (Course Reserve) Innovative Interfaces, Inc; (ILL) Innovative Interfaces, Inc; (Media Booking) Innovative Interfaces, Inc; (OPAC) Innovative Interfaces, Inc; (Serials) Innovative Interfaces, Inc
Wireless access
Function: Adult bk club, Adult literacy prog, Digital talking bks, Handicapped accessible, Homebound delivery serv, ILL available, Prog for children & young adult, Spoken cassettes & CDs, VHS videos
Mem of Mid-Hudson Library System
Special Services for the Blind - Bks on cassette; Bks on CD; Large print bks; Talking bks
Open Tues-Fri 11-6, Sat 10-3, Sun (Fall & Winter) 1-4

MILTON

P SARAH HULL HALLOCK FREE LIBRARY*, Milton Library, 56-58 Main St, 12547. (Mail add: PO Box 802, 12547-0802), SAN 311-5062. Tel: 845-795-2200. FAX: 845-795-1005. E-mail: miltonlibrary@hvc.rr.com. Web Site: www.hallock.milton.lib.ny.us. *Dir,* Cheryl Bennin; Staff 2 (MLS 1, Non-MLS 1)
Founded 1887. Circ 12,943
Library Holdings: Bk Vols 18,849; Per Subs 41
Mem of Mid-Hudson Library System
Open Mon & Thurs 12-8, Wed & Fri 10-6, Sat 10-2

MINEOLA

P MINEOLA MEMORIAL LIBRARY*, 195 Marcellus Rd, 11501. SAN 311-5089. Tel: 516-746-8488. FAX: 516-294-6459. E-mail: mineola@nassaulibrary.org. Web Site: www.nassaulibrary.org/mineola. *Dir,* Charles Sleefe, *Ch Serv,* Meredith Minkoff; *Ref Serv,* Cathy Sagevick
Pop 20,757; Circ 77,219
Library Holdings: Bk Vols 85,000; Per Subs 150
Automation Activity & Vendor Info: (Acquisitions) Innovative Interfaces, Inc; (Cataloging) Innovative Interfaces, Inc; (Circulation) Innovative Interfaces, Inc; (ILL) Innovative Interfaces, Inc; (Media Booking) Innovative Interfaces, Inc; (OPAC) Innovative Interfaces, Inc; (Serials) Innovative Interfaces, Inc
Wireless access
Mem of Nassau Library System
Open Mon, Wed & Thurs 10-9, Tues & Fri 10-5:30, Sat (Winter) 10-5
Friends of the Library Group

GL NASSAU COUNTY SUPREME COURT*, Law Library, 100 Supreme Court Dr, 11501. SAN 352-8243. Tel: 516-442-8580. FAX: 516-442-8578. *Principal Law Librn,* Jean-Paul Vivian; E-mail: jvivian@courts.state.ny.us; Staff 4 (MLS 1, Non-MLS 3)
Founded 1902
Library Holdings: Bk Vols 408,782
Special Collections: Four Departments of the Appellate & Court of Appeals Records & Briefs
Database Vendor: HeinOnline, LexisNexis, Westlaw
Wireless access
Function: Copy machines, Microfiche/film & reading machines, Pub access computers, Scanner
Partic in Long Island Library Resources Council
Open Mon-Fri 9-5
Restriction: Lending to staff only, Open to pub for ref only

M WINTHROP UNIVERSITY HOSPITAL*, Hollis Health Sciences Library, 259 First St, 11501. SAN 311-5100. Tel: 516-663-2802. FAX: 516-663-8171. Web Site: www.winthrop.org. *Dir,* Barbara Elish; Tel: 516-663-2783, E-mail: belish@winthrop.org; Staff 6 (MLS 2, Non-MLS 4)
Founded 1925
Library Holdings: Bk Titles 5,000; Per Subs 500
Subject Interests: Allied health, Computer instruction, Med, Nursing, Surgery
Automation Activity & Vendor Info: (OPAC) SirsiDynix
Database Vendor: OCLC FirstSearch, OVID Technologies
Wireless access
Publications: Acquisition List (Quarterly)
Partic in Long Island Library Resources Council
Open Mon-Thurs 8:30am-9pm, Fri 8:30-6, Sat 10-5, Sun 12-5
Restriction: Staff use only

MINOA

P MINOA LIBRARY*, 242 N Main St, 13116. SAN 311-5119. Tel: 315-656-7401. FAX: 315-656-7033. Web Site: www.minoalibrary.org. *Dir,* Laura Ravera; E-mail: lpravera@googlemail.com; Staff 7 (Non-MLS 7)
Founded 1936. Pop 3,640; Circ 38,569
Library Holdings: DVDs 222; Large Print Bks 200; Bk Titles 15,318; Bk Vols 16,325; Per Subs 55; Talking Bks 322; Videos 689
Automation Activity & Vendor Info: (Cataloging) Innovative Interfaces, Inc; (Circulation) Innovative Interfaces, Inc; (OPAC) Innovative Interfaces, Inc
Wireless access
Mem of Onondaga County Public Library
Open Mon 10-6, Tues-Thurs 10-8:30, Fri 10-5, Sat 10-3

MODENA

P PLATTEKILL PUBLIC LIBRARY*, 2047 State Rte 32, 12548. SAN 376-6977. Tel: 845-883-7286. FAX: 845-883-7295. E-mail: plattekill_lib@hotmail.com. Web Site: plattekill.lib.ny.us. *Dir,* John Georghiou; Staff 9 (MLS 1, Non-MLS 8)
Founded 1973. Pop 10,500; Circ 14,000
Jan 2007-Dec 2007 Income $234,000, State $2,000, City $232,000. Mats Exp $42,000, Books $35,000, Per/Ser (Incl. Access Fees) $1,000, AV Mat $6,000
Library Holdings: Audiobooks 271; Bks on Deafness & Sign Lang 50; Braille Volumes 12; CDs 455; DVDs 766; High Interest/Low Vocabulary Bk Vols 190; Large Print Bks 665; Bk Titles 19,910; Per Subs 87; Talking Bks 794; Videos 821
Special Collections: Library of America Books
Subject Interests: Careers, Parenting, Regional, Spanish (Children & Adults)
Automation Activity & Vendor Info: (Circulation) Innovative Interfaces, Inc
Wireless access
Function: Adult bk club, After school storytime, Audiobks via web, Bilingual assistance for Spanish patrons, Bk club(s), Bks on cassette, Bks on CD, CD-ROM, Children's prog, Computer training, Computers for patron use, Copy machines, Digital talking bks, e-mail & chat, Electronic databases & coll, Fax serv, Homework prog, ILL available, Mail & tel request accepted, Music CDs, Online cat, Online searches, Photocopying/Printing, Preschool outreach, Prog for adults, Prog for children & young adult, Pub access computers, Ref serv available, Senior computer classes, Senior outreach, Story hour, Summer reading prog, Tax forms, Teen prog, VHS videos, Web-catalog, Workshops
Mem of Mid-Hudson Library System
Special Services for the Deaf - Bks on deafness & sign lang; Closed caption videos; Deaf publ; High interest/low vocabulary bks; Staff with knowledge of sign lang
Special Services for the Blind - Audio mat; Bks & mags in Braille, on rec, tape & cassette; Bks on cassette; Bks on CD; Braille bks; Children's Braille; Large print bks; Large screen computer & software; Screen enlargement software for people with visual disabilities
Open Mon & Fri 1-6, Tues 1-8, Wed & Thurs 10-8, Sat 10-3
Friends of the Library Group

MOHAWK

P WELLER PUBLIC LIBRARY*, 41 W Main St, 13407. SAN 311-5127. Tel: 315-866-2983. FAX: 315-866-2983. E-mail: mohawk@midyork.org. *Mgr,* Marie Marrone
Circ 22,295
Library Holdings: Bk Vols 33,000; Per Subs 4
Wireless access
Mem of Mid-York Library System
Open Mon-Wed 2-7, Thurs 10-2 & 2-7, Fri 2-5, Sat 10-2

MONROE

P MONROE FREE LIBRARY*, 44 Millpond Pkwy, 10950. SAN 311-5135. Tel: 845-783-4411. FAX: 845-782-4707. E-mail: mfl@rcls.org, mmcintos@rcls.org. Web Site: www.monroelibrary.org. *Dir,* Marilyn McIntosh; *Asst Dir,* Suzanne Skeels; *Automation Syst Coordr, Circ,* Carol Bezkorowajny; *Ch Serv,* Melissa Quarles; *Ref,* Catina Strauss
Founded 1908. Pop 23,035; Circ 115,000
Library Holdings: AV Mats 3,637; Bk Vols 50,106; Per Subs 135
Subject Interests: Local hist
Automation Activity & Vendor Info: (Acquisitions) SirsiDynix; (Cataloging) SirsiDynix; (Circulation) SirsiDynix; (ILL) SirsiDynix; (Media Booking) SirsiDynix; (OPAC) SirsiDynix; (Serials) SirsiDynix
Wireless access
Publications: Annual Report; Calendar of Events (Monthly); Newsletter (Quarterly)
Mem of Ramapo Catskill Library System
Open Mon 10-8, Tues & Thurs 10-9, Wed 1-9, Fri 10-5, Sat 10-4, Sun 12-5
Friends of the Library Group

MONTAUK

P MONTAUK LIBRARY, 871 Montauk Hwy, 11954. (Mail add: PO Box 700, 11954-0500), SAN 325-5204. Tel: 631-668-3377. FAX: 631-668-3468. E-mail: contact@montauklibrary.org, mntklib@suffolk.lib.ny.us. Web Site: www.montauklibrary.org. *Dir,* Karen A Rade; E-mail: karade@suffolk.lib.ny.us; Staff 2 (MLS 1, Non-MLS 1)
Founded 1980. Pop 3,848; Circ 33,648
Jul 2012-Jun 2013 Income $710,880, State $1,200, City $684,800, Locally Generated Income $7,680, Other $17,200. Mats Exp $60,638, Books $18,225, Per/Ser (Incl. Access Fees) $7,964, Other Print Mats $619, AV Equip $11,591, AV Mat $11,567, Electronic Ref Mat (Incl. Access Fees) $10,672. Sal $299,504 (Prof $91,847)
Library Holdings: Audiobooks 1,223; AV Mats 202; Bks on Deafness & Sign Lang 16; CDs 323; DVDs 1,844; e-books 56,141; Large Print Bks 686; Bk Titles 33,100; Bk Vols 33,550; Per Subs 63; Talking Bks 870; Videos 696
Special Collections: Archival Rm; Long Island Coll; Shakespeare Coll. Oral History
Automation Activity & Vendor Info: (Cataloging) Innovative Interfaces, Inc; (Circulation) Innovative Interfaces, Inc - Millenium; (ILL) Innovative Interfaces, Inc; (OPAC) Innovative Interfaces, Inc
Database Vendor: Baker & Taylor, EBSCOhost, Gale Cengage Learning, Grolier Online, Innovative Interfaces, Inc, Overdrive, Inc, TumbleBookLibrary
Wireless access
Function: Adult bk club, Archival coll, Art exhibits, Bk club(s), Bks on CD, Children's prog, Computers for patron use, Copy machines, e-mail serv, Fax serv, Handicapped accessible, Homebound delivery serv, ILL available, Mail & tel request accepted, Microfiche/film & reading machines, Mus passes, Music CDs, Online cat, OverDrive digital audio bks, Photocopying/Printing, Preschool reading prog, Printer for laptops & handheld devices, Prog for adults, Pub access computers, Spanish lang bks, Story hour, Summer reading prog, Tax forms, Video lending libr, Wheelchair accessible
Mem of Suffolk Cooperative Library System
Open Mon, Tues & Fri 11-6, Wed 11-8, Sat 10-5, Sun 2-5
Friends of the Library Group

MONTGOMERY

P MONTGOMERY FREE LIBRARY*, 133 Clinton St, 12549. SAN 311-5151. Tel: 845-457-5616. FAX: 845-457-5616. Web Site: www.rcls.org/mng. *Dir,* Betsy Comizio; *Asst Dir,* Barbara Meyer
Founded 1911. Pop 2,318; Circ 17,219
Library Holdings: Bk Vols 18,393
Automation Activity & Vendor Info: (Acquisitions) SirsiDynix; (Cataloging) SirsiDynix; (Circulation) SirsiDynix; (ILL) SirsiDynix; (Media Booking) SirsiDynix; (OPAC) SirsiDynix; (Serials) SirsiDynix
Mem of Ramapo Catskill Library System
Open Mon-Fri 10-12 & 2-6, Sat 10-1
Friends of the Library Group

MONTICELLO

P ETHELBERT B CRAWFORD PUBLIC LIBRARY*, 393 Broadway, 12701. SAN 311-516X. Tel: 845-794-4660. FAX: 845-794-4602. Web Site: www.rcls.org/mtc. *Dir,* Alan Barrish; E-mail: abarrish@rcls.org; Staff 6 (MLS 1, Non-MLS 5)
Pop 20,000; Circ 80,000
Library Holdings: Bk Titles 18,210; Bk Vols 20,170; Per Subs 88
Automation Activity & Vendor Info: (Cataloging) Horizon; (Circulation) Horizon; (OPAC) Horizon
Wireless access

Mem of Ramapo Catskill Library System
Open Mon, Tues, Thurs & Fri 10-6, Wed 10-7:30, Sat 11-5

MONTOUR FALLS

P MONTOUR FALLS MEMORIAL LIBRARY*, 406 Main St, 14865. (Mail add: PO Box 486, 14865-0486), SAN 376-3048. Tel: 607-535-7489. FAX: 607-535-7489. E-mail: montourfalls@stls.org. Web Site: www.stls.org/montourfalls/. *Dir,* Luke Rondinaro; E-mail: rondinarol@stls.org
Library Holdings: Large Print Bks 200; Bk Vols 4,000; Per Subs 40
Mem of Southern Tier Library System
Open Mon Wed & Fri 10-4, Tues 10-4 & 6-8, Thurs 1-7

MONTROSE

P HENDRICK HUDSON FREE LIBRARY*, 185 Kings Ferry Rd, 10548. SAN 311-5186. Tel: 914-739-5654. FAX: 914-739-5659. Web Site: www.henhudfreelibrary.org. *Dir,* M Jill Davis; E-mail: jdavis@wlsmail.org; *Head, Ref & Adult Serv,* Risa Getman; E-mail: rgetman@wlsmail.org; *Bus & Finance Mgr,* Jenny Kolesar; E-mail: jkolesar@wlsmail.org; *Ch,* Elizabeth Dewey; Staff 28 (MLS 8, Non-MLS 20)
Founded 1937. Pop 15,642; Circ 229,642
Jul 2009-Jun 2010 Income $1,286,825. Mats Exp $117,500, Books $90,000, Per/Ser (Incl. Access Fees) $5,500, AV Mat $22,000. Sal $545,425
Library Holdings: Bk Vols 55,479; Per Subs 97
Automation Activity & Vendor Info: (Cataloging) SirsiDynix; (Circulation) SirsiDynix; (ILL) SirsiDynix; (OPAC) SirsiDynix
Database Vendor: EBSCOhost, ProQuest, SirsiDynix
Wireless access
Function: Homebound delivery serv, ILL available, Online searches, Prog for adults, Prog for children & young adult, Summer reading prog, Wheelchair accessible
Publications: Newsletter
Mem of Westchester Library System

GM VA HUDSON VALLEY HEALTH CARE SYSTEM*, Castle Point & Franklin Delano Roosevelt Medical Center Libraries, PO Box 100, 10548-0100. SAN 311-5194. Tel: 914-737-4400, Ext 2360. FAX: 914-737-4400, Ext 2754. *Chief Librn,* Jeffrey Nicholas; E-mail: jeffrey.nicholas@va.gov
Library Holdings: CDs 200; e-journals 3,500; Large Print Bks 200; Bk Titles 2,000; Per Subs 35; Videos 750
Subject Interests: AIDS, Alzheimers disease, Geriatrics, Geropshychiat, Med, Nursing, Post-traumatic stress, Psychiat, Psychol, Soc work
Database Vendor: MD Consult, OVID Technologies, ProQuest, STAT!Ref (Teton Data Systems), UpToDate
Wireless access
Publications: Medical Library News
Partic in National Network of Libraries of Medicine; Southeastern New York Library Resources Council
Open Mon-Fri 9-4

MOOERS

P MOOERS FREE LIBRARY, 2430 Rte 11, 12958. (Mail add: PO Box 286, 12958-0286), SAN 311-5208. Tel: 518-236-7744. FAX: 518-236-7744. E-mail: moorlib@primelink1.net. Web Site: www.cefls.org. *Dir,* Jacqueline Madison
Founded 1917. Circ 6,911
Library Holdings: Audiobooks 10; CDs 180; DVDs 140; e-journals 5; Large Print Bks 118; Bk Vols 9,046; Per Subs 47; Videos 40
Special Collections: Local History (Information on Mooers); Local History (Towns in Clinton County)
Subject Interests: Adirondack, Andrew Wyeth, Genealogy, Local hist
Automation Activity & Vendor Info: (Cataloging) Horizon; (OPAC) Horizon
Wireless access
Mem of Clinton-Essex-Franklin Library System
Open Tues & Wed 10-7, Thurs 2-5, Sat 9-1
Friends of the Library Group

MORAVIA

P POWERS LIBRARY*, 29 Church St, 13118. (Mail add: PO Box 71, 13118-0071), SAN 311-5216. Tel: 315-497-1955. FAX: 315-497-3284. Web Site: powerslibrary.org. *Dir,* Lori A Cochran
Founded 1880. Circ 18,219
Library Holdings: Bk Vols 20,000; Per Subs 14
Wireless access
Mem of Finger Lakes Library System
Open Mon & Wed 2-8, Tues & Fri 10-5, Sat 10-2

MORRIS

P VILLAGE LIBRARY OF MORRIS, 152 Main St, 13808. (Mail add: PO Box 126, 13808), SAN 311-5224. Tel: 607-263-2080. FAX: 607-263-2080. E-mail: mo.ill@4cls.org. *Mgr,* Gary Norman; E-mail: mo.gary@4cls.org
Founded 1919. Pop 2,800; Circ 7,943
Library Holdings: Audiobooks 25; DVDs 79; Large Print Bks 320; Bk Titles 7,100; Bk Vols 7,138; Per Subs 12; Videos 400
Subject Interests: Local hist
Wireless access
Mem of Four County Library System
Open Mon, Wed, Fri & Sat 1-5, Tues & Thurs 1-7

MORRISTOWN

P MORRISTOWN PUBLIC LIBRARY*, 200 Main St, 13664. (Mail add: PO Box 206, 13664-0206). Tel: 315-375-8833. FAX: 315-375-8266. E-mail: mtnlib@ncls.org. Web Site: www.morristownpubliclibrary.org. *Dir,* Bridget Whalen-Nevin
Library Holdings: AV Mats 50; Bk Vols 8,000; Talking Bks 40
Mem of North Country Library System
Open Mon & Wed 1-8, Tues 10-5, Thurs 11-5, Sat 9-1
Friends of the Library Group

MORRISVILLE

P MORRISVILLE PUBLIC LIBRARY*, 87 E Main St, 13408. (Mail add: PO Box 37, 13408-0037), SAN 311-5240. Tel: 315-684-9130. FAX: 315-684-9132. E-mail: morrisville@midyork.org. Web Site: www.midyork.org/morrisville. *Mgr,* Michelle Rounds; Staff 5 (Non-MLS 5)
Founded 1903. Pop 6,137; Circ 35,587
Library Holdings: Bk Vols 15,810; Per Subs 45
Automation Activity & Vendor Info: (Cataloging) SIRSI WorkFlows; (Circulation) SIRSI WorkFlows; (OPAC) SIRSI WorkFlows
Wireless access
Mem of Mid York Library System
Open Mon, Wed, Thurs & Fri 12-8, Tues 10-6, Sat 10-4
Friends of the Library Group

C STATE UNIVERSITY OF NEW YORK*, Morrisville State College Library, PO Box 902, 13408-0902. SAN 311-5259. Tel: 315-684-6055. FAX: 315-684-6115. Web Site: library.morrisville.edu. *Dir of Libr,* Christine Rudecoff; *Assoc Librn, Head, Circ, Ref Serv,* Colleen Stella; E-mail: stellac@morrisville.edu; *Asst Librn, Electronic Res & Syst Librn,* Angela Rhodes; E-mail: rhodesam@morrisville.edu; *Instrul Serv Librn,* Wenli Gao; E-mail: gaow@morrisville.edu; *Instrul Design/Online Serv,* Position Currently Open; Staff 7 (MLS 4, Non-MLS 3)
Founded 1908. Enrl 3,000; Highest Degree: Bachelor
Library Holdings: Audiobooks 331; DVDs 2,520; e-books 14,080; e-journals 6,055; Electronic Media & Resources 50; Microforms 6,762; Bk Titles 88,725; Bk Vols 110,000; Per Subs 223
Special Collections: New York State Historical Coll
Subject Interests: Agr, Animal husbandry-horses, Automotive tech, Environ studies, Hort, Journalism, Natural res, Nursing, Renewable energy
Automation Activity & Vendor Info: (Cataloging) OCLC; (Circulation) Ex Libris Group; (Course Reserve) Docutek; (ILL) OCLC; (OPAC) Ex Libris Group; (Serials) Ex Libris Group
Database Vendor: CredoReference, EBSCOhost, Gale Cengage Learning, H W Wilson, LexisNexis, OCLC ArticleFirst, OCLC FirstSearch, OCLC WorldShare Interlibrary Loan, ReferenceUSA, ScienceDirect
Wireless access
Function: Art exhibits, Computers for patron use, Copy machines, e-mail & chat, E-Reserves, Electronic databases & coll, Online cat, Online info literacy tutorials on the web & in blackboard, Online ref, Online searches, Ref serv in person, Telephone ref
Partic in Central New York Library Resources Council; OCLC Online Computer Library Center, Inc; SUNYConnect
Open Mon-Thurs (Winter) 8am-Midnight, Fri 8-5, Sat 1-6, Sun 1-10; Mon-Fri (Summer) 8-4

MOUNT KISCO

P MOUNT KISCO PUBLIC LIBRARY*, 100 E Main St, 10549. SAN 311-5267. Tel: 914-666-8041. FAX: 914-666-3899. Web Site: www.mountkiscolibrary.org. *Dir,* Kathryn Feeley; E-mail: kfeeley@wlsmail.org; *Head, Ref,* Amy Ayers; E-mail: mayers@wlsmail.org; *Head, Circ,* Coleen Carpenter; *Head, Youth Serv,* Deirdre Johnson; E-mail: djohnson@wlsmail.org; *Media Librn,* Martha Iwan; E-mail: miwan@wlsmail.org; *Spanish Lang Librn,* Juliana Biro; *Youth Serv Librn,* Laria Ciccone; Staff 17 (MLS 5, Non-MLS 12)
Founded 1913. Pop 10,000
Library Holdings: AV Mats 6,096; Electronic Media & Resources 33; Large Print Bks 200; Bk Vols 74,292; Per Subs 148; Talking Bks 500; Videos 2,402
Special Collections: State Document Depository
Subject Interests: Job info, Local hist

Automation Activity & Vendor Info: (Cataloging) SirsiDynix; (Circulation) SirsiDynix; (OPAC) SirsiDynix
Database Vendor: Dun & Bradstreet
Wireless access
Mem of Westchester Library System
Open Mon & Thurs 10-6, Tues & Wed 10-8, Sat 10-4
Friends of the Library Group

M NORTHERN WESTCHESTER HOSPITAL*, Hal Federman, MD Health Sciences Library, 400 E Main St, 10549-0802. SAN 311-5275. Tel: 914-666-1259. FAX: 914-666-1940. Web Site: www.nwhc.net. *Dir,* Janie Kaplan; E-mail: JKaplan1@nwhc.net; Staff 1 (MLS 1)
Founded 1960
Library Holdings: e-books 35; e-journals 200; Bk Titles 600; Bk Vols 800; Per Subs 90
Subject Interests: Clinical med, Med libr
Automation Activity & Vendor Info: (OPAC) Professional Software; (Serials) TDNet
Database Vendor: Cinahl, EBSCO Information Services, Elsevier MDL, Gale Cengage Learning, Majors, Marcive, Inc, McGraw-Hill, Medline, Micromedex, Natural Standard, OVID Technologies, Oxford Online, PubMed, ScienceDirect, STAT!Ref (Teton Data Systems), TDNet, UpToDate, Wiley
Wireless access
Partic in Basic Health Sciences Library Network; Health Info Librs of Westchester (HILOW); Metropolitan New York Library Council
Open Mon & Tues 9-5

MOUNT MORRIS

P MOUNT MORRIS LIBRARY*, 121 Main St, 14510-1596. SAN 311-5283. Tel: 585-658-4412. FAX: 585-658-3642. E-mail: mmorris@pls-net.org. Web Site: www.mmorris.pls-net.org. *Dir,* Sharon Stanley
Founded 1910. Pop 4,478; Circ 25,412
Library Holdings: Bk Titles 17,923; Per Subs 24
Subject Interests: English as a second lang
Wireless access
Mem of Pioneer Library System
Open Mon & Fri 2-5, Tues 9-12 & 2-8, Thurs 2-8, Sat (Sept-June) 11-3

MOUNT VERNON

P MOUNT VERNON PUBLIC LIBRARY, 28 S First Ave, 10550. SAN 311-5313. Tel: 914-668-1840. Interlibrary Loan Service Tel: 914-668-1840, Ext 216. Administration Tel: 914-668-1840, Ext 223. Information Services Tel: 914-668-1840, Ext 219. FAX: 914-668-1018. Web Site: www.mountvernonpubliclibrary.org, www.mtvpl.org. *Exec Dir,* Carolyn Karwoski; E-mail: ckarwoski@wlsmail.org; *Head, Ref,* Gary Newman; Tel: 914-668-1840, Ext 209, E-mail: newman@wlsmail.org; *Coll Mgr,* Nishan Stepak; Tel: 914-668-1840, Ext 228, E-mail: nstepak@wlsmail.org; *Circ Supvr,* Christopher Williams; E-mail: cwilliams@wlsmail.org; *Supvr, Per,* Maxine Grandison; Tel: 914-668-1840, Ext 206, E-mail: mgrandison@wlsmail.org; *Youth Serv Coordr,* Denise Lyles; Tel: 914-668-1840, Ext 212, E-mail: dlyles@wlsmail.org; *Teen Prog,* Catherine Webb; Tel: 914-668-1840, Ext 236, E-mail: cwebb@wlsmail.org; Staff 13 (MLS 13)
Founded 1854. Pop 67,153; Circ 239,186
Jul 2014-Jun 2015 Income $4,350,000. Mats Exp $250,000
Library Holdings: Bk Vols 615,000; Per Subs 4,320
Special Collections: Black Heritage (Haines Coll); Mills Law Coll. Oral History; State Document Depository; US Document Depository
Subject Interests: African-Am hist, Behav sci, Foreign lang, Law, Local hist, Music, Soc sci
Automation Activity & Vendor Info: (Acquisitions) SirsiDynix; (Cataloging) SirsiDynix; (Circulation) SirsiDynix; (ILL) SirsiDynix; (Media Booking) SirsiDynix; (OPAC) SirsiDynix; (Serials) SirsiDynix
Wireless access
Mem of Westchester Library System
Open Mon-Fri 10-8:30, Sat 10-5, Sun 1-5
Friends of the Library Group

NANUET

P NANUET PUBLIC LIBRARY*, 149 Church St, 10954. SAN 311-5364. Tel: 845-623-4281. FAX: 845-623-2415. E-mail: nan@rcls.org. Web Site: www.rcls.org/nan. *Dir,* Gretchen Bell; *Automation Librn,* William Finnigan; *Adult Serv,* Julie Marallo; *Adult Serv,* Richard Piattelli; *Ch Serv,* Tracy Suffecool
Founded 1894. Pop 13,000; Circ 274,238
Library Holdings: AV Mats 4,600; Bk Titles 135,000; Per Subs 249; Talking Bks 3,400
Automation Activity & Vendor Info: (Acquisitions) Horizon; (Cataloging) Horizon; (Circulation) Horizon; (Course Reserve) Horizon; (ILL) Horizon; (Media Booking) Horizon; (OPAC) Horizon; (Serials) Horizon
Database Vendor: EBSCOhost
Wireless access
Mem of Ramapo Catskill Library System
Open Mon-Thurs 10-9, Fri & Sat 10-5, Sun 12-5
Friends of the Library Group

NAPANOCH

S EASTERN CORRECTIONAL FACILITY LIBRARY*, PO Box 338, 12458-0338. SAN 325-8955. Tel: 845-647-7400, Ext 4600. FAX: 845-647-7400, Ext 5099. *Sr Librn,* Janet Dymond; Staff 1 (MLS 1)
Library Holdings: Bk Vols 11,000; Per Subs 88
Automation Activity & Vendor Info: (Cataloging) Follett Software; (Circulation) Follett Software
Special Services for the Blind - Audio mat
Open Mon-Fri 8am-9:30pm

NAPLES

P NAPLES LIBRARY*, 118 S Main, 14512. SAN 311-5372. Tel: 585-374-2757. FAX: 585-374-6493. Web Site: www.naples.pls-net.org. *Dir,* Blanche Warner; E-mail: bwarner@pls-net.org
Founded 1962. Pop 3,563; Circ 17,367
Library Holdings: Bk Titles 17,000; Per Subs 50
Automation Activity & Vendor Info: (Acquisitions) SirsiDynix; (Cataloging) SirsiDynix; (Circulation) SirsiDynix; (Course Reserve) SirsiDynix; (ILL) SirsiDynix; (Media Booking) SirsiDynix; (OPAC) SirsiDynix; (Serials) SirsiDynix
Wireless access
Mem of Pioneer Library System
Open Mon-Wed 10-7, Thurs 2-7, Fri 10-8, Sat 10-2
Friends of the Library Group

NARROWSBURG

P WESTERN SULLIVAN PUBLIC LIBRARY*, Tusten-Cochecton Branch, 198 Bridge St, 12764-6402. (Mail add: PO Box 129, 12764-0129), SAN 376-6985. Tel: 845-252-3360. FAX: 845-252-3331. E-mail: plohr@rcls.org. Web Site: www.wsplonline.org. *Mgr,* Penelope Morgan-Lohr
Library Holdings: Bk Vols 13,700; Per Subs 30
Subject Interests: Local hist
Wireless access
Mem of Ramapo Catskill Library System
Open Mon, Wed & Fri 10-8, Tues & Sat 10-1

NASSAU

P NASSAU FREE LIBRARY*, 18 Church St, 12123. (Mail add: PO Box 436, 12123-0436), SAN 311-5380. Tel: 518-766-2715. FAX: 518-766-2715. E-mail: nassaufreelibrary@gmail.com. Web Site: www.nassaufreelibrary.org. *Dir,* Katherine Chansky; E-mail: director@nassaufreelibrary.org; *Asst Dir,* Kristine Moxon
Founded 1893. Pop 4,800; Circ 19,249
Library Holdings: Bk Vols 20,442
Automation Activity & Vendor Info: (Cataloging) Horizon; (Circulation) Horizon; (ILL) Horizon; (OPAC) Horizon; (Serials) Horizon
Wireless access
Mem of Upper Hudson Library System
Open Mon, Tues, Thurs & Fri 2-8, Wed 10-12 & 2-8, Sat 10-1
Friends of the Library Group

NEW BERLIN

P NEW BERLIN LIBRARY*, 15 S Main St, 13411-2905. (Mail add: PO Box J, 13411-0610), SAN 311-5399. Tel: 607-847-8564. FAX: 607-847-8564. *Dir,* Darlene LaBrie
Founded 1896. Pop 4,519; Circ 24,362
Library Holdings: CDs 150; DVDs 100; Large Print Bks 300; Bk Titles 32,000; Per Subs 100; Talking Bks 250; Videos 400
Special Collections: Literacy Service Center Museum; New Berlin Gazettes, microfilm; Oral History Project
Subject Interests: Genealogy, Local hist
Automation Activity & Vendor Info: (Cataloging) SirsiDynix; (Circulation) SirsiDynix
Wireless access
Mem of Four County Library System
Special Services for the Blind - Talking bks
Open Mon & Wed 10-9, Tues, Thurs & Fri 10-5, Sat 10-1

NEW CITY

S HISTORICAL SOCIETY OF ROCKLAND COUNTY LIBRARY*, 20 Zukor Rd, 10956. SAN 328-4271. Tel: 845-634-9629. FAX: 845-634-8690. E-mail: info@rocklandhistory.org. Web Site: rocklandhistory.org. *Exec Dir,* Erin L Martin; E-mail: emartin@rocklandhistory.org
Library Holdings: AV Mats 20; Bk Vols 1,200

Special Collections: Oral History
Subject Interests: Local genealogy, Local hist
Function: Ref serv available, Res libr
Publications: South of the Mountain (Quarterly)
Restriction: Non-circulating, Open by appt only

P NEW CITY LIBRARY, 220 N Main St, 10956. SAN 311-5402. Tel: 845-634-4997. Circulation Tel: 845-634-4997, Ext 124. Reference Tel: 845-634-4997, Ext 126. Administration Tel: 845-634-4997, Ext 112. Reference FAX: 845-634-4401. Administration FAX: 845-634-0173. Web Site: www.newcitylibrary.org. *Dir,* Mitch Freedman; E-mail: mfreedman@rcls.org; *Head, Adult Serv,* Marianne Silver; E-mail: msilver@rcls.org; *Head, Ch,* Janet Makoujy; E-mail: jmakoujy@rcls.org; *Head, Circ,* Gail Seidenfrau; E-mail: gseidenfrau@rcls.org; *Head, Tech Serv,* Sue Telesca; E-mail: stelesca@rcls.org; *Ch,* Kathy Bachor; E-mail: kbachor@rcls.org; *Ch,* Marie McDermott; E-mail: mmcdermott@rcls.org; *Coll Develop Librn,* Nancy Moskowitz; E-mail: nmoskowi@rcls.org; *Coll Develop Librn,* Karen Ostertag; E-mail: kosterta@rcls.org; *Coll Develop Librn,* Harriet Wollenberg; E-mail: hwollenb@rcls.org; *Teen Serv Librn,* Mary Phillips; E-mail: mphillip@rcls.org; *Coordr, Commun Relations,* Veronica Reynolds; E-mail: vreynolds@rcls.org; Staff 47 (MLS 14, Non-MLS 33)
Founded 1933. Pop 46,708; Circ 589,876
Jul 2007-Jun 2008 Income $4,102,300, State $12,300, Locally Generated Income $4,090,000. Mats Exp $519,600, Books $275,500, Per/Ser (Incl. Access Fees) $44,000, Other Print Mats $1,500, AV Mat $152,100, Electronic Ref Mat (Incl. Access Fees) $45,000, Presv $1,500. Sal $2,273,000 (Prof $972,000)
Library Holdings: AV Mats 28,574; CDs 5,480; DVDs 3,683; Electronic Media & Resources 49,479; Large Print Bks 3,479; Bk Vols 171,209; Per Subs 634; Talking Bks 4,979; Videos 6,959
Special Collections: Rockland County (NY) Information & Genealogy
Subject Interests: Korean (Lang), Local hist, Russian (Lang), Spanish (Lang)
Automation Activity & Vendor Info: (Cataloging) SirsiDynix; (Circulation) SirsiDynix; (OPAC) SirsiDynix
Database Vendor: EBSCOhost, Gale Cengage Learning, ProQuest
Wireless access
Function: Adult bk club, Art exhibits, Audiobks via web, AV serv, Bk club(s), Bks on cassette, Bks on CD, Children's prog, Computer training, Computers for patron use, Copy machines, Digital talking bks, E-Reserves, Electronic databases & coll, Free DVD rentals, Genealogy discussion group, Health sci info serv, Holiday prog, ILL available, Mail & tel request accepted, Mus passes, Music CDs, Newsp ref libr, Notary serv, OverDrive digital audio bks, Photocopying/Printing, Prog for adults, Prog for children & young adult, Ref serv available, Summer reading prog, Tax forms, Teen prog, Telephone ref, VHS videos
Publications: Fine Print (Newsletter)
Mem of Ramapo Catskill Library System
Open Mon-Thurs 9-9, Fri 11-6, Sat 9-5, Sun 12-5; Mon-Thurs (Summer) 9-9, Fri 12-6, Sat 11-3

NEW HAMPTON

G MID-HUDSON FORENSIC PSYCHIATRIC CENTER LIBRARY, 2834 Rte 17M, 10958-5011. (Mail add: PO Box 158, 10958-0158), SAN 327-8700. Tel: 845-374-8700, Ext 3625, 845-374-8842. FAX: 845-374-8853. E-mail: mhrsemh@omh.ny.gov. *Librn,* Elizabeth Horvath; Staff 1 (MLS 1)
Library Holdings: Bk Vols 9,000; Per Subs 60
Partic in Southeastern New York Library Resources Council
Open Mon-Fri 8-4:30

NEW HARTFORD

P NEW HARTFORD PUBLIC LIBRARY*, Two Library Lane, 13413-2815. SAN 326-5358. Tel: 315-733-1535. FAX: 315-733-0795. E-mail: newhartford@midyork.org. Web Site: www.newhartfordpubliclibrary.org. *Dir,* Elina Shneyder; E-mail: Eshneyder@midyork.org; *Ch,* Ruth Cook; *Ref Librn, YA Librn,* Mary Javorsky; *Ref Librn,* Margaret Preston; *Info Tech,* Roy Senn; E-mail: rsenn@midyork.org; Staff 20.5 (MLS 2.5, Non-MLS 18)
Founded 1976. Pop 22,166; Circ 166,409
Jan 2013-Dec 2013 Income $504,280, State $5,187, City $400,000, County $19,934, Other $79,159. Mats Exp $494,499. Sal $337,101
Library Holdings: AV Mats 7,844; e-books 649; Bk Vols 74,532; Per Subs 67
Automation Activity & Vendor Info: (Acquisitions) SirsiDynix; (Cataloging) SirsiDynix; (Circulation) SirsiDynix; (Course Reserve) SirsiDynix; (ILL) SirsiDynix; (Media Booking) SirsiDynix; (OPAC) SirsiDynix; (Serials) SirsiDynix
Wireless access
Function: Adult bk club, Art exhibits, Audiobks via web, Bks on cassette, Bks on CD, Children's prog, Copy machines, Fax serv, Homebound delivery serv, Senior computer classes, Summer reading prog
Publications: Footnotes; Friends (Newsletter)
Mem of Mid-York Library System
Open Mon & Tues 10-9, Thurs & Fri 10-6, Sat 10-5, Sun 1-5
Friends of the Library Group

NEW HYDE PARK

P HILLSIDE PUBLIC LIBRARY*, 155 Lakeville Rd, 11040-3003. SAN 311-5453. Tel: 516-355-7850. FAX: 516-355-7855. E-mail: hillsidelibrary@yahoo.com. Web Site: www.nassaulibrary.org/hillside. *Dir,* Charlene Noll; Staff 39 (MLS 7, Non-MLS 32)
Founded 1962. Pop 22,000; Circ 318,504
Library Holdings: Audiobooks 1,347; AV Mats 207; CDs 1,674; DVDs 2,392; Large Print Bks 2,173; Bk Titles 94,159; Per Subs 122; Videos 1,484
Special Collections: Career Resource Center; Greater New Hyde Park Chamber of Commerce Coll; Palma Pursino New Fiction Coll; Patricia Ching Science Fiction Coll; Stanley L. Itkin War Memorial Coll; Teachers' Resource Center
Automation Activity & Vendor Info: (Acquisitions) Innovative Interfaces, Inc; (Cataloging) Innovative Interfaces, Inc; (Circulation) Innovative Interfaces, Inc; (Course Reserve) Innovative Interfaces, Inc; (ILL) Innovative Interfaces, Inc; (Media Booking) Innovative Interfaces, Inc; (OPAC) Innovative Interfaces, Inc; (Serials) Innovative Interfaces, Inc
Database Vendor: Baker & Taylor, Gale Cengage Learning, Innovative Interfaces, Inc, LearningExpress, LexisNexis, Natural Standard, OCLC FirstSearch, OCLC WorldShare Interlibrary Loan, Overdrive, Inc, ProQuest, TumbleBookLibrary
Wireless access
Open Mon-Fri (Winter) 10-8:45, Sat 10-4:45, Sun 12-3:45; Mon-Fri (Summer) 10-8:45, Sat 10-2
Restriction: ID required to use computers (Ltd hrs)
Friends of the Library Group

M LONG ISLAND JEWISH MEDICAL CENTER, Health Sciences Library, 270-05 76th Ave, 11040. SAN 311-5461. Tel: 718-470-7070. FAX: 718-470-6150. Web Site: www.nslij.com/library. *Ref & Educ Librn,* Janice Lester; E-mail: jlester1@nshs.edu; *Mgr, Libr Syst,* Barbara Sacks; E-mail: bsacks@lij.edu; *Project Coordr,* Raquel Fereres-Moskowitz; E-mail: rfereres@nshs.edu; Staff 4 (MLS 3, Non-MLS 1)
Founded 1954
Subject Interests: Dentistry, Geriatrics, Med, Nursing, Pharm
Automation Activity & Vendor Info: (Cataloging) SirsiDynix; (Circulation) SirsiDynix; (OPAC) SirsiDynix; (Serials) SirsiDynix
Database Vendor: OVID Technologies
Partic in Metropolitan New York Library Council
Open Mon-Fri 8:30-6:30

NEW LEBANON

P NEW LEBANON LIBRARY*, 550 State Rte 20, 12125. SAN 311-418X. Tel: 518-794-8844. E-mail: leb@taconic.net. Web Site: www.newlebanon.lib.ny.us. *Libr Dir,* Jeannie Bogino; Staff 1.75 (MLS 1, Non-MLS 0.75)
Founded 1804. Pop 2,271; Circ 27,000
Library Holdings: Audiobooks 693; AV Mats 551; DVDs 2,107; Bk Vols 17,063; Per Subs 37
Special Collections: Local History Coll; Shaker Coll
Wireless access
Mem of Mid-Hudson Library System
Open Mon-Wed & Fri 10-6, Thurs 10-7, Sat 10-1

NEW PALTZ

P ELTING MEMORIAL LIBRARY*, 93 Main St, 12561-1593. SAN 311-5488. Tel: 845-255-5030. FAX: 845-255-5818. Web Site: elting.newpaltz.lib.ny.us. *Dir,* John A Giralico; Staff 4 (MLS 1, Non-MLS 3)
Founded 1909. Pop 14,000; Circ 100,000
Library Holdings: Audiobooks 325; CDs 1,000; DVDs 2,000; Large Print Bks 1,500; Bk Titles 50,000; Per Subs 75; Videos 800
Special Collections: Mid-Hudson History (Haviland-Heidgerd Coll). Municipal Document Depository; Oral History
Automation Activity & Vendor Info: (Acquisitions) Baker & Taylor; (Circulation) Innovative Interfaces, Inc - Millenium; (OPAC) Innovative Interfaces, Inc - Millenium; (Serials) EBSCO Online
Wireless access
Mem of Mid-Hudson Library System
Open Mon, Wed & Fri 10-8, Tues & Thurs 1-5:30, Sat 10-4, Sun 1-4

S HISTORIC HUGUENOT STREET LIBRARY & ARCHIVES, 88 Huguenot St, 12561. SAN 311-5496. Tel: 845-255-1660. FAX: 845-255-0376. E-mail: library@huguenotstreet.org. Web Site: www.huguenotstreet.org. *Librn & Archivist,* Carrie Allmendinger
Founded 1974
Library Holdings: Bk Titles 2,500; Bk Vols 5,000

Special Collections: Bible Coll; Biographies; County Documents; Genealogical Chart Coll; Map Coll; Personal & Family Papers Coll; Photograph Coll; Rare Books Coll
Subject Interests: Dutch hist, Genealogy, Huguenot hist, Immigration to Am, 17th-19th centuries, Local hist, NY State hist
Wireless access
Function: Ref serv available
Restriction: Not open to pub, Open by appt only
Friends of the Library Group

C STATE UNIVERSITY OF NEW YORK AT NEW PALTZ, Sojourner Truth Library, 300 Hawk Dr, 12561-2493. SAN 311-550X. Circulation Tel: 845-257-3714. Interlibrary Loan Service Tel: 845-257-3680. Reference Tel: 845-257-3710. Administration Tel: 845-257-3719. Interlibrary Loan Service FAX: 845-257-3670. Administration FAX: 845-257-3718. Web Site: library.newpaltz.edu. *Dean,* William Mark Colvson; E-mail: colvsonm@newpaltz.edu; *Head, Info Syst,* Kristy Lee; Tel: 845-257-3769, E-mail: leek@newpaltz.edu; *ILL Librn,* Corinne Nyquist; Tel: 845-257-3681, E-mail: nyquistc@newpaltz.edu; *Ser/Accounts Librn,* Elizabeth Strickland; Tel: 845-257-3662, Fax: 845-257-3888, E-mail: strickle@newpaltz.edu; *Coll Develop Coordr,* Valerie Mittenberg; Tel: 845-257-3703, E-mail: mittenbv@newpaltz.edu; Staff 28 (MLS 15, Non-MLS 13)
Founded 1886. Enrl 7,600; Fac 350; Highest Degree: Master
Jul 2013-Jul 2014 Income $2,670,520, State $2,362,471, Other $308,049. Mats Exp $803,077, Books $204,666, Per/Ser (Incl. Access Fees) $86,084, Electronic Ref Mat (Incl. Access Fees) $507,024, Presv $5,303. Sal $1,461,028 (Prof $850,306)
Library Holdings: AV Mats 3,000; CDs 1,233; DVDs 1,370; e-books 122,481; e-journals 83,863; Microforms 40,821; Bk Vols 399,762; Per Subs 410
Special Collections: State Document Depository; US Document Depository
Automation Activity & Vendor Info: (Acquisitions) Ex Libris Group; (Cataloging) Ex Libris Group; (Circulation) Ex Libris Group; (Course Reserve) Ex Libris Group; (ILL) OCLC ILLiad; (OPAC) Ex Libris Group; (Serials) Ex Libris Group
Database Vendor: Alexander Street Press, American Chemical Society, American Mathematical Society, American Psychological Association (APA), ARTstor, CountryWatch, ebrary, EBSCOhost, Elsevier, Ex Libris Group, Gale Cengage Learning, IEEE (Institute of Electrical & Electronics Engineers), JSTOR, LexisNexis, Mergent Online, OCLC, OCLC WorldShare Interlibrary Loan, Oxford Online, Paratext, Project MUSE, ProQuest, PubMed, Sage, ScienceDirect, ValueLine
Wireless access
Publications: The Latest @ The Library (Newsletter)
Member Libraries: State University of New York
Partic in Southeastern New York Library Resources Council
Open Mon-Thurs 8am-12:30am, Fri 8am-9pm, Sat 10-9, Sun 1-12:30
Friends of the Library Group

NEW ROCHELLE

C THE COLLEGE OF NEW ROCHELLE*, Gill Library, 29 Castle Pl, 10805-2308. SAN 311-5518. Tel: 914-654-5345. Circulation Tel: 914-654-5340. Interlibrary Loan Service Tel: 914-654-5491. Reference Tel: 914-654-5342. FAX: 914-654-5884. E-mail: gillrefdesk@cnr.edu. Web Site: cnr.edu/home/library/index.htm. *Dean,* Ana E Fontoura; *Assoc Dean, Coll Develop, Tech Serv,* Margaret Lynn; *Instrul Serv Librn, Ref Serv,* Mark Haber; *Syst Librn,* Susan Acampora; *Coordr, Libr Serv,* Yvette Page; *Archivist,* Martha Counihan; *ILL, Ref,* Kathleen Mannino; Tel: 914-654-5357; *Ref,* Jennifer Ransom; Staff 15 (MLS 14, Non-MLS 1)
Founded 1904. Enrl 5,811; Fac 799; Highest Degree: Master
Library Holdings: Bk Vols 150,000; Per Subs 1,100
Special Collections: Early English Text Society; English Literature (Thomas More); James Joyce; Religious History (Ursuline Coll)
Subject Interests: Educ, Psychol
Automation Activity & Vendor Info: (Acquisitions) Innovative Interfaces, Inc; (Cataloging) OCLC; (Circulation) Innovative Interfaces, Inc; (Course Reserve) Innovative Interfaces, Inc; (ILL) OCLC; (OPAC) Innovative Interfaces, Inc; (Serials) Innovative Interfaces, Inc
Database Vendor: EBSCOhost, Gale Cengage Learning, OCLC FirstSearch, OCLC WorldShare Interlibrary Loan, OVID Technologies, SerialsSolutions, Wilson - Wilson Web
Wireless access
Publications: Acquisitions List
Partic in Metropolitan New York Library Council; OCLC Online Computer Library Center, Inc; Westchester Academic Library Directors Organization (WALDO)
Open Mon-Thurs 9am-11pm, Fri 9-5, Sat 10-6, Sun 1-11

Departmental Libraries:
BROOKLYN CAMPUS, 1368 Fulton St, Brooklyn, 11216. Tel: 718-638-2500. FAX: 914-654-5080. *Librn,* Lilith Newby; *Librn,* Marie Octobre
Library Holdings: Bk Vols 1,000; Per Subs 25
Open Mon-Thurs 10-9, Fri 10-3, Sat 11-4
CARDINAL JOHN O'CONNOR CAMPUS, 332 E 149 St, Bronx, 10451. Tel: 718-665-1310. FAX: 718-292-2906. *Librn,* Yvette Page
Open Mon-Thurs 10-9, Fri 10-4, Sat 10-2
CO-OP CITY CAMPUS, 755 Co-op City Blvd, Bronx, 10475. Tel: 718-320-0300, Ext 232. FAX: 718-379-1680. *Librn,* Yvonne Hamilton
Library Holdings: Bk Vols 3,000
Open Mon-Thurs 10-9, Fri 10-3, Sat 10-2
ROSA PARKS CAMPUS, 144 W 125th St, New York, 10027. Tel: 212-662-7500. FAX: 212-864-9469. *Librn,* Mario A Charles
Library Holdings: Bk Vols 1,000
Open Mon-Thurs 10-9, Fri 10-6, Sat 11-3

C IONA COLLEGE*, Ryan Library, 715 North Ave, 10801-1890. SAN 311-5534. Tel: 914-633-2351. Circulation Tel: 914-633-2343. Interlibrary Loan Service Tel: 914-633-2352. Reference Tel: 914-637-7716. FAX: 914-633-2136. Web Site: www.iona.edu/library. *Dir of Libr,* Richard L Palladino; E-mail: rpalladino@iona.edu; *Asst Dir, Libr for Pub Serv & Syst,* Natalka Sawchuk; Tel: 914-633-2220, E-mail: nsawchuk@iona.edu; *Sr Ref & Instrul Serv Librn,* Adrienne Franco; Tel: 914-633-2348, E-mail: afranco@iona.edu; *Media & Digital Res Librn,* Jill Strykowski; Tel: 914-633-2353, E-mail: jstrykowski@iona.edu; *Ref & Instrul Serv Librn,* Callie Bergeris; Tel: 914-633-2227, E-mail: cbergeris@iona.edu; *Ref & Instrul Serv Librn,* Cynthia Denesevich; Tel: 914-633-2525, E-mail: cdenesevich@iona.edu; *Ser Librn,* Valerie Masone; Tel: 914-633-2449, E-mail: vmasone@iona.edu; *Asst Help Desk Mgr/Circ Supvr,* Kathleen Pascuzzi; E-mail: kpascuzzi@iona.edu; *Mgr, Ctr for the Enhancement of Learning & Teaching,* Anthony Iodice; Tel: 914-633-2347, E-mail: aiodice@iona.edu; *Doc Delivery Mgr,* Ed Helmrich; E-mail: ehelmrich@iona.edu; *Acq, Supvr,* Anthony Mastantuoni; Tel: 914-633-2028, E-mail: amastantuoni@iona.edu; *Coll Develop, Coordr, Tech Serv,* Diana Kiel; Tel: 914-633-2417, E-mail: dkiel@iona.edu
Founded 1940. Highest Degree: Master
Special Collections: Brother Edmund Rice Coll; Committee on the Art of Teaching Coll; Sean McBride Coll; Thomas Paine National Historical Association Coll (TPNHA)
Subject Interests: Bus, Hist, Irish lang, Lit, Relig studies
Automation Activity & Vendor Info: (Acquisitions) OCLC WorldShare Interlibrary Loan; (Cataloging) OCLC; (Circulation) OCLC; (ILL) Clio; (OPAC) OCLC; (Serials) OCLC
Database Vendor: ACM (Association for Computing Machinery), Agricola, American Chemical Society, American Psychological Association (APA), Annual Reviews, Baker & Taylor, Blackwell, CountryWatch, CQ Press, Dialog, EBSCOhost, Elsevier, Gale Cengage Learning, Gallup, Greenwood Publishing Group, Haworth Pres Inc, IEEE (Institute of Electrical & Electronics Engineers), Inspire, JSTOR, LexisNexis, Mergent Online, OCLC, OCLC FirstSearch, OCLC WorldShare Interlibrary Loan, OVID Technologies, Oxford Online, ProQuest, PubMed, Sage, ScienceDirect, SerialsSolutions, ValueLine, Westlaw, Wiley, Wilson - Wilson Web
Wireless access
Partic in Metropolitan New York Library Council; New York State Higher Education Initiative; OCLC Online Computer Library Center, Inc; Westchester Academic Library Directors Organization (WALDO)
Open Mon-Thurs 8am-Midnight, Fri 8-8, Sat 11-7, Sun 10am-Midnight

Departmental Libraries:
HELEN T ARRIGONI LIBRARY-TECHNOLOGY CENTER, 715 North Ave, 10801-1890. Tel: 914-637-2791. FAX: 914-633-2136. *Supvr, Pub Serv,* Manuel Alvia; Tel: 914-633-2000, Ext 4165, E-mail: malvia@iona.edu; Staff 2 (MLS 1, Non-MLS 1)
Subject Interests: Computer sci, Educ, Mass communications
ROCKLAND GRADUATE CENTER, Two Blue Hill Plaza, Concourse Level, Pearl River, 10965. (Mail add: PO Box 1522, Pearl River, 10965-8522), SAN 375-5460. Tel: 845-620-1350. FAX: 845-620-1260. E-mail: rockland@iona.edu. *Librn,* Eileen Layman; E-mail: elayman@iona.edu; *Librn,* Claire Morrissey; Staff 1 (MLS 1)
Subject Interests: Bus, Computer sci, Educ

P NEW ROCHELLE PUBLIC LIBRARY*, One Library Plaza, 10801. SAN 352-8308. Tel: 914-632-7878, Ext 1000. Circulation Tel: 914-632-7878, Ext 1700. Reference Tel: 914-632-7878, Ext 2000. FAX: 914-632-0262. Web Site: www.nrpl.org. *Dir,* Tom Geoffino; Tel: 914-632-7878, Ext 1200, E-mail: tgeoffino@nrpl.org; *Commun Relations Librn,* Barbara Davis; *Adult Serv,* Daniel Ogyiri; *Ch Serv,* Kathleen Cronin; *Ref Serv,* Beth Mills; *Tech Serv,* Kira Aiello; Staff 34 (MLS 16, Non-MLS 18)
Founded 1894. Pop 72,182; Circ 498,412
Jul 2007-Jun 2008 Income (Main Library and Branch(s)) $3,356,789. Mats Exp $254,000. Sal $2,043,187
Library Holdings: Bk Vols 270,989; Per Subs 3,055

Special Collections: Fine Art Books (Retrospective); Libretti Scores; Local History Coll; Local Newspapers from 1861; Opera; Picture Coll
Automation Activity & Vendor Info: (Cataloging) SirsiDynix; (Circulation) SirsiDynix; (ILL) SirsiDynix; (OPAC) SirsiDynix
Database Vendor: EBSCOhost, Gale Cengage Learning
Wireless access
Publications: Bi-Monthly Newsletter; Monthly Calendar
Mem of Westchester Library System
Open Mon, Tues & Thurs 9-8, Wed 19-6, Fri & Sat 9-5, Sun (Sep-June) 1-5
Friends of the Library Group
Branches: 1
HUGUENOT CHILDREN'S LIBRARY, 794 North Ave, 10801, SAN 377-6484. Tel: 914-632-8954. *Mgr,* Susan Moorhead; *Head, Ch,* Kathleen Cronin; Tel: 914-632-7878, Fax: 914-632-0262, E-mail: kcronin@wlsmail.org; Staff 2 (MLS 1, Non-MLS 1)
Library Holdings: Bk Titles 4,000; Bk Vols 4,400
Automation Activity & Vendor Info: (Circulation) SIRSI WorkFlows
Open Mon & Thurs 10-6, Tues, Fri & Sat 10-5, Wed 10-8

M SOUND SHORE HEALTH SYSTEM OF WESTCHESTER*, Medical Library, 16 Guion Pl, 10802. SAN 311-5550. Tel: 914-365-3566. FAX: 914-576-4028. *Dir,* Mary Saramak; Staff 1 (MLS 1)
Founded 1950. Highest Degree: Doctorate
Library Holdings: Bk Vols 1,000; Per Subs 75
Subject Interests: Allied health, Med, Nursing
Automation Activity & Vendor Info: (Acquisitions) Basch Subscriptions, Inc; (Cataloging) Professional Software; (Circulation) Professional Software; (Course Reserve) Aurora Information Technology; (Serials) Basch Subscriptions, Inc
Database Vendor: Cinahl, EBSCO Information Services, OVID Technologies
Wireless access
Function: Computers for patron use, Electronic databases & coll, Online searches, Outside serv via phone, mail, e-mail & web, Ref & res
Publications: New York State Database (Index to periodicals); Newsletter (Online only)
Partic in National Network of Libraries of Medicine; Regional Med Libr
Restriction: Authorized patrons

R TEMPLE ISRAEL OF NEW ROCHELLE, Edith H Handelman Library, 1000 Pinebrook Blvd, 10804. SAN 311-5569. Tel: 914-235-1800. FAX: 914-235-1854. Web Site: www.tinr.org. *Librn,* Stephanie Krasner; Tel: 914-636-1204, E-mail: stephkras11@gmail.com; Staff 1 (Non-MLS 1)
Library Holdings: Bk Vols 6,500; Spec Interest Per Sub 5
Special Collections: Judaica
Automation Activity & Vendor Info: (Cataloging) Surpass
Database Vendor: Surpass
Wireless access
Function: Adult bk club, Bk club(s), Children's prog, Electronic databases & coll, Exhibits, Family literacy, Handicapped accessible, Holiday prog, Magazines, Prog for children & young adult, Wheelchair accessible
Open Mon-Fri 10-4, Sun 10-Noon
Restriction: Authorized patrons, Borrowing privileges limited to fac & registered students, Congregants only, Open to authorized patrons, Open to fac, students & qualified researchers, Open to students, fac & staff
Friends of the Library Group

NEW WOODSTOCK

P NEW WOODSTOCK FREE LIBRARY*, 2106 Main St, 13122-8718. (Mail add: PO Box 340, 13122-0340), SAN 311-5577. Tel: 315-662-3134. Web Site: www.midyork.org/newwoodstock. *Dir,* Norm Parry; *Libr Mgr,* Renee Beardsley; *Asst Librn,* Janine English; *Asst Librn,* Rebecca Noble; *Coordr, Ch Serv,* Kelly Roberts
Founded 1939
Library Holdings: Bk Vols 30,000; Per Subs 12
Open Mon & Wed 1-5 & 7-9, Tues, Thurs & Fri 1-5, Sat 10-1

NEW YORK

C ADELPHI UNIVERSITY*, Manhattan Center Library, 75 Varick St, 10013. SAN 352-4787. Tel: 212-965-8340. FAX: 212-965-8367. Web Site: www.adelphi.edu/library/branches.html. *Librn,* Kristin Hart; Staff 1 (MLS 1)
Library Holdings: Bk Vols 7,451; Per Subs 117
Subject Interests: Counseling, Educ, Psychol
Automation Activity & Vendor Info: (Acquisitions) Innovative Interfaces, Inc; (Cataloging) Innovative Interfaces, Inc; (Circulation) Innovative Interfaces, Inc; (Course Reserve) Innovative Interfaces, Inc; (ILL) Innovative Interfaces, Inc; (Media Booking) Innovative Interfaces, Inc; (OPAC) Innovative Interfaces, Inc; (Serials) Innovative Interfaces, Inc
Database Vendor: EBSCOhost
Partic in Metropolitan New York Library Council
Open Mon 9am-10pm, Tues-Thurs 11-10, Fri 9-9, Sat & Sun 9-5:30

S AESTHETIC REALISM FOUNDATION LIBRARY*, 141 Greene St, 10012-3201. SAN 328-8706. Tel: 212-777-4490. FAX: 212-777-4426. *Librn,* Richita Anderson; Staff 1 (Non-MLS 1)
Founded 1973
Library Holdings: Bk Vols 4,800
Special Collections: Books & Periodicals Containing Poems, Essays, Lectures by Eli Siegel & Works by Aesthetic Realism Consultants
Subject Interests: Aesthetics, Art, Drama, Lit, Poetry, Soc sci
Publications: The Right of Aesthetic Realism To Be Known (Periodical)
Restriction: Open to fac, students & qualified researchers
Branches:
ELI SIEGEL COLLECTION, 141 Greene St, 10012-3201, SAN 328-8722. Tel: 212-777-4490. FAX: 212-777-4426. Web Site: www.aestheticrealism.org. *Librn,* Richita Anderson; *Librn,* Leila Rosen; *Librn,* Meryl Simon; Staff 3 (Non-MLS 3)
Founded 1982
Library Holdings: Bk Vols 25,000; Per Subs 500
Special Collections: 19th Century Periodical Literature; British & American Poetry; Early American History; French, German & Spanish Literature; Lessons & Lectures by Eli Siegel, Founder of Aesthetic Realism; Poetry & Prose of Eli Siegel, original ms, holograph
Subject Interests: Art, Econ, Hist, Labor, Literary criticism, Philos, Poetry, Sciences
Restriction: Open to fac, students & qualified researchers

L ALSTON & BIRD, LLP LIBRARY*, 90 Park Ave, 12th Flr, 10016. SAN 325-5255. Tel: 212-210-9526. Interlibrary Loan Service Tel: 212-210-9531. FAX: 212-210-9444. *Libr Mgr,* John H Davey; E-mail: john.davey@alston.com; *Ref Librn,* Tina Zoccali; E-mail: tina.zoccali@alston.com; Staff 2 (MLS 2)
Library Holdings: Bk Vols 15,000
Special Collections: German Law Materials
Automation Activity & Vendor Info: (Acquisitions) SydneyPlus; (Cataloging) SydneyPlus; (Circulation) SydneyPlus; (ILL) SydneyPlus; (OPAC) SydneyPlus; (Serials) SydneyPlus
Database Vendor: Dun & Bradstreet, HeinOnline, LexisNexis, OCLC FirstSearch, Westlaw, Westlaw Business
Open Mon-Fri 9-5

S AMERICAN ACADEMY OF ARTS & LETTERS LIBRARY*, 633 W 155th St, 10032. SAN 311-564X. Tel: 212-368-6361. FAX: 212-491-4615. E-mail: academy@artsandletters.org. Web Site: www.artsandletters.org. *Exec Dir,* Virginia Dajani; Staff 10 (MLS 10)
Library Holdings: Bk Vols 21,000
Subject Interests: Art, Lit, Manuscripts, Memorabilia, Music
Wireless access
Restriction: Not open to pub

S AMERICAN ACADEMY OF DRAMATIC ARTS LIBRARY*, 120 Madison Ave, 10016. SAN 311-5658. Tel: 212-686-9244, Ext 337. FAX: 212-545-7934. Web Site: www.aada.org. *Librn,* Deborah Picone; Staff 1 (MLS 1)
Founded 1978
Library Holdings: Bk Titles 8,000
Wireless access
Partic in Metropolitan New York Library Council
Open Mon-Thurs 10-7:30, Fri 10-6:30

S AMERICAN ASSOCIATION OF ADVERTISING AGENCIES*, Research Services, 405 Lexington Ave, 18th Flr, 10174. SAN 311-5690. Tel: 212-682-2500. Web Site: www.aaaa.org. *Mgr,* Marge Morris; *Mgr,* Julie Zilavy; Staff 9 (MLS 9)
Founded 1938
Library Holdings: Bk Titles 1,800; Bk Vols 2,000; Per Subs 200
Subject Interests: Advertising, Advertising agency bus, Mkt
Publications: Index to AAAA Bulletins, Newsletters & Press Releases
Open Mon-Fri 8:30-5:30

SR AMERICAN BIBLE SOCIETY LIBRARY*, 1865 Broadway, 10023-9980. SAN 311-5712. Tel: 212-408-1203. FAX: 212-408-8724. Web Site: americanbible.org. *Curator,* Liana Lupas; Tel: 212-408-1204, E-mail: llupas@americanbible.org; *Archivist,* Kristin Miller; Staff 4 (MLS 2, Non-MLS 2)
Founded 1816
Library Holdings: Bk Vols 60,000; Per Subs 150
Special Collections: Book Volumes in 2287 Languages (Historic Bibles Coll); The Bible and/or Its Parts (Chicago Bible Society Scripture Coll)
Subject Interests: Bible, Publ, Relig hist, Relig in Am, Translation
Automation Activity & Vendor Info: (Acquisitions) Ex Libris Group; (Cataloging) Ex Libris Group; (ILL) OCLC; (OPAC) Ex Libris Group; (Serials) Ex Libris Group

Publications: A Concise History of the English Bible; English Bible in America; Portraits: An American Bible Society Catalog; Scriptures of the World; The Book of a Thousand Tongues
Partic in OCLC Online Computer Library Center, Inc
Restriction: Open by appt only

S AMERICAN FEDERATION OF JEWS FROM CENTRAL EUROPE, INC*, Research Foundation for Jewish Immigration, Inc Library, 15 W 16th St, 4th Flr, 10011. SAN 326-3460. Tel: 212-921-3871. FAX: 212-921-3860. E-mail: amfederation@yahoo.com. *Archivist, Librn,* Dennis E Rohrbaugh
Founded 1971
Library Holdings: Bk Titles 150
Special Collections: Biographical Data on German-Speaking Emigres from Central Europe Worldwide, 1933-1945 (Archival Coll), bks, published mats, questionnaires; Jewish-German-Speaking Emigres in US (Oral Hist Coll), bks, transcribed taped interviews
Function: Mail & tel request accepted
Restriction: Open by appt only

S AMERICAN HUNGARIAN LIBRARY & HISTORICAL SOCIETY, 215 E 82nd St, 10028. SAN 375-7277. Tel: 212-744-5298. E-mail: info@americanhungarianlibrary.org. Web Site: www.americanhungarianlibrary.org. *Librn,* Zsuzsi Simon Borbiro
Founded 1955
Library Holdings: Bk Titles 5,000
Special Collections: Hungarian Subject Matters & Fiction in English
Subject Interests: Hungarian culture, Hungarian hist, Hungarian lit
Automation Activity & Vendor Info: (Cataloging) Inmagic, Inc.
Open Sat 9-Noon
Friends of the Library Group

S AMERICAN INTERNATIONAL GROUP*, Corporate Information Center, 70 Pine St, 6th Flr, 10270. SAN 370-727X. Tel: 212-770-7911. FAX: 212-742-0949. *Sr Mgr,* Sharon Smith
Founded 1977
Library Holdings: Bk Vols 5,000; Per Subs 100
Open Mon-Fri 9-5

S AMERICAN IRISH HISTORICAL SOCIETY LIBRARY*, 991 Fifth Ave, 10028. SAN 311-5860. Tel: 212-288-2263. FAX: 212-628-7927. E-mail: aihs@aihs.org. Web Site: www.aihs.org. *Managing Dir,* John Devlin
Founded 1897
Library Holdings: Bk Vols 10,000
Special Collections: Daniel Cohalan Papers; Friends of Irish Freedom Papers
Subject Interests: Am Irish, Gaelic lit, Irish hist, Lit
Publications: Newsletter (Quarterly); The Recorder (Semi-annual)

R AMERICAN JEWISH CONGRESS*, Shad Polier Memorial Library, 825 Third Ave, Ste 1800, 10022. SAN 326-2332. Tel: 212-879-4500. Interlibrary Loan Service Tel: 212-360-1549. FAX: 212-758-1633. Web Site: ajcongress.org.
Founded 1977
Library Holdings: Bk Titles 1,000; Per Subs 40
Special Collections: AJ Congress court briefs; Commission on Law & Social Action Archives
Subject Interests: Civil rights
Partic in Westlaw
Restriction: Authorized scholars by appt, Staff use only

S AMERICAN KENNEL CLUB INC LIBRARY*, 260 Madison Ave, 4th Flr, 10016. SAN 311-5895. Tel: 212-696-8245, 212-696-8246. FAX: 212-696-8281. E-mail: library@akc.org. Web Site: www.akc.org/about/library/index.cfm. *Librn,* Barbara Kolk; Staff 1 (MLS 1)
Founded 1934
Library Holdings: Bk Vols 18,000; Per Subs 300; Videos 350
Subject Interests: Art about dogs, Breeding, Care, Domestic, Foreign studies bks, Training of dogs
Automation Activity & Vendor Info: (Cataloging) OCLC CatExpress; (OPAC) EOS International
Function: Ref serv available, Res libr
Partic in Metropolitan New York Library Council
Open Mon-Fri 9-4
Restriction: Not a lending libr

S AMERICAN MUSEUM OF NATURAL HISTORY LIBRARY*, Research Library, 79th St & Central Park W, 10024-5192. SAN 352-8510. Tel: 212-769-5400. FAX: 212-769-5009. E-mail: libref@amnh.org. Web Site: library.amnh.org. *Harold Boeschenstein Dir,* Tom Baione; Tel: 212-769-5417, E-mail: tbaione@amnh.org; *Asst Dir, Acq,* Matthew Bolin; Tel: 212-769-5409; Staff 15 (MLS 9, Non-MLS 6)
Founded 1869
Library Holdings: Bk Titles 153,000; Bk Vols 550,000; Per Subs 4,004
Special Collections: Art & Memorabilia; Natural History Film Archives; Photograph & Archives Coll; Rare Books & Manuscripts Coll
Subject Interests: Anthrop, Astronomy, Biol, Expedition, Geol, Hist of sci, Mineralogy, Museology, Paleontology, Travel, Zoology
Wireless access
Function: Archival coll, Electronic databases & coll, Exhibits, Handicapped accessible, ILL available, Online cat, Online ref, Online searches, Photocopying/Printing, Pub access computers, Ref serv in person, Scanner, Telephone ref
Publications: Anthropological Papers; Bull of the American Museum of Natural History Library; James Arthur Lecture Series; Novitates, Natural History
Partic in Med Libr Consortium; OCLC Online Computer Library Center, Inc
Open Tues-Thurs 2-5:30
Restriction: Authorized scholars by appt, Circulates for staff only, Open to qualified scholars
Branches:
BASHFORD DEAN MEMORIAL LIBRARY, 79th St at Central Park W, 10024-5192, SAN 352-857X. Tel: 212-769-5798. FAX: 212-769-5009. Web Site: research.amnh.org/ichthyology. *Curator,* Melanie Stiassny; Tel: 212-769-5796, Fax: 212-769-5642, E-mail: mljs@amnh.org
Subject Interests: Biol of fishes
Restriction: Staff use only
HENRY FAIRFIELD OSBORN LIBRARY, Central Park W at 79th St, 10024, SAN 352-8545. Tel: 212-769-5803. Administration Tel: 212-769-5821. *Adminr,* Susan K Bell; Fax: 212-769-5842, E-mail: skbell@amnh.org
Founded 1908
Library Holdings: Bk Vols 4,500
Subject Interests: Vertebrate paleontology
Restriction: Open by appt only

S AMERICAN NUMISMATIC SOCIETY LIBRARY*, The Harry W Bass Jr Library, 75 Varick St, 10013. SAN 311-5941. Tel: 212-571-4470. FAX: 212-571-4479. Web Site: www.numismatics.org. *Librn,* Francis D Campbell; E-mail: campbell@numismatics.org; Staff 2 (MLS 2)
Founded 1858
Library Holdings: Bk Titles 100,000; Per Subs 270
Special Collections: Auction catalogs; Numismatics
Open Tues-Fri 9:30-4:30
Friends of the Library Group

S AMERICAN SOCIETY FOR PSYCHICAL RESEARCH INC, LIBRARY*, Five W 73rd St, 10023. SAN 311-5984. Tel: 212-799-5050. FAX: 212-496-2497. Web Site: www.aspr.com. *Exec Dir,* Patrice Keane; *Librn,* Jeff Twine
Founded 1885
Library Holdings: Bk Titles 15,000; Bk Vols 18,500; Per Subs 300
Special Collections: Archives (Rare bks, correspondence, drawings & photos); Shaker Bks & Ms
Subject Interests: Alternative med, Parapsychol, Philos, Psychol, Relig studies, Spiritualism
Automation Activity & Vendor Info: (Cataloging) Inmagic, Inc.; (Circulation) Inmagic, Inc.
Restriction: Open by appt only

S AMERICAN STANDARDS TESTING BUREAU, INC*, Sam Tour Memorial Library, 40 Wall St, 28th Flr, 10005-2672. (Mail add: PO Box 583, 10274-0583), SAN 311-5992. Tel: 212-943-3160. FAX: 212-825-2250. *Dir,* Dr Charles Coleman; *Asst Librn,* Arthur Baylor
Founded 1916
Library Holdings: Bk Titles 25,000; Per Subs 300
Special Collections: National & International Standards
Subject Interests: Applied sci, Applied sci manual, Eng, Forensic eng, Govt standards, Indust, Texts
Restriction: Staff use only

M ANDERSON, KILL & OLICK*, Law Library, 1251 Avenue of the Americas, 10020-1182. SAN 325-5026. Tel: 212-278-1069. FAX: 212-278-1733. E-mail: akony@andersonkill.com. Web Site: andersonkill.com. *Librn,* Esther Quiles
Library Holdings: Bk Titles 2,500; Bk Vols 20,100; Per Subs 150
Database Vendor: Dun & Bradstreet, Hoovers, LexisNexis
Publications: Newsletter
Partic in Dialog Corp; Dow Jones News Retrieval; Westlaw
Restriction: Staff use only

S ANTHOLOGY FILM ARCHIVES*, Jerome Hill Reference Library, 32 Second Ave, 10003. SAN 321-9003. Tel: 212-505-5181. FAX: 212-477-2714. *Dir,* Robert A Haller; E-mail: robert@anthologyfilmarchives.org; Staff 1 (MLS 1)
Founded 1970
Library Holdings: Bk Titles 12,000; Per Subs 250

Subject Interests: Avant garde film, Avant garde video
Publications: Legend of Maya Deren
Restriction: Closed stack, Open by appt only

S ANTI-DEFAMATION LEAGUE*, Rita & Leo Greenland Library & Archive, 605 Third Ave, 10158. SAN 311-6050. Tel: 212-885-5844, 212-885-7823. FAX: 212-885-5882. E-mail: librarian@adl.org. Web Site: www.adl.org. *Librn,* Marianne Benjamin; E-mail: mbenjamin@adl.org; Staff 3 (MLS 1, Non-MLS 2)
Founded 1939
Library Holdings: Bk Titles 10,000; Bk Vols 15,000; Per Subs 300
Special Collections: Anti-Defamation League Historic & Research Materials
Subject Interests: Anti-Semitism, Civil rights, Discrimination, Human relations, Intergroup relations, Political extremism
Automation Activity & Vendor Info: (Acquisitions) Inmagic, Inc.; (Cataloging) Inmagic, Inc.; (Circulation) Inmagic, Inc.; (OPAC) Inmagic, Inc.; (Serials) Inmagic, Inc.
Function: Archival coll
Restriction: Staff use only

SR ARMENIAN APOSTOLIC CHURCH OF AMERICA*, Saint Nerses Shnorhali Library, 138 E 39th St, 10016. SAN 371-5663. Tel: 212-689-7810. FAX: 212-689-7168. *Librn,* Houri Ghougassian
Founded 1975
Library Holdings: Bk Vols 12,000

L ASSOCIATION OF THE BAR OF THE CITY OF NEW YORK LIBRARY*, 42 W 44th St, 10036. SAN 311-6166. Tel: 212-382-6666. Reference Tel: 212-302-8219. FAX: 212-382-6790. E-mail: library@nycbar.org. Web Site: www.abcny.org/library/index.htm. *Dir,* Richard Tuske; *Head, Ref, Librn,* Ronald Mirvis
Founded 1870
Library Holdings: Bk Titles 200,000; Bk Vols 600,000; Per Subs 2,500
Special Collections: Major coll of legal materials including appellate court records & briefs, domestic law, early Am session laws, foreign & int law
Database Vendor: HeinOnline, LexisNexis, Westlaw
Wireless access
Open Mon-Thurs 9-9, Fri 9-7
Restriction: Mem only

S AUSTRIAN CULTURAL FORUM LIBRARY, 11 E 52nd St, 10022. SAN 311-6204. Tel: 212-319-5300. FAX: 212-644-8660. E-mail: library@acfny.org. Web Site: www.acfny.org. *Librn,* Alexandra Riener; E-mail: alexandra.riener@bmeia.gv.at
Founded 1962
Library Holdings: Bk Vols 10,000; Per Subs 22
Special Collections: Austriaca Coll
Subject Interests: Archit, Art, Educ, Hist, Lit, Music, Performing arts
Wireless access
Open Mon, Wed & Fri 10-5, Tues & Thurs 10-8

L BAKER & MCKENZIE LLP*, 114 Avenue of the Americas, 10036. SAN 311-6263. Tel: 212-626-4100. FAX: 212-310-1600. Web Site: www.bakernet.com. *Dir, Libr Serv,* Leslee I Budlong; E-mail: leslee.i.budlong@bakernet.com; Staff 4 (MLS 2, Non-MLS 2)
Founded 1971
Library Holdings: Bk Titles 4,500; Bk Vols 25,000; Per Subs 70
Subject Interests: Arbitration, Banking, Captive ins, Corporate law, Intellectual property, Securities, Tax
Automation Activity & Vendor Info: (Acquisitions) Sydney; (Cataloging) Sydney; (Circulation) Sydney; (OPAC) Sydney; (Serials) Sydney
Database Vendor: LexisNexis
Wireless access
Publications: TOC Bulletin
Restriction: Not open to pub

C BANK STREET COLLEGE OF EDUCATION LIBRARY*, 610 W 112th St, 5th Flr, 10025. SAN 311-628X. Tel: 212-875-4455. Interlibrary Loan Service Tel: 212-875-4458. Reference Tel: 212-875-4456. FAX: 212-875-4558. E-mail: library@bankstreet.edu. Web Site: www.bankstreet.edu. *Dir of Libr Serv,* Kristin Freda; E-mail: kfreda@bankstreet.edu; *Dir, Ctr for Children's Lit,* Jenny Brown; *Acq & Electronic Reserves Librn,* Nora Gaines; Tel: 212-875-4457, E-mail: ngaines@bankstreet.edu; *Archivist & Spec Coll Librn,* Lindsey Wyckoff; E-mail: lwyckoff@bankstreet.edu; *Ch,* Position Currently Open; *Interim Ch,* Allie Bruce; *Ref Librn,* Maureen Garvey; *Ref Librn,* Peter Hare; E-mail: phare@bankstreet.edu; *Tech Serv Librn,* Jackie DeQuinzio; *Acq Asst,* Debbie Taybron; *Circ Asst,* Alex Iwachiw; *Circ Asst,* Yesenia Pedraza; *Tech Serv Asst,* Audrey Pryce; *Tech Serv Asst,* Micheline Thomas; Staff 10.5 (MLS 5.5, Non-MLS 5)
Founded 1916. Enrl 1,007; Fac 125; Highest Degree: Master
Library Holdings: Bk Titles 85,168; Bk Vols 150,000; Per Subs 325; Talking Bks 400; Videos 647
Subject Interests: Adolescence, Bilingual educ, Children's lit, Early childhood educ, Spec educ
Automation Activity & Vendor Info: (Acquisitions) SirsiDynix; (Cataloging) SirsiDynix; (Circulation) SirsiDynix; (ILL) OCLC; (OPAC) SirsiDynix; (Serials) SirsiDynix
Database Vendor: EBSCOhost, LexisNexis, OCLC FirstSearch, OCLC WorldShare Interlibrary Loan, ProQuest, SerialsSolutions, Wilson - Wilson Web, World Book Online
Wireless access
Function: Archival coll, Copy machines, ILL available, Online ref, Orientations, Telephone ref, Wheelchair accessible
Publications: Multicultural Education: A Bibliographic Essay & AIDS Education
Partic in Metropolitan New York Library Council; Nylink
Open Mon-Thurs 9am-9:50pm, Fri 9-5, Sat 10-5
Restriction: In-house use for visitors, Open to pub by appt only

C BARD GRADUATE CENTER LIBRARY*, 38 W 86th St, 10024. SAN 374-5848. Tel: 212-501-3025. FAX: 212-501-3098. E-mail: reference@bgc.bard.edu. Web Site: www.bgc.bard.edu/research/library.html. *Chief Librn,* Heather Topcik; Tel: 212-501-3036, E-mail: topcik@bgc.bard.edu; *Reader Serv Librn,* Karyn Hinkle; Tel: 212-501-3035, E-mail: hinkle@bgc.bard.edu; *Tech Serv Librn,* Cory Rockliff; Tel: 212-501-3037, E-mail: rockliff@bgc.bard.edu; Staff 6.5 (MLS 3, Non-MLS 3.5)
Founded 1992. Enrl 60; Highest Degree: Doctorate
Library Holdings: Bk Titles 35,000; Per Subs 190
Subject Interests: Decorative art, Design, Mat culture
Automation Activity & Vendor Info: (Acquisitions) Innovative Interfaces, Inc; (Cataloging) Innovative Interfaces, Inc; (Course Reserve) Innovative Interfaces, Inc; (OPAC) Innovative Interfaces, Inc; (Serials) Innovative Interfaces, Inc
Database Vendor: OCLC FirstSearch, OVID Technologies, Wilson - Wilson Web
Wireless access
Function: Res libr
Publications: Exhibition Catalogs
Partic in Metropolitan New York Library Council; OCLC Online Computer Library Center, Inc; OCLC Research Library Partnership
Open Mon-Thurs 9-7, Fri 9-5, Sat & Sun 12-5

C BARNARD COLLEGE*, Wollman Library, 3009 Broadway, 10027-6598. SAN 353-037X. Tel: 212-854-3953. E-mail: refdesk@barnard.edu. Web Site: library.barnard.edu. *Dean,* Lisa Norberg; E-mail: lnorberg@barnard.edu; *Res & Instruction Librn,* Lois Coleman; Tel: 212-854-9095, E-mail: lcoleman@barnard.edu; *Res & Instruction Librn,* Jenna Freedman; Tel: 212-854-4615, E-mail: jfreedma@barnard.edu; *Res & Instruction Librn,* Vani Natarajan; Tel: 212-854-8595; *Res & Instruction Librn,* Heather Van Volkingburg; Tel: 212-851-9692, E-mail: hvanvolk@barnard.edu; *Res & Instruction Librn,* Megan Wacha; Tel: 212-854-7652, E-mail: mwacha@barnard.edu; *Res & Instruction Librn,* Heidi Winston; Tel: 212-854-9096, E-mail: hwinston@barnard.edu; *Archives,* Shannon O'Neill; Tel: 212-854-4079, E-mail: soneill@barnard.edu; *Tech Serv,* Michael Elmore; E-mail: melmore@barnard.edu. Subject Specialists: *Info serv,* Lisa Norberg; *Eng, Math, Sci, Tech,* Lois Coleman; *Gender studies, Women's studies,* Jenna Freedman; *Humanities,* Vani Natarajan; *Psychol, Soc sci,* Heather Van Volkingburg; *Media, Performing arts,* Megan Wacha, *Archit, Fine arts, Urban studies,* Heidi Winston; Staff 9.5 (MLS 9.5)
Founded 1889. Enrl 2,295; Fac 240; Highest Degree: Bachelor
Jul 2007-Jun 2008 Income $1,800,445, Parent Institution $1,764,875. Mats Exp $444,293, Books $133,454, Per/Ser (Incl. Access Fees) $106,158, Manu Arch $11,961, Micro $8,498, AV Equip $84,848, AV Mat $26,045, Electronic Ref Mat (Incl. Access Fees) $60,203, Presv $13,126. Sal $1,237,600 (Prof $652,316)
Library Holdings: AV Mats 19,747; Microforms 18,780; Bk Titles 157,835; Bk Vols 209,883; Per Subs 419
Special Collections: American Women Writers (Overbury Coll); Zines
Automation Activity & Vendor Info: (Acquisitions) Ex Libris Group; (Cataloging) Ex Libris Group; (Circulation) Ex Libris Group; (Course Reserve) Ex Libris Group; (OPAC) Ex Libris Group; (Serials) EBSCO Online
Wireless access
Function: Archival coll, Art exhibits, Audio & video playback equip for onsite use, AV serv, e-mail & chat, Electronic databases & coll, Equip loans & repairs, Handicapped accessible, ILL available, Photocopying/Printing, Scanner
Partic in Metropolitan New York Library Council; New York State Interlibrary Loan Network (NYSILL); OCLC Research Library Partnership
Restriction: Access at librarian's discretion, Authorized patrons, Authorized scholars by appt, Open to students, fac & staff

C BARUCH COLLEGE-CUNY*, William & Anita Newman Library, 151 E 25 St, Box H-0520, 10010-2313. SAN 311-6395. Tel: 646-312-1610. Circulation Tel: 646-312-1660. Interlibrary Loan Service Tel:

646-312-1674. Administration Tel: 646-312-1655. Circulation FAX: 646-312-1662. Administration FAX: 646-312-1651. Information Services FAX: 646-312-1601. Web Site: newman.baruch.cuny.edu. *Chief Librn,* Dr Arthur Downing; Tel: 646-312-1654, E-mail: arthur.downing@baruch.cuny.edu; *Head, Archives & Spec Coll,* Sandra Roff; Tel: 646-312-1623, E-mail: sandra.roff@baruch.cuny.edu; *Head, Coll Mgt,* Michael Waldman; Tel: 646-312-1689, Fax: 646-312-1691, E-mail: michael.waldman@baruch.cuny.edu; *Grad Serv Librn,* Linda Rath; Tel: 646-312-1622, E-mail: Linda.Rath@baruch.cuny.edu; *Mgr, Access Serv,* Monique Prince; Tel: 646-312-1670, E-mail: monique.prince@baruch.cuny.edu; *Coordr, Info Serv,* Randy B Hensley; Tel: 646-312-1609, E-mail: randy.hensley@baruch.cuny.edu. Subject Specialists: *Math, Statistics,* Dr Arthur Downing; *Hist,* Sandra Roff; *Communication studies, Healthcare admin, Polit sci,* Michael Waldman; *Anthrop, Sociol, Women's studies,* Linda Rath; *Pub affairs,* Randy B Hensley; Staff 47 (MLS 25, Non-MLS 22)
Founded 1968. Enrl 17,373; Fac 472; Highest Degree: Master
Jul 2012-Jun 2013. Mats Exp $1,640,844. Sal $2,908,294 (Prof $2,171,641)
Library Holdings: DVDs 2,001; e-books 236,358; Microforms 2,066,739; Bk Titles 633,231; Bk Vols 606,448
Subject Interests: Financial, Tax serv
Automation Activity & Vendor Info: (Acquisitions) Ex Libris Group; (Cataloging) Ex Libris Group; (Circulation) Ex Libris Group; (Course Reserve) Docutek; (ILL) OCLC; (OPAC) Ex Libris Group; (Serials) Ex Libris Group
Database Vendor: ABC-CLIO, Alexander Street Press, American Chemical Society, American Psychological Association (APA), Annual Reviews, Blackwell, Cambridge Scientific Abstracts, CIOS (Communication Institute for Online Scholarship), CQ Press, CredoReference, Dialog, ebrary, EBSCOhost, Emerald, Ex Libris Group, Factiva.com, Facts on File, Gale Cengage Learning, IBISWorld, infoUSA, ISI Web of Knowledge, JSTOR, LexisNexis, Marquis Who's Who, Medline, Mergent Online, Modern Language Association, OCLC FirstSearch, OCLC WorldShare Interlibrary Loan, Oxford Online, Project MUSE, ProQuest, PubMed, ReferenceUSA, RefWorks, ScienceDirect, SerialsSolutions, Springer-Verlag, Standard & Poor's, Thomson - Web of Science, ValueLine, Westlaw, Wiley, Wiley InterScience, Wilson - Wilson Web
Wireless access
Special Services for the Blind - Assistive/Adapted tech devices, equip & products
Restriction: Open to students, fac, staff & alumni
Friends of the Library Group

S BAYVIEW CORRECTIONAL FACILITY LIBRARY*, 550 W 20th St, 10011. SAN 327-1455. Tel: 212-255-7590. FAX: 212-255-7590, Ext 2099. *Librn,* Edna Crespo
Library Holdings: Bk Vols 6,000
Partic in NY Pub Libr Syst
Open Mon-Sat 11-1 & 5-9

M BELLEVUE MEDICAL LIBRARY*, Clarence E de la Chapelle Medical Library, 462 First Ave & 27th St, 14N12, 10016. SAN 352-8812. Tel: 212-562-6535. Administration Tel: 212-562-2933. FAX: 212-562-3506. E-mail: hsl_bellevue@nyumc.org. Web Site: library.med.nyu.edu/bellevue. Staff 2.35 (MLS 1, Non-MLS 1.35)
Founded 1941
Library Holdings: Bk Titles 3,000
Subject Interests: Allied health, Med, Nursing
Partic in Basic Health Sciences Library Network
Restriction: Hospital employees & physicians only
Branches:
PATIENTS LIBRARY, 462 First Ave & 27th St, 10016. Tel: 212-562-3833. *Mgr,* Judith Gonzalez-Rahming
Library Holdings: Bk Vols 5,000; Per Subs 50
Open Mon-Fri 8-4

C BERKELEY COLLEGE*, New York City Campus, Three E 43rd St, 10017. SAN 329-9260. Tel: 212-986-4343. FAX: 212-661-2940. Web Site: www.berkeleycollege.edu. Staff 4 (MLS 3, Non-MLS 1)
Founded 1936. Fac 100; Highest Degree: Bachelor
Library Holdings: AV Mats 1,200; e-books 4,000; Electronic Media & Resources 21; Bk Vols 18,000; Per Subs 100
Subject Interests: Acctg, Bus admin, Fashion mkt, Info syst mgt, Mgt, Mkt
Automation Activity & Vendor Info: (Cataloging) TLC (The Library Corporation); (Circulation) TLC (The Library Corporation); (OPAC) TLC (The Library Corporation)
Database Vendor: EBSCOhost, Gale Cengage Learning, LexisNexis, Westlaw
Wireless access
Partic in Metropolitan New York Library Council; Nylink; OCLC Online Computer Library Center, Inc
Open Mon-Thurs 8am-9:30pm, Fri 8am-9pm, Sat 9-5

M BETH ISRAEL MEDICAL CENTER*, Seymour J Phillips Health Sciences Library, 317 E 17th, 10003. (Mail add: First Ave at 16th St, 10003), SAN 311-6417. Tel: 212-420-2855. FAX: 212-420-4640. E-mail: library@chpnet.org. *Dir,* Maria Astifidis; *Asst Tech Serv Librn,* Robert Payne; Staff 4 (MLS 1, Non-MLS 3)
Founded 1946
Library Holdings: Bk Vols 15,000; Per Subs 600
Subject Interests: Alcohol, Allied health sci, Behav sci, Drug, Med, Nursing, Nursing educ, Psychiat, Psychol, Soc sci, Surgery
Wireless access
Partic in Metropolitan New York Library Council
Restriction: Staff use only

L BLANK ROME LLP*, Law Library, Chrysler Bldg, 15th Fl, 405 Lexington Ave, 10174. SAN 371-5361. Tel: 212-885-5000. FAX: 212-885-5001. E-mail: librarygroup@blankrome.com. Web Site: www.blankrome.com. *Dir,* Mary Newman; *Coordr,* Arah Joseph
Library Holdings: Bk Titles 3,000; Bk Vols 20,000; Per Subs 800
Automation Activity & Vendor Info: (Cataloging) Inmagic, Inc.; (Circulation) Inmagic, Inc.
Database Vendor: LexisNexis, Westlaw
Wireless access
Publications: Newsletter
Open Mon-Fri 8:30-5:30

C BORICUA COLLEGE*, Library & Learning Resources Center, 3755 Broadway, 10032. Tel: 212-694-1000, Ext 666 or 667. FAX: 212-694-1015. Web Site: www.boricuacollege.edu. *Dir,* Liza Rivera; Staff 1 (MLS 1)
Founded 1974. Enrl 1,095; Fac 50; Highest Degree: Master
Library Holdings: Bk Vols 121,000
Special Collections: Baoillo Papers; Puerto Rican Repository
Subject Interests: Latin Am, Maps, Music, Puerto Rico
Automation Activity & Vendor Info: (Cataloging) JayWil Software Development, Inc; (OPAC) JayWil Software Development, Inc
Database Vendor: EBSCOhost
Wireless access
Partic in Metrop Regional Res & Ref Librs; Metropolitan New York Library Council

J BOROUGH OF MANHATTAN COMMUNITY COLLEGE LIBRARY, A Philip Randolph Memorial Library, 199 Chambers St, 10007. SAN 311-6484. Tel: 212-220-1442. Interlibrary Loan Service Tel: 212-220-1444. Reference Tel: 212-220-8139. FAX: 212-748-7466. Web Site: lib1.bmcc.cuny.edu. *Chief Librn,* Sidney Eng; Tel: 212-220-1499, E-mail: seng@bmcc.cuny.edu; *Head, Access Serv,* Joy Dunkley; Tel: 212-220-8000, Ext 5259, E-mail: jdunkley@bmcc.cuny.edu; *Head, Coll Develop,* Joanna Bevecqua; Tel: 212-220-1446, E-mail: jbevecqua@bmcc.cuny.edu; *Head, ILL, Media Serv, Ref,* Dorothea Coiffe; E-mail: dcoiffe@bmcc.cuny.edu; *Archivist, Head, Per,* Phyllis Niles; Tel: 212-220-1450, E-mail: pniles@bmcc.cuny.edu; *Head, Tech Serv,* Taian Zhao; Tel: 212-220-1452, E-mail: tzhao@bmcc.cuny.edu; *Electronic Res Librn,* Kanu Nagra; Tel: 212-220-8000, Ext 7487, E-mail: knagra@bmcc.cuny.edu; *Evening Ref Librn,* Lane Glisson; Tel: 212-220-8000, Ext 7112, E-mail: lglisson@bmcc.cuny.edu; *Info Literacy Librn, Instruction Coordr,* Robin Brown; Tel: 212-220-1445, E-mail: rbrown@bmcc.cuny.edu; *Outreach Librn,* Jean Amaral; Tel: 212 220-8000, Ext 5114, E-mail: jamaral@bmcc.cuny.edu; *Ref Librn,* Barbara Linton; Tel: 212-220-1448, E-mail: blinton@bmcc.cuny.edu; *Ref Librn,* Dr Wambui Mbugua; Tel: 212-220-1447, E-mail: wmbugua@bmcc.cuny.edu; *Ref Librn,* Vicente Revilla; Tel: 212-220-1498, E-mail: vrevilla@bmcc.cuny.edu; *Website & E-Reserve Mgr,* Derek Stadler; Tel: 212-220-8000, Ext 5293, E-mail: dstadler@bmcc.cuny.edu; *Acq,* Linda Wadas; Tel: 212-220-1443, E-mail: lwadas@bmcc.cuny.edu; *Stacks & Media Coll Coordr,* Guerda Baucicaut; Tel: 212-220-8000, Ext 7211, E-mail: gbaucicaut@bmcc.cuny.edu. Subject Specialists: *Syst mgt,* Sidney Eng; Staff 17 (MLS 15, Non-MLS 2)
Founded 1964. Enrl 26,606; Fac 2,007; Highest Degree: Associate
Library Holdings: DVDs 992; e-books 220,000; e-journals 73,583; Microforms 18,445; Bk Titles 102,669; Bk Vols 132,305; Per Subs 261; Videos 1,394
Subject Interests: Allied health, Computer info syst, Educ, Ethnic studies, Med, Nursing
Automation Activity & Vendor Info: (Acquisitions) Ex Libris Group; (Cataloging) Ex Libris Group; (Circulation) Ex Libris Group; (Course Reserve) Ex Libris Group; (ILL) Ex Libris Group; (OPAC) Ex Libris Group; (Serials) Ex Libris Group
Database Vendor: ABC-CLIO, ACM (Association for Computing Machinery), Alexander Street Press, ARTstor, Baker & Taylor, Bowker, College Source, Coutts Information Service, CQ Press, CredoReference, ebrary, EBSCOhost, Facts on File, Gale Cengage Learning, Grolier Online, H W Wilson, IBISWorld, JSTOR, LearningExpress, LexisNexis, Mergent Online, OCLC FirstSearch, OVID Technologies, Oxford Online, Project MUSE, ProQuest, PubMed, RefWorks, Sage, ScienceDirect, Scopus,

SerialsSolutions, Springer-Verlag, Wiley InterScience, Wilson - Wilson Web
Wireless access
Function: 24/7 Online cat, Copy machines, e-mail & chat, E-Reserves, Electronic databases & coll, ILL available, Magazines, Online cat, Photocopying/Printing, Ref serv in person, Scanner, Study rm, Telephone ref, VHS videos, Wheelchair accessible
Publications: Media List; Newsletter
Partic in Metropolitan New York Library Council
Special Services for the Blind - Reader equip
Open Mon-Thurs 8am-10pm, Fri 8-7, Sat 10-6, Sun 12-5
Restriction: Open to students, fac & staff

L BRIGER & ASSOCIATES LIBRARY*, 230 Park Ave, Ste 950, 10169. SAN 329-8469. Tel: 212 953 4400. FAX: 212-953-2266. *Librn,* Erika Soldano
Library Holdings: Bk Vols 4,000

L BRYAN CAVE LLP*, Law Library, 1290 Avenue of the Americas, 10104. SAN 324-1157. Tel: 212-541-2165. Interlibrary Loan Service Tel: 212-541-2166. Reference Tel: 212-541-2167. FAX: 212-541-1465. Web Site: www.bryancave.com. *Mgr, Libr Serv,* Christine M Wierzba; E-mail: cmwierzba@bryancave.com; *Res Librn,* Roxanne Griffin Hamberry; E-mail: rhamberry@bryancave.com; *Tech Serv,* Kimberly August; Tel: 212-541-2032, E-mail: kimberly.august@bryancave.com; *Libr Spec,* Solomon K Berry; E-mail: solomon.berry@bryancave.com; Staff 5 (MLS 3, Non-MLS 2)
Founded 1873
Library Holdings: Bk Titles 3,500; Bk Vols 10,000; Per Subs 300
Subject Interests: Law
Automation Activity & Vendor Info: (Cataloging) Inmagic, Inc.; (Serials) Inmagic, Inc.
Database Vendor: LexisNexis, Westlaw
Wireless access
Partic in Amigos Library Services, Inc; RLIN (Research Libraries Information Network)
Open Mon-Fri 9-5

L CADWALADER, WICKERSHAM & TAFT LIBRARY*, One World Financial Ctr, 10281. SAN 311-6670. Tel: 212-504-6767. FAX: 212-993-3351. Web Site: www.cadwalader.com. *Libr Dir,* Rissa Peckar; *Asst Dir,* Joseph L Biagiotti; Staff 14 (MLS 6, Non-MLS 8)
Subject Interests: Banking, Commodities, Gen corp, Healthcare, Insolvency, Litigation, Mergers, Project finance, Real estate, Securities, Tax
Restriction: Staff use only

L CAHILL, GORDON & REINDEL LIBRARY*, 80 Pine St, 10005. SAN 311-6689. Tel: 212-701-3542. FAX: 212-269-5420. E-mail: library@cahill.com. Web Site: www.cahill.com. *Dir, Info Serv,* Caren Biberman; Tel: 212-701-3540, E-mail: cbiberman@cahill.com
Library Holdings: Bk Vols 45,000
Special Collections: Legislative Histories & Law Reports Coll
Subject Interests: Antitrust, Corporate, Corporate finance, Securities, Tax law
Database Vendor: LexisNexis, Loislaw, Westlaw
Open Mon-Fri 9-5

S CANADIAN CONSULATE GENERAL LIBRARY*, The Research Centre, 1251 Avenue of the Americas, 10020-1175. SAN 311-6700. Tel: 212-596-1623. FAX: 212-596-1646. Web Site: www.newyork.gc.ca. *Dir,* Curtis Field; E-mail: curtis.field@international.gc.ca
Founded 1945
Library Holdings: Bk Vols 3,500; Per Subs 120
Special Collections: Can; Statistics Canada, Annual Reports of Canadian Companies
Subject Interests: Cultural affairs, Econ, Geog, Govt, Hist, Indust, Law, Politics, Trade
Wireless access
Partic in Dialog Corp; Dow Jones News Retrieval; Info Globe; Infomart
Restriction: Employees only

S CARIBBEAN CULTURAL CENTER LIBRARY*, 408 W 58th St, 10019. SAN 371-2419. Tel: 212-307-7420. FAX: 212-315-1086. Web Site: www.caribecenter.org. *Exec Dir,* Marta Moreno-Vega
Library Holdings: Bk Vols 1,075
Automation Activity & Vendor Info: (Cataloging) ComPanion Corp
Wireless access
Open Mon-Fri 10-6

L CARTER, LEDYARD & MILBURN LIBRARY*, Two Wall St, 10005. SAN 311-6727. Tel: 212-238-8851. FAX: 212-732-3232. *Libr Dir,* Emily Moog; E-mail: moog@clm.com; *Asst Librn,* Nora Gardner; Tel: 212-238-8691, E-mail: gardner@clm.com. Subject Specialists: *Law,* Emily Moog; *Law,* Nora Gardner; Staff 2 (MLS 2)
Library Holdings: Bk Vols 20,000; Per Subs 30
Open Mon-Fri 9:30-5:30

S CBS NEWS REFERENCE LIBRARY*, 524 W 57th St, Ste 533/2, 10019. SAN 311-6654. Tel: 212-975-2877. FAX: 212-975-3940. E-mail: st4@cbsnews.com. *Mgr,* Cryder H Bankes, III; *Mgr,* Carole D Parnes; Staff 2 (MLS 2)
Founded 1940
Library Holdings: Bk Titles 24,000; Bk Vols 31,000; Per Subs 250
Special Collections: Transcripts of CBS News Broadcasts
Subject Interests: Broadcasting, Current events, Govt, Hist, Politics
Automation Activity & Vendor Info: (Acquisitions) EOS International; (Cataloging) EOS International; (Circulation) EOS International; (ILL) EOS International; (OPAC) EOS International; (Serials) EOS International
Restriction: Open by appt only

S CENTER FOR FICTION*, 17 E 47th St, 10017. SAN 311-8908. Tel: 212-755-6710. FAX: 212-824-0831. E-mail: info@centerforfiction.org. Web Site: www.centerforfiction.org. *Dir,* Noreen Tomassi; *Head of Libr,* Brenda Wegener; Staff 6 (MLS 1, Non-MLS 5)
Founded 1820
Library Holdings: Bk Vols 75,000; Per Subs 66
Special Collections: 19th Century Fiction & Nonfiction
Subject Interests: Lit
Publications: Newsletter (Bi-monthly)
Open Mon-Thurs 10:30-7:30, Fri 9-5, Sat 11-3
Restriction: Circ to mem only
Friends of the Library Group

S CENTER FOR JEWISH HISTORY*, Leo Baeck Institute Library, 15 W 16 St, 10011-6301. SAN 311-6255. Tel: 212-744-6400. Interlibrary Loan Service Tel: 212-744-6400, Ext 8404. FAX: 212-988-1305. E-mail: lbaeck@lbi.cjh.org. Web Site: www.lbi.org. *Exec Dir,* Carol Kahn Strauss; *Dir,* Dr Frank Mecklenburg; *Admin Dir,* Norma Kirschen; *Head Librn,* Renate Evers; *Curator,* Renata Stein. Subject Specialists: *Archives,* Dr Frank Mecklenburg
Founded 1955
Library Holdings: Bk Vols 80,000; Per Subs 200
Special Collections: Art Coll; Extensive Coll of Literature by Jews in German Language; History & Archives of German-speaking Jewry of Central Europe, 18th-20th Century
Automation Activity & Vendor Info: (Acquisitions) Ex Libris Group; (Cataloging) Ex Libris Group; (Circulation) Ex Libris Group; (OPAC) Ex Libris Group; (Serials) Ex Libris Group
Database Vendor: Ex Libris Group
Wireless access
Publications: Exhibition Catalogs; Judischer Almanach des Leo Baeck Institute; LBI News; Leo Baeck Institute Yearbook; Memorial Lectures; Schriftenreihe Wissenschaftlicher Abhandlungen des Leo Baeck Instituts
Partic in Asn of Jewish Librs
Open Mon-Thurs 9:30-4:30
Restriction: Closed stack
Friends of the Library Group

S CENTER FOR MODERN PSYCHOANALYTIC STUDIES LIBRARY*, 16 W Tenth St, 10011. SAN 320-2119. Tel: 212-260-7050, Ext 15. FAX: 212-228-6410. E-mail: librarian@cmps.edu. Web Site: www.cmps.edu. *Librn,* Laura Covino
Founded 1972
Library Holdings: Bk Titles 2,500; Bk Vols 2,800; Per Subs 10
Special Collections: Psychoanalysts Research Projects Coll
Subject Interests: Psychiat, Psychoanalysis, Psychol, Sociol
Automation Activity & Vendor Info: (Cataloging) Surpass; (Circulation) Surpass; (ILL) OCLC FirstSearch; (OPAC) Surpass
Wireless access
Function: Res libr
Partic in Metropolitan New York Library Council
Restriction: Borrowing privileges limited to fac & registered students
Friends of the Library Group

S THE CENTURY ASSOCIATION LIBRARY*, Seven W 43rd St, 10036. SAN 311-6778. Tel: 212-944-0090. FAX: 212-840-3609. E-mail: library@thecentury.org. *Librn,* W Gregory Gallagher; Staff 2 (MLS 2)
Founded 1847
Library Holdings: Bk Titles 25,000
Partic in Metropolitan New York Library Council
Restriction: Mem only

S CHANCELLOR ROBERT R LIVINGSTON MASONIC LIBRARY OF GRAND LODGE*, 71 W 23rd St, 14th Flr, 10010-4171. SAN 311-7901. Tel: 212-337-6620. FAX: 212-633-2639. E-mail: info@nymasoniclibrary.org. Web Site: www.nymasoniclibrary.org. *Dir,* Thomas M Savini; Tel: 212-337-6619; *Cat,* Georgia Hershfeld; E-mail:

ghershfeld@nymasoniclibrary.org; *Curator,* Catherine Walter; E-mail: cwalter@nymasoniclibrary.org. Subject Specialists: *Classical mythology, Masonic hist,* Thomas M Savini; *Anthrop,* Catherine Walter; Staff 4 (MLS 1, Non-MLS 3)
Founded 1856
Library Holdings: Bk Titles 16,000; Bk Vols 60,000; Per Subs 150
Special Collections: 18th & 19th Century Freemasons (Charles Looney Coll), engravings; Early 19th Century Anti-Masonic Movement (Victory Birdseye Coll); Early 20th Century African American Freemasonry (Edward Cusick Coll), docs
Subject Interests: Comparative relig, Freemasonry
Automation Activity & Vendor Info: (Cataloging) Follett Software
Wireless access
Partic in Metropolitan New York Library Council
Open Mon & Wed-Fri 8:30-4:30, Tues 12-8
Restriction: Closed stack, Non-circulating to the pub, Open to pub for ref only

S CHILDREN'S BOOK COUNCIL LIBRARY, 54 W 39th St, 14th Flr, 10018-2039. SAN 311-6840. Tel: 212-966-1990. FAX: 212-966-2073. E-mail: cbc.info@cbcbooks.org. Web Site: www.cbcbooks.org. *Interim Dir,* Nicole Deming; *Librn,* Ayanna Coleman; E-mail: ayanna.coleman@cbcbooks.org
Founded 1945
Library Holdings: Bk Titles 8,000; Per Subs 20
Special Collections: Children's Book Week Posters 1919-2009; Newbery & Caldecott Medal & Honor Books Coll; Young People's Poetry Week Posters 1999-2006
Subject Interests: Bks about children's bks, Current children's trade bks, Selected prize winning children's bks
Open Mon-Thurs 10-4:30, Fri 10-12:30
Restriction: Non-circulating

G CITIZENS UNION FOUNDATION LIBRARY*, 299 Broadway, Ste 700, 10007. SAN 323-6013. Tel: 212-227-0342. FAX: 212-227-0345. E-mail: info@citizensunion.org. Web Site: www.citizenunion.org. *Dir, Communications & Develop,* Sara Stuart
Founded 1948
Library Holdings: Bk Titles 400; Bk Vols 1,000
Special Collections: NY City Charter Revision Commission
Restriction: Open by appt only

C CITY COLLEGE OF THE CITY UNIVERSITY OF NEW YORK, Morris Raphael Cohen Library, North Academic Ctr, 160 Convent Ave, 10031. SAN 352-9177. Tel: 212-650-7155, 212-650-7292. Interlibrary Loan Service Tel: 212-650-7616. Reference Tel: 212-650-7611, 212-650-7612. Administration Tel: 212-650-7271. FAX: 212-650-7604. Interlibrary Loan Service FAX: 212-650-7648. E-mail: reference@ccny.cuny.edu. Web Site: library.ccny.cuny.edu. *Actg Chief Librn,* Chip Stewart; E-mail: cstewart@ccny.cuny.edu; *Actg Chief, Tech Serv,* Rob Laurich; Tel: 212-650-7152, E-mail: rlaurich@yahoo.fr; *Head, Cat,* Yoko Inagi; Tel: 212-650-7623, E-mail: inagoo@gmail.com; *Head, Govt Doc, Head, Ser,* Helena Marvin; Tel: 212-650-5073, E-mail: lena.marvin@gmail.com; *Head, Info Serv,* Amrita Dhawan; Tel: 212-650-5763, E-mail: adhawan@ccny.cuny.edu; *Head, Ref,* William Gibbons; Tel: 212-650-7602, E-mail: wgibbons@ccny.cuny.edu; *Access Serv Librn,* Trevar Riley-Reid; Tel: 212-650-7601, Fax: 212-650-7388, E-mail: trileyreid@ccny.cuny.edu; *Acq,* Anita Meyers; Tel: 212-650-7620, Fax: 212-650-7618, E-mail: ameyers@ccny.cuny.edu; *Archivist,* Sydney Van Nort; Tel: 212-650-7609, E-mail: svannort@ccny.cuny.edu; *ILL,* Evelyn Bodden; E-mail: ill@ccny.cuny.edu; Staff 38 (MLS 21, Non-MLS 17)
Founded 1847. Enrl 16,100; Fac 540; Highest Degree: Doctorate
Library Holdings: AV Mats 1,292,000; CDs 19,825; DVDs 8,013; e-books 564,000; e-journals 105,000; Microforms 1,081,268; Music Scores 7,158; Bk Titles 966,966; Bk Vols 1,639,342; Per Subs 2,476
Special Collections: 18th & Early 19th Century Plays; Astronomy (Newcomb Coll); Costume Coll; English Civil War Pamphlets; Harlem Development Archive; Metropolitan Applied Research Center (MARC) Archives; Poetry (Library of Contemporary Poets: Readings from 1932-1941), rec; Russell Sage Coll; Socio-Economic Broadsides before 1800 (Gitelson Coll), microfilm. Oral History; State Document Depository; US Document Depository
Subject Interests: Educ, Humanities
Automation Activity & Vendor Info: (Acquisitions) Ex Libris Group; (Cataloging) Ex Libris Group; (Circulation) Ex Libris Group; (Course Reserve) Docutek; (ILL) Ex Libris Group; (OPAC) Ex Libris Group; (Serials) SerialsSolutions
Database Vendor: ACM (Association for Computing Machinery), Alexander Street Press, American Chemical Society, American Geophysical Union, American Mathematical Society, American Physical Society, American Psychological Association (APA), Annual Reviews, ARTstor, ASCE Research Library, Atlas Systems, BioOne, Cinahl, CISTI Source, Corbis, Coutts Information Service, CQ Press, ebrary, EBSCOhost, Elsevier, Emerald, Ex Libris Group, Foundation Center, Gale Cengage Learning, H W Wilson, HeinOnline, IEEE (Institute of Electrical & Electronics Engineers), IOP, ISI Web of Knowledge, JSTOR, LexisNexis, Modern Language Association, Nature Publishing Group, OCLC WorldShare Interlibrary Loan, Oxford Online, Project MUSE, ProQuest, PubMed, RefWorks, Sage, ScienceDirect, SerialsSolutions, Springer-Verlag, STN International, Thomson - Web of Science, Wiley InterScience, Wilson - Wilson Web
Wireless access
Function: Archival coll, Art exhibits, Copy machines, Doc delivery serv, Govt ref serv, Handicapped accessible, ILL available, Magnifiers for reading, Music CDs, Online searches, Orientations, Outside serv via phone, mail, e-mail & web, Photocopying/Printing, Ref serv available, Referrals accepted, Res libr, Telephone ref, VHS videos, Wheelchair accessible
Publications: Circumspice (Newsletter)
Partic in Metropolitan New York Library Council; New York Online Virtual Electronic Library (NOVEL); New York State Higher Education Initiative; OCLC Online Computer Library Center, Inc
Special Services for the Blind - Braille equip; Braille servs; Cassette playback machines; Closed circuit TV; Computer with voice synthesizer for visually impaired persons; Magnifiers; Reader equip; Screen reader software
Open Mon-Fri 7am-Midnight, Sat 9-6, Sun 12-6
Restriction: Authorized patrons, Limited access for the pub, Photo ID required for access
Friends of the Library Group

Departmental Libraries:

ARCHITECTURE LIBRARY, Spitzer Bldg, Rm 101, 160 Convent Ave, 10031, SAN 352-9207. Tel: 212-650-8767. FAX: 212-650-7214. Web Site: library.ccny.cuny.edu/index/?page_id=23. *Librn,* Judith Connorton; E-mail: jconnorton@ccny.cuny.edu. Subject Specialists: *Archit, Art,* Judith Connorton; Staff 2 (MLS 1, Non-MLS 1)
Subject Interests: Archit, Art, Urban landscape planning, Urban planning
Open Mon, Wed & Thurs 10-8, Tues 12-8, Fri 10-5, Sat 12-5

ARCHITECTURE VISUAL RESOURCES LIBRARY, Spitzer 104, 160 Convent Ave, 10031. Tel: 212-650-8754. FAX: 212-650-7604. E-mail: archimage@ccny.cuny.edu. Web Site: libguides.ccny.cuny.edu/content.php?pid=350985&sid=2943662. *Librn,* Dr Ching-jung Chen; E-mail: cchen@ccny.cuny.edu; Staff 1 (MLS 0.5, Non-MLS 0.5)
Open Mon-Thurs 9-6, Fri 9-5

CENTER FOR WORKER EDUCATION LIBRARY, 25 Broadway, 7th Flr, 10004. Tel: 212-925-6625, Ext 228. FAX: 212-925-0963. Web Site: libguides.ccny.cuny.edu/content.php?pid=350985&sid=2873391. *Actg Librn,* Nilda Sanchez; E-mail: nsanchez@ccny.cuny.edu; Staff 1 (MLS 1)
Open Mon-Fri 12-8, Sat 10-5

COLLEGE ARCHIVES & SPECIAL COLLECTIONS, North Academic Ctr-Cohen Library, 160 Convent Ave, 10031, SAN 352-9231. Tel: 212-650-7609. FAX: 212-650-7604. E-mail: archives@ccny.cuny.edu. Web Site: library.ccny.cuny.edu/index/?page_id=458. *Archivist,* Sydney Van Nort; E-mail: svannort@ccny.cuny.edu; Staff 2 (MLS 1, Non-MLS 1)
Special Collections: First Editions & Rare Books; Harlem Development Archive; Harlem Development Archive; Papers of Cleveland Abbe, R R Bowker, Townsend Harris, J H Finley, Waldemar Kaempffert, L F Mott, Edward M Shepard, Alexander Webb & Everett Wheeler; Source Material Relating to Free Higher Education in New York since 1847; William Butler Yeats Coll, printed editions

DOMINICAN STUDIES INSTITUTE RESEARCH LIBRARY & ARCHIVES, NAC 2/204, 160 Convent Ave, 10031-0198. Tel: 212-650-7170, 212-650-7496. FAX: 212-650-7489. E-mail: dsi@ccny.cuny.edu. Web Site: www.ccny.cuny.edu/dsi/dominican-library.cfm. *Librn,* Sarah Aponte; E-mail: aponte@ccny.cuny.edu; *Archivist,* Idilio Garcia-Pena; E-mail: igpconsulting@gmail.com; Staff 2 (MLS 1, Non-MLS 1)
Founded 1994
Library Holdings: Bk Vols 15,500
Open Mon & Thurs 9-8:30, Tues, Wed & Fri 9-5, Sat 12-5

MUSIC LIBRARY, Shepard Hall, Rm 160, 160 Convent Ave, 10031, SAN 352-9355. Tel: 212-650-7174. FAX: 212-650-7231. Web Site: libguides.ccny.cuny.edu/aecontent.php?pid=350985&sid=2873356. *Actg Music Librn,* Michael Crowley; Tel: 212-650-7120, E-mail: rcrowley@ccny.cuny.edu; Staff 2 (MLS 1, Non-MLS 1)
Open Mon 10-6, Tues-Thurs 10-7, Fri 10-5

SCIENCE-ENGINEERING, Marshak Bldg, Rm 29, 160 Convent Ave, 10031, SAN 352-938X. Tel: 212-650-8246. Reference Tel: 212-650-5712. FAX: 212-650-7626. Web Site: library.ccny.cuny.edu/index/?page_id=25. *Head of Libr,* Loren Mendelsohn; Tel: 212-650-8244, E-mail: lmend@ccny.cuny.edu; *Librn,* Philip Barnett; Tel: 212-650-8243, E-mail: pbsci@ccny.cuny.edu; *Librn,* Claudia Lascar; Tel: 212-650-6826, E-mail: clascar@ccny.cuny.edu; Staff 5 (MLS 3, Non-MLS 2)
Subject Interests: Atmospheric sci, Biochem, Biol, Chem, Computer sci, Earth sci, Eng, Magnetic resonance imaging, Math, Spectroscopy, Transportation, Waste treatment

Open Mon-Thurs 9am-11pm, Fri & Sat 9-6, Sun 12-6
Friends of the Library Group

S CITY OF NEW YORK DEPARTMENT OF RECORDS & INFORMATION SERVICES*, City Hall Library, 31 Chambers St, Rm 112, 10007. SAN 353-202X. Tel: 212-788-8590. FAX: 212-788-8589. E-mail: chlibrary@records.nyc.gov. Web Site: www.nyc.gov/html/records. *Supv Librn,* Christine Bruzzese; Staff 2 (MLS 1, Non-MLS 1)
Founded 1913
Library Holdings: Bk Vols 66,000; Per Subs 10
Special Collections: Municipal Document Depository; State Document Depository
Subject Interests: Civil serv, Consul studies, Hist of NY City, Legislation, Local govt, Municipal mgt, Politicians, Pub health, State doc, Urban affairs
Automation Activity & Vendor Info: (Cataloging) Mandarin Library Automation; (OPAC) Mandarin Library Automation
Open Mon-Thurs 9-4:30, Fri, 9-1

C CITY UNIVERSITY OF NEW YORK*, Mina Rees Library of Graduate School & University Center, 365 Fifth Ave, 10016-4309. SAN 311-6883. Tel: 212-817-7040. Circulation Tel: 212-817-7083. Reference Tel: 212-817-7077. FAX: 212-817-2982. Web Site: library.gc.cuny.edu. *Actg Chief Librn,* Polly Thistlethwaite; E-mail: pthistlethwaite@gc.cuny.edu; *Head, Circ & Reserves,* Matthew Curtis; E-mail: mcurtis@gc.cuny.edu; *Head, Tech Serv,* Mike Handis; Tel: 212-817-7075, E-mail: mhandis@gc.cuny.edu; *Acq,* Jane Fitzpatrick; Tel: 212-817-7056, E-mail: jfitzpatrick@gc.cuny.edu; *Acq,* Rose Ochoa; *Archives,* John Rothman; *Cat,* Dalia Leonardo; Tel: 212-817-7067, E-mail: ldalia@gc.cuny.edu; *Cat,* Joel Singer; Tel: 212-817-7072, E-mail: jsinger@gc.cuny.edu; *ILL,* Jessica McGivney; *ILL,* Beth Posner; Tel: 212-817-7051, E-mail: bposner@gc.cuny.edu; *Ref,* Michael Adams; Tel: 212-817-7055, E-mail: madams@gc.cuny.edu; *Ref,* Amy Ballmer; Tel: 212-817-7059, E-mail: aballmer@gc.cuny.edu; *Ser,* Melissa Longhi; *Syst,* Stephen Klein; Tel: 212-817-7074; Staff 15 (MLS 11, Non-MLS 4)
Founded 1964. Enrl 4,000; Highest Degree: Doctorate
Library Holdings: Bk Vols 285,000; Per Subs 11,000
Special Collections: American History (US Presidential Papers), microfilm; City University of New York; Old York Library (Seymour Durst Coll)
Automation Activity & Vendor Info: (Acquisitions) Ex Libris Group; (Cataloging) Ex Libris Group; (Circulation) Ex Libris Group; (Course Reserve) Docutek; (ILL) OCLC ILLiad; (OPAC) Ex Libris Group; (Serials) Ex Libris Group
Database Vendor: ABC-CLIO, ACM (Association for Computing Machinery), Alexander Street Press, American Chemical Society, American Mathematical Society, American Psychological Association (APA), Annual Reviews, ARTstor, Baker & Taylor, Blackwell, Cambridge Scientific Abstracts, Cinahl, CISTI Source, ebrary, EBSCOhost, Elsevier, Ex Libris Group, Foundation Center, Gale Cengage Learning, Greenwood Publishing Group, H W Wilson, Haworth Pres Inc, IEEE (Institute of Electrical & Electronics Engineers), Infotrieve, Ingenta, ISI Web of Knowledge, JSTOR, LexisNexis, Marquis Who's Who, Modern Language Association, Nature Publishing Group, OCLC FirstSearch, OCLC WorldShare Interlibrary Loan, OVID Technologies, Oxford Online, Paratext, Project MUSE, ProQuest, PubMed, RefWorks, Sage, ScienceDirect, Scopus, SerialsSolutions, Springer-Verlag, Thomson - Web of Science, Wiley, Wiley InterScience, Wilson - Wilson Web
Wireless access
Partic in Metropolitan New York Library Council; Nylink; Westchester Academic Library Directors Organization (WALDO)
Special Services for the Deaf - Assistive tech
Special Services for the Blind - Assistive/Adapted tech devices, equip & products; Computer with voice synthesizer for visually impaired persons
Open Mon-Fri 9am-11pm, Sat 10-8, Sun 12-8
Restriction: Open to students, fac & staff
Friends of the Library Group

L CLEARY, GOTTLIEB, STEEN & HAMILTON LLP LIBRARY*, One Liberty Plaza, 10006. SAN 311-6913. Tel: 212-225-3444. FAX: 212-225-3999. *Dir, Libr Serv,* Susan M Burrows; Staff 12 (MLS 6, Non-MLS 6)
Library Holdings: Bk Titles 22,000
Subject Interests: Foreign, Intl law, Intl taxation
Automation Activity & Vendor Info: (Cataloging) SirsiDynix; (OPAC) SirsiDynix
Restriction: Staff use only

L CLIFFORD CHANCE LLP LIBRARY*, 31 W 52nd St, 10019. SAN 312-0368. Tel: 212-878-8095. Reference Tel: 212-878-8211. FAX: 212-878-3474. Web Site: www.cliffordchance.com. *Dir,* Grace McLaughlin; *Tech Serv,* Rosalinda Rupel; Tel: 212-878-3238; Staff 10 (MLS 6, Non-MLS 4)
Founded 1871
Library Holdings: Bk Vols 25,000; Per Subs 250
Automation Activity & Vendor Info: (Acquisitions) SydneyPlus; (Cataloging) SydneyPlus; (Circulation) SydneyPlus; (OPAC) SydneyPlus; (Serials) SydneyPlus
Database Vendor: Dialog, LexisNexis, Westlaw
Wireless access
Restriction: Staff use only

S COLLECTORS CLUB LIBRARY*, 22 E 35th St, 10016-3806. SAN 311-6948. Tel: 212-683-0559. FAX: 212-481-1269. Web Site: www.collectorsclub.org. *Librn,* Miklos Tinther
Founded 1896
Library Holdings: Bk Titles 30,000; Per Subs 30
Subject Interests: Philately
Publications: Collectors Club Philatelist
Open Wed 10-5

C COLLEGE OF NEW ROCHELLE*, District Council 37 Library, 125 Barclay, Rm 211, 10007. Tel: 212-815-1699. FAX: 212-815-7529. *Librn,* Ken Nash; E-mail: knash@dc37.net
Library Holdings: Bk Vols 12,000; Per Subs 50
Special Collections: Harry Gray Labor Coll
Automation Activity & Vendor Info: (Cataloging) Follett Software; (Circulation) Follett Software; (OPAC) Follett Software
Open Mon-Thurs 10-9, Fri 11:30-7:30, Sat 10-3

C COLUMBIA UNIVERSITY*, Butler Library, Rm 517, 535 W 114th St, 10027. SAN 352-941X. Tel: 212-854-7309. Circulation Tel: 212-854-2235. Interlibrary Loan Service Tel: 212-854-2533, 212-854-7535. Reference Tel: 212-854-2241. FAX: 212-854-9099. E-mail: butler@library.columbia.edu, lio@columbia.edu. Web Site: library.columbia.edu. *Univ Librn, VPres for Info Serv,* James G Neal; *Assoc Univ Librn, Bibliog Serv & Coll Develop,* Robert Wolven; *Assoc Univ Librn, Coll Develop,* Damon Jaggars; Tel: 212-854-0025, E-mail: djaggars@columbia.edu; *Dir, Presv Serv,* Janet Gertz; *Dir, Coll Develop,* Jeffrey D Carroll; *Dir, Libr Info Tech,* Breck White. Subject Specialists: *Info serv,* James G Neal; Staff 328 (MLS 328)
Founded 1761. Enrl 23,422; Fac 1,401; Highest Degree: Doctorate
Library Holdings: Bk Vols 10,296,816
Special Collections: Oral History; State Document Depository; UN Document Depository; US Document Depository
Automation Activity & Vendor Info: (Acquisitions) Ex Libris Group; (Cataloging) Ex Libris Group; (Circulation) Ex Libris Group
Publications: Books & Bytes
Partic in Association of Research Libraries (ARL); Metropolitan New York Library Council; Northeast Research Libraries Consortium (NERL); OCLC Research Library Partnership
Friends of the Library Group

Departmental Libraries:

ACCESS SERVICES, Butler Library 207 C, 535 W 114th St, 10027. Tel: 212-854-2245. Circulation Tel: 212-854-4734. *Dir, Access Serv,* Francie Mrkich

AFRICAN STUDIES, Lehman Library, 420 W 118th St, 10027, SAN 377-0044. Tel: 212-854-8045. FAX: 212-854-3834. E-mail: africa@library.columbia.edu. Web Site: library.columbia.edu/locations/global/africa.html. *Librn,* Yuusuf Caruso; E-mail: caruso@columbia.edu

ARCHIVES, Butler Library, 6th Flr, 114th St, MC 1127, 10027, SAN 353-0191. Tel: 212-854-5590. FAX: 212-854-1365. E-mail: rbml@library.columbia.edu. Web Site: library.columbia.edu/locations/cuarchives.html. *Curator of Ms & Univ Archivist,* Susan Hamson; Tel: 212-854-1331, E-mail: sgh2105@columbia.edu; *Pub Serv Archivist,* Jocelyn K Wilk; Tel: 212-854-1338, E-mail: jkw19@columbia.edu; *Ref Serv Supvr,* Tara Craig; Staff 3 (MLS 2, Non-MLS 1)
Founded 1883
Library Holdings: Bk Vols 45,000
Function: Archival coll
Open Mon 9-7:45, Tues-Fri 9-4:45
Restriction: Non-circulating

AVERY ARCHITECTURAL & FINE ARTS LIBRARY, 1172 Amsterdam Ave, MC 0301, 10027. Tel: 212-854-6199. E-mail: avery@library.columbia.edu. Web Site: library.columbia.edu/locations/avery.html. *Dir,* Carole Ann Fabian; Tel: 212-854-3068, E-mail: caf2140@columbia.edu; *Assoc Dir, Head, Access Serv,* Kitty Chibnik; Tel: 212-854-3506, E-mail: krc1@columbia.edu; *Archit Librn,* Christine Sala; *Fine Arts Librn,* Paula Gabbard; *Project Librn,* Margaret Smithglass; *Indexer, Ref Librn,* Jeffrey Ross; *Supvr, Access Serv,* Zachary Rouse; *Archivist,* Shelley Hayreh; Staff 21 (MLS 9, Non-MLS 12)
Founded 1890
Library Holdings: Bk Vols 450,000; Per Subs 1,700
Open Mon-Thurs 9am-11pm, Fri 9-9, Sat 10-7, Sun 12-10
Restriction: Non-circulating, Open to students, fac & staff

CR THE BURKE LIBRARY AT UNION THEOLOGICAL SEMINARY, 3041 Broadway, 10027, SAN 312-1054. Tel: 212-851-5606. Interlibrary Loan Service Tel: 212-851-5623. Administration Tel: 212-851-5611. FAX:

212-851-5613. E-mail: burke@libraries.cul.columbia.edu. Web Site: library.columbia.edu/indiv/burke.html. *Dir,* Beth Bidlack; *Coll Serv Librn,* Matthew Baker; *Pub Serv Librn,* Elizabeth Call; *Archivist,* Ruth Tonkiss Cameron; *Project Archivist,* Brigette Kamsler; Staff 4 (MLS 4)
Founded 1836. Enrl 226; Fac 20; Highest Degree: Doctorate
Library Holdings: AV Mats 1,781; Music Scores 1,812; Bk Vols 604,361; Per Subs 1,719; Videos 34
Special Collections: Americana Coll; Archive of Women in Theology; Archives; Auburn Coll; Bonhoeffer Coll; British History & Theology (McAlpin Coll); Christian Science Coll; Ecumenics & Church Union (William Adams Brown Coll); Gillett Coll; Hymnology; Missionary Research Library Coll; Reformation Tracts; Thompson; Van Ess Coll
Subject Interests: Bible, Christian ethics, Church hist, Communication, Ecumenics, Missions
Automation Activity & Vendor Info: (Cataloging) Ex Libris Group; (Circulation) Ex Libris Group; (Course Reserve) Ex Libris Group; (OPAC) Ex Libris Group; (Serials) Ex Libris Group
Partic in New England Law Library Consortium, Inc; New York State Interlibrary Loan Network (NYSILL); OCLC Online Computer Library Center, Inc; OCLC Research Library Partnership; RLIN (Research Libraries Information Network)
Friends of the Library Group

BUTLER LIBRARY REFERENCE DEPARTMENT, 301 Butler Library, 535 W 114th St, 10027, SAN 352-9568. Tel: 212-854-2241. E-mail: ref-ref@columbia.edu. Web Site: library.columbia.edu/locations/butler-reference.html. *Dept Head,* Barbara Rockenbach; *Librn,* Mary Cargill; Staff 12 (MLS 10, Non-MLS 2)
Library Holdings: Bk Vols 57,981

CL ARTHUR W DIAMOND LAW LIBRARY, 435 W 116th St, 10027, SAN 353-0256. Tel: 212-854-3922. Reference Tel: 212-854-3743. Web Site: www.law.columbia.edu/library. *Dir,* Kent McKeever; Tel: 212-854-4228, E-mail: mckeever@law.columbia.edu; *Assoc Dir,* Jody Armstrong; *Head, Pub Serv,* Jennifer Wertkin; *Head, Tech Serv,* Mary Burgos; *Ref Librn,* Deborah Heller; *Ref Librn,* Dana Neacsu; *Spec Coll Librn,* Sabrina Sondhi; Staff 41 (MLS 18, Non-MLS 23)
Library Holdings: e-journals 26,742; Microforms 24,694; Bk Titles 398,028; Bk Vols 1,197,430; Per Subs 6,103
Special Collections: UN Document Depository; US Document Depository
Subject Interests: Foreign law, Intl law
Database Vendor: Innovative Interfaces, Inc
Open Mon-Fri (Winter) 8am-Midnight, Sat 10-8, Sun 10am-Midnight; Mon-Fri (Summer) 9-5

GEOLOGY, 601 Schermerhorn, 1190 Amsterdam Ave, 10027, SAN 352-9835. Tel: 212-854-4713. FAX: 212-854-4716. E-mail: geology@libraries.cul.columbia.edu. Web Site: library.columbia.edu/indiv/geology.html. *Librn,* Amanda Bielskas; Tel: 212-854-6767, E-mail: asb2154@columbia.edu. Subject Specialists: *Geol, Geoscience,* Amanda Bielskas; Staff 2 (MLS 1, Non-MLS 1)
Library Holdings: Bk Vols 96,021
Special Collections: State & Foreign Geological Surveys & Societies Dating Back to 18th Century
Subject Interests: Hydrol, Mineralogy, Paleontology, Petrology, Sedimentology, Stratigraphy, Traditional terrestrial geol
Friends of the Library Group

GLOBAL STUDIES, Lehman Library, 420 W 118th St, 10027, SAN 377-0141. Tel: 212-854-3630. FAX: 212-854-3834. E-mail: global@library.columbia.edu. Web Site: library.columbia.edu/locations/global.html. *Dir,* Pamela Graham, PhD; E-mail: graham@columbia.edu; *Librn,* Michelle Chesner; *Librn,* Yuusuf Curuso; *Librn,* Robert H Davis, Jr; *Librn,* Gary Hausman; *Librn,* Sean Knowlton; *Librn,* Peter Magierski
Database Vendor: ABC-CLIO, Ex Libris Group

LAMONT-DOHERTY GEOSCIENCE LIBRARY, Lamont-Doherty Earth Observatory, 61 Rte 9 W, Palisades, 10964. (Mail add: PO Box 1000, Palisades, 10964-8000), SAN 352-986X. Tel: 845-365-8808. FAX: 845-365-8151. E-mail: geology@libraries.cul.columbia.edu. Web Site: library.columbia.edu/indiv/geosci.html. *Librn,* Amanda Bielskas; Tel: 845-365-8809, E-mail: asb2154@columbia.edu; *Libr Spec,* Miriam Colwell. Subject Specialists: *Geol, Geoscience,* Amanda Bielskas; Staff 2.5 (MLS 1, Non-MLS 1.5)
Library Holdings: Bk Vols 30,000; Per Subs 500
Special Collections: Earth Science Journals
Subject Interests: Climatology, Geochemistry, Geophysics, Marine biol, Paleomagnetics, Phys geog, Rock mechanics
Open Mon-Fri 9-5
Friends of the Library Group

LATIN AMERICAN & IBERIAN STUDIES, 309 International Affairs Bldg, 420 W 118th St, 10027, SAN 377-0060. Tel: 212-854-1679. FAX: 212-854-3834. E-mail: latam@library.columbia.edu. Web Site: library.columbia.edu/locations/global/latinamerica.html. *Interim Librn,* Pamela Graham

LEHMAN LIBRARY, 300 International Affairs, 420 W 118th St, 10027, SAN 377-0125. Tel: 212-854-3794. FAX: 212-854-2495. E-mail: lehman@library.columbia.edu. Web Site: library.columbia.edu/locations/lehman.html. *Dir,* Mary Giunta; E-mail: mg201@columbia.edu; *Head, Libr Operations,* Peguy Jean-Pierre; *Metadata Librn,* Eric Glass; *Ref & Coll Develop Librn,* Fadi Dagher; E-mail: fd2102@columbia.edu; *Coordr,* Jeremiah Trinidad-Christensen; *Libr Spec I,* Emily McNeil
Founded 1971

CM AUGUSTUS C LONG HEALTH SCIENCES LIBRARY, 701 W 168th St, Lobby Level, 10032, SAN 353-0221. Tel: 212-305-3605. Reference Tel: 212-305-3692. FAX: 212-234-0595. E-mail: hs-library@columbia.edu. Web Site: library.cumc.columbia.edu. *Dir of Libr Operations,* Michael Koehn; Tel: 212-305-9216, E-mail: mdk2126@columbia.edu; *Head, Archives & Spec Coll,* Stephen Novak; E-mail: sen13@columbia.edu; *Knowledge Mgt Spec,* Susan Kimley; *Archivist,* Jennifer McGillan
Library Holdings: Bk Vols 551,000; Per Subs 4,416
Special Collections: Anatomy (Huntington Coll); Cancer Research; Physiology (Curtis Coll); Plastic Surgery (Jerome P Webster Coll)
Automation Activity & Vendor Info: (Acquisitions) Ex Libris Group; (Cataloging) Ex Libris Group; (Circulation) Ex Libris Group; (Course Reserve) Ex Libris Group; (OPAC) Ex Libris Group; (Serials) Ex Libris Group
Function: Distance learning, Doc delivery serv, ILL available, Photocopying/Printing, Ref serv available
Open Mon-Thurs (Fall & Spring) 8am-11pm, Fri 8-8, Sat 10am-11pm, Sun 12-11; Mon-Thurs (Summer) 8-8, Fri 8-6, Sat 10-6, Sun 12-8

MATHEMATICS, 303 Mathematics, 2990 Broadway, MC 4702, 10027, SAN 352-9894. Tel: 212-854-4712. E-mail: math@library.columbia.edu. Web Site: library.columbia.edu/locations/math.html. *Tech Serv Supvr,* Jim Babcock; Tel: 212-854-4181, E-mail: jrb55@columbia.edu
Library Holdings: Bk Vols 126,004

MIDDLE EAST & ISLAMIC STUDIES/AREA STUDIES, 309 Lehman Social Sciences Library, 420 W 118th St, 10027, SAN 377-0087. Tel: 212-854-3995. FAX: 212-854-3834. E-mail: mideast@library.columbia.edu. Web Site: library.columbia.edu/locations/global/mideast.html. *Librn,* Peter Magierski; E-mail: pm2650@columbia.edu. Subject Specialists: *Middle Eastern hist,* Peter Magierski
Jul 2005-Jun 2006. Mats Exp $250,000, Books $210,000, Micro $20,000, Electronic Ref Mat (Incl. Access Fees) $20,000
Library Holdings: CDs 300; DVDs 100; e-books 1,000; e-journals 300; Bk Titles 300,000; Bk Vols 500,000; Per Subs 400; Videos 300
Special Collections: Oral History; US Document Depository
Friends of the Library Group

PHILIP L MILSTEIN FAMILY COLLEGE LIBRARY, 208 Butler Library, 535 W 114th St, 10027, SAN 352-9479. Tel: 212-854-5327. Reference Tel: 212-854-0520. E-mail: undergrad@library.columbia.edu. Web Site: library.columbia.edu/locations/undergraduate.html. *Undergrad Serv Librn,* Anice Mills; E-mail: amills@columbia.edu; *Reserves Supvr,* Insaf M Ali; E-mail: ima2104@columbia.edu; Staff 2 (MLS 1, Non-MLS 1)
Founded 1998
Library Holdings: Bk Vols 92,000
Friends of the Library Group

ORIGINAL & SPECIAL MATERIALS CATALOGING, 102 Butler Library, 535 W 114th St, 10027, SAN 352-9487. Tel: 212-854-2714. FAX: 212-854-5167. *Dir,* Kate Harcourt; E-mail: harcourt@columbia.edu

RARE BOOK & MANUSCRIPT, Butler Library, 6th Flr E, 535 W 114th St, 10027, SAN 353-0167. Tel: 212-854-2231, 212-854-5590. Information Services Tel: 212-854-5153. FAX: 212-854-1365. E-mail: rbml@library.columbia.edu. Web Site: library.columbia.edu/locations/rbml.html. *Dir,* Sean Quimby; *Head, Access Serv, Univ Archivist,* Susan Hamson; Tel: 212-854-1331, E-mail: sgh2105@columbia.edu; *Bibliog Serv, Rare Bk Librn,* Jane Rogers Siegel; Tel: 212-854-8482, E-mail: jrs19@columbia.edu; *Ref Serv Supvr,* Tara Craig; *Curator, Bakhmeteff Archives,* Tanya Chebatarev; Tel: 212-854-3986, E-mail: tc241@columbia.edu; *Curator, Medieval & Renaissance Ms,* Consuelo Dutschke; Tel: 212-854-4139, E-mail: cwd3@columbia.edu; *Curator, Performing Arts & Exhibitions,* Jennifer B Lee; Tel: 212-854-4048, E-mail: jbl100@columbia.edu; *Lehman Curator, Am Hist,* Thai Jones; Tel: 212-854-9616, E-mail: tsj2001@columbia.edu. Subject Specialists: *Rare bks,* Jane Rogers Siegel; *Russian,* Tanya Chebatarev; Staff 14 (MLS 8, Non-MLS 6)
Special Collections: Carnegie Coll; Columbia Center for Oral History; Columbia University Archives; Herbert H Lehman Coll; Manuscripts Coll; Rare Book Coll; Russian & East European History & Culture (Bakhmeteff Archive). Oral History
Function: Res libr
Restriction: Non-circulating coll
Friends of the Library Group

RUSSIAN, EURASIAN & EAST EUROPEAN STUDIES, 306 International Affairs Bldg, 420 W 118th St, 10027, SAN 377-0109. Tel: 212-854-4701. FAX: 212-854-3834. E-mail: slavic@library.columbia.edu. Web Site: library.columbia.edu/locations/global/slavic.html. *Librn,* Robert H Davis, Jr

SCIENCE & ENGINEERING, 401 Northwest Corner Bldg, 550 W 120th St, MC 4707, 10027, SAN 352-9800. Tel: 212-854-2976. FAX: 212-854-3323. E-mail: scieng@library.columbia.edu. *Dir,* Jane Winland; E-mail: winland@columbia.edu

SOCIAL WORK LIBRARY, Columbia University School of Social Work, 1255 Amsterdam Ave, 2nd Flr, 10027, SAN 353-0078. Tel: 212-851-2194. Reference Tel: 212-851-2196. FAX: 212-851-2199. E-mail: socwk@library.columbia.edu. Web Site: www.columbia.edu/locations/social-work.html. *Head of Libr,* Alysse Jordan; Tel: 212-851-2195, E-mail: aj204@columbia.edu; *Libr Spec,* Dionne Harris-Jackman; Tel: 212-851-2197, E-mail: dch2001@columbia.edu; Staff 4 (MLS 1, Non-MLS 3)
Highest Degree: Doctorate
Special Collections: Gerontology (Brookdale Memorial Coll); Social Work Agency Coll
Function: AV serv, Handicapped accessible, ILL available, Ref serv available, Res libr, Telephone ref, Wheelchair accessible, Workshops
Open Mon 10-8, Tues-Thurs 10-9, Fri & Sat 10-6, Sun 12-8
Restriction: Open to students, fac & staff
Friends of the Library Group

C V STARR EAST ASIAN LIBRARY, 300 Kent Hall, MC 3901, 1140 Amsterdam Ave, 10027, SAN 353-0132. Tel: 212-854-4318. FAX: 212-662-6286. E-mail: starr@libraries.cul.columbia.edu. Web Site: library.columbia.edu/locations/eastasian.html. *Dir,* Jim Cheng; E-mail: jc3685@columbia.edu; *Head, Pub Serv,* Ria Koopmans-de Bruijn; *Head, Tech Serv,* Sarah S Elman; *Coll Develop/Ref Librn,* Lauran Hartley; *Coll Develop/Ref Librn,* Sachie Noguchi; *Coll Develop/Ref Librn,* Hee-sook Shin; *Coll Develop/Ref Librn,* Chengzhi Wang; *Evening/Weekend Librn,* Rongxiang Zhang; *Access Serv,* Kenneth Harlin; *Archivist, Pub Serv,* Beth Katzoff; Staff 14 (MLS 10, Non-MLS 4)
Founded 1902
Library Holdings: Bk Vols 1,000,000; Per Subs 7,500
Special Collections: Rare Book Coll
Subject Interests: Humanities, Lang, Lit, Soc sci

TEACHERS COLLEGE, GOTTESMAN LIBRARIES
See Separate Entry under Teachers College, Columbia University

THOMAS J WATSON LIBRARY OF BUSINESS & ECONOMICS, 130 Uris Hall, 3022 Broadway, 10027, SAN 352-9983. Tel: 212-854-7804. Reference Tel: 212-854-3383. FAX: 212-854-5723. E-mail: business@library.columbia.edu. Web Site: library.columbia.edu/locations/business.html. *Head of Libr,* Kathleen M Dreyer; Tel: 212-854-7804, E-mail: kd2145@columbia.edu; *Head, Access/Tech Serv,* Yasmin Saira; *Electronic Serv & Res Librn,* Peng Xu; E-mail: px2108@columbia.edu; *Access/Reserves Supvr,* Michael Lillard; Staff 23 (MLS 5, Non-MLS 18)
Highest Degree: Doctorate
Library Holdings: Bk Vols 400,000
Subject Interests: Bus, Econ
Database Vendor: EBSCOhost, LexisNexis, OCLC FirstSearch, ProQuest, Standard & Poor's, STN International, Wilson - Wilson Web
Function: Res libr
Open Mon-Wed 8am-12am, Thurs 8am-10pm, Fri 8am-9pm, Sat 10-9, Sun 10am-11pm
Restriction: Open to pub upon request, Residents only

THE GABE M WIENER MUSIC & ARTS LIBRARY, 701 Dodge Hall, 2960 Broadway, 10027, SAN 352-9657. Tel: 212-854-4711. FAX: 212-854-4748. E-mail: music@library.columbia.edu. Web Site: library.columbia.edu/locations/music.html. *Head Librn,* Elizabeth Davis; Tel: 212 854-7604, E-mail: davise@columbia.edu; *Music Librn,* Nick Patterson; E-mail: njp2@columbia.edu
Library Holdings: Bk Vols 80,000
Open Mon-Thurs 9-9, Fri 9-5, Sat 12-6, Sun 3-8

S CONDE NAST PUBLICATIONS LIBRARY*, Four Times Sq, 10036. SAN 311-7022. Tel: 212-286-8245. FAX: 212-286-6763. E-mail: library@condenast.com. Web Site: www.condenast.com. *Dir,* Cynthia Cathcart; *Librn,* Stanford Friedman; *Librn,* Deirdre Nolan; *Librn,* Florence Palomo
Founded 1935
Library Holdings: Bk Titles 3,000; Bk Vols 3,500; Per Subs 150
Subject Interests: Fashion
Automation Activity & Vendor Info: (Cataloging) TLC (The Library Corporation)
Restriction: Open by appt only

S CONDON & FORSYTH LIBRARY*, Seven Times Sq, 18th Flr, 10036. SAN 326-1875. Tel: 212-490-9100. FAX: 212-370-4453. Web Site: www.condonlaw.com. *Librn,* Antonietta Tatta
Founded 1922
Library Holdings: Bk Vols 10,000; Per Subs 76
Subject Interests: Aviation, Ins, Law
Restriction: Staff use only

R CONGREGATION EMANU-EL OF THE CITY OF NEW YORK*, Ivan M Stettenheim Library, One E 65th St, 10065-6596. SAN 312-0864. Tel: 212-744-1400. Circulation Tel: 212-744-1400, Ext 360. FAX: 212-570-0826. Web Site: www.emanuelnyc.org. *Librn,* Elizabeth F Stabler; E-mail: establer@emanuelnyc.org; Staff 1 (MLS 1)
Founded 1906
Library Holdings: Bk Vols 11,000; Per Subs 45; Spec Interest Per Sub 45; Talking Bks 75
Subject Interests: Judaica
Automation Activity & Vendor Info: (Acquisitions) Mandarin Library Automation; (Cataloging) Mandarin Library Automation; (Circulation) Mandarin Library Automation; (Course Reserve) Mandarin Library Automation; (Media Booking) Mandarin Library Automation; (OPAC) Mandarin Library Automation; (Serials) Mandarin Library Automation
Special Services for the Blind - Audio mat; Bks available with recordings; Bks on cassette; Bks on CD; Cassette playback machines; Cassettes; Large print bks; Sound rec; Soundproof reading booth
Open Mon-Thurs 10-6, Fri 10-2, Sun 10-4
Restriction: Non-circulating to the pub

S CONGREGATION SHEARITH ISRAEL ARCHIVES*, Eight W 70th St, 10023. SAN 327-2362. Tel: 212-873-0300. FAX: 212-724-6165. E-mail: office@shearithisrael.org. Web Site: www.shearithisrael.org. *In Charge,* Maria Caputo; E-mail: maria.caputo@shearithisrael.org
Founded 1840
Library Holdings: Bk Vols 500
Special Collections: Early Jewish Docs; Congregation Hist 1654-1900
Subject Interests: Orthodox theol
Restriction: Non-circulating, Ref only

L COOLEY LLP*, Law Library, 1114 Avenue of the Americas, 10036. SAN 372-2457. Tel: 212-479-6000. Interlibrary Loan Service Tel: 212-479-6025. Reference Tel: 212-479-6027. FAX: 212-479-6275. Web Site: www.cooley.com. *Firmwide Libr Mgr,* Gary Jaskula; E-mail: gjaskula@cooley.com; Staff 2 (Non-MLS 2)
Library Holdings: Bk Titles 2,000; Bk Vols 10,000; Per Subs 100
Automation Activity & Vendor Info: (Acquisitions) Softlink America; (Cataloging) Softlink America; (Serials) Softlink America
Restriction: Staff use only

C COOPER UNION FOR ADVANCEMENT OF SCIENCE & ART LIBRARY*, Seven E Seventh St, 10003. (Mail add: 30 Cooper Sq, 10003-8001), SAN 311-7081. Tel: 212-353-4186. Circulation Tel: 212-353-4188. Interlibrary Loan Service Tel: 212-353-4189. FAX: 212-353-4017. Web Site: www.cooper.edu/facilities/library/library.html. *Actg Libr Dir, Librn,* Carol Solomon; E-mail: solomo@cooper.edu; *Dir, Libr Serv,* Position Currently Open; *Librn,* Julie Castelluzzo; Tel: 212-353-4178, E-mail: juliec@cooper.edu; *Librn,* Claire Gunning; E-mail: gunning@cooper.edu; *Librn,* Thomas Micchelli; E mail: micche@cooper.edu. Subject Specialists: *Computer sci, Electrical eng,* Julie Castelluzzo; *Archit, Art,* Claire Gunning; *Art,* Thomas Micchelli; Staff 9 (MLS 6, Non-MLS 3)
Founded 1859. Enrl 967; Fac 54; Highest Degree: Master
Library Holdings: Bk Vols 136,711; Per Subs 170
Special Collections: Cooperana, bk & mss. US Document Depository
Subject Interests: Archit, Art, Eng
Automation Activity & Vendor Info: (Circulation) Ex Libris Group; (Course Reserve) Ex Libris Group; (OPAC) Ex Libris Group
Database Vendor: American Chemical Society, ARTstor, Dialog, Elsevier, H W Wilson, IEEE (Institute of Electrical & Electronics Engineers), Knovel, Material ConneXion, OCLC ArticleFirst, OCLC FirstSearch, OCLC WorldShare Interlibrary Loan, Project MUSE, ProQuest, Safari Books Online, Wilson - Wilson Web
Wireless access
Publications: Acquisitions Lists; Databases List; Faculty Guide
Partic in Metropolitan New York Library Council; Research Library Association of South Manhattan
Open Mon-Thurs 8:30am-9pm, Fri 9-6, Sat 11-5, Sun 12-5

S COPPER DEVELOPMENT ASSOCIATION*, Technical Reference Library, 260 Madison Ave, 16th Flr, 10016. SAN 311-7103. Tel: 212-251-7200. FAX: 212-251-7234. Web Site: www.copper.org. *VPres,* Harold Michels
Founded 1963
Subject Interests: Copper, Copper alloy tech
Publications: Accessions; Bulletin; Patent Brief; Thesaurus of Terms on Copper Technology
Open Mon-Fri 9-5

S COUNCIL ON FOREIGN RELATIONS LIBRARY*, 58 E 68th St, 10065. SAN 311-7154. Tel: 212-434-9400. Reference Tel: 212-434-9583. FAX: 212-434-9824. E-mail: clibrary@cfr.org. Web Site: www.cfr.org. *Dir, Libr & Res Serv,* Dr Lilita Gusts; E-mail: lgusts@cfr.org; Staff 6 (MLS 4, Non-MLS 2)
Founded 1930

Library Holdings: Bk Titles 11,000; Per Subs 210
Subject Interests: Econ, Hist, Intl law, Intl relations, Polit sci
Automation Activity & Vendor Info: (Cataloging) Softlink America
Database Vendor: Dialog, EBSCOhost, HeinOnline, Hoovers, JSTOR, LexisNexis, Marquis Who's Who, OCLC FirstSearch, Project MUSE, ProQuest
Partic in Lyrasis; Metropolitan New York Library Council; OCLC Online Computer Library Center, Inc
Restriction: Staff use only

L CRAVATH, SWAINE & MOORE LLP*, Law Library, 825 Eighth Ave, 10019. SAN 311-7162. Tel: 212-474-3500. FAX: 212-474-3556. Web Site: www.cravath.com. *Dir, Libr Serv,* Deborah Panella; E-mail: dspanella@cravath.com; *Assoc Dir,* Katherine Kenworthy
Founded 1819
Library Holdings: Bk Vols 50,000; Per Subs 400
Subject Interests: Antitrust, Corporate, Litigation, Tax
Automation Activity & Vendor Info: (Acquisitions) EOS International; (Cataloging) EOS International; (Circulation) EOS International; (Serials) EOS International
Database Vendor: Dialog, Factiva.com, LexisNexis, OCLC FirstSearch, Westlaw
Restriction: By permission only

L CURTIS, MALLET-PREVOST, COLT & MOSLE LIBRARY*, 101 Park Ave, 10178-0061. SAN 311-7197. Tel: 212-696-6138. FAX: 212-697-1559. Web Site: www.curtis.com. *Librn,* Heather Striebel; E-mail: hstriebel@curtis.com
Founded 1900
Library Holdings: Bk Vols 16,000
Special Collections: Central & South American Law
Automation Activity & Vendor Info: (Cataloging) SydneyPlus
Database Vendor: LexisNexis, Westlaw
Wireless access
Partic in Westlaw
Open Mon-Fri 9-5

S DANCE NOTATION BUREAU LIBRARY*, 111 John St, Ste 704, 10038. SAN 324-8054. Tel: 212-571-7011. FAX: 212-571-7012. E-mail: library@dancenotation.org. Web Site: www.dancenotation.org. *Dir of Libr Serv,* Mei-Chen Lu; Staff 1 (Non-MLS 1)
Founded 1940
Library Holdings: CDs 400; DVDs 600; Music Scores 150; Bk Titles 770; Videos 300
Special Collections: Audiotapes for Notated Dances; Benesh Notation Scores; Isaac Archive (Original Pencil Labanotation Scores); Music Scores & Supplementary Items for Individual Dances; Technical Papers on Labanotation
Subject Interests: Dance notation, Labanotation
Function: Archival coll, Mail & tel request accepted, Ref serv available
Publications: Notated Theatrical Dances: A Listing of Theatrical Dance Scores Housed at the Dance Notation Bureau (free catalogue)
Restriction: Open by appt only

L DAVIS POLK & WARDWELL LIBRARY*, 450 Lexington Ave, 10017. SAN 311-7235. Tel: 212-450-4266. FAX: 212-450-5522. Web Site: www.dpw.com. *Librn,* Daniel J Hanson; E-mail: hanson@dpw.com; *Online Serv,* Joseph Florio; *Tech Serv,* Laurie Wilson
Founded 1891
Library Holdings: Bk Vols 60,000; Per Subs 700
Special Collections: International Law; Legislature
Subject Interests: Antitrust, Banking, Securities, Taxation
Automation Activity & Vendor Info: (Acquisitions) Livelink for Libraries; (Cataloging) Livelink for Libraries; (Circulation) Livelink for Libraries
Database Vendor: Dialog, LexisNexis, Westlaw
Partic in Dialog Corp; OCLC Online Computer Library Center, Inc; Westlaw
Restriction: Staff use only

S DDB WORLDWIDE*, Information Center, 437 Madison Ave, 10022. SAN 311-7391. Tel: 212-415-2546. Web Site: www.ddb.com. *Dir,* Carmela Cangialosi
Founded 1958
Library Holdings: Bk Vols 6,000; Per Subs 300
Subject Interests: Advertising, Mkt
Database Vendor: Dialog, Factiva.com, LexisNexis, ProQuest, Wilson - Wilson Web
Restriction: Staff use only

L DEBEVOISE & PLIMPTON*, Law Library, 919 Third Ave, 10022. SAN 311-7251. Tel: 212-909-6275. FAX: 212-909-1025. Web Site: www.debevoise.com. *Dir, Libr Serv,* Steven A Lastres; Tel: 212-909-6279
Library Holdings: Bk Vols 30,000; Per Subs 150
Subject Interests: Aviation, Corp law, Litigation, Real estate, Securities, Taxation law
Automation Activity & Vendor Info: (Acquisitions) EOS International; (Cataloging) EOS International; (Circulation) EOS International; (ILL) EOS International; (OPAC) EOS International; (Serials) EOS International
Database Vendor: LexisNexis, Westlaw
Wireless access
Function: For res purposes
Restriction: Staff use only

L DECHERT LAW LIBRARY*, 1095 Ave of the Americas, 30th Fl, 10036. SAN 372-4549. Tel: 212-698-3500. FAX: 212-698-3599. Web Site: www.dechert.com. *Librn,* Brian Deaver; Tel: 212-698-3515, E-mail: brian.deaver@dechert.com; Staff 3 (MLS 2, Non-MLS 1)
Library Holdings: Bk Titles 1,500; Per Subs 150
Subject Interests: Corporate securities
Automation Activity & Vendor Info: (Cataloging) SirsiDynix; (Serials) SirsiDynix
Restriction: Staff use only

GM DEPARTMENT OF VETERANS AFFAIRS, NEW YORK HARBOR HEALTHCARE SYSTEM*, New York Campus Library, 423 E 23rd St, 10010. SAN 353-829X. Tel: 212-686-7500, Ext 7682. FAX: 212-951-3367. *Chief Librn,* Lori Winterfeldt; Tel: 212-686-7500, Ext 7675, E-mail: lori.winterfeldt@va.gov; Staff 4 (MLS 2, Non-MLS 2)
Founded 1956
Library Holdings: Bk Titles 10,000; Per Subs 420
Subject Interests: Patient health educ
Automation Activity & Vendor Info: (Cataloging) Follett Software; (Circulation) Follett Software
Partic in Metropolitan New York Library Council
Special Services for the Blind - Reader equip; Talking bks

J DEVRY COLLEGE OF NEW YORK LIBRARY*, 180 Madison Ave, 16th Flr, 10016-5267. SAN 375-4200. Tel: 212-312-4414. *Libr Dir,* Emily Turner; E-mail: eturner@devry.edu; *Ref Serv,* Grace Bazile; E-mail: gbazile@devry.edu; Staff 2 (MLS 2)
Subject Interests: Bus mgt, Electronics
Automation Activity & Vendor Info: (Cataloging) Ex Libris Group; (Circulation) Ex Libris Group; (OPAC) Ex Libris Group
Database Vendor: EBSCOhost
Wireless access
Open Mon-Fri 8am-9pm, Sat 10-3

L DLA PIPER US LLP*, Law Library, 1251 Avenue of Americas, 45th Flr, 10020-1104. SAN 372-4395. Tel: 212-776-3940. Web Site: www.dlapiper.com. *Head Librn,* Justine Kalka; E-mail: justine.kalka@dlapiper.com
Library Holdings: Bk Vols 8,000; Per Subs 50
Automation Activity & Vendor Info: (Acquisitions) Innovative Interfaces, Inc; (Cataloging) Innovative Interfaces, Inc; (Serials) Innovative Interfaces, Inc
Restriction: Staff use only

S DREYFUS CORP LIBRARY*, 200 Park Ave, 7th Flr, 10166. SAN 311-7405. Tel: 212-922-6087. FAX: 212-922-7018. E-mail: library@dreyfus.com. *Dir,* Clara Keriotis; *Librn,* Shirin Menon; Staff 4 (MLS 3, Non-MLS 1)
Founded 1962
Library Holdings: Bk Titles 300; Per Subs 400
Special Collections: Investment Companies
Subject Interests: Corp bus, Econ, Finance, Invest co
Automation Activity & Vendor Info: (Serials) EOS International
Database Vendor: LexisNexis
Function: Res libr
Restriction: Staff use only

S ENGLISH-SPEAKING UNION*, Ruth M Shellens Memorial Library, 144 E 39th St, 10016. SAN 311-7510. Tel: 212-818-1200. FAX: 212-867-4177. E-mail: info@esuus.org. Web Site: www.esuus.org. *Exec Dir,* Alice Boyne
Founded 1944
Library Holdings: Bk Titles 7,500
Special Collections: Ambassador Book Awards Winners; Biographies & Autobiographies of British & American Authors, 1900-1964 (Winifred Nerney Coll)
Subject Interests: Britain, United Kingdom
Restriction: Mem only

G ENVIRONMENTAL PROTECTION AGENCY*, Region 2 Library, 290 Broadway, 16th Flr, 10007. SAN 311-7529. Tel: 212-637-3185. FAX: 212-637-3086. E-mail: library.region2@epa.gov. Web Site: www.epa.gov/region2/library/. *Mgr,* Rebecca Garvin; Staff 2 (MLS 2)
Founded 1965

Library Holdings: CDs 58; Bk Titles 50,000; Videos 44
Special Collections: Hazardous Waste Coll
Subject Interests: Chem risk assessment, Drinking water, Environ law, Groundwater protection, Hazardous waste, Pesticides, Superfund, Toxic substance, Wetlands
Partic in Dialog Corp; OCLC Online Computer Library Center, Inc
Open Mon-Thurs 9-4
Restriction: Circulates for staff only, In-house use for visitors

L EPSTEIN, BECKER & GREEN*, Law Library, 250 Park Ave, 12th Flr, 10177. SAN 372-2414. Tel: 212-351-4695. FAX: 212-661-0989. Web Site: www.ebglaw.com. *Mgr, Libr Serv,* Janet Hefferle; *Ref Librn,* Nancy Moore
Library Holdings: Bk Vols 7,000; Per Subs 100
Automation Activity & Vendor Info: (Cataloging) Inmagic, Inc.; (Circulation) Inmagic, Inc.
Database Vendor: LexisNexis, Westlaw
Restriction: Staff use only

S THE EXPLORERS CLUB, Research Collections & James B Ford Library, 46 E 70th St, 10021. SAN 311-7553. Tel: 212-628-8383. FAX: 212-288-4449. E-mail: researchcollections@explorers.org. Web Site: www.explorers.org. *Chmn,* Rodney Hilton Brown; *Archivist & Curator of Res Col, Librn,* Lacey Flint; E-mail: lflint@explorers.org; Staff 2 (MLS 2)
Founded 1904
Library Holdings: Bk Titles 13,000; Per Subs 50
Special Collections: 18th - 20th Century Travel Coll; Polar Exploration Coll
Subject Interests: Exploration, Geog, Travel
Wireless access
Function: Ref serv available
Restriction: Not a lending libr, Open to pub by appt only

C FASHION INSTITUTE OF TECHNOLOGY-SUNY*, Gladys Marcus Library, Seventh Ave at 27th St, 10001-5992. SAN 311-7596. Tel: 212-217-4340. Circulation Tel: 212-217-4360. Interlibrary Loan Service Tel: 212-217-4364. Reference Tel: 212-217-4400. Administration Tel: 212-217-4370. FAX: 212-217-4371. Web Site: www.fitnyc.edu/library. *Dir,* NJ Wolfe; E-mail: nj_wolfe@fitnyc.edu; *Acq, Asst Dir, Coll Develop Officer,* Greta K Earnest; Tel: 212-217-4366, E-mail: greta_earnest@fitnyc.edu; *Head, Acq,* Leslie Preston; Tel: 212-217-4346, E-mail: leslie_preston@fitnyc.edu; *Head, Cat,* Janette M Rozene; Tel: 212-217-4358, E-mail: janette_rozene@fitnyc.edu; *Head, Res & Instrul Serv,* Helen Taylor Lane; Tel: 212-217-4407, E-mail: helen_lane@fitnyc.edu; *Head, Spec Coll & Archives,* Karen T Cannell; Tel: 212-217-4386, E-mail: karen_cannell@fitnyc.edu; *Electronic Res & Per Librn,* Lana Bittman; Tel: 212-217-4382, E-mail: lana_bittman@fitnyc.edu; *Access Serv Mgr/Day,* Lydia Gwyn; Tel: 212-217-4363, E-mail: lydia_gwyn@fitnyc.edu; *ILL Access & Serv Mgr/Evening,* Paul Lajoie; Tel: 212-217-4362, E-mail: paul_lajoie@fitnyc.edu; *Ref Fac,* Stephen Rosenberger; Tel: 212-217-4396, E-mail: stephen_rosenberger@fitnyc.edu; *Ref,* Beryl Rentof; Tel: 212-217-4401, E-mail: beryl_rentof@fitnyc.edu; *Syst,* Lorraine Weberg; Tel: 212-217-4398, E-mail: lorraine_weberg@fitnyc.edu; Staff 68 (MLS 23, Non-MLS 45)
Founded 1944. Enrl 10,065; Fac 989; Highest Degree: Master
Jul 2009-Jun 2010 Income $3,230,818, State $12,000, Locally Generated Income $40,000, Other $3,178,818. Mats Exp $308,458, Books $30,487, Per/Ser (Incl. Access Fees) $43,000, AV Equip $15,960, Electronic Ref Mat (Incl. Access Fees) $96,380. Sal $3,118,258 (Prof $1,375,380)
Library Holdings: Bk Vols 188,780; Per Subs 500; Videos 3,684
Special Collections: Fashion (sketch bks of fashion designs); Interviews of Members of the Fashion Industry. Oral History
Subject Interests: Fashion design, Fine arts, Gallery, Merchandising, Mus studies, Retail art admin
Automation Activity & Vendor Info: (Cataloging) Ex Libris Group; (Circulation) Ex Libris Group; (ILL) OCLC ILLiad; (OPAC) Ex Libris Group; (Serials) EBSCO Online
Database Vendor: 3M Library Systems, ARTstor, Atlas Systems, EBSCOhost, Ex Libris Group, Gale Cengage Learning, Greenwood Publishing Group, Hoovers, Ingenta, JSTOR, Material ConneXion, Mergent Online, OCLC FirstSearch
Publications: Acquisitions List; Bibliographies; Brochures/Pathfinders; Faculty Handbook; Library News & Notes; Subject Heading Brochures
Partic in Metropolitan New York Library Council; OCLC Online Computer Library Center, Inc
Restriction: Open to students, fac, staff & alumni, Photo ID required for access, Pub by appt only, Visitors must make appt to use bks in the libr

C FORDHAM UNIVERSITY LIBRARY AT LINCOLN CENTER*, Quinn Library, Leon Lowenstein Bldg, 113 W 60th St, 10023-7480. SAN 311-7731. Tel: 212-636-6050. Circulation Tel: 212-636-6062. FAX: 212-636-6766. Web Site: www.library.fordham.edu. *Dir of Libr,* Linda LoSchiavo; Tel: 718-817-3570; *Dep Dir,* Robert Allen; Tel: 212-636-6058, E-mail: rallen@fordham.edu; *Ref & Info Serv,* Nicholas Alongi; *Ref & Info Serv,* Bethany Jarret; *Ref & Info Serv,* David Vassar; Staff 6 (MLS 6)
Founded 1969. Enrl 6,841; Fac 262; Highest Degree: Doctorate
Library Holdings: Bk Vols 450,000; Per Subs 30,000; Videos 11,000
Special Collections: Education (ERIC Documents); Holocaust. US Document Depository
Subject Interests: Bus, Educ, Soc serv
Automation Activity & Vendor Info: (Circulation) SirsiDynix; (OPAC) SirsiDynix
Wireless access
Publications: Inside Fordham Libraries (Semi-annual)
Partic in Metropolitan New York Library Council; Westchester Academic Library Directors Organization (WALDO)
Open Mon-Thurs 8am-2am, Fri 8-8, Sat 9-7, Sun Noon-2am

CL FORDHAM UNIVERSITY SCHOOL OF LAW, The Maloney Library, 150 W 62nd St, 10023. SAN 311-7723. Tel: 212-636-6900. Circulation Tel: 212-636-7820. Interlibrary Loan Service Tel: 212-636-6909. Reference Tel: 212-636-6908. Administration Tel: 212-636-6904. FAX: 212-930-8818. Interlibrary Loan Service FAX: 212-636-7192. E-mail: refdesk@law.fordham.edu. Web Site: law.fordham.edu/library.htm. *Dir,* Robert J Nissenbaum; Tel: 212-636-7609, E-mail: rnissenbaum@law.fordham.edu; *Dep Dir,* Mary McKee; Tel: 212-636-6903, E-mail: mmckee@law.fordham.edu; *Head, Cat,* Yael Mandelstam; Tel: 212-636-7971, E-mail: ymandelstam@law.fordham.edu; *Head, Electronic Serv,* Jacob Sayward; Tel: 212-930-8882, E-mail: sayward@law.fordham.edu; *Head, Instrul Serv,* Lawrence Abraham; E-mail: labraham@law.fordham.edu; *Head, Ref,* Alissa Black-Dorward; Tel: 212-636-7968, E-mail: blackdorward@law.fordham.edu; *Assoc Librn, Pub Serv,* Todd Melnick; Tel: 212-636-7677, E-mail: tmelnick@law.fordham.edu; *Circ Librn,* David Goodwin; Tel: 212-636-6901, E-mail: dgoodwin@law.fordham.edu; *Foreign & Intl Law Librn,* Victor Essien; Tel: 212-636-6913, E-mail: vessien@law.fordham.edu; *Ref Librn,* Sarah Jaramillo; Tel: 212-636-7005, E-mail: sjaramillo@law.fordham.edu; *Foreign & Intl Law Spec, Ref Librn,* Alison Shea; Tel: 212-636-6751, E-mail: aashea@law.fordham.edu; *Cataloger,* Theodore Pitts; Tel: 212-636-7684, E-mail: tpitts@fordham.edu. Subject Specialists: *Estates, Trusts, Wills,* Robert J Nissenbaum; *Advan legal res, Legal res,* Jacob Sayward; *Advan legal res, Legal res,* Lawrence Abraham; *Advan legal res, Legal res,* Alissa Black-Dorward; *Advan legal res, Legal res,* Todd Melnick; *Advan legal res, Intl law, Intl trade,* Victor Essien; *Advan legal res, Legal res,* Sarah Jaramillo; *Advan legal res, Foreign/Intl law,* Alison Shea; Staff 15 (MLS 12, Non-MLS 3)
Founded 1905. Enrl 1,630; Fac 79; Highest Degree: Doctorate
Jul 2013-Jun 2014. Mats Exp $1,863,406, Books $232,686, Per/Ser (Incl. Access Fees) $1,126,506, Micro $12,556, Electronic Ref Mat (Incl. Access Fees) $432,821, Presv $58,837. Sal $1,738,726 (Prof $1,399,693)
Library Holdings: Bk Titles 372,513; Bk Vols 608,948; Per Subs 6,172; Videos 179
Special Collections: State Document Depository; US Document Depository
Subject Interests: Antitrust law, Banking law, Comparative law, Corporate law, European commun law, Foreign law, Human rights, Intl law, Legal ethics, Securities law
Automation Activity & Vendor Info: (Acquisitions) Innovative Interfaces, Inc - Millenium; (Cataloging) Innovative Interfaces, Inc - Millenium; (Circulation) Innovative Interfaces, Inc - Millenium; (Course Reserve) Innovative Interfaces, Inc - Millenium; (ILL) OCLC ILLiad; (OPAC) Innovative Interfaces, Inc - Millenium; (Serials) Innovative Interfaces, Inc - Millenium
Database Vendor: Bloomberg, Bowker, Cassidy Cataloguing Services, Inc, CQ Press, ebrary, EBSCOhost, Fastcase, Gale Cengage Learning, H W Wilson, Haworth Pres Inc, HeinOnline, Innovative Interfaces, Inc, JSTOR, LexisNexis, Marcive, Inc, OCLC FirstSearch, OCLC WorldShare Interlibrary Loan, OCLC-RLG, Oxford Online, Paratext, ProQuest, Sage, SerialsSolutions, Swets Information Services, Thomson Carswell, Westlaw, Wilson - Wilson Web, YBP Library Services
Wireless access
Function: Art exhibits, Copy machines, Exhibits, ILL available, Online cat, Ref serv in person, Scanner
Publications: Law Library Guide (Library handbook); Learned Handy Research Guides
Partic in American Association of Law Libraries (AALL); Association of Jesuit Colleges & Universities (AJCU); Legal Information Preservation Alliance (LIPA); New England Law Library Consortium, Inc; OCLC Online Computer Library Center, Inc; Westchester Academic Library Directors Organization (WALDO)
Open Mon-Sun 8am-1am
Restriction: Borrowing privileges limited to fac & registered students, Open to students, fac, staff & alumni

S FOUNDATION CENTER LIBRARY*, 79 Fifth Ave, 10003-3076. SAN 311-774X. Tel: 212-620-4230. Toll Free Tel: 800-424-9836. FAX: 212-691-1828. E-mail: library@foundationcenter.org. Web Site: www.foundationcenter.org. *Dir,* Jimmy Tom; Staff 9 (MLS 6, Non-MLS 3)
Founded 1956
Library Holdings: Bk Titles 4,600; Bk Vols 5,000; Per Subs 85

Special Collections: Foundation Annual Reports; Foundation Directory Online Database
Subject Interests: Corporate grants, Found grants, Fundraising, Nonprofit mgt, Philanthropy, Pvt found
Publications: A Nonprofit Organization Operating Manual; America's Voluntary Spirit; Foundation 1000; Foundation Directory; Foundation Directory Part II; Foundation Fundamentals; Foundation Grants Index (Quarterly); Foundation Grants to Individuals; Foundations Today Series; Grant Guides; Guide to US Foundation, their Trustees Officers & Donors; Literature of the Nonprofit Sector; Managing for Profit in the Nonprofit World; National Directory of Corporate Giving; New York State Foundations; Philanthropy & Volunteerism; Philanthropy in Action; Promoting Issues & Ideas; Securing Your Organization's Future; The Board Members Book; The Foundation Center's Guide to Proposal Writing; The Foundation Center's User-Friendly Guide; The Twenty-First Century Nonprofit
Partic in Consortium of Foundation Libraries; Dialog Corp
Special Services for the Blind - Computer with voice synthesizer for visually impaired persons
Open Tues & Thurs-Sat 10-5, Wed 10-8
Restriction: Circ limited

S FRENCH INSTITUTE-ALLIANCE FRANCAISE LIBRARY*, Haskell Library, 22 E 60th St, 10022-1077. SAN 311-7774. Tel: 212-355-6100. Circulation Tel: 646-388-6655. Information Services Tel: 646-388-6656. FAX: 212-935-4119. E-mail: library@fiaf.org. Web Site: www.fiaf.org. *Dir,* Katharine Branning; Tel: 646-388-6614, E-mail: kbranning@fiaf.org; *Libr Serv Coordr,* Ronda Murdock; Tel: 646-388-6636, E-mail: rmurdock@fiaf.org; *Libr Assoc,* Jessica Feinman; Tel: 646-388-6638, E-mail: jfeinman@fiaf.org; *Lit Develop Assoc,* Yann Carmona; Tel: 646-388-6639, E-mail: ycarmona@fiaf.org; Staff 4 (MLS 1, Non-MLS 3)
Founded 1911
Jul 2006-Jun 2007. Mats Exp $40,000, Books $9,000, Per/Ser (Incl. Access Fees) $12,000, AV Equip $2,000, AV Mat $8,000, Electronic Ref Mat (Incl. Access Fees) $7,000, Presv $2,000. Sal $180,400
Library Holdings: AV Mats 9,000; CDs 2,500; Large Print Bks 500; Bk Vols 45,000; Per Subs 102; Videos 2,500
Subject Interests: Archit, Art, Civilization, Fr speaking countries, Geog, Hist, Lit, Philos, Tourism
Automation Activity & Vendor Info: (Acquisitions) BiblioMondo; (Cataloging) BiblioMondo; (Circulation) BiblioMondo; (Course Reserve) BiblioMondo; (ILL) BiblioMondo; (Media Booking) BiblioMondo; (OPAC) BiblioMondo; (Serials) BiblioMondo
Wireless access
Publications: Acquisitions List; Newsletter
Partic in Metropolitan New York Library Council
Open Mon-Thurs 11:30-8, Sat 9:30-3
Restriction: Open to pub for ref only
Friends of the Library Group

L FRESHFIELDS BRUCKHAUS DERINGER US LLP*, 520 Madison Ave, 34th Flr, 10022. Tel: 212-277-4084. Interlibrary Loan Service Tel: 212-284-4933. FAX: 646-521-5684. *Info Serv Mgr, Librn,* Benjamin Toby; E-mail: benjamin.toby@freshfields.com; *Asst Librn,* Elizabeth Nicholson; Tel: 212-284-4933, Fax: 646-521-5733, E-mail: elizabeth.nicholson@freshfields.com; Staff 2 (MLS 1, Non-MLS 1)
Founded 1999
Function: Online cat, Ref serv available, Res performed for a fee
Restriction: Authorized patrons, Borrowing requests are handled by ILL, Circ limited, Co libr, Employees & their associates, External users must contact libr, Internal circ only, Not open to pub, Private libr, Use of others with permission of librn

S THE FRICK COLLECTION, Frick Art Reference Library, Ten E 71st St, 10021. SAN 311-7782. Tel: 212-288-8700. Reference Tel: 212-547-0641. Administration Tel: 212-547-0656. Information Services Tel: 212-547-6889. FAX: 212-879-2091. Web Site: www.frick.org. *Chief Librn,* Stephen Bury; *Coll Develop,* Inge Reist; *Coll Mgt,* Deborah Kempe; Staff 21 (MLS 12, Non-MLS 9)
Founded 1920
Jul 2013-Jun 2014 Income $3,500,000. Mats Exp $478,000, Books $250,000, Per/Ser (Incl. Access Fees) $40,000, Electronic Ref Mat (Incl. Access Fees) $38,000, Presv $150,000. Sal $2,400,000 (Prof $1,800,000)
Library Holdings: CDs 350; e-journals 120; Electronic Media & Resources 70; Microforms 170; Bk Titles 450,000; Bk Vols 453,000; Per Subs 530
Special Collections: Artist Files; Auction Catalogs; Exhibition Catalogs. Oral History
Subject Interests: Decorative art, Drawing, Hist of collecting, Hist of painting, Sculpture
Automation Activity & Vendor Info: (Acquisitions) Innovative Interfaces, Inc; (Cataloging) Innovative Interfaces, Inc; (Circulation) Innovative Interfaces, Inc; (ILL) OCLC; (OPAC) Innovative Interfaces, Inc; (Serials) Innovative Interfaces, Inc
Function: Res libr
Publications: Frick Art Reference Library Original Index to Art Periodicals (1983); Frick Art Reference Library Sales Catalogue Index (1992); Spanish Artists from the Fourth to the Twentieth Century; The Story of the Frick Art Reference Library: The Early Years (1979); Vol 1 (A-F) (1993)
Partic in Metropolitan New York Library Council; New York Art Resources Consortium (NYARC); OCLC Research Library Partnership
Open Mon-Fri 10-5, Sat (Sept-May) 9:30-1
Restriction: Closed stack, Non-circulating, Photo ID required for access

L FRIED, FRANK, HARRIS, SHRIVER & JACOBSON LIBRARY*, One New York Plaza, 10004. SAN 311-7790. Tel: 212-859-4886. FAX: 212-859-8000. E-mail: nylibrary@ffhsj.com. Web Site: www.ffhsj.com. *Dir,* Nancy Rine; *Ref Librn,* Marcy Cabanas
Founded 1960
Library Holdings: Bk Vols 30,000; Per Subs 110
Subject Interests: Corporate, Fed, Securities, State law
Database Vendor: LexisNexis, Westlaw
Open Mon-Fri 9:30-7

CM HELENE FULD COLLEGE OF NURSING*, Learning Center Library, 1879 Madison Ave, 10035. SAN 327-1919. Tel: 212-616-7200, 212-616-7269. FAX: 212-616-7269. Web Site: www.helenefuld.edu. *Dir,* Indrajeet Singh
Library Holdings: AV Mats 688; Bk Vols 6,000; Per Subs 101
Automation Activity & Vendor Info: (Cataloging) Surpass; (Circulation) Surpass
Database Vendor: EBSCOhost
Wireless access
Open Mon-Thurs 8-7:45, Fri 8-4

S THE GENERAL SOCIETY OF MECHANICS & TRADESMEN LIBRARY*, 20 W 44th St, 10036. SAN 311-7839. Tel: 212-921-1767. FAX: 212-840-2046. E-mail: library@generalsociety.org.
Founded 1820
Library Holdings: Bk Titles 110,000; Per Subs 30
Special Collections: General Society of Mechanics & Tradesmen Archives
Subject Interests: Archit, Arts, Construction, Hist of work & tech, Labor hist, NY, Urban trades & crafts
Automation Activity & Vendor Info: (Acquisitions) Softlink America; (Cataloging) Softlink America; (Circulation) Softlink America; (OPAC) Softlink America
Wireless access
Function: Archival coll, Photocopying/Printing, Res libr
Partic in Metropolitan New York Library Council
Open Mon & Thurs 11-7, Tues & Wed 11-5, Fri 9-5
Restriction: Sub libr
Friends of the Library Group
Branches:
THE NEW YORK CENTER FOR INDEPENDENT PUBLISHING, 20 W 44th St, 10036. Tel: 212-764-7021. Web Site: www.generalsociety.org. *In Charge,* Malena Rogers; E-mail: mrogers@generalsociety.org
Library Holdings: Bk Titles 1,600
Restriction: Mem only

SR GENERAL THEOLOGICAL SEMINARY*, Christoph Keller Jr Library, 440 West 21st St, 10011. SAN 311-7847. Tel: 212-243-5150. FAX: 212-924-6304. E-mail: library@gts.edu. Web Site: library.gts.edu. *Dir,* Fr Andrew Kadel; *Archives, Ref & Info Serv,* Mary Robison; E-mail: robison@gts.edu; *Circ,* Dr Laura Moore; Tel: 646-717-9784, E-mail: moore@gts.edu; *Tech Serv,* Patrick Cates; E-mail: cates@gts.edu; Staff 3 (MLS 3)
Founded 1819. Enrl 120; Fac 20; Highest Degree: Doctorate
Library Holdings: Bk Titles 150,000; Bk Vols 180,000; Per Subs 250
Special Collections: Clement Clarke Moore Coll; Early English Church Theology Coll; Episcopal Church Hist (coll on the Protestant Episcopal Church in the United States); Latin Bible Coll; Liturgics
Subject Interests: Anglican, Christian hist, Liturgics, Spirituality, Theol
Automation Activity & Vendor Info: (Acquisitions) Ex Libris Group; (Cataloging) Ex Libris Group; (Circulation) Ex Libris Group; (Course Reserve) Ex Libris Group; (OPAC) Ex Libris Group; (Serials) Ex Libris Group
Database Vendor: EBSCOhost, JSTOR, OCLC WorldShare Interlibrary Loan, SerialsSolutions
Wireless access
Function: Archival coll, Audio & video playback equip for onsite use, Computers for patron use, Copy machines, Electronic databases & coll, Exhibits, ILL available, Microfiche/film & reading machines, Online cat
Partic in Metropolitan New York Library Council; NY Area Theol Libr Asn; OCLC Online Computer Library Center, Inc
Open Mon-Thurs 8am-11pm, Fri 8-8, Sat 9-7, Sun 2-10

Restriction: Borrowing privileges limited to fac & registered students, Non-circulating of rare bks, Non-circulating to the pub, Open to students, fac, staff & alumni
Friends of the Library Group

S HENRY GEORGE SCHOOL OF SOCIAL SCIENCE*, Research Library, 121 E 30th St, 10016. SAN 374-5767. Tel: 212-889-8020. FAX: 212-889-8953. E-mail: hengeoschool@worldnet.att.net. Web Site: www.henrygeorgeschool.org. *Librn,* Vesa J Nelson
Founded 1937
Library Holdings: Bk Titles 5,000
Special Collections: Henry George & Family, bks (incl rare ed), clippings, letters; Land Value Tax/Single Tax (Georgist Authors Coll), bks, journal-art, clippings, theses
Automation Activity & Vendor Info: (Cataloging) JayWil Software Development, Inc; (Circulation) JayWil Software Development, Inc
Wireless access
Open Mon-Thurs 10-6

L GIBSON, DUNN & CRUTCHER*, Research & Information Management Department, 200 Park Ave, 48th Flr, 10166-0193. SAN 323-5688. Tel: 212-351-4005. Interlibrary Loan Service Tel: 212-351-4006. FAX: 212-351-6262. E-mail: nylibrary@gibsondunn.com. Web Site: www.gibsondunn.com. *Librn,* Steven Raber; E-mail: sraber@gibsondunn.com; Staff 3 (MLS 3)
Founded 1987
Library Holdings: Bk Titles 600
Subject Interests: Litigation, Securities
Automation Activity & Vendor Info: (OPAC) EOS International
Database Vendor: Bloomberg, Checkpoint Systems, Inc, CQ Press, Dun & Bradstreet, EOS International, HeinOnline, Hoovers, JSTOR, LexisNexis, OCLC FirstSearch, Westlaw
Wireless access
Partic in American Association of Law Libraries (AALL); SLA
Open Mon-Fri 9:30-6

S GLOBAL INTELLIGENCE GROUP*, 285 Madison Ave, 10th Flr, 10017. SAN 312-150X. Tel: 212-210-3983. FAX: 212-210-3918. *Dir,* Stephen Fleming; *Res Spec,* Joshua Chodakowsky; *Res Spec,* Matthew Flynn; Staff 4 (MLS 3, Non-MLS 1)
Founded 1953
Library Holdings: Bk Vols 4,000; Per Subs 220
Subject Interests: Advertising, Mkt

J GLOBE INSTITUTE OF TECHNOLOGY*, Library & Information Center, 500 Seventh Ave, 10018. Tel: 212-349-4330. Toll Free Tel: 877-394-5623. Web Site: www.globe.institute.edu. *Mgr,* Alicia Kobak; E-mail: akobak@globe.edu
Founded 1985
Library Holdings: Electronic Media & Resources 20; Bk Titles 7,000; Bk Vols 16,000; Per Subs 56
Special Collections: Black Experience; Classics; Popular Fiction
Automation Activity & Vendor Info: (Acquisitions) Follett Software; (Cataloging) Follett Software; (Circulation) Follett Software; (Course Reserve) Follett Software; (ILL) Follett Software; (OPAC) Follett Software; (Serials) Follett Software
Database Vendor: EBSCOhost, Gale Cengage Learning
Wireless access
Open Mon-Fri 9-9, Sat & Sun 9-4
Restriction: Open to students, fac & staff

S GOETHE-INSTITUT NEW YORK*, German Cultural Center Library, 72 Spring St, 11th Flr, 10012. SAN 311-7871. Tel: 212-439-8688. Toll Free Tel: 877-463-8431. FAX: 212-439-8705. E-mail: library@newyork.goethe.org. Web Site: www.goethe.de/newyork. *Dir,* Elisabeth Pyroth; Tel: 212-439-8700; *Ref Serv,* Katherine Lorimer; Staff 3 (MLS 2, Non-MLS 1)
Founded 1957
Library Holdings: Audiobooks 500; AV Mats 1,500; CDs 1,000; DVDs 700; e-books 1,000; e-journals 5; Bk Vols 9,000; Per Subs 60
Subject Interests: German (Lang)
Database Vendor: OCLC FirstSearch
Wireless access
Function: Adult bk club, Art exhibits, Audio & video playback equip for onsite use, Bks on CD, Computers for patron use, Copy machines, e-mail serv, Free DVD rentals, ILL available, Magnifiers for reading, Mail & tel request accepted, Mail loans to mem, Music CDs, Online cat, Online ref, Photocopying/Printing, Prof lending libr, Pub access computers, Ref serv available, Ref serv in person, Spoken cassettes & CDs, Spoken cassettes & DVDs, Telephone ref, Video lending libr, Web-catalog
Open Mon & Fri 12-5, Tues-Thurs 12-6:30
Restriction: Circ to mem only, In-house use for visitors, Open to pub for ref & circ; with some limitations, Open to students

M GOLDWATER MEMORIAL HOSPITAL*, Health Sciences Library, 900 Main, Roosevelt Island, 10001. SAN 311-7898. Tel: 212-318-4800. Reference Tel: 212-318-4376. FAX: 212-318-4628. *Dir,* William Jones; *Asst Dir,* Frank Pavel; E-mail: frank.pavel@nychhc.org
Founded 1939
Library Holdings: Bk Vols 13,680; Per Subs 386
Subject Interests: Chronic disease, Geriatrics, Hearing, Med, Rehabilitation med, Speech
Wireless access
Publications: Acquisition List
Partic in Metropolitan New York Library Council; OCLC Online Computer Library Center, Inc
Restriction: Open by appt only

L GREENBERG TRAURIG LLP*, Research Center Law Library, 200 Park Ave, 10166. SAN 372-4476. Tel: 212-801-9200. FAX: 212-801-6400. Web Site: www.gtlaw.com. *Mgr,* Position Currently Open
Library Holdings: Bk Vols 10,000
Automation Activity & Vendor Info: (Acquisitions) Ex Libris Group; (Cataloging) Ex Libris Group; (Circulation) Ex Libris Group; (Course Reserve) Ex Libris Group; (ILL) Ex Libris Group; (Media Booking) Ex Libris Group; (OPAC) Ex Libris Group; (Serials) Ex Libris Group
Database Vendor: HeinOnline, Hoovers, LexisNexis, Westlaw
Open Mon-Fri 9-8

S GROLIER CLUB OF NEW YORK LIBRARY*, 47 E 60th St, 10022. SAN 311-7952. Tel: 212-838-6690. FAX: 212-838-2445. Web Site: www.grolierclub.org. *Librn,* Meghan Constantinou; Tel: 212-838-6690, Ext 5, E-mail: mconstantinou@grolierclub.org; Staff 6 (MLS 1, Non-MLS 5)
Founded 1884
Library Holdings: Bk Vols 100,000; Per Subs 200
Special Collections: Archives of Book Collectors, Bookish Societies & Antiquarian Bookdealers; Book Trade & Auction Catalogs; Examples of Fine Printing & Binding; History of Printing & Book Collecting; Inventories of Private Libraries; Portraits of Authors, Printers & Artists; Rare Bibliography
Automation Activity & Vendor Info: (Cataloging) Innovative Interfaces, Inc; (OPAC) Innovative Interfaces, Inc
Wireless access
Partic in RLIN (Research Libraries Information Network)
Open Mon-Fri (Sept-July) 10-5

S THE HAMPDEN BOOTH THEATRE LIBRARY AT THE PLAYERS*, 16 Gramercy Park S, 10003. SAN 312-0015. Tel: 212-228-1861. FAX: 212-253-6473. *Librn,* Raymond Wemmlinger
Founded 1957
Library Holdings: Bk Titles 10,000; Per Subs 25
Special Collections: 18th-19th Century English Playbills (William Henderson Coll); Burlesque (Chuck Callahan Coll); Cabinet; Edwin Booth; Franklin; George M Cohan; Heller; La Mama Experimental Theatre Club Coll, playbills, doc; Maurice Evans; Off-Off Broadway Theatre; Photographs; Pipenight; Players; Robert B Mantell; Stage Charities (British Actors Orphanage Fund Coll), correspondence, doc; Union Square Theatre; Walter Hampden
Subject Interests: Hist of Am stage, Hist of English stage

M HARLEM HOSPITAL MEDICAL CENTER*, Health Sciences Library, 506 Lenox Ave, KP6108, 10037. SAN 353-1066. Tel: 212-939-1685. *Dir,* James Swanton; E-mail: swantonj@nychhc.org
Founded 1907
Library Holdings: Bk Titles 5,000; Per Subs 30
Subject Interests: Med, Nursing
Automation Activity & Vendor Info: (Cataloging) Professional Software; (Circulation) Professional Software; (Serials) Professional Software
Wireless access
Partic in Basic Health Sciences Library Network; Manhattan-Bronx Health Sciences Libraries Group; Metropolitan New York Library Council
Open Mon-Fri 8:30-4:45

S HARVARD LIBRARY IN NEW YORK*, 35 W 44th St, 10036. SAN 311-8002. Tel: 212-827-1246. FAX: 212-827-1251, Ext 1246. *Librn,* Adrienne G Fischier; Staff 2 (MLS 2)
Founded 1978
Library Holdings: Bk Vols 24,000
Special Collections: Harvardiana
Open Mon-Fri 10-9

S HATCH-BILLOPS COLLECTION, INC LIBRARY*, Archive of Black American Cultural History, 491 Broadway, 7th Flr, 10012. SAN 326-551X. Tel: 212-966-3231. FAX: 212-966-3231. E-mail: hatchbillops@gmail.com. Web Site: hatch-billopscollection.org. *Archivist,* Camille Billops; *Archivist,* James Hatch
Founded 1975
Library Holdings: AV Mats 600; Bk Vols 3,000

Special Collections: Oral History
Wireless access
Publications: Artist & Influence
Restriction: Open by appt only

L HAWKINS, DELAFIELD & WOOD*, Law Library, One Chase Manhattan Plaza, 10005. SAN 311-8010. Tel: 212-820-9444. FAX: 212-344-6258. *Libr Dir,* Kathryn McRae; Staff 4 (MLS 1, Non-MLS 3)
Library Holdings: Bk Vols 10,000; Per Subs 50
Automation Activity & Vendor Info: (Cataloging) Inmagic, Inc.; (Circulation) Inmagic, Inc.; (OPAC) Inmagic, Inc.
Restriction: Not open to pub

S HAZEN & SAWYER, PC*, Information Research Center, 498 Seventh Ave, 10018. Tel: 212-539-7093. FAX: 212-614-9049. E-mail: irc@hazenandsawyer.com. Web Site: www.hazenandsawyer.com. *Managing Librn,* Sara J Steen; Tel: 212-539-7164, E-mail: ssteen@hazenandsawyer.com; Staff 2 (MLS 2)
Founded 1951
Library Holdings: AV Mats 117; Electronic Media & Resources 50; Bk Titles 3,400; Per Subs 82
Subject Interests: Civil eng, Construction, Environ eng, Mechanical eng, Structural eng, Waste water treatment, Water, Water treatment
Automation Activity & Vendor Info: (Acquisitions) Inmagic, Inc.; (Cataloging) Inmagic, Inc.; (Circulation) Inmagic, Inc.; (OPAC) Inmagic, Inc.; (Serials) Inmagic, Inc.
Wireless access
Publications: IRC Digest (Newsletter)
Partic in Metropolitan New York Library Council
Restriction: Co libr

S THE HEALTHCARE CHAPLAINCY*, Spears Center for Pastoral Research Library, 307 E 60th St, 10022. Tel: 212-644-1111, Ext 235. FAX: 212-486-7060. E-mail: library@healthcarechaplaincy.org. Web Site: www.healthcarechaplaincy.org. *Librn,* Sandra Lee Jamison; E-mail: sjamison@healthcarechaplaincy.org; Staff 1 (MLS 1)
Founded 1997
Library Holdings: Bk Titles 3,000; Bk Vols 4,000; Per Subs 100
Subject Interests: Pastoral care, Spirituality
Automation Activity & Vendor Info: (Cataloging) EOS International; (Circulation) EOS International; (OPAC) EOS International
Database Vendor: EBSCOhost
Wireless access
Partic in Metropolitan New York Library Council
Restriction: Open by appt only

CR HEBREW UNION COLLEGE-JEWISH INSTITUTE OF RELIGION*, Klau Library, Brookdale Ctr, HUC-JIR, One W Fourth St, 10012-1186. SAN 353-1120. Tel: 212-674-5300. FAX: 212-388-1720. Web Site: huc.edu/libraries/NY. *Librn,* Yoram Bitton; Tel: 212-674-5300, Ext 2261, E-mail: ybitton@huc.edu; *Assoc Librn,* Tina Weiss; E-mail: tweiss@huc.edu; Staff 3 (MLS 2, Non-MLS 1)
Founded 1922
Library Holdings: Bk Titles 135,000; Per Subs 250
Subject Interests: Hebrew lit, Hist, Relig studies
Automation Activity & Vendor Info: (Cataloging) Innovative Interfaces, Inc; (Circulation) Innovative Interfaces, Inc; (OPAC) Innovative Interfaces, Inc; (Serials) Innovative Interfaces, Inc
Wireless access
Open Mon-Thurs 9-5, Fri 9-3

S HISPANIC SOCIETY OF AMERICA LIBRARY, 613 W 155th St, 10032. SAN 311-8061. Tel: 212-926-2234, Ext 229. Reference Tel: 212-926-2234, Ext 260. FAX: 212-690-0743. E-mail: library@hispanicsociety.org. Web Site: www.hispanicsociety.org. *Curator,* Dr John O'Neill; Tel: 212-926-2234, Ext 251, E-mail: oneill@hispanicsociety.org; *Asst Curator,* Edwin Xavier Rolon; Tel: 212-926-2234, Ext 262, E-mail: rolon@hispanicsociety.org; *Asst Librn,* William Delgado; *Asst Librn,* Vanessa Pintado; E-mail: pintado@hispanicsociety.org. Subject Specialists: *Manuscripts, Rare bks,* Dr John O'Neill; *Modern bks,* Edwin Xavier Rolon; *Rare bks,* Vanessa Pintado; Staff 6 (MLS 3, Non-MLS 3)
Founded 1904
Library Holdings: Bk Vols 300,000; Per Subs 142
Special Collections: Golden Age Drama Manuscript Coll; Medieval Manuscripts Coll; Rare Book Coll
Subject Interests: Archaeology, Art, Customs, Hist, Lit
Automation Activity & Vendor Info: (Acquisitions) Mandarin Library Automation; (Cataloging) Mandarin Library Automation; (OPAC) Mandarin Library Automation
Function: Ref serv available, Res libr
Open Tues-Sat 10-4:15
Restriction: Closed stack, Non-circulating

L HOGAN & HARTSON LLP LAW LIBRARY*, 875 Third Ave, 25th Flr, 10022. SAN 326-1212. Tel: 212-918-3000, 212-918-6117. FAX: 212-918-3100. Web Site: www.hhlaw.com. *Librn,* Elizabeth Ohman; E-mail: etohman@hhlaw.com
Founded 1980
Library Holdings: Bk Titles 400; Bk Vols 6,500; Per Subs 27
Automation Activity & Vendor Info: (Cataloging) Sydney; (Circulation) Sydney; (OPAC) Sydney
Database Vendor: Dialog, LexisNexis, Westlaw
Open Mon-Fri 8-6

L HOLLAND & KNIGHT LLP*, Law Library, 31 W 52nd St, 10019. SAN 311-7987. Tel: 212-513-3580. FAX: 212-385-9010. E-mail: library@hklaw.com. Web Site: www.hklaw.com. *Head Librn,* Helen Akulich; Tel: 212-513-3581
Subject Interests: Admiralty, Aviation
Database Vendor: HeinOnline, Westlaw
Restriction: Mem only

S HOLLAND SOCIETY OF NEW YORK LIBRARY*, 20 W 44th St, 5th Fl, 10036. SAN 311-807X. Tel: 212-758-1871. FAX: 212-758-2232. E-mail: hsnylibrary@gmail.com. Web Site: www.hollandsociety.org/library.html. *Librn,* Mary Collins; Staff 1 (MLS 1)
Founded 1885
Library Holdings: Bk Titles 7,000; Per Subs 20
Special Collections: Genealogy & Related Subjects Focusing on Dutch Culture & Heritage (Dutch American Colonial History Coll)
Subject Interests: Am colonial hist, Dutch Am genealogy, New Netherland
Automation Activity & Vendor Info: (Cataloging) JayWil Software Development, Inc
Wireless access
Publications: De Halve Maen Journal; New York Historical Manuscripts
Open Tues-Thurs 11:30-5
Restriction: Fee for pub use

S HORTICULTURAL SOCIETY OF NEW YORK, INC LIBRARY*, 148 W 37th St, 13th Flr, 10018. SAN 311-810X. Tel: 212-757-0915, Ext 109. FAX: 212-246-1207. Web Site: www.hsny.org. *In Charge,* George Pisegna; Tel: 212-757-0915, Ext 115; Staff 1 (MLS 1)
Founded 1922
Library Holdings: Bk Titles 10,000; Per Subs 95
Special Collections: Golden Age of American Gardens 1890-1940 (incl Garden, Landscape & Horticulture Index), archives, per
Subject Interests: Botanical illustration, Garden design, Gardening, Landscape design
Automation Activity & Vendor Info: (Cataloging) OCLC CatExpress; (OPAC) SydneyPlus
Database Vendor: EBSCOhost, OCLC FirstSearch
Wireless access
Partic in Council on Botanical & Horticultural Libraries, Inc (CBHL); Metropolitan New York Library Council
Open Mon-Fri 10-6
Restriction: Open to pub for ref only

M HOSPITAL FOR SPECIAL SURGERY*, Kim Barrett Memorial Library, 535 E 70th St, 10021. SAN 311-8126. Tel: 212-606-1000, 212-606-1210. FAX: 212-774-2779. *Librn,* Tim Roberts; Staff 1 (Non-MLS 1)
Founded 1952
Library Holdings: Bk Titles 4,200; Per Subs 112
Subject Interests: Orthopaedic surgery, Orthopedics, Rheumatic diseases
Database Vendor: OVID Technologies
Wireless access
Partic in Metropolitan New York Library Council
Restriction: Open to staff only
Friends of the Library Group

L HUGHES, HUBBARD & REED LIBRARY*, Law Library, One Battery Park Plaza, 16th Flr, 10004. SAN 311-8142. Tel: 212-837-6666. Interlibrary Loan Service Tel: 212-837-6670. FAX: 212-422-4726. E-mail: library@hugheshubbard.com. *Dir, Libr Serv,* Patricia E Barbone; Tel: 212-837-6594, E-mail: barbone@hugheshubbard.com; Staff 6 (MLS 3, Non-MLS 3)
Founded 1942
Library Holdings: Bk Titles 5,500; Bk Vols 30,000; Per Subs 1,200
Subject Interests: Corporate securities, Labor, Litigation, Product liability, Securities law, Tax
Automation Activity & Vendor Info: (Cataloging) Cassidy Cataloguing Services, Inc; (Serials) EOS International
Database Vendor: Dialog, Dun & Bradstreet, Factset, HeinOnline, Hoovers, LexisNexis, OCLC FirstSearch, Westlaw, Westlaw Business
Function: ILL available
Partic in RLIN (Research Libraries Information Network)
Restriction: Not open to pub

S HUGUENOT SOCIETY OF AMERICA LIBRARY*, 20 W 44th St, Ste 510, 10036. SAN 327-1935. Tel: 212-755-0592. FAX: 212-317-0676. *In Charge,* Mary Bertschmann
Founded 1883
Library Holdings: Bk Vols 3,000
Subject Interests: Genealogy, Manuscripts
Restriction: Open by appt only

C HUNTER COLLEGE LIBRARIES*, Leon & Toby Cooperman Library, 695 Park Ave, 10065. SAN 353-1155. Tel: 212-772-4146. Circulation Tel: 212-772-4166. Interlibrary Loan Service Tel: 212-772-4192. Reference Tel: 212-772-4180. FAX: 212-772-4142. Web Site: library.hunter.cuny.edu. *Chief Librn,* Dan Cherubin; Tel: 212-772-4143, E-mail: daniel.cherubin@hunter.cuny.edu; *Actg Dep Chief Librn,* Clay Williams; Tel: 212-772-4144, E-mail: clwillia@hunter.cuny.edu; *Head Librn, Art Slide Libr,* Steven Kowalik; Tel: 212-772-5054, E-mail: skowalik@hunter.cuny.edu; *Head, Access Serv,* David Donabedian; Tel: 212-772-4176; *Head, Res & Instruction,* Philip Swan; Tel: 212-396-6733, E-mail: pswan@hunter.cuny.edu; *Head, Syst,* Ilan Zelazny; Tel: 212-772-4171, E-mail: izelazny@hunter.cuny.edu; *Acq/Coll Develop Librn,* Linda Dickinson; Tel: 212-772-4168, E-mail: ldickins@hunter.cuny.edu; *Instrul Design Librn,* Stephanie Margolin; *Ref/Outreach Librn,* Sarah Laleman Ward; Tel: 212-772-4108, E-mail: sara.ward@hunter.cuny.edu; *Sci Librn,* Mason Brown; Tel: 212-772-4191, E-mail: mbr0010@hunter.cuny.edu; *Ser Librn,* Lisa Finder; Tel: 212-772-4186, E-mail: lfinder@hunter.cuny.edu; *Coordr, Ref Serv (Acting),* Patricia Woodard; Tel: 212-650-3653, E-mail: pwoodard@hunter.cuny.edu; *Archivist,* Julio Hernandez-Delgado; Tel: 212-772-4149, E-mail: jhernand@hunter.cuny.edu; *Cat,* Wendy Tan; Tel: 212-772-4173; *ILL,* Gowen Campbell; Tel: 212-396-6168, E-mail: gcampbel@hunter.cuny.edu; *Pub Serv,* Danise Hoover; Tel: 212-772-4190, E-mail: dhoover@hunter.cuny.edu; Staff 48 (MLS 26, Non-MLS 22)
Founded 1870. Enrl 21,295; Fac 1,568; Highest Degree: Master
Jul 2007-Jun 2008 Income (Main and Other College/University Libraries) $4,586,343. Mats Exp $1,602,394, Books $207,130, Per/Ser (Incl. Access Fees) $937,000, Other Print Mats $17,376, Micro $35,876, AV Mat $9,772, Electronic Ref Mat (Incl. Access Fees) $367,290, Presv $27,950. Sal $2,957,685 (Prof $2,420,780)
Library Holdings: AV Mats 14,055; e-books 6,240; e-journals 46,131; Electronic Media & Resources 156; Bk Vols 798,148; Per Subs 962; Videos 432
Special Collections: Archives of the Hunter College Alumni Association; Early English Novels (Stonehill Coll); Eileen Cowe Historical Textbooks; Lenox Hill Neighborhood Coll; Women's City Club of NY Coll
Automation Activity & Vendor Info: (Acquisitions) Ex Libris Group; (Cataloging) Ex Libris Group; (Circulation) Ex Libris Group; (Course Reserve) Ex Libris Group; (ILL) OCLC; (OPAC) Ex Libris Group; (Serials) Ex Libris Group
Database Vendor: 3M Library Systems, ARTstor, Cambridge Scientific Abstracts, Dialog, EBSCOhost, Gale Cengage Learning, ISI Web of Knowledge, JSTOR, LexisNexis, OCLC FirstSearch, OCLC WorldShare Interlibrary Loan, OVID Technologies, ProQuest, PubMed, ScienceDirect, Wilson - Wilson Web
Wireless access
Function: Archival coll, Computers for patron use, Copy machines, Doc delivery serv, E-Reserves, Electronic databases & coll, Handicapped accessible, ILL available, Learning ctr, Magnifiers for reading, Online cat, Online ref, Orientations, Outreach serv, Prof lending libr, Pub access computers, Ref & res, Ref serv available, Ref serv in person, Referrals accepted, Res libr, Spoken cassettes & CDs, Spoken cassettes & DVDs, Telephone ref, VHS videos, Video lending libr, Web-catalog, Wheelchair accessible
Partic in Metropolitan New York Library Council; OCLC Online Computer Library Center, Inc
Restriction: Authorized patrons, Borrowing privileges limited to fac & registered students, Circ privileges for students & alumni only, Open to fac, students & qualified researchers
Friends of the Library Group

Departmental Libraries:

CENTRO - CENTER FOR PUERTO RICAN STUDIES LIBRARY, 2180 Third Ave, Rm 121, 10035, SAN 325-7533. Tel: 212-396-7874. FAX: 212-396-7707. E-mail: centro.library@hunter.cuny.edu. Web Site: centropr.hunter.cuny.edu. *Assoc Dir, Chief Librn,* Alberto Hernandez; Tel: 212-396-7876, E-mail: alberto.hernandez@hunter.cuny.edu; *Ref & Flm Librn,* Felix A Rivera; Tel: 212-396-7880, E-mail: xrivera@hunter.cuny.edu; *Cataloger/Ref Librn,* Helvetia M Martell; *Digitization Coordr,* Diego F Valencia; *Sr Archivist,* Pedro Juan Hernandez; Tel: 212-396-7877, E-mail: dhernand@hunter.cuny.edu; *Libr Asst,* Yosenex Orengo; Staff 9 (MLS 5, Non-MLS 4)
Founded 1973
Library Holdings: AV Mats 500; Bk Vols 25,000
Special Collections: Archival Holdings on the Puerto Rican Diaspora; Dissertations on Puerto Rican Subjects; Film Coll on Puerto Rican Themes; Microforms on Latino Periodicals in New York; Monographs on Puerto Rican/Latino Studies Subjects; Oral History Coll; Periodicals/Microforms on Puerto Rico; Photographic Coll of the Puerto Rican Migration
Subject Interests: Latino studies, Puerto Rican studies
Function: Art exhibits, Bilingual assistance for Spanish patrons, CD-ROM, Computers for patron use, Copy machines, e-mail serv, Electronic databases & coll, Newsp ref libr, Online ref, Online searches, Orientations, Outside serv via phone, mail, e-mail & web, Photocopying/Printing, Pub access computers, Ref serv available, Serves mentally handicapped consumers, Telephone ref, VHS videos, Wheelchair accessible
Open Mon-Fri 10-5
Restriction: Non-circulating coll, Non-circulating to the pub, Not a lending libr, Open to pub for ref only, Open to students, fac & staff, Photo ID required for access, Pub ref by request

CM HEALTH PROFESSIONS LIBRARY, Hunter College Brookdale Campus, 425 E 25th St, 10010, SAN 353-118X. Tel: 212-481-5117. FAX: 212-772-5116. *Head of Libr,* John Carey; E-mail: john.carey@hunter.cuny.edu; *Instrul & Ref Librn,* John Pell; E-mail: jpell@hunter.cuny.edu; Staff 5 (MLS 3, Non-MLS 2)
Founded 1909. Highest Degree: Doctorate
Library Holdings: Bk Vols 26,000; Per Subs 330
Automation Activity & Vendor Info: (Circulation) Ex Libris Group

SCHOOLS OF SOCIAL WORK & PUBLIC HEALTH LIBRARY, 2180 Third Ave, 10035, SAN 353-121X. Tel: 212-396-7654. *Asst Prof, Interim Head of Libr,* Margaret Bausman; E-mail: mbausman@hunter.cuny.edu; Staff 4 (MLS 2, Non-MLS 2)
Founded 1969
Library Holdings: Bk Vols 47,386; Per Subs 139

L HUNTON & WILLIAMS*, Law Library, 200 Park Ave, 10166. SAN 371-8433. Tel: 212-309-1000. Interlibrary Loan Service Tel: 212-309-1077. FAX: 212-309-1100. *Librn,* Alina Alvarez-Lenda; Tel: 212-309-1078, E-mail: aalvarez-lenda@hunton.com; Staff 2 (Non-MLS 2)
Library Holdings: Bk Titles 25,000; Per Subs 5,000
Subject Interests: Legal
Automation Activity & Vendor Info: (Acquisitions) Sydney; (Cataloging) Sydney; (Circulation) Sydney; (OPAC) Sydney; (Serials) Sydney
Database Vendor: Bloomberg, HeinOnline, Hoovers, LexisNexis, Westlaw, Westlaw Business
Function: ILL available
Restriction: Co libr

S INSURANCE INFORMATION INSTITUTE LIBRARY*, 110 William St, 10038. SAN 324-6272. Tel: 212-346-5533. FAX: 212-267-9591. Web Site: www.iii.org. *Librn,* Madine Singer; E-mail: madines@iii.org
Founded 1960
Library Holdings: Bk Titles 1,500; Bk Vols 2,000; Per Subs 130
Subject Interests: Casualty ins, Property ins
Automation Activity & Vendor Info: (Acquisitions) Inmagic, Inc.; (Cataloging) Inmagic, Inc.; (Circulation) Inmagic, Inc.; (Course Reserve) Inmagic, Inc.; (ILL) Inmagic, Inc.; (Media Booking) Inmagic, Inc.; (OPAC) Inmagic, Inc.; (Serials) Inmagic, Inc.
Database Vendor: Factiva.com, LexisNexis
Wireless access
Restriction: Open by appt only

SR INTERCHURCH CENTER*, Ecumenical Library, 475 Riverside Dr, Rm 900, 10115. SAN 311-8266. Tel: 212-870-3804. FAX: 212-870-2440. Web Site: www.interchurch-center.org/ecumenical_library.html. *Librn,* Tracey Del Duca; E-mail: tdelduca@interchurch-center.org; Staff 2 (MLS 1, Non-MLS 1)
Founded 1978
Library Holdings: Bk Titles 15,500; Per Subs 95
Special Collections: Denominational Yearbooks; Religious Research Projects (H Paul Douglass), micro
Subject Interests: Missions, Nonprofit mgt, Relig, Soc problems
Automation Activity & Vendor Info: (ILL) OCLC; (OPAC) TLC (The Library Corporation)
Database Vendor: OCLC FirstSearch
Function: Res libr
Partic in Metropolitan New York Library Council; NY Area Theol Libr Asn
Restriction: Mem only, Open to others by appt

S INTERNATIONAL CENTER OF PHOTOGRAPHY LIBRARY*, Concourse, 1114 Avenue of the Americas, 10036-7703. SAN 324-1823. Tel: 212-857-0004. FAX: 212-857-0091. E-mail: library@icp.org. Web Site: www.icp.org. *Chief Librn,* Deirdre Donohue; E-mail: ddonohue@icp.org; Staff 2 (MLS 1.5, Non-MLS 0.5)
Founded 1977
Library Holdings: Bk Vols 18,000; Per Subs 75
Special Collections: Oral History
Automation Activity & Vendor Info: (Cataloging) OCLC; (OPAC) LibraryWorld, Inc

Wireless access
Restriction: Open to pub by appt only
Friends of the Library Group

S INTERNATIONAL TRADEMARK ASSOCIATION LIBRARY*, 655 Third Ave 10th Flr, 10017. SAN 312-1208. Tel: 212-768-9887. FAX: 212-768-7796. Web Site: www.inta.org. *Supvr,* Melissa Starr
Founded 1878
Library Holdings: Bk Titles 2,000; Per Subs 18
Subject Interests: Trademarks
Open Mon-Fri 9-5

S ISTITUTO ITALIANO DI CULTURA, BIBLIOTECA*, 686 Park Ave, 10065. SAN 311-8347. Tel: 212-879-4242. FAX: 212-861-4018. E-mail: visualarts.iicnewyork@esteri.it. Web Site: www.iicnewyork.esteri.it. *Actg Librn, In Charge,* Vincent Fuccillo
Founded 1959
Library Holdings: Bk Titles 8,000
Subject Interests: Italy
Open Mon-Fri 9-4

L JACKSON LEWIS LLP*, Law Library, 666 Third Ave, 29th Flr, 10017-4030. SAN 372-4247. Tel: 212-545-4033. *Dir, Info Serv,* Catherine M Dillon
Library Holdings: Bk Vols 10,000
Automation Activity & Vendor Info: (Acquisitions) Inmagic, Inc.; (Cataloging) Inmagic, Inc.
Wireless access

S JAPAN SOCIETY*, C V Starr Library, 333 E 47th St, 10017. SAN 311-8355. Tel: 212-715-1273. FAX: 212-715-1279. Web Site: www.japansociety.org. *Dir,* Reiko Sassa; Staff 1 (MLS 1)
Library Holdings: Bk Titles 14,000; Per Subs 116
Subject Interests: Archit, Art, Econ, Hist, Lang arts
Restriction: Authorized patrons, Employees only, Mem only

S JBI INTERNATIONAL*, Jewish Braille Institute of America, 110 E 30th St, 10016. SAN 327-1994. Tel: 212-889-2525. Toll Free Tel: 800-433-1531. FAX: 212-689-3692. E-mail: library@jbilibrary.org. Web Site: www.jbilibrary.org. *Librn,* Arlene Arfe; *Librn,* Inna Suholutsky; *Libr Distribution Mgr,* Barry Pelofsky
Founded 1931
Library Holdings: Audiobooks 13,000; Braille Volumes 68,000; Large Print Bks 1,000; Bk Titles 13,000; Spec Interest Per Sub 4; Talking Bks 13,000
Subject Interests: Jewish bks, Jewish per
Publications: Concert, Lecture & Poetry Series - Audio (Monthly); JBI Voice - Audio (Monthly); Jewish Braille Review - Braille (Monthly); The JBI Periodicals Series - Audio (Monthly)
Special Services for the Blind - Bks & mags in Braille, on rec, tape & cassette; Bks on cassette; Braille & cassettes; Children's Braille; Club for the blind; Digital talking bk; Extensive large print coll; Home delivery serv; Large print bks; Large print bks & talking machines; Production of talking bks; Rec of textbk mat; Student ref mat taped; Talking bks
Open Mon-Fri 9-5

S JEWISH BOARD OF FAMILY & CHILDREN SERVICES*, Mary & Louis Robinson Library, 120 W 57th St, 10019. SAN 327-1978. Tel: 212-582-9100, Ext 1504. FAX: 212-956-0526. *Librn,* Melanie Meyers Cushman; E-mail: mcushman@jbfcs.org; Staff 1 (MLS 1)
Founded 1968
Library Holdings: Bk Vols 5,000; Per Subs 60
Subject Interests: Mental health
Automation Activity & Vendor Info: (Cataloging) JayWil Software Development, Inc; (Circulation) JayWil Software Development, Inc
Wireless access
Restriction: Staff use only

S JEWISH EDUCATION SERVICE*, Resource Center, 318 W 39th St, 5th Flr, 10018. SAN 327-201X. Tel: 212-284-6950. FAX: 212-284-6951. Web Site: www.jesna.org. *Head, Tech Serv,* Stephan Gross
Subject Interests: Jewish educ
Wireless access

S THE JEWISH MUSEUM*, National Jewish Archive of Broadcasting, 1109 Fifth Ave, 10128. SAN 326-3274. Tel: 212-423-3234. FAX: 212-423-3232. E-mail: njab@thejm.org. Web Site: www.thejewishmuseum.org. *Assoc Curator,* Aviva Weintraub; *Asst Curator,* Andrew Ingall; *AV Coordr,* Niger Miles; Staff 3 (Non-MLS 3)
Founded 1981
Library Holdings: Bk Titles 4,300
Special Collections: Holocaust (Israel State Archives & Eichmann Trial Coll), v-tapes; The Jewish Experience (Television & Radio Program AV Recordings)
Wireless access
Publications: A Subject Guide to the Collection of the National Jewish Archive of Broadcasting; Annotated Catalogue of Selected Holdings of the Jewish Museum's National Jewish Archive of Broadcasting; Brochures
Restriction: Non-circulating to the pub

R JEWISH THEOLOGICAL SEMINARY LIBRARY*, 3080 Broadway, 10027. SAN 311-8398. Tel: 212-678-8075. Circulation Tel: 212-678-8082. Interlibrary Loan Service Tel: 212-678-8963. Reference Tel: 212-678-8081. FAX: 212-678-8891, 212-678-8998. E-mail: library@jtsa.edu, srr@jtsa.edu. Web Site: www.jtsa.edu/library. *Dir, Libr Serv,* Naomi M Steinberger; Tel: 212-678-8982, E-mail: nsteinberger@jtsa.edu; *Librn,* Dr David Kraemer; E-mail: drkramer@jtsa.edu; *Pub Serv Librn,* Rena Borow; Tel: 212-678-8970, E-mail: reborow@jtsa.edu; *Spec Coll Librn,* Jerry Schwarzbard; Tel: 212-678-8973, E-mail: jschwarzbard@jtsa.edu; *Tech Serv Librn,* Sara Spiegel; Tel: 212-678-8093, E-mail: saspiegel@jtsa.edu; Staff 14.5 (MLS 11, Non-MLS 3.5)
Founded 1903. Enrl 450; Fac 30; Highest Degree: Doctorate
Library Holdings: AV Mats 8,000; CDs 150; DVDs 45; e-books 250; e-journals 100; Music Scores 6,000; Bk Vols 400,000; Per Subs 788; Videos 1,250
Special Collections: Bible Coll; Hebrew Incunabula, archives; Hebrew Manuscripts, micro; Liturgical Works; Rabbinics; Rare Books
Subject Interests: Bible, Hebrew lit, Israel, Jewish hist, Judaism, Liturgy, Rabbinics
Automation Activity & Vendor Info: (Acquisitions) Ex Libris Group; (Cataloging) Ex Libris Group; (Circulation) Ex Libris Group; (Course Reserve) Ex Libris Group; (ILL) Ex Libris Group; (OPAC) Ex Libris Group; (Serials) Ex Libris Group
Wireless access
Function: Archival coll, Audio & video playback equip for onsite use, Copy machines, Distance learning, Doc delivery serv, e-mail & chat, e-mail serv, E-Reserves, Electronic databases & coll, Exhibits, ILL available, Mail & tel request accepted, Online cat, Online ref, Online searches, Ref & res, Ref serv available, Ref serv in person, Scanner, Web-catalog
Publications: News from the Library
Partic in Metropolitan New York Library Council; OCLC Online Computer Library Center, Inc
Open Mon-Thurs 8-8, Sun 10-7:30
Restriction: Photo ID required for access
Friends of the Library Group

C JOHN JAY COLLEGE OF CRIMINAL JUSTICE*, Lloyd George Sealy Library, 899 Tenth Ave, 10019. SAN 311-8401. Tel: 212-237-8246, 212-237-8265. Circulation Tel: 212-237-8225. Interlibrary Loan Service Tel: 212-237-8257. Reference Tel: 212-237-8247. FAX: 212-237-8221. Web Site: www.lib.jjay.cuny.edu. *Chief Librn,* Dr Larry E Sullivan; E-mail: lsullivan@jjay.cuny.edu; *Assoc Librn, Info Syst,* Bonnie R Nelson; Tel: 212-237-8267, E-mail: bnelson@jjay.cuny.edu; *Assoc Librn, Pub Serv,* Janice Dunham; Tel: 212-237-8256, E-mail: jdunham@jjay.cuny.edu; *Circ Librn,* Jeffrey Kroessler; Tel: 212-237-8236, E-mail: jkroessler@jjay.cuny.edu; *Coll Develop Librn,* Maria Kiriakova; Tel: 212-237-8260, E-mail: mkiriakova@jjay.cuny.edu; *Electronic Res Librn, Media Librn,* Nancy Egan; Tel: 212-237-8269, E-mail: negan@jjay.cuny.edu; *ILL Librn,* Karen Okamoto; *Instruction Librn,* Marvelous Brooks; Tel: 212-237-8261, E-mail: mbrooks@jjay.cuny.edu; *Reserves Librn,* Kathleen Collins; Tel: 212-237-8242, E-mail: kcollins@jjay.cuny.edu; *Ser Librn,* Dolores Grande; Tel: 212-237-8235, E-mail: dgrande@jjay.cuny.edu; *Archives, Spec Coll Librn,* Ellen Belcher; Tel: 212-237-8238, E-mail: ebelcher@jjay.cuny.edu; *Tech Serv Coordr,* Marlene Kandel; Tel: 212-237-8237, E-mail: mkandel@jjay.cuny.edu; *Info Literacy,* Ellen Sexton; Tel: 212-237-8258, E-mail: esexton@jjay.cuny.edu. Subject Specialists: *Info syst,* Bonnie R Nelson; Staff 15.7 (MLS 14.4, Non-MLS 1.3)
Founded 1965. Enrl 11,000; Fac 325; Highest Degree: Master
Jul 2005-Jun 2006. Mats Exp $668,070, Books $90,424, Per/Ser (Incl. Access Fees) $542,000, Presv $10,445
Library Holdings: e-books 42,062; e-journals 26,000; Bk Vols 247,969; Per Subs 14,374
Special Collections: Flora R Schreiber Papers; New York Criminal Court Transcripts & Records 1890-1920; NYC Police Dept Blotters, Manhatten 1920-1933; Police Department Annual Reports; Sing Sing Prison (Warden Lewis E Lawes Papers)
Subject Interests: Criminal justice, Fire serv admin, Forensic psychol, Pub admin, Sci
Automation Activity & Vendor Info: (Acquisitions) Ex Libris Group; (Cataloging) Ex Libris Group; (Circulation) Ex Libris Group; (Course Reserve) Docutek; (ILL) OCLC; (OPAC) Ex Libris Group; (Serials) Ex Libris Group
Wireless access
Publications: Newsletter; Research Guides; Self-Guided Workbooks
Partic in Criminal Justice Info Exchange; OCLC Online Computer Library Center, Inc
Restriction: Limited access for the pub, Open to students, fac, staff & alumni

S JUILLIARD SCHOOL*, Lila Acheson Wallace Library, 60 Lincoln Center Plaza, 10023-6588. SAN 311-8436. Tel: 212-799-5000, Ext 265. FAX: 212-769-6421. E-mail: library@juilliard.edu. Web Site: www.juilliard.edu/library/lib.html. *VPres, Libr & Info Serv,* Jane Gottlieb; E-mail: gottlieb@juilliard.edu; *Head, Cat,* Patricia Thomson; E-mail: pthomson@juilliard.edu; *Head, Tech Serv,* Alan Klein; E-mail: aklein@juilliard.edu; *Archivist,* Jeni Dahmus; Tel: 212-799-5000, Ext 367, E-mail: jdahmus@juilliard.edu; *Cat,* Brien Weiner; E-mail: bweiner@juilliard.edu; *Media Spec, Ad,* Sandra Czajkowski; E-mail: sczajkowski@juilliard.edu; Staff 13 (MLS 6, Non-MLS 7)
Founded 1905. Enrl 1,769; Fac 300; Highest Degree: Doctorate
Library Holdings: AV Mats 700; CDs 14,000; DVDs 700; Music Scores 70,000; Bk Titles 25,000; Per Subs 230; Videos 1,385
Special Collections: First & Early Editions of Liszt Piano Works; Flutes (Julius Baker & Samuel Boeran Colls); Juilliard Manuscript Coll, autographs, first eds, sketchbks; Kneisel Hall Archives; Opera Librettos of 19th Century; Opera Piano-Vocal Scores; Soulima & Igor Stravinsky Coll
Subject Interests: Dance, Drama, Music
Automation Activity & Vendor Info: (Acquisitions) Innovative Interfaces, Inc; (Cataloging) Innovative Interfaces, Inc; (Circulation) Innovative Interfaces, Inc; (Course Reserve) Innovative Interfaces, Inc; (ILL) Innovative Interfaces, Inc; (Media Booking) Innovative Interfaces, Inc; (OPAC) Innovative Interfaces, Inc; (Serials) Innovative Interfaces, Inc
Database Vendor: Alexander Street Press, ARTstor, EBSCOhost, Innovative Interfaces, Inc, JSTOR, OCLC FirstSearch
Wireless access
Publications: Guide to The Juilliard School Archives
Partic in Metropolitan New York Library Council; OCLC Online Computer Library Center, Inc
Open Mon-Thurs (Winter) 8:30am-9pm, Fri 8:30-7, Sat 9-5, Sun 2-7; Mon-Thurs (Summer) 9-5
Restriction: Open to researchers by request, Open to students, fac & staff
Friends of the Library Group

L JULIEN & SCHLESINGER, PC*, Attorneys at Law Library, One Whitehall St, 10004. SAN 311-8444. Tel: 212-962-8020. *In Charge,* Michael Schlesinger; E-mail: michaels@jstriallaw.com
Library Holdings: Bk Vols 6,000; Per Subs 32
Subject Interests: Litigation
Restriction: Not open to pub

L KATTEN MUCHIN ROSENMAN LLP*, Law Library, 575 Madison Ave, 10022-2585. SAN 312-0384. Tel: 212-940-8800. Reference Tel: 212-940-7017. FAX: 212-940-8776. Web Site: www.kattenlaw.com. *Ref Librn,* Monica Shenkerman; Staff 3 (MLS 3)
Founded 1946
Library Holdings: Bk Vols 50,000; Per Subs 700
Automation Activity & Vendor Info: (Acquisitions) EOS International; (Cataloging) EOS International; (Circulation) EOS International; (ILL) EOS International; (Serials) EOS International
Database Vendor: LexisNexis, Westlaw
Wireless access
Restriction: Staff use only

L KAYE SCHOLER LLP*, Information Resource Center, 425 Park Ave, 10022. SAN 311-8479. Tel: 212-836-8000, 212-836-8312. FAX: 212-836-6613. *Dir,* Shabeer Khan; *Info Spec,* Brian Blaho; Tel: 212-836-8550; *Info Spec,* Heather Hochstatter; *Info Spec,* Cherryl Stephen; Tel: 212-836-7217; *ILL,* Sabrina Busgith; Staff 12 (MLS 5, Non-MLS 7)
Subject Interests: Banking, Bankruptcy, Copyright, Corporate, Emerging markets, Estates, Labor, Latin Am, Law antitrust, Real estate, Tax, Trademarks, Wills
Automation Activity & Vendor Info: (Acquisitions) EOS International; (Cataloging) EOS International; (Circulation) EOS International; (Course Reserve) EOS International; (ILL) EOS International; (Media Booking) EOS International; (OPAC) EOS International; (Serials) EOS International
Database Vendor: Bloomberg, Carroll Publishing, Checkpoint Systems, Inc, Dialog, Dun & Bradstreet, Elsevier, EOS International, Factiva.com, HeinOnline, IEEE (Institute of Electrical & Electronics Engineers), LexisNexis, MD Consult, MicroPatent, OCLC FirstSearch, ProQuest, ScienceDirect, Westlaw, Wiley InterScience
Wireless access
Restriction: Open by appt only

L KELLEY DRYE & WARREN*, Law Library, 101 Park Ave, 10178. SAN 327-2052. Tel: 212-808-7800. FAX: 212-808-7897. Web Site: www.kelleydrye.com. *Mgr, Libr Serv,* Patricia Renze; E-mail: prenze@kelleydrye.com; *Asst Librn,* Ann Caulfield; *Ref,* Sandra Stuart
Library Holdings: Bk Vols 25,000; Per Subs 100
Automation Activity & Vendor Info: (Cataloging) EOS International; (Circulation) EOS International; (OPAC) EOS International
Wireless access
Open Mon-Fri 8-4

L KENYON & KENYON LLP, Law Library, One Broadway, 10th Flr, 10004-1007. SAN 372-4409. Tel: 212-425-7200. Administration Tel: 212-908-6122. FAX: 212-908-6113. Administration FAX: 212-425-5288. Web Site: www.kenyon.com. *Dir, Libr & Info Serv,* Lucy Curci-Gonzalez; E-mail: lcurcigonzalez@kenyon.com; *Bus Info Spec,* Diane M Leo; Tel: 212-908-6100, E-mail: dleo@kenyon.com; *Info Spec, ILL,* Timothy Butler; Tel: 212-908-6166, E-mail: tbutler@kenyon.com; *Info Spec,* Richard A Matula; Tel: 212-908-6123, E-mail: rmatula@kenyon.com; *Cataloger,* Robin Johnson; Tel: 212-908-6045, E-mail: rjohnson@kenyon.com. Subject Specialists: *Bus res,* Diane M Leo; *Doc delivery,* Timothy Butler; *Patent, Sci,* Richard A Matula; Staff 4.5 (MLS 1.5, Non-MLS 3)
Founded 1979
Library Holdings: Bk Vols 21,000; Per Subs 200
Subject Interests: Intellectual property law
Automation Activity & Vendor Info: (Cataloging) Inmagic, Inc.; (Circulation) Inmagic, Inc.; (OPAC) Inmagic, Inc.
Database Vendor: Bloomberg, Dun & Bradstreet, HeinOnline, Hoovers, IEEE (Institute of Electrical & Electronics Engineers), LexisNexis, Loislaw, MicroPatent, OCLC FirstSearch, OCLC WorldShare Interlibrary Loan, ProQuest, Springer-Verlag, STN International, Westlaw
Wireless access
Restriction: Private libr

L KIRKLAND & ELLIS*, Law Library, 153 E 53rd St, 10022. SAN 372-2317. Tel: 212-446-4990. FAX: 212-446-4900. Web Site: www.kirkland.com. *Libr Serv Mgr,* Paulette Toth; E-mail: paulette.Toth@kirkland.com
Automation Activity & Vendor Info: (Cataloging) SirsiDynix; (OPAC) SirsiDynix
Database Vendor: Bloomberg, Dialog, HeinOnline, Hoovers, LexisNexis, Westlaw
Open Mon-Fri 9-7

L KRAMER, LEVIN, NAFTALIS & FRANKEL LLP*, Law Library, 1177 Avenue of the Americas, 10036. SAN 372-4212. Tel: 212-715-9321. FAX: 212-715-8000. E-mail: librarygroup@kramerlevin.com. Web Site: www.kramerlevin.com. *Dir,* Daniel J Pelletier; E-mail: dpelletier@kramerlevin.com; *Head, Ref Serv,* Brian Boyle; *Asst Librn,* Eileen Dolan; *Ref Librn,* Elise Ng; *Ref,* Evelyn Gomez
Library Holdings: Bk Titles 5,000; Bk Vols 15,000; Per Subs 300
Automation Activity & Vendor Info: (Acquisitions) Sydney; (Cataloging) Sydney; (Circulation) Sydney; (Course Reserve) Sydney; (ILL) Sydney; (Media Booking) Sydney; (OPAC) Sydney; (Serials) Sydney
Database Vendor: HeinOnline, LexisNexis, Westlaw
Open Mon-Fri 9-7

L LATHAM & WATKINS*, Law Library, 885 Third Ave, Ste 1000, 10022. SAN 372-4522. Tel: 212-906-1200. FAX: 212-751-4864. Web Site: www.lw.com. *Mgr,* Anne Lewis
Library Holdings: Bk Vols 20,000; Per Subs 150
Restriction: Staff use only

S LEAGUE OF AMERICAN ORCHESTRAS, Knowledge Center, 33 W 60th St, 5th Flr, 10023. SAN 329-2975. Tel: 212-262-5161. FAX: 212-262-5198. Web Site: www.americanorchestras.org. *Mgr,* Position Currently Open
Library Holdings: Bk Titles 300
Special Collections: League Publications; Orchestra Program, bks
Subject Interests: Am orchestras, Govt, Orchestra mgt
Open Mon-Fri 10-5:30

S LEGAL AID SOCIETY*, Central Library & Information Center, 199 Water St, 10038. SAN 371-1722. Tel: 212-298-5258; 212-577-3300. FAX: 212-693-1149. Web Site: www.legal-aid.org. *Librn,* Olive Reznik
Library Holdings: Bk Vols 64,000; Per Subs 80
Restriction: Staff use only

M LENOX HILL HOSPITAL, Health Sciences Library, Achelis Fifth Flr, 100 E 77th St, 10075. SAN 311-8614. Tel: 212-434-2077. *Dir,* William Self; E-mail: wself@nshs.edu; Staff 1 (MLS 1)
Founded 1925
Library Holdings: e-journals 9,200; Bk Titles 6,452
Subject Interests: Dentistry, Med, Nursing
Database Vendor: PubMed
Wireless access
Function: Health sci info serv
Partic in Brooklyn-Queens-Staten Island-Manhattan-Bronx Health Sciences Librarians; Medical Library Association (MLA); Metropolitan New York Library Council; NY & NJ Regional Med Libr
Restriction: Staff use only

C LIM COLLEGE LIBRARY*, 216 E 45th St, 2nd Flr, 10017. SAN 311-855X. Tel: 646-218-4126. Reference Tel: 646-218-7737. Administration Tel: 646-218-4695. FAX: 212-750-3453. E-mail:

library@limcollege.edu. Web Site: www.limcollege.edu. *Dir,* Lou Acierno; *Ref Librn,* Lisa Ryan; *Tech Serv,* Amy Wolfe
Founded 1939
Library Holdings: Bk Vols 19,000; Per Subs 240
Special Collections: Merchandising (B Earl Puckett Fund for Retail Education)
Subject Interests: Advertising, Current affairs, Econ, Fashion buying, Lang arts, Math, Mkt, Psychol, Retailing, Visual merchandising
Automation Activity & Vendor Info: (Cataloging) SirsiDynix; (Circulation) SirsiDynix; (OPAC) SirsiDynix
Database Vendor: ARTstor, CQ Press, CredoReference, ebrary, EBSCOhost, LexisNexis, Mergent Online, OCLC, Oxford Online, ProQuest, SerialsSolutions, SirsiDynix
Open Mon-Thurs 8am-9pm, Fri 8-5

L LINKLATERS*, Law Library, 1345 Sixth Ave, 19th Flr, 10105. SAN 372-4166. Tel: 212-424-9000. FAX: 212-424-9100. Web Site: www.linklaters.com. *Librn,* Peter Valentine; *Res Librn,* Sonal Pandya
Library Holdings: Bk Titles 1,000; Bk Vols 10,000; Per Subs 100
Automation Activity & Vendor Info: (Circulation) SirsiDynix
Wireless access
Open Mon-Fri 9:30-5:30

L LOEB & LOEB LLP*, Law Library, 345 Park Ave, 18th flr, 10154-0037. SAN 372-2325. Tel: 212-407-4000, 212-407-4961. FAX: 212-407-4990. Web Site: www.loeb.com. *Librn,* Joanne Camejo
Library Holdings: Bk Vols 10,000; Per Subs 500

C MANHATTAN SCHOOL OF MUSIC*, The Peter Jay Sharp Library, 120 Claremont Ave, 10027. SAN 311-8770. Tel: 917-493-4507, 917-493-4511. Circulation Tel: 917-493-4512. FAX: 212-749-5471. E-mail: library@lists.msmnyc.edu. Web Site: library.msmnyc.edu. *Dir,* Peter Caleb; E-mail: pcaleb@msmnyc.edu; Staff 8 (MLS 4, Non-MLS 4)
Founded 1925. Enrl 900; Highest Degree: Doctorate
Library Holdings: CDs 2,000; DVDs 3,000; Music Scores 50,000; Bk Vols 180,000; Per Subs 107
Special Collections: Mischa Elman Coll; Nicolas Flagello Coll, scores
Subject Interests: Music
Automation Activity & Vendor Info: (Acquisitions) Innovative Interfaces, Inc
Wireless access
Partic in Nylink; OCLC Online Computer Library Center, Inc
Open Mon-Thurs (Winter) 9-9, Fri 9-6, Sat 9-5, Sun 2-8; Mon-Thurs (Summer) 9-5
Restriction: In-house use for visitors, Students only

S KRISTINE MANN LIBRARY*, C G Jung Center of New York, 28 E 39th St, 10016. SAN 311-6018. Tel: 212-697-7877. FAX: 212-986-1743. Web Site: www.junglibrary.org. *Libr Dir,* Position Currently Open; Staff 3 (MLS 1, Non-MLS 2)
Founded 1945
Library Holdings: Audiobooks 1,200; CDs 200; DVDs 60; Bk Titles 10,000; Bk Vols 21,000; Per Subs 40; Videos 100
Special Collections: Carl Gustav Jung (Jung Press Archive), photostats of press clippings
Subject Interests: Alchemy, Analytical psychol, Jungian psychol, Mythology, Occult, Relig, Symbolism
Wireless access
Function: Res libr
Open Mon 10-8, Tues & Wed 10-7, Thurs 10-5
Restriction: Circ to mem only, In-house use for visitors, Private libr, Sub libr

S MARLBOROUGH GALLERY LIBRARY*, 40 W 57th St, 10019. SAN 373-1162. Tel: 212-541-4900. FAX: 212-541-4948. E-mail: mny@marlboroughgallery.com. Web Site: www.marlboroughgallery.com. *Archivist,* Rochfort Annie; E-mail: arochfort@marlboroughgallery.com
Library Holdings: Bk Vols 10,000
Wireless access
Restriction: Staff use only

C MARYMOUNT MANHATTAN COLLEGE*, Thomas J Shanahan Library, 221 E 71st St, 10021. SAN 311-886X. Tel: 212-774-4806. Reference Tel: 212-774-4808. FAX: 212-458-8207. Web Site: www.marymount.mmm.edu. *Dir,* Donna Hurwitz; Tel: 212-774-4801, E-mail: dhurwitz@mmm.edu; *Head, Ref,* Henry Blanke; E-mail: hblanke@mmm.edu; *Circ Mgr,* Brian Soto; Tel: 212-774-4804, E-mail: bsoto@mmm.edu; *Coordr, Media Serv,* Jordon Horsley; Tel: 212-774-4854, E-mail: jhorsley@mmm.edu; *Archivist,* Mary Brown; Tel: 212-774-4817, E-mail: mbrown1@mmm.edu; *Cataloger,* Teresa Yip; Tel: 212-774-4818, E-mail: tyip@mmm.edu; *ILL,* Tammy Wofsey; Tel: 212-774-4803, E-mail: twofsey@mmm.edu; *Media Spec,* Sean Smith; Tel: 212-774-4805, E-mail: ssmith@mmm.edu; *Media Serv,* Jonathan Warren; E-mail: jwarren@mmu.edu; *Ref,* Tammy Wofsey; E-mail: twofsey@mmm.edu; *Ser,* Kunchog Dolma; Tel: 212-774-4807, E-mail: kdolma@mmm.edu; *Tech Serv,* Brian Rocco; Tel: 212-774-4802, E-mail: brocco@mmm.edu. Subject Specialists: *Hist,* Donna Hurwitz; *Arts, Polit sci,* Henry Blanke; Staff 18 (MLS 6, Non-MLS 12)
Founded 1948. Fac 52; Highest Degree: Bachelor
Library Holdings: Bk Titles 65,000; Bk Vols 80,000; Per Subs 650
Special Collections: Geraldine A Ferraro Archives; William Harris Coll
Subject Interests: Communications, Theatre, Women's studies
Automation Activity & Vendor Info: (Cataloging) LibLime; (Circulation) LibLime; (ILL) LibLime; (OPAC) LibLime; (Serials) LibLime
Database Vendor: EBSCOhost, Gale Cengage Learning, LexisNexis, OCLC FirstSearch, ProQuest, Wilson - Wilson Web
Wireless access
Publications: Resource Aids & Bulletins
Partic in OCLC Online Computer Library Center, Inc; Westchester Academic Library Directors Organization (WALDO)
Special Services for the Deaf - Bks on deafness & sign lang
Open Mon-Thurs 8am-10pm, Fri 8am-9pm, Sat 11-5, Sun 12-6
Friends of the Library Group

S ANDREW W MELLON FOUNDATION*, Nathan Marsh Pusey Library, 140 E 62nd St, 10065. SAN 375-7188. Tel: 212-838-8400. FAX: 212-888-4172. Web Site: www.mellon.org. *Librn,* Susanne Pichler; E-mail: scp@mellon.org; *Assoc Librn,* Ellen Nasto; E-mail: ejn@mellon.org; *Asst Librn,* Lisa Bonifacic; E-mail: lmb@mellon.org; Staff 3 (MLS 3)
Library Holdings: Bk Titles 7,600; Per Subs 150
Subject Interests: Higher educ, Humanities
Automation Activity & Vendor Info: (Cataloging) Inmagic, Inc.; (OPAC) Inmagic, Inc.; (Serials) Inmagic, Inc.
Database Vendor: JSTOR, Oxford Online, ProQuest
Partic in Nylink
Restriction: Not open to pub

M MEMORIAL SLOAN-KETTERING CANCER CENTER MEDICAL LIBRARY*, Nathan Cummings Center, 430 East 67th St, 10065. (Mail add: 1275 York Ave, 10065), SAN 311-8886. Tel: 212-639-2109. Circulation Tel: 212-639-7439. Interlibrary Loan Service Tel: 212-639-7441. FAX: 212-717-3048. Web Site: library.mskcc.org. *Mgr,* Donna Gibson; E-mail: gibsond@mskcc.org; Staff 11 (MLS 11)
Library Holdings: e-books 600; e-journals 2,100; Bk Vols 5,000; Per Subs 150
Special Collections: Memorial Sloan-Kettering Cancer Center Archives
Subject Interests: Oncology
Partic in Metropolitan New York Library Council; OCLC Online Computer Library Center, Inc
Restriction: Staff use only, Use of others with permission of librn

L MENDES & MOUNT, LLP*, Law Library, 750 Seventh Ave, 10019-6829. SAN 372-4239. Tel: 212-261-8000, 212-261-8338. FAX: 212-261-8750. Web Site: www.mendes.com. *Dir,* Ray Jassin; E-mail: ray.jassin@mendes.com; *Sr Librn,* Steven M Cohen; E-mail: mendes.librarian@mendes.com; *Asst Librn,* Linda Banta; Staff 3 (MLS 1, Non-MLS 2)
Library Holdings: Bk Vols 10,000
Restriction: Co libr

C METROPOLITAN COLLEGE OF NEW YORK LIBRARY*, 431 Canal St, 12th Flr, 10013. SAN 311-6956. Tel: 212-343-1234, Ext 2001. Interlibrary Loan Service Tel: 212-343-1234, Ext 2008. Reference Tel: 212-343-1234, Ext 2010. FAX: 212-343-7398. E-mail: library@metropolitan.edu. Web Site: www.metropolitan.edu. *Dir,* Lou Acierno; E-mail: lacierno@mcny.edu; *Libr Mgr,* Gregory Lewis; Tel: 212-343-1234, Ext 2007, E-mail: glewis@metropolitan.edu; *Head, Circ,* Sandra Green; Tel: 212-343-1234, Ext 2003, E-mail: greenes@metropolitan.edu; *Head, Ref, ILL,* Judith Mavodza; E-mail: jmavodza@metropolitan.edu; *Head, Tech Serv,* Jonathan Frater; Tel: 212-343-1234, Ext 2017, E-mail: jfrater@metropolitan.edu; *Circ,* Blondel Brown; Tel: 212-343-1234, Ext 2002, E-mail: brownb@metropolitan.edu. Subject Specialists: *Mgt,* Judith Mavodza; Staff 5 (MLS 5)
Founded 1966. Enrl 1,000; Highest Degree: Master
Library Holdings: Bk Titles 26,000; Bk Vols 32,000; Per Subs 400
Special Collections: Audrey Cohen Archives
Subject Interests: Bus, Culinary arts, Mgt, Res mgt
Automation Activity & Vendor Info: (Circulation) SirsiDynix; (Course Reserve) SirsiDynix; (OPAC) SirsiDynix; (Serials) EBSCO Online
Database Vendor: EBSCOhost, Gale Cengage Learning, H W Wilson, LexisNexis, OCLC FirstSearch, TLC (The Library Corporation), Wilson - Wilson Web
Function: For res purposes, ILL available
Publications: Library Matters (Newsletter)
Partic in Metropolitan New York Library Council; OCLC Online Computer Library Center, Inc; Westchester Academic Library Directors Organization (WALDO)
Open Mon-Thurs 9am-10pm, Fri 1-10, Sat 10-7
Restriction: Access for corporate affiliates

M METROPOLITAN HOSPITAL CENTER*, Frederick M Dearborn Library, 1901 First Ave & 97th St, 10029. SAN 353-1694. Tel: 212-423-6055. Interlibrary Loan Service Tel: 212-423-6270. FAX: 212-423-7961. E-mail: mhclibrary@yahoo.com. *Dir,* Antoinette Drago; Staff 2 (MLS 1, Non-MLS 1)
Founded 1906
Library Holdings: Bk Titles 5,000; Bk Vols 8,000; Per Subs 90
Subject Interests: Med, Surgery
Automation Activity & Vendor Info: (Cataloging) Professional Software; (Circulation) Professional Software
Wireless access
Partic in Docline; National Network of Libraries of Medicine
Restriction: Open to pub upon request

THE METROPOLITAN MUSEUM OF ART

S CLOISTERS LIBRARY*, Fort Tryon Park, 10040, SAN 353-1848. Tel: 212-396-5319. FAX: 212-795-3640. E-mail: cloisters.library@metmuseum.org. *Librn,* Michael K Carter; Tel: 212-396-5365, E-mail: michael.carter@metmuseum.org
Founded 1938
Library Holdings: Bk Vols 13,000; Per Subs 50
Special Collections: Archives of The Cloisters; George Grey Barnard Papers; Harry Bober Papers; Sumner McKnight Crosby Papers
Subject Interests: European medieval art, Medieval archit, Middle ages
Automation Activity & Vendor Info: (Cataloging) Innovative Interfaces, Inc; (Circulation) Innovative Interfaces, Inc; (OPAC) Innovative Interfaces, Inc
Open Tues-Fri 10-4:30

S ROBERT GOLDWATER LIBRARY*, 1000 Fifth Ave, 10028-0198, SAN 353-1872. Tel: 212-570-3707. FAX: 212-570-3879. E-mail: goldwater.library@metmuseum.org. Web Site: library.metmuseum.org. *Head of Libr,* Ross Day; Staff 3 (MLS 1, Non-MLS 2)
Founded 1982
Library Holdings: Bk Titles 15,000; Bk Vols 20,000; Per Subs 224
Subject Interests: African, Am Indian, Pacific
Database Vendor: Innovative Interfaces, Inc
Partic in RLIN (Research Libraries Information Network)
Publications: Catalog of The Robert Goldwater Library
Restriction: Non-circulating, Open by appt only, Open to fac, students & qualified researchers, Photo ID required for access

S ROBERT LEHMAN COLLECTION LIBRARY*, 1000 Fifth Ave, 10028, SAN 353-1937. Tel: 212-570-3915. FAX: 212-650-2542. E-mail: lehman.library@metmuseum.org. *Librn,* Meg Black; Staff 2 (MLS 1, Non-MLS 1)
Library Holdings: Bk Vols 18,500
Special Collections: Archives of bk, mss, reproductions, correspondence; Photograph Coll, photogs, negatives
Subject Interests: Decorative art, Old master drawings, Renaissance, Western European Arts from the 13th to 20th centuries
Function: Res libr
Restriction: Open by appt only, Open to qualified scholars, Open to researchers by request

S THE IRENE LEWISOHN COSTUME REFERENCE LIBRARY, COSTUME INSTITUTE*, 1000 Fifth Ave, 10028, SAN 353-1961. Tel: 212-396-5233, 212-650-2723. FAX: 212-570-3970. E-mail: thecostumeinstitute@metmuseum.org. Web Site: www.metmuseum.org. *In Charge,* Julie Le; E-mail: juliele@metmuseum.org; Staff 3 (MLS 1, Non-MLS 2)
Founded 1951
Library Holdings: Bk Titles 20,000; Bk Vols 40,000; Per Subs 75
Special Collections: Mainbocher Archive; Norman Norell Coll, scrap bks
Subject Interests: Fashion, Hist of costume
Automation Activity & Vendor Info: (OPAC) Innovative Interfaces, Inc
Function: Res libr
Partic in Metropolitan New York Library Council; OCLC Research Library Partnership; RLIN (Research Libraries Information Network)
Restriction: Non-circulating coll, Open by appt only

S LIBRARY & TEACHER RESOURCE CENTER IN THE URIS CENTER FOR EDUCATION*, 1000 Fifth Ave, 10028-0198. Tel: 212-570-3788. E-mail: education@metmuseum.org. Web Site: www.metmuseum.org. *Assoc Librn,* Naomi Niles; Staff 2 (MLS 2)
Founded 1941
Library Holdings: AV Mats 1,000; Bk Vols 6,000; Per Subs 20
Special Collections: Art & Architecture Coll
Subject Interests: Archaeology, Art educ, Art lit, Fine arts, Illustrators, Metrop Mus of Art, Mythology, Visual arts
Partic in RLIN (Research Libraries Information Network)
Restriction: Open to pub for ref only

S THOMAS J WATSON LIBRARY*, 1000 Fifth Ave, 10028-0198, SAN 353-1813. Tel: 212-650-2225. Circulation Tel: 212-650-2175. Interlibrary Loan Service Tel: 212-396-5221. Administration Tel: 212-570-3933. FAX: 212-570-3847. E-mail: watson.library@metmuseum.org. Web Site: library.metmuseum.org. *Dir, Tech Serv,* Daniel Starr; Tel: 212-650-2582, E-mail: daniel.starr@metmuseum.org; *Chief Librn,* Kenneth Soehner; Tel: 212-570-3934, E-mail: ken.soehner@metmuseum.org; *Conserv Librn,* Mindell Dubansky; Tel: 212-570-3220, E-mail: mindell.dubansky@metmuseum.org; *Syst Librn,* Oleg Kreymer; Tel: 212-650-2438, E-mail: oleg.kreymer@metmuseum.org; *Assoc Mgr, Circ & Coll,* Lisa Harms; Tel: 212-650-2344, E-mail: lisa.harms@metmuseum.org; *Acq,* Ross Day; Tel: 212-650-2949, E-mail: ross.day@metmuseum.org; *Electronic Res,* Deborah Vincelli; Tel: 212 650-2912, E-mail: deborah.vincelli@metmuseum.org; *ILL,* Robyn Fleming; E-mail: robyn.fleming@metmuseum.org; *Reader Serv,* Linda Seckelson; Tel: 212-570-3759, E-mail: linda.seckelson@metmuseum.org; Staff 42 (MLS 17, Non-MLS 25)
Founded 1880
Library Holdings: e-books 30,000; e-journals 2,000; Bk Vols 600,000; Per Subs 2,500
Special Collections: Auction-Sale Catalogs, Autograph Letters; Ephemera on Individual Artists; Museum History Coll
Subject Interests: Archaeology, Archit
Automation Activity & Vendor Info: (Acquisitions) Innovative Interfaces, Inc; (Cataloging) Innovative Interfaces, Inc; (Circulation) Innovative Interfaces, Inc; (ILL) OCLC ILLiad; (OPAC) Innovative Interfaces, Inc; (Serials) Innovative Interfaces, Inc
Database Vendor: ARTstor, Backstage Library Works, Blackwell, Cambridge Scientific Abstracts, Checkpoint Systems, Inc, Duncan Systems Specialists Inc, ebrary, EBSCOhost, H W Wilson, Innovative Interfaces, Inc, JSTOR, Marcive, Inc, Marquis Who's Who, OCLC FirstSearch, OCLC WorldShare Interlibrary Loan, OCLC-RLG, OVID Technologies, Oxford Online, ProQuest, SerialsSolutions, Wilson - Wilson Web, YBP Library Services
Function: Res libr
Partic in OCLC Online Computer Library Center, Inc
Publications: Library Catalog of the Metropolitan Museum of Art
Open Tues-Fri 10-4:45
Friends of the Library Group

S THE MORGAN LIBRARY*, 225 Madison Ave, 10016. SAN 311-998X. Tel: 212-685-0008. Web Site: www.themorganlibrary.org. *Dir of Coll, Dir, Info Syst,* Elizabeth OKeefe; E-mail: eokeefe@themorgan.org; *Head, Cat & Database Mgt,* Maria Oldal; *Head, Reader Serv,* Inge Dupont; *Head, Ref & Coll Develop,* Heidi Hass
Founded 1924
Subject Interests: Drawings, Early children's bks, Manuscripts, Prints
Automation Activity & Vendor Info: (Acquisitions) Ex Libris Group; (Cataloging) Ex Libris Group; (Circulation) Ex Libris Group; (OPAC) Ex Libris Group
Function: Res libr
Publications: Exhibition Catalogues; Newsletter
Partic in RLIN (Research Libraries Information Network)
Restriction: Open by appt only
Friends of the Library Group

CM MOUNT SINAI SCHOOL OF MEDICINE*, Gustave L & Janet W Levy Library, One Gustave L Levy Pl, 10029. (Mail add: PO Box 1102, 10029-6574), SAN 311-9033. Tel: 212-241-7892. Interlibrary Loan Service Tel: 212-241-7795. FAX: 212-831-2625. Web Site: www.mssm.edu/library. *Dir,* Position Currently Open; *Interim Dir,* Alan Krissoff; E-mail: alan.krissoff@mssm.edu; Staff 52 (MLS 17, Non-MLS 35)
Enrl 624, Fac 3,530; Highest Degree: Doctorate
Library Holdings: AV Mats 2,512; e-books 5,938; e-journals 23,979; Bk Vols 36,133; Per Subs 24,152
Special Collections: Biomedical Audiovisual & Computer software
Subject Interests: Archives, Med
Automation Activity & Vendor Info: (Acquisitions) SirsiDynix; (Cataloging) SirsiDynix; (Circulation) SirsiDynix; (Course Reserve) SirsiDynix; (ILL) OCLC ILLiad; (OPAC) SirsiDynix; (Serials) SirsiDynix
Database Vendor: 3M Library Systems, American Psychological Association (APA), Annual Reviews, Blackwell, Cinahl, ebrary, EBSCOhost, Elsevier, Foundation Center, IEEE (Institute of Electrical & Electronics Engineers), ISI Web of Knowledge, JSTOR, LexisNexis, MD Consult, Medline, Micromedex, Nature Publishing Group, OCLC FirstSearch, OCLC WorldShare Interlibrary Loan, OVID Technologies, ProQuest, PubMed, Sage, ScienceDirect, SerialsSolutions, SirsiDynix, STAT!Ref (Teton Data Systems), UpToDate, Wiley InterScience
Wireless access
Partic in National Network of Libraries of Medicine; New York State Higher Education Initiative; Nylink; OCLC Online Computer Library Center, Inc
Restriction: Not open to pub

S MUSEUM OF JEWISH HERITAGE*, 36 Battery Pl, 10280. SAN 326-162X. Tel: 646-437-4248. FAX: 646-437-4372. Web Site: www.mjhnyc.org. *Coll, Sr Curator,* Esther Brumberg; Staff 1 (MLS 1)
Founded 1986
Library Holdings: Bk Titles 8,000
Special Collections: Holocaust, bks, flm, learning ctr, oral history tapes & videotapes

Subject Interests: World War II
Automation Activity & Vendor Info: (Acquisitions) Mandarin Library Automation; (Cataloging) Mandarin Library Automation; (Circulation) Mandarin Library Automation; (ILL) OCLC
Restriction: Not a lending libr, Not open to pub

S MUSEUM OF MODERN ART LIBRARY*, 11 W 54th St, 10019-5498. SAN 311-9076. Tel: 212-708-9433. Interlibrary Loan Service Tel: 212-708-9441. FAX: 212-333-1122. Web Site: library.moma.org. *Chief Librn,* Milan R Hughston; Tel: 212-708-9409, E-mail: milan_hughston@moma.org; *Reader Serv Librn,* Jennifer Tobias; E-mail: jennifer_tobias@moma.org; *Archivist,* Michelle Elligott; Tel: 212-708-9436, E-mail: michelle_elligott@moma.org; Staff 5 (MLS 4, Non-MLS 1)
Founded 1929
Library Holdings: Bk Titles 300,000; Per Subs 250
Special Collections: Artist Files; Artists' Books; Dada & Surrealism (Eluard-Dausse Coll); Latin American Art; Museum of Modern Art Publications; Political Art Documentation & Distribution (PADD) Archives
Subject Interests: Archit, Archives, Art, Design, Drawing, Film, Mixed media, Painting, Sculpture, Video from 1880 to present
Automation Activity & Vendor Info: (Acquisitions) Innovative Interfaces, Inc - Millenium; (Cataloging) Innovative Interfaces, Inc - Millenium; (Circulation) Innovative Interfaces, Inc - Millenium; (OPAC) Innovative Interfaces, Inc - Millenium; (Serials) Innovative Interfaces, Inc - Millenium
Wireless access
Partic in Metropolitan New York Library Council; New York Art Resources Consortium (NYARC); OCLC Research Library Partnership
Friends of the Library Group

S MUSEUM OF THE CITY OF NEW YORK*, Theatre Collection Library, 1220 Fifth Ave, 10029. SAN 325-7371. Tel: 212-534-1672. FAX: 212-423-0758. E-mail: collections@mcny.org, info@mcny.org. Web Site: www.mcny.org. *Pres,* Susan Henshaw Jones; *Dir,* Ronay Menschel; *Curator,* Marty Jacobs
Special Collections: New York City Stage Productions & Personalities, clippings, correspondence, costume designs, costumes, doc, drawings, memorabilia, paintings, photog, programs, props, scores, scripts, set models & designs
Wireless access
Restriction: Open by appt only, Open to researchers by request

G NASA GODDARD INSTITUTE FOR SPACE STUDIES LIBRARY*, 2880 Broadway, Rm 710, 10025. SAN 311-9092. Tel: 212-678-5613. FAX: 212-678-5552. *Mgr,* Zoe Wai; *Librn,* Josefina Mora; Staff 1 (MLS 1)
Founded 1961
Library Holdings: Bk Vols 7,000
Subject Interests: Astronomy, Astrophysics, Climate, Geophysics, Global warming, Math, Meteorology, Physics, Planetary atmospheres, Remote sensing of environ
Automation Activity & Vendor Info: (Acquisitions) SirsiDynix; (Cataloging) SirsiDynix; (Circulation) SirsiDynix; (OPAC) SirsiDynix; (Serials) SirsiDynix
Database Vendor: OCLC FirstSearch
Wireless access
Publications: Booklist
Partic in OCLC Online Computer Library Center, Inc
Restriction: Staff use only

S NATIONAL BUREAU OF ECONOMIC RESEARCH, INC LIBRARY*, 365 Fifth Ave, 5th Flr, 10016-4309. SAN 311-9173. Tel: 212-817-7955. FAX: 212-817-1597. E-mail: nber@gc.cuny.edu. Web Site: www.nber.org. *Librn,* Marinella Moscheni
Founded 1920
Library Holdings: Bk Vols 2,000; Per Subs 35
Subject Interests: Bus cycle, Gen econ
Wireless access
Restriction: Open to students, fac & staff

L NATIONAL CENTER FOR LAW & ECONOMIC JUSTICE*, 275 Seventh Ave, Ste 1205, 10001-6708. SAN 325-9544. Tel: 212-633-6967. FAX: 212-633-6371. Web Site: www.nclej.org. *Prog Dir,* Gina Mannix
Library Holdings: Bk Vols 2,000; Per Subs 150
Special Collections: Publications & Case Materials on Welfare Law
Wireless access
Publications: Welfare Bulletin (Monthly), Welfare News (Bimonthly)
Open Mon-Fri 9-6
Restriction: Staff use only

L NATIONAL EMPLOYMENT LAW PROJECT LIBRARY*, 75 Maiden lane, Ste 601, 10038. SAN 325-7355. Tel: 212-285-3025, Ext 100. FAX: 212-285-3044. E-mail: nelp@nelp.org. Web Site: www.nelp.org. *Librn,* Deborah Buchanan-Taylor
Library Holdings: Bk Vols 1,200

S NATIONAL MULTIPLE SCLEROSIS SOCIETY*, Professional Resource Center, 733 Third Ave, 10017. SAN 326-5838. Tel: 212-986-3240. FAX: 212-986-7981. E-mail: healthprof_info@nmss.org. Web Site: www.nationalmssociety.org. *Dir,* Rosalind Kalb; *Librn,* Ann Palmer; E-mail: a.palmer@nmss.org; Staff 3 (MLS 1, Non-MLS 2)
Library Holdings: Bk Titles 1,018; Bk Vols 1,300; Per Subs 25
Special Collections: Multiple Sclerosis, bks, reprints & pamphlets
Subject Interests: Neurology, Nursing
Wireless access
Publications: Online Compendium of MS Information
Partic in Dialog Corp
Open Mon-Fri 9-5
Restriction: Non-circulating

S NATIONAL PSYCHOLOGICAL ASSOCIATION FOR PSYCHOANALYSIS, INC*, George Lawton Memorial Library, 40 W 13th St, 10011. SAN 311-9254. Tel: 212-924-7440. FAX: 212-989-7543. E-mail: info@npap.org. Web Site: www.npap.org. *In Charge,* Doris Mare
Founded 1958
Library Holdings: Bk Titles 5,000; Per Subs 25
Wireless access

THE NEW SCHOOL

C RAYMOND FOGELMAN LIBRARY*, 55 W 13th St, 10011, SAN 311-9319. Tel: 212-229-5307. Circulation Tel: 212-229-5307, Ext 3056. Interlibrary Loan Service Tel: 212-229-5307, Ext 3152. Reference Tel: 212-229-5307, Ext 3058. Administration Tel: 212-229-5307, Ext 3054. FAX: 212-229-5306. E-mail: reference@newschool.edu. Web Site: library.newschool.edu. *Dir,* John Aubry; E-mail: aubryj@newschool.edu; *Undergrad Serv Librn,* Brita Servaes; Tel: 212-229-5307, Ext 3163, E-mail: servaesb@newschool.edu; *Ref & Instrul Serv, Instr Coordr,* Paul Abruzzo; Tel: 212-229-5307, Ext 3055, E-mail: abruzzop@newschool.edu; *Ref Serv,* Carmen Hendershott; Tel: 212-229-5307, Ext 3053, E-mail: hendersh@newschool.edu; Staff 12 (MLS 4, Non-MLS 8)
Founded 1919. Enrl 6,500; Fac 1,100; Highest Degree: Doctorate
Jul 2005-Jun 2006. Mats Exp $482,000, Books $90,000, Per/Ser (Incl. Access Fees) $140,000, AV Mat $2,000, Electronic Ref Mat (Incl. Access Fees) $250,000
Library Holdings: Bk Vols 194,000; Per Subs 220
Automation Activity & Vendor Info: (Acquisitions) Ex Libris Group; (Cataloging) Ex Libris Group; (Circulation) Ex Libris Group; (Course Reserve) Ex Libris Group; (OPAC) Ex Libris Group; (Serials) Ex Libris Group
Function: Audio & video playback equip for onsite use, Computers for patron use, Copy machines, Distance learning, E-Reserves, Electronic databases & coll, For res purposes, Homebound delivery serv, ILL available, Online searches, Orientations, Referrals accepted, Telephone ref, VCDs
Partic in Metropolitan New York Library Council; Research Library Association of South Manhattan
Open Mon-Thurs 8:30am-10:30pm, Fri 8:30-7:30, Sat 9:30-7:30, Sun 10-8:30
Restriction: In-house use for visitors, Off-site coll in storage - retrieval as requested, Open to others by appt, Open to researchers by request, Open to students, fac, staff & alumni, Photo ID required for access

C ADAM & SOPHIE GIMBEL DESIGN LIBRARY*, Two W 13th St, 2nd Flr, 10011, SAN 311-9890. Tel: 212-229-8914. Circulation Tel: 212-229-8914, Ext 4121. Interlibrary Loan Service Tel: 212-229-8914, Ext 4288. Reference Tel: 212-229-8914, Ext 4286. FAX: 212-229-2806. Web Site: library.newschool.edu/gimbel/. *Dir,* John Aubry; Tel: 212-229-5307, E-mail: aubryj@newschool.edu; *Ref & Instrul Serv Librn,* Jennifer Yao; Tel: 212-229-8914, Ext 4285, E-mail: yaoj@newschool.edu; Staff 8 (MLS 3, Non-MLS 5)
Founded 1896. Enrl 15,479; Fac 2,220; Highest Degree: Master
Library Holdings: CDs 170; DVDs 200; Bk Titles 52,600; Bk Vols 56,000; Per Subs 222
Special Collections: Fashion Design (Claire McCardell Coll), sketchbks; Parsons Archives
Subject Interests: Archit, Costume, Fashion, Fine arts, Graphic, Indust design, Interior design, Lighting, Textiles design
Automation Activity & Vendor Info: (Acquisitions) Ex Libris Group; (Cataloging) Ex Libris Group; (Circulation) Ex Libris Group; (Course Reserve) Ex Libris Group; (OPAC) Ex Libris Group; (Serials) Ex Libris Group
Function: Archival coll, Art exhibits, Audio & video playback equip for onsite use, Electronic databases & coll, ILL available, Online ref, Online searches, Orientations, Photocopying/Printing, Ref & res, Ref serv available, Telephone ref, VHS videos
Partic in Metropolitan New York Library Council; OCLC Research Library Partnership; RLIN (Research Libraries Information Network)
Restriction: Access at librarian's discretion, Open to students, fac & staff

C HARRY SCHERMAN LIBRARY*, 150 W 85th St, 10024-4499, SAN 311-8797. Tel: 212-580-0210, Ext 4803. FAX: 212-580-1738. Web Site: library.newschool.edu. *Dir,* Ed Scarcelle; Tel: 212-580-0210, Ext 4828, E-mail: scarcele@newschool.edu; *Asst Dir,* Arsi Ioannidou; Tel: 212-580-0210, Ext 4827, E-mail: ioannida@newschool.edu; *Head, Circ,* Gregory Briggler; E-mail: briggleg@newschool.edu; Staff 3.5 (MLS 2, Non-MLS 1.5)
Founded 1954. Enrl 320; Highest Degree: Master
Library Holdings: AV Mats 5,000; CDs 6,500; DVDs 450; Music Scores 31,000; Bk Vols 8,100; Per Subs 74
Special Collections: Konstantin Ivanov Viola Coll; Leopald Mannes Compositions; Salzedo Harp Coll; Sylvia Marlowe Harpsichord Coll
Subject Interests: Classical music
Partic in OCLC Online Computer Library Center, Inc; Research Library Association of South Manhattan

S NEW YORK ACADEMY OF ART LIBRARY*, 111 Franklin St, 10013-2911. SAN 375-4421. Tel: 212-966-0300. FAX: 212-966-3217. *Librn,* Holly Frisbee; Tel: 212-966-0300, Ext 964
Founded 1990. Enrl 125; Fac 21; Highest Degree: Master
Library Holdings: Bk Titles 6,300; Per Subs 50
Subject Interests: Art hist, Drawing, Painting, Sculpture
Automation Activity & Vendor Info: (Acquisitions) Book Systems; (Cataloging) Book Systems; (Circulation) Book Systems; (Course Reserve) Book Systems; (ILL) Book Systems; (Media Booking) Book Systems; (OPAC) Book Systems; (Serials) Book Systems
Database Vendor: ARTstor, ProQuest
Wireless access
Open Mon-Fri 9-9, Sat & Sun 12-5
Restriction: Non-circulating to the pub, Open to others by appt
Friends of the Library Group

M NEW YORK ACADEMY OF MEDICINE LIBRARY*, 1216 Fifth Ave, 10029-5293. SAN 311-9327. Tel: 212-822-7327. Interlibrary Loan Service Tel: 212-822-7296. Reference Tel: 212-822-7315. FAX: 212-423-0266. Web Site: www.nyam.org/library/index.shtml. *Dir,* Janice Kaplan; *Doc Delivery Mgr,* Steve Chiaffone; *Mrg, Tech Res,* Ying Jia; Tel: 212-822-7334; *Spec Projects Librn,* Danielle Aloia; Tel: 212-822-7323, E-mail: daloia@nyam.org; *Tech Serv Librn,* Latrina Keith; Tel: 212-822-7331, E-mail: lkeith@nyam.org; *Libr Asst,* Walter Linton; Tel: 212-822-7362, E-mail: wlinton@nyam.org; Staff 37 (MLS 25, Non-MLS 12)
Founded 1847
Library Holdings: Bk Vols 650,000; Per Subs 1,000
Special Collections: 16-19th Century Medals (Greenwald Coll), medals; Anatomy & Surgery (Lambert Coll); Cardiology (Levy Coll), bks, mss; Engravings of Medical Men (Ladd Coll), prints; Foods & Cookery (Wilson Coll); Francesco Redi & Contemporaries (Cole Coll); German Psychology & Psychiatry (Harms Coll); Medical Americana By & About J & W Hunter (Beekman Coll); Medical Coll; Medical Economics (Michael Davis Coll), VF; Plague (Neinken Coll), bks, broadsides; Rare Medical Works (Friends of Rare Book Room), bk, mss; Theses-16th-18th Century (Gamble-Cranefield), pamphlets
Subject Interests: AIDS, Epidemiology, Health policy, Med, Pub health
Automation Activity & Vendor Info: (Cataloging) OCLC Connexion; (OPAC) LibLime
Database Vendor: Annual Reviews, Cinahl, EBSCOhost, Elsevier, LibLime, MD Consult, Medline, Nature Publishing Group, OCLC FirstSearch, OCLC WorldShare Interlibrary Loan, OVID Technologies, PubMed, RefWorks, ScienceDirect
Wireless access
Function: Res libr
Publications: Author Catalog of the Library & first supplement; Catalog of Biographies in the Library; History of Medicine Series; Illustration Catalog of the Library; Subject Catalog of the Library & first supplement
Partic in Westchester Academic Library Directors Organization (WALDO)
Open Tues-Fri 10-4:45
Friends of the Library Group

GL NEW YORK CITY LAW DEPARTMENT*, Office of Corporation Counsel Law Library, 100 Church St, Rm 6-310, 10007. SAN 311-9394. Tel: 212-788-1609, 212-788-1610. FAX: 212-788-1239. *Chief Librn,* Catherine Fitzgerald; Tel: 212-788-1669, E-mail: cfitzger@law.nyc.gov; *Dep Librn,* James H Meece; Tel: 212-788-0858; *Sr Librn,* Tamar Raum; Tel: 212-788-1608; Staff 3 (MLS 3)
Founded 1856
Library Holdings: Bk Titles 71,600; Per Subs 3,000
Subject Interests: Case law, Legal, Legis hist, State & fed statutes
Function: ILL available
Partic in Metropolitan New York Library Council
Restriction: Not open to pub

CM NEW YORK COLLEGE OF PODIATRIC MEDICINE*, Sidney Druskin Memorial Library, 53 E 124th St, 10035. SAN 311-9416. Tel: 212-410-8020. Circulation Tel: 212-410-8018. Interlibrary Loan Service Tel: 212-410-8142. FAX: 212-876-9426. Web Site: www.nycpm.edu/library.asp. *Dir,* Thomas Paul Walker; E-mail: twalker@nycpm.edu; Staff 5 (MLS 2, Non-MLS 3)
Founded 1911. Fac 5; Highest Degree: Doctorate
Library Holdings: Bk Titles 1,300; Per Subs 250; Spec Interest Per Sub 250
Subject Interests: Dermatology, Family practice, Orthopedics, Podiatry
Automation Activity & Vendor Info: (Acquisitions) Follett Software; (Circulation) Follett Software; (Media Booking) Follett Software; (OPAC) Follett Software; (Serials) Follett Software
Database Vendor: 3M Library Systems, Blackwell, Dialog, Gale Cengage Learning, Infotrieve, OVID Technologies, PubMed, ScienceDirect, STAT!Ref (Teton Data Systems)
Wireless access
Partic in Brooklyn-Queens Staten Island Manhattan-Bronx Health Sciences Librarians; Greater NE Regional Med Libr Program; Metropolitan New York Library Council
Restriction: Not open to pub

GL NEW YORK COUNTY DISTRICT ATTORNEY'S OFFICE LIBRARY*, One Hogan Pl, 10013. SAN 311-9424. Tel: 212-335-4292. FAX: 212-335-4266. Web Site: www.manhattanda.org. *Dir, Libr Serv,* Mary E Matuszak; E-mail: matuszakm@dany.nyc.gov; Staff 2 (MLS 2)
Library Holdings: Bk Titles 26,970; Per Subs 56
Subject Interests: Criminal law
Database Vendor: LexisNexis, Westlaw
Restriction: Staff use only

M NEW YORK DOWNTOWN HOSPITAL*, Elisha Walker Staff Library, 170 William St, 10038. SAN 311-6352. Tel: 212-312-5000, 212-312-5229. FAX: 212-312-5929. Web Site: www.downtownhospital.org.
Founded 1944
Library Holdings: Bk Vols 300
Subject Interests: Med, Surgery
Partic in Metropolitan New York Library Council; Regional Med Libr
Restriction: Med staff only

M NEW YORK EYE & EAR INFIRMARY*, Medical Library, 310 E 14th St, 10003. SAN 311-9483. Tel: 212-979-4000. FAX: 212-979-4179. *Dir,* Mary Ann Lach; E-mail: mlach@nyee.edu
Founded 1954
Library Holdings: Bk Vols 1,650; Per Subs 68
Subject Interests: Head, Neck surgery, Ophthalmology, Otolaryngology, Plastic surgery
Wireless access
Partic in Manhattan-Bronx Health Sciences Libraries Group
Restriction: Staff use only

S NEW YORK HISTORICAL SOCIETY LIBRARY*, 170 Central Park W, 10024. SAN 311-9521. Tel: 212-873-3400. Interlibrary Loan Service Tel: 212-873-3400, Ext 225. FAX: 212-875-1591. E-mail: reference@nyhistory.org. Web Site: www.nyhistory.org. *Dir,* Jean W Ashton; *Dir of Libr Operations,* Nina Nazionale; *Ref Librn,* Joseph Ditta; Staff 10 (MLS 8, Non-MLS 2)
Founded 1804
Library Holdings: Bk Titles 350,000
Special Collections: 18th & 19th Century New York City & New York State Newspapers; American Almanacs; American Genealogy; American Indian (Accounts of & Captivities); Among the Manuscript Coll: Horatio Gates, Alexander McDougall, Rufus King, American Fur Company, Livingston Family, American Art Union, American Academy of Fine Arts; Circus in America (Leonidas Westervelt); Civil War Regimental Histories & Muster Rolls; Early American; Early American Trials; Early Travels in America; Imprints; Jenny Lind (Leonidas Westervelt); Maps; Military History & Science (Seventh Regiment Military Library); Military History (Military Order of the Loyal Legion of the United States, Commandery of the State of New York); Naval & Marine History (Naval History Society); Slavery & the Civil War; Spanish American War (Harper)
Subject Interests: Am art, Hist of N Am continent, Hist of NY City, Hist of US, Naval hist, NY genealogy, State
Automation Activity & Vendor Info: (Cataloging) Ex Libris Group
Database Vendor: ProQuest
Wireless access
Publications: Catalogs; Indexes; Special Publications
Partic in RLIN (Research Libraries Information Network)
Open Tues-Sat (Winter) 10-5; Tues-Fri (Summer) 10-5
Friends of the Library Group

C NEW YORK INSTITUTE OF TECHNOLOGY*, Manhattan Campus, 1855 Broadway, 10023-7692. SAN 353-2291. Tel: 212-261-1526. Reference Tel: 212-261-1527. FAX: 212-261-1681. Web Site: www.nyit.edu/library. *Dir,* Elisabete Ferretti; Tel: 212-261-1525, E-mail:

eferrett@nyit.edu; *Librn III,* Sebastian Marion; E-mail: smarion@nyit.edu; *Librn III,* Jennifer Tsao; E-mail: jtsao@nyit.edu; Staff 6 (MLS 6)
Founded 1958
Library Holdings: Bk Vols 43,282; Per Subs 764
Subject Interests: Archit, Art, Computer sci
Automation Activity & Vendor Info: (Acquisitions) SirsiDynix; (Cataloging) SirsiDynix; (Circulation) SirsiDynix; (Course Reserve) SirsiDynix; (ILL) SirsiDynix; (OPAC) SirsiDynix; (Serials) SirsiDynix
Database Vendor: EBSCOhost, OCLC FirstSearch, ProQuest, Wilson - Wilson Web
Wireless access
Publications: Library News; New Acquisitions
Partic in Metropolitan New York Library Council; Westchester Academic Library Directors Organization (WALDO)
Open Mon-Fri 8am-11pm, Sat 10-7, Sun 1-7

L NEW YORK LAW INSTITUTE LIBRARY*, 120 Broadway, Rm 932, 10271-0043. SAN 311-9548. Tel: 212-732-8720. FAX: 212-406-1204. Web Site: www.nyli.org. *Chief Librn,* Ralph Monaco; *Res Librn,* Mikhail Koulikov; *Ref,* Ralph Caiazzo; Staff 11 (MLS 3, Non-MLS 8)
Founded 1828
Library Holdings: Bk Vols 300,000
Special Collections: Appellate Divisions, 1st, 2nd & 3rd Departments; Records & Briefs for New York Court of Appeals; United States Court of Appeals for Second Circuit; United States Supreme Court, fiche
Subject Interests: Colonies, Former possessions
Automation Activity & Vendor Info: (Circulation) Innovative Interfaces, Inc - Millenium; (OPAC) Innovative Interfaces, Inc - Millenium; (Serials) Innovative Interfaces, Inc - Millenium
Database Vendor: HeinOnline, LexisNexis, Westlaw
Wireless access
Publications: Newsletter
Partic in OCLC Online Computer Library Center, Inc
Restriction: Mem only

L NEW YORK LAW SCHOOL LIBRARY*, 185 W Broadway, 10013. SAN 311-9564. Tel: 212-431-2332. FAX: 212-965-8839. Web Site: www.nyls.edu/library. *Librn,* Camille Broussard; E-mail: camille.broussard@nyls.edu; *Assoc Librn,* Bill Mills; Tel: 212-431-2380
Founded 1891
Library Holdings: Bk Vols 435,000; Per Subs 1,450
Subject Interests: Anglo-Am, Intl law, NY
Wireless access
Publications: Current Acquisitions (Bi-monthly); Table of Contents
Partic in Dialog Corp; Metropolitan New York Library Council; OCLC Online Computer Library Center, Inc; Westlaw
Open Mon-Thurs 9am-11pm, Fri 9am-10pm, Sat & Sun 9-9
Restriction: Mem only

L NEW YORK LEGISLATIVE SERVICE, INC LIBRARY, 14 Vesey St, 3rd Flr, 10007. SAN 372-4328. Tel: 212-962-2826. FAX: 212-962-1420. E-mail: nylegal@nyls.org. Web Site: www.nyls.org. *Exec Dir,* Steven Harvey
Founded 1932
Library Holdings: Bk Vols 10,000
Special Collections: Governor's Bill Jackets (1905-present); New York City Local Law Bill Jackets (1954-present); New York State Constitution (Contitutional Convention docs); New York State Legislative Documents
Publications: New York City Legislative (Annual); New York State Legislative (Annual)

M NEW YORK ORTHOPAEDIC HOSPITAL-COLUMBIA UNIVERSITY COLLEGE OF PHYSICIANS & SURGEONS*, Russell A Hibbs Memorial Library, 622 W 168th St, 10032. SAN 370-5536. Tel: 212-305-3294. FAX: 212-305-6193. *Librn,* Meret Anca; Staff 1 (MLS 1)
Founded 1927
Library Holdings: Bk Titles 4,000; Per Subs 25
Special Collections: Rare Books on Orthopaedics
Subject Interests: Orthopedics
Automation Activity & Vendor Info: (Cataloging) Clio
Wireless access
Restriction: Open to students, fac & staff

M NEW YORK PSYCHOANALYTIC SOCIETY & INSTITUTE*, Abraham A Brill Library, 247 E 82nd St, 10028-2701. SAN 311-9599. Tel: 212-879-6900. FAX: 212-879-0588. E-mail: library@nypsi.org. Web Site: www.nypsi.org. *Libr Dir,* Matthew von Unwerth; *Asst Librn,* Adrian Thomas; E-mail: athomas@nypsi.org
Library Holdings: Bk Titles 40,000; Per Subs 55
Special Collections: Art (Arieti Papers); Freud's Writings in all Editions & Languages (Sigmund Freud Coll); History, Literature, Languages & Linguistics Coll; Sociology (Ernst Kris Coll). Oral History
Subject Interests: Behav sci, Humanities, Psychiat, Psychoanalysis, Psychol, Soc sci
Automation Activity & Vendor Info: (Cataloging) Inmagic, Inc.; (Circulation) Inmagic, Inc.; (OPAC) Inmagic, Inc.
Database Vendor: Dialog
Wireless access
Partic in Dialog Corp
Open Mon-Thurs 1-9, Fri 1-5

P THE NEW YORK PUBLIC LIBRARY - ASTOR, LENOX & TILDEN FOUNDATIONS, 476 Fifth Ave, (@ 42nd St), 10018-2788. SAN 353-2410. Tel: 212-930-0800. Administration Tel: 212-704-8600. FAX: 212-592-7440. Web Site: www.nypl.org. *Pres,* Dr Anthony W Marx; Tel: 212-930-0736, Fax: 212-930-9299; *Chief Tech Officer, VPres,* Jane Aboyoun; Tel: 212-621-0661, E-mail: janeaboyoun@nypl.org; *VPres, Capital Planning & Fac Operations,* Joanna M Pestka; Tel: 212-930-0071, E-mail: jpestka@nypl.org; *VPres, Develop,* Ryan Cairns; Tel: 212-930-0630, E-mail: ryancairns@nypl.org; *VPres, Strategic Planning,* Jeffrey Roth; Tel: 212-621-0241, E-mail: jeffreyroth@nypl.org; *VPres, Communications & Mkt,* Ken Weine; Tel: 212-592-7714, E-mail: kenweine@nypl.org; *VPres, Pub Serv,* Anne L Coriston; Tel: 212-930-0953, Fax: 212-930-9217, E-mail: annecoriston@nypl.org; *VPres, Human Res,* Louise Shea; Tel: 212-592-7302, E-mail: louiseshea@nypl.org; *VPres/Gen Counsel,* Michele Coleman Mayes; Tel: 212-642-0115, E-mail: michelemayes@nypl.org; *Actg VPres, Pub Serv,* Christopher Platt; Tel: 917-229-9503, E-mail: christopherplatt@bookops.org; *Andrew W Mellon Dir of the New York Pub Libr,* Thornton Ann; Tel: 212-930-0674, E-mail: annthornton@nypl.org; *Dir, Adult Educ Serv,* Swarthout Luke; Tel: 212-592-7574, E-mail: lukeswarthout@nypl.org; *Dir, Digital Experience,* Frank Migliorelli; Tel: 212-621-0547, E-mail: frankmigliorelli@nypl.org; *Dir, Educ Prog,* Jacobs Maggie; Fax: 212-592-7567, E-mail: maggiejacobs@nypl.org; *Dir, Res & Ref Serv,* Jennifer Engstrom; Tel: 212-930-0585, E-mail: jenniferengstrom@nypl.org; *Dep Dir, Libr Sites & Serv,* Position Currently Open; *Chief Operating Officer,* Iris Wienshall; Tel: 212-930-0600, E-mail: irisweinshall@nypl.org; *Exec Coordr for the Andrew W Mellon Dir,* Daniel Wong; Tel: 212-930-0710, E-mail: danielwong@nypl.org
Founded 1895
Publications: Biblion; NYPL News; Staff News; Various Books
Partic in Metropolitan New York Library Council; New York State Interlibrary Loan Network (NYSILL); OCLC Online Computer Library Center, Inc; OCLC Research Library Partnership; Southeastern New York Library Resources Council; Urban Libraries Council (ULC)
Friends of the Library Group
Branches: 91
AGUILAR BRANCH, 174 E 110th St, (Between Lexington & Third Aves), 10029-3212, SAN 353-4065. Tel: 212-534-2930. FAX: 212-860-4580. Web Site: www.nypl.org/branch/local/man/ag.cfm. *Libr Mgr,* Christina Park; E-mail: christinapark@nypl.org
Library Holdings: Bk Vols 60,830
Function: Wheelchair accessible
Open Mon & Wed 11-6, Tues & Thurs 11-7, Fri & Sat 10-5
ALLERTON BRANCH, 2740 Barnes Ave, (Between Allerton & Arnow Aves), Bronx, 10467, SAN 353-409X. Tel: 718-881-4240. E-mail: allerton@nypl.org. Web Site: www.nypl.org/branch/local/bx/al.cfm. *Libr Mgr,* Manuel Martinez; E-mail: manuelmartinez@nypl.org
Library Holdings: Bk Vols 40,847
Function: Wheelchair accessible
Open Mon, Tues & Thurs 10-6, Wed 11-7, Fri & Sat 10-5
BATTERY PARK CITY LIBRARY, 175 North End Ave, 10282. Tel: 212-790-3499. Web Site: www.nypl.org/locations/battery-park-city. *Libr Mgr,* Anne Barreca; E-mail: annebarreca@nypl.org
Open Mon & Wed 10-6, Tues & Thurs 12-8, Fri & Sat 10-5
BAYCHESTER BRANCH, 2049 Asch Loop N, (North of Bartow Ave), Bronx, 10475, SAN 353-412X. Tel: 718-379-6700. FAX: 718-671-2836. E-mail: baychester@nypl.org. Web Site: www.nypl.org/branch/local/bx/bar.cfm. *Libr Mgr,* Leslie Brown; E-mail: lesliebrown@nypl.org
Library Holdings: Bk Vols 59,902
Function: Wheelchair accessible
Special Services for the Blind - Closed circuit TV; Reader equip
Open Mon & Wed 10-7, Tues & Thurs 10-6, Fri & Sat 10-5
BELMONT BRANCH, 610 E 186th St, (@ Hughes Ave), Bronx, 10458, SAN 353-4154. Tel: 718-933-6410. FAX: 718-365-8756. E-mail: belmont@nypl.org. Web Site: www.nypl.org/branch/local/bx/ber.cfm. *Libr Mgr,* Danielle Youmeni; Tel: 718-933-6439, E-mail: daniellewansi@nypl.org
Library Holdings: Bk Vols 74,680
Subject Interests: Italian
Function: Wheelchair accessible
Open Mon-Tues 10-6, Wed-Thurs 12-8, Fri & Sat 10-5
BLOOMINGDALE BRANCH, 150 W 100th St, (Between Amsterdam & Columbus Aves), 10025-5196, SAN 353-4189. Tel: 212-222-8030. FAX: 212-932-2421. Web Site: www.nypl.org/branch/local/man/blr.cfm. *Libr Mgr,* Yajaira Mejia; Tel: 212-749-5240, E-mail: yajairamejia@nypl.org
Library Holdings: Bk Vols 83,825

Function: Wheelchair accessible
Open Mon & Tues 10-6, Wed & Thurs 12-7, Fri & Sat 10-5

BRONX LIBRARY CENTER, 310 E Kingsbridge Rd, (At Briggs Ave), Bronx, 10458, SAN 353-3522. Tel: 718-579-4244. Circulation Tel: 718-579-4243. Reference Tel: 718-579-4257. Administration Tel: 718-579-4240. FAX: 718-579-4264. TDD: 718-773-4315. Web Site: www.nypl.org/branch/local/bx/fdc.cfm. *Chief Librn,* Michael Alvarez; E-mail: michaelalvarez@nypl.org
Library Holdings: Bk Vols 183,681
Function: Wheelchair accessible
Special Services for the Deaf - TTY equip
Special Services for the Blind - Closed circuit TV; Reader equip
Open Mon-Sat 9-9, Sun 12-6

GEORGE BRUCE BRANCH, 518 W 125th St, 10027, SAN 353-4758. Tel: 212-662-9727. Web Site: www.nypl.org/branch/local/man/br.cfm. *Libr Mgr,* Junelle Carter-Bowman; Tel: 212-662-0416, E-mail: junellecarter@nypl.org
Library Holdings: Bk Vols 51,189
Function: Wheelchair accessible
Open Mon & Wed Noon-7, Tues & Thurs 11-6, Fri & Sat 10-5

CASTLE HILL BRANCH, 947 Castle Hill Ave, (@ Bruckner Blvd), Bronx, 10473, SAN 353-4243. Tel: 718-824-3838. FAX: 718-824-9812. E-mail: castle_hill@nypl.org. Web Site: www.nypl.org/branch/local/bx/ct.cfm. *Libr Mgr,* Yilda L Rodriguez; E-mail: yildarodriguez@nypl.org
Library Holdings: Bk Vols 40,449
Function: Wheelchair accessible
Open Mon & Wed 11-7, Tues & Thurs 10-6, Fri & Sat 10-5

CHATHAM SQUARE BRANCH, 33 E Broadway, (Near Catherine St), 10002-6804, SAN 353-4367. Tel: 212-964-6598. E-mail: chatham_square@nypl.org. Web Site: www.nypl.org/locations/chatham-square. *Actg Libr Mgr,* Sean Ferguson; E-mail: seanferguson@nypl.org
Function: Wheelchair accessible
Open Mon-Thurs 10-7, Fri & Sat 10-5

CITY ISLAND BRANCH, 320 City Island Ave, (Between Bay & Fordham Sts), Bronx, 10464, SAN 353-4391. Tel: 718-885-1703. FAX: 718-885-3051. E-mail: city_island@nypl.org. Web Site: www.nypl.org/branch/local/bx/ci.cfm. *Libr Mgr,* Judd Karlman; E-mail: juddkarlman@nypl.org
Library Holdings: Bk Vols 35,000
Function: Wheelchair accessible
Open Mon & Thurs 11-7, Tues & Wed 11-6, Fri & Sat 10-5

CLASON'S POINT BRANCH, 1215 Morrison Ave, (Near Westchester Ave), Bronx, 10472, SAN 353-4421. Tel: 718-842-1235. FAX: 718-861-4041. E-mail: clasons_point@nypl.org. Web Site: www.nypl.org/branch/local/bx/cp.cfm. *Libr Mgr,* Melissa Davis; E-mail: melissadavis@nypl.org
Library Holdings: Bk Vols 51,823
Function: Wheelchair accessible
Open Mon & Thurs 10-7, Tues & Wed 10-6, Fri & Sat 10-5

COLUMBUS BRANCH, 742 Tenth Ave, (Between E 50th & 51st Sts), 10019-7019, SAN 353-4480. Tel: 212-586-5098. E-mail: columbus@nypl.org. Web Site: www.nypl.org/locations/columbus. *Actg Libr Mgr,* Sandra Chambers; E-mail: sandrachambers@nypl.org
Library Holdings: Bk Vols 22,639
Function: Wheelchair accessible
Open Mon, Tues & Thurs 10-6, Wed 10-7, Fri & Sat 10-5

COUNTEE CULLEN BRANCH, 104 W 136th St, (Near Lenox Ave), 10030-2695, SAN 353-4510. Tel: 212-491-2070. Web Site: www.nypl.org/branch/local/man/htr.cfm. *Libr Mgr,* Victor Simmons; Tel: 212-491-2071, E-mail: victorsimmons@nypl.org
Library Holdings: Bk Vols 65,092
Function: Wheelchair accessible
Special Services for the Blind - Closed circuit TV; Reader equip
Open Mon-Thurs 10-8, Fri & Sat 10-5

DONGAN HILLS BRANCH, 1617 Richmond Rd, (Between Seaview & Liberty Aves), Staten Island, 10304, SAN 353-4545. Tel: 718-351-1444. FAX: 718-987-6883. E-mail: donganhills@nypl.org. Web Site: www.nypl.org/branch/local/si/dh.cfm. *Libr Mgr,* Colleen Castellani; E-mail: colleencastellani@nypl.org
Library Holdings: Bk Vols 54,507
Function: Wheelchair accessible
Special Services for the Blind - Closed circuit TV; Reader equip
Open Mon & Wed 12-7, Tues & Thurs 11-6, Fri & Sat 10-5

EASTCHESTER BRANCH, 1385 E Gun Hill Rd, (Near Eastchester Rd), Bronx, 10469, SAN 353-457X. Tel: 718-653-3292. FAX: 718-881-8977. E-mail: eastchester@nypl.org. Web Site: www.nypl.org/branch/local/bx/ea.cfm. *Libr Mgr,* Joan Aikens; E-mail: joanaikens@nypl.org
Library Holdings: Bk Vols 49,648
Function: Wheelchair accessible
Open Mon & Tues 10-6, Wed & Thurs 11-7, Fri & Sat 10-5

EDENWALD BRANCH, 1255 E 233rd St, (@ DeReimer Ave), Bronx, 10466, SAN 353-460X. Tel: 718-798-3355. FAX: 718-882-5449. E-mail: edenwald@nypl.org. Web Site: www.nypl.org/branch/local/bx/ew.cfm. *Libr Mgr,* Charity Goh; E-mail: charitygoh@nypl.org
Library Holdings: Bk Vols 39,673
Function: Wheelchair accessible
Open Mon & Wed 11-7, Tues & Thurs 10-6, Fri & Sat 10-5

EPIPHANY BRANCH, 228 E 23rd St, (Near Second Ave), 10010-4672, SAN 353-4634. Tel: 212-679-2645. E-mail: epiphany@nypl.org. Web Site: www.nypl.org/locations/epiphany. *Libr Mgr,* Omisha Covington-Isidore; Tel: 212-726-9756, E-mail: omishacovington@nypl.org
Library Holdings: Bk Vols 56,563
Function: Wheelchair accessible
Open Mon & Wed 12-7, Tues & Thurs 10-6, Fri & Sat 10-5

58TH STREET BRANCH, 127 E 58th St, (Between Park & Lexington Aves), 10022-1211, SAN 353-4669. Tel: 212-759-7358. Web Site: www.nypl.org/locations/58th-street. *Libr Mgr,* John Bhagwandin; Tel: 212-758-6848, E-mail: johnbhagwandin@nypl.org; Staff 9 (MLS 2, Non-MLS 7)
Founded 1907. Pop 50,000; Circ 375,000
Jul 2012-Jun 2013 Income $865,000, City $850,000, Locally Generated Income $15,000. Mats Exp $165,000, Books $150,000, AV Equip $10,000, AV Mat $5,000. Sal $446,709 (Prof $446,709)
Library Holdings: Audiobooks 1,000; AV Mats 200; Bks-By-Mail 500; CDs 2,000; DVDs 3,000; Large Print Bks 1,000; Bk Vols 60,145
Special Collections: World Languages; Test materials; Large print
Automation Activity & Vendor Info: (Acquisitions) BiblioCommons
Database Vendor: Baker & Taylor, BiblioCommons, EBSCO - WebFeat, OCLC, SerialsSolutions
Function: Adult bk club, Adult literacy prog, Art exhibits, Audio & video playback equip for onsite use, Bk club(s), Bk reviews (Group), Bks on CD, Bus archives, CD-ROM, Citizenship assistance, Computer training, Computers for patron use, Copy machines, Digital talking bks, Distance learning, e-mail & chat, e-mail serv, E-Reserves, Electronic databases & coll, Exhibits, Family literacy, Free DVD rentals, Health sci info serv, Home delivery & serv to Sr ctr & nursing homes, Homebound delivery serv, Homework prog, ILL available, Instruction & testing, Large print keyboards, Learning ctr, Literacy & newcomer serv, Magnifiers for reading, Music CDs, Newsp ref libr, Online cat, Online searches, Outreach serv, OverDrive digital audio bks, Photocopying/Printing, Printer for laptops & handheld devices, Prof lending libr, Prog for adults, Pub access computers, Ref & res, Ref serv available, Ref serv in person, Referrals accepted, Res libr, Scanner, Senior computer classes, Senior outreach, Serves mentally handicapped consumers, Spanish lang bks, Spoken cassettes & CDs, Spoken cassettes & DVDs, Summer & winter reading prog, Summer reading prog, Tax forms, Telephone ref, Video lending libr, Web-catalog, Workshops, Writing prog
Special Services for the Deaf - Assisted listening device
Special Services for the Blind - Ref in Braille
Open Mon & Wed 11-7, Tues & Thurs 10-6, Fri & Sat 10-5
Friends of the Library Group

FORT WASHINGTON BRANCH, 535 W 179th St, (Between St Nicholas & Audubon Aves), 10033-5799, SAN 353-4693. Tel: 212-927-3533. Web Site: www.nypl.org/branch/local/man/fw.cfm. *Libr Mgr,* Lyman Clayborn; E-mail: lymanclayborn@nypl.org
Library Holdings: Bk Vols 70,441
Open Mon & Wed 10-6, Tues & Thurs 12-7, Fri & Sat 10-5

GRAND CENTRAL LIBRARY, 135 E 46th St, 10017. Tel: 212-621-0670. Web Site: www.nypl.org/locations/grand-central. *Managing Librn,* Genoveve Stowell; E-mail: genovevestowell@nypl.org
Open Mon 11-7, Tues 10-6, Wed-Fri 11-6, Sat 10-5

GRAND CONCOURSE BRANCH, 155 E 173rd St, (East of Grand Concourse), Bronx, 10457, SAN 353-4782. Tel: 718-583-6611. E-mail: grand_concourse@nypl.org. Web Site: www.nypl.org/branch/local/bx/gd.cfm. *Network Mgr,* Gesille A Dixon; Tel: 718-583-6625, E-mail: gesilledixon@nypl.org
Library Holdings: Bk Vols 52,590
Function: Wheelchair accessible
Open Mon & Wed 10-8, Tues & Thurs 10-6, Fri & Sat 10-5

GREAT KILLS BRANCH, 56 Giffords Lane, (@ Margaret St), Staten Island, 10308, SAN 353-4812. Tel: 718-984-6670. FAX: 718-317-1011. E-mail: greatkills@nypl.org. Web Site: www.nypl.org/branch/local/si/gk.cfm. *Actg Libr Mgr,* Peter Hegel; E-mail: peterhegel@nypl.org
Library Holdings: Bk Vols 27,243
Function: Wheelchair accessible
Open Mon & Thurs 11-6, Tues & Wed 12-7, Fri & Sat 10-5

HAMILTON FISH PARK BRANCH, 415 E Houston St, (Near Avenue D), 10002-1197, SAN 353-4847. Tel: 212-673-2290. E-mail: hamilton_fish@nypl.org. Web Site: www.nypl.org/locations/hamilton-fish-park. *Libr Mgr,* Norma Acevedo; Tel: 212-673-3290, E-mail: normaacevedo@nypl.org
Library Holdings: Bk Vols 43,374

Function: Wheelchair accessible
Open Mon & Wed 10-6, Tues & Thurs 12-7, Fri & Sat 10-5
HAMILTON GRANGE BRANCH, 503 W 145th St, 10031-5101, SAN 353-4871. Tel: 212-926-2147. Web Site: www.nypl.org/branch/local/man/hg.cfm. *Libr Mgr,* Yolounda S Bennett-Reid; E-mail: yoloundabennett@nypl.org
Library Holdings: Bk Vols 52,247
Function: Wheelchair accessible
Open Mon & Wed 11-7, Tues & Thurs 11-6, Fri & Sat 10-5
HARLEM BRANCH, Nine W 124th St, 10027-5699, SAN 353-4901. Tel: 212-348-5620. Web Site: www.nypl.org/branch/local/man/hl.cfm. *Libr Mgr,* Donna Murphy; E-mail: donnamurphy@nypl.org
Library Holdings: Bk Vols 42,016
Function: Wheelchair accessible
Open Mon & Wed 11-6, Tues & Thurs 12-7, Fri & Sat 10-5
P ANDREW HEISKELL BRAILLE & TALKING BOOK LIBRARY, 40 W 20th St, (Between Fifth & Sixth Aves), 10011-4211, SAN 353-3913. Tel: 212-206-5400, 212-206-5425. Toll Free Tel: 855-697-6975. FAX: 212-206-5418. E-mail: talkingbooks@nypl.org. Web Site: www.nypl.org/talkingbooks. *Managing Librn,* Jill Rothstein; Tel: 212-621-0637, E-mail: jillrothstein@nypl.org
Automation Activity & Vendor Info: (Cataloging) Keystone Systems, Inc (KLAS); (Circulation) Keystone Systems, Inc (KLAS); (OPAC) Keystone Systems, Inc (KLAS)
Function: Wheelchair accessible
Publications: NewsLion (Newsletter)
Special Services for the Blind - Accessible computers; Braille bks; Braille equip; Closed circuit TV magnifier; Digital talking bk; Digital talking bk machines; Internet workstation with adaptive software; Large print bks; Magnifiers; Newsletter (in large print, Braille or on cassette); Scanner for conversion & translation of mats; Screen enlargement software for people with visual disabilities; Screen reader software
Open Mon, Wed, Fri & Sat 10-5, Tues & Thurs Noon-7
Friends of the Library Group
HIGH BRIDGE BRANCH, 78 W 168th St, (@ Woodycrest Ave), Bronx, 10452, SAN 353-4936. Tel: 718-293-7800. FAX: 718-588-3898. E-mail: highbridge@nypl.org. Web Site: www.nypl.org/branch/local/bx/hb.cfm. *Libr Mgr,* Margaret Fleesak; E-mail: margaretfleesak@nypl.org
Library Holdings: Bk Vols 39,521
Function: Wheelchair accessible
Open Mon & Wed 11-7, Tues & Thurs 10-6, Sat & Sun 10-5
HUDSON PARK BRANCH, 66 Leroy St, (Off Seventh Ave, South), 10014-3929, SAN 353-4960. Tel: 212-243-6876. E-mail: hudson_park@nypl.org. Web Site: www.nypl.org/locations/hudson-park. *Libr Mgr,* Miranda Murray; E-mail: mirandamurray@nypl.org
Library Holdings: Bk Vols 43,074
Open Mon & Wed 11-6, Tues & Thurs 12-7, Fri & Sat 10-5
HUGUENOT PARK BRANCH, 830 Huguenot Ave, (@ Dumgole Rd), Staten Island, 10312, SAN 353-4995. Tel: 718-984-4636. FAX: 718-966-9163. E-mail: huguenot_park@nypl.org. Web Site: www.nypl.org/branch/local/si/hk.cfm. *Libr Mgr,* Steven Horvath; Tel: 718-605-0703, E-mail: stevenhorvath@nypl.org
Library Holdings: Bk Vols 61,676
Function: Wheelchair accessible
Open Mon & Wed 11-6, Tues 10-6, Thurs 12-8, Fri & Sat 10-5
HUNT'S POINT BRANCH, 877 Southern Blvd, (@ Tiffany St), Bronx, 10459, SAN 353-5029. Tel: 718-617-0338. FAX: 718-893-3491. E-mail: hunts_point@nypl.org. Web Site: www.nypl.org/branch/local/bx/hsr.cfm. *Libr Mgr,* Liana Acevedo; E-mail: lianaacevedo@nypl.org
Library Holdings: Bk Vols 74,424
Function: Wheelchair accessible
Open Mon & Thurs 10-7, Tues & Wed 10-6, Fri & Sat 10-5
INWOOD BRANCH, 4790 Broadway, (Near Dyckman St), 10034-4916, SAN 353-5053. Tel: 212-942-2445. Web Site: www.nypl.org/branch/local/man/inr.cfm. *Libr Mgr,* Danita R Nichols; E-mail: danitanichols@nypl.org
Library Holdings: Bk Vols 90,298
Function: Wheelchair accessible
Open Mon & Wed 11-7, Tues & Thurs 11-6, Fri & Sat 10-5
JEFFERSON MARKET BRANCH, 425 Avenue of the Americas, (@ Tenth St), 10011-8454, SAN 353-5088. Tel: 212-243-4334. Web Site: www.nypl.org/locations/jefferson-market. *Libr Mgr,* Frank Collerius; Tel: 212-242-5233, E-mail: frankcollerius@nypl.org
Library Holdings: Bk Vols 79,977
Function: Wheelchair accessible
Special Services for the Blind - Closed circuit TV; Reader equip
Open Mon & Wed 10-8, Tues & Thurs 11-6, Fri & Sat 10-5
JEROME PARK BRANCH, 118 Eames Pl, Bronx, 10468, SAN 353-5118. Tel: 718-549-5200. E-mail: jerome_park@nypl.org. Web Site: www.nypl.org/branch/local/bx/jp.cfm. *Libr Mgr,* Nicola McDonald; E-mail: nicolamcdonald@nypl.org
Library Holdings: Bk Vols 42,371
Function: Wheelchair accessible
Open Mon 12-8, Tues-Thurs 10-6, Fri & Sat 10-5
KINGSBRIDGE BRANCH, 291 W 231st St, (@ Corlear Ave), Bronx, 10463, SAN 353-5142. Tel: 718-548-5656. FAX: 718-796-4065. E-mail: kingsbridge@nypl.org. Web Site: www.nypl.org/branch/local/bx/kbr.cfm. *Libr Mgr,* Martha Gonzalez-Buitrago; Tel: 718-548-5980, E-mail: marthagonzalezbuitrago@nypl.org
Library Holdings: Bk Vols 61,939
Function: Wheelchair accessible
Special Services for the Blind - Closed circuit TV; Reader equip
Open Mon & Wed 11-7, Tues & Thurs 10-6, Fri & Sat 10-5
KIPS BAY BRANCH, 446 Third Ave, (@ E 31st St), 10016-6025, SAN 353-5177. Tel: 212-683-2520. E-mail: kips_bay@nypl.org. Web Site: www.nypl.org/locations/kips-bay. *Libr Mgr,* Kaydene Humphrey; E-mail: kaydenehumphrey@nypl.org
Library Holdings: Bk Vols 50,329
Function: Wheelchair accessible
Open Mon & Wed 11-6, Tues & Thurs 12-7, Fri & Sat 10-5
MACOMB'S BRIDGE BRANCH, 2650 Adam Clayton Powell Jr Blvd, (Between W 152nd & 153rd Sts), 10039-2004, SAN 353-5207. Tel: 212-281-4900. Web Site: www.nypl.org/branch/local/man/mb.cfm. *Libr Mgr,* Alison Williams; E-mail: alisonwilliams@nypl.org
Library Holdings: Bk Vols 11,772
Function: Wheelchair accessible
Open Mon 12-7, Tues, Wed & Thurs 11-6, Fri & Sat 10-5
MARINERS HARBOR LIBRARY, 206 South Ave, (Between Arlington Pl & Brabant St), Staten Island, 10303. *Libr Mgr,* Elizabete Pata; Tel: 212-621-0690, E-mail: elizabetepata@nypl.org
FRANCIS MARTIN BRANCH, 2150 University Ave, (@ 181st St), Bronx, 10453, SAN 353-4723. Tel: 718-295-5287. FAX: 718-365-8979. E-mail: francis_martin@nypl.org. Web Site: www.nypl.org/branch/local/bx/fxr.cfm. *Libr Mgr,* Linda Jones; Tel: 718-295-5944, E-mail: lindajones@nypl.org
Library Holdings: Bk Vols 65,995
Function: Wheelchair accessible
Open Mon 11-7, Tues-Thurs 10-6, Fri & Sat 10-5
MELROSE BRANCH, 910 Morris Ave, (@ E 162nd St), Bronx, 10451, SAN 353-5231. Tel: 718-588-0110. FAX: 718-588-1432. E-mail: melrose@nypl.org. Web Site: www.nypl.org/branch/local/bx/me.cfm. *Libr Mgr,* Sadeqwa Atkinson; E-mail: sadeqwaatkinson@nypl.org
Library Holdings: Bk Vols 48,551
Open Mon & Wed 10-7, Tues & Thurs 10-6, Fri & Sat 10-5
MID-MANHATTAN LIBRARY, 455 Fifth Ave, (at 40th St), 10016-0122, SAN 353-5266. Tel: 212-340-0849. Web Site: www.nypl.org/locations/mid-manhattan-library. *Chief Librn,* Caryl Soriano; Tel: 212-340-0830, E-mail: carylsoriano@nypl.org
Library Holdings: Bk Vols 1,554,578
Special Collections: Picture Coll
Function: Wheelchair accessible
Special Services for the Deaf - TTY equip
Special Services for the Blind - Reader equip
Open Mon-Thurs 8-11, Fri 8-8, Sat & Sun 10-6
MORNINGSIDE HEIGHTS BRANCH, 2900 Broadway, (@ W 113th St), 10025-7822, SAN 353-4456. Tel: 212-864-2530. Web Site: www.nypl.org/branch/local/man/cl.cfm. *Libr Mgr,* Thaddeus Krupo; Tel: 212-666-5099, E-mail: thaddeuskrupo@nypl.org
Library Holdings: Bk Vols 65,255
Function: Wheelchair accessible
Open Mon-Thurs 10-7, Fri & Sat 10-5
MORRIS PARK BRANCH, 985 Morris Park, (Between Radcliff & Colden Aves), Bronx, 10462. Tel: 718-931-0636. FAX: 718-931-1637. Web Site: www.nypl.org/branch/local/bx/mp.cfm. *Libr Mgr,* Dawn M Holloway; Tel: 718-931-0892, E-mail: dawnholloway@nypl.org
Library Holdings: Bk Vols 25,000
Function: Wheelchair accessible
Open Mon & Wed 10-7, Tues & Thurs 10-6, Fri & Sat 10-5
MORRISANIA BRANCH, 610 E 169th St, (@ Franklin Ave), Bronx, 10456, SAN 353-5479. Tel: 718-589-9268. FAX: 718-861-0394. E-mail: morrisania@nypl.org. Web Site: www.nypl.org/branch/local/bx/mr.cfm. *Libr Mgr,* Colbert Nembhard; Tel: 718-861-0372, E-mail: colbertnembhard@nypl.org
Library Holdings: Bk Vols 44,026
Function: Wheelchair accessible
Open Mon & Wed 10-6, Tues & Thurs 11-7, Fri & Sat 10-5
MOSHOLU BRANCH, 285 E 205th St, (Near Perry Ave), Bronx, 10467, SAN 353-5509. Tel: 718-882-8239. FAX: 718-547-0434. E-mail: mosholu@nypl.org. Web Site: www.nypl.org/branch/local/bx/mo.cfm. *Libr Mgr,* Jane Addison-Amoyaw; E-mail: janeaddisonamoyaw@nypl.org
Library Holdings: Bk Vols 61,560
Function: Wheelchair accessible
Open Mon 12-8, Tues-Thurs 10-6, Fri & Sat 10-5
MOTT HAVEN BRANCH, 321 E 140th St, (@ Alexander Ave), Bronx, 10454, SAN 353-5533. Tel: 718-665-4878. FAX: 718-585-8059. E-mail: mott_haven@nypl.org. Web Site: www.nypl.org/branch/local/bx/mh.cfm. *Libr Mgr,* Jeanine Thomas-Cross; E-mail: jeaninethomas@nypl.org
Library Holdings: Bk Vols 60,212

Function: Wheelchair accessible
Open Mon & Thurs 10-6, Tues & Wed 10-7, Fri & Sat 10-5
MUHLENBERG BRANCH, 209 W 23rd St, (Near Seventh Ave), 10011-2379, SAN 353-5568. Tel: 212-924-1585. E-mail: muhlenberg@nypl.org. Web Site: www.nypl.org/locations/muhlenberg. *Libr Mgr,* Ashley Curran; Tel: 646-230-6784, E-mail: ashleycurran@nypl.org
Library Holdings: Bk Vols 41,815
Function: Wheelchair accessible
Open Mon & Wed 10-6, Tues & Thurs 10-7, Fri & Sat 10-5
MULBERRY STREET BRANCH, 10 Jersey St, (Between Lafayette & Mulberry Sts), 10012-3332. Tel: 212-966-3424. Web Site: www.nypl.org/locations/mulberry-street. *Libr Mgr,* Jennifer Craft; Tel: 212-966-4894, E-mail: jennifercraft@nypl.org
Library Holdings: Bk Vols 32,655
Function: Wheelchair accessible
Open Mon & Wed 12-7, Tues & Thurs 10-6, Fri & Sat 10-5
NEW AMSTERDAM BRANCH, Nine Murray St, (Between Broadway and Church St), 10007-2223, SAN 371-3423. Tel: 212-732-8186. E-mail: new_amsterdam@nypl.org. Web Site: www.nypl.org/locations/new-amsterdam. *Libr Mgr,* Kimberly Spring; E-mail: kimberlyspring@nypl.org
Library Holdings: Bk Vols 58,231
Function: Wheelchair accessible
Open Mon & Wed 11-7, Tues & Thurs 10-6, Fri & Sat 10-5
NEW DORP BRANCH, 309 New Dorp Lane, Staten Island, 10306, SAN 353-5622. Tel: 718-351-2977. E-mail: newdorp@nypl.org. Web Site: www.nypl.org/locations/new-dorp. *Supv Librn,* Janet L Klucevsek; E-mail: janklucevsek@nypl.org
Function: Wheelchair accessible
Open Mon-Wed 10-6, Thurs 12-8, Fri & Sat 10-5
NEW YORK PUBLIC LIBRARY FOR THE PERFORMING ARTS, Library for the Performing Arts, 40 Lincoln Center Plaza, 10023-7498, SAN 353-3824. Tel: 212-870-1605. FAX: 212-870-1860. *Dir,* Jacqueline Z Davis; Tel: 212-870-1643, E-mail: jacquelinedavis@nypl.org; *Asst Dir,* Don Francis Baldini; Tel: 212-870-1644, E-mail: dbaldini@nypl.org
Subject Interests: Classical music, Comedy, Dance, Drama, Exercise rec, Folk, Jazz, Monologues, Performing arts, Plays, Popular music, Sound effects, Theatre, World music
96TH STREET BRANCH, 112 E 96th St, (Near Lexington Ave), 10128-2597, SAN 353-5657. Tel: 212-289-0908. Web Site: www.nypl.org/branch/local/man/nsr.cfm. *Libr Mgr,* William J Seufert; Tel: 212-289-0909, E-mail: williamseufert@nypl.org
Library Holdings: Bk Vols 59,156
Function: Wheelchair accessible
Open Mon-Thurs 10-7, Fri & Sat 10-5
115TH STREET BRANCH, 203 W 115th St, 10026, SAN 353-5681. Tel: 212 666 9393. Web Site: www.nypl.org/branch/local/man/hu.cfm. *Libr Mgr,* Tequila A Davis; E-mail: tequiladavis@nypl.org
Library Holdings: Bk Vols 26,430
Function: Wheelchair accessible
Open Mon & Wed 12-7, Tues & Thurs 11-6, Fri & Sat 10-5
125TH STREET BRANCH, 224 E 125th St, (Near Third Ave), 10035-1786, SAN 353-5711. Tel: 212-534-5050. Web Site: www.nypl.org/branch/local/man/hd.cfm. *Actg Libr Mgr,* Velma Morton; E-mail: velmamorton@nypl.org
Library Holdings: Bk Vols 34,090
Open Mon & Wed 11-6, Tues & Thurs 12-7, Fri & Sat 10-5
OTTENDORFER BRANCH, 135 Second Ave, (Near E 8th St - St Marks Place), 10003-8304, SAN 353-5746. Tel: 212 674-0947. E-mail: ottendorfer@nypl.org. Web Site: www.nypl.org/locations/ottendorfer. *Libr Mgr,* Kristin Kuehl; E-mail: kristinkuehl@nypl.org
Library Holdings: Bk Vols 40,824
Open Mon & Wed 11-6, Tues & Thurs 12-7, Fri & Sat 10-5
PARKCHESTER BRANCH, 1985 Westchester Ave, (@ Pugsley Ave), Bronx, 10462, SAN 353-5770. Tel: 718-829-7830. FAX: 718-824-0397. E-mail: parkchester@nypl.org. Web Site: www.nypl.org/branch/local/bx/pkr.cfm. *Libr Mgr,* Wendy Archer; E-mail: wendyarcher@nypl.org
Library Holdings: Bk Vols 46,562
Function: Wheelchair accessible
Open Mon-Thurs 8-8, Fri & Sat 10-5
PELHAM BAY BRANCH, 3060 Middletown Rd, (North of Crosby Ave), Bronx, 10461, SAN 353-5800. Tel: 718-792-6744. FAX: 718-892-4329. E-mail: pelham_bay@nypl.org. Web Site: www.nypl.org/branch/local/bx/pm.cfm. *Libr Mgr,* Debra Acosta; E-mail: debraacosta@nypl.org
Library Holdings: Bk Vols 56,629
Function: Wheelchair accessible
Open Mon & Wed 11-7, Tues & Thurs 10-6, Fri & Sat 10-5
PORT RICHMOND BRANCH, 75 Bennett St, (@ Heberton Ave), Staten Island, 10302, SAN 353-5835. Tel: 718-442-0158. E-mail: port_richmond@nypl.org. Web Site: www.nypl.org/locations/port-richmond. *Libr Mgr,* Patricia Kettles; E-mail: patriciakettles@nypl.org
Library Holdings: Bk Vols 38,310
Function: Wheelchair accessible
Open Mon-Wed 10-6, Thurs 12-8, Fri & Sat 10-5
RICHMONDTOWN BRANCH, 200 Clarke Ave, (@ Amber St), Staten Island, 10306, SAN 377-6891. Tel: 718-668-0413. E-mail: richmondtown@nypl.org. Web Site: www.nypl.org/locations/richmondtown. *Libr Mgr,* Bridget Salvato; Tel: 718-668-0414, E-mail: bridgetsalvato@nypl.org
Library Holdings: Bk Vols 65,740
Function: Wheelchair accessible
Open Mon 12-8, Tues-Thurs 10-6, Fri & Sat 10-5
RIVERDALE BRANCH, 5540 Mosholu Ave, (@ W 256th St), Bronx, 10471, SAN 353-5894. Tel: 718-549-1212. E-mail: riverdale@nypl.org. Web Site: www.nypl.org/branch/local/bx/rd.cfm. *Libr Mgr,* Rebecca Brown-Barbier; Tel: 718-432 9415, E-mail: rebeccabrown@nypl org
Library Holdings: Bk Vols 46,218
Function: Wheelchair accessible
Open Mon & Wed 10-6, Tues & Thurs 11-7, Fri & Sat 10-5
RIVERSIDE BRANCH, 127 Amsterdam Ave, (@ W 65th St), 10023-6447, SAN 353-5924. Tel: 212-870-1810. Web Site: www.nypl.org/branch/local/man/rs.cfm. *Libr Mgr,* Magally Gomila; E-mail: magallygomila@nypl.org
Library Holdings: Bk Vols 69,248
Function: Wheelchair accessible
Open Mon & Wed 11-7, Tues & Thurs 10-6, Fri & Sat 10-5
ROOSEVELT ISLAND BRANCH, 524 Main St, 10044-0001, SAN 377-6875. Tel: 212-308-6243. E-mail: roosevelt_island@nypl.org. Web Site: www.nypl.org/locations/roosevelt-island. *Libr Mgr,* Nicole Nelson; E-mail: nicolenelson@nypl.org
Library Holdings: Bk Vols 25,878
Function: Wheelchair accessible
Open Mon & Wed 10-8, Tues & Thurs 10 6, Fri & Sat 10-5
ST AGNES BRANCH, 444 Amsterdam Ave, (@ 81st St), 10024-5506, SAN 353-5959. Tel: 212-621-0619. Web Site: www.nypl.org/branch/local/man/sa.cfm. *Libr Mgr,* Jennifer Ann Zarr; E-mail: jenniferzarr@nypl.org
Library Holdings: Bk Vols 72,517
Open Mon & Wed 11-6, Tues 11-7, Thurs 12-7, Fri & Sat 10-5
ST GEORGE LIBRARY CENTER, Five Central Ave, (Near Borough Hall), Staten Island, 10301, SAN 353-4006. Tel: 718-442-8560. FAX: 718-447-2703. E-mail: stgeorge@nypl.org. Web Site: www.nypl.org/branch/local/si/sgc.cfm. *Libr Mgr,* Lorraine Ruiz; E-mail: lorraineruiz@nypl.org
Library Holdings: Bk Vols 85,806
Function: Wheelchair accessible
Special Services for the Blind - Closed circuit TV; Reader equip
Open Mon-Thurs 8-8, Fri & Sat 10-5
SCHOMBURG CENTER FOR RESEARCH IN BLACK CULTURE, 515 Malcolm X Blvd, 10037-1801, SAN 353-3468. Tel: 212-491-2263. FAX: 212-491-6760. *Dir,* Dr Khalil Gibran Muhammad; Tel: 212-491-2208, E-mail: khalilmuhammad@nypl.org; *Dep Dir,* Dr Kara Olidge; Tel: 212-491-2258, E-mail: karaolidge@nypl.org
Founded 1926
Library Holdings: Bk Vols 150,000
Special Collections: African Sculpture & Artifacts; Afro-American Paintings, Prints & Sculpture; Haitian Manuscripts (Kurt Fisher & Eugene Maximilien Coll); Harry A Williamson Library of the Negro in Masonry; Malcolm X Coll; Manuscripts of W E B DuBois, Langston Hughes, Claude McKay, Arthur Schomburg, George & Philippa Schuyler, Robert C Weaver, Clarence Cameron White, Richard Wright, Piri Thomas & Amiri Baraka; Papers of John E Bruce, Civil Rights Congress, International Labor Defense, Carnegie-Myrdal Research Memoranda, Alexander Crummell, Oakley Johnson, National Association of Colored Graduate Nurses, National Negro Congress, Phelps-Stokes Fund, Central Africa Project, William Pickens, Richard Parrish New York Urban League, Universal Negro Improvement Association, Paul Robeson, Hugh Smythe & Robert Weaver; Photographs; Rare Books; Tape & Phonograph Records, incl Interviews & Music
Subject Interests: Africa, African-Am throughout the world, with major emphasis on Afro-Am, Caribbean
Function: Res libr
Publications: Bibliographies; Exhibition catalogs; Schomburg Center Journal
Restriction: Non-circulating
Friends of the Library Group
STEPHEN A SCHWARZMAN BUILDING, Fifth Ave & 42nd St, 10018. Tel: 917-275-6975. *Dir,* Theresa Myrhol; Tel: 212-930-0716, E-mail: theresamyrhol@nypl.org
Special Collections: English & American Literature (Berg Coll); English Romanticism (Pforzheimer Coll); Manuscripts & Archives Division; Photography Coll; Print Coll; Rare Book Division; Spencer Coll; Tobacco (Arents Coll)

SCIENCE, INDUSTRY & BUSINESS LIBRARY, 188 Madison Ave, 10016-4314, SAN 371-3415. Tel: 917-275-6975. FAX: 212-592-7082. *Dir,* Kristin McDonough; E-mail: kristinmcdonough@nypl.org
Special Collections: Government Publications (United States, United Nations, European Union, New York State); Patent & Trademark Gazettes (European Patent Office & Patent Cooperation Treaty, United States, British & German Patents). US Document Depository
Subject Interests: Advertising, Astronautics, Astronomy, Automobiles, Banking, Beverages, Chem, Communications, Computer sci, Demography, Earth sci, Econ, Electricity, Electronics, Eng, Finance, Food tech, Indust relations, Labor, Manufacturing, Math, Metallurgy, Mining, Mkt, Navigation, Paper, Physics, Plastics, Railroads, Rubber, Sci hist, Shipbuilding, Small bus, Soc statistics, Tech aspects of transportation, Textiles
Special Services for the Deaf - TTY equip

SEDGWICK BRANCH, 1701 University Ave, (@ W 176th St)), Bronx, 10453, SAN 353-5983. Tel: 718-731-2074. FAX: 718-299-2608. E-mail: sedgwick@nypl.org. Web Site: www.nypl.org/branch/local/bx/sd.cfm. *Libr Mgr,* Samuel O Ansah; E-mail: samuelansah@nypl.org
Library Holdings: Bk Vols 36,813
Function: Wheelchair accessible
Open Mon-Wed 10-6, Thurs 11-7, Fri & Sat 10-5

SEWARD PARK BRANCH, 192 E Broadway, (@ Jefferson St), 10002-5597, SAN 353-6017. Tel: 212-477-6770. E-mail: seward_park@nypl.org. Web Site: www.nypl.org/locations/seward-park. *Libr Mgr,* Lakisha Brown; E-mail: lakishabrown@nypl.org
Library Holdings: Bk Vols 59,049
Function: Wheelchair accessible
Open Mon & Wed 11-7, Tues & Thurs 10-8, Fri & Sat 10-5

SIXTY-SEVENTH STREET BRANCH, 328 E 67th St, (Near First Ave), 10021-6296, SAN 353-6041. Tel: 212-734-1717. Web Site: www.nypl.org/branch/local/man/ss.cfm. *Libr Mgr,* Rebecca Donsky; E-mail: rebeccadonsky@nypl.org
Library Holdings: Bk Vols 23,981
Function: Wheelchair accessible
Open Mon & Wed 11-6, Tues & Thurs 12-7, Fri & Sat 10-5

SOUNDVIEW BRANCH, 660 Soundview Ave, (@ Seward Ave), Bronx, 10473, SAN 353-6076. Tel: 718-589-0880. FAX: 718-589-5869. E-mail: soundview@nypl.org. Web Site: www.nypl.org/branch/local/bx/sv.cfm. *Libr Mgr,* Tanya F Willis; E-mail: tanyawillis@nypl.org
Library Holdings: Bk Vols 52,479
Function: Wheelchair accessible
Open Mon & Thurs 10-6, Tues & Wed 11-7, Fri & Sat 10-5

SOUTH BEACH BRANCH, 21-25 Robin Rd, (@ Ocean Ave & Father Capodanno Blvd), Staten Island, 10305, SAN 353-6106. Tel: 718-816-5834. FAX: 718-816-5936. E-mail: south_beach@nypl.org. Web Site: www.nypl.org/branch/local/si/sb.cfm. *Libr Mgr,* Susan Hansen; Tel: 718-816-5836, E-mail: susanhansen@nypl.org
Library Holdings: Bk Vols 24,953
Function: Wheelchair accessible
Open Mon, Tues & Wed 11-6, Thurs 12-7, Fri & Sat 10-5

SPUYTEN DUYVIL BRANCH, 650 W 235th St, (@ Independence Ave), Bronx, 10463, SAN 353-6165. Tel: 718-796-1202. FAX: 718-796-2351. E-mail: spuyten_duyvil@nypl.org. Web Site: www.nypl.org/branch/local/bx/dy.cfm. *Libr Mgr,* Tim Tureski; E-mail: timtureski@nypl.org
Library Holdings: Bk Vols 56,596
Function: Wheelchair accessible
Open Mon & Wed 11-7, Tues & Thurs 10-6, Fri & Sat 10-5

STAPLETON BRANCH, 132 Canal St, Staten Island, 10304, SAN 353-619X. Tel: 718-727-0427. E-mail: stapleton@nypl.org. Web Site: www.nypl.org/locations/stapleton. *Libr Mgr,* Robert Gibbs; Tel: 718-442-6725, E-mail: robertgibbs@nypl.org
Library Holdings: Bk Vols 29,960
Open Mon, Wed & Thurs 10-6, Tues 12-8, Fri & Sat 10-5

TERENCE CARDINAL COOKE-CATHEDRAL BRANCH, 560 Lexington Ave, (@ E 50th St, Lower Level), 10022-6828, SAN 353-4278. Tel: 212-752-3824. E-mail: cathedral@nypl.org. Web Site: www.nypl.org/locations/cathedral.
Library Holdings: Bk Vols 26,328
Function: Wheelchair accessible
Closed for renovation
Open Mon-Thurs 10-6, Fri 10-5

THROG'S NECK BRANCH, 3025 Cross Bronx Expressway Exten, (@ East Tremont Ave), Bronx, 10465, SAN 353-622X. Tel: 718-792-2612. FAX: 718-671-1495. E-mail: throgs_neck@nypl.org. Web Site: www.nypl.org/branch/local/bx/tg.cfm. *Libr Mgr,* Leida Torres; E-mail: leidatorres@nypl.org
Library Holdings: Bk Vols 43,789
Function: Wheelchair accessible
Open Mon & Wed 10-6, Tues & Thurs 11-7, Fri & Sat 10-5

TODT HILL-WESTERLEIGH BRANCH, 2550 Victory Blvd, (Past Willowbrook Rd), Staten Island, 10314, SAN 353-6254. Tel: 718-494-1642. E-mail: todt_hill@nypl.org. Web Site: www.nypl.org/locations/todt-hill-westerleigh. *Libr Mgr,* Jeanise LaBrew; E-mail: jeaniselabrew@nypl.org
Library Holdings: Bk Vols 97,766
Function: Wheelchair accessible
Open Mon, Wed & Thurs 10-6, Tues 12-8, Fri & Sat 10-5, Sun 1-5

TOMPKINS SQUARE BRANCH, 331 E Tenth St, (Near Avenue B), 10009-5099, SAN 353-6289. Tel: 212-228-4747. E-mail: tompkins_square@nypl.org. Web Site: www.nypl.org/locations/tompkins-square. *Libr Mgr,* Tyler Smith; E-mail: tylersmith@nypl.org
Library Holdings: Bk Vols 54,057
Function: Wheelchair accessible
Open Mon & Wed Noon-7, Tues & Thurs 11-6, Fri & Sat 10-5

TOTTENVILLE BRANCH, 7430 Amboy Rd, Staten Island, 10307, SAN 353-6319. Tel: 718-984-0945. FAX: 718-967-8817. E-mail: tottenville@nypl.org. Web Site: www.nypl.org/branch/local/si/tv.cfm. *Libr Mgr,* Courtney Castellane; Tel: 718-608-9389, E-mail: courtneycastellane@nypl.org
Library Holdings: Bk Vols 31,757
Function: Wheelchair accessible
Open Mon 12-8, Tues, Wed & Thurs 11-6, Fri & Sat 10-5

TREMONT BRANCH, 1866 Washington Ave, (@ E 176th St), Bronx, 10457, SAN 353-6343. Tel: 718-299-2155, 718-299-5177. FAX: 718-466-9589. E-mail: tremont@nypl.org. Web Site: www.nypl.org/branch/local/bx/tm.cfm. *Libr Mgr,* Sandra Pugh; E-mail: sandrapugh@nypl.org
Library Holdings: Bk Vols 29,837
Function: Wheelchair accessible
Open Mon & Wed 10-6, Tues & Thurs 11-7, Fri & Sat 10-5

VAN CORTLANDT BRANCH, 3874 Sedgwick Ave, (South of Mosholu Pkwy), 10463, SAN 353-6378. Tel: 718-543-5150. E-mail: van_cortlandt@nypl.org. Web Site: www.nypl.org/branch/local/bx/vc.cfm. *Libr Mgr,* Peter Pamphile; E-mail: peterpamphile@nypl.org
Library Holdings: Bk Vols 31,997
Function: Wheelchair accessible
Open Mon, Tues, & Thurs 10-6, Wed 11-7, Fri & Sat 10-5

VAN NEST BRANCH, 2147 Barnes Ave, (Near Pelham Pkwy South), Bronx, 10462, SAN 353-6408. Tel: 718-829-5864. Web Site: www.nypl.org/branch/local/bx/vn.cfm. *Libr Mgr,* David Nochimson; E-mail: davidnochimson@nypl.org
Library Holdings: Bk Vols 51,512
Function: Wheelchair accessible
Open Mon-Wed 10-6, Thurs 11-7, Fri & Sat 10-5

WAKEFIELD BRANCH, 4100 Lowerre Pl, Bronx, 10466, SAN 353-6432. Tel: 718-652-4663. FAX: 718-652-0425. E-mail: wakefield@nypl.org. Web Site: www.nypl.org/branch/local/bx/wk.cfm. *Libr Mgr,* Maribel Ramos-Lugo; E-mail: maribelramoslugo@nypl.org
Library Holdings: Bk Vols 47,638
Function: Wheelchair accessible
Open Mon & Wed 11-7, Tues & Thurs 10-6, Fri & Sat 10-5

WASHINGTON HEIGHTS BRANCH, 1000 St Nicholas Ave, (@ W 160th St), 10032-5202, SAN 353-6467. Tel: 212-923-6054. Web Site: www.nypl.org/branch/local/man/wh.cfm. *Libr Mgr,* Vianela Rivas; E-mail: vianelarivas@nypl.org
Library Holdings: Bk Vols 52,826
Library closed for partial renovation

WEBSTER BRANCH, 1465 York Ave, (Near E 78th St), 10021-8895, SAN 353-6491. Tel: 212-288-5049. FAX: 676-422-0428. Web Site: www.nypl.org/branch/local/man/wb.cfm. *Libr Mgr,* Jean F Pamphile; E-mail: jeanpamphile@nypl.org
Library Holdings: Bk Vols 41,261
Function: Wheelchair accessible
Open Mon & Wed 11-6, Tues & Thurs 12-7, Fri & Sat 10-5

WEST FARMS BRANCH, 2085 Honeywell Ave, (Between E 179th & 180th Sts), Bronx, 10460, SAN 353-6521. Tel: 718-367-5376. FAX: 718-220-4262. E-mail: west_farms@nypl.org. Web Site: www.nypl.org/branch/local/bx/wf.cfm. *Libr Mgr,* Tambra Gill; E-mail: tambragill@nypl.org
Library Holdings: Bk Vols 43,117
Function: Wheelchair accessible
Open Mon & Tues 10-6, Wed & Thurs 11-7, Fri & Sat 10-5

WEST NEW BRIGHTON BRANCH, 976 Castleton Ave, (@ North Burgher Ave), Staten Island, 10310, SAN 353-6556. Tel: 718-442-1416. Web Site: www.nypl.org/locations/west-new-brighton. *Libr Mgr,* Tanisha Litrell; Tel: 718-448-9655, E-mail: tanishalitrell@nypl.org
Library Holdings: Bk Vols 35,105
Function: Wheelchair accessible
Open Mon, Tues & Thurs 11-6, Wed 12-8, Fri & Sat 10-5

WESTCHESTER SQUARE BRANCH, 2521 Glebe Ave, Bronx, 10461, SAN 353-6580. Tel: 718-863-0436. FAX: 718-931-4751. E-mail: westchester_square@nypl.org. Web Site: www.nypl.org/branch/local/bx/wt.cfm. *Libr Mgr,* Kathleen Carrasco; E-mail: kathleencarrasco@nypl.org
Library Holdings: Bk Vols 42,721
Open Mon & Wed 10-6, Tues & Thurs 11-7, Fri & Sat 10-5

WOODLAWN HEIGHTS BRANCH, 4355 Katonah Ave, (@ E 239th St), Bronx, 10470, SAN 353-6610. Tel: 718-519-9627. FAX: 718-519-9628. E-mail: woodlawn@nypl.org. Web Site: www.nypl.org/branch/local/bx/wl.cfm. *Libr Mgr,* Rana Smith; E-mail: ranasmith@nypl.org
Library Holdings: Bk Vols 26,336
Function: Wheelchair accessible
Open Mon, Wed & Thurs 10-6, Tues 11-7, Fri & Sat 10-5

WOODSTOCK BRANCH, 761 E 160th St, (West of Prospect Ave), Bronx, 10456, SAN 353-6645. Tel: 718-665-6255. FAX: 718-665-9403. E-mail: woodstock@nypl.org. Web Site: www.nypl.org/branch/local/bx/wo.cfm.
Library Holdings: Bk Vols 40,000
Closed for Renovations

YORKVILLE BRANCH, 222 E 79th St, (Between Second & Third Aves), 10021-1295, SAN 353-667X. Tel: 212-744-5824. FAX: 212-744-5929. Web Site: www.nypl.org/branch/local/man/yv.cfm. *Libr Mgr,* Leslie Tabor; E-mail: leslietabor@nypl.org
Library Holdings: Bk Vols 57,721
Open Mon & Wed 12-7, Tues & Thurs 10-6, Fri & Sat 10-5

C NEW YORK SCHOOL OF INTERIOR DESIGN LIBRARY*, 170 E 70th St, 10021. SAN 321-0545. Tel: 212-472-1500, Ext 214. Circulation Tel: 212-452-4169. Administration Tel: 212-472-1500, Ext 216. Toll Free Tel: 800-336-9743, Ext 214. FAX: 212-472-8175. E-mail: libraryinfo@nysid.edu. Web Site: library.nysid.edu/library. *Dir,* Billy Kwan; Tel: 212-452-4171, E-mail: bkwan@nysid.edu; *Librn,* Meg Donabedian; Tel: 212-452-4174, E-mail: mdonabedian@nysid.edu; *Asst Librn,* Katie Knight; Tel: 212-452-4160, E-mail: kknight@nysid.edu; Staff 2 (MLS 2)
Founded 1924. Enrl 700; Fac 85; Highest Degree: Master
Library Holdings: AV Mats 100; Bk Vols 15,000; Per Subs 104
Special Collections: Architecture & Interiors; Digitized Images of Interiors, architecture and decorative arts; History of Furniture
Subject Interests: Archit, Interior design
Automation Activity & Vendor Info: (Acquisitions) Ex Libris Group; (Cataloging) Ex Libris Group; (Circulation) Ex Libris Group; (Course Reserve) Ex Libris Group; (OPAC) Ex Libris Group; (Serials) Ex Libris Group
Database Vendor: OCLC FirstSearch
Wireless access
Function: Photocopying/Printing
Partic in Metropolitan New York Library Council
Open Mon-Thurs 9-9, Fri 9-5, Sat 10-6
Restriction: Open to fac, students & qualified researchers

S THE NEW YORK SOCIETY LIBRARY, 53 E 79th St, 10075. SAN 311-9602. Tel: 212-288-6900. Interlibrary Loan Service Tel: 212-288-6900, Ext 215. Reference Tel: 212-288-6900, Ext 201. FAX: 212-744-5832. E-mail: reference@nysoclib.org. Web Site: www.nysoclib.org. *Head Librn,* Mark Bartlett; E-mail: mark@nysoclib.org; *Asst Head Librn,* Carolyn Waters; Tel: 212-288-6900, Ext 244, E-mail: carolyn@nysoclib.org; *Dir of Develop,* Joan Zimmett; Tel: 212-288-6900, Ext 202, E-mail: jzimmett@nysoclib.org; *Head, Cat & Spec Coll,* Laura OKeefe; Tel: 212-288-6900, Ext 240, Fax: 212-288-6870, E-mail: laura@nysoclib.org; *Head, Children's Libr,* Carrie Silberman; Tel: 212-288-6900, Ext 234, E-mail: carrie@nysoclib.org; *Head, Exhibitions,* Harriet Shapiro; Tel: 212-288-6000, Ext 221, E-mail: harriet@nysoclib.org; *Head, Acq,* Steve McGuirl; Tel: 212-288-6900, Ext 247, Fax: 212-585-0227, E-mail: smcguirl@nysoclib.org, *Head, Syst,* Syed Rasool; Tel: 212 288-6900, Ext 241, E-mail: syed@nysoclib.org; *Spec Coll Librn,* Erin Schreiner; Tel: 212-288-6900, Ext 242, E-mail: erin@nysoclib.org; *Conservator,* George Munoz; Tel: 212-288-6900, Ext 249, E-mail: george@nysoclib.org; Staff 18 (MLS 12, Non-MLS 6)
Founded 1754
Library Holdings: Audiobooks 1,700; e-books 40,000; e-journals 400; Electronic Media & Resources 22; Large Print Bks 1,700; Microforms 750; Bk Vols 320,000; Per Subs 240
Special Collections: Irene Sharaff/Mai-Mai Sze Coll; John Hammond Coll, early gothic fiction & literature; John Winthrop Coll; Lorenzo Da Ponte Coll; Reverend John Sharpe Coll
Subject Interests: Art & archit, Biog, Criticism, Exploration, Fiction, Hist, NY City, Poetry, Travel
Automation Activity & Vendor Info: (Acquisitions) Innovative Interfaces, Inc; (Cataloging) Innovative Interfaces, Inc; (Circulation) Innovative Interfaces, Inc; (ILL) OCLC WorldShare Interlibrary Loan; (OPAC) Innovative Interfaces, Inc; (Serials) Innovative Interfaces, Inc
Wireless access
Publications: Annual Report; Books & People (Newsletter); E-news (Online only); Events (Newsletter); New Book List (Monthly)
Open Mon, Wed, Fri & Sat 9-5, Tues & Thurs 9-7, Sun 1-5

GL NEW YORK STATE DEPARTMENT OF LAW LIBRARY*, 120 Broadway, 25th Flr, 10271. SAN 311-9610. Tel: 212-416-8012. FAX: 212-416-6130. E-mail: nyc.library@oag.state.ny.us. Web Site: www.oag.state.ny.us. *Sr Librn,* Fran Sheinwald
Library Holdings: Bk Titles 25,000
Subject Interests: Attorney Generals' opinions, NY State law
Automation Activity & Vendor Info: (Acquisitions) SirsiDynix; (Cataloging) SirsiDynix
Database Vendor: LexisNexis, Westlaw
Wireless access
Restriction: Open to staff only

GM NEW YORK STATE PSYCHIATRIC INSTITUTE*, Research Library, 1051 Riverside Dr, Box 114, 10032. SAN 311-9629. Tel: 212-543-5675. FAX: 212-543-5092. Web Site: nyspi.org/library. *Asst Librn,* Alfa J Garcia. Subject Specialists: *Bibliog instruction, Internet,* Alfa J Garcia
Founded 1896
Library Holdings: Bk Titles 15,000; Bk Vols 30,000; Per Subs 400
Subject Interests: Neurology, Neuropathology, Psychiat, Psychoanalysis, Psychol
Database Vendor: PubMed
Publications: Acquisition (Newsletter)
Open Mon-Fri 9-5

NEW YORK STATE SUPREME COURT

L FIRST JUDICIAL DISTRICT CIVIL LAW LIBRARY*, 60 Centre St, 10007, SAN 353-6793. Tel: 646-386-3670. FAX: 212-374-8159. *Librn,* Julie Gick; E-mail: jgick@courts.state.ny.us
Library Holdings: Bk Vols 60,000
Special Collections: New York City Codes; New York State Statutes; Records & Briefs NY Court of Appeals & Appellate Divisions, 1984-present, micro
Database Vendor: LexisNexis, Westlaw
Publications: Newsletter (Quarterly)
Open Mon-Fri 9-5

GL FIRST JUDICIAL DISTRICT CRIMINAL LAW LIBRARY*, 100 Centre St, 17th Flr, 10013, SAN 353-6769. Tel: 646-386-3890, 646-386-3891. FAX: 212-748-7908. E-mail: reflibny@courts.state.ny.us. Web Site: www.nycourts.gov/library/nyc_criminal/. *Sr Law Librn,* Ted Pollack; E-mail: tpollack@courts.state.ny.us; *Spec Asst, Budget & Payment Proc,* Felicia Barratsingh; Tel: 646-386-3889, E-mail: fbarrats@courts.state.ny.us; *Online Serv,* Walter Moy. Subject Specialists: *Law,* Ted Pollack
Library Holdings: Bk Titles 35,000; Bk Vols 109,000
Special Collections: Trial Transcripts for New York State, First JD Supreme Court-Criminal Branch
Subject Interests: Court admin, Criminology, Law
Automation Activity & Vendor Info: (Acquisitions) SirsiDynix; (Cataloging) SirsiDynix; (Circulation) SirsiDynix; (ILL) SirsiDynix; (OPAC) SirsiDynix; (Serials) SirsiDynix
Database Vendor: LexisNexis, Westlaw
Partic in Metropolitan New York Library Council; OCLC Online Computer Library Center, Inc
Restriction: Open to pub by appt only

NEW YORK TIMES

S PHOTO LIBRARY*, 620 Eighth Ave, 5th Flr, 10018, SAN 353-6882. Tel: 212-556-1642. FAX: 646-428-6366. *Dir,* James J Mones; E-mail: jmones@nytimes.com
Special Collections: Photographic Coll
Restriction: Staff use only

S REFERENCE LIBRARY*, 620 Eighth Ave, 5th Flr, 10018, SAN 353-6912. Tel: 212-556-7428. FAX: 212 556 4448. *Dir, Res,* Barbara Gray; Staff 10 (MLS 8, Non-MLS 2)
Library Holdings: Bk Titles 35,000; Bk Vols 40,000; Per Subs 200
Subject Interests: Biog, Journalism, Politics
Database Vendor: EBSCOhost, Factiva.com, LexisNexis
Function: Res libr
Restriction: Employees only

C NEW YORK UNIVERSITY*, Elmer Holmes Bobst Library, 70 Washington Sq S, 10012-1019. SAN 353-6947. Tel: 212-998-2500. Interlibrary Loan Service Tel: 212-998-2511. FAX: 212-995-4070. Web Site: library.nyu.edu. *Dean of Libr,* Carol A Mandel; Tel: 212-998-2444; *Pub Serv Dir,* Lucinda Covert-Vail; *Head, Bus & Doc,* Alicia Estes; *Head, Humanities & Soc Sci,* Evelyn Ehrlich; *Head, Media Serv,* Kent Underwood; *Head, Sci Libr,* Kara Whatley; *Spec Coll Librn,* Marvin Taylor; *Cat,* Susan Hayes; *Tech Serv,* Amy Lucker; Staff 113 (MLS 113)
Founded 1831. Enrl 36,719; Fac 2,380; Highest Degree: Doctorate
Library Holdings: e-journals 49,987; Bk Vols 3,816,019
Special Collections: Alfred C Berol Lewis Carroll Coll, bks, letters, ms, photog; Erich Maria Remarque Library Coll; Rare Judaica & Hebraica; Robert Frost Library Coll; Tamiment Institute-Ben Josephson Library & Robert F Wagner Labor Archives; Toumlilene Monastery (Morocco) Library of North Africana; Wiet Coll of Islamic Materials
Publications: New York Labor Heritage; Progressions, Library Division Newsletter
Partic in Metropolitan New York Library Council; OCLC Research Library Partnership

Open Mon-Thurs 9am-10:45pm, Fri 9-7:45, Sat 11-7:45, Sun 1-9:45
Friends of the Library Group
Departmental Libraries:
JACK BRAUSE LIBRARY, 11 W 42nd St, Ste 510, 10036-8002, SAN 353-7080. Tel: 212-992-3627. FAX: 212-992-3684. Web Site: guides.nyu.edu/jackbrauselibrary. *Head Librn,* Alicia Estes
Founded 1984
Library Holdings: Bk Titles 2,000; Per Subs 245
Subject Interests: Real estate
Partic in RLIN (Research Libraries Information Network)
Open Mon-Thurs 10-7, Fri 10-5
Restriction: Closed stack, In-house use for visitors, Limited access based on advanced application, Non-circulating coll, Open to others by appt, Pub by appt only
STEPHEN CHAN LIBRARY OF FINE ARTS, One E 78th St, 10021, SAN 353-7099. Tel: 212-992-5825. FAX: 212-992-5807. E-mail: ifa.library@nyu.edu. Web Site: www.nyu.edu/gsas/dept/fineart/research/library-ifa.htm. *Head Librn,* Amy Lucker; E-mail: amy.lucker@nyu.edu; Staff 4 (MLS 3, Non-MLS 1)
Library Holdings: Bk Vols 200,000; Per Subs 508
Subject Interests: Archaeology, Art hist, Conserv
Partic in RLIN (Research Libraries Information Network)
Open Mon & Fri (Fall & Spring) 9-5, Tues-Thurs 9-7: Mon-Fri (Summer) 9-5
COURANT INSTITUTE OF MATHEMATICAL SCIENCES, 251 Mercer St, 12th Flr, 10012-1110, SAN 353-7129. Tel: 212-998-3315. FAX: 212-995-4808. Web Site: cims.nyu.edu/library. *Librn,* Carol Hutchins; E-mail: hutchins@nyu.edu
Founded 1954. Enrl 2,000
Library Holdings: Bk Vols 66,014; Per Subs 300
Special Collections: Mathematics (Courant, Bohr & Friedricks Reprints)
Subject Interests: Computer sci, Fluid mechanics, Math, Robotics
Open Mon-Thurs (Fall-Spring) 9am-9:30pm, Fri 9-7, Sat 10-6; Mon-Thurs (Summer) 10-9. Fri 10-6
FALES LIBRARY & SPECIAL COLLECTIONS, 70 Washington Sq S, 10012. Tel: 212-998-2596. FAX: 212-995-3835. E-mail: fales.library@nyu.edu. Web Site: www.nyu.edu/library/bobst/research/fales. *Dir,* Marvin Taylor; Tel: 212-998-2599; *Librn,* Charlotte Priddle. Subject Specialists: *Experimental writing, Victorian lit,* Marvin Taylor; Staff 3 (MLS 3)
Founded 1957
Library Holdings: Bk Vols 200,000
Special Collections: American Cookbooks from the 18th Century to the Present (Cecily Brownstone Cookbook Coll); British & American Fiction from 1750 to the Present (Fales Library); Printed & Archival Materials Documenting the Downtown New York Art, Literary, Performance & Music Scene from 1973 to the Present (Downtown Coll)
Subject Interests: Am lit, Art, British lit, Cookery, Experimental writing, Film, Video
Automation Activity & Vendor Info: (Cataloging) Innovative Interfaces, Inc; (OPAC) Innovative Interfaces, Inc
Function: Archival coll, For res purposes, Prog for adults, Res libr
Publications: Fales Library Checklist (Collection catalog)
Open Mon-Thurs 10-4:45
Restriction: Authorized scholars by appt, Closed stack, Non-circulating coll, Open to fac, students & qualified researchers, Photo ID required for access
Friends of the Library Group
INSTITUTE OF FINE ARTS CONSERVATION CENTER LIBRARY, 14 E 78th St, 10075, SAN 353-7110. Tel: 212-992-5854. FAX: 212-992-5851. Web Site: www.nyu.edu/gsas/dept/fineart/research/library-conservation.htm. *Supvr,* Daniel Biddle; E-mail: daniel.biddle@nyu.edu; Staff 1 (Non-MLS 1)
Library Holdings: Bk Vols 14,000; Per Subs 202
Subject Interests: Art conserv
Partic in RLIN (Research Libraries Information Network)
TAMIMENT LIBRARY/ROBERT F WAGNER LABOR ARCHIVES, Elmer Holmes Bobst Library, 70 Washington Sq S, 10th Flr, 10012. Tel: 212-998-2630. E-mail: tamiment.wagner@library.nyu.edu. Web Site: www.nyu.edu/library/bobst/research/tam/. *Actg Head,* Chela Scott Weber; *Curator,* Erika Gottfried
Library Holdings: Bk Vols 60,502
Special Collections: Oral History
Subject Interests: Labor, Soc liberalism, Utopianism
Publications: New York Labor Heritage
Open Mon & Wed-Fri 10-5, Tues 9-6
UNITED NATIONS COLLECTION, Elmer Holmes Bobst Library, 70 Washington Sq S, 10012. Tel: 212-998-2610. FAX: 212-995-4442. E-mail: intl.doc@nyu.edu. Web Site: nyu.libguides.com/internationaldocs. *Librn,* Alicia Estes
Library Holdings: Bk Vols 4,000; Per Subs 530
Partic in Metropolitan New York Library Council
Special Services for the Deaf - Assistive tech
Special Services for the Blind - Assistive/Adapted tech devices, equip & products
Open Mon-Fri 10-6
Friends of the Library Group

CL NEW YORK UNIVERSITY SCHOOL OF LAW*, 40 Washington Sq S, 10012-1099. SAN 353-7218. Tel: 212-998-6300. Circulation Tel: 212-998-6312. Reference Tel: 212-998-6600. Administration Tel: 212-998-6321. FAX: 212-995-4559. Web Site: www.law.nyu.edu/library/. *Asst Dean, Libr Serv, Dir, Law Libr,* Radu D Popa; *Assoc Dir, Coll Serv,* Ron Brown; *Assoc Dir, Res & Online Serv,* Jay Shuman; *Assoc Dir, Tech,* Leslie Rich; Staff 41 (MLS 14, Non-MLS 27)
Library Holdings: Bk Vols 1,101,672
Automation Activity & Vendor Info: (ILL) OCLC ILLiad
Wireless access
Partic in RLIN (Research Libraries Information Network)
Open Mon-Thurs 8am-11:30pm, Fri 8am-10pm, Sat 9-9, Sun 10am-11:30pm

S NEWSWEEK, INC*, Research Center, 395 Hudson St, 10014. SAN 353-7366. Tel: 212-445-4680. FAX: 212-445-4107. *Dir,* Madeline Cohen; Staff 10 (MLS 9, Non-MLS 1)
Founded 1933
Library Holdings: Bk Titles 8,000; Per Subs 100
Subject Interests: Current affairs, Politics
Automation Activity & Vendor Info: (Cataloging) Inmagic, Inc.; (Circulation) Inmagic, Inc.
Database Vendor: Dialog, Factiva.com, LexisNexis, ProQuest
Wireless access
Partic in OCLC Online Computer Library Center, Inc
Restriction: Staff use only

M NORTH GENERAL HOSPITAL*, Medical Library, 1879 Madison Ave, 10035. SAN 311-8118. Tel: 212-423-4476. *Dir,* Judith Wilkinson; E-mail: nghlibrarian@gmail.com; Staff 1 (MLS 1)
Founded 1957
Library Holdings: Bk Vols 8,000; Per Subs 40
Special Collections: Audiovisual Coll on Medicine, Surgery & Podiatry
Subject Interests: Med, Podiatry, Surgery
Function: Health sci info serv
Partic in Metropolitan New York Library Council; National Network of Libraries of Medicine South Central Region
Open Mon-Fri 8-4:30
Restriction: Access at librarian's discretion, Staff & prof res

L O'MELVENY & MYERS LLP*, Law Library, Times Square Tower, Seven Times Sq, 10036. SAN 371-6074. Reference Tel: 212-326-2008. FAX: 212-326-2061. E-mail: nylibrary@omm.com. *Br Mgr,* Heide-Marie Bliss; E-mail: hbliss@omm.com; *Res Librn,* Mary-Lynne Bancone; *Tech Serv,* Jill Lanier; Tel: 212-326-2022, E-mail: jlanier@omm.com; Staff 4 (MLS 3, Non-MLS 1)
Library Holdings: Bk Vols 15,000
Subject Interests: Law
Automation Activity & Vendor Info: (Course Reserve) Sydney
Database Vendor: Bloomberg, Checkpoint Systems, Inc, Dialog, Factset, Gale Cengage Learning, HeinOnline, Hoovers, LexisNexis, OCLC-RLG, Westlaw, Westlaw Business
Function: ILL available
Restriction: Authorized personnel only

S OMNICOM*, BBDO, Inc Information Resource Center, 1285 Avenue of the Americas, 10019. SAN 311-6328. Tel: 212-459-5103. Information Services Tel: 212-459-6311. FAX: 212-459-6417. *Mgr,* Sylvia Wachtel
Founded 1965
Library Holdings: Bk Titles 1,200; Per Subs 100
Subject Interests: Advertising, Gen bus, Mkt
Database Vendor: Dialog, Factiva.com, LexisNexis
Restriction: Staff use only

S ORIGAMI USA LIBRARY*, 15 W 77th St, 10024-5192. SAN 326-2170. Tel: 212-769-5635. FAX: 212-769-5668. Web Site: www.origami-usa.org. *Pres,* Ziechner Wendy
Library Holdings: Bk Vols 1,750
Special Collections: Historical Manuscripts; Original Origami Creations; Unpublished Diagrams
Wireless access
Restriction: Mem only, Open by appt only

L ORRICK, HERRINGTON & SUTCLIFFE*, Law Library, 666 Fifth Ave, 10103. SAN 372-4425. Tel: 212-506-5340. FAX: 212-506-5151. *Res Spec,* Wilson Addo; *Res Spec,* Alan Dubin; Staff 5 (MLS 2, Non-MLS 3)
Library Holdings: Bk Vols 15,000
Automation Activity & Vendor Info: (Acquisitions) SydneyPlus; (Cataloging) SydneyPlus; (Circulation) SydneyPlus; (OPAC) SydneyPlus; (Serials) SydneyPlus
Database Vendor: LexisNexis, Westlaw

Wireless access
Restriction: Staff use only

C PACE UNIVERSITY LIBRARY*, Henry Birnbaum Library, New York Civic Ctr, One Pace Plaza, 10038-1502. SAN 353-7420. Tel: 212-346-1332. FAX: 212-346-1615. Web Site: www.pace.edu/library. *Assoc Univ Librn,* Rey Racelis; Tel: 212-346-1598, E-mail: rracelis@pace.edu; *Asst Dir, Libr Tech,* Milton David Almodovar; *Head, Access Serv,* Ann Wilberton; *Head, Info Serv & Res,* Sue Hunter; *Head, Tech Serv,* Adele Artola; Staff 9 (MLS 9)
Founded 1934. Highest Degree: Doctorate
Library Holdings: Bk Titles 319,000; Bk Vols 424,000; Per Subs 500
Subject Interests: Acctg, Computer sci, Educ, Finance, Liberal arts, Mkt, Nursing, Real estate, Taxation
Automation Activity & Vendor Info: (Acquisitions) Innovative Interfaces, Inc; (Cataloging) Innovative Interfaces, Inc; (Circulation) Innovative Interfaces, Inc; (Course Reserve) Innovative Interfaces, Inc; (ILL) Innovative Interfaces, Inc; (Media Booking) Innovative Interfaces, Inc; (OPAC) Innovative Interfaces, Inc; (Serials) Innovative Interfaces, Inc
Wireless access
Partic in Metropolitan New York Library Council; OCLC Online Computer Library Center, Inc; Westchester Academic Library Directors Organization (WALDO)
Open Mon-Fri 8am-11pm, Sat 10-8, Sun 12-8

R PARK AVENUE SYNAGOGUE, Edmond de Rothschild Library, 50 E 87th St, 10128. SAN 311-9874. Tel: 212-369-2600, Ext 127. FAX: 212-410-7879. *Librn,* Marga Hirsch; E-mail: mhirsch@pasyn.org; Staff 1 (MLS 1)
Founded 1956
Library Holdings: Bk Vols 9,000; Per Subs 10
Special Collections: Judaica Picture Books
Subject Interests: 15th-20th Century, Bible, Childrens' bks, Fiction, Holocaust, Israel, Jewish cookbks, Judaica, Judaica novels, Judaica ref, Juv Judaica
Automation Activity & Vendor Info: (Cataloging) OPALS (Open-source Automated Library System); (Circulation) OPALS (Open-source Automated Library System)
Database Vendor: OPALS (Open-source Automated Library System)
Wireless access
Open Mon 12-6, Tues-Thurs 12-6:30, Fri 10-1

S PAT PARKER-VITO RUSSO CENTER LIBRARY*, Lesbian & Gay Community Serv Ctr, 208 W 13th St, 10011. Tel: 212-620-7310. Web Site: www.gaycenter.org/library. *Co-Dir,* David Chase; Staff 30 (MLS 5, Non-MLS 25)
Library Holdings: AV Mats 700; Bk Titles 12,396; Bk Vols 20,138; Per Subs 20; Videos 1,595
Subject Interests: Fiction, Film, Gay liberation, Non-fiction
Automation Activity & Vendor Info: (Cataloging) Follett Software; (Circulation) Follett Software; (OPAC) Follett Software
Wireless access
Open Mon-Thurs 6pm-9pm, Fri & Sat 1-4

L PATTERSON, BELKNAP, WEBB & TYLER LLP LIBRARY*, 1133 Avenue of the Americas, 10036. SAN 311-9904. Tel. 212-336-2930. Interlibrary Loan Service Tel: 212-336-2325. Reference Tel: 212-336-2103. FAX: 212-336-2222. *Mgr, Libr Serv,* Christina Senezak; E-mail: cmsenezak@pbwt.com; *Asst Librn,* Betty Hunter-Beatty; Tel: 212-336-2326; Staff 4 (MLS 2, Non-MLS 2)
Library Holdings: e-books 27; Bk Vols 5,000; Per Subs 75
Subject Interests: Bankruptcy, Corporate, Equal rights amendments, Estates, Intellectual property, Libel, Litigation, Product liability, Tax
Automation Activity & Vendor Info: (Cataloging) EOS International; (Circulation) EOS International; (ILL) EOS International; (Serials) EOS International
Database Vendor: Bloomberg, Checkpoint Systems, Inc, Dialog, Dun & Bradstreet, EOS International, HeinOnline, LexisNexis, OCLC WorldShare Interlibrary Loan
Wireless access
Restriction: Staff use only

L PAUL, WEISS, RIFKIND, WHARTON & GARRISON LIBRARY*, 1285 Avenue of the Americas, 10019-6064. SAN 311-9912. Tel: 212-373-2401. FAX: 212-373-2268. *Managing Librn,* Armando Gonzalez; *Librn,* Theresa O'Leary; Staff 19 (MLS 10, Non-MLS 9)
Library Holdings: Bk Vols 80,000
Subject Interests: Law
Database Vendor: LexisNexis, Westlaw
Wireless access
Partic in RLIN (Research Libraries Information Network)
Open Mon-Fri 8:30-7

S THE PHILATELIC FOUNDATION*, Archives & Library, 70 W 40th St, 15th Flr, 10018-2615. SAN 325-9439. Tel: 212-221-6555. FAX: 212-867-6208. E-mail: philatelicfoundation@verizon.net. Web Site: www.philatelicfoundation.org. *Archivist,* Robert Waterman
Library Holdings: Bk Vols 6,000
Wireless access
Open Mon-Fri 9-4:30

L PILLSBURY WINTHROP SHAW PITTMAN LLP*, Law Library, 1540 Broadway, 10036-4039. SAN 312-1410. Tel: 212-858-1000. FAX: 212-858-1500. Web Site: pillsburylaw.com. *Dir, Libr Serv,* Linda Becker; Staff 5 (MLS 3, Non-MLS 2)
Library Holdings: Bk Titles 38,000; Bk Vols 40,000
Subject Interests: Law
Wireless access
Restriction: Staff use only

S PILSUDSKI INSTITUTE OF AMERICA LIBRARY*, 180 Second Ave, 10003-5778. SAN 325-9358. Tel: 212-505-9077. FAX: 212-505-9052. E-mail: office@pilsudski.org. Web Site: www.pilsudskilibrary.org. *In Charge,* Iwona Korga
Library Holdings: Bk Vols 22,000
Open Mon-Fri 9-5

S PKF LIBRARY*, 29 Broadway, 4th Flr, 10006. SAN 322-9149. Tel: 212-867-8000. Administration Tel: 212-867-8000, Ext 352. FAX: 212-687-4346. *In Charge,* Ann Delia; Tel: 212-867-8000, Ext 437
Founded 1945
Library Holdings: Bk Titles 1,000; Per Subs 50
Subject Interests: Acctg, Hospitality, Hotels, Real estate, Restaurants, Tourism
Automation Activity & Vendor Info: (Cataloging) EOS International
Restriction: Clients only, Staff use only

S PLANNED PARENTHOOD FEDERATION OF AMERICA, INC, Katharine Dexter McCormick Library, 434 W 33rd St, 10001. SAN 311-9998. Tel: 212-261-4716. Web Site: www.plannedparenthood.org. *Librn,* Jennie Correia; E-mail: jennie.correia@ppfa.org; Staff 1 (MLS 1)
Founded 1964
Library Holdings: Bk Vols 4,000; Per Subs 35
Special Collections: Margaret Sanger Coll; Photo Archives
Subject Interests: Abortion, Birth control, Contraception, Contraceptives, Reproductive health, Sexuality, Sexuality educ, Training in family planning
Automation Activity & Vendor Info: (Serials) EBSCO Online
Database Vendor: LexisNexis, ScienceDirect, Wiley
Wireless access
Function: Res libr
Publications: Family Planning Library Manual
Partic in Metropolitan New York Library Council
Restriction: Circulates for staff only, Open to researchers by request

S POLISH INSTITUTE OF ARTS & SCIENCES IN AMERICA, INC*, Research Library, 208 E 30th St, 10016. SAN 312-004X. Tel: 212-686-4164. FAX: 212-545-1130. E-mail: piasany@verizon.net. Web Site: www.piasa.org. *Librn,* Krystyna Baron; Staff 5 (MLS 3, Non-MLS 2)
Founded 1942
Library Holdings: Bk Titles 24,000; Per Subs 400
Special Collections: Jan Lechon Coll; Translators Coll; Urbanski Polish-Latin American Coll; Workshops
Open Mon-Thurs 10-3

S POPULATION COUNCIL LIBRARY*, One Dag Hammarskjold Plaza, 10017. SAN 320-4049. Tel: 212-339-0533. FAX: 212-755-6052. Web Site: www.popcouncil.org. *Librn,* H Neil Zimmerman; E-mail: nzimmerman@popcouncil.org; Staff 2 (MLS 1, Non-MLS 1)
Founded 1953
Library Holdings: Bk Titles 25,000; Bk Vols 28,000; Per Subs 350
Subject Interests: Demography, Develop countries, Develop economics, Family planning
Automation Activity & Vendor Info: (Acquisitions) EOS International; (Cataloging) EOS International; (Circulation) EOS International; (ILL) EOS International; (OPAC) EOS International; (Serials) EOS International
Database Vendor: JSTOR
Wireless access
Partic in Consortium of Foundation Libraries
Open Mon-Fri 9-5

M PRESBYTERIAN HOSPITAL*, John M Wheeler Library, Edward S Harkness Eye Institute, 635 W 165th St, 10032. SAN 353-751X. Tel: 212-305-2916, 212-305-9855. FAX: 212-305-3173. *Dir,* Lijun Tian
Founded 1933
Library Holdings: Bk Titles 14,121; Per Subs 90
Special Collections: Ophthalmology Memorabilia; Rare Book Coll
Wireless access

Partic in Greater NE Regional Group; Med Libr Res Librs Group; New Mexico Consortium of Biomedical & Hospital Libraries
Restriction: Staff use only

S PRINCETON LIBRARY IN NEW YORK*, 15 W 43rd St, 10036. SAN 312-0104. Tel: 212-596-1250. FAX: 212-596-1399. E-mail: library@princetonclub.com. *Librn,* Erin Tahaney; Staff 2 (Non-MLS 2)
Founded 1962
Library Holdings: Bk Vols 10,000; Per Subs 70
Special Collections: Princetoniana; Woodrow Wilson Coll
Subject Interests: Histories of NY
Automation Activity & Vendor Info: (OPAC) Mandarin Library Automation
Wireless access
Open Mon-Fri 7am-11pm, Sat & Sun 10-6

S PROJECT FOR PUBLIC SPACES, INC*, Media Library, 419 Lafayette St, 7th Flr, 10003. SAN 370-7415. Tel: 212-620-5660. FAX: 212-620-5660. E-mail: info@pps.org. Web Site: www.pps.org. *Pres,* Fred Kent; *VPres,* Ethan Kent; Staff 1 (MLS 1)
Founded 1975
Library Holdings: Bk Titles 1,000
Restriction: Open by appt only

L PROSKAUER ROSE LLP LIBRARY*, 1585 Broadway, Concourse Level, 10036. SAN 312-0139. Tel: 212-969-5001. FAX: 212-969-2931. E-mail: library@proskauer.com. Web Site: www.proskauer.com/library. *Libr Mgr,* Karen Provost; *Head, Ref,* Alma De Jesus; *Ref,* Megan D'Errico; *Ref,* Joann Doria; *Ref,* Sarah Kagen; *Ref,* Maria Maida; *Ref,* Ruthie McGonagil; Staff 16 (MLS 7, Non-MLS 9)
Founded 1875
Library Holdings: Bk Titles 40,000; Per Subs 400
Special Collections: Labor Law Coll
Wireless access
Restriction: Open by appt only

L PRYOR, CASHMAN LLP*, Law Library, Seven Times Square, 10036-6569. SAN 372-4433. Tel: 212-421-4100. FAX: 212-326-0806. *Librn,* Robert Corallo
Library Holdings: Bk Vols 10,000; Per Subs 78
Open Mon-Fri 8-4

S RACQUET & TENNIS CLUB LIBRARY*, 370 Park Ave, 10022-5968. SAN 312-0171. Tel: 212-753-9700. *Head Librn,* Gerard J Belliveau, Jr; *Asst Librn,* Todd M Thompson; Staff 2 (MLS 2)
Founded 1905
Library Holdings: Bk Titles 21,000; Per Subs 40
Special Collections: Court Tennis (Jeu de Paume Coll); Early American Sports; Lawn Tennis
Subject Interests: Sports
Wireless access
Publications: Annual Report to Members
Friends of the Library Group

S REAL ESTATE BOARD OF NEW YORK*, Seymour B Durst Library, 570 Lexington Ave, 2nd Flr, 10022. SAN 312-0201. Tel: 212-532-3100. FAX: 212-481-0420. Web Site: www.rebny.com. *Librn,* Carolyn Dunn; E-mail: cdunn@rebny.com; Staff 3 (Non-MLS 3)
Founded 1896
Library Holdings: Bk Titles 850; Per Subs 100
Wireless access
Restriction: Mem only

S REHABILITATION INTERNATIONAL, Collection on Disability-Handicap Library, 165 Broadway, Office 2342, 10006. SAN 329-1359. Tel: 212-420-1500. FAX: 212-505-0871. E-mail: info@riglobal.org. Web Site: www.riglobal.org. *Secy Gen,* Venus Ilagan
Founded 1922
Library Holdings: Bk Vols 3,500
Subject Interests: Barrier free designs, Childhood disability in developing countries, Developing countries, Disability, Legis, Soc policy, Soc security disability progs, Women
Wireless access
Restriction: Mem only

R RIVERSIDE CHURCH LIBRARY*, 490 Riverside Dr, 10027. SAN 312-0325. Tel: 212-870-6728. FAX: 212-870-6800. Web Site: www.theriversidechurchny.org/about/?library. *Coordr,* Michelle Abbott-Smith; E-mail: mabbott-smith@theriversidechurchny.org
Library Holdings: AV Mats 800; Large Print Bks 50; Bk Vols 9,000
Special Collections: Books by South African Writers; Emancipation from Poverty; Works of Harry Emerson Fosdick
Subject Interests: Environ studies, Fiction, Fine arts, Juv, Multicultural, Philos, Psychol, Relig, Sociol, Youth
Automation Activity & Vendor Info: (Cataloging) Follett Software; (Circulation) Follett Software; (OPAC) Follett Software
Wireless access
Partic in CSLA
Open Mon & Wed 2-7, Tues 10-7, Thurs 10-4, Sun 9-3

C THE ROCKEFELLER UNIVERSITY*, Rita & Frits Markus Library & Scientific Commons, 1222 York Ave, Welch Hall, 10065. (Mail add: 1230 York Ave, Box 263, 10065), SAN 312-035X. Tel: 212-327-8904. Interlibrary Loan Service Tel: 212-327-8916. Toll Free Tel: 800-980-6922. FAX: 212-327-8802. Interlibrary Loan Service FAX: 212-327-7840. E-mail: libref@rockefeller.edu, librequest@rockefeller.edu. Web Site: markuslibrary.rockefeller.edu. *Univ Librn,* Carol Feltes; Tel: 212-327-8909, Fax: 212-327-7349, E-mail: cfeltes@rockefeller.edu; *Outreach Librn, Spec Coll,* Olga Nilova; Tel: 212-327-8868, E-mail: nilovao@rockefeller.edu; *Coll Mgr,* Jeanine McSweeney; Tel: 212-327-8980, E-mail: mcsweej@rockefeller.edu; *Mgr, Libr Syst,* Douglas Many; Tel: 212-327-8906, E-mail: many@rockefeller.edu; *ILL,* Alisa Jackson; E-mail: jacksoa@rockefeller.edu. Subject Specialists: *Biol,* Jeanine McSweeney; *Libr syst & software,* Douglas Many; Staff 6 (MLS 4, Non-MLS 2)
Founded 1906. Enrl 204; Fac 350; Highest Degree: Doctorate
Library Holdings: Bk Titles 53,453; Bk Vols 59,823; Per Subs 576
Special Collections: Science & General Interest Books published between 1787 & 1926
Subject Interests: Biochem, Chem, Human genetics, Immunology, Med sci, Microbiology, Physics, Virology
Automation Activity & Vendor Info: (Acquisitions) Innovative Interfaces, Inc; (Cataloging) Innovative Interfaces, Inc; (Circulation) Innovative Interfaces, Inc; (Course Reserve) Innovative Interfaces, Inc; (OPAC) Innovative Interfaces, Inc; (Serials) Innovative Interfaces, Inc
Database Vendor: 3M Library Systems, American Chemical Society, American Mathematical Society, American Physical Society, Annual Reviews, BioOne, Blackwell, Community of Science (COS), Ex Libris Group, Innovative Interfaces, Inc, IOP, ISI Web of Knowledge, JSTOR, Nature Publishing Group, OCLC WorldShare Interlibrary Loan, OVID Technologies, PubMed, Sage, ScienceDirect, Scopus, Springer-Verlag, Thomson - Web of Science, Wiley
Wireless access
Function: Res libr
Publications: Brochures
Partic in Cas; Metropolitan New York Library Council
Restriction: Use of others with permission of librn

S ROMANIAN CULTURAL INSTITUTE*, 200 E 38th St, 10016. SAN 320-2143. Tel: 212-687-0180. FAX: 212-687-0181. E-mail: icrny@icrny.org, roculture@aol.com. Web Site: www.icrny.org. *Dir,* Corina Suteu; *Librn,* Stefania Ferchedau
Founded 1969
Library Holdings: Bk Titles 22,000; Per Subs 60
Special Collections: Bibliographies (Romanian Topics Coll)
Subject Interests: Romania
Wireless access
Open Mon & Wed 3-6, Tues, Thurs & Fri 10-1

M ROOSEVELT HOSPITAL*, Medical Library, 1000 Tenth Ave, 10019. SAN 312-0376. Tel: 212-523-6100. FAX: 212-523-6108. *Librn,* Paul Barth
Founded 1955
Library Holdings: Bk Titles 1,500; Per Subs 400
Subject Interests: Med, Pediatrics, Surgery
Partic in Docline; Metrop Consortium
Restriction: Staff use only

L ROPES & GRAY LLP LIBRARY*, 1211 Avenue of the Americas, 10036. SAN 371-0467. Tel: 212-596-9000. FAX: 212-596-9090.
Library Holdings: Bk Vols 15,500; Per Subs 78
Automation Activity & Vendor Info: (Cataloging) Inmagic, Inc.; (Circulation) Inmagic, Inc.; (ILL) OCLC; (OPAC) Inmagic, Inc.
Database Vendor: Dialog, LexisNexis, Westlaw
Open Mon-Fri 9-6

S RUSSELL SAGE FOUNDATION LIBRARY*, 112 E 64th St, 10065. SAN 324-1815. Tel: 212-752-8641. FAX: 212-688-2684. E-mail: library@rsage.org. Web Site: www.russellsage.org. *Dir, Info Serv,* Claire Gabriel; *Res Librn,* Catherine Winograd; Tel: 212-752-8640; Staff 3 (MLS 2, Non-MLS 1)
Founded 1982
Library Holdings: Bk Vols 1,300; Per Subs 68
Special Collections: Russell Sage Foundation Publications
Automation Activity & Vendor Info: (Cataloging) OCLC; (ILL) OCLC; (OPAC) EOS International
Database Vendor: LexisNexis, ProQuest
Wireless access
Function: ILL available

Partic in Consortium of Foundation Libraries; Metropolitan New York Library Council
Restriction: Open to pub upon request

M ST LUKE'S-ROOSEVELT HOSPITAL CENTER*, Richard Walker Bolling Memorial Medical Library, 1111 Amsterdam Ave, 10025. SAN 312-0422. Tel: 212-523-4315. FAX: 212-523-4313. *Librn,* Dr Nancy Panella; E-mail: npanella@panix.com; *ILL,* Geeta Mathur; *Per,* Carroll Otis
Founded 1876
Library Holdings: Bk Vols 10,000; Per Subs 150
Special Collections: Photographs & Other Memorabilia; Surgical & Medical Historical Instruments
Subject Interests: Hist of med
Wireless access
Partic in Metropolitan New York Library Council
Restriction: Staff use only

S SAINT MATTHEW'S & SAINT TIMOTHY'S NEIGHBORHOOD CENTER, INC LIBRARY*, Star Learning Center, 26 W 84th St, 10024. SAN 320-2151. Tel: 212-362-2369, Ext 303. *Dir,* Deena Hellman; E-mail: dhellma@goddard.org
Founded 1971
Library Holdings: Bk Vols 11,000
Subject Interests: Children's lit, Remedial reading
Wireless access
Open Mon-Fri 10-6
Friends of the Library Group

S SALMAGUNDI CLUB LIBRARY*, 47 Fifth Ave, 10003. SAN 312-0473. Tel: 212-255-7740. FAX: 212-229-0172. Web Site: www.salmagundi.org. *In Charge,* John Morehouse
Founded 1899
Library Holdings: Bk Vols 6,500
Subject Interests: Art, Coronations, Costumes, Uniforms
Wireless access
Open Mon-Fri 9-5

L SATTERLEE, STEPHENS, BURKE & BURKE*, Law Library, 230 Park Ave, 10169. SAN 311-6603. Tel: 212-818-9200. FAX: 212-818-9606. E-mail: info@ssbb.com. Web Site: www.ssbb.com. *Librn,* Dolores Fusik; E-mail: dfusik@ssbb.com
Library Holdings: Bk Vols 13,000; Per Subs 25
Database Vendor: LexisNexis, Westlaw
Wireless access
Restriction: Staff use only

S SCHOLASTIC INC LIBRARY, 557 Broadway, 10012. SAN 312-0511. Tel: 212-343-6171. Administration Tel: 212-343-6188. FAX: 212-389-3317. E-mail: library@scholastic.com. *Assoc Librn,* Deimosa Webber-Bey; E-mail: deimosa@scholastic.com; *Sr Info Spec,* Karen Van Rossem; E-mail: kvanrossem@scholastic.com; Staff 3 (MLS 2, Non-MLS 1)
Founded 1929
Library Holdings: Bk Vols 150,000; Per Subs 25
Automation Activity & Vendor Info: (Acquisitions) SirsiDynix; (Cataloging) SirsiDynix; (Circulation) SirsiDynix; (OPAC) SIRSI-iBistro
Database Vendor: Children's Literature Comprehensive Database Company (CLCD), Factiva.com, Facts on File, Grolier Online, LexisNexis, ProQuest, SirsiDynix, World Book Online
Wireless access
Partic in Metropolitan New York Library Council

C SCHOOL OF VISUAL ARTS LIBRARY, SVA Library, 380 Second Ave, 2nd Flr, 10010-3994. SAN 312-052X. Tel: 212-592-2660. FAX: 212-592-2655. E-mail: reference@sva.edu. Web Site: www.sva.edu/library. *Dir, Libr Serv,* Robert Lobe; Tel: 212-592-2661, E-mail: rlobe@sva.edu; *Assoc Dir,* Caitlin Kilgallen; Tel: 212-592-2663, E-mail: ckilgallen@sva.edu; *Head, Tech Serv,* Zimra Panitz; Tel: 212-592-2662, E-mail: zpanitz@sva.edu; *Visual Res Curator,* Lorraine Gerety; Tel: 212-592-2667, E-mail: lgerety@sva.edu; Staff 11 (MLS 5, Non-MLS 6)
Founded 1962. Enrl 3,350; Fac 440; Highest Degree: Master
Library Holdings: AV Mats 1,600; DVDs 5,000; Bk Vols 80,000; Per Subs 400
Special Collections: Design Archives; Picture Coll
Subject Interests: Art, Art hist, Design, Film, Illustration, Photog
Automation Activity & Vendor Info: (Acquisitions) Ex Libris Group; (Cataloging) Ex Libris Group; (Circulation) Ex Libris Group; (OPAC) Ex Libris Group; (Serials) Ex Libris Group
Database Vendor: ARTstor, EBSCO Discovery Service, EBSCO Information Services
Wireless access
Function: 24/7 Online cat, Art exhibits, Computers for patron use, Copy machines, Electronic databases & coll, ILL available, Magazines, Online ref

Partic in Association of Independent Colleges of Art & Design (AICAD); Metropolitan New York Library Council; OCLC Online Computer Library Center, Inc
Open Mon-Thurs 8:30am-10pm, Fri 8:30-7:30, Sat 12-5:30, Sun 12-8
Restriction: Open to students, fac, staff & alumni, Photo ID required for access, Researchers by appt only

L SCHULTE ROTH & ZABEL LLP*, Law Library, 919 Third Ave, 10022. SAN 372-4573. Tel: 212-756-2000. Interlibrary Loan Service Tel: 212-756-2303. FAX: 212-593-5955. Web Site: www.srz.com. *Dir, Libr Serv,* Carol K Sergis; Tel: 212-756-2302, E-mail: carol.sergis@srz.com; *Asst Dir,* Wood Reid; Tel: 212-756-2305, E-mail: linda.reid@srz.com; *Electronic Res,* Ellyn Freeman; Tel: 212-756-2321, E-mail: ellyn.freeman@srz.com; *Res,* Jeffrey Giles; Tel: 212-756-2304, E-mail: jeffrey.giles@srz.com; *Res,* Laraine Ginsberg; Tel: 212-756-2309, E-mail: laraine.ginsburg@srz.com; *Res,* Karen Heusel; Tel: 212-756-2274, E-mail: karen.heusel@srz.com; *Tech Serv,* Daniel Pappas; Tel: 212-756-2237, E-mail: daniel.pappas@srz.com; Staff 14 (MLS 7, Non-MLS 7)
Founded 1969
Library Holdings: AV Mats 100; Bk Titles 8,392; Per Subs 499
Subject Interests: Corporate law, Human rights, Securities indust
Automation Activity & Vendor Info: (Acquisitions) Sydney; (Cataloging) Sydney; (Circulation) Sydney; (ILL) Sydney; (OPAC) Sydney; (Serials) Sydney
Wireless access
Partic in American Association of Law Libraries (AALL); SLA
Restriction: Staff use only

L SEWARD & KISSEL LLP*, Law Library, One Battery Park Plaza, 10004. SAN 325-9471. Tel: 212-574-1478. FAX: 212-480-8421. Web Site: www.sewkis.com. *Dir,* Robert J Davis; E-mail: davis@sewkis.com
Library Holdings: Bk Titles 1,200; Bk Vols 18,000; Per Subs 100
Database Vendor: Bloomberg, LexisNexis
Wireless access
Partic in Westlaw
Restriction: Staff use only

L SEYFARTH & SHAW NEW YORK LIBRARY*, 620 Eighth Ave Flr 32, 10018-1405. SAN 327-0211. Tel: 212-218-5500. FAX: 212-218-5526. Web Site: www.seyfarth.com. *Libr Mgr,* Oi-May Wong
Library Holdings: Bk Vols 10,000; Per Subs 100
Subject Interests: Employment, Labor, Securities, Tax
Restriction: Staff use only

L SHEARMAN & STERLING LLP LIBRARY*, 599 Lexington Ave, 10022-6069. SAN 353-7900. Tel: 212-848-4627. Interlibrary Loan Service Tel: 212-848-5400. FAX: 646-848-4627. *In Charge,* Eleanor Gonzalez
Founded 1873
Library Holdings: Bk Vols 35,000; Per Subs 700
Subject Interests: Antitrust, Capital markets, Intl, Litigation, Securities, Tax
Automation Activity & Vendor Info: (Cataloging) SydneyPlus
Database Vendor: Bloomberg, Dialog, Dun & Bradstreet, Factset, HeinOnline, Hoovers, LexisNexis, Standard & Poor's, Westlaw, Westlaw Business
Wireless access
Restriction: Not open to pub

S SHEVCHENKO SCIENTIFIC SOCIETY INC*, Library & Archives, 63 Fourth Ave, 10003. SAN 326-0976. Tel: 212-254-5130. FAX: 212-254-5239. E-mail: library@shevchenko.org. Web Site: www.shevchenko.org. *Dir,* Svitlana Andrushkiw; *Bibliographer, Librn,* Sergiy Panko; *Archivist,* Ostap Kin; Staff 3 (MLS 1, Non-MLS 2)
Founded 1952
Library Holdings: Bk Titles 45,000; Videos 400
Special Collections: The Immigration of Ukrainians to North & South America, archives & docs, av rare bks
Subject Interests: Ukrainian civilization, Ukrainian culture, Ukrainian hist, Ukrainian lit
Wireless access
Function: Archival coll, Photocopying/Printing, Res libr
Open Mon-Fri 9-4:30
Restriction: Access at librarian's discretion, Not a lending libr

L SIDLEY, AUSTIN, BROWN & WOOD LLP*, Law Library, 787 Seventh Ave, 24th Flr, 10019. SAN 372-2554. Tel: 212-839-5300. Interlibrary Loan Service Tel: 212-839-5445. FAX: 212-839-5599. *Librn,* Christa Lang; *Ref Librn,* Amy Weiner
Library Holdings: Bk Vols 50,000; Per Subs 250
Restriction: Staff use only

S SIECUS - SEXUALITY INFORMATION & EDUCATION COUNCIL OF THE UNITED STATES*, Mary S Calderone Library, 90 John St, Ste 402, 10038. SAN 326-8756. Tel: 212-819-9770. FAX: 212-819-9776. Web Site: www.siecus.org. *In Charge,* Kurt Conklin; Staff 1 (MLS 1)

Founded 1964
Library Holdings: Bk Titles 6,500; Per Subs 50
Subject Interests: Human sexuality, Sexuality educ
Restriction: Non-circulating, Open by appt only

L SIMPSON, THACHER & BARTLETT*, Law Library, 425 Lexington Ave, 10017-3954. SAN 312-0619. Tel: 212-455-2800. FAX: 212-455-2502. *Dir,* Peggy Martin; Staff 14 (MLS 9, Non-MLS 5)
Founded 1884
Library Holdings: Bk Vols 50,000
Subject Interests: Antitrust, Banking, Corp, Labor, Taxation
Automation Activity & Vendor Info: (Cataloging) SirsiDynix; (OPAC) SirsiDynix; (Serials) SirsiDynix
Database Vendor: LexisNexis, Westlaw, Westlaw Business
Wireless access
Partic in OCLC Online Computer Library Center, Inc; RLIN (Research Libraries Information Network)
Restriction: Staff use only

L SKADDEN, ARPS, SLATE, MEAGHER & FLOM LIBRARY*, Four Times Sq, 10036. SAN 312-0627. Tel: 212-735-3000. FAX: 212-735-3244. *Dir,* Janet Accardo; *Head Librn,* Carrie Hirtz; Staff 26 (MLS 8, Non-MLS 18)
Founded 1948
Library Holdings: Bk Vols 75,000
Subject Interests: Law
Restriction: Staff use only

S SKIDMORE, OWINGS & MERRILL*, Resource Library, 14 Wall St, 10005. SAN 327-6937. Tel: 212-298-9300. FAX: 212-298-9500. Web Site: www.som.com. *Head Librn,* Lynn Chen; E-mail: lynn.chen@som.com; *Librn, Mat,* Lauren Haber; E-mail: lauren.haber@som.com
Library Holdings: Bk Vols 3,000; Per Subs 85
Special Collections: Design Reports
Automation Activity & Vendor Info: (Cataloging) Inmagic, Inc.; (Circulation) Inmagic, Inc.; (OPAC) Inmagic, Inc.
Database Vendor: Factiva.com
Wireless access
Open Mon-Fri 9-5:30

L SNR DENTON*, Law Library, 1221 Avenue of the Americas, 24th Flr, 10020. SAN 372-2473. Tel: 212-768-6700. FAX: 212-768-6800. *Head Librn,* Patricia A Garvey
Library Holdings: Bk Vols 4,500; Per Subs 15
Restriction: Staff use only

S SPORTS ILLUSTRATED LIBRARY*, 1271 Ave of the Ameicas, Rm 32-319, 10020. SAN 353-8052. Tel: 212-522-3046. FAX: 212-522-1719. *Chief Librn,* Joy Birdsong
Founded 1960
Library Holdings: Bk Titles 5,200; Per Subs 150
Special Collections: College & Professional Team Media Guides; Olympic Games Resource Coll
Automation Activity & Vendor Info: (Cataloging) Inmagic, Inc.
Database Vendor: Dialog, Factiva.com, LexisNexis, ProQuest
Wireless access
Publications: Sports Source
Partic in Dialog Corp
Restriction: Not open to pub, Staff use only

S STACKS RARE COIN COMPANY OF NY*, Technical Information Center Library, 123 W 57th St, 10019-2280. SAN 327-0270. Tel: 212-582-2580. Toll Free Tel: 800-566-2580. FAX: 212-245-5018. E-mail: info@stacks.com. Web Site: www.stacks.com. *In Charge,* Scott Mitchell
Founded 1858
Library Holdings: Bk Vols 5,200
Subject Interests: Numismatics, Syngraphics
Open Mon-Fri 10-5

CM STATE UNIVERSITY OF NEW YORK, STATE COLLEGE OF OPTOMETRY*, Harold Kohn Vision Science Library, 33 W 42nd St, 10036-8003. SAN 312-0759. Tel: 212-938-5690. Interlibrary Loan Service Tel: 212-938-5693. Reference Tel: 212-938-5691. FAX: 212-938-5696. Web Site: www.sunyopt.edu/library. *Dir,* Elaine Wells; E-mail: ewells@sunyopt.edu; *Asst Librn,* Kadri Niider; E-mail: kniider@sunyopt.edu; *ILL,* Clementine Perez; E-mail: perez@sunyopt.edu. Subject Specialists: *Tech assistance, Tech educ,* Kadri Niider; Staff 5 (MLS 2, Non-MLS 3)
Founded 1971. Enrl 283; Fac 150; Highest Degree: Doctorate
Library Holdings: e-books 1,246; Bk Vols 38,000; Per Subs 483
Special Collections: Learning Disabilities & Optometry
Subject Interests: Ophthalmology, Optics, Optometry, Physiological optics
Automation Activity & Vendor Info: (Cataloging) Ex Libris Group; (Circulation) Ex Libris Group; (ILL) OCLC Online; (OPAC) Ex Libris Group
Wireless access
Publications: Kohn Library Holdings (Index to science materials); Newsletter; Tip Sheets (Reference guide)
Partic in Metropolitan New York Library Council; Nylink
Open Mon-Fri 8am-9:30pm
Restriction: Circ limited

L STROOCK & STROOCK & LAVAN LIBRARY*, 180 Maiden Lane, 10038. SAN 312-0791. Tel: 212-806-5700. FAX: 212-806-6006. Web Site: www.stroock.com. *Dir,* June Berger; E-mail: jberger@stroock.com
Library Holdings: Bk Vols 20,000; Per Subs 500
Automation Activity & Vendor Info: (Cataloging) EOS International
Database Vendor: LexisNexis, Westlaw
Restriction: Staff use only

L SULLIVAN & CROMWELL LLP*, Information Resources Center, 125 Broad St, 10004. SAN 312-0805. Tel: 212-558-3780. FAX: 212-558-3346. E-mail: library@sullcrom.com. Web Site: www.sullcrom.com. *Dir, Info Res,* Jennifer G Rish; Tel: 212-558-3715, E-mail: rishj@sullcrom.com; *Assoc Dir, Info Res,* Alison F Alifano; Tel: 212-558-4896, E-mail: alifanoa@sullcrom.com; *Sr Ref Librn,* Evelyn Seeger; E-mail: seegere@sullcrom.com; *Intranet Librn,* Michael Cho; E-mail: chom@sullcrom.com; *Ref Librn,* Joseph Boston; E-mail: bostonj@sullcrom.com; *Ref Librn,* Kimberly Council; E-mail: councilk@sullcrom.com; *Ref Librn,* Teresa Gorman; E-mail: gormant@sullcrom.com; *Ref Librn,* Tariq Khwaja; E-mail: khwajat@sullcrom.com; *Ref Librn,* Michael Pearson; E-mail: pearsonm@sullcrom.com; *Ref Librn,* Marshall Voizard; E-mail: voizardm@sullcrom.com; *Tech Serv Librn,* Pauline Webster; E-mail: websterp@sullcrom.com; *Mgr, Precedent Res,* Brian Nolan; E-mail: nolanb@sullcrom.com; *Mgr, Ref Serv,* Lucy Redmond; E-mail: redmondl@sullcrom.com; Staff 17 (MLS 13, Non-MLS 4)
Founded 1879
Library Holdings: Bk Titles 24,282; Bk Vols 96,273
Automation Activity & Vendor Info: (Acquisitions) Cuadra Associates, Inc; (Cataloging) Cuadra Associates, Inc; (Circulation) Cuadra Associates, Inc; (ILL) Cuadra Associates, Inc; (OPAC) Cuadra Associates, Inc; (Serials) Cuadra Associates, Inc
Database Vendor: Bloomberg, Checkpoint Systems, Inc, CQ Press, Dialog, Dun & Bradstreet, Factset, HeinOnline, LexisNexis, Mergent Online, MicroPatent, OCLC FirstSearch, OCLC WorldShare Interlibrary Loan, OneSource, Oxford Online, ProQuest, Westlaw, Westlaw Business

GL SUPREME COURT, APPELLATE DIVISION*, First Department Law Library, 27 Madison Ave, 10010. SAN 312-0813. Tel: 212-340-0478. *Librn,* Gene Preudhomme
Founded 1901
Library Holdings: Bk Vols 70,000; Per Subs 60
Database Vendor: LexisNexis, Westlaw
Wireless access
Restriction: Not open to pub

S TAIWAN RESOURCE LIBRARY*, Press Division, One E 42nd St, 5th Flr, 10017-6904. SAN 325-7517. Tel: 212-317-7342. FAX: 212-557-3043. Web Site: www.taipei.org. *Dir,* Brian Su; *Librn,* Ching-yi Ting; Staff 1 (MLS 1)
Founded 1991
Library Holdings: Bk Vols 6,000; Per Subs 20
Special Collections: Republic of China Government Document Coll
Subject Interests: Art, Econ, Hist, Lit, Philos, Politics, Relig
Open Mon-Fri 10-4
Restriction: Access at librarian's discretion

J TCI COLLEGE OF TECHNOLOGY*, 320 W 31st St, 10001. SAN 325-2752. Tel: 212-594-4000, Ext 5279. FAX: 212-330-0894. Web Site: www.tcicollege.edu/resources/college-library/. *Dir,* Asha Unni; E-mail: aunni@tcicollege.edu; Staff 2 (MLS 1, Non-MLS 1)
Library Holdings: AV Mats 263; CDs 1,000; e-books 20,000; Bk Vols 20,000; Per Subs 160; Videos 587
Subject Interests: Electrical eng, Electronics, Math
Automation Activity & Vendor Info: (Acquisitions) EOS International; (Cataloging) EOS International; (Circulation) EOS International; (Serials) EOS International
Database Vendor: CredoReference, EBSCO Auto Repair Reference, EBSCOhost, Gale Cengage Learning, Grolier Online, LexisNexis, Medline, ProQuest, ReferenceUSA
Wireless access
Open Mon-Thurs 8am-9:30pm, Fri 8-7, Sat 9-4

C TEACHERS COLLEGE, COLUMBIA UNIVERSITY*, The Gottesman Libraries of Teachers College, Columbia University, 525 W 120th St, 10027-6696. SAN 353-0345. Tel: 212-678-3494. Interlibrary Loan Service

Tel: 212-678-3495. Interlibrary Loan Service FAX: 212-678-3092. Web Site: library.tc.columbia.edu. *Dir,* Dr Gary J Natriello; Tel: 212-678-3087, E-mail: gjn6@columbia.edu; *Assoc Dir, Head Knowledge Ctr,* Hui Soo Chae; Tel: 212-678-3448, E-mail: chae@tc.columbia.edu; *Assoc Dir, Head, Media Design Ctr,* Dr Brian Hughes; Tel: 212-678-3069, E-mail: bhughes@tc.columbia.edu; *Asst Dir, Res Info Serv,* Jennifer L Govan; Tel: 212-678-3022, E-mail: govan@tc.columbia.edu; *Sr Librn,* Allen Foresta; Tel: 212-678-3026, E-mail: foresta@tc.columbia.edu; Staff 16 (MLS 6, Non-MLS 10)
Founded 1887. Enrl 5,000; Fac 140; Highest Degree: Doctorate
Library Holdings: AV Mats 5,651; CDs 986; e-journals 17,000; Electronic Media & Resources 4,766; Bk Vols 430,432; Per Subs 789; Videos 3,174
Special Collections: 18th-20th Century K-12 Textbooks, American & Foreign; Annie E Moore Illustrated Children's Books (18th & 19th Century); Art Education (including Children's Artworks in the Arthur W Dow, Edwin Ziegfeld & Israeli Children's Peace Art Colls); Black History Series (Educational Coll); Children's Village Records, ms; Education (Historical Photograph Coll); Education (Rare Books of 15th-19th Century); Educational Software Coll (K-12); Educational Tests & Manuals (TC Guidance Laboratory 1915-1960 & Papers of Edward L Thordike & Will McCall); English Children's Books, 18th & 19th Century (Harvey Darton Coll); International Mathematics Education (David E Smith Coll); National Council of Social Studies Records Coll, ms; National Kindergarten Association Records, ms; Nursing Education (Adelaid Nutting History of Nursing Coll); Papers of Prominent Educators; Teachers College Archives
Subject Interests: Adult educ, Applied health sci, Applied linguistics, Art educ, Audiology, Bilingual educ, Clinical psychol, Communications, Computing, Curric, Early childhood educ, Econ, Educ, Educ admin, Educ psychol, English, Evaluation, Health educ, Higher educ, Hist of educ, Intl educ, Math, Nursing educ, Nutrition, Philos, Psychol, Sci educ, Secondary educ, Soc studies, Sociol, Spanish, Speech-lang pathology
Automation Activity & Vendor Info: (Acquisitions) Innovative Interfaces, Inc; (Cataloging) Innovative Interfaces, Inc; (Circulation) Innovative Interfaces, Inc; (OPAC) Innovative Interfaces, Inc; (Serials) Innovative Interfaces, Inc
Database Vendor: Cambridge Scientific Abstracts, EBSCOhost, Factiva.com, Gale Cengage Learning, Innovative Interfaces, Inc, JSTOR, LexisNexis, OCLC FirstSearch, OVID Technologies, ProQuest, TLC (The Library Corporation), Westlaw, Wilson - Wilson Web
Function: For res purposes
Publications: Library Bookmarks; Russia & Other Former Soviet Republics
Partic in Metropolitan New York Library Council; OCLC Research Library Partnership; RLIN (Research Libraries Information Network); Wilsonline
Special Services for the Deaf - Assistive tech; Bks on deafness & sign lang; Spec interest per
Special Services for the Blind - Assistive/Adapted tech devices, equip & products; Braille equip; Compressed speech equip; Magnifiers; Thermoform Brailon duplicator
Open Mon-Fri 8am-11pm, Sat 8-8, Sun 9am-10pm
Restriction: In-house use for visitors, Open to students, fac & staff, Photo ID required for access, Restricted access
Friends of the Library Group

L TORYS LAW LIBRARY*, 237 Park Ave, 20th Flr, 10017. SAN 372-4530. Tel: 212-880-6177. FAX: 212-682-0200. E-mail: info@torys.com. Web Site: www.torys.com. *Librn,* Michael B Hoffman; E-mail: mhoffman@torys.com; *Asst Librn,* Claudette Wellington
Library Holdings: Bk Vols 10,000; Per Subs 50
Wireless access

C TOURO COLLEGE LIBRARIES*, 43 W 23rd St, Fifth Fl, 10010. SAN 312-0937. Tel: 212-463-0400, Ext 5321. Interlibrary Loan Service Tel: 718-252-7800, Ext 338. FAX: 212-627-3696. Interlibrary Loan Service FAX: 718-338-7732. Web Site: www.touro.edu/library. *Dir of Libr,* Bashe Simon; Tel: 718-252-7800, Ext 226, E-mail: simonb@touro.edu; *Assoc Dir of Libr,* Michoel Ronn; Tel: 212-463-0400, Ext 224, Fax: 212-627-9144, E-mail: michoelr@touro.edu; *Asst Dir, Pub Serv,* Russo Salvatore; Tel: 212-463-0400, Ext 222, E-mail: salvator@touro.edu; *Chief Librn,* Agalliu Edlira; Tel: 718-252-7800, Ext 217, E-mail: edlira.agalliu@touro.edu; *Chief Librn,* Myra Reisman; E-mail: myrar@touro.edu; *Librn,* Eileen M DeSimone; Tel: 631-665-1600, Ext 6224, Fax: 631-665-6263, E-mail: eileen.desimone@touro.edu; *Librn,* Lauri Kelly; E-mail: lori.kelly@touro.edu; *Librn,* Leib Klein; Tel: 718-871-6187, Ext 17, Fax: 718-686-7071, E-mail: leibk@touro.edu; *Librn,* David B Levy; Tel: 212-287-3531, E-mail: david.levy@touro.edu; *Librn,* Zhanna Marina; *Librn,* Amram S Rister; E-mail: amram.rister@touro.edu; *Librn,* Carol Schapiro; *Librn,* Rita Stravets; *Bus Librn,* Annette Carr; E-mail: annette.carr@touro.edu; *Info Literacy Librn,* Sara Tabaei; E-mail: sara.tabaei@touro.edu; *Cat,* Liping Wang; *Tech Serv,* Philip R Papas; Tel: 212-463-0400, E-mail: philip.pappas@touro.edu. Subject Specialists: *Judaica,* Amram S Rister; Staff 54 (MLS 27, Non-MLS 27)
Highest Degree: Doctorate
Library Holdings: AV Mats 31,616; CDs 1,770; DVDs 295; e-books 38,460; e-journals 26,510; Bk Vols 286,727; Per Subs 550; Videos 1,145
Subject Interests: Bus, Educ, Health sci, Jewish studies, Psychol
Automation Activity & Vendor Info: (Course Reserve) Docutek; (ILL) OCLC; (OPAC) Innovative Interfaces, Inc
Wireless access
Publications: Library Guide; Newsletter; Research & Writing Guide
Partic in Long Island Library Resources Council; Metropolitan New York Library Council
Open Mon-Thurs 9-9, Fri 9-2

SR TRINITY CHURCH ARCHIVES*, 74 Trinity Pl, 4th Flr, 10006-2088. SAN 320-4405. Tel: 212-602-9652, 212-602-9687. FAX: 212-602-9641. E-mail: archives@trinitywallstreet.org. Web Site: www.trinitywallstreet.org. *Archivist,* Ann Petrimoulx; E-mail: apetrimoulx@trinitywallstreet.org; Staff 2 (MLS 2)
Founded 1980
Library Holdings: Bk Titles 500
Subject Interests: Episcopal church, Theol
Open Mon-Fri 9-5

S TURTLE BAY MUSIC SCHOOL LIBRARY*, 244 E 52nd St, 10022-6201. SAN 370-5234. Tel: 212-753-8811. FAX: 212-752-6228. Web Site: www.tbms.org. *Head Librn,* Bruce Potterton; Tel: 212-753-8811, Ext 13
Founded 1925
Library Holdings: Music Scores 12,000; Bk Titles 1,500
Special Collections: 19th Century & Early 20th Sheet Music; Out of Print Editions of Music; Walter Trampler Viola Coll, scores featuring notations, fingerings & bowings
Open Mon-Fri 9am-10pm, Sat 9-4

S UBS WARBURG LIBRARY*, 299 Park Ave, 10171-0099. SAN 311-6468. Tel: 212-821-3000. *Dir,* Katherine Cray; *Assoc Dir,* Melissa Daley; *Assoc Dir,* Pattie Noonan; Staff 44 (MLS 21, Non-MLS 23)
Founded 1967
Library Holdings: Bk Titles 7,000; Per Subs 200
Subject Interests: Banking, Bus conditions, Econ, Finance, Indust, Investing, Money
Restriction: Not open to pub

S UKRANIAN INSTITUTE OF AMERICA /RESEARCH & DEVELOPMENT CENTER*, Research & Development Center, Two E 79th St, 10021. SAN 374-7824. Tel: 212-288-8660. FAX: 212-288-2918. Web Site: www.ukrainianinstitute.org. *In Charge,* Victoria Kurchenko
Library Holdings: Bk Vols 1,000
Special Collections: Ukranian Engineers Society of America Journal Coll
Subject Interests: Emigration & immigration, Ukrainian hist
Function: Archival coll, For res purposes, Photocopying/Printing, Res libr, Telephone ref
Restriction: Access at librarian's discretion, Not a lending libr, Open to others by appt, Open to students

S UNION LEAGUE CLUB LIBRARY, 38 E 37th St, 10016. SAN 312-102X. Tel: 212-685-3800. FAX: 212-545-0130. *Librn,* Steele Hearne; E-mail: shearne@unionleagueclub.org
Founded 1863
Library Holdings: Bk Titles 20,000; Per Subs 38
Subject Interests: Am biog, Civil War
Restriction: Not open to pub

S UNITED HOSPITAL FUND OF NEW YORK*, Reference Library, 350 Fifth Ave, 23rd Flr, 10118. SAN 312-1070. Tel: 212-494-0720. FAX: 212-494-0800. Web Site: www.uhfnyc.org. *Librn,* Will Yates
Founded 1941
Library Holdings: Bk Titles 2,000; Per Subs 120
Subject Interests: Healthcare econ, Healthcare mgt
Automation Activity & Vendor Info: (OPAC) LibraryWorld, Inc
Database Vendor: PubMed
Wireless access
Partic in Manhattan-Bronx Health Sciences Libraries Group; Metropolitan New York Library Council
Restriction: Open by appt only

S UNITED LODGE OF THEOSOPHISTS*, Theosophy Hall Library, 347 E 72nd St, 10021. SAN 312-1089. Tel: 212-535-2230. FAX: 212-628-3430. *Librn,* Rosemary Jourdan
Founded 1922
Library Holdings: Bk Titles 6,800
Subject Interests: Ancient philos, Ancient psychol, Comparative mythology, Comparative relig, Modern philos, Original writings of H P Blavatsky, Original writings of Wm Q Judge, Parapsychol, Reincarnation res in relig, Reincarnation res in sci, Theosophical hist
Restriction: Open by appt only

S UNITED NATIONS CHILDRENS FUND LIBRARY*, Three UN Plaza, H-12C UNICEF House, 10017. SAN 374-7557. Tel: 212-326-7064. FAX: 212-303-7989. Web Site: www.unicef.org. *Chief, Info Mgt Spec,* Howard Dale; *Prog Serv,* Shannon OShea
Library Holdings: Bk Vols 25,000; Per Subs 200
Partic in Consortium of Foundation Libraries; Metropolitan New York Library Council
Restriction: Open to pub by appt only, Open to researchers by request

S UNITED NATIONS DAG HAMMARSKJOLD LIBRARY, United Nations, 10017. (Mail add: UN Headquarters, Rm L-105, First Ave @ 46th St, 10017). SAN 353-8176. Tel: 212-963-3000. FAX: 212-963-2261. E-mail: library-ny@un.org. *Chief, Libr User Serv,* Iain Watt; *Coll Develop,* Kikuko Maeyama; Tel: 917-367-9415, Fax: 212-263-2608; Staff 61 (MLS 28, Non-MLS 33)
Founded 1946
Library Holdings: Bk Vols 400,000; Per Subs 9,800
Special Collections: Activities & History of the United Nations; Government Documents of Member States; International Affairs 1918-1945 (Woodrow Wilson Memorial Library); League of Nations Documents; Maps Coll; UN Specialized Agencies Documents; United Nations Documents. Oral History; UN Document Depository; US Document Depository
Subject Interests: Disarmament, Econ, Environ, Intl law, Intl relations, Legis, Nat law, Peace-keeping, Polit sci, Sustainable develop, Women
Automation Activity & Vendor Info: (Acquisitions) SirsiDynix; (Cataloging) SirsiDynix; (Circulation) SirsiDynix; (OPAC) SirsiDynix; (Serials) SirsiDynix
Database Vendor: SirsiDynix
Wireless access
Publications: Indexes to Proceedings of General Assembly, Economic & Social Council, Security Council; United Nations Documents Index
Partic in United Nations System Electronic Information Acquisitions Consortium

GL UNITED STATES COURT OF INTERNATIONAL TRADE*, Court Library, One Federal Plaza, 10278. SAN 312-1151. Tel: 212-264-2816. FAX: 212-264-3242. Web Site: www.cit.uscourts.gov. *Dir,* Daniel Campbell; *Dep Dir,* Anna Djirdjirian; *Asst Librn,* Frederick Frankel; Staff 6 (MLS 4, Non-MLS 2)
Library Holdings: Bk Titles 5,000; Bk Vols 50,000; Per Subs 100
Subject Interests: Customs law, Law
Automation Activity & Vendor Info: (OPAC) SIRSI WorkFlows
Wireless access
Publications: United States Court of International Trade Reports: Cases Adjudged in the US Court of International Trade (Annual)
Partic in OCLC Online Computer Library Center, Inc
Restriction: Not open to pub

G UNITED STATES DEPARTMENT OF LABOR*, Bureau of Labor Statistics, 201 Varick St, Rm 808, 10014. SAN 312-1194. Tel: 646-264-3600. FAX: 212-337-2532. E-mail: blsinfony@bls.gov. *In Charge,* Martin Kohli; E-mail: kohli.martin@bls.gov; Staff 4 (Non-MLS 4)
Founded 1949
Library Holdings: Bk Vols 5,000; Per Subs 10
Subject Interests: Consumer prices, Earnings, Econ growth, Employment, Indexes, Occupational outlook, Occupational safety, Producer prices, Productivity, Unemployment, Wages

S UNIVERSITY CLUB LIBRARY*, One W 54th St, 10019. SAN 312-1224. Tel: 212-572-3418. FAX: 212-572-3452. E-mail: library@universityclubny.org. Web Site: www.universityclubny.org. *Curator, Dir,* Andrew J Berner; *Assoc Dir,* Scott Overall; *Librn,* Laurie Bolger; *Asst Curator, Asst Librn,* Position Currently Open; *Tech Serv,* Maureen Manning. Subject Specialists: *Conserv,* Laurie Bolger; Staff 5 (MLS 5)
Founded 1865
Library Holdings: Bk Vols 90,000; Per Subs 125
Special Collections: Civil War Ante-bellum Southern History (New York Southern Society Coll); Fine Printing & Limited Editions Coll; George Cruikshank (H Gregory Thomas Coll); Illustrated Books (Tinker Coll); Publishing History (Whitney Darrow Coll); Rare Book Coll
Subject Interests: 1st World War, 2nd World War, Archit, Art, Biog, Civil War, English lit
Automation Activity & Vendor Info: (Cataloging) EOS International; (Circulation) EOS International; (ILL) OCLC; (OPAC) EOS International
Wireless access
Publications: The Illuminator
Partic in Metropolitan New York Library Council
Open Mon-Fri 9-6
Friends of the Library Group

L WACHTELL, LIPTON, ROSEN & KATZ*, Law Library, 51 W 52nd St, 10019. SAN 372-2422. Tel: 212-403-1521. FAX: 212-403-2000. E-mail: alllibrary@wlrk.com. Web Site: www.wlrk.com. *Dir,* Susan Hesse
Library Holdings: Bk Vols 2,000; Per Subs 400
Subject Interests: Corporate law
Automation Activity & Vendor Info: (Cataloging) Horizon; (Circulation) Horizon; (OPAC) Horizon
Database Vendor: Bloomberg, Factset, HeinOnline, Hoovers, LexisNexis, Westlaw, Westlaw Business
Wireless access
Open Mon-Fri 8:30-7:30, Sat & Sun 11-4:30

L WARSHAW BURSTEIN, LLP, Law Library, 555 Fifth Ave, 11th Flr, 10017. SAN 372-4220. Tel: 212-984-7700. FAX: 212-972-9150. Web Site: www.wbcsk.com. *In Charge,* Shari Beckerman; Staff 1 (Non-MLS 1)
Library Holdings: Bk Vols 1,000
Subject Interests: Corporate law, Estates, Litigation, Mergers, Real estate law, Securities law, Tax, Trusts
Open Mon-Fri 9:30-5:30

L WEIL, GOTSHAL & MANGES LLP*, Law Library, 767 Fifth Ave, 10153. SAN 312-1283. Tel: 212-310-8626. Interlibrary Loan Service Tel: 212-735-4560. FAX: 212-310-8007. E-mail: libts@weil.com. Web Site: www.weil.com. *Dir,* Deborah G Cinque; E-mail: deborah.cinque@weil.com; *Head, Res Serv,* Bonnie Fox Schwartz; E-mail: bonnie.schwartz@weil.com; *Head, Syst,* Rosalie Piscitelli; E-mail: rosalie.piscitelli@weil.com; *Asst Librn, ILL,* Daniela Pugh; E-mail: daniela.pugh@weil.com; *Tech Serv Librn,* Meredith Mulligan; E-mail: meredith.mulligan@weil.com; *Res,* Philip Barahona; E-mail: philip.barahona@weil.com; *Res,* Sadys Espitia; E-mail: sadys.espitia@weil.com; *Res,* Daniel McLaughlin; E-mail: daniel.mclaughlin@weil.com; *Syst,* John Terhorst; E-mail: john.terhorst@weil.com; Staff 11 (MLS 10, Non-MLS 1)
Subject Interests: Law
Automation Activity & Vendor Info: (Acquisitions) Sydney; (Cataloging) Sydney; (Circulation) Sydney; (ILL) Sydney; (OPAC) Sydney; (Serials) Sydney
Database Vendor: Dialog, Dun & Bradstreet, LexisNexis, Westlaw, Westlaw Business
Wireless access
Publications: SmartSearching
Partic in OCLC Online Computer Library Center, Inc; RLIN (Research Libraries Information Network)

L WHITE & CASE LAW LIBRARY*, 1155 Avenue of the Americas, 10036. SAN 353-8419. Tel: 212-819-8200. FAX: 212-354-8113. *Dir, Libr Serv,* Ruth Carter Armstrong
Founded 1901

S WHITNEY MUSEUM OF AMERICAN ART*, Frances Mulhall Achilles Library, 945 Madison Ave, 10021. SAN 312-1380. Tel: 212-570-3648. E-mail: library@whitney.org. Web Site: www.whitney.org. *Benjamin & Irma Weiss Librn,* Carol Rusk; Tel: 215-570-3649, E-mail: carol_rusk@whitney.org; *Asst Librn, Cataloger,* Ivy Blackman; Tel: 212-570-3682, E-mail: ivy_blackman@whitney.org; *Asst Archivist,* Kristen Leipert; Tel: 212-671-5335, E-mail: kristen_leipert@whitney.org; Staff 4 (MLS 3, Non-MLS 1)
Founded 1931
Library Holdings: Bk Titles 50,000; Per Subs 100
Special Collections: American Art Research Concil Papers; Edward Hopper Research Coll; Museum Archives
Subject Interests: 20th Century art, 21st Century art, Am artists
Automation Activity & Vendor Info: (Acquisitions) Ex Libris Group; (Cataloging) Ex Libris Group; (Circulation) Ex Libris Group; (OPAC) Ex Libris Group; (Serials) Ex Libris Group
Database Vendor: OCLC FirstSearch, Wilson - Wilson Web
Function: Res libr
Restriction: Authorized scholars by appt, Circulates for staff only, Closed stack, Not a lending libr, Open by appt only, Photo ID required for access, Restricted access
Friends of the Library Group

L WILLKIE FARR & GALLAGHER LLP*, Law Library, 787 Seventh Ave, 10019. SAN 312-1399. Tel: 212-728-8700. Interlibrary Loan Service Tel: 212-728-8709. FAX: 212-728-3303. E-mail: library@willkie.com. *Dir, Libr Serv,* Debra Glessner; E-mail: dglessner@willkie.com; *Assoc Dir,* Elise Lilly; Staff 15 (MLS 8, Non-MLS 7)
Library Holdings: Bk Titles 50,000; Per Subs 200
Subject Interests: Securities law, Taxation
Publications: Bulletin
Partic in Dialog Corp; Dow Jones News Retrieval; OCLC Online Computer Library Center, Inc; Westlaw
Open Mon-Fri 9-6

L WILSON ELSER MOSKOWITZ EDELMAN & DICKER LLP*, Law Library, 150 E 42nd St, 10017. SAN 372-2430. Tel: 212-490-3000. FAX: 212-490-3038. *Dir, Libr & Info Serv,* Jin Qian; E-mail: jin.qian@wilsonelser.com; *Res Serv Librn,* Larisa Zakiene; E-mail: larisa.zakiene@wilsonelser.com; *Electronic Res,* Yi Sheng; E-mail: yi.sheng@wilsonelser.com; Staff 4 (MLS 3, Non-MLS 1)
Library Holdings: Bk Vols 5,000; Per Subs 20
Database Vendor: LexisNexis, Westlaw
Function: For res purposes
Open Mon-Fri 9-5

S WINDELS MARX LANE & MITTENDORF, LLP LIBRARY*, 156 W 56th St, 10019. SAN 312-1402. Tel: 212-237-1000. Reference Tel: 212 237-1136. FAX: 212-262-1215. Web Site: www.windelsmarx.com. *Mgr, Libr Serv,* Joel Solomon; E-mail: jsolomon@windelsmarx.com
Library Holdings: Bk Titles 10,000
Subject Interests: Banking law, Corp law, Litigation
Function: ILL available
Restriction: Staff use only

L WINSTON & STRAWN LIBRARY*, 200 Park Ave, 10166. SAN 312-1356. Tel: 212-294-4648, 212-294-6700. Interlibrary Loan Service Tel: 212-294-4713. FAX: 212-294-4700. Web Site: www.winston.com. *Res Librn,* Rebecca Wright; Staff 5 (MLS 2, Non-MLS 3)
Founded 1993
Library Holdings: Bk Vols 100,000; Per Subs 150
Subject Interests: Law
Automation Activity & Vendor Info: (Cataloging) SIRSI Unicorn; (Circulation) SIRSI Unicorn; (OPAC) SIRSI Unicorn
Wireless access
Partic in Dialog Corp; Illinois Library & Information Network; Westlaw
Open Mon-Fri 8:30-6:30

SR STEPHEN WISE FREE SYNAGOGUE*, Rabbi Edward E Klein Memorial Library, 30 W 68th St, 10023. SAN 371-6260. Tel: 212-877-4050, Ext 238. FAX: 212-787-7108. E-mail: library@swfs.org. Web Site: www.swfs.org. *Ch Serv,* Jill Goldin
Founded 1985
Library Holdings: AV Mats 100; Bks on Deafness & Sign Lang 30; Bk Vols 6,000; Talking Bks 2,002
Special Collections: Stephen Wise Archives, docs, letters
Subject Interests: Judaica
Automation Activity & Vendor Info: (Cataloging) EOS International; (Circulation) EOS International; (OPAC) EOS International
Wireless access
Open Mon-Fri 8:30-3, Sun 10-1
Friends of the Library Group

M WOLTERS KLUWER/AMERICAN JOURNAL OF NURSING, Sophia F Palmer Library, (Formerly WKH/LWW American Journal of Nursing), 333 Seventh Ave, 19th Flr, 10001. SAN 311-5887. Tel: 646-674-6601. FAX: 212-886-1206. *Librn,* Joanne Jahr; E-mail: joanne.jahr@wolterskluwer.com. Subject Specialists: *Health sci,* Joanne Jahr; Staff 1 (MLS 1)
Founded 1951
Library Holdings: Bk Vols 6,000; Per Subs 10
Special Collections: International Nursing Index, 1966-2000
Subject Interests: Nursing, Nursing admin, Nursing educ
Wireless access
Function: Doc delivery serv, Health sci info serv, ILL available, Ref & res
Partic in Brooklyn-Queens-Staten Island-Manhattan-Bronx Health Sciences Librarians; Docline
Restriction: Borrowing requests are handled by ILL, Not open to pub

S XAVIER SOCIETY FOR THE BLIND, National Catholic Press & Lending Library for the Visually Impaired, Two Penn Plaza, Ste 1102, 10121. SAN 328-3577. Tel: 212-473-7800. Toll Free Tel: 800-637-9193. FAX: 212-473-7801. E-mail: library@xaviersocietyfortheblind.org. Web Site: www.xaviersocietyfortheblind.org. Staff 2 (Non-MLS 2)
Founded 1900
Library Holdings: Audiobooks 5,107; Braille Volumes 1,903; CDs 737; Bk Titles 3,474; Bk Vols 8,366; Per Subs 11; Talking Bks 17,443
Subject Interests: Braille, Catholicism, Inspirational, Spirituals
Publications: Annual Print Calendar (Annual); Annual Report; Braille Calendars (Annual); Catholic Review (Quarterly); Large Print & Audio Books; Xavier Review (Quarterly); XSB Lending Library Catalog of Braille (Collection catalog)
Special Services for the Blind - Bks & mags in Braille, on rec, tape & cassette; Bks on cassette; Bks on CD; Bks on flash-memory cartridges; Braille bks; Children's Braille; Info on spec aids & appliances; Newsletter (in large print, Braille or on cassette); Newsline for the Blind; Rec of textbk mat; Recorded bks; Talking bk & rec for the blind cat; Talking bks
Open Mon-Fri 8:30-4:30

S YALE CLUB LIBRARY*, 50 Vanderbilt Ave, 10017. SAN 312-1488. Tel: 212-716-2129. FAX: 212-716-2158. E-mail: librarian@yaleclubnyc.org. Web Site: www.yaleclubnyc.org. *Librn,* Dana Gerschel; Staff 2 (MLS 1, Non-MLS 1)
Library Holdings: Bk Vols 45,500
Special Collections: Yale Memorabilia & Publications
Wireless access
Open Mon-Sun 7am-11pm

C YESHIVA UNIVERSITY LIBRARIES*, 2520 Amsterdam Ave, Rm 405, 10033. SAN 353-8508. Tel: 212-960-5363. Interlibrary Loan Service Tel: 212-960-5491. FAX: 212-960-0066. Web Site: www.yu.edu/libraries. *Dean of Libr,* Pearl Berger; Staff 84 (MLS 37, Non-MLS 47)
Founded 1897. Highest Degree: Doctorate
Library Holdings: AV Mats 8,690; e-books 175,447; e-journals 35,000; Bk Vols 1,083,079
Special Collections: Archives Coll; Manuscripts Coll; Rare Books Coll. US Document Depository
Subject Interests: Jewish studies, Law, Med, Psychol, Soc work
Automation Activity & Vendor Info: (Course Reserve) Docutek; (OPAC) Innovative Interfaces, Inc
Database Vendor: American Chemical Society, American Mathematical Society, American Psychological Association (APA), Annual Reviews, CQ Press, ebrary, EBSCOhost, Elsevier, Elsevier MDL, Factiva.com, Facts on File, Gale Cengage Learning, Haworth Pres Inc, HeinOnline, Innovative Interfaces, Inc, IOP, ISI Web of Knowledge, JSTOR, LexisNexis, Nature Publishing Group, OCLC FirstSearch, OCLC WorldShare Interlibrary Loan, OCLC-RLG, OVID Technologies, Oxford Online, ProQuest, PubMed, RefWorks, ScienceDirect, SerialsSolutions, Springer-Verlag, Standard & Poor's, Westlaw, Wiley, Wilson - Wilson Web
Wireless access
Publications: Inventories to Collections (Archives guide); Rabbinic Manuscripts - Mendel Gottesman Library (Collection catalog)
Partic in Lyrasis; OCLC Online Computer Library Center, Inc; Westchester Academic Library Directors Organization (WALDO)

Departmental Libraries:

ALBERT EINSTEIN COLLEGE OF MEDICINE
See Separate Entry in Bronx

CL DR LILLIAN & DR REBECCA CHUTICK LAW LIBRARY, Benjamin N Cardozo School of Law, 55 Fifth Ave, 10003-4301, SAN 353-8567. Tel: 212-790-0223. Circulation Tel: 212-790-0285. Reference Tel: 212-790-0220. FAX: 212-790-0236. E-mail: lawref@yu.edu. Web Site: www.cardozo.yu.edu/library. *Dir,* Lynn Wishart; E-mail: wishart@yu.edu; *Asst Librn,* Norma Feld; E-mail: feld@yu.edu; *Instrul Serv Librn,* Kay Mackey; E-mail: mackey@yu.edu; *Acq,* Grace Collins; E-mail: grace.collins@yu.edu; *Cat,* Linda Aschkenasy; E-mail: aschkena@yu.edu; *Circ,* Peter Walenta; E-mail: walenta@yu.edu; *Doc,* Beth Gordon; E-mail: bagordon@yu.edu; Staff 21 (MLS 9, Non-MLS 12)
Founded 1976. Enrl 1,076; Fac 45; Highest Degree: Doctorate
Library Holdings: Bk Titles 98,751; Bk Vols 530,698; Per Subs 6,407
Special Collections: US Document Depository
Subject Interests: Intellectual property, Israeli law, Law, Lit
Automation Activity & Vendor Info: (Acquisitions) Innovative Interfaces, Inc; (Cataloging) Innovative Interfaces, Inc; (Circulation) Innovative Interfaces, Inc; (OPAC) Innovative Interfaces, Inc; (Serials) Innovative Interfaces, Inc
Database Vendor: Gale Cengage Learning, JSTOR, LexisNexis, ProQuest, Westlaw, Wilson - Wilson Web
Partic in Lyrasis; Metropolitan New York Library Council; New England Law Library Consortium, Inc; Nylink; OCLC Online Computer Library Center, Inc
Publications: Current Contents; Research Guides
Open Mon-Thurs 8am-Midnight, Fri 8-6, Sun 10am-Midnight

MENDEL GOTTESMAN LIBRARY OF HEBRAICA-JUDAICA, 2520 Amsterdam Ave, 10033. (Mail add: 500 W 185th St, 10033). Tel: 212-960-5382. Circulation Tel: 212-960-5379. FAX: 212-960-0066. Web Site: www.yu.edu/libraries/about/mendel-gottesman-library. *Librn,* Leah Adler; *Coll Develop,* Zvi Erenyi; *Per,* Zalman Alpert; *Ref,* Moshe Schapiro; Staff 3 (MLS 3)
Founded 1897. Highest Degree: Doctorate
Library Holdings: AV Mats 2,996; e-books 304,779; e-journals 44,616; Microforms 3,046; Bk Vols 293,561; Per Subs 1,069
Special Collections: Hebraica Rare Books & Manuscripts; Sephardic Studies Coll
Subject Interests: Bible, Jewish hist, Jewish lit, Jewish philos, Rabbinics
Automation Activity & Vendor Info: (Acquisitions) Innovative Interfaces, Inc; (Cataloging) Innovative Interfaces, Inc; (Circulation) Innovative Interfaces, Inc; (Course Reserve) Docutek; (OPAC) Innovative Interfaces, Inc; (Serials) Innovative Interfaces, Inc
Partic in Metropolitan New York Library Council; OCLC Online Computer Library Center, Inc; RLIN (Research Libraries Information Network)
Open Mon-Thurs & Sun 9am-1am, Fri 9-12:30, Sat 7pm-1am

POLLACK LIBRARY-LANDOWNE BLOOM LIBRARY, Wilf Campus, 2520 Amsterdam Ave, 10033, SAN 353-8656. Tel: 212-960-5378, 212-960-5379, 212-960-5380. Interlibrary Loan Service Tel: 212-960-5491. FAX: 212-960-0066. Web Site: www.yu.edu/libraries/index.aspx?id=33. *Chief Librn,* John Moryl; *Electronic Coll Librn,* Shulamis Landesman; *Electronic Reserves Librn,* Stephanie Gross; *Pub Serv Librn,* Linda Miles; E-mail: lmiles@yu.edu; *ILL,* Mary Ann Linahan; Staff 4 (MLS 4)
Founded 1938
Library Holdings: AV Mats 1,801; Bk Vols 311,885
Special Collections: US Document Depository
Subject Interests: Soc work
Automation Activity & Vendor Info: (Acquisitions) Innovative Interfaces, Inc; (Circulation) Innovative Interfaces, Inc; (Course Reserve) Innovative Interfaces, Inc; (ILL) OCLC; (OPAC) Innovative Interfaces, Inc; (Serials) Innovative Interfaces, Inc
Partic in Metropolitan New York Library Council; OCLC Online Computer Library Center, Inc
Open Mon-Thurs & Sun 9am-1am, Fri 9-12:30

SIMON WIESENTHAL CENTER LIBRARY & ARCHIVES
See Separate Entry under Simon Wiesenthal Center & Museum of Tolerance, Los Angeles, CA

HEDI STEINBERG LIBRARY, 245 Lexington Ave, 10016, SAN 353-8680. Tel: 212-340-7720. Reference Tel: 212-340-7785. Information Services Tel: 212-340-7725. FAX: 212-340-7808. Web Site: www.yu.edu/libraries/about/steinberg. *Head Librn,* Edith Lubetski; E-mail: lubetski@yu.edu; *Ref,* Elinor Grumet; *Ref,* Vivian Moskowitz; Staff 3 (MLS 3)
Founded 1954
Library Holdings: AV Mats 2,380; Bk Vols 149,000; Per Subs 558
Subject Interests: Hebraica, Judaica
Partic in Metropolitan New York Library Council
Open Mon-Thurs 8:30am-1am, Fri & Sun 9-1

S YIVO INSTITUTE FOR JEWISH RESEARCH*, Library & Archives, 15 W 16th St, 10011. SAN 312-1496. Tel: 212-246-6080, Ext 5102. FAX: 212-292-1892. E-mail: yivomail@yivo.cjh.org. Web Site: www.yivo.org. *Head Librn,* Aviva E Astrinsky; Tel: 212-294-6134, E-mail: avastrinsky@yivo.cjh.org; *Archivist,* Fruma Mohrer; Tel: 212-294-6143, E-mail: fmohrer@yivo.cjh.org. Subject Specialists: *E European hist,* Fruma Mohrer; Staff 15 (MLS 8, Non-MLS 7)
Founded 1925
Library Holdings: Bk Vols 350,000; Per Subs 200
Special Collections: Hebrew Immigrant Aid Society Coll; Jewish Music Coll; Jewish Sheet Music; Manuscript Coll; Milwitzki Coll of Ladino Literature; Nazi Coll; Rabbinics (Vilna Coll); Yiddish Linguistics (Weinreich Library Coll)
Subject Interests: Eastern European Jewish hist, Holocaust, Lit, Yiddish (Lang)
Publications: YIVO Bleter (Yiddish); YIVO News/Yedies (English & Yiddish)
Partic in Asn of Jewish Librs; Metropolitan New York Library Council; RLIN (Research Libraries Information Network)
Restriction: Not a lending libr

NEW YORK MILLS

P NEW YORK MILLS PUBLIC LIBRARY*, 399 Main St, 13417. SAN 312-1577. Tel: 315-736-5391. Web Site: www.midyork.org/newyorkmills. *Librn,* Nancy Carey
Circ 32,949
Library Holdings: Bk Vols 37,036
Automation Activity & Vendor Info: (Cataloging) SIRSI WorkFlows; (Circulation) SIRSI WorkFlows; (OPAC) SIRSI WorkFlows
Mem of Mid-York Library System; Viking Library System
Open Mon-Fri 12-8, Sat 10-2
Friends of the Library Group

NEWARK

P NEWARK PUBLIC LIBRARY*, 121 High St, 14513-1492. SAN 312-1585. Tel: 315-331-4370. FAX: 315-331-0552. *Dir,* Elaine B Dawson; E-mail: edawson@pls-net.org; *Ch Serv,* Dorothy Morehouse
Founded 1897. Pop 9,849; Circ 215,000
Library Holdings: Bk Vols 42,000; Per Subs 57
Special Collections: Local History Coll. State Document Depository
Automation Activity & Vendor Info: (Circulation) SirsiDynix
Wireless access
Partic in OCLC Online Computer Library Center, Inc
Open Mon-Thurs 9:30-9, Fri 9:30-6, Sat 9:30-5
Friends of the Library Group

NEWARK VALLEY

P TAPPAN-SPAULDING MEMORIAL LIBRARY, Six Rock St, 13811. (Mail add: PO Box 397, 13811-0397), SAN 312-1615. Tel: 607-642-9960. FAX: 607-642-9960. E-mail: tslibrary@stny.rr.com. *Dir,* Carol Forde
Founded 1908. Pop 5,260; Circ 20,615
Wireless access
Function: Bks on cassette, Bks on CD, Children's prog, Computers for patron use, Copy machines, e-mail & chat, e-mail serv, Electronic databases & coll, Family literacy, Fax serv, Free DVD rentals, Holiday prog, Home delivery & serv to Sr ctr & nursing homes, Homebound delivery serv, ILL available, Instruction & testing, Music CDs, Newsp ref libr, Online cat, Online ref, Online searches, Outreach serv, OverDrive digital audio bks, Photocopying/Printing, Preschool outreach, Prog for children & young adult, Pub access computers, Ref & res, Story hour, Summer reading prog, Tax forms, Teen prog, VHS videos, Video lending libr
Mem of Finger Lakes Library System
Restriction: Authorized patrons

NEWBURGH

S LIBRARY OF HISTORICAL SOCIETY OF NEWBURGH BAY & THE HIGHLANDS*, 189 Montgomery St, 12550. SAN 326-579X. Tel: 845-561-2585. E-mail: historicalsocietynb@yahoo.com. Web Site: www.newburghhistoricalsociety.com. *Librn,* Pat Favata
Founded 1951
Library Holdings: Bk Vols 3,000
Special Collections: Art & Architecture; Charitible Organizations; Civil War; Environmental Affairs; Ethnic Groups, English, German, Irish; Local History, Newburgh, NY area; Military; Natural Resources; Revolutionary War; Social Science
Partic in Southeastern New York Library Resources Council
Open Sun 1-4

C MOUNT SAINT MARY COLLEGE, Kaplan Family Library, 330 Powell Ave, 12550-3494. SAN 312-1623. Tel: 845-569-3600. Reference Tel: 845-569-3200. FAX: 845-561-0999. E-mail: library@msmc.edu. Web Site: www.msmc.edu/library. *Dir,* Barbara Petruzzelli; Tel: 845-569-3601; *Coll Develop/E-Res Librn,* Vivian Milczarski; Tel: 845-569-3523; *Syst & Cat Serv Librn,* Denise A Garofalo; Tel: 845-569-3519, E-mail: garofalo@msmc.edu
Founded 1959
Library Holdings: Bk Vols 80,000; Per Subs 250
Subject Interests: Grad educ programs, Nursing, Sci
Automation Activity & Vendor Info: (Acquisitions) Innovative Interfaces, Inc; (Cataloging) Innovative Interfaces, Inc; (Circulation) Innovative Interfaces, Inc; (Course Reserve) Innovative Interfaces, Inc; (ILL) Innovative Interfaces, Inc; (OPAC) Innovative Interfaces, Inc; (Serials) Innovative Interfaces, Inc
Database Vendor: EBSCOhost, OCLC FirstSearch, ProQuest, Wilson - Wilson Web
Wireless access
Publications: Faculty Handbook-Student Handbook; Library Subject Resource Guides
Partic in Southeastern New York Library Resources Council
Open Mon-Thurs 7:30am-Midnight, Fri 7:30-7, Sat 10-6, Sun 1-Midnight

G NEW YORK STATE OFFICE OF PARKS, RECREATION & HISTORIC PRESERVATION*, Washington's Headquarters State Historic Site Library, 84 Liberty St, 12550-5603. (Mail add: PO Box 1783, 12551), SAN 326-5404. Tel: 845-562-1195. FAX: 845-561-1789. *In Charge,* Melvin Johnson; E-mail: melvin.johnson@oprhp.state.ny.us
Founded 1850
Library Holdings: Bk Titles 800; Bk Vols 1,000
Special Collections: George Washington Coll, mss, papers; Revolutionary War Colls, mss; Timothy Pickering Coll, mss
Wireless access
Open Tues-Sat 9-5
Restriction: Non-circulating to the pub

P NEWBURGH FREE LIBRARY*, 124 Grand St, 12550. SAN 353-880X. Tel: 845-563-3600. Interlibrary Loan Service Tel: 845-563-3630. Information Services Tel: 845-563-3625. FAX: 845-563-3602. Web Site: www.newburghlibrary.org. *Dir,* Muriel Verdibello; *Automation Serv,* Anne McCarthy Kennedy; *Ch Serv,* Lisa Kochik; *Circ,* Ann Kennedy; *Doc,* Heather Henricksen-Georghiou; *Ref,* Jeanne Stiller; Staff 22 (MLS 22)
Founded 1852. Pop 63,410; Circ 309,070
Jul 2007-Jun 2008 Income $4,035,000. Mats Exp $488,000. Sal $2,274,765
Library Holdings: Bk Titles 220,937; Per Subs 430
Special Collections: Children's Lit Coll; Genealogy, bk, micro. State Document Depository; US Document Depository
Subject Interests: Bibliographies, Local hist, Parenting coll
Automation Activity & Vendor Info: (Cataloging) SirsiDynix

Database Vendor: Dialog, Gale Cengage Learning, OCLC FirstSearch, SirsiDynix
Wireless access
Mem of Ramapo Catskill Library System
Partic in New York Online Virtual Electronic Library (NOVEL)
Special Services for the Deaf - Bks on deafness & sign lang; Spec interest per
Open Mon-Thurs (Winter) 9-9, Fri & Sat 9-5, Sun 1-5; Mon & Thurs (Summer) 9-9, Tues, Wed, Fri & Sat 9-5
Friends of the Library Group

M ST LUKE'S CORNWALL HOSPITAL*, Medical Library, 70 Dubois St, 12550-9986. SAN 353-8869. Tel: 845-568-2220. FAX: 845-568-2913. E-mail: library@slchospital.org. Web Site: www.slchlibrary.org. *Libr Mgr,* Twila Snead
Founded 1957
Library Holdings: e-books 150; e-journals 10,000; Bk Titles 350; Per Subs 50
Subject Interests: Med
Database Vendor: EBSCOhost, Elsevier, OCLC FirstSearch, OVID Technologies, PubMed, SerialsSolutions
Partic in Basic Health Sciences Library Network; Health Info Librs of Westchester (HILOW); Southeastern New York Library Resources Council
Open Mon-Fri 8-2:30

NEWFANE

P NEWFANE FREE LIBRARY*, 2761 Maple Ave, 14108. SAN 312-164X. Tel: 716-778-9344. FAX: 716-778-9344. E-mail: newfanelibrary@nioga.org. Web Site: www.newfanelibrary.org. *Dir,* Kristine DeGlopper-Banks; E-mail: kdegl@nioga.org
Founded 1911. Pop 9,833; Circ 42,431
Library Holdings: Audiobooks 425; CDs 287; DVDs 673; Large Print Bks 1,040; Bk Vols 20,165; Per Subs 23; Videos 525
Automation Activity & Vendor Info: (Cataloging) SirsiDynix; (Circulation) SirsiDynix; (OPAC) SirsiDynix
Wireless access
Function: Adult bk club, Bk club(s), Bks on cassette, Bks on CD, Children's prog, Computers for patron use, Copy machines, Exhibits, Fax serv, Free DVD rentals, Handicapped accessible, Holiday prog, ILL available, Music CDs, Outreach serv, Photocopying/Printing, Pub access computers, Story hour, Summer reading prog, Tax forms
Mem of Nioga Library System
Open Mon, Wed & Fri 10-5, Tues & Thurs 12-8, Sat 11-2
Friends of the Library Group

NEWFIELD

P NEWFIELD PUBLIC LIBRARY*, 198 Main St, 14867. (Mail add: PO Box 154, 14867-0154), SAN 312-1658. Tel: 607-564-3594. FAX: 607-564-3594. E-mail: newfieldpubliclibrary@yahoo.com. Web Site: www.flls.org. *Librn,* Tina Winstead; *Asst Librn,* Vicky Cody
Founded 1882. Circ 13,739
Library Holdings: Bk Titles 8,824; Bk Vols 10,500; Per Subs 35
Automation Activity & Vendor Info: (Circulation) Innovative Interfaces, Inc; (OPAC) Innovative Interfaces, Inc
Wireless access
Mem of Finger Lakes Library System
Open Mon-Thurs 2-8, Sat 10-2

NEWPORT

P NEWPORT FREE LIBRARY*, 7390 Main St, 13416-3500. (Mail add: PO Box 359, 13416-0359), SAN 312-1666. Tel: 315-845-8533. E-mail: newport@midyork.org. *Co-Dir,* Betty Dodge; *Co-Dir,* Charlene Grossett
Founded 1923. Pop 3,614; Circ 18,784
Library Holdings: Bk Titles 18,000; Per Subs 23
Subject Interests: Cooking, Educ, Fiction, Hist
Wireless access
Mem of Mid-York Library System
Open Mon 1-8, Tues 1-7, Wed 9-12, Thurs 4-7, Fri 1-5

NIAGARA FALLS

P NIAGARA FALLS PUBLIC LIBRARY*, Earl W Brydges Bldg, 1425 Main St, 14305. SAN 353-8958. Tel: 716-286-4894. Reference Tel: 716-286-4881. FAX: 716-286-4912. Web Site: www.niagarafallspubliclib.org. *Dir,* Michelle Petrazzoulo; E-mail: mpetra@nioga.org; Staff 11 (MLS 11)
Founded 1838. Pop 55,593; Circ 340,000
Jan 2005-Dec 2005 Income (Main Library and Branch(s)) $2,254,678, State $124,572, City $2,063,292, County $64,481, Other $2,333. Mats Exp $247,111. Sal $1,183,122
Library Holdings: AV Mats 25,000; Bk Vols 325,000
Special Collections: US Document Depository
Subject Interests: Local hist
Automation Activity & Vendor Info: (Acquisitions) Horizon; (Cataloging) Horizon; (Circulation) Horizon; (Course Reserve) Horizon; (ILL) Horizon; (Media Booking) Horizon; (OPAC) Horizon; (Serials) Horizon
Wireless access
Publications: Newsletter
Mem of Nioga Library System
Open Mon-Wed 9-9, Thurs-Sat 9-5
Friends of the Library Group
Branches: 1
LASALLE, 8728 Buffalo Ave, 14304, SAN 353-8982. Tel: 716-283-8309. *Dir,* Michelle Petrazzoulo; E-mail: mpetra@nioga.org
Open Mon-Wed 10-8, Thurs-Sat 10-5
Friends of the Library Group

NIAGARA UNIVERSITY

C NIAGARA UNIVERSITY LIBRARY*, 5795 Lewiston Rd, 14109. SAN 312-1712. Tel: 716-286-8000. Circulation Tel: 716-286-8020. Interlibrary Loan Service Tel: 716-286-8013. Reference Tel: 716-286-8022. FAX: 716-286-8030. E-mail: reflib@niagara.edu. Web Site: www.niagara.edu/library. *Dir,* David Schoen; Tel: 716-286-8001, E-mail: schoen@niagara.edu; *Head, Pub Serv,* Jonathan Coe; Tel: 716-286-8005, E-mail: jcoe@niagara.edu; *Head, Acq,* Charles Dabkowski; Tel: 716-286-8007, E-mail: dabkowski@niagara.edu; *Head, Cat,* Joseph Umhauer; Tel: 716-286-8015, E-mail: jumhauer@niagara.edu; Staff 23 (MLS 11, Non-MLS 12)
Founded 1856. Enrl 3,548; Fac 198; Highest Degree: Master
Library Holdings: Bks on Deafness & Sign Lang 60; e-books 117; Bk Titles 202,402; Bk Vols 232,135; Per Subs 22,000
Special Collections: 15th-17th Century Religious Materials
Automation Activity & Vendor Info: (Cataloging) SirsiDynix; (Circulation) SirsiDynix; (OPAC) SirsiDynix
Database Vendor: EBSCOhost, ProQuest
Wireless access
Partic in Nylink; Western New York Library Resources Council
Open Mon-Thurs 8am-Midnight, Fri 8am-9pm, Sat 10-6, Sun 11am-Midnight

NICHOLS

P GEORGE P & SUSAN PLATT CADY LIBRARY*, 42 E River St, 13812. (Mail add: PO Box 70, 13812-0070), SAN 312-1720. Tel: 607-699-3835. FAX: 607-699-3835. E-mail: clibrary3@stny.rr.com. Web Site: cadylibrary.lib.ny.us. *Dir,* Ronnette Councilman
Founded 1927. Circ 14,500
Library Holdings: Bks on Deafness & Sign Lang 17; Bk Vols 10,000; Per Subs 25
Subject Interests: Health
Automation Activity & Vendor Info: (Cataloging) Innovative Interfaces, Inc; (Circulation) Innovative Interfaces, Inc; (ILL) Innovative Interfaces, Inc
Wireless access
Mem of Finger Lakes Library System
Open Mon 2-8:30, Tues, Wed & Fri 2-5, Thurs 2-8, Sat 10-Noon
Friends of the Library Group

NINEVEH

P NINEVEH PUBLIC LIBRARY OF COLESVILLE TOWNSHIP*, 3029 NY State Hwy 7, 13813. (Mail add: PO Box 124, 13813-0124), SAN 312-1739. Tel: 607-693-1858. FAX: 607-693-1858. E-mail: ni.ill@4cls.org. *Dir,* Tracie Livermore; *Asst Dir,* Pat Carpenter
Founded 1901. Pop 5,441
Library Holdings: Bk Titles 11,000
Wireless access
Mem of Four County Library System
Open Mon-Thurs 12:30-7:30, Fri 10-4, Sat 9-3

NISKAYUNA

S GENERAL ELECTRIC GLOBAL RESEARCH*, Whitney Knowledge Center-Niskayuna, One Research Circle, 12309. SAN 354-1177. Tel: 518-387-4952, 518-387-5000. E-mail: library@crd.ge.com. *Access Serv & Syst, Ref Serv,* Louise Macuirles; *Access Serv & Syst, Syst Coordr,* Dr James Lommel; Tel: 518-387-6162, E-mail: lommel@crd.ge.com; *Tech Info Spec,* Carolyn Warden; *Acq, Tech Serv,* Andrea Langhurst; Staff 4 (MLS 3, Non-MLS 1)
Founded 1905
Library Holdings: e-books 450; Bk Titles 26,000; Per Subs 400
Subject Interests: Biol, Ceramics, Chem, Electronics, Eng, Finance, Info sci, Math, Metallurgy, Physics, Polymers
Automation Activity & Vendor Info: (Acquisitions) Livelink for Libraries; (Cataloging) Livelink for Libraries; (Circulation) Livelink for Libraries; (ILL) OCLC Online; (OPAC) Livelink for Libraries
Database Vendor: Dialog, LexisNexis, Open Text Corporation, ProQuest

Function: For res purposes
Publications: Bibliogram; Intranet Web Page
Partic in Cap District Libr Coun for Ref & Res Resources; OCLC Online Computer Library Center, Inc
Restriction: Internal circ only, Restricted access

NORFOLK

P HEPBURN LIBRARY OF NORFOLK*, One Hepburn St, 13667. (Mail add: PO Box 530, 13667-0530), SAN 312-1747. Tel: 315-384-3052. FAX: 315-384-3841. Web Site: www.nc3r.org/norfolk. *Librn,* Vicky Brothers; Staff 1 (MLS 1)
Pop 4,258; Circ 13,023
Library Holdings: Bk Vols 14,000; Per Subs 75
Automation Activity & Vendor Info: (Acquisitions) Mandarin Library Automation; (Cataloging) Mandarin Library Automation; (Circulation) Mandarin Library Automation; (Course Reserve) Mandarin Library Automation; (ILL) Mandarin Library Automation; (Media Booking) Mandarin Library Automation; (OPAC) Mandarin Library Automation; (Serials) Mandarin Library Automation
Database Vendor: Baker & Taylor
Wireless access
Mem of North Country Library System
Partic in Northern New York Library Network
Open Mon-Fri 10-12 & 2-9, Sat 10-12
Friends of the Library Group

NORTH BABYLON

P NORTH BABYLON PUBLIC LIBRARY, 815 Deer Park Ave, 11703-3812. SAN 312-1755. Tel: 631-669-4020. FAX: 631-669-3432. TDD: 631-669-4140. E-mail: nbablib@suffolk.lib.ny.us. Web Site: www.northbabylonpl.org. *Dir,* Marc David Horowitz; E-mail: horowm@suffolk.lib.ny.us; *Librn III,* Maureen Nicolazzi; E-mail: mnicolaz@suffolk.lib.ny.us; *Ch Serv,* Elizabeth Arena; E-mail: earena@suffolk.lib.ny.us; *Circ,* Kathy Costello; *Computer Serv,* James Jenkins; E-mail: jenkinsj@suffolk.lib.ny.us; *Tech Serv,* Arleen Schwenker; Staff 9 (MLS 9)
Founded 1960. Pop 30,666; Circ 224,915
Library Holdings: Bk Vols 113,739; Per Subs 205
Special Collections: Newsday, 1944-2007, microfilm
Automation Activity & Vendor Info: (Cataloging) Innovative Interfaces, Inc; (Circulation) Innovative Interfaces, Inc; (ILL) Innovative Interfaces, Inc; (OPAC) Innovative Interfaces, Inc; (Serials) Innovative Interfaces, Inc
Database Vendor: Baker & Taylor, Checkpoint Systems, Inc, ebrary, EBSCO Information Services, Gale Cengage Learning, Innovative Interfaces, Inc, OVID Technologies, Wilson - Wilson Web
Wireless access
Publications: News & Notes (Bi-monthly)
Mem of Suffolk Cooperative Library System
Special Services for the Blind - Talking bks plus
Open Mon-Fri 9-9, Sat 9-5, Sun (Oct-May) 1-5

NORTH BELLMORE

P NORTH BELLMORE PUBLIC LIBRARY*, 1551 Newbridge Rd, 11710. SAN 312-1763. Tel: 516-785-6260. FAX: 516-785-7204. Web Site: www.nassaulibrary.org. *Dir,* Tom Bazzicalupo; Staff 17 (MLS 17)
Founded 1946. Pop 25,856; Circ 199,042
Library Holdings: AV Mats 6,188; Bk Titles 106,772; Bk Vols 112,744; Per Subs 348
Automation Activity & Vendor Info: (Circulation) Innovative Interfaces, Inc; (OPAC) Innovative Interfaces, Inc
Database Vendor: Innovative Interfaces, Inc
Publications: Inklings (Monthly Newsletter)
Mem of Nassau Library System
Open Mon-Thurs 9-9, Fri 9-6, Sat 9-5, Sun 1-5

NORTH CHATHAM

P NORTH CHATHAM FREE LIBRARY, PO Box 907, 12132-0907. SAN 312-1771. Tel: 518-766-3211. FAX: 518-766-3211. E-mail: nclibrary@fairpoint.net. Web Site: northchatham.lib.ny.us. *Dir,* Vicki Kurashige
Founded 1915. Pop 1,083; Circ 15,868
Library Holdings: Bk Titles 11,000; Per Subs 21
Subject Interests: Local hist
Function: Bk club(s), Bks on CD, Children's prog, Computer training, Computers for patron use, Copy machines, Fax serv, Free DVD rentals, Handicapped accessible, ILL available, Online cat, Online ref, Online searches, Photocopying/Printing, Prog for adults, Pub access computers, Ref serv available, Senior computer classes, Story hour, Summer reading prog, Wheelchair accessible
Mem of Mid-Hudson Library System
Open Mon-Thurs 2-8, Fri 2-6, Sat 10-2

NORTH COLLINS

P TOWN OF NORTH COLLINS PUBLIC LIBRARY*, 2095 School St, 14111. (Mail add: PO Box 730, 14111-0730), SAN 312-178X. Tel: 716-337-3211. FAX: 716-337-0647. Web Site: www.buffalolib.org. *Dir,* Mary Muscarella; E-mail: muscarellam@buffalolib.org
Founded 1878. Circ 18,772
Library Holdings: Bk Vols 8,000; Per Subs 102
Special Collections: Local Historical & Geneological Resources
Mem of Buffalo & Erie County Public Library System
Open Mon (Winter) 11-8, Wed 2-8, Fri 10-4, Sun 1-5; Mon (Summer) 11-8, Tues & Thurs 11-3, Wed 2-8, Fri 10-4;
Friends of the Library Group

NORTH CREEK

P TOWN OF JOHNSBURG LIBRARY*, 219 Main St, 12853. (Mail add: PO Box 7, 12853-0007). Tel: 518-251-4343. FAX: 518-251-9991. Web Site: www.sals.edu/johnsburg.shtml. *Dir,* Susan Schmidt
Library Holdings: AV Mats 1,200; Bk Vols 44,000; Per Subs 35; Talking Bks 400
Automation Activity & Vendor Info: (Cataloging) Innovative Interfaces, Inc; (Circulation) Innovative Interfaces, Inc; (OPAC) Innovative Interfaces, Inc
Wireless access
Mem of Southern Adirondack Library System
Open Wed & Fri (Sept-June) 11-5, Thurs 11-7, Sat 10-2; Mon (July & Aug) 9-12, Wed & Fri 11-5, Thurs 11-7, Sat 10-2
Friends of the Library Group

NORTH MERRICK

P NORTH MERRICK PUBLIC LIBRARY*, 1691 Meadowbrook Rd, 11566. SAN 312-1798. Tel: 516-378-7474. FAX: 516-378-0876. Administration FAX: 516-378-2523. Web Site: www.northmerrickpubliclibrary.org. *Dir,* Thomas Witt; *Head, Ch,* Ilene Leibowitz; *Head, Circ,* Anne Flynn; *Head, Ref,* Anibal Salazar; *Head, Tech Serv,* Diane Burkhardt; *Ref Librn,* Donna Elliott; *Ref Librn,* Nicholas Olijnyk; *Ch Serv,* Helen Friedman; *Ch Serv,* Janet Wasserman; *Pub Relations,* Marilyn Flynn; *Pub Relations,* Linda Vasconi; *YA Serv,* Kelly Rechsteiner; Staff 8 (MLS 8)
Founded 1965. Pop 12,498; Circ 124,054
Library Holdings: Audiobooks 1,100; AV Mats 2,547; Bks on Deafness & Sign Lang 20; CDs 1,680; DVDs 2,850; e-books 432; e-journals 3,500; Electronic Media & Resources 98; High Interest/Low Vocabulary Bk Vols 36; Large Print Bks 1,050; Music Scores 200; Bk Vols 84,334; Per Subs 218
Subject Interests: Art, Cookery
Automation Activity & Vendor Info: (Cataloging) Innovative Interfaces, Inc; (Circulation) Innovative Interfaces, Inc; (OPAC) Innovative Interfaces, Inc
Wireless access
Publications: Yesterday in the Merricks (Local historical information)
Mem of Nassau Library System
Open Mon-Thurs 10-9, Fri 10-6, Sat 10-5 (9:30-1 Summer), Sun 1-5
Friends of the Library Group

NORTH SALEM

P RUTH KEELER MEMORIAL LIBRARY*, North Salem Free Library, 276 Titicus Rd, 10560-1708. SAN 353-9016. Tel: 914-669-5161. FAX: 914-669-5173. E-mail: keelerlibrary@wlsmail.org. Web Site: www.keelerlibrary.org/. *Dir,* Carolyn Reznick; Staff 10 (MLS 3, Non-MLS 7)
Founded 1932. Pop 5,264; Circ 62,614
Jan 2014-Dec 2014 Income $432,915, State $1,391, City $311,000, Locally Generated Income $105,146, Other $15,378. Mats Exp $31,900, Books $21,000, Per/Ser (Incl. Access Fees) $3,900, AV Mat $7,000. Sal $238,791 (Prof $142,249)
Library Holdings: AV Mats 5,800; e-books 264; Electronic Media & Resources 141; Bk Titles 34,500; Per Subs 60
Special Collections: Helen Ferris Tibbets Children's Books; Hellen Whitman Herbal Coll
Automation Activity & Vendor Info: (Circulation) SIRSI WorkFlows
Database Vendor: Booksite, Overdrive, Inc, ProQuest, TumbleBookLibrary
Wireless access
Function: Adult bk club, Art exhibits, Audiobks via web, Bk club(s), Bks on CD, Children's prog, Computer training, Computers for patron use, Copy machines, Digital talking bks, e-mail serv, E-Reserves, Electronic databases & coll, Exhibits, Fax serv, Free DVD rentals, Handicapped accessible, Health sci info serv, Holiday prog, Home delivery & serv to Sr ctr & nursing homes, Homebound delivery serv, ILL available, Mus passes, Online cat, Online ref, Online searches, OverDrive digital audio bks, Preschool reading prog, Prog for adults, Prog for children & young adult, Pub access computers, Ref serv available, Scanner, Spanish lang bks, Spoken cassettes & DVDs, Story hour, Summer reading prog, Tax forms,

Teen prog, Telephone ref, VHS videos, Wheelchair accessible, Workshops, Writing prog
Publications: Newsletter (Monthly); North Salem Literary Review (Annual)
Mem of Westchester Library System
Special Services for the Blind - Bks on CD; Copier with enlargement capabilities; Free checkout of audio mat; Home delivery serv; Large print bks; Recorded bks
Open Mon 12-7, Tues, Wed, Fri & Sat 10-5, Thurs 10-7
Restriction: Lending limited to county residents
Friends of the Library Group

NORTH SYRACUSE

P NORTHERN ONONDAGA PUBLIC LIBRARY*, North Syracuse, 100 Trolley Barn Lane, 13212. SAN 377-8398. Tel: 315-458-6184. FAX: 315-458-7026. Web Site: www.nopl.org. *Dir,* Kate McCaffrey; E-mail: kmccaffrey@nopl.org; *Asst Dir/Mgr,* William Hastings; E-mail: whastings@nopl.org
Founded 1929. Pop 51,000; Circ 244,902
Automation Activity & Vendor Info: (Acquisitions) SirsiDynix; (Cataloging) SirsiDynix; (Circulation) SirsiDynix; (Course Reserve) SirsiDynix; (ILL) SirsiDynix; (Media Booking) SirsiDynix; (OPAC) SirsiDynix
Mem of Onondaga County Public Library
Open Mon-Thurs 9-8, Fri 9-5, Sat 9-3
Friends of the Library Group
Branches: 2
BREWERTON BRANCH, 5437 Library St, Brewerton, 13029-8719, SAN 310-8880. Tel: 315-676-7484. FAX: 315-676-7463. *Mgr,* Nancy Boisseau; E-mail: nboisseau@nopl.org
Pop 6,000; Circ 60,000
Subject Interests: Genealogy, Local hist
Open Mon-Thurs 10-8, Fri 10-5, Sat 10-3
Friends of the Library Group
CICERO BRANCH, 8686 Knowledge Lane, Cicero, 13039, SAN 311-0494. Tel: 315-699-2032. FAX: 315-699-2302. *Mgr,* Jill Youngs; E-mail: jyoungs@nopl.org
Founded 1924. Pop 7,500; Circ 24,742
Library Holdings: Bk Titles 12,400; Per Subs 62
Open Mon-Thurs 10-8, Fri 10-5, Sat 10-3
Friends of the Library Group

NORTH TONAWANDA

P NORTH TONAWANDA PUBLIC LIBRARY*, 505 Meadow Dr, 14120-2888. SAN 312-1836. Tel: 716-693-4132. Reference Tel: 716-693-3009. FAX: 716-693-0719. E-mail: ntwref@nioga.org. Web Site: www.ntlibrary.org. *Dir,* Margaret A Waite; E-mail: mwaite@nioga.org; *Coordr, Circ,* Lorri Corbin-Lewis; E-mail: lcorbin@nioga.org; *Coordr, Tech Serv,* Sylvia Grace; E-mail: sgrace@nioga.org; *Acq, Ref,* Jane Olstad; E-mail: jolstad@nioga.org; *Ch Serv,* Rebecca Stutzman; E-mail: rstutzma@nioga.org; Staff 23 (MLS 9, Non-MLS 14)
Founded 1893. Pop 33,262; Circ 464,000
Jul 2005-Jun 2006 Income $1,210,508, State $9,336, County $63,000, Locally Generated Income $1,079,672, Other $58,500. Mats Exp $236,050, Books $159,000, Per/Ser (Incl. Access Fees) $27,000, AV Mat $45,000, Electronic Ref Mat (Incl. Access Fees) $4,050, Presv $1,000. Sal $667,261 (Prof $310,461)
Library Holdings: AV Mats 31,518; CDs 10,499; DVDs 3,230; Bk Titles 146,904; Bk Vols 163,272; Per Subs 268; Videos 7,056
Special Collections: Carousels Coll
Subject Interests: Antiques, Handicraft, Local hist
Automation Activity & Vendor Info: (Cataloging) SirsiDynix; (Circulation) SirsiDynix; (OPAC) SirsiDynix
Publications: North Tonawanda Public Library Log (Newsletter)
Mem of Nioga Library System
Open Mon-Thurs 9:30-9, Fri & Sat 9:30-5, Sun 1-5
Friends of the Library Group

NORTHPORT

GM DEPARTMENT OF VETERANS AFFAIRS*, Medical Library, 79 Middleville Rd, 11768-2290. SAN 312-1852. Tel: 631-261-4400, Ext 2962. FAX: 631-754-7992. *Chief Librn,* Marylou Glazer; Tel: 631-261-4400, Ext 2966, E-mail: marylou.glazerl@med.va.gov
Library Holdings: Bk Titles 4,000; Per Subs 250
Subject Interests: Allied health, Geriatrics, Hospital admin, Med, Psychiat, Psychol, Surgery
Automation Activity & Vendor Info: (Cataloging) EOS International; (Circulation) EOS International; (OPAC) EOS International; (Serials) EOS International
Database Vendor: OCLC FirstSearch, OVID Technologies
Publications: Library Line (Quarterly)
Partic in Medical & Scientific Libraries of Long Island; Veterans Affairs Libr Network (VALNET)
Restriction: Staff & patient use

P NORTHPORT-EAST NORTHPORT PUBLIC LIBRARY*, 151 Laurel Ave, 11768. SAN 353-9075. Tel: 631-261-6930. FAX: 631-261-6718. Administration FAX: 631-754-6613. E mail: nenpl@suffolk.lib.ny.us. Web Site: www.nenpl.org. *Libr Dir,* James Olney; *Asst Libr Dir,* Nancy Morcerf; *Local Hist Librn,* Barbara Johnson; *Network & Syst Adminr,* Anthony Martocello; *Adult Serv,* Michelle Epstein; *Circ,* Frances Byrne; *Circ,* Emily McNamara; *Commun Serv,* Mary Ellen Moll; *Tech Serv,* Carol Senatore; *Youth Serv,* Doris Gebel; Staff 34 (MLS 34)
Founded 1914. Pop 36,499; Circ 563,466
Library Holdings: Bk Vols 237,110; Per Subs 820
Special Collections: Jack Kerouac Coll; Kerovac-Off the Shelf (Bibliography); Milton E Brasher Portfolio; Rosemary Wells Coll. Oral History
Subject Interests: Archit, Art, Boating
Automation Activity & Vendor Info: (Acquisitions) Innovative Interfaces, Inc - Millenium; (Cataloging) Innovative Interfaces, Inc - Millenium; (Circulation) Innovative Interfaces, Inc - Millenium; (Course Reserve) Innovative Interfaces, Inc - Millenium; (ILL) Innovative Interfaces, Inc - Millenium; (OPAC) Innovative Interfaces, Inc - Millenium; (Serials) Innovative Interfaces, Inc - Millenium
Database Vendor: ALLDATA Online, Baker & Taylor, BWI, College Source, EBSCO - WebFeat, EBSCO Information Services, Facts on File, Grolier Online, Hoovers, Innovative Interfaces, Inc, Marquis Who's Who, Mergent Online, OCLC WorldShare Interlibrary Loan, Overdrive, Inc, Westlaw
Wireless access
Publications: Bibliographies; Booklists; Living in Northport & East Northport; Special Loan Service to Our Schools; The Library (Newsletter); Welcome (Brochure)
Mem of Suffolk Cooperative Library System
Special Services for the Deaf - Adult & family literacy prog; Assisted listening device; Assistive tech; Bks on deafness & sign lang; Closed caption videos; High interest/low vocabulary bks
Special Services for the Blind - Assistive/Adapted tech devices, equip & products; Audio mat; BiFolkal kits; Bks on cassette; Bks on CD; Closed circuit TV magnifier; Computer with voice synthesizer for visually impaired persons; Copier with enlargement capabilities; Home delivery serv; Info on spec aids & appliances; Internet workstation with adaptive software; Large print bks; Large screen computer & software; Low vision equip; Magnifiers; Networked computers with assistive software; Playaways (bks on MP3); Recorded bks; Screen enlargement software for people with visual disabilities; Screen reader software; Talking bks; Talking bks & player equip; ZoomText magnification & reading software
Open Mon-Fri 9-9, Sat 9-5, Sun (Winter) 1-5
Friends of the Library Group
Branches: 1
EAST NORTHPORT PUBLIC, 185 Larkfield Rd, East Northport, 11731, SAN 353-9105. Tel: 631-261-2313. FAX: 631-261-3523. E-mail: netwalk@suffolk.lib.ny.us. *Asst Libr Dir,* Nancy Morcerf
Database Vendor: Wilson - Wilson Web
Friends of the Library Group

S NORTHPORT HISTORICAL SOCIETY*, 215 Main St, 11768. (Mail add: PO Box 545, 11768-0545), SAN 372-5677. Tel: 631-757-9859. FAX: 631-757-9398. E-mail: info@northporthistorical.org. Web Site: www.northporthistorical.org. *Dir,* Rosemary S Feeney; Staff 1 (MLS 1)
Founded 1962
Library Holdings: Bk Titles 350
Special Collections: Northport Area History Coll, doc, photog

NORTHVILLE

P NORTHVILLE PUBLIC LIBRARY*, 341 S Third St, 12134-4231. (Mail add: PO Box 1259, 12134-1259), SAN 376-3099. Tel: 518-863-6922. FAX: 518-863-6922. E-mail: norlib@mvls.info. Web Site: northville.mvls.info. *Dir,* Michael S Burnett; E-mail: mburnett@mvls.info
Founded 1986. Pop 3,047; Circ 39,130
Library Holdings: Bk Vols 16,813; Per Subs 60
Automation Activity & Vendor Info: (Acquisitions) Innovative Interfaces, Inc; (Cataloging) Innovative Interfaces, Inc; (Circulation) Innovative Interfaces, Inc; (OPAC) Innovative Interfaces, Inc; (Serials) Innovative Interfaces, Inc
Wireless access
Mem of Mohawk Valley Library System
Open Mon & Sat 9-12, Tues 9-8, Wed-Fri 9-4
Friends of the Library Group

NORWICH

M CHENANGO MEMORIAL HOSPITAL*, Medical Library, 179 N Broad St, 13815. SAN 312-1860. Tel: 607-337-4111, 607-337-4577. FAX: 607-334-2024. *Librn,* Hedy Messineo
Founded 1972
Library Holdings: Bk Vols 2,000; Per Subs 230
Subject Interests: Clinical med, Geriatric nursing, Nursing
Partic in National Network of Libraries of Medicine; OCLC Online Computer Library Center, Inc; South Central Regional Library Council
Open Mon-Fri 8:30-4

P GUERNSEY MEMORIAL LIBRARY*, Three Court St, 13815. SAN 312-1879. Tel: 607-334-4034. FAX: 607-336-3901. E-mail: guernsey@4cls.org. Web Site: www.guernseylibrary.org. *Dir,* Connie Dalrymple; *Ch,* Kim Hazen; *ILL,* Carol Manwarren; *Local Hist/Genealogy,* Kathryn Barton; *Ref Serv,* Sue Morehead. Subject Specialists: *Local hist,* Kathryn Barton; Staff 18 (MLS 2, Non-MLS 16)
Founded 1902. Pop 13,600; Circ 133,000
Library Holdings: AV Mats 3,038; Bk Vols 79,116; Per Subs 109
Subject Interests: Genealogy, Health, Job info, Local hist
Automation Activity & Vendor Info: (Acquisitions) SirsiDynix; (Cataloging) SirsiDynix; (Circulation) SirsiDynix; (ILL) SirsiDynix; (OPAC) SirsiDynix
Wireless access
Publications: Glance at Guernsey (Newsletter)
Mem of Four County Library System
Open Mon-Thurs 9-8:30, Fri 9-6, Sat 9-4, Sun 1-4

GL NEW YORK STATE SUPREME COURT SIXTH DISTRICT LAW LIBRARY*, David L Follett Memorial Library, Five W Main St, 13815-1899. SAN 312-1887. Tel: 607-334-9463. *Librn,* Lorraine Knapp
Founded 1902
Library Holdings: Bk Vols 10,000
Automation Activity & Vendor Info: (Cataloging) SirsiDynix
Database Vendor: LexisNexis, Westlaw
Wireless access
Partic in South Central Regional Library Council
Open Mon, Thurs & Fri 9-5

NORWOOD

P NORWOOD LIBRARY, One Morton St, 13668-1100. SAN 312-1909. Tel: 315-353-6692. FAX: 315-353-4688. E-mail: nowlib@ncls.org. Web Site: www.norwoodnylibrary.org. *Dir,* Rebecca Donnelly
Founded 1912. Circ 21,120
Library Holdings: AV Mats 1,205; Large Print Bks 750; Bk Vols 17,884; Per Subs 60; Talking Bks 230
Automation Activity & Vendor Info: (Cataloging) SirsiDynix; (Circulation) SirsiDynix
Wireless access
Mem of North Country Library System
Open Tues & Thurs 2-8, Wed & Fri 10-4, Sat 10-2
Friends of the Library Group

NUNDA

P BELL MEMORIAL LIBRARY*, 16 East St, 14517. (Mail add: PO Box 725, 14517-0725), SAN 312-1917. Tel: 585-468-2266. FAX: 585-468-2266. Web Site: www.nunda.pls-net.org. *Managing Librn,* Patricia Galbraith; E-mail: pgalbraith@pls-net.org; Staff 3 (Non-MLS 3)
Founded 1912. Pop 5,119; Circ 21,484
Library Holdings: AV Mats 534; CDs 240; Bk Vols 15,078; Per Subs 32; Videos 365
Automation Activity & Vendor Info: (Cataloging) SirsiDynix; (Circulation) SirsiDynix; (OPAC) SirsiDynix; (Serials) SirsiDynix
Mem of Pioneer Library System
Open Tues-Thurs 12-8, Fri 9-12 & 2-5, Sat 9-2

NYACK

C NYACK COLLEGE LIBRARY*, Bailey Library, One South Blvd, 10960-3698. SAN 312-1925. Interlibrary Loan Service Tel: 845-675-4437. Reference Tel: 845-675-4435. Administration Tel: 845-675-4434. FAX: 845-353-0817. Circulation FAX: 845-675-4580. Web Site: www.nyack.edu/library. *Dean, Libr Serv,* Linda Poston; E-mail: linda.poston@nyack.edu; *Dir,* Sunya Notley; E-mail: sunya.notley@nyack.edu; *Asst Dir,* Mick Williams; E-mail: mick.williams@nyack.edu; *Tech & Info Syst Librn,* Christy Choi; E-mail: christy.choi@nyack.edu; Staff 5 (MLS 3, Non-MLS 2)
Founded 1882. Enrl 2,400; Fac 140; Highest Degree: Master
Jul 2012-Jun 2013 Income $1,115,545. Mats Exp $613,895, Books $146,042, Per/Ser (Incl. Access Fees) $14,316, AV Mat $3,870, Electronic Ref Mat (Incl. Access Fees) $449,667. Sal $547,384 (Prof $392,735)
Library Holdings: AV Mats 12,000; e-books 60,000; Bk Vols 175,000; Per Subs 500
Subject Interests: Bible, Missions, Theol
Automation Activity & Vendor Info: (ILL) OCLC Connexion
Database Vendor: Alexander Street Press, American Psychological Association (APA), Atlas Systems, Bowker, Cinahl, CountryWatch, CredoReference, ebrary, EBSCOhost, Gale Cengage Learning, Gallup, Grolier Online, JSTOR, Medline, Mergent Online, Modern Language Association, OCLC, OCLC WorldShare Interlibrary Loan, Oxford Online, ProQuest, SerialsSolutions, Springshare, LLC, STAT!Ref (Teton Data Systems), YBP Library Services
Wireless access
Partic in OCLC Online Computer Library Center, Inc; Southeastern New York Library Resources Council; Westchester Academic Library Directors Organization (WALDO)
Open Mon-Thurs 8am-Midnight, Fri 8-4:30, Sat 10:30-9, Sun 1-10

M NYACK HOSPITAL*, Memorial Library, 160 N Midland Ave, 10960. Tel: 845-348-2514, 854-348-2000. FAX: 845-348-2515. Web Site: www.nyackhospital.org. *Dir,* Maria V Kwon; E-mail: Kwonm@nyackhospital.org; Staff 4 (MLS 1, Non-MLS 3)
Founded 1960
Library Holdings: e-books 240; e-journals 300; Bk Titles 1,250
Subject Interests: Med, Nursing, Pediatrics
Automation Activity & Vendor Info: (Cataloging) Marcive, Inc; (Circulation) Marcive, Inc; (OPAC) Marcive, Inc
Database Vendor: Elsevier, MD Consult, OVID Technologies, STAT!Ref (Teton Data Systems), UpToDate
Wireless access
Function: ILL available, Res libr
Publications: Acquisitions List
Partic in Basic Health Sciences Library Network; BRS; Health Info Librs of Westchester (HILOW); National Network of Libraries of Medicine; Southeastern New York Library Resources Council
Restriction: Med staff only

P THE NYACK LIBRARY*, 59 S Broadway, 10960. SAN 312-1933. Tel: 845-358-3370. Circulation Tel: 845-358-3370, Ext 211, 845-358-3370, Ext 216. Reference Tel: 845-358-3370, Ext 214. FAX: 845-358-6429. E-mail: info@nyacklibrary.org. Web Site: www.nyacklibrary.org. *Dir,* Jane Marino; Tel: 845-358-3370, Ext 221, E-mail: jmarino@nyacklibrary.org; *Bus Mgr,* Sharon Alfano; Tel: 845-358-3370, Ext 233, E-mail: salfano@nyacklibrary.org; *Mgr, Ref Serv,* Thomas Berman; Tel: 845-358-3370, Ext 217, E-mail: tberman@nyacklibrary.org; *Head, Ch,* Aldona Pilmanis; Tel: 845-358-3370, Ext 231, E-mail: apilmanis@nyacklibrary.org; *Teen Librn,* Elizabeth Hobson; Tel: 845-358-3370, Ext 236, E-mail: ehobson@nyacklibrary.org; *Youth Librn,* Claudia Uccellani; Tel: 845-358-3370, Ext 239, E-mail: cuccellani@nyacklibrary.org; Staff 28.5 (MLS 8, Non-MLS 20.5)
Founded 1879. Pop 14,699; Circ 203,876
Jul 2012-Jun 2013 Income $2,736,834, State $19,231, County $3,301, Locally Generated Income $2,714,302. Mats Exp $198,396, Books $104,230, Per/Ser (Incl. Access Fees) $10,000, AV Mat $37,328, Electronic Ref Mat (Incl. Access Fees) $46,838. Sal $1,643,636
Library Holdings: AV Mats 17,861; e-books 4,423; Microforms 1,555; Bk Vols 104,664; Per Subs 209
Special Collections: Local History Coll
Automation Activity & Vendor Info: (Acquisitions) SirsiDynix; (Cataloging) SirsiDynix; (Circulation) SirsiDynix; (OPAC) SirsiDynix
Database Vendor: EBSCO Information Services, Newsbank, ProQuest
Wireless access
Mem of Ramapo Catskill Library System
Open Mon (Winter) 11-9, Tues-Thurs 10-9, Fri 10-6, Sat 10-5, Sun 12-5; Mon (Summer) 11-8, Tues-Thurs 10-8, Fri 10-6, Sat 10-5, Sun 12-4
Friends of the Library Group

OAKDALE

C DOWLING COLLEGE LIBRARY*, 150 Idle Hour Blvd, 11769-1999. SAN 312-1968. Tel: 631-244-3280. Interlibrary Loan Service Tel: 631-244-3488. Reference Tel: 631-244-3282. Administration Tel: 631-244-3343. FAX: 631-244-3374. E-mail: reference@dowling.edu. Web Site: library.dowling.edu. *Mgr, Libr Syst & Serv,* Priscilla Powers; E-mail: powersp@dowling.edu; *Digital Res Librn,* Chris Kretz; Tel: 631-244-3396, E-mail: kretzc@dowling.edu; *Archives,* Diane Holliday; Tel: 631-244-3397, E-mail: hollidad@dowling.edu; *Cat, Tech Serv,* Michael Aloi; Tel: 631-244-3219; *Coll Develop,* Kami Convery; Tel: 631-244-3283, E-mail: converyk@dowling.edu; *Info Instruction, Distance Learning,* David Jank; Tel: 631-244-3081, E-mail: jankd@dowling.edu; *ILL, Web Coordr,* Laura Pope Robbins; Tel: 631-244-5023, E-mail: pope-rol@dowling.edu; *Outreach & Promotion,* Joyce Gotsch; Tel: 631-244-3150, E-mail: gotschj@dowling.edu; *Res, Outcomes & Assessment,* Marjorie Fusco; Tel: 631-244-3284, E-mail: fuscom@dowling.edu; *Spec Coll,* Suzanne Terry; Tel: 631-244-3285, E-mail: gterrys@dowling.edu; Staff 42 (MLS 22, Non-MLS 20)
Founded 1955. Enrl 7,000; Fac 130; Highest Degree: Doctorate

Library Holdings: e-books 9,423; Bk Titles 139,450; Bk Vols 215,273; Per Subs 961
Special Collections: Long Island History; Vanderbilt Family Coll
Subject Interests: Aviation, Educ, Transportation
Automation Activity & Vendor Info: (Acquisitions) Innovative Interfaces, Inc; (Cataloging) Innovative Interfaces, Inc; (Circulation) Innovative Interfaces, Inc; (Course Reserve) Innovative Interfaces, Inc; (ILL) Innovative Interfaces, Inc; (OPAC) Innovative Interfaces, Inc; (Serials) Innovative Interfaces, Inc
Database Vendor: American Chemical Society, College Source, CredoReference, Dialog, EBSCOhost, Elsevier, Gale Cengage Learning, Innovative Interfaces, Inc, LexisNexis, OCLC FirstSearch, OVID Technologies, ProQuest, Sage, Wilson - Wilson Web
Wireless access
Function: Ref serv available
Partic in Long Island Library Resources Council; OCLC Online Computer Library Center, Inc; Westchester Academic Library Directors Organization (WALDO)
Friends of the Library Group

OAKFIELD

P HAXTON MEMORIAL LIBRARY*, Three N Pearl St, 14125. SAN 312-1976. Tel: 585-948-9900. FAX: 585-948-9900. Web Site: www.nioga.org/oak.html. *Dir,* Jen Magee
Founded 1963. Pop 3,213; Circ 5,900
Library Holdings: Bk Vols 47,000; Per Subs 60
Wireless access
Mem of Nioga Library System
Open Mon 10-12 & 2-5, Tues & Fri 1-5, Wed & Thurs 1-5 & 6:30-8:30
Friends of the Library Group

OCEANSIDE

P OCEANSIDE LIBRARY*, 30 Davison Ave, 11572-2299. SAN 312-1984. Tel: 516-766-2360. FAX: 516-766-1895. Web Site: www.oceansidelibrary.com. *Dir,* Evelyn Rothschild; E-mail: erothschild@oceansidelibrary.com; *Asst Dir,* Barbara Markowitz; *Head, Ref,* Marcia Ratcliff; *Ch Serv,* Kathy Heaney; *ILL,* Susan Urban; *Tech Serv,* Barbara Chicco; *YA Serv,* Barbara Mickowski
Founded 1938. Pop 36,847; Circ 393,206
Jul 2012-Jun 2013 Income $4,190,451. Mats Exp $415,500, Books $258,500, Per/Ser (Incl. Access Fees) $20,000, AV Mat $83,000, Electronic Ref Mat (Incl. Access Fees) $54,000. Sal $1,992,626
Library Holdings: Bk Vols 174,027
Wireless access
Publications: Oceanside Library (Newsletter)
Mem of Nassau Library System
Partic in Long Island Library Resources Council
Special Services for the Deaf - Assistive tech
Special Services for the Blind - Magnifiers; Talking bks; ZoomText magnification & reading software

M SOUTH NASSAU COMMUNITIES HOSPITAL*, Jules Redish Memorial Medical Library, One Healthy Way, 11572. SAN 312-1992. Tel: 516-632-3452. FAX: 516-766-3857. *Dir,* Claire Joseph; E-mail: cjoseph@snch.org; Staff 1 (MLS 1)
Founded 1958
Library Holdings: Bk Titles 1,100; Per Subs 120
Subject Interests: Med, Nursing, Surgery
Partic in Long Island Library Resources Council
Restriction: Staff use only

ODESSA

P DUTTON S PETERSON MEMORIAL LIBRARY*, 106 First St, 14869. (Mail add: PO Box 46, 14869-0046), SAN 376-3064. Tel: 607-594-2791. FAX: 607-594-2791. E-mail: odessa@stls.org. Web Site: www.stls.org/odessa. *Dir,* Gayle Greuber; E-mail: greuberg@stls.org
Founded 1986
Library Holdings: AV Mats 950; Bk Titles 7,000; Per Subs 12
Automation Activity & Vendor Info: (Cataloging) SirsiDynix; (Circulation) SirsiDynix; (OPAC) SirsiDynix
Wireless access
Mem of Southern Tier Library System
Open Mon-Thurs 2-8, Fri 10-12 & 2-6, Sat 10-12
Friends of the Library Group

OGDENSBURG

M CLAXTON-HEPBURN MEDICAL CENTER LIBRARY*, 214 King St, 13669. SAN 312-2018. Tel: 315-393-3600, Ext 5632. FAX: 315-393-8506. Web Site: www.claxtonhepburn.org. *Adminr,* Mark Webster; *Circuit Librn,* Leslie Beale; *Circuit Librn,* Ellen Darabaner; E-mail: edarabaner@shsny.com
Founded 1958
Library Holdings: Bk Vols 300; Per Subs 30
Partic in Northern New York Library Network
Restriction: Med staff only

S NEW YORK STATE DEPARTMENT OF CORRECTIONAL SERVICES*, Ogdensburg Correctional Facility General Library, One Correction Way, 13669. SAN 327-1870. Tel: 315-393-0281. FAX: 315-393-0281, Ext 3299. *Librn,* Thomas E Lawrence; Staff 1 (MLS 1)
Founded 1982
Apr 2010-Mar 2011 Income $76,265, State $2,765, Parent Institution $73,500. Mats Exp $5,000, Books $1,250, Per/Ser (Incl. Access Fees) $3,750. Sal $68,200
Library Holdings: AV Mats 2,968; CDs 1; DVDs 40; High Interest/Low Vocabulary Bk Vols 513; Large Print Bks 35; Microforms 239; Bk Titles 16,076; Bk Vols 19,207; Per Subs 65, Talking Bks 365; Videos 890
Special Collections: Black Culture History & Spanish Language Coll
Automation Activity & Vendor Info: (Acquisitions) Follett Software; (Cataloging) Follett Software; (Circulation) Follett Software; (OPAC) Follett Software
Mem of North Country Library System
Restriction: Inmate patrons, facility staff & vols direct access. All others through ILL only, Not open to pub

P OGDENSBURG PUBLIC LIBRARY*, 312 Washington St, 13669-1518. SAN 312-2034. Tel: 315-393-4325. FAX: 315-393-4344. E-mail: ogdlib@ncls.org. Web Site: www.ogdensburgpubliclibrary.org, www.ogdlib.org. *Dir,* Wayne L Miller; E-mail: wmiller@ncls.org; *Adult Serv,* Stephanie Young; E-mail: syoung@ncls.org; *Ch Serv,* Position Currently Open; Staff 11 (MLS 3, Non-MLS 8)
Founded 1893. Pop 12,364; Circ 66,407
Jan 2008-Dec 2008 Income $444,575, State $73,279, City $319,171, County $17,709, Locally Generated Income $34,416. Mats Exp $63,300, Books $45,000, Per/Ser (Incl. Access Fees) $5,800, Micro $200, AV Mat $5,000, Electronic Ref Mat (Incl. Access Fees) $7,300. Sal $261,872 (Prof $136,988)
Library Holdings: Audiobooks 3,042; AV Mats 29,820; e-books 620; Bk Vols 81,765; Per Subs 236; Videos 6,792
Special Collections: General Newton Martin Curtis Civil War Coll; Ogdensburg History (Ogdensburg Archives), bks, flm, ms. Municipal Document Depository; Oral History
Subject Interests: Local hist
Automation Activity & Vendor Info: (Circulation) SirsiDynix; (OPAC) SirsiDynix
Wireless access
Function: Archival coll, Bks on cassette, Bks on CD, Children's prog, Computer training, Computers for patron use, Copy machines, e-mail & chat, e-mail serv, Electronic databases & coll, Exhibits, Fax serv, Free DVD rentals, Handicapped accessible, Home delivery & serv to Sr ctr & nursing homes, ILL available, Mail & tel request accepted, Music CDs, Online cat, Online ref, Online searches, Prog for adults, Prog for children & young adult, Provide serv for the mentally ill, Pub access computers, Ref serv available, Ref serv in person, Scanner, Senior computer classes, Story hour, Summer reading prog, Tax forms, Teen prog, Video lending libr
Publications: Between a Book & a Tech Place (Newsletter)
Mem of North Country Library System
Open Mon, Tues & Thurs 9-8, Fri & Sat 9-5
Friends of the Library Group

OLD CHATHAM

SR SHAKER MUSEUM & LIBRARY*, Emma B King Library, 88 Shaker Museum Rd, 12136. SAN 312-2069. Tel: 518-794-9100, Ext 211. FAX: 518-794-8621. Web Site: www.shakermuseumandlibrary.org. *Dir, Res Serv,* Jerry Grant; E-mail: jgrant@shakerml.org; Staff 2 (MLS 1, Non-MLS 1)
Founded 1950
Library Holdings: Bk Titles 2,500
Special Collections: Paper Artifacts, drawings, broadsides, advertising labels, product packages, watercolors; Photograph Coll; Society of Shakers: Their Arts, Crafts, Theology, Philosophy, includes membership rolls, patents, deeds, diaries, account books
Subject Interests: Archit, Art, Furniture, Relig, Shakers, Women
Publications: Making His Mark: The World of Shaker Craftsman Orren Haskins; Noble But Plain: The Shaker Meetinghouse at Mount Lebanon; Shaker Adventure; Shaker Museum & Library Broadside (to members); Shakerism & Feminism: Reflections on Women's Religion & the Early Shakers; The Shaker Museum Guide to Shaker Collections & Libraries
Restriction: Open by appt only

OLD FORGE

P OLD FORGE LIBRARY*, 220 Crosby Blvd, 13420. (Mail add: PO Box 128, 13420-0128), SAN 312-2077. Tel: 315-369-6008. FAX: 315-369-2754. Web Site: www.midyork.org/oldforge. *Dir,* Isabella P Worthen; E-mail: iworthen@midyork.org

Founded 1914. Pop 1,637; Circ 19,326
Library Holdings: Bk Titles 20,000; Per Subs 25
Subject Interests: Adirondack hist
Publications: Adirondack Reflections
Mem of Mid-York Library System
Open Tues-Fri (Winter) 11-8, Sat 11-3, Tues-Fri (Summer) 11-9, Sat 11-3
Friends of the Library Group

OLD WESTBURY

C NEW YORK INSTITUTE OF TECHNOLOGY*, Wisser Library, PO Box 8000, 11568-8000. SAN 329-1774. Tel: 516-686-7657. FAX: 516-686-1320. Web Site: www.nyit.edu/library. *Librn,* Gerri Flanzraich; *Online Serv,* Clare Cohn; Staff 17 (MLS 17)
Founded 1955. Enrl 8,555; Fac 734; Highest Degree: Master
Library Holdings: e-books 21,264; e-journals 55,122; Bk Vols 166,983; Per Subs 477
Special Collections: Center for Prejudice Reduction
Subject Interests: Archit, Computer sci, Culinary arts, Educ, Eng
Automation Activity & Vendor Info: (Cataloging) SirsiDynix
Publications: New Acquisitions; Newsletter; Resource Guides
Partic in OCLC Online Computer Library Center, Inc
Open Mon-Thurs 8am-10pm, Fri 8-5, Sat 9-5, Sun 1-6
Departmental Libraries:
EDUCATION HALL LIBRARY ART & ARCHITECTURE COLLECTION, PO Box 8000, 11568. Tel: 516-686-7422, 516-686-7579. FAX: 516-686-7814. Web Site: iris.nyit.edu/library/campus/edhall/index.html. *Librn,* Linda Heslin; E-mail: lheslin@nyit.edu
Library Holdings: Bk Vols 26,500; Per Subs 215; Spec Interest Per Sub 217
Automation Activity & Vendor Info: (Acquisitions) SirsiDynix
Open Mon-Fri 8-4

M NEW YORK INSTITUTE OF TECHNOLOGY*, New York College of Osteopathic Medicine Medical Library, Northern Blvd, 11568-8000. SAN 326-1697. Tel: 516-686-3743. FAX: 516-686-3709. *Chief Librn,* Jeanne Strausman; Tel: 516-686-3779, E-mail: jstrausm@nyit.edu; *ILL,* Mahnaz Tehrani; E-mail: mtehrani@nyit.edu; *Tech Serv,* Adrienne Lippmann; E-mail: lippmann@nyit.edu; Staff 6 (MLS 3, Non-MLS 3)
Founded 1978
Library Holdings: Bk Vols 10,000; Per Subs 415
Automation Activity & Vendor Info: (Cataloging) SirsiDynix; (Circulation) SirsiDynix; (OPAC) SirsiDynix; (Serials) SirsiDynix
Wireless access
Partic in Medical & Scientific Libraries of Long Island
Open Mon-Fri 8am-9pm, Sat 9am-Midnight, Sun 1pm-Midnight
Restriction: Open to students, fac & staff

C STATE UNIVERSITY OF NEW YORK*, College at Old Westbury Library, 223 Store Hill Rd, 11568. (Mail add: PO Box 229, 11568-0229), SAN 312-2093. Tel: 516-876-3156. Circulation Tel: 516-876-3150. Interlibrary Loan Service Tel: 516-876-3152. Reference Tel: 516-876-3151. FAX: 516-876-3325. E-mail: libraryreference@oldwestbury.edu. Web Site: www.oldwestbury.edu/library. *Dir,* Stephen Kirkpatrick; E-mail: kirkpatricks@oldwestbury.edu; *Assoc Librn, Per/Acq,* Barbara Walsh; Tel: 516-876-3164, E-mail: walshb@oldwestbury.edu; *Sr Asst Librn, Access Serv,* Antonia DiGregorio; Tel: 516-876-3226, E-mail: digregorioa@oldwestbury.edu; *Sr Asst Librn, Cat/Syst,* Werner Sbaschnik; Tel: 516-876-3154, E-mail: sbaschnikw@oldwestbury.edu; *Sr Asst Librn, Ref,* Curt Friehs; Tel: 516-876-2895, E-mail: friehsc@oldwestbury.edu; *Sr Asst Librn, Ref,* Joanne Spadaro; Tel: 516-876-2896, E-mail: spadaroj@oldwestbury.edu. Subject Specialists: *Bus,* Curt Friehs; *Educ,* Joanne Spadaro; Staff 7 (MLS 7)
Founded 1967. Enrl 4,200; Highest Degree: Master
Special Collections: Slavery Source Material Coll, micro; Underground Press Coll, micro; Women's Studies Coll
Subject Interests: Behav sci, Bus, Educ, Ethnic studies, Feminism, Soc sci
Function: AV serv, Computers for patron use, Copy machines, e-mail serv, Electronic databases & coll, ILL available, Online cat, Online ref, Online searches, Orientations
Publications: Focus Bibliographies; Library Information (Pamphlets); Research Guides; Subject List of Periodicals
Partic in OCLC Online Computer Library Center, Inc
Open Mon-Fri 7:30-6
Restriction: Pub use on premises

OLEAN

P OLEAN PUBLIC LIBRARY*, 134 N Second St, 14760-2583. SAN 312-2115. Tel: 716-372-0200. FAX: 716-372-8651. E-mail: info@oleanlibrary.org. Web Site: www.oleanlibrary.org. *Dir,* Lance Chaffee; E-mail: director@oleanlibrary.org; *Ref Librn,* Kim Mahar; *Ch Serv,* Kathy Price; *Tech Serv,* Sheryl Soborski; Staff 5 (MLS 5)
Founded 1871. Pop 16,818; Circ 203,585
Jan 2005-Dec 2005 Income $1,051,689, State $44,736, City $882,388, Locally Generated Income $70,688, Other $53,877. Mats Exp $137,803, Books $91,207, Per/Ser (Incl. Access Fees) $18,147, Other Print Mats $512, AV Mat $13,145, Electronic Ref Mat (Incl. Access Fees) $12,927, Presv $1,270. Sal $432,742 (Prof $149,964)
Library Holdings: AV Mats 8,231; Bk Vols 99,241; Per Subs 373
Subject Interests: Agr, Archit, Art, Educ
Automation Activity & Vendor Info: (Circulation) SirsiDynix; (OPAC) SirsiDynix
Wireless access
Mem of Chautauqua-Cattaraugus Library System
Open Mon-Thurs 9-9, Fri 9-6, Sat 10-5, Sun (Oct-Apr) 1-4
Friends of the Library Group

ONEIDA

S MADISON COUNTY HISTORICAL SOCIETY LIBRARY*, 435 Main St, 13421. SAN 325-0741. Tel: 315-361-9735, 315-363-4136. E-mail: history@mchs1900.org. Web Site: www.mchs1900.org. *Dir,* Sydney Loftus; Staff 2 (Non-MLS 2)
Founded 1900
Library Holdings: Bk Vols 2,000
Special Collections: Gerrit Smith Coll; Marshall Hope Coll
Subject Interests: City of Oneida, Genealogy, Hist, Madison County, NY
Wireless access
Function: Archival coll
Restriction: Open to pub by appt only

P ONEIDA PUBLIC LIBRARY*, 220 Broad St, 13421. SAN 312-2123. Tel: 315-363-3050. E-mail: oneida@midyork.org. Web Site: www.midyork.org/oneida. *Dir,* Carolyn Gerakopoulos
Founded 1924. Pop 15,300; Circ 94,738
Library Holdings: Bk Vols 58,000; Per Subs 110
Special Collections: Local History & Genealogy, bks, clippings, Cemetery rec; Madison County History; Oneida Community, bks, newsp; Oneida Indian Nation History
Wireless access
Publications: Life at Oneida Library (Quarterly)
Mem of Mid-York Library System
Partic in OCLC Online Computer Library Center, Inc
Open Mon-Thurs 9-8, Fri 9-5, Sat 10-4
Friends of the Library Group

ONEONTA

C HARTWICK COLLEGE, Stevens-German Library, One Hartwick Dr, 13820. SAN 312-214X. Tel: 607-431-4441. FAX: 607-431-4457. E-mail: reference@hartwick.edu. Web Site: hartwick.edu/academics/stevens-german-library. *Dir, Libr & Info Res,* Paul Coleman; Tel: 607-431-4449, E-mail: colemanp@hartwick.edu; *Head, Pub Serv,* Peter Rieseler; Tel: 607-431-4395, E-mail: rieselerp@hartwick.edu; *Acq & Cat Librn,* David Heyduk; Tel: 607-431-4459, E-mail: heydukd@hartwick.edu; *Ref & Instrul Serv Librn,* Mike Friery; Tel: 607-431-4475, E-mail: frieryj@hartwick.edu; *Circ Mgr,* Deanna Meadowcroft; E-mail: meadowcroftd@hartwick.edu; *Mgr, Libr Media Serv,* Ray Cesnavicius; Tel: 607-431-4446, E-mail: cesnaviciusr@hartwick.edu; *Archivist & Curator of Rare Bks, Rec Mgr,* Rebekah Ambrose-Dalton; Tel: 607-431-4450, E-mail: ambroser@hartwick.edu; *ILL Spec,* Dawn Baker; Tel: 607-431-4454, E-mail: bakerd0@hartwick.edu; Staff 10 (MLS 7, Non-MLS 3)
Founded 1928. Enrl 1,450; Fac 113; Highest Degree: Bachelor
Library Holdings: Bk Vols 315,227; Per Subs 2,300
Special Collections: Judge William Cooper Papers, ms; North American Indians (Yager Coll), bk, micro
Subject Interests: N Am Indians
Automation Activity & Vendor Info: (Acquisitions) Innovative Interfaces, Inc; (Cataloging) Innovative Interfaces, Inc; (Circulation) Innovative Interfaces, Inc; (Course Reserve) Docutek; (ILL) OCLC ILLiad; (Media Booking) Innovative Interfaces, Inc; (OPAC) Innovative Interfaces, Inc
Database Vendor: Cambridge Scientific Abstracts, Dialog, EBSCOhost, Gale Cengage Learning, JSTOR, LexisNexis, Newsbank, OCLC FirstSearch, OCLC WorldShare Interlibrary Loan, ProQuest, PubMed, ScienceDirect, SerialsSolutions, STN International
Wireless access
Function: AV serv, Copy machines, E-Reserves, Electronic databases & coll, Handicapped accessible, ILL available, Ref serv available, Wheelchair accessible, Workshops
Publications: Stevens-German Library (Newsletter)
Partic in OCLC Online Computer Library Center, Inc; South Central Regional Library Council
Open Mon & Tues 8am-1am, Wed & Thurs 8am-11-pm, Fri 8-6, Sat 12-5, Sun Noon-1am

P HUNTINGTON MEMORIAL LIBRARY, 62 Chestnut, 13820-2498. SAN 312-2158. Tel: 607-432-1980. Web Site: hmloneonta.org, www.4cls.org. *Dir,* Tina Winstead; *Librn,* Sarah Livingston; E-mail: on.sarah@4cls.org; *Ch Serv,* Debra Hansen; Staff 3 (MLS 2, Non-MLS 1)
Founded 1893. Pop 25,000; Circ 177,541
Library Holdings: AV Mats 2,795; DVDs 1,067; Large Print Bks 3,000; Bk Vols 79,000; Per Subs 115
Special Collections: DAR Lineage Coll; Railroads (Beach Coll), pictures
Automation Activity & Vendor Info: (Acquisitions) SirsiDynix; (Circulation) SirsiDynix; (ILL) SirsiDynix; (OPAC) SirsiDynix
Wireless access
Mem of Four County Library System
Open Mon-Thurs 9-8, Fri 9-5:30, Sat 9-4
Friends of the Library Group

C STATE UNIVERSITY OF NEW YORK, COLLEGE AT ONEONTA, James M Milne Library, 108 Ravine Pkwy, 13820. (Mail add: Milne Library, SUNY Oneonta, 13820), SAN 312-2166. Tel: 607-436-3702. Circulation Tel: 607-436-2720. Interlibrary Loan Service Tel: 607-436-2726. Reference Tel: 607-436-2722. FAX: 607-436-3081. Web Site: www.oneonta.edu/library. *Dir,* Charles R O'Bryan; E-mail: charles.obryan@oneonta.edu; *Head, Bibliog & Digital Serv,* James Coan; Tel: 607-436-3454, E-mail: James.Coan@oneonta.edu; *Head, Access Serv,* Andrea Gerberg; Tel: 607-436-2774, E-mail: Andrea.Gerberg@oneonta.edu; *Head, Ref & Instruction,* Mary Lynn Bensen; Tel: 607-436-2729, E-mail: bensenml@oneonta.edu; *Circ,* Kathy Croft; Tel: 607-436-2725, E-mail: croftkc@oneonta.edu; Staff 22.65 (MLS 9.525, Non-MLS 13.125)
Founded 1889. Enrl 6,055; Fac 494; Highest Degree: Master
Jul 2013-Jun 2014 Income $2,228,133, State $2,169,306, Other $58,827. Mats Exp $767,670, Books $132,630, Per/Ser (Incl. Access Fees) $275,438, AV Mat $6,170, Electronic Ref Mat (Incl. Access Fees) $347,841, Presv $5,591. Sal $1,330,996 (Prof $639,620)
Library Holdings: Audiobooks 158; AV Mats 12,035; Bks on Deafness & Sign Lang 342; CDs 1,960; DVDs 1,814; e-books 362,898; e-journals 127,413; Electronic Media & Resources 230; High Interest/Low Vocabulary Bk Vols 25; Large Print Bks 57; Music Scores 3,807; Bk Titles 1,082,591; Bk Vols 833,741; Per Subs 406; Videos 1,188
Special Collections: 19th & Early 20th Century Popular Fiction; Early Textbooks & Early Educational Theory; Faculty Publications Coll; James Fenimore Cooper Coll; John Burroughs & Nature Writing (Cornell-Gladstone-Hanlon-Kaufmann Coll); Lantern Slide Coll; Martha Chambers Memorial Coll; Masters Theses; New York State History Coll; New York State Verse Coll; Private Press Publs; SCC Miscellanies; SUNY Oneonta Archives. State Document Depository; US Document Depository
Subject Interests: Educ, Music indust
Automation Activity & Vendor Info: (Acquisitions) Ex Libris Group; (Cataloging) Ex Libris Group; (Circulation) Ex Libris Group; (ILL) OCLC ILLiad; (OPAC) Ex Libris Group; (Serials) Ex Libris Group
Database Vendor: Agricola, Alexander Street Press, American Chemical Society, CQ Press, ebrary, EBSCOhost, Ex Libris Group, Gale Cengage Learning, Greenwood Publishing Group, JSTOR, LexisNexis, OCLC FirstSearch, Paratext, Project MUSE, ProQuest, ScienceDirect, Standard & Poor's, ValueLine, Wiley, Wiley InterScience
Wireless access
Publications: Milne Library Blog (Current awareness service)
Partic in New York State Higher Education Initiative; South Central Regional Library Council
Special Services for the Deaf - Bks on deafness & sign lang
Special Services for the Blind - Computer with voice synthesizer for visually impaired persons; Scanner for conversion & translation of mats
Open Mon-Thurs 8am-1am, Fri 8am-9pm, Sat Noon-9, Sun Noon-1am

ONTARIO

P ONTARIO PUBLIC LIBRARY*, 1850 Ridge Rd, 14519. SAN 312-2174. Tel: 315-524-8381. FAX: 315-524-5838. E-mail: ontariolibrarydirector@owwl.org. Web Site: www.ontariopubliclibrary.org. *Dir,* Sandra Hylen; E-mail: shylen@pls-net.org; *Youth Serv Librn,* Anne Rehor; E-mail: arehor@pls-net.org; Staff 15 (MLS 2, Non-MLS 13)
Founded 1914. Pop 9,778; Circ 159,385
Jan 2011-Dec 2011 Income $550,475, State $4,600, City $518,875, County $8,100, Locally Generated Income $13,900, Other $5,000. Mats Exp $65,700, Books $41,000, Per/Ser (Incl. Access Fees) $5,400, AV Equip $100, AV Mat $19,200. Sal $294,000 (Prof $95,000)
Library Holdings: Audiobooks 2,600; Bks on Deafness & Sign Lang 15; CDs 350; DVDs 3,245; e-books 212; High Interest/Low Vocabulary Bk Vols 86; Large Print Bks 2,000; Bk Titles 39,600; Per Subs 115; Videos 160
Automation Activity & Vendor Info: (Cataloging) Evergreen; (Circulation) Evergreen; (OPAC) Evergreen
Wireless access
Function: Adult bk club, Art exhibits, Bk club(s), Bk reviews (Group), Bks on cassette, Bks on CD, Children's prog, Computer training, Computers for patron use, Copy machines, Electronic databases & coll, Exhibits, Fax serv, Free DVD rentals, Genealogy discussion group, Holiday prog, Home delivery & serv to Sr ctr & nursing homes, Homebound delivery serv, ILL available, Instruction & testing, Jazz prog, Magnifiers for reading, Mail & tel request accepted, Music CDs, Newsp ref libr, Online cat, Online ref, Outreach serv, Outside serv via phone, mail, e-mail & web, OverDrive digital audio bks, Photocopying/Printing, Preschool outreach, Prog for adults, Prog for children & young adult, Pub access computers, Ref serv available, Ref serv in person, Senior computer classes, Story hour, Tax forms, Teen prog, Telephone ref, VHS videos, Wheelchair accessible, Workshops
Partic in Rochester Regional Library Council
Special Services for the Deaf - Bks on deafness & sign lang; High interest/low vocabulary bks
Open Mon-Thurs 10-8:30, Fri 10-5:30, Sat 10-3
Friends of the Library Group

ORANGEBURG

GM NATHAN S KLINE INSTITUTE FOR PSYCHIATRIC RESEARCH, Health Sciences Library, 140 Old Orangeburg Rd, Bldg 35, 10962. SAN 312-2204. Tel: 845-398-6575. FAX: 845-398-5551. Web Site: nki.hospitalservices.senylrc.org. *Dir,* Stuart Moss; Tel: 845-398-6576, E-mail: moss@nki.rfmh.org; Staff 2 (MLS 1, Non-MLS 1)
Founded 1952
Library Holdings: Bk Titles 10,000; Bk Vols 25,000
Special Collections: Family Resource Center
Subject Interests: Biochem, Mental health, Neuroscience, Psychiat, Psychol, Psychopharmacology
Database Vendor: EBSCOhost, Gale Cengage Learning
Function: Archival coll, For res purposes, Photocopying/Printing
Partic in National Network of Libraries of Medicine; OCLC Online Computer Library Center, Inc; Southeastern New York Library Resources Council
Restriction: In-house use for visitors, Pub use on premises

C LONG ISLAND UNIVERSITY*, Rockland Graduate Campus Library, 70 Rte 340, 10962. Tel: 845-359-7200, Ext 5411. FAX: 845-359-2804. Web Site: library.liu.edu. *Dir,* Kara Sheridan; E-mail: kara.sheridan@liu.edu
Library Holdings: Bk Vols 10,000; Per Subs 350
Wireless access
Open Mon-Thurs 12-9, Fri 11-5, Sat 9-3

P ORANGEBURG LIBRARY, 20 S Greenbush Rd, 10962-1311. SAN 312-2190. Tel: 845-359-2244. FAX: 845-359-8692. E-mail: org@rcls.org. Web Site: www.orangeburg-library.org. *Dir,* Mary Kane; E-mail: mkane@rcls.org; *Ad,* Cheryl McNeil; E-mail: cmcneil@rcls.org; *Ch Serv,* Angela Krajcar; E-mail: akrajcar@rcls.org; Staff 4 (MLS 3, Non-MLS 1)
Founded 1962. Pop 3,388; Circ 111,657
Jan 2012-Dec 2012 Income $647,615. Mats Exp $88,500, Books $56,000, Per/Ser (Incl. Access Fees) $6,000, AV Mat $23,000, Electronic Ref Mat (Incl. Access Fees) $5,000. Sal $336,000 (Prof $160,000)
Library Holdings: Audiobooks 2,870; Bks on Deafness & Sign Lang 25; CDs 1,000; DVDs 2,870; e-books 1,350; Electronic Media & Resources 49,896; High Interest/Low Vocabulary Bk Vols 15; Large Print Bks 250; Bk Vols 36,319; Per Subs 100; Talking Bks 1,139; Videos 200
Subject Interests: Mystery
Automation Activity & Vendor Info: (Cataloging) SIRSI WorkFlows; (Circulation) SIRSI WorkFlows, (OPAC) SirsiDynix; (Serials) SirsiDynix
Database Vendor: Bowker, EBSCOhost, Evanced Solutions, Inc, Gale Cengage Learning, Newsbank, Overdrive, Inc, ProQuest, ReferenceUSA, SirsiDynix
Wireless access
Function: Adult bk club, After school storytime, Art exhibits, CD-ROM, E-Reserves, Electronic databases & coll, Fax serv, Handicapped accessible, Homebound delivery serv, ILL available, Magnifiers for reading, Mail & tel request accepted, Music CDs, Online searches, Photocopying/Printing, Prog for adults, Prog for children & young adult, Ref serv available, Summer reading prog, Tax forms, Telephone ref, VHS videos, Workshops
Publications: Newsletter (Quarterly)
Mem of Ramapo Catskill Library System
Partic in Southeastern New York Library Resources Council
Special Services for the Deaf - Closed caption videos
Special Services for the Blind - Large print bks
Open Mon-Thurs 10-9, Fri & Sat 10-5, Sun 1-5

ORCHARD PARK

J ERIE COMMUNITY COLLEGE-SOUTH CAMPUS, Library Resource Center, 4041 Southwestern Blvd, 14127. SAN 353-913X. Tel: 716-851-1772. Interlibrary Loan Service Tel: 716-270-5358. Reference Tel: 716-270-5212. FAX: 716-851-1778. Web Site: elinks.ecc.edu/library. *Chair,* Melissa Peterson; E-mail: petersonm@ecc.edu; *Acq,* Margaret Lew; E-mail: lewm@ecc.edu; *ILL,* Elaine Mazurkiewicz; E-mail: mazurkiewicz@ecc.edu; Staff 9 (MLS 5, Non-MLS 4)
Founded 1974. Enrl 4,800; Fac 120; Highest Degree: Associate
Sept 2014-Aug 2015. Mats Exp $73,000, Books $66,000, AV Mat $7,000

Library Holdings: AV Mats 1,910; Bk Titles 57,300; Bk Vols 60,180; Per Subs 188
Automation Activity & Vendor Info: (Cataloging) Ex Libris Group; (OPAC) Ex Libris Group
Database Vendor: EBSCOhost, Gale Cengage Learning, LexisNexis, OCLC FirstSearch
Wireless access
Publications: LRC News; Periodical Holdings List; Study Guides
Partic in Western New York Library Resources Council
Open Mon-Thurs 7:30am-10pm, Fri 7:30-4, Sat 9-3

P ORCHARD PARK PUBLIC LIBRARY*, S-4570 S Buffalo St, 14127. SAN 312-2212. Tel: 716-662-9851. FAX: 716-667-3098. Web Site: www.buffalolib.org. *Dir,* Dawn Peters; E-mail: petersd@buffalolib.org; *Ch Serv,* Jude Jacobs; E-mail: jacobsj@buffalolib.org; Staff 3 (MLS 3)
Founded 1935. Pop 27,637; Circ 365,637
Library Holdings: Bk Titles 71,837; Per Subs 286
Automation Activity & Vendor Info: (Cataloging) SirsiDynix; (Circulation) SirsiDynix; (OPAC) SirsiDynix; (Serials) SirsiDynix
Wireless access
Mem of Buffalo & Erie County Public Library System
Open Mon-Thurs 10-9, Fri & Sat 10-5, Sun 1-5
Friends of the Library Group

ORIENT

S OYSTERPONDS HISTORICAL SOCIETY*, Donald H Boerum Research Library, Village Lane, 11957. (Mail add: PO Box 70, 11957-0070), SAN 312-2220. Tel: 631-323-2480. E-mail: ohsorient@optonline.net. Web Site: www.oysterpondshistoricalsociety.org. *Archivist, Coll Mgr,* Amy Folk; E-mail: ohsarchives@optonline.net
Founded 1944
Library Holdings: Bk Vols 450
Special Collections: Art (William Steeple Davis Coll), paintings; Local Historical Research (Clarence Ashton Wood Coll); Photography (William Steeple Davis & Vinton Richard Colls), black & white glass plates
Subject Interests: 19th Century, Educ, Genealogy, Local hist, Long Island, Relig
Partic in Asn for Conservation
Restriction: Closed stack, Open by appt only
Friends of the Library Group

ORISKANY

P ORISKANY PUBLIC LIBRARY*, 621 Utica St, 13424. (Mail add: PO Box 428, 13424-0428), SAN 312-2239. Tel: 315-736-2532. FAX: 315-736-2532. *Mgr,* Michelle McGrath
Founded 1938. Pop 1,500; Circ 10,900
Library Holdings: Bk Titles 12,664; Per Subs 55
Wireless access
Mem of Mid-York Library System
Open Mon-Fri 1-6:30
Friends of the Library Group

ORISKANY FALLS

P C W CLARK MEMORIAL LIBRARY*, 160 N Main St, 13425. SAN 312-2247. Tel: 315-821-7850. FAX: 315-821-7850. E-mail: oriskanyfalls@midyork.org. Web Site: www.midyork.org/oriskanyfalls. *Dir,* Susan Tice; *Circ,* Michelle Hynes; *Circ,* Cory Merckle; *Circ,* Roy Sarvey
Pop 1,600; Circ 10,000
Library Holdings: Bk Vols 12,000; Per Subs 70
Automation Activity & Vendor Info: (Cataloging) SirsiDynix; (Circulation) SirsiDynix; (OPAC) SirsiDynix; (Serials) SirsiDynix
Wireless access
Mem of Mid-York Library System
Open Mon, Wed & Fri 9:30-5:30, Tues & Thurs 2-8, Sat 9:30-11:30

ORWELL

P COGSWELL FREE PUBLIC LIBRARY*, 1999 County Rte 2, 13426. (Mail add: PO Box 35, 13426-0035), SAN 312-2255. Tel: 315-298-5563. FAX: 315-298-5859. Web Site: www.cogswellfreelibrary.org. *Dir & Librn,* Erin Kimball-Salzman
Circ 9,926
Library Holdings: Bk Vols 8,075; Per Subs 27
Mem of North Country Library System
Open Tues (Winter) 12-8, Wed & Thurs 12-5, Sat 9-2; Tues-Thurs (Summer) 12-5, Sat 9-2

OSSINING

S NEW YORK STATE DEPARTMENT OF CORRECTIONAL SERVICES*, Sing Sing Correctional Facility Library, 354 Hunter St, 10562. SAN 327-0718. Tel: 914-941-0108. FAX: 914-941-6583. *Sr Librn,* Robert Richter; Staff 1 (MLS 1)
Founded 1840. Pop 1,700
Library Holdings: High Interest/Low Vocabulary Bk Vols 1,475; Microforms 236; Bk Vols 18,545; Per Subs 58
Restriction: Staff & inmates only

S OSSINING HISTORICAL SOCIETY MUSEUM*, 196 Croton Ave, 10562. SAN 323-4525. Tel: 914-941-0001. FAX: 914-941-0001. E-mail: ohsm@bestweb.net. Web Site: ossinghistorical.org. *Exec Dir,* Roberta Y Arminio
Founded 1931
Library Holdings: Bk Vols 2,000; Per Subs 6
Special Collections: Croton Aquaduct; Hudson River Fishing; Local Newspapers (Late 18th Century to Present); Sing Sing Prison. Oral History
Subject Interests: Genealogy, Local hist
Function: Res libr
Publications: A Memorial 1775-1983; A Primer of Ossining History; Ossining in the 1940's; Ossining in the 1950's; Ossining Remembered (Quarterly); Sing Sing Prison Electrecutions 1891-1963; Sparta Cemetery Book 1764; William Dolphin's Civil War Diary
Restriction: Non-circulating, Open by appt only

P OSSINING PUBLIC LIBRARY*, 53 Croton Ave, 10562-4903. SAN 312-2263. Tel: 914-941-2416. Circulation Tel: 914-941-2416, Ext 305. Reference Tel: 914-941-2416, Ext 320. FAX: 914-941-7464. Web Site: ossininglibrary.org. *Dir,* James L Farrell, Jr; E-mail: opldirector@wlsmail.org; *Asst Dir,* Molly Robbins; E-mail: mrobbins@wlsmail.org; *Head, Adult Serv,* Molly Robbins; *Head, Ch,* Marci Dressler; E-mail: mdressler@wlsmail.org; *Head, Pub Serv,* James Trapasso; E-mail: jtrapasso@wlsmail.org; *Adult Ref Librn, Media Spec,* Bonnie Katz; *Ch,* Deborah Fletcher; *Ch,* Tricia Sabini; *Ref & Coll Develop Librn,* John Hawkins; Tel: 914-941-2416, Ext 316; *Ref & Educ Serv Librn,* Cheryl Cohen; Tel: 914-941-2416, Ext 315; *Teen Librn,* Mallory Harlen; E-mail: mharlen@wlsmail.org; Staff 45 (MLS 20, Non-MLS 25)
Founded 1893. Pop 33,273; Circ 420,000
Library Holdings: AV Mats 13,231; e-books 767; Electronic Media & Resources 923; Bk Vols 110,654
Special Collections: Job Info Center
Automation Activity & Vendor Info: (Circulation) SirsiDynix
Wireless access
Function: Adult literacy prog, Art exhibits, AV serv, Bilingual assistance for Spanish patrons, Bk club(s), Bks on cassette, Bks on CD, Children's prog, Computer training, Computers for patron use, Copy machines, Free DVD rentals, Handicapped accessible, Home delivery & serv to Sr ctr & nursing homes, Homebound delivery serv, ILL available, Mus passes, Music CDs, Newsp ref libr, Online cat, Photocopying/Printing, Preschool outreach, Prog for children & young adult, Pub access computers, Ref serv available, Scanner, Senior computer classes, Serves mentally handicapped consumers, Spanish lang bks, Story hour, Summer reading prog, Tax forms, Teen prog, Telephone ref, Wheelchair accessible
Publications: Update (Monthly)
Open Mon & Thurs 9-9, Tues & Fri 10-6, Wed 1-9, Sat 11-5, Sun 1-5
Friends of the Library Group

OSWEGO

S NEW YORK STATE OFFICE OF PARKS, RECREATION & HISTORIC PRESERVATION*, Fort Ontario State Historic Site Research Library, One E Fourth St, 13126. SAN 326-324X. Tel: 315-343-4711. FAX: 315-343-1430. Web Site: www.fortontario.com. *Mgr,* Paul Lear; E-mail: paul.lear@oprhp.state.ny.us
Library Holdings: Bk Titles 1,500; Per Subs 10
Subject Interests: Archit, Hist
Wireless access
Open Mon-Fri 9-5
Friends of the Library Group

L OSWEGO COUNTY SUPREME COURT*, Law Library, 25 E Oneida St, 13126. Tel: 315-349-3297. FAX: 315-349-3273. *Librn,* Anne Thomas
Library Holdings: Bk Vols 10,000
Automation Activity & Vendor Info: (Circulation) Horizon; (OPAC) Horizon
Wireless access
Open Mon-Fri 8:30-4

P OSWEGO SCHOOL DISTRICT PUBLIC LIBRARY*, 120 E Second St, 13126. SAN 312-2271. Tel: 315-341-5867. FAX: 315-216-6492. E-mail: oswegopl@northnet.org. Web Site: www.oswegopubliclibrary.org. *Dir,* Carol Ferlito; *Librn,* Martha Lyon
Founded 1854. Pop 19,195; Circ 108,980
Library Holdings: Bk Vols 55,000; Per Subs 1,188
Special Collections: Local Cemetery Records; Local Oswego County Historical Society Coll, per
Automation Activity & Vendor Info: (Acquisitions) Follett Software; (Cataloging) Follett Software; (Circulation) Follett Software; (Course

Reserve) Follett Software; (ILL) Follett Software; (Media Booking) Follett Software; (OPAC) Follett Software; (Serials) Follett Software
Mem of North Country Library System
Open Mon-Thurs 10-8, Fri 10-5, Sat & Sun 12-5
Friends of the Library Group

C STATE UNIVERSITY OF NEW YORK AT OSWEGO, Penfield Library, SUNY Oswego, 7060 State Rte 104, 13126-3514. SAN 312-228X. Tel: 315-312-4232. Circulation Tel: 315-312-2560. Interlibrary Loan Service Tel: 315-312-4546. Reference Tel: 315-312-4267. FAX: 315-312-3194. Web Site: www.oswego.edu/library. *Dir,* Barbara Shaffer; Tel: 315-312-3557, E-mail: barbara.shaffer@oswego.edu; *Head, Acq,* Deborah Curry; Tel: 315-312-3545, E-mail: deborah.curry@oswego.edu; *Head, Cat & Ser,* Kathryn Johns-Masten; Tel: 315-312-3553, E-mail: kathryn.johnsmasten@oswego.edu; *Head, Circ,* Ray Morrison; Tel: 315-312-3567, E-mail: ray.morrison@oswego.edu; *Archives & Spec Coll Librn,* Elizabeth Young; Tel: 315-312-3537, E-mail: archives@oswego.edu; *Distance Educ Librn,* Jim Nichols; Tel: 315-312-3549, E-mail: jim.nichols@oswego.edu; *First Year Experience Librn,* Michelle Bishop; Tel: 315-312-3564, E-mail: michelle.bishop@oswego.edu; *Learning Tech Librn,* Emily Thompson; Tel: 315-312-3563, E-mail: emily.thompson@oswego.edu; *Online Instruction/Instrul Design Librn,* Brandon West; Tel: 315-312-3539, E-mail: brandon.west@oswego.edu; *Res Sharing Librn,* Anita Calderon; E-mail: ill@oswego.edu; *Coordr of Ref Serv,* Christopher Hebblethwaite; Tel: 315-312-3060, E-mail: chris.hebblethwaite@oswego.edu; *Libr Instruction Coordr,* Karen Shockey; Tel: 315-312-3566, E-mail: karen.shockey@oswego.edu; *Coordr, Libr Tech,* Natalie Sturr; Tel: 315-312-3565, E-mail: natalie.sturr@oswego.edu; *Asst Coordr, Ref Serv,* Tina Chan; Tel: 315-312-3010, E-mail: tina.chan@oswego.edu; Staff 35 (MLS 17, Non-MLS 18)
Founded 1861. Enrl 8,117; Fac 318; Highest Degree: Master
Jul 2013-Jun 2014. Mats Exp $533,057, Books $115,008, Per/Ser (Incl. Access Fees) $128,086, AV Mat $11,096, Electronic Ref Mat (Incl. Access Fees) $278,867
Library Holdings: e-books 127,834; Bk Vols 448,318
Special Collections: College Archives; Local & State History (Safe Haven Coll); Local History (Marshall Family Coll); Presidential Papers (Millard Fillmore Coll). Oral History; State Document Depository; US Document Depository
Subject Interests: Bus admin, Educ, Liberal arts
Automation Activity & Vendor Info: (Acquisitions) Ex Libris Group; (Cataloging) Ex Libris Group; (Circulation) Ex Libris Group; (Course Reserve) Atlas Systems; (ILL) OCLC ILLiad; (OPAC) Ex Libris Group; (Serials) Ex Libris Group
Wireless access
Partic in Northern New York Library Network; OCLC Online Computer Library Center, Inc; SUNYConnect
Friends of the Library Group

OTEGO

P HARRIS MEMORIAL LIBRARY*, 334 Main St, 13825. (Mail add: PO Box 470, 13825-0470), SAN 312-2298. Tel: 607-988-6661. FAX: 607-988-6661. E-mail: ot_ill@4cls.org. *Librn,* Dorothy Wilber; Staff 1 (MLS 1)
Founded 1923. Pop 3,000; Circ 13,000
Library Holdings: Bk Titles 10,000; Per Subs 45
Database Vendor: SirsiDynix
Mem of Four County Library System
Open Tues & Thurs 10-12 & 2-5, Wed & Fri 2-5 & 6-9, Sat 10-1

OTISVILLE

S OTISVILLE STATE CORRECTIONAL FACILITY LIBRARY*, PO Box 8, 10963-0008. SAN 327-1811. Tel: 845-386-1490, Ext 4600. *Sr Librn,* Karrie Torres; Staff 1 (MLS 1)
Library Holdings: Bk Vols 7,500; Per Subs 41
Automation Activity & Vendor Info: (Cataloging) Follett Software; (Circulation) Follett Software; (OPAC) Follett Software
Restriction: Staff & inmates only

OVID

P EDITH B FORD MEMORIAL LIBRARY*, 7169 N Main St, 14521. (Mail add: PO Box 410, 14521), SAN 312-2301. Tel: 607-869-3031. FAX: 607-869-3031. E-mail: ovidlib@rochester.rr.com. Web Site: www.ovidlibrary.org. *Dir,* Shannon O'Connor
Founded 1899. Pop 6,627; Circ 20,485
Library Holdings: Audiobooks 150; Bk Vols 34,127; Per Subs 30; Videos 150
Automation Activity & Vendor Info: (Acquisitions) Innovative Interfaces, Inc; (Cataloging) Innovative Interfaces, Inc; (OPAC) Innovative Interfaces, Inc
Wireless access
Mem of Finger Lakes Library System
Open Mon & Fri 9-5, Tues & Wed 11-8, Thurs 1-7, Sat 10-2

OWEGO

P COBURN FREE LIBRARY, 275 Main St, 13827. SAN 312-231X. Tel: 607-687-3520. E-mail: coburnlibrary@clarityconnect.com. Web Site: www.flls.org/memberpages/owego.htm. *Dir,* Karen Bernardo; Staff 2.5 (Non-MLS 2.5)
Founded 1895
Library Holdings: Bk Vols 30,614; Per Subs 28
Special Collections: Genealogy (Dr Hyde Room)
Wireless access
Mem of Finger Lakes Library System
Open Mon, Wed & Fri 10-5, Tues & Thurs 1-5 & 6:30-8:30, Sat (Sept-June) 1-5
Friends of the Library Group

S LOCKHEED MARTIN SYSTEMS INTEGRATION - OWEGO*, Library & Information Research Center, 1801 State Rte 17C, Maildrop 0409, 13827. SAN 312-2328. Tel: 607-751-2000. FAX: 607-751-6171. *In Charge,* Edwina Jhingan; Tel: 607-751-2128; Staff 2 (MLS 1, Non-MLS 1)
Founded 1955
Library Holdings: Bk Vols 1,500
Subject Interests: Aeronaut, Astronautics, Computers, Electricity, Electronics, Math, Undersea (naval)
Wireless access
Open Mon-Fri 9-4

S TIOGA COUNTY HISTORICAL SOCIETY MUSEUM LIBRARY*, 110-112 Front St, 13827. SAN 312-2336. Tel: 607-687-2460. E-mail: info@tiogahistory.org. Web Site: www.tiogahistory.org.
Founded 1914
Library Holdings: Bk Vols 3,000
Special Collections: Local Newspapers, microfilm
Subject Interests: Genealogy, Hist of NY
Function: Res libr
Restriction: Non-circulating

OXFORD

G NEW YORK STATE VETERANS HOME LIBRARY*, 4207 St Hwy 220, 13830. SAN 376-0774. Tel: 607-843-3100. FAX: 607-843-3199. *Dir,* Heeyoun Cho; E-mail: hcho@nysvets.org
Library Holdings: Bk Vols 700
Open Mon-Fri 8-4

P OXFORD MEMORIAL LIBRARY*, Eight Fort Hill Park, 13830. (Mail add: PO Box 552, 13830-0552), SAN 312-2344. Tel: 607-843-6146. FAX: 607-843-9157. *Dir,* Nancy Wilcox; Staff 5 (Non-MLS 5)
Founded 1900. Pop 5,408; Circ 33,500
Library Holdings: Bk Titles 20,500; Per Subs 44
Automation Activity & Vendor Info: (Acquisitions) SirsiDynix; (Cataloging) SirsiDynix; (Circulation) SirsiDynix
Wireless access
Mem of Four County Library System
Open Mon-Thurs 9:30-8:30 Fri 9:30-5, Sat 9:30-1

OYSTER BAY

P OYSTER BAY-EAST NORWICH PUBLIC LIBRARY*, 89 E Main St, 11771. SAN 312-2352. Tel: 516-922-1212. FAX: 516-922-6453. Administration FAX: 516-624-8693. E-mail: oysterbay@nassaulibrary.org. Web Site: www.oysterbaylibrary.org. *Dir,* Suzanne Koch; E-mail: suznkoch@aol.com; *Head, Ref Serv,* Dorothy Moore; *Ch Serv,* Barbara Grodin; *Circ,* Jane Byrd McCurdy; *Tech Serv,* Margaret Wanser; *YA Serv,* Daniel Huber; Staff 25 (MLS 8, Non-MLS 17)
Founded 1901. Pop 13,458; Circ 155,000
Library Holdings: Bk Titles 77,993; Per Subs 253; Talking Bks 4,313
Special Collections: Presidential (Theodore Roosevelt Coll)
Subject Interests: Career develop, Local hist
Automation Activity & Vendor Info: (Acquisitions) Innovative Interfaces, Inc; (Cataloging) Innovative Interfaces, Inc; (Circulation) Innovative Interfaces, Inc; (OPAC) Innovative Interfaces, Inc
Database Vendor: ALLDATA Online, CQ Press, Electric Library, Gale Cengage Learning, Greenwood Publishing Group, Grolier Online, LearningExpress, OCLC FirstSearch, OCLC WorldShare Interlibrary Loan, Oxford Online, ProQuest
Wireless access
Publications: Newsletter (Bi-monthly)
Mem of Nassau Library System
Special Services for the Deaf - Assistive tech
Special Services for the Blind - Closed circuit TV magnifier
Open Mon, Tues & Thurs 9:30-9, Wed 10-9, Fri 9:30-6, Sat 9-5 (9-1 July-Aug), Sun 1-5
Friends of the Library Group

S OYSTER BAY HISTORICAL SOCIETY LIBRARY*, 20 Summit St, 11771. (Mail add: PO Box 297, 11771-0297), SAN 326-1999. Tel: 516-922-5032. FAX: 516-922-6892. E-mail: obhistory@aol.com. Web Site: www.oysterbayhistory.org. *Dir,* Thomas A Kuehhas; *Archivist, Librn,* Philip D Blocklyn; *Curator,* Yvonne Noonan-Cifarelli; Staff 3 (MLS 1, Non-MLS 2)
Founded 1960
Library Holdings: Bk Titles 1,015; Bk Vols 1,028
Special Collections: Early American Tools & Trades (Reichman Coll); Theodore Roosevelt Coll
Subject Interests: Genealogy, Local hist
Publications: Magazine for members (Quarterly); The Freeholder (Quarterly history journal)
Open Mon-Fri 10-2, Sat 9-1, Sun 1-4
Restriction: Non-circulating to the pub

S SAGAMORE HILL NATIONAL HISTORIC SITE LIBRARY*, 20 Sagamore Hill Rd, 11771-1899. SAN 324-4393. Tel: 516-922-4788. FAX: 516-922-4792. Web Site: www.nps.gov/sahi. *Curator,* Amy Verone
Library Holdings: Bk Titles 850; Bk Vols 950
Special Collections: Theodore Roosevelt Life & Career
Subject Interests: Nat park area, Sagamore Hill
Function: Res libr
Restriction: Non-circulating, Open by appt only

PAINTED POST

P SOUTHERN TIER LIBRARY SYSTEM*, 9424 Scott Rd, 14870-9598. SAN 352-3861. Tel: 607-962-3141. FAX: 607-962-5356. E-mail: stls@stls.org. Web Site: www.stls.org. *Dir,* Ristiina Wigg; E-mail: wiggr@stls.org; *Tech Coordr,* Ken Behn; *Adult Serv,* Mary Passage; *Tech Serv,* Shelley MacFeiggan; *Youth Serv,* Lorie Brown; Staff 19 (MLS 4, Non-MLS 15)
Founded 1958. Pop 286,225
Library Holdings: Bk Vols 48,000; Per Subs 15
Subject Interests: NY State county hist
Automation Activity & Vendor Info: (Acquisitions) SirsiDynix; (Cataloging) SirsiDynix; (Circulation) SirsiDynix; (OPAC) SirsiDynix
Database Vendor: SirsiDynix
Wireless access
Member Libraries: Addison Public Library; Andover Free Library; Angelica Free Library; Arkport Village Book Center; Avoca Free Library; Belfast Public Library; Belmont Literary & Historical Society Free Library; Bolivar Free Library; Chemung County Historical Society, Inc; Chemung County Library District; Cohocton Public Library; Colonial Library; Cuba Circulating Library; David A Howe Public Library; Dormann Library; Dundee Library; Dutton S Peterson Memorial Library; E J Cottrell Memorial Library; Elizabeth B Pert Library; Essential Club Free Library; Fred & Harriett Taylor Memorial Library; Friendship Free Library; Genesee Public Library; Greenwood Reading Center; Hornell Public Library; Howard Public Library; Jasper Free Library; Mabel D Blodgett Memorial Library; Middlesex Reading Center; Modeste Bedient Memorial Library; Montour Falls Memorial Library; Penn Yan Public Library; Prattsburgh Library; Pulteney Free Library; Rushford Free Library; Savona Free Library; Scio Memorial Library; Southeast Steuben County Library; Twentieth Century Club Library; Watkins Glen Public Library; Wayland Free Library; Whitesville Public Library; Wide Awake Club Library; Wimodaughsian Free Library
Open Mon-Fri 9-5

PALISADES

P PALISADES FREE LIBRARY*, 19 Closter Rd, 10964. SAN 312-2379. Tel: 845-359-0136. FAX: 845-359-6124. E-mail: pal@rcls.org. Web Site: www.palisadeslibrary.org. *Dir,* Maria Gagliardi; *ILL,* Marie Firestone; *Ref,* Johanna Lo; Staff 6 (MLS 2, Non-MLS 4)
Founded 1891. Pop 1,282; Circ 21,471
Library Holdings: AV Mats 3,285; Bks on Deafness & Sign Lang 10; Electronic Media & Resources 78,050; Bk Vols 23,956
Special Collections: Local History, bks, microflm, maps
Automation Activity & Vendor Info: (Circulation) Horizon; (OPAC) Horizon
Database Vendor: LearningExpress, ProQuest
Wireless access
Mem of Ramapo Catskill Library System
Open Mon-Thurs 11-9, Fri & Sat 11-5, Sun 1-5

PALMYRA

P PALMYRA COMMUNITY LIBRARY*, 127 Cuyler St, 14522. SAN 312-2387. Tel: 315-597-5276. FAX: 315-597-1375. Web Site: www.palmyra.pls-net.org. *Dir,* Patricia Baynes; E-mail: pbaynes@pls-net.org; Staff 5 (MLS 1, Non-MLS 4)
Founded 1901. Pop 7,652; Circ 55,672
Jan 2010-Dec 2010 Income $386,155, State $75,482, City $291,000, County $7,367, Locally Generated Income $8,172, Other $4,134. Mats Exp $28,652, Books $17,620, Per/Ser (Incl. Access Fees) $1,813, AV Mat $9,219. Sal $89,302 (Prof $47,500)
Library Holdings: Audiobooks 442; DVDs 1,403; Large Print Bks 260; Bk Vols 18,605; Per Subs 51
Special Collections: Local History (Genealogy & Palmyra)
Automation Activity & Vendor Info: (Acquisitions) Baker & Taylor; (Cataloging) Evergreen; (Circulation) Evergreen; (OPAC) Evergreen
Wireless access
Function: Adult literacy prog, After school storytime, Audiobks via web, Bks on cassette, Bks on CD, Children's prog, Computers for patron use, Copy machines, e-mail & chat, Electronic databases & coll, Fax serv, Handicapped accessible, Holiday prog, Home delivery & serv to Sr ctr & nursing homes, Homebound delivery serv, ILL available, Mail & tel request accepted, Online cat, OverDrive digital audio bks, Photocopying/Printing, Preschool outreach, Prog for adults, Prog for children & young adult, Pub access computers, Ref serv in person, Story hour, Summer reading prog, Tax forms, Teen prog, Telephone ref, VHS videos, Wheelchair accessible
Special Services for the Blind - BiFolkal kits; Bks on cassette; Bks on CD; Home delivery serv; Large print bks; Magnifiers; Playaways (bks on MP3)
Open Mon-Thurs 10-8, Fri 10-5, Sat 10-2
Friends of the Library Group

PARISH

P PARISH PUBLIC LIBRARY*, Three Church St, 13131. SAN 312-2395. Tel: 315-625-7130. Web Site: www.parishpubliclibrary.org. *Dir,* Bridget Swartz; *Asst Librn,* Verna Henderson
Pop 1,700; Circ 7,071
Library Holdings: Bk Titles 10,500; Per Subs 47
Wireless access
Mem of North Country Library System
Open Mon 9-5, Wed 12-5, Thurs 7pm-9pm, Sat 11-4
Friends of the Library Group

PATCHOGUE

M BROOKHAVEN MEMORIAL HOSPITAL MEDICAL LIBRARY*, 101 Hospital Rd, 11772-4897. SAN 312-2409. Tel: 631-654-7774. FAX: 631-447-3723. *Dir,* Valerie Rankow
Founded 1975
Library Holdings: e-journals 200; Bk Titles 400
Subject Interests: Allied health, Med, Nursing
Automation Activity & Vendor Info: (Cataloging) Professional Software; (OPAC) Professional Software
Database Vendor: MD Consult, Micromedex, UpToDate
Wireless access
Open Mon-Thurs 10-5:30

SR CONGREGATIONAL CHURCH OF PATCHOGUE*, Stuart VanCott Memorial Library & Virginia Crowell Children's Library, 95 E Main St, 11772. SAN 371-9405. Tel: 631-475-1235. FAX: 631-207-9470. E-mail: office@churchonmainstreet.org. Web Site: www.churchonmainstreet.org. *Librn,* Sherley Werner; *Ch Serv,* Toni Dean; Staff 6 (MLS 1, Non-MLS 5)
Founded 1967
Library Holdings: Bk Titles 4,530; Bk Vols 5,350
Subject Interests: Church hist, Local hist, Relig
Partic in Church & Synagogue Libr Asn
Open Mon-Fri 9-1, Sun 10-12

P PATCHOGUE-MEDFORD LIBRARY*, 54-60 E Main St, 11772. SAN 312-2417. Tel: 631-654-4700. Reference Tel: 631-654-4700, Ext 221. Administration Tel: 631-654-4700, Ext 302. FAX: 631-289-3999. E-mail: info@pmlib.org. Web Site: pmlib.org. *Dir,* Lauren Nichols; Tel: 631-654-4700, Ext 300, E-mail: lnichols@pmlib.org; *Head of Digital Serv & Tech Serv,* Rona Dressler; E-mail: rdressler@pmlib.org; *Head, Automation & Tech Serv,* Bruce Silverstein; E-mail: bsilverstein@pmlib.org; *Head, Ch,* Jane Drake; E-mail: jdrake@pmlib.org; *Head, Circ,* Patricia Lach; E-mail: plach@pmlib.org; *Head, Ref,* June Cerveny; E-mail: jcerveny@pmlib.org; *Head, Young Adult Serv/AV Serv,* Jeri Cohen; E-mail: jcohen@pmlib.org; *Head, Young Adult Serv/AV Serv,* Danielle Paisley; E-mail: dpaisley@pmlib.org; Staff 28 (MLS 27, Non-MLS 1)
Founded 1900. Pop 52,929; Circ 655,516
Jul 2011-Jun 2012 Income $8,416,272, State $12,304, Locally Generated Income $7,893,879, Other $510,089. Mats Exp $8,505,209, Books $800,006, Other Print Mats $26,929, AV Mat $91,452. Sal $4,378,555
Library Holdings: AV Mats 395; CDs 12,786; DVDs 18,889; High Interest/Low Vocabulary Bk Vols 531; Bk Vols 284,451; Per Subs 36,450
Special Collections: Martial Arts (Maccarrone-Kresge Coll); Opera (Sara Courant Coll)
Subject Interests: Adult educ, Consumer health, Foreign lang, Law, Local genealogies, Local hist, Music
Automation Activity & Vendor Info: (Acquisitions) Innovative Interfaces, Inc; (Cataloging) Innovative Interfaces, Inc; (Circulation) Innovative

Interfaces, Inc; (ILL) Innovative Interfaces, Inc; (OPAC) Innovative Interfaces, Inc; (Serials) Innovative Interfaces, Inc
Database Vendor: Dialog, EBSCOhost, Gale Cengage Learning, LexisNexis, OCLC FirstSearch, Wilson - Wilson Web
Wireless access
Publications: An Index to Selected Popular Song Books; An Index to the Records-Town of Brookhaven up to 1800; Centennial Research Digest; Classical Music Index; Guide to Senior Citizen Services; Newsletter (Bi-monthly); Patchogue-Medford Library Community Directory; Songs in Collections; The Library Story: A Patchogue-Medford Library Centennial Story for Children & Parents; The Maccarrone-Kresge Martial Arts Book Collection
Mem of Suffolk Cooperative Library System
Special Services for the Blind - Closed circuit TV; Magnifiers
Open Mon-Fri 9:30-9, Sat 9:30-5:30, Sun (Oct-May) 1-5
Friends of the Library Group

C SAINT JOSEPH'S COLLEGE*, Callahan Library, 25 Audubon Ave, 11772-2399. SAN 352-2067. Tel: 631-447-3232. Administration Tel: 631-447-3226. FAX: 631-654-3255. E-mail: callahan@sjcny.edu. Web Site: libraries.sjcny.edu. *Dir,* Elizabeth Pollicino-Murphy; E-mail: epollicino@sjcny.edu; *Ref Librn,* Mary Keller; E-mail: mkeller@sjcny.edu; Staff 13 (MLS 6, Non-MLS 7)
Founded 1972. Enrl 4,368; Fac 370; Highest Degree: Master
Library Holdings: AV Mats 1,540; e-books 1,918; e-journals 399; Microforms 3,755; Bk Vols 118,040; Per Subs 258
Special Collections: Archives; Curriculum Library
Subject Interests: Child study, Liberal arts
Automation Activity & Vendor Info: (Acquisitions) Ex Libris Group; (Cataloging) Ex Libris Group; (Circulation) Ex Libris Group; (Course Reserve) Docutek; (ILL) OCLC; (OPAC) Ex Libris Group; (Serials) Ex Libris Group
Database Vendor: Alexander Street Press, Annual Reviews, ARTstor, BioOne, CQ Press, EBSCOhost, Gale Cengage Learning, Hoovers, JSTOR, OCLC WorldShare Interlibrary Loan, Oxford Online, ProQuest, SerialsSolutions, Wilson - Wilson Web
Wireless access
Function: Audio & video playback equip for onsite use, Computers for patron use, Copy machines, E-Reserves, Electronic databases & coll, Handicapped accessible, ILL available, Photocopying/Printing, Ref serv available, Wheelchair accessible
Partic in Nylink; OCLC Online Computer Library Center, Inc; Westchester Academic Library Directors Organization (WALDO)
Special Services for the Blind - ZoomText magnification & reading software
Open Mon-Thurs 7:30am 9pm, Fri 7:30-5, Sat & Sun 11-5
Restriction: Open to students, fac, staff & alumni, Pub use on premises

PATTERSON

P PATTERSON LIBRARY*, 1167 Rte 311, 12563-2801. (Mail add: PO Box 418, 12563-0418), SAN 312-2425. Tel: 845-878-6121. FAX: 845-878-3116. E-mail: reference@pattersonlibrary.org. Web Site: pattersonlibrary.org. *Dir,* Patti Haar
Founded 1947. Pop 12,000; Circ 54,738
Library Holdings: AV Mats 2,100; Large Print Bks 500; Bk Titles 23,037; Bk Vols 24,999; Per Subs 45; Talking Bks 700
Special Collections: Maxwell Weaner Music Book Coll
Automation Activity & Vendor Info: (Circulation) Innovative Interfaces, Inc; (OPAC) Innovative Interfaces, Inc
Database Vendor: Gale Cengage Learning, ProQuest
Wireless access
Mem of Chautauqua-Cattaraugus Library System; Mid-Hudson Library System
Open Mon, Wed & Thurs 10-8, Tues & Fri 10-5, Sat 10-4

SR WATCHTOWER BIBLE SCHOOL OF GILEAD LIBRARY*, 100 Watchtower Dr, 12563-9204. (Mail add: 25 Columbia Heights, Brooklyn, 11201-2483), SAN 310-9542. Tel: 718-560-5000. Web Site: www.watchtower.org. *Librn,* Sarah Hall; *Librn,* Gene Smalley
Library Holdings: Bk Vols 33,000; Per Subs 30
Subject Interests: Relig matters
Automation Activity & Vendor Info: (Cataloging) Inmagic, Inc.; (Circulation) Inmagic, Inc.; (OPAC) Inmagic, Inc.
Wireless access
Open Mon-Fri 8-5

PAUL SMITHS

C PAUL SMITHS COLLEGE OF ARTS & SCIENCES*, Joan Weill Adirondack Library, Rte's 30 & 86, 12970. SAN 312-2433. Tel: 518-327-6313. FAX: 518-327-6350. Web Site: www.paulsmiths.edu. *Dir, Educ Res,* Neil Surprenant; Tel: 518-327-6353; *Pub Serv Librn,* Meggan Frost; Tel: 518-327-6462; *Syst Librn,* Mike Beccaria; Tel: 518-327-6376; *Tech Serv Librn,* Andrew Kelly; Tel: 518-327-6354; Staff 7 (MLS 4, Non-MLS 3)
Founded 1946. Enrl 1,080; Fac 53; Highest Degree: Bachelor
Library Holdings: Bk Vols 62,000; Per Subs 400
Subject Interests: Arboriculture, Culinary arts, Environ studies, Fisheries mgt, Forestry, Hotel mgt, Outdoor recreation, Restaurant mgt, Surveying, Sustainability, Wildlife mgt
Automation Activity & Vendor Info: (Cataloging) OCLC; (Circulation) SirsiDynix; (OPAC) SirsiDynix
Wireless access
Partic in Northern New York Library Network; OCLC Online Computer Library Center, Inc

PAVILION

P PAVILION PUBLIC LIBRARY*, Five Woodrow Dr, 14525. (Mail add: PO Box 422, 14525-0422). Tel: 585-584-8843. FAX: 585-584-8801. Web Site: www.nioga.org/pav.html. *Dir,* Suzanne Schauf
Pop 2,476
Library Holdings: DVDs 723; Large Print Bks 150; Bk Vols 13,000; Per Subs 35; Talking Bks 115; Videos 553
Automation Activity & Vendor Info: (Cataloging) SIRSI WorkFlows; (Circulation) SIRSI WorkFlows; (OPAC) SIRSI WorkFlows; (Serials) SIRSI WorkFlows
Wireless access
Function: Handicapped accessible, ILL available, Photocopying/Printing, Prog for adults, Prog for children & young adult, Serves mentally handicapped consumers, Summer reading prog, Wheelchair accessible
Mem of Nioga Library System
Open Mon & Wed 1-5 & 6-8, Tues & Sat 10-12:30, Fri 1-5
Friends of the Library Group

PAWLING

S AKIN FREE LIBRARY*, 378 Old Quaker Hill Rd, 12564-3411. (Mail add: PO Box 345, 12564-0345), SAN 371-0165. Tel: 845-855-5099. E-mail: akinlibrary@sbcglobal.net. *Librn,* James Mandracchia; Tel: 860-354-2822
Founded 1898
Jul 2005-Jun 2006. Mats Exp $300
Library Holdings: Bk Vols 7,000
Special Collections: Historical Research, Quakers-Pawling 1740-1800; Quaker Hill Series & Ledgers Coll; Quaker Local history 1730-1740
Open Fri-Sun 1-4

P PAWLING FREE LIBRARY*, 11 Broad St, 12564. SAN 312-2441. Tel: 845-855-3444. FAX: 845-855-8138. Web Site: www.pawlinglibrary.org. *Dir,* tTracy Priest; E-mail: director@pawlinglibrary.org; *Adult Prog,* Donald Partelow; E-mail: dpartelow@pawlinglibrary.org; *Ch Serv,* Karen DeGennaro; E-mail: children@pawlinglibrary.org; *Circ, Youth Serv,* Evelina Simoes; E-mail: ya@pawlinglibrary.org; Staff 3 (Non-MLS 3)
Founded 1926. Pop 8,377; Circ 100,000
Library Holdings: Bk Vols 40,000
Wireless access
Function: Adult bk club, After school storytime, Archival coll, Art exhibits, Audio & video playback equip for onsite use, Audiobks via web, Bk club(s), Bks on cassette, Bks on CD, CD-ROM, Children's prog, Computer training, Computers for patron use, Copy machines, Electronic databases & coll, Exhibits, Fax serv, Free DVD rentals, Handicapped accessible, Holiday prog, Home delivery & serv to Sr ctr & nursing homes, Homebound delivery serv, Homework prog, ILL available, Literacy & newcomer serv, Music CDs, Newsp ref libr, Online cat, Online ref, Online searches, Outreach serv, Outside serv via phone, mail, e-mail & web, Photocopying/Printing, Preschool outreach, Prog for adults, Prog for children & young adult, Pub access computers, Ref & res, Scanner, Senior computer classes, Senior outreach, Spoken cassettes & CDs, Spoken cassettes & DVDs, Story hour, Summer reading prog, Tax forms, Teen prog, VHS videos, Video lending libr, Web-catalog, Wheelchair accessible, Workshops
Mem of Mid-Hudson Library System
Open Mon & Fri 12-5, Tues-Thurs 10-8, Sat 10-4, Sun 12-4
Friends of the Library Group

PEARL RIVER

P PEARL RIVER PUBLIC LIBRARY*, 80 Franklin Ave, 10965. SAN 312-2468. Tel: 845-735-4084. FAX: 845-735-4041. E-mail: prl@rcls.org. Web Site: www.pearlriverlibrary.org. *Dir,* Kathleen W Rose; E-mail: prpldirector@rcls.org; *Head, Adult Serv,* Vicki Biehl; *Youth Serv Dept Head,* Pamela Gunning; *Circ Supvr,* Ellen Frawley; Staff 8 (MLS 8)
Founded 1935. Pop 15,300; Circ 203,311
Library Holdings: AV Mats 16,703; Bk Vols 103,584; Per Subs 288
Automation Activity & Vendor Info: (Cataloging) SirsiDynix; (Circulation) SirsiDynix; (OPAC) SirsiDynix
Wireless access
Mem of Ramapo Catskill Library System

Open Mon-Thurs 9-9, Fri & Sat 10-5, Sun 1-5
Friends of the Library Group

PEEKSKILL

P THE FIELD LIBRARY*, Four Nelson Ave, 10566-2138. SAN 312-2476. Tel: 914-737-1212. FAX: 914-737-0714. E-mail: pek@westchesterlibraries.org. Web Site: www.peekskill.org. *Dir,* Laura Wolven; E-mail: lwolven@wlsmail.org; *Head, Ref,* Robert Boyle; E-mail: rboyle@westchesterlibraries.org; *Ch,* Sara A Bentley; E-mail: sbentley@wlsmail.org; *Ch,* Jody Sitts; E-mail: jsitts@wlsmail.org; *Ref Librn, YA Librn,* Elizabeth Anastasi; *Ref Librn & Local Hist Spec,* Kim Stucko; E-mail: kstucko@wlsmail.org; *Spanish Literacy Coordr,* Tanya Soto; E-mail: tsoto@wlsmail.org; *Gallery Curator,* Alicia Morgan; E-mail: amorgan@wlsmail.org; Staff 21 (MLS 6, Non-MLS 15)
Founded 1887. Pop 23,500
Jan 2007-Dec 2007 Income $954,318. Mats Exp $246,663. Sal Prof $698,337
Library Holdings: Bk Vols 95,498; Per Subs 135
Special Collections: Lincoln Coll; Local History (Peekskill Historical Coll)
Automation Activity & Vendor Info: (Acquisitions) SirsiDynix; (Cataloging) SirsiDynix; (Circulation) SirsiDynix; (Course Reserve) SirsiDynix; (ILL) SirsiDynix; (Media Booking) SirsiDynix; (OPAC) SirsiDynix; (Serials) SirsiDynix
Wireless access
Function: Adult bk club, Archival coll, Art exhibits, Audiobks via web, Bks on CD, Children's prog, Computer training, Computers for patron use, Copy machines, Digital talking bks, Doc delivery serv, e-mail serv, Electronic databases & coll, Exhibits, Fax serv, Free DVD rentals, Handicapped accessible, Homebound delivery serv, ILL available, Microfiche/film & reading machines, Music CDs, Online cat, Photocopying/Printing, Prog for adults, Prog for children & young adult, Pub access computers, Ref serv available, Ref serv in person, Res performed for a fee, Scanner, Senior computer classes, Spoken cassettes & CDs, Summer reading prog, Teen prog, Telephone ref, Wheelchair accessible
Mem of Westchester Library System
Open Mon, Tues & Thurs (Winter) 9-9, Wed 11-9, Fri 9-5, Sat 10-5, Sun 1-4; Mon, Tues & Thurs (Summer) 9-9, Wed 11-9, Fri 9-5, Sat 10-2
Friends of the Library Group

PELHAM

P TOWN OF PELHAM PUBLIC LIBRARY*, 530 Colonial Ave, 10803. SAN 312-1801. Tel: 914-738-1234. FAX: 914-738-0809. E-mail: contactus@pelhamlibrary.org. Web Site: www.pelhamlibrary.org. *Dir,* Patricia Perito
Founded 1915. Pop 11,866; Circ 115,000
Library Holdings: e-books 800; Bk Titles 35,000; Per Subs 70
Special Collections: Mysteries
Automation Activity & Vendor Info: (Acquisitions) SirsiDynix; (Cataloging) SirsiDynix; (Circulation) SirsiDynix; (OPAC) SirsiDynix; (Serials) SirsiDynix
Wireless access
Mem of Westchester Library System
Open Mon & Thurs 1-9, Tues, Wed & Fri 10-5, Sat 10-4
Friends of the Library Group

PENFIELD

P PENFIELD PUBLIC LIBRARY*, 1985 Baird Rd, 14526. SAN 312-2506. Tel: 585-340-8720. FAX: 585-340-8748. Web Site: www.penfieldlibrary.org. *Dir,* Bernadette Brinkman; *Librn,* Carol Bond; *Librn,* Camille DelVecchio; *Librn,* Margaret O'Neil; *Librn,* Todd Randall; *Librn,* Lily Shung; *Ch,* Jennifer Caccavale; *Ch,* Judy Carpenter; *YA Librn,* Lyla Grills
Pop 36,242
Library Holdings: Audiobooks 18,589; CDs 5,045; DVDs 13,966; Electronic Media & Resources 1,735; Bk Vols 135,044; Per Subs 387
Special Collections: Russian Language Coll
Automation Activity & Vendor Info: (Acquisitions) Baker & Taylor; (Circulation) CARL.Solution (TLC); (OPAC) CARL.Solution (TLC)
Database Vendor: EBSCOhost, ReferenceUSA
Wireless access
Mem of Monroe County Library System
Open Mon-Thurs (Winter) 10-9, Fri 10-6, Sat 10-5, Sun 2-5; Mon-Thurs (Summer) 10-9, Fri 10-6, Sat 10-1
Friends of the Library Group

PENN YAN

P PENN YAN PUBLIC LIBRARY*, 214 Main St, 14527. SAN 312-2514. Tel: 315-536-6114. FAX: 315-536-0131. Web Site: www.pypl.org. *Dir,* Angela Gonzalez; *Info & Referral,* John Creamer; E-mail: jcreamer@pypl.org; *Youth Serv Coordr,* Andrea Wheeler; E-mail: afwheeler@pypl.org; Staff 10 (MLS 2, Non-MLS 8)
Founded 1895. Pop 15,060; Circ 122,582
Library Holdings: AV Mats 4,038; Bk Titles 51,515; Per Subs 100
Subject Interests: Local hist
Automation Activity & Vendor Info: (Acquisitions) Innovative Interfaces, Inc; (Cataloging) Innovative Interfaces, Inc; (Circulation) Innovative Interfaces, Inc; (OPAC) Innovative Interfaces, Inc
Wireless access
Mem of Southern Tier Library System
Open Mon-Fri 9-7:30, Sat 9-1
Friends of the Library Group

PERRY

P PERRY PUBLIC LIBRARY, 70 N Main St, 14530-1299. SAN 312-2522. Tel: 585-237-2243. FAX: 585-237-2008. E-mail: perrylibrary@owwl.org, perrylibrarydirector@owwl.org. Web Site: www.perry.pls-net.org. *Libr Dir,* Margaret S Parker; E-mail: pparker@pls-net.org; *Youth Serv Librn,* Janet N Rossman; E-mail: jrossman@pls-net.org; Staff 2 (MLS 2)
Founded 1914. Pop 6,214; Circ 45,532
Jan 2013-Dec 2013 Income $195,311, State $4,731, Locally Generated Income $175,000, Parent Institution $416, Other $15,164. Mats Exp $20,651, Books $11,426, Per/Ser (Incl. Access Fees) $1,614, AV Equip $3,802, AV Mat $3,255, Electronic Ref Mat (Incl. Access Fees) $554. Sal $97,581 (Prof $74,810)
Library Holdings: Audiobooks 326; DVDs 670; Electronic Media & Resources 18; Bk Vols 22,431; Per Subs 47
Special Collections: Lemuel M Wiles, Artist (Stowell-Wiles Coll), oil paintings; Local History (Clark Rice Coll), photog; Local History (Henry Page Coll)
Automation Activity & Vendor Info: (Cataloging) Evergreen; (Circulation) Evergreen; (OPAC) Evergreen
Wireless access
Mem of Pioneer Library System
Open Mon & Wed 1-7, Tues & Thurs 10-7, Fri 1-5, Sat 9-1
Friends of the Library Group

PERU

P PERU FREE LIBRARY*, 3024 N Main St, 12972. SAN 312-2530. Tel: 518-643-8618. E-mail: perulib@gmail.com. *Librn,* Rebecca Pace
Circ 14,119
Library Holdings: Bk Vols 16,000; Per Subs 40
Automation Activity & Vendor Info: (Cataloging) Horizon; (Circulation) Horizon; (ILL) Horizon; (OPAC) Horizon; (Serials) Horizon
Wireless access
Mem of Clinton-Essex-Franklin Library System
Open Tues-Thurs 11-7, Fri 10-4, Sat 10-3
Friends of the Library Group

PETERSBURGH

P PETERSBURGH PUBLIC LIBRARY*, 69 Main St, 12138-5010. (Mail add: PO Box 250, 12138-0250), SAN 312-2549. Tel: 518-658-2927. FAX: 518-658-2927. *Dir,* Sharon Hodges
Circ 24,000
Library Holdings: Bk Vols 23,601; Per Subs 12
Automation Activity & Vendor Info: (Cataloging) Horizon; (Circulation) Horizon; (OPAC) Horizon
Wireless access
Mem of Upper Hudson Library System
Open Mon-Fri 2-5, Wed 2-9, Sat 9:30-12:30

PHELPS

P PHELPS COMMUNITY MEMORIAL LIBRARY*, Eight Banta St, Ste 200, 14532. SAN 312-2557. Tel: 315-548-3120. FAX: 315-548-5314. Web Site: phelpslibrary.org/. *Dir,* Louise Furber; Staff 1 (MLS 1)
Founded 1948. Pop 7,017; Circ 34,000
Library Holdings: Bk Vols 20,000; Per Subs 54
Special Collections: Historical (Bellamy Partridge Coll); Local History/Genealogy
Automation Activity & Vendor Info: (Cataloging) SirsiDynix; (Circulation) SirsiDynix
Function: Bk club(s), Bks on CD, Chess club, Computers for patron use, Copy machines, e-mail & chat, E-Reserves, Electronic databases & coll, Exhibits, Fax serv, Free DVD rentals, Genealogy discussion group, Handicapped accessible, Home delivery & serv to Sr ctr & nursing homes, ILL available, Instruction & testing, Music CDs, Online searches, Photocopying/Printing, Prog for adults, Prog for children & young adult, Pub access computers, Ref serv available, Scanner, Story hour, Summer reading prog, Tax forms, Teen prog, VHS videos, Video lending libr, Wheelchair accessible
Mem of Pioneer Library System
Open Mon & Wed 1-8, Tues & Thurs 10-8, Fri 1-5, Sat 10-2

PHILADELPHIA

P BODMAN MEMORIAL LIBRARY, Eight Aldrich St, 13673. SAN 312-2565. Tel: 315-642-3323. FAX: 315-642-0617. E-mail: philib@ncls.org. Web Site: www.bodmanmemoriallibrary.org. *Libr Mgr,* Jacinda Gagnon; Staff 1 (Non-MLS 1)
Founded 1917. Pop 1,947; Circ 8,361
Jan 2014-Dec 2014 Income $43,096, State $125, County $2,850, Locally Generated Income $6,121, Other $34,000. Mats Exp Books $1,550
Automation Activity & Vendor Info: (Cataloging) SirsiDynix; (Circulation) SirsiDynix; (OPAC) SirsiDynix
Wireless access
Function: 24/7 Electronic res, 24/7 Online cat, Accessibility serv available based on individual needs, Audiobks via web, Bks on CD, Children's prog, Computer training, Computers for patron use, Copy machines, Handicapped accessible, Home delivery & serv to Sr ctr & nursing homes, Homebound delivery serv, ILL available, Life-long learning prog for all ages, Magazines, Mail & tel request accepted, Microfiche/film & reading machines, Movies, Mus passes, Notary serv, Online cat, Online ref, Online searches, Outreach serv, OverDrive digital audio bks, Photocopying/Printing, Prog for adults, Prog for children & young adult, Pub access computers, Ref & res, Ref serv available, Ref serv in person, Referrals accepted, Scanner, Senior computer classes, Senior outreach, Serves mentally handicapped consumers, Story hour, Summer reading prog, Tax forms, VHS videos, Wheelchair accessible
Mem of North Country Library System
Special Services for the Blind - Audio mat; Bks on cassette; Bks on CD; Copier with enlargement capabilities; Free checkout of audio mat; Large print bks
Open Mon, Tues & Thurs 2-7, Wed & Fri 2-5, Sat 10-Noon
Restriction: ID required to use computers (Ltd hrs)
Friends of the Library Group

PHILMONT

S ANTHROPOSOPHICAL SOCIETY IN AMERICA, Rudolf Steiner Library, 139 Main St, 12565. (Mail add: PO Box 800, 12565-0800), SAN 373-1197. Tel: 518-672-7690. E-mail: rsteinerlibrary@taconic.net. Web Site: www.anthroposophy.org/rudolf-steiner-library. *Interim Librn,* Judith Kiely; Staff 0.75 (Non-MLS 0.75)
Founded 1928
Library Holdings: Bk Vols 25,000; Spec Interest Per Sub 30
Subject Interests: Anthroposophy, Liberal arts, Waldorf educ, World spirituality
Automation Activity & Vendor Info: (OPAC) OPALS (Open-source Automated Library System)
Wireless access
Function: Mail loans to mem, Res libr
Partic in Capital District Library Council
Restriction: Circ to mem only, Fee for pub use

P PHILMONT PUBLIC LIBRARY*, 101 Main St, 12565-1001. (Mail add: PO Box 816, 12565-0816), SAN 312-2573. Tel: 518-672-5010. FAX: 518-672-5010. E-mail: library@philmont.org. Web Site: www.philmont.org. *Interim Dir,* Karen A Garafalo; *Circ,* Karen Beinkampen; Staff 2 (MLS 1, Non-MLS 1)
Founded 1898. Pop 1,500; Circ 21,600
Library Holdings: Bks on Deafness & Sign Lang 10, High Interest/Low Vocabulary Bk Vols 250; Bk Vols 25,000
Special Collections: Main Street Coll
Automation Activity & Vendor Info: (Cataloging) Innovative Interfaces, Inc; (Circulation) Innovative Interfaces, Inc; (OPAC) Innovative Interfaces, Inc
Database Vendor: Innovative Interfaces, Inc, ProQuest
Wireless access
Function: ILL available
Mem of Mid-Hudson Library System
Special Services for the Deaf - TTY equip
Special Services for the Blind - Talking bks
Open Mon & Wed 12-5 & 6-8, Thurs & Sat 10-12, Fri 12-5
Friends of the Library Group

PHOENICIA

P PHOENICIA LIBRARY*, 48 Main St, 12464-5213. (Mail add: PO Box 555, 12464-0555), SAN 312-2581. Tel: 845-688-7811. E-mail: phoenicialibrary@gmail.com. Web Site: phoenicia.lib.ny.us/. *Dir,* Regina Johnson
Founded 1909. Pop 3,200; Circ 13,000
Library Holdings: Bk Vols 12,000
Automation Activity & Vendor Info: (Cataloging) Innovative Interfaces, Inc; (Circulation) Innovative Interfaces, Inc; (OPAC) Innovative Interfaces, Inc
Wireless access
Mem of Mid-Hudson Library System
Open Mon & Wed-Fri 1-6, Tues 10-4, Sat 10-3
Friends of the Library Group

PHOENIX

P PHOENIX PUBLIC LIBRARY*, 34 Elm St, 13135. SAN 312-259X. Tel: 315-695-4355. FAX: 315-695-4355. *Dir,* Noreen Patterson
Founded 1920. Circ 27,659
Library Holdings: Bk Vols 24,100
Subject Interests: Civil War hist, Job info, Local hist
Wireless access
Mem of North Country Library System
Open Mon & Wed 11-8, Tues, Thurs & Fri 11-5, Sat 10-1

PIERMONT

P DENNIS P MCHUGH PIERMONT PUBLIC LIBRARY*, 25 Flywheel Park W, 10968. SAN 312-2603. Tel: 845-359-4595. E-mail: info@piermontlibrary.org. Web Site: piermontlibrary.org. *Dir,* Jessica Bowen; *Asst Dir, Prog Coordr,* Grace Mitchell. Subject Specialists: *Local hist,* Grace Mitchell; Staff 3 (MLS 2, Non-MLS 1)
Library Holdings: Bk Vols 15,500
Special Collections: Local History Coll
Wireless access
Mem of Ramapo Catskill Library System
Open Mon-Thurs 10-8, Fri 12-5, Sat 10-4
Friends of the Library Group

PIKE

P PIKE LIBRARY*, 65 Main St, 14130. (Mail add: PO Box 246, 14130-0246), SAN 312-262X. Tel: 585-493-5900. FAX: 585-493-5900. *Dir,* Tammy Hopkins
Circ 7,617
Library Holdings: Bk Vols 12,700; Per Subs 42
Wireless access
Mem of Pioneer Library System
Open Mon 1-7, Wed 10-6, Sat 10-4

PINE BUSH

P PINE BUSH AREA LIBRARY*, 227 Maple Ave, 12566. (Mail add: PO Box 63, 12566-0063), SAN 312-2638. Tel: 845-744-3375. FAX: 845-744-3375. E-mail: pbl@rcls.org. Web Site: www.rcls.org/pbl. *Dir,* Doris Callan
Circ 61,000
Library Holdings: Electronic Media & Resources 2,002, Bk Vols 22,715; Videos 1,275
Automation Activity & Vendor Info: (Cataloging) Horizon; (Circulation) Horizon; (OPAC) Horizon; (Serials) Horizon
Wireless access
Open Mon & Wed 9-7, Tues & Thurs 12-8, Fri 9-5, Sat 10-2
Friends of the Library Group

PINE HILL

P MORTON MEMORIAL LIBRARY*, 22 Elm St, 12465. SAN 312-2646. Tel: 845-254-4222. FAX: 845-254-4222. Web Site: www.mhls.org. *Dir,* Charlis Weiss; E-mail: charlisweiss@yahoo.com
Founded 1903. Pop 308; Circ 5,000
Library Holdings: AV Mats 200; High Interest/Low Vocabulary Bk Vols 20; Bk Vols 9,000
Automation Activity & Vendor Info: (OPAC) Innovative Interfaces, Inc
Mem of Mid-Hudson Library System
Special Services for the Blind - Talking bks
Open Tues & Thurs 2-6, Wed 5-8, Fri 5-9, Sat 1-6

PINE PLAINS

P PINE PLAINS FREE LIBRARY*, 7775 S Main St, 12567-5653. (Mail add: PO Box 325, 12567-0325), SAN 312-2654. Tel: 518-398-1927. FAX: 518-398-6085. E-mail: pinelib@fairpoint.net. Web Site: pineplains.lib.ny.us. *Librn,* Marguerite Hill
Pop 2,287; Circ 10,000
Library Holdings: Bk Vols 10,000; Per Subs 28
Automation Activity & Vendor Info: (Cataloging) Innovative Interfaces, Inc - Millenium; (Circulation) Innovative Interfaces, Inc - Millenium; (OPAC) Innovative Interfaces, Inc - Millenium
Wireless access
Mem of Mid-Hudson Library System
Open Mon, Wed & Thurs 7pm-9pm, Tues & Fri 2-5:30 & 7-9, Sat 9-12 & 2-5:30

PITTSFORD

L HARRIS, BEACH PLLC*, Law Library, 99 Garnsey Rd, 14534. SAN 371-5205. Tel: 585-419-8800, Ext 8917. FAX: 585-419-8814. Web Site: www.harrisbeach.com. *Dir, Libr Serv,* Joan Pedzich; E-mail: jpedzich@harrisbeach.com; *Coll Develop,* Marie Calvaruso; *Computer Serv, Ref,* Cyndi Trembley
Library Holdings: Bk Vols 21,334; Per Subs 450
Automation Activity & Vendor Info: (Cataloging) Inmagic, Inc.; (Circulation) Inmagic, Inc.; (OPAC) Inmagic, Inc.
Database Vendor: LexisNexis, Westlaw
Wireless access
Publications: Harris Beach & Wilcox Library Guide
Restriction: Staff use only

P PITTSFORD COMMUNITY LIBRARY*, 24 State St, 14534. SAN 353-9164. Tel: 585-248-6275. FAX: 585-248-6259. *Dir,* Marjorie Shelly; E-mail: mshelly@townofpittsford.org; *Asst Dir,* Liz Barrett; *Adult Serv, AV,* Mary Kopczynski; *YA Serv,* Rhonda Rossman; Staff 5 (MLS 5)
Founded 1920. Pop 27,219; Circ 378,604
Library Holdings: Bk Vols 90,920
Automation Activity & Vendor Info: (Circulation) TLC (The Library Corporation); (OPAC) TLC (The Library Corporation)
Database Vendor: TLC (The Library Corporation)
Wireless access
Mem of Monroe County Library System
Open Mon-Thurs 9-9, Fri 9-6, Sat 10-5, Sun 1-5
Friends of the Library Group

PLAINVIEW

SR CHURCH OF JESUS CHRIST OF LATTER-DAY SAINTS*, Family History Center, 160 Washington Ave, 11803. SAN 377-5631. Tel: 516-433-0122. Web Site: www.familysearch.org. *Dir,* Roberta Olson
Library Holdings: Bk Vols 500
Open Tues & Thurs 10-2 & 7-9:30, Wed & Fri 10-2, Sat 11-3

P PLAINVIEW-OLD BETHPAGE PUBLIC LIBRARY*, 999 Old Country Rd, 11803-4995. SAN 312-2689. Tel: 516-938-0077. FAX: 516-433-4645. E-mail: website@poblib.org. Web Site: www.poblib.org. *Dir,* Gretchen Browne; E-mail: gbrowne@poblib.org; Staff 106 (MLS 24, Non-MLS 82)
Founded 1955. Pop 28,676; Circ 454,881
Jul 2012-Jun 2013 Income $6,313,650, State $7,800, Locally Generated Income $6,305,850. Mats Exp $430,000, Books $300,000, Per/Ser (Incl. Access Fees) $22,000, Electronic Ref Mat (Incl. Access Fees) $63,000. Sal $3,437,600 (Prof $1,300,000)
Library Holdings: Audiobooks 2,918; AV Mats 26,455; Bks on Deafness & Sign Lang 60; CDs 3,989; DVDs 9,653; e-books 26,652; Bk Vols 183,605; Per Subs 3,925; Talking Bks 1,217
Special Collections: Career; Career-Job Learning; Consumer Information; Law; LI Jewish Genealogical Society Coll; New & Used Automobiles; Plainview Old Bethpage Coll
Subject Interests: Bus info, Career info, College catalogs, Educ opportunities, Employment, Law, Local hist, Med
Automation Activity & Vendor Info: (Acquisitions) Innovative Interfaces, Inc; (Cataloging) Innovative Interfaces, Inc; (Circulation) Innovative Interfaces, Inc; (Course Reserve) Innovative Interfaces, Inc; (ILL) Innovative Interfaces, Inc; (Media Booking) Innovative Interfaces, Inc; (OPAC) Innovative Interfaces, Inc; (Serials) Innovative Interfaces, Inc
Wireless access
Function: Homebound delivery serv
Publications: Library World (Bi-monthly)
Mem of Nassau Library System
Partic in Dialog Corp; OCLC Online Computer Library Center, Inc
Special Services for the Blind - Home delivery serv; Talking bks
Open Mon-Fri 9-9, Sat 9:30-5:30, Sun 1-9
Friends of the Library Group

PLATTSBURGH

M CHAMPLAIN VALLEY PHYSICIANS HOSPITAL MEDICAL CENTER LIBRARY*, 75 Beekman St, 12901. SAN 312-2700. Tel: 518-562-7325. FAX: 518-562-7129. *Librn,* Christina Ransom; E-mail: cransom@cvph.org; Staff 2 (MLS 2)
Founded 1930
Library Holdings: Bk Titles 1,000; Per Subs 500
Publications: Library Newsletter (Quarterly)
Partic in Health Sci Libr & Info Consortium; National Network of Libraries of Medicine; Northern New York Library Network; OCLC Online Computer Library Center, Inc
Open Mon-Fri 7:30-3:30
Restriction: Open to pub for ref only

J CLINTON COMMUNITY COLLEGE*, LeRoy M Douglas Sr Library, 136 Clinton Point Dr, 12901-5690. SAN 312-2719. Tel: 518-562-4241. Reference Tel: 518-562-4240. Administration Tel: 518-562-4237. FAX: 518-562-4116. Web Site: www.clinton.edu/douglaslibrary. *Libr Dir,* Mary Ann Weighlhofer; E-mail: maryann.weiglhofer@clinton.edu; *Electronic Serv & Emerging Tech Librn,* Anne de la Chapelle; Tel: 518-562-4244, E-mail: anne.delachapelle@clinton.edu; *Ref & Instruction Librn,* Catherine Figlioli; Tel: 518-562-4249, E-mail: catherine.figlioli@clinton.edu; *Syst & Tech Serv Librn,* Jill M Tarabula; Tel: 518-562-4247, E-mail: jill.tarabula@clinton.edu; Staff 7 (MLS 4, Non-MLS 3)
Founded 1969. Enrl 1,686; Fac 145; Highest Degree: Associate
Sept 2012-Aug 2013 Income $95,800. Mats Exp $69,150, Books $25,000, Per/Ser (Incl. Access Fees) $13,500, AV Mat $7,650, Electronic Ref Mat (Incl. Access Fees) $23,000. Sal $269,000 (Prof $215,000)
Library Holdings: Bks on Deafness & Sign Lang 17; CDs 640; DVDs 1,930; e-books 401,712; e-journals 58,693; Electronic Media & Resources 1; Large Print Bks 6; Music Scores 26; Bk Titles 41,512; Bk Vols 41,875; Per Subs 40
Special Collections: Adirondack Coll; Special Coll
Subject Interests: Local hist, Regional hist
Automation Activity & Vendor Info: (Acquisitions) Baker & Taylor; (Cataloging) Ex Libris Group; (Circulation) Ex Libris Group; (Course Reserve) Ex Libris Group; (ILL) OCLC ILLiad; (OPAC) Ex Libris Group; (Serials) Ex Libris Group
Database Vendor: American Psychological Association (APA), EBSCOhost, Gale Cengage Learning, OCLC, Project MUSE, ProQuest, ScienceDirect, SerialsSolutions, Springshare, LLC, Wilson - Wilson Web
Wireless access
Partic in Northern New York Library Network; OCLC Online Computer Library Center, Inc; SUNYConnect; Westchester Academic Library Directors Organization (WALDO)
Open Mon-Thurs 8-7, Fri 8-4

P CLINTON-ESSEX-FRANKLIN LIBRARY SYSTEM, 33 Oak St, 12901-2810. SAN 312-2727. Tel: 518-563-5190. Toll Free Tel: 800-221-1980. FAX: 518-563-0421. Web Site: www.cefls.org. *Dir,* Ewa Jankowska; Tel: 518-563-5190, Ext 11; *Head, Tech Serv & ILL,* Elizabeth S Rogers; Tel: 518-563-5190, Ext 14, E-mail: erogers@cefls.org; *Outreach & Youth Serv Librn,* Julie Wever; Tel: 518-563-5190, Ext 18, E-mail: jwever@cefls.org; *Automation Syst Coordr,* Betsy Brooks; Tel: 518-563-5190, Ext 35, E-mail: bbrooks@cefls.org; *AV,* Karen Batchelder; Tel: 518-563-5190, Ext 20, E-mail: kbatchelder@cefls.org; *Outreach Serv,* Chad Chase; Tel: 518-563-5190, Ext 22, E-mail: cchase@cefls.org; *Tech Serv,* Kimberly Fletcher; Tel: 518-563-5190, Ext 16, E-mail: kfletcher@cefls.org; Staff 10 (MLS 4, Non-MLS 6)
Founded 1954. Pop 169,661
Jan 2012-Dec 2012 Income $1,500,000. Mats Exp $60,000
Library Holdings: Audiobooks 2,286; AV Mats 7,368; CDs 1,834; DVDs 2,074; e-books 1,985; Electronic Media & Resources 20; High Interest/Low Vocabulary Bk Vols 7,281; Large Print Bks 10,045; Bk Titles 54,976; Bk Vols 55,554; Per Subs 6; Talking Bks 1,790; Videos 4,294
Automation Activity & Vendor Info: (Cataloging) SirsiDynix; (Circulation) SirsiDynix; (ILL) OCLC; (OPAC) SirsiDynix
Database Vendor: EBSCO Auto Repair Reference, OCLC FirstSearch, OCLC WorldShare Interlibrary Loan, SirsiDynix
Wireless access
Function: Audiobks via web, AV serv, Bks on cassette, Bks on CD, E-Reserves, Electronic databases & coll, Equip loans & repairs, Handicapped accessible, Home delivery & serv to Sr ctr & nursing homes, ILL available, Jail serv, Mail loans to mem, Online cat, Online searches, Outreach serv, Photocopying/Printing, Senior outreach, Summer reading prog, Telephone ref, VHS videos, Web-catalog, Wheelchair accessible, Workshops
Publications: Trailblazer (Newsletter)
Member Libraries: Akwesasne Cultural Center Library; Altona Reading Center; Au Sable Forks Free Library; Beldon Noble Memorial Library; Black Watch Memorial Library; Champlain Memorial Library; Chateaugay Memorial Library; Chazy Public Library; Dannemora Free Library; Dodge Library; Dodge Memorial Library; E M Cooper Memorial Library; Elizabethtown Library Association; Ellenburg Center Library; Ellenburg Sarah A Munsil Free Library; Goff-Nelson Memorial Library; Hammond Library of Crown Point NY; Keene Public Library; Keene Valley Library Association; Keeseville Free Library; Lake Placid Public Library; Mooers Free Library; New York State Department of Corrections & Community Supervision; Paine Memorial Free Library; Peru Free Library; Plattsburgh Public Library; Saranac Lake Free Library; Schroon Lake Public Library; Sherman Free Library; Wadhams Free Library; Waverly Reading Center; Wead Library; Wells Memorial Library; Westport Library Association
Partic in Northern New York Library Network
Special Services for the Deaf - TDD equip
Special Services for the Blind - Aids for in-house use; BiFolkal kits; Large print bks; Magnifiers; Talking bks & player equip
Open Mon-Fri 8-5

GL NEW YORK STATE SUPREME COURT FOURTH DISTRICT*, Law Library, 72 Clinton St, 12901. SAN 312-2735. Tel: 518-565-4808. FAX: 518-562-1193. Web Site: www.courts.state.ny.us. *Librn,* Lynn Bezio; E-mail: lbezio@courts.state.ny.us

Library Holdings: Bk Vols 12,000
Database Vendor: LexisNexis, Loislaw, Westlaw
Wireless access
Open Mon-Fri 9-5

P PLATTSBURGH PUBLIC LIBRARY*, 19 Oak St, 12901-2810. SAN 312-2743. Tel: 518-563-0921. Circulation Tel: 518-536-7446. Reference Tel: 518-536-7447. Administration Tel: 518-536-7442. FAX: 518-563-1681. Administration FAX: 518-324-6556. Web Site: www.plattsburghlib.org. *Dir,* Anne de la Chapelle; E-mail: delachapellea@cityofplattsburgh-ny.gov; *Ad,* Caleb Moshier; *Ch Serv,* Sharon Bandhold; *ILL,* Mary Heffernan; *Tech Serv,* Colleen Pelletier; Staff 4 (MLS 4)
Founded 1894. Pop 19,163; Circ 134,687
Jan 2008-Dec 2008 Income $753,270, State $102,900, City $639,715. Mats Exp $75,000, Books $70,000. Sal $451,700 (Prof $152,769)
Library Holdings: Bk Titles 100,000
Special Collections: Clinton County & Plattsburgh History Coll
Automation Activity & Vendor Info: (Circulation) Horizon
Mem of Clinton-Essex-Franklin Library System
Partic in Northern New York Library Network
Open Mon, Fri & Sat 9-5, Tues-Thurs 9-8
Friends of the Library Group

C STATE UNIVERSITY OF NEW YORK COLLEGE AT PLATTSBURGH*, Benjamin F Feinberg Library, Two Draper Ave, 12901-2697. SAN 312-2751. Tel: 518-564-5180. Circulation Tel: 518-564-5182. Interlibrary Loan Service Tel: 518-564-4427. Reference Tel: 518-564-5190. Information Services Tel: 518-564-5191. FAX: 518-564-5100. Reference FAX: 518-564-3059. E-mail: library@plattsburgh.edu. Web Site: www.plattsburgh.edu/library. *Dean of Libr & Info Serv,* Holly H Heller-Ross; E-mail: hellerhh@plattsburgh.edu; *Asst Dean, Libr & Info Serv,* Mark Mastrean; Tel: 518-564-5307, E-mail: mastrems@plattsburgh.edu; *Instruction/Ref Serv, Sr Asst Librn, Spec Coll Librn,* Debra Kimok; Tel: 518-564-5206, Fax: 518-564-5325, E-mail: debra.kimok@plattsburgh.edu; *Assoc Librn, Coordr, Coll Develop & Delivery,* Gordon Muir; Tel: 518-564-5304, E-mail: gordon.muir@plattsburgh.edu; *Assoc Librn, Instrul & Ref Serv Coordr,* Karen Volkman; Tel: 518-564-5305, E-mail: volkmake@plattsburgh.edu; *Assoc Librn, Coordr, Libr Courses,* Michelle Toth; Tel: 518-564-5225, E-mail: michelle.toth@plattsburgh.edu; Staff 22.05 (MLS 11.5, Non-MLS 10.55)
Founded 1889. Fac 469; Highest Degree: Master
Jul 2012-Jun 2013 Income $2,512,825. Mats Exp $677,016, Books $69,504, Per/Ser (Incl. Access Fees) $400,190, AV Mat $8,000, Electronic Ref Mat (Incl. Access Fees) $192,322, Presv $7,000. Sal $1,327,587 (Prof $140,393)
Library Holdings: CDs 944; DVDs 1,288; e-books 114,144; e-journals 5,089; Electronic Media & Resources 102; Microforms 711,342; Bk Titles 226,187; Bk Vols 295,056; Per Subs 5,343; Videos 670
Special Collections: College Archives; North Country History (Adirondack & Lake Champlain Regions; Clinton, Essex & Franklin Counties), bks, ms, maps, newsp, pamphlets, per, photog; Rockwell Kent Coll. Can & Prov; Oral History; State Document Depository; US Document Depository
Subject Interests: Adirondack hist, N Country hist
Automation Activity & Vendor Info: (Acquisitions) Ex Libris Group; (Cataloging) Ex Libris Group; (Circulation) Ex Libris Group; (Course Reserve) Docutek; (ILL) OCLC ILLiad; (OPAC) Ex Libris Group; (Serials) Ex Libris Group
Database Vendor: ACM (Association for Computing Machinery), Alexander Street Press, American Mathematical Society, ARTstor, BioOne, Bowker, CredoReference, EBSCOhost, Gale Cengage Learning, JSTOR, LexisNexis, Mergent Online, OCLC FirstSearch, Oxford Online, Project MUSE, ProQuest, PubMed, ScienceDirect, Springer-Verlag, Wiley InterScience, Wilson - Wilson Web
Wireless access
Function: Doc delivery serv
Publications: Access The World
Partic in New York State Higher Education Initiative; New York State Interlibrary Loan Network (NYSILL); SUNYConnect
Open Mon-Thurs 7:30am-Midnight, Fri 7:30am-8pm, Sat 11-8, Sun Noon-Midnight

PLEASANT VALLEY

P PLEASANT VALLEY FREE LIBRARY*, 1584 Main St, 12569. (Mail add: PO Box 633, 12569-0633), SAN 312-276X. Tel: 845-635-8460. FAX: 845-635-9556. E-mail: PVFLibrary@gmail.com. Web Site: www.pleasantvalleylibrary.org. *Dir,* Daniela L Pulice; E-mail: danielapulice@gmail.com; *Head, Ch,* Julie A Poplees; *Head, Circ,* Valerie Britton; Staff 4 (MLS 1, Non-MLS 3)
Founded 1903. Pop 9,864; Circ 142,000
Jan 2012-Dec 2012 Income $385,000, State $2,500, Locally Generated Income $360,000, Other $15,000. Mats Exp $51,000, Books $32,500, Per/Ser (Incl. Access Fees) $1,500, AV Mat $15,000, Electronic Ref Mat (Incl. Access Fees) $2,000. Sal $180,000 (Prof $70,000)
Library Holdings: AV Mats 500; Bks on Deafness & Sign Lang 15; CDs 2,000; DVDs 10,000; Large Print Bks 2,500; Bk Vols 50,000; Per Subs 20; Talking Bks 1,000
Automation Activity & Vendor Info: (Acquisitions) Innovative Interfaces, Inc; (Cataloging) Innovative Interfaces, Inc; (Circulation) Innovative Interfaces, Inc; (Course Reserve) Innovative Interfaces, Inc; (OPAC) Innovative Interfaces, Inc; (Serials) Innovative Interfaces, Inc
Wireless access
Mem of Mid-Hudson Library System
Open Mon-Thurs 10-8:30, Fri 1-6, Sat 10-4
Friends of the Library Group

PLEASANTVILLE

P MOUNT PLEASANT PUBLIC LIBRARY, 350 Bedford Rd, 10570-3099. SAN 353-9253. Tel: 914-769-0548. FAX: 914-769-6149. E-mail: info@mountpleasantlibrary.org. Web Site: www.mountpleasantlibrary.org. *Dir,* John Fearon; E-mail: jfearon@mountpleasantlibrary.org; *Asst Dir,* Vivian Gufarotti; E-mail: vgufarotti@mountpleasantlibrary.org; *Head, Ch,* Susan Chajes; *Head, Circ & Tech Serv,* Matt DiTomasso; Staff 20 (MLS 5, Non-MLS 15)
Founded 1893. Pop 33,323; Circ 392,812
Jan 2013-Dec 2013 Income (Main Library and Branch(s)) $2,588,134. Mats Exp $230,460, Books $139,898, Per/Ser (Incl. Access Fees) $10,700, AV Mat $69,066, Electronic Ref Mat (Incl. Access Fees) $10,796. Sal $1,187,035
Library Holdings: Audiobooks 2,750; CDs 4,987; DVDs 8,481; Bk Vols 90,013; Per Subs 150
Special Collections: Jacob Burns Film Center Curated Coll of DVDs; Local History Coll; Pleasantville SEPTA Parenting Coll
Automation Activity & Vendor Info: (Cataloging) SirsiDynix; (Circulation) SirsiDynix; (ILL) SirsiDynix
Database Vendor: EBSCOhost, Gale Cengage Learning, SirsiDynix
Wireless access
Publications: Inklings; Newsletter (Quarterly)
Open Mon, Tues & Thurs 10-9, Wed 10-6, Fri & Sat 10-5, Sun 1-5
Friends of the Library Group
Branches: 1
MOUNT PLEASANT BRANCH, 125 Lozza Dr, Valhalla, 10595-1268, SAN 353-9288. Tel: 914-741-0276. FAX: 914-495-3864. *Br Mgr,* Martha Mesiti; *Circ Supvr,* Donna Coppola. Subject Specialists: *Local hist,* Martha Mesiti
Open Mon, Tues & Thurs 10-5, Wed 10-8, Fri & Sat 10-2
Friends of the Library Group

C PACE UNIVERSITY*, Edward & Doris Mortola Library, 861 Bedford Rd, 10570-2799. SAN 353-9318. Tel: 914-773-3380. Interlibrary Loan Service Tel: 914-773-3853. Reference Tel: 914-773-3381. Web Site: www.pace.edu/library. *Access Serv Coordr, Admin Dir,* MacDonald Nadine; Tel: 914-773-3854, E-mail: nmacdonald@pace.edu; *Assoc Univ Librn,* Steven Feyl; Tel: 914-773-3233, E-mail: sfeyl@pace.edu; *Asst Univ Librn,* Sarah K Burns-Feyl; Tel: 914-773-3220, E-mail: sburnsfeyl@pace.edu; *Asst Univ Librn,* Noreen McGuire; Tel: 914-773-3815, E-mail: nmcguire@pace.edu; *Asst Univ Librn,* Medaline Philbert; Tel: 914-773-3945, E-mail: mphilbert@pace.edu; *Head, Info & Res Serv,* Gillen Rose; Tel: 914-773-3382, E-mail: rgillen@pace.edu; *Electronic Res Librn,* Christina Blenke; Tel: 914-773-3222, E-mail: cblenke@pace.edu; *Instrul Serv Librn,* Douglas Heimbigner; Tel: 917-773-3244, E-mail: dheimbigner@pace.edu; *Cat,* June Pang; Tel: 914-773-3255, E-mail: jpang@pace.edu; *Coll Develop,* Harriet Huang; Tel: 914-773-3240, E-mail: hhuang@pace.edu; *ILL,* Sheila Hu; Tel: 914-773-3853, E-mail: shu@pace.edu; Staff 16 (MLS 10, Non-MLS 6)
Founded 1963. Enrl 3,300; Fac 438; Highest Degree: Doctorate
Library Holdings: AV Mats 13,787; DVDs 1,100; e-books 8,352; e-journals 62,417; Microforms 12,971; Bk Titles 195,502; Bk Vols 194,405; Per Subs 41; Videos 359
Special Collections: Rene Dubos; Saint Joan of Arc
Subject Interests: Computer sci, Educ, Lit, Nursing
Automation Activity & Vendor Info: (Acquisitions) Innovative Interfaces, Inc; (Cataloging) Innovative Interfaces, Inc; (Circulation) Innovative Interfaces, Inc; (Course Reserve) Innovative Interfaces, Inc; (ILL) Innovative Interfaces, Inc; (OPAC) Innovative Interfaces, Inc; (Serials) Innovative Interfaces, Inc
Database Vendor: EBSCOhost, Gale Cengage Learning, LexisNexis, OCLC FirstSearch, OVID Technologies, ProQuest
Wireless access
Publications: Information Edge (Newsletter); Printed & Online Bibliographic Handouts
Partic in Metropolitan New York Library Council; New England Law Library Consortium, Inc; OCLC Online Computer Library Center, Inc; Westchester Academic Library Directors Organization (WALDO)
Open Mon-Thurs 8:30am-2am, Fri 8am-11pm, Sat 10-8, Sun 10am-2am

POESTENKILL

P POESTENKILL PUBLIC LIBRARY*, Nine Plank Rd, 12140. (Mail add: PO Box 305, 12140-0305). Tel: 518-283-3721. FAX: 518-283-5618. E-mail: info@poestenkilllibrary.org. Web Site: www.poestenkilllibrary.org. *Dir,* Margie Ann Morris; E-mail: margie@poestenkilllibrary.org
Pop 4,054
Library Holdings: AV Mats 850; Large Print Bks 200; Bk Vols 16,000; Talking Bks 350
Automation Activity & Vendor Info: (Cataloging) SirsiDynix; (Circulation) SirsiDynix; (OPAC) SirsiDynix
Wireless access
Mem of Upper Hudson Library System
Open Mon, Fri & Sat 10-1, Tues-Thurs 1-8:30
Friends of the Library Group

POLAND

P POLAND PUBLIC LIBRARY*, 8849 Main St, 13431. (Mail add: PO Box 140, 13431-0140), SAN 312-2786. Tel: 315-826-3112. FAX: 315-826-5677. *Librn,* Paula Johnson
Circ 31,288
Library Holdings: AV Mats 800; Bk Vols 15,000; Per Subs 30
Automation Activity & Vendor Info: (Cataloging) SirsiDynix; (Circulation) SirsiDynix; (OPAC) SirsiDynix
Wireless access
Mem of Mid-York Library System
Open Mon & Wed 3:30-6:30, Tues & Thurs 8:30-4:30

POPLAR RIDGE

P HAZARD LIBRARY ASSOCIATION*, 2487 Rte 34 B, 13139. (Mail add: PO Box 3, 13139-0003), SAN 312-2794. Tel: 315-364-7975. FAX: 315-364-6704. E-mail: librarian@hazardlibrary.org. Web Site: www.flls.org/poplar/. *Dir,* Lisa Semenza; *Asst Librn,* Linda Shaw Bush
Founded 1887. Pop 1,286; Circ 14,776
Library Holdings: Bk Titles 6,542
Special Collections: Quaker Coll
Subject Interests: Local hist
Automation Activity & Vendor Info: (Cataloging) Innovative Interfaces, Inc; (Circulation) Innovative Interfaces, Inc; (OPAC) Innovative Interfaces, Inc
Wireless access
Mem of Finger Lakes Library System
Open Tues 9-12 & 2-8, Thurs 1-8, Sat 9-2
Friends of the Library Group

PORT BYRON

P PORT BYRON LIBRARY*, 12 Sponable Dr, 13140. (Mail add: PO Box 520, 13140-0520). Tel: 315-776-5694. FAX: 315-776-5693. E-mail: portbyro@twcny.rr.com. Web Site: www.flls.org/portbyron/. *Dir,* Evelyn Taylor; *Asst Dir,* Anna Chappell; Staff 2 (MLS 1, Non-MLS 1)
Pop 2,446
Jul 2009-Jun 2010 Income $818,300. Mats Exp $110,000. Sal $382,500
Library Holdings: AV Mats 140; Bk Titles 15,000
Special Collections: Local History Coll
Automation Activity & Vendor Info: (Cataloging) Horizon; (Circulation) Horizon; (ILL) Horizon; (OPAC) Horizon; (Serials) Horizon
Wireless access
Mem of Finger Lakes Library System
Open Mon, Wed & Fri 3-8, Tues & Thurs 10-6, Sat 10-2
Friends of the Library Group

PORT CHESTER

P PORT CHESTER-RYE BROOK PUBLIC LIBRARY, One Haseco Ave, 10573. SAN 312-2816. Tel: 914-939-6710. Circulation Tel: 914-939-6710, Ext 101. Reference Tel: 914-939-6710, Ext 103, 914-939-6710, Ext 110. FAX: 914-939-4735. Administration FAX: 914-937-2580. Web Site: www.portchester-ryebrooklibrary.org. *Dir,* Robin Lettieri; Tel: 914-939-6710, Ext 114, E-mail: rlettieri@wlsmail.org; *Asst Dir,* Mayra Hernandez; Tel: 914-939-6710, Ext 111; *Ch Serv,* Teresa Cotter; Tel: 914-939-6710, Ext 108; *Ref & Info Serv,* Stacey Harris; *Tech Serv,* Tomasa Rodriguez; Tel: 914-939-6710, Ext 107; Staff 20 (MLS 5, Non-MLS 15)
Founded 1876. Pop 38,314; Circ 263,275
Jun 2012-May 2013 Income $1,486,770, State $12,309, Locally Generated Income $1,342,732, Other $131,682. Mats Exp $61,518, Books $55,114, AV Mat $6,404. Sal $793,456 (Prof $348,312)
Library Holdings: Audiobooks 1,295; AV Mats 12,737; DVDs 2,443; Bk Titles 70,488; Per Subs 1,997
Special Collections: Genealogy, bks & original ms; Job Information Center; Local & County History Coll
Subject Interests: Foreign lang
Automation Activity & Vendor Info: (Acquisitions) SirsiDynix; (Cataloging) SirsiDynix; (Circulation) SirsiDynix; (ILL) SirsiDynix; (OPAC) SirsiDynix; (Serials) SirsiDynix
Wireless access
Function: Adult bk club, Adult literacy prog, After school storytime, AV serv, BA reader (adult literacy), Bilingual assistance for Spanish patrons, Bks on cassette, Bks on CD, Chess club, Children's prog, Citizenship assistance, Computer training, Computers for patron use, Copy machines, e-mail serv, E-Reserves, Electronic databases & coll, Family literacy, For res purposes, Free DVD rentals, Handicapped accessible, Holiday prog, Home delivery & serv to Sr ctr & nursing homes, Homebound delivery serv, ILL available, Mail & tel request accepted, Online cat, Online info literacy tutorials on the web & in blackboard, Online ref, Online searches, Orientations, Outreach serv, OverDrive digital audio bks, Photocopying/Printing, Preschool outreach, Prog for adults, Prog for children & young adult, Ref & res, Ref serv available, Ref serv in person, Senior computer classes, Senior outreach, Serves mentally handicapped consumers, Spoken cassettes & CDs, Spoken cassettes & DVDs, Story hour, Summer reading prog, Tax forms, Teen prog, Telephone ref, Wheelchair accessible, Workshops
Mem of Westchester Library System
Special Services for the Blind - Bks on cassette; Bks on CD
Open Mon 9-9, Tues 9-8, Wed-Sat 9-5
Friends of the Library Group

PORT EWEN

P TOWN OF ESOPUS PUBLIC LIBRARY*, 128 Canal St, 12466. (Mail add: PO Box 1167, 12466-1167), SAN 312-2832. Tel: 845-338-5580. FAX: 845-338-5583. E-mail: esopuslibrary@hvc.rr.com. Web Site: www.esopuslibrary.org. *Dir,* Kelly L Tomaseski; E-mail: gibbersbu@yahoo.com; Staff 1 (MLS 1)
Founded 1922. Pop 9,331; Circ 45,000
Jan 2009-Dec 2009 Income $290,250, State $10,000, City $8,000, Locally Generated Income $231,900, Other $40,000. Sal $400,000 (Prof $110,200)
Library Holdings: Bk Vols 25,000; Per Subs 82
Special Collections: John Burrough Coll
Subject Interests: Art, Cooking, Ecology, Health, Hudson River Valley hist, Local hist
Automation Activity & Vendor Info: (Acquisitions) Innovative Interfaces, Inc; (Cataloging) Innovative Interfaces, Inc; (Circulation) Innovative Interfaces, Inc; (ILL) Innovative Interfaces, Inc; (Media Booking) Innovative Interfaces, Inc; (OPAC) Innovative Interfaces, Inc; (Serials) Innovative Interfaces, Inc
Wireless access
Mem of Mid-Hudson Library System
Special Services for the Deaf - Bks on deafness & sign lang
Special Services for the Blind - Audio mat; Bks available with recordings; Bks on cassette; Bks on CD; Large print bks; Talking bks
Open Mon, Tues & Thurs 10-5:30, Wed 10-8, Fri 10-7, Sat 10-4, Sun (May-Sept) 1-4
Friends of the Library Group

PORT HENRY

P SHERMAN FREE LIBRARY, 20 Church St, 12974. SAN 312-2840. Tel: 518-546-7461. FAX: 518-546-7461. E-mail: flibrar1@nycap.rr.com. Web Site: www.shermanfreelibrary.org. *Libr Dir,* Andrea Ancsi
Founded 1887. Pop 4,978; Circ 7,778
Library Holdings: Bk Vols 10,500; Per Subs 10
Subject Interests: Local hist, Mining
Automation Activity & Vendor Info: (Cataloging) Horizon; (Circulation) Horizon; (ILL) Horizon; (OPAC) Horizon; (Serials) Horizon
Wireless access
Mem of Clinton-Essex-Franklin Library System
Open Tues & Thurs 12-7, Wed 12-4, Fri 12-5, Sat 10-2
Friends of the Library Group

PORT JEFFERSON

P PORT JEFFERSON FREE LIBRARY*, 100 Thompson St, 11777-1897. SAN 312-2867. Tel: 631-473-0022. Administration Tel: 631-473-0631. FAX: 631-473-4765. Administration FAX: 631-473-8661. Web Site: www.portjefflibrary.org. *Libr Dir,* Robert Goykin; *Media Serv,* Earlene O'Hare; E-mail: eohare@suffolk.lib.ny.us; *Ch Serv,* Joann Muscardin; E-mail: jmuscard@suffolk.lib.ny.us; *Ref (Adult Prog),* Robert Konoski; E-mail: rkonoski@aol.com; *Ref,* Robert Maggio; E-mail: rmaggio@suffolk.lib.ny.us; *YA Serv,* Erin Schaarschmidt; E-mail: pjteen@gmail.com; Staff 7 (MLS 7)
Founded 1908. Pop 7,705; Circ 278,000
Library Holdings: Audiobooks 4,655; AV Mats 24,669; CDs 4,023; DVDs 7,683; High Interest/Low Vocabulary Bk Vols 350; Large Print Bks 2,957; Bk Vols 147,143; Per Subs 250; Spec Interest Per Sub 17; Videos 7,477
Special Collections: Long Island History

Automation Activity & Vendor Info: (Cataloging) Innovative Interfaces, Inc; (Circulation) Innovative Interfaces, Inc; (ILL) Innovative Interfaces, Inc; (OPAC) Innovative Interfaces, Inc
Wireless access
Publications: The Yeoman (Newsletter)
Mem of Suffolk Cooperative Library System
Special Services for the Blind - Closed circuit TV magnifier; Reader equip; Talking bks
Open Mon & Wed-Fri 9:30-9, Tues 10-9, Sat 9:30-5, Sun 1-5
Friends of the Library Group

PORT JEFFERSON STATION

P COMSEWOGUE PUBLIC LIBRARY*, 170 Terryville Rd, 11776. SAN 312-2883. Tel: 631-928-1212. FAX: 631-928-6307. Web Site: www.cplib.org. *Dir,* Brandon Pantorno; *Circ,* Elizabeth Washburn; *Ref Serv, Ad,* Susan Guerin; *Ref Serv, Ch,* Carol O'Connell; *Network Serv,* Len Frosina; *Tech Serv,* Dianne Hall
Founded 1966. Pop 22,288; Circ 557,486
Library Holdings: Audiobooks 8,125; CDs 15,117; DVDs 13,555; Bk Vols 156,724; Per Subs 386
Automation Activity & Vendor Info: (Cataloging) Innovative Interfaces, Inc; (Circulation) Innovative Interfaces, Inc; (OPAC) Innovative Interfaces, Inc
Wireless access
Mem of Suffolk Cooperative Library System
Open Mon-Thurs 9:30-9, Fri & Sat 9:30-5, Sun (Oct-May) 12-4

PORT JERVIS

S MINISINK VALLEY HISTORICAL SOCIETY LIBRARY*, 127 W Main St, 12771-1808. (Mail add: PO Box 659, 12771-0659), SAN 325-4607. Tel: 845-856-2375. FAX: 845-856-1049. Web Site: www.minisink.org. *Archives, Exec Dir,* Peter Osborne, III; Staff 1 (MLS 1)
Founded 1889
Library Holdings: Bk Titles 30,000; Bk Vols 31,000
Subject Interests: Genealogy, Local hist
Publications: Newsletter (Quarterly)
Restriction: Open by appt only

P PORT JERVIS FREE LIBRARY*, 138 Pike St, 12771. SAN 312-2891. Tel: 845-856-7313, 845-856-9154. FAX: 845-858-8710. E-mail: pjj@rcls.org. Web Site: www.portjervislibrary.org. *Dir,* Beverly Arlequeeuw; E-mail: barlequeeuw@rcls.org; Staff 18 (MLS 1, Non-MLS 17)
Founded 1892. Pop 18,000; Circ 147,646
Jul 2005-Jun 2006 Income $700,000. Mats Exp $155,000, Books $110,000, Per/Ser (Incl. Access Fees) $5,000, Manu Arch $2,000, Micro $1,500, AV Mat $5,500, Electronic Ref Mat (Incl. Access Fees) $31,000. Sal $366,000
Library Holdings: Bk Titles 46,155; Per Subs 107; Talking Bks 1,201; Videos 2,210
Special Collections: Local Newspaper (115 years of the Port Jervis Union Gazette), microflm; Stephen Crane Materials; Zane Grey Coll
Automation Activity & Vendor Info: (Circulation) SIRSI WorkFlows
Wireless access
Mem of Ramapo Catskill Library System
Open Mon, Tues & Thurs 10-9, Wed & Fri 10-6, Sat 10-5
Friends of the Library Group

PORT LEYDEN

P PORT LEYDEN COMMUNITY LIBRARY*, 3145 Canal St, 13433. (Mail add: PO Box 97, 13433), SAN 312-2913. Tel: 315-348-6077. FAX: 315-348-4234. E-mail: plylib@ncls.org. Web Site: www.portleydenlibrary.org. *Dir,* Lyn Cyr
Founded 1925. Pop 665; Circ 9,402
Library Holdings: Large Print Bks 463; Bk Titles 8,458; Per Subs 20
Automation Activity & Vendor Info: (Cataloging) SirsiDynix; (Circulation) SirsiDynix; (OPAC) SirsiDynix; (Serials) SirsiDynix
Wireless access
Function: Handicapped accessible, Homebound delivery serv, ILL available, Magnifiers for reading, Photocopying/Printing, Prog for children & young adult, Summer reading prog, Wheelchair accessible
Mem of North Country Library System
Open Mon 9-1 & 6-9, Tues & Fri 1-5, Wed 6-9, Sat 10-Noon

PORT WASHINGTON

S NASSAU COUNTY MUSEUM RESEARCH LIBRARY*, Jesse Merritt Memorial Library, Sands Point Preserve, 127 Middleneck Rd, 11050. SAN 311-1458. Tel: 516-571-7901. FAX: 516-571-7909. *In Charge,* Gary Hammond; E-mail: ghammond@nassaucountyny.gov. Subject Specialists: *Long Island hist,* Gary Hammond; Staff 1 (MLS 1)
Founded 1962
Library Holdings: Bk Titles 8,500; Bk Vols 9,000; Per Subs 175
Special Collections: Long Island Maps; Long Island Newspapers, microfilm; Long Island Photographs; Queens County Deeds, microfilm; Queens County Estate Inventories, microfilm; Queens, Nassau & Suffolk Censuses, microfilm; Vertical Files, Arranged by Community, Subject or Biographical. Municipal Document Depository
Subject Interests: Genealogy, Long Island hist, Nassau County hist, Suffolk County
Wireless access
Function: Archival coll, Res libr, Telephone ref
Partic in Long Island Library Resources Council
Restriction: Closed stack, Non-circulating coll, Open to pub by appt only

P PORT WASHINGTON PUBLIC LIBRARY*, One Library Dr, 11050. SAN 312-2921. Tel: 516-883-4400. FAX: 516-883-7927. E-mail: library@pwpl.org. Web Site: www.pwpl.org. *Dir,* Nancy Curtin; *Asst Dir,* Corinne Camarata; E-mail: camarata@pwpl.org; *Adult Serv,* Lee Fertitta; *Ch Serv,* Rachel Fox; *Media Spec,* Jonathan Guildroy; *YA Serv,* Suzanne Ponzini; *Ref Serv,* Janet West
Founded 1892. Pop 29,064; Circ 354,891
Library Holdings: Bk Vols 171,086; Per Subs 474
Special Collections: Long Island Coll; Nautical Center Coll; Sinclair Lewis. Oral History
Automation Activity & Vendor Info: (Circulation) Innovative Interfaces, Inc; (OPAC) Innovative Interfaces, Inc
Wireless access
Publications: Flight of Memory: Long Island's Aeronautical Past; It Looks Like Yesterday to Me: Port Washington's Afro-American Heritage; Particles of the Past: Sandmining on Long Island 1870's-1980's; Workers on the Grand Estates of Long Island 1980's-1940's
Mem of Nassau Library System
Partic in OCLC Online Computer Library Center, Inc
Open Mon-Tues & Thurs-Fri 9-9, Wed 11-9, Sat 9-5 (9-1 Summer), Sun 1-5
Friends of the Library Group

PORTVILLE

P PORTVILLE FREE LIBRARY*, Two N Main St, 14770-9530. (Mail add: PO Box 768, 14770-0768), SAN 312-293X. Tel. 716-933-8441. FAX: 716-933-7020. *Dir,* Charles F Bretzin
Founded 1902. Pop 3,952; Circ 19,712
Jan 2007-Dec 2007 Income $175,596, State $2,500, City $3,000, Other $170,096. Mats Exp $14,336, Books $12,118, Per/Ser (Incl. Access Fees) $1,632, AV Mat $586. Sal $87,569 (Prof $30,000)
Library Holdings: Audiobooks 2,936; DVDs 201; Bk Vols 42,530; Per Subs 89; Videos 515
Special Collections: Dusenbury Coll; Portville Newspaper Coll
Subject Interests: Local hist
Wireless access
Mem of Chautauqua-Cattaraugus Library System
Open Mon & Thurs 1-8, Tues 10-5, Fri 9-5, Sat 10-1
Friends of the Library Group

POTSDAM

C CLARKSON UNIVERSITY LIBRARIES*, Harriet Call Burnap Memorial Library (Main Library), Andrew S Schuler Educational Resources Center, CU Box 5590, Eight Clarkson Ave, 13699-5590. SAN 312-2948. Tel: 315-268-2292. FAX: 315-268-7655. E-mail: refdesk@clarkson.edu. Web Site: libguides.library.clarkson.edu. *Dir of Libr,* Michelle L Young; Tel: 315-268-4268, E-mail: myoung@clarkson.edu; *Coll Mgt Librn,* Gayle C Berry; Tel: 315-268-4452, E-mail: gberry@clarkson.edu; *Ref & Instruction Librn,* Mary K Cabral; Tel: 315-268-4462, E-mail: mcabral@clarkson.edu; *Syst Librn,* Peter J Morris; Tel: 315-268-4459, E-mail: pmorris@clarkson.edu; Staff 7 (MLS 4, Non-MLS 3)
Founded 1896. Enrl 3,339; Fac 214; Highest Degree: Doctorate
Jul 2011-Jun 2012 Income (Main Library Only) $1,406,343. Mats Exp $879,079. Sal $412,021 (Prof $336,972)
Library Holdings: AV Mats 3; CDs 1,496; DVDs 139; e-books 40,177; e-journals 22,059; Microforms 256,647; Bk Vols 264,347; Per Subs 21; Videos 233
Special Collections: US Document Depository
Subject Interests: Bus, Eng, Sci
Automation Activity & Vendor Info: (Acquisitions) Innovative Interfaces, Inc; (Cataloging) Innovative Interfaces, Inc; (Circulation) Innovative Interfaces, Inc; (Course Reserve) Innovative Interfaces, Inc; (ILL) OCLC; (OPAC) Innovative Interfaces, Inc; (Serials) Innovative Interfaces, Inc
Database Vendor: 3M Library Systems, ACM (Association for Computing Machinery), American Chemical Society, American Mathematical Society, American Physical Society, American Psychological Association (APA), Annual Reviews, ASCE Research Library, Elsevier, Gale Cengage Learning, IEEE (Institute of Electrical & Electronics Engineers), Ingenta, IOP, ISI Web of Knowledge, JSTOR, Knovel, LexisNexis, Nature Publishing Group, OCLC, OCLC ArticleFirst, OCLC FirstSearch, OCLC WorldShare Interlibrary Loan, ProQuest, PubMed, RefWorks, Sage,

ScienceDirect, SerialsSolutions, Springshare, LLC, Standard & Poor's, Thomson - Web of Science, Wiley InterScience
Wireless access
Partic in New York State Higher Education Initiative; Northeast Research Libraries Consortium (NERL); Northern New York Library Network; OCLC Online Computer Library Center, Inc; Westchester Academic Library Directors Organization (WALDO)
Special Services for the Blind - Assistive/Adapted tech devices, equip & products; Computer access aids; Copier with enlargement capabilities; Low vision equip; ZoomText magnification & reading software
Open Mon-Thurs 7am-2am, Fri 7-5, Sat 12-8, Sun Noon-2am

Departmental Libraries:

CM HEALTH SCIENCES LIBRARY, Clarkson Hall - 2nd Flr, CU Box 5880, Eight Clarkson Ave, 13699-5880. Tel: 315-268-3760. FAX: 315-268-7655. Web Site: libguides.library.clarkson.edu/content.php?pid=172857&sid=1454685. *Dir of Libr,* Michelle L Young; Tel: 315-268-4268, E-mail: myoung@clarkson.edu; *Health Sci Librn,* Regan DeFranza; E-mail: rdefranz@clarkson.edu; Staff 0.75 (MLS 0.75)
Founded 1999. Enrl 75; Fac 13; Highest Degree: Doctorate
Jul 2011-Jun 2012 Income $48,612. Mats Exp $26,000. Sal $22,612 (Prof $21,112)
Library Holdings: AV Mats 7; CDs 15; e-journals 613; Bk Vols 2,652; Per Subs 24; Videos 179
Automation Activity & Vendor Info: (ILL) Innovative Interfaces, Inc
Database Vendor: Cinahl, DynaMed
Open Mon-Fri 8-4:30

P POTSDAM PUBLIC LIBRARY*, Civic Center, Ste 1, Two Park St, 13676. SAN 312-2956. Tel: 315-265-7230. FAX: 315-268-0306. Web Site: potsdamlibrary.org. *Dir,* Patricia Musante; E-mail: musante@potsdamlibrary.org; Staff 16 (MLS 3, Non-MLS 13)
Founded 1896. Pop 14,736; Circ 134,891
Library Holdings: Bk Vols 60,339; Per Subs 70
Special Collections: Adult Literacy; Employment Information & Micro-Enterprize Coll
Subject Interests: Local hist
Automation Activity & Vendor Info: (OPAC) SirsiDynix
Wireless access
Mem of North Country Library System
Partic in Northern New York Library Network
Open Mon-Thurs 9-8, Fri & Sat 9-5, Sun Noon-5
Friends of the Library Group
Bookmobiles: 3

C STATE UNIVERSITY OF NEW YORK COLLEGE AT POTSDAM*, Frederick W Crumb Memorial Library, 44 Pierrepont Ave, 13676-2294. SAN 353-9342. Tel: 315-267-2485. Interlibrary Loan Service Tel: 315-267-2489. Administration Tel: 315-267-2482. FAX: 315-267-2744. E-mail: libcrumb@potsdam.edu. Web Site: www.potsdam.edu/library. *Dir of Libr Serv,* Jenica P Rogers-Urbanek; Tel: 315-267-3328, E-mail: rogersjp@potsdam.edu; *Archives & Spec Coll Librn,* Jane Subramanian; Tel: 315-267-3326, E-mail: subramjm@potsdam.edu; *Automation Syst Librn,* Marianne Hebert; Tel: 315-267-3308, E-mail: hebertm@potsdam.edu; *Coll Develop Coordr, Syst,* Marianne Hebert; E-mail: hebertm@potsdam.edu; *Govt Doc Coordr,* David Trithart; Tel: 315-267-3311, E-mail: trithadi@potsdam.edu; *Ref Serv Coordr,* Nancy Alzo; Tel: 315-267-3317, E-mail: alzona@potsdam.edu; *Distance Educ,* Holly Chambers; Tel: 315-267-3312, E-mail: chambehe@potsdam.edu; *Info Literacy,* Carol Franck; Tel: 315-267-3310, E-mail: franckcr@potsdam.edu; Staff 11.25 (MLS 9, Non-MLS 2.25)
Founded 1816. Enrl 4,445; Fac 345; Highest Degree: Master
Library Holdings: AV Mats 1,805; Bk Titles 238,473; Per Subs 499
Special Collections: College Archives; St Lawrence Seaway (Bertrand H Snell Papers). State Document Depository; US Document Depository
Subject Interests: Educ
Partic in Northern New York Library Network; Nylink; SUNYConnect
Special Services for the Blind - Assistive/Adapted tech devices, equip & products
Open Mon-Thurs 7:45am-11pm, Fri 7:45-6, Sat 10-6, Sun Noon-11
Restriction: Open to pub for ref & circ; with some limitations

Departmental Libraries:

JULIA E CRANE MEMORIAL LIBRARY, Crane School of Music, 44 Pierrepont Ave, 13676-2294, SAN 353-9377. Tel: 315-267-2451. *Music Librn,* Edward Komara; Tel: 315-267-3227, Fax: 315-267-3115, E-mail: komaraem@potsdam.edu; Staff 3 (MLS 1, Non-MLS 2)
Founded 1927. Enrl 620; Fac 70; Highest Degree: Master
Library Holdings: AV Mats 10,792; Music Scores 19,907; Bk Titles 11,103; Per Subs 45
Subject Interests: Music, Music scores, Sound rec

POUGHKEEPSIE

J DUTCHESS COMMUNITY COLLEGE LIBRARY*, Francis U & Mary F Ritz Library, 53 Pendell Rd, 12601-1595. SAN 312-2964. Tel: 845-431-8630. Circulation Tel: 845-431-8639. Interlibrary Loan Service Tel: 845-431-8636. Reference Tel: 845-431-8634. FAX: 845-431-8995. Web Site: www.sunydutchess.edu/library. *Dir,* Barbara Liesenbein; Tel: 845-431-8635, E-mail: liesenbe@sunydutchess.edu; *Bibliog Instr, Ref,* Ron Crovisier; Tel: 845-431-8642, E-mail: crovisie@sunydutchess.edu; *ILL,* Christine Craig; E-mail: craig@sunydutchess.edu; *Tech Serv,* Alice McGovern; Tel: 845-431-8640, E-mail: mcgovern@sunydutchess.edu; Staff 7 (MLS 7)
Founded 1957. Enrl 7,700; Fac 119; Highest Degree: Associate
Library Holdings: Bk Titles 76,394; Bk Vols 83,457; Per Subs 312
Automation Activity & Vendor Info: (Cataloging) Ex Libris Group; (Circulation) Ex Libris Group; (ILL) OCLC; (OPAC) Ex Libris Group
Database Vendor: Gale Cengage Learning, ProQuest, Westlaw
Wireless access
Publications: Periodical List (Annual)
Partic in Southeastern New York Library Resources Council
Open Mon-Thurs 8am-9pm, Fri 8-5, Sat 11-3
Restriction: Circ limited

S DUTCHESS COUNTY GENEALOGICAL SOCIETY LIBRARY*, 204 Spackenkill Rd, 12603-5135. (Mail add: PO Box 708, 12602-0708), SAN 370-2316. Tel: 845-462-4168. Web Site: www.dcgs-gen.org. *Librn,* Mary Colbert
Founded 1972
Jul 2013-Jun 2014 Income $700. Mats Exp $500
Library Holdings: Bk Titles 900; Spec Interest Per Sub 6
Subject Interests: Genealogy, Heraldry, Hist
Wireless access
Function: Res libr
Publications: The Dutchess (Quarterly)
Open Tues 9-2 & 5-9, Wed 7pm-9pm, Thurs 9-Noon
Restriction: Not a lending libr, Pub use on premises

P LA GRANGE ASSOCIATION LIBRARY, 488 Freedom Plains Rd, Ste 109, 12603. SAN 376-5849. Tel: 845-452-3141. FAX: 845-452-1974. E-mail: lagrangelibrary@laglib.org. Web Site: www.laglib.org. *Dir,* Sarah Potwin
Library Holdings: Bk Vols 77,000
Automation Activity & Vendor Info: (Cataloging) Innovative Interfaces, Inc; (Circulation) Innovative Interfaces, Inc; (OPAC) Innovative Interfaces, Inc; (Serials) Innovative Interfaces, Inc
Wireless access
Mem of Mid-Hudson Library System
Open Mon & Wed 9:30-8, Tues & Thurs 9:30-5, Fri 2-8, Sat 9:30-2
Friends of the Library Group

C MARIST COLLEGE*, James A Cannavino Library, 3399 North Rd, 12601-1387. SAN 312-3014. Tel: 845-575-3199. FAX: 845-575-3150. Web Site: library.marist.edu. *Libr Dir,* Verne Newton; E-mail: verne.newton@marist.edu; *Assoc Dir,* Mark Colvson; E-mail: mark.colvson@marist.edu; *Head, Acq,* Judy Diffenderfer; E-mail: judy.diffenderfer@marist.edu; *Head, Archives & Spec Coll,* John Ansley; E-mail: john.ansley@marist.edu; *Head, Automation,* Kathryn Silberger; E-mail: kathryn.silberger@marist.edu; *Head, Instruction & Extn Serv,* Ruth Boetcker; E-mail: ruth.boetcker@marist.edu; *Head, Cat,* Marta Cwik; E-mail: marta.cwik@marist.edu; *Pub Serv Coordr,* Elena Filchagina; E-mail: elena.filchagina@marist.edu; Staff 10 (MLS 9, Non-MLS 1)
Founded 1929. Enrl 5,218; Fac 232; Highest Degree: Master
Jul 2009-Jun 2010 Income $1,753,035. Mats Exp $676,405
Library Holdings: AV Mats 5,939; e-books 56,747; e-journals 31,316; Bk Vols 240,500
Special Collections: Hudson River Environmental Society Coll; John Tillman Newscasts; Lowell Thomas Coll; Maristiana; Rick Whitsell R&B Rec Coll
Subject Interests: Hudson Valley Regional studies
Automation Activity & Vendor Info: (Acquisitions) Ex Libris Group; (Cataloging) Ex Libris Group; (Circulation) Ex Libris Group; (Course Reserve) Ex Libris Group; (ILL) OCLC ILLiad; (OPAC) Ex Libris Group
Database Vendor: ACM (Association for Computing Machinery), American Chemical Society, American Psychological Association (APA), ARTstor, Bloomberg, CQ Press, ebrary, EBSCOhost, Gale Cengage Learning, H W Wilson, JSTOR, LexisNexis, OCLC WorldShare Interlibrary Loan, Project MUSE, ProQuest, Sage, SBRnet (Sports Business Research Network), ScienceDirect, Standard & Poor's, Westlaw
Wireless access
Partic in Southeastern New York Library Resources Council; Westchester Academic Library Directors Organization (WALDO)

S MENTAL HEALTH AMERICA LIBRARY*, 230 North Rd, 12601. SAN 312-2980. Tel: 845-486-2896. FAX: 845-486-2897. E-mail: mhadclib@senylrc.org. *Librn,* Janet Caruso; Staff 2 (MLS 1, Non-MLS 1)
Founded 1969
Library Holdings: Bk Titles 2,500; Per Subs 40
Subject Interests: Alcoholism, Child psychiat, Child study, Drug abuse, Psychiat, Psychol, Psychotherapy
Wireless access
Publications: Accessions List; Audio-Visual Catalog; Brochure
Partic in Southeastern New York Library Resources Council
Open Mon, Wed, Thurs & Fri 9-5, Tues 11-2:30

P MID-HUDSON LIBRARY SYSTEM*, 103 Market St, 12601-4098. SAN 312-3022. Tel: 845-471-6060. Interlibrary Loan Service Tel: 845-471-6060, Ext 224. Information Services Tel: 845-471-6060, Ext 239. FAX: 845-454-5940. Web Site: www.midhudson.org. *Exec Dir,* Tom Sloan; E-mail: tsloan@midhudson.org; Staff 26 (MLS 4, Non-MLS 22)
Founded 1959. Pop 650,704
Library Holdings: Bk Vols 2,294,554
Automation Activity & Vendor Info: (Cataloging) Innovative Interfaces, Inc; (Circulation) Innovative Interfaces, Inc; (OPAC) Innovative Interfaces, Inc
Publications: Mid-Hudson Library System (Weekly Bulletin); Multi-Media Catalog; Newsletter (Quarterly); NYSAVE
Member Libraries: Alice Curtis Desmond & Hamilton Fish Library; Amenia Free Library; Beekman Library; Blodgett Memorial Library; Brewster Public Library; Cairo Public Library; Catskill Public Library; Chatham Public Library; Claverack Free Library; Clinton Community Library; D R Evarts Library; Dover Plains Library; East Fishkill Public Library District; Elting Memorial Library; Germantown Library; Greenville Public Library; Grinnell Library; Heermance Memorial Library; Highland Public Library; Howland Public Library; Hudson Area Library; Hunter Public Library; Hurley Library District; Hyde Park Free Library; Julia L Butterfield Memorial Library; Kent Public Library; Kinderhook Memorial Library; Kingston Library; La Grange Association Library; Livingston Free Library; Mahopac Public Library; Marlboro Free Library; Millbrook Free Library; Morton Memorial Library; Morton Memorial Library & Community House; Mountain Top Library; New Lebanon Library; North Chatham Free Library; NorthEast-Millerton Library; Olive Free Library Association; Patterson Library; Pawling Free Library; Philmont Public Library; Phoenicia Library; Pine Plains Free Library; Plattekill Public Library; Pleasant Valley Free Library; Poughkeepsie Public Library District; Putnam Valley Free Library; Red Hook Public Library; Reed Memorial Library; Roeliff Jansen Community Library Association, Inc; Rosendale Library; Sarah Hull Hallock Free Library; Saugerties Public Library; Staatsburg Library; Stanford Free Library; Starr Library; Stone Ridge Public Library; Tivoli Free Library; Town of Esopus Public Library; Town of Ulster Public Library; Valatie Free Library; West Hurley Public Library; Windham Public Library; Woodstock Library
Partic in Southeastern New York Library Resources Council
Open Mon-Fri 8:30-4:30

GL NEW YORK STATE SUPREME COURT*, Law Library, Family Court House, Ninth Judicial District, 50 Market St, 12601-3203. SAN 312-3030. Tel: 845 431-1859. *In Charge,* Karen Boback
Founded 1904
Library Holdings: Bk Titles 15,000
Special Collections: Legal Reference Material
Subject Interests: Law
Database Vendor: LexisNexis
Wireless access
Open Mon-Fri 9-1 & 2-5

P POUGHKEEPSIE PUBLIC LIBRARY DISTRICT, Adriance Memorial Library, 93 Market St, 12601. SAN 353-9407. Tel: 845-485-3445. Circulation Tel: 845-485-3445, Ext 3701. Reference Tel: 845-485-3445, Ext 3702. Administration Tel: 845-485-3445, Ext 3306. FAX: 845-485-3789. E-mail: info@poklib.org. Web Site: www.poklib.org. *Libr Dir,* Thomas A Lawrence; E-mail: tlawrence@poklib.org; *Asst Dir,* Janet Huen; Tel: 845-485-3445, Ext 3308, E-mail: jhuen@poklib.org; *Asst Dir,* Lauren Muffs; Tel: 845-485-3445, Ext 3310, E-mail: lmuffs@poklib.org; *Head, Ref & Adult Serv,* Deborah Weltsch; E-mail: dweltsch@poklib.org; *Head, Youth Serv,* Nicole Guenkel; Tel: 845-485-3445, Ext 3320, E-mail: nguenkel@poklib.org; *Bus Mgr,* Barbara Lynch; E-mail: blynch@poklib.org; *Network Adminr,* Bruce Sullivan; E-mail: bsullivan@poklib.org; Staff 62 (MLS 18, Non-MLS 44)
Founded 1841. Pop 73,500
Library Holdings: Bk Vols 180,000; Per Subs 460
Special Collections: Foundation Center
Subject Interests: Genealogy, Local hist
Automation Activity & Vendor Info: (Acquisitions) Innovative Interfaces, Inc; (Cataloging) Innovative Interfaces, Inc; (Circulation) Innovative Interfaces, Inc; (ILL) Innovative Interfaces, Inc; (OPAC) Innovative Interfaces, Inc
Database Vendor: Gale Cengage Learning, OCLC FirstSearch, ProQuest, TLC (The Library Corporation)
Wireless access
Mem of Mid-Hudson Library System
Partic in Southeastern New York Library Resources Council
Open Mon-Thurs 9-9, Fri & Sat 9-5, Sun 2-5
Friends of the Library Group
Branches: 1
ARLINGTON, 504 Haight Ave, 12603, SAN 353-9466. Tel: 845-485-3445. FAX: 845-454-9308. *Asst Dir,* Lauren Muffs; Tel: 845-485-3445, Ext 3310, E-mail: lmuffs@poklib.org
Library Holdings: Bk Titles 10,800; Bk Vols 11,100
Open Mon, Wed & Fri 9-8, Tues, Thurs & Sat 9-5

M SAINT FRANCIS HOSPITAL*, Health Science Library, 241 North Rd, 12601. SAN 320-7234. Tel: 845-431-8132. FAX: 845-485-2964. *Librn,* Valerie C Roberts
Library Holdings: Bk Titles 1,200; Per Subs 158
Subject Interests: Allied health prof, Med, Orthopedics
Partic in BRS; Long Island Library Resources Council; NY Libr Res Coun
Open Mon-Fri 8-4:30

M VASSAR BROTHERS MEDICAL CENTER, Medical Library, 45 Reade Pl, 12601. SAN 312-3049. Tel: 845-437-3121. FAX: 845-437-3002. E-mail: vbmclibrary@health-quest.org. Web Site: vbmc.libguides.com/library. *Mgr, Libr Serv,* Mary Jo Russell; E-mail: mrussell2@health-quest.org; Staff 2 (MLS 1, Non-MLS 1)
Founded 1951
Library Holdings: e-books 250; e-journals 300; Electronic Media & Resources 24; Bk Titles 100; Per Subs 15
Special Collections: Medical Center Archives
Subject Interests: Cardiology, Internal med, Nursing, Oncology, Pediatrics, Surgery
Automation Activity & Vendor Info: (OPAC) LibLime; (Serials) OVID Technologies
Database Vendor: Cinahl, OCLC FirstSearch, OVID Technologies, PubMed
Wireless access
Function: 24/7 Electronic res, 24/7 Online cat, Archival coll, Computers for patron use, Electronic databases & coll, Ref serv available, Res libr
Partic in Basic Health Sciences Library Network; Health Info Librs of Westchester (HILOW); National Network of Libraries of Medicine Middle Atlantic Region; Southeastern New York Library Resources Council
Special Services for the Deaf - Assistive tech
Restriction: Badge access after hrs, Hospital employees & physicians only, Non circulating coll, Not a lending libr, Open to pub by appt only

C VASSAR COLLEGE LIBRARY*, 124 Raymond Ave, Maildrop 20, 12604-0020. SAN 312-3057. Tel: 845-437-5760. FAX: 845-437-5864. Web Site: library.vassar.edu. *Dir Gen, Publ Br,* Sabrina L Pape; Tel: 845-437-5787, E-mail: sapape@vassar.edu; *Asst Dir, Spec Coll, Outreach Prog,* Ronald Patkus; *Assoc Dir, Tech Serv,* Joan Pirie; *Head, Reader Serv,* Barbara Durniak; *Coll Develop Librn,* Debra Bucher; *Monographs Tech Serv Librn,* Emily Ray; *Music Librn,* Sarah Canino; *Ref Librn,* Kathleen Kurosman; *Ref Librn,* Gretchen Lieb; *Ref Librn,* Carol Lynn Marshall; *Ref Librn, Sci Librn,* Flora Grabowska; *Spec Coll Librn,* Laura Finkel; *Govt Doc, Tech Serv Librn,* Christine Fitchett; *Visual Res Librn,* Sarah Goldstein; Staff 18 (MLS 15, Non-MLS 3)
Founded 1861. Enrl 2,414; Fac 246; Highest Degree: Bachelor
Library Holdings: Bk Vols 890,304
Special Collections: College History & Archives; Early Atlases & Maps; Elizabeth Bishop Papers; Incunabula; John Burroughs Journals; Mark Twain Coll, mss; Mary McCarthy Papers; Robert Owens Coll; Ruth Benedict Papers; Village Press; Women, bks, mss. State Document Depository; US Document Depository
Automation Activity & Vendor Info: (Acquisitions) Innovative Interfaces, Inc; (Cataloging) Innovative Interfaces, Inc; (Circulation) Innovative Interfaces, Inc; (Course Reserve) Docutek; (ILL) Innovative Interfaces, Inc; (Media Booking) Innovative Interfaces, Inc; (OPAC) Innovative Interfaces, Inc; (Serials) Innovative Interfaces, Inc
Partic in Southeastern New York Library Resources Council
Departmental Libraries:
ART LIBRARY, 124 Raymon Ave, 12604-0022, SAN 321-4230. Tel: 845-437-5790. Web Site: artlibrary.vassar.edu/. *Librn,* Thomas E Hill; E-mail: thill@vassar.edu
GEORGE SHERMAN DICKINSON MUSIC LIBRARY, 12604-0038, SAN 320-0507. Tel: 845-437-7492. FAX: 845-437-7335. E-mail: musiclib@vassar.edu. Web Site: musiclibrary.vassar.edu. *Music Librn,* Sarah Canino
Library Holdings: Music Scores 30,000; Bk Vols 20,000
Restriction: Open to pub by appt only

POUND RIDGE

P POUND RIDGE LIBRARY*, Hiram Halle Memorial Library, 271 Westchester Ave, 10576-1714. SAN 312-3065. Tel: 914-764-5085. FAX: 914-764-5319. Web Site: www.poundridgelibrary.org. *Dir,* Marilyn Tinter; E-mail: mtinter@wlsmail.org
Founded 1953. Pop 4,700; Circ 74,484
Library Holdings: Bk Vols 57,152; Per Subs 98
Special Collections: Art; Phonograph Records
Automation Activity & Vendor Info: (Cataloging) SirsiDynix; (Circulation) SirsiDynix; (OPAC) SirsiDynix
Wireless access
Mem of Westchester Library System
Open Tues & Thurs 10-8, Wed, Fri & Sat 10-5 (10-1 May-Sept)

PRATTSBURGH

P PRATTSBURGH LIBRARY*, 26 Main St, 14873. (Mail add: PO Box 426, 14873-0426), SAN 376-6969. Tel: 607-522-3490. FAX: 607-522-3490. Web Site: www.stls.org/prattsburg. *Dir,* Kathy Plate; E-mail: platek@stls.org; Staff 1 (Non-MLS 1)
Founded 1981. Pop 2,000; Circ 6,200
Library Holdings: Bk Vols 8,533
Automation Activity & Vendor Info: (Circulation) SirsiDynix; (OPAC) SirsiDynix
Mem of Southern Tier Library System
Open Tues 1-5, Wed 12-7, Thurs 9-5, Fri 11:30-2:30, Sat 9-1

PROSPECT

P PROSPECT FREE LIBRARY*, 915 Trenton Falls St, 13435. (Mail add: PO Box 177, 13435-0177), SAN 376-3080. Tel: 315-896-2736. FAX: 315-896-4045. E-mail: prospect@midyork.org. *Dir,* Betsy Mack
Pop 300
Library Holdings: Bk Vols 8,000; Per Subs 40
Wireless access
Mem of Mid-York Library System
Special Services for the Blind - Bks on cassette
Open Mon (Nov-May) 4-7, Tues 2-7, Wed & Sat 10-12, Thurs 2-8; Mon (June-Oct) 4-9, Tues & Thurs 4:30-9, Wed 10-12 & 7-9, Fri 1-3, Sat 10-12

PULASKI

P PULASKI PUBLIC LIBRARY, 4917 N Jefferson St, 13142. SAN 312-3073. Tel: 315-298-2717. FAX: 315-298-2717. E-mail: pullib@ncls.org. Web Site: www.pulaskinypubliclibrary.org. *Dir,* Margaret Weigel
Circ 22,189
Library Holdings: Bk Vols 22,000; Per Subs 35
Automation Activity & Vendor Info: (Cataloging) SIRSI Unicorn; (Circulation) SIRSI WorkFlows; (OPAC) SIRSI Unicorn
Wireless access
Mem of North Country Library System
Special Services for the Blind - Bks & mags in Braille, on rec, tape & cassette
Open Mon, Wed & Fri 9-5, Tues & Thurs 9-7, Sat 9-1
Friends of the Library Group

PULTENEY

P PULTENEY FREE LIBRARY, 9226 Rte 74, 14874. (Mail add: PO Box 215, 14874-0215), SAN 312-3081. Tel: 607-868-3652. FAX: 607-868-3652. Web Site: pulteney.org. *Dir,* Barbara Radiganb; E-mail: radiganb@stls.org
Founded 1881. Pop 1,274; Circ 8,760
Library Holdings: Audiobooks 313; DVDs 550; Bk Titles 13,500; Per Subs 13
Automation Activity & Vendor Info: (Circulation) SirsiDynix; (OPAC) SirsiDynix
Wireless access
Mem of Southern Tier Library System
Special Services for the Deaf - Bks on deafness & sign lang; High interest/low vocabulary bks
Special Services for the Blind - Large print bks
Open Tues & Thurs 12-8, Wed 12-6, Sat 9-1

PURCHASE

C MANHATTANVILLE COLLEGE LIBRARY*, 2900 Purchase St, 10577. SAN 312-309X. Tel: 914-323-5207. Reference Tel: 914-323-5282. Information Services Tel: 914-323-5275. FAX: 914-323-8139. E-mail: library@mville.edu. Web Site: www.mville.edu/library. *Dir,* Position Currently Open; *Actg Dir,* Jeff Rosedale; Tel: 914-323-5277, E-mail: jeff.rosedale@mville.edu; *Head, Coll Serv,* Mary Elizabeth Schaub; E-mail: maryelizabeth.schaub@mville.edu; *Head, Pub Serv,* Position Currently Open; *Acad Tech Librn,* Catherine Medeot; Tel: 914-323-5424, E-mail: catherine.medeot@mville.edu; *Digital Serv Librn,* Christina Ostroff; Tel: 914-323-5385, E-mail: christina.ostroff@mville.edu; *Educ Librn, Learning Res Coordr,* Lynda Hanley; Tel: 914-323-5314, E-mail: lynda.hanley@mville.edu; *Fac Librn,* Maureen Kindilien; Tel: 914-323-3132, E-mail: maureen.kindilien@mville.edu; *Spec Coll Librn,* Lauren Ziarko; Tel: 914-323-5422, E-mail: lauren.ziarko@mville.edu; *Admin & Outreach Coordr,* Elaine Provenzano; *Coordr, Info Literacy,* Paula Moskowitz; Tel: 914-323-3159, E-mail: paula.moskowitz@mville.edu; *Digital Serv Coordr,* Kevin Sullivan; Tel: 914-323-5453, E-mail: kevin.sullivan@mville.edu. Subject Specialists: *Art hist,* Catherine Medeot; *Educ,* Lynda Hanley; *Bus, Econ,* Maureen Kindilien; *English, Music, Rare bks,* Elaine Provenzano; *Students with disabilities,* Paula Moskowitz; Staff 17.5 (MLS 10.5, Non-MLS 7)
Founded 1841. Fac 92; Highest Degree: Master
Library Holdings: Bk Titles 183,576; Bk Vols 238,700; Per Subs 1,010
Special Collections: Alexander Stephens Letters; Allain Biography; Buddhism & Hinduism (Zigmund Cerbu Coll)
Subject Interests: Archit, Art, Asian studies, Biog, Educ, Music
Automation Activity & Vendor Info: (Acquisitions) Ex Libris Group; (Cataloging) Ex Libris Group; (Circulation) Ex Libris Group; (Course Reserve) Docutek; (ILL) OCLC Online; (OPAC) Ex Libris Group; (Serials) SerialsSolutions
Database Vendor: 3M Library Systems, ABC-CLIO, ACM (Association for Computing Machinery), American Mathematical Society, American Psychological Association (APA), ARTstor, Baker & Taylor, BioOne, Blackwell, Cambridge Scientific Abstracts, Children's Literature Comprehensive Database Company (CLCD), CIOS (Communication Institute for Online Scholarship), CQ Press, Dun & Bradstreet, EBSCOhost, Elsevier, Emerald, Ex Libris Group, Factiva.com, Facts on File, Gale Cengage Learning, Greenwood Publishing Group, Grolier Online, IEEE (Institute of Electrical & Electronics Engineers), JSTOR, LexisNexis, Newsbank, OCLC FirstSearch, OVID Technologies, ProQuest, RefWorks, SerialsSolutions, Swets Information Services, TLC (The Library Corporation), Wilson - Wilson Web, YBP Library Services
Wireless access
Partic in Metropolitan New York Library Council; New York State Higher Education Initiative; OCLC Online Computer Library Center, Inc; Westchester Academic Library Directors Organization (WALDO)
Special Services for the Blind - Computer with voice synthesizer for visually impaired persons
Friends of the Library Group

P PURCHASE FREE LIBRARY*, 3093 Purchase St, 10577. SAN 312-3103. Tel: 914-948-0550. FAX: 914-328-3405. *Dir,* Anne Collins; Staff 5 (MLS 1, Non-MLS 4)
Founded 1928. Pop 3,480; Circ 31,649
Library Holdings: Bk Titles 11,700; Per Subs 32
Subject Interests: Bus mat, Local hist
Automation Activity & Vendor Info: (Acquisitions) SirsiDynix; (Circulation) SirsiDynix; (ILL) SirsiDynix
Wireless access
Mem of Westchester Library System
Open Mon-Fri 9:30-5:30, Sat 10:30-3:30
Friends of the Library Group

C STATE UNIVERSITY OF NEW YORK, Purchase College Library, 735 Anderson Hill Rd, 10577-1400. SAN 312-3111. Tel: 914-251-6400. Circulation Tel: 914-251-6401. Interlibrary Loan Service Tel: 914-251-6428. Reference Tel: 914-251-6410. Administration Tel: 914-251-6435. FAX: 914-251-6437. E-mail: lib.reference@purchase.edu. Web Site: www.purchase.edu/library. *Dir,* Patrick F Callahan; Tel: 914-251-6436, E-mail: patrick.callahan@purchase.edu; *Dir, Teaching, Learning & Tech Ctr,* Keith Landa; Tel: 914-251-6450, E-mail: keith.landa@purchase.edu; *Head, Access Serv, Performing Arts Librn,* Mark Smith; Tel: 914-251-6431, E-mail: mark.smith@purchase.edu; *Head, Instrul Serv,* Rebecca Oling; Tel: 914-251-6417, E-mail: rebecca.oling@purchase.edu; *Head, Ref,* Leah Massar Bloom; Tel: 914-251-6413, E-mail: leah.massar@purchase.edu; *Art Librn,* Kimberly Detterbeck; Tel: 914-251-6406, E-mail: kimberly.detterbeck@purchase.edu; *Digital Serv Librn,* Susanne Markgren; Tel: 914-251-6415, E-mail: susanne.markgren@purchase.edu; *Ref & Instruction Librn,* Darcy Gervasio; Tel: 914-251-6423, E-mail: darcy.gervasio@purchase.edu; *Ref Librn & Stacks Mgr,* Joseph Swatski; Tel: 914-251-6411, E-mail: joseph.swatski@purchase.edu; *Res Sharing Librn,* Carrie Marten; E-mail: carrie.marten@purchase.edu. Subject Specialists: *Asian studies, Hist, Journalism,* Patrick F Callahan; *Biol, Instrul tech,* Keith Landa; *Dance, Music, Theatre,* Mark Smith; *Film, Jewish studies, Lit,* Rebecca Oling; *Econ, Nat sci, Polit sci,* Leah Massar Bloom; *Art hist, Design, Visual arts,* Kimberly Detterbeck; *Computer sci, Math,* Susanne Markgren; *Anthrop, Gender studies, Sociol,* Darcy Gervasio; *Archives,* Joseph Swatski; *Philos,* Carrie Marten; Staff 22.5 (MLS 8.5, Non-MLS 14)
Founded 1967. Enrl 4,006; Fac 150; Highest Degree: Master
Jul 2013-Jun 2014. Mats Exp $359,439, Books $58,850, Per/Ser (Incl. Access Fees) $19,791, AV Mat $14,456, Electronic Ref Mat (Incl. Access Fees) $268,342. Sal $1,386,605

Library Holdings: DVDs 6,465; e-journals 73,615; Bk Vols 237,674; Per Subs 128
Special Collections: US Document Depository
Subject Interests: Art, Film, Music, Theatre
Automation Activity & Vendor Info: (Cataloging) Ex Libris Group; (Circulation) Ex Libris Group; (ILL) OCLC ILLiad; (OPAC) Ex Libris Group; (Serials) Ex Libris Group
Database Vendor: ABC-CLIO, Alexander Street Press, American Mathematical Society, American Psychological Association (APA), ARTstor, CredoReference, EBSCOhost, Elsevier, Ex Libris Group, Gale Cengage Learning, JSTOR, LexisNexis, OCLC WorldShare Interlibrary Loan, Project MUSE, ProQuest, RefWorks, ScienceDirect, Springshare, LLC, YBP Library Services
Wireless access
Function: Art exhibits, Computers for patron use, Copy machines, e mail & chat, Electronic databases & coll, Handicapped accessible, ILL available, Online cat, Pub access computers, Ref serv in person, Scanner, Telephone ref
Partic in Metropolitan New York Library Council; SUNYConnect; Westchester Academic Library Directors Organization (WALDO)
Special Services for the Blind - Assistive/Adapted tech devices, equip & products; Computer with voice synthesizer for visually impaired persons; Low vision equip; Reader equip
Open Mon-Thurs 8am-2am, Fri 8am-10pm, Sat 10-8, Sun 12pm-2am
Friends of the Library Group

PUTNAM VALLEY

P PUTNAM VALLEY FREE LIBRARY*, 30 Oscawana Lake Rd, 10579. SAN 312-312X. Tel: 845-528-3242. FAX: 845-528-3297. Web Site: www.putnamvalleylibrary.org. *Dir,* Kathleen McLaughlin
Founded 1936. Circ 60,060
Library Holdings: AV Mats 4,516; Bk Vols 41,298
Special Collections: Fine Arts (Harry N Abrams Coll)
Automation Activity & Vendor Info: (Cataloging) Innovative Interfaces, Inc - Millenium; (Circulation) Innovative Interfaces, Inc - Millenium; (OPAC) Innovative Interfaces, Inc - Millenium
Wireless access
Mem of Mid-Hudson Library System
Open Mon 10-6, Tues & Wed 10-8, Thurs & Fri 10-5, Sat 10-4, Sun 1-5

QUEENS

C ST JOHN'S UNIVERSITY LIBRARY*, St Augustine Hall, 8000 Utopia Pkwy, 11439. SAN 352-7700. Tel: 718-990-6201. Circulation Tel: 718-990-6850. Interlibrary Loan Service Tel: 718-990-6441. Reference Tel: 718-990-6727. E-mail: eservices@stjohns.edu. Web Site: www.stjohns.edu. *Dean of Libr,* Theresa Maylone; Tel: 718-990-2517, Fax: 718-990-2044, E-mail: maylonet@stjohns.edu; *Dir, Coll & Info Mgt,* Andrew Sankowski; Tel: 718-990-6712, Fax: 718-990-5938, E-mail: sankowsa@stjohns.edu; *Assoc Univ Librn, Coll & Access, Univ Archivist,* Blythe Roveland-Brenton; Tel: 718-990-6734, E-mail: rovelanb@stjohns.edu; *Head, Ref,* Lucy Heckman; Tel: 718-990-6571, E-mail: heckmanl@stjohns.edu; *Circ Supvr,* Marilyn Narson; Tel: 718-990-6202, Fax: 718-990-8090, E-mail: narsonm@stjohns.edu; *Syst Coordr,* Shilpa Karnik; Tel: 718-990-5819, E-mail: karniks@stjohns.edu; *Info Mgt,* Cynthia Chambers; Tel: 718-990-1355, Fax: 718-990-5938, E-mail: chambers@stjohns.edu; *Ser Mgt,* Tian Zhang; Tel: 718 990 5082, Fax: 718-990-5938, E-mail: zhangt@stjohns.edu; *Libr Develop,* Joan D'Andrea; Tel: 718-990-6054, E-mail: dandreaj@stjohns.edu; Staff 23 (MLS 23)
Founded 1870. Enrl 21,082; Fac 663; Highest Degree: Doctorate
Library Holdings: e-books 310,062; e-journals 70,533; Bk Titles 240,530; Bk Vols 374,415; Per Subs 1,671
Special Collections: Alfred Politz Papers (1942-83); American Friends of Irish Neutrality Records (1938-41); American League for an Undivided Ireland Records (1947-63); Art Exhibition Catalogs; Asian Art Coll; Chin Ying Asian Library; Edward Carofano Apothecary Jar Coll; Joseph C Meyer Accounting Coll; Paul O'Dwyer Coll; Rare & Limited Edition Books; Saul Heller Shorthand Coll; Sen James L Buckley Papers (1970-71); University Archives; Wm M Fischer Lawn Tennis Coll. Oral History
Subject Interests: Humanities, Pharm, Relig studies, Sciences, Soc sci
Automation Activity & Vendor Info: (Acquisitions) LibLime; (Cataloging) LibLime; (Circulation) LibLime; (Course Reserve) LibLime; (ILL) LibLime; (Media Booking) LibLime; (OPAC) LibLime; (Serials) LibLime
Wireless access
Publications: Campus Guides; Library Guides
Partic in Metropolitan New York Library Council
Friends of the Library Group
Departmental Libraries:
KATHRYN & SHELBY CULLOM DAVIS LIBRARY, 101 Murray St, New York, 10007. Tel: 212-277-5135. FAX: 212-277-5140. E-mail: davislibrary@stjohns.edu. Web Site: www.stjohns.edu/academics/libraries/campus/davis. *Cataloger & Acq, Dir,* Ismael Rivera-Sierra; Tel: 212-277-5137, E-mail: riverasi@stjohns.edu; *Head, Digital Info Serv & ILL,* Richard Waller; Tel: 212-277-5136, E-mail: wallerr@stjohns.edu; *Tech Serv/Ref Librn,* Galina Spicehandler; E-mail: spicehag@stjohns.edu. Subject Specialists: *Actuarial sci, Ins, Risk mgt,* Ismael Rivera-Sierra; Staff 4 (MLS 3, Non-MLS 1)
Founded 1901. Enrl 400; Fac 8; Highest Degree: Master
Library Holdings: Bk Vols 125,000; Per Subs 290
Special Collections: Actuarial Science; American Academy of Insurance Medicine, rec, 1889 to present; Automatic Fire Sprinkler Coll (19th Century to present); Children's Risks Coll; Disaster Images Coll; Fire Marks; Insurance (1569 to present); Insurance Company Signages (19th Century to present); Insurance Policies (17th Century to present); Risk Management - Disasters & Hazards. US Document Depository
Subject Interests: Actuarial sci, Ins, Risk mgt
Automation Activity & Vendor Info: (Acquisitions) Horizon; (Cataloging) Horizon; (Circulation) Horizon; (Course Reserve) Horizon; (ILL) OCLC; (OPAC) Horizon; (Serials) Horizon
Database Vendor: Bloomberg, EBSCO Information Services, EBSCOhost, Factset, MITINET, Inc, Progressive Technology Federal Systems, Inc (PTFS), SirsiDynix, Standard & Poor's, WebClarity Software Inc
Function: Archival coll, For res purposes, ILL available, Res libr, Web-catalog
Restriction: Access for corporate affiliates, Authorized patrons, Authorized scholars by appt, Borrowing privileges limited to fac & registered students, Borrowing requests are handled by ILL, Circ to mem only, External users must contact libr, Not open to pub, Open to fac, students & qualified researchers, Open to qualified scholars
LORETTO MEMORIAL
See Separate Entry in Staten Island

CL RITTENBERG LAW LIBRARY, 8000 Utopia Pkwy, 11439. SAN 352-776X. Tel: 718-990-1896. Circulation Tel: 718-990-1580. Reference Tel: 718-990-6651. FAX: 718-990-6649. Circulation FAX: 718-990-6649. Reference FAX: 718-990-6649. Web Site: lawlibrary.stjohns.edu. *Assoc Dean for Libr & Tech Serv,* Martin Cerjan; Tel: 718-990-1578, E-mail: cerjanm@stjohns.edu; *Dir, Tech Serv,* Joseph Hinger; Tel: 718-990-1582, E-mail: hingerj@stjohns.edu; *Asst Dir, Tech Serv,* Allan Ryan; Tel: 718-990-5074, E-mail: ryana@stjohns.edu; *Circ Librn,* Astrid Emel; Tel: 718-990-6826, E-mail: emela@stjohns.edu; *Ref/Govt Coll Librn,* Rosemary LaSala; Tel: 718-990-1896, E-mail: lasalar@stjohns.edu; *Tech Asst II,* Samantha Jialal; Tel: 718-990-8258, E-mail: jialalk@stjohns.edu; *Tech Asst III,* Jeff Munoz; Tel: 718-990-6660, E-mail: munozj@stjohns.edu
Founded 1925. Highest Degree: Master
Library Holdings: Bk Titles 344,440; Bk Vols 379,456; Per Subs 14,277
Special Collections: State Document Depository; UN Document Depository; US Document Depository
Automation Activity & Vendor Info: (Acquisitions) Innovative Interfaces, Inc; (Cataloging) Innovative Interfaces, Inc; (Circulation) Innovative Interfaces, Inc; (Course Reserve) Innovative Interfaces, Inc; (ILL) Innovative Interfaces, Inc; (Media Booking) Innovative Interfaces, Inc; (OPAC) Innovative Interfaces, Inc; (Serials) Innovative Interfaces, Inc
Database Vendor: HeinOnline, LexisNexis, Westlaw

QUEENSBURY

J ADIRONDACK COMMUNITY COLLEGE LIBRARY*, Scoville Learning Center, 640 Bay Rd, 12804. SAN 311-2462. Tel: 518-743-2260. FAX: 518-745-1442. E-mail: librarian@sunyacc.edu. Web Site: www.sunyacc.edu. *Chair, Dir,* Teresa Ronning; Tel: 518-743-2200, Ext 2261, E-mail: ronningt@sunyacc.edu; *Instrul Serv Librn, Ref,* Joyce Miller; Tel: 518-743-2200, Ext 2485, E-mail: millerja@sunyacc.edu; *Media Spec,* David Ofiara; Tel: 518-743-2200, Ext 2484, E-mail: ofiarad@sunyacc.edu; Staff 11 (MLS 7, Non-MLS 4)
Founded 1961. Enrl 2,400; Fac 100; Highest Degree: Associate
Library Holdings: e-books 5,700; e-journals 10,570; Bk Titles 51,400; Bk Vols 5,900; Per Subs 370
Special Collections: Local History (Hill Coll)
Subject Interests: Criminal justice, Liberal arts, Nursing
Automation Activity & Vendor Info: (Cataloging) Ex Libris Group; (Circulation) Ex Libris Group; (Course Reserve) Ex Libris Group; (ILL) OCLC ILLiad; (OPAC) Ex Libris Group
Database Vendor: ARTstor, Baker & Taylor, CQ Press, CredoReference, EBSCOhost, Elsevier, Ex Libris Group, Facts on File, Faulkner Information Services, Gale Cengage Learning, H W Wilson, JSTOR, OCLC FirstSearch, OCLC WorldShare Interlibrary Loan, ProQuest, ScienceDirect, SerialsSolutions, Westlaw, Wilson - Wilson Web
Wireless access
Function: ILL available, Telephone ref
Publications: Subject Pathfinders (Research guide)

Partic in Cap District Libr Coun for Ref & Res Resources; OCLC Online Computer Library Center, Inc
Open Mon-Thurs 8-8, Fri 8-4, Sat 9-1, Sun 5pm-9pm

QUOGUE

P QUOGUE LIBRARY*, 90 Quogue St, 11959. (Mail add: PO Box 5036, 11959-5036), SAN 312-3138. Tel: 631-653-4224. FAX: 631-653-6151. E-mail: quoguelibrary@gmail.com. Web Site: www.quoguelibrary.org. *Dir,* Christine Clifton; E-mail: cclifton@suffolk.lib.ny.us; Staff 1 (MLS 1)
Founded 1897. Circ 40,689
Library Holdings: Audiobooks 672; DVDs 2,718; e-books 9,733; Bk Vols 29,795; Per Subs 50
Wireless access
Mem of Suffolk Cooperative Library System
Partic in Partnership of Automated Librs in Suffolk
Special Services for the Blind - Large print bks & talking machines
Open Sun & Mon 12-5, Tues & Thurs 10-8, Wed, Fri & Sat 10-5

RANDOLPH

P RANDOLPH FREE LIBRARY*, 26 Jamestown St, 14772. SAN 312-3146. Tel: 716-358-3712. FAX: 716-358-2039. E-mail: randolphfreelibrary@windstream.net. Web Site: www.cclslib.org/randolph. *Librn,* Ellen Beck; Staff 1 (Non-MLS 1)
Founded 1909. Pop 1,393; Circ 32,719
Library Holdings: Bk Titles 20,350; Bk Vols 22,700; Per Subs 40
Special Collections: Garden Club Coll, bks, pamphlets & per; Local Newspaper 1876-1979, micro. State Document Depository; UN Document Depository; US Document Depository
Subject Interests: Antiques, Local genealogy
Wireless access
Mem of Chautauqua-Cattaraugus Library System
Open Mon, Tues & Thurs 1-9, Wed 7-9, Fri & Sat 10-5

RANSOMVILLE

P RANSOMVILLE FREE LIBRARY*, 3733 Ransomville Rd, 14131. SAN 312-3154. Tel: 716-791-4073. FAX: 716-791-4073. Web Site: ran.nioga.org. *Dir,* Phila Ibaugh
Circ 32,714
Library Holdings: Bk Vols 25,000; Per Subs 75
Wireless access
Mem of Nioga Library System
Open Mon & Wed 2-8, Tue & Thurs 10-8, Sat 2-5
Friends of the Library Group

RAQUETTE LAKE

P RAQUETTE LAKE FREE LIBRARY*, One Dillon Rd, 13436. (Mail add: PO Box 129, 13436-0129), SAN 312-3162. Tel: 315-354-4005. FAX: 315-354-4005. Web Site: www.sals.edu. *Librn,* Carolynn Dufft
Pop 125; Circ 11,280
Library Holdings: Bk Vols 9,400; Per Subs 50
Special Collections: Adirondack Region
Subject Interests: Adirondack hist
Automation Activity & Vendor Info: (Cataloging) Innovative Interfaces, Inc; (Circulation) Innovative Interfaces, Inc; (OPAC) Innovative Interfaces, Inc; (Serials) Innovative Interfaces, Inc
Wireless access
Publications: Winter Newsletter
Mem of Southern Adirondack Library System
Open Mon (Winter) 4:30-7:30, Tues 1-8:30, Thurs 12-6, Sat 3-5; Mon (Summer) 2-8, Tues 10-6, Thurs 11-7, Sat & Sun 11-3

RAVENA

P RCS COMMUNITY LIBRARY*, 95 Main St, 12143. SAN 312-3170. Tel: 518-756-2053. FAX: 518-756-8595. E-mail: info@rcscommunitylibrary.org. Web Site: www.rcscommunitylibrary.org. *Dir,* Judith Felsten; *Circ Mgr,* Carol Melewski; *Ch Serv, Coll Develop,* Barbara Goetschius; *Tech Serv,* Bryan L Rowzee; Staff 4 (MLS 3, Non-MLS 1)
Founded 1994. Pop 14,505; Circ 56,000
Special Collections: Hudson River Valley Coll
Automation Activity & Vendor Info: (Cataloging) SirsiDynix; (Circulation) SirsiDynix; (ILL) SirsiDynix; (OPAC) SirsiDynix
Wireless access
Publications: Newsletter
Mem of Upper Hudson Library System
Open Mon-Thurs 10-8:30, Fri & Sat 10-5
Friends of the Library Group

RAY BROOK

S ADIRONDACK CORRECTIONAL FACILITY LIBRARY*, PO Box 110, 12977-0110. SAN 327-1749. Tel: 518-891-1343. FAX: 518-891-1343. *Sr Librn,* Suzanne Orlando; Staff 1 (MLS 1)
Library Holdings: High Interest/Low Vocabulary Bk Vols 12; Bk Vols 6,000; Per Subs 37
Subject Interests: Spanish lang
Automation Activity & Vendor Info: (Cataloging) Follett Software; (Circulation) Follett Software; (OPAC) Follett Software
Open Mon-Fri 7-3

S RAY BROOK FEDERAL CORRECTIONAL INSTITUTION LIBRARY*, 128 Ray Brook Rd, 12977. (Mail add: PO Box 300, 12977-0300). Tel: 518-897-4167. FAX: 518-897-4220. *Librn,* Kathy Snyder
Library Holdings: Bk Vols 6,000
Special Collections: Britannica of the Western World
Wireless access
Open Mon-Thurs 7:30am-8:30pm, Fri & Sat 7:30-3:30

RED CREEK

P RED CREEK FREE LIBRARY*, 6817 Main St, 13143. (Mail add: PO Box 360, 13143-0360), SAN 312-3189. Tel: 315-754-6679. FAX: 315-754-6679. *Dir,* Allen Tompkins
Pop 5,600; Circ 32,000
Library Holdings: Bk Vols 8,000
Subject Interests: Children's bks, Local hist
Automation Activity & Vendor Info: (Cataloging) SirsiDynix; (Circulation) SirsiDynix; (OPAC) SirsiDynix; (Serials) SirsiDynix
Wireless access
Mem of Pioneer Library System
Open Mon & Fri 10-12 & 1-6, Tues & Thurs 1-6, Wed 10-12 & 1-7

RED HOOK

P RED HOOK PUBLIC LIBRARY*, 7444 S Broadway, 12571. SAN 312-3197. Tel: 845-758-3241. E-mail: director@redhooklibrary.org. Web Site: www.redhooklibrary.org. *Libr Dir,* Erica Freudenberger
Founded 1898. Pop 1,903; Circ 71,366
Jan 2011-Dec 2011 Income $172,414, State $2,414, City $145,000, Other $25,000. Mats Exp $26,450, Books $20,650, AV Mat $5,800. Sal $114,000 (Prof $38,000)
Library Holdings: Audiobooks 1,090; DVDs 711; e-books 1,576; Bk Titles 15,860
Wireless access
Function: Adult bk club, Audiobks via web, Bk club(s), Bks on cassette, Bks on CD, Children's prog, Computers for patron use, Copy machines, e-mail serv, Electronic databases & coll, Free DVD rentals, Handicapped accessible, Homebound delivery serv, ILL available, Mail & tel request accepted, Music CDs, Online cat, Online searches, Outreach serv, Outside serv via phone, mail, e-mail & web, Prog for adults, Prog for children & young adult, Pub access computers, Ref serv available, Spoken cassettes & CDs, Spoken cassettes & DVDs, Story hour, Summer reading prog, Tax forms, Teen prog, VHS videos, Wheelchair accessible, Workshops
Publications: Octagon (Newsletter)
Mem of Mid-Hudson Library System
Special Services for the Deaf - Bks on deafness & sign lang; Staff with knowledge of sign lang
Open Mon-Fri 10-7, Sat 10-4
Friends of the Library Group

REMSEN

P DIDYMUS THOMAS LIBRARY*, 9639 Main St, 13438. (Mail add: PO Box 410, 13438-0410), SAN 312-3200. Tel: 315-831-5651. FAX: 315-831-5651. E-mail: remsen@midyork.org. Web Site: www.didymusthomaslibrary.cnynorthcountry.com. *Dir,* Linda Horn; E-mail: lhorn@midyork.org
Founded 1899. Pop 531; Circ 9,141
Library Holdings: AV Mats 391; Bk Titles 12,914; Per Subs 37
Automation Activity & Vendor Info: (Cataloging) SirsiDynix; (Circulation) SirsiDynix
Wireless access
Publications: History of Remsen, by Millard Roberts
Mem of Mid-York Library System
Open Mon 1-5, Tues & Thurs 2-6, Wed & Fri 2-5, Sat 10-12

RENSSELAER

M HEALTHCARE ASSOCIATION OF NEW YORK STATE*, Lillian R Hayt Memorial Library, One Empire Dr, 12144. SAN 310-7558. Tel: 518-431-7600. FAX: 518-431-7812. *In Charge,* Lynne Donnelly; Tel: 518-431-7834; Staff 1 (MLS 1)
Founded 1965
Library Holdings: Bk Titles 2,000; Per Subs 150

Subject Interests: Econ, Finance, Planning
Automation Activity & Vendor Info: (Cataloging) LibraryWorld, Inc
Wireless access
Function: Res libr
Partic in Capital District Library Council
Restriction: Employees & their associates

P RENSSELAER PUBLIC LIBRARY*, 676 East St, 12144. SAN 312-3227. Tel: 518-462-1193. FAX: 518-462-2819. *Libr Dir,* Jane Chirgwin; Staff 3 (MLS 1, Non-MLS 2)
Founded 1920. Pop 9,047; Circ 20,619
Library Holdings: Bk Vols 20,000; Per Subs 20
Wireless access
Function: Fax serv, Free DVD rentals, Music CDs, Online cat, OverDrive digital audio bks, Prog for children & young adult, Pub access computers, Tax forms
Mem of Upper Hudson Library System
Partic in OCLC Online Computer Library Center, Inc
Open Tues & Fri 10-5, Wed & Thurs 10-8, Sat 11-2
Friends of the Library Group

RENSSELAERVILLE

P RENSSELAERVILLE LIBRARY*, 1459 County Rte 351, 12147. (Mail add: PO Box 188, 12147-0188), SAN 312-3251. Tel: 518-797-3949. FAX: 518-797-5211. Web Site: rensselaervillelibrary.org. *Dir,* Kimberly Graff; E-mail: director@rensselaervillelibrary.org; *Assoc Librn,* Katie Caprio; Staff 5 (MLS 1, Non-MLS 4)
Founded 1896. Pop 2,000; Circ 12,482
Library Holdings: Bk Vols 23,123; Per Subs 44
Automation Activity & Vendor Info: (Circulation) Horizon; (OPAC) Horizon
Wireless access
Mem of Upper Hudson Library System
Open Tues & Wed 10-12 & 4-9, Thurs & Fri 4-9, Sat 9-1
Friends of the Library Group

RHINEBECK

P CLINTON COMMUNITY LIBRARY, 1215 Centre Rd, 12572. Tel: 845-266-5530. FAX: 845-266-5748. E-mail: clintonlib1215@gmail.com. Web Site: www.clinton.lib.ny.us. *Dir,* Alice Graves; Staff 4 (MLS 1, Non-MLS 3)
Founded 1965
Library Holdings: Bk Titles 12,000; Per Subs 18
Special Collections: Local History, Alice & Martin Provensen (Clinton Coll), Illustrators, Local authors
Automation Activity & Vendor Info: (Cataloging) Innovative Interfaces, Inc; (Circulation) Innovative Interfaces, Inc; (OPAC) Innovative Interfaces, Inc
Wireless access
Function: Digital talking bks, Doc delivery serv, Handicapped accessible, ILL available, Orientations, Photocopying/Printing, Prog for adults, Prog for children & young adult, Ref serv available, Spoken cassettes & CDs, Summer reading prog, VHS videos
Mem of Mid-Hudson Library System
Open Mon, Tues & Thurs 9-5, Fri 12-8, Sat 9-1

P STARR LIBRARY*, 68 W Market St, 12572. SAN 312-3278. Tel: 845-876-4030. FAX: 845-876-4030. E-mail: starrdirector@me.com. Web Site: starrlibrary.org. *Dir,* Steven Cook; *Asst Librn,* David Wanzer; *Ch,* Brooke Stevens; Staff 5 (MLS 1, Non-MLS 4)
Founded 1862. Pop 7,762; Circ 90,000
Library Holdings: Bk Vols 35,000
Special Collections: Franklin D Roosevelt Coll; Large Print Coll; Local History (DAR Coll); Rare Book Coll
Automation Activity & Vendor Info: (Cataloging) Innovative Interfaces, Inc - Millenium; (Circulation) Innovative Interfaces, Inc - Millenium; (OPAC) Innovative Interfaces, Inc - Millenium
Wireless access
Function: Adult bk club, Archival coll, Art exhibits, Audiobks via web, Bk club(s), Bks on cassette, Bks on CD, Children's prog, Computers for patron use, Copy machines, Electronic databases & coll, Fax serv, Handicapped accessible, ILL available, Music CDs, Newsp ref libr, Online cat, Online searches, Photocopying/Printing, Prog for adults, Prog for children & young adult, Spoken cassettes & CDs, Teen prog, VHS videos, Web-catalog, Wheelchair accessible, Workshops
Mem of Mid-Hudson Library System
Open Mon & Fri 10-5, Tues-Thurs 10-7, Sat 10-4, Sun 1-4
Friends of the Library Group

RHINECLIFF

P MORTON MEMORIAL LIBRARY & COMMUNITY HOUSE*, 82 Kelly St, 12574. (Mail add: PO Box 157, 12574-0157), SAN 312-3286. Tel: 845-876-2903. FAX: 845-876-1584. E-mail: mortonrhinecliff@gmail.com. Web Site: morton.rhinecliff.lib.ny.us. *Librn,* Joanne A Meyer
Circ 7,643
Library Holdings: Bk Vols 7,600; Per Subs 20
Automation Activity & Vendor Info: (Cataloging) Innovative Interfaces, Inc; (Circulation) Innovative Interfaces, Inc; (OPAC) Innovative Interfaces, Inc
Wireless access
Mem of Mid-Hudson Library System
Open Tues 2:30-6, Wed 2:30-7:30, Thurs & Fri 10-12:30 & 2:30-5:30, Sat 10-12:30
Friends of the Library Group

RICHBURG

P COLONIAL LIBRARY*, 160 Main St, 14774. SAN 312-3294. Tel: 585-928-2694. FAX: 585-928-2694. *Librn,* Judy Johnson; E-mail: johnsonj@stls.org
Founded 1913. Pop 1,200
Library Holdings: Bk Titles 19,250; Per Subs 25
Automation Activity & Vendor Info: (Cataloging) SirsiDynix; (Circulation) SirsiDynix; (OPAC) SirsiDynix
Wireless access
Mem of Southern Tier Library System
Open Mon & Thurs 9-5, Tues 3-7

RICHFIELD SPRINGS

P RICHFIELD SPRINGS PUBLIC LIBRARY*, 102 Main St, 13439. (Mail add: PO Box 1650, 13439-1650), SAN 312-3308. Tel: 315-858-0230. FAX: 315-858-0230. E-mail: rs.ill@4cls.org. Web Site: www.4cls.org. *Librn,* Alice Mahardy; *Asst Librn,* Joyce Urtz
Founded 1909. Pop 1,561; Circ 22,362
Library Holdings: Bk Vols 15,000; Per Subs 63
Special Collections: Microfilm Coll of RS Mercury 1867-1972, (incl Summer Daily 1888-1917)
Wireless access
Mem of Four County Library System
Open Mon & Thurs 11:30-4:30 & 7-9, Tues, Wed & Fri 11:30-4:30

RICHVILLE

P RICHVILLE FREE LIBRARY, 87 Main St, 13681-3102. (Mail add: PO Box 42, 13681-0042), SAN 312-3316. Tel: 315-287-1481. FAX: 315-287-0956. E-mail: riclib@ncls.org. Web Site: www.richvillefreelibrary.org. *Dir,* Lila M Youngs; Staff 0.2 (Non-MLS 0.2)
Founded 1926. Pop 500; Circ 3,500
Jan 2008-Dec 2008 Income $11,000
Library Holdings: DVDs 18; Large Print Bks 124; Bk Vols 5,000; Per Subs 30; Talking Bks 38; Videos 200
Special Collections: Adirondack Mountains; St Lawrence County Topographical Maps
Wireless access
Function: Audio & video playback equip for onsite use, Bks on cassette, Bks on CD, Children's prog, Computer training, Computers for patron use, Copy machines, e-mail & chat, Fax serv, Free DVD rentals, Genealogy discussion group, Holiday prog, ILL available, Instruction & testing, Literacy & newcomer serv, Online cat, Photocopying/Printing, Prog for children & young adult, Scanner, Summer reading prog, Tax forms, VHS videos, Wheelchair accessible
Mem of North Country Library System
Open Mon-Wed 6pm-8pm, Thurs 10-1, Fri 6pm-9pm
Friends of the Library Group

RIPLEY

P RIPLEY FREE LIBRARY, 64 W Main St, 14775. (Mail add: PO Box 808, 14775-0808), SAN 312-3324. Tel: 716-736-3913. FAX: 716-736-3923. E-mail: riplylib@fairpoint.net. *Dir,* Rhonda Thompson
Founded 1938. Pop 2,460; Circ 29,600
Library Holdings: Bk Titles 10,430; Bk Vols 10,573; Per Subs 47
Wireless access
Mem of Chautauqua-Cattaraugus Library System
Open Mon & Fri 10-5, Tues & Thurs 10-7:30, Sat 9-2
Friends of the Library Group

RIVERDALE

C MANHATTAN COLLEGE, Mary Alice & Tom O'Malley Library, 4513 Manhattan College Pkwy, 10471. SAN 351-9244. Tel: 718-862-7166, 718-862-7743. FAX: 718-862-8028. Web Site: lib.manhattan.edu. *Exec Dir,* Dr William H Walters; E-mail: william.walters@manhattan.edu; *Asst Dir,*

Dr Catherine M Shanley; E-mail: catherine.shanley@manhattan.edu; *Info Serv Librn,* Sarah Cohn; E-mail: sarah.cohn@manhattan.edu; *Info Serv Librn,* Bernadette M Lopez-Fitzsimmons; E-mail: bernadette.lopez@manhattan.edu; *Access Serv,* Amy Handfield; E-mail: amy.handfield@manhattan.edu; *Archivist,* Amy Surak; E-mail: amy.surak@manhattan.edu; *Cat,* Maire Duchon; E-mail: maire.duchon@manhattan.edu; *Electronic Res,* Stacy Pober; E-mail: stacy.pober@manhattan.edu; *ILL,* John C Gormley; E-mail: john.gormley@manhattan.edu; Staff 9 (MLS 8, Non-MLS 1)
Founded 1853. Enrl 3,500; Highest Degree: Master
Special Collections: American Culture (Library of American Civilization), micro; English Literature (Library of English Literature), micro; Lydia Cabrera Coll (Spanish)
Automation Activity & Vendor Info: (Cataloging) ByWater Solutions; (Circulation) ByWater Solutions; (Course Reserve) ByWater Solutions; (ILL) OCLC; (OPAC) ByWater Solutions; (Serials) OCLC
Wireless access
Partic in Metropolitan New York Library Council; Oberlin Group; OCLC Online Computer Library Center, Inc; Westchester Academic Library Directors Organization (WALDO)
Restriction: Authorized personnel only

RIVERHEAD

M PECONIC BAY MEDICAL CENTER*, Medical Library, 1300 Roanoke Ave, 11901-2058. SAN 312-3332. Tel: 631-548-6000. FAX: 631-727-0772. E-mail: info@pbmedicalcenter.org. Web Site: www.peconicbaymedicalcenter.org. *Coordr,* Lisa Squicciarini
Founded 1973
Library Holdings: Bk Titles 850; Per Subs 85
Restriction: Staff use only

P RIVERHEAD FREE LIBRARY*, 330 Court St, 11901-2885. SAN 312-3340. Tel: 631-727-3228. FAX: 631-727-4762. Web Site: www.riverheadlibrary.org. *Dir,* Lisa Jacobs; E-mail: director@riverheadlibrary.org; *Head, Ch,* Laurie Harrison; E-mail: lhharris@suffolk.lib.ny.us; *Head, Circ,* Elizabeth Stokes; E-mail: estokes@suffolk.lib.ny.us; *Head, Tech Serv,* Elva Zeichner; E-mail: evictori@suffolk.lib.ny.us; *Ch,* Karen DeLisa; *Ch,* Linda Nelson; *Outreach Serv Librn, YA Serv,* Laura LaSita; E-mail: llasita@suffolk.lib.ny.us; *Ref Librn,* Mary Lee Gaylor; *Ref Librn,* James Provencher; *Adult Prog Coordr,* Nancy Whitt; E-mail: nwhitt@suffolk.lib.ny.us; *Ref Coordr,* Susan Bergmann; E-mail: bergmann@suffolk.lib.ny.us; *Tech Coordr,* Sean Myrden; E-mail: smyrden@suffolk.lib.ny.us; Staff 60 (MLS 10, Non-MLS 50)
Founded 1896. Pop 32,270; Circ 322,875
Library Holdings: AV Mats 18,318; Bk Vols 165,522; Per Subs 334
Special Collections: Long Island Coll; Tanger Wellness Coll
Automation Activity & Vendor Info: (Cataloging) Innovative Interfaces, Inc; (Circulation) Innovative Interfaces, Inc; (Course Reserve) Innovative Interfaces, Inc; (OPAC) Innovative Interfaces, Inc
Database Vendor: American Physical Society, Bowker, CredoReference, EBSCOhost, Gale Cengage Learning, Greenwood Publishing Group, Grolier Online, infoUSA, ReferenceUSA, TumbleBookLibrary, Wilson - Wilson Web, World Book Online
Wireless access
Function: Adult bk club, After school storytime, Art exhibits, Audiobks via web, Bk club(s), Bks on cassette, Bks on CD, CD-ROM, Children's prog, Computer training, Computers for patron use, Copy machines, Digital talking bks, e-mail serv, E-Reserves, Electronic databases & coll, Free DVD rentals, Handicapped accessible, Health sci info serv, Home delivery & serv to Sr ctr & nursing homes, Homebound delivery serv, Homework prog, ILL available, Magnifiers for reading, Mail & tel request accepted, Music CDs, Notary serv, Online cat, Online ref, Online searches, OverDrive digital audio bks, Photocopying/Printing, Preschool outreach, Prog for adults, Prog for children & young adult, Ref serv available, Senior computer classes, Summer reading prog, Tax forms, Teen prog, Telephone ref, VHS videos, Wheelchair accessible
Publications: Newsletter
Mem of Suffolk Cooperative Library System
Open Mon-Fri 9-9, Sat 9-5, Sun (Oct-April) 1-5
Friends of the Library Group

J SUFFOLK COUNTY COMMUNITY COLLEGE*, Eastern Campus Library, 121 Speonk Riverhead Rd, 11901-9990. SAN 320-8907. Tel: 631-548-2536. FAX: 631-369-2641. Web Site: depthome.sunysuffolk.edu/library/index.asp. *Head Librn,* Dana Antonucci-Durgan; Tel: 631-548-2540, E-mail: antonud@sunysuffolk.edu; *Coll Develop, Info Literacy,* Dr Penny J Bealle; Tel: 631-548-2541, E-mail: beallep@sunysuffolk.edu; *Info Literacy/Ref,* Johanna M MacKay; Tel: 631-548-2569, E-mail: mackayj@sunysuffolk.edu; *Media Serv,* Susan Wood; Tel: 631-548-2544, E-mail: woods@sunysuffolk.edu. Subject Specialists: *Art hist,* Dr Penny J Bealle; *English as a second lang,* Johanna M MacKay; Staff 12 (MLS 7, Non-MLS 5)
Founded 1977. Enrl 3,937; Fac 85; Highest Degree: Associate
Sept 2012-Aug 2013. Mats Exp $61,900, Books $23,000, Per/Ser (Incl. Access Fees) $30,000, AV Equip $7,000, AV Mat $1,500, Presv $400
Library Holdings: AV Mats 300; High Interest/Low Vocabulary Bk Vols 75; Bk Titles 36,001; Bk Vols 37,542; Per Subs 200
Subject Interests: Culinary, Graphic design
Wireless access
Function: Handicapped accessible
Partic in Information Delivery Services Project (IDS); New York State Interlibrary Loan Network (NYSILL); OCLC-LVIS
Open Mon-Thurs 8am-9:15pm, Fri 8-5, Sat 10:30-4:30

S SUFFOLK COUNTY HISTORICAL SOCIETY LIBRARY, 300 W Main St, 11901-2894. SAN 312-3359. Tel: 631-727-2881, Ext 103. FAX: 631-727-3467. E-mail: librarian@schs-museum.org. Web Site: www.suffolkcountyhistoricalsociety.org. *Librn,* Edward Smith, III; *Asst Librn,* Wendy Polhemus-Annibell
Founded 1886
Library Holdings: Bk Titles 9,400; Bk Vols 15,400; Per Subs 16
Special Collections: Daughters of the Revolution of 1776 Membership Records; Deeds; Federal & State Censuses, microfilm; Fullerton Coll; Long Island History Coll; Military Coll; Shipwreck Coll; Suffolk County History, biographies, diaries, genealogies, maps, newsp, per, photogs, etc; The Talmage Weaving Coll; Towns & Wills Coll
Subject Interests: Agr, Genealogy, General Long Island mat, Specifically Suffolk County events, Specifically Suffolk County people
Wireless access
Publications: Booklist; Index of the Munsell; Register (Quarterly)
Open Wed-Sat 12:30-4:30

ROCHESTER

SR ALDERSGATE UNITED METHODIST CHURCH LIBRARY*, 4115 Dewey Ave, 14616. SAN 327-0157. Tel: 585-663-3665. FAX: 585-865-8442. *Librn,* Frances Crabtree; *Librn,* Shirley Tschorke; *Librn,* Helen Wolter
Library Holdings: Bk Vols 3,300

R ASBURY FIRST UNITED METHODIST CHURCH LIBRARY*, 1050 East Ave, 14607. SAN 312-3375. Tel: 585-271-1050. FAX: 585-271-3743. *Librn,* Sharon Crouch
Library Holdings: Bk Vols 2,500
Wireless access

R BETHANY PRESBYTERIAN CHURCH LIBRARY*, 3000 Dewey Ave, 14616. SAN 312-3391. Tel: 585-663-3000. FAX: 585-663-5325. *Librn,* Judy Dick; *Coordr,* Betty Joyce
Founded 1958
Jan 2005-Dec 2005 Income $700, Parent Institution $300, Other $400. Mats Exp $300
Library Holdings: AV Mats 157; High Interest/Low Vocabulary Bk Vols 581; Large Print Bks 17; Bk Titles 1,760; Bk Vols 1,828
Automation Activity & Vendor Info: (Cataloging) JayWil Software Development, Inc
Restriction: Restricted pub use

P BRIGHTON MEMORIAL LIBRARY*, 2300 Elmwood Ave, 14618. SAN 312-3405. Tel: 585-784-5300. FAX: 585-784-5333. TDD: 585 784 5302. E-mail: brirefl@libraryweb.org. Web Site: www.brightonlibrary.org. *Exec Dir,* Jennifer Ries-Taggart; *Access Serv, YA Serv,* Deena Lipomi; *Adult Serv,* Lynne Fretz; *Ch Serv, Prog Coordr,* Tonia Burton; *Media Spec,* Jennifer Lenio; *Network Serv, Ref,* Mathew Bashore; Staff 12 (MLS 12)
Founded 1953. Pop 35,588; Circ 517,147
Library Holdings: Bk Vols 111,482
Subject Interests: Brighton local hist, Judaica
Automation Activity & Vendor Info: (Acquisitions) TLC (The Library Corporation); (Circulation) TLC (The Library Corporation); (OPAC) TLC (The Library Corporation); (Serials) TLC (The Library Corporation)
Wireless access
Mem of Monroe County Library System
Special Services for the Deaf - TDD equip
Special Services for the Blind - Reader equip; Screen reader software; ZoomText magnification & reading software
Open Mon-Thurs 10-9, Fri 10-6, Sat 10-4, Sun 1-4
Friends of the Library Group

P CHILI PUBLIC LIBRARY*, 3333 Chili Ave, 14624-5494. SAN 311-0478. Tel: 585-889-2200. FAX: 585-889-5819. Web Site: www.chililibrary.org. *Dir,* Jeff Baker; E-mail: jbaker@libraryweb.org; *Ch Serv,* Jennifer Lindsey; *Ref,* Jeanne Austin; *Ref,* Richard Gagnier; *Teen Serv,* Cathy Kyle
Founded 1962. Pop 27,000; Circ 350,000
Library Holdings: Bk Titles 84,620; Bk Vols 85,948; Per Subs 198; Videos 4,328
Subject Interests: Local hist

Automation Activity & Vendor Info: (Circulation) TLC (The Library Corporation)
Mem of Monroe County Library System
Open Mon-Thurs 9-9, Fri & Sat 9-5, Sun 1-4
Friends of the Library Group

SR CHRIST EPISCOPAL CHURCH*, Christ Church Library, 141 East Ave, 14604. SAN 323-8474. Tel: 585-454-3878. FAX: 585-730-5646. E-mail: office@christchurchrochester.org. Web Site: www.christchurchrochester.org.
Library Holdings: Bk Titles 1,200; Per Subs 33
Subject Interests: Relig
Open Mon-Fri 8:30-2:30

CR COLGATE ROCHESTER CROZER DIVINITY SCHOOL*, Ambrose Swasey Library, 1100 S Goodman St, 14620-2592. SAN 312-3421. Tel: 585-340-9602. Web Site: www.crcds.edu/AmbroseSwaseyLibrary.asp. *Dir,* Marge Nead
Founded 1817. Enrl 120; Fac 21; Highest Degree: Doctorate
Library Holdings: Bk Vols 40,000; Per Subs 103
Special Collections: Bible Coll; Church History
Subject Interests: Behav sci, Relig studies, Soc sci
Automation Activity & Vendor Info: (Cataloging) Ex Libris Group; (Circulation) Ex Libris Group; (Course Reserve) Ex Libris Group; (ILL) OCLC; (OPAC) Ex Libris Group; (Serials) Ex Libris Group
Partic in Rochester Regional Library Council
Open Mon-Fri (Winter) 9-8, Sat 10-1; Mon-Thurs (Summer) 9-4

J EVEREST INSTITUTE*, Betty Cronk Memorial Library, 1630 Portland Ave, 14621. SAN 312-3715. Tel: 585-266-0430, Ext 108. FAX: 585-266-8243. Web Site: www.everestinstitute.com. *Dir,* Kyle E Daniels; E-mail: kdaniels@cci.edu; *Asst Dir,* Lynn Beh-Zahn, Staff 1 (MLS 1)
Founded 1925
Library Holdings: Bk Titles 6,200; Per Subs 35
Special Collections: Annual Report Coll, bklet; College Catalog Coll; Rochester Business Institute School Catalogs Coll, 1860 to date
Subject Interests: Bus admin, Computer sci, Med asst, Mkt, Paralegal, Rochester Bus Inst sch hist
Wireless access
Publications: Library Brochure
Partic in Rochester Regional Library Council
Open Mon-Thurs 8:30-7, Fri 9-2

P GATES PUBLIC LIBRARY*, 902 Elmgrove Rd, 14624. SAN 353-9881. Tel: 585-247-6446. FAX: 585-426-5733. Web Site: www.gateslibrary.org. *Libr Dir,* Greg Benoit; *Adult Serv,* Paula Blackburn; *Ch Serv,* Mary Jo Smith; *Internet Serv,* Cathy Carstens; *Media Spec,* Melissa McHenry; *Spec Projects, Tech Serv,* Susan Saylor; *YA Serv,* Heidi Jung; Staff 45 (MLS 7, Non-MLS 38)
Founded 1960. Pop 29,275; Circ 403,055
Jan 2006-Dec 2006 Income $1,208,422. Mats Exp $145,011. Sal $676,491 (Prof $290,384)
Library Holdings: AV Mats 16,867; Bk Vols 126,786; Per Subs 236
Special Collections: Italian Coll, bks
Automation Activity & Vendor Info: (Circulation) TLC (The Library Corporation), (OPAC) TLC (The Library Corporation)
Wireless access
Publications: Gates Business Directory; Gates Human Services Directory
Mem of Monroe County Library System
Special Services for the Deaf - Assistive tech
Open Mon-Thurs 9-9, Fri 9-6, Sat 10-5
Friends of the Library Group

L HARTER, SECREST & EMERY LLP*, Law Library, 1600 Bausch & Lomb Pl, 14604. SAN 372-2406. Tel: 585-231-1230. FAX: 585-232-2152. *Law Librn,* Lisa Pipia; Tel: 585-231-1228; *Mgr, Info Serv,* Robert Stivers; Staff 2 (MLS 2)

M HIGHLAND HOSPITAL LIBRARY*, John R Williams Health Sciences Library, Highland Hospital, 1000 South Ave, 14620. (Mail add: Box 49, 14620), SAN 312-3529. Tel: 585-341-6761. E-mail: hh_library@urmc.rochester.edu. Web Site: www.urmc.rochester.edu/hh/library. *Librn,* Lorraine Porcello; Tel: 585-341-0378, E-mail: lorraine_porcello@urmc.rochester.edu; Staff 2 (MLS 1, Non-MLS 1)
Founded 1967
Special Collections: Highland Hospital Archives Coll, papers, photog, yearbks & other memorabilia
Subject Interests: Allied health, Consumer health, Family med, Geriatrics, Med, Nursing, Obstetrics & gynecology, Oncology, Orthopedics, Women's health
Automation Activity & Vendor Info: (Acquisitions) Ex Libris Group; (Cataloging) Ex Libris Group; (Circulation) Ex Libris Group; (OPAC) Ex Libris Group; (Serials) Ex Libris Group
Database Vendor: OVID Technologies, PubMed
Wireless access
Function: Archival coll, Computers for patron use, Copy machines, E-Reserves, Electronic databases & coll, Health sci info serv, ILL available, Online cat, Online searches, Photocopying/Printing, Ref serv available
Partic in Rochester Regional Library Council
Open Tues-Thurs 8:30-12, Fri 8:30-4:30
Restriction: Badge access after hrs, Hospital staff & commun, In-house use for visitors, Lending to staff only

M INTERLAKES ONCOLOGY MEDICAL LIBRARY*, Unity Hospital Medical Library, 1555 Long Pond Rd, 14626. SAN 327-2338. Tel: 585-723-7755. FAX: 585-723-7078. *Dir,* Raymond W Curtin; E-mail: rcurtin@unityhealth.org; *Med Librn,* Steven F Buckley; E-mail: sbuckley@unityhealth.org; Staff 1.5 (MLS 1.5)
Founded 1946
Library Holdings: Bk Vols 1,900; Per Subs 140
Automation Activity & Vendor Info: (Cataloging) EOS International; (Circulation) EOS International; (OPAC) EOS International; (Serials) EOS International
Database Vendor: OVID Technologies
Wireless access
Function: Health sci info serv
Partic in OCLC Online Computer Library Center, Inc
Restriction: Open to staff, patients & family mem

P IRONDEQUOIT PUBLIC LIBRARY*, Pauline Evans Branch, 45 Cooper Rd, 14617. SAN 312-3545. Tel: 585-336-6062. FAX: 585-336-6066. Web Site: libraryweb.org/irondequoit. *Dir,* Terrence Buford; *Br Mgr,* Carla Robbins; *Acq,* Nora Pelish; Staff 9 (MLS 9)
Founded 1947. Pop 52,354; Circ 771,623
Library Holdings: Bk Vols 156,718; Per Subs 250
Automation Activity & Vendor Info: (Cataloging) TLC (The Library Corporation); (Circulation) TLC (The Library Corporation); (OPAC) TLC (The Library Corporation)
Database Vendor: Gale Cengage Learning
Mem of Monroe County Library System
Open Mon-Thurs 10-9, Tues & Wed 10-5, Fri 10-6
Friends of the Library Group
Branches: 1
HELEN MCGRAW BRANCH, 2180 Ridge Rd E, 14622, SAN 320-3808. Tel: 585-336-6060. FAX: 585-336-6067. *Br Mgr,* Karen Hultz
Open Mon & Thurs 10-5, Tues & Wed 10-9, Fri 10-6, Sat (Winter) 10-5
Friends of the Library Group

R JEWISH COMMUNITY CENTER OF GREATER ROCHESTER*, Philip Feinbloom Library, 1200 Edgewood Ave, 14618-5408. SAN 325-6790. Tel: 585-461-2000, Ext 607. FAX: 585-461-0805. Web Site: www.jccrochester.org. *Librn,* Anna Gossin; Staff 1 (Non-MLS 1)
Founded 1973
Library Holdings: Bk Vols 10,000; Per Subs 20
Special Collections: Dr Saul Moress Peace Coll; Holocaust Coll; Jewish Children Coll; Jewish Genealogy, print microfiche; Jewish Themes, videos, audio cassettes
Subject Interests: Judaica
Wireless access
Open Mon & Wed 3-5:30, Tues 10-2:30, Thurs 10-12:30
Friends of the Library Group
Branches:
ISRAEL EMIOT MEMORIAL YIDDISH LIBRARY, 1200 Edgewood Ave, 14618-5408. Tel: 585-461-2000, Ext 607. FAX: 585-461-0805. *Librn,* Anna Gossin
Founded 1981
Library Holdings: Bk Vols 1,500
Subject Interests: Yiddish
Open Mon & Wed 3-5:30, Tues 10-2:30, Thurs 10-12:30

S LANDMARK SOCIETY OF WESTERN NEW YORK, INC*, Wenrich Memorial Library, 133 S Fitzhugh St, 14608-2204. SAN 312-3561. Tel: 585-546-7029, Ext 10. FAX: 585-546-4788. Web Site: www.landmarksociety.org. *Coordr,* Cynthia Howk; Tel: 585-546-7029, Ext 24, E-mail: chowk@landmarksociety.org. Subject Specialists: *Presv,* Cynthia Howk; Staff 2 (MLS 1, Non-MLS 1)
Founded 1970
Library Holdings: Bk Titles 3,600
Special Collections: Information on Local Architecture; Local Architectural Surveys
Subject Interests: Bldg techniques, Hist rehabilitation, Hort, Landscape design, Regional archit
Function: Res libr
Partic in RLIN (Research Libraries Information Network)
Open Wed-Fri 9-5
Restriction: Non-circulating

MONROE COMMUNITY COLLEGE

J DAMON CITY CAMPUS LIBRARY*, 228 E Main St, 4th Flr 4-101, 14604. Tel: 585-262-1413. Reference Tel: 585-262-1420. Administration Tel: 585-292-2307. FAX: 585-262-1516. E-mail: dcclibrary@monroecc.edu. Web Site: www.monroecc.edu/go/library. *Managing Librn,* Mary Timmons; E-mail: mtimmons@monroecc.edu; *Instrul Serv Librn,* Michael McCullough; E-mail: mmccullough@monroecc.edu; *Ref Serv,* Stephanie Hranjec; E-mail: shranjec@monroecc.edu; *Ref Serv,* William Johnson; E-mail: wjohnson@monroecc.edu; Staff 4 (MLS 4)
Highest Degree: Associate
Library Holdings: Bk Titles 10,000
Partic in Rochester Regional Library Council
Restriction: Open to students, fac & staff, Pub use on premises

J LEROY V GOOD LIBRARY, 1000 E Henrietta Rd, 14692. (Mail add: PO Box 92810, 14692-8910), SAN 312-3596. Tel: 585-292-2665. Circulation Tel: 585-292-2303. Interlibrary Loan Service Tel: 585-292-2318. Reference Tel: 585-292-2319. Administration Tel: 585-292-2307. Interlibrary Loan Service FAX: 585-292-3823. Administration FAX: 585-292-3859. E-mail: shr_ill@monroecc.edu. Web Site: www.monroecc.edu/go/library. *Dir,* Mark McBride; Tel: 585-292-2321, E-mail: mmcbride17@monroecc.edu; *Asst Dir,* Alice Wilson; Tel: 585-292-2304, E-mail: awilson@monroecc.edu; *Coll Develop Librn,* Richard Squires; Tel: 585-292-2314, E-mail: rsquires@monroecc.edu; *Database Control Librn,* Deborah Mohr; Tel: 585-292-2316, E-mail: dmohr@monroecc.edu; *Database Mgt Librn,* Charlene Rezabek; Tel: 585-292-2330, E-mail: crezabek@monroecc.edu; *Ref Librn/Distance Learning,* Pamela Czaja; Tel: 585-292-2308, E-mail: pczaja@monroecc.edu; *Ref Librn/Spec Coll,* Lori Annesi; Tel: 585-292-2338, E-mail: lannesi@monroecc.edu; Staff 16.5 (MLS 10.5, Non-MLS 6)
Founded 1962. Enrl 37,929; Fac 341; Highest Degree: Associate
Library Holdings: Bk Vols 115,531; Per Subs 435
Special Collections: Historical Genocide, Human Rights Issues & Peace Studies (Holocaust & Human Rights Center)
Automation Activity & Vendor Info: (Cataloging) Ex Libris Group; (Circulation) Ex Libris Group; (Course Reserve) Blackboard Inc; (ILL) OCLC ILLiad; (OPAC) Ex Libris Group; (Serials) Ex Libris Group
Database Vendor: American Psychological Association (APA), ARTstor, CredoReference, ebrary, EBSCOhost, Gale Cengage Learning, JSTOR, OCLC WorldShare Interlibrary Loan, OVID Technologies, Project MUSE, ProQuest, ScienceDirect, SerialsSolutions
Function: Distance learning, e-mail & chat, Exhibits, ILL available, Scanner
Partic in OCLC Online Computer Library Center, Inc; Rochester Regional Library Council; SUNYConnect
Publications: Point of Use Guides
Special Services for the Deaf - Bks on deafness & sign lang
Special Services for the Blind - Low vision equip
Open Mon-Thurs 8am-9pm, Fri 8-4

P MONROE COUNTY LIBRARY SYSTEM*, 115 South Ave, 14604. SAN 312-3626. Tel: 585-428-8000. Reference Tel: 585-428-8160. FAX: 585-428-8353. Reference FAX: 585-428-8166. Web Site: www.libraryweb.org. *Dir,* Patricia Uttaro; E-mail: patricia.uttaro@libraryweb.org; *Asst Dir,* Sally Snow; E-mail: sally.snow@libraryweb.org
Founded 1952. Pop 729,308
Special Collections: US Document Depository
Database Vendor: Gale Cengage Learning, OCLC FirstSearch, ProQuest, TLC (The Library Corporation)
Member Libraries: Brighton Memorial Library; Chili Public Library; East Rochester Public Library; Fairport Public Library; Gates Public Library; Greece Public Library; Hamlin Public Library; Henrietta Public Library; Irondequoit Public Library; Newman Riga Library; Ogden Farmers' Library; Parma Public Library; Penfield Public Library; Pittsford Community Library; Rochester Public Library; Rush Public Library; Scottsville Free Library; Seymour Library; Town of Mendon Public Library; Webster Public Library
Partic in Rochester Regional Library Council
Open Mon-Fri 9-5

S MONROE COUNTY SENECA PARK ZOO*, Marion C Barry Memorial Library, 2222 St Paul St, 14621-1097. SAN 329-2819. Tel: 585-266-6591. FAX: 585-266-5775. Web Site: www.senecaparkzoo.org. *Dir,* Lawrence J Sorel; E-mail: lsorel@monroecounty.gov
Founded 1980
Library Holdings: Bk Titles 2,080; Per Subs 75
Subject Interests: Veterinary med, Zoology
Wireless access
Restriction: Staff use only

C NAZARETH COLLEGE OF ROCHESTER LIBRARY*, Lorette Wilmot Library, 4245 East Ave, 14618-3790. (Mail add: PO Box 18950, 14618-0950), SAN 312-3634. Tel: 585-389-2129. FAX: 585-389-2145. Web Site: www.naz.edu/library. *Libr Dir,* Catherine Doyle; Tel: 585-389-2123, E-mail: cdoyle0@naz.edu; *Col Archivist, Head, Cat,* Diane Riley; Tel: 585-389-2152, E-mail: driley9@naz.edu; *Head, Circ Serv,* Jody Barker; Tel: 585-389-2160, E-mail: jbarker8@naz.edu; *Electronic Res Librn, Syst, Webmaster,* Heather Lagoy; Tel: 585-389-2121, E-mail: hlagoy7@naz.edu; *Bibliog Instr, Ref & Info Serv, Team Leader,* Jennifer S Burr; Tel: 585-389-2133, E-mail: jburr0@naz.edu; *Acq,* Janet B Smith; Tel: 585-389-2124, E-mail: jsmith12@naz.edu; *ILL, Ser,* Christine A Sisak; Tel: 585-389-2184, E-mail: csisak5@naz.edu; Staff 16 (MLS 8, Non-MLS 8)
Founded 1924. Enrl 2,910; Fac 175; Highest Degree: Master
Jul 2011-Jun 2012 Income State $6,800. Mats Exp $912,397
Library Holdings: Bk Titles 235,155; Per Subs 27,149
Special Collections: Thomas Merton Coll
Automation Activity & Vendor Info: (Cataloging) Innovative Interfaces, Inc; (Circulation) Innovative Interfaces, Inc; (Course Reserve) Innovative Interfaces, Inc; (ILL) OCLC ILLiad; (OPAC) Innovative Interfaces, Inc
Database Vendor: ABC-CLIO, ACM (Association for Computing Machinery), Alexander Street Press, American Chemical Society, ARTstor, Dialog, EBSCOhost, Gale Cengage Learning, Greenwood Publishing Group, LexisNexis, OCLC FirstSearch, OCLC WorldShare Interlibrary Loan, OVID Technologies
Wireless access
Publications: Acquisitions List; Periodicals; Special Collections Brochure; Subject Guides
Partic in Information Delivery Services Project (IDS); Lyrasis; Rochester Regional Library Council; Westchester Academic Library Directors Organization (WALDO)
Open Mon-Thurs 7:45-Midnight, Fri 7:45am-10pm, Sat 10-6, Sun 10-Midnight

GL NEW YORK STATE JUDICIAL DEPARTMENT*, Appellate Division Law Library, M Dolores Denman Courthouse, 50 East Ave, Ste 100, 14604-2214. SAN 312-3642. Tel: 585-530-3250. Interlibrary Loan Service Tel: 585-530-3254. Reference Tel: 585-530-3251. Administration Tel: 585-530-3252. FAX: 585-530-3270. Web Site: www.courts.state.ny.us/ad4/lib/. *Dir,* David Voisinet; *Head, Teen Serv,* Joan Hoolihan; *Librn,* Robert Cunningham; E-mail: rcunnin@courts.state.ny.us; *Pub Serv,* Betsy Vipperman; Staff 12 (MLS 6, Non-MLS 6)
Founded 1849
Apr 2005-Mar 2006 Income $1,342,479. Mats Exp $686,480. Sal $655,999
Library Holdings: Bk Vols 310,000; Per Subs 650
Special Collections: Pre-1850 Law Books; Regional Directories & Plat Books; Women in the Law
Subject Interests: Admin rules, Appeal papers, Citators, Court rpt, Decisions, Indexes, Monographs, Statutes
Automation Activity & Vendor Info: (Acquisitions) SirsiDynix; (Circulation) SirsiDynix; (ILL) SirsiDynix; (OPAC) SirsiDynix
Database Vendor: LexisNexis, Westlaw
Wireless access
Partic in Rochester Regional Library Council
Open Mon & Thurs 9-8, Tues, Wed & Fri 9-5
Restriction: Non-circulating to the pub

CR ROBERTS WESLEYAN COLLEGE & NORTHEASTERN SEMINARY*, B Thomas Golisano Library, 2301 Westside Dr, 14624-1997. SAN 312-3693. Tel: 585-594-6280. Interlibrary Loan Service Tel: 585-594-6017. Reference Tel: 585-594-6499. FAX: 585-594-6543. Web Site: www.roberts.edu/library. *Dir, Libr Serv,* Alfred Krober; Tel: 585-594-6501, E-mail: krobera@roberts.edu; *Librn,* Dr Barry Hamilton; Tel: 585-594-6893, E-mail: hamilton_barry@roberts.edu; *Coordr, Pub Serv, Ref Librn,* Esther Gillie; Tel: 585-594-6141, E-mail: gillie_esther@roberts.edu; *Operations Mgr,* Elizabeth Specht; Tel: 585-594-6816, E-mail: specht_elizabeth@roberts.edu; *Archivist, Coll Serv,* Charles H Canon, III; Tel: 585-594-6016, E-mail: canonc@roberts.edu; *Bibliog Instr, Ref,* Linda Jones; Tel: 585-594-6044, E-mail: jones_linda@roberts.edu; *Digital Serv & Syst,* Lynn Brown; Tel: 585-594-6064, E-mail: brown_lynn@roberts.edu.
Subject Specialists: *Theol,* Dr Barry Hamilton; Staff 6 (MLS 6)
Enrl 1,703; Fac 259; Highest Degree: Master
Jul 2010-Jun 2011. Mats Exp $442,507, Books $130,722, Per/Ser (Incl. Access Fees) $173,471, Micro $993, Electronic Ref Mat (Incl. Access Fees) $135,592, Presv $1,729. Sal $440,778 (Prof $259,323)
Library Holdings: CDs 1,464; DVDs 510; e-books 3,086; e-journals 1,466; Electronic Media & Resources 127; Bk Titles 111,000; Bk Vols 126,000; Per Subs 650; Videos 292
Special Collections: Benjamin Titus Roberts Coll, bks, ms & photog; Free Methodist Church History, bks, per, photog; Roberts Wesleyan College Historical Materials
Subject Interests: Art, Biblical studies, Educ, Mgt, Music, Nursing, Psychol, Soc work, Theol
Automation Activity & Vendor Info: (Acquisitions) Ex Libris Group; (Cataloging) Ex Libris Group; (Circulation) Ex Libris Group; (Course Reserve) Ex Libris Group; (ILL) OCLC; (OPAC) Ex Libris Group; (Serials) Ex Libris Group

Database Vendor: Alexander Street Press, American Psychological Association (APA), Cinahl, CQ Press, Dun & Bradstreet, EBSCOhost, Ex Libris Group, Gale Cengage Learning, Grolier Online, H W Wilson, Hoovers, JSTOR, LexisNexis, Medline, Modern Language Association, Newsbank, OCLC ArticleFirst, OCLC FirstSearch, OCLC WorldShare Interlibrary Loan, OVID Technologies, Oxford Online, Project MUSE, ProQuest, Sage, Standard & Poor's, Wiley InterScience, Wilson - Wilson Web
Wireless access
Function: Audio & video playback equip for onsite use, Computers for patron use, Copy machines, e-mail & chat, E-Reserves, Electronic databases & coll, Handicapped accessible, Music CDs, Online cat, Photocopying/Printing, Pub access computers, VHS videos
Partic in Christian Library Consortium; OCLC Online Computer Library Center, Inc; Rochester Regional Library Council; Westchester Academic Library Directors Organization (WALDO)
Special Services for the Blind - Reader equip
Open Mon-Thurs 8am-Midnight, Fri 8am-9pm, Sat 10-6, Sun 2-Midnight

M ROCHESTER ACADEMY OF MEDICINE LIBRARY*, 1441 East Ave, Ste 100, 14610-1665. SAN 312-3707. Tel: 585-271-1313. E-mail: raom@frontier.com. Web Site: www.raom.org. *Exec Dir,* Suzanne D Welch; Tel: 585-271-1314, E-mail: suzanne.welch@frontier.com
Founded 1900
Library Holdings: Bk Vols 31,300
Wireless access
Open Mon-Fri 8-4
Restriction: Closed stack

S ROCHESTER CIVIC GARDEN CENTER, INC LIBRARY, Five Castle Park, 14620. SAN 312-3480. Tel: 716-473-5130. FAX: 716-473-8136. E-mail: rcgclib@frontiernet.net. Web Site: www.rcgc.org. *Coll Develop, Librn,* Carolyn VanNess; Staff 8 (MLS 1, Non-MLS 7)
Founded 1945
Jan 2007-Dec 2007 Income $2,200, Locally Generated Income $1,200, Parent Institution $1,000. Mats Exp $2,400, Books $1,600, Per/Ser (Incl. Access Fees) $400, AV Mat $200, Presv $200
Library Holdings: DVDs 4; Bk Titles 4,500; Bk Vols 4,800; Per Subs 23; Spec Interest Per Sub 23; Videos 27
Special Collections: 19th Century Garden, bks, cat
Subject Interests: Garden hist, Hort, Landscaping, Natural crafts, Related facets incl flower arrangements
Automation Activity & Vendor Info: (Cataloging) JayWil Software Development, Inc; (OPAC) JayWil Software Development, Inc
Wireless access
Publications: RCGC Class Catalog (Current awareness service); Upstate Gardeners Journal (Bi-monthly)
Partic in Rochester Regional Library Council
Open Tues-Thurs 9-4
Restriction: Non-circulating to the pub, Open to pub for ref only

M ROCHESTER GENERAL HOSPITAL*, Lillie B Werner Medical Library, 1425 Portland Ave, 14621. SAN 312-3723. Tel: 585-922-4743. FAX: 585-544-1504. E-mail: wellness@rochestergeneral.org. Web Site: www.rochestergeneral.org/MedicalLibrary. *Dir,* Elizabeth Mamo; *Librn,* Tami Hartzell, *Librn,* Mary Ann Howie; *Librn,* Edward Lewek; Tel: 585-922-4045, E-mail: ed.lewek@rochestergeneral.org; *Librn,* Lana Rudy; *Librn,* Karen Sampone; *Librn,* Eileen Shirley; *Syst Librn,* James Goff; Tel: 585-922-4702; *ILL, Ref,* Cathy Carey; *Ref,* Mary McVicar-Keim; Tel: 585-922-4723. Subject Specialists: *Wellness,* Mary Ann Howie; Staff 10 (MLS 6, Non-MLS 4)
Founded 1883
Library Holdings: AV Mats 2,000; Bk Titles 5,000; Per Subs 300
Special Collections: History of Medicine Coll
Automation Activity & Vendor Info: (Cataloging) CyberTools for Libraries; (Circulation) CyberTools for Libraries; (OPAC) CyberTools for Libraries; (Serials) EBSCO Online
Database Vendor: EBSCOhost
Wireless access
Publications: Libra Links (Monthly newsletter)
Partic in Docline; OCLC Online Computer Library Center, Inc; Rochester Regional Library Council
Open Mon-Fri 8am-9pm, Sat 8:30-5, Sun 12-5
Friends of the Library Group

S ROCHESTER HISTORICAL SOCIETY LIBRARY*, 115 South Ave, 14604. SAN 312-3731. Tel: 716-428-8470. FAX: 716-588-8478. Web Site: www.rochesterhistory.org. *Archivist, Librn,* William Keeler; E-mail: wkeeler@rochesterhistory.org
Library Holdings: Bk Vols 15,000
Special Collections: Rochester & Genesee Valley History Coll, bks, mss, photog; Rochester City Directories; Rochester Historical Society Publications
Function: ILL available
Restriction: Non-circulating to the pub, Open by appt only

C ROCHESTER INSTITUTE OF TECHNOLOGY*, Wallace Library, 90 Lomb Memorial Dr, 14623-5604. SAN 354-012X. Circulation Tel: 585-475-2562. Interlibrary Loan Service Tel: 585-475-2560. Reference Tel: 585-475-2563. Administration Tel: 585-475-2550, 585-475-2565. FAX: 585-475-7007. Web Site: library.rit.edu. *Dir,* Shirley Bower; Tel: 585-475-5034, E-mail: slbwm@rit.edu; *Head, Acq & Ser,* Sheila Smokey; Tel: 585-475-7283, E-mail: scswml@rit.edu; *Head, Circ,* Jason Stryker; Tel: 585-475-5819; *Head, ILL, Head, Info Serv,* Morna Hilderbrand; Tel: 585-475-7667, E-mail: mbhwml@rit.edu; *Head, Publ & Scholarship Support Serv,* Nicholas Paulus; Tel: 585-475-7934, E-mail: nipwml@rit.edu; *Mgr, Instruction & Educ Serv,* Margaret Bartlett, Tel: 585-475-2559, E-mail: mbbwml@rit.edu; *Archivist,* Rebecca Simmons; Tel: 585-475-2557, E-mail: raswml@rit.edu; *Curator, Melbert B Cary Graphic Arts Coll & Mgr Cultural Coll,* Amelia Hugill-Fontanel; Staff 46 (MLS 17, Non-MLS 29)
Founded 1829. Enrl 12,600; Fac 1,095; Highest Degree: Doctorate
Library Holdings: Bk Titles 245,277; Bk Vols 271,876; Per Subs 3,217
Special Collections: Melbert B Cary Graphic Arts Library
Subject Interests: Allied health, Applied art, Archives, Bus, Computer graphics, Computers, Deafness, Electronics, Eng, Graphic arts, Imaging sci, Mat sci, Optics, Printing
Partic in Rochester Regional Library Council
Special Services for the Deaf - Bks on deafness & sign lang; Spec interest per; Staff with knowledge of sign lang; TTY equip
Open Mon-Thurs 7:30am-3am, Fri 7:30am-Midnight, Sat 10am-Midnight, Sun 11am-3am

S ROCHESTER MUSEUM & SCIENCE CENTER LIBRARY, Schuyler C Townson Library, 657 East Ave, 14607. SAN 354-0189. Tel: 585-271-4320, Ext 315. FAX: 585-271-0492. Web Site: www.rmsc.org. *Archivist, Librn,* Leatrice Kemp; E-mail: lea_kemp@rmsc.org; Staff 1 (MLS 1)
Founded 1917
Library Holdings: AV Mats 50; Bk Titles 30,000; Per Subs 60
Special Collections: 19th Century Periodicals, Almanacs, Posters, Greeting Cards; African American History (Howard W Coles Coll); Domestic Architecture (Barrows, Thomas Boyd & William H Richardson Coll), architectural drawings; Flour Milling Industry (Moseley & Motley Coll), mss; Rochester Button Company, mss; Rochester History; Stone Coll - Glass Plate Negatives
Subject Interests: Anthrop, Antiques, Archaeology, Costume, Local hist, Native Am especially Iroquois, Natural hist
Automation Activity & Vendor Info: (Cataloging) OCLC; (ILL) OCLC
Wireless access
Partic in OCLC Online Computer Library Center, Inc; Rochester Regional Library Council
Open Tues-Thurs 9-5
Restriction: Open to pub for ref only

P ROCHESTER PUBLIC LIBRARY*, 115 South Ave, 14604-1896. SAN 354-0243. Tel: 585-428-7300. FAX: 585-428-8353. TDD: 585-428-8023. Web Site: www3.libraryweb.org. *Dir,* Uttaro Patricia; Tel: 585-428-8045; *Asst Dir,* David Creek; Tel: 585-428-8345; *Automation Spec,* Mary Jane Wright; *Outreach Serv,* Larry Taylor
Founded 1911. Pop 713,968; Circ 1,779,111
Library Holdings: Bk Titles 950,000; Per Subs 5,620
Special Collections: Black History (Wheatley Branch Coll); Department Coll, flm; Local History, bks, photogs, newsp; Reynolds Audio Visual. US Document Depository
Automation Activity & Vendor Info: (Acquisitions) TLC (The Library Corporation); (Cataloging) OCLC; (Circulation) TLC (The Library Corporation); (OPAC) TLC (The Library Corporation); (Serials) TLC (The Library Corporation)
Wireless access
Publications: Directory of Associations in Monroe County; Directory of Clubs in Monroe County; Guide to Grant Markers; Human Services Directory; Neighborhood Associations; Visiting Artists Directory
Mem of Monroe County Library System
Partic in OCLC Online Computer Library Center, Inc; Rochester Regional Library Council; Southeastern Libraries Cooperating
Special Services for the Deaf - Bks on deafness & sign lang; Captioned film dep; Spec interest per; Staff with knowledge of sign lang
Open Mon-Wed & Fri 10-6, Thurs 11-7, Sat (Sept-June) 10-5, Sun (Oct-May) 1-5
Friends of the Library Group
Branches: 9
ARNETT, 310 Arnett Blvd, 14619, SAN 354-0278. Tel: 585-428-8214. *Br Mgr,* Bruce Tehan; E-mail: bruce.tehan@libraryweb.org
Subject Interests: African-Am hist
Open Mon & Wed 11-6, Tues & Thurs 11-7, Fri 11-5, Sat 10-2

CHARLOTTE, 3557 Lake Ave, 14612, SAN 354-0332. Tel: 585-428-8216. *Br Mgr,* Paul Tantillo
Subject Interests: Boating, Local hist
Open Mon-Thurs 11:30-7, Fri 11:30-5:30, Sat 10-2
HIGHLAND, 971 South Ave, 14620, SAN 354-0510. Tel: 585-428-8206. *Br Mgr,* Erin Clarke
Open Mon 1-7, Tues & Thurs 10-6, Wed & Fri 1-6, Sat 10-2
LINCOLN, 851 Joseph Ave, 14621, SAN 354-0421. Tel: 585-428-8210. *Br Mgr,* Jason Gogniat; E-mail: jason.gogniat@libraryweb.org
Subject Interests: African-Am hist, Spanish lang
Open Mon-Wed 10-6, Thurs & Fri 12-6, Sat 12-4
LYELL, 956 Lyell Ave, 14606, SAN 325-4356. Tel: 585-428-8218. *Br Mgr,* Patricia Connor; E-mail: patricia.connor@libraryweb.com
Open Mon 12-8, Tues & Fri 12-6, Sat 10-2
MAPLEWOOD, 1111 Dewey Ave, 14613, SAN 354-0456. Tel: 585-428-8220. *Br Mgr,* Johanna Buran; E-mail: johanna.buran@libraryweb.org
Open Mon-Thurs 11:30-7, Fri 11:30-5:30, Sat 10-2
MONROE, 809 Monroe Ave, 14607, SAN 354-0480. Tel: 585-428-8202. *Supvr,* Mary Clare Scheg; E-mail: Mary.Scheg@libraryweb.org
Open Mon 12-8, Tues 10-6, Wed 12-6, Thurs & Fri 11-6, Sat 10-2
PHILLIS WHEATLEY COMMUNITY, 33 Dr Samuel McCree Way, 14608, SAN 354-057X. Tel: 585-428-8212. *Br Mgr,* Lori Frankunas; E-mail: lfrankunas@libraryweb.org
Special Collections: Oral History
Subject Interests: African-Am hist
Open Mon & Wed Noon-7, Tues & Thurs 10-6, Fri Noon-6, Sat 10-2
WINTON, 611 Winton Rd N, 14609, SAN 354-060X. Tel: 585-428-8204. *Br Mgr,* Barbara Nichols; E-mail: barbara.nichols@libraryweb.org
Subject Interests: Russian lang
Open Mon 11-8, Tues-Fri 11-6, Sat 11-2
Bookmobiles: 1

C SAINT JOHN FISHER COLLEGE, Lavery Library, 3690 East Ave, 14618-3599. SAN 312-2662. Tel: 585-385-8165. Interlibrary Loan Service Tel: 585-385-8106. Reference Tel: 585-385-8141. Administration Tel: 585-385-8164. FAX: 585-385-8445. Web Site: www.sjfc.edu/library. *Dir,* Melissa Jadlos; E-mail: mjadlos@sjfc.edu; *Head, Ref & Ser,* Marianne Simmons; Tel: 585-385-7399, E-mail: msimmons@sjfc.edu; *Acq Librn, Head, Tech Serv,* Kate Ross; Tel: 585-385-8136, E-mail: kross@sjfc.edu; *Access Serv Librn,* Kourtney Blackburn; Tel: 585-385-7340, E-mail: kblackburn@sjfc.edu; *Assessment & Online Prog Librn,* Christina Hillman; Tel: 585-385-8493, E-mail: chillman@sjfc.edu; *Educ Librn,* Kathi Sigler; Tel: 585-385-8140, E-mail: ksigler@sjfc.edu; *Instruction & Archives Librn,* Nancy Greco; Tel: 585-385-8139, E-mail: ngreco@sjfc.edu; *Outreach & Spec Coll Librn,* Michelle Price; Tel: 585-899-3743, E-mail: mprice@sjfc.edu; *Syst Librn,* Benjamin Hockenberry; Tel: 585-385-8382, E-mail: bhockenberry@sjfc.edu; *Circ Coordr,* Stacy Celata; E-mail: sdupuis@sjfc.edu; *ILL Coordr,* Alicia Marrese; E-mail: amarrese@sjfc.edu. Subject Specialists: *Nursing, Pharm, Sci,* Michelle Price; Staff 9 (MLS 9)
Founded 1951. Enrl 3,997; Fac 430; Highest Degree: Doctorate
Library Holdings: AV Mats 9,948; e-books 136,437; Bk Vols 162,694; Per Subs 148,365
Special Collections: Anti-Slavery Newspapers; Frederick Douglass Newspapers; George P Decker Papers; Theodore C. Cazeau Grand Army of the Republic Coll
Subject Interests: Bus, Educ, Liberal arts, Nursing, Pharm
Automation Activity & Vendor Info: (Acquisitions) Innovative Interfaces, Inc; (Cataloging) Innovative Interfaces, Inc; (Circulation) Innovative Interfaces, Inc; (Course Reserve) Innovative Interfaces, Inc; (ILL) OCLC ILLiad; (OPAC) Innovative Interfaces, Inc; (Serials) Innovative Interfaces, Inc
Wireless access
Partic in Information Delivery Services Project (IDS); Rochester Regional Library Council
Special Services for the Blind - Assistive/Adapted tech devices, equip & products
Open Mon-Thurs 7:45am-Midnight, Fri 7:45am-10pm, Sat 8:45am-10pm, Sun 8:45am-Midnight
Restriction: In-house use for visitors, Non-circulating to the pub

S THE STRONG MUSEUM LIBRARY*, One Manhattan Sq, 14607. SAN 312-3790. Tel: 585-263-2700. FAX: 585-263-2493. Web Site: www.museumofplay.org. *Dir,* Carol Sandler; E-mail: csandler@museumofplay.org; Staff 2 (MLS 1, Non-MLS 1)
Founded 1972
Library Holdings: Bk Titles 80,000
Special Collections: 19th & 20th Century Trade Catalogs; 19th & Early 20th Century Children's; Fore-Edge Paintings Coll; Patent Papers for Dolls & Toys; Winslow Homer Coll
Subject Interests: 19th Century Am domestic life bks inc socio-cultural hist, Decorative art, Early 20th Century Am domestic life bks inc socio-cultural hist
Automation Activity & Vendor Info: (Cataloging) OCLC; (OPAC) EOS International
Wireless access
Partic in Nylink; Rochester Regional Library Council
Restriction: Open by appt only

R TEMPLE BETH EL LIBRARY*, 139 Winton Rd S, 14610. SAN 312-3804. Tel: 585-473-1770, Ext 27. FAX: 585-473-2689.
Founded 1946
Library Holdings: Bk Titles 6,900; Bk Vols 10,000; Per Subs 29

R TEMPLE B'RITH KODESH LIBRARY*, 2131 Elmwood Ave, 14618-1021. SAN 312-3812. Tel: 585-244-7060. FAX: 585-244-0557. *Librn,* Shelly Weinstein
Founded 1962
Library Holdings: Bk Vols 3,700
Wireless access
Open Mon-Thurs 9-4:15

R TEMPLE SINAI LIBRARY*, 363 Penfield Rd, 14625. SAN 312-3820. Tel: 585-381-6890. FAX: 585-381-4921. Web Site: www.tsinai.org. *Librn,* Heidi Davis
Founded 1974
Library Holdings: Bk Vols 5,000
Subject Interests: Judaica
Wireless access
Open Sun (Sept-May) 9-1:30

L UNDERBERG & KESSLER LAW LIBRARY*, 300 Bausch & Lomb Pl, 14604. SAN 372-252X. Tel: 585-258-2800. FAX: 585-258-2821. *Librn,* Jane Snyder
Library Holdings: Bk Vols 8,000

C UNIVERSITY OF ROCHESTER*, Rush Rhees Library, River Campus Libraries, 755 Library Rd, 14627. SAN 354-0693. Tel: 585-275-4461. Interlibrary Loan Service Tel: 585-275-4454. FAX: 585-273-5309. Web Site: www.library.rochester.edu. *Dean of Libr, Vice Provost, Andrew H & Janet Dayton Neilly,* Mary Ann Mavrinac; *Head, Acq,* Sharon Briggs; *Head, Coll Develop,* Helen Anderson; *Head, Ref,* LeRoy Lafleur; *Rare Bks & Spec Coll Librn,* Jim Kuhn; *Spec Coll Librn,* Melissa Mead; *Cat,* Walt Nickeson; *Ser,* Erin DeGroff; *Syst Coordr,* Denise Dunham; *Syst Coordr,* Stephen O'Connor; Staff 65 (MLS 33, Non-MLS 32)
Founded 1850. Enrl 10,290; Fac 1,347; Highest Degree: Doctorate
Library Holdings: Bk Vols 3,259,159; Per Subs 44,175
Special Collections: 19th & 20th Century Public Affairs Colls (Papers of William Henry Seward, Thurlow Weed, David Jayne Hill, Susan B Anthony, Rev William C Gannett, Thomas E Dewey, Marion Folsom, Kenneth Keating & Frank Horton); 19th Century Botany & Horticulture Colls (Ellwanger & Barry Nursery Papers & Library, Historian Christopher Lasch Archives, Political Scientist William Riker); American Literature Coll (Washington Irving, Henry James, Mark Twain, William Dean Howells, Edward Everett Hale (filmed bks), William Heyen (filmed bks, historical children's bks, ms & printed works), Christopher Morley, Adelaide Crapsey (ms & printed works), Henry W Clune (ms & printed works), Frederick Exley (ms & printed works), John A Williams (ms & printed works), John Gardner (ms & printed works), Jerre Mangione (ms & printed works), Plutzik Library (ms & printed works), Paul Zimmer Papers); Art & Architecture Colls (Claude Bragdon Papers, Drawings & Printed Works; Dyrer & Dryer Papers); English History & Literature Colls (Eikon Basilike, John Dryden, Restoration Drama, John Ruskin, John Masefield, Benjamin Disraeli, Sean O'Casey, Edward Gorey, 19th & 20th Century Theatre Manuscripts, Robert Southey (ms & printed works), Arnold Bennett); Leonardo da Vinci Coll; Optical Industry Trade Catalogs; Regional History (New York State Settlement, Land Development & Local History, especially Rochester & Monroe County, Native Americans, Early Upstate New York Printing, Manuscript Records of Rochester Benevolent Organizations, Businesses & Industry); Social & Natural Science Colls (Papers of Anthropologist Lewis Henry Morgan & Scientists Herman LeRoy Fairchild, Henry A Ward, Carl E Akeley, Printed Works of Charles Darwin). State Document Depository; US Document Depository
Partic in Association of Research Libraries (ARL); Nylink; Rochester Regional Library Council
Friends of the Library Group

Departmental Libraries:

CHARLOTTE WHITNEY ALLEN LIBRARY, Memorial Art Gallery, 500 University Ave, 14607, SAN 354-0758. Tel: 585-276-8999. FAX: 585-473-6266. E-mail: maglibinfo@mag.rochester.edu. Web Site: mag.rochester.edu/library. *Librn,* Lu Harper; Tel: 585-276-8997, E-mail: lharper@mag.rochester.edu; *Libr Asst,* Kathleen Nicastro; Tel: 585-276-8901, E-mail: knicastr@mag.rochester.edu; Staff 1.5 (MLS 1, Non-MLS 0.5)
Founded 1913
Library Holdings: Bk Vols 45,408; Per Subs 60
Special Collections: Fritz Trautmann Coll, scrapbks; MAG Archives; Rochester Art Club Coll, 1880-present, exhibition cats

Subject Interests: Art hist, Museology
Open Wed-Fri 1-5
ART-MUSIC, Rush Rhees Library, 14627, SAN 354-0723. Tel: 585-275-4476. FAX: 585-273-1032. E-mail: artlib@library.rochester.edu. Web Site: www.lib.rochester.edu/artmusic/home. *Librn,* Stephanie Frontz; E-mail: sfrontz@library.rochester.edu
Library Holdings: CDs 2,500; Bk Titles 70,000; Per Subs 200
Special Collections: Robert MacCameron Coll, papers & photos, Artists' Books
Subject Interests: Archit, Art hist, Cultural studies, Mus, Sound rec
Friends of the Library Group
BUSINESS & GOVERNMENT INFORMATION LIBRARY, Rush Rhees Library, 14627, SAN 354-0847. Tel: 585-275-4482. FAX: 585-273-5316. Web Site: www.library.rochester.edu/bgil/home. *Librn,* Suzanne Bell; *Librn,* Kathy Wu; Staff 4 (MLS 2, Non-MLS 2)
Special Collections: State Document Depository; US Document Depository
Subject Interests: Acctg, Econ, Finance, Govt info, Manufacturing mgt, Mkt, Operations mgt
Friends of the Library Group
CARLSON SCIENCE & ENGINEERING LIBRARY, 160 Trustee Rd, 14627-0236, SAN 327-9138. Tel: 585-275-4488. FAX: 585-273-4656. Web Site: www.library.rochester.edu/carlson/home. *Dir,* Zahra Kamarei; Staff 6 (MLS 6)
Special Collections: USGS Topographic Maps
Subject Interests: Biol, Chem, Computer sci, Eng, Geol, Maps, Math, Statistics
Friends of the Library Group
LABORATORY FOR LASER ENERGETICS LIBRARY, 250 E River Rd, 14623, SAN 327-9219. Tel: 585-275-4479. FAX: 585-273-3663. Web Site: www.library.rochester.edu/lle/home. *Librn,* Delores Baxter; E-mail: dbax@lle.rochester.edu
Special Collections: DOE Energyfiche
Subject Interests: Applied optics, Lasers, Plasma physics, Thermonuclear fusion
Friends of the Library Group
PHYSICS-OPTICS-ASTRONOMY LIBRARY - RIVER CAMPUS, 374 Bausch & Lomb Hall, 14627-0171, SAN 327-9197. Tel: 585-275-4469. FAX: 585-273-5321. Web Site: www.library.rochester.edu/poalibrary/home. *Dean of Libr,* Mary Ann Mavrinac; *Head of Libr,* Tyler Dzuba; Tel: 585-275-7659, E-mail: tdzuba@library.rochester.edu; Staff 1 (MLS 1)
Highest Degree: Doctorate
Special Collections: History of Optics
Subject Interests: Astronomy, Optics, Physics
Friends of the Library Group
ROSSELL HOPE ROBBINS LIBRARY, Rush Rhees Library, Rm 416, 14627, SAN 372-509X. Tel: 585-275-0110. Web Site: www.library.rochester.edu/robbins/home. *Dir,* Alan Lupack; E-mail: alupack@library.rochester.edu; *Supvr,* Rosemary Paprocki; E-mail: rpaprocki@library.rochester.edu
Founded 1987
Library Holdings: Bk Titles 15,000
Special Collections: Medieval Literature (Offprint Coll)
Subject Interests: Medieval English lit, Medieval studies
Open Mon & Thurs 9-9, Tues, Wed & Fri 9-5
Restriction: Non-circulating to the pub
Friends of the Library Group
SIBLEY MUSIC LIBRARY, 27 Gibbs St, 14604-2596, SAN 354-0901. Tel: 585-274-1350. Circulation Tel: 585-274-1300. Reference Tel: 585-274-1320. FAX: 585-274-1380. Web Site: www.esm.rochester.edu/sibley. *Assoc Dean,* Daniel Zager; *Head, Pub Serv,* James Farrington; *Spec Coll & Archives Librn,* David Peter Coppen; Staff 8 (MLS 6, Non-MLS 2)
Founded 1904. Enrl 853; Fac 96; Highest Degree: Doctorate
Library Holdings: AV Mats 105,731; Microforms 14,403; Bk Titles 240,524; Bk Vols 387,752; Per Subs 620
Special Collections: 17th Century Sacred Music (Olschki Coll); Books & Scores (Oscar Sonneck Library); Chamber Music; Folk Music (Krehbiel Coll); Music Biography, Theatre & Librettos (Pougin Coll); Music Manuscripts (Howard Hanson, Gardner Read, Burrill Philips, Weldon Hart Coll, Karl Weigl & Alec Wilder Colls); Music Publishing (Sengstack Archives); Performers' Coll (Malcolm Frager, Jan DeGaetani & Jacques Gordon Colls)
Subject Interests: Chamber music, Hist of music, Libretti, Music theory, Musical theatre, Opera, Solo lit
Automation Activity & Vendor Info: (Acquisitions) Ex Libris Group; (Cataloging) Ex Libris Group; (Circulation) Ex Libris Group; (OPAC) Ex Libris Group; (Serials) Ex Libris Group
Partic in OCLC Online Computer Library Center, Inc; Rochester Regional Library Council

CM UNIVERSITY OF ROCHESTER MEDICAL CENTER*, Edward G Miner Library, 601 Elmwood Ave, 14642. Tel: 585-275-3361. Reference Tel: 716-275-2487. FAX: 585-756-7762. Web Site: www.urmc.rochester.edu/libraries/miner. *Dir,* Julia Sollenberger; Tel: 716-275-5194, E-mail: julia_sollenberger@urmc.rochester.edu; *Asst Dir,* Donna Berryman; E-mail: Donna_Berryman@urmc.rochester.edu; *Asst Dir,* Michele Shipley; E-mail: Michele_Shipley@urmc.rochester.edu; Staff 31 (MLS 9, Non-MLS 22)
Library Holdings: e-journals 1,100; Bk Titles 58,000; Bk Vols 240,000; Per Subs 1,200
Subject Interests: Hist of med, Med, Nursing
Automation Activity & Vendor Info: (Acquisitions) Ex Libris Group; (Cataloging) Ex Libris Group; (Circulation) Ex Libris Group; (OPAC) Ex Libris Group; (Serials) Ex Libris Group
Database Vendor: OVID Technologies
Wireless access
Partic in Miraclenet; Northeast Research Libraries Consortium (NERL); Rochester Regional Library Council
Open Mon-Thurs (Winter) 7:30am-Midnight, Fri 7:30am-10pm, Sat 10-10, Sun 10am-Midnight; Mon-Thurs (Summer) 7:30am-10pm, Fri 7:30am-8pm, Sat 10-5, Sun Noon-10
Departmental Libraries:
BASIL G BIBBY LIBRARY, Eastman Dental, 625 Elmwood Ave, 14620, SAN 312-3456. Tel: 585-275-5010. FAX: 585-273-1230. Web Site: www.urmc.rochester.edu/libraries/bibby. *Librn,* Lorraine Porcello; E-mail: lorraine_porcello@urmc.rochester.edu; *Sr Libr Asst,* Bonnie Archer; E-mail: barcher@urmc.rochester.edu; Staff 2 (MLS 1, Non-MLS 1)
Founded 1947
Library Holdings: Bk Vols 2,100; Per Subs 35
Special Collections: Eastman Dental & Dentistry History Coll, archives
Subject Interests: Dentistry
Automation Activity & Vendor Info: (Course Reserve) Blackboard Inc
Function: Archival coll, Computers for patron use, Copy machines, Electronic databases & coll, For res purposes, Health sci info serv, ILL available, Online cat, Photocopying/Printing
Partic in New York State Interlibrary Loan Network (NYSILL); Rochester Regional Library Council
Publications: Basil G Bibby Library Gazette (Online only)
Open Mon 8-5, Tues 8-4:30, Wed 1:30-5, Thurs 8:30-4:30, Fri 8:30-Noon
Restriction: Badge access after hrs, Hospital staff & commun, In-house use for visitors, Lending to staff only

ROCKVILLE CENTRE

P LAKEVIEW PUBLIC LIBRARY*, 1120 Woodfield Rd, 11570. SAN 312-3855. Tel: 516-536-3071. FAX: 516-536-6260. E-mail: lakeview@nassaulibrary.org. Web Site: www.nassaulibrary.org/lakeview. *Librn,* Ruby Boykins; E-mail: rboykins@nassaulibrary.org; *Librn,* Mamta Mehta; E-mail: lklref@nassaulibrary.org; *YA Librn,* Jennifer Dunlop; E-mail: jdunlop@nassaulibrary.org; *Admin Serv,* Barbara Walker; E-mail: bwalker@nassaulibrary.org; *Circ,* Diana Walker; *Treas,* Opal Ramdial; Staff 10 (MLS 10)
Founded 1973. Pop 6,500
Library Holdings: Bks on Deafness & Sign Lang 15; CDs 450; DVDs 1,200; e-journals 109; Bk Vols 60,000; Videos 1,127
Special Collections: Black Experience, bks, micro, per
Subject Interests: Foreign lang bks
Automation Activity & Vendor Info: (Cataloging) Innovative Interfaces, Inc; (Circulation) Innovative Interfaces, Inc; (OPAC) Innovative Interfaces, Inc
Wireless access
Publications: Community Directory of Community Organizations; Community Library (Newsletter)
Mem of Nassau Library System
Partic in Long Island Library Resources Council; New York State Interlibrary Loan Network (NYSILL)
Open Mon-Thurs 10-8, Fri & Sat 9-5
Friends of the Library Group

C MOLLOY COLLEGE*, James Edward Tobin Library, 1000 Hempstead Ave, 11571. (Mail add: PO Box 5002, 11571-5002), SAN 312-3871. Tel: 516-678-5000. Interlibrary Loan Service Tel: 516-678-5000, Ext 6461. Reference Tel: 516-678-5000, Ext 6236. Administration Tel: 516-678-5000, Ext 6819. FAX: 516-678-8908. Web Site: www.molloy.edu/library1. *Dir, Libr & Media Serv,* Robert D Martin; E-mail: rmartin@molloy.edu; *Asst Dir, Assoc Librn, Instrul Serv,* Patricia Sullivan; Tel: 516-678-5000, Ext 6386, E-mail: psullivan1@molloy.edu; *Assoc Librn, Access Serv/Grad Studies,* Theresa Rienzo; Tel: 516-678-5000, Ext 6967, E-mail: trienzo@molloy.edu; *Media Librn,* Cori Miller; Tel: 516-678-5000, Ext 6159, E-mail: clmiller@molloy.edu; *Ref Librn,* Wenhui Chen; Tel: 516-678-5000, Ext 6461, E-mail: wchen@molloy.edu; *Ref Librn,* Norman Weil; Tel: 516-678-5000, Ext 6567, E-mail: nweil@molloy.edu; Staff 30 (MLS 10, Non-MLS 20)
Founded 1955. Enrl 3,700; Fac 350; Highest Degree: Master
Jul 2006-Jun 2007. Mats Exp $374,400, Books $70,000, Per/Ser (Incl. Access Fees) $130,000, AV Equip $28,000, AV Mat $15,000, Electronic

Ref Mat (Incl. Access Fees) $130,000, Presv $1,400. Sal $700,071 (Prof $376,330)
Library Holdings: Bk Vols 110,000; Per Subs 700; Videos 650
Automation Activity & Vendor Info: (Acquisitions) Ex Libris Group; (Cataloging) Ex Libris Group; (Circulation) Ex Libris Group; (Course Reserve) Docutek; (ILL) OCLC Connexion; (OPAC) Ex Libris Group; (Serials) Ex Libris Group
Database Vendor: Cambridge Scientific Abstracts, EBSCOhost, Gale Cengage Learning, LexisNexis, OCLC FirstSearch, OCLC WorldShare Interlibrary Loan, OVID Technologies, ProQuest, PubMed, SerialsSolutions, SirsiDynix, Wilson - Wilson Web
Wireless access
Publications: Annual Media Holdings; Annual Periodical Holdings
Partic in Long Island Library Resources Council; Westchester Academic Library Directors Organization (WALDO)
Open Mon-Thurs 8am-10pm, Fri 8-8, Sat 10-6, Sun 11-6

P ROCKVILLE CENTRE PUBLIC LIBRARY*, 221 N Village Ave, 11570. SAN 312-388X. Tel: 516-766-6257. Circulation Tel: 516-766-6257, Ext 10. Reference Tel: 516-766-6257, Ext 5. Administration Tel: 516-766-6257, Ext 15. FAX: 516-766-6090. E-mail: reference@rvcpl.org. Web Site: www.rvclibrary.org. *Dir,* Maureen Chiofalo; E-mail: mchiofalo@rvcpl.org; *Head, Ref,* Ellen Berman; *Ch Serv,* Anita La Spina; *Tech Serv,* Ruth Black; *YA Serv,* Terry Ain; Staff 65 (MLS 20, Non-MLS 45)
Founded 1882. Pop 24,747; Circ 307,986
Library Holdings: Large Print Bks 4,379; Bk Vols 179,320; Per Subs 300
Special Collections: Rockville Centre History, bks, pictures, newsp
Subject Interests: Civil War, Educ, Hist
Automation Activity & Vendor Info: (Circulation) Innovative Interfaces, Inc; (OPAC) Innovative Interfaces, Inc
Database Vendor: Baker & Taylor, CredoReference, EBSCOhost, Gale Cengage Learning, OCLC FirstSearch, ProQuest, SirsiDynix, TLC (The Library Corporation)
Wireless access
Function: Adult bk club, After school storytime, Art exhibits, Copy machines, e-mail serv, E-Reserves, Electronic databases & coll, Handicapped accessible, Homebound delivery serv, ILL available, Large print keyboards, Magnifiers for reading, Online ref, Photocopying/Printing, Prog for adults, Prog for children & young adult, Summer reading prog, Tax forms, Video lending libr, Wheelchair accessible, Workshops
Publications: Library Newsletter
Mem of Nassau Library System
Open Mon, Wed & Thurs 9-9, Tues 10-9, Fri 9-6, Sat 9-5, Sun (Sept-June) 1-5
Friends of the Library Group

RODMAN

P RODMAN PUBLIC LIBRARY*, Town Hall, 13682. (Mail add: PO Box B, 13682-0002), SAN 312-3898. Tel: 315-232-2522. FAX: 315-232-3853. *Mgr,* Karen Marriott
Circ 7,000
Library Holdings: Bk Vols 2,700
Open Mon-Fri 9-5, Sat 10-4
Friends of the Library Group

ROME

P JERVIS PUBLIC LIBRARY ASSOCIATION, INC*, 613 N Washington St, 13440-4296. SAN 312-3901. Tel: 315-336-4570. Web Site: www.jervislibrary.org. *Dir,* Lisa M Matte; *Asst Dir,* Kari Tucker; *Chief Librn, Ch,* Lorie O'Donnell; *Chief Librn, Local Hist/Genealogy & Ref Serv,* Lori Chien; E-mail: lchien@midyork.org; *Chief Librn, Pub Digital Literacy,* Peter Chien; *Sr Librn, Adult Engagement & Outreach,* Mary Beth Portley; *Teen Serv Librn,* Lisa Kinna. Subject Specialists: *Genealogy, Local hist,* Lori Chien; Staff 8 (MLS 7, Non-MLS 1)
Founded 1894. Pop 33,125; Circ 264,533
Jan 2012-Dec 2012 Income $1,740,713, State $28,983, City $322,932, County $201,482, Locally Generated Income $69,775, Other $817,000. Mats Exp $149,267, Books $109,849, Per/Ser (Incl. Access Fees) $7,200, AV Mat $16,990, Electronic Ref Mat (Incl. Access Fees) $14,428, Presv $800. Sal $759,451
Library Holdings: Audiobooks 5,908; AV Mats 73; Bks on Deafness & Sign Lang 108; CDs 5,908; DVDs 4,610; e-books 772; Electronic Media & Resources 335; Large Print Bks 2,660; Microforms 2,603; Bk Vols 104,658; Per Subs 199; Videos 858
Special Collections: Civil Engineering Canals, Aqueducts, Railroads (John B Jervis Papers), letters, ms, microfilm, bks; Revolutionary War (Bright-Huntington Coll), ms
Automation Activity & Vendor Info: (Acquisitions) SirsiDynix; (Cataloging) SirsiDynix; (Circulation) SirsiDynix; (ILL) SirsiDynix; (OPAC) SirsiDynix; (Serials) SirsiDynix
Wireless access
Function: Adult bk club, Bk club(s), Bks on CD, Children's prog, Computer training, Computers for patron use, Copy machines, Electronic databases & coll, Fax serv, Free DVD rentals, Handicapped accessible, ILL available, Microfiche/film & reading machines, Music CDs, Online cat, OverDrive digital audio bks, Photocopying/Printing, Prog for adults, Prog for children & young adult, Pub access computers, Ref & res, Story hour, Summer reading prog, Tax forms, Teen prog, Telephone ref, Wheelchair accessible
Mem of Mid-York Library System
Special Services for the Deaf - Staff with knowledge of sign lang
Special Services for the Blind - Bks on CD; Large print bks
Open Mon-Thurs 9:30-8:30, Fri 9:30-5:30, Sat 9:30-5
Friends of the Library Group

S MOHAWK CORRECTIONAL FACILITY LIBRARY*, 6100 School Rd, 13440. (Mail add: PO Box 8450, 13442-8450). Tel: 315-339-5232. FAX: 315-339-5232, Ext 2099. *Sr Librn,* Martin Willetts, Jr
Library Holdings: Per Subs 70
Automation Activity & Vendor Info: (Cataloging) Follett Software; (Circulation) Follett Software
Open Mon-Fri 8-8

S ONEIDA CORRECTIONAL FACILITY LIBRARY*, 6100 School Rd, 13440. Tel: 315-339-6880, Ext 4600. FAX: 315-339-6880, Ext 3299. *Sr Librn,* Bruce Thompson
Founded 1988
Library Holdings: Audiobooks 100; Bk Vols 9,000; Per Subs 65; Spec Interest Per Sub 2
Open Mon & Fri 8-2, Tues-Thurs 8-2 & 5-9, Sat 5-9

S ROME HISTORICAL SOCIETY, William E & Elaine Scripture Memorial Library, 200 Church St, 13440. SAN 312-391X. Tel: 315-336-5870. FAX: 315-336-5912. E-mail: info@romehistoricalsociety.org. Web Site: www.romehistoricalsociety.org. *Dir,* Arthur Simmons; Staff 2 (Non-MLS 2)
Founded 1936
Library Holdings: Bk Vols 3,500
Special Collections: Audio-visual presentation - Built of Iron, Copper & Steel: The Industrial Development of Rome; From Portage to Cross Road: The Changing Face of Rome; Journals, letters, ephemery of local heritage; Oral Histories; Our Goodly Heritage, maps, photogs, newsp, prog for schools; Rome Turney Radiator Company Records Coll 1905-33; The Ill-fated Village of Delta. Oral History
Subject Interests: Canals & railroads, Civil War, Genealogy, Local hist to date, Revolutionary period
Wireless access
Function: Res libr
Open Tues-Fri 9-3

A UNITED STATES AIR FORCE*, Air Force Research Laboratory-Information Directorate Technical Library, Air Force Research Lab RIOIL, Bldg 3, 525 Brooks Rd, 13441-4505. SAN 352-5031. Tel: 315-330-7600. Reference Tel: 315-330-7607. FAX: 315-330-3086. *Chief Librn,* Rodney M Heines; Staff 1 (MLS 1)
Founded 1952
Library Holdings: Bk Vols 19,548; Per Subs 358
Subject Interests: Computer sci, Electronics, Math, Radar
Automation Activity & Vendor Info: (Acquisitions) CyberTools for Libraries; (Cataloging) OCLC CatExpress; (Circulation) CyberTools for Libraries; (ILL) OCLC WorldShare Interlibrary Loan; (OPAC) CyberTools for Libraries
Database Vendor: ACM (Association for Computing Machinery), Cambridge Scientific Abstracts, Dialog, EBSCOhost, Gale Cengage Learning, IEEE (Institute of Electrical & Electronics Engineers), Nature Publishing Group, OCLC FirstSearch, OCLC WorldShare Interlibrary Loan, SerialsSolutions
Function: Res libr
Publications: Accessions Lists - Open Literature & Documents
Partic in Air Force Res Lab Virtual Libr Team; Central New York Library Resources Council; Fedlink
Restriction: Staff use only

ROOSEVELT

P ROOSEVELT PUBLIC LIBRARY*, 27 W Fulton Ave, 11575. SAN 354-1029. Tel: 516-378-0222. FAX: 516-378-1011. Web Site: www.nassaulibrary.org/roosevelt. *Dir,* Joy L Rankin; Staff 4 (MLS 4)
Founded 1934. Pop 15,564
Library Holdings: Bk Titles 48,000; Bk Vols 60,000
Subject Interests: African-Am studies
Wireless access
Publications: Four Seasons Library News Bulletin
Mem of Nassau Library System
Open Mon & Wed Noon-8, Tues & Thurs 9-8, Fri & Sat 9-5
Friends of the Library Group

Branches: 1
CHILDREN'S ROOM, 27 W Fulton Ave, 11575. Tel: 516-378-0222. FAX: 516-378-1011. *Youth Serv,* Alisa Neumayer
Library Holdings: Bk Titles 12,702; Bk Vols 13,074
Subject Interests: African-Am studies
Open Mon & Wed 12-8, Tues & Thurs 9-8, Fri & Sat 9-5

ROSCOE

P ROSCOE FREE LIBRARY*, 85 Highland Ave, 12776. (Mail add: PO Box 339, 12776-0339), SAN 312-3928. Tel: 607-498-5574. FAX: 607-498-5574. Web Site: www.rcls.org/ros/. *Dir,* Dr Joyce Conroy
Founded 1920. Pop 2,100; Circ 15,000
Library Holdings: Bk Vols 15,000; Per Subs 23
Special Collections: Local History Coll, newsp on microfilm (1894-1942)
Mem of Ramapo Catskill Library System
Open Mon, Tues & Thurs 10-12 & 1-5, Fri 11-1 & 2-6, Sat 10-2

ROSE

P ROSE FREE LIBRARY*, 4069 Main St, 14542. (Mail add: PO Box 67, 14542-0067), SAN 312-3936. Tel: 315-587-2335. FAX: 315-587-2335. Web Site: www.rose.pls-net.org. *Dir,* Donna J Norris; E-mail: dnorris@pls-net.org
Founded 1912. Pop 2,684; Circ 15,325
Library Holdings: Bk Vols 10,635; Per Subs 25
Automation Activity & Vendor Info: (Cataloging) Evergreen; (Circulation) Evergreen; (OPAC) Evergreen; (Serials) Evergreen
Wireless access
Mem of Pioneer Library System
Open Mon, Wed & Fri 2-8, Tues 9-12, Sat 10-12

ROSENDALE

P ROSENDALE LIBRARY*, 264 Main St, 12472. (Mail add: PO Box 482, 12472-0482), SAN 312-3944. Tel: 845-658-9013. FAX: 845-658-3752. E-mail: rosendalelibrary@hvi.net. Web Site: rosendalelibrary.org. *Dir,* Wendy Alexander; E-mail: wpa_roslib@yahoo.com; Staff 5 (MLS 1, Non-MLS 4)
Founded 1958. Pop 6,352; Circ 35,162
Jan 2010-Dec 2010 Income $242,156
Library Holdings: Bk Titles 22,826
Subject Interests: Local hist
Automation Activity & Vendor Info: (Circulation) Innovative Interfaces, Inc; (ILL) Innovative Interfaces, Inc; (OPAC) Innovative Interfaces, Inc
Wireless access
Function: AV serv, Bks on cassette, Bks on CD, Children's prog, Citizenship assistance, Computers for patron use, Copy machines, Electronic databases & coll, Exhibits, Handicapped accessible, ILL available, Online cat, Online searches, Senior computer classes, Story hour, Summer reading prog, Wheelchair accessible
Mem of Mid-Hudson Library System
Open Mon, Tues & Thurs 11-7:30, Wed & Fri 11-5, Sat 10-3
Friends of the Library Group

ROSLYN

P BRYANT LIBRARY*, Two Paper Mill Rd, 11576-2193. SAN 312-3952. Tel: 516-621-2240. FAX: 516-621-7211. Administration FAX: 516-621-2542. E-mail: info@bryantlibrary.org. Web Site: www.nassaulibrary.org/bryant. *Dir,* Cathleen Mealing; *Asst Dir,* Joan Casson Sauer; *Archivist,* Myrna Sloam; *AV,* Kathleen Micucci; *Ch Serv,* J Scheuering; *Ch Serv, Computer Serv,* Ann Secter; *Circ,* Barbara Federman; *Pub Relations,* Victor Caputo; *Per, Ref Serv,* Barbara Campbell Czekala; *Tech Serv,* Paulette Palumbo; *YA Serv,* Susan Owens
Founded 1878. Pop 18,221; Circ 285,140
Library Holdings: AV Mats 51,141; DVDs 1,481; Electronic Media & Resources 55; Large Print Bks 1,671; Bk Titles 155,027; Bk Vols 164,188; Videos 9,666
Special Collections: Christopher Morley Coll; Local History Coll, photog; Roslyn Architecture Coll; William Cullen Bryant Coll. Oral History
Automation Activity & Vendor Info: (Circulation) Innovative Interfaces, Inc; (OPAC) Innovative Interfaces, Inc
Publications: Pathways to the Past; Regular Newsletter; W C Bryant in Roslyn
Mem of Nassau Library System
Friends of the Library Group

M SAINT FRANCIS HOSPITAL*, Medical Library, 100 Port Washington Blvd, 11576. SAN 312-3960. Tel: 516-562-6673. FAX: 516-562-6695. *Libr Mgr,* Rita Neri; E-mail: rita.neri@chsli.org. Subject Specialists: *Med, Nursing,* Rita Neri; Staff 1 (MLS 1)
Founded 1949
Library Holdings: Bk Titles 1,600; Per Subs 80
Subject Interests: Cardiology, Cardiovascular
Database Vendor: Cinahl, MD Consult, OCLC FirstSearch, UpToDate
Wireless access
Publications: New Book List; Newsletter; Periodicals Holding List
Partic in Basic Health Sciences Library Network; Medical & Scientific Libraries of Long Island; National Network of Libraries of Medicine Middle Atlantic Region
Restriction: Access for corporate affiliates

ROSLYN HEIGHTS

R TEMPLE SINAI LIBRARY*, 425 Roslyn Rd, 11577. SAN 312-3979. Tel: 516-621-6800. FAX: 516-625-6020. Web Site: mysinai.org. *Librn,* Burnette Groveman
Library Holdings: Bk Vols 10,000
Subject Interests: Judaica
Open Mon-Fri 9-5

ROUND LAKE

P ROUND LAKE LIBRARY*, 31 Wesley Ave, 12151. (Mail add: PO Box 665, 12151-0665), SAN 312-3987. Tel: 518-899-2285. Administration Tel: 518-641-2799. FAX: 518-899-0006. E-mail: roundlake@sals.edu. Web Site: www.roundlakelibrary.org. *Dir,* Denise Lynn Coblish; Staff 8 (MLS 3, Non-MLS 5)
Founded 1897. Pop 15,000; Circ 23,000
Library Holdings: Bk Vols 15,000; Per Subs 20
Special Collections: Centennial Coll; Round Lake Historical Coll; Victoriana Coll
Automation Activity & Vendor Info: (Acquisitions) Innovative Interfaces, Inc; (Cataloging) Innovative Interfaces, Inc; (Circulation) Innovative Interfaces, Inc
Database Vendor: EBSCOhost
Wireless access
Mem of Southern Adirondack Library System
Open Tues Noon-8, Wed-Fri 10-5, Sat 10-12
Friends of the Library Group
Branches: 1
MALTA COMMUNITY CENTER, One Bayberry Dr, Malta, 12020. Tel: 518-682-2495. FAX: 518-682-2492. *Br Mgr,* Jennifer Hurd
Library Holdings: DVDs 250; Bk Vols 5,000; Per Subs 20; Talking Bks 110
Open Mon-Fri 10-8, Sat 9-Noon

ROUSES POINT

P DODGE MEMORIAL LIBRARY*, 144 Lake St, 12979. SAN 312-4002. Tel: 518-297-6242. E-mail: rpdml1907@gmail.com. Web Site: www.cefls.org/rousespoint.htm. *Librn,* Donna Boumil
Founded 1922. Pop 2,377; Circ 10,640
Library Holdings: Bk Vols 10,000; Per Subs 59
Automation Activity & Vendor Info: (Cataloging) Horizon; (Circulation) Horizon; (OPAC) Horizon
Wireless access
Mem of Clinton-Essex-Franklin Library System
Open Mon, Tues & Thurs 12-4 & 7-9, Wed & Fri 12-4, Sat 9-3

ROXBURY

S ROXBURY LIBRARY ASSOCIATION*, 53742 State Hwy 30, 12474. (Mail add: PO Box 186, 12474 0186), SAN 312-4010. Tel: 607-326-7901. FAX: 607-326-7901. E-mail: ro.ill@4cls.org. Web Site: www.roxburylibraryonline.org. *Dir,* Dian Seiler; E-mail: dian@roxburylibraryonline.org; Staff 2 (Non-MLS 2)
Founded 1903. Pop 2,509; Circ 5,604
Jan 2007-Dec 2007. Mats Exp $3,162, Books $2,600, Per/Ser (Incl. Access Fees) $150, Other Print Mats $50, AV Mat $362. Sal $16,155
Library Holdings: AV Mats 256; Bk Titles 12,723; Per Subs 13; Talking Bks 62; Videos 298
Special Collections: John Burroughs Coll, bks, pictures; Local History, bks, ledgers, maps. Oral History
Subject Interests: Natural sci
Automation Activity & Vendor Info: (ILL) SIRSI WorkFlows
Wireless access
Function: Adult literacy prog, Archival coll, Art exhibits
Publications: History of the Town of Roxbury
Mem of Four County Library System
Open Mon & Wed 10-6, Thurs 11-5, Sat 11-2
Restriction: Authorized patrons

RUSH

P RUSH PUBLIC LIBRARY*, 5977 E Henrietta Rd, 14543. SAN 312-4029. Tel: 585-533-1370. FAX: 585-533-1546. Web Site: www.libraryweb.org/rush. *Dir,* Kirsten Flass; E-mail: kflass@libraryweb.org; Staff 11 (Non-MLS 11)
Founded 1914. Pop 3,604; Circ 30,461
Library Holdings: Bk Vols 19,427; Per Subs 48

Subject Interests: Archit, Art, Craft, Hist
Automation Activity & Vendor Info: (Cataloging) CARL.Solution (TLC); (Circulation) CARL.Solution (TLC); (OPAC) CARL.Solution (TLC); (Serials) CARL.Solution (TLC)
Wireless access
Function: Adult bk club, Bks on CD, Children's prog, Computers for patron use, Copy machines, Fax serv, Free DVD rentals, Homebound delivery serv, ILL available, Mus passes, Music CDs, OverDrive digital audio bks, Photocopying/Printing, Preschool outreach, Prog for adults, Prog for children & young adult, Ref & res, Summer reading prog, Tax forms, Teen prog, Telephone ref, Web-catalog, Wheelchair accessible, Workshops
Mem of Monroe County Library System
Open Mon, Wed & Fri 1-8, Tues & Thurs 11-8, Sat 10-2
Friends of the Library Group

RUSHFORD

P RUSHFORD FREE LIBRARY*, 9012 Main St, 14777-9700. (Mail add: PO Box 8, 14777-0008), SAN 312-4037. Tel: 585-437-2533. FAX: 585-437-9940. Web Site: www.members.aol.com/rushweb. *Dir,* Rebecca Cole; *Asst Librn,* Bernie Armison
Circ 8,223
Library Holdings: Bk Vols 16,815
Publications: Newsletter
Mem of Southern Tier Library System
Open Mon & Sat 9-12, Tues & Thurs 1-5 & 6-8, Fri 9-12 & 1-5

RUSHVILLE

P MABEL D BLODGETT MEMORIAL LIBRARY*, 35 S Main St, 14544-9648. SAN 352-3950. Tel: 585-554-3939. *Dir,* Betty Clark; E-mail: clarkb@stls.org; Staff 1 (Non-MLS 1)
Library Holdings: Bk Vols 7,500
Special Collections: Local history
Function: Homebound delivery serv, Prog for children & young adult
Mem of Southern Tier Library System
Open Mon, Wed & Fri 1-4:30

RUSSELL

P RUSSELL PUBLIC LIBRARY*, 24 Pestle St, 13684. (Mail add: PO Box 510, 13684-0510). Tel: 315-347-2115. FAX: 315-347-2115. E-mail: ruslib@ncls.org. Web Site: www.russellny.org/library.html. *Librn,* Brenda Hale
Pop 1,794
Mem of North Country Library System
Open Mon, Tues & Thurs 10-6

RYE

P RYE FREE READING ROOM*, 1061 Boston Post Rd, 10580. SAN 312-4053. Tel: 914-967-0480. Circulation Tel: 914-967-0481. Administration Tel: 914-231-3160. Information Services Tel: 914-231-3161. FAX: 914-967-5522. Web Site: www.ryelibrary.org. *Dir,* Kitty Little; *Managing Librn,* Maria Lagonia; Tel: 914-231-3165, E-mail: mlagonia@ryelibrary.org; *Teen Librn,* Bettyjane Surabian; *Bus Mgr,* Maria Ryen; Staff 34 (MLS 14, Non-MLS 20)
Founded 1884. Pop 14,955; Circ 228,000
Library Holdings: AV Mats 89,217; Bk Vols 75,818; Per Subs 1,252
Subject Interests: Rye hist
Automation Activity & Vendor Info: (Circulation) SirsiDynix; (OPAC) SirsiDynix
Wireless access
Function: Handicapped accessible, Homebound delivery serv, ILL available, Photocopying/Printing, Prog for children & young adult, Ref serv available, Summer reading prog, Telephone ref
Publications: Annual Report (Newsletter)
Mem of Westchester Library System
Open Mon & Wed-Fri 9:30-5, Tues 12-8, Sun 12-4

S RYE HISTORICAL SOCIETY, Knapp House Library & Archives, 265 Rye Beach Ave, 10580. (Mail add: One Purchase St, 10580), SAN 312-4061. Tel: 914-967-7588. FAX: 914-967-6253. E-mail: info@ryehistoricalsociety.org. Web Site: ryehistory.org. *Exec Dir,* Sheri Jordan
Founded 1964
Library Holdings: Bk Titles 920; Bk Vols 1,100
Special Collections: Rye History, photogs, slides (manuscripts 557.25 cu ft). Oral History
Subject Interests: Genealogy, Local hist
Publications: Estates of Grace; Father Burke's Dream to Rescue Children of the Inner City: St Benedict's Home, Rye, NY, 1891-1941; One Hundred Years of Health Care: 1889-1989; Read about Rye 1660-1960; Rye in the Twenties; Silent Companions: Dummy Board Figures of the 17th through 19th Centuries; The Art of Lauren Ford
Open Tues-Fri 10-3

SACKETS HARBOR

P HAY MEMORIAL LIBRARY*, 105 S Broad, 13685. (Mail add: PO Box 288, 13685-0288), SAN 312-4088. Tel: 315-646-2228. FAX: 315-646-2228. E-mail: sahlib@ncls.org. Web Site: haymemoriallibrary.org. *Mgr,* Antonette Joan Ellinger; Staff 1 (Non-MLS 1)
Founded 1900. Pop 3,323; Circ 9,505
Library Holdings: Electronic Media & Resources 11; Bk Vols 6,267; Per Subs 32; Talking Bks 527; Videos 487
Automation Activity & Vendor Info: (Circulation) SIRSI WorkFlows; (OPAC) SIRSI WorkFlows
Wireless access
Function: Adult bk club, Bks on cassette, Bks on CD, Children's prog, Computers for patron use, Copy machines, Fax serv, Free DVD rentals, Holiday prog, Homebound delivery serv, ILL available, Online cat, OverDrive digital audio bks, Prog for adults, Story hour, Summer reading prog, Tax forms, VHS videos, Wheelchair accessible
Mem of North Country Library System
Open Mon 12-7, Tues, Wed & Fri 12-5, Thurs 10-3, Sat 9-12
Friends of the Library Group

SAG HARBOR

P JOHN JERMAIN MEMORIAL LIBRARY*, 201 Main St, 11963. SAN 312-4096. Tel: 631-725-0049. FAX: 631-725-0597. E-mail: jjlib@suffolk.lib.ny.us. Web Site: johnjermain.org. *Dir,* Catherine Creedon; Tel: 631-725-0049, Ext 23, E-mail: ccreedon@johnjermain.org
Pop 5,944; Circ 48,000
Library Holdings: Bk Vols 45,000; Per Subs 117
Subject Interests: Whaling
Automation Activity & Vendor Info: (Cataloging) Innovative Interfaces, Inc
Wireless access
Mem of Suffolk Cooperative Library System
Open Mon-Wed 10-7, Thurs 10-9, Fri & Sat 10-5, Sun 12-4
Friends of the Library Group

SAINT BONAVENTURE

C SAINT BONAVENTURE UNIVERSITY, Friedsam Memorial Library, 3261 W State Rd, 14778. SAN 312-410X. Tel: 716-375-2323. FAX: 716-375-2389. Web Site: www.sbu.edu/library. *Dir, Spec Coll Librn,* Paul J Spaeth; E-mail: pspaeth@sbu.edu; *Assoc Dir,* Ann M Tenglund; Tel: 716-375-2378, E-mail: ateng@sbu.edu; *Head, Ref, ILL,* Theresa Shaffer; *Archivist,* Dennis Frank; Tel: 716-375-2322, E-mail: dfrank@sbu.edu; *Cat,* John Anderson; Tel: 716-375-2340, E-mail: janderso@sbu.edu; *Govt Doc, Ref & Instruction,* Mary Ellen Ash; Tel: 716-375-2343, E-mail: mash@sbu.edu; *Ref & Instruction,* Cathy Maldonado; Tel: 716-375-2153, E-mail: cmaldona@sbu.edu; Staff 12 (MLS 7, Non-MLS 5)
Founded 1858. Enrl 2,100; Fac 155; Highest Degree: Master
Library Holdings: Bk Titles 225,000; Bk Vols 494,088; Per Subs 881
Special Collections: Franciscan Institute; Jim Bishop Coll, ms; Rare Books, incunabula & ms; Robert Lax Coll, ms; Thomas Merton Coll, ms. State Document Depository; US Document Depository
Automation Activity & Vendor Info: (Acquisitions) SirsiDynix; (Cataloging) SirsiDynix; (Circulation) SirsiDynix; (Course Reserve) SirsiDynix; (ILL) OCLC ILLiad; (OPAC) SirsiDynix; (Serials) SirsiDynix
Wireless access
Partic in Western New York Library Resources Council
Open Mon-Thurs 8am-1am, Fri 8am-10pm, Sat 10-10, Sun 10am-1am

SAINT JOHNSVILLE

P MARGARET REANEY MEMORIAL LIBRARY*, 19 Kingsbury Ave, 13452. SAN 312-4126. Tel: 518-568-7822. FAX: 518-568-7822. E-mail: margaretreaneylibrary@gmail.com. *Dir,* Dawn Lamphere; *Asst Dir,* Marta Zimmerman
Circ 20,436
Library Holdings: Bk Titles 31,000; Bk Vols 31,200; Per Subs 22
Special Collections: Local Hist Coll, genealogies, newspapers, & hist ref
Automation Activity & Vendor Info: (Circulation) SirsiDynix
Wireless access
Mem of Mohawk Valley Library System
Open Mon & Fri 9:30-5 & 6:30-8:30, Tues & Wed 9:30-5, Sat 9:30-Noon

SALAMANCA

P SALAMANCA PUBLIC LIBRARY, 155 Wildwood Ave, 14779. SAN 312-4134. Tel: 716-945-1890. FAX: 716-945-2741. Web Site: www.salmun.com. *Dir,* Thomas L Sharbaugh; E-mail: tsharbaugh@salmun.com; Staff 3 (MLS 1, Non-MLS 2)
Founded 1920. Pop 5,895; Circ 66,617
Apr 2012-Mar 2013 Income $287,196, City $277,196, Locally Generated Income $10,000. Mats Exp $23,000, Books $15,000, Per/Ser (Incl. Access Fees) $4,500, AV Mat $3,500. Sal $144,357 (Prof $61,000)

Library Holdings: AV Mats 5,676; Bk Titles 39,410; Bk Vols 42,602; Per Subs 118
Special Collections: Iroquois & Seneca Indians (Iroquoia); Salamanca Historical Coll
Automation Activity & Vendor Info: (Circulation) Follett Software; (OPAC) Follett Software
Wireless access
Mem of Chautauqua-Cattaraugus Library System
Open Mon & Fri 9-5:30, Tues & Thurs 11-7, Sat 9-1
Friends of the Library Group

S SENECA NATION LIBRARY*, 830 Broad St, 14779. SAN 375-166X. Tel: 716-945-3157. FAX: 716-945-9770. E-mail: Alleg.Library@sni.org. Web Site: senecanationlibrary.wordpress.com/. *Dir,* Krista Jacobs; E-mail: Krista.Jacobs@sni.org; *Libr Supvr,* Jayde Lichy
Founded 1979
Library Holdings: Bk Vols 18,000; Per Subs 374
Special Collections: Native American Materials
Wireless access
Mem of Chautauqua-Cattaraugus Library System
Open Mon-Wed (Winter) 8-8, Thurs & Fri 8-4:30, Sat 10-1; Mon-Thurs (Summer) 8:30-8:30, Fri 8:30-5
Friends of the Library Group

SALEM

P BANCROFT PUBLIC LIBRARY*, 181 Main St, 12865. (Mail add: PO Box 515, 12865), SAN 312-4142. Tel: 518-854-7463. FAX: 518-854-7463. Web Site: www.slibrary.org. *Libr Dir,* Peg Culver; E-mail: pculver@sals.edu; Staff 1 (Non-MLS 1)
Pop 9,877; Circ 13,298
Library Holdings: Bk Vols 18,000; Per Subs 10
Automation Activity & Vendor Info: (Acquisitions) Innovative Interfaces, Inc; (Circulation) Innovative Interfaces, Inc; (Media Booking) Innovative Interfaces, Inc; (OPAC) Innovative Interfaces, Inc; (Serials) Innovative Interfaces, Inc
Open Mon & Fri 12:30-4:30, Tues & Thurs 12:30-4:30 & 6:30-8:30, Wed & Sat 10-1
Friends of the Library Group

SALISBURY CENTER

P KIRBY FREE LIBRARY OF SALISBURY CENTER*, 105 Rte 29A, 13454. (Mail add: PO Box 322, 13454-0322), SAN 376-3137. Tel: 315-429-9006. FAX: 315-429-9006. E-mail: salisbury@midyork.org. Web Site: www.midyork.org/salisburycenter. *Dir,* Holly Eckler; *Librn,* Sue Jorrey
Pop 1,954
Library Holdings: Bk Vols 8,000
Special Collections: Christian Coll
Wireless access
Mem of Mid-York Library System
Open Mon 3:30-7:30, Tues & Thurs 10-12 & 1-5, Wed 4-7, Fri 10-Noon

SANBORN

J NIAGARA COUNTY COMMUNITY COLLEGE*, Library Learning Center, 3111 Saunders Settlement Rd, 14132. SAN 312-4150. Tel: 716-614-6705, 716-614-6780. Circulation Tel: 716-614-6783. Reference Tel: 716-614-6786. FAX: 716-614-6816, 716-614-6828. Web Site: niagaracc.suny.edu/library. *Chair,* Tamara Anderson; Tel: 716-614-6788, E-mail: tanderson@niagaracc.suny.edu; *Tech Serv Librn,* Nancy Kennedy; Tel: 716-614-6792, E-mail: verstrea@niagaracc.suny.edu; *Cat,* Karen Ferington; Tel: 716-614-6787, E-mail: feringtk@niagaracc.suny.edu; *Ref & Instrul Serv, Instr Coordr,* Lillian Passanese; Tel: 716-614-6790, E-mail: passanli@niagaracc.suny.edu; *Ref,* Jeanne Tuohey; Tel: 716-614-6791, E-mail: tuohey@niagaracc.suny.edu; Staff 12 (MLS 6, Non-MLS 6)
Founded 1963. Enrl 5,000; Highest Degree: Associate
Sept 2005-Aug 2006. Mats Exp $229,730, Books $77,070, Per/Ser (Incl. Access Fees) $127,000, Micro $21,160, AV Mat $4,500
Library Holdings: Bk Titles 85,042; Bk Vols 94,921; Per Subs 500
Subject Interests: Archives
Automation Activity & Vendor Info: (Acquisitions) Ex Libris Group; (Circulation) Ex Libris Group; (Course Reserve) Ex Libris Group; (OPAC) Ex Libris Group; (Serials) Ex Libris Group
Database Vendor: ARTstor, Dialog, EBSCOhost, Gale Cengage Learning, JSTOR, OCLC FirstSearch, ProQuest, ScienceDirect, Wilson - Wilson Web
Wireless access
Publications: Pathfinders; Periodicals in the LLC; What's New
Partic in OCLC Online Computer Library Center, Inc; Western New York Library Resources Council
Open Mon-Thurs (Fall & Spring) 8am-9pm, Fri 8-4, Sat 11-3

P SANBORN-PEKIN FREE LIBRARY*, 5884 West St, 14132. SAN 312-4169. Tel: 716-731-9933. FAX: 716-731-9933. Web Site: www.nioga.org. *Librn,* Sallie Ditzel; E-mail: sditz@nioga.org
Pop 4,000; Circ 52,966
Library Holdings: Bk Vols 45,000; Per Subs 64
Automation Activity & Vendor Info: (Cataloging) SirsiDynix; (Circulation) SirsiDynix; (OPAC) SirsiDynix; (Serials) SirsiDynix
Wireless access
Mem of Nioga Library System
Open Mon, Wed & Thurs 2-8, Tues & Fri 2-6, Sat 10-1

SANDY CREEK

P ANNIE PORTER AINSWORTH MEMORIAL LIBRARY*, 6064 S Main St, 13145. (Mail add: PO Box 69, 13145-0069), SAN 312-4177. Tel: 315-387-3732. FAX: 315-387-2005. *Dir,* Valerie Cascanet; *Libr Asst,* Dianna Stanton-Jones
Founded 1928
Special Collections: Hollis Coll
Automation Activity & Vendor Info: (Acquisitions) SIRSI WorkFlows; (Cataloging) SIRSI WorkFlows; (Circulation) SIRSI WorkFlows; (ILL) SIRSI WorkFlows; (OPAC) SIRSI WorkFlows; (Serials) SIRSI WorkFlows
Wireless access
Mem of North Country Library System
Open Tues & Wed 11-6, Thurs 11-6 & 7-9, Fri 10-6, Sat 10-1

SARANAC LAKE

J NORTH COUNTRY COMMUNITY COLLEGE LIBRARIES*, Saranac Lake Campus Library, 23 Santanoni Ave, 12983-2046. (Mail add: PO Box 89, 12983-0089), SAN 312-4185. Tel: 518-891-2915, Ext 1314. Web Site: www.nccc.edu. *Interim Dir, Libr Serv,* Brian O'Connor; E-mail: boconnor@nccc.edu; *Librn,* Christen Cardina; E-mail: ccardina@nccc.edu; *Acq & Cat,* Phil Gallos; E-mail: pgallos@nccc.edu; *ILL & Circ,* Irene Finlayson; E-mail: ifinlayson@nccc.edu; Staff 1 (MLS 1)
Founded 1967. Enrl 1,672; Fac 50; Highest Degree: Associate
Sept 2007-Aug 2008 Income $321,649, State $5,649, Parent Institution $316,000. Mats Exp $384,020, Books $349,369, Per/Ser (Incl. Access Fees) $13,606, Micro $5,445, AV Mat $1,081, Electronic Ref Mat (Incl. Access Fees) $14,156, Presv $363
Library Holdings: Bks on Deafness & Sign Lang 34; e-books 4,600; e-journals 18,000; Electronic Media & Resources 36; Bk Titles 62,517; Bk Vols 64,451; Per Subs 130; Videos 641
Special Collections: Adirondack History (Adirondack Coll), bks, maps & prints; Nettie Marie Jones Fine Arts Coll. State Document Depository
Subject Interests: Adirondack hist, Criminal justice, Nursing, Radiologic tech
Automation Activity & Vendor Info: (Cataloging) OCLC; (Circulation) Follett Software; (ILL) OCLC; (OPAC) Ex Libris Group
Database Vendor: Baker & Taylor, CQ Press, CredoReference, Dialog, EBSCO Information Services, EBSCOhost, Elsevier, Ex Libris Group, Gale Cengage Learning, H W Wilson, LexisNexis, OCLC ArticleFirst, OCLC FirstSearch, OCLC WorldShare Interlibrary Loan, Oxford Online, ProQuest, PubMed, ScienceDirect, TLC (The Library Corporation), WebMD, Wilson - Wilson Web
Wireless access
Publications: From the Top of the Hill (Newsletter)
Partic in New York Online Virtual Electronic Library (NOVEL); Northern New York Library Network; Nylink; OCLC Online Computer Library Center, Inc; SUNYConnect; Westchester Academic Library Directors Organization (WALDO)
Special Services for the Deaf - Accessible learning ctr; Assistive tech; Bks on deafness & sign lang
Special Services for the Blind - Aids for in-house use; Bks on cassette; Bks on CD; Computer with voice synthesizer for visually impaired persons; Copier with enlargement capabilities; Dragon Naturally Speaking software; Magnifiers; Rec; Recorded bks; Screen enlargement software for people with visual disabilities; Sound rec; Talking bk & rec for the blind cat; Talking bks; Talking bks & player equip; Text reader
Open Mon-Thurs 7:30am-8pm, Fri 7:30-4:30, Sun 1-6

Departmental Libraries:

MALONE CAMPUS LIBRARY, 75 William St, Malone, 12953. Tel: 518-483-4550. *Campus Librn,* Katherine White; E-mail: kwhite@nccc.edu
Open Mon-Thurs 8:30-4:30

TICONDEROGA CAMPUS LIBRARY, 11 Hawkeye Trail, Ticonderoga, 12883. Tel: 518-585-4454. *Campus Librn,* Mary Ann Rockwell; E-mail: marockwell@nccc.edu
Open Mon-Thurs 8:30-4:30

P SARANAC LAKE FREE LIBRARY*, 109 Main St, 12983. SAN 312-4207. Tel: 518-891-4190. FAX: 518-891-5931. Web Site: www.saranaclakelibrary.org. *Dir,* Peter Benson
Founded 1907. Circ 66,207
Library Holdings: AV Mats 7,553; Bk Titles 33,232; Bk Vols 36,171

Special Collections: Adirondack History Coll; Mounted Wildlife Museum
Automation Activity & Vendor Info: (Cataloging) SirsiDynix; (Circulation) SirsiDynix; (OPAC) SirsiDynix
Wireless access
Publications: Newsletter
Mem of Clinton-Essex-Franklin Library System
Open Mon-Fri 10-5:30
Friends of the Library Group

M TRUDEAU INSTITUTE LIBRARY*, 154 Algonquin Ave, 12983. SAN 312-4215. Tel: 518-891-3084, Ext 127. FAX: 518-891-5126. Web Site: www.trudeauinstitute.org. *Info Spec,* Kelly Stanyon; E-mail: kstanyon@trudeauinstitute.org; Staff 1 (MLS 1)
Founded 1964
Library Holdings: Bk Vols 15,000; Per Subs 110
Subject Interests: Immunology, Virology
Wireless access
Function: Archival coll, Doc delivery serv, For res purposes, ILL available
Restriction: Open by appt only

SARATOGA SPRINGS

E EMPIRE STATE COLLEGE*, Three Union Ave, 12866. Tel: 518-587-2100. FAX: 518-581-9526. E-mail: librarian@esc.edu. Web Site: www.esc.edu/library. *Asst Dir, Libr Instruction & Info Literacy,* Dana Longley; *Info Res Coordr,* Sarah Morehouse; Staff 4 (MLS 4)
Library Holdings: e-books 65,000; e-journals 38,000
Database Vendor: Alexander Street Press, ARTstor, Career Guidance Foundation, College Source, CQ Press, ebrary, EBSCOhost, Gale Cengage Learning, Greenwood Publishing Group, JSTOR, Mergent Online, OCLC WorldShare Interlibrary Loan, Oxford Online, ProQuest, RefWorks, ScienceDirect, SerialsSolutions, Springshare, LLC, Westlaw
Partic in SUNYConnect; Westchester Academic Library Directors Organization (WALDO)

S NATIONAL MUSEUM OF RACING & HALL OF FAME*, John A Morris Library, 191 Union Ave, 12866. SAN 312-4231. Tel: 518-584-0400. Reference Tel: 518-584-0400, Ext 122. FAX: 518-584-4574. *Dir,* Peter Hammell; *Curator,* Lori Ann Fisher; Tel: 518-584-0400, Ext 109, E-mail: nmrcollect@racingmuseum.net; *Coll Mgr,* Beth Sheffer; Tel: 518-584-0400, Ext 141, E-mail: nmrasstcollect@racingmuseum.net; Staff 4 (MLS 2, Non-MLS 2)
Founded 1950
Library Holdings: Bk Titles 1,700; Bk Vols 2,300; Per Subs 12
Subject Interests: Horses, Thoroughbred horse racing
Database Vendor: OCLC FirstSearch
Publications: Horses & Members in the National Racing Hall of Fame; The Race Horses of America 1832-1872
Partic in Capital District Library Council; OCLC Online Computer Library Center, Inc
Restriction: Open by appt only

M SARATOGA HOSPITAL*, Medical Library, 211 Church St, 12866. SAN 328-316X. Tel: 518-583-8301. FAX: 518-580-4285. E-mail: shlibry@saratogacare.org. Web Site: www.saratogacare.org. *Dir,* Jill H Lewis; *Librn,* Jane Lindberg; *Librn,* Jean A Richards; Staff 10 (MLS 2, Non-MLS 8)
Library Holdings: Bk Titles 481; Per Subs 60
Database Vendor: EBSCOhost
Wireless access
Partic in Capital District Library Council
Open Mon-Fri 9-4

P SARATOGA SPRINGS PUBLIC LIBRARY*, 49 Henry St, 12866. SAN 312-424X. Tel: 518-584-7860. FAX: 518-584-7866. Web Site: www.sspl.org. *Dir,* A Issac Pulver; E-mail: ipulver@sals.edu; *Head, Circ, Head, Tech Serv,* Mary Ann Hunter; *Adult Serv,* Dan Hubbs; *Ch Serv,* Jennifer Ogrodowski; *ILL,* Cathy Stevens; Staff 12 (MLS 12)
Founded 1950. Pop 46,000; Circ 630,000
Library Holdings: Bk Titles 85,000; Bk Vols 207,000; Per Subs 400
Special Collections: Balneology; Hydrotherapy; Saratogiana
Wireless access
Publications: Bibliography of Research Materials on Saratoga Springs
Mem of Southern Adirondack Library System
Open Mon-Thurs 9-9, Fri 9-6, Sat 9-5, Sun 12-5
Friends of the Library Group

C SKIDMORE COLLEGE*, Lucy Scribner Library, 815 N Broadway, 12866. SAN 312-4266. Tel: 518-580-5000. Circulation Tel: 518-580-5502. Interlibrary Loan Service Tel: 518-580-5520. Reference Tel: 518-580-5503. FAX: 518-580-5541. Interlibrary Loan Service FAX: 518-580-5540. E-mail: illdesk@skidmore.edu. Web Site: www.skidmore.edu. *Col Librn, Spec Coll Librn,* Ruth Copans; Tel: 518-580-5506, E-mail: rcopans@skidmore.edu; *Assoc Col Librn,* Susan Zappen; E-mail: szappen@skidmore.edu; *Acq Librn,* Dung Lam Chen; Staff 22.17 (MLS 9.17, Non-MLS 13)
Founded 1911. Enrl 2,468; Fac 169; Highest Degree: Master
Library Holdings: Bk Vols 400,000
Special Collections: College Archives; Edith Wharton Coll; Edna St Vincent Millay Coll; Hebraica-Judaica (Leo Usdan Coll); Late 19th Century Illustrated Books Coll; Max Beerbohm Coll; Saratogiana (Anita P Yates Coll), bks, photogs. State Document Depository; US Document Depository
Subject Interests: Art
Automation Activity & Vendor Info: (Acquisitions) Ex Libris Group; (Cataloging) Ex Libris Group; (Circulation) Ex Libris Group; (ILL) OCLC ILLiad; (OPAC) Ex Libris Group; (Serials) Ex Libris Group
Wireless access
Partic in Capital District Library Council; OCLC Online Computer Library Center, Inc
Open Mon-Thurs 8am-1am, Fri 8am-10pm, Sat 9am-10pm, Sun 11am-1am
Friends of the Library Group

P SOUTHERN ADIRONDACK LIBRARY SYSTEM*, 22 Whitney Pl, 12866-4596. SAN 312-4274. Tel: 518-584-7300. FAX: 518-587-5589. Web Site: www.sals.edu. *Dir,* Sara Dallas; *Librn,* Jill Ryder; *Tech Serv,* Jennifer Ferriss; Staff 4 (MLS 4)
Founded 1958. Pop 302,933
Library Holdings: Bk Vols 94,023; Per Subs 25
Automation Activity & Vendor Info: (Acquisitions) Innovative Interfaces, Inc; (Cataloging) Innovative Interfaces, Inc; (Circulation) Innovative Interfaces, Inc; (ILL) Innovative Interfaces, Inc; (OPAC) Innovative Interfaces, Inc; (Serials) Innovative Interfaces, Inc
Database Vendor: Overdrive, Inc
Wireless access
Publications: Newsletter
Member Libraries: Argyle Free Library; Ballston Spa Public Library; Bancroft Public Library; Bolton Free Library; Caldwell-Lake George Library; Cambridge Public Library; Clifton Park-Halfmoon Public Library; Corinth Free Library; Crandall Public Library; Easton Library; Fort Edward Free Library; Galway Public Library; Great Meadow Correctional Facility Library; Greenwich Free Library; Hadley-Luzerne Public Library; Hillview Free Library; Horicon Free Public Library; Hudson Falls Free Library; Long Lake Library; Mechanicville District Public Library; Mount McGregor Correctional Facility Library; Pember Library & Museum of Natural History; Raquette Lake Free Library; Richards Library; Round Lake Library; Saratoga Springs Public Library; Schuylerville Public Library; Stillwater Free Library; Stony Creek Free Library; The Whitehall Free Library; Town of Ballston Community Library; Town of Chester Public Library; Town of Indian Lake Public Library; Town of Inlet Public Library; Town of Johnsburg Library; Town of Lake Pleasant Public Library; Washington Correctional Facility Library; Waterford Public Library
Partic in Capital District Library Council
Special Services for the Deaf - ADA equip
Open Mon-Fri 8:30-4:30

GL SUPREME COURT LIBRARY AT SARATOGA SPRINGS*, Fourth Judicial District, 474 Broadway, Ste 10, 12866-2297. SAN 312-4282. Tel: 518-451-8777. E-mail: lawlibrarysaratoga@nycourts.gov. *Librn,* Vicki Heidelberger
Founded 1866
Library Holdings: Bk Vols 20,000
Special Collections: Directories of Saratoga Springs (1884-present)
Subject Interests: Law
Automation Activity & Vendor Info: (Acquisitions) SIRSI WorkFlows; (Cataloging) SIRSI WorkFlows; (Circulation) SIRSI WorkFlows; (Serials) SIRSI WorkFlows
Database Vendor: LexisNexis, Loislaw, Westlaw
Open Mon-Fri 8-12 & 1-4

SAUGERTIES

P SAUGERTIES PUBLIC LIBRARY*, 91 Washington Ave, 12477. SAN 312-4304. Tel: 845-246-4317. FAX: 845-246-0858. Web Site: www.saugertiespubliclibrary.org. *Dir,* Sukrit Goswami; E-mail: director@saugertiespubliclibrary.org; Staff 10 (MLS 3, Non-MLS 7)
Founded 1894. Pop 19,000; Circ 75,282
Library Holdings: AV Mats 3,354; Bk Vols 43,308; Per Subs 82
Special Collections: Local Newspapers Coll, microfilm; New York State, Ulster County & Local History Coll, bks, newsp, pamphlet
Automation Activity & Vendor Info: (Cataloging) Innovative Interfaces, Inc; (Circulation) Innovative Interfaces, Inc; (ILL) Innovative Interfaces, Inc; (OPAC) Innovative Interfaces, Inc
Wireless access
Mem of Mid-Hudson Library System
Open Mon & Wed 10-8, Tues, Thurs & Fri 10-6, Sat 10-2
Friends of the Library Group

SAVONA

P SAVONA FREE LIBRARY*, 15 McCoy St, 14879. (Mail add: PO Box 475, 14879-0475), SAN 312-4312. Tel: 607-583-4426. FAX: 607-583-4426. Web Site: www.stls.org/savona/index.htm.
Pop 860; Circ 17,000
Library Holdings: Bk Titles 11,000; Per Subs 20
Automation Activity & Vendor Info: (Cataloging) SirsiDynix; (Circulation) SirsiDynix; (OPAC) SirsiDynix; (Serials) SirsiDynix
Wireless access
Mem of Southern Tier Library System
Open Mon-Fri 2-7
Friends of the Library Group

SAYVILLE

P SAYVILLE LIBRARY*, 11 Collins Ave, 11782-3199. SAN 312-4320. Tel: 631-589-4440. FAX: 631-589-6128. E-mail: sayvlib@suffolk.lib.ny.us. Web Site: www.sayville.suffolk.lib.ny.us. *Dir,* Alice Lepore; *Head, Circ,* Debbie Pouletsos; *Automation Syst Coordr,* William Olson; *Ref,* Jonathan Pryer; *Youth Serv,* Donna DiBerardino; Staff 14 (MLS 14)
Founded 1914. Pop 18,131
Library Holdings: AV Mats 19,808; CDs 3,147; DVDs 2,050; e-journals 16,549; Large Print Bks 2,600; Bk Vols 108,683; Per Subs 255; Talking Bks 3,369; Videos 6,890
Special Collections: Local History Coll; Long Island Coll
Automation Activity & Vendor Info: (Acquisitions) Innovative Interfaces, Inc; (Cataloging) Innovative Interfaces, Inc; (Circulation) Innovative Interfaces, Inc; (Course Reserve) Innovative Interfaces, Inc; (OPAC) Innovative Interfaces, Inc
Wireless access
Mem of Suffolk Cooperative Library System
Open Mon-Fri 10-9, Sat 9:30-5, Sun (Sept-June) 1-5
Friends of the Library Group

SCARSDALE

P SCARSDALE PUBLIC LIBRARY*, 54 Olmsted Rd, 10583. SAN 312-4339. Tel: 914-722-1300. FAX: 914-722-1305. Web Site: www.scarsdalelibrary.org. *Dir,* Elizabeth Bermel; E-mail: scadirector@wlsmail.org; *Asst Dir,* Leni Glauber; E-mail: scasstdirector@wls.mail.org; *Head, Ch,* Karen Zielinski; *Head, Ref,* Jennifer Friedman; *Outreach Serv Librn,* Judith Reinfeld-Bruno; *Bus & Human Res Mgr,* Roberta Stein-Ham; *Ch Serv,* Aisha Bell; *Info Tech,* Anne-Marie Cutul; *Reader Serv, YA Serv,* Nancy Zachary; *Ref Serv,* Daniel Glauber; *Ref Serv,* Barbara Kokot; *YA Serv,* Claudette Gassler; Staff 56 (MLS 26, Non-MLS 30)
Founded 1928. Pop 17,823; Circ 409,034
Jun 2010-May 2011 Income $3,202,332, State $12,362, City $3,189,970. Mats Exp $299,670, Books $226,370, Per/Ser (Incl. Access Fees) $25,500, AV Mat $47,800. Sal $2,614,600 (Prof $1,903,135)
Library Holdings: Audiobooks 7,397; AV Mats 11,965; e-books 4,581; Bk Vols 122,758; Per Subs 300
Subject Interests: Japanese (Lang), Local hist, Newsp items
Automation Activity & Vendor Info: (Acquisitions) SirsiDynix; (Circulation) SirsiDynix; (OPAC) SirsiDynix
Database Vendor: EBSCOhost, Gale Cengage Learning, JSTOR, Overdrive, Inc, ProQuest, SirsiDynix
Wireless access
Mem of Westchester Library System
Partic in Westlynx
Friends of the Library Group

S WEINBERG NATURE CENTER LIBRARY*, 455 Mamaroneck Rd, 10583. SAN 328-364X. Tel: 914-722-1289. FAX: 914-723-4784. Web Site: www.weinbergnaturecenter.org. *Exec Dir,* Walter D Terrell, Jr
Library Holdings: Bk Titles 500; Bk Vols 521; Per Subs 12
Special Collections: Birds & Local Mammals Coll; Native American/Woodland Indian Artifacts Coll
Subject Interests: Environ, Local hist, Native Am, Nature
Wireless access
Open Wed-Sun (Fall-Spring) 9-5; Mon-Fri (Summer) 9-5
Friends of the Library Group

R WESTCHESTER REFORM TEMPLE LIBRARY*, 255 Mamaroneck Rd, 10583. SAN 312-4347. Tel: 914-723-7727. FAX: 914-723-5946. E-mail: office@wrtemple.org. Web Site: www.wrtemple.org. *Librn,* Florence Gross; Staff 4 (MLS 2, Non-MLS 2)
Founded 1960
Library Holdings: Bk Titles 3,000; Bk Vols 3,080; Per Subs 10
Special Collections: Jacks/Scheye; Torah Study
Subject Interests: Judaica
Wireless access
Open Mon-Sat 9-5
Friends of the Library Group

SCHAGHTICOKE

P ARVILLA E DIVER MEMORIAL LIBRARY*, 136 Main St, 12154. SAN 312-4355. Tel: 518-753-4344. FAX: 518-753-4344. E-mail: info@diverlibrary.org. Web Site: diverlibrary.org. *Dir,* Rebekah Jarvis; *Assoc Dir,* Laura Twombly; Staff 1 (MLS 1)
Founded 1939. Circ 5,708
Library Holdings: Audiobooks 223; DVDs 458; Large Print Bks 22; Bk Vols 7,000; Per Subs 20
Wireless access
Function: After school storytime, Archival coll, Audio & video playback equip for onsite use, Audiobks via web, Bks on cassette, Bks on CD, Children's prog, Computer training, Computers for patron use, Fax serv, Free DVD rentals, Handicapped accessible, Holiday prog, ILL available, Music CDs, OverDrive digital audio bks, Photocopying/Printing, Prog for adults, Prog for children & young adult, Pub access computers, Scanner, Summer reading prog, VHS videos, Workshops
Mem of Upper Hudson Library System
Open Mon-Fri 1-7, Sat 10-1
Friends of the Library Group

SCHENECTADY

S DUDLEY OBSERVATORY LIBRARY*, 15 Nott Terrace Heights, 12308. SAN 354-1509. Tel: 518-382-7583. FAX: 518-382-7584. E-mail: info@dudleyobservatory.org. Web Site: www.dudleyobservatory.org. *Exec Dir,* Elissa Kane; E-mail: ekane@dudleyobservatory.org; Staff 1 (MLS 1)
Founded 1852
Library Holdings: Bk Titles 5,000; Per Subs 10
Special Collections: Archives of Dudley Observatory; Benjamin A Gould Jr Library
Subject Interests: Astronomy, Astrophysics, Hist of astronomy, Space sci
Automation Activity & Vendor Info: (ILL) OCLC
Partic in Capital District Library Council
Restriction: Circ limited, Open by appt only

GL JOSEPH F EGAN MEMORIAL SUPREME COURT LIBRARY*, Schenectady County Judicial Bldg, 612 State St, 12305. SAN 312-4363. Tel: 518-285-8518. FAX: 518-451-8730. E-mail: 4JDLawLibrary@nycourts.gov. *Sr Law Librn,* Dana Wantuch; Staff 3 (MLS 1, Non-MLS 2)
Library Holdings: Bk Vols 27,650
Automation Activity & Vendor Info: (Acquisitions) SirsiDynix; (Cataloging) SirsiDynix; (Circulation) SirsiDynix; (ILL) SirsiDynix; (OPAC) SirsiDynix; (Serials) SirsiDynix
Database Vendor: LexisNexis, Loislaw, Westlaw
Wireless access
Open Mon-Fri 9-4:45

M ELLIS HOSPITAL*, Medical-Nursing Library, 1101 Nott St, 12308. SAN 312-4371. Tel: 518-243-4000, 518-243-4381. FAX: 518-243-1429. Web Site: www.ellishospital.org. *Dir,* Christopher Stater
Founded 1930
Library Holdings: Bk Titles 2,815; Bk Vols 3,150; Per Subs 210
Special Collections: Nursing History
Database Vendor: EBSCOhost
Partic in Cap District Libr Coun for Ref & Res Resources; New York State Interlibrary Loan Network (NYSILL)
Restriction: Staff use only

SR FIRST REFORMED CHURCH OF SCHENECTADY*, Norman B Johnson Memorial Library, Eight N Church St, 12305-1699. SAN 371-7712. Tel: 518-377-2201. FAX: 518-374-4098. E-mail: 1streformed@gmail.com. Web Site: www.1streformed.com. *Dir,* Virginia Laumeister; *Cat,* Alice B Reed; Staff 13 (MLS 3, Non-MLS 10)
Founded 1838
Jan 2005-Dec 2005 Income $1,645, Locally Generated Income $20, Parent Institution $1,400, Other $200. Mats Exp $1,375, Books $1,105, Per/Ser (Incl. Access Fees) $150, Presv $120
Library Holdings: Bk Titles 7,600
Special Collections: Children's Coll; Christmas Coll
Subject Interests: Art, Hist, Lit, Music, Relig
Special Services for the Deaf - Bks on deafness & sign lang
Open Mon-Fri 7-3, Sun 10-Noon

S KNOLLS ATOMIC POWER LABORATORY INC, LIBRARY*, 35 Front St, 12305. (Mail add: PO Box 7400, 12301-7400), SAN 371-0998. Tel: 518-395-4918. FAX: 518-395-7761. *Mgr,* Denise Gladding; *Mgr,* Tony Oliveira; *Librn,* Patricia Oliver; Tel: 518-395-4918; Staff 5 (MLS 1, Non-MLS 4)
Founded 1946
Library Holdings: Bk Titles 6,729; Bk Vols 18,955; Per Subs 250
Restriction: Not open to pub

P MOHAWK VALLEY LIBRARY SYSTEM, 858 Duanesburg Rd, 12306-1057. SAN 312-438X. Tel: 518-355-2010. FAX: 518-355-0674. E-mail: mvls@mvls.info. Web Site: www.mvls.info. *Dir,* Eric Trahan; E-mail: etrahan@mvls.info; *Asst Dir, Ch Serv,* Sue Z Rokos; E-mail: srokos@mvls.info; *Mem Serv Librn,* Sharon O'Brien; E-mail: sobrien@mvls.info; *Outreach Serv Librn,* Lois Gordon; E-mail: lgordon@mvls.info; Staff 6.5 (MLS 4, Non-MLS 2.5)
Founded 1959. Pop 293,226
Library Holdings: Bk Vols 56,761
Wireless access
Member Libraries: Amsterdam Free Library; Canajoharie Library & Art Gallery; Community Library; Fort Hunter Free Library; Fort Plain Free Library; Frothingham Free Library; Gloversville Public Library; Johnstown Public Library; Margaret Reaney Memorial Library; Middleburgh Library Association; Northville Public Library; Schenectady County Public Library; Schoharie Free Association Library; Sharon Springs Free Library
Partic in Cap District Libr Coun for Ref & Res Resources
Restriction: Staff use only

J SCHENECTADY COUNTY COMMUNITY COLLEGE*, Begley Library & Instructional Technology Center, 78 Washington Ave, 12305. SAN 312-4428. Tel: 518-381-1235. Reference Tel: 518-381-1239. Administration Tel: 518-381-1240. FAX: 518-381-1252. Web Site: www.sunysccc.edu/library. *Dir, Libr Serv,* Lynne King; *Head, Tech Serv,* David Moore; *Pub Serv,* Caroline Laier; Staff 7 (MLS 5, Non-MLS 2)
Founded 1968. Enrl 2,901; Highest Degree: Bachelor
Library Holdings: Bks on Deafness & Sign Lang 50; Bk Titles 74,000; Bk Vols 81,000; Per Subs 400
Special Collections: College Memorabilia Coll
Subject Interests: Culinary arts, Fire sci, Hotel tech, Paralegal, Travel & tourism
Automation Activity & Vendor Info: (Cataloging) OCLC Connexion; (Circulation) Ex Libris Group; (ILL) OCLC ILLiad; (OPAC) Ex Libris Group
Database Vendor: EBSCOhost, Gale Cengage Learning, LexisNexis, OCLC FirstSearch, OCLC WorldShare Interlibrary Loan, ScienceDirect, Westlaw
Wireless access
Publications: A Guide to Begley Library & the Instructional Technology Center
Partic in Cap District Libr Coun for Ref & Res Resources; OCLC Online Computer Library Center, Inc
Open Mon-Thurs (Winter) 8am-8:30pm, Fri 8-4:30, Sat 10-2; Mon-Fri (Summer) 9-4

S SCHENECTADY COUNTY HISTORICAL SOCIETY*, Grems-Doolittle Library, 32 Washington Ave, 12305. SAN 321-0030. Tel: 518-374-0263. FAX: 518-688-2825. E-mail: librarian@schist.org. Web Site: www.schenectadyhistory.net. *Archivist, Librn,* Melissa Tacke; Staff 1 (MLS 1)
Founded 1905
Library Holdings: Bk Vols 5,000
Special Collections: Archives (Carl Company Coll); Diaries of Harriet Mumford Paige; Personal Papers (Charles P Steinmetz Coll). Oral History
Subject Interests: Genealogy, Local hist
Wireless access
Publications: A History of the Schenectady PATENT; Duanesburg Memorial Census, rev; Images of America: Glennville, Images of America: Rotterdam; The Markers Speak
Open Mon-Fri 9-5, Sat 10-2
Restriction: Non-circulating

P SCHENECTADY COUNTY PUBLIC LIBRARY*, 99 Clinton St, 12305-2083. SAN 354-1266. Tel: 518-388-4500. Circulation Tel: 518-388-4538. Interlibrary Loan Service Tel: 518-388-4518. Reference Tel: 518-388-4511. FAX: 518-386-2241. Web Site: www.scpl.org/. *Dir,* Karen Bradley; Tel: 518-388-4543; *Asst Dir, Youth Serv Coordr,* Serena Butch; Tel: 518-388-4545, E-mail: sbutch@sals.edu; *Outreach Librn,* Paula Carosella; Tel: 518-388-4521, E-mail: pcarosella@sals.edu; *Adult Serv Coordr,* Mary Ann Warner; Tel: 518-388-4573, E-mail: mwarner@sals.edu; *AV,* Kenneth Wagner; Tel: 518-388-4502, E-mail: kwagner@sals.edu; Staff 84 (MLS 24, Non-MLS 60)
Founded 1894. Pop 146,555; Circ 1,231,567
Jan 2005-Dec 2005 Income (Main Library and Branch(s)) $5,005,405, State $211,625, County $4,532,310, Other $261,470. Mats Exp $746,500, Books $479,500, Per/Ser (Incl. Access Fees) $68,000, AV Mat $169,000, Electronic Ref Mat (Incl. Access Fees) $18,000, Presv $12,000. Sal $2,968,092 (Prof $1,194,192)
Library Holdings: AV Mats 58,736; CDs 9,484; DVDs 10,399; Large Print Bks 9,030; Music Scores 1,811; Bk Titles 186,165; Bk Vols 549,789; Per Subs 1,652; Videos 15,943
Automation Activity & Vendor Info: (Cataloging) Innovative Interfaces, Inc; (Circulation) Innovative Interfaces, Inc; (OPAC) Innovative Interfaces, Inc; (Serials) Innovative Interfaces, Inc
Database Vendor: EBSCOhost, Gale Cengage Learning, ProQuest
Mem of Mohawk Valley Library System
Partic in Capital District Library Council
Open Mon-Thurs 9-9, Fri & Sat 9-5, Sun 1-5
Friends of the Library Group
Branches: 9
DUANE, 1331 State St, 12304, SAN 354-1290. Tel: 518-386-2242. FAX: 518-386-2242. *In Charge,* Sandy Anderson
Open Mon-Sat 12-6
GLENVILLE, 20 Glenridge Rd, Scotia, 12302, SAN 370-9299. Tel: 518-386-2243. FAX: 518-386-2243. *In Charge,* Carolyn Morin
Open Mon-Thurs 10-8:30, Fri & Sat 10-5
HAMILTON HILL, 700 Craig St, 12307. Tel: 518-386-2244. *In Charge,* Peggy Stringer
Open Mon-Thurs 1-6
MONT PLEASANT, 1026 Crane St, 12303, SAN 354-1320. Tel: 518-386-2245. FAX: 518-386-2245. *Librn,* Kaela Wallman
Open Mon & Wed 10-6, Fri 10-5, Sat 12-5
NISKAYUNA, 2400 Nott St E, Niskayuna, 12309, SAN 370-128X. Tel: 518-386-2249. FAX: 518-386-2249. *In Charge,* Susan Garrett
Open Mon-Thurs 10-8:30, Fri & Sat 10-5
QUAKER STREET BRANCH, 133 Bull St, Quaker Street, 12141. (Mail add: PO Box 157, Quaker Street, 12056-0157), SAN 354-1339. Tel: 518-895-2719. FAX: 518-895-2719. *Dir,* Karen Bradley
Open Mon & Tues 2-7, Wed 10-6, Thurs 2-6, Sat 10-4
ROTTERDAM, 1100 N Westcott Rd, Rotterdam, 12306, SAN 354-138X. Tel: 518-356-3440. FAX: 518-356-3467. *In Charge,* Judy Fitzmaurice
Open Mon-Thurs 10-8:30, Fri & Sat 10-5
SCOTIA BRANCH, 14 Mohawk Ave, Scotia, 12302, SAN 354-1355. Tel: 518-386-2247. FAX: 518-366-2247. *Librn,* Nancy Gifford
Founded 1929
Open Mon, Tues, Thurs & Fri 10:30-5:30, Sat 10-4
Friends of the Library Group
WOODLAWN, Two Sanford St, 12304, SAN 354-141X. Tel: 518-386-2248. FAX: 518-386-2248. *In Charge,* Lois Miller
Open Mon & Thurs 12-8, Tues 10-8, Fri & Sat 10-5

S SI GROUP, INC*, Henry Howard Wright Research Center Library, 2750 Balltown Rd, 12309-1094. SAN 312-441X. Tel: 518-347-4401. FAX: 518-347-6401. Web Site: www.siigroup.com. *Head, Tech Serv,* Marsha J Shea; E-mail: marsha.shea@siigroup.com; Staff 2 (MLS 1, Non-MLS 1)
Founded 1968
Library Holdings: Bk Vols 1,610
Subject Interests: Polymer chem
Partic in Cap District Libr Coun for Ref & Res Resources
Open Mon-Fri 8-4

C UNION COLLEGE*, Schaffer Library, 807 Union St, 12308. SAN 354-1479. Tel: 518-388-6277. Circulation Tel: 518-388-6280. Interlibrary Loan Service Tel: 518-388-6282. Reference Tel: 518-388-6281. FAX: 518-388-6619, 518-388-6641. Web Site: www.union.edu/library. *Dir,* Frances G Maloy; Staff 28 (MLS 13, Non-MLS 15)
Founded 1795. Enrl 2,189; Fac 203
Jul 2006-Jun 2007. Mats Exp $1,965,574, Books $391,637, Per/Ser (Incl. Access Fees) $1,498,448, AV Mat $26,654, Electronic Ref Mat (Incl. Access Fees) $31,307, Presv $17,528. Sal $1,371,822 (Prof $950,250)
Library Holdings: AV Mats 11,943; Bk Titles 367,348; Bk Vols 614,490; Per Subs 6,248
Special Collections: 19th Century American Wit & Humor (Bailey Coll); French Civilization to End of 19th Century (John Bigelow Library Coll); Local History (Schenectady Coll); Manuscript Coll; Microscopy (Kellert Coll); Rare Book Coll; Science & Technology (Schenectady Archives of Science & Technology Coll), personal papers of various General Electric Co Scientists; Union College Archives; William J Stillman Coll. US Document Depository
Automation Activity & Vendor Info: (Acquisitions) Innovative Interfaces, Inc; (Cataloging) Innovative Interfaces, Inc; (Circulation) Innovative Interfaces, Inc
Database Vendor: Cambridge Scientific Abstracts, Dialog, EBSCOhost, Gale Cengage Learning, JSTOR, LexisNexis, OCLC FirstSearch, OCLC WorldShare Interlibrary Loan, OVID Technologies, ProQuest, SerialsSolutions, Wilson - Wilson Web
Wireless access
Publications: Friends of the Library; Occasional Publications; Union College Faculty Bibliography
Partic in OCLC Online Computer Library Center, Inc
Friends of the Library Group

SCHOHARIE

S SCHOHARIE COUNTY HISTORICAL SOCIETY*, Historical Museum Reference Library, 145 Fort Rd, 12157. SAN 312-4452. Tel: 518-295-7192. FAX: 518-295-7187. Web Site: www.schohariehistory.net. *Dir,* Carle Kopecky
Founded 1889

Library Holdings: Bk Titles 1,600; Bk Vols 2,000
Special Collections: Area Business Papers; Area Town/County/Village Papers; Civil War Papers; Folklore & Folklife
Subject Interests: Genealogy, Local hist, NY State hist
Wireless access
Publications: Schoharie County Historical Review
Open Mon-Sat 10-4:30, Sun 12-4:30
Restriction: Not a lending libr, Open to pub with supv only

P SCHOHARIE FREE ASSOCIATION LIBRARY*, Mary Beatrice Cushing Memorial Library, 103 Knower Ave, 12157. (Mail add: PO Box 519, 12157-0519), SAN 312-4460. Tel: 518-295-7127. FAX: 518-295-7127. E-mail: sholib@midtel.net. Web Site: www.schoharielibrary.org. *Dir,* Catherine Caiazzo
Founded 1916. Pop 1,016; Circ 15,148
Library Holdings: Bk Vols 20,000; Per Subs 44
Automation Activity & Vendor Info: (Cataloging) Innovative Interfaces, Inc; (Circulation) Innovative Interfaces, Inc; (OPAC) Innovative Interfaces, Inc; (Serials) Innovative Interfaces, Inc
Wireless access
Mem of Mohawk Valley Library System
Open Mon & Thurs 1-5 & 6-9, Tues & Fri 10-5, Sat 10-2

SCHROON LAKE

P SCHROON LAKE PUBLIC LIBRARY*, 15 Leland Ave, 12870. (Mail add: PO Box 398, 12870-0398), SAN 312-4479. Tel: 518-532-7737. FAX: 518-532-9474. E-mail: library@schroon.net. *Dir,* Jane A Bouchard; Staff 2 (Non-MLS 2)
Founded 1979
Library Holdings: Bk Vols 30,000; Per Subs 35
Automation Activity & Vendor Info: (Cataloging) SirsiDynix; (Circulation) SirsiDynix; (OPAC) SirsiDynix; (Serials) SirsiDynix
Wireless access
Mem of Clinton-Essex-Franklin Library System
Open Tues & Wed 10-4, Thurs 10-6, Fri & Sat 10-2

SCHUYLERVILLE

P SCHUYLERVILLE PUBLIC LIBRARY, 52 Ferry St, 12871. SAN 312-4487. Tel: 518-695-6641. FAX: 518 695 3619. Web Site: schuylervillelibrary.sals.edu. *Dir,* Julia Martin; E-mail: jmartin1@sals.edu; Staff 2 (Non-MLS 2)
Founded 1905. Pop 9,881; Circ 37,340
Library Holdings: AV Mats 703; DVDs 1,425; Large Print Bks 118; Bk Titles 20,853; Per Subs 54; Talking Bks 531
Special Collections: Battle of Saratoga
Automation Activity & Vendor Info: (Cataloging) Innovative Interfaces, Inc; (Circulation) Innovative Interfaces, Inc; (OPAC) Innovative Interfaces, Inc; (Serials) Innovative Interfaces, Inc
Wireless access
Mem of Southern Adirondack Library System
Open Mon, Wed & Fri 10-12 & 2-8, Tues & Thurs 10-12 & 2-5, Sat 9-1
Friends of the Library Group

SCIO

P SCIO MEMORIAL LIBRARY*, PO Box 77, 14880-0075. SAN 312-4495. Tel: 585-593-4816. FAX: 585-593-4816. Web Site: stls.org/scio. *Librn,* Sue Moyer; E-mail: moyers@stls.org; Staff 1 (Non-MLS 1)
Founded 1906. Pop 1,900; Circ 7,500
Library Holdings: Bk Vols 6,100; Per Subs 20
Subject Interests: Civil War, Genealogy, Quilting
Wireless access
Mem of Southern Tier Library System
Open Tues 3-7, Wed 10-2, Thurs 5-9, Fri Noon-5, Sat 9-Noon
Friends of the Library Group

SCOTTSVILLE

P SCOTTSVILLE FREE LIBRARY*, 28 Main St, 14546. SAN 312-4509. Tel: 585-889-2023. FAX: 585-889-7938. E-mail: scotts@libraryweb.org. Web Site: www.libraryweb.org. *Dir,* Laurie Leo; E-mail: lleo@libraryweb.org
Founded 1917. Pop 5,149; Circ 60,315
Library Holdings: Bk Vols 42,391; Per Subs 51
Automation Activity & Vendor Info: (Circulation) TLC (The Library Corporation)
Wireless access
Mem of Monroe County Library System
Open Mon, Wed & Thurs 1-8:30, Tues 10-8:30, Fri 10-5, Sat 10-1
Friends of the Library Group

Branches: 1
MUMFORD BRANCH, 883 George St, Mumford, 14511. (Mail add: PO Box 89, Mumford, 14511-0089). Tel: 718-538-6124. Web Site: www.rochester.lib.ny.us/scottsville/mumford.html. *Br Mgr,* Kathy Smith
Open Mon, Wed & Fri 2-8, Sat 10-1

SEA CLIFF

P SEA CLIFF VILLAGE LIBRARY*, Sea Cliff & Central Ave, 11579-0280. (Mail add: PO Box 280, 11579-0280), SAN 312-4517. Tel: 516-671-4290. FAX: 516-759-6613. E-mail: scinfo@seaclifflibrary.org. Web Site: www.seaclifflibrary.org. *Dir,* Arlene Nevens; E-mail: anevens@seaclifflibrary.org; *Librn,* Denise Ambrosait
Founded 1905. Circ 39,390
Library Holdings: AV Mats 1,998; Bk Vols 30,000; Per Subs 80
Automation Activity & Vendor Info: (Cataloging) Innovative Interfaces, Inc; (Circulation) Innovative Interfaces, Inc; (OPAC) Innovative Interfaces, Inc
Wireless access
Publications: Newsletter
Mem of Nassau Library System
Open Mon 1-9, Tues, Wed & Fri 9-5, Thurs 9-9, Sat 10-4 (10-1 July & Aug)
Friends of the Library Group

SEAFORD

P SEAFORD PUBLIC LIBRARY*, 2234 Jackson Ave, 11783. SAN 312-4525. Tel: 516-221-1334. FAX: 516-826-8133. Web Site: www.seafordlibrary.org. *Dir,* Frank J McKenna; E-mail: fjmckiii@aol.com; Staff 30 (MLS 8, Non-MLS 22)
Founded 1956. Pop 16,687; Circ 162,398
Library Holdings: Bk Vols 83,747
Automation Activity & Vendor Info: (Acquisitions) Innovative Interfaces, Inc - Millenium; (Cataloging) Innovative Interfaces, Inc - Millenium; (Circulation) Innovative Interfaces, Inc - Millenium; (ILL) OCLC FirstSearch; (OPAC) Innovative Interfaces, Inc - Millenium
Wireless access
Publications: Newsletter (Monthly)
Mem of Nassau Library System
Partic in Long Island Library Resources Council
Open Mon, Tues & Thurs 10-9, Wed 1-9, Fri 10-6, Sat 10-5 (9-1 Summer)
Friends of the Library Group

SELDEN

J SUFFOLK COUNTY COMMUNITY COLLEGE*, Ammerman Campus Library, 533 College Rd, 11784-2899. SAN 354-1568. Tel: 631-451-4800. FAX: 631-451-4697. Web Site: www.sunysuffolk.edu/library/ammerman. *Libr Dir,* Susan Lieberthal; E-mail: liebers@sunysuffolk.edu; *Head, Bibliog Serv, Head of Instruction,* Jennifer Farquahar; *Head, Circ,* Rebecca Turner; *Head, Coll Develop,* Marya Shephero; *Head, Per,* Krista Gruber; *Electronic Res Librn,* Joyce Gabriele; *Syst Librn,* Kevin McCoy; *Coll Develop,* Deborah Provenzano; *Media Spec,* Susan DeMasi; Staff 7 (MLS 7)
Founded 1960. Enrl 12,700; Fac 300; Highest Degree: Associate
Library Holdings: Bk Titles 100,000; Bk Vols 105,610; Per Subs 500
Special Collections: Long Island Coll
Subject Interests: Allied health, Nursing
Automation Activity & Vendor Info: (Acquisitions) Ex Libris Group; (Cataloging) OCLC Connexion; (Circulation) Ex Libris Group; (OPAC) Ex Libris Group; (Serials) Ex Libris Group
Wireless access
Publications: Centralized Media & Periodicals Catalog; Newsletter; Student Handbook
Partic in Long Island Library Resources Council
Open Mon-Thurs 8am-10pm, Fri 8-6, Sat 9-4

SENECA FALLS

CM NEW YORK CHIROPRACTIC COLLEGE LIBRARY*, 2360 State Rte 89, 13148-9460. (Mail add: PO Box 800, 13148-0800), SAN 320-457X. Tel: 315-568-3244. Reference Tel: 315-568-3249. FAX: 315-568-3119. Web Site: www.nycc.edu/library. *Dir,* Bethyn A Boni; E-mail: bboni@nycc.edu; *Media & Digital Res Librn,* Suellen Christopoulos-Nutting; *Ref/Syst Librn,* Chris Sheldon; Staff 3 (MLS 3)
Founded 1919. Enrl 763; Fac 47; Highest Degree: Doctorate
Library Holdings: Bk Vols 16,521; Per Subs 407; Spec Interest Per Sub 52
Subject Interests: Acupuncture, Anatomy, Chiropractic & Oriental med, Nutrition, Radiology
Automation Activity & Vendor Info: (Cataloging) SirsiDynix; (Circulation) SirsiDynix; (OPAC) SirsiDynix
Database Vendor: EBSCOhost, SirsiDynix
Wireless access

Partic in Chiropractic Libr Consortium; South Central Regional Library Council
Open Mon-Fri 7:45am-11pm, Sat & Sun 11-11

S SENECA FALLS HISTORICAL SOCIETY LIBRARY*, 55 Cayuga St, 13148. SAN 329-4307. Tel: 315-568-8412. FAX: 315-568-8426. E-mail: sfhs@rochester.rr.com. *Coll Mgt,* Kathy Jans-Duffy
Founded 1896
Library Holdings: Bk Titles 1,500; Per Subs 10
Special Collections: Civil War Coll; Women's Rights Coll
Subject Interests: Seneca County hist, Seneca Falls hist, Victorian era
Wireless access
Function: Res libr
Open Mon-Fri 9-4
Restriction: In-house use for visitors

P SENECA FALLS LIBRARY*, 47 Cayuga St, 13148. SAN 312-455X. Tel: 315-568-8265. FAX: 315-568-1606. E-mail: myndersl@rochester.rr.com. Web Site: www.senecafallslibrary.org. *Dir,* Michael Caraher; Tel: 315-568-8265, Ext 3, E-mail: myndersl@rochester.rr.com; *Dir, Support Serv,* Jackie Grey; Tel: 315-568-8265, Ext 4, E-mail: jgrey@rochester.rr.com
Founded 1881. Pop 6,861; Circ 38,048
Jan 2007-Dec 2007 Income $273,000. Mats Exp $30,000, Books $27,000, Per/Ser (Incl. Access Fees) $3,000. Sal $148,986
Library Holdings: AV Mats 524; e-books 1,851; Bk Vols 27,047; Per Subs 44; Talking Bks 1,839
Special Collections: DAR Coll; Genealogy Coll
Automation Activity & Vendor Info: (Circulation) Innovative Interfaces, Inc
Wireless access
Mem of Finger Lakes Library System
Open Mon-Fri 10-8, Sat 10-5, Sun 2-5
Friends of the Library Group

SETAUKET

P EMMA S CLARK MEMORIAL LIBRARY*, 120 Main St, 11733-2868. SAN 312-4568. Tel: 631-941-4080. FAX: 631-941-4541. E-mail: reference@emmaclark.org. Web Site: www.emmaclark.org. *Dir,* Ted Gutmann; *Circ Mgr,* Aileen Clark; *Tech Serv Mgr,* Ruth Crane; *Head, Adult Serv,* Joan Kahnhauser; *Head, Ch,* Marge Bengston; Staff 49 (MLS 15, Non-MLS 34)
Founded 1892. Pop 45,668; Circ 760,743
Jan 2008-Dec 2008 Income $4,629,000. Mats Exp $577,000. Sal $2,902,000 (Prof $1,291,000)
Library Holdings: Bk Vols 196,000; Per Subs 400
Subject Interests: Long Island hist
Automation Activity & Vendor Info: (Cataloging) Innovative Interfaces, Inc; (Circulation) Innovative Interfaces, Inc; (OPAC) Innovative Interfaces, Inc
Wireless access
Mem of Suffolk Cooperative Library System
Open Mon-Fri 9:30-9, Sat 9-5, Sun Noon-5

SHARON SPRINGS

P SHARON SPRINGS FREE LIBRARY*, Main St, Rte 10, 13459. (Mail add: PO Box 268, 13459-0268), SAN 312-4576. Tel: 518-284-2625. FAX: 518-284-3126. *Dir,* Mary Ellen Wolfe; E-mail: mwolfe@sals.edu; *Asst Librn,* C Alfred Santillo
Circ 5,527
Library Holdings: Bk Vols 7,000
Automation Activity & Vendor Info: (Cataloging) Innovative Interfaces, Inc; (Circulation) Innovative Interfaces, Inc; (OPAC) Innovative Interfaces, Inc
Wireless access
Mem of Mohawk Valley Library System
Open Mon 10-4 & 6-9, Wed 5-9, Fri 12-5, Sat 9-1

SHELTER ISLAND

P SHELTER ISLAND PUBLIC LIBRARY*, 37 N Ferry Rd, 11964. (Mail add: PO Box 2016, 11964-2016), SAN 312-4584. Tel: 631-749-0042. FAX: 631-749-1575. E-mail: info@shelterislandpubliclibrary.org. Web Site: www.shelterislandpubliclibrary.org. *Libr Dir,* Denise DiPaolo; E-mail: ddipaolo@sheltrtislandpubliclibrary.org; *Asst Dir,* Laura Dickerson; E-mail: ldickerson@silibrary.org
Founded 1885. Circ 23,565
Wireless access
Mem of Suffolk Cooperative Library System
Open Mon & Wed 10-5, Tues, Thurs & Fri 10-7, Sat 10-4
Friends of the Library Group

SHERBURNE

P SHERBURNE PUBLIC LIBRARY*, Two E State St, 13460. (Mail add: PO Box 702, 13460-0702), SAN 312-4592. Tel: 607-674-4242. FAX: 607-674-4242. E-mail: sh.ill@4cls.org. Web Site: sherburnelibrary.org. *Librn,* Nancy Simerl
Pop 3,903; Circ 29,384
Library Holdings: Bk Vols 17,000; Per Subs 40
Automation Activity & Vendor Info: (Cataloging) SIRSI WorkFlows; (Circulation) SIRSI WorkFlows; (OPAC) SIRSI WorkFlows; (Serials) SIRSI WorkFlows
Wireless access
Mem of Four County Library System
Open Mon-Wed 1-8, Thurs & Fri 10-5, Sat 10-12

SHERMAN

P MINERVA FREE LIBRARY*, 116 Miller St, 14781-9783. (Mail add: PO Box 588, 14781-0588), SAN 312-4606. Tel: 716-761-6378. FAX: 716-761-6335. E-mail: shermlib@cecomet.net. Web Site: www2.cecomet.net/shermlib/. *Librn,* Shellie Williams
Founded 1907. Pop 1,505; Circ 6,738
Library Holdings: Bk Vols 14,500; Per Subs 15
Automation Activity & Vendor Info: (Cataloging) SirsiDynix; (Circulation) SirsiDynix; (OPAC) SirsiDynix; (Serials) SirsiDynix
Wireless access
Mem of Chautauqua-Cattaraugus Library System
Open Tues 4-8, Thurs 9-4 & 6-8, Fri 9-3, Sat 9-Noon
Friends of the Library Group

SHERRILL

P SHERRILL-KENWOOD FREE LIBRARY*, 543 Sherrill Rd, 13461-1263. SAN 312-4614. Tel: 315-363-5980. FAX: 315-363-4133. E-mail: sherrill@midyork.org. Web Site: www.sherrillkenwoodlibrary.org. *Dir,* Jennifer Milligan; Staff 3 (MLS 1, Non-MLS 2)
Founded 1912. Pop 3,583; Circ 36,490
Jan 2012-Dec 2012 Income $109,089, City $53,000, County $5,214, Locally Generated Income $20,115, Other $30,760. Mats Exp $18,689, Books $13,500, Other Print Mats $1,400, AV Mat $3,764, Presv $25. Sal $70,000 (Prof $30,680)
Library Holdings: Audiobooks 622; CDs 40; DVDs 602; e-books 26; Electronic Media & Resources 9; Large Print Bks 400; Bk Titles 20,180; Bk Vols 20,180; Per Subs 102
Automation Activity & Vendor Info: (Circulation) SirsiDynix; (OPAC) SirsiDynix
Wireless access
Function: Adult bk club, Audiobks via web, Bks on cassette, Bks on CD, Children's prog, Computer training, Computers for patron use, Copy machines, Digital talking bks, E-Reserves, Electronic databases & coll, Exhibits, Family literacy, Fax serv, Free DVD rentals, Holiday prog, ILL available, Mail & tel request accepted, Music CDs, Online cat, Online ref, Online searches, Outside serv via phone, mail, e-mail & web, OverDrive digital audio bks, Photocopying/Printing, Preschool reading prog, Prog for adults, Prog for children & young adult, Pub access computers, Ref serv available, Ref serv in person, Scanner, Senior computer classes, Spoken cassettes & CDs, Story hour, Summer & winter reading prog, Summer reading prog, Tax forms, Teen prog, Telephone ref, VHS videos, Video lending libr, Web-catalog, Wheelchair accessible, Winter reading prog, Workshops
Mem of Mid-York Library System
Open Mon & Wed 1-8, Tues & Thurs 11-8, Fri 1-6, Sat (Sept-June) 10-2
Friends of the Library Group

SHIRLEY

P MASTICS-MORICHES-SHIRLEY COMMUNITY LIBRARY*, 407 William Floyd Pkwy, 11967. SAN 312-4622. Tel: 631-399-1511. FAX: 631-281-4442. E-mail: mmshlib@suffolk.lib.ny.us. Web Site: www.communitylibrary.org. *Dir,* Kerri Rosalia; *Asst Dir,* Tara D'Amato; *Bus Mgr,* Christopher Nowak; *Adult Serv, Ref,* Josephine Wuthenow; *Children's & Parents' Serv,* Rachel Catan; *Circ,* Anne Marie Hoffman; *Tech Serv,* Judy Corso; *YA Serv,* Lorraine Squires; Staff 22 (MLS 22)
Founded 1974. Pop 63,000; Circ 758,971
Library Holdings: AV Mats 116,145; Bk Vols 272,319; Per Subs 27,141
Subject Interests: Italian lang, Local hist, Spanish
Automation Activity & Vendor Info: (Acquisitions) Innovative Interfaces, Inc; (Cataloging) Innovative Interfaces, Inc; (Circulation) Innovative Interfaces, Inc; (ILL) Innovative Interfaces, Inc; (OPAC) Innovative Interfaces, Inc
Wireless access
Publications: Newsletter
Mem of Suffolk Cooperative Library System
Partic in Long Island Library Resources Council
Open Mon-Thurs 9-9, Fri 9-6, Sat 9-5, Sun (Sept-June) 12-4

SHOREHAM

P NORTH SHORE PUBLIC LIBRARY*, 250 Rte 25A, 11786-9677. SAN 320-4960. Tel: 631-929-4488. FAX: 631-929-4551. E-mail: nspl@suffolk.lib.ny.us. Web Site: www.nspl.suffolk.lib.ny.us. *Dir,* Laura Hawney; *Asst Dir,* J O'Hare; *Ch Serv,* L Blend; *Ch Serv,* J Tousey; *Circ,* A Caravello; *Computer Serv,* T Donton; *ILL,* M Clark; *Ref,* R Hawkins; *Ser, Tech Serv,* J Gatto; *YA Serv,* K Welch; Staff 34 (MLS 12, Non-MLS 22)
Founded 1975. Pop 22,933; Circ 287,780
Library Holdings: Bk Titles 97,506; Per Subs 342
Automation Activity & Vendor Info: (Acquisitions) Innovative Interfaces, Inc; (Cataloging) Innovative Interfaces, Inc; (Circulation) Innovative Interfaces, Inc; (OPAC) Innovative Interfaces, Inc; (Serials) Innovative Interfaces, Inc
Wireless access
Mem of Suffolk Cooperative Library System
Open Mon-Fri 10-9, Sat 10-5, Sun 1-5
Friends of the Library Group

SHORTSVILLE

P RED JACKET COMMUNITY LIBRARY*, Seven Lehigh Ave, 14548. (Mail add: PO Box 370, 14548-0370). Tel: 585-289-3559. FAX: 585-289-9845. Web Site: redjacket.pls-net.org. *Dir,* Andrea Tillinghast-Thompson
Founded 1998
Library Holdings: AV Mats 1,260; Large Print Bks 669; Bk Vols 30,000; Per Subs 13; Talking Bks 487
Automation Activity & Vendor Info: (Cataloging) Mandarin Library Automation; (Circulation) Mandarin Library Automation; (OPAC) Mandarin Library Automation
Wireless access
Mem of Pioneer Library System
Open Mon-Thurs (Winter) 3-9, Fri 3-7, Sat 10-5; Mon, Wed & Fri (Summer) 9-4, Tues & Thurs 1-8, Sat 9-1
Friends of the Library Group

SHRUB OAK

P JOHN C HART MEMORIAL LIBRARY*, 1130 Main St, 10588. SAN 354-1622. Tel: 914-245-5262. FAX: 914-245-2216. Web Site: www.yorktownlibrary.org. *Dir,* Patricia Barresi; Tel: 914-245-1598, Fax: 914-245-5936, E-mail: pbarresi@wlsmail.org; *Circ Supvr,* Catherine Capone; *Adult Serv,* Maureen Davis; *Ch Serv,* Irena Goss; *Ch Serv,* Christine Piattelli; *Circ,* Sandra Norman; *Circ,* Margaret O'Riley; *Circ,* Deborah Sarno; *ILL,* Reva Queler; *Ref,* Patricia Hallinan; *Tech Serv,* Shirley Mccord; *Tech Serv,* Maria Stolfi; *YA Serv,* Maureen Connelly; Staff 24 (MLS 10, Non-MLS 14)
Founded 1920. Pop 35,000; Circ 490,273
Jan 2008-Dec 2008 Income $2,210,163. Mats Exp $215,000
Library Holdings: Bk Titles 156,717
Special Collections: Special Education Jerome Thaler Weather Coll
Automation Activity & Vendor Info: (Circulation) SirsiDynix; (ILL) SirsiDynix; (OPAC) SirsiDynix
Database Vendor: Newsbank
Wireless access
Mem of Westchester Library System
Open Mon-Thurs (Sept-Apr) 9:30-8, Fri & Sat 9:30-5, Sun 1-5
Friends of the Library Group

SIDNEY

P SIDNEY MEMORIAL PUBLIC LIBRARY*, Eight River St, 13838. SAN 312-4649. Tel: 607-563-1200, 607-563-8021. FAX: 607-563-7675. Web Site: sidneylibrary.org. *Dir,* Conner Roz; E-mail: si.roz@4cls.org; *Ch Serv,* Linda Shea; *Circ,* Ann Philpott; *Computer Serv,* Marcie Gifford; *ILL,* Dawn Rogers Kroll; *Youth Serv,* Jennifer Mech
Founded 1887. Pop 8,088
Library Holdings: Bk Vols 57,887; Per Subs 197
Subject Interests: Local hist
Automation Activity & Vendor Info: (Cataloging) SirsiDynix; (Circulation) SirsiDynix; (OPAC) SirsiDynix
Wireless access
Publications: Newsletter
Mem of Four County Library System
Open Mon-Thurs 9-8:30, Fri 9-6, Sat 9:30-4, Sun 1-4
Friends of the Library Group
Branches: 2
MASONVILLE BRANCH, 15565 State Hwy 8, 13838-2721. Tel: 607-265-3330. FAX: 607-265-3330. *Libr Dir,* Rosalind Conner
Open Mon & Wed 3:30-7, Tues, Thurs & Sat 10-2
SIDNEY CENTER BRANCH, 10599 County Hwy 23, Unadilla, 13849. Tel: 607-369-7500.
Open Mon-Fri 1-5, Tues & Thurs 3:30-8, Wed & Sat 10-2

SILVER CREEK

P ANDERSON-LEE LIBRARY*, 43 Main St, 14136. SAN 312-4657. Tel: 716-934-3468. FAX: 716-934-3037. Web Site: andersonleelibrary.com. *Interim Librn,* Linda Beach; Staff 1 (MLS 1)
Founded 1924. Circ 57,028
Library Holdings: Bk Vols 25,000
Mem of Chautauqua-Cattaraugus Library System
Open Mon & Tues 12-8, Thurs 10-8, Fri 12-5, Sat 10-2
Friends of the Library Group

SILVER SPRINGS

P TOWN OF GAINESVILLE PUBLIC LIBRARY*, Ten Church St, 14550. (Mail add: PO Box 321, 14550-0321), SAN 312-4665. Tel: 585-493-2970. FAX: 585-493-2970. E-mail: SilverSpringsLibraryDirector@owwl.org. *Dir,* Angel Wright-Sackett
Pop 2,288; Circ 12,289
Library Holdings: Bk Vols 12,500; Per Subs 47
Automation Activity & Vendor Info: (Cataloging) SirsiDynix; (Circulation) SirsiDynix; (OPAC) SirsiDynix
Wireless access
Mem of Pioneer Library System
Open Mon & Fri 2-5, Tues & Thurs 2-5 & 6-8:30, Sat 9-Noon

SINCLAIRVILLE

P SINCLAIRVILLE FREE LIBRARY*, 15 Main St, 14782. (Mail add: PO Box 609, 14782-0609), SAN 312-4673. Tel: 716-962-5885. FAX: 716-962-5885. E-mail: sincfrlb@gmail.com. Web Site: www.cclslib.org/sinclairville. *Libr Mgr,* Beth Hadley; *Libr Asst,* Cynthia Pagano; Staff 1 (Non-MLS 1)
Founded 1870. Pop 665; Circ 17,264
Library Holdings: Bk Vols 12,159; Per Subs 50
Subject Interests: Local hist
Wireless access
Mem of Chautauqua-Cattaraugus Library System
Open Mon 2-8, Wed 9-6, Thurs 4-8, Fri 10-4

SKANEATELES

P SKANEATELES LIBRARY ASSOCIATION*, 49 E Genesee St, 13152. SAN 312-4681. Tel: 315-685-5135. Web Site: www.skaneateleslibrary.com. *Libr Dir,* Nickie Marquis; Tel: 315-685-5135, E-mail: nmarquis@skaneateleslibrary.org; Staff 1 (MLS 1)
Founded 1878. Circ 75,759
Library Holdings: Large Print Bks 978; Bk Titles 31,417; Bk Vols 32,946; Per Subs 100; Talking Bks 1,643
Special Collections: Barrow Art Gallery (local artist's work late 19th century); Large Print Books Coll; Unabridged Book-on-Tapes
Subject Interests: Art, Arts, Gardening, Local hist
Automation Activity & Vendor Info: (Cataloging) Innovative Interfaces, Inc; (Circulation) Innovative Interfaces, Inc; (OPAC) Innovative Interfaces, Inc
Wireless access
Special Services for the Blind - Talking bks
Open Mon, Wed & Fri (Winter) 10-5, Tues & Thurs 10-8, Sat 10-4; Mon, Wed & Fri (Summer) 9-5, Tues & Thurs 9-8, Sat 9-4

SLOATSBURG

P SLOATSBURG PUBLIC LIBRARY*, One Liberty Rock Rd, 10974-2392. SAN 322-8355. Tel: 845-753-2001. FAX: 845-753-2144. Web Site: sloatsburglibrary.org/. *Dir,* Mary Blake; Staff 1 (Non-MLS 1)
Founded 1959. Pop 3,124; Circ 49,000
Jan 2005-Dec 2005 Income $282,875, Provincial $2,500, County $2,700, Locally Generated Income $26,325, Parent Institution $1,500, Other $249,850. Mats Exp $59,800, Books $35,000, Per/Ser (Incl. Access Fees) $4,000, AV Mat $7,700, Electronic Ref Mat (Incl. Access Fees) $13,100. Sal $141,670 (Prof $42,590)
Library Holdings: AV Mats 5,992; Bk Titles 30,209; Bk Vols 31,587; Per Subs 87; Talking Bks 3,154
Subject Interests: Local hist
Automation Activity & Vendor Info: (Circulation) SirsiDynix; (ILL) SirsiDynix; (OPAC) SirsiDynix
Wireless access
Publications: Books & Beyond (Newsletter)
Mem of Ramapo Catskill Library System
Special Services for the Deaf - TTY equip
Open Mon-Thurs 10-9, Fri & Sat 10-5, Sun (Sept-June) 12-4
Friends of the Library Group

SMITHTOWN

P SMITHTOWN LIBRARY*, One N Country Rd, 11787. SAN 354-1657. Tel: 631-265-2072. FAX: 631-265-2044. Web Site: www.smithlib.org. *Dir,* Robert Lusak; *Asst Dir,* Robert Goykin; *Head of Acq/Cataloging,* Cynthia Guzzo; *Head, Ch,* Maria Barlin; *Ref Librn,* Karen Baudouin; *Circ Supvr,* Sandra Altas; Staff 108 (MLS 38, Non-MLS 70)
Founded 1905. Pop 112,762; Circ 895,374
Library Holdings: AV Mats 47,032; Bk Vols 299,153; Per Subs 9,319
Special Collections: Long Island (Richard Handley & Charles E Lawrence Coll), bk, mss, fiche, microflm
Subject Interests: Behav sci, Soc sci
Automation Activity & Vendor Info: (Acquisitions) Innovative Interfaces, Inc; (Cataloging) Innovative Interfaces, Inc; (Circulation) Innovative Interfaces, Inc; (Course Reserve) Innovative Interfaces, Inc; (ILL) Innovative Interfaces, Inc; (OPAC) Innovative Interfaces, Inc; (Serials) Innovative Interfaces, Inc
Database Vendor: Baker & Taylor, CQ Press, CredoReference, EBSCO Auto Repair Reference, EBSCOhost, Facts on File, Gale Cengage Learning, Grolier Online, H W Wilson, Hoovers, infoUSA, Innovative Interfaces, Inc, LearningExpress, Medline, OCLC ArticleFirst, OCLC FirstSearch, OCLC WorldShare Interlibrary Loan, Olive Software, Inc, Overdrive, Inc, ProQuest, ReferenceUSA, SerialsSolutions, Standard & Poor's, Wilson - Wilson Web
Wireless access
Function: Adult literacy prog, Govt ref serv, Handicapped accessible, Home delivery & serv to Sr ctr & nursing homes, Homebound delivery serv, ILL available, Newsp ref libr, Outside serv via phone, mail, e-mail & web, Photocopying/Printing, Prof lending libr, Prog for children & young adult, Ref serv available, Summer reading prog, Telephone ref, Wheelchair accessible
Publications: Inside Your Library (Monthly)
Mem of Suffolk Cooperative Library System
Special Services for the Deaf - ADA equip; Bks on deafness & sign lang; Closed caption videos; Coll on deaf educ; High interest/low vocabulary bks Special Services for the Blind - Accessible computers; BiFolkal kits; Bks on cassette; Bks on CD; Cassette playback machines; Cassettes; Closed circuit TV magnifier; Copier with enlargement capabilities; Extensive large print coll; Home delivery serv; Internet workstation with adaptive software; Large print bks; Large screen computer & software; PC for handicapped; Photo duplicator for making large print; Recorded bks; Ref serv; Screen enlargement software for people with visual disabilities; Talking bk & rec for the blind cat; Talking bk serv referral; Talking bks; Talking bks & player equip; Talking bks from Braille Inst; Talking bks plus; Videos on blindness & phys handicaps; ZoomText magnification & reading software
Open Mon-Thurs 10-9, Fri 10-6, Sat 9-5, Sun (Sept-May) 1-5
Friends of the Library Group
Branches: 3
COMMACK BRANCH, Three Indian Head Rd, Commack, 11725, SAN 354-1681. Tel: 631-543-0998. FAX: 631-543-0661.
Friends of the Library Group
KINGS PARK BRANCH, One Church St, Kings Park, 11754, SAN 354-1711. Tel: 631-269-9191. FAX: 631-269-0807. *Librn,* Suzanne McManus
Friends of the Library Group
NESCONSET BRANCH, 127-20 Smithtown Blvd, Nesconset, 11767, SAN 354-1746. Tel: 631-265-3994. FAX: 631-265-8158. *Asst Dir,* Robert Goykin
Friends of the Library Group

SMYRNA

P SMYRNA PUBLIC LIBRARY*, Seven E Main St, 13464-1932. (Mail add: PO Box 202, 13464-0202), SAN 312-472X. Tel: 607-627-6271. FAX: 607-627-6271. *Dir,* Stacie Beers
Pop 1,418
Library Holdings: Bk Vols 4,500; Per Subs 25
Wireless access
Mem of Four County Library System
Open Mon, Wed, & Fri 10-2, Tues & Thurs 2-6, Sat 10-Noon

SODUS

P SODUS COMMUNITY LIBRARY, 17 Maple Ave, 14551. SAN 312-4738. Tel: 315-483-9292. FAX: 315-483-9616. E-mail: soduslibrary@owwl.org. Web Site: www.soduslibrary.org. *Mgr,* Carol Garland; Staff 1 (Non-MLS 1)
Founded 1907. Pop 7,686; Circ 60,000
Library Holdings: Bk Vols 31,000; Per Subs 105
Special Collections: Antique Books & Periodicals of Collectibles; Crocks; Glass (Clyde); Jars (Lyons); Jugs
Automation Activity & Vendor Info: (Acquisitions) Baker & Taylor; (Cataloging) Evergreen; (Circulation) Evergreen; (OPAC) Evergreen; (Serials) Evergreen
Wireless access
Function: 24/7 Electronic res, 24/7 Online cat, Adult bk club, Audiobks via web, Bks on CD, Children's prog, Computers for patron use, Copy machines, Electronic databases & coll, Fax serv, Free DVD rentals, Handicapped accessible, ILL available, Magazines, Online cat, OverDrive digital audio bks, Photocopying/Printing, Preschool reading prog, Prog for adults, Prog for children & young adult, Pub access computers, Story hour, Study rm, Summer reading prog, Tax forms, Teen prog, Web-catalog, Wheelchair accessible
Mem of Pioneer Library System
Open Mon-Thurs 10-8, Fri & Sat 10-5, Sun 2-5
Friends of the Library Group

SOLVAY

P SOLVAY PUBLIC LIBRARY*, 615 Woods Rd, 13209-1697. SAN 312-4754. Tel: 315-468-2441. FAX: 315-468-0373. Web Site: solvaylibrary.org. *Interim Dir,* Elizabeth Loftus; *Librn,* Ann L Moore; Staff 15 (MLS 3, Non-MLS 12)
Founded 1903. Pop 6,584; Circ 95,000
Library Holdings: Bk Vols 34,000; Per Subs 75
Special Collections: Local History; Solvay Process Co
Automation Activity & Vendor Info: (Cataloging) Innovative Interfaces, Inc; (Circulation) Innovative Interfaces, Inc; (OPAC) Innovative Interfaces, Inc
Wireless access
Mem of Onondaga County Public Library
Open Mon-Wed (Winter) 9-8, Thurs-Fri 9-5, Sat 10-5, Sun 1-5; Mon-Wed (Summer) 9-8, Thurs-Fri 9-5, Sat 9-1
Friends of the Library Group

SOMERS

S SOMERS HISTORICAL SOCIETY LIBRARY*, 335 Rte 202, 10589-3204. (Mail add: PO Box 336, 10589-0336), SAN 328-333X. Tel: 914-277-4977. E-mail: somershistoricalsoc@yahoo.com. Web Site: www.somerhistoricalsoc.org. *Pres,* Emil Antonaccio; Staff 1 (Non-MLS 1)
Library Holdings: Bk Vols 900; Per Subs 5
Subject Interests: Circus hist, Genealogy, Local hist
Wireless access
Function: Ref & res, Ref serv available, Ref serv in person, Referrals accepted, Res libr
Restriction: Open by appt only

P SOMERS LIBRARY*, 80 Primrose St, Rte 139 & Reis Park, 10589. (Mail add: PO Box 443, 10589), SAN 312-4762. Tel: 914-232-5717. Administration Tel: 914-232-1285. FAX: 914-232-1035. E-mail: somers@wlsmail.org. Web Site: www.somerslibrary.org. *Dir,* Patricia Miller; E-mail: miller@wlsmail.org; *Adult Serv, Ref Librn,* Valerie Herman; *Teen Librn,* Tara Ferretti; *Ch Serv,* Betsy Bishop; *Ch Serv,* Vicki DiSanto; Staff 7 (MLS 5, Non-MLS 2)
Founded 1876. Pop 18,346; Circ 218,241
Jan 2009-Dec 2009 Income $992,348, State $4,600, City $955,748, Locally Generated Income $32,000. Mats Exp $97,000, Books $62,000, Per/Ser (Incl. Access Fees) $7,000, Other Print Mats $9,000, AV Mat $19,000. Sal $545,117 (Prof $46,000)
Library Holdings: CDs 3,943; DVDs 4,841; e-books 1,140; Bk Titles 54,875; Per Subs 113
Subject Interests: Circus bks, Somers local hist
Automation Activity & Vendor Info: (Cataloging) SirsiDynix; (Circulation) SirsiDynix; (ILL) SirsiDynix; (OPAC) SirsiDynix
Database Vendor: Baker & Taylor, ProQuest, SirsiDynix, WT Cox
Wireless access
Function: Accelerated reader prog, Adult bk club, After school storytime, Archival coll, Art exhibits, Audiobks via web, Bk club(s), Bks on CD, CD-ROM, Children's prog, Computer training, Computers for patron use, Copy machines, e-mail & chat, Exhibits, For res purposes, Free DVD rentals, Genealogy discussion group, Handicapped accessible, Holiday prog, Home delivery & serv to Sr ctr & nursing homes, Homebound delivery serv, Homework prog, ILL available, Instruction & testing, Mail & tel request accepted, Music CDs, Newsp ref libr, Online cat, Online ref, Online searches, Orientations, Outreach serv, OverDrive digital audio bks, Photocopying/Printing, Prog for adults, Prog for children & young adult, Pub access computers, Ref & res, Ref serv available, Ref serv in person, Senior computer classes, Senior outreach, Spoken cassettes & CDs, Spoken cassettes & DVDs, Story hour, Summer reading prog, Tax forms, Teen prog, Telephone ref, VHS videos, Video lending libr, Wheelchair accessible, Workshops, Writing prog
Publications: Somers Library Friends (Newsletter)
Mem of Westchester Library System
Partic in Westlynx
Open Mon 1-8, Tues & Thurs 11-6, Wed & Fri 10-5, Sat 12-5, Sun 1-5
Friends of the Library Group

SONYEA

S GROVELAND CORRECTIONAL FACILITY LIBRARY*, 7000 Rte 36, Sonyea Rd, 14556-0001. SAN 327-2354. Tel: 585-658-2871. *Librn,* Doug Petric
Library Holdings: Bk Titles 23,000
Automation Activity & Vendor Info: (Cataloging) Follett Software; (Circulation) Follett Software
Wireless access

S LIVINGSTON CORRECTIONAL FACILITY LIBRARY*, PO Box 49, 14556. Tel: 585-658-3710. FAX: 585-658-4841. *Librn,* Amy Kelley
Library Holdings: Bk Vols 9,500; Per Subs 45
Automation Activity & Vendor Info: (Circulation) Follett Software; (Course Reserve) Follett Software; (OPAC) Follett Software
Wireless access
Open Mon-Wed 1-8, Thurs & Fri 8-11 & 1-8

SOUTH FALLSBURG

P FALLSBURG LIBRARY INC*, 12 Railroad Plaza, 12779. (Mail add: PO Box 730, 12779-0730). Tel: 845-436-6067. FAX: 845-434-1254. E-mail: fbr@rcls.org. Web Site: rcls.org/fbl. *Dir,* David J Phillips; Staff 2 (MLS 1, Non-MLS 1)
Founded 1999. Pop 10,217; Circ 36,000
Library Holdings: AV Mats 3,000; Bk Vols 25,000; Per Subs 40
Automation Activity & Vendor Info: (Acquisitions) Horizon; (Cataloging) Horizon; (Circulation) Horizon; (ILL) Horizon; (OPAC) Horizon
Database Vendor: Gale Cengage Learning, PubMed
Mem of Ramapo Catskill Library System
Open Mon & Thurs (Winter) 10-6, Tues & Wed 10-7, Fri 10-5, Sun 10-2; Mon & Fri (Summer) 9:30-4, Tues & Thurs 9:30-7, Wed 9:30-6, Sun 9:30-1
Friends of the Library Group

SOUTH NEW BERLIN

P SOUTH NEW BERLIN FREE LIBRARY*, 3320 State Hwy 8, 13843. (Mail add: PO Box 9, 13843), SAN 312-4789. Tel: 607-859-2420. FAX: 607-859-2660. E-mail: sn.ill@4cls.org. Web Site: libraries.4cls.org/southnewberlin. *Librn,* Donna Henderson
Founded 1921. Pop 600; Circ 13,829
Library Holdings: AV Mats 882; Bk Vols 7,393; Per Subs 21
Wireless access
Mem of Four County Library System
Open Mon & Thurs 11-8, Tues, Wed & Fri 3-6
Friends of the Library Group

SOUTH SALEM

P LEWISBORO LIBRARY*, 15 Main St, 10590-1413. (Mail add: PO Box 477, 10590-0477), SAN 312-4797. Tel: 914-763-3857. FAX: 914-763-2193. E-mail: lewisborolibrary@gmail.com. Web Site: www.lewisborolibrary.org. *Dir,* Cynthia Rubino; *Head, Circ,* Susan Hamiton; *Ch Serv,* Catherine Lim; Staff 12 (MLS 4, Non-MLS 8)
Founded 1798. Pop 12,300; Circ 126,600
Library Holdings: AV Mats 3,247; e-books 264; Electronic Media & Resources 127; Large Print Bks 400; Bk Vols 48,000; Per Subs 100; Talking Bks 4,171
Special Collections: Early Childhood Development (Ethel Horn Memorial Coll)
Automation Activity & Vendor Info: (Circulation) SirsiDynix; (OPAC) SirsiDynix
Wireless access
Function: Homebound delivery serv, Prog for children & young adult, Spoken cassettes & CDs, Summer reading prog, VHS videos
Publications: Newsletter
Mem of Westchester Library System
Partic in OCLC Online Computer Library Center, Inc
Open Mon, Wed & Thurs 10-6, Tues 10-9, Fri 10-5, Sat 10-4 (10-1 Summer), Sun 1-4

SOUTHAMPTON

P ROGERS MEMORIAL LIBRARY*, 91 Coopers Farm Rd, 11968. SAN 312-4819. Tel: 631-283-0774. FAX: 631-287-6539. Reference FAX: 631-287-6537. Web Site: www.myrml.org. *Dir,* Liz Burns; Tel: 631-283-0774, Ext 501, E-mail: liz@myrml.org; *Head, Tech Serv,* Sue Ann Taylor; *Head, Computer Serv,* David Janku; *Circ Mgr,* Connie Gaud; *ILL,* Ann Ernst; *YA Serv,* Laurie Ridgeway; Staff 10 (MLS 10)
Founded 1895. Pop 14,500; Circ 182,000
Library Holdings: Bk Vols 100,000; Per Subs 275
Special Collections: Long Island Coll
Automation Activity & Vendor Info: (Acquisitions) Innovative Interfaces, Inc; (Cataloging) Innovative Interfaces, Inc; (Circulation) Innovative Interfaces, Inc; (OPAC) Innovative Interfaces, Inc; (Serials) Innovative Interfaces, Inc
Wireless access
Function: Adult literacy prog, Archival coll, AV serv, BA reader (adult literacy), Games & aids for the handicapped, Handicapped accessible, Homebound delivery serv, ILL available, Large print keyboards, Magnifiers for reading, Online searches, Photocopying/Printing, Prog for adults, Prog for children & young adult, Ref serv available, Summer reading prog, Telephone ref, Wheelchair accessible, Workshops
Mem of Suffolk Cooperative Library System
Open Mon-Thurs 10-9, Fri 10-7, Sat 10-5, Sun 1-5
Friends of the Library Group

SOUTHOLD

P SOUTHOLD FREE LIBRARY, 53705 Main Rd, 11971. (Mail add: PO Box 697, 11971-0697), SAN 312-4843. Tel: 631-765-2077. FAX: 631-765-2197. E-mail: southoldlibrary@gmail.com. Web Site: southoldlibrary.org. *Dir,* Caroline MacArthur; E-mail: cmmacarth@optonline.net; Staff 15 (MLS 3, Non-MLS 12)
Founded 1797. Pop 6,000; Circ 93,267
Library Holdings: High Interest/Low Vocabulary Bk Vols 30; Bk Titles 38,598; Per Subs 80
Special Collections: Southold History & Genealogy (Whitaker Coll)
Automation Activity & Vendor Info: (Cataloging) Innovative Interfaces, Inc - Sierra; (Circulation) Innovative Interfaces, Inc - Sierra; (Course Reserve) Innovative Interfaces, Inc - Sierra; (ILL) Innovative Interfaces, Inc - Sierra; (Media Booking) Innovative Interfaces, Inc - Sierra; (OPAC) Innovative Interfaces, Inc - Sierra
Wireless access
Mem of Suffolk Cooperative Library System
Special Services for the Blind Dep for Braille Inst; Talking bks
Open Mon-Fri 9:30-9, Sat 9:30-5, Sun (Sept-May) 1-5
Friends of the Library Group

S SOUTHOLD HISTORICAL SOCIETY MUSEUM LIBRARY*, 54325 Main Rd, 11971. (Mail add: PO Box 1, 11971-0001), SAN 327-2192. Tel: 631-765-5500. FAX: 631-765-8510. E-mail: sohissoc@optonline.net. Web Site: www.southoldhistoricalsociety.org. *Dir,* Geoffrey K Fleming; *Coll Mgr,* Amy Folk; *Adminr,* Deanna Witte-Walker
Founded 1965
Library Holdings: Bk Vols 1,500
Subject Interests: Local hist
Wireless access
Open Tues 9-3

SPARKILL

C SAINT THOMAS AQUINAS COLLEGE*, Lougheed Library, 125 Rte 340, 10976. SAN 312-4851. Tel: 845-398-4219. Reference Tel: 845-398-4218. FAX: 845-359-9537. Web Site: www.stac.edu. *Dir,* Mary Anne Lenk; E-mail: mlenk@stac.edu; *Head, Tech Serv,* Stan Plozaj; Tel: 845-398-4222, E-mail: splozaj@stac.edu; *Head, Ser Acq,* Nancy Cosgrove; Tel: 845-398-4214, E-mail: ncosgrov@stac.edu; *Head, Info Serv,* Kenneth Donohue; E-mail: kdonohue@stac.edu; *Govt Doc,* Virginia Dunnigan; Tel: 845-398-4216, E-mail: vdunniga@stac.edu; Staff 10 (MLS 5, Non-MLS 5)
Founded 1952. Enrl 1,400; Highest Degree: Master
Library Holdings: Bk Titles 98,978; Bk Vols 110,000; Per Subs 450
Automation Activity & Vendor Info: (Cataloging) LibLime; (Circulation) LibLime
Database Vendor: Dialog, EBSCOhost, OCLC FirstSearch, OVID Technologies, ProQuest, Wilson - Wilson Web
Wireless access
Function: ILL available
Publications: Library Guide
Partic in Southeastern New York Library Resources Council; Westchester Academic Library Directors Organization (WALDO)
Open Mon-Thurs 8am-11pm, Fri 8-4, Sat 10-5, Sun 1-9

SPECULATOR

P TOWN OF LAKE PLEASANT PUBLIC LIBRARY, 2864 State Hwy 8, 12164. (Mail add: PO Box 300, 12164). Tel: 518-548-4411. FAX: 518-548-8395. E-mail: lkplibrary@gmail.com. *Dir,* Deborah Desrochers; E-mail: ddesrochers@sals.edu
Library Holdings: Bk Vols 14,000
Automation Activity & Vendor Info: (Acquisitions) Innovative Interfaces, Inc; (Cataloging) Innovative Interfaces, Inc; (Circulation) Innovative Interfaces, Inc; (Course Reserve) Innovative Interfaces, Inc; (ILL) Innovative Interfaces, Inc; (Media Booking) Innovative Interfaces, Inc; (OPAC) Innovative Interfaces, Inc; (Serials) Innovative Interfaces, Inc
Wireless access
Mem of Southern Adirondack Library System
Open Mon, Wed & Fri 1-4 & 7-9, Tues, Thurs & Sat 10-2

SPENCER

P SPENCER LIBRARY*, 41 N Main St, 14883-9100. (Mail add: PO Box 305, 14883-0305), SAN 312-486X. Tel: 607-589-4496. FAX: 607-589-4271. E-mail: splibrary@htva.net. *Dir,* Elizabeth Helmetsie
Founded 1830. Circ 22,689
Library Holdings: Bk Vols 16,427; Per Subs 10
Special Collections: Spencer Needles Coll 1888-1977
Automation Activity & Vendor Info: (Acquisitions) Innovative Interfaces, Inc
Wireless access
Mem of Finger Lakes Library System

SPENCERPORT

P OGDEN FARMERS' LIBRARY*, 269 Ogden Center Rd, 14559. SAN 312-4878. Tel: 585-617-6181. FAX: 585-352-3406. E-mail: library@ogdenlibrary.com. Web Site: www.ogdenlibrary.com. *Libr Dir,* John Cohen; E-mail: jcohen@ogdenlibrary.com; *Ch,* Anne Strang; *Genealogy & Outreach Librn,* Laura Richardson; *Adult Serv,* Kate Vreeland; *YA Serv,* Roberta Voelkl; Staff 17 (MLS 4, Non-MLS 13)
Founded 1817. Pop 16,912; Circ 179,579
Library Holdings: Bk Vols 63,648; Per Subs 136
Special Collections: Genealogy Coll; Local History Coll
Automation Activity & Vendor Info: (Circulation) TLC (The Library Corporation); (OPAC) TLC (The Library Corporation)
Database Vendor: EBSCOhost, Gale Cengage Learning, TLC (The Library Corporation)
Wireless access
Function: Adult bk club, Archival coll, Art exhibits, Audio & video playback equip for onsite use, Audiobks via web, AV serv, Bk reviews (Group), Bks on cassette, Bks on CD, CD-ROM, Children's prog, Computer training, Computers for patron use, Copy machines, e-mail & chat, e-mail serv, E-Reserves, Electronic databases & coll, Exhibits, Family literacy, Fax serv, Free DVD rentals, Genealogy discussion group, Handicapped accessible, Holiday prog, Home delivery & serv to Sr ctr & nursing homes, Homebound delivery serv, ILL available, Instruction & testing, Magnifiers for reading, Mail & tel request accepted, Music CDs, Newsp ref libr, Notary serv, Online cat, Online info literacy tutorials on the web & in blackboard, Online ref, Online searches, Outreach serv, Outside serv via phone, mail, e-mail & web, OverDrive digital audio bks, Photocopying/Printing, Preschool outreach, Prog for adults, Prog for children & young adult, Pub access computers, Ref & res, Ref serv available, Ref serv in person, Res libr, Scanner, Senior outreach, Serves mentally handicapped consumers, Spoken cassettes & CDs, Spoken cassettes & DVDs, Story hour, Summer & winter reading prog, Tax forms, Teen prog, Telephone ref, VHS videos, Video lending libr, Web-catalog, Wheelchair accessible, Workshops
Mem of Monroe County Library System
Open Mon-Thurs 9-9, Fri & Sat 9-5
Friends of the Library Group

SPRING VALLEY

P FINKELSTEIN MEMORIAL LIBRARY*, 24 Chestnut St, 10977-5594. SAN 312-4886. Tel: 845-352-5700. FAX: 845-352-2319. Web Site: finkelsteinlibrary.org. *Dir,* Robert S Devino; *Asst Dir,* Karen LaRocca-Fels; *Head, Tech Serv,* Erica Grodin; *Bus Mgr,* Howard Heffler; *Adult Serv,* Tracy Allen; *Automation Librn,* Vera Curry; *Ch Serv,* Mildred Rivers; *Circ Supvr,* Dora Pizzoli; *Circ, Media Spec,* Fred Sandner; *Coll Develop, Ref,* John Dempsey; *ILL,* Christine Ball; *Prog Coordr,* Evelyn Daks; *YA Serv,* Laura Wolven; Staff 45 (MLS 19, Non-MLS 26)
Founded 1917. Pop 95,335; Circ 646,020
Library Holdings: AV Mats 20,000; Bk Vols 225,000; Per Subs 518; Talking Bks 3,000
Subject Interests: Educ, Foreign lang, Holocaust, Local hist
Automation Activity & Vendor Info: (Cataloging) SirsiDynix; (Circulation) SirsiDynix; (ILL) SirsiDynix; (OPAC) SirsiDynix
Database Vendor: EBSCOhost, Gale Cengage Learning, Newsbank, ProQuest, SirsiDynix
Wireless access
Publications: ADLIB (Quarterly Newsletter)
Mem of Ramapo Catskill Library System
Partic in Southeastern New York Library Resources Council
Special Services for the Deaf - Assistive tech; Bks on deafness & sign lang
Special Services for the Blind - Aids for in-house use; Assistive/Adapted tech devices, equip & products; Audio mat; Bks on cassette; Bks on CD; Computer with voice synthesizer for visually impaired persons; Home delivery serv; Large print & cassettes; Talking bks
Open Mon-Thurs 9-9, Fri 9-6, Sat 10-5, Sun 12-5
Friends of the Library Group
Bookmobiles: 1

SPRINGFIELD CENTER

S SPRINGFIELD LIBRARY*, 129 County Hwy 29A, 13468. (Mail add: PO Box 142, 13468). Tel: 315-858-5802. FAX: 315-858-5876. *Dir,* Nancy Sloan
Library Holdings: Bk Titles 2,700
Wireless access
Mem of Four County Library System
Partic in Central & Western Massachusetts Automated Resource Sharing
Open Mon & Thurs 2-8, Wed 9-2, Sat 9-12

SPRINGVILLE

P HULBERT PUBLIC LIBRARY OF THE TOWN OF CONCORD, Concord Public, 18 Chapel St, 14141. SAN 312-4908. Tel: 716-592-7742. E-mail: con@buffalolib.org. Web Site: www.buffalolib.org/content/library-locations/area-libraries?lib=Concord+Public+Library, www.townofconcordny.com/hulbert_library.php3. *Dir,* Bridgette Heintz; Staff 3 (MLS 1, Non-MLS 2)
Library Holdings: Bk Vols 34,000; Per Subs 52
Wireless access
Mem of Buffalo & Erie County Public Library System
Open Mon (Winter) 1-8, Tues & Thurs 10-7, Fri 12-7, Sat 10-1; Mon (Summer) 12-8, Tues, Thurs & Fri 10-7

STAATSBURG

P STAATSBURG LIBRARY*, 70 Old Post Rd, 12580. SAN 312-4916. Tel: 845-889-4683. FAX: 845-889-8414. E-mail: staatslibrary@gmail.com. Web Site: staatsburg.library.org. *Dir,* Lorraine Rothman
Founded 1894. Pop 3,840; Circ 9,550
Library Holdings: Bk Vols 12,023; Per Subs 21
Automation Activity & Vendor Info: (Cataloging) Innovative Interfaces, Inc - Millenium; (Circulation) Innovative Interfaces, Inc - Millenium; (OPAC) Innovative Interfaces, Inc - Millenium
Wireless access
Mem of Mid-Hudson Library System
Open Mon & Wed 10-12 & 2-8, Thurs 2-5, Fri 2-8, Sat 10-2
Friends of the Library Group

STAMFORD

P STAMFORD VILLAGE LIBRARY, 117 Main St, 12167. SAN 312-4924. Tel: 607-652-5001. FAX: 607-652-5001. E-mail: st.ill@4cls.org. *Dir,* Erin Larucci; *Libr Asst,* Pat Parks; Staff 1 (MLS 1)
Founded 1908. Pop 1,286; Circ 18,181
Library Holdings: Bk Vols 22,007; Per Subs 29
Special Collections: Local Historical Papers & Memorabilia
Automation Activity & Vendor Info: (Circulation) SirsiDynix; (OPAC) SirsiDynix
Wireless access
Mem of Four County Library System
Open Mon, Wed & Fri 10-5, Tues & Thurs 1-7, Sat 12-6

STANFORDVILLE

P STANFORD FREE LIBRARY*, 14 Creamery Rd, 12581. SAN 312-4932. Tel: 845-868-1341. FAX: 845-868-7482. E-mail: stanfordlibrary@optonline.net. Web Site: www.stanfordlibrary.org. *Librn,* Arlene Christensen
Pop 3,495; Circ 16,601
Library Holdings: Bk Vols 12,000; Per Subs 10
Automation Activity & Vendor Info: (Cataloging) Innovative Interfaces, Inc - Millenium; (Circulation) Innovative Interfaces, Inc - Millenium; (OPAC) Innovative Interfaces, Inc - Millenium; (Serials) Innovative Interfaces, Inc - Millenium
Wireless access
Mem of Mid-Hudson Library System
Open Mon, Tues, Thurs & Fri 2-8, Wed 9-11 & 2-8, Sat 9-2

STATEN ISLAND

S ARTHURKILL CORRECTIONAL FACILITY LIBRARY*, 2911 Arthurkill Rd, 10309. SAN 327-1145. Tel: 718-356-7333, Ext 4600. FAX: 718-356-7333, Ext 2099. *Librn,* Carl Romalis; Staff 1 (MLS 1)
Founded 1976
Apr 2006-Mar 2007 Income $10,000
Library Holdings: High Interest/Low Vocabulary Bk Vols 2,200; Large Print Bks 45; Per Subs 35
Restriction: Not open to pub

C COLLEGE OF STATEN ISLAND LIBRARY*, 2800 Victory Blvd, 10314-6609. SAN 354-1770. Tel: 718-982-4001. Circulation Tel: 718-982-4011. Interlibrary Loan Service Tel: 718-982-4014. Reference Tel: 718-982-4010. FAX: 718-982-4002. Interlibrary Loan Service FAX: 718-982-4015. TDD: 718-982-4096. E-mail: library@csi.cuny.edu. Web

Site: www.library.csi.cuny.edu. *Chief Librn,* Wilma L Jones; E-mail: wilma.jones@csi.cuny.edu; Staff 51 (MLS 19, Non-MLS 32)
Founded 1976. Enrl 12,600; Fac 823; Highest Degree: Doctorate
Library Holdings: AV Mats 7,726; e-books 3,000; e-journals 15,000; Electronic Media & Resources 143; Bk Vols 232,510; Per Subs 8,215
Special Collections: Staten Island Coll
Subject Interests: Computer sci, Educ, Eng, Hist, Media culture, Nursing, Polymer chem
Automation Activity & Vendor Info: (Acquisitions) Ex Libris Group; (Cataloging) Ex Libris Group; (Circulation) Ex Libris Group; (Course Reserve) Ex Libris Group; (ILL) OCLC; (OPAC) Ex Libris Group; (Serials) Ex Libris Group
Database Vendor: Cambridge Scientific Abstracts, EBSCOhost, Elsevier MDL, Gale Cengage Learning, JSTOR, LexisNexis, OCLC FirstSearch, OCLC WorldShare Interlibrary Loan, OVID Technologies, Oxford Online, ProQuest, ScienceDirect, Wiley, Wilson - Wilson Web
Wireless access
Function: Archival coll, Art exhibits, Audio & video playback equip for onsite use, AV serv, CD-ROM, Copy machines, Distance learning, Doc delivery serv, Electronic databases & coll, Equip loans & repairs, Fax serv, Handicapped accessible, Health sci info serv, ILL available, Online ref, Online searches, Orientations, Ref & res, Ref serv available, VHS videos
Publications: CSI Library (Newsletter)
Partic in Metropolitan New York Library Council; Nylink; OCLC Online Computer Library Center, Inc
Special Services for the Deaf - Assisted listening device; Assistive tech; Closed caption videos; TDD equip
Special Services for the Blind - Assistive/Adapted tech devices, equip & products; Computer with voice synthesizer for visually impaired persons
Open Mon-Thurs 8am-10pm, Fri 8-8, Sat 8:30-7, Sun 12-7
Restriction: Authorized patrons, Authorized scholars by appt, Borrowing privileges limited to fac & registered students, In-house use for visitors, Non-circulating coll, Photo ID required for access

S JACQUES MARCHAIS MUSEUM OF TIBETAN ART LIBRARY*, 338 Lighthouse Ave, 10306. SAN 312-4959. Tel: 718-987-3500. FAX: 718-351-0402. Web Site: www.tibetanmuseum.org. *Dir,* Meg Ventrudo; E-mail: mventrudo@tibetanmuseum.org
Founded 1945
Library Holdings: Bk Vols 1,200
Subject Interests: Archit, Art, Asia, Ethical philos, Lang arts, Oriental culture, Relig studies, Tibet
Wireless access
Restriction: Authorized scholars by appt

GM NEW YORK STATE OFFICE OF MENTAL RETARDATION & DEVELOPMENTAL DISABILITIES*, Institute for Basic Research in Developmental Disabilities Library, 1050 Forest Hill Rd, 10314. SAN 312-4967. Tel: 718-494-5119. FAX: 718-494-6660. *Librn,* Lawrence Black; E-mail: lawrence.black@opwdd.ny.gov; Staff 1 (MLS 1)
Founded 1969
Library Holdings: Bk Titles 5,900; Bk Vols 6,000; Per Subs 100
Subject Interests: Biochem, Genetics, Immunology, Neurology, Neuropathology, Physiological psychol, Virology
Wireless access
Partic in Brooklyn-Queens-Staten Island-Manhattan-Bronx Health Sciences Librarians

M RICHMOND UNIVERSITY MEDICAL CENTER*, Dimitrios Fournarakis Medical Library, 355 Bard Ave, 10310-1664. SAN 312-4991. Tel: 718-818-3117. FAX: 718-727-2456. E-mail: library@rumcsi.org. *Med Librn,* Andrea Rudner; E-mail: arudner@rumcsi.org; Staff 0.6 (MLS 0.6)
Founded 1925
Library Holdings: AV Mats 168; CDs 67; e-books 63; e-journals 50; Bk Vols 3,000; Per Subs 160
Subject Interests: Cardiology, Gynecology, Internal med, Nursing, Obstetrics, Pathology, Pediatrics, Psychiat, Radiology, Surgery
Automation Activity & Vendor Info: (Cataloging) Professional Software; (OPAC) Professional Software
Database Vendor: EBSCOhost, Gale Cengage Learning, OVID Technologies, PubMed, STAT!Ref (Teton Data Systems), UpToDate
Wireless access
Function: ILL available
Partic in Basic Health Sciences Library Network; Brooklyn-Queens-Staten Island-Manhattan-Bronx Health Sciences Librarians; National Network of Libraries of Medicine
Restriction: Open to staff only

C ST JOHN'S UNIVERSITY*, Loretto Memorial Library, Staten Island Campus, 300 Howard Ave, 10301. SAN 312-4983. Tel: 718-390-4456. Circulation Tel: 718-390-4457. Interlibrary Loan Service Tel: 718-390-4362. Reference Tel: 718-390-4460. FAX: 718-390-4290. Web Site: www.stjohns.edu/academics/libraries. *Dir,* Dr Mark Meng; Tel: 718-390-4458, E-mail: mengm@stjohns.edu; *Ref,* Lois Cherepon; Tel: 718-390-4521, E-mail: cherepol@stjohns.edu; *Ref,* Andrea McElrath; E-mail: mcelrata@stjohns.edu; Staff 6 (MLS 4, Non-MLS 2)
Founded 1972. Enrl 1,200; Fac 4; Highest Degree: Master
Library Holdings: e-books 18,547; Bk Titles 130,013; Bk Vols 153,566; Per Subs 129
Subject Interests: Educ
Automation Activity & Vendor Info: (Acquisitions) LibLime; (Cataloging) LibLime; (Circulation) LibLime; (Course Reserve) LibLime; (ILL) OCLC ILLiad; (OPAC) LibLime; (Serials) LibLime
Wireless access
Partic in Metropolitan New York Library Council; Minitex Library Information Network; Minnesota Theological Library Association; OCLC Online Computer Library Center, Inc; Westchester Academic Library Directors Organization (WALDO)
Open Mon-Thurs 8am-11pm, Fri 8-6, Sat 9-5, Sun 12-6
Friends of the Library Group

S STATEN ISLAND HISTORICAL SOCIETY LIBRARY*, 441 Clarke Ave, 10306. SAN 312-5025. Tel: 718-351-1611, Ext 299. FAX: 718-979-6102. Web Site: www.historicrichmondtown.org. *In Charge,* Carlotta DeFillo; E-mail: cdefillo@historicrichmondtown.org
Founded 1933
Library Holdings: Bk Vols 5,000
Special Collections: Staten Island Manuscript Coll (1670 to present), 18th & 19th Century History
Subject Interests: Local hist
Wireless access
Function: Archival coll, Bus archives, Photocopying/Printing, Ref serv available
Publications: Staten Island Historian
Restriction: Non-circulating, Not a lending libr, Open by appt only, Open to pub for ref only

S STATEN ISLAND INSTITUTE OF ARTS & SCIENCES*, Archives & Library, Snug Harbor Cultural Center, 1000 Richmond Terrace, Bldg H, 10301. SAN 354-1835. Tel: 718-727-1135. FAX: 718-273-5683. Web Site: www.statenislandmuseum.org. *Curator of Hist,* Patricia Salmon; E-mail: psalmon@statenislandmuseum.org; *Asst Archivist, Res,* Cara Dellate; E-mail: cdellate@statenislandmesem.org. Subject Specialists: *Hist,* Patricia Salmon; Staff 1 (MLS 1)
Founded 1881
Library Holdings: Bk Vols 30,000
Special Collections: Black Community on Staten Island (Crooke Coll & Gravelle Coll); Britton, Desosway & Gratacap Family (Charles G Hine Coll); Conservation History Coll, bks, clippings, letters; Daguerreotypes (H H Cleaves Coll); Davis, Hollick & Anthon Archives; Environmental Coll; Kreischer Family (Chapin Coll); Leng (Harry B Weiss Coll); Manuscript Coll, Staten Island & Environments Coll, docs, maps, photogs, scrapbks; Staten Island Newspaper (Curtis Coll), maps, photogs, print; Staten Island Newspapers from 1828 to 1945, micro; Steele Family (Mabel Abbott Coll); Women's Suffrage (Delvan Coll)
Subject Interests: Archaeology, City planning, Conserv of mat, Environ, Local Black hist, Museology, Natural sci, Staten Island
Wireless access
Open Tues, Thurs & Fri 10-4

M STATEN ISLAND UNIVERSITY HOSPITAL*, Medical Library, 475 Seaview Ave, 10305. SAN 312-5033. Tel: 718-226-9545. Interlibrary Loan Service Tel: 718-226-9547. FAX: 718-226-8582. E-mail: siuhlibrary@siuh.edu. Web Site: www.siuh.edu. *Dir,* Yelena Friedman; E-mail: yfriedman@siuh.edu; *Coordr,* Bridget Scanlon; E-mail: bscanlon@siuh.edu; Staff 2 (MLS 1, Non-MLS 1)
Founded 1938
Library Holdings: e-books 600; e-journals 550; Bk Titles 800; Per Subs 620
Partic in Brooklyn-Queens-Staten Island-Manhattan-Bronx Health Sciences Librarians; BSHL; Docline; Metropolitan New York Library Council; National Network of Libraries of Medicine Middle Atlantic Region; NY NJ-MLA
Open Mon-Fri 9-5

GL SUPREME COURT LIBRARY, Richmond County Court House, 25 Hyatt St, Rm 515, 10301-1968. SAN 312-505X. Tel: 718-675-8711. FAX: 718-447-6104. *Principal Law Librn,* Philip A Klingle; Staff 1 (MLS 1)
Founded 1920
Library Holdings: Bk Titles 1,600; Bk Vols 66,500; Per Subs 200
Partic in OCLC Online Computer Library Center, Inc

C WAGNER COLLEGE*, Horrmann Library, One Campus Rd, 10301-4495. SAN 312-5076. Tel: 718-390-3401. Interlibrary Loan Service Tel: 718-390-4110. Reference Tel: 718-390-3402. FAX: 718-420-4218. Interlibrary Loan Service FAX: 718-420-4363. E-mail: library@wagner.edu. Web Site: www.wagner.edu/library. *Dean of Libr,* Dorothy Davison; Tel: 718-420-4221, E-mail: ddavison@wagner.edu; *Acq, Per, Sr Librn, Ref,*

Denis Schaub; E-mail: dshaub@wagner.edu; *Access Serv/ILL Librn,* Timothy Hickey; *Archives Supvr, Instrul Serv Librn,* Catherine Perkins; E-mail: catherine.perkins@wagner.edu; *Syst & Tech Serv Librn,* Yan Ye Lee; Tel: 718-420-4219, E-mail: ylee@wagner.edu; *Archivist,* Lisa Holland; Staff 14 (MLS 5, Non-MLS 9)
Founded 1889. Enrl 2,280; Fac 206; Highest Degree: Master
Sept 2006-Aug 2007 Income $334,050, State $6,750, Parent Institution $327,300. Mats Exp $301,053, Books $70,000, Per/Ser (Incl. Access Fees) $140,000, AV Mat $8,753, Electronic Ref Mat (Incl. Access Fees) $82,300
Library Holdings: CDs 968; e-journals 11,879; Music Scores 1,000; Bk Titles 137,138; Bk Vols 208,642; Per Subs 548; Talking Bks 136; Videos 1,616
Special Collections: Literature (Edwin Markham Coll), bks & monographs
Subject Interests: Chem, Educ, Nursing
Automation Activity & Vendor Info: (Acquisitions) OCLC CatExpress; (Cataloging) OCLC CatExpress; (Circulation) Ex Libris Group; (Course Reserve) OpenAccess Software, Inc; (ILL) OCLC ILLiad
Database Vendor: EBSCOhost, JSTOR, LexisNexis, OCLC FirstSearch, OCLC WorldShare Interlibrary Loan, OVID Technologies, ProQuest
Wireless access
Publications: College Workstudy Handbook; Faculty Guide; Periodicals Holdings List; Student Guide
Partic in Metropolitan New York Library Council
Special Services for the Blind - Computer with voice synthesizer for visually impaired persons
Restriction: Private libr
Friends of the Library Group

STEPHENTOWN

P STEPHENTOWN MEMORIAL LIBRARY, 472 State Rte 43, 12168. SAN 312-5092. Tel: 518-733-5750. E-mail: director@stephentownlibrary.org. Web Site: www.stephentownlibrary.org. *Dir,* Laurenne Teachout; *Libr Spec,* Erica Bingham-Green; Staff 0.5 (MLS 0.5)
Founded 1946. Pop 2,676; Circ 24,771
Library Holdings: Audiobooks 900; Bks on Deafness & Sign Lang 20; CDs 300; DVDs 2,100; Large Print Bks 200; Bk Titles 14,400; Per Subs 24; Videos 100
Special Collections: Grant Seeking (Foundation Center Coll)
Wireless access
Function: Accessibility serv available based on individual needs, Adult bk club, Art exhibits, Audio & video playback equip for onsite use, Audiobks via web, Bks on cassette, Bks on CD, Children's prog, Computer training, Computers for patron use, Copy machines, Digital talking bks, e-mail serv, Electronic databases & coll, Family literacy, Fax serv, Free DVD rentals, Handicapped accessible, Homebound delivery serv, ILL available, Magnifiers for reading, Mus passes, Music CDs, Newsp ref libr, Online cat, Online info literacy tutorials on the web & in blackboard, Online ref, Online searches, Outreach serv, OverDrive digital audio bks, Photocopying/Printing, Preschool reading prog, Printer for laptops & handheld devices, Prog for adults, Prog for children & young adult, Pub access computers, Ref serv available, Ref serv in person, Scanner, Senior computer classes, Senior outreach, Serves mentally handicapped consumers, Spanish lang bks, Spoken cassettes & CDs, Spoken cassettes & DVDs, Story hour, Summer reading prog, Tax forms, Teen prog, Telephone ref, VHS videos, Video lending libr, Web-catalog, Wheelchair accessible
Mem of Upper Hudson Library System
Special Services for the Deaf - Bks on deafness & sign lang
Special Services for the Blind - Bks on cassette; Bks on CD; Braille bks; Cassette playback machines; Cassettes; Children's Braille; Copier with enlargement capabilities; Extensive large print coll; Free checkout of audio mat; Handicapped awareness prog; Home delivery serv; Large print bks; Low vision equip; Playaways (bks on MP3)
Open Mon-Thurs 12-6, Fri 12-8, Sat 10-2
Friends of the Library Group

STILLWATER

S NATIONAL PARK SERVICE*, Saratoga National Historical Park Archives, 648 Rte 32, 12170. SAN 312-5114. Tel: 518-664-9821, Ext 221. FAX: 518-664-9830. Web Site: www.nps.gov/sara. *Curator,* Chris Valosin
Founded 1941
Library Holdings: Bk Vols 1,000
Special Collections: Northern Campaign of 1777
Subject Interests: Am Revolution
Wireless access
Restriction: Open by appt only

P STILLWATER FREE LIBRARY*, 72 S Hudson Ave, 12170. (Mail add: PO Box 485, 12170-0485), SAN 312-5122. Tel: 518-664-6255. FAX: 518-664-6826. Web Site: stillwater.sals.edu. *Dir,* Sara Kipp; E-mail: skipp@sals.edu; Staff 2 (MLS 1, Non-MLS 1)
Founded 1949. Pop 7,522; Circ 20,311
Library Holdings: Bk Vols 19,354; Per Subs 10
Mem of Southern Adirondack Library System
Open Tues & Wed 11-8, Thurs & Fri 10-5, Sat 10-1
Friends of the Library Group

STOCKTON

P MARY E SEYMOUR MEMORIAL FREE LIBRARY*, 22 N Main St, 14784-0432. (Mail add: PO Box 128, 14784-0128), SAN 354-1959. Tel: 716-595-3323. FAX: 716-595-3323. E-mail: stocasslib@yahoo.com. Web Site: www.cclslib.org/cassadaga. *Dir,* Catherine Heath
Founded 1899. Pop 2,301; Circ 17,928
Library Holdings: Bk Titles 17,000; Bk Vols 19,000; Per Subs 25
Special Collections: Local History (Town of Stockton), bks, church records, military records
Mem of Chautauqua-Cattaraugus Library System
Special Services for the Blind - Bks on cassette
Open Mon & Wed 2-7, Fri 9-5
Friends of the Library Group
Branches: 1
CASSADAGA BRANCH, 18 Maple Ave, Cassadaga, 14718, SAN 354-1983. Tel: 716-595-3822. FAX: 716-595-3822. *Dir,* Catherine Heath
Special Services for the Blind - Bks on cassette
Open Tues & Thurs 11-8, Fri 4-8, Sat 10-2
Friends of the Library Group

STONE RIDGE

P STONE RIDGE PUBLIC LIBRARY*, Rte 209, 12484. (Mail add: Box 188, 12484), SAN 312-5130. Tel: 845-687-7023. FAX: 845-687-0094. E-mail: stoneridgelibrary@hvc.rr.com. Web Site: stoneridgelibrary.org. *Dir,* Jody Ford; *Asst Dir,* Sandy Zinaman; *Ch Serv,* Julianna Muth; Staff 8 (MLS 2, Non-MLS 6)
Founded 1909. Pop 7,500; Circ 66,718
Library Holdings: Bk Vols 33,426; Per Subs 85
Special Collections: Oral History
Automation Activity & Vendor Info: (Circulation) Innovative Interfaces, Inc; (OPAC) Innovative Interfaces, Inc
Wireless access
Mem of Mid-Hudson Library System
Open Mon 1:30-8, Tues, Thurs & Fri-Sat 10-5:30, Wed 10-8
Friends of the Library Group

J ULSTER COUNTY COMMUNITY COLLEGE*, Macdonald DeWitt Library, 12484. SAN 312-5149. Tel: 845-687-5213. Interlibrary Loan Service Tel: 845-687-5212. Reference Tel: 845-687-5208. FAX: 845-687-5220. Web Site: www.sunyulster.edu/library. *Dir, Libr Serv,* Kari Mack; *Instrul Serv Librn,* Judith Capurso; *Tech Serv & Syst Librn,* Judy Kuhns; *Circ Supvr,* Lisa Fabiano; *Ref Serv,* Cheri Gerstung; Staff 4 (MLS 4)
Founded 1963
Library Holdings: e-books 92,417; e-journals 47,000; Bk Titles 73,365; Bk Vols 80,767
Subject Interests: Local hist
Automation Activity & Vendor Info: (Cataloging) OCLC Connexion; (Circulation) Ex Libris Group; (ILL) OCLC ILLiad; (OPAC) Ex Libris Group; (Serials) Ex Libris Group
Wireless access
Partic in OCLC Online Computer Library Center, Inc; Southeastern New York Library Resources Council; SUNYConnect
Open Mon-Thurs 8-7, Fri 8-4, Sat & Sun 9-3

STONY BROOK

THE LONG ISLAND MUSEUM OF AMERICAN ART, HISTORY & CARRIAGES

S GERSTENBURG CARRIAGE REFERENCE LIBRARY, 1200 Rte 25A, 11790-1992, SAN 323-5610. Tel: 631-751-0066, Ext 232. FAX: 631-751-0353. E-mail: mail@longislandmuseum.org. Web Site: www.longislandmuseum.org. *Coll Mgr,* Christa Zaros; Staff 0.5 (MLS 0.5)
Founded 1950
Library Holdings: Bk Titles 5,000
Subject Interests: Accoutrements, Carriage archives, Carriage decoration, Carriage design, Carriage per, Horse drawn transportation, Horses
Restriction: Open by appt only

S KATE STRONG HISTORICAL LIBRARY, 1200 Rte 25A, 11790, SAN 312-5157. Tel: 631-751-0066. FAX: 631-751-0353. E-mail: mail@longislandmuseum.org. Web Site: www.longislandmuseum.org. *Coll Mgr,* Christa Zaros
Founded 1942
Library Holdings: Bk Titles 4,000
Special Collections: Decoys (Otto Johs Memorial Library)
Subject Interests: 19th Cent trade cat, Am art hist, Costumes, Decoys, Hunting, Local Long Island mat
Restriction: Open by appt only

C STONY BROOK UNIVERSITY*, Frank Melville Jr Memorial Library, W-1502 Melville Library, John S Toll Rd, 11794-3300. SAN 354-2017. Tel: 631-632-7100. Circulation Tel: 631-632-7115. Interlibrary Loan Service Tel: 631-632-7133. Reference Tel: 631-632-7110. FAX: 631-632-7116. Web Site: www.library.stonybrook.edu. *Dean of Libr,* Constantia Constantinou; E-mail: Constantia.Constantinou@stonybrook.edu; Staff 70 (MLS 30, Non-MLS 40)
Founded 1957. Enrl 19,487; Fac 1,900; Highest Degree: Doctorate
Jul 2007-Jun 2008. Mats Exp $5,376,129, Books $581,869, Per/Ser (Incl. Access Fees) $4,298,265. Sal $4,644,418 (Prof $3,633,355)
Library Holdings: CDs 40,910; e-books 2,500; e-journals 62,000; Electronic Media & Resources 300; Microforms 3,837,093; Bk Vols 1,976,172; Per Subs 35,222; Videos 8,087
Special Collections: 19th Century Children's Books; AIDC (Barcoding Industry) Coll; Current Fine Publishing & Printing (Perlshable Press Coll); Environmental Defense Coll; Ezra Pound Coll; Fielding Dawson Coll; Hispanic Literature & Culture (Jorge Carrera Andrade Coll); Jacob K Javits Papers; Jacqueline Newman Chinese Cookbook Coll; Long Island Historical Documents (Pre Revolutionary War - Civil War); Robert Creeley Coll; Robert Payne Coll; William Butler Yeats Papers, microform. State Document Depository; US Document Depository
Subject Interests: Behav sci, Eng, Environ studies, Music, Nat sci, Soc sci
Automation Activity & Vendor Info: (Acquisitions) Ex Libris Group; (Cataloging) Ex Libris Group; (Circulation) Ex Libris Group; (Course Reserve) Ex Libris Group; (ILL) OCLC; (Media Booking) OCLC; (OPAC) Ex Libris Group; (Serials) Ex Libris Group
Database Vendor: ARTstor, Blackwell, EBSCO Information Services, Elsevier, Gale Cengage Learning, LexisNexis, Nature Publishing Group, OCLC FirstSearch, OVID Technologies, ProQuest, PubMed, ScienceDirect, SerialsSolutions
Wireless access
Publications: Daily Bulletin (Newsletter); Library Connections (Bi-annually); The Screen Porch
Partic in Association of Research Libraries (ARL); Long Island Library Resources Council; OCLC Online Computer Library Center, Inc; RLIN (Research Libraries Information Network)
Special Services for the Deaf - Assistive tech; Staff with knowledge of sign lang
Special Services for the Blind - Assistive/Adapted tech devices, equip & products; Audio mat; Copier with enlargement capabilities; Large print bks; Reader equip
Open Mon-Thurs 8:30am-Midnight, Fri 8:30-8, Sat 10-6, Sun Noon-Midnight
Friends of the Library Group

Departmental Libraries:

CHEMISTRY, Chemistry Bldg, C-299, 11794-3425. Tel: 631-632-7150. FAX: 631-632-9191. *Head Librn,* Position Currently Open; Staff 2 (MLS 1, Non-MLS 1)
Open Mon-Fri 8:30-5
Friends of the Library Group

CM HEALTH SCIENCES LIBRARY, HST Level 3, Rm 136, 8034 SUNY Stony Brook, 11794-8034, SAN 354-2165. Tel: 631-444-2512. Interlibrary Loan Service Tel: 631-444-3105. FAX: 631-444-6649. Web Site: www.library.stonybrook.edu/healthsciences. *Interim Dean of Libr,* Andrew White; Tel: 631-444-3101; Staff 24 (MLS 5, Non-MLS 19)
Founded 1969. Enrl 2,293; Fac 557; Highest Degree: Doctorate
Library Holdings: e-books 4,200; e-journals 10,000; Bk Vols 280,000; Per Subs 20
Special Collections: History of Medicine, Dentistry & Nursing
Subject Interests: Allied health, Basic health sci, Dentistry, Med, Nursing, Soc welfare
Automation Activity & Vendor Info: (Acquisitions) Ex Libris Group; (Cataloging) Ex Libris Group; (Circulation) Ex Libris Group; (Course Reserve) Ex Libris Group; (OPAC) Ex Libris Group; (Serials) Ex Libris Group
Partic in National Network of Libraries of Medicine; OCLC Online Computer Library Center, Inc
Open Mon-Thurs 8:30am-12:30am, Fri 8am-9pm, Sat 10-7, Sun 1pm-12:30am

MARINE & ATMOSPHERIC SCIENCES INFORMATION CENTER, 165 Challenger Hall, 11794-5000. Tel: 631-632-8679. FAX: 631-632-2364. Web Site: www.msrc.sunysb.edu/pages/library.html. *Mgr,* Maria Riegert
Open Mon-Thurs 8:30am-10pm, Fri 8:30-5, Sun 2-10

MATHEMATICS-PHYSICS-ASTRONOMY, Physics Bldg C-124, 11794-3855. Tel: 631-632-7145. FAX: 631-632-9192. Web Site: www.sunysb.edu/sciencelibs/ldmath.htm. *Head Librn,* Sherry Chang
Open Mon-Thurs 8:30am-10pm, Fri 8:30-5, Sat 2-6, Sun 2-10

MUSIC, Melville Library, Rm W1530, 11794-3333. Tel: 631-632-7097. FAX: 631-632-1741. *Head Librn,* Gisele Ira Schierhorst; E-mail: gschierhorst@notes.cc.sunysb.edu; *Cataloger,* Celeste Hessler; Tel: 631-632-7541, E-mail: chessler@notes.cc.sunysb.edu
Open Mon-Thurs 8:30am-9pm, Fri 8:30-5, Sat 2-6, Sun 2-6

SCIENCE & ENGINEERING LIBRARY, Frank Melville Jr Memorial Library N-1001, 11794-3301. Tel: 631-632-7148. FAX: 631-632-7186. *In Charge,* Elsa Gonzalez; E-mail: elsa.gonzalez@stonybrook.edu

STONY CREEK

P STONY CREEK FREE LIBRARY*, 37 Harrisburg Rd, 12878-1622. (Mail add: PO Box 0064, 12878-0064), SAN 312-5165. Tel: 518-696-5911. FAX: 518-696-5911. Web Site: www.sals.edu. *Dir,* Lisa Bartow; Staff 0.5 (Non-MLS 0.5)
Founded 1916. Pop 734; Circ 4,803
Jan 2005-Dec 2005 Income $37,571, State $6,150, County $1,605, Locally Generated Income $17,500, Other $12,316. Mats Exp $1,343. Sal $16,118
Library Holdings: AV Mats 1,058; Bk Vols 8,052
Wireless access
Mem of Southern Adirondack Library System
Open Mon & Wed 5pm-9pm, Tues & Thurs 1-5:30, Sat 9-12

STONY POINT

P ROSE MEMORIAL LIBRARY*, 79 E Main St, 10980-1699. SAN 312-5173. Tel: 845-786-2100. FAX: 845-786-6042. Web Site: www.rosememoriallibrary.org. *Dir,* Benjamin Reid; E-mail: breid@rcls.org; *Ch,* Danielle Connolly; *Teen & Adult Librn,* Jennifer Russell; Staff 1 (MLS 1)
Founded 1950. Pop 12,838; Circ 29,455
Library Holdings: AV Mats 5,450; Bk Titles 26,143; Per Subs 78
Subject Interests: Local hist
Automation Activity & Vendor Info: (Cataloging) Horizon; (Circulation) Horizon; (OPAC) Horizon
Wireless access
Mem of Ramapo Catskill Library System
Open Mon-Thurs 10-9, Fri & Sat 10-5, Sun 1-5

STORMVILLE

S NEW YORK STATE DEPARTMENT OF CORRECTIONAL SERVICES*, Green Haven Correctional Facility Library, 594 Rte 216, 12582. SAN 354-2254. Tel: 845-221-2711, Ext 4562. *In Charge,* Eileen Pucci; Staff 1.5 (MLS 1, Non-MLS 0.5)
Founded 1942
Apr 2005-Mar 2006. Mats Exp $26,000, Books $16,000, Per/Ser (Incl. Access Fees) $10,000. Sal $45,000
Library Holdings: AV Mats 200; Large Print Bks 30; Bk Vols 7,000; Per Subs 99; Spec Interest Per Sub 30; Talking Bks 50
Special Collections: Black History Coll; Spanish Coll
Subject Interests: Coping skills mat, Occult
Automation Activity & Vendor Info: (Cataloging) Follett Software; (Circulation) Follett Software
Wireless access
Partic in Northern New York Library Network
Special Services for the Blind - Bks on cassette
Restriction: Not open to pub

SUFFERN

J ROCKLAND COMMUNITY COLLEGE LIBRARY*, 145 College Rd, 10901. SAN 312-519X. Tel: 845-574-4000. Circulation Tel: 845-574-4408. Interlibrary Loan Service Tel: 845-574-4414. Reference Tel: 845-574-4409. FAX: 845-574-4424. E-mail: library@sunyrockland.edu. Web Site: www.sunyrockland.edu/library. *Dir,* Position Currently Open; *Head Librn,* Dr Xi Shi; Tel: 845-574-4402, E-mail: xshi@sunyrockland.edu; *Access Serv,* Sarah Levy; Tel: 845-574-4472, E-mail: slevy@sunyrockland.edu; *Tech Serv,* Kim Weston; Tel: 845-574-4407, E-mail: kweston@sunyrockland.edu; Staff 7 (MLS 7)
Founded 1959. Enrl 4,600; Fac 240; Highest Degree: Associate
Library Holdings: Bk Titles 120,000; Per Subs 23,000
Automation Activity & Vendor Info: (Acquisitions) Ex Libris Group; (Cataloging) Ex Libris Group; (Circulation) Ex Libris Group; (Course Reserve) Ex Libris Group; (ILL) OCLC Online; (OPAC) Ex Libris Group
Database Vendor: EBSCOhost, Gale Cengage Learning, JSTOR, LexisNexis, Newsbank, OCLC FirstSearch, ProQuest, Wilson - Wilson Web
Publications: Bibliographic Instruction Aids; Bibliographies
Partic in OCLC Online Computer Library Center, Inc; Southeastern New York Library Resources Council
Open Mon-Thurs 8am-10pm, Fri 8-5, Sat 9-6, Sun 11-6

S SALVATION ARMY SCHOOL FOR OFFICER TRAINING*, Brengle Library, 201 Lafayette Ave, 10901. SAN 312-5203. Tel: 845-368-7228. FAX: 845-357-6644. Web Site: www.sfotusa.org. *Libr Dir,* Robin Rader; E-mail: rrader@use.salvationarmy.org; Staff 3 (MLS 1, Non-MLS 2)
Founded 1936. Enrl 90
Library Holdings: Bk Titles 22,000; Bk Vols 27,000; Per Subs 225
Special Collections: Salvation Army Publications
Automation Activity & Vendor Info: (Cataloging) CASPR; (Circulation) CASPR; (OPAC) CASPR
Database Vendor: Gale Cengage Learning, OCLC FirstSearch
Wireless access

Partic in Southeastern New York Library Resources Council
Open Mon-Thurs 8:30-10, Fri & Sat 8:30-4

P SUFFERN FREE LIBRARY*, 210 Lafayette Ave, 10901. SAN 312-5211. Tel: 845-357-1237. FAX: 845-357-3156. Web Site: www.suffernfreelibrary.org. *Dir,* Carol Connell-Connor; *Head, Ch,* Jennifer Smith; E-mail: jknoerze@rcls.org; *Coll Develop, Head, Ref,* Delys DeZwaan; E-mail: ddezwaan@rcls.org; *Commun Relations Librn,* Miguelina Molina; E-mail: mmolina@rcls.org; *Mgr, Circ Serv,* Nancy Wendt; E-mail: nwendt@rcls.org; *YA Serv,* Pauline Brower; E-mail: pbrower@rcls.org; Staff 38 (MLS 9, Non-MLS 29)
Founded 1926. Pop 27,426; Circ 518,043
Jul 2008-Jun 2009 Income $2,797,473, City $5,500, Locally Generated Income $199,708, Other $2,065,816. Mats Exp $360,572, Books $172,496, Per/Ser (Incl. Access Fees) $10,066, Micro $10,043, AV Equip $8,421, AV Mat $76,819, Electronic Ref Mat (Incl. Access Fees) $44,253. Sal $1,241,476 (Prof $541,971)
Library Holdings: AV Mats 19,599; DVDs 9,438; Electronic Media & Resources 41,108; Bk Vols 137,639; Per Subs 280
Subject Interests: Local hist
Automation Activity & Vendor Info: (Acquisitions) SirsiDynix; (Cataloging) SirsiDynix
Database Vendor: ALLDATA Online, Baker & Taylor, Booksite, CountryWatch, EBSCOhost, Gale Cengage Learning, Grolier Online, Overdrive, Inc, ProQuest, ReferenceUSA, SirsiDynix
Wireless access
Publications: Newsletter (Bi-monthly)
Mem of Ramapo Catskill Library System
Open Mon-Thurs 10-9, Fri & Sat 10-5

SYOSSET

R NORTH SHORE SYNAGOGUE*, Charles Cohn Memorial Library, 83 Muttontown Rd, 11791. SAN 312-5246. Tel: 516-921-2282. FAX: 516-921-2393. Web Site: www.northshoresynagogue.org. *In Charge,* Carol Joseph; Staff 1 (MLS 1)
Founded 1972
Library Holdings: Bk Titles 4,200; Per Subs 24
Special Collections: Sound Filmstrip Coll
Subject Interests: Holocaust, Judaica
Wireless access

SR ORTHODOX CHURCH IN AMERICA*, Department of History & Archives, 6850 Rte 25A, 11791. (Mail add: PO Box 675, 11791-0675), SAN 327-2176. Tel: 516-922-0550. FAX: 516-922-0954. Web Site: oca.org. *Archivist,* Alexis Liberovsky; E-mail: alex@oca.org
Library Holdings: Bk Vols 1,000; Per Subs 200
Wireless access
Restriction: Open by appt only
Friends of the Library Group

P SYOSSET PUBLIC LIBRARY*, 225 S Oyster Bay Rd, 11791-5897. SAN 312-5254. Tel: 516-921-7161. Reference Tel: 516-921-7161, Ext 217. FAX: 516-921-8771. E-mail: spladministration@syossetlibrary.org. Web Site: www.syossetlibrary.org. *Dir,* Karen Liebman; *Asst Dir, Head, Adult Serv,* Lisa Caputo; *Head, Ch,* Sue Ann Reale; *Head, Prog,* Pam Martin; *Syst Adminr,* Christine Belling; Staff 79 (MLS 34, Non-MLS 45)
Founded 1961. Pop 33,716; Circ 237,693
Library Holdings: Bk Vols 247,155; Per Subs 339
Subject Interests: Local hist
Automation Activity & Vendor Info: (Acquisitions) Innovative Interfaces, Inc - Millenium
Wireless access
Publications: Newsletter
Mem of Nassau Library System
Open Mon-Thurs 9-9, Fri 10-9, Sat 9-5, Sun 12-5
Friends of the Library Group

SYRACUSE

L BOND, SCHOENECK & KING, PLLC*, Law Library, One Lincoln Ctr, 13202-1355. SAN 372-2384. Tel: 315-218-8000. FAX: 315-218-8100. Web Site: www.bsk.com. *Dir,* Maureen T Kays; *Librn,* Allison Perry; Staff 3 (MLS 2, Non-MLS 1)
Library Holdings: Bk Vols 25,000; Per Subs 100
Partic in Central New York Library Resources Council
Open Mon-Fri 9-5

G CENTRAL NEW YORK REGIONAL PLANNING & DEVELOPMENT BOARD*, Library & Information Center, 126 N Salina St, Ste 200, 13202. SAN 327-2370. Tel: 315-422-8276. FAX: 315-422-9051. Web Site: www.cnyrpdb.org. *Dir,* David Bottar; Tel: 315-422-8276, Ext 207, E-mail: dbottar@cnyrpdb.org
Founded 1966
Library Holdings: Bk Titles 3,000; Per Subs 25
Partic in NY State Data Ctr Network
Open Mon-Fri 8:30-4:30

M CROUSE HOSPITAL LIBRARY*, 736 Irving Ave, 13210. SAN 312-5327. Tel: 315-470-7380. FAX: 315-470-7443. E-mail: library@crouse.org. Web Site: www.crouse.org/library. *Libr Mgr,* Kristine Delaney; E-mail: kristinedelaney@crouse.org; *Librn,* Ellen Owens; Staff 3 (MLS 2, Non-MLS 1)
Founded 1916
Library Holdings: AV Mats 300; Bk Titles 2,000; Per Subs 40
Special Collections: Nursing Archives
Subject Interests: Healthcare, Med, Nursing
Automation Activity & Vendor Info: (OPAC) LibraryWorld, Inc
Database Vendor: OVID Technologies
Wireless access
Partic in National Network of Libraries of Medicine

S ERIE CANAL MUSEUM RESEARCH LIBRARY*, 318 Erie Blvd E, 13202. SAN 312-5289. Tel: 315-471-0593. FAX: 315-471-7220. E-mail: curator@eriecanalmuseum.org. Web Site: www.eriecanalmuseum.org. *Curator,* Daniel Ward
Library Holdings: Bk Titles 500; Bk Vols 5,000; Per Subs 50
Special Collections: Erie Canal (State Engineers & Surveyors), doc
Subject Interests: NY State canal hist
Open Mon-Fri 10-5
Restriction: Non-circulating, Researchers only

S EVERSON MUSEUM OF ART LIBRARY*, Richard V Smith Art Reference Library, 401 Harrison St, 13202. SAN 312-5335. Tel: 315-474-6064. FAX: 315-474-6943. Web Site: www.everson.org. *Actg Librn,* Mary Iversen
Founded 1896
Library Holdings: Bk Vols 16,400; Per Subs 20
Special Collections: American Ceramics, mss; Archives of Ceramic National Exhibitions, 1932-present
Subject Interests: Am, Ceramics, Exhibition catalogs, Oriental art
Open Mon & Thurs 9-3

P FAIRMOUNT COMMUNITY LIBRARY*, 406 Chapel Dr, 13219. SAN 312-5343. Tel: 315-487-8933. FAX: 315-484-9475. E-mail: fairmountcommunitylibrary@gmail.com. Web Site: www.fairmountlibrary.org. *Dir,* Paul Morrell; *Asst Dir,* Janet Hayduke
Founded 1957. Pop 6,106; Circ 68,551
Library Holdings: Bk Vols 27,667; Per Subs 40
Subject Interests: Adult fiction
Automation Activity & Vendor Info: (Cataloging) Innovative Interfaces, Inc; (Circulation) Innovative Interfaces, Inc; (OPAC) Innovative Interfaces, Inc
Wireless access
Mem of Onondaga County Public Library
Open Mon-Thurs 10-8, Fri 10-5, Sat (Sept-June) 10-2
Friends of the Library Group

L HANCOCK ESTABROOK, LLP, Law Library, 1500 AXA Tower One, 100 Madison St, 13202. SAN 327-5302. Tel: 315-565-4500. FAX: 315-565-4600. Web Site: www.hancocklaw.com. *Law Librn,* Donna Byrne; Tel: 315-565-4706, Fax: 315-565-4806, E-mail: dbyrne@hancocklaw.com; Staff 3 (MLS 1, Non-MLS 2)
Founded 1889
Library Holdings: Bk Titles 2,128; Per Subs 50
Subject Interests: Employment, Environ, Estates, Health law, Intellectual property, Labor, Real estate, Tax, Trial practice law
Automation Activity & Vendor Info: (Acquisitions) Inmagic, Inc.; (Cataloging) Inmagic, Inc.; (Circulation) Inmagic, Inc.
Database Vendor: LexisNexis, Westlaw
Function: Doc delivery serv, Ref serv available
Restriction: Private libr

C LE MOYNE COLLEGE, Noreen Reale Falcone Library, 1419 Salt Springs Rd, 13214-1301. SAN 312-536X. Tel: 315-445-4153. Circulation Tel: 315-445-4330. Interlibrary Loan Service Tel: 315-445-4333. Administration Tel: 315-445-4320. FAX: 315-445-4642. Web Site: www.lemoyne.edu/library. *Dir,* Robert C Johnston; Tel: 315-445-4321, E-mail: johnstrc@lemoyne.edu; *Access Serv Librn,* Lisa Doyle; Tel: 315-445-4681, E-mail: doylel@lemoyne.edu; *Coll & Res Sharing Librn,* Inga H Barnello; Tel: 315-445-4326, E-mail: barnello@lemoyne.edu; *Electronic Syst & Res Librn,* Thomas H Keays; Tel: 315-445-4322, E-mail: keaysht@lemoyne.edu; *Instrul Serv/CORE Librn,* Kelly Delevan; Tel: 315-445-4154, E-mail: delevakk@lemoyne.edu; *Ref Librn,* Cathleen O Scott; Tel: 315-445-4627, E-mail: scottco@lemoyne.edu; *Ref Librn,* Karen Zhe-Heimerman; E-mail: zheheikm@lemoyne.edu; *Tech Serv Librn,* I-Chene Tai; Tel: 315-445-4331, E-mail: tai@lemoyne.edu. Subject Specialists: *Foreign lang, Visual arts,* Robert C Johnston; *Educ,* Lisa Doyle; *Anthrop, Econ, Polit sci, Soc sci,* Inga H Barnello; *Computer sci,*

Info syst, Math, Thomas H Keays; *Eng, Hist,* Kelly Delevan; *Acctg, Bus admin, Health sci,* Cathleen O Scott; *Bio, Chem, Physics,* Karen Zhe-Heimerman; *Communications, Music, Theatre,* I-Chene Tai; Staff 14 (MLS 8, Non-MLS 6)
Founded 1946. Enrl 2,922; Fac 326; Highest Degree: Master
Jun 2012-May 2013 Income $1,701,645, State $6,251, Federal $50,155, Locally Generated Income $9,672, Parent Institution $1,635,567. Mats Exp $864,109, Books $66,943, Per/Ser (Incl. Access Fees) $55,956, Other Print Mats $10,339, Micro $1,012, AV Equip $635, AV Mat $21,223, Electronic Ref Mat (Incl. Access Fees) $703,293, Presv $4,708. Sal $721,546 (Prof $653,842)
Library Holdings: AV Mats 13,366; CDs 985; DVDs 3,673; e-books 29,127; e-journals 140,418; Microforms 277,313; Music Scores 527; Bk Titles 180,254; Bk Vols 223,345; Per Subs 1,355; Videos 3,704
Special Collections: Danny Biasone Syracuse Nationals Coll; Irish Literature (Father William Noon, S J Coll); Jesuitica (Jesuit History); McGrath Music Coll
Subject Interests: Archives, Philos, Relig
Automation Activity & Vendor Info: (Acquisitions) Innovative Interfaces, Inc; (Cataloging) Innovative Interfaces, Inc; (Circulation) Innovative Interfaces, Inc; (Course Reserve) Innovative Interfaces, Inc; (ILL) OCLC WorldShare Interlibrary Loan; (Media Booking) Innovative Interfaces, Inc; (OPAC) Innovative Interfaces, Inc; (Serials) Innovative Interfaces, Inc
Database Vendor: ABC-CLIO, ACM (Association for Computing Machinery), Alexander Street Press, American Physical Society, Annual Reviews, BioOne, Blackwell, Coutts Information Service, CQ Press, Emerald, Facts on File, Gale Cengage Learning, Grolier Online, Haworth Pres Inc, Hoovers, IEEE (Institute of Electrical & Electronics Engineers), Ingenta, IOP, JSTOR, Knovel, LexisNexis, MD Consult, Mergent Online, Modern Language Association, Nature Publishing Group, Newsbank, OCLC FirstSearch, OCLC WorldShare Interlibrary Loan, OVID Technologies, ProQuest, RefWorks, Sage, ScienceDirect, SerialsSolutions, Springer-Verlag, ValueLine, Westlaw, Wiley, YBP Library Services
Wireless access
Function: Adult bk club, Archival coll, Art exhibits, Audio & video playback equip for onsite use, AV serv, Bk club(s), Computers for patron use, Copy machines, Doc delivery serv, e-mail & chat, e-mail serv, E-Reserves, Electronic databases & coll, Handicapped accessible, Health sci info serv, ILL available, Music CDs, Online cat, Online ref, Online searches, Photocopying/Printing, Pub access computers, Ref serv available, Ref serv in person, Scanner, Telephone ref, VHS videos, Web-catalog, Wheelchair accessible
Publications: AlphaBYTES (Newsletter); Bibliography of Le Moyne College Authors (1946-1992); Library Guides
Partic in Center for Research Libraries; Central New York Library Resources Council; Connect NY; OCLC Online Computer Library Center, Inc
Special Services for the Deaf - Accessible learning ctr
Open Mon-Thurs 8am-2am, Fri 8-8, Sat 9-8, Sun Noon-2am

S LOCKHEED MARTIN CORP*, Maritime Systems & Sensors-Syracuse, Bldg 6, 497 Electronics Pkwy, E7-G92, 13221. SAN 375-8176. Tel: 315-456-2269. FAX: 315-456-0099. *Dir,* Lori Scoones
Library Holdings: Bk Titles 5,000; Per Subs 125
Subject Interests: Avionics, Radar
Database Vendor: Jane's, OCLC FirstSearch
Wireless access
Partic in Central New York Library Resources Council
Restriction: Staff use only

L MACKENZIE, HUGHES LLP*, Law Library, 101 S Salina St, Ste 600, 13202-1399. (Mail add: PO Box 4967, 13221-4967), SAN 312-5378. Tel: 315-474-7571. FAX: 315-474-6409. Web Site: www.mackenziehughes.com. *In Charge,* Mike Campbell
Library Holdings: Bk Vols 16,500; Per Subs 110
Subject Interests: Civil litigation, Corporate, Employment law, Estates, Labor law, Real estate, Tax, Worker compensation
Database Vendor: Westlaw
Partic in Dialog Corp; Westlaw
Open Mon-Fri 9-5

S MANUFACTURERS ASSOCIATION OF CENTRAL NEW YORK LIBRARY*, 5788 Widewaters Pkwy, 13214. SAN 312-5386. Tel: 315-474-4201. FAX: 315-474-0524. Web Site: www.macny.org. *In Charge,* Patty Clark
Library Holdings: Bk Vols 2,100; Per Subs 25
Subject Interests: Collective bargaining, Human resources, Unions
Open Mon-Thurs 8:30-5, Fri 8:30-4

GL NEW YORK STATE UNIFIED COURT SYSTEM*, Syracuse Supreme Court Law Library, 401 Montgomery St, 13202. SAN 312-5424. Tel: 315-671-1150. Interlibrary Loan Service Tel: 315-671-1143. Reference Tel: 315-671-1151. Toll Free Tel: 800-268-7869. FAX: 315-671-1160. *Principal Librn,* Cynthia Kesler; Staff 8 (MLS 4, Non-MLS 4)
Founded 1849
Library Holdings: Bk Titles 15,556; Bk Vols 165,000; Per Subs 600
Special Collections: Native American Law Materials. State Document Depository
Subject Interests: Extensive NY state, Fed legal mats, Shared fed dep
Database Vendor: LexisNexis, SirsiDynix, Westlaw
Wireless access
Publications: Articles of Interest & Subject Bibliographies; Library Guide; Microform Guide; New Book List; New Doc Topic Finders; Records & Briefs Guide
Partic in NY Cent Libr Resources Coun; Nylink
Open Mon-Fri 8:30-4:30

J ONONDAGA COMMUNITY COLLEGE, Sidney B Coulter Library, 4585 W Seneca Tpk, 13215-4585. SAN 312-5432. Tel: 315-498-2334. Interlibrary Loan Service Tel: 315-498-2338. FAX: 315-498-7213. E-mail: library@sunyocc.edu. Web Site: library.sunyocc.edu. *Chair,* Pauline Lynch Shostack; Tel: 315-498-2708, E-mail: shostacp@sunyocc.edu; *Distance Learning & Outreach Librn,* Fantasia Thorne-Ortiz; Tel: 315-498-2337, E-mail: f.a.thorne-ortiz@sunyocc.edu; *Ref & ILL Librn,* Angela Weiler; Tel: 315-498-2340, E-mail: weilera@sunyocc.edu; *Acq & Tech Serv,* Jeffrey Harr; Tel: 315-498-2144, E-mail: shostacp@sunyocc.edu; *Electronic Res & Pub Serv,* Penelope Klein; Tel: 315-498-2135, E-mail: kleinp@sunyocc.edu; Staff 5 (MLS 5)
Founded 1962. Enrl 12,834; Fac 407; Highest Degree: Associate
Sept 2012-Aug 2013 Income $1,088,988. Mats Exp $179,310, Books $56,400, Per/Ser (Incl. Access Fees) $61,410, Micro $12,000, AV Equip $1,500, AV Mat $28,000, Electronic Ref Mat (Incl. Access Fees) $20,000. Sal $872,902 (Prof $343,353)
Library Holdings: Audiobooks 162; Bks on Deafness & Sign Lang 250; CDs 4,160; DVDs 2,383; e-books 32,297; e-journals 9; Microforms 601; Bk Titles 88,448; Bk Vols 152,286; Per Subs 305; Talking Bks 167; Videos 3,420
Special Collections: Berrigan Brothers Coll; Central New York History; Faculty Authors; Local History Coll; Onondaga Community College Archives
Subject Interests: Careers, Health, Humanities, Technologies
Automation Activity & Vendor Info: (Acquisitions) Ex Libris Group; (Cataloging) Ex Libris Group; (Circulation) Ex Libris Group; (Course Reserve) Ex Libris Group; (ILL) OCLC ILLiad; (Media Booking) Ex Libris Group; (OPAC) Ex Libris Group; (Serials) EBSCO Online
Database Vendor: Alexander Street Press, CQ Press, ebrary, EBSCOhost, Elsevier, Gale Cengage Learning, Newsbank, OCLC FirstSearch, OVID Technologies, Oxford Online, ProQuest, World Trade Press
Wireless access
Publications: Library Brochure; Library Newsletter; Periodical Holdings
Partic in Central New York Library Resources Council; OCLC Online Computer Library Center, Inc; Westchester Academic Library Directors Organization (WALDO)
Special Services for the Deaf - Bks on deafness & sign lang; Closed caption videos
Special Services for the Blind - Accessible computers; Dragon Naturally Speaking software; Large screen computer & software; Sound rec; Variable speed audiotape players; VisualTek equip; ZoomText magnification & reading software
Open Mon-Thurs 8am-9pm, Fri 8-4:30, Sun 12-6
Restriction: Circ limited

P ONONDAGA COUNTY PUBLIC LIBRARY, Robert P Kinchen Central Library, The Galleries of Syracuse, 447 S Salina St, 13202-2494. SAN 354-2319. Circulation Tel: 315-435-1904. Reference Tel: 315-435-1900. FAX: 315-435-8533. TDD: 315-435-1872. E-mail: reference@onlib.org. Web Site: www.onlib.org. *Exec Dir,* Susan Mitchell; E-mail: director@onlib.org; *Cent Libr Adminr,* Doreen Milcarek; *Br Serv Adminr & Initiatives,* Susan Reckhow; *Pub Info Officer,* Kathy Osmond; *Syst & Mem Serv,* Deb Lewis; Staff 52 (MLS 52)
Founded 1852. Pop 467,026; Circ 1,569,383
Library Holdings: Bk Vols 1,700,000
Special Collections: Foundation Center; Historic Syracuse, microfiche. US Document Depository
Subject Interests: Genealogy, Literacy, Local hist
Automation Activity & Vendor Info: (Cataloging) Innovative Interfaces, Inc; (Circulation) Innovative Interfaces, Inc; (OPAC) Innovative Interfaces, Inc
Database Vendor: EBSCOhost, Gale Cengage Learning, Hoovers, Newsbank, ReferenceUSA
Wireless access
Member Libraries: Baldwinsville Public Library; DeWitt Community Library; East Syracuse Free Library; Elbridge Free Library; Fairmount Community Library; Fayetteville Free Library; Jordan Bramley Library; Liverpool Public Library; Manlius Library; Marcellus Free Library; Maxwell Memorial Library; Minoa Library; Northern Onondaga Public Library; Onondaga Free Library; Salina Free Library; Solvay Public Library; Tully Free Library

Partic in Central New York Library Resources Council; OCLC Online Computer Library Center, Inc
Special Services for the Deaf - TDD equip; TTY equip; Videos & decoder
Special Services for the Blind - Reader equip
Friends of the Library Group
Branches: 10
BEAUCHAMP, 2111 S Salina St, 13205, SAN 354-2343. Tel: 315-435-3395. FAX: 315-435-2729. *Br Mgr,* Dawn Marmor
Open Mon, Wed, Fri & Sat 9-5, Tues & Thurs 9-7:30
BETTS, 4862 S Salina St, 13205, SAN 354-2378. Tel: 315-435-1940. FAX: 315-435-1944. *Br Mgr,* Elyse Meltz
Open Mon & Wed 9-7:30, Tues, Thurs, Fri & Sat 9-5, Sun (Winter) 1-5
HAZARD, 1620 W Genesee St, 13204, SAN 354-2408. Tel: 315-435-5326. FAX: 315-435-5329. *Br Mgr,* George Konder
Open Mon, Wed, Fri & Sat 9-5, Tues & Thurs 9-7:30
Friends of the Library Group
MUNDY, 1204 S Geddes St, 13204, SAN 354-2432. Tel: 315-435-3797. FAX: 315-435-8557. *Br Mgr,* Janet Park
Open Mon, Tues, Thurs, Fri & Sat 9-5, Wed 9-7:30
Friends of the Library Group
NORTHEAST COMMUNITY CENTER, 716 Hawley Ave, 13203, SAN 354-2580. Tel: 315-472-6343, Ext 208. FAX: 315-472-8332. *Librn,* Tatiana Sahm
Open Mon-Fri 10-5
PAINE, 113 Nichols Ave, 13206, SAN 354-2467. Tel: 315-435-5442. FAX: 315-435-3553. *Br Mgr,* Renate Dunsmore
Open Mon & Tues 9-7:30, Wed-Sat 9-5
PETIT, 105 Victoria Pl, 13210, SAN 354-2491. Tel: 315-435-3636. FAX: 315-435-2731. *Br Mgr,* Marilyn Smith
Open Mon & Thurs 9-7:30, Tues, Wed, Fri & Sat 9-5
SOULE, 101 Springfield Rd, 13214, SAN 354-2521. Tel: 315-435-5320. FAX: 315-435-5322. *Br Mgr,* Mitch Tiegel
Open Mon, Thurs & Fri & Sat 9-5, Tues & Wed 9-7:30, Sun (Winter) 1-5
SOUTHWEST COMMUNITY CENTER, 401 South Ave, 13204, SAN 354-2610. Tel: 315-671-5814. *Librn,* Dan Smith
Open Mon-Thurs 11-5
WHITE BRANCH, 763 Butternut St, 13208, SAN 354-2556. Tel: 315-435-3519. FAX: 315-435-3367. *Br Mgr,* Renate Dunsmore
Open Mon, Tues, Fri & Sat 9-5, Wed & Thurs 9-7:30

P ONONDAGA FREE LIBRARY*, 4840 W Seneca Tpk, 13215. SAN 312-5440. Tel: 315-492-1727. FAX: 315-492-1323. E-mail: onondagafree@yahoo.com. Web Site: www.oflibrary.org. *Dir,* Susan Morgan; E-mail: smorgan@onlib.org; *Asst Dir,* Alyssa Newton; *Ch Serv,* Holly Hart; *Ch Serv,* Betty Tucker; Staff 4 (MLS 2, Non-MLS 2)
Founded 1961. Pop 26,000; Circ 139,010
Library Holdings: AV Mats 5,086; Bk Vols 31,459; Per Subs 173
Automation Activity & Vendor Info: (Cataloging) Innovative Interfaces, Inc; (Circulation) Innovative Interfaces, Inc
Wireless access
Mem of Onondaga County Public Library
Open Mon-Thurs (Winter) 10-8:30, Fri 10-5, Sat 11-4, Sun 1-4; Mon-Thurs (Summer) 10-8:30, Fri 10-5, Sat 10-2
Friends of the Library Group

S PROLITERACY*, 104 Marcellus St, 13204. SAN 324-2218. Tel: 315-422-9121. FAX: 315-422-6369. Web Site: www.proliteracy.org. *Dir,* Katie Bova; Tel: 315-422-9121, Ext 2459, E-mail: kbova@proliteracy.org; Staff 1 (MLS 1)
Library Holdings: Bk Titles 6,950; Per Subs 152
Special Collections: Literacy (Frank Laubach Coll)
Subject Interests: Adult illiteracy, Adult literacy, English as a second lang, Nonprofit mgt, Nontraditional adult basic educ, Publ for adult new readers, Reading, Voluntarism
Wireless access

M SAINT JOSEPH'S HOSPITAL HEALTH CENTER*, College of Nursing & Medical Library, 206 Prospect Ave, 13203. SAN 312-5467. Tel: 315-448-5053. FAX: 315-423-6804. Web Site: www.sjhsyr.org. *Mgr,* Sandra Zajac; E-mail: sandra.zajac@sjhsyr.org; *Librn,* Peter Mathe; E-mail: peter.mathe@sjhsyr.org; *Computer Serv,* Andrew Yackel; E-mail: andrew.yackel@sjhsyr.org; Staff 4 (MLS 3, Non-MLS 1)
Founded 1948
Library Holdings: DVDs 20; e-books 60; e-journals 500; Bk Vols 4,500; Per Subs 100; Videos 250
Subject Interests: Nursing, Nursing hist
Automation Activity & Vendor Info: (Cataloging) EOS International; (Circulation) EOS International; (OPAC) EOS International
Database Vendor: Cinahl, MD Consult, PubMed, UpToDate
Wireless access
Publications: Accession List (Monthly)
Partic in Central New York Library Resources Council
Open Mon-Fri 8am-9pm, Sat & Sun 12:30-9

L SCOLARO, SHULMAN, COHEN, FETTER & BURSTEIN, PC*, Law Library, 507 Plum St, Ste 300, 13204. SAN 372-2376. Tel: 315-471-8111, Ext 238. FAX: 315-425-3638. *Librn,* Richard J Powell; E-mail: rpowell@scolaro.com; Staff 1 (MLS 1)
Founded 1979
Library Holdings: Bk Vols 5,000; Per Subs 20
Automation Activity & Vendor Info: (Acquisitions) Inmagic, Inc.; (Cataloging) Inmagic, Inc.; (OPAC) Inmagic, Inc.; (Serials) Inmagic, Inc.
Database Vendor: LexisNexis
Function: For res purposes
Restriction: Staff use only

C STATE UNIVERSITY OF NEW YORK, COLLEGE OF ENVIRONMENTAL SCIENCE & FORESTRY*, F Franklin Moon Library, One Forestry Dr, 13210. SAN 312-5483. Tel: 315-470-6711. Interlibrary Loan Service Tel: 315-470-6729. FAX: 315-470-4766. Web Site: www.esf.edu/moonlib. *Dir,* Stephen P Weiter; E-mail: spweiter@esf.edu; *ILL,* James Williamson; Staff 5 (MLS 5)
Founded 1911. Enrl 2,000; Fac 125; Highest Degree: Doctorate
Library Holdings: Bk Vols 135,258; Per Subs 2,022
Subject Interests: Environ studies, Forestry, Landscape archit, Natural res, Outdoor recreation, Paper sci, Plant pathology, Polymer chem
Automation Activity & Vendor Info: (Acquisitions) Ex Libris Group; (Cataloging) Ex Libris Group; (Circulation) Ex Libris Group; (ILL) OCLC ILLiad; (OPAC) Ex Libris Group; (Serials) Ex Libris Group
Database Vendor: Agricola, American Chemical Society, Cambridge Scientific Abstracts, CIOS (Communication Institute for Online Scholarship), Dialog, EBSCO Information Services, EBSCOhost, Elsevier, Gale Cengage Learning, ISI Web of Knowledge, LexisNexis, ProQuest, ScienceDirect, Wiley
Wireless access
Publications: Point of Use Guides (Newsletter)
Partic in Central New York Library Resources Council; OCLC Online Computer Library Center, Inc
Open Mon-Thurs 8am-11:30pm, Fri 8-5, Sat 11-6, Sun 11am-11:30pm
Friends of the Library Group

CM SUNY UPSTATE MEDICAL UNIVERSITY, Health Sciences Library, 766 Irving Ave, 13210-1602. SAN 312-5475. Tel: 315-464-4582. Interlibrary Loan Service Tel: 315-464-5116. Reference Tel: 315-464-4581. FAX: 315-464-4584. Interlibrary Loan Service FAX: 315-464-7199. E-mail: library@upstate.edu. Web Site: library.upstate.edu. *Dir,* Cristina Pope; E-mail: popec@upstate.edu; *Dep Dir,* Wendi Ackerman; Tel: 315-464-8141, E-mail: ackermaw@upstate.edu; *Asst Dir, Customer Serv,* Darlene Ford; Tel: 315-464-7114, E-mail: fordd@upstate.edu; *Digital Content Librn,* Laura Schlueter; Tel: 315-464-7195, E-mail: schluetL@upstate.edu; *Family Res Ctr Librn,* Clare Rauch; Tel: 315-464-7204, E-mail: rauchc@upstate.edu; *Ref Librn,* James Capodagli; Tel: 315-464-7193, E-mail: capodagj@upstate.edu; *Ref Librn,* Christine Kucharski; Tel: 315-464-7199, E-mail: kucharsC@upstate.edu; *Ref Librn,* Amy Slutzky; Tel: 315-464-7104, E-mail: slutzkya@upstate.edu; *Ref Librn,* Virginia Young; Tel: 315-464-7084, E-mail: youngv@upstate.edu; *Info Res Mgr,* Rebecca Kindon; E-mail: kindonr@upstate.edu; Staff 15 (MLS 13, Non-MLS 2)
Founded 1912
Library Holdings: e-books 1,049; e-journals 33,816; Bk Titles 47,725; Bk Vols 210,858; Per Subs 8; Videos 2,138
Special Collections: Geneva Coll; Medicine (Americana Coll); Rare Books Coll; Stephen Smith Coll
Subject Interests: Behav sci, Med, Pre-clinical sci, Soc sci
Automation Activity & Vendor Info: (Circulation) Ex Libris Group; (ILL) Atlas Systems; (OPAC) Ex Libris Group; (Serials) SerialsSolutions
Database Vendor: American Chemical Society, American Psychological Association (APA), Annual Reviews, Atlas Systems, Cambridge Scientific Abstracts, Cinahl, EBSCOhost, Elsevier, Ingenta, Lexi-Comp, McGraw-Hill, MD Consult, Micromedex, Nature Publishing Group, Newsbank, OCLC FirstSearch, OCLC WorldShare Interlibrary Loan, OVID Technologies, ProQuest, PubMed, RefWorks, Sage, ScienceDirect, Scopus, SerialsSolutions, Springer-Verlag, STAT!Ref (Teton Data Systems), UpToDate, WebMD, Wiley
Wireless access
Partic in Central New York Library Resources Council; National Network of Libraries of Medicine Middle Atlantic Region; OCLC Online Computer Library Center, Inc

CL SYRACUSE UNIVERSITY COLLEGE OF LAW LIBRARY*, H Douglas Barclay Law Library, Dineen Hall, 950 Irving Ave, 13244-6070. SAN 354-2793. Tel: 315-443-9560, 315-443-9582. Circulation Tel: 315-443-9570. Reference Tel: 315-443-9572. FAX: 315-443-9567. E-mail: library@law.syr.edu. Web Site: www.law.syr.edu/library. *Assoc Dean,* Thomas R French; Tel: 315-443-9571, E-mail: trfrench@law.syr.edu; *Assoc Dir, Head, Info Serv,* Jan Fleckenstein; E-mail: jflecken@law.syr.edu; Staff 22 (MLS 10, Non-MLS 12)
Founded 1899

Library Holdings: Bk Titles 59,785; Bk Vols 228,392; Per Subs 3,592
Special Collections: US Document Depository
Subject Interests: Family law, Intl law, Law mgt, Legal hist, Trial practice
Automation Activity & Vendor Info: (Cataloging) Ex Libris Group; (Circulation) Ex Libris Group; (Course Reserve) Ex Libris Group; (OPAC) Ex Libris Group; (Serials) Ex Libris Group
Wireless access
Publications: Acquisitions Bulletin; Electronic Newsletter; Law Library Guide; Library Update
Partic in OCLC Online Computer Library Center, Inc; OCLC Research Library Partnership

C SYRACUSE UNIVERSITY LIBRARY*, E S Bird Library, 222 Waverly Ave, 13244-2010. SAN 354-2645. Tel: 315-443-2573. Interlibrary Loan Service Tel: 315-443-3725. Reference Tel: 315-443-4792. Interlibrary Loan Service FAX: 315-443-4507. Reference FAX: 315-443-2060. Web Site: library.syr.edu. *Dean, Libr & Univ Librn,* Position Currently Open; *Interim Dean & Univ Librn,* K Matthew Dames; E-mail: kmdames@syr.edu; *Assoc Dean, Access & Res Mgt,* Roberta Gwilt; Tel: 315-443-9773, E-mail: rbgwilt@syr.edu; *Assoc Dean, Undergrad Educ,* Lisa Moeckel; Tel: 315-443-9790, E-mail: lemoecke@syr.edu; *Interim Assoc Dean for Res & Scholarship,* Scott Warren; Tel: 315-443-8339, E-mail: sawarr01@syr.edu; *Asst Dean, Admin Serv,* Dale King; Tel: 315-443-5781, E-mail: dking01@syr.edu; *Asst Dean, Prog, Analytics & Fac Mgt,* Terriruth Carrier; Tel: 315-443-8456, E-mail: tecarrie@syr.edu; *Asst Dean, Advan,* Ronald L Thiele; Tel: 315-443-2537, E-mail: rlthiele@syr.edu; *Sr Dir, Spec Coll Res Ctr,* Position Currently Open; *Dir, Communications & External Relations,* Pamela Whiteley McLaughlin; Tel: 315-443-9788, E-mail: pwmclaug@syr.edu; *Dir, Info Syst,* DeAnn Buss; Tel: 315-443-2977, E-mail: dmbuss@syr.edu; Staff 147 (MLS 55, Non-MLS 92)
Founded 1871. Enrl 20,829; Fac 1,546; Highest Degree: Doctorate
Library Holdings: Bk Vols 3,431,056; Per Subs 39,153
Special Collections: Albert Schweitzer Papers; Anna Hyatt Huntington Papers; Arna Bontemps Papers; Averill Harriman Gubernatorial Papers; Benjamin Spock Papers; C P Huntington Papers; Cartoonist Coll; Continuing Education Coll; Dorothy Thompson Papers; Earl R Browder Papers; Gerrit & Peter Smith Coll; Grove Press Archive; Leopold Von Ranke Library; Marcel Breuer Coll; Margaret Bourke-White Coll; Mary Walker Papers; Modern American Private Press Books; Morris Lapidus Papers; Novotny Library of Economic History; Oneida Community Coll; Peggy Bacon Papers; Revolution; Rudyard Kipling First Editions; Science Fiction Books & Manuscripts; Shaker Coll; Sol Feinstone Library; Spire Collection on Loyalists in the American; Stephen Crane First Editions & Manuscripts; Street & Smith Archive; William Hobart Royce Balzac Coll; William Safire Coll; William Safire Papers. State Document Depository; US Document Depository
Automation Activity & Vendor Info: (Acquisitions) Ex Libris Group; (Cataloging) Ex Libris Group; (Circulation) Ex Libris Group; (Course Reserve) Ex Libris Group; (ILL) OCLC ILLiad; (OPAC) Ex Libris Group; (Serials) Ex Libris Group
Wireless access
Publications: Library Connection (Newsletter)
Partic in Association of Research Libraries (ARL); Central New York Library Resources Council; OCLC Online Computer Library Center, Inc
Special Services for the Blind - Computer with voice synthesizer for visually impaired persons; Talking bks
Friends of the Library Group

Departmental Libraries:

CARNEGIE LIBRARY, Carnegie Bldg, 13244-2010. (Mail add: 222 Waverly Ave, 13244-5040). Tel: 315-443-2160. Web Site: library.syr.edu/about/locations/carnegie/index.php. *Librn,* Mary DeCarlo; Tel: 315-443-9771; *Librn,* Linda Galloway; *Librn,* Anne Rauh. Subject Specialists: *Math,* Mary DeCarlo; *Biol, Chem, Forensic sci,* Linda Galloway; *Computer sci, Eng,* Anne Rauh; Staff 7 (MLS 4, Non-MLS 3)
Subject Interests: Biol, Chem, Computer sci, Eng, Health & wellness, Libr & info sci, Math, Mil sci, Naval sci, Nutrition, Photog, Physics, Tech arts
Function: Computers for patron use, Copy machines, E-Reserves, Electronic databases & coll, Online ref, Ref serv in person, Res libr, Telephone ref
Open Mon-Thurs 8am-11pm, Fri 8-6, Sat 10-5, Sun 10-10
Restriction: Borrowing privileges limited to fac & registered students, Borrowing requests are handled by ILL, Open to students, fac, staff & alumni, Pub use on premises

GEOLOGY, 300 Heroy Geology Lab, 13244-1070, SAN 354-2769. Tel: 315-443-3337. FAX: 315-443-3363. Web Site: library.syr.edu/about/locations/geology. *Libr Tech,* Carol Cavalluzzi; E-mail: cacavall@syr.edu; Staff 2 (MLS 1, Non-MLS 1)
Subject Interests: Geol, Hydrogeology, Paleontology
Open Mon-Thurs (Winter) 8:30am-10pm, Fri 8:30-5, Sat 12-5, Sun 1-10; Mon-Fri (Summer) 8-4:30

TANNERSVILLE

P MOUNTAIN TOP LIBRARY, (Formerly Haines Falls Free Library), 6093 Main St, 12485. (Mail add: PO Box 427, 12485-0427), SAN 311-2810. Tel: 518-589-5707. FAX: 518-589-5707. E-mail: tanmttoplib@yahoo.com. Web Site: mountaintoplibrary.org. *Libr Dir,* Elaine Farley
Founded 1900. Pop 1,358; Circ 17,156
Library Holdings: AV Mats 1,360; Electronic Media & Resources 21; Large Print Bks 258; Microforms 8; Bk Vols 12,664; Per Subs 190; Talking Bks 210
Special Collections: Postcards
Subject Interests: Local hist
Automation Activity & Vendor Info: (Circulation) Innovative Interfaces, Inc; (Course Reserve) Innovative Interfaces, Inc; (ILL) Innovative Interfaces, Inc; (Media Booking) Innovative Interfaces, Inc; (OPAC) Innovative Interfaces, Inc
Wireless access
Publications: Library Cookbook
Mem of Mid-Hudson Library System
Open Mon-Fri 10-7, Sat 10-2

TAPPAN

P TAPPAN LIBRARY*, 93 Main St, 10983. SAN 312-5548. Tel: 845-359-3877. E-mail: tapl@rcls.org. Web Site: www.taplib.org. *Dir,* Sara Nugent; *Head, Circ,* Susan Coppola; *Adult Serv,* Jill Gross; *Ch Serv,* Nancy Russell; *Tech Serv,* Maureen Cunningham; Staff 2 (MLS 2)
Founded 1956. Pop 6,867
Library Holdings: Bk Vols 48,140
Special Collections: Major John Andre Coll; Sean McCarthy Poetry Coll
Subject Interests: Local hist, Poetry
Automation Activity & Vendor Info: (Circulation) Horizon; (ILL) Horizon; (OPAC) Horizon
Database Vendor: College Source, EBSCOhost, Gale Cengage Learning, LearningExpress, Newsbank, OCLC FirstSearch, OCLC WorldShare Interlibrary Loan, ProQuest, PubMed
Wireless access
Function: Adult literacy prog, ILL available, Magnifiers for reading, Prog for adults, Prog for children & young adult, Ref serv available, Summer reading prog, Telephone ref, Wheelchair accessible
Publications: Newsletter
Mem of Ramapo Catskill Library System
Open Mon-Thurs 10-9, Fri & Sat 10-5, Sun 1-5
Friends of the Library Group

TARRYTOWN

S HISTORIC HUDSON VALLEY LIBRARY*, 639 Bedford Rd, 10591. SAN 312-5599. Tel: 914-366-6901, 914-366-6902. FAX: 914-631-0089. E-mail: librarian@hudsonvalley.org. Web Site: www.hudsonvalley.org/education/library. *Librn,* Catalina Hannan; *Mgr, Libr & Archival Serv,* Karen Walton Morse; Staff 1.5 (MLS 1.5)
Founded 1951
Library Holdings: Bk Titles 22,000; Bk Vols 25,000; Per Subs 90
Special Collections: Washington Irving Editions; Washington Irving's Personal Library
Subject Interests: 17th Century, 18th Century, 19th Century Hudson River Valley hist, Archit, Decorative art, Slavery
Function: Archival coll, Bus archives, Exhibits, Handicapped accessible, Microfiche/film & reading machines, Ref serv available, Ref serv in person, Res libr
Restriction: Open by appt only

S HISTORICAL SOCIETY SERVING SLEEPY HOLLOW & TARRYTOWN*, Society Library, One Grove St, 10591. SAN 312-5564. Tel: 914-631-8374. FAX: 914-631-8374. E-mail: historyatgrove@aol.com. *Curator,* Sara Mascia
Founded 1889
Library Holdings: Bk Titles 3,500
Special Collections: Children's Books of Earlier Times & Related History Books for Children; Civil War Memorabilia; Civil War Papers of Capt Charles H Rockwell; Indians (Leslie V Case Coll), artifacts; John Paulding, Isaac Van Wart & David Williams Coll, artifacts, docs; Life Along the Hudson River Valley, art, bks, per, photogs; Local Families & Their History, bks, genealogies, micro, records, VF; Local Newspapers, micro; Local Photographs Coll, 1800s- Present; Local Schools & Churches, art, bks; Local Writers, bks, mss; Major Andre: His Capture & His Captors, bks, pictures; Maps (Tarrytown, North Tarrytown, Pocantico Hills, Westchester County & New York State 1700 - Present); Old Dutch Church History & Burying Ground; Revolutionary War Memorabilia; Ward B Burnett Post GAR Coll, records; World War I & World War II Coll
Subject Interests: Am Revolutionary War, Genealogy, Local hist, Regional newspapers, State

Publications: Postcards of Local Historic Sites & Events; The Capture of Major John Andre, September 23, 1780 (An Excerpt from Westchester County During the American Revolution by Otto Hufeland); The Chronicle
Open Wed, Thurs & Sat 2-4

P WARNER LIBRARY*, 121 N Broadway, 10591. SAN 312-5610. Tel: 914-631-7734. FAX: 914-631-2324. Web Site: westchesterlibraries.org. *Dir,* Maureen Petry; E-mail: director@warnerlibrary.org; *Sr Librn, Ch Serv,* Patricia Cohn; *Head, Ref (Info Serv),* Robert Mannion; *Ch,* Barbara Cespo; *Outreach Serv Librn,* Elizabeth Siracusa; *Pub Info,* Jeanne Reid; Staff 21 (MLS 6, Non-MLS 15)
Founded 1929. Pop 20,300; Circ 146,083
Library Holdings: High Interest/Low Vocabulary Bk Vols 300; Bk Vols 88,218; Per Subs 170
Special Collections: Rockwell Kent Coll; Washington Irving Coll, large print
Subject Interests: Literacy, Local hist
Automation Activity & Vendor Info: (Acquisitions) SirsiDynix; (Cataloging) SirsiDynix; (Circulation) SirsiDynix; (OPAC) SirsiDynix; (Serials) SirsiDynix
Wireless access
Function: Adult literacy prog, Handicapped accessible, ILL available, Prog for adults, Prog for children & young adult, Ref serv available, Wheelchair accessible
Publications: Warner Library Newsletter
Mem of Westchester Library System
Open Mon & Thurs 1-9, Tues & Wed 10-6, Fri & Sat 10-5, Sun 1-5
Friends of the Library Group

P WESTCHESTER LIBRARY SYSTEM, 540 White Plains Rd, Ste 200, 10591-5110. SAN 311-2942. Tel: 914-674-3600. FAX: 914-674-4185. Web Site: www.westchesterlibraries.org. *Exec Dir,* Terry Kirchner; *Dir, Info Tech,* Rob Caluori; Tel: 914-231-8642, E-mail: robc@wlsmail.org; *Outreach Serv Librn,* Elena Falcone; Tel: 914-231-3240, E-mail: elena@wlsmail.org; *Mgr, Cat Serv,* Douglas Wray; Tel: 914-231-3243, Fax: 914-674-4186, E-mail: dwray@westchesterlibraries.org; *Mgr, E-Coll & Res Sharing,* Hui Sheng; Tel: 914-231-3258, E-mail: hsheng@westchesterlibraries.org
Founded 1958
Automation Activity & Vendor Info: (Acquisitions) SirsiDynix; (Cataloging) OCLC; (Circulation) SirsiDynix; (ILL) OCLC ILLiad; (OPAC) SirsiDynix; (Serials) SirsiDynix
Database Vendor: Baker & Taylor, Brodart, BWI, EBSCOhost, Gale Cengage Learning, Library Ideas, LLC, Overdrive, Inc, SirsiDynix, TumbleBookLibrary
Wireless access
Publications: Assorted Bookmarks & Brochures Describing Specific Services & Bibliographies; WLS Members Directory; WLS Members Library Statistics (Annual)
Member Libraries: Ardsley Public Library; Bedford Free Library; Bedford Hills Free Library; Briarcliff Manor Public Library; Bronxville Public Library; Chappaqua Public Library; Croton Free Library; Dobbs Ferry Public Library; Eastchester Public Library; Greenburgh Public Library; Hastings-on-Hudson Public Library; Hendrick Hudson Free Library; Irvington Public Library; John C Hart Memorial Library; Katonah Village Library; Larchmont Public Library; Lewisboro Library; Mamaroneck Public Library District; Mount Kisco Public Library; Mount Vernon Public Library; New Rochelle Public Library; North Castle Public Library; Port Chester-Rye Brook Public Library; Pound Ridge Library; Purchase Free Library; Ruth Keeler Memorial Library; Rye Free Reading Room; Scarsdale Public Library; Somers Library; The Field Library; Town of Pelham Public Library; Tuckahoe Public Library; Warner Library; White Plains Public Library; Yonkers Public Library
Partic in Coop Libr Agency for Syst & Servs; Metropolitan New York Library Council; New York State Interlibrary Loan Network (NYSILL); OCLC Online Computer Library Center, Inc
Open Mon-Fri 9-5

THERESA

P THERESA FREE LIBRARY*, 301 Main St, 13691. SAN 312-5629. Tel: 315-628-5972. FAX: 315-628-4839. *Librn,* Christine Rajner; E-mail: crajner@ncls.org
Pop 1,853; Circ 12,132
Library Holdings: Bk Vols 7,000
Wireless access
Mem of North Country Library System
Open Tues, Thurs & Fri 1:30-5 & 7-9, Sat 9-12:30
Friends of the Library Group

THOUSAND ISLAND PARK

P THOUSAND ISLAND PARK LIBRARY*, Saint Lawrence Ave, 13692. (Mail add: PO Box 1115, 13692-1115), SAN 312-5637. Tel: 315-482-9098. FAX: 315-482-9098. *Librn,* Mabel Heath
Circ 6,247
Library Holdings: Bk Vols 6,750
Wireless access
Mem of North Country Library System
Open Mon-Fri 9-12 & 1-4:30, Sat (June-Sept) 9-12
Friends of the Library Group

TICONDEROGA

P BLACK WATCH MEMORIAL LIBRARY, 99 Montcalm St, 12883. SAN 312-5645. Tel: 518-585-7380. FAX: 518-585-3209. E-mail: blackwatch@townofticonderoga.org. *Librn,* Heather Johns; *Asst Librn,* Beth Nadeau
Founded 1906. Pop 5,486; Circ 19,421
Library Holdings: Bk Titles 14,110; Per Subs 32
Special Collections: State Document Depository; UN Document Depository; US Document Depository
Automation Activity & Vendor Info: (Cataloging) SirsiDynix; (Circulation) SirsiDynix; (OPAC) SirsiDynix
Wireless access
Mem of Clinton-Essex-Franklin Library System
Open Tues 10-7, Wed-Fri 10-5, Sat 10-3
Friends of the Library Group

S FORT TICONDEROGA MUSEUM*, Thompson-Pell Research Center, Fort Rd, 12883. (Mail add: PO Box 390, 12883-0390), SAN 312-5653. Tel: 518-585-2821. FAX: 518-585-2210. E-mail: fort@fort-ticonderoga.org. Web Site: www.fort-ticonderoga.org. *Curator,* Christopher D Fox; Tel: 518-585-2821, Ext 229, E-mail: cfox@fort-ticonderoga.org
Founded 1908
Jan 2006-Dec 2006 Income $2,291,633. Mats Exp $30,000, Books $3,000, Per/Ser (Incl. Access Fees) $1,000, Manu Arch $20,000, Micro $1,000, Presv $5,000
Library Holdings: Bk Vols 13,000; Per Subs 20; Spec Interest Per Sub 20
Special Collections: 18th Century English & American Newspapers & Literary Magazines; 18th Century Military Weapons & Artillery Coll; Archival Coll, diaries, mss, maps, orderly bks & photos; Military Manuals, 18th-early 19th Century; William L Stone Coll
Subject Interests: Colonial, Fr & Indian War, Mil hist 1609-1780, Revolutionary wars in Champlain Valley, Upper Hudson valleys
Wireless access
Publications: Bulletin of the Fort Ticonderoga Museum, Vol 1 (1927 - present)
Partic in Northern New York Library Network
Open Mon-Fri 9:30-12 & 1-4:30
Restriction: Non-circulating to the pub, Open by appt only

S TICONDEROGA HISTORICAL SOCIETY LIBRARY*, Hancock House, Six Moses Circle, 12883. SAN 325-9668. Tel: 518-585-7868. FAX: 518-585-6367. E-mail: tihistory@bridgepoint.com. Web Site: www.thehancockhouse.org/research_library.htm. *In Charge,* Robin Trudeau
Founded 1898
Library Holdings: Bk Titles 8,000; Bk Vols 10,000
Special Collections: Account Books; Diaries; Local History Books; Manuscripts; Newspapers; Photos
Wireless access
Publications: Patches & Patterns Extended
Open Wed-Sat (June-Dec) 10-4
Restriction: Non-circulating to the pub

TIVOLI

P TIVOLI FREE LIBRARY*, 86 Broadway, 12583. (Mail add: PO Box 400, 12583-0400), SAN 312-5661. Tel: 845-757-3771. Interlibrary Loan Service Tel: 845-471-6060. E-mail: tivolilibrary@gmail.com. Web Site: www.tivolilibrary.org. *Librn,* Bonnie Corrado
Founded 1919. Circ 3,536
Library Holdings: Bk Vols 8,000
Automation Activity & Vendor Info: (Circulation) Innovative Interfaces, Inc - Millenium; (OPAC) Innovative Interfaces, Inc - Millenium
Wireless access
Mem of Mid-Hudson Library System
Open Mon & Thurs (Winter) 4-8, Tues & Wed 10-2 & 4-8, Sat 10-2; Mon, Fri (Summer) 2-8, Tues-Thurs 10-8, Sat 10-2

TOMKINS COVE

P TOMKINS COVE PUBLIC LIBRARY*, 419 Liberty Dr N, 10986. SAN 312-567X. Tel: 845-786-3060. FAX: 845-947-5572. Web Site: www.tomkinscovelibrary.org. *Libr Dir,* Janet Lukas; E-mail: jlukas@rcls.org; Staff 7 (MLS 1, Non-MLS 6)

Founded 1896. Pop 1,800; Circ 12,000
Library Holdings: Bk Vols 22,000; Per Subs 49
Special Collections: Birds & Conservation (Margaret Tomkins Memorial Coll)
Wireless access
Publications: Newsletter (Quarterly)
Mem of Ramapo Catskill Library System
Open Mon-Thurs 1-9, Fri 3-6, Sat 1-4, Sun (Oct-May) 2-5

TONAWANDA

P CITY OF TONAWANDA PUBLIC LIBRARY*, 333 Main St, 14150. SAN 312-5696. Tel: 716-693-5043. FAX: 716-693-0825. Web Site: www.buffalolib.org. *Dir,* Beverly Federspiel; *Ch,* Carol L Veach; Staff 2 (MLS 2)
Pop 16,136; Circ 134,515
Library Holdings: Bk Vols 35,388; Per Subs 75
Automation Activity & Vendor Info: (Cataloging) SirsiDynix; (Circulation) SirsiDynix; (OPAC) SirsiDynix
Wireless access
Mem of Buffalo & Erie County Public Library System
Open Mon, Tues & Thurs (Winter) 10-8, Fri 10-4, Sat 10-2; Mon, Tues & Thurs (Summer) 10-8, Wed 10-2, Fri 10-4
Friends of the Library Group

S PRAXAIR, INC LIBRARY*, 175 E Park Dr, 14151. (Mail add: PO Box 44, 14151-0044), SAN 312-570X. Tel: 716-879-2031. FAX: 716-879-3101. *Sr Librn,* Yvonne Curry; E-mail: yvonne_curry@praxair.com; Staff 1 (MLS 1)
Founded 1939
Library Holdings: Bk Vols 1,000; Per Subs 200
Subject Interests: Chem, Indust gases
Database Vendor: Dialog, Ingenta, STN International
Function: ILL available
Partic in Western New York Library Resources Council
Restriction: Staff use only, Use of others with permission of librn

TROY

P BRUNSWICK COMMUNITY LIBRARY*, 4118 State Hwy 2, 12180-9029. Tel: 518-279-4023. FAX: 518-279-0527. E-mail: library@brunswicklibrary.org. Web Site: www.brunswicklibrary.org. *Dir,* Julie Zelman; Staff 1 (MLS 1)
Library Holdings: Audiobooks 632; AV Mats 1,461; CDs 121; DVDs 200; Large Print Bks 633; Bk Titles 8,836; Per Subs 55
Automation Activity & Vendor Info: (Acquisitions) SirsiDynix; (Cataloging) SirsiDynix; (Circulation) SirsiDynix; (Course Reserve) SirsiDynix; (ILL) SirsiDynix; (OPAC) SirsiDynix; (Serials) SirsiDynix
Wireless access
Function: Adult bk club, ILL available, Photocopying/Printing, Prog for adults, Prog for children & young adult, Ref serv available, Spoken cassettes & CDs, Spoken cassettes & DVDs, Summer reading prog, VHS videos
Mem of Upper Hudson Library System
Open Mon-Wed 12-8, Thurs & Fri 12-6, Sat 10-4
Friends of the Library Group

J HUDSON VALLEY COMMUNITY COLLEGE, Dwight Marvin Library, 80 Vandenburgh Ave, 12180. SAN 312-5742. Tel: 518-629-7330. Interlibrary Loan Service Tel: 518-629-7387. Reference Tel: 518-629-7337. Information Services Tel: 518-629-7336. FAX: 518-629-7509. Web Site: library.hvcc.edu. *Dir,* Brenda Hazard; Tel: 518-629-7388; *Asst Admin,* Patricia Kaiser; Tel: 518-629-7333, E-mail: p.kaiser@hvcc.edu; *Cat & Syst Librn,* Katie Jezik; Tel: 518-629-7395, E-mail: k.jezik@hvcc.edu; *Circ/ILL Librn,* Sue Grayson; Tel: 518-629-7555, E-mail: s.grayson@hvcc.edu; *Electronic Ser & Ref Librn,* Valerie Waldin; Tel: 518-629-7319, E-mail: v.waldin@hvcc.edu; *Ref Librn,* Cynthia Koman; Tel: 518-629-7360, E-mail: c.koman@hvcc.edu; *Coordr, Ref & Electronic Serv,* Anne La Belle; Tel: 518-629-7384, E-mail: a.labelle@hvcc.edu; *Acq,* Cheryl Trantham; Tel: 518-629-7391, E-mail: c.trantham@hvcc.edu; *Bibliog Instr,* Robert Matthews; Tel: 518-629-7392, E-mail: r.matthews@hvcc.edu; *Circ,* Tylan Nino; E-mail: t.nino@hvcc.edu; *Info Res,* John Staerker; Tel: 518-629-7323, E-mail: j.staerker@hvcc.edu; *ILL,* Jennifer Acker; E-mail: j.acker1@hvcc.edu; *Per,* Sherry LaMarche; Tel: 518-629-7322, E-mail: s.lamarche@hvcc.edu; Staff 10 (MLS 10)
Founded 1953. Enrl 8,808; Fac 310
Library Holdings: AV Mats 5,776; Bk Titles 97,624; Bk Vols 9,213; Per Subs 110
Special Collections: History (Microbook Library Journal of American Civilization Coll), micro; History of Western Civilization (Microbook); Video Encyclopedia of the 20th Century
Subject Interests: Automotive tech, Bus, Child develop, Dental, Eng tech, Liberal arts, Med, Mortuary sci
Wireless access
Publications: Dwight Marvin LRC Guide; Faculty LRC Handbook; From the Library (Acquisitions); Kaleidoscope; Policies & Procedures Manual; Previews (from the Media Center); Student Guide; Worksheets & Bibliographic
Partic in Capital District Library Council; OCLC Online Computer Library Center, Inc
Open Mon-Thurs (Winter) 7am-10pm, Fri 7-4:30, Sat 9-4; Mon, Tues & Fri (Summer) 7-4, Wed & Thurs 7am-10pm

GL NEW YORK STATE SUPREME COURT LIBRARY*, Court House Second St Annex, 86 Second St, 12180-4098. SAN 312-5769. Tel: 518-285-6183. FAX: 518-274-0590. Web Site: www.nycourts.gov. *Principal Law Librn,* Laura Barber; Staff 3 (MLS 1, Non-MLS 2)
Founded 1909
Apr 2005-Mar 2006 Income $244,620. Sal $175,000
Library Holdings: Bk Titles 1,100; Bk Vols 43,000
Subject Interests: Law, NY State
Automation Activity & Vendor Info: (Acquisitions) SirsiDynix; (Cataloging) SirsiDynix; (Circulation) SirsiDynix; (OPAC) SirsiDynix; (Serials) SirsiDynix
Database Vendor: LexisNexis, Westlaw
Wireless access
Open Mon-Fri 9-5
Restriction: Open to pub for ref only

S RENSSELAER COUNTY HISTORICAL SOCIETY*, Dean P Taylor Research Library, 57 Second St, 12180. SAN 312-5785. Tel: 518-244-6846. FAX: 518-273-1264. Web Site: www.rchsonline.org/library.htm. *Curator,* Stacy P Draper; E-mail: spdraper@rchsonline.org
Founded 1927
Library Holdings: Bk Titles 3,000; Per Subs 23
Special Collections: Burden Iron Company Papers; Cable Flax Mill Papers; Cluett, Peabody & Co Papers; Congressman Dean P Taylor Papers; Hart Family Papers; Marshall Mills Papers; Organizational Papers (Troy Chromatics, Thursday Morning Club, Troy Day Home, etc); Rensselaer County Families Papers; Samaritan Hospital School of Nursing Papers
Subject Interests: Archit, Archives, Genealogy, Manuscripts, Rensselaer County hist
Publications: Rensselaer County History Research at the RCHS Research Library
Open Thurs-Sat (Feb-Dec) 12-5
Restriction: Non-circulating

C RENSSELAER LIBRARIES*, Folsom Library, Rensselaer Polytechnic Inst, 110 Eighth St, 12180-3590. SAN 354-2971. Tel: 518-276-8300. Circulation Tel: 518-276-8310. Interlibrary Loan Service Tel: 973-276-8330. Reference Tel: 518-276-8320. FAX: 518-276-2044. Web Site: library.rpi.edu. *Dir of Libr,* Bob Mayo; *Head, Coll Mgt, Inst Archivist,* John Dojka; *Covering Supvr, Pub Serv & Acq, Electronic Res Librn,* Tanis Kreiger; *IT Librn,* Matt Benzing; *Mgt Librn,* Colette Holmes; *Media & Digital Assets Librn,* Jeanne Keefe; *Sci Librn,* Connie Fritz; *Tech & Metadata Librn,* Kathryn Dunn; *Mgr, Archit Libr/Ref & Instrul Serv,* Fran Scott; *Mgr, Tech Serv,* Patricia Hults; *Automation Archivist,* Tammy Gobert; *Sr Syst Adminr,* George Biggar; Staff 22 (MLS 12, Non-MLS 10)
Founded 1824. Enrl 6,559; Fac 400; Highest Degree: Doctorate
Jul 2010-Jun 2011. Mats Exp $2,148,987, Books $332,293, Per/Ser (Incl. Access Fees) $1,310,813. Sal $1,150,346 (Prof $821,334)
Library Holdings: e-books 69,757; e-journals 19,241; Bk Vols 338,687
Special Collections: Architecture Coll
Subject Interests: Archit, Eng, Experimental media, Hist of sci & tech, Info tech
Automation Activity & Vendor Info: (Acquisitions) Innovative Interfaces, Inc - Millenium; (Cataloging) Innovative Interfaces, Inc - Millenium; (Circulation) Innovative Interfaces, Inc - Millenium; (ILL) OCLC ILLiad; (OPAC) Innovative Interfaces, Inc - Millenium; (Serials) Innovative Interfaces, Inc - Millenium
Wireless access
Function: Handicapped accessible, ILL available, Ref serv available
Partic in Capital District Library Council; Connect NY; New York State Higher Education Initiative
Special Services for the Blind - Closed circuit TV magnifier; Reader equip
Restriction: Pub use on premises
Friends of the Library Group

C THE SAGE COLLEGES*, James Wheelock Clark Library, 45 Ferry St, 12180. SAN 354-303X. Tel: 518-244-2249. Interlibrary Loan Service Tel: 518-244-2320. Reference Tel: 518-244-2431. FAX: 518-244-2400. E-mail: libref@sage.edu. Web Site: www.sage.edu. *Dir,* Kingsley W Greene; Tel: 518-244-2346, E-mail: greenk@sage.edu; *Access Serv Librn,* Lisa Brainard; Tel: 518-292-1959, Fax: 518-292-1904, E-mail: brainl@sage.edu; *Archivist, Tech Serv Librn,* Terrance Wasielewski; Tel: 518-224-2435, E-mail: wasiet@sage.edu; *Info Literacy Librn,* Amy Pass; Tel: 518-292-1701, E-mail: passa@sage.edu; *Syst Librn,* Christopher White; Tel: 518-244-4521, E-mail: whitec2@sage.edu; *Web Librn,* Kelly MacWatters;

Tel: 518-292-1784, E-mail: macwak@sage.edu; Staff 11 (MLS 4, Non-MLS 7)
Founded 1916. Enrl 900; Fac 150; Highest Degree: Doctorate
Library Holdings: AV Mats 6,093; e-books 10,000; e-journals 50,000; Microforms 7,100; Bk Titles 134,378; Bk Vols 154,101; Per Subs 284
Special Collections: 20th Century Poetry (Carol Ann Donahue Memorial Coll). State Document Depository
Subject Interests: Allied health, Women's studies
Automation Activity & Vendor Info: (Acquisitions) SirsiDynix; (Cataloging) SirsiDynix; (Circulation) SirsiDynix; (Course Reserve) SirsiDynix; (ILL) OCLC ILLiad; (OPAC) SirsiDynix; (Serials) SirsiDynix
Database Vendor: ARTstor, Bowker, CredoReference, EBSCOhost, Elsevier, Gale Cengage Learning, JSTOR, LexisNexis, OCLC FirstSearch, OCLC WorldShare Interlibrary Loan, ProQuest, PubMed, ReferenceUSA, Safari Books Online, ScienceDirect, SerialsSolutions, Westlaw, Wilson - Wilson Web
Wireless access
Publications: Newsletter
Partic in Cap District Libr Coun for Ref & Res Resources; OCLC Online Computer Library Center, Inc; Westchester Academic Library Directors Organization (WALDO)

M SAMARITAN HOSPITAL*, Health Science Library, School of Nursing, 2215 Burdett Ave, 12180. SAN 312-5807. Tel: 518-271-3285, 518-271-3320. FAX: 518-271-3303. Web Site: www.nehealth.com/SON. *Libr Asst,* Valorie Vogel
Founded 1950
Library Holdings: Bk Vols 420; Per Subs 24
Special Collections: Health Sciences (Spafford)
Subject Interests: Gynecology, Internal med, Obstetrics, Pediatrics, Surgery
Publications: The Book Bag
Open Mon, Tues & Thurs (Fall & Spring) 7:30-3:30, Wed 7:30-6, Fri 7:30-4, Sun 12-4; Mon-Fri (Summer) 7:30-3

M SETON HEALTH SYSTEMS*, Health Sciences Library, 1300 Massachusetts Ave, 12180. SAN 312-5793. Tel: 518-268-5210. FAX: 518-268-5806. *Dir,* Beverly Cook
Founded 1955
Library Holdings: Electronic Media & Resources 4; Bk Titles 500; Per Subs 21
Subject Interests: Med, Nursing
Partic in Capital District Library Council
Open Mon-Fri 8-5
Restriction: Open to staff, patients & family mem

P TROY PUBLIC LIBRARY*, 100 Second St, 12180-4005. SAN 354-3064. Tel: 518-274-7071. FAX: 518-271-9154. E-mail: troyref@thetroylibrary.org. Web Site: www.thetroylibrary.org. *Dir,* Paul Hicok; Staff 25 (MLS 5, Non-MLS 20)
Founded 1835. Pop 44,169; Circ 278,453
Library Holdings: Bk Titles 89,240; Bk Vols 131,000; Per Subs 412
Special Collections: US Document Depository
Subject Interests: Genealogy, Local hist
Automation Activity & Vendor Info: (Circulation) SirsiDynix
Database Vendor: ValueLine
Wireless access
Publications: Annual Report; Friends Newsletter
Mem of Upper Hudson Library System
Partic in Suburban Library Cooperative
Open Mon-Thurs 9-8, Fri 9-5, Sat 9-5 (9-1 Summer), Sun (Sept-May) 1-5
Friends of the Library Group
Branches: 2
LANSINGBURGH BRANCH, Fourth Ave & 114th St, 12182, SAN 354-3129. Tel: 518-235-5310. *Dir,* Paul Hicok
Library Holdings: Bk Vols 11,983
Open Mon & Wed 1-7, Fri & Sat 10-4
Friends of the Library Group
SYCAWAY BRANCH, Hoosick St & Lee Ave, 12180, SAN 354-3153. Tel: 518-274-1822. *Dir,* Paul Hicok
Library Holdings: Bk Vols 5,000
Open Tues & Wed 2-6, Thurs 12-4
Friends of the Library Group

TRUMANSBURG

P ULYSSES PHILOMATHIC LIBRARY, 74 E Main St, 14886. SAN 312-5815. Tel: 607-387-5623. FAX: 607-387-3823. E-mail: director@trumansburglibrary.org. Web Site: www.trumansburglibrary.org. *Dir,* Annette Birdsall; Staff 3 (MLS 1, Non-MLS 2)
Founded 1935. Pop 4,775; Circ 49,531
Jan 2005-Dec 2005 Income $163,932, State $1,521, County $27,967, Locally Generated Income $14,250, Other $120,194. Mats Exp $19,446. Sal $65,085 (Prof $24,388)
Library Holdings: AV Mats 228; Electronic Media & Resources 16; Bk Titles 19,400; Per Subs 47; Talking Bks 501
Automation Activity & Vendor Info: (Cataloging) Innovative Interfaces, Inc; (Circulation) Innovative Interfaces, Inc; (OPAC) Innovative Interfaces, Inc
Wireless access
Mem of Finger Lakes Library System
Open Mon, Wed & Fri 10-5, Tues & Thurs 10-8, Sat 10-2
Friends of the Library Group

TUCKAHOE

P TUCKAHOE PUBLIC LIBRARY*, 71 Columbus Ave, 10707. SAN 312-5823. Tel: 914-961-2121. FAX: 914-961-3832. Web Site: www.tuckahoelibrary.org. *Dir,* Swadesh Pachnanda; E-mail: spachnan@wlsmail.org; Staff 17 (MLS 6, Non-MLS 11)
Founded 1912. Pop 6,486; Circ 84,960
Library Holdings: Bk Vols 66,000; Per Subs 100
Special Collections: Tuckahoe History (files, newsps on microfilm 1918-1931, pamphlets, photogs)
Automation Activity & Vendor Info: (Cataloging) SirsiDynix; (Circulation) SirsiDynix; (OPAC) SirsiDynix
Wireless access
Publications: Monthly calendar of events; newsletter
Mem of Westchester Library System
Open Mon & Wed 10:30-8:30, Tues, Thurs & Fri 10:30-5:30, Sat 10-2
Friends of the Library Group

TULLY

P TULLY FREE LIBRARY*, 12 State St, 13159-3254. (Mail add: PO Box 250, 13159-0250), SAN 312-5858. Tel: 315-696-8606. FAX: 315-696-8120. Web Site: www.tullyfreelibrary.com. *Dir,* Matthew DeLaney; E-mail: mdelaney@onlib.org; *YA Librn,* Kelly Chambala; E-mail: kchambala@onlib.org; *Ch Serv,* Sonja Shepherd; E-mail: sshepherd@onlib.org; *Coll Mgt,* Irene Maskelony; *Outreach Coordr,* Lorraine Tickner
Founded 1936. Pop 6,067; Circ 49,862
Jan 2005-Dec 2005 Income $95,566, State $5,158, Locally Generated Income $85,000, Other $5,408. Mats Exp $26,917, Books $19,000, Per/Ser (Incl. Access Fees) $897, AV Mat $7,020. Sal $45,415
Library Holdings: AV Mats 720; Bks on Deafness & Sign Lang 10; Large Print Bks 375; Bk Titles 15,930; Per Subs 100; Talking Bks 900
Special Collections: Civil War
Automation Activity & Vendor Info: (Cataloging) Innovative Interfaces, Inc; (Circulation) Innovative Interfaces, Inc; (OPAC) Innovative Interfaces, Inc
Wireless access
Mem of Onondaga County Public Library
Open Mon & Wed 10-8, Tues, Thurs & Fri 10-6, Sat 10-2

TUPPER LAKE

P GOFF-NELSON MEMORIAL LIBRARY*, 41 Lake St, 12986. SAN 354-3188. Tel: 518-359-9421. FAX: 518-359-9421. E-mail: goffnelson@adelphia.net. *Head Librn,* Peg Mauer
Founded 1932. Pop 6,712; Circ 76,888
Library Holdings: Bk Vols 50,000; Per Subs 150
Automation Activity & Vendor Info: (Circulation) Horizon; (OPAC) Horizon
Wireless access
Mem of Clinton-Essex-Franklin Library System
Open Mon-Thurs 10-5:30 & 7-9, Fri 10-5:30

TURIN

P B ELIZABETH STRONG MEMORIAL LIBRARY*, Turin Library, 6312 E Main St, 13473-9998. (Mail add: PO Box 27, 13473-0027), SAN 312-5866. Tel: 315-348-6433. FAX: 315-348-6433. Web Site: www.turinlibrary.org. *Librn,* Sharon Stewart
Founded 1947. Circ 7,699
Library Holdings: Bk Vols 2,200; Per Subs 50
Wireless access
Mem of North Country Library System
Open Mon 4-6, Wed 1-9, Thurs 7pm-9pm

TUXEDO PARK

P TUXEDO PARK LIBRARY*, 227 Rte 17, 10987-4405. (Mail add: PO Box 776, 10987-0776), SAN 312-5882. Tel: 845-351-2207. FAX: 845-351-2213. E-mail: tuxpl@rcls.org. Web Site: tuxedoparklibrary.org. *Dir,* Claudia Depkin; *Asst Dir,* Florence Brady; Staff 11 (MLS 1, Non-MLS 10)
Founded 1901. Pop 3,334; Circ 56,697
Library Holdings: AV Mats 7,607; Bk Titles 30,072; Per Subs 129

Special Collections: Tuxedo Park Library Local History Coll, oral hist, photos, doc, & slides
Automation Activity & Vendor Info: (Cataloging) Horizon; (Circulation) Horizon; (OPAC) Horizon
Wireless access
Publications: Newsletter (Quarterly)
Mem of Ramapo Catskill Library System
Open Mon, Tues & Fri 9-5:30, Wed & Thurs 9-9, Sat 10-4, Sun (Sept-Jun) 11-3
Friends of the Library Group

UNADILLA

P UNADILLA PUBLIC LIBRARY*, 193 Main, 13849. (Mail add: PO Box 632, 13849-0632), SAN 312-5904. Tel: 607-369-3131. FAX: 607-369-4500. *Dir,* Andrea Edwards; E-mail: sawcem@yahoo.com
Pop 1,489; Circ 6,116
Library Holdings: Bk Vols 12,000; Per Subs 18
Automation Activity & Vendor Info: (OPAC) SIRSI WorkFlows
Wireless access
Mem of Four County Library System
Open Mon & Wed 10-12, 1-5 & 7-9, Tues & Thurs 7pm-9pm, Sat 10-2

UNION SPRINGS

P SPRINGPORT FREE LIBRARY*, 171 Cayuga St, 13160. (Mail add: PO Box 501, 13160), SAN 312-5912. Tel: 315-889-7766. FAX: 315-889-7766. Web Site: www.flls.org. *Dir,* Carla Piperno-Jones; E-mail: ctpjones@yahoo.com
Pop 2,198; Circ 18,078
Library Holdings: Bk Titles 11,000; Per Subs 24
Automation Activity & Vendor Info: (Cataloging) Innovative Interfaces, Inc; (Circulation) Innovative Interfaces, Inc; (OPAC) Innovative Interfaces, Inc; (Serials) Innovative Interfaces, Inc
Wireless access
Mem of Finger Lakes Library System
Open Mon, Tues & Thurs 2-8, Fri & Sat 10-2

UNIONDALE

P NASSAU LIBRARY SYSTEM, 900 Jerusalem Ave, 11553-3039. SAN 354-3242. Tel: 516-292-8920. Interlibrary Loan Service Tel: 516-292-8920, Ext 253. FAX: 516-565-0950. Interlibrary Loan Service FAX: 516-481-4777. E-mail: nls@nassaulibrary.org. Web Site: www.nassaulibrary.org. *Dir,* Jacquelyn Thresher; Tel: 516-292-8920, Ext 220, E-mail: jthresher@nassaulibrary.org; *Asst Dir,* Caroline Ashby; Tel: 516-292-8920, Ext 237, E-mail: cashby@nassaulibrary.org; *ILS Consortium Dir,* Brenda Giovanncillo; Tel: 516-292-8920, Ext 241, Fax: 516-483-4726, E-mail: brenda@alisnet.info; *Bus Off Mgr,* Jan Heinlein; Tel: 516-292-8920, Ext 246, Fax: 516-292-8944, E-mail: heinlein@nassaulibrary.org; *Mgr, Cat Dept,* Michele Zwierski; Tel: 516-292-8920, Ext 269, E-mail: mzwierski@nassaulibrary.org; *Mgr, Online Serv & Tech,* Marianne Malagon; Tel: 516-292-8920, Ext 282, E-mail: mmalagon@nassaulibrary.org; *Mgr, Youth Serv,* Renee McGrath; Tel: 516-292-8920, Ext 230, E-mail: rmcgrath@nassaulibrary.org; *ILL,* Lori Summerhayes; Tel: 516-292-8920, Ext 261, E-mail: summerh@nassaulibrary.org; *Online Serv & Tech Spec,* James McHugh; Tel: 516-292-8920, Ext 244, E-mail: jmchugh@nassaulibrary.org; *Outreach Serv Spec,* Andrea Snyder; Tel: 516-292-8920, Ext 273, E-mail: asnyder@nassaulibrary.org; Staff 23 (MLS 8, Non-MLS 15)
Founded 1959. Pop 1,334,544
Automation Activity & Vendor Info: (Cataloging) Innovative Interfaces, Inc; (Circulation) Innovative Interfaces, Inc; (ILL) OCLC; (OPAC) Innovative Interfaces, Inc
Wireless access
Function: 24/7 Electronic res, 24/7 Online cat, e-mail serv, Electronic databases & coll, ILL available, Jail serv, Libr develop
Member Libraries: Baldwin Public Library; Bayville Free Library; Bellmore Memorial Library; Bethpage Public Library; Bryant Library; East Meadow Public Library; East Rockaway Public Library; East Williston Public Library; Elmont Public Library; Farmingdale Public Library; Floral Park Public Library; Franklin Square Public Library; Freeport Memorial Library; Glen Cove Public Library; Gold Coast Public Library; Great Neck Library; Hempstead Public Library; Henry Waldinger Memorial Library; Hewlett-Woodmere Public Library; Hicksville Public Library; Hillside Public Library; Island Park Public Library; Island Trees Public Library; Jericho Public Library; Lakeview Public Library; Levittown Public Library; Locust Valley Library; Long Beach Public Library; Lynbrook Public Library; Malverne Public Library; Manhasset Public Library; Massapequa Public Library; Merrick Library; Mineola Memorial Library; North Bellmore Public Library; North Merrick Public Library; Oceanside Library; Oyster Bay-East Norwich Public Library; Peninsula Public Library; Plainedge Public Library; Plainview-Old Bethpage Public Library; Port Washington Public Library; Rockville Centre Public Library; Roosevelt Public Library; Sea Cliff Village Library; Seaford Public Library; Shelter Rock Public Library; Syosset Public Library; Uniondale Public Library; Wantagh Public Library; West Hempstead Public Library; Westbury Memorial Public Library; Williston Park Public Library
Restriction: Not a lending libr, Not open to pub

L RIVKIN RADLER LLP*, Law Library, 926 RexCorp Plaza, 11556-0926. SAN 372-2368. Tel: 516-357-3453, 516-357-3454, 516-357-3455. FAX: 516-357-3333. *Librn,* Kathy Greco; *Asst Librn,* Aurelia Sanchez; *Tech Serv Librn,* Therese Villella; Staff 3 (MLS 3)
Library Holdings: Bk Vols 10,000; Per Subs 50
Restriction: Staff use only

L RUSKIN, MOSCOU & FALTISCHEK PC*, Law Library, 1425 RXR Plaza, 11556-0190. SAN 374-4868. Tel: 516-663-6525. FAX: 516-663-6725. *Librn,* Paul Nardone
Founded 1968
Library Holdings: Bk Titles 893; Bk Vols 10,000

P UNIONDALE PUBLIC LIBRARY*, 400 Uniondale Ave, 11553-1995. SAN 312-5920. Tel: 516-489-2220. FAX: 516-489-4005. Web Site: www.nassaulibrary.org/uniondale. *Dir,* Trina Reed; *Adult Serv,* Guo Ilgar; Tel: 516-489-2220, Ext 208, E-mail: iguo@uniondalelibrary.org; *Ch Serv,* Deirdre Escoffier; Tel: 516-489-2220, Ext 215, E-mail: descoffier@uniondalelibrary.org; *Circ Serv,* Chris Marra; Tel: 516-489-2220, Ext 235, E-mail: cmarra@uniondalelibrary.org
Founded 1954. Pop 25,000; Circ 160,000
Library Holdings: Bk Vols 115,000
Wireless access
Publications: Uniondale Public Library (Newsletter)
Mem of Nassau Library System
Friends of the Library Group

UPPER JAY

P WELLS MEMORIAL LIBRARY, 12230 NYS Rte 9N, Box 57, 12987-0057. SAN 312-5939. Tel: 518-946-2644. FAX: 518-946-2644. E-mail: wellslib@primelink1.net. Web Site: wellsmemoriallibrary.com. *Libr Dir,* Karen Rappaport; Staff 0.5 (MLS 0.5)
Founded 1906. Pop 2,506
Library Holdings: AV Mats 1,000; Large Print Bks 200; Bk Vols 12,000; Per Subs 35; Talking Bks 120
Special Collections: Adirondack-NY Coll
Wireless access
Mem of Clinton-Essex-Franklin Library System
Partic in Northern New York Library Network
Open Tues-Fri 12-5, Sat 11-4

UPPER NYACK

R TEMPLE BETH TORAH LIBRARY*, Rte 9 W, 330 N Highland Ave, 10960. SAN 312-5947. Tel: 845-358-2248. FAX: 845-358-3450. Web Site: www.templebethtorah.org. *Actg Librn,* Seth Schlanger
Library Holdings: Bk Titles 1,200; Bk Vols 1,250; Per Subs 14
Wireless access
Open Tues 4:15-8:15, Sun 9-1

UPTON

S BROOKHAVEN NATIONAL LABORATORY*, Information Services Division, Research Library, Bldg 477, 11973-5000. SAN 312-5955. Tel: 631-344-3483. Interlibrary Loan Service Tel: 631-344-3138, 631-344-3802. FAX: 631-344-2090. Web Site: www.bnl.gov/bnl.html. *Mgr,* Mary Petersen; Tel: 631-344-3489; *Syst Librn,* Betsy Schwartz; Tel: 631-344-2758, E-mail: bjs@bnl.gov; *Tech Serv,* Leah Donley; Tel: 631-344-5069; Staff 18 (MLS 5, Non-MLS 13)
Founded 1947
Library Holdings: e-books 3,900; e-journals 10,600; Bk Titles 31,560; Bk Vols 45,220; Per Subs 465
Subject Interests: Biol, Chem, Energy, Eng, Med, Nuclear sci, Physics
Automation Activity & Vendor Info: (Acquisitions) SirsiDynix; (Cataloging) SirsiDynix
Database Vendor: ISI Web of Knowledge
Publications: Newsletter (Monthly)
Partic in Dialog Corp; Long Island Library Resources Council; OCLC Online Computer Library Center, Inc
Restriction: Open by appt only

UTICA

M FAXTON SAINT LUKE'S HEALTH CARE*, Saint Luke's Campus, 1656 Champlin Ave, 13502. (Mail add: PO Box 479, 13503-0479), SAN 373-6148. Tel: 315-624-6059. FAX: 315-624-6947. *Dir, Libr Serv,* Deborah Hailston; E-mail: dhailsto@mvnhealth.com
Library Holdings: e-books 19; e-journals 120; Bk Titles 810; Per Subs 143

Subject Interests: Cardiology, Long term care, Nursing, Obstetrics, Oncology, Pediatrics
Partic in Central New York Library Resources Council

M MASONIC MEDICAL RESEARCH LABORATORY LIBRARY*, Max L Kamiel Library, 2150 Bleecker St, 13501-1787. SAN 312-598X. Tel: 315-735-2217, Ext 135. FAX: 315-724-0963. E-mail: lib@mmrl.edu. Web Site: www.mmrl.edu. *Head of Libr,* Rebecca Warren; Staff 1 (MLS 1)
Founded 1959
Library Holdings: Bk Vols 13,300; Per Subs 60
Subject Interests: Cardiac, Cardiology, Molecular biol, Molecular genetics, Pharmacology, Physiology
Wireless access
Function: ILL available, Telephone ref
Partic in Central New York Library Resources Council; New York State Interlibrary Loan Network (NYSILL)
Open Mon-Fri 9-5
Restriction: Open to others by appt

P MID-YORK LIBRARY SYSTEM*, 1600 Lincoln Ave, 13502. SAN 312-5998. Tel: 315-735-8328. FAX: 315-735-0943. Web Site: www.midyork.org. *Exec Dir,* Wanda Bruchis; Staff 7 (MLS 3, Non-MLS 4)
Founded 1960. Pop 369,377
Library Holdings: Bk Vols 85,000; Per Subs 20
Automation Activity & Vendor Info: (Acquisitions) Baker & Taylor; (Cataloging) OCLC Connexion; (Circulation) SirsiDynix; (ILL) OCLC; (OPAC) SIRSI-iBistro
Database Vendor: Dialog, EBSCOhost, Gale Cengage Learning, Newsbank, OCLC FirstSearch, SirsiDynix
Wireless access
Publications: Book Buying Lists; Core Collection Reference Buying Guide; Get Ready Sheet; Headhunters Guide to Genealogical Resources in Central NY; MYLS Reporter; Union List of Periodicals
Member Libraries: Barneveld Free Library; Bridgewater Free Library; C W Clark Memorial Library; Camden Public Library; Canastota Public Library; Cazenovia Public Library; Clayville Library Association; DeRuyter Free Library; Didymus Thomas Library; Dolgeville-Manheim Public Library; Dunham Public Library; Earlville Free Library; Erwin Library & Institute; Frank J Basloe Library of Herkimer New York; Frankfort Free Library; Holland Patent Free Library; Ilion Free Public Library; Jervis Public Library Association, Inc; Jordanville Public Library; Kirby Free Library of Salisbury Center; Kirkland Town Library; Middleville Free Library; Morrisville Public Library; New Hartford Public Library; New York Mills Public Library; Newport Free Library; Old Forge Library; Oneida County Historical Society Library; Oneida Public Library; Oriskany Public Library; Poland Public Library; Prospect Free Library; Sherrill-Kenwood Free Library; Sullivan Free Library; Utica Public Library; Vernon Public Library; Waterville Public Library; Weller Public Library; West Winfield Library; Western Town Library; Westmoreland Reading Center; Woodgate Free Library
Partic in Central New York Library Resources Council; OCLC Online Computer Library Center, Inc
Restriction: Not open to pub

J MOHAWK VALLEY COMMUNITY COLLEGE LIBRARY*, 1101 Sherman Dr, 13501-5394. SAN 312-6005. Tel: 315-792-5408. Interlibrary Loan Service Tel: 315-792-5669. Reference Tel: 315-792-5561. Administration Tel: 315-792-5399. FAX: 315-792-5666. Web Site: www.mvcc.edu/academics/library. *Dir of Libr,* Stephen Frisbee; E-mail: sfrisbee@mvcc.edu; *Br Librn,* Barbara Evans; Tel: 315-334-7714; *Ref & Info Serv, Web Coordr,* Colleen Kehoe-Robinson; Tel: 315-731-5737; *Cataloger,* Krista Hartman; *Circ,* Anne Ichihana; Tel: 315-731-5735; *Electronic Res, ILL & Ser,* Louise Charbonneau; Tel: 315-731-5793; *ILL,* Sherry Day; Staff 13 (MLS 13)
Founded 1946. Enrl 6,000
Library Holdings: Bk Titles 62,022; Bk Vols 92,000; Per Subs 650
Special Collections: Career Center; Children's Books
Automation Activity & Vendor Info: (Acquisitions) Ex Libris Group; (Cataloging) Ex Libris Group; (Circulation) Ex Libris Group; (Course Reserve) Ex Libris Group; (ILL) OCLC ILLiad; (OPAC) Ex Libris Group; (Serials) Ex Libris Group
Database Vendor: College Source, CQ Press, CredoReference, EBSCOhost, Facts on File, Newsbank, OCLC FirstSearch, ProQuest, ScienceDirect, SerialsSolutions, Westlaw
Wireless access
Publications: Newsletter
Partic in Central New York Library Resources Council; OCLC Online Computer Library Center, Inc
Open Mon-Thurs 8am-9pm, Fri 8-4, Sat 12-5, Sun 1-6
Friends of the Library Group

M MOHAWK VALLEY PSYCHIATRIC CENTER*, George M Lein Information Center, 1400 Noyes St at York, 13502-3852. SAN 354-3420. Tel: 315-738-4033. *In Charge,* Frances Service
Founded 1843
Library Holdings: Bk Titles 3,300; Per Subs 10
Subject Interests: Hist med, Med, Nursing, Psychiat
Partic in Central New York Library Resources Council; Greater NE Regional Med Libr Program
Open Mon-Fri 8-4:30
Restriction: Staff & patient use

S MUNSON-WILLIAMS-PROCTOR ARTS INSTITUTE LIBRARY*, Art Reference Library, 310 Genesee St, 13502. SAN 354-3307. Tel: 315-797-0000, Ext 2123. FAX: 315-797-5608. E-mail: library@mwpai.edu. Web Site: www.mwpai.org/museum/library/. *Archives Dir, Libr Serv Dir, Mus Librn,* Kathryn L Corcoran; Tel: 315-797-0000, Ext 2228, E-mail: kcorcoran@mwpai.org; *Bibliog Instr, Circ, Ref Serv,* Kathleen Salsbury; E-mail: ksalsbur@mwpai.edu. Subject Specialists: *Art,* Kathryn L Corcoran; Staff 3 (MLS 1, Non-MLS 2)
Founded 1960
Library Holdings: CDs 2,400; DVDs 330; Bk Vols 26,000; Per Subs 50; Videos 1,017
Special Collections: Autographs & Bookplates (Proctor Families Coll); Rare Books (Fountain Elms Coll)
Subject Interests: Art hist, Fine arts
Automation Activity & Vendor Info: (Cataloging) Mandarin Library Automation; (Circulation) Mandarin Library Automation; (Course Reserve) Mandarin Library Automation; (ILL) OCLC WorldShare Interlibrary Loan; (OPAC) Mandarin Library Automation; (Serials) Mandarin Library Automation
Database Vendor: Cambridge Scientific Abstracts, OCLC FirstSearch, OCLC WorldShare Interlibrary Loan, Wilson - Wilson Web
Function: Adult bk club, Archival coll, CD-ROM, Copy machines, e-mail serv, Electronic databases & coll, Mail & tel request accepted, Ref & res, Telephone ref, VHS videos
Partic in Central New York Library Resources Council
Open Mon-Fri 9-5, Sat 9-12 & 1-5, Sun 12-5
Restriction: Circ limited, In-house use for visitors, Non-circulating of rare bks

GL NEW YORK SUPREME COURT*, Law Library-Oneida County, 235 Elizabeth St, 13501. SAN 312-6013. Tel: 315-798-5703. FAX: 315-798-6470. *Sr Librn,* Paula J Eannace; E-mail: peannace@courts.state.ny.us; Staff 4 (MLS 1, Non-MLS 3)
Library Holdings: Bk Titles 250,000; Per Subs 500
Special Collections: Legal Treatises for Practitioners, 18th & 19th Centuries
Subject Interests: Am legal mats, NY legal mats
Database Vendor: LexisNexis, Westlaw
Wireless access
Partic in OCLC Online Computer Library Center, Inc; Westlaw
Open Mon-Fri 8:30-4:30

S ONEIDA COUNTY HISTORICAL SOCIETY LIBRARY*, 1608 Genesee St, 13502. SAN 325-9684. Tel: 315-735-3642. FAX: 315-732-0806. E-mail: ochs@oneidacountyhistory.org. Web Site: oneidacountyhistory.org. *Exec Dir,* Brian J Howard
Founded 1876
Jan 2010-Dec 2010 Income $2,500. Mats Exp $1,500
Library Holdings: Bk Titles 2,500; Bk Vols 4,000
Special Collections: Journals & Letters, family & business recos
Subject Interests: Genealogy, Indust, Local bus, Oneida County hist
Wireless access
Function: Archival coll, Computers for patron use, Copy machines, Exhibits, Handicapped accessible, Photocopying/Printing, Ref serv available, Ref serv in person
Mem of Mid-York Library System
Open Tues-Thurs 10-4, Sat 11-3
Restriction: Access for corporate affiliates, Authorized patrons, Fee for pub use, Non-circulating, Not a lending libr

M SAINT ELIZABETH MEDICAL CENTER*, College of Nursing Library, 2215 Genesee St, 13501. SAN 324-539X. Tel: 315-798-8209. *Librn,* Michael Garcia; Staff 1 (MLS 1)
Library Holdings: Bk Vols 5,005; Per Subs 48
Subject Interests: Nursing
Partic in Central New York Library Resources Council
Restriction: Staff use only

C STATE UNIVERSITY OF NEW YORK INSTITUTE OF TECHNOLOGY*, Peter J Cayan Library, Rte 12 N & Horatio St, 13502. (Mail add: PO Box 3050, 13504-3050), SAN 312-6021. Tel: 315-792-7245. Circulation Tel: 315-792-7245. Interlibrary Loan Service Tel: 315-792-7249. Reference Tel: 315-792-7251. Administration Tel: 315-792-7308. FAX: 315-792-7517. Web Site: www.sunyit.edu/library. *Assoc Librn,* Ron Foster; E-mail: ron.foster@sunyit.edu; *Assoc Librn,* Barbara Grimes; E-mail: barbara.grimes@sunyit.edu; *Sr Asst Librn,* Nancy

Kaiser; Tel: 315-792-7307, E-mail: nancy.kaiser@sunyit.edu; Staff 7 (MLS 6, Non-MLS 1)
Founded 1969. Enrl 2,450; Fac 200; Highest Degree: Master
Library Holdings: e-journals 1,400; Bk Vols 177,839; Per Subs 181
Special Collections: State Document Depository; US Document Depository
Subject Interests: Bus, Computer sci, Health, Technologies
Automation Activity & Vendor Info: (Cataloging) Ex Libris Group; (Circulation) Ex Libris Group; (ILL) OCLC ILLiad; (OPAC) Ex Libris Group
Database Vendor: EBSCOhost, Elsevier, ProQuest, ScienceDirect
Wireless access
Function: E-Reserves, Handicapped accessible, ILL available, Online ref, Online searches, Ref serv available, Telephone ref
Partic in New York State Higher Education Initiative; Nylink; Westchester Academic Library Directors Organization (WALDO)
Open Mon-Thurs 8am-11pm, Fri 8-5, Sat 10-5, Sun 1-11
Restriction: Open to pub for ref & circ; with some limitations

C UTICA COLLEGE*, Frank E Gannett Memorial Library, 1600 Burrstone Rd, 13502-4892. SAN 312-603X. Tel: 315-792-3041. Interlibrary Loan Service Tel: 315-792-3262. Information Services Tel: 315-792-3044. FAX: 315-792-3361. E-mail: library@utica.edu. Web Site: www.utica.edu/academic/library/index.cfm. *Asst Libr Dir, Ref Librn,* Nancy Virgil-Call; Tel: 315-792-3151, E-mail: navirgil@utica.edu; *Head, Circ,* Elizabeth Caraco; Tel: 315-792-3218, E-mail: ecaraco@utica.edu; *Cat Librn, Coordr, Tech Serv,* Herb LaGoy; Tel: 315-792-3217, E-mail: hllagoy@utica.edu; *Distance Learning Librn,* Lisa Rogers; Tel: 315-792-3342, E-mail: lrogers@utica.edu; *Ref Librn,* Janis VanCourt, Tel: 315-792-3351, E-mail: jvancourt@utica.edu; *Ref Librn & Coordr of Electronic Res,* Jan Malcheski; Tel: 315-792-3388, E-mail: jamalche@utica.edu; *Tech Serv Technician,* Lynn M Guca; Tel: 315-233-2485, E-mail: lmguca@utica.edu. Subject Specialists: *Humanities,* Nancy Virgil-Call; Staff 13 (MLS 6, Non-MLS 7)
Founded 1946. Enrl 2,468; Fac 111; Highest Degree: Master
Library Holdings: Bk Vols 180,000; Per Subs 1,400
Special Collections: Fiction-Scene in Upstate New York Since 1929; Walter Edmonds; Welsh Language Imprints of New York State
Automation Activity & Vendor Info: (Cataloging) OCLC; (Circulation) SirsiDynix; (OPAC) SirsiDynix
Wireless access
Partic in Central New York Library Resources Council; Nylink; OCLC Online Computer Library Center, Inc
Open Mon-Thurs 8am-Midnight, Fri 8am-10pm (8-7 Summer), Sun Noon-Midnight

P UTICA PUBLIC LIBRARY, 303 Genesee St, 13501. SAN 354-348X. Tel: 315-735-2279. FAX: 315-734-1034. Web Site: www.uticapubliclibrary.org. *Dir,* Darby O'Brien; E-mail: dobrien@uticapubliclibrary.org; *Asst Dir,* Heidi McManus; *Youth Serv Dir,* Joshua Carlson; *Digital Literacy Librn,* Jocelyn Ireland; *Early Literacy Coordr,* Amanda Stewart; *Circ,* Joan Stalloch; *Info Tech,* Fritz Meeusen; *Ref,* Carl Antonucci; *Ref,* Robert Lalli; *Ref,* Angela Sweet Cloud; *Youth Serv,* Marjorie Cobane; *Youth Serv,* Lisa Renz; Staff 9.5 (MLS 6.3, Non-MLS 3.2)
Founded 1893. Pop 62,235; Circ 142,360
Apr 2014-Mar 2015 Income $1,209,076, State $43,015, City $10,000, County $201,460, Locally Generated Income $214,571, Other $740,000. Mats Exp $75,123, Books $28,805, Per/Ser (Incl. Access Fees) $6,883, Micro $3,117, AV Mat $24,318, Electronic Ref Mat (Incl. Access Fees) $12,000. Sal $600,326 (Prof $369,930)
Library Holdings: AV Mats 18,755; e-books 417; Electronic Media & Resources 163; Microforms 8,905; Bk Vols 145,073; Per Subs 63
Subject Interests: Genealogy, Local hist
Automation Activity & Vendor Info: (Acquisitions) SirsiDynix; (Cataloging) SirsiDynix; (Circulation) SirsiDynix; (ILL) SirsiDynix; (OPAC) SirsiDynix
Wireless access
Function: 24/7 Online cat, Adult bk club, Art exhibits, Bks on CD, Chess club, Children's prog, Computer training, Computers for patron use, Copy machines, Electronic databases & coll, Exhibits, Fax serv, Free DVD rentals, Handicapped accessible, ILL available, Magazines, Mail & tel request accepted, Mango lang, Microfiche/film & reading machines, Movies, Music CDs, Notary serv, Online cat, Online ref, Online searches, Orientations, Outreach serv, Outside serv via phone, mail, e-mail & web, OverDrive digital audio bks, Photocopying/Printing, Preschool outreach, Prog for adults, Prog for children & young adult, Pub access computers, Ref serv available, Ref serv in person, Scanner, Senior computer classes, Spanish lang bks, Story hour, Summer reading prog, Tax forms, Teen prog, Telephone ref, Wheelchair accessible, Writing prog
Open Mon & Tues 8:30-8, Wed-Fri 8:30-5:30, Sat 8:30-5

VALATIE

P VALATIE FREE LIBRARY*, 3203 Church St, 12184-2301. (Mail add: PO Box 336, 12184-0336), SAN 312-6056. Tel: 518-758-9321. FAX: 518-758-6497. E-mail: valatielibrary@fairpoint.net. Web Site: valatielibrary.org. *Dir,* Jean Pallas
Circ 7,459
Library Holdings: Bk Vols 10,243
Automation Activity & Vendor Info: (Cataloging) Innovative Interfaces, Inc; (Circulation) Innovative Interfaces, Inc; (OPAC) Innovative Interfaces, Inc
Wireless access
Mem of Mid-Hudson Library System
Open Mon Noon-7, Tues & Wed Noon-5

VALHALLA

CM NEW YORK MEDICAL COLLEGE*, Health Sciences Library, Basic Science Bldg, 95 Grasslands Rd, 10595. SAN 312-6064. Tel: 914-594-4200. Interlibrary Loan Service Tel: 914-594-4201. Reference Tel: 914-594-4210. Administration Tel: 914-594-4208. FAX: 914-594-3171. Administration FAX: 914-594-4191. E-mail: hsl_nymc@nymc.edu. Web Site: library.nymc.edu. *Assoc Dean, Dir,* Diana Cunningham; *Circ,* Marta Ambroziak; Tel: 914-594-4204; *Media Spec,* Michael Cotter; Tel: 914-594-3675; *Ref,* Marie Ascher; Tel: 914-594-3168; *Tech Serv,* Cheryl Silver; Tel: 914-594-4205; Staff 17 (MLS 9, Non-MLS 8)
Founded 1976. Enrl 1,100; Fac 1,294; Highest Degree: Doctorate
Library Holdings: e-journals 8,319; Bk Titles 29,838; Bk Vols 198,025; Per Subs 9,351
Special Collections: History of Medicine & Homeopathy (Historical Coll); History of Orthopedics (Alfred Haas Coll); Rare Books (J Alexander van Heuven Coll)
Subject Interests: Biomed sci, Health policy, Homeopathy, Med, Pub health
Automation Activity & Vendor Info: (Cataloging) SirsiDynix; (Circulation) SirsiDynix; (Course Reserve) SirsiDynix; (ILL) OCLC ILLiad; (Media Booking) SirsiDynix; (OPAC) SirsiDynix; (Serials) SirsiDynix
Database Vendor: Dialog, EBSCOhost, Gale Cengage Learning, LexisNexis, OCLC FirstSearch, OVID Technologies, SirsiDynix
Function: Archival coll, Doc delivery serv, Res libr
Partic in Nylink
Restriction: Not open to pub
Friends of the Library Group

J SUNY WESTCHESTER COMMUNITY COLLEGE*, Harold L Drimmer Library/Learning Resource Center, 75 Grasslands Rd, 10595-1693. SAN 312-6080. Tel: 914-785-6960. Circulation Tel: 914-785-6965. FAX: 914-785-6513. Circulation FAX: 914-606-6531. Web Site: www.sunywcc.edu/library. *Electronic Res Librn,* Jessica Tagliaferro; Tel: 914-606-6808; *User Educ Librn,* Gloria Meisel; Tel: 914-785-6968, E-mail: gloria.meisel@sunywcc.edu; *Virtual Serv Coordr,* Sandy Schepis; Tel: 914-606-6629, E-mail: sandy.schepis@sunywcc.edu; *Acq,* Diana Matson; Tel: 914-606-6819, E-mail: dorothy.freeman@sunywcc.edu; *Circ,* Anna Pierce; Tel: 914-606-7847, E-mail: anne.pierce@sunywcc.edu; *Electronic Res,* Karen Vanterpool; Tel: 914-783-8536, E-mail: karen.vanterpool@sunywcc.edu; *ILL, Res,* Una Shih; Tel: 914-606-6573, E-mail: una.shih@sunywcc.edu; *Outreach/Educ,* Beth Seelick; *Per,* Mathurin Towanda; Tel: 914-606-8529, E-mail: towanda.mathurin@sunywcc.edu; Staff 27 (MLS 17, Non-MLS 10)
Founded 1946. Enrl 11,981; Fac 157; Highest Degree: Associate
Library Holdings: Bk Titles 105,501; Bk Vols 138,000; Per Subs 362
Special Collections: College & Career Coll; Legal Coll New York State
Automation Activity & Vendor Info: (Circulation) Ex Libris Group; (OPAC) Ex Libris Group; (Serials) Ex Libris Group
Wireless access
Function: Distance learning, ILL available, Ref serv available
Publications: Periodicals List
Partic in Metropolitan New York Library Council; Nylink; Westchester Academic Library Directors Organization (WALDO)
Open Mon-Thurs 8am-9:30pm, Fri 8-5, Sat 9-5, Sun 1-5

VALLEY COTTAGE

S TOLSTOY FOUNDATION, INC*, Alexandra Tolstoy Memorial Library, 104 Lake Rd, 10989-2339. (Mail add: PO Box 578, 10989-0578), SAN 371-1072. Tel: 845-268-6722. FAX: 845-268-6937. E-mail: info@tolstoyfoundation.org, tfhq@aol.com. Web Site: www.tolstoyfoundation.org. *Librn,* Robert Whitaker; E-mail: rwhittaker@rusinc.net
Library Holdings: Bk Vols 52,000
Wireless access
Open Mon 9-4

P VALLEY COTTAGE FREE LIBRARY*, 110 Rte 303, 10989. SAN 312-6102. Tel: 845-268-7700. FAX: 845-268-7760. Web Site: www.vclib.org. *Dir,* Amelia Kalin; *Head, Tech Serv,* Veta Binkley; *Ref Librn,* Liene Chaudhuri; *Adult Serv,* Christy Blanchette; *Ch Serv,* Melinda Watkins; Staff 30 (MLS 8, Non-MLS 22)
Founded 1959. Pop 23,805; Circ 201,957
Library Holdings: DVDs 1,000; Bk Titles 68,985; Per Subs 6,140; Talking Bks 3,795; Videos 2,767
Special Collections: Local History Photog Coll
Subject Interests: Art, Local hist
Automation Activity & Vendor Info: (Acquisitions) SirsiDynix; (Cataloging) SirsiDynix; (Circulation) SirsiDynix; (ILL) SirsiDynix; (OPAC) SirsiDynix
Wireless access
Function: BA reader (adult literacy), Homebound delivery serv, ILL available, Outside serv via phone, mail, e-mail & web, Photocopying/Printing, Prog for children & young adult, Ref serv available, Summer reading prog, Wheelchair accessible
Publications: Focus (Newsletter)
Mem of Ramapo Catskill Library System
Open Mon-Thurs 10-9, Fri & Sat 10-5, Sun 12-4
Friends of the Library Group

VALLEY FALLS

P VALLEY FALLS FREE LIBRARY*, 42 State St, 12185. (Mail add: PO Box 296, 12185-0296), SAN 312-6110. Tel: 518-753-4230. FAX: 518-753-4230. *Dir,* Sandi Goodwin
Founded 1907. Pop 5,000; Circ 7,094
Library Holdings: Bk Vols 9,000; Per Subs 20
Wireless access
Mem of Upper Hudson Library System
Open Tues 10-12 & 2-8, Wed 2-8, Thurs & Fri 2-6, Sat 9-12:30

VALLEY STREAM

P HENRY WALDINGER MEMORIAL LIBRARY*, 60 Verona Pl, 11582-3011. SAN 312-6137. Tel: 516-825-6422. FAX: 516-825-6551. E-mail: hwmlcontact@hotmail.com. Web Site: www.nassaulibrary.org/valleyst. *Dir,* Mamie Eng; E-mail: director24@nassaulibrary.org; Staff 6 (MLS 5, Non-MLS 1)
Founded 1932. Pop 40,601; Circ 143,268
Jun 2010-May 2011 Income $1,248,807, State $26,813, City $1,180,880, Locally Generated Income $41,114. Mats Exp $169,183, Books $98,239, Electronic Ref Mat (Incl. Access Fees) $50,000. Sal $737,924 (Prof $330,246)
Library Holdings: AV Mats 8,069; Bk Vols 121,127; Per Subs 182
Special Collections: Oral History
Subject Interests: Valley Stream hist
Automation Activity & Vendor Info: (Cataloging) Innovative Interfaces, Inc; (Circulation) Innovative Interfaces, Inc; (OPAC) Innovative Interfaces, Inc
Database Vendor: ABC-CLIO, ALLDATA Online, CQ Press, CredoReference, EBSCOhost, Gale Cengage Learning, Greenwood Publishing Group, Innovative Interfaces, Inc, OCLC FirstSearch, Oxford Online, ProQuest, ReferenceUSA, TumbleBookLibrary, Westlaw
Wireless access
Function: Adult bk club, After school storytime, Art exhibits, Audio & video playback equip for onsite use, Bk club(s), Bks on cassette, Bks on CD, CD-ROM, Children's prog, Computer training, Computers for patron use, Copy machines, e-mail serv, E-Reserves, Electronic databases & coll, Exhibits, Family literacy, Free DVD rentals, Handicapped accessible, Homebound delivery serv, ILL available, Magnifiers for reading, Mus passes, Music CDs, Online cat, Online searches, OverDrive digital audio bks, Photocopying/Printing, Preschool outreach, Prog for children & young adult, Pub access computers, Ref & res, Ref serv available, Spoken cassettes & CDs, Story hour, Summer reading prog, Tax forms, Teen prog, Telephone ref, VHS videos, Video lending libr, Wheelchair accessible
Mem of Nassau Library System
Open Mon, Tues, Thurs & Fri 10-9, Wed 10-5:30, Sat 10-4

VERNON

P VERNON PUBLIC LIBRARY*, 4441 Peterboro St, 13476-3643. (Mail add: PO Box 1048, 13476-1048), SAN 312-6145. Tel: 315-829-2463. *Librn,* Gary Seelman; *Asst Librn,* Robert Seelman
Pop 1,300; Circ 32,841
Library Holdings: Bk Vols 8,500; Per Subs 16
Wireless access
Mem of Mid-York Library System
Open Tues-Fri 3-7, Sat Noon-4
Friends of the Library Group

VESTAL

P FOUR COUNTY LIBRARY SYSTEM*, 304 Clubhouse Rd, 13850-3713. SAN 310-866X. Tel: 607-723-8236. FAX: 607-723-1722. Web Site: www.4cls.org. *Exec Dir,* Steven J Bachman; *Dep Exec Dir,* Pamela Brown; Tel: 607-723-8236, Ext 303, E-mail: pbrown@4cls.org; *Automation Syst Coordr,* Jeff Henry; Tel: 607-723-8236, Ext 310, E-mail: jbhenry@4cls.org; *Ch Serv,* M Starr LaTronica; Tel: 607-723-8236, Ext 350, E-mail: slatronica@4cls.org; Staff 18 (MLS 6, Non-MLS 12)
Founded 1960. Pop 361,668; Circ 38,153
Library Holdings: Bk Vols 170,044
Automation Activity & Vendor Info: (Acquisitions) SirsiDynix; (Cataloging) SirsiDynix; (Circulation) SirsiDynix; (ILL) SirsiDynix; (OPAC) SirsiDynix
Database Vendor: SirsiDynix
Function: ILL available
Publications: Directory of Member Libraries; Newsletter
Member Libraries: Afton Free Library; Andes Public Library; Bainbridge Free Library; Bovina Library Association; Broome County Public Library; Cannon Free Library; Cherry Valley Memorial Library; Deposit Free Library; Edmeston Free Library & Museum; Fairview Public Library; Fenton Free Library; Franklin Free Library; George F Johnson Memorial Library; Gilbertsville Free Library; Guernsey Memorial Library; Harris Memorial Library; Huntington Memorial Library; Kinney Memorial Library; Lisle Free Library; Louise Adelia Read Memorial Library; Mary Wilcox Memorial Library; Milford Free Library; Moore Memorial Library; New Berlin Library; Nineveh Public Library of Colesville Township; Oxford Memorial Library; Richfield Springs Public Library; Roxbury Library Association; Sherburne Public Library; Sidney Memorial Public Library; Skene Memorial Library; Smyrna Public Library; South New Berlin Free Library; Springfield Library; Stamford Village Library; Unadilla Public Library; Vestal Public Library; Village Library of Cooperstown; Village Library of Morris; William B Ogden Free Library; Worcester Free Library; Your Home Public Library
Partic in New York State Interlibrary Loan Network (NYSILL)
Open Mon-Fri 8-4:30
Bookmobiles: 1

R TEMPLE ISRAEL LIBRARY*, 4737 Deerfield Pl, 13850-3762. SAN 324-0290. Tel: 607-723-7461. *Librn,* Barbara Gilbert; Staff 5 (MLS 1, Non-MLS 4)
Founded 1968
Library Holdings: Bk Titles 2,000; Bk Vols 2,600; Talking Bks 50
Subject Interests: Holocaust, Jewish authors, Jewish fiction, Jewish hist, Jewish lit, Jewish-Am hist, Judaica
Friends of the Library Group

P VESTAL PUBLIC LIBRARY*, 320 Vestal Pkwy E, 13850-1632. SAN 312-6153. Tel: 607-754-4243. Reference Tel: 607-754-4244. FAX: 607-754-7936. E-mail: ve.ref@4cls.org. Web Site: lib.4cty.org/vestal-r.html. *Dir,* Carol Boyce; *Ad, Asst Dir,* Scott Clark; *Ch,* Kathy Kretzmer; Staff 6 (MLS 6)
Founded 1970. Pop 26,733; Circ 309,799
Library Holdings: Bk Titles 96,000; Bk Vols 116,412; Per Subs 256
Special Collections: David Ross Locke Book Coll
Automation Activity & Vendor Info: (Circulation) SirsiDynix
Wireless access
Function: Mail loans to mem
Publications: Friends (Newsletter)
Mem of Four County Library System
Open Mon (Winter) 2-9, Tues-Thurs 9-9, Fri 9-6, Sat 9-2; Mon-Thurs (Summer) 9-9, Fri 9-5
Friends of the Library Group

VICTOR

P VICTOR FREE LIBRARY*, 15 W Main, 14564. SAN 312-6161. Tel: 585-924-2637. FAX: 585-924-1893. Web Site: www.victor.pls-net.org. *Dir,* Patricia Evans; *Ch Serv,* Lynne Madden; Staff 2 (MLS 1, Non-MLS 1)
Founded 1939. Pop 17,010; Circ 211,902
Jan 2007-Dec 2007 Income $418,182, City $319,025. Mats Exp $56,806, Books $39,660, Per/Ser (Incl. Access Fees) $4,770, Other Print Mats $7, AV Mat $12,369. Sal $205,146 (Prof $89,795)
Library Holdings: Audiobooks 1,952; Bk Vols 46,633; Per Subs 121
Automation Activity & Vendor Info: (Circulation) SirsiDynix; (OPAC) SirsiDynix
Wireless access
Mem of Pioneer Library System
Open Mon-Thurs 10-9, Fri 10-6, Sat 10-4, Sun (Oct-April) 2-4
Friends of the Library Group

VOORHEESVILLE

P VOORHEESVILLE PUBLIC LIBRARY*, 51 School Rd, 12186. SAN 312-617X. Tel: 518-765-2791. FAX: 518-765-3007. E-mail: reference@voorheesvillelibrary.org. Web Site:

www.voorheesvillelibrary.org. *Libr Dir,* Gail Alter Sacco; E-mail: gail.sacco@voorheesvillelibrary.org; *Asst Dir, Circ,* Rebecca Lubin; E-mail: rebecca.lubin@voorheesvillelibrary.org; *Automation Serv,* John Love; E-mail: voorheesvilleIT@voorheesvillelibrary.org; *ILL,* Kathleen Tyrrell; E-mail: kathleen.tyrrell@voorheesvillelibrary.org; *Pub Relations,* Lynn Kohler; E-mail: lynn.kohler@voorheesvillelibrary.org; *Youth Serv,* Gail Brown; E-mail: gail.brown@voorheesvillelibrary.org; Staff 13 (MLS 6, Non-MLS 7)
Founded 1915. Pop 7,131; Circ 105,681
Library Holdings: Bk Titles 45,968
Subject Interests: Local hist
Automation Activity & Vendor Info: (Cataloging) SirsiDynix; (Circulation) SirsiDynix; (ILL) SirsiDynix; (OPAC) SirsiDynix
Wireless access
Publications: Bookworm (Bi-monthly)
Mem of Upper Hudson Library System
Open Mon-Thurs 10-9, Fri 10-6, Sat 10-5, Sun (Sept-May) 1-5
Friends of the Library Group

WADDINGTON

P HEPBURN LIBRARY OF WADDINGTON*, 30 Main St, 13694. (Mail add: PO Box 205, 13694-0205), SAN 312-6188. Tel: 315-388-4454. FAX: 315-388-4050. E-mail: waddingtonlib@twcny.rr.com. Web Site: www.waddingtonlibrary.org. *Dir,* Theresa Hill; Staff 2 (Non-MLS 2)
Founded 1919. Pop 2,000
Library Holdings: Bk Vols 10,125; Per Subs 38
Special Collections: New York State Regional Heritage Coll
Automation Activity & Vendor Info: (Cataloging) SirsiDynix; (Circulation) SirsiDynix; (ILL) SirsiDynix; (OPAC) SirsiDynix; (Serials) SirsiDynix
Wireless access
Mem of North Country Library System
Special Services for the Blind - Talking bks
Open Mon 12-6, Tues & Thurs 12-5, Wed 2-8, Fri 9-2, Sat 10-12
Friends of the Library Group

WADHAMS

P WADHAMS FREE LIBRARY*, 763 NYS Rte 22, 12993. SAN 312-6196. Tel: 518-962-8717. E-mail: wadh2@westelcom.com. *Dir,* Elizabeth Rapalee; Staff 2 (Non-MLS 2)
Founded 1897. Pop 250
Library Holdings: Bk Vols 5,000; Per Subs 12
Wireless access
Mem of Clinton-Essex-Franklin Library System
Open Tues-Thurs 3-9, Sat 9-12

WALDEN

P JOSEPHINE-LOUISE PUBLIC LIBRARY*, Five Scofield St, 12586. SAN 312-620X. Tel: 845-778-7621. FAX: 845-778-1946. E-mail: wal@rcls.org. Web Site: www.rcls.org/wal. *Dir,* Virginia Neidmier
Founded 1904. Pop 5,277; Circ 35,261
Library Holdings: Bk Titles 20,000; Bk Vols 26,428; Per Subs 42
Mem of Ramapo Catskill Library System
Open Mon, Tues & Thurs 10-8, Wed & Fri 10-6, Sat 10-2
Friends of the Library Group

WALLKILL

S SHAWANGUNK CORRECTIONAL FACILITY LIBRARY*, Quick Rd, 12589. (Mail add: PO Box 750, 12589-0750), SAN 327-2559. Tel: 845-895-2081, Ext 4600. *Sr Librn,* Halyna Barannik; Staff 1 (MLS 1)
Library Holdings: Bk Titles 16,000
Subject Interests: Fiction
Automation Activity & Vendor Info: (Cataloging) Follett Software; (Circulation) Follett Software
Mem of Ramapo Catskill Library System
Partic in Southeastern New York Library Resources Council
Restriction: Staff & inmates only

P WALLKILL PUBLIC LIBRARY*, Seven Bona Ventura Ave, 12589-4422. (Mail add: PO Box C, 12589-0258), SAN 312-6218. Tel: 845-895-3707. FAX: 845-895-8659. E-mail: wak@rcls.org. Web Site: www.rcls.org/wak. *Dir,* Mary Lou Carolan; *Asst Librn,* Linda Going
Founded 1906. Circ 18,460
Library Holdings: Bk Vols 13,200; Per Subs 162
Special Collections: Regional History Coll, rare bks, pamphlets
Publications: Newsletter (Newsletter)
Mem of Ramapo Catskill Library System
Open Mon 12-5, Tues & Thurs 12-8, Wed 10-8, Fri 10-5, Sat 10-2

WALTON

M DELAWARE VALLEY HOSPITAL*, One Titus Pl, 13856. SAN 325-0873. Tel: 607-865-2100, Ext 2171. FAX: 607-865-2114. *Dir,* Cindy Gardepe
Library Holdings: Bk Vols 308; Per Subs 36
Subject Interests: Med
Database Vendor: OVID Technologies
Open Mon-Fri 8-4:30

P WILLIAM B OGDEN FREE LIBRARY*, 42 Gardiner Pl, 13856. SAN 312-6226. Tel: 607-865-5929. FAX: 607-865-6821. *Dir,* Sally Cranston; E-mail: wa.sally@4cls.org; *Ch Serv,* Tara Dwyer; *Ch Serv,* Carly Finn; *ILL,* Anna Sulgar; Staff 1 (MLS 1)
Founded 1809. Pop 3,329; Circ 35,553
Library Holdings: Bk Vols 18,691; Per Subs 87
Special Collections: Local History (Loose Coll)
Automation Activity & Vendor Info: (Cataloging) SIRSI WorkFlows; (Circulation) SIRSI WorkFlows; (OPAC) SIRSI WorkFlows; (Serials) SIRSI WorkFlows
Wireless access
Mem of Four County Library System
Open Mon, Wed & Thurs 2-8, Tues & Fri 10-5, Sat 10-4
Friends of the Library Group

WALWORTH

P WALWORTH-SEELY PUBLIC LIBRARY*, 3600 Lorraine Dr, 14568. SAN 312-6234. Tel: 315-986-1511. FAX: 315-986-5917. Web Site: www.walworth.pls-net.org. *Dir,* Jeff Davignon; E-mail: walworthlibrarydirector@owwl.org; Staff 11 (MLS 1, Non-MLS 10)
Founded 1960. Pop 8,402; Circ 79,111
Library Holdings: Bk Titles 42,230
Automation Activity & Vendor Info: (Cataloging) SirsiDynix; (Circulation) SirsiDynix; (OPAC) SirsiDynix; (Serials) SirsiDynix
Wireless access
Mem of Pioneer Library System
Open Mon-Thurs 10-8, Fri 10-6, Sat 10-2, Sun (Sept-June) 1-3
Friends of the Library Group

WANTAGH

P WANTAGH PUBLIC LIBRARY*, 3285 Park Ave, 11793. SAN 312-6250. Tel: 516-221-1200. FAX: 516-826-9357. E-mail: wantaghpl@yahoo.com. Web Site: www.wantaughlibrary.org. *Head, Ref,* Joan Filberman; *Head, Circ,* Vickie LiPetri; Staff 34 (MLS 7, Non-MLS 27)
Founded 1962. Pop 18,610; Circ 160,000
Library Holdings: Bk Titles 104,302; Bk Vols 124,678; Per Subs 388
Subject Interests: Local hist
Automation Activity & Vendor Info: (Circulation) Innovative Interfaces, Inc; (OPAC) Innovative Interfaces, Inc
Database Vendor: ABC-CLIO, ALLDATA Online, Baker & Taylor, BWI, Career Guidance Foundation, College Source, CountryWatch, CQ Press, Dialog, Dun & Bradstreet, EBSCOhost, Electric Library, Facts on File, Gale Cengage Learning, Greenwood Publishing Group, infoUSA, OCLC FirstSearch, OCLC WorldShare Interlibrary Loan, P4 Performance Management, Inc, ProQuest, ReferenceUSA
Wireless access
Publications: News & Notes (Monthly newsletter)
Mem of Nassau Library System
Open Mon-Thurs 9:30-9, Fri 9:30-6, Sat 10-5, Sun 1-5
Friends of the Library Group

WAPPINGERS FALLS

P GRINNELL LIBRARY*, 2642 E Main St, 12590. SAN 312-6277. Tel: 845-297-3428. FAX: 845-297-1506. Web Site: www.grinnell-library.org. *Exec Dir,* Laura Stein; E-mail: ldirector@grinnell-library.org; *Head, Ch,* Christine Pattantyus; *Outreach Coordr,* Jessica Simmons; *Teen Coordr,* Natasha Scalice
Founded 1867. Pop 26,008; Circ 123,025
Library Holdings: High Interest/Low Vocabulary Bk Vols 100; Bk Vols 47,000; Per Subs 3,100
Special Collections: Civil War (Ferris Coll), bks, pamphlets
Automation Activity & Vendor Info: (Cataloging) Innovative Interfaces, Inc; (Circulation) Innovative Interfaces, Inc; (OPAC) Innovative Interfaces, Inc
Wireless access
Mem of Mid-Hudson Library System
Open Mon-Thurs 9:30-8:30, Fri 9:30-6, Sat 9:30-5, Sun 1-4
Friends of the Library Group

WARRENSBURG

P RICHARDS LIBRARY*, 36 Elm St, 12885. SAN 312-6293. Tel: 518-623-3011. FAX: 518-623-3011. Web Site: www.sals.edu/warrensburg.shtml. *Dir,* Sarah M Farrar
Founded 1901. Pop 4,255; Circ 14,951
Library Holdings: Bk Vols 15,000; Per Subs 10
Subject Interests: Local hist
Wireless access
Mem of Southern Adirondack Library System
Open Mon, Wed & Fri (Winter) 10-1 & 2-5, Tues & Thurs 10-1, 2-5 & 7-9, Sat 10-1; Mon, Wed & Fri (Summer) 9-1 & 3-5, Tues & Thurs 9-1 & 7-9, Sat 9-1

WARSAW

P WARSAW PUBLIC LIBRARY*, 130 N Main St, 14569. SAN 312-6307. Tel: 585-786-5650. FAX: 585-786-8706. E-mail: warsawlibrarydirector@owwl.org. Web Site: warsawpubliclibrary.blogspot.com. *Dir,* Angela Gonzale
Founded 1870. Pop 5,074; Circ 75,753
Library Holdings: Bk Vols 35,000; Per Subs 35
Special Collections: Film Depot; Job Info Center; Large Print Coll
Automation Activity & Vendor Info: (Cataloging) SirsiDynix; (Circulation) SirsiDynix; (OPAC) SirsiDynix; (Serials) SirsiDynix
Wireless access
Mem of Reaching Across Illinois Library System (RAILS)
Open Mon & Tues 10-8, Wed & Thurs 1-8, Fri & Sat 1-5
Friends of the Library Group

WARWICK

M AMERICAN RHINOLOGIC SOCIETY LIBRARY*, PO Box 495, 10990-0495. SAN 376-1835. Tel: 845-988-1631. FAX: 845-986-1527. Web Site: www.american-rhinologic.org. *Exec Dir,* Wendi Perez; E-mail: wendi.perez@gmail.com; *Officer,* Dr Peter Hwang
Library Holdings: Bk Vols 500

P ALBERT WISNER PUBLIC LIBRARY*, Two Colonial Ave, 10990-1191. SAN 312-6323. Tel: 845-986-1047. FAX: 845-987-1228. E-mail: warref@rcls.org. Web Site: www.albertwisnerlibrary.org. *Dir,* Rosemary Cooper; E-mail: rcooper@rcls.org; *Head, Adult Serv,* Laurie Angle; Staff 5 (MLS 5)
Founded 1974. Pop 21,900; Circ 150,000
Jul 2005-Jun 2006 Income $880,812, Other $716,765. Mats Exp $95,500, Books $68,000, Per/Ser (Incl. Access Fees) $7,500, AV Mat $20,000. Sal $392,035 (Prof $184,000)
Library Holdings: AV Mats 9,544; Bk Vols 50,111; Per Subs 84
Subject Interests: Local hist
Automation Activity & Vendor Info: (OPAC) Horizon
Database Vendor: Gale Cengage Learning
Mem of Ramapo Catskill Library System
Open Mon-Thurs 9-8, Fri & Sat 9-5, Sun (Sept-June) 12-4
Friends of the Library Group

WATER MILL

S PARRISH ART MUSEUM LIBRARY*, 270 Montauk Hwy, 11976. SAN 312-4800. Tel: 631-283-2118. FAX: 631-283-7006. Web Site: www.parrishart.org. *Dir,* Susan Galardi
Founded 1955
Library Holdings: Bk Titles 5,000
Special Collections: Aline B Saarinen Library Coll; Moses & Ida Soyer Library Coll; William Merritt Chase Archives Coll
Wireless access
Function: Res libr
Restriction: Open by appt only

WATERFORD

P WATERFORD PUBLIC LIBRARY*, 117 Third St, 12188. SAN 312-6358. Tel: 518-237-0891. FAX: 518-237-2568. E-mail: watpublibrary@gmail.com. Web Site: www.waterfordlibrary.net. *Dir,* Timothy McDonough; E-mail: tmcdonough@sals.edu; *Ch Serv Librn,* Elizabeth Liddington; E-mail: lliddington@sals.edu; Staff 5 (MLS 2, Non-MLS 3)
Founded 1895. Pop 6,800; Circ 60,000
Library Holdings: AV Mats 4,532; Bk Vols 21,587; Per Subs 132; Talking Bks 1,340
Automation Activity & Vendor Info: (Acquisitions) Innovative Interfaces, Inc; (Cataloging) Innovative Interfaces, Inc; (Circulation) Innovative Interfaces, Inc; (ILL) Innovative Interfaces, Inc; (OPAC) Innovative Interfaces, Inc
Database Vendor: EBSCOhost
Wireless access
Mem of Southern Adirondack Library System
Open Mon & Thurs 9-8, Tues & Wed 9-6, Fri 9-5, Sat 10-3 (9-1 July & Aug), Sun (Sept-June) 12-4
Friends of the Library Group

WATERLOO

P WATERLOO LIBRARY & HISTORICAL SOCIETY*, 31 E Williams St, 13165. SAN 312-6366. Tel: 315-539-3313. FAX: 315-539-7798. *Dir,* Anne Stincic
Founded 1876. Pop 5,116; Circ 31,998
Library Holdings: Bk Titles 26,449; Per Subs 20
Subject Interests: Genealogy, Local hist
Automation Activity & Vendor Info: (Cataloging) Innovative Interfaces, Inc; (Circulation) Innovative Interfaces, Inc; (OPAC) Innovative Interfaces, Inc
Wireless access
Mem of Finger Lakes Library System
Open Mon-Wed 11-8, Thurs & Fri 11-5, Sat (Sept-June) 9-12

WATERTOWN

P EAST HOUNSFIELD FREE LIBRARY*, 19438 NYS Rte 3, 13601. SAN 312-6374. Tel: 315-788-0637. FAX: 315-836-3172. Web Site: www.easthounsfieldlibrary.org. *Dir,* Sandra Bliss; *Asst Librn,* Lois Boshane
Circ 3,879
Library Holdings: Bk Vols 3,892
Wireless access
Mem of North Country Library System
Open Tues & Thurs 5-8, Wed 1-4, Sat 10-1

P ROSWELL P FLOWER MEMORIAL LIBRARY*, 229 Washington St, 13601-3388. SAN 312-6382. Tel: 315-785-7705. FAX: 315-788-2584. E-mail: watlib@ncls.org. Web Site: www.flowermemoriallibrary.org. *Dir,* Maggie Waggoner; E-mail: mwaggoner@ncls.org; *Ch,* Ginger Tebo; *Ref Librn,* Yvonne Reff; Staff 11 (MLS 4, Non-MLS 7)
Founded 1904. Pop 26,705; Circ 140,893
Library Holdings: e-journals 28; Electronic Media & Resources 17; Bk Vols 193,616; Per Subs 140; Talking Bks 1,405; Videos 2,800
Subject Interests: Genealogy, Local hist
Automation Activity & Vendor Info: (Circulation) SirsiDynix; (OPAC) SirsiDynix
Wireless access
Mem of North Country Library System
Partic in Northern New York Library Network
Open Mon, Tues & Thurs (Winter) 9-8, Wed, Fri & Sat 9-5; Mon-Thurs (Summer) 8-8, Fri 8-4
Friends of the Library Group

S JEFFERSON COUNTY HISTORICAL SOCIETY LIBRARY*, 228 Washington St, 13601. SAN 325-9765. Tel: 315-782-3491. FAX: 315-782-2913. Web Site: www.jeffersoncountyhistory.org. *Dir,* Bill Wood; *Educ Curator,* Melissa Widrick; E-mail: educator@jeffersoncountyhistory.org
Library Holdings: Bk Vols 1,000
Special Collections: City Directories Coll (1830-1985); Nineteenth Century Maps of Jefferson County; Water Turbines Catalogue
Wireless access
Function: Ref serv available, Res libr
Publications: Exhibition Catalogues; JCHS Bulletin; Newsletter
Open Tues-Fri 10-5, Sat (May-Nov) 12-5

G NEW YORK STATE DEPARTMENT OF CORRECTIONAL SERVICES*, Watertown Correctional Facility Library, 23147 Swan Rd, 13601-9340. SAN 322-8185. Tel: 315-782-7490, Ext 4600. FAX: 315-782-7490, Ext 2099. *Librn,* Ken Hodosy; Staff 1 (MLS 1)
Library Holdings: Bk Titles 9,000; Bk Vols 9,500; Per Subs 84
Special Collections: Spanish Language & Culture
Subject Interests: African-Am hist
Automation Activity & Vendor Info: (Cataloging) Follett Software; (Circulation) Follett Software; (OPAC) Follett Software
Wireless access
Function: ILL available
Open Sun-Thurs 8-4

GL NEW YORK STATE SUPREME COURT*, Law Library at Watertown, Court House, 163 Arsenal St, 13601. SAN 312-6404. Tel: 315-785-3064. FAX: 315-785-3330. *In Charge,* Catherine Miller
Founded 1914
Library Holdings: Bk Titles 850; Bk Vols 45,000; Per Subs 34
Database Vendor: LexisNexis, Westlaw
Wireless access
Open Mon-Fri 8:30-4:30
Restriction: Circ limited

P NORTH COUNTRY LIBRARY SYSTEM*, 22072 County Rte 190, 13601-1066. SAN 312-6412. Tel: 315-782-5540. FAX: 315-782-6883. Web Site: www.nclsweb.org. *Dir,* Stephen B Bolton; *Bus Mgr,* Linda Lawler; Staff 8 (MLS 5, Non-MLS 3)
Founded 1947. Pop 372,990
Jul 2005-Jun 2006 Income $1,886,987. Mats Exp $157,153, Books $138,767, AV Mat $9,950, Electronic Ref Mat (Incl. Access Fees) $8,436. Sal $762,912 (Prof $283,202)
Library Holdings: AV Mats 2,585; Bk Vols 239,363; Per Subs 40; Talking Bks 2,403
Automation Activity & Vendor Info: (Cataloging) SirsiDynix; (Circulation) SirsiDynix; (OPAC) SirsiDynix
Database Vendor: SirsiDynix
Publications: Netbrary System Outreach Services (Newsletter); North Country Library News (Newsletter)
Member Libraries: Adams Center Free Library; Adams Free Library; Annie Porter Ainsworth Memorial Library; B Elizabeth Strong Memorial Library; Beaver Falls Library; Belleville Public Library; Bodman Memorial Library; Brownville-Glen Park Library; Canton Free Library; Cape Vincent Community Library; Carthage Free Library; Central Square Library; Clifton Community Library; Cogswell Free Public Library; Colton Hepburn Library; Constableville Village Library; Croghan Free Library; Crosby Public Library; Depauville Free Library; Dexter Free Library; East Hounsfield Free Library; Ellisburg Free Library; Evans Mills Public Library; Fulton Public Library; Hammond Free Library; Hannibal Free Library; Harrisville Free Library; Hawn Memorial Library; Hay Memorial Library; Henderson Free Library; Hepburn Library of Edwards; Hepburn Library of Hermon; Hepburn Library of Lisbon; Hepburn Library of Madrid; Hepburn Library of Norfolk; Hepburn Library of Waddington; Heuvelton Free Library; Hopkinton Town Library; Lowville Free Library; Lyme Free Library; Lyons Falls Free Library; Macsherry Library; Mannsville Free Library; Massena Public Library; Mexico Public Library; Morristown Public Library; New York State Department of Correctional Services; Norwood Library; Ogdensburg Public Library; Orleans Public Library; Oswego School District Public Library; Parish Public Library; Phoenix Public Library; Port Leyden Community Library; Potsdam Public Library; Pulaski Public Library; Reading Room Association of Gouverneur; Richville Free Library; Roswell P Flower Memorial Library; Russell Public Library; Sally Ploof Hunter Memorial Library; Theresa Free Library; Thousand Island Park Library; Town of Lewis Library; William H Bush Memorial Library
Partic in Northern New York Library Network; NY Libr Asn; OCLC Online Computer Library Center, Inc
Special Services for the Deaf - Bks on deafness & sign lang; Closed caption videos
Special Services for the Blind - BiFolkal kits; Bks on cassette; Bks on CD; Home delivery serv; Large print bks; Talking bks
Open Mon-Fri 8-4:30

M SAMARITAN MEDICAL CENTER*, Health Sciences Library, 830 Washington St, 13601. SAN 373-6962. Tel: 315-785-4191. FAX: 315-779-5173. Web Site: www.samaritanhealth.com/library.htm. *Dir, Libr Serv,* Jeffrey M Garvey; E-mail: jgarvey@shsny.com; *Librn,* Ellen Darabaner; *Tech Serv,* Michael Chartrand; Staff 5 (MLS 3, Non-MLS 2)
Library Holdings: Bk Titles 1,000; Per Subs 200
Automation Activity & Vendor Info: (Cataloging) LibLime; (Circulation) LibLime
Database Vendor: MD Consult, UpToDate
Wireless access
Open Mon-Fri 8-5:30

J STATE UNIVERSITY OF NEW YORK - JEFFERSON COMMUNITY COLLEGE*, Melvil Dewey Library, 1220 Coffeen St, 13601-1897. SAN 312-6390. Tel: 315-786-2225. FAX: 315-788-0716. Web Site: sunyjefferson.edu/library. *Dir,* Constance Holberg; Tel: 315-786-2224, E-mail: cholberg@sunyjefferson.edu; *Info Literacy,* John Thomas; Tel: 315-786-2314, E-mail: jthomas@sunyjefferson.edu; *Media Spec,* Jacquelyn Young; Tel: 315-786-2413, E-mail: jyoung@sunyjefferson.edu; *Ref Serv,* Carleen Huxley; E-mail: chuxley@sunnyjeferson.edu; Staff 4 (MLS 4)
Founded 1963. Enrl 3,700; Fac 70; Highest Degree: Associate
Library Holdings: DVDs 200; e-books 7,000; e-journals 7,000; Electronic Media & Resources 65; Bk Titles 54,000; Bk Vols 60,000; Per Subs 230; Videos 4,000
Subject Interests: Jefferson County local hist
Automation Activity & Vendor Info: (Cataloging) Ex Libris Group; (Circulation) Ex Libris Group; (Course Reserve) Ex Libris Group; (OPAC) Ex Libris Group; (Serials) Ex Libris Group
Database Vendor: Dialog, EBSCOhost, Gale Cengage Learning, JSTOR, LexisNexis, OCLC FirstSearch, OVID Technologies, ProQuest, Wilson - Wilson Web
Wireless access
Function: Archival coll, Doc delivery serv, Handicapped accessible, ILL available, Online searches, Orientations, Ref serv available, Telephone ref, VHS videos, Wheelchair accessible
Publications: Annual Report
Partic in Northern New York Library Network; Nylink; OCLC Online Computer Library Center, Inc; Westchester Academic Library Directors Organization (WALDO)
Special Services for the Deaf - Assistive tech; Bks on deafness & sign lang; Closed caption videos; Deaf publ
Special Services for the Blind - ZoomText magnification & reading software
Restriction: Open to students, fac & staff, Pub use on premises

S WATERTOWN DAILY TIMES LIBRARY*, 260 Washington St, 13601. SAN 322-9106. Tel: 315-782-1000, Ext 345. FAX: 315-661-2523. E-mail: news@wdt.net. Web Site: www.watertowndailytimes.com, www.wdt.net. *Chief Librn,* Lisa Carr; Staff 3 (MLS 1, Non-MLS 2)
Special Collections: Other Northern New York Newspapers, microfilm
Subject Interests: Northern NY hist
Open Tues-Thurs 1-3

WATERVILLE

P WATERVILLE PUBLIC LIBRARY*, 206 White St, 13480. SAN 312-6420. Tel: 315-841-4651. FAX: 315-841-4258. E-mail: waterville@midyork.org. Web Site: www.midyork.org/waterville/. *Dir,* Jeffrey Reynolds; *Asst Dir,* Amanda Briggs; Staff 1 (MLS 1)
Founded 1874. Pop 5,500; Circ 39,983
Library Holdings: CDs 1,121; Bk Vols 25,835; Per Subs 41; Videos 1,995
Special Collections: Waterville Times (local newspaper) 1855-1990, microfilm
Automation Activity & Vendor Info: (Cataloging) SirsiDynix; (Circulation) SirsiDynix
Wireless access
Mem of Mid-York Library System
Open Mon, Wed & Fri 10-5:30, Tues 2-5:30, Thurs 2-8, Sat 10-2
Friends of the Library Group
Branches: 1
DEANSBORO BRANCH, Marshall Community Ctr, Deansboro, 13328, SAN 329-5680. Tel: 315-841-4888. E-mail: waterville@midyork.org. Web Site: www.uhls.org/watervliet. *Br Mgr,* Margery Wilson
Library Holdings: Bk Vols 5,183; Per Subs 8; Videos 450
Open Mon 5:30-7:30, Tues 2-6, Thurs & Sat 9:30-11:30, Fri 9:30-11:30 & 2-4
Friends of the Library Group

WATERVLIET

P WATERVLIET PUBLIC LIBRARY*, 1501 Broadway, 12189-2895. SAN 312-6455. Tel: 518-274-4471. FAX: 518-271-0667. Web Site: www.watervlietpubliclibrary.org. *Dir,* Samantha Fagan; Staff 2 (MLS 1, Non-MLS 1)
Founded 1953. Pop 10,207; Circ 15,052
Library Holdings: Bk Vols 16,738; Per Subs 15
Special Collections: City Directories (1855 to present)
Automation Activity & Vendor Info: (Circulation) SirsiDynix; (OPAC) SirsiDynix
Wireless access
Mem of Upper Hudson Library System
Open Mon, Wed & Thurs 2-8, Tues 11-8, Fri 2-6, Sat 11-3

WATKINS GLEN

P WATKINS GLEN PUBLIC LIBRARY, 610 S Decatur St, 14891. SAN 312-6463. Tel: 607-535-2346. FAX: 607-535-7338. E-mail: watkins@stls.org. Web Site: www.watkinsglenlibrary.org. *Dir,* Harriet Eisman; *Asst Dir,* Linda Fowler; Staff 2.6 (MLS 0.6, Non-MLS 2)
Founded 1870. Pop 8,579; Circ 51,231
Jul 2013-Jun 2014 Income $175,138. Mats Exp $28,300, Books $22,500, Other Print Mats $2,300, AV Mat $3,500. Sal $89,508
Library Holdings: AV Mats 4,969; Bk Vols 32,984; Per Subs 42
Automation Activity & Vendor Info: (Circulation) SirsiDynix; (ILL) SirsiDynix; (OPAC) SirsiDynix; (Serials) SirsiDynix
Wireless access
Function: Art exhibits, Audio & video playback equip for onsite use, Bk reviews (Group), Bks on cassette, Bks on CD, Children's prog, Computer training, Computers for patron use, Copy machines, Electronic databases & coll, Fax serv, Free DVD rentals, Handicapped accessible, Holiday prog, ILL available, Instruction & testing, Mail & tel request accepted, Music CDs, Online cat, Online ref, Online searches, Photocopying/Printing, Prog for adults, Prog for children & young adult, Pub access computers, Scanner, Senior computer classes, Serves mentally handicapped consumers, Spoken cassettes & CDs, Spoken cassettes & DVDs, Story hour, Summer reading prog, Tax forms, Telephone ref, VHS videos, Web-catalog, Wheelchair accessible, Writing prog
Mem of Southern Tier Library System
Open Mon-Fri 11-5 & 7-9, Sat 10-2, Sun 2-4

WAVERLY

P WAVERLY READING CENTER*, 18 Elizabeth St, 14892. SAN 312-6471. Tel: 607-565-9341. FAX: 607-565-3960. Web Site: www.cefls.org/waverly.htm. *Dir,* Judy Wever; E-mail: jwever@westelcom.com; *Librn,* Todd Williams; Staff 1 (MLS 1)
Founded 1929. Pop 4,607; Circ 30,087
Jan 2006-Dec 2006 Income $110,422, State $1,500, City $12,000, County $7,561, Locally Generated Income $60,111, Other $29,250. Mats Exp $18,314, Books $16,646, AV Mat $1,668. Sal $53,271 (Prof $27,566)
Library Holdings: AV Mats 1,154; CDs 85; DVDs 89; Large Print Bks 746; Bk Vols 40,265; Per Subs 40; Videos 1,009
Special Collections: Tioga County Law Library
Subject Interests: Civil War, Local hist
Automation Activity & Vendor Info: (Cataloging) Innovative Interfaces, Inc; (Circulation) Innovative Interfaces, Inc; (OPAC) Innovative Interfaces, Inc
Database Vendor: EBSCOhost, Gale Cengage Learning, infoUSA, LearningExpress, OCLC FirstSearch, ProQuest, ReferenceUSA, TLC (The Library Corporation)
Wireless access
Function: Art exhibits, Audio & video playback equip for onsite use, Bks on cassette, Bks on CD, Children's prog, Computers for patron use, Copy machines, Digital talking bks, Electronic databases & coll, Handicapped accessible, ILL available, Music CDs, Online cat, Photocopying/Printing, Prog for adults, Prog for children & young adult, Summer reading prog, Tax forms, VHS videos
Mem of Clinton-Essex-Franklin Library System
Special Services for the Deaf - Closed caption videos
Special Services for the Blind - Bks on cassette
Open Tues, 11-6, Wed 10-6, Thurs 11-9, Fri 11-5, Sat 11-2

WAYLAND

P WAYLAND FREE LIBRARY*, Gunlocke Memorial Library, 101 W Naples St, 14572. SAN 312-648X. Tel: 585-728-5380. FAX: 585-728-5002. Web Site: www.gunlockelibrary.org. *Dir,* Karen Deutsch; E-mail: deutschk@stls.org; Staff 1 (MLS 1)
Founded 1913. Pop 5,000; Circ 35,477
Jan 2012-Dec 2012 Income $430,156, State $4,019, City $105,000, Federal $97,038, Locally Generated Income $20,214, Other $56,202. Mats Exp $19,599, Books $14,308, Per/Ser (Incl. Access Fees) $1,700, AV Mat $3,114, Electronic Ref Mat (Incl. Access Fees) $397. Sal $101,174 (Prof $36,720)
Library Holdings: Audiobooks 1,508; Bks on Deafness & Sign Lang 40; CDs 420; DVDs 1,821; e-books 4,336; Electronic Media & Resources 218; High Interest/Low Vocabulary Bk Vols 80; Large Print Bks 1,636; Bk Titles 28,052; Per Subs 87; Videos 348
Special Collections: Children with Developmental Disabilities (Parent Reference Coll); Local Newspapers, Microfilm; Railroad Coll
Subject Interests: Local hist
Automation Activity & Vendor Info: (Cataloging) SirsiDynix; (Circulation) SirsiDynix; (OPAC) SirsiDynix; (Serials) SirsiDynix
Database Vendor: EBSCO Information Services, Medline, OCLC WorldShare Interlibrary Loan
Wireless access
Function: Adult bk club, Bks on CD, Children's prog, Computer training, Computers for patron use, Copy machines, Family literacy, Fax serv, Free DVD rentals, Handicapped accessible, ILL available, Large print keyboards, Microfiche/film & reading machines, Music CDs, Online cat, OverDrive digital audio bks, Photocopying/Printing, Preschool outreach, Preschool reading prog, Printer for laptops & handheld devices, Prog for adults, Prog for children & young adult, Scanner, Senior computer classes, Senior outreach, Story hour, Summer reading prog, Tax forms, Wheelchair accessible
Mem of Southern Tier Library System
Partic in New York Online Virtual Electronic Library (NOVEL)
Special Services for the Deaf - TTY equip
Special Services for the Blind - Braille bks

WEBSTER

P WEBSTER PUBLIC LIBRARY*, Webster Plaza, 980 Ridge Rd, 14580. SAN 312-6501. Tel: 585-872-7075. Web Site: www.websterlibrary.org. *Dir,* Theresa Bennett; E-mail: tbennett@mcls.rochester.lib.ny.us; *Asst Dir,* Diane Kozlowski; *Adult Serv,* Greg Benoit; *Ch Serv,* Adrienne Furness; *Ch Serv,* Jason Poole; *Electronic Res,* Patricia Ligozio; *Teen Serv, YA Serv,* Olivia Durant; Staff 24 (MLS 7, Non-MLS 17)
Founded 1929. Pop 37,926; Circ 645,314
Library Holdings: Bk Titles 92,702; Bk Vols 138,053; Per Subs 243
Automation Activity & Vendor Info: (Circulation) CARL.Solution (TLC); (OPAC) CARL.Solution (TLC)
Database Vendor: ReferenceUSA
Wireless access
Mem of Monroe County Library System
Open Mon-Thurs (Winter) 10-9, Fri 10-6, Sat 10-5, Sun 1-4; Mon-Thurs (Summer) 10-9, Fri 10-6, Sat 10-1
Friends of the Library Group

WEEDSPORT

P WEEDSPORT LIBRARY*, 2795 E Brutus St, 13166-8720. (Mail add: PO Box 1165, 13166-1165), SAN 325-9781. Tel: 315-834-6222. FAX: 315-834-8621. E-mail: weedlib@twcny.rr.com. Web Site: www.flls.org/weedsport. *Dir,* Cheryl Austin; *Asst Dir,* Diana Grant
Library Holdings: Bk Vols 10,000; Per Subs 15
Special Collections: Local History; References, clips, docs, maps; School Texts & Photographs
Subject Interests: Genealogy, Local govt
Automation Activity & Vendor Info: (Cataloging) Innovative Interfaces, Inc; (Circulation) Innovative Interfaces, Inc; (OPAC) Innovative Interfaces, Inc
Wireless access
Mem of Finger Lakes Library System
Open Mon-Thurs 10-9, Sat 10-2
Friends of the Library Group

WELLSVILLE

P DAVID A HOWE PUBLIC LIBRARY*, 155 N Main St, 14895. SAN 312-6544. Tel: 585-593-3410. FAX: 585-593-4176. E-mail: wellsville@stls.org. Web Site: www.davidahowelibrary.org. *Dir,* Michelle La Voie; Staff 1 (MLS 1)
Founded 1894. Pop 5,241; Circ 127,417
Library Holdings: AV Mats 8,111; Bk Vols 102,476; Per Subs 91
Special Collections: Bird's Egg Coll (Charles Munson Coll); Children's Reference Books; Currier & Ives Coll; Indian Artifacts (Avery Mosher Coll); Lincoln Pictures (Coyle Coll). State Document Depository
Automation Activity & Vendor Info: (Circulation) SirsiDynix; (OPAC) SirsiDynix
Wireless access
Mem of Southern Tier Library System
Open Mon-Tues & Thurs 10-9, Fri 10-6, Sat (Sept-May) 10-5
Friends of the Library Group

C STATE UNIVERSITY OF NEW YORK, SCHOOL OF APPLIED TECHNOLOGY*, 2530 River Rd, 14895. SAN 351-8132. Tel: 585-593-6270, Ext 3115. FAX: 607-587-3120. Web Site: www.alfredstae.edu. *Librn,* Cindy Flurschutz
Library Holdings: Bk Vols 3,300
Subject Interests: Automotive, Bldg, Construction trades, Culinary trades
Open Mon-Fri (Sept-May) 8-12 & 1-4

WEST BABYLON

P WEST BABYLON PUBLIC LIBRARY*, 211 Rte 109, 11704. SAN 324-4873. Tel: 631-669-5445. FAX: 631-669-6539. Web Site: wbab.suffolk.lib.ny.us. *Dir,* Anne Marie Dolan; *Ad, Computer Serv Librn,* Jill Ballou; *Ch Serv Librn,* Ilana Silver; *Ref Serv Librn,* Nicole Haas; *YA Librn,* Azuree Agnello; Staff 31 (MLS 12, Non-MLS 19)
Founded 1982. Pop 28,271; Circ 323,739
Jul 2009-Jun 2010 Income $3,058,748, Locally Generated Income $2,972,937, Other $85,811. Mats Exp $328,340, Books $174,937, Per/Ser (Incl. Access Fees) $12,925, AV Mat $57,722, Electronic Ref Mat (Incl. Access Fees) $82,756. Sal $1,497,771 (Prof $819,945)
Library Holdings: Audiobooks 8,704; AV Mats 5,841; e-books 5,623; Electronic Media & Resources 5,010; Bk Vols 97,687; Per Subs 227; Videos 3,736
Wireless access
Publications: Newsletter (Monthly)
Mem of Suffolk Cooperative Library System
Special Services for the Deaf - TTY equip; Videos & decoder
Open Mon-Thurs 10-9, Fri & Sat 10-5, Sun (Oct-May) 1-5
Friends of the Library Group

WEST BRENTWOOD

PILGRIM PSYCHIATRIC CENTER

M MEDICAL LIBRARY, BLDG 82*, 998 Crooked Hill Rd, 11717-1087, SAN 311-3914. Tel: 631-761-3500. *Librn,* Irving Treadwell
Founded 1958
Library Holdings: Bk Titles 1,800; Per Subs 70
Special Collections: History of Psychiatry
Subject Interests: Behav sci, Med, Nursing, Philos, Psychiat, Psychol, Soc sci
Partic in Long Island Library Resources Council; Medical & Scientific Libraries of Long Island

M PILGRIM READING ROOM & PATIENTS LIBRARY*, Bldg 102, 998 Crooked Hill Rd, 11717-1087, SAN 354-3609. Tel: 631-761-3813. FAX: 631-761-3103. E-mail: pgetjxm@omh.state.ny.us. *Coordr,* Jeanne Murphy; Staff 2 (Non-MLS 2)

Founded 1933
Library Holdings: Audiobooks 100; High Interest/Low Vocabulary Bk Vols 50; Large Print Bks 35; Bk Vols 8,000; Per Subs 26
Subject Interests: Gen interest
Special Services for the Blind - Closed circuit TV; Reader equip
Open Mon-Thurs 9-11:30, 1-3 & 5:30-8, Fri 9-11:30 & 1-3, Sat 9-11 & 1-3

WEST CHAZY

P DODGE LIBRARY*, Nine Fisk Rd, 12992. (Mail add: PO Box 226, 12992-0226), SAN 312-6560. Tel: 518-493-6131. FAX: 518-493-3393. E-mail: dodge_library@yahoo.com. Web Site: www.nnyln.org/dodgewestchazy/. *Dir,* Larry Hahn
Circ 9,097
Library Holdings: Bk Vols 7,500; Per Subs 15
Special Collections: New England, New York, Pennsylvania & New Jersey Genealogy (Nell B Sullivan Memorial Coll)
Subject Interests: Local hist
Automation Activity & Vendor Info: (Cataloging) Horizon; (Circulation) Horizon; (OPAC) Horizon
Wireless access
Mem of Clinton-Essex-Franklin Library System
Open Tues & Thurs 12:30-6, Sat 9-12

WEST HARRISON

C FORDHAM UNIVERSITY WESTCHESTER LIBRARY*, 400 Westchester Ave, 10604. SAN 312-5572. Tel: 914-367-3426. Reference Tel: 914-367-3061. Web Site: www.library.fordham.edu. *Head Librn,* Diane Deery; Tel: 914-367-3058; *Cat,* Dympna Haber, Sr; Tel: 914-367-3056, E-mail: dhaber@fordham.edu; *Circ,* Robert Jensen; E-mail: rjensen@fordham.edu; *Circ,* Stephen J Lalli; *Circ,* Eileen Reid; E-mail: eireid@fordham.edu; *Ref Serv,* Diane Batemarco; *Ref Serv,* Deirdre Corwin; Tel: 914-367-3055; *Ref Serv,* Tony Iodice; Staff 6 (MLS 4, Non-MLS 2)
Founded 2008. Enrl 2,472; Fac 173; Highest Degree: Master
Library Holdings: Bk Titles 22,029; Bk Vols 23,071
Automation Activity & Vendor Info: (Acquisitions) SirsiDynix; (Cataloging) SirsiDynix; (Circulation) SirsiDynix; (ILL) OCLC ILLiad; (OPAC) SirsiDynix; (Serials) SirsiDynix
Database Vendor: EBSCOhost, Gale Cengage Learning, LexisNexis, OCLC FirstSearch, OVID Technologies, ProQuest, Wilson - Wilson Web
Function: For res purposes
Partic in Metropolitan New York Library Council; Westchester Academic Library Directors Organization (WALDO)
Restriction: Open to students, fac & staff

WEST HAVERSTRAW

M HELEN HAYES HOSPITAL*, Medical Library, Rte 9 W, 10993. SAN 312-6579. Tel: 845-786-4185. Interlibrary Loan Service Tel: 845-786-4188. FAX: 845-786-4978. Web Site: hospitalservices.senylrc.org/hhh. *Dir,* Kathleen Fiola; E-mail: fiolak@helenhayeshosp.org; Staff 2 (MLS 1, Non-MLS 1)
Founded 1960
Library Holdings: Bk Vols 1,500; Per Subs 100
Subject Interests: Arthritis, Hearing, Neurology, Occupational therapy, Orthopedics, Phys therapy, Rehabilitation med, Speech
Database Vendor: EBSCOhost
Wireless access
Partic in Health Info Librs of Westchester (HILOW); Middle Atlantic Regional Med Libr Prog; Southeastern New York Library Resources Council
Open Mon-Fri 12-4

WEST HEMPSTEAD

P WEST HEMPSTEAD PUBLIC LIBRARY*, 500 Hempstead Ave, 11552. SAN 312-6587. Tel: 516-481-6591. FAX: 516-481-2608. E-mail: reference@whplibrary.org. Web Site: www.whplibrary.org. *Dir,* Regina Mascia; E-mail: regina.mascia@whnypl.org; Staff 45 (MLS 15, Non-MLS 30)
Founded 1965. Pop 16,931; Circ 173,152
Jul 2006-Jun 2007 Income $2,988,403. Mats Exp $202,272, Books $130,772, Per/Ser (Incl. Access Fees) $8,500, AV Equip $2,500, AV Mat $28,500, Electronic Ref Mat (Incl. Access Fees) $32,000. Sal $963,410 (Prof $475,744)
Library Holdings: Audiobooks 829; CDs 3,800; DVDs 1,372; Large Print Bks 1,000; Bk Vols 86,368; Per Subs 156; Videos 2,500
Automation Activity & Vendor Info: (Acquisitions) Innovative Interfaces, Inc - Millenium; (Cataloging) Innovative Interfaces, Inc - Millenium; (Circulation) Innovative Interfaces, Inc; (OPAC) Innovative Interfaces, Inc - Millenium
Database Vendor: CountryWatch, CredoReference, EBSCOhost, Electric Library, Facts on File, Gale Cengage Learning, Grolier Online, OCLC FirstSearch, Oxford Online, ProQuest, ReferenceUSA
Wireless access
Publications: Quarterly Newsletter
Mem of Nassau Library System
Partic in Long Island Library Resources Council; New York State Interlibrary Loan Network (NYSILL)
Special Services for the Blind - Large print bks
Friends of the Library Group

WEST HURLEY

P WEST HURLEY PUBLIC LIBRARY*, 42 Clover St, 12491. SAN 312-6595. Tel. 845-679-6405. FAX: 845-679-2144. E mail: mailbox@westhurleylibrary.org. Web Site: westhurleylibrary.org. *Dir,* Kara Lustiber; Staff 2 (MLS 1, Non-MLS 1)
Pop 3,504; Circ 35,760
Jan 2009-Dec 2009 Income $166,610, State $1,220, Locally Generated Income $165,390. Mats Exp $25,022, Books $15,041, Other Print Mats $905, AV Mat $9,076. Sal $49,540 (Prof $23,154)
Library Holdings: Audiobooks 1,103; AV Mats 770; Bk Titles 20,114; Per Subs 22
Subject Interests: Local hist
Automation Activity & Vendor Info: (Cataloging) Innovative Interfaces, Inc; (OPAC) Innovative Interfaces, Inc
Database Vendor: EBSCOhost, Gale Cengage Learning, Overdrive, Inc, ProQuest
Wireless access
Function: Adult bk club, Bks on CD, Children's prog, Computer training, Computers for patron use, Copy machines, Digital talking bks, Electronic databases & coll, Fax serv, Handicapped accessible, Holiday prog, ILL available, Music CDs, Online ref, Photocopying/Printing, Prog for adults, Prog for children & young adult, Spoken cassettes & CDs, Spoken cassettes & DVDs, Story hour, Summer reading prog, Tax forms
Mem of Mid-Hudson Library System
Open Mon & Wed 1-7, Tues & Fri 10-6, Sat 10-4
Friends of the Library Group

WEST ISLIP

M GOOD SAMARITAN HOSPITAL*, Medical Library, 1000 Montauk Hwy, 11795. SAN 312-6609. Tel: 631-376-3380. FAX: 631-376-4166. *Librn,* Maryann Emsig; E-mail: maryann.emsig@chsli.org; Staff 1 (MLS 1)
Founded 1961
Library Holdings: Bk Titles 600; Per Subs 80
Special Collections: Medical Coll, texts & journals
Database Vendor: PubMed
Function: Ref serv available
Partic in Medical & Scientific Libraries of Long Island
Restriction: Staff use only

P WEST ISLIP PUBLIC LIBRARY*, Three Higbie Lane, 11795-3999. SAN 312-6617. Tel: 631-661-7080. FAX: 631-661-7137. Administration FAX: 631-661-6573. Web Site: www.wipublib.org. *Dir,* Andrew Hamm; *Ch Serv,* A McGrory; *Coll Develop, Ref,* Grace O'Connor; Staff 12 (MLS 12)
Founded 1957. Pop 28,907
Library Holdings: AV Mats 23,130; Bk Vols 201,383; Per Subs 361
Special Collections: Career Center (Grace O'Connor)
Automation Activity & Vendor Info: (Acquisitions) Innovative Interfaces, Inc; (Cataloging) Innovative Interfaces, Inc; (Circulation) Innovative Interfaces, Inc; (Course Reserve) Innovative Interfaces, Inc; (ILL) Innovative Interfaces, Inc; (OPAC) Innovative Interfaces, Inc
Database Vendor: Gale Cengage Learning, Innovative Interfaces, Inc, OCLC FirstSearch
Wireless access
Publications: Library Newsletter; The Source
Mem of Suffolk Cooperative Library System
Friends of the Library Group

WEST LEYDEN

P TOWN OF LEWIS LIBRARY*, 5213 Osceola Rd, 13489. Tel: 315-942-6813. Web Site: westleyden.northcountrylibraries.org. *Dir,* Susan Kornatowski
Mem of North Country Library System
Open Tues 10:30am-11:30am, Thurs 2-4 & 6:30-8

WEST NYACK

P WEST NYACK FREE LIBRARY*, 65 Strawtown Rd, 10994. SAN 312-6633. Tel: 845-358-6081. FAX: 845-358-4071. E-mail: staff@westnyacklib.org. Web Site: www.westnyacklib.org. *Dir,* Eugenia Schatoff; *Head, Circ, Tech Serv Supvr,* Vicki Ernst; *Prog Coordr,* Susan Ferber; *Admin Serv,* Jennifer Visione; *Ch Serv,* Myrna Sigal; *Coll Develop,*

Eva Gruenebaum; *ILL,* Ellen Kardon; *Ref,* Olga Bell; Staff 3.9 (MLS 3.3, Non-MLS 0.6)
Founded 1959. Pop 7,649; Circ 94,433
Jan 2008-Dec 2008 Income $948,055. Mats Exp $106,750
Library Holdings: AV Mats 9,201; Bk Vols 48,892; Per Subs 155
Automation Activity & Vendor Info: (Cataloging) Horizon; (Circulation) Horizon; (ILL) Horizon; (OPAC) Horizon
Wireless access
Publications: Newsletter
Mem of Ramapo Catskill Library System
Partic in Library Association of Rockland County; NY Libr Asn
Open Mon-Thurs 9:30-9, Fri 9:30-5, Sat 10-5, Sun 1-5
Friends of the Library Group

WEST POINT

UNITED STATES ARMY

AM USA MEDDAC*, Keller Army Community Hospital, Bldg 900, US Military Academy, 10996-1197, SAN 354-3676. Tel: 845-938-4883. FAX: 845-938-0114. *Librn,* Joan M Stehn; E-mail: joan.stehn@us.army.mil; Staff 1 (MLS 1)
Library Holdings: e-books 500; e-journals 325; Bk Vols 50; Per Subs 16; Spec Interest Per Sub 16
Special Collections: Sports Medicine Coll
Subject Interests: Sports med
Function: Web-Braille, Web-catalog
Partic in Army Medical Department - Medical Library & Information Network (AMEDD MEDLI-NET); Federal Library & Information Center Committee (FLICC); Southeastern New York Library Resources Council
Restriction: Mil only
Friends of the Library Group

A WEST POINT POST LIBRARY*, 622 Swift Rd, 10996-1981, SAN 354-3668. Tel: 845-938-2974. FAX: 845-938-3019. *Librn,* Suzanne Moskala
Library Holdings: Bk Titles 33,000; Bk Vols 37,000; Per Subs 65
Subject Interests: Mil hist
Automation Activity & Vendor Info: (Circulation) EOS International
Partic in OCLC Online Computer Library Center, Inc

C UNITED STATES MILITARY ACADEMY LIBRARY*, Jefferson Hall Library & Learning Center, 758 Cullum Rd, 10996. SAN 312-6641. Tel: 845-938-3833. Circulation Tel: 845-938-2230. Interlibrary Loan Service Tel: 845-938-3752. Reference Tel: 845-938-8325. FAX: 845-938-4000. Web Site: www.library.usma.edu. *Assoc Dean, Librn,* Christopher Barth; E-mail: christopher.barth@usma.edu; *Assoc Dir, Access Serv,* Deborah DiSalvo; *Assoc Dir, Info Gateway,* Dan Pritchard; *Assoc Dir, Mat Proc,* David Stockton; *Assoc Dir, Spec Coll & Archives,* Suzanne Christoff; *Assoc Dir, Syst Mgt,* Christine Bassett; *Access Serv Librn,* Darrell Hankins; *Access Serv Librn,* Karen Shea; *Admin Serv Librn,* Melinda Mosley; *AV Librn,* Michael Arden; *Cat Librn,* Dawn L Crumpler; *Cat Librn,* Marie Dennett; *Cat Librn,* Heather Goyette; *Doc Librn,* Paul Nergelovic; *Ref Librn,* Alan Aimone; *Ref Librn,* Edward Dacey; *Ref Librn,* Celeste Evans; *Ref Librn,* Laura Mosher; *Syst Librn,* Justin Kovalcik; *Syst Librn,* Tietze Larry; *Admin Supvr,* Pam Long; *Curator of Archives,* Alicia Mauldin-Ware; *Curator, Rare Bks,* Elaine McConnell; *Ms Curator,* Susan Lintelmann. Subject Specialists: *Humanities,* Dawn L Crumpler
Founded 1802. Highest Degree: Bachelor
Special Collections: Cadet Textbooks; Chess Coll; Hudson Highlands History; Military Arts & Sciences; Omar N Bradley Papers; Orientalia; Papers & Writings of Academy Graduates; US Army History; West Pointiana. US Document Depository
Automation Activity & Vendor Info: (OPAC) Innovative Interfaces, Inc - Millenium; (Serials) Innovative Interfaces, Inc - Millenium
Wireless access
Publications: Archives & Manuscript Inventory Lists; Friends of the West Point Library Newsletter (Large print newspapers); Library Handbook; New Accessions; Subject Bibliographies
Partic in Connect NY; OCLC Online Computer Library Center, Inc; Southeastern New York Library Resources Council
Open Mon-Thurs 7am-10:45pm, Fri & Sat 7am-9pm, Sun 11-10:45
Restriction: Authorized patrons

WEST SAYVILLE

S LONG ISLAND MARITIME MUSEUM LIBRARY*, 86 West Ave, 11796-1908. (Mail add: PO Box 184, 11796-0184), SAN 312-665X. Tel: 631-447-8679, 631-854-4974. FAX: 631-854-4979. E-mail: limm@limaritime.org. Web Site: www.limaritime.org. *Dir,* Natasha Alexenko; *Librn,* Barbara Forde; E-mail: barbaralimm@gmail.com
Founded 1966
Library Holdings: Bk Titles 2,500
Special Collections: Photograph Coll, copy prints, glass plates, original & copy negatives, original historic prints, slides
Subject Interests: America's Cup races, Boatbuilding, Groundings, Lifesaving, Local captains, Local hist, Local shipwrecks, Racing, Shellfishing, Ship models, Vessels, Wildfowling, Yachting
Wireless access
Restriction: Open by appt only

WEST SENECA

P WEST SENECA PUBLIC LIBRARY*, 1300 Union Rd, 14224. SAN 312-6676. Tel: 716-674-2928. FAX: 716-674-9206. Web Site: www.buffalolib.org/libraries/WestSeneca/index.asp. *Dir,* Cathy Foertch; Staff 3 (MLS 3)
Founded 1935. Circ 332,994
Library Holdings: Bk Vols 65,000
Automation Activity & Vendor Info: (Cataloging) SirsiDynix; (Circulation) SirsiDynix; (OPAC) SirsiDynix
Mem of Buffalo & Erie County Public Library System
Open Mon-Thurs 10-9, Fri 10-6, Sat 10-4
Friends of the Library Group

WEST SHOKAN

P OLIVE FREE LIBRARY ASSOCIATION*, 4033 Rte 28A, 12494. SAN 312-6684. Tel: 845-657-2482. FAX: 845-657-2664. E-mail: helpdesk@olivefreelibrary.org. Web Site: olivefreelibrary.org. *Dir,* Katie Scott-Childress; *Asst Dir,* Ruth Anne Muller
Founded 1952. Pop 4,000
Library Holdings: Bk Titles 35,000; Per Subs 52
Automation Activity & Vendor Info: (Cataloging) Innovative Interfaces, Inc; (Circulation) Innovative Interfaces, Inc; (ILL) Innovative Interfaces, Inc; (Media Booking) Innovative Interfaces, Inc; (OPAC) Innovative Interfaces, Inc
Wireless access
Mem of Mid-Hudson Library System
Open Mon & Wed 10-8, Tues & Thurs 10-5, Sat 10-4

WEST WINFIELD

P WEST WINFIELD LIBRARY*, 179 South St, 13491-2826. (Mail add: PO Box 487, 13491-0487), SAN 312-6692. Tel: 315-822-6394. FAX: 315-822-6394. E-mail: westwinfield@midyork.org. Web Site: www.midyork.org/westwinfield. *Dir,* Ruth Rowe
Founded 1895. Pop 871; Circ 25,196
Library Holdings: Bk Vols 22,000; Per Subs 16
Automation Activity & Vendor Info: (Cataloging) SirsiDynix; (Circulation) SirsiDynix; (OPAC) SirsiDynix; (Serials) SirsiDynix
Wireless access
Mem of Mid-York Library System
Open Mon, Tues, Thurs & Fri 12:30-5:30, Wed 10-12 & 6-8, Sat 10-12
Friends of the Library Group

WESTBURY

P WESTBURY MEMORIAL PUBLIC LIBRARY*, 445 Jefferson St, 11590. SAN 354-3870. Tel: 516-333-0176. FAX: 516-333-1752. E-mail: contactus@westburylibrary.org. Web Site: www.westburylibrary.org. *Dir,* Cathleen Towey; E-mail: cathleentowey@westburylibrary.org; *Asst Dir, Head, Ref,* Colleen McCrea; E-mail: colleenmccrea@westburylibrary.org; Staff 32 (MLS 8, Non-MLS 24)
Founded 1924. Pop 25,488
Library Holdings: Bk Vols 99,500; Per Subs 100
Special Collections: Old English & American Children's Books
Automation Activity & Vendor Info: (Acquisitions) Innovative Interfaces, Inc - Millenium; (Cataloging) Innovative Interfaces, Inc - Millenium; (Circulation) Innovative Interfaces, Inc - Millenium; (Course Reserve) Innovative Interfaces, Inc - Millenium; (ILL) Innovative Interfaces, Inc - Millenium; (OPAC) Innovative Interfaces, Inc - Millenium; (Serials) Innovative Interfaces, Inc - Millenium
Wireless access
Publications: Bi-Monthly Program Schedules; Newsletters
Mem of Nassau Library System
Open Mon 10-9, Tues-Fri 9-9, Sat 9-5 (9-1 July-Aug), Sun 1-5
Branches: 1
CHILDREN'S LIBRARY, 374 School St, 11590, SAN 354-3900. Tel: 516-333-0176. E-mail: contactus@westburylibrary.org. *Head, Children's Libr,* Emily Farrell; E-mail: emilyfarrell@westburylibrary.org
Library Holdings: Bk Vols 18,500; Per Subs 17
Special Collections: Old Children's Books
Open Mon 10-9, Tues-Thurs 9-9, Fri & Sat 9-5, Sat (9-1 July-Aug), Sun 1-5

WESTERLO

P WESTERLO PUBLIC LIBRARY*, 604 State Rte 143, 12193. (Mail add: PO Box 267, 12193), SAN 376-3072. Tel: 518-797-3415. FAX: 518-797-3415. Web Site: www.westerlolibrary.org. *Dir,* Sue A Hoadley; E-mail: director@westerlolibrary.org; Staff 1 (MLS 1)
Founded 1986. Pop 3,466; Circ 15,997
Jan 2010-Dec 2010 Income $74,017. Mats Exp $6,812, Books $5,052, AV Mat $1,760. Sal $46,145 (Prof $25,000)
Library Holdings: Audiobooks 513; CDs 230; DVDs 1,415; Large Print Bks 87; Bk Titles 10,345; Per Subs 24
Automation Activity & Vendor Info: (Cataloging) SirsiDynix; (OPAC) SirsiDynix
Database Vendor: SirsiDynix
Wireless access
Mem of Upper Hudson Library System
Open Mon 2-6, Tues 2-8, Wed & Sat 9-2, Thurs 3-8, Fri 4-8

WESTERNVILLE

P WESTERN TOWN LIBRARY*, 9172 Main St, 13486. (Mail add: PO Box 247, 13486-0247), SAN 312-6730. Tel: 315-827-4118. FAX: 315-827-4118. *Librn,* Kathryn Dorr; *Asst Librn,* Rebecca Barnes; *Asst Librn,* Sandrine Copeland
Founded 1921. Pop 2,029
Library Holdings: Bk Titles 7,214; Per Subs 69
Database Vendor: EBSCOhost
Mem of Mid-York Library System
Open Tues-Thurs 2-8, Sat 10-Noon
Friends of the Library Group

WESTFIELD

S CHAUTAUQUA COUNTY HISTORICAL SOCIETY & MCCLURG MUSEUM LIBRARY*, Main & Portage St, 14787-0007. (Mail add: PO Box 7, 14787-0007), SAN 312-6749. Tel: 716-326-2977. E-mail: mcclurg@fairpoint.net. Web Site: www.mcclurgmuseum.org. *Pres,* James O'Brien
Founded 1950
Library Holdings: Bk Titles 2,000
Special Collections: Correspondence (Albion Tourgee Coll), micro; Diaries (E T Foote Papers)
Subject Interests: Chautauqua County hist, Genealogy
Publications: History of Chautauqua County, 1938-1978
Open Tues-Sat 10-4
Restriction: Open to pub for ref only

P PATTERSON LIBRARY*, 40 S Portage St, 14787. SAN 312-6757. Tel: 716-326-2154. FAX: 716-326-2554. E-mail: pattersondirector@gmail.com. Web Site: www.pattersonlibrary.info. *Dir,* Eli Guinnee; *Ref,* Janice Hogenboom; Staff 10 (MLS 2, Non-MLS 8)
Founded 1896. Pop 5,194; Circ 69,694
Library Holdings: Bk Vols 38,812; Per Subs 3,063
Special Collections: Genealogy & Local History (Crandall Coll); Mounted Birds; Photographs (Mateer Coll & Sherman Coll); Shell Coll; World War I Posters. Oral History
Subject Interests: Antiques, Collectibles, Cooking, Gardening, Local hist
Automation Activity & Vendor Info: (Cataloging) SIRSI Unicorn; (Circulation) SIRSI Unicorn; (OPAC) SIRSI Unicorn
Wireless access
Publications: Patterson Library; Westfield's Magnificent Legacy by M Poshka
Friends of the Library Group

WESTHAMPTON BEACH

P WESTHAMPTON FREE LIBRARY*, Seven Library Ave, 11978-2697. SAN 312-6773. Tel: 631-288-3335. FAX: 631-288-5715. E-mail: whamlib@suffolk.lib.ny.us. Web Site: www.westhamptonfreelibrary.org. *Libr Dir,* Matthew Bollerman; *Head, Circ,* Jan Camarda; *Head, Ref,* Dave Jones; *Ch Serv,* Leslie Milrod; Staff 7 (MLS 4, Non-MLS 3)
Founded 1897. Pop 9,405; Circ 175,000
Library Holdings: AV Mats 4,728; Bk Vols 43,345; Per Subs 181
Automation Activity & Vendor Info: (Cataloging) PALS; (Circulation) PALS; (OPAC) PALS
Wireless access
Function: ILL available
Publications: Newsletter
Mem of Suffolk Cooperative Library System
Open Mon-Fri 9:30-9, Sat 9:30-5, Sun 1-5
Friends of the Library Group

WESTMORELAND

P WESTMORELAND READING CENTER*, 50 Station Rd, 13490. (Mail add: PO Box 310, 13490-0310). Tel: 315-853-8001, Ext 5. Web Site: www.midyork.org/librarylist/libraryinfo/westmoreland.html. *Dir,* Riley McFadden
Library Holdings: AV Mats 900; Bk Titles 1,100; Talking Bks 100
Mem of Mid-York Library System
Open Mon & Fri (Winter) 2-5, Tues 5-8, Wed 8-12, Thurs 1-7; Mon (Summer) 2-5, Tues 5-9, Wed 8-12, Thurs 1-7

WESTPORT

P WESTPORT LIBRARY ASSOCIATION*, PO Box 436, 12993-0436. SAN 312-6781. Tel: 518-962-8219. FAX: 518-962-8219. E-mail: library12993@gmail.com. Web Site: www.westportnylibrary.org. *Libr Dir,* Daniel Van Olpen
Founded 1887. Circ 7,980
Library Holdings: Bk Titles 15,000; Bk Vols 16,000
Automation Activity & Vendor Info: (Cataloging) Horizon; (Circulation) Horizon; (OPAC) Horizon; (Serials) Horizon
Wireless access
Mem of Clinton-Essex-Franklin Library System
Partic in Connecticut Library Consortium
Open Mon-Tues & Thurs 10-6, Sat 10-2

WHITE PLAINS

J BERKELEY COLLEGE*, White Plains Campus, 99 Church St, 10601. SAN 378-3979. Tel: 914-694-1122, Ext 3371. Web Site: www.berkeleycollege.edu. *Dir,* James B Leftwich; Tel: 914-694-1122, Ext 3370, E-mail: jbl@berkeleycollege.edu; *Instrul Serv Librn, Ref Librn,* Ed Rivera; Staff 2 (MLS 2)
Library Holdings: Bk Titles 12,000; Per Subs 100
Subject Interests: Bus, Computers, Fashion, Mkt
Automation Activity & Vendor Info: (Circulation) TLC (The Library Corporation); (OPAC) TLC (The Library Corporation)
Wireless access
Function: AV serv, ILL available
Partic in Metrop Wash Libr Coun
Open Mon-Thurs 8am-10pm, Fri 8-4, Sat 9-3:30

L LIBRARY OF THE LEGAL AID SOCIETY OF WESTCHESTER COUNTY*, One N Broadway, Ste 910, 10601-2352. SAN 312-6838. Tel: 914-286-3400. FAX: 914-682-4112. *Librn,* Mina Pease; E-mail: mbpease@laswest.org; *Coll Develop,* S Pittari
Founded 1936
Library Holdings: Bk Vols 6,200; Per Subs 12
Subject Interests: Criminology, Matrimonial legal mat
Database Vendor: LexisNexis, Westlaw
Open Mon-Fri 9-5

MERCY COLLEGE
See Dobbs Ferry

S NATIONAL ECONOMIC RESEARCH ASSOCIATES, INC*, 360 Hamilton Ave, 10th Flr, 10601. SAN 311-922X. Tel: 914-448-4000. FAX: 914-448-4040. *Dir, Info Res & Knowledge Mgt,* Barbara Hirsh; Tel: 914-448-4090, E-mail: barbara.hirsh@nera.com; *Mgr, Info Res N Am,* Jennifer Bennett; Tel: 212-345-2993, E-mail: jennifer.bennett@nera.com; *Mgr, Knowledge Mgt,* Janice Keeler; Tel: 312-573-2813, E-mail: janice.keeler@nera.com; *Sr Assoc, Info Res N Am,* William Chamis; Tel: 212-345-9304, E-mail: william.chamis@nera.com; *Sr Assoc, Info Res N Am,* Barbara Eames; Tel: 202-466-9271, E-mail: barbara.eames@nera.com; *Sr Assoc, Info Res N Am,* Joan Wolff; Tel: 213-346-3028, E-mail: joan.wolff@nera.com; *Assoc, Info Res,* Taj Parmesar; Tel: 914-448-4064, E-mail: taj.parmesar@nera.com; Staff 6.9 (MLS 5.9, Non-MLS 1)
Founded 1961
Library Holdings: Bk Titles 7,000; Per Subs 350
Subject Interests: Antitrust, Bus, Econ, Energy economics, Environment, Financial, Intellectual property, Securities, Transfer pricing, Utilities
Automation Activity & Vendor Info: (Cataloging) Livelink for Libraries; (Circulation) Livelink for Libraries; (OPAC) Livelink for Libraries; (Serials) Livelink for Libraries
Database Vendor: Altarama Systems & Services, Bloomberg, Dialog, Dun & Bradstreet, EBSCO Information Services, EBSCOhost, Factiva.com, Factset, Gale Cengage Learning, HeinOnline, Hoovers, IHS, LexisNexis, OCLC FirstSearch, OCLC WorldShare Interlibrary Loan, OneSource, ProQuest, Standard & Poor's, ValueLine, Westlaw

M NEW YORK PRESBYTERIAN HOSPITAL-WEILL CORNELL*, Westchester Division Medical Library, 21 Bloomingdale Rd, 10605. SAN 312-6870. Tel: 914-997-5897. FAX: 914-997-5861. Web Site: library.med.cornell.edu. *Librn,* Marcia A Miller; Staff 1 (MLS 1)
Founded 1823

Library Holdings: Bk Vols 1,000; Per Subs 100
Subject Interests: Clinical psychol, Psychiat, Psychiat nursing
Wireless access
Partic in National Network of Libraries of Medicine
Open Mon-Fri 9-5

S NEXANT INC*, Information Center, 44 S Broadway, 4th Flr, 10601. SAN 311-6794. Tel: 914-609-0375. FAX: 914-609-0399. E-mail: whiteplains-library@nexant.com. Web Site: www.nexant.com. *Head, Info Serv,* Lorraine Moneypenny; E-mail: lmoneypenny@nexant.com; Staff 1 (Non-MLS 1)
Founded 1966
Library Holdings: Bk Titles 1,000; Per Subs 40
Subject Interests: Energy, Environment, Petrochem, Plastics, Refining, Specialty chem
Automation Activity & Vendor Info: (Cataloging) Softlink America; (Circulation) Softlink America; (OPAC) Softlink America
Database Vendor: LexisNexis
Wireless access
Open Mon-Fri 8:30-5:15

GL NYS SUPREME COURT LIBRARY*, Ninth Judicial District, 9th Flr, 111 Dr Martin Luther King Blvd, 10601. SAN 354-3994. Tel: 914-824-5660. *Dir,* Zoya Golban; *Sr Librn,* Ed Murphy; Staff 2 (MLS 2)
Founded 1908
Library Holdings: Bk Vols 300,000; Per Subs 45
Special Collections: Records on Appeal (Second Department & Court of Appeals), micro
Automation Activity & Vendor Info: (Cataloging) SirsiDynix
Database Vendor: LexisNexis, Loislaw, Westlaw
Wireless access
Open Mon-Fri 9-5
Restriction: Open to pub for ref only

CL PACE UNIVERSITY, School of Law Library, 78 N Broadway, 10603. SAN 312-6897. Tel: 914-422-4273. Interlibrary Loan Service Tel: 914-422-4137. Reference Tel: 914-422-4208. Administration Tel: 914-422-4249. Web Site: www.law.pace.edu/library. *Dir, Prof,* Marie S Newman; Tel: 914-422-4169, E-mail: mnewman@law.pace.edu; *Assoc Dir,* John McNeill; Tel: 914-422-4414, E-mail: jmcneill@law.pace.edu; *Head, Cat,* Jindi Zhang; Tel: 914-422-4649, E-mail: jzhang@law.pace.edu; *Head, Circ,* Vicky Gannon; Tel: 914-422-4369, E-mail: vgannon@law.pace.edu; *Head, Ref,* Cynthia Pittson; Tel: 914-422-4482, E-mail: cpittson@law.pace.edu; *Head, Tech Serv,* Alice Pidgeon; Tel: 914-422-4280, E-mail: apidgeon@law.pace.edu; *Electronic Serv Librn, Ref Librn,* Lucie Olejnikova; Tel: 914-422-4339, E-mail: lolejnikova@law.pace.edu; *Ref Librn,* Taryn Rucinski; Tel: 914-422-4358, E-mail: trucinski2@law.pace.edu; *Ref Librn, Spec Coll Librn,* Gail Whittemore; E-mail: gwhittemore@law.pace.edu; *Cataloger,* Helen Choi; Tel: 914-422-4648, E-mail: hchoi@law.pace.edu. Subject Specialists: *Intl law,* Marie S Newman; *Health law,* John McNeill; *Admin law,* Vicky Gannon; *Intellectual property,* Cynthia Pittson; *Intl law,* Lucie Olejnikova; *Environ law,* Taryn Rucinski; *Corporate law, Govt doc,* Gail Whittemore; Staff 20 (MLS 10, Non-MLS 10)
Founded 1976. Enrl 555; Fac 40; Highest Degree: Doctorate
Jul 2013-Jun 2014 Income $2,837,267, Locally Generated Income $5,846, Parent Institution $2,831,421. Mats Exp $1,132,571, Books $143,643, Per/Ser (Incl. Access Fees) $608,048, Micro $16,153, AV Equip $11,770, AV Mat $2,444, Electronic Ref Mat (Incl. Access Fees) $303,934. Sal $1,232,922 (Prof $874,117)
Library Holdings: DVDs 909; Microforms 62,322; Bk Titles 141,697; Bk Vols 399,986; Per Subs 1,631
Special Collections: David Sive Archive; Pace Law School Archives; Papers of the Hon John Carey; Yonkers Archives. US Document Depository
Subject Interests: Energy, Environ law, Health law, Intl law
Automation Activity & Vendor Info: (Acquisitions) Innovative Interfaces, Inc; (Cataloging) Innovative Interfaces, Inc; (Circulation) Innovative Interfaces, Inc; (Course Reserve) Innovative Interfaces, Inc; (ILL) OCLC ILLiad; (OPAC) Innovative Interfaces, Inc; (Serials) Innovative Interfaces, Inc
Database Vendor: Innovative Interfaces, Inc
Wireless access
Function: Res libr
Publications: Environmental Notes (Online only); LibGuides (Research guide); Pace Law Library Blog (Online only)
Partic in Connect NY; Metropolitan New York Library Council; New England Law Library Consortium, Inc; OCLC Online Computer Library Center, Inc; Westchester Academic Library Directors Organization (WALDO)
Open Mon-Thurs 8am-10:30pm, Fri 8am-9pm, Sat 9-9, Sun 11-9
Restriction: Open to students, fac & staff
Friends of the Library Group

S READER'S DIGEST ASSOCIATION INC LIBRARY*, Editorial Research Library, Reader's Digest Rd, 44 S Broadway, 10601. SAN 353-7692. Tel: 646-244-7846. *Head Librn,* Ann DiCesare; Staff 1 (MLS 1)
Library Holdings: Bk Vols 6,000; Per Subs 200
Special Collections: Reader's Digest Magazine
Subject Interests: Current news, Journalism
Restriction: Employees & their associates

P WHITE PLAINS PUBLIC LIBRARY*, 100 Martine Ave, 10601-2599. SAN 312-6927. Tel: 914-422-1400. FAX: 914-422-1462. E-mail: cybrary@wppl.lib.ny.us. Web Site: www.whiteplainslibrary.org. *Dir,* Brian Kenney; Tel: 914-422-1406; *Asst Dir,* Kathleen Degyansky; *Head, Tech Serv,* John Lolis; *Ch Serv,* Rosemary Rasmussen; *Coll Develop,* Christiane Deschamps; Staff 18 (MLS 18)
Founded 1899. Pop 53,000; Circ 600,947
Library Holdings: Bk Vols 309,000; Per Subs 2,300
Special Collections: Children's Literature Research Coll; Folklore/Fairy Tale Coll; Percy Grainger Music Coll; Westchester County/White Plains Local History Coll
Subject Interests: Local hist
Automation Activity & Vendor Info: (Acquisitions) SirsiDynix; (Cataloging) SirsiDynix; (Circulation) SirsiDynix; (Course Reserve) SirsiDynix; (ILL) SirsiDynix; (Media Booking) SirsiDynix; (OPAC) SirsiDynix; (Serials) SirsiDynix
Wireless access
Publications: Annual Report
Mem of Westchester Library System
Special Services for the Deaf - TTY equip
Open Mon & Wed 10-9, Tues, Thurs & Fri 10-6, Sun 1-5
Friends of the Library Group

WHITEHALL

P THE WHITEHALL FREE LIBRARY*, 12 William St, 12887. Tel: 518-499-1366. FAX: 518-499-1366. Web Site: whitehall.sals.edu. *Dir,* Karen Gordon; E-mail: kgordon@sals.edu
Library Holdings: AV Mats 615; Bk Vols 14,000; Per Subs 15; Talking Bks 365
Automation Activity & Vendor Info: (Cataloging) Innovative Interfaces, Inc; (Circulation) Innovative Interfaces, Inc; (OPAC) Innovative Interfaces, Inc
Mem of Southern Adirondack Library System
Open Mon, Wed & Fri 4-8:30, Tues 4-7, Thurs 1:30-6, Sat 10-2

WHITESBORO

P DUNHAM PUBLIC LIBRARY*, 76 Main St, 13492. SAN 312-6943. Tel: 315-736-9734. FAX: 315-736-3265. Web Site: www.whitesborolibrary.org. *Dir,* April R Bliss; E-mail: abliss@midyork.org; *Ref Librn,* Susan Hansen; E-mail: shansen@midyork.org; *Ref Librn,* Dennis Kininger; E-mail: dkininger@midyork.org; *Youth Serv Librn,* Sharon Trodler; E-mail: strodler@midyork.org; Staff 17.5 (MLS 4, Non-MLS 13.5)
Founded 1926. Pop 26,133; Circ 161,395
Oct 2012-Sept 2013 Income $860,459. Mats Exp $82,761. Sal $402,229 (Prof $193,900)
Library Holdings: e-books 140; Bk Vols 65,907; Per Subs 179
Special Collections: Helen Dunham Coll
Automation Activity & Vendor Info: (Acquisitions) SirsiDynix; (Cataloging) SirsiDynix; (Circulation) SirsiDynix; (OPAC) SirsiDynix
Database Vendor: EBSCOhost, FileMaker, Gale Cengage Learning, OCLC FirstSearch, Overdrive, Inc, SirsiDynix
Wireless access
Function: Adult literacy prog, ILL available, Prog for adults, Prog for children & young adult, Summer reading prog
Mem of Mid-York Library System
Partic in New York Online Virtual Electronic Library (NOVEL)
Open Mon-Wed 9:30-8, Thurs & Fri 9:30-5:30, Sat 9-5
Friends of the Library Group

WHITESVILLE

P WHITESVILLE PUBLIC LIBRARY*, 500 Main St, 14897-9703. (Mail add: PO Box 158, 14897-0158). Tel: 607-356-3645. FAX: 607-356-3645. E-mail: whitesville@stls.org. *Dir,* Karen M Smith; E-mail: smithk@stls.org
Founded 1923
Library Holdings: CDs 50; DVDs 25; Bk Titles 4,500; Per Subs 20; Videos 250
Subject Interests: Local hist
Wireless access
Function: Homebound delivery serv
Mem of Southern Tier Library System
Open Mon & Wed 10-4, Tues & Thurs 2-8, Fri 2-6, Sat 10-2

WHITNEY POINT

P MARY WILCOX MEMORIAL LIBRARY*, 2630 Main St, 13862. SAN 312-696X. Tel: 607-692-3159. FAX: 607-692-3159. Web Site: www.4cls.org. *Dir,* Juanita Aleba; E-mail: jaa3124@aol.com; *Asst Librn,* Amy Beardsley
Founded 1959. Pop 1,008; Circ 25,555
Library Holdings: Bk Vols 15,430; Per Subs 23
Automation Activity & Vendor Info: (Acquisitions) SirsiDynix; (Cataloging) SirsiDynix; (Circulation) SirsiDynix; (Course Reserve) SirsiDynix; (ILL) SirsiDynix; (Media Booking) SirsiDynix; (OPAC) SirsiDynix; (Serials) SirsiDynix
Wireless access
Mem of Four County Library System
Open Mon, Wed & Thurs 11-5, Tues & Fri 11-8, Sat 11-3
Friends of the Library Group

WILLIAMSON

P WILLIAMSON FREE PUBLIC LIBRARY, 6380 Rte 21, Ste 1, 14589. SAN 312-6978. Tel: 315-589-2048. FAX: 315-589-5077. E-mail: williamson@pls-net.org. Web Site: www.williamson.pls-net.org. *Dir,* Kim Iraci; *Ch Serv,* Michelle Byrne; Staff 11 (MLS 1, Non-MLS 10)
Founded 1911. Pop 6,777; Circ 168,807
Library Holdings: AV Mats 7,098; Bk Titles 30,684; Per Subs 182
Automation Activity & Vendor Info: (Circulation) Evergreen
Wireless access
Function: Handicapped accessible, Home delivery & serv to Sr ctr & nursing homes, Homebound delivery serv, ILL available, Magnifiers for reading, Online searches, Photocopying/Printing, Prog for adults, Prog for children & young adult, Ref serv available, Referrals accepted, Summer reading prog, Telephone ref, Wheelchair accessible
Mem of Pioneer Library System
Open Mon-Thurs 9:30-8:30, Fri 9:30-5, Sat 10-2
Friends of the Library Group

WILLIAMSVILLE

J ERIE COMMUNITY COLLEGE-NORTH*, R R Dry Memorial Library, 6205 Main St, 14221-7095. SAN 310-9712. Tel: 716-851-1273. FAX: 716-851-1277. Web Site: www.ecc.edu. *Librn, Prof,* Jane Ashwill; Tel: 716-851-1265, E-mail: ashwill@ecc.edu; *Head, Acq, Prof,* Lynnette Mende; Tel: 716-851-1271, E-mail: mende@ecc.edu. Subject Specialists: *Health sci, Lit, Relig,* Lynnette Mende; Staff 13 (MLS 6, Non-MLS 7)
Founded 1946. Enrl 8,900; Fac 278; Highest Degree: Associate
Library Holdings: Bks on Deafness & Sign Lang 50; Bk Vols 78,244; Per Subs 380
Special Collections: College Archives
Subject Interests: Allied health
Automation Activity & Vendor Info: (Acquisitions) Ex Libris Group; (Cataloging) Ex Libris Group; (Circulation) Ex Libris Group; (Course Reserve) Ex Libris Group; (ILL) Ex Libris Group; (Media Booking) Ex Libris Group; (OPAC) Ex Libris Group; (Serials) Ex Libris Group
Database Vendor: Gale Cengage Learning, LexisNexis, OCLC FirstSearch
Wireless access
Function: ILL available
Publications: Faculty Handbook; Library Guidebook; Library Handbook; Workbook in Library Skills
Partic in Western New York Library Resources Council
Special Services for the Deaf - Bks on deafness & sign lang
Open Mon-Thurs 8am-9pm, Fri 9-4, Sat 9-3

WILLISTON PARK

P WILLISTON PARK PUBLIC LIBRARY*, 494 Willis Ave, 11596. SAN 312-6986. Tel: 516-742-1820. FAX: 516-294-5004. E-mail: willistonparklibrary@yahoo.com. Web Site: www.willistonparklibrary.org. *Dir,* Donna McKenna; *Youth Serv Librn,* James Pagano
Founded 1937. Pop 7,261; Circ 77,206
Library Holdings: Bk Vols 35,000; Per Subs 88
Automation Activity & Vendor Info: (Acquisitions) Innovative Interfaces, Inc - Millenium; (Cataloging) Innovative Interfaces, Inc - Millenium; (Circulation) Innovative Interfaces, Inc - Millenium; (ILL) Innovative Interfaces, Inc - Millenium; (OPAC) Innovative Interfaces, Inc - Millenium
Wireless access
Mem of Nassau Library System
Open Mon 10:30-8:30, Tues, Thurs & Fri 10:30-5:30, Wed 1-8:30, Sat 10-4
Friends of the Library Group

WILLSBORO

P PAINE MEMORIAL FREE LIBRARY*, Two Gilliland Ln, 12996. SAN 312-6994. Tel: 518-963-4478. E-mail: painefreelib@willex.com. *Librn,* Cheryl Blanchard; *Asst Librn,* Alice Wand
Pop 1,800; Circ 46,051
Library Holdings: Bk Vols 20,000; Per Subs 40
Automation Activity & Vendor Info: (Acquisitions) SirsiDynix; (Cataloging) SirsiDynix; (Circulation) SirsiDynix; (Course Reserve) SirsiDynix; (ILL) SirsiDynix; (Media Booking) SirsiDynix; (OPAC) SirsiDynix; (Serials) SirsiDynix
Wireless access
Mem of Clinton-Essex-Franklin Library System
Open Mon, Tues, Thurs & Fri 9-5, Wed 9-7, Sat 9-2
Friends of the Library Group

WILMINGTON

P E M COOPER MEMORIAL LIBRARY*, 5751 Rte 86, 12997. (Mail add: PO Box 29, 12997-0029), SAN 376-6896. Tel: 518-946-7701. FAX: 518-946-7701. E-mail: library@wilmingtoncooperlibrary.net. Web Site: www.wilmingtoncooperlibrary.org. *Dir,* Samantha Baer
Library Holdings: Bk Titles 7,000
Automation Activity & Vendor Info: (Cataloging) Horizon; (Circulation) Horizon; (OPAC) Horizon
Wireless access
Mem of Clinton-Essex-Franklin Library System
Open Wed & Thurs 9-12 & 1-5, Fri 9-12 & 1-3, Sat 9-2
Friends of the Library Group

WILSON

P WILSON FREE LIBRARY*, 265 Young St, 14172-9500. (Mail add: PO Box 579, 14172-0579), SAN 312-7001. Tel: 716-751-6070. FAX: 716-751-6526. Web Site: www.nioga.org. *Mgr,* Marjorie Clark; E-mail: mclar@nioga.org; Staff 2 (Non-MLS 2)
Pop 5,640; Circ 25,754
Library Holdings: Bk Vols 15,500
Automation Activity & Vendor Info: (Circulation) SirsiDynix; (OPAC) SirsiDynix
Wireless access
Function: Art exhibits, CD-ROM, Home delivery & serv to Sr ctr & nursing homes, ILL available, Magnifiers for reading, Music CDs, Online searches, Photocopying/Printing, Prog for adults, Prog for children & young adult, Ref serv available, Spoken cassettes & CDs, Summer reading prog, VCDs, VHS videos, Wheelchair accessible
Mem of Nioga Library System
Open Mon 10-8, Tues & Wed 2-8, Thurs & Fri 10-5, Sat 10-1
Friends of the Library Group

WILTON

S MOUNT MCGREGOR CORRECTIONAL FACILITY LIBRARY*, 1000 Mount McGregor Rd, 12831-1223. (Mail add: PO Box 2071, 12831), SAN 321-0669. Tel: 518-587-3960. FAX: 518-587-3960. *Librn,* Pamela Raymond
Library Holdings: Bk Vols 7,600; Per Subs 63
Subject Interests: Law
Automation Activity & Vendor Info: (Cataloging) Follett Software; (Circulation) Follett Software
Wireless access
Mem of Southern Adirondack Library System
Restriction: Staff & inmates only

WINDHAM

P WINDHAM PUBLIC LIBRARY*, Church & Main Sts, 12496. (Mail add: PO Box 158, 12496-0158), SAN 312-701X. Tel: 518-734-4405. FAX: 518-734-4405. E-mail: windham@mhcable.com. Web Site: www.windham.lib.ny.us. *Dir,* Candace Begley; E-mail: windham@mhcable.com; *Asst Librn,* Elfrieda Benjamin; *Asst Librn,* Joan Sheridan; Staff 3 (Non-MLS 3)
Founded 1922. Pop 1,660; Circ 30,671
Library Holdings: Bks on Deafness & Sign Lang 10; CDs 168; DVDs 208; Large Print Bks 343; Bk Titles 11,704; Per Subs 60; Videos 887
Database Vendor: Gale Cengage Learning, ProQuest
Wireless access
Publications: TOPS Booklist
Mem of Mid-Hudson Library System
Special Services for the Deaf - Bks on deafness & sign lang; Closed caption videos
Special Services for the Blind - Bks on cassette; Bks on CD; Large print bks
Open Tues, Wed & Fri 10-5, Thurs 10-8, Sat 10-1

WINGDALE

P DOVER PLAINS LIBRARY*, Dover Veterans Memorial, 1797 Rte 22, 12594-1444. (Mail add: PO Box 534, 12594-0534), SAN 311-130X. Tel: 845-832-6605. FAX: 845-832-6616. E-mail: library@doverlib.org. Web Site: dover.lib.ny.us. *Dir,* Susan Totter; Staff 1 (MLS 1)
Founded 1904. Pop 7,778; Circ 23,000

Library Holdings: Bk Titles 20,335; Per Subs 40
Database Vendor: TLC (The Library Corporation)
Wireless access
Mem of Mid-Hudson Library System
Open Mon-Fri 10-8, Sat 10-4
Friends of the Library Group

WOLCOTT

P WOLCOTT CIVIC FREE LIBRARY*, 5890 New Hartford St, 14590. SAN 312-7028. Tel: 315-594-2265. FAX: 315-594-2681. Web Site: www.wolcott.pls-net.org. *Libr Dir,* Dottie Patt
Pop 1,496; Circ 222,584
Library Holdings: Bk Vols 16,300; Per Subs 32
Automation Activity & Vendor Info: (Cataloging) SirsiDynix; (Circulation) SirsiDynix
Wireless access
Mem of Pioneer Library System
Open Mon, Wed & Fri 2-8, Tues & Thurs 10-3, Sat 1-3

WOODBOURNE

S WOODBOURNE CORRECTIONAL FACILITY LIBRARY*, 99 Prison Rd, 12788-1000. SAN 327-1706. Tel: 845-434-7730. FAX: 845-434-7730, Ext 2099. *Librn,* Jane Ward
Library Holdings: Bk Titles 17,000; Per Subs 70
Automation Activity & Vendor Info: (Cataloging) Follett Software; (Circulation) Follett Software; (OPAC) Follett Software; (Serials) Follett Software
Wireless access
Open Mon-Tues & Thurs-Fri 8-11 & 12:45-3, Wed 12:30-3:30 & 6:30-8:25

WOODGATE

P WOODGATE FREE LIBRARY*, Woodgate Dr, 13494. (Mail add: PO Box 52, 13494-0052), SAN 312-7060. Tel: 315-392-4814. FAX: 315-392-4814. *Librn,* Kathy Lawrence
Founded 1932. Pop 1,700; Circ 4,485
Library Holdings: Bk Vols 3,100
Subject Interests: Adirondack Mountain hist
Wireless access
Mem of Mid-York Library System
Open Mon 2-8, Wed 3-6, Thurs & Sat 9-3
Friends of the Library Group

WOODSTOCK

P WOODSTOCK LIBRARY*, Five Library Lane, 12498-1299. SAN 312-7079. Tel: 845-679-2213. FAX: 845-679-7149. E-mail: info@woodstock.org. Web Site: www.woodstock.org. *Dir,* Diana B Stern; *Asst Dir,* Amy Raff; Staff 7 (MLS 2, Non-MLS 5)
Founded 1913. Pop 6,823; Circ 90,000
Library Holdings: Bk Vols 60,000
Subject Interests: Archit, Art, Belles lettres, Hist, Music
Automation Activity & Vendor Info: (Acquisitions) Innovative Interfaces, Inc; (Cataloging) Innovative Interfaces, Inc; (Circulation) Innovative Interfaces, Inc; (OPAC) Innovative Interfaces, Inc
Wireless access
Mem of Mid-Hudson Library System
Open Tues, Thurs & Fri 10-6, Wed 10-8, Sat 10-5

WORCESTER

P WORCESTER FREE LIBRARY*, 168 Main St, Ste 2, 12197. (Mail add: PO Box 461, 12197-0461), SAN 312-7087. Tel: 607-397-7309. *Librn,* Christine Gartung; *Librn,* Melinda McTaggart
Founded 1909. Pop 2,337
Library Holdings: Bk Vols 5,573; Per Subs 23
Wireless access
Mem of Four County Library System
Open Tues 9-6:30, Thurs 9-5:30, Sat 9-4

WURTSBORO

P MAMAKATING LIBRARY*, 128 Sullivan St, 12790. (Mail add: PO Box 806, 12790), SAN 370-3576. Tel: 845-888-8004. FAX: 845-888-8008. Web Site: www.mamakatinglibrary.org. *Dir,* Greg Wirszyla
Library Holdings: Bk Vols 19,000
Open Thurs & Fri 11-6, Sat 10-4
Friends of the Library Group

WYANDANCH

P WYANDANCH PUBLIC LIBRARY*, 14 S 20th St, 11798. SAN 312-7095. Tel: 631-643-4848. Administration Tel: 631-643-4848, Ext 227. FAX: 631-643-9664. E-mail: wyandanchlib@gmail.com. Web Site: www.suffolk.lib.ny.us/libraries/wyan. *Dir,* Silvia Archibalb
Founded 1974. Pop 11,005
Library Holdings: Bk Titles 58,000; Bk Vols 60,282; Per Subs 96
Database Vendor: OCLC FirstSearch
Wireless access
Mem of Suffolk Cooperative Library System
Open Mon & Fri 10-6, Tues-Thurs 10-9, Sat 10-5, Sun 1-5
Friends of the Library Group

WYNANTSKILL

P NORTH GREENBUSH PUBLIC LIBRARY*, 141 Main Ave, 12198. SAN 321-0995. Tel: 518-283-0303. FAX: 518-283-0303. *Dir,* Daryl McCarthy; Staff 1 (MLS 1)
Founded 1964. Pop 10,304; Circ 63,500
Library Holdings: Bk Titles 36,000; Bk Vols 40,000; Per Subs 50
Automation Activity & Vendor Info: (Cataloging) Horizon; (Circulation) Horizon; (OPAC) Horizon
Wireless access
Mem of Upper Hudson Library System
Open Mon-Fri 11-8, Sat 10-2
Friends of the Library Group

WYOMING

P WYOMING FREE CIRCULATING LIBRARY*, 114 S Academy St, 14591. (Mail add: PO Box 248, 14591-0248), SAN 312-7117. Tel: 585-495-6840. FAX: 585-495-6840. Web Site: www.wyoming.pls-net.org. *Dir,* Cheryl Ebel-Northup
Circ 4,703
Library Holdings: Bk Titles 7,000; Per Subs 22
Wireless access
Mem of Pioneer Library System
Open Mon & Sat 9:30-1, Tues 1-7, Wed & Thurs 1-4:30
Friends of the Library Group

YONKERS

S CONSUMER REPORTS*, Information Services, 101 Truman Ave, 10703-1057. SAN 311-5291. Tel: 914-378-2000. FAX: 914-378-2913. Web Site: www.consumerreports.org. *Dir,* Elena Falcone; Tel: 914-378-2265, E-mail: falcel@consumer.org; Staff 13 (MLS 11, Non-MLS 2)
Founded 1936
Library Holdings: Bk Titles 1,500; Per Subs 250
Special Collections: History of the Consumer Movement Coll. Oral History
Subject Interests: Consumer products testing, Consumer protection
Wireless access
Function: Archival coll, Res libr
Restriction: Co libr, Lending to staff only, Restricted access

M SAINT JOHN'S RIVERSIDE HOSPITAL*, Andrus Pavilion, Medical Library 4th Flr, 967 N Broadway, 10701. SAN 327-2133. Tel: 914-964-4281. FAX: 914-964-4971. Web Site: www.riversidehealth.org. *Dir, Med Libr,* Paul Hersh; Staff 7 (MLS 2, Non-MLS 5)
Library Holdings: CDs 92; DVDs 100; Bk Vols 2,000; Per Subs 113; Videos 360
Subject Interests: Med, Nursing
Automation Activity & Vendor Info: (Acquisitions) EBSCO Online
Database Vendor: 3M Library Systems, Cinahl, EBSCOhost, OCLC WorldShare Interlibrary Loan, OVID Technologies
Wireless access
Function: Audio & video playback equip for onsite use, CD-ROM, Computers for patron use, Copy machines, Electronic databases & coll, Instruction & testing, Online searches, Res libr, Telephone ref, VHS videos
Partic in Basic Health Sciences Library Network; Health Info Librs of Westchester (HILOW)
Restriction: Authorized patrons, In-house use for visitors, Non-circulating to the pub, Not open to pub, Open to hospital affiliates only, Open to students, fac, staff & alumni

CR SAINT JOSEPH'S SEMINARY*, Corrigan Memorial Library, 201 Seminary Ave, 10704. SAN 312-7184. Tel: 914-968-6200, Ext 8255. FAX: 914-968-8787. *Dir,* Sister Monica Wood; Tel: 914-367-8256, E-mail: mwood@corriganlibrary.org; *Librn,* Barbara Carey; Tel: 914-367-8262, E-mail: bcarey@corriganlibrary.org; *Per,* Sister Joan Ahl; E-mail: jahl@corriganlibrary.org; *ILL,* Sister Mary Elizabeth Rathgeb; Staff 4 (MLS 3, Non-MLS 1)
Founded 1896. Enrl 71; Fac 29; Highest Degree: Master
Library Holdings: e-journals 7; Microforms 10,750; Bk Vols 103,329; Per Subs 273
Subject Interests: Canon law, Liturgy, Relig studies, Scriptures, Theol
Automation Activity & Vendor Info: (Cataloging) TLC (The Library Corporation); (ILL) OCLC; (OPAC) TLC (The Library Corporation)
Database Vendor: EBSCOhost, OCLC FirstSearch
Wireless access

Partic in OCLC Online Computer Library Center, Inc
Open Mon, Wed & Fri 8-5, Tues & Thurs 8-8, Sat 10-3
Restriction: Open to students

CR SAINT VLADIMIR'S ORTHODOX THEOLOGICAL SEMINARY LIBRARY, Father Georges Florovsky Library, 575 Scarsdale Rd, 10707-1699. SAN 312-7192. Tel: 914 961 8313. Interlibrary Loan Service Tel: 914-961-8313, Ext 334. FAX: 914-961-4507. E-mail: librarian@svots.edu. Web Site: www.svots.edu/library. *Librn,* Eleana Silk; E-mail: es@svots.edu
Founded 1938. Enrl 72; Fac 11; Highest Degree: Doctorate
Jul 2009-Jun 2010 Income $203,000. Mats Exp $54,500, Books $15,000, Per/Ser (Incl. Access Fees) $35,000, Micro $500, Presv $4,000. Sal $129,000
Library Holdings: Bk Vols 181,000; Per Subs 355
Special Collections: Byzantine History & Art; Russian History & Culture (incl 19th Century Russian Theological Periodicals); Theology, History & Culture of the Orthodox Church
Subject Interests: Liturgical music, Rec
Automation Activity & Vendor Info: (Cataloging) LibLime; (Circulation) LibLime; (Course Reserve) LibLime; (ILL) OCLC; (OPAC) LibLime
Database Vendor: LibLime, OCLC FirstSearch
Wireless access
Function: Online ref, Ref serv available, Wheelchair accessible
Open Mon-Thurs 9-1, 3-5 & 6:30-9:30
Restriction: Open to pub for ref & circ; with some limitations

S YONKERS HISTORICAL SOCIETY*, Grinton I Will Library, 1500 Central Park Ave, 10710. (Mail add: PO Box 190, 10710-0181), SAN 371-4381. Tel: 914-961-8940. FAX: 914-961-8945. Web Site: www.yonkershistory.org. *Pres,* Mary Hoar
Library Holdings: Bk Titles 225
Special Collections: City Directory Coll (1890-1930); Photograph Coll
Publications: Yonkers History (Quarterly)
Restriction: Open by appt only

P YONKERS PUBLIC LIBRARY*, One Larkin Ctr, 10701. SAN 354-4230. Tel: 914-337-1500. FAX: 914-376-3004. Web Site: www.ypl.org. *Dir,* Stephen E Force; *Dep Dir,* Edward Falcone; *Bus Mgr,* Donna Marino
Founded 1893. Pop 198,000; Circ 985,176
Jul 2007-Jun 2008 Income (Main Library and Branch(s)) $8,768,891, State $61,992, City $8,299,961, Other $406,938. Mats Exp $321,263. Sal $5,159,111
Library Holdings: AV Mats 62,706; Bk Titles 322,448; Per Subs 743
Special Collections: Jewish Interest (Kogan Coll); Theatre & Dramatic Arts (John G Jutkowitz Memorial Coll). US Document Depository
Subject Interests: Agr, Archit, Art, Hist, Indust, Music
Automation Activity & Vendor Info: (Cataloging) SirsiDynix; (Circulation) SirsiDynix; (OPAC) SirsiDynix
Wireless access
Mem of Westchester Library System
Friends of the Library Group
Branches: 3
CRESTWOOD, 16 Thompson St, 10707, SAN 354-432X. Tel: 914-779-3774. *Adminr,* Sandy Amoyaw
Friends of the Library Group
RIVERFRONT, One Larkin Ctr, 10701, SAN 375-8656. Tel: 914-337-1500. FAX: 914-376-3004. *Adminr,* Susan Thaler
Friends of the Library Group
GRINTON I WILL BRANCH, 1500 Central Park Ave, 10710, SAN 354-4389. Tel: 914-337-1500. FAX: 914-337-9114. *Adminr,* Sandy Amoyaw
Library Holdings: Bk Vols 140,000
Subject Interests: Dramatic arts, Fine arts, Music
Friends of the Library Group
Bookmobiles: 1

YORKTOWN HEIGHTS

S IBM CORP*, Thomas J Watson Research Center Library, 1101 Kitchawan Rd, 10598. SAN 312-7206. Tel: 914-945-1415. E-mail: watlib@us.ibm.com. *Staff Librn,* Kathleen Falcigno; E-mail: mcck@us.ibm.com; Staff 1 (MLS 1)
Subject Interests: Bus, Chem, Computer sci, Eng, Info tech, Math, Phys sci
Automation Activity & Vendor Info: (Cataloging) Horizon; (Circulation) Horizon; (ILL) OCLC
Wireless access
Restriction: Employees only, Not open to pub

S GEORGE KURIAN REFERENCE BOOKS, Editorial Library, 3689 Campbell Ct, 10598-1808. (Mail add: PO Box 519, Baldwin Place, 10505-0519), SAN 322-6573. Tel: 914-962-3287. FAX: 914-962-3287. *Librn,* Sarah Claudine
Jul 2007-Jun 2008 Income $82,500. Mats Exp $46,000, Books $40,000, Per/Ser (Incl. Access Fees) $6,000. Sal $36,500
Library Holdings: Bk Titles 34,004; Per Subs 41
Subject Interests: Educ, Hist, Humanities, Law
Open Mon-Fri 9-5

MERCY COLLEGE
See Dobbs Ferry

S PUTNAM NORTHERN WESTCHESTER BOCES*, Professional Library, 200 BOCES Dr, 10598. SAN 371-0181. Tel: 914-248-2392. FAX: 914-248-2419. Web Site: www.pnwboces.org/library/default.htm. *Coordr,* Judy Ashby; E-mail: jashby@pnwboces.org; Staff 3 (MLS 1, Non-MLS 2)
Library Holdings: Bk Titles 8,265; Bk Vols 10,937; Per Subs 180
Automation Activity & Vendor Info: (Cataloging) Mandarin Library Automation; (Circulation) Mandarin Library Automation
Wireless access

YOUNGSTOWN

S OLD FORT NIAGARA ASSOCIATION LIBRARY & ARCHIVES, Old Fort Niagara Visitor Ctr, Fort Niagara State Park, 14174. (Mail add: PO Box 169, 14174-0169), SAN 325-9803. Tel: 716-745-7611. FAX: 716-745-9141. Web Site: www.oldfortniagara.org. *Curator & Asst Site Dir,* Jerome P Brubaker; E-mail: jbrubaker@oldfortniagara.org; Staff 3 (MLS 1, Non-MLS 2)
Founded 1927
Library Holdings: Bk Titles 2,650; Bk Vols 3,000
Special Collections: Archaeological Specimens; Historical Objects Coll; Historical Photographic Images; History of Western New York & the Niagara region in general & Fort Niagara (1678-1963), with specific focus on 18th & early 19th centuries; Manuscript Items
Wireless access
Function: Res libr
Publications: Fortress Niagara, Journal of the Old Fort Niagara Association (Newsletter)
Restriction: Non-circulating, Open by appt only
Friends of the Library Group

P YOUNGSTOWN FREE LIBRARY*, 240 Lockport St, 14174. SAN 312-7222. Tel: 716-745-3555. FAX: 716-745-7122. E-mail: yfl@nioga.org. Web Site: youngstownfreelibrary.org. *Dir,* Jan Gilgore; E-mail: jgilg@nioga.org
Founded 1949. Circ 37,523
Library Holdings: Bk Vols 24,000; Per Subs 53
Automation Activity & Vendor Info: (Cataloging) SIRSI WorkFlows; (Circulation) SIRSI WorkFlows; (ILL) SIRSI WorkFlows; (OPAC) SIRSI WorkFlows; (Serials) SIRSI WorkFlows
Wireless access
Mem of Nioga Library System
Open Mon-Thurs 1:30-8:30, Fri & Sat (Winter) 10-2
Friends of the Library Group

NORTH CAROLINA

Date of Statistics: FY 2012-2013
Population, 2010 U.S. Census: 9,535,483
Population Served by Public Libraries: 9,765,229
Total Volumes in Public Libraries: 16,516,721
Volumes Per Capita: 1.69
Total Public Library Circulation: 52,705,420
Circulation Per Capita: 5.40
Total Public Library Income (including Grants-in-Aid): $206,160,285
Source of Income Local: 86% public funds; 7% state aid; 1% federal; 6% other
Expenditures Per Capita: $19.96
Grants-in-Aid to Public Libraries:
Federal (LSTA): $1,675,778
State Aid: $13,491,030
Formula for State Aid: One half of appropriation in block grants; one half per capita income equalization grants
Number of County or Multi-County (regional libraries): 58 county, 12 regional, 10 municipal
Counties Served: 100
Number of Bookmobiles in State: 26

AHOSKIE

J ROANOKE-CHOWAN COMMUNITY COLLEGE, Learning Resources Center, 109 Community College Rd, 27910. SAN 312-7249. Tel: 252-862-1209. FAX: 252-862-1358. E-mail: lrc@roanokechowan.edu. Web Site: www.roanokechowan.edu. *Dir,* Monique Mitchell; Tel: 252-862-1250; Staff 1 (MLS 1)
Founded 1967. Enrl 900; Fac 38; Highest Degree: Associate
Library Holdings: Bk Titles 23,731; Per Subs 38
Automation Activity & Vendor Info: (Acquisitions) SirsiDynix; (Cataloging) SirsiDynix; (Circulation) SirsiDynix; (Course Reserve) SirsiDynix; (ILL) SirsiDynix; (Media Booking) SirsiDynix; (OPAC) SirsiDynix; (Serials) SirsiDynix
Wireless acccss
Partic in Community Colleges Libraries in North Carolina (CCLINC); NC State ILL Network

ALBEMARLE

J STANLY COMMUNITY COLLEGE*, Learning Resources Center, Snyder Bldg, 28001. (Mail add: 141 College Dr, 28001), SAN 354-4621. Tel: 704-991-0259. Interlibrary Loan Service Tel: 704-991-0261. FAX: 704-991-0112. Web Site: www.stanly.edu. *Dir, Media Serv,* Mark Sample; E-mail: jsample7479@stanly.edu; *Dir, Libr Serv,* Elizabeth W Estes; Tel: 704-991-0337, E-mail: eestes7421@stanly.edu; *Librn,* Michael Hicks; Tel: 704-991-0261, E-mail: mhicks7497@stanly.edu; *Libr Tech,* Virginia Yandle; E-mail: vyandle7840@stanly.edu; Staff 4 (MLS 2, Non-MLS 2)
Founded 1972. Enrl 2,000; Highest Degree: Associate
Library Holdings: Bk Titles 20,000; Bk Vols 22,000; Per Subs 185
Subject Interests: Computer lang, Nursing, Respiratory therapy
Automation Activity & Vendor Info: (Cataloging) SirsiDynix; (Circulation) SirsiDynix; (OPAC) SirsiDynix
Special Services for the Blind - Computer with voice synthesizer for visually impaired persons
Open Mon-Thurs 7:30am-9pm (7:30am-8pm Summer), Fri 7:45-4

P STANLY COUNTY PUBLIC LIBRARY*, 133 E Main St, 28001. SAN 354-4478. Tel: 704-986-3759. Circulation Tel: 704-986-3755. Administration Tel: 704-986-3765. FAX: 704-983-6713. Web Site: www.stanlycountylibrary.org. *Dir,* Melanie Holles; Tel: 704-986-3766, E-mail: m-holles@stanlycountylibrary.org; *Ch Serv,* Alan Pozyck; *Ref,* Joyce Morgan; Staff 27 (MLS 5, Non-MLS 22)
Founded 1927. Pop 59,078; Circ 224,037
Library Holdings: Bk Titles 71,313; Per Subs 100
Subject Interests: Local hist
Automation Activity & Vendor Info: (Cataloging) Innovative Interfaces, Inc; (Circulation) Innovative Interfaces, Inc; (OPAC) Innovative Interfaces, Inc
Wireless access
Open Mon-Thurs 9-8, Fri & Sat 9-5, Sat (Summer) 9-1
Friends of the Library Group

Branches: 4
BADIN BRANCH, 62 Pine St, Badin, 28009, SAN 354-4508. Tel: 704-422-3218. *In Charge,* Jenny Allen; Staff 2 (Non-MLS 2)
Open Mon, Wed & Fri 1-5, Tues 10-2, Thurs 3-7
Friends of the Library Group
LOCUST BRANCH, 213 Towne Centre Dr, Locust, 28097. (Mail add: PO Box 400, Locust, 28097-0400), SAN 375-2909. Tel: 704-888-0103. *In Charge,* Karen Hartsell; Staff 3 (Non-MLS 3)
Open Mon-Thurs 1-7, Fri 1-5, Sat 9-1
Friends of the Library Group
NORWOOD BRANCH, 207 Pee Dee Ave, Norwood, 28128. (Mail add: PO Box 1217, Norwood, 28128-1217), SAN 354-4532. Tel: 704-474-3625. *In Charge,* Julie Russell; Staff 3 (Non-MLS 3)
Open Mon-Thurs 1-7, Fri & Sat 9-1
Friends of the Library Group
OAKBORO BRANCH, 214 S Main St, Oakboro, 28129, SAN 354-4567. Tel: 704-485-4310. *In Charge,* Glenda Austin; Staff 2 (Non-MLS 2)
Open Mon 9-1, Wed-Fri 1-5, Tues 3-7
Friends of the Library Group

ANDREWS

P ANDREWS PUBLIC LIBRARY*, 871 Main St, 28901. (Mail add: PO Box 700, 28901-0700), SAN 312-7257. Tel: 828-321-5956. FAX: 828-321-3256. Web Site: www.nantahalalibrary.org. *Br Mgr,* Jane Blue; *Asst Librn,* Kelly Bryant; *Asst Librn,* Jacqueline Hulse; Staff 3 (MLS 1, Non-MLS 2)
Founded 1915. Circ 40,070
Library Holdings: Bk Vols 15,000
Special Collections: African American Books (Purel Miller Coll)
Mem of Nantahala Regional Library
Open Mon, Wed & Fri 9-6, Tues & Thurs 9-9, Sat 9-3
Friends of the Library Group

ASHEBORO

J RANDOLPH COMMUNITY COLLEGE*, Learning Resources Center, 629 Industrial Park Ave, 27205-7333. (Mail add: PO Box 1009, 27204-1009), SAN 312-7273. Tel: 336-633-0204. FAX: 336-629-4695. E-mail: library@randolph.edu. Web Site: library.randolph.edu. *Dean of Libr Serv,* Deborah Scott Luck; Tel: 336-633-0272, E-mail: dsluck@randolph.edu; *Info Tech,* Mario Ramos; E-mail: msramos@randolph.edu; *Info Tech,* Elizabeth Vidrine; E-mail: eevidrine@randolph.edu; *Instrul Serv Librn,* Donna Windish; E-mail: dcwindish@randolph.edu; Staff 7 (MLS 3, Non-MLS 4)
Founded 1963. Highest Degree: Associate
Library Holdings: AV Mats 5,000; Bk Titles 39,000; Per Subs 278
Special Collections: Bienenstock Furniture Library (High Point, North Carolina), microfiche
Subject Interests: Archit, Art, Interior design, Nursing, Pottery, Tech educ, Vocational

Automation Activity & Vendor Info: (Cataloging) SirsiDynix; (Circulation) SirsiDynix; (Course Reserve) SirsiDynix; (ILL) SirsiDynix; (OPAC) SirsiDynix; (Serials) SirsiDynix
Database Vendor: Gale Cengage Learning, ProQuest
Function: AV serv, Distance learning, For res purposes, ILL available, Photocopying/Printing, Ref serv available, Telephone ref
Partic in Community Colleges Libraries in North Carolina (CCLINC); North Carolina Libraries for Virtual Education
Open Mon-Thurs 8am-10pm, Fri 8-5
Restriction: Open to pub for ref & circ; with some limitations, Open to students, fac & staff

P RANDOLPH COUNTY PUBLIC LIBRARY*, Headquarters, 201 Worth St, 27203. SAN 354-4745. Tel: 336-318-6800. Circulation Tel: 336-318-6801. Reference Tel: 336-318-6803. FAX: 336-318-6823. Web Site: www.randolphlibrary.org. *Dir,* Ross A Holt; Staff 43.34 (MLS 10, Non-MLS 33.34)
Founded 1936. Pop 139,399; Circ 547,371
Jul 2009-Jun 2010 Income $2,349,130, State $190,781, City $487,568, County $1,358,843, Locally Generated Income $311,938. Mats Exp $258,986, Books $173,283, Per/Ser (Incl. Access Fees) $19,217, AV Mat $10,909, Electronic Ref Mat (Incl. Access Fees) $55,577. Sal $1,442,191 (Prof $450,355)
Library Holdings: Audiobooks 5,097; AV Mats 823; CDs 1,487; DVDs 7,749; e-books 3; Large Print Bks 7,119; Bk Vols 424,936; Per Subs 244; Videos 7,106
Special Collections: Microfilm; NC History Coll
Subject Interests: Local hist
Automation Activity & Vendor Info: (Acquisitions) Horizon; (Cataloging) Horizon; (Circulation) Horizon; (OPAC) Horizon
Database Vendor: Baker & Taylor, EBSCO Auto Repair Reference, EBSCOhost, Facts on File, Newsbank, OCLC FirstSearch, ProQuest, ReferenceUSA, SirsiDynix, TLC (The Library Corporation), Westlaw, WT Cox
Wireless access
Function: Accelerated reader prog, Adult bk club, After school storytime, Archival coll, Art exhibits, Audiobks via web, Bilingual assistance for Spanish patrons, Bk club(s), Bks on cassette, Bks on CD, CD-ROM, Chess club, Children's prog, Computer training, Computers for patron use, Copy machines, e-mail & chat, e-mail serv, Electronic databases & coll, Free DVD rentals, Genealogy discussion group, Handicapped accessible, Holiday prog, Home delivery & serv to Sr ctr & nursing homes, Homebound delivery serv, ILL available, Large print keyboards, Magnifiers for reading, Mail & tel request accepted, Music CDs, Newsp ref libr, Online cat, Online ref, Online searches, Orientations, Outreach serv, Outside serv via phone, mail, e-mail & web, Photocopying/Printing, Preschool outreach, Prog for adults, Prog for children & young adult, Provide serv for the mentally ill, Pub access computers, Ref serv available, Ref serv in person, Senior computer classes, Senior outreach, Serves mentally handicapped consumers, Spoken cassettes & CDs, Story hour, Summer reading prog, Tax forms, Teen prog, Telephone ref, VHS videos, Wheelchair accessible
Publications: Randolph County Public Library News
Special Services for the Deaf - Bks on deafness & sign lang; High interest/low vocabulary bks
Special Services for the Blind - Assistive/Adapted tech devices, equip & products; Audio mat; Bks on cassette; Bks on CD; Cassettes; Extensive large print coll; Home delivery serv; Large print bks; Low vision equip; Magnifiers; Ref serv; Talking bks; VisualTek equip
Open Mon-Thurs 9-9, Fri 9-6, Sat 9-5
Restriction: Non-circulating of rare bks
Friends of the Library Group

ASHEVILLE

J ASHEVILLE-BUNCOMBE TECHNICAL COMMUNITY COLLEGE*, Holly Library, 340 Victoria Rd, 28801. SAN 312-7281. Tel: 828-254-1921, Ext 301. FAX: 828-251-6074. Web Site: www.abtech.edu/lrc. *Dir,* Carol Fleming; E-mail: cfleming@abtech.edu; *Syst Librn,* Terry Wyszynski; Staff 8 (MLS 3, Non-MLS 5)
Founded 1959. Highest Degree: Associate
Library Holdings: Audiobooks 600; DVDs 2,000; Bk Titles 49,000; Per Subs 290; Videos 2,000
Subject Interests: Allied health, Eng tech, Law enforcement
Automation Activity & Vendor Info: (Acquisitions) SirsiDynix; (Cataloging) SirsiDynix; (Circulation) SirsiDynix; (Course Reserve) SirsiDynix; (ILL) OCLC; (OPAC) SirsiDynix; (Serials) EBSCO Online
Database Vendor: SirsiDynix
Wireless access
Partic in NC Dept of Commun Cols
Open Mon-Thurs 8-8, Fri 8-4:30, Sat 12-4

P BUNCOMBE COUNTY PUBLIC LIBRARIES*, 67 Haywood St, 28801. SAN 354-5040. Tel: 828-250-4700. Administration Tel: 828-250-4711. FAX: 828-250-4746. TDD: 828-255-5216. E-mail: library@buncombecounty.org. Web Site: www.buncombecounty.org/library. *Dir,* Edward J Sheary; E-mail: ed.sheary@buncombecounty.org; *Admin Librn,* Georgianna J Francis; *Spec Coll Librn,* Ann Wright; *Ch Serv,* Patricia Glazener; *Ref,* Laura Gaskin; *Tech Serv,* Mary Bunner; Staff 78 (MLS 14, Non-MLS 64)
Founded 1879. Pop 210,550; Circ 1,372,547
Library Holdings: AV Mats 47,235; Bk Vols 495,117; Per Subs 830
Special Collections: Thomas Wolfe Coll
Subject Interests: NC
Automation Activity & Vendor Info: (Acquisitions) SirsiDynix; (Cataloging) SirsiDynix; (Circulation) SirsiDynix; (OPAC) SirsiDynix
Database Vendor: SirsiDynix
Publications: Happenings (Monthly newsletter)
Friends of the Library Group
Branches: 11
BLACK MOUNTAIN BRANCH, 105 Dougherty St, Black Mountain, 28711, SAN 354-5067. Tel: 828-250-4756. *Librn,* Ann Butler
Library Holdings: Bk Vols 41,576
Open Mon & Wed-Fri 10-6, Tues 10-8, Sat 10-5
Friends of the Library Group
EAST ASHEVILLE, 902 Tunnel Rd, 28805, SAN 354-5075. Tel: 828-250-4738. *Librn,* Alexandra Duncan; *Libr Assoc,* Malcolm Bruce
Library Holdings: Bk Vols 32,006
Open Tues & Thurs 9-8, Wed & Fri 9-6, Sat 9-5
ENKA-CANDLER BRANCH, 1404 Sandhill Rd, Enka, 28715. (Mail add: PO Box 1559, Enka, 28728-1559), SAN 377-5941. Tel: 828-250-4758. *Librn,* Leisa Stamey
Library Holdings: Bk Vols 31,682
Open Mon & Wed-Fri 10-6, Tues 10-8, Sat 10-5
Friends of the Library Group
FAIRVIEW BRANCH, One Taylor Rd, Fairview, 28730. Tel: 828-250-6484. *Librn,* Elizabeth Parker
Library Holdings: Bk Vols 22,838
Open Mon & Wed-Fri 10-6, Tues 10-8, Sat 10-5
Friends of the Library Group
LEICESTER BRANCH, 1561 Alexander Rd, Leicester, 28748. Tel: 828-250-6480. FAX: 828-683-8874. *Br Mgr,* Mary McLean
Library Holdings: Bk Vols 16,816
Open Mon & Wed-Fri 10-6, Tues 10-8, Sat 10-5
Friends of the Library Group
NORTH ASHEVILLE, 1030 Merrimon Ave, 28804, SAN 354-5105. Tel: 828-250-4752. *In Charge,* Ann Mayeux
Library Holdings: Bk Vols 30,064
Open Mon, Wed & Fri 10-6, Tues & Thurs 10-8, Sat 10-5
Friends of the Library Group
SOUTH ASHEVILLE OAKLEY, 749 Fairview Rd, 28803, SAN 354-513X. Tel: 828-250-4754. *Librn,* Cheryl Middelton
Library Holdings: Bk Vols 25,045
Open Tues & Thurs 9-8, Wed & Fri 9-6, Sat 9-5
Friends of the Library Group
SOUTH BUNCOMBE SKYLAND, 260 Overlook Rd, 28803, SAN 354-5121. Tel: 828-250-6488. *Librn,* Marsha Lockwood
Library Holdings: Bk Vols 45,727
Open Mon & Wed-Fri 10-6, Tues 10-8, Sat 10-5
Friends of the Library Group
WEAVERVILLE BRANCH-SPRINKLE MEMORIAL LIBRARY, 41 N Main St, Weaverville, 28787. (Mail add: PO Box 633, Weaverville, 28787), SAN 354-5156. Tel: 828-250-6482. *Librn,* Jill Totman
Library Holdings: Bk Vols 38,726
Open Mon & Wed-Fri 10-6, Tues 10-8, Sat 10-5
Friends of the Library Group
SWANNANOA BRANCH, 101 W Charleston St, Swannanoa, 28778, SAN 354-5148. Tel: 828-250-6486. FAX: 828-686-5516. E-mail: swannanoa.library@buncombecounty.org. *Asst Librn,* Griff Ford
Library Holdings: Bk Vols 17,596
Open Tues 10-8, Wed-Fri 10-6, Sat 10-2
Friends of the Library Group
WEST ASHEVILLE, 942 Haywood Rd, 28806, SAN 354-5164. Tel: 828-250-4750. *Librn,* Julie Niwinski
Library Holdings: Bk Vols 49,682
Open Mon & Wed-Fri 10-6, Tues 10-8, Sat 10-5
Friends of the Library Group

GM DEPARTMENT OF VETERANS AFFAIRS*, Medical Center Library, 1100 Tunnel Rd, 28805. SAN 312-732X. Tel: 828-299-2525. FAX: 828-299-2500. *Libr Tech,* Franklin DeJarnette; E-mail: franklin.dejarnette@va.gov; *Med Media,* Thomas Whiteside; Tel: 828-299-5360, E-mail: tom.whiteside@va.gov
Library Holdings: Bk Titles 1,500
Subject Interests: Cardiovascular, Gen med, Thoracic surgery
Database Vendor: EBSCOhost, ProQuest
Partic in Docline; Veterans Affairs Libr Network (VALNET)
Open Mon-Fri 8-4:30

R EPISCOPAL DIOCESE OF WESTERN NORTH CAROLINA*, Episcopal Resource Center, 900B Centre Park Dr, 28805. SAN 328-1213. Tel: 828-225-6656. FAX: 828-225-6657. Web Site: www.diocesewnc.org. *Dir,* Thomas Murphy; E-mail: tlm1322@gmail.com; Staff 1 (MLS 1)
Founded 1974
Library Holdings: Bks on Deafness & Sign Lang 12; DVDs 10; Bk Vols 4,500; Per Subs 12; Videos 500
Special Collections: Archives of Diocese & 62 Parishes
Open Mon-Fri 8:30-4:30

M MOUNTAIN AREA HEALTH EDUCATION CENTER*, Library & Knowledge Services, 121 Hendersonville Rd, 28803. SAN 354-4982. Tel: 828-257-4444. FAX: 828-257-4712. E-mail: library@mahec.net. Web Site: www.mahec.net/library. *Dir,* Joan Colburn; Tel: 828-257-4438, E-mail: joan.colburn@mahec.net; *Librn,* Debbie Skolnik; Tel: 828-257-4441, E-mail: debbie.skolnik@mahec.net; *Librn,* Sue Stigleman; Tel: 828-257-4451, E-mail: sue.stigleman@mahec.net; *Librn,* Jennifer Stuart; Tel: 828-257-4449, E-mail: jennifer.stuart@mahec.net; *ILL/Doc Delivery Serv,* Violet Rickey; Tel: 828-257-4446, E-mail: violet.rickey@mahec.net; *Tech Asst,* Chris Russell; Tel: 828-257-4445, E-mail: chris.russell@mahec.net; Staff 5.25 (MLS 3.25, Non-MLS 2)
Founded 1972
Library Holdings: AV Mats 100; e-journals 750; Bk Vols 1,500
Subject Interests: Allied health, Cultural diversity, Dentistry, Family practice, Med, Nursing, Obstetrics & gynecology, Pharm, Pub health
Automation Activity & Vendor Info: (Cataloging) EOS International; (Circulation) EOS International; (OPAC) EOS International; (Serials) EOS International
Database Vendor: EBSCO - WebFeat, EBSCO Information Services, EOS International, NC LIVE, OCLC FirstSearch, OVID Technologies, PubMed
Wireless access
Function: Doc delivery serv, Electronic databases & coll, Health sci info serv, Mail loans to mem, Online cat, Online searches, Outreach serv, Prof lending libr, Ref serv available, Web-catalog, Wheelchair accessible
Partic in Western North Carolina Library Network
Open Mon-Fri 8-5

G NATIONAL OCEANIC & ATMOSPHERIC ADMINISTRATION, National Climatic Data Center Library, 151 Patton Ave, 28801-5001. SAN 312-729X. Tel: 828-271-4677. FAX: 828-271-4009. *Librn,* Mara Sprain; E-mail: mara.sprain@noaa.gov; Staff 1 (MLS 1)
Founded 1961
Library Holdings: Bk Vols 7,000; Per Subs 20
Subject Interests: Climatology, Meteorology, Oceanography
Automation Activity & Vendor Info: (OPAC) SirsiDynix
Partic in Fedlink; OCLC Online Computer Library Center, Inc
Restriction: By permission only, Staff use only

S SOUTHERN HIGHLAND CRAFT GUILD*, Robert W Gray Library Collection-Folk Art Center, Blue Ridge Pkwy, Milepost 382, 370 Riceville Rd, 28805. (Mail add: PO Box 9545, 28815-0545), SAN 325-7657. Tel: 828-298-7928. FAX: 828-298-7962. E-mail: library@craftguild.org. Web Site: www.southernhighlandguild.org. *Librn,* Deborah Schillo; Staff 2 (MLS 1, Non-MLS 1)
Founded 1930
Library Holdings: CDs 15; DVDs 55; Bk Vols 10,900; Per Subs 45; Videos 150
Special Collections: Hand Crafts & History of Southern Highlands Region, rare & out-of-print bks; Manuscript Colls of Mountain Craft Persons, 1892-; Southern Highland Craft Guild Archival Records, 1929-
Wireless access
Function: Ref serv available
Open Mon-Sun 9-6 (9-5 Winter)
Restriction: Non-circulating

C UNIVERSITY OF NORTH CAROLINA AT ASHEVILLE*, D Hiden Ramsey Library, One University Heights, CPO 1500, 28804-8504. SAN 312-7311. Tel: 828-251-6336. Interlibrary Loan Service Tel: 828-251-6436. Reference Tel: 828-251-6111. Administration Tel: 828-251-6729. Interlibrary Loan Service FAX: 828-251-6012. TDD: 828-251-6301. Web Site: www.unca.edu/library. *Univ Librn,* Leah Dunn; Tel: 828-251-6545, E-mail: dunn@unca.edu; *Head, Spec Coll, Univ Archivist,* Gene Hyde; *Access Serv Librn,* Leith Tate; *Pub Serv Librn,* Anita White-Carter; *Tech Serv Librn,* Barbara Svenson; Tel: 828-251-6547; *Web Serv Librn,* Brandy Bourne; Tel: 828-251-6639, E-mail: bbourne@unca.edu; Staff 24 (MLS 10, Non-MLS 14)
Founded 1928. Enrl 3,460; Fac 207; Highest Degree: Master
Jul 2007-Jun 2008 Income $2,015,560, State $1,955,297, Federal $14,533, Locally Generated Income $45,730. Mats Exp $799,134, Books $189,963, Per/Ser (Incl. Access Fees) $539,972, Other Print Mats $88, Micro $23,318, AV Equip $1,300, AV Mat $33,880, Electronic Ref Mat (Incl. Access Fees) $2,110, Presv $8,503. Sal $1,059,201 (Prof $512,078)
Library Holdings: AV Mats 13,850; CDs 2,670; DVDs 2,871; e-books 24,805; e-journals 43,083; Microforms 860,972; Bk Titles 297,985; Bk Vols 384,383; Per Subs 7,246; Videos 4,398
Special Collections: Harrison Coll of Early American History; Manuscript & Photograph Coll, documents the history of Western North Carolina; Peckham Coll of WWI Narratives; Speculation Land Materials; University Archives. State Document Depository; US Document Depository
Subject Interests: Liberal arts
Automation Activity & Vendor Info: (Acquisitions) Innovative Interfaces, Inc; (Cataloging) Innovative Interfaces, Inc; (Circulation) Innovative Interfaces, Inc; (Course Reserve) Innovative Interfaces, Inc; (OPAC) Innovative Interfaces, Inc; (Serials) Innovative Interfaces, Inc
Database Vendor: 3M Library Systems, ACM (Association for Computing Machinery), Agricola, Alexander Street Press, American Chemical Society, American Mathematical Society, American Physical Society, American Psychological Association (APA), Amigos Library Services, ARTstor, Baker & Taylor, BioOne, Blackwell, Cinahl, CIOS (Communication Institute for Online Scholarship), CountryWatch, CQ Press, EBSCOhost, Elsevier, Gale Cengage Learning, H W Wilson, Ingenta, Innovative Interfaces, Inc, IOP, ISI Web of Knowledge, JSTOR, LearningExpress, LexisNexis, Marcive, Inc, McGraw-Hill, NC LIVE, Newsbank-Readex, OCLC CAMIO, OCLC FirstSearch, OCLC WorldShare Interlibrary Loan, OVID Technologies, Oxford Online, Project MUSE, ProQuest, PubMed, Safari Books Online, Sage, ScienceDirect, Springer-Verlag, Thomson - Web of Science, Wiley, Wiley InterScience, Wilson - Wilson Web
Wireless access
Publications: Making Sense of Library Research (Research guide)
Partic in Lyrasis; Western North Carolina Library Network
Open Mon-Thurs 8am-Midnight, Fri 8-6, Sat 10-6, Sun 1-Midnight
Friends of the Library Group

AYDEN

P QUINERLY OLSCHNER PUBLIC LIBRARY*, 451 Second St, 28513-7179. (Mail add: PO Box 40, 28513-0040), SAN 312-7354. Tel: 252-746-7026. FAX: 252-746-7041. E-mail: library@ayden.com. Web Site: www.ayden.com. *Dir,* Pat Nichols
Pop 4,500; Circ 16,800
Library Holdings: Bk Vols 18,000; Per Subs 15
Open Mon-Fri 8:30-1 & 2-5:30

BAKERSVILLE

P MITCHELL COUNTY PUBLIC LIBRARY*, 18 N Mitchell Ave, 28705. (Mail add: PO Box 26, 28705-0026), SAN 312-7370. Tel: 828-688-2511. E-mail: mcpl@amyregionallibrary.org. Web Site: www.amy.regionllibray.org/mitchell/index.html. *Head Librn,* Linda B Gouge; *Asst Librn,* Cynthia Burleson
Founded 1948. Pop 14,391
Library Holdings: Bk Vols 35,000; Per Subs 39
Special Collections: North Carolina Mineral & Geology Coll
Function: Prog for children & young adult, Summer reading prog
Mem of Avery-Mitchell-Yancey Regional Library System
Open Mon, Wed & Fri 9-5, Tues & Thurs 9-8, Sat 9-12
Friends of the Library Group
Bookmobiles: 1

BANNER ELK

C LEES-MCRAE COLLEGE*, James H Carson Library & Information Center, 191 Main St W, 28604-9238. (Mail add: PO Box 128, 28604-0128), SAN 312-7389. Tel: 828-898-8727. Circulation Tel: 828-898-2419. Administration Tel: 828-898-8770. Toll Free Tel: 800-280-4562. FAX: 828-898-8710. Web Site: www.lmc.edu/sites/library. *Dir of Libr,* Russell Taylor; E-mail: taylorrg@lmc.edu; *Assoc Librn,* Charlotte Presswood; E-mail: preswood@lmc.edu; *Circ Mgr,* Faye Williams; E-mail: williamsf@lmc.edu; *Cat, Ref Serv,* Donese Preswood; E-mail: preswood@lmc.edu; Staff 5 (MLS 2, Non-MLS 3)
Founded 1900. Highest Degree: Bachelor
Library Holdings: Bk Vols 98,000; Per Subs 343
Special Collections: Southern Appalachian Region (A B Stirling Coll)
Database Vendor: SirsiDynix
Publications: Puddingstone Press
Partic in Mountain College Libr Network
Open Mon-Thurs 8am-11pm, Fri 8-5, Sat 1-5, Sun 4-11

BARCO

P CURRITUCK COUNTY PUBLIC LIBRARY*, 4261 Caratoke Hwy, 27917-9707. SAN 312-7966. Tel: 252-453-8345. FAX: 252-453-8717. Web Site: www.earlibrary.org. *Librn,* Vicky Hagemeister; *Ch Serv,* Brenda Miller; Staff 5 (MLS 1, Non-MLS 4)
Founded 1948. Pop 19,000; Circ 66,000
Library Holdings: Bk Titles 36,000; Per Subs 100
Special Collections: Family Genealogy Coll. Oral History
Subject Interests: Genealogy
Mem of East Albemarle Regional Library
Open Mon-Fri 9-6, Sat 8:30-5

Branches: 2

COROLLA BRANCH, 1123 Ocean Trail, Corolla, 27927-9998. (Mail add: PO Box 123, Corolla, 27927-0123). Tel: 252-453-0496. FAX: 252-453-6960. *Br Mgr,* Kathleen Burns
Library Holdings: AV Mats 130; Bk Vols 4,200; Per Subs 15; Talking Bks 200
Open Mon-Wed & Fri 9-5, Thurs 10-6
Friends of the Library Group

MOYOCK PUBLIC LIBRARY, 126 Campus Dr, Moyock, 27958. Tel: 252-435-6419. FAX: 252-435-0680. *Mgr,* Patsy Howard

BAYBORO

P PAMLICO COUNTY LIBRARY*, 603 Main St, 28515. SAN 312-7400. Tel: 252-745-3515. FAX: 252-745-3847. E-mail: pamlicolibrary@hotmail.com. Web Site: newbern.cpclib.org/pamlico. *Librn,* Katherine Clowers; *Asst Librn,* Fran Benninger; Staff 12 (MLS 2, Non-MLS 10)
Founded 1964. Pop 13,000
Library Holdings: Bks on Deafness & Sign Lang 25; High Interest/Low Vocabulary Bk Vols 275; Bk Titles 23,592; Per Subs 123
Subject Interests: Genealogy, Local hist, Spanish
Automation Activity & Vendor Info: (Circulation) SirsiDynix
Database Vendor: SirsiDynix
Function: Ref serv available
Mem of Craven-Pamlico-Carteret Regional Library System
Special Services for the Blind - Large print bks
Open Mon-Thurs (Winter) 9-8, Fri 9-6, Sat 9-1; Mon, Wed & Fri (Summer) 9-6, Tues & Thurs 9-8, Sat 9-1
Friends of the Library Group

BEAUFORT

P CARTERET COUNTY PUBLIC LIBRARY*, 1702 Live Oak St, 28516. SAN 312-7419. Tel: 252-728-2050. FAX: 252-728-1857. Web Site: carteret.cpclib.org. *Librn,* Susan W Simpson
Founded 1939. Pop 57,050; Circ 149,840
Library Holdings: Bk Vols 60,000; Per Subs 112
Subject Interests: County hist, Genealogy
Automation Activity & Vendor Info: (Cataloging) Horizon; (Circulation) Horizon; (OPAC) Horizon
Wireless access
Function: Homebound delivery serv
Mem of Craven-Pamlico-Carteret Regional Library System
Open Mon-Thurs 8:30am-9pm, Fri 8:30-6, Sat 8:30-5
Friends of the Library Group

Branches: 2

BOGUE BANKS, 320 Salter Path Rd, Ste W, Pine Knoll Shores, 28512, SAN 321-9569. Tel: 252-247-4660. FAX: 252-247-2802. *Librn,* Susan W Simpson
Circ 7,325
Library Holdings: Bk Vols 11,447; Per Subs 36
Open Mon-Sat 8:30-5
Friends of the Library Group

WESTERN CARTERET, 230 Taylor Notion Rd, Cape Carteret, 28584, SAN 377-7987. Tel: 252-393-6500. FAX: 252-393-6660. *Librn,* Susan W Simpson
Library Holdings: Bk Vols 9,260
Open Mon, Wed, Fri & Sat 8:30-5, Tues & Thurs 8:30-8
Friends of the Library Group

BELMONT

C BELMONT ABBEY COLLEGE*, Abbot Vincent Taylor Library, 100 Belmont-Mt Holly Rd, 28012. SAN 312-7443. Tel: 704-461-6748. Circulation Tel: 704-461-6737. Interlibrary Loan Service Tel: 704-461-6744. Reference Tel: 704-461-6741. Administration Tel: 704-461-6740. FAX: 704-461-6743. Web Site: www.belmontabbeycollege.edu. *Dir, Libr & Info Serv,* Donald Beagle; E-mail: donaldbeagle@bac.edu; *Cat Librn,* Susan Mayes; E-mail: susanmayes@bac.edu; *Per Librn,* Margaret Vickers; Tel: 704-461-6747, E-mail: meginvickers@bac.edu; *Ref Librn,* Christine Pasour; E-mail: christinepasour@bac.edu; *Ref Librn,* Sandra Williams; E-mail: sandrawilliams@bac.edu; *Circ Mgr,* Bradley Baker; E-mail: bradleybaker@bac.edu; *Circ Supvr,* Margrete Anderson; Tel: 704-461-6565, E-mail: maggieanderson@bac.edu; *Admin Serv,* Vickie Jenkins; E-mail: vickiejenkins@bac.edu; *Cat,* Mary Burazer; Tel: 704-461-6745, E-mail: maryburazer@bac.edu; *Ref Serv,* Komal Sodha; Tel: 704-461-6742, E-mail: komalsodha@bac.edu; *Ref Spec,* Brother Andrew Spivey; E-mail: brotherandrew@bac.edu; *Ref Asst,* Ronald Pruett; E-mail: ronaldpruett@bac.edu; Staff 12 (MLS 6, Non-MLS 6)
Founded 1876. Enrl 1,642; Fac 74
Library Holdings: Bk Titles 130,000; Per Subs 600
Special Collections: Autographed Books; Benedictine Coll; Napoleonic Coll; North & South Carolina Coll, old & rare bks; Valuable Books from 15th-18th Centuries, brought by Monks from Europe
Subject Interests: Hist, Relig studies
Automation Activity & Vendor Info: (Cataloging) OCLC Online; (ILL) OCLC Online
Database Vendor: Annual Reviews, BioOne, Cambridge Scientific Abstracts, Dialog, EBSCOhost, Gale Cengage Learning, JSTOR, LexisNexis, Modern Language Association, NC LIVE, Newsbank, OCLC FirstSearch, OCLC WorldShare Interlibrary Loan, OVID Technologies, ProQuest, Wilson - Wilson Web, WT Cox
Wireless access
Publications: Friends Newsletter; Library Handbook; Operational Manual of the Library; Periodicals Holdings List
Open Mon-Thurs 8am-Midnight, Fri 8-5, Sat 10-5, Sun 1:30-Midnight
Friends of the Library Group

BENSON

P MARY DUNCAN PUBLIC LIBRARY*, 100 W Main St, 27504. SAN 355-1733. Tel: 919-894-3724. FAX: 919-894-1283. E-mail: info@mdpl-nc.org. Web Site: mdpl-nc.org. *Librn,* Linda Haynes; Staff 1 (Non-MLS 1)
Pop 3,500; Circ 10,000
Library Holdings: Bk Vols 25,000
Automation Activity & Vendor Info: (Circulation) Innovative Interfaces, Inc; (OPAC) Innovative Interfaces, Inc
Partic in North Carolina Libraries for Virtual Education
Open Mon & Wed 9-5:30, Tues & Thurs 9-8, Fri 9-3, Sat 9-12

BOILING SPRINGS

C GARDNER-WEBB UNIVERSITY*, John R Dover Memorial Library, 110 S Main St, 28017. (Mail add: PO Box 836, 28017-0836), SAN 312-7508. Tel: 704-406-4290. Interlibrary Loan Service Tel: 704-406-3050. FAX: 704-406-4623. Web Site: www.library.gardner-webb.edu. *Dean of Libr,* Valerie M Parry; Tel: 704-406-4293, E-mail: vparry@gardner-webb.edu; *Assoc Dean,* Mary Roby; Tel: 704-406-4298, E-mail: mroby@gardner-webb.edu; *Instruction Librn,* Natalie Edwards; Tel: 704-406-3274, E-mail: nedwards@gardner-webb.edu; *Ref Librn,* David Dunham; Tel: 704-406-3051, E-mail: ddunham@gardner-webb.edu; *Circ Mgr,* Boyd Harris; Tel: 704-406-4295, E-mail: brharris@gardner-webb.edu; *Libr Syst Mgr,* Daniel Jolley; Tel: 704-406-4297, E-mail: djolley@gardner-webb.edu; *AV,* Margaret Christopher; Tel: 704-406-4291, E-mail: mchristopher@gardner-webb.edu; *ILL,* Denise McKee; Tel: 704-406-3050, E-mail: dmckee@gardner-webb.edu; *Pub Serv,* Mary Thompson; Tel: 704-406-4294, E-mail: mthompson@gardner-webb.edu; *Tech Serv,* Frank Newton; E-mail: fnewton@gardner-webb.edu; Staff 8 (MLS 6, Non-MLS 2)
Founded 1928. Enrl 3,800; Fac 250; Highest Degree: Doctorate
Jul 2006-Jun 2007 Income $854,465. Mats Exp $266,848, Books $108,280, Per/Ser (Incl. Access Fees) $139,588, Other Print Mats $48, AV Equip $3,729, AV Mat $15,103, Presv $100. Sal $425,142 (Prof $263,407)
Library Holdings: AV Mats 10,540; e-books 24,000; Bk Titles 185,000; Bk Vols 223,000; Per Subs 450
Special Collections: Church Curriculum Laboratory Coll; Thomas Dixon Coll. US Document Depository
Subject Interests: Relig
Automation Activity & Vendor Info: (Acquisitions) Innovative Interfaces, Inc; (Cataloging) Innovative Interfaces, Inc; (Circulation) Innovative Interfaces, Inc; (Course Reserve) Innovative Interfaces, Inc; (ILL) OCLC; (OPAC) Innovative Interfaces, Inc; (Serials) Innovative Interfaces, Inc
Database Vendor: EBSCOhost, Gale Cengage Learning, Newsbank, OCLC FirstSearch, ProQuest, Wilson - Wilson Web
Wireless access
Partic in Lyrasis; Metrolina Libr Asn; Mountain College Libr Network; NC Libr Asn
Special Services for the Deaf - Bks on deafness & sign lang; Coll on deaf educ
Special Services for the Blind - Assistive/Adapted tech devices, equip & products; Computer with voice synthesizer for visually impaired persons

BOONE

C APPALACHIAN STATE UNIVERSITY*, Carol Grotnes Belk Library, 218 College St, 28608. (Mail add: PO Box 32026, 28608-2026), SAN 354-5199. Circulation Tel: 828-262-2818. Reference Tel: 828-262-2820. FAX: 828-262-3001. Web Site: www.library.appstate.edu. *Dean of Libr,* Joyce Ogburn; E-mail: ogburnjl@appstate.edu; *Assoc Dean of Libr,* Georgie Donovan; E-mail: donovangl@appstate.edu
Founded 1903. Enrl 13,500; Fac 34; Highest Degree: Doctorate
Library Holdings: AV Mats 56,703; Electronic Media & Resources 81,220; Bk Titles 576,497; Bk Vols 823,377; Per Subs 5,306
Special Collections: Appalachian Mountains Regional Materials. Oral History; US Document Depository
Subject Interests: Educ
Automation Activity & Vendor Info: (Acquisitions) Innovative Interfaces, Inc; (Cataloging) Innovative Interfaces, Inc; (Circulation) Innovative Interfaces, Inc; (Course Reserve) Innovative Interfaces, Inc; (ILL)

Innovative Interfaces, Inc; (Media Booking) Innovative Interfaces, Inc; (OPAC) Innovative Interfaces, Inc; (Serials) Innovative Interfaces, Inc
Database Vendor: Dialog, EBSCOhost, Gale Cengage Learning, LexisNexis, OCLC FirstSearch, OVID Technologies, ProQuest, Wilson - Wilson Web
Publications: Appalnotes (Newsletter)
Partic in Western North Carolina Library Network
Open Mon-Thurs 7:30am-Midnight, Fri 7:30-9, Sat 10-6, Sun 12:30-12
Friends of the Library Group

Departmental Libraries:

WILLIAM LEONARD EURY APPALACHIAN COLLECTION, 218 College St, 28608. (Mail add: ASU Box 32026, 28608). Tel: 828-262-2186. FAX: 828-262-2553. Web Site: www.library.appstate.edu/appcoll/. *Librn, W L Eury Appalachian Coll,* Dr Fred J Hay; E-mail: hayfj@appstate.edu; *Dir, Rec Mgt,* Norma Riddle; E-mail: riddlenm@appstate.edu; *Ref Librn,* Greta Browning; Tel: 828-262-7974, E-mail: browningge@appstate.edu; *Libr Spec,* Dean Williams; E-mail: willmsda@appstate.edu. Subject Specialists: *African diaspora, Appalachia,* Dr Fred J Hay; Staff 5 (MLS 3, Non-MLS 2)
Founded 1968. Fac 3
Library Holdings: CDs 1,500; DVDs 35; Bk Vols 40,000; Per Subs 200; Videos 1,500
Special Collections: William Leonard Eury Appalachian Coll
Subject Interests: Appalachian studies
Function: For res purposes
Publications: Appalachian Journal (College journal)
Open Mon-Thurs 8am-10pm, Fri 8-5, Sat 10-5, Sun 1-10
Friends of the Library Group

MUSIC LIBRARY, 813 Rivers St, 28608-2097. (Mail add: PO Box 32097, 28608-2097). Tel: 828-262-2388. FAX: 828-265-8642. Web Site: www.library.appstate.edu/music. *Mgr,* Tom Byland; E-mail: bylandtp@appstate.edu; *Music Librn,* Gary Boye; Tel: 828-262-2389, E-mail: boyegr@appstate.edu. Subject Specialists: *Music,* Tom Byland
Open Mon-Thurs 8am-10pm, Fri 8-5, Sat 1-5, Sun 4-10

M NORTHWEST AREA HEALTH EDUCATION CENTER LIBRARY AT BOONE*, Watauga Medical Ctr, 336 Deerfield Rd, 28607-5008. (Mail add: PO Box 2600, 28607-2600), SAN 325-7711. Tel: 828-262-4300. FAX: 828-265-5048. *Dir,* Karen Martinez; *Libr Mgr,* Robin Daniel; Staff 3 (MLS 1, Non-MLS 2)
Library Holdings: Bk Titles 1,100; Per Subs 30
Subject Interests: Allied health, Med, Nursing

P WATAUGA COUNTY PUBLIC LIBRARY*, 140 Queen St, 28607. SAN 320-8338. Tel: 828-264-8784. FAX: 828-264-1794. Web Site: www.arlibrary.org. *County Librn,* Monica Caruso; *Adult Serv, Mgr, Ref Serv,* Evelyn Johnson; E-mail: ejohnson@arlibrary.org; *Youth Serv Librn,* Judith Winecoff; E-mail: jwinecoff@arlibrary.org; Staff 6 (MLS 1, Non-MLS 5)
Founded 1932. Pop 44,000; Circ 286,303
Library Holdings: Bk Vols 86,000; Per Subs 110
Special Collections: Boone Historical Society Papers
Subject Interests: NC
Automation Activity & Vendor Info: (Cataloging) SirsiDynix; (Circulation) SirsiDynix; (OPAC) SirsiDynix
Database Vendor: NC LIVE
Wireless access
Mem of Appalachian Regional Library
Special Services for the Deaf - Bks on deafness & sign lang
Special Services for the Blind - Computer with voice synthesizer for visually impaired persons
Open Mon-Thurs 9-7, Fri & Sat 9-5
Friends of the Library Group

Branches: 1

WESTERN WATAUGA, 1085 Old US Hwy 421, Sugar Grove, 28692, SAN 376-8120. Tel: 828-297-5515. FAX: 828-297-7805. *Outreach Serv Librn,* Jackie Cornette; E-mail: jcornette@arlibrary.org; Staff 2 (Non-MLS 2)
Founded 1986
Open Mon & Wed 10-5, Tues-Thurs 10-7
Friends of the Library Group

BOONVILLE

P BOONVILLE COMMUNITY PUBLIC LIBRARY*, 121 W Main St, 27011-9125. (Mail add: PO Box 786, 27011-0786). Tel: 336-367-7737. FAX: 336-367-7767. E-mail: bnv@nwrl.org. *Librn,* Gaye Layel; *Asst Librn,* Annie Ellis; *Asst Librn,* Angie Walker; Staff 2 (Non-MLS 2)
Founded 1999. Pop 3,372
Library Holdings: Bk Vols 5,000
Automation Activity & Vendor Info: (Acquisitions) SirsiDynix; (Cataloging) SirsiDynix; (Circulation) SirsiDynix
Mem of Northwestern Regional Library
Open Mon & Thurs 10-7, Tues, Wed & Fri 12-4
Friends of the Library Group

BREVARD

C BREVARD COLLEGE*, James Addison Jones Library, One Brevard College Dr, 28712-4283. SAN 312-7516. Tel: 828-884-8268. Interlibrary Loan Service Tel: 828-883-8292, Ext 2223. E-mail: library@brevard.edu. Web Site: www.brevard.edu/library. *Libr Dir,* Michael M McCabe; Tel: 828-884-8248; *Cat,* Melodie Farnhan; Tel: 828-884-8368; *ILL,* Brenda G Spillman; E-mail: brendas@brevard.edu; *Acq/Res Mgt Asst,* Kathy A Wilson; Tel: 828-884-8298; Staff 5 (MLS 2.5, Non-MLS 2.5)
Founded 1934. Enrl 700; Fac 52; Highest Degree: Bachelor
Jun 2011-May 2012. Mats Exp $60,808, Books $16,481, Per/Ser (Incl. Access Fees) $23,622, AV Equip $320, AV Mat $2,117, Electronic Ref Mat (Incl. Access Fees) $16,238, Presv $2,030. Sal $155,176
Library Holdings: AV Mats 4,508; CDs 2,243; DVDs 268; e-books 130,000; e-journals 30,000; Electronic Media & Resources 200, Microforms 3,325; Music Scores 1,497; Bk Titles 45,944; Bk Vols 58,718; Per Subs 120; Videos 1,101
Subject Interests: Art, Ecology, Environ studies, Music, Outdoor wilderness educ, Psychol, Southern lit, Teacher licensure
Automation Activity & Vendor Info: (Acquisitions) Innovative Interfaces, Inc; (Cataloging) Innovative Interfaces, Inc; (Circulation) Innovative Interfaces, Inc; (Course Reserve) Innovative Interfaces, Inc; (ILL) OCLC Online; (OPAC) Innovative Interfaces, Inc; (Serials) Innovative Interfaces, Inc
Database Vendor: ABC-CLIO, Alexander Street Press, ARTstor, Baker & Taylor, CQ Press, EBSCOhost, Gale Cengage Learning, Ingram Library Services, Innovative Interfaces, Inc, JSTOR, LearningExpress, NC LIVE, OCLC, OCLC ArticleFirst, OCLC CAMIO, OCLC FirstSearch, OCLC WorldShare Interlibrary Loan, ProQuest, PubMed, ReferenceUSA, TDNet
Wireless access
Function: Copy machines, e-mail & chat, e-mail serv, E-Reserves, Electronic databases & coll, Handicapped accessible, ILL available, Online cat, Online ref, Photocopying/Printing, Pub access computers, Ref & res, Ref serv in person, Scanner, Web-catalog
Partic in Appalachian Col Asn; Carolina Consortium; Lyrasis; Mid-Atlantic Library Alliance (MALiA); NC Asn of Independent Cols & Univs; North Carolina Libraries for Virtual Education
Open Mon-Thurs 8am-11pm, Fri 8-5, Sun 3-10

SR FIRST BAPTIST CHURCH*, Media Center, 122 Gaston St, 28712. SAN 329-9813. Tel: 828-883-8251. FAX: 828-883-8573. *Chair,* Betty Light
Library Holdings: Bk Vols 3,860; Per Subs 20

P TRANSYLVANIA COUNTY LIBRARY*, 212 S Gaston, 28712. SAN 312-7524. Tel: 828-884-3151. Circulation Tel: 828-884-3151, Ext 232. Interlibrary Loan Service Tel: 828-884-3151, Ext 241. Reference Tel: 828-884-3151, Ext 229. Administration Tel: 828-884-3151, Ext 240. FAX: 828-877-4230. Web Site: library.transylvaniacounty.org. *Libr Dir,* Anna Yount; Tel: 828-884-3151, Ext 239, E-mail: anna.yount@transylvaniacounty.org; *Admin Serv,* Saronda Morgan; E-mail: saronda.morgan@transylvaniacounty.org; *Access Serv Librn,* Edwin Arnaudin; Tel: 828-884-3151, Ext 223, E-mail: edwin.arnaudin@transylvaniacounty.org; *Local Hist Librn,* Marcy Thompson; E-mail: marcy.thompson@transylvaniacounty.org; *Youth Serv Librn,* Carrie Foreman; Tel: 828-884-3151, Ext 233, E-mail: carrie.foreman@transylvaniacounty.org, *Adult Serv Coordr,* Lisa Sheffield; Tel: 828-884-3151, Ext 226, E-mail: lisa.sheffield@transylvaniacounty.org; *Bkmobile/Outreach Serv,* Brenda Ivers; Tel: 828-884-3151, Ext 246, E-mail: brenda.ivers@transylvaniacounty.org; Staff 15 (MLS 6, Non-MLS 9)
Founded 1912. Pop 31,091; Circ 352,980
Jul 2010-Jun 2011 Income $1,133,116
Library Holdings: Bk Vols 109,785
Automation Activity & Vendor Info: (Cataloging) TLC (The Library Corporation); (Circulation) TLC (The Library Corporation); (OPAC) TLC (The Library Corporation)
Database Vendor: TLC (The Library Corporation)
Wireless access
Publications: Library Herald (Newsletter)
Open Mon & Thurs 9:30-8, Tues, Wed, Fri & Sat 9:30-5:30
Friends of the Library Group
Bookmobiles: 1

BRYSON CITY

P MARIANNA BLACK LIBRARY*, 33 Fryemont St, 28713. SAN 312-7532. Tel: 828-488-3030. FAX: 828-488-9857. Web Site: www.fontanalib.org. *County Librn,* Jeffrey Delfield; E-mail: jdelfield@fontanalib.org; Staff 6 (MLS 1, Non-MLS 5)
Founded 1929. Pop 12,000
Library Holdings: Bk Titles 44,000
Subject Interests: Genealogy
Wireless access
Mem of Fontana Regional Library

Partic in North Carolina Libraries for Virtual Education
Open Mon & Wed 10-5:30, Tues & Thurs 10-7, Fri & Sat 10-4
Friends of the Library Group

P FONTANA REGIONAL LIBRARY*, 33 Fryemont St, 28713. SAN 312-7540. Tel: 828-488-2382. Automation Services Tel: 828-488-6983. FAX: 828-488-2638. E-mail: info@fontanalib.org. Web Site: www.fontanalib.org. *Dir,* Karen Wallace; *Mgr, Info Tech,* John Tyndall; *Cataloger,* Rachel Carey; *Outreach Serv Librn,* Carol Grise; Staff 42 (MLS 8, Non-MLS 34)
Founded 1944. Pop 82,102; Circ 325,996
Jul 2005-Jun 2006 Income $2,040,486, State $408,698, City $36,000, County $1,160,550, Locally Generated Income $290,009, Other $145,229. Mats Exp $198,087, Books $141,713, Per/Ser (Incl. Access Fees) $22,552, Micro $132, AV Mat $28,143, Electronic Ref Mat (Incl. Access Fees) $5,436. Sal $1,324,998 (Prof $395,527)
Library Holdings: Bks on Deafness & Sign Lang 100; CDs 1,773; DVDs 1,474; High Interest/Low Vocabulary Bk Vols 489; Large Print Bks 4,630; Bk Titles 106,183; Bk Vols 167,278; Per Subs 459; Talking Bks 6,025; Videos 7,801
Automation Activity & Vendor Info: (Cataloging) TLC (The Library Corporation); (Circulation) SirsiDynix; (ILL) OCLC; (OPAC) SirsiDynix
Database Vendor: EBSCOhost, NC LIVE, OCLC FirstSearch
Member Libraries: Albert Carlton-Cashiers Community Library; Jackson County Public Library; Macon County Public Library; Marianna Black Library
Friends of the Library Group
Bookmobiles: 1

BUIES CREEK

C CAMPBELL UNIVERSITY*, Wiggins Memorial Library, 113 Main St, 27506. (Mail add: PO Box 98, 27506-0098), SAN 312-7559. Tel: 910-893-1460. Circulation Tel: 910-893-1462. Reference Tel: 910-893-1467. FAX: 910-893-1470. E-mail: reference@campbell.edu. Web Site: www.lib.campbell.edu. *Dean of Libr,* Borree Kwok; E-mail: kwokb@campbell.edu; *Head, Access Serv,* Marie Berry; E-mail: berrym@campbell.edu; *Head, Res & Instruction,* Sarah Steele; E-mail: steeles@campbell.edu; *Head, Tech Serv,* Siu-Ki Wong; E-mail: wong@campbell.edu; *Bus Librn,* Daniel Maynard; E-mail: maynard@campbell.edu; *Cat Librn,* Jacquelynn Sherman; E-mail: shermanj@campbell.edu; *Curric/Media Librn,* LaKeshia Darden; E-mail: dardenl@campbell.edu; *Electronic Res Librn, Ref,* Steve Bahnaman; E-mail: bahnamans@campbell.edu; *Ref & Instruction Librn,* Brooke Taxakis; E-mail: taxakisb@campbell.edu; *Ref & Print Res Librn,* W Ron Epps; E-mail: eppsw@campbell.edu; *Circ Mgr,* Elizabeth Dobbins; E-mail: dobbinse@campbell.edu; Staff 18 (MLS 10, Non-MLS 8)
Founded 1887. Enrl 4,539; Fac 155; Highest Degree: Doctorate
Library Holdings: AV Mats 8,772; e-books 210,127; e-journals 55,265; Electronic Media & Resources 77,377; Microforms 602,312; Bk Titles 187,655; Bk Vols 229,608; Per Subs 318
Special Collections: US Document Depository
Automation Activity & Vendor Info: (Acquisitions) SirsiDynix; (Cataloging) SirsiDynix; (Circulation) SirsiDynix; (Course Reserve) SirsiDynix; (ILL) OCLC ILLiad; (OPAC) SirsiDynix; (Serials) SirsiDynix
Database Vendor: 3M Library Systems, ABC-CLIO, Alexander Street Press, American Chemical Society, American Psychological Association (APA), Annual Reviews, Baker & Taylor, BioOne, Blackwell, Bowker, Cinahl, CountryWatch, CQ Press, CRC Press/Taylor & Francis Group, CredoReference, Dialog, Dun & Bradstreet, ebrary, EBSCO - WebFeat, EBSCO Auto Repair Reference, EBSCOhost, Elsevier, Facts on File, Gale Cengage Learning, Greenwood Publishing Group, Haworth Pres Inc, HeinOnline, Hoovers, IBISWorld, JSTOR, LearningExpress, Lexi-Comp, LexisNexis, McGraw-Hill, MD Consult, Mergent Online, Micromedex, Modern Language Association, NC LIVE, Newsbank, OCLC, OCLC CAMIO, OCLC FirstSearch, OCLC WorldShare Interlibrary Loan, OVID Technologies, Oxford Online, Project MUSE, ProQuest, PubMed, ReferenceUSA, RefWorks, Sage, ScienceDirect, SerialsSolutions, SirsiDynix, Springer-Verlag, Springshare, LLC, UpToDate, Westlaw, Wiley, Wiley InterScience
Wireless access
Publications: History of Carrie Rich Memorial; Newsline (Friends Newsletter)
Partic in Docline; North Carolina Libraries for Virtual Education; OCLC Online Computer Library Center, Inc
Open Mon-Thurs 8am-Midnight, Fri 8-6, Sat 10-5:30, Sun 2-Midnight
Friends of the Library Group
Departmental Libraries:
CL NORMAN ADRIAN WIGGINS SCHOOL OF LAW LIBRARY, 225 Hillsborough St, Ste 203, Raleigh, 27603, SAN 321-7124. Tel: 919-865-5869. FAX: 919-865-5995. E-mail: library@law.campbell.edu. Web Site: www.law.campbell.edu/page.cfm?id=6&n=law-library. *Dir, Law Libr,* Olivia L Weeks; E-mail: weeks@law.campbell.edu; *Asst Dir, Info Serv, Educ Tech Librn,* Stephen S Chan; E-mail: chans@law.campbell.edu; *Head, Access Serv,* Kimberly Hocking; E-mail: hockingk@law.campbell.edu; *Cat Librn,* Sophia Gregory; E-mail: gregory@law.campbell.edu; *Ref Librn,* Swift Caitlin; E-mail: swiftc@law.campbell.edu; *Asst Librn, Tech Serv,* Teresa Teague; Tel: 919-865-5872, E-mail: teague@law.campbell.edu; Staff 8 (MLS 5, Non-MLS 3)
Founded 1976. Enrl 465; Fac 27; Highest Degree: Doctorate
Library Holdings: Bk Titles 21,231; Bk Vols 196,328; Per Subs 2,584
Automation Activity & Vendor Info: (ILL) SirsiDynix
Database Vendor: Bloomberg, EBSCOhost, Fastcase, Gale Cengage Learning, Haworth Pres Inc, JSTOR, LexisNexis, Marcive, Inc, Newsbank-Readex, OCLC FirstSearch, OCLC WorldShare Interlibrary Loan, ProQuest, SerialsSolutions, SirsiDynix, Westlaw, Wilson - Wilson Web
Open Mon-Thurs 7am-Midnight, Fri 7am-9pm, Sat 9-6, Sun 1-Midnight
Restriction: Open to pub for ref only

BURGAW

P PENDER COUNTY PUBLIC LIBRARY*, 103 S Cowan St, 28425. (Mail add: PO Box 879, 28425-0879), SAN 312-7567. Tel: 910-259-1234. FAX: 910-259-0656. E-mail: infodesk@pendercountync.gov. Web Site: www.youseemore.com/penderpl. *Dir,* Michael Taylor; *Br Mgr,* Marsha Dees; *Tech Coordr,* Cindy Goodin; *Circ,* Misty Smith; *Mkt,* Nancy Lukens; *Ref,* Aimee Mitchell; *Youth Serv,* Ann Mendenhall; Staff 12 (MLS 1, Non-MLS 11)
Founded 1942. Pop 53,000; Circ 271,688
Library Holdings: AV Mats 5,279; Bk Vols 110,472; Per Subs 116
Special Collections: Dallas Herring Heritage Coll
Automation Activity & Vendor Info: (Cataloging) TLC (The Library Corporation); (Circulation) TLC (The Library Corporation); (OPAC) TLC (The Library Corporation)
Wireless access
Partic in Lyrasis
Open Mon, Wed & Fri 10-6, Tues & Thurs 10-7, Sat 10-2
Friends of the Library Group
Branches: 1
HAMPSTEAD BRANCH, 75 Library Dr, Hampstead, 28443. Tel: 910-270-4603. FAX: 910-270-5015. *Br Mgr,* Marsha Dees
Library Holdings: Bk Vols 90,000; Per Subs 65
Special Collections: North Carolina Coll
Open Mon, Wed & Fri 9-6, Tues & Thurs 9-8, Sat 9-5
Friends of the Library Group

BURLINGTON

P ALAMANCE COUNTY PUBLIC LIBRARIES*, 342 S Spring St, 27215. SAN 354-5288. Tel: 336-229-3588. FAX: 336-229-3592. Web Site: www.alamancelibraries.org. *Dir,* MJ Wilkerson; *Tech Serv & Automation,* Martha Sink; Tel: 336-513-4754, E-mail: msink@alamancelibraries.org; Staff 24 (MLS 10, Non-MLS 14)
Founded 1962. Pop 150,000; Circ 855,115
Jul 2012-Jun 2013 Income (Main Library and Branch(s)) $2,571,116, State $240,600, City $10,000, County $2,201,269, Other $119,247. Mats Exp $183,661, Books $109,411, Per/Ser (Incl. Access Fees) $17,750, Micro $1,000, AV Mat $50,000, Electronic Ref Mat (Incl. Access Fees) $5,500. Sal $1,385,773
Library Holdings: Bk Vols 226,842; Per Subs 309
Subject Interests: Local hist
Automation Activity & Vendor Info: (Acquisitions) TLC (The Library Corporation); (Cataloging) TLC (The Library Corporation); (Circulation) TLC (The Library Corporation); (OPAC) TLC (The Library Corporation)
Function: Adult bk club, After school storytime, Art exhibits, Bk club(s), Bks on CD, Children's prog, Computer training, Copy machines, E-Reserves, Family literacy, Fax serv, Handicapped accessible, Holiday prog, Homebound delivery serv, ILL available, Microfiche/film & reading machines, Music CDs, Online cat, Photocopying/Printing, Preschool outreach, Preschool reading prog, Prog for adults, Prog for children & young adult, Pub access computers, Ref & res, Ref serv available, Ref serv in person, Scanner, Spanish lang bks, Story hour, Summer reading prog, Tax forms, Teen prog, Telephone ref, Wheelchair accessible
Open Mon-Thurs 9-9, Fri & Sat 9-6, Sun 1-5
Friends of the Library Group
Branches: 4
GRAHAM PUBLIC LIBRARY, 211 S Main St, Graham, 27253, SAN 354-5296. Tel: 336-570-6730. FAX: 336-570-6732. *Br Mgr,* Jennifer Beach; E-mail: jbeach@alamancelibraries.org; *Mgr, Br Serv,* Heather Holley-Hall; E-mail: hhhall@alamancelibraries.org; Staff 7.6 (MLS 2, Non-MLS 5.6)
Pop 12,833
Library Holdings: Bk Titles 47,049; Per Subs 62
Open Mon & Tues 9-8, Wed-Sat 9-6, Sun (Sept-May) 2-5
Friends of the Library Group
MAY MEMORIAL LIBRARY, 342 S Spring St, 27215, SAN 354-5342. Tel: 336-229-3588. FAX: 336-229-3592. *Br Mgr,* Susan Benning; E-mail: sbenning@alamancelibraries.org; *Head, Ref (Info Serv),* Lisa Kobrin;

E-mail: lkobrin@alamancelibraries.org; *Youth Serv Coordr,* Julia Walker; E-mail: jwalker@alamancelibraries.org; *Ref,* Dawn-Michelle Oliver; E-mail: doliver@alamancelibraries.org; *Ref,* Becky Peterson; E-mail: bpeterson@alamancelibraries.org; Staff 16 (MLS 5, Non-MLS 11)
Founded 1938. Pop 130,800; Circ 289,514
Library Holdings: Bk Titles 96,065; Per Subs 154
Subject Interests: Genealogy, Local hist
Open Mon-Thurs 9-9, Fri & Sat 9-6, Sun 1-5
Friends of the Library Group

MEBANE PUBLIC LIBRARY, 101 S First St, Mebane, 27302, SAN 354-5318. Tel: 919-563-6431. FAX: 919-563-5098. *Br Mgr,* Katherine Arends; E-mail: karends@alamancelibraries.org; Staff 10.1 (MLS 1, Non-MLS 9.1)
Founded 1936. Pop 7,284; Circ 133,560
Library Holdings: Bk Titles 42,026; Per Subs 71
Open Mon & Tues 9-8, Wed-Sat 9-6, Sun (Sept-May) 2-5
Friends of the Library Group

NORTH PARK, North Park Community Ctr, 849 Sharpe Rd, 27217, SAN 354-5377. Tel: 336-226-7185. FAX: 336-513-5425. *Librn,* Risha Bigelow; Staff 0.6 (Non-MLS 0.6)
Library Holdings: Bk Titles 9,123; Per Subs 22
Open Mon-Thurs (Sept-May) 3:30-8; Mon-Fri (June-Aug) 9-5:30

M ALAMANCE REGIONAL MEDICAL CENTER*, Medical Library, 1240 Huffman Mill Rd, 27216. SAN 371-2850. Tel: 336-538-7574. FAX: 336-538-7571. *Librn,* Marian Blecker; E-mail: blecmari@armc.com
Library Holdings: Bk Vols 500; Per Subs 50
Wireless access
Open Mon-Fri 8-4:30

BURNSVILLE

P AVERY-MITCHELL-YANCEY REGIONAL LIBRARY SYSTEM*, 289 Burnsville School Rd, 28714. (Mail add: PO Drawer 310, 28714-0310), SAN 313-0037. Tel: 828-682-4476. FAX: 828-682-6277. Web Site: www.amyregionallibrary.org. *Dir,* Dr Daniel Barron; *Tech Serv Mgr,* Rella Dale; *Outreach Librn,* Jane Crowder; *Ch Serv,* Karen Dobrogosz; *Fiscal Officer,* Mitchell Allen; *Spec Projects,* James C Byrd; Staff 10 (MLS 2, Non-MLS 8)
Founded 1961. Pop 42,979; Circ 256,933
Library Holdings: Audiobooks 1,899; CDs 1,074; Electronic Media & Resources 3,667; Large Print Bks 9,876; Microforms 2,487; Bk Vols 160,786; Per Subs 198; Talking Bks 1,897
Special Collections: Census Records on microfilm; Genealogy Holdings; North Carolina Mineral & Geology; Precious Stones Book Coll; Video Collections for all levels
Subject Interests: Local hist, NC hist
Automation Activity & Vendor Info: (Acquisitions) TLC (The Library Corporation); (Cataloging) TLC (The Library Corporation); (Circulation) TLC (The Library Corporation); (OPAC) TLC (The Library Corporation); (Serials) TLC (The Library Corporation)
Database Vendor: TLC (The Library Corporation)
Member Libraries: Avery County Morrison Public Library; Mitchell County Public Library; Spruce Pine Public Library; Yancey County Public Library
Partic in Lyrasis, OCLC Online Computer Library Center, Inc
Special Services for the Blind - Bks on cassette; Large print bks
Open Mon, Tues & Thurs 9-8, Wed & Fri 9-5, Sat 10 1
Restriction: Restricted borrowing privileges
Friends of the Library Group
Bookmobiles: 1. Librn, Sylvia Archer

P YANCEY COUNTY PUBLIC LIBRARY, 321 School Circle, 28714. (Mail add: PO Box 1659, 28714), SAN 312-7575. Tel: 828-682-2600. FAX: 828-682-3060. E-mail: ycpl@amyregionallibrary.org. Web Site: www.amyregionallibrary.org. *Librn,* Melanie Stallings; *Asst Librn,* Amber W Briggs; Staff 2 (MLS 2)
Founded 1945. Pop 14,955; Circ 84,483
Library Holdings: Bk Vols 40,000
Subject Interests: Genealogy, Local hist
Automation Activity & Vendor Info: (Circulation) TLC (The Library Corporation); (OPAC) TLC (The Library Corporation); (Serials) TLC (The Library Corporation)
Wireless access
Function: Accessibility serv available based on individual needs, Adult bk club, Archival coll, Art exhibits, Audiobks via web, AV serv, Bk club(s), Bks on CD, Children's prog, Computers for patron use, Copy machines, Digital talking bks, e-mail serv, Electronic databases & coll, Exhibits, Family literacy, Fax serv, Free DVD rentals, Games & aids for the handicapped, Handicapped accessible, Home delivery & serv to Sr ctr & nursing homes, Homebound delivery serv, Literacy & newcomer serv, Magnifiers for reading, Mail & tel request accepted, Microfiche/film & reading machines, Music CDs, Online cat, Online searches, Outreach serv, Outside serv via phone, mail, e-mail & web, Photocopying/Printing, Preschool outreach, Prog for children & young adult, Pub access computers, Scanner, Senior outreach, Serves mentally handicapped consumers, Spanish lang bks, Spoken cassettes & CDs, Spoken cassettes & DVDs, Story hour, Summer & winter reading prog, Tax forms, Teen prog, Web-catalog, Wheelchair accessible, Writing prog
Mem of Avery-Mitchell-Yancey Regional Library System
Open Mon, Wed & Fri 9-5, Tues & Thurs 9-8, Sat 10-1
Friends of the Library Group

CAMP LEJEUNE

A UNITED STATES MARINE CORPS*, Harriotte B Smith Library, 1401 West Rd, Bldg 1220, 28547-2539. SAN 354-5466. Tel: 910-451-5724. FAX: 910-451-1871. Web Site: library.usmc-mccs.org, www.mccslejeune.com/library.html. *Dir,* Janice Woodward; *Ref Serv,* Linda Hopkins; Staff 22 (MLS 3, Non-MLS 19)
Founded 1942
Library Holdings: DVDs 300; Bk Vols 150,000; Per Subs 308; Talking Bks 5,300; Videos 4,000
Special Collections: Military History Coll
Automation Activity & Vendor Info: (Acquisitions) SirsiDynix; (Cataloging) OCLC; (Circulation) SirsiDynix; (ILL) SirsiDynix; (OPAC) SirsiDynix; (Serials) SirsiDynix
Database Vendor: ProQuest
Restriction: Mil only

AM UNITED STATES NAVY*, Medical Library, Naval Hospital, 100 Brewster Blvd, 28547. SAN 354-5490. Tel: 910-450-4076. FAX: 910-450-3941. *Dir, Libr Serv,* JoAnn T Hall; E-mail: joann.hall@med.navy.mil. Subject Specialists: *Med res,* JoAnn T Hall; Staff 1 (MLS 1)
Founded 1942
Library Holdings: Bk Titles 300; Bk Vols 600; Per Subs 15
Subject Interests: Med, Sci
Function: ILL available
Restriction: Staff use only

CARTHAGE

P MOORE COUNTY LIBRARY*, 101 Saunders St, 28327. (Mail add: PO Box 400, 28327-0400), SAN 312-7591. Tel: 910-947-5335. FAX: 910-947-3660. *Dir,* Catherine Roche; *Libr Serv Supvr,* Carol Cowe; *Acq,* Diana Belvin; *AV,* Sue Aklus; Staff 1 (MLS 1)
Founded 1969. Pop 74,769
Library Holdings: Large Print Bks 1,724; Bk Vols 85,816; Per Subs 88, Talking Bks 1,973
Subject Interests: Genealogy, Local hist, Spanish lang mat
Database Vendor: TLC (The Library Corporation)
Function: ILL available
Open Mon-Fri 8:30-6, Sat 10-4
Friends of the Library Group
Branches: 4

PAGE MEMORIAL, 100 N Poplar St, Aberdeen, 28315, SAN 376-2874. Tel: 910-944-1200.
Open Mon-Fri 2-6

PINEBLUFF BRANCH, 305 E Baltimore Ave, Pinebluff, 28373-8903. (Mail add: PO Box 758, Pinebluff, 28373-0758), SAN 312-9454. Tel: 910-281-3004
Open Mon-Fri 2 6
Friends of the Library Group

ROBBINS BRANCH, 161 E Magnolia Dr, Robbins, 27325. (Mail add: PO Box 159, Robbins, 27325). Tel: 910-948-4000.
Open Tues 10-1 & 2-8, Wed, Thurs & Fri 8-1 & 2-6, Sat 10-2
Friends of the Library Group

VASS BRANCH, 128 Seaboard St, Vass, 28394. (Mail add: PO Box 1349, Vass, 28394). Tel: 910-245-2200. FAX: 910-245-2200.
Open Tues 9:30-8, Wed-Fri 8:30-5:30, Sat 8:30-1
Friends of the Library Group

Bookmobiles: 1. Librn, Ann Gibbon. Bk titles 1,600

CARY

S LORD CORP*, Research Center Library, 110 Lord Dr, 27511-7900. SAN 328-2465. Tel: 919-469-2500. FAX: 919-460-9648. Web Site: www.lord.com. *Librn,* Pamela Lacy; E-mail: pamela.lacy@lord.com; Staff 3 (MLS 2, Non-MLS 1)
Library Holdings: Bk Titles 2,800; Per Subs 200
Special Collections: Audio-visuals, Rpts
Subject Interests: Chem, Eng, Polymer chem
Partic in Lyrasis
Open Mon-Fri 8-5

R SHEPHERDS THEOLOGICAL SEMINARY LIBRARY, Paul K Jackson Memorial Library, 6051 Tryon Rd, 27518. Administration Tel: 919-390-1104. Web Site: www.weblibrary.shepherdsseminary.org/opac/shepherds/#menuHome. *Dir of*

Libr Serv, William Coberly; E-mail: wcoberly@shepherds.edu. Subject Specialists: *Hermeneutics,* William Coberly
Founded 2003. Enrl 75; Fac 12; Highest Degree: Master
Jul 2009-Jun 2010 Income $55,000, Locally Generated Income $5,000, Parent Institution $50,000. Mats Exp $3,000
Library Holdings: Bk Titles 22,000; Per Subs 15
Automation Activity & Vendor Info: (Cataloging) Book Systems; (Circulation) Book Systems; (Course Reserve) Book Systems; (ILL) OCLC WorldShare Interlibrary Loan; (OPAC) Book Systems
Database Vendor: EBSCOhost, OCLC WorldShare Interlibrary Loan
Wireless access
Function: Audio & video playback equip for onsite use, Computers for patron use, Distance learning, Electronic databases & coll, Handicapped accessible, Online cat, Online searches, Orientations, Web-catalog, Wheelchair accessible
Partic in Carolinas Theological Library Consortium
Restriction: Authorized patrons

CASHIERS

P ALBERT CARLTON-CASHIERS COMMUNITY LIBRARY*, 249 Frank Allen Rd, 28717-9561. (Mail add: PO Box 2127, 28717-2127), SAN 375-5037. Tel: 828-743-0215. FAX: 828-743-1638. Web Site: www.fontanalib.org/cashiers/index.htm. *Br Mgr, Librn,* Serenity Richards; E-mail: srichards@fontanalib.org; *Circ,* Hedy Okolichany; E-mail: hokolichany@fontanalib.org; Staff 5 (MLS 1, Non-MLS 4)
Founded 1994. Pop 1,700; Circ 25,000
Library Holdings: AV Mats 300; Bks on Deafness & Sign Lang 15; CDs 50; DVDs 200; Large Print Bks 500; Bk Vols 25,029; Per Subs 59; Talking Bks 1,017
Automation Activity & Vendor Info: (Acquisitions) Baker & Taylor; (Cataloging) Evergreen; (Circulation) Evergreen; (OPAC) Evergreen; (Serials) Evergreen
Database Vendor: NC LIVE
Wireless access
Function: Story hour, Summer reading prog, Tax forms, Teen prog, Telephone ref, Wheelchair accessible, Workshops
Mem of Fontana Regional Library
Open Tues & Wed 10-5:30, Thurs 10-8, Fri & Sat 10-4
Restriction: Non-circulating of rare bks, Non-resident fee
Friends of the Library Group

CHAPEL HILL

S CAROLINA POPULATION CENTER LIBRARY*, University of North Carolina at Chapel Hill, 302 University Sq E, 123 W Franklin St, 27516-2524. SAN 312-7621. Tel: 919-962-3081. FAX: 919-962-7217. E-mail: cpclib@unc.edu. Web Site: www.cpc.unc.edu/services/infoserv/library.html. *Head Librn,* Lori Delaney; E-mail: lori_delaney@unc.edu; *Ref,* Laurie Leadbetter; E-mail: laurie_leadbetter@unc.edu; Staff 2 (MLS 2)
Founded 1967. Highest Degree: Doctorate
Library Holdings: Bk Titles 6,000; Per Subs 175
Subject Interests: Adolescent sexuality, Demography, Developing countries, Family planning, Human sexual behavior
Automation Activity & Vendor Info: (OPAC) SirsiDynix
Database Vendor: EBSCOhost, LexisNexis, OCLC FirstSearch, OVID Technologies, SirsiDynix, TLC (The Library Corporation)
Function: Res libr
Publications: In-house documentation for the Internet & other automated services
Partic in Dialog Corp; SDC Info Servs
Open Mon-Fri 8:30-5:30

P CHAPEL HILL PUBLIC LIBRARY, 100 Library Dr, 27514. SAN 312-763X. Tel: 919-968-2777. Circulation Tel: 919-968-2779. Reference Tel: 919-968-2780. FAX: 919-968-2838. E-mail: library@townofchapelhill.org. Web Site: www.chapelhillpubliclibrary.org. *Dir,* Susan Brown; *Asst Dir,* Mark S Bayles; Tel: 919-969-2036, E-mail: mbayles@townofchapelhill.org; *Asst Dir, Head, Tech Serv,* Meeghan Rosen; Tel: 919-969-2046, E-mail: mrosen@townofchapelhill.org; *Head, Ref,* Luba Sawczyn; Tel: 919-969-2032, E-mail: lsawczyn@townofchapelhill.org; *Head, Youth Serv,* Karin Michel; *Youth Serv Librn,* Krystal Black; *Circ Supvr,* Tim Logue; Staff 8 (MLS 8)
Founded 1958. Pop 54,904; Circ 1,018,000
Automation Activity & Vendor Info: (Cataloging) Innovative Interfaces, Inc; (Circulation) Innovative Interfaces, Inc; (OPAC) Innovative Interfaces, Inc
Open Mon-Thurs 10-8, Fri & Sat 10-6, Sun 12-6
Friends of the Library Group

SR CHAPEL OF THE CROSS EPISCOPAL LIBRARY*, 304 E Franklin St, 27514. SAN 375-054X. Tel: 919-929-2193. FAX: 919-933-9187. Web Site: www.thechapelofthecross.org.
Library Holdings: Bk Vols 3,000
Open Mon-Fri 9-5
Restriction: Non-circulating to the pub

C UNIVERSITY OF NORTH CAROLINA AT CHAPEL HILL*, University Library, Davis Library, 208 Raleigh St, Campus Box 3900, 27515-8890. SAN 354-5520. Circulation Tel: 919-962-1053. Interlibrary Loan Service Tel: 919-962-1326. Reference Tel: 919-962-1151. Administration Tel: 919-962-1301. Circulation FAX: 919-962-0484. Reference FAX: 919-962-5537. Administration FAX: 919-843-8936. E-mail: reference@unc.edu. Web Site: library.unc.edu. *Univ Librn & Assoc Provost for Libr,* Sarah Michalak; E-mail: smichala@email.unc.edu; *Assoc Univ Librn, Coll & Serv, Dep Univ Librn,* Carol Hunter; E-mail: cfhunter@email.unc.edu; *Assoc Univ Librn, Financial Planning & Admin Serv,* Catherine Gerdes; Tel: 919-962-1255, E-mail: cagerdes@email.unc.edu; *Assoc Univ Librn, Spec Coll, Dir, Louis Round Wilson Libr,* Rich Szary; Tel: 919-962-8125, E-mail: szary@email.unc.edu; *Assoc Univ Librn, Tech Serv & Syst,* Will Owen; E-mail: owen@email.unc.edu; *Dir, Pub Serv,* Joe Williams; E-mail: joewilliams@unc.edu; *Head, Circ,* Mitchell Whichard; E-mail: mlwhicha@email.unc.edu; *Head, Libr Syst,* Timothy McGeary; Tel: 919-962-1288, E-mail: tim.mcgeary@unc.edu; *Interim Head, Res & Instrul Serv,* Robert Dalton; E-mail: rdalton@email.unc.edu; Staff 131 (MLS 128, Non-MLS 3)
Founded 1796. Enrl 29,278; Fac 3,221; Highest Degree: Doctorate
Jul 2012-Jun 2013. Mats Exp $41,369,628
Library Holdings: Bk Vols 4,665,658; Per Subs 113,065
Special Collections: North Carolina Coll; Rare Book Coll; Southern Folklife Coll; Southern Historical Coll; University Archives. State Document Depository; UN Document Depository; US Document Depository
Wireless access
Publications: Windows (Newsletter)
Partic in Association of Research Libraries (ARL); Association of Southeastern Research Libraries; Carolina Consortium; Lyrasis; OCLC Online Computer Library Center, Inc; Triangle Research Libraries Network
Friends of the Library Group

Departmental Libraries:

COUCH BIOLOGY (BOTANY SECTION), 301 Coker Hall, CB No 3280, 27599, SAN 354-561X. Tel: 919-962-3783. FAX: 919-843-8393. *Librn,* William Burk; Tel: 919-962-4785, E-mail: billburk@email.unc.edu
Library Holdings: Bk Vols 36,189
Open Mon-Fri 8-5

COUCH BIOLOGY (ZOOLOGY SECTION), 213 Wilson Hall, CB No 3280, 27599, SAN 354-5822. Tel: 919-962-2264. FAX: 919-843-8393. *Librn,* David Romito; E-mail: dromito@email.unc.edu
Library Holdings: Bk Vols 30,939
Open Mon-Thurs 8-8, Fri 8-5, Sat 10-2, Sun 1-6

CL KATHRINE R EVERETT LAW LIBRARY, UNC Law Library, 160 Ridge Rd, CB No 3385, 27599-3385, SAN 354-5695. Tel: 919-962-1321. Circulation Tel: 919-962-1191. Interlibrary Loan Service Tel: 919-962-1196. Reference Tel: 919-962-1194. Administration Tel: 919-962-1322. Reference FAX: 919-843-7810. Administration FAX: 919-962-1193. E-mail: law_reference@unc.edu. Web Site: www.library.law.unc.edu. *Dir,* Anne Klinefelter; E-mail: klinefel@email.unc.edu; *Dep Dir,* Sara Sampson; Tel: 919-962-6202, E-mail: sasampso@email.unc.edu; *Asst Dir, Coll Serv,* Julie Kimbrough; Tel: 919-962 1199, Fax: 919-962-2294, E-mail: jlkimbro@email.unc.edu; *Asst Dir, Pub Serv,* Leslie Street; Tel: 919-843-5949, E-mail: lastreet@email.unc.edu; Staff 18 (MLS 11, Non-MLS 7)
Library Holdings: Bk Titles 74,721; Bk Vols 315,325; Per Subs 6,277
Subject Interests: Law
Automation Activity & Vendor Info: (Acquisitions) SirsiDynix; (Cataloging) Innovative Interfaces, Inc; (Media Booking) Innovative Interfaces, Inc
Database Vendor: LexisNexis, OCLC FirstSearch, Westlaw
Partic in OCLC Online Computer Library Center, Inc; TRLN

GEOLOGICAL SCIENCES, 121 Mitchell Hall, CB No 3315, 27599-3315, SAN 354-5679. Tel: 919-962-2386. FAX: 919-966-4519. Web Site: www.lib.unc.edu/geolib. *Librn,* Miriam Kennard; Tel: 919-962-0681, E-mail: kennard@email.unc.edu
Library Holdings: Bk Vols 48,000; Per Subs 850
Open Mon-Thurs (Winter) 8-8, Fri 8-5; Mon-Fri (Summer) 8-5

CM HEALTH SCIENCES, 355 S Columbia St, 27599. (Mail add: Campus Box 7585, 27599-7585), SAN 354-5857. Tel: 919-966-2111. Interlibrary Loan Service Tel: 919-966-4998. Reference Tel: 919-962-0800. FAX: 919-966-5592. Web Site: www.hsl.unc.edu. *Dir,* Position Currently Open; Staff 65 (MLS 27, Non-MLS 38)
Founded 1952. Highest Degree: Doctorate
Library Holdings: Bk Titles 128,737; Bk Vols 310,978; Per Subs 4,193
Subject Interests: Allied health, Dentistry, Med, Nursing, Pub health, Rare bks
Automation Activity & Vendor Info: (Acquisitions) Innovative Interfaces, Inc; (Cataloging) SirsiDynix; (Circulation) SirsiDynix; (OPAC) SirsiDynix

Partic in Center for Research Libraries; Lyrasis; National Network of Libraries of Medicine South Central Region; OCLC Online Computer Library Center, Inc
Publications: Annual Report; Brochures; Friends (Newsletter); News & Views (Newsletter)
Open Mon-Thurs 7:30am-1am, Fri 7:30am-8pm, Sat 10-6, Sun 10am-1am
Friends of the Library Group

HIGHWAY SAFETY RESEARCH CENTER, 730 Martin Luther King Jr Blvd, Ste 300, CB 3430, 27599-3430, SAN 312-7656. Tel: 919-962-2202. FAX: 919-962-8710. Web Site: www.hsrc.unc.edu/research_library/index.cfm. *Dir,* David L Harkey; E-mail: david_harkey@unc.edu; Staff 3 (MLS 1, Non-MLS 2)
Founded 1970
Subject Interests: Bicycle safety, Driver behav, Driver educ, Evaluation of hwy safety prog, Licensing, Pedestrian safety, Traffic records
Partic in Eastern Transportation Knowledge Network (ETKN); OCLC Online Computer Library Center, Inc
Publications: Research Publications of the University of NC Highway Safety Research Center
Open Mon-Fri 8-5
Restriction: Open to pub for ref only

ROBERT B HOUSE UNDERGRADUATE, 203 South Rd, CB No 3942, 27514-8890, SAN 354-5555. Tel: 919-962-1355. FAX: 919-962-2697. Web Site: www.lib.unc.edu/house. *Dir,* Suchi Mohanty; E-mail: smohanty@email.unc.edu
Library Holdings: Bk Vols 84,903
Partic in TRLN

INFORMATION & LIBRARY SCIENCE, 114 Manning Hall, CB No 3360, 27599, SAN 354-5709. Tel: 919-962-8361. FAX: 919-962-8071. E-mail: library@ils.unc.edu. Web Site: library.unc.edu/sils. *Librn,* Rebecca Vargha; E-mail: vargha@email.unc.edu; Staff 2 (MLS 1, Non-MLS 1)
Founded 1931
Library Holdings: Bk Vols 100,000
Subject Interests: Children's lit, Libr & info sci
Automation Activity & Vendor Info: (Cataloging) Innovative Interfaces, Inc; (OPAC) Innovative Interfaces, Inc
Open Mon-Thurs 7:45am-10pm, Fri 7:45-6, Sun Noon-10

INSTITUTE OF GOVERNMENT, Knapp-Sanders Bldg, CB No 3330, 27599-3330, SAN 354-5687. Tel: 919-966-4172. FAX: 919-966-4762. Web Site: www.sog.unc.edu/library. *Librn,* Alex Hess, III; E-mail: hess@sog.unc,edu; *Asst Librn,* Marsha Lobacz; E-mail: lobacz@sog.unc.edu
Library Holdings: Bk Vols 16,498
Open Mon-Fri 8-5

KENAN SCIENCE LIBRARY, G301 Venable Hall, CB No 3290, 27599, SAN 354-5644. Tel: 919-962-1188. E-mail: kenan-library@listserv.unc.edu. Web Site: library.unc.edu/science. *Head, Info Serv,* Danianne Mizzy; E-mail: mizzy@email.unc.edu; *Librn,* David Romito; E-mail: dromito@email.unc.edu
Partic in Dialog Corp

MUSIC, 300 Wilson Library, Campus Box 3906, 27514-8890, SAN 354-5768. Tel: 919-966-1113. FAX: 919-843-0418. Web Site: www.lib.unc.edu/music. *Head of Libr,* Philip Vandermeer; E-mail: vanderme@email.unc.edu
Library Holdings: AV Mats 43,000; Music Scores 81,000; Bk Vols 54,000
Open Mon-Thurs (Winter) 8:30am-9:30pm, Fri 8:30-5, Sat Noon-4, Sun 1-9:30; Mon-Thurs (Summer) 9-6, Fri 9-5

JOSEPH CURTIS SLOANE ART LIBRARY, 102 Hanes Art Ctr, CB No 3405, 27599-3405, SAN 354-558X. Tel: 919-962-2397. FAX: 919-962-0722. Web Site: www.lib.unc.edu/art. *Libr Tech,* Joshua Hockensmith; E-mail: hockensm@email.unc.edu
Library Holdings: Bk Vols 100,357
Open Mon-Thurs (Winter) 8am-9pm, Fri 8-5, Sat Noon-5, Sun 3-9; Mon-Fri (Summer) 9-4

CHARLOTTE

J CENTRAL PIEDMONT COMMUNITY COLLEGE LIBRARY*, 1201 Elizabeth Ave, 28235. (Mail add: PO Box 35009, 28235-5009), SAN 312-7680. Tel: 704-330-6885. Reference Tel: 704-330-6884. FAX: 704-330-6887. Web Site: www.cpcc.edu/library. *Dean,* Gloria Kelley; Tel: 704-330-6441, E-mail: Gloria.Kelley@cpcc.edu; *Dir,* Jennifer Arnold; Tel: 704-330-6635, E-mail: Jennifer.Arnold@cpcc.edu; *Asst Dir, Campus Serv,* Victoria Tsai; Tel: 704-330-6106, E-mail: vicky.tsai@cpcc.edu; *Asst Dir, Pub Serv,* Martin House; Tel: 704-330-6752, E-mail: martin.house@cpcc.edu; *Asst Dir, Tech Serv,* Kimberley Balcos; Tel: 704-330-6023, E-mail: kimberley.balcos@cpcc.edu; *Sr Librn,* Amy Burns; Tel: 704-330-4212, E-mail: amy.burns@cpcc.edu; *Sr Librn,* Retha Hall; Tel: 704-330-4816, E-mail: retha.hall@cpcc.edu; *Sr Librn,* Elaine Kushmaul; Tel: 704-330-6113, E-mail: elaine.kushmaul@cpcc.edu; *Sr Librn,* Erin Payton; Tel: 704-330-6814, E-mail: erin.payton@cpcc.edu; *Sr Librn,* Yan Wang; Tel: 704-330-6041, E-mail: yan.wang@cpcc.edu; *Librn,* Denise Keating; Tel: 704-330-4418, E-mail: denise.keating@cpcc.edu; *Librn,* Abigail Rovner; Tel: 704-330-4103, E-mail: abby.rovner@cpcc.edu; *Librn,* Melanie Wood; Tel: 704-330-7695, E-mail: melanie.wood@cpcc.edu; *E-Librn,* Julie Obst; Tel: 704-330-6498, E-mail: julie.obst@cpcc.edu; *Online Serv Librn,* Doug Short; Tel: 704-330-6845, E-mail: doug.short@cpcc.edu; *Syst Librn,* Gena Craig; Tel: 704-330-6755, E-mail: gena.craig@cpcc.edu; *Libr Serv Supvr,* Gloria Onukwufor; Tel: 704-330-3844, E-mail: gloria.onukwufor@cpcc.edu; *Libr Serv Supvr,* Martha Taylor; Tel: 704-330-6872, E-mail: martha.taylor@cpcc.edu; *Archivist,* Catherine Howell; Tel: 704-330-6373, E-mail: katie.howell@cpcc.edu; Staff 32 (MLS 17, Non-MLS 15)
Founded 1963. Highest Degree: Associate
Library Holdings: Bk Vols 100,000; Per Subs 4,350
Automation Activity & Vendor Info: (Acquisitions) SirsiDynix; (Cataloging) SirsiDynix; (Circulation) SirsiDynix; (OPAC) SirsiDynix
Database Vendor: CredoReference, EBSCOhost, Hoovers, LearningExpress, Medline, OCLC FirstSearch, Westlaw
Wireless access
Publications: Periodicals Holdings; Search Guides
Special Services for the Deaf - Assistive tech; TTY equip
Special Services for the Blind - Accessible computers
Open Mon-Thurs 7:30-8, Fri 7:30-5

M CHARLOTTE AHEC LIBRARY*, Medical Education Bldg, 1000 Blythe Blvd, 28203. (Mail add: PO Box 32861, 28232), SAN 312-7818. Tel: 704-355-3129. FAX: 704-355-7138. E-mail: charlotteaheclibrary@charlotteahec.org. Web Site: www.charlotteahec.org. *Dir, AHEC Med Media & Libr Serv,* Charles R Troutman; *Asst Dir,* Alan T Williams; *Med Librn,* Caroline Harzewski; *Med Librn,* Laura Leach; *Med Librn,* John Swearingen; *Educ Spec,* Nick Vukovich
Founded 1909
Library Holdings: AV Mats 2,000; Bk Titles 6,000; Per Subs 520
Subject Interests: Allied health, Clinical med, Nursing
Automation Activity & Vendor Info: (Cataloging) EOS International; (Circulation) EOS International; (OPAC) EOS International; (Serials) EOS International
Database Vendor: OVID Technologies
Partic in Dialog Corp; National Network of Libraries of Medicine
Open Mon-Thurs 8:30-6:30, Fri 8:30-5

P CHARLOTTE MECKLENBURG LIBRARY*, 310 N Tryon St, 28202-2176. SAN 354-6039. Tel: 704-416-0101. Circulation Tel: 704-416-0304. Interlibrary Loan Service Tel: 704-416-0105. Administration Tel: 704-416-0600. FAX: 704-416-0130. Administration FAX: 704-416-0677. Web Site: www.cmlibrary.org. *Chief Exec Officer,* Lenoir C Keesler, Jr; *Dir,* David Singleton; E-mail: dsingleton@cmlibrary.org; *Web Coordr,* Paul Devillo; *Educ Spec,* Julia Bowers Hanson; *Govt Doc, Ser,* Mimi Curlee, *ILL,* John Camenga; *Ref,* Barbara Gwynn; *Ser,* David Waters; *YA Serv,* Craig Angela; Staff 363.5 (MLS 107, Non-MLS 256.5)
Founded 1903. Pop 940,697; Circ 5,743,699
Jul 2012-Jun 2013 Income (Main Library and Branch(s)) $33,428,798, State $549,223, City $2,500, Federal $70,680, County $26,872,941, Other $5,933,454
Library Holdings: Bk Vols 1,159,957
Special Collections: Business Management Coll; Census; Genealogy Coll; Local History Coll; Mecklenburg Research Room. State Document Depository; US Document Depository
Subject Interests: Bus, Children's lit, Hist, Popular culture, Textiles
Automation Activity & Vendor Info: (Acquisitions) SirsiDynix; (Cataloging) SirsiDynix; (Circulation) SirsiDynix; (ILL) SirsiDynix; (OPAC) SirsiDynix; (Serials) SirsiDynix
Database Vendor: NC LIVE
Wireless access
Publications: African-American Album, Vol II (CD-ROM); An African-American Album; CIO (Monthly); Novello: Ten Years of Great American Writing (Anthology); Plum Thickets & Field Daisies; Trapping Time Between the Branches (Poetry Book)
Partic in Lyrasis; OCLC Online Computer Library Center, Inc
Open Tues-Thurs 10-7, Fri & Sat 10-5, Sun (Sept-May) 1-5
Friends of the Library Group
Branches: 19

BEATTIES FORD ROAD BRANCH, 2412 Beatties Ford Rd, 28216, SAN 377-5968. Tel: 704-416-3000. FAX: 704-416-3100. *Libr Mgr,* Irish McNair
Founded 1957
Special Collections: African-American Resource Coll
Open Mon-Thurs 10-8, Fri & Sat 10-5, Sun 1-5

CORNELIUS BRANCH, 21105 Catawba Ave, Cornelius, 28031, SAN 354-6128. Tel: 704-416-3800. FAX: 704-416-3900. *Libr Mgr,* Ellen Giduz
Open Mon-Wed 10-8, Fri & Sat 10-5

DAVIDSON BRANCH, 119 Main St, Davidson, 28036, SAN 354-6152. Tel: 704-416-4000. *Mgr,* Ellen Giduz
Founded 1995
Open Mon-Wed 10-8, Fri & Sat 10-5

HICKORY GROVE BRANCH, 5935 Hickory Grove Rd, 28215, SAN 328-6940. Tel: 704-416-4400. *Mgr,* April Wallace
Founded 1986
Open Mon-Wed 10-8, Fri & Sat 10-5

IMAGINON: THE JOE & JOAN MARTIN CENTER, 300 E Seventh St, 28202. Tel: 704-416-4600. FAX: 704-416-4700. Web Site: www.imaginon.org. *Libr Mgr,* Jason Hyatt; Tel: 704-416-4601, E-mail: jhyatt@cmlibrary.org; *Children's Mgr,* Ervin Seth; E-mail: servin@cmlibrary.org; *Circ Mgr,* Frank Mendoza; E-mail: fmendoza@cmlibrary.org; *Teen Serv,* Angela Craig; E-mail: acraig@cmlibrary.org
Founded 2005
Special Collections: Children's Book Illustrators Coll; Interactive Exhibits
Subject Interests: Animation, Children's lit, Film, Gaming, Music creation, Scripts, Teen lit
Open Tues-Thurs 10-7, Fri & Sat 10-5, Sun 1-5

INDEPENDENCE REGIONAL, 6000 Conference Dr, 28212, SAN 354-6241. Tel: 704-416-4800. *Br Mgr,* LaJuan Pringle
Founded 1996
Open Mon-Thurs 10-8, Fri & Sat 10-5, Sun 1-5

MATTHEWS BRANCH, 230 Matthews Station St, Matthews, 28105, SAN 354-6276. Tel: 704-416-5000. FAX: 704-416-5100. *Br Mgr,* Laura Highfill
Founded 1985
Open Mon-Wed 10-8, Fri & Sat 10-5

MINT HILL BRANCH, 6840 Matthews-Mint Hill Rd, Mint Hill, 28227, SAN 354-6306. Tel: 704-416-5200. FAX: 704-416-5300. *Br Mgr,* Mark Engelbrecht
Founded 1999
Open Mon-Wed 10-8, Fri & Sat 10-5

MORRISON REGIONAL LIBRARY, 7015 Morrison Blvd, 28211, SAN 354-642X. Tel: 704-416-5400. *Br Mgr,* Susan Green
Founded 1991
Open Mon-Thurs 10-8, Fri & Sat 10-5, Sun 1-5

MOUNTAIN ISLAND BRANCH, 4420 Hoyt Galvin Way, 28214, SAN 354-6365. Tel: 704-416-5600. FAX: 704-416-5710. *Br Mgr,* Helen McDowell
Founded 2005
Open Mon-Wed 10-8, Fri & Sat 10-5

MYERS PARK BRANCH, 1361 Queens Rd, 28207, SAN 354-6454. Tel: 704-416-5800. FAX: 704-416-5900. *Br Mgr,* Trilby Meeks
Founded 1956
Open Mon-Wed 10-8, Fri & Sat 10-5

NORTH COUNTY REGIONAL, 16500 Holly Crest Lane, Huntersville, 28078, SAN 377-600X. Tel: 704-416-6000. FAX: 704-416-6100. *Br Mgr,* Jo Ann Rodgers
Founded 1997
Open Mon-Thurs 10-8, Fri & Sat 10-5, Sun 1-5

PLAZA MIDWOOD BRANCH, 1623 Central Ave, 28205, SAN 354-6187. Tel: 704-416-6200. FAX: 704-416-6300. *Br Mgr,* Peter Jareo
Founded 1995
Open Mon-Wed 10-8, Fri & Sat 10-5

SCALEYBARK BRANCH, 101 Scaleybark Rd, 28209, SAN 325-4275. Tel: 704-416-6400. FAX: 704-416-6500. *Br Mgr,* Staci Falkowitz
Founded 1985
Open Mon-Wed 10-8, Fri & Sat 10-5

SOUTH COUNTY REGIONAL, 5801 Rea Rd, 28277, SAN 377-6026. Tel: 704-416-6600. *Mgr,* Susan McDonald
Founded 1998
Open Mon-Thurs 10-8, Fri & Sat 10-5, Sun 1-5

STEELE CREEK, 13620 Steele Creek Rd, 28273, SAN 373-7187. Tel: 704-416-6800. FAX: 704-416-6900. *Mgr,* Rhonda Pinkney
Founded 1994
Open Mon-Wed 10-8, Fri & Sat 10-5

SUGAR CREEK, 4045 N Tryon St, 28206, SAN 354-6489. Tel: 704-416-7000. FAX: 704-416-7100. *Br Mgr,* Kevin Bittle
Open Mon-Wed 10-8, Fri & Sat 10-5

UNIVERSITY CITY REGIONAL, 301 East W T Harris Blvd, 28262, SAN 372-008X. Tel: 704-416-7200. FAX: 704-416-7300. *Mgr,* Julia Smith
Founded 1999
Open Mon-Thurs 10-8, Fri & Sat 10-5, Sun 1-5

WEST BOULEVARD BRANCH, 2157 West Blvd, 28208, SAN 322-5003. Tel: 704-416-7400. FAX: 704-416-7500. *Br Mgr,* Alecia Mitchell
Founded 1996
Open Mon-Wed 10-8, Fri & Sat 10-5

S CHARLOTTE MUSEUM OF HISTORY*, Hezekiah Alexander Homesite - Lassiter Research Library, 3500 Shamrock Dr, 28215. SAN 325-7592. Tel: 704-568-1774. FAX: 704-566-1817. Web Site: www.charlottemuseum.org. *Curator, Historian,* Leslie Kesler
Library Holdings: Bk Titles 3,000; Bk Vols 3,500; Per Subs 10
Special Collections: Alexander Geneology (Hez Alexander)
Restriction: Open by appt only

S CHARLOTTE OBSERVER NEWSROOM LIBRARY*, 600 S Tryon, 28202. (Mail add: PO Box 30308, 28230-0308), SAN 312-7788. Tel: 704-358-5212. FAX: 704-358-5203. E-mail: lib@charlotteobserver.com. Web Site: www.charlotte.com. *Mgr,* Maria David
Founded 1956
Library Holdings: Bk Vols 2,000
Restriction: Not open to pub

S CHIQUITA BRANDS INTERNATIONAL, INC*, Law Library, 550 S Caldwell St, 28202. SAN 374-5783. Tel: 980-636-5000. FAX: 704-919-5230. *In Charge,* Deresa Sherrill; Staff 1 (MLS 1)
Founded 1990
Library Holdings: Bk Titles 1,000
Database Vendor: Westlaw
Partic in Westlaw
Restriction: Staff use only

R CHRIST EPISCOPAL CHURCH LIBRARY*, 1412 Providence Rd, 28207. SAN 312-7710. Tel: 704-333-0378. FAX: 704-333-8420. Web Site: www.christchurchcharlotte.org. *Librn,* Elizabeth Preston
Library Holdings: Bk Vols 2,425

S DUKE ENERGY CORP*, David Nabow Library, 526 S Church St, NC EC06H, 28202. (Mail add: PO Box 1006, 28201-1006), SAN 354-5946. Tel: 704-382-4095. FAX: 704-382-7826. E-mail: corporate_library_services@duke-energy.com. *Mgr, Libr Serv,* Lynn Helms; Tel: 704-382-2803; Staff 3 (Non-MLS 3)
Founded 1967
Library Holdings: Bk Titles 50,000; Per Subs 200
Special Collections: Standards (ANSI, NEMA, IEEE, EPRI, INPOS, ASTM)
Subject Interests: Automation, Civil, Electrical, Environ, Humanities, Mechanical, Nuclear eng, Soc sci
Automation Activity & Vendor Info: (Acquisitions) SirsiDynix; (Cataloging) SirsiDynix; (Circulation) SirsiDynix; (OPAC) SirsiDynix; (Serials) SirsiDynix
Wireless access
Function: For res purposes
Restriction: Co libr

C ECPI UNIVERSITY*, Charlotte Campus, 4800 Airport Center Pkwy, 28208. Tel: 704-399-1010, Ext 244. Toll Free Tel: 866-708-6167. FAX: 704-399-9144. Web Site: www.ecpi.edu. *Campus Librn,* Judith Cousar; E-mail: jcousar@ecpi.edu; *Evening Librn,* Carol Camenga; Staff 2 (MLS 1, Non-MLS 1)
Enrl 500; Fac 30; Highest Degree: Associate
Library Holdings: Bk Titles 5,461; Bk Vols 6,109
Subject Interests: Computer sci, Computer tech, Nursing
Automation Activity & Vendor Info: (Cataloging) Follett Software; (Circulation) Follett Software; (OPAC) Follett Software
Database Vendor: Gale Cengage Learning
Partic in Libr & Info Resources Network (LIRN)
Open Mon, Wed & Thurs 8:45am-9:30pm, Tues 8:45-5:30, Fri 8:45-1:30

R FIRST PRESBYTERIAN CHURCH LIBRARY*, 200 W Trade St, 28202-1623. SAN 312-7737. Tel: 704-332-5123, Ext 269. FAX: 704-334-4135. Web Site: www.firstpres-charlotte.org. *In Charge,* Patricia Spearman
Founded 1821
Library Holdings: CDs 25; DVDs 15; Large Print Bks 50; Bk Titles 4,500; Bk Vols 4,800; Per Subs 12; Spec Interest Per Sub 4; Videos 10
Special Collections: Church Histories, Mecklenburg County & Other Southern Counties
Subject Interests: Christianity, Spiritual issues
Automation Activity & Vendor Info: (Cataloging) Follett Software; (Circulation) Follett Software
Open Mon-Fri 8-5, Sat 8-12, Sun 7-7
Friends of the Library Group

C JOHNSON & WALES UNIVERSITY*, Charlotte Campus Library, 801 W Trade St, 28202. Tel: 980-598-1611. Administration Tel: 908-598-1603. Administration FAX: 980-598-1606. Web Site: www.library.jwu.edu. *Dir of Libr Serv,* Richard Moniz; Tel: 980-598-1604; *Coll Mgt Librn,* Jean Moats; Tel: 980-598-1608; *Ref & Instruction Librn,* Joe Eshleman; Tel: 980-598-1605; *Ref Librn,* Justin Herman; Tel: 980-598-1607; *Ref Librn,* Melanie Wood; *Ref Librn,* Valerie Freeman; Tel: 980-598-1609
Library Holdings: Bk Vols 29,041
Automation Activity & Vendor Info: (Cataloging) Innovative Interfaces, Inc; (Circulation) Innovative Interfaces, Inc; (ILL) Innovative Interfaces, Inc; (OPAC) Innovative Interfaces, Inc; (Serials) Innovative Interfaces, Inc
Database Vendor: EBSCOhost, LexisNexis
Open Mon-Wed 8am-10pm, Thurs 8am-9pm, Fri 8-4, Sat 12-4, Sun 1-8

C JOHNSON C SMITH UNIVERSITY*, James B Duke Memorial Library, 100 Beatties Ford Rd, 28216. SAN 312-7753. Tel: 704-371-6740. Circulation Tel: 704-371-6745. Interlibrary Loan Service Tel: 704-371-6732. FAX: 704-378-1191. E-mail: refdesk@jcsu.edu. Web Site: library.jcsu.edu. *Dir of Libr Serv,* Monika Rhue; Tel: 704-371-6730, E-mail: mrhue@jcsu.edu; *Archival Serv Librn,* Brandon Lunsford; E-mail: bdlunsford@jcsu.edu; *Coll Develop, Digitization Librn,* Michelle Orr; E-mail: morr@jcsu.edu; *Educ Tech Librn,* Geneen Clinkscales; E-mail: gclinkscales@jcsu.edu; *Instrul Tech Librn,* Position Currently Open; *Info Literacy, Ref Librn,* Brenda Almeyda; E-mail: balmeyda@jcsu.edu; *Syst Librn,* Andrea Hylton; E-mail: ahylton@jcsu.edu; *Cat,* Barbara Carr; *Instrul Electronic Res, Ser,* Marcella McGowan; E-mail: mmcgowan@jcsu.edu. Subject Specialists: *Archives, Digitization, Info literacy,* Monika Rhue; Staff 14 (MLS 8, Non-MLS 6)
Founded 1867. Enrl 1,500; Fac 105; Highest Degree: Bachelor
Library Holdings: AV Mats 1,239; e-books 22,000; Electronic Media & Resources 59; Microforms 179,616; Bk Vols 105,249; Per Subs 227
Special Collections: Black Heritage Rare Book Coll; Black Life & Literature (Schomburg Coll), microfilm; Black Presbyterian Coll (Inez Moore Parker Archives); Charlotte REACH 2010; Eva M Clayton Coll. Oral History
Automation Activity & Vendor Info: (Acquisitions) Innovative Interfaces, Inc - Millenium; (Cataloging) OCLC; (Circulation) Innovative Interfaces, Inc - Millenium; (Course Reserve) Innovative Interfaces, Inc - Millenium; (ILL) OCLC; (OPAC) Innovative Interfaces, Inc - Millenium; (Serials) Innovative Interfaces, Inc - Millenium
Database Vendor: 3M Library Systems, ACM (Association for Computing Machinery), CQ Press, EBSCOhost, JSTOR, LexisNexis, Medline, NC LIVE, OCLC FirstSearch, OCLC WorldShare Interlibrary Loan, Project MUSE, ProQuest, ReferenceUSA, Wilson - Wilson Web, YBP Library Services
Wireless access
Function: Archival coll, Computers for patron use, Copy machines, Distance learning, Doc delivery serv, e-mail & chat, E-Reserves, Electronic databases & coll, Exhibits, Fax serv, ILL available, Instruction & testing, Learning ctr, Online info literacy tutorials on the web & in blackboard, Online searches, Orientations, Ref serv in person, Scanner, Web-catalog
Publications: The Informer (Bi-annually)
Partic in Charlotte Area Educ Consortium
Special Services for the Deaf - Accessible learning ctr
Open Mon-Thurs 7:30am-1am, Fri 7:30-5:30, Sat 10-2, Sun 2-Midnight

L K&L GATES LAW LIBRARY*, Hearst Tower, 214 N Tryon St, 47th Flr, 28202. SAN 372-2104. Tel: 704-331-7553. FAX: 704-353-3253. Web Site: www.klgates.com. *Libr Mgr,* Lee Elliott Carnes; E-mail: lee.carnes@klgates.com; *Ref Librn,* Stephanie Dooley; Staff 2 (MLS 2)
Founded 1957
Library Holdings: Bk Titles 4,000; Per Subs 125
Automation Activity & Vendor Info: (Cataloging) SIRSI WorkFlows
Database Vendor: Dialog, Dun & Bradstreet, HeinOnline, Hoovers, LexisNexis, OneSource, Westlaw, Westlaw Business
Wireless access

R LEVINE-SKLUT JUDAIC LIBRARY & RESOURCE CENTER*, 5007 Providence Rd, Ste 107, 28226. SAN 312-7893. Tel: 704-944-6763. Reference Tel: 704-944-6783. FAX: 704-362-4171. E-mail: library@shalomcharlotte.org. *Dir,* Amalia Warshenbrot; Staff 4 (MLS 2, Non-MLS 2)
Founded 1986
Library Holdings: CDs 50; DVDs 100; Large Print Bks 50; Bk Titles 15,000; Bk Vols 17,000; Per Subs 20; Videos 400
Special Collections: Judaica Coll. Oral History
Automation Activity & Vendor Info: (Cataloging) Follett Software; (Circulation) Follett Software
Friends of the Library Group

S MINT MUSEUM LIBRARY*, 2730 Randolph Rd, 28207. SAN 326-4599. Tel: 704-337-2000, 704-337-2023. FAX: 704-337-2101. E-mail: library@mintmuseum.org. Web Site: www.mintmuseum.org/libraries.html. *Dir of Educ,* Cheryl Palmer; Tel: 704-337-2031, E-mail: cheryl.palmer@mintmuseum.org; *Librn,* Joyce Weaver; E-mail: joyce.weaver@mintmuseum.org; *Cataloger,* Nancy Mosley; E-mail: nancy.mosley@mintmuseum.org; Staff 1.5 (MLS 1.5)
Library Holdings: Bk Vols 18,000; Per Subs 75
Special Collections: Decorative Arts & Ceramics Primary Source Material, 17th-19th Centuries
Subject Interests: Craft, Design, Fashion, Fine arts
Automation Activity & Vendor Info: (Acquisitions) Innovative Interfaces, Inc; (Cataloging) Innovative Interfaces, Inc; (Circulation) Innovative Interfaces, Inc; (OPAC) Innovative Interfaces, Inc; (Serials) Innovative Interfaces, Inc
Function: Copy machines, Online cat, Ref & res, Scanner
Open Tues-Fri 10-5
Restriction: Non-circulating

L MOORE & VAN ALLEN PLLC*, Law Library, Bank of America Corporate Ctr, 100 N Tryon, Ste 4700, 28202. SAN 372-235X. Tel: 704-331-1000. FAX: 704-339-5946. E-mail: librarians@mvalaw.com. *Dir, Legal Res,* Tamara Reno; E-mail: tamarareno@mvalaw.com
Library Holdings: Bk Titles 5,000; Bk Vols 11,000; Per Subs 200
Automation Activity & Vendor Info: (Acquisitions) EOS International; (Cataloging) EOS International; (Circulation) EOS International; (Serials) EOS International

M PRESBYTERIAN HOSPITAL*, Learning Resource Center, 200 Hawthorne Lane, 28204-2528. (Mail add: PO Box 33549, 28233-3549), SAN 312-7869. Tel: 704-384-4258. FAX: 704-384-5058. E-mail: lrc@novanthealth.org. *Librn,* Mary Wallace Berry; *Media Spec,* William Barfield
Library Holdings: Bk Vols 6,500; Per Subs 150
Subject Interests: Med, Nursing
Automation Activity & Vendor Info: (Cataloging) EOS International; (Circulation) EOS International; (OPAC) EOS International; (Serials) EOS International
Database Vendor: OVID Technologies

C QUEENS UNIVERSITY OF CHARLOTTE*, Everett Library, 1900 Selwyn Ave, 28274-0001. SAN 354-6543. Tel: 704-337-2401. Reference Tel: 704-337-7127. FAX: 704-337-2517. Web Site: www.queens.edu/library. *Univ Librn,* Dr Carol Walker Jordan; Tel: 704-337-2400, E-mail: jordanc@queens.edu; *Pub Serv Librn,* Elaine Wood; E-mail: woode@queens.edu; *Syst Instruction Librn,* John Norris; Tel: 704-337-2278, E-mail: norrisj@queens.edu; *Acq, Ser,* Carolyn Patterson; E-mail: pattersc@queens.edu; *Cat,* Harold Newfield; E-mail: newfieldh@queens.edu; *ILL,* Sharon Barham; E-mail: barhams@queens.edu; *Ref Serv,* Lew Hermann; Tel: 704-337-2470, E-mail: hermanl@queens.edu; Staff 10 (MLS 5, Non-MLS 5)
Founded 1857. Enrl 1,610; Fac 120; Highest Degree: Master
Library Holdings: Bk Titles 106,090; Bk Vols 131,365; Per Subs 632
Special Collections: Hicks Asia Coll; North Carolina Coll; Queens College memorabilia & archives. Oral History
Subject Interests: 18th Century Charlotte, Local hist, Queen's College hist
Automation Activity & Vendor Info: (Acquisitions) SirsiDynix; (Cataloging) SirsiDynix; (Circulation) SirsiDynix; (Course Reserve) SirsiDynix; (ILL) SirsiDynix; (Media Booking) SirsiDynix; (OPAC) SirsiDynix; (Serials) SirsiDynix
Publications: Friends of the Library Newsletter (3 per yr); Rena Herald Newsletter (10 per yr)
Partic in Charlotte Area Educ Consortium; Lyrasis
Open Mon-Thurs (Winter) 8am-Midnight, Fri 8:30-6, Sat 10-5, Sun 1-Midnight; Mon-Thurs (Summer) 1-9, Fri 1-5, Sat 10-2
Friends of the Library Group

C UNIVERSITY OF NORTH CAROLINA AT CHARLOTTE*, J Murrey Atkins Library, 9201 University City Blvd, 28223-0001. SAN 312-7907. Tel: 704-687-0494. Circulation Tel: 704-687-0491. Interlibrary Loan Service Tel: 704-687-2416. Reference Tel: 704-687-2241. FAX: 704-687-3050. Interlibrary Loan Service FAX: 704-687-3473. Reference FAX: 704-687-2232. Web Site: library.uncc.edu. *Univ Librn,* Position Currently Open; *Assoc Univ Librn, Coll Develop,* Chuck Hamaker; Tel: 704-687-1106, E-mail: cahamake@uncc.edu; *Assoc Univ Librn, Tech Serv,* Michael Winecoff, Tel: 704-687-1126, E-mail: mkwineco@uncc.edu; Staff 32 (MLS 32)
Founded 1946. Highest Degree: Doctorate
Library Holdings: AV Mats 110,870; e-books 24,380; Bk Titles 551,399; Bk Vols 969,680; Per Subs 34,486
Special Collections: 17th & 18th Century English Drama; Contemporary, Social & Political History of Charlotte & Mecklenburg County; NC state & county document. Oral History; UN Document Depository; US Document Depository
Automation Activity & Vendor Info: (Acquisitions) OCLC WorldShare Interlibrary Loan; (Cataloging) OCLC WorldShare Interlibrary Loan; (Circulation) OCLC WorldShare Interlibrary Loan; (Course Reserve) OCLC WorldShare Interlibrary Loan; (ILL) OCLC WorldShare Interlibrary Loan; (Media Booking) OCLC WorldShare Interlibrary Loan; (OPAC) OCLC WorldShare Interlibrary Loan; (Serials) OCLC WorldShare Interlibrary Loan
Publications: Atlis
Partic in OCLC Online Computer Library Center, Inc
Open Mon-Thurs 7:30am-Midnight, Fri 7:30am-8pm, Sat 10-8, Sun 11am-Midnight

CHEROKEE

S MUSEUM OF THE CHEROKEE INDIAN*, Archives Library, 589 Tsali Blvd, 28719. (Mail add: PO Box 1599, 28719-1599), SAN 325-7630. Tel: 828-497-3481. FAX: 828-497-4985. Web Site: www.cherokeemuseum.org. *Archivist,* James Taylor; E-mail: botaylor@cherokeemuseum.org
Founded 1948

Library Holdings: Bk Vols 4,000
Open Mon-Fri (Winter) 9-5; Mon-Fri (Summer) 9-7

P QUALLA BOUNDARY PUBLIC LIBRARY*, 810 Acquoni Rd, Cherokee Indian Reservation, 28719. (Mail add: PO Box 1839, 28719-1839), SAN 354-6632. Tel: 828-497-1764. FAX: 828-497-1763. *Libr Mgr,* Robin Swayney
Founded 1970. Pop 13,000; Circ 20,000
Library Holdings: Bk Titles 26,000; Per Subs 55
Special Collections: Genealogy (Cherokee Coll); Native Americans (Indian Coll)
Automation Activity & Vendor Info: (Cataloging) Follett Software; (Circulation) Follett Software; (OPAC) Follett Software
Wireless access
Open Mon, Tues & Thurs 8-7, Wed 8-5, Fri 7:45-4:30

CHERRY POINT

A UNITED STATES MARINE CORPS*, Air Station Library, Bldg 298, Marine Corps Air Station, 28533-0009. (Mail add: PSC Box 8009, 28533-8009), SAN 354-6691. Tel: 252-466-3552. Administration Tel: 252-466-3532. FAX: 252-466-5402. Administration FAX: 252-466-6418. Web Site: library.usmc-mccs.org, mccs.ent.sirsi.net/client/cherry_point. *Dir,* Suzanne L Shell; E-mail: shells@usmc-mccs.org; *Ref Librn,* David Conlin; Fax: 252-466-2476, E-mail: conlindb@usmc-mccs.org; *Cataloger,* Thomas Donaldson; E-mail: donaldsontm@usmc-mccs.org; Staff 10 (MLS 3, Non-MLS 7)
Founded 1942
Library Holdings: AV Mats 14,747; e-books 100,095; Bk Vols 35,350; Per Subs 158
Subject Interests: Mil hist (US), Mil sci
Automation Activity & Vendor Info: (Cataloging) SirsiDynix; (Circulation) SirsiDynix; (ILL) OCLC FirstSearch; (OPAC) SirsiDynix; (Serials) SirsiDynix
Database Vendor: ABC-CLIO, Baker & Taylor, Booklist Online, College Source, CountryWatch, ebrary, EBSCOhost, Evanced Solutions, Inc, Facts on File, Gale Cengage Learning, Grolier Online, Ingram Library Services, Jane's, LearningExpress, Newsbank, Overdrive, Inc, ProQuest, Safari Books Online, SirsiDynix, World Book Online, WT Cox
Wireless access
Open Mon-Sat 10-7, Sun 1-7

CLINTON

P SAMPSON-CLINTON PUBLIC LIBRARY*, J C Holliday Memorial Library, 217 Graham St, 28328. SAN 354-6721. Tel: 910-592-4153. FAX: 910-590-3504. Web Site: sites.google.com/site/sampsonclintonpubliclibrary. *Dir,* Heather Bonney; E-mail: hbonney@sampsonnc.com; *Ch Serv,* Addie Hodges; E-mail: ahodges@sampsonnc.com; Staff 13 (MLS 2, Non-MLS 11)
Founded 1935
Library Holdings: AV Mats 15; DVDs 141; Large Print Bks 1,261; Bk Vols 46,454; Per Subs 103; Talking Bks 523; Videos 1,554
Special Collections: North Carolina & Local History Coll, bks & microflm
Subject Interests: Local hist
Automation Activity & Vendor Info: (Cataloging) Innovative Interfaces, Inc; (Circulation) Innovative Interfaces, Inc; (OPAC) Innovative Interfaces, Inc
Database Vendor: EBSCOhost, Gale Cengage Learning, LexisNexis, OCLC FirstSearch, OVID Technologies, ProQuest
Wireless access
Function: After school storytime, AV serv, Homebound delivery serv, ILL available, Photocopying/Printing, Prog for adults, Prog for children & young adult, Ref serv available, Spoken cassettes & CDs, Summer reading prog, VHS videos
Open Mon-Fri 9-6, Sat 11-5
Restriction: Non-circulating coll, Photo ID required for access
Branches: 3
BRYAN MEMORIAL, 302 W Wecksdale St, Newton Grove, 28366. (Mail add: PO Box 188, Newton Grove, 28366-0188), SAN 354-673X. Tel: 910-594-1260. *Br Mgr,* Jean Simmons
Library Holdings: AV Mats 8; DVDs 172; Large Print Bks 239; Bk Vols 17,083; Per Subs 21; Talking Bks 160; Videos 977
Open Mon, Tues, Thurs & Fri 9-6
MIRIAM B LAMB MEMORIAL, 144 S Church Ave, Garland, 28441. (Mail add: PO Box 426, Garland, 28441-0426), SAN 354-6780. Tel: 910-529-2441. *Br Mgr,* Connie Guyton; E-mail: cguyton@sampsonnc.com; Staff 1 (Non-MLS 1)
Library Holdings: AV Mats 7; DVDs 139; Large Print Bks 186; Bk Vols 7,692; Per Subs 15; Talking Bks 81; Videos 217
Open Mon-Wed & Fri 9-6
ROSEBORO BRANCH, 300 W Roseboro St, Roseboro, 28382. (Mail add: PO Box 2066, Roseboro, 28382-2066), SAN 354-6810. Tel: 910-525-5436. *Br Mgr,* Deborah Dudley; E-mail: ddudley@sampsonnc.com; *Circ,* Rachel Corbin
Library Holdings: AV Mats 8; DVDs 143; Large Print Bks 89; Bk Vols 16,404; Talking Bks 245; Videos 480
Open Mon & Wed-Fri 9-6
Bookmobiles: 1. In Charge, Stephanie Johnson. Bk vols 7,259

J SAMPSON COMMUNITY COLLEGE LIBRARY*, 1801 Sunset Ave, Hwy 24 W, 28328. (Mail add: PO Box 318, 28329-0318), SAN 312-794X. Tel: 910-592-8081. FAX: 910-592-8048. Web Site: www.sampson.cc.nc.us. *Dir,* Mark Rushing; Tel: 910-592-8081, Ext 5002, E-mail: mrushing@sampsoncc.edu; Staff 2 (MLS 1, Non-MLS 1)
Founded 1966. Enrl 1,330; Fac 44
Library Holdings: Bk Titles 30,000; Per Subs 250
Automation Activity & Vendor Info: (Acquisitions) SirsiDynix; (Cataloging) SirsiDynix; (Circulation) SirsiDynix
Publications: AV Handbook; LRC Handbook; Manual of Policies & Procedures
Open Mon-Thurs 8am-9pm, Fri 8-4

CLYDE

J HAYWOOD COMMUNITY COLLEGE*, Learning Resource Center, 185 Freedlander Dr, 28721. SAN 312-7958. Tel: 828-627-4550. FAX: 828-627-4553. Web Site: www.haywood.edu. *Dir,* Bill Kinyon; Tel: 828-627-4551, E-mail: wrkinyon@haywood.edu; *Librn,* Heather Cyre; Tel: 828-565-4083, E-mail: hmcyre@haywood.edu; Staff 2 (MLS 2)
Founded 1967. Enrl 1,600; Fac 59; Highest Degree: Associate
Jul 2012-Jun 2013. Mats Exp $50,000, Books $35,165, Per/Ser (Incl. Access Fees) $13,500, AV Mat $78
Library Holdings: Bk Vols 40,000; Per Subs 160
Special Collections: Folkmoot
Subject Interests: Auto trades, Bldg construction, Bus admin, Cosmetology, Criminal justice, Electrical installation, Fish, Forest mgt, Machinist, Manufacturing eng tech, Med off asst, Nursing educ, Production crafts, Welding
Automation Activity & Vendor Info: (Acquisitions) SirsiDynix; (Cataloging) SirsiDynix; (Circulation) SirsiDynix; (Course Reserve) SirsiDynix; (ILL) SirsiDynix; (Media Booking) SirsiDynix; (OPAC) SirsiDynix; (Serials) SirsiDynix
Database Vendor: EBSCOhost, OCLC FirstSearch
Wireless access
Function: Prof lending libr
Partic in CCLINK; North Carolina Community College System; North Carolina Libraries for Virtual Education; OCLC Online Computer Library Center, Inc

COLUMBIA

P TYRRELL COUNTY PUBLIC LIBRARY*, 414 Main St, 27925. (Mail add: PO Box 540, 27925-0540), SAN 312-7974. Tel: 252-796-3771. FAX: 252-796-1167. *Librn,* Douglas Hoffman; Staff 1 (MLS 1)
Pop 4,000; Circ 33,703
Library Holdings: Bk Vols 21,000; Per Subs 30
Subject Interests: Genealogy, Local hist
Automation Activity & Vendor Info: (Cataloging) TLC (The Library Corporation); (Circulation) TLC (The Library Corporation); (OPAC) TLC (The Library Corporation)
Mem of Pettigrew Regional Library
Open Mon-Thurs 10-8, Fri 10-6, Sat 10-1

COLUMBUS

P POLK COUNTY PUBLIC LIBRARY*, 1289 W Mills St, 28722. SAN 312-7982. Tel: 828-894-8721. FAX: 828-894-2761. E-mail: pcpl@polklibrary.org. Web Site: polklibrary.org. *Dir,* Rishara Finsel; E-mail: rfinsel@publib.polknc.org; *Outreach Serv Librn,* Rita Owens; E-mail: rowens@polklibrary.org; *Coordr, Ch Serv,* Jen Pace; E-mail: jpace@polklibrary.org; *Pub Serv,* Sharon Spurlin; E-mail: sspurlin@polklibrary.org; *Tech Serv,* Wannangwa Dever; E-mail: wdever@polklibrary.org; Staff 6 (MLS 1, Non-MLS 5)
Founded 1960. Circ 92,604
Library Holdings: Bk Vols 45,624; Per Subs 190
Subject Interests: Genealogy, Literacy, Local hist
Wireless access
Publications: Friends of the Polk County Library (Newsletter)
Open Mon & Fri 9-6, Tues-Thurs 9-8, Sat 9-4
Friends of the Library Group
Branches: 1
SALUDA BRANCH, 44 W Main St, Saluda, 28773-0398. Tel: 828-749-2117. FAX: 828-749-2118. *Br Mgr,* Bob McCall; E-mail: bmccall@publib.polknc.org; *Circ,* Margaret Easley
Open Mon-Fri 9-6, Sat 9-1
Friends of the Library Group
Bookmobiles: 1. Outreach Servs Librn, Rita Owens

CONCORD

C BARBER SCOTIA COLLEGE*, Sage Memorial Library, 145 Cabarrus Ave W, 28025. SAN 312-7990. Tel: 704-789-2953. FAX: 704-789-2955. Web Site: www.b-sc.edu. *Pub Serv,* Flora Allison; *Cat,* Joanne Gresham; Staff 4 (MLS 2, Non-MLS 2)
Founded 1867. Enrl 700; Fac 60; Highest Degree: Bachelor
Library Holdings: Bk Vols 49,000; Per Subs 102
Subject Interests: African-Am
Automation Activity & Vendor Info: (Circulation) Ex Libris Group
Publications: The Sageline (Newsletter)
Open Mon-Thurs 8am-10pm, Fri 8-5, Sun 5-9

P CABARRUS COUNTY PUBLIC LIBRARY*, 27 Union St N, 28025-4793. SAN 312-8016. Tel: 704-920-2050. FAX: 704-784-3822. E-mail: library@cabarruscounty.us. Web Site: www.cabarruscounty.us/library. *Dir of Libr,* Thomas W Dillard, Jr; E-mail: twdillard@cabarruscounty.us; *Br Mgr,* JoAnn H Gresham; *Acq,* Janet S Barbee; *Adult Serv,* Kristine Benshoff; *Ch Serv,* Leslie Cook; *Circ,* Loretta Barringer; *ILL,* Timothy Auten; Staff 3 (MLS 3)
Founded 1911. Pop 140,000; Circ 58,000
Library Holdings: AV Mats 8,399; Electronic Media & Resources 11; Large Print Bks 3,000; Bk Vols 260,000; Per Subs 537; Videos 7,122
Special Collections: Concord & Cabarrus County History Coll; Holt Coll, original art
Automation Activity & Vendor Info: (Cataloging) SirsiDynix; (Circulation) SirsiDynix; (ILL) OCLC; (OPAC) SirsiDynix
Database Vendor: OCLC FirstSearch, SirsiDynix
Publications: Conspectus (Newsletter)
Open Mon-Thurs 9-9, Fri & Sat 9-5
Restriction: Lending limited to county residents
Friends of the Library Group
Branches: 3
HARRISBURG BRANCH, 201 Sims Pkwy, Harrisburg, 28075. Tel: 704-920-2080. FAX: 704-455-2017. *Br Mgr,* Adele Fitzgerald; E-mail: arfitzgerald@cabarruscounty.us; *Br Mgr,* Patricia Lowder; Staff 1 (MLS 1)
Open Mon-Thurs 10-8, Fri 10-5, Sat 10-2
KANNAPOLIS BRANCH, 850 Mountain St, Kannapolis, 28081, SAN 325-3813. Tel: 704-920-1180. FAX: 704-938-3512. *Br Mgr,* Terry B Prather; *Adult Serv,* Annie Gardner; Staff 7 (MLS 2, Non-MLS 5)
Founded 1985
Special Collections: Local History Coll
Open Mon-Thurs 9-8, Fri & Sat 9-5
Friends of the Library Group
MT PLEASANT BRANCH, 8556 Cook St, Mount Pleasant, 28124, SAN 377-6050. Tel: 704-436-2202. FAX: 704-436-8205. *Br Mgr,* Kate Moore; E-mail: khmoore@cabarruscounty.us
Open Mon & Wed 10-6, Tues & Thurs 10-8, Fri 10-5, Sat 10-2
Friends of the Library Group
Bookmobiles: 1

M NORTHEAST MEDICAL CENTER*, Cabarrus Health Sciences Library, 920 Church St N, 28025. SAN 312-8008. Tel: 704-403-1798. FAX: 704-403-1776. Web Site: www.cabarruscollege.edu/library/index.html. *Librn,* Emily Patridge; E-mail: emily.patridge@cabarruscollege.edu; Staff 2 (MLS 1, Non-MLS 1)
Founded 1966
Library Holdings: Bk Vols 6,300; Per Subs 150
Special Collections: Health Care & Medical Subjects, V-tapes
Subject Interests: Allied health, Med, Nursing
Open Mon-Thurs 8:30am-9pm, Fri 8:30-4:30, Sun 1-9

CONOVER

S HARTSHORN FAMILY ASSOCIATION LIBRARY*, 1204 Fourth St Dr SE, 28613-1847. SAN 371-5140. Tel: 828-464-4981. FAX: 828-464-4981. *Librn,* Lana C Hartshorn
Founded 1985
Library Holdings: Bk Titles 466; Bk Vols 500; Per Subs 31
Special Collections: Genealogy (Hartshorn Coll), bks & doc copies
Publications: Hartshorn Hotline
Restriction: Open by appt only

COVE CITY

P COVE CITY PUBLIC LIBRARY*, 102 N Main St, 28523. (Mail add: PO Box 399, 28523-0399), SAN 320-4995. Tel: 252-638-6363. FAX: 252-638-4639. *Librn,* Nancy Chase; E-mail: ncchase45@yahoo.com; *Ch Serv,* Barbara Avery
Founded 1979. Pop 600; Circ 8,020
Library Holdings: Bk Titles 7,500; Per Subs 13; Talking Bks 28
Automation Activity & Vendor Info: (Cataloging) Horizon; (Circulation) Horizon; (OPAC) Horizon
Mem of Craven-Pamlico-Carteret Regional Library System
Open Mon-Thurs 2-8, Fri 2-6
Friends of the Library Group

CULLOWHEE

C WESTERN CAROLINA UNIVERSITY*, Hunter Library, 176 Central Dr, 28723. SAN 312-8024. Tel: 828-227-7307. Circulation Tel: 828-227-7485. Reference Tel: 828-227-7465. Toll Free Tel: 866-928-5424. FAX: 828-227-7015. Web Site: www.wcu.edu/library. *Dean,* Dana Sally; E-mail: dsally@email.wcu.edu; *Assoc Dir,* Tim Carstens; Tel: 828-227-3399, E-mail: carstens@email.wcu.edu; *Head, Access Serv,* Peter Johnson; Tel: 828-227-3405; *Head, Ref,* Becky Kornegay; Tel: 828-227-3417, E-mail: kornegay@email.wcu.edu; *Head, Spec Coll,* George Frizzell; Tel: 828-227-7474, E-mail: gfrizzell@email.wcu.edu; *Head, Syst,* Gillian Ellern; Tel: 828-227-3746, E-mail: ellern@email.wcu.edu; *Ref Librn/Bus Liaison,* Sheri Edwards; Tel: 828-227-3413, E-mail: sedwards@email.wcu.edu; *Ref Librn/Educ Liaison,* Beth McDonough; Tel: 828-227-3423, E-mail: bmcdono@email.wcu.edu; *Ref Librn/Geosciences Liaison,* Bart Voskuil; Tel: 828-227-3493, E-mail: voskuil@email.wcu.edu; *Ref Librn/Health Sci Liaison,* Ann Hallyburton; Tel: 828-227-3418, E-mail: ahallyb@email.wcu.edu; *Ref Librn/Info Literacy Coordr,* Heidi Buchanan; Tel: 828-227-3408, E-mail: hbuchanan@email.wcu.edu; *Ref Librn/Sci Liaison,* Krista Schmidt; Tel: 828-227-2215, E-mail: schmidt@email.wcu.edu; *Ref Librn/Soc Sci Liaison,* Susan Metcalf; Tel: 828-227-3416, E-mail: metcalf@email.wcu.edu. Subject Specialists: *Philos, Relig,* Tim Carstens; *Law,* Becky Kornegay; *Eng, Math,* Gillian Ellern; *Bus,* Sheri Edwards; *Geol,* Bart Voskuil; *Nursing,* Ann Hallyburton; *English,* Heidi Buchanan; *Biol, Chem, Physics,* Krista Schmidt; Staff 50 (MLS 18, Non-MLS 32)
Founded 1922. Enrl 8,665; Fac 433; Highest Degree: Doctorate
Library Holdings: AV Mats 14,000; e-books 23,000; Bk Vols 702,000; Per Subs 3,330
Special Collections: Southern Highlands; Spider Coll. State Document Depository; US Document Depository
Subject Interests: Acad support, Appalachia, Cherokee Indians, Maps
Automation Activity & Vendor Info: (Acquisitions) Innovative Interfaces, Inc; (Cataloging) Innovative Interfaces, Inc; (Circulation) Innovative Interfaces, Inc; (Course Reserve) Innovative Interfaces, Inc; (ILL) Innovative Interfaces, Inc; (OPAC) Innovative Interfaces, Inc; (Serials) Innovative Interfaces, Inc
Database Vendor: ARTstor, EBSCOhost, Gale Cengage Learning, Innovative Interfaces, Inc, ISI Web of Knowledge, JSTOR, LexisNexis, OCLC FirstSearch, OCLC WorldShare Interlibrary Loan, ProQuest, PubMed
Wireless access
Partic in Lyrasis; WNCLN
Friends of the Library Group

CURRIE

S US NATIONAL PARK SERVICE*, Moores Creek Battlefield Library, 40 Patriots Hall Dr, 28435. SAN 370-310X. Tel: 910-283-5591. FAX: 910-283-5351. Web Site: www.nps.gov/mocr. *Superintendent,* Tyrone Brandyburg; E-mail: tyrone_brandyburg@nps.gov
Library Holdings: Bk Vols 800
Open Mon-Sun 9-5
Restriction: Not a lending libr

DALLAS

J GASTON COLLEGE, Morris Library & Media Center, 201 Hwy 321 S, 28034-1499. SAN 312-8040. Tel: 704-922-6359. Interlibrary Loan Service Tel: 704-922-6358. Reference Tel: 704-922-6357. Administration Tel: 704-922-6355. FAX: 704-922-2342. Web Site: www.gaston.edu. *Dir of Libr,* Dr Harry Cooke; E-mail: cooke.harry@gaston.edu; *Circ,* Annette Mintz; *ILL, Pub Serv Spec,* Pat Hull; E-mail: hull.patricia@gaston.edu; *ILL, Pub Serv,* Libby Stone; E-mail: stone.libby@gaston.edu; *Libr Tech,* Harriet Dameron; Tel: 704-922-6356, E-mail: dameron.harriet@gaston.edu; *Ref Serv,* Calvin Craig; E-mail: craig.calvin@gaston.edu; *Tech Serv,* Sharon Hedgepeth; Tel: 704-922-6361, E-mail: day-lowe.sharon@gaston.edu; Staff 8 (MLS 4, Non-MLS 4)
Founded 1964. Enrl 5,000; Fac 106; Highest Degree: Associate
Jul 2013-Jun 2014. Mats Exp $67,000. Sal $360,994
Library Holdings: AV Mats 4,528; CDs 450; Bk Titles 44,965; Bk Vols 50,272; Per Subs 192
Special Collections: Civil War Coll
Subject Interests: Local hist
Automation Activity & Vendor Info: (Cataloging) SirsiDynix; (Circulation) SirsiDynix; (ILL) SirsiDynix; (OPAC) SirsiDynix; (Serials) SirsiDynix
Database Vendor: EBSCOhost, Gale Cengage Learning, OCLC FirstSearch, ProQuest
Wireless access
Partic in Community Colleges Libraries in North Carolina (CCLINC)
Open Mon-Thurs 7:45am-9pm, Fri (Summer) 7:45-4

Departmental Libraries:

HARVEY A JONAS LIBRARY, 511 S Aspen St, Lincolnton, 28092. Tel: 704-748-1050. FAX: 704-748-1068. *Dir of Libr,* Dr Harry Cooke; E-mail: cooke.harry@gaston.edu; *Coordr, Libr Serv,* Bointa King; E-mail: king.bonita@gaston.edu
Library Holdings: Bk Titles 1,000
Open Mon-Thurs 8am-9pm, Fri 8-4 (8-Noon Summer)

KIMBRELL CAMPUS & TEXTILE CENTER LIBRARY, 7220 Wilkinson Blvd, Belmont, 28012. (Mail add: PO Box 1044, Belmont, 28012). Tel: 704-825-6278. FAX: 704-825-6345. *Coordr, Libr Serv,* Jody Mosteller; E-mail: mosteller.jody@gaston.edu
Database Vendor: LexisNexis, NC LIVE, OCLC WorldShare Interlibrary Loan

DANBURY

P DANBURY PUBLIC LIBRARY*, 1007 N Main St, 27016. SAN 312-8059. Tel: 336-593-2419. FAX: 336-593-3232. E-mail: dnb@nwrl.org. *Librn,* Nora Lankfort
Founded 1945
Library Holdings: Large Print Bks 300; Bk Vols 25,000; Per Subs 10
Automation Activity & Vendor Info: (Acquisitions) SirsiDynix; (Cataloging) SirsiDynix; (Circulation) SirsiDynix
Mem of Northwestern Regional Library
Open Mon, Wed & Fri 9-5:30, Tues & Thurs 9-8, Sat 9-1
Friends of the Library Group

DAVIDSON

C DAVIDSON COLLEGE*, E H Little Library, 209 Ridge Rd, 28035-0001. (Mail add: PO Box 7200, 28035-7200), SAN 312-8067. Tel: 704-894-2331. Interlibrary Loan Service Tel: 704-894-2159. Reference Tel: 704-894-2425. FAX: 704-894-2625. E-mail: referencedesk@davidson.edu. Web Site: www.davidson.edu. *Libr Dir,* Jill Gremmels; E-mail: jigremmels@davidson.edu; *Asst Dir, Access & Acq,* Jean Coates; Tel: 704-894-2332, E-mail: jecoates@davidson.edu; *Asst Dir, Discovery Syst,* Craig Milberg; E-mail: crmilberg@davidson.edu; *Asst Dir, Libr Instructions & Coll Develop,* Susanna Boylston; E-mail: suboylston@davidson.edu; *Asst Dir, Operations, Finance & Fac,* Denise Sherrill; E-mail: desherrill@davidson.edu; *Cat/Metadata Librn,* Kim Sanderson; E-mail: kisanderson@davidson.edu; *Info Literacy Librn,* Sara Swanson; *Spec Coll Outreach Librn,* Sharon H Byrd; E-mail: shbyrd@davidson.edu; *Syst Librn,* Susan Kerr; E-mail: sukerr@davidson.edu; *Music Libr Mgr,* Katy Hoffler; Tel: 704-894-2721, E-mail: kahoffler@davidson.edu; *Col Archivist & Rec Mgt Coordr,* Dr Jan Blodgett; Tel: 704-894-2632, E-mail: jablodgett@davidson.edu; *ILL Coordr,* Joe Gutekanst; E-mail: jogutekanst@davidson.edu; Staff 11 (MLS 10, Non-MLS 1)
Founded 1837. Enrl 1,668; Fac 162; Highest Degree: Bachelor
Jul 2007-Jun 2008. Mats Exp $1,683,111, Books $336,101, Per/Ser (Incl. Access Fees) $697,737, Micro $86,452, AV Mat $21,496, Electronic Ref Mat (Incl. Access Fees) $506,575, Presv $31,747. Sal $1,012,167 (Prof $662,250)
Special Collections: Bruce Rogers Coll; Davidsoniana Coll; Mecklenburg Declaration of Independence Coll; Peter S Ney Coll; Robert Burns Coll; W P Cumming Map Coll; Woodrow Wilson Coll. Oral History; US Document Depository
Automation Activity & Vendor Info: (Acquisitions) SirsiDynix; (Cataloging) SirsiDynix; (Circulation) SirsiDynix; (Course Reserve) SirsiDynix; (ILL) OCLC ILLiad; (OPAC) SirsiDynix; (Serials) SirsiDynix
Database Vendor: ABC-CLIO, American Chemical Society, American Mathematical Society, ARTstor, Baker & Taylor, Blackwell, Bowker, Dialog, EBSCO Information Services, EBSCOhost, Gale Cengage Learning, H W Wilson, ISI Web of Knowledge, JSTOR, LexisNexis, Marcive, Inc, NC LIVE, OCLC FirstSearch, OCLC WorldShare Interlibrary Loan, OVID Technologies, Project MUSE, ProQuest, RefWorks, Sage, SerialsSolutions, SirsiDynix, Thomson - Web of Science, Westlaw, Wiley, Wilson - Wilson Web, YBP Library Services
Wireless access
Partic in Carolina Consortium; Lyrasis; North Carolina Libraries for Virtual Education; Oberlin Group
Open Mon-Thurs 8am-1am, Fri & Sat 10-9, Sun 10am-1am

DOBSON

P DOBSON COMMUNITY LIBRARY*, 113 S Crutchfield St, 27017. (Mail add: PO Box 1264, 27017-1264), SAN 312-8091. Tel: 336-386-8208. FAX: 336-386-4086. *Br Librn,* Cindy Brannak; *Asst Librn,* Gaye Layell
Library Holdings: Large Print Bks 300; Bk Titles 7,500; Bk Vols 8,000; Per Subs 20
Automation Activity & Vendor Info: (Acquisitions) SirsiDynix; (Cataloging) SirsiDynix; (Circulation) SirsiDynix
Mem of Northwestern Regional Library
Open Mon-Fri 9-6
Friends of the Library Group

J SURRY COMMUNITY COLLEGE*, Learning Resources Center, 630 S Main St, 27017-8432. Tel: 336-386-8121. Circulation Tel: 336-386-3259. Interlibrary Loan Service Tel: 336-386-3317. Reference Tel: 336-386-3260. Administration Tel: 336-386-3252. FAX: 336-386-3692. Web Site: depts.surry.edu/lrc. *Libr Dir,* Dr David Wright; E-mail: wrightd@surry.edu; *Ref & Web Serv Librn,* Alan Unsworth; Tel: 336-386-3317, E-mail: unswortha@surry.edu; *Archives, Genealogy Serv,* Sebrina Mabe; *Tech Serv,* Faye Ireland; Tel: 336-386-3501, E-mail: irelandf@surry.edu; Staff 10 (MLS 4, Non-MLS 6)
Founded 1965. Enrl 3,029; Fac 88; Highest Degree: Associate
Library Holdings: AV Mats 3,492; Bk Titles 42,800; Bk Vols 46,580; Per Subs 344
Special Collections: Genealogy & Local History (Surratt Room)
Subject Interests: Enology, Local hist, Viticulture
Partic in Lyrasis; North Carolina Libraries for Virtual Education
Open Mon-Thurs 7:30-9, Fri 7:30-3

DUBLIN

J BLADEN COMMUNITY COLLEGE LIBRARY, 7418 NC HWY 41 W, 28332. (Mail add: PO Box 266, 28332-0266), SAN 312-8105. Tel: 910-879-5641. FAX: 910-879-5642. E-mail: library@bladencc.edu. Web Site: www.bladencc.edu/lrc. *Dir, Libr Serv,* Sherwin Rice; E-mail: srice@bladencc.edu; Staff 5 (MLS 1, Non-MLS 4)
Founded 1967. Enrl 1,400; Fac 28; Highest Degree: Associate
Library Holdings: AV Mats 1,992; e-books 185; Bk Vols 20,000; Per Subs 120; Talking Bks 400
Automation Activity & Vendor Info: (Cataloging) SirsiDynix; (Circulation) SirsiDynix; (OPAC) SirsiDynix
Wireless access
Open Mon-Thurs 8-8:30, Fri 8-3

DURHAM

GM DEPARTMENT OF VETERANS AFFAIRS*, Library Service, 508 Fulton St, 27705. SAN 312-8172. Tel: 919-286-6929. FAX: 919-286-6859. Web Site: www.durham.va.gov, www.va.gov. *Chief Librn,* Jeff Kager; E-mail: jeff.kager@med.va.gov; *Librn,* Steven Perlman; Tel: 919-286-6929, Ext 6656, E-mail: stephen.perlman@med.va.gov; *Tech Serv,* Pathenia Hawthorne; Tel: 919-286-6929, Ext 6654, E-mail: pathenia.hawthorne@med.va.gov; Staff 3 (MLS 2, Non-MLS 1)
Founded 1952
Library Holdings: Bk Titles 2,500; Bk Vols 3,200; Per Subs 300
Subject Interests: Patient educ
Database Vendor: OVID Technologies
Function: Ref serv available
Restriction: Not open to pub

C DUKE UNIVERSITY LIBRARIES*, William R Perkins Library System, 411 Chapel Dr, 27708. (Mail add: PO Box 90193, 27708-0193), SAN 354-6845. Tel: 919-660-5800. Circulation Tel: 919-660-5870. Interlibrary Loan Service Tel: 919-660-5890. Reference Tel: 919-660-5880. FAX: 919-660-5923. Circulation FAX: 919-660-5964. Reference FAX: 919-684-2855. E-mail: asklib@duke.edu. Web Site: www.library.duke.edu. *Univ Librn & Vice Provost for Libr Affairs,* Deborah Jakubs, PhD; E-mail: deborah.jakubs@duke.edu; *Assoc Univ Librn, Coll & User Serv,* Robert Byrd; Tel: 919-660-5821, E-mail: robert.byrd@duke.edu; *Assoc Univ Librn, Info Tech,* Position Currently Open; *Dir of Communications,* Aaron Welborn; *Dir of Develop,* Tom Hadzor; Tel: 919-660-5940, E-mail: t.hadzor@duke.edu; *Dir, Acad Tech & Instrul Serv,* Lynne O'Brien, PhD; Tel: 919-660-5862, E-mail: lynne.obrien@duke.edu; *Dir, Admin Serv,* Ann Elsner; Tel: 919-660-5947, E-mail: ann.elsner@duke.edu; *Dir, Copyright & Scholarly Communication,* Kevin L Smith; Tel: 919-668-4451, E-mail: kevin.l.smith@duke.edu; *Head, Access Serv & Doc Delivery,* Michael Finigan; Tel: 919-660-5872, E-mail: michael.finigan@duke.edu; *Head, Acq,* Teddy Gray; Tel: 919-660-5971, E-mail: teddy.gray@duke.edu; *Head, Cat & Metadata Serv,* Rosalyn Raeford; Tel: 919-660-5892, E-mail: ros.raeford@duke.edu; *Head, Coll Develop,* Jeff Kosokoff; Tel: 919-660-7892; *Head, Coll Develop & Curator of Coll, RBMSCL,* Andrew Armacost; Tel: 919-660-5835, Fax: 919-660-5934, E-mail: andrew.armacost@duke.edu; *Head, Core Serv, IT,* Brad Williams; *Head, Data & GIS Serv,* Joel Herndon, PhD; Tel: 919-660-5946, E-mail: joel.herndon@duke.edu; *Head, Digital Projects,* Will Sexton; Tel: 919-660-5888; *Head, Digital Scholarship Serv,* Liz Milewicz, PhD; Tel: 919-660-5911; *Head, Electronic Res & Ser Mgt,* Beverly Dowdy; Tel: 919-613-5185, E-mail: beverly.dowdy@duke.edu; *Head, Intl & Area Studies,* Kristina Troost, PhD; Tel: 919-660-5844, E-mail: kktroost@duke.edu; *Head, Libr Serv Ctr,* Marvin Tillman; Tel: 919-596-3962, Fax: 919-598-3103, E-mail: marvin.tillman@duke.edu; *Head, Lilly Libr,* Kelley Lawton; Tel: 919-660-5990, Fax: 919-660-5999, E-mail: kelley.lawton@duke.edu; *Head Music Libr,* Laura Williams; Tel: 919-660-5952, E-mail: laura.williams@duke.edu; *Head, RBMSCL Res Serv,* David Pavelich; *Head, RBMSCL Tech Serv,* Katherine Stefko; *Head, Res & Instrul Serv,* Jean Ferguson; Tel: 919-660-5928, E-mail: jean.ferguson@duke.edu; *Mgr, Libr Human Res,* Kimberly Burhop; Tel:

919-660-5937, E-mail: kim.burhop@duke.edu; *Perkins Mail Ctr Mgr,* Charles Beck; Tel: 919-660-5868, E-mail: karl.beck@duke.edu; *Univ Archivist,* Valerie Gillispie; Tel: 919-684-8929; *Presv Officer,* Winston Atkins; Tel: 919-660-5843, E-mail: winston.atkins@duke.edu. Subject Specialists: *Manuscripts, Rare bks,* Andrew Armacost; *Data serv, Soc sci, Statistics,* Joel Herndon, PhD; *Japan,* Kristina Troost, PhD; *US hist,* Kelley Lawton; *Music,* Laura Williams; *Humanities,* Jean Ferguson; Staff 137 (MLS 80, Non-MLS 57)
Founded 1838. Enrl 14,600; Fac 1,784; Highest Degree: Doctorate
Jul 2012-Jun 2013. Mats Exp $14,162,443. Sal $16,040,842
Library Holdings: AV Mats 147,727; DVDs 16,699; e-books 203,442; e-journals 91,695; Microforms 4,359,354; Bk Vols 6,073,696
Special Collections: African & African Americana Coll; American History Coll; American Literature Coll; Art & Architecture Coll; British & Commonwealth History Coll; Cartography Coll; Classics Coll; Comics & Pulp Culture Coll; Documentary Photography Coll; Drama Coll; English Literature Coll; German Literature & Culture Coll; History of Advertising Coll; History of Economics Coll; History of Science Coll; Iconology Coll; Italian Literature & Culture Coll; Judaica Coll; Latin Americana Coll; Medieval & Renaissance Culture Coll; Music Coll; Religion Coll; Southern Americana Coll; Travel Coll; Women's Studies & History of Feminism Coll. US Document Depository
Automation Activity & Vendor Info: (Acquisitions) Ex Libris Group; (Cataloging) Ex Libris Group; (Circulation) Ex Libris Group
Database Vendor: Ex Libris Group
Wireless access
Publications: Duke University Libraries
Partic in Asn of College & Res Libr; Association of Research Libraries (ARL); Association of Southeastern Research Libraries; Carolina Consortium; Lyrasis; OCLC Online Computer Library Center, Inc
Friends of the Library Group

Departmental Libraries:

CR DIVINITY SCHOOL LIBRARY, 407 Chapel Dr, 27708. (Mail add: PO Box 90972, 27708-0972), SAN 354-6969. Tel: 919-660-3453. Circulation Tel: 919-660-3450. FAX: 919-681-7594. Web Site: library.divinity.duke.edu. *Dir,* Beth Sheppard; E-mail: bsheppard@div.duke.edu; *Ref & Pub Serv Librn,* Shanee Murrain; Tel: 919-660-3549, E-mail: smurrian@div.duke.edu; *Circ Mgr,* Melissa Harrel; Tel: 919-660-3449, E-mail: melissa.h@duke.edu; *Asst Mgr, Circ,* Anne Marie Boyd; Tel: 919-660-3546, E-mail: anne.marie.boyd@duke.edu; Staff 5 (MLS 3, Non-MLS 2)
Library Holdings: Bk Vols 370,000; Per Subs 708
Subject Interests: Biblical studies, Methodism
Open Mon-Thurs (Winter) 8am-11pm, Fri 8-5, Sat 10-6, Sun 2-10; Mon-Fri (Summer) 8-5

FORD LIBRARY, 100 Fuqua Dr, 27708. (Mail add: Fuqua School of Business, PO Box 90122, 27708-0122). Tel: 919-660-7870. FAX: 919-660-7950. Web Site: library.fuqua.duke.edu. *Dir,* Meg Trauner; Tel: 919-660-7869, E-mail: mtrauner@duke.edu; *Librn, Research, Planning & Evaluation,* Bethany Costello; E-mail: bethany.koestner@duke.edu; *Syst Librn,* Carlton Brown; Tel: 919-660-7871, E-mail: carlton.brown@duke.edu; *Access Serv,* Amy Brenan; Tel: 919-660-7873, E-mail: amy.brenan@duke.edu; *Cat,* Linda McCormick; Tel: 919-660-8016, E-mail: linda.mccormick@duke.edu; *Pub Serv,* Jane Day; Tel: 919-660-7874, E-mail: jnday@duke.edu; *Ref,* Paula Robinson; Tel: 919-660-7942, E-mail: robinson@duke.edu; Staff 10 (MLS 7, Non-MLS 3)
Founded 1983. Enrl 1,600; Fac 120; Highest Degree: Doctorate
Library Holdings: AV Mats 3,000; Microforms 450,000; Bk Vols 40,000; Per Subs 300
Subject Interests: Bus
Automation Activity & Vendor Info: (OPAC) Ex Libris Group; (Serials) Ex Libris Group
Database Vendor: EBSCOhost, OCLC FirstSearch
Open Mon-Thurs 7:30am-Midnight, Fri 7:30am-10pm, Sat 10-8, Sun 10-Midnight

CL J MICHAEL GOODSON LAW LIBRARY, 210 Science Dr, 27708. (Mail add: PO Box 90361, 27708-0361), SAN 354-7051. Circulation Tel: 919-613-7128. Interlibrary Loan Service Tel: 919-613-7122. Reference Tel: 919-613-7121. Administration Tel: 919-613-7114. FAX: 919-613-7237. Web Site: www.law.duke.edu/lib. *Sr Assoc Dean for Info Serv,* Richard A Danner; Tel: 919-613-7115, E-mail: danner@law.duke.edu; *Asst Dean, Libr Serv,* Melanie J Dunshee; Tel: 919-613-7119, E-mail: dunshee@law.duke.edu; *Head, Coll Serv,* Karen B Douglas; Tel: 919-613-7116, E-mail: douglas@law.duke.edu; *Head, Ref Serv,* Jennifer L Behrens; Tel: 919-613-7198, E-mail: behrens@law.duke.edu; *Acq Librn,* Shyama Agrawal; Tel: 919-613-7070, E-mail: agrawal@law.duke.edu; *Digital Res Librn,* Sean Chen; Tel: 919-613-7028, E-mail: schen@law.duke.edu; *Foreign & Intl Law Ref Librn,* Kristina J Alayan; Tel: 919-613-7118, E-mail: alayan@law.duke.edu; *Ref Librn,* Jane Bahnson; Tel: 919-613-7113, E-mail: bahnson@law.duke.edu; *Ref Librn,* Kelly Leong; Tel: 919-613-7041, E-mail: leong@law.duke.edu; *Ref Librn,* Marguerite Most; Tel: 919-613-7120, E-mail: most@law.duke.edu; *Ref Librn,* Laura M Scott; Tel: 919-613-7164, E-mail: scott@law.duke.edu; *Empirical Res Analyst,* Guangya Liu; Tel: 919-613-7178, E-mail: guangya.liu@law.duke.edu; Staff 13 (MLS 12, Non-MLS 1)
Founded 1931. Enrl 730; Highest Degree: Doctorate
Special Collections: US Document Depository
Database Vendor: Ex Libris Group
Partic in Legal Information Preservation Alliance (LIPA); New England Law Library Consortium, Inc; Triangle Research Libraries Network
Restriction: Circ limited

CM MEDICAL CENTER LIBRARY & ARCHIVES, DUMC Box 3702, Ten Searle Dr, 27710-0001, SAN 354-7116. Tel: 919-660-1100. Interlibrary Loan Service Tel: 919-660-1138. Administration Tel: 919-660-1150. FAX: 919-681-7599. Interlibrary Loan Service FAX: 919-660-1188. E-mail: medical-librarian@dm.duke.edu. Web Site: www.mclibrary.duke.edu. *Assoc Dean, Libr Serv,* Patricia Thibodeau; Tel: 919-660-1148, E-mail: patricia.thibodeau@duke.edu; *Dep Dir,* Rick Peterson; E-mail: rick.peterson@duke.edu; *Dir, Archives & Digital Initiatives,* Russell Koonts; Tel: 919-383-2653, E-mail: russell.koonts@duke.edu; *Assoc Dir, Coll Serv,* Emma Cryer; Tel: 919-660-1140, E-mail: emma.cryer@duke.edu; *Assoc Dir, Res & Educ,* Megan Von Isenburg; Tel: 919-660-1131, E-mail: megan.vonisenburg@duke.edu; *Asst Dir, Archival Coll & Serv,* Jolie Braun; E-mail: jolie.braun@duke.edu; *Asst Dir, Adm Serv, Bus Mgr,* Vanessa Sellars; Tel: 919-660-1149, E-mail: vanessa.sellars@duke.edu; *Asst Dir, Communications & Web Content Mgt,* Beverly Murphy; Tel: 919-660-1127, E-mail: beverly.murphy@duke.edu; *Mgr, Access Serv,* Elizabeth Berney; E-mail: elizabeth.berney@duke.edu; *Doc Delivery & ILL Mgr/Access Serv,* Louis Wiethe; Tel: 919-660-1179, E-mail: Louis.Wiethe@duke.edu; Staff 46 (MLS 16, Non-MLS 30)
Founded 1930. Fac 1,800; Highest Degree: Doctorate
Jul 2006-Jun 2007. Mats Exp $1,525,274, Books $96,693, Per/Ser (Incl. Access Fees) $1,331,183
Library Holdings: Bk Vols 296,491
Special Collections: Duke Medical Authors. Oral History
Partic in Docline; National Network of Libraries of Medicine; New England Law Library Consortium, Inc; OCLC Online Computer Library Center, Inc; Triangle Research Libraries Network
Publications: Archives (Newsletter); Medical Center Library News (Newsletter)
Open Mon-Fri 7:30am-Midnight, Sat 12-8, Sun Noon-Midnight

P DURHAM COUNTY LIBRARY*, Headquarters, 300 N Roxboro St, 27701. (Mail add: PO Box 3809, 27702-3809), SAN 354-7205. Tel: 919-560-0100. Circulation Tel: 919-560-0131. Interlibrary Loan Service Tel: 919-560-0104. Reference Tel: 919-560-0110. Administration Tel: 919-560-0163. Automation Services Tel: 919-560-0189. FAX: 919-560-0137. Reference FAX: 919-560-0106. Web Site: www.durhamcountylibrary.org. *Dir,* Tammy Baggett; *Dep Dir,* Terry Hill; *Mgr, Mkt & Develop,* Gina Rozier; Tel: 919-560-0151, E-mail: grozier@durhamcountync.gov; Staff 120.79 (MLS 40, Non-MLS 80.79)
Founded 1897. Circ 1,513,603
Jul 2007-Jun 2008 Income (Main Library and Branch(s)) $10,142,203, State $258,686, County $9,646,850, Other $236,667. Mats Exp $2,828,097, Books $1,267,608, Per/Ser (Incl. Access Fees) $89,269, Other Print Mats $1,101,372, AV Mat $267,897, Electronic Ref Mat (Incl. Access Fees) $101,951. Sal $5,999,926
Library Holdings: Audiobooks 26,174; AV Mats 17,392; Bk Vols 554,598; Per Subs 1,219
Special Collections: African-American History & Literature Coll, bks, per; Durham Biography & History Coll, including Durham County Library History; Durham Historical Photographs (Archival); North Carolina History & Literature, bks, microfilm, per, newsp, rec, v-tapes, slides, CDs
Automation Activity & Vendor Info: (Cataloging) SirsiDynix; (Circulation) SirsiDynix; (OPAC) SirsiDynix
Database Vendor: ProQuest, TLC (The Library Corporation)
Wireless access
Publications: Branching Out (library newsletter and events) (Quarterly); Seasons Readings; The Best of Friends (Friends Newsletter); The Grapevine (Staff newsletter) (Bi-monthly)
Partic in Lyrasis; OCLC Online Computer Library Center, Inc
Special Services for the Deaf - TTY equip
Open Mon-Fri 8:30-5
Friends of the Library Group

Branches: 6

BRAGTOWN, 3200 Dearborn Dr, 27704, SAN 354-723X. Tel: 919-560-0210. *Mgr,* DeLois Cue; E-mail: dcue@dconc.gov
Open Mon-Fri 2-6
Friends of the Library Group

EAST REGIONAL, 211 Lick Creek Lane, 27703-6746. Tel: 919-560-0203. Reference Tel: 919-560-0213. FAX: 919-598-8673. *Mgr,* Anita Hasty-Speed; Tel: 919-560-0128, E-mail: ahspeed@dconc.gov
Founded 2006
Open Mon, Tues & Thurs 9-9, Wed 9-6, Fri & Sun 2-6, Sat 9:30-6

NORTH REGIONAL, 221 Milton Rd, 27712-2223, SAN 354-7302. Tel: 919-560-0231. Reference Tel: 919-560-0236. FAX: 919-560-0246. *Mgr,* Susan Wright; Tel: 919-560-0243, E-mail: swright@dconc.gov
Open Mon, Tues & Thurs 9-9, Wed 9-6
SOUTH REGIONAL, 4505 S Alston Ave, 27713, SAN 354-7329. Tel: 919-560-7409. *Mgr,* Sandra Lovely; Tel: 919-560-0262, E-mail: slovely@durhamcountync.gov
Open Mon, Tues & Thurs 9-9, Wed 9-6, Fri & Sun 2-6, Sat 9:30-6
SOUTHWEST, 3605 Shannon Rd, 27707, SAN 354-7264. Tel: 919-560-8590. FAX: 919-560-0542. *Mgr,* Lynne Barnette
Founded 1992
Library Holdings: Large Print Bks 500; Bk Vols 69,000; Per Subs 120
Subject Interests: Children's videos
Function: Photocopying/Printing
Open Mon, Tues & Thurs 9-9, Wed 9-6, Fri & Sun 2-6, Sat 9:30-6
STANFORD L WARREN BRANCH, 1201 Fayetteville St, 27707, SAN 354-7388. Tel: 919-560-0270. FAX: 919-560-0283. E-mail: slwarren@dclnc.gov. *Mgr,* Myrtle Darden; Tel: 919-560-0274
Library Holdings: Bk Vols 29,492; Per Subs 40
Special Collections: African-American Cultural History Coll
Open Mon, Tues & Thurs 9-9, Wed 9-6, Fri 2-6, Sat 9:30-6
Friends of the Library Group
Bookmobiles: 1. Outreach & Mobile Serv Mgr, Kathi Sippen

J DURHAM TECHNICAL COMMUNITY COLLEGE*, 1637 Lawson St, 27703. (Mail add: PO Box 11307, 27703-0307), SAN 312-8148. Tel: 919-536-7211. FAX: 919-686-3471. E-mail: library@durhamtech.edu. Web Site: www.durhamtech.edu/library.htm. *Asst Dean of Libr,* Irene H Laube; E-mail: laubei@durhamtech.edu; *Pub Serv Librn,* Wendy Ramseur; E-mail: ramseurw@durhamtech.edu; *Ref Librn,* Susan Baker; E-mail: bakers@durhamtech.edu; *Ref Librn, Tech Serv Librn,* Julie Humphrey; E-mail: humphrej@durhamtech.edu; Staff 5.33 (MLS 5.33)
Founded 1961. Enrl 1,776
Library Holdings: Bk Vols 44,998; Per Subs 16,569
Subject Interests: Educ, Law, Liberal arts, Med
Automation Activity & Vendor Info: (Circulation) SirsiDynix; (OPAC) SirsiDynix
Database Vendor: American Psychological Association (APA), EBSCOhost, Gale Cengage Learning, JSTOR, ProQuest, Sage, ScienceDirect, SirsiDynix, Westlaw
Wireless access
Publications: Library Handbook; News from the Library; Periodical Holdings
Partic in Community Colleges Libraries in North Carolina (CCLINC); OCLC Online Computer Library Center, Inc
Open Mon-Thurs (Winter) 8am-8:30pm, Fri 8-5, Sat 9-1; Mon-Thurs (Summer) 8-6:30, Fri 8-Noon

Departmental Libraries:

NORTHERN DURHAM CENTER, 2401 Snow Hill Rd, 27712, SAN 377-0524. Tel: 919-536-7240. FAX: 919-686-3519. *Librn,* Santosh Shonek
Open Mon-Thurs 9-6
ORANGE COUNTY CAMPUS, 525 College Park Rd, Hillsborough, 27278. Tel: 919-536-7211. FAX: 919-536-7297.
Open Mon-Thurs 9-6

S FHI360 LIBRARY SERVICES*, 2224 E NC Hwy 54, 27713. (Mail add: PO Box 13950, Research Triangle Park, 27709-3950), SAN 322-8762. Tel: 919-544-7040. FAX: 919-544-7261. E-mail: library.helpdesk@fhi360.org. *Assoc Dir,* Margaret Shiels; Staff 4 (MLS 3, Non-MLS 1)
Founded 1971
Library Holdings: Bk Titles 10,000; Per Subs 700
Subject Interests: Demography, Family planning, HIV-AIDS, Pub health
Publications: Library Handbook; Serials Holdings (Annual)

S FOREST HISTORY SOCIETY LIBRARY, 701 William Vickers Ave, 27701-3162. SAN 301-5807. Tel: 919-682-9319. FAX: 919-682-2349. Web Site: www.foresthistory.org/research/library.html. *Librn,* Cheryl Oakes; E-mail: coakes@duke.edu. Subject Specialists: *Environ hist,* Cheryl Oakes; Staff 2 (MLS 2)
Founded 1946
Library Holdings: AV Mats 500; Bk Vols 9,500; Per Subs 200; Spec Interest Per Sub 100; Videos 250
Special Collections: American Forest Council Archives; American Forestry Association Archives; Interview Coll, tapes & transcripts; National Forest Products Association Archives; Society of American Foresters Archives; United States Forest Service. Oral History
Subject Interests: Conserv, Environ hist, Forestry
Wireless access
Function: Archival coll, ILL available, Online searches, Res libr
Open Mon-Fri 8-5
Restriction: Non-circulating coll

C NORTH CAROLINA CENTRAL UNIVERSITY*, James E Shepard Memorial Library, 1801 Fayetteville St, 27707-3129. (Mail add: PO Box 19436, 27707-0019), SAN 354-7590. Tel: 919-530-6475. Circulation Tel: 919-530-6426. Interlibrary Loan Service Tel: 919-530-7469. Reference Tel: 919-530-6473. Toll Free Tel: 800-662-7644 (NC only). FAX: 919-530-7612. Web Site: www.nccu.edu/shepardlibrary. *Dir of Libr Serv,* Dr Theodosia Shields; Tel: 919-530-5233, E-mail: tshields@nccu.edu; *Head, Cat, Head, Tech Serv,* Gouri Dutta; Tel: 919-560-6430, E-mail: goudutta@nccu.edu; *Head, Circ, Reserves,* Vickie V Spencer; Tel: 919-530-7305, E-mail: vspencer@nccu.edu; *Head, Govt Doc,* Victoria Silver; Tel: 919-530-7307, E-mail: vsilver@nccu.edu; *Head, Ser, Interim Head, Ref,* Christine Covington; Tel: 919-530-7311, E-mail: ccovington@nccu.edu; *Cat Librn,* Vanessa Lennon; Tel: 919-530-7309, E-mail: vlennon@nccu.edu; *Curric Mat Librn,* Yash Garg; Tel: 919-530-6383, E-mail: ygarg@nccu.edu; *Info Literacy Librn,* Hafsa Murad; Tel: 919-530-7315, E-mail: hmurad@nccu.edu; *Ref Librn,* Ife B Grady; Tel: 919-530-7314, E-mail: igrady@nccu.edu; *Ref Librn,* Carolene Griffin; Tel: 919-530-5237, E-mail: cgriffin@nccu.edu; *Ser Librn,* Doris Sigl; Tel: 919-530-7317, E-mail: dsigl@nccu.edu; *Syst Librn,* Yan Wang; Tel: 919-530-5240, E-mail: ywang@nccu.edu; Staff 31 (MLS 15, Non-MLS 16)
Founded 1923. Enrl 5,482; Fac 284; Highest Degree: Master
Library Holdings: Bk Titles 450,000; Bk Vols 500,597; Per Subs 1,928
Special Collections: African American (Martin Coll). US Document Depository
Subject Interests: Local hist
Automation Activity & Vendor Info: (Cataloging) SirsiDynix; (Circulation) SirsiDynix
Database Vendor: EBSCOhost, Gale Cengage Learning, OCLC FirstSearch, OVID Technologies, ProQuest, SirsiDynix
Publications: Annual Reports; SNN: Shepard News Network
Partic in Lyrasis
Open Mon-Sat (Winter) 8am-1am, Sun 2pm-1am; Mon-Thurs (Summer) 8am-10pm, Fri 8-5, Sat 10-5, Sun 2-10
Friends of the Library Group

Departmental Libraries:

MUSIC, 1801 Fayetteville St, 27707. Tel: 919-530-6220. FAX: 919-530-7979. Web Site: www.nccu.edu/library/music.html. *Librn,* Vernice Faison; E-mail: vfaison@nccu.edu
Library Holdings: Bk Vols 12,000
CL SCHOOL OF LAW LIBRARY, 640 Nelson St, 27707, SAN 354-768X. Tel: 919-530-6333. Circulation Tel: 919-530-5189. Interlibrary Loan Service Tel: 919-530-6608. Reference Tel: 919-530-6715. Administration Tel: 919-530-6244. FAX: 919-530-7926. Web Site: law.nccu.edu/library. *Interim Dir,* Nichelle Perry; Tel: 919-530-5188, E-mail: nperry@nccu.edu; *Access Serv Librn,* Jonathan Beeker; E-mail: jbeeker@nccu.edu; *Sr Ref Librn,* Michelle T Cosby; Tel: 919-530-5241, E-mail: mcosby@nccu.edu; *Cataloger,* Wadad Giles; Tel: 919-530-7177, E-mail: wgiles@nccu.edu; Staff 15 (MLS 7, Non-MLS 8)
Founded 1939. Enrl 362; Highest Degree: Doctorate
Library Holdings: Bk Vols 450,000
Special Collections: Civil Rights (McKissick Coll)
Subject Interests: Civil rights, NC law, Tax
Database Vendor: HeinOnline, LexisNexis, Loislaw, NC LIVE, OCLC WorldShare Interlibrary Loan, Westlaw, YBP Library Services
Function: Ref serv available
Partic in Consortium of Southeastern Law Libraries; OCLC Online Computer Library Center, Inc; Triangle Research Libraries Network; Westlaw
Restriction: Limited access for the pub
SCHOOL OF LIBRARY & INFORMATION SCIENCES, James E Shepard Memorial Library, 3rd Flr, 1801 Fayetteville St, 27707. Tel: 919-530-7323. FAX: 919-530-6402. Web Site: www.nccuslis.org/slislib. *Univ Librn,* Virginia Purefoy Jones; E-mail: vpjones@nccu.edu; *Libr Tech,* Marie Preston; Tel: 919-530-6400, E-mail: mpreston@nccu.edu; Staff 2 (MLS 2)
Founded 1939. Highest Degree: Master
Library Holdings: Bk Vols 46,000
Special Collections: Black Librarian's Coll; William Tucker Coll
Subject Interests: Children's lit, Info sci, Libr sci
Partic in OCLC Online Computer Library Center, Inc
Open Mon-Thurs 8am-10pm, Fri & Sat 8-5, Sun 2-5

S NORTH CAROLINA MUSEUM OF LIFE & SCIENCE LIBRARY*, 433 W Murray Ave, 27704-3101. (Mail add: PO Box 15190, 27704-0190), SAN 328-1833. Tel: 919-220-5429. FAX: 919-220-5575. Web Site: www.ncmls.org. *Mgr,* Nancy A Dragotta; E-mail: nancyd@ncmls.org; Staff 1 (MLS 1)
Founded 1980
Library Holdings: Bk Titles 3,550; Per Subs 11
Open Tues-Sat (Sept-Jan) 10-5, Sun 12-5; Mon-Sat (Feb-Aug) 10-5, Sun 12-5

S NORTH CAROLINA SCHOOL OF SCIENCE & MATHEMATICS LIBRARY, Borden Mace Library, Library, Instructional Technologies & Communications, 1219 Broad St, 27705. Tel: 919-416-2929. Circulation

Tel: 919-416-2917. Interlibrary Loan Service Tel: 919-416-2916. Automation Services Tel: 919-416-2914. Information Services Tel: 919-416-2920. FAX: 919-416-2890. Automation Services FAX: 919-416-2955. E-mail: library@ncssm.edu. Web Site: www.ncssm.edu/library. *Dir, Libr Instrul Tech & Communications,* Dr Robin Boltz; E-mail: boltz@ncssm.edu; *Librn,* Stephanie Barnwell; Tel: 919-416-2657, E-mail: stephanie.barnwell@ncssm.edu; *Librn,* Melissa Cox; E-mail: cox@ncssm.edu; *Librn,* Andrea Smythe; E-mail: smythe@ncssm.edu; *Tech Asst II,* Anthony Myles; E-mail: myles@ncssm.edu; Staff 4 (MLS 3, Non-MLS 1)
Founded 1980. Enrl 650; Fac 2; Highest Degree: Certificate
Library Holdings: Audiobooks 200; AV Mats 500; Bks on Deafness & Sign Lang 5; CDs 300; DVDs 500; e-books 10; e-journals 20,000; Electronic Media & Resources 25; High Interest/Low Vocabulary Bk Vols 2; Large Print Bks 10; Microforms 10,000; Music Scores 50; Bk Titles 22,000; Bk Vols 24,000; Per Subs 100; Spec Interest Per Sub 20; Talking Bks 2; Videos 300
Automation Activity & Vendor Info: (Acquisitions) Follett Software; (Cataloging) Follett Software; (Circulation) Follett Software; (ILL) OCLC WorldShare Interlibrary Loan; (OPAC) Follett Software; (Serials) EBSCO Online
Database Vendor: 3M Library Systems, Baker & Taylor, Bowker, BWI, Cinahl, Discovery Education, EBSCO - WebFeat, EBSCOhost, Electric Library, Elsevier, Greenwood Publishing Group, H W Wilson, Hoovers, JSTOR, LexisNexis, Medline, NC LIVE, ProQuest, PubMed, ScienceDirect, Thomson - Web of Science, WebMD
Function: Archival coll, Audio & video playback equip for onsite use, Audiobks via web, AV serv, Bk club(s), Bks on cassette, Bks on CD, CD-ROM, Computer training, Computers for patron use, Copy machines, Digital talking bks, E-Reserves, Electronic databases & coll, Equip loans & repairs, Exhibits, Fax serv, Free DVD rentals, ILL available, Instruction & testing, Learning ctr, Libr develop, Literacy & newcomer serv, Music CDs, Online cat, Online info literacy tutorials on the web & in blackboard, Online ref, Online searches, Orientations, Photocopying/Printing, Prof lending libr, Prog for children & young adult, Pub access computers, Ref & res, Ref serv available, Ref serv in person, Res libr, Scanner, Summer reading prog, Teen prog, VCDs, VHS videos, Video lending libr, Web-catalog, Workshops
Open Mon-Fri 8am-10pm, Fri 8-5, Sun 5-10
Restriction: Authorized patrons, Borrowing privileges limited to fac & registered students, Borrowing requests are handled by ILL, External users must contact libr, In-house use for visitors, Lending limited to county residents, Limited access for the pub, Mem organizations only, Non-circulating of rare bks, Non-circulating to the pub, Open to fac, students & qualified researchers, Open to pub upon request, Open to researchers by request, Open to students, fac & staff, Open to students, fac, staff & alumni, Photo ID required for access, Pub ref by request, Researchers by appt only, Secured area only open to authorized personnel, Visitors must make appt to use bks in the libr

S ORGANIZATION FOR TROPICAL STUDIES LIBRARY*, Duke University, 410 Swift Ave, 27705. SAN 377-5259. Tel: 919-684-5774. FAX: 919-684-5661. E-mail: ots@duke.edu. Web Site: www.ots.duke.edu. *Chief Exec Officer, Pres,* Dr Elizabeth Losos; E-mail: elosos@duke.edu
Founded 1963
Library Holdings: Bk Vols 1,000
Subject Interests: Natural res

M RHINE RESEARCH CENTER*, Institute for Parapsychology, 2741 Campus Walk Ave, Bldg 500, 27705-3707. SAN 322-8851. Tel: 919-309-4600. FAX: 919-309-4700. Web Site: www.rhine.org. *Asst Librn,* Conway Christopher; Tel: 919-309-4600, Ext 204
Founded 1930
Library Holdings: Bk Vols 10,000; Per Subs 70
Special Collections: Foreign language books on parapsychology; J B Rhine & Louisa Rhine Archival Coll, unpublished mss, theses & dissertations
Subject Interests: Parapsychol, Psychol res, Related areas
Open Mon-Fri 10-4

SR WATTS STREET BAPTIST CHURCH LIBRARY*, 800 Watts St, 27701. SAN 328-4433. Tel: 919-688-1366. FAX: 919-688-7255. Web Site: www.wattsstreet.org.
Library Holdings: Bk Titles 1,000
Open Mon-Fri 8:30-5

EAST BEND

P EAST BEND PUBLIC LIBRARY*, 332 W Main St, 27018. (Mail add: PO Box 69, 27018-0069), SAN 376-2882. Tel: 336-699-3890. FAX: 336-699-2359. E-mail: ebn@nwrl.org. Web Site: www.nwrl.org/ebn.asp. *Librn,* Susan Hutchens; E-mail: shutchens@nwrl.org; *Asst Librn,* Darlene Novakowski
Founded 1985
Library Holdings: Bk Vols 15,000; Per Subs 18
Automation Activity & Vendor Info: (Acquisitions) SirsiDynix; (Cataloging) SirsiDynix; (Circulation) SirsiDynix; (Course Reserve) SirsiDynix; (ILL) SirsiDynix; (Media Booking) SirsiDynix; (OPAC) SirsiDynix; (Serials) SirsiDynix
Mem of Northwestern Regional Library
Open Mon 9-7, Tues-Thurs 9-5:30, Fri 9-2, Sat 9-12
Friends of the Library Group

EDEN

P ROCKINGHAM COUNTY PUBLIC LIBRARY*, 527 Boone Rd, 27288. SAN 354-7744. Tel: 336-627-1106. FAX: 336-623-1258. Web Site: www.rcpl.org. *Dir,* Michael Roche; E-mail: mproche@rcpl.org; *Ch Serv,* Jacky Miller; E-mail: jmiller@library.rcpl.org; *Extn Serv, Pub Serv,* Calvert Mason; E-mail: cmason@library.rcpl.org; *Ref,* Summer Cox; Staff 33 (MLS 9, Non-MLS 24)
Founded 1934. Pop 91,928; Circ 513,241
Jul 2005-Jun 2006 Income $1,987,569, State $202,548, City $2,600, Federal $44,226, County $1,689,545. Mats Exp $295,909. Sal $1,215,030
Library Holdings: Bk Vols 293,724; Per Subs 624
Subject Interests: African-Am, Bus, Genealogy, State hist
Automation Activity & Vendor Info: (Cataloging) Innovative Interfaces, Inc; (Circulation) Innovative Interfaces, Inc
Function: AV serv, Handicapped accessible, Home delivery & serv to Sr ctr & nursing homes, Homebound delivery serv, ILL available, Online searches, Photocopying/Printing, Prof lending libr, Prog for children & young adult, Ref serv available, Summer reading prog, Telephone ref, Wheelchair accessible
Publications: Genealogy Bibliography; Rockingham County Public Library Patron Brochure; Suggested Reading List for Home Extension Groups (Annual)
Open Mon-Fri 8-5
Friends of the Library Group
Branches: 5
EDEN BRANCH, 598 S Pierce St, 27288, SAN 354-7779. Tel: 336-623-3168. FAX: 336-623-1171. *Br Mgr,* Connie Whitt; E-mail: cwhitt@library.rcpl.org
Open Mon & Thurs 9-8, Tues, Wed & Fri 9-6, Sat 9-4
Friends of the Library Group
MADISON BRANCH, 140 E Murphy St, Madison, 27025, SAN 354-7809. Tel: 336-548-6553. FAX: 336-548-2010. *Librn/Mgr,* Joan Waynick; *Libr Asst,* Shirley Brim-Jones. Subject Specialists: *Genealogy,* Shirley Brim-Jones
Subject Interests: Genealogy, Local hist
Open Tues 9-6, Thurs 9-8, Sat 9-4
Friends of the Library Group
MAYODAN BRANCH, 101 N Tenth Ave, Mayodan, 27027, SAN 354-7833. Tel: 336-548-6951. FAX: 336-548-2015. *Librn/Mgr,* Joan Waynick
Open Mon 9-8, Wed & Fri 9-6
Friends of the Library Group
REIDSVILLE BRANCH, 204 W Morehead St, Reidsville, 27320, SAN 354 7868. Tel: 336-349-8476. FAX: 336-342-4824. *Br Mgr,* Calvert Smith
Subject Interests: African-Am
Automation Activity & Vendor Info: (OPAC) Innovative Interfaces, Inc
Database Vendor: Innovative Interfaces, Inc
Open Mon & Thurs 9-8, Tues, Wed & Fri 9-6, Sat 9-4
Friends of the Library Group
STONEVILLE BRANCH, 201 E Main St, Stoneville, 27048-8714. (Mail add: PO Box 26, Stoneville, 27048-0026), SAN 354-7892. Tel: 336-573-9040. FAX: 336-573-2774. *Librn/Mgr,* Joan Waynick
Open Mon & Wed 12-5, Tues 1-6, Thurs 1-8, Fri 10-6
Friends of the Library Group
Bookmobiles: 1

EDENTON

P SHEPARD-PRUDEN MEMORIAL LIBRARY, 106 W Water St, 27932. SAN 312-8199. Tel: 252-482-4112. FAX: 252-482-5451. E-mail: shepard-pruden@pettigrewlibraries.org. *Librn,* Jennifer Finlay; E-mail: jfinlay@pettigrewlibraries.org; *Asst Librn,* Naomi White; Staff 6 (MLS 1, Non-MLS 5)
Founded 1921. Pop 14,368; Circ 48,748
Library Holdings: Bk Titles 24,697; Bk Vols 29,379; Per Subs 69
Subject Interests: Local hist
Wireless access
Mem of Pettigrew Regional Library
Open Mon & Tues 10-7, Wed-Fri 10-5, Sat 10-1
Friends of the Library Group

ELIZABETH CITY

J COLLEGE OF THE ALBEMARLE LIBRARY*, 1208 N Road St, 27906. (Mail add: PO Box 2327, 27906-2327), SAN 354-7922. Tel: 252-335-0821, Ext 2270. FAX: 252-335-0649. Web Site: www.albemarle.edu/library.php. *Dir,* Robert Schenck; E-mail: rschenck@albemarle.edu; *Pub Serv,* Ruth E Balf; Tel: 252-335-0821, Ext 2371, E-mail: rbalf@albemarle.edu; *Tech Serv,* Shirley Gray Outlaw; Tel: 252-335-0821, Ext 2271, E-mail: soutlaw@albemarle.edu
Founded 1961
Library Holdings: Bk Titles 28,000; Bk Vols 35,000; Per Subs 232
Subject Interests: N Caroliniana
Partic in North Carolina Information Network (NCIN); OCLC Online Computer Library Center, Inc
Open Mon & Wed (Winter) 1-5, Tues & Thurs 8-Noon; Mon-Thurs (Summer) 8-5

P EAST ALBEMARLE REGIONAL LIBRARY*, 100 E Colonial Ave, 27909-0303. SAN 312-8202. Tel: 252-335-2511. FAX: 252-335-2386. Web Site: earlibrary.org. *Exec Dir,* Becky Callison; E-mail: bcallison@earlibrary.org; *Dir,* Jackie King; E-mail: jking@earlibrary.org; *Librn,* Jonathan Wark; Staff 31 (MLS 4, Non-MLS 27)
Founded 1964. Pop 89,939; Circ 390,995
Library Holdings: Bk Vols 170,000; Per Subs 350
Subject Interests: NC
Automation Activity & Vendor Info: (Cataloging) TLC (The Library Corporation); (Circulation) TLC (The Library Corporation); (OPAC) TLC (The Library Corporation)
Database Vendor: EBSCOhost, OCLC FirstSearch, ProQuest
Wireless access
Member Libraries: Currituck County Public Library; Dare County Library; Pasquotank-Camden Library
Open Mon-Fri 8:30-5
Bookmobiles: 1

C ELIZABETH CITY STATE UNIVERSITY*, G R Little Library, 1704 Weeksville Rd, 27909. SAN 312-8210. Tel: 252-335-3427. Circulation Tel: 252-335-8511, 252-335-8741. Interlibrary Loan Service Tel: 252-335-8513. Administration Tel: 252-335-3586. FAX: 252-335-3446. Reference FAX: 252-335-3094. Web Site: www.ecsu.edu/library/index.cfm. *Dir, Libr Serv,* Dr Juanita Midgette Spence; Tel: 252-335-3585, E-mail: jmidgette@mail.ecsu.edu; *Acq Librn,* Raeshawn MuGuffie; Tel: 252-335-3431, E-mail: rmcguffie@mail.ecsu.edu; *Circ Librn,* Amy Bondy; E-mail: aesbondy@mail.ecsu.edu; *ILL Librn,* Cheryl Leigh; E-mail: celeigh@mail.ecsu.edu; *Music Librn,* Stephanie Lewin-Lane; Tel: 252-335-3632, E-mail: splewin-lane@mail.ecsu.edu; *Ser Librn,* Burnella Griffin; Tel: 252-335-3432, E-mail: bwgriffin@mail.ecsu.edu; *Computer Tech,* Jerin Jefferson; Tel: 252-335-3905, E-mail: jmjefferson@mail.ecsu.edu; *Distance Educ, Info Literacy,* Dennis Brown; Tel: 252-335-3577, Fax: 252-335-3469, E-mail: djmbrown@mail.ecsu.edu; *Libr Tech,* Matisha Artis; Tel: 252-335-8511, E-mail: maartis@mail.ecsu.edu; *Libr Tech,* Leah Banks; Tel: 252-335-3429, E-mail: lcbanks@mail.ecsu.edu; *Libr Tech,* Pernell Bartlett; Tel: 252-335-8537, E-mail: pdbartlett@mail.ecsu.edu; *Libr Tech,* Claudia Davis; Tel: 252-335-8512, Fax: 252-335-3552, E-mail: ccdavis@mail.ecsu.edu; *Libr Tech,* Michael Marts; Tel: 252-335-8514, E-mail: mlmarts@mail.ecsu.edu; *Libr Tech,* Chiquita Mitchell; Tel: 252-335-8519, E-mail: cdmitchell@mail.ecsu.edu; *Libr Tech,* Sharon Owens; Tel: 252-335-8515, E-mail: ssowens@mail.ecsu.edu; *Univ Archivist,* Jean B Bischoff; Tel: 252-335-3647, E-mail: jbbischoff@mail.ecsu.edu. Subject Specialists: *Music,* Stephanie Lewin-Lane; Staff 17 (MLS 10, Non-MLS 7)
Founded 1892. Enrl 2,513; Fac 156; Highest Degree: Master
Jul 2011-Jun 2012. Mats Exp $682,265. Sal $770,000 (Prof $436,943)
Library Holdings: AV Mats 9,334; e-books 33; e-journals 41,919; Microforms 7,912; Bk Titles 170,787; Bk Vols 213,449; Per Subs 898
Special Collections: Children's Vintage Coll; State Normal School Coll (Coll contains books collected by the College library between the years of 1891-1939); State Teacher's College Coll (Coll contains books collected by the College library between the years of 1939-1963); Walter N Ridley Heritage Coll (Coll consists of books from Walter Ridley's, a former college president, personal library)
Automation Activity & Vendor Info: (Acquisitions) SIRSI WorkFlows; (Cataloging) SIRSI WorkFlows; (Circulation) SIRSI WorkFlows; (Course Reserve) SIRSI WorkFlows; (OPAC) SIRSI WorkFlows; (Serials) SIRSI WorkFlows
Database Vendor: ABC-CLIO, Alexander Street Press, American Chemical Society, BioOne, Bowker, Cambridge Scientific Abstracts, Cinahl, CQ Press, CRC Press/Taylor & Francis Group, EBSCOhost, Elsevier, Facts on File, Gale Cengage Learning, H W Wilson, Hoovers, IEEE (Institute of Electrical & Electronics Engineers), LearningExpress, LexisNexis, NC LIVE, Newsbank, OCLC, OCLC FirstSearch, OCLC WebJunction, OCLC WorldShare Interlibrary Loan, OneSource, ProQuest, PubMed, RefWorks, Sage, ScienceDirect, SerialsSolutions, SirsiDynix, Springshare, LLC, Wiley InterScience, Wilson - Wilson Web, WT Cox, YBP Library Services
Wireless access
Partic in Carolina Consortium; Eastern Carolina Libr Network; Lyrasis; NC State Libr Info Network; OCLC Online Computer Library Center, Inc
Open Mon-Thurs (Fall & Spring) 7:30am-11pm, Fri 7:30-6, Sat 11-5, Sun 2-10; Mon-Thurs (Summer) 8-9, Fri 8-5, Sat 9-2
Friends of the Library Group

CR MID-ATLANTIC CHRISTIAN UNIVERSITY, Watson-Griffith Library, 715 N Poindexter St, 27909-4054. SAN 312-8237. Tel: 252-334-2057. Administration Tel: 252-334-2046. FAX: 252-334-2577. Web Site: www.macuniversity.edu. *Dir,* Ken Gunselman; E-mail: ken.gunselman@macuniversity.edu; *Asst Dir,* Alice K Andrews; Tel: 252-334-2027, E-mail: alice.andrews@macuniversity.edu; Staff 3 (MLS 1, Non-MLS 2)
Founded 1948. Enrl 185; Fac 17; Highest Degree: Bachelor
Library Holdings: Bk Vols 35,000; Per Subs 188
Special Collections: Creationism Coll; Deaf Coll; Discipliana Coll
Subject Interests: Christian educ, Deaf studies, Prof life, Relig
Automation Activity & Vendor Info: (Cataloging) Mandarin Library Automation; (Circulation) Mandarin Library Automation; (OPAC) Mandarin Library Automation
Wireless access
Function: ILL available
Partic in Christian Libr Network; Lyrasis
Open Mon-Thurs 7:30am-8pm, Fri 7:30-5, Sat 12:30-2:30

S NORTH CAROLINA DEPARTMENT OF CORRECTION*, Pasquotank Correctional Institution Library, 527 Commerce Dr, Caller No 5005, 27906-5005. Tel: 252-331-4881. FAX: 252-331-4867. *Supv Librn,* Andre Williams; *Librn,* Farah Parks
Library Holdings: Bk Vols 12,000; Per Subs 20
Automation Activity & Vendor Info: (Cataloging) Brodart; (Circulation) Brodart
Open Mon-Thurs 8-3:30

P PASQUOTANK-CAMDEN LIBRARY*, 100 E Colonial Ave, 27909. SAN 312-8229. Tel: 252-335-2473, 252-335-7536. FAX: 252-331-7449. Web Site: www.earlibrary.org/pasquotank-camden/index.html. *Dir,* Jackie King; Fax: 252-331-7440, E-mail: jking@earlibrary.org; *Tech Serv Librn,* Charline Meads; E-mail: cmeads@earlibrary.org; *Ch Serv,* Peggy Brabble; E-mail: pbrabble@earlibrary.org; *Circ,* Karen Dicioccio; E-mail: kdicioccio@earlibrary.org; *Circ,* Sarah Halstead; E-mail: shalstead@earlibrary.org; *Info Serv,* Beatheia Jackson; E-mail: bjackson@earlibrary.org; *Ref,* Carrie Taylor; E-mail: ctaylor@earlibrary.org; *Tech Serv,* Christina Williams; E-mail: cwilliams@earlibrary.org
Founded 1930. Pop 36,732; Circ 131,140
Library Holdings: AV Mats 1,041; Large Print Bks 1,911; Bk Vols 62,000; Per Subs 88; Talking Bks 1,795
Subject Interests: NC hist
Automation Activity & Vendor Info: (Cataloging) TLC (The Library Corporation); (Circulation) TLC (The Library Corporation); (ILL) OCLC; (OPAC) TLC (The Library Corporation)
Database Vendor: ProQuest, TLC (The Library Corporation)
Wireless access
Mem of East Albemarle Regional Library
Open Mon, Wed & Fri 8:30-6:30, Tues & Thurs 8:30-7, Sat 9-6
Friends of the Library Group
Bookmobiles: 1. Librn, Monek Adams

ELIZABETHTOWN

P BLADEN COUNTY PUBLIC LIBRARY*, 111 N Cyprus St, 28337. (Mail add: PO Box 1419, 28337-1419), SAN 354-7981. Tel: 910-862-6990. FAX: 910-862-8777. Web Site: www2.youseemore.com/bladen. *Dir,* Rhea Hebert; E-mail: rhebert@bladenco.org; Staff 10 (MLS 1, Non-MLS 9)
Founded 1939. Pop 32,000; Circ 200,591
Jul 2005-Jun 2006 Income (Main Library and Branch(s)) $476,519, State $108,234, City $13,000, County $355,285. Mats Exp $36,635, Books $23,935, Per/Ser (Incl. Access Fees) $4,200, AV Mat $8,000, Electronic Ref Mat (Incl. Access Fees) $500. Sal $285,497
Library Holdings: Large Print Bks 3,000; Bk Vols 76,413; Per Subs 85; Talking Bks 539
Special Collections: North Carolina Genealogy
Subject Interests: Bladen County genealogy, Local hist, NC genealogy
Automation Activity & Vendor Info: (Cataloging) TLC (The Library Corporation); (Circulation) TLC (The Library Corporation); (OPAC) TLC (The Library Corporation)
Wireless access
Open Mon, Wed & Fri 8:30-6, Tues & Thurs 8:30-8:30, Sat 8:30am-12:30pm
Friends of the Library Group

Branches: 2
BRIDGER MEMORIAL, 313 S Main St, Bladenboro, 28320. (Mail add: PO Box 1259, Bladenboro, 28320-1259), SAN 354-8015. Tel: 910-863-4586. E-mail: bml@bladenco.org. *Br Mgr,* Kayla Parker
Library Holdings: Bk Titles 4,000
Open Mon 9-7, Tues 9-6, Wed-Fri 1-6
CLARKTON PUBLIC, 10413 N College St, Clarkton, 28433. (Mail add: PO Box 665, Clarkton, 28433-0665), SAN 354-804X. Tel: 910-647-3661. *Dir,* Rhea Hebert
Library Holdings: Bk Vols 5,000
Open Mon 9-6, Tues 9-7, Wed-Fri 1-6
Bookmobiles: 1

ELKIN

P NORTHWESTERN REGIONAL LIBRARY*, 111 N Front St, 28621. SAN 312-8253. Tel: 336-835-4894. Administration Tel: 336-835-2609. FAX: 336-526-2270. Administration FAX: 336-835-1356. E-mail: nwrl@nwrl.org. Web Site: www.nwrl.org/mta.asp. *Dir,* John Hedrick; E-mail: jhedrick@nwrl.org; *Br Supvr, Tech Coordr,* Joan Sherif; E-mail: jsherif@nwrl.org; *Acq, Info Serv,* Marie Simonelli; E-mail: msimonelli@nwrl.org; *Cataloger, ILL,* Claudia Humiston; E-mail: chumiston@nwrl.org; *Cat, Info Serv,* Steve McKinney; E-mail: smckinney@nwrl.org; *Info Serv,* Tonya Triplett; E-mail: triplett@nwrl.org; Staff 46 (MLS 4, Non-MLS 42)
Founded 1959. Pop 163,573; Circ 593,828
Library Holdings: DVDs 445; Large Print Bks 18,853; Bk Vols 319,272; Per Subs 225; Talking Bks 17,024; Videos 47,963
Subject Interests: Local hist
Automation Activity & Vendor Info: (Cataloging) SirsiDynix; (Circulation) SirsiDynix; (OPAC) SirsiDynix
Member Libraries: Alleghany County Public Library; Boonville Community Public Library; Charles H Stone Memorial Library; Danbury Public Library; Dobson Community Library; East Bend Public Library; Elkin Public Library; Jonesville Public Library; Lowgap Public Library; Mount Airy Public Library; Walnut Cove Public Library; Yadkin County Public Library
Friends of the Library Group
Bookmobiles: 1

ELON

C ELON UNIVERSITY*, Carol Grotnes Belk Library, 308 N O'Kelly Ave, 27244-0187. (Mail add: 2550 Campus Box, 27244), SAN 354-8074. Tel: 336-278-6600. Interlibrary Loan Service Tel: 336-278-6580. Administration Tel: 336-278-6579. Information Services Tel: 336-278-6599. FAX: 336-278-6637. Interlibrary Loan Service FAX: 336-278-6639. Web Site: www.elon.edu/library. *Dean & Univ Librn,* Joan Ruelle; Tel: 336-278-6572, E-mail: jruelle@elon.edu; *Archives Librn,* Shaunta Alvarez; Tel: 336-278-6531, E-mail: salvarez@elon.edu; *Archivist & Spec Coll Librn,* Katie Nash; Tel: 226-278-6681, E-mail: knash@elon.edu; *Cat Librn,* Shannon Tennant; Tel: 336-278-6585, E-mail: stennant@elon.edu; *Circ Serv Librn,* Chris Benton; Tel: 336-278-6593, E-mail: cbenton@elon.edu; *Evening Librn,* Sundeep Mahendra; E-mail: smahendra@elon.edu; *Non-Print Librn,* Lynne Bisko, Tel: 336-278-6587, E-mail: lbisko@elon.edu; *Ref & Instruction Librn,* Randall Bowman; Tel: 336-278-6571, E-mail: rbowman@elon.edu, *Ref/Bus Librn,* Betty L Garrison; Tel: 336-278-6581, E-mail: bgarrison@elon.edu; *Ref/Electronic Serv Librn,* Jamane Yeager; Tel: 336-278-6576, E-mail: jyeager@elon.edu; *Coordr, Pub Serv & Ref Librn,* Teresa LePors; Tel: 336-278-6577, E-mail: lepors@elon.edu; *Coordr, Ser/Govt Doc,* Dianne Ford; Tel: 336-278-6584, E-mail: dford@elon.edu; *Coordr, Tech Serv & Syst,* Connie Keller; Tel: 336-278-6578, E-mail: keller@elon.edu; *Coordr, Access Serv,* Patrick Rudd; E-mail: prudd@elon.edu; *Coordr, Acq,* Sandra Kilpatrick; E-mail: skilpatrick@elon.edu; *ILL Coordr,* Lynn Melchor; Staff 13 (MLS 13)
Founded 1889. Enrl 5,230; Fac 357; Highest Degree: Doctorate
Jun 2006-May 2007 Income $2,995,062. Mats Exp $1,482,426, Books $522,701, Per/Ser (Incl. Access Fees) $439,499, AV Mat $77,243, Electronic Ref Mat (Incl. Access Fees) $418,172, Presv $24,811. Sal $944,474 (Prof $619,400)
Library Holdings: AV Mats 23,781; CDs 5,181; DVDs 6,155; e-books 30,392; e-journals 25,646; Music Scores 4,497; Bk Vols 278,268; Per Subs 7,401; Talking Bks 2,078; Videos 10,109
Special Collections: Church History Coll (United Church of Christ-Southern Conference Archives), bks, mss, memorabilia; Civil War (McClendon Coll); Elon University Archives; Faculty Publications; North Carolina Authors (Johnson Coll), autographed first editions. Oral History; State Document Depository; US Document Depository
Subject Interests: Bus admin, Hist, Lit, Music, N Caroliniana, Phys therapy, Relig
Automation Activity & Vendor Info: (Acquisitions) Innovative Interfaces, Inc; (Cataloging) Innovative Interfaces, Inc; (Circulation) Innovative Interfaces, Inc; (Course Reserve) Innovative Interfaces, Inc; (ILL) OCLC; (OPAC) Innovative Interfaces, Inc; (Serials) Innovative Interfaces, Inc
Database Vendor: 3M Library Systems, Alexander Street Press, Baker & Taylor, Cambridge Scientific Abstracts, EBSCOhost, Gale Cengage Learning, Grolier Online, ISI Web of Knowledge, JSTOR, LexisNexis, Newsbank, OCLC FirstSearch, OCLC WorldShare Interlibrary Loan, OVID Technologies, ProQuest, PubMed, ReferenceUSA, SirsiDynix
Wireless access
Function: Archival coll, Audio & video playback equip for onsite use, Govt ref serv, Handicapped accessible, ILL available, Photocopying/Printing, Ref serv available
Publications: Brochures; Friends of the Libr Newsletter
Partic in Lyrasis; NC Asn of Independent Cols & Univs; OCLC Online Computer Library Center, Inc
Special Services for the Blind - Reader equip
Open Mon-Thurs 7:30am-1am, Fri 7:30am-9pm, Sat 9-9, Sun 10am-1am
Restriction: Open to fac, students & qualified researchers, Open to pub for ref & circ; with some limitations
Friends of the Library Group

ENFIELD

P LILLY PIKE SULLIVAN MUNICIPAL LIBRARY*, 103 Railroad St, 27823. SAN 312-8261. Tel: 252-445-5203. FAX: 252-445-4321. *Librn,* Cheryl Sumner; E-mail: csumner26@hotmail.com
Founded 1938. Pop 3,000; Circ 40,570
Library Holdings: Bk Vols 30,000; Per Subs 20
Special Collections: Commonwealth Microfilms 1908-1995; NC History Coll, AV
Wireless access
Open Mon-Fri 8:30-5, Sat 9-12

FAIRMONT

R FAIRMONT FIRST BAPTIST CHURCH*, Stinceon Ivey Memorial Library, 416 S Main, 28340. (Mail add: PO Box 663, 28340-0663), SAN 312-8296. Tel: 910-628-0626. FAX: 910-628-0627. E-mail: contact1baptist@yahoo.com. Web Site: www.fairmontsouth.com. *In Charge,* Charlotte Mitchell
Founded 1956
Library Holdings: Bk Vols 5,000

FARMVILLE

P FARMVILLE PUBLIC LIBRARY*, 4276 W Church St, 27828. SAN 312-8318. Tel: 252-753-3355. FAX: 252-753-2855. Web Site: www.farmvillelibrary.org. *Libr Dir,* David Robert Miller; Tel: 252-753-6713, E-mail: dmiller@farmville-nc.com; *Ch,* Connie Widney; *Libr Tech II,* Garris Edwards; *Libr Tech I,* Judy Andrews; Staff 1 (MLS 0.5, Non-MLS 0.5)
Founded 1930. Pop 5,090; Circ 16,500
Library Holdings: AV Mats 300; Large Print Bks 300; Bk Vols 35,000; Per Subs 120
Automation Activity & Vendor Info: (Acquisitions) Follett Software; (Cataloging) Follett Software; (Circulation) Follett Software
Function: After school storytime, Archival coll
Open Mon-Fri 9-6, Sat 9-1
Restriction: Authorized patrons
Friends of the Library Group

FAYETTEVILLE

M CAPE FEAR VALLEY HEALTH SYSTEM*, Library Services, 1638 Owen Dr, 28304. (Mail add: PO Box 2000, 28302-2000), SAN 321-4559. Tel: 910-615-5746. FAX: 910-609-7710. *Librn,* Sharon Barbiaux; Staff 1 (MLS 1)
Library Holdings: Bk Titles 225; Per Subs 200
Subject Interests: Allied health, Med, Nursing
Partic in National Network of Libraries of Medicine
Open Mon-Fri 8:30-5

P CUMBERLAND COUNTY PUBLIC LIBRARY & INFORMATION CENTER*, Headquarters, 300 Maiden Lane, 28301-5000. SAN 354-8139. Tel: 910-483-7727. Reference Tel: 910-483-7727, Ext 210. Administration Tel: 910-483-1580, Ext 102. FAX: 910-486-5372. Interlibrary Loan Service FAX: 910-486-6661. TDD: 910-483-7878. E-mail: library@cumberland.lib.nc.us. Web Site: www.cumberland.lib.nc.us. *Dir,* Jody A Risacher; *Dep Dir,* Brian Manning; *Commun Relations Librn,* Susan Parrish; E-mail: sparrish@cumberland.lib.nc.us; *Mgr,* Jane Casto; E-mail: jcasto@cumberland.lib.nc.us; *Circ Mgr,* Kathy Cotton; E-mail: kcotton@cumberland.lib.nc.us; *Div Mgr,* Catherine Rudelich; E-mail: crudelic@cumberland.lib.nc.us; *Info Serv Mgr,* Nora Armstrong; E-mail: narmstro@cumberland.lib.nc.us; *Mkt & Communications Mgr,* Kellie Tomita; E-mail: ktomita@cumberland.lib.nc.us; *Youth Serv Coordr,* Sheila Rider; E-mail: srider@cumberland.lib.nc.us; *Cat,* Martha Crawley; E-mail: mcrawley@cumberland.lib.nc.us; *Computer Serv,* Kenneth Young; E-mail: kyoung@cumberland.lib.nc.us; *Genealogy Serv,* Wanda Hunter; E-mail:

whunter@cumberland.lib.nc.us; *YA Serv,* Melissa Lang; E-mail: mlang@cumberland.lib.nc.us; Staff 200 (MLS 32, Non-MLS 168)
Founded 1932. Pop 305,851; Circ 1,715,574
Jul 2008-Jun 2009 Income (Main Library and Branch(s)) $9,384,139, State $389,489, County $8,459,717, Other $534,933. Mats Exp $947,038, Books $739,538, Micro $7,500, AV Mat $100,000, Electronic Ref Mat (Incl. Access Fees) $100,000. Sal $4,472,158
Library Holdings: AV Mats 46,264; Bk Vols 610,616; Per Subs 1,102
Special Collections: Foreign Language Center, bks, compact disc, DVD, newsp, per, tapes, video
Subject Interests: Commun agencies, Foreign lang mat, Law, Local hist
Automation Activity & Vendor Info: (Circulation) Innovative Interfaces, Inc; (OPAC) Innovative Interfaces, Inc
Function: Handicapped accessible, Home delivery & serv to Sr ctr & nursing homes, ILL available, Online searches, Photocopying/Printing, Prog for adults, Prog for children & young adult, Ref serv available, Summer reading prog, Telephone ref, Wheelchair accessible
Special Services for the Deaf - Staff with knowledge of sign lang; TTY equip
Open Mon-Thurs 9-9, Fri & Sat 9-6, Sun 2-6
Friends of the Library Group
Branches: 7
BORDEAUX, 3711 Village Dr, 28304-1530, SAN 354-8198. Tel: 910-424-4008. FAX: 910-423-1456. Web Site: www.cumberland.lib.nc.us/locations/bor/bordeaux.htm. *Br Mgr,* Robin Deffendall; E-mail: rdeffend@cumberland.lib.nc.us; *Librn,* Robin Imperial; E-mail: rimperia@cumberland.lib.nc.us; *Info Serv Librn,* Jean Boyer
Founded 1986
Library Holdings: Bk Vols 50,534
Open Mon & Tues 9-9, Wed-Sat 11-6
CLIFFDALE, 6882 Cliffdale Rd, 28314-1936, SAN 371-1374. Tel: 910-864-3800. FAX: 910-487-9090. Web Site: www.cumberland.lib.nc.us/locations/clf/cliffdale.htm. *Br Mgr,* Pamela Kource; E-mail: pkource@cumberland.lib.nc.us; *Head, Ref,* Marna Martin; E-mail: mmartin@cumberland.lib.nc.us; *Youth Serv,* Suzanne Miles; E-mail: smiles@cumberland.lib.nc.us
Founded 1991
Library Holdings: Bk Vols 78,725
Open Mon-Thurs 9-9, Fri & Sat 9-6, Sun 2-6

L CUMBERLAND COUNTY LAW LIBRARY, Courthouse, Rm 341, 117 Dick St, 28301, SAN 354-8163. Tel: 910-321-6600. FAX: 910-485-5291. Web Site: www.cumberland.lib.nc.us/locations/law/lawlibrary.htm. *Br Mgr,* Lisa O'Connor; E-mail: loconnor@cumberland.lib.nc.us
Library Holdings: Bk Vols 12,030
Publications: Due Process
Open Mon-Fri 8-1 & 2-5

EAST REGIONAL, 4809 Clinton Rd, 28301-8992, SAN 378-150X. Tel: 910-485-2955. FAX: 910-485-5492. Web Site: www.cumberland.lib.nc.us/locations/erl/eastregional.htm. *Br Mgr,* Judy Brown; E-mail: jmbrown@cumberland.lib.nc.us; *Info Serv Librn,* MaryAnne Sommer
Founded 1999
Library Holdings: Bk Vols 71,009
Open Mon-Wed 9-9, Thurs & Fri 11-6, Sat 9-6
HOPE MILLS BRANCH, 3411 Golfview Rd, Hope Mills, 28348-2266, SAN 354-8317. Tel: 910-425-8455. FAX: 910-423-0997. E-mail: hpm@cumberland.lib.nc.us. *Br Mgr,* Meg Smith; E-mail: msmith@cumberland.lib.nc.us
Founded 1992
Library Holdings: Bk Vols 56,447
Open Mon-Wed 9-9, Thurs-Sat 9-6
Friends of the Library Group
NORTH REGIONAL, 855 McArthur Rd, 28311-1961, SAN 378-1488. Tel: 910-822-1998. FAX: 910-480-0030. E-mail: nrl@cumberland.lib.nc.us. Web Site: www.cumberland.lib.nc.us/Locations/nrl/northregional. *Br Mgr,* Mary Campbell; E-mail: mcampbel@cumberland.lib.nc.us; *Head, Ref,* Mark Wilson; E-mail: mwilson@cumberland.lib.nc.us; *Youth Serv Mgr,* Susan Weigel; E-mail: sweigel@cumberland.lib.nc.us; Staff 30 (MLS 5, Non-MLS 25)
Founded 1998
Library Holdings: AV Mats 6,344; Bk Vols 92,315
Function: After school storytime, Computer training, Computers for patron use, Copy machines, e-mail serv, Free DVD rentals, Spoken cassettes & CDs, Summer reading prog, Web-catalog
Open Mon-Thurs 9-9, Fri & Sat 9-6, Sun 2-6
Restriction: Pub access for legal res only
SPRING LAKE BRANCH, 101 Laketree Blvd, Spring Lake, 28390-3189, SAN 354-8341. Tel: 910-497-3650. FAX: 910-497-0523. Web Site: www.cumberland.lib.nc.us/locations/spl/springlake.htm. *Br Mgr,* Gloria Nelson; E-mail: gnelson@cumberland.lib.nc.us; *Info Serv Librn,* Heather Heady
Founded 1999
Library Holdings: Bk Vols 44,871
Open Mon & Tues 9-9, Wed-Sat 11-6
Bookmobiles: 1

GM DEPARTMENT OF VETERANS AFFAIRS*, Medical Center Library Service, 2300 Ramsey St, 28301. SAN 312-8369. Tel: 910-822-7072. Toll Free Tel: 800-771-6106. Web Site: www.fayettevillenc.va.gov/index.asp. *Tech Serv,* Karen March; Staff 1 (Non-MLS 1)
Founded 1939
Library Holdings: Bk Titles 500; Per Subs 80; Videos 50
Subject Interests: Allied health, Med, Nursing
Open Mon-Fri 8-4:30

S FAYETTEVILLE PUBLISHING CO*, Newspaper Library, 458 Whitfield St, 28306. (Mail add: PO Box 849, 28302), SAN 325-7819. Tel: 910-486-3584. Toll Free Tel: 800-682-3476. FAX: 910-486-3545. Web Site: www.fayobserver.com. *Dir,* Michelle Luther; E-mail: lutherm@fayobserver.com; *Res,* Cathy Barnes; *Res,* Michelle Luther; Staff 4 (MLS 1, Non-MLS 3)
Library Holdings: Bk Vols 3,200; Per Subs 72
Special Collections: Fayetteville Observer (Newspaper)
Subject Interests: Local hist
Restriction: Staff use only

C FAYETTEVILLE STATE UNIVERSITY*, Charles W Chesnutt Library, 1200 Murchison Rd, 28301-4298. SAN 312-8334. Tel: 910-672-1231. Reference Tel: 910-672-1233. FAX: 910-672-1746. Administration FAX: 910-672-1312. Web Site: library.uncfsu.edu. *Dir,* Bobby C Wynn; Tel: 910-672-1232, E-mail: bwynn@uncfsu.edu; *Assoc Dir, Coll Develop,* Evelyn Council; Tel: 910-672-1520, E-mail: ecouncil@uncfsu.edu; *Head, Pub Serv, Head, Ref Serv,* Jan Whitfield; Tel: 910-672-1750, E-mail: jwhitfield@uncfsu.edu; *Head, Tech Serv, Info Tech,* Matthew Lawson; Tel: 910-672-1546, E-mail: mlawson@uncfsu.edu; *Acq Librn,* Betty Washington; Tel: 910-672-1642, E-mail: bwashington@uncfsu.edu; *Cat Librn,* Lewis Trott; Tel: 910-672-1549, E-mail: ltrott@uncsfu.edu; *Ref Librn,* Bernadette Ross; E-mail: bross@uncfsu.edu; *Coordr, ILL, Ref Coordr,* Linette Neal; Tel: 910-672-1230, E-mail: lneal3@uncfsu.edu; *Archivist,* Craig Tuttle; Tel: 910-672-1613; *Circ,* Gloria Garner; Tel: 910-672-1236, E-mail: ggarner@uncfsu.edu; *Govt Doc,* Jinong Sun; Tel: 910-672-1752, E-mail: jsun@uncfsu.edu; *ILL,* Laura Wright; *Ser,* Vera Hooks; Tel: 910-672-1539, E-mail: vhooks@uncfsu.edu; Staff 33 (MLS 15, Non-MLS 18)
Founded 1867. Enrl 6,300; Fac 200; Highest Degree: Doctorate
Jul 2005-Jun 2006 Income $1,517,502, Federal $514,597, Parent Institution $1,002,905. Mats Exp $1,505,320, Books $400,905, Per/Ser (Incl. Access Fees) $444,855, Micro $85,000, AV Mat $30,000, Electronic Ref Mat (Incl. Access Fees) $534,560, Presv $10,000. Sal $1,449,783 (Prof $703,788)
Library Holdings: AV Mats 1,200,000; CDs 1,115; e-books 13,000; e-journals 994; Electronic Media & Resources 252; Bk Vols 291,718; Per Subs 2,742; Videos 4,974
Special Collections: US Govt Doc, Archives. US Document Depository
Subject Interests: African-Am, Ethnic studies
Automation Activity & Vendor Info: (Acquisitions) Innovative Interfaces, Inc; (Cataloging) Innovative Interfaces, Inc; (Circulation) Innovative Interfaces, Inc; (Course Reserve) Innovative Interfaces, Inc; (ILL) OCLC PromptCat; (OPAC) Innovative Interfaces, Inc
Wireless access
Publications: Acquisitions List; Ches-Notes
Partic in Lyrasis
Open Mon-Thurs (Winter) 7am-12am, Fri 7am-9pm, Sat 8am-9pm, Sun 2-11; Mon-Thurs (Summer) 7am-10pm, Fri 7-6, Sat 8-5, Sun 1-10
Friends of the Library Group

J FAYETTEVILLE TECHNICAL COMMUNITY COLLEGE*, Paul H Thompson Library, 2201 Hull Rd, 28303. SAN 312-8342. Tel: 910-678-8247. FAX: 910-678-8401. E-mail: library@faytechcc.edu. Web Site: www.faytechcc.edu/library_services. *Dir, Libr Serv,* Robert Antill; Tel: 910-678-8382, E-mail: antillr@faytechcc.edu; *Access Serv, Pub Serv,* Deborah Foster; Tel: 910-678-8257, E-mail: fosterd@faytechcc.edu; *Tech Serv,* Tammy Stewart; Tel: 910-678-8253, E-mail: stewartt@faytechcc.edu; Staff 9 (MLS 3, Non-MLS 6)
Founded 1961. Enrl 8,000; Fac 250; Highest Degree: Associate
Library Holdings: Bk Titles 64,000; Per Subs 100
Subject Interests: Health occupation, Law
Automation Activity & Vendor Info: (Circulation) SirsiDynix; (Serials) SirsiDynix
Wireless access
Function: Telephone ref
Partic in Cape Fear Health Sciences Information Consortium; Community Colleges Libraries in North Carolina (CCLINC); Westlaw
Open Mon-Thurs 7:45am-9pm, Fri 7:45-7

C METHODIST COLLEGE*, Davis Memorial Library, 5400 Ramsey St, 28311. SAN 312-8350. Tel: 910-630-7123. Circulation Tel: 910-630-7645. Interlibrary Loan Service Tel: 910-630-7415. Administration Tel:

910-630-7587. FAX: 910-630-7119. E-mail: reference@methodist.edu. Web Site: www.methodist.edu/library/davis.htm. *Dir, Libr Serv,* Tracey Pearson; Tel: 910-630-7587, E-mail: tpearson@methodist.edu; *Circ,* David Hodgins; Tel: 910-630-7618, E-mail: chodgins@methodist.edu; Staff 14 (MLS 5, Non-MLS 9)
Founded 1960. Enrl 2,255; Fac 150; Highest Degree: Master
Library Holdings: AV Mats 13,799; e-books 22,700; e-journals 14,275; Bk Vols 109,578; Per Subs 470
Special Collections: Lafayette Coll
Automation Activity & Vendor Info: (Acquisitions) Ex Libris Group; (Cataloging) Ex Libris Group; (Circulation) Ex Libris Group; (Media Booking) Ex Libris Group; (OPAC) Ex Libris Group; (Serials) Ex Libris Group
Database Vendor: EBSCOhost, Gale Cengage Learning, LexisNexis, OCLC FirstSearch, OCLC WorldShare Interlibrary Loan, OVID Technologies, ProQuest, Westlaw
Partic in Cape Fear Health Sciences Information Consortium
Open Mon-Thurs 7:45am-11pm, Fri 7:45-6, Sat 11-7, Sun 1-11

M SOUTHERN REGIONAL AREA HEALTH EDUCATION CENTER*, Information Access Center, Library Services, 1601 Owen Dr, 28304. SAN 312-8326. Tel: 910-678-7273. Interlibrary Loan Service Tel: 910-678-7204. FAX: 910-323-4007. E-mail: ill@sr-ahec.org, reference@sr-ahec.org. Web Site: www.southernregionalahec.org. *Dir, Info Access Libr Serv,* Rebecca Johnston; Tel: 910-678-7270, E-mail: rebecca.johnston@sr-ahec.org; Staff 3 (MLS 2, Non-MLS 1)
Founded 1977
Jul 2011-Jun 2012. Mats Exp $62,000
Library Holdings: AV Mats 150; e-books 200; e-journals 2,000; Bk Titles 2,500; Per Subs 15
Subject Interests: Allied health, Consumer health, Family med, Med, Mental health, Nursing, Osteopathic med
Automation Activity & Vendor Info: (Cataloging) EOS International; (Circulation) EOS International; (OPAC) EOS International
Database Vendor: Cinahl, EBSCO - WebFeat, EBSCOhost, EOS International, Majors, Medline, NC LIVE, OCLC FirstSearch, OVID Technologies, PubMed, UpToDate
Wireless access
Partic in Medical Library Association (MLA); Mid-Atlantic Chapter-Med Libr Asn; National Network of Libraries of Medicine Southeastern Atlantic Region; US National Library of Medicine
Open Mon-Fri 8-5
Restriction: Med & health res only

FLAT ROCK

J BLUE RIDGE COMMUNITY COLLEGE LIBRARY*, 180 W Campus Dr, 28731. SAN 312-8377. Tel: 828-694-1879. FAX: 828-694-1692. E-mail: library@blueridge.edu. Web Site: library.blueridge.edu. *Dir,* Susan D Williams; Tel: 828-694-1824, E-mail: susanw@blueridge.edu; *Librn,* Marianne Campbell; E-mail: marianc@blueridge.edu; *Electronic Res Librn,* Alison A Norvell; Tel: 828-694-1636; Staff 2.5 (MLS 2.5)
Founded 1969. Fac 55; Highest Degree: Associate
Library Holdings: Bk Vols 34,000; Per Subs 120
Automation Activity & Vendor Info: (Cataloging) SirsiDynix; (Circulation) SirsiDynix; (Course Reserve) SirsiDynix; (OPAC) SirsiDynix
Database Vendor: SirsiDynix
Wireless access
Function: Bks on cassette, Bks on CD, Computers for patron use, Copy machines, ILL available, Pub access computers, Ref serv available
Partic in NC Dept of Commun Cols
Open Mon-Thurs 8am-9pm & Fri 8-4:30
Restriction: Open to pub for ref & circ; with some limitations, Open to students, fac & staff

FOREST CITY

P MOONEYHAM PUBLIC LIBRARY*, 240 E Main St, 28043. SAN 355-1288. Tel: 828-248-5224. FAX: 828-248-5224. E-mail: fclib@townofforestcity.com. Web Site: www.cmclibraries.org, www.townofforestcity.com/library.html. *Dir,* Denise Strickland; *Asst Librn,* Diane Bailey
Library Holdings: AV Mats 200; Bks on Deafness & Sign Lang 10; Large Print Bks 60; Bk Vols 15,600; Per Subs 40; Talking Bks 100
Wireless access
Open Mon-Thurs 9-6, Fri 9-5:30

FORT BRAGG

UNITED STATES ARMY

A MARQUAT MEMORIAL LIBRARY*, Bank Hall, Bldg D-3915, 3004 Ardennes St, 28310-9610, SAN 354-8430. Tel: 910-396-5370. FAX: 910-432-7788. *Chief, Libr Serv,* Margaret Harrison; Tel: 910-396-3958; *Sr Librn,* Jane Crabill; Tel: 910-432-8184, E-mail: jane.crabill@us.army.mil; *Acq, Cat,* C Labsan; Tel: 910-432-6503; *ILL,* Eva Murphy; Tel: 910-432-9222, E-mail: eva.murphy@us.army.mil; *Ref,* Nan Kutulas; Tel: 910-432-8920, E-mail: nancy.kutulas@us.army.mil; Staff 5 (MLS 2, Non-MLS 3)
Founded 1952
Library Holdings: Bk Vols 33,000; Per Subs 126
Subject Interests: Area studies, Civil affairs, Geopolitics, Intl relations, Lang, Mil assistance, Polit sci, Psychol operations, Regional studies, Spec forces, Spec operations, Terrorism, Unconventional warfare
Automation Activity & Vendor Info: (Cataloging) TLC (The Library Corporation); (Circulation) TLC (The Library Corporation); (ILL) OCLC; (OPAC) TLC (The Library Corporation)
Partic in OCLC Online Computer Library Center, Inc
Publications: (Accession list); Bibliographics (2/yr); Library Guide; Periodicals Holdings List
Open Mon-Fri 9-4:30
Restriction: Circ to mil employees only

A JOHN L THROCKMORTON LIBRARY*, IMSE-BRG-MWR-L Bldg 1-3346, Randolph St, 28310-5000, SAN 354-8406. Tel: 910-396-2665. Circulation Tel: 910-396-1691. Reference Tel: 910-396-3523. FAX: 910-907-2274. Web Site: www.fortbraggmwr.com/library.php. *Chief Librn,* Philip Quinones; *Ref Librn,* Ron Jackson; *Ref Librn,* Bernadette Ross; Staff 13 (MLS 3, Non-MLS 10)
Founded 1941
Library Holdings: Bk Vols 125,000; Per Subs 200
Subject Interests: Current affairs, Hist, Intl relations, Mil sci, Testing
Automation Activity & Vendor Info: (Acquisitions) SirsiDynix; (Cataloging) SirsiDynix; (Circulation) SirsiDynix; (ILL) OCLC; (OPAC) SirsiDynix; (Serials) SirsiDynix
Database Vendor: EBSCOhost, ProQuest
Partic in Fedlink; OCLC Online Computer Library Center, Inc
Publications: Bibliographies
Open Mon-Thurs 9-8, Fri & Sat 10-6

AM WOMACK ARMY MEDICAL CENTER, MEDICAL LIBRARY*, WAMC Stop A, 2817 Reilly Rd, 28310-7301. Tel: 910-907-7323. FAX: 910-907-7449. *Librn,* Jennifer Kuntz
Library Holdings: Bk Vols 3,800; Per Subs 179
Function: ILL available, Photocopying/Printing
Partic in Fedlink
Restriction: Not open to pub

FRANKLIN

P MACON COUNTY PUBLIC LIBRARY*, 149 Siler Farm Rd, 28734. SAN 312-8385. Tel: 828-524-3600, 828-524-3700. FAX: 828-524-9550. Web Site: www.fontanalib.org. *Dir,* Karen Wallace; E-mail: kwallace@fontanalib.org; Staff 23 (MLS 2, Non-MLS 21)
Founded 1890. Pop 34,000
Library Holdings: Bk Vols 75,000
Automation Activity & Vendor Info: (Cataloging) Evergreen; (Circulation) Evergreen; (OPAC) Evergreen
Database Vendor: NC LIVE, Overdrive, Inc
Wireless access
Function: Distance learning
Mem of Fontana Regional Library
Open Mon-Thurs 9-8, Fri & Sat 9-5
Friends of the Library Group
Branches: 2
HUDSON LIBRARY, 554 Main St, Highlands, 28741. (Mail add: PO Box 430, Highlands, 28741-0430), SAN 312-8830. Tel: 828-526-3031. FAX: 828-526-5278. *Librn,* Mary Lou Worley; E-mail: mworley@fontanalib.org; Staff 5 (MLS 1, Non-MLS 4)
Founded 1884
Library Holdings: Bk Vols 22,367; Per Subs 80; Talking Bks 650; Videos 800
Open Tues-Fri 10-5:30, Sat 10-4
NANTAHALA COMMUNITY, 128 Nantahala School Rd, Topton, 28781. Tel: 828-321-3020. FAX: 828-488-9857. Web Site: www.fontanalib.org/nantahala/index.htm. *Br Mgr,* Teresa Bryant; E-mail: tbryant@fontanalib.org
Founded 1986
Library Holdings: AV Mats 100; Bk Vols 800; Per Subs 13; Talking Bks 60
Open Tues-Sat 10-5
Friends of the Library Group

GASTONIA

R FLINT-GROVES BAPTIST CHURCH LIBRARY*, 2017 E Ozark Ave, 28054. SAN 312-8393. Tel: 704-865-4068. FAX: 704-865-8008. Web Site: www.flintgroves.org. *Librn,* Pam Grindstaff; E-mail: pgrindstaff@carolina.rr.com
Automation Activity & Vendor Info: (Acquisitions) Book Systems; (Cataloging) Book Systems; (Circulation) Book Systems; (OPAC) Book Systems
Wireless access

Open Mon-Fri 8:30-4:30
Friends of the Library Group

P GASTON COUNTY PUBLIC LIBRARY*, 1555 E Garrison Blvd, 28054. SAN 312-8407. Tel: 704-868-2164. FAX: 704-853-0609. Web Site: www.gastonlibrary.org. *Dir,* Laurel Hicks; E-mail: laurel.hicks@gastongov.com; *Asst Dir,* Paul Ward, Jr; *Supvr, Automation Serv,* Chad Eller; *Supvr, Ch Serv,* Sarah Miller; *Supvr, Circ,* Tanya Jones; *Supvr, Circ,* Jane Kaylor; *Supvr, Extn Serv,* Marty Wilson; *Ref Supvr,* Anne Gometz
Mem of Gaston-Lincoln Regional Library
Open Mon, Tues & Thurs 10-9, Wed & Sat 10-6, Fri 10-2
Friends of the Library Group
Branches: 9
BELMONT BRANCH, 125 Central Ave, Belmont, 28012, SAN 312-7451. Tel: 704-825-5426. FAX: 704-825-5426. *Br Mgr,* Shannon Potter
Open Mon & Sat 10-2, Tues & Thurs 10-6
BESSEMER CITY BRANCH, 207 N 12th St, Bessemer City, 28016, SAN 312-7478. Tel: 704-629-3321. FAX: 704-629-3321. *Br Mgr,* Traci Pollitt
Open Wed & Fri 10-6
CHERRYVILLE BRANCH, 605 E Main St, Cherryville, 28021, SAN 312-7923. Tel: 704-435-6767. FAX: 704-435-6767. *Br Mgr,* Traci Pollitt
Open Mon & Sat 10-2, Tues & Thurs 10-6
Friends of the Library Group
DALLAS BRANCH, 105 S Holland St, Dallas, 28034, SAN 312-8032. Tel: 704-922-3621. FAX: 704-922-3621. *Br Mgr,* Dianne Navey
Open Mon, Wed & Fri 10-6
Friends of the Library Group
FERGUSON BRANCH, Erwin Center, 913 N Pryor St, 28052, SAN 372-5189. Tel: 704-868-8046. FAX: 704-868-8046. *Br Supvr,* Kyle Hearns; *Br Supvr,* Michael Webb
Open Mon, Tues & Thurs 4-9, Sat 10-2
Friends of the Library Group
LOWELL BRANCH, 203 McAdenville Rd, Lowell, 28098, SAN 312-908X. Tel: 704-824-1266. FAX: 704-824-1266. *Br Mgr,* Shannon Potter
Open Mon, Wed & Fri 10-6
MOUNT HOLLY BRANCH, 245 W Catawba Ave, Mount Holly, 28120, SAN 312-925X. Tel: 704-827-3581. FAX: 704-827-8573. *Br Mgr,* Debra Livingston
Open Mon & Sat 10-2, Tues & Thurs 10-6
Friends of the Library Group
STANLEY BRANCH, 205 N Peterson St, Stanley, 28164, SAN 320-9083. Tel: 704-263-4166. FAX: 704-263-4166. *Br Mgr,* Debra Livingston
Open Mon, Wed & Fri 10-6
UNION ROAD, 5800 Union Rd, 28056. Tel: 704-852-4073. FAX: 704-852-9631. *Br Mgr,* Rene Crump
Open Mon, Wed & Fri 10-6

S SCHIELE MUSEUM OF NATURAL HISTORY LIBRARY*, 1500 E Garrison Blvd, 28054-5199. SAN 328-0691. Tel: 704-869-1009. FAX: 704-866-6041. *Coll Mgr,* Carrie Duran; E-mail: carried@cityofgastonia.com
Library Holdings: Bk Titles 7,000; Bk Vols 7,600; Per Subs 20
Subject Interests: Archaeology, Astronomy, Mus studies, Natural hist
Function: Res libr
Restriction: Open to others by appt, Staff use only

GOLDSBORO

S CHERRY HOSPITAL*, Learning Resource Center Library, U-4 Bldg, 1st Flr, 201 Stevens Mill Rd, 27530. SAN 325-7827. Tel: 919-731-3447, Ext 232. FAX: 919-731-3429. Web Site: www.esn.net/win/cherry.htm. *Librn,* Brian Curry; E-mail: brian.curry@ncmail.net
Library Holdings: Bk Vols 3,000; Per Subs 30
Automation Activity & Vendor Info: (Cataloging) Follett Software; (Circulation) Follett Software; (Serials) Follett Software
Partic in Wayne Info Network
Open Mon-Fri 8-12 & 1-5

J WAYNE COMMUNITY COLLEGE LIBRARY*, 3000 Wayne Memorial Dr, 27533. (Mail add: PO Box 8002, 27533-8002), SAN 312-8431. Tel: 919-735-5151, Ext 293. Interlibrary Loan Service Tel: 919-735-5151, Ext 295. Reference Tel: 919-735-5151, Ext 390. FAX: 919-736-3204. E-mail: wcc-library@waynecc.edu. Web Site: www.waynecc.edu. *Dir of Libr Serv,* Dr Aletha Andrew; Tel: 919-735-5151, Ext 292, E-mail: raandrew@waynecc.edu; Staff 6 (MLS 3, Non-MLS 3)
Founded 1965. Enrl 3,000; Fac 115; Highest Degree: Associate
Jul 2005-Jun 2006 Income $401,235. Mats Exp $112,570, Books $53,030, Per/Ser (Incl. Access Fees) $31,200, AV Mat $28,000, Presv $340
Library Holdings: AV Mats 3,305; Bk Vols 50,000; Per Subs 317
Special Collections: Children's Literature Coll; North Carolina Genealogy Coll; Wayne Community College Historical Archives
Automation Activity & Vendor Info: (Cataloging) SirsiDynix; (Circulation) SirsiDynix; (OPAC) SirsiDynix
Function: Computers for patron use, Copy machines, Distance learning, e-mail serv, Electronic databases & coll, Fax serv, ILL available, Online cat, Photocopying/Printing, Ref serv available, Telephone ref
Partic in Community Colleges Libraries in North Carolina (CCLINC); Wayne Info Network
Open Mon & Thurs 7:45am-8pm, Tues & Wed 7:45-5, Fri 7:45-4

P WAYNE COUNTY PUBLIC LIBRARY, 1001 E Ash St, 27530. SAN 354-849X. Tel: 919-735-1824. FAX: 919-731-2889. Web Site: www.wcpl.org. *Dir,* Donna Phillips; E-mail: donna.phillips@waynegov.com; *Asst Dir,* Rosemary Loomis; *Head, Children's Dept,* Laura Rachel Barwick; *Head, Ref Serv,* Johnnie Pippin; *Head, Tech Serv,* Marion Waters; E-mail: marion.waters@waynegov.com; Staff 27 (MLS 4, Non-MLS 23)
Founded 1907. Pop 140,000
Library Holdings: Bk Vols 100,000; Per Subs 212
Subject Interests: Genealogy, Local hist
Automation Activity & Vendor Info: (Acquisitions) Innovative Interfaces, Inc; (Cataloging) Innovative Interfaces, Inc; (Circulation) Innovative Interfaces, Inc; (ILL) Innovative Interfaces, Inc; (OPAC) Innovative Interfaces, Inc
Database Vendor: Gale Cengage Learning, ProQuest
Publications: Calendar; Friend Reminders; Friends Newsletter
Open Mon-Thurs 9-9, Fri & Sat 9-5:30
Friends of the Library Group
Branches: 3
FREMONT PUBLIC, 202 N Goldsboro St, Fremont, 27830, SAN 354-8554. Tel: 919-705-1893. *Mgr,* Cathy Bannister
Open Mon & Thurs 2-6, Tues & Wed 9-1
PIKEVILLE PUBLIC, 107 W Main St, Pikeville, 27863. (Mail add: PO Box 909, Pikeville, 27863-0909), SAN 354-8589. Tel: 919-705-1892. *Mgr,* Lisa Stevens
Open Mon, Thurs & Sat 9-1, Tues & Wed 2-6
STEELE MEMORIAL, 119 W Main St, Mount Olive, 28365, SAN 354-8643. Tel: 919-299-8105. *Br Mgr,* Jerylin Lee; Staff 1 (MLS 1)
Special Collections: Marion Hargrove Coll, ms
Function: Bilingual assistance for Spanish patrons, Children's prog, Computers for patron use, Copy machines, Free DVD rentals, Handicapped accessible, ILL available, Notary serv, Story hour, Summer reading prog
Open Mon & Wed-Sat 9-5:30, Tues 9-8
Restriction: Open to pub for ref & circ; with some limitations
Friends of the Library Group

GRAHAM

J ALAMANCE COMMUNITY COLLEGE*, Learning Resources Center, 1247 Jimmie Kerr Rd, 27253. (Mail add: PO Box 8000, 27253-8000), SAN 312-8733. Tel: 336-506-4116. FAX: 336-578-5561. Web Site: www.alamancecc.edu/library. *Dir,* Sheila Street; Tel: 336-506-4186, E-mail: sheila.street@alamancecc.edu; *Tech Serv Librn,* Mary Davis; Tel: 336-506-4198, E-mail: mary.davis@alamancecc.edu
Founded 1960. Enrl 4,300; Fac 250; Highest Degree: Associate
Library Holdings: AV Mats 1,200; Bk Vols 39,000; Per Subs 200
Subject Interests: Applied arts, Econ, Educ, Eng tech, Mechanical occupations
Wireless access
Open Mon-Thurs 7:45am-9:30pm, Fri 7:45-4, Sat (Fall & Spring) 8-Noon

S ALAMANCE COUNTY HISTORIC PROPERTIES COMMISSION*, Historic Restoration Resources Library, 217 College St, Ste C, 27253. SAN 325-7886. Tel: 336-228-1312. FAX: 336-570-4055. *Dir,* Jason Martin; E-mail: jason.martin@alamance-nc.com
Library Holdings: Bk Vols 200
Special Collections: Municipal Document Depository
Subject Interests: Genealogy
Open Mon-Fri 8-5

GRANTSBORO

J PAMLICO COMMUNITY COLLEGE*, Library Services & Cultural Enrichment, 5049 Hwy 306 S, 28529. (Mail add: PO Box 185, 28529-0185), SAN 312-8474. Tel: 252-249-1851, Ext 3034. FAX: 252-249-2377. Web Site: www.pamlicocc.edu/library. *Chair, Libr Serv,* Leigh Russell; Tel: 252-249-1851, Ext 3033, E-mail: lrussell@pamlicocc.edu; *Libr Tech,* Erlinda Leggett; E-mail: eleggett@pamlicocc.edu; Staff 4 (MLS 1, Non-MLS 3)
Founded 1963. Enrl 1,500; Fac 50; Highest Degree: Associate
Library Holdings: Bk Titles 10,000; Per Subs 6,000
Special Collections: Black History Coll. State Document Depository
Subject Interests: African-Am hist, Econ, Ethnic studies, Health, Local hist, Vocational
Automation Activity & Vendor Info: (Acquisitions) SirsiDynix; (Cataloging) SirsiDynix; (Circulation) SirsiDynix; (Course Reserve)

SirsiDynix; (ILL) SirsiDynix; (Media Booking) SirsiDynix; (OPAC) SirsiDynix; (Serials) SirsiDynix
Database Vendor: EBSCOhost, Gale Cengage Learning, OCLC FirstSearch, OVID Technologies, ProQuest
Partic in Community Colleges Libraries in North Carolina (CCLINC); OCLC Online Computer Library Center, Inc
Open Mon-Thurs 7:30am-9:30pm, Fri 7:30am-1pm
Friends of the Library Group
Bookmobiles: 1

GREENSBORO

C BENNETT COLLEGE*, Thomas F Holgate Library, 900 E Washington St, 27401-3239. SAN 312 8482. Tel: 336-517-2139. FAX: 336-517-2144. Web Site: library.bennett.edu. *Libr Dir,* Joan Williams; Tel: 336-517-2141, E-mail: jwilliams@bennett.edu; *Circ Librn,* Julia Scott; E-mail: jscott@bennett.edu; *Cataloger,* Addie Harrison; Tel: 336-517-2143, E-mail: aharrison@bennett.edu; Staff 5 (MLS 3, Non-MLS 2)
Founded 1939. Enrl 672; Fac 45; Highest Degree: Bachelor
Library Holdings: AV Mats 2,400; e-books 36,000; Bk Vols 98,000; Per Subs 150
Special Collections: Art (Carnegie Art Coll), bks, repro; Bennett College Archives, bks, clippings, photog; Bennett College History; Black Studies, Women (Afro-American Women's Coll), bks, clippings, photog; Individual Biography (Norris Wright Cuney Papers), clippings, correspondence; Palmer Coll
Subject Interests: African-Am women
Automation Activity & Vendor Info: (Cataloging) SirsiDynix; (Circulation) SirsiDynix; (OPAC) SirsiDynix; (Serials) SirsiDynix
Database Vendor: EBSCOhost, JSTOR, NC LIVE, Newsbank, OCLC WorldShare Interlibrary Loan
Wireless access
Partic in OCLC Online Computer Library Center, Inc
Open Mon-Thurs 8am-Midnight, Fri 8-5, Sat 1-5, Sun 6pm-Midnight; Mon-Fri (Summer) 8-5
Friends of the Library Group

S CENTER FOR CREATIVE LEADERSHIP LIBRARY*, One Leadership Pl, 27410. (Mail add: PO Box 26300, 27438-6300), SAN 321-0553. Tel: 336-286-4083. FAX: 336-286-4087. E-mail: library@ccl.org. Web Site: www.ccl.org. *Sr Librn,* Peggy Cartner; *Sr Librn,* Mary Schwartz; *Cat Librn,* Chris Arney; *Ref Librn,* Felecia Corbett; *Libr Assoc,* Marie Tretiakova; Staff 5 (MLS 4, Non-MLS 1)
Founded 1970
Library Holdings: Electronic Media & Resources 12; Bk Vols 8,000; Per Subs 150
Subject Interests: Indust/organizational psychol
Partic in Lyrasis
Open Mon-Fri 8-5
Restriction: In-house use for visitors

R CURRIE LIBRARY*, Shelter Bldg, Rm 100, Elm St & Fisher Ave, 27401. SAN 312-8547. Tel: 336-373-0445. Circulation Tel: 336-478-4732. FAX: 336-275-9398. Web Site: www.fpcgreensboro.org. *Librn,* Nancy Fuller; Tel: 336-478-4712, E-mail: nfuller@fpcgreensboro.org; Staff 1 (MLS 1)
Founded 1925
Library Holdings: Bk Titles 18,000; Bk Vols 18,000; Per Subs 21
Subject Interests: Music
Open Mon-Thurs 9:30-3:30, Fri 9:30-Noon, Sun 9am-10:20pm

C ECPI UNIVERSITY*, Greensboro Campus, 7802 Airport Center Dr, 27409. Tel: 336-665-1400. FAX: 336-664-0801. Web Site: www.ecpi.edu. *Librn,* Melissa Graham; E-mail: mgraham@ecpi.edu; *Syst Librn,* Beth Seufer; E-mail: bseufer@ecpi.edu; Staff 2 (MLS 2)
Enrl 380; Fac 30; Highest Degree: Associate
Library Holdings: Bk Titles 4,400; Bk Vols 5,100; Per Subs 75
Subject Interests: Computer sci, Computer tech, Nursing
Automation Activity & Vendor Info: (Cataloging) Follett Software; (Circulation) Follett Software; (OPAC) Follett Software
Database Vendor: Gale Cengage Learning
Partic in Libr & Info Resources Network (LIRN)
Open Mon-Thurs 7:30am-10pm, Fri 8-5, Sat 9-1

R FIRST BAPTIST CHURCH LIBRARY*, 100 W Friendly Ave, 27401. SAN 312-8539. Tel: 336-274-3286. FAX: 336-274-3288. E-mail: media@fbcgso.org. Web Site: www.fbcgso.org/library.html. *Dir,* Kelly Stephens; Staff 1 (MLS 1)
Founded 1947
Library Holdings: Bk Vols 16,000; Per Subs 20
Subject Interests: Children's lit, Relig
Open Mon-Fri 9-1:30, Wed 5:45-7:15, Sun 8:45am-10-30am

C GREENSBORO COLLEGE*, James Addison Jones Library, 815 W Market St, 27401. SAN 312-8555. Tel: 336-272-7102, Ext 241. Web Site: www.greensboro.edu/library. *Dir,* William Ritter; Tel: 336-272-7102, Ext 377, E-mail: will.ritter@greensboro.edu; *Ref Serv,* Al-don Schraeder; Tel: 336-272-7102, Ext 378; Staff 6 (MLS 3, Non-MLS 3)
Founded 1838. Enrl 1,200; Fac 103; Highest Degree: Master
Library Holdings: High Interest/Low Vocabulary Bk Vols 11; Bk Titles 80,000; Bk Vols 110,000; Per Subs 302
Subject Interests: Music, Spec educ
Database Vendor: EBSCOhost, LexisNexis, OCLC WorldShare Interlibrary Loan, OVID Technologies, ProQuest, SirsiDynix, Wilson - Wilson Web
Wireless access
Publications: Friends of the Greensboro College Newsletter; Guide to the James Addison Jones Library
Partic in Lyrasis
Open Mon-Thurs 8:30am-Midnight, Fri 8:30-5, Sat 12-5, Sun 2-Midnight
Friends of the Library Group

S GREENSBORO HISTORICAL MUSEUM ARCHIVES LIBRARY*, 130 Summit Ave, 27401-3004. SAN 326-4521. Tel: 336-373-2043, 336-373-2976. FAX: 336-373-2204. Web Site: www.greensborohistory.org. *Dir,* Carol Ghiorsi Hart; Tel: 336-373-2306, E-mail: carol.hart@greensboro-nc.gov; *Archivist,* Elise Allison; E-mail: elise.allison@greensboro-nc.gov; *Curator of Coll,* Jon Zachman; Tel: 336-373-4589, E-mail: jon.zachman@greensboro-nc.gov; Staff 1 (MLS 1)
Founded 1924
Library Holdings: Bk Titles 5,000; Per Subs 12
Special Collections: Dolley Madison Coll, bks, letters, docs; O Henry Coll, bks, newsp clippings
Open Tues-Sat 10-5, Sun 2-5
Restriction: Staff use only

P GREENSBORO PUBLIC LIBRARY*, 219 N Church St, 27402-3178. SAN 354-8678. Tel: 336-373-2471. Interlibrary Loan Service Tel: 336-373-2159. Reference Tel: 336-373-2471, Ext 2. FAX: 336-333-6781. Reference FAX: 336-335-5416. Web Site: www.greensborolibrary.org. *Dir,* Sandra M Neerman; Tel: 336-373-2699, E-mail: sandy.neerman@ci.greensboro.nc.us; *Asst Dir,* Brigette Blanton; *Asst Dir, Commun Relations Librn,* Steven L Sumerford; Tel: 336-373-3636, E-mail: steve.sumerford@ci.greensboro.nc.us; *Ch Serv,* Jim B Young; Tel: 336-373-4103, Fax: 336-335-5415, E-mail: jim.young@ci.greensboro.nc.us; *Ref,* Shearin Antonowicz; Tel: 336-373-2466, E-mail: sherrie.antonowicz@ci.greensboro.nc.us; *Ref Serv,* Helen M Snow; Tel: 336-373-2706, E-mail: helen.snow@ci.greensboro.nc.us; Staff 32 (MLS 32)
Founded 1902. Pop 294,964; Circ 1,358,996
Library Holdings: Bk Vols 541,858; Per Subs 790
Special Collections: Oral History
Subject Interests: Genealogy, Local hist
Automation Activity & Vendor Info: (Acquisitions) SirsiDynix; (Cataloging) SirsiDynix; (Circulation) SirsiDynix; (Serials) SirsiDynix
Wireless access
Publications: Clubs & Organizations Directory; Globa Greensboro Directory
Special Services for the Deaf - Bks on deafness & sign lang; Captioned film dep; High interest/low vocabulary bks; Spec interest per; Staff with knowledge of sign lang; TTY equip
Open Mon-Fri 9-9, Sat 9-6, Sun 2-6
Friends of the Library Group
Branches: 6
BLANCHE S BENJAMIN BRANCH, 1530 Benjamin Pkwy, 27408, SAN 354-8708. Tel: 336-373-7540. FAX: 336-545-5954.
Library Holdings: Bk Vols 54,693
Open Mon-Thurs 9-9, Fri & Sat 9-6, Sun 2-6
Friends of the Library Group
VANCE H CHAVIS LIFELONG LEARNING BRANCH, 900 S Benbow Rd, 27406, SAN 354-8791. Tel: 336-373-5838. FAX: 336-333-6781. *Librn,* Wanda Phifer; Tel: 336-373-5841, Fax: 336-412-5960, E-mail: wanda.phifer@ci.greensboro.nc.us
Library Holdings: Bk Vols 33,000
Open Mon-Thurs 9-9, Fri & Sat 9-6, Sun 2-6
Friends of the Library Group
KATHLEEN CLAY EDWARDS FAMILY BRANCH, 1420 Price Park Rd, 27410, SAN 354-8767. Tel: 336-373-2923. FAX: 336-851-5047. *Mgr,* Susan Vermeulen
Library Holdings: Bk Vols 53,000; Per Subs 70
Open Mon-Thurs 9-9, Fri & Sat 9-6, Sun 2-6
Friends of the Library Group
GLENWOOD COMMUNITY LIBRARY, 1901 W Florida St, 27403, SAN 375-5517. Tel: 336-297-5000. FAX: 336-297-5005.
Library Holdings: Bk Vols 32,800
Open Mon-Thurs 9-9, Fri & Sat 9-6, Sun 2-6
Friends of the Library Group
HEMPHILL, 2301 W Vandalia Rd, 27407, SAN 354-8821. Tel: 336-373-2925. FAX: 336-855-6635. *Mgr,* Brian Johnson; E-mail: brian.johnson@greensboro-nc.gov
Library Holdings: Bk Vols 41,771

Open Mon-Thurs 9-9, Fri & Sat 9-6, Sun 2-6
Friends of the Library Group
MCGIRT-HORTON, 2509 Phillips Ave, 27405, SAN 354-8732. Tel: 336-373-5810. FAX: 336-332-6458. *Librn,* Delores Lawrence; E-mail: delores.lawrence@greensboro-nc.gov
Library Holdings: Bk Vols 27,000; Per Subs 35
Open Mon-Thurs 9-9, Fri & Sat 9-6, Sun 2-6
Friends of the Library Group
Bookmobiles: 1

C GUILFORD COLLEGE*, Hege Library, 5800 W Friendly Ave, 27410-4175. SAN 312-8563. Tel: 336-316-2450. Interlibrary Loan Service Tel: 336-316-2439. Reference Tel: 336-316-2265. FAX: 336-316-2950. E-mail: hegelib@guilford.edu. Web Site: www.guilford.edu. *Dir, Libr Serv & Instrul Tech,* Suzanne M Bartels; Tel: 336-316-2046, E-mail: bartelssm@guilford.edu; *Access & Info Serv Librn,* Elizabeth J Wade; Tel: 336-316-2368, E-mail: wadeej@guilford.edu; *Friends Librn & Col Archivist,* Gwendolyn Gosney Erickson; Tel: 336-316-2264, E-mail: gerickso@guilford.edu; *Instrul Design & Assessment Librn,* James L Parrigin; Tel: 336-316-2340, E-mail: parriginjl@guilford.edu; *Instrul Tech Librn,* Jessica S Sender; Tel: 336-316-2113, Fax: 336-316-2113, E-mail: senderjs@guilford.edu; *Res & Instrul Serv Librn, Weekend Supvr & Personal Librn for Continuing Educ,* Martha E Davis; Tel: 336-316-2044, E-mail: mdavis2@guilford.edu; *Access & Info Serv Assoc, Evening Serv Supvr & ILL Coordr,* Nicklaus C McCollister; E-mail: mccollisternc@guilford.edu; *Coordr, Coll Mgt,* Susan McClanahan; Tel: 336-316-2251, E-mail: smcclana@guilford.edu; *Access & Info Assoc/Cat & Coll Develop Asst,* Leslie M Perry; Tel: 336-316-2362, E-mail: perrylm@guilford.edu; *Access & Info Serv Assoc/Coll Mgt Asst,* Monesha Staton; Tel: 336-316-2252, E-mail: mstaton@guilford.edu; *Access & Info Serv Assoc/Tech Serv,* Jonathan Carter; E-mail: jcarter@guilford.edu; Staff 6.5 (MLS 5.5, Non-MLS 1)
Founded 1837. Enrl 2,138; Fac 145; Highest Degree: Bachelor
Special Collections: Religious Society of Friends (Quaker)
Subject Interests: Civil War, Genealogy, Hist, N Caroliniana
Automation Activity & Vendor Info: (Acquisitions) OCLC; (Cataloging) OCLC; (Circulation) OCLC
Database Vendor: OCLC
Publications: Bibliographies
Partic in Lyrasis; NC-PALS
Special Services for the Blind - Reader equip
Open Mon-Thurs (Winter) 8:30am-10:30pm, Fri 8:30-5, Sat 10-6, Sun Noon-10:30; Mon-Thurs (Summer) 8:30am-2am, Fri 8:30-6, Sat 10-9, Sun Noon-2am;
Friends of the Library Group

S LANDMARK COMMUNICATIONS*, News & Record Library & Archives, 200 E Market St, 27401-2910. (Mail add: PO Box 20848, 27420-0848), SAN 312-858X. Tel: 336-373-7169. Toll Free Tel: 800-553-6880. FAX: 336-373-4437. E-mail: newslibrary@newsbank.com. Web Site: www.news-record.com. *Librn,* Diane Lamb; E-mail: diane.lamb@news-record.com
Founded 1969
Library Holdings: Bk Titles 1,000; Bk Vols 1,075; Per Subs 25
Database Vendor: Newsbank
Wireless access
Restriction: Private libr

MOSES CONE HEALTH SYSTEM
M MOSES H CONE MEMORIAL HOSPITAL LIBRARY*, 1200 N Elm St, 27401, SAN 312-8520. Tel: 336-832-7484. FAX: 336-832-7328. Web Site: www.gahec.org/library. *Dir,* Edward Donnald; Staff 3.5 (MLS 2.5, Non-MLS 1)
Founded 1952
Library Holdings: e-books 70; e-journals 511; Bk Titles 7,071; Per Subs 200
Special Collections: Greensboro Medical History Library; Local History of Medicine
Subject Interests: Life sci, Med
Database Vendor: EBSCOhost, OCLC WorldShare Interlibrary Loan, OVID Technologies, PubMed, UpToDate
Partic in National Network of Libraries of Medicine
Publications: Newsletter-Offline
Open Mon-Thurs 8-6, Fri 8-5
Restriction: Circulates for staff only
M WESLEY LONG COMMUNITY HOSPITAL MEDICAL LIBRARY*, 501 N Elam Ave, 27403, SAN 325-3120. Tel: 336-832-1299. FAX: 336-832-0370. Web Site: www.gahec.org/library.
Founded 1978
Library Holdings: Bk Titles 410; Per Subs 10
Subject Interests: Allied health, Healthcare, Med, Nursing
Partic in Docline
Open Mon-Wed & Fri 8:30-2

M WOMEN'S HOSPITAL OF GREENSBORO LIBRARY*, 801 Green Valley, 27408. Tel: 336-832-6878. FAX: 336-832-6893. Web Site: www.gahec.org/library. *Librn,* Monica Williamson Young
Library Holdings: Bk Vols 700; Per Subs 250
Automation Activity & Vendor Info: (Cataloging) Horizon; (Circulation) Horizon; (OPAC) Horizon
Database Vendor: EBSCOhost, OVID Technologies
Open Mon-Thurs 8-5

C NORTH CAROLINA AGRICULTURAL & TECHNICAL STATE UNIVERSITY*, F D Bluford Library, 1601 E Market St, 27411-0002. SAN 312-8598. Tel: 336-334-7159. Interlibrary Loan Service Tel: 336-334-7617. Administration Tel: 336-334-7158, 336-334-7782. Automation Services Tel: 336-334-7640. Toll Free Tel: 888-246-1271. FAX: 336-334-7783. Reference FAX: 336-334-7157. Administration FAX: 336-334-7281. E-mail: refemail@ncat.edu. Web Site: www.library.ncat.edu. *Dean, Libr Serv,* Waltrene M Canada; Tel: 336-334-7782, Ext 3202, E-mail: canadaw@ncat.edu; *Assoc Dean,* Doris F Mitchell; Tel: 336-334-7158, Ext 3204, E-mail: mitcheld@ncat.edu; *Head, Access Serv,* Octavious Spruill; Tel: 336-334-7617, Ext 3221, E-mail: odspruil@ncat.edu; *Head, Coll Mgt,* Ednita Bullock; Tel: 336-334-7668, Ext 3232, E-mail: bullocke@ncat.edu; *Head, Govt Info,* Inez Lyons; Tel: 336-334-7617, Ext 3223, E-mail: lyonsi@ncat.edu; *Head, Pub Serv,* Jean Williams; Tel: 336-334-7618, Ext 3211, E-mail: williamj@ncat.edu; *Head, Tech Serv,* Euthena Newman; Tel: 336-334-7867, Ext 3225, E-mail: newman@ncat.edu; *Ref Librn,* Nina Exner; Tel: 336-334-7159, Ext 3257, E-mail: ninae@ncat.edu; *Ref Librn,* Jacquelyn McGirt; Tel: 336-334-7159, Ext 3214, E-mail: jmcgirt@ncat.edu; *Ref Librn,* Cassandra Plater; Tel: 336-334-7159, Ext 3205, E-mail: ceplater@ncat.edu; *Ref Librn,* Clifton Sawyerr; Tel: 336-334-7159, Ext 3217, E-mail: sawyerrc@ncat.edu; *Ref Librn,* John Teleha; Tel: 336-334-7159, Ext 3213, E-mail: teleha@ncat.edu; *Archives Mgr,* Gloria Pitts; Tel: 336-334-7159, Ext 3235, E-mail: gloriap@ncat.edu; *Cat Mgr,* Arneice Bowen; Tel: 336-334-7669, Ext 3228, E-mail: abowen@ncat.edu; *Cat,* Teresa Coons; Tel: 336-334-7669, Ext 3234, E-mail: coons@ncat.edu; *Cat,* Donna Royster; E-mail: droyster@ncat.edu; *Electronic Res,* Iyanna Sims; Tel: 336-334-7640, Ext 3261, E-mail: iyanna@ncat.edu; *Ref Serv,* Francene Moore; Tel: 336-334-7159, Ext 3216, E-mail: efmoore@ncat.edu. Subject Specialists: *Math, Physics,* Ednita Bullock; *Acctg,* Inez Lyons; *Computer sci, Psychol,* Jean Williams; *Hist, Polit sci,* Euthena Newman; *Bus,* Nina Exner; *Archit eng, Civil eng, Environ eng,* Jacquelyn McGirt; *Curric,* Cassandra Plater; *Biol,* Clifton Sawyerr; *Mechanical eng,* John Teleha; *Human develop, Music,* Gloria Pitts; *Animal sci, Natural res,* Arneice Bowen; *Visual arts,* Teresa Coons; *African-Am studies, English,* Iyanna Sims; *Sociol, Theatre arts,* Francene Moore; Staff 49 (MLS 19, Non-MLS 30)
Founded 1892. Enrl 10,386; Fac 502; Highest Degree: Doctorate
Library Holdings: AV Mats 36,715; e-books 44,450; e-journals 50,688; Electronic Media & Resources 100,778; Bk Vols 580,312; Per Subs 5,466; Talking Bks 800
Special Collections: Black Studies Coll; University Archives. State Document Depository; US Document Depository
Subject Interests: Agr, Educ, Eng, Nursing
Automation Activity & Vendor Info: (Acquisitions) Innovative Interfaces, Inc; (Cataloging) Innovative Interfaces, Inc; (Circulation) Innovative Interfaces, Inc; (Course Reserve) Innovative Interfaces, Inc; (ILL) Innovative Interfaces, Inc; (Media Booking) Innovative Interfaces, Inc; (OPAC) Innovative Interfaces, Inc; (Serials) Innovative Interfaces, Inc
Database Vendor: 3M Library Systems, Agricola, Alexander Street Press, ARTstor, Baker & Taylor, Blackwell, BookStore Library Systems, Cambridge Scientific Abstracts, Career Guidance Foundation, Community of Science (COS), EBSCOhost, Elsevier MDL, Gale Cengage Learning, Infotrieve, Innovative Interfaces, Inc, ISI Web of Knowledge, JSTOR, LexisNexis, Newsbank, OCLC FirstSearch, OCLC WorldShare Interlibrary Loan, OVID Technologies, ProQuest, PubMed, ReferenceUSA, ScienceDirect, Scopeware, SerialsSolutions, STAT!Ref (Teton Data Systems), TLC (The Library Corporation), Wiley, Wilson - Wilson Web
Wireless access
Function: Archival coll, Audio & video playback equip for onsite use, AV serv, Bk club(s), Computer training, Copy machines, Distance learning, Doc delivery serv, E-Reserves, Electronic databases & coll, For res purposes, ILL available, Mail & tel request accepted, Online info literacy tutorials on the web & in blackboard, Online ref, Orientations, Outside serv via phone, mail, e-mail & web, Photocopying/Printing, Ref & res, Ref serv available, Telephone ref, VHS videos, Workshops
Publications: Bluford Notes & Quotes (Newsletter); Public Service (Newsletter)
Partic in Central North Carolina Library Consortium; Lyrasis; OCLC Online Computer Library Center, Inc
Special Services for the Deaf - Assistive tech
Special Services for the Blind - Assistive/Adapted tech devices, equip & products
Restriction: Limited access for the pub, Non-circulating coll, Non-circulating of rare bks, Open to pub for ref & circ; with some limitations

L SMITH MOORE, LLP*, Law Library, 300 N Greene St, 27401. (Mail add: PO Box 21927, 27420-1927), SAN 325-7908. Tel: 336-378-5272. FAX: 336-433-7566. *Mgr, Libr Serv,* Anne Washburn; E-mail: anne.washburn@smithmoorelaw.com; *Asst Librn,* Carolyn Santanella; Staff 2 (MLS 2)
Library Holdings: Bk Vols 15,000; Per Subs 280

S SYNGENTA CROP PROTECTION LIBRARY*, 410 Swing Rd, 27409. SAN 312-8504. Tel: 336-632-7570. FAX: 336-299-8318. Web Site: www.syngenta.com. *Librn,* Kathryn Schlee; Tel: 336-632-5696; *Info Spec,* Jeff Stabnau; E-mail: jeff.stabnau@syngenta.com; Staff 2 (MLS 2)
Founded 1973
Library Holdings: e-journals 600; Bk Vols 2,000
Subject Interests: Agr, Environ sci, Organic chem, Toxicology
Function: ILL available
Restriction: Staff use only

C UNIVERSITY LIBRARIES, UNIVERSITY OF NORTH CAROLINA AT GREENSBORO, Walter Clinton Jackson Library & Harold Schiffman Music Library, 320 Spring Garden St, 27402. (Mail add: PO Box 26170, 27402-6170), SAN 312-8628. Tel: 336-334-5880. Circulation Tel: 336-334-5304. Interlibrary Loan Service Tel: 336-334-5849. Reference Tel: 336-334-5419. Automation Services Tel: 336-334-4238. FAX: 336-334-5399. Interlibrary Loan Service FAX: 336-334-5097. Web Site: library.uncg.edu. *Dean,* Rosann Bazirjian; E-mail: rvbazirj@uncg.edu; *Assoc Dean, Pub Serv,* Kathryn Crowe; E-mail: kmcrowe@uncg.edu; *Asst Dean, Admin Serv,* Michael Crumpton; E-mail: macrumpt@uncg.edu; *Asst Dean, Coll Mgt & Scholarly Communications,* Beth Bernhardt; Tel: 336-256-1210, E-mail: beth_bernhardt@uncg.edu; *Asst Dean, Info Tech & Electronic Res,* Tim Bucknall; E-mail: bucknall@uncg.edu; *Dir, Communications & External Relations,* Barry Miller; *Dir of Develop,* Linda Burr; Tel: 336-256-0184, E-mail: lgburr@uncg.edu; *Head of Ref & Instrul Serv,* Mary Krautter; E-mail: mmkrautt@uncg.edu; *Head, Access Serv,* Cathy Griffith; Tel: 336-334-5492, E-mail: cathy_griffith@uncg.edu; *Head, Acq,* Christine Fischer; E-mail: cmfische@uncg.edu; *Head, Cat,* Mary Jane Conger; E-mail: maryjane_conger@uncg.edu; *Head, Spec Coll & Univ Archives,* Dr Keith Gorman; E-mail: k_gorman@uncg.edu; *Asst Head, Ref & Instrul Serv,* Nancy Ryckman; Tel: 336-256-0345, E-mail: nancy_ryckman@uncg.edu; *Bus Librn,* Steve Cramer; Tel: 336-256-0346, E-mail: steve_cramer@uncg.edu; *Data Serv & Govt Info Librn,* Lynda Kellam; Tel: 336-334-5241, E-mail: lmkellam@uncg.edu; *Distance Educ Librn,* Beth Filar-Williams; Tel: 336-256-1232, E-mail: efwilli3@uncg.edu; *Diversity Resident Librn,* Orolando Duffus; E-mail: oaduffus@uncg.edu; *Health Sci Ref Librn,* Lea Leininger; Tel: 336-256-0215, E-mail: laleinin@uncg.edu; *Human Res Librn,* Kathy Bradshaw; Tel: 336-334-3741, E-mail: akbradsh@uncg.edu; *IT Librn,* Terry Brandsma, Tel: 336-256-1218, E-mail: twbrands@uncg.edu; *Music Librn,* Sarah Dorsey; E-mail: sarah_dorsey@uncg.edu; *First Year Instruction Coordr, Ref Librn,* Jenny Dale; Tel: 336-256-0240, E-mail: jedale@uncg.edu; *Ref Librn, Sci Librn,* Karen Grigg; E-mail: ksgrigg@uncg.edu; *Info Literacy, Ref Librn,* Amy Harris Houk; Tel: 336-256-0275, E-mail: a_harri2@uncg.edu; *Diversity Coordr, Ref Librn,* Gerald Holmes; Tel: 336-256-0273, E-mail: gerald_holmes@uncg.edu; *Ref Librn,* Mark Schumacher; Tel: 336-334-3215, E-mail: mark_schumacher@uncg.edu; *IT Operations Mgr,* Franklin Graves; Tel: 336-256-1211, E-mail: franklin_mckee@uncg.edu; *Digital Projects Coordr,* David Gwynn; Tel: 336-256-2606, E-mail: jdgwynn@uncg.edu; *Ms Archivist,* Jennifer Motszko; E-mail: j_motszk@uncg.edu; *Univ Archivist,* Erin Lawrimore; E-mail: erlawrim@uncg.edu; *Cello Music Cataloger,* Mac Nelson; Tel: 336-334-5781, E-mail: wmnelson@uncg.edu; *Metada Cataloger,* Anna Craft; E-mail: arcraft@uncg.edu; *Spec Coll/Chief Monographic Cataloger,* Paul Hessling; *Curator, Women Vet Hist Project,* Beth Ann Koelsch; E-mail: bakoelsc@uncg.edu; *Web Applications Developer,* Danny Nanez; Tel: 336-256-1215, E-mail: d_nanez@uncg.edu; Staff 89 (MLS 35, Non-MLS 54)
Founded 1892. Enrl 17,707; Fac 1,005; Highest Degree: Doctorate
Jul 2013-Jun 2014. Mats Exp $4,086,743. Sal $6,418,168 (Prof $2,461,995)
Library Holdings: AV Mats 52,507; DVDs 16,144; e-books 473,878; e-journals 53,284; Microforms 733,462; Bk Vols 2,235,868; Per Subs 1,100
Special Collections: American Trade Bindings; Cello Music & Literature, artifacts, ms, textiles; Children's Authors Coll, bks, ms; Children's Books (Lois Lenski Coll), bks, ms; Creative Writers Coll, bks, ms, photog; Early Dance Book Coll; Early Juvenile Literature Coll; Emily Dickinson Coll; George Herbert Coll, bks, ms; Girls' Series Books; Greensboro & Guilford County Civil Rights Oral History, ms, tapes; Home Economics Pamphlet Coll; Joseph Bryan Coll, ms; Papermaking; Physical Education Coll, bks, ms; Private Presses & Book Arts; Randall Jarrell Coll, bks, music, tapes; Rare Book Coll; Robbie Emily Dunn Coll of American Detective Fiction; Rupert Brooke Coll; T E Lawrence Coll; University Archives; Way & Williams Coll, artwork, bks, ms; Women Veterans Coll; Women's Studies (Woman's Coll), bks, ms, pamphlets. Oral History; State Document Depository; US Document Depository
Automation Activity & Vendor Info: (Acquisitions) OCLC WorldShare Interlibrary Loan; (Cataloging) OCLC WorldShare Interlibrary Loan; (Circulation) OCLC WorldShare Interlibrary Loan; (Course Reserve) Blackboard Inc; (ILL) OCLC ILLiad; (OPAC) OCLC WorldShare Interlibrary Loan; (Serials) OCLC WorldShare Interlibrary Loan
Database Vendor: ABC-CLIO, ACM (Association for Computing Machinery), Agricola, Alexander Street Press, American Chemical Society, American Mathematical Society, American Psychological Association (APA), Annual Reviews, ARTstor, Baker & Taylor, Blackwell, Cambridge Scientific Abstracts, Cinahl, CQ Press, CRC Press/Taylor & Francis Group, Dun & Bradstreet, EBSCOhost, Elsevier, Emerald, Gale Cengage Learning, H W Wilson, Ingram Library Services, IOP, JSTOR, LearningExpress, LexisNexis, Mergent Online, Modern Language Association, Nature Publishing Group, NC LIVE, Newsbank-Readex, OCLC FirstSearch, OCLC WorldShare Interlibrary Loan, OVID Technologies, Oxford Online, Project MUSE, ProQuest, PubMed, Safari Books Online, Sage, ScienceDirect, Springer-Verlag, Wiley, YBP Library Services
Wireless access
Function: Archival coll, Art exhibits, Audiobks via web, Bks on cassette, Bks on CD, Computers for patron use, Copy machines, Distance learning, Doc delivery serv, e-mail serv, E-Reserves, Electronic databases & coll, Equip loans & repairs, Exhibits, Govt ref serv, Handicapped accessible, Music CDs, Online info literacy tutorials on the web & in blackboard, Online ref, Outside serv via phone, mail, e-mail & web, Ref serv available, Wheelchair accessible
Publications: Library Columns (Newsletter)
Partic in Association of Southeastern Research Libraries; Carolina Consortium; Coalition for Networked Information (CNI); Lyrasis; North Carolina Libraries for Virtual Education; North Carolina Preservation Consortium; OCLC Online Computer Library Center, Inc; OCLC Research Library Partnership; Scholarly Publ & Acad Resources Coalition
Special Services for the Deaf - Bks on deafness & sign lang
Friends of the Library Group

SR WESTMINISTER PRESBYTERIAN CHURCH LIBRARY*, 3906 W Friendly Ave, 27410. SAN 375-1996. Tel: 336-299-3785. FAX: 336-299-5837. E-mail: info@westpreschurch.org. Web Site: www.westpreschurch.org. *Dir, Adult Ministries,* Melinda Billings
Library Holdings: Bk Titles 250

GREENVILLE

EAST CAROLINA UNIVERSITY

C J Y JOYNER LIBRARY*, E Fifth St, 27858-4353, SAN 378-4509. Tel: 252-328-6518. Interlibrary Loan Service Tel: 252-328-6068. Reference Tel: 252-328-6677. Administration Tel: 252-328-6514. Toll Free Tel: 866-291-5581. FAX: 252-328-6892. Interlibrary Loan Service FAX: 252 328 6618. Reference FAX: 252-328-2271. E-mail: askref@ecu.edu. Web Site: www.ecu.edu/lib. *Dean, Acad Libr & Learning Res,* Dr Larry Boyer, E-mail: boyerl@ecu.edu; *Assoc Dean,* Janice Steed Lewis; Tel: 252-328-2267, E-mail: lewisja@ecu.edu; *Asst Dir, Adm Serv,* Robert James; Tel: 252-328-6114, E-mail: jamesr@ecu.edu; *Asst Dir, Coll & Tech Serv,* Eleanor Cook; Tel: 252-328-2598, E-mail: cooke@ecu.edu; *Ast Dir, Libr Tech & Digital Initiatives,* May Chang; Tel: 252-328-2780, E-mail: changm@ecu.edu; *Asst Dir, Pub Serv,* Mark Sanders; Tel: 242-328-2900, E-mail: sandersm@ecu.edu; *Asst Dir, Spec Coll,* Maurice York; Tel: 252-328-0252, E-mail: yorkm@ecu.edu; *Copyright Officer,* Beth Winstead; Tel: 252-328-0247, E-mail: winsteade@ecu.edu; Staff 40 (MLS 38, Non-MLS 2)
Founded 1907. Enrl 27,783; Fac 1,882; Highest Degree: Doctorate
Jul 2010-Jun 2011 Income $12,972,276. Mats Exp $5,067,825, Books $615,520, Per/Ser (Incl. Access Fees) $2,778,574, Micro $30,369, AV Mat $24,263. Sal $5,928,000 (Prof $2,561,436)
Library Holdings: AV Mats 31,780; DVDs 17,830; e-books 270,000; e-journals 68,000; Electronic Media & Resources 450; Microforms 2,117,313; Music Scores 30,857; Bk Titles 1,437,277; Bk Vols 2,290,197; Per Subs 44,955
Special Collections: Local History (North Carolina Coll); Regional History (East Carolina Manuscript Coll); Southern Authors (Stuart Wright Coll). Oral History; State Document Depository; US Document Depository
Automation Activity & Vendor Info: (Acquisitions) SirsiDynix; (Cataloging) SirsiDynix; (Circulation) SirsiDynix; (Course Reserve) SirsiDynix; (ILL) OCLC ILLiad; (OPAC) SirsiDynix; (Serials) SerialsSolutions
Database Vendor: ABC-CLIO, ACM (Association for Computing Machinery), Alexander Street Press, American Chemical Society, American Geophysical Union, American Mathematical Society, American Physical Society, American Psychological Association (APA), Annual Reviews, ARTstor, Backstage Library Works, BioOne, Blackwell, Cambridge Scientific Abstracts, Community of Science (COS), CQ Press, CredoReference, EBSCOhost, Elsevier, Emerald, Facts on File, Foundation Center, Gale Cengage Learning, Greenwood Publishing Group, H W Wilson, Haworth Pres Inc, HeinOnline, IBISWorld, IEEE (Institute of Electrical & Electronics Engineers), IOP, ISI Web of Knowledge, JSTOR, Knovel, LexisNexis, Marcive, Inc, McGraw-Hill, Mergent Online, Modern Language Association, Nature Publishing

Group, NC LIVE, Newsbank-Readex, OCLC FirstSearch, OCLC WorldShare Interlibrary Loan, Oxford Online, Paratext, Project MUSE, ProQuest, RefWorks, Sage, ScienceDirect, SerialsSolutions, SirsiDynix, Springer-Verlag, Springshare, LLC, Standard & Poor's, Thomson - Web of Science, Wiley InterScience, YBP Library Services
Function: Computers for patron use, Distance learning, Doc delivery serv, e-mail & chat, E-Reserves, Electronic databases & coll, Exhibits, Free DVD rentals, Govt ref serv, Handicapped accessible, ILL available, Libr develop, Music CDs, Online cat, Online info literacy tutorials on the web & in blackboard, Online ref, Orientations, Outreach serv, Photocopying/Printing, Pub access computers, Ref & res, Ref serv in person, Scanner, Telephone ref, Web-catalog
Partic in Association of Southeastern Research Libraries; Carolina Consortium; Lyrasis; OCLC Research Library Partnership; Scholarly Publ & Acad Resources Coalition
Open Mon-Thurs (Winter) 7:30am-2am, Fri 7:30am-8pm, Sat 10-7, Sun Noon-2am); Mon-Thurs (Summer) 7:30am-10pm, Fri 7:30-5, Sat 10-5, Sun 1-10
Friends of the Library Group

CM WILLIAM E LAUPUS HEALTH SCIENCES LIBRARY*, 500 Health Sciences Dr, 27834, SAN 354-8880. Tel: 252-744-2219. Reference Tel: 252-744-2230. Administration Tel: 252-744-2212. Toll Free Tel: 888-820-0522. FAX: 252-744-2672. Administration FAX: 252-744-2300. Web Site: www.ecu.edu/laupuslibrary. *Dir,* Position Currently Open; *Interim Dir,* Gregg Hassler; *Dir, Eastern AHEC Libr Serv/Head, Outreach Serv,* Jeffrey G Coghill; Tel: 252-744-2066, E-mail: coghillj@ecu.edu; *Asst Dir, Coll,* Elizabeth Ketterman; Tel: 252-744-3056, E-mail: kettermane@ecu.edu; *Asst Dir, Admin,* Teresa D Tripp; Tel: 252-744-3495, E-mail: trippt@ecu.edu; *Asst Dir, User Serv,* Roger G Russell; Tel: 252-744-3215, E-mail: russellr@ecu.edu; *Head, Access Serv & Doc Delivery,* Vicki Daughtridge; Fax: 252-744-3311, E-mail: daughtridgev@ecu.edu; *Spec Projects Librn,* Susan N Simpson; Tel: 252-744-2904, E-mail: simpsons@ecu.edu; *Coordr, Ser,* Janet P Heath; Tel: 252-744-2234, E-mail: heathj@ecu.edu; Staff 15 (MLS 15)
Founded 1969. Highest Degree: Doctorate
Library Holdings: AV Mats 4,428; Bk Titles 33,365; Bk Vols 35,094; Per Subs 346
Special Collections: History of Medicine Special Coll
Subject Interests: Allied health, Med, Nursing
Automation Activity & Vendor Info: (Acquisitions) SirsiDynix
Database Vendor: EBSCOhost, Gale Cengage Learning, JSTOR, OCLC FirstSearch, OVID Technologies, ProQuest, PubMed, ScienceDirect, STAT!Ref (Teton Data Systems), UpToDate
Partic in Lyrasis
Special Services for the Deaf - TDD equip
Open Mon-Thurs 7:30am-Midnight, Fri 7:30am-8pm, Sat 9-8, Sun Noon-10; Mon-Thurs (Summer) 7:30am-10pm, Fri 7:30-5, Sat 9-5, Sun Noon-10
Friends of the Library Group

C MUSIC LIBRARY, A J Fletcher Music Ctr, Rm A110, 27858, SAN 354-8899. Tel: 252-328-6250. E-mail: musiclibrary@ecu.edu. Web Site: www.ecu.edu/cs-lib/music.cfm. *Head Librn,* David Hursh; Tel: 252-328-1239, E-mail: hurshd@ecu.edu; *Head, Access Serv,* Dorthea Taylor; Tel: 252-328-1242, E-mail: taylordor14@ecu.edu; *Head, Tech Serv,* Judith Barber; Tel: 252-328-1240, E-mail: barberju@ecu.edu; *Asst Music Librn,* Christopher Holden; Tel: 252-328-1241, E-mail: holdenc@ecu.edu; *Evening & Weekend Access Serv Mgr,* Kevin-Andrew Cronin; Tel: 252-328-1238, E-mail: cronink@ecu.edu; Staff 5 (MLS 2, Non-MLS 3)
Founded 1958. Highest Degree: Doctorate
Library Holdings: AV Mats 30,444; Music Scores 43,375; Bk Titles 19,626; Bk Vols 25,248
Database Vendor: SirsiDynix
Function: Audio & video playback equip for onsite use, Computers for patron use, Handicapped accessible, ILL available, Music CDs, Ref serv in person, Wheelchair accessible
Open Mon-Thurs 8am-10pm, Fri 8-5, Sat 1-5, Sun 1-10

J PITT COMMUNITY COLLEGE*, Learning Resources Center, Hwy 11 S, 27835. (Mail add: PO Box 7007, 27835-7007), SAN 312-8652. Tel: 252-493-7357. Interlibrary Loan Service Tel: 252-493-7352. FAX: 252-321-4404. Web Site: www.pitt.cc.nc.us/lrc/lrc.htm. *Dir, Libr Serv,* Xudong Jin; *Re/Ser Librn,* Stephanie Bowers; *Circ,* Arthur Stevenson; Staff 20 (MLS 6, Non-MLS 14)
Founded 1964. Enrl 5,300; Fac 240; Highest Degree: Associate
Library Holdings: Bk Titles 35,000; Bk Vols 45,000; Per Subs 575
Database Vendor: EBSCOhost, Gale Cengage Learning, OCLC FirstSearch, OVID Technologies, ProQuest
Partic in Community Colleges Libraries in North Carolina (CCLINC)

P SHEPPARD MEMORIAL LIBRARY*, 530 S Evans St, 27858-2308. SAN 312-8660. Tel: 252-329-4580. Circulation Tel: 252-329-4063, 252-329-4579. Reference Tel: 252-329-4376. Administration Tel: 252-329-4586. FAX: 252-329-4587. Administration FAX: 252-329-4255. Web Site: www.sheppardlibrary.org. *Dir,* Greg Needham; Tel: 252-329-4585, E-mail: gneedham@sheppardlibrary.org; *Adult Serv, Head, Tech Serv,* Tammy Fulcher; Tel: 252-329-4254, E-mail: tfulcher@sheppardlibrary.org; *Outreach Serv Librn,* Amber Winstead; Tel: 252-329-4311, Fax: 252-329-4521, E-mail: awinstead@sheppardlibrary.org; *Bus & Finance Mgr,* Lynn Woolard; E-mail: lwoolard@sheppardlibrary.org; *Ch Serv,* Phyllis Conner; Tel: 252-329-4878, E-mail: pconner@sheppardlibrary.org; *Circ,* Amanda Prokop; E-mail: aprokop@sheppardlibrary.org; *Ref,* Sharon Vaughn; E-mail: svaughn@sheppardlibrary.org; *Ser,* Kim Averette; E-mail: kaverette@sheppardlibrary.org; Staff 5 (MLS 3, Non-MLS 2)
Founded 1929. Pop 194,274; Circ 481,611
Jul 2005-Jun 2006 Income (Main Library and Branch(s)) $1,911,005, State $204,818, City $914,415, Federal $24,840, County $457,207, Locally Generated Income $168,857, Other $139,768. Mats Exp $277,906, Books $201,862, Other Print Mats $49,804, Micro $1,400, AV Equip $24,840. Sal $1,124,280
Library Holdings: CDs 7,453; DVDs 9,182; Electronic Media & Resources 98; Bk Vols 237,000; Per Subs 377; Talking Bks 1,842
Automation Activity & Vendor Info: (Cataloging) TLC (The Library Corporation); (Circulation) TLC (The Library Corporation)
Database Vendor: OCLC FirstSearch, ProQuest, TLC (The Library Corporation)
Wireless access
Function: ILL available
Publications: The Bookmark (Newsletter)
Open Mon-Thurs 9-9, Fri & Sat 9-6, Sun 2-5
Friends of the Library Group
Branches: 4
MARGARET LITTLE BLOUNT LIBRARY, 201 Ives St, Bethel, 27812. (Mail add: PO Box 1170, Bethel, 27812), SAN 373-5370. Tel: 252-825-0782. FAX: 252-825-0782. *Br Coordr,* Mildred Elliott; E-mail: melliott@sheppardlibrary.org
Open Mon-Fri 1-5
Friends of the Library Group
GEORGE WASHINGTON CARVER LIBRARY, 618 W 14th Ave, 27834-3016, SAN 374-678X. Tel: 252-329-4583. FAX: 252-329-4126. *Librn,* Mildred Elliott; E-mail: melliott@sheppardlibrary.org
Open Mon-Thurs 9-8, Fri 9-6, Sat 11-3
Friends of the Library Group
EAST, 2000 Cedar Lane, 27858-4845, SAN 374-6798. Tel: 252-329-4582. FAX: 252-329-4127. *Br Mgr,* Mildred Elliot; E-mail: melliot@sheppardlibrary.org
Open Mon-Thurs 9-8, Fri 9-6, Sat 11-3
Friends of the Library Group
WINTERVILLE PUBLIC, 2613 Railroad St, Winterville, 28590-9760, SAN 373-5389. Tel: 252-756-1786. FAX: 252-355-0287. *Br Coordr,* Mildred Elliott; E-mail: melliott@sheppardlibrary.org
Open Mon-Thurs 9-8, Fri 9-6, Sat 1-5
Friends of the Library Group
Bookmobiles: 1

GRIFTON

P GRIFTON PUBLIC LIBRARY*, 568 Queen St, 28530. (Mail add: PO Box 579, 28530-0579), SAN 312-8679. Tel: 252-524-0345. FAX: 252-524-5545. *Librn,* Bernell Skinner
Pop 4,500; Circ 6,602
Library Holdings: Large Print Bks 150; Bk Vols 20,000; Per Subs 75
Automation Activity & Vendor Info: (Acquisitions) Follett Software; (Cataloging) Follett Software; (Circulation) Follett Software
Open Mon-Thurs 11:30-6:30, Fri 11:30-5:30

HALIFAX

P HALIFAX COUNTY LIBRARY*, 33 S Granville St, 27839. (Mail add: PO Box 97, 27839-0097), SAN 312-8687. Tel: 252-583-3631. FAX: 252-583-8661. Web Site: www.halifaxnc.com. *Dir,* Virginia Orvedahl; E-mail: orvedahlg@halifaxnc.com; *Tech Serv,* Barbara Valdes; Staff 11 (MLS 1, Non-MLS 10)
Founded 1941. Pop 55,432
Library Holdings: Bk Vols 65,000; Per Subs 180
Subject Interests: Genealogy, Local hist
Automation Activity & Vendor Info: (Cataloging) Innovative Interfaces, Inc; (Circulation) Innovative Interfaces, Inc; (OPAC) Innovative Interfaces, Inc
Wireless access
Publications: Monthly Newsletter
Open Mon, Wed & Fri 8:30-5, Tues & Thurs 8:30-8, Sat 9-12:30
Friends of the Library Group
Branches: 3
W C JONES JR MEMORIAL, 127 W South Main St, Littleton, 27850. (Mail add: PO Box 455, Littleton, 27850), SAN 328-6983. Tel: 252-586-3608. FAX: 252-586-3495. *Librn,* Sheila Milan
Open Mon-Fri 9-5, Sat 9-12:30
Friends of the Library Group

SCOTLAND NECK MEMORIAL, 1600 Main St, Scotland Neck, 27874-1438. (Mail add: PO Box 126, Scotland Neck, 27874-0126), SAN 371-3679. Tel: 252-826-5578. FAX: 252-826-5037. *Librn,* Martha Leach
Library Holdings: Bk Vols 13,000; Per Subs 25
Subject Interests: Genealogy
Open Mon, Wed & Fri 8:30-5, Tues & Thurs 8:30-7, Sat 9-12
Friends of the Library Group

WELDON MEMORIAL, Six W First St, Weldon, 27890, SAN 328-6967. Tel: 252-536-3837. FAX: 252-536-2477. *Librn,* LaTarsha Thomas
Open Mon-Fri 8:30-5, Sat 9-12:30

Bookmobiles: 1

HAMLET

J RICHMOND COMMUNITY COLLEGE LIBRARY*, 1042 W Hamlet Ave, 28345. (Mail add: PO Box 1189, 28345-1189), SAN 312-8709. Tel: 910-410-1700, 910-410-1752. Interlibrary Loan Service Tel: 910-410-1753. FAX: 910-582-7045. Web Site: www.richmondcc.edu. *Dean, Learning Res,* Carolyn Theresa Bittle; E-mail: ctbittle@richmondcc.edu; *Librn,* Gail Booth-Riley; E-mail: gailb@richmondcc.edu; *Librn,* Amanda Caudill; E-mail: abcaudill@richmondcc.edu; *Libr Tech,* Shevonne Lockhart; Tel: 910-410-1755, E-mail: slockhart@richmondcc.edu; *Circ & ILL,* Sarah Anderson; E-mail: sanderson@richmondcc.edu; Staff 4.5 (MLS 3, Non-MLS 1.5)
Founded 1964. Enrl 2,570; Fac 60; Highest Degree: Associate
Jul 2012-Jun 2013. Mats Exp $70,133, Books $33,542, Per/Ser (Incl. Access Fees) $34,500, AV Mat $2,091. Sal $290,164 (Prof $172,020)
Library Holdings: Audiobooks 239; AV Mats 318; Bks on Deafness & Sign Lang 250; DVDs 2,731; Large Print Bks 57; Bk Titles 28,718; Bk Vols 27,842; Per Subs 104; Videos 3,268
Special Collections: Easy Books for Early Childhood Program; North Carolina Coll
Subject Interests: Col transfer, Vocational
Automation Activity & Vendor Info: (Acquisitions) SirsiDynix; (Cataloging) SirsiDynix; (Circulation) SirsiDynix; (Course Reserve) SirsiDynix; (ILL) OCLC Online; (Media Booking) SirsiDynix; (OPAC) SirsiDynix; (Serials) SirsiDynix
Database Vendor: Baker & Taylor, NC LIVE, SirsiDynix
Wireless access
Function: Archival coll, Bks on cassette, Bks on CD, Computers for patron use, Digital talking bks, Distance learning, Doc delivery serv, e-mail & chat, Electronic databases & coll, Exhibits, Fax serv, Handicapped accessible, Health sci info serv, ILL available, Instruction & testing, Magnifiers for reading, Online cat, Online info literacy tutorials on the web & in blackboard, Online searches, Orientations, Outreach serv, Outside serv via phone, mail, e-mail & web, Photocopying/Printing, Pub access computers, Ref serv available, Scanner, Spoken cassettes & DVDs, Telephone ref, VHS videos, Web-catalog, Wheelchair accessible, Workshops
Partic in Cape Fear Health Sciences Information Consortium; Community Colleges Libraries in North Carolina (CCLINC); North Carolina Libraries for Virtual Education
Special Services for the Blind - Audio mat; Bks on cassette; Bks on CD; Cassette playback machines; Copier with enlargement capabilities; Large print bks; Magnifiers; Ref serv
Open Mon-Thurs 8am-9pm, Fri 8-2:30
Restriction: ID required to use computers (Ltd hrs), Non-circulating coll, Non-circulating of rare bks, Open to pub for ref & circ; with some limitations, Photo ID required for access, Restricted borrowing privileges, Restricted loan policy

HAVELOCK

P HAVELOCK-CRAVEN COUNTY PUBLIC LIBRARY*, 301 Cunningham Blvd, 28532. Tel: 252-447-7509. FAX: 252-447-7422. Web Site: www.havelocklibrary.org. *Librn,* Margie Garrison; E-mail: mmgarrison@live.com; Staff 1 (MLS 1)
Founded 1974. Pop 21,000; Circ 44,723
Library Holdings: Audiobooks 1,920; AV Mats 2,072; Bk Vols 26,700; Per Subs 45
Wireless access
Function: Art exhibits, Audiobks via web, AV serv, Bks on cassette, Bks on CD, Children's prog, Computers for patron use, Copy machines, Digital talking bks, e-mail serv, E-Reserves, Electronic databases & coll, Exhibits, Fax serv, Handicapped accessible, ILL available, Magnifiers for reading, Music CDs, Online cat, Online searches, Photocopying/Printing, Pub access computers, Scanner, Spoken cassettes & CDs, Spoken cassettes & DVDs, Story hour, Summer reading prog, Tax forms, VHS videos, Web-catalog, Wheelchair accessible
Mem of Craven-Pamlico-Carteret Regional Library System
Open Mon-Wed 10-8, Thurs & Fri 10-6, Sat 10-4
Friends of the Library Group

HAYESVILLE

P MOSS MEMORIAL LIBRARY*, 26 Anderson St, 28904-7371. (Mail add: PO Box 900, 28904-0900), SAN 312-8741. Tel: 828-389-8401. FAX: 828-389-3734. Web Site: www.nantahalalibrary.org. *Br Librn,* Mary Fonda; E-mail: mfonda@nantahalalibrary.org
Founded 1942
Library Holdings: Large Print Bks 3,000; Bk Vols 35,000; Per Subs 50
Automation Activity & Vendor Info: (Cataloging) TLC (The Library Corporation); (Circulation) TLC (The Library Corporation); (OPAC) TLC (The Library Corporation)
Mem of Nantahala Regional Library
Open Wed, Fri & Sat 9-6, Tues & Thurs 9-8
Friends of the Library Group

HENDERSON

P H LESLIE PERRY MEMORIAL LIBRARY*, 205 Breckenridge St, 27536. SAN 354-8910. Tel: 252-438-3316. FAX: 252-438-3744. Web Site: www.perrylibrary.org. *Dir,* Jay Stephens; E-mail: jstephens@perrylibrary.org; *Tech Coordr,* Thomas Milan; *Adult Serv,* Jennifer Brax; *Tech Serv,* Beth Lyles; Staff 15 (MLS 3, Non-MLS 12)
Founded 1924. Pop 44,000; Circ 168,135
Jul 2006-Jun 2007 Income $895,213, State $123,753, City $300,000, County $411,329, Locally Generated Income $53,000, Other $7,131. Mats Exp $122,019, Books $92,086, Per/Ser (Incl. Access Fees) $7,500, AV Mat $12,910, Electronic Ref Mat (Incl. Access Fees) $9,523. Sal $475,201
Library Holdings: Bk Vols 103,661; Per Subs 200; Talking Bks 4,280
Subject Interests: Local hist
Automation Activity & Vendor Info: (Acquisitions) TLC (The Library Corporation); (Cataloging) TLC (The Library Corporation); (Circulation) TLC (The Library Corporation); (ILL) OCLC; (OPAC) TLC (The Library Corporation)
Wireless access
Publications: Children's Newsletter; Friends Newsletter
Partic in Lyrasis
Open Mon & Tues 12-8, Wed-Sat 10-6
Friends of the Library Group

J VANCE-GRANVILLE COMMUNITY COLLEGE*, Learning Resources Center, 200 Community College Rd, 27536. (Mail add: PO Box 917, 27536-0917), SAN 312-875X. Tel: 252-492-2061. Circulation Tel: 252-738-3279. Interlibrary Loan Service Tel: 252-738-3331. Administration Tel: 252-738-3352. FAX: 252-738-3372. Web Site: www.vgcc.edu. *Dir,* Dave Trudeau; E-mail: trudeaud@vgcc.edu; *Librn,* Annette Clark; *Librn,* Jennie Davis; *Ref Serv,* Nicole Robertson; Staff 7 (MLS 4, Non-MLS 3)
Founded 1970. Highest Degree: Associate
Jul 2012-Jun 2013. Mats Exp $153,000, Books $68,000, Per/Ser (Incl. Access Fees) $60,000, AV Mat $25,000
Library Holdings: Bk Titles 38,000; Bk Vols 43,443; Per Subs 250
Subject Interests: Children's bks, Current novels
Automation Activity & Vendor Info: (Cataloging) SirsiDynix; (Circulation) SirsiDynix; (ILL) SirsiDynix; (OPAC) SirsiDynix
Database Vendor: Gale Cengage Learning, ProQuest
Wireless access
Publications: LRC Brochure; Student Handbook
Partic in Community Colleges Libraries in North Carolina (CCLINC); North Carolina Libraries for Virtual Education; OCLC Online Computer Library Center, Inc
Open Mon-Thurs 7:30am-8pm, Fri 7:30-3

Departmental Libraries:

FRANKLIN CAMPUS, 8100 NC 56 Hwy, Louisburg, 27549. (Mail add: PO Box 777, Louisburg, 27549-0777). Tel: 919-496-1567, Ext 3606. FAX: 919-496-6604. Web Site: lrc.vgcc.edu/home. *Br Coordr,* Julie Sterling; E-mail: sterling@vgcc.edu; Staff 1 (Non-MLS 1)
Library Holdings: Bk Vols 2,000
Open Mon-Thurs 8-8, Fri 8-3

SOUTH CAMPUS, 1547 S Campus Dr, Creedmoor, 27522-7381. (Mail add: PO Box 39, Creedmoor, 27522-0039). Tel: 919-528-1752. FAX: 919-528-1752. *Ref Librn,* Nicole Robertson; E-mail: robertson@vgcc.edu; *Libr Asst,* Rebecca Hayes; Tel: 252-738-3510, E-mail: rhayes5021@vgcc.edu; Staff 5 (MLS 1, Non-MLS 4)
Fac 5; Highest Degree: Associate
Library Holdings: Bk Vols 10,000; Per Subs 50
Open Mon & Tues 8:30-8, Wed 10-8, Thurs & Fri 8:30-5, Sat 10-2

WARREN CAMPUS, 210 W Ridgeway St, Warrenton, 27589-1838. (Mail add: PO Box 207, Warrenton, 27589-0207). Tel: 252-738-3685. FAX: 252-257-3612. *Br Coordr,* Lauren Hurley; Staff 1 (Non-MLS 1)
Library Holdings: Bk Vols 5,000

HENDERSONVILLE

SR FRUITLAND BAPTIST BIBLE INSTITUTE*, Randy Kilby Memorial Library, 1455 Gillaim Rd, 28792. SAN 312-8768. Tel: 828-685-8886. FAX: 828-685-8888. Web Site: www.fruitland.edu. *Interim Librn,* Ansel Pace; Staff 2 (MLS 1, Non-MLS 1)

Founded 1949
Library Holdings: Bk Vols 27,000; Per Subs 50
Open Mon-Fri 8:30-4:30

P HENDERSON COUNTY PUBLIC LIBRARY*, 301 N Washington St, 28739. SAN 354-897X. Tel: 828-697-4725. FAX: 828-692-8449, 828-697-4700. E-mail: reference@henderson.lib.nc.us. Web Site: www.henderson.lib.nc.us. *Dir,* William E Snyder; *Acq Librn,* Trina Rushing; *Youth/Young Adult Librn,* Tina Stepp; *Adult Serv,* Simon Coultas; *AV,* Kathryn Conlon; *ILL,* Chris Kersten; *Tech Serv,* Sharon Arnette; Staff 8 (MLS 8)
Founded 1914. Pop 95,824; Circ 948,000
Library Holdings: Bk Vols 250,000; Per Subs 250
Automation Activity & Vendor Info: (Acquisitions) SirsiDynix; (Cataloging) SirsiDynix; (Circulation) SirsiDynix
Open Mon-Thurs 9-9, Fri & Sat 9-6, Sun 2-6
Friends of the Library Group
Branches: 4
EDNEYVILLE BRANCH, Two Firehouse Lane, 28792, SAN 377-8312. Tel: 828-685-0110. FAX: 828-685-0110. *Librn,* Theresa Weaver
Founded 1989
Open Mon 9-8, Tues-Thurs 9-5:30, Sat 9-1
Friends of the Library Group
ETOWAH BRANCH, 101 Brickyard Rd, Etowah, 28729, SAN 354-8988. Tel: 828-891-6577. FAX: 828-890-7798. *Librn,* Joyce Crain
Founded 1982
Library Holdings: Bk Vols 18,302
Open Mon, Tues & Thurs 9-5:30, Wed 1:30-5:30, Fri & Sat 9-1
Friends of the Library Group
FLETCHER BRANCH, 120 Library Rd, Fletcher, 28732, SAN 354-9003. Tel: 828-687-1218. FAX: 828-684-9446. Web Site: www.henderson.lib.nc.us/fletcher.htm. *Librn,* Position Currently Open
Founded 1977
Library Holdings: Bk Vols 15,000
Open Mon 9-8, Tues-Thurs 9-5:30, Fri & Sat 9-1
Friends of the Library Group
GREEN RIVER, 50 Green River Rd, Zirconia, 28790, SAN 377-8339. Tel: 828-697-4969. FAX: 828-697-4969. *Librn,* Carol Case
Founded 1990
Open Mon & Thurs 9-12 & 1-5:30, Tues & Wed 9-5:30, Fri & Sat 9-1
Friends of the Library Group

HERTFORD

P PERQUIMANS COUNTY LIBRARY*, 110 W Academy St, 27944. SAN 312-8776. Tel: 252-426-5319. FAX: 252-426-1556. E-mail: perquimans@pettigrewlibraries.org. *Libr Dir,* Position Currently Open; Staff 1 (MLS 1)
Founded 1937. Pop 12,000; Circ 46,728
Library Holdings: Audiobooks 1,191; AV Mats 3,680; Bks on Deafness & Sign Lang 10; Braille Volumes 2; CDs 528; DVDs 682; Large Print Bks 2,476; Bk Titles 32,395; Bk Vols 33,814; Per Subs 47; Videos 1,307
Special Collections: CCR&R, games, puzzles & toys for young children
Subject Interests: Genealogy, Local hist
Automation Activity & Vendor Info: (Acquisitions) TLC (The Library Corporation); (Cataloging) TLC (The Library Corporation); (Circulation) TLC (The Library Corporation); (OPAC) TLC (The Library Corporation)
Database Vendor: NC LIVE, TLC (The Library Corporation)
Wireless access
Function: Accelerated reader prog, Bks on cassette, Bks on CD, Children's prog, Computers for patron use, Copy machines, Electronic databases & coll, Free DVD rentals, Handicapped accessible, Home delivery & serv to Sr ctr & nursing homes, ILL available, Magnifiers for reading, Music CDs, Online cat, Photocopying/Printing, Preschool outreach, Prog for adults, Pub access computers, Ref serv available, Scanner, Spoken cassettes & CDs, Story hour, Summer reading prog, Tax forms, Telephone ref, VHS videos, Wheelchair accessible
Mem of Pettigrew Regional Library
Open Mon, Tues & Thurs 9:30-8, Wed & Fri 9:30-6, Sat 9:30-1:30
Friends of the Library Group

HICKORY

J CATAWBA VALLEY COMMUNITY COLLEGE*, Learning Resource Center, 2550 Hwy 70 SE, 28602-9699. SAN 312-8784. Tel: 828-327-7000, Ext 4229. FAX: 828-324-5130. Web Site: www.cvcc.edu. *Dir,* Ari Sigal; E-mail: asigal@cvcc.edu; *Ref Librn,* Brad Vogler; Tel: 828-327-7000, Ext 4457, E-mail: bvolger@cvcc.edu; Staff 1 (MLS 1)
Founded 1960. Enrl 2,049; Fac 180
Library Holdings: Bk Titles 28,000; Bk Vols 30,000; Per Subs 200
Subject Interests: Decoration, Furniture
Automation Activity & Vendor Info: (Acquisitions) Keystone Systems, Inc (KLAS); (Cataloging) Keystone Systems, Inc (KLAS); (Circulation) Keystone Systems, Inc (KLAS)
Publications: Library Information Pamphlet
Open Mon-Thurs 7:30am-9pm, Fri 7:30-4:30

P HICKORY PUBLIC LIBRARY, Patrick Beaver Memorial Library, 375 Third St NE, 28601-5126. SAN 354-9038. Tel: 828-304-0500. FAX: 828-304-0023. Web Site: www.hickorync.gov/library. *Dir,* Louise Humphrey; Tel: 828-304-0500, Ext 7275, E-mail: lhumphrey@hickorync.gov; *Head, Ref & Tech Serv,* Beth Bradshaw; *Youth Serv Librn,* Lisa Neal; *Circ Supvr,* Amy Horn; Staff 7 (MLS 7)
Founded 1922. Pop 40,020; Circ 326,443
Library Holdings: AV Mats 14,874; Bk Vols 112,490; Per Subs 354
Special Collections: Career Enhancement
Subject Interests: Baseball, Genealogy, Learning disabilities, Local hist
Automation Activity & Vendor Info: (Cataloging) TLC (The Library Corporation); (Circulation) TLC (The Library Corporation); (OPAC) TLC (The Library Corporation)
Database Vendor: NC LIVE
Wireless access
Function: Outreach serv
Publications: Calendar (Monthly)
Special Services for the Blind - Computer with voice synthesizer for visually impaired persons
Open Mon-Thurs 9-9, Fri & Sat 9-5
Friends of the Library Group
Branches: 1
RIDGEVIEW, 706 First St SW, 28602, SAN 354-9062. Tel: 828-345-6037. FAX: 828-267-0485. *Br Mgr,* Terressa Jefferson; Staff 2 (MLS 2)
Circ 5,215
Library Holdings: Bk Vols 7,500
Subject Interests: African-Am
Open Mon-Thurs 9-9, Fri & Sat 9-5
Friends of the Library Group

C LENOIR-RHYNE UNIVERSITY LIBRARY*, Carl A Rudisill Library, 625 7th Ave NE, 28601. (Mail add: PO Box 7548, 28603-7548), SAN 312-8806. Tel: 828-328-7236. FAX: 828-328-7338. Web Site: library.lr.edu. *Dean of Libr Serv,* Rita Johnson; Tel: 828-328-7235, E-mail: rita.johnson@lr.edu; *Asst Dir, Coll Develop Instruction & Ref Librn,* Burl McCuiston; E-mail: mccuiston@lr.edu; *ILL,* Vicki Woodrich; E-mail: vicki.woodrich@lr.edu; *Libr Spec,* Greg Callahan; E-mail: callahang@lr.edu; *Libr Spec for Tech & Learning Support,* Jessica O'Brien; E-mail: jessica.obrien@lr.edu; Staff 8.7 (MLS 4, Non-MLS 4.7)
Founded 1891. Enrl 1,446; Fac 90; Highest Degree: Master
Jun 2006-May 2007. Mats Exp $167,524, Books $44,046, Per/Ser (Incl. Access Fees) $61,111, AV Mat $13,358, Electronic Ref Mat (Incl. Access Fees) $47,551, Presv $1,458. Sal $326,876 (Prof $222,345)
Library Holdings: AV Mats 38,533; Bks on Deafness & Sign Lang 4,372; e-books 125,000; e-journals 20,000; Bk Titles 119,121; Bk Vols 150,152; Per Subs 70
Special Collections: Martin Luther Works Coll (Wiemar Edition); Quetzalcoatl Coll
Automation Activity & Vendor Info: (Acquisitions) Innovative Interfaces, Inc; (Cataloging) Innovative Interfaces, Inc; (Circulation) Innovative Interfaces, Inc; (Course Reserve) Innovative Interfaces, Inc; (ILL) OCLC ILLiad; (OPAC) Innovative Interfaces, Inc; (Serials) Innovative Interfaces, Inc
Database Vendor: Alexander Street Press, American Psychological Association (APA), ARTstor, CQ Press, EBSCO - WebFeat, EBSCOhost, Gale Cengage Learning, Greenwood Publishing Group, JSTOR, Modern Language Association, NC LIVE, Newsbank, OCLC FirstSearch, OCLC WorldShare Interlibrary Loan, ProQuest, PubMed, SerialsSolutions, Wiley
Wireless access
Partic in Appalachian Col Asn; Carolina Consortium; Lyrasis; Mountain College Libr Network; NC Asn of Independent Cols & Univs; OCLC Online Computer Library Center, Inc
Special Services for the Deaf - Bks on deafness & sign lang; Captioned film dep; High interest/low vocabulary bks; Spec interest per; Staff with knowledge of sign lang
Special Services for the Blind - Computer with voice synthesizer for visually impaired persons
Open Mon-Thurs 8am-Midnight, Fri 8-5, Sat 11-5, Sun 2-Midnight
Restriction: Open to pub for ref only, Open to students, fac & staff
Friends of the Library Group

CM NORTHWEST AREA HEALTH EDUCATION CENTER*, Catawba Valley Medical Center, 810 Fairgrove Church Rd, 28602. SAN 325-7738. Tel: 828-326-3662, Ext 3482. FAX: 828-326-3484. *Coordr,* Karen Lee Martinez; Tel: 828-326-3482, E-mail: martinez@wfubmc.edu; Staff 1 (MLS 1)
Jul 2007-Jun 2008. Mats Exp $20,000. Sal $76,000
Library Holdings: Bk Titles 2,200; Bk Vols 2,300
Subject Interests: Allied health, Med, Nursing
Wireless access
Partic in Northwest AHEC Library Information Network

Open Mon-Fri 8-5
Friends of the Library Group

HIGH POINT

S BERNICE BIENENSTOCK FURNITURE LIBRARY*, 1009 N Main St, 27262. SAN 325-7967. Tel: 336-883-4011. FAX: 336-883-6579. E-mail: info@furniturelibrary.com. Web Site: www.furniturelibrary.com. *Curator,* Carl Vuncannon
Founded 1970
Library Holdings: Bk Vols 7,000; Per Subs 10
Open Mon-Fri 9-5

P HIGH POINT PUBLIC LIBRARY*, 901 N Main St, 27262. (Mail add: PO Box 2530, 27261-2530), SAN 354-9097. Tel: 336-883-3660. Circulation Tel: 336-883-3661. Reference Tel: 336-883-3641. Administration Tel: 336-883-3631. Automation Services Tel: 336-883-9317. Information Services Tel: 336-883-3693. FAX: 336-883-3636. TDD: 336-883-3675. Web Site: highpointpubliclibrary.com. *Dir,* Mary M Sizemore; Tel: 336-883-3694, E-mail: mary.sizemore@highpointnc.gov; *Asst Dir,* Lorrie Russell; Tel: 336-883-3644, E-mail: lorrie.russell@highpointnc.gov; *Div Mgr, Children's Serv,* Jim Zola; Tel: 336-883-3668, E-mail: jim.zola@highpointnc.gov; *Div Mgr, Reader Serv,* Nancy Metzner; Tel: 336-883-3650, E-mail: nancy.metzner@highpointnc.gov; *Div Mgr, Res Serv,* Ginny Lewis; Tel: 336-883-3643, E-mail: ginny.lewis@highpointnc.gov; *Div Mgr, Tech Serv,* Kim Coleman; Tel: 336-883-3645, E-mail: kim.coleman@highpointnc.gov; *Supvr, AV & Media Serv,* Julie Raynor; Tel: 336-883-3093, E-mail: julie.raynor@highpointnc.gov; *Supvr, Computer Serv & Ref (Info Serv),* Mario Ramos; Tel: 336-883-3633, E-mail: mario.ramos@highpointnc.gov; *Genealogy Serv,* Larry Cates; Tel: 336-883-3637, E-mail: larry.cates@highpointnc.gov; *ILL, Ref,* John Hedstrom; Tel: 336-883-8585, E-mail: john.hedstrom@highpointnc.gov; *Tech Serv,* Megan Joyce; Tel: 336-883-3648, E-mail: megan.joyce@highpointnc.gov; *Ref,* John Raynor; Tel: 336-883-3216, E-mail: john.raynor@highpointnc.gov; *Syst Adminr,* Jamie Beck; E-mail: jamie.beck@highpointnc.gov; Staff 15.5 (MLS 15.5)
Founded 1926. Pop 95,630; Circ 817,752
Jul 2012-Jun 2013 Income $4,655,924, State $77,917, City $4,198,047, Federal $20,000, County $359,960. Mats Exp $410,510. Sal $2,765,143
Library Holdings: AV Mats 45,877; Bk Vols 327,003; Per Subs 566
Subject Interests: Design, Furniture, Genealogy, Local hist, NC
Automation Activity & Vendor Info: (Acquisitions) TLC (The Library Corporation); (Cataloging) TLC (The Library Corporation); (Circulation) TLC (The Library Corporation); (OPAC) TLC (The Library Corporation); (Serials) TLC (The Library Corporation)
Wireless access
Function: Adult bk club, Adult literacy prog, Computer training, Copy machines, E-Reserves, Electronic databases & coll, Fax serv, Handicapped accessible, Home delivery & serv to Sr ctr & nursing homes, Homebound delivery serv, ILL available, Magnifiers for reading, Mail & tel request accepted, Preschool outreach, Prog for adults, Prog for children & young adult, Satellite serv, Summer reading prog, Tax forms, Telephone ref, VHS videos, Wheelchair accessible
Publications: Business Research (Newsletter); Library Daycare Connections; Library Whispers (Newsletter); Minority Business Directory; North Carolina Collection (Newsletter); Share Stories (Newsletter); Teacher Times (Newsletter)
Partic in North Carolina Libraries for Virtual Education
Special Services for the Blind - Assistive/Adapted tech devices, equip & products; Bks on cassette; Bks on CD; Extensive large print coll; Large print & cassettes; Large print bks; Magnifiers
Open Mon-Thurs 10-8, Fri 10-6, Sat 12-6, Sun 1:30-5:30
Restriction: Non-resident fee
Friends of the Library Group
Bookmobiles: 1. Libr Assoc, Kim Wilks

C HIGH POINT UNIVERSITY*, Smith Library, 833 Montlieu Ave, 27262-4221. SAN 312-8814. Tel: 336-841-9102. Circulation Tel: 336-841-8102. Interlibrary Loan Service Tel: 336-841-9170. Reference Tel: 336-841-9101. Administration Tel: 336-841-9215. FAX: 336-841-5123. Web Site: library.highpoint.edu. *Dir,* David L Bryden; Tel: 336-841-9215, E-mail: dbryden@highpoint.edu; *Ref/ILL,* Robert Fitzgerald, Jr; Tel: 336-841-9170, E-mail: rfitzger@highpoint.edu; *Acq, Supvr,* Karen Harbin; Tel: 336-841-9100, E-mail: kharbin@highpoint.edu; *Syst Coordr, Tech Serv,* Michael Ingram; Tel: 336-841-9152, E-mail: mingram@highpoint.edu; *Cat, Ser,* Sheri Teleha; Tel: 336-841-4549, E-mail: steleha@highpoint.edu; *Circ Serv,* La-Nita Williams; E-mail: nwilliam@highpoint.edu; *Media Spec,* Samantha Harlow; Staff 9 (MLS 5, Non-MLS 4)
Founded 1924. Enrl 2,500; Fac 130; Highest Degree: Master
Library Holdings: e-books 54,000; Bk Vols 310,000; Per Subs 25,000
Special Collections: Home Furnishings Marketing Coll; Methodist Archives; North Carolina Coll
Subject Interests: Liberal arts
Automation Activity & Vendor Info: (Acquisitions) SirsiDynix; (Cataloging) SirsiDynix
Database Vendor: 3M Library Systems, Baker & Taylor, Blackwell, Dialog, EBSCOhost, Gale Cengage Learning, Grolier Online, JSTOR, LexisNexis, Newsbank, OCLC FirstSearch, OCLC WorldShare Interlibrary Loan, OVID Technologies, ProQuest, ReferenceUSA, SirsiDynix, Wiley
Wireless access
Partic in Carolina Consortium; North Carolina Libraries for Virtual Education; OCLC Online Computer Library Center, Inc
Restriction: Authorized patrons
Friends of the Library Group

C LAUREL UNIVERSITY LIBRARY*, Temple Library, 1215 Eastchester Drive, 27265 3197. SAN 312-8822. Tel: 336-889-2262. FAX: 336-889-2261. Web Site: www.laureluniversity.edu. *Dir,* April Lindsey; Tel: 336-889-2262, Ext 146, E-mail: alindsey@laureluniversity.edu
Founded 1936. Highest Degree: Bachelor
Library Holdings: AV Mats 2,886; Bk Vols 39,111; Per Subs 200
Special Collections: John Wesley Coll
Subject Interests: Gen educ, Music, Relig studies
Wireless access
Open Mon & Tues 8-5 & 6-8:30, Wed & Thurs 8-5, Fri 10-12

HILLSBOROUGH

P HYCONEECHEE REGIONAL LIBRARY*, 300 W Tryon St, 27278. SAN 313-0649. Tel: 919-644-3011. FAX: 919-644-3003. *Dir,* Brenda W Stephens
Founded 1948. Pop 178,129; Circ 492,376
Library Holdings: Bk Vols 210,632; Per Subs 907
Subject Interests: Antiques, Genealogy, Geog, Local hist
Automation Activity & Vendor Info: (Cataloging) Innovative Interfaces, Inc; (Circulation) Innovative Interfaces, Inc; (OPAC) Innovative Interfaces, Inc
Database Vendor: Baker & Taylor, Bowker, ProQuest
Wireless access
Member Libraries: Gunn Memorial Public Library; Orange County Public Library; Person County Public Library
Friends of the Library Group

P ORANGE COUNTY PUBLIC LIBRARY*, 137 W Margaret Lane, 27278. SAN 312-8849. Tel: 919-245-2525. FAX: 919-644-3003. Web Site: www.co.orange.nc.us/library. *Dir,* Lucinda Munger; Tel: 919-245-2528, E-mail: lmunger@co.orange.nc.us; *Ch,* Ginger Holler; E-mail: gholler@co.orange.nc.us; *Outreach Serv Librn,* Kevin Delaney; E-mail: kdelaney@co.orange.nc.us; *Ref Librn,* Kim Sholar; E-mail: ksholar@co.orange.nc.us; *Circ Supvr,* Theresa Quiner; E-mail: tquiner@co.orange.nc.us; *Syst Adminr,* Amber Campbell; E-mail: acampbell@co.orange.nc.us; *ILL,* Oliver Collier; E-mail: ocollier@co.orange.nc.us; Staff 14 (MLS 7, Non-MLS 7)
Founded 1912. Pop 118,227; Circ 154,873
Library Holdings: Bk Vols 86,369; Per Subs 420
Subject Interests: Genealogy, Local hist
Automation Activity & Vendor Info: (Cataloging) Innovative Interfaces, Inc; (Circulation) Innovative Interfaces, Inc; (OPAC) Innovative Interfaces, Inc
Database Vendor: Baker & Taylor, Bowker, ProQuest
Wireless access
Mem of Hyconeechee Regional Library
Open Mon-Thurs 9-8, Fri & Sat 9-5, Sun 1-5
Friends of the Library Group
Branches: 2
CARRBORO BRANCH, McDougle Middle School, 900 Old Fayetteville Rd, Chapel Hill, 27516, SAN 377-7901. Tel: 919-969-3006. FAX: 919-969-3008. *Br Mgr,* Anne Pusey; E-mail: apusey@co.orange.nc.us; *Circ,* Janet Caudle; E-mail: jcaudle@co.orange.nc.us; Staff 6 (MLS 2, Non-MLS 4)
Library Holdings: Bk Vols 19,450; Per Subs 75
Automation Activity & Vendor Info: (Cataloging) ComPanion Corp; (Circulation) ComPanion Corp
Open Mon-Thurs 3:30-8, Sat 10-2, Sun 1-5
Friends of the Library Group
CARRBORO CYBRARY BRANCH, Carrboro Century Ctr, 100 N Greensboro St, Carrboro, 27510. Tel: 919-918-7387. FAX: 919-918-3960. E-mail: cybrary@co.orange.nc.us. *Br Mgr,* Ann Pusey; *Circ Supvr,* Vanessa Soleic; Staff 1.25 (MLS 1.25)
Founded 2004
Library Holdings: Bk Vols 369; Per Subs 23
Function: Adult bk club, Adult literacy prog, Bk club(s), Bks on cassette, Bks on CD, Computer training, Computers for patron use, Copy machines, Digital talking bks, Fax serv, Handicapped accessible, ILL available, Magnifiers for reading, Online cat, Photocopying/Printing, Prog for adults, Pub access computers, Ref serv available, Scanner, Spoken cassettes & CDs, Wheelchair accessible

Open Mon-Fri 9-4, Sat 10-2
Friends of the Library Group

HUDSON

J CALDWELL COMMUNITY COLLEGE & TECHNICAL INSTITUTE, Broyhill Center for Learning Resources, 2855 Hickory Blvd, 28638. SAN 312-9020. Tel: 828-726-2309. FAX: 828-726-2603. E-mail: reference@cccti.edu. Web Site: www.cccti.edu/LRC/library.htm. *Dir,* Deborah Joyner; Tel: 828-726-2311, E-mail: dwjoyner@cccti.edu; Staff 8 (MLS 3, Non-MLS 5)
Founded 1966. Highest Degree: Associate
Library Holdings: DVDs 536; Bk Vols 43,285; Per Subs 112; Videos 1,408
Automation Activity & Vendor Info: (Cataloging) SirsiDynix; (Circulation) SirsiDynix; (ILL) OCLC; (OPAC) SirsiDynix
Database Vendor: ABC-CLIO, Alexander Street Press, Cinahl, CQ Press, ebrary, EBSCOhost, Facts on File, Gale Cengage Learning, Greenwood Publishing Group, Hoovers, JSTOR, LearningExpress, NC LIVE, OCLC, ProQuest, SirsiDynix, STAT!Ref (Teton Data Systems), Westlaw
Wireless access
Publications: Audio-visual & book acquisitions lists; Audio-visual catalog
Partic in Community Colleges Libraries in North Carolina (CCLINC); Northwest AHEC Library Information Network
Open Mon-Thurs 8-8, Fri 8-4

JACKSONVILLE

J COASTAL CAROLINA COMMUNITY COLLEGE, Learning Resources Center, 444 Western Blvd, 28546. SAN 312-8865. Tel: 910-938-6237. FAX: 910-455-7027. Web Site: www.coastalcarolina.edu. *Head Librn,* Sally Goodman; Tel: 910-938-6793, E-mail: goodmans@coastalcarolina.edu; *Pub Serv Librn,* Maria Fesz; Tel: 910-938-6239, E-mail: feszm@coastalcarolina.edu; *Pub Serv Librn,* Libby Garrison; Tel: 910-938-6278, E-mail: libbyg@coastalcarolina.edu; *Tech Asst,* Marilyn Gresham; Tel: 910-938-6114, E-mail: greshamm@coastalcarolina.edu; *Tech Asst,* Teresa Ortega; Tel: 910-938-6147, E-mail: ortegat@coastalcarolina.edu; *Acq,* Kerry Brinker; Tel: 910-938-6844, E-mail: brinkerk@coastalcarolina.edu. Subject Specialists: *Allied health, Nursing,* Sally Goodman; *Fine arts, Hist, Nat sci,* Maria Fesz; *English, Soc & behav sci,* Libby Garrison; Staff 6 (MLS 3, Non-MLS 3)
Founded 1965. Enrl 1,745; Fac 125; Highest Degree: Associate
Library Holdings: CDs 1,837; DVDs 7,172; Microforms 20,758; Bk Titles 45,000; Per Subs 53
Special Collections: Oral History
Automation Activity & Vendor Info: (Cataloging) SirsiDynix; (Circulation) SirsiDynix; (Course Reserve) SirsiDynix; (ILL) SirsiDynix; (OPAC) SirsiDynix
Partic in Community Colleges Libraries in North Carolina (CCLINC); North Carolina Libraries for Virtual Education; OCLC Online Computer Library Center, Inc
Open Mon-Thurs 7am-9:30pm, Fri 7-5, Sat 9-5

P ONSLOW COUNTY PUBLIC LIBRARY*, 58 Doris Ave E, 28540. SAN 354-9186. Tel: 910-455-7350. Circulation Tel: 910-455-7350, Ext 1412. Administration Tel: 910-455-7350, Ext 1419. FAX: 910-455-1661. E-mail: library@onslowcountync.gov. Web Site: www.onslowcountync.gov/library. *Dir,* Estell Carter; Tel: 910-455-7350, Ext 1425, E-mail: estell_carter@onslowcountync.gov; *Asst Dir,* Emery Ortiz; Tel: 910-455-7350, Ext 1416, E-mail: emery_ortiz@onslowcountync.gov; *Pub Serv Librn,* Karen Moore; Tel: 910-455-7350, Ext 1421, E-mail: karen_moore@onslowcountync.gov; *Youth Serv Librn,* Valerie Suttee; Tel: 910-455-7350, Ext 1420, E-mail: valerie_suttee@onslowcountync.gov; *Tech Serv Mgr,* Deborah Wadleigh; Tel: 910-455-7350, Ext 1415, E-mail: deborah_wadleigh@onslowcountync.gov; Staff 40 (MLS 4, Non-MLS 36)
Founded 1936. Pop 152,424
Jul 2006-Jun 2007 Income (Main Library and Branch(s)) $2,125,738, State $265,995, Federal $1,000, County $1,690,006, Locally Generated Income $168,737. Mats Exp $250,914, Books $191,000, Per/Ser (Incl. Access Fees) $14,914, AV Mat $37,000, Electronic Ref Mat (Incl. Access Fees) $8,000. Sal $1,263,651 (Prof $184,944)
Library Holdings: AV Mats 3,695; Bks on Deafness & Sign Lang 33; Large Print Bks 2,472; Bk Titles 59,618; Bk Vols 75,026; Per Subs 131; Talking Bks 1,347
Special Collections: Oral History Coll Relating to Building Camp Lejeune Marine Base
Subject Interests: Genealogy, Local hist
Automation Activity & Vendor Info: (Cataloging) Innovative Interfaces, Inc; (Circulation) Innovative Interfaces, Inc; (OPAC) Innovative Interfaces, Inc
Database Vendor: Comprise Technologies Inc, NC LIVE, World Book Online
Wireless access
Publications: Civic Club Roster; Human Resources Manual; Page Break (Newsletter)
Partic in NCIN; North Carolina Libraries for Virtual Education; OCLC Online Computer Library Center, Inc
Open Mon-Thurs 9-9, Fri & Sat 9-6, Sun 1-5
Friends of the Library Group
Branches: 4
LAW LIBRARY, 109 Old Bridge St, 28540, SAN 329-5656. Tel: 910-455-4458, Ext 307. FAX: 910-989-2079. *Br Mgr,* David Dalimonte; E-mail: david_dalimonte@onslowcountync.gov; Staff 1 (Non-MLS 1)
Library Holdings: Bk Vols 5,621
Open Mon-Fri 8-12 & 1-5
RICHLANDS BRANCH, 299 S Wilmington St, Richlands, 28574, SAN 354-9216. Tel: 910-324-5321. FAX: 910-324-4682. E-mail: lib_rl@onslowcountync.gov. *Br Mgr,* Michelle King; Tel: 910-324-5321, Ext 3179, E-mail: michelle_king@onslowcountync.gov
Library Holdings: AV Mats 1,644; Large Print Bks 361; Bk Titles 22,182; Bk Vols 23,445; Talking Bks 551
Open Mon-Wed & Fri 9-6, Thurs 10-7, Sat 9-3
Friends of the Library Group
SNEADS FERRY BRANCH, 242 Sneads Ferry Rd, Sneads Ferry, 28460, SAN 354-9232. Tel: 910-327-6471. FAX: 910-327-0284. *Br Mgr,* Elizabeth Barrett; E-mail: liza_barrett@onslowcountync.gov
Library Holdings: AV Mats 1,666; Bks on Deafness & Sign Lang 11; Large Print Bks 225; Bk Titles 19,876; Bk Vols 20,759; Per Subs 33; Talking Bks 493
Open Mon-Wed & Fri 9-6, Thurs 10-7, Sat 9-3
Friends of the Library Group
SWANSBORO BRANCH, 1460 W Corbett Ave, Swansboro, 28584, SAN 354-9240. Tel: 910-326-4888. FAX: 910-326-6682. *Br Mgr,* Michelle King; E-mail: michelle_king@onslowcountync.gov
Library Holdings: AV Mats 1,953; Bks on Deafness & Sign Lang 13; Large Print Bks 643; Bk Titles 21,833; Bk Vols 223,199; Per Subs 29; Talking Bks 641
Open Mon-Wed & Fri 9-6, Thurs 10-7, Sat 9-3
Friends of the Library Group

A UNITED STATES MARINE CORPS*, MCAS Station Library, Bldg AS-201, 28540. (Mail add: PO Box 4128, 28545), SAN 354-9275. Tel: 910-449-6715. FAX: 910-449-6037. Web Site: library.usmc-mccs.org. *Dir,* Trent Reynolds
Founded 1956
Library Holdings: AV Mats 1,000; Bk Titles 23,000; Per Subs 74
Subject Interests: Alcohol abuse control, Automobile maintenance repair, Drug abuse, Human relations, Juv picture bks, Microcomputer, Mil preparedness, Sports, Vietnam conflict, World War II
Automation Activity & Vendor Info: (Cataloging) SirsiDynix; (Circulation) SirsiDynix; (OPAC) SirsiDynix
Database Vendor: ProQuest
Open Mon-Thurs 9-8:30, Fri 9-5, Sat 10-4

JAMESTOWN

J GUILFORD TECHNICAL COMMUNITY COLLEGE*, Mertys W Bell Library, 601 High Point Rd, 27282. (Mail add: PO Box 309, 27282-0309), SAN 354-9305. Tel: 336-334-4822, Ext 2292. FAX: 336-841-4350. Web Site: www.gtcc.edu/library. *Dir, Libr Serv,* Mary S Lane; E-mail: mslane@gtcc.edu; *Extn Serv,* Keith Burkhead; E-mail: burkheadk@gtcc.edu; *Ref Serv,* Belinda S Daniels-Richardson, Tel: 336-334-4822, Ext 2636, E-mail: brichardson@gtcc.edu; *Ref Serv,* Alisha Webb; Tel: 336-334-4822, Ext 2287; *Tech Serv,* Jennifer Noga; Tel: 336-334-4822, Ext 2232, E-mail: jhnoga@gtcc.edu; Staff 7 (MLS 7)
Founded 1958. Enrl 11,884; Fac 231; Highest Degree: Associate
Library Holdings: AV Mats 7,585; e-books 25,000; Bk Titles 70,120; Bk Vols 84,134; Per Subs 300
Subject Interests: Archit, Automotive tech, Commercial art, Commun col, Dental sci, Eng, Nursing, Paralegal, Surgical tech
Automation Activity & Vendor Info: (Acquisitions) SirsiDynix; (Cataloging) SirsiDynix; (Circulation) SirsiDynix; (Course Reserve) SirsiDynix; (Media Booking) SirsiDynix; (OPAC) SirsiDynix; (Serials) SirsiDynix
Database Vendor: NC LIVE
Publications: Faculty Guide; Newsletter; Periodicals List; Student-How-To-Bookmarks
Partic in NC Dept of Commun Cols
Open Mon-Thurs (Fall & Spring) 7:30am-9pm, Fri 7:30-5, Sat 9-1; Mon-Thurs (Summer) 7:30-6, Fri 8-12
Friends of the Library Group

P JAMESTOWN PUBLIC LIBRARY*, 200 W Main St, 27282. SAN 370-6648. Tel: 336-454-4815. FAX: 336-454-0630. Web Site: jamestownpubliclibrary.com. *Libr Mgr,* Eleanor Ratterman; *Ch Serv,* Carol Reed; *Genealogy Serv, Ref Serv,* John Ebel; *Tech Serv,* Audrey Kendrick; Staff 5 (MLS 2, Non-MLS 3)
Founded 1988. Pop 18,000; Circ 20,000; Fac 5

Jul 2008-Jun 2009 Income $123,500, City $50,000, County $55,500, Other $18,000. Mats Exp $15,500, Books $14,500, Per/Ser (Incl. Access Fees) $1,000. Sal $65,000
Library Holdings: Audiobooks 351; Bks on Deafness & Sign Lang 12; DVDs 414; High Interest/Low Vocabulary Bk Vols 423; Large Print Bks 449; Bk Titles 16,016; Bk Vols 17,613; Per Subs 54
Automation Activity & Vendor Info: (Acquisitions) Follett Software; (Cataloging) Follett Software; (Circulation) Follett Software
Wireless access
Function: Adult bk club, After school storytime, Art exhibits, Bks on cassette, Bks on CD, Children's prog, Computer training, Computers for patron use, Copy machines, Fax serv, Free DVD rentals, ILL available, Online cat, Photocopying/Printing, Summer reading prog, Tax forms, VHS videos
Publications: FOL (Newsletter); Library News Article (Newsletter)
Special Services for the Deaf - Closed caption videos
Open Mon-Fri 9-5:30, Sat 10-12:30
Restriction: Authorized patrons, Lending limited to county residents
Friends of the Library Group

JONESVILLE

P JONESVILLE PUBLIC LIBRARY*, 150 W Main St, 28642. SAN 312-8873. Tel: 336-835-7604. FAX: 336-526-4226. E-mail: jva@nwrl.org. Web Site: www.nwrl.org/jva.asp. *Librn,* Cynthia Allred; E-mail: callred@nwrl.org; *Asst Librn, Ch Serv,* Barbara Gilpin; E-mail: bgilpin@nwrl.org; Staff 3 (Non-MLS 3)
Founded 1962. Pop 5,000; Circ 68,000
Library Holdings: Bks on Deafness & Sign Lang 10; Bk Titles 20,000
Automation Activity & Vendor Info: (Circulation) SirsiDynix; (OPAC) SirsiDynix
Wireless access
Function: Bks on cassette, Bks on CD, Children's prog, Copy machines, Fax serv, Free DVD rentals, ILL available, Prog for children & young adult, Pub access computers, Senior outreach, Spoken cassettes & CDs, Story hour, Summer reading prog, Tax forms, VHS videos, Wheelchair accessible
Mem of Northwestern Regional Library
Open Mon, Wed & Fri 8:30-5:30, Tues & Thurs 8:30-7:30, Sat 9-1
Friends of the Library Group

KENANSVILLE

P DUPLIN COUNTY LIBRARY*, Dorothy Wightman Library, 107 Bowden Dr, 28349. (Mail add: PO Box 930, 28349-0930), SAN 312-889X. Tel: 910-296-2117. FAX: 910-296-2172. Web Site: www2.youseemore.com/duplin. *Dir,* Elizabeth Watson; E-mail: elizabeth.watson@duplincountync.com; *Br Coordr,* Shannon Sutton; E-mail: shannon.sutton@duplincountync.com; *Youth Serv Coordr,* Donna Jones; E-mail: djones@duplincountync.com
Founded 1920. Pop 39,995
Library Holdings: Large Print Bks 400; Bk Titles 42,600; Bk Vols 75,000; Per Subs 200
Subject Interests: NC hist
Automation Activity & Vendor Info: (Acquisitions) TLC (The Library Corporation); (Cataloging) TLC (The Library Corporation); (Circulation) TLC (The Library Corporation)
Open Mon-Fri 9-6
Friends of the Library Group
Branches: 5
FLORENCE GALLIER LIBRARY, 104 W Main St, Magnolia, 28453. (Mail add: PO Box 333, Magnolia, 28453-0333). Tel: 910-289-7056. FAX: 910-289-7056. *Br Librn,* Glendoria Boney; E-mail: gboney@duplincountync.com
Library Holdings: Bk Vols 1,600
Open Mon-Fri 2-6
Friends of the Library Group
EMILY S HILL LIBRARY, 106 Park Circle Dr, Faison, 28341. (Mail add: PO Box 129, Faison, 28341-0129), SAN 376-2912. Tel: 910-267-0601. FAX: 910-267-0601. *Br Librn,* Glenda Hooks; E-mail: ghooks@duplincountync.com
Library Holdings: Bk Titles 45,000; Bk Vols 50,000
Automation Activity & Vendor Info: (Acquisitions) TLC (The Library Corporation); (Cataloging) TLC (The Library Corporation); (Circulation) TLC (The Library Corporation)
Open Mon-Fri 2-6
Friends of the Library Group
PHILLIP LEFF MEMORIAL LIBRARY, 807 Broad St, Beulaville, 28518. (Mail add: PO Box 721, Beulaville, 28518-0721), SAN 376-2920. Tel: 910-298-4677. FAX: 910-298-5069. *Br Librn,* Jennifer Wade; E-mail: jwade@duplincountync.com
Library Holdings: Bk Titles 20,000; Bk Vols 30,000; Per Subs 10
Automation Activity & Vendor Info: (Acquisitions) TLC (The Library Corporation); (Cataloging) TLC (The Library Corporation); (Circulation) TLC (The Library Corporation)
Open Mon, Tues, Thurs & Fri 10-12:30 & 2-6, Wed 2-6
Friends of the Library Group
ROSE HILL COMMUNITY MEMORIAL LIBRARY, 113 S Walnut St, Rose Hill, 28458. (Mail add: PO Box 940, Rose Hill, 28458-0940), SAN 320-8311. Tel: 910-289-2490. FAX: 910-289-2186. *Br Head,* Maggie Casteen; E-mail: maggie.casteen@dublincountync.com
Pop 1,500; Circ 11,000
Library Holdings: Bk Vols 7,150
Automation Activity & Vendor Info: (Circulation) TLC (The Library Corporation)
Open Tues & Fri 9-1 & 2-6, Wed & Thurs 2-6
Friends of the Library Group
WARSAW-KORNEGAY LIBRARY, 117 E College St, Warsaw, 28398, SAN 376-2904. Tel: 910-293-4664. FAX: 910-293-4664. *Br Librn,* Karen Martin; E-mail: karen.martin@duplincountync.com
Library Holdings: Bk Vols 6,000
Open Mon & Fri 9-1 & 2-6, Tues & Thurs 2-6
Friends of the Library Group

J JAMES SPRUNT COMMUNITY COLLEGE LIBRARY*, Boyette Bldg, 133 James Sprunt Dr, 28349-0398. (Mail add: PO Box 398, 28349), SAN 312-8903. Tel: 910-296-2519. FAX: 910-296-6038. E-mail: jscclibrary@jamessprunt.edu. Web Site: www.sprunt.com/library.html. *Dir, Libr & Info Serv,* Patricia Lynn Klimschot; Tel: 910-296-2474, E-mail: pklimschot@jamessprunt.edu; Staff 3 (MLS 1, Non-MLS 2)
Founded 1966. Enrl 1,200; Highest Degree: Associate
Library Holdings: Bk Titles 2,500; Per Subs 200
Special Collections: Local History (Duplin County NC))
Function: Handicapped accessible, ILL available, Online searches, Photocopying/Printing, Wheelchair accessible
Partic in North Carolina Community College System
Open Mon & Thurs (Fall & Spring) 8-6.30, Tues & Wed 8-8, Fri 8 Noon; Mon-Thurs (Summer) 8-6:30
Restriction: Open to pub for ref only, Open to students, fac & staff, Pub use on premises

KERNERSVILLE

S NORTH AMERICAN YOUTH SPORT INSTITUTE*, News, Information & Resource Center, 4985 Oak Garden Dr, 27284-9520. (Mail add: PO Box 957, 27285), SAN 326-3479. Tel: 336-784-4926. FAX: 336-784-5546. Web Site: www.naysi.com. *Dir,* Dr Jack Hutslar; E-mail: jack@naysi.com
Founded 1979
Library Holdings: Bk Titles 1,000
Special Collections: Youth Sport Coll
Subject Interests: Educ, Fitness, Health, Recreation, Sports
Publications: Ask Jack; Beyond Xs & Os; KIDbits (Annual); Munchkin Tennis, NAYSI Activity Tip; NAYSI News FYI; NAYSI On-Line Course; Player Evaluation Forms; Sport Scene
Restriction: Open by appt only

KING

P KING PUBLIC LIBRARY*, 101 Pilot View Dr, 27021-9180. (Mail add: PO Box 629, 27021-0629), SAN 312-8911. Tel: 336-983-3868. FAX: 336-983-0769. Web Site: www.nwrl.org. *Librn,* Ann Nichols; *Asst Librn,* Gretchen Parker
Library Holdings: Bk Vols 30,000; Per Subs 35
Automation Activity & Vendor Info: (Acquisitions) SirsiDynix; (Cataloging) SirsiDynix; (Circulation) SirsiDynix; (Course Reserve) SirsiDynix; (ILL) SirsiDynix; (Media Booking) SirsiDynix; (OPAC) SirsiDynix; (Serials) SirsiDynix
Open Mon-Thurs 9-8, Fri 9-6, Sat 10-3
Friends of the Library Group

KINGS MOUNTAIN

P MAUNEY MEMORIAL LIBRARY*, 100 S Piedmont Ave, 28086. SAN 312-892X. Tel: 704-739-2371. FAX: 704-734-4499. E-mail: info@mauneylibrary.org. *Dir,* Sharon Stack; Tel: 704-739-2371, Ext 1678, E-mail: sstack@mauneylibrary.org; *Ch,* Christy Conner; E-mail: chconner@mauneylibrary.org; *Circ Supvr,* Christina Martin; E-mail: charmon@mauneylibrary.org; Staff 8.12 (MLS 1, Non-MLS 7.12)
Founded 1936. Pop 12,000; Circ 74,374
Library Holdings: Bk Vols 58,000; Per Subs 45
Subject Interests: Local family hist
Automation Activity & Vendor Info: (Acquisitions) SirsiDynix; (Cataloging) SirsiDynix; (Circulation) SirsiDynix; (ILL) OCLC FirstSearch; (OPAC) SirsiDynix
Database Vendor: Baker & Taylor, OCLC WorldShare Interlibrary Loan
Wireless access
Function: Handicapped accessible, Homebound delivery serv, ILL available, Prog for children & young adult, Summer reading prog, Telephone ref
Partic in CLEVE-NET; NCIN

Open Mon & Tues 9-8, Wed & Thurs 9-6, Fri 9-5, Sat 9-1
Friends of the Library Group

KINSTON

C LENOIR COMMUNITY COLLEGE*, Learning Resources Center, 231 Hwy 58 S, 28504-6836. (Mail add: PO Box 188, 28502-0188), SAN 312-8954. Tel: 252-527-6223, Ext 507. FAX: 252-527-0192. E-mail: lrcinfo@lenoircc.edu. Web Site: www.lenoircc.edu/Library/index.htm. *Interim Dir, Libr Serv Coordr,* Carenado V Davis; Tel: 252-527-6223, Ext 504, E-mail: cdavis@lenoircc.edu; Staff 4.5 (MLS 1.5, Non-MLS 3)
Founded 1964. Fac 184
Library Holdings: Bk Titles 38,000; Bk Vols 50,000; Per Subs 300
Special Collections: Local eastern North Carolina
Subject Interests: Distance learning classroom, Genealogy, Local hist, Writing across the curric
Wireless access
Publications: Annual Report; Book Mark Schedules; Local History Brochure; LRC Handbook; Operations Report; Periodical Holdings Brochure
Partic in Community Colleges Libraries in North Carolina (CCLINC); North Carolina Community College System
Open Mon-Thurs (Winter) 7:45am-9pm, Fri 7:45-3; Mon-Thurs (Summer) 7:30am-9pm
Friends of the Library Group

P NEUSE REGIONAL LIBRARY*, Kinston-Lenoir County Public Library (Headquarters), 510 N Queen St, 28501. SAN 312-8962. Tel: 252-527-7066. Circulation Tel: 252-527-7066, Ext 120. Reference Tel: 252-527-7066, Ext 134. Administration Tel: 252-527-7066, Ext 130. FAX: 252-527-8220. Circulation FAX: 252-527-9235. E-mail: nrl@neuselibrary.org. Web Site: www.neuselibrary.org. *Dir,* Agnes W Ho; Tel: 252-527-7066, Ext 131, E-mail: aho@neuselibrary.org; *Ch Serv,* Amber Hargett; Tel: 252-527-7066, Ext 133, E-mail: ahargett@neuselibrary.org; *Circ,* Shannon Riggs; E-mail: sriggs@neuselibrary.org; *Ref Serv, Ad,* Beth Boone; Tel: 252-527-7066, Ext 122, E-mail: bboone@neuselibrary.org; Staff 10 (MLS 4, Non-MLS 6)
Founded 1962. Pop 90,915; Circ 339,864
Jul 2011-Jun 2012 Income (Main Library and Branch(s)) $2,211,947, State $326,079, City $194,000, Federal $19,955, County $966,893, Other $705,020. Mats Exp $183,532, Books $98,000, Per/Ser (Incl. Access Fees) $4,432, AV Mat $75,405, Electronic Ref Mat (Incl. Access Fees) $5,695. Sal $889,020 (Prof $678,000)
Library Holdings: AV Mats 6,599; CDs 243; DVDs 12,019; e-books 89; Electronic Media & Resources 71; Large Print Bks 4,109; Bk Vols 197,187; Per Subs 401; Videos 675
Special Collections: Eastern North Carolina Genealogy (Sybil Hyatt Coll); Foreign Language Coll; Henry Pearson Art Coll; Modern Fiction on Cassette and CD; North Carolina - Specialized in Eastern North Carolina; North Carolina Original Art Coll; Piranesi Art Print Coll
Automation Activity & Vendor Info: (Acquisitions) TLC (The Library Corporation); (Cataloging) TLC (The Library Corporation); (Circulation) TLC (The Library Corporation); (OPAC) TLC (The Library Corporation); (Serials) TLC (The Library Corporation)
Database Vendor: EBSCOhost, Gale Cengage Learning, Ingram Library Services, NC LIVE, OCLC WorldShare Interlibrary Loan, ProQuest, Sage, TLC (The Library Corporation)
Wireless access
Function: Adult bk club, After school storytime, Art exhibits, Bks on cassette, Bks on CD, CD-ROM, Children's prog, Computer training, Computers for patron use, Copy machines, e-mail & chat, Electronic databases & coll, Exhibits, Fax serv, Handicapped accessible, Holiday prog, ILL available, Instruction & testing, Music CDs, Newsp ref libr, Notary serv, Online cat, Orientations, Photocopying/Printing, Prog for adults, Prog for children & young adult, Pub access computers, Ref serv in person, Spoken cassettes & CDs, Spoken cassettes & DVDs, Story hour, Summer reading prog, Tax forms, Teen prog, Wheelchair accessible, Workshops
Publications: A Trip to the Library; African American Bibliography; Neuse Regional Library Upcoming Events (Monthly); Personnel Policies Manual; School Video Annotated Catalog; Security Guard Manual; Statistical Report (Quarterly)
Open Mon-Thurs 9-9, Fri & Sat 9-6, Sun 2-6
Friends of the Library Group
Branches: 7
COMFORT PUBLIC LIBRARY, 4889 Hwy 41 W, Trenton, 28585, SAN 320-5959. Tel: 910-324-5061. E-mail: comfort@neuselibrary.org. *Head of Libr,* Teffiney Maready
Pop 360
Library Holdings: Bk Vols 9,000
Open Tues & Thurs 2:30-7:30, Sat 11-3
GREENE COUNTY PUBLIC LIBRARY, 229 Kingold Blvd, Snow Hill, 28580, SAN 312-9985. Tel: 252-747-3437. FAX: 252-747-7489. E-mail: greeneco@neuselibrary.org. *Librn,* Laquita Davis
Open Mon-Thurs 9-9, Fri & Sat 9-6
Friends of the Library Group
LA GRANGE PUBLIC LIBRARY, 119 E Washington St, La Grange, 28551, SAN 312-8989. Tel: 252-566-3722. FAX: 252-566-9768. E-mail: lagrange@neuselibrary.org. *In Charge,* Laquita Davis
Special Collections: Law Books
Open Mon 9-8, Tues-Sat 9-6
Friends of the Library Group
MAYSVILLE PUBLIC LIBRARY, 605 Seventh St, Maysville, 28555. (Mail add: PO Box 205, Maysville, 28555), SAN 320-5924. Tel: 910-743-3796. FAX: 910-743-3796. E-mail: maysville@neuselibrary.org. *Libr Asst,* Donna Renee Portolese
Pop 900
Library Holdings: Bk Titles 1,000; Per Subs 24
Open Mon 2-8, Tues 10-6, Wed & Fri 1-6, Sat 10-2
PINK HILL PUBLIC LIBRARY, 114 W Broadway, Pink Hill, 28572, SAN 312-9470. Tel: 252-568-3631. FAX: 252-568-3631. E-mail: pinkhill@neuselibrary.org. *Librn,* Carmen Fernandez
Open Mon-Fri 9-6, Sat 9-5
Friends of the Library Group
POLLOCKSVILLE PUBLIC LIBRARY, 415 Green Hill St, Pollocksville, 28573. (Mail add: PO Box 6, Pollocksville, 28573-0006), SAN 320-5932. Tel: 252-224-5011. FAX: 252-224-5011. E-mail: pollocksville@neuselibrary.org. *Libr Asst,* Kathy Fagan
Library Holdings: Bk Vols 3,800; Per Subs 12
Special Collections: North Carolina Coll
Open Tues 2-8, Wed 2-6, Thurs & Fri 11-6, Sat 10-2
TRENTON PUBLIC LIBRARY, 204 Lakeview Dr, Trenton, 28585-0610. (Mail add: PO Box 610, Trenton, 28585-0610), SAN 320-5940. Tel: 252-448-4261. FAX: 252-448-4261. E-mail: trenton@neuselibrary.org. *Libr Asst,* Carol Lee
Founded 1974. Pop 1,048
Library Holdings: Bk Vols 5,000; Per Subs 17
Open Mon & Thurs 2-7, Tues 9-6, Wed & Fri 2-6, Sat 10-2

KNIGHTDALE

S NATIONAL HUNTERS ASSOCIATION INC LIBRARY*, 590 Wendell Blvd, 27545-7886. (Mail add: PO Box 820, 27545-0820), SAN 375-1651. Tel: 919-365-7157. FAX: 919-366-2142. E-mail: nhadvs@bellsouth.net. Web Site: www.nationalhunters.com. *Pres,* D V Smith
Library Holdings: Bk Titles 1,000; Per Subs 100
Open Mon-Fri 9-5

LAURINBURG

C ST ANDREWS UNIVERSITY, DeTamble Library, 1700 Dogwood Mile, 28352. SAN 312-9012. Tel: 910-277-5049. Interlibrary Loan Service Tel: 910-277-5023. Automation Services Tel: 910-277-5047. Web Site: www.sapc.edu/detamble. *Libr Dir,* Mary McDonald; E-mail: mhm@sapc.edu; *Project Mgr,* Louise Mabry; Tel: 910-277-5044; *Tech Mgr,* Diane Hanke; E-mail: dch@sapc.edu; *Libr Res Coordr,* Thomas Waage; Tel: 910-277-5025, E-mail: waagetf@sapc.edu; Staff 3 (MLS 1, Non-MLS 2)
Founded 1896. Enrl 500; Fac 35; Highest Degree: Master
Library Holdings: Audiobooks 1,485; CDs 53; DVDs 1,078; e-books 171,902; e-journals 54,227; Microforms 14,960; Bk Titles 96,862; Bk Vols 105,000; Per Subs 79
Special Collections: University Archives. US Document Depository
Automation Activity & Vendor Info: (Acquisitions) Innovative Interfaces, Inc; (Cataloging) Innovative Interfaces, Inc; (Circulation) Innovative Interfaces, Inc; (Course Reserve) Innovative Interfaces, Inc; (ILL) Innovative Interfaces, Inc; (OPAC) Innovative Interfaces, Inc; (Serials) Innovative Interfaces, Inc
Wireless access
Partic in Carolina Consortium; Lyrasis; OCLC Online Computer Library Center, Inc
Open Mon-Thurs (Winter) 8:30am-11pm, Fri 8-5, Sun 2-11; Mon-Fri (Summer) 8:30-Noon

P SCOTLAND COUNTY MEMORIAL LIBRARY*, 312 W Church St, 28352-3720. SAN 354-933X. Tel: 910-276-0563. FAX: 910-276-4032. Web Site: www.scotlandcolibrary.com. *Dir,* Leon L Gyles; E-mail: lgyles@scotlandcounty.org; Staff 1 (MLS 1)
Founded 1941. Pop 35,600; Circ 135,119
Library Holdings: Large Print Bks 4,000; Bk Vols 65,000; Per Subs 40; Talking Bks 3,200
Special Collections: Heritage Room (North Carolina Coll)
Automation Activity & Vendor Info: (Acquisitions) TLC (The Library Corporation); (Cataloging) TLC (The Library Corporation); (Circulation) TLC (The Library Corporation); (Course Reserve) TLC (The Library Corporation); (OPAC) TLC (The Library Corporation)

Database Vendor: Gale Cengage Learning
Wireless access
Publications: Annual Report; Brochures
Special Services for the Deaf - Deaf publ
Special Services for the Blind - Audio mat; Bks on CD; Talking bks
Open Mon, Wed & Fri 9:30-6, Tues & Thurs 9:30-7, Sat 9-5
Branches: 1
WAGRAM BRANCH, PO Box 118, Wagram, 28396-0118, SAN 354-9399. Tel: 910-369-2966. *Librn,* Joy Davis
Founded 1976
Library Holdings: Bk Titles 5,500; Bk Vols 6,000
Open Mon, Wed & Fri 1:30-5:30
Friends of the Library Group
Bookmobiles: 1. Librn, Hedy Taylor

LENOIR

P CALDWELL COUNTY PUBLIC LIBRARY*, 120 Hospital Ave, 28645-4454. SAN 312-9039. Tel: 828-757-1270. Administration Tel: 828-757-1288. Automation Services Tel: 828-757-1274. FAX: 828-757-1413. Information Services FAX: 828-757-1484. Web Site: www.ccpl.us. *Dir,* Sarah Greene; E-mail: ssgreene@caldwellcounty.nc.org; *Ref Librn,* Forrest Tate; Staff 19 (MLS 5, Non-MLS 14)
Founded 1930. Pop 77,415; Circ 305,342
Library Holdings: CDs 1,500; DVDs 500; Bk Vols 84,735; Per Subs 399; Talking Bks 3,112; Videos 4,018
Subject Interests: Caldwell county hist
Automation Activity & Vendor Info: (Circulation) Evergreen; (OPAC) Evergreen
Wireless access
Open Mon, Wed & Fri 8:30-5:30, Tues & Thurs 8:30-8:30, Sat 9-4
Friends of the Library Group
Branches: 2
GRANITE FALLS PUBLIC, 24 S Main St, Granite Falls, 28630, SAN 312-8466. Tel: 828-396-7703. FAX: 828-396-2723. *Br Librn,* Susan Dudley; E-mail: sdudley@caldwellcountync.org
Library Holdings: CDs 300; DVDs 300; Large Print Bks 1,000; Bk Vols 21,426; Per Subs 92; Talking Bks 300
Open Mon, Tues, Thurs & Fri 8:30-5:30, Wed 11-1 & 2-5:30, Sat 9-12
Friends of the Library Group
HUDSON PUBLIC, 530 Central St, Hudson, 28638-1230, SAN 324-5802. Tel: 828-728-4207. FAX: 828-726-1325. *Br Librn,* Susan Dudley; E-mail: sdudley@caldwellcountync.org
Library Holdings: CDs 300; DVDs 300; Large Print Bks 1,000; Bk Vols 20,326; Talking Bks 300; Videos 300
Open Mon, Tues, Thurs & Fri 8:30-5:30, Wed 11-5:30, Sat 9-1
Friends of the Library Group

LEXINGTON

P DAVIDSON COUNTY PUBLIC LIBRARY SYSTEM, 602 S Main St, 27292. SAN 312-9055. Tel: 336-242-2040. Administration Tel: 336-242-2063. Information Services Tel: 336-242-2005. FAX: 336-248-4122. Administration FAX: 336-249-8161. Web Site: www.co.davidson.nc.us/library. *Dir,* Ruth Ann Copley; Tel: 336-242-2064, E-mail: ruth.copley@davidsoncountync.gov; *Asst Dir,* Sarah H Hudson; Tel: 336-474-2696, Fax: 336-472-4690, E-mail: sarah.hudson@davidsoncountync.gov; Staff 47 (MLS 7, Non MLS 40)
Founded 1928. Pop 158,158; Circ 514,056
Jul 2013-Jun 2014 Income $3,300,998, State $179,045, County $3,027,558, Other $94,395. Mats Exp $277,646, Books $202,248, Per/Ser (Incl. Access Fees) $22,999, Other Print Mats $11,550, AV Mat $20,872, Electronic Ref Mat (Incl. Access Fees) $19,977. Sal $1,586,461
Library Holdings: Audiobooks 30,446; e-books 55,171; e-journals 84; Bk Vols 307,740; Per Subs 3,627; Videos 22,543
Special Collections: Literature (Gerald R Johnson & Richard Walser Colls); North Carolina Coll, bks, microfilm. US Document Depository
Subject Interests: Genealogy, Local hist
Automation Activity & Vendor Info: (Acquisitions) Evergreen; (Cataloging) Evergreen; (Circulation) Evergreen; (ILL) OCLC Online; (OPAC) Evergreen; (Serials) EBSCO Online
Database Vendor: Baker & Taylor, Booklist Online, EBSCOhost, Gale Cengage Learning, Ingram Library Services, LearningExpress, NC LIVE, OCLC, OCLC FirstSearch, OCLC WorldShare Interlibrary Loan, Overdrive, Inc, ProQuest, ReferenceUSA, TumbleBookLibrary, Westlaw, WT Cox
Wireless access
Function: Adult literacy prog, AV serv, Govt ref serv, Handicapped accessible, Homebound delivery serv, ILL available, Magnifiers for reading, Newsp ref libr, Online searches, Photocopying/Printing, Prog for adults, Prog for children & young adult, Ref serv available, Referrals accepted, Summer reading prog, Telephone ref, Wheelchair accessible, Workshops
Special Services for the Deaf - Bks on deafness & sign lang; Closed caption videos; High interest/low vocabulary bks; Staff with knowledge of sign lang
Special Services for the Blind - BiFolkal kits; Bks on cassette; Bks on CD; Braille bks; Copier with enlargement capabilities; Large print bks; Magnifiers; Talking bks
Open Mon-Fri 8:30-5
Friends of the Library Group
Branches: 4
DENTON PUBLIC, 310 W Salisbury St, Denton, 27239-6944. (Mail add: PO Box 578, Denton, 27239-0578), SAN 312-8075. Tel: 336-859-2215. FAX: 336-859-5006. *Br Mgr,* Christina Adams; E-mail: christina.adams@davidsoncountync.gov; Staff 3 (Non-MLS 3)
Founded 1946
Open Mon & Thurs 9-8, Tues, Wed & Fri 9-5:30, Sat 10-2
NORTH DAVIDSON PUBLIC, 559 Critcher Dr, Welcome, 27374. (Mail add: PO Box 1749, Welcome, 27374-1749), SAN 313-0304. Tel: 336-242-2050. FAX: 336-731-3719. *Br Mgr,* Sheila Killebrew, Tel: 336-242-3051, E-mail: sheila.killebrew@davidsoncountync.gov; Staff 5 (MLS 1, Non-MLS 4)
Founded 1955
Open Mon 9:30-8, Tues-Thurs 9:30-7, Fri 9-5:30, Sat 10-2
Friends of the Library Group
THOMASVILLE PUBLIC, 14 Randolph St, Thomasville, 27360-4638, SAN 313-0142. Tel: 336-474-2690. FAX: 336-472-4690. *Asst Dir,* Sarah Hudson; E-mail: sarah.hudson@davidsoncountync.gov
Founded 1928
Special Collections: Gerald R Johnson Coll; History of Thomasville; Wint Capel
Open Mon-Thurs 9-8, Fri 9-5:30, Sat 9:30-3
Friends of the Library Group
WEST DAVIDSON PUBLIC, 246 Tyro School Rd, 27295-6006. Tel: 336-853-4800. FAX: 336-853-4803. *Br Mgr,* Jan Beck; E-mail: jan.beck@davidsoncountync.gov
Founded 2000
Open Mon & Thurs 9-8, Tues & Wed 9-6, Fri 9-5:30, Sat 10-2
Bookmobiles: 1. Librn, Donna Phelps. Bk titles 5,264

LILLINGTON

P HARNETT COUNTY PUBLIC LIBRARY*, 601 S Main St, 27546-6107. (Mail add: PO Box 1149, 27546-1149), SAN 354-9429. Tel: 910-893-3446. FAX: 910-893-3001. Web Site: www.harnett.org/library. *Dir,* Patrick Fitzgerald; E-mail: pfitzgerald@harnett.org; *Tech Serv Librn,* Angela McCauley; E-mail: amccauley@harnett.org; *Ref Serv,* Barbara MacLean; E-mail: bmaclean@harnett.org; Staff 9 (MLS 3, Non-MLS 6)
Founded 1941. Pop 101,737; Circ 337,529
Jul 2005-Jun 2006 Income $831,599. Mats Exp $108,669. Sal $552,074
Library Holdings: AV Mats 9,101; High Interest/Low Vocabulary Bk Vols 30; Bk Vols 200,000; Per Subs 412; Talking Bks 5,182
Special Collections: Photo Coll
Subject Interests: Cooking, Local hist
Automation Activity & Vendor Info: (Acquisitions) Infor Library & Information Solutions; (Cataloging) Infor Library & Information Solutions; (Circulation) Infor Library & Information Solutions; (OPAC) Infor Library & Information Solutions; (Serials) Infor Library & Information Solutions
Database Vendor: OCLC FirstSearch
Wireless access
Function: Homebound delivery serv
Partic in North Carolina Libraries for Virtual Education
Open Mon-Thurs 9-8, Sat 9-1
Friends of the Library Group
Branches: 5
ANDERSON CREEK PUBLIC, 914 Anderson Creek School Rd, Bunn Level, 28323. Tel: 910-814-4012. FAX: 910-814-0262. *Dir,* Carolyn Norris; E-mail: cnorris@harnett.org
Founded 1998
Open Tues-Thurs (Fall) 4-8, Sat 10-2; Mon-Sat (Summer) 10-2
Friends of the Library Group
ANGIER PUBLIC, 28 N Raleigh St, Angier, 27501-6073, SAN 354-9453. Tel: 919-639-4413. FAX: 919-639-2412. Web Site: www.angier.org/library. *Br Head,* Amanda Davis; E-mail: abdavis@angier.org
Library Holdings: Bk Vols 21,000
Open Mon, Wed & Fri 9-5, Tues & Thurs 9-6:30
Friends of the Library Group
COATS BRANCH, 243 S McKinley St, Coats, 27521, SAN 354-9488. Tel: 910-230-1944. E-mail: coatslibrary@harnett.org. ; Staff 1 (Non-MLS 1)
Library Holdings: Bk Vols 5,033
Friends of the Library Group
DUNN PUBLIC, 110 E Divine St, Dunn, 28334, SAN 312-8113. Tel: 910-892-2899. Administration Tel: 910-892-2560. FAX: 910-892-8385. Web Site: www.dunn-nc.org/library. *Dir,* Michael B Williams; E-mail: mwilliams@dunn-nc.org; Staff 4 (MLS 1, Non-MLS 3)
Founded 1921. Pop 24,908; Circ 66,484
Jul 2013-Jun 2014 Income $243,200. Mats Exp $38,500, Books $35,000, Per/Ser (Incl. Access Fees) $3,500. Sal $137,900

Library Holdings: Audiobooks 300; DVDs 800; Large Print Bks 1,650; Bk Vols 25,000; Per Subs 64
Function: Adult bk club, Bks on CD, Children's prog, Computers for patron use, Copy machines, Exhibits, Fax serv, Free DVD rentals, Online cat, Preschool reading prog, Printer for laptops & handheld devices, Prog for adults, Prog for children & young adult, Pub access computers, Ref serv available, Scanner, Story hour, Summer reading prog, Tax forms, Telephone ref
Open Mon & Wed 9-6, Tues 9-8, Thurs 11-8, Fri 9-5, Sat 9-1; Tues (Summer) 9-6, Thurs 11-6
Friends of the Library Group

ERWIN PUBLIC, 110 West F St, Erwin, 28339. (Mail add: PO Box 459, Erwin, 28339), SAN 354-9518. Tel: 910-897-5780. FAX: 910-897-4474. Web Site: www.erwin-nc.org/dept-library.cfm. *Librn,* Betsy L Pollard; E-mail: bpollard@harnett.org; *Asst Librn,* Heather Honeycutt; E-mail: honeycuttheather@yahoo.com
Founded 1973. Pop 4,697; Circ 59,342
Library Holdings: Bk Vols 8,400; Per Subs 15
Open Mon-Fri 8-5
Friends of the Library Group

LINCOLNTON

P LINCOLN COUNTY PUBLIC LIBRARY*, Charles R Jonas Library, 306 W Main St, 28092. SAN 312-9063. Tel: 704-735-8044. FAX: 704-732-9042. Web Site: www.mylincolnlibrary.org. *Dir,* Jennifer Sackett; Staff 16 (MLS 1, Non-MLS 15)
Founded 1925. Pop 78,265; Circ 329,072
Jul 2008-Jun 2009 Income (Main Library and Branch(s)) $919,022
Library Holdings: AV Mats 12,337; Bk Vols 121,121
Special Collections: Lincoln County Historical & Genealogical Coll
Automation Activity & Vendor Info: (Circulation) Innovative Interfaces, Inc; (OPAC) Innovative Interfaces, Inc; (Serials) Innovative Interfaces, Inc
Open Mon, Tues & Thurs 9-9, Wed 10-6, Fri & Sat 9-6
Friends of the Library Group
Branches: 2

FLORENCE SOULE SHANKLIN MEMORIAL, 7837 Fairfield Forest Rd, Denver, 28037, SAN 329-5885. Tel: 704-483-3589. FAX: 704-483-8317. *Br Mgr,* Pamela Sweezy; E-mail: psweezy@lincolncounty.org; Staff 4 (MLS 4)
Founded 1980. Circ 113,790
Open Mon 10-8, Tues, Thurs & Fri 9-6, Wed 10-6, Sat 10-2
Friends of the Library Group

WEST LINCOLN, 5545 W Hwy 27, Vale, 28168. Tel: 704-276-9946. FAX: 704-276-1243. *Br Mgr,* Helena Brittain; E-mail: hbrittain@lincolncounty.org; Staff 2 (Non-MLS 2)
Founded 2002. Circ 31,421
Open Mon 10-8, Tues-Fri 10-6, Sat 10-1
Friends of the Library Group
Bookmobiles: 1

LOUISBURG

P FRANKLIN COUNTY LIBRARY*, Louisburg Main Library, 906 N Main St, 27549-2199. SAN 354-9542. Tel: 919-496-2111. Interlibrary Loan Service Tel: 919-496-6764. FAX: 919-496-1339. Interlibrary Loan Service FAX: 919-497-5821. Web Site: www.fcnclibrary.org. *Dir,* Holt Kornegay; *Adult Serv, Ref Serv,* Scott Mumford; *Tech Serv,* Bill Morrison; *YA Serv, Youth Serv,* Betty Ball; Staff 16 (MLS 2, Non-MLS 14)
Founded 1937. Pop 50,000; Circ 21,932
Library Holdings: Bk Vols 105,000; Per Subs 183
Function: ILL available, Online searches, Photocopying/Printing, Prog for children & young adult, Ref serv available, Summer reading prog, Wheelchair accessible
Open Mon-Fri 10-7, Sat 10-5
Restriction: Open to pub for ref & circ; with some limitations
Friends of the Library Group
Branches: 3

BUNN BRANCH, 610 Main St, Bunn, 27508. (Mail add: PO Box 213, Bunn, 27508-0213), SAN 375-3336. Tel: 919-496-6764. FAX: 919-497-5821. *Br Coordr,* Alyce Kidd; E-mail: librarykidd@yahoo.com
Library Holdings: Bk Vols 5,000; Per Subs 20
Open Mon, Tues, Thurs & Fri 1-7, Sat 1-5

FRANKLINTON BRANCH, Nine W Mason St, Franklinton, 27525, SAN 354-9577. Tel: 919-494-2736. FAX: 919-494-2466. *Br Coordr,* Alyce Kidd; E-mail: librarykidd@yahoo.com
Library Holdings: Bk Vols 4,000; Per Subs 20
Open Mon-Fri 12-7

YOUNGSVILLE BRANCH, 218 US 1A Hwy S, Youngsville, 27596, SAN 354-9607. Tel: 919-556-1612. FAX: 919-556-9633. *Br Coordr,* Alyce Kidd; E-mail: librarykidd@yahoo.com
Open Mon-Fri 10-7, Sat 1-5
Friends of the Library Group
Bookmobiles: 1

J LOUISBURG COLLEGE*, Cecil W Robbins Library, 501 N Main St, 27549-7704. SAN 312-9071. Tel: 919-497-3269. Administration Tel: 919-497-3217. FAX: 919-496-5444. Web Site: www.louisburg.edu. *Head Librn,* Patricia G Hinton; E-mail: phinton@louisburg.edu; *Asst Librn,* Candace Jones; Tel: 919-497-3237, E-mail: cjones@louisburg.edu; *AV,* Linda Robertson; Tel: 919-497-3253, E-mail: lrobertson@louisburg.edu; *Cat, ILL,* Curtis Edgerton; E-mail: cedgerton@louisburg.edu; Staff 6 (MLS 3, Non-MLS 3)
Founded 1890. Enrl 690; Fac 40
Library Holdings: Bk Titles 51,000; Per Subs 55
Special Collections: Louisburg College & Town Archives, mixed
Subject Interests: Relig in Am
Automation Activity & Vendor Info: (Cataloging) TLC (The Library Corporation); (Circulation) TLC (The Library Corporation); (Course Reserve) TLC (The Library Corporation); (ILL) TLC (The Library Corporation); (Media Booking) TLC (The Library Corporation); (OPAC) TLC (The Library Corporation)
Wireless access
Partic in North Carolina Libraries for Virtual Education
Open Mon-Thurs 8:30am-10:30pm, Fri 8:30-4, Sun 6pm-10:30pm

LOWGAP

P LOWGAP PUBLIC LIBRARY*, 9070 W Pine St, 27024. SAN 376-6837. Tel: 336-352-3000. FAX: 336-352-3000. E-mail: lwg@nwrl.org. Web Site: www.nwrl.org/lwg.asp. *Librn,* Linda Hice
Library Holdings: Bk Vols 6,500; Per Subs 50
Automation Activity & Vendor Info: (Cataloging) SirsiDynix; (Circulation) SirsiDynix
Function: Bks on CD, Children's prog, Copy machines, Fax serv, ILL available
Mem of Northwestern Regional Library
Open Tues & Thurs 2:30-8
Friends of the Library Group

LUMBERTON

J ROBESON COMMUNITY COLLEGE LIBRARY*, 5160 Fayetteville Rd, 28360-2158. (Mail add: PO Box 1420, 28359), SAN 312-9098. Tel: 910-272-3700, Ext 3321. FAX: 910-618-5685. E-mail: library@robeson.edu. Web Site: robeson.edu. *Dir,* Maryellen O'Brien; E-mail: mclarke@robeson.edu; *Librn,* Margaret Honeycutt; E-mail: mhoneycutt@robeson.edu; *Evening Librn,* Shamella Cromartie; E-mail: scromartie@robeson.edu; Staff 3 (MLS 3)
Founded 1965. Enrl 2,100; Fac 50
Library Holdings: Bk Titles 18,000; Per Subs 112
Subject Interests: Vocational tech
Automation Activity & Vendor Info: (Acquisitions) SirsiDynix; (Cataloging) SirsiDynix; (Circulation) SirsiDynix; (Course Reserve) SirsiDynix; (ILL) SirsiDynix; (OPAC) SirsiDynix; (Serials) SirsiDynix
Partic in Cape Fear Health Sciences Information Consortium
Open Mon-Thurs 7:30am-8pm, Fri 7:30-3

P ROBESON COUNTY PUBLIC LIBRARY*, 101 N Chestnut St, 28358-5639. (Mail add: PO Box 988, 28359-0988), SAN 354-9631. Tel: 910-738-4859. FAX: 910-739-8321. Web Site: www.robesoncountylibrary.org. *Interim Dir, Youth Serv Librn,* Katie Huneycutt; E-mail: khuneycutt@robesoncountylibrary.org; *Dir,* Position Currently Open; *Tech Serv Librn,* Kelly Mecifi; E-mail: techserv@robesoncountylibrary.org; Staff 19 (MLS 3, Non-MLS 16)
Founded 1967. Pop 130,000; Circ 198,083
Library Holdings: AV Mats 10,429; Bk Titles 92,000; Bk Vols 142,846; Per Subs 129
Special Collections: Genealogy (Biggs Coll, Hodgin Coll, Rhodes Coll); Local History (McLean Coll)
Subject Interests: Indian mats
Automation Activity & Vendor Info: (Cataloging) Innovative Interfaces, Inc; (Circulation) Innovative Interfaces, Inc; (OPAC) Innovative Interfaces, Inc
Wireless access
Open Mon, Wed, Fri & Sat 9-6, Tues & Thurs 9-9
Friends of the Library Group
Branches: 6

HECTOR MACLEAN PUBLIC, 106 S Main St, Fairmont, 28340. (Mail add: PO Box 458, Fairmont, 28340-0458), SAN 354-9682. Tel: 910-628-9331. FAX: 910-628-9331. *Mgr,* Tony Hargett; Staff 1 (Non-MLS 1)
Library Holdings: Bk Titles 4,000
Open Mon 1-5, Tues 9-1, Wed 2-6, Thurs & Fri 1:30-5:30
Friends of the Library Group

ANNIE HUBBARD MCEACHERN PUBLIC, 221 W Broad St, Saint Pauls, 28384, SAN 312-9888. Tel: 910-865-4002. FAX: 910-865-4002. *Mgr,* Mary Jane Butler; Staff 2 (Non-MLS 2)
Pop 2,130; Circ 5,304

Library Holdings: Bk Vols 20,000; Per Subs 25
Open Mon-Wed 11-6, Thurs 12-5:30, Fri 9-12:30
MCMILLAN MEMORIAL LIBRARY, 205 E Second Ave, Red Springs, 28377, SAN 312-9675. Tel: 910-843-4205. *Librn,* Jacky Rentz
Founded 1964. Pop 5,000; Circ 12,000
Library Holdings: Bk Titles 13,000; Per Subs 24
Open Tues-Fri 2:30-6
GILBERT PATTERSON MEMORIAL, 210 N Florence St, Maxton, 28364, SAN 354-9666. Tel: 910-844-3884. FAX: 910-844-3884. *Mgr,* Pat Middleton; Staff 1 (Non-MLS 1)
Library Holdings: Bk Vols 6,500
Open Mon 12-8, Tues 2-8, Wed-Fri 12-6
Friends of the Library Group
PEMBROKE PUBLIC, 413 S Blaine St, Pembroke, 28372. (Mail add: PO Box 1295, Pembroke, 28372), SAN 373-1839. Tel: 910-521-1554. FAX: 910-521-1554. *Mgr,* Mattie Locklear; Staff 2 (Non-MLS 2)
Open Mon & Wed 9-12:30 & 1-5:30, Tues & Fri 1:30-5:30, Thurs 2-8
ROWLAND PUBLIC, 113 E Main St, Rowland, 28383, SAN 328-6770. *Mgr,* Lisa Matthews; Staff 1 (Non-MLS 1)
Open Mon 2-6, Tues & Wed 2:30-5:30, Thurs 9-6
Bookmobiles: 1

M SOUTHEASTERN REGIONAL MEDICAL CENTER*, J Irvin Biggs Information Resource Center, 300 W 27th St, 28358. (Mail add: PO Box 1408, 28358-1408), SAN 312-9101. Tel: 910-671-5046. FAX: 910-671-5337. *Dir,* Kathy McGinniss; E-mail: mcginn01@srmc.org
Founded 1953
Library Holdings: Bk Vols 1,345; Per Subs 92
Subject Interests: Med, Nursing, Surgery
Partic in Cape Fear Health Sciences Information Consortium; SC Health Info Network
Open Mon-Fri 8:30-5

MANTEO

G CAPE HATTERAS NATIONAL SEASHORE*, Technical Library, 1401 National Park Dr, 27954-9708. SAN 312-911X. Tel: 252-473-2111. FAX: 252-473-2595. Web Site: nps.gov/caha. *In Charge,* Jamie Lanier; Tel: 252-473-2111, Ext 153, E-mail: jamie_p_lanier@nps.gov
Founded 1955
Library Holdings: Bk Titles 4,200; Per Subs 10
Special Collections: Cape Hatteras National Seashore; Fort Raleigh NHS; Wright Brothers NMEM. Oral History; US Document Depository
Subject Interests: Hist, Natural hist of NC Outer Banks
Open Mon-Fri 9-4

P DARE COUNTY LIBRARY*, 700 N Hwy 64-264, 27954. (Mail add: PO Box 1000, 27954), SAN 354-9690. Tel: 252-473-2372. FAX: 252-473-6034. Web Site: www.youseemore.com/earl. *Dir,* Jonathan Wark; *Mgr,* Veronica Brickhouse; *Ch Serv,* Julia McPherson; Staff 2 (MLS 2)
Founded 1935. Pop 36,000; Circ 230,000
Library Holdings: Bk Titles 85,000; Per Subs 100
Special Collections: North Carolina & Dare County Maps
Automation Activity & Vendor Info: (Cataloging) TLC (The Library Corporation); (Circulation) TLC (The Library Corporation); (Course Reserve) TLC (The Library Corporation); (ILL) OCLC Connexion; (OPAC) TLC (The Library Corporation)
Database Vendor: EBSCOhost, OCLC WorldShare Interlibrary Loan, ProQuest
Wireless access
Mem of East Albemarle Regional Library
Open Mon & Thurs 10-7, Tues, Wed & Fri 10-5:30, Sat 10-4
Branches: 2
HATTERAS BRANCH, PO Box 309, Hatteras, 27943-0309, SAN 354-9720. Tel: 252-986-2385. FAX: 252-986-2952. *Br Mgr,* Helen Hudson
Open Tues, Thurs & Fri 9:30-5:30, Wed 1-7, Sat 9:30-12:30
KILL DEVIL HILLS BRANCH, 400 Mustian St, Kill Devil Hills, 27948, SAN 370-5994. Tel: 252-441-4331. FAX: 252-441-0608. *Br Mgr,* Kathy Lassiter; *Ref Serv,* Naomi Rhodes
Open Mon, Thurs & Fri 9-5:30, Tues & Wed 10-7, Sat 10-4

G NORTH CAROLINA AQUARIUM LIBRARY*, 374 Airport Rd, 27954-9485. (Mail add: PO Box 967, 27954-0967), SAN 325-7983. Tel: 252-473-3494. Toll Free Tel: 866-332-3475. FAX: 252-473-1980. E-mail: rimail@ncaquariums.com. Web Site: www.ncaquariums.com.
Founded 2000
Library Holdings: Bk Titles 1,200; Bk Vols 1,500; Per Subs 20
Subject Interests: Marine biol
Open Mon-Sun 9-5
Restriction: Open to pub for ref only

G NORTH CAROLINA OFFICE OF ARCHIVES & HISTORY*, Outer Banks History Center, One Festival Park Blvd, 27954. (Mail add: PO Box 250, 27954-0250), SAN 373-1138. Tel: 252-473-2655. FAX: 252-473-1483. E-mail: obhc@ncdcr.gov. Web Site: www.obhistorycenter.ncdcr.gov. *Archivist, Curator, Site Mgr,* KaeLi Schurr; E-mail: kaeli.schurr@ncdcr.gov; *Asst Curator, Cataloger, Librn,* Sarah Downing; E-mail: sarah.downing@ncdcr.gov; *Archivist,* Tama Creef; E-mail: tama.creef@ncdcr.gov; *Archivist,* Stuart Parks; E-mail: stuart.parks@ncdcr.gov; Staff 4 (MLS 1, Non-MLS 3)
Founded 1988
Library Holdings: Bk Vols 30,000; Per Subs 75
Special Collections: African American History; Civil War History; Colonial American History; Early Exploration; Lighthouses; Maritime History & Culture; US Life Saving Service, Shipwrecks; Wright Brothers. Oral History
Subject Interests: Civil War, Genealogy, Local hist, Maritime hist, Native Am, Oral hist, Tourism, Weather
Open Mon-Fri 9-5
Restriction: Non-circulating
Friends of the Library Group
Branches:
NORTH CAROLINA MARITIME MUSEUM, CHARLES R MCNEILL MARITIME LIBRARY, 315 Front St, Beaufort, 28516, SAN 374-9894. Tel: 252-728-7317. FAX: 252-728-2108. E-mail: maritime@ncmail.net. Web Site: www.ah.dcr.state.nc.us/sections/maritime/default.htm. *Actg Librn,* Frances Diane Hayden; E-mail: frances.hayden@ncdcr.gov
Founded 1985
Library Holdings: Bk Titles 4,000; Per Subs 27; Spec Interest Per Sub 26
Subject Interests: Boatbuilding, Maritime hist, Natural hist, NC hist
Function: Res libr
Open Mon-Fri 9-5, Sat 10-5, Sun 1-5
Restriction: Non-circulating

MARION

R FIRST BAPTIST CHURCH*, Witherspoon Memorial Library, 99 N Main St, 28752. SAN 312-9128. Tel: 828-652-6030. FAX: 828-659-9111. Web Site: www.fbcmarion.org. *Librn,* Kearson Al
Founded 1950
Library Holdings: Bk Vols 5,200
Subject Interests: Relig
Open Sun 10-12

P MCDOWELL COUNTY PUBLIC LIBRARY*, 90 W Court St, 28752. SAN 354-9755. Tel: 828-652-3858. FAX: 828-652-2098. E-mail: mcdowellcountypubliclibrary@yahoo.com. Web Site: www.mcdowellpubliclibrary.org. *Dir,* Elizabeth House; E-mail: ehouse@mcdowellpubliclibrary.org; *Ch Serv,* Allison Hollifield; Staff 13 (MLS 1, Non MLS 12)
Founded 1960. Pop 45,000
Library Holdings: Bk Titles 53,000; Bk Vols 109,546; Per Subs 252
Subject Interests: Genealogy, Local hist
Automation Activity & Vendor Info: (Acquisitions) Evergreen; (Cataloging) Evergreen; (Circulation) Evergreen; (OPAC) Evergreen
Wireless access
Open Mon, Wed & Fri 10-5:30, Tues & Thurs 10-7
Friends of the Library Group
Branches: 1
MARION DAVIS MEMORIAL BRANCH, 65 Mitchell St, Old Fort, 28762, SAN 354-978X. Tel: 828-668-7111. FAX: 828-668-4013. *Br Mgr,* Dee Daughtridge; E-mail: lddaughtridge@mcdowellpubliclibrary.org; Staff 2 (Non-MLS 2)
Founded 1960
Open Tues, Wed & Fri 10-5:30, Thurs 10-8, Sat 12:30-5:30
Friends of the Library Group

J MCDOWELL TECHNICAL COMMUNITY COLLEGE LIBRARY*, 54 College Dr, 28752-8728. SAN 312-9136. Tel: 828-652-6021. Circulation Tel: 828-652-0604. Administration Tel: 828-652-0697. FAX: 828-652-1014. Web Site: www.mcdowelltech.edu/newlib.html, www.mcdowelltech.libguides.com. *Dir,* Sharon Smith; E-mail: sharons@mcdowelltech.edu; Staff 3 (MLS 1, Non-MLS 2)
Founded 1964. Enrl 1,200; Fac 49; Highest Degree: Associate
Jul 2012-Jun 2013 Income $225,332. Mats Exp $31,623, Books $16,539, Per/Ser (Incl. Access Fees) $7,603, AV Mat $2,741, Electronic Ref Mat (Incl. Access Fees) $4,740. Sal $142,501 (Prof $66,792)
Library Holdings: AV Mats 8,572; CDs 23; DVDs 187; Bk Vols 28,789; Per Subs 121; Videos 1,011
Automation Activity & Vendor Info: (Cataloging) SirsiDynix; (Circulation) SirsiDynix; (Course Reserve) SirsiDynix; (ILL) SirsiDynix; (OPAC) SirsiDynix
Database Vendor: EBSCOhost, Facts on File, Gale Cengage Learning, OCLC FirstSearch, ProQuest
Wireless access
Publications: Handbook (Online only)

Partic in Community Colleges Libraries in North Carolina (CCLINC); OCLC Online Computer Library Center, Inc
Open Mon-Thurs 8am-9pm, Fri 8-4

MARS HILL

C MARS HILL UNIVERSITY, Renfro Library, 124 Cascade St, 28754. (Mail add: PO Box 220, 28754-0220), SAN 312-9144. Tel: 828-689-1244. Circulation Tel: 828-689-1518. Interlibrary Loan Service Tel: 828-689-1443. Reference Tel: 828-689-1468. Web Site: library.mhu.edu. *Dir, Libr Serv,* Bev Robertson; Tel: 828-689-1561, E-mail: brobertson@mhu.edu; *Cat Librn,* Jennifer Brown; Tel: 828-689-1448, E-mail: jabrown@mhu.edu; *Electronic Res & Ref Librn,* Rachel Mitchell; E-mail: rmitchell@mhu.edu; *Pub Serv/Ref Librn,* Daniel Koster; Tel: 828 689-1454, E-mail: dkoster@mhu.edu; *Ref & Instrul Serv Librn,* Shannon Lucas; Tel: 828-689-1391, E-mail: slucas@mhu.edu; *Acq Mgr,* Jill Nelson; Tel: 828-689-1452, E-mail: jnelson@mhu.edu; *Supvr, Pub Serv,* Louise Robinson; Tel: 828-689-1492, E-mail: lrobinsonl@mhu.edu; Staff 7 (MLS 5, Non-MLS 2)
Founded 1856. Enrl 1,100; Fac 88; Highest Degree: Master
Library Holdings: AV Mats 4,597; CDs 374; DVDs 108; e-books 109,800; e-journals 21,850; Microforms 178,000; Music Scores 4,628; Bk Titles 85,000; Bk Vols 92,700; Per Subs 170; Videos 400
Special Collections: Folk Music (Bascom Lamar Lunsford Southern Appalachia Music); Southern Appalachia (Southern Appalachia Photo Archives). Oral History
Subject Interests: Educ, Music
Automation Activity & Vendor Info: (Acquisitions) Innovative Interfaces, Inc - Millenium; (Cataloging) Innovative Interfaces, Inc - Millenium; (Circulation) Innovative Interfaces, Inc - Millenium; (Course Reserve) Innovative Interfaces, Inc - Millenium; (ILL) Innovative Interfaces, Inc - Millenium; (OPAC) Innovative Interfaces, Inc - Millenium; (Serials) Innovative Interfaces, Inc - Millenium
Database Vendor: ABC-CLIO, Alexander Street Press, American Psychological Association (APA), ARTstor, BioOne, Bowker, CountryWatch, CQ Press, EBSCOhost, Gale Cengage Learning, infoUSA, JSTOR, LearningExpress, NC LIVE, Newsbank-Readex, OCLC CAMIO, OCLC FirstSearch, OCLC WorldShare Interlibrary Loan, OVID Technologies, Oxford Online, ProQuest, ReferenceUSA, SerialsSolutions, Wiley InterScience
Wireless access
Partic in Appalachian Col Asn; Lyrasis; Mountain College Libr Network; NC Asn of Independent Cols & Univs
Open Mon-Thurs (Fall & Spring) 7:45am-10pm, Fri 7:45-4, Sat 12-4, Sun 2-10; Mon-Thurs (Summer) 8-5, Fri 8-4

MARSHALL

P MADISON COUNTY PUBLIC LIBRARY*, 1335 N Main St, 28753-6901. SAN 354-981X. Tel: 828-649-3741. FAX: 828-649-3504. Web Site: www.madisoncountylibrary.org. *Dir,* Sallie Klipp; E-mail: sklipp@MadisonCountyLibrary.org; Staff 8 (MLS 1, Non-MLS 7)
Founded 1955. Pop 19,976; Circ 114,611
Library Holdings: Bk Vols 60,156; Per Subs 63; Talking Bks 3,762
Automation Activity & Vendor Info: (Cataloging) TLC (The Library Corporation); (Circulation) TLC (The Library Corporation); (OPAC) TLC (The Library Corporation)
Wireless access
Function: Homebound delivery serv, ILL available, Photocopying/Printing, Prog for adults, Prog for children & young adult, Spoken cassettes & CDs, Summer reading prog, Wheelchair accessible
Open Mon 9-7, Tues-Thurs 9-6, Fri 9-5:30, Sat 9-1
Friends of the Library Group
Branches: 2
HOT SPRINGS BRANCH, 88 Bridge St, Hot Springs, 28743-9645. (Mail add: PO Box 175, Hot Springs, 28743-0175), SAN 354-9879. Tel: 828-622-3584. Administration Tel: 828-649-3741. FAX: 828-622-3584. Administration FAX: 828-649-3504. *Librn,* Lisa Ledford; E-mail: lledford@madisoncountylibrary.org; Staff 1 (Non-MLS 1)
Library Holdings: AV Mats 201; CDs 90; DVDs 700; Large Print Bks 125; Bk Vols 5,464; Per Subs 20; Talking Bks 47; Videos 300
Database Vendor: TLC (The Library Corporation)
Open Mon 10-7, Tues & Thurs 10-6, Wed & Sat 10-2, Fri 10-5
Friends of the Library Group
MARS HILL BRANCH, 25 Dogwood St, Mars Hill, 28754-9783. (Mail add: PO Box 28, Mars Hill, 28754), SAN 354-9909. Tel: 828-689-5183. FAX: 828-689-5183. *Librn,* Ann Parks; Staff 1 (Non-MLS 1)
Library Holdings: AV Mats 999; Large Print Bks 1,615; Bk Vols 17,653; Per Subs 32; Talking Bks 290
Open Mon & Wed 10-6, Tues & Thurs 10-8, Fri 10-5:30, Sat 10-1
Friends of the Library Group

MAURY

S NORTH CAROLINA DEPARTMENT OF CORRECTION*, Eastern Correctional Institution Library, PO Box 215, 28554-0215. Tel: 252-747-8101, Ext 2186. FAX: 252-747-5697.
Library Holdings: Bk Vols 8,500
Automation Activity & Vendor Info: (Cataloging) Book Systems
Open Mon-Fri 8:30-4

MISENHEIMER

C PFEIFFER UNIVERSITY, G A Pfeiffer Library, 48380 US Hwy 52 N, 28109. (Mail add: PO Box 930, 28109-0930), SAN 312-9160. Tel: 704-463-3350. Interlibrary Loan Service Tel: 704-463-3353. Web Site: library.pfeiffer.edu. *Libr Dir, Ref & ILL Librn,* Lara B Little; E-mail: lara.little@pfeiffer.edu; *Archives Librn, Syst Adminr,* Jonathan C Hutchinson; Tel: 704-463-3361, E-mail: jonathan.hutchinson@pfeiffer.edu; *Acq, Coll Develop Librn,* Damion Miller; Tel: 704-463-3352, E-mail: damion.miller@pfeiffer.edu; *Coordr, Circ,* Cindy Newport; Tel: 704-463-3363, E-mail: cindy.newport@pfeiffer.edu; *Cat,* Jennifer Cease; Tel: 704-463-3351, E-mail: jennifer.cease@pfeiffer.edu; Staff 5 (MLS 4, Non-MLS 1)
Founded 1917. Enrl 1,500; Fac 70; Highest Degree: Master
Library Holdings: AV Mats 2,368; e-books 20,000; Electronic Media & Resources 60; Bk Vols 131,000; Per Subs 230
Special Collections: Pfeiffer University Archival Materials
Subject Interests: Am, Educ, English lit, Music, Relig studies
Automation Activity & Vendor Info: (Acquisitions) Innovative Interfaces, Inc; (Cataloging) Innovative Interfaces, Inc; (Circulation) Innovative Interfaces, Inc; (Course Reserve) Innovative Interfaces, Inc; (OPAC) Innovative Interfaces, Inc
Database Vendor: Alexander Street Press, BioOne, CQ Press, EBSCOhost, Gale Cengage Learning, Greenwood Publishing Group, Hoovers, JSTOR, LearningExpress, NC LIVE, OCLC WorldShare Interlibrary Loan, ProQuest, ReferenceUSA
Wireless access
Function: 24/7 Electronic res, Archival coll, Computers for patron use, Copy machines, Distance learning, eReaders, ILL available, Microfiche/film & reading machines, Music CDs, Photocopying/Printing
Partic in Lyrasis
Friends of the Library Group
Departmental Libraries:
PFEIFFER LIBRARY AT CHARLOTTE, 4701 Park Rd, Charlotte, 28209, SAN 375-4324. Tel: 704-945-7305. FAX: 704-521-8617. *Dir of Info Support Serv, Charlotte Campus,* Jeri Brentlinger; E-mail: jeri.brentlinger@pfeiffer.edu; *Evening Librn,* Linda Fidelle; Staff 1.75 (MLS 1.75)
Highest Degree: Master
Library Holdings: Bk Vols 12,000; Per Subs 35
Subject Interests: Acctg, Bus admin, Christian educ, Criminal justice, Health admin, Liberal arts, Marriage & family therapy, Organizational mgt
Automation Activity & Vendor Info: (Serials) Innovative Interfaces, Inc
Database Vendor: H W Wilson, OCLC FirstSearch
Open Mon-Thurs 2-10, Sat 10-2
Friends of the Library Group

MOCKSVILLE

P DAVIE COUNTY PUBLIC LIBRARY, 371 N Main St, 27028-2115. SAN 354-9933. Tel: 336-753-6030. FAX: 336-751-1370. Web Site: www.library.daviecounty.org. *Dir,* Jane McAllister; E-mail: jmcallister@daviecountync.gov; *Youth Serv,* Julie Whittaker; E-mail: jwhittaker@daviecountync.gov; Staff 4 (MLS 4)
Founded 1943. Pop 40,970; Circ 147,088
Jul 2009-Jun 2010 Income (Main Library and Branch(s)) $700,284, State $96,693, City $46,143, County $497,050, Other $60,398. Mats Exp $695,957, Books $85,806, Other Print Mats $17,170, AV Mat $17,170, Electronic Ref Mat (Incl. Access Fees) $5,820. Sal $383,829
Library Holdings: Audiobooks 3,908; DVDs 1,756; Large Print Bks 5,056; Bk Vols 69,271; Per Subs 116
Subject Interests: Local hist
Automation Activity & Vendor Info: (Cataloging) Evergreen; (Circulation) Evergreen; (OPAC) Evergreen
Database Vendor: NC LIVE
Wireless access
Publications: History of Davie County; The Historic Architecture of Davie County
Special Services for the Blind - Bks on cassette; Bks on CD; Large print bks; Low vision equip
Open Mon-Thurs 9-8:30, Fri 9-5:30, Sat 9-3, Sun 2-5
Friends of the Library Group

Branches: 1
COOLEEMEE BRANCH, 7796 NC Hwy 801 S, Cooleemee, 27014. (Mail add: PO Box 25, Cooleemee, 27014-0025). Tel: 336-284-2805. FAX: 336-284-2805. *Dir,* Ruth Hoyle; Tel: 336-751-2023, E-mail: ruth.hoyle@co.davie.nc.us; *Asst Dir,* Janie Neely
Automation Activity & Vendor Info: (OPAC) SIRSI-iBistro
Database Vendor: NC LIVE
Open Mon 12-6, Tues-Fri 10-12:30 & 1:30-5

MONROE

P UNION COUNTY PUBLIC LIBRARY*, 316 E Windsor St, 28112. SAN 354-9992. Tel: 704-283-8184. FAX: 704-282-0657. TDD: 704-225-8554. Web Site: www.union.lib.nc.us. *Dir,* Martie Smith; E-mail: msmith@union.lib.nc.us; *Asst Dir,* Nina Zanjani; E-mail: nzanjani@union.lib.nc.us; *Head, Automation,* Beverly Osborn; E-mail: bosborn@union.lib.nc.us; *Head, Ref,* Tim Speasl; E-mail: tspeasl@union.lib.nc.us; *Hist Coll Librn,* Patricia Poland; E-mail: ppoland@union.lib.nc.us; *Circ Mgr,* Rosanna Thompson; E-mail: rthompson@union.lib.nc.us; *Juv Serv Coordr,* Kacy Vega; E-mail: kvega@union.lib.nc.us; *Tech Serv Coordr,* Seth Ervin; E-mail: servin@union.lib.nc.us; *Reader Serv,* Shelley Fearn; E-mail: sfearn@union.lib.nc.us; Staff 64 (MLS 10, Non-MLS 54)
Founded 1930. Pop 138,928; Circ 646,976
Jul 2008-Jun 2009 Income (Main Library and Branch(s)) $4,224,189, State $274,585, County $3,765,629, Other $183,975. Mats Exp $453,289, Books $401,892, Other Print Mats $24,393, Electronic Ref Mat (Incl. Access Fees) $27,004. Sal $3,047,893
Library Holdings: Audiobooks 6,997; CDs 5,203; DVDs 5,868; e-books 116; Large Print Bks 6,130; Bk Vols 191,640; Per Subs 330; Videos 2,040
Subject Interests: Genealogy, Local hist
Automation Activity & Vendor Info: (Cataloging) TLC (The Library Corporation); (Circulation) TLC (The Library Corporation); (OPAC) TLC (The Library Corporation)
Database Vendor: EBSCOhost, Gale Cengage Learning, Newsbank, OCLC FirstSearch, TLC (The Library Corporation)
Wireless access
Function: Adult bk club, Bilingual assistance for Spanish patrons, Bks on CD, CD-ROM, Children's prog, Computer training, Computers for patron use, Copy machines, Electronic databases & coll, Family literacy, Fax serv, Free DVD rentals, Handicapped accessible, Music CDs, Online cat, Photocopying/Printing, Prog for adults, Prog for children & young adult, Pub access computers, Ref serv in person, Scanner, Story hour, Summer reading prog, Tax forms
Special Services for the Deaf - Bks on deafness & sign lang; High interest/low vocabulary bks; TDD equip; TTY equip
Special Services for the Blind - Assistive/Adapted tech devices, equip & products; Descriptive video serv (DVS); Home delivery serv; Large print bks; Talking bks
Open Mon-Thurs 10-7, Fri 10-6, Sat 1-5, Sun 2-5
Friends of the Library Group
Branches: 3
LOIS MORGAN EDWARDS MEMORIAL, 414 Hasty St, Marshville, 28103, SAN 355-0052. Tel: 704-624-2828. FAX: 704-624-2055. *Br Mgr,* Position Currently Open
Automation Activity & Vendor Info: (Acquisitions) TLC (The Library Corporation)
Database Vendor: Alexander Street Press, EBSCO - WebFeat, EBSCO Auto Repair Reference, EBSCO Information Services, Facts on File, Greenwood Publishing Group, H W Wilson, infoUSA, LearningExpress, NC LIVE, OCLC WorldShare Interlibrary Loan, ProQuest, ReferenceUSA, Wilson - Wilson Web
Open Mon & Tues 9-8, Wed & Thurs 9-7, Fri 9-6, Sat 9-5, Sun 2-5
Friends of the Library Group
UNION WEST REGIONAL, 123 Unionville-Indian Trail Rd, Indian Trail, 28079, SAN 355-0028. Tel: 704-821-7475. FAX: 704-821-4279. *Br Mgr,* Betsy Cullen; E-mail: bcullen@union.lib.nc.us
Database Vendor: Alexander Street Press, EBSCO - WebFeat, EBSCO Auto Repair Reference, EBSCO Information Services, Facts on File, ProQuest, ReferenceUSA, Wilson - Wilson Web
Open Mon & Tues 9-8, Wed & Thurs 9-7, Fri 9-6, Sat 9-5, Sun 2-5
Friends of the Library Group
WAXHAW BRANCH, 509 S Providence St, Waxhaw, 28173, SAN 355-0087. Tel: 704-843-3131. FAX: 704-843-5538. *Br Mgr,* Beth Myles; E-mail: bmyles@union.lib.nc.us
Database Vendor: Alexander Street Press, EBSCO - WebFeat, EBSCO Auto Repair Reference, EBSCO Information Services, Facts on File, Greenwood Publishing Group, infoUSA, NC LIVE, OCLC WorldShare Interlibrary Loan, ProQuest, ReferenceUSA, Wilson - Wilson Web
Open Mon & Thurs 9-8, Tues, Wed & Fri 9-6, Sat 9-5
Friends of the Library Group

MONTREAT

C MONTREAT COLLEGE, L Nelson Bell Library, 310 Gaither Circle, 28757. (Mail add: PO Box 1297, 28757-1297), SAN 312-9187. Tel: 828-669-8012, Ext 3504. FAX: 828-350-2083. Web Site: www.montreat.edu. *Dir,* Elizabeth Pearson; Tel: 828-669-8012, Ext 3502, E-mail: epearson@montreat.edu; *Dir, Pub Serv,* Martha Martin; Tel: 828-669-8012, Ext 3503, E-mail: mlmartin@montreat.edu; *IT Librn,* Nathan King; Tel: 828-669-8012, Ext 3508, E-mail: nking@montreat.edu; *Libr Serv Mgr,* Rebecca Shaw; Tel: 828-669-8012, Ext 3505, E-mail: shawrr@montreat.edu; Staff 4 (MLS 3, Non-MLS 1)
Founded 1898. Enrl 800; Fac 44; Highest Degree: Master
Library Holdings: AV Mats 7,612; CDs 150; DVDs 150; e-books 132,470; Electronic Media & Resources 40; Microforms 117,155; Bk Vols 79,000; Per Subs 26
Special Collections: College Archives; Crosby Adams Music Coll
Subject Interests: Bus, Clinical mental health counseling, Environ educ, Outdoor educ, Psychol, Theol studies
Automation Activity & Vendor Info: (Acquisitions) Innovative Interfaces, Inc; (Cataloging) OCLC Connexion; (Circulation) Innovative Interfaces, Inc - Millenium; (ILL) OCLC WorldShare Interlibrary Loan; (OPAC) Innovative Interfaces, Inc - Millenium
Database Vendor: ABC-CLIO, Alexander Street Press, American Chemical Society, American Psychological Association (APA), ARTstor, CQ Press, ebrary, EBSCOhost, Gale Cengage Learning, Innovative Interfaces, Inc, JSTOR, LearningExpress, LexisNexis, Modern Language Association, NC LIVE, OCLC WorldShare Interlibrary Loan, ProQuest, Springshare, LLC, Wiley
Wireless access
Function: Adult bk club, Copy machines
Publications: Friends (Newsletter)
Partic in Appalachian Col Asn; Carolina Consortium; Lyrasis; OCLC Online Computer Library Center, Inc
Open Mon-Thurs (Winter) 8am-Midnight, Fri 8-5, Sat 1-5, Sun 2-11; Mon-Fri (Summer) 8-5
Friends of the Library Group

MOORESVILLE

P MOORESVILLE PUBLIC LIBRARY*, 304 S Main St, 28115. SAN 312-9195. Tel: 704-664-2927. FAX: 704-660-3292. Web Site: www.ci.mooresville.nc.us/library. *Dir,* John Pritchard; E-mail: jpritchard@ci.mooresville.nc.us; *Syst Librn, Tech Serv,* Neal Martin; E-mail: nmartin@ci.mooresville.nc.us; *Circ,* Kim Parker; E-mail: kparker@ci.mooresville.nc.us; *Ref Serv,* Brenda Scoggins; E-mail: bscoggins@ci.mooresville.nc.us; *Youth Serv,* Snow Wildsmith; E-mail: swildsmith@ci.mooresville.nc.us; Staff 4 (MLS 4)
Founded 1894. Pop 26,000; Circ 220,000
Jul 2005-Jun 2006 Income $1,800,000, State $22,000, City $400,000, County $1,300,000, Other $78,000. Mats Exp $335,000, Books $250,000, AV Mat $85,000. Sal $650,000
Library Holdings: DVDs 1,300; Large Print Bks 2,000; Bk Vols 73,000; Per Subs 198; Talking Bks 1,228; Videos 3,500
Automation Activity & Vendor Info: (Acquisitions) SirsiDynix; (Cataloging) SirsiDynix; (Circulation) SirsiDynix; (OPAC) SirsiDynix
Wireless access
Open Mon-Thurs 9-9, Fri & Sat 9-6, Sun 2-6
Friends of the Library Group

MOREHEAD CITY

J CARTERET COMMUNITY COLLEGE LIBRARY*, 201 College Circle, 28557. SAN 312-9209. Tel: 252-222-6213. Interlibrary Loan Service Tel: 252-222-6194. Reference Tel: 252-222-6247. FAX: 252-222-6219. E-mail: library@carteret.edu. Web Site: www.carteret.edu/library.htm. *Dir,* Elizabeth Baker; Tel: 252-222-6216, E-mail: bakere@carteret.edu; *Ref Librn/Instrul Serv,* Eva Earles; Staff 6 (MLS 2, Non-MLS 4)
Founded 1965. Enrl 1,800; Fac 225; Highest Degree: Associate
Library Holdings: AV Mats 1,726; Bk Titles 19,000; Bk Vols 21,000; Per Subs 120; Talking Bks 430; Videos 1,100
Special Collections: Consumer Health Coll; Law Library; Spanish Coll
Publications: Staff, Faculty & Student Handbooks
Partic in OCLC Online Computer Library Center, Inc
Open Mon-Thurs 8am-9:30pm, Fri 8-5

MORGANTON

M BROUGHTON HOSPITAL*, Sarah D Merrill Patients' Library, 1000 S Sterling St, 28655. SAN 312-9217. Tel: 828-433-2435. FAX: 828-433-2097. Web Site: www.broughtonhospital.org. *Librn,* Tina Girgo
Library Holdings: Bk Vols 4,729; Per Subs 38
Subject Interests: Patient educ, Self improvement
Publications: Announcements of new materials

Branches:
JOHN S MCKEE JR MEMORIAL LIBRARY, 1000 S Sterling St, 28655, SAN 372-4948. Tel: 828-433-2303. FAX: 828-433-2097. *Librn,* Karen Gilliam; E-mail: karen.gilliam@ncmail.net
Library Holdings: Bk Vols 1,100; Per Subs 35
Database Vendor: OVID Technologies

P BURKE COUNTY PUBLIC LIBRARY*, 204 S King St, 28655-3535. SAN 312-9225. Tel: 828-437-5638. FAX: 828-433-1914. E-mail: library@bcpls.org. Web Site: www.bcpls.org. *Asst Dir,* Jim Wilson; Tel: 828-437-5638, Ext 219, E-mail: jwilson@bcpls.org; Staff 18 (MLS 3, Non-MLS 15)
Founded 1924. Pop 89,148; Circ 210,000
Library Holdings: Bk Vols 97,921; Per Subs 210
Special Collections: North Carolina History, bks, micro & VF. Oral History
Subject Interests: Art, Environ studies, Genealogy, Local hist
Database Vendor: SirsiDynix
Publications: Brochure on services
Special Services for the Deaf - TDD equip
Open Mon & Wed 9-8, Tues & Thurs 9-6, Fri 12-6, Sat 9-5
Friends of the Library Group
Branches: 2
C B HILDEBRAND PUBLIC, 201 S Center St, Hildebran, 28637. (Mail add: PO Box 643, Hildebran, 28637), SAN 378-1798. Tel: 828-397-3600. FAX: 828-397-3600. *Br Mgr,* Betty Riley
Founded 1997
Open Mon 3-8, Tues-Fri 10-5, Sat 10-2
Friends of the Library Group
VALDESE BRANCH, 213 St Germain Ave SE, Valdese, 28690-2846, SAN 321-9283. Tel: 828-874-2421. FAX: 828-874-1211. *Br Mgr,* Betty Riley; E-mail: briley@bcpls.org
Open Mon & Wed 9-6, Tues & Thurs 9-8, Fri 12-6, Sat 9-5
Friends of the Library Group
Bookmobiles: 1

NORTH CAROLINA DEPARTMENT OF CORRECTION
S FOOTHILLS CORRECTIONAL INSTITUTION LIBRARY*, 5150 Western Ave, 28655. Tel: 828-438-5585. FAX: 828-438-6281. *Librn,* LeeAnn McRary
Library Holdings: Bk Vols 5,500; Per Subs 24
Automation Activity & Vendor Info: (Cataloging) Brodart; (Circulation) Brodart
Open Mon-Fri 8-10:45 & 1-3:45
S WESTERN YOUTH INSTITUTION LIBRARY*, 5155 Western Ave, 28655-9696. (Mail add: PO Box 1439, 28680-1439), SAN 372-5464. Tel: 828-438-6037, Ext 270. FAX: 828-438-6076. *Librn,* Bill Smith
Founded 1971
Library Holdings: Bk Vols 13,000; Per Subs 161
Special Collections: NC DOC Educational Services Video Coll
Automation Activity & Vendor Info: (Cataloging) Follett Software; (Circulation) Follett Software
Special Services for the Deaf - Bks on deafness & sign lang; High interest/low vocabulary bks

SR PRESBYTERY OF WESTERN NORTH CAROLINA*, Resource Center, 114 Silver Creek Rd, 28655. SAN 375-202X. Tel: 828-438-4217. FAX: 828-437-8655. Web Site: www.presbyterywnc.org.
Library Holdings: Bk Vols 2,300
Open Mon-Fri 8-4:30

J WESTERN PIEDMONT COMMUNITY COLLEGE*, Phifer Learning Resources Center, 1001 Burkemont Ave, 28655-4504. SAN 312-9233. Tel: 828-448-6195. Administration Tel: 828-448-6036. FAX: 828-448-6173. E-mail: library@wpcc.edu. Web Site: www.wpcc.edu/academics.php?cat=88. *Admin Dir, Dean, Tech Serv Adminr,* Dr Daniel R Smith; E-mail: dsmith@wpcc.edu; *Acq Librn, Asst Dean, Coll Develop Librn,* Susan C Keller; Tel: 828-448-6037, E-mail: skeller@wpcc.edu; *Archivist, Ref & Instrul Serv Librn, Res Librn,* Nancy L Daniel; Tel: 828-448-3160, E-mail: ndaniel@wpcc.edu; *Circ Mgr, ILL, Learning Res Ctr Spec,* Ruth Ann Brisson; E-mail: rbrisson@wpcc.edu; *Ser & Archival Spec,* Carmen D Melinn; Tel: 828-448-6039, E-mail: cmelinn@wpcc.edu; Staff 5 (MLS 3, Non-MLS 2)
Founded 1966. Enrl 3,939; Fac 156; Highest Degree: Associate
Library Holdings: AV Mats 6,203; Bks on Deafness & Sign Lang 51; e-books 1,604; Bk Vols 42,105; Per Subs 167
Special Collections: Grace DiSanto Poetry Coll; Mark Twain (Dr Jean C Ervin Coll); Senator Sam J Ervin, Jr, Coll
Automation Activity & Vendor Info: (Cataloging) EOS International; (Circulation) EOS International; (ILL) OCLC; (OPAC) EOS International; (Serials) EOS International
Database Vendor: EBSCOhost, Faulkner Information Services, Gale Cengage Learning, McGraw-Hill, NC LIVE, Westlaw
Wireless access
Function: Art exhibits, Distance learning, Electronic databases & coll, Handicapped accessible, ILL available, Wheelchair accessible
Publications: Learning Resources (Annual report); Library & Media Services for Faculty & Staff Handbook; Periodical Holdings (Serials catalog); Videotape Collection Catalog
Partic in NC Info Hwy; North Carolina Community College System; Northwest AHEC Library Information Network
Special Services for the Deaf - Bks on deafness & sign lang
Open Mon-Thurs (Winter) 7:30am-9pm, Fri 7:30-5; Mon-Thurs (Summer) 7:30-7, Fri 7:30-5

MOUNT AIRY

P MOUNT AIRY PUBLIC LIBRARY*, 145 Rockford St, 27030-4759. SAN 312-9241. Tel: 336-789-5108. FAX: 336-786-5838. E-mail: mta@nwrl.org. Web Site: www.nwrl.org. *Librn,* Pat Gwyn; E-mail: pgwyn@nwrl.org; *Asst Librn,* Tommie Smith; E-mail: tsmith@nwrl.org; Staff 7 (Non-MLS 7)
Founded 1930
Library Holdings: Bk Vols 57,500; Per Subs 25
Automation Activity & Vendor Info: (Acquisitions) SirsiDynix; (Cataloging) SirsiDynix; (Circulation) SirsiDynix; (OPAC) SIRSI-iBistro
Wireless access
Mem of Northwestern Regional Library
Open Mon-Thurs 8:30-8, Fri 8:30-5, Sat 10-1
Friends of the Library Group

MOUNT OLIVE

C MOUNT OLIVE COLLEGE*, Moye Library, 634 Henderson St, 28365-1699. (Mail add: 644 Henderson St, 28365), SAN 312-9268. Tel: 919-658-7869. Toll Free Tel: 800-653-0854, Ext 1412. FAX: 919-658-8934. Web Site: www.moc.edu. *Dir, Libr Serv,* Pamela R Wood; Tel: 919-658-7753, E-mail: pwood@moc.edu; *Curator,* Gary Barefoot; Tel: 919-658-7869, Ext 1416, E-mail: gbarefoot@moc.edu; *Cat,* Cynthia D Hughes; Tel: 919-658-7869, Ext 1414, E-mail: chughes@moc.edu; *Circ,* Gwin L Cox; Tel: 919-658-7869, Ext 1413, E-mail: gwcox@moc.edu; *Ref,* Susan G Ryberg; Tel: 919-658-7869, Ext 1411, E-mail: sryberg@moc.edu; *Tech Serv,* Heather Braswell; E-mail: hbraswell@moc.edu; Staff 3 (MLS 3)
Founded 1951. Enrl 3,700; Highest Degree: Bachelor
Library Holdings: Bks on Deafness & Sign Lang 25; CDs 141; DVDs 161; e-books 11,056; Large Print Bks 17; Music Scores 34; Bk Titles 57,164; Bk Vols 66,375; Per Subs 3,755; Videos 345
Special Collections: Free Will Baptist History, bks, flm, micro, mss, pamphlets, clippings
Automation Activity & Vendor Info: (Cataloging) TLC (The Library Corporation); (Circulation) Mandarin Library Automation; (OPAC) Mandarin Library Automation
Partic in OCLC Online Computer Library Center, Inc
Open Mon-Thurs (Winter) 8am-10pm, Fri 8-4:30, Sat 10-2, Sun 6-10; Mon-Thurs (Summer) 8-8, Fri 8-4:30, Sat 10-2

MURFREESBORO

C CHOWAN UNIVERSITY, Whitaker Library, One University Pl, 27855. SAN 312-9276. Tel: 252-398-6212. FAX: 252-398-1301. E-mail: library@chowan.edu. Web Site: www.chowan.edu/lib. *Univ Librn,* Georgia E Williams; Tel: 252-398-6439, E-mail: willig@chowan.edu; *Assoc Dir,* Linda Hassell; Tel: 252-398-6293, E-mail: hassel@chowan.edu; *Acq,* William Metcalfe; Tel: 252-398-1194, E-mail: metcaw@chowan.edu; *Instruction Coordr, Ref Librn,* Sarah Bonner; Tel: 252-398-6533, E-mail: bonnes@chowan.edu; *Pub Serv,* Deborah Baugham; Tel: 252-398-6202, E-mail: baughd@chowan.edu; *Pub Serv,* Frances Cole; E-mail: frances@chowan.edu; Staff 6.5 (MLS 3, Non-MLS 3.5)
Founded 1848. Enrl 1,400; Highest Degree: Master
Special Collections: McDowell Coll of Archives & Antiquities (Chowan & local history); Oscar Creech Baptist Coll; Subject Specific Coll for Educ Students & Music Students Housed in Teacher Resource Center & Daniel Hall Music Media Center
Automation Activity & Vendor Info: (Acquisitions) Innovative Interfaces, Inc; (Cataloging) Innovative Interfaces, Inc; (Circulation) Innovative Interfaces, Inc; (Course Reserve) Innovative Interfaces, Inc; (ILL) Innovative Interfaces, Inc; (OPAC) Innovative Interfaces, Inc; (Serials) Innovative Interfaces, Inc
Database Vendor: American Psychological Association (APA), Annual Reviews, CredoReference, ebrary, EBSCO Discovery Service, EBSCOhost, Gale Cengage Learning, JSTOR, LexisNexis, NC LIVE, Project MUSE, ProQuest, ScienceDirect, WT Cox, YBP Library Services
Wireless access
Open Mon-Thurs 7:45am-11pm, Fri 7:45-4, Sat 10-4, Sun 2-11
Restriction: Open to pub for ref & circ; with some limitations
Friends of the Library Group

MURPHY

P MURPHY PUBLIC LIBRARY*, Nine Blumenthal St, 28906. SAN 312-9284. Tel: 828-837-2417. FAX: 828-837-6416. Web Site: nantahalalibrary.org. *Librn,* Jeffrey L Murphy; E-mail: jeffmurphy@hotmail.com; *Asst Librn, ILL,* Melissa Barker. Subject Specialists: *Genealogy,* Jeffrey L Murphy; Staff 6 (MLS 1, Non-MLS 5)
Founded 1919. Circ 161,172
Library Holdings: Bk Vols 24,132; Per Subs 92
Subject Interests: Genealogy
Automation Activity & Vendor Info: (Acquisitions) TLC (The Library Corporation); (Cataloging) TLC (The Library Corporation); (Circulation) TLC (The Library Corporation); (OPAC) TLC (The Library Corporation)
Mem of Nantahala Regional Library
Open Mon-Wed & Fri 9-6, Thurs 9-9, Sat 9-2
Friends of the Library Group

P NANTAHALA REGIONAL LIBRARY*, 11 Blumenthal St, 28906. SAN 312-9292. Tel: 828-837-2025. FAX: 828-837-6416. Web Site: www.nantahalalibrary.org. *Dir,* Marcia Joyner Clontz; Fax: 828-837-6406, E-mail: mclontz@nantahalalibrary.org; *Ch Serv,* Pamela Ashbrook; E-mail: pashbroo@nantahalalibrary.org; Staff 19 (MLS 5, Non-MLS 14)
Founded 1942. Pop 41,753; Circ 255,691
Library Holdings: Bk Vols 14,000; Per Subs 250
Special Collections: Cherokee Indian Coll
Database Vendor: EBSCOhost, OCLC FirstSearch, ProQuest
Function: ILL available, Photocopying/Printing, Prog for children & young adult, Summer reading prog
Member Libraries: Andrews Public Library; Graham County Public Library; Moss Memorial Library; Murphy Public Library
Partic in NC Online Libr Network; North Carolina Libraries for Virtual Education; OCLC Online Computer Library Center, Inc
Open Mon-Fri 8-4:30
Friends of the Library Group
Bookmobiles: 1

J TRI-COUNTY COMMUNITY COLLEGE*, Dr Carl D Dockery Library, 4600 E Hwy 64, 28906. SAN 312-9306. Tel: 828-835-4314, 828-837-6810. Administration Tel: 828-835-4288. FAX: 828-837-0028. E-mail: library@tricountycc.edu. Web Site: www.tricountycc.edu/library.php. *Dir,* Linda J Kressal; E-mail: lkressal@tricountycc.edu; Staff 2 (MLS 2)
Founded 1974. Enrl 1,193; Fac 60; Highest Degree: Associate
Library Holdings: Bk Titles 8,000; Per Subs 169
Automation Activity & Vendor Info: (Cataloging) SIRSI WorkFlows; (Circulation) SirsiDynix; (Course Reserve) SIRSI WorkFlows; (ILL) SIRSI WorkFlows; (OPAC) SIRSI-iLink; (Serials) SIRSI WorkFlows
Database Vendor: EBSCOhost, Facts on File, Medline, OCLC FirstSearch, OCLC WorldShare Interlibrary Loan
Wireless access
Function: Audio & video playback equip for onsite use, Bks on cassette, Bks on CD, CD ROM, Computers for patron use, Copy machines, Distance learning, Doc delivery serv, Electronic databases & coll, Music CDs, Online cat, Online searches, Orientations, Photocopying/Printing, Pub access computers, Ref & res, Ref serv available, Scanner, Spoken cassettes & CDs, Spoken cassettes & DVDs, VHS videos, Video lending libr, Web catalog
Partic in Community Colleges Libraries in North Carolina (CCLINC)
Open Mon-Thurs 8am-9pm, Fri 8-3
Restriction: Hospital employees & physicians only

NASHVILLE

P NASHVILLE PUBLIC LIBRARY*, Harold D Cooley Library, 114 W Church St, 27856. (Mail add: Drawer 987, 27856). Tel: 252-459-2106. FAX: 252-459-8819. Web Site: www.townofnashville.com/library.html. *Dir,* Kent Oliver; Staff 1 (MLS 1)
Founded 1942
Library Holdings: AV Mats 650; Bk Vols 28,000; Per Subs 57; Talking Bks 250
Automation Activity & Vendor Info: (Cataloging) TLC (The Library Corporation); (Circulation) TLC (The Library Corporation); (OPAC) TLC (The Library Corporation)
Database Vendor: World Book Online
Open Mon 9-8, Tues-Fri 9-6
Friends of the Library Group

NEW BERN

J CRAVEN COMMUNITY COLLEGE*, R C Godwin Memorial Library, 800 College Ct, 28562. SAN 312-9314. Tel: 252-638-7272. Interlibrary Loan Service Tel: 252-638-7276. FAX: 252-672-5091. E-mail: library@cravencc.edu. Web Site: www.cravencc.edu/library. *Dir,* Catherine Campbell; Tel: 252-638-7271, E-mail: campbelc@cravencc.edu; Staff 3 (MLS 3)
Founded 1966. Enrl 2,974; Fac 100; Highest Degree: Associate
Library Holdings: Bk Titles 28,150; Bk Vols 30,200; Per Subs 75
Automation Activity & Vendor Info: (Acquisitions) SirsiDynix; (Cataloging) SirsiDynix; (Circulation) SirsiDynix; (ILL) SirsiDynix
Database Vendor: ABC-CLIO, CredoReference, Gale Cengage Learning, NC LIVE, STAT!Ref (Teton Data Systems)
Wireless access
Partic in Community Colleges Libraries in North Carolina (CCLINC)
Open Mon-Thurs 8-7, Fri 8-1

P CRAVEN-PAMLICO-CARTERET REGIONAL LIBRARY SYSTEM*, 400 Johnson St, 28560. SAN 312-9322. Tel: 252-638-7800. FAX: 252-638-7817. Web Site: newbern.cpclib.org. *Dir,* Susan Simpson; E-mail: susansimpson@carteretcountylibrary.org; Staff 4 (MLS 4)
Founded 1962. Pop 163,753; Circ 598,496
Library Holdings: AV Mats 6,000; Bk Vols 260,000; Per Subs 200
Special Collections: Genealogy East North Carolina; North Carolina Coll
Automation Activity & Vendor Info: (Cataloging) Horizon; (Circulation) Horizon; (ILL) Horizon
Member Libraries: Carteret County Public Library; Cove City Public Library; Havelock-Craven County Public Library; New Bern-Craven County Public Library; Newport Public Library; Pamlico County Library; Vanceboro Public Library
Open Mon-Thurs 9-9, Fri & Sat 9-6, Sun (Oct-May) 2-6
Friends of the Library Group
Bookmobiles: 2

P NEW BERN-CRAVEN COUNTY PUBLIC LIBRARY*, 400 Johnson St, 28560-4098. SAN 312-9330. Tel: 252-638-7800. Reference Tel: 252-638-7807. FAX: 252-638-7817. Web Site: newbern.cpclib.org. *Head Librn,* Cassandra Hunsucker; E-mail: chunsucker@nbccpl.org; *Ref Librn,* Wendy L Rosen; *Spec Coll Librn,* Victor T Jones, Jr; Tel: 252-638-7808; *Circ Supvr,* Joan Robbins; *Ch Serv,* Pam Jenkins; Tel: 252-638-7815
Founded 1906. Pop 27,650; Circ 244,522
Library Holdings: Bk Vols 99,821; Per Subs 223
Special Collections: North Carolina Coll
Automation Activity & Vendor Info: (Cataloging) OCLC GovDoc; (Circulation) OCLC; (OPAC) OCLC WorldShare Interlibrary Loan
Database Vendor: Baker & Taylor, EBSCOhost, Gale Cengage Learning, NC LIVE, OCLC, OCLC WorldShare Interlibrary Loan, ProQuest
Wireless access
Function: Archival coll, Art exhibits, Bk club(s), Bks on cassette, Bks on CD, Children's prog, Computer training, Computers for patron use, Copy machines, Electronic databases & coll, Exhibits, Free DVD rentals, Handicapped accessible, ILL available, Magnifiers for reading, Mail & tel request accepted, Music CDs, Newsp ref libr, Notary serv, Online cat, Photocopying/Printing, Prog for adults, Prog for children & young adult, Pub access computers, Ref serv available, Ref serv in person, Spoken cassettes & CDs, Story hour, Summer reading prog, Tax forms, Teen prog, Telephone ref, VHS videos, Video lending libr, Web-catalog
Mem of Craven-Pamlico-Carteret Regional Library System
Special Services for the Deaf - Staff with knowledge of sign lang; TTY equip
Special Services for the Blind - Bks on cassette; Bks on CD; Large print bks; Magnifiers
Open Mon-Thurs 9-9, Fri & Sat 9-6, Sun (Fall-Spring) 2-6
Friends of the Library Group

S TRYON PALACE, Gertrude Carraway Research Library, 529 S Front St, 28562-5614. (Mail add: PO Box 1007, 28563-1007), SAN 325-8009. Tel: 252-639-3500, 252-639-3542. FAX: 252-514-4876. E-mail: info@tryonpalace.org. Web Site: www.tryonpalace.org. *Conserv Spec,* R Baker; E-mail: richard.baker@ncdcr.gov
Founded 1959
Library Holdings: Bk Titles 4,750
Subject Interests: Archit, Decorative art, Gardening, Mus studies, NC hist
Automation Activity & Vendor Info: (Cataloging) OCLC Connexion
Function: Archival coll, ILL available, Pub access computers, Wheelchair accessible
Open Mon-Fri 8-5
Restriction: Circulates for staff only

NEWLAND

P AVERY COUNTY MORRISON PUBLIC LIBRARY*, 150 Library Pl, 28657. (Mail add: PO Box 250, 28657), SAN 312-9349. Tel: 828-733-9393. FAX: 828-682-6277. E-mail: acpl@amyregionallibrary.org. Web Site: www.amyregionallibrary.org. *Head Librn,* Phyllis Burroughs; *Asst Librn,* Debbie Mclean
Pop 17,946
Library Holdings: Large Print Bks 500; Bk Vols 10,000; Per Subs 30; Talking Bks 300
Special Collections: Robert Morrison Reference Coll
Subject Interests: Genealogy, Local hist
Automation Activity & Vendor Info: (Cataloging) TLC (The Library Corporation); (Circulation) TLC (The Library Corporation)

Wireless access
Mem of Avery-Mitchell-Yancey Regional Library System
Open Mon & Tues 9-8, Wed-Fri 9-5, Sat 10-1

NEWPORT

P NEWPORT PUBLIC LIBRARY*, 210 Howard Blvd, 28570. (Mail add: PO Box 727, 28570), SAN 312-9357. Tel: 252-223-5108. FAX: 252-223-6116. *Librn,* Alice Chavez
Circ 10,621
Library Holdings: Bk Vols 15,000; Per Subs 21
Mem of Craven-Pamlico-Carteret Regional Library System
Open Mon-Thurs 9-8, Fri 9-6, Sat 9-4
Friends of the Library Group

NEWTON

S CATAWBA COUNTY HISTORICAL MUSEUM*, Library & Archives, 30 N College Ave, 28658. (Mail add: CCHA, PO Box 73, 28658-0073), SAN 312-9365. Tel: 828-465-0383. FAX: 828-465-9813. E-mail: cchamuseum@bellsouth.net. Web Site: www.catawbahistory.org. *Exec Dir,* Melinda Herzog; *Librn,* Marian Stearns; E-mail: cchamstearns@gmail.com
Founded 1954
Library Holdings: Bk Titles 4,713; Bk Vols 5,200
Special Collections: 19th Century Law (Shipp Coll) 1750-1885; Civil War (Long Island Coll), family papers; Clapp Family Letters; Col Cilley papers; Decorative Arts (Mrs Eaton Coll), 1920-1930 magazines. Oral History
Subject Interests: Family hist, Regional hist
Friends of the Library Group

P CATAWBA COUNTY LIBRARY*, 115 West C St, 28658. SAN 355-0117. Tel: 828-465-8664. FAX: 828-465-8983. Web Site: www.catawbacountync.gov/library/. *Dir,* Suzanne White; E-mail: Suzanne@catawbacountync.gov; *Asst Dir,* Siobhan Loendorf; Staff 9 (MLS 9)
Founded 1936. Pop 110,123; Circ 666,069
Jul 2006-Jun 2007 Income (Main Library and Branch(s)) $2,222,073, State $176,940, City $66,889, Federal $5,808, County $1,907,176. Mats Exp $394,387, Books $352,029, AV Mat $37,668, Electronic Ref Mat (Incl. Access Fees) $4,690. Sal $1,511,232
Library Holdings: Bk Vols 206,818; Per Subs 763; Talking Bks 11,893; Videos 12,652
Special Collections: State Document Depository
Publications: Newsletter
Open Mon-Thurs 9-8, Fri & Sat 9-6
Friends of the Library Group
Branches: 6
CLAREMONT BRANCH, 3288 E Main St, Claremont, 28610-1248. Tel: 828-459-9311. *Librn,* Brytani Fraser
Library Holdings: Bk Vols 8,813
Open Tues-Fri 12-6, Sat 9-2
Friends of the Library Group
CONOVER EXPRESS BRANCH, 101 First St E, Conover, 28613. (Mail add: PO Box 1299, Conover, 28613-1299). Tel: 828-466-5108. FAX: 828-466-5109. *Librn,* Brytani Fraser
Library Holdings: Bk Vols 6,000; Per Subs 20
Open Mon, Wed & Thurs 9-6, Tues 12-8, Sun 2-6
MAIDEN BRANCH, 11 S A Ave, Maiden, 28650, SAN 355-0133. Tel: 828-428-2712. FAX: 828-428-3845. *Librn,* Betty Jean Stinson; *YA Serv,* Keri Adams
Library Holdings: AV Mats 1,000; Large Print Bks 200; Bk Titles 15,000; Bk Vols 16,000; Per Subs 50
Open Tues 12-8, Wed-Fri 9-6, Sat 9-2
SAINT STEPHENS, 3225 Springs Rd, Hickory, 28601-9700, SAN 329-6490. Tel: 828-256-3030. FAX: 828-256-6029. *Librn,* Debbie Hosford
Library Holdings: AV Mats 6,522; Large Print Bks 8,000; Bk Vols 78,000; Per Subs 46
Open Mon & Tues 12-8, Wed, Fri & Sat 9-6, Thurs 9-8, Sun 2-6
SHERRILLS FORD BRANCH, 8456 Sherrills Ford Rd, Sherrills Ford, 28673, SAN 355-0141. Tel: 828-478-2729. FAX: 828-478-5837. *Librn,* Sandy Cooke
Library Holdings: Bk Titles 3,000
Open Tues 12-8, Wed 9-6, Sat 9-2
SOUTHWEST, West Over Plaza, 2944 Hwy 127 S, Hickory, 28602, SAN 376-9283. Tel: 828-294-2343. FAX: 828-294-2477. *Librn,* Glenda Ramsey
Library Holdings: AV Mats 3,000; Large Print Bks 300; Bk Vols 35,000; Per Subs 30
Open Mon & Tues 12-8, Wed & Fri 9-6, Thurs 9-8, Sat 9-2, Sun 2-6

NORTH WILKESBORO

P WILKES COUNTY PUBLIC LIBRARY*, 215 Tenth St, 28659. SAN 312-9381. Tel: 336-838-2818. FAX: 336-667-2638. Web Site: www.arlibrary.org. *Librn,* Jennifer Lee Murphy; *Circ Mgr,* Laurie Love; E-mail: llove@arlibrary.org; *Adult Serv,* Jordan Welborn; *Tech Serv,* Janet R Kilby; E-mail: jkilby@arlibrary.org; *Youth Serv,* Maria Parker; Staff 24 (MLS 4, Non-MLS 20)
Founded 1909. Pop 65,632; Circ 325,807
Library Holdings: CDs 4,931; DVDs 682; Large Print Bks 2,654; Bk Vols 99,254; Per Subs 110; Talking Bks 3,061; Videos 3,649
Special Collections: Spanish Language Coll
Subject Interests: Genealogy, Local hist
Automation Activity & Vendor Info: (Circulation) SirsiDynix
Database Vendor: SirsiDynix
Function: Handicapped accessible, Homebound delivery serv, ILL available, Online searches, Photocopying/Printing, Prog for children & young adult, Ref serv available, Summer reading prog, Telephone ref, Wheelchair accessible
Mem of Appalachian Regional Library
Special Services for the Blind - Computer with voice synthesizer for visually impaired persons
Open Mon-Thurs 9-8, Fri & Sat 9-5
Friends of the Library Group
Branches: 1
TRAPHILL BRANCH, 6938 Traphill Rd, Traphill, 28685. (Mail add: PO Box 113, Traphill, 28685). Tel: 336-957-2534. FAX: 336-957-2534. *Br Mgr,* Ola K Norman; E-mail: onorman@arlibrary.org; Staff 1 (Non-MLS 1)
Library Holdings: AV Mats 926; Bk Vols 8,275
Special Services for the Deaf - Closed caption videos
Special Services for the Blind - Audio mat; Bks on cassette; Bks on CD; Large print bks
Open Tues & Thurs 10-1 & 2-6, Sat 9-4:30
Friends of the Library Group
Bookmobiles: 2. Bkmobile Spec, Wesley Knight

OXFORD

P GRANVILLE COUNTY LIBRARY SYSTEM*, Richard H Thornton Library, 210 Main St, 27565-3321. (Mail add: PO Box 339, 27565), SAN 355-0176. Tel: 919-693-1121. FAX: 919-693-2244. Web Site: www.granville.lib.nc.us. *Dir,* Tresia Dodson; E-mail: tresia.dodson@granvillecounty.org; *Adult Serv,* Deana Cunningham; E-mail: deanacunningham@granvillecounty.org; *Ch Serv,* Margaret Duckworth; E-mail: margaret.duckworth@granvillecounty.org; Staff 19 (MLS 3, Non-MLS 16)
Founded 1935. Pop 51,852
Library Holdings: AV Mats 4,905; Bks on Deafness & Sign Lang 43; High Interest/Low Vocabulary Bk Vols 188; Large Print Bks 1,479; Bk Vols 71,716; Per Subs 267; Talking Bks 1,992; Videos 5,593
Special Collections: Granville County History; North Carolina History & Genealogy Coll
Automation Activity & Vendor Info: (Cataloging) SirsiDynix; (Circulation) SirsiDynix; (OPAC) SirsiDynix
Database Vendor: EBSCOhost, Gale Cengage Learning
Open Mon-Thurs 10-8, Fri & Sat 10-5
Friends of the Library Group
Branches: 3
BEREA BRANCH, 1211 Hwy 158, Berea, 27565. (Mail add: PO Box 339, 27565-0339), SAN 329-6326. Tel: 919-693-1231. FAX: 919-693-1231. *Br Mgr,* Margaret Adcock; Staff 1 (Non-MLS 1)
Open Mon-Fri 2:30-5:30
SOUTH, 1547 S Campus Dr, Creedmoor, 27522-7381, SAN 355-0230. Tel: 919-528-1752. FAX: 919-528-1752. *Br Mgr,* Kate Pearce; E-mail: kate.pearce@granvillecounty.org
Function: Handicapped accessible, ILL available, Photocopying/Printing, Prog for children & young adult, Summer reading prog, Wheelchair accessible
Open Mon-Thurs 9-8, Fri 9-3, Sat 9-1
STOVALL BRANCH, 101 Hwy 15, Stovall, 27582, SAN 355-0265. Tel: 919-693-5722. FAX: 919-693-5722. *Br Mgr,* Angelina Cromer; Staff 1 (Non-MLS 1)
Function: Photocopying/Printing, Summer reading prog
Open Mon-Thurs. 2-6:30
Friends of the Library Group

PEMBROKE

C UNIVERSITY OF NORTH CAROLINA AT PEMBROKE*, Mary Livermore Library, Faculty Row, 28372. (Mail add: PO Box 1510, 28372-1510), SAN 312-9438. Tel: 910-521-6516. FAX: 910-521-6547. Web Site: www.uncp.edu/library. *Dean, Libr Serv,* Elinor Foster; *Assoc Dean Coll Mgt,* Susan Whitt; *Asst Dean for Res Serv,* Anne Coleman; *Access Serv Librn,* June Power; *Cat Librn,* David W Young; *Coll Develop Librn,* Carl Danis; *Distance Educ & Outreach Librn,* Michael Alewine; *Govt Doc/Develop Librn,* Karen Orr Fritts; *Instrul Serv/Ref Librn,* Anthony Holdried; *Media Cat Serv Librn,* Rachel Holderied; *Ref Serv Librn,* Robert Arndt; *Coordr, Cat,* Jean Sexton; *Ser & Digital Operations Coordr,* Robert Wolf; Staff 13 (MLS 13)

Founded 1887. Enrl 6,661; Fac 436; Highest Degree: Master
Jul 2008-Jun 2009 Income $3,113,171. Mats Exp $1,607,148, Books $588,891, Per/Ser (Incl. Access Fees) $360,337, Micro $20,202, AV Mat $98,071, Electronic Ref Mat (Incl. Access Fees) $533,308, Presv $6,339. Sal $1,370,871 (Prof $737,367)
Library Holdings: AV Mats 8,774; e-books 59,858; Electronic Media & Resources 165; Bk Titles 376,901; Bk Vols 370,900; Per Subs 33,163
Special Collections: Lumbee Indian History Coll. State Document Depository; US Document Depository
Automation Activity & Vendor Info: (Acquisitions) Innovative Interfaces, Inc; (Cataloging) Innovative Interfaces, Inc; (Circulation) Innovative Interfaces, Inc; (Course Reserve) Innovative Interfaces, Inc; (ILL) OCLC; (OPAC) Innovative Interfaces, Inc; (Serials) Innovative Interfaces, Inc
Database Vendor: Innovative Interfaces, Inc, OCLC FirstSearch
Wireless access
Publications: Informational Handouts; Library Lines (Newsletter)
Partic in Cape Fear Health Sciences Information Consortium; Lyrasis; OCLC Online Computer Library Center, Inc
Open Mon-Thurs 7:30am-Midnight, Fri 7:30am-11pm, Sat 9am-11pm, Sun 2-Midnight
Friends of the Library Group

PILOT MOUNTAIN

P CHARLES H STONE MEMORIAL LIBRARY*, 319 W Main St, 27041. (Mail add: PO Box 10, 27041-0010), SAN 312-9446. Tel: 336-368-2370. FAX: 336-368-9587. Web Site: www.nwrl.org. *Librn,* Anna L Nichols; E-mail: annanichols@nwrl.org; *Asst Librn,* Sandra P Phillips; E-mail: sphillips@nwrl.org
Pop 6,000
Library Holdings: Bk Vols 70,000; Per Subs 75
Automation Activity & Vendor Info: (Acquisitions) SirsiDynix; (Cataloging) SirsiDynix; (Circulation) SirsiDynix; (Course Reserve) SirsiDynix; (ILL) SirsiDynix; (Media Booking) SirsiDynix; (OPAC) SirsiDynix; (Serials) SirsiDynix
Wireless access
Mem of Northwestern Regional Library
Partic in NW Regional Libr Syst
Open Mon 9-8, Tues-Thurs 8:30-5:30, Fri 12-5:30, Sat 9-1

PINEHURST

J SANDHILLS COMMUNITY COLLEGE*, Katharine L Boyd Library, 3395 Airport Rd, 28374. SAN 312-7605. Tel: 910-695-3819. FAX: 910-695-3947. E-mail: info@sandhills.edu. Web Site: www.sandhills.edu/lib/library0.html. *Dir, Learning Res,* Dr John W Stacey; Tel: 910-695-3820, E-mail: staceyj@sandhills.edu; *Librn,* Deborah Ashby; Tel: 910-695-3821, E-mail: ashbyd@sandhills.edu; *Librn,* Alice Wilkins; Tel: 910-695-3822, E-mail: wilkinsa@sandhills.edu; *Circ Supvr,* Brenda Quick; Tel: 910-695-3969, E-mail: quickb@sandhills.edu; *LRC Supvr,* Judy Hines; Tel: 910-695-3890, E-mail: hinesj@sandhills.edu; *Tech Serv Supvr,* Windie Barnes; Tel: 910-695-3818, E-mail: barnesw@sandhills.edu
Founded 1965. Enrl 4,000; Fac 123
Library Holdings: Bk Titles 78,000; Per Subs 358
Wireless access
Open Mon-Thurs (Fall & Spring) 7:45am-9pm, Fri 7:45-5, Sat 8:30-2:30; Mon-Thurs (Summer) 7:45am-8:30pm, Fri 7:45-5, Sat 8:30-1:30

PLYMOUTH

P PETTIGREW REGIONAL LIBRARY*, 201 E Third St, 27962. SAN 355-029X. Tel: 252-793-2875. FAX: 252-793-2818. E-mail: headquarters@pettigrewlibraries.org. Web Site: www.pettigrewlibraries.org. *Regional Dir,* Judi Bugniazet; E-mail: jbugniazet@pettigrewlibraries.org; Staff 26 (MLS 5, Non-MLS 21)
Founded 1955. Pop 44,184; Circ 187,172
Jul 2009-Jun 2010 Income $1,051,006, State $377,382, Federal $65,133, County $530,342, Locally Generated Income $78,149. Mats Exp $79,446, Books $69,700, Per/Ser (Incl. Access Fees) $8,761, Electronic Ref Mat (Incl. Access Fees) $985. Sal $585,630
Library Holdings: Audiobooks 5,029; Bk Vols 118,554; Per Subs 196; Videos 5,715
Subject Interests: Local hist
Automation Activity & Vendor Info: (Acquisitions) TLC (The Library Corporation); (Cataloging) TLC (The Library Corporation); (Circulation) TLC (The Library Corporation); (OPAC) TLC (The Library Corporation)
Database Vendor: NC LIVE, ProQuest
Wireless access
Function: Adult bk club, Adult literacy prog, AV serv, Bks on cassette, Bks on CD, Children's prog, Computers for patron use, Copy machines, E-Reserves, Electronic databases & coll, Fax serv, Free DVD rentals, Handicapped accessible, Holiday prog, Home delivery & serv to Sr ctr & nursing homes, Homebound delivery serv, ILL available, Music CDs, Notary serv, Online cat, Online ref, Outreach serv, Photocopying/Printing, Prog for adults, Prog for children & young adult, Pub access computers, Ref serv in person, Scanner, Senior outreach, Spoken cassettes & CDs, Spoken cassettes & DVDs, Story hour, Summer reading prog, Tax forms, Telephone ref, VHS videos, Web-catalog, Wheelchair accessible
Member Libraries: Perquimans County Library; Shepard-Pruden Memorial Library; Tyrrell County Public Library
Friends of the Library Group

P WASHINGTON COUNTY LIBRARY*, 201 E Third St, 27962. SAN 320-4081. Tel: 252-793-2113. FAX: 252-793-2818. E-mail: washington@pettigrewlibraries.org. Web Site: www.pettigrewlibraries.org. *Librn,* Amy O'Neal; Staff 1 (MLS 1)
Founded 1918. Pop 12,946; Circ 47,700
Library Holdings: Bk Vols 40,000; Per Subs 67
Special Collections: Local History Coll
Automation Activity & Vendor Info: (Acquisitions) TLC (The Library Corporation); (Cataloging) TLC (The Library Corporation); (Circulation) TLC (The Library Corporation); (ILL) TLC (The Library Corporation); (OPAC) TLC (The Library Corporation)
Partic in Metropolitan Library Service Agency
Open Mon-Thurs 10-7, Fri 10-5:30, Sat 10-1
Friends of the Library Group

POLKTON

J SOUTH PIEDMONT COMMUNITY COLLEGE*, Horne Library, Cyber Center, 680 Hwy 74 W, 28135. (Mail add: PO Box 126, 28135), SAN 354-4710. Tel: 704-272-5389. Administration Tel: 704-272-5300. FAX: 704-272-5384. E-mail: library@spcc.edu. Web Site: www.spcc.edu. *Dir,* Lynn Gambon; Tel: 704-290-5855, Fax: 704-290-5880; *Libr Tech,* Barbara Chewning; Tel: 704-272-5387, E-mail: bchewning@spcc.edu; *Ref Serv, Ad,* Christopher Meister. Subject Specialists: *Mus,* Christopher Meister; Staff 7 (MLS 4, Non-MLS 3)
Founded 1967. Enrl 1,893; Highest Degree: Associate
Library Holdings: Bk Titles 18,614; Per Subs 225
Special Collections: Civil War (Linn D Garibaldi Coll), bks, docs, pictures; Historical & Personal Memorabilia (D Garibaldi Coll), bks, docs, pictures; Survey Maps (Frank Clarke Coll)
Subject Interests: Early childhood, Law, Lit, Nursing, Relig, Sociol
Database Vendor: EBSCOhost, Gale Cengage Learning, OCLC FirstSearch, OVID Technologies, ProQuest, TLC (The Library Corporation)
Partic in Community Colleges Libraries in North Carolina (CCLINC); NC Dept of Commun Cols
Open Mon-Thurs (Winter) 8-7:30, Fri 8-3; Mon-Thurs (Summer) 8-5:30, Fri 8-3

Departmental Libraries:

CARPENTER LIBRARY, Technical Education Bldg, 4209 Old Charlotte Hwy, Monroe, 28110. Tel: 704-290-5851. FAX: 704-290-5880. *Libr Tech,* Marion Sabin
Library Holdings: Bk Vols 25,000
Open Mon-Thurs 8-7:30, Fri 8-3

RAEFORD

P HOKE COUNTY PUBLIC LIBRARY*, 334 N Main St, 28376. SAN 312-9500. Tel: 910-875-2502. FAX: 910-875-2207. Web Site: www.srls.info/hoke/hokeindex.html. *Dir,* Sheila Evans
Founded 1934. Pop 24,939; Circ 14,565
Library Holdings: Bk Titles 38,000; Bk Vols 40,000
Automation Activity & Vendor Info: (Cataloging) TLC (The Library Corporation); (Circulation) TLC (The Library Corporation)
Open Mon, Wed & Fri 9-6, Tues & Thurs 9-8, Sat 9-5

RALEIGH

C ECPI UNIVERSITY*, Raleigh Campus Library, 4101 Doie Cope Rd, 27613. Tel: 919-571-0057, Ext 210. FAX: 919-571-0780. Web Site: www.ecpi.edu. *Chief Librn,* Sojourna Cunningham; E-mail: Scunningham@ecpi.edu; Staff 3 (MLS 1, Non-MLS 2)
Founded 1990. Highest Degree: Associate
Library Holdings: AV Mats 160; Bk Vols 6,439; Per Subs 108
Automation Activity & Vendor Info: (Cataloging) Follett Software; (Circulation) Follett Software; (OPAC) Follett Software
Database Vendor: Gale Cengage Learning
Function: Photocopying/Printing
Open Mon-Thurs 7:30am-10pm, Fri 7:30-4:30

L HUNTON & WILLIAMS*, Law Library, One Bank of America Plaza, Ste 1400, 421 Fayetteville St, 27601. SAN 372-2538. Tel: 919-899-3000. FAX: 919-833-6352. Web Site: www.hunton.com. *In Charge,* Elizabeth Byerly; Staff 2 (MLS 1, Non-MLS 1)
Founded 1980
Library Holdings: Bk Vols 10,000; Per Subs 70
Database Vendor: LexisNexis, OCLC FirstSearch, Westlaw
Wireless access
Function: Res libr
Open Mon-Fri 9-6

C MEREDITH COLLEGE*, Carlyle Campbell Library, 3800 Hillsborough St, 27607-5298. SAN 312-9543. Tel: 919-760-8531. Circulation Tel: 919-760-8532. Interlibrary Loan Service Tel: 919-760-8446. Reference Tel: 919-760-8095. Automation Services Tel: 919-760-8381. FAX: 919-760-2830. E-mail: library@meredith.edu. Web Site: www.meredith.edu/library. *Dean of Libr,* Laura Davidson; E-mail: davidson@meredith.edu; *Head, Archives, Head, Tech Serv,* Ted Waller; E-mail: wallert@meredith.edu; *Head, Circ,* Donna Garner; E-mail: garnerd@meredith.edu; *Head, Media Serv,* John Kincheloe; Tel: 919-760-8457, E-mail: kincheloej@meredith.edu; *Head, Ref,* Susan Kincheloe McClintock; Tel: 919-760-8382, E-mail: mcclinto@meredith.edu; *ILL,* Dianne Andrews; E-mail: andrewsd@meredith.edu; Staff 8 (MLS 7, Non-MLS 1)
Founded 1899. Enrl 2,168; Fac 130; Highest Degree: Master
Jul 2009-Jun 2010 Income $1,370,000. Mats Exp $431,000. Sal $770,000 (Prof $463,400)
Library Holdings: Audiobooks 97; AV Mats 18,990; CDs 2,576; DVDs 2,601; e-books 119,885; e-journals 27,000; Microforms 5,496; Music Scores 8,849; Bk Titles 252,000; Per Subs 2,867; Videos 5,441
Special Collections: Clyde Edgerton Coll
Subject Interests: Educ, Music, Women's studies
Automation Activity & Vendor Info: (Acquisitions) Innovative Interfaces, Inc; (Cataloging) Innovative Interfaces, Inc; (Circulation) Innovative Interfaces, Inc; (Course Reserve) Innovative Interfaces, Inc; (OPAC) Innovative Interfaces, Inc; (Serials) Innovative Interfaces, Inc
Database Vendor: ABC-CLIO, Alexander Street Press, American Physical Society, American Psychological Association (APA), Backstage Library Works, BioOne, Booklist Online, Bowker, Cambridge Scientific Abstracts, Career Guidance Foundation, Cinahl, CQ Press, CRC Press/Taylor & Francis Group, CredoReference, ebrary, EBSCOhost, Emerald, Gale Cengage Learning, H W Wilson, infoUSA, Innovative Interfaces, Inc, IOP, ISI Web of Knowledge, JSTOR, LexisNexis, McGraw-Hill, Modern Language Association, NC LIVE, Newsbank, OCLC CAMIO, OCLC FirstSearch, OCLC WorldShare Interlibrary Loan, Oxford Online, Paratext, ProQuest, PubMed, ReferenceUSA, ScienceDirect, Springer-Verlag, STN International, Thomson - Web of Science, ValueLine, Westlaw, Wiley, Wiley InterScience, Wilson - Wilson Web, WT Cox
Wireless access
Publications: Friends of the Carlyle Campbell Library (Newsletter)
Partic in Carolina Consortium; Lyrasis
Open Mon-Thurs (Fall-Spring) 7:45am-Midnight, Fri 7:45-5, Sat 11-5, Sun 1-Midnight
Friends of the Library Group

S NEWS & OBSERVER PUBLISHING CO*, News Research Department Library, 215 S McDowell St, 27602. SAN 371-2664. Tel: 919-829-4580. Toll Free Tel: 800-365-6115. FAX: 919-829-8916. E-mail: research@nando.com. *Dir,* Teresa G Leonard; Tel: 919-829-4866, E-mail: tleonard@nando.com; Staff 10 (MLS 4, Non-MLS 6)
Founded 1964
Library Holdings: Bk Titles 4,000; Per Subs 50
Special Collections: Public Records Databases
Subject Interests: Journalism
Database Vendor: Dialog, Factiva.com, LexisNexis, Newsbank, ProQuest
Function: Newsp ref libr
Partic in News Bank
Restriction: Staff use only

G NORTH CAROLINA DEPARTMENT OF LABOR*, Charles H Livengood Jr Memorial Library, 111 Hillsborough St, Rm C510, 27603-1762. (Mail add: 1101 Mail Service Ctr, 27699-1101), SAN 322-7782. Tel: 919-807-2848, 919-807-2850. Toll Free Tel: 800-625-2267. FAX: 919-807-2849. E-mail: dol.library@labor.nc.gov. Web Site: www.nclabor.com. *Head Librn,* Nick J Vincelli; Staff 2 (MLS 1, Non-MLS 1)
Founded 1973
Library Holdings: AV Mats 1,000; Bk Vols 8,000; Per Subs 60
Special Collections: Labor Law (Charles H Livengood, Jr Coll), bks, arbitrations
Subject Interests: Labor law, Occupational law, Occupational safety
Automation Activity & Vendor Info: (Circulation) Ex Libris Group; (OPAC) Ex Libris Group
Partic in National Network of Libraries of Medicine
Open Mon-Fri 8-5

GL NORTH CAROLINA LEGISLATIVE LIBRARY*, 500 Legislative Office Bldg, 300 N Salisbury St, 27603-5925. SAN 321-0863. Tel: 919-733-9390. FAX: 919-715-5460. Web Site: www.ncleg.net/leglibrary. *Legis Librn,* Cathy L Martin; E-mail: cathy.martin@ncleg.net; *Ref Librn,* Jane W Basnight; E-mail: jane.basnight@ncleg.net; *Ref Librn,* Julia B Covington; E-mail: julia.covington@ncleg.net; *Tech Librn & Indexer,* Brian M Peck; E-mail: brian.peck@ncleg.net; *Boards Comn Asst,* Becky K R Cook; E-mail: becky.cook@ncleg.net; Staff 5.75 (MLS 5, Non-MLS 0.75)
Founded 1967
Library Holdings: Bk Vols 20,000
Special Collections: Legislation (Committee Notebooks); Legislative Reports; State & County History
Subject Interests: Hist, Law, Legislation
Partic in Lyrasis; North Carolina Information Network (NCIN)
Open Mon-Fri 8-5:30

G NORTH CAROLINA MUSEUM OF ART*, Art Reference Library, 2110 Blue Ridge Rd, 27607-6494. (Mail add: 4630 Mail Service Ctr, 27699-4630), SAN 312-956X. Tel: 919-664-6769, 919-664-6770. FAX: 919-733-8034. Web Site: ncartmuseum.org/collection/library. *Libr Dir,* Natalia J Lonchyna; E-mail: natalia.lonchyna@ncdcr.gov. Subject Specialists: *Fine arts,* Natalia J Lonchyna; Staff 1 (MLS 1)
Founded 1956
Library Holdings: Bk Titles 43,000; Bk Vols 44,500; Per Subs 90
Subject Interests: Decorative art, Fine arts
Automation Activity & Vendor Info: (Cataloging) Ex Libris Group; (OPAC) Ex Libris Group
Database Vendor: ARTstor, JSTOR, NC LIVE, Oxford Online, Wilson - Wilson Web
Wireless access
Function: Res libr
Partic in OCLC Online Computer Library Center, Inc
Open Tues-Fri 10-4
Restriction: Not a lending libr

P NORTH CAROLINA REGIONAL LIBRARY FOR THE BLIND & PHYSICALLY HANDICAPPED, 1841 Capital Blvd, 27635. SAN 312-9578. Tel: 919-733-4376. Toll Free Tel: 888-388-2460. FAX: 919-733-6910. TDD: 919-733-1462. E-mail: nclbph@ncdcr.gov. Web Site: statelibrary.dcr.state.nc.us/lbph/lbph.htm. *Regional Librn,* Carl Keehn; E-mail: carl.keehn@ncdcr.gov; *Asst Regional Librn,* Catherine Rubin; E-mail: catherine.rubin@ncdcr.gov; *Mat Mgt Librn,* Josh Berkov; E-mail: joshua.berkov@ncdcr.gov; *Outreach & Vols Serv Librn,* Gina Powell; E-mail: gina.powell@ncdcr.gov; *Syst & Digital Serv Librn,* Craig Hayward; E-mail: craig.hayward@ncdcr.gov; Staff 5 (MLS 5)
Founded 1959. Pop 12,000; Circ 499,000
Library Holdings: Bk Titles 80,000; Bk Vols 311,000
Subject Interests: NC
Publications: Newsletter, Braille, large type & tape (4 issues annually)
Special Services for the Deaf - TDD equip
Special Services for the Blind - Braille bks; Digital talking bk; Large print bks
Friends of the Library Group

S NORTH CAROLINA STATE MUSEUM OF NATURAL SCIENCES*, H H Brimley Memorial Library, 11 W Jones St, 27601-1029. SAN 312-9594. Tel: 919-733-7450, Ext 208. FAX: 919-715-2356. *Chief Librn,* Janet G Edgerton; E-mail: janet.edgerton@ncmail.net; *Asst Librn,* Margaret Cotrufo; Staff 2 (MLS 1, Non-MLS 1)
Founded 1941
Library Holdings: Bk Titles 10,000; Bk Vols 12,000; Per Subs 80
Subject Interests: Ecology, Environ studies, Natural hist, Paleontology, Sci educ, Systematics, Vertebrate zool
Automation Activity & Vendor Info: (Cataloging) Follett Software; (Circulation) Follett Software
Function: For res purposes
Partic in Lyrasis
Open Mon-Fri 9-5

C NORTH CAROLINA STATE UNIVERSITY LIBRARIES*, Two Broughton Dr, 27695. (Mail add: NC State University, Campus Box 7111, 27695-7111), SAN 355-0443. Tel: 919-515-7188. Circulation Tel: 919-515-3364. Interlibrary Loan Service Tel: 919-515-2116. Reference Tel: 919-515-2935. FAX: 919-515-3628. Information Services FAX: 919-515-8264. Web Site: www.lib.ncsu.edu. *Vice Provost & Dir,* Susan K Nutter; E-mail: susan_nutter@ncsu.edu; *Dep Dir,* Carolyn Argentati; E-mail: carolyn_argentati@ncsu.edu; *Assoc Dir, Coll & Scholarly Communication,* Gregory Raschke; E-mail: greg_raschke@ncsu.edu; *Assoc Dir, Digital Libr,* Kristin Antelman; E-mail: kristin_antelman@ncsu.edu; *Assoc Dir, Mat Mgt,* David Goldsmith; E-mail: david_goldsmith@ncsu.edu; *Head, Access & Delivery Serv,* Nancy Kress, E-mail: nancy_kress@ncsu.edu; *Head, Acq & Discovery,* Maria Collins; Tel: 919-515-3150, E-mail: maria_collins@ncsu.edu; *Head, Coll Mgt,* Annette Day; Tel: 919-515-3833, E-mail: annette_day@ncsu.edu; *Head, Digital Libr Initiatives,* Steven Morris; Tel: 919-515-1361, E-mail: steven_morris@ncsu.edu; *Head, Info Tech,* Maurice York; Tel: 919-515-2339, E-mail: maurice_york@ncsu.edu; *Head, Res & Info Serv,* Rob Rucker; E-mail: rob_rucker@ncsu.edu; *Head, Spec Coll,* Eli Brown; Tel: 919-515-2273, E-mail: eleanor_brown@ncsu.edu; Staff 229 (MLS 134, Non-MLS 95)
Founded 1887. Enrl 34,000; Fac 1,733; Highest Degree: Doctorate
Library Holdings: Bk Vols 4,500,000; Per Subs 66,000
Special Collections: Animal Welfare & Rights (Tom Regan Coll); Architecture & Design Coll; Entomology (Tippman & Metcalf Coll); NTIS

Research Reports, micro; Plant & Forestry Genetics & Genomics; Textiles Coll; United States Patent Coll. State Document Depository; US Document Depository
Subject Interests: Agr, Archit, Biol sci, Computer sci, Design, Eng, Math, Natural res, Phys sci, Soc sci, Statistics, Textiles, Veterinary med
Automation Activity & Vendor Info: (Acquisitions) SirsiDynix; (Cataloging) SirsiDynix; (OPAC) SirsiDynix
Wireless access
Publications: Annual Report; Focus
Partic in Association of Research Libraries (ARL); Association of Southeastern Research Libraries; Coop Raleigh Col; Digital Libr Fedn; Lyrasis
Friends of the Library Group

Departmental Libraries:

BURLINGTON TEXTILES LIBRARY, 4411 College of Textiles, Campus Box 8301, 27695-8301, SAN 355-0508. Tel: 919-515-3043. FAX: 919-515-3926. *Head of Libr,* Honora Eskridge; Tel: 919-515-6120, E-mail: honora_eskridge@ncsu.edu; Staff 5 (MLS 3, Non-MLS 2)
Library Holdings: Bk Vols 18,000; Per Subs 200
Special Collections: Harriss Fabrics & Speizman Hosiery
Subject Interests: Polymers, Textiles

COLLEGE OF EDUCATION MEDIA CENTER, 400 Poe Hall, Campus Box 7801, 27695-7801, SAN 366-0524. Tel: 919-515-3191. FAX: 919-515-7634. *Asst Dir,* Nathan Stevens; E-mail: nathan_stevens@ncsu.edu; Staff 3 (MLS 2, Non-MLS 1)
Library Holdings: Bk Vols 12,000; Per Subs 80
Special Collections: North Carolina State Adopted Textbooks; Standardized Test Library
Subject Interests: Middle sch, Psychol, Secondary educ
Publications: Information Brochure; Newsletter

CM KENAN VETERINARY MEDICAL LIBRARY, 1060 William Moore Dr, Campus Box 8401, 27607, SAN 355-0516. Tel: 919-513-6218. FAX: 919-513-6400. *Head of Libr,* Kristine Alpi; Tel: 919-513-6219, E-mail: kristine_alpi@ncsu.edu; Staff 4 (MLS 2, Non-MLS 2)
Library Holdings: Bk Vols 24,000
Subject Interests: Biochem, Biol, Med, Veterinary med
Partic in Triangle Research Libraries Network

HARRYE B LYONS DESIGN LIBRARY, 209 Brooks Hall, Campus Box 7701, 27695-7701, SAN 355-0532. Tel: 919-515-2207. FAX: 919-515-7330. Web Site: www.lib.ncsu.edu/design. *Head of Libr,* Karen DeWitt; Tel: 919-513-3860, E-mail: karen_dewitt@ncsu.edu; Staff 4 (MLS 2, Non-MLS 2)
Library Holdings: Bk Vols 30,000
Special Collections: Slide Coll, pamphlet file, product file
Subject Interests: Archit, Art, Graphic, Indust design, Landscape archit, Visual design

NATURAL RESOURCES LIBRARY, Jordan Hall, Rm 1102, 2800 Faucette Dr, Campus Box 7114, 27695-7114, SAN 355-0478. Tel: 919-515-2306. FAX: 919-515-3687. *Head of Libr,* Karen Ciccone; Tel: 919-515-3513, E-mail: karen_ciccone@ncsu.edu; Staff 3 (MLS 1, Non-MLS 2)
Library Holdings: Bk Vols 22,000; Per Subs 150
Subject Interests: Forestry, GIS, Natural res, Paper sci, Recreation, Tourism mgt, Wood sci
Publications: Newsletter (Monthly)

GL NORTH CAROLINA SUPREME COURT LIBRARY*, 500 Justice Bldg, Two E Morgan St, 27601-1428. SAN 312-9608. Tel: 919-831-5709. FAX: 919-831-5732. Web Site: www.aoc.state.nc.us/www/public/html/sc_library.htm. *Librn,* Thomas Davis; E-mail: tpd@sc.state.nc.us; *Asst Librn, Ref,* Barrett Fish; *Asst Librn, Tech Serv,* Jennifer McLean; E-mail: jlm@sc.nccourts.org; Staff 5 (MLS 3, Non-MLS 2)
Founded 1812
Library Holdings: Bk Vols 159,774; Per Subs 881
Special Collections: US Document Depository
Automation Activity & Vendor Info: (Cataloging) SirsiDynix; (OPAC) SirsiDynix; (Serials) SirsiDynix
Database Vendor: HeinOnline, LexisNexis, SirsiDynix, Westlaw
Wireless access
Open Mon-Fri 8:30-4:30
Restriction: Non-circulating to the pub

L PARKER, POE, ADAMS & BERNSTEIN, LLP, Law Library, PNC Plaza, 301 Fayetteville St, Ste 1400, 27601. SAN 372-2546. Tel: 919-828-0564. FAX: 919-834-4564. E-mail: info@parkerpoe.com. Web Site: www.parkerpoe.com. *Dir, Libr & Res Serv,* Lisa W Williams; E-mail: lisawilliams@parkerpoe.com
Founded 1990
Library Holdings: Bk Vols 9,000; Per Subs 39
Wireless access
Restriction: Not open to pub

S PROGRESS ENERGY CORP*, Corporate Library, 410 S Wilmington St, 27601-1849. (Mail add: PO Box 1551, 27602-1551), SAN 324-6450. Tel: 919-546-7573. FAX: 919-546-5365. *In Charge,* Richard Warren; Staff 2 (MLS 1, Non-MLS 1)
Founded 1908
Library Holdings: Bk Titles 20,000; Per Subs 40
Special Collections: EPRI Reports; Industrial Standards
Database Vendor: Factiva.com, LexisNexis
Open Mon-Fri 8-5

M REX HEALTHCARE LIBRARY*, 4420 Lake Boone Trail, 27607. SAN 312-9624. Tel: 919-784-3032. FAX: 919-784-1670. E-mail: library.administrator@rexhealth.com. Web Site: www.rexhealth.com/classes_and_resources/medical_library. *Managing Librn,* Mrs Deniz Ender; Staff 1 (MLS 1)
Library Holdings: AV Mats 100; e-books 50; e-journals 200; High Interest/Low Vocabulary Bk Vols 100; Bk Vols 1,500; Per Subs 200; Talking Bks 50
Subject Interests: Med, Nursing
Automation Activity & Vendor Info: (Acquisitions) EOS International; (Cataloging) EOS International; (Circulation) EOS International; (OPAC) EOS International; (Serials) EOS International
Wireless access
Partic in Retit
Special Services for the Blind - Talking bks
Restriction: Staff use only

C SAINT AUGUSTINE'S COLLEGE*, The Prezell R Robinson Library, 1315 Oakwood Ave, 27610-2298. SAN 312-9632. Tel: 919-516-4145. Automation Services Tel: 919 516-4148. FAX: 919-516-4758. *Interim Dir, Libr Serv,* Clevell S Roseboro, II; *Dir, Spec Coll & Info Tech,* Linda Simmons-Henry; E-mail: lshenry@st-aug.edu; *Pub Serv Librn, Syst Librn,* Sukamoy Dutta; *Cat Librn,* Greeta Dave; Staff 9 (MLS 4, Non-MLS 5)
Founded 1974. Enrl 1,600; Highest Degree: Master
Library Holdings: Bk Vols 100,000; Per Subs 200
Special Collections: Curriculum Materials; James Boyer; Prezell R Robinson Papers (Delany Coll); Saint Agnes Coll. Oral History
Subject Interests: African-Am hist, Econ, Ethnic studies, Music, Soc sci
Publications: Library newsletter
Partic in Coop Raleigh Col; NC Asn of Independent Cols & Univs
Open Mon-Thurs 8am-11pm, Fri 8-5, Sat 12-6, Sun 3-11
Friends of the Library Group

C SHAW UNIVERSITY, James E Cheek Learning Resources Center, 118 E South St, 27601. SAN 312-9659. Tel: 919-546-8407. Interlibrary Loan Service Tel: 919-546-8427. Reference Tel: 919-546-8391, 919-546-8450. Administration Tel: 919-582-3750. Toll Free Tel: 800-214-6683. FAX: 919-831-1161. Web Site: thelibrary@shawu.edu, www.shawu.edu. *Dir of Libr Serv,* Carolyn Peterson; E-mail: cpeterson@shawu.edu; *Circ Librn,* Lizzette Tapp; E-mail: ltapp@shawu.edu; *Curric Center Librn,* Wendi Mair; Tel: 919-546-8555, Fax: 919-546-8554, E-mail: wmair@shawu.edu; *Divinity Sch Librn,* Tom Clarke; Tel: 919-716-5518, E-mail: tclark@shawu.edu; *Ref Librn,* Jahala Simuel; E-mail: jsimuel@shawu.edu; *Cataloger,* Musette McKelvey; Tel: 919-546-8406, E-mail: mmckelvey@shawu.edu; *Circ Asst,* Velma Williams; Tel: 919-546-8438, E-mail: vwilliams@shawu.edu; *Libr Asst,* Michael Allen; Tel. 919-546-8526, E-mail: mallen@shawu.edu; *Libr Asst,* Ayana Knight; Tel: 919-582-4985, E-mail: aknight@shawu.edu; *Libr Asst,* Patricia Powell, Tel. 919-546-8324, E-mail: ppowell@shawu.edu; *Libr Asst,* Tanya Williams; E-mail: twilliams@shawu.edu; Staff 10 (MLS 5, Non-MLS 5)
Founded 1865. Enrl 2,300; Fac 120; Highest Degree: Master
Library Holdings: Bk Titles 94,000; Bk Vols 102,000; Per Subs 100
Special Collections: John Wilson Fleming African-American Coll; Mollie Huston Lee African-American Coll; Schomburg Microfilm Coll
Automation Activity & Vendor Info: (Cataloging) SirsiDynix; (Circulation) SirsiDynix; (OPAC) SirsiDynix
Function: Prof lending libr
Publications: Cheek CD & DVD Collection (Film catalog); Circulation Manual (Library handbook); Collection Development Policies Manual (Library handbook); Curriculum Materials Library Manual (Library handbook); Divinity School Library Manual (Library handbook); Library Annual Reports (Library statistics & report); Reference & Information Literacy Instruction Manual (Reference guide)
Partic in Coop Raleigh Col; NC Asn of Independent Cols & Univs
Special Services for the Deaf - Coll on deaf educ
Open Mon-Thurs 8am-11pm, Fri 8-5, Sat 10-6, Sun 3-11

P STATE LIBRARY OF NORTH CAROLINA*, 109 E Jones St, 27601. (Mail add: 4640 Mail Service Ctr, 27699-4640), SAN 355-0389. Tel: 919-807-7400. Reference Tel: 919-807-7450. FAX: 919-733-8748. Reference FAX: 919-733-5679. Web Site: statelibrary.ncdcr.gov. *State Librn,* Cal Shepard; *Asst State Librn,* Laura O'Donoghue; *Libr Develop Section Chief,* Jennifer Pratt; Tel: 919-807-7415, E-mail: jennifer.pratt@ncdcr.gov; *Libr Serv Section Chief,* Jan Reagan; Tel:

919-807-7443, E-mail: jan.reagan@ncdcr.gov; Staff 75.5 (MLS 37, Non-MLS 38.5)
Founded 1812
Library Holdings: AV Mats 1,000; Braille Volumes 11,318; Large Print Bks 23,187; Bk Vols 170,229; Per Subs 125; Talking Bks 312,955
Special Collections: State Document Depository; US Document Depository
Subject Interests: Demographics, Genealogy, N Caroliniana, Statistics
Automation Activity & Vendor Info: (Acquisitions) Ex Libris Group; (Cataloging) Ex Libris Group; (Circulation) Ex Libris Group; (ILL) OCLC; (OPAC) Ex Libris Group; (Serials) Ex Libris Group
Wireless access
Publications: Checklist of Official North Carolina State Publications; State Library Update
Partic in Lyrasis
Open Mon-Fri 8:30-5
Branches: 1
LIBRARY FOR THE BLIND & PHYSICALLY HANDICAPPED
See Separate Entry under North Carolina Regional Library for the Blind & Physically Handicapped

P WAKE COUNTY PUBLIC LIBRARY SYSTEM*, Library Administration Building, 4020 Carya Dr, 27610-2900. SAN 355-0567. Tel: 919-250-1200. Circulation Tel: 919-250-3972. Interlibrary Loan Service Tel: 919-250-1205, 919-250-1238. Reference Tel: 919-856-6868. Automation Services Tel: 919-250-1220, 919-250-1246. Circulation FAX: 919-250-1239. Administration FAX: 919-250-1209. Automation Services FAX: 919-250-1115. Web Site: www.wakegov.com/libraries. *Dir,* Michael Wasilick; Tel: 919-250-4532, E-mail: libraryadministration@wakegov.com; *Dep Dir,* Ann Burlingame; Tel: 919-212-7820; *Coll Develop Serv Mgr,* Betty Utley; Tel: 919-250-3972, E-mail: butley@wakegov.com; *IT Mgr,* Theresa Cummings; Tel: 919-250-1220, E-mail: theresa.cummings@wakegov.com; Staff 212.5 (MLS 105, Non-MLS 107.5)
Founded 1898. Pop 866,410; Circ 10,998,242
Jul 2008-Jun 2009 Income (Main Library and Branch(s)) $5,062,117, State $550,839, County $4,439,110, Other $72,168. Mats Exp $2,415,279, Books $2,185,279, Other Print Mats $130,000, Electronic Ref Mat (Incl. Access Fees) $100,000. Sal $12,177,007
Library Holdings: Bk Vols 1,714,645
Special Collections: African American (Mollie Houston Lee Coll), bks, clippings, fiche; North Carolina History Coll
Automation Activity & Vendor Info: (Acquisitions) SirsiDynix; (Cataloging) OCLC; (Circulation) SirsiDynix; (ILL) OCLC ILLiad; (OPAC) SirsiDynix
Database Vendor: Booksite, EBSCOhost, Facts on File, Gale Cengage Learning, Grolier Online, infoUSA, NC LIVE, OCLC FirstSearch, OCLC WorldShare Interlibrary Loan, ReferenceUSA
Wireless access
Friends of the Library Group
Branches: 20
ATHENS DRIVE COMMUNITY LIBRARY, 1420 Athens Dr, 27606, SAN 355-0605. Tel: 919-233-4000. FAX: 919-233-4082. *Br Mgr,* Kerri-Ann Ruthven; E-mail: Kerri-Ann.Ruthven@wakegov.com
Circ 109,302
Library Holdings: Bk Vols 46,848
Open Mon-Thurs 10-8, Fri 10-6, Sat 10-2
Friends of the Library Group
CAMERON VILLAGE REGIONAL LIBRARY, 1930 Clark Ave, 27605, SAN 355-0621. Tel: 919-856-6710. Circulation Tel: 919-856-6711. FAX: 919-856-6722. Circulation FAX: 919-856-6755. *Regional Libr Supvr,* Position Currently Open; *Lifelong Learning Mgr,* Susan Neilson; Tel: 919-856-6718, E-mail: susan.neilson@wakegov.com; *Reader Serv Mgr,* Jean Ells; Tel: 919-856-6727, E-mail: jells@wakegov.com; *Youth Serv Mgr,* Benjie Hester; Tel: 919-856-6725, E-mail: mhester@wakegov.com; Staff 24 (MLS 10, Non-MLS 14)
Founded 1974. Circ 1,051,833
Library Holdings: Bk Vols 176,724
Special Collections: North Carolina Coll
Open Mon-Thurs 9-9, Fri 10-6, Sat 10-5, Sun 1-5
Friends of the Library Group
CARY COMMUNITY LIBRARY, 310 S Academy St, Cary, 27511, SAN 355-0656. Tel: 919-460-3350. FAX: 919-460-3362. *Br Mgr,* Liz Bartlett; E-mail: lbartlett@wakegov.com; Staff 9 (MLS 2, Non-MLS 7)
Circ 809,933
Library Holdings: Bk Vols 108,303
Open Mon-Thurs 9-8, Fri 10-6, Sat 10-5
Friends of the Library Group
DURALEIGH ROAD COMMUNITY LIBRARY, 5800 Duraleigh Rd, 27612, SAN 372-4123. Tel: 919-881-1344. FAX: 919-881-1317. *Br Mgr,* Linda Cooper; Tel: 919-881-1318, E-mail: lcooper@wakegov.com; Staff 7 (MLS 2, Non-MLS 5)
Circ 531,473
Library Holdings: Bk Vols 70,272
Open Mon-Thurs 10-8, Fri 10-6, Sat 10-2
Friends of the Library Group
EAST REGIONAL LIBRARY, 946 Steeple Square Ct, Knightdale, 27545, SAN 355-0869. Tel: 919-217-5300. FAX: 919-217-5327. *Regional Libr Supvr,* Carol Laing; Tel: 919-217-5305, E-mail: carol.laing@wakegov.com; *Adult Serv Mgr,* Cathy Nowell; Tel: 919-217-5323, E-mail: cnowell@wakegov.com; *Youth Serv Mgr,* Judy Packer; Tel: 919-217-5316, E-mail: judy.packer@wakegov.com; Staff 16 (MLS 8, Non-MLS 8)
Circ 506,799
Library Holdings: Bk Vols 110,075
Open Mon-Thurs 9-9, Fri 10-6, Sat 10-5, Sun 1-5
Friends of the Library Group
EXPRESS LIBRARY FAYETTEVILLE STREET, Wake County Off Bldg, 334 Fayetteville St, 27602, SAN 376-9259. Tel: 919-856-6690. FAX: 919-856-6206. *Br Mgr,* Christie Starnes; Tel: 919-856-6898, E-mail: christie.starnes@wakegov.com; Staff 3 (MLS 2, Non-MLS 1)
Circ 16,473
Library Holdings: Bk Vols 5,016
Open Mon-Fri 8:30-5:30
FUQUAY-VARINA COMMUNITY LIBRARY, 133 S Fuquay Ave, Fuquay-Varina, 27526, SAN 355-0710. Tel: 919-557-2788. FAX: 919-557-2792. *Br Mgr,* Lucinda McConnell; Tel: 919-557-2793, E-mail: lmcconnell@wakegov.com; Staff 4 (MLS 1, Non-MLS 3)
Circ 360,753
Library Holdings: Bk Vols 47,534
Open Mon-Thurs 10-8, Fri 10-6, Sat 10-2
Friends of the Library Group
GREEN ROAD COMMUNITY LIBRARY, 4101 Green Rd, 27604, SAN 376-9267. Tel: 919-790-3200. FAX: 919-790-3250. *Br Mgr,* Travis Horton; Tel: 919-790-3242, E-mail: thorton@wakegov.com; Staff 7 (MLS 3, Non-MLS 4)
Circ 288,640
Library Holdings: Bk Vols 61,892
Open Mon-Thurs 9-8, Fri 10-6, Sat 10-5
Friends of the Library Group
RICHARD B HARRISON COMMUNITY LIBRARY, 1313 New Bern Ave, 27610, SAN 355-0834. Tel: 919-856-5720. FAX: 919-856-6943. *Br Mgr,* Wanda Cox-Bailey; Tel: 919-856-5724, E-mail: wcox-bailey@wakegov.com; Staff 5.5 (MLS 2, Non-MLS 3.5)
Circ 68,288
Library Holdings: Bk Vols 37,397
Special Collections: Black Literature (Mollie H Lee Coll)
Open Mon-Thurs 9-8, Fri 10-6, Sat 10-5
Friends of the Library Group
HOLLY SPRINGS COMMUNITY LIBRARY, 300 W Ballentine St, Holly Springs, 27540. Tel: 919-577-1660. FAX: 919-577-1671. *Br Mgr,* Elena Owens; Tel: 919-577-1665, E-mail: eowens@wakegov.com; Staff 8 (MLS 3, Non-MLS 5)
Circ 514,487
Library Holdings: Bk Vols 70,962
Open Mon-Thurs 9-8, Fri 10-6, Sat 10-5
Friends of the Library Group
LEESVILLE COMMUNITY LIBRARY, 5105 Country Trail, 27613. Tel: 919-571-6661. FAX: 919-571-6666. *Br Mgr,* Jean Fargo; Tel: 919-571-6665, E-mail: jean.fargo@wakegov.com; Staff 7.5 (MLS 3, Non-MLS 4.5)
Founded 2009
Library Holdings: Bk Vols 57,149
Open Mon-Thurs 9-8, Fri 10-6, Sat 10-5
Friends of the Library Group
NORTH REGIONAL LIBRARY, 7009 Harps Mill Rd, 27615, SAN 355-0893. Tel: 919-870-4000. FAX: 919-870-4007. *Regional Libr Supvr,* Robin Hemrick; Tel: 919-870-4021, E-mail: rhemrick@wakegov.com; *Adult Serv Mgr,* Kevin Bourque; Tel: 919-870-4022, E-mail: kevin.bourque@wakegov.com; *Youth Serv Mgr,* Sally Baron; Tel: 919-870-4020, E-mail: sbaron@wakegov.com; Staff 23 (MLS 10, Non-MLS 13)
Circ 1,690,651
Library Holdings: Bk Vols 207,137
Open Mon-Thurs 9-9, Fri 10-6, Sat 10-5, Sun 1-5
Friends of the Library Group
EVA H PERRY REGIONAL LIBRARY, 2100 Shepherd's Vineyard Dr, Apex, 27502, SAN 355 0591. Tel: 919-387-2100. FAX. 919-387-4320. *Regional Libr Supvr,* Christina Piscitello; Tel: 919-387-4305, E-mail: Christina.Piscitello@wakegov.com; *Lifelong Learning Mgr,* Mary McNabb-Graham; Tel: 919-387-4317, E-mail: mmcnabb@wakegov.com; *Readers' Serv Manager,* Elizabeth Caran; Tel: 919-387-4304, E-mail: elizabeth.caran@wakegov.com; *Youth Serv Mgr,* Honey Trippensee; Tel: 919-387-4311, E-mail: honey.trippensee@wakegov.com; Staff 20 (MLS 9, Non-MLS 11)
Founded 1996. Circ 1,496,036
Library Holdings: Bk Vols 178,679
Open Mon-Thurs 9-9, Fri 10-6, Sat 10-5, Sun 1-5
Friends of the Library Group

OLIVIA RANEY LOCAL HISTORY LIBRARY, 4016 Carya Dr, 27610, SAN 376-9275. Tel: 919-250-1196. FAX: 919-212-0476. *Br Mgr,* Karen-Marie Allen; Tel: 919-250-1229, E-mail: Karen.Allen@wakegov.com; Staff 3 (MLS 2, Non-MLS 1)
Circ 1,686
Library Holdings: Bk Vols 39,983
Subject Interests: Family hist, Local hist
Open Mon-Fri 10-6, Sat 10-2

SOUTHEAST REGIONAL LIBRARY, 908 Seventh Ave, Garner, 27529, SAN 329-6415. Tel: 919-662-2250. FAX: 919-662-2270. *Regional Libr Supvr,* Gail Harrell; Tel: 919-662-2255, E-mail: Gail.Harrell@wakegov.com; *Lifelong Learning Mgr,* Pat Rogers; Tel: 919-662-2264, E-mail: progers@wakegov.com; *Readers' Serv Manager,* Brandy Hamilton; Tel: 919-662-2269, E-mail: brandy.hamilton@wakegov.com; *Youth Serv Mgr,* Susan Adams; Tel: 919-662-2265, E-mail: sadams@wakegov.com; Staff 17 (MLS 8, Non-MLS 9)
Circ 726,007
Library Holdings: Bk Vols 126,526
Open Mon-Thurs 9-9, Fri 10-6, Sat 10-5, Sun 1-5
Friends of the Library Group

SOUTHGATE COMMUNITY LIBRARY, 1601-14 Cross Link Rd, 27610, SAN 355-0958. Tel: 919-856-6598. FAX: 919-856-6762. *Br Mgr,* Avis Jones; Tel: 919-856-6691, E-mail: Avis.Jones@wakegov.com; Staff 3.5 (MLS 2, Non-MLS 1.5)
Circ 48,047
Library Holdings: Bk Vols 22,671
Open Mon-Thurs 10-8, Fri 10-6, Sat 10-2
Friends of the Library Group

WAKE FOREST COMMUNITY LIBRARY, 400 E Holding Ave, Wake Forest, 27587, SAN 355-0982. Tel: 919-554-8498. FAX: 919-554-8499. *Br Mgr,* Yvonne T Allen; Tel: 919-554-3308, E-mail: yallen@wakegov.com; Staff 4 (MLS 2, Non-MLS 2)
Founded 1961. Circ 574,186
Library Holdings: Bk Vols 64,048
Open Mon-Thurs 10-8, Fri 10-6, Sat 10-2
Friends of the Library Group

WENDELL COMMUNITY LIBRARY, 207 S Hollybrook Rd, Wendell, 27591, SAN 355-1016. Tel: 919-365-2600. FAX: 919-365-2602. *Br Mgr,* Linda Wilkes; Tel: 919-365-2601, E-mail: Linda.Wilkes@wakegov.com; Staff 3 (MLS 1, Non-MLS 2)
Founded 1950. Circ 86,091
Library Holdings: Bk Vols 21,713
Open Mon-Thurs 10-8, Fri 10-6, Sat 10-2

WEST REGIONAL LIBRARY, 4000 Louis Stephens Dr, Cary, 27519. Tel: 919-463-8500, 919-463-8533. *Regional Libr Supvr,* Terri Luke; Tel: 919-463-8505, E-mail: tluke@wakegov.com; *Lifelong Learning Mgr,* Suzanne France; Tel: 919-463-8507, E-mail: suzanne.france@wakegov.com; *Readers' Serv Manager,* Kathryn Gundlach; Tel: 919-463-8506, E-mail: kathryn.gundlach@wakegov.com; *Youth Serv Mgr,* Bridget Daniel; Tel: 919-463-8524, E-mail: bdaniel@wakegov.com; Staff 24 (MLS 11, Non-MLS 13)
Circ 1,367,192
Library Holdings: Bk Vols 155,582
Open Mon-Thurs 9-9, Fri 10-6, Sat 10-5, Sun 1-5
Friends of the Library Group

ZEBULON COMMUNITY LIBRARY, 1000 Dogwood Ave, Zebulon, 27597, SAN 355-1040. Tel: 919-404-3610. FAX: 919-404-3619. *Br Mgr,* Suzanna O'Donnell; Tel: 919-404-3611, E-mail: suzanna.o'donnell@wakegov.com; Staff 3 (MLS 1, Non-MLS 2)
Circ 113,958
Library Holdings: Bk Vols 32,419
Open Mon-Thurs 10-8, Fri 10-6, Sat 10-2
Friends of the Library Group

Bookmobiles: 1. In Charge, Judy Packer

J WAKE TECHNICAL COMMUNITY COLLEGE*, Bruce I Howell Library, 9101 Fayetteville Rd, 27603-5696. SAN 312-9667. Tel: 919-866-5644. Reference Tel: 919-866-5643. FAX: 919-662-3575. Web Site: library.waketech.edu. *Dir, Libr Serv,* Jackie Case; Tel: 919-662-3607; *Circ,* Lorraine Krichko; E-mail: lpkrichk@waketech.edu; *Instrul Serv/Ref Librn,* Suvanida Duangudom; E-mail: sduangudom@waketech.edu; *Coll Develop Spec,* Pat Sexton; Tel: 919-866-5650, E-mail: phsexton@waketech.edu; *Ser,* Marilyn Carney; Tel: 919-866-5642, E-mail: mmcarney@waketech.edu; *Tech Serv,* Jim Gray; E-mail: jegray@waketech.edu; Staff 6 (MLS 6)
Founded 1962. Enrl 15,000; Highest Degree: Certificate
Library Holdings: AV Mats 5,254; CDs 750; DVDs 101; Bk Vols 68,902; Per Subs 299
Subject Interests: Arts, Bus, Health sci, Sciences, Vocational tech
Automation Activity & Vendor Info: (Acquisitions) ADLiB; (Cataloging) SirsiDynix; (Circulation) SirsiDynix; (ILL) SirsiDynix; (OPAC) SirsiDynix
Database Vendor: EBSCOhost, Gale Cengage Learning, JSTOR, ProQuest, ScienceDirect
Wireless access
Function: Distance learning, Doc delivery serv, Handicapped accessible, Online searches, Photocopying/Printing, Ref serv available, Telephone ref, Wheelchair accessible
Publications: Library Handbook
Partic in Community Colleges Libraries in North Carolina (CCLINC)
Special Services for the Deaf - TTY equip
Open Mon-Thurs 7:30am-9pm, Fri 7:30-5, Sat 9-1

Departmental Libraries:

HEALTH SCIENCES, 2901 Holston Lane, 27610-2092. Tel: 919-747-0002. *Health Sci Librn, Ser,* Marilyn Carney; Tel: 919-747-0003, E-mail: mmcarney@waketech.edu; *Ref Librn,* Burnette Bell; Tel: 919-747-0016, E-mail: blbell@waketech.edu; *Pub Serv Librn,* Kathleen Kessel; Tel: 919-747-0013, E-mail: kekessel@waketech.edu; *Circ,* Brittany Boynton; Staff 3 (MLS 3)
Library Holdings: AV Mats 1,850; DVDs 350; Bk Vols 9,965; Per Subs 97
Function: Health sci info serv
Open Mon-Thurs 7:30am-9pm, Fri 7:30-5, Sat 9-1

NORTHERN WAKE LIBRARY, 6600 Louisburg Rd, Bldg B, Rm 239, 27616. Tel: 919-532-5550. *Campus Librn,* Savanida Duangudom; Tel: 919-532-5553; *Evening Librn,* Jennifer Mincey; *Pub Serv Librn,* Anita Young; *Ref & Instruction Librn,* Julia Mielish; Staff 13.5 (MLS 7.75, Non-MLS 5.75)
Highest Degree: Associate
Library Holdings: e-books 24,000; Bk Titles 90,000; Per Subs 14
Automation Activity & Vendor Info: (Cataloging) SIRSI Unicorn; (Circulation) SIRSI Unicorn
Function: e-mail & chat, E-Reserves, Electronic databases & coll, Online cat, Online info literacy tutorials on the web & in blackboard, Online ref, Online searches, Photocopying/Printing, Pub access computers
Open Mon-Thurs 7:30am-9pm, Fri 7:30-5, Sat 9-1
Restriction: 24-hr pass syst for students only, Open to pub for ref & circ; with some limitations, Open to students, fac & staff

WESTERN WAKE LIBRARY, 3434 Kildaire Farms Rd, Cary, 27518-2277. Tel: 919-335-1029. *Librn,* Rachel Vidrine; E-mail: rbvidrine@waketech.edu; Staff 1 (MLS 1)
Founded 2006. Enrl 2,000; Highest Degree: Associate
Library Holdings: Bk Titles 3,000; Bk Vols 3,100
Special Collections: Curriculum Support
Automation Activity & Vendor Info: (Course Reserve) SirsiDynix
Database Vendor: NC LIVE
Function: Electronic databases & coll, Ref serv available
Publications: Wake Tech Libraries (Library handbook)
Open Mon-Thurs 8-4, Fri 8-1
Restriction: Open to students, fac & staff

C WILLIAM PEACE UNIVERSITY*, Lucy Cooper Finch Library, 15 E Peace St, 27604-1194. SAN 312-9616. Tel: 919-508-2302. Reference Tel: 919-508-2304. FAX: 919-508-2787. E-mail: library@peace.edu. Web Site: www.peace.edu/academics/library. *Dir,* Nathan Hellmers; Tel: 919-508-2303, E-mail: njhellmers@peace.edu; *Managing Librn, Tech Serv Librn,* Diane Jensen; Tel: 919-508-2305, E-mail: djensen@peace.edu; *Re/Ser Librn,* Paul King; E-mail: pfking@peace.edu; Staff 4 (MLS 4)
Founded 1856. Enrl 700; Fac 35; Highest Degree: Bachelor
Library Holdings: AV Mats 120; CDs 694; DVDs 327; e-books 100,000; e-journals 140,000, Microforms 525; Music Scores 760; Bk Titles 45,000; Bk Vols 49,000; Per Subs 42,000
Subject Interests: Liberal arts
Automation Activity & Vendor Info: (Acquisitions) Mandarin Library Automation; (Cataloging) Mandarin Library Automation; (Circulation) Mandarin Library Automation; (ILL) OCLC FirstSearch; (OPAC) Mandarin Library Automation
Database Vendor: Baker & Taylor, Brodart, EBSCOhost, JSTOR, LexisNexis, MITINET, Inc, NC LIVE, Newsbank, OCLC, OCLC ArticleFirst, OCLC FirstSearch, OCLC WorldShare Interlibrary Loan, ProQuest, WebClarity Software Inc, YBP Library Services
Wireless access
Function: Archival coll, Audio & video playback equip for onsite use, Computers for patron use, Copy machines, e-mail serv, Electronic databases & coll, Equip loans & repairs, Exhibits, Free DVD rentals, ILL available, Microfiche/film & reading machines, Online cat, Online ref, Online searches, Photocopying/Printing, Ref & res, Ref serv in person, Scanner
Partic in Coop Raleigh Col
Open Mon-Thurs 7:30am-11pm, Fri 7:30am-8pm, Sat 10-6, Sun 2-11
Restriction: Badge access after hrs, Borrowing privileges limited to fac & registered students, Borrowing requests are handled by ILL, Circ privileges for students & alumni only, Non-circulating to the pub

L WILLIAMS MULLEN LIBRARY*, 301 Fayetteville St, Ste 1700, 27601. (Mail add: PO Box 1000, 27601-1000), SAN 372-2341. Tel: 919-981-4038. FAX: 919-981-4300. *Librn,* Catherine V Lambe; E-mail: clambe@williamsmullen.com; Staff 1 (MLS 1)
Library Holdings: Bk Titles 3,000; Bk Vols 12,000; Per Subs 200

Subject Interests: Legal mat
Automation Activity & Vendor Info: (Cataloging) EOS International; (OPAC) EOS International; (Serials) EOS International
Database Vendor: EOS International, HeinOnline, LexisNexis, OCLC FirstSearch, Westlaw Business
Wireless access
Restriction: External users must contact libr, Not open to pub

L YOUNG, MOORE, HENDERSON, PA LIBRARY, 3101 Glenwood Ave, 27622. (Mail add: PO Box 31627, 27622), SAN 323-6862. Tel: 919-782-6860. FAX: 919-782-6753. *Librn,* Carolyn Scott; E-mail: cs@ymh.com; Staff 1 (MLS 1)
Library Holdings: Bk Vols 2,500; Per Subs 25
Subject Interests: Law
Restriction: Staff use only

RESEARCH TRIANGLE PARK

S AMERICAN ASSOCIATION OF TEXTILE CHEMISTS & COLORISTS LIBRARY*, One Davis Dr, 27709. (Mail add: PO Box 12215, 27709-2215), SAN 329-8353. Tel: 919-549-3534. FAX: 919-549-8933. Web Site: www.aatcc.org. *Adminr,* Tricia F Day; E-mail: dayt@aatcc.org
Library Holdings: Bk Vols 2,500; Per Subs 15
Restriction: Not a lending libr, Not open to pub, Open by appt only, Use of others with permission of librn

S BECTON, DICKINSON & CO*, Research Information Center, 21 Davis Dr, 27709. (Mail add: PO Box 12016, Durham, 27709-2016), SAN 312-9683. Tel: 919-597-6194. FAX: 919-597-6406. Web Site: www.bd.com. *Info Spec,* Sandra Morris; E-mail: smorris@bd.com
Founded 1973
Library Holdings: Bk Vols 850; Per Subs 55
Subject Interests: Applied physics, Immunology, Mat sci, Microbiology, Organic chem, Polymer chem
Automation Activity & Vendor Info: (Cataloging) SirsiDynix; (Circulation) SirsiDynix
Partic in Dialog Corp; National Network of Libraries of Medicine
Open Mon-Fri 8-5

G ENVIRONMENTAL PROTECTION AGENCY LIBRARY*, MD C267-01, 109 Alexander Dr, 27711. SAN 354-7507. Tel: 919-541-2777. FAX: 919-541-1405. Web Site: www.epa.gov/rtp/library. *Dir,* Tamika Barnes; *Asst Dir,* Susan Forbes; *Head, Tech Serv,* Thea Allen; Staff 8.5 (MLS 4, Non-MLS 4.5)
Library Holdings: e-journals 425; Bk Vols 18,000; Per Subs 400
Special Collections: APTIC File
Subject Interests: Air chem, Air pollution, Eng, Health effects of pollution
Publications: Check It Out (Newsletter)
Partic in Fedlink; OCLC Online Computer Library Center, Inc
Open Mon-Fri 9-3

G EPA-RTP LIBRARY, 109 T W Alexander Dr, Rm C261, 27711. SAN 312-9748. Tel: 919-541-2777. FAX: 919-685-3110. E-mail: library.rtp@epa.gov. Web Site: www2.epa.gov/libraries/research-triangle-park-library-services. *Librn,* Susan Forbes; E-mail: forbes.susan@epa.gov; Staff 5.5 (MLS 4, Non-MLS 1.5)
Library Holdings: Bk Vols 6,000; Per Subs 3,000
Subject Interests: Air pollution, Toxicology
Open Mon-Fri 9-3

S THE HAMNER INSTITUTES FOR HEALTH SCIENCES*, Golberg Library & Resource Center, Six Davis Dr, 27709. (Mail add: PO Box 12137, 27709-2137), SAN 325-4577. Tel: 919-558-1402. Interlibrary Loan Service Tel: 919-558-1257. FAX: 919-558-1300. E-mail: library@thehamner.org. *Mgr,* Mason Baldwin; E-mail: mbaldwin@thehamner.org; Staff 1 (MLS 1)
Founded 1974
Library Holdings: AV Mats 300; Bk Titles 6,300; Per Subs 240
Subject Interests: Toxicology
Automation Activity & Vendor Info: (Acquisitions) Inmagic, Inc.; (Cataloging) Inmagic, Inc.; (Circulation) Inmagic, Inc.; (ILL) Inmagic, Inc.; (OPAC) Inmagic, Inc.; (Serials) Inmagic, Inc.
Partic in Docline; National Network of Libraries of Medicine
Open Mon & Tues 7:30-4, Wed-Fri 9-5

S ISA - THE INTERNATIONAL SOCIETY OF AUTOMATION*, Albert F Sperry Library, 67 Alexander Dr, 27709. (Mail add: PO Box 12277, 27709-2277), SAN 315-0763. Tel: 919-549-8411. FAX: 919-549-8288. Web Site: www.isa.org. *Librn/Standards Adminr,* Linda Wolffe; Tel: 910-990-9257, E-mail: lwolffe@isa.org; Staff 0.25 (MLS 0.25)
Founded 1950
Library Holdings: CDs 250; Bk Vols 3,600
Special Collections: ISA Archives; Measurement, Process Control Theory & Application; Process Control Engineering, journals & references
Subject Interests: Computer, Control tech, Electronic eng, Instrumentation
Function: Archival coll
Publications: Intech (Monthly); ISA Transactions (Quarterly); Process Control Engineering Reference Books
Restriction: Staff use only

S NATIONAL HUMANITIES CENTER LIBRARY*, Seven Alexander Dr, 27709. (Mail add: PO Box 12256, 27709-2256), SAN 320-9334. Tel: 919-549-0661. FAX: 919-990-8535. E-mail: nhclib@nationalhumanitiescenter.org. Web Site: www.nhc.rtp.nc.us. *Dir,* Eliza S Robertson; E-mail: erobertson@nationalhumanitiescenter.org; *Circ,* Jean Houston; *ILL, Ref,* Brooke P Andrade; E-mail: bandrade@nationalhumanitiescenter.org; Staff 3 (MLS 2, Non-MLS 1)
Founded 1978
Library Holdings: Bk Titles 2,200; Bk Vols 2,500; Per Subs 20
Special Collections: Robert F & Margaret S Goheen Coll of Fellows' Works
Database Vendor: OCLC FirstSearch
Wireless access
Publications: Library Guide for Users
Partic in Lyrasis; OCLC Online Computer Library Center, Inc

G NATIONAL INSTITUTE OF ENVIRONMENTAL HEALTH SCIENCES LIBRARY*, 111 TW Alexander Dr, Bldg 101, 27709. (Mail add: PO Box 12233, Mail Drop A0-01, 27709), SAN 312-973X. Tel: 919-541-3426. FAX: 919-541-0669. Web Site: www.niehs.nih.gov/research/resources/library/index.cfm. *Libr Mgr,* Erin Knight; E-mail: knighten@mail.nih.gov; Staff 5 (MLS 3, Non-MLS 2)
Founded 1967
Library Holdings: e-books 300; e-journals 9,000; Bk Titles 15,000; Bk Vols 20,000; Per Subs 40
Subject Interests: Carcinogenesis, Environ health, Epigenetics, Molecular biol, Toxicology
Automation Activity & Vendor Info: (Cataloging) Innovative Interfaces, Inc - Millenium; (Circulation) Innovative Interfaces, Inc - Millenium; (OPAC) Innovative Interfaces, Inc - Millenium
Database Vendor: Cambridge Scientific Abstracts, Elsevier, Innovative Interfaces, Inc, ISI Web of Knowledge, JSTOR, LexisNexis, OCLC FirstSearch, OCLC WorldShare Interlibrary Loan, PubMed, ScienceDirect, Scopus, STN International, Thomson - Web of Science, Wiley InterScience
Wireless access
Function: Res libr
Partic in Coalition for Networked Information (CNI); Fedlink; National Network of Libraries of Medicine; OCLC Online Computer Library Center, Inc
Open Mon-Fri 8:30-5

S NORTH CAROLINA BIOTECHNOLOGY CENTER LIBRARY*, 15 Alexander Dr, 27709. (Mail add: PO Box 13547, 27709-3547), SAN 329-1111. Tel: 919-541-9366. Information Services Tel: 919-549-8880. FAX: 919-990-9521. E-mail: library@ncbiotech.org. Web Site: www.ncbiotech.org. *VPres,* Susan Corbett; *Data Mgr,* Howard Franklin, III; *Res,* Sperry Krueger; *Res,* Karin Shank; Staff 5 (MLS 4, Non-MLS 1)
Founded 1986
Library Holdings: AV Mats 210; Bk Titles 1,200; Per Subs 180
Automation Activity & Vendor Info: (Cataloging) Inmagic, Inc.; (Circulation) Inmagic, Inc.; (OPAC) Inmagic, Inc.; (Serials) Inmagic, Inc.
Database Vendor: BioPharm Insight, Factiva.com, ScienceDirect, UTEK Knowledge Express
Wireless access
Function: Res libr
Open Mon-Fri 9-4:30
Restriction: Not a lending libr

S RTI INTERNATIONAL*, Information Services, 3040 Cornwallis Rd, 27709. (Mail add: PO Box 12194, 27709-2194), SAN 312-9756. Tel: 919-541-8787. FAX: 919-541-1221. Web Site: www.rti.org. *Dir,* Mariel Christian; Tel: 919-541-6303; *Librn,* Mark E Howell; Tel: 919-541-6364; Staff 5 (MLS 2, Non-MLS 3)
Founded 1958
Library Holdings: Per Subs 1,125
Subject Interests: Chem, Educ, Energy, Eng, Environ eng, Environ studies, Med
Branches:
MCNC CAMPUS TECHNICAL LIBRARY, 3021 Cornwallis Rd, 27709-3910. (Mail add: PO Box 12194, 27709-2914). Tel: 919-248-1985. FAX: 919-248-1455. *Mgr,* Bonnie Crotty Nelson; Tel: 919-248-1853, E-mail: bnelson@rti.org; Staff 1.5 (MLS 1, Non-MLS 0.5)
Founded 1986
Library Holdings: Electronic Media & Resources 200; Bk Titles 1,500; Per Subs 25
Function: Bus archives, For res purposes, ILL available

Partic in Soline
Restriction: Access at librarian's discretion, Access for corporate affiliates, Co libr, Employees & their associates, In-house use for visitors, Secured area only open to authorized personnel

A UNITED STATES ARMY RESEARCH OFFICE*, Technical Library, 4300 S Miami Blvd, 27703-9142. (Mail add: PO Box 12211, 27709-2211), SAN 328-8102. Tel: 919-549-4220. FAX: 919-549-4310. Web Site: www.aro.army.mil.
Library Holdings: Bk Titles 500; Per Subs 241

ROANOKE RAPIDS

P ROANOKE RAPIDS PUBLIC LIBRARY, 319 Roanoke Ave, 27870. SAN 312-9764. Tel: 252-533-2890. FAX: 252-533-2892. E-mail: rrpl@roanokerapidsnc.com. Web Site: www.youseemore.com/roanokerapids. *Head Librn,* Jeff Watson; Staff 1 (MLS 1)
Founded 1933. Pop 15,900
Library Holdings: Bk Titles 40,000
Automation Activity & Vendor Info: (Cataloging) TLC (The Library Corporation); (Circulation) TLC (The Library Corporation); (OPAC) TLC (The Library Corporation)
Wireless access
Partic in CORE; Lyrasis; North Carolina Information Network (NCIN)
Open Mon & Tues 10-7, Wed-Fri 10-6, Sat 10-3
Friends of the Library Group

ROBBINSVILLE

P GRAHAM COUNTY PUBLIC LIBRARY*, 80 Knight St, 28771. SAN 312-9772. Tel: 828-479-8796. FAX: 828-479-3156. *Br Librn,* Gary James Pressley; E-mail: gpressley@nantahalalibrary.org; Staff 4.5 (MLS 1, Non-MLS 3.5)
Founded 1984. Pop 7,500; Circ 33,000
Library Holdings: CDs 250; DVDs 300; Large Print Bks 1,600; Bk Titles 22,000; Bk Vols 22,500; Per Subs 47; Talking Bks 1,020; Videos 1,580
Automation Activity & Vendor Info: (Circulation) TLC (The Library Corporation)
Database Vendor: NC LIVE
Wireless access
Function: Bks on cassette, Bks on CD, Children's prog, Computers for patron use, Copy machines, Electronic databases & coll, Fax serv, Free DVD rentals, ILL available, Large print keyboards, Mail & tel request accepted, Music CDs, Newsp ref libr, Online cat, Online searches, Photocopying/Printing, Prog for children & young adult, Scanner, Tax forms, Telephone ref, VHS videos
Mem of Nantahala Regional Library
Open Mon-Thurs 8:30-9, Fri 8:30-6, Sat 8:30-2
Friends of the Library Group

ROBERSONVILLE

P ROBERSONVILLE PUBLIC LIBRARY*, 119 S Main St, 27871. (Mail add: PO Box 1060, 27871-1060), SAN 312-9780. Tel: 252-795-3591. FAX: 252-795-3359. *Librn,* Margaret Partin
Pop 14,000
Library Holdings: Bk Vols 6,000; Per Subs 20
Wireless access
Partic in North Carolina Libraries for Virtual Education
Open Mon-Fri 9-5, Sat 9-Noon
Friends of the Library Group

ROCKINGHAM

P THOMAS H LEATH MEMORIAL LIBRARY*, 412 E Franklin St, 28379-4995. SAN 312-9802. Tel: 910-895-6337. FAX: 910-895-5851. Web Site: www.srls.info/richmond/richmondindex.html. *Dir,* Jesse Gibson; *Supvr,* Gladys Sheppard; *Dir, Tech Serv,* Bonita Collins; Staff 6 (MLS 1, Non-MLS 5)
Founded 1962. Pop 9,171; Circ 44,384
Library Holdings: Audiobooks 949; AV Mats 2,426; Bk Titles 44,249; Per Subs 57; Videos 1,229
Special Collections: Local & State Genealogy Coll
Automation Activity & Vendor Info: (Cataloging) TLC (The Library Corporation); (Circulation) TLC (The Library Corporation); (OPAC) TLC (The Library Corporation)
Function: Bks on CD, Children's prog, Computer training, Computers for patron use, Copy machines, Electronic databases & coll, Fax serv, ILL available, Newsp ref libr, Notary serv, Online cat, Online ref, Online searches, Outreach serv, Photocopying/Printing, Preschool outreach, Prog for adults, Prog for children & young adult, Pub access computers, Ref & res, Ref serv available, Senior outreach, Spoken cassettes & CDs, Story hour, Summer reading prog, Tax forms, Teen prog, Telephone ref, VHS videos, Video lending libr, Web-catalog, Wheelchair accessible, Workshops
Publications: Statistical & Financial Reports
Special Services for the Deaf - Bks on deafness & sign lang
Special Services for the Blind - Audio mat; Bks on cassette; Bks on CD; Braille & cassettes; Braille bks; Large print & cassettes; Large print bks
Open Mon-Thurs 8:30-7, Fri 8:30-6, Sat 8:30-5
Friends of the Library Group
Branches: 2
HAMLET PUBLIC, 302 Main St, Hamlet, 28345-3304, SAN 312-8695. Tel: 910-582-3477. FAX: 910-582-3478. Web Site: www.srls.info/richmond/richmondbranches.html. *Mgr,* Patsy Hardee; Staff 3 (Non-MLS 3)
Founded 1922. Pop 6,800; Circ 39,517
Library Holdings: Bk Vols 25,000; Per Subs 50
Subject Interests: Fiction, Local hist
Automation Activity & Vendor Info: (Acquisitions) TLC (The Library Corporation); (Cataloging) TLC (The Library Corporation); (Circulation) TLC (The Library Corporation); (OPAC) TLC (The Library Corporation)
Open Mon-Fri 9:30-6, Sat 9:30-12:30
Friends of the Library Group
KEMP-SUGG MEMORIAL, 279 Second St, Ellerbe, 28338-9001, SAN 320-5002. Tel: 910-652-6130. FAX: 910-652-6130. Web Site: www.srls.info/richmond/richmondbranches.html. *Supvr,* Sami Poore; E-mail: samikemp@yahoo.com; Staff 1 (Non-MLS 1)
Founded 1978. Pop 1,500; Circ 7,983
Library Holdings: Bk Vols 6,254; Per Subs 13
Subject Interests: Artifacts, Local hist
Open Mon, Tues, Thurs & Fri 9-12:30 & 2-5:30, Sat 10-Noon
Friends of the Library Group

ROCKY MOUNT

P BRASWELL MEMORIAL PUBLIC LIBRARY*, 727 N Grace St, 27804-4842. Tel: 252-442-1951. Administration Tel: 252-442-1951, Ext 254. FAX: 252-442-7366. Information Services FAX: 252-442-7180. Web Site: www.braswell-library.org. *Dir,* Catherine Roche; E-mail: croche@braswell-library.org; *Asst Dir,* Gloria Sutton; E-mail: gsutton@braswell-library.org; *Assoc Dir, Support Serv,* Phillip Whitford; E-mail: pwhitford@braswell-library.org; Staff 27 (MLS 7, Non-MLS 20)
Founded 1922. Pop 106,000; Circ 402,000
Library Holdings: Audiobooks 6,187; AV Mats 10,000; e-books 20,899; Microforms 1,069; Bk Vols 122,671; Per Subs 150; Videos 4,492
Special Collections: Parent-Teacher Coll
Subject Interests: African-Am, Civil War, Genealogy
Automation Activity & Vendor Info: (Acquisitions) TLC (The Library Corporation); (Cataloging) TLC (The Library Corporation); (Circulation) TLC (The Library Corporation); (OPAC) TLC (The Library Corporation); (Serials) TLC (The Library Corporation)
Database Vendor: Gale Cengage Learning, infoUSA, LearningExpress, ProQuest, ReferenceUSA
Wireless access
Publications: Braswell Memorial Library (Newsletter)
Special Services for the Blind - Audio mat; Bks on cassette; Bks on CD; Large print bks
Open Mon-Thurs 10-8, Fri & Sat 10-6
Friends of the Library Group

J NASH COMMUNITY COLLEGE LIBRARY*, 522 N Old Carriage Rd, 27804-9441. (Mail add: PO Box 7488, 27804-0788), SAN 312-9837. Tel: 252-451-8244. FAX: 252-451-8401. Web Site: www.nashcc.edu. *Dir,* Lynette Finch; E-mail: lfinch@nashcc.edu; Staff 2 (MLS 1, Non-MLS 1)
Founded 1968. Enrl 2,000; Fac 100; Highest Degree: Associate
Library Holdings: Bk Vols 42,000; Per Subs 130
Subject Interests: NC
Automation Activity & Vendor Info: (Cataloging) SirsiDynix; (Circulation) SirsiDynix; (OPAC) SirsiDynix
Database Vendor: Gale Cengage Learning
Partic in North Carolina Libraries for Virtual Education
Open Mon-Thurs 7:30am-9pm, Fri 7:30-4

C NORTH CAROLINA WESLEYAN COLLEGE*, Elizabeth Braswell Pearsall Library, 3400 N Wesleyan Blvd, 27804. SAN 312-9845. Tel: 252-985-5350. Circulation Tel: 252-985-5231. Interlibrary Loan Service Tel: 252-985-5234. FAX: 252-985-5235. E-mail: reference@ncwc.edu. Web Site: www.ncwc.edu/library. *Dir,* Katherine R Winslow; Tel: 252-985-5134, E-mail: kwinslow@ncwc.edu; *Electronic Res & Ref Librn,* Rachel McWilliams; Tel: 252-985-5343, E-mail: rmcwilliams@ncwc.edu; *Instruction & Assessment Librn,* Amy Brake; Tel: 252-985-5233, E-mail: abrake@ncwc.edu; *Circ Supvr,* Sue Pellegrino; E-mail: spellegrino@ncwc.edu; *Tech Serv Assoc,* Grace Wallace; E-mail: gwallace@ncwc.edu. Subject Specialists: *Bus,* Katherine R Winslow; *Art, Art hist,* Amy Brake; Staff 5 (MLS 3, Non-MLS 2)
Founded 1960. Enrl 1,350; Fac 50; Highest Degree: Bachelor
Jun 2010-May 2011 Income $418,500. Mats Exp $418,500
Library Holdings: AV Mats 2,820; e-books 30,760; e-journals 30,600; Microforms 36,000; Bk Titles 77,800; Bk Vols 80,000; Per Subs 32,100

Special Collections: Black Mountain College Coll, bks & art prints; Music Coll; United Methodist Church & North Caroliniana (Hardee-Rives Coll), rare bks, fine eds. US Document Depository
Automation Activity & Vendor Info: (Acquisitions) TLC (The Library Corporation); (Cataloging) TLC (The Library Corporation); (Circulation) TLC (The Library Corporation); (OPAC) TLC (The Library Corporation)
Database Vendor: BioOne, Bowker, EBSCOhost, Gale Cengage Learning, JSTOR, LearningExpress, LexisNexis, Mergent Online, NC LIVE, OCLC FirstSearch, ProQuest, PubMed, Springer-Verlag, TLC (The Library Corporation), Wiley InterScience, WT Cox
Wireless access
Function: Computers for patron use, Copy machines, Doc delivery serv, e-mail & chat, Electronic databases & coll, Free DVD rentals, ILL available, Online cat, Online ref, Ref serv available, Telephone ref
Open Mon-Thurs (Fall & Spring) 8am-Midnight, Fri 8-5, Sat 11-5, Sun 1-Midnight; Mon-Thurs (Summer) 8-7, Fri 8-3
Friends of the Library Group

ROSE HILL

S DUPLIN COUNTY HISTORICAL FOUNDATION*, Leora H McEachern Library of Local History, PO Box 130, 28458. SAN 375-1244. Tel: 910-289-2430. *Librn,* William Dallas Herring
Library Holdings: Bk Vols 5,000
Special Collections: Leslie H Brown Jr Coll, index cards
Open Mon-Sun 2-Midnight
Restriction: Restricted access

ROWLAND

P ROWLAND PUBLIC LIBRARY*, 113 W Main St, 28383. (Mail add: PO Box 10, 28383-0010), SAN 312-9853. Tel: 910-422-3996. Web Site: robesoncountylibrary.com. *Mgr,* Lisa Matthews
Pop 1,460; Circ 2,173
Library Holdings: Bk Vols 7,000
Open Mon 2-6, Tues & Wed 2:30-5:30, Thurs 9-6

ROXBORO

P PERSON COUNTY PUBLIC LIBRARY*, 319 S Main St, 27573. SAN 312-9861. Tel: 336-597-7881. FAX: 336-597-5081. Web Site: www.personcounty.net. *Dir,* Linda Howerton; E-mail: lhowerton@personcounty.net; *Asst Dir,* Vicki Solomon; E-mail: vsolomon@personcounty.net; *Outreach Coordr,* Susanne Satterfield; E-mail: ssatterfield@personcounty.net; *Ch Serv,* Christie Bondy; E-mail: cbondy@personcounty.net; *Ref Serv,* Vickie Clayton; E-mail: vclayton@personcounty.net; Staff 7 (MLS 1, Non-MLS 6)
Founded 1936. Pop 36,000; Circ 12,000
Library Holdings: Bks on Deafness & Sign Lang 28; Bk Titles 51,161; Per Subs 177
Special Collections: Large Print Books; Local History Coll; North Carolina Room (geneology, local hist)
Automation Activity & Vendor Info: (Acquisitions) Innovative Interfaces, Inc; (Cataloging) Innovative Interfaces, Inc; (Circulation) Innovative Interfaces, Inc; (OPAC) Innovative Interfaces, Inc; (Serials) Innovative Interfaces, Inc
Wireless access
Function: ILL available
Mem of Hyconeechee Regional Library
Open Mon-Thurs 9-6, Fri 9-5, Sat 9-3
Friends of the Library Group

J PIEDMONT COMMUNITY COLLEGE*, Gordon P Allen Learning Resources Center, 1715 College Dr, 27573. (Mail add: PO Box 1197, 27573-1197), SAN 376-5822. Tel: 336-599-1181, Ext 489. FAX: 336-599-9146. Web Site: www.piedmont.cc.nc.us. *Dean of Libr,* Gretchen M Bell; Tel: 336-599-1181, Ext 267, E-mail: bellg@piedmontcc.edu; *Circ,* Deborah Brown; Tel: 336-599-1181, Ext 446, E-mail: brownd@piedmontcc.edu; *Distance Educ,* Joseph Solomon; Tel: 336-599-1181, Ext 253, E-mail: solomoj@piedmontcc.edu; *Instr,* Libbie McPhaul-Moore; Tel: 336-599-1181, Ext 445, E-mail: mcphaul@piedmontcc.edu; *Ref Librn,* Vanessa L Nwanze; Tel: 336-599-1181, Ext 235, E-mail: nwanzev@piedmontcc.edu; *Tech Serv Librn,* Ernest Avery; Tel: 336-599-1181, Ext 231, E-mail: averye@piedmontcc.edu; Staff 3 (MLS 2, Non-MLS 1)
Founded 1970
Library Holdings: Bk Titles 16,906; Bk Vols 18,354; Per Subs 165
Automation Activity & Vendor Info: (Acquisitions) SirsiDynix; (Cataloging) SirsiDynix; (Circulation) SirsiDynix; (ILL) SirsiDynix; (Media Booking) SirsiDynix; (Serials) SirsiDynix
Open Mon-Thurs (Winter) 7:30am-9pm, Fri 7:30-5, Sat 8-3; Mon-Thurs (Summer) 7:30-8, Fri 7:30-12:30
Departmental Libraries:
CASWELL LEARNING RESOURCES CENTER, 331 Piedmont Dr, Yanceyville, 27379. (Mail add: PO Box 1150, Yanceyville, 27379). Tel: 336-694-5707, Ext 231, 336-694-5707, Ext 286. FAX: 336-694-5893. Web Site: www.piedmontcc.edu/lrc. *Dir,* Lionell Parker; Tel: 336-599-1181, Ext 248, E-mail: parkerl@piedmontcc.edu
Open Mon & Wed 7:30-5, Tues & Thurs 7:30-6, Fri (Summer) 7:30-12:30

RUTHERFORDTON

P NORRIS PUBLIC LIBRARY*, 132 N Main, 28139. SAN 355-1318. Tel: 828-287-4981. FAX: 828-287-0660. E-mail: nplibrary@rutherfordton.net. *Librn,* Patricia A Hardin; *Libr Assoc,* Cindy Bowlin; *Libr Assoc,* Vanessa Harbison
Library Holdings: Large Print Bks 600; Bk Vols 44,000; Per Subs 60; Talking Bks 500
Subject Interests: Local hist
Automation Activity & Vendor Info: (Cataloging) TLC (The Library Corporation); (Circulation) TLC (The Library Corporation); (OPAC) TLC (The Library Corporation)
Open Mon-Fri 9-5:30, Sat 10-Noon
Friends of the Library Group

SALEMBURG

G NORTH CAROLINA JUSTICE ACADEMY*, Learning Resource Center, 200 W College St, 28385. (Mail add: PO Box 99, 28385), SAN 321-0154. Tel: 910-525-4151, Ext 267. FAX: 910-525-4491. Web Site: www.ncja.ncdoj.gov/NCJAHome.aspx. *Librn,* Anthony Aycock; Tel: 910-525-4158, Ext 267, E-mail: aaycock@ncdoj.gov; Staff 3 (MLS 1, Non-MLS 2)
Founded 1975
Library Holdings: AV Mats 2,300; Bk Vols 23,000; Per Subs 150
Special Collections: Criminal Justice; Law Enforcement Policy & Procedures Manuals
Subject Interests: Law, Law enforcement
Wireless access
Function: ILL available
Publications: Acquisitions List (Monthly); AV catalog (Irregular)
Open Mon-Thurs 8am-9pm, Fri 8-5
Restriction: Open to pub for ref & circ; with some limitations

SALISBURY

C CATAWBA COLLEGE*, Corriher-Linn-Black Library, 2300 W Innes St, 28144-2488. SAN 312-9896. Tel: 704-637-4448. Interlibrary Loan Service Tel: 704-637-4214. FAX: 704-637-4304. Interlibrary Loan Service E-mail: ill@catawba.edu. Web Site: www.lib.catawba.edu. *Libr Dir,* Steve McKinzie; Tel: 704-637-4449, E-mail: smckinzi@catawba.edu; *Head, Info Serv,* Jacquelyn Sims; Tel: 704-637-4379, E-mail: jsims@catawba.edu; *Head, Syst,* Issac Meadows; Tel: 704-637-4212, E-mail: smeadows@catawba.edu; *Head, Tech Serv,* Constance Grant; Tel: 704-637-4228, E-mail: cbgrant@catawba.edu; *Circ Supvr,* Suzanne Wilson; E-mail: swilson@catawba.edu; *Circ Asst,* Whitney Owens; *Info Serv,* Billie Cunningham; E-mail: mwcunnin@catawba.edu; *Info Serv, ILL,* Jean Wurster; E-mail: jwurster@catawba.edu; *Info Serv, Tech Serv,* Mark Wurster; Tel: 704-637-4783, E-mail: mwurster@catawba.edu; *Tech Serv,* Ray Porter; Tel: 704-637-4215; *Tech Serv,* Winnell Short; Tel: 704-637-4209, E-mail: wbshort@catawba.edu; Staff 11.5 (MLS 5.5, Non-MLS 6)
Founded 1851. Enrl 1,270; Fac 90; Highest Degree: Master
Jun 2006-May 2007. Mats Exp $266,111, Books $38,085, Per/Ser (Incl. Access Fees) $139,480, AV Mat $6,142, Electronic Ref Mat (Incl. Access Fees) $42,300, Presv $1,190. Sal $414,960 (Prof $266,907)
Library Holdings: CDs 185; DVDs 245; Music Scores 444; Bk Titles 126,483; Bk Vols 167,452; Per Subs 594; Videos 1,200
Special Collections: Catawba College Archives; Poetry Council of North Carolina Coll; Wolfe Coll. State Document Depository; US Document Depository
Subject Interests: Environ sci, Intl bus, NC poetry, Teacher educ, Theatre arts
Automation Activity & Vendor Info: (Acquisitions) Ex Libris Group; (Cataloging) Ex Libris Group; (Circulation) Ex Libris Group; (Course Reserve) Ex Libris Group; (OPAC) Ex Libris Group; (Serials) Ex Libris Group
Database Vendor: Alexander Street Press, American Chemical Society, American Psychological Association (APA), Bowker, EBSCOhost, Greenwood Publishing Group, Grolier Online, JSTOR, Modern Language Association, NC LIVE, Newsbank, OCLC WorldShare Interlibrary Loan, Oxford Online, Project MUSE, ProQuest, ReferenceUSA, Wiley InterScience
Wireless access
Partic in Asn Col & Res Librs; Charlotte Area Educ Consortium; Lyrasis; Metrolina Libr Asn; NC Libr Asn; North Carolina Libraries for Virtual Education
Open Mon-Thurs (Fall & Spring) 8am-11pm, Fri 8-5, Sat 10-5, Sun 1:30-11; Mon-Thurs (Summer) 8am-9pm, Fri 8-5, Sat 12-5, Sun 2-6
Friends of the Library Group

GM DEPARTMENT OF VETERANS AFFAIRS*, W G Hefner VA Medical Center Library, 1601 Brenner Ave, 28144. SAN 312-9926. Tel: 704-638-9000, Ext 3403. FAX: 704-638-3483. *Chief Librn,* Nancy Martino
Founded 1953
Library Holdings: CDs 150; DVDs 78; Bk Vols 800; Per Subs 120
Special Collections: Business/Careers
Subject Interests: Geriatrics, Med, Nursing, Psychiat, Psychol, Surgery
Open Mon-Fri 7-3:30
Restriction: Staff use only

C LIVINGSTONE COLLEGE*, Andrew Carnegie Library, 701 W Monroe St, 28144. SAN 355-1377. Tel: 704-216-6030. Reference Tel: 704-216-6033. Toll Free Tel: 800-835-3435. FAX: 704-216-6798. Web Site: www.livingstone.edu/lib/index.html. *Dir,* Dr G Peart, Tel. 704-216-6029; Staff 4 (MLS 2, Non-MLS 2)
Founded 1908. Enrl 900; Fac 60; Highest Degree: Bachelor
Library Holdings: Bk Vols 75,000; Spec Interest Per Sub 15
Special Collections: African-American Coll. Oral History
Subject Interests: African-Am hist
Automation Activity & Vendor Info: (Acquisitions) Ex Libris Group; (Cataloging) Ex Libris Group; (Circulation) Ex Libris Group; (Course Reserve) Ex Libris Group; (ILL) Ex Libris Group; (OPAC) Ex Libris Group; (Serials) Ex Libris Group
Database Vendor: EBSCOhost, OCLC FirstSearch
Wireless access
Function: ILL available
Publications: Newsletter
Partic in Charlotte Area Educ Consortium; Metrolina Libr Asn
Open Mon-Thurs (Fall & Spring) 8am-10pm, Fri 8-5, Sat 9-1, Sun 6pm-10pm; Mon-Fri (Summer) 8-5
Friends of the Library Group

Departmental Libraries:

CR HOOD THEOLOGICAL SEMINARY LIBRARY, 1810 Lutheran Synod Dr, 28144, SAN 355-1407. Tel: 704-636-6779, 704-636-6840. Administration Tel: 704-636-6823. FAX: 704-636-7699. Web Site: www.hoodseminary.edu. *Dir,* Cynthia D Keever; E-mail: ckeever@hoodseminary.edu; *Asst Librn,* Sonia Edgar; E-mail: sedgar@hoodseminary.edu; Staff 1 (MLS 1)
Founded 1885. Enrl 212; Pop 300; Fac 9; Highest Degree: Doctorate
Library Holdings: Electronic Media & Resources 175; Bk Vols 32,000; Per Subs 360
Special Collections: The AME Zion Coll
Subject Interests: Philos, Psychol, Sociol, Theol
Function: ILL available, Ref serv available
Partic in Charlotte Theological Library Consortium
Open Mon & Thurs 8-5, Tues & Wed 8-7, Fri 8am-9pm, Sat 9-5
Restriction: Open to pub for ref & circ; with some limitations

SR NORTH CAROLINA SYNOD OF THE ELCA*, Heilig Resource Center, 1988 Lutheran Synod Dr, 28144. SAN 327-6422. Tel: 704-633-4861. Toll Free Tel: 800-560-7292. FAX: 704-638-0508. Web Site: www.nclutheran.org/heilig_resource_center.201.html. *Dir,* Catherine Fink; Tel: 704-633-4861, Ext 121, E-mail: cfink@nclutheran.org; Staff 1 (Non-MLS 1)
Founded 1955
Library Holdings: CDs 138; DVDs 489, Bk Titles 3,135; Per Subs 24; Videos 2,106
Open Mon-Fri 9-5

M NORTHWEST AHEC*, Rowan Regional Medical Center Library, 612 Mocksville Ave, 28144. SAN 312-990X. Tel: 704-210-5069. FAX: 704-636-5050. Web Site: www1.wfubmc.edu/nwahec/library/library+locations.htm. *Librn,* Position Currently Open; Staff 3 (MLS 1, Non-MLS 2)
Founded 1976
Library Holdings: e-books 60; e-journals 800; Bk Titles 1,034; Bk Vols 1,093; Per Subs 20
Subject Interests: Med, Nursing
Wireless access
Publications: Northwest AHEC Periodicals List (Union list of periodicals)
Open Mon-Fri 8-5

J ROWAN-CABARRUS COMMUNITY COLLEGE*, Learning Resource Center-North Campus, 1333 Jake Alexander Blvd, 28145. (Mail add: PO Box 1595, 28145-1595), SAN 377-788X. Tel: 704-216-3691. FAX: 704-216-3827. *Dir, Learning Res,* Rodney Lippard; E-mail: rodney.lippard@rccc.edu; Staff 7 (MLS 3, Non-MLS 4)
Founded 1964. Enrl 2,900; Fac 80; Highest Degree: Associate
Library Holdings: Bk Titles 40,000; Per Subs 425
Subject Interests: Archives, Early childhood, Liberal arts, Med, Small bus
Automation Activity & Vendor Info: (Cataloging) SirsiDynix; (Circulation) SirsiDynix; (OPAC) SirsiDynix
Database Vendor: NC LIVE, SirsiDynix, Wilson - Wilson Web
Wireless access
Partic in OCLC Online Computer Library Center, Inc
Open Mon-Thurs 7:45am-9pm, Fri 7:45-5, Sat 9-1

Departmental Libraries:

SOUTH CAMPUS, 1531 Trinity Church Rd, Concord, 28027-7601. Tel: 704-216-3694. FAX: 704-788-2169. Web Site: www.rowancabarrus.edu/lrc. *Coordr, Libr Sci,* Timothy Hunter; E-mail: timothy.hunter@rccc.edu; Staff 2.5 (MLS 2.5)
Highest Degree: Associate
Library Holdings: Bk Vols 7,000; Per Subs 75
Database Vendor: ProQuest
Open Mon-Thurs 7:45am-8pm, Fri 7:45-5, Sat 9-1

P ROWAN PUBLIC LIBRARY*, 201 W Fisher St, 28144-4935. (Mail add: PO Box 4039, 28145-4039), SAN 355-1431. Tel: 704-216-8228. Circulation Tel: 704-216-8256. Interlibrary Loan Service Tel: 704-216-8253. Information Services Tel: 704-216-8243. FAX: 704-216-8237. Information Services FAX: 704-216-8246. TDD: 704-216-8251. E-mail: info@rowancountync.gov. Web Site: www.rowanpubliclibrary.org. *Libr Serv Dir,* Jeff Hall; Tel: 704-216-8231, E-mail: jeff.hall@rowancountync.gov; *Librn I,* Paul Birkhead; *Librn I,* Dara Cain; *Librn I,* Marissa Creamer; *Librn I,* April Everett; *Librn I,* Edward Hirst; *Librn I,* Rebecca Hyde; *Librn I,* Amy Notarius; *Librn II,* Lynn Denison; Tel: 704-216-8242, E-mail: lynn.denison@rowancountync.gov; *Librn II,* Gretchen Witt; Tel: 704-216-8232, E-mail: gretchen.witt@rowancountync.gov; *Libr Serv Mgr,* Erika Kosin. Subject Specialists: *Genealogy, Local hist,* Gretchen Witt; Staff 47 (MLS 10, Non-MLS 37)
Founded 1911. Pop 133,134; Circ 683,414
Library Holdings: Bk Vols 226,661; Per Subs 386
Special Collections: Oral History
Subject Interests: Genealogy, Local hist
Automation Activity & Vendor Info: (Acquisitions) TLC (The Library Corporation); (Cataloging) TLC (The Library Corporation); (Circulation) TLC (The Library Corporation); (ILL) OCLC Connexion; (OPAC) TLC (The Library Corporation)
Database Vendor: ALLDATA Online, Oxford Online, ProQuest
Function: After school storytime, AV serv, Electronic databases & coll, Handicapped accessible, Home delivery & serv to Sr ctr & nursing homes, Homebound delivery serv, ILL available, Magnifiers for reading, Mail & tel request accepted, Newsp ref libr, Online searches, Photocopying/Printing, Preschool outreach, Prog for adults, Prog for children & young adult, Ref serv available
Publications: News Etc Newsletter (Monthly)
Special Services for the Deaf - TDD equip; TTY equip
Open Mon-Thurs 9-9, Fri & Sat 9-5, Sun (Sept-May) 1-5
Friends of the Library Group

Branches: 2

EAST BRANCH, 110 Broad St, Rockwell, 28138. (Mail add: PO Box 550, Rockwell, 28138), SAN 312-9810. Tel: 704-279-5014. FAX: 704-216-7838. *Librn,* Paul Birkhead; E-mail: paul.birkhead@rowancountync.gov
Open Mon-Wed 9-8, Thurs 9-5, Fri 10-5, Sat 9-1
Friends of the Library Group

SOUTH, 920 Kimball Rd, China Grove, 28023, SAN 355-1466. Tel: 704-216-7727. FAX: 704-855-2449.
Open Mon-Thurs 9-9, Fri & Sat 9-5, Sun (Sept-May) 1-5
Friends of the Library Group

Bookmobiles: 1

SANFORD

J CENTRAL CAROLINA COMMUNITY COLLEGE LIBRARIES*, 1105 Kelly Dr, 27330. SAN 312-9934. Tel: 919-718-7244. FAX: 919-718-7378. Web Site: www.cccc.edu/library. *Dir of Libr Serv,* Tara Guthrie; Tel: 919-718-7245, E-mail: tguthrie@cccc.edu; *Pub Serv Librn,* Position Currently Open; *Ref, Instruction & Emerging Technologies Librn,* Amy Gustavson; Tel: 919-718-7435, E-mail: agustavson@cccc.edu; *Lead Libr Asst,* BJ Thompson; Tel: 919-718-7375, E-mail: bthompson@cccc.edu; *Libr Asst,* Jessica Walshaw; Tel: 919-718-7207, E-mail: jwalshaw@cccc.edu; *Libr, Circ,* Peggy Cotten; E-mail: pcotten@cccc.edu; *Evening Libr Asst,* Elizabeth Kelly; E-mail: lkelly@cccc.edu; Staff 6.4 (MLS 3, Non-MLS 3.4)
Founded 1962. Enrl 4,949; Highest Degree: Associate
Library Holdings: AV Mats 1,697; Bk Vols 25,666; Per Subs 82
Subject Interests: Automotive mechanics, Biofuels, Bus admin, Cosmetology, Culinary, Dental tech, Dentistry, Early childhood, Electro optics, Electronics, Human resources, Indust maintenance tech, Internet, Laser, Law, Law enforcement, Libr sci, Machining, Microcomputers, Motorcycles, Networks, Nursing, Radio, Sustainability, Telecommunication, TV broadcasting, Veterinary med
Automation Activity & Vendor Info: (Acquisitions) SirsiDynix; (Cataloging) SirsiDynix; (Circulation) SirsiDynix; (Course Reserve) SirsiDynix; (ILL) SirsiDynix; (Media Booking) SirsiDynix; (OPAC) SirsiDynix; (Serials) SirsiDynix
Wireless access

Publications: Library Newsletter
Partic in Community Colleges Libraries in North Carolina (CCLINC); North Carolina Community College System
Open Mon-Thurs 7:30am-8pm, Fri 7:30-3:30
Departmental Libraries:
LILLINGTON CAMPUS, 1075 E Cornelius Harnett Blvd, Lillington, 27546, SAN 378-1259. Tel: 910-814-8843. *Evening Ref Librn,* Peggy Christian; E-mail: pchristian@cccc.edu; *Evening Ref Librn,* Paula Fish; E-mail: pfish@cccc.edu; *Libr Asst/Circ, Acq & Cat,* Barbara Wood; E-mail: bwood@cccc.edu; Staff 1.6 (MLS 0.6, Non-MLS 1)
Highest Degree: Associate
Library Holdings: AV Mats 67; Bk Vols 4,332; Per Subs 41
Subject Interests: Bus, Cosmetology, Criminal justice, Laser & photonics, Law enforcement, Machining, Med asst, Nursing, Off admin
Open Mon-Thurs 7:30-7, Fri 7:30-3:30

P LEE COUNTY LIBRARY*, Suzanne Reeves Library, 107 Hawkins Ave, 27331-4399. SAN 355-1490. Tel: 919-718-4665. FAX: 919-775-1832. Web Site: www.leecountync.gov/Departments/LibraryMain.asp. *Dir,* Michael J Matochik; E-mail: michael.matochik@leecountync.gov; *Ch Serv, YA Serv,* Doris Powell; E-mail: doris.powell@leecountync.gov; *Circ, ILL,* Michael Williams; E-mail: michael.williams@leecountync.gov; Staff 17 (MLS 3, Non-MLS 14)
Founded 1933. Pop 54,417; Circ 173,964
Library Holdings: Bk Titles 135,000; Per Subs 150
Special Collections: Central North Carolina Historic Newspapers (microfilm)
Automation Activity & Vendor Info: (Cataloging) SirsiDynix; (Circulation) SirsiDynix
Wireless access
Open Mon-Thurs 9-9, Fri & Sat 9-6, Sun 2-6
Friends of the Library Group
Branches: 1
BROADWAY BRANCH, 206 S Main St, Broadway, 27505. (Mail add: 107 Hawkins Ave, 27330), SAN 355-1520. Tel: 919-258-6513. *Br Head,* Kim McIver
Open Mon-Wed 2-6
Friends of the Library Group

SEYMOUR JOHNSON AFB

A UNITED STATES AIR FORCE*, Seymour Johnson Air Force Base Library FL4809, 4FSS/FSDL, 1520 Goodson St, Bldg 3660, 27531. SAN 355-158X. Tel: 919-722-5825. FAX: 919-722-5835. Web Site: library.seymourjohnson.accqolnet.org. *Dir,* Kim Huskins Webb; *Computer Serv,* Mark Lee; Staff 5 (MLS 1, Non-MLS 4)
Founded 1956
Library Holdings: Bk Vols 41,000; Per Subs 50
Subject Interests: Aeronaut, Biog, Educ, Humanities, Mil sci, Polit sci
Automation Activity & Vendor Info: (Acquisitions) SIRSI WorkFlows; (Cataloging) SirsiDynix; (Circulation) SirsiDynix; (ILL) OCLC; (OPAC) SirsiDynix
Wireless access
Partic in Dialog Corp; OCLC Online Computer Library Center, Inc; Wayne Info Network
Open Mon-Thurs 10-8, Fri 10-6, Sat 10-5

SHELBY

J CLEVELAND COMMUNITY COLLEGE*, Jim & Patsy Rose Library, 137 S Post Rd, 28152. SAN 312-9950. Tel: 704-669-4024. Interlibrary Loan Service Tel: 704-669-4086. Reference Tel: 704-669-4053. FAX: 704-669-4036. E-mail: library@clevelandcc.edu. Web Site: library.clevelandcc.edu. *Dean, Learning Res,* Barbara McKibbin; Tel: 704-669-4116, E-mail: mckibbin@clevelandcc.edu; *Instruction & Ref Librn,* Jessica Crowe; E-mail: crowej@clevelandcc.edu; *Tech Serv Librn,* Emily Von Pfahl; Tel: 704-669-4042, E-mail: vonpfahle@clevelandcc.edu; *Coordr, AV,* Roger Perry; Tel: 704-669-4032, E-mail: perryr@clevelandcc.edu; *Libr Serv Coordr,* Victoria Linder; E-mail: linderv@clevelandcc.edu. Subject Specialists: *Ins, Instrul design,* Jessica Crowe; *AV,* Roger Perry; Staff 6 (MLS 3, Non-MLS 3)
Founded 1965. Enrl 3,400; Fac 90; Highest Degree: Associate
Library Holdings: Bk Titles 22,951; Bk Vols 27,594; Per Subs 312
Automation Activity & Vendor Info: (Acquisitions) SirsiDynix; (Cataloging) SirsiDynix; (Circulation) SirsiDynix; (Course Reserve) SirsiDynix; (ILL) OCLC ILLiad; (Media Booking) SirsiDynix; (OPAC) SirsiDynix; (Serials) SirsiDynix
Database Vendor: ABC-CLIO, Alexander Street Press, CredoReference, EBSCOhost, JSTOR, NC LIVE, Oxford Online, ProQuest, Safari Books Online, STAT!Ref (Teton Data Systems)
Wireless access
Open Mon-Thurs 7:30am-9pm, Fri 7:30-2

P CLEVELAND COUNTY LIBRARY SYSTEM*, 104 Howie Dr, 28150. (Mail add: PO Box 1120, 28151-1120), SAN 312-9942. Tel: 704-487-9069. FAX: 704-487-4856. Web Site: www.ccml.org. *Dir,* Carol H Wilson; E-mail: cwilson@ccml.org; *Asst Dir,* JoAnne Owens; *Tech Serv,* Kathy Alexander; Staff 20 (MLS 3, Non-MLS 17)
Founded 1909. Pop 86,158; Circ 330,000
Library Holdings: AV Mats 9,058; Bk Vols 140,000; Per Subs 96
Subject Interests: Genealogy, Local hist
Automation Activity & Vendor Info: (Cataloging) SirsiDynix; (Circulation) SirsiDynix
Publications: Libri Amicus (Newsletter)
Open Mon-Thurs 10-8, Fri & Sat 10-2
Friends of the Library Group
Branches: 1
SPANGLER LIBRARY, 112 Piedmont Dr, Lawndale, 28090, SAN 370-0127. Tel: 704-538-7005. FAX: 704-538-0801. *Librn,* Deborah Page; E-mail: dpage@ccml.org
Founded 1990
Open Mon-Thurs 2-6, Sat 9-1
Friends of the Library Group
Bookmobiles: 1

SILER CITY

P CHATHAM COUNTY PUBLIC LIBRARIES*, 500 N Second Ave, 27344. Tel: 919-742-2016. FAX: 919-742-5546. Web Site: www.chathamlibraries.org. *Dir,* Linda Berry Clarke; E-mail: lclarke@chathamlibraries.org; Staff 1 (MLS 1)
Branches: 3
CHATHAM COMMUNITY LIBRARY, 197 NC Hwy 87 N, Pittsboro, 27312, SAN 354-5326. Tel: 919-545-8084. FAX: 919-545-8080. *Br Mgr,* Jennifer Gillis; E-mail: jgillis@chathamlibraries.org; Staff 3 (Non-MLS 3)
Founded 1943
Library Holdings: AV Mats 2,265; CDs 764; DVDs 650; Large Print Bks 325; Bk Vols 40,000; Videos 2,625
Automation Activity & Vendor Info: (Acquisitions) Innovative Interfaces, Inc; (Cataloging) Innovative Interfaces, Inc; (Circulation) Innovative Interfaces, Inc; (ILL) OCLC FirstSearch; (OPAC) Innovative Interfaces, Inc
Open Mon-Thurs 9-8, Fri 9-6, Sat 9-5
Friends of the Library Group
GOLDSTON PUBLIC LIBRARY, 9235 Pittsboro-Goldston Rd, Goldston, 27252-0040. (Mail add: PO Box 40, Goldston, 27252-0040), SAN 354-530X. Tel: 919-898-4522. *Br Mgr,* Sharon Brewer; E-mail: sbrewer@chathamlibraries.org; Staff 1 (Non-MLS 1)
Founded 1952
Library Holdings: AV Mats 100; CDs 125; DVDs 100; Large Print Bks 100; Bk Titles 12,000; Per Subs 30; Videos 450
Database Vendor: TLC (The Library Corporation)
Open Mon & Wed 10-1 & 2-6, Thurs 10-1 & 2-8, Fri 1-5, Sat 9-1
Friends of the Library Group
WREN MEMORIAL LIBRARY, 500 N Second Ave, 27344, SAN 354-5334. Tel: 919-742-2016. FAX: 919-742-5546. *Br Mgr,* Mike Cowell; E-mail: mcowell@chathamlibraries.org; Staff 3 (Non-MLS 3)
Founded 1941. Pop 17,000; Circ 45,000
Library Holdings: AV Mats 2,593; Large Print Bks 350; Bk Titles 37,000; Bk Vols 39,000; Per Subs 55
Automation Activity & Vendor Info: (Acquisitions) Innovative Interfaces, Inc
Partic in North Carolina Libraries for Virtual Education
Open Mon 12-8, Tues-Fri 10-6, Sat 9-5
Bookmobiles: 1. Librn, Edna Johnson

SMITHFIELD

J JOHNSTON COMMUNITY COLLEGE LIBRARY*, Learning Resource Ctr, 245 College Rd, 27577. (Mail add: PO Box 2350, 27577-2350), SAN 312-9977. Tel: 919-464-2251. FAX: 919-464-2250. E-mail: jcclibraryhelp@johnstoncc.edu. Web Site: www.johnstoncc.libguides.com/libraryhome1. *Libr Adminr,* Jaxie Bryan; *Librn,* Letoria Gales Lewis; *Librn,* Debby Warrick; *Libr Spec,* April Bass; Staff 5.5 (MLS 3.5, Non-MLS 2)
Founded 1969
Library Holdings: Bk Vols 36,000; Per Subs 350
Special Collections: Children's Coll; Jane Dillard Music Coll; North Carolina Hist & JCC Archives
Automation Activity & Vendor Info: (Cataloging) SirsiDynix; (Circulation) SirsiDynix
Wireless access
Partic in CCLINK
Open Mon-Thurs (Fall & Spring) 7:30am-8pm, Fri 9:30-3; Mon-Thurs (Summer) 7:30-6
Friends of the Library Group

P PUBLIC LIBRARY OF JOHNSTON COUNTY & SMITHFIELD*, 305 E Market St, 27577-3919. SAN 355-1644. Tel: 919-934-8146. Reference Tel: 919-934-8146, Ext 3. FAX: 919-934-8084. Web Site: www.pljcs.org. *Dir,* Margaret Marshall; E-mail: mmarshall@pljcs.org; *Ref, YA Librn,* Morgan Paty; E-mail: mpaty@pljcs.org; *Bus Mgr,* Vickie Duren; E-mail: vduren@pljcs.org; *Circ Supvr,* Brenda Burton; E-mail: bburton@pljcs.org; *Ref Supvr,* Ruby Smith; E-mail: rsmith@pljcs.org; *Tech Serv Supvr,* Joy Vaughn; E-mail: jvaughn@pljcs.org; *Tech Coordr,* Dustin Mobley; E-mail: dmobley@pljcs.org; *Cat,* Laura Marciniak; E-mail: lmarciniak@pljcs.org; *Ch Serv,* Elaine Forman; E-mail: eforman@pljcs.org; *Ch Serv,* Nancy Wigmore; Staff 4 (MLS 3, Non-MLS 1)
Founded 1966. Pop 168,878; Circ 464,444
Library Holdings: Audiobooks 13,156; AV Mats 8,562; Bk Titles 206,901; Bk Vols 251,038; Per Subs 75
Subject Interests: Genealogy, Local hist
Automation Activity & Vendor Info: (Acquisitions) Innovative Interfaces, Inc; (Cataloging) Innovative Interfaces, Inc; (Circulation) Innovative Interfaces, Inc; (OPAC) Innovative Interfaces, Inc; (Serials) Innovative Interfaces, Inc
Wireless access
Function: Adult bk club, Art exhibits, Bk club(s), Bks on cassette, Bks on CD, Chess club, Children's prog, Computer training, Computers for patron use, Copy machines, Fax serv, Magnifiers for reading, Music CDs, Online cat, Photocopying/Printing, Preschool outreach, Prog for adults, Prog for children & young adult, Pub access computers, Ref & res, Ref serv in person, Scanner, Senior computer classes, Story hour, Summer reading prog, Teen prog, Telephone ref, VHS videos, Web-catalog
Open Mon & Thurs 9-8, Tues, Wed & Fri 9-5:30, Sat 9-5
Friends of the Library Group
Branches: 5
JAMES BRYAN CREECH PUBLIC LIBRARY, Black Creek Rd, Four Oaks, 27524, SAN 355-1768. Tel: 919-963-6013. *Librn,* Jean Adams
Circ 5,047
Library Holdings: AV Mats 536; Large Print Bks 76; Bk Vols 10,110; Talking Bks 115
Open Wed 10-6, Thurs 2-6, Sat 2-5
HOCUTT-ELLINGTON MEMORIAL, 100 S Church St, Clayton, 27520, SAN 355-1709. Tel: 919-553-5542. FAX: 919-553-1529. *Dir,* Christie Starnes; Tel: 919-359-9366, E-mail: clstarnes@townofclaytonnc.org; Staff 6 (MLS 1, Non-MLS 5)
Automation Activity & Vendor Info: (Acquisitions) Innovative Interfaces, Inc
Database Vendor: Ingram Library Services
Function: Adult bk club, Bk club(s), Children's prog, Computers for patron use, Copy machines, Outreach serv, Pub access computers, Ref serv available, Senior outreach, Story hour, Summer reading prog, Tax forms, Web-catalog, Workshops
Open Mon-Wed 10-6, Thurs 1-8, Fri 10-5, Sat 9-12
Friends of the Library Group
KENLY PUBLIC, 205 Edgerton St, Kenly, 27542, SAN 355-1792. Tel: 919-284-4217. *Librn,* Betty B Pope; Staff 1 (Non-MLS 1)
Circ 8,731
Library Holdings: Large Print Bks 220; Bk Vols 14,156; Per Subs 27; Talking Bks 44
Open Mon & Wed 9-5:30, Tues & Thurs 9-7, Fri 9-5, Sat 9-12
PRINCETON PUBLIC, 101 Dr Donnie Jones Blvd, Princeton, 27569. Tel: 919-936-9996. FAX: 919-936-2962. *Librn,* Angie Proctor
Circ 717
Library Holdings: Large Print Bks 13; Bk Vols 910; Per Subs 69; Talking Bks 67
Partic in North Carolina Libraries for Virtual Education
Open Mon, Tues & Thurs 4-7, Sun 2-5
SELMA PUBLIC, 301 N Pollock, Selma, 27576, SAN 355-1857. Tel: 919-965-8613. *Librn,* Chris Markley; Staff 1 (MLS 1)
Circ 23,039
Library Holdings: AV Mats 861; Large Print Bks 1,549; Bk Vols 23,888; Per Subs 23; Talking Bks 453
Open Mon-Wed 9-6, Thurs 9-8, Fri 9-5, Sat 9-Noon
Bookmobiles: 1. Supvr, Pam Viars

SOUTHERN PINES

P SOUTHERN PINES PUBLIC LIBRARY*, 170 W Connecticut Ave, 28387-4819. SAN 312-9993. Tel: 910-692-8235. Circulation Tel: 910-692-8235, Ext 231. Reference Tel: 910-692-8235, Ext 232. FAX: 910-695-1037. Web Site: www.sppl.net. *Dir,* D Lynn Thompson; *Asst Dir, Pub Serv,* Alice Thomas; *Asst Dir, Tech Serv,* Kelley Loftis; Staff 10.35 (MLS 4, Non-MLS 6.35)
Founded 1922. Pop 12,717; Circ 117,667
Jul 2010-Jun 2011 Income $754,558, State $8,420, City $684,234, Other $41,904. Mats Exp $104,755. Sal $420,029
Library Holdings: AV Mats 9,278; e-books 23,694; Bk Vols 65,752; Per Subs 129
Special Collections: English as a Second Language (ESL); Large Print Coll
Automation Activity & Vendor Info: (Cataloging) TLC (The Library Corporation); (Circulation) TLC (The Library Corporation); (ILL) OCLC; (OPAC) TLC (The Library Corporation)
Database Vendor: TLC (The Library Corporation)
Wireless access
Publications: Bookends (Newsletter)
Open Mon-Thurs 10-7, Fri & Sat 10-5, Sun 2-5
Friends of the Library Group

SOUTHPORT

P BRUNSWICK COUNTY LIBRARY*, Margaret & James Harper Library, 109 W Moore St, 28461. SAN 355-1881. Tel: 910-457-6237. Web Site: library.brunsco.net. *Dir,* Maurice T Tate; *Mgr,* Nancy Price; *Ch Serv,* Simpson Signa; Staff 1 (MLS 1)
Founded 1912. Pop 75,000; Circ 200,000
Library Holdings: AV Mats 3,600; Bk Vols 100,000
Automation Activity & Vendor Info: (Cataloging) Innovative Interfaces, Inc; (Circulation) Innovative Interfaces, Inc; (OPAC) Innovative Interfaces, Inc
Open Mon-Fri 9-6, Sat 9-1, Sun 2-6
Friends of the Library Group
Branches: 4
G V BARBEE SR BRANCH, 8200 E Oak Island Dr, Oak Island, 28465, SAN 375-2925. Tel: 910-278-4283. FAX: 910-278-4049. *Br Mgr,* Susan Angelow
Library Holdings: Large Print Bks 3,000; Bk Vols 20,000; Per Subs 20; Talking Bks 1,000
Open Mon-Fri 9-6, Sat 9-1, Sun 2-6
Friends of the Library Group
HICKMANS CROSSROADS LIBRARY, 1040 Calabash Rd, Calabash, 28467. Tel: 910-575-0173. FAX: 910-575-0176. *Br Mgr,* Christi Iffergan; E-mail: ciffergan@brunsco.net
Founded 2004
Library Holdings: Bk Vols 9,000; Per Subs 30
Open Mon-Fri 9-6
Friends of the Library Group
LELAND BRANCH, 487 Village Rd, Leland, 28451, SAN 355-1911. Tel: 910-371-9442. FAX: 910-371-1856. *Br Mgr,* Lisa Milligan
Library Holdings: Bk Vols 10,000
Open Mon-Fri 9-6, Sat 9-1, Sun 2-6
Friends of the Library Group
ROURK LIBRARY, 5068 Main St, Shallotte, 28459, SAN 355-1946. Tel: 910-754-6578. FAX: 910-754-6874. *Mgr,* Felecia Hardy
Open Mon-Fri 8:30-6, Sat 9-1, Sun 2-6
Friends of the Library Group

SPARTA

P ALLEGHANY COUNTY PUBLIC LIBRARY*, 122 N Main St, 28675. (Mail add: PO Box 656, 28675-0656), SAN 313-0002. Tel: 336-372-5573. FAX: 336-372-4912. E-mail: alg@nwrl.org. Web Site: www.nwrl.org. *Librn,* Debra Brewer; E-mail: dbrewer@nwrl.org
Pop 10,000
Library Holdings: Bk Vols 40,000; Per Subs 25
Subject Interests: Genealogy, Local hist
Automation Activity & Vendor Info: (Acquisitions) SirsiDynix; (Cataloging) SirsiDynix; (Circulation) SirsiDynix; (Course Reserve) SirsiDynix; (ILL) SirsiDynix; (Media Booking) SirsiDynix; (OPAC) SirsiDynix; (Serials) SirsiDynix
Wireless access
Mem of Northwestern Regional Library
Open Mon & Thurs 8:30-6, Tues, Wed & Fri 8:30-5:30, Sat 8:30-1:30
Friends of the Library Group

SPENCER

P SPENCER PUBLIC LIBRARY*, 300 Fourth St, 28159. (Mail add: PO Box 152, 28159-0152), SAN 313-0010. Tel: 704-636-9072. *Librn,* Sarah Pruett
Founded 1943. Pop 3,075; Circ 13,497
Library Holdings: Bk Vols 10,500; Per Subs 40
Open Mon & Thurs 2-6, Tues & Fri 2-5, Sat 11-4

SPINDALE

J ISOTHERMAL COMMUNITY COLLEGE LIBRARY*, 286 ICC Loop Rd, 28160. (Mail add: PO Box 804, 28160-0804), SAN 313-0029. Tel: 828-286-3636. Interlibrary Loan Service Tel: 828-286-3636, Ext 301. Reference Tel: 828-286-4636. FAX: 828-286-8208. Web Site: www.isothermal.edu/library. *Dir of Libr Serv,* Charles P Wiggins; Tel: 828-286-3636, Ext 216, E-mail: cpwiggins@isothermal.edu; *Evening Librn,* Becky Cleland; Tel: 828-286-3636, Ext 309, E-mail: rcleland@isothermal.edu; *Circ, Ref Serv,* Engle Troxler; Tel: 828-286-3636, Ext 217, E-mail: etroxler@isothermal.edu; Staff 5 (MLS 3, Non-MLS 2)
Founded 1965. Enrl 2,987; Highest Degree: Associate

Library Holdings: AV Mats 3,292; Bk Titles 36,726; Bk Vols 40,913; Per Subs 146
Special Collections: Old Tryon Historical Coll
Subject Interests: Genealogy, Local hist
Automation Activity & Vendor Info: (Acquisitions) TLC (The Library Corporation); (Cataloging) TLC (The Library Corporation); (Circulation) TLC (The Library Corporation); (Course Reserve) TLC (The Library Corporation); (ILL) OCLC; (OPAC) TLC (The Library Corporation)
Database Vendor: ABC-CLIO, Alexander Street Press, CQ Press, EBSCOhost, Facts on File, Gale Cengage Learning, Ingram Library Services, LearningExpress, NC LIVE, OCLC CAMIO, OCLC FirstSearch, OCLC WorldShare Interlibrary Loan, Overdrive, Inc, ProQuest, ReferenceUSA, STAT!Ref (Teton Data Systems)
Wireless access
Publications: Library Handbook; Periodical Holdings List (Collection catalog)
Partic in CMC Library Consortium
Special Services for the Blind - Assistive/Adapted tech devices, equip & products; Audio mat; Copier with enlargement capabilities; Magnifiers; Ref serv; Talking bks
Open Mon-Thurs 7:45am-9pm, Fri 7:45-4:15

P RUTHERFORD COUNTY LIBRARY*, 255 Callahan Koon Rd, 28160. SAN 355-1229. Tel: 828-287-6115. FAX: 828-287-6119. Web Site: www.rutherfordcountylibrary.org. *Dir,* Martha Schatz; Tel: 828-287-6117, E-mail: martha.schatz@rutherfordcountync.gov; Staff 1 (MLS 1)
Founded 1938. Pop 63,432; Circ 224,561
Jul 2006-Jun 2007 Income (Main Library and Branch(s)) $518,465, State $137,700, Federal $13,500, County $367,265. Mats Exp $101,696, Books $70,000, Per/Ser (Incl. Access Fees) $11,000, AV Mat $12,500, Electronic Ref Mat (Incl. Access Fees) $8,196. Sal $254,642 (Prof $53,875)
Library Holdings: AV Mats 9,857; e-books 22,693; Bk Vols 74,229; Per Subs 58; Talking Bks 2,812
Special Collections: North Carolina History & Genealogy Coll
Subject Interests: Genealogy, Rutherford county hist
Automation Activity & Vendor Info: (Cataloging) TLC (The Library Corporation); (Circulation) TLC (The Library Corporation); (ILL) OCLC; (OPAC) TLC (The Library Corporation)
Database Vendor: TLC (The Library Corporation)
Wireless access
Publications: Booklist; Horn Book; Library Journal
Open Mon-Fri 9-5:30, Sat 10-1
Branches: 2
HAYNES BRANCH, 141 N Main St, Ste 110, Henrietta, 28076, SAN 355-1253. Tel: 828-657-5278, 828-657-9110. FAX: 828-657-5278. *Br Mgr,* Deb Womack
Library Holdings: Bk Vols 25,000
Open Mon-Fri 9-5, Sat 10-Noon
MOUNTAINS BRANCH, 150 Bills Creek Rd, Lake Lure, 28746, SAN 377-0249. Tel: 828-625-0456. FAX: 828-625-0453. Web Site: www.mountainsbranchlibrary.org. *Br Librn,* April Young; *Asst Librn,* Angela Turner; Staff 2 (MLS 1, Non-MLS 1)
Founded 1995
Library Holdings: CDs 1,061; DVDs 2,225; Large Print Bks 341; Bk Titles 21,422; Talking Bks 1,453
Function: Accelerated reader prog, Adult bk club, Audio & video playback equip for onsite use, Audiobks via web, Bks on CD, Children's prog, Computers for patron use, Copy machines, e-mail serv, Fax serv, Free DVD rentals, Genealogy discussion group, Handicapped accessible, ILL available, Music CDs, OverDrive digital audio bks, Photocopying/Printing, Preschool reading prog, Prog for adults, Prog for children & young adult, Pub access computers, Senior outreach, Story hour, Summer reading prog, Tax forms, VHS videos, Web-catalog, Wheelchair accessible
Open Mon-Fri 9-5, Sat 10-12
Friends of the Library Group

P SPINDALE PUBLIC LIBRARY, 131 Tanner St, 28160. SAN 355-1342. Tel: 828-286-3879. FAX: 828-286-8338. E-mail: spinlib@yahoo.com. Web Site: www.cmclibraries.org. *Librn,* Amy Taylor; *Asst Librn,* Sharon Melton; Staff 2 (Non-MLS 2)
Founded 1926
Library Holdings: Bk Vols 25,000
Database Vendor: TLC (The Library Corporation)
Wireless access
Open Mon-Fri 8:30-5

SPRING HOPE

S INTERNATIONAL WILD WATERFOWL ASSOCIATION, Lee Ridge Aviaries Reference Library, 1633 Bowden Rd, 27882. (Mail add: PO Box 1251, 27882-1251), SAN 372-6444. Tel: 252-478-5610. FAX: 252-478-7286. *Librn,* Walter B Sturgeon
Founded 1975
Library Holdings: Bk Titles 1,500
Special Collections: Natural History, bks, videos & slides
Subject Interests: Arctic, Govt aid & subsidies, Natural hist
Restriction: Private libr

SPRUCE PINE

J MAYLAND COMMUNITY COLLEGE*, Carolyn Munro Wilson Learning Resources Center, 200 Mayland Dr, 28777. (Mail add: PO Box 547, 28777-0547), SAN 373-8698. Tel: 828-765-7351, Ext 243. FAX: 828-765-0728. E-mail: lrc@mayland.edu. Web Site: www.mayland.edu/lrc. *Dean,* Jon Wilmesherr; E-mail: jwilmesherr@mayland.edu; *Assoc Librn,* Debra Barnett; E-mail: dbarnett@mayland.edu; *Tech Serv,* Eric King; E-mail: eking@mayland.edu; Staff 3 (MLS 1, Non-MLS 2)
Founded 1972
Library Holdings: Bk Titles 20,000; Bk Vols 25,000; Per Subs 125
Automation Activity & Vendor Info: (Cataloging) SirsiDynix; (Circulation) SirsiDynix
Function: ILL available
Partic in Community Colleges Libraries in North Carolina (CCLINC)
Open Mon-Thurs 8-7, Fri 8-4

P SPRUCE PINE PUBLIC LIBRARY*, 142 Walnut Ave, 28777. SAN 313-0045. Tel: 828-765-4673. E-mail: sppl@amyregionallibrary.org. Web Site: www.amyregionallibrary.org/sprucepine/index.html. *Head Librn,* Cathy Silver; *Asst Librn,* Meredith Hayes
Founded 1952. Pop 2,333
Library Holdings: Bk Vols 45,000; Per Subs 60
Subject Interests: Genealogy, Local hist
Database Vendor: TLC (The Library Corporation)
Function: Homebound delivery serv, Prog for children & young adult, Summer reading prog
Mem of Avery-Mitchell-Yancey Regional Library System
Open Mon & Tues 9-8, Wed-Fri 9-5, Sat 10-1
Friends of the Library Group

STATESVILLE

P IREDELL COUNTY PUBLIC LIBRARY*, 201 N Tradd St, 28677. (Mail add: PO Box 1810, 28687-1810), SAN 313-0061. Tel: 704-878-3090. Circulation Tel: 704-878-3134. Interlibrary Loan Service Tel: 704-878-5423. Reference Tel: 704-928-2400. FAX: 704-878-5449. Web Site: www.iredell.lib.nc.us. *Dir,* Steve L Messick; Tel: 704-878-3092, E-mail: smessick@co.iredell.nc.us; *Asst Dir,* Peggy Carter; Tel: 704-878-3098, E-mail: pcarter@co.iredell.nc.us; *Local Hist Librn,* Joel Reese; Tel: 704-878-3093, E-mail: jreese@co.iredell.nc.us; *Outreach Serv Librn,* Bernie Ipsen-Tompkins; Tel: 704-878-3099, E-mail: btompkins@co.iredell.nc.us; *Acq,* Zelma Flowers; Tel: 704-878-5448, E-mail: zflowers@co.iredell.nc.us; *Circ,* Gary Elam; Tel: 704-928-2405, E-mail: gelam@co.iredell.nc.us; *Info Tech,* Myra Patterson; Tel: 704-878-3148, E-mail: mpatterson@co.iredell.nc.us; *Ref,* Mardi J Durham; Tel: 704-878-3109, E-mail: mdurham@co.iredell.nc.us; *Tech Serv,* Kimberly Crawford; Tel: 704-878-3147, E-mail: kcrawford@co.iredell.nc.us; *Youth Serv,* Reitha Z Morrison; Tel: 704-928-2414, E-mail: rmorrison@co.iredell.nc.us; Staff 31 (MLS 7, Non-MLS 24)
Founded 1967. Pop 122,660; Circ 973,305
Library Holdings: Bks on Deafness & Sign Lang 65; Bk Titles 142,000; Bk Vols 186,000; Per Subs 290; Spec Interest Per Sub 43
Subject Interests: Genealogy, Local hist
Automation Activity & Vendor Info: (Cataloging) SirsiDynix
Database Vendor: SirsiDynix
Special Services for the Deaf - TDD equip
Open Mon-Thurs 9-9, Fri & Sat 9-6, Sun 2-6
Friends of the Library Group
Branches: 1
HARMONY BRANCH, 3393 Harmony Hwy, Harmony, 28634. (Mail add: PO Box 419, Harmony, 28634-0419). Tel: 704-546-7086. FAX: 704-546-7549. *Br Mgr,* Melissa Spivey; E-mail: mspivey@iredell.lib.nc.us
Founded 2003
Library Holdings: Bk Vols 15,000; Per Subs 43
Open Mon, Wed, Fri & Sat 9-6, Tues & Thurs 11-7
Friends of the Library Group
Bookmobiles: 1

J MITCHELL COMMUNITY COLLEGE*, Mildred & J P Huskins Library, 500 W Broad St, 28677. SAN 313-007X. Tel: 704-878-3271. Web Site: www.mitchellcc.edu. *Dir,* Vicki Caldwell; Tel: 704-978-3107, E-mail: vcaldwell@mitchellcc.edu; *Libr Spec,* Joan Jordan; Tel: 704-878-3249, E-mail: jjordan@mitchellcc.edu; *Ref Spec,* Jennifer Warren; Tel: 704-878-3270, E-mail: jwarren@mitchellcc.edu
Founded 1852
Library Holdings: Bk Titles 40,000; Bk Vols 42,000; Per Subs 180
Subject Interests: Criminal justice, Lit, Nursing, Soc sci

Automation Activity & Vendor Info: (Cataloging) Ex Libris Group; (Circulation) Ex Libris Group; (OPAC) Ex Libris Group; (Serials) Ex Libris Group
Function: ILL available, Photocopying/Printing
Partic in Charlotte Area Educ Consortium
Open Mon-Thurs 8am-10pm, Fri 8-5, Sun 6pm-10pm

SUPPLY

J BRUNSWICK COMMUNITY COLLEGE LIBRARY*, 50 College Rd, 28462. (Mail add: PO Box 30, 28462-0030). Tel: 910-755-7331. Toll Free Tel: 800-754-1050, Ext 331. Web Site: www.brunswickcc.edu/library. *Dir, Learning Res,* Carmen B Blanton; E-mail: blantonc@brunswickcc.edu; *Librn,* Brett O Riggs, E-mail: riggsb@brunswickcc.edu; *Libr Tech,* Delois Hines; E-mail: williamsdh@brunswickcc.edu
Founded 1979. Enrl 1,119
Library Holdings: Bk Vols 20,000; Per Subs 80
Special Collections: North Carolina Records Coll, microfilm
Subject Interests: Genealogy, Local hist
Automation Activity & Vendor Info: (Acquisitions) SirsiDynix; (Cataloging) SirsiDynix; (Circulation) SirsiDynix; (Course Reserve) SirsiDynix; (OPAC) SirsiDynix
Wireless access

SWANNANOA

C WARREN WILSON COLLEGE*, Pew Learning Center & Ellison Library, 701 Warren Wilson Rd, 28778. (Mail add: Campus Box 6358, PO Box 9000, Asheville, 28815-9000), SAN 313-0088. Tel: 828-771-3061. Circulation Tel: 828-771-3058. Reference Tel: 828-771-3035. FAX: 828-771-7085. Web Site: www.warren-wilson.edu/~library/. *Dir,* Chris Nugent; E-mail: nugent@warren-wilson.edu; *Acq,* Joy Pastucha; Tel: 828-771-3063, E-mail: jpastuch@warren-wilson.edu; *Archivist,* Diana Sanderson; Tel: 828-771-3055, E-mail: dsanderson@warren-wilson.edu; *Cat,* Yoke Mei Mah; Tel: 828-771-3054, E-mail: mmah@warren-wilson.edu; *Circ,* B K Segall; Tel: 828-771-3064, E-mail: bksegall@warren.wilson.edu; *Electronic Res,* David O Bradshaw; Tel: 828-771-3059, E-mail: dobrshaw@warren-wilson.edu; *ILL,* Mary O Brown; Tel: 828-771-3062, E-mail: mbrown@warren-wilson.edu; *Per,* Judy Tizzard; Tel: 828-771-3060, E-mail: jtizzard@warren-wilson.edu; Staff 6 (MLS 5, Non-MLS 1)
Founded 1894. Enrl 858; Fac 76; Highest Degree: Master
Library Holdings: AV Mats 2,588; CDs 308; DVDs 308; e-books 50,000; Bk Titles 95,000; Bk Vols 106,837; Per Subs 11,076; Spec Interest Per Sub 48; Videos 2,478
Special Collections: Arthur S Link Library of American History; James McClure Clarke Papers
Subject Interests: Appalachian studies, Archives, Environ studies, Gay & lesbian, Intl area studies, Local hist, Peace studies, Women studies
Automation Activity & Vendor Info: (Cataloging) SirsiDynix; (Circulation) SirsiDynix; (OPAC) SirsiDynix
Database Vendor: EBSCOhost, Gale Cengage Learning, OCLC FirstSearch, OVID Technologies, ProQuest
Publications: Library Lines (Accession list)
Partic in Appalachian Col Asn; Lyrasis; Mountain College Libr Network; North Carolina Libraries for Virtual Education; OCLC Online Computer Library Center, Inc
Open Mon-Thurs 8am-10:30pm, Fri 8-5, Sat 12:30-5, Sun 1-10:30
Friends of the Library Group

SYLVA

P JACKSON COUNTY PUBLIC LIBRARY*, 310 Keener St, 28779-3241. SAN 313-010X. Tel: 828-586-2016. FAX: 828-586-3423. Web Site: www.fontanalib.org/sylva/index.htm. *County Librn,* Dottie Brunette; Tel: 828-586-2016, Ext 303, E-mail: dbrunette@fontanalib.org; *Asst County Librn,* Liz Gregg; Tel: 828-586-2016, Ext 313, E-mail: egregg@fontanalib.org; Staff 20 (MLS 2, Non-MLS 18)
Founded 1928. Pop 40,000; Circ 100,000
Jul 2013-Jun 2014 Income $842,000, County $800,000, Locally Generated Income $40,000, Other $2,000. Mats Exp $69,040, Books $50,000, Per/Ser (Incl. Access Fees) $6,000, Micro $40, AV Equip $7,000, AV Mat $6,000. Sal $650,000 (Prof $45,752)
Library Holdings: Audiobooks 2,000; CDs 1,500; DVDs 2,500; Large Print Bks 2,200; Microforms 150; Bk Vols 65,000; Per Subs 93; Videos 300
Special Collections: Jean Nations Lefler Appalachian Coll
Subject Interests: Appalachia, Genealogy, Local hist
Automation Activity & Vendor Info: (Acquisitions) Baker & Taylor; (Cataloging) Evergreen; (Circulation) Evergreen; (ILL) OCLC; (OPAC) Evergreen; (Serials) Evergreen
Database Vendor: Baker & Taylor, NC LIVE
Wireless access
Function: After school storytime, Archival coll, Art exhibits, Audiobks via web, Bks on CD, Chess club, Children's prog, Computer training, Computers for patron use, Copy machines, e-mail & chat, e-mail serv, Electronic databases & coll, Equip loans & repairs, Exhibits, Holiday prog, ILL available, Mail & tel request accepted, Mail loans to mem, Music CDs, Notary serv, Online cat, Online ref, Online searches, Outside serv via phone, mail, e-mail & web, OverDrive digital audio bks, Photocopying/Printing, Preschool outreach, Preschool reading prog, Printer for laptops & handheld devices, Prog for adults, Prog for children & young adult, Pub access computers, Ref & res, Ref serv available, Ref serv in person, Res libr, Scanner, Senior computer classes, Spanish lang bks, Spoken cassettes & CDs, Spoken cassettes & DVDs, Story hour, Summer & winter reading prog, Tax forms, Teen prog, Telephone ref, Web-catalog, Wheelchair accessible, Workshops, Writing prog
Publications: Fontana Flyer (Newsletter)
Mem of Fontana Regional Library
Special Services for the Blind - Bks on CD; Large print bks; Screen enlargement software for people with visual disabilities
Open Mon & Wed 10-6, Tues & Thurs 10-8, Fri & Sat 10-5
Restriction: Photo ID required for access
Friends of the Library Group
Bookmobiles: 1

J SOUTHWESTERN COMMUNITY COLLEGE LIBRARY*, 447 College Dr, 28779. SAN 313-0118. Tel: 828-586-4091, Ext 268. Toll Free Tel: 800-447-4091, Ext 269. FAX: 828-586-3129. Web Site: www.southwesterncc.edu. *Dir,* Nelda M Reid; E-mail: nelda@southwesterncc.edu; *Librn,* Dianne J Lindgren; E-mail: diannel@southwesterncc.edu
Founded 1964
Library Holdings: Bk Vols 30,000; Per Subs 250
Wireless access
Open Mon-Thurs 8am-9pm, Fri 8-12, Sat (Summer) 9-2

TARBORO

J EDGECOMBE COMMUNITY COLLEGE*, Learning Resources Center, 2009 W Wilson St, 27886. SAN 312-9829. Tel: 252-823-5166. FAX: 252-823-6817. Web Site: www.edgecombe.edu. *Dir of Libr Serv,* Rejeanor H Scott; E-mail: scottr@edgecombe.edu; Staff 8 (MLS 3, Non-MLS 5)
Founded 1968. Enrl 2,500; Fac 134
Library Holdings: Bk Titles 36,929; Bk Vols 41,687; Per Subs 245
Special Collections: North Carolina County Records & History, bks, micro
Subject Interests: Acctg, Admin off tech, Autobody, Computer prog, Cosmetology, Health info tech, Imaging tech, Indust electrical-electronics tech, Indust maintenance tech, Law enforcement, Manufacturing eng tech, Mechanical drafting tech, Nursing, Radiology, Respiratory care, Soc work, Surgical tech, Teacher associates
Automation Activity & Vendor Info: (Acquisitions) SirsiDynix; (Cataloging) SirsiDynix; (Circulation) SirsiDynix; (Course Reserve) SirsiDynix, (ILL) SirsiDynix; (Media Booking) SirsiDynix; (OPAC) SirsiDynix; (Serials) SirsiDynix
Database Vendor: Gale Cengage Learning, OCLC FirstSearch, ProQuest
Partic in OCLC Online Computer Library Center, Inc
Open Mon-Thurs (Fall-Spring) 7:30am-9pm, Fri 7:30-4; Mon-Thurs (Summer) 7:15am-9pm
Departmental Libraries:
ROCKY MOUNT CAMPUS, 225 Tarboro St, Rocky Mount, 27801, SAN 373-6210. Tel: 252-446-0436. FAX: 252-985-2212. *Dir of Libr Serv,* Rejeanor H Scott; E-mail: scottr@edgecombe.edu
Open Mon-Thurs (Fall-Spring) 7:30am-9pm, Fri 7:30-4; Mon-Thurs (Summer) 7:15am-9pm

P EDGECOMBE COUNTY MEMORIAL LIBRARY*, 909 Main St, 27886. SAN 313-0126. Tel: 252-823-1141. FAX: 252-823-7699. Web Site: www.edgecombelibrary.org. *Dir,* Roman Leary; E-mail: rleary@edgecombelibrary.org; *Asst Dir,* Sue Howard; *Adult Serv Coordr,* Anna Adams; E-mail: aadams@edgecombelibrary.org; *Children's Coordr,* Carol Hayes; *Ref Asst,* Brian Everett; Staff 12 (MLS 2, Non-MLS 10)
Founded 1920. Pop 56,000; Circ 126,468
Library Holdings: Large Print Bks 10,000; Bk Vols 101,708; Per Subs 300; Talking Bks 4,000; Videos 178
Special Collections: NC History Coll
Automation Activity & Vendor Info: (Cataloging) TLC (The Library Corporation); (Circulation) TLC (The Library Corporation); (OPAC) TLC (The Library Corporation)
Database Vendor: ProQuest
Wireless access
Publications: Newsletter
Partic in NC State Libr Info Network; OCLC Online Computer Library Center, Inc
Open Mon-Thurs 9-9, Fri 9-6, Sat 9-5
Friends of the Library Group
Branches: 1
PINETOPS BRANCH, 201 S First St, Pinetops, 27864. (Mail add: PO Box 688, Pinetops, 27864-0688), SAN 377-0338. Tel: 252-827-4621. FAX: 252-827-0426. *Br Mgr,* Kathy Causway; E-mail: kcausway@edgecombelibrary.org

Library Holdings: Bk Vols 7,200
Open Mon, Wed & Fri 9-6, Tues & Thurs 9-8
Friends of the Library Group

TAYLORSVILLE

P ALEXANDER COUNTY LIBRARY*, 77 First Ave SW, 28681. SAN 313-0134. Tel: 828-632-4058. FAX: 828-632-1094. Web Site: www.alexanderlibrary.org. *Dir,* Laura Crooks
Founded 1967. Pop 35,000; Circ 115,000
Library Holdings: Bk Vols 57,000; Per Subs 149
Special Collections: Local History Room
Automation Activity & Vendor Info: (Acquisitions) SirsiDynix; (Cataloging) SirsiDynix; (Circulation) SirsiDynix; (Course Reserve) SirsiDynix; (ILL) SirsiDynix; (Media Booking) SirsiDynix; (OPAC) SirsiDynix; (Serials) SirsiDynix
Open Mon & Thurs 9-7, Tues, Wed & Fri 9-6, Sat 9-3
Friends of the Library Group

THOMASVILLE

J DAVIDSON COUNTY COMMUNITY COLLEGE*, Grady E Love Learning Resources Center, 297 DCCC Rd, 27360-7385. (Mail add: PO Box 1287, Lexington, 27293-1287), SAN 312-9047. Tel: 336-249-8186. Reference Tel: 336-224-4727. FAX: 336-248-8531. E-mail: dccclibrary@gmail.com. Web Site: www.davidsonccc.edu. *Dir, Libr Serv,* Jason Setzer; Tel: 336-249-8186, Ext 6207, E-mail: Jason_Setzer@davidsonccc.edu; Staff 3 (MLS 3)
Founded 1963. Enrl 2,100; Fac 66
Library Holdings: Bk Titles 57,000; Per Subs 236
Special Collections: Furniture Design & Decoration
Subject Interests: Archit, Arts, Automotive, Criticism, Furniture, Law, Local hist
Automation Activity & Vendor Info: (Acquisitions) SirsiDynix; (Cataloging) SirsiDynix; (Circulation) SirsiDynix; (Course Reserve) SirsiDynix; (OPAC) SirsiDynix; (Serials) SirsiDynix
Database Vendor: EBSCOhost, Gale Cengage Learning, OCLC FirstSearch, OVID Technologies, ProQuest, Westlaw
Publications: Cooleemee Plantation and Its People (monograph); Country College on the Yadkin: A Historical Narrative (monograph); Index to Centennial History of Davidson County; Index to Dutch Settlement on Abbotts Creek; Index to Saints & Sinners; Index to Wheels of Faith & Courage: History of Thomasville NC; Records of the Evangelical Lutheran Congregation at Sandy Creek; Topical Index to Homespun Magazine
Open Mon-Thurs 7:45am-9pm, Fri 7:45-4, Sat 9-2

TROY

J MONTGOMERY COMMUNITY COLLEGE LIBRARY*, 1011 Page St, 27371. SAN 313-0150. Tel: 910-576-6222, Ext 395. FAX: 910-576-2176. Web Site: www.montgomery.edu. *Dir, Learning Res,* Sharon Faulkner; Tel: 910-576-6222, Ext 201, E-mail: faulkners@montgomery.edu; *Pub Serv,* Billie Durham; Tel: 910-576-6222, Ext 520, E-mail: durhamb@montgomery.edu
Founded 1967. Highest Degree: Associate
Library Holdings: CDs 140; Bk Vols 18,300; Per Subs 100; Videos 300
Subject Interests: Forestry, Gunsmithing, Pottery, Taxidermy
Automation Activity & Vendor Info: (Cataloging) SirsiDynix; (Circulation) SirsiDynix; (Course Reserve) SirsiDynix; (ILL) SirsiDynix; (OPAC) SirsiDynix
Partic in NC State Ref Libr
Open Mon-Thurs 8am-9pm, Fri 8-3

P MONTGOMERY COUNTY PUBLIC LIBRARY*, 215 W Main, 27371. SAN 355-2004. Tel: 910-572-1311. FAX: 910-576-5565. Web Site: www.srls.info/montgomery/montindex.html. *Libr Dir,* David R Atkins; E-mail: david.atkins@ncmail.net
Pop 26,822; Circ 119,681
Library Holdings: Bk Vols 62,009; Per Subs 200
Subject Interests: Local hist
Open Mon, Wed & Fri 9:30-6, Tues & Thurs 9:30-8, Sat 9:30-3, Sun (Sept-May) 2-5
Friends of the Library Group
Branches: 4
ALLEN LIBRARY-BISCOE BRANCH, 307 Page St, Biscoe, 27209-0518, SAN 355-2039. Tel: 910-428-2551. FAX: 910-428-2551. *Br Mgr,* Dianne Saunders; Staff 1 (Non-MLS 1)
Circ 28,499
Open Mon & Tues 2:30-6, Wed & Fri 9:30-1
Friends of the Library Group
JOHN C CURRIE MEMORIAL LIBRARY CANDOR BRANCH, 138 S School Rd, Candor, 27229, SAN 355-2063. Tel: 910-974-4033. FAX: 910-974-4033. *Br Mgr,* Diana Steed; Staff 1 (Non-MLS 1)
Circ 44,657
Open Mon, Wed & Fri 1-5
Friends of the Library Group
MOUNT GILEAD BRANCH, 110 W Allenton St, Mount Gilead, 27306, SAN 355-2098. Tel: 910-439-6651. FAX: 910-439-6651. *Br Mgr,* Nancy Hurley; Staff 1 (Non-MLS 1)
Circ 15,262
Open Mon, Tues, Thurs & Fri 1-5
Friends of the Library Group
STAR BRANCH, 222 S Main St, Star, 27356, SAN 355-2128. Tel: 910-428-2338. FAX: 910-428-2338. *Br Mgr,* Claudia McIntosh; Staff 1 (Non-MLS 1)
Circ 28,156
Open Mon, Wed & Thurs 2-6, Tues & Fri 9:30-1:30
Friends of the Library Group

TRYON

S THE LANIER LIBRARY ASSOCIATION*, 72 Chestnut St, 28782. SAN 313-0169. Tel: 828-859-9535. E-mail: lanierlib@windstream.net. Web Site: www.lanierlib.org. *Exec Dir,* Vonda Krahn
Founded 1890
Library Holdings: Bk Titles 27,000; Per Subs 63
Special Collections: Sidney Lanier Coll; Tryon Area Authors
Wireless access
Publications: New Book List (Monthly); Newsletter (Quarterly)
Open Tues & Thurs 9:30-4:30, Wed 3-6, Sat 9:30-1, Sun 1-4
Restriction: Mem only

VANCEBORO

P VANCEBORO PUBLIC LIBRARY*, 7931 Main St, 28586. (Mail add: PO Box 38, 28586-0038), SAN 313-0177. Tel: 252-244-0571. FAX: 252-244-0571. Web Site: cpclib.org. *Librn,* Marlene Copeland
Circ 12,546
Library Holdings: Bk Vols 12,222; Per Subs 10
Mem of Craven-Pamlico-Carteret Regional Library System
Open Mon-Thurs 2-8, Fri 2-6

WADESBORO

P HAMPTON B ALLEN LIBRARY*, 120 S Greene St, 28170. SAN 313-0185. Tel: 704-694-5177. FAX: 704-694-5178. Web Site: www.srls.info/anson/ansonindex.html. *Dir,* Phoebe Midlan
Founded 1923. Pop 25,000; Circ 44,000
Library Holdings: Bk Vols 52,000; Per Subs 120
Subject Interests: Genealogy, Local hist
Automation Activity & Vendor Info: (Cataloging) TLC (The Library Corporation); (Circulation) TLC (The Library Corporation); (OPAC) TLC (The Library Corporation)
Partic in OCLC Online Computer Library Center, Inc
Open Mon 9:30-5:30, Wed & Fri 8:30-5:30, Tues & Thurs 8:30-6:30, Sat 9-12
Friends of the Library Group
Bookmobiles: 1

WAKE FOREST

R SOUTHEASTERN BAPTIST THEOLOGICAL SEMINARY LIBRARY*, 114 N Wingate St, 27587. SAN 313-0193. Tel: 919-556-3104. Circulation Tel: 919-863-8251. Interlibrary Loan Service Tel: 919-863-8323. Reference Tel: 919-863-8258. FAX: 919-863-8150. Web Site: www.library.sebts.edu. *Dir,* Shawn C Madden; Tel: 919-863-2250, E-mail: smadden@sebts.edu; *Asst Dir, Ref,* Terese Jerose; E-mail: tjerose@sebts.edu; *Supvr, Circ,* michele Shinholser; *Acq,* Steve Frary; *Archivist,* Bill Youngmark; *Cat,* Donna Wells; *Coll Develop,* Steve Jones; *Ser,* Jeannie Beck. Subject Specialists: *Hebrew,* Shawn C Madden; Staff 9 (MLS 4, Non-MLS 5)
Founded 1951. Enrl 1,915; Fac 54; Highest Degree: Doctorate
Library Holdings: Bk Titles 156,654; Bk Vols 177,000; Per Subs 781
Special Collections: Baptists (Baptist Documents Coll); Education Curriculum Lab; Lifeway Curriculum
Subject Interests: Baptist hist, Biblical studies, Christianity, Doctrine, Philos, Relig studies, Theol
Automation Activity & Vendor Info: (Acquisitions) SirsiDynix; (Cataloging) SirsiDynix; (Circulation) SirsiDynix; (Course Reserve) SirsiDynix; (OPAC) SirsiDynix; (Serials) SirsiDynix
Database Vendor: EBSCOhost, OCLC FirstSearch
Function: ILL available
Partic in Lyrasis; OCLC Online Computer Library Center, Inc
Open Mon, Tues & Thurs 7am-10pm, Wed 7-6, Fri 7-4, Sat 10-5

WALLACE

P THELMA DINGUS BRYANT LIBRARY*, 409 W Main St, 28466. (Mail add: PO Box 995, 28466), SAN 313-0207. Tel: 910-285-3796. FAX: 910-285-8224. E-mail: tdblibrary@townofwallace.com. *Dir,* Kris Bryant; *Ch Serv,* Sharon Robison; Staff 3 (Non-MLS 3)

Founded 1969. Circ 42,000
Library Holdings: DVDs 65; Large Print Bks 244; Bk Titles 30,300; Per Subs 35; Talking Bks 634; Videos 666
Subject Interests: English (Lang), Spanish
Automation Activity & Vendor Info: (Circulation) Follett Software
Wireless access
Friends of the Library Group

WALNUT COVE

P WALNUT COVE PUBLIC LIBRARY*, 106 W Fifth St, 27052. (Mail add: PO Box 706, 27052-0706), SAN 313-0215. Tel: 336-591-7496. FAX: 336-591-8494. E-mail: wco@nwrl.org. Web Site: www.nwrl.org. *Librn,* Christine Boles; E-mail: cboles@nwrl.org
Founded 1970. Pop 3,500
Library Holdings: Bk Vols 28,000
Special Collections: Danbury Reporter, bd vols; Stokes News, bd vols
Automation Activity & Vendor Info: (Acquisitions) SIRSI WorkFlows; (Cataloging) SirsiDynix; (Circulation) SirsiDynix; (OPAC) SirsiDynix
Wireless access
Mem of Northwestern Regional Library
Open Mon, Wed & Fri 9-5:30, Tues & Thurs 9-8, Sat 9-1
Friends of the Library Group

WARRENTON

P WARREN COUNTY MEMORIAL LIBRARY*, 119 South Front St, 27589. SAN 313-0223. Tel: 252-257-4990. FAX: 252-257-4089. E-mail: admin@co.warren.nc.us. Web Site: www.wcplnc.org. *Dir,* Cheryl Reddish; E-mail: creddish@co.warren.nc.us; *Outreach & Youth Serv Librn,* Mary Bullock; *Circ Supvr,* Jacqueline Sneed; *Cat,* Terry Henderson; *Coll Develop,* Terry Henderson; *Human Res,* Beth Perkinson; Staff 1 (MLS 1)
Founded 1937
Jul 2005-Jun 2006 Income $295,851, State $96,971, County $197,132, Other $3,748. Mats Exp $44,301, Books $32,507, AV Mat $8,735, Electronic Ref Mat (Incl. Access Fees) $3,059. Sal $188,448 (Prof $47,128)
Library Holdings: CDs 187; DVDs 1,574; e-books 24; Large Print Bks 1,396; Bk Vols 20,105; Per Subs 49; Talking Bks 810
Automation Activity & Vendor Info: (Cataloging) Follett Software; (Circulation) Follett Software; (OPAC) Follett Software
Database Vendor: NC LIVE
Open Mon-Thurs 10-7, Fri & Sat 10-6
Friends of the Library Group

WASHINGTON

J BEAUFORT COUNTY COMMUNITY COLLEGE LIBRARY*, Hwy 264 E, 27889. (Mail add: PO Box 1069, 27889-1069), SAN 313-024X. Tel: 252-940-6282. FAX: 252-946-9575. Web Site: www.beaufort.cc.nc.us/lrc/library/library.htm. *Dir, Libr Res Ctr,* Penny Sermons; Tel: 252-940-6243, E-mail: pennys@beaufortccc.edu; *Librn,* Betty Ferrell; Tel: 252-940-6253, E-mail: bettyf@beaufortccc.edu; Staff 5 (MLS 2, Non-MLS 3)
Founded 1968
Library Holdings: Bk Vols 30,000; Per Subs 222
Automation Activity & Vendor Info: (Cataloging) SirsiDynix; (Circulation) SirsiDynix; (OPAC) SirsiDynix
Database Vendor: Bowker, Cinahl, EBSCOhost, Gale Cengage Learning, NC LIVE, OCLC FirstSearch, ProQuest
Function: Audio & video playback equip for onsite use, AV serv, Bks on CD, CD-ROM, Computers for patron use, Copy machines, Distance learning, Equip loans & repairs, Free DVD rentals, Handicapped accessible, ILL available, Online searches, Orientations, Outside serv via phone, mail, e-mail & web, Photocopying/Printing, Ref serv available, Scanner
Partic in Community Colleges Libraries in North Carolina (CCLINC)
Open Mon-Thurs 8am-9:30pm, Fri 8-4, Sat 9-2

P BEAUFORT, HYDE & MARTIN COUNTY REGIONAL LIBRARY*, Old Court House, 158 N Market St, 27889. SAN 313-0258. Tel: 252-946-6401. FAX: 252-946-0352. Web Site: www.bhmlib.org. *Dir,* Susan Benning; E-mail: sbenning@bhmlib.org; Staff 19 (MLS 3, Non-MLS 16)
Founded 1941. Pop 76,024; Circ 195,802
Library Holdings: Bk Vols 117,000; Per Subs 275
Automation Activity & Vendor Info: (Cataloging) Evergreen; (Circulation) Evergreen; (OPAC) Evergreen
Wireless access
Member Libraries: Martin Memorial Library
Open Mon, Wed & Fri 9-5
Friends of the Library Group
Branches: 7
BATH COMMUNITY, Main & Carteret Sts, Bath, 27808. (Mail add: PO Box 160, Bath, 27808-0160), SAN 377-6352. Tel: 252-923-6371. FAX: 252-923-0497. *Br Mgr,* Winnifred Webster; E-mail: wwebster@bhmlib.org
Library Holdings: Bk Vols 5,000; Per Subs 15
Open Mon, Wed & Fri 9-5, Sat 9-12
Friends of the Library Group
BELHAVEN PUBLIC, 333 E Main St, Belhaven, 27810. (Mail add: PO Box 130, Belhaven, 27810-0130), SAN 312-7435. Tel: 252-943-2993. FAX: 252-943-2606. *Librn,* Joan Bogun
Library Holdings: Large Print Bks 500; Bk Vols 6,000; Per Subs 20
Open Mon-Fri 9:30-5:30, Sat 10-1
Friends of the Library Group
HAZEL W GUILFORD MEMORIAL, 524 Main St, Aurora, 27806. (Mail add: PO Box 489, Aurora, 27806-0489), SAN 377-6417. Tel: 252-322-5046. FAX: 252-322-7109. *Librn,* Robina Norman
Library Holdings: Large Print Bks 150; Bk Vols 2,000; Per Subs 20
Open Tues & Thurs 9-5, Wed & Sat 9-12
Friends of the Library Group
MARTIN MEMORIAL, 200 N Smithwick St, Williamston, 27892, SAN 377-6433. Tel: 252-792-7476. FAX: 252-792-8964. *Head Librn,* Ann Phelps; Staff 5 (MLS 1, Non-MLS 4)
Library Holdings: Audiobooks 100; DVDs 150; Large Print Bks 750; Microforms 200; Bk Vols 40,000; Per Subs 70; Videos 25
Special Collections: Local Genealogy Coll; North Carolina Coll
Function: Accelerated reader prog, Adult bk club, Bks on CD, Children's prog, Computers for patron use, Copy machines, e-mail & chat, Electronic databases & coll, Free DVD rentals, Handicapped accessible, Holiday prog, ILL available, Online cat, Photocopying/Printing, Preschool outreach, Prog for adults, Prog for children & young adult, Pub access computers, Ref & res, Ref serv available, Ref serv in person, Story hour, Summer reading prog, Tax forms, Teen prog
Open Mon, Tues, Fri & Sat 9:30-5:30, Wed & Thurs 9:30-8, Sun 2-5
Friends of the Library Group
MATTAMUSKEET, 20418 US 264, Swan Quarter, 27885. Tel: 252-926-0310. FAX: 252-926-0311. *Librn,* Ruth O'Neal Harrell
Library Holdings: AV Mats 400; Bk Titles 22,000; Bk Vols 25,000; Per Subs 40
Open Mon-Fri 3-6, Sat 9-1
OCRACOKE BRANCH, 225 Back Rd, Ocracoke, 27960. (Mail add: PO Box 130, Ocracoke, 27960-0130), SAN 376-2890. Tel: 252-928-4436. FAX: 252-928-4436. Web Site: www.bhmlib.org/bhm/ocracoke.htm. *Br Head,* Ingeborg Frye; Fax: 252-928-2633
Pop 1,000
Library Holdings: Large Print Bks 120; Bk Vols 5,000; Per Subs 25
Special Collections: North Carolina Fiction, Nonfiction & Reference Coll. Municipal Document Depository
Open Mon, Wed & Fri 12-4, Tues 12-3, Thurs 12-6, Sat 9-1
Friends of the Library Group
ROBERSONVILLE PUBLIC, 119 S Main St, Robersonville, 27871. (Mail add: PO Box 1060, Robersonville, 27871-1060), SAN 377-6468. Tel: 252-508-0342. FAX: 252-795-3359. *Br Mgr,* Madge Partin
Library Holdings: Bk Titles 6,000; Bk Vols 16,000
Open Mon-Fri 9-5, Sat 9-12
Friends of the Library Group
Bookmobiles: 2

P GEORGE H & LAURA E BROWN LIBRARY*, 122 Van Norden St, 27889. SAN 313-0266. Tel: 252-946-4300. FAX: 252 975 2015. Web Site: washington-nc.com/library.aspx. *Dir,* Gloria Moore; *Coordr, Ch Serv,* Rose Ann Fennell; *Coordr, Libr Serv,* Carol Newman; Staff 2 (MLS 2)
Founded 1911. Pop 15,000; Circ 72,000
Library Holdings: Bk Titles 50,000; Bk Vols 55,000; Per Subs 75
Special Collections: Bellamy Papers; Bible Translations Coll; C F Warren Coll; Cemetery Records; County Newspapers Found & Filmed by North Carolina State Archives, dated prior to 1900; Current Local Newspaper, microfilm; Dunstan Papers; E J Warren Coll; Ernest Harding Civil War Coll; Fowle Papers; Gould Marsh Ledger, 1805-11; Havens Ledgers; John Respess Papers, copy; Jonathan Havens Coll; Josiah Fowle Ledger, 1808-47, copy; Local Daughters of the American Revolution Records, copies; Wiswall Papers. Oral History
Subject Interests: Career Information Center, Carolina hist, Civil War, Genealogy
Automation Activity & Vendor Info: (Cataloging) TLC (The Library Corporation); (Circulation) TLC (The Library Corporation)
Wireless access
Partic in North Carolina Information Network (NCIN); OCLC Online Computer Library Center, Inc
Open Mon-Thurs 9-9, Fri 9-5, Sat 9-1
Friends of the Library Group

WAYNESVILLE

P HAYWOOD COUNTY PUBLIC LIBRARY*, 678 S Haywood St, 28786-4398. SAN 355-2152. Tel: 828-452-5169. FAX: 828-452-6746. Web Site: www.haywoodlibrary.org. *Dir,* Sharon Woodrow; Tel: 828-356-2504, E-mail: swoodrow@haywoodnc.net; *Asst Dir,* Kim Garmon; Tel: 828-356-2513, E-mail: kgarmon@haywoodnc.net; *Head, Youth Serv,* Lisa

Hartzell; *Ad,* Kathy Olsen; Tel: 828-356-2507, E-mail: kolsen@haywoodnc.net; *Outreach Librn,* Donna Surles; Tel: 828-356-2519, E-mail: dsurles@haywoodnc.net; Staff 25 (MLS 5, Non-MLS 20)
Founded 1891. Pop 52,000; Circ 465,000
Library Holdings: Bk Vols 14,000; Per Subs 500
Subject Interests: NC genealogy
Automation Activity & Vendor Info: (Acquisitions) SirsiDynix; (Cataloging) SirsiDynix; (Circulation) SirsiDynix; (Course Reserve) SirsiDynix; (ILL) SirsiDynix; (Media Booking) SirsiDynix; (OPAC) SirsiDynix; (Serials) SirsiDynix
Database Vendor: Dialog, Gale Cengage Learning, OCLC FirstSearch, ProQuest, SirsiDynix, Wilson - Wilson Web
Function: ILL available
Publications: Paperclips: Haywood County Public Library & Friends (Newsletter)
Open Mon-Wed & Fri 9-6, Thurs 9-7, Sat 9-5
Friends of the Library Group
Branches: 3
CANTON BRANCH, 11 Pennsylvania Ave, Canton, 28716, SAN 355-2187. Tel: 828-648-2924. FAX: 828-648-0377. *Ad, Mgr,* Mannie Dalton Crone; Tel: 828-648-2924, E-mail: mcrone@haywood.net; Staff 3 (MLS 1, Non-MLS 2)
Library Holdings: Bk Vols 25,000; Per Subs 75
Function: Art exhibits, Audiobks via web, Bks on cassette, Bks on CD, CD-ROM, Children's prog, Computer training, Computers for patron use, Copy machines, e-mail & chat, e-mail serv, Electronic databases & coll, Fax serv, Free DVD rentals, Handicapped accessible, Holiday prog, ILL available, Music CDs, Notary serv, Online cat, Online searches, OverDrive digital audio bks, Photocopying/Printing, Printer for laptops & handheld devices, Prog for adults, Prog for children & young adult, Pub access computers, Senior computer classes, Serves mentally handicapped consumers, Spoken cassettes & CDs, Story hour, Summer reading prog, Tax forms, VHS videos
Open Mon, Wed & Fri 9-6, Tues & Thurs 9-7, Sun 1:30-5
Friends of the Library Group
FINES CREEK, Fines Creek Community Bldg, 190 Fines Creek Rd, Clyde, 28721. Tel: 828-627-0146. *Br Mgr,* Kim Garmon; E-mail: kgarmon@haywoodnc.net
Library Holdings: Bk Vols 3,654
Open Mon & Wed 9-5
Friends of the Library Group
MAGGIE VALLEY, Town Hall, 3987 Soco Rd, Maggie Valley, 28751. Tel: 828-356-2541. *Br Mgr,* Kim Garmon; E-mail: kgarmon@haywoodnc.net
Founded 2002
Library Holdings: Bk Vols 6,544; Per Subs 15
Open Tues & Thurs 9-5
Friends of the Library Group
Bookmobiles: 1

WELDON

J HALIFAX COMMUNITY COLLEGE LIBRARY*, 100 College Dr, 27890. (Mail add: PO Drawer 809, 27890-0700), SAN 313-0312. Tel: 252-536-7237. Circulation Tel: 252-536-7236. FAX: 252-536-0474. Web Site: www.halifaxcc.edu. *Dir,* Marc L Finney; E-mail: finneym@halifaxcc.edu; Staff 6 (MLS 1, Non-MLS 5)
Founded 1968. Enrl 1,721; Fac 12; Highest Degree: Associate
Library Holdings: Bk Titles 30,000; Per Subs 100
Special Collections: News Bank Library 1979-present
Subject Interests: Archit, Art, Dental hygiene, Econ, Govt, Hist, Lit, Nursing, Paralegal
Wireless access
Open Mon-Thurs 8-5, Fri (Summer) 8-4

WENTWORTH

J ROCKINGHAM COMMUNITY COLLEGE*, Gerald B James Library, 315 Wrenn Memorial Rd, 27375. (Mail add: PO Box 38, 27375-0038), SAN 313-0339. Tel: 336-342-4261, Ext 2247. FAX: 336-342-1203. E-mail: library@rockinghamcc.edu. Web Site: www.rockinghamcc.edu/library. *Dir of Libr Serv,* Kimberly Shireman; Tel: 336-342-4261, Ext 2250, E-mail: shiremank@rockinghamcc.edu; *Pub Serv Librn,* Michael Rose; Tel: 336-342-4261, Ext 2271, E-mail: rosem@rockinghamcc.edu; *Tech Serv Librn,* Mary Gomez; Tel: 336-342-4261, Ext 2320, E-mail: gomezm@rockinghamcc.edu; Staff 8 (MLS 3, Non-MLS 5)
Founded 1966. Enrl 2,200; Fac 140; Highest Degree: Associate
Library Holdings: Bk Titles 37,500; Bk Vols 45,500; Per Subs 145
Special Collections: Rockingham County Historical Coll, County hist bks, family/genealogy files, local newsp, maps, micro, oral hist, photog, realia
Subject Interests: Rockingham county
Automation Activity & Vendor Info: (Cataloging) SirsiDynix; (Circulation) SirsiDynix; (OPAC) SirsiDynix
Database Vendor: EBSCOhost, Gale Cengage Learning, OCLC FirstSearch, ProQuest
Wireless access
Partic in Community Colleges Libraries in North Carolina (CCLINC); Lyrasis; OCLC Online Computer Library Center, Inc
Open Mon-Thurs 7:45-9, Fri 7:45-3

WEST JEFFERSON

P APPALACHIAN REGIONAL LIBRARY, 148 Library Dr, 28694. SAN 375-5932. Tel: 336-846-2041. FAX: 336-846-7503. Web Site: www.arlibrary.org. *Dir of Libr,* Jane W Blackburn; E-mail: jblackburn@arlibrary.org; Staff 45.7 (MLS 11.6, Non-MLS 34.1)
Founded 1962. Pop 149,423; Circ 693,130
Library Holdings: Audiobooks 9,148; AV Mats 20,213; CDs 9,148; DVDs 11,065; e-books 3,075; Bk Vols 250,672; Per Subs 279; Talking Bks 9,148
Special Collections: Local Histories of Ashe, Watauga & Wilkes Counties
Subject Interests: Genealogy, Local hist
Automation Activity & Vendor Info: (Cataloging) Evergreen; (Circulation) Evergreen; (OPAC) Evergreen
Wireless access
Function: 24/7 Electronic res, 24/7 Online cat, Activity rm, Adult bk club, Adult literacy prog, After school storytime, Archival coll, Art exhibits, Audiobks via web, AV serv, Bk club(s), Bks on CD, Children's prog, Citizenship assistance, Computer training, Computers for patron use, Copy machines, Electronic databases & coll, eReaders, Exhibits, Family literacy, Fax serv, Free DVD rentals, Handicapped accessible, Holiday prog, Home delivery & serv to Sr ctr & nursing homes, Homebound delivery serv, Homework prog, ILL available, Life-long learning prog for all ages, Magazines, Magnifiers for reading, Mail & tel request accepted, Microfiche/film & reading machines, Movies, Music CDs, Notary serv, Online cat, Online searches, Outreach serv, Outside serv via phone, mail, e-mail & web, OverDrive digital audio bks, Photocopying/Printing, Preschool outreach, Printer for laptops & handheld devices, Prog for adults, Prog for children & young adult, Pub access computers, Ref & res, Ref serv available, Ref serv in person, Scanner, Senior computer classes, Senior outreach, Serves mentally handicapped consumers, Story hour, Study rm, Summer reading prog, Tax forms, Teen prog, Telephone ref, Wheelchair accessible, Workshops, Writing prog
Member Libraries: Ashe County Public Library; Watauga County Public Library; Wilkes County Public Library
Open Mon-Thurs 9-7, Fri & Sat 9-5
Friends of the Library Group

P ASHE COUNTY PUBLIC LIBRARY*, 148 Library Dr, 28694. SAN 320-5010. Tel: 336-846-2041. FAX: 336-846-7503. Web Site: www.arlibrary.org. *County Librn,* Suzanne Moore; E-mail: smoore@arlibrary.org; *Adult Serv,* Kim Grindrod; *Youth Serv,* Peggy Bailey; Staff 5 (MLS 3, Non-MLS 2)
Founded 1932. Pop 26,000; Circ 174,978
Library Holdings: AV Mats 6,008; Bk Vols 46,769; Per Subs 90
Special Collections: Business & Career; Local History & Genealogy. Oral History
Automation Activity & Vendor Info: (Cataloging) Evergreen; (Circulation) Evergreen; (OPAC) Evergreen; (Serials) EBSCO Online
Database Vendor: NC LIVE
Wireless access
Mem of Appalachian Regional Library
Open Mon-Thurs 9-7, Fri & Sat 9-5
Friends of the Library Group
Bookmobiles: 1. Outreach Servs, Janis DeBord

WHITEVILLE

P COLUMBUS COUNTY PUBLIC LIBRARY*, Carolyn T High Memorial Library, 407 N Powell Blvd, 28472. SAN 355-2217. Tel: 910-642-3116. Reference Tel: 910-641-3976. FAX: 910-642-3839. Web Site: www.columbusco.org. *Dir, Libr Serv,* Morris D Pridgen, Jr; Fax: 910-642-7271, E-mail: mpridgen@columbusco.org; *Cat, Tech Serv,* Faye King; *Ch Serv,* Lizette Dixon; *Circ,* Annie Bowen; *ILL,* Alice Soles; *Ref Serv,* Ann White; *Ser,* Diane Worley; *Syst Adminr,* Chad Benton; Staff 25 (MLS 1, Non-MLS 24)
Founded 1921. Pop 50,198; Circ 257,350
Library Holdings: AV Mats 3,698; Bk Titles 115,000; Bk Vols 120,000; Per Subs 321
Special Collections: Genealogy & Local History; Local newspapers on microfilm; North Carolina
Subject Interests: Genealogy, Local hist
Automation Activity & Vendor Info: (Circulation) Innovative Interfaces, Inc
Function: Homebound delivery serv
Publications: Columbus County, North Carolina: Recollections & Records
Open Mon-Thurs 9-8, Fri 9-5, Sat 10:30-5
Friends of the Library Group

Branches: 5
CHADBOURN COMMUNITY, 301 N Wilson St, Chadbourn, 28431, SAN 377-8479. Tel: 910-654-3322. FAX: 910-654-4392. *Br Mgr,* Dianne Milliken; E-mail: millikendianne@hotmail.com
Library Holdings: Bk Vols 2,000; Per Subs 33
Automation Activity & Vendor Info: (Acquisitions) Innovative Interfaces, Inc; (Cataloging) Innovative Interfaces, Inc
Open Mon-Thurs 11-6, Fri 11-5
Friends of the Library Group
EAST COLUMBUS LIBRARY, 103 Church Rd, Riegelwood, 28456, SAN 355-2233. Tel: 910-655-4157. FAX: 910-655-9414. *Br Mgr,* Robin Creech; *Asst Librn,* Sarah Clifton; Staff 2 (Non-MLS 2)
Library Holdings: Large Print Bks 150; Bk Vols 11,000; Per Subs 30
Open Mon-Thurs 11-6, Fri 11-5
Friends of the Library Group
FAIR BLUFF COMMUNITY, 315 Railroad St, Fair Bluff, 28469. (Mail add: PO Box 428, Fair Bluff, 28439-0428), SAN 355-2241. Tel: 910-649-7098. FAX: 910-649-7733. *Br Mgr,* Teresa Fountain; Staff 2 (Non-MLS 2)
Library Holdings: Bk Vols 11,000; Per Subs 40; Talking Bks 32; Videos 126
Open Mon-Thurs 11-6, Fri 11-5
Friends of the Library Group
RUBE MCCRAY MEMORIAL, 301 Flemington Dr, Lake Waccamaw, 28450, SAN 375-2933. Tel: 910-646-4616. FAX: 910-646-4747. *Br Mgr,* Kim Jenerette; Staff 2 (Non-MLS 2)
Library Holdings: AV Mats 200; Large Print Bks 175; Bk Vols 10,000; Per Subs 250
Open Mon-Thurs 11-6, Fri 11-5, Sun 2-5
Friends of the Library Group
TABOR CITY PUBLIC, 101 E Fifth St, Tabor City, 28463, SAN 355-2276. Tel: 910-653-3774. FAX: 910-653-3788. *Br Mgr,* Patricia Strickland; Staff 2 (Non-MLS 2)
Library Holdings: Bk Vols 17,118; Per Subs 23
Open Mon-Thurs 11-6, Fri 11-5
Friends of the Library Group
Bookmobiles: 1

J SOUTHEASTERN COMMUNITY COLLEGE LIBRARY*, 4564 Chadbourne Hwy, 28472. (Mail add: PO Box 151, 28472-0151), SAN 313-0347. Tel: 910-642-7141, Ext 386. FAX: 910-642-4513. Web Site: www.sccnc.edu/library.htm. *Librn,* Kay Houser; Tel: 910-642-7141, Ext 219, E-mail: khouser@sccnc.edu; Staff 6 (MLS 2, Non-MLS 4)
Founded 1965. Enrl 1,600; Fac 80
Library Holdings: Bk Vols 74,000; Per Subs 236
Special Collections: North Carolina Colonial Records 1662-1789; North Carolina Genealogy & History Coll; Official Records of the Union & Confederate Armies; Southeastern North Carolina Records, micro; War of the Rebellion
Publications: Library Handbook
Partic in Community Colleges Libraries in North Carolina (CCLINC); Lyrasis; North Carolina Community College System; OCLC Online Computer Library Center, Inc; State of Iowa Libraries Online
Open Mon-Thurs (Winter) 8am-9pm, Fri 8-3; Mon-Thurs (Summer) 7:30am-9pm

WILKESBORO

J WILKES COMMUNITY COLLEGE*, Learning Resources Center/Pardue Library, 1328 S Collegiate Dr, 28697. (Mail add: PO Box 120, 28697-0120), SAN 313-0363. Tel: 336-838-6114. Interlibrary Loan Service Tel: 336-838-6117. FAX: 336-838-6515. E-mail: wccparduelibrary@gmail.com. Web Site: www.wilkescc.edu. *Dir,* Christy Earp; Tel: 336-838-6117, E-mail: christy.earp@wilkescc.edu; *Libr Asst,* Vickie L Cothren; Tel: 336-838-6513, E-mail: vickie.cothren@wilkescc.edu; Staff 5 (MLS 3, Non-MLS 2)
Founded 1966
Jul 2005-Jun 2006 Income $343,985. Mats Exp $66,915, Books $51,991, Per/Ser (Incl. Access Fees) $10,364, Other Print Mats $367, Micro $370, AV Mat $62, Electronic Ref Mat (Incl. Access Fees) $3,761
Library Holdings: AV Mats 6,867; Bk Titles 60,000; Per Subs 127
Special Collections: James Larkin Pearson Coll; Wilkes County Coll, bks & tapes. Oral History
Automation Activity & Vendor Info: (Acquisitions) SirsiDynix; (Cataloging) SirsiDynix; (Circulation) SirsiDynix; (OPAC) SirsiDynix
Database Vendor: EBSCOhost, OCLC FirstSearch
Partic in North Carolina Library & Information Network

WILLIAMSTON

J MARTIN COMMUNITY COLLEGE LIBRARY*, 1161 Kehukee Park Rd, 27892-4425. SAN 313-038X. Tel: 252-789-0238, 252-792-1521. FAX: 252-792-4425. Web Site: www.martin.cc.nc.us. *Interim Dir,* Mrs Sudie Reason; E-mail: sreason@martincc.edu; Staff 2 (MLS 2)
Founded 1968
Library Holdings: High Interest/Low Vocabulary Bk Vols 150; Large Print Bks 250; Bk Vols 40,000; Per Subs 228; Talking Bks 2,000
Special Collections: Martin County History Coll
Subject Interests: Equine tech, Indust lab tech, Phys therapy
Automation Activity & Vendor Info: (Acquisitions) TLC (The Library Corporation); (Cataloging) TLC (The Library Corporation); (Circulation) TLC (The Library Corporation)
Wireless access
Partic in NC Dept of Commun Cols

WILMINGTON

J CAPE FEAR COMMUNITY COLLEGE*, Learning Resource Center, 415 N Second St, 28401-3993. (Mail add: 411 N Front St, 28401-3993), SAN 313-0401. Tel: 910-362-7030. Reference Tel: 910-362-7034. Administration Tel: 910-362-7033. FAX: 910-362-7005. E-mail: lrcref@cfcc.edu. Web Site: cfcc.edu/lrc. *Dean,* Catherine Lee; *N Campus Librn,* Bill Keach; Tel: 910-362-7530, Fax: 910-362-7549, E-mail: bkeach@cfcc.edu; *Ref Serv,* Cathy Burwell; Tel: 910-362-7456, E-mail: cburwell@cfcc.edu; *Tech Serv,* Deanna Lewis; Tel: 910-362-7039, E-mail: dllewis@cfcc.edu; Staff 8 (MLS 6, Non-MLS 2)
Founded 1964. Enrl 7,100; Fac 254; Highest Degree: Associate
Library Holdings: AV Mats 7,175; e-books 24,990; Microforms 31,227; Bk Vols 47,352; Per Subs 581
Subject Interests: Local hist, NC hist
Automation Activity & Vendor Info: (Cataloging) SirsiDynix; (Circulation) SirsiDynix; (ILL) SirsiDynix; (OPAC) SirsiDynix; (Serials) SirsiDynix
Database Vendor: Alexander Street Press, ALLDATA Online, CQ Press, EBSCOhost, Gale Cengage Learning, JSTOR, Micromedex, NC LIVE, ProQuest, SirsiDynix, Westlaw, Wilson - Wilson Web
Wireless access
Partic in Carolina Consortium; North Carolina Libraries for Virtual Education
Open Mon-Thurs 7:30am-9pm, Fri 7:30-5, Sat 10-2; Mon-Thurs (Summer) 7:30am-9pm, Fri 7:30-Noon

P NEW HANOVER COUNTY PUBLIC LIBRARY*, 201 Chestnut St, 28401. SAN 355-2306. Tel: 910-798-6300. Circulation Tel: 910-798-6302. Interlibrary Loan Service Tel: 910-798-6359. Reference Tel: 910-798-6301. Administration Tel: 910-798-6309. FAX: 910-798-6312. TDD: 910-798-6306. Web Site: www.nhclibrary.org. *Dir,* Harry Tuchmayer; Tel: 910-798-6321, E mail: htuchmayer@nhcgov.com; *Asst Dir,* Paige Owens; Tel: 910-798-6322, E-mail: powens@nhcgov.com; *Sr Librn,* Dorothy Hodder; Tel: 910-798-6323, E-mail: dhodder@nhcgov.com; *Sr Librn,* Margaret Miles; Tel: 910-798-6361, E-mail: mmiles@nhcgov.com; *Sr Librn,* Jennifer Daugherty; Tel: 910-798-6305, E-mail: jdaugherty@nhcgov.com; *Librn,* Stephanie Carver; Tel: 910-798-6352, E-mail: scarver@nhcgov.com; *Librn,* Julie Criser; Tel: 910-798-6362, E-mail: jcriser@nhcgov.com; *Librn,* Susan DeMarco; Tel: 910-798-6353, E-mail: sdemarco@nhcgov.com; *Librn,* Scooter Hayes; Tel: 910-798-6348, E-mail: shayes@nhcgov.com; *Librn,* Janet Oliver; Tel: 910-798-6341, E-mail: joliver@nhcgov.com; *Librn,* Mary Ellen Nolan; Tel: 910-798-6358, E-mail: mnolan@nhcgov.com; *Librn,* Justine Roach; Tel: 910-798-6355, E-mail: jroach@nhcgov.com; *Supv Librn, Ref,* James Rider; Tel: 910-798-6351, E-mail: jrider@nhcgov.com. Subject Specialists: *Genealogy, Local hist,* Jennifer Daugherty; *Ch,* Julie Criser; *Ch,* Susan DeMarco, *Ch,* Scooter Hayes; *Consumer health,* Mary Ellen Nolan; *Bus, Law,* Justine Roach; Staff 39 (MLS 16, Non-MLS 23)
Founded 1906. Pop 165,000; Circ 1,110,308
Special Collections: Civil War Materials; Fales Coll; Historic Wilmington Plaques; New Hanover County & City of Wilmington, North Carolina; North Carolina History; Old New Hanover Genealogical Society Publications
Automation Activity & Vendor Info: (Circulation) TLC (The Library Corporation); (OPAC) TLC (The Library Corporation)
Wireless access
Partic in North Carolina Information Network (NCIN)
Open Mon & Tues 9-8, Wed & Thurs 9-6, Fri & Sat 9-5, Sun 1-5
Friends of the Library Group
Branches: 4
CAROLINA BEACH BRANCH, 300 Cape Fear Blvd, Carolina Beach, 28428, SAN 355-2314. Tel: 910-798-6385. FAX: 910-458-9422. *Libr Asst,* Sharon Walters; E-mail: swalters@nhcgov.com; *Libr Assoc,* Cathy Wahnefried; E-mail: cwahnefried@nhcgov.com
Function: Adult bk club
Open Mon, Wed, Fri & Sat 9-1, Tues & Thurs 1-5
L LAW LIBRARY, 201 Chestnut St, 28401. Tel: 910-798-6306. Circulation Tel: 910-798-6302. Interlibrary Loan Service Tel: 910-798-6359. Reference Tel: 910-798-6301. Administration Tel: 910-798-6324, 910-798-6325. Administration FAX: 910-798-6312. *Librn,* Justine Roach; E-mail: jroach@nhcgov.com
Special Collections: Law
Automation Activity & Vendor Info: (Acquisitions) TLC (The Library Corporation); (Cataloging) TLC (The Library Corporation); (Circulation)

TLC (The Library Corporation); (ILL) OCLC WorldShare Interlibrary Loan; (OPAC) TLC (The Library Corporation)
Database Vendor: Booklist Online, CQ Press, Evanced Solutions, Inc, Ingram Library Services, Medline, NC LIVE, OCLC WorldShare Interlibrary Loan, PubMed, ReferenceUSA, TLC (The Library Corporation), ValueLine, Westlaw
Friends of the Library Group

MYRTLE GROVE, 5155 S College Rd, 28412, SAN 372-8323. Tel: 910-798-6390. FAX: 910-452-6417. *Sr Librn,* Teresa Bishop; E-mail: tbishop@nhcgov.com
Open Mon-Wed 9-8, Thurs-Sat 9-5

NORTHEAST REGIONAL LIBRARY, 1241 Military Cutoff Rd, 28403, SAN 355-2330. Tel: 910-798-6370. Circulation Tel: 910-798-6372. Reference Tel: 910-798-6371. FAX: 910-256-1238. *Supv Librn,* Jimi Rider; E-mail: jrider@nhcgov.com; *Librn,* Linda Clover
Library Holdings: Bk Vols 9,828
Open Mon-Wed 9-8, Thurs-Sat 9-5

C WILLIAM MADISON RANDALL LIBRARY*, 601 S College Rd, 28403-5616. SAN 313-0428. Tel: 910-962-3000. Circulation Tel: 910-962-3272. Interlibrary Loan Service Tel: 910-962-3273. Reference Tel: 910-962-3760. Administration Tel: 910-962-3270. Toll Free Tel: 866-377-8309. FAX: 910-962-3078. Interlibrary Loan Service FAX: 910-962-3863. Web Site: library.uncw.edu. *Univ Librn,* Sarah Barbara Watstein; E-mail: Watsteins@uncw.edu; *Head, Ref,* Lisa Williams; E-mail: williamsl@uncw.edu; *Spec Coll Librn,* Jerry Parnell; E-mail: parnellg@uncw.edu; *Syst Coordr,* Daniel Pfohl; E-mail: pfohld@uncw.edu; *Circ,* Joyce Johnson; E-mail: johnsonjj@uncw.edu; *Doc,* Eileen Brown; E-mail: browne@uncw.edu; *ILL,* Madeleine Bombeld; E-mail: bombeldm@uncw.edu; Staff 42 (MLS 19, Non-MLS 23)
Founded 1947. Enrl 13,000; Highest Degree: Doctorate
Jul 2008-Jun 2009. Mats Exp $2,059,860, Books $122,799, Per/Ser (Incl. Access Fees) $1,937,061. Sal $2,088,567 (Prof $1,150,027)
Library Holdings: Bk Vols 962,717; Per Subs 40,000; Videos 23,851
Special Collections: Audiovisuals. Oral History; State Document Depository; US Document Depository
Subject Interests: Educ, Hist, Marine biol
Automation Activity & Vendor Info: (Acquisitions) Innovative Interfaces, Inc; (Cataloging) Innovative Interfaces, Inc; (Circulation) Innovative Interfaces, Inc; (Course Reserve) Innovative Interfaces, Inc; (ILL) Innovative Interfaces, Inc; (Media Booking) Innovative Interfaces, Inc; (OPAC) Innovative Interfaces, Inc; (Serials) EBSCO Online
Wireless access
Partic in Lyrasis
Special Services for the Blind - Reader equip
Restriction: Borrowing requests are handled by ILL

M SOUTH EAST AREA HEALTH EDUCATION CENTER MEDICAL LIBRARY*, Robert M Fales Health Sciences Library, 2131 S 17th St, 28402. (Mail add: PO Box 9025, 28402-9025), SAN 324-6418. Tel: 910-343-2180. Circulation Tel: 910-667-9226. Administration Tel: 910-343-0161. FAX: 910-762-7600. Web Site: www.seahec.net. *Dir,* Donna Bunting Flake; Tel: 910-667-9227, E-mail: donna.flake@seahec.net; *Educ & Ref Librn,* Allison Paige Matthews; E-mail: allison.matthews@seahec.net; *Tech Serv,* Sharon Llewellyn Welsh; E-mail: sharon.welsh@seahec.net; Staff 4 (MLS 3, Non-MLS 1)
Founded 1971
Library Holdings: AV Mats 500; Bk Titles 3,100; Per Subs 330
Special Collections: Children's Health; Consumer Health; History of Medicine; Pastoral Care
Subject Interests: Allied health, Dental, Med, Nursing, Pharm, Psychol, Rehabilitation
Automation Activity & Vendor Info: (Cataloging) EOS International; (Circulation) EOS International; (OPAC) EOS International; (Serials) EOS International
Database Vendor: EOS International, OCLC FirstSearch, OCLC WorldShare Interlibrary Loan, OVID Technologies
Wireless access
Function: Audio & video playback equip for onsite use, AV serv, CD-ROM, Computer training, Computers for patron use, Copy machines, Doc delivery serv, e-mail serv, Electronic databases & coll, Handicapped accessible, Health sci info serv, ILL available, Mail loans to mem, Online cat, Online searches, Orientations, Outreach serv, Photocopying/Printing, Pub access computers, Ref serv available, Ref serv in person, Spanish lang bks, Telephone ref, VHS videos, Web-catalog, Wheelchair accessible
Partic in National Network of Libraries of Medicine; National Network of Libraries of Medicine Greater Midwest Region
Open Mon-Fri 8-5
Friends of the Library Group

WILSON

C BARTON COLLEGE*, Hackney Library, 400 Atlantic Christian College Dr NE, 27893. (Mail add: PO Box 5000, 27893-7000), SAN 313-0444. Tel: 252-399-6500. Reference Tel: 252-399-6502. FAX: 252-399-6571. E-mail: reference@barton.edu. Web Site: library.barton.edu. *Interim Dir,* Jason Fleming; Tel: 252-399-6505, E-mail: jtfleming@barton.edu; *Coll & Access Serv Librn,* Richard Fulling; Tel: 252-399-6504, E-mail: rfulling@barton.edu; *Outreach/Pub Serv Librn,* Ann Dolman; Tel: 252-399-6507, E-mail: adolman@barton.edu; *Libr Assoc for Outreach & Pub Serv, Weekend Librn,* Cynthia Collins; Tel: 252-399-6503, E-mail: cecollins@barton.edu; *Weekend Librn,* Tempie Hayes; E-mail: tahayes@bartone.du; *Libr Assoc for Coll & Access Serv,* Norma Williams; Tel: 252-399-6506, E-mail: nwilliam@barton.edu; *Libr Tech Assoc for Outreach & Pub Serv,* Steven Stewart; E-mail: sgstewart@barton.edu; Staff 4 (MLS 3, Non-MLS 1)
Founded 1902. Enrl 1,050; Fac 80; Highest Degree: Master
Library Holdings: AV Mats 3,581; e-books 22,581; Bk Vols 192,417; Per Subs 13,437
Special Collections: Discipliana Coll. State Document Depository; US Document Depository
Subject Interests: Deaf educ
Automation Activity & Vendor Info: (Acquisitions) Innovative Interfaces, Inc; (Cataloging) Innovative Interfaces, Inc; (Circulation) Innovative Interfaces, Inc; (OPAC) Innovative Interfaces, Inc; (Serials) Innovative Interfaces, Inc
Database Vendor: ABC-CLIO, Alexander Street Press, Bowker, Cinahl, CQ Press, EBSCOhost, Gale Cengage Learning, H W Wilson, Haworth Pres Inc, Innovative Interfaces, Inc, JSTOR, LearningExpress, Medline, NC LIVE, OCLC CAMIO, OCLC FirstSearch, OCLC WorldShare Interlibrary Loan, Oxford Online, Project MUSE, ProQuest, PubMed, Sage, Wilson - Wilson Web, WT Cox
Wireless access
Partic in Carolina Consortium; Lyrasis; OCLC Online Computer Library Center, Inc
Restriction: Restricted loan policy
Friends of the Library Group

J WILSON COMMUNITY COLLEGE LIBRARY*, 902 Herring Ave, 27893. (Mail add: PO Box 4305, 27893-4305), SAN 313-0452. Tel: 252-246-1235. Information Services Tel: 252-246-1337. FAX: 252-243-7148. E-mail: library_support@wilsoncc.edu. Web Site: www.wilsoncc.edu/library.cfm. *Head Librn,* Gerard O'Neill; E-mail: goneill@wilsoncc.edu; *Librn,* Kelly Letourneau; Tel: 252-246-1251, E-mail: kletourneau@wilsoncc.edu; Staff 6 (MLS 3, Non-MLS 3)
Founded 1958. Enrl 1,285; Fac 65
Library Holdings: Bk Vols 33,000; Per Subs 420
Automation Activity & Vendor Info: (Cataloging) SirsiDynix; (Circulation) SirsiDynix
Database Vendor: Gale Cengage Learning, NC LIVE, ProQuest, Westlaw
Wireless access
Partic in Community Colleges Libraries in North Carolina (CCLINC)
Special Services for the Deaf - Bks on deafness & sign lang; High interest/low vocabulary bks

P WILSON COUNTY PUBLIC LIBRARY, 249 Nash St W, 27893-3801. SAN 355-2365. Tel: 252-237-5355. Reference FAX: 252-243-4311. Administration FAX: 252-265-5569. *Dir,* Becky Callison; Tel: 252-237-5355, Ext 5024, E-mail: bcallison@wilson-co.com; *Head, Ch,* Rebecca Tighe; E-mail: rtighe@wilson-co.com; Staff 32.69 (MLS 8, Non-MLS 24.69)
Founded 1937. Pop 82,020; Circ 305,872
Library Holdings: Audiobooks 2,055; DVDs 4,383; e-books 461; Bk Vols 189,582; Per Subs 189
Special Collections: Genealogy Coll; North Carolina Coll, bks, microfilm
Automation Activity & Vendor Info: (Cataloging) TLC (The Library Corporation); (Circulation) TLC (The Library Corporation); (OPAC) TLC (The Library Corporation)
Database Vendor: NC LIVE
Wireless access
Publications: Wilson County Public Library: A History
Special Services for the Deaf - Bks on deafness & sign lang; High interest/low vocabulary bks
Open Mon-Wed 9-9, Thurs-Sat 9-6
Friends of the Library Group
Branches: 5

BLACK CREEK BRANCH, 103 Central Ave, Black Creek, 27813, SAN 370-9450. Tel: 252-237-3715. FAX: 252-237-3715. *Br Mgr,* Sarah Packard; E-mail: spackard@wilson-co.com; Staff 1 (Non-MLS 1)
Library Holdings: Bk Vols 11,390; Per Subs 14
Open Mon, Wed & Thurs 2-5:30, Tues 3-6:30

CROCKER-STANTONSBURG BRANCH, 114 S Main St, Stantonsburg, 27883, SAN 355-2519. Tel: 252-238-3758. FAX: 252-238-3758. *Br Mgr,* Megan Proctor; E-mail: mrproctor@wilson-co.com; Staff 1 (Non-MLS 1)
Library Holdings: Bk Vols 11,776; Per Subs 15
Open Mon-Thurs 2-5:30

EAST WILSON BRANCH, 6000-C Ward Blvd, 27893-6488, SAN 355-239X. Tel: 252-237-2627. FAX: 252-237-2627. *Br Mgr,* Brenda Edmondson; E-mail: bedmondson@wilson-co.com; Staff 1 (Non-MLS 1)
Library Holdings: Bk Vols 13,819
Open Mon-Thurs 2-5:30

ELM CITY BRANCH, 114 N Railroad St, Elm City, 27822-0717. (Mail add: PO Box 717, Elm City, 27822-0717), SAN 355-242X. Tel: 252-236-4269. FAX: 252-236-4269. *Br Mgr,* Sue Young; E-mail: syoung@wilson-co.com; Staff 1 (Non-MLS 1)
Library Holdings: Bk Vols 19,101
Open Mon-Fri 10-6

LUCAMA BRANCH, 103 E Spring St, Lucama, 27851, SAN 355-2489. Tel: 252-239-0046. FAX: 252-239-0046. *Br Mgr,* Alison Howard; E-mail: ahoward@wilson-co.com; Staff 2 (Non-MLS 2)
Library Holdings: Bk Vols 14,057; Per Subs 15
Open Mon-Fri 10-6

M WILSON MEDICAL CENTER LIBRARY*, Bell-Pittman Library Resource Center, 1705 Tarboro St SW, 27893-3428. SAN 320-409X. Tel: 252-399-8253. FAX: 252-399-8119. *Coordr,* Rosa Edwards; E-mail: rosa.edwards@wilmed.org; Staff 2 (MLS 1, Non-MLS 1)
Founded 1964
Library Holdings: Bk Titles 1,766; Per Subs 75
Special Collections: Leadership Coll; Wellness/Consumer Health Coll
Automation Activity & Vendor Info: (Cataloging) Winnebago Software Co; (Serials) Winnebago Software Co
Database Vendor: UpToDate
Publications: Bibliography of Resources; Library Links
Partic in Docline
Special Services for the Deaf - Staff with knowledge of sign lang
Open Mon, Tues, Thurs & Fri 8:30-5

WINGATE

R WINGATE BAPTIST CHURCH LIBRARY*, 109 E Elm St, 28174. (Mail add: P0 Box 339, 28174-0339), SAN 313-0479. Tel: 704-233-4256. FAX: 704-233-0598. Web Site: www.wingatebaptistchurch.com. *Librn,* Alice Coleman; Staff 6 (MLS 1, Non-MLS 5)
Founded 1962
Library Holdings: AV Mats 70; Bk Vols 2,566
Subject Interests: Biog, Children's bks, Fiction
Open Sun 9:30-11:30

C WINGATE UNIVERSITY*, Ethel K Smith Library, Campus Box 3067-WU, 28174-1202. SAN 313-0487. Tel: 704-233-8089. Reference Tel: 704-233-8097. FAX: 704-233-8254. E-mail: library_info@wingate.edu. Web Site: library.wingate.edu. *Libr Dir,* Amee Huneycutt Odom; E-mail: ameeodom@wingate.edu; *Cat Librn,* Marilyn Brown; E-mail: marbrown@wingate.edu; *Coll Develop Librn,* Richard Pipes; E-mail: rpipes@wingate.edu; *E-Res & Spec Coll Librn,* Debbie Hargett; E-mail: dhargett@wingate.edu; *Ref & Instruction Librn,* Ashley Shealy; E-mail: a.shealy@wingate.edu; *Access Serv Mgr,* Christy Inge; E-mail: c.inge@wingate.edu; *Evening Fac Mgr,* Carrie Keziah; E-mail: c.r.keziah@wingate.edu; *Pub Serv Mgr,* Alison Simpson; E-mail: a.simpson@wingate.edu; *Network & Syst Adminr,* Jimm Wetherbee; E-mail: jimm@wingate.edu; Staff 8.5 (MLS 6, Non-MLS 2.5)
Founded 1896. Enrl 2,159, Fac 140; Highest Degree: Doctorate
Special Collections: Charles A Cannon Personal Papers; Mary Ann Kincaid Children's Coll; Wingate University Archives
Automation Activity & Vendor Info: (Acquisitions) Ex Libris Group; (Cataloging) Ex Libris Group; (Circulation) Ex Libris Group; (Course Reserve) Ex Libris Group; (OPAC) Ex Libris Group
Wireless access
Function: Archival coll, Computer training, Computers for patron use, Copy machines, e-mail & chat, E-Reserves, Electronic databases & coll, Exhibits, Handicapped accessible, ILL available, Music CDs, Online cat, Online ref, Orientations, Outside serv via phone, mail, e-mail & web, Photocopying/Printing, Pub access computers, Ref & res, Ref serv available, Ref serv in person, Satellite serv, Scanner, Telephone ref, VHS videos, Web-catalog, Wheelchair accessible, Workshops
Publications: The Bookmark (Newsletter)
Partic in Carolina Consortium; Charlotte Area Educ Consortium; Lyrasis; NC Asn of Independent Cols & Univs; OCLC Online Computer Library Center, Inc
Open Mon-Thurs 7:30am-11pm, Fri 7:30-5, Sat 10-5, Sun 3-11
Friends of the Library Group

WINSTON-SALEM

R FIRST BAPTIST CHURCH*, John Davis Memorial Library, 700 N Highland Ave, 27101. SAN 313-0495. Tel: 336-722-5605. FAX: 336-722-6266. *In Charge,* Selena Nichols
Founded 1958
Library Holdings: Bk Vols 1,250
Subject Interests: Archit, Art, Hist, Recreation

P FORSYTH COUNTY PUBLIC LIBRARY*, 660 W Fifth St, 27101. SAN 355-2543. Tel: 336-703-2665. Interlibrary Loan Service Tel: 336-703-3030. Administration Tel: 336-703-3011. Information Services Tel: 336-703-3020. FAX: 336-727-2549. Web Site: www.forsythlibrary.org. *Dir,* Sylvia Sprinkle-Hamlin; E-mail: hamlinss@forsythlibrary.org; *Assoc Dir,* Elizabeth Skinner; Staff 105 (MLS 43, Non-MLS 62)
Founded 1903. Pop 358,137; Circ 1,887,526
Library Holdings: AV Mats 62,121; e-books 5,895; Bk Vols 674,902; Per Subs 700
Special Collections: African American Coll; Foreign Language Coll; Frank Jones Photographic Print Coll; Generation Teen; H Kapp Ogburn Philatelic Coll; Nonprofit Resource Center; North Caroliniana, genealogy; Small Business Center. US Document Depository
Subject Interests: Bus, Children's lit, Humanities
Automation Activity & Vendor Info: (Acquisitions) SirsiDynix; (Cataloging) SirsiDynix; (Circulation) SirsiDynix; (Course Reserve) SirsiDynix; (ILL) SirsiDynix; (Media Booking) SirsiDynix; (OPAC) SirsiDynix; (Serials) SirsiDynix
Wireless access
Publications: Annual Report; Bookshelf (Newsletter); Children's Calendar (Monthly); FirstLine Community Directory (Business & organization papers & directories); Jobseeker's Resource Guide: Your Guide to Surviving Unemployment (Research guide); Monthly Calendar of Events; Periodical Holdings (Serials catalog)
Partic in BRS; Lyrasis; OCLC Online Computer Library Center, Inc
Special Services for the Deaf - Assistive tech; Videos & decoder
Special Services for the Blind - Assistive/Adapted tech devices, equip & products; Computer with voice synthesizer for visually impaired persons; Home delivery serv
Open Mon-Wed 9-9, Thurs & Fri 9-6, Sat 9-5, Sun (Sept-May) 1-5
Friends of the Library Group
Branches: 9

CARVER SCHOOL ROAD BRANCH, 4915 Lansing Dr W, 27105, SAN 378-1917. Tel: 336-703-2910. FAX: 336-661-4919. *Br Mgr,* Melisa Williams; E-mail: william2@forsythlibrary.org
Library Holdings: e-books 40; Bk Vols 28,518; Per Subs 104
Open Mon-Wed 10-9, Thurs & Fri 10-6, Sat 10-5
Friends of the Library Group

CLEMMONS BRANCH, 3554 Clemmons Rd, Old Hwy 158, Clemmons, 27012, SAN 355-2578. Tel: 336-703-2920. FAX: 336-712-4452. *Br Mgr,* Carolyn Price; E-mail: pricecp@forsythlibrary.org; Staff 5 (MLS 2, Non-MLS 3)
Library Holdings: Bk Vols 43,465; Per Subs 100
Open Mon-Wed 10-9, Thurs & Fri 10-6, Sat 10-5
Friends of the Library Group

KERNERSVILLE BRANCH, 130 E Mountain St, Kernersville, 27284, SAN 355-2632. Tel: 336-703-2930. FAX: 336-993-5216. *Br Mgr,* William Durham; E-mail: durhamwe@forsythlibrary.org
Library Holdings: e-books 33; Bk Vols 56,053; Per Subs 102
Open Mon-Wed 10-9, Thurs & Fri 10-6, Sat 10-5
Friends of the Library Group

LEWISVILLE BRANCH, 6490 Shallowford Rd, Lewisville, 27023, SAN 355-2667. Tel: 336-703-2940. FAX: 336-945-9745. *Br Mgr,* Merrikay Brown; E-mail: brownme@forsythlibrary.org
Library Holdings: Bk Vols 31,362; Per Subs 78
Open Mon-Wed 10-9, Thurs & Fri 10-6, Sat 10-5
Friends of the Library Group

MALLOY/JORDON EAST WINSTON HERITAGE CENTER, 1110 E Seventh St, 27101, SAN 355-2608. Tel: 336-703-2950. FAX: 336-727-8498. *Br Mgr,* Yolanda F Bolden; E-mail: boldenyf@forsythlibrary.org
Library Holdings: Bk Vols 24,966; Per Subs 106
Special Collections: Storytime Kits. Oral History
Subject Interests: African-Am hist, Early childhood
Open Mon-Wed 12-9, Thurs & Fri 9-6, Sat 10-2
Friends of the Library Group

REYNOLDA MANOR, 2839 Fairlawn Dr, 27106, SAN 355-2691. Tel: 336-703-2960. FAX: 336-748-3318. *Br Mgr,* Jennifer Boneno; E-mail: barretjs@forsythlibrary.org
Library Holdings: e-books 40; Bk Vols 57,260; Per Subs 100
Open Mon-Wed 10-9, Thurs & Fri 10-6, Sat 10-5
Friends of the Library Group

RURAL HALL BRANCH, 7125 Broad St, Rural Hall, 27045, SAN 355-2721. Tel: 336-703-2970. FAX: 336-969-9401. *Br Head,* Lara Luck; Tel: 336-703-2971, E-mail: luckla@forsyth.cc; Staff 3 (MLS 2, Non-MLS 1)
Library Holdings: Bk Vols 39,490; Per Subs 104
Open Mon-Wed 10-9, Thurs & Fri 10-6, Sat 10-5
Friends of the Library Group

SOUTHSIDE, 3185 Buchanan St, 27127, SAN 355-2756. Tel: 336-703-2980. FAX: 336-771-4724. *Br Mgr,* Decca Slaughter; E-mail: slaughdr@forsyth.cc; Staff 5 (MLS 3, Non-MLS 2)
Library Holdings: Bk Vols 54,647; Per Subs 166

Automation Activity & Vendor Info: (Acquisitions) Evergreen; (Cataloging) Evergreen; (Circulation) Evergreen; (ILL) Brodart; (OPAC) Evergreen; (Serials) Evergreen
Database Vendor: Baker & Taylor, Brodart, EBSCO Auto Repair Reference, EBSCO Information Services, EBSCOhost, Gale Cengage Learning, NC LIVE, OCLC WorldShare Interlibrary Loan, ProQuest, ReferenceUSA, WT Cox
Function: Adult bk club, Bks on CD, Children's prog, Computer training, Computers for patron use, Copy machines, Distance learning, Electronic databases & coll, Exhibits, Free DVD rentals, Handicapped accessible, Holiday prog, Homework prog, ILL available, Instruction & testing, Music CDs, Online cat, Online ref, Online searches, Outreach serv, OverDrive digital audio bks, Photocopying/Printing, Preschool outreach, Preschool reading prog, Prog for adults, Prog for children & young adult, Pub access computers, Ref & res, Ref serv available, Ref serv in person, Senior computer classes, Spanish lang bks, Story hour, Summer & winter reading prog, Summer reading prog, Tax forms, Teen prog, Telephone ref, VHS videos, Wheelchair accessible, Winter reading prog, Workshops
Open Mon-Wed 10-9, Thurs & Fri 10-6, Sat 10-5
Friends of the Library Group

WALKERTOWN BRANCH, 2969 Main St, Walkertown, 27051, SAN 374-4167. Tel: 336-703-2990. FAX: 336-595-9080. *Br Mgr,* Natalia Tuchina; E-mail: tuchinnb@forsythlibrary.org
Library Holdings: Bk Vols 33,630; Per Subs 96
Open Mon & Tues 10-9, Wed-Fri 10-6, Sat 10-2
Friends of the Library Group

Bookmobiles: 1. Bk vols 3000

M FORSYTH MEDICAL CENTER*, John C Whitaker Library, 3333 Silas Creek Pkwy, 27103-3090. SAN 355-2810. Tel: 336-718-5995. *Mgr,* Margaret Cobb; Staff 2.5 (MLS 1, Non-MLS 1.5)
Founded 1964
Library Holdings: AV Mats 50; e-books 70; e-journals 4,000; Bk Titles 1,892; Bk Vols 3,000; Per Subs 48
Subject Interests: Allied health, Clinical med, Nursing
Automation Activity & Vendor Info: (Acquisitions) EOS International; (Cataloging) EOS International; (Circulation) EOS International; (Course Reserve) EOS International; (Media Booking) EOS International; (OPAC) EOS International; (Serials) EOS International
Database Vendor: EBSCOhost, MD Consult, Medline, Micromedex, OCLC FirstSearch, OCLC WorldShare Interlibrary Loan, OVID Technologies, PubMed
Wireless access
Function: Audio & video playback equip for onsite use, AV serv, Bks on CD, Computers for patron use, Copy machines, Doc delivery serv, ILL available, Online cat, Online searches, Photocopying/Printing, Ref serv available
Open Mon-Fri 8:30-6
Restriction: Access for corporate affiliates, Circulates for staff only, In-house use for visitors, Med & health res only, Non-circulating to the pub

J FORSYTH TECHNICAL COMMUNITY COLLEGE LIBRARY*, 2100 Silas Creek Pkwy, 27103. SAN 355-287X. Tel: 336-734-7219. Reference Tel: 336-734-7415. Administration Tel: 336-734-7217. Information Services Tel: 336-734-7218. FAX: 336-761-2465. Web Site: www1.forsythtech.edu/students/lrc. *Dean,* J Randel Candelaria; Tel: 336-734-7216, E-mail: rcandelaria@forsythtech.edu; *Coll Develop Librn,* Carol Freeman; Tel: 336-734-7176, E-mail: cfreeman@forsythtech.edu; *Circ,* Gay Lynn Briggs; E-mail: gbriggs@forsythtech.edu; *Media Spec,* John Briggs; Tel: 336-734-7378, E-mail: jbriggs@forsythtech.edu; *Pub Serv,* Tom Gordon; E-mail: tgordon@forsythtech.edu; *Ser, Tech Serv,* Ted Labosky; Tel: 336-734-7508, E-mail: tlabosky@forsythtech.edu; Staff 9 (MLS 4, Non-MLS 5)
Founded 1964. Enrl 7,800; Highest Degree: Associate
Library Holdings: e-books 22,000; Bk Titles 42,000; Per Subs 240
Special Collections: Guy Blynn Holocaust Coll
Subject Interests: Eng, Health, Hort
Automation Activity & Vendor Info: (Acquisitions) SirsiDynix; (Cataloging) SirsiDynix; (Circulation) SirsiDynix; (ILL) OCLC Online; (OPAC) Horizon; (Serials) SirsiDynix
Database Vendor: Cinahl, EBSCOhost, Gale Cengage Learning, LexisNexis, NC LIVE, OCLC FirstSearch, ProQuest
Wireless access
Function: Audio & video playback equip for onsite use, Audiobks via web, AV serv, Bks on cassette, Computer training, Computers for patron use, Copy machines, Distance learning, e-mail serv, Electronic databases & coll, Equip loans & repairs, Fax serv, ILL available, Instruction & testing, Learning ctr, Magnifiers for reading, Music CDs, Online cat, Online ref, Orientations, Photocopying/Printing, Pub access computers, Ref & res, Referrals accepted, Spoken cassettes & CDs, Telephone ref, VHS videos, Wheelchair accessible, Workshops
Partic in Lyrasis
Open Mon-Thurs 7:30am-9pm, Fri 7:30-3, Sat (Fall & Spring) 9-12
Restriction: Open to pub for ref & circ; with some limitations, Open to students, fac & staff

SR MORAVIAN CHURCH IN AMERICA, SOUTHERN PROVINCE*, Archives & Research Library, 457 S Church St, 27101-5314. SAN 326-341X. Tel: 336-722-1742. FAX: 336-725-4514. E-mail: moravianarchives@mcsp.org. Web Site: moravianarchives.org. *Archivist,* Dr C Daniel Crews; Tel: 336-722-1742, Ext 1501; Staff 3 (Non-MLS 3)
Founded 1753
Library Holdings: Bk Titles 2,500; Bk Vols 3,000; Per Subs 50
Function: Res libr
Publications: Annotations (Newsletter)
Open Mon-Fri 9:30-12 & 1:30-4:30
Restriction: Non-circulating to the pub
Friends of the Library Group

S MORAVIAN MUSIC FOUNDATION*, Peter Memorial Library, 457 S Church St, 27101. SAN 313-0517. Tel: 336-725-0651. FAX: 336-725-4514. Web Site: www.moravianmusic.org. *Dir,* Dr Nola R Knouse
Founded 1961
Library Holdings: AV Mats 800; Bk Titles 6,000; Per Subs 10
Special Collections: Music (Lowens Coll of Musical Americana & Manuscripts of Early American Music), bk, mss
Subject Interests: 18th Century music, 19th Century music, Am music, Hymnology, Moravian music
Publications: Catalogs of Music Collection; Newsletter (Quarterly); Publications
Open Mon-Fri 9:30-12 & 1:30-4:30
Restriction: Open to pub for ref only

S OLD SALEM MUSEUMS & GARDENS LIBRARY*, Frank L Horton Museum Center, 924 S Main St, 27101. SAN 325-8084. Tel: 336-721-7365, 336-721-7372. FAX: 336-721-7367. E-mail: Library@oldsalem.org. *Assoc Curator,* Daniel Ackerman; Staff 1 (MLS 1)
Library Holdings: Bk Vols 20,000; Per Subs 125
Automation Activity & Vendor Info: (Cataloging) Re:discovery Software, Inc; (OPAC) Re:discovery Software, Inc
Wireless access
Restriction: Open by appt only

CR PIEDMONT BAPTIST COLLEGE & GRADUATE SCHOOL*, George M Manuel Memorial Library, 420 S Broad St, 27101. SAN 313-055X. Tel: 336-725-8344, Ext 7009. Toll Free Tel: 800-937-5097. FAX: 336-725-5522. Web Site: www.pbc.edu/ps/ps_ac_library.aspx. *Librn,* Delores G Fulton; *Archivist, Per, Ref Librn,* Roger L Barnes; Tel: 336-725-8344, Ext 7952, E-mail: barnesrl@pbc.edu; *Res Serv,* Catherine Chantmon; Tel: 336-725-8344, Ext 7953, E-mail: chatmonc@pbc.edu; Staff 3 (MLS 2, Non-MLS 1)
Founded 1945. Enrl 290; Fac 41; Highest Degree: Doctorate
Library Holdings: CDs 20; DVDs 66; e-books 977; e-journals 3,808; Electronic Media & Resources 4; Microforms 6,000; Music Scores 300; Bk Titles 48,000; Bk Vols 58,000; Per Subs 225; Videos 601
Subject Interests: Educ, Hist, Music, Relig studies
Automation Activity & Vendor Info: (Acquisitions) JayWil Software Development, Inc; (Cataloging) JayWil Software Development, Inc; (Circulation) JayWil Software Development, Inc; (OPAC) JayWil Software Development, Inc; (Serials) EBSCO Online
Database Vendor: BCR; Christian Periodical Index, EBSCOhost, H W Wilson, JayWil Software Development, Inc, NC LIVE
Wireless access
Function: Photocopying/Printing
Open Mon, Tues & Thurs 7:30am-9pm, Wed & Fri 7:30-5, Sat 10-2

C SALEM COLLEGE*, Dale H Gramley Library, 626 S Church St, 27108. (Mail add: PO Box 10548, 27108), SAN 313-0576. Tel: 336-721-2649. Interlibrary Loan Service Tel: 336-917-5420. FAX: 336-917-5339. Web Site: www.salem.edu. *Dir,* Dr Rose Simon; Tel: 336-917-5421, E-mail: simon@salem.edu; *Circ Supvr,* Donna Melton; Tel: 336-917-5419, E-mail: melton@salem.edu; *Pub Serv,* Sarah Rothstein; E-mail: rothstei@salem.edu; *Tech Serv,* Peter Austin; Tel: 336-917-5422, E-mail: austin@salem.edu
Founded 1772. Enrl 1,019; Fac 90; Highest Degree: Master
Library Holdings: Bk Vols 129,577; Per Subs 5,500
Special Collections: Moravian Church Coll; Salem Academy & College Coll
Subject Interests: Lit, Women's hist
Automation Activity & Vendor Info: (Acquisitions) SirsiDynix; (Cataloging) SirsiDynix; (Circulation) SirsiDynix; (Course Reserve) SirsiDynix; (ILL) SirsiDynix; (OPAC) SirsiDynix; (Serials) SirsiDynix
Database Vendor: ProQuest
Partic in Lyrasis; NC-PALS
Open Mon-Thurs 8:30am-11:45pm, Fri 8:30-8, Sat 9-5, Sun 1-11:45
Friends of the Library Group

Departmental Libraries:
LORRAINE F RUDOLPH FINE ARTS CENTER LIBRARY, 601 S Church St, 27101. Tel: 336-721-2738. FAX: 336-721-2683. *Librn,* Donna Rothrock; Tel: 336-917-5475, E-mail: rothrock@salem.edu
Library Holdings: CDs 1,957; DVDs 85; Music Scores 9,335; Bk Titles 785; Videos 339
Open Mon-Thurs 8am-10pm, Fri 8-4:30, Sun 2-10

C UNIVERSITY OF NORTH CAROLINA SCHOOL OF THE ARTS*, Semans Library, 1533 S Main St, 27127. SAN 313-0541. Tel: 336-770-3270. Interlibrary Loan Service Tel: 336-770-3257. Reference Tel: 336-770-1479. FAX: 336-770-3271. Web Site: library.uncsa.edu/home/. *Dir of Libr Serv,* Vicki Weavil; E-mail: weavilv@uncsa.edu; *Head, Access Serv & Doc Delivery,* Rebecca Brown; E-mail: rebeccab@ncarts.edu; *Cat & Digital Res Librn,* Christia Thomason; E-mail: thomasonc@ncarts.edu; *Music Librn,* Leslie Kamtman; E-mail: kamtml@ncarts.edu; *Syst & Web Develop Librn,* Benjamin Morgan; E-mail: morganb@ncarts.edu; *Archivist,* Patrice Slattery; E-mail: slatteryp@ncarts.edu; *Bibliog Instr, Ref,* Susan Keely; E-mail: keelys@ncarts.edu; *Cataloger,* Sylvia Koontz; E-mail: koontzs@ncarts.edu. Subject Specialists: *Music,* Christia Thomason; *Music,* Leslie Kamtman; *Archives,* Patrice Slattery; Staff 15 (MLS 7, Non-MLS 8)
Founded 1965. Enrl 1,100; Fac 152; Highest Degree: Master
Jul 2011-Jun 2012 Income $102,023, State $99,023, Other $3,000. Mats Exp $201,085, Books $28,065, Per/Ser (Incl. Access Fees) $47,364, Manu Arch $1,000, Other Print Mats $41,794, AV Equip $3,000, AV Mat $19,718, Electronic Ref Mat (Incl. Access Fees) $53,738, Presv $6,406. Sal $629,536 (Prof $371,281)
Library Holdings: AV Mats 7,000; CDs 7,000; DVDs 4,000; Electronic Media & Resources 45; Music Scores 60,000; Bk Vols 110,000; Per Subs 450; Spec Interest Per Sub 200; Videos 4,000
Special Collections: School Archives; Music Scores; Sound Recordings; Moving Image Materials. Oral History
Subject Interests: Art, Dance, Drama, Film, Music
Automation Activity & Vendor Info: (Acquisitions) Innovative Interfaces, Inc; (Cataloging) Innovative Interfaces, Inc; (Circulation) Innovative Interfaces, Inc; (Course Reserve) Innovative Interfaces, Inc; (ILL) OCLC; (OPAC) Innovative Interfaces, Inc; (Serials) Innovative Interfaces, Inc
Database Vendor: Alexander Street Press, ARTstor, Career Guidance Foundation, College Source, Commonwealth Business Media, EBSCOhost, Facts on File, Gale Cengage Learning, H W Wilson, JSTOR, LexisNexis, NC LIVE, OCLC WorldShare Interlibrary Loan, Oxford Online, ProQuest, Wilson - Wilson Web
Wireless access
Partic in Carolina Consortium; Central North Carolina Library Consortium; Lyrasis; North Carolina Libraries for Virtual Education; OCLC Online Computer Library Center, Inc
Open Mon-Thurs 8am-11pm, Fri 8-6, Sat 2-6, Sun 2-11
Restriction: Open to pub for ref & circ; with some limitations, Open to students, fac & staff

C WAKE FOREST UNIVERSITY*, Z Smith Reynolds Library, PO Box 7777, 27109-7777. SAN 355-3116. Tel: 336-758-5478. Circulation Tel: 336-758-4931. Interlibrary Loan Service Tel: 336-758-5006. Reference Tel: 336-758-5475. FAX: 336-758-3694, 336-758-8831. Circulation FAX: 336 758 5605. Web Site: zsr.wfu.edu. *Dean,* Lynn Sutton; Tel: 335-758-5480, E-mail: suttonls@wfu.edu; *Assoc Dean,* Wanda Brown; Tel: 336-758-5094, E-mail: brown@wfu.edu; *Assoc Dean,* Susan Smith; Tel: 336-758-5828, E-mail: smithss@wfu.edu; *Dir, Access Serv,* Mary Beth Lock; Tel: 336-758-6140, E-mail: lockmb@wfu.edu; *Dir, Res & Instruction Serv,* Rosalind Tedford; Tel: 336-758-5910, E-mail: tedforrl@wfu.edu; *Dir, Res Serv,* Lauren Corbett; Tel: 336-758-6136, E-mail: corbetle@wfu.edu; *ILL,* Cristina Yu; Tel: 336-758-5675, E-mail: yu@wfu.edu; Staff 36 (MLS 28, Non-MLS 8)
Founded 1834. Enrl 6,707; Fac 1,438; Highest Degree: Doctorate
Jul 2009-Jun 2010. Mats Exp $4,001,389, Books $576,576, Per/Ser (Incl. Access Fees) $2,938,444, Micro $26,496, Electronic Ref Mat (Incl. Access Fees) $426,074, Presv $33,799. Sal $2,869,817 (Prof $2,100,510)
Library Holdings: AV Mats 37,259; e-books 445,782; e-journals 36,505; Microforms 696,798; Bk Vols 1,398,364; Per Subs 4,738; Videos 19,665
Special Collections: Anglo-Irish Literature; Dolman Press Archives; Gertrude Stein Coll; Giuseppe De Santis Film Archives; Harold Hayes Manuscripts; History Books & Printing; Holocaust Coll; Joseph E Smith Music Coll; Mark Twain Coll; Maya Angelou Film & Theatre Coll; North Carolina Baptist History; Ronald Watkins Library & Personal Papers; Selected English & American Authors of the 20th Century; W J Cash Manuscripts; Wayne Oates Manuscripts. State Document Depository; US Document Depository
Automation Activity & Vendor Info: (Acquisitions) Ex Libris Group; (Cataloging) Ex Libris Group; (Circulation) Ex Libris Group; (Course Reserve) Ex Libris Group; (ILL) Ex Libris Group; (OPAC) Ex Libris Group; (Serials) Ex Libris Group
Database Vendor: Cambridge Scientific Abstracts, Dialog, EBSCOhost, Gale Cengage Learning, JSTOR, LexisNexis, OCLC FirstSearch, OCLC WorldShare Interlibrary Loan, OVID Technologies, ProQuest, SerialsSolutions, Wilson - Wilson Web
Wireless access
Publications: ZSReads (Newsletter)
Partic in Association of Southeastern Research Libraries; Lyrasis; North Carolina Libraries for Virtual Education
Departmental Libraries:

CM COY C CARPENTER SCHOOL OF MEDICINE LIBRARY, Medical Center Blvd, 27157-1069, SAN 355-3205. Tel: 336-716-4691. Circulation Tel: 336-716-4414. Reference Tel: 336-713-7100. FAX: 336-716-2186. Web Site: www.wfubmc.edu/library. *Dir,* Parks Welch; Tel: 336-716-2299, E-mail: pwelch@wfubmc.edu; *Coll Develop,* Bonnie Poston; E-mail: bposton@wfubmc.edu; *Pub Serv,* David Stewart; E-mail: dstewart@wfubmc.edu; *Tech Serv,* Molly Barnett; E-mail: mbarnett@wfubmc.edu; Staff 10 (MLS 10)
Founded 1941. Enrl 847; Highest Degree: Doctorate
Library Holdings: AV Mats 2,531; e-books 134; e-journals 1,543; Bk Titles 30,729; Bk Vols 153,077; Per Subs 2,156
Special Collections: Arts in Medicine; History of Medicine & Neurology (Rare Book Coll); Samuel Johnson Coll. Oral History
Subject Interests: Life sci, Med
Partic in OCLC Online Computer Library Center, Inc
Open Mon-Thurs 7am-Midnight, Fri 7-7, Sat 10-7, Sun 1-Midnight

CL PROFESSIONAL CENTER LIBRARY, Worrell Professional Ctr for Law & Management, 1834 Wake Forest Rd, 27106. (Mail add: PO Box 7206, 27109-7206), SAN 355-3140. Tel: 336-758-5438. Reference Tel: 336-758-4520. FAX: 336-758-6077. Web Site: www.pcl.wfu.edu. *Dir,* Position Currently Open; *Assoc Dir,* Maureen Eggert; Tel: 336-758-5072; *Assoc Dir,* Alan Keely; *Assoc Dir,* Sally Irvin; Tel: 336-758-5442; *Mgt Librn,* Robert Hebert; Tel: 336-758-4567; *Ref Librn,* Kate Irwin-Smiler; Tel: 336-758-4009; *Ref Librn,* Liz M Johnson; *Tech Serv Librn,* Jennifer Noga; *Tech Serv Librn,* Leslie Wakeford; Tel: 336-758-5932; *Circ Supvr,* Jean Reader; *Coordr, Acq,* Gina Jarrett; *Ref Coordr,* Angie Hobbs; *Ser,* Michael Greene; Staff 8 (MLS 8)
Founded 1894. Enrl 1,149; Fac 75; Highest Degree: Doctorate
Library Holdings: Bk Vols 217,490
Special Collections: State Document Depository; US Document Depository
Subject Interests: Law
Partic in Association of Southeastern Research Libraries; OCLC Online Computer Library Center, Inc
Open Mon-Thurs 7am-Midnight, Fri 7am-9pm, Sat 9-9, Sun 10am-Midnight

S WINSTON-SALEM JOURNAL LIBRARY*, 418 N Marshall St, 27101. (Mail add: PO Box 3159, 27102-3159), SAN 313-0568. Tel: 336-727-7275. E-mail: library@wsjournal.com. *Librn,* Craig Rhyne; Staff 2 (MLS 1, Non-MLS 1)
Founded 1947
Library Holdings: Bk Titles 1,500; Per Subs 40
Special Collections: Winston Salem Journal Text & Photo Archives
Function: Newsp ref libr
Restriction: Co libr, Not open to pub

C WINSTON-SALEM STATE UNIVERSITY, C G O'Kelly Library, 601 Martin Luther King Jr Dr, 27110. (Mail add: 227 O'Kelly Library, 27110), SAN 313-0592. Tel: 336-750-2440. Circulation Tel: 336-750-2449. Interlibrary Loan Service Tel: 336-750-2124. Reference Tel: 336-750-2454. Administration Tel: 336-750-2446. Automation Services Tel: 336-414-9327. FAX: 336-750-2459. Web Site: www.wssu.edu/library. *Dir,* Mae L Rodney; E-mail: rodneyml@wssu.edu; *Asst Dir, Archives & Spec Coll,* Thomas Flynn; Tel: 336-750-2426, E-mail: flynnth@wssu.edu; *Assoc Dir, Res & Instruction,* Carl Leak; Tel: 336-750-2453, E-mail: leakca@wssu.edu; *Distance Serv Librn,* Melinda Livas; Tel: 336-750-8933, E-mail: livasmm@wssu.edu; *Electronic Res Librn,* Ian Hertz; Tel: 336-750-2532, E-mail: hertzis@wssu.edu; *Life Sci Librn,* Michael Frye; E-mail: fryema@wssu.edu; *Coordr, Evening-Weekend Serv,* Lizzie Alston-Reeder; Tel: 336-750-2447, E-mail: reederl@wssu.edu; *Info Commons Coordr,* Forrest Foster. Subject Specialists: *Computer sci,* Thomas Flynn; *Fine arts,* Carl Leak; *Math,* Melinda Livas; *Bus,* Ian Hertz; *Chem, Life sci,* Michael Frye; Staff 21 (MLS 13, Non-MLS 8)
Founded 1920. Enrl 5,400; Fac 325; Highest Degree: Doctorate
Jul 2012-Jun 2013 Income $3,487,075, State $3,387,075, Federal $100,000. Mats Exp $3,487,075, Books $175,856, Per/Ser (Incl. Access Fees) $227,174, Micro $126,798, AV Equip $1,104,546, AV Mat $49,821, Electronic Ref Mat (Incl. Access Fees) $866,646. Sal $1,426,980
Library Holdings: AV Mats 2,334; DVDs 11,932; e-books 96,933; e-journals 76,514; Microforms 430,664; Bk Titles 210,000; Bk Vols 257,005; Per Subs 1,648
Special Collections: Black Studies (Curriculum Materials Center)
Automation Activity & Vendor Info: (Acquisitions) Innovative Interfaces, Inc; (Cataloging) Innovative Interfaces, Inc; (Circulation) Innovative Interfaces, Inc; (Course Reserve) Innovative Interfaces, Inc; (ILL) Innovative Interfaces, Inc; (OPAC) Innovative Interfaces, Inc; (Serials) Innovative Interfaces, Inc
Database Vendor: ACM (Association for Computing Machinery), Alexander Street Press, American Psychological Association (APA),

Cinahl, CQ Press, EBSCOhost, H W Wilson, LexisNexis, OCLC FirstSearch, OCLC WorldShare Interlibrary Loan, ProQuest, Wilson - Wilson Web
Wireless access
Function: ILL available, Ref serv available
Publications: WSSU Friends of the Library (Newsletter)
Partic in Central North Carolina Library Consortium; OCLC Online Computer Library Center, Inc
Open Mon-Thurs (Fall & Spring) 8am-1am, Fri 8-6, Sat 10-4, Sun Noon-1am; Mon-Thurs (Summer) 8-8, Fri 8-5, Sat 10-2, Sun 2-6
Friends of the Library Group

L WOMBLE, CARLYLE, SANDRIDGE & RICE*, Law Library, One W Fourth St, 27101. SAN 372-2333. Tel: 336-747-4757. FAX: 336-721-3660. Web Site: www.wcsr.com. *In Charge,* Susan Garrison
Library Holdings: Bk Vols 20,000; Per Subs 50
Restriction: Staff use only

WINTON

P ALBEMARLE REGIONAL LIBRARY*, 303 W Tryon St, 27986. (Mail add: PO Box 68, 27986-0068), SAN 313-0606. Tel: 252-358-7832. FAX: 252-358-7868. Web Site: www.arlnc.org. *Dir,* Gary Hoyle; E-mail: ghoyle@arlnc.org; *Financial Serv,* Betty Massie; Tel: 252-358-7834; *Syst Adminr,* Tamy Lewter; Tel: 252-358-7864, E-mail: tlewter@arlnc.org; *Tech Serv,* Brenda Jones; Tel: 252-358-7854; Staff 19 (MLS 2, Non-MLS 17)
Founded 1948. Pop 76,200; Circ 148,745
Jul 2012-Jun 2013 Income (Main Library and Branch(s)) $1,436,194, State $378,579, City $215,348, Federal $24,795, County $443,795, Locally Generated Income $139,314, Other $234,363. Mats Exp $83,630, Books $49,667, Per/Ser (Incl. Access Fees) $5,573, AV Mat $24,880, Electronic Ref Mat (Incl. Access Fees) $3,510. Sal $746,786 (Prof $68,978)
Library Holdings: AV Mats 24,374; Bks on Deafness & Sign Lang 32; Bk Vols 195,264; Per Subs 319
Special Collections: Care Givers Coll; Grandparents as Parents Coll; Historic Murfreesboro, North Carolina (Paul Ronald Jenkins Photographs Coll); World War II Scrapbook
Subject Interests: Genealogy, Local hist
Automation Activity & Vendor Info: (Acquisitions) Evergreen; (Cataloging) Evergreen; (Circulation) Evergreen; (OPAC) Evergreen
Database Vendor: Facts on File, NC LIVE, ProQuest
Wireless access
Function: Homebound delivery serv, ILL available, Music CDs, Photocopying/Printing, Prog for children & young adult, Spoken cassettes & CDs, Summer reading prog
Partic in OCLC Online Computer Library Center, Inc
Special Services for the Deaf - Bks on deafness & sign lang; High interest/low vocabulary bks
Special Services for the Blind - Bks on cassette; Bks on CD; Copier with enlargement capabilities; Home delivery serv; Large print bks; Talking bks
Branches: 7
AHOSKIE PUBLIC LIBRARY, 210 E Church St, Ahoskie, 27910, SAN 354-4419. Tel: 252-332-5500. FAX: 252-332-6435. *Br Mgr,* Cindy Henderson; *Asst Librn,* Shiwanda Bishop; *Asst Librn,* Annette Perry
Library Holdings: Bk Vols 16,000; Per Subs 28
Open Mon 10-8, Tues & Thurs 10-6, Wed & Fri 2-6, Sat 9-12
GATES COUNTY PUBLIC LIBRARY, 14 Cypress Creek Dr, Gatesville, 27938-9507. (Mail add: PO Box 27, Gatesville, 27938 0027), SAN 312-8423. Tel: 252-357-0110. FAX: 252-357-1285. *Br Mgr,* Patricia B Familar; *Asst Librn,* Sarah Doughtie; *Asst Librn,* Mylinda Eure; Staff 3 (MLS 1, Non-MLS 2)
Open Mon, Tues, Thurs & Fri 10:30-6, Wed 1-8:30, Sat 9:30-12:30
HERTFORD COUNTY LIBRARY, 303 W Tryon St, 27986. (Mail add: PO Box 68, 27986-0068), SAN 313-0614. Tel: 252-358-7855. FAX: 252-358-0368. *Br Mgr,* Hal Scott; E-mail: hscott@arlnc.org; *Asst Librn,* Amber Moore; *Asst Librn,* Nancy Wall; Staff 1.63 (Non-MLS 1.63)
Founded 1948. Pop 20,000; Circ 12,382
Subject Interests: Genealogy, Local hist
Open Mon, Wed, Fri & Sat 10-6, Tues & Thurs 10-8
SALLIE HARRELL JENKINS MEMORIAL LIBRARY, 302 Broad St, Aulander, 27805. (Mail add: PO Box 189, Aulander, 27805-0189), SAN 312-7338. Tel: 252-345-4461. FAX: 252-345-8000. *Br Mgr,* Sarah Davis
Open Mon & Wed 9-12:30 & 1-6, Tues & Thurs 1-6
LAWRENCE MEMORIAL PUBLIC LIBRARY, 204 E Dundee St, Windsor, 27983, SAN 313-0460. Tel: 252-794-2244. FAX: 252-794-1546. *Br Mgr,* Nancy B Hughes; *Asst Librn,* Lillian Harden; *Asst Librn,* Vashti Holley
Special Collections: Genealogy Coll; Local History Coll
Subject Interests: County hist, World War II
Open Mon-Wed & Fri 10-6, Thurs 10-8, Sat 9-12
NORTHAMPTON MEMORIAL LIBRARY, 207 W Jefferson St, Jackson, 27845. (Mail add: PO Box 427, Jackson, 27845-0427), SAN 312-8857. Tel: 252-534-3571. FAX: 252-534-1017. *Br Mgr,* Barbara Davis; *Asst Librn,* Pam Cox; *Asst Librn,* Cheryl Kee
Open Mon-Wed & Fri 10-6, Thurs 10-8, Sat 9-12
ELIZABETH SEWELL PARKER MEMORIAL LIBRARY, 213 E Main, Murfreesboro, 27855. (Mail add: PO Drawer 186, Murfreesboro, 27855-0186), SAN 354-4443. Tel: 252-398-4494. FAX: 252-398-5724. *Br Mgr,* Beverly Warrick; *Asst Librn,* Karen Cavin; *Asst Librn,* Shirley Kwasikpui
Special Collections: Murfreesboro, North Carolina (Paul Ronald Jenkins Photographs)
Open Mon-Wed & Fri 10-6, Thurs 10-7:30, Sat 9-12

YADKINVILLE

P YADKIN COUNTY PUBLIC LIBRARY*, 233 E Main St, 27055. (Mail add: PO Box 607, 27055-0607), SAN 313-0622. Tel: 336-679-8792. FAX: 336-679-4625. E-mail: ydk@nwrl.org. Web Site: www.nwrl.org. *Librn,* Malinda S Sells; *Asst Librn,* Christy E Ellington
Founded 1942. Pop 32,000; Circ 58,000
Library Holdings: Bk Titles 57,000; Bk Vols 58,000; Per Subs 10
Special Collections: Local History Coll. Oral History
Automation Activity & Vendor Info: (Cataloging) SirsiDynix; (Circulation) SirsiDynix; (OPAC) SirsiDynix
Mem of Northwestern Regional Library
Open Mon & Thurs 8:30-6:30, Tues, Wed & Fri 8:30-5:30
Friends of the Library Group

YANCEYVILLE

P GUNN MEMORIAL PUBLIC LIBRARY*, 161 Main St E, 27379. SAN 313-0630. Tel: 336-694-6241. Administration Tel: 336-694-9673. FAX: 336-694-9846. E-mail: gunnpublibrary@gmail.com. *Dir,* Rhonda Griffin; E-mail: rgriffin@caswellcountync.gov; Staff 7 (MLS 1, Non-MLS 6)
Founded 1937. Pop 23,248; Circ 66,989
Library Holdings: Bk Vols 43,460; Per Subs 107
Special Collections: Local History/Genealogy Coll
Subject Interests: Genealogy, Local hist
Wireless access
Mem of Hyconeechee Regional Library
Open Mon & Thurs 9-7, Tues & Wed 9-6, Fri 9-5, Sat 10-1
Friends of the Library Group

NORTH DAKOTA

Date of Statistics: FY 2013
Population, 2010 U.S. Census: 672,591
Population, 2013 Census: 723,393
Population Served by Public Libraries: 640,923
Unserved: 82,470
Total Volumes in Public Libraries: 3,011,687
Volumes Per Capita: 4.16
Total Public Library Circulation: 4,168,369
Circulation Per Capita: 5.76
Total Public Library Income (including Grants-in-Aid): $17,044,517
Source of Income: Mainly public funds
Expenditure Per Capita: $22.20
Grants-in-Aid for Public Libraries: $118,750
State Aid: $750,000
Number of Bookmobiles in State: 11
Number of County or Multi-county Libraries: 31
Counties Served: 31
Counties Unserved: 22

ASHLEY

P ASHLEY PUBLIC LIBRARY*, 113 First Ave NW, 58413-7037. (Mail add: PO Box 185, 58413-0185). Tel: 701-288-3510. *Librn,* Janice Rott; *Asst Librn,* Barbara Nitschke
Founded 1913. Pop 882; Circ 2,185
Library Holdings: AV Mats 52; DVDs 50; Large Print Bks 50; Bk Vols 10,600; Talking Bks 25; Videos 42
Wireless access
Open Wed 10-12 & 1-7:30, Thurs 1-5, Fri 10-12 & 1-5, Sat 10-Noon
Friends of the Library Group

BEACH

P GOLDEN VALLEY COUNTY LIBRARY*, 54 Central Ave S, 58621. (Mail add: PO Box 579, 58621-0579), SAN 313-0665. Tel: 701-872-4627. *Dir,* Joanne Tescher
Founded 1910. Pop 2,108; Circ 21,343
Library Holdings: Bk Vols 19,500; Per Subs 35
Open Tues & Fri 1-5, Wed 10-12 & 1-5, Thurs 1-5 & 6-8, Sat 9-Noon

BELCOURT

J TURTLE MOUNTAIN COMMUNITY COLLEGE LIBRARY*, PO Box 340, 58316-0340. SAN 313-0673. Tel: 701-477-7862, Ext 2084. FAX: 701-477-7805. Web Site: www.tm.edu/library.aspx. *Dir,* Laisee Allery, Tel: 701-477-7854, Ext 2081, E-mail: lallery@tm.edu; Staff 2 (MLS 1, Non-MLS 1)
Founded 1977. Enrl 911; Fac 44; Highest Degree: Bachelor
Library Holdings: AV Mats 1,462; Bks on Deafness & Sign Lang 11; Large Print Bks 54; Bk Titles 22,535; Bk Vols 31,248; Per Subs 135
Special Collections: Anishanabe Coll (materials about Native Americans); Elementary Education Coll; Erdrich Coll (Books written and dontated by Louise Erdrich)
Subject Interests: Native Am
Automation Activity & Vendor Info: (Acquisitions) Follett Software; (Cataloging) Follett Software; (Circulation) Follett Software; (Course Reserve) Follett Software; (Media Booking) Follett Software; (OPAC) Follett Software
Database Vendor: EBSCOhost, Gale Cengage Learning
Wireless access
Function: ILL available, Photocopying/Printing, Ref serv available, Referrals accepted, Telephone ref
Partic in Online Dakota Info Network (ODIN)
Open Mon-Fri 8-6

BISMARCK

C BISMARCK STATE COLLEGE LIBRARY*, 1500 Edwards Ave, 58501. (Mail add: PO Box 5587, 58506-5587), SAN 313-069X. Tel: 701-224-5450. Interlibrary Loan Service Tel: 701-224-5503. Toll Free Tel: 800-445-5073. FAX: 701-224-5551. E-mail: bsc.library@bismarckstate.edu. Web Site: www.bismarckstate.edu/library. *Coll Develop, Dir of Libr Serv,* Marlene Anderson; Tel: 701-224-5578, E-mail: marlene.anderson@bismarckstate.edu; *ILL, Ref & Instruction Librn, Ser,* Sandi Bates; Tel: 701-224-5451; *Archives, Ref & Instruction Librn,* Johanna Bjork; Tel: 701-224-5738, E-mail: johanna.bjork@bismarckstate.edu; *Circ, ILL, Reserves,* Laura Kalvoda; Tel: 701-224-5483, E-mail: laura.kalvoda@bismarckstate.edu; *Tech Serv,* Liz Mason; E-mail: liz.mason@bismarckstate.edu; Staff 6 (MLS 3, Non-MLS 3)
Founded 1955. Enrl 3,887; Fac 135; Highest Degree: Bachelor
Jul 2012-Jun 2013 Income $586,575. Sal $373,366
Special Collections: BSC Archives (Institutional history)
Subject Interests: Energy, NDak hist
Automation Activity & Vendor Info: (Acquisitions) Ex Libris Group; (Cataloging) Ex Libris Group; (Circulation) Ex Libris Group; (Course Reserve) Ex Libris Group; (ILL) Ex Libris Group; (Media Booking) Ex Libris Group; (OPAC) Ex Libris Group; (Serials) Ex Libris Group
Database Vendor: Alexander Street Press, Cinahl, College Source, CredoReference, EBSCO Auto Repair Reference, EBSCOhost, Facts on File, Gale Cengage Learning, McGraw-Hill, Newsbank, OCLC, Overdrive, Inc, ProQuest
Wireless access
Function: Art exhibits, Audio & video playback equip for onsite use, Audiobks via web, Bks on cassette, Bks on CD, Computers for patron use, Copy machines, Electronic databases & coll, Exhibits, Fax serv, Handicapped accessible, ILL available, Microfiche/film & reading machines, Music CDs, Online ref, Online searches, Orientations, Outside serv via phone, mail, e-mail & web, Pub access computers, Ref serv available, Ref serv in person, Telephone ref, VHS videos, Web-catalog, Winter reading prog, Workshops
Partic in Online Dakota Info Network (ODIN)
Special Services for the Blind - Magnifiers
Open Mon-Thurs 7:30am-9pm, Fri 7:30-4, Sun 3-7
Restriction: In-house use for visitors, Restricted pub use

P BISMARCK VETERANS MEMORIAL PUBLIC LIBRARY*, 515 N Fifth St, 58501-4081. SAN 313-0789. Tel: 701-355-1480. Interlibrary Loan Service Tel: 701-355-1485. FAX: 701-221-3729. Web Site: www.bismarcklibrary.org. *Dir,* Mary Jane Schmaltz; Tel: 701-355-1482, E-mail: mjschmaltz@cdln.info; *Asst Dir,* Christine Kujawa; Tel: 701-355-1483, E-mail: ckujawa@cdln.info; *Head, Children's Dept,* Traci Juhala; Tel: 701-355-1489, E-mail: tjuhala@cdln.info; *Head, Ref,* Kate Waldera; Tel: 701-355-1492, E-mail: kwaldera@cdln.info; *Head, Tech Serv,* Jennifer Jones; Tel: 701-355-1488, E-mail: jjones@cdln.info; *ILL Librn,* Sarah Matthews; E-mail: smatthews@cdln.info; *Ref & Teen Serv,* Kathleen Vandervorst; Tel: 701-355-1487, E-mail: kavandervorst@cdln.info; Staff 9.4 (MLS 9.4)
Founded 1917. Pop 77,000; Circ 537,337
Jan 2013-Dec 2013 Income $2,578,541, State $55,000, City $2,313,356, County $200,185, Locally Generated Income $10,000. Mats Exp $372,000, Books $251,000, Per/Ser (Incl. Access Fees) $37,000, Micro $2,000, AV Mat $29,000, Electronic Ref Mat (Incl. Access Fees) $52,000, Presv $1,000. Sal $1,412,815

Library Holdings: CDs 8,515; DVDs 7,707; e-books 12,000; Bk Vols 201,811; Per Subs 420
Subject Interests: Northern Mo river hist
Automation Activity & Vendor Info: (Cataloging) SirsiDynix; (Circulation) SirsiDynix; (OPAC) SirsiDynix
Database Vendor: Alexander Street Press, EBSCO Auto Repair Reference, EBSCO Information Services, EBSCOhost, Electric Library, OCLC FirstSearch, OCLC WorldShare Interlibrary Loan, ProQuest, SirsiDynix
Wireless access
Partic in OCLC Online Computer Library Center, Inc
Open Mon-Thurs 9-9, Fri & Sat 9-6, Sun 1-6
Restriction: Open to pub for ref & circ; with some limitations
Friends of the Library Group
Bookmobiles: 1. Librn, Keli Trowbridge

GL NORTH DAKOTA LEGISLATIVE COUNCIL LIBRARY*, 600 E Boulevard Ave, 58505-0660. Tel: 701-328-4900. FAX: 701-328-3615. *Mgr,* Kylah Aull; E-mail: kaull@nd.gov
Library Holdings: Bk Vols 20,000; Per Subs 120
Wireless access
Open Mon-Fri 8-5

S NORTH DAKOTA PREVENTION RESOURCE CENTER LIBRARY*, 1237 W Divide Ave, Ste 1D, 58501-1208. Tel: 701-328-8919. Toll Free Tel: 800-642-6744 (ND only). FAX: 701-328-8979. Web Site: nd.gov/dhs/prevention. *Librn,* Stacey Orso; E-mail: sorso@nd.gov
Library Holdings: Bk Vols 500
Open Mon-Fri 8-5

P NORTH DAKOTA STATE LIBRARY*, Library Memorial Bldg, 604 East Blvd Ave, Dept 250, 58505-0800. SAN 313-0746. Tel: 701-328-2492. Circulation Tel: 701-328-4657. Interlibrary Loan Service Tel: 701-328-3252. Reference Tel: 701-328-4622. Automation Services Tel: 701-328-4658. Toll Free Tel: 800-472-2104. FAX: 701-328-2040. TDD: 701-328-4923. E-mail: statelib@nd.gov. Web Site: www.library.nd.gov. *State Librn,* Mary Soucie; *Asst State Librn,* Cynthia Clairmont-Schmidt; Tel: 701-328-4652, E-mail: ccclairmont@nd.gov; *Head, Doc Delivery/ILL,* Shari Mosser; Tel: 701-328-3252, E-mail: ssandwick@nd.gov; *Head, Info Tech,* Ryan Kroh; Tel: 701-328-4658, E-mail: rkroh@nd.gov; *Head, Pub Serv,* Al Peterson; Tel: 701-328-4021, E-mail: alpeterson@nd.gov; *Head, Serv for Blind & Handicapped,* Susan Hammer-Schneider; Tel: 701-328-2185, E-mail: sbschneider@nd.gov; *Head, Statewide Cat Develop,* Stacey Goldade; Tel: 701-328-1860, E-mail: sgoldade@nd.gov; *Head, Tech Serv,* Kristen Northrup; Tel: 701-328-2491, E-mail: knorthrup@nd.gov; *Coordr, Digital Mat,* Stephanie Baltzer-Kom; E-mail: baltzer@nd.gov; *Coordr, Field Serv Prog,* Eric Stroshane; Tel: 701-328-4661, E-mail: estroshane@nd.gov; *Coordr, Training Prog,* Steve Axtman; Tel: 701-328-3495, E-mail: saxtman@nd.gov; *Pub Relations Coordr,* Adam Emter; Tel: 701-328-4656, E-mail: aemter@nd.gov; Staff 14 (MLS 10, Non-MLS 4)
Founded 1907
Library Holdings: CDs 396; e-books 11,068; Large Print Bks 10,392; Bk Titles 150,819; Per Subs 146; Talking Bks 60,781; Videos 3,734
Special Collections: North Dakota Coll; State Documents. State Document Depository; US Document Depository
Automation Activity & Vendor Info: (Acquisitions) Ex Libris Group; (Cataloging) Ex Libris Group; (Circulation) Ex Libris Group; (ILL) Ex Libris Group; (OPAC) Ex Libris Group, (Serials) Ex Libris Group
Database Vendor: Ex Libris Group, OCLC WorldShare Interlibrary Loan
Wireless access
Publications: Discovery (Newsletter); Library Statistics; ND Flickertale (Monthly newsletter); State Library Biennial Report
Partic in Minitex Library Information Network
Special Services for the Deaf - TDD equip
Special Services for the Blind - Radio reading serv; Talking bks
Open Mon-Fri 8-5

GL NORTH DAKOTA SUPREME COURT, Law Library, Judicial Wing, 2nd Flr, 600 E Boulevard Ave, Dept 182, 58505-0540. SAN 313-0762. Tel: 701-328-2227, 701-328-4496, 701-328-4594. FAX: 701-328-3609. Web Site: www.court.state.nd.us/lawlib/www6.htm. *Librn,* Ted Smith
Founded 1889
Library Holdings: Bk Vols 72,000
Special Collections: North Dakota Legal Materials
Automation Activity & Vendor Info: (ILL) Ex Libris Group; (OPAC) Ex Libris Group
Database Vendor: LexisNexis, Westlaw
Wireless access
Partic in Online Dakota Info Network (ODIN)
Open Mon-Fri 8-5

M SANFORD HEALTH*, Sanford Health Sciences Library, 622 Ave A East, 58501. SAN 313-0770. Tel: 701-323-5390, 701-323-5392. FAX: 701-323-6967. Web Site: bismarck.sanfordhealth.org. *Dir,* Travis Schulz; Tel: 701-323-5391, E-mail: t.schulz@sanfordhealth.org; Staff 3 (MLS 2, Non-MLS 1)
Founded 1927
Library Holdings: Bk Vols 6,000; Per Subs 6
Subject Interests: Clinical med, Nursing
Automation Activity & Vendor Info: (Circulation) Ex Libris Group; (ILL) Ex Libris Group
Database Vendor: EBSCOhost, Elsevier, ProQuest
Wireless access
Function: Archival coll, Doc delivery serv, For res purposes, ILL available, Photocopying/Printing, Ref serv available, Telephone ref
Partic in Online Dakota Info Network (ODIN)
Open Mon-Fri 8-5
Restriction: Circ limited, In-house use for visitors, Private libr

S STATE HISTORICAL SOCIETY OF NORTH DAKOTA, State Archives, North Dakota Heritage Ctr, 612 E Boulevard Ave, 58505-0830. SAN 313-072X. Tel: 701-328-2668. Reference Tel: 701-328-2091. FAX: 701-328-2650. E-mail: archives@nd.gov. Web Site: history.nd.gov/archives/index.html. *State Archivist,* Ann Jenks; E-mail: ajenks@nd.gov; *Dep State Archivist,* Shane Molander; Tel: 701-328-3570, E-mail: smolander@nd.gov; *Dept Head, Ref,* Jim Davis; Tel: 701-328-2539, E-mail: jidavis@nd.gov; *Dept Head, Tech Serv,* Rachel White; Tel: 701-328-3571, E-mail: rewhite@nd.gov; Staff 13 (MLS 3, Non-MLS 10)
Founded 1895
Library Holdings: Bk Titles 40,000; Bk Vols 105,000; Per Subs 570
Special Collections: Oral History; State Document Depository; US Document Depository
Subject Interests: Archaeology, Hist of Northern Great Plains, NDak hist, Presv
Automation Activity & Vendor Info: (Cataloging) OCLC Online; (ILL) OCLC Online; (OPAC) Ex Libris Group
Database Vendor: OCLC FirstSearch, OCLC WorldShare Interlibrary Loan
Wireless access
Function: Archival coll, Handicapped accessible, ILL available, Microfiche/film & reading machines, Newsp ref libr, Photocopying/Printing, Ref serv available, Res performed for a fee, Telephone ref
Publications: North Dakota History (Quarterly); PlainsTalk (Quarterly)
Partic in Minitex Library Information Network; OCLC Online Computer Library Center, Inc
Open Mon-Fri 8-4:30
Restriction: Closed stack, In-house use for visitors, Non-circulating coll

J UNITED TRIBES TECHNICAL COLLEGE LIBRARY*, Education Bldg, 3315 University Dr, 58504-7565. Tel: 701-255-3285, Ext 1282. FAX: 701-530-0625. Web Site: www.uttc.edu. *Dir,* Charlene Weis; E-mail: cweis@uttc.edu
Library Holdings: Bk Vols 9,000
Special Collections: Native American Coll
Automation Activity & Vendor Info: (Cataloging) SirsiDynix; (Circulation) SirsiDynix; (OPAC) SirsiDynix
Database Vendor: EBSCOhost, ProQuest
Open Mon-Fri 8-4:30

C UNIVERSITY OF MARY*, Welder Library, 7500 University Dr, 58504-9652. SAN 313-0711. Tel: 701-355-8070. FAX: 701-355-8255. Web Site: www.umary.edu. *Dir,* Cheryl M Bailey; Staff 4 (MLS 4)
Founded 1959. Enrl 2,552; Highest Degree: Doctorate
Library Holdings: Bk Vols 70,000; Per Subs 525
Subject Interests: Educ, Nursing, Theol
Automation Activity & Vendor Info: (Acquisitions) SirsiDynix; (Cataloging) Horizon; (Circulation) Horizon; (OPAC) Horizon
Database Vendor: EBSCOhost, JSTOR, ProQuest, SirsiDynix
Partic in OCLC Online Computer Library Center, Inc
Open Mon-Thurs 8am-10pm, Fri 8-4:30, Sat 1-5, Sun 2-10

BOTTINEAU

P BOTTINEAU COUNTY PUBLIC LIBRARY*, 314 W Fifth St, 58318-9600. SAN 375-4537. Tel: 701-228-2967. FAX: 701-228-2171. E-mail: bottineaulibrary@yahoo.com. *Dir,* Beth Reitan; Staff 3 (MLS 1, Non-MLS 2)
Founded 1922
Library Holdings: Bk Vols 30,000; Per Subs 30
Automation Activity & Vendor Info: (Circulation) Follett Software; (Serials) Follett Software
Function: ILL available
Partic in Online Dakota Info Network (ODIN)
Open Mon-Fri 11:30-5:30, Sat 10-2
Bookmobiles: 1

J DAKOTA COLLEGE AT BOTTINEAU LIBRARY*, 105 Simrall Blvd, 58318. SAN 313-0797. Tel: 701-228-5454. FAX: 701-228-5438. Web Site: www.dakotacollege.edu. *Dir,* Deb M Syvertson; Tel: 701-228-5425, E-mail: deb.syvertson@dakotacollege.edu; *Assoc Librn,* Terri Hauge
Founded 1907. Enrl 644; Fac 26; Highest Degree: Associate
Library Holdings: Audiobooks 110; AV Mats 1,300; e-books 8,075; Bk Titles 25,325; Bk Vols 27,200; Per Subs 180
Subject Interests: Forestry, Hort, Natural sci, Recreation
Database Vendor: Ex Libris Group
Wireless access
Partic in Online Dakota Info Network (ODIN)
Open Mon-Thurs 7:30am-10pm, Fri 7:30-4, Sun 6pm-10pm

BOWMAN

P BOWMAN REGIONAL PUBLIC LIBRARY*, 18 E Divide St, 58623. (Mail add: PO Box 179, 58623-0179), SAN 313-0800. Tel: 701-523-3797. E-mail: bowlib@ndsupernet.com. Web Site: www.bowmanlibrary.org. *Dir,* Sarah Snavely; *Librn,* Amy Bergquist
Founded 1913
Library Holdings: Bk Vols 11,000; Per Subs 50
Automation Activity & Vendor Info: (Cataloging) Follett Software; (Circulation) Follett Software; (OPAC) Follett Software
Open Mon 10-6, Tues-Thurs 9-7, Fri 10-5, Sat 9-1

CANDO

P CANDO COMMUNITY LIBRARY*, 523 Main St, 58324. (Mail add: PO Box 798, 58324-0798). Tel: 701-968-4549. Web Site: www.candond.com. *Librn,* Hazel Krack
Library Holdings: Bk Titles 25,000
Open Tues & Thurs 3-8, Wed & Sat 11-2

CARRINGTON

P CARRINGTON CITY LIBRARY*, 55 Ninth Ave S, 58421-1198. SAN 313-0819. Tel: 701-652-3921. FAX: 701-652-3922. E-mail: cgtnlib@daktel.com. *Librn,* Lenore Franchuk
Founded 1916. Pop 2,267; Circ 9,982
Library Holdings: Bk Vols 12,718; Per Subs 33; Talking Bks 225; Videos 499
Partic in NDak Network for Knowledge
Open Mon-Wed & Fri 10:30-5:30, Thurs 10:30-7:30, Sat 10:30-3:30

CASSELTON

P CASSELTON PUBLIC LIBRARY*, 701 First St N, 58012. (Mail add: PO Box 1090, 58012-1090), SAN 313-0827. Tel: 701-347-4861, Ext 13. FAX: 701-347-4505. E-mail: cassndlibrary@casselton.net. *Dir,* Beverly Drager; *Actg Asst Librn,* Harriet Gruel
Pop 2,200
Jan 2007-Dec 2007 Income $26,385, State $886, City $24,760, Locally Generated Income $539. Mats Exp $5,861. Sal $14,256
Library Holdings: CDs 80; DVDs 24; Bk Titles 25,000; Per Subs 4; Spec Interest Per Sub 5; Talking Bks 356; Videos 288
Partic in Online Dakota Info Network (ODIN)
Special Services for the Blind - Audio mat; Bks on cassette; Bks on CD; Home delivery serv; Recorded bks; Talking bk serv referral; Talking bks; Talking bks & player equip; Talking bks from Braille Inst
Open Mon 10-7, Tues-Fri 10-5, Sat 10-2; Mon (Summer) 9-7, Tues-Fri 9-4
Friends of the Library Group

CAVALIER

P CAVALIER PUBLIC LIBRARY*, 106 W Second Ave S, 58220. SAN 313-0835. Tel: 701-265-4746. E-mail: cavlibry@polarcomm.com. *Librn,* Janet Morrison; *Ch,* Rebecca Ratchenski; Tel: 701-265-4016; Staff 1 (Non-MLS 1)
Founded 1915. Pop 1,300; Circ 20,000
Jan 2007-Dec 2007 Income $33,079, State $1,102, City $8,740, County $7,000, Locally Generated Income $5,272, Other $10,965. Mats Exp $7,235, Books $6,500, Per/Ser (Incl. Access Fees) $650, Other Print Mats $85. Sal $14,965
Library Holdings: Audiobooks 249; DVDs 183; Large Print Bks 180; Bk Vols 12,039; Per Subs 35; Videos 582
Automation Activity & Vendor Info: (Acquisitions) Follett Software
Database Vendor: OCLC WorldShare Interlibrary Loan
Wireless access
Partic in Online Dakota Info Network (ODIN)
Open Mon-Fri 12:30-5:30

COOPERSTOWN

P GRIGGS COUNTY PUBLIC LIBRARY*, 902 Burrell Ave, 58425. (Mail add: PO Box 546, 58425-0546), SAN 313-0843. Tel: 701-797-2214. E-mail: gcplibrary@mlgc.com. Web Site: griggscountypubliclibrary.com. *Dir,* Bonnie Krenz; Staff 2 (Non-MLS 2)
Founded 1944. Pop 1,500; Circ 34,887
Library Holdings: AV Mats 300; Large Print Bks 500; Bk Titles 30,000; Per Subs 52; Talking Bks 300
Special Collections: North Dakota Historical Coll
Automation Activity & Vendor Info: (Cataloging) Follett Software; (Circulation) Follett Software
Database Vendor: World Book Online
Open Mon 9-12 & 1-5, Tues-Thurs 9-6, Fri 9-5, Sat 9-1
Bookmobiles: 1. In Charge, Bonnie Krenz. Bk titles 4,000

CROSBY

P DIVIDE COUNTY PUBLIC LIBRARY*, 204 First St NE, 58730. (Mail add: PO Box 90, 58730), SAN 313-0851. Tel: 701-965-6305. E-mail: dcl@nccray.net. Web Site: www.dividecountyndlibrary.com. *Dir,* Traci Petry
Founded 1912. Pop 2,283
Jan 2005-Dec 2005 Income $46,000. Mats Exp $43,000, Books $6,000
Library Holdings: Bks-By-Mail 50; Bks on Deafness & Sign Lang 10; Large Print Bks 200; Bk Vols 38,000; Per Subs 44; Talking Bks 100; Videos 350
Special Collections: Local Geneology Coll. Oral History
Subject Interests: Local hist, State hist
Automation Activity & Vendor Info: (Acquisitions) Follett Software; (ILL) Follett Software
Wireless access
Open Mon-Fri 8:30-5

DEVILS LAKE

P LAKE REGION PUBLIC LIBRARY, 423 Seventh St NE, 58301-2529. SAN 313-086X. Tel: 701-662-2220. FAX: 701-662-2281. E-mail: lakeregion.pl@sendit.nodak.edu. Web Site: www.dvlnd.com/departments/library.html. *Dir,* Jim Chattin; Staff 1 (Non-MLS 1)
Founded 1908. Pop 11,536; Circ 24,065
Jan 2013-Dec 2013 Income $164,743, State $14,434, City $74,682, County $60,761, Locally Generated Income $14,866. Mats Exp $16,249, Books $8,651, Per/Ser (Incl. Access Fees) $2,079, AV Mat $1,259, Electronic Ref Mat (Incl. Access Fees) $4,260. Sal $80,620 (Prof $29,894)
Library Holdings: Audiobooks 510; CDs 203; DVDs 544; e-books 8,436; Electronic Media & Resources 56; Large Print Bks 1,423; Microforms 293; Bk Vols 35,199; Per Subs 57; Videos 715
Special Collections: George Johnson Genealogy Coll; Germans-From-Russia Coll; Local History Coll; North Dakota Coll; Special Scandinavian Coll
Subject Interests: Hist, Needlework, Recipes
Automation Activity & Vendor Info: (Acquisitions) Book Systems; (Cataloging) Book Systems; (Circulation) Book Systems; (OPAC) Book Systems
Database Vendor: EBSCO Information Services, Electric Library, LearningExpress, Medline, ProQuest
Wireless access
Function: Audiobks via web, Bks on cassette, Bks on CD, Children's prog, Computers for patron use, Copy machines, Digital talking bks, e-mail serv, Electronic databases & coll, Fax serv, Free DVD rentals, Handicapped accessible, ILL available, Magazines, Microfiche/film & reading machines, Music CDs, Outreach serv, Photocopying/Printing, Prog for adults, Prog for children & young adult, Pub access computers, Scanner, Spoken cassettes & CDs, Spoken cassettes & DVDs, Story hour, Summer reading prog, Tax forms, VHS videos, Wheelchair accessible
Special Services for the Deaf - ADA equip; Closed caption videos
Special Services for the Blind - Bks on cassette; Bks on CD; Cassettes; Copier with enlargement capabilities; Extensive large print coll; Free checkout of audio mat; Large print bks
Open Mon-Wed & Fri 10:30-6, Thurs 10:30-7, Sat 10:30-3
Restriction: Non-resident fee

C LAKE REGION STATE COLLEGE, Paul Hoghaug Library, 1801 College Dr N, 58301. SAN 313-0878. Tel: 701-662-1533. FAX: 701-662-1570. Web Site: www.lrsc.nodak.edu. *Libr Dir,* Celeste Ertelt; E-mail: celeste.m.ertelt@lrsc.edu; Staff 1 (MLS 1)
Founded 1966. Enrl 1,300; Highest Degree: Associate
Library Holdings: Audiobooks 500; Bks on Deafness & Sign Lang 25; CDs 25; DVDs 500; e-books 18,000; Bk Vols 35,000; Per Subs 100; Videos 400
Special Collections: Irish History & Culture
Automation Activity & Vendor Info: (Acquisitions) Ex Libris Group; (Cataloging) Ex Libris Group; (Circulation) Ex Libris Group; (Course

Reserve) Ex Libris Group; (ILL) Ex Libris Group; (Media Booking) Ex Libris Group; (OPAC) Ex Libris Group; (Serials) Ex Libris Group
Database Vendor: EBSCO Auto Repair Reference, EBSCOhost, Facts on File, Gale Cengage Learning, ProQuest
Wireless access
Open Mon-Thurs 8am-9pm, Fri 8-4

S NORTH DAKOTA SCHOOL FOR THE DEAF LIBRARY*, 1401 College Dr N, 58301. SAN 313-0886. Tel: 701-665-4400. FAX: 701-665-4409. Web Site: www.nd.gov/ndsd. *Librn,* Susan Schwab-Kjelland; Tel: 701-665-4433, E-mail: susan.schwab-kjelland.1@sendit.nodak.edu
Library Holdings: Bk Vols 4,000; Per Subs 20
Wireless access
Open Mon-Fri 8-4

DICKINSON

P DICKINSON AREA PUBLIC LIBRARY*, 139 Third St W, 58601. SAN 313-0894. Tel: 701-456-7700. FAX: 701-456-7702. E-mail: dickinson.library@sendit.nodak.edu. Web Site: www.dickinsonlibrary.org. *Dir,* Renee Paasch; *Tech Serv,* Mary Lovell; Staff 6 (Non-MLS 6)
Founded 1908. Pop 28,000; Circ 130,000
Jan 2011-Dec 2011 Income (Main Library and Branch(s)) $502,241, State $28,000, City $262,900, Federal $1,500, County $184,920, Locally Generated Income $24,921. Mats Exp $72,614, Books $44,614, Per/Ser (Incl. Access Fees) $6,000, AV Mat $12,000, Electronic Ref Mat (Incl. Access Fees) $10,000. Sal $301,041 (Prof $243,529)
Library Holdings: CDs 1,000; DVDs 1,100; e-books 8,000; Large Print Bks 3,500; Bk Titles 85,000; Per Subs 100; Talking Bks 3,000; Videos 3,056
Special Collections: Dickinson Press, 1883-present
Automation Activity & Vendor Info: (Acquisitions) Ex Libris Group; (Cataloging) Ex Libris Group; (Circulation) Ex Libris Group; (ILL) Ex Libris Group; (OPAC) Ex Libris Group; (Serials) Ex Libris Group
Database Vendor: Gale Cengage Learning, OCLC FirstSearch, OCLC WorldShare Interlibrary Loan
Wireless access
Publications: Library Skills for Adult Education
Partic in NDak Network for Knowledge; OCLC Online Computer Library Center, Inc; Online Dakota Info Network (ODIN)
Open Mon-Thurs 9-9, Fri 9-6, Sat 9-5, Sun 1-4
Friends of the Library Group
Branches: 1
BILLINGS COUNTY RESOURCE CENTER, PO Box 307, Medora, 58645-0307. Tel: 701-623-4604. FAX: 701-623-4941. *Dir,* Renee Paasch; *Pub Serv,* Tina Kuntz
Library Holdings: Bk Vols 15,000
Partic in Online Dakota Info Network (ODIN)
Open Mon & Tues 3:15-6, Wed 10-6
Bookmobiles: 1. Dir, Renee Paasch. Bk titles 3,000

C DICKINSON STATE UNIVERSITY, Stoxen Library, 291 Campus Dr, 58601. SAN 313-0908. Tel: 701-483-2135. FAX: 701-483-2006. Web Site: www.dickinsonstate.edu. *Dir, Libr Serv,* Mary Sheahan; Tel: 701-483-2883, E-mail: mary.sheahan@dickinsonstate.edu; *Asst Dir,* Keri Youngstrand; Tel: 701-483-2561, E-mail: keri.youngstrand@dickinsonstate.edu; Staff 6 (MLS 3, Non-MLS 3)
Founded 1918. Enrl 1,500; Fac 70; Highest Degree: Bachelor
Jul 2013-Jun 2014. Mats Exp $307,078, Books $77,357, Per/Ser (Incl. Access Fees) $143,943, Micro $684, AV Mat $12,892, Electronic Ref Mat (Incl. Access Fees) $72,202. Sal $267,156 (Prof $156,320)
Library Holdings: AV Mats 7,300; e-books 13,046; Bk Vols 96,000; Per Subs 400
Special Collections: Teddy Roosevelt Coll
Subject Interests: Educ
Automation Activity & Vendor Info: (Acquisitions) Ex Libris Group; (Cataloging) Ex Libris Group; (Circulation) Ex Libris Group; (Course Reserve) Ex Libris Group; (ILL) Ex Libris Group; (OPAC) Ex Libris Group; (Serials) Ex Libris Group
Database Vendor: EBSCOhost, Gale Cengage Learning, Overdrive, Inc, ProQuest
Wireless access
Partic in Online Dakota Info Network (ODIN)

DRAKE

P DRAKE PUBLIC LIBRARY*, 411 Main St, 58736. (Mail add: PO Box 407, 58736-0407). Tel: 701-465-3732. FAX: 701-465-3634. *Librn,* Kim Meckle
Library Holdings: CDs 25; Bk Vols 5,000; Per Subs 10
Partic in Online Dakota Info Network (ODIN)

DUNN CENTER

P DUNN CENTER PUBLIC LIBRARY*, PO Box 14, 58626-0014. Tel: 701-548-8400. E-mail: dclibrary@ndsupernet.com. *In Charge,* Linda Brown
Library Holdings: Bk Vols 30,000
Automation Activity & Vendor Info: (Cataloging) JayWil Software Development, Inc
Open Tues, Fri & Sat 10-3

EDGELEY

P SOUTH CENTRAL AREA LIBRARY*, Edgeley Public, 530 Main St, 58433. (Mail add: PO Box 218, 58433-0218), SAN 355-323X. Tel: 701-493-2769. FAX: 701-493-2959. E-mail: library@drtel.net. *Dir,* Lynda Dunn
Founded 1958. Pop 10,075; Circ 88,000
Library Holdings: AV Mats 350; Large Print Bks 5,000; Bk Titles 30,000; Bk Vols 15,000; Per Subs 12; Talking Bks 400
Special Collections: North Dakota Coll
Automation Activity & Vendor Info: (Cataloging) Follett Software; (Circulation) Follett Software; (OPAC) Follett Software
Open Mon-Fri 1-5 (9-12 Summer)
Bookmobiles: 1

ELGIN

P ELGIN PUBLIC LIBRARY*, PO Box 153, 58533-0153. Tel: 701-584-2181. E-mail: elginlibrary@westriv.com. *Pres,* Debbie Michaels
Library Holdings: Bk Titles 9,500
Open Mon-Fri 9-5

ELLENDALE

P ELLENDALE PUBLIC LIBRARY*, 75 First St S, 58436. (Mail add: PO Box 113, 58436-0113), SAN 313-0916. Tel: 701-349-3852. *Dir,* Marian Crautmann
Circ 18,000
Library Holdings: Bk Vols 25,000; Per Subs 10
Open Mon 6-8, Tues & Wed 1-5, Thurs 1-8, Sat 9-Noon
Friends of the Library Group

CR TRINITY BIBLE COLLEGE*, The Graham Library, 50 Sixth Ave S, 58436-7150. SAN 313-0924. Tel: 701-349-5407. Toll Free Tel: 800-523-1603. FAX: 701-349-5443. E-mail: tbclibrary@trinitybiblecollege.edu. Web Site: www.trinitybiblecollege.edu/library. *Librn,* Diane Olson
Founded 1948. Enrl 250; Fac 25; Highest Degree: Bachelor
Library Holdings: e-books 11,730; Bk Titles 57,604; Bk Vols 89,690; Per Subs 175; Videos 518
Special Collections: College & Denomination Archives; Juvenile Coll; North Dakota History (Graham Coll); Rare Coll
Subject Interests: Biblical studies, Evangelism, Missions, Relig studies, Soc sci
Automation Activity & Vendor Info: (Circulation) Ex Libris Group
Database Vendor: EBSCOhost, Gale Cengage Learning, OCLC FirstSearch, ProQuest
Wireless access
Function: Copy machines, Electronic databases & coll, ILL available, Photocopying/Printing, Pub access computers, Tax forms
Partic in Minitex Library Information Network; Online Dakota Info Network (ODIN)
Open Mon, Tues & Thurs 9am-10pm, Wed 9-5 & 8:30-10, Fri 9-5, Sat 12-5
Restriction: Borrowing requests are handled by ILL, Non-circulating of rare bks

ENDERLIN

P ENDERLIN MUNICIPAL LIBRARY, 303 Railway St, 58027. SAN 313-0932. Tel: 701-437-2953. FAX: 701-437-2104. E-mail: enderlinlibrary@mlgc.com. *Librn,* Myrene Peterson
Founded 1911. Pop 986; Circ 5,895
Library Holdings: Bk Vols 12,000; Per Subs 17
Special Collections: SooLine Railroad Resources
Subject Interests: NDak
Automation Activity & Vendor Info: (Acquisitions) Follett Software; (Circulation) Follett Software; (Course Reserve) Follett Software; (ILL) Follett Software
Wireless access
Open Tues 12-7, Wed-Fri 12-6, Sat 9-1
Friends of the Library Group

FARGO

GM DEPARTMENT OF VETERANS AFFAIRS*, Medical Library, 2101 N Elm St, 58102. SAN 313-1041. Tel: 701-239-3755. FAX: 701-239-3775. Web Site: medicine.nodak.edu/va. *Librn,* Diane Nordeng; E-mail: diane.nordeng@med.va.gov; *Tech Serv,* Joyce Nicholas; E-mail: joyce.nicholas@med.va.gov
Founded 1930
Library Holdings: e-books 65; Bk Titles 860; Per Subs 50
Subject Interests: Clinical med
Automation Activity & Vendor Info: (Cataloging) Ex Libris Group; (ILL) Ex Libris Group
Database Vendor: Elsevier, PubMed, STAT!Ref (Teton Data Systems), UpToDate
Partic in Online Dakota Info Network (ODIN)
Open Mon-Fri 7:30-4

P FARGO PUBLIC LIBRARY*, 102 N Third St, 58102. SAN 313-0959. Tel: 701-241-1472. Reference Tel: 701-241-1492. Administration Tel: 701-241-8277. FAX: 701-241-8581. E-mail: askreference@cityoffargo.com. Web Site: www.fargolibrary.org. *Dir,* Timothy Dirks; Tel: 701-241-1493, E-mail: tdirks@cityoffargo.com; *Dep Dir,* Beth E Postema; Tel: 701-241-8198, E-mail: bpostema@cityoffargo.com; *Syst Librn,* Edie M Discher; E-mail: edischer@cityoffargo.com; *Tech Librn,* Benjamin Daeuber; E-mail: bdaeuber@cityoffargo.com; *Coll Develop Mgr,* Elizabeth Madson; Tel: 701-241-1498; *Mgr, Br Serv,* Lori West; Tel: 701-476-4040; *Ch Serv,* Amber Emery; Tel: 701-241-1495, E-mail: aemery@cityoffargo.com; *Ref,* J Stephen Hubbard; *Tech Serv,* Jacqueline Lang; Tel: 701-241-6673, E-mail: jlang@cityoffargo.com; Staff 40 (MLS 7, Non-MLS 33)
Founded 1900. Pop 105,549
Jan 2011-Dec 2011 Income $3,110,022. Mats Exp $530,853. Sal $1,664,588
Library Holdings: Audiobooks 2,944; CDs 7,443; DVDs 10,121; e-books 1,437; Electronic Media & Resources 862; Large Print Bks 7,053; Bk Vols 131,025; Per Subs 410
Special Collections: North Dakota Coll
Automation Activity & Vendor Info: (Acquisitions) Ex Libris Group; (Cataloging) Ex Libris Group; (Circulation) Ex Libris Group; (ILL) OCLC; (OPAC) Ex Libris Group; (Serials) Ex Libris Group
Database Vendor: ebrary, EBSCO Auto Repair Reference, EBSCO Information Services, Gale Cengage Learning, OCLC WorldShare Interlibrary Loan, ValueLine
Wireless access
Partic in OCLC Online Computer Library Center, Inc; Online Dakota Info Network (ODIN)
Open Mon-Thurs 9-9, Fri 11-6, Sat 9-6, Sun (Sept-May) 1-6
Friends of the Library Group
Branches: 2
DR JAMES CARLSON BRANCH, 2801 32nd Ave S, 58103. Tel: 701-476-4040. Reference Tel: 701-476-5980. FAX: 701-364-2852. *Br Mgr,* Lori K West
Founded 2002
Library Holdings: Audiobooks 1,687; CDs 3,608; DVDs 5,553; Large Print Bks 1,560; Bk Vols 49,683; Per Subs 122
Function: AV serv, ILL available, Ref serv available
Open Mon-Thurs 10-8, Fri 11-6, Sat 9-6, Sun (Sept-May) 1-6
NORTHPORT, 2714 Broadway, 58102. Tel: 701-476-4026. *Librn,* Jenilee Kanenwisher; *Br Mgr,* Lori West
Library Holdings: Audiobooks 472; CDs 1,953; DVDs 2,755; Bk Titles 16,262; Per Subs 56
Open Mon-Thurs 10-8, Fri 11-6, Sat 9-6

S MASONIC GRAND LODGE LIBRARY*, 201 14th Ave N, 58102. SAN 313-0975. Tel: 701-235-8321. FAX: 701-235-8323. E-mail: grandlodgend@yahoo.com. Web Site: www.ndmasons.com. *Mgr,* Harlan Pratt; E-mail: hdpratt@far.midco.net
Founded 1889
Library Holdings: Bk Vols 4,000
Subject Interests: Masonic heritage, Philos lit
Publications: North Dakota Mason
Open Mon-Fri 8-12 & 1-4

C NORTH DAKOTA STATE UNIVERSITY LIBRARIES, 1201 Albrecht Blvd, 58108. (Mail add: PO Box 6050, NDSU Dept 2080, 58108-6050), SAN 355-3329. Tel: 701-231-8888. Interlibrary Loan Service Tel: 701-231-7699, 701-231-8890. Reference Tel: 701-231-8886. FAX: 701-231-6128. Web Site: library.ndsu.edu. *Dean of Libr,* Bridget Burke; *Dir,* Michael Robinson; Tel: 701-231-8878, E-mail: michael.robinson@ndsu.edu; *Access Serv Librn,* Chris Martin; Tel: 701-231-8915, E-mail: chris.a.martin@ndsu.edu; *Acq & Ser Librn,* Position Currently Open; *Agr Sci Librn,* Nicole Mason; Tel: 701-231-8879, E-mail: nicole.k.mason@ndsu.edu; *Cat/Metadata Librn,* Christa Welty; Tel: 701-231-9677, E-mail: christa.welty@ndsu.edu; *Eng Librn,* Carolyn Harvey; Tel: 701-231-5912, E-mail: carolyn.mead.harvey@ndsu.edu; *Govt Doc Librn,* Alicia Koubas; Tel: 701-231-8863, E-mail: alicia.koubas@ndsu.edu; *Humanities Librn,* Lisa Eggebraaten; Tel: 701-231-8394, E-mail: lisa.eggebraaten@ndsu.edu; *Interim Tech Serv Librn,* Jenny Grasto; Tel: 701-231-6462; 701-231-8191, E-mail: jenny.grasto@ndsu.edu; *Sci Librn,* Robert Correll; Tel: 701-231-9746, E-mail: robert.correll@ndsu.edu; *Sr Ref & Instruction Librn,* Beth Twomey; Tel: 701-231-8141, E-mail: beth.twomey@ndsu.edu; *Soc Sci Librn,* Jylisa Doney; Tel: 701-231-8817, E-mail: jylisa.doney@ndsu.edu; *Syst & Emerging Tech Librn,* Amy Reese; Tel: 701-231-7288, E-mail: amy.reese@ndsu.edu; *Undergrad Instruction & Outreach Librn,* Alejandro Marquez; Tel: 701-231-8396, E-mail: alejandro.marquez@ndsu.edu; *Archivist,* Trista Raezer; Tel: 701-231-8877, E-mail: trista.raezer@ndsu.edu; *Bibliographer,* Michael Miller; Tel: 701-231-8416, E-mail: michael.miller@ndsu.edu; Staff 41 (MLS 18, Non-MLS 23)
Founded 1891. Enrl 14,000; Fac 41; Highest Degree: Doctorate
Special Collections: Bonanza Farming; Fred Hultstrand History in Pictures Coll; Germans from Russia Heritage Coll; North Dakota Biography Index; North Dakota Historical Manuscript; North Dakota Pioneer Reminiscences; Senator Milton R Young Photograph Coll; Shott Coll; University Archives. State Document Depository; US Document Depository
Automation Activity & Vendor Info: (Acquisitions) Ex Libris Group; (Cataloging) Ex Libris Group; (Circulation) Ex Libris Group; (Course Reserve) Ex Libris Group; (ILL) Ex Libris Group; (Media Booking) Ex Libris Group; (OPAC) Ex Libris Group; (Serials) Ex Libris Group
Database Vendor: Cambridge Scientific Abstracts, EBSCOhost, Gale Cengage Learning, JSTOR, OCLC FirstSearch, OCLC WorldShare Interlibrary Loan, OVID Technologies, ProQuest, ScienceDirect, STN International
Wireless access
Function: Archival coll, Computers for patron use, Copy machines, Doc delivery serv, e-mail & chat, e mail serv, E-Reserves, Electronic databases & coll, Fax serv, Free DVD rentals, Govt ref serv, Health sci info serv, ILL available, Literacy & newcomer serv, Music CDs, Online cat, Online info literacy tutorials on the web & in blackboard, Online ref, Online searches, Photocopying/Printing, Ref serv available, Ref serv in person, Tax forms, Wheelchair accessible
Publications: North Dakota Institute for Regional Studies Guide to Manuscripts & Archives; Researching the Germans from Russia; Visual Images from the Northern Prairies
Special Services for the Deaf - TDD equip
Open Mon-Thurs 7:30am-Midnight, Fri 7:30-5, Sat 11-5, Sun 1-Midnight
Restriction: Authorized personnel only
Departmental Libraries:
ARCHITECTURE & LANDSCAPE ARCHITECTURE, 711 Second Ave N, 58102. (Mail add: PO Box 6050, NDSU Dept 2080, 58108-6050). Tel: 701-231-8616. FAX: 701-231-6128. Web Site: guides.lib.ndsu.nodak.edu/content.php?pid=239579&sid=2021421. *Archit & Visual Arts Librn,* Jenny Grasto; E-mail: jenny.grasto@ndsu.edu. Subject Specialists: *Archit, Art,* Jenny Grasto
Subject Interests: Archit, Landscape archit
Open Mon-Thurs (Winter) 8-7, Fri 8-5; Mon-Fri (Summer) 7:30-4:30
RICHARD H BARRY BUSINESS LIBRARY, 811 Second Ave N, 58102. (Mail add: PO Box 6050, NDSU Dept 2080, 58108-6050). Tel: 701-231-8616. FAX: 701-231-6128. *Bus Librn,* Laura Trude; Tel: 701-231-8462, E-mail: laura.trude@ndsu.edu
CM PHILIP N HAAKENSON HEALTH SCIENCES LIBRARY, 3551 Seventh Ave N, 58102. (Mail add: PO Box 6050, NDSU Dept 2080, 58108-6050). Tel: 701-231-7748, 791-231-7965. FAX: 701-231-7606. *Health Sci Librn,* Merete Christianson; *Libr Assoc,* Diana Kowalski
Library Holdings: e-journals 108; Bk Vols 4,600; Per Subs 20
Subject Interests: Nursing, Pharm
Partic in Tri-College University Libraries Consortium
Open Mon-Fri 8-4:30
H J KLOSTERMAN CHEMISTRY LIBRARY, 209 Ladd Hall, 58108. Tel: 701-231-8888. FAX: 701-231-6128.
Library Holdings: Bk Vols 7,300
Subject Interests: Chem, Coatings, Polymers

SR PRESENTATION CENTER LIBRARY*, 1101 32nd Ave S, 58103-6092. SAN 313-1009. Tel: 701-237-4857. FAX: 701 237-9822. *Actg Librn,* Sister Mary Margaret Mooney; Staff 0.25 (Non-MLS 0.25)
Jul 2005-Jun 2006 Income $3,500. Mats Exp $3,500, Per/Ser (Incl. Access Fees) $1,500, Manu Arch $2,000
Library Holdings: Bk Titles 5,000; Bk Vols 7,067; Per Subs 15
Function: Adult literacy prog
Restriction: Authorized scholars by appt, Co libr

M SANFORD HEALTH LIBRARY*, 801 Broadway N, 58102. (Mail add: PO Box 2010, 58122-0212), SAN 355-3442. Tel: 701-234-5571. FAX: 701-234-5927. *Librn,* Eileen Chamberlain; Staff 3 (MLS 1, Non-MLS 2)
Founded 1955
Subject Interests: Allied health, Med, Nursing
Open Mon-Fri 8-4

G US COURTS BRANCH LIBRARY*, 655 First Ave N, Ste 310, 58102. SAN 371-6538. Tel: 701-297-7280. FAX: 701-297-7285. *Librn,* Suzanne Morrison; E-mail: suzanne_morrison@ca8.uscourts.gov; Staff 3 (MLS 1, Non-MLS 2)
Founded 1986
Library Holdings: Bk Titles 28,000; Per Subs 150
Subject Interests: Law
Open Mon-Fri 8-4:30

FINLEY

P FINLEY-SHARON LIBRARY*, 302 Broadway, 58230. (Mail add: PO Box 453, 58230-0453). Tel: 701-524-2495. *Librn,* Judy Gray; Tel: 701-524-2420, E-mail: Judy.Gray@sendit.nodak.edu
Library Holdings: Bk Titles 7,000
Open Thurs 6:30-8, Fri 2-5

FLASHER

P FLASHER PUBLIC LIBRARY*, 104 Fifth Ave E, 58535. (Mail add: PO Box 227, 58535-0227). Tel: 701-597-3127. FAX: 701-597-3127. E-mail: cityofflasher@westriv.com. *Librn,* Jeanne Conti
Library Holdings: Bk Vols 3,133
Special Collections: Old West Books Coll
Open Mon-Thurs 9-11 & 1-4

FORMAN

P FORMAN PUBLIC LIBRARY*, 382 Main St, 58032. (Mail add: PO Box 382, 58032-0382), SAN 372-5359. Tel: 701-724-3986.
Founded 1972. Pop 1,000
Jan 2008-Dec 2008 Income $12,645. Mats Exp $12,600. Sal $4,500
Library Holdings: Audiobooks 100; AV Mats 150; CDs 100; DVDs 200; Large Print Bks 300; Bk Titles 10,000; Per Subs 12; Talking Bks 40; Videos 200
Wireless access
Open Mon, Wed & Fri 1-5
Friends of the Library Group

FORT TOTTEN

S VALERIE MERRICK MEMORIAL LIBRARY*, PO Box 479, 58335-0479. Tel: 701-766-1353. FAX: 701-766-1307. Web Site: www.littlehoop.edu. *Libr Dir,* Antoinette McDonald
Library Holdings: Bk Titles 12,500; Per Subs 20
Database Vendor: ProQuest
Open Mon-Thurs 8-7, Fri 8-4:30, Sat 10-3

FORT YATES

C SITTING BULL COLLEGE LIBRARY*, 1341 92nd St, 58538. SAN 313-1068. Tel: 701-854-3861, Ext 8024. FAX: 701-854-3403. Web Site: www.sittingbull.edu. *Librn,* Mark Holman; E-mail: markh@sbci.edu
Founded 1972. Fac 35
Library Holdings: Bk Titles 17,500; Per Subs 70
Special Collections: College Archives; Sioux Indians Coll; Standing Rock Sioux Tribal Archives. Oral History
Wireless access
Open Mon, Wed & Fri 8-4:30, Tues & Thurs 8-8

GACKLE

P GACKLE PUBLIC LIBRARY*, 302 Main St, 58442. (Mail add: PO Box 141, 58442-0141). Tel: 701-485-3374. *Librn,* Nedina Denning
Library Holdings: Bk Vols 800; Per Subs 10
Open Wed (Winter) 1-4, Sat 9-11; Mon-Fri (Summer) 9:30-11:30

GLEN ULLIN

P GLEN ULLIN PUBLIC LIBRARY*, 114 S Main St, 58631. Tel: 701-348-3951. *Librn,* Shirley Kastner
Pop 865
Library Holdings: Audiobooks 289; AV Mats 247; Bk Vols 6,389; Videos 288
Open Fri 1:30-3, Sat 1:30-3:30

GRAFTON

P CARNEGIE REGIONAL LIBRARY*, 630 Griggs Ave, 58237. SAN 355-3531. Tel: 701-352-2754. FAX: 701-352-2757. E-mail: crldir@polarcomm.com. *Dir,* Jill Bjerke; Staff 8 (MLS 1, Non-MLS 7)
Founded 1972. Pop 22,648
Library Holdings: Bk Titles 75,000; Per Subs 58
Subject Interests: NDak hist
Automation Activity & Vendor Info: (Cataloging) Winnebago Software Co; (Circulation) Follett Software
Wireless access
Open Mon-Fri 10-6, Sat 10-2
Branches: 2
ANETA PUBLIC, 309 Main Ave, Aneta, 58212. (Mail add: PO Box 198, Aneta, 58212). Tel: 701-326-4107. E-mail: anetalib@polarcomm.com. *Librn,* Karen Retzlaff; E-mail: karen.e.retzlaff@sendit.nodak.edu
Library Holdings: Audiobooks 150; AV Mats 300; DVDs 55; Large Print Bks 250; Bk Vols 15,000; Videos 75
Database Vendor: EBSCOhost, OCLC FirstSearch, Wilson - Wilson Web
Open Mon-Fri 5-6
MICHIGAN PUBLIC, PO Box 331, Michigan, 58259. Tel: 701-259-2122. *Librn,* Bernice Ferguson
Library Holdings: Bk Vols 400
Open Wed 9-2:30

GRAND FORKS

M ALTRU HEALTH SYSTEM*, Altru Medical Library, 1200 S Columbia Rd, 58201. (Mail add: PO Box 6002, 58206-6002), SAN 313-1092. Tel: 701-780-5186. FAX: 701-780-5772. *Dir,* Ann Pederson; E-mail: apederson@altru.org; Staff 1 (MLS 1)
Founded 1958
Library Holdings: e-books 24; Bk Vols 3,000; Per Subs 20
Special Collections: Archives
Subject Interests: Consumer health
Automation Activity & Vendor Info: (Cataloging) Ex Libris Group; (ILL) Ex Libris Group; (OPAC) Ex Libris Group
Database Vendor: EBSCOhost, Elsevier, OCLC WorldShare Interlibrary Loan, PubMed
Wireless access
Partic in Minitex Library Information Network
Open Mon-Fri 8-4:30

P GRAND FORKS PUBLIC LIBRARY*, Grand Forks City/County Public Library, 2110 Library Circle, 58201-6324. SAN 313-1084. Tel: 701-772-8116. Circulation Tel: 701-772-8116, Ext 11. Interlibrary Loan Service Tel: 701-772-8116, Ext 19. Reference Tel: 701-772-8116, Ext 12. Automation Services Tel: 701-772-8116, Ext 15. FAX: 701-772-1379. E-mail: reference@gflibrary.com. Web Site: www.gflibrary.com. *Dir,* Wendy Wendt; E-mail: wendy.wendt@gflibrary.com; *Circ Supvr,* Carol Junk; *Adult Serv, Ref Supvr (Info Serv),* Toni Engelhardt Vonasek; *Ch Serv,* Aaron Stefanich; Tel: 701-772-8116, Ext 13, E-mail: aaron.stefanich@gflibrary.com; *Tech Serv,* David Haney; Tel: 701-772-8116, Ext 16, E-mail: david.haney@gflibrary.com. Subject Specialists: *Computer,* David Haney; Staff 12 (MLS 7, Non-MLS 5)
Founded 1900. Pop 67,000; Circ 855,000
Jan 2007-Dec 2007 Income $1,603,000, State $75,000, City $1,124,000, County $350,000, Locally Generated Income $42,000. Mats Exp $349,500, Books $198,000, Per/Ser (Incl. Access Fees) $5,000, Micro $1,500, AV Equip $35,000, AV Mat $75,000, Electronic Ref Mat (Incl. Access Fees) $35,000. Sal $744,000 (Prof $300,000)
Library Holdings: AV Mats 39,315; Bks-By-Mail 3,000; DVDs 10,000; Bk Titles 327,961; Bk Vols 370,000; Per Subs 349; Talking Bks 6,000; Videos 15,315
Special Collections: Local History (Grand Forks Coll), bks & pictures
Subject Interests: Agr
Automation Activity & Vendor Info: (Cataloging) OCLC; (Circulation) Ex Libris Group; (ILL) Ex Libris Group; (OPAC) Ex Libris Group; (Serials) Ex Libris Group
Database Vendor: EBSCO Information Services, Gale Cengage Learning, LearningExpress, ProQuest
Wireless access
Function: Adult bk club, Bk club(s), Bks on CD, CD-ROM, Children's prog, Computer training, Computers for patron use, Copy machines, Electronic databases & coll, Fax serv, Free DVD rentals, Handicapped accessible, ILL available, Mail & tel request accepted, Microfiche/film & reading machines, Music CDs, Online cat, Online ref, Orientations, Outside serv via phone, mail, e-mail & web, OverDrive digital audio bks, Prog for adults, Prog for children & young adult, Pub access computers, Ref & res, Ref serv in person, Scanner, Story hour, Summer & winter reading prog, Tax forms, Teen prog, Telephone ref
Publications: Check It Out (Monthly newsletter)
Partic in OCLC Online Computer Library Center, Inc; Online Dakota Info Network (ODIN)
Special Services for the Blind - Bks on cassette; Bks on CD; Large print bks
Open Mon-Thurs 9-9, Fri & Sat 9-5, Sun 1-5
Restriction: Non-resident fee
Friends of the Library Group

S NORTH DAKOTA VISION SERVICES-SCHOOL FOR THE BLIND, Vision Resource Center, 500 Stanford Rd, 58203. Tel: 701-795-2700. Toll Free Tel: 800-421-1181 (ND only). FAX: 701-795-2727. Web Site:

www.ndivisionservices.com. *Librn,* Emily Stenberg; Tel: 701-795-2709, E-mail: estenberg@nd.gov
Founded 1908
Library Holdings: AV Mats 550; Large Print Bks 750; Bk Vols 1,350
Special Collections: Teachers Reference Coll; Toy Library; Vision Equipment Library
Automation Activity & Vendor Info: (Cataloging) OCLC
Database Vendor: Gale Cengage Learning
Wireless access
Publications: Reaching Out (Quarterly newsletter)
Special Services for the Blind - Braille bks; Large print bks
Open Mon-Fri 8-4:30

C UNIVERSITY OF NORTH DAKOTA*, Chester Fritz Library, 3051 University Ave, Stop 9000, 58202-9000. SAN 355-3655. Tel: 701-777-2617. Circulation Tel: 701-777-4644. Interlibrary Loan Service Tel: 701-777-4631. Reference Tel: 701-777-4629. FAX: 701-777-3319. TDD: 701-777-3313. E-mail: library@mail.und.edu. Web Site: www.library.und.edu. *Dir,* Wilbur Stolt; Tel: 701-777-2189, E-mail: wilbur.stolt@library.und.edu; *Asst Libr Dir, Head, Coll Develop,* Mary Hegle Drewes; Tel: 701-777-4630, E-mail: mary.drewes@library.und.edu; *Head, Access & Br Serv,* Naomi Frantes; Tel: 701-777-4648, E-mail: naomi.frantes@library.und.edu; *Head, Ref,* Sally Dockter; Tel: 701-777-4640, E-mail: sally.dockter@library.und.edu; *Head, Spec Coll,* Curt Hanson; Tel: 701-777-4626, E-mail: curt.hanson@library.und.edu; *Head, Syst,* Randy Pederson; Tel: 701-777-4643, E-mail: randy.pederson@library.und.edu; *Head, Tech Serv,* Shelby Harken; Tel: 701-777-4634, E-mail: shelby.harken@library.und.edu; *Mgr, Access Serv,* Stan Johnson; Fax: 701-777-6745, E-mail: stan.johnson@library.und.edu; Staff 21 (MLS 16, Non-MLS 5)
Founded 1883. Enrl 15,250; Fac 821; Highest Degree: Doctorate
Jul 2012-Jun 2013. Mats Exp $2,658,459, Books $288,449, Per/Ser (Incl. Access Fees) $1,867,992, AV Mat $17,860, Electronic Ref Mat (Incl. Access Fees) $467,564, Presv $16,594. Sal $2,017,863 (Prof $1,289,745)
Library Holdings: Audiobooks 319; AV Mats 82,329; Braille Volumes 165; CDs 3,711; DVDs 1,305; e-books 78,083; e-journals 58,087; Electronic Media & Resources 128,524; Large Print Bks 59; Microforms 902,163; Music Scores 24,002; Bk Titles 616,366; Bk Vols 712,030; Per Subs 3,029; Videos 1,382
Special Collections: Great Plains (Fred G Aandahl Coll); North Dakota Ethnic Heritage/Family History; North Dakota History (Orin G Libby Coll), ms; Norwegian Local History. Oral History; State Document Depository; US Document Depository
Subject Interests: Educ, Western hist
Automation Activity & Vendor Info: (Acquisitions) Ex Libris Group; (Cataloging) Ex Libris Group; (Circulation) Ex Libris Group; (Course Reserve) Ex Libris Group; (ILL) Ex Libris Group; (OPAC) Ex Libris Group; (Serials) Ex Libris Group
Database Vendor: ACM (Association for Computing Machinery), American Chemical Society, Dialog, EBSCOhost, Gale Cengage Learning, JSTOR, OCLC WorldShare Interlibrary Loan, Project MUSE, ProQuest, ScienceDirect
Wireless access
Publications: Guides to Collections; Lux et Lex
Partic in EPSCoR Science Information Group; Minitex Library Information Network; Online Dakota Info Network (ODIN)
Special Services for the Deaf - TDD equip
Special Services for the Blind - Scanner for conversion & translation of mats
Open Mon-Thurs 7:45am-Midnight, Fri 7:45-4:30, Sat 1-5, Sun 1-Midnight

Departmental Libraries:

ENERGY & ENVIRONMENTAL RESEARCH CENTER LIBRARY, 15 N 23rd St, Stop 9018, 58202-9018, SAN 313-1114. Tel: 701-777-5132. FAX: 701-777-5181. Web Site: library.und.edu/eerc. *Librn,* Rosemary Pleva Flynn; E-mail: rflynn@undeerc.org; Staff 1 (MLS 1)
Library Holdings: CDs 105; Bk Titles 4,429; Bk Vols 18,657; Per Subs 60
Special Collections: US Bureau of Mines Materials; US Department of Energy Reports
Subject Interests: Air quality, Climate change, Coal, Geothermal energy, Mining rec, Natural gas, Oil, Solar energy, Synthetic fuels, Toxic wastes, Water

GORDON ERICKSON MUSIC LIBRARY, Hughes Fine Arts Ctr 170, 3350 Campus Rd, Stop 7125, 58202-7125, SAN 371-3261. Tel: 701-777-2817. FAX: 701-777-3319. Web Site: library.und.edu/music. *Br Mgr,* Felecia Clifton; E-mail: felecia.clifton@library.und.edu; Staff 1 (Non-MLS 1)
Founded 1983. Enrl 170; Fac 30; Highest Degree: Doctorate
Library Holdings: Bks on Deafness & Sign Lang 13; CDs 3,550; DVDs 109; Music Scores 24,002; Bk Titles 33,257; Bk Vols 42,687; Per Subs 38; Videos 387
Special Services for the Deaf - Staff with knowledge of sign lang
Special Services for the Blind - Braille bks
Open Mon-Thurs 9-8, Fri 9-4, Sun 4-8
Restriction: Open to fac, students & qualified researchers

F D HOLLAND JR GEOLOGY LIBRARY, 81 Cornell St, Stop 8358, 58202-8358, SAN 371-327X. Tel: 701-777-3221. Interlibrary Loan Service Tel: 701-777-4631. FAX: 701-777-4449. Web Site: library.und.edu/geology. *Br Mgr,* Darin Buri; Tel: 701-777-2408, E-mail: darin.buri@engr.und.edu; Staff 1 (Non-MLS 1)
Library Holdings: CDs 472; Microforms 13,622; Bk Titles 32,144; Bk Vols 88,227; Per Subs 227
Special Collections: Map Coll. US Document Depository
Subject Interests: Environ geol, Geol eng, Hydrogeology, Mining, Petroleum geol
Open Mon-Thurs (Winter) 8am-9pm, Fri 8-4:30; Mon-Fri (Summer) 8-4:30
Friends of the Library Group

UNIVERSITY OF NORTH DAKOTA

CM HARLEY E FRENCH LIBRARY OF THE HEALTH SCIENCES, School of Medicine & Health Sciences, 501 N Columbia Rd, Stop 9002, 58202-9002, SAN 355-368X. Tel: 701-777-3993. Interlibrary Loan Service Tel: 701-777-2606. Reference Tel: 701-777-3994. FAX: 701-777-4790. Web Site: undmedlibrary.org. *Dir,* Lila Pedersen; E-mail: lila.pedersen@med.und.edu; *Asst Dir,* Kelly Thirmodson; Tel: 701-777-4129; *Automation Syst Coordr,* Theresa Norton; Tel: 701-777-2946, E-mail: theresa.norton@med.und.edu; *Cat,* Michael Safratowich; Tel: 701-777-2602, E-mail: michael.safratowich@med.und.edu; *Circ,* Jan Gunderson; *ILL,* Allison Ranisate; E-mail: allison.ranisate@med.und.edu; Staff 11 (MLS 10, Non-MLS 1)
Founded 1950. Enrl 1,500; Fac 156; Highest Degree: Doctorate
Library Holdings: e-books 915; e-journals 12,000; Bk Titles 34,000; Bk Vols 43,000; Per Subs 300
Special Collections: History of Medicine (Dr French Coll); History of Pathology (Dr Barger Coll)
Subject Interests: Med, Nursing, Occupational therapy, Phys therapy
Automation Activity & Vendor Info: (Acquisitions) Ex Libris Group; (Cataloging) Ex Libris Group; (Circulation) Ex Libris Group; (Course Reserve) Ex Libris Group; (ILL) Ex Libris Group; (Media Booking) Ex Libris Group; (OPAC) Ex Libris Group; (Serials) Ex Libris Group
Database Vendor: Cinahl, DynaMed, EBSCOhost, Gale Cengage Learning, JSTOR, Medline, OCLC FirstSearch, OVID Technologies, ProQuest, PubMed, RefWorks, ScienceDirect, Scopus
Function: ILL available
Partic in OCLC Online Computer Library Center, Inc
Open Mon-Thurs 7:30am-Midnight, Fri 7:30-6, Sat 10-6, Sun 1-Midnight

CL THORMODSGARD LAW LIBRARY*, 215 Centennial Dr, 58202. (Mail add: PO Box 9004, 58202-9004), SAN 355-371X. Tel: 701-777-2204. Interlibrary Loan Service Tel: 701-777-3538. Reference Tel: 701-777-3354. FAX: 701-777-2217. Web Site: www.law.und.nodak.edu. *Dir,* Rhonda Schwartz; E-mail: schwartz@law.und.edu; *Head, Student Serv,* David Haberman; E-mail: haberman@law.und.edu; *Acq, Head, Tech Serv, Ser,* Kaaren Pupino; E-mail: pupino@law.und.edu; *Head, Fac Serv,* Jan Stone; *Circ Mgr, ILL,* Jane Oakland; E-mail: oakland@law.und.edu; *Cat Librn,* Dorrene Devos; E-mail: devos@law.und.edu; *Syst Adminr,* Carl Warrene; E-mail: warrene@law.und.edu; *User Support Serv Coordr,* Kasey Hanson; *Computer Support Spec, Web Serv,* Mark Conway; Staff 7 (MLS 5, Non-MLS 2)
Founded 1899. Enrl 224; Highest Degree: Doctorate
Library Holdings: AV Mats 456; e-journals 726; Electronic Media & Resources 10; Bk Titles 33,253; Bk Vols 159,447; Per Subs 2,001; Videos 332
Automation Activity & Vendor Info: (Acquisitions) Ex Libris Group; (Cataloging) Ex Libris Group; (Circulation) Ex Libris Group; (Course Reserve) Ex Libris Group; (ILL) Ex Libris Group; (Media Booking) Ex Libris Group; (OPAC) Ex Libris Group; (Serials) Ex Libris Group
Database Vendor: EBSCOhost, LexisNexis, Westlaw
Partic in OCLC Online Computer Library Center, Inc
Open Mon-Thurs 7:30am-11pm, Fri 7:30am-9pm, Sat 10-9, Sun 10am-11pm

GRAND FORKS AFB

A UNITED STATES AIR FORCE*, Grand Forks Air Force Base Library FL4659, 319 FSS/FSDL, 511 Holzapple St, Bldg 201, 58205. SAN 355-3744. Tel: 701-747-3046. Interlibrary Loan Service Tel: 701-747-3047. Administration Tel: 701-747-3048. FAX: 701-747-4584. Web Site: www.forksupport.com/library.html. *Libr Dir,* Arlene Ott; E-mail: arlene.ott@us.af.mil; Staff 5.7 (MLS 1.2, Non-MLS 4.5)
Founded 1968
Library Holdings: AV Mats 1,704; e-books 7,100; Electronic Media & Resources 33; Bk Vols 33,000; Per Subs 60; Talking Bks 1,620
Special Collections: Chief of Staff Reading Coll
Automation Activity & Vendor Info: (Cataloging) SirsiDynix; (Circulation) SIRSI WorkFlows; (ILL) OCLC; (OPAC) SIRSI-iBistro
Database Vendor: CountryWatch, EBSCOhost, Gale Cengage Learning, Jane's, OCLC FirstSearch, OCLC WorldShare Interlibrary Loan, Overdrive, Inc, ProQuest, Safari Books Online, SirsiDynix, TumbleBookLibrary

Wireless access
Function: Audio & video playback equip for onsite use, Audiobks via web, Bks on CD, CD-ROM, Children's prog, Citizenship assistance, Computer training, Computers for patron use, Copy machines, Digital talking bks, Distance learning, Doc delivery serv, e-mail & chat, Electronic databases & coll, Equip loans & repairs, Exhibits, Fax serv, Free DVD rentals, Handicapped accessible, Holiday prog, Homebound delivery serv, ILL available, Instruction & testing, Learning ctr, Mail & tel request accepted, Music CDs, Online cat, Orientations, OverDrive digital audio bks, Photocopying/Printing, Preschool outreach, Prof lending libr, Prog for adults, Prog for children & young adult, Pub access computers, Ref & res, Ref serv in person, Scanner, Story hour, Summer reading prog, Teen prog, Telephone ref, Web-catalog, Wheelchair accessible
Partic in Fedlink; OCLC Online Computer Library Center, Inc
Special Services for the Blind - Bks on CD; Playaways (bks on MP3)
Open Mon-Thurs 10-8, Fri-Sun 12-5

HANKINSON

P HANKINSON PUBLIC LIBRARY*, City Hall, 58041. (Mail add: PO Box 244, 58041-0244), SAN 313-1130. Tel: 701-242-7929. *Librn,* Andrea Stein
Founded 1905. Pop 1,038; Circ 6,846
Library Holdings: Bk Vols 9,000; Per Subs 14
Open Mon-Fri 10-6

HARVEY

P HARVEY PUBLIC LIBRARY*, 119 E Tenth St, 58341. SAN 313-1149. Tel: 701-324-2156. FAX: 701-324-2156. E-mail: hpublib@gondtc.com. *Librn,* Marlene Ripplinger; *Asst Librn,* Stephina Gisi
Founded 1952. Pop 2,700; Circ 44,000
Library Holdings: Bk Titles 22,000; Per Subs 100
Special Collections: Regional Coll, bks
Automation Activity & Vendor Info: (Cataloging) Follett Software; (Circulation) Follett Software
Open Mon & Fri 1:30-5:30, Tues & Wed 11:30-5:30, Thurs 1:30-5:30 & 7-9, Sat 11:30-3:30, Sun 1-4

HATTON

P HATTON SCHOOL & PUBLIC LIBRARY*, 503 Fourth St, 58240. (Mail add: PO Box 200, 58240-0200). Tel: 701-543-3456. FAX: 701-543-3459. *Librn,* Curt Schaff; *Librn,* Sarah Johnson
Library Holdings: AV Mats 100; Bk Vols 5,500; Per Subs 40; Talking Bks 600
Open Thurs 7pm-9pm, Sat 2-4

HEBRON

P HEBRON PUBLIC LIBRARY*, 606 Lincoln Ave, 58638-7050. (Mail add: PO Box R, 58638-0448), SAN 375-5967. Tel: 701-878-4110. E-mail: hebronpubliclibrary@gmail.com. Web Site: www.hebronnd.org. *Dir,* Jean D Pascual
Founded 1938. Pop 850; Circ 2,213
Jan 2006-Dec 2006 Income $6,118, State $356, City $4,607, Other $1,155. Mats Exp $4,347, Books $616, Other Print Mats $3,700, AV Mat $31. Sal $5,560
Library Holdings: AV Mats 330; Bks-By-Mail 84; Large Print Bks 90; Bk Titles 14,000; Talking Bks 110
Database Vendor: EBSCO Information Services, OCLC FirstSearch, OCLC WebJunction, OCLC WorldShare Interlibrary Loan, ProQuest
Wireless access
Partic in Online Dakota Info Network (ODIN)
Open Mon & Thurs 1-7, Tues & Wed 10-4, Fri 8-2

HETTINGER

P ADAMS COUNTY LIBRARY*, 103 N Sixth St, 58639-7015. (Mail add: PO Box 448, 58639-0448), SAN 355-3868. Tel: 701-567-2741. FAX: 701-567-2741. E-mail: adams.countylibrary@sendit.nodak.edu. Web Site: www.adamscountylibrary.com. *Dir,* Pat A Anderson; E-mail: pat.anderson@sendit.nodak.edu; *Ch Serv,* Berniece Marion; Staff 4 (Non-MLS 4)
Founded 1961. Pop 2,750; Circ 7,890
Library Holdings: AV Mats 750; Large Print Bks 700; Bk Vols 22,789; Per Subs 21; Talking Bks 204
Subject Interests: Norwegian hist
Automation Activity & Vendor Info: (Cataloging) Follett Software; (Circulation) Follett Software
Function: ILL available
Mem of South Central Library System
Open Mon-Thurs 3:30-7, Fri 3:30-5:30
Friends of the Library Group

HOPE

P HOPE CITY LIBRARY*, PO Box 115, 58046-0115. SAN 313-1157. Tel: 701-945-2796. *Librn,* Carol Elston
Founded 1910
Library Holdings: Bk Titles 15,000
Open Fri 1-6
Friends of the Library Group

JAMESTOWN

S ANNE CARLSEN LEARNING CENTER*, 701 Third St NW, 58401-2971. Tel: 701-952-5169. Toll Free Tel: 800-568-5175. FAX: 701-952-5154. Web Site: www.annecenter.org. *Mgr,* Mark Coppin; Tel: 701-952-5125, E-mail: mark.coppin@annecenter.org; *Tech Spec,* Theresa Hanson; E-mail: theresa.hanson@annecenter.org
Library Holdings: AV Mats 2,000; Bk Vols 10,000; Per Subs 23
Automation Activity & Vendor Info: (Cataloging) Winnebago Software Co; (Circulation) Winnebago Software Co; (OPAC) Winnebago Software Co
Wireless access
Open Mon-Fri 7:30-5

P ALFRED DICKEY PUBLIC LIBRARY*, 105 SE Third St, 58401. SAN 313-1165. Tel: 701-252-2990. FAX: 701-252-6030. E-mail: adpl@daktel.com. Web Site: www.adpl.org. *Dir,* Daphne Drewello
Pop 16,000; Circ 120,000
Library Holdings: Bk Vols 51,000; Per Subs 119
Special Collections: Louis L'Amour Memorial Coll
Automation Activity & Vendor Info: (Acquisitions) Follett Software
Open Mon-Thurs 10-8:30, Fri & Sat 10-5:30, Sun (Sept-May) 2-5

GM NORTH DAKOTA STATE HOSPITAL*, Health Science Library, 2605 Circle Dr, 58401-6905. SAN 355-3922. Tel: 701-253-3679. FAX: 701-253-3204. *Mgr,* Gene A Haugen; E-mail: haugeg@nd.gov; Staff 1 (Non-MLS 1)
Founded 1958
Library Holdings: e-books 10,000; Bk Titles 4,500; Bk Vols 5,000; Per Subs 40
Special Collections: North Dakota State Hospital Biennial Reports, 1890 to date; North Dakota State Hospital Newsletter (employee newsletter)
Subject Interests: Activity therapy, Adolescence, Alcoholism, Ch, Counseling, Families of alcoholics, Forensic psychiat, Geriatrics, Psychiat treatment, Psychol, Psychopharmacology, Psychotherapy, Soc work, Vocational rehabilitation
Automation Activity & Vendor Info: (Acquisitions) EBSCO Online; (Cataloging) Ex Libris Group; (Circulation) Ex Libris Group; (ILL) Ex Libris Group; (OPAC) Ex Libris Group; (Serials) EBSCO Online
Database Vendor: Gale Cengage Learning, OCLC FirstSearch, OVID Technologies
Publications: PsychINFO
Partic in Midwest Health Sci Libr Network
Open Mon & Wed 9-12, 1-5 & 7-9, Thurs & Fri 8-12 & 1-5, Sun 1-5
Branches:
PATIENTS' LIBRARY, 2605 Circle Dr, 58401-6905. Tel: 701-253-3678. *Mgr,* Gene A Haugen; E-mail: haugeg@nd.gov
Library Holdings: Bk Vols 3,500
Special Collections: Audio Cassettes; LP Records; ND Newspapers; Patient Education Video Coll
Subject Interests: Art, Biog, Consumer awareness, Health, Native Am, Patient educ, Substance abuse, Westerns
Open Mon & Wed 9-12, 1-5 & 7-9, Thurs & Fri 8-12 & 1-5, Sun 1-5

P STUTSMAN COUNTY LIBRARY*, 910 Fifth St SE, 58401. SAN 313-119X. Tel: 701-252-1531. FAX: 701-252-2217. E-mail: ill@daktel.com. *Dir,* Joe Rector; *Asst Dir,* Jennifer Senger; Staff 1 (MLS 1)
Founded 1954. Pop 6,381; Circ 44,080
Library Holdings: AV Mats 13,960; High Interest/Low Vocabulary Bk Vols 20; Large Print Bks 2,627; Bk Titles 20,000; Bk Vols 26,273; Per Subs 20; Talking Bks 31
Open Mon-Fri 9-5
Bookmobiles: 1. Librn, Doreen Brophy & Jean Zachrison. Bk vols 3,500

G UNITED STATES GEOLOGICAL SURVEY*, Northern Prairie Wildlife Research Center Library, 8711 37th St SE, 58401-9736. SAN 313-1203. Tel: 701-253-5566. FAX: 701-253-5553. Web Site: library.npwrc.cr.usgs.gov. *Librn,* Reagen A Thalacker; Staff 1 (MLS 1)
Founded 1965
Oct 2005-Sept 2006. Mats Exp $40,000, Books $5,000, Per/Ser (Incl. Access Fees) $30,000, Electronic Ref Mat (Incl. Access Fees) $5,000. Sal $82,000
Library Holdings: AV Mats 120; Bk Titles 11,000; Per Subs 125
Special Collections: Waterfowl Management (Unpublished Papers of Merrill C Hammond)

Subject Interests: Ecology, Global climate change, Mgt of waterfowl, Plant ecology, Predation, Wetland ecology
Automation Activity & Vendor Info: (Acquisitions) Cuadra Associates, Inc; (Cataloging) Cuadra Associates, Inc; (Circulation) Cuadra Associates, Inc; (OPAC) Cuadra Associates, Inc; (Serials) Cuadra Associates, Inc
Database Vendor: Cambridge Scientific Abstracts, Dialog, JSTOR, OCLC FirstSearch, OCLC WorldShare Interlibrary Loan, ScienceDirect
Function: Res libr
Partic in OCLC Online Computer Library Center, Inc
Open Mon-Fri 8-4:30

C UNIVERSITY OF JAMESTOWN, Raugust Library, 6070 College Lane, 58405-0001. SAN 313-1173. Tel: 701-252-3467. Circulation Tel: 701 252 3467, Ext 5530. Interlibrary Loan Service Tel: 701-252-3467, Ext 5441. Reference Tel: 701-252-3467, Ext 5433. FAX: 701-253-4446. Web Site: www.uj.edu/library. *Dir,* Phyllis Ann K Bratton; E-mail: pbratton@uj.edu; *Acq,* Daphne Drewello; Tel: 701-252-3467, Ext 5432, E-mail: Daphne.Drewello@uj.edu; *Cataloger,* Jasmine Lee; Tel: 701-252-3467, Ext 5431, E-mail: jlee@uj.edu; *Circ,* Brenda Fischer; E-mail: bfischer@uj.edu; *ILL,* Anthoula Hanse; E-mail: ahanse@uj.edu; Staff 5 (MLS 2, Non-MLS 3)
Enrl 1,045; Fac 66; Highest Degree: Doctorate
Jul 2005-Jun 2006 Income $267,320. Mats Exp $160,280, Books $34,000, Per/Ser (Incl. Access Fees) $38,000, Other Print Mats $10,000, AV Equip $1,080, AV Mat $6,000, Electronic Ref Mat (Incl. Access Fees) $38,050. Sal $85,000 (Prof $43,280)
Library Holdings: AV Mats 6,484; Bks on Deafness & Sign Lang 104; e-books 15,000; e-journals 22,000; Bk Titles 110,000; Bk Vols 110,869; Per Subs 125; Talking Bks 559
Special Collections: Children's materials; Western Americana Coll
Subject Interests: NDak hist, Regional poets
Automation Activity & Vendor Info: (Acquisitions) Ex Libris Group; (Cataloging) Ex Libris Group; (Circulation) Ex Libris Group; (Course Reserve) Ex Libris Group; (ILL) Ex Libris Group; (OPAC) Ex Libris Group
Database Vendor: Alexander Street Press, American Chemical Society, Cinahl, CIOS (Communication Institute for Online Scholarship), EBSCOhost, Electric Library, Facts on File, Gale Cengage Learning, JSTOR, Medline, OCLC, ProQuest, Sage, STAT!Ref (Teton Data Systems), YBP Library Services
Wireless access
Partic in GMRMLN - Region 3 of NLM Network; Minitex Library Information Network; Online Dakota Info Network (ODIN)
Open Mon-Thurs 8am-Midnight, Fri 8-5, Sun 2-Midnight

KILLDEER

P KILLDEER PUBLIC LIBRARY*, PO Box 579, 58640-0579. SAN 355-4015. Tel: 701-764-5877. FAX: 701-764-5648. *Librn,* Fayleen Fischer; E-mail: fayleen.fischer@sendit.nodak.edu
Pop 815; Circ 3,804
Library Holdings: Bk Titles 19,000; Per Subs 45
Automation Activity & Vendor Info: (Cataloging) Follett Software; (Circulation) Follett Software; (OPAC) Follett Software
Open Mon-Fri 8:30-3

KINDRED

P KINDRED PUBLIC LIBRARY*, 330 Elm St, 58051. (Mail add: PO Box 63, 58051-0063). Tel: 701-428-3456. E-mail: kindredpubliclibrary@gmail.com. Web Site: www.kindredpubliclibrary.com. *Dir,* Linda Otterson
Library Holdings: Bk Vols 9,000
Automation Activity & Vendor Info: (Cataloging) Brodart; (Circulation) Brodart
Open Mon, Fri & Sat 10:30-12:30, Tues-Thurs 3:30-7:30
Friends of the Library Group

LA MOURE

P LA MOURE SCHOOL & PUBLIC LIBRARY*, PO Box 656, 58458-0656. SAN 313-1211. Tel: 701-883-5396. FAX: 701-883-5144. *Librn,* Becky Bockwoldt
Circ 17,671
Library Holdings: Bk Vols 23,000
Automation Activity & Vendor Info: (Cataloging) Follett Software; (Circulation) Follett Software; (OPAC) Follett Software
Open Mon-Thurs 8:30-5:30, Fri 8:30-3:30, Sat 9:30-11:30
Friends of the Library Group

LAKOTA

P LAKOTA CITY LIBRARY*, A M Tofthagen Library & Museum, 116 West B Ave, 58344. (Mail add: PO Box 307, 58344-0307). Tel: 701-247-2543. *Librn,* Gerry Wagness; E-mail: gerry.wagness@sendit.nodak.edu
Founded 1927. Pop 781; Circ 12,379
Library Holdings: Large Print Bks 1,350; Bk Vols 12,915; Per Subs 10; Talking Bks 463; Videos 727
Special Collections: Municipal Document Depository; Oral History
Open Tues (Sept-May) 2-7, Thurs 2-5, Sat 1-5; Tues (June-Aug) 2-5 & 7-9, Thurs 2-5, Sat 1-5

LANGDON

P CAVALIER COUNTY LIBRARY*, 600 Fifth Ave, 58249. SAN 371-5973. Tel: 701-256-5353. FAX: 701-256-5361. *Dir,* Shannon Nuelle; *Asst Librn,* Dawn Borgen; *Asst Librn,* Linda Economy; *Asst Librn,* Lori Neubert; Staff 2 (Non-MLS 2)
Founded 1940. Pop 4,800; Circ 26,000
Library Holdings: Bk Titles 27,000; Bk Vols 30,000; Per Subs 40; Talking Bks 640
Open Mon, Tues, Thurs & Fri 10-5, Wed 10-7, Sat 10-3
Friends of the Library Group

LARIMORE

P EDNA RALSTON PUBLIC LIBRARY*, 116 1/2 Towner Ave, 58251. (Mail add: PO Box 6, 58251-0006), SAN 313-122X. Tel: 701-343-2181. *Librn,* Ashley Turner
Pop 1,400; Circ 3,700
Library Holdings: Bk Vols 10,000; Talking Bks 37
Open Wed 1:30-4:30, Sat 9-Noon

LEEDS

P LEEDS PUBLIC LIBRARY*, PO Box 295, 58346. Tel: 701-466-2930. *Librn,* Diane Hoffmann
Library Holdings: Bk Titles 4,500; Per Subs 15
Open Thurs 3-5, Sat 2-4

LIDGERWOOD

P LIDGERWOOD CITY LIBRARY*, 15 Wiley Ave S, 58053-4001. (Mail add: PO Box 280, 58053-0280), SAN 313-1238. Tel: 701-538-4669. *Librn,* Orva Krause
Pop 996; Circ 10,795
Library Holdings: Bk Vols 17,021; Per Subs 29
Open Tues-Sat 2-4:30
Friends of the Library Group

LINTON

P LINTON PUBLIC LIBRARY*, Harry L Petrie Public Library, 101 NE First St, 58552-7123. (Mail add: PO Box 416, 58552-0416), SAN 313-1246. Tel: 701-254-4737. FAX: 701-254-4727. E-mail: hlplib@bektel.com. Web Site: lintonndlibrary.com. *Dir,* Carla Frison
Founded 1937. Pop 7,000; Circ 8,000
Library Holdings: Bk Vols 15,000; Per Subs 17
Special Collections: Local Newspaper Bound Copies 1905-present; North Dakota Coll
Function: ILL available, Ref serv available
Open Mon & Thurs 10-6, Wed & Fri 2-5, Sat (Summer) 11-2

LISBON

P LISBON PUBLIC LIBRARY*, 409 Forest St, 58054. (Mail add: PO Box 569, 58054-0569), SAN 313-1254. Tel: 701-683-5174. FAX: 701-683-5174. E-mail: lisbonpl@pioneer.state.nd.us. Web Site: www.lisbonpubliclibrary.com. *Dir,* Bonnie Mattson
Founded 1911. Pop 2,400; Circ 21,500
Library Holdings: Bk Vols 19,000; Per Subs 35
Function: Alaskana res
Open Mon & Fri 2-6, Tues & Wed 10-1 & 2-6, Thurs 2-8

S NORTH DAKOTA VETERANS HOME LIBRARY*, 1400 Rose St, 58054. (Mail add: PO Box 673, 58054-0673). Tel: 701-683-6541. FAX: 701-683-6550. *In Charge,* Jann Neameyer; Tel: 701-683-6534
Library Holdings: Bk Vols 1,000; Per Subs 40
Wireless access
Restriction: Residents only

MADDOCK

P MADDOCK COMMUNITY LIBRARY*, Second & Dakota Ave, 58348. (Mail add: PO Box 188, 58348-0188). Tel: 701-438-2235. FAX: 701-438-2202. *Dir,* Priscilla Backstrom
Pop 498; Circ 1,590
Library Holdings: Large Print Bks 50; Bk Titles 5,700
Wireless access
Open Mon-Fri 9-5

MANDAN

P MORTON MANDAN PUBLIC LIBRARY*, 609 W Main St, 58554. SAN 313-1262. Tel: 701-667-5365. FAX: 701-667-5368. E-mail: mortonmandanlibrary@cdln.info. Web Site: www.cdln.info, www.mortonmandanlibrary.org. *Dir,* Kelly Steckler; E-mail: ksteckler@cdln.info; *Asst Dir,* Mary Henderson; E-mail: mhenderson@cdln.info; *Bkmobile/Outreach Serv Dir,* Sheila Berreth; E-mail: sberreth@cdln.info; Staff 2 (MLS 2)
Founded 1904. Pop 16,969; Circ 64,429
Library Holdings: Bk Titles 30,000; Per Subs 150
Special Collections: Indians of North America; Large Print Books; Railroads
Subject Interests: Local hist, Railroads
Automation Activity & Vendor Info: (Cataloging) SirsiDynix; (Circulation) SirsiDynix; (OPAC) SirsiDynix
Database Vendor: EBSCOhost, SirsiDynix
Open Mon-Thurs 9:30-9, Fri & Sat 9:30-5, Sun 1-5
Friends of the Library Group
Bookmobiles: 1

S NORTH DAKOTA DEPARTMENT OF CORRECTIONS*, North Dakota Youth Correctional Center Library, 701 16 Ave SW, 58554-5800. Tel: 701-667-1479. FAX: 701-667-1414. *Librn,* Judy Ringgenberg; E-mail: judy.ringgenberg@sendit.nodak.edu
Library Holdings: AV Mats 100; Bk Vols 3,600; Per Subs 40
Partic in Online Dakota Info Network (ODIN)
Open Mon-Fri 8-4:30

S NORTHERN GREAT PLAINS RESEARCH LABORATORY LIBRARY*, PO Box 459, 58554-0459. Tel: 701-667-3000. FAX: 701-667-3054. Web Site: www.mandan.ars.usda.gov. *Admin Assoc,* Jeremy Will; E-mail: jeremy.will@ars.usda.gov
Library Holdings: Bk Vols 1,000; Per Subs 50
Function: Res libr
Partic in Minitex Library Information Network
Open Mon-Fri 8-4:30
Restriction: Non-circulating coll

MAYVILLE

P MAYVILLE PUBLIC LIBRARY*, 52 Center Ave N, 58257. SAN 313-1300. Tel: 701-788-3388. *Dir,* M Rice
Founded 1900. Pop 4,900; Circ 13,000
Library Holdings: AV Mats 30; Bk Vols 18,000; Per Subs 10
Special Collections: Norwegian Book Coll
Mem of Mid-Wisconsin Federated Library System
Open Tues, Wed & Fri 12-5, Thurs 12-5 & 6-9, Sat 9-12
Friends of the Library Group

C MAYVILLE STATE UNIVERSITY*, Byrnes-Quanbeck Library, 330 Third St NE, 58257. SAN 313-1319. Tel: 701-788-4815. Toll Free Tel: 800-437-4104, Ext 34814. FAX: 701-788-4846. Web Site: www.mayvillestate.edu. *Dir,* Kelly Kornkven; Tel: 701-788-4816, E-mail: kelly.kornkven@mayvillestate.edu; *Asst Dir, Tech Serv,* Aubrey Madler; E-mail: aubrey.madler@mayvillestate.edu; *Circ/Acq, ILL,* Shannon Hofer; E-mail: shannon.hofer@mayvillestate.edu; *Per,* Marjorie Fugleberg; Tel: 701-788-4817, E-mail: marjorie.fugleberg@mayvillestate.edu. Subject Specialists: *Bus admin,* Shannon Hofer; *Math,* Marjorie Fugleberg; Staff 5 (MLS 1, Non-MLS 4)
Founded 1889. Enrl 644; Fac 43; Highest Degree: Bachelor
Library Holdings: Bk Vols 105,000; Per Subs 497
Special Collections: North Dakota Coll
Automation Activity & Vendor Info: (Cataloging) Ex Libris Group; (Circulation) Ex Libris Group; (Course Reserve) Ex Libris Group; (ILL) Ex Libris Group; (OPAC) Ex Libris Group; (Serials) Ex Libris Group
Database Vendor: EBSCOhost, OCLC FirstSearch
Wireless access
Partic in OCLC Online Computer Library Center, Inc; Online Dakota Info Network (ODIN)
Open Mon-Thurs 8am-10pm, Fri 8-5, Sun 6-10

MEDORA

G THEODORE ROOSEVELT NATIONAL PARK LIBRARY*, PO Box 7, 58645-0007. SAN 323-6846. Tel: 701-623-4466. FAX: 701-623-4840. *Coordr,* Eileen Andes
Library Holdings: Bk Titles 2,800; Per Subs 30
Special Collections: Theodore Roosevelt Coll
Subject Interests: Northern Great Plains nat hist, Western Americana
Open Mon-Fri 8-4:30

MILNOR

P SATRE MEMORIAL LIBRARY*, 528 Fifth St, 58060. (Mail add: PO Box 225, 58060-0225). Tel: 701-427-5295. E-mail: satrelib@drtel.net. *Librn,* Melissa Lynn Bryant
Founded 1973. Pop 711; Circ 10,404
Library Holdings: AV Mats 483; Large Print Bks 100; Bk Vols 11,000; Talking Bks 18
Special Collections: World War II TimeLife Books
Automation Activity & Vendor Info: (Acquisitions) LibraryWorld, Inc; (Cataloging) LibraryWorld, Inc; (Circulation) LibraryWorld, Inc
Database Vendor: LibraryWorld, Inc
Wireless access
Open Wed 10-4, Thurs 10-5

MINNEWAUKAN

P MINNEWAUKAN PUBLIC LIBRARY*, 130 Main St, 58351. (Mail add: PO Box 261, 58351-0261). Tel: 701-473-5735. FAX: 701-473-5377. E-mail: mwkncity@gondtc.com. Web Site: www.minnewaukan.com/Library.htm. *Librn,* Cathy Burkhardsmeier
Library Holdings: Bk Vols 13,000
Open Mon 2-5, Tues, Wed & Fri 10-12 & 2-5, Thurs 2-7, Sat 10-12

MINOT

P MINOT PUBLIC LIBRARY*, 516 Second Ave SW, 58701-3792. SAN 313-1335. Tel: 701-852-1045. FAX: 701-852-2595. Web Site: www.minotlibrary.org. *Dir,* Jerry Kaup; E-mail: jkaup@srt.com; *Cat,* Judith Toelle; E-mail: jtoelle@srt.com; *Ch Serv,* Paulette Nelson; Tel: 701-838-0606, E-mail: pnelson@srt.com; *Circ/Tech,* Jeanne Narum; E-mail: jnarum@srt.com; *ILL,* Marci Julson; E-mail: mjulson@srt.com; *Info Spec,* Darla Schaeffer; Tel: 701-852-0333, E-mail: daschaef@srt.com; *Ref,* Marilyn Holbach; E-mail: mholbach@srt.com; Staff 5 (MLS 4, Non-MLS 1)
Founded 1908. Pop 36,567; Circ 301,172
Jan 2005-Dec 2005 Income $896,192, State $50,750, City $785,539, Other $59,903. Mats Exp $167,488, Books $129,003, Per/Ser (Incl. Access Fees) $18,125, Electronic Ref Mat (Incl. Access Fees) $20,360. Sal $463,770
Library Holdings: AV Mats 10,590; e-books 13,500; Large Print Bks 4,050; Bk Vols 134,416; Per Subs 300
Special Collections: Minot Daily News, 1895-present, micro; North Dakota Census, micro & CD
Subject Interests: Genealogy, Literacy
Automation Activity & Vendor Info: (Cataloging) Follett Software; (Circulation) Follett Software; (ILL) OCLC; (OPAC) Follett Software
Function: Homebound delivery serv
Publications: Directory of Clubs & Organizations; Peddler (Newsletter)
Special Services for the Deaf - Videos & decoder
Special Services for the Blind - Talking bks
Open Mon-Thurs 9-9, Fri 9-6, Sat 10-5, Sun (Sept-May) 1-5
Friends of the Library Group

C MINOT STATE UNIVERSITY*, Gordon B Olson Library, 500 University Ave W, 58707. SAN 313-1343. Tel: 701-858-3200. Circulation Tel: 701-858-3201. Interlibrary Loan Service Tel: 701-858-3094. Reference Tel: 701-858-3296. FAX: 701-858-3581. Web Site: www.minotstateu.edu/library/. *Access Serv,* Sarah Henderson; *Bibliog Instr, Ref,* Ben Bruton; *Bibliog Instr, Ref,* Patty Hunt; *Bibliog Instr, Ref,* Jane LaPlante; *Cat,* David Iversen; *Coll Develop, Ser,* Susan Podrygula; Staff 11.5 (MLS 6, Non-MLS 5.5)
Founded 1913. Enrl 3,649; Fac 272; Highest Degree: Master
Special Collections: Dakota Territory and North Dakota History Coll; Indians of the North Central States Coll. State Document Depository; US Document Depository
Subject Interests: Educ, Geol
Automation Activity & Vendor Info: (Acquisitions) Ex Libris Group; (Cataloging) Ex Libris Group; (Circulation) Ex Libris Group; (Course Reserve) Docutek; (ILL) Ex Libris Group; (OPAC) Ex Libris Group; (Serials) Ex Libris Group
Partic in Minitex Library Information Network; OCLC Online Computer Library Center, Inc; Online Dakota Info Network (ODIN)

M TRINITY HEALTH*, Angus L Cameron Medical Library, 20 Burdick Expressway W, Health Center E, 58701. SAN 355-4074. Tel: 701-857-5435. *Dir,* Karen Anderson; Staff 1 (MLS 1)
Founded 1928
Library Holdings: Bk Titles 2,000; Per Subs 100
Subject Interests: Clinical med
Automation Activity & Vendor Info: (Cataloging) Ex Libris Group; (Circulation) Ex Libris Group; (OPAC) Ex Libris Group
Partic in Greater Midwest Regional Medical Libr Network
Open Mon-Fri 8-4:30

P WARD COUNTY PUBLIC LIBRARY*, 405 Third Ave SE, 58701-4020. SAN 355-4139. Tel: 701-852-5388. Toll Free Tel: 800-932-8932. FAX: 701-837-4960. E-mail: library@co.ward.nd.us. Web Site: www.co.ward.nd.us/library. *Adminr,* Jan Murphy; Staff 3 (Non-MLS 3)
Founded 1960. Pop 22,228; Circ 101,000
Library Holdings: AV Mats 1,200; Bks on Deafness & Sign Lang 10; CDs 50; DVDs 50; Large Print Bks 1,000; Bk Vols 52,800; Per Subs 35; Talking Bks 500; Videos 2,500
Automation Activity & Vendor Info: (Cataloging) OCLC; (Circulation) ComPanion Corp; (OPAC) ComPanion Corp
Database Vendor: EBSCOhost, Gale Cengage Learning
Partic in NDak Network for Knowledge
Open Mon-Fri 8-4:30
Branches: 1
KENMARE BRANCH, Five NE Third, Memorial Hall, Kenmare, 58746. (Mail add: PO Box 104, Kenmare, 58746-0104), SAN 355-4163. Tel: 701-385-4090. FAX: 701-385-4090. *Librn,* Pauline Nielsen; Staff 1 (Non-MLS 1)
Founded 1976. Pop 2,500; Circ 30,000
Library Holdings: AV Mats 200; Large Print Bks 300; Bk Vols 6,000
Open Mon, Wed & Thurs 9:30-5
Bookmobiles: 1

MINOT AFB

A UNITED STATES AIR FORCE*, Minot Air Force Base Library FL4528, 156 Missel Ave, Ste 1, 58705-5026. SAN 355-4198. Tel: 701-723-3344. FAX: 701-727-9850. Web Site: www.minot.af.mil/library. *Dir,* Julie Reiten; E-mail: julie.reiten@us.af.mil; Staff 5.625 (MLS 1, Non-MLS 4.625)
Founded 1961
Library Holdings: Bk Vols 30,000; Per Subs 20
Special Collections: Air War College Coll; Defense Logistics Studies Information Exchange (DLSIE); Defense Technical Information Center (DTIC); McNaughton Rental Coll; Video Coll
Subject Interests: Aviation, Mil hist, Space studies
Automation Activity & Vendor Info: (Cataloging) SirsiDynix; (Circulation) SirsiDynix; (OPAC) SirsiDynix
Database Vendor: EBSCO Auto Repair Reference, EBSCOhost, Jane's, Knovel, Marcive, Inc, Newsbank, OCLC ArticleFirst, OCLC FirstSearch, OCLC WorldShare Interlibrary Loan, Overdrive, Inc, ProQuest, Safari Books Online
Wireless access
Open Mon-Wed 10-5, Thurs 10-8, Sat 12-5

MOHALL

P MOHALL PUBLIC LIBRARY, 115 W Main, 58761. (Mail add: PO Box 159, 58761-0159), SAN 313-1378. Tel: 701-756-7242. E-mail: mplibrary@srt.com. *Librn,* Sarah Jensen
Pop 931; Circ 3,589
Library Holdings: Bk Vols 15,670
Open Mon-Thurs 11-5

MOTT

P MOTT PUBLIC LIBRARY*, 203 Third St E, 58646-7525. (Mail add: PO Box 57, 58646-0057), SAN 313-1386. Tel: 701-824-2163. FAX: 701-824-4008. *Librn,* Pam Steinke
Founded 1912. Pop 1,019; Circ 5,513
Library Holdings: Bk Titles 12,065
Open Mon 9-6, Wed 9-1, Fri 9-2

NEW ENGLAND

P NEW ENGLAND PUBLIC LIBRARY*, 726 McKenzie Ave, 58647-7105. (Mail add: PO Box 266, 58647-0266). Tel: 701-579-4223. E-mail: nepl@ndsupernet.com. *Dir,* Donna Mae Jirges
Pop 555; Circ 6,649
Library Holdings: Audiobooks 55; CDs 75; Large Print Bks 175; Bk Vols 5,980; Per Subs 25
Open Mon (Winter) 5-6, Tues-Fri 3:30-5; Mon-Fri (Summer) 10-12

NEW ROCKFORD

P NEW ROCKFORD PUBLIC LIBRARY*, 10 Eight St N, 58356. SAN 313-1408. Tel: 701-947-5540. FAX: 701-947-5540. *Librn,* Susie Sharp
Pop 2,000; Circ 4,241
Library Holdings: Bk Vols 15,000
Automation Activity & Vendor Info: (Cataloging) Winnebago Software Co; (Circulation) Winnebago Software Co; (OPAC) Winnebago Software Co
Wireless access
Open Mon 2-8, Tues-Fri 11-6
Friends of the Library Group

NEW TOWN

J FORT BERTHOLD LIBRARY*, 220 Eighth Ave N, 58763. (Mail add: PO Box 788, 58763), SAN 371-7275. Tel: 701-627-4738. FAX: 701-627-4677. *Dir,* Quincee Baker; Staff 3 (MLS 1, Non-MLS 2)
Founded 1985. Enrl 185; Fac 7
Library Holdings: Bk Titles 16,000; Per Subs 150
Special Collections: Indians of North America
Database Vendor: EBSCOhost, Gale Cengage Learning
Open Mon-Fri 8-5

P NEW TOWN PUBLIC LIBRARY*, PO Box 309, 58763-0309. Tel: 701-627-4812. FAX: 701-627-4316. *In Charge,* Geri Bretvold
Library Holdings: Bk Titles 12,000
Open Mon-Fri 4:30-6:30

NORTHWOOD

P NORTHWOOD CITY LIBRARY*, 420 Trojan Rd, 58267-3001. Tel: 701-587-5221. FAX: 701-587-5423. Web Site: www.northwood.k12.nd.us. *Librn,* Wendy Holkesvig
Library Holdings: Bk Vols 10,000; Per Subs 10
Automation Activity & Vendor Info: (Acquisitions) Ex Libris Group; (Cataloging) Ex Libris Group; (Circulation) Ex Libris Group; (ILL) Ex Libris Group; (OPAC) Ex Libris Group; (Serials) Ex Libris Group
Partic in Online Dakota Info Network (ODIN)
Open Mon-Fri 8-4, Sat 10-12

OAKES

P OAKES PUBLIC LIBRARY*, 804 Main Ave, 58474. SAN 313-1432. Tel: 701-742-3234. FAX: 701-742-2812. *Librn,* Jeanine Pahl; E-mail: pahl@oakes.k12.nd.us
Founded 1927. Pop 2,500; Circ 20,000
Jan 2007-Dec 2007 Income $11,000. Mats Exp $5,000, Books $3,700, Per/Ser (Incl. Access Fees) $500, Other Print Mats $300, AV Mat $300, Electronic Ref Mat (Incl. Access Fees) $200. Sal $6,000
Library Holdings: AV Mats 50; Bks-By-Mail 25; Bks on Deafness & Sign Lang 10; Electronic Media & Resources 40; High Interest/Low Vocabulary Bk Vols 60; Large Print Bks 75; Bk Titles 31,181; Per Subs 35; Talking Bks 45
Automation Activity & Vendor Info: (Cataloging) Chancery SMS; (Circulation) Chancery SMS; (OPAC) Chancery SMS
Database Vendor: World Book Online
Open Tues, Thurs & Sat 2:30-5:30, Wed 2:30-7:30

PARK RIVER

P PARK RIVER PUBLIC LIBRARY*, 605 Sixth St W, 58270. (Mail add. PO Box 240, 58270-0240), SAN 313-1440. Tel: 701-284-6116. *Librn,* Rochelle Kovarik; Staff 1 (Non-MLS 1)
Founded 1900. Pop 2,000; Circ 4,800
Library Holdings: AV Mats 855; DVDs 70; Bk Titles 17,000; Bk Vols 20,500; Per Subs 50; Videos 740
Automation Activity & Vendor Info: (Cataloging) ComPanion Corp; (Circulation) ComPanion Corp
Open Mon & Thurs 8-4 & 6:30 8:30, Tues, Wed & Fri 8-4, Sat 9-1
Friends of the Library Group

PEMBINA

P PEMBINA CITY LIBRARY*, Pembina Public School, 155 S Third St, 58271. SAN 313-1467. Tel: 701-825-6217. E-mail: Pembina.Library@sendit.nodak.edu. *City Librn,* Marcy Cleem
Pop 700; Circ 5,400
Library Holdings: Audiobooks 70; DVDs 75; Large Print Bks 50; Bk Vols 5,500; Per Subs 30; Videos 100
Subject Interests: State hist
Wireless access
Function: Accelerated reader prog, After school storytime, Computers for patron use, ILL available, Online cat, Pub access computers, Story hour, Summer reading prog
Partic in Online Dakota Info Network (ODIN)
Open Mon & Fri 6:30pm-8:30pm, Tues 3:30-6:30, Thurs 3:30-5:30, Sat 9:30-11:30
Restriction: Borrowing requests are handled by ILL, Open to pub for ref & circ; with some limitations

RICHARDTON

SR ASSUMPTION ABBEY LIBRARY, 418 Third Ave W, 58652-7100. (Mail add: PO Box A, 58652-0901), SAN 313-1475. Tel: 701-974-3315. FAX: 701-974-3317. *Librn,* Brother Michael Taffe
Founded 1899
Jul 2013-Jun 2014. Mats Exp $8,098, Books $2,660, Per/Ser (Incl. Access Fees) $3,975, Presv $1,463

Library Holdings: Bk Vols 104,000; Per Subs 58
Subject Interests: Church hist, Germans from Russia, Monastic hist, NDak hist
Automation Activity & Vendor Info: (Cataloging) Book Systems
Function: ILL available, Res libr
Partic in NDak Network for Knowledge
Restriction: Circ limited, In-house use for visitors, Open by appt only, Private libr

RIVERDALE

P MCLEAN-MERCER REGIONAL LIBRARY*, Downtown Plaza, Second St, 58565. (Mail add: PO Box 505, 58565-0505), SAN 355-4228. Tel: 701-654-7652. FAX: 701-654-7526. E-mail: mmrlib@westriv.com. *Dir,* Beth Bruestle
Founded 1959. Pop 26,316; Circ 106,622
Library Holdings: Bk Vols 30,000
Automation Activity & Vendor Info: (Cataloging) SirsiDynix; (Circulation) SirsiDynix; (Course Reserve) SirsiDynix; (ILL) SirsiDynix; (Media Booking) SirsiDynix; (OPAC) SirsiDynix; (Serials) SirsiDynix
Database Vendor: EBSCOhost, Gale Cengage Learning
Open Mon-Fri 8-12 & 1-5
Branches: 8
BEULAH BRANCH, Beulah City Hall, 120 Central Ave N, Beulah, 58523-6964. (Mail add: PO Box 239, Beulah, 58523-0239), SAN 355-4252. Tel: 701-873-2884. FAX: 701-873-2885. E-mail: beulahlibrary@cdln.info. Web Site: www.beulahlibrary.org. *Librn,* Colleen Wiest
Open Mon-Fri 9-6, Sat (Oct-April) 9-Noon
GARRISON BRANCH, 32 S Main, Garrison, 58540. (Mail add: PO Box 67, Garrison, 58540-0067), SAN 355-4287. Tel: 701-463-7336. E-mail: garplib@cdln.info. *Librn,* Mercedes Sayler
Open Mon 1-8, Tues & Fri 10-1 & 2-6
HAZEN BRANCH, Main St, Hazen, 58545. (Mail add: PO Box 471, Hazen, 58545-0471), SAN 355-4317. Tel: 701-748-2977. E-mail: hazenlibrary@cdln.info. *Librn,* Val Albrecht
Open Mon-Fri 9-6
Friends of the Library Group
MAX BRANCH, 215 Main St, Max, 58759. (Mail add: PO Box 102, Max, 58759), SAN 322-6212. Tel: 701-679-2263. E-mail: maxlib@rtc.coop. *In Charge,* Amy Hauf
Open Mon, Tues & Thurs 9:30-12 & 1-5
STANTON BRANCH, 312 Harmon Ave, Stanton, 58571. (Mail add: PO Box 130, Stanton, 58571-0130), SAN 370-9078. Tel: 701-745-3235. E-mail: stpl@westriv.com. *Librn,* Nancy Miller
Open Mon & Thurs 12-6, Wed 11:30-6:30
TURTLE LAKE PUBLIC LIBRARY, City Hall, Turtle Lake, 58575. (Mail add: PO Box 540, Turtle Lake, 58575-0540), SAN 355-4341. Tel: 701-448-9170. E-mail: tlpublic@westriv.com. *Librn,* Kelly Voth
Library Holdings: Audiobooks 90; DVDs 198; Bk Vols 8,571; Per Subs 199
Open Mon & Wed-Fri 1-5, Tues 1-7
UNDERWOOD PUBLIC LIBRARY, 88 Lincoln Ave, Underwood, 58576. (Mail add: PO Box 304, Underwood, 58576-0304), SAN 370-9086. Tel: 701-442-3441. FAX: 701-442-5482. E-mail: underwoodlibrary@westriv.com. Web Site: www.underwoodndlibrary.com. *Libr Dir,* Harmony Higbie; Staff 0.6 (Non-MLS 0.6)
Pop 750
Automation Activity & Vendor Info: (Acquisitions) SirsiDynix
Database Vendor: SirsiDynix
Open Mon & Fri 10-2, Tues & Thurs 3-7, Wed 10-2 & 3-7
Restriction: Pub access for legal res only
WASHBURN BRANCH, 705 Main St, Washburn, 58577. (Mail add: PO Box 637, Washburn, 58577-0637), SAN 355-4376. Tel: 701-462-8180. E-mail: washlib@westriv.com. *Librn,* Elizabeth Patterson
Open Mon 1-8, Tues & Wed 10-6, Thurs 1-6, Sat 10-1
Bookmobiles: 1. Librn, Dawn Grannis

ROLETTE

P ROLETTE PUBLIC LIBRARY*, 1015 First Ave, 58366. (Mail add: PO Box 175, 58366-0175). Tel: 701-246-3849. *Librn,* Elaine Ellingson; *Asst Librn,* Fern Beaver
Library Holdings: Bk Vols 3,136
Open Mon 5:30-7:30, Sat 10-Noon

ROLLA

P ROLLA PUBLIC LIBRARY*, 14 SE First St, 58367. (Mail add: PO Box 1200, 58367-1200), SAN 313-1491. Tel: 701-477-3849. FAX: 701-477-9633. E-mail: rollandlibrary@rollapubliclibrary.net. Web Site: www.rollapubliclibrary.net. *Dir,* Peggy Johnson; E-mail: pjohnson@utma.com; *Asst Dir,* Lois Menard
Library Holdings: Bk Vols 20,000; Per Subs 20; Talking Bks 1,000; Videos 400
Wireless access
Open Mon-Wed & Fri 2:30-6, Thurs 9:30am-10:30am, Sat 11-2

RUGBY

P HEART OF AMERICA LIBRARY*, 201 Third St SW, 58368-1793. SAN 313-1505. Tel: 701-776-6223. FAX: 701-776-6897. *Dir,* Amy Bryn; E-mail: amy.bryn@sendit.nodak.edu; *Asst Librn,* Dianne Tuff
Founded 1911. Pop 4,675; Circ 33,609
Jan 2009-Dec 2009 Income $128,025, State $8,117, City $34,651, County $59,525, Locally Generated Income $17,704, Other $8,028. Mats Exp $23,044, Books $19,444, Per/Ser (Incl. Access Fees) $1,800, AV Mat $1,800. Sal $66,354
Library Holdings: AV Mats 690; Electronic Media & Resources 56; Bk Vols 28,260; Per Subs 73; Videos 670
Automation Activity & Vendor Info: (Cataloging) Book Systems; (Circulation) Book Systems; (OPAC) Book Systems
Wireless access
Partic in NDak Network for Knowledge
Open Mon-Wed, Fri & Sat 10-5:30, Thurs 10-9

STANLEY

P STANLEY PUBLIC LIBRARY*, 116 Main St, 58784-4051. (Mail add: PO Box 249, 58785), SAN 313-1513. Tel: 701-628-2223. Web Site: www.stanleyndlibrary.com. *Libr Dir,* Kelly Kudrna
Pop 1,371; Circ 8,000
Library Holdings: Audiobooks 125; DVDs 550; Large Print Bks 60; Bk Vols 11,000; Videos 500
Wireless access
Open Mon & Wed-Fri 12:30-5:30, Tues 1-7
Friends of the Library Group

STEELE

P KIDDER COUNTY LIBRARY*, 115 W Broadway, 58482. (Mail add: PO Box 227, 58482-0227), SAN 313-1521. Tel: 701-475-2855. *Librn,* Paulette Fischer
Founded 1964. Pop 3,800; Circ 11,860
Library Holdings: Bk Vols 24,000; Per Subs 15
Open Mon-Fri 9-12 & 1-5

STREETER

P STREETER CENTENNIAL LIBRARY*, 5280 50th Ave SE, 58483. (Mail add: 114 Helen St N, No 7, 58483). Tel: 701-424-3602. *Chmn,* Judith Williams; *Asst Librn,* Janet Patton
Library Holdings: Bk Titles 3,000
Open Wed 3-5

VALLEY CITY

P VALLEY CITY BARNES COUNTY PUBLIC LIBRARY, 410 N Central Ave, 58072-2949. SAN 313-1564. Tel: 701-845-3821. Toll Free Tel: 800-532-8600 (ND only). FAX: 701-845-4884. E-mail: vcbclibrary@outlook.com. Web Site: www.vcbclibrary.org. *Libr Dir,* Steve Hammel; *Adult Serv Coordr,* Liz Hoskisson; *Youth Serv Coordr,* Melissa Lloyd; Staff 5 (MLS 1, Non-MLS 4)
Founded 1903. Pop 11,075; Circ 39,700
Jan 2014-Dec 2014 Income $247,214
Library Holdings: Audiobooks 970; CDs 518; DVDs 1,093; Large Print Bks 4,405; Bk Vols 40,622
Special Collections: North Dakota Coll
Automation Activity & Vendor Info: (Acquisitions) Biblionix/Apollo; (Cataloging) Biblionix/Apollo; (Circulation) Biblionix/Apollo; (OPAC) Biblionix/Apollo; (Serials) Biblionix/Apollo
Database Vendor: Biblionix/Apollo, Overdrive, Inc
Wireless access
Function: Accelerated reader prog, Adult bk club, Audiobks via web, Bks on cassette, Bks on CD, Computers for patron use, Copy machines, Electronic databases & coll, Fax serv, Free DVD rentals, Genealogy discussion group, Handicapped accessible, ILL available, Life-long learning prog for all ages, Magazines, Movies, Music CDs, Online cat, OverDrive digital audio bks, Photocopying/Printing, Preschool reading prog, Prog for adults, Prog for children & young adult, Pub access computers, Ref serv available, Senior outreach, Story hour, Summer reading prog, Tax forms, Teen prog, Wheelchair accessible
Partic in Online Dakota Info Network (ODIN)
Open Mon 10-7, Tues-Fri 10-5, Sat 10-2
Friends of the Library Group

C VALLEY CITY STATE UNIVERSITY LIBRARY*, Allen Memorial Library, 101 College St SW, 58072-4098. SAN 313-1572. Tel: 701-845-7276. Reference Tel: 701-845-7277. Administration Tel: 701-845-7275. Automation Services Tel: 701-845-7279. Toll Free Tel: 800-532-8641, Ext 37276. FAX: 701-845-7437. E-mail:

library.office@vcsu.edu. Web Site: library.vcsu.edu. *Dir, Libr Serv, Distance Educ, Info Literacy,* Donna James; E-mail: donna.james@vcsu.edu; *Acq Librn, Ser Librn,* Patricia Fisher; *Circ Supvr,* Jennifer Porter; *Syst Spec,* Benjamin Ferguson; E-mail: benjamin.ferguson@vcsu.edu; Staff 4 (MLS 4)
Founded 1890. Enrl 855; Fac 59; Highest Degree: Master
Library Holdings: e-books 15,000; Bk Titles 85,677; Bk Vols 95,197; Per Subs 246
Special Collections: North Dakota Coll; Valley City State University Historical Coll; Woiwode Manuscripts Coll. US Document Depository
Subject Interests: Educ
Automation Activity & Vendor Info: (Acquisitions) Ex Libris Group; (Cataloging) Ex Libris Group; (Circulation) Ex Libris Group; (Course Reserve) Docutek; (ILL) Ex Libris Group; (OPAC) Ex Libris Group; (Serials) Ex Libris Group
Database Vendor: Agricola, Baker & Taylor, EBSCOhost, Gale Cengage Learning, LexisNexis, OCLC FirstSearch, OCLC WorldShare Interlibrary Loan, ProQuest, PubMed, ScienceDirect, SerialsSolutions, Wilson - Wilson Web
Wireless access
Function: Adult bk club, Audio & video playback equip for onsite use, Audiobks via web, Bks on CD, Computers for patron use, Copy machines, Doc delivery serv, E-Reserves, Electronic databases & coll, Equip loans & repairs, Handicapped accessible, ILL available, Instruction & testing, Music CDs, Online cat, Online info literacy tutorials on the web & in blackboard, Online ref, Online searches, Ref & res, Ref serv available, Satellite serv, Scanner, Telephone ref, VHS videos, Wheelchair accessible
Partic in Minitex Library Information Network; NDak Network for Knowledge; OCLC Online Computer Library Center, Inc; Online Dakota Info Network (ODIN)
Open Mon-Thurs 7:45am-10pm, Fri 7:45-4, Sun 6pm-10pm
Restriction: Open to pub for ref & circ; with some limitations, Open to students, fac & staff
Friends of the Library Group

VELVA

P VELVA SCHOOL & PUBLIC LIBRARY*, 101 W Fourth St, 58790-7045. (Mail add: PO Box 179, 58790-0179), SAN 313-1580. Tel: 701-338-2022. FAX: 701-338-2023. *Librn,* Iris Swedlund; E-mail: iris.swedlund@sendit.nodak.edu; Staff 2 (Non-MLS 2)
Founded 1913. Pop 1,300; Circ 26,779
Library Holdings: Bk Titles 18,000; Per Subs 120
Automation Activity & Vendor Info: (OPAC) OVID Technologies
Open Mon & Wed-Fri 8-4, Tues 8-4 & 7-9

WAHPETON

P LEACH PUBLIC LIBRARY*, 417 Second Ave N, 58075. SAN 313-1599. Tel: 701-642-5732. FAX: 701-642-5732. E-mail: leachplib@702com.net. Web Site: www.wahpeton.com. *Dir,* Bonnie R MacIver; E-mail: bonnie.leachplib@midconetwork.com
Founded 1924. Pop 9,000; Circ 36,100
Jan 2008-Dec 2008 Income $218,994, State $16,926, City $188,168, County $10,000, Locally Generated Income $3,900. Mats Exp $27,000, Books $16,000, Per/Ser (Incl. Access Fees) $3,500, AV Mat $4,500, Electronic Ref Mat (Incl. Access Fees) $3,000. Sal $95,731 (Prof $33,800)
Library Holdings: Audiobooks 1,768; Bks on Deafness & Sign Lang 15; DVDs 837; Large Print Bks 600; Bk Vols 30,233; Per Subs 75; Videos 557
Special Collections: Local Paper back to 1890, microfilm
Automation Activity & Vendor Info: (Cataloging) Ex Libris Group; (Circulation) Ex Libris Group; (ILL) Ex Libris Group; (OPAC) Ex Libris Group; (Serials) Ex Libris Group
Database Vendor: EBSCOhost, Gale Cengage Learning
Partic in Online Dakota Info Network (ODIN)
Open Mon, Tues & Thurs 9-7, Wed 9-5:30, Fri 9-4, Sat (Winter) 9-1
Friends of the Library Group

J NORTH DAKOTA STATE COLLEGE OF SCIENCE*, Mildred Johnson Library, 800 Sixth St N, 58076-0001. SAN 313-1602. Tel: 701-671-2298, 701-671-2618. Administration Tel: 701-671-2385. Toll Free Tel: 800-342-4325. FAX: 701-671-2674. E-mail: ndscs.library@ndscs.edu. Web Site: www.ndscs.edu/library. *Dir,* Karen M Chobot; E-mail: karen.chobot@ndscs.edu; *Access Serv Librn,* Daniel Gaghan; Tel: 701-671-2611, E-mail: daniel.gaghan@ndscs.edu; *Coll Mgt Librn,* Tina M Grenier; Tel: 701-671-2612, E-mail: tina.grenier@ndscs.edu; Staff 4 (MLS 2, Non-MLS 2)
Founded 1903. Enrl 2,100; Fac 135; Highest Degree: Associate
Library Holdings: Audiobooks 500; AV Mats 3,700; e-books 11,842; e-journals 1; Bk Vols 70,000; Per Subs 120
Subject Interests: Automotive, Behav sci, Electronics, Foods mgt, Health sci, Soc sci
Automation Activity & Vendor Info: (Acquisitions) Ex Libris Group; (Cataloging) Ex Libris Group; (Circulation) Ex Libris Group; (Course Reserve) Ex Libris Group; (ILL) OCLC Connexion; (OPAC) Ex Libris Group; (Serials) Ex Libris Group
Database Vendor: ALLDATA Online, Baker & Taylor, Cinahl, CredoReference, EBSCO Auto Repair Reference, EBSCOhost, Ex Libris Group, Gale Cengage Learning, Micromedex, OCLC, OCLC FirstSearch, OCLC WebJunction, OCLC WorldShare Interlibrary Loan, Overdrive, Inc, ProQuest, PubMed, Springshare, LLC
Wireless access
Function: Adult bk club, CD-ROM, Copy machines, Electronic databases & coll, Fax serv, Handicapped accessible, ILL available, Photocopying/Printing, Telephone ref, VHS videos, Wheelchair accessible
Partic in Minitex Library Information Network; OCLC Online Computer Library Center, Inc; Online Dakota Info Network (ODIN)
Open Mon-Thurs 7:30am-10pm, Fri 7:30-4, Sun 5pm-10pm
Restriction: In-house use for visitors

WALHALLA

P WALHALLA PUBLIC LIBRARY*, 1010 Central Ave, 58282-4015. (Mail add: PO Box 587, 58282-0587), SAN 313-1610. Tel: 701-549-3794. FAX: 701-549-3794. E-mail: wlibrary@utma.com. *Librn,* Diana Yeado
Circ 5,798
Library Holdings: Bk Vols 17,865
Automation Activity & Vendor Info: (Cataloging) Follett Software; (Circulation) Follett Software
Open Mon, Tues & Fri 12-6, Wed 12-8, Thurs 10-6

WATFORD CITY

P MCKENZIE COUNTY PUBLIC LIBRARY*, 112 Second Ave NE, 58854. (Mail add: PO Box 990, 58854-0990), SAN 313-1629. Tel: 701-444-3785. FAX: 701-444-3730. E-mail: librarian@co.mckenzie.nd.us. *Dir,* Dr Kelly Dionysus; *Head Asst Librn,* Crystal Slaubaugh; *Asst Librn,* Tam Engelbrecht; *Asst Librn,* Diane M Oswald; Staff 4 (MLS 2, Non-MLS 2)
Founded 1958. Pop 18,000; Circ 26,880
Jan 2011-Dec 2012 Income $99,590. Mats Exp $10,855. Sal $54,900
Library Holdings: Audiobooks 550; DVDs 401; Large Print Bks 900; Bk Titles 25,000; Bk Vols 26,185; Per Subs 35
Automation Activity & Vendor Info: (Cataloging) Book Systems; (Circulation) Book Systems; (OPAC) Book Systems; (Serials) Book Systems
Database Vendor: Baker & Taylor
Wireless access
Publications: Booklist
Partic in NW Regional Libr Coop
Open Mon, Tues, Thurs & Fri 10-6, Wed 10-8, Sat (Winter) 9-12
Friends of the Library Group
Bookmobiles: 1

WEST FARGO

P WEST FARGO PUBLIC LIBRARY*, 109 Third St E, 58078. SAN 313-1637. Tel: 701-433-5460. FAX: 701-433-5479. E-mail: askus@westfargolibrary.org. Web Site: www.westfargolibrary.org. *Dir,* Sandra Hannahs; *Asst Dir,* Carrie Scarr; Staff 7 (MLS 3, Non-MLS 4)
Founded 1971. Pop 25,830
Library Holdings: Audiobooks 3,477; CDs 507; DVDs 4,270; e-books 8,557; Bk Titles 55,080; Per Subs 142
Special Collections: United States (State & Local History)
Automation Activity & Vendor Info: (Cataloging) Ex Libris Group; (Circulation) Ex Libris Group; (OPAC) Ex Libris Group
Wireless access
Open Mon-Thurs 10-9, Fri 10-6, Sat 10-5, Sun 1-6
Friends of the Library Group

WILLISTON

P WILLISTON COMMUNITY LIBRARY*, 1302 Davidson Dr, 58801. SAN 313-1645. Tel: 701-774-8805. Toll Free Tel: 800-932-8934 (ND only). FAX: 701-572-1186. Web Site: www.willistonlibrary.org. *Dir,* Debbie Slais; Staff 5.5 (Non-MLS 5.5)
Founded 1983. Pop 19,000; Circ 225,000
Jan 2008-Dec 2008 Income (Main Library Only) $353,166. Mats Exp $79,000, Books $55,000, Per/Ser (Incl. Access Fees) $12,000, AV Mat $12,000. Sal $163,000
Library Holdings: AV Mats 350; CDs 1,000; DVDs 900; Electronic Media & Resources 156; Large Print Bks 2,200; Microforms 100; Bk Vols 56,100; Per Subs 100; Talking Bks 1,000; Videos 2,200
Special Collections: American Indian Coll; Genealogy Coll; North Dakota Coll
Automation Activity & Vendor Info: (Cataloging) OCLC Connexion; (Circulation) Follett Software; (ILL) OCLC FirstSearch; (OPAC) Follett Software
Database Vendor: EBSCOhost, Gale Cengage Learning, OCLC FirstSearch, ProQuest
Wireless access

Function: Bks on cassette, Bks on CD, CD-ROM, Children's prog, Computers for patron use, Copy machines, Fax serv, Free DVD rentals, Handicapped accessible, Home delivery & serv to Sr ctr & nursing homes, ILL available, Magnifiers for reading, Music CDs, Online cat, Outreach serv, Pub access computers, Spoken cassettes & CDs, Story hour, Summer reading prog, Tax forms, VHS videos, Web-catalog
Partic in Minitex Library Information Network
Open Mon-Thurs 9-8, Fri 9-5, Sat 1-5, Sun 2-5
Friends of the Library Group
Branches: 1
TIOGA COMMUNITY LIBRARY, 321 N Benson St, Tioga, 58852. (Mail add: PO Box 279, Tioga, 58852-0279), SAN 313-153X. Tel: 701-664-3627. *Librn*, Dorothy Placek; Staff 1 (Non-MLS 1)
Pop 1,200
Library Holdings: AV Mats 163; Large Print Bks 67; Bk Titles 10,000; Per Subs 19; Talking Bks 53; Videos 421
Friends of the Library Group
Bookmobiles: 1

C WILLISTON STATE COLLEGE LIBRARY*, 1410 University Ave, 58801. Tel: 701-774-4226. FAX: 701-774-4547. Web Site: www.willistonstate.edu/classes/library.html. *Dir, Learning Commons,* Betty Lahn; Staff 1 (MLS 1)
Founded 1966
Library Holdings: AV Mats 600; e-books 6,500; Bk Vols 13,000
Wireless access
Partic in Online Dakota Info Network (ODIN)
Open Mon-Thurs 8-5, Fri 8-4:30

OHIO

Date of Statistics: FY 2013
Population, 2010 U.S. Census: 11,536,504
Population, 2013 U.S. Census: 11,570,808
Total Volumes in Public Libraries: 43,186,348
Volumes Per Capita: 3.73
Total Public Library Circulation: 185,348,458
Circulation Per Capita: 16.01
Total Public Library Income (including State Aid): $1,071,429.939
Source of Income: Public Library Fund. Note: All public libraries receive PLF; 182 public libraries also have local property tax levy
Income Per Capita: $92.59
Expenditure Per Capita: $75.52
Total Operating Expenditures: $873,918,626
Grants-in-Aid to Public Libraries:
Federal: LSTA: $1,509,317
State Aid: $1,856,663
Formula & amount for apportionment for State Aid: Library must meet certain performance standards; amount received determined by formula based on local tax collection & distribution
Number of County or Multi-County Regional Libraries: 4
Chartered Regional Library Systems: Countywide service in all 88 counties

ADA

P ADA PUBLIC LIBRARY*, 320 N Main St, 45810-1199. SAN 313-1688. Tel: 419-634-5246. FAX: 419-634-9747. Web Site: www.adalibrary.org. *Dir,* Amanda Bennett; E-mail: abennett@oplin.org; Staff 2 (MLS 1, Non-MLS 1)
Founded 1916. Pop 7,300; Circ 41,447
Library Holdings: Bk Vols 25,000; Per Subs 82
Special Collections: City, County & State History
Automation Activity & Vendor Info: (Cataloging) SIRSI WorkFlows; (Circulation) SIRSI WorkFlows; (OPAC) SIRSI WorkFlows
Wireless access
Function: Adult bk club, After school storytime, Audiobks via web, Bk club(s), Bks on CD, Children's prog, Computer training, Computers for patron use, Copy machines, Digital talking bks, Fax serv, Free DVD rentals, Holiday prog, Microfiche/film & reading machines, Music CDs, Newsp ref libr, Notary serv, Online cat, OverDrive digital audio bks, Preschool outreach, Preschool reading prog, Prog for adults, Prog for children & young adult, Pub access computers, Scanner, Story hour, Summer reading prog, Tax forms, Teen prog, Wheelchair accessible, Writing prog
Partic in NORWELD
Special Services for the Deaf - Bks on deafness & sign lang
Special Services for the Blind - Bks on CD; Large print bks
Open Mon-Thurs 10-8, Fri 10-5, Sat 10-2
Friends of the Library Group

C OHIO NORTHERN UNIVERSITY*, Heterick Memorial Library, 525 S Main St, 45810. SAN 355-4406. Tel: 419-772-2181. Reference Tel: 419-772-2185. FAX: 419-772-1927. Web Site: www.onu.edu/library. *Dir/Ref Librn,* Position Currently Open; *Coll & Electronic Res Librn, Interim Dir,* Kathleen Baril; Tel: 419-772-2188, E-mail: k-baril@onu.edu; *Cat Librn,* Jennifer Donley; *Pub Serv Librn,* Traci Welch Moritz; E-mail: t-mortiz@onu.edu; *Syst Librn,* Kelly Kobiela; Tel: 419-772-2183, E-mail: k-kobiela@onu.edu
Founded 1915. Enrl 3,228; Fac 225; Highest Degree: Doctorate
Library Holdings: AV Mats 12,802; e-books 72,022; Microforms 224,869; Bk Vols 277,193; Per Subs 9,000
Special Collections: Ohio Northern University Authors
Automation Activity & Vendor Info: (Acquisitions) Innovative Interfaces, Inc; (Cataloging) Innovative Interfaces, Inc; (Circulation) Innovative Interfaces, Inc; (Course Reserve) Innovative Interfaces, Inc; (OPAC) Innovative Interfaces, Inc
Publications: Bookmarks; Library Handbook; Subject Bibliographies
Partic in OCLC Online Computer Library Center, Inc; OHIONET
Open Mon-Thurs 7:30am-Midnight, Fri 8am-9pm, Sat 10-6, Sun 10am-Midnight
Departmental Libraries:
CL TAGGART LAW LIBRARY, 525 S Main St, 45810. Tel: 419-772-2250. Circulation Tel: 419-772-2239. Interlibrary Loan Service Tel: 419-772-2255. FAX: 419-772-1875. Web Site: www.law.onu.edu/library.html. *Dir,* Nancy A Armstrong; Tel: 419-772-2692, E-mail: n-armstrong@onu.edu; Staff 10 (MLS 4, Non-MLS 6)
Founded 1885. Enrl 300
Library Holdings: Bk Titles 53,096; Bk Vols 210,640; Per Subs 3,023
Special Collections: Anthony J Celebrezze Papers. US Document Depository
Automation Activity & Vendor Info: (Acquisitions) Innovative Interfaces, Inc
Database Vendor: Gale Cengage Learning, LexisNexis, OCLC FirstSearch, Westlaw
Function: Res libr
Partic in Ohio Library & Information Network

AKRON

S AKRON ART MUSEUM*, Martha Stecher Reed Art Reference Library, One S High, 44308-1801. SAN 313-1696. Tel: 330-376-9186, Ext 221. FAX: 330-376-1180. Web Site: www.akronartmuseum.org/library. *Libr & Archives Mgr,* Ellie Ward; E-mail: eward@akronartmuseum.org; Staff 1 (MLS 1)
Library Holdings: Bk Titles 12,000; Per Subs 37
Special Collections: Edwin C Shaw Archives
Subject Interests: Am Impressionism, Contemporary painting, Photog, Sculpture
Restriction: Non-circulating, Open by appt only, Photo ID required for access

G AKRON DEPARTMENT OF PLANNING & URBAN DEVELOPMENT LIBRARY*, 403 Municipal Bldg, 166 S High St, 44308. SAN 328-5871. Tel: 330-375-2084. FAX: 330-375-2387. E-mail: planlib@ci.akron.oh.us. *Librn,* Claudia A Burdge; *Asst Librn,* Mary Denise Robb
Library Holdings: Bk Vols 2,000; Per Subs 80
Restriction: Open by appt only

M AKRON GENERAL MEDICAL CENTER*, Medical Library, 400 Wabash Ave, 44307. SAN 313-1726. Tel: 330-344-6242. FAX: 330-344-1834. E-mail: library@agmc.org. Web Site: www.akrongeneral.org. *Librn,* Judy Knight; E-mail: jknight@agmc.org
Library Holdings: Bk Titles 3,000; Per Subs 300
Automation Activity & Vendor Info: (Acquisitions) Innovative Interfaces, Inc; (Cataloging) Innovative Interfaces, Inc; (Circulation) Innovative Interfaces, Inc; (OPAC) Innovative Interfaces, Inc; (Serials) Innovative Interfaces, Inc
Restriction: Staff use only

L AKRON LAW LIBRARY*, 209 S High St, 4th Flr, 44308-1675. SAN 313-1734. Tel: 330-643-2804. FAX: 330-535-0077. Web Site: www.akronlawlib.org. *Dir,* Alan Canfora; E-mail: acanfora@akronlawlib.org; *Asst Dir,* Amber Repp; E-mail: arepp@akronlawlib.org; Staff 4 (MLS 2, Non-MLS 2)
Founded 1888

Library Holdings: Bk Titles 7,953; Bk Vols 81,797; Per Subs 254
Automation Activity & Vendor Info: (Cataloging) EOS International; (Circulation) EOS International; (OPAC) EOS International; (Serials) EOS International
Database Vendor: Checkpoint Systems, Inc, LexisNexis, OCLC FirstSearch, OCLC WorldShare Interlibrary Loan, Westlaw
Wireless access
Open Mon-Fri 8-4:30

P AKRON-SUMMIT COUNTY PUBLIC LIBRARY*, 60 S High St, 44326. SAN 355-4465. Tel: 330-643-9000. Information Services Tel: 330-643-9010. FAX: 330-643-9160. TDD: 330-643-9005. Web Site: www.akronlibrary.org. *Dir, Cent Libr Serv,* David Jennings; Tel: 330-643-9100, E-mail: djennings@akronlibrary.org; *Dep Dir,* Pam Hickson-Stevenson; Tel: 330-643-9102, E-mail: phickson@akronlibrary.org; *Dir, Human Res,* Lisa Peercy; Tel: 330-643-9106, E-mail: lpeercy@akronlibrary.org; *Dir, Mkt,* Carla Davis; Tel: 330-643-9090, E-mail: cdavis@akronlibrary.org; *Fac Dir,* Carol Roxbury; *Tech Dir,* Ann Hutchison; E-mail: ahutchison@akronlibrary.org; *Br Mgr,* Barbara White; Tel: 330-643-9082, Fax: 330-643-9167, E-mail: bwhite@akronlibrary.org; *Fiscal Officer,* Michelle Scarpitti; E-mail: mscarpitti@akronlibrary.org; *Coll Develop Coordr,* Valerie Sherman; *Coordr, Youth Serv,* Carrie Burrier; E-mail: cburrier@akronlibrary.org; Staff 309 (MLS 118, Non-MLS 191)
Founded 1874. Pop 384,632; Circ 5,155,296
Library Holdings: AV Mats 275,126; Bk Titles 461,283; Bk Vols 1,640,985; Per Subs 1,838
Special Collections: Lighter-than-Air. State Document Depository; US Document Depository
Subject Interests: Genealogy, Local hist, Patents trademarks, Sci fair projects
Automation Activity & Vendor Info: (Acquisitions) SirsiDynix; (Cataloging) SirsiDynix; (Circulation) SirsiDynix; (OPAC) SirsiDynix; (Serials) SirsiDynix
Database Vendor: Gale Cengage Learning, SirsiDynix
Function: Govt ref serv, Health sci info serv, ILL available, Prog for adults, Prog for children & young adult, Ref serv available, Summer reading prog
Publications: Shelf Life (Newsletter)
Partic in Northeast Ohio Regional Library System; OCLC Online Computer Library Center, Inc
Special Services for the Deaf - High interest/low vocabulary bks; TTY equip
Special Services for the Blind - Reader equip
Open Mon-Thurs 9-9, Fri 9-6, Sat 9-5, Sun 1-5
Friends of the Library Group

Branches: 17

ELLET, 2470 E Market St, 44312, SAN 355-4619. Tel: 330-784-2019. FAX: 330-784-6692. *Br Mgr,* Marianna DiGiacomo; E-mail: mdigiacomo@akronlibrary.org; Staff 3 (MLS 3)
Circ 246,446
Library Holdings: Bk Vols 75,000
Open Mon, Tues & Thurs 10-8, Wed & Fri 12-6, Sat 10-5
Friends of the Library Group

FAIRLAWN-BATH, 3101 Smith Rd, 44333, SAN 355-4708. Tel: 330-666-4888. FAX: 330-666-8741. *Br Mgr,* Jane Scott; E-mail: jscott@akronlibrary.org; Staff 3 (MLS 3)
Circ 283,232
Library Holdings: Bk Vols 56,471
Open Mon, Tues & Thurs 10-8, Wed & Fri 12-6, Sat 10-5
Friends of the Library Group

FIRESTONE PARK, 1486 Aster Ave, 44301-2104, SAN 355-452X. Tel: 330-724-2126. FAX: 330-724-4391. *Br Mgr,* Michelle Alleman; E-mail: malleman@akronlibrary.org; Staff 3 (MLS 3)
Circ 135,905
Library Holdings: Bk Vols 41,729
Open Mon-Thurs 10-8:30, Fri 12-6, Sat 10-5
Friends of the Library Group

GOODYEAR, 60 Goodyear Blvd, 44305-4487, SAN 355-4589. Tel: 330-784-7522. FAX: 330-784-6599. *Br Mgr,* Deborah Catrone; E-mail: dcatrone@akronlibrary.org; Staff 3 (MLS 3)
Circ 112,462
Library Holdings: Bk Vols 50,103
Open Mon-Thurs 10-8:30, Fri 12-6, Sat 10-5
Friends of the Library Group

GREEN, 4046 Massillon Rd, Uniontown, 44685-4046, SAN 355-4643. Tel: 330-896-9074. FAX: 330-896-9412. *Br Mgr,* Sherry Swisher; E-mail: sswisher@akronlibrary.org; Staff 3 (MLS 3)
Circ 362,518
Library Holdings: Bk Vols 59,875
Open Mon, Tues & Thurs 10-8, Wed & Fri 12-6, Sat 10-5
Friends of the Library Group

HIGHLAND SQUARE, 807 W Market St, 44303-1010, SAN 355-497X. Tel: 330-376-2927. FAX: 330-376-9025. *Br Mgr,* Fred Baerkircher; E-mail: fbaerkircher@akronlibrary.org; Staff 2 (MLS 2)
Circ 135,644
Library Holdings: Bk Vols 48,106
Open Mon-Thurs 10-8:30, Fri 12-6, Sat 10-5
Friends of the Library Group

KENMORE, 969 Kenmore Blvd, 44314-2302, SAN 355-4678. Tel: 330-745-6126. FAX: 330-745-9947. *Br Mgr,* Mary Hickman; E-mail: mhickman@akronlibrary.org; Staff 2 (MLS 2)
Circ 169,179
Library Holdings: Bk Vols 53,218
Open Mon, Tues & Thurs 10-8, Wed & Fri 12-6, Sat 10-5
Friends of the Library Group

MAPLE VALLEY, 1187 Copley Rd, 44320-2766, SAN 355-4767. Tel: 330-864-5721. FAX: 330-864-8971. *Br Mgr,* Tonya Wright; E-mail: twright@akronlibrary.org; Staff 3 (MLS 3)
Circ 111,244
Library Holdings: Bk Vols 49,810
Open Mon-Thurs 10-8:30, Fri 12-6, Sat 10-5
Friends of the Library Group

MOGADORE BRANCH, 144 S Cleveland Ave, Mogadore, 44260, SAN 355-4791. Tel: 330-628-9228. FAX: 330-628-3256. *Br Mgr,* Kimberlie DeBenedictis; E-mail: kdebenedictis@akronlibrary.org; Staff 7 (MLS 3, Non-MLS 4)
Circ 200,509
Library Holdings: Bk Vols 56,529
Special Services for the Blind - Vantage closed circuit TV magnifier
Open Mon, Tues & Thurs 10-8, Wed & Fri 12-6, Sat 10-5
Friends of the Library Group

NORDONIA HILLS, 9458 Olde Eight Rd, Northfield, 44067-1952, SAN 355-4856. Tel: 330-467-8595. FAX: 330-467-4332. *Br Mgr,* Patrick Manning; E-mail: pmanning@akronlibrary.org; Staff 3 (MLS 3)
Circ 272,393
Library Holdings: Bk Vols 60,153
Open Mon, Tues & Thurs 10-8, Wed & Fri 12-6, Sat 10-5
Friends of the Library Group

NORTH HILL, 183 E Cuyahoga Falls Ave, 44310-3078, SAN 355-4821. Tel: 330-535-9423. FAX: 330-376-5661. *Br Mgr,* Lisa Weiser; E-mail: lweiser@akronlibrary.org; *Early Childhood Librn,* Sally Bailey; E-mail: sbailey@akronlibrary.org; *Teen/Intermediate Librn,* Emily Yohn; E-mail: eyohn@akronlibrary.org; Staff 3 (MLS 3)
Circ 64,339
Open Mon-Thurs 10-8:30, Fri 12-6, Sat 10-5
Friends of the Library Group

NORTHWEST AKRON, 1720 Shatto Ave, 44313, SAN 355-449X. Tel: 330-836-1081. FAX: 330-836-1574. *Br Mgr,* Tricia Twarogowski; E-mail: ttwarogowski@akronlibrary.org; Staff 3 (MLS 3)
Circ 343,977
Library Holdings: Bk Vols 59,145
Open Mon, Tues & Thurs 10-8, Wed & Fri 12-6, Sat 10-5
Friends of the Library Group

NORTON BRANCH, 3930 S Cleveland-Massillon Rd, Norton, 44203-5563, SAN 355-4880. Tel: 330-825-7800. FAX: 330-825-5155. *Br Mgr,* Catherine Clements; E-mail: cclement@akronlibrary.org; Staff 3 (MLS 3)
Circ 232,531
Library Holdings: Bk Vols 58,360
Open Mon-Thurs 10-8:30, Fri 12-6, Sat 10-5
Friends of the Library Group

ODOM BOULEVARD, 600 Vernon Odom Blvd, 44307-1828, SAN 355-5003. Tel: 330-434-8726. FAX: 330-434-3750. *Br Mgr,* Cheryl Chlysta, E-mail: cchlysta@akronlibrary.org; Staff 9 (MLS 2, Non-MLS 7)
Founded 1923. Circ 118,199
Library Holdings: Bk Vols 61,827
Open Mon, Tues & Thurs 10-8, Wed & Fri 12-6, Sat 10-5
Friends of the Library Group

PORTAGE LAKES, 4261 Manchester Rd, 44319-2659, SAN 370-3509. Tel: 330-644-7050. FAX: 330-644-0977. *Br Mgr,* Cheryl Luck; Staff 2 (MLS 2)
Circ 189,524
Library Holdings: Bk Vols 51,177
Open Mon, Tues & Thurs 10-8, Wed & Fri 12-6, Sat 10-5
Friends of the Library Group

RICHFIELD BRANCH, 3761 S Grant St, Richfield, 44286-9603, SAN 355-4910. Tel: 330-659-4343. FAX: 330-659-6205. *Br Mgr,* Jennifer Stencel; E-mail: jstencel@akronlibrary.org; Staff 3 (MLS 3)
Circ 199,729
Library Holdings: Bk Vols 50,388
Open Mon, Tues & Thurs 10-8, Wed & Fri 12-6, Sat 10-5
Friends of the Library Group

TALLMADGE BRANCH, 90 Community Rd, Tallmadge, 44278, SAN 355-4945. Tel: 330-633-4345. FAX: 330-633-6324. *Br Mgr,* Denise Lee; E-mail: dlee@akronlibrary.org; Staff 3 (MLS 3)
Circ 236,361
Library Holdings: Bk Vols 54,613
Subject Interests: Local hist
Open Mon, Tues & Thurs 10-8, Wed & Fri 12-6, Sat 10-5

Friends of the Library Group
Bookmobiles: 2

S BRIDGESTONE/FIRESTONE RESEARCH LLC*, Bridgestone Americas Center for Research & Technology, 1200 Firestone Pkwy, 44317. SAN 355-5062. Tel: 330-379-7630. FAX: 330-379-7530. *Sr Res Librn,* David Koo
Founded 1945
Library Holdings: Bk Titles 6,000; Bk Vols 15,000; Per Subs 100
Database Vendor: American Chemical Society, Dialog, Gale Cengage Learning, ScienceDirect, STN International
Partic in Dialog Corp
Restriction: Staff use only

R CHRIST UNITED METHODIST CHURCH LIBRARY*, The Helen Stahler Library, 380 Mineola Ave, 44320-1935. SAN 328-1574. Tel: 330-836-5563. FAX: 330-836-7209. *Librn,* Marilyn Frank; Staff 10 (MLS 1, Non-MLS 9)
Founded 1959
Library Holdings: DVDs 32; High Interest/Low Vocabulary Bk Vols 28; Large Print Bks 28; Bk Vols 3,791; Talking Bks 89; Videos 345
Special Collections: Children's books
Subject Interests: Fiction, Relig
Automation Activity & Vendor Info: (Acquisitions) Book Systems; (Cataloging) Book Systems
Wireless access
Open Mon-Fri 8:30-12 & 12:30-4
Friends of the Library Group

S FIRSTENERGY CORP*, Business Information Center, 76 S Main St, A-GO-17, 44308. SAN 321-3951. Tel: 330-384-4934. FAX: 330-255-1099. *Res,* Susan R Lloyd; E-mail: lloyds@firstenergycorp.com; Staff 1 (Non-MLS 1)
Founded 1981
Library Holdings: Bk Vols 17,000; Per Subs 10
Special Collections: Edison Electric Institute Reports; Electric Power Research Institute Reports; Industry Standards
Subject Interests: Electric power, Energy, Utilities industry
Database Vendor: Dialog, EBSCOhost, Factiva.com, Westlaw
Function: ILL available
Restriction: Employees & their associates, Open to others by appt

M MARY HOWER MEDICAL LIBRARY*, One Perkins Sq, 44308-1062. SAN 329-8566. Tel: 330-543-8250. *Libr Mgr,* Alyssa Portwood; Staff 3.75 (MLS 1, Non-MLS 2.75)
Library Holdings: Per Subs 200
Subject Interests: Pediatrics & burn injuries
Function: Res libr
Restriction: Staff use only

S NORTHEAST OHIO FOUR COUNTY REGIONAL PLANNING & DEVELOPMENT ORGANIZATION*, 180 E South St, 44311. SAN 328-5340. Tel: 330-252-0337. FAX: 330-252-0664. *Exec Dir,* Joseph Hadley
Library Holdings: Bk Titles 3,500

S OMNOVA SOLUTIONS INC*, Technical Information Center, 2990 Gilchrist Rd, 44305. SAN 313-1742. Tel: 330-794-6382. Toll Free Tel: 888-253-5454. FAX: 330-794-6375. Web Site: www.omnova.com. *Librn,* Barbara Hubal
Founded 1946
Library Holdings: Bk Vols 9,000; Per Subs 50
Subject Interests: Adhesives, Plastics, Polymer chem, Rubber
Database Vendor: Dialog
Partic in Dialog Corp

M SUMMA HEALTH SYSTEM*, Medical Library, 55 N Arch, Ste G-3, 44304. SAN 313-1718. Tel: 330-375-3260. FAX: 330-375-3978. *Syst Librn,* Wendy Hess; *Ref,* Heather Holme; Staff 5 (MLS 3, Non-MLS 2)
Founded 1930
Library Holdings: Bk Titles 2,500; Per Subs 280
Subject Interests: Ethics
Automation Activity & Vendor Info: (Cataloging) Innovative Interfaces, Inc; (Circulation) Innovative Interfaces, Inc
Open Mon-Fri 8-4:30

C UNIVERSITY OF AKRON LIBRARIES*, Bierce Library, 315 Buchtel Mall, 44325-1701. SAN 355-5127. Tel: 330-972-7495. Circulation Tel: 330-972-7656. Interlibrary Loan Service Tel: 330-972-6275. Information Services Tel: 330-972-3056. FAX: 330-972-5106. Interlibrary Loan Service FAX: 330-972-6383. Reference FAX: 330-972-6059. Web Site: www.uakron.edu/libraries. *Interim Dean,* Phyllis G O'Connor; Tel: 330-972-6057, E-mail: oconnor@uakron.edu; *Asst Dean, Univ Libr,* Nancy L Stokes; Tel: 330-972-7017, E-mail: nstokes@uakron.edu; *Head, Acq,* Julia A Gammon; Tel: 330-972-6254, E-mail: jgammon@uakron.edu; *Head, Archival Serv,* Victor S Fleischer; Tel: 330-972-6253, Fax: 330-972-6170, E-mail: svfleis@uakron.edu; *Head, Circ,* Melanie F Smith; Tel: 330-972-7047, E-mail: melani6@uakron.edu; *Head, Coll Mgt,* Peter Linberger; Tel: 330-972-8230, E-mail: pl@uakron.edu; *Head, Libr Syst,* Susan DiRenzo Ashby; Tel: 330-972-7240, E-mail: direnzo@uakron.edu; *Head, Ref,* Jeffrey Franks; Tel: 330-972-6052, Fax: 330-972-2317, E-mail: jfranks@uakron.edu; *Head, Teaching & Training,* Michael P Tosko; Tel: 330-972-2648, E-mail: tosko@uakron.edu; Staff 62 (MLS 29, Non-MLS 33)
Founded 1872. Enrl 26,257; Fac 797; Highest Degree: Doctorate
Jul 2006-Jun 2007. Mats Exp $5,019,784, Books $915,499, Per/Ser (Incl. Access Fees) $2,210,198, Electronic Ref Mat (Incl. Access Fees) $1,894,087. Sal $3,164,711 (Prof $1,743,291)
Library Holdings: AV Mats 48,423; Bks on Deafness & Sign Lang 884; CDs 4,022; DVDs 928; e-books 2,789; e-journals 1,655,555; Electronic Media & Resources 263; Microforms 168,381; Music Scores 27,960; Bk Vols 1,259,804; Per Subs 15,266
Special Collections: B-26 Archives; Brozek Coll; Herman Muehlstein Rare Book Coll; Paul Belcher Coll; Propaganda Coll, flm; Sylvia Smith Archives; The Archives of the History of American Psychology & the American History Research Center; The University of Akron Archives. State Document Depository; US Document Depository
Subject Interests: Hist of psychol, Polymer, Polymer chem, Rubber indust
Automation Activity & Vendor Info: (Acquisitions) Innovative Interfaces, Inc; (Cataloging) Innovative Interfaces, Inc; (Circulation) Innovative Interfaces, Inc; (Course Reserve) Docutek; (ILL) OCLC; (Media Booking) Innovative Interfaces, Inc; (OPAC) Innovative Interfaces, Inc; (Serials) Innovative Interfaces, Inc
Database Vendor: ARTstor
Wireless access
Partic in BRS; Center for Research Libraries; OCLC Online Computer Library Center, Inc; OHIONET
Friends of the Library Group

Departmental Libraries:

CL SCHOOL OF LAW LIBRARY, 150 University Ave, 44325. (Mail add: 302 Buchtel Common, 44325). Tel: 330-972-7330. FAX: 330-972-4948. Web Site: www.uakron.edu/law. *Dir,* Paul Richert; E-mail: richert@uakron.edu; *Dep Law Librn,* Kyle Passmore; E-mail: passmore@uakron.edu; *Circ Supvr,* Tiffanie Nevins
Library Holdings: AV Mats 1,772; Electronic Media & Resources 7,459; Microforms 19,458; Bk Titles 46,195
Partic in Ohio Library & Information Network
Open Mon-Fri 7am-11pm, Sat 9-9, Sun 10am-11pm
Friends of the Library Group

SCIENCE & TECHNOLOGY, Auburn Science Engineering Center, No 104, 44325-3907. (Mail add: 244 Sumner St, 44325-3907). Tel: 330-972-8323. Reference Tel: 330-972-7195. Administration Tel: 330-972-8196. FAX: 330-972-7033. E-mail: scilib@uakron.edu. *Head Librn,* Jo Ann Calzonetti; E-mail: jc44@uakron.edu; Staff 7.5 (MLS 4.5, Non-MLS 3)
Enrl 26,000; Fac 4; Highest Degree: Doctorate
Special Collections: Rubber
Function: Handicapped accessible
Open Mon & Thurs 7:30am-11pm, Fri 7:30-6, Sat 9-6, Sun 1-11
Restriction: Badge access after hrs
Friends of the Library Group

ALEXANDRIA

P ALEXANDRIA PUBLIC LIBRARY, Ten Maple Dr, 43001. (Mail add: PO Box 67, 43001-0067), SAN 313-1815. Tel: 740-924-3561. Automation Services Toll Free Tel: 877-772-6657. FAX: 740-924-3007. Web Site: www.alexandrialibrary.org. *Dir of Libr,* Denise Shedloski; E-mail: dshedloski@alexandria.lib.oh.us
Founded 1935. Pop 5,800; Circ 86,500
Library Holdings: Audiobooks 800; AV Mats 7,300; CDs 2,500; DVDs 1,000; Large Print Bks 2,850; Bk Titles 47,000; Per Subs 90; Talking Bks 800; Videos 3,000
Subject Interests: Local hist
Database Vendor: Baker & Taylor, Checkpoint Systems, Inc, Comprise Technologies Inc, EBSCOhost, Gale Cengage Learning, OHIONET, Overdrive, Inc, ProQuest
Wireless access
Function: Accelerated reader prog, Adult bk club, After school storytime, AV serv, Bk club(s), Bks on cassette, Bks on CD, Children's prog, Computers for patron use, Copy machines, Fax serv, Free DVD rentals, Handicapped accessible, ILL available, Mail & tel request accepted, Music CDs, Online cat, Online ref, Online searches, Prog for adults, Prog for children & young adult, Pub access computers, Story hour, Summer reading prog, Tax forms, Teen prog, VHS videos, Web-catalog
Publications: Inside the Alexandria Public Library (Newsletter)
Partic in Central Library Consortium (CLC)
Special Services for the Deaf - Bks on deafness & sign lang

Special Services for the Blind - Bks on cassette; Bks on CD; Cassettes; Copier with enlargement capabilities; Extensive large print coll; Large print bks
Open Mon, Tues & Thurs 10-8, Wed & Sat 10-4
Friends of the Library Group

ALGER

P ALGER PUBLIC LIBRARY*, 100 W Wagner St, 45812. (Mail add: PO Box 18, 45812-0018), SAN 313-1823. Tel: 419-757-7755. FAX: 419-757-0290. Web Site: www.algerlibrary.org. *Dir,* Kathy Herfurth; E-mail: herfurka@oplin.org
Pop 2,500
Library Holdings: Large Print Bks 300; Bk Vols 10,000; Per Subs 14; Videos 850
Wireless access
Function: AV serv, Bks on CD, Children's prog, Computers for patron use, Copy machines, Online cat, Photocopying/Printing, Prog for children & young adult, Summer reading prog, Wheelchair accessible
Partic in SEO (Serving Every Ohioan) Library Center
Open Mon-Thurs 1-7, Fri 1-5, Sat 10-1

ALLIANCE

P RODMAN PUBLIC LIBRARY*, 215 E Broadway St, 44601-2694. SAN 313-1858. Tel: 330-821-2665. FAX: 330-821-5053. Web Site: www.rodmanlibrary.com. *Dir,* Patricia Stone; E-mail: pstone@rodmanlibrary.com; *Head, Ref,* Penny Neubauer; *Adult Serv Mgr,* JoAnn Hodgekin; *Tech Serv & Syst Mgr,* Karen Perone; Staff 20 (MLS 8, Non-MLS 12)
Founded 1900. Pop 38,827; Circ 429,169
Library Holdings: CDs 3,729; DVDs 1,361; Large Print Bks 6,292; Bk Titles 123,736; Bk Vols 169,123; Per Subs 589; Talking Bks 6,489; Videos 7,932
Special Collections: Original Drawings by Brinton Turkle. Oral History
Automation Activity & Vendor Info: (Acquisitions) Innovative Interfaces, Inc; (Cataloging) Innovative Interfaces, Inc; (Circulation) Innovative Interfaces, Inc; (OPAC) Innovative Interfaces, Inc; (Serials) Innovative Interfaces, Inc
Wireless access
Function: AV serv, Homebound delivery serv, ILL available, Magnifiers for reading, Photocopying/Printing, Prog for children & young adult, Ref serv available, Summer reading prog
Publications: Bibliographies; Genealogies
Partic in Ohio Public Library Information Network; OHIONET
Special Services for the Deaf - Bks on deafness & sign lang; Closed caption videos; Coll on deaf educ
Special Services for the Blind - Assistive/Adapted tech devices, equip & products; BiFolkal kits; Bks & mags in Braille, on rec, tape & cassette; Bks on cassette; Bks on CD; Computer with voice synthesizer for visually impaired persons; Copier with enlargement capabilities; Extensive large print coll; Large print bks & talking machines; Large screen computer & software; PC for handicapped; Screen enlargement software for people with visual disabilities; Screen reader software; Talking bks & player equip
Open Mon-Wed 9-9, Thurs-Sat 9-5:30
Restriction: Residents only
Friends of the Library Group
Branches: 1
BRANCH IN THE MALL, 2500 W State St, 44601, SAN 374-4485. Tel: 330-821-1313. *Br Mgr,* Charlene Duro; Staff 3 (MLS 1, Non-MLS 2)
Founded 1990. Pop 38,525; Circ 95,806
Open Mon & Tues 10-8, Wed & Fri 10-5:30, Sat 10-3:30
Friends of the Library Group
Bookmobiles: 1

C UNIVERSITY OF MOUNT UNION LIBRARY*, 1972 Clark Ave, 44601-3993. SAN 313-184X. Tel: 330-823-3844. Circulation Tel: 330-823-4140. Interlibrary Loan Service Tel: 330-829-6659. Reference Tel: 330-823-3795. FAX: 330-823-3963. Web Site: www.mountunion.edu/library. *Dir,* Robert Garland; E-mail: garlanrr@mountunion.edu; *Cat,* Linda Scott; *Circ,* Gina Maida; *ILL,* Christine Cochran; *Ser,* Rebekah Bosler; Staff 6 (MLS 6)
Founded 1846. Enrl 2,110; Fac 125; Highest Degree: Bachelor
Library Holdings: Bk Vols 185,000; Per Subs 174
Special Collections: Graphic Arts (Shilts Rare Books); Greek & Latin Classics (Charles Sutherin). US Document Depository
Subject Interests: Secondary educ
Automation Activity & Vendor Info: (Acquisitions) Innovative Interfaces, Inc; (Cataloging) Innovative Interfaces, Inc; (Circulation) Innovative Interfaces, Inc; (Course Reserve) Innovative Interfaces, Inc; (ILL) Innovative Interfaces, Inc; (OPAC) Innovative Interfaces, Inc; (Serials) Innovative Interfaces, Inc
Wireless access
Partic in Dialog Corp; Mideastern Ohio Libr Orgn; OCLC Online Computer Library Center, Inc; Ohio Library & Information Network; Ohio Private Academic Libraries (OPAL); OHIONET
Open Mon-Thurs 7am-Midnight, Fri 7:30-5, Sat 9-5, Sun Noon-Midnight

AMHERST

P AMHERST PUBLIC LIBRARY*, 221 Spring St, 44001. SAN 313-1866. Tel: 440-988-4230. FAX: 440-988-4115. Web Site: amherst.lib.oh.us. *Dir,* Donald Dovala; E-mail: dovalado@oplin.org; *Circ Mgr,* Dorene Sweet; *Ref Serv Mgr,* Janet Turner; *Tech Serv Mgr,* Mary Geer; *Youth Serv Mgr,* Cheryl Ashton; *Fiscal Officer,* Kathi Blakey; Staff 12 (MLS 2, Non-MLS 10)
Founded 1906. Pop 22,545; Circ 240,700
Library Holdings: Bk Vols 57,000; Per Subs 142
Automation Activity & Vendor Info: (Cataloging) TLC (The Library Corporation); (Circulation) TLC (The Library Corporation); (OPAC) TLC (The Library Corporation)
Wireless access
Partic in Ohio Public Library Information Network
Open Mon-Thurs 9-8:30, Fri & Sat 10-5, Sun (Sept-May) 1-5
Friends of the Library Group

ANDOVER

P ANDOVER PUBLIC LIBRARY, 142 W Main St, 44003-9318. (Mail add: PO Box 1210, 44003-1210), SAN 313-1882. Tel: 440-293-6792. FAX: 440-293-5720. E-mail: info@andoverlibrary.com. Web Site: www.andover.lib.oh.us. *Dir,* Susan Hill; E-mail: hillsu@andoverlibrary.com; *Head, Ch,* Betsy Paul; *Head, Ref,* Laura York; Staff 7 (MLS 1, Non-MLS 6)
Founded 1934. Pop 7,600; Circ 99,117
Library Holdings: Audiobooks 3,571; AV Mats 1,424; Bks on Deafness & Sign Lang 3; CDs 240; DVDs 349; e-books 783; Electronic Media & Resources 260; Large Print Bks 1,722; Bk Titles 29,726; Per Subs 83; Talking Bks 624; Videos 1,362
Special Collections: Local History Coll
Automation Activity & Vendor Info: (Acquisitions) SirsiDynix; (Cataloging) SirsiDynix; (Circulation) BiblioCommons; (ILL) BiblioCommons; (OPAC) SirsiDynix
Database Vendor: SirsiDynix
Wireless access
Open Mon-Thurs 10-7, Fri 10-6, Sat 10-2
Friends of the Library Group

ARCANUM

P ARCANUM PUBLIC LIBRARY*, 101 W North St, 45304-1126. SAN 313-1890. Tel: 937-692-8484. FAX: 937-692-8916. Web Site: www.arcanumpubliclibrary.org. *Dir,* Marilyn Walden; E-mail: waldenm1@oplin.org; *Assoc Dir,* Deborah Fourman; E-mail: deb_4man@yahoo.com
Founded 1911. Pop 9,000; Circ 68,341
Library Holdings: Bk Vols 54,325; Per Subs 204
Automation Activity & Vendor Info: (Cataloging) Follett Software; (Circulation) Follett Software
Partic in Miami Valley Librs
Open Mon-Thurs 9-8, Fri 9-5, Sat 9-1

ARCHBOLD

P ARCHBOLD COMMUNITY LIBRARY*, 205 Stryker St, 43502-1142. SAN 313-1904. Tel: 419-446-2783. FAX: 419-446-2142. Web Site: www.archboldlibrary.org. *Dir,* Joyce Klingelsmith; E-mail: joyce.k@archboldlibrary.org; *Fiscal Officer,* Jennifer Harkey; E-mail: jennifer.h@archboldlibrary.org; *Mgr, Circ Serv,* Muriel King; *Mgr, Tech Serv,* Ruth Grieser; *Youth Serv,* Brenda Sensenig; E-mail: brenda.s@archboldlibrary.org; Staff 11 (Non-MLS 11)
Founded 1917. Pop 6,500; Circ 160,439
Library Holdings: Bk Vols 27,000; Per Subs 110
Subject Interests: Local hist
Automation Activity & Vendor Info: (Cataloging) TLC (The Library Corporation); (Circulation) TLC (The Library Corporation); (OPAC) TLC (The Library Corporation)
Wireless access
Publications: Update (Newsletter)
Partic in NORWELD; Ohio Libr Coun
Open Mon, Tues & Thurs 9:30-8:30, Wed & Fri 9:30-5:30, Sat 9:30-3

J NORTHWEST STATE COMMUNITY COLLEGE LIBRARY*, 22600 State Rte 34, 43502-9517. SAN 313-1912. Tel: 419-267-1272. FAX: 419-267-5657. E-mail: library@northweststate.edu. *Dir,* Kristi Rotroff; E-mail: krotroff@northweststate.edu; Staff 1 (MLS 1)
Founded 1969. Enrl 3,000; Fac 137; Highest Degree: Associate
Library Holdings: Bk Titles 20,000; Per Subs 375

Automation Activity & Vendor Info: (Acquisitions) Innovative Interfaces, Inc; (Circulation) Innovative Interfaces, Inc; (Course Reserve) Innovative Interfaces, Inc; (ILL) Innovative Interfaces, Inc; (Media Booking) Innovative Interfaces, Inc; (OPAC) Innovative Interfaces, Inc; (Serials) Innovative Interfaces, Inc
Wireless access
Partic in OCLC Online Computer Library Center, Inc; Ohio Library & Information Network; OHIONET
Open Mon-Thurs 7:30am-8:30pm, Fri 7:30-4, Sat 9-2

ASHLAND

P ASHLAND PUBLIC LIBRARY*, 224 Claremont Ave, 44805. SAN 313-1920. Tel: 419-289-8188. Circulation Tel: 419-289-8188, Ext 13, 14. Reference Tel: 419-289-8188, Ext 15. FAX: 419-281-8552. Web Site: www.ashland.lib.oh.us. *Dir,* William Rutger; E-mail: wrutger@ashland.lib.oh.us; *Head, Ad Ref Serv,* Theresa Schenk-Webster; E-mail: twebster@ashland.lib.oh.us; *Head, Circ,* Susan Brown; E-mail: sbrown@ashland.lib.oh.us; *Head, Tech Serv,* Jennifer Bull; Tel: 419-289-8188, Ext 19, E-mail: jbull@ashland.lib.oh.us; *Librn,* Kristie Morrison; E-mail: kmorris@ashland.lib.oh.us; *Youth Serv,* Brenda Guggenbiller; Tel: 419-289-8188, Ext 16, E-mail: bhogan@ashland.lib.oh.us; Staff 7 (MLS 4, Non-MLS 3)
Founded 1893. Pop 52,000; Circ 614,000
Library Holdings: AV Mats 15,000; Bk Vols 130,000; Per Subs 250
Subject Interests: Genealogy, Local hist
Automation Activity & Vendor Info: (Cataloging) SirsiDynix; (Circulation) SirsiDynix; (OPAC) SirsiDynix
Database Vendor: EBSCOhost, SirsiDynix
Partic in Northeast Ohio Regional Library System; Ohio Public Library Information Network
Open Mon-Thurs 9-9, Fri & Sat 9-5
Friends of the Library Group
Bookmobiles: 1

R ASHLAND THEOLOGICAL SEMINARY*, Roger E Darling Memorial Library, 910 Center St, 44805. SAN 313-1939. Tel: 419-289-5169. Reference Tel: 419-289-5434. FAX: 419-289-5969. Web Site: library.ashland.edu. *Dir,* Sylvia L Locher; Tel: 419-289-5168, E-mail: slocher@ashland.edu; *Digital Serv Librn,* Sarah Thomas; E-mail: sthomas4@ashland.edu; Staff 6 (MLS 2, Non-MLS 4)
Founded 1930. Enrl 801; Highest Degree: Doctorate
Library Holdings: Bk Titles 70,980; Bk Vols 82,212; Per Subs 480
Special Collections: artifacts; Mary, Queen of Scots (Ronk Coll); Religious Debates (Darling Debate)
Automation Activity & Vendor Info: (Cataloging) Innovative Interfaces, Inc; (Circulation) Innovative Interfaces, Inc; (OPAC) Innovative Interfaces, Inc; (Serials) Innovative Interfaces, Inc
Database Vendor: EBSCOhost
Partic in Ohio Library & Information Network
Open Mon-Thurs (Winter) 7:45am-10pm, Fri 7:45-5, Sat 10-5; Mon-Thurs (Summer) 8-7, Fri 8-4

C ASHLAND UNIVERSITY LIBRARY, 509 College Ave, 44805-3796. SAN 355-5186. Tel: 419-289-5400. Reference Tel: 419-289-5402. FAX: 419-289-5422. E-mail: library@ashland.edu. Web Site: www.ashland.edu/students/library. *Co-Dir,* Janice Marotta; E-mail: jmarotta@ashland.edu; *Co-Dir,* Sue Ellen Ronk; E-mail: sronk@ashland.edu; *Instrul Serv Librn,* Diane Schrecker; E-mail: dschreck@ashland.edu; *Ref Librn,* Kathern Venditti; E-mail: kvenditt@ashland.edu; *Acq,* Joan Hignett; E-mail: jhignett@ashland.edu; *Ref,* Jeffrey Pinkham; E-mail: jpinkham@ashland.edu; Staff 8 (MLS 6, Non-MLS 2)
Founded 1878. Enrl 5,979; Fac 257; Highest Degree: Doctorate
Library Holdings: CDs 2,186; DVDs 618; e-books 249,000; e-journals 114,007; Bk Titles 174,296; Bk Vols 202,533; Per Subs 280
Special Collections: 19th Century English Literature (Andrews Special Books Coll), 1st editions; 19th Century Historical Children's Literature (Lulu Wood Coll), 1st editions; American Studies (Libr of American Civilization), microbk; Bibles. State Document Depository; US Document Depository
Subject Interests: Art, Chem, Criminal justice, Econ, Educ, Geol, Health educ, Human serv home econ, Math, Music, Philos, Physics, Radio-TV, Relig, Speech comm, Theatre, Toxicology
Automation Activity & Vendor Info: (Cataloging) Innovative Interfaces, Inc; (Circulation) Innovative Interfaces, Inc; (OPAC) Innovative Interfaces, Inc
Database Vendor: EBSCOhost, Gale Cengage Learning, LexisNexis, OCLC FirstSearch
Wireless access
Publications: Friends of Library (Newsletter)
Partic in OCLC Online Computer Library Center, Inc; Ohio Library & Information Network; OHIONET
Open Mon-Thurs 8am-11pm, Fri 8-5, Sat 11-4, Sun 2-11
Friends of the Library Group

ASHLEY

P WORNSTAFF MEMORIAL PUBLIC LIBRARY*, 302 E High St, 43003-9703. (Mail add: PO Box 358, 43003-0358), SAN 313-1947. Tel: 740-747-2085. FAX: 740-747-2085. E-mail: wornstaff@oplin.org. Web Site: www.wornstafflibrary.blogspot.com. *Dir,* Jane Horn; *Ch Serv,* Megan Burns; Staff 8 (MLS 2, Non-MLS 6)
Founded 1928. Pop 2,500; Circ 32,434
Jan 2010-Dec 2010 Income $187,021, State $118,218, Federal $2,494, Locally Generated Income $6,916, Other $56,392. Mats Exp $15,485, Books $11,503, AV Equip $500, AV Mat $3,482. Sal $93,972 (Prof $29,545)
Library Holdings: AV Mats 3,885; Large Print Bks 1,016; Bk Vols 35,535; Per Subs 105; Talking Bks 367
Subject Interests: Local hist, Mysteries, Old westerns
Automation Activity & Vendor Info: (Cataloging) Follett Software; (Circulation) Follett Software; (OPAC) Follett Software
Function: Handicapped accessible, Home delivery & serv to Sr ctr & nursing homes, Homebound delivery serv, ILL available, Photocopying/Printing, Prog for adults, Prog for children & young adult, Ref serv available, Telephone ref, Wheelchair accessible
Publications: Newsletter (Monthly)
Partic in Ohio Public Library Information Network
Open Mon-Fri 10-8, Sat 10-5

ASHTABULA

P ASHTABULA COUNTY DISTRICT LIBRARY, 335 W 44th St, 44004-6897. SAN 355-5305. Tel: 440-997-9341. FAX: 440-992-7714. Administration FAX: 440-998-1198. TDD: 440-992-8066. E-mail: ashref@oplin.org. Web Site: www.acdl.info. *Dir,* William J Tokarczyk; Tel: 440-997-9341, Ext 224, Fax: 440-998-6098, E-mail: tokarcwi@oplin.org; *Asst Dir,* Penny Neubauer; Tel: 440-997-9341, Ext 222, E-mail: pneubauer@oplin.org; *Head, Ref,* Douglas Anderson; Tel: 440-997-9341, Ext 225, E-mail: andersodo@oplin.org; *Head, Youth Serv,* Barbara Tack; Tel: 440-997-9341, Ext 230, E-mail: tackba@oplin.org; Staff 29.83 (MLS 7, Non-MLS 22.83)
Founded 1813. Pop 52,668; Circ 239,710
Jan 2013-Dec 2013 Income (Main Library and Branch(s)) $1,568,691, State $1,208,708, Locally Generated Income $83,000. Mats Exp $195,851, Books $110,112, Per/Ser (Incl. Access Fees) $16,000, Manu Arch $1,031, Micro $3,100, AV Mat $45,608, Electronic Ref Mat (Incl. Access Fees) $20,000. Sal $750,181 (Prof $340,000)
Library Holdings: AV Mats 16,439; CDs 726; DVDs 5,955; e-books 616; Bk Vols 182,517; Talking Bks 5,299; Videos 4,459
Special Collections: Ohio Room Local History Coll. State Document Depository
Automation Activity & Vendor Info: (Acquisitions) SirsiDynix; (Cataloging) SirsiDynix; (Circulation) SirsiDynix; (ILL) OCLC WorldShare Interlibrary Loan; (OPAC) SirsiDynix
Database Vendor: Baker & Taylor, EBSCOhost, Gale Cengage Learning, Ingram Library Services, OCLC WorldShare Interlibrary Loan, Overdrive, Inc, ProQuest
Wireless access
Function: ILL available, Outside serv via phone, mail, e-mail & web, OverDrive digital audio bks, Photocopying/Printing, Preschool outreach, Prog for adults, Prog for children & young adult, Pub access computers, Ref serv in person, Senior computer classes, Story hour, Summer reading prog, Tax forms, Teen prog, Telephone ref, VHS videos, Web-catalog, Wheelchair accessible, Workshops
Publications: (Your) Library Matters (Quarterly)
Partic in Northeast Ohio Regional Library System; OCLC Online Computer Library Center, Inc
Special Services for the Deaf - Closed caption videos; TDD equip; TTY equip
Special Services for the Blind - Aids for in-house use; BiFolkal kits; Bks on cassette; Bks on CD; Cassette playback machines; Copier with enlargement capabilities; Descriptive video serv (DVS); Extensive large print coll; Home delivery serv; Large print bks; Magnifiers; Talking bks; Text reader
Open Mon-Wed 10-8, Thurs 10-6, Fri 10-5, Sat 10-4
Friends of the Library Group
Branches: 1
GENEVA PUBLIC, 860 Sherman St, Geneva, 44041. (Mail add: 335 W 44th St, 44004-6897), SAN 355-533X. Tel: 440-466-4521. FAX: 440-466-0162. TDD: 440-466-9268. E-mail: genref@oplin.org. *Librn,* Mary Stokes; E-mail: stokesma@oplin.org
Founded 1832
Special Collections: Archie Bell Materials; Ashtabula County Geneological Society; Leander Lyon Coll; Platt R Spencer Materials
Function: Archival coll, Bks on CD, Children's prog, Computer training, Computers for patron use, Copy machines, Electronic databases & coll, Fax serv, Free DVD rentals, Handicapped accessible, Holiday prog, Home delivery & serv to Sr ctr & nursing homes, Homebound delivery

serv, ILL available, Magnifiers for reading, Mail & tel request accepted, Music CDs, Online cat, Online ref, OverDrive digital audio bks, Photocopying/Printing, Preschool outreach, Prog for adults, Prog for children & young adult, Pub access computers, Ref serv in person, Story hour, Summer reading prog, Tax forms, Teen prog, Telephone ref, Web-catalog, Wheelchair accessible, Workshops
Special Services for the Deaf - TTY equip
Open Mon-Thurs (Winter) 9:30-8, Fri & Sat 9:30-4:30, Sun 1-4; Mon-Thurs (Summer) 9:30-8, Fri 9:30-4:30, Sat 9:30-1:30
Friends of the Library Group
Bookmobiles: 1. Branch Extension Servs Coord, Mary Stokes

P HARBOR-TOPKY MEMORIAL LIBRARY*, 1633 Walnut Blvd, 44004. SAN 313-1963. Tel: 440-964-9645. FAX: 440-964-6701. E-mail: harbor@oplin.org. Web Site: www.harbortopky.lib.oh.us. *Dir,* Joseph Zappitello; *Head, Ref & Adult Serv,* Andy Pochatko; E-mail: pochana@oplin.org; *Head, Youth Serv,* Kathy Eames; E-mail: eameska@oplin.org; Staff 11 (MLS 3, Non-MLS 8)
Founded 1924. Pop 4,200; Circ 150,009
Library Holdings: AV Mats 7,135; CDs 2,608; Bk Vols 50,364; Per Subs 126
Automation Activity & Vendor Info: (Acquisitions) Horizon; (Cataloging) LibLime; (Circulation) LibLime; (ILL) SirsiDynix; (OPAC) Horizon
Database Vendor: EBSCOhost, Gale Cengage Learning, Newsbank, SirsiDynix
Function: Homebound delivery serv, ILL available, Photocopying/Printing, Prog for adults, Prog for children & young adult, Ref serv available, Summer reading prog
Partic in Coun of Ashtabula County Librs; Northeastern Ohio Libr Asn
Open Mon-Thurs 10-8, Fri 10-6
Friends of the Library Group

C KENT STATE UNIVERSITY*, Ashtabula Campus Library, 3431 W 13th St, 44004-2298. SAN 313-1955. Tel: 440-964-4239. FAX: 440-964-4271. Web Site: www.ashtabula.kent.edu/library/index.cfm. *Dir,* Amy Thomas; Tel: 440-964-4237; *Libr Assoc,* Bethany Tackett; Tel: 440-964-4215; Staff 3 (MLS 1, Non-MLS 2)
Founded 1961. Enrl 706; Fac 32
Library Holdings: Bk Vols 50,000; Per Subs 150
Open Mon-Thurs 8:30am-9pm, Fri 8:30-2, Sat 11-3

ATHENS

APPALACHIAN BEHAVIORAL HEALTHCARE

L ATHENS COUNTY LAW LIBRARY*, Court House, 4th Flr, 45701. SAN 327-8964. Tel: 740-593-8893. FAX: 740-592-3282. *Librn,* Edward Kruse
Library Holdings: Bk Vols 10,000; Per Subs 10
Open Mon-Fri 8-4

C OHIO UNIVERSITY LIBRARIES*, Vernon R Alden Library, 30 Park Pl, 45701-2978. SAN 355-5429. Tel: 740-593-2702. Circulation Tel: 740-593-2695. Interlibrary Loan Service Tel: 740-593-2690. Reference Tel: 740-593-2699. Automation Services Tel: 740-593-0981. FAX: 740-593-2708. Interlibrary Loan Service FAX: 740-593-2659. Reference FAX: 740-593-0138. Web Site: www.library.ohiou.edu/find/index.html. *Dean of Libr,* Scott Seaman; Tel: 740-593-2705, E-mail: seaman@ohio.edu; *Asst Dean, Coll & Access,* Jan Maxwell; Tel: 740-593-2707, E-mail: maxwelj2@ohio.edu; *Actg Asst Dean, Pub Serv,* Wanda Weinberg; Tel: 740-593-9685, E-mail: weinberg@ohio.edu; *Head, Circ,* Annette Talbert; Tel: 740-593-2906, E-mail: talbert@ohio.edu; *Head, Govt Doc,* Doreen Hockenberry; Tel: 740-593-2718, E-mail: hockenbe@ohio.edu; *Dir, Info Tech,* David Dudding; Tel: 740-593-0981, E-mail: duddingd@ohio.edu; *Media Libr Mgr,* Robin Krivesti; Tel: 740-593-2665, E-mail: krivesti@ohio.edu; *Human Res,* Eileen Theodore-Shusta; Tel: 740-593-2989, E-mail: theodore@ohio.edu; Staff 103.75 (MLS 51.75, Non-MLS 52)
Founded 1804. Enrl 20,461; Fac 1,188; Highest Degree: Doctorate
Jul 2005-Jun 2006. Mats Exp $4,566,463, Books $1,077,550, Per/Ser (Incl. Access Fees) $1,157,303, Other Print Mats $49,502, Electronic Ref Mat (Incl. Access Fees) $2,264,989, Presv $17,119. Sal $4,937,565 (Prof $2,651,037)
Library Holdings: AV Mats 86,574; Bk Vols 2,468,497; Per Subs 25,557
Special Collections: Cornelius Ryan World War II Papers; E W Scripps Papers; George Voinovich Papers; Morgan History of Chemistry Coll; Nikolais/Louis Dance Coll; Romantic & Georgian Literature (Edmund Blunden Coll); Southeast Asia Coll. State Document Depository; UN Document Depository; US Document Depository
Automation Activity & Vendor Info: (Acquisitions) Innovative Interfaces, Inc; (Cataloging) Innovative Interfaces, Inc; (Circulation) Innovative Interfaces, Inc; (Course Reserve) Innovative Interfaces, Inc; (ILL) OCLC; (Media Booking) Innovative Interfaces, Inc; (OPAC) Innovative Interfaces, Inc; (Serials) Innovative Interfaces, Inc
Wireless access
Publications: Gatherings
Partic in OCLC Online Computer Library Center, Inc
Special Services for the Deaf - Staff with knowledge of sign lang
Special Services for the Blind - Computer with voice synthesizer for visually impaired persons
Open Mon-Thurs 8-7, Fri (Summer) 8-5
Friends of the Library Group
Departmental Libraries:
MAHN CENTER FOR ARCHIVES & SPECIAL COLLECTIONS, Vernon R Alden Library, 30 Park Pl, Fifth Flr, 45701-2978. Tel: 740-593-2710. FAX: 740-593-2708. *Rec Mgr, Univ Archivist,* William Kimok; Tel: 740-593-2712, E-mail: kimok@ohio.edu; *Archivist/Librn,* Sara Harrington; E-mail: harrings@ohio.edu; *Curator of Ms,* Douglas McCabe; Tel: 740-593-2715, E-mail: mccabe@ohio.edu; *Spec Coll Librn,* Miriam Intrator; E-mail: intrator@ohio.edu; Staff 6 (MLS 5, Non-MLS 1)
Founded 1963
Library Holdings: Bk Vols 54,000; Per Subs 115
Subject Interests: Georgian lit, Hist of chem, Journalism, Performing arts, Romantic, World War II
Open Mon-Fri 9-5, Sat 12-4
Friends of the Library Group
MUSIC-DANCE, Robert Gidden Hall, Fifth Flr, 45701-2978. Tel: 740-593-4255. FAX: 740-593-9190. *Libr Spec,* Gregory Sigman; E-mail: sigman@ohio.edu
Library Holdings: CDs 10,000; Music Scores 30,000; Bk Vols 50,000; Videos 1,500
Special Collections: LP Record Coll; Microfiche/Microfilm
Open Mon-Thurs (Winter) 8am-11pm, Fri 8-6, Sat 12-6, Sun 1-11; Mon-Fri (Summer) 8-5
Friends of the Library Group

ATTICA

P SENECA EAST PUBLIC LIBRARY*, 14 N Main St, 44807. (Mail add: PO Box 572, 44807-0572), SAN 313-1971. Tel: 419-426-3825. FAX: 419-426-3701. E-mail: seneca@oplin.org. Web Site: www.seneca-east.lib.oh.us. *Dir,* Barbara Ann Bayer; Tel: 419-426-8205, E-mail: bayerba@oplin.org; Staff 2 (MLS 1, Non-MLS 1)
Founded 1924. Pop 5,811; Circ 60,134
Library Holdings: AV Mats 4,005; Bk Titles 33,044; Per Subs 99
Special Collections: Attica Area Historical Room (Attica Area Museum); Attica Area Local History (Archives)
Automation Activity & Vendor Info: (Acquisitions) SirsiDynix; (Cataloging) SirsiDynix; (Circulation) SirsiDynix; (Course Reserve) SirsiDynix; (ILL) SirsiDynix; (OPAC) SirsiDynix; (Serials) SirsiDynix
Database Vendor: EBSCOhost, Newsbank, OCLC FirstSearch, SirsiDynix, TLC (The Library Corporation)
Wireless access
Function: Adult bk club, After school storytime, Audio & video playback equip for onsite use, Bk club(s), CD-ROM, Copy machines, Doc delivery serv, Electronic databases & coll, Fax serv, Home delivery & serv to Sr ctr & nursing homes, ILL available, Music CDs, Online ref, Online searches, Orientations, Outside serv via phone, mail, e-mail & web, Photocopying/Printing, Preschool outreach, Prog for children & young adult, Ref & res, Ref serv available, Spoken cassettes & CDs, Spoken cassettes & DVDs, Summer reading prog, Tax forms, Telephone ref, VHS videos, Video lending libr, Workshops
Partic in NORWELD; SEO (Serving Every Ohioan) Library Center
Open Mon-Thurs 10-8:30, Fri 10-5:30, Sat 10-2:30
Friends of the Library Group

AVON LAKE

P AVON LAKE PUBLIC LIBRARY*, 32649 Electric Blvd, 44012-1669. SAN 313-198X. Tel: 440-933-8128. Administration Tel: 440-933-7857. FAX: 440-933-5659. Administration FAX: 440-933-6406. E-mail: refdesk@avonlake.lib.oh.us. Web Site: www.alpl.org, www.avonlake.lib.oh.us. *Dir,* Mary Crehore; Tel: 440-933-3851, E-mail: mcrehore@avonlake.lib.oh.us; *Asst Dir,* Gerald Vogel; E-mail: gvogel@avonlake.lib.oh.us; *Mgr, Ch Serv,* Paula Shadle; *Support Serv Mgr,* Judy Means; *Tech Mgr,* Nick Kelley; *Pub Relations Coordr,* Jill Ralston; Staff 14 (MLS 7, Non-MLS 7)
Founded 1930. Pop 22,602; Circ 620,000
Jan 2012-Dec 2012 Income $3,050,000, State $600,000, County $2,100,000, Locally Generated Income $60,000, Other $290,000. Mats Exp $293,000, Books $155,000, Per/Ser (Incl. Access Fees) $14,000, Micro $300, AV Equip $2,000, AV Mat $95,000, Electronic Ref Mat (Incl. Access Fees) $17,000, Presv $2,000. Sal $1,250,000 (Prof $830,000)
Library Holdings: Audiobooks 5,700; AV Mats 34,000; CDs 9,000; DVDs 19,500; e-books 19,000; Large Print Bks 4,500; Bk Vols 104,000; Per Subs 300
Special Collections: DiscoveryWorks Center; Local History & Genealogy (Avon Lake Coll), bks, doc, flm, newsp, photg, videos. Oral History

Subject Interests: Art, Gardening, Multicultural kits, Pre-sch concept kits, Sci kits
Automation Activity & Vendor Info: (Acquisitions) SirsiDynix; (Cataloging) SirsiDynix; (Circulation) SirsiDynix; (ILL) OCLC FirstSearch; (OPAC) SIRSI-iBistro
Database Vendor: ALLDATA Online, EBSCO Auto Repair Reference, EBSCOhost, Gale Cengage Learning, Grolier Online, Ingram Library Services, LearningExpress, Newsbank, Overdrive, Inc, Oxford Online, ReferenceUSA, TumbleBookLibrary, World Book Online
Wireless access
Function: Art exhibits, Audiobks via web, Bks on cassette, Bks on CD, Children's prog, Computer training, Computers for patron use, Copy machines, e-mail serv, Electronic databases & coll, Exhibits, Fax serv, Free DVD rentals, Handicapped accessible, Holiday prog, Home delivery & serv to Sr ctr & nursing homes, Homebound delivery serv, ILL available, Large print keyboards, Magnifiers for reading, Mail & tel request accepted, Music CDs, Notary serv, Online cat, Online ref, Online searches, Orientations, Outreach serv, Outside serv via phone, mail, e-mail & web, OverDrive digital audio bks, Photocopying/Printing, Prog for adults, Prog for children & young adult, Pub access computers, Ref & res, Ref serv available, Ref serv in person, Scanner, Senior computer classes, Senior outreach, Story hour, Summer reading prog, Tax forms, Teen prog, Telephone ref, Web-catalog, Wheelchair accessible
Partic in Northeast Ohio Regional Library System
Special Services for the Deaf - Closed caption videos
Special Services for the Blind - Low vision equip; Playaways (bks on MP3); Recorded bks
Open Mon-Thurs 9-9, Fri & Sat 9-5, Sun (Sept-May) 1-5
Friends of the Library Group

BARBERTON

P BARBERTON PUBLIC LIBRARY*, 602 W Park Ave, 44203-2458. SAN 313-2021. Tel: 330-745-1194. FAX: 330-745-8261. Web Site: www.barbertonlibrary.org. *Dir,* Julianne Bedel; E-mail: julianne.bedel@barbertonlibrary.org; *AV Librn,* Dia Thomas; E-mail: dia.thomas@barbertonlibrary.org; *Ch,* Alison Huey; E-mail: alison.huey@barbertonlibrary.org; *Local Hist Librn,* Allan Harjala; E-mail: allan.harjala@barbertonlibrary.org; *Ref Librn,* Mary Kay Ball; E-mail: marykay.ball@barbertonlibrary.org; *Teen Serv Librn,* Sarah Granville; E-mail: sarah.granville@barbertonlibrary.org; *Ch Mgr,* Lisa Gilgenbach; E-mail: lisa.gilgenbach@barbertonlibrary.org; *Customer Serv Mgr & Outreach Librn,* Mary Eritano; E-mail: mary.eritano@barbertonlibrary.org; *Ref Mgr,* Susanne Nirschl Cogar; E-mail: susanne.cogar@barbertonlibrary.org; *Tech Serv Mgr,* Jennifer O'Neill; E-mail: jennifer.oneill@barbertonlibrary.org. Subject Specialists: *Consumer health info,* Mary Kay Ball; Staff 7.06 (MLS 7.06)
Founded 1903. Pop 26,385; Circ 326,950
Jan 2012-Dec 2012 Income (Main Library and Branch(s)) $1,304,450. Mats Exp $154,128. Sal $627,148
Library Holdings: e-books 79,089; Bk Vols 72,579; Videos 8,683
Special Collections: Barberton History (William A Johnston Coll)
Automation Activity & Vendor Info: (Cataloging) SirsiDynix; (Circulation) SirsiDynix; (ILL) OCLC; (OPAC) SirsiDynix; (Serials) SirsiDynix
Database Vendor: Grolier Online, LibLime
Wireless access
Function: Adult bk club, After school storytime, Audiobks via web, AV serv, Bi-weekly Writer's Group, Bk club(s), Bk reviews (Group), Bks on cassette, Bks on CD, CD-ROM, Children's prog, Computer training, Computers for patron use, Copy machines, Digital talking bks, e-mail & chat, e-mail serv, E-Reserves, Electronic databases & coll, Family literacy, Fax serv, Free DVD rentals, Handicapped accessible, Health sci info serv, Holiday prog, Home delivery & serv to Sr ctr & nursing homes, Homebound delivery serv, ILL available, Mail & tel request accepted, Microfiche/film & reading machines, Music CDs, Online cat, Online ref, Online searches, Outreach serv, Outside serv via phone, mail, e-mail & web, OverDrive digital audio bks, Photocopying/Printing, Preschool outreach, Preschool reading prog, Prog for adults, Prog for children & young adult, Pub access computers, Ref & res, Ref serv available, Ref serv in person, Scanner, Senior computer classes, Senior outreach, Spoken cassettes & CDs, Spoken cassettes & DVDs, Story hour, Summer & winter reading prog, Summer reading prog, Tax forms, Teen prog, Telephone ref, VHS videos, Video lending libr, Web-catalog, Wheelchair accessible, Winter reading prog, Writing prog
Publications: Enchanted Times (Newsletter)
Partic in CLEVNET
Special Services for the Blind - Bks on cassette; Bks on CD; Copier with enlargement capabilities; Home delivery serv; Large print & cassettes; Large print bks; Recorded bks
Open Mon-Thurs 10-8, Fri 10-6, Sat 12-6, Sun (Sept-May) 1-5
Friends of the Library Group

Branches: 1
COMMUNITY HEALTH LIBRARY, Summa Barberton Hospital, 155 Fifth St NE, 1st Flr, 44203-3398. Tel: 330-615-3105. FAX: 330-615-3103. *Librn,* Mary Kay Ball; E-mail: marykay.ball@barbertonlibrary.org. Subject Specialists: *Consumer health info,* Mary Kay Ball; Staff 1 (MLS 1)
Founded 2000
Open Mon-Fri 10-3

M SUMMA BARBERTON CITIZENS HOSPITAL*, Morris Medical Library, 155 Fifth St NE, 44203. SAN 313-2013. Tel: 330-615-3104. FAX: 330-615-3103. *Med Librn,* Charlotte Sievert; E-mail: csievert@summahealth.org; Staff 1 (MLS 1)
Founded 1955
Library Holdings: Bk Titles 1,281; Bk Vols 1,553; Per Subs 90
Subject Interests: Clinical med, Nursing
Automation Activity & Vendor Info: (Cataloging) Innovative Interfaces, Inc; (Circulation) Innovative Interfaces, Inc; (OPAC) Innovative Interfaces, Inc; (Serials) Innovative Interfaces, Inc
Function: Health sci info serv
Partic in National Network of Libraries of Medicine; Ohio Library & Information Network
Open Mon-Fri 8-4
Restriction: Limited access for the pub

BARNESVILLE

P BARNESVILLE HUTTON MEMORIAL LIBRARY*, 308 E Main St, 43713-1410. SAN 313-2048. Tel: 740-425-1651. FAX: 740-425-3504. Web Site: www.barnesvillehutton.lib.oh.us. *Dir,* Brenda G Brown; E-mail: brownbr@oplin.org; Staff 2 (MLS 2)
Founded 1924. Pop 12,000; Circ 200,075
Library Holdings: Bk Titles 54,000
Subject Interests: Ohio hist, Relig studies
Automation Activity & Vendor Info: (Cataloging) SirsiDynix; (Circulation) SirsiDynix; (OPAC) SirsiDynix
Wireless access
Open Mon & Thurs 9-8, Tues, Wed & Fri 9-6, Sat 9-5

BATAVIA

GL CLERMONT COUNTY LAW LIBRARY ASSOCIATION*, 270 Main St, 45103. SAN 327-716X. Tel: 513-732-7109. FAX: 513-732-0974. E-mail: cclaw@cclla.org. Web Site: www.clermontlawlibrary.com. *Dir,* Carol A Suhre
Library Holdings: Bk Vols 18,000; Per Subs 88
Automation Activity & Vendor Info: (Cataloging) Sydney; (OPAC) Sydney
Database Vendor: LexisNexis, Westlaw
Partic in OHIONET; Westlaw
Open Mon-Fri 8:30-4:30
Restriction: Non-circulating to the pub

P CLERMONT COUNTY PUBLIC LIBRARY*, 326 Broadway St, 45103. SAN 355-5542. Tel: 513-732-2736. FAX: 513-732-3177. Web Site: www.clermont.lib.oh.us. *Dir,* Chris Wick; Tel: 513-735-7190, E-mail: cwick@clermontlibrary.org; Staff 182 (MLS 19, Non-MLS 163)
Founded 1955. Pop 195,385; Circ 1,689,696
Jan 2009-Dec 2009 Income (Main Library and Branch(s)) $8,508,420. Mats Exp $1,105,691, Books $692,000, Per/Ser (Incl. Access Fees) $43,656, AV Mat $305,000. Sal $3,659,962
Library Holdings: Audiobooks 26,723; CDs 26,485; DVDs 49,924; e-books 212; Electronic Media & Resources 52; Large Print Bks 24,990; Microforms 246; Bk Vols 448,708; Per Subs 1,084; Videos 9,098
Special Collections: Oral History; State Document Depository
Subject Interests: Genealogy, Local hist
Automation Activity & Vendor Info: (Acquisitions) Innovative Interfaces, Inc; (Cataloging) Innovative Interfaces, Inc; (Circulation) Innovative Interfaces, Inc; (Course Reserve) Innovative Interfaces, Inc; (ILL) Innovative Interfaces, Inc; (OPAC) Innovative Interfaces, Inc; (Serials) Innovative Interfaces, Inc
Database Vendor: Booksite, EBSCO Auto Repair Reference, EBSCOhost, Gale Cengage Learning, H W Wilson, infoUSA, LearningExpress, McGraw-Hill, Medline, Newsbank, Overdrive, Inc, Oxford Online, ReferenceUSA, Wilson - Wilson Web
Wireless access
Function: Adult bk club, Audiobks via web, Bks on cassette, Bks on CD, Children's prog, Computer training, Computers for patron use, Copy machines, e-mail serv, Electronic databases & coll, Family literacy, Free DVD rentals, Genealogy discussion group, Handicapped accessible, Holiday prog, ILL available, Large print keyboards, Magnifiers for reading, Music CDs, Notary serv, Online cat, Online ref, Outreach serv, OverDrive digital audio bks, Photocopying/Printing, Preschool outreach, Prog for adults, Prog for children & young adult, Pub access computers, Ref serv in person, Senior outreach, Spoken cassettes & CDs, Spoken cassettes &

DVDs, Story hour, Summer reading prog, Tax forms, Teen prog, Telephone ref, Web-catalog, Wheelchair accessible
Partic in Ohio Public Library Information Network; SouthWest Ohio & Neighboring Libraries
Open Mon & Tues 12-8, Wed & Thurs 10-6, Fri & Sat 9-5
Friends of the Library Group
Branches: 10
AMELIA BRANCH, 58 Maple St, Amelia, 45102, SAN 329-594X. Tel: 513-752-5580. FAX: 513-752-5266. *Br Mgr,* Beth Lammrish; E-mail: lammribe@oplin.org
Open Mon-Thurs 9-9, Fri & Sat 9-5:30
BATAVIA-DORIS WOOD BRANCH, 180 S Third St, 45103-2806, SAN 355-5550. Tel: 513-732-2128. FAX: 513-732-2498. *Br Mgr,* Leslie Jacobs; E-mail: jacobsle@oplin.org
Open Mon & Tues 12-8, Wed & Thurs 10-6, Fri & Sat 9-5
BETHEL BRANCH, 611 W Plane St, Bethel, 45106-1302, SAN 355-5577. Tel: 513-734-2619. FAX: 513-734-1321. *Br Mgr,* Allison Schultz; E-mail: aschultz@clermontlibrary.org
Open Mon-Thurs 9-9, Fri & Sat 9-5:30
FELICITY BRANCH, 209 Prather Rd, Felicity, 45120, SAN 374-4299. Tel: 513-876-4134. FAX: 513-876-3619. *Br Mgr,* Lucinda Chandler; E-mail: chandllu@oplin.org
Database Vendor: Innovative Interfaces, Inc
Open Mon & Tues 12-8, Wed & Thurs 10-6, Fri & Sat 9-5
GOSHEN BRANCH, 6678 State Rte 132, Goshen, 45122, SAN 323-777X. Tel: 513-722-1221. FAX: 513-722-2158. *Br Mgr,* Lisa Breithaupt; E-mail: breithli@oplin.org
Open Mon-Thurs 9-9, Fri & Sat 9-5:30
MILFORD-MIAMI TOWNSHIP BRANCH, 1099 State Rte 131, Milford, 45150-2700, SAN 355-5607. Tel: 513-248-0700. FAX: 513-248-4579. *Br Mgr,* Joann Kiser; E-mail: kiserjo@oplin.org; *Br Supvr,* Emily Wichman; E-mail: wichmanme@oplin.org
Open Mon & Tues 12-8, Wed & Thurs 10-6, Fri & Sat 9-5
NEW RICHMOND BRANCH, 103 River Valley Blvd, New Richmond, 45157, SAN 355-5615. Tel: 513-553-0570. FAX: 513-553-0574. *Br Mgr,* Amy Buskey; E-mail: buskeyam@oplin.org
Open Mon-Thurs 9-9, Fri & Sat 9-5:30
Friends of the Library Group
OWENSVILLE BRANCH, 2548 US Rte 50, Owensville, 45160. (Mail add: PO Box 875, Owensville, 45160-0875), SAN 377-7197. Tel: 513-732-6084. FAX: 513-732-9168. *Br Mgr,* Chris Rich; E-mail: richch@oplin.org
Open Mon-Thurs 9-9, Fri & Sat 9-5:30
UNION TOWNSHIP, 4462 Mt Carmel-Tobasco Rd, Cincinnati, 45244-2224, SAN 355-5631. Tel: 513-528-1744. FAX: 513-528-0539. *Br Mgr,* Garria Blundell; E-mail: blundega@oplin.org
Open Mon-Thurs 9-9, Fri & Sat 9-5:30
WILLIAMSBURG BRANCH, 594 Main St, Williamsburg, 45176, SAN 329-5966. Tel: 513-724-1070. FAX: 513-724-5549. *Br Mgr,* Shawn Fry; E-mail: frysha@oplin.org
Open Mon-Thurs 9-9, Fri & Sat 9-5:30

C UNIVERSITY OF CINCINNATI*, Clermont College Library, 4200 Clermont College Dr, 45103-1785. SAN 355-9149. Tel: 513-732-5233. FAX: 513-732-5237. Web Site: www.ucclermont.edu/library. *Instruction Coordr, Interim Dir, Libr Serv,* Katie Foran-Mulcahy; Tel: 513-558-5164, E-mail: katie.foran-mulcahy@uc.edu; *Pub Serv Mgr,* Natalie Winland; *Tech Serv Mgr,* Penny McGinnis; Tel: 513-732-5206, E-mail: penny.mcginnis@uc.edu; *Assoc Librn, Ref & Instruction,* Kathleen Epperson; Tel: 513-558-7010, E-mail: kathleen.epperson@uc.edu; Staff 4 (MLS 2, Non-MLS 2)
Founded 1972. Enrl 3,000; Fac 170
Jul 2007-Jun 2008 Income $413,210. Mats Exp $133,875, Books $93,439, Per/Ser (Incl. Access Fees) $8,850, Micro $500, Electronic Ref Mat (Incl. Access Fees) $29,856, Presv $1,230. Sal $178,280
Library Holdings: AV Mats 1,000; e-books 400,000; e-journals 60,000; Bk Vols 30,000; Per Subs 75
Subject Interests: Career
Wireless access
Function: AV serv, ILL available, Photocopying/Printing, Ref serv available, Wheelchair accessible
Open Mon-Thurs (Winter) 7:30am-9pm, Fri 7:30-4, Sat 10-2; Mon-Thurs (Summer) 7:30-6:30, Fri 7:30-3
Restriction: Open to pub for ref & circ; with some limitations

BEACHWOOD

R ANSHE CHESED FAIRMOUNT TEMPLE*, Arthur J Lelyveld Center for Jewish Learning, 23737 Fairmount Blvd, 44122-2296. SAN 313-3443. Tel: 216-464-1330, Ext 123. FAX: 216-464-3628. E-mail: mail@fairmounttemple.org. Web Site: www.fairmounttemple.org. *Librn,* Julie Moss; E-mail: jmoss@fairmounttemple.org; Staff 3 (MLS 1, Non-MLS 2)
Library Holdings: Bk Titles 16,232; Per Subs 45; Videos 200
Special Collections: Celia Smith Rogovin Children's Library
Subject Interests: Archit, Bible, Feminism, Festivals, Hist, Holidays, Holocaust, Jewish art, Jewish fiction, Jewish philos, Judaica, Theol, Women's studies
Automation Activity & Vendor Info: (Cataloging) Follett Software; (OPAC) Follett Software
Wireless access
Partic in Asn of Jewish Librs
Open Tues & Thurs 10-3

R LEE & DOLORES HARTZMARK LIBRARY*, 26000 Shaker Blvd, 44122. SAN 313-3842. Tel: 216-831-3233. FAX: 216-831-4216. *Librn,* Andrea Davidson; Tel: 216-455-1724, E-mail: adavidson@ttti.org
Founded 1896
Library Holdings: Bk Titles 12,000; Per Subs 75
Special Collections: Abba Hillel Silver Archives
Subject Interests: Judaica
Publications: The Loom & the Cloth
Friends of the Library Group

SR SUBURBAN TEMPLE*, Gries Library, 22401 Chagrin Blvd, 44122-5345. SAN 328-3291. Tel: 216-991-0700. FAX: 216-991-0705. Web Site: www.suburbantemple.org. *Librn,* Eileen Kollins
Founded 1954
Library Holdings: Bk Titles 6,000; Bk Vols 6,500; Per Subs 15
Subject Interests: Judaism (religion)
Database Vendor: JayWil Software Development, Inc

BEDFORD

S BEDFORD HISTORICAL SOCIETY LIBRARY*, 30 S Park St, 44146-3635. (Mail add: PO Box 46282, 44146-0282), SAN 328-5057. Tel: 440-232-0796. Web Site: www.bedfordohiohistory.org. *Dir,* Dana Best-Mizsak; *Librn,* Paul Pojman; *Curator,* Janet Caldwell; *Archivist,* Debra Grubb
Founded 1955
Library Holdings: Bk Titles 12,000
Special Collections: 1876 Centennial Coll; Civil War Coll; Early Aviation; Lincolniana Coll; Local Archives Coll; Photograph Coll; Railroads Coll. Municipal Document Depository; Oral History
Open Mon & Wed 7:30pm-10pm, Thurs 10-4

BELLAIRE

P BELLAIRE PUBLIC LIBRARY*, 330 32nd St, 43906. SAN 313-2099. Tel: 740-676-9421. FAX: 740-676-7940. E-mail: bellaire@oplin.org. Web Site: www.bellaire.lib.oh.us. *Libr Dir,* Laura Cramblet; E-mail: lcramblet@oplin.org; *Asst Dir,* Mary DeGenova; E-mail: degenoma@oplin.org; Staff 6 (MLS 1, Non-MLS 5)
Founded 1927. Pop 18,000
Library Holdings: AV Mats 3,746; CDs 2,500; Bk Vols 80,000; Per Subs 120
Database Vendor: EBSCO Auto Repair Reference, EBSCO Information Services, EBSCOhost, OCLC WorldShare Interlibrary Loan, OHIONET, Overdrive, Inc, Project MUSE, ProQuest, Wiley, World Book Online
Wireless access
Function: Adult bk club, After school storytime, Audiobks via web, Bks on cassette, Bks on CD, CD-ROM, Children's prog, Computer training, Computers for patron use, Copy machines, Digital talking bks, e-mail & chat, e-mail serv, E-Reserves, Electronic databases & coll, Equip loans & repairs, Exhibits, Fax serv, Handicapped accessible, Holiday prog, ILL available, Instruction & testing, Magnifiers for reading, Microfiche/film & reading machines, Music CDs, Newsp ref libr, Online cat, Online info literacy tutorials on the web & in blackboard, Online ref, Online searches, Orientations, Outreach serv, OverDrive digital audio bks, Photocopying/Printing, Preschool outreach, Preschool reading prog, Printer for laptops & handheld devices, Prof lending libr, Prog for adults, Prog for children & young adult, Pub access computers, Ref & res, Ref serv available, Ref serv in person, Referrals accepted, Spoken cassettes & CDs, Spoken cassettes & DVDs, Story hour, Summer & winter reading prog, Summer reading prog, Tax forms, Telephone ref, VHS videos, Video lending libr, Web-catalog, Wheelchair accessible, Winter reading prog
Partic in Ohio Public Library Information Network; SEO (Serving Every Ohioan) Library Center
Special Services for the Deaf - Captioned film dep
Special Services for the Blind - Recorded bks
Open Mon-Wed 9-7, Thurs 9-6, Fri 9-5, Sat 9-2
Friends of the Library Group

BELLE CENTER

P BELLE CENTER FREE PUBLIC LIBRARY*, 103 S Elizabeth St, 43310. (Mail add: PO Box 336, 43310-9780). Tel: 937-464-3611. FAX: 937-464-3611. E-mail: bellectr@oplin.org. Web Site: bellecenterlibrary.com. *Dir,* Amy Bowdle; E-mail: amy@bellecenterlibrary.com; *Asst Dir,* Susan Johns; *Librn,* Beth Karshner
Pop 2,865

Library Holdings: AV Mats 2,150; Bk Vols 20,415; Per Subs 30
Open Mon-Wed 1-8, Thurs 9-5, Sat 9-2

BELLEFONTAINE

P LOGAN COUNTY LIBRARIES*, 220 N Main St, 43311-2228. SAN 355-5666. Tel: 937-599-4189. FAX: 937-599-5503. E-mail: lcdlref@oplin.org. Web Site: www.logancountylibraries.org. *Dir,* Judith A Goodrich; E-mail: jgoodrich@logancountylibraries.org; *Ch Serv,* Nancy Kuta; E-mail: kutana@oplin.org
Founded 1901. Pop 45,688
Library Holdings: Bk Titles 122,264; Bk Vols 168,864; Per Subs 205
Automation Activity & Vendor Info: (Cataloging) SIRSI-iBistro; (Circulation) SirsiDynix; (OPAC) SirsiDynix
Database Vendor: ALLDATA Online, Booksite, EBSCOhost, LearningExpress, OCLC WorldShare Interlibrary Loan, OHIONET, Overdrive, Inc, ProQuest, SirsiDynix, TumbleBookLibrary, World Book Online
Wireless access
Partic in NORWELD; Ohio Public Library Information Network
Special Services for the Blind - Aids for in-house use; Bks on cassette; Bks on CD; Free checkout of audio mat; Home delivery serv; Large print & cassettes; Large print bks; Large print bks & talking machines; Magnifiers; Playaways (bks on MP3)
Open Mon-Thurs (Winter) 9-8, Fri & Sat 9-4; Mon-Thurs (Summer) 9-8, Fri 9-4, Sat 9-2
Branches: 5
DEGRAFF BRANCH, One S Main St, DeGraff, 43318, SAN 355-5690. Tel: 937-585-5010. *Librn,* Angela Leatherman; E-mail: aleatherrman@logancountylibraries.org
Library Holdings: Bk Vols 2,900
Open Tues & Thurs 1-4:30, Wed 4-7, Fri 9-12 & 1-4:30
LAKEVIEW BRANCH, 130 N Main, Lakeview, 43331. (Mail add: PO Box 197, Lakeview, 43331-0197), SAN 355-5755. Tel: 937-842-4144. *Librn,* Elaine Castle; E-mail: ecastle@logancountylibraries.org
Library Holdings: Bk Vols 3,100
Open Mon & Wed 4-7, Tues & Thurs 9:30-12 & 1-5
RUSHSYLVANIA BRANCH, 113 N Sandusky, Rushsylvania, 43347. (Mail add: PO Box 115, Rushsylvania, 43347-0115), SAN 355-578X. Tel: 937-468-9963. *Librn,* Nikki Johnson; E-mail: njohnson@logancountylibraries.org
Open Mon 3-7, Tues & Thurs 10-12 & 1-6, Sat 9:30-12
WEST LIBERTY BRANCH, 117 N Detroit, West Liberty, 43357. (Mail add: PO Box 702, West Liberty, 43357-0702), SAN 355-581X. Tel: 937-465-3656. *Librn,* Nancy Spragen; E-mail: nspragen@logancountylibraries.org
Library Holdings: Bk Vols 4,850
Database Vendor: SirsiDynix
Open Mon 1-7, Tues & Thurs 9-12 & 1-5:30, Fri 10-12 & 1-4, Sat 9-12
WEST MANSFIELD BRANCH, 127 N Main, West Mansfield, 43358, SAN 355-5844. Tel: 937-355-0033. *Librn,* Bonnie Brose; E-mail: bbrose@logancountylibraries.org
Automation Activity & Vendor Info: (Cataloging) SirsiDynix; (OPAC) SIRSI-iBistro
Database Vendor: SirsiDynix
Open Mon 4-7, Tues & Wed 11-5, Thurs 11-2

BELLEVUE

P BELLEVUE PUBLIC LIBRARY, 224 E Main St, 44811-1467. SAN 313-2102. Tel: 419-483-4769. FAX: 419-483-0158. Web Site: www.bellevue.lib.oh.us. *Dir,* Position Currently Open; *Adult Serv Mgr,* Tracy Marr; *Tech Serv & Spec Projects Mgr,* Shayna Muckerheide; *Youth Serv Mgr,* JoEllen Boos; Staff 4 (MLS 4)
Founded 1891. Pop 13,339; Circ 193,968
Library Holdings: Audiobooks 2,238; CDs 3,139; DVDs 4,796; e-books 79,089; Electronic Media & Resources 313; Large Print Bks 1,707; Microforms 306; Bk Vols 62,751; Per Subs 218; Videos 1,001
Special Collections: Genealogy; Local history
Wireless access
Partic in CLEVNET; Northeast Ohio Regional Library System
Open Mon, Tues & Thurs 9-8:30, Wed 9-5:30, Fri & Sat 9-5

BELLVILLE

S OHIO GENEALOGICAL SOCIETY LIBRARY, 611 State Rte 97 W, 44813-8813. SAN 313-5934. Tel: 419-886-1903. FAX: 419-886-0092. E-mail: ogs@ogs.org. Web Site: www.ogs.org. *Dir,* Thomas Stephen Neel; E-mail: tneel@ogs.org; Staff 1 (MLS 1)
Founded 1959
Jan 2013-Dec 2013 Income $570,883. Mats Exp $508,627, Books $10,818, Manu Arch $1,892, Electronic Ref Mat (Incl. Access Fees) $4,968. Sal $104,983
Library Holdings: Bk Titles 57,007; Bk Vols 59,000; Per Subs 130
Special Collections: County & State Source Material, ms; First Families of Ohio; Ohio Bible Records File; Society of Civil War Families of Ohio (pre-1820 settler lineage society)
Subject Interests: Genealogy, Hist
Automation Activity & Vendor Info: (Cataloging) Mandarin Library Automation; (OPAC) Mandarin Library Automation
Wireless access
Publications: Ohio Civil War Genealogy Journal; Ohio Genealogy News; Ohio Records & Pioneer Families; The OGS Quarterly
Open Tues-Sat 9-5

BEREA

C BALDWIN WALLACE UNIVERSITY*, Ritter Library, 57 E Bagley Rd, 44017. SAN 355-5879. Tel: 440-826-2204. Reference Tel: 440-826-2206. FAX: 440-826-8558. E-mail: wwwlib@bw.edu. Web Site: www.bw.edu/academics/libraries/ritter. *Dir,* John DiGennaro; E-mail: jdigenna@bw.edu; *Pub Serv,* Richard Densmore; E-mail: rdensmor@bw.edu; Staff 4 (MLS 4)
Founded 1845. Enrl 3,000; Fac 166; Highest Degree: Master
Library Holdings: Bk Titles 160,000; Bk Vols 200,000; Per Subs 800
Special Collections: Folksongs (Harry E Ridenour Coll); Paul & Josephine Mayer Rare Book Coll; Religion (Methodist Historical Coll) bks, artifacts
Subject Interests: Educ, Hist, Music
Automation Activity & Vendor Info: (Circulation) Innovative Interfaces, Inc; (OPAC) Innovative Interfaces, Inc; (Serials) Innovative Interfaces, Inc
Database Vendor: Gale Cengage Learning
Partic in Libr Coun of Greater Cleveland; Northeast Ohio Regional Library System; OCLC Online Computer Library Center, Inc; OHIONET
Open Mon Thurs 8:30am-Midnight, Fri 8:30-6, Sat 10-6, Sun 12:30-Midnight
Friends of the Library Group
Departmental Libraries:
CHEMISTRY READING ROOM, Wilker Hall, 320 Front St, 44017-1732. (Mail add: Department of Chemistry, 275 Eastland Rd, 44017-2088), SAN 355-5909. Tel: 440-826-2312. FAX: 440-826-2399. *In Charge,* Jackie Yavornitzky; E-mail: jayavorn@bw.edu
Library Holdings: Bk Vols 875; Per Subs 30
Open Mon-Fri 8:30-5
JONES MUSIC LIBRARY, 49 Seminary St, 44017-1905. (Mail add: 275 Eastland Rd, 44017-2005), SAN 355-5968. Tel: 440-826-2375. E-mail: jonesml@bw.edu. Web Site: www.bw.edu/academics/libraries/jones. *Dir,* Paul Cary; *Access Serv,* Timothy Collins; *Tech Serv,* Timothy Keller. Subject Specialists: *Music,* Paul Cary; Staff 4 (MLS 2, Non-MLS 2)
Founded 1976. Enrl 4,000; Fac 165; Highest Degree: Master
Jul 2011-Jun 2012 Income $204,107. Mats Exp $29,150, Books $4,550, Per/Ser (Incl. Access Fees) $5,300, Other Print Mats $5,500, AV Mat $6,600, Electronic Ref Mat (Incl. Access Fees) $3,000, Presv $4,200. Sal $121,357 (Prof $62,747)
Library Holdings: AV Mats 15,368; CDs 5,626; DVDs 429; Electronic Media & Resources 100; Music Scores 17,754; Bk Vols 10,692; Per Subs 30
Special Collections: Cleveland Music Therapy Consortium Coll; Mildred Kerschner Music Education Curriculum Center
Subject Interests: Music, Music educ, Music therapy
Automation Activity & Vendor Info: (Cataloging) Innovative Interfaces, Inc; (Course Reserve) Innovative Interfaces, Inc; (ILL) Innovative Interfaces, Inc
Database Vendor: EBSCOhost
Partic in Ohio Private Academic Libraries (OPAL)
Open Mon-Thurs 8:30am-9pm, Fri 8:30-5, Sat 1-4, Sun 2-7
Restriction: Open to pub for ref only
RIEMENSCHNEIDER BACH INSTITUTE, Boesel Musical Arts Bldg., 49 Seminary St, 44017-2088. (Mail add: 275 Eastland Rd, 44017-2088). Tel: 440-826-2207. FAX: 440-826-8138. E-mail: bachinst@bw.edu. Web Site: www.bw.edu/academics/libraries/bach. *Dir,* Dr Melvin P Unger; E-mail: munger@bw.edu; *Music,* Sandra Eichenberg; Tel: 440-826-2044, E-mail: seichenb@bw.edu; Staff 4 (Non-MLS 4)
Founded 1969
Library Holdings: CDs 450; DVDs 6; Music Scores 3,500; Bk Vols 12,643; Per Subs 27
Special Collections: Emmy Martin Coll incl many 1st editions & presentation copies; Hans David's Coll mainly from the Baroque Era; J S Bach & His Contemporaries, bks, mss; Riemenschneider's Bach Coll; Tom Villella's Recording & Book Coll
Subject Interests: 17th Century music, 18th Century music, Albert Riemenschneider, J S Bach, Unpublished papers of Hans T David
Function: Archival coll
Partic in Ohio Library & Information Network; Ohio Private Academic Libraries (OPAL)
Publications: BACH: Journal of the Riemenschneider Bach Institute (Periodical)
Open Mon, Tues, Thurs & Fri 9-4
Restriction: Not a lending libr

BETTSVILLE

P BETTSVILLE PUBLIC LIBRARY*, 233 State St, 44815-9999. (Mail add: PO Box 385, 44815), SAN 313-2110. Tel: 419-986-5198. FAX: 419-986-6012. *Librn,* Angie Kliss
Library Holdings: Bk Vols 26,000
Partic in Ohio Public Library Information Network
Open Mon-Thurs 10-8, Fri & Sat 9-4

BEXLEY

R AGUDAS ACHIM CONGREGATION*, Stein Memorial Library, 2767 E Broad St, 43209. SAN 313-4008. Tel: 614-237-2747. FAX: 614-237-3576.
Founded 1961
Library Holdings: Bk Vols 3,500
Restriction: Not open to pub

P BEXLEY PUBLIC LIBRARY*, 2411 E Main St, 43209. SAN 313-4032. Tel: 614-231-9709. Circulation Tel: 614-231-8741. Reference Tel: 614-231-8795. Information Services Tel: 614-231-2793. E-mail: bexleydirector@bexleylibrary.org. Web Site: www.bexlib.org. *Dir,* Rachel Rubin; *Head, AV,* Sharon Short; E-mail: sshort@bexleylibrary.org; *Head, Ch,* Brenda Stenberg; E-mail: bstenberg@bexleylibrary.org; *Head, Circ,* Carl Kline; E-mail: cklein@bexleylibrary.org; *Head, Ref,* Christine Atzberger; E-mail: catzberger@bexleylibrary.org; Staff 11 (MLS 5, Non-MLS 6)
Founded 1924. Circ 769,707
Jan 2008-Dec 2008 Income $1,954,244, County $1,856,026, Locally Generated Income $98,218. Mats Exp $230,743, Books $106,491, Per/Ser (Incl. Access Fees) $39,837, AV Mat $71,654, Electronic Ref Mat (Incl. Access Fees) $12,646
Library Holdings: AV Mats 31,933; Bk Vols 205,768; Per Subs 179
Special Collections: Bexley Author Coll
Automation Activity & Vendor Info: (Cataloging) Innovative Interfaces, Inc; (Circulation) Innovative Interfaces, Inc; (OPAC) Innovative Interfaces, Inc; (Serials) Innovative Interfaces, Inc
Database Vendor: Gale Cengage Learning, OCLC FirstSearch
Function: Adult bk club, Bks on CD, CD-ROM, Children's prog, Copy machines, Electronic databases & coll, Free DVD rentals, Handicapped accessible, Music CDs, Newsp ref libr, Photocopying/Printing, Pub access computers, Story hour, Summer reading prog, Wheelchair accessible
Partic in OCLC Online Computer Library Center, Inc
Open Mon-Thurs 9-9, Fri & Sat 9-6, Sun 1-5
Restriction: Lending limited to county residents
Friends of the Library Group

BLANCHESTER

P BLANCHESTER PUBLIC LIBRARY, 110 N Broadway, 45107-1250. SAN 313-2129. Tel: 937-783-3585. FAX: 937-783-2910. Web Site: www.blanlibrary.org. *Dir,* Chris Owens; E-mail: cowens@blanlibrary.org; Staff 9 (MLS 1, Non-MLS 8)
Founded 1935. Pop 8,920; Circ 120,189
Library Holdings: Audiobooks 2,353; AV Mats 6,884; DVDs 3,908; e-books 99,491; Electronic Media & Resources 128,464; Large Print Bks 787; Bk Vols 55,381; Per Subs 135; Videos 623
Automation Activity & Vendor Info: (Cataloging) Evergreen; (Circulation) Evergreen; (OPAC) Evergreen
Database Vendor: Baker & Taylor, EBSCO Auto Repair Reference, EBSCOhost, Facts on File, Gale Cengage Learning, LearningExpress, OHIONET, Overdrive, Inc, ProQuest, Wilson - Wilson Web, World Book Online
Wireless access
Function: Adult bk club, Audiobks via web, Bks on CD, Children's prog, Computers for patron use, Copy machines, Electronic databases & coll, Free DVD rentals, Handicapped accessible, ILL available, Mail & tel request accepted, Online cat, OverDrive digital audio bks, Photocopying/Printing, Prog for adults, Prog for children & young adult, Pub access computers, Ref serv in person, Story hour, Summer reading prog, Tax forms, Telephone ref, VHS videos, Web-catalog
Partic in SouthWest Ohio & Neighboring Libraries
Open Mon-Fri 10-8, Sat 10-4
Friends of the Library Group

BLOOMVILLE

P BLISS MEMORIAL PUBLIC LIBRARY, 20 S Marion St, 44818-9201. (Mail add: PO Box 39, 44818-0039), SAN 313-2137. Tel: 419-983-4675. FAX: 419-983-4675. Web Site: www.blisslibrary.org. *Dir,* Elizabeth Fry; *Fiscal Officer,* Jane Lewis; Staff 4 (Non-MLS 4)
Founded 1935. Pop 1,799; Circ 24,888
Jan 2013-Dec 2013 Income $121,061. Mats Exp $20,674, Books $11,647, Per/Ser (Incl. Access Fees) $3,623, AV Mat $5,183. Sal $46,221
Library Holdings: Bk Titles 25,569; Per Subs 115
Special Collections: Bloomville Gazette (1928), microfilm
Subject Interests: Seneca County hist
Automation Activity & Vendor Info: (Cataloging) SIRSI WorkFlows; (Circulation) SIRSI WorkFlows; (ILL) SIRSI WorkFlows; (Serials) SIRSI WorkFlows
Database Vendor: SirsiDynix
Wireless access
Function: Bks on cassette, Bks on CD, CD-ROM, Children's prog, Computers for patron use, Copy machines, Fax serv, Free DVD rentals, Handicapped accessible, ILL available, Laminating, Magazines, Microfiche/film & reading machines, Movies, Music CDs, Online cat, OverDrive digital audio bks, Photocopying/Printing, Preschool reading prog, Printer for laptops & handheld devices, Scanner, Story hour, Summer & winter reading prog, Tax forms, VHS videos, Wheelchair accessible
Partic in NORWELD; SEO (Serving Every Ohioan) Library Center
Open Mon-Wed 11-8, Thurs & Fri 11-5, Sat 9-Noon
Friends of the Library Group

BLUFFTON

P BLUFFTON PUBLIC LIBRARY*, 145 S Main St, 45817. SAN 313-2161. Tel: 419-358-5016. FAX: 419-358-9653. Web Site: www.blufftonpubliclibrary.org. *Dir,* Jessica Hermiller; E-mail: hermiller@blufftonpubliclibrary.org; Staff 5 (MLS 1, Non-MLS 4)
Founded 1935. Pop 6,800; Circ 87,000
Jan 2008-Dec 2008 Income $430,109, State $282,456, Locally Generated Income $111,596, Other $36,057. Mats Exp $58,457, Books $28,019, Per/Ser (Incl. Access Fees) $4,441, AV Mat $14,147, Electronic Ref Mat (Incl. Access Fees) $11,850. Sal $175,795 (Prof $45,800)
Library Holdings: AV Mats 2,592; Bks on Deafness & Sign Lang 15; High Interest/Low Vocabulary Bk Vols 159; Large Print Bks 2,021; Bk Vols 32,084; Per Subs 116
Automation Activity & Vendor Info: (Cataloging) SirsiDynix; (Circulation) SirsiDynix; (ILL) SIRSI WorkFlows; (OPAC) SIRSI Unicorn; (Serials) SIRSI WorkFlows
Database Vendor: EBSCOhost, Facts on File, Gale Cengage Learning, LearningExpress, Medline, Newsbank, OCLC FirstSearch, OCLC WebJunction, OCLC WorldShare Interlibrary Loan, OHIONET, ProQuest, SirsiDynix, TLC (The Library Corporation), ValueLine, World Book Online
Wireless access
Function: Accelerated reader prog, Adult bk club, Bk club(s), Bks on cassette, Bks on CD, Children's prog, Computers for patron use, Copy machines, Electronic databases & coll, Fax serv, Free DVD rentals, Handicapped accessible, Holiday prog, Home delivery & serv to Sr ctr & nursing homes, Homebound delivery serv, ILL available, Magnifiers for reading, Mail & tel request accepted, Music CDs, Online cat, Online ref, Online searches, Outreach serv, Photocopying/Printing, Prog for adults, Prog for children & young adult, Pub access computers, Ref serv available, Story hour, Summer reading prog, Tax forms, Teen prog, Telephone ref, VHS videos, Web-catalog, Wheelchair accessible
Publications: Off the Shelf (Newsletter)
Partic in NORWELD
Special Services for the Blind - BiFolkal kits; Bks on cassette; Bks on CD; Extensive large print coll; Large print bks; Large screen computer & software; Low vision equip; Magnifiers
Open Mon-Thurs 9:30-8, Fri 9:30-5:30, Sat 9:30-2
Friends of the Library Group

CR BLUFFTON UNIVERSITY*, Musselman Library, One University Dr, 45817-2104. SAN 313-2153. Tel: 419-358-3271. Circulation Tel: 419-358-3262. Reference Tel: 419-358-3450. FAX: 419-358-3384. E-mail: referencedesk@bluffton.edu. Web Site: www.bluffton.edu/library. *Dir,* Mary Jean Johnson; Tel: 419-358-3396, E-mail: johnsonmj@bluffton.edu; *Archives & Spec Coll Librn,* Carrie Phillips; Tel: 419-358-3275, E-mail: phillipsc@bluffton.edu; *Ref Librn,* Paul Weaver; Tel: 419-358-3448, E-mail: weaverp@bluffton.edu; *Syst Librn,* Kathleen Aufderhaar; Tel: 419-358-3414, E-mail: aufderhaark@bluffton.edu; *Access Serv Coordr, Circ Supvr,* Audra Hammond; Staff 7 (MLS 4, Non-MLS 3)
Founded 1930. Enrl 1,000; Fac 70; Highest Degree: Master
Library Holdings: Bk Titles 94,451; Bk Vols 156,334; Per Subs 700
Special Collections: Mennonite Historical Libr. US Document Depository
Automation Activity & Vendor Info: (Acquisitions) Innovative Interfaces, Inc; (Cataloging) Innovative Interfaces, Inc; (Circulation) Innovative Interfaces, Inc; (Course Reserve) Innovative Interfaces, Inc; (OPAC) Innovative Interfaces, Inc; (Serials) Innovative Interfaces, Inc
Function: Bus archives
Partic in Ohio Private Academic Libraries (OPAL); OHIONET
Open Mon-Thurs 8am-11pm, Fri 8-5, Sat 1-5, Sun 1-11

BOARDMAN

SR BOARDMAN UNITED METHODIST CHURCH LIBRARY*, 6809 Market St, 44512. SAN 372-4859. Tel: 330-758-4527. FAX: 330-758-7348. E-mail: boardmanmethodist@sbcglobal.net. Web Site: www.boardmanumc.org. *Librn,* Mary Lou Henneman
Library Holdings: AV Mats 150; Bk Vols 2,000; Per Subs 10

Automation Activity & Vendor Info: (Cataloging) Book Systems
Open Mon-Fri 8:30-4, Sun 9-12

BOWERSTON

P BOWERSTON PUBLIC LIBRARY*, 200 Main St, 44695. (Mail add: PO Box 205, 44695-0205), SAN 313-217X. Tel: 740-269-8531. FAX: 740-269-8503. Web Site: www.bowerstonlibrary.org. *Dir,* Deborah Allen; E-mail: dallen@bowerstonlibrary.org
Founded 1935. Circ 87,005
Library Holdings: Bk Titles 40,000; Per Subs 100
Subject Interests: Local hist, Ohio, Pottery
Automation Activity & Vendor Info: (Cataloging) Horizon; (Circulation) Horizon; (OPAC) Horizon
Partic in Mideastern Ohio Libr Orgn
Open Mon & Thurs 10-8, Tues & Wed 10-5, Fri 10-2, Sat 9-1

BOWLING GREEN

C BOWLING GREEN STATE UNIVERSITY LIBRARIES, 204 Wm T Jerome Library, 43403-0170. SAN 355-6026. Circulation Tel: 419-372-2051. Interlibrary Loan Service Tel: 419-372-8726. Reference Tel: 419-372-6943. Administration Tel: 419-372-2856. Information Services Tel: 419-372-8664. Toll Free Tel: 866-542-2478. Circulation FAX: 419-372-0475. Interlibrary Loan Service FAX: 419-372-6877. Administration FAX: 419-372-0188. E-mail: libadmin@bgsu.edu. Web Site: www.bgsu.edu/colleges/library. *Dean,* Sara A Bushong; *Assoc Dean,* Colleen Boff; *Chair, Access Serv,* Mary Beth Zachary; *Chair, Archival Coll & Br,* Susannah Cleveland; *Chair, Coll & Tech Serv, Coordr, Cat & Acq,* Julie Rabine; *Chair, Libr Teaching & Learning, Coordr of Ref Serv,* Linda Rich; *Mgr, Libr Info Tech,* John Eggenton; *Coordr, Electronic Res,* Amy Fry; *Coordr, First Year Experience,* Robert Snyder; *Coordr, Libr Instruction,* Eileen Bosch; *ILL,* Sherri Long; Staff 40 (MLS 20, Non-MLS 20)
Founded 1910. Enrl 19,408; Fac 750; Highest Degree: Doctorate
Jul 2012-Jun 2013. Mats Exp $2,678,182. Sal $3,837,558
Special Collections: Browne Popular Culture Coll; Center for Archival Coll; Curriculum Resource Center; Great Lakes Historical Coll; Music Library & Sound Recordings Archives. State Document Depository; US Document Depository
Automation Activity & Vendor Info: (Acquisitions) Innovative Interfaces, Inc; (Cataloging) Innovative Interfaces, Inc; (Circulation) Innovative Interfaces, Inc; (Course Reserve) Docutek; (ILL) OCLC ILLiad; (OPAC) Innovative Interfaces, Inc; (Serials) Innovative Interfaces, Inc
Wireless access
Partic in Ohio Library & Information Network; Ohio Network of American History Research Centers; OHIONET
Friends of the Library Group

Departmental Libraries:

RAY & PAT BROWNE POPULAR CULTURE LIBRARY, Jerome Library, 4th Flr, 43403. Tel: 419-372-2450. FAX: 419-372-7996. *Head Librn,* Nancy Down; Tel: 419-372-6054, E-mail: ndown@bgsu.edu
Special Collections: Allen & John Saunders Coll; Archives of the Romance Writers of America; E T Ned Guymon Detective Fiction Coll; H James Horovitz Science Fiction Coll; Papers of Noted Fiction Authors such as Ruth Rendell, Joanna Russ, Dorothy Daniels & Marcia Muller
Subject Interests: Comic arts, Comic bks, Leisure, Movies, Popular fiction, Radio, Recreation, Romances, Sci fict

CENTER FOR ARCHIVAL COLLECTIONS, Jerome Library, 5th Flr, 43403. Tel: 419-372-2411. FAX: 419-372-0155. E-mail: archive@bgsu.edu. *Head Univ Archivist,* Stephen M Charter; E-mail: scharte@bgsu.edu
Founded 1968
Special Collections: Delbert Latta Papers; Lud Ashley Papers; Rare Books (Ray Bradbury Coll); Sam Pollock Labor Coll
Subject Interests: Genealogy, Labor hist, State hist

CURRICULUM RESOURCE CENTER, Jerome Library, 43403-0178. Tel: 419-372-2956. Web Site: www.bgsu.edu/colleges/library/crc. *Head Librn,* Jennifer Harvey
Special Collections: Pre-k through 12 Curriculum Materials
Subject Interests: Educ K-12 curriculum, Juv lit
Friends of the Library Group

MUSIC LIBRARY & SOUND RECORDINGS ARCHIVES, Jerome Library, 3rd Flr, 43403. (Mail add: 1001 E Wooster St, 43403). Tel: 419-372-2307. FAX: 419-372-7996. E-mail: mlsra@bgsu.edu. Web Site: www.bgsu.edu/colleges/library/music. *Head Librn,* Susannah Cleveland; Tel: 419-372-9929, E-mail: clevels@bgsu.edu; *Music Cat & Metadata Librn,* Patty Falk; Tel: 419-372-0266, E-mail: pkfalk@bgsu.edu; *Sound Rec Archivist,* William Schurk; Tel: 419-372-2308, E-mail: wschurk@bgsu.edu; Staff 4.5 (MLS 3, Non-MLS 1.5)
Founded 1967. Enrl 19,000; Fac 600; Highest Degree: Doctorate
Library Holdings: CDs 50,000; DVDs 800; Music Scores 65,000; Bk Titles 35,000
Special Collections: New Music Festival; Sound Recordings Archives
Subject Interests: Contemporary music, Popular music, Sound rec hist
Function: Archival coll, Audio & video playback equip for onsite use, Computers for patron use, Copy machines, e-mail & chat, e-mail serv, Electronic databases & coll, Exhibits, Free DVD rentals, ILL available, Instruction & testing, Music CDs, Online cat, Online ref, Online searches, Orientations, Outside serv via phone, mail, e-mail & web, Photocopying/Printing, Ref & res, Ref serv available, Ref serv in person, Scanner, VHS videos, Video lending libr, Web-catalog
Friends of the Library Group

P WOOD COUNTY DISTRICT PUBLIC LIBRARY, 251 N Main St, 43402-2477. SAN 355-6085. Tel: 419-352-5104. FAX: 419-354-0405. Administration FAX: 419-353-8013. E-mail: woodcirc@oplin.org, woodref@oplin.org. Web Site: wcdpl.org. *Dir,* Michael Penrod; E-mail: michaelpenrod@wcdpl.org; Staff 41 (MLS 4, Non-MLS 37)
Founded 1875. Pop 60,000; Circ 605,000
Jan 2014-Dec 2014 Income (Main Library and Branch(s)) $2,322,000, State $1,198,000, Locally Generated Income $979,000, Other $145,000. Mats Exp $373,000, Books $165,000, Per/Ser (Incl. Access Fees) $8,000, AV Mat $165,000, Electronic Ref Mat (Incl. Access Fees) $35,000. Sal $888,000
Library Holdings: Audiobooks 4,925; CDs 2,945; DVDs 9,872; e-books 40,000; Large Print Bks 4,965; Bk Vols 168,500; Per Subs 239
Subject Interests: Local hist, Mysteries, Parenting, Shakespeare studies
Automation Activity & Vendor Info: (Acquisitions) Baker & Taylor; (Cataloging) SirsiDynix; (Circulation) SirsiDynix; (ILL) SirsiDynix; (OPAC) SirsiDynix; (Serials) SirsiDynix
Database Vendor: EBSCOhost, ProQuest, ReferenceUSA, SirsiDynix
Wireless access
Function: Adult bk club, Archival coll, Audiobks via web, AV serv, Bks on CD, Children's prog, Computer training, Computers for patron use, Copy machines, E-Reserves, Family literacy, Handicapped accessible, Home delivery & serv to Sr ctr & nursing homes, Homebound delivery serv, Homework prog, ILL available, Jail serv, Magnifiers for reading, Notary serv, Online cat, Online ref, Online searches, Outreach serv, OverDrive digital audio bks, Photocopying/Printing, Preschool outreach, Prog for adults, Prog for children & young adult, Pub access computers, Ref serv available, Ref serv in person, Scanner, Spanish lang bks, Story hour, Summer reading prog, Tax forms, Teen prog, Telephone ref, Web-catalog, Wheelchair accessible
Partic in NORWELD; Ohio Public Library Information Network; SEO (Serving Every Ohioan) Library Center
Special Services for the Blind - Talking bks; Talking bks & player equip
Open Mon-Thurs 9-8:30, Fri 9-6, Sat 9-5, Sun 1-5
Friends of the Library Group

Branches: 1

WALBRIDGE BRANCH, 108 N Main, Walbridge, 43465, SAN 355-614X. Tel: 419-666-9900. FAX: 419-666-8217. *Br Supvr,* Matt Mehling, E-mail: mattmehling@wcdpl.org; Staff 2.5 (Non-MLS 2.5)
Founded 1987. Pop 15,200; Circ 58,000
Open Mon & Wed 1-7, Tues & Thurs 11-7, Fri 1-5, Sat 11-3

Bookmobiles: 1. Librn, Jessica Troyer. Bk titles 2,000

GL WOOD COUNTY LAW LIBRARY*, One Courthouse Sq, 43402. SAN 313-2188. Tel: 419-353-3921. FAX: 419-352-9269. *Librn,* Dorrie Cramer-Rumple; E-mail: dcramer-rumple@co.wood.oh.us
Library Holdings: Bk Vols 6,000; Per Subs 40
Open Mon-Fri 8:30-4:30

BRADFORD

P BRADFORD PUBLIC LIBRARY*, 138 E Main St, 45308-1108. SAN 313-2196. Tel: 937-448-2612. FAX: 937-448-2615. E-mail: bradfordpublic@gmail.com. Web Site: www.bradfordpubliclibrary.org. *Dir,* Cherie Roeth; E-mail: cherie_roeth@darke.k12.oh.us; *Librn,* Deborah Barger; *Librn,* Carolene Coy; *Librn,* Linda Moore; Staff 4 (MLS 1, Non-MLS 3)
Founded 1935. Pop 8,000; Circ 73,041
Library Holdings: AV Mats 2,975; Large Print Bks 300; Bk Vols 34,865; Per Subs 149; Talking Bks 794
Special Collections: Local History Room (Darke & Miami Co Information); Old Newspaper on Microfilm & CD. Oral History
Automation Activity & Vendor Info: (Cataloging) Innovative Interfaces, Inc; (Circulation) Innovative Interfaces, Inc
Wireless access
Function: Audio & video playback equip for onsite use, Bk club(s), Copy machines, Electronic databases & coll, Fax serv, Handicapped accessible, ILL available, Photocopying/Printing, Prog for children & young adult, Summer reading prog, VHS videos
Partic in Miami Valley Librs; SouthWest Ohio & Neighboring Libraries
Special Services for the Blind - Talking bks
Open Mon 9-7, Tues & Thurs 11-7, Fri 11-5, Sat 10-1

BRISTOLVILLE

P BRISTOL PUBLIC LIBRARY, 1855 Greenville Rd, 44402-9700. (Mail add: PO Box 220, 44402-0220), SAN 313-2218. Tel: 330-889-3651. FAX: 330-889-9794. E-mail: bristol@oplin.org. Web Site: www.bristol-libraryoh.org. *Dept Head, Adult Serv,* Cheryl French; E-mail: frenchch@oplin.org; *Youth Serv Dept Head,* Deborah Imhoff; E-mail: Deb.Imhoff@bristol-libraryoh.org; *Fiscal Officer,* Ida Mansfield; Staff 8 (Non-MLS 8)
Founded 1912. Pop 3,000; Circ 177,710; Highest Degree: Bachelor
Automation Activity & Vendor Info: (Acquisitions) SIRSI WorkFlows; (Cataloging) SIRSI WorkFlows; (Circulation) SIRSI WorkFlows; (ILL) SIRSI WorkFlows; (OPAC) SIRSI WorkFlows; (Serials) SIRSI WorkFlows
Database Vendor: EBSCOhost
Wireless access
Function: Adult bk club, Bks on CD, Children's prog, Computers for patron use, Copy machines, Digital talking bks, e-mail serv, Electronic databases & coll, Exhibits, Fax serv, Free DVD rentals, Holiday prog, Laminating, Magazines, Music CDs, Notary serv, Online cat, OverDrive digital audio bks, Photocopying/Printing, Prog for adults, Prog for children & young adult, Pub access computers, Ref serv available, Story hour, Summer & winter reading prog, Tax forms, Teen prog
Partic in CLEVNET
Special Services for the Deaf - Bks on deafness & sign lang; Closed caption videos
Special Services for the Blind - Audio mat; Bks on cassette; Bks on CD; Large print bks; Talking bks; Videos on blindness & phys handicaps
Open Mon & Thurs 8-7, Tues, Wed & Fri 8-5
Friends of the Library Group

BRYAN

GL WILLIAMS COUNTY LAW LIBRARY ASSOCIATION*, One Courthouse Sq, 43506. SAN 313-2226. Tel: 419-636-4600. FAX: 419-636-9886. *In Charge,* John Shaffer
Library Holdings: Bk Vols 8,000; Per Subs 10

P WILLIAMS COUNTY PUBLIC LIBRARY*, 107 E High St, 43506-1702. SAN 355-6174. Tel: 419-636-6734. FAX: 419-636-3970. Administration FAX: 419-630-0408. Web Site: www.williamsco.lib.oh.us. *Dir,* Jeffrey A Yahraus; E-mail: yahrauje@oplin.org; *Asst Dir,* Susan K Irwin; E-mail: irwinsu@oplin.org; *Coordr,* Jane Kelly; E-mail: kellyja@oplin.org; *Adult Serv,* Donna Kneipp; E-mail: kneippdo@oplin.org; *Ch Serv,* Vickie Zippay; E-mail: zippayvi@oplin.org; *Ref Serv,* Nancy Bryce; E-mail: brycena@oplin.org; *Syst Adminr,* Tyson Horton; *Tech Serv,* Cindy Riter; E-mail: riterci@oplin.org. Subject Specialists: *Local hist,* Jane Kelly; Staff 4 (MLS 3, Non-MLS 1)
Founded 1882. Pop 38,000; Circ 500,000
Library Holdings: Bk Titles 102,000; Bk Vols 120,000; Per Subs 610
Subject Interests: Genealogy, Local hist, Ohio
Automation Activity & Vendor Info: (Cataloging) SirsiDynix; (Circulation) SirsiDynix
Database Vendor: EBSCOhost, OCLC FirstSearch, SirsiDynix
Wireless access
Publications: Open Book (Newsletter)
Open Mon-Thurs (Winter) 9-8, Fri & Sat 9-5; Mon-Thurs (Summer) 9-8, Fri 9-5, Sat 9-1
Friends of the Library Group
Branches: 5
EDGERTON BRANCH, 319 N Michigan Ave, Edgerton, 43517. (Mail add: PO Box 488, Edgerton, 43517-0488), SAN 355-6204. Tel: 419-298-3230. FAX: 419-298-3230. *Br Mgr,* Anne Trail; E-mail: trailan@oplin.org
Founded 1936
Library Holdings: Bk Vols 12,000
Open Mon & Tues 1-7, Wed & Thurs 11-6, Fri 11-5
Friends of the Library Group
EDON BRANCH, 103 N Michigan St, Edon, 43518. (Mail add: PO Box 185, Edon, 43518-0185), SAN 355-6239. Tel: 419-272-2839. FAX: 419-272-2839. *Br Mgr,* Cynthia Jewell; E-mail: jewellcy@oplin.org
Founded 1936
Library Holdings: Bk Vols 11,000
Open Mon & Wed 10-8, Tues, Thurs & Fri 10-5, Sat 9-1
Friends of the Library Group
PIONEER BRANCH, 106 Baubice St, Pioneer, 43554. (Mail add: PO Box 155, Pioneer, 43554-0155), SAN 355-6263. Tel: 419-737-2833. FAX: 419-737-2833. *Br Mgr,* Rose King; E-mail: kingro@oplin.org
Founded 1936
Library Holdings: Bk Vols 10,000
Open Mon-Thurs 10-7, Fri 10-4, Sat 10-1
Friends of the Library Group
STRYKER BRANCH, 304 S Defiance St, Stryker, 43557. (Mail add: PO Box 137, Stryker, 43557-0137), SAN 355-6298. Tel: 419-682-5081. FAX: 419-682-5081. *Br Mgr,* Connie Aeschliman; E-mail: aeschico@oplin.org
Founded 1936
Library Holdings: Bk Vols 12,000
Open Mon & Tues 1-7, Wed & Thurs 11-6, Fri 11-5
Friends of the Library Group
WEST UNITY BRANCH, 109 S High St, West Unity, 43570. (Mail add: PO Box 522, West Unity, 43570-0522), SAN 355-6328. Tel: 419-924-5237. FAX: 419-924-5237. *Br Mgr,* Ruth Meyer; E-mail: meyerru@oplin.org; Staff 1 (MLS 1)
Founded 1936
Library Holdings: Bk Vols 12,000
Open Mon, Wed & Thurs 10-8, Tues & Fri 10-5, Sat 9-1
Friends of the Library Group

BUCYRUS

P BUCYRUS PUBLIC LIBRARY*, 200 E Mansfield St, 44820-2381. SAN 313-2234. Tel: 419-562-7327. FAX: 419-562-7437. Web Site: www.youseemore.com/bucyrus. *Dir,* Matthew Ross; Tel: 419-562-7327, Ext 102, E-mail: mross@bucyruslibrary.org; Staff 4 (MLS 1, Non-MLS 3)
Founded 1906. Pop 26,000; Circ 114,144
Library Holdings: Bk Vols 54,000; Per Subs 125
Subject Interests: Genealogy, Local hist
Automation Activity & Vendor Info: (Cataloging) TLC (The Library Corporation); (Circulation) TLC (The Library Corporation); (OPAC) TLC (The Library Corporation)
Wireless access
Open Mon-Thurs 11-8, Fri 11-6, Sat 9-2
Friends of the Library Group

BURTON

P BURTON PUBLIC LIBRARY*, 14588 W Park St, 44021. (Mail add: PO Box 427, 44021-0427), SAN 313-2242. Tel: 440-834-4466. FAX: 440-834-0128. E-mail: email@burton.lib.oh.us. Web Site: www.burton.lib.oh.us. *Dir,* Holly Manning Lynn; *Coordr, Ch Serv,* Linda Baker; *Coordr, Circ,* Kathy Schaefer; *Tech Serv Coordr,* Rochelle Baker; *Fiscal Officer,* Rebecca Herrick; Staff 10.3 (MLS 2.8, Non-MLS 7.5)
Founded 1910. Pop 10,000; Circ 319,159
Library Holdings: Bk Titles 64,300; Bk Vols 72,005; Per Subs 201
Subject Interests: Amish, Local hist, Ohio hist, Puppets
Automation Activity & Vendor Info: (Acquisitions) SirsiDynix; (Cataloging) SirsiDynix; (Circulation) SirsiDynix; (OPAC) SirsiDynix
Database Vendor: SirsiDynix
Wireless access
Function: Adult bk club, Bks on cassette, Bks on CD, CD-ROM, Children's prog, Computers for patron use, Copy machines, Electronic databases & coll, Handicapped accessible, Home delivery & serv to Sr ctr & nursing homes, Homebound delivery serv, ILL available, Music CDs, Notary serv, Prog for adults, Prog for children & young adult, Ref & res, Summer reading prog, Tax forms, Telephone ref, VHS videos, Wheelchair accessible
Publications: Friends (Newsletter)
Partic in CLEVNET; Northeast Ohio Regional Library System
Open Mon-Thurs 9-8, Fri 9-5, Sat 10-2, Sun (Sept-May) 1-5
Friends of the Library Group

S GEAUGA COUNTY HISTORICAL SOCIETY*, Shanower Library, 14653 E Park St, 44021. (Mail add: PO Box 153, 44021-0153), SAN 325-4739. Tel: 440-834-1492. FAX: 440-834-4012. E-mail: info@geaugahistorical.org. Web Site: www.geaugahistorical.org.
Founded 1941
Library Holdings: Bk Titles 2,000
Special Collections: Geauga County, Ohio History, corresp, ms, photog; Hitchcock Family Papers. Oral History
Subject Interests: Genealogy, Local hist
Function: Res libr
Publications: Geauga County Historical Quarterly (Newsletter)
Restriction: Open by appt only

C KENT STATE UNIVERSITY*, Geauga Campus Library, 11411 Claridon-Troy Rd, 44021-9535. SAN 324-4407. Tel: 440-834-3722, 440-834-4187. FAX: 440-834-3766. E-mail: library@kent.edu. Web Site: www.geauga.kent.edu. *Dir,* Dr Mary Hricko, PhD; Tel: 440-834-3717, Fax: 440-834-3786, E-mail: mhricko@kent.edu. Subject Specialists: *Acad support, Assessment, Educ tech,* Dr Mary Hricko, PhD; Staff 2 (MLS 2)
Founded 1976. Enrl 2,800; Highest Degree: Bachelor
Library Holdings: Bk Vols 18,000
Open Mon-Thurs 9-8, Fri 9-1, Sat 10-2

CADIZ

P PUSKARICH PUBLIC LIBRARY*, 200 E Market St, 43907-1185. SAN 313-2250. Tel: 740-942-2623. FAX: 740-942-8047. Web Site: www.harrison.lib.oh.us. *Dir,* Sandi Thompson; E-mail: sthompson@oplin.org; Staff 3 (MLS 1, Non-MLS 2)
Founded 1880. Pop 13,874; Circ 126,168

Library Holdings: Bk Titles 50,537; Bk Vols 50,591; Per Subs 185
Subject Interests: Coal, Genealogy, Local hist
Automation Activity & Vendor Info: (Acquisitions) SirsiDynix; (Cataloging) SirsiDynix; (Circulation) SirsiDynix; (Course Reserve) SirsiDynix; (ILL) SirsiDynix; (OPAC) SirsiDynix
Partic in SEO (Serving Every Ohioan) Library Center
Open Mon-Thurs 9-8, Fri 9-6, Sat 9-5
Friends of the Library Group
Branches: 2
CLARK MEMORIAL, 102 W Main St, Freeport, 43973. Tel: 740-658-3855. FAX: 740-658-3798. *Br Mgr,* Patricia Spain
Library Holdings: Bk Vols 10,000; Per Subs 30
Open Mon & Fri 10-5, Tues & Thurs 10-7, Sat 9-1
SCIO BRANCH, 331 W Main St, Scio, 43988. Tel: 740-945-6811. FAX: 740-945-9515. *Librn,* Kathryn Birney
Library Holdings: Bk Vols 12,000; Per Subs 40; Videos 1,600
Open Mon & Fri 10-5, Tues & Thurs 10-7, Sat 9-1

CALDWELL

P CALDWELL PUBLIC LIBRARY*, 517 Spruce St, 43724-1135. (Mail add: PO Box 230, 43724-0230), SAN 313-2269. Tel: 740-732-4506. FAX: 740-732-4795. Web Site: www.caldwell.lib.oh.us. *Dir,* Belinda West; E-mail: westbe@oplin.org; Staff 12 (Non-MLS 12)
Founded 1930. Pop 15,000; Circ 98,511
Library Holdings: Bk Vols 39,026; Per Subs 162
Subject Interests: Genealogy
Automation Activity & Vendor Info: (Circulation) SirsiDynix; (OPAC) SirsiDynix
Database Vendor: SirsiDynix
Partic in SEO (Serving Every Ohioan) Library Center
Open Mon-Wed 9-8, Thurs & Fri 9-5, Sat 9-2
Friends of the Library Group

S STATE OF OHIO DEPARTMENT OF CORRECTIONS*, Noble Correctional Institution Library, 15708 Collinsville Rd, 43724. Tel: 740-748-5188. FAX: 740-748-5010. *Librn,* Julie Hupp; E-mail: julie.hupp@odrc.state.oh.us
Library Holdings: Bk Vols 12,000; Per Subs 60
Automation Activity & Vendor Info: (Cataloging) Autolib Library & Information Management Systems; (Circulation) Autolib Library & Information Management Systems; (ILL) Autolib Library & Information Management Systems; (OPAC) Autolib Library & Information Management Systems
Open Mon-Sun 8-10:30, 12:30-3:30 & 6-8

CAMBRIDGE

P GUERNSEY COUNTY DISTRICT PUBLIC LIBRARY*, 800 Steubenville Ave, 43725-2385. SAN 355-6352. Tel: 740-432-5946. FAX: 740-432-7142. Web Site: www.gcdpl.lib.oh.us. *Dir,* Richard E Goodwin; E-mail: goodwinr@oplin.org; *Asst Dir,* Melissa Essex; E-mail: essexme@oplin.org; *Ch,* Donna King; E-mail: kingdo@oplin.org; Staff 25 (MLS 2, Non-MLS 23)
Founded 1832. Pop 40,000; Circ 350,000
Library Holdings: Bk Vols 130,162; Per Subs 320
Special Collections: Local History & Genealogy (Finley Coll Room)
Automation Activity & Vendor Info: (Cataloging) SirsiDynix; (Circulation) SirsiDynix; (OPAC) SirsiDynix
Database Vendor: ALLDATA Online, EBSCOhost, Electric Library
Wireless access
Partic in Ohio Public Library Information Network; SEO (Serving Every Ohioan) Library Center
Open Mon 9-8, Tues-Fri 9-6:30, Sat 9-5
Friends of the Library Group
Branches: 2
BYESVILLE BRANCH, 100 Glass Ave, Byesville, 43723, SAN 355-6387. Tel: 740-685-2236. FAX: 740-685-6105. *Dir,* Richard Goodwin; E-mail: goodwinr@oplin.org; *Br Mgr,* Linda Kostelnik; E-mail: kostell1@oplin.org
Open Mon-Fri 9-5:30, Sat 9-5
Friends of the Library Group
CROSSROADS, 63500 Byesville Rd, 43725. Tel: 740-432-7536. FAX: 740-435-3426.
Open Mon-Thurs 9-8, Fri 9-6:30, Sat 9-5, Sun 1-5
Bookmobiles: 1. In Charge, Susie Clark. Bk titles 2,500

L GUERNSEY COUNTY LAW LIBRARY*, Guernsey County Court House, 801 Wheeling Ave, Rm D 301, 43725. SAN 325-4747. Tel: 740-432-9258. *Librn,* Richard A Baker; *Asst Librn,* Margot A Ringer
Library Holdings: Bk Vols 15,000
Subject Interests: Fed law, Ohio law
Open Mon-Fri 8:30-12 & 1-4
Restriction: Restricted pub use

CANAL FULTON

P CANAL FULTON PUBLIC LIBRARY*, 154 Market St NE, 44614-1196. SAN 313-2285. Tel: 330-854-4148. FAX: 330-854-9520. E-mail: info@canalfultonlibrary.org. Web Site: www.canalfultonlibrary.org. *Libr Dir,* David Brown; E-mail: david@canalfultonlibrary.org; *Head, Circ,* Janet Deans; E-mail: janet@canalfultonlibrary.org; *Head, ILL,* Tracey Hayward; E-mail: tracey@canalfultonlibrary.org; *Head, Ref Serv,* Cheryl Mullins; E-mail: cheryl@canalfultonlibrary.org; *Mgr, Children's Dept,* Jennifer Hendricks; E-mail: jennifer@canalfultonlibrary.org; Staff 15.11 (MLS 4, Non-MLS 11.11)
Founded 1937. Pop 13,329; Circ 305,262
Jan 2012-Dec 2012 Income $777,545, State $425,047, Locally Generated Income $250,761, Other $101,737. Mats Exp $129,597, Books $72,957, Per/Ser (Incl. Access Fees) $9,000, Other Print Mats $7,164, AV Mat $34,476, Electronic Ref Mat (Incl. Access Fees) $6,000. Sal $442,862 (Prof $110,335)
Library Holdings: AV Mats 516; CDs 2,117; DVDs 4,819; e-books 24,578; Electronic Media & Resources 284; Bk Vols 55,258; Per Subs 3,859
Automation Activity & Vendor Info: (Acquisitions) SIRSI WorkFlows; (Cataloging) SIRSI WorkFlows; (Circulation) SIRSI WorkFlows
Database Vendor: ALLDATA Online, Booksite, EBSCO Auto Repair Reference, EBSCOhost, Facts on File, H W Wilson, LearningExpress, Marquis Who's Who, Medline, Newsbank, OHIONET, Overdrive, Inc, Oxford Online, ProQuest, SirsiDynix, Wilson - Wilson Web, World Book Online
Wireless access
Function: Accelerated reader prog, Adult bk club, Audiobks via web, Bk club(s), Bks on CD, Children's prog, Computer training, Computers for patron use, Copy machines, Electronic databases & coll, Equip loans & repairs, Exhibits, Fax serv, Free DVD rentals, Handicapped accessible
Special Services for the Deaf - Bks on deafness & sign lang
Special Services for the Blind - BiFolkal kits; Bks on CD; Cassettes; Home delivery serv; Large print bks; Magnifiers; Playaways (bks on MP3); Recorded bks
Open Mon-Thurs 9-8, Fri & Sat 10-5
Friends of the Library Group

CANTON

M AULTMAN HOSPITAL*, Health Sciences Library, Aultman Education Ctr, C2-230, 2600 Seventh St SW, 44710-1799. SAN 313-2293. Tel: 330-363-5000. Administration Tel: 330-363-3833. FAX: 330-363-2604. E-mail: hlibrary@aultman.com. Web Site: www.neoucom.edu/audience/library. *Chief Med Librn,* Krystal K Slivka; E-mail: kslivka@aultman.com; *Libr Asst,* Elaine Ott; E-mail: hlibrary@aultman.com; Staff 2 (MLS 1, Non-MLS 1)
Library Holdings: Bk Titles 4,000; Per Subs 50
Subject Interests: Med, Nursing
Automation Activity & Vendor Info: (Cataloging) Innovative Interfaces, Inc - Millenium; (Circulation) Innovative Interfaces, Inc - Millenium; (Course Reserve) Innovative Interfaces, Inc - Millenium); (OPAC) Innovative Interfaces, Inc - Millenium; (Serials) Innovative Interfaces, Inc - Millenium
Database Vendor: ACM (Association for Computing Machinery), Agricola, Blackwell, Cinahl, EBSCOhost, Elsevier, Innovative Interfaces, Inc, ISI Web of Knowledge, LearningExpress, Lexi-Comp, LexisNexis, Medline, Modern Language Association, OCLC ArticleFirst, OCLC WorldShare Interlibrary Loan, Oxford Online, ProQuest, PubMed, Safari Books Online, UpToDate, Wiley
Wireless access
Partic in Ohio Library & Information Network
Special Services for the Blind - Bks & mags in Braille, on rec, tape & cassette
Open Mon-Fri 8-4:30
Restriction: External users must contact libr, Open to pub by appt only, Use of others with permission of librn

S CANTON MUSEUM OF ART LIBRARY*, 1001 Market Ave N, 44702. SAN 313-2307. Tel: 330-453-7666. FAX: 330-453-1034. Web Site: www.cantonart.org. *Exec Dir,* M J Albacete; E-mail: al@cantonart.org
Founded 1941
Library Holdings: Bk Vols 2,000; Per Subs 20
Special Collections: Victorian Art (John Hemming Fry Coll), bks, portfolios
Subject Interests: Art, Music
Function: Res libr
Restriction: Open to pub upon request

CR MALONE UNIVERSITY*, Everett L Cattell Library, 2600 Cleveland Ave NW, 44709-3897. SAN 313-234X. Tel: 330-471-8317. Interlibrary Loan Service Tel: 330-471-8319. Reference Tel: 330-471-8314. FAX: 330-471-8655. E-mail: libcirc@malone.edu, reference@malone.edu. Web Site: www.malone.edu/library. *Acq, Actg Dir, Libr Serv, Pub Serv,* Rebecca

Fort; Tel: 330-471-8313, E-mail: rfort@malone.edu; *Per, Ref Librn,* Troy Alpeter; Tel: 330-471-8334, E-mail: talpeter@malone.edu; *Cataloger, Ref Librn,* Janice L Anderson; Tel: 330-471-8312, E-mail: janderson@malone.edu; *Archivist, Ref Librn,* Amy Yuncker; Tel: 330-471-8233, E-mail: ayuncker@malone.edu; *Ref Librn/Electronic Serv/Instruction,* Kris Owens; Tel: 330-471-8557, E-mail: kowens@malone.edu; *Weekend Ref Librn,* Stephanie Livengood; E-mail: slivengood@malone.edu; *Circ Supvr, ILL,* Mary-Ann Frischkorn; E-mail: mfrischkorn@malone.edu; *Circ Support,* Peggy Sluss; Tel: 330-471-8215, E-mail: psluss@malone.edu; Staff 6.75 (MLS 4.125, Non-MLS 2.625)
Founded 1892. Enrl 2,113; Fac 139; Highest Degree: Master
Jul 2012-Jun 2013 Income $782,715. Mats Exp $244,833, Per/Ser (Incl. Access Fees) $70,958, Micro $19,601, Electronic Ref Mat (Incl. Access Fees) $145,452, Presv $8,822. Sal $280,655 (Prof $240,688)
Library Holdings: AV Mats 9,306; CDs 3,237; DVDs 1,842; e-books 81,514; e-journals 45,619; Microforms 654,486; Music Scores 2,477; Bk Titles 137,121; Bk Vols 156,079; Per Subs 240; Videos 1,910
Special Collections: Evangelical Friends Church-Eastern Region Archives; Friends Library (Quakers)
Subject Interests: Soc of Friends
Automation Activity & Vendor Info: (Acquisitions) Innovative Interfaces, Inc; (Cataloging) Innovative Interfaces, Inc; (Circulation) Innovative Interfaces, Inc; (OPAC) Innovative Interfaces, Inc; (Serials) Innovative Interfaces, Inc
Database Vendor: ABC-CLIO, ACM (Association for Computing Machinery), Alexander Street Press, American Chemical Society, American Psychological Association (APA), Annual Reviews, Blackwell, Children's Literature Comprehensive Database Company (CLCD), CIOS (Communication Institute for Online Scholarship), College Source, CQ Press, EBSCOhost, Elsevier, Emerald, Gale Cengage Learning, H W Wilson, Hoovers, Ingenta, Innovative Interfaces, Inc, Innovative Interfaces, Inc, IOP, ISI Web of Knowledge, JSTOR, LexisNexis, Mergent Online, OCLC WorldShare Interlibrary Loan, OHIONET, OVID Technologies, Oxford Online, Project MUSE, ProQuest, Safari Books Online, Sage, SerialsSolutions, Springer-Verlag, Thomson - Web of Science, Wiley, Wilson - Wilson Web
Wireless access
Function: ILL available
Partic in OCLC Online Computer Library Center, Inc; Ohio Library & Information Network; Ohio Private Academic Libraries (OPAL); OHIONET
Open Mon-Thurs (Winter) 7:30am-11:30pm, Fri 8-7, Sat 10-5, Sun 2-10; Mon, Tues & Thurs (Summer) 8-7, Wed 8am-9pm, Fri 8-5, Sat 10-5
Restriction: Badge access after hrs

S WILLIAM MCKINLEY PRESIDENTIAL LIBRARY & MUSEUM*, Ramsayer Research Library, 800 McKinley Monument Dr NW, 44708. SAN 327-683X. Tel: 330-455-7043. FAX: 330-455-1137. E-mail: library@mckinleymuseum.org. Web Site: www.mckinleymuseum.org. *Librn,* Fr Karl W Ash; Staff 1 (MLS 1)
Founded 1946
Library Holdings: Bk Vols 10,000
Special Collections: Don Mellett Murder & Trial Records, papers & photos; McKinley Presidential Papers, microfilm; Primary & Secondary Sources Focusing on the Life & Legacy of 25th President William McKinley; Stark County, Ohio History Coll. Oral History
Subject Interests: City hist, State hist
Function: Archival coll, Bus archives, For res purposes, Handicapped accessible, Magnifiers for reading, Photocopying/Printing, Ref serv available, Res libr
Open Mon-Fri 9-4
Restriction: Access at librarian's discretion, In-house use for visitors, Non-circulating, Not a lending libr, Open to pub with supv only, Open to researchers by request, Open to students, fac & staff

M MERCY MEDICAL CENTER*, Medical Library, 1320 Mercy Dr NW, 44708. SAN 355-6689. Tel: 330-489-1462. FAX: 330-489-1127. *Dir,* Marlene Derrick; E-mail: marlene.derrick@csauh.com; Staff 1 (MLS 1)
Founded 1960
Library Holdings: Bk Titles 1,500; Per Subs 88
Subject Interests: Allied health, Health admin, Med
Publications: Core Reference Collection (Accession list); Journals Listing

P STARK COUNTY DISTRICT LIBRARY, 715 Market Ave N, 44702-1018. SAN 355-6441. Tel: 330-452-0665. FAX: 330-455-9596. E-mail: contactus@starklibrary.org. Web Site: www.thesmartstore.org. *Exec Dir,* Tena Wilson; E-mail: twilson@starklibrary.org; *Libr Dir,* Jean McFarren; Tel: 330-458-2702, E-mail: jmcfarren@starklibrary.org; *Dir, Commun Serv,* Marianna DiGiacomo; Tel: 330-458-2769, E-mail: mdigiacomo@starklibrary.org; *Dir of Coll,* Gregory Burlingame; Tel: 330-458-2832, E-mail: gburlingame@starklibrary.org; *Dir, Mkt & Develop,* Stacey Giammarco; E-mail: sgiammarco@starklibrary.org; *Commun Libr Dir,* Patty Marsh; Tel: 330-458-2703, E-mail: pmarsh@starklibrary.org; *Human Res Dir,* Linda Wilkins; Tel: 330-458-2701, E-mail: lwilkins@starklibrary.org; *IT Dir,* Bryan Harris; Tel: 330-458-3145; *Fiscal Officer,* Russ Humerickhouse; Tel: 330-458-2690, E-mail: rhumerickhouse@starklibrary.org; *Knowledge Officer,* Suzette Burlingame; Tel: 330-458-2720, E-mail: sburlingame@starklibrary.org; Staff 165.25 (MLS 54.75, Non-MLS 110.5)
Founded 1884. Pop 240,131; Circ 3,506,134
Jan 2013-Dec 2013 Income (Main Library and Branch(s)) $14,203,471, State $6,390,872, Federal $3,720, County $7,225,346, Other $583,533. Mats Exp $1,616,406, Books $793,021, Per/Ser (Incl. Access Fees) $102,793, Other Print Mats $7,880, AV Mat $415,512, Electronic Ref Mat (Incl. Access Fees) $297,200. Sal $6,101,755
Library Holdings: AV Mats 410,546; Bks on Deafness & Sign Lang 202; Braille Volumes 159; CDs 78,516; DVDs 79,425; e-books 100,214; Large Print Bks 26,506; Music Scores 357; Bk Vols 599,293; Per Subs 1,411; Talking Bks 168,151; Videos 86,979
Special Collections: Genealogy, African-American Coll. Oral History; State Document Depository
Subject Interests: Career, Grants
Automation Activity & Vendor Info: (Circulation) Innovative Interfaces, Inc
Database Vendor: Gale Cengage Learning, OCLC FirstSearch, ProQuest
Wireless access
Function: Adult bk club, After school storytime, AV serv, Bk club(s), Bks on cassette, Bks on CD, Chess club, Children's prog, Computer training, Computers for patron use, Copy machines, Doc delivery serv, Fax serv, Handicapped accessible, Holiday prog, Home delivery & serv to Sr ctr & nursing homes, Homebound delivery serv, Homework prog, ILL available, Music CDs, Notary serv, Online cat, Online ref, Prog for adults, Prog for children & young adult, Ref & res, Ref serv available, Senior computer classes, Spoken cassettes & CDs, Story hour, Summer reading prog, Tax forms, Teen prog, Wheelchair accessible, Workshops
Publications: Stark Scene (Newsletter)
Partic in OHIONET
Special Services for the Blind - Bks on CD; Braille bks; Talking bks
Open Mon-Thurs 9-8, Fri 9-6, Sat 9-5, Sun (Sept-May) 1-5
Friends of the Library Group
Branches: 9
DEHOFF MEMORIAL BRANCH, 216 Hartford Ave SE, 44707, SAN 355-6476. Tel: 330-452-9014. FAX: 330-452-8224. E-mail: dehoff@starklibrary.org. *Br Mgr,* Linda Bennett; E-mail: lbennett@starklibrary.org; Staff 5 (MLS 1, Non-MLS 4)
Circ 64,256
Special Collections: Oral History; State Document Depository
Function: Computers for patron use, Copy machines, Prog for children & young adult, Summer reading prog, Teen prog
Open Mon & Tues 10-8, Wed-Fri 10-6, Sat 10-5
Friends of the Library Group
EAST CANTON BRANCH, 224 N Wood St, East Canton, 44730, SAN 355-6506. Tel: 330-488-1501. FAX: 330-488-2509. E-mail: eastcanton@starklibrary.org. *Br Mgr,* Rebecca Baldwin; E-mail: rbaldwin@starklibrary.org; Staff 3.75 (MLS 1, Non-MLS 2.75)
Circ 85,681
Special Collections: Oral History; State Document Depository
Function: Adult bk club, After school storytime, Children's prog, Computers for patron use, Copy machines, Prog for adults, Summer reading prog, Teen prog
Open Mon & Tues 9-8, Wed-Fri 9-6, Sat 10-5
JACKSON TOWNSHIP BRANCH, 7487 Fulton Dr NW, Massillon, 44646, SAN 373-5583. Tel: 330-833-1010. FAX: 330-833-3491. E-mail: jackson@starklibrary.org. *Br Mgr,* Kathy Kibler; E-mail: kkibler@starklibrary.org; Staff 10 (MLS 4, Non-MLS 6)
Circ 301,643
Special Collections: Oral History; State Document Depository
Function: Adult bk club, Children's prog, Computers for patron use, Copy machines, Prog for adults, Summer reading prog, Teen prog
Open Mon-Thurs 9-8, Fri 9-6, Sat 9-5, Sun (Sept-May) 1-5
Friends of the Library Group
LAKE COMMUNITY BRANCH, 565 Market Ave SW, Uniontown, 44685, SAN 355-6530. Tel: 330-877-9975. FAX: 330-877-7568. E-mail: lake@starklibrary.org. *Br Mgr,* Jennifer Welsh; E-mail: jwelsh@starklibrary.org; Staff 9.5 (MLS 3, Non-MLS 6.5)
Circ 317,744
Special Collections: Oral History; State Document Depository
Function: Adult bk club, Children's prog, Computers for patron use, Copy machines, Prog for adults, Summer reading prog, Teen prog
Open Mon-Thurs 9-8, Fri 9-6, Sat 9-5
Friends of the Library Group
NORTH BRANCH, 189 25th St NW, 44709, SAN 355-6565. Tel: 330-456-4356. FAX: 330-580-1806. E-mail: north@starklibrary.org. *Br Mgr,* Robyn Guedel; E-mail: rguedel@starklibrary.org; Staff 8.5 (MLS 3, Non-MLS 5.5)
Founded 1960. Circ 330,454
Special Collections: Oral History; State Document Depository
Function: Adult bk club, Children's prog, Computers for patron use, Copy machines, Prog for adults, Summer reading prog, Teen prog

Open Mon-Thurs 9-8, Fri 9-6, Sat 9-5
Friends of the Library Group
PERRY SIPPO BRANCH, 5710 12th St NW, 44708, SAN 355-659X. Tel: 330-477-8482. FAX: 330-479-0015. E-mail: perry@starklibrary.org. *Br Mgr,* Lisa Szeles; E-mail: lszeles@starklibrary.org; Staff 10 (MLS 3, Non-MLS 7)
Circ 259,599
Special Collections: Oral History; State Document Depository
Function: Adult bk club, Children's prog, Computers for patron use, Copy machines, Prog for adults, Summer reading prog, Teen prog
Open Mon-Thurs 9-8, Fri 9-6, Sat 9-5, Sun (Sept-May) 1-5
Friends of the Library Group
PLAIN COMMUNITY BRANCH, 1803 Schneider St NE, 44721. Tel: 330-494-3399. FAX: 330-497-0466. E-mail: plain@starklibrary.org. *Br Mgr,* Megan Johnson; E-mail: mjohnson@starklibrary.org; Staff 8.5 (MLS 4, Non-MLS 4.5)
Circ 147,206
Function: Adult bk club, Computers for patron use, Copy machines, Prog for adults, Prog for children & young adult, Summer reading prog, Teen prog
Open Mon-Thurs (Sept-May) 7:30am-8pm, Fri 7:30-6, Sat 9-5, Sun 1-5; Mon-Thurs (June-Aug) 9-8, Fri 9-6, Sat 9-5
Friends of the Library Group
SANDY VALLEY BRANCH, 9754 Cleveland Ave SE, Magnolia, 44643, SAN 355-662X. Tel: 330-866-3366. FAX: 330-866-9859. E-mail: sandyvalley@starklibrary.org. *Br Mgr,* Lisa Murray; E-mail: lmurray@starklibrary.org; Staff 4.5 (MLS 1, Non-MLS 3.5)
Circ 133,888
Special Collections: Oral History; State Document Depository
Function: Adult bk club, After school storytime, Children's prog, Computers for patron use, Copy machines, Prog for adults, Summer reading prog, Teen prog
Open Mon & Tues 10-8, Wed-Fri 10-6, Sat 10-5
Friends of the Library Group
MADGE YOUTZ BRANCH, 2921 Mahoning Rd NE, 44705, SAN 355-6654. Tel: 330-452-2618. FAX: 330-580-1807. E-mail: madgeyoutz@starklibrary.org. *Br Mgr,* Kathy Clay; E-mail: kclay@starklibrary.org; Staff 4.5 (MLS 3, Non-MLS 1.5)
Circ 85,992
Special Collections: Oral History; State Document Depository
Function: Adult bk club, Chess club, Children's prog, Computers for patron use, Copy machines, Prog for adults, Summer reading prog, Teen prog
Open Mon & Tues 10-8, Wed-Fri 10-6, Sat 10-5
Friends of the Library Group
Bookmobiles: 5. Librn, Tammy Long. Bk vols 97,448

L STARK COUNTY LAW LIBRARY, 110 Central Plaza S, Ste 401, 44702. SAN 328-5812. Tel: 330-451-7380. FAX: 330-451-7381. E-mail: inform@starkcountyohio.gov. Web Site: www.starkcountyohio.gov/law-library. *Dir,* Kendel Croston; Staff 4 (MLS 1, Non-MLS 3)
Founded 1890
Jan 2014-Dec 2014 Income (Main Library and Branch(s)) $639,000, County $96,000, Locally Generated Income $498,000, Other $45,000. Mats Exp $407,000, Books $312,000, Electronic Ref Mat (Incl. Access Fees) $95,000. Sal $100,000
Library Holdings: CDs 193; DVDs 2; Microforms 301,613; Bk Titles 4,905; Bk Vols 66,582; Per Subs 40; Videos 1
Subject Interests: Ohio law
Automation Activity & Vendor Info: (Cataloging) SirsiDynix; (Circulation) SirsiDynix; (OPAC) SirsiDynix; (Serials) SirsiDynix
Database Vendor: LexisNexis, Loislaw, Westlaw
Function: 24/7 Online cat, Electronic databases & coll
Publications: Legally Speaking (Newsletter)
Partic in Consortium of Ohio County Law Libraries
Open Mon-Fri 8:30-4:30
Restriction: Circ to mem only
Branches:
MASSILLON BRANCH, Two James Duncan Plaza, Massillon, 44646. (Mail add: 110 Central Plaza S, Ste 401, 44702), SAN 329-3807. Tel: 330-451-7380. FAX: 330-451-7381.
Library Holdings: Bk Titles 115; Bk Vols 2,295
Subject Interests: Ohio law
Restriction: Restricted access

CARDINGTON

P CARDINGTON-LINCOLN PUBLIC LIBRARY*, 128 E Main St, 43315. (Mail add: PO Box 38, 43315-0038), SAN 313-2404. Tel: 419-864-8181. FAX: 419-864-8184. E-mail: cardlinc@oplin.org. Web Site: www.cardingtonlibrary.org. *Dir,* Lisa Murray; E-mail: murrayli@oplin.org; *Ad,* Lisa Ebert; E-mail: ebertli@oplin.org; *Youth Serv Librn,* Jennifer Gliebe; E-mail: gliebeje@oplin.org; Staff 3.38 (MLS 1.14, Non-MLS 2.24)
Founded 1896. Pop 6,516; Circ 46,922
Jan 2011-Dec 2011 Income $251,806, State $218,872, Other $32,934. Mats Exp $29,324, Books $16,834, Per/Ser (Incl. Access Fees) $2,771, Other Print Mats $648, AV Mat $3,107, Electronic Ref Mat (Incl. Access Fees) $5,964. Sal $116,156
Library Holdings: Audiobooks 654; DVDs 2,458; Bk Vols 32,393; Per Subs 118
Automation Activity & Vendor Info: (Acquisitions) Evergreen; (Cataloging) Evergreen; (Circulation) Evergreen; (ILL) Evergreen; (OPAC) Evergreen
Database Vendor: EBSCOhost
Wireless access
Function: Adult bk club, Adult literacy prog, Art exhibits, Audiobks via web, Bks on CD, Children's prog, Computer training, Computers for patron use, Copy machines, E-Reserves, Electronic databases & coll, Fax serv, Free DVD rentals, Govt ref serv, Handicapped accessible, ILL available, Mail & tel request accepted, Music CDs, Online info literacy tutorials on the web & in blackboard, Online ref, Online searches, Orientations, Outreach serv, OverDrive digital audio bks, Photocopying/Printing, Preschool outreach, Preschool reading prog, Printer for laptops & handheld devices, Prog for adults, Prog for children & young adult, Pub access computers, Ref serv available, Ref serv in person, Scanner, Senior computer classes, Story hour, Summer reading prog, Tax forms, Teen prog, Telephone ref, Web-catalog, Wheelchair accessible
Partic in Ohio Public Library Information Network; OHIONET
Special Services for the Deaf - Bks on deafness & sign lang
Special Services for the Blind - Bks on CD; Large print bks
Open Mon-Thurs 10:30-7, Sat 10:30-2

CAREY

P DORCAS CAREY PUBLIC LIBRARY*, 236 E Findlay St, 43316-1250. SAN 313-2412. Tel: 419-396-7921. FAX: 419-396-3046. Web Site: www.dorcus-carey.lib.oh.us. *Dir,* Laura Toland; *Asst Librn,* Rosemary Unverferth
Founded 1905. Pop 5,800; Circ 84,328
Library Holdings: Bk Vols 38,000; Per Subs 112
Automation Activity & Vendor Info: (Cataloging) SirsiDynix; (Circulation) SirsiDynix; (OPAC) SirsiDynix
Database Vendor: EBSCOhost
Function: AV serv, Homebound delivery serv, ILL available
Partic in Northwestern Libr District
Open Mon-Thurs 9-8, Fri 9-5, Sat 9-1

CARROLLTON

P CARROLL COUNTY DISTRICT LIBRARY*, 70 Second St NE, 44615. SAN 355-6743. Tel: 330-627-2613. FAX: 330-627-2523. E-mail: carroll@oplin.org. Web Site: www.carroll.lib.oh.us. *Dir,* Ellen Finnicum
Founded 1935. Pop 28,836; Circ 251,859
Library Holdings: Bk Vols 79,786; Per Subs 200
Subject Interests: Local hist, Sports
Automation Activity & Vendor Info: (Cataloging) SirsiDynix; (Circulation) SirsiDynix; (OPAC) SirsiDynix
Database Vendor: SirsiDynix
Wireless access
Open Mon-Thurs 9-8, Fri 9-6, Sat 9-4:30
Branches: 1
MALVERN BRANCH, 710 E Porter St, Malvern, 44644, SAN 355-6778. Tel: 330-863-0636. FAX: 330-863-0419. *Dir,* Ellen Finnicum; E-mail: finnicumel@oplin.org; *Br Head,* Roof Kay
Library Holdings: Bk Vols 55,000; Per Subs 65
Open Mon-Thurs 10-7, Fri 9-6, Sat 9-4:30
Bookmobiles: 1

CEDARVILLE

CR CEDARVILLE UNIVERSITY, Centennial Library, 251 N Main St, 45314-0601. SAN 313-2420. Tel: 937-766-7840. Reference Tel: 937-766-7850. FAX: 937-766-2337. E-mail: library@cedarville.edu. Web Site: www.cedarville.edu/Academics/Library.aspx. *Dean, Libr Serv,* Lynn Alan Brock; Tel: 937-766-7846; *Dir, Pub Serv,* Joshua Michael; *Dir, Coll Serv,* Julie Deardorff; *Digital Commons Dir,* Gregory Martin; *Curric Center Librn,* Sharon Kerestes; *Info Serv Librn,* Lynne Funtik; *Info Serv Librn,* Jeffery Gates; *Instrul Serv Librn,* Joe Fox; Staff 20 (MLS 9, Non-MLS 11)
Founded 1887. Enrl 3,400; Fac 235; Highest Degree: Doctorate
Jul 2013-Jun 2014 Income $1,829,598, Locally Generated Income $24,245, Parent Institution $1,805,353. Mats Exp $1,724,321, Books $215,881, Per/Ser (Incl. Access Fees) $256,010, Manu Arch $1,007, AV Equip $3,152, AV Mat $25,632, Electronic Ref Mat (Incl. Access Fees) $147,433, Presv $9,481. Sal $873,312 (Prof $502,428)
Library Holdings: AV Mats 11,347; CDs 4,670; DVDs 3,671; e-books 85,122; e-journals 25,012; Electronic Media & Resources 192; Microforms 16,479; Bk Titles 154,742; Bk Vols 178,573; Per Subs 816; Videos 371
Special Collections: English Bible Coll; University Archives
Subject Interests: Baptist hist, Theol studies

Automation Activity & Vendor Info: (Acquisitions) Innovative Interfaces, Inc; (Cataloging) Innovative Interfaces, Inc; (Circulation) Innovative Interfaces, Inc; (ILL) OCLC; (OPAC) Innovative Interfaces, Inc; (Serials) Innovative Interfaces, Inc
Database Vendor: 3M Library Systems, Agricola, American Chemical Society, American Psychological Association (APA), ARTstor, BCR: Christian Periodical Index, Bowker, Cinahl, CIOS (Communication Institute for Online Scholarship), CQ Press, CRC Press/Taylor & Francis Group, Dun & Bradstreet, DynaMed, EBSCO Information Services, EBSCOhost, Elsevier, Emerald, Facts on File, Gale Cengage Learning, Hoovers, Innovative Interfaces, Inc, ISI Web of Knowledge, JSTOR, Lexi-Comp, LexisNexis, McGraw-Hill, Mergent Online, Natural Standard, Newsbank, OCLC, OCLC FirstSearch, OCLC WorldShare Interlibrary Loan, OHIONET, ProQuest, PubMed, RefWorks, Safari Books Online, Scopus, ValueLine, YBP Library Services
Wireless access
Function: Ref serv available
Partic in OCLC Online Computer Library Center, Inc; Ohio Library & Information Network; OHIONET; Southwestern Ohio Council for Higher Education
Special Services for the Deaf - Am sign lang & deaf culture; Bks on deafness & sign lang
Open Mon-Thurs 7:45am-11:30pm, Fri 7:45-7, Sat 10-7, Sun 7:30pm-11:30pm

CELINA

P MERCER COUNTY DISTRICT LIBRARY*, 303 N Main St, 45822. SAN 355-6808. Tel: 419-586-4442. FAX: 419-586-3222. E-mail: mercer@oplin.org. Web Site: www.mercer.lib.oh.us. *Dir,* Elizabeth Muether; E-mail: muetheel@oplin.org; *Assoc Dir,* Vicki DeBolt; *AV,* Jean Shaw; *Ch Serv,* Amy Broering; Staff 15 (MLS 3, Non-MLS 12)
Founded 1899. Pop 39,000; Circ 240,000
Library Holdings: Bk Vols 98,000; Per Subs 125
Subject Interests: Children's lit
Automation Activity & Vendor Info: (Circulation) SirsiDynix
Database Vendor: SirsiDynix
Open Mon, Tues, Thurs & Fri 9-6, Wed 9-8, Sat 9-5
Friends of the Library Group
Branches: 3
MENDON BRANCH, 105 W Market St, Mendon, 45862. (Mail add: PO Box 302, Mendon, 45862-0302), SAN 355-6832. Tel: 419-795-6472. FAX: 419-795-6472. E-mail: mendon@mercerlibrary.org. *Librn,* Leigh Ann Shaffer
Library Holdings: Bk Vols 5,353
Open Mon & Tues 12-6, Wed 12-8, Thurs 9:30-11 & 12-6, Sat 9-1
Friends of the Library Group
SAINT HENRY GRANVILLE TOWNSHIP, 200 E Main St, Saint Henry, 45883. (Mail add: PO Box 320, Saint Henry, 45883), SAN 355-6867. Tel: 419-678-3128. FAX: 419-678-3128. E-mail: sthenry@mercerlibrary.org. *Librn,* Judy Gelhaus
Library Holdings: Bk Vols 10,721
Open Mon, Tues & Thurs 1-8, Wed 9-8, Sat 9-12
Friends of the Library Group
ZAHN-MARION TOWNSHIP BRANCH, Five East Franklin St, Chickasaw, 45826. (Mail add: PO Box 219, Chickasaw, 45826-0219), SAN 355-6824. Tel: 419-925-4966. FAX: 419-925-4227. E-mail: marion@mercerlibrary.org. *Librn,* Karen Hoying; Staff 5 (Non-MLS 5)
Founded 1982
Library Holdings: Audiobooks 50; CDs 400; DVDs 100; Large Print Bks 100; Bk Titles 11,058; Per Subs 45; Videos 300
Open Mon-Wed 1-7, Thurs 10-12 & 1-7, Sat 9-12
Friends of the Library Group

L MERCER COUNTY LAW LIBRARY*, Court House, Rm 206, 101 N Main St, 45822. SAN 329-8841. Tel: 419-584-2572. FAX: 419-586-4000. E-mail: lawlibrary@mercercountyohio.org. *Librn,* Carol Forsthoefel; Staff 1 (Non-MLS 1)
Library Holdings: Bk Vols 4,000; Per Subs 2
Subject Interests: Law, Tax
Open Tues & Thurs 9-1

C WRIGHT STATE UNIVERSITY*, Lake Campus Library, 7600 State Rte 703 E, 45822-2952. SAN 313-2439. Tel: 419-586-0360. Circulation Tel: 419-586-0333. Toll Free Tel: 800-237-1477. FAX: 419-586-8334. Web Site: www.libraries.wright.edu, www.wright.edu/lake. *Dir, Br Serv,* Alex Pittman; Tel: 937-775-8360, E-mail: alex.pittman@wright.edu; Staff 1 (MLS 1)
Founded 1962. Enrl 763; Fac 17; Highest Degree: Master
Library Holdings: Bk Titles 21,107; Bk Vols 30,000; Per Subs 300
Special Collections: Material on History of the American Frontier
Subject Interests: Bibliog instruction, Mat on hist of the Am frontier, Modern lang
Database Vendor: EBSCOhost, JSTOR, LexisNexis, Newsbank, OCLC FirstSearch, OVID Technologies
Function: ILL available, Online searches, Photocopying/Printing, Prog for children & young adult, Ref serv available, Summer reading prog, Telephone ref
Partic in Ohio Library & Information Network
Special Services for the Blind - Computer with voice synthesizer for visually impaired persons
Open Mon-Thurs (Fall-Spring) 9-8, Fri & Sat 9-4; Mon-Thurs (Summer) 9-7, Fri 9-5
Restriction: Circ limited
Friends of the Library Group

CENTERBURG

P CENTERBURG PUBLIC LIBRARY*, 49 E Main St, 43011. (Mail add: PO Box 609, 43011-0609), SAN 313-2447. Tel: 740-625-6538. FAX: 740-625-7311. E-mail: cburglibrary@yahoo.com. Web Site: www.centerburg.lib.oh.us. *Dir,* Karen Pritchard; E-mail: pritchka@oplin.org; *Asst Dir,* Chriss White
Founded 1924. Pop 6,500; Circ 86,693
Library Holdings: Bk Vols 33,000; Per Subs 114
Automation Activity & Vendor Info: (Cataloging) Follett Software; (Circulation) Follett Software
Open Mon-Thurs 10-8, Fri 10-5, Sat 10-3

CENTERVILLE

P WASHINGTON-CENTERVILLE PUBLIC LIBRARY*, 111 W Spring Valley Rd, 45458. SAN 355-6891. Tel: 937-433-8091. FAX: 937-433-1366. E-mail: cvref@wcpl.lib.oh.us. Web Site: www.wclibrary.info. *Libr Dir,* Kim Ann Senft-Paras; Tel: 937-610-4420, E-mail: kparas@wcpl.lib.oh.us; *Libr Mgr,* D Elizabeth Fultz; Tel: 937-610-4480, Fax: 937-610-4481, E-mail: lfultz@wcpl.lib.oh.us; Staff 17.35 (MLS 16.35, Non-MLS 1)
Founded 1930. Pop 56,607; Circ 2,301,657
Jan 2012-Dec 2012 Income (Main Library and Branch(s)) $6,244,215, State $2,007,293, Locally Generated Income $3,811,140, Other $425,782. Mats Exp $971,819, Books $527,067, Per/Ser (Incl. Access Fees) $31,796, Other Print Mats $18,249, AV Mat $270,227, Electronic Ref Mat (Incl. Access Fees) $124,480. Sal $3,275,688 (Prof $1,414,444)
Library Holdings: Audiobooks 7,684; AV Mats 59,774; Bks on Deafness & Sign Lang 67; CDs 10,864; DVDs 33,620; e-books 48,239; Electronic Media & Resources 67,140; High Interest/Low Vocabulary Bk Vols 10; Large Print Bks 9,833; Bk Titles 197,605; Bk Vols 303,425; Per Subs 287; Spec Interest Per Sub 89
Automation Activity & Vendor Info: (Acquisitions) Innovative Interfaces, Inc - Millenium; (Cataloging) Innovative Interfaces, Inc - Millenium; (Circulation) Innovative Interfaces, Inc - Millenium; (OPAC) Innovative Interfaces, Inc - Millenium
Database Vendor: EBSCOhost, Gale Cengage Learning, infoUSA, Mergent Online, OHIONET, ProQuest, Standard & Poor's, TumbleBookLibrary
Wireless access
Mem of Miami Valley Libraries
Partic in OCLC Online Computer Library Center, Inc; Ohio Library & Information Network
Open Mon-Thurs 10-9, Fri 10-6, Sat 10-5, Sun (Sept-May) 1-5
Friends of the Library Group
Branches: 1
WOODBOURNE, 6060 Far Hills Ave, 45459-1924, SAN 374-681X. Tel: 937-435-3700. FAX. 937-435-6812. E-mail: wbref@wcpl.lib.oh.us. *Libr Mgr,* Kristi Hale; Tel: 937-610-4484, E-mail: khale@wcpl.lib.oh.us

CHARDON

L GEAUGA COUNTY LAW LIBRARY RESOURCES BOARD*, 100 Short Court St, Ste BA, 44024. SAN 327-6813. Tel: 440-279-2087. FAX: 440-285-3603. E-mail: gcll@nls.net. Web Site: www.co.geauga.oh.us. *Librn,* Susan McGrew; Staff 1 (MLS 1)
Library Holdings: Bk Vols 20,000; Per Subs 100
Wireless access
Partic in Westlaw
Open Mon-Fri 8-4:30

P GEAUGA COUNTY PUBLIC LIBRARY, 12701 Ravenwood Dr, 44024-1336. SAN 355-6956. Tel: 440-286-6811. FAX: 440-286-7419. E-mail: administration.center@geaugalibrary.info. Web Site: www.geaugalibrary.net. *Dir,* Deborah F O'Connor; Tel: 440-286-6811, Ext 101, E-mail: oconnode@oplin.org; *Asst Dir,* Therese Feicht; E-mail: therese.feicht@geaugalibrary.info; *Head, Tech Serv,* Connie Pekar; E-mail: connie.pekar@geaugalibrary.info; Staff 106 (MLS 17, Non-MLS 89)
Founded 1963. Pop 84,057; Circ 2,117,792
Library Holdings: Audiobooks 48,359; DVDs 57,729; e-books 142,248; Electronic Media & Resources 36,890; Bk Vols 467,881; Per Subs 1,031
Special Collections: US Document Depository
Subject Interests: Local genealogy
Automation Activity & Vendor Info: (Acquisitions) Innovative Interfaces, Inc; (Cataloging) Innovative Interfaces, Inc; (Circulation) Innovative

Interfaces, Inc; (ILL) Innovative Interfaces, Inc; (OPAC) Innovative Interfaces, Inc; (Serials) Innovative Interfaces, Inc
Database Vendor: OHIONET
Wireless access
Partic in Northeast Ohio Regional Library System; OHIONET
Special Services for the Blind - BiFolkal kits; Bks on cassette; Bks on CD; Cassette playback machines; Cassettes; Extensive large print coll; Home delivery serv; Magnifiers
Open Mon-Fri 9-9, Sat 9-5
Friends of the Library Group
Branches: 6
BAINBRIDGE LIBRARY, 17222 Snyder Rd, Chagrin Falls, 44023, SAN 355-6980. Tel: 440-543-5611. FAX: 440-543-4734. E-mail: bainbridge.library@geaugalibrary.info. *Mgr,* Kris Carroll; E-mail: kris.carroll@geaugalibrary.info
Open Mon-Thurs 9-9, Fri & Sat 9-5, Sun 1-5
Friends of the Library Group
CHARDON LIBRARY, 110 E Park St, 44024, SAN 328-7025. Tel: 440-285-7601. FAX: 440-285-3808. E-mail: chardon.library@geaugalibrary.info. *Mgr,* Judith Smith; E-mail: judi.smith@geaugalibrary.info
Subject Interests: Genealogy, Local hist
Open Mon-Thurs 9-9, Fri & Sat 9-5, Sun 1-5
Friends of the Library Group
GEAUGA WEST LIBRARY, 13455 Chillicothe Rd, Chesterland, 44026, SAN 355-7014. Tel: 440-729-4250. FAX: 440-729-7517. E-mail: geauga.west@geaugalibrary.info. *Mgr,* Linda Yanko; E-mail: linda.yanko@geaugalibrary.info
Open Mon-Thurs 9-9, Fri & Sat 9-5, Sun 1-5
Friends of the Library Group
MIDDLEFIELD LIBRARY, 16167 E High St, Middlefield, 44062, SAN 355-7049. Tel: 440-632-1961. FAX: 440-632-1407. E-mail: middlefield.library@geaugalibrary.info. Web Site: geaugalibrary.net/newsite/locations/middlefield-library. *Mgr,* Rachael Hartman; E-mail: rachael.hartman@geaugalibrary.info
Open Mon-Fri 9-9, Sat 9-5, Sun (Fall-Spring) 1-5
Friends of the Library Group
NEWBURY PUBLIC LIBRARY STATION, 14775 Auburn Rd, Newbury, 44065, SAN 376-9151. Tel: 440-564-7552. FAX: 440-564-7117. E-mail: newbury.librarystation@geaugalibrary.info. *Supvr,* Jane Zimmerman; E-mail: jane.zimmerman@geaugalibrary.info
Open Mon-Wed 4-8, Thurs 9-1 & 4-8, Sat & Sun 12-4
Friends of the Library Group
THOMPSON LIBRARY STATION, 16200 Burrows Rd, Thompson, 44086, SAN 328-7041. Tel: 440-298-3831. FAX: 440-298-3921. E-mail: thompson.librarystation@geaugalibrary.info. *Supvr,* Robin Kuhlman; E-mail: robin.kuhlman@geaugalibrary.info
Open Mon, Tues & Thurs 4-8, Wed 10-8, Sat & Sun 12-4
Friends of the Library Group
Bookmobiles: 1. Head of Outreach, Leah Schmidt

CHESTERVILLE

P SELOVER PUBLIC LIBRARY*, 31 State Rte 95, 43317-0025. (Mail add: PO Box 25, 43317-0025), SAN 313-2455. Tel: 419-768-3431. FAX: 419-768-2249. Web Site: www.selover.lib.oh.us. *Dir,* Suzi Lyle; E-mail: lylesu@oplin.org; *Librn,* Nancy Alspaugh; *Librn,* Joyce Biggs; *Librn,* Louella Chapman; *Librn,* Teri Hartwell; *Librn,* Connie Henthorn; *Librn,* Nancy Witzel
Founded 1926. Pop 8,000; Circ 47,896
Library Holdings: Bk Titles 19,460; Per Subs 165
Special Collections: National Geographic Coll
Subject Interests: Local hist
Wireless access
Open Mon-Sat 10-8

CHILLICOTHE

P CHILLICOTHE & ROSS COUNTY PUBLIC LIBRARY*, 140 S Paint St, 45601. (Mail add: PO Box 185, 45601-0185), SAN 355-7073. Tel: 740-702-4145. FAX: 740-702-4153. E-mail: crcpl@oplin.org. Web Site: www.crcpl.org. *Dir,* C Nicholas Tepe; E-mail: tepecn@oplin.org; *Adult Serv Mgr,* Leslie Hartley; E-mail: hartlele@oplin.org; *Circ Mgr, County Br Mgr,* Teresa Myers; E-mail: hardbate@oplin.org; *Digital Serv Mgr,* Julie VanHoose; E-mail: jvanhoose@oplin.org; *IT Mgr,* Bruce Landis; E-mail: landisbr@oplin.org; *Pub Relations Mgr,* Debbie Nunziato; E-mail: nunziade@oplin.org; *Tech Proc Mgr,* Rebecca McClain; E-mail: mcclaire@oplin.org; *Spec Serv Mgr,* Mike Jones; E-mail: jonesmi@oplin.org; *Youth Serv Mgr,* Cheilon Preston; E-mail: prestoch@oplin.org; Staff 11 (MLS 6, Non-MLS 5)
Founded 1859. Pop 78,064; Circ 571,668
Jan 2012-Dec 2012 Income (Main Library and Branch(s)) $3,270,411, State $2,029,400, County $1,151,361, Other $89,650. Mats Exp $355,950, Books $183,750, Per/Ser (Incl. Access Fees) $20,000, Micro $2,200, AV Mat $90,000, Electronic Ref Mat (Incl. Access Fees) $60,000. Sal $1,373,907
Library Holdings: AV Mats 17,575; Electronic Media & Resources 29,510; Bk Vols 129,901; Per Subs 116
Special Collections: Burton E Stevenson Coll; Ross County Census Records, 1820-1900, micro
Subject Interests: Genealogy
Automation Activity & Vendor Info: (Acquisitions) SirsiDynix; (Cataloging) SirsiDynix; (Circulation) SirsiDynix; (OPAC) SirsiDynix; (Serials) SirsiDynix
Wireless access
Partic in SEO (Serving Every Ohioan) Library Center
Special Services for the Blind - Talking bks
Open Mon-Thurs 9-9, Fri & Sat 9-5:30
Friends of the Library Group
Branches: 6
BAINBRIDGE PAXTON TOWNSHIP, 204 N Quarry St, Bainbridge, 45612. (Mail add: PO Box 185, 45601), SAN 355-7162. Tel: 740-702-4185. FAX: 740-702-4186.
Library Holdings: CDs 234; DVDs 289; Large Print Bks 73; Bk Vols 7,653; Videos 117
Open Mon 1-8, Tues-Thurs 1-6, Fri 1-5:30
KINGSTON BRANCH, 17 Main St, Kingston, 45644. (Mail add: PO Box 185, 45601), SAN 355-7138. Tel: 740-702-4180. FAX: 740-702-4181.
Circ 18,999
Library Holdings: CDs 271; DVDs 218; Large Print Bks 46; Bk Vols 7,585; Videos 107
Open Mon 1-8, Tues-Thurs 1-6, Fri 1-5:30
NORTHSIDE BRANCH, 550 Buckeye St, 45601. (Mail add: PO Box 185, 45601), SAN 377-0206. Tel: 740-702-4100. FAX: 740-702-4117.
Library Holdings: CDs 1,298; DVDs 2,034; Large Print Bks 3,960; Bk Vols 48,649; Videos 536
Open Mon-Thurs 10-9, Fri & Sat 10-5:30, Sun 1-5
RICHMOND DALE COMMUNITY BRANCH, 770 Main St, Richmond Dale, 45673. (Mail add: PO Box 185, 45601), SAN 355-7197. Tel: 740-702-4190. FAX: 740-702-4191.
Circ 15,342
Library Holdings: CDs 168; DVDs 272; Large Print Bks 60; Bk Vols 6,333; Videos 78
Open Mon 1-8, Tues-Thurs 1-6, Fri 1-5:30
SOUTH SALEM BRANCH, Buckskin Elementary School, 770 Main St, South Salem, 45681. (Mail add: PO Box 185, 45601), SAN 355-7227. Tel: 937-981-2400. FAX: 937-981-3194.
Circ 18,633
Library Holdings: CDs 199; DVDs 180; Large Print Bks 48; Bk Vols 9,862; Videos 103
Open Mon-Thurs 4-8, Sat 1-5
HOWARD S YOUNG BRANCH, 167 Springfield St, Frankfort, 45628. (Mail add: PO Box 185, 45601), SAN 355-7103. Tel: 740-702-4175. FAX: 740-702-4176.
Circ 18,591
Library Holdings: CDs 171; DVDs 265; Large Print Bks 80; Bk Vols 5,403
Open Mon 1-8, Tues-Thurs 1-6, Fri 1-5:30

S CHILLICOTHE CORRECTIONAL INSTITUTION*, 15802 State Rte 104 N, 45601. (Mail add: PO Box 5500, 45601-5500), SAN 325-0156. Tel. 740-774-7080, Ext 2381. FAX: 740-774-7082. *Libr Asst II,* Cathy Pummill; Staff 1 (Non-MLS 1)
Library Holdings: Bk Titles 14,000; Bk Vols 15,000; Per Subs 100
Open Mon-Sun 8-8

GM DEPARTMENT OF VETERANS AFFAIRS*, Library Service, 17273 State Rte 104, 45601. SAN 313-248X. Tel: 740-773-1141, Ext 7627. FAX: 740-772-7041. *Libr Tech,* Tina M Fore; E-mail: tbubbles4u@yahoo.com; *Libr Tech,* Charles Tackett; Tel: 740-773-1141 Ext 7623, E-mail: charles.tackett@med.va.gov. Subject Specialists: *Med ref,* Tina M Fore
Library Holdings: Bk Vols 6,506; Per Subs 373
Subject Interests: Nursing, Psychiat
Automation Activity & Vendor Info: (Cataloging) EOS International; (OPAC) EOS International
Partic in OHIONET; Veterans Affairs Libr Network (VALNET)
Open Mon-Fri 8-4
Restriction: Staff use only

C OHIO UNIVERSITY CHILLICOTHE CAMPUS*, Quinn Library, 101 University Dr, 45601-0629. SAN 313-2471. Tel: 740-774-7201. Administration Tel: 740-774-7202, 740-774-7203. FAX: 740-774-7268. E-mail: ouc.quinnlibrary@ohio.edu. *Dir,* Brandi Weaver; *Sr Libr Assoc,* Chris Hicks; E-mail: ch034713@ohio.edu; Staff 2 (MLS 1, Non-MLS 1)
Founded 1974. Enrl 2,000; Fac 70; Highest Degree: Bachelor
Library Holdings: AV Mats 79; Bks on Deafness & Sign Lang 156; Bk Titles 47,766; Bk Vols 56,157; Per Subs 247
Special Collections: Dard Hunter Coll; Religious Tolerance Coll, incl rare bks

Automation Activity & Vendor Info: (Acquisitions) Innovative Interfaces, Inc; (Cataloging) Innovative Interfaces, Inc; (Circulation) Innovative Interfaces, Inc; (Course Reserve) Innovative Interfaces, Inc; (ILL) Innovative Interfaces, Inc; (Media Booking) Innovative Interfaces, Inc; (OPAC) Innovative Interfaces, Inc; (Serials) Innovative Interfaces, Inc
Database Vendor: Gale Cengage Learning, LexisNexis, OCLC FirstSearch
Wireless access
Publications: QuinnEssentials (Newsletter)
Partic in Ohio Library & Information Network; OHIONET

S US NATIONAL PARK SERVICE*, Hopewell Culture National Historical Park Library, 16062 State Rte 104, 45601. SAN 370-3096. Tel: 740-774-1126. FAX: 740-774-1140. Web Site: www.nps.gov/hocu. *Curator,* Kathy Brady; E-mail: Kathy_Brady@nps.gov
Founded 1992
Library Holdings: Bk Vols 1,000
Special Collections: Hopewell Archeological Conference Papers
Subject Interests: Archaeology
Restriction: Open by appt only

CINCINNATI

R ADATH ISRAEL CONGREGATION*, The Nancy Petricoff Meisel Library, 3201 E Galbraith Rd, 45236. SAN 313-2498. Tel: 513-793-1800. FAX: 513-792-5085. E-mail: info@adath-israel.org. Web Site: www.adath-israel.org. *Head of Libr,* Barbara Bresler; Tel: 517-793-1800, Ext 162, E-mail: barbara@adath-israel.org; *Dir of Educ,* Dara Wood; Tel: 517-793-1800, Ext 104
Founded 1927
Library Holdings: DVDs 30; Bk Titles 5,800; Per Subs 12
Special Collections: Cookbooks (Kosher); Dr Seuss (Hebrew version); Talmud (& commentaries)
Subject Interests: Culture, Hebrew lit, Jewish hist, Jewish lit, Russian lang, Yiddish
Wireless access
Publications: AJL Newsletter; Biblical Archaeology; Commentary Magazine; Eretz Magazine; Haddasah Magazine; Jerusalem Report; Moment Magazine; The Forward
Open Wed 4-6:15, Sun 9-12:30
Friends of the Library Group

SR ATHENAEUM OF OHIO, Eugene H Maly Memorial Library, 6616 Beechmont Ave, 45230-2091. SAN 321-1177. Tel: 513-231-2223, Ext 136. FAX: 513-231-3254. E-mail: circ@athenaeum.edu. Web Site: www.athenaeum.edu. *Dir,* Connie Song; *Pub Serv Librn,* Claire Ballinger; *Ser,* Donna Vanderbosch; Staff 5 (MLS 2, Non-MLS 3)
Founded 1829. Enrl 250; Fac 26; Highest Degree: Master
Jul 2009-Jun 2010 Income $283,336. Mats Exp $81,002, Books $40,000, Per/Ser (Incl. Access Fees) $29,542, AV Mat $750, Electronic Ref Mat (Incl. Access Fees) $9,830, Presv $900. Sal $142,415 (Prof $116,150)
Library Holdings: AV Mats 951; Braille Volumes 30; CDs 171; e-books 7,100; Bk Titles 91,111; Bk Vols 114,243; Per Subs 287; Videos 247
Special Collections: American Catholic Church History (Archbishop Purcell Special Coll); Rare Books & Manuscripts; Roman Catholic Liturgy Coll; Unusual Bibles (Rare Book Coll)
Subject Interests: Biblical studies, Canon law, Church hist, Pastoral counseling, Roman Catholic theol
Automation Activity & Vendor Info: (Acquisitions) Innovative Interfaces, Inc; (Cataloging) Innovative Interfaces, Inc; (Circulation) Innovative Interfaces, Inc; (Course Reserve) Innovative Interfaces, Inc; (ILL) OCLC WorldShare Interlibrary Loan; (OPAC) Innovative Interfaces, Inc; (Serials) Innovative Interfaces, Inc
Database Vendor: Innovative Interfaces, Inc
Wireless access
Partic in Ohio Library & Information Network; Ohio Private Academic Libraries (OPAL); SouthWest Ohio & Neighboring Libraries
Open Mon-Thurs 8-12 & 1-10, Fri 8-12 & 1-5, Sat 9-11 & 1-5, Sun 2-6

M BETHESDA NORTH HOSPITAL*, Medical Library, 10500 Montgomery Rd, 45242. Tel: 513-745-1129. FAX: 513-745-1220. *Librn,* Michael Douglas; Tel: 513-872-2443
Library Holdings: e-journals 227; Bk Vols 3,550
Automation Activity & Vendor Info: (Circulation) EOS International
Database Vendor: OVID Technologies, PubMed
Open Mon-Fri 8-5

J BROWN MACKIE COLLEGE-CINCINNATI LIBRARY*, 1011 Glendale-Milford Rd, 45215. SAN 321-7094. Tel: 513-771-2424. Circulation Tel: 513-672-1595. FAX: 513-771-3413. Web Site: brownmackielibrary.com. *Librn,* Melanie Moon; E-mail: mmoon@brownmackie.edu; Staff 3 (MLS 2, Non-MLS 1)
Founded 1978
Library Holdings: DVDs 340; e-journals 8,000; Bk Titles 12,300; Bk Vols 13,000; Per Subs 149; Videos 428

Automation Activity & Vendor Info: (Cataloging) LibraryWorld, Inc; (Circulation) LibraryWorld, Inc; (Course Reserve) LibraryWorld, Inc; (OPAC) LibraryWorld, Inc; (Serials) LibraryWorld, Inc
Database Vendor: ProQuest, Westlaw
Wireless access
Partic in SouthWest Ohio & Neighboring Libraries
Open Mon, Tues & Thurs 8am-9pm, Wed 8-4, Fri 8-5

G CENTERS FOR DISEASE CONTROL*, National Institute for Occupational Safety & Health Library, Robert A Taft Laboratories, 4676 Columbia Pkwy, 45226. SAN 313-2943. Tel: 513-533-8321. FAX: 513-533-8382. *Librn,* Kathy Connick; Staff 3 (MLS 1, Non-MLS 2)
Founded 1971
Library Holdings: Bk Vols 10,000; Per Subs 100
Subject Interests: Health res, Occupational safety
Partic in OCLC Online Computer Library Center, Inc

S CINCINNATI ART MUSEUM, Mary R Schiff Library & Archives, 953 Eden Park Dr, 45202-1557. SAN 313-2544. Tel: 513-639-2978. Administration Tel: 513-639-2976. FAX: 513-721-0129. E-mail: library@cincyart.org. Web Site: www.cincinnatiartmuseum.org/visit/plan/mary-r-schiff-library-a-archives. *Head of Libr & Archives,* Galina Lewandowicz; E-mail: galinal@cincyart.org; *Asst Librn,* Jennifer Hardin; Staff 4 (MLS 3, Non-MLS 1)
Founded 1882
Library Holdings: Bk Vols 85,000; Per Subs 70
Special Collections: Art In Cincinnati (bks, files, archival materials); Auction Catalogs (Christie's & Sotheby's starting from the 1930s, miscellaneous other); Cincinnati Art Museum Coll (archives, bks, files); Cincinnati Artists Coll (artist files, bks, archival materials)
Subject Interests: Exhibition catalogs, Japanese prints, Rookwood pottery
Automation Activity & Vendor Info: (Cataloging) OCLC Connexion; (ILL) OCLC WorldShare Interlibrary Loan; (OPAC) Innovative Interfaces, Inc
Database Vendor: ARTstor, JSTOR, OCLC FirstSearch
Wireless access
Function: Archival coll, Electronic databases & coll, Handicapped accessible, Web-catalog
Partic in OCLC Online Computer Library Center, Inc; SouthWest Ohio & Neighboring Libraries
Open Tues-Fri 11-5
Restriction: Circulates for staff only, In-house use for visitors

CINCINNATI CHILDREN'S HOSPITAL

M EDWARD L PRATT LIBRARY, S9.125 ML 3012, 3333 Burnet Ave, 45229-3039, SAN 313-2528. Tel: 513-636-4230. FAX: 513-559-9669. E-mail: prattlibrary@cchmc.org. Web Site: prattlibrary.cchmc.org, www.cincinnatichildrens.org/research/cincinnati/support/pratt/library-services. *Dir,* Melida Busch; E-mail: Melida.Busch@cchmc.org; *Clinical Librn,* Elaine Dean; E-mail: elaine.dean@cchmc.org; *Res Librn,* Alison Kissling; E-mail: alison.kissling@cchmc.org; *Res Librn,* Holly Spindler; E-mail: Holly.Spindler@cchmc.org; *Coordr,* Cristen Ross; E-mail: Cristen.Ross@cchmc.org; Staff 6 (MLS 4, Non-MLS 2)
Founded 1931
Library Holdings: e-books 1,217; e-journals 76,945; Bk Titles 330
Subject Interests: Developmental biol, Genetics, Pediatrics, Teratology
Database Vendor: Dialog, EBSCOhost, Gale Cengage Learning, OVID Technologies
Partic in National Network of Libraries of Medicine; OCLC Online Computer Library Center, Inc
Publications: Studies of the Cincinnati Children's Research Foundation
Restriction: Staff use only

M JACK H RUBINSTEIN LIBRARY*, 3430 Burnet Ave, MOB 2 MLC 3000, 45229, SAN 355-8789. Tel: 513-636-4626. FAX: 513-636-0107. Web Site: www.cincinnatichildrens.org. *Mgr,* Barbara Ann Johnson; E-mail: barbara.johnson@chmcc.org; Staff 1 (MLS 1)
Founded 1957
Library Holdings: Bk Vols 8,000; Per Subs 1; Videos 300
Special Collections: Bibliotherapy Coll; Developmental Disability Research Library; Parents' Library, bks, pamphlets & videos; Toy Library for Children with Special Needs
Subject Interests: Genetics, Handicapping conditions, Learning disabilities, Mental retardation, Pediatrics, Rehabilitation

CR CINCINNATI CHRISTIAN UNIVERSITY, G M Elliott Library, 2700 Glenway Ave, 45204-3200. SAN 313-2552. Tel: 513-244-8680. Interlibrary Loan Service Tel: 513-244-8679. Administration Tel: 513-244-8197. FAX: 513-244-8434. E-mail: library@ccuniversity.edu. Web Site: library.ccuniversity.edu. *Dir,* James H Lloyd; Tel: 513-244-8138, E-mail: jim.lloyd@ccuniversity.edu; *Asst Dir,* Scott Lloyd; E-mail: scott.lloyd@ccuniversity.edu; *Tech Serv Librn,* Carissa Thatcher; Tel: 513-244-8139, E-mail: carissa.thatcher@ccuniversity.edu; *Pub Serv Mgr,* Deanna Hansee; E-mail: deanna.hansee@ccuniversity.edu. Subject

Specialists: *Old Testament, Theol,* James H Lloyd; *New Testament, Theol,* Scott Lloyd; Staff 4 (MLS 3, Non-MLS 1)
Founded 1924. Enrl 1,198; Fac 38; Highest Degree: Master
Jul 2005-Jun 2006. Mats Exp $55,000. Sal $275,000
Library Holdings: Bk Titles 95,000; Bk Vols 115,000; Per Subs 625
Special Collections: Restoration Movement
Subject Interests: Biblical studies, Theol
Automation Activity & Vendor Info: (Cataloging) Innovative Interfaces, Inc; (Circulation) Innovative Interfaces, Inc; (Course Reserve) Innovative Interfaces, Inc; (OPAC) Innovative Interfaces, Inc
Wireless access
Partic in Ohio Library & Information Network; OHIONET; SouthWest Ohio & Neighboring Libraries
Open Mon-Thurs 7am-11pm, Fri 8-6, Sat 11-8

C CINCINNATI COLLEGE OF MORTUARY SCIENCE LIBRARY, 645 W North Bend Rd, 45224-1428. SAN 327-6791. Tel: 513-761-2020. Administration Tel: 513-618-1933. Toll Free Tel: 888-377-8433. FAX: 513-761-3333. Web Site: www.ccms.edu/view/home/about-us/library.aspx. *Dir, Libr & Info Tech,* Molly Jones; E-mail: mjones@ccms.edu; Staff 1 (MLS 1)
Founded 1882. Enrl 100; Fac 12; Highest Degree: Bachelor
Library Holdings: DVDs 50; Electronic Media & Resources 10; Bk Titles 2,300; Per Subs 30; Spec Interest Per Sub 20; Videos 50
Special Collections: Funeral Sciences & Grief Counseling (Rare Book Coll)
Subject Interests: Bereavement, Mortuary sci
Automation Activity & Vendor Info: (Cataloging) Follett Software; (Circulation) Follett Software
Wireless access
Function: 24/7 Online cat, Bks on CD, Computer training, Computers for patron use, Copy machines, Exhibits, Instruction & testing, Magazines, Online cat, Online ref, Orientations, Outside serv via phone, mail, e-mail & web, Photocopying/Printing, Prog for adults, Res libr, Video lending libr, Web-catalog
Partic in SouthWest Ohio & Neighboring Libraries
Open Mon-Fri 8-4
Restriction: Students only

S CINCINNATI MUSEUM CENTER AT UNION TERMINAL*, Cincinnati History Library & Archives, 1301 Western Ave, 45203. SAN 313-2587. Tel: 513-287-7030. Interlibrary Loan Service Tel: 513-287-7089. Toll Free Tel: 800-733-2077. FAX: 513-287-7095. E-mail: library@cincymuseum.org. Web Site: www.cincymuseum.org. *Dir,* Scott Gampfer; Tel: 513-287-7084, E-mail: sgampfer@cincymuseum.org; *Ref Librn,* Anne B Shepherd; Tel: 513-287-7069, E-mail: ashepherd@cincymuseum.org; *Archives Mgr,* Christine Engels; Tel: 513-287-7066, E-mail: cengels@cincymuseum.org; *Mgr, Ref Serv,* M'Lissa Kesterman; E-mail: mkesterman@cincymuseum.org; *Curator, Photog & Prints,* Linda Bailey; Tel: 513-287-7094, E-mail: lbailey@cincymuseum.org; *Curator, Printed Works,* Barbara J Dawson; Tel: 513-287-7098, E-mail: bdawson@cincymuseum.org. Subject Specialists: *River hist,* M'Lissa Kesterman; Staff 10 (MLS 3, Non-MLS 7)
Founded 1831
Library Holdings: AV Mats 1,000,000; Bk Vols 90,000; Per Subs 300
Special Collections: Cornelius J Hauck Botanical Coll; Peter G Thomson Northwest Territory Coll; Photograph & Manuscript Colls; William H Harrison Coll
Subject Interests: Metrop Cincinnati, Miami purchase, Ohio, Old Northwest territory
Automation Activity & Vendor Info: (Cataloging) Cuadra Associates, Inc; (OPAC) Cuadra Associates, Inc; (Serials) Cuadra Associates, Inc
Wireless access
Function: Res libr
Partic in OCLC Online Computer Library Center, Inc; SouthWest Ohio & Neighboring Libraries
Open Mon-Fri 12-5, Sat 10-5
Restriction: Open to pub for ref only

Branches:

GEIER SCIENCE LIBRARY, 760 W Fifth St, 45203, SAN 313-2633. Tel: 513-455-7183. FAX: 513-455-7169. E-mail: sciencelibrary@cincymuseum.org. *Librn,* Phil Yannarella
Library Holdings: Bk Vols 7,500; Per Subs 80
Subject Interests: Natural hist
Restriction: Open by appt only

S CINCINNATI PSYCHOANALYTIC INSTITUTE*, Frederic T Kapp Memorial Library, 3001 Highland Ave, 45219. SAN 328-1558. Tel: 513-961-8886. FAX: 513-961-0308. Web Site: cps-i.org/library/. *Librn,* Mary Kroeger Vuyk; E-mail: mkroegervuyk@3001.us; Staff 1 (Non-MLS 1)
Founded 1981
Library Holdings: Bk Titles 4,400; Per Subs 48
Subject Interests: Psychoanalysis, Psychotherapy
Restriction: Mem only
Friends of the Library Group

J CINCINNATI STATE TECHNICAL & COMMUNITY COLLEGE*, Johnnie Mae Berry Library, 3520 Central Pkwy, 45223-2612. SAN 375-2771. Tel: 513-569-1606. Circulation Tel: 513-569-1699. FAX: 513-559-1527. E-mail: rdl@cincinnatistate.edu. Web Site: www.cincinnatistate.edu/library. *Dir,* Cindy C Sefton; *Coll Develop, Instrul Serv Librn, Ref,* Kathleen Pickens; Tel: 513-569-1611; *Acq,* Karen Douglas; Tel: 513-569-1607; *Archives, Database Coordr, Tech Serv,* Tracey Stivers; Tel: 513-569-1608; *Circ,* Ginna Witte; *ILL,* Myra Justus; Tel: 513-569-4690; *Ser,* Thelma Barnes; Tel: 513-569-1610
Highest Degree: Associate
Library Holdings: Bk Vols 26,131; Per Subs 339
Partic in OCLC Online Computer Library Center, Inc; Ohio Library & Information Network; SouthWest Ohio & Neighboring Libraries
Open Mon-Thurs 7:30am-10pm, Fri 7:30-4:30, Sat 8-4

CR COLLEGE OF MOUNT SAINT JOSEPH*, Archbishop Alter Library, 5701 Delhi Rd, 45233-1671. SAN 313-6299. Tel: 513-244-4216. Reference Tel: 513-244-4307. FAX: 513-244-4355. E-mail: library@mail.msj.edu. Web Site: inside.msj.edu/departments/library. *Dir, Libr Serv,* Paul Owen Jenkins; Tel: 513-244-4351, E-mail: paul_jenkins@mail.msj.edu; *Head, Electronic Res,* Cynthia Gregory; Tel: 513-244-4762, E-mail: cynthia_gregory@mail.msj.edu; *Head, Pub Serv,* Susan Falgner; Tel: 513-244-4352, E-mail: susan_falgner@mail.msj.edu; *Head, Tech Serv,* Julie Flanders; Tel: 513-244-4798, E-mail: julie_flanders@mail.msj.edu; Staff 7 (MLS 5, Non-MLS 2)
Founded 1920. Enrl 1,800; Fac 120; Highest Degree: Doctorate
Jul 2011-Jun 2012. Mats Exp $217,030, Books $58,000, Per/Ser (Incl. Access Fees) $140,000, AV Mat $8,000, Electronic Ref Mat (Incl. Access Fees) $8,000, Presv $3,030. Sal $300,000 (Prof $222,000)
Library Holdings: AV Mats 1,500; CDs 640; e-books 55,000; e-journals 10,000; Bk Titles 56,985; Bk Vols 97,000; Per Subs 195
Special Collections: Post 1945 American Poetry (Aaron Levine Coll)
Automation Activity & Vendor Info: (Acquisitions) Innovative Interfaces, Inc; (Cataloging) Innovative Interfaces, Inc; (Circulation) Innovative Interfaces, Inc; (Course Reserve) Docutek; (OPAC) Innovative Interfaces, Inc; (Serials) Innovative Interfaces, Inc
Database Vendor: EBSCOhost, Gale Cengage Learning, Innovative Interfaces, Inc, LexisNexis, OCLC FirstSearch, OCLC WorldShare Interlibrary Loan
Wireless access
Partic in Ohio Library & Information Network
Open Mon-Thurs 7:30am-10pm, Fri 8-5, Sat 10-5, Sun 12-10

GM DEPARTMENT OF VETERANS AFFAIRS*, Medical Center Library, 3200 Vine St, 45220-2213. SAN 313-296X. Tel: 513-475-6315. FAX: 513-475-6454. *Chief Librn,* Sandra Mason; *Librn, Ref Serv,* Catherine Constance; Staff 2 (MLS 2)
Library Holdings: e-journals 125; Bk Vols 1,200; Per Subs 180
Automation Activity & Vendor Info: (OPAC) EOS International
Database Vendor: OVID Technologies, PubMed
Partic in Cincinnati Area Health Sci Libr Asn
Restriction: Staff use only

L DINSMORE & SHOHL LIBRARY*, 255 E Fifth St, 1900 Chemed Ctr, 45202-3172. SAN 313-2668. Tel: 513-977-8486. FAX: 513-977-8141. E-mail: library@dinslaw.com. *Dir,* Mary Jo Merkowitz; E-mail: maryjo.merkowitz@dinslaw.com; *Law Librn,* Tim Hennies; Staff 5 (MLS 3, Non-MLS 2)
Library Holdings: Bk Vols 24,000
Subject Interests: Law
Automation Activity & Vendor Info: (Acquisitions) EOS International; (Cataloging) EOS International; (Circulation) EOS International; (OPAC) EOS International; (Serials) EOS International
Database Vendor: LexisNexis, OCLC FirstSearch, Westlaw
Wireless access
Function: For res purposes
Restriction: Private libr

L FROST BROWN TODD LLC, Law Library, 3300 Great American Tower, 301 E Fourth St, 45202. SAN 372-2147. Tel: 513-651-6982. FAX: 513-651-6981. Web Site: www.frostbrowntodd.com. *Librn,* Tracie Tiegs; Staff 2 (MLS 1, Non-MLS 1)
Wireless access
Open Mon-Fri 8:30-5

CR GOD'S BIBLE SCHOOL & COLLEGE LIBRARY*, R G Flexon Memorial Library, 513 Ringgold St, 45202. (Mail add: 1810 Young St, 45202-6838), SAN 313-2722. Tel: 513-721-7944, Ext 5113. Information Services Tel: 513-721-7944, Ext 5111. E-mail: library@gbs.edu. *Head Librn,* Elisabeth A Tyler; Tel: 513-721-7944, Ext 261. Subject Specialists: *Bible, Music,* Elisabeth A Tyler; Staff 1 (MLS 1)

Founded 1900. Enrl 500; Fac 26; Highest Degree: Bachelor
Library Holdings: AV Mats 2,200; CDs 449; DVDs 209; Electronic Media & Resources 12; Music Scores 400; Bk Titles 41,257; Bk Vols 45,309; Per Subs 210; Spec Interest Per Sub 150; Talking Bks 30; Videos 1,556
Special Collections: Oral History
Subject Interests: Relig
Automation Activity & Vendor Info: (Circulation) Follett Software; (OPAC) Follett Software; (Serials) Follett Software
Wireless access
Function: Archival coll, Audio & video playback equip for onsite use, Bks on CD, Children's prog, Copy machines, Distance learning, e-mail serv, Fax serv, For res purposes, Free DVD rentals, ILL available, Learning ctr, Libr develop, Magnifiers for reading, Mail & tel request accepted, Mail loans to mem, Music CDs, Orientations, Outside serv via phone, mail, e-mail & web, Photocopying/Printing, Prog for children & young adult, Ref serv available, Res libr, Spoken cassettes & CDs, Spoken cassettes & DVDs, Story hour, Telephone ref, VHS videos, Video lending libr
Partic in SouthWest Ohio & Neighboring Libraries
Open Mon-Thurs 8am-10pm, Fri 8-5, Sat 11-2

L HAMILTON COUNTY LAW LIBRARY*, Hamilton County Court House, 1000 Main St, Rm 601, 45202. SAN 313-2595. Tel: 513-946-5300. Circulation Tel: 513-946-5303. Administration Tel: 513-946-5263. FAX: 513-946-5252. E-mail: reference@cms.hamilton-co.org. Web Site: www.hamilton-co.org/cinlawlib. *Dir, Law Librn,* Mary Jenkins; E-mail: mjenkins@cms.hamilton-co.org; *Ref Librn,* Laura Dixon-Caldwell; E-mail: ldixoncaldwell@cms.hamilton.co.org; *Syst Librn,* Julie Koehne; E-mail: jkoehne@cms.hamilton-co.org; *Tech Serv Librn,* Melissa Barney; E-mail: mbarney@cms.hamilton-co.org; Staff 4 (MLS 3, Non-MLS 1)
Founded 1834
Library Holdings: Bk Vols 184,000; Per Subs 400
Special Collections: Rare Legal Treatises; United States Session Laws
Subject Interests: Loose-leaf serv, Reporters treatises, Statutes
Automation Activity & Vendor Info: (Cataloging) SirsiDynix; (Circulation) SirsiDynix; (OPAC) SirsiDynix; (Serials) SirsiDynix
Function: Web-catalog, Workshops
Partic in OCLC Online Computer Library Center, Inc; OHIONET
Open Mon-Fri 7:30-4:30
Restriction: Circ limited, Circ to mem only, Circulates for staff only, Pub access for legal res only, Pub use on premises, Vols & interns use only

CR HEBREW UNION COLLEGE-JEWISH INSTITUTE OF RELIGION, Klau Library, 3101 Clifton Ave, 45220-2488. SAN 355-7316. Tel: 513-221-1875. Interlibrary Loan Service Tel: 513-487-3281. Reference Tel: 513-487-3287. Administration Tel: 513-487-3276. Information Services Tel: 513-487-3278. FAX: 513-221-0519. E-mail: librarian@huc.edu. Web Site: huc.edu/research/libraries. *Dir of Libr,* Dr David J Gilner; Tel: 513-487-3273, E-mail: dgilner@huc.edu; *Admin Librn,* Laurel S Wolfson; Tel: 513-487-3274, E-mail: lwolfson@huc.edu; *Sr Assoc Librn,* Sarah Barnard; *Sr Assoc Librn,* Allan D Satin; *Sr Assoc Librn for Pub Serv,* Arnona Rudavsky; E-mail: nrudavsk@huc.edu; *Sr Assoc Librn for Tech Serv,* Ellen S Kovacic; Tel: 513-487-3298, E-mail: ekovacic@huc.edu; Staff 14 (MLS 6, Non-MLS 8)
Founded 1875. Enrl 81; Fac 18; Highest Degree: Doctorate
Library Holdings: e-journals 200; Electronic Media & Resources 200; Microforms 38,000; Bk Vols 500,000; Per Subs 1,600
Special Collections: 16th Century Hebrew Printing Coll; Assyriology Coll; Broadside Coll; Hebrew Manuscripts; Inquisition Coll; Jewish Americana to 1850; Jewish Music Coll; Josephus Coll; Printed Bible Coll; Spinoza Coll; Yiddish Theater Coll
Subject Interests: Ancient & Near Eastern studies, Hebraica, Incunabula, Judaica, Rabbinics
Automation Activity & Vendor Info: (Cataloging) Innovative Interfaces, Inc; (Circulation) Innovative Interfaces, Inc; (Course Reserve) Innovative Interfaces, Inc; (OPAC) Innovative Interfaces, Inc; (Serials) Innovative Interfaces, Inc
Wireless access
Function: ILL available, Ref serv available
Publications: Bibliographica Judaica; Studies in Bibliography & Booklore
Partic in OCLC Online Computer Library Center, Inc
Open Mon-Thurs 8am-9pm, Fri 8-3, Sun 2-6

SR HOME MISSIONERS OF AMERICA*, Glenmary Novitiate Library, PO Box 465618, 45246-5618. SAN 328-5723. Tel: 513-874-8900. FAX: 513-874-1690. *Archivist,* Lucy Putnam; Tel: 513-881-7439
Library Holdings: Bk Vols 900
Restriction: Open by appt only

S ANDREW JERGENS CO*, Research Library, 2535 Spring Grove Ave, 45214. SAN 313-2757. Tel: 513-421-1400, 513-455-5362. FAX: 513-455-5363. Web Site: www.jergens.com. *Asst Admin,* Joan Gordon
Library Holdings: Bk Vols 1,500; Per Subs 50
Subject Interests: Chem, Cosmetics, Personal products
Restriction: Staff use only

M JEWISH HOSPITAL*, Health Sciences Library, 4777 E Galbraith Rd, 45236. SAN 355-7340. Tel: 513-686-5173. FAX: 513-686-5418. *Mgr, Libr Serv,* Lisa McCormick; Staff 3 (MLS 1, Non-MLS 2)
Founded 1959
Library Holdings: Bk Titles 2,500; Bk Vols 3,000; Per Subs 180
Special Collections: Leisurely Medical Reading Coll; Medical History Coll
Subject Interests: Internal med, Nursing, Surgery
Automation Activity & Vendor Info: (Cataloging) Marcive, Inc; (OPAC) LibraryWorld, Inc
Database Vendor: OVID Technologies
Partic in Docline; Greater Midwest Regional Medical Libr Network; Kentucky Medical Library Association
Restriction: Staff use only

S KATZEN INTERNATIONAL INC LIBRARY*, 2300 Wall St, Ste K, 45212-2789. SAN 375-6475. Tel: 513-351-7500. FAX: 513-351-0810. E-mail: projects@katzen.com. Web Site: www.katzen.com. *Pres,* Philip W Madson
Library Holdings: Per Subs 30
Subject Interests: Chem eng, Mechanical eng
Open Mon-Fri 8-5

S KZF DESIGN LIBRARY*, 655 Eden Park Dr, 45202. SAN 324-0606. Tel: 513-621-6211. FAX: 513-621-6530. *Adminr,* Karen Green; E-mail: karen.green@kzf.com; Staff 1 (MLS 1)
Founded 1974
Library Holdings: Bk Titles 2,000; Per Subs 80
Subject Interests: Archit, Eng, Interior design, Planning
Automation Activity & Vendor Info: (Cataloging) Inmagic, Inc.; (Circulation) Inmagic, Inc.; (Serials) Inmagic, Inc.
Database Vendor: Dialog
Restriction: Access at librarian's discretion, Closed stack, Co libr, Open by appt only

S LLOYD LIBRARY & MUSEUM, 917 Plum St, 45202. SAN 313-2781. Tel: 513-721-3707. FAX: 513-721-6575. Reference E-mail: reference@lloydlibrary.org. Web Site: www.lloydlibrary.org. *Exec Dir,* Maggie Heran; E-mail: mheran@lloydlibrary.org; *Librn,* Alex Herrlein; E-mail: aherrlein@lloydlibrary.org; *Librn, Rare Bk Cataloger,* Betsy Kruthoffer; E-mail: betsy@lloydlibrary.org; *Ref Librn,* Erin Campbell; E-mail: ecampbell@lloydlibrary.org; *Educ & Outreach Coordr, IT Spec, Webmaster,* Anna Heran; E-mail: aheran@lloydlibrary.org; *Archivist,* Devhra BennettJones; E-mail: dbjones@lloydlibrary.org; Staff 4.75 (MLS 4.25, Non-MLS 0.5)
Founded 1885
Library Holdings: Bk Titles 200,000; Per Subs 250
Special Collections: Botanical Art; Botany with an Emphasis on Morphology & Taxonomy; Eclectic Medicine Coll; Linnean Literature Original Editions; Materia Medica, bks, journals; Mycology, bks, ms; Natural History Coll; Pharmacognosy, History of Pharmacy; Pharmacy (Pharmacopeias & Related Subjects); Plant Chemistry & Floras
Subject Interests: Botany, Hist, Nat hist, Pharm
Wireless access
Function: Archival coll, Art exhibits, Copy machines, Doc delivery serv, e-mail serv, Exhibits, Fax serv, Handicapped accessible, Online cat, Online ref, Online searches, Orientations, Outreach serv, Outside serv via phone, mail, e-mail & web, Photocopying/Printing, Pub access computers, Ref serv available, Res libr, Res performed for a fee, Telephone ref, Wheelchair accessible
Publications: Lloydiana: A Publication of the Friends of the Lloyd Library (Quarterly)
Partic in OCLC Online Computer Library Center, Inc; OHIONET
Open Mon-Fri 8:30-4
Restriction: Closed stack, Non-circulating
Friends of the Library Group

S MERCANTILE LIBRARY ASSOCIATION*, 414 Walnut St, 45202. SAN 313-3028. Tel: 513-621-0717. FAX: 513-621-2023. Web Site: www.mercantilelibrary.com. *Exec Dir,* Albert Pyle; E-mail: apyle@mercantilelibrary.com; *Lit Prog Mgr,* Mary Gruber; E-mail: mgruber@mercantilelibrary.com
Founded 1835
Library Holdings: Bk Titles 150,000; Per Subs 80
Open Mon-Fri 9-5:30, Sat 10-3

SR MONTGOMERY PRESBYTERIAN CHURCH LIBRARY*, 9994 Zig Zag Rd, 45242. SAN 328-414X. Tel: 513-891-8670. FAX: 513-891-8673. Web Site: www.mpchurch.net.
Library Holdings: Bk Vols 2,250
Special Collections: Audiovisual Materials; Children's bks

Subject Interests: Relig
Open Mon-Thurs 9:30-4:30

R NORTHMINSTER PRESBYTERIAN CHURCH LIBRARY*, 703 Compton Rd, 45231. SAN 328-2910. Tel: 513-931-0243. FAX: 513-931-0260. Web Site: www.nmpchurch.org. *Dir,* Mary Hensey; E-mail: mhensey@nmpchurch.org; *Adult Serv,* Ruth Ann Heusinvelt; *Ch Serv,* Marilyn Spreen
Library Holdings: Bk Titles 3,000
Open Mon-Fri 11:30-4:30, Sun 8-1

P PUBLIC LIBRARY OF CINCINNATI & HAMILTON COUNTY, Cincinnati & Hamilton County Public Library, 800 Vine St, 45202-2009. SAN 355-7588. Tel: 513-369-6900. FAX: 513-369-6993. E-mail: info@cincinnatilibrary.org. Web Site: www.cincinnatilibrary.org. *Eva Jane Romaine Coombe Dir,* Kimber L Fender; Tel: 513-369-6972; *Dep Dir,* Greg Edwards; Tel: 513-369-4418; *Dir, Human Res,* Mary Bennett-Brown; Tel: 513-369-6968; *Mgr, Serv Operations-Cent,* Angela Farmer; Tel: 513-665-3358; *Mgr, Serv Operations-E,* Chris Holt; Tel: 513-369-4417; *Mgr, Serv Operations-W,* Maria Sferra; Tel: 513-369-4419; *Mgr, Serv Operations-Syst-Wide,* Holbrook Sample; Tel: 513-369-4408; *Serv Operations Mgr,* Paula Brehm-Heeger; Tel: 513-369-6941; *Tech Operations Mgr,* Marty Beets; Tel: 513-369-4568; *Fiscal Officer,* Molly DeFosse; Tel: 513-369-6967; *Mkt Communications Strategist,* Maelynn Foster; *Mat Selection & Acq,* Holly Varley; Tel: 513-369-6952; Staff 726 (MLS 157, Non-MLS 569)
Founded 1853. Pop 802,374; Circ 17,884,498
Jan 2013-Dec 2013 Income (Main Library and Branch(s)) $57,348,050, State $36,324,165, County $17,911,703, Locally Generated Income $3,112,182. Mats Exp $8,294,515, Books $3,225,187, Per/Ser (Incl. Access Fees) $551,660, AV Mat $1,875,724, Electronic Ref Mat (Incl. Access Fees) $2,629,408, Presv $12,536. Sal $25,204,241
Library Holdings: AV Mats 914,399; Large Print Bks 124,156; Bk Vols 4,467,664; Per Subs 7,831
Special Collections: US Document Depository
Automation Activity & Vendor Info: (Acquisitions) Innovative Interfaces, Inc; (Circulation) Innovative Interfaces, Inc; (OPAC) Innovative Interfaces, Inc; (Serials) Innovative Interfaces, Inc
Database Vendor: Alexander Street Press, Auto-Graphics, Inc, Facts on File, Gale Cengage Learning, LexisNexis, Newsbank, OHIONET, ProQuest, ReferenceUSA
Wireless access
Publications: @the Library (Newsletter); eLinks (Newsletter); Links (Newsletter); New For You (Newsletter); Ohioana Author List & Program (Bibliographies)
Partic in OCLC Online Computer Library Center, Inc; OHIONET; SouthWest Ohio & Neighboring Libraries
Special Services for the Deaf - TDD equip
Special Services for the Blind - Aids for in-house use; Assistive/Adapted tech devices, equip & products; Audio mat; BiFolkal kits; Braille bks; Descriptive video serv (DVS); Extensive large print coll; Large print bks; Newsletter (in large print, Braille or on cassette)
Open Mon-Wed 9-9, Thurs-Sat 9-6, Sun 1-5
Friends of the Library Group
Branches: 49
ANDERSON, 7450 State Rd, 45230, SAN 355-7685. Tel: 513-369-6030. FAX: 513-369-4444. *Br Mgr,* Katie Greifenkamp; E-mail: katie.greifenkamp@cincinnatilibrary.org
Library Holdings: AV Mats 30,890; Bk Vols 116,972
Open Mon-Thurs 10-9, Fri & Sat 10-6
Friends of the Library Group
AVONDALE, 3566 Reading Rd, 45229, SAN 355-7677. Tel: 513-369-4440. FAX: 513-369-4539. *Br Mgr,* Ella Mulford-Chinn; E-mail: ella.mulford-chinn@cincinnatilibrary.org
Library Holdings: AV Mats 13,447; Bk Vols 17,637
Open Mon & Tues 12-8, Wed & Thurs 12-6, Fri & Sat 10-6
Friends of the Library Group
BLUE ASH BRANCH, 4911 Cooper Rd, Blue Ash, 45242, SAN 355-8630. Tel: 513-369-6051. FAX: 513-369-4464. *Br Mgr,* Lisa Salyers; E-mail: lisa.salyers@cincinnatilibrary.org
Library Holdings: AV Mats 22,801; Bk Vols 77,756
Open Mon-Thurs 10-9, Fri & Sat 10-6
Friends of the Library Group
BOND HILL, 1740 Langdon Farm Rd at Jordan Crossing, 45237, SAN 355-7707. Tel: 513-369-4445. FAX: 513-369-4532. *Br Mgr,* Melissa Davis; E-mail: melissa.davis@cincinnatilibrary.org
Library Holdings: AV Mats 19,852; Bk Vols 44,847
Open Mon, Tues & Thurs 12-8, Wed, Fri & Sat 10-6
Friends of the Library Group
CHEVIOT, 3711 Robb Ave, 45211, SAN 355-7766. Tel: 513-369-6015. FAX: 513-369-6048. *Br Mgr,* Tom Gardner; E-mail: tom.gardner@cincinnatilibrary.org
Library Holdings: AV Mats 11,793; Bk Vols 33,522
Open Mon, Tues & Thurs 12-8, Wed, Fri & Sat 10-6
Friends of the Library Group
CHILDREN'S LEARNING CENTER, North Bldg, 1st Flr, 800 Vine St, 45202-2009. Tel: 513-369-6922. FAX: 513-369-3123. *Mgr,* Garrette Smith; E-mail: garrette.smith@cincinnatilibrary.org
Special Collections: Goldsmith Coll
CIRCULATION SERVICES, 800 Vine St, 45202-2009. FAX: 513-369-6902. *Mgr,* Paul Burch; E-mail: paul.burch@cincinnatilibrary.org
CLIFTON, 351 Ludlow Ave, 45220, SAN 355-7790. Tel: 513-369-4447. FAX: 513-369-4448. *Br Mgr,* Jill Beitz; E-mail: jill.beitz@cincinnatilibrary.org
Library Holdings: AV Mats 11,717; Bk Vols 23,456
Open Mon, Tues & Thurs 12-8, Wed, Fri & Sat 10-6, Sun 1-5
Friends of the Library Group
COLLEGE HILL, 1400 W North Bend Rd, 45224, SAN 355-8339. Tel: 513-369-6036. FAX: 513-369-6043. *Br Mgr,* Travis Castleberry; E-mail: travis.castleberry@cincinnatilibrary.org
Library Holdings: AV Mats 13,096; Bk Vols 35,634
Open Mon, Tues & Thurs 12-8, Wed, Fri & Sat 10-6
Friends of the Library Group
CORRYVILLE, 2802 Vine St, 45219, SAN 355-8304. Tel: 513-369-6034. FAX: 513-369-4471. *Mgr,* Brad Wedig; E-mail: brad.wedig@cincinnatilibrary.org
Library Holdings: AV Mats 11,516; Bk Vols 30,599
Open Mon, Tues & Thurs 12-8, Wed, Fri & Sat 10-6
Friends of the Library Group
COVEDALE, 4980 Glenway Ave, 45238, SAN 355-8428. Tel: 513-369-4460. FAX: 513-369-4461. *Br Mgr,* Casey Titschinger; E-mail: casey.titschinger@cincinnatilibrary.org
Library Holdings: AV Mats 19,205; Bk Vols 55,899
Open Mon, Tues & Thurs 12-8, Wed, Fri & Sat 10-6
Friends of the Library Group
DEER PARK, 3970 E Galbraith Rd, 45236, SAN 355-7855. Tel: 513-369-4450. FAX: 513-369-4451. *Br Mgr,* Natalie Fields; E-mail: natalie.fields@cincinnatilibrary.org
Library Holdings: AV Mats 15,743; Bk Vols 40,030
Open Mon, Tues & Thurs 12-8, Wed, Fri & Sat 10-6
Friends of the Library Group
DELHI TOWNSHIP, 5095 Foley Rd, 45238, SAN 355-788X. Tel: 513-369-6019. FAX: 513-369-4453. *Br Mgr,* Mary Beth Brestel; E-mail: marybeth.brestel@cincinnatilibrary.org
Library Holdings: AV Mats 25,243; Bk Vols 76,586
Open Mon-Thurs 10-9, Fri & Sat 10-6
Friends of the Library Group
ELMWOOD PLACE, 6120 Vine St, 45216, SAN 355-791X. Tel: 513-369-4452. FAX: 513-369-4534. *Br Mgr,* Deborah Carrico; E-mail: debby.carrico@cincinnatilibrary.org
Library Holdings: AV Mats 7,886; Bk Vols 12,847
Open Mon & Tues 12-8, Wed & Thurs 12-6, Fri & Sat 10-6
Friends of the Library Group
FOREST PARK BRANCH, 655 Waycross Rd, Forest Park, 45240, SAN 355-8452. Tel: 513-369-4478. FAX: 513-369-4480. *Br Mgr,* Denise Scretchen; E-mail: denise.scretchen@cincinnatilibrary.org
Library Holdings: AV Mats 15,124; Bk Vols 40,430
Open Mon, Tues & Thurs 12-8, Wed, Fri & Sat 10-6
Friends of the Library Group
GENEALOGY & LOCAL HISTORY, South Bldg, 3rd Flr, 800 Vine St, 45202-2009. Tel: 513-369-6905. FAX: 513-369-3123. *Mgr,* Patricia Van Skaik; E-mail: patricia.skaik@cincinnatilibrary.org
Special Collections: A Edward Newton Coll; Artist Illustrated Books, (19th & 20th Century); Bible Coll; Book Arts; Charles Dickens Coll; Christopher Morley Coll; Cincinnati Coll; City Directories; Cruikshank Coll; Discovery & Exploration of America Coll; Edgar Rice Burroughs Coll; English Language Dictionary Coll; Ernest Hemingway Coll; Fleischmann Coll; Frank & Dick Merriwell Coll; Glueck Coll; Hatfield Coll; Huenefeld Coll; Inland River Library; J Richard Abell Coll; John Steinbeck Coll; Kahn Dictionary Coll; Lafeadio Hearn Coll; Langstroth Lithograph Coll; Lazarus Coll; Lewis Coll; Loeb Coll; Map Coll; Mark Twain Coll; Mudge Coll; Nora May Nolan Irish Coll; Ohio Valley Coll; Postcard Coll; Posters; Rockwell Kent Coll; Sackett Coll; School Yearbooks; Sir Winston Churchill Coll; Sports Coll; Trager Memorial Coll; US Census Records, (1790-1930); Veterans History Project Archives; W Somerset Maugham Coll; Walpole Coll; Willa Cather Coll; William Faulkner Coll; William Makepeace Thackeray Coll
Subject Interests: African-Am res, Genealogy, Local hist, River hist
GREEN TOWNSHIP, 6525 Bridgetown Rd, 45248, SAN 370-0968. Tel: 513-369-6095. FAX: 513-369-4482. *Br Mgr,* Kathy Taylor; E-mail: kathy.taylor@cincinnatilibrary.org
Library Holdings: AV Mats 22,437; Bk Vols 66,060
Open Mon & Thurs 10-9, Fri & Sat 10-6
Friends of the Library Group
GREENHILLS, Seven Endicott St, 45218, SAN 355-7979. Tel: 513-369-4441. FAX: 513-369-4535. *Br Mgr,* Jennifer Weikert; E-mail: jennifer.weikert@cincinnatilibrary.org
Library Holdings: AV Mats 9,854; Bk Vols 25,334

Open Mon & Tues 12-8, Wed & Thurs 12-6, Fri & Sat 10-6
Friends of the Library Group
GROESBECK, 2994 W Galbraith Rd, 45239, SAN 355-8002. Tel: 513-369-4454. FAX: 513-369-4455. *Br Mgr,* Ned Heeger-Brehm; E-mail: ned.heeger-brehm@cincinnatilibrary.org
Library Holdings: AV Mats 32,641; Bk Vols 95,645
Open Mon-Thurs 10-9, Fri & Sat 10-6
Friends of the Library Group
HARRISON BRANCH, 10398 New Haven Rd, Harrison, 45030, SAN 355-8037. Tel: 513-369-4442. FAX: 513-369-4443. *Br Mgr,* Michelle Elliott; E-mail: michelle.elliott@cincinnatilibrary.org
Library Holdings: AV Mats 26,534; Bk Vols 74,444
Open Mon-Thurs 10-9, Fri & Sat 10-6
Friends of the Library Group
HOMEWORK CENTRAL, North Bldg, 1st Flr, 800 Vine St, 45202. *Mgr,* Keith Armour; Tel: 513-369-3121, Fax: 513-369-4412, E-mail: keith.armour@cincinnatilibrary.org
HYDE PARK, 2747 Erie Ave, 45208, SAN 355-8061. Tel: 513-369-4456. FAX: 513-369-4458. *Br Mgr,* Blossom Smith; E-mail: blossom.smith@cincinnatilibrary.org
Library Holdings: AV Mats 19,254; Bk Vols 55,329
Open Mon, Tues & Thurs 12-8, Wed, Fri & Sat 10-6
Friends of the Library Group
INFORMATION & REFERENCE, South Bldg, 2nd Flr, 800 Vine St, 45202-2009. FAX: 513-665-3388. *Mgr,* Ben Lathrop; E-mail: ben.lathrop@cincinnatilibrary.org
Special Collections: ANSI Standards Coll; ASTM Standards Coll; Cincinnati Freie Presse 1874-1964; Cincinnati Volksblatt 1846-1918; Cincinnati Volksfreunt 1850-1908; Doane Coll; Dr Martin Luther King Jr Coll; Foundation Center Regional Coll; Grants Resource Center; Kane/Merton Coll; Keller Coll; Langstroth Lithograph Coll; Lenke Coll; Orpheus & Apollo Clubs Choral Coll; Plaut Coll; Roedter Coll; Russel Alger Frager Coll; Sackett Coll; Sackett Coll; Schild-SCORE Coll; Seasongood Coll; Straus Mayer Coll; Striker Coll; Theater, Dance & Music Programs; Theological & Religious Library Coll; Trager Memorial Coll; Trager Memorial Coll; Tragger Coll; Twentieth Century Artists Books; Valerio Coll
Subject Interests: Antiques, Applied sci, Archit, Art, Bronzes, Chem, Computer use in bus, Consumer info, Cookery, Costume hist, Dance, Decorative art, Educ, Employment, Eng, Film, Finance, Govt, Graphics, Hort, Intl relations, Libr sci, Mil sci, Music, Natural hist, Occult, Ornithology, Painting, Philos, Politics, Porcelain, Pottery, Psychol, Pure, Real estate, Recreation, Relig, Sculpture, Sociol, Sports
LOVELAND BRANCH, 649 Loveland-Madeira Rd, Loveland, 45140, SAN 355-8126. Tel: 513-369-4476. FAX: 513-369-4477. *Br Mgr,* Karen Davis; E-mail: karen.davis@cincinnatilibrary.org
Library Holdings: AV Mats 16,188; Bk Vols 65,005
Open Mon, Tues & Thurs 12-8, Wed, Fri & Sat 10-6
Friends of the Library Group
MADEIRA BRANCH, 7200 Miami Ave, Madeira, 45243, SAN 355-8150. Tel: 513-369-6028. FAX: 513-369-4501. *Br Mgr,* Kathy Kennedy-Brunner; E-mail: kathy.kennedy-brunner@cincinnatilibrary.org
Library Holdings: AV Mats 31,221; Bk Vols 89,913
Open Mon-Thurs 10-9, Fri & Sat 10-6
Friends of the Library Group
MADISONVILLE, 4830 Whetsel Ave, 45227, SAN 355-8185. Tel: 513-369-6029. FAX: 513-369-4537. *Br Mgr,* Mari Randolph; E-mail: mari.randolph@cincinnatilibrary.org; Staff 4 (MLS 1, Non-MLS 3)
Library Holdings: AV Mats 8,472; Bk Vols 17,299
Open Mon & Tues 12-8, Wed & Thurs 12-6, Fri & Sat 10-6
Friends of the Library Group
MARIEMONT BRANCH, 3810 Pocahontas Ave, Mariemont, 45227, SAN 355-8215. Tel: 513-369-4467. FAX: 513-369-4468. *Br Mgr,* Mary Sanker; E-mail: mary.sanker@cincinnatilibrary.org
Library Holdings: AV Mats 13,091; Bk Vols 40,738
Open Mon, Tues & Thurs 12-8, Wed, Fri & Sat 10-6
Friends of the Library Group
MIAMI TOWNSHIP, Eight N Miami Ave, Cleves, 45002, SAN 355-8223. Tel: 513-369-6050. FAX: 513-369-4487. *Br Mgr,* Carrie Vale; E-mail: carrie.vale@cincinnatilibrary.org
Library Holdings: AV Mats 8,679; Bk Vols 22,998
Open Mon & Tues 12-8, Wed & Thurs 12-6, Fri & Sat 10-6
Friends of the Library Group
MONFORT HEIGHTS, 3825 W Fork Rd, 45247, SAN 355-872X. Tel: 513-369-4472. FAX: 513-369-4473. *Br Mgr,* Lisa Cappel; E-mail: lisa.cappel@cincinnatilibrary.org
Library Holdings: AV Mats 16,060; Bk Vols 51,227
Open Mon, Tues & Thurs 12-8, Wed, Fri & Sat 10-6, Sun 1-5
Friends of the Library Group
MOUNT HEALTHY, 7608 Hamilton Ave, 45231, SAN 355-824X. Tel: 513-369-4469. FAX: 513-369-4470. *Br Mgr,* Elizabeth Sullivan; E-mail: elizabeth.sullivan@cincinnatilibrary.org
Library Holdings: AV Mats 10,789; Bk Vols 29,172
Open Mon, Tues & Thurs 12-8, Wed, Fri & Sat 10-6
Friends of the Library Group
MOUNT WASHINGTON, 2049 Beechmont Ave, 45230, SAN 355-8274. Tel: 513-369-6033. FAX: 513-369-6044. *Br Mgr,* Larry Richmond; E-mail: larry.richmond@cincinnatilibrary.org
Library Holdings: AV Mats 20,146; Bk Vols 52,788
Open Mon, Tues & Thurs 12-8, Wed, Fri & Sat 10-6
Friends of the Library Group
NORTH CENTRAL, 11109 Hamilton Ave, 45231, SAN 370-0976. Tel: 513-369-6068. FAX: 513-369-4459. *Br Mgr,* Lisa Hamrick; E-mail: lisa.hamrick@cincinnatilibrary.org
Library Holdings: AV Mats 23,412; Bk Vols 58,323
Open Mon-Thurs 10-9, Fri & Sat 10-6, Sun 1-5
Friends of the Library Group
NORTHSIDE, 4219 Hamilton Ave, 45223, SAN 355-7820. Tel: 513-369-4449. FAX: 513-369-4533. *Br Mgr,* Sarah Schellenger; E-mail: sarah.schellenger@cincinnatilibrary.org
Library Holdings: AV Mats 12,898; Bk Vols 24,830
Open Mon & Tues 12-8, Wed & Thurs 12-6, Fri & Sat 10-6
Friends of the Library Group
NORWOOD, 4325 Montgomery Rd, 45212, SAN 355-8363. Tel: 513-369-6037. FAX: 513-369-6039. *Br Mgr,* Maggi Jackson; E-mail: maggi.jackson@cincinnatilibrary.org
Library Holdings: AV Mats 18,687; Bk Vols 39,609
Open Mon, Tues & Thurs 12-8, Wed, Fri & Sat 10-6
Friends of the Library Group
OAKLEY, 4033 Gilmore Ave, 45209, SAN 355-8398. Tel: 513-369-6038. FAX: 513-369-6055. *Br Mgr,* Melissa Fasanella; E-mail: melissa.fasanella@cincinnatilibrary.org
Library Holdings: AV Mats 14,439; Bk Vols 36,561
Open Mon, Tues & Thurs 12-8, Wed, Fri & Sat 10-6
Friends of the Library Group
OUTREACH SERVICES, 800 Vine St, 45202-2009, SAN 355-7596. Tel: 513-369-6963. FAX: 513-369-4586. *Outreach Serv Mgr,* Drew D Pearson; Tel: 513-665-3352, E-mail: drew.pearson@cincinnatilibrary.org
Library Holdings: AV Mats 12,543; Bk Vols 358,093
Special Collections: Dwyer Special Needs Coll; Large Print Coll
Friends of the Library Group
PLEASANT RIDGE, 6233 Montgomery Rd, 45213, SAN 355-8487. Tel: 513-369-4488. FAX: 513-369-4489. *Br Mgr,* Kate Denier; E-mail: kate.denier@cincinnatilibrary.org
Library Holdings: AV Mats 14,683; Bk Vols 35,038
Open Mon, Tues & Thurs 12-8, Wed, Fri & Sat 10-6
Friends of the Library Group
POPULAR, South Bldg, 1st Flr, 800 Vine St, 45202-2009. Tel: 513-369-6919. FAX: 513-369-3123. *Mgr,* David Siders; E-mail: david.siders@cincinnatilibrary.org
Special Collections: Adler Coll; American International Music Fund Tapes; Dr Martin Luther King Jr Coll; Marsh Coll; Meister Coll; Oscar Treadwell Coll
PRICE HILL, 3215 Warsaw Ave, 45205, SAN 355-8517. Tel: 513-369-4490. FAX: 513-369-4538. *Br Mgr,* Megan Brandmaier; E-mail: megan.brandmaier@cincinnatilibrary.org
Library Holdings: AV Mats 13,864; Bk Vols 21,209
Open Mon & Tues 12-8, Wed & Thurs 12-6, Fri & Sat 10-6
Friends of the Library Group
READING BRANCH, 9001 Reading Rd, Reading, 45215, SAN 355-8665. Tel: 513-369-4465. FAX: 513-369-4466. *Br Mgr,* Liz Anderson; E-mail: liz.anderson@cincinnatilibrary.org
Library Holdings: AV Mats 9,007; Bk Vols 22,003
Open Mon & Tues 12-8, Wed & Thurs 12-6, Fri & Sat 10-6
Friends of the Library Group
SAINT BERNARD, 4803 Tower Ave, 45217, SAN 355-8576. Tel: 513-369-4462. FAX: 513-369-4463. *Br Mgr,* Katheryn Toren-Jones; E-mail: katheryn.toren-jones@cincinnatilibrary.org
Library Holdings: AV Mats 9,485; Bk Vols 19,599
Open Mon & Tues 12-8, Wed & Thurs 12-6, Fri & Sat 10-6
Friends of the Library Group
SHARONVILLE, 10980 Thornview Dr, 45241, SAN 355-8606. Tel: 513-369-6049. FAX: 513-369-4504. *Br Mgr,* Tina Riehle; E-mail: tina.riehle@cincinnatilibrary.org
Library Holdings: AV Mats 23,960; Bk Vols 70,881
Open Mon-Thurs 10-9, Fri & Sat 10-6, Sun 1-5
Friends of the Library Group
SYMMES TOWNSHIP, 11850 E Enyart Rd, Loveland, 45140, SAN 370-0984. Tel: 513-369-6001. FAX: 513-369-4481. *Br Mgr,* Tara Kressler; E-mail: tara.kressler@cincinnatilibrary.org
Library Holdings: AV Mats 36,171; Bk Vols 121,017
Open Mon-Thurs 10-9, Fri & Sat 10-6
Friends of the Library Group
TECHCENTER, South Bldg, 2nd Flr, 800 Vine St, 45202-2009. FAX: 513-369-3123. *Mgr,* Bill Hyden; E-mail: bill.hyden@cincinnatilibrary.org
TEENSPOT, North Bldg, 2nd Flr, 800 Vine St, 45202-2009. Tel: 513-369-6960. FAX: 513-369-3123. *Mgr,* Jennifer Korn; E-mail: jennifer.korn@cincinnatilibrary.org

WALNUT HILLS, 2533 Kemper Lane, 45206, SAN 355-869X. Tel: 513-369-6053. FAX: 513-369-4492. *Br Mgr,* Kate Kraus; E-mail: kate.kraus@cincinnatilibrary.org
Library Holdings: AV Mats 10,966; Bk Vols 21,249
Open Mon & Tues 12-8, Wed & Thurs 12-6, Fri & Sat 10-6
Friends of the Library Group

WEST END, 805 Ezzard Charles Dr, 45203, SAN 355-8096. Tel: 513-369-6026. FAX: 513-369-4536. *Br Mgr,* Patty Peterson; E-mail: patty.peterson@cincinnatilibrary.org
Library Holdings: AV Mats 8,826; Bk Vols 16,473
Open Mon & Tues 12-8, Wed & Thurs 12-6, Fri & Sat 10-6
Friends of the Library Group

WESTWOOD, 3345 Epworth Ave, 45211, SAN 355-8754. Tel: 513-369-4474. FAX. 513-369-4475. *Br Mgr,* Kathy Bach; E mail: kathy.bach@cincinnatilibrary.org
Library Holdings: AV Mats 17,735; Bk Vols 46,429
Open Mon, Tues & Thurs 12-8, Wed, Fri & Sat 10-6
Friends of the Library Group

WYOMING BRANCH, 500 Springfield Pike, Wyoming, 45215, SAN 355-7731. Tel: 513-369-6014. FAX: 513-369-6052. *Br Mgr,* Aimee Pennington; E-mail: aimee.pennington@cincinnatilibrary.org
Library Holdings: AV Mats 15,119; Bk Vols 48,214
Open Mon, Tues & Thurs 12-8, Wed, Fri & Sat 10-6
Friends of the Library Group

R ROCKDALE TEMPLE*, Sidney G Rose Library, 8501 Ridge Rd, 45236. SAN 313-2846. Tel: 513-891-9900. FAX: 513-891-0515. E-mail: library@rockdaletemple.org. Web Site: www.rockdaletemple.org. *Vols Librn,* Karen Zanger
Founded 1960
Library Holdings: Bk Vols 5,000; Per Subs 4
Subject Interests: Judaica
Automation Activity & Vendor Info: (Cataloging) Library Concepts
Wireless access
Open Mon-Thurs 9-5, Fri 9-8, Sat & Sun 9-Noon
Restriction: Open to pub for ref & circ; with some limitations

R ST JOHN'S WESTMINSTER UNION CHURCH*, John H Holmes Library, 1085 Neeb Rd, 45233. SAN 313-2986. Tel: 513-347-4613. FAX: 513-347-4615. E-mail: info@sjwuc.org. Web Site: www.sjwuc.org. *Librn,* Carolyn Brinkerhoff
Founded 1960
Library Holdings: Bk Titles 2,000; Bk Vols 5,500; Per Subs 10
Special Collections: Old Bibles
Subject Interests: Bible study, Devotional, Geriatrics, Relig educ

S TAFT MUSEUM OF ART LIBRARY*, 316 Pike St, 45202-4293. SAN 313-2897. Tel: 513-241-0343. FAX: 513-241-2266. E-mail: taftmuseum@taftmuseum.org. Web Site: www.taftmuseum.org. *Chief Curator,* Lynne D Ambrosini; Tel: 513-684-4513, E-mail: lambrosini@taftmuseum.org; *Asst Curator,* Tamera Lenz Muente; Tel: 513-352-5136, E-mail: tmuente@taftmuseum.org; *Curatorial Asst,* Katie Gephart; Tel: 513-684-4524, E-mail: kgephart@taftmuseum.org
Founded 1932
Library Holdings: Bk Vols 3,000
Special Collections: Taft Art Coll Archives
Subject Interests: Archit, Art, Decorative arts of 16th to 19th centuries
Publications: Taft Museum: Collections & Its History (4 vols)
Restriction: Open by appt only

L TAFT, STETTINIUS & HOLLISTER LIBRARY*, 425 Walnut St, Ste 1800, 45202-3957. SAN 313-2900. Tel: 513-381-2838. FAX: 513-381-0205. *Dir, Libr Serv,* Stephanie Woebkenberg; Tel: 513-357-9416, E-mail: woebkenberg@taftlaw.com; Staff 3 (MLS 2, Non-MLS 1)
Library Holdings: Bk Vols 30,000

L THOMPSON HINE LLP*, Law Library, 1400 Scripps Ctr, 312 Walnut St, 45202. SAN 372-2112. Tel: 513-352-6528. FAX: 513-241-4771. *Assoc Dir, Libr Operations,* Barbara Silbersack; E-mail: barbara.silbersack@thompsonhine.com; Staff 2 (MLS 2)
Library Holdings: Bk Vols 2,000; Per Subs 100
Automation Activity & Vendor Info: (Cataloging) Horizon; (Circulation) Horizon; (OPAC) Horizon; (Serials) Horizon
Wireless access
Restriction: Not open to pub

M TRIHEALTH, INC*, Good Samaritan Hospital Library, 375 Dixmyth Ave, 45220-2489. SAN 313-2730. Tel: 513-862-2433. FAX: 513-862-4984. E-mail: library@trihealth.com. *Dir,* Michael Douglas; E-mail: michael_douglas@trihealth.com; Staff 5 (MLS 1, Non-MLS 4)
Founded 1915
Library Holdings: Bk Titles 9,000; Bk Vols 9,500
Special Collections: History of Nursing
Subject Interests: Biomed, Nursing, Obstetrics, Perinatology, Surgery
Automation Activity & Vendor Info: (Cataloging) EOS International; (Circulation) EOS International; (OPAC) EOS International; (Serials) EOS International
Publications: Library News

SR UNITED METHODIST CHURCH*, Armstrong Chapel Church Library, 5125 Drake Rd, 45243. SAN 374-9908. Tel: 513-561-4220. FAX: 513-561-3062. *In Charge,* Michelle Terry
Library Holdings: Bk Vols 3,000; Per Subs 10

L US COURT OF APPEALS FOR THE SIXTH CIRCUIT LIBRARY*, 312 Potter Stewart US Courthouse, 45202. (Mail add: 317 Potter Stewart US Courthouse, 45202), SAN 313-2927. Tel: 513-564-7321. FAX: 513-564-7329. Web Site: www.ca6.uscourts.gov. *Circuit Librn,* Owen G Smith; E-mail: owen_smith@ca6.uscourts.gov; *Dep Circuit Librn,* Pam Schaffner; E-mail: pam_schaffner@ca6.uscourts.gov; *Chattanooga Satellite Librn,* Philleatra Gaylord; Tel: 423-752-5331; *Cleveland Satellite Librn,* Irene Milan; Tel: 216-357-7275; *Columbus Satellite Librn,* Ellen Smith; Tel: 614-719-3181; *Detroit Satellite Librn,* Elise Keller; Tel: 313-234-5255; *Asst Detroit Satellite Librn,* Michelle LaLonde-Reaume; *Digital Serv Librn,* Tom Vanderloo; *Grand Rapids Satellite Librn,* Mary Andrews; Tel: 616-456-2068; *Louisville Satellite Librn,* Bonnie Robinson; Tel: 502-625-3850; *Memphis Satellite Librn,* Karen Kalnins; Tel: 901-495-1357; *Nashville Satellite Librn,* Molly McCluer; *Syst & Cat Librn,* Joseph Orth; *Toledo Satellite Librn,* Marianne Mussett; Tel: 419-259-7539; *Archivist,* Rita Wallace; Tel: 513-564-7304; *Ref Serv,* Barbara Overshiner; Staff 27 (MLS 15, Non-MLS 12)
Founded 1895
Library Holdings: Bk Vols 250,000
Special Collections: Primarily Anglo-American Legal Coll
Automation Activity & Vendor Info: (Acquisitions) SirsiDynix; (Cataloging) SirsiDynix; (Serials) SirsiDynix
Publications: Sixth Circuit History (Online only)
Partic in Fedlink; OCLC Online Computer Library Center, Inc
Satellite libraries located in Louisville, Kentucky; Detroit & Grand Rapids, Michigan; Cleveland, Columbus & Toledo, Ohio; Chattanooga, Nashville & Memphis, Tennessee
Open Mon-Fri 8-5
Restriction: Access at librarian's discretion

C UNIVERSITY OF CINCINNATI*, Blue Ash College Library, Muntz 113, 9555 Plainfield Rd, 45236. SAN 355-9173. Tel: 513-745-5710. FAX: 513-745-5767. E-mail: ucbalibrary@ucblueash.edu. Web Site: www.libraries.uc.edu/ucba. *Dir,* Heather Maloney; Tel: 513-936-1541, E-mail: heather.maloney@uc.edu; Staff 4 (MLS 4)
Founded 1967. Enrl 2,000; Fac 95
Library Holdings: Bk Vols 50,000; Per Subs 450
Automation Activity & Vendor Info: (Acquisitions) Innovative Interfaces, Inc
Partic in Dialog Corp; OCLC Online Computer Library Center, Inc; Ohio Library & Information Network; SouthWest Ohio & Neighboring Libraries
Open Mon-Thurs (Winter) 7:30am-9pm, Fri 7:30-5, Sat 12-4; Mon-Thurs (Summer) 8-6:30, Fri 8-4

CL UNIVERSITY OF CINCINNATI*, Robert S Marx Law Library, 2540 Clifton Ave, 45219. (Mail add: PO Box 210142, 45221-0142), SAN 355-905X. Tel: 513-556-0163. Circulation Tel: 513-556-3016. Reference Tel: 513-556-8078. Administration Tel: 513-556-0159. FAX: 513-556-6265. E-mail: marxlawlib@ucmail.uc.edu. Web Site: www.law.uc.edu. *Dir, Law Libr & Info Tech,* Kenneth Hirsh; E-mail: ken.hirsh@uc.edu; *Dir, Info Tech,* John Hopkins; Tel: 513-556-0153, E-mail: john.hopkins@uc.edu; *Assoc Dir, Pub & Res Serv,* Susan Boland; Tel: 513-556-4407, E-mail: susan.boland@uc.edu; *Cat Librn,* Akram Sadeghi Pari; Tel: 513-556-0154, E-mail: akram.sadeghipari@uc.edu; *Coll & Access Serv Librn,* Lisa Britt-Wernke; Tel: 513-556-0156, E-mail: lisa.britt@uc.edu; *Electronic Serv/Ref Librn,* Ronald Jones; Tel: 513-556-0158, E-mail: ronald.jones@uc.edu; *Ref Librn,* James Hart; Tel: 513-556-0160, E-mail: james.hart@uc.edu; *Ref Librn,* Shannon Kemen; Tel: 513-556-6407, E-mail: kemensl@uc.edu; *Syst Adminr,* William Kimbelton; Tel: 513-556-0430, E-mail: william.kimbelton@uc.edu; *Computer Support Spec,* Alan Wheeler; Tel: 513-556-4419, E-mail: j.alan.wheeler@uc.edu; *Media Serv Spec,* Mike Mimms; Tel: 513-556-0161, E-mail: michael.mimms@uc.edu; *Tech Serv Assoc,* Rhonda Wiseman; Tel: 513-556-0165, E-mail: rhonda.wiseman@uc.edu; Staff 12 (MLS 8, Non-MLS 4)
Founded 1833. Enrl 415; Fac 34; Highest Degree: Doctorate
Special Collections: Church & State Coll; Cincinnati Legal History & Reports of Various Courts; Early Ohio Legal Coll, history reports; Human Rights; Land Use & Planning. US Document Depository
Subject Interests: Human rights, Intl law, Law
Automation Activity & Vendor Info: (Acquisitions) Innovative Interfaces, Inc; (Cataloging) Innovative Interfaces, Inc; (Circulation) Innovative Interfaces, Inc; (ILL) OCLC; (OPAC) Innovative Interfaces, Inc; (Serials) Innovative Interfaces, Inc

Wireless access
Function: Copy machines, e-mail serv, Electronic databases & coll, ILL available, Online cat, Online searches, Ref serv available
Partic in OCLC Online Computer Library Center, Inc
Open Mon-Fri 8am-10pm, Sat 9am-10pm, Sun 10-10
Restriction: 24-hr pass syst for students only

C UNIVERSITY OF CINCINNATI LIBRARIES, Walter C Langsam Library, PO Box 210033, 45221-0033. SAN 355-8843. Tel: 513-556-1515. Circulation Tel: 513-556-1424. Interlibrary Loan Service Tel: 513-556-1461. Reference Tel: 513-556-1867. FAX: 513-556-0325. Interlibrary Loan Service FAX: 513-556-1505. Reference FAX: 513-556-3141. Web Site: www.libraries.uc.edu. *Dean & Univ Librn,* Xuemao Wang; E-mail: xuemao.wang@uc.edu; *Assoc Dean, Spec Coll,* Steve Marine; Tel: 513-558-0166, E-mail: steve.marine@uc.edu; *Assoc Dean, Libr Serv,* Cheryl Albrecht; Tel: 513-556-1784; *Assoc Dean, Libr Serv, Dir, Health Sci Libr,* Leslie Schick; Tel: 513-558-4321, Fax: 513-558-2682; Staff 93 (MLS 42, Non-MLS 51)
Founded 1819. Enrl 43,598; Fac 1,166; Highest Degree: Doctorate
Library Holdings: e-books 148,082; e-journals 121,649; Bk Vols 4,439,265
Special Collections: 18th Century British Anonymous Poetical Pamphlets (Dobell Coll); 19th & 20th Century Astronomy (Cincinnati Observatory Coll), journals, monographs, recs; 19th & 20th Century German-Americana (Fick Coll); 20th Century English Language Poetry (Elliston Coll); American Labor History (McNamara Coll); Celtic Studies (Knott-Radner Coll); Classical Studies, incl Art, Language, Literature, History, Civilization, Philosophy, Religion, Archaeology, Greek & Latin Paleography (Burnam Classical Library); D H Lawrence Manuscripts & Dorothy Brett Correspondence (D H Lawrence Coll); Dale Warland Singers Coll; History of Chemistry (Oesper Coll); Modern Greek Studies Coll; Urban Studies Coll. US Document Depository
Automation Activity & Vendor Info: (Acquisitions) Innovative Interfaces, Inc; (Cataloging) Innovative Interfaces, Inc; (Circulation) Innovative Interfaces, Inc; (Course Reserve) Docutek; (ILL) OCLC ILLiad
Wireless access
Function: Copy machines, e-mail serv, E-Reserves, Equip loans & repairs, Govt ref serv, Handicapped accessible, ILL available, Libr develop, Newsp ref libr, Photocopying/Printing, Workshops
Publications: Source (Newsletter)
Partic in Asn Col & Res Librs; Association of Research Libraries (ARL); Center for Research Libraries; Ohio Library & Information Network; OHIONET
Special Services for the Blind - Assistive/Adapted tech devices, equip & products; Audio mat; Braille equip; Closed circuit TV; Computer with voice synthesizer for visually impaired persons; Copier with enlargement capabilities; Magnifiers
Friends of the Library Group

Departmental Libraries:

ARCHIVES & RARE BOOKS, 808 Blegen Library, 45221. (Mail add: PO Box 210113, 45221-0113), SAN 323-5734. Tel: 513-556-1959. FAX: 513-556-2113. Web Site: www.libraries.uc.edu/arb. *Head of Libr,* Kevin Grace; *Ref/Coll Librn,* Suzanne Maggard Reller; Tel: 513-556-7016; *Digital Archivist/Rec Mgr,* Eira Tansey; Tel: 513-556-1958
Special Collections: German-Americana Coll; Ohio Network Coll; Rare Book Coll; University Archives; Urban Studies Coll
Open Mon-Fri 8-5

CHEMISTRY-BIOLOGY, 503 Rieveschl, A 3, 45221. (Mail add: PO Box 210151, 45221-0151), SAN 355-8878. Tel: 513-556-1498. FAX: 513-556-1103. Web Site: www.libraries.uc.edu/chem-bio. *Head of Libr,* Ted Baldwin; Tel: 513-556-4211
Special Collections: The Oesper History of Chemistry Coll

CLASSICS, 417 Blegen Library, 45221. (Mail add: PO Box 210191, 45221-0191), SAN 355-8908. Tel: 513-556-1315. FAX: 513-556-6244. Web Site: www.libraries.uc.edu/classics. *Head of Libr,* Jacquelene Riley; Tel: 513-556-1316
Special Collections: Modern Greek Coll

COLLEGE-CONSERVATORY OF MUSIC, 600 Blegen Library, 45221. (Mail add: PO Box 210152, 45221-0152), SAN 355-8932. Tel: 513-556-1970. FAX: 513-556-3777. Web Site: www.libraries.uc.edu/ccm. *Head of Libr,* Mark Palkovic; Tel: 513-556-1964; *Asst Music Librn,* Paul Cauthen; Tel: 513-556-1965, E-mail: paul.cauthen@uc.edu
Special Collections: Dale Warland Singers Coll; Everett Helm Coll; Parvin Titus Coll; Thomas Cobbe Coll of Composer Portraits

COLLEGE OF EDUCATION, CRIMINAL JUSTICE & HUMAN SERVICES LIBRARY, 400 Teachers College, 45221. (Mail add: PO Box 210219, 45221-0219), SAN 329-0166. Tel: 513-556-1430. FAX: 513-556-2122. Web Site: www.libraries.uc.edu/cech. *Head of Libr,* Cheryl Ghosh; Tel: 513-556-1758, E-mail: cheryl.ghosh@uc.edu

COLLEGE OF ENGINEERING & APPLIED SCIENCE LIBRARY, 850 Baldwin Hall, 45221. (Mail add: PO Box 210018, 45221-0018), SAN 355-8991. Tel: 513-556-1550. FAX: 513-556-2654. Web Site: www.libraries.uc.edu/ceas. *Head of Libr,* Ted Baldwin; Tel: 513-556-4211, E-mail: ted.baldwin@uc.edu; *Asst Eng & Applied Sci Librn,* James Clasper; Tel: 513-556-1452, E-mail: jim.clasper@uc.edu

DESIGN, ARCHITECTURE ART & PLANNING, 5480 Aronoff Ctr, 45221. (Mail add: PO Box 210016, 45221-0016), SAN 355-8967. Tel: 513-556-1335. FAX: 513-556-3006. Web Site: www.libraries.uc.edu/daap. *Head of Libr,* Jennifer Krivickas; Tel: 513-556-1319, E-mail: jennifer.krivickas@uc.edu; *Visual Res Librn,* Elizabeth Meyer; Tel: 513-556-0279, E-mail: elizabeth.meyer@uc.edu

GEOLOGY-MATHEMATICS-PHYSICS, 240 Braunstein Hall, 45221. (Mail add: PO Box 210153, 45221-0153), SAN 355-9025. Tel: 513-556-1324. FAX: 513-556-1930. Web Site: www.libraries.uc.edu/gmp. *Head of Libr,* Ted Baldwin; Tel: 513-556-4211, E-mail: ted.baldwin@uc.edu
Founded 2004

CM DONALD C HARRISON HEALTH SCIENCES LIBRARY, PO Box 670574, 45267-0574, SAN 355-9238. Tel: 513-558-0127. Interlibrary Loan Service Tel: 513-558-0173. Administration Tel: 513-558-4321. Information Services Tel: 513-558-5628. FAX: 513-558-2682. Interlibrary Loan Service FAX: 513-558-4899. Web Site: www.libraries.uc.edu/hsl. *Assoc Dean, Dir,* Leslie Schick; E-mail: leslie.schick@uc.edu; *Exec Dir, Winkler Ctr for the Hist of Health Professions,* Stephen Marine; Tel: 513-558-0166, E-mail: steve.marine@uc.edu; *Dir, Winkler Ctr for the Hist of Health Professions,* Doris Haag; Tel: 513-558-0123, E-mail: doris.haag@uc.edu; *Dir, IT Serv & Circ,* Birsen Kaya; Tel: 513-558-0345, E-mail: birsen.kaya@uc.edu; *Head, ILL & Doc Delivery,* Gerald Wagner; Tel: 513-558-8389, E-mail: gerald.wagner@uc.edu; *Mgr, Cat & Coll Serv,* Sharon Ann Purtee; Tel: 513-558-1019, E-mail: sharon.purtee@uc.edu; *Info Spec,* Kristen Burgess; Tel: 513-558-3071; *Info Spec,* Tiffany Grant; Tel: 513-558-9153
Founded 1974
Subject Interests: Allied health, Basic med sci, Clinical med sci, Healthcare delivery, Hist of med, Non-print instrul mat in med, Nursing, Patient educ, Pharm
Partic in Dialog Corp; OCLC Online Computer Library Center, Inc; SouthWest Ohio & Neighboring Libraries
Publications: University of Cincinnati Serials Holdings List

HENRY R WINKLER CENTER FOR THE HISTORY OF THE HEALTH PROFESSIONS, PO Box 670574, 45267-0574. Tel: 513-558-5120. FAX: 513-558-2199. E-mail: CHHP@uc.edu. Web Site: www.libraries.uc.edu/winkler-center.html. *Dir,* Doris Haag; Tel: 513-558-5123, E-mail: doris.haag@uc.edu
Founded 1974
Special Collections: 63 Archives (including Robert A Kehoe & Albert S Sabin Archives); History of Laser Medicine; History of Medicine in West (Daniel Drake, Reuben Dimond Mussey & David A Tucker Colls), bks & ms; Local & State Medical Archives, photog & portraits. Oral History
Restriction: Open by appt only

R WESTWOOD FIRST PRESBYTERIAN CHURCH LIBRARY, 3011 Harrison Ave, 45211. SAN 313-2994. Tel: 513-661-6846. FAX: 513-389-3683. E-mail: wfpci@zoomtown.com. *Librn,* Eleanor Owens; Staff 8 (MLS 3, Non-MLS 5)
Founded 1957
Library Holdings: Bk Titles 4,000; Bk Vols 4,200; Per Subs 16
Special Collections: Anchor Bible Series; Books & Materials on Cincinnati; General (Henderson Coll); Large Print Coll, bks & pers; New Interpreter's Bible Series; Presbyterian Church College Catalogue Coll
Subject Interests: Bible ref, Relig bks
Automation Activity & Vendor Info: (Cataloging) Follett Software; (Circulation) Follett Software
Publications: Adult Education Class (Bibliographies); Church Curriculum Materials Lists; Holiday Bibliographies; Newsletter (Annual)
Special Services for the Blind - Large print bks
Open Mon-Fri 9-5, Sat & Sun 8-1

R ISAAC M WISE TEMPLE LIBRARY*, 8329 Ridge Rd, 45236. SAN 313-3001. Tel: 513-793-2556, Ext 123. FAX: 513-793-3322. Web Site: wisetemple.org. *Librn,* Andrea Rapp; E-mail: arapp@wisetemple.org. Subject Specialists: *Israel, Jewish holocaust, Judaica,* Andrea Rapp; Staff 1 (MLS 1)
Founded 1931
Library Holdings: Bk Titles 15,000; Bk Vols 20,000; Per Subs 35
Subject Interests: Holocaust, Judaica
Automation Activity & Vendor Info: (Cataloging) Surpass; (Circulation) Surpass; (OPAC) Surpass
Open Mon 12-7, Tues 9-3, Wed 12-5, Thurs 9-12

CR XAVIER UNIVERSITY*, McDonald Memorial Library, 3800 Victory Pkwy, 45207-5211. SAN 313-301X. Tel: 513-745-3884. Circulation Tel: 513-745-3881. Interlibrary Loan Service Tel: 513-745-4812. Reference Tel: 513-745-4808. Automation Services Tel: 513-745-4819, 513-745-4822. Information Services Tel: 513-745-4811. FAX: 513-745-1932. E-mail: xulib@xavier.edu. Web Site: www.xavier.edu/library. *Asst Dir,* Alison Morgan; *Head, Circ,* Lindsey Ritzert; *Head, Ref & Instruction,* Vicki Young; Staff 26 (MLS 13, Non-MLS 13)
Founded 1831. Enrl 6,666; Fac 373; Highest Degree: Doctorate

Jun 2005-May 2006. Mats Exp $1,110,091, Books $261,689, Per/Ser (Incl. Access Fees) $405,931, Micro $19,585, AV Mat $44,457, Electronic Ref Mat (Incl. Access Fees) $359,791, Presv $18,638. Sal $1,067,870 (Prof $722,228)
Library Holdings: AV Mats 6,353; Bks on Deafness & Sign Lang 112; e-books 8,209; High Interest/Low Vocabulary Bk Vols 52; Bk Titles 215,311; Bk Vols 303,721; Per Subs 1,631; Talking Bks 137
Special Collections: Bibles, Incunabula & Jesuitica; Catholic Boy's Fiction (Francis Finn, SJ, Coll)
Subject Interests: Gen, Philos, Theol
Automation Activity & Vendor Info: (Acquisitions) Innovative Interfaces, Inc; (Cataloging) Innovative Interfaces, Inc; (Circulation) Innovative Interfaces, Inc; (ILL) Innovative Interfaces, Inc; (OPAC) Innovative Interfaces, Inc; (Serials) Innovative Interfaces, Inc
Database Vendor: Dialog, Gale Cengage Learning, LexisNexis, OCLC FirstSearch, OVID Technologies, ProQuest, TLC (The Library Corporation), Wilson - Wilson Web
Wireless access
Function: Archival coll, Doc delivery serv, ILL available, Telephone ref
Publications: Update (Newsletter)
Partic in OCLC Online Computer Library Center, Inc; Ohio Library & Information Network; OHIONET; SouthWest Ohio & Neighboring Libraries
Open Mon-Thurs (Sept-April) 8-1, Fri 8-7, Sat 10-6, Sun Noon-1am; Mon-Thurs (May-Aug) 8am-10pm, Fri 8am-7pm, Sat 10-6
Friends of the Library Group
Departmental Libraries:
INSTRUCTIONAL TECHNOLOGY SERVICES, 3800 Victory Pkwy, 45207-5211, SAN 370-7067. Tel: 513-745-3183. FAX: 513-745-1932. *Dir,* Robert M Cotter; E-mail: cotter@xavier.edu
Friends of the Library Group

S ZOOLOGICAL SOCIETY OF CINCINNATI LIBRARY*, 3400 Vine St, 45220-1399. (Mail add: PO Box 198073, 45219-8073), SAN 327-6759. Tel: 513-559-7760. FAX: 513-475-6101, 513-559-7776. E-mail: info@cincinnatizoo.org. Web Site: www.cincinnatizoo.org. *Coordr,* Jan Dietrich
Founded 1873
Library Holdings: Bk Titles 3,300; Per Subs 15; Videos 324
Subject Interests: Ecology, Hort, Zoology
Function: Ref serv available
Publications: Newsletters; Pamphlets
Open Mon-Fri 9-5
Restriction: Open to pub for ref only

CIRCLEVILLE

CR OHIO CHRISTIAN UNIVERSITY*, Melvin & Laura Maxwell Library, 1476 Lancaster Pike, 43113. SAN 313-3036. Tel: 740-477-7737, 740-477-7858. Interlibrary Loan Service Tel: 740-477-7747. FAX: 740-477-7855. E-mail: library@ohiochristian.edu. Web Site: ohiochristian.edu/maxwell_library/index.htm. *Libr Dir,* Barbara Meister; E-mail: bmeister@ohiochristian.edu; Staff 3 (MLS 1.5, Non-MLS 1.5)
Founded 1947. Highest Degree: Master
Library Holdings: Bk Vols 53,000; Per Subs 153
Special Collections: Stout Bible Coll
Subject Interests: Bible, Missions, Theol
Automation Activity & Vendor Info: (Cataloging) Innovative Interfaces, Inc - Millenium; (Circulation) Innovative Interfaces, Inc - Millenium; (ILL) OCLC FirstSearch; (OPAC) Innovative Interfaces, Inc - Millenium
Database Vendor: Agricola, Cinahl, EBSCOhost, LexisNexis, Oxford Online, Safari Books Online
Wireless access
Publications: New Books List
Partic in Ohio Library & Information Network
Open Mon-Thurs 7:30am-Midnight, Fri 7:30-5, Sat Noon-8, Sun 8pm-Midnight

P PICKAWAY COUNTY DISTRICT PUBLIC LIBRARY*, 1160 N Court St, 43113-1725. SAN 313-3052. Tel: 740-477-1644. FAX: 740-474-2855. Web Site: www.pickawaylib.org. *Dir,* Jim Guenther; Tel: 740-477-1644, Ext 223, E-mail: jguenther@pickawaylib.org; *Supvr, Ch Serv,* Cathy Hartwick; Tel: 740-477-1644, Ext 228, E-mail: chartwick@pickawaylib.org; *Supvr, Circ,* Mary Stanton; Tel: 740-477-1644, Ext 225, E-mail: mstanton@pickawaylib.org; *Supvr, Coll Develop,* Shelah Star; E-mail: sstahr@pickawaylib.org; *IT Supvr,* Shane Ian Hoffman; Tel: 740-477-1644, Ext 232, E-mail: shoffman@pickawaylib.org; *Supvr, Outreach Serv,* Karen Wheeler; Tel: 740-477-1644, Ext 226, E-mail: kwheeler@pickawaylib.org; *Ref Supvr,* Sarah Hintz; Tel: 740-477-1644, Ext 227, E-mail: shintz@pickawaylib.org; Staff 17 (MLS 8, Non-MLS 9)
Founded 1834. Pop 50,325
Library Holdings: Per Subs 168
Automation Activity & Vendor Info: (Acquisitions) SirsiDynix; (Cataloging) SirsiDynix; (Circulation) SirsiDynix; (ILL) SirsiDynix; (OPAC) SirsiDynix; (Serials) SirsiDynix
Wireless access
Partic in Cent Libr Consortium; OCLC Online Computer Library Center, Inc; OHIONET
Open Mon-Thurs 9:30-8, Fri & Sat 9:30-5, Sun (Sept-May) 1-5
Friends of the Library Group
Branches: 1
FLOYD E YOUNKIN BRANCH, 51 Long St, Ashville, 43103. Tel: 740-983-8856. Circulation Tel: 740-983-8856, Ext 21. FAX: 740-983-4287. *Br Mgr,* Joy Jewett; Tel: 740-983-8856, Ext 23, E-mail: jjewett@pickawaylib.org
Open Mon-Thurs (Fall & Spring) 9:30-8, Sat 9:30-5, Sun 1-5; Mon (Summer) 9:30-8, Tues-Thurs 9:30-6, Sat 9:30-5
Friends of the Library Group
Bookmobiles: 1. Supvr, Karen Wheeler

GL PICKAWAY COUNTY LAW LIBRARY ASSOCIATION*, 207 S Court St, 43113. (Mail add: PO Box 727, 43113-0727), SAN 313-3060. Tel: 740-474-6026. FAX: 740-477-6334. *Librn,* Alice Milott
Open Mon 9-12

CLEVELAND

L BAKER & HOSTETLER LLP LIBRARY*, 3200 National City Ctr, 1900 E Ninth St, 44114-3485. SAN 313-3133. Tel: 216-621-0200, 216-861-7101. FAX: 216-696-0740. Web Site: www.bakerlaw.com. *Librn,* Susan Miljinovic; Staff 2 (MLS 2)
Founded 1916. Circ 39,795
Library Holdings: Bk Vols 54,000
Automation Activity & Vendor Info: (Acquisitions) SirsiDynix; (Cataloging) SirsiDynix; (Circulation) SirsiDynix; (Course Reserve) SirsiDynix; (ILL) SirsiDynix; (Media Booking) SirsiDynix; (OPAC) SirsiDynix; (Serials) SirsiDynix
Database Vendor: LexisNexis, Westlaw
Partic in Westlaw
Restriction: Staff use only

C CASE WESTERN RESERVE UNIVERSITY*, Kelvin Smith Library, 11055 Euclid Ave, 44106. (Mail add: 10900 Euclid Ave, 44106-7151), SAN 355-9416. Tel: 216-368-3506. Interlibrary Loan Service Tel: 216-368-3517. Reference Tel: 216-368-6596. Administration Tel: 216-368-2992. FAX: 216-368-6950. E-mail: asksl@case.edu. Web Site: www.case.edu/dir/libraries.html. *Assoc Provost, Univ Librn,* Arnold Hirshon; E-mail: arnold.hirshon@case.edu; *Assoc Dir, Acad Engagement Serv,* Timothy D Robson; Tel: 216-368-6508, E-mail: timothy.robson@case.edu; *Assoc Dir, Pub Engagement Serv & Libr Admin,* E Gail Reese; Tel: 216-368-5291, E-mail: evangeline.reese@case.edu; *Acq & Metadata Serv Team Leader,* Dr Richard Wisneski; Tel: 216-368-6599, E-mail: richard.wisneski@case.edu; *Acq & Metadata Serv Librn,* Earnestine Adeyemon; Tel: 216-368-4248, E-mail: earnestine.adeyemon@case.edu; *Res Serv Librn,* William Claspy; Tel: 216-368-3595, E-mail: william.claspy@case.edu; *Res Serv Librn,* Karen Thornton; Tel: 216-368-6511, E-mail: karen.thornton@case.edu; *Res Serv Librn,* Stephen Toombs; Tel: 216-368-2403, E-mail: stephen.toombs@case.edu. Subject Specialists: *Sci tech,* Earnestine Adeyemon; *English, Hist,* William Claspy; *Sciences,* Karen Thornton; *Classics, Dance, Music,* Stephen Toombs; Staff 34 (MLS 24, Non-MLS 10)
Enrl 10,130; Highest Degree: Doctorate
Library Holdings: Bk Vols 1,753,623
Special Collections: Bookplates (Lemperly & Sherwin Coll); British & American Autographs & Letters; Chemistry Periodicals (Morley Coll); French Revolution & Napoleonic Period (Bourne Coll); German Literature & Philology (Sherer Coll); Henry Adams Library; History of Printing (Eastman Coll); History of Science & Technology; Letters of Junius (Doty Coll); Medieval History (Severance Coll); Natural History (Kirtland Coll); Public Housing & Urban Development (Bohn Coll); Science Fiction; Thoreau (Bailey Coll); Victorian Illustrated Literature (Haskell Coll). US Document Depository
Automation Activity & Vendor Info: (Acquisitions) Innovative Interfaces, Inc; (Cataloging) Innovative Interfaces, Inc; (Circulation) Innovative Interfaces, Inc; (OPAC) Innovative Interfaces, Inc; (Serials) Innovative Interfaces, Inc
Wireless access
Partic in OCLC Online Computer Library Center, Inc; Ohio Library & Information Network; OHIONET
Special Services for the Blind - Assistive/Adapted tech devices, equip & products
Departmental Libraries:
ASTRONOMY, Sears Bldg, 10900 Euclid Ave, 44106, SAN 355-9440. Tel: 216-368-6701. FAX: 216-368-5406. Web Site: library.case.edu/ksl/collections/astronomy/index.html. *Sci Librn,* Karen Thornton; E-mail: karen.thornton@case.edu; *Libr Asst,* Agnes Torontali; Staff 1 (MLS 1)
Library Holdings: Bk Vols 3,000; Per Subs 210
Subject Interests: Astronomy, Astrophysics

LILLIAN & MILFORD HARRIS LIBRARY, Jack Joseph & Morton Mandel School of Applied Social Sciences, 11235 Bellflower Rd, 44106-7164, SAN 355-9564. Tel: 216-368-2302. FAX: 216-368-2106. E-mail: harrisref@case.edu. Web Site: msass.case.edu/harrislibrary. *Dir,* Samantha C Skutnik; Tel: 216-368-2283, E-mail: samantha.skutnik@case.edu; *Ref & Instrul Serv Librn,* Kristen J Kirchgesler; E-mail: kristen1@case.edu; *Tech Serv Librn,* June Hund; E-mail: june.hund@case.edu; *Access Serv, Circ Serv,* Lena Ford; E-mail: lena.ford@case.edu; Staff 5 (MLS 3, Non-MLS 2)
Founded 1916. Enrl 600; Fac 30; Highest Degree: Doctorate
Library Holdings: AV Mats 979; Bk Vols 40,421; Per Subs 267
Subject Interests: Soc work
Automation Activity & Vendor Info: (Acquisitions) Innovative Interfaces, Inc - Millenium; (Cataloging) Innovative Interfaces, Inc - Millenium; (Circulation) Innovative Interfaces, Inc - Millenium; (Course Reserve) Innovative Interfaces, Inc - Millenium; (ILL) OCLC ILLiad; (OPAC) Innovative Interfaces, Inc - Millenium; (Serials) Innovative Interfaces, Inc - Millenium
Special Services for the Blind - Accessible computers; Assistive/Adapted tech devices, equip & products; Magnifiers
Open Mon-Thurs 8-7, Fri 8-5, Sat & Sun 11-5

KULAS MUSIC LIBRARY, Hayden Hall, 11118 Bellflower Rd, 44106-7106, SAN 355-953X. Tel: 216-368-2403. Web Site: library.case.edu/ksl/collections/kulas/index.html. *Music Librn,* Stephen Toombs; E-mail: stephen.toombs@case.edu

CL SCHOOL OF LAW LIBRARY, 11075 East Blvd, 44106-7148, SAN 355-9599. Tel: 216-368-2792. Interlibrary Loan Service Tel: 216-368-8862. Reference Tel: 216-368-5206. FAX: 216-368-1002. Web Site: law.cwru.edu. *Dir, Law Libr,* C Andrew Plumb-Larrick; E-mail: cap95@case.edu; *Assoc Dir for Operations,* Robert Myers; Tel: 216-368-8656, E-mail: rrm8@case.edu; *Head, Cat,* Deborah Dennison; Tel: 216-368-6040, E-mail: dsd2@case.edu; *Head, Circ,* Donna Ertin; Tel: 216-368-8510, E-mail: dme@case.edu; *Head, Ref,* Andy Dorchak; Tel: 216-368-2842, E-mail: axd10@case.edu; *Access Serv,* Lisa Peters; Tel: 216-368-2793, E-mail: lkp@case.edu; *Electronic Res,* Megan Allen; Tel: 216-368-5223, E-mail: mja5@case.edu; *Electronic Res,* Judy Kaul; Tel: 216-368-8570, E-mail: jak4@case.edu; *Govt Doc,* Petite Sarajean; Tel: 216-368-6356, E-mail: sjw3@case.edu; *Ref,* Cheryl Cheatham; Tel: 216-368-1611, E-mail: csc4@case.edu; Staff 25 (MLS 11, Non-MLS 14)
Founded 1893. Enrl 747; Fac 54; Highest Degree: Doctorate
Library Holdings: Bk Titles 96,000; Bk Vols 297,786; Per Subs 9,962
Special Collections: Anglo-American Common Law; Audiovisual Coll; Government Documents Coll; Legal Clinic; Microforms Coll; Rare Book Coll
Subject Interests: Comparative law, Computers, Foreign, Law, Med
Automation Activity & Vendor Info: (Acquisitions) Innovative Interfaces, Inc; (Cataloging) Innovative Interfaces, Inc; (Circulation) Innovative Interfaces, Inc; (Course Reserve) Innovative Interfaces, Inc; (OPAC) Innovative Interfaces, Inc; (Serials) Innovative Interfaces, Inc
Database Vendor: LexisNexis, Westlaw
Partic in Lexis, OCLC Online Computer Libr Ctr, Inc; Quicklaw Inc; Westlaw; Worldcat
Publications: Acquisitions List; Computer Lab Manual, 2nd ed; Guide to Periodicals; Research Guides & Pathfinder Series
Open Mon-Thurs 7:30am-Midnight, Fri 7:30am-10pm, Sat 8:30-8, Sun Noon-Midnight

S CLEVELAND BOTANICAL GARDEN*, Eleanor Squire Library, 11030 East Blvd, 44106. SAN 313-3486. Tel: 216-707-2812. Reference Tel: 216-721-1600, Ext 140. FAX: 216-721-1694, 216-721-2056. Web Site: www.cbgarden.org. *Head Librn,* Gary Esmonde; E-mail: gesmonde@cbgarden.org; *Head, Cat,* Christopher Thornton; Staff 2 (MLS 1, Non-MLS 1)
Founded 1930
Jan 2006-Dec 2006. Mats Exp $2,500, Books $1,000, Per/Ser (Incl. Access Fees) $1,500
Library Holdings: Bk Titles 16,000; Per Subs 45
Special Collections: Botany (Warren H Corning Coll); Flowering Plant Index of Illustration & Information
Subject Interests: Garden hist, Gardening, Hort, Landscape design
Database Vendor: OCLC FirstSearch
Wireless access
Function: Res libr
Partic in OCLC Online Computer Library Center, Inc
Open Mon-Sat 10-5, Sun 12-5
Restriction: Circ limited

M CLEVELAND CLINIC ALUMNI LIBRARY, 9500 Euclid Ave, NA30, 44195-5243. SAN 313-3184. Tel: 216-444-5697. FAX: 216-444-0271. E-mail: library@ccf.org. Web Site: www.clevelandclinic.org/library. *Dir,* Gretchen Hallerberg; Tel: 216-445-7333, E-mail: hallerg@ccf.org; Staff 8.6 (MLS 8.6)
Library Holdings: Per Subs 850
Subject Interests: Clinical med, Med res
Automation Activity & Vendor Info: (Acquisitions) Innovative Interfaces, Inc
Wireless access
Partic in Med Libr Asn of NE Ohio; National Network of Libraries of Medicine; Ohio Library & Information Network
Open Mon-Fri 7:30-6:30, Sat 8:30-4:30

CM CLEVELAND HEALTH SCIENCES LIBRARY, Health Center Library, School of Medicine, Robbins Bldg, 2109 Adelbert Rd, 44106. (Mail add: Health Center Library/CWRU, 10900 Euclid Ave, 44106-4914), SAN 355-9351. Circulation Tel: 216-368-4540. Interlibrary Loan Service Tel: 216-368-6424. Reference Tel: 216-368-3218. Administration Tel: 216-368-1361. FAX: 216-368-3008. Interlibrary Loan Service FAX: 216-368-3008. E-mail: hclref@case.edu. Web Site: www.case.edu/chsl/library/index.html. *Dir,* Position Currently Open; *Asst Dir, Interim Dir,* Kathleen Blazar; E-mail: kathleen.blazar@case.edu; *Assoc Dir,* Dzwinka Holian; Tel: 216-368-3642, E-mail: dzwinka.holian@case.edu; *Curator,* James Edmonson; Tel: 216-368-6391, E-mail: james.edmonson@case.edu; Staff 6 (MLS 6)
Founded 1965
Special Collections: Cole Coll of Venereals; Darwin Coll; Freud Coll; History of Medicine Dittrick Museum of Medical History, all media, archival mat; Marshall Herbal Coll
Subject Interests: Biol, Dentistry, Med, Nursing, Nutrition
Automation Activity & Vendor Info: (Acquisitions) Innovative Interfaces, Inc; (Cataloging) Innovative Interfaces, Inc; (Circulation) Innovative Interfaces, Inc; (Course Reserve) Innovative Interfaces, Inc; (ILL) OCLC ILLiad; (OPAC) Innovative Interfaces, Inc; (Serials) Innovative Interfaces, Inc
Wireless access
Publications: Cleveland Medical Library Association (Newsletter)
Partic in National Network of Libraries of Medicine Greater Midwest Region; OCLC Online Computer Library Center, Inc; Ohio Library & Information Network; OHIONET
Open Mon-Thurs (Winter) 8am-Midnight, Fri 8-7, Sat 9-5, Sun 1-9; Mon-Thurs (Summer) 8am-9pm, Fri 8-7, Sat 9-5

Departmental Libraries:

ALLEN MEMORIAL MEDICAL LIBRARY, 11000 Euclid Ave, 44106-7130, SAN 355-9386. Tel: 216-368-3643. Circulation Tel: 216-368-3641. *Assoc Dir,* Dzwinka Holian; Staff 1 (MLS 1)
Open Mon-Fri 8:30-7, Sat 9-5, Sun (Sept-May) 1-6

DITTRICK MEDICAL HISTORY CENTER, 11000 Euclid Ave, 44106-7130. Tel: 216-368-3648. FAX: 216-368-0165. Web Site: www.case.edu/artsci/dittrick/site2. *Chief Curator,* James Edmonson; Staff 2 (Non-MLS 2)
Open Mon-Fri 8:30-5
Friends of the Library Group

C CLEVELAND INSTITUTE OF ART*, Jessica Gund Memorial Library, 11141 East Blvd, 44106. SAN 313-3214. Tel: 216-421-7440, 216-421-7441. FAX: 216-421-7439. E-mail: referencehelp@gate.cia.edu. Web Site: www.cia.edu/library. *Dir, Libr Serv,* Cristine C Rom; E-mail: crom@cia.edu; *Image & Instrul Serv Librn,* Laura M Ponikvar; Tel: 216-421-7442, E-mail: lponikvar@cia.edu; *Patron Serv Librn,* Beth Owens; E-mail: bowens@cia.edu; *Tech Serv Librn,* Dana M Bjorklund; Tel: 216-421-7446, E-mail: dbjorklund@cia.edu; Staff 7 (MLS 4, Non-MLS 3)
Founded 1882. Enrl 500; Fac 70; Highest Degree: Bachelor
Jul 2009-Jun 2010. Mats Exp $53,637, Books $22,334, Per/Ser (Incl. Access Fees) $12,405, AV Equip $1,206, AV Mat $1,823, Electronic Ref Mat (Incl. Access Fees) $11,277, Presv $4,592. Sal $231,231
Library Holdings: AV Mats 133,000; CDs 184; DVDs 221; Electronic Media & Resources 15; Bk Vols 45,403; Per Subs 140; Videos 460
Special Collections: Books Made by Artists Coll
Subject Interests: Artists bks, Contemporary intl art, Craft, Design, Modern art, Photog
Automation Activity & Vendor Info: (Cataloging) Innovative Interfaces, Inc; (Circulation) Innovative Interfaces, Inc; (Course Reserve) Innovative Interfaces, Inc; (OPAC) Innovative Interfaces, Inc
Database Vendor: ARTstor, H W Wilson, Innovative Interfaces, Inc, Material ConneXion, Oxford Online, ProQuest, Wilson - Wilson Web
Wireless access
Partic in OCLC Online Computer Library Center, Inc

S CLEVELAND INSTITUTE OF MUSIC*, Robinson Music Library, 11021 East Blvd, 44106-1776. SAN 313-3222. Tel: 216-795-3114. FAX: 216-791-3063. Web Site: www.cim.edu/library. *Dir,* Jean Toombs; Tel: 216-795-3181, E-mail: jean.toombs@case.edu; *Media Librn,* Denise Green; Tel: 216-707-4503; *Acq,* Janet Winzenburger; *Music Cataloger,* Anne Lockard; Tel: 216-795-3115; *Ref,* Laurie Lake; Tel: 216-795-3151; Staff 7 (MLS 5, Non-MLS 2)
Founded 1922. Highest Degree: Doctorate
Library Holdings: AV Mats 28,609; Music Scores 42,902; Bk Vols 10,726; Per Subs 110
Special Collections: Audio Visual
Subject Interests: Music

Automation Activity & Vendor Info: (Cataloging) OCLC; (OPAC) Innovative Interfaces, Inc
Wireless access
Partic in OHIONET
Restriction: Private libr

L CLEVELAND LAW LIBRARY ASSOCIATION*, One W Lakeside Ave, 4th Flr, 44113-1023. SAN 313-3230. Tel: 216-861-5070. FAX: 216-861-1606. E-mail: lawlib@clelaw.lib.oh.us. Web Site: www.clevelandlawlibrary.org. *Chief Admin Officer, Librn,* Kathleen M Dugan; E-mail: ksasala@clelaw.lib.oh.us; *Tech Serv Librn,* Terri Faulhaber; E-mail: tfaulhaber@clelaw.lib.oh.us; *Circ,* Sharla Johnston; E-mail: sjohnston@clelaw.lib.oh.us; *Network Serv,* Eric Hess; E-mail: ehess@clelaw.lib.oh.us; Staff 5 (MLS 3, Non-MLS 2)
Founded 1869
Library Holdings: Bk Vols 110,000; Per Subs 90
Special Collections: Ohio Records & Briefs
Subject Interests: Law
Automation Activity & Vendor Info: (Acquisitions) SirsiDynix; (Cataloging) SirsiDynix; (Circulation) SirsiDynix; (ILL) OCLC; (OPAC) SirsiDynix; (Serials) SirsiDynix
Database Vendor: Gale Cengage Learning, LexisNexis, Newsbank, ProQuest, SirsiDynix, Westlaw
Wireless access
Publications: Research Guide Series; FAQ's; Ohio Legal Periodical Index
Partic in CLEVNET; OCLC Online Computer Library Center, Inc; Ohio Law Library Consortium
Open Mon-Fri 8:30-5:30
Restriction: Mem only

S CLEVELAND METROPARKS ZOO LIBRARY*, 3900 Wildlife Way, 44109. SAN 327-7631. Tel: 216-635-3333. FAX: 216-661-3312. *Librn,* Jason Schafer; E-mail: jcs1@clevelandmetroparks.com. Subject Specialists: *Biol, Conserv, Zoology,* Jason Schafer; Staff 1 (MLS 1)
Founded 1992
Jan 2008-Dec 2008 Income $10,000. Mats Exp $10,000, Books $3,000, Per/Ser (Incl. Access Fees) $7,000
Library Holdings: Bk Vols 6,000; Per Subs 100
Subject Interests: Conserv, Educ, Zoology
Automation Activity & Vendor Info: (Cataloging) LibraryWorld, Inc
Function: Res libr
Open Mon-Fri 9-4, Sat & Sun 9-1
Restriction: Non-circulating, Open to others by appt, Staff use only

S CLEVELAND MUSEUM OF ART*, Ingalls Library, 11150 East Blvd, 44106-1797. SAN 313-3257. Tel: 216-707-2530. Administration Tel: 216-421-7340. FAX: 216-421-0921. E-mail: library@clevelandart.org. Web Site: www.clevelandart.org. *Dir, Libr & Archives,* Elizabeth A Lantz; E-mail: blantz@clevelandart.org; *Head, Access Serv,* Matthew Gengler; E-mail: mgengler@clevelandart.org; *Head, Res & Pub Prog,* Louis V Adrean; E-mail: ladrean@clevelandart.org; *Cat Librn,* Margaret Castellani; E-mail: mcastellani@clevelandart.org; *Ref Librn,* Christine Edmonson; E-mail: cedmonson@clevelandart.org; *Ser & Electronic Res Librn,* Jane Kirkland; E-mail: jkirkland@clevelandart.org; *Archivist, Rec Mgr,* Leslir Cade; E-mail: lcade@clevelandart.org; *Electronic Rec Archivist,* Susan Miller; E-mail: smiller@clevelandart.org; *Art Bibliogr/Western Lang,* Anne Trenholme; Tel: 216-707-2557, E-mail: atrenholme@clevelandart.org; Staff 20 (MLS 10, Non-MLS 10)
Founded 1916
Library Holdings: AV Mats 862,000; e-journals 2,247; Electronic Media & Resources 95; Bk Titles 346,755; Bk Vols 462,090; Per Subs 1,232
Special Collections: American Committee on South Asian Art Coll; Arndt-Brunn Greek & Roman Portraits Coll; Asian Art Photographic Distribution, photog; Bartsch Coll; Biblioteca Berenson Archive, photog; Christie's Coll, micro; Cicognara Fiche; Courtauld Institute of Art: The Witt Library, The Conway Library; Decimal Index to Art of the Low Countries (DIAL), photog; Foto Marburg; National Palace Museum; Victoria & Albert Museum
Subject Interests: Art, Asian art, Decorative art
Automation Activity & Vendor Info: (Acquisitions) Ex Libris Group; (Cataloging) Ex Libris Group; (Circulation) Ex Libris Group; (ILL) OCLC WorldShare Interlibrary Loan; (OPAC) Ex Libris Group; (Serials) Ex Libris Group
Database Vendor: ARTstor, Blackwell, EBSCOhost, Ex Libris Group, LexisNexis, Luna Imaging/Insight, OCLC CAMIO, OCLC FirstSearch, OCLC WorldShare Interlibrary Loan, OCLC-RLG, OHIONET, YBP Library Services
Wireless access
Function: Res libr
Partic in Northeast Ohio Regional Library System; OCLC Online Computer Library Center, Inc; OCLC Research Library Partnership; OHIONET
Open Tues, Thurs & Fri (Winter) 10-5, Wed 10-7:30; Tues-Fri (Summer) 10-5
Restriction: Non-circulating

S CLEVELAND MUSEUM OF NATURAL HISTORY*, Harold T Clark Library, One Wade Oval Dr, University Circle, 44106-1767. SAN 313-3265. Tel: 216-231-4600, Ext 3222. FAX: 216-231-5919. E-mail: library@cmnh.org. Web Site: www.cmnh.org/site/researchandcollections_library.aspx. *Librn,* Wendy Wasman; E-mail: wwasman@cmnh.org; Staff 1 (MLS 1)
Founded 1922
Library Holdings: Bk Vols 60,000; Per Subs 650
Special Collections: Rare Book Coll
Subject Interests: Anthrop, Archaeology, Astronomy, Botany, Ecology, Geol, Mineralogy, Natural hist, Paleontology, Zoology
Wireless access
Restriction: Circulates for staff only, Open by appt only, Open to pub for ref only

P CLEVELAND PUBLIC LIBRARY*, 325 Superior Ave, 44114-1271. SAN 355-9688. Tel: 216-623-2800. Circulation Tel: 216-623-2872. Interlibrary Loan Service Tel: 216-623-2901. Reference Tel: 216-623-2856. Administration Tel: 216-623-2827. Circulation FAX: 216-902-4958. Interlibrary Loan Service FAX: 216-623-7078. Reference FAX: 216-623-2972. Administration FAX: 216-623-7015. E-mail: info@cpl.org. Web Site: www.cpl.org. *Exec Dir, CEO,* Felton Thomas, Jr; E-mail: Felton.Thomas@cpl.org; *Dep Dir, COO,* Cindy Lombardo; E-mail: cindy.lombardo@cpl.org; *Dir, Pub Serv,* John Skrtic; Tel: 216-623-2878, E-mail: john.skrtic@cpl.org; *Dir, Tech Serv,* Patricia Lowrey; Tel: 216-623-2817, E-mail: patricia.lowrey@cpl.org; *Chief Knowledge Officer,* Timothy R Diamond; Tel: 216-623-2832, E-mail: timothy.Diamond@cpl.org; Staff 133 (MLS 133)
Founded 1869. Pop 400,787; Circ 6,799,839
Jan 2011-Dec 2011 Income (Main Library and Branch(s)) $57,382,429, State $27,338,496, Locally Generated Income $26,214,496, Other $3,829,437. Mats Exp $10,250,362, Books $4,438,443, Per/Ser (Incl. Access Fees) $1,374,955, Micro $239,000, AV Mat $2,731,426, Electronic Ref Mat (Incl. Access Fees) $1,270,538, Presv $189,000. Sal $27,647,262 (Prof $11,166,991)
Library Holdings: Audiobooks 33,398; CDs 173,795; DVDs 184,333; e-books 50,687; Microforms 4,596,870; Music Scores 18,000; Bk Vols 3,337,617; Per Subs 11,827
Special Collections: Baseball History Coll; Cleveland Theatre History Coll; Cookbook Coll; Dog Coll; Historical Photograph Coll; History of Architecture, drawings, photos, plans; History of Business (Corporate Annual Reports); History of Children's Literature Coll; Industrial Standards; John G White Chess & Checkers Coll; John G White Folklore Coll; Local History & Genealogy Coll; Map Coll; Music Coll, performance parts, sheet music; Rare Books; Visual & Modern Arts (Lockwood Thompson Coll). State Document Depository; UN Document Depository; US Document Depository
Automation Activity & Vendor Info: (Acquisitions) SirsiDynix; (Cataloging) SirsiDynix; (Circulation) SirsiDynix; (ILL) SirsiDynix; (OPAC) BiblioCommons; (Serials) SirsiDynix
Database Vendor: SirsiDynix
Wireless access
Function: Archival coll, Children's prog, Computer training, Computers for patron use, Electronic databases & coll, Handicapped accessible, Homebound delivery serv, ILL available, Online cat, OverDrive digital audio bks, Prog for adults, Prog for children & young adult, Pub access computers, Ref & res, Story hour, Summer reading prog, Tax forms, Telephone ref
Partic in CLEVNET; OCLC Online Computer Library Center, Inc; OHIONET
Special Services for the Deaf - Bks on deafness & sign lang
Special Services for the Blind - Accessible computers; Assistive/Adapted tech devices, equip & products; Digital talking bk; Digital talking bk machines
Friends of the Library Group
Branches: 28
ADDISON, 6901 Superior Ave, 44103, SAN 370-9345. Tel: 216-623-6906. FAX: 216-623-6909. E-mail: Addison.Branch@cpl.org. *Br Mgr,* Magnolia Peters
Circ 183,093
BROOKLYN, 3706 Pearl Rd, 44109, SAN 356-0287. Tel: 216-623-6920. FAX: 216-623-6970. E-mail: Brooklyn.Branch@cpl.org. *Br Mgr,* Ron Antonucci
Circ 108,922
CARNEGIE WEST, 1900 Fulton Rd, 44113, SAN 356-0317. Tel: 216-623-6927. FAX: 216-623-6929. E-mail: Carnegie.West.Branch@cpl.org. *Br Mgr,* Angela Guinther
Circ 164,735
COLLINWOOD, 856 E 152nd St, 44110, SAN 356-0376. Tel: 216-623-6934. FAX: 216-623-6936. E-mail: Collinwood.Branch@cpl.org. *Br Mgr,* Caroline Peak
Circ 126,298

EAST 131ST STREET, 3830 E 131st St, 44120, SAN 356-0430. Tel: 216-623-6941. FAX: 216-623-6978. *Br Mgr,* Ginaya Willoughby
Circ 70,499

EASTMAN, 11602 Lorain Ave, 44111, SAN 356-049X. Tel: 216-623-6955. FAX: 216-623-6957. *Br Mgr,* Kenneth Knape
Circ 233,862

FLEET, 7224 Broadway Ave, 44105, SAN 356-052X. Tel: 216-623-6962. FAX: 216-623-6964. *Br Mgr,* Rekiat Olayiwola
Circ 161,990

FULTON, 3545 Fulton Rd, 44109, SAN 356-0538. Tel: 216-623-6969. FAX: 216-623-6972. *Br Mgr,* Cheryl Diamond
Circ 148,064

GARDEN VALLEY, 7201 Kinsman Rd, Ste 101, 44104, SAN 356-0554. Tel: 216-623-6976. FAX: 216-623-7186. *Br Mgr,* Rena Hunter
Circ 57,095

GLENVILLE, 11900 St Clair Ave, 44108, SAN 356-0589. Tel: 216-623-6983. FAX: 216-623-6985. *Br Mgr,* Sharon Jefferson
Circ 106,841

HARVARD-LEE, 16918 Harvard Ave, 44128, SAN 356-0619. Tel: 216-623-6990. FAX: 216-623-6992. *Br Mgr,* Harriette Parks
Circ 122,398

HOUGH, 1566 Crawford Rd, 44106, SAN 325-3368. Tel: 216-623-6997. FAX: 216-623-6999. *Br Mgr,* Donna Willingham
Circ 79,029

LANGSTON HUGHES BRANCH, 10200 Superior Ave, 44106, SAN 377-8029. Tel: 216-623-6975. FAX: 216-623-6974. *Br Mgr,* William Bradford
Circ 94,860

JEFFERSON, 850 Jefferson Ave, 44113, SAN 356-0643. Tel: 216-623-7004. FAX: 216-623-7007. *Br Mgr,* Jaime DeClet
Circ 125,293

MARTIN LUTHER KING JR BRANCH, 1962 Stokes Blvd, 44106, SAN 356-0678. Tel: 216-623-7018. FAX: 216-623-7020. *Br Mgr,* Toni Parker
Circ 108,668

LORAIN, 8216 Lorain Ave, 44102, SAN 356-0708. Tel: 216-623-7011. FAX: 216-623-7014. *Br Mgr,* Oliver Hoge
Circ 150,565

MEMORIAL-NOTTINGHAM, 17109 Lake Shore Blvd, 44110, SAN 356-0732. Tel: 216-623-7039. FAX: 216-623-7042. *Br Mgr,* Paula Logan Reid
Circ 210,316

MOUNT PLEASANT, 14000 Kinsman Rd, 44120, SAN 356-0791. Tel: 216-623-7032. FAX: 216-623-7035. *Br Mgr,* Cal Zunt
Circ 87,799

P OHIO LIBRARY FOR THE BLIND & PHYSICALLY HANDICAPPED, 17121 Lake Shore Blvd, 44110-4006, SAN 313-3303. Tel: 216-623-2911. Toll Free Tel: 800-362-1262. FAX: 216-623-7036. E-mail: olbpd@cpl.org. *Librn,* William Reed; E-mail: William.Reed@cpl.org
Founded 1931. Circ 691,237
Special Collections: Talking Books,Braille Books & Musical Scores, Print Braille Books, Described DVDs & Blu-Rays, Described Video Cassettes, Playaways
Publications: Bibliographies; Catalogs of Locally Produced Cassettes & Braille; Juvenile Patrons Newsletter (Quarterly); Ohioana; Patrons Newsletter (Quarterly)
Special Services for the Blind - Digital talking bk; Home delivery serv; Internet workstation with adaptive software; Local mags & bks recorded; Low vision equip; Magnifiers; Micro-computer access & training; PC for handicapped; Playaways (bks on MP3); Recorded bks; Scanner for conversion & translation of mats; Screen enlargement software for people with visual disabilities; Screen reader software; Spanish Braille mags & bks; Web-Braille; ZoomText magnification & reading software
Open Mon-Fri 9-5

RICE, 11535 Shaker Blvd, 44120, SAN 356-0856. Tel: 216-623-7046. FAX: 216-623-7049. *Br Mgr,* Ali Boyd
Circ 162,701

ROCKPORT, 4421 W 140th St, 44135, SAN 356-0880. Tel: 216-623-7053. FAX: 216-623-7055. *Br Mgr,* Position Currently Open
Circ 283,241

SOUTH, 3096 Scranton Rd, 44113, SAN 356-0910. Tel: 216-623-7060. FAX: 216-623-7063. *Br Mgr,* Jaime Declet
Circ 118,840

SOUTH BROOKLYN, 4303 Pearl Rd, 44109, SAN 356-0945. Tel: 216-623-7067. FAX: 216-623-7069. *Br Mgr,* Position Currently Open
Circ 266,329

STERLING, 2200 E 30th St, 44115, SAN 356-097X. Tel: 216-623-7074. FAX: 216-623-7072. *Br Mgr,* Position Currently Open
Circ 75,907

UNION, 3463 E 93rd St, 44104, SAN 356-1062. Tel: 216-623-7088. FAX: 216-623-7082. *Br Mgr,* Marcie Williams
Circ 85,174

WALZ, 7910 Detroit Ave, 44102, SAN 356-1097. Tel: 216-623-7095. FAX: 216-623-7099. *Br Mgr,* Kathleen Lefkowitz
Circ 217,726

WEST PARK, 3805 W 157th St, 44111, SAN 356-1127. Tel: 216-623-7102. FAX: 216-623-7104. *Br Mgr,* Michael Dalby
Circ 309,415

WOODLAND, 5806 Woodland Ave, 44104, SAN 356-1186. Tel: 216-623-7109. FAX: 216-623-7113. *Br Mgr,* Rena Hunter
Circ 126,053

Bookmobiles: 1. Librn, Linda Sperry

CLEVELAND STATE UNIVERSITY

CL CLEVELAND-MARSHALL LAW LIBRARY*, Cleveland-Marshall College of Law, 1801 Euclid Ave, 44115-2223, SAN 356-1240. Tel: 216-687-2250. Circulation Tel: 216-687-2251. Reference Tel: 216-687-6877. FAX: 216-687-6881. Web Site: www.law.csuohio.edu/lawlibrary. *Assoc Prof of Law, Dir,* Lauren M Collins; Tel: 216-687-3547, E-mail: l.m.collins36@csuohio.edu; *Dir of Tech,* Dan Thomas; Tel: 216-523-7372; *Assoc Dir,* Jan R Babbit; Tel: 216-687-6913, E-mail: j.babbit@csuohio.edu; *Access & Fac Serv Librn,* Amy Burchfield; Tel: 216-687-6885, E-mail: amy.burchfield@law.csuohio.edu; *Digital Content Serv/Ref Librn,* Jacquelyn McCloud; Tel: 216-523-7364, E-mail: jacquelyn.mccloud@law.csuohio.edu; *Educ Prog Librn,* Laura Ray; Tel: 216-687-6880, E-mail: laura.ray@law.csuohio.edu; *Electronic Serv Librn,* Sue Altmeyer; Tel: 216-687-4894, E-mail: sue.altmeyer@law.csuohio.edu; Staff 22 (MLS 9, Non-MLS 13)
Founded 1897. Enrl 752; Fac 43; Highest Degree: Doctorate
Jul 2009-Jun 2010 Income $2,591,785. Mats Exp $987,147, Books $31,162, Per/Ser (Incl. Access Fees) $690,347, AV Mat $1,261, Electronic Ref Mat (Incl. Access Fees) $261,247, Presv $3,130. Sal $1,183,440 (Prof $606,392)
Library Holdings: Bk Titles 172,599; Bk Vols 538,239
Special Collections: Briefs & Records of Ohio Supreme Court, microform; Briefs & Records of US Supreme Court, microform; CIS Index & US Legislative Hist microfiche
Automation Activity & Vendor Info: (Acquisitions) Innovative Interfaces, Inc; (Cataloging) Innovative Interfaces, Inc; (Circulation) Innovative Interfaces, Inc; (Course Reserve) Innovative Interfaces, Inc; (ILL) Clio; (OPAC) Innovative Interfaces, Inc; (Serials) Innovative Interfaces, Inc
Database Vendor: HeinOnline, Innovative Interfaces, Inc, LexisNexis, Loislaw, OCLC WorldShare Interlibrary Loan, OHIONET, Westlaw, YBP Library Services
Partic in OCLC Online Computer Library Center, Inc; Ohio Library & Information Network
Open Mon-Thurs 8am-11pm, Fri 8am-9pm, Sat 8-8, Sun 10-10

C MICHAEL SCHWARTZ LIBRARY*, Rhodes Tower, Ste 501, 2121 Euclid Ave, 44115-2214, SAN 356-1216. Tel: 216-687-2475. Circulation Tel: 216-687-2478. Interlibrary Loan Service Tel: 216-687-2445. Reference Tel: 216-687-5300. Automation Services Tel: 216-687-6956. FAX: 216-687-9380. Interlibrary Loan Service FAX: 216-687-2383. Reference FAX: 216-687-2403. Web Site: library.csuohio.edu. *Dir,* Dr Glenda A Thornton; E-mail: g.thornton@csuohio.edu; *Asst Dir, Admin & Syst,* David Lodwick; E-mail: d.lodwick@csuohio.edu; *Asst Dir, Discovery Support Services,* Barbara Strauss; Tel: 216-687-2362, E-mail: b.strauss@csuohio.edu; *Asst Dir, Pub Serv,* Kathyanne Dobda; Tel: 216-875-9738, E-mail: k.dobda@csuohio.edu; *Head, Coll Mgt,* Carol Zsulya; Tel: 216-523-7373, E-mail: c.zsulya@csuohio.edu; *Cat Librn,* Yuezeng Shen Yang; Tel: 216-687-5274, E-mail: y.s.yang@csuohio.edu; *Digital Initiatives Librn,* Marsha Miles; Tel: 216-687-2369, E-mail: m.a.miles24@csuohio.edu; *First Year Experience Librn,* Ann Marie Smeraldi; Tel: 216-687-5020, E-mail: a.smeraldi@csuohio.edu; *Librn,* Diane Kolosionek; Tel: 216-802-3358, E-mail: d.kolosionek44@csuohio.edu; *Librn,* Gail Marredeth; Tel: 216-687-2291, E-mail: g.marredeth@csuohio.edu; *Librn,* Fran Mentch; Tel: 216-687-2365, E-mail: f.mentch@csuohio.edu; *Librn,* Theresa Nawalaniec; Tel: 216-687-3504, E-mail: t.nawalaniec@csuohio.edu; *Spec Coll Librn,* William Barrow; Tel: 216-687-6998, E-mail: w.barrow@csuohio.edu; *Coordr, Fac & Admin Serv,* Bob Cieslik; Tel: 216-687-2256, E-mail: r.cieslik@csuohio.edu. Subject Specialists: *Middle Eastern studies, Music, Urban agr,* Barbara Strauss; *Educ,* Kathyanne Dobda; *Bus, Communication, Econ,* Carol Zsulya; *Contemporary poetry, English lang, Lit,* Ann Marie Smeraldi; *Educ, Polit sci, Urban,* Diane Kolosionek; *Biog, Environ studies, Nursing,* Gail Marredeth; *Biomed, Health sci, Nursing,* Fran Mentch; *Eng, Sciences,* Theresa Nawalaniec; *Dance, Local hist, Theatre,* William Barrow; Staff 23 (MLS 15, Non-MLS 8)
Founded 1928. Enrl 12,957; Fac 564; Highest Degree: Doctorate
Jul 2007-Jun 2008. Mats Exp $1,769,000. Sal $2,874,836
Library Holdings: AV Mats 134,118; e-books 30,579; e-journals 43,072; Microforms 730,210; Music Scores 13,906; Bk Titles 516,463; Bk Vols 1,083,843; Per Subs 10,944
Special Collections: Black History (Walker Coll); Bridge Engineering (Watson Bridge Coll); Cleveland Memory; Cleveland Press Coll; Cleveland Union Terminal Coll; French-American/Great Lakes Industrial History Coll; Hazel Hutchison Collister Contemporary Poetry Coll; Marquis de Lafayette Microfilm Coll. US Document Depository

Automation Activity & Vendor Info: (ILL) Innovative Interfaces, Inc
Partic in OCLC Online Computer Library Center, Inc; OHIONET
Special Services for the Deaf - Assisted listening device
Special Services for the Blind - Assistive/Adapted tech devices, equip & products
Open Mon-Thurs 7:30am-10pm, Fri 7:30-6, Sat 8-5, Sun 2-10
Friends of the Library Group

CUYAHOGA COMMUNITY COLLEGE
J EASTERN CAMPUS LIBRARY*, 4250 Richmond Rd, Highland Hills, 44122-6195, SAN 320-9202. Tel: 216-987-2085. Information Services Tel: 216-987-2088. FAX: 216-987-2054. Web Site: www.tri-c.edu/library. *Dir,* Terry Hancox; Tel: 216-987-2087, E-mail: terry.hancox@tri-c.edu; *Librn,* Anna Lauer; Tel: 216-987-2091, E-mail: anna.lauer@tri-c.edu; *Librn,* John Rasel; Tel: 216-987-2321, E-mail: John.Rasel@tri-c.edu; Staff 4 (MLS 3, Non-MLS 1)
Founded 1971. Enrl 6,168; Fac 110; Highest Degree: Associate
Library Holdings: Bk Titles 38,000; Bk Vols 40,100; Per Subs 200
Automation Activity & Vendor Info: (Acquisitions) Innovative Interfaces, Inc; (Cataloging) Innovative Interfaces, Inc; (Circulation) Innovative Interfaces, Inc; (Course Reserve) Innovative Interfaces, Inc; (ILL) Innovative Interfaces, Inc; (OPAC) Innovative Interfaces, Inc; (Serials) Innovative Interfaces, Inc
Partic in OCLC Online Computer Library Center, Inc
Open Mon-Thurs 8-8, Fri & Sat 9am-2pm

J LIBRARY TECHNICAL SERVICES*, 2900 Community College Ave, MRC507, 44115-3123, SAN 322-5747. Tel: 216-987-3383. FAX: 216-987-4404. E-mail: tpd-acquisitions@tri-c.edu. *Supvr,* Constance Clemons; *Supvr,* Laquodra Simmons; Staff 4 (MLS 1, Non-MLS 3)
Automation Activity & Vendor Info: (Acquisitions) Innovative Interfaces, Inc; (Cataloging) Innovative Interfaces, Inc; (Circulation) Innovative Interfaces, Inc; (OPAC) Innovative Interfaces, Inc; (Serials) Innovative Interfaces, Inc
Partic in Northeast Ohio Regional Library System; OCLC Online Computer Library Center, Inc; Ohio Library & Information Network; OHIONET
Open Mon-Fri 8:30-5

J METROPOLITAN CAMPUS LIBRARY*, 2900 Community College Ave, 44115, SAN 356-1275. Tel: 216-987-4296. FAX: 216-987-4404. *Asst Dean,* Tonya Briggs; E-mail: tonya.briggs@tri-c.edu; *Asst Prof, Librn,* Daniel Overfield; E-mail: Daniel.Overfield@tri-c.edu; Staff 13 (MLS 4, Non-MLS 9)
Founded 1968. Enrl 4,194; Fac 205
Library Holdings: Bk Titles 49,877; Bk Vols 53,883; Per Subs 391
Automation Activity & Vendor Info: (Acquisitions) Innovative Interfaces, Inc; (Cataloging) Innovative Interfaces, Inc; (Circulation) Innovative Interfaces, Inc; (Course Reserve) Innovative Interfaces, Inc; (ILL) Innovative Interfaces, Inc; (OPAC) Innovative Interfaces, Inc; (Serials) Innovative Interfaces, Inc
Open Mon-Thurs 8am-10pm, Fri 8-5, Sat 8:30-4

J WESTERN CAMPUS LIBRARY*, 11000 Pleasant Valley Rd, Parma, 44130-5199, SAN 320-9210. Tel: 216-987-5416. FAX: 216-987-5050. *Asst Dean,* Michael Collura; E-mail: michael.collura@tri-c.edu; *Asst Prof, Librn,* Paula DuPerow; E-mail: paula.duperow@tri-c.edu; Staff 13 (MLS 4, Non-MLS 9)
Founded 1966. Enrl 5,049
Library Holdings: Bk Titles 55,372; Bk Vols 62,570; Per Subs 377
Automation Activity & Vendor Info: (Acquisitions) Innovative Interfaces, Inc; (Cataloging) Innovative Interfaces, Inc; (Circulation) Innovative Interfaces, Inc; (Course Reserve) Innovative Interfaces, Inc; (ILL) Innovative Interfaces, Inc; (OPAC) Innovative Interfaces, Inc; (Serials) Innovative Interfaces, Inc
Partic in Northeast Ohio Regional Library System; OCLC Online Computer Library Center, Inc
Open Mon-Thurs 8am-10pm, Fri 8-5, Sat 8:30-4

G CUYAHOGA COUNTY ARCHIVES LIBRARY*, The Robert Russell Rhodes House, 2905 Franklin Blvd NW, 44113. SAN 313-3362. Tel: 216-443-7250. FAX: 216-443-3636. E-mail: archive@cuyahogacounty.us. *Archivist,* Judith G Cetina, PhD
Founded 1975
Library Holdings: Bk Titles 2,150
Subject Interests: Cleveland, Cuyahoga County, Genealogy
Open Mon, Wed & Fri 8:30-3

S DUNHAM TAVERN MUSEUM LIBRARY*, 6709 Euclid Ave, 44103-3913. SAN 321-0871. Tel: 216-431-1060. FAX: 216-431-1060. Web Site: www.dunhamtavern.org. *Librn,* Germain Gibian; E-mail: germaingibian@sbeglobal.net
Founded 1954
Library Holdings: Bk Titles 750
Subject Interests: Antiques, Cleveland hist, Ohio
Open Wed & Sun 1-4

M FAIRVIEW HOSPITAL*, Medical Library, 18101 Lorain Ave, 44111. SAN 356-2115. Tel: 216-476-7117. FAX: 216-476-7803. E-mail: librarywest@ccf.org. *Librn,* Irene Szentkiralyi; Staff 2 (MLS 1, Non-MLS 1)
Library Holdings: Bk Vols 3,000; Per Subs 150
Subject Interests: Med, Nursing, Surgery
Automation Activity & Vendor Info: (Cataloging) Follett Software; (Circulation) Follett Software
Wireless access
Partic in MLANO; National Network of Libraries of Medicine
Restriction: Staff use only

S FEDERAL RESERVE BANK OF CLEVELAND*, Research Library, 1455 E Sixth St, 44114. (Mail add. PO Box 5620, 44101 0620), SAN 313-3451. Tel: 216-579-2052, 216-579-2961. Reference Tel: 216-579-2050. FAX: 216-579-3172. E-mail: 4D.Library@clev.frb.org. *Librn,* Lee D Faulhaber; *Assoc Librn,* Diane Mogren; *Assoc Librn,* Lynn Sniderman; Staff 5 (MLS 2, Non-MLS 3)
Founded 1918
Library Holdings: Bk Titles 20,000; Bk Vols 22,000; Per Subs 600
Subject Interests: Banking, Econ, Finance, Reserve syst
Publications: Acquisitions list; Bibliography of Bank Publications
Partic in OCLC Online Computer Library Center, Inc; OHIONET
Open Mon-Fri 8-4:30

G FEDERAL TRADE COMMISSION*, Cleveland Regional Office, 1111 Superior Ave, Ste 200, 44114. SAN 313-346X. Tel: 216-263-3455. FAX: 216-263-3426. *Dir,* John Steiger
Library Holdings: Bk Vols 2,500; Per Subs 15
Restriction: Staff use only

S FOUNDATION CENTER-CLEVELAND LIBRARY*, 1422 Euclid Ave, Ste 1600, 44115-2001. SAN 313-3478. Tel: 216-861-1934. FAX: 216-861-1936. Web Site: www.foundationcenter.org/cleveland. *Dir,* Cynthia Bailie; *Librn,* Melissa Pulis; *Training/Coll Librn,* David Holmes; Staff 5 (MLS 3, Non-MLS 2)
Founded 1977
Library Holdings: Bk Vols 2,000; Spec Interest Per Sub 50
Special Collections: Foundations (Annual Reports & Tax Returns), mss, micro
Subject Interests: Fundraising, Grantsmanship, Philanthropy
Automation Activity & Vendor Info: (Serials) EBSCO Online
Publications: Library Brochure, Worksheets For Grantseekers
Partic in Dialog Corp; Northeast Ohio Regional Library System
Open Mon, Wed & Fri 12-4:30, Tues & Thurs 9:30-4:30
Restriction: Open to pub for ref only
Friends of the Library Group

S GRAFTECH INTERNATIONAL HOLDINGS, INC*, Information Services, 12900 Snow Rd, 44130. SAN 313-668X. Tel: 216-676-2000. *Librn,* Deb Klembara; Staff 1 (Non-MLS 1)
Founded 1945
Library Holdings: Bk Titles 16,000; Bk Vols 20,000; Per Subs 100
Subject Interests: Carbon, Graphite tech, High performance non-metallic mat
Database Vendor: EOS International

L HAHN, LOESER & PARKS*, Law Library, 200 Public Sq, Ste 3300, 44114-2301. SAN 372-2139. Tel: 216-621-0150. FAX: 216-241-2824. *Librn,* Susan B Hersch
Library Holdings: Bk Vols 3,600; Per Subs 40
Open Mon-Fri 9-5

L HOUSING ADVOCATES, INC*, Law & Consumer Affairs Library, 3655 Prospect Ave E, 44115. SAN 320-4138. Tel: 216-391-5444. FAX: 216-391-5404. *Dir,* Ed Kramer; E-mail: kramere7@aol.com
Founded 1979
Library Holdings: Bk Titles 6,000; Per Subs 80
Special Collections: Housing Law Coll
Restriction: Staff use only

L JONES DAY*, Law Library, 901 Lakeside Ave, 44114. SAN 313-3575. Tel: 216-586-3939. FAX: 216-579-0212. *Res Serv Librn,* Rachel Kusmik; *Libr Res Serv Mgr,* Jo Ann Fisher; *Libr Serv Mgr,* Suzanne Young; Staff 4 (MLS 3, Non-MLS 1)
Library Holdings: Bk Vols 2,500; Per Subs 50
Subject Interests: Corp law, Law, Taxation
Wireless access
Restriction: Staff use only

L MCDONALD HOPKINS, LPA*, Law Library, 600 Superior Ave E, Ste 2100, 44114. SAN 372-2279. Tel: 216-348-5400. FAX: 216-348-5474. *Libr Assoc,* Mike Melillo; E-mail: mmelillo@mcdonaldhopkins.com; Staff 1 (Non-MLS 1)

Library Holdings: Bk Vols 10,000; Per Subs 100
Automation Activity & Vendor Info: (Serials) TLC (The Library Corporation)

M METROHEALTH MEDICAL CENTER*, Harold H Brittingham Memorial Library, 2500 MetroHealth Dr, 44101-1998. SAN 313-3249. Tel: 216-778-5623. FAX: 216-778-8242. E-mail: library@metrohealth.org. Web Site: www.metrohealth.org. *Chief Librn,* Laura A Frater; E-mail: lfrater@metrohealth.org; Staff 6 (MLS 2, Non-MLS 4)
Founded 1937
Library Holdings: Bk Vols 9,000; Per Subs 300
Special Collections: Arthritis & Rheumatism (Stecher Coll); Heritage Recognition Coll; Highland View Hospital Library Coll. Oral History
Subject Interests: Med, Nursing
Automation Activity & Vendor Info: (Cataloging) SydneyPlus; (Circulation) SydneyPlus; (OPAC) SydneyPlus
Database Vendor: Brodart, EBSCOhost, Elsevier, Ingenta, Majors, MD Consult, OVID Technologies, PubMed, Swets Information Services, UpToDate
Wireless access
Partic in Med Libr Asn of NE Ohio; National Network of Libraries of Medicine Greater Midwest Region

G NASA*, John H Glenn Research Center at Lewis Field, 21000 Brookpark Rd, MS142-3, 44135. SAN 313-3664. Circulation Tel: 216-433-5761. Interlibrary Loan Service Tel: 216-433-8305. FAX: 216-433-8139. Web Site: www.nasa.gov/centers/glenn/home. *Chief Librn,* Kate Dunlap; *Supv Librn,* Don Reams; *Sci Librn,* Robin Pertz; *Sci Librn,* Jaime Scibelli; *Doc Delivery,* Janis Dick; *ILL,* Marcia Stegenga; Staff 6 (MLS 4, Non-MLS 2)
Founded 1941. Pop 5,000
Library Holdings: Bk Titles 25,000; Bk Vols 80,500; Per Subs 300
Special Collections: NACA Documents
Subject Interests: Aeronaut, Eng, Power, Propulsion, Space communications mat, Space sci, Space shuttles, Space sta, Structures
Automation Activity & Vendor Info: (Cataloging) SirsiDynix; (Circulation) SirsiDynix; (ILL) OCLC; (OPAC) SirsiDynix; (Serials) SirsiDynix
Database Vendor: Dialog, OCLC FirstSearch
Wireless access
Function: Res libr
Partic in Nat Res Libr Alliance (NRLA); OHIONET
Restriction: Staff use only

S PLAIN DEALER PUBLISHING CO*, News Research Center, 1801 Superior Ave, 44114-2198. SAN 313-3745. Tel: 216-999-4195. FAX: 216-999-6363. E-mail: library@plaind.com. Web Site: www.cleveland.com. *Dir,* Patti A Graziano; Staff 3 (MLS 3)
Founded 1842
Library Holdings: Bk Vols 3,970; Per Subs 25
Subject Interests: Cleveland, Clippings from 1920 to present, Ohio hist, Photog from 1858 to present
Database Vendor: Dialog, LexisNexis, Newsbank, ProQuest

S ROMANIAN ETHNIC ARTS MUSEUM LIBRARY*, 3256 Warren Rd, 44111. SAN 321-0561. Tel: 216-941-5550. FAX: 216-941-3068. *In Charge,* Fr Remus Grama; Staff 1 (MLS 1)
Founded 1928
Library Holdings: Bk Titles 5,500
Subject Interests: Culture, Romanian art
Restriction: Open by appt only

S ST ANDREW'S ABBEY*, Slovak Institute Library & Museum, 10510 Buckeye Rd, 44104. SAN 328-3674. Tel: 216-721-5300, Ext 294. FAX: 216-791-8268. E-mail: slovakinstitute@csnmail.net. *Dir,* Andrew F Hudak, Jr
Library Holdings: Bk Vols 11,000; Per Subs 200
Function: Archival coll

M SAINT VINCENT CHARITY HOSPITAL*, Medical Library, 2351 E 22nd St, 44115-3197. SAN 313-3818. Tel: 216-241-5118. FAX: 216-363-3337. *Librn,* Joanne Billiar; E-mail: joanne.billiar@csauh.com
Library Holdings: Bk Vols 2,200; Per Subs 100
Subject Interests: Med, Nursing, Psychiat, Surgery
Restriction: Open to pub for ref only

S SHERWIN-WILLIAMS AUTOMOTIVE FINISHES CORP LIBRARY*, 4440 Warrensville Center Rd, 44128. SAN 375-9644. Tel: 216-332-8427. FAX: 216-332-8800. *Librn,* Beth Maher Rinz; E-mail: elizabeth.m.rinz@sherwin.com. Subject Specialists: *Chem,* Beth Maher Rinz; Staff 1 (MLS 1)
Library Holdings: Bk Titles 6,000; Per Subs 50
Automation Activity & Vendor Info: (Cataloging) EOS International; (Circulation) EOS International; (OPAC) EOS International; (Serials) EOS International
Restriction: Staff use only

M SIEGAL COLLEGE OF JUDAIC STUDIES*, Aaron Garber Library, 26500 Shaker Blvd, 44122. SAN 327-6856. Tel: 216-371-0446. Toll Free Tel: 888-336-2257. *In Charge,* Heather Lenson; Staff 2 (MLS 2)
Library Holdings: Bk Vols 34,000; Per Subs 150
Automation Activity & Vendor Info: (Cataloging) Innovative Interfaces, Inc; (Circulation) Innovative Interfaces, Inc; (OPAC) Innovative Interfaces, Inc
Database Vendor: EBSCOhost
Partic in Ohio Library & Information Network
Open Mon-Thurs 9-8, Fri 9-3
Friends of the Library Group

L THOMPSON, HINE LLP*, Law Library, 3900 Key Ctr, 127 Public Sq, 44114-1291. SAN 372-2295. Tel: 216-566-5651. FAX: 216-566-8565.
Library Holdings: Bk Vols 30,000; Per Subs 150

L TUCKER ELLIS LLP*, Law Library, 950 Main Avenue, Ste 1100, 44113-7213. SAN 313-3125. Tel: 216-592-5000. FAX: 216-592-5009. *Librn,* Ellen Smith; *Libr Asst,* Joseph Lara; Staff 2 (MLS 1, Non-MLS 1)
Library Holdings: Bk Vols 20,000
Database Vendor: Westlaw
Restriction: Private libr

S UKRAINIAN MUSEUM-ARCHIVES INC*, 1202 Kenilworth Ave, 44113. SAN 323-5270. Tel: 216-781-4329. E-mail: staff@umacleveland.org. Web Site: www.umacleveland.org. *Exec Dir,* Taras Szmagala; *Curator,* Aniza Kraus; E-mail: aniza@umacleveland.org. Subject Specialists: *Ethnography, Ukrainian traditional mat culture,* Aniza Kraus
Founded 1952
Library Holdings: Bk Vols 25,000; Per Subs 40
Special Collections: Taras Shevchenko, Ukrainian Revolution, Ukrainian Religion Periodical Coll outside of Ukraine, 1900-present
Wireless access
Open Tues-Sat 10-3

SR UNITED CHURCH OF CHRIST*, Wider Church Ministries Library, 700 Prospect Ave, 44115. SAN 327-0416. Tel: 216-736-3200. Toll Free Tel: 866-822-8224, Ext 3200. FAX: 216-736-3203. E-mail: wcm@ucc.org. Web Site: www.ucc.org.
Library Holdings: Bk Vols 3,500; Per Subs 50

S UNITED STATES BOOK EXCHANGE LIBRARY*, 2969 W 25th St, 44113-5393. SAN 370-6370. Tel: 216-241-6960. FAX: 216-241-6966. E-mail: usbe@usbe.com. Web Site: usbe.com. *Pres,* John T Zubal; *Coll Develop,* Robert Farkas; *Librn,* Thomas A Zubal; *Circ,* Jean Marie Vovos; E-mail: jean@usbe.com; *ILL, Per,* Marilyn Zubal; Staff 9 (MLS 3, Non-MLS 6)
Founded 1948
Library Holdings: Bk Titles 20,000
Publications: USBE: For Members Only
Partic in OCLC Online Computer Library Center, Inc

CM UNIVERSITY HOSPITALS CASE MEDICAL CENTER*, Core Library, 11100 Euclid Ave, Lakeside 3119, 44106. SAN 371-859X. Tel: 216-844-1208. FAX: 216-844-1207. E-mail: corelibrary@uhhospitals.org. *Dir,* Esther Gutow; Staff 4.5 (MLS 3.5, Non-MLS 1)
Library Holdings: Bk Titles 5,000; Per Subs 750
Partic in MLANO
Restriction: Employees only, Med & health res only, Med staff only, Non-circulating

S URS CORPORATION*, Resource Center, 1375 Euclid Ave, Ste 600, 44115-1808. SAN 328-1477. Tel: 216-622-2400. FAX: 216-622-2428. Web Site: www.urscorp.com. *In Charge,* Shirley Peavy; Staff 2 (MLS 1, Non-MLS 1)
Library Holdings: Bk Vols 300; Per Subs 10
Subject Interests: Archit, Eng, Interior design, Planning
Partic in OCLC Online Computer Library Center, Inc; OHIONET
Restriction: Staff use only

L WALTER & HAVERFIELD LLP*, Law Library, The Tower at Erieview, Ste 3500, 1301 E Ninth St, 44114-1821. SAN 325-5387. Tel: 216-781-1212. FAX: 216-575-0911. E-mail: info@walterhav.com. Web Site: www.walterhav.com. *Librn,* Leon Stevens; E-mail: lstevens@walterhav.com; Staff 2 (MLS 1, Non-MLS 1)
Founded 1932
Subject Interests: Bus, Labor

S WESTERN RESERVE HISTORICAL SOCIETY RESEARCH LIBRARY, 10825 East Blvd, 44106-1777. SAN 313-3915. Tel: 216-721-5722. Reference Tel: 216-721-5722, Ext 1509. FAX: 216-721-0891. E-mail: reference@wrhs.org. Web Site: www.wrhs.org. *Res Libr Dir,* Richard Shrake; Tel: 216-721-5722, Ext 1522, E-mail: rshrake@wrhs.org; Staff 5.5 (MLS 1, Non-MLS 4.5)
Founded 1867
Library Holdings: Bk Titles 238,000
Special Collections: Automobile Marque Files; Presidential Campaign Memorabilia; Wallace H Cathcart Shaker Coll; William Palmer Civil War Coll. Oral History
Subject Interests: Abolitionism, African-Am, Am genealogy, Family hist, Irish hist, Italian, Jewish hist, Local hist, Philanthropy, Relig hist, Slavery, Sports
Automation Activity & Vendor Info: (Cataloging) Cuadra Associates, Inc; (OPAC) Cuadra Associates, Inc
Wireless access
Function: Archival coll, Computers for patron use, Handicapped accessible, Microfiche/film & reading machines, Online cat, Photocopying/Printing, Ref serv available, Res libr, Res performed for a fee
Partic in OCLC Online Computer Library Center, Inc
Open Thurs-Sat 10-5
Restriction: Non-circulating
Friends of the Library Group

L WESTON HURD, LLP*, Law Library, The Tower at Erieview, Ste 1900, 1301 E Ninth St, 44114-1862. SAN 371-9057. Tel: 216-241-6602, Ext 3383. Toll Free Tel: 800-336-4952. FAX: 216-621-8369. Web Site: www.westonhurd.com. *Mkt Mgr,* Maria Murphy; E-mail: mmurphy@westonhurd.com
Library Holdings: Bk Titles 15,000
Special Collections: Insurance Law; Products Liability Law; Tax Law
Wireless access
Restriction: Staff use only

CLEVELAND HEIGHTS

P CLEVELAND HEIGHTS-UNIVERSITY HEIGHTS PUBLIC LIBRARY*, 2345 Lee Rd, 44118-3493. SAN 356-2387. Tel: 216-932-3600. FAX: 216-932-0932. TDD: 216-321-0739. Web Site: www.heightslibrary.org. *Dir,* Nancy S Levin; Tel: 216-932-3600, Ext 240, E-mail: nlevin@heightslibrary.org; *Dep Dir,* Kim DeNero-Ackroyd; Staff 108.7 (MLS 27.45, Non-MLS 81.25)
Founded 1916. Pop 61,194; Circ 1,816,766
Jan 2007-Dec 2007 Income (Main Library and Branch(s)) $7,926,450, State $3,136,269, Locally Generated Income $4,527,452, Other $262,729. Mats Exp $701,877, Books $284,276, AV Mat $416,568, Electronic Ref Mat (Incl. Access Fees) $1,033. Sal $4,034,365
Library Holdings: Audiobooks 58,368; AV Mats 24,597; Bks on Deafness & Sign Lang 1,000; e-books 15,944; Electronic Media & Resources 223; Bk Vols 284,276; Per Subs 1,033; Talking Bks 5,174; Videos 26,875
Special Collections: Parenting Coll
Automation Activity & Vendor Info: (Cataloging) SirsiDynix; (Circulation) SirsiDynix; (OPAC) SirsiDynix
Database Vendor: ALLDATA Online, Baker & Taylor, Booklist Online, Booksite, Bowker, BWI, Comprise Technologies Inc, CQ Press, Dun & Bradstreet, EBSCO - WebFeat, EBSCO Auto Repair Reference, EBSCO Information Services, EBSCOhost, Facts on File, Gale Cengage Learning, Greenwood Publishing Group, Grolier Online, H W Wilson, Hoovers, infoUSA, Ingram Library Services, Jane's, LearningExpress, Library Automation Technologies, Inc. (LAT), Marquis Who's Who, McGraw-Hill, Medline, Newsbank, OCLC FirstSearch, OCLC WorldShare Interlibrary Loan, Overdrive, Inc, Oxford Online, ProQuest, ReferenceUSA, SerialsSolutions, SirsiDynix, Standard & Poor's, ValueLine, WebMD, Wiley, Wilson - Wilson Web
Wireless access
Function: Adult bk club, Adult literacy prog, After school storytime, Art exhibits, Audiobks via web, AV serv, Bk club(s), Bk reviews (Group), Bks on cassette, Bks on CD, Children's prog, Computer training, Computers for patron use, Copy machines, Doc delivery serv, E-Reserves, Electronic databases & coll, Fax serv, Free DVD rentals, Games & aids for the handicapped, Handicapped accessible, Homebound delivery serv, ILL available, Instruction & testing, Large print keyboards, Mail & tel request accepted, Music CDs, Online cat, Online ref, Online searches, Outreach serv, OverDrive digital audio bks, Photocopying/Printing, Preschool outreach, Prog for adults, Prog for children & young adult, Pub access computers, Ref serv available, Referrals accepted, Scanner, Senior computer classes, Senior outreach, Spoken cassettes & CDs, Spoken cassettes & DVDs, Story hour, Summer reading prog, Tax forms, Teen prog, Telephone ref, VHS videos, Web-catalog, Wheelchair accessible, Workshops
Publications: Check Us Out; CH-UH Organizations; CH-UH Quick Information; Potamus Press; YAZine
Partic in CLEVNET; Northeast Ohio Regional Library System
Special Services for the Deaf - High interest/low vocabulary bks; TTY equip
Open Mon-Fri 9-9, Sat 9-5:30, Sun 1-5
Friends of the Library Group
Branches: 3
COVENTRY VILLAGE, 1925 Coventry Rd, 44118-2001, SAN 356-2417. Tel: 216-321-3400. Circulation Tel: 216-321-3600, Ext 610. Reference Tel: 216-321-3600, Ext 600. FAX: 216-321-0739. TDD: 216-321-0739. *Br Mgr,* Patricia Gray; Tel: 216-932-3600, Ext 620, E-mail: pgray@heightslibrary.org
Library Holdings: Bks on Deafness & Sign Lang 1,000; Bk Vols 32,808
Open Mon, Tues & Thurs 12-8:30, Wed, Fri & Sat 9-5:30, Sun 1-5
Friends of the Library Group
NOBLE NEIGHBORHOOD, 2800 Noble Rd, 44121-2208, SAN 356-2441. Tel: 216-291-5665. FAX: 216-291-1798. *Br Mgr,* Constance Dickerson; Tel: 216-932-3600, Ext 721, E-mail: cdickers@heightslibrary.org
Library Holdings: Bk Vols 41,275
Open Mon, Tues & Thurs 1-9, Wed, Fri & Sat 9-5:30
Friends of the Library Group
UNIVERSITY HEIGHTS, 13866 Cedar Rd, University Heights, 44118-3201, SAN 356-2476. Tel: 216-321-4700. FAX: 216-321-3049. *Br Mgr,* Aurora Martinez; E-mail: amartine@heightslibrary.org
Library Holdings: Bk Vols 42,370
Open Mon, Tues & Thurs 12:30-9, Wed, Fri & Sat 9-5:30, Sun 1-5
Friends of the Library Group

M CLEVELAND PSYCHOANALYTIC CENTER LIBRARY*, 2460 Fairmount Blvd, Ste 312, 44106. SAN 324-6922. Tel: 216-229-5959. FAX: 216-229-7321. E-mail: library@psychoanalysiscleveland.org. Web Site: www.psychoanalysiscleveland.org. *Librn,* Mary Ellen Kollar; E-mail: mekollarcpc@sbcglobal.net; Staff 2 (MLS 1, Non-MLS 1)
Founded 1962
Library Holdings: DVDs 2; Bk Titles 2,500; Per Subs 20; Videos 1
Special Collections: Manuscript Coll; Sigmund Freud (Complete Psychological Works)
Subject Interests: Child analysis, Psychoanalysis
Open Mon-Fri 8-4:30

CLYDE

P CLYDE PUBLIC LIBRARY*, 222 W Buckeye St, 43410. SAN 313-394X. Tel: 419-547-7174. FAX: 419-547-0480. E-mail: deskre@oplin.org. Web Site: clydelibrary.org. *Dir,* Beth Leibengood; E-mail: beth.leibengood@clyde.lib.oh.us; *Ad,* Jill McCullough; *Ch,* Deborah Meyer; Staff 3 (MLS 1, Non-MLS 2)
Founded 1903. Pop 6,200; Circ 118,429
Jan 2009-Dec 2009 Income $562,496, State $354,372, Locally Generated Income $131,400, Other $76,724. Mats Exp $64,897, Books $22,335, Other Print Mats $7,131, AV Mat $4,918, Electronic Ref Mat (Incl. Access Fees) $25,733. Sal $291,853
Library Holdings: AV Mats 5,203; CDs 560; DVDs 2,838; Large Print Bks 603; Bk Titles 33,532; Bk Vols 33,565; Per Subs 111; Videos 37
Special Collections: Clyde Coll; Maj Gen James B McPherson Coll; Roger Young Coll; Sherwood Anderson Coll
Automation Activity & Vendor Info: (Circulation) SirsiDynix
Database Vendor: EBSCOhost, Gale Cengage Learning, OCLC FirstSearch, SirsiDynix
Wireless access
Function: Adult bk club, Adult literacy prog, After school storytime, Archival coll, Audiobks via web, AV serv, Bk club(s), Bks on cassette, Bks on CD, CD-ROM, Children's prog, Computer training, Computers for patron use, Copy machines, Digital talking bks, e-mail & chat, Electronic databases & coll, Exhibits, Fax serv, Free DVD rentals, Games & aids for the handicapped, Handicapped accessible, Holiday prog, Home delivery & serv to Sr ctr & nursing homes, Homebound delivery serv, ILL available, Literacy & newcomer serv, Magnifiers for reading, Mail & tel request accepted, Music CDs, Online cat, Online ref, Online searches, Outreach serv, OverDrive digital audio bks, Photocopying/Printing, Preschool outreach, Prog for adults, Prog for children & young adult, Pub access computers, Ref & res, Ref serv available, Ref serv in person, Scanner, Senior outreach, Spoken cassettes & CDs, Story hour, Summer reading prog, Tax forms, Teen prog, Telephone ref, Web-catalog, Wheelchair accessible
Partic in CLEVNET; NORWELD
Special Services for the Deaf - Bks on deafness & sign lang
Special Services for the Blind - Aids for in-house use; Audio mat; BiFolkal kits; Bks on cassette; Bks on CD; Cassettes; Home delivery serv; Large print & cassettes; Large print bks; Large print bks & talking machines; Playaways (bks on MP3); Recorded bks; Talking bk & rec for the blind cat; Talking bks; Talking bks & player equip
Open Mon-Thurs 10-7:30, Fri 10-4, Sat 10-3

COLDWATER

P COLDWATER PUBLIC LIBRARY*, 305 W Main St, 45828-1604. SAN 313-3958. Tel: 419-678-2431. FAX: 419-678-8516. Web Site: www.coldwaterpubliclibrary.org. *Dir,* Carol Evers; E-mail: eversca@oplin.org
Founded 1936
Special Collections: Census, microfilm; Local Newspaper, microfilm
Automation Activity & Vendor Info: (Circulation) SirsiDynix; (ILL) SirsiDynix; (OPAC) SirsiDynix
Database Vendor: SirsiDynix
Wireless access
Partic in NORWELD
Open Mon-Wed 10-7, Thurs & Fri 10-5, Sat 10-12:30

COLUMBIANA

P COLUMBIANA PUBLIC LIBRARY, 332 N Middle St, 44408. SAN 313-3966. Tel: 330-482-5509. FAX: 330-482-9669. E-mail: columlib@oplin.org. Web Site: www.columbiana.lib.oh.us. *Dir, Fiscal Officer,* Carol Cobbs; E-mail: cobbsca@oplin.org; *Ad,* Kathryn Clewell; E-mail: kclewell@oplin.org; *Tech & Syst Librn,* Marceile Kaiser; E-mail: kaiserma@oplin.org; *YA Librn,* Amy Geary; E-mail: gearyam@oplin.org; *Youth Serv Mgr,* Carrie Radman; E-mail: radmanca@oplin.org; Staff 13 (MLS 4, Non-MLS 9)
Founded 1934. Pop 7,857; Circ 323,171
Jan 2013-Dec 2013 Income $850,001, State $724,647, Locally Generated Income $125,354. Mats Exp $150,783, Books $87,111, Per/Ser (Incl. Access Fees) $10,357, AV Mat $45,973, Electronic Ref Mat (Incl. Access Fees) $3,809
Library Holdings: Audiobooks 4,222; CDs 2,572; DVDs 5,663; Bk Vols 62,910; Per Subs 181; Videos 621
Automation Activity & Vendor Info: (Cataloging) TLC (The Library Corporation); (Circulation) TLC (The Library Corporation); (OPAC) TLC (The Library Corporation)
Wireless access
Open Mon-Sat 9-8
Friends of the Library Group

COLUMBUS

S THE AMERICAN SOCIETY FOR NONDESTRUCTIVE TESTING LIBRARY*, 1711 Arlingate Lane, 43228. (Mail add: PO Box 28518, 43228-0518), SAN 372-7963. Tel: 614-274-6003, Ext 245. Toll Free Tel: 800-222-2768, Ext 245. FAX: 614-274-6899. Web Site: www.asnt.org. *Librn,* Brian Geary
Founded 1990
Library Holdings: Bk Titles 2,000; Per Subs 100
Open Mon-Fri 8:30-5

L BAILEY CAVALIERI LLC*, Law Library, Ten W Broad St, Ste 2100, 43215-3422. SAN 372-2058. Tel: 614-221-3155. FAX: 614-221-0479. Web Site: www.baileycavalieri.com. *Librn,* Pamela Muller; E-mail: pamela.muller@baileycavalieri.com
Library Holdings: Bk Vols 15,000; Per Subs 45
Database Vendor: LexisNexis, Westlaw
Restriction: Staff use only

L BAKER & HOSTETLER LIBRARY*, 65 E State St, Ste 2100, 43215-4260. SAN 329-0603. Tel: 614-228-1541, Ext 2608. FAX: 614-462-2616. *Librn,* Ben Gaul; E-mail: bgaul@bakerlaw.com; Staff 2 (MLS 1, Non-MLS 1)
Library Holdings: Bk Vols 15,000; Per Subs 95
Subject Interests: Legal mat
Automation Activity & Vendor Info: (OPAC) SirsiDynix
Database Vendor: LexisNexis
Partic in OHIONET
Restriction: Staff use only

S BATTELLE MEMORIAL INSTITUTE*, Battelle Library, 505 King Ave, 43201. SAN 356-2506. Tel: 614-424-6302. Interlibrary Loan Service Tel: 614-424-6305. Administration Tel: 614-424-7835. Interlibrary Loan Service FAX: 614-458-3605. E-mail: library@battelle.org. *Actg Libr Mgr,* Curt Flemming; E-mail: flemmingc@battelle.org; *Cat, Online Serv,* David Blum; Tel: 614-424-5138; *Coll Mgt, Online Serv,* Melissa Gustafson; Tel: 614-397-9014; *Doc Delivery,* Darlene Fields; *Online Serv, Ref,* Carol Staudenheimer; Tel: 614-424-3526; Staff 4 (MLS 3, Non-MLS 1)
Founded 1929
Library Holdings: CDs 10; e-books 4,000; e-journals 710; Microforms 149; Bk Vols 26,377; Per Subs 601
Subject Interests: Chem, Eng, Math, Metallurgy, Physics
Automation Activity & Vendor Info: (Cataloging) SirsiDynix; (Circulation) SirsiDynix; (OPAC) SirsiDynix; (Serials) SirsiDynix
Database Vendor: Dialog, EBSCOhost, Infotrieve, Jane's, Knovel, LexisNexis, OCLC, OHIONET, ProQuest, Safari Books Online, ScienceDirect, SirsiDynix, STN International, Wiley InterScience
Wireless access
Function: Doc delivery serv, ILL available, Online searches, Ref serv available
Partic in OCLC Online Computer Library Center, Inc; OHIONET
Restriction: Co libr, Open to pub by appt only

C BYRD POLAR RESEARCH CENTER*, Goldthwait Polar Library, 176 Scott Hall, 1090 Carmack Rd, 43210-1002. SAN 313-4202. Tel: 614-292-6715. FAX: 614-292-4697. Web Site: www.library.osu.edu/sites/libinfo/PLR.html. *Librn,* Lynn B Lay; E-mail: lay.1@osu.edu; Staff 3 (MLS 1, Non-MLS 2)
Library Holdings: Bk Titles 8,000; Bk Vols 12,000; Per Subs 215
Special Collections: Reprint Coll
Subject Interests: Climatology, Geol, Geomorphology, Glaciology, Global change, Meteorology, Polar regions
Function: Res libr
Partic in Ohio Library & Information Network

C CAPITAL UNIVERSITY*, Blackmore Library, One College & Main, 43209. SAN 356-2565. Tel: 614-236-6614. Interlibrary Loan Service Tel: 614-236-6436. Reference Tel: 614-236-6351. FAX: 614-236-6490. E-mail: refdesk@capital.edu. Interlibrary Loan Service E-mail: ill@capital.edu. Web Site: www.capital.edu. *Mgr,* Scott Bates; Tel: 614-236-6475, E-mail: sbates@capital.edu; *Head, Tech Serv,* Stephen Long; Tel: 614-236-6470, E-mail: slong@capital.edu; Staff 12 (MLS 9, Non-MLS 3)
Founded 1876. Enrl 2,500; Fac 146; Highest Degree: Master
Library Holdings: AV Mats 18,868; CDs 6,169; DVDs 1,099; e-books 19,014; e-journals 9,297; Electronic Media & Resources 28,643; Microforms 148,202; Music Scores 6,030; Bk Titles 132,007; Bk Vols 146,310; Per Subs 268; Videos 2,643
Special Collections: Archives (University Archives); Juvenile Literature (Lois Lenski Coll), bk & mss. US Document Depository
Subject Interests: Art, Educ, Music, Relig studies
Automation Activity & Vendor Info: (Acquisitions) Innovative Interfaces, Inc; (Cataloging) Innovative Interfaces, Inc; (Circulation) Innovative Interfaces, Inc; (OPAC) Innovative Interfaces, Inc; (Serials) Innovative Interfaces, Inc
Database Vendor: Cambridge Scientific Abstracts, EBSCOhost, Gale Cengage Learning, JSTOR, LexisNexis, OCLC FirstSearch, OVID Technologies, ProQuest, Wilson - Wilson Web
Wireless access
Partic in Ohio Libr Coun; OHIONET
Open Mon-Thurs 7:30am-Midnight, Fri 7:30-6, Sat 1-5, Sun 1-11

Departmental Libraries:

CL LAW SCHOOL LIBRARY, 303 E Broad St, 43215, SAN 356-259X. Tel: 614-236-6464. FAX: 614-236-6957. Web Site: www.law.capital.edu. *Dir,* Donald A Hughes, Jr; E-mail: dhughes@law.capital.edu; *Assoc Dir,* Jacqueline Orlando; *Ref Librn,* Daniel Baker; Tel: 614-236-6463, E-mail: dbaker3@law.capital.edu; *Circ Supvr,* Tracey Newman; *Acq, Tech Serv,* Wendy Medvetz; *Tech Serv,* Phyllis Post; Staff 9 (MLS 6, Non-MLS 3)
Founded 1903. Enrl 735; Fac 40; Highest Degree: Doctorate
Library Holdings: Bk Vols 266,901; Per Subs 2,405
Automation Activity & Vendor Info: (Acquisitions) Innovative Interfaces, Inc; (Cataloging) Innovative Interfaces, Inc; (Circulation) Innovative Interfaces, Inc; (Course Reserve) Innovative Interfaces, Inc; (OPAC) Innovative Interfaces, Inc; (Serials) Innovative Interfaces, Inc
Function: Copy machines, Electronic databases & coll, Handicapped accessible, ILL available, Online cat, Ref & res, Ref serv in person, Telephone ref, Web-catalog
Partic in OCLC Online Computer Library Center, Inc; Ohio Library & Information Network; Westlaw
Open Mon-Thurs 8am-11pm, Fri 8am-9pm, Sat 9-6, Sun 11-11
Restriction: 24-hr pass syst for students only, Authorized patrons, Badge access after hrs, Borrowing privileges limited to fac & registered students, Not open to pub, Open to students, fac, staff & alumni

S CENTER ON EDUCATION & TRAINING FOR EMPLOYMENT*, 1900 Kenny Rd, 43210-1016. SAN 327-7674. Tel: 614-292-6991. FAX: 614-292-1260. Web Site: cete.osu.edu/. *Librn,* Steve Chambers; E-mail: chambers.2@osu.edu; Staff 2 (MLS 1, Non-MLS 1)
Founded 1965
Library Holdings: Bk Titles 68,000; Per Subs 171
Special Collections: High Schools That Work
Subject Interests: Adult educ, Career educ, Vocational educ
Open Mon-Fri 8-5

S MINNIE COBEY MEMORIAL LIBRARY*, 1354 E Broad St, 43205. SAN 313-4083. Tel: 614-253-8523. FAX: 614-253-6323. *Librn,* Helen Chronister; E-mail: hchronister@tiferethisrael.org
Founded 1950
Library Holdings: Bk Titles 4,500; Bk Vols 6,500; Per Subs 30

Special Collections: Talmud (Babylonian Talmud Coll)
Subject Interests: Bible, Judaism, Prayer bks, Relig studies, Talmud

C COLUMBUS COLLEGE OF ART & DESIGN*, Packard Library, 107 N Ninth St, 43215-3875. SAN 313-4091. Tel: 614-222-3273, 614-224-9101. FAX: 614-222-6193. Web Site: www.ccad.edu. *Dir,* Gail Storer; *Librn,* Ann Shifflet
Founded 1931. Highest Degree: Bachelor
Library Holdings: Bk Vols 50,000; Per Subs 275
Subject Interests: Art & archit
Automation Activity & Vendor Info: (Acquisitions) Innovative Interfaces, Inc; (Cataloging) Innovative Interfaces, Inc; (Circulation) Innovative Interfaces, Inc; (Course Reserve) Innovative Interfaces, Inc; (OPAC) Innovative Interfaces, Inc; (Serials) Innovative Interfaces, Inc
Open Mon-Thurs (Winter) 8am-9:30pm, Fri 8-5, Sat 1-5; Mon-Fri (Summer) 8:30-5

P COLUMBUS METROPOLITAN LIBRARY*, Main Library, 96 S Grant Ave, 43215-4702. SAN 356-3790. Tel: 614-645-2275. Circulation Tel: 614-849-1201. FAX: 614-849-1157. Circulation FAX: 614-849-1389. Web Site: www.columbuslibrary.org. *Chief Operating Officer,* Nate Oliver; E-mail: noliver@columbuslibrary.org; *Pub Serv Dir,* Tony Howard; *Managing Librn,* Jay Kegley; E-mail: jkegley@columbuslibrary.org; *Librn,* Chuck Cody; E-mail: ccody@columbuslibrary.org; *Tech Serv Mgr,* Heidi Dowling; E-mail: hdowling@columbuslibrary.org. Subject Specialists: *Bus, News, Sci,* Jay Kegley; *Fine arts, Humanities, Recreation,* Chuck Cody; Staff 612 (MLS 110, Non-MLS 502)
Founded 1872. Pop 846,761; Circ 15,360,000
Jan 2013-Dec 2013 Income (Main Library and Branch(s)) $67,877,332. Mats Exp $56,100,232. Sal $35,370,453
Library Holdings: Bk Vols 1,928,112; Per Subs 2,513
Special Collections: Black Heritage Coll; ESOL; Local History (Columbus & Ohio), bks, micro, VF. State Document Depository; US Document Depository
Database Vendor: Gale Cengage Learning
Wireless access
Publications: Check It Out (Quarterly)
Partic in Discovery Place Librs; OCLC Online Computer Library Center, Inc
Special Services for the Deaf - Bks on deafness & sign lang; High interest/low vocabulary bks; Spec interest per; Staff with knowledge of sign lang; TDD equip; TTY equip
Open Mon-Thurs 9-9, Fri & Sat 9-6, Sun 1-5
Friends of the Library Group
Branches: 22
DRIVING PARK, 1422 E Livingston Ave, 43205, SAN 356-3944. Tel: 614-645-2275. Reference Tel: 614-479-3371. FAX: 614-479-4379. *Managing Librn,* Mel Jones; E-mail: mjones@columbuslibrary.org
Circ 71,081
Library Holdings: Bk Vols 29,000
Special Services for the Deaf - TDD equip
Open Mon-Thurs 10-8, Fri & Sat 10-6
Friends of the Library Group
DUBLIN BRANCH, 75 N High St, Dublin, 43017, SAN 356-3979. Tel: 614-645-2275. Reference Tel: 614-479-3171. FAX: 614-479-4179. *Br Mgr,* Michael Blackwell
Circ 1,558,342
Library Holdings: Bk Vols 140,000
Special Services for the Deaf - TDD equip
Open Mon-Thurs 9-9, Fri & Sat 9-6, Sun 1-5
Friends of the Library Group
FRANKLINTON, 1061 W Town St, 43222, SAN 356-4002. Tel: 614-645-2275. Circulation Tel: 614-479-3410. Reference Tel: 614-479-3411. FAX: 614-479-4419. *Managing Librn,* Steve Pullen; E-mail: spullen@columbuslibrary.org
Founded 1995. Circ 124,123
Special Collections: Local History Books & Clippings
Function: Copy machines, Electronic databases & coll, Fax serv, Handicapped accessible, Prog for adults, Prog for children & young adult, Ref serv available, Summer reading prog, Tax forms
Special Services for the Deaf - TDD equip
Open Mon-Thurs 10-8, Fri & Sat 10-6
Friends of the Library Group
GAHANNA BRANCH, 310 Granville St, Gahanna, 43230, SAN 356-4037. Tel: 614-645-2275. Circulation Tel: 614-479-3270. Reference Tel: 614-479-3271. FAX: 614-479-4279. *Managing Librn,* Mary Campanelli; E-mail: mcampanelli@columbuslibrary.org
Founded 1969. Circ 1,174,913
Library Holdings: Bk Vols 143,103
Function: Res libr
Special Services for the Deaf - TDD equip
Open Mon-Thurs 9-9, Fri & Sat 9-6, Sun 1-5
Friends of the Library Group
HILLIARD BRANCH, 4772 Cemetery Rd, Hilliard, 43026, SAN 356-4061. Tel: 614-645-2275. Circulation Tel: 614-479-3140. Reference Tel: 614-479-3141. FAX: 614-479-4149. *Managing Librn,* Robin Nesbitt; E-mail: rnesbitt@columbuslibrary.org
Circ 1,591,721
Library Holdings: Bk Vols 170,000
Special Services for the Deaf - TDD equip
Open Mon-Thurs 9-9, Fri & Sat 9-6, Sun 1-5
Friends of the Library Group
HILLTOP, 511 S Hague Ave, 43204, SAN 356-4126. Tel: 614-645-2275. Circulation Tel: 614-479-3430. Reference Tel: 614-479-3431. FAX: 614-479-4439. *Managing Librn,* John Tetzloff
Circ 519,700
Library Holdings: Bk Vols 119,719
Special Services for the Deaf - TDD equip
Open Mon-Thurs 9-9, Fri & Sat 9-6, Sun 1-5
Friends of the Library Group
KARL ROAD, 5590 Karl Rd, 43229, SAN 356-424X. Tel: 614-645-2275. Circulation Tel: 614-479-3250. Reference Tel: 614-479-3251. FAX: 614-479-4259. *Mgr,* Keith Hanson
Founded 1988. Circ 720,080
Library Holdings: Bk Vols 170,000
Special Services for the Deaf - TDD equip
Open Mon-Thurs 9-9, Fri & Sat 9-6, Sun 1-5
Friends of the Library Group
MARTIN LUTHER KING BRANCH, 1600 E Long St, 43203, SAN 356-4150. Tel: 614-645-2275. Circulation Tel: 614-479-3210. Reference Tel: 614-479-3211. FAX: 614-479-4219. *Managing Librn,* Keisha Gibbs; E-mail: kgibbs@columbuslibrary.org
Founded 1953. Circ 127,794
Library Holdings: Bk Vols 30,000
Special Services for the Deaf - TDD equip
Open Mon-Thurs 10-8, Fri & Sat 10-6
Friends of the Library Group
LINDEN BRANCH, 2223 Cleveland Ave, 43211, SAN 356-4185. Tel: 614-645-2275. Circulation Tel: 614-479-3230. Reference Tel: 614-479-3231. FAX: 614-479-4239. *Managing Librn,* Karen Richardson-Rogers; E-mail: krichardson@columbuslibrary.org
Founded 1928. Circ 135,494
Library Holdings: Bk Vols 52,050
Special Services for the Deaf - TDD equip
Open Mon-Thurs 10-8, Fri & Sat 10-6
Friends of the Library Group
LIVINGSTON BRANCH, 3434 E Livingston Ave, 43227, SAN 356-4215. Tel: 614-645-2275. Circulation Tel: 614-479-3330. Reference Tel: 614-479-3331. FAX: 614-479-4339. *Managing Librn,* Sheryl Owens; E-mail: sowens@columbuslibrary.org; Staff 7 (MLS 5, Non-MLS 2)
Founded 1963. Circ 234,540
Library Holdings: Bk Vols 90,000
Special Services for the Deaf - TDD equip
Open Mon-Thurs 10-9, Fri & Sat 10-6
Friends of the Library Group
NEW ALBANY BRANCH, 200 Market St, New Albany, 43054, SAN 378-0333. Tel: 614-645-2275. Circulation Tel: 614-479-3540. Reference Tel: 614-479-3541. FAX: 614-479-4549. *Managing Librn,* Joe Yersavich; E-mail: jyersavich@columbuslibrary.org
Founded 2003. Circ 880,868
Library Holdings: Bk Vols 120,000
Special Services for the Deaf - TDD equip
Open Mon-Thurs 9-9, Fri & Sat 9-6, Sun 1-5
Friends of the Library Group
NORTHERN LIGHTS, 4093 Cleveland Ave, 43224, SAN 356-4274. Tel: 614-645-2275. Circulation Tel: 614-479-3240. Reference Tel: 614-479-3241. FAX: 614-479-4249. *Managing Librn,* Rick Catrone
Founded 1956. Circ 326,299
Library Holdings: Bk Vols 72,926
Open Mon-Thurs 10-9, Fri & Sat 10-6
Friends of the Library Group
NORTHSIDE, 1423 N High St, 43201, SAN 356-4304. Tel: 614-645-2275. Circulation Tel: 614-479-3110. Reference Tel: 614-479-3111. FAX: 614-479-4119. *Managing Librn,* Candy Princehorn; E-mail: cprincehorn@columbuslibrary.org
Founded 1940. Circ 357,420
Library Holdings: Bk Vols 48,000
Special Services for the Deaf - TDD equip
Open Mon-Thurs 10-8, Fri & Sat 10-6
Friends of the Library Group
NORTHWEST, 2280 Hard Rd, 43235, SAN 378-035X. Tel: 614-807-2650. Reference Tel: 614-807-2656. FAX: 614-807-2659. Web Site: www.worthingtonlibraries.org. *Managing Librn,* Jeff Regensburger; Tel: 614-807-2659, E-mail: jregensb@worthingtonlibraries.org; *Circ Mgr,* Jessi Tisdale; Tel: 614-807-2655, E-mail: jtisdale@worthingtonlibraries.org
Founded 1996. Pop 359,412; Circ 840,039

Library Holdings: CDs 17,000; DVDs 12,000; Bk Vols 162,000; Per Subs 200; Videos 1,200
Special Services for the Deaf - TDD equip
Open Mon-Thurs 9-9, Fri & Sat 9-6, Sun (Sept-May) 1-5
Friends of the Library Group

OUTREACH DIVISION, 101 S Stygler Rd, Gahanna, 43230, SAN 356-4312. Tel: 614-645-2275. FAX: 614-849-1390. *Co-Mgr,* Mike Conner; E-mail: mconnor@columbuslibrary.org; *Co-Mgr,* Wendy Ramsey; E-mail: wramsey@columbuslibrary.org
Circ 51,907
Library Holdings: Bk Vols 38,848
Special Services for the Deaf - TDD equip
Friends of the Library Group

PARSONS, 845 Parsons Ave, 43206, SAN 356-4339. Tel: 614-645-2275. Circulation Tel: 614-479-3310. Reference Tel: 614-479-3311. FAX: 614-479-4319. *Managing Librn,* Anne Heidrich; E-mail: aheidrich@columbuslibrary.org
Founded 1956. Circ 164,471
Library Holdings: Bk Vols 37,000
Special Services for the Deaf - TDD equip
Open Mon-Thurs 10-8, Fri & Sat 10-6
Friends of the Library Group

REYNOLDSBURG BRANCH, 1402 Brice Rd, Reynoldsburg, 43068, SAN 356-4363. Tel: 614-645-2275. Circulation Tel: 614-479-3340. Reference Tel: 614-479-3341. FAX: 614-479-4349. *Managing Librn,* Dave Dennison; E-mail: ddennison@columbuslibrary.org
Founded 1980. Circ 1,157,804
Library Holdings: Bk Vols 170,000
Special Services for the Deaf - TDD equip
Open Mon-Thurs 9-9, Fri & Sat 9-6, Sun 1-5
Friends of the Library Group

SHEPARD BRANCH, 790 N Nelson Rd, 43219, SAN 356-4398. Tel: 614-645-2275. Circulation Tel: 614-479-3220. Reference Tel: 614-479-3221. FAX: 614-479-4229. *Managing Librn,* Jen Hess; E-mail: jhess@columbuslibrary.org
Founded 1939. Pop 112,501
Library Holdings: Bk Vols 33,000
Special Services for the Deaf - TDD equip
Open Mon-Thurs 10-8, Fri & Sat 10-6
Friends of the Library Group

SOUTH HIGH, 3540 S High St, 43207, SAN 356-4428. Tel: 614-645-2275. Circulation Tel: 614-479-3360. Reference Tel: 614-479-3361. FAX: 614-479-4369. *Managing Librn,* Summer Sherman; E-mail: ssherman@columbuslibrary.org
Founded 1971. Circ 274,358
Library Holdings: Bk Vols 84,000
Special Services for the Deaf - TDD equip
Open Mon-Thurs 10-9, Fri & Sat 10-6
Friends of the Library Group

SOUTHEAST, 3980 S Hamilton Rd, Groveport, 43125, SAN 370-9418. Tel: 614-645-2275. Circulation Tel: 614-479-3350. Reference Tel: 614-479-3351. FAX: 614-479-4359. *Managing Librn,* Sandee Wagle; E-mail: swagle@columbuslibrary.org
Founded 1991. Circ 853,097
Library Holdings: Bk Vols 112,346
Database Vendor: EBSCOhost, OCLC WorldShare Interlibrary Loan, ProQuest, ReferenceUSA
Function: Copy machines, Handicapped accessible, Prog for children & young adult, Summer reading prog, Tax forms
Special Services for the Deaf - TDD equip
Open Mon-Thurs 9-9, Fri & Sat 9-6, Sun 1-5
Friends of the Library Group

WHETSTONE BRANCH, 3909 N High St, 43214, SAN 326-7938. Tel: 614-645-2275. Circulation Tel: 614-479-3150. Reference Tel: 614-479-3151. FAX: 614-479-4159. *Managing Librn,* Greg Denby; E-mail: gdenby@columbuslibrary.org
Founded 1997. Circ 1,408,640
Library Holdings: Bk Vols 170,000
Special Services for the Deaf - TDD equip
Open Mon-Thurs 9-9, Fri & Sat 9-6, Sun 1-5
Friends of the Library Group

WHITEHALL BRANCH, 4371 E Broad St, 43213, SAN 356-4452. Tel: 614-645-2275. Circulation Tel: 614-479-3320. Reference Tel: 614-479-3321. FAX: 614-479-4329. *Managing Librn,* Shirley Freeman; E-mail: sfreeman@columbuslibrary.org
Founded 1950. Circ 317,757
Library Holdings: Bk Vols 63,000
Special Services for the Deaf - TDD equip
Open Mon-Thurs 10-9, Fri & Sat 10-6
Friends of the Library Group
Bookmobiles: 2

J COLUMBUS STATE COMMUNITY COLLEGE LIBRARY*, 550 E Spring St, 43215. SAN 313-4121. Tel: 614-287-2465. Reference Tel: 614-287-2460. Toll Free Tel: 800-621-6407. FAX: 614-287-2457. E-mail: information@cscc.edu. Web Site: www.cscc.edu/library. *Dir of Libr,* Bruce Massis; Tel: 614-287-5484, Fax: 614-287-6029, E-mail: bmassis@cscc.edu; *Asst Dir,* Kim Leggett; Tel: 614-287-5879, E-mail: kleggett@cscc.edu; *Supvr, Multimedia Support Ctr/Circ,* Angel Gondek; Tel: 614-287-2267, E-mail: agondek@cscc.edu; *Ref Supvr,* Tracy Kemp; Tel: 614-287-5380, E-mail: tkemp@cscc.edu; *Supvr, Tech Serv/DMS,* Robin Buser; Tel: 614-287-2469, E-mail: rbuser@cscc.edu. Subject Specialists: *Admin, Mgt,* Bruce Massis; *Admin, Mgt,* Kim Leggett; Staff 17 (MLS 12, Non-MLS 5)
Founded 1965. Enrl 30,000; Fac 320; Highest Degree: Associate
Jul 2013-Jun 2014. Mats Exp $235,347, Books $115,423, Per/Ser (Incl. Access Fees) $70,924, Electronic Ref Mat (Incl. Access Fees) $49,000. Sal $988,515 (Prof $806,008)
Library Holdings: Bk Titles 30,244; Bk Vols 40,973; Per Subs 450
Subject Interests: Allied health tech, Nursing, Pub serv tech
Automation Activity & Vendor Info: (Acquisitions) Innovative Interfaces, Inc; (Cataloging) Innovative Interfaces, Inc; (Circulation) Innovative Interfaces, Inc; (OPAC) Innovative Interfaces, Inc
Database Vendor: Dialog, EBSCOhost, Innovative Interfaces, Inc, LexisNexis, OCLC FirstSearch, OVID Technologies, Wilson - Wilson Web
Wireless access
Function: Ref serv available
Publications: Handbook
Partic in Ohio Library & Information Network; OHIONET
Open Mon-Thurs 7:30am-10pm, Fri 7:30-6, Sat 9-4

C DEVRY UNIVERSITY LIBRARY*, Columbus Campus Community Library, 1350 Alum Creek Dr, 43209. SAN 313-430X. Tel: 614-257-4625. FAX: 614-252-4108. Web Site: www.devrycols.edu/library. *Librn,* Brittany Tesar; E-mail: btesar@devry.edu; *Librn,* Oliva Riley; Tel: 614-253-7291, Ext 1365, E-mail: oriley@devry.edu; Staff 3 (MLS 2, Non-MLS 1)
Founded 1970. Enrl 3,000; Fac 80; Highest Degree: Master
Library Holdings: e-books 13,000; Bk Titles 21,805; Bk Vols 24,996; Per Subs 70
Special Collections: SAMS Schematics
Automation Activity & Vendor Info: (Acquisitions) Ex Libris Group; (Cataloging) Ex Libris Group; (Circulation) Ex Libris Group; (OPAC) Ex Libris Group
Database Vendor: EBSCOhost, ProQuest
Partic in OHIONET
Open Mon-Thurs 9-8, Fri 9-5, Sat 10-1
Restriction: Open to students, fac & staff

C FRANKLIN UNIVERSITY LIBRARY*, Phillips Hall, 1st Flr, 303 S Grant Ave, 43215. (Mail add: 201 S Grant Ave, 43215), SAN 313-4164. Tel: 614-341-6252. Toll Free Tel: 866-341-6252. FAX: 614-461-0957. E-mail: library@franklin.edu. Web Site: www.franklin.edu/students/library. *Dir,* Tiffany Lipstreu; Tel: 614-947-6558, E-mail: tiffany.lipstreu@franklin.edu; *Acq Librn,* Amber Bice; *Instrul Res Librn,* Daron Larson; *Pub Serv Librn,* Carmen Byg; *Ref Librn,* David Migerney; *Syst Librn,* Kristi Lobrano; *Circ Coordr,* Brandon Houseman; Staff 15 (MLS 7, Non-MLS 8)
Founded 1966. Enrl 6,100; Highest Degree: Master
Library Holdings: Bk Titles 12,200; Bk Vols 15,200; Per Subs 350
Subject Interests: Bus
Automation Activity & Vendor Info: (Acquisitions) Innovative Interfaces, Inc; (Cataloging) Innovative Interfaces, Inc; (Circulation) Innovative Interfaces, Inc; (Course Reserve) Innovative Interfaces, Inc; (ILL) OCLC Online; (OPAC) Innovative Interfaces, Inc, (Serials) Innovative Interfaces, Inc
Wireless access
Partic in Columbus Area Library & Information Council of Ohio; Ohio Library & Information Network; OHIONET
Open Mon-Thurs 8-10, Fri 8-5, Sat 8-4, Sun 1-5

P GRANDVIEW HEIGHTS PUBLIC LIBRARY*, 1685 W First Ave, 43212. SAN 313-4172. Tel: 614-486-2951. Administration Tel: 614-486-2954. FAX: 614-481-7021. Web Site: www.ghpl.org. *Dir,* Ryan McDonnell; E-mail: rmcdonnell@ghpl.org; *Asst Dir,* Rebecca Felkner; E-mail: rfelkner@ghpl.org; *Circ Serv Mgr,* Anne Richards; *Coll Develop, Ref Mgr, Tech Serv Mgr,* Wendy Greenwood; *Youth Serv Mgr,* Eileen McNeil; *Tech Coordr,* Nate Nguyen; *Fiscal Officer,* Terri McKeown; *Teen Serv,* Jennifer Lawson; Staff 32 (MLS 6, Non-MLS 26)
Founded 1924. Pop 7,000; Circ 772,000
Jan 2011-Dec 2011 Income $2,878,000. Mats Exp $297,200. Sal $1,221,000
Library Holdings: CDs 10,000; DVDs 13,000; e-books 38,000; Bk Vols 129,000; Per Subs 253
Subject Interests: Archit, Art, Behav sci, Bus info, Computer, Cookery, Relig studies, Soc sci
Automation Activity & Vendor Info: (Acquisitions) Innovative Interfaces, Inc; (Cataloging) Innovative Interfaces, Inc; (Circulation) Innovative Interfaces, Inc; (ILL) Innovative Interfaces, Inc; (OPAC) Innovative Interfaces, Inc; (Serials) Innovative Interfaces, Inc
Database Vendor: EBSCOhost, Gale Cengage Learning, ReferenceUSA
Wireless access

Partic in Cent Libr Consortium; OHIONET
Open Mon-Thurs 10-8:30, Fri 10-6, Sat 10-5, Sun 1-5
Friends of the Library Group

L JONES DAY*, Law Library, 325 John H McConnell Blvd, Ste 600, 43215-2673. (Mail add: PO Box 165017, 43216-5017). Tel: 614-469-3939. FAX: 614-461-4198. Web Site: www.jonesday.com. *Libr Serv Mgr,* Nancy S Seymour; *Res Librn,* Morris Jackson

L KEGLER BROWN HILL & RITTER, Law Library, 65 E State St, Ste 1800, 43215. SAN 372-1949. Tel: 614-255-5502. FAX: 614-464-2634. *Dir of Libr Serv,* Keith S Knopf; E-mail: kknopf@keglerbrown.com; Staff 1.5 (MLS 1, Non-MLS 0.5)
Library Holdings: DVDs 2; e-books 10; Bk Titles 1,000; Bk Vols 10,000; Per Subs 25; Videos 20
Automation Activity & Vendor Info: (Cataloging) TLC (The Library Corporation); (Serials) TLC (The Library Corporation)
Database Vendor: Dun & Bradstreet, HeinOnline, LexisNexis, Overdrive, Inc, TLC (The Library Corporation), Westlaw
Wireless access
Function: AV serv, Copy machines, Online searches, Orientations, Res libr, Tax forms, Telephone ref, VHS videos
Restriction: Not open to pub

M MOUNT CARMEL*, Health Sciences Library, 127 S Davis Ave, 43222. SAN 313-4229. Tel: 614-234-5214. FAX: 614-234-1257. E-mail: library@mchs.com. Web Site: www.mccn.edu/library. *Dir,* Stevo Roksandic; Tel: 614-234-1644, E-mail: sroksandic@mchs.com; Staff 7 (MLS 5, Non-MLS 2)
Founded 1964
Library Holdings: Bk Vols 10,000; Per Subs 500
Subject Interests: Allied health, Med, Nursing
Automation Activity & Vendor Info: (Acquisitions) Innovative Interfaces, Inc; (Cataloging) Innovative Interfaces, Inc; (OPAC) Innovative Interfaces, Inc
Wireless access
Partic in GMR; Medical Library Association (MLA); Michigan Health Sciences Libraries Association; Ohio Library & Information Network; Ohio Private Academic Libraries (OPAL); OHIONET; Oregon Health Sciences Libraries Association
Open Mon-Thurs 8am-9pm, Fri 8-5, Sat 8:30-12:30

S NATIONWIDE LIBRARY*, One Nationwide Plaza 1-01-05, 43215. SAN 313-4237. Tel: 614-249-6414. FAX: 614-249-2218. *Mgr, Libr Serv,* John W Holtzclaw; E-mail: holtzcj@nationwide.com; *Librn,* Karen Hoyt; *Librn,* David Schneider; Staff 6 (MLS 3, Non-MLS 3)
Founded 1935
Library Holdings: Bk Vols 10,000; Per Subs 150
Subject Interests: Ins
Automation Activity & Vendor Info: (Cataloging) SirsiDynix; (Circulation) SirsiDynix; (OPAC) SirsiDynix; (Serials) SirsiDynix
Database Vendor: Factiva.com, LexisNexis, SirsiDynix
Partic in OHIONET
Restriction: Restricted access

GL OHIO ATTORNEY GENERAL*, Law Library, 30 E Broad St, 15th Flr, 43215. SAN 313-4245. Tel: 614-466-2465, 614-466-4534. FAX: 614-752-9867. *Dir, Libr Serv,* Carol Ottolenghi; *Principal Librn,* Madelaine A Gordon; *Sr Res Librn,* Jonathan Chagat; Staff 3 (MLS 3)
Founded 1846
Subject Interests: Cases, Law statutes
Partic in Ohio Library & Information Network
Restriction: Staff use only

G OHIO BUREAU OF WORKER'S COMPENSATION*, Division of Safety & Hygiene Library, 30 W Spring St, 3rd Flr, 43215-2256. SAN 356-2891. Tel: 614-466-7388. Toll Free Tel: 800-644-6292. FAX: 614-644-9634. E-mail: library@bwc.state.oh.us. Web Site: www.ohiobwc.com. *Adminr,* Melissa Hatfield; E-mail: melissa.hatfield@bwc.state.oh.us; *Librn,* Karen Jensen; E-mail: karen.jensen@bwc.state.oh.us; *Librn,* Sharon Roney; E-mail: sharon.roney@bwc.state.oh.us; Staff 3 (MLS 2, Non-MLS 1)
Founded 1974
Library Holdings: Bk Vols 5,000; Per Subs 260
Subject Interests: Accident prevention, Indust hygiene, Indust toxicology, Noise control, Occupational med, Occupational rehab, Occupational safety
Database Vendor: Dialog, EBSCOhost
Function: Res libr
Open Mon-Fri 8-4:45

C OHIO DOMINICAN UNIVERSITY LIBRARY*, 1216 Sunbury Rd, 43219. SAN 356-2808. Tel: 614-251-4752. Interlibrary Loan Service Tel: 614-251-4637. Reference Tel: 614-251-4754. Toll Free Tel: 888-681-8044. Reference Toll Free Tel: 888-681-8044. FAX: 614-252-2650. E-mail: library@ohiodominican.edu. Web Site: library.ohiodominican.edu, www.ohiodominican.edu/library. *Dir,* James E Layden; Tel: 614-251-4758, E-mail: laydenj@ohiodominican.edu; *Head, Access Serv,* Timothy Sandusky; Tel: 614-251-4676, E-mail: sanduskt@ohiodominican.edu; *Head, Ref & Instruction,* Christina Bonner; Tel: 614-251-4585, E-mail: bonnerc@ohiodominican.edu; *Head, Tech Serv,* Matilda Davis-Northrup; Tel: 614-251-4757, E-mail: davisnom@ohiodominican.edu; *Coll & Liaison Serv Librn,* Shaunda Tichgelaar; Tel: 614-251-4755, E-mail: tichgels@ohiodominican.edu; *Electronic Res Librn,* Christopher Casey; E-mail: caseyc2@ohiodominican.edu; *Ref Serv Librn,* Matthew Heller; E-mail: hellerm@ohiodominican.edu; Staff 10 (MLS 6, Non-MLS 4)
Founded 1924. Enrl 2,700; Highest Degree: Master
Special Collections: Anne O'Hara McCormick Coll; Catholic Diocese of Columbus Newspaper Coll; Mary Teeter Zimmerman Coll
Subject Interests: Bus, Educ, Health, Humanities, Philos, Theol
Automation Activity & Vendor Info: (Acquisitions) Innovative Interfaces, Inc; (Cataloging) Innovative Interfaces, Inc; (Circulation) Innovative Interfaces, Inc; (Course Reserve) Innovative Interfaces, Inc; (ILL) OCLC; (OPAC) Innovative Interfaces, Inc; (Serials) Innovative Interfaces, Inc
Database Vendor: 3M Library Systems, ABC-CLIO, ACM (Association for Computing Machinery), Agricola, American Mathematical Society, American Psychological Association (APA), Atlas Systems, Baker & Taylor, BioOne, Cambridge Scientific Abstracts, CQ Press, Dun & Bradstreet, EBSCO Information Services, EBSCOhost, Elsevier, Gale Cengage Learning, Greenwood Publishing Group, Grolier Online, H W Wilson, Haworth Pres Inc, Hoovers, infoUSA, Ingenta, Innovative Interfaces, Inc, ISI Web of Knowledge, JSTOR, LearningExpress, LexisNexis, McGraw-Hill, Medline, Mergent Online, OCLC, OCLC FirstSearch, OCLC WorldShare Interlibrary Loan, OHIONET, Oxford Online, Project MUSE, ProQuest, PubMed, Safari Books Online, Sage, Springer-Verlag, Standard & Poor's, Thomson - Web of Science, YBP Library Services
Wireless access
Partic in OCLC Online Computer Library Center, Inc; OHIONET

M OHIO HEALTH-RIVERSIDE METHODIST HOSPITAL, D J Vincent Medical Library, 3535 Olentangy River Rd, 43214-3998. SAN 313-4407. Tel: 614-566-5230. FAX: 614-544-6967. E-mail: medlib@ohiohealth.com. *Dir,* Stacy Gall; Staff 5 (MLS 3, Non-MLS 2)
Founded 1946
Library Holdings: Bk Titles 5,000; Per Subs 1,000
Automation Activity & Vendor Info: (Acquisitions) EOS International; (Cataloging) EOS International; (Circulation) EOS International; (OPAC) EOS International; (Serials) EOS International
Database Vendor: EBSCOhost, Elsevier, EOS International, Natural Standard, OVID Technologies, PubMed, UpToDate
Wireless access
Function: For res purposes, ILL available, Online searches, Photocopying/Printing, Ref serv available, Res libr
Partic in Columbus Area Library & Information Council of Ohio; OCLC Online Computer Library Center, Inc; OHIONET
Restriction: Hospital employees & physicians only

S OHIO HISTORICAL SOCIETY*, Archives-Library, 800 E 17th Ave, 43211. SAN 313-4296. Tel: 614-297-2510. FAX: 614-297-2546. E-mail: reference@ohiohistory.org. Web Site: www.ohiohistory.org. *Dir, Mus & Libr Serv,* Jackie Barton; E-mail: jbarton@ohiohistory.org
Founded 1885
Library Holdings: Bk Titles 140,000; Bk Vols 144,043
Special Collections: Ohio Memory (images from Ohio libraries); State Archives of Ohio. Oral History; State Document Depository
Subject Interests: Archaeology, Genealogy, Natural hist, Ohio hist
Automation Activity & Vendor Info: (Cataloging) Cuadra Associates, Inc; (ILL) OCLC FirstSearch; (OPAC) Cuadra Associates, Inc; (Serials) Cuadra Associates, Inc
Wireless access
Partic in OCLC Online Computer Library Center, Inc; Ohio Network of American History Research Centers; OHIONET
Open Wed-Sat 10-5
Restriction: Non-circulating to the pub

G OHIO LEGISLATIVE SERVICE COMMISSION LIBRARY*, 77 S High St, 9th Flr, 43215-6136. SAN 313-4326. Tel: 614-466-5312. FAX: 614-644-1721. *Adminr,* Debbie Tavenner; Tel: 614-466-2241, E-mail: dtavenner@lsc.state.oh.us; *Asst Librn,* Kelly Pickett; Tel: 614-466-2242, E-mail: kpickett@lsc.state.oh.us; Staff 3 (MLS 2, Non-MLS 1)
Founded 1953
Library Holdings: Bk Titles 15,000
Special Collections: Bulletins of the Ohio General Assembly; Journals of the Ohio House & Senate; Laws of Ohio
Subject Interests: Legis mat, Ohio legal mat
Automation Activity & Vendor Info: (Cataloging) Inmagic, Inc.
Restriction: Open to others by appt, Open to staff only, Restricted access

S OHIO SCHOOL FOR THE DEAF LIBRARY*, 500 Morse Rd, 43214. SAN 373-1073. Tel: 614-728-1414. Administration Tel: 614-728-4030. FAX: 614-728-4060. TDD: 614-728-1415. Web Site: www.ohioschoolforthedeaf.org/library.aspx. *Librn,* Nancy Boone; E-mail: boone@osd.oh.gov; Staff 2 (MLS 1, Non-MLS 1)
Library Holdings: Bk Vols 10,000; Per Subs 45
Special Collections: Deafness Coll, bks, videos, CDs; Ohio Chronicle 1868-1999
Special Services for the Deaf - TDD equip
Restriction: Open by appt only

THE OHIO STATE UNIVERSITY LIBRARIES

C AGRICULTURAL TECHNICAL INSTITUTE LIBRARY, Halterman Hall, 1328 Dover Rd, Wooster, 44691-4000, SAN 313-8143. Tel: 330-287-1294. Toll Free Tel: 800-647-8283 (Ohio only). FAX: 330-287-1333. E-mail: atilibrary@osu.edu. Web Site: library.osu.edu. *Libr Dir,* Kathy Yoder; E-mail: yoder.332@osu.edu; *Mgr, Tech Serv,* Kristen Purdy; Tel: 330-287-1225, E-mail: purdy.23@osu.edu; *Circ Supvr,* Position Currently Open; Staff 3 (MLS 2, Non-MLS 1)
Founded 1972. Enrl 704; Fac 44
Library Holdings: Bk Vols 6,700; Per Subs 205
Special Collections: ATI Historical Archives (Through Ohio State Knowledge Bank)
Subject Interests: Agr, Animal sci, Cattle production, Construction, Dairy production, Eng, Environ sci, Floral design, Golf course mgt, Hort
Automation Activity & Vendor Info: (Acquisitions) Innovative Interfaces, Inc; (Cataloging) Innovative Interfaces, Inc; (Circulation) Innovative Interfaces, Inc; (Course Reserve) Innovative Interfaces, Inc; (ILL) Innovative Interfaces, Inc; (OPAC) Innovative Interfaces, Inc; (Serials) Innovative Interfaces, Inc
Open Mon-Thurs 8-8, Fri 8-5

C ARCHIVES*, 2700 Kenny Rd, 43210, SAN 326-6869. Tel: 614-292-2409. FAX: 614-688-4150. Web Site: library.osu.edu/sites/archives/index.php. *Archivist,* Tamar Chute; Tel: 614-292-3271, E-mail: chute.6@osu.edu; *Archivist,* Laura Kissel; Tel: 614-688-8173, E-mail: kissel.4@osu.edu; *Ref,* Bertha Ihnat; Tel: 614-292-2409, E-mail: ihnat.1@osu.edu; Staff 6 (MLS 5, Non-MLS 1)
Founded 1965. Enrl 48,000; Fac 2,800; Highest Degree: Doctorate
Special Collections: Papers of Admiral Richard E Byrd; Papers of Sir Hubert Wilkins; Records of Dr Frederick A Cook Society; Senator John Glenn Archives. Oral History
Database Vendor: Innovative Interfaces, Inc, OCLC FirstSearch
Function: Archival coll
Partic in OCLC Online Computer Library Center, Inc
Open Mon-Fri 9-12 & 1-4:30
Restriction: Non-circulating
Friends of the Library Group

C BIOLOGICAL SCIENCES & PHARMACY*, 102 Riffe Bldg, 496 W 12th Ave, 43210-1214, SAN 356-3049. Tel: 614-292-1744. FAX: 614-688-3123. Web Site: library.osu.edu/sites/biosci. *Head of Libr,* Natalie Kupferberg; E-mail: kupferberg.1@osu.edu; *Head, Sci Libr,* Bruce A Leach; E-mail: leach.5@osu.edu; Staff 6 (MLS 2, Non-MLS 4)
Founded 1994
Library Holdings: Bk Vols 120,000; Per Subs 1,300
Subject Interests: Biochem, Biophysics, Botany, Chem, Entomology, Genetics, Med chem, Microbiology, Pharmaceutics, Pharmacology, Zoology
Function: Res libr
Partic in OCLC Online Computer Library Center, Inc

C LOUIS BROMFIELD LIBRARY - MANSFIELD CAMPUS*, 1660 University Dr, Mansfield, 44906-1599, SAN 313-5950. Tel: 419-755-4324. Circulation Tel: 419-755-4331. Interlibrary Loan Service Tel: 419-755-4398. Reference Tel: 419-755-4326. FAX: 419-755-4327. Web Site: library.mansfield.ohio-state.edu. *Head Librn,* Position Currently Open; *Interim Libr Mgr,* Kay Foltz; Tel: 419-755-4013, E-mail: foltz.2@osu.edu; Staff 5 (MLS 2, Non-MLS 3)
Founded 1966. Enrl 1,640; Fac 90; Highest Degree: Master
Library Holdings: CDs 100; Bk Vols 50,000; Per Subs 300; Talking Bks 50; Videos 2,000
Function: Handicapped accessible, ILL available, Ref serv available, Telephone ref, Wheelchair accessible
Partic in Committee on Institutional Cooperation; Ohio Library & Information Network
Restriction: Open to pub for ref & circ; with some limitations

C FINE ARTS*, Wexner Center for the Arts, 1871 N High St, 43210, SAN 356-3251. Tel: 614-292-6184. FAX: 614-292-4573. Web Site: library.osu.edu/sites/finearts. *Libr Mgr,* Gretchen Donelson; E-mail: donelson.9@osu.edu; *Circ,* Clint Tomlinson; E-mail: tomlinson.42@osu.edu; *Ref,* Leta Hendricks; E-mail: hendricks.3@osu.edu; Staff 3 (MLS 1, Non-MLS 2)
Library Holdings: Bk Vols 140,000; Per Subs 400
Subject Interests: Art, Art educ, Design, Hist of art
Function: Res libr
Publications: New acquisitions list (Quarterly)
Open Mon-Thurs 8am-10pm, Fri 8-6, Sat 12-6, Sun 2-10
Restriction: Circ limited

C FOOD, AGRICULTURAL & ENVIRONMENTAL SCIENCES*, 045 Agriculture Administration Bldg, 2120 Fyffe Rd, 43210-1066, SAN 356-3014. Tel: 614-292-6125. Reference Tel: 614-292-9563. FAX: 614-292-0590. *Librn,* Florian Diekmann, PhD; E-mail: diekmann.4@osu.edu; *Librn,* Jessica R Page; Tel: 614-688-8474, E-mail: page.84@osu.edu; *Circ Supvr,* Anutosh Datta. Subject Specialists: *Agr sci, Environ sci, Food sci,* Florian Diekmann, PhD; *Environ sci, Food sci, Veterinary med,* Jessica R Page; Staff 2 (MLS 1, Non-MLS 1)
Founded 1956. Highest Degree: Doctorate
Library Holdings: Bk Vols 89,304; Per Subs 1,138
Subject Interests: Agr econ, Agr environ, Agronomy, Animal sci, Crop sci, Food sci, Forestry, Hort, Natural res, Plant pathology, Rural sociol
Automation Activity & Vendor Info: (Acquisitions) Innovative Interfaces, Inc; (Cataloging) OCLC; (Circulation) Innovative Interfaces, Inc; (Course Reserve) Innovative Interfaces, Inc; (ILL) OCLC ILLiad; (OPAC) Innovative Interfaces, Inc; (Serials) Innovative Interfaces, Inc
Database Vendor: Agricola, Cambridge Scientific Abstracts, EBSCOhost, Factiva.com, Gale Cengage Learning, JSTOR, LexisNexis, ProQuest, Wilson - Wilson Web
Partic in Council of Independent Colleges (CIC); OCLC Online Computer Library Center, Inc
Special Services for the Blind - Assistive/Adapted tech devices, equip & products
Open Mon-Wed 8-8, Thurs & Fri 8-5, Sun 4-8
Restriction: In-house use for visitors, Open to students, fac & staff
Friends of the Library Group

CM PHILIP B HARDYMON MEDICAL LIBRARY*, 1492 E Broad St, 43205, SAN 324-5888. Tel: 614-257-3248. FAX: 614-257-3904. *Librn,* Rebecca Mehling
Founded 1956
Library Holdings: Bk Titles 4,000
Subject Interests: Med
Partic in Greater Midwest Regional Medical Libr Network
Open Mon-Fri 7:30-4

C HILANDAR RESEARCH LIBRARY & RESEARCH CENTER FOR MEDIEVAL SLAVIC STUDIES, 119 Thompson Library, 1858 Neil Avenue Mall, 43210, SAN 326-9353. Tel: 614-292-0634. FAX: 614-292-8417. E-mail: hilandar@osu.edu. Web Site: rcmss.osu.edu. *Curator,* Dr Predrag Matejic; E-mail: matejic.1@osu.edu; *Assoc Curator,* Mary-Allen Johnson. Subject Specialists: *Medieval Slavic studies,* Dr Predrag Matejic; *Slavic linguistics,* Mary-Allen Johnson; Staff 2 (MLS 2)
Founded 1978. Fac 2
Library Holdings: Microforms 4,000; Bk Vols 8,000; Per Subs 10
Special Collections: Early Cyrrillic Coll, bks, microfilm; Hilandar Monastery (Mt Athos, Greece), mss, microfilm
Subject Interests: Medieval Slavic studies
Function: Res libr
Publications: Cyrrillic Manuscript Heritage (Newsletter)
Open Mon-Fri 9-5
Restriction: Non-circulating
Friends of the Library Group

C BILLY IRELAND CARTOON LIBRARY & MUSEUM*, 27 W 17th Ave Mall, 43210-1393, SAN 326-6656. Tel: 614-292-0538. FAX: 614-292-9101. E-mail: cartoons@osu.edu. Web Site: cartoons.osu.edu. *Curator,* Jenny E Robb; Staff 4 (MLS 2, Non-MLS 2)
Founded 1977
Library Holdings: Bk Vols 50,000
Special Collections: Original American Cartoon Art & Related Published Works
Database Vendor: Innovative Interfaces, Inc, OHIONET
Function: Res libr
Partic in Consortium of Popular Culture Collections in the Midwest
Open Mon-Fri 9-5
Restriction: Non-circulating
Friends of the Library Group

C JEROME LAWRENCE & ROBERT E LEE THEATRE RESEARCH INSTITUTE LIBRARY*, 1430 Lincoln Tower, 1800 Cannon Dr, 43210-1230, SAN 327-8913. Tel: 614-292-6614. FAX: 614-688-8417. Web Site: library.osu.edu/sites/tri. *Dir,* Carol Pitts Diedrichs; *Ref Librn,* Orville Martin; E-mail: martin.369@osu.edu; *Curator,* Nena Couch; E-mail: couch.1@osu.edu; *Assoc Curator,* Beth Kattelman; E-mail: kattelman.1@osu.edu; *Asst Curator,* Kathleen Kopp; E-mail: kopp.1@osu.edu. Subject Specialists: *18th Century culture, Dance, Performing arts,* Nena Couch; Staff 3.5 (MLS 3, Non-MLS 0.5)
Founded 1951. Highest Degree: Doctorate
Library Holdings: Bk Vols 5,000
Special Collections: Company Organization Archives: Alpha Psi Omega, American Playwrights Theatre, American Theatre Critics Association, Best Plays, Black Theatre Network, Columbus Symphony Orchestra, Contemporary American Theatre Company, Cupola, Curtiss Show Print (Nyle Stateler), Dalcroze School of Music (Hilda Schuster), Dalcroze Society of America, East Lynne Company, Ensemble Theatre of Cincinnati, Gallery Players, Grandparents Living Theatre, Harmount

Company, Hartman Theatre, Horse Cave Theatre, International Al Jolson Society, Los Angeles Theatre Center, Lancton Lucier Vaudeville, Players Theatre, Washington Theatre, Windsor Indoor Chautauqua; Czech Theatre: Jarka Burian Papers; Designs by Helen Anyzova, Jan Dusek, Marie Frankova, Josef Jelinek, Jaroslav Malina, Petr Matasek, Marta Roskopfova, Jan Sladek, Katerina Stefkova, Zuzana Stefunkova, Frantisek Troster, Ladislav Vychodil, Jana Zborilova; Designs, Artwork & Photographs Colls: Boris Anisfeld, Armbruster Scenic Studio, William Barclay, Alexandre Benois, Daphne Dare, Raoul Pene Du Bois, Alexandra Exter, Robert Fletcher, Peter Flinsch, French Theatre Prints, Ella Gerber, Mordecai Gorelik, George Hall, Russell Hastings, David Hays, Edith Head, Al Hirschfeld, Donald Horton, Norris Houghton, Ray Lee Jackson, Toni-Leslie James, Robert Edmond Jones, Gerald Kahan, Simon Lissim, Mircea Marosin, Gordon Micunis, Jo Mielziner, Tanya Moiseiwitsch, Motley, Sam Norkin, Dennis Parker, William Pitkin, Helene Pons, Sanford Roth, Tom Skelton, Robert Slusser Dance Photographs, Leandro Soto, Paul Stiga, Tony Straiges, Sophie Vielle, Sylvia Westerman; Personal Papers: Doris Cole Abrahams, Hollis Alpert, Isabel Bigley Barnett, Mary Bishop, Robert Breen, Jarka Burian, Lucien Bonheur, Sam Coit, John Colman, Paul Denis, Nelson Eddy & Jeanette MacDonald, Tom Eyen, Paulette Goddard/Burgess Meredith, Jed Harris, Eileen Heckart, Mary Henderson, Norris Houghton, Nancy Kelly, Madge Kendal, William F Kilmer Vaudeville, Sidney Kingsley, Ted Lange, Jerome Lawrence & Robert E Lee, Katherine Locke, Sam Locke, Charles H McCaghy Coll of Exotic Dance from Burlesque to Clubs, Bebe Miller, Don Nigro, Ethel Outland, Oysher Family, John Patrick, Robert Post, Peter Rankin, Louis Robin, Randy Skinner, Irwin Spector, Meridee Stein, Twyla Tharp, Robert A Wachsman, Clifton Webb, Ella Richey Wells, Earl Wilson, Luke Yankee; Script Colls: As the World Turns, Dramatists Play Service, International Centre for Women Playwrights, Playwrights, Samuel French; Theatre Critics: American Theatre Critics Association, Alice T Carter, Tish Dace, Marianne Evett, Bill Fark, Michael Grossberg, Henry Hewes, Holly Hill, Jeffrey Eric Jenkins, Larry Ledford, Elizabeth Maupin, E B Radcliffe, Jean Reed, Maxine Rose, Cathern Stadem, Caldwell Titcomb, Gerald Weales; Vertical Files: Artists, Japanese Theatre, Music & Opera, Dance Company, Production, Theatre Companies. Oral History
Subject Interests: Costume design, Lighting, Performing arts, Regional theatre, Theatrical dance
Function: Archival coll
Partic in Consortium of Popular Culture Collections in the Midwest
Restriction: Non-circulating
Friends of the Library Group

C LIMA CAMPUS LIBRARY*, 4240 Campus Dr, Lima, 45804, SAN 313-5721. Tel: 419-995-8401. Interlibrary Loan Service Tel: 419-995-8336. Reference Tel: 419-995-8326. FAX: 419-995-8138. E-mail: lima-library@osu.edu. Web Site: www.lima.ohio-state.edu/library/index.php. *Dir, Libr Serv,* Tina Schneider; E-mail: schneider.290@osu.edu; *Circ Supvr,* Kathy Stedke; Tel: 419-995-8361, E-mail: stedke.1@osu.edu; *Ref Librn/Instrul Serv,* Calvin Cleary
Founded 1966. Enrl 4,100; Fac 199; Highest Degree: Master
Library Holdings: Bk Vols 80,000; Per Subs 517
Publications: Library Handbook for Faculty; Student Assistants Handbook; User Instruction Sheets
Open Mon-Thurs (Winter) 8-8, Fri 8-5, Sat 10-2; Mon, Thurs & Fri (Summer) 8-5, Tues & Wed 8-7

C MARION CAMPUS LIBRARY*, 1469 Mount Vernon Ave, Marion, 43302, SAN 313-6027. Tel: 740-725-6254. Administration Tel: 740-725-6231. FAX: 740-725-6309. E-mail: marionlibrary@osu.edu. Web Site: marionlibrary.osu.edu. *Dir,* Betsy L Blankenship; E-mail: blankenship.5@osu.edu; *Circ, Tech Serv,* Patricia Wood; Tel: 740-725-6335, E-mail: wood.360@osu.edu; Staff 3 (MLS 2, Non-MLS 1)
Founded 1957. Enrl 3,757; Fac 130
Library Holdings: AV Mats 2,785; CDs 307; DVDs 144; e-books 467,034; e-journals 118,713; Microforms 3,498; Bk Vols 52,599; Per Subs 160; Videos 1,293
Special Collections: Richard Myers Music Coll (Sheet Music); Warren G Harding - Norman Thomas Research Coll
Subject Interests: Children's lit, Educ, Lit, Nursing, Psychol
Automation Activity & Vendor Info: (Acquisitions) Innovative Interfaces, Inc; (Cataloging) Innovative Interfaces, Inc; (Circulation) Innovative Interfaces, Inc; (Course Reserve) Innovative Interfaces, Inc; (ILL) OCLC ILLiad; (Media Booking) Innovative Interfaces, Inc; (OPAC) Innovative Interfaces, Inc; (Serials) Innovative Interfaces, Inc
Database Vendor: ABC-CLIO, Bowker, EBSCO Information Services, EBSCOhost, H W Wilson, Innovative Interfaces, Inc, OHIONET, ProQuest, PubMed, RefWorks, Safari Books Online, Sage, SerialsSolutions, Thomson - Web of Science, Wiley InterScience, Wilson - Wilson Web
Open Mon-Thurs 8am-9pm, Fri 8-5

CL MICHAEL E MORITZ LAW LIBRARY*, 55 W 12th Ave, 43210-1391, SAN 313-4350. Tel: 614-292-6691. Circulation Tel: 614-292-3987. Reference Tel: 614-292-9463. FAX: 614-292-3202. E-mail: lawlibref@osu.edu. Web Site: www.moritzlaw.osu.edu/library/. *Asst Dir, Tech Serv, Interim Dir,* Mary Hamburger; Tel: 614-292-9466, E-mail: hamburger.11@osu.edu; *Asst Dir, Pub Serv,* Matt Cooper; *Circ Mgr,* Kaylie Vermillion; E-mail: vermillion.41@osu.edu; Staff 17 (MLS 7, Non-MLS 10)
Founded 1891. Enrl 727; Fac 49; Highest Degree: Doctorate
Library Holdings: Bk Titles 175,681; Bk Vols 789,615; Per Subs 7,192
Special Collections: Ohio Legal Materials
Subject Interests: Dispute resolution
Database Vendor: Gale Cengage Learning, Innovative Interfaces, Inc, JSTOR, LexisNexis, OCLC FirstSearch, Westlaw
Function: ILL available
Partic in OCLC Online Computer Library Center, Inc; OHIONET
Open Mon-Thurs (Winter) 7:15am-Midnight, Fri 7:15-9, Sat 9-9, Sun 10am-Midnight; Mon-Thurs (Summer) 7:15am-11pm, Fri 7:15-6, Sat 9-5, Sun 12-6

CM GRANT MORROW III MD LIBRARY AT NATIONWIDE CHILDREN'S HOSPITAL*, 700 Children's Dr, Rm ED-244, 43205, SAN 356-3707. Tel: 614-722-3200. FAX: 614-722-3205. Web Site: library.osu.edu/sites/chi. *Dir,* Linda DeMuro; Tel: 614-722-3203, E-mail: linda.demuro@nationwidechildrens.org; Staff 4 (MLS 2, Non-MLS 2)
Founded 1953
Library Holdings: Bk Titles 10,000; Bk Vols 25,000; Per Subs 225
Special Collections: Consumer Health in Pediatrics
Subject Interests: Pediatrics
Automation Activity & Vendor Info: (Circulation) Innovative Interfaces, Inc; (OPAC) Innovative Interfaces, Inc
Database Vendor: EBSCOhost, Innovative Interfaces, Inc, ISI Web of Knowledge, JSTOR, LexisNexis, MD Consult, Micromedex, OHIONET, RefWorks, UpToDate, YBP Library Services
Partic in Association of Research Libraries (ARL); OSU Librs
Open Mon-Thurs 8:30-7, Fri 8:30-5

C MUSIC & DANCE*, 166 Sullivant Hall, 1813 N High St, 43210-1307, SAN 356-3499. Tel: 614-292-2319. Reference Tel: 614-688-0163. Administration Tel: 614-688-0106. FAX: 614-247-6794. Web Site: library.osu.edu/sites/music. *Head of Libr,* Alan Green; Staff 6 (MLS 2, Non-MLS 4)
Founded 1949
Library Holdings: CDs 28,000; Bk Vols 140,000; Per Subs 615; Videos 3,441
Special Collections: American Popular Songs; Dance V-tapes; Medieval Chant microfilm; Nordic Music Archive; Renaissance Music microfilm
Subject Interests: Dance, Hist, Music educ, Music indust, Performance, Therapy, World music
Partic in OCLC Online Computer Library Center, Inc; OHIONET
Publications: Newsletter
Open Mon-Thurs (Winter) 8-8, Fri 8-6, Sat 12-6, Sun 2-8; Mon-Fri (Summer) 10-5

C NEWARK CAMPUS LIBRARY*, Warner Library & Student Center, 1179 University Dr, Newark, 43055-1797, SAN 313-6442. Tel: 740-366-9307. Interlibrary Loan Service Tel: 740-364-9501. Reference Tel: 740-366-9306, 740-366-9308. Administration Tel: 740-364-9513. FAX: 740-366-9264. E-mail: askus@cotc.edu, askus@osu.edu. Web Site: www.cotc.edu/library, www.newark.osu.edu/library. *Dir,* Susan Scott; E-mail: scott.37@osu.edu; *Ref Librn,* Katie Blocksidge; E-mail: blocksidge.3@osu.edu; *Evening Circ Supvr,* Mrs Shawn Brookbank; Tel: 740-366-9183, E-mail: brookbank.14@osu.edu; *Weekend Supvr,* Mrs Jesse Higel; *Archivist, Ref,* John Crissinger; E-mail: crissinger.5@osu.edu; *Circ, ILL, Reserves,* Tauni Graham; E-mail: graham.151@osu.edu; Staff 6 (MLS 4, Non-MLS 2)
Founded 1957. Enrl 6,900; Fac 350; Highest Degree: Master
Library Holdings: Bk Vols 47,000; Per Subs 250; Videos 2,000
Special Collections: Newark Earthworks
Subject Interests: Native Am
Database Vendor: Innovative Interfaces, Inc
Open Mon-Thurs (Winter) 8am-10pm, Fri 8-5, Sat 10-4, Sun 1-5; Mon-Thurs (Summer) 7:30am-9pm, Fri 7:30-5, Sat 10-4

C ORTON MEMORIAL LIBRARY OF GEOLOGY*, 180 Orton Hall, 155 S Oval Mall, 43210, SAN 356-3316. Tel: 614-292-2428. Web Site: library.osu.edu/about/locations/geology-library. *Libr Mgr,* Patti Dittoe; Tel: 614-292-6549, E-mail: dittoe.1@osu.edu; Staff 2 (MLS 1, Non-MLS 1)
Founded 1923
Library Holdings: Bk Vols 111,000; Per Subs 651
Subject Interests: Geol, Mineralogy, Paleontology, Polar studies
Automation Activity & Vendor Info: (OPAC) Innovative Interfaces, Inc
Partic in Center for Research Libraries; Committee on Institutional Cooperation (CIC); OCLC Online Computer Library Center, Inc; OHIONET
Open Mon-Thur 8-8, Fri 8-5, Sun 2-6

CM JOHN A PRIOR HEALTH SCIENCES LIBRARY*, 376 W Tenth Ave, 43210-1240, SAN 356-3677. Tel: 614-292-4861. Reference Tel: 614-292-4869. FAX: 614-292-1920. E-mail: hslinfo@osumc.edu. Web Site: library.med.ohio-state.edu. *Dir,* Pamela S Bradigan; Tel: 614-292-4866, E-mail: bradigan.1@osu.edu; *Asst Dir,* Lynda J Hartel;

Tel: 614-292-4892, E-mail: hartel.642@osu.edu; *Curator,* Judith A Wiener; Tel: 614-292-9273, Fax: 614-292-9919, E-mail: wiener3@osu.edu; *Info Tech,* Eric H Schnell; Tel: 614-292-4870, E-mail: schnell.9@osu.edu; Staff 40 (MLS 10, Non-MLS 30)
Founded 1849. Enrl 3,462; Fac 791
Library Holdings: AV Mats 1,905; e-books 953; Bk Vols 215,686; Per Subs 19,106
Special Collections: US Document Depository
Subject Interests: Allied med professions, Cancer, Dentistry, Med, Nursing, Optometry
Automation Activity & Vendor Info: (Cataloging) OCLC; (OPAC) Innovative Interfaces, Inc
Database Vendor: EBSCOhost, Gale Cengage Learning, Innovative Interfaces, Inc, LexisNexis, OCLC FirstSearch, OVID Technologies
Publications: Health Science Library Service Bulletin (Monthly); Health Sciences Library List of Serials
Open Mon-Thurs 7:30am-11:45pm, Fri 7:30am-7:45pm, Sat 10-5:45
Friends of the Library Group

C SCIENCE & ENGINEERING*, 175 W 18th Ave, 43210, SAN 373-5923. Tel: 614-292-0211. Interlibrary Loan Service Tel: 614-292-6211. Reference Tel: 614-292-3022. FAX: 614-292-3062. Interlibrary Loan Service FAX: 614-292-3061. Web Site: library.osu.edu/sites/sel. ; Staff 5 (MLS 5)
Library Holdings: Bk Vols 370,283; Per Subs 2,600
Special Collections: US Document Depository
Subject Interests: Archit, Astronomy, Chem, Computer, Eng genetic sci, Info serv, Landscape archit, Math, Physics, Statistics
Partic in OCLC Online Computer Library Center, Inc

C WILLIAM OXLEY THOMPSON LIBRARY*, 1858 Neil Ave Mall, 43210-1286, SAN 356-2921. Tel: 614-292-6785. FAX: 614-292-7859. Web Site: library.osu.edu. *Dir,* Carol Diedrichs; Tel: 614-292-2365, Fax: 614-292-2443, E-mail: diedrichs.1@osu.edu; *Assoc Dir, Coll & Tech Serv,* Karla Strieb; *Assoc Dir, Info Tech,* Beth Warner; *Assoc Dir, Res & Educ,* Alison Armstrong; Staff 166 (MLS 68, Non-MLS 98)
Founded 1873. Enrl 56,867; Fac 2,930; Highest Degree: Doctorate
Jul 2011-Jun 2012. Mats Exp $15,178,158
Library Holdings: e-books 526,075; Bk Titles 4,921,972; Bk Vols 7,117,102
Special Collections: 19th Century Paperback Coll; Admiral Richard E Byrd Papers; American Association of Editorial Cartoonist Archives; American Fiction 18th Century through Contemporary (William Charvat Coll); American Playwrights' Theatre Records; American Sheet Music (ABC & Fanny Arms Colls); Arion Press Coll; Armbruster Scenic Design; Australiana; Author Collections: Nelson Algren, W H Auden, Samuel Beckett, Robert Breen, William S Burroughs, Frederick Busch, Milton Caniff, Raymond Carver, Miguel de Cervantes, Hart Crane, Emily Dickinson, Will Eisner, T S Eliot, John Gardner, Nathaniel Hawthorne, Ernest Hemingway, Chester Hines, Eileen Heckart, T J Holmes, Jerome Lawrence & Robert E Lee, Richard Lewis, Jack London, Ralph D Mershon, Anais Nin, Jessica Mitford, James Purdy, Jesse Stuart, Twyla Tharp, Dylan Thomas, James Thurber, F L Utley, William T Vollman, Edith Wharton, Jon Whitcom; Book Plate Literature; Conjunctions Literary Journal Archive; Daguerrotypes & Ambrotypes (Floyd & Marion Rinhart Coll); Dance Notation Coll; Emanuel Rudolph Children's Science Coll; English Drama Coll; European Econ Community; Film Scripts; Little Magazines; Mather Bibliography (T J Holmes Papers); Medieval Slavic Manuscripts; Northprint Press German; Ohio News Photographers Association Archives; Oriole Press Coll; Peter D Franklin Cookbook Coll; Philip Sills Coll, film posters & stills; Reformation History Coll; Renaissance to 18th Century Coll; Science Fiction Paperbacks & Magazines; Secondary School Curricula (W W Charters Papers); Stanley J Kahrl 17th Century Drama Coll; UFO Coll. State Document Depository; UN Document Depository; US Document Depository
Automation Activity & Vendor Info: (Acquisitions) Innovative Interfaces, Inc - Millenium; (Cataloging) Innovative Interfaces, Inc - Millenium; (Circulation) Innovative Interfaces, Inc - Millenium; (ILL) OCLC ILLiad; (OPAC) Innovative Interfaces, Inc - Millenium; (Serials) Innovative Interfaces, Inc - Millenium
Function: Archival coll, Audio & video playback equip for onsite use, Computers for patron use, Copy machines, Distance learning, Doc delivery serv, E-Reserves, Electronic databases & coll, Exhibits, ILL available, Microfiche/film & reading machines, Online cat, Online ref, Photocopying/Printing, Ref & res, Res libr, Telephone ref, Web-catalog
Partic in Association of Research Libraries (ARL); OCLC Online Computer Library Center, Inc
Open Mon-Thurs 7:30am-Midnight, Fri 7:30am-10pm, Sat 8am-10pm, Sun 11am-Midnight
Friends of the Library Group

CM VETERINARY MEDICINE*, 225 Veterinary Medicine Academic Bldg, 1900 Coffey Rd, 43210, SAN 356-3618. Tel: 614-292-6107. FAX: 614-292-7476. Web Site: library.osu.edu/sites/vetmed. *Veterinary Med Librn,* Jessica Page; E-mail: page.84@osu.edu; *Circ Supvr,* David Sharp; E-mail: sharp.20@osu.edu; Staff 3 (MLS 1, Non-MLS 2)
Library Holdings: Bk Vols 40,000; Per Subs 630
Automation Activity & Vendor Info: (ILL) OVID Technologies
Database Vendor: OVID Technologies
Partic in OCLC Online Computer Library Center, Inc
Open Mon-Thurs 8am-10pm, Fri 8-6, Sat 10-6, Sun 12-9

S OHIOANA LIBRARY, 274 E First Ave, Ste 300, 43201. SAN 313-413X. Tel: 614-466-3831. FAX: 614-728-6974. E-mail: ohioana@ohioana.org. Web Site: www.ohioana.org. *Dir,* David Weaver; *Librn,* Stephanie Michaels; Staff 4 (MLS 1, Non-MLS 3)
Founded 1929
Jul 2006-Jun 2007 Income $586,806. Sal $233,022
Library Holdings: Bk Titles 43,500; Bk Vols 46,000
Special Collections: Books written by Ohioans or about Ohio & Ohioans; Dawn Powell Coll; George Randolph Chester Coll; James Thurber Coll; Louis Bromfield Coll; Martha Finley Coll; Mildred Wirt Benson Coll; R L Stine Coll; Rollo W Brown Coll; Sherwood Anderson Coll; W D Howells Coll; Women's History in Ohio; Zane Gray Coll
Subject Interests: Bks by Ohioans or about Ohio, Music by Ohio composers, Rare bks, Scrapbks of biog info
Automation Activity & Vendor Info: (OPAC) Innovative Interfaces, Inc
Publications: Educational Resource List; Ohioana Quarterly; Ohioana-Ohio Literary Map
Partic in Ohio Library & Information Network; OHIONET
Open Mon-Fri 8:30-4:30
Restriction: In-house use for visitors, Not a lending libr

M OHIOHEALTH GRANT MEDICAL CENTER*, Medical Library, 285 E State St, Ste 210, 43215. (Mail add: 111 S Grant Ave, 43215), SAN 313-4180. Tel: 614-566-9468. FAX: 614-566-8451. *Libr Supvr,* Katherine Vaughan; E-mail: kvaugha2@ohiohealth.com; Staff 1.5 (MLS 1, Non-MLS 0.5)
Founded 1960
Subject Interests: Allied health, Med, Nursing
Automation Activity & Vendor Info: (Cataloging) EOS International; (Circulation) EOS International; (OPAC) EOS International
Database Vendor: EBSCOhost, EOS International, McGraw-Hill, MD Consult, Natural Standard, OVID Technologies, PubMed, STAT!Ref (Teton Data Systems), UpToDate
Wireless access
Partic in National Network of Libraries of Medicine Greater Midwest Region
Restriction: Hospital employees & physicians only, Not open to pub

SR PONTIFICAL COLLEGE JOSEPHINUM*, A T Wehrle Memorial Library, 7625 N High St, 43235-1498. SAN 313-8178. Tel: 614-985-2295. FAX: 614-885-2307. E-mail: libreqs@pcj.edu. Web Site: libguides.pcj.edu/pcjlibrary. *Dir,* Peter G Veracka; E-mail: pveracka@pcj.edu; *Asst Librn,* Beverly S Lane; E-mail: bslane@pcj.edu; Staff 2 (MLS 2)
Founded 1888. Enrl 205; Fac 24; Highest Degree: Master
Jul 2012-Jun 2013 Income $295,360. Mats Exp $78,874, Books $28,198, Per/Ser (Incl. Access Fees) $29,545, Electronic Ref Mat (Incl. Access Fees) $16,984, Presv $4,147. Sal $181,559
Library Holdings: e-books 68,722; e-journals 7,456; Microforms 1,895; Bk Titles 175,254; Bk Vols 213,547; Per Subs 312
Subject Interests: Philos, Relig studies, Theol
Automation Activity & Vendor Info: (Acquisitions) Innovative Interfaces, Inc; (Cataloging) Innovative Interfaces, Inc; (Circulation) Innovative Interfaces, Inc; (Course Reserve) Innovative Interfaces, Inc; (ILL) Innovative Interfaces, Inc; (Media Booking) Innovative Interfaces, Inc; (OPAC) Innovative Interfaces, Inc; (Serials) Innovative Interfaces, Inc
Database Vendor: EBSCO Information Services, EBSCOhost, Gale Cengage Learning, OCLC FirstSearch, OCLC WorldShare Interlibrary Loan, ProQuest
Wireless access
Partic in OCLC Online Computer Library Center, Inc; Ohio Library & Information Network; Ohio Private Academic Libraries (OPAL); OHIONET; Theol Consortium of Greater Columbus

L PORTER, WRIGHT, MORRIS & ARTHUR, LLP*, Law Library, Huntington Ctr, 41 S High St, 43215-6194. SAN 326-1727. Tel: 614-227-2152. Reference Tel: 614-227-1927. Administration Tel: 614-227-2090. Toll Free Tel: 800-533-2794. FAX: 614-227-2100. Web Site: www.porterwright.com. *Mgr, Libr Serv,* Susan M Schaefgen; E-mail: sschaefgen@porterwright.com; Staff 4 (MLS 2, Non-MLS 2)
Founded 1846
Library Holdings: Bk Titles 6,000; Bk Vols 28,000; Per Subs 1,000
Automation Activity & Vendor Info: (Acquisitions) Softlink America; (Cataloging) Softlink America; (Circulation) Softlink America; (OPAC) Softlink America; (Serials) Softlink America
Database Vendor: Checkpoint Systems, Inc, Dun & Bradstreet, HeinOnline, Loislaw, Westlaw
Partic in OHIONET
Restriction: Not open to pub

L SQUIRE, SANDERS & DEMPSEY*, Law Library, 1300 Huntington Ctr, 41 S High St, Ste 1300, 43215. SAN 323-8539. Tel: 614-365-2700. FAX: 614-365-2499. *Librn,* Patricia Christian; E-mail: pchristian@ssd.com; Staff 3 (MLS 2, Non-MLS 1)
Library Holdings: Bk Titles 1,200; Bk Vols 13,000; Per Subs 50

P STATE LIBRARY OF OHIO*, 274 E First Ave, Ste 100, 43201. SAN 356-4487. Tel: 614-644-7061. Circulation Tel: 614-644-6950. Interlibrary Loan Service Tel: 614-387-1189. Reference Tel: 614-644-7051. Toll Free Tel: 800-686-1532 (Ohio only). FAX: 614-466-3584. Reference FAX: 614-644-7004. E-mail: refhelp@library.ohio.gov. Web Site: www.library.ohio.gov. *State Librn,* Beverly Cain; E-mail: bcain@library.ohio.gov; *Assoc State Librn, Libr Develop,* Melissa Lodge; Tel: 614-644-6914, E-mail: mlodge@library.ohio.gov; *Assoc State Librn, Libr Serv,* Ann M Watson; E-mail: awatson@library.ohio.go; *Head, Fiscal Serv,* Jamie Pardee; Tel: 614-644-6879, E-mail: jpardee@library.ohio.gov; Staff 28 (MLS 19, Non-MLS 9)
Founded 1817. Pop 11,478,006
Jul 2010-Jun 2011 Income $22,544,296, State $6,188,398, Federal $5,543,747, Other $10,812,151. Mats Exp $2,133,413, Books $283,134, Per/Ser (Incl. Access Fees) $76,985, Other Print Mats $4,489, Micro $5,672, AV Mat $48,257, Electronic Ref Mat (Incl. Access Fees) $1,714,876. Sal $4,610,416
Library Holdings: AV Mats 1,558; Bks on Deafness & Sign Lang 1,218; e-books 38,950; Microforms 212,563; Bk Titles 888,865; Bk Vols 962,840; Per Subs 407
Special Collections: Rare Books Coll. State Document Depository; US Document Depository
Subject Interests: Admin, Behav sci, Econ, Educ, Soc sci
Automation Activity & Vendor Info: (Acquisitions) Innovative Interfaces, Inc; (Cataloging) Innovative Interfaces, Inc; (Circulation) Innovative Interfaces, Inc; (ILL) OCLC; (Media Booking) Innovative Interfaces, Inc; (OPAC) OCLC WorldShare Interlibrary Loan; (Serials) Innovative Interfaces, Inc
Wireless access
Function: For res purposes
Publications: Directory of Ohio Libraries; State Library News; Statistics Categorized by Income; Statistics of Ohio Libraries
Partic in Ohio Library & Information Network; Ohio Public Library Information Network
Special Services for the Blind - Talking bks
Open Mon-Fri 8-5

GL SUPREME COURT OF OHIO*, Law Library, 65 S Front St, 11th Flr, 43215-3431. SAN 313-4431. Tel: 614-387-9650. Circulation Tel: 614-387-9680. Reference Tel: 614-387-9682. FAX: 614-387-9689. E-mail: libref@sc.ohio.gov. Web Site: www.supremecourtofohio.gov/legalresources/lawlibrary. *Dir,* Ken Kozlowski; Tel: 614-387-9666, E-mail: ken.kozlowski@sc.ohio.gov; *Pub Serv Mgr,* Erin Waltz; Tel: 614-387-9668, E-mail: erin.waltz@sc.ohio.gov; *Tech Serv Mgr,* Marlys Bradshaw; Tel: 614-387-9661, E-mail: marlys.bradshaw@sc.ohio.gov; Staff 10.5 (MLS 6, Non-MLS 4.5)
Founded 1860
Library Holdings: Bk Vols 400,000; Per Subs 1,740
Special Collections: Ohio & US Legal Treatises, Cases & Statutes
Wireless access
Publications: The Supreme Court of Ohio Law Library Handbook
Partic in OCLC Online Computer Library Center, Inc; OHIONET
Open Mon-Fri 8-5
Restriction: Open to pub for ref & circ; with some limitations

R TEMPLE ISRAEL*, Meta Marx Lazarus Memorial Library, 5419 E Broad St, 43213. SAN 313-444X. Tel: 614-866-0010. FAX: 614-866-9046.
Founded 1932
Library Holdings: Bk Titles 5,000
Subject Interests: Judaica
Open Mon-Thurs 9-5, Fri 9-4

R TRINITY LUTHERAN SEMINARY*, Hamma Library, 2199 E Main St, 43209-2334. SAN 313-4466. Tel: 614-384-4645. Reference Tel: 614-384-4644. FAX: 614-238-0263. E-mail: tlslibrary@tlsohio.edu. Web Site: www.tlsohio.edu. *Dir,* Ray A Olson; Tel: 614-384-4640, E-mail: rolson@tlsohio.edu; Staff 5 (MLS 2, Non-MLS 3)
Founded 1830. Enrl 100; Fac 20; Highest Degree: Master
Library Holdings: Bk Vols 131,358; Per Subs 185
Special Collections: Ecola Christian Music Coll; New Testament studies (Lenski Memorial Coll); Simmons Gospel Music Coll; The Dr Donald L Huber Rare Book Room
Subject Interests: Theol
Automation Activity & Vendor Info: (Acquisitions) Innovative Interfaces, Inc - Millenium; (Cataloging) Innovative Interfaces, Inc; (Circulation) Innovative Interfaces, Inc - Millenium; (Course Reserve) Innovative Interfaces, Inc - Millenium; (ILL) OCLC; (OPAC) Innovative Interfaces, Inc - Millenium; (Serials) Innovative Interfaces, Inc - Millenium
Database Vendor: EBSCO Discovery Service, EBSCOhost, OHIONET, ProQuest
Wireless access
Partic in OCLC Online Computer Library Center, Inc; Ohio Library & Information Network; Ohio Private Academic Libraries (OPAL); OHIONET; Theological Consortium of Greater Columbus
Open Mon-Thurs 8am-10pm, Fri 8-5, Sat (Sept-May) 9-5

TWIN VALLEY BEHAVIORAL HEALTHCARE
M FORENSIC PATIENTS' LIBRARY*, 2200 W Broad St, 43223, SAN 320-3565. Tel: 614-752-0333, Ext 5451. FAX: 614-752-0385. *In Charge,* Liz Smith
Library Holdings: Bk Vols 5,500; Per Subs 21
Subject Interests: Med, Psychiat
M MARLIN R WEDEMEYER STAFF LIBRARY*, 2200 W Broad St, 43223, SAN 313-4067. Tel: 614-752-0333, Ext 5454. FAX: 614-752-0385.
Library Holdings: Bk Titles 3,366; Per Subs 80
Subject Interests: Med, Psychiat

P UPPER ARLINGTON PUBLIC LIBRARY, 2800 Tremont Rd, 43221. SAN 357-282X. Tel: 614-486-9621. Reference Tel: 614-486-3342. Administration Tel: 614-486-0900. FAX: 614-486-4530. Web Site: www.ualibrary.org. *Dir,* Chris Taylor; E-mail: ctaylor@ualibrary.org; *Asst Dir,* Kate Porter; E-mail: kporter@ualibrary.org; *Fiscal Officer,* Kate Hemleben; E-mail: khemleben@ualibrary.org; *Adult Serv Mgr,* Vita Marinello; E-mail: vmarinello@ualibrary.org; *Circ Mgr,* Annette Heffernan; E-mail: aheffernan@ualibrary.org; *Fac Mgr,* Sherman Wallace; E-mail: swallace@ualibrary.org; *Human Res Mgr,* Julie Whitt; E-mail: jwhitt@ualibrary.org; *Mgr, Info Tech,* Gregory Ramage; E-mail: gramagc@ualibrary.org; *Mkt & Commun Relations Mgr,* Christine Minx; E-mail: cminx@ualibrary.org; *Media Serv Mgr,* Shahin Shoar; E-mail: sshoar@ualibrary.org; *Ref Mgr,* Mark Mangini; Fax: 614-486-2043, E-mail: mmangini@ualibrary.org; *Tech Serv Mgr,* Jennifer Christensen; E-mail: jchristensen@ualibrary.org; *Youth Serv Mgr,* Dena Little; E-mail: dlittle@ualibrary.org; Staff 17.65 (MLS 15.78, Non-MLS 1.87)
Founded 1967. Pop 34,150; Circ 2,006,003
Jan 2012-Dec 2012 Income (Main Library and Branch(s)) $5,223,634. Mats Exp $962,199, Books $427,089, Per/Ser (Incl. Access Fees) $51,519, AV Mat $243,343, Electronic Ref Mat (Incl. Access Fees) $240,248. Sal $2,703,274
Library Holdings: AV Mats 38,188; DVDs 59,799; e-books 72,158; Electronic Media & Resources 488; Bk Vols 334,759; Per Subs 626
Special Collections: School Reading; UA Archives (Digital Coll); Upper Arlington High School Digital Yearbooks; Upper Arlington Hist & Authors Coll
Subject Interests: Foreign lang
Automation Activity & Vendor Info: (Acquisitions) Innovative Interfaces, Inc; (Cataloging) Innovative Interfaces, Inc; (Circulation) Innovative Interfaces, Inc; (ILL) OCLC WorldShare Interlibrary Loan; (OPAC) Innovative Interfaces, Inc; (Serials) Innovative Interfaces, Inc
Database Vendor: ABC-CLIO, American Psychological Association (APA), Baker & Taylor, Booksite, College Source, EBSCO Information Services, EBSCOhost, Facts on File, Gale Cengage Learning, Greenwood Publishing Group, H W Wilson, infoUSA, LearningExpress, Newsbank, OCLC FirstSearch, OCLC WorldShare Interlibrary Loan, OHIONET, Overdrive, Inc, Oxford Online, ProQuest, PubMed, ReferenceUSA, Standard & Poor's, ValueLine, Wilson - Wilson Web
Wireless access
Partic in Central Library Consortium (CLC); OCLC Online Computer Library Center, Inc; OHIONET
Open Mon-Thurs 10-9, Fri 10-6, Sat 10-5, Sun 1-5
Friends of the Library Group
Branches: 2
LANE ROAD BRANCH, 1945 Lane Rd, Upper Arlington, 43220, SAN 357-2854. Tel: 614-459-0273. FAX: 614-459-3437. *Br Mgr,* Pam Cole; E-mail: pcole@ualibrary.org; *Ch Serv,* Sue Emrick; E-mail: semrick@ualibrary.org
Open Mon-Thurs 10-9, Fri 10-6, Sat 10-5, Sun 1-5
Friends of the Library Group
MILLER PARK BRANCH, 1901 Arlington Ave, Upper Arlington, 43212, SAN 357-2889. Tel: 614-488-5710. FAX: 614-487-2032. *Br Mgr,* Kate Albers; E-mail: kalbers@ualibrary.org; *Ch Serv,* Sarah Manley; E-mail: smanley@ualibrary.org
Open Mon-Thurs 10-9, Fri 10-6, Sat 10-5, Sun 1-5
Friends of the Library Group

M VICTORIAN VILLAGE HEALTH CENTER*, William S Konold Memorial Library, 1087 Dennison Ave, 43201. SAN 356-2743. Tel: 614-544-5819. FAX: 614-299-2475. *Supvr,* Julie Spaulding; Tel: 614-544-2016, Fax: 614-544-2015; *Cat,* Sheila Knapik-Fields; E-mail: sfieldsk@ohiohealth.com; Staff 3 (MLS 1, Non-MLS 2)
Founded 1973
Library Holdings: Bk Vols 4,113
Special Collections: History of Medicine; History of Osteopathy

Subject Interests: Med
Function: Archival coll, For res purposes
Partic in CORE; Tri State Col Libr Coop
Open Mon-Thurs 10:30-8:30
Restriction: Lending to staff only, Non-circulating to the pub

CONNEAUT

P CONNEAUT PUBLIC LIBRARY*, 304 Buffalo St, 44030-2658. SAN 356-4630. Tel: 440-593-1608. FAX: 440-593-4470. E-mail: conneaut@oplin.org. Web Site: www.conneaut.lib.oh.us. *Dir,* Kathy Pape; E-mail: papeka@oplin.org; *Asst Dir/Ref Librn,* Michael Speer; E-mail: speermi@oplin.org; *Tech Serv,* Cindy Prather; E-mail: pratheci@oplin.org; *Youth Serv,* Stephanie Gildone; E-mail: gildonst@oplin.org
Founded 1908. Pop 17,000
Library Holdings: AV Mats 17,686; Bk Vols 52,513; Per Subs 127
Special Collections: Large Print Coll; Local History Coll, newspapers 1835-1982, micro; Media, audios; New Grove Directory of Music & Musicians Coll; Old Radio Shows Coll, cassettes; Young Adult Coll
Subject Interests: Local hist, Local newsp, Music, Self help
Automation Activity & Vendor Info: (Cataloging) LibLime; (Circulation) LibLime; (OPAC) LibLime
Database Vendor: ALLDATA Online, Brodart, EBSCOhost, Facts on File, infoUSA, Ingram Library Services, OCLC WorldShare Interlibrary Loan, OHIONET
Wireless access
Publications: Annual Report; Brochure of Services
Partic in Northeast Ohio Regional Library System
Special Services for the Deaf - TDD equip
Special Services for the Blind - Audio mat; Bks on CD; Cassettes; Computer with voice synthesizer for visually impaired persons; Copier with enlargement capabilities; Home delivery serv; Large print bks; Magnifiers; Reading & writing aids
Open Mon-Thurs 10-7, Fri 10-6
Friends of the Library Group

COSHOCTON

P COSHOCTON PUBLIC LIBRARY*, 655 Main St, 43812-1697. SAN 323-679X. Tel: 740-622-0956. FAX: 740-622-4331. E-mail: coshpl@oplin.org. Web Site: www.coshoctonlibrary.org. *Dir,* Eric D Taggart; E-mail: etaggart@coshoctonlibrary.org; *Outreach Serv Librn,* Holli Rainwater; E-mail: hrainwater@coshoctonlibrary.org; *Ref Librn,* Mike Ontko; E-mail: montko@coshoctonlibrary.org; *YA Librn,* Jennifer Ricketts; E-mail: jricketts@coshoctonlibrary.org; *Br Mgr,* Andrea Schweitzer Smith; E-mail: aschweitzer@coshoctonlibrary.org; *Children's Coordr,* Barb Custer; E-mail: bcuster@coshoctonlibrary.org; *Pub Relations Coordr,* Cathy Haynes; E-mail: chaynes@coshoctonlibrary.org; *Genealogy/Local Hist Spec,* Deborah Crowdy; E-mail: dcrowdy@coshoctonlibrary.org; Staff 18.9 (MLS 3, Non-MLS 15.9)
Founded 1904. Pop 36,901; Circ 375,175
Library Holdings: e-books 99,491; Bk Vols 116,490; Per Subs 193
Special Collections: State Document Depository
Subject Interests: Genealogy, Local hist
Automation Activity & Vendor Info: (Acquisitions) SirsiDynix; (Cataloging) SirsiDynix; (Circulation) SirsiDynix; (OPAC) SirsiDynix
Database Vendor: EBSCOhost, OCLC WebJunction, SirsiDynix
Wireless access
Publications: Library Connections (Newsletter)
Partic in Northeast Ohio Regional Library System
Special Services for the Deaf - Bks on deafness & sign lang; High interest/low vocabulary bks
Special Services for the Blind - Talking bks
Open Mon-Wed 10-8, Thurs & Fri 10-5, Sat 10-3
Friends of the Library Group
Branches: 1
WEST LAFAYETTE BRANCH, 601 E Main St, West Lafayette, 43845, SAN 323-6811. Tel: 740-545-6672. FAX: 740-545-6418. E-mail: wlbranch@coshoctonlibrary.org. Web Site: www.coshoctonpl.org/west-lafayette/index.php. *Br Mgr,* Andrea Schweitzer
Circ 62,163
Library Holdings: Bk Vols 13,000
Partic in SEO (Serving Every Ohioan) Library Center; State Libr of Ohio
Open Mon-Wed 11-7, Thurs & Fri 12-5, Sat 11-2
Friends of the Library Group
Bookmobiles: 1. Mgr, Kris Ringwalt. Bk titles 3,000

COVINGTON

P J R CLARKE PUBLIC LIBRARY*, 102 E Spring St, 45318. SAN 313-4512. Tel: 937-473-2226. FAX: 937-473-8118. *Dir,* Krista Gibson; E-mail: kgibson@oplin.org; Staff 9 (Non-MLS 9)
Founded 1917. Pop 5,124; Circ 174,350
Library Holdings: AV Mats 2,476; Large Print Bks 633; Bk Vols 59,738; Per Subs 131; Talking Bks 698
Special Collections: J R Clarke Family Coll; Obituary Index
Subject Interests: Civil War, Hist
Automation Activity & Vendor Info: (Acquisitions) Follett Software; (Cataloging) Follett Software; (Circulation) Follett Software
Database Vendor: EBSCOhost
Wireless access
Publications: Newsletter (Monthly)
Partic in Miami Valley Librs
Open Mon, Wed & Thurs 9-8, Tues & Fri 9-5, Sat 9-2
Friends of the Library Group

CRESTLINE

P CRESTLINE PUBLIC LIBRARY*, 324 N Thoman St, 44827-1410. SAN 313-4520. Tel: 419-683-3909. FAX: 419-683-3022. Web Site: crestlinepubliclibrary.org. *Librn,* Cheryl Swihart; E-mail: swiharch@oplin.org; *Ch Serv,* Lynn Altftadt; *Circ,* Linda McClurg; Staff 6 (MLS 6)
Founded 1925. Pop 8,400; Circ 110,148
Library Holdings: Bk Vols 68,636; Per Subs 215
Special Collections: Books on Cassette; County Census Records; County Court Records; County Death Records, micro; Filmed Periodicals; Historical Picture Coll; Large Print Books; Ohio Local Newspaper, 113 years, micro; Read-Alongs; Videos
Subject Interests: Railroad printed mat
Automation Activity & Vendor Info: (Cataloging) TLC (The Library Corporation); (Circulation) TLC (The Library Corporation); (OPAC) TLC (The Library Corporation)
Special Services for the Deaf - Captioned film dep; High interest/low vocabulary bks
Special Services for the Blind - Bks on cassette; Large print bks
Open Mon 9-9, Tues-Fri 9-8, Sat 9-5, Sun (Oct-April) 1-4

CUYAHOGA FALLS

S ALMOND TEA GALLERY LIBRARY*, 2250 Front St, 44221. SAN 313-4539. Tel: 330-929-1575. FAX: 330-929-2285. Web Site: www.jackorchard.com. *Dir,* Jack Richard
Founded 1961
Library Holdings: Bk Vols 2,000; Per Subs 30; Videos 400
Subject Interests: Art
Open Tues 11:30-5 & 7-10, Wed-Fri 11:30-5

P CUYAHOGA FALLS LIBRARY*, Taylor Memorial Association, 2015 Third St, 44221-3294. SAN 313-4563. Tel: 330-928-2117. FAX: 330-928-2535. E-mail: mail@cuyahogafallslibrary.org. Web Site: www.cuyahogafallslibrary.org. *Dir,* Kevin M Rosswurm; E-mail: krosswurm@cuyahogafallslibrary.org; *Cat,* David Allen; Tel: 330-928-2117, Ext 111, E-mail: dallen@cuyahogafallslibrary.org; *Ch Serv,* Joyce Bigam; Tel: 330-928-2117, Ext 122, E-mail: joyceb@cuyahogafallslibrary.org; *Circ,* Donna Dixon; Tel: 330-928-2117, Ext 108, E-mail: dixon@cuyahogafallslibrary.org; *Commun Relations Librn,* Valerie Moirano; Tel: 330-928-2117, Ext 102, E-mail: vmoirano@cuyahogafallslibrary.org; *Ref Serv, Ad,* Nancy Milford; E-mail: nmilford@cuyahogafallslibrary.org; *Tech Coordr,* Philip Shirley; Tel: 330-928-2117, Ext 109, E-mail: pshirley@cuyahogafallslibrary.org; Staff 43 (MLS 6, Non-MLS 37)
Founded 1911. Pop 44,832; Circ 772,326
Library Holdings: AV Mats 24,835; Bk Vols 146,620; Per Subs 363
Subject Interests: Local hist
Automation Activity & Vendor Info: (Circulation) Innovative Interfaces, Inc; (ILL) OCLC; (OPAC) Innovative Interfaces, Inc
Database Vendor: EBSCOhost, Gale Cengage Learning, Innovative Interfaces, Inc
Wireless access
Publications: Newsletter (Monthly)
Special Services for the Deaf - TDD equip
Open Mon-Thurs 9-9, Fri 9-6, Sat 9-5, Sun 12-5
Friends of the Library Group

R PILGRIM UNITED CHURCH OF CHRIST MEMORIAL LIBRARY*, 130 Broad Blvd, 44221. SAN 313-4555. Tel: 330-928-4847. FAX: 330-928-1017. E-mail: pilgrimoffice@ameritech.net. Web Site: www.pilgrimcf.org. *Dir,* Marilyn Freeman; E-mail: pilgrimce@ameritech.ne
Library Holdings: Bk Vols 400
Open Mon-Fri 9-5

DAYTON

M CHILDREN'S MEDICAL CENTER*, Medical Library, One Children's Plaza, 45404-1815. SAN 313-4571. Tel: 937-641-3307. Interlibrary Loan Service Tel: 937-641-5072. FAX: 937-461-5409. Web Site: www.childrensdayton.org. *Librn,* Luzviminda Navarro Sinha; E-mail: sinhal@childrensdayton.org; Staff 2 (MLS 1, Non-MLS 1)
Founded 1967

Library Holdings: Bk Vols 1,720; Per Subs 180
Database Vendor: Gale Cengage Learning, Innovative Interfaces, Inc, LexisNexis
Restriction: Not open to pub

S DAYTON ART INSTITUTE*, Louis Lott Memorial Art Reference Library, 456 Belmonte Park N, 45405-4700. SAN 313-458X. Tel: 937-223-5277. FAX: 937-223-3140. E-mail: library@daytonartinstitute.org. Web Site: www.daytonartinstitute.org. *In Charge,* Eric Brockman; Tel: 937-223-5277, Ext 242; Staff 2 (MLS 1, Non-MLS 1)
Founded 1922
Library Holdings: Electronic Media & Resources 2; Bk Titles 16,047; Bk Vols 20,059; Per Subs 50
Special Collections: Architecture (Lott-Schaeffer Memorial Architecture Library); Institutional Archives
Subject Interests: Archit, Art
Automation Activity & Vendor Info: (Cataloging) OCLC; (Circulation) Innovative Interfaces, Inc; (ILL) OCLC; (OPAC) Innovative Interfaces, Inc
Database Vendor: Oxford Online
Function: Adult bk club, Archival coll, Copy machines, Online cat, Ref serv available
Partic in OCLC Online Computer Library Center, Inc; OHIONET
Restriction: Open to pub by appt only, Open to pub for ref only

L DAYTON LAW LIBRARY*, 41 N Perry St, Rm 505, 45402. (Mail add: PO Box 972, 45422-2490), SAN 372-1981. Tel: 937-225-4496. FAX: 937-225-5056. *Librn,* Joanne Beal
Library Holdings: Bk Vols 141,260; Per Subs 4,214
Open Mon-Fri 8:30-5

P DAYTON METRO LIBRARY*, 215 E Third St, 45402-2103. SAN 356-4754. Tel: 937-463-2665. Circulation Tel: 937-496-8905. Reference Tel: 937-496-8910. FAX: 937-496-4300. Web Site: www.daytonmetrolibrary.org. *Exec Dir,* Timothy Kambitsch; *Asst Dir,* David Slivken; *Asst Dir,* Letitia Wilson; *Asst Dir, Br Serv,* Miriam Morris; *Asst Dir, Tech,* Barbara Kuhns; *Commun Relations Librn,* Mark Willis; *Mgr, Ad Serv,* Jennifer Spillman; *Circ Mgr,* Charles Romine; *Mgr, Per,* Jamie McQuinn; *Syst Mgr,* Rich Simmerman; Staff 545 (MLS 76, Non-MLS 469)
Founded 1847. Pop 458,677; Circ 644,768
Library Holdings: Bk Vols 2,206,735; Per Subs 919
Special Collections: Local History (Dayton Room). State Document Depository; US Document Depository
Automation Activity & Vendor Info: (Acquisitions) Innovative Interfaces, Inc; (Cataloging) Innovative Interfaces, Inc; (Circulation) Innovative Interfaces, Inc; (OPAC) Innovative Interfaces, Inc
Wireless access
Special Services for the Deaf - High interest/low vocabulary bks; TTY equip
Open Mon, Tues & Thurs 9:30-8:30, Wed, Fri & Sat 9:30-6
Friends of the Library Group
Branches: 21
BELMONT, 1041 Watervliet Ave, 45420, SAN 356-4789. Tel: 937-496-8920. *Mgr,* Mark Roma
Library Holdings: Bk Vols 36,853
Open Mon, Tues & Thurs 9:30-8:30, Wed, Fri & Sat 9:30-6
Friends of the Library Group
BROOKVILLE BRANCH, 425 Rona Pkwy, Brookville, 45309. Tel: 937-496-8922. FAX: 937-496-4322. *Mgr,* Elaine Lindstrom
Open Mon, Tues & Thurs 9:30-8:30, Wed, Fri & Sat 9:30-6
Friends of the Library Group
BURKHARDT, 4680 Burkhardt Ave, 45431, SAN 356-4843. Tel: 937-496-8924. FAX: 937-496-4324. *Mgr,* Francesca Hary
Open Mon, Tues & Thurs 9:30-8:30, Wed, Fri & Sat 9:30-6
Friends of the Library Group
DAYTON VIEW, 1515 Salem Ave, 45406, SAN 356-4878. Tel: 937-496-8926. FAX: 937-496-4326. *Mgr,* Sharon Taste
Open Mon, Tues & Thurs 9:30-8:30, Wed, Fri & Sat 9:30-6
Friends of the Library Group
ELECTRA C DOREN BRANCH, 701 Troy St, 45404, SAN 356-4908. Tel: 937-496-8928. FAX: 937-496-4328. *Br Mgr,* Jonathan Cline
Founded 1927
Open Mon, Tues & Thurs 9:30-8:30, Wed, Fri & Sat 9:30-6
Friends of the Library Group
EAST, 2008 Wyoming St, 45410, SAN 356-4932. Tel: 937-496-8930. FAX: 937-496-4330. *Mgr,* Cindy Butcher
Open Mon, Tues & Thurs 9:30-8:30, Wed, Fri & Sat 9:30-6
Friends of the Library Group
FORT MCKINLEY, 3735 Salem Ave, 45406, SAN 356-4967. Tel: 937-496-8932. FAX: 937-496-4332. *Mgr,* Tracy Phillips
Open Mon, Tues & Thurs 9:30-8:30, Wed, Fri & Sat 9:30-6
Friends of the Library Group
HUBER HEIGHTS, 6160 Chambersburg Rd, 45424, SAN 356-4991. Tel: 937-496-8934. FAX: 937-496-4334. *Mgr,* Paula Dale; *Asst Mgr,* Karen Findlay
Open Mon, Tues & Thurs 9:30-8:30, Wed, Fri & Sat 9:30-6
Friends of the Library Group
KETTERING-MORAINE, 3496 Far Hills Ave, Kettering, 45429, SAN 356-5025. Tel: 937-496-8938. FAX: 937-496-4338. *Mgr,* Teresa Huntley
Open Mon, Tues & Thurs 9:30-8:30, Wed, Fri & Sat 9:30-6
Friends of the Library Group
MADDEN HILLS, 2542 Germantown St, 45408, SAN 356-505X. Tel: 937-496-8942. FAX: 937-496-4342. *Mgr,* Winnie Johnson
Open Mon, Tues & Thurs 9:30-8:30, Wed, Fri & Sat 9:30-6
Friends of the Library Group
MIAMI TOWNSHIP, 2718 Lyons Rd, Miamisburg, 45342. Tel: 937-496-8944. FAX: 937-496-4344. *Mgr,* Cheryl C Wirtley; E-mail: cwirtley@daytonmetrolibrary.org
Open Mon, Tues & Thurs 9:30-8:30, Wed, Fri & Sat 9:30-6
MIAMISBURG BRANCH, 35 S Fifth St, Miamisburg, 45342, SAN 356-5084. Tel: 937-496-8946. FAX: 937-496-4346. *Mgr,* Brielle Maynor
Open Mon, Tues & Thurs 9:30-8:30, Wed, Fri & Sat 9:30-6
Friends of the Library Group
NEW LEBANON BRANCH, 715 W Main St, New Lebanon, 45345, SAN 356-5114. Tel: 937-496-8948. *Br Mgr,* Carol Macmann
Open Mon, Tues & Thurs 9:30-8:30, Wed, Fri & Sat 9:30-6
Friends of the Library Group
NORTHMONT, 333 W National Rd, Englewood, 45322, SAN 356-5149. Tel: 937-496-8950. *Mgr,* Donna Brown
Open Mon, Tues & Thurs 9:30-8:30, Wed, Fri & Sat 9:30-6
Friends of the Library Group
NORTHTOWN-SHILOH, 35 Bennington Dr, 45405, SAN 356-5173. Tel: 937-496-8954. FAX: 937-496-4354. *Mgr,* Sammie Allen
Open Mon, Tues & Thurs 9:30-8:30, Wed, Fri & Sat 9:30-6
Friends of the Library Group
OUTREACH SERVICES, 2293 Arbor Blvd, 45439. Tel: 937-496-8956. FAX: 937-496-4356. *Mgr, Outreach Serv,* Rachel Gut; Tel: 937-227-9520
Open Mon, Tues & Thurs 9:30-8:30, Wed, Fri & Sat 9:30-6
TROTWOOD BRANCH, 651 E Main St, Trotwood, 45426, SAN 356-5203. Tel: 937-496-8958. FAX: 937-496-4358. *Mgr,* Luellen Wilson
Open Mon, Tues & Thurs 9:30-8:30, Wed, Fri & Sat 9:30-6
Friends of the Library Group
VANDALIA BRANCH, 500 S Dixie Dr, Vandalia, 45377, SAN 356-5238. Tel: 937-496-8960. FAX: 937-496-4360. *Mgr,* Doris Pettit
Open Mon, Tues & Thurs 9:30-8:30, Wed, Fri & Sat 9:30-6
Friends of the Library Group
WEST CARROLLTON BRANCH, 300 E Central Ave, West Carrollton, 45449, SAN 356-5262. Tel: 937-496-8962. FAX: 937-496-4362. *Mgr,* Karri Marshall; Staff 3 (MLS 2, Non-MLS 1)
Open Mon, Tues & Thurs 9:30-8:30, Wed, Fri & Sat 9:30-6
Friends of the Library Group
WESTWOOD, 3207 Hoover Ave, 45407, SAN 356-5297. Tel: 937-496-8964. FAX: 937-496-4364. *Mgr,* Noland Lester
Open Mon, Tues & Thurs 9:30-8:30, Wed, Fri & Sat 9:30-6
Friends of the Library Group
WILMINGTON-STROOP, 3980 Wilmington Pike, 45429. Tel: 937-496-8966. FAX: 937-496-4366. *Br Mgr,* Cara Kouse; Staff 4 (MLS 4)
Founded 1976. Circ 550,000
Open Mon, Tues & Thurs 9:30-8:30, Wed, Fri & Sat 9:30-6
Friends of the Library Group
Bookmobiles: 1

M GOOD SAMARITAN HOSPITAL LIBRARY*, 2222 Philadelphia Dr, 45406-1891. SAN 313-4644. Tel: 937-734-2141. FAX: 937-734-2634. Web Site: www.goodsamdayton.org. *Dir,* Candy Winteregg; E-mail: cswinteregg@premierhealth.org
Founded 1965
Library Holdings: Bk Titles 6,200; Per Subs 136
Subject Interests: Psychiat
Automation Activity & Vendor Info: (Cataloging) Innovative Interfaces, Inc; (Circulation) Innovative Interfaces, Inc; (ILL) Innovative Interfaces, Inc; (OPAC) Innovative Interfaces, Inc; (Serials) Innovative Interfaces, Inc
Partic in Docline
Open Mon-Fri 8-5

M GRANDVIEW HOSPITAL*, Medical Library, 405 Grand Ave, 45405. SAN 324-6280. Tel: 937-226-3379. FAX: 937-226-3609. *Librn,* Stephen Sadler; Staff 3 (Non-MLS 3)
Library Holdings: Bk Titles 7,000; Per Subs 326
Subject Interests: Anesthesiology, Cardiology, Internal med, Neurology, Oncology, Ophthalmology, Orthopedics, Pediatrics, Radiology, Surgery, Urology
Automation Activity & Vendor Info: (Cataloging) Innovative Interfaces, Inc; (Circulation) Innovative Interfaces, Inc; (OPAC) Innovative Interfaces, Inc
Mem of Miami Valley Libraries

Partic in BRS
Restriction: Staff use only

S KETTERING FOUNDATION LIBRARY, 200 Commons Rd, 45459. SAN 374-9320. Tel: 937-439-9806. Toll Free Tel: 800-221-3657. FAX: 937-439-9837. E-mail: library@kettering.org. Web Site: www.kettering.org. *Archivist, Prog Officer,* Libby Kingseed; Staff 2 (MLS 1, Non-MLS 1)
Library Holdings: Bk Vols 3,500; Per Subs 60
Special Collections: Abstracts Coll, staff-written abstracts, articles
Subject Interests: Democracy
Function: ILL available
Partic in OCLC Online Computer Library Center, Inc
Restriction: Not open to pub, Staff use only

J MIAMI-JACOBS COLLEGE*, Learning Resource Center, 110 N Patterson, 45402. SAN 313-4679. Tel: 937-461-5174. Web Site: www.miamijacobs.edu. *Dir,* Michael Stone; Staff 5 (Non-MLS 5)
Founded 1920. Enrl 700; Fac 32; Highest Degree: Associate
Special Collections: Miami - Jacobs Archives; Miami Commercial & Jacobs Business Historical Information
Subject Interests: Info tech
Function: For res purposes, Govt ref serv, Health sci info serv, Homebound delivery serv, Online searches, Ref serv available
Restriction: Clients only

M MIAMI VALLEY HOSPITAL*, Craig Memorial Library, One Wyoming St, 45409. SAN 313-4687. Tel: 937-208-2612. FAX: 937-208-2569. *Dir,* Shirley Sebald-Kinder; Tel: 937-208-6236, E-mail: sjsebald@mvh.org; *Assoc Librn,* Janet Petty; Tel: 937-208-2624, E-mail: jlpetty@mvh.org; Staff 5 (MLS 2, Non-MLS 3)
Founded 1926
Library Holdings: Bk Titles 10,000; Bk Vols 42,000; Per Subs 500
Subject Interests: Hospital admin, Med, Nursing, Nutrition
Automation Activity & Vendor Info: (Serials) Innovative Interfaces, Inc
Database Vendor: EBSCOhost, Innovative Interfaces, Inc
Partic in National Network of Libraries of Medicine Greater Midwest Region; Ohio Library & Information Network
Open Mon-Fri 7:30-5

SR NORTH AMERICAN CENTER FOR MARIANIST STUDIES LIBRARY, University of Dayton, River Campus, 1700 S Patterson Blvd, 45409-2106. (Mail add: North American Ctr for Marianist Studies, University of Dayton, 300 College Park, 45469-7022). Tel: 937-229-1889. Administration Tel: 937-229-1880. FAX: 937-229-1888. E-mail: trimbotz@udayton.edu. Web Site: nacms.org. *Librn,* Teresa Trimboli; Staff 1 (MLS 1)
Founded 1986
Library Holdings: Bk Titles 2,034; Bk Vols 3,170
Special Collections: Marianist history & spirituality
Database Vendor: ComPanion Corp
Open Mon-Fri 9-5
Restriction: Non-circulating, Open to pub for ref only

J SINCLAIR COMMUNITY COLLEGE LIBRARY*, 444 W Third St, 45402-1460. SAN 313-475X. Tel: 937-512-2855. Circulation Tel: 937-512-3007. Reference Tel: 937-512-3004. Toll Free Tel: 800-315-3000. FAX: 937-512-4564. E-mail: ereferen@sinclair.edu. Web Site: library.sinclair.edu. *Dir,* Douglas Kaylor; Tel: 937-512-2107, E-mail: douglas.kaylor@sinclair.edu; *Librn,* Austin Pevler; Tel: 937-512-3925, E-mail: austin.pevler@sinclair.edu; *Tech Serv & Syst Librn,* Andrea Christman; Tel: 937-512-4513, E-mail: andrea.christman@sinclair.edu; *Coll Develop, Ref,* Marlene Bundy; Tel: 937-512-3003, E-mail: marlene.bundy@sinclair.edu; *ILL, Online Serv, Ref,* Sonya Kirkwood; Tel: 937-512-3005, E-mail: sonya.kirkwood@sinclair.edu; *Ref Serv,* Debra Oswald; E-mail: debra.oswald@sinclair.edu. Subject Specialists: *Bus, Info tech, Paralegal,* Austin Pevler; *Criminal justice, Liberal arts, Soc sci,* Marlene Bundy; *Health sci, Life sci,* Sonya Kirkwood; *English, Lang,* Debra Oswald; Staff 7 (MLS 7)
Founded 1887. Enrl 23,241; Fac 1,129; Highest Degree: Associate
Library Holdings: Bk Vols 147,613; Per Subs 509
Subject Interests: Computer sci, Early childhood educ, Multicultural studies, Ohio law, Prof develop, Quality in higher educ
Automation Activity & Vendor Info: (Acquisitions) Innovative Interfaces, Inc; (Circulation) Innovative Interfaces, Inc
Database Vendor: EBSCOhost, Innovative Interfaces, Inc, ProQuest
Partic in Ohio Library & Information Network; OHIONET; Southwestern Ohio Council for Higher Education
Special Services for the Deaf - Bks on deafness & sign lang
Open Mon-Thurs (Winter) 7:30am-9:30pm, Fri 7:30-5, Sat 9-4; Mon-Thurs (Summer) 7:30am-9:30pm, Fri 7:30-4:30

R TEMPLE ISRAEL LIBRARY*, One Riverbend, 45405. SAN 313-4792. Tel: 937-496-0050. FAX: 937-496-0060.
Library Holdings: Bk Titles 5,000
Subject Interests: Judaica

L THOMPSON, HINE LLP*, Law Library, Austin Landing 1, 10050 Innovation Dr, Ste 400, 45342-4934. SAN 328-3690. Tel: 937-443-6600. FAX: 937-443-6635. Web Site: www.thompsonhine.com. *Librn,* Janie Hack; Tel: 937-443-6823, E-mail: janie.hack@thompsonhine.com
Founded 1911
Library Holdings: Bk Vols 35,000; Per Subs 216

GM US VETERANS AFFAIRS MEDICAL CENTER*, Health Sciences Library, 4100 W Third St, 45428. SAN 356-5475. Tel: 937-268-6511, Ext 2379. FAX: 937-262-2181. *Chief Librn,* Niki Conca; E-mail: niki.conca@med.va.gov; Staff 7 (MLS 4, Non-MLS 3)
Founded 1871
Library Holdings: Bk Titles 2,000; Per Subs 300
Subject Interests: Chronic disease, Dentistry, Extended care facilities, Geriatrics, Rehabilitation
Publications: Monthly Newsletter; Quarterly Acquisitions List
Partic in Docline; Miami Valley Librs; Veterans Affairs Libr Network (VALNET)
Restriction: Staff use only

R UNITED THEOLOGICAL SEMINARY LIBRARY*, 4501 Denlinger Rd, 45426. SAN 313-4806. Tel: 937-529-2201, Ext 3400. FAX: 937-529-2292. E-mail: obrienlibrary@united.edu. Web Site: united.edu/obrien-library. *Dir,* Sarah D Brooks Blair; E-mail: sblair@united.edu; *Asst Dir,* Ken Cochrane; *Acq,* Lesia Harvey; E-mail: lesiah@united.edu; *Circ Coordr,* Caryn Dalton; E-mail: cdalton@united.edu; *ILL, Per,* Brillie Scott; E-mail: brscott@united.edu; Staff 3 (MLS 3)
Founded 1871
Library Holdings: Bk Vols 144,000; Per Subs 500
Special Collections: Edmund S Lorenz Hymnal Coll; Evangelical Church Coll; Evangelical United Brethren Church Coll; J Allan Ranck Coll of Friendship Press; United Brethren in Christ Church Coll; United Methodist Church Coll; Waldensian-Methodist Coll. Oral History
Partic in OCLC Online Computer Library Center, Inc; OHIONET

C UNIVERSITY OF DAYTON LIBRARIES*, Roesch Library, 300 College Park Dr, 45469-1360. SAN 356-5416. Tel: 937-229-4221. Circulation Tel: 937-229-4234. Interlibrary Loan Service Tel: 937-229-4284. Reference Tel: 937-229-4270. Administration Tel: 937-229-4265. Automation Services Tel: 937-229-3551. FAX: 937-229-4215. E-mail: ref@udayton.edu. Web Site: library.udayton.edu. *Dean, Univ Libr,* Kathleen Webb; E-mail: kwebb1@udayton.edu; *Assoc Dean, Coll & Operations,* Dr Fred Jenkins; Tel: 937-229-4272, E-mail: fjenkins1@udayton.edu; *Dir, Educ & Info Delivery,* Hector Escobar; Tel: 937-229-5141, Fax: 937-229-4590, E-mail: hescobar1@udayton.edu; *Dir, Info Acq & Organization,* Emily Anne Hicks; Tel: 937-229-1558, E-mail: ehicks1@udayton.edu; *Dir, Info Syst & Digital Access,* Fran Rice; E-mail: frice1@udayton.edu; *Dir, Spec Libr,* Fr Thomas Thompson; Tel: 937-229-4252, E-mail: tthompson2@udayton.edu; *Coordr, Access Serv,* Amanda Black; E-mail: ablack2@udayton.edu; *Coordr, Instruction & Ref,* Heidi Gauder; Tel: 937-229-4259, E-mail: hgauder1@udayton.edu; *Univ Archivist & Coordr of Spec Coll,* Jennifer Brancato; Tel: 937-229-4267, E-mail: jbrancato1@udayton.edu; Staff 51 (MLS 14, Non-MLS 37)
Founded 1850. Enrl 10,856; Fac 507; Highest Degree: Doctorate
Library Holdings: AV Mats 4,500; e-books 381,236; e-journals 71,286; Microforms 747,871; Bk Vols 1,238,889
Special Collections: Charles W Whalen Jr Congressional Papers; Doris Speyer J F Kennedy Coll; Marian Library; Science Fiction & Fantasy Writers of America Coll; Si Burick & Miriam Joseph Baseball Colls; US Catholic Coll. US Document Depository
Subject Interests: Catholicism, Educ, Theol
Automation Activity & Vendor Info: (Acquisitions) Innovative Interfaces, Inc; (Cataloging) Innovative Interfaces, Inc; (Circulation) Innovative Interfaces, Inc; (ILL) OCLC ILLiad; (OPAC) Innovative Interfaces, Inc; (Serials) Innovative Interfaces, Inc
Database Vendor: ACM (Association for Computing Machinery), Alexander Street Press, American Chemical Society, American Mathematical Society, Annual Reviews, ARTstor, ebrary, EBSCO Discovery Service, EBSCOhost, Gale Cengage Learning, Greenwood Publishing Group, IBISWorld, IEEE (Institute of Electrical & Electronics Engineers), IOP, JSTOR, LexisNexis, Newsbank, OCLC FirstSearch, OCLC WorldShare Interlibrary Loan, OVID Technologies, Project MUSE, ProQuest, RefWorks, Safari Books Online, SBRnet (Sports Business Research Network), Springshare, LLC, Thomson - Web of Science, Wilson - Wilson Web
Wireless access
Function: Archival coll, Art exhibits, Doc delivery serv, e-mail & chat, Pub access computers, Tax forms
Publications: Libraries' Update (Newsletter); Marian Library Studies (Journal)
Partic in Lyrasis; Ohio Library & Information Network; OHIONET; Southwestern Ohio Council for Higher Education

Departmental Libraries:

CR MARIAN LIBRARY, 300 College Park Dr, 45469-1390, SAN 313-4814. Tel: 937-229-4214. FAX: 937-229-4258. *Dir,* Fr Thomas A Thompson; E-mail: tthompson2@udayton.edu. Subject Specialists: *Relig hist,* Fr Thomas A Thompson
Library Holdings: Bk Vols 99,500; Per Subs 160
Partic in Ohio Library & Information Network
Publications: Marian Library (Newsletter)
Open Mon-Fri 8:30-4:30
Friends of the Library Group

CL UNIVERSITY OF DAYTON SCHOOL OF LAW*, Zimmerman Law Library, 300 College Park, 45469-2780. SAN 356-5440. Tel: 937-229-2314. Information Services Tel: 937-229-4810. FAX: 937-229-2555. Web Site: community.udayton.edu/law/library. *Dir,* Thomas L Hanley; Tel: 937-229-2444, E-mail: hanley@udayton.edu; *Asst Dir, Pub Serv,* Susan N Elliott; *Access Serv Librn,* Maureen H Anderson; *Ref Librn,* Paul D Venard; *Acq,* Jackie J Johnston; Staff 5 (MLS 4, Non-MLS 1)
Founded 1974. Enrl 424; Fac 34; Highest Degree: Doctorate
Library Holdings: Bk Vols 337,943; Per Subs 4,278
Automation Activity & Vendor Info: (Acquisitions) Innovative Interfaces, Inc; (Cataloging) Innovative Interfaces, Inc; (Circulation) Innovative Interfaces, Inc; (Serials) Innovative Interfaces, Inc
Database Vendor: LexisNexis, Westlaw
Wireless access
Publications: Aquisitions Update
Partic in Ohio Library & Information Network; Southwestern Ohio Council for Higher Education
Open Mon-Fri 8am-Midnight, Sat 10-10, Sun Noon-Midnight
Restriction: Circ limited, Restricted pub use

P WRIGHT MEMORIAL PUBLIC LIBRARY*, 1776 Far Hills Ave, 45419-2598. SAN 313-4830. Tel: 937-294-7171. Administration Tel: 937-294-8572. FAX: 937-294-8578. Web Site: www.wrightlibrary.org. *Interim Dir,* Debra Schenk; E-mail: schenk@wrightlibrary.org; *Youth Serv Coordr,* Jennifer Sommer; *Ref Serv,* Margaret Peters; *Tech Serv,* Kate Chalfant; Staff 9.78 (MLS 6.78, Non-MLS 3)
Founded 1913. Pop 9,120; Circ 391,185
Library Holdings: Bk Vols 148,000
Automation Activity & Vendor Info: (Cataloging) Innovative Interfaces, Inc; (Circulation) Innovative Interfaces, Inc; (OPAC) Innovative Interfaces, Inc
Database Vendor: EBSCOhost, Gale Cengage Learning, Wilson - Wilson Web
Wireless access
Function: Accelerated reader prog, Adult bk club, Audiobks via web, AV serv, Bks on CD, Children's prog, Computer training, Computers for patron use, Copy machines, Electronic databases & coll, Free DVD rentals, Homebound delivery serv, ILL available, Mus passes, Music CDs, OverDrive digital audio bks, Preschool reading prog, Prog for adults, Prog for children & young adult, Pub access computers, Ref serv available, Story hour, Summer reading prog, Tax forms, Teen prog, Telephone ref
Partic in Miami Valley Librs; OCLC Online Computer Library Center, Inc; Ohio OPLIN GOSIP Network; OHIONET
Friends of the Library Group

C WRIGHT STATE UNIVERSITY LIBRARIES*, 126 Dunbar Library, 3640 Colonel Glenn Hwy, 45435-0001. SAN 356-553X. Tel: 937-775-4125. Circulation Tel: 937-775-2525. Interlibrary Loan Service Tel: 937-775-2289. Reference Tel: 937-775-2925. Administration Tel: 937-775-2380. Automation Services Tel: 937-775-3889. FAX: 937-775-4109. Interlibrary Loan Service FAX: 937-775-2356. Web Site: www.libraries.wright.edu. *Dir of Libr Serv,* Position Currently Open; *Interim Dir,* Sheila Shellabarger; Tel: 937-775-2685, E-mail: sheila.shellabarger@wright.edu; *Assoc Univ Librn, Coll & Serv,* Karen Wilhoit; Tel: 937-775-3039, E-mail: karen.wilhoit@wright.edu; *Head, Automation,* Kathi Herick; E-mail: kathi.herick@wright.edu; *Head, Digital Libr Serv,* Jane Wildermuth; Tel: 937-775-3927, E-mail: jane.wildermuth@wright.edu; *Head, Info Serv,* Susan Wehmeyer; Tel: 937-775-3565, E-mail: susan.wehmeyer@wright.edu; *Head, Ref (Info Serv),* Sue Polanka; Tel: 937-775-3142, E-mail: sue.polanka@wright.edu; *Head, Ref (Info Serv),* Bette Sydelko; Tel: 937-775-3840, E-mail: bette.sydelko@wright.edu; *Head, Spec Coll & Archives,* Dawne Dewey; Tel: 937-775-2011, E-mail: dawne.dewey@wright.edu; *Head, Tech Serv,* Marty Jenkins; Tel: 937-775-4983, E-mail: martin.jenkins@wright.edu; Staff 40.16 (MLS 23.5, Non-MLS 16.66)
Founded 1967. Enrl 16,952; Fac 831; Highest Degree: Doctorate
Library Holdings: e-journals 6,500; Bk Titles 573,914; Bk Vols 870,792; Per Subs 4,320
Special Collections: Aerospace Medical Association Archives; Aerospace Medicine & Human Factors Engineering (Ross A McFarland Coll); Andrews S Iddings Papers; Anthropometry (HTE Hertzburg Coll); Aviation Crash Research (Howard Hashbrook Coll); Children's Literature, including Books Illustrated by Arthur Rackham; Cincinnati Coll (Dayton Ballet Co, Overholser Civil War Diary, Glenn Curtiss Photographs, Springfield Urban League Records, Clayton Bruckner Papers, Early Local Records from Auglaize, Champaign, Clark, Darke, Greene & Mercer Counties); Dayton Urban League Papers; Early Aviation Coll; Glenn Thompson Papers; Governor James M Cox Papers; History of Medicine; Local & Regional History Coll, includes Miami Valley Genealogical Society Library; Miami Conservancy District Papers; Miami Valley Area & Early Aviation Photograph Coll; Miami, Montgomery, Logan, Preble & Shelby Counties; O S Kelly Company Papers; Paul Laurence Dunbar Coll; Space & Life Sciences (William Rhornton Coll); Unpublished Manuscripts Coll: Wright Brothers Papers, Governor James M Cox Papers, Dayton Urban League Papers; Wright Brothers Papers
Subject Interests: Biochem, Cardiology, Med, Microbiology, Nursing, Physiology
Automation Activity & Vendor Info: (Acquisitions) Innovative Interfaces, Inc; (Cataloging) Innovative Interfaces, Inc; (Circulation) Innovative Interfaces, Inc; (Course Reserve) Docutek; (ILL) OCLC ILLiad; (Media Booking) Innovative Interfaces, Inc; (OPAC) Innovative Interfaces, Inc; (Serials) Innovative Interfaces, Inc
Wireless access
Publications: Access; Diaries: 1857-1917 by Bishop Milton Wright; Guide to Local Government Records & Newspapers at WSU; Guide to Manuscripts
Partic in OCLC Online Computer Library Center, Inc; Ohio Library & Information Network; OHIONET
Friends of the Library Group

DEFIANCE

C DEFIANCE COLLEGE*, Pilgrim Library, 201 College Pl, 43512-1667. SAN 313-4849. Tel: 419-783-2481. FAX: 419-783-2594. Web Site: library.defiance.edu. *Dir,* Michelle Blank; Tel: 419-783-2484, E-mail: mblank@defiance.edu; *Metadata & Archives Librn,* Barbara Sedlock; Tel: 419-783-2487, E-mail: bsedlock@defiance.edu; *Ref Librn,* Alex Hauser; Tel: 419-783-2483, E-mail: ahauser@defiance.edu; *Coordr, Circ,* Collette Knight; Tel: 419-783-2482, E-mail: knightc@defiance.edu; Staff 5 (MLS 4, Non-MLS 1)
Enrl 861; Fac 57; Highest Degree: Master
Library Holdings: AV Mats 2,826; Bk Vols 107,454; Per Subs 375
Special Collections: American History (Indian Wars of Northwest Ohio, 1785-1815), bk & micro
Function: ILL available, Ref serv available, Telephone ref
Partic in NOLC; Ohio Library & Information Network; Ohio Private Academic Libraries (OPAL); OHIONET
Restriction: Open to pub for ref & circ; with some limitations, Open to students, fac & staff

P DEFIANCE PUBLIC LIBRARY*, 320 Fort St, 43512-2186. SAN 356-5653. Tel: 419-782-1456. FAX: 419-782-6235. Web Site: www.defiancelibrary.org. *Dir,* Marilyn Hite; E-mail: hitema@oplin.org; Staff 3 (MLS 3)
Founded 1895. Pop 39,825; Circ 234,998
Library Holdings: Bk Vols 141,149; Per Subs 283
Special Collections: Ohioana; Slocum
Subject Interests: Local hist
Automation Activity & Vendor Info: (Cataloging) SirsiDynix; (Circulation) SirsiDynix; (OPAC) SirsiDynix
Publications: Holding The Fort
Partic in NORWELD; Ohio Public Library Information Network
Open Mon-Thurs 9:30-8:30, Sat 9:30-3:30, Sun 1-5
Friends of the Library Group
Branches: 2
JOHNSON MEMORIAL, 116 W High St, Hicksville, 43526, SAN 356-5688. Tel: 419-542-6200. FAX: 419-542-1015. *Br Mgr,* Zachary Bowling
Open Mon & Tues 12-8, Wed 10-8, Fri 12-6, Sat 10-1
Friends of the Library Group
SHERWOOD BRANCH, 117 Harrison St, Sherwood, 43556. (Mail add: PO Box 4586, Sherwood, 43556-0586), SAN 374-7190. Tel: 419-899-4343. FAX: 419-899-4343. *Br Mgr,* Kathy Holtsberry
Open Mon & Wed 12-8, Tues & Thurs 9-6, Fri & Sat 9-12
Friends of the Library Group

DELAWARE

P DELAWARE COUNTY DISTRICT LIBRARY*, 84 E Winter St, 43015. SAN 313-4857. Tel: 740-362-3861. Administration Tel: 740-363-7277. FAX: 740-369-0196. Administration FAX: 740-362-0391. E-mail: askus@delawarelibrary.org. Web Site: www.delawarelibrary.org. *Dir,* Mary Jane Santos; E-mail: mjsantos@delawarelibrary.org; *Dep Dir,* Donald Yarman; *Br Mgr,* Harla Lawson; Tel: 740-666-1410; *Br Mgr,* Julie Standish; Tel: 614-888-9160; *Adult Serv Mgr,* Joseph O'Rourke; *Communications Mgr,* Shea Alltmont; *Outreach Serv Mgr,* Robbie Apt; *Youth Serv Mgr,* Connie Pottle; *Circ Supvr,* Pam Taylor; *Tech Serv,* Kyle Halstead; Staff 9 (MLS 8, Non-MLS 1)

Founded 1906. Pop 114,913; Circ 779,677
Library Holdings: Bk Vols 228,226; Per Subs 284
Special Collections: Harness Racing Coll
Subject Interests: Local hist
Automation Activity & Vendor Info: (Cataloging) OCLC; (Circulation) Innovative Interfaces, Inc; (ILL) OCLC; (OPAC) Innovative Interfaces, Inc
Wireless access
Function: Adult bk club, Art exhibits, Audio & video playback equip for onsite use, Bk reviews (Group), Bks on cassette, Bks on CD, Chess club, Children's prog, Computer training, Computers for patron use, Copy machines, Digital talking bks, e-mail serv, E-Reserves, Electronic databases & coll, Handicapped accessible, Home delivery & serv to Sr ctr & nursing homes, Homebound delivery serv, ILL available, Large print keyboards, Magnifiers for reading, Mail & tel request accepted, Online cat, Online ref, Online searches, OverDrive digital audio bks, Photocopying/Printing, Preschool outreach, Prog for adults, Prog for children & young adult, Ref serv available, Senior outreach, Spoken cassettes & CDs, Spoken cassettes & DVDs, Summer reading prog, Tax forms, Teen prog, Telephone ref, VHS videos, Wheelchair accessible
Partic in Southeast Regional Library System
Open Mon-Thurs 9-9, Fri 9-6, Sat 9-5, Sun 12-5
Friends of the Library Group
Branches: 2
OSTRANDER BRANCH, 75 N Fourth St, Ostrander, 43061. (Mail add: PO Box 6, Ostrander, 43061), SAN 372-5618. Tel: 740-666-1410. FAX: 740-666-1437. *Br Mgr,* Harla Lawson
Open Tues-Thurs 10-8, Fri & Sat 10-4
Friends of the Library Group
POWELL BRANCH, 460 S Liberty Rd, Powell, 43065, SAN 373-2908. Tel: 614-888-9160. FAX: 614-888-7358. *Br Mgr,* George Morrison
Open Mon-Thurs 9-9, Fri 9-6, Sat 9-5, Sun 12-5
Bookmobiles: 1. Outreach Servs Mgr, Robbie Apt. Bk titles 5,000

GL DELAWARE COUNTY LAW LIBRARY, 20 W Central Ave, 43015. SAN 327-3806. Tel: 740-833-2545. FAX: 740-833-2548. *Librn,* J R Maxwell; E-mail: JMaxwell@co.delaware.oh.us; Staff 1 (Non-MLS 1)
Library Holdings: Bk Vols 6,000
Database Vendor: Westlaw
Function: Computers for patron use, Copy machines
Partic in Ohio Regional Asn of Law Librs
Restriction: Open to pub for ref only

CR METHODIST THEOLOGICAL SCHOOL, Dickhaut Library, 3081 Columbus Pike, 43015. SAN 313-4873. Tel: 740-363-1146. Circulation Tel: 740-362-3450. FAX: 740-362-3456. E-mail: library@mtso.edu. Web Site: www.mtso.edu/academics/dickhaut-library. *Dir,* Paul Burnam; Tel: 740-362-3435, E-mail: pburnam@mtso.edu; *Asst Librn, Ref,* David Powell; Tel: 740-362-3438, E-mail: dpowell@mtso.edu; *Pub Serv Asst,* Beth Bringman; Tel: 740-362-3439, E-mail: bbringman@mtso.edu. Subject Specialists: *Church hist, Church leadership, Counseling,* Paul Burnam; *Biblical studies, Theol,* David Powell; Staff 3 (MLS 2, Non-MLS 1)
Founded 1960. Enrl 153; Fac 18; Highest Degree: Doctorate
Jul 2011-Jun 2012. Mats Exp $116,890, Books $31,100, Per/Ser (Incl. Access Fees) $22,000, Electronic Ref Mat (Incl. Access Fees) $4,300. Sal $96,100 (Prof $96,100)
Library Holdings: AV Mats 4,582; Microforms 1,862; Bk Titles 135,306; Per Subs 142
Special Collections: Denominational Coll of the United Methodist Church & its Predecessor Bodies, bks & micro; Philip Gatch Manuscripts
Subject Interests: Biblical studies, Church hist, Theol
Automation Activity & Vendor Info: (Acquisitions) Innovative Interfaces, Inc; (Cataloging) Innovative Interfaces, Inc; (Circulation) Innovative Interfaces, Inc; (Course Reserve) Innovative Interfaces, Inc; (ILL) OCLC; (OPAC) Innovative Interfaces, Inc; (Serials) Innovative Interfaces, Inc
Database Vendor: EBSCOhost, Innovative Interfaces, Inc, ProQuest
Wireless access
Function: Audio & video playback equip for onsite use, AV serv, Computers for patron use, Copy machines, Doc delivery serv, e-mail serv, Electronic databases & coll, Exhibits, ILL available, Music CDs, Online cat, Online ref, Online searches, Orientations, Outside serv via phone, mail, e-mail & web, Ref & res, Ref serv available, Ref serv in person, Scanner, Telephone ref, VHS videos, Wheelchair accessible
Partic in OCLC Online Computer Library Center, Inc; Ohio Library & Information Network; Ohio Private Academic Libraries (OPAL); OHIONET; Theological Consortium of Greater Columbus
Restriction: Access for corporate affiliates, Authorized scholars by appt, Open to researchers by request, Open to students, fac, staff & alumni, Pub use on premises, Restricted borrowing privileges, Restricted loan policy

C OHIO WESLEYAN UNIVERSITY*, L A Beeghly Library, 43 Rowland, 43015-2370. SAN 313-4881. Tel: 740-368-3225. Interlibrary Loan Service Tel: 740-368-3234. Reference Tel: 740-368-3242. Administration Tel: 740-368-3247. FAX: 740-368-3222. E-mail: refdesk@owu.edu. Web Site: lis.owu.edu. *Dir, Libr Serv,* Catherine Cardwell; Tel: 740-368-3246, E-mail: cacardwe@owu.edu; *Digital Librn,* Emily Gattozzi; Tel: 740-368-3233; *Music Librn, Ref,* Peter Szabo; Tel: 740-368-3709, E-mail: paszabo@owu.edu; *Pub Serv Librn, Govt Doc,* Joy Gao; Tel: 740-368-3238, E-mail: yyhe@owu.edu; *Pub Serv Librn, Info Literacy,* Jillian Maruskin; Tel: 740-368-3237, E-mail: jbmarusk@owu.edu; *Pub Serv Librn, Ref,* Dee Peterson; Tel: 740-368-3240, E-mail: dmpeters@owu.edu; *Sci Librn,* Deborah Peoples; Tel: 740-368-3241, E-mail: dapeople@owu.edu; *Ser Librn,* Melissa Hill; Tel: 740-368-3252; *Archivist,* Carol Holliger; Tel: 740-368-3285, E-mail: chhollig@owu.edu; Staff 10.5 (MLS 9.8, Non-MLS 0.7)
Founded 1842. Enrl 1,879; Fac 163; Highest Degree: Bachelor
Library Holdings: AV Mats 12,913; e-journals 20,406; Bk Vols 514,932; Per Subs 21,221
Special Collections: Archive of Ohio United Methodism; Browning (Gunsaulus Coll); James Joyce (Staples Coll); Schubert (20th Century Imprints Coll); Walt Whitman (Bayley Coll). US Document Depository
Database Vendor: ARTstor, EBSCOhost, Innovative Interfaces, Inc, JSTOR, LexisNexis, Wilson - Wilson Web
Wireless access
Partic in OCLC Online Computer Library Center, Inc; Ohio Library & Information Network; OHIONET; The Five Colleges of Ohio

S STATE OF OHIO DEPARTMENT OF CORRECTIONS*, Scioto Juvenile Correctional Facility Library, 5993 Home Rd, 43015. Tel: 740-881-3250. FAX: 740-881-1324. *Librn,* Charles Steinbower; E-mail: chuck.steinbower@dys.ohio.gov
Library Holdings: Bk Vols 5,000; Per Subs 30
Automation Activity & Vendor Info: (Cataloging) SirsiDynix; (Circulation) SirsiDynix; (OPAC) SirsiDynix
Open Mon-Fri 7-4

DELPHOS

P DELPHOS PUBLIC LIBRARY, 309 W Second St, 45833-1695. SAN 313-489X. Tel: 419-695-4015. FAX: 419-695-4025. Web Site: www.delphos.lib.oh.us. *Dir,* Kelly Rist; E-mail: ristke@oplin.org; *Ch Serv,* Denise Cressman; E-mail: cressmande@oplin.org; Staff 6 (MLS 2, Non-MLS 4)
Founded 1912. Pop 12,000; Circ 226,287
Library Holdings: Bk Vols 77,000; Per Subs 230
Special Collections: Delphos Newspapers, 1872-2012
Subject Interests: Local hist
Automation Activity & Vendor Info: (Cataloging) SIRSI WorkFlows; (Circulation) SIRSI WorkFlows; (OPAC) SirsiDynix; (Serials) SIRSI WorkFlows
Database Vendor: SirsiDynix
Wireless access
Partic in NORWELD; Ohio Public Library Information Network
Open Mon, Tues & Thurs 9-8, Wed 12-8, Fri 9-5, Sat 9-12

DELTA

P DELTA PUBLIC LIBRARY*, 402 Main St, 43515-1304. SAN 313-4903. Tel: 419-822-3110. FAX: 419-822-5310. Web Site: www.deltaohio.com/library. *Dir,* Patricia Grover; *Asst Dir,* Candy Baird
Founded 1911. Pop 7,000; Circ 79,840
Library Holdings: Bk Vols 53,000; Per Subs 180
Automation Activity & Vendor Info: (Cataloging) Follett Software; (Circulation) Follett Software; (OPAC) Follett Software
Partic in NW Ohio Libr District
Open Mon-Wed 9:30-8:30, Thurs-Sat 9:30-5:30
Friends of the Library Group

DESHLER

P PATRICK HENRY SCHOOL DISTRICT PUBLIC LIBRARY*, Deshler Edwin Wood Memorial Library, 208 North East Ave, 43516. SAN 356-5718. Tel: 419-278-3616. FAX: 419-278-3616. Web Site: phlibraries.oplin.org. *Dir,* Lori Tietje; E-mail: tietjelo@oplin.org; *Br Mgr,* Debra Wensink; E-mail: wensinde@oplin.org; *Ch,* Tamara Johnson; E-mail: johnsota@oplin.org; *Libr Asst,* Lauri Phillips
Founded 1924. Pop 5,000
Library Holdings: Bk Vols 22,027; Per Subs 150
Special Collections: Genealogy, bks, flm; Ohio & Local History, bks, fs, slides
Open Mon, Tues, Thurs & Fri (Winter) 8:30-5, Wed 8:30-8, Sat 10-2; Mon, Tues, Thurs & Fri (Summer) 9-5, Wed 9-8, Sat 10-2
Branches: 2
HAMLER BRANCH, 230 Randolph St, Hamler, 43524, SAN 356-5742. Tel: 419-274-3821. FAX: 419-274-3821. *Br Mgr,* Ramona Malinowski
Founded 1941
Library Holdings: Bk Vols 13,760
Open Mon Noon-5, Tues & Thurs 9-2, Wed Noon-8, Fri Noon-6, Sat 10-2
Friends of the Library Group

MALINTA BRANCH, 204 N Henry St, Malinta, 43535, SAN 356-5777. Tel: 419-256-7223. FAX: 419-256-7223. *Br Mgr,* Gwenn Maas
Founded 1964
Library Holdings: Bk Vols 18,147
Open Thurs (Winter) 8-3; Tues & Thurs (Summer) 9-2

DOVER

P DOVER PUBLIC LIBRARY*, 525 N Walnut St, 44622. SAN 313-4911. Tel: 330-343-6123. FAX: 330-343-2087. Web Site: www.doverlibrary.org. *Dir,* Jim Gill; E-mail: director@doverlibrary.org
Founded 1923. Pop 20,000; Circ 226,778
Jan 2006-Dec 2006 Income $841,000. Mats Exp $198,000. Sal $504,000
Library Holdings: Bk Vols 93,000; Per Subs 320
Automation Activity & Vendor Info: (Cataloging) Innovative Interfaces, Inc; (Circulation) Innovative Interfaces, Inc; (OPAC) Innovative Interfaces, Inc
Wireless access
Partic in Mideastern Ohio Libr Orgn; Ohio Public Library Information Network
Open Mon-Thurs 9-8, Fri 9-6, Sat 9-5
Friends of the Library Group

DUBLIN

S OCLC LIBRARY*, 6565 Kilgour Pl, 43017. (Mail add: PO Box 7777, 43017), SAN 320-9253. Tel: 614-764-6000. Circulation Tel: 614-761-5100. Reference Tel: 614-761-5054. Administration Tel: 614-764-6293. Toll Free Tel: 800-848-5878. FAX: 614-718-7313. Administration FAX: 614-718-7336. E-mail: oclclibrary@oclc.org. Web Site: oclclibrary.worldcat.org. *Dir,* Lawrence Olszewski; E-mail: olszewsl@oclc.org; *Sr Electronic Res Librn,* Terry Butterworth; Tel: 614-764-4300, E-mail: butterw@oclc.org; *Access Serv Coordr,* Paula Julien; E-mail: julienp@oclc.org; *Sr Info Serv Spec,* Tam Dalrymple; E-mail: dalrymt@oclc.org; *Curator, Corporate Heritage,* Kem Lang; Tel: 614-761-5217, E-mail: langk@oclc.org. Subject Specialists: *Archives,* Kem Lang; Staff 5 (MLS 4, Non-MLS 1)
Founded 1977
Library Holdings: Audiobooks 60; CDs 70; DVDs 436; e-books 23,392; e-journals 603; Microforms 54; Bk Titles 11,776; Bk Vols 15,987; Per Subs 42
Special Collections: Historic Dewey Decimal Coll; Library Network Newsletters; OCLC Archives; OCLC Museum; State Library & State Library Association Newsletters
Subject Interests: Info sci, Libr sci
Automation Activity & Vendor Info: (Acquisitions) OCLC; (Cataloging) OCLC Connexion; (Circulation) OCLC; (ILL) OCLC; (OPAC) OCLC
Database Vendor: OCLC, OCLC FirstSearch, OCLC WebJunction, OCLC WorldShare Interlibrary Loan, OCLC Worldshare Management Services
Wireless access
Function: Archival coll, Exhibits, ILL available
Restriction: Open to others by appt

DUNKIRK

P HARDIN NORTHERN PUBLIC LIBRARY*, 153 N Main St, 45836-1064. (Mail add: PO Box 114, 45836-0114), SAN 313-4938. Tel: 419-759-3558 FAX: 419-759-3558. Web Site: www.hardin-northern.lib.oh.us. *Librn,* Rebecca Coker; E-mail: cokerre@oplin.org
Library Holdings: Bk Vols 10,000; Per Subs 60
Automation Activity & Vendor Info: (Cataloging) SirsiDynix; (Circulation) SirsiDynix; (OPAC) SirsiDynix
Partic in NORWELD
Open Mon, Tues & Thurs 1-8, Wed 10-5, Fri 12-5, Sat 9-1

EAST CLEVELAND

P EAST CLEVELAND PUBLIC LIBRARY*, 14101 Euclid Ave, 44112-3891. SAN 356-5807. Tel: 216-541-4128. FAX: 216-541-1790. E-mail: ecplweb@ecpl.lib.oh.us. Web Site: www.ecpl.lib.oh.us. *Exec Dir,* Sheba Marcus-Bey; E-mail: sheba.marcus-bey@ecpl.lib.oh.us; *Ch,* Pamela Henderson; E-mail: phenderson@ecpl.lib.oh.us; *Ref Librn,* Sara Phillips; E-mail: sphillips@ecpl.lib.oh.us; *Tech,* Theresa Flood; E-mail: tflood@ecpl.lib.oh.us; Staff 33 (MLS 7, Non-MLS 26)
Founded 1916. Pop 37,000; Circ 211,743
Library Holdings: Bk Vols 210,000; Per Subs 200
Special Collections: Black Heritage Coll; Holograph Letters of the Presidents from George Washington to James E Carter; Illustrated Children's Book (W H Quinby Coll). State Document Depository
Subject Interests: African-Am lit, Behav sci, Soc sci
Automation Activity & Vendor Info: (Acquisitions) SirsiDynix; (Cataloging) SirsiDynix; (Circulation) SirsiDynix; (Course Reserve) SirsiDynix; (ILL) SirsiDynix; (Media Booking) SirsiDynix; (OPAC) SirsiDynix; (Serials) SirsiDynix
Publications: Annual Report; Black Heritage Bibliography
Partic in Northeast Ohio Regional Library System
Open Mon-Fri 10-7, Sat 10-6
Friends of the Library Group
Branches: 2
CALEDONIA BRANCH, 960 Caledonia Rd, Cleveland Heights, 44112, SAN 356-5831. Tel: 216-268-6280. FAX: 216-268-6294. *Librn,* Linda Umbayemake
Library Holdings: Bk Vols 25,032
Open Mon & Thurs 12-8, Tues, Wed, Fri & Sat 9-5
Friends of the Library Group
NORTH BRANCH LIBRARY & TECHNOLOGY CENTER, 1425 Hayden Ave, 44112, SAN 356-5866. Tel: 216-268-6283. FAX: 216-268-6297. *Librn,* Monisa Ramseur
Library Holdings: Bk Vols 17,464
Open Mon & Thurs 12-8, Tues, Wed, Fri & Sat 9-5
Friends of the Library Group

EAST LIVERPOOL

P CARNEGIE PUBLIC LIBRARY, 219 E Fourth St, 43920-3143. SAN 313-4946. Tel: 330-385-2048. Circulation Tel: 330-385-2048, Ext 100. Reference Tel: 330-385-2048, Ext 102. FAX: 330-385-7600. E-mail: eastliv@oplin.org. Web Site: www.carnegie.lib.oh.us. *Dir,* Melissa A W Percic; *Asst Dir, Fiscal Officer,* Mary Deem; Tel: 330-385-2048, Ext 103, E-mail: deemma@oplin.org; *Circ,* Jackie Hicks; *Tech Serv & Automation,* Tom Marlatt; *Youth Serv,* Kim Blevins; Staff 7.775 (MLS 2.65, Non-MLS 5.125)
Founded 1900. Pop 11,062; Circ 100,000
Library Holdings: Bk Vols 70,652; Per Subs 104
Special Collections: State Document Depository
Subject Interests: Local hist
Automation Activity & Vendor Info: (Cataloging) SirsiDynix; (Circulation) SirsiDynix; (OPAC) SirsiDynix; (Serials) SirsiDynix
Database Vendor: EBSCOhost, Overdrive, Inc
Wireless access
Function: 24/7 Online cat, Activity rm, Adult bk club, Audiobks via web, Bks on cassette, Bks on CD, Children's prog, Computers for patron use, Copy machines, E-Reserves, Electronic databases & coll, Fax serv, Free DVD rentals, Handicapped accessible, Home delivery & serv to Sr ctr & nursing homes, Homebound delivery serv, ILL available, Magazines, Mango lang, Microfiche/film & reading machines, Online cat, OverDrive digital audio bks, Prog for adults, Prog for children & young adult, Pub access computers, Ref serv in person, Story hour, Summer reading prog, Tax forms, VHS videos, Wheelchair accessible
Partic in SEO (Serving Every Ohioan) Library Center
Open Mon & Thurs 9-7, Tues & Wed 9-5, Fri & Sat 9-1
Restriction: Non-resident fee

C KENT STATE UNIVERSITY*, Blair Memorial Library, 400 E Fourth St, Rm 216, 43920-5769. SAN 313-4954. Tel: 330-382-7401, 330-382-7421. Administration Tel: 330-382-7432. FAX: 330-382-7561. *Dir,* Susan Weaver; E-mail: sweaver@kent.edu; Staff 2 (MLS 1, Non-MLS 1)
Founded 1968. Enrl 798; Fac 35; Highest Degree: Bachelor
Library Holdings: Bk Vols 31,320; Per Subs 44
Database Vendor: JSTOR, OVID Technologies
Partic in Northeast Ohio Regional Library System; Ohio Library & Information Network
Open Mon-Thurs 8-8, Fri 8-1

EAST PALESTINE

P EAST PALESTINE MEMORIAL PUBLIC LIBRARY*, 309 N Market St, 44413. SAN 313-4962. Tel: 330-426-3778. FAX: 330-426-4950. E-mail: eplibmail@yahoo.com. Web Site: www.east-palestine.lib.oh.us. *Dir,* Tamra Hess; *Asst Dir, Youth Serv Librn,* Noreen McBride; Staff 6 (MLS 2, Non-MLS 4)
Founded 1920. Pop 4,721; Circ 110,521
Jan 2011-Dec 2011 Income $372,685, State $352,080, Locally Generated Income $20,605. Mats Exp $61,569. Sal $172,080
Library Holdings: Bk Titles 41,391; Bk Vols 45,556; Per Subs 66
Subject Interests: Local hist
Automation Activity & Vendor Info: (Cataloging) Follett Software; (Circulation) Follett Software; (OPAC) Follett Software
Wireless access
Function: Bk club(s), Children's prog, Copy machines, Fax serv, Free DVD rentals, Homebound delivery serv, ILL available, Online cat, Pub access computers, Ref serv available, Tax forms, Wheelchair accessible
Partic in Northeast Ohio Regional Library System
Open Mon-Thurs 9-8, Fri & Sat 9-5
Restriction: Non-resident fee
Friends of the Library Group

EATON

P PREBLE COUNTY DISTRICT LIBRARY*, 450 S Barron St, 45320-2402. SAN 356-5890. Tel: 937-456-4250. FAX: 937-456-6092. TDD: 937-456-6804. E-mail: pcdllibrary@oplin.org. Web Site:

www.pcdl.lib.oh.us. *Dir,* Abigail Noland; E-mail: nolandab@oplin.org; *Outreach Serv Librn,* Danita Cook; E-mail: prebleoutreach@oplin.org; *Syst Librn,* Jen Thomas; E-mail: thomasjen@oplin.org; *Cat,* Diane Knaff; E-mail: knaffdi@oplin.org; *Ch Serv,* Teresa Deaton; Tel: 937-456-4331, E-mail: deatonte@oplin.org; *Network Adminr,* Doug Montgomery; E-mail: montgodo@oplin.org; *Res,* Lauren Robinson; Fax: 937-456-4774, E-mail: prebleref@oplin.org; *Teen Serv,* Christina Jones; E-mail: jonesch@oplin.org; Staff 39 (MLS 6, Non-MLS 33)
Founded 1959. Pop 39,605; Circ 269,953
Library Holdings: Bk Titles 150,000; Bk Vols 174,000; Per Subs 980
Special Collections: ASL Coll
Subject Interests: Genealogy, Local hist
Automation Activity & Vendor Info: (Cataloging) SirsiDynix; (Circulation) SirsiDynix; (OPAC) SirsiDynix
Database Vendor: ProQuest
Wireless access
Publications: Library Ink (Newsletter)
Partic in Miami Valley Librs; Ohio Public Library Information Network; OHIONET; SouthWest Ohio & Neighboring Libraries
Special Services for the Deaf - Bks on deafness & sign lang; Closed caption videos; Coll on deaf educ; Deaf publ; Described encaptioned media prog; High interest/low vocabulary bks; Interpreter on staff; Sign lang interpreter upon request for prog; Sorenson video relay syst; Staff with knowledge of sign lang
Special Services for the Blind - Accessible computers; Assistive/Adapted tech devices, equip & products; Audio mat; BiFolkal kits; Bks & mags in Braille, on rec, tape & cassette; Bks on CD; Braille & cassettes; Braille alphabet card; Braille bks; Children's Braille; Dep for Braille Inst; Descriptive video serv (DVS); Extensive large print coll; Handicapped awareness prog; Home delivery serv; Large print & cassettes; Large print bks; Large print bks & talking machines; Large type calculator; Lending of low vision aids; Magnifiers; Reader equip; Ref serv; Sound rec; Soundproof reading booth; Talking bk & rec for the blind cat; Talking bk serv referral; Talking bks & player equip; Talking machines
Friends of the Library Group
Branches: 9
BROOKE-GOULD MEMORIAL, 301 N Barron St, 45320-1705, SAN 356-5955. Tel: 937-456-4331. FAX: 937-456-4774. *Librn,* Phyllis Bennett
Founded 1815
Library Holdings: AV Mats 10,000; Bks on Deafness & Sign Lang 200; Braille Volumes 50; Bk Titles 140,000; Per Subs 307; Videos 14,000
Special Services for the Deaf - Interpreter on staff
CAMDEN, 104 S Main St, 45311, SAN 356-5920. Tel: 937-452-3142. FAX: 937-452-7365. *Librn,* Toni Keesler
Founded 1837
Special Collections: Eleanor I Jones Archives
Friends of the Library Group
ELDORADO BRANCH, 150 N Main St, 45321. (Mail add: PO Box 244, Eldorado, 45321-0244), SAN 356-598X. Tel: 937-273-4933. FAX: 937-273-5673. *Librn,* Pam Kessler
LIBRARY ADMINISTRATION & RESOURCE CENTER, 450 S Barron St, 45320-2402. Tel: 937-456-4520. Toll Free FAX: 937-456-6092. Web Site: www.pcdl.lib.oh.us/genealogy/index.htm. *Dir,* Abigail Noland
Special Collections: Preble County Historical Society & Preble County Genealogical Society Genealogy
Subject Interests: Local hist
Publications: Library Ink (Monthly newsletter)
Friends of the Library Group
NEW PARIS BRANCH, 115 N Washington St, New Paris, 45347, SAN 356-6013. Tel: 937-437-7242. FAX: 937-437-0772. *Librn,* Lisa Stall
Founded 1902
Friends of the Library Group
PREBLE COUNTY ROOM, 450 S Barron St, 45320-2402. Tel: 937-456-4970. E-mail: pcroom@oplin.org. *Supvr,* Marlene Ressler
Special Collections: Genealogical & Historian Resources
WEST ALEXANDRIA BRANCH, 16 N Main St, West Alexandria, 45381, SAN 356-6048. Tel: 937-839-4915. FAX: 937-839-4209. *Br Librn,* Michelle Laughlin
Founded 1896
Special Collections: West Alexandria Archives
Friends of the Library Group
WEST ELKTON BRANCH, PO Box 100, West Elkton, 45070, SAN 328-7068. Tel: 937-787-4873. FAX: 937-787-3153. *Librn,* Pam Kessler
Founded 1935
Friends of the Library Group
WEST MANCHESTER BRANCH, 212 S High St, West Manchester, 45382. (Mail add: PO Box 138, West Manchester, 45382-0138), SAN 371-3032. Tel: 937-678-8503. FAX: 937-678-4030. *Br Librn,* Pamela Kessler
Founded 1961
Friends of the Library Group

ELMORE

P HARRIS-ELMORE PUBLIC LIBRARY*, 328 Toledo St, 43416. (Mail add: PO Box 45, 43416-0045), SAN 356-6072. Tel: 419-862-2482. FAX: 419-862-2123. E-mail: elmorelibrary@gmail.com. Web Site: library.norweld.lib.oh.us/harris-elmore. *Dir,* Amy Laity; E-mail: laityam@oplin.org; Staff 19 (MLS 2, Non-MLS 17)
Founded 1947. Pop 15,000; Circ 124,663
Library Holdings: Bk Vols 40,000; Per Subs 75
Special Collections: Local History
Subject Interests: Genealogy
Automation Activity & Vendor Info: (Cataloging) SirsiDynix; (Circulation) SirsiDynix
Database Vendor: EBSCOhost, SirsiDynix, TLC (The Library Corporation)
Function: Accelerated reader prog, Adult bk club, Archival coll, Audiobks via web, Bks on cassette, Bks on CD, Children's prog, Computers for patron use, Copy machines, E-Reserves, Electronic databases & coll, Fax serv, Free DVD rentals, Handicapped accessible, Holiday prog, Home delivery & serv to Sr ctr & nursing homes, ILL available, Magnifiers for reading, Music CDs, Notary serv, Online cat, Online ref, Online searches, Outside serv via phone, mail, e-mail & web, OverDrive digital audio bks, Preschool outreach, Prog for adults, Prog for children & young adult, Spoken cassettes & CDs, Spoken cassettes & DVDs, Tax forms, Teen prog, Telephone ref, VHS videos, Video lending libr, Web-catalog, Wheelchair accessible
Partic in NORWELD; SEO (Serving Every Ohioan) Library Center
Branches: 1
GENOA BRANCH, 602 West St, Genoa, 43430, SAN 356-6102. Tel: 419-855-3380. FAX: 419-855-7012. Web Site: www.library.norweld.lib.oh.us/harris-elmore/br.htm. *Br Mgr,* Mimi Fintel; Staff 8 (MLS 1, Non-MLS 7)
Library Holdings: Bk Vols 35,000; Per Subs 60
Function: AV serv, Home delivery & serv to Sr ctr & nursing homes, Homebound delivery serv, ILL available, Prog for adults, Prog for children & young adult, Ref serv available, Summer reading prog, Telephone ref, Wheelchair accessible
Friends of the Library Group

ELYRIA

P ELYRIA PUBLIC LIBRARY SYSTEM*, 320 Washington Ave, 44035-5199. SAN 313-4997. Tel: 440-323-5747. Reference Tel: 440-322-0461. Administration Tel: 440-322-0175. FAX: 440-323-5788. Administration FAX: 440-323-1078. TDD: 440-323-1322. E-mail: epl@elyria.lib.oh.us. Web Site: www.elyria.lib.oh.us. *Dir,* Lyn Crouse; E-mail: lcrouse@elyria.lib.oh.us; *Assoc Dir,* Jennifer Jung Gallant; *Outreach Serv Librn,* Virginia Suda; *AV,* Celeste Brlas; E-mail: cbrlas@elyria.lib.oh.us; *Ch Serv,* Margaret Savoy; E-mail: msavoy@elyria.lib.oh.us; *ILL, Ref,* Rose Burton; E-mail: rburton@elyria.lib.oh.us; *Tech Serv,* Kathy Webb; E-mail: kwebb@elyria.lib.oh.us
Founded 1870. Pop 66,977; Circ 866,995
Library Holdings: Bk Vols 383,862; Per Subs 715
Special Collections: Local History (Ely Papers); Nonprofit Information Center
Automation Activity & Vendor Info: (Cataloging) SirsiDynix; (Circulation) SirsiDynix; (OPAC) SirsiDynix
Publications: A Friendly Word (Newsletter); The Next Chapter (Newsletter)
Partic in CLEVNET; Northeast Ohio Regional Library System
Open Mon-Thurs 10-8:30, Fri & Sat 10-6, Sun 1-5
Friends of the Library Group
Branches: 3
KEYSTONE-LAGRANGE BRANCH, 101 West St, LaGrange, 44050. Tel: 440-355-6323. FAX: 440-355-8082. *Mgr,* Jill Warren
Library Holdings: Bk Vols 9,679
Open Mon & Thurs 1-8, Tues, Wed, Fri & Sat 10-5:30
Friends of the Library Group
SOUTH BRANCH, 1215 Middle Ave, 44035. Tel: 440-323-7519. FAX: 440-323-7518.
Library Holdings: Bk Vols 4,251
Open Mon & Thurs 1-5, Tues, Wed & Fri 9-3
Friends of the Library Group
WEST RIVER, 1194 West River Rd N, 44035. Tel: 440-324-2270. Administration Tel: 440-324-9812. FAX: 440-324-4766. Administration FAX: 440-324-5549. *Assoc Dir,* Jennifer Jung Gallant
Library Holdings: Bk Vols 146,962
Open Mon-Thurs 10-8:30, Fri & Sat 10-6, Sun 1-5
Bookmobiles: 1. Mgr, Charlene Hartman. Bk vols 11,397

M EMH REGIONAL HEALTHCARE SYSTEM*, Dr Joseph M Strong Memorial Library, 630 E River St, 44035. SAN 313-4989. Tel: 440-326-4321. FAX: 440-329-7405. *Mgr, Libr Serv,* Terry Kyrios; Staff 1 (MLS 1)

Founded 1927
Library Holdings: Bk Vols 2,500; Per Subs 120
Subject Interests: Hospital admin, Med, Nursing, Nutrition, Pub health
Automation Activity & Vendor Info: (Acquisitions) LibraryWorld, Inc; (Cataloging) LibraryWorld, Inc; (Circulation) LibraryWorld, Inc
Database Vendor: EBSCOhost, UpToDate
Function: For res purposes, ILL available, Res libr
Partic in Northeast Ohio Regional Library System
Restriction: Lending to staff only

S LORAIN COUNTY HISTORICAL SOCIETY*, Gerald Hicks Memorial Library, 509 Washington Ave, 44035. SAN 327-3822. Tel: 440-322-3341. FAX: 440-322-2817. E-mail: library@lchs.org. *Exec Dir,* William Bird; *Librn,* Kies Bill; *Archivist,* Eric Greenly; Staff 4 (Non-MLS 4)
Library Holdings: Bk Vols 3,500
Open Tues-Fri 10-4

GL LORAIN COUNTY LAW LIBRARY*, 226 Middle Ave, 44035. SAN 313-5012. Tel: 440-329-5567. FAX: 440-322-1724. Web Site: www.lorainlawlib.org. *Librn,* Mary Kovacs; E-mail: mkovacs@lorainlawlib.org; Staff 2 (MLS 1, Non-MLS 1)
Founded 1889
Library Holdings: Bk Titles 18,000; Per Subs 25
Subject Interests: Law
Restriction: Mem only

EUCLID

P EUCLID PUBLIC LIBRARY*, 631 E 222nd St, 44123-2091. SAN 356-6137. Tel: 216-261-5300. FAX: 216-261-0575. Web Site: www.euclidlibrary.org. *Dir,* Kacie Armstrong; Tel: 216-261-5300, Ext 111, E-mail: karmstrong@euclidlibrary.org; *YA Librn,* Dawn Sardes; E-mail: dsardes@euclidlibrary.org; *Tech Mgr,* Matthew Augustine; Tel: 216-261-5300, Ext 126, E-mail: maugustine@euclidlibrary.org; *Adult Serv,* Karla Bowman; Tel: 216-261-5300, Ext 134, Fax: 216-261-9559, E-mail: dsardes@euclidlibrary.org; *Ch Serv,* Teresa Smith; Tel: 216-261-5300, Ext 143, Fax: 216-261-9559, E-mail: tsmith@euclidlibrary.org; *Circ,* Cheryl Burley; Tel: 216-261-5300, Ext 153, E-mail: cburley@euclidlibrary.org; Staff 98 (MLS 16, Non-MLS 82)
Founded 1935. Pop 52,717; Circ 1,236,314
Library Holdings: AV Mats 57,586; Bk Vols 279,392; Per Subs 472
Special Collections: Oral History
Automation Activity & Vendor Info: (Cataloging) SirsiDynix; (Circulation) SirsiDynix; (OPAC) SirsiDynix
Database Vendor: Gale Cengage Learning, OCLC FirstSearch
Function: ILL available
Publications: Library Lines (Newsletter)
Partic in CLEVNET; Northeast Ohio Regional Library System
Open Mon-Thurs 10-9, Fri 10-5, Sat 9-5, Sun (Oct-May) 1-5
Friends of the Library Group

FAIRPORT HARBOR

P FAIRPORT HARBOR PUBLIC LIBRARY*, 335 Vine St, 44077-5799. SAN 313-5020. Tel: 440-354-8191. Interlibrary Loan Service Tel: 440-354-8191, Ext 24. Reference Tel: 440-354-8191, Ext 21. Administration Tel: 440-354-8191, Ext 22. FAX: 440-354-6059. E-mail: director@fairport.lib.oh.us. Web Site: www.fairport.lib.oh.us. *Dir,* Carol L Lipscomb Butsko; E-mail: clipscomb@fairport.lib.oh.us; *Asst Librn,* Cheryl Rymer; E-mail: crymer@fairport.lib.oh.us; *Cat, Tech Serv,* Melanee Simpson; Tel: 440-358-0119, E-mail: melanee.simpson@fairport.lib.oh.us; *Computer Librn,* Vance Todd; *Youth Serv,* Catherine Norman; Tel: 440-354-8191, Ext 23, E-mail: cathy.norman@fairport.lib.oh.us; Staff 9 (Non-MLS 9)
Founded 1922. Pop 3,180; Circ 83,000
Subject Interests: Finnish (Lang), Hungarian (Lang), Local hist
Automation Activity & Vendor Info: (Cataloging) SirsiDynix; (Circulation) SirsiDynix; (ILL) SirsiDynix
Database Vendor: EBSCOhost, Gale Cengage Learning, OCLC FirstSearch, ProQuest, SirsiDynix
Wireless access
Function: ILL available
Partic in CLEVNET; Northeast Ohio Regional Library System
Open Mon-Thurs 10-8, Fri 10-6, Sat 12-5
Friends of the Library Group

FAYETTE

P NORMAL MEMORIAL LIBRARY*, Fayette Library, 301 N Eagle St, 43521. (Mail add: PO Box 100, 43521-0100), SAN 313-5039. Tel: 419-237-2115. FAX: 419-237-2002. Web Site: www.fayette-nml.org. *Dir,* Sally Canfield; *Ch Serv,* Denise Jensen; *Tech Serv,* Susan Stuckey
Founded 1929. Pop 2,500; Circ 31,608
Library Holdings: Bk Vols 22,500; Per Subs 100
Automation Activity & Vendor Info: (Cataloging) SirsiDynix; (Circulation) SirsiDynix; (OPAC) SirsiDynix
Wireless access
Open Mon & Wed 10-8, Tues 10-5, Thurs & Fri 1-5, Sat 10-1

FINDLAY

S BLACK HERITAGE LIBRARY & MULTICULTURAL CENTER*, 817 Harmon St, 45840. Tel: 419-423-4954. *Exec Dir,* Nina Parker; *Librn,* Sharon Mason
Library Holdings: AV Mats 500; Bk Vols 3,500
Subject Interests: African-Am art, African-Am culture, African-Am hist, Multicultural art, hist & culture
Database Vendor: OVID Technologies, PubMed
Open Mon, Tues, Thurs & Fri 4-6
Friends of the Library Group

P FINDLAY-HANCOCK COUNTY DISTRICT PUBLIC LIBRARY*, 206 Broadway, 45840-3382. SAN 356-6226. Tel: 419-422-1712. Reference Tel: 419-422-1737. FAX: 419-422-0638. Web Site: www.findlaylibrary.org. *Dir,* Jeff Winkle; E-mail: winkleje@findlaylibrary.org; *Adult Serv Mgr, Asst Dir,* Sarah Clevidence; *Children's Mgr,* Cynthia Romick; *Tech Serv Mgr,* Sharon Mason; Staff 72 (MLS 4, Non-MLS 68)
Founded 1888. Pop 73,824; Circ 804,668
Jan 2007-Dec 2007 Income $3,000,000. Mats Exp $303,500, Books $173,500, Per/Ser (Incl. Access Fees) $13,000, AV Mat $80,500, Electronic Ref Mat (Incl. Access Fees) $28,000. Sal $1,800,000 (Prof $191,000)
Library Holdings: Bk Vols 176,405; Per Subs 306
Special Collections: Foreign Language DVDs; Genealogy Coll; Local History Coll
Automation Activity & Vendor Info: (Cataloging) SirsiDynix; (Circulation) SirsiDynix; (OPAC) SirsiDynix
Database Vendor: SirsiDynix
Wireless access
Function: Adult bk club, After school storytime, Audiobks via web, AV serv, Bk club(s), Bks on CD, CD-ROM, Chess club, Computer training, Computers for patron use, Copy machines, Digital talking bks, E-mail & chat, E-mail serv, E-Reserves, Electronic databases & coll, Family literacy, Free DVD rentals, Home delivery & serv to Sr ctr & nursing homes, ILL available, Jail serv, Magnifiers for reading, Music CDs, Online cat, Online searches, Outreach serv, OverDrive digital audio bks, Photocopying/Printing, Prog for adults, Prog for children & young adult, Pub access computers, Ref & res, Ref serv available, Ref serv in person, Senior computer classes, Spoken cassettes & CDs, Spoken cassettes & DVDs, Story hour, Summer reading prog, Tax forms, Teen prog, Telephone ref, VHS videos, Video lending libr, Web-catalog, Wheelchair accessible
Publications: Book Ends (Newsletter)
Partic in SEO (Serving Every Ohioan) Library Center
Open Mon-Thurs 9:30-8:30, Fri & Sat 9:30-5, Sun 1-5
Friends of the Library Group
Bookmobiles: 1. Contact, Jill Hendricks

L HANCOCK COUNTY LAW LIBRARY ASSOCIATION*, 300 S Main St, 4th Flr, 45840. SAN 313-5055. Tel: 419-424-7077. FAX: 419-425-4136. *Exec Dir,* Deborah L Ward
Library Holdings: Bk Vols 24,500
Open Mon-Fri 8:30-4:30

C THE UNIVERSITY OF FINDLAY, Shafer Library, 1000 N Main St, 45840-3695. SAN 313-5047. Tel: 419-434-4627. E-mail: library@findlay.edu. Web Site: www.findlay.edu/offices/academic/shaferlibrary. *Univ Librn & Col Librn for Bus,* Andrew Whitis; Tel: 419-434-5735, E-mail: whitis@findlay.edu; *Col Librn for Educ,* Margaret Hirschy; Tel: 419-434-4262, E-mail: hirschym@findlay.edu; *Col Librn for Health Professions, Pharm & Sci,* Rebecca Quintus; Tel: 419-434-4549, E-mail: quintus@findlay.edu; *Col Librn for Liberal Arts & Info Literacy,* Jenny Denen; Tel: 419-434-5880, E-mail: denen@findlay.edu; *Acq & Per Mgr,* Nancy Bickford; Tel: 419-434-4617, E-mail: bickford@findlay.edu; *Access Serv Coordr,* Pam Carles; Tel: 419-434-4612, E-mail: carlesp@findlay.edu; *Univ Archivist,* Robert W Schirmer; Tel: 419-434-4767, E-mail: schirmer@findlay.edu; Staff 8 (MLS 5, Non-MLS 3)
Founded 1882. Enrl 3,722; Fac 225; Highest Degree: Doctorate
Library Holdings: e-journals 38,338; Bk Titles 82,000; Bk Vols 136,000; Per Subs 472
Special Collections: State Document Depository; US Document Depository
Automation Activity & Vendor Info: (Acquisitions) Innovative Interfaces, Inc
Database Vendor: ACM (Association for Computing Machinery), American Chemical Society, American Mathematical Society, American Physical Society, American Psychological Association (APA), BioOne, Bloomberg, EBSCOhost, Elsevier, Emerald, Factiva.com, Gale Cengage Learning, Innovative Interfaces, Inc, JSTOR, Lexi-Comp, LexisNexis,

Mergent Online, Newsbank, OCLC FirstSearch, OCLC WorldShare Interlibrary Loan, OHIONET, Oxford Online, ProQuest, PubMed, Safari Books Online, Sage, ScienceDirect, Scopus, SerialsSolutions, Springer-Verlag, Springshare, LLC, Wiley InterScience
Partic in OCLC Online Computer Library Center, Inc; OHIONET

R WINEBRENNER THEOLOGICAL SEMINARY LIBRARY, 950 N Main St, 45840-3652. SAN 313-5071. Tel: 419-434-4200. Toll Free Tel: 800-992-4987. FAX: 419-434-4267. E-mail: library@winebrenner.edu. Web Site: www.winebrenner.edu. *Librn,* Margaret Hirschy; Tel: 419-434-4260; Staff 0.5 (MLS 0.5)
Founded 1942. Enrl 119; Fac 7; Highest Degree: Doctorate
Jul 2006-Jun 2007. Mats Exp $22,755, Books $18,114, Per/Ser (Incl. Access Fees) $3,721, Electronic Ref Mat (Incl. Access Fees) $920. Sal $66,132
Library Holdings: AV Mats 692; Bk Vols 43,582; Per Subs 110
Automation Activity & Vendor Info: (Acquisitions) Innovative Interfaces, Inc; (Cataloging) OCLC; (Circulation) Innovative Interfaces, Inc; (Course Reserve) Innovative Interfaces, Inc; (ILL) OCLC; (OPAC) Innovative Interfaces, Inc; (Serials) Innovative Interfaces, Inc
Database Vendor: Innovative Interfaces, Inc
Wireless access
Partic in Ohio Library & Information Network; Ohio Private Academic Libraries (OPAL)
Open Mon, Tues & Thurs 8-6, Wed & Fri 8-4

FOREST

P FOREST-JACKSON PUBLIC LIBRARY*, 102 W Lima St, 45843-1128. SAN 313-508X. Tel: 419-273-2400. FAX: 419-273-8007. Web Site: www.forestlibrary.org. *Dir,* Karen Moore; E-mail: mooreka@oplin.org; Staff 6 (Non-MLS 6)
Founded 1936. Pop 5,700; Circ 51,742
Library Holdings: Bk Vols 12,244
Automation Activity & Vendor Info: (Cataloging) SirsiDynix; (Circulation) SirsiDynix; (OPAC) SirsiDynix
Database Vendor: EBSCOhost, SirsiDynix
Wireless access
Function: Adult bk club, After school storytime, Archival coll, Audiobks via web, Bks on cassette, Bks on CD, Children's prog, Computers for patron use, Copy machines, Fax serv, Free DVD rentals, ILL available, Music CDs, Online cat, Online ref, Outreach serv, Photocopying/Printing, Preschool outreach, Prog for adults, Prog for children & young adult, Pub access computers, Story hour, Summer reading prog, Tax forms, VHS videos
Open Mon, Wed & Fri 10-5, Tues & Thurs 10-8, Sat (Sept-May) 10-1
Friends of the Library Group

FORT RECOVERY

P FORT RECOVERY PUBLIC LIBRARY*, 113 N Wayne St, 45846. (Mail add: PO Box 309, 45846-0309), SAN 313-5098. Tel: 419-375-2869. FAX: 419-375-2525. Web Site: www.fortrecoverylibrary.org. *Librn,* Linda Nietfeld; Staff 5 (Non-MLS 5)
Founded 1928. Circ 55,246
Library Holdings: Bk Vols 53,625; Per Subs 71
Automation Activity & Vendor Info: (Cataloging) SIRSI WorkFlows; (Circulation) SIRSI WorkFlows; (OPAC) SIRSI WorkFlows
Wireless access
Partic in SEO (Serving Every Ohioan) Library Center
Open Mon & Wed 10-5:30, Tues 10-7, Fri 9-5:30, Sat 9-1
Friends of the Library Group

FOSTORIA

P KAUBISCH MEMORIAL PUBLIC LIBRARY*, 205 Perry St, 44830-2265. SAN 313-5101. Tel: 419-435-2813. FAX: 419-435-5350. E-mail: kaubisch@oplin.org. Web Site: www.fostoria.lib.oh.us. *Dir,* Michael Limer; *Head, Circ Serv,* Julie Beeson; *Head, Tech Serv,* Kelli Foster; *Head, Youth Serv,* Joan Kendall-Sperry; *Fiscal Officer,* Nancy Whipple; Staff 7 (MLS 1, Non-MLS 6)
Founded 1892. Pop 25,000; Circ 178,410
Library Holdings: Bk Vols 84,748; Per Subs 189
Special Services for the Blind - Audio mat; Bks available with recordings; Bks on CD; Large print bks; Talking bks & player equip
Open Mon-Thurs 9-8, Sat 9-2
Friends of the Library Group

FRANKLIN

P FRANKLIN-SPRINGBORO PUBLIC LIBRARY*, 44 E Fourth St, 45005. SAN 313-511X. Tel: 937-746-2665. FAX: 937-746-2846. E-mail: fspl@oplin.org. Web Site: www.franklin.lib.oh.us. *Libr Dir,* Martha M Bush; E-mail: bushma@oplin.org; *Libr Mgr,* Susan Horner; Staff 17 (MLS 5, Non-MLS 12)
Founded 1923. Pop 55,770; Circ 458,171
Library Holdings: AV Mats 1,328; CDs 1,674; DVDs 2,495; Large Print Bks 3,382; Bk Vols 150,535; Per Subs 381; Talking Bks 5,375; Videos 7,432
Automation Activity & Vendor Info: (Acquisitions) Innovative Interfaces, Inc; (Cataloging) Innovative Interfaces, Inc; (Circulation) Innovative Interfaces, Inc; (OPAC) Innovative Interfaces, Inc
Wireless access
Function: Audio & video playback equip for onsite use, Audiobks via web, Bk club(s), Bks on cassette, Bks on CD, Children's prog, Computers for patron use, Copy machines, Electronic databases & coll, Fax serv, Handicapped accessible, Home delivery & serv to Sr ctr & nursing homes, ILL available, Music CDs, Notary serv, Online cat, Photocopying/Printing, Preschool outreach, Pub access computers, Summer reading prog, Tax forms, Web-catalog
Partic in Miami Valley Librs; SouthWest Ohio & Neighboring Libraries
Special Services for the Deaf - Sorenson video relay syst
Special Services for the Blind - Assistive/Adapted tech devices, equip & products; Bks on cassette; Bks on CD; Home delivery serv; Large print bks; Low vision equip; Talking bks
Open Mon-Thurs 9-8, Fri 10-6, Sat 9-5, Sun 1-5
Friends of the Library Group
Branches: 1
SPRINGBORO BRANCH, 125 Park Lane, Springboro, 45066-9801, SAN 370-5765. Tel: 937-748-3200. FAX: 937-748-4831. E-mail: fspl@oplin.org. *Asst Dir, Libr Mgr,* Vicky Sweeney; Staff 11 (MLS 1, Non-MLS 10)
Founded 1990
Open Mon-Thurs 9-8, Fri 10-6, Sat 9-5
Friends of the Library Group

FREMONT

P BIRCHARD PUBLIC LIBRARY OF SANDUSKY COUNTY*, 423 Croghan St, 43420. SAN 356-6315. Tel: 419-334-7101. FAX: 419-334-4788. Web Site: www.birchard.lib.oh.us. *Dir,* Pam Hoesman; E-mail: pam.hoesman@birchard.lib.ih.us; *Network Adminr,* Larry Gundy; *Adult & Tech Serv Coordr,* Angie Lorensen; *Outreach Coordr, Youth Serv Coordr,* Melinda Baty; *YA Serv,* Nancy Koebel
Founded 1873. Pop 48,087; Circ 506,099
Library Holdings: Bk Vols 154,660
Subject Interests: Local hist, Pres Rutherford B Hayes
Automation Activity & Vendor Info: (Acquisitions) SirsiDynix; (Cataloging) SirsiDynix; (Circulation) SirsiDynix; (ILL) SirsiDynix; (OPAC) BiblioCommons; (Serials) SirsiDynix
Wireless access
Partic in CLEVNET
Open Mon-Thurs 9-8:30, Fri 9-5:30, Sat 9-5, Sun 1-5
Friends of the Library Group
Branches: 3
GIBSONBURG BRANCH, 100 N Webster St, Gibsonburg, 43431, SAN 356-634X. Tel: 419-637-2173. *Br Supvr,* Carol Montgomery
Circ 44,889
Open Mon & Wed 12-8, Tues 9-5:30, Thurs 12-5:30, Fri 12-4, Sat 10-3
GREEN SPRINGS MEMORIAL, 217 N Broadway, Green Springs, 44836, SAN 356-6374. Tel: 419-639-2014. *Br Supvr,* Zeferina Anguiano
Circ 21,834
Open Mon & Wed 12-8, Tues 9-5:30, Thurs 12-5:30, Fri 12-4, Sat 10-3
WOODVILLE BRANCH, 101 E Main, Woodville, 43469, SAN 356-6404. Tel: 419-849-2744. *Br Supvr,* Rene Dix
Circ 36,525
Open Mon & Wed 12-8, Tues 9-5:30, Thurs 12-5:30, Fri 12-4, Sat 10-3
Friends of the Library Group

S RUTHERFORD B HAYES PRESIDENTIAL CENTER LIBRARY*, Spiegel Grove, 43420-2796. SAN 313-5128. Tel: 419-332-2081. FAX: 419-332-4952. E-mail: hayeslib@rbhayes.org. Web Site: www.rbhayes.org. *Exec Dir,* Christie Weininger; Tel: 419-332-2081, Ext 220, E-mail: cweininger@rbhayes.org; *Head Librn,* Rebecca B Hill; Tel: 419-332-2081, Ext 231, E-mail: bhill@rbhayes.org; *Archivist,* Nan Card; Tel: 419-332-2081, Ext 239, E-mail: ncard@rbhayes.org; *Libr Tech,* John Ransom; Tel: 419-332-2081, Ext 232, E-mail: jransom@rbhayes.org; *Res,* Gilbert Gonzalez; Tel: 419-332-2081, Ext 222, E-mail: ggonzalez@rbhayes.org. Subject Specialists: *Genealogy,* Rebecca B Hill; *Manuscripts,* Nan Card; Staff 3 (MLS 1, Non-MLS 2)
Founded 1911
Library Holdings: Bk Vols 75,000; Per Subs 221
Special Collections: Abraham Lincoln Coll; Benson J Lossing Coll, ms; David Ross Locke Coll, ms; History of the United States, 19th-20th Century (Rutherford B Hayes Personal Library); Nineteenth Century Cookbooks; Rutherford B Hayes Family Coll, ms; Sandusky River Valley & the Great Lakes Coll; Thomas Nast Coll, ms; William & Mary B Claflin Coll, ms; William Dean Howells Coll, ms; William M Evarts Coll, ms
Subject Interests: Croquet, Econ hist (1865-1917), Genealogy, Gilded Age US (1865-1917), Local hist, Ohio, Presidents, Reconstruction in the South, US political soc

Automation Activity & Vendor Info: (OPAC) Innovative Interfaces, Inc
Database Vendor: ProQuest
Wireless access
Function: ILL available
Publications: The Statesman (Newsletter)
Partic in Ohio Library & Information Network; OHIONET
Open Tues-Sat 9-5
Restriction: Non-circulating to the pub

M MEMORIAL HOSPITAL*, Medical Library, 715 S Taft Ave, 43420. SAN 370-6060. Tel: 419-332-7321, Ext 3497. FAX: 419-334-6691. *Librn,* Linda Stricker; Staff 1 (Non-MLS 1)
Library Holdings: Bk Titles 1,000; Per Subs 100
Special Services for the Deaf - Bks on deafness & sign lang; Staff with knowledge of sign lang
Open Mon-Fri 8-4:30

GL SANDUSKY COUNTY LAW LIBRARY*, 100 N Park Ave, No 106, 43420-2493. SAN 327-3849. Tel: 419-334-6165. FAX: 419-334-6156. E-mail: lawlibrary@co.sandusky.oh.us. *Librn,* Cyndi Zienta

J TERRA STATE COMMUNITY COLLEGE LIBRARY*, 2830 Napoleon Rd, 43420-9670. SAN 313-5136. Tel: 419-559-2318. Interlibrary Loan Service Tel: 419-559-2316. Reference Tel: 419-559-2383. Administration Tel: 419-559-2317. Toll Free Tel: 800-334-3886. FAX: 419-334-3667. E-mail: library@terra.edu. Web Site: www.terra.edu/support/library.html. *Librn,* Claire Keating; E-mail: ckeating01@terra.edu; Staff 4 (MLS 2, Non-MLS 2)
Founded 1971. Enrl 3,485; Highest Degree: Associate
Library Holdings: Bk Titles 20,000; Bk Vols 28,000; Per Subs 375
Automation Activity & Vendor Info: (Acquisitions) Innovative Interfaces, Inc - Millenium; (Cataloging) Innovative Interfaces, Inc - Millenium; (Circulation) Innovative Interfaces, Inc - Millenium; (Course Reserve) Innovative Interfaces, Inc - Millenium; (ILL) Innovative Interfaces, Inc - Millenium; (OPAC) Innovative Interfaces, Inc - Millenium; (Serials) Innovative Interfaces, Inc - Millenium
Database Vendor: Baker & Taylor, EBSCOhost, Innovative Interfaces, Inc, Innovative Interfaces, Inc, OHIONET, Safari Books Online, YBP Library Services
Wireless access
Function: Archival coll, Audio & video playback equip for onsite use, Bks on CD, Computers for patron use, Copy machines, Fax serv, Handicapped accessible, ILL available, Music CDs, Ref & res, Scanner, Tax forms, Wheelchair accessible
Partic in Ohio Library & Information Network

GALION

P GALION PUBLIC LIBRARY ASSOCIATION*, 123 N Market St, 44833. SAN 313-5144. Tel: 419-468-3203. FAX: 419-468-7298. E-mail: galion@galionlibrary.org. Web Site: www.galion.lib.oh.us, www.galionlibrary.org. *Dir,* J Victoria Eckenrod; Staff 14 (MLS 2, Non-MLS 12)
Founded 1901. Pop 12,000; Circ 230,244
Jan 2010-Dec 2010 Income $743,310, State $486,106, Locally Generated Income $8,034, Parent Institution $57,172. Mats Exp $732,785, Books $39,032, Per/Ser (Incl. Access Fees) $6,480, AV Equip $3,255, AV Mat $14,895, Electronic Ref Mat (Incl. Access Fees) $3,722. Sal $273,513 (Prof $45,000)
Library Holdings: Audiobooks 2,617; AV Mats 13,621; CDs 2,462; DVDs 4,503; Electronic Media & Resources 2; Large Print Bks 3,016; Bk Vols 86,871; Per Subs 102
Special Collections: Local & Ohio History (Ohio Room)
Automation Activity & Vendor Info: (Cataloging) Innovative Interfaces, Inc; (Circulation) Innovative Interfaces, Inc; (OPAC) Innovative Interfaces, Inc
Database Vendor: EBSCOhost, Electric Library, Gale Cengage Learning, ProQuest
Wireless access
Open Mon-Thurs 9-8:30, Fri 9-6, Sat 9-5
Friends of the Library Group

GALLIPOLIS

P GALLIA COUNTY DISTRICT LIBRARY, Dr Samuel L Bossard Memorial Library, Seven Spruce St, 45631. SAN 313-5152. Tel: 740-446-7323. Administration Tel: 740-446-7323, Ext 235. FAX: 740-446-1701. E-mail: bossard@oplin.org. Web Site: www.bossard.lib.oh.us. *Dir,* Deborah Saunders; E-mail: saundede@oplin.org; *Ref Librn,* Randall Fulks; *Circ Mgr,* Susan Randolph; *Mobile Serv Mgr,* Jack Mowery; *Youth Serv Prog Coordr,* Rachael Barker; *Dep Fiscal Officer,* Kimberely Trout; Staff 1 (MLS 1)
Founded 1899. Pop 32,000; Circ 196,006
Library Holdings: AV Mats 39,008; DVDs 4,934; e-books 142,285; Bk Vols 88,851; Per Subs 2,949
Special Collections: Depression Era Fiction (O O McIntyre Coll); Genealogy, local & surrounding counties. Municipal Document Depository
Subject Interests: Genealogy, Local hist
Automation Activity & Vendor Info: (Acquisitions) Innovative Interfaces, Inc; (Cataloging) Innovative Interfaces, Inc; (Circulation) Innovative Interfaces, Inc; (OPAC) Innovative Interfaces, Inc; (Serials) Innovative Interfaces, Inc
Database Vendor: EBSCOhost, Gale Cengage Learning
Wireless access
Function: 24/7 Online cat, Activity rm, Adult bk club, Bks on CD, Children's prog, Computer training, Computers for patron use, Copy machines, Electronic databases & coll, Equip loans & repairs, Fax serv, Handicapped accessible, Home delivery & serv to Sr ctr & nursing homes, Homebound delivery serv, ILL available, Magazines, Music CDs, Notary serv, Outreach serv, OverDrive digital audio bks, Photocopying/Printing, Preschool outreach, Prog for adults, Prog for children & young adult, Pub access computers, Ref & res, Senior computer classes, Senior outreach, Story hour, Summer & winter reading prog, Summer reading prog, Tax forms, Web-catalog, Wheelchair accessible
Partic in Southeast Regional Library System
Special Services for the Deaf - Assistive tech
Open Mon-Fri 9am-8pm, Sat 9-5, Sun 1-5
Restriction: 24-hr pass syst for students only
Friends of the Library Group

GAMBIER

C KENYON COLLEGE LIBRARY & INFORMATION SERVICES*, Olin Library & Gordon Keith Chalmers Memorial Library, 103 College Dr, 43022-9624. SAN 313-5187. Tel: 740-427-5186. Circulation Tel: 740-427-5187. Interlibrary Loan Service Tel: 740-427-5692. Reference Tel. 740-427-5691. Administration Tel: 740-427-5571. FAX: 740-427-5272. Administration FAX: 740-427-5941. Web Site: lbis.kenyon.edu. *VPres, Libr & Info Serv,* Ronald Griggs; *Dir, Info Syst,* Janice R Kijak; *Dir of Libr Serv,* Amy E Badertscher; *Dir, User Serv,* Paul Mollard; Staff 21 (MLS 9, Non-MLS 12)
Founded 1824. Enrl 1,640; Fac 176; Highest Degree: Bachelor
Library Holdings: Bk Vols 420,385; Per Subs 8,185
Special Collections: Kenyon College Archives; Kenyon Review Archives; Letters of Charles Pettit McIlvane; Letters of Philander Chase; Typography Coll; William Butler Yeats Publications (Riker Coll). Oral History; US Document Depository
Wireless access
Function: Accelerated reader prog
Partic in Ohio Library & Information Network; OHIONET; The Five Colleges of Ohio
Restriction: Hospital employees & physicians only

GARRETTSVILLE

P PORTAGE COUNTY DISTRICT LIBRARY*, 10482 South St, 44231. SAN 356-6854. Tel: 330-527-5082. Toll Free Tel: 800-500-5179. FAX: 330-527-4370. TDD: 330-677-4278. Web Site: www.portagecounty.lib.oh.us. *Dir,* Cecilia Swanson; *Asst Dir, Coll Develop Mgr,* Corrine Alldridge
Founded 1935. Pop 85,000
Library Holdings: Bk Vols 259,361; Per Subs 530
Automation Activity & Vendor Info: (Acquisitions) Innovative Interfaces, Inc; (Cataloging) Innovative Interfaces, Inc; (Circulation) Innovative Interfaces, Inc; (ILL) Innovative Interfaces, Inc; (OPAC) Innovative Interfaces, Inc; (Serials) Innovative Interfaces, Inc
Partic in Northeast Ohio Regional Library System
Open Mon-Wed 10-8, Thurs & Sat 10-5, Fri 12-5
Friends of the Library Group
Branches: 5
AURORA MEMORIAL, 115 E Pioneer Trail, Aurora, 44202-9349, SAN 356-6889. Tel: 330-562-6502. FAX: 330-562-2084. *Mgr,* Cheryl Chlysta
Founded 1966
Library Holdings: Bk Vols 76,000
Open Mon, Tues & Thurs 10-8, Wed & Sat 10-5, Fri 12-5
Friends of the Library Group
GARRETTSVILLE BRANCH, 10482 South St, 44231. Tel: 330-527-4378. Toll Free Tel: 800-500-6504. FAX: 330-527-4370. *Mgr,* Kathleen Kozup
Founded 1936
Library Holdings: Bk Vols 65,000
Open Mon-Wed 10-8, Thurs & Sat 10-5, Fri 12-5
Friends of the Library Group
PIERCE STREETSBORO, 8990 Kirby Lane, Streetsboro, 44241-1723, SAN 356-6943. Tel: 330-626-4458. FAX: 330-626-1737. *Mgr,* Michelle Dillon
Founded 1976
Library Holdings: Bk Vols 42,179
Open Mon-Wed 10-8, Thurs & Sat 10-5, Fri 12-5
Friends of the Library Group

RANDOLPH BRANCH, 1639 State Rte 44, Randolph, 44265. (Mail add: PO Box 368, Randolph, 44265-0368), SAN 356-6927. Tel: 330-325-7003. FAX: 330-325-7740. *Mgr,* Norma McDonough
Founded 1981
Library Holdings: Bk Vols 22,699
Open Mon & Tues 10-8, Wed-Fri 10-5, Sat 10-2
Friends of the Library Group

WINDHAM BRANCH, 9647 E Center St, Windham, 44288, SAN 356-6978. Tel: 330-326-3145. FAX: 330-326-2490. *Mgr,* Kathleen Baum
Founded 1945
Library Holdings: Bk Vols 22,985
Open Mon 9-6, Tues & Fri 9-5, Wed 10-6, Thurs 10-5
Friends of the Library Group

Bookmobiles: 2

GERMANTOWN

P GERMANTOWN PUBLIC LIBRARY*, 51 N Plum St, 45327. SAN 313-5209. Tel: 937-855-4001. FAX: 937-855-6098. E-mail: germantown@oplin.org. Web Site: www.germantown.lib.oh.us. *Dir,* Joe Knueven; *Asst Dir,* Gillian Izor; *Youth Serv Coordr,* Savannah McCoy; Staff 3 (MLS 2, Non-MLS 1)
Founded 1888. Pop 11,500; Circ 216,012
Library Holdings: Bk Titles 94,993; Per Subs 79
Special Collections: Local History (Germantown Historical Coll), bks, pamphlets
Automation Activity & Vendor Info: (Cataloging) Evergreen; (Circulation) Evergreen; (ILL) OCLC FirstSearch; (OPAC) Evergreen
Wireless access
Function: After school storytime, AV serv, CD-ROM, Computer training, Copy machines, Digital talking bks, E-Reserves, Fax serv, Handicapped accessible, Home delivery & serv to Sr ctr & nursing homes, Homebound delivery serv, Homework prog, ILL available, Mail & tel request accepted, Music CDs, Outside serv via phone, mail, e-mail & web, Photocopying/Printing, Preschool outreach, Prog for adults, Prog for children & young adult, Ref & res, Spoken cassettes & CDs, Summer reading prog, Tax forms, Telephone ref, VHS videos, Video lending libr, Wheelchair accessible
Partic in Miami Valley Librs; Ohio Public Library Information Network
Open Mon-Thurs 10-8, Fri & Sat 10-5

GIRARD

P GIRARD FREE LIBRARY*, 105 E Prospect St, 44420-1899. SAN 313-5217. Tel: 330-545-2508. Circulation Tel: 330-545-2508, Ext 308. Reference Tel: 330-545-2508, Ext 301. Administration Tel: 330-545-2508, Ext 303. FAX: 330-545-8213. Web Site: www.girard.lib.oh.us. *Dir,* Rose Ann Lubert; E-mail: lubertro@oplin.org; *Asst Dir, Syst Adminr,* Sondra K Fisher; E-mail: fisherso@oplin.org; *Acq Librn,* Michelle H Ducklin; E-mail: michaelene0911@yahoo.com; *Ch,* Maria F Selak; E-mail: selakma@oplin.org; *Ref Librn, Web Coordr,* Colleen A Keller; E-mail: kellerco@oplin.org; *YA Librn,* Sarah H Gilpin; E-mail: soundnfury98@yahoo.com; *Cataloger,* Mary C Barnes; E-mail: barnesma@oplin.org; *Fiscal Officer,* Pamela S D'Amore; E-mail: psdamore@aol.com; Staff 15 (MLS 2, Non-MLS 13)
Founded 1919. Pop 11,000; Circ 133,491
Jul 2010-Jun 2011 Income $915,302, State $661,732, Locally Generated Income $218,770. Mats Exp $95,085, Books $41,893, Per/Ser (Incl. Access Fees) $9,022, AV Mat $7,494, Electronic Ref Mat (Incl. Access Fees) $36,676. Sal $382,639
Library Holdings: AV Mats 7,578; Bk Vols 67,706; Per Subs 120
Special Collections: World War II Coll
Subject Interests: Biographies, Cooking, Hist, Lit, Music, Soc issues
Automation Activity & Vendor Info: (Cataloging) SirsiDynix; (Circulation) SirsiDynix; (OPAC) SirsiDynix
Database Vendor: ProQuest
Wireless access
Function: Adult bk club, Copy machines, e-mail serv, Electronic databases & coll, Fax serv, Handicapped accessible, Homebound delivery serv, ILL available, Music CDs, Online ref, Online searches, Preschool outreach, Prog for children & young adult, Spoken cassettes & CDs, Summer reading prog, Tax forms, VHS videos, Wheelchair accessible
Partic in Northeast Ohio Regional Library System
Open Mon-Thurs 9-8, Fri 9-5, Sat 10-4
Friends of the Library Group

GNADENHUTTEN

P GNADENHUTTEN PUBLIC LIBRARY*, 160 N Walnut St, 44629. (Mail add: PO Box 216, 44629-0216), SAN 313-5225. Tel: 740-254-9224. FAX: 740-254-9841. Web Site: www.gnaden.lib.oh.us. *Dir,* Erin Barlow; E-mail: barlower@oplin.org; *Youth Serv,* Emily Crilley; Staff 5 (Non-MLS 5)
Founded 1936. Pop 5,082; Circ 37,000
Jul 2005-Jun 2006 Income $151,000. Mats Exp $28,500, Books $15,000, Per/Ser (Incl. Access Fees) $2,500, AV Equip $7,000, AV Mat $4,000. Sal $79,000
Library Holdings: AV Mats 700; Large Print Bks 220; Bk Titles 22,197; Bk Vols 25,082; Per Subs 72; Talking Bks 477
Subject Interests: Early Ohio hist, Indians, Moravian missions
Automation Activity & Vendor Info: (Cataloging) Follett Software; (Circulation) Follett Software; (OPAC) Follett Software
Wireless access
Partic in Molo Regional Library System
Open Mon-Thurs 9-8, Fri 9-5, Sat 9-12

GRAFTON

P GRAFTON - MIDVIEW PUBLIC LIBRARY*, 983 Main St, 44044-1492. SAN 313-5233. Tel: 440-926-3317. FAX: 440-926-3000. Web Site: www.graftonpl.lib.oh.us. *Dir,* Adele Infante; Staff 13 (MLS 1, Non-MLS 12)
Founded 1944. Pop 21,000; Circ 190,000
Jan 2009-Dec 2009 Income $507,012, State $503,000, Locally Generated Income $4,012. Mats Exp $86,294. Sal $281,565 (Prof $66,788)
Library Holdings: Audiobooks 1,169; AV Mats 8,818; Bks on Deafness & Sign Lang 28; CDs 1,591; DVDs 4,083; Electronic Media & Resources 78; Large Print Bks 1,253; Bk Titles 60,024; Videos 1,897
Special Collections: Automotive Repair Manuals Coll; Local Author Coll; Local History Coll
Automation Activity & Vendor Info: (Cataloging) TLC (The Library Corporation); (Circulation) TLC (The Library Corporation); (OPAC) TLC (The Library Corporation)
Database Vendor: ProQuest
Wireless access
Function: After school storytime, Bks on cassette, Bks on CD, Children's prog, Computer training, Computers for patron use, Copy machines, e-mail serv, E-Reserves, Electronic databases & coll, Family literacy, Fax serv, Free DVD rentals, Handicapped accessible, Homework prog, ILL available, Music CDs, Online cat, Online ref, Outreach serv, Photocopying/Printing, Preschool outreach, Prog for adults, Prog for children & young adult, Pub access computers, Ref serv available, Ref serv in person, Scanner, Senior computer classes, Story hour, Summer reading prog, Tax forms, Teen prog, Telephone ref, VHS videos, Web-catalog, Wheelchair accessible
Partic in Northeast Ohio Regional Library System; Ohio Public Library Information Network
Open Mon-Thurs 10-8, Fri 10-5, Sat 1-5
Friends of the Library Group

GRANVILLE

C DENISON UNIVERSITY LIBRARIES, William Howard Doane Library, Seeley G Mudd Learning Center, 400 W Loop, 43023. (Mail add: PO Box 805, 43023-0805), SAN 313-5241. Tel: 740-587-6235. Interlibrary Loan Service Tel: 740-587-6431. Reference Tel: 740-587-6682. Administration Tel: 740-587-6225. FAX: 740-587-6285. Circulation FAX: 740-587-8280. E-mail: rector@denison.edu, reference@denison.edu. *Dir of Libr,* BethAnn Zambella; Tel: 740-587-6215, Fax: 740-587-6285, E-mail: zambellab@denison.edu; *Dep Dir,* Mary Webb Prophet; Tel: 740-587-6512, Fax: 740-587-6285, E-mail: prophet@denison.edu; *Asst Dir, Coll & Scholarly Res,* Earl Griffith; Tel: 740-587-6619, Fax: 740-587-6285, E-mail: griffith@denison.edu; *Asst Dir, Educ & Res Serv,* Debra Andreadis; Tel: 740-587-5653, Fax: 740-587-6285, E-mail: andreadisd@denison.edu; *Fine Arts Liaison Librn,* Shannon Robinson; Tel: 740-587-6688, Fax: 740-587-6285, E-mail: robinsons@denison.edu, *Humanities Liaison Librn,* Josh Finnell; Tel: 740-587-8651, Fax: 740-587-6285, E-mail: finnellj@denison.edu; *Natural Sci Liaison Librn,* Dr Moriana Garcia; Tel: 740-587-5714, Fax: 740-587-6285, E-mail: garciam@denison.edu; *Soc Sci Liaison Librn,* Roger Kosson; Tel: 740-587-6389, Fax: 740-587-6285, E-mail: kossonr@denison.edu; *Spec Coll Librn, Univ Archivist,* Sasha Griffin; Tel: 740-587-6399, Fax: 740-587-6285, E-mail: griffins@denison.edu; Staff 9 (MLS 9)
Founded 1831. Enrl 2,166; Fac 226; Highest Degree: Bachelor
Jul 2013-Jun 2014 Income $3,559,630. Mats Exp $1,380,930, Books $449,994, Per/Ser (Incl. Access Fees) $678,958, Other Print Mats $40,500, Micro $35,775, AV Mat $31,844, Electronic Ref Mat (Incl. Access Fees) $157,012, Presv $27,347. Sal $1,185,428 (Prof $611,191)
Library Holdings: AV Mats 40,617; CDs 32,027; DVDs 8,590; e-books 912,952; e-journals 24,154; Electronic Media & Resources 394; Microforms 128,390; Bk Vols 323,851; Per Subs 24,154
Special Collections: US Document Depository
Automation Activity & Vendor Info: (Acquisitions) Innovative Interfaces, Inc; (Cataloging) Innovative Interfaces, Inc; (Circulation) Innovative Interfaces, Inc; (Course Reserve) Innovative Interfaces, Inc; (ILL) Innovative Interfaces, Inc; (OPAC) Innovative Interfaces, Inc; (Serials) Innovative Interfaces, Inc
Database Vendor: ABC-CLIO, Alexander Street Press, ARTstor, Cambridge Scientific Abstracts, Cinahl, CIOS (Communication Institute for Online Scholarship), CQ Press, Dialog, EBSCO Information Services, EBSCOhost, Gale Cengage Learning, ISI Web of Knowledge, JSTOR, LexisNexis, McGraw-Hill, OCLC FirstSearch, ProQuest, Wilson - Wilson Web

Wireless access
Function: Archival coll, Art exhibits, Audio & video playback equip for onsite use, Audiobks via web, AV serv, CD-ROM, Computers for patron use, Copy machines, Doc delivery serv, e-mail & chat, Electronic databases & coll, Equip loans & repairs, Exhibits, Free DVD rentals, ILL available, Learning ctr, Music CDs, Online cat, Online info literacy tutorials on the web & in blackboard, Online ref, Online searches, Orientations, Photocopying/Printing, Ref serv available, Telephone ref, VHS videos, Web-catalog
Partic in OCLC Online Computer Library Center, Inc; Ohio Library & Information Network; OHIONET; The Five Colleges of Ohio
Open Mon-Thurs 8:30am-2am, Fri 8:30am-9pm, Sat 10:30-9, Sun 10:30am-2am
Restriction: Open to students, fac & staff, Use of others with permission of librn

P GRANVILLE PUBLIC LIBRARY*, 217 E Broadway, 43023-1398. SAN 313-525X. Tel: 740-587-0196. FAX: 740-587-0197. Web Site: www.granvillelibrary.org. *Dir,* Charlie Hansen; E-mail: chansen@granvillelibrary.org; *Head, Info & Prog Serv,* Julia Walden; E-mail: jwalden@granvillelibrary.org; *Ch,* Sarah Simpson; E-mail: ssimpson@granvillelibrary.org; *Circ Mgr,* Amy Deeds; E-mail: adeeds@granvillelibrary.org; *Ref & Teen Librn,* Emily Shellhouse; E-mail: eshellhouse@granvillelibrary.org; *Fiscal Officer,* Patrick McGonagle; *Tech Serv,* Sarah Baker; E-mail: sbaker@granvillelibrary.org; Staff 11.5 (MLS 3, Non-MLS 8.5)
Founded 1912. Pop 12,939; Circ 295,634
Library Holdings: AV Mats 5,305; Bk Titles 65,323; Per Subs 150
Automation Activity & Vendor Info: (Cataloging) SirsiDynix; (Circulation) SirsiDynix; (ILL) OCLC WorldShare Interlibrary Loan; (OPAC) SirsiDynix
Wireless access
Partic in SEO (Serving Every Ohioan) Library Center
Open Mon-Thurs 9-9, Fri & Sat 9-6
Friends of the Library Group

GRATIS

P MARION LAWRENCE MEMORIAL LIBRARY*, 15 E Franklin St, 45330. Tel: 937-787-3502. FAX: 937-787-3502. *Librn,* Penny Johnston
Circ 5,101
Library Holdings: Bk Vols 14,426; Per Subs 58
Automation Activity & Vendor Info: (Cataloging) SirsiDynix; (Circulation) SirsiDynix; (OPAC) SirsiDynix
Partic in Miami Valley Librs
Open Mon-Thurs 10-8, Sat 10-3

GREENVILLE

GL GREENVILLE LAW LIBRARY ASSOCIATION*, Darke County Law Library, 124 W Fifth St, 45331. SAN 327-3865. Tel: 937-547-9741. FAX: 937-547-9743. *Librn,* Eileen Litchfield; Staff 1 (Non-MLS 1)
Founded 1875
Library Holdings: Bk Vols 8,500
Open Tues & Thurs 9am-11am, Wed 11-1
Restriction: Non-circulating to the pub

P GREENVILLE PUBLIC LIBRARY*, 520 Sycamore St, 45331-1438. SAN 313-5284. Tel: 937-548-3915. FAX: 937-548-3837. Web Site: www.greenville-publiclibrary.org. *Dir,* John L Vehre, Jr; E-mail: vehrejjo@oplin.org; *Asst Dir,* Susi Halley; Staff 3 (MLS 1, Non-MLS 2)
Founded 1883. Pop 25,000; Circ 268,000
Jan 2006-Dec 2006 Income $1,047,000, State $968,000, Parent Institution $79,000. Mats Exp $213,000, Books $160,000, Per/Ser (Incl. Access Fees) $15,000, AV Mat $20,000, Electronic Ref Mat (Incl. Access Fees) $15,000, Presv $3,000. Sal $490,000 (Prof $60,000)
Library Holdings: Bk Vols 100,000; Per Subs 211
Special Collections: Annie Oakley Coll; Genealogy of Darke County Coll; Saint Clair Coll; Sheet Music Coll; Signed Limited Editions Coll. State Document Depository
Automation Activity & Vendor Info: (Cataloging) Innovative Interfaces, Inc; (Circulation) Innovative Interfaces, Inc; (OPAC) Innovative Interfaces, Inc
Wireless access
Function: AV serv, Games & aids for the handicapped, Home delivery & serv to Sr ctr & nursing homes, Homebound delivery serv, ILL available, Magnifiers for reading, Online searches, Photocopying/Printing, Prog for children & young adult, Summer reading prog
Mem of Miami Valley Libraries
Special Services for the Deaf - TTY equip
Special Services for the Blind - Magnifiers; Production of talking bks
Open Mon-Thurs 9-8, Fri 9-6, Sat 9-4
Friends of the Library Group
Bookmobiles: 1

GROVE CITY

P SOUTHWEST PUBLIC LIBRARIES*, SPL Admin, 3359 Park St, 43123. SAN 356-6439. Tel: 614-875-6716. FAX: 614-875-2219. Web Site: www.swpl.org/. *Dir,* Mark M Shaw; Tel: 614-875-6716, Ext 119, E-mail: mshaw@swpl.org; *Head, Tech Serv,* Patrick Crossen; E-mail: pcrossen@swpl.org; *Circ Serv Librn,* Katie Geddes; *Tech Serv Librn,* Debra Wittkop; E-mail: dwittkop@swpl.org; *Adult Serv, Ref Serv,* Bethanne Johnson; E-mail: bjohnson@swpl.org; *Youth Serv,* Lore Lehr; E-mail: llehr@swpl.org; Staff 15 (MLS 11, Non-MLS 4)
Founded 1891. Pop 120,900; Circ 1,200,000
Library Holdings: Bk Vols 267,000; Per Subs 380
Special Collections: Local History Coll. Oral History
Publications: Happenings (Newsletter); The Update
Partic in Discovery Place Librs; OCLC Online Computer Library Center, Inc; Ohio Public Library Information Network; OHIONET
Open Mon-Thurs 9:30-9, Fri & Sat 9:30-6
Friends of the Library Group
Branches: 1
WESTLAND AREA LIBRARY, 4740 W Broad St, Columbus, 43228, SAN 356-6498. Tel: 614-878-1301. FAX: 614-878-3454. *Libr Mgr,* Michele Lowe; *Ad,* John Kazalia; *Circ Serv Librn,* Denise Southworth; *Youth Serv Librn,* Mary Allen
Friends of the Library Group

HAMILTON

L BUTLER COUNTY LAW LIBRARY ASSOCIATION*, Ten Journal Sq, Ste 200, 45011. SAN 313-5292. Tel: 513-887-3455. FAX: 513-887-3696. Web Site: www.bclawlib.org. *Dir,* Joe D Hodnicki; E-mail: hodnickija@butlercountyohio.org; Staff 1 (MLS 1)
Founded 1889
Library Holdings: Bk Vols 40,000; Per Subs 150
Automation Activity & Vendor Info: (Cataloging) EOS International; (Circulation) EOS International; (OPAC) EOS International; (Serials) EOS International
Publications: Bibliographies; Newsletter (Bi-monthly); User's Guide
Partic in OHIONET
Open Mon-Fri 8:30-4:30

M FORT HAMILTON HOSPITAL*, Sohn Memorial Library, 630 Eaton Ave, 45013. SAN 313-5306. Tel: 513-867-2248, 513-867-2870. FAX: 513-867-2558. *Mgr,* Tracie Neal
Library Holdings: Bk Vols 1,109; Per Subs 28
Database Vendor: UpToDate
Partic in Cincinnati Area Health Sci Libr Asn
Restriction: Staff use only

P LANE PUBLIC LIBRARIES*, 300 N Third St, 45011-1629. SAN 356-6587. Tel: 513-894-7156. Reference Tel: 513-894-7158. Administration Tel: 513-894-0113. FAX: 513-894-2718. Administration FAX: 513-844-6535. E-mail: comments@lanepl.org. Web Site: www.lanepl.org. *Dir,* Joseph Greenward; E-mail: j.greenward@lanepl.org; *Libr Mgr,* Carol Bowling; Tel: 513-894-7156, Ext 110, E-mail: c.bowling@lanepl.org, Staff 13.81 (MLS 13.81)
Founded 1866. Pop 185,142; Circ 2,364,966
Jan 2009-Dec 2009 Income (Main Library and Branch(s)) $5,205,085, State $4,853,549, Locally Generated Income $310,586, Other $40,950. Mats Exp $790,998, Books $545,535, Per/Ser (Incl. Access Fees) $35,431, AV Mat $157,704, Electronic Ref Mat (Incl. Access Fees) $52,328. Sal $2,531,840
Library Holdings: CDs 3,234; DVDs 49,552; e-books 1,919; Bk Vols 505,816; Per Subs 643; Videos 4,135
Special Collections: George Cummins Local History Room; Smith Library of Regional History
Automation Activity & Vendor Info: (Acquisitions) SirsiDynix; (Cataloging) SirsiDynix; (Circulation) SirsiDynix; (OPAC) SirsiDynix
Database Vendor: EBSCOhost, Gale Cengage Learning, OCLC FirstSearch, SirsiDynix, Wilson - Wilson Web
Wireless access
Function: Adult bk club, Bk club(s), Bk reviews (Group), Bks on cassette, Bks on CD, CD-ROM, Children's prog, Computer training, Computers for patron use, Copy machines, Digital talking bks, E-Reserves, Electronic databases & coll, Fax serv, Free DVD rentals, Handicapped accessible, Holiday prog, ILL available, Jazz prog, Music CDs, Online cat, Online ref, Online searches, Prog for adults, Prog for children & young adult, Ref serv available, Senior computer classes, Spoken cassettes & CDs, Spoken cassettes & DVDs, Story hour, Summer reading prog, Tax forms, Teen prog, Telephone ref, VHS videos, Web-catalog, Wheelchair accessible
Partic in OCLC Online Computer Library Center, Inc; OHIONET
Open Mon-Thurs 10-8, Fri & Sat 10-5, Sun 1-5
Friends of the Library Group

Branches: 2
FAIRFIELD LANE LIBRARY, 1485 Corydale Dr, Fairfield, 45014, SAN 356-6641. Tel: 513-858-3238. FAX: 513-858-3298. *Br Mgr,* Cynthia Stafford; E-mail: c.stafford@lanepl.org; Staff 3.74 (MLS 2.8, Non-MLS 0.94)
Circ 1,255,531
Open Mon-Thurs 9-8, Fri & Sat 9-6, Sun 1-5
Friends of the Library Group
SMITH LIBRARY OF REGIONAL HISTORY
See Separate Entry in Oxford, Ohio
Bookmobiles: 2

HARRISON

S AMERICAN WATCHMAKERS-CLOCKMAKERS INSTITUTE LIBRARY*, 701 Enterprise Dr, 45030-1696. SAN 324-573X. Tel: 513-367-9800. Toll Free Tel: 866-367-2924. FAX: 513-367-1414. Web Site: www.awi-net.org. *Mem Serv Librn,* Maureen Seals; E-mail: mseals@awci.com
Founded 1960
Library Holdings: Bk Vols 1,400; Per Subs 6
Subject Interests: Clock historical, Hist of time, Jewelry, Repair, Watch
Publications: AWI Library Index; Horological Times
Restriction: Mem only

HIGHLAND HILLS

S GLOBAL ISSUES RESOURCE CENTER LIBRARY*, Cuyahoga Community College, Education Ctr Bldg, Rm 115, 4250 Richmond Rd, 44122. SAN 323-4274. Tel: 216-987-2231. Web Site: www.tri-c.edu/community/globalissues/pages/home.aspx. *Dir,* Joanne Lewis; E-mail: joanne.lewis@tri-c.edu; Staff 3 (MLS 3)
Library Holdings: Bk Titles 2,000; Per Subs 30
Special Collections: Conflict Resolution; Curricula; Energy; Environment; Global Education
Publications: Audio-Visual Catalog; Bibliographies On Energy Issues, Enviromental Concerns & Global Education; Games & Simulations Catalog; Resources to Teach About Conflict Resolution
Partic in CLEVE-NET; Northeast Ohio Regional Library System
Friends of the Library Group

HILLSBORO

P HIGHLAND COUNTY DISTRICT LIBRARY, Ten Willettsville Pike, 45133. SAN 356-6730. Tel: 937-393-3114. FAX: 937-393-2985. E-mail: highlandco@highlandco.org. Web Site: www.highlandco.org. *Dir,* Jennifer West; E-mail: westje@oplin.org; Staff 23 (MLS 3, Non-MLS 20)
Founded 1898. Pop 42,833; Circ 672,197
Library Holdings: AV Mats 16,808; Bk Vols 158,215; Per Subs 371
Special Collections: State Document Depository
Subject Interests: Genealogy, Investment, Local hist
Automation Activity & Vendor Info: (Cataloging) SirsiDynix; (Circulation) SirsiDynix
Database Vendor: SirsiDynix
Wireless access
Function: ILL available
Special Services for the Blind - Bks on cassette; Bks on CD; Large print bks
Open Mon-Thurs 10-8, Fri & Sat 10-5
Branches: 3
GREENFIELD BRANCH, 1125 W Jefferson St, Greenfield, 45123, SAN 356-6765. Tel: 937-981-3772. FAX: 937-981-5177. *Mgr,* Margaret Magee
Open Mon-Thurs 10-7, Fri 10-5, Sat 10-3
LEESBURG BRANCH, 240 E Main, Leesburg, 45135, SAN 356-679X. Tel: 937-780-7295. FAX: 937-780-7295. *Mgr,* Sharon Aukeman
Pop 4,000
Open Mon-Thurs 10-7, Fri 10-5, Sat 10-3
LYNCHBURG BRANCH, 102 S Main St, Lynchburg, 45142, SAN 356-682X. Tel: 937-364-2511. FAX: 937-364-2511. *Mgr,* Elaine Williams
Open Mon-Thurs 10-7, Fri 10-5, Sat 10-3

GL HIGHLAND COUNTY LAW LIBRARY*, Courthouse, 105 N High St, 45133. SAN 327-3903. Tel: 937-393-4863. FAX: 937-393-6878. *Librn,* Michelle Vanzant-Salyer; Staff 1 (Non-MLS 1)
Library Holdings: Bk Vols 8,000; Per Subs 25
Subject Interests: Civil law, Criminal law, Domestic law
Partic in Ohio Asn of Regional Law Libr
Open Mon-Fri 9-3
Restriction: Open to pub with supv only

J SOUTHERN STATE COMMUNITY COLLEGE LIBRARY, 100 Hobart Dr, 45133-9487. SAN 325-3260. Tel: 937-393-3431, Ext 2680, 937-695-0307, Ext 3680. Toll Free Tel: 800-628-7722, Ext 2680 (Ohio only). FAX: 937-393-9370, 937-695-8093. Web Site: lrc.sscc.edu. *Librn,* Angel Mootispaw; Tel: 740-333-5115, E-mail: amootispaw@sscc.edu; *Mgr, Libr Serv,* ReBecca Griffith; Tel: 937-393-3431, Ext 2684, E-mail: rgriffith@sscc.edu; *Mgr, Libr Serv,* Kari Jones; Tel: 740-333-5115, Ext 5681, E-mail: kjones@sscc.edu; *ILL,* Amanda Lyons; Tel: 937-393-3431, Ext 2681, E-mail: alyons@sscc.edu; Staff 4 (MLS 1, Non-MLS 3)
Founded 1985. Enrl 2,200; Fac 47; Highest Degree: Associate
Library Holdings: AV Mats 995; e-books 5,904; Bk Titles 40,856; Bk Vols 42,512; Per Subs 214
Special Collections: Gateway to Appalachia Resources Center; Southern Ohio Genealogical Society Coll
Subject Interests: Children's lit, Educ, Genealogy, Med, Nursing, Teaching
Automation Activity & Vendor Info: (Acquisitions) Innovative Interfaces, Inc; (Cataloging) OCLC; (Circulation) Innovative Interfaces, Inc; (Course Reserve) Innovative Interfaces, Inc; (ILL) OCLC; (OPAC) Innovative Interfaces, Inc; (Serials) Innovative Interfaces, Inc
Database Vendor: EBSCOhost, Innovative Interfaces, Inc, LexisNexis, Newsbank, OCLC FirstSearch, Wilson - Wilson Web
Wireless access
Function: AV serv, Distance learning, Doc delivery serv, For res purposes, Handicapped accessible, Health sci info serv, Homebound delivery serv, ILL available, Large print keyboards, Online searches, Photocopying/Printing, Prog for children & young adult, Ref serv available, Satellite serv, Telephone ref, Wheelchair accessible, Workshops
Partic in Ohio Library & Information Network; OHIONET; SouthWest Ohio & Neighboring Libraries; Southwestern Ohio Council for Higher Education

HIRAM

C HIRAM COLLEGE LIBRARY, 11694 Hayden St, 44234. (Mail add: PO Box 67, 44234-0067), SAN 313-5330. Tel: 330-569-5354, 330-569-5489. Interlibrary Loan Service Tel: 330-569-5359. Administration Tel: 330-569-5353. FAX: 330-569-5491. Web Site: library.hiram.edu. *Dir,* David Everett; E-mail: everettdd@hiram.edu; *Archivist, Spec Coll Librn,* Jennifer Morrow; Tel: 330-569-5361, E-mail: morrowjs@hiram.edu; *Syst/Electronic Res Librn,* Chris Schmidt; Tel: 330-569-5363, E-mail: schmidtcj@hiram.edu; *Doc, Ref,* Jeffery Wanser; Tel: 330-569-5358, E-mail: wanserjc@hiram.edu; *ILL,* Terri Foy; E-mail: foytm@hiram.edu; Staff 6 (MLS 4, Non-MLS 2)
Founded 1900. Enrl 1,281; Fac 82; Highest Degree: Master
Jul 2013-Jun 2014 Income $828,064. Mats Exp $289,754, Books $42,489, Per/Ser (Incl. Access Fees) $182,591, AV Mat $2,321, Electronic Ref Mat (Incl. Access Fees) $62,353. Sal $313,657 (Prof $179,973)
Library Holdings: CDs 15,723; DVDs 1,736; e-books 83,598; e-journals 9,028; Bk Vols 225,766; Per Subs 159; Videos 9,714
Special Collections: Education (Burke Aaron Hinsdale Coll, Textbooks 1773 to present & E B Wakefield Coll), corresp, ms; History (James A Garfield Coll & Henry Family Papers), corresp, ms; Literature (Nicholas Vachel Lindsay Coll & Juvenile Literature Coll 1828 to present), bks, corresp, ms, per. State Document Depository; US Document Depository
Subject Interests: Biol, Humanities
Automation Activity & Vendor Info: (Acquisitions) Innovative Interfaces, Inc; (Cataloging) Innovative Interfaces, Inc; (Circulation) Innovative Interfaces, Inc; (OPAC) Innovative Interfaces, Inc; (Serials) Innovative Interfaces, Inc
Database Vendor: Alexander Street Press, EBSCOhost, Innovative Interfaces, Inc, ISI Web of Knowledge, JSTOR, LexisNexis, Mergent Online, Newsbank, OCLC WorldShare Interlibrary Loan, RefWorks, Safari Books Online, YBP Library Services
Wireless access
Function: Archival coll, ILL available, Photocopying/Printing, Ref serv available, Telephone ref
Publications: The Flyleaf (Newsletter)
Partic in Ohio Library & Information Network; OHIONET
Open Mon-Thurs 8am-11pm, Fri 8-5, Sat 9-5, Sun 3-11
Restriction: Circ limited, Non-circulating to the pub
Friends of the Library Group

HOLGATE

P HOLGATE COMMUNITY LIBRARY*, 204 Railway Ave, 43527. SAN 313-5349. Tel: 419-264-7965. FAX: 419-264-1261. Web Site: library.norweld.lib.oh.us/holgate. *Librn,* Lynn Swary
Founded 1921. Pop 3,000; Circ 31,273
Library Holdings: Bk Titles 25,000; Per Subs 170
Automation Activity & Vendor Info: (Cataloging) SirsiDynix; (Circulation) SirsiDynix; (OPAC) SirsiDynix
Partic in NORWELD
Open Mon-Wed 12-7, Thurs & Sat 9-12, Fri 12-5

HOMER

P HOMER PUBLIC LIBRARY*, 385 South St NW, 43027. (Mail add: PO Box 49, 43027-0049), SAN 313-5357. Tel: 740-892-2020. FAX: 740-892-2036. E-mail: homer@oplin.org. Web Site: www.homer.lib.oh.us. *Dir,* Chet Geiger; E-mail: geigerch@oplin.org; Staff 3 (Non-MLS 3)
Founded 1895. Circ 36,600
Library Holdings: AV Mats 3,100; Bk Titles 30,000; Bk Vols 35,000; Per Subs 115
Special Collections: Antique Tractors; Homer History; Victoria Claflin Woodhull
Subject Interests: Agr
Automation Activity & Vendor Info: (Circulation) Follett Software; (OPAC) Follett Software
Open Mon, Tues & Thurs 10-8, Wed 10-6, Fri 10-5, Sat 10-2

HUBBARD

P HUBBARD PUBLIC LIBRARY, 436 W Liberty St, 44425. SAN 313-5365. Tel: 330-534-3512. FAX: 330-534-7836. Web Site: www.beyond-books.org. *Dir,* Lorena Ferne Williams; E-mail: lorena@beyond-books.org; *Asst Dir,* Leslie Kimble; E-mail: leslie@beyond-books.org; *Tech Adminr,* Chris Wisniewski; E-mail: chris@beyond-books.org; *Youth Serv,* Mary Anne Russo; E-mail: maryanne@beyond-books.org; Staff 5 (MLS 4, Non-MLS 1)
Founded 1937. Pop 13,552; Circ 261,309
Subject Interests: Local hist
Automation Activity & Vendor Info: (Cataloging) SIRSI WorkFlows; (Circulation) SIRSI WorkFlows; (OPAC) BiblioCommons
Database Vendor: ALLDATA Online, Booklist Online, Brodart, EBSCOhost, Gale Cengage Learning, Ingram Library Services, LearningExpress, Newsbank, OHIONET, Overdrive, Inc, ReferenceUSA, SirsiDynix
Wireless access
Function: Bks on CD, Children's prog, Computer training, Computers for patron use, Copy machines, Digital talking bks, E-Reserves, Electronic databases & coll, Fax serv, Free DVD rentals, Govt ref serv, Handicapped accessible, Homebound delivery serv, ILL available, Microfiche/film & reading machines, Music CDs, Notary serv, Online cat, OverDrive digital audio bks, Photocopying/Printing, Printer for laptops & handheld devices, Prog for adults, Prog for children & young adult, Pub access computers, Story hour, Summer reading prog, Tax forms, Teen prog, Telephone ref, Wheelchair accessible
Partic in Northeast Ohio Regional Library System; Ohio Public Library Information Network
Special Services for the Deaf - TTY equip
Open Mon-Thurs 9-8, Fri & Sat 9-5
Friends of the Library Group

HUDSON

P HUDSON LIBRARY & HISTORICAL SOCIETY*, 96 Library St, 44236-5122. SAN 313-5373. Tel: 330-653-6658. FAX: 330-650-3373. Web Site: www.hudsonlibrary.org. *Dir,* E Leslie Polott; *Asst Dir,* Position Currently Open; *Head, Ch, Head, Youth Serv,* Amelia Yunker; *Head, Circ,* Marcy Shipley; *Head, Ref,* Ellen Smith; *Head, Tech Serv,* Gretchen Myers; *Tech Coordr,* Marylyn Stanko; Staff 18 (MLS 13, Non-MLS 5)
Founded 1910. Pop 25,000, Circ 502,000
Library Holdings: Bk Vols 99,302; Per Subs 681
Special Collections: John Brown, Abolitionist Leader (Clarence S Gee), bks, holographs, pictures, clippings
Subject Interests: Genealogy
Automation Activity & Vendor Info: (Acquisitions) SirsiDynix; (Cataloging) SirsiDynix; (Circulation) SirsiDynix; (OPAC) SirsiDynix
Function: Archival coll, Art exhibits, CD-ROM, Handicapped accessible, Homebound delivery serv, ILL available, Music CDs, Online searches, Photocopying/Printing, Prog for adults, Prog for children & young adult, Ref serv available, Summer reading prog, VHS videos
Publications: Books to Bytes (Newsletter)
Partic in CLEVNET; Northeast Ohio Regional Library System
Open Mon-Thurs 9-9, Fri & Sat 9-5, Sun 12-5
Friends of the Library Group

HURON

C BOWLING GREEN STATE UNIVERSITY*, Firelands College Library, One University Dr, 2nd Flr, 44839-9791. SAN 313-5381. Tel: 419-433-5560, Ext 20739. Toll Free Tel: 800-322-4787 (Limited to area codes 419, 216, 440). FAX: 419-433-9696. E-mail: firelib@bgnet.bgsu.edu. Web Site: www.firelands.bgsu.edu/library/index.html. *Dir,* Sharon Britton; E-mail: sbritto@bgsu.edu; *Librn,* Pat Antonelli; E-mail: antonel@bgsu.edu; Staff 5 (MLS 2, Non-MLS 3)
Founded 1968. Enrl 2,055; Fac 49; Highest Degree: Bachelor
Jul 2005-Jun 2006 Income $317,277. Mats Exp $65,687, Books $31,057, Per/Ser (Incl. Access Fees) $21,248, Micro $6,640, AV Mat $232, Electronic Ref Mat (Incl. Access Fees) $6,510. Sal $251,456 (Prof $105,104)
Library Holdings: AV Mats 1,475; Bks on Deafness & Sign Lang 10; DVDs 13; Bk Titles 31,175; Bk Vols 41,340; Per Subs 249; Videos 734
Special Collections: Holocaust Teaching Resource Coll. State Document Depository
Subject Interests: Firelands of the Conn Western Reserve
Automation Activity & Vendor Info: (Cataloging) OCLC; (Circulation) Innovative Interfaces, Inc; (Course Reserve) Innovative Interfaces, Inc; (ILL) OCLC; (OPAC) Innovative Interfaces, Inc; (Serials) Innovative Interfaces, Inc
Database Vendor: ABC-CLIO, ACM (Association for Computing Machinery), Agricola, American Psychological Association (APA), ARTstor, BioOne, Cambridge Scientific Abstracts, CQ Press, ebrary, EBSCOhost, H W Wilson, infoUSA, JSTOR, LexisNexis, OCLC FirstSearch, Oxford Online, ProQuest, ReferenceUSA, SerialsSolutions, Wilson - Wilson Web
Wireless access
Function: Archival coll, Audio & video playback equip for onsite use, Computers for patron use, Copy machines, Doc delivery serv, E-Reserves, Electronic databases & coll, ILL available, Instruction & testing, Online ref, Online searches, Photocopying/Printing, Ref & res, Ref serv available, VHS videos
Publications: Firelands College Library Newsletter
Partic in Ohio Library & Information Network; OHIONET
Open Mon-Thurs (Winter) 8am-8:30pm, Fri 8-5, Sat 9-1; Mon-Thurs (Summer) 7:30-6, Fri 7:30am-11:30am

P HURON PUBLIC LIBRARY, 333 Williams St, 44839. SAN 313-539X. Tel: 419-433-5009. FAX: 419-433-7228. E-mail: huron@huronlibrary.org. Web Site: www.huronlibrary.org. *Dir,* Benjamin Reid; E-mail: breid@huronlibrary.org; *Adult Serv,* Shirley Mann; *Circ, Tech Serv,* Cindy Carruthers; Staff 13 (MLS 3, Non-MLS 10)
Founded 1933. Pop 10,551; Circ 176,310
Wireless access
Partic in CLEVNET
Special Services for the Deaf - TTY equip
Special Services for the Blind - Bks & mags in Braille, on rec, tape & cassette; Cassette playback machines
Open Mon-Thurs 9-8:30, Fri & Sat 9-5, Sun 1-5
Friends of the Library Group

INDEPENDENCE

CM KENT STATE UNIVERSITY COLLEGE OF PODIATRIC MEDICINE*, Morton & Norma Seidman Memorial Library, 6000 Rockside Woods Blvd, 44131. SAN 313-3710. Tel: 216-916-7505. Web Site: www2.kent.edu/library. *Dir, Libr Serv,* Donna Perzeski; Tel: 216-916-7506, E-mail: dperzesk@kent.edu; *Med Librn,* Leo Mallias
Enrl 300; Fac 25; Highest Degree: Doctorate
Library Holdings: Bk Vols 17,000; Per Subs 105
Automation Activity & Vendor Info: (Cataloging) Professional Software; (Circulation) Professional Software; (OPAC) Professional Software
Open Mon-Fri 7am-10pm, Sat 9am-10pm, Sun 12-10

IRONTON

P BRIGGS LAWRENCE COUNTY PUBLIC LIBRARY*, Ironton Library, 321 S Fourth St, 45638. SAN 313-5446. Tel: 740-532-1124. FAX: 740-532-4948. E-mail: irontonbranch@briggslibrary.org. Web Site: www.briggslibrary.com. *Exec Dir,* Joseph Jenkins; E-mail: jjenkins@briggslibrary.org; *Ch Serv,* Cheryl Blankenship; *Adult Serv,* Lori Shafer; *Youth Serv Librn,* Rachel Webb; Staff 49 (MLS 4, Non-MLS 45)
Founded 1881. Pop 61,834; Circ 402,481
Library Holdings: Bk Titles 128,604; Bk Vols 141,133; Per Subs 293
Subject Interests: Genealogy, Local hist
Automation Activity & Vendor Info: (Cataloging) TLC (The Library Corporation); (Circulation) TLC (The Library Corporation); (OPAC) TLC (The Library Corporation)
Publications: Book Mark (Newsletter)
Partic in Ohio Public Library Information Network
Special Services for the Blind - Lending of low vision aids; Talking bks & player equip
Open Mon-Thurs 9-8:30, Fri & Sat 9-5:30
Friends of the Library Group
Branches: 4
CHESAPEAKE BRANCH, 11054 County Rd 1, Cheseapeake, 45619. Tel: 740-867-3390. FAX: 740-867-4881. *Br Mgr,* Pam Murphy; E-mail: pammurphy@briggslibrary.org; *Ch Serv Librn,* Cheryl Blankenship; Staff 2 (MLS 2)
Pop 60,000; Circ 66,000
Library Holdings: CDs 1,200; Bk Titles 20,000; Per Subs 30
Open Mon, Wed & Thurs 10-5:30, Tues 10-7:30, Fri & Sat 10-5

PROCTORSVILLE BRANCH, 410 Elizabeth St, Proctorville, 45669. Tel: 740-886-6697. FAX: 740-886-7175. Web Site: www.briggslibrary.org. *Librn,* Pam Murphy; E-mail: pmurphy@briggslibrary.org
Founded 1990
Open Mon, Tues & Wed 10-5:30, Thurs 10-7:30, Fri & Sat 10-5
Friends of the Library Group

SOUTHERN, 317 Solida Rd, South Point, 45680. Tel: 740-377-2288. FAX: 740-377-9298. E-mail: aut@briggslibrary.org. *Br Mgr,* Alda Wagner; E-mail: awagner@briggslibrary.org
Open Mon 10-7:30, Tues-Thurs 10-5:30, Fri & Sat 10-5
Friends of the Library Group

SYMMES VALLEY BRANCH, 14778 State Rte 141, Willow Wood, 45696. Tel: 740-643-2086. FAX: 740-643-2086. *Br Mgr,* Tami Jones; E-mail: tjones@briggslibrary.org
Open Mon-Thurs (Winter) 3-8, Sat 10-3; Mon & Tues (Summer) 10-5:30, Wed, Thurs & Fri 10-3

Bookmobiles: 1

L LAWRENCE COUNTY LAW LIBRARY ASSOCIATION*, Lawrence County Courthouse, 4th Flr Annex, 111 S Fourth St, 45638-1586. SAN 313-5454. Tel: 740-533-0582. FAX: 740-533-1084. *Libr Dir,* Sharon K Bradshaw
Founded 1911
Library Holdings: Bk Titles 15,000

C OHIO UNIVERSITY*, Southern Campus, 1804 Liberty Ave, 45638-2296. SAN 313-5462. Tel: 740-533-4622. FAX: 740-533-4631. Web Site: www.southern.ohiou.edu/pages/s-library/index.htm. *Libr Dir,* Mary J Stout; Tel: 740-533-4649, E-mail: stout@ohio.edu; *Libr Assoc,* Cheryl Seals; E-mail: seals@ohio.edu; *Libr Asst,* Brian Kelley; E-mail: kelleyb2@ohio.edu; *Libr Spec,* Carmeleeta Stewart; E-mail: stewartc@ohio.edu; Staff 4 (MLS 1, Non-MLS 3)
Founded 1956. Enrl 1,903; Highest Degree: Master
Jul 2005-Jun 2006. Mats Exp $72,007. Sal $199,376
Library Holdings: Bk Vols 25,000; Per Subs 200
Special Collections: Catherine Toothman Coll; David E Carter Coll
Automation Activity & Vendor Info: (Acquisitions) Innovative Interfaces, Inc; (Cataloging) Innovative Interfaces, Inc; (Circulation) Innovative Interfaces, Inc; (OPAC) Innovative Interfaces, Inc; (Serials) Innovative Interfaces, Inc
Database Vendor: EBSCOhost, Innovative Interfaces, Inc, LexisNexis, OCLC FirstSearch, ProQuest
Wireless access
Partic in OCLC Online Computer Library Center, Inc
Special Services for the Blind - ZoomText magnification & reading software
Open Mon-Thurs 8am-9pm, Fri 8-5, Sat 8-Noon

JACKSON

P JACKSON CITY LIBRARY*, 21 Broadway St, 45640-1695. SAN 313-5470. Tel: 740-286-4111. FAX: 740-286-3438. E-mail: jackson@oplin.org. Web Site: www.youseemore.com/jacksoncity. *Dir,* Laura Thorne; E-mail: thornela@oplin.org; *Youth Serv,* Sharon Leali; E-mail: lealish@oplin.org; Staff 1 (MLS 1)
Founded 1901. Pop 27,181; Circ 73,210
Library Holdings: Bk Vols 45,000; Per Subs 135
Special Collections: Appalachian Children's Books; Jackson County History & Genealogy
Subject Interests: Appalachian children's books, Genealogy, Jackson County hist
Open Mon-Thurs 9-8, Fri & Sat 9-5

L JACKSON COUNTY LAW LIBRARY*, 226 E Main St, 45640-1764. (Mail add: PO Box 882, 45640-0882). Tel: 740-286-8054. *In Charge,* Ann Callahan
Open Mon-Fri 8-4

JEFFERSON

L ASHTABULA COUNTY LAW LIBRARY*, County Courthouse, 25 W Jefferson St, 44047. SAN 372-1957. Tel: 440-576-3690. FAX: 440-576-1506. *Librn,* Jennifer Lynn Feher; Staff 40 (Non-MLS 40)
Automation Activity & Vendor Info: (Cataloging) LibraryWorld, Inc
Database Vendor: Westlaw
Wireless access
Open Mon-Fri 8:30-4:30
Restriction: Non-circulating

P HENDERSON MEMORIAL PUBLIC LIBRARY ASSOCIATION*, 54 E Jefferson St, 44047-1198. SAN 313-5489. Tel: 440-576-3761. FAX: 440-576-8402. Web Site: www.henderson.lib.oh.us. *Dir,* Edward Worso; E-mail: worsoed@oplin.org; Staff 3 (MLS 3)
Founded 1883. Pop 5,500; Circ 100,000
Library Holdings: Bk Vols 55,000
Automation Activity & Vendor Info: (Cataloging) BiblioCommons; (Circulation) BiblioCommons; (OPAC) BiblioCommons
Database Vendor: ALLDATA Online
Wireless access
Partic in Northeast Ohio Regional Library System
Open Mon-Thurs 9-8, Fri 9-5, Sat & Sun 1-5
Friends of the Library Group

KENT

P KENT FREE LIBRARY*, 312 W Main, 44240-2493. SAN 313-5497. Tel: 330-673-4414. FAX: 330-673-0226. Web Site: www.kentfreelibrary.org. *Dir,* Stacey Richardson; E-mail: stacey.richardson@kentfreelibrary.org; *Commun Serv, Spec Serv Mgr,* Kristen Pool; Staff 10 (MLS 10)
Founded 1892. Pop 33,704
Jan 2008-Dec 2008 Income $1,659,981, State $1,609,881, Other $50,100. Mats Exp $254,691, Books $192,337, Per/Ser (Incl. Access Fees) $26,068, AV Mat $36,286. Sal $832,665 (Prof $540,061)
Library Holdings: AV Mats 15,976; Bk Titles 160,686; Per Subs 363
Automation Activity & Vendor Info: (Acquisitions) Innovative Interfaces, Inc; (Cataloging) Innovative Interfaces, Inc; (Circulation) Innovative Interfaces, Inc; (OPAC) Innovative Interfaces, Inc; (Serials) Innovative Interfaces, Inc
Database Vendor: Innovative Interfaces, Inc
Wireless access
Partic in Northeast Ohio Regional Library System; Portage Library Consortium
Open Mon-Thurs 10-8, Fri & Sat 10-6, Sun 1-5

C KENT STATE UNIVERSITY LIBRARIES*, 1125 Risman Dr, 44242. (Mail add: PO Box 5190, 44242-0001), SAN 356-7001. Tel: 330-672-2962. Circulation Tel: 330-672-7905. Interlibrary Loan Service Tel: 330-672-2670. Reference Tel: 330-672-3150. Information Services Tel: 330-672-3045. FAX: 330-672-4811. Interlibrary Loan Service FAX: 330-672-2265. Reference FAX: 330-672-3964. E-mail: library@kent.edu. Web Site: www.kent.edu/library. *Dean,* James K Bracken; *Asst Dean, Admin Serv,* Mark Pike; Tel: 330-672-1841, E-mail: jmpike@kent.edu; *Asst Dean, Learning & Outreach Serv,* Ken Burhanna; Tel: 330-672-1660, E-mail: kburhann@kent.edu; *Asst Dean, Tech Serv,* Tom Klingler; Tel: 330-672-1646, E-mail: tk@kent.edu; *Head, Access Serv,* Cindy Kristof; Tel: 330-672-1641, E-mail: ckristof@kent.edu; *Head, Cat,* Margaret Maurer; Tel: 330-672-1702, E-mail: mbmaurer@kent.edu; *Head, Ref Serv,* Kara Robinson; Tel: 330-672-1664, E-mail: krobinso@kent.edu; *Acq Librn,* Melissa Spohn; Tel: 330-672-1682, Fax: 330-672-3463, E-mail: mspohn@kent.edu; *Circ Mgr,* Robert Opper; Tel: 330-672-1671, E-mail: ropper@kent.edu; *Coll Mgt,* Maria Downey; Tel: 330-672-5000, E-mail: mdowney1@kent.edu; *Curator, Spec Coll & Univ Archives,* Cara Gilgenbach; Tel: 330-672-1677, E-mail: cgilgenb@kent.edu; *ILL,* Elizabeth Richardson; Tel: 330-672-2177, E-mail: earicha1@kent.edu; Staff 84 (MLS 36, Non-MLS 48)
Founded 1913. Enrl 26,980; Fac 881; Highest Degree: Doctorate
Library Holdings: Bk Vols 2,853,965; Per Subs 60,015
Special Collections: 19th & 20th Century American Literature Coll; Borowitz True Crime Coll; Contemporary American Poetry - especially James Broughton, Robert Duncan, Robert Frost, W C Williams; History of Books & Printing; Local Historical Archives Coll; May 4 Coll; Open Theater; Queen Marie of Rumania Coll; University Archives Coll. State Document Depository; UN Document Depository; US Document Depository
Automation Activity & Vendor Info: (Acquisitions) Innovative Interfaces, Inc; (Cataloging) Innovative Interfaces, Inc; (Circulation) Innovative Interfaces, Inc; (Course Reserve) Docutek; (ILL) OCLC; (Media Booking) Innovative Interfaces, Inc; (OPAC) Innovative Interfaces, Inc; (Serials) Innovative Interfaces, Inc
Database Vendor: EBSCOhost, LexisNexis, OCLC FirstSearch, OVID Technologies, ProQuest
Wireless access
Function: Res libr
Publications: Footnotes
Partic in Association of Research Libraries (ARL); Center for Research Libraries; OCLC Online Computer Library Center, Inc; Ohio Library & Information Network
Restriction: 24-hr pass syst for students only
Friends of the Library Group

Departmental Libraries:

FASHION, 131 Rockwell Hall, 44242-0001, SAN 377-6344. Tel: 330-672-9500. FAX: 330-672-9578. E-mail: fashionlibrary@kent.edu. Web Site: www.kent.edu/library/fashion. *Librn,* Tom Gates; Staff 1.5 (MLS 1.5)

MAP, 410 McGilvery Hall, 44242-0001. (Mail add: PO Box 5190, 44242-5190), SAN 356-701X. Tel: 330-672-2017. E-mail: maplibrary@kent.edu. Web Site: www.kent.edu/library/map. *Head of Libr,* Edith Scarletto. Subject Specialists: *Geog, Geol,* Edith Scarletto; Staff 0.5 (MLS 0.5)

Library Holdings: Bk Vols 3,000
Special Collections: California AAA Map Coll (Depository); GeoDEX AGS (Milwaukee); Sanborn Insurance Map & Atlas Coll
Subject Interests: Climate, Geog, Geol, Soils, Topography, Urban geog
Database Vendor: Innovative Interfaces, Inc

JOSEPH F MORBITO ARCHITECTURE LIBRARY, 309 Taylor Hall, 44242-0001. (Mail add: PO Box 5190, 44242-5190), SAN 328-7572. Tel: 330-672-2876. E-mail: archlibrary@kent.edu. Web Site: www.kent.edu/library/architecture. *Head, Archit Libr,* Tom Gates; Tel: 330-672-0931, E-mail: tgates@kent.edu; Staff 2 (MLS 1, Non-MLS 1)
Founded 1987. Enrl 550; Highest Degree: Master
Library Holdings: AV Mats 300; CDs 50; DVDs 25; Bk Vols 15,000; Per Subs 87
Special Collections: HABS & HAER Documentation, micro, print; HABS & HAER, print, micro; Historic Urban Plans & Views; Sanborn Fire Insurance Maps (online)
Subject Interests: Archit, Architects & firms, Architectural hist, Architectural styles, Bldg types, Drawing & model making, Historic presv, Landscape archit, Mat & methods, Prof practice, Site planning, Structures, Sustainable architecture, Urban planning
Database Vendor: YBP Library Services
Open Mon-Thurs 9-8, Fri 9-5, Sun (Fall & Spring) 4-8

PERFORMING ARTS, D-004 Music & Speech Ctr, 1325 Theatre Dr, 44242-0001. (Mail add: PO Box 5190, 44242), SAN 356-7052. Tel: 330-672-2004. FAX: 330-672-4482. E-mail: performingartslibrary@kent.edu. Web Site: www.kent.edu/library/performingarts. *Librn,* Joe Clark; Tel: 330-672-1667; Staff 3 (MLS 2, Non-MLS 1)
Enrl 400; Fac 40; Highest Degree: Doctorate
Library Holdings: CDs 5,000; DVDs 200; Music Scores 50,000; Bk Vols 90,000; Per Subs 150; Videos 600
Special Collections: Choralist Coll
Function: AV serv, Electronic databases & coll, Music CDs, Ref & res, VHS videos
Restriction: Open to students, fac & staff

KENTON

P MARY LOU JOHNSON HARDIN COUNTY DISTRICT LIBRARY, 325 E Columbus St, 43326-1546. SAN 313-5500. Tel: 419-673-2278. FAX: 419-674-4321. Web Site: mljlibrary.org. *Dir,* Samuel Norris; E-mail: norrissa@oplin.org; *Asst Dir,* Sharon Newman; *Cat,* Marilyn Holland; Staff 1 (MLS 1)
Founded 1853. Pop 34,000; Circ 174,000
Library Holdings: Bk Vols 56,000; Per Subs 120
Special Collections: Circulating Hand Puppets
Subject Interests: Genealogy
Wireless access
Partic in NORWELD
Open Mon-Thurs 9-8, Fri & Sat 9-5

KETTERING

CM KETTERING COLLEGE*, Learning Commons, 3737 Southern Blvd, 45429-1299. SAN 356-7060. Tel: 937-395-8053. FAX: 937-395-8861. Web Site: www.kcma.edu/library. *Dir,* John kissinger; E-mail: john.kissinger@kc.edu; *Cat,* Teresa Simmons; Tel: 937-395-8053, Ext 4, E-mail: teresa.simmons@kcma.edu; *Circ,* Ellen Mosher; Tel: 937-395-8053, Ext 3, E-mail: ellenmosher@kcma.edu; *Ref,* Kathy Salgado; Tel: 937-395-8053, Ext 6, E-mail: kathy.salgado@kcma.edu; Staff 3 (MLS 3)
Founded 1967. Enrl 900; Fac 45; Highest Degree: Master
Jan 2011-Dec 2011. Mats Exp $85,000, Books $55,000, AV Mat $30,000
Library Holdings: Bk Titles 24,065; Bk Vols 26,401; Per Subs 253
Subject Interests: Allied health, Nursing, Seventh Day Adventists
Automation Activity & Vendor Info: (Cataloging) Innovative Interfaces, Inc; (Circulation) Innovative Interfaces, Inc; (OPAC) Innovative Interfaces, Inc; (Serials) Innovative Interfaces, Inc
Database Vendor: EBSCOhost, Gale Cengage Learning, LexisNexis, OCLC FirstSearch, ProQuest
Wireless access
Partic in Ohio Library & Information Network; OHIONET; Southwestern Ohio Council for Higher Education
Open Mon-Thurs 8am-9pm, Fri 8-4:30, Sun Noon-5
Friends of the Library Group

KINGSVILLE

P KINGSVILLE PUBLIC LIBRARY*, 6006 Academy St, 44048-0057. (Mail add: PO Box 57, 44048-0057), SAN 313-5535. Tel: 440-224-0239. FAX: 440-224-0029. Web Site: www.kingsville.lib.oh.us. *Dir,* Mariana Branch; E-mail: branchma@oplin.org
Founded 1886. Circ 114,214
Library Holdings: Audiobooks 1,355; DVDs 2,307; Bk Vols 46,530; Per Subs 148; Videos 300
Special Collections: Local Estate Memoriabilia; Local History
Subject Interests: Circulating per, Current best sellers, Hobbies
Wireless access
Function: Handicapped accessible, Homebound delivery serv, Prog for children & young adult
Partic in Independently Cooperating Ashtabula Network (ICAN); Ohio Libr Coun
Special Services for the Deaf - TDD equip
Open Mon-Thurs 10-7, Fri & Sat 10-4
Friends of the Library Group

KINSMAN

P KINSMAN FREE PUBLIC LIBRARY*, 6420 Church St, 44428-9702. (Mail add: PO Box 166, 44428-0166), SAN 313-5543. Tel: 330-876-2461. FAX: 330-876-3335. Reference E-mail: Reference@kinsmanlibrary.org. Web Site: www.kinsmanlibrary.org. *Dir,* Darla Bates
Founded 1885. Pop 6,496; Circ 152,379
Special Collections: Clarence Darrow Coll; Dr Ernest L Scott Coll
Wireless access
Open Mon, Wed & Fri 9-5, Tues & Thurs 11-7, Sat 9-1
Friends of the Library Group

KIRTLAND

S HERB SOCIETY OF AMERICA LIBRARY*, 9019 Kirtland Chardon Rd, 44094. SAN 329-4978. Tel: 440-256-0514. FAX: 440-256-0541. E-mail: library@herbsociety.org. Web Site: www.herbsociety.org/library/index.php. *Librn,* Tara Coulter; Staff 1 (MLS 1)
Founded 1944
Library Holdings: Bk Vols 3,800; Per Subs 24; Videos 30
Special Collections: Rare Herbals
Subject Interests: Ethnobotany, Folklore, Herbs, Hort
Function: e-mail serv, Online cat, Ref serv in person
Special Services for the Blind - Braille bks
Open Mon-Thurs 9-5
Restriction: Circ to mem only, In-house use for visitors, Non-circulating of rare bks
Friends of the Library Group

S HOLDEN ARBORETUM*, Warren H Corning Library, 9500 Sperry Rd, 44094. SAN 313-6116. Tel: 440-946-4400, Ext 225. FAX: 440-256-5836. E-mail: holden@holdenarb.org. Web Site: www.holdenarb.org. *Librn,* Susan Swisher; E-mail: sswisher@holdenarb.org; Staff 2 (MLS 2)
Founded 1963
Library Holdings: Bk Titles 8,000; Bk Vols 9,000; Per Subs 60
Special Collections: Warren H Corning Horticulture Classics, 1200 vols
Subject Interests: Botany, Environ studies, Hort, Natural hist, Natural sci
Automation Activity & Vendor Info: (Cataloging) EOS International; (Circulation) EOS International; (OPAC) EOS International; (Serials) EOS International
Database Vendor: OCLC FirstSearch
Publications: Arbor Day Resources (List of materials available for use at the Corning Library); Native Woody Plant Resources (List of materials for use at the Corning Library)
Partic in Northeast Ohio Regional Library System
Open Tues-Sat 10-5

P KIRTLAND PUBLIC LIBRARY*, 9267 Chillicothe Rd, 44094. SAN 313-5551. Tel: 440-256-7323. FAX: 440-256-1372. E-mail: reference@kirtland.lib.oh.us. Web Site: www.kirtland.lib.oh.us. *Dir,* Jane R Carle; E-mail: jcarle@kirtland.lib.oh.us; *Ref Serv, Ad,* Jamie Breitsch; E-mail: jreitsch@kirtland.lib.oh.us; Staff 10 (MLS 3, Non-MLS 7)
Founded 1936. Pop 7,600; Circ 207,879
Library Holdings: AV Mats 5,177; Large Print Bks 2,130; Bk Titles 65,597; Per Subs 265; Talking Bks 2,343
Subject Interests: Local hist
Automation Activity & Vendor Info: (Circulation) SirsiDynix
Database Vendor: EBSCOhost, Gale Cengage Learning, OCLC FirstSearch, ProQuest, SirsiDynix
Function: Accessibility serv available based on individual needs
Partic in CLEVNET; Northeast Ohio Regional Library System
Open Mon-Thurs 9-9, Fri 9-6, Sat 9-5, Sun 12-4
Friends of the Library Group

J LAKELAND COMMUNITY COLLEGE LIBRARY*, 7700 Clocktower Dr, 44094-5198. SAN 313-6132. Tel: 440-525-7067. Circulation Tel: 440-525-7424. Reference Tel: 440-525-7425. FAX: 440-525-7602. E-mail: lakelandlibrary@lakelandcc.edu. Web Site: library.lakelandcc.edu. *Chairperson, Ref,* Michelle Rossman; E-mail: mrossman@lakelandcc.edu; Staff 10 (MLS 3, Non-MLS 7)
Founded 1967. Enrl 4,300
Library Holdings: Bk Titles 46,000; Bk Vols 57,000; Per Subs 600
Automation Activity & Vendor Info: (Acquisitions) Innovative Interfaces, Inc; (Cataloging) Innovative Interfaces, Inc; (Circulation) Innovative Interfaces, Inc; (Course Reserve) Innovative Interfaces, Inc; (Media

Booking) Innovative Interfaces, Inc; (OPAC) Innovative Interfaces, Inc; (Serials) Innovative Interfaces, Inc
Partic in Northeast Ohio Regional Library System; Ohio Library & Information Network

LAKEWOOD

S LAKEWOOD HISTORICAL SOCIETY LIBRARY*, 14710 Lake Ave, 44107. SAN 329-9546. Tel: 216-221-7343. E-mail: lakewoodhistory@bge.net. Web Site: lakewoodhistory.org. *Exec Dir,* Gregory Palumbo; *Curator,* Amanda Francazio; E-mail: curator@lakewoodhistory.org
Library Holdings: Bk Vols 200
Subject Interests: Lakewood, Rockport Township
Publications: Lakewood: The First Hundred Years
Restriction: Open by appt only

P LAKEWOOD PUBLIC LIBRARY*, 15425 Detroit Ave, 44107-3890. SAN 356-7125. Tel: 216-226-8275. Web Site: www.lakewoodpubliclibrary.org. *Dir,* James Crawford
Founded 1916. Pop 56,646
Wireless access
Open Mon-Sat 9-9, Sun 1-9
Friends of the Library Group
Branches: 1
MADISON, 13229 Madison Ave, 44107, SAN 356-715X. Tel: 216-228-7428.
Open Mon-Sat 9-9, Sun 1-5

LANCASTER

P FAIRFIELD COUNTY DISTRICT LIBRARY*, 219 N Broad St, 43130-3098. SAN 356-7184. Tel: 740-653-2745. FAX: 740-653-4199. TDD: 740-653-8282. Web Site: www.fcdlibrary.org. *Libr Dir,* Marilyn C Steiner; E-mail: msteiner@fcdlibrary.org; *Coordr, Circ & Customer Serv,* Rita Hiles; E-mail: rhiles@fcdlibrary.org; *Coordr, Info Tech & Tech Serv,* Ruchie Rice; E-mail: rrice@fcdlibrary.org; *Coordr, Pub Serv,* Rebecca Schaade; E-mail: bschaade@fcdlibrary.org; *Asst Coordr, Adult Serv,* Melanie McCormack; E-mail: mmccormack@fcdlibrary.org; *Asst Coordr, Youth Serv,* Shannon Smith; E-mail: ssmith@fcdlibrary.org; *Fiscal Officer,* Cathy Woodruff; E-mail: cwood@fcdlibrary.org; Staff 42 (MLS 8, Non-MLS 34)
Founded 1878. Pop 97,138; Circ 1,120,298
Jan 2011-Dec 2011 Income (Main Library and Branch(s)) $3,485,217, Locally Generated Income $949,953, Other $195,923. Mats Exp $367,000, Books $178,672, Per/Ser (Incl. Access Fees) $32,000, AV Equip $19,515, AV Mat $123,234, Electronic Ref Mat (Incl. Access Fees) $13,579. Sal $1,303,012
Library Holdings: Audiobooks 26,413; AV Mats 35,832; e-books 37,008; Electronic Media & Resources 1,309; Bk Vols 228,461; Per Subs 263
Special Collections: History of Fairfield County & Lancaster
Automation Activity & Vendor Info: (Acquisitions) Innovative Interfaces, Inc; (Cataloging) Innovative Interfaces, Inc; (Circulation) Innovative Interfaces, Inc; (ILL) OCLC; (OPAC) Innovative Interfaces, Inc; (Serials) Innovative Interfaces, Inc
Database Vendor: EBSCOhost, Gale Cengage Learning, Ingram Library Services, LearningExpress, Newsbank, OCLC WebJunction, OHIONET, Overdrive, Inc, World Book Online
Wireless access
Function: Adult bk club, Archival coll, Audiobks via web, Bk club(s), Bks on CD, CD-ROM, Children's prog, Computer training, Computers for patron use, Copy machines, E-Reserves, Electronic databases & coll, Exhibits, Free DVD rentals, Handicapped accessible, Holiday prog, Home delivery & serv to Sr ctr & nursing homes, ILL available, Magnifiers for reading, Mail & tel request accepted, Music CDs, Online cat, Online ref, Orientations, Outreach serv, OverDrive digital audio bks, Photocopying/Printing, Preschool outreach, Prog for adults, Prog for children & young adult, Pub access computers, Ref serv available, Ref serv in person, Senior computer classes, Story hour, Summer & winter reading prog, Tax forms, Teen prog, Telephone ref, Wheelchair accessible
Publications: Keywords (Quarterly)
Partic in Central Library Consortium (CLC); OCLC Online Computer Library Center, Inc
Special Services for the Deaf - Bks on deafness & sign lang; TDD equip
Special Services for the Blind - Bks on CD; Copier with enlargement capabilities; Extensive large print coll; Low vision equip; Playaways (bks on MP3)
Open Mon, Tues & Thurs 10-8, Wed & Sat 10-5, Fri 12-5, Sun 1-5
Friends of the Library Group
Branches: 4
BALTIMORE BRANCH, 205 E Market St, Baltimore, 43105, SAN 356-7214. Tel: 740-862-8505. *Br Mgr,* Debbie Fields; E-mail: dfields@fcdlibrary.org
Circ 118,761
Library Holdings: Bk Vols 28,176
Function: Bks on CD, CD-ROM, Computers for patron use, Copy machines, Free DVD rentals, Handicapped accessible, Holiday prog, ILL available, Music CDs, Photocopying/Printing, Prog for children & young adult, Ref serv available, Spoken cassettes & CDs, Summer & winter reading prog, Telephone ref, Wheelchair accessible
Open Mon & Wed 10-8, Fri 12-5, Sat 10-5
JOHNS MEMORIAL BRANCH, 116 E High St, Amanda, 43102. (Mail add: PO Box 279, Amanda, 43102-0279), SAN 329-2258. Tel: 740-969-2785. *Br Mgr,* Brenda Johnson; E-mail: bjohnson@fcdlibrary.org
Function: Bks on CD, CD-ROM, Computers for patron use, Copy machines, Digital talking bks, E-Reserves, Free DVD rentals, Handicapped accessible, Holiday prog, ILL available, Music CDs, Online cat, OverDrive digital audio bks, Prog for children & young adult, Ref serv available, Summer & winter reading prog, Tax forms
Open Tues & Thurs 10-8, Sat 10-5
Friends of the Library Group
NORTHWEST BRANCH, 2855 Helena Dr NW, Carroll, 43112. Tel: 740-756-4391. *Mgr, Tech Serv,* Samantha Betts; E-mail: sbetts@fcdlibrary.org
Circ 51,165
Function: Bks on CD, Computers for patron use, Copy machines, Free DVD rentals, Handicapped accessible, Holiday prog, ILL available, Music CDs, Online cat, OverDrive digital audio bks, Prog for children & young adult, Ref serv available, Summer & winter reading prog, Tax forms
Open Tues & Thurs 10-8, Fri 12-5
BREMEN RUSHCREEK MEMORIAL BRANCH, 200 School St, Bremen, 43107, SAN 356-7249. Tel: 740-569-7246. *Br Mgr,* Brenda Johnson; E-mail: bjohnson@fcdlibrary.org
Function: Bks on CD, CD-ROM, Computers for patron use, Copy machines, Free DVD rentals, Handicapped accessible, Holiday prog, ILL available, Music CDs, Online cat, OverDrive digital audio bks, Prog for children & young adult, Ref serv available, Summer & winter reading prog
Open Mon & Wed 10-8, Fri 10-5
Friends of the Library Group

C OHIO UNIVERSITY-LANCASTER LIBRARY*, Hannah V McCauley Library, 1570 Granville Pike, 43130-1097. SAN 313-5608. Tel: 740-654-6711, Ext 236. Reference Tel: 740-681-2609. Administration Toll Free Tel: 888-446-4468, Ext 221. FAX: 740-687-9497. E-mail: oul-library@ohio.edu. Web Site: www.lancaster.ohiou.edu/library. *Dir, Libr Serv,* Judy A Carey Nevin; Tel: 740-681-2611, E-mail: careynev@ohio.edu; *Coll Develop, Libr Instruction, Ref Librn,* Julia Robinson; Tel: 740-654-6711, Ext 222, E-mail: robinsj1@ohio.edu; *Acq, Instrul Media, Ser,* Joyce Mohler; Tel: 740-654-6711, Ext 621, E-mail: mohler@ohiou.edu; Staff 4 (MLS 3, Non-MLS 1)
Founded 1956. Enrl 2,300; Fac 150; Highest Degree: Master
Library Holdings: AV Mats 1,000; Bks on Deafness & Sign Lang 322; e-books 2,000; Bk Titles 55,000; Per Subs 267; Talking Bks 20
Special Collections: Charles Goslin Coll; Herbert M Turner Pioneer Coll
Automation Activity & Vendor Info: (Cataloging) OCLC; (Circulation) Innovative Interfaces, Inc; (Course Reserve) Innovative Interfaces, Inc; (OPAC) Innovative Interfaces, Inc; (Serials) Innovative Interfaces, Inc
Database Vendor: Innovative Interfaces, Inc
Function: AV serv, Computers for patron use, Copy machines, Doc delivery serv, E-Reserves, Equip loans & repairs, Exhibits, Free DVD rentals, Handicapped accessible, ILL available, Instruction & testing, Learning ctr, Online cat, Photocopying/Printing, Pub access computers, Ref serv in person, Scanner
Partic in OCLC Online Computer Library Center, Inc; Ohio Library & Information Network; OHIONET
Open Mon-Thurs 8am-9pm, Fri 8-3, Sat 10-2, Sun 1-5
Friends of the Library Group

S STATE OF OHIO DEPARTMENT OF CORRECTIONS*, Southeastern Correctional Institution Library, 5900 Bis Rd, 43130. Tel: 740-653-4324, Ext 2728. FAX: 740-654-4511. *Librn,* Lisa Carlisle; E-mail: lisa.carlisle@odrc.state.oh.us
Library Holdings: Bk Vols 6,000; Per Subs 30
Open Mon, Wed & Fri-Sun 8-4, Tues & Thurs 8-8

LEAVITTSBURG

S STATE OF OHIO DEPARTMENT OF CORRECTIONS*, Trumbull Correctional Institution Library, 5701 Burnette Rd, 44430. (Mail add: PO Box 901, 44430-0901). Tel: 330-898-0820, Ext 7408. FAX: 330-898-2011. *Librn,* Diane Filkorn; E-mail: diane.filkorn@odrc.state.oh.us
Library Holdings: Bk Vols 10,344; Per Subs 66
Restriction: Not open to pub

LEBANON

S LEBANON CORRECTIONAL INSTITUTION LIBRARY*, 3791 State Rd 63, PO Box 56, 45036. SAN 313-5624. Tel: 513-932-1211, Ext 3728. FAX: 513-932-5803. *Librn,* Billy Bailey; Staff 1 (MLS 1)
Founded 1961
Library Holdings: Bk Vols 12,000
Subject Interests: Law

P LEBANON PUBLIC LIBRARY*, 101 S Broadway, 45036. SAN 313-5632. Tel: 513-932-2665. FAX: 513-932-7323. Web Site: www.lebanonlibrary.org. *Dir,* Julie S Florence; *Adult Serv,* Mary Ann Mulford; *Ch Serv,* Connie LaVallee; *Ch Serv,* Lou Ann Studer; *Circ,* Paula Bradley
Founded 1904. Pop 45,000; Circ 408,000
Library Holdings: Bk Vols 153,000; Per Subs 70
Wireless access
Open Mon & Wed 10-8, Tues & Thurs 10-6, Fri & Sat 9-5

S WARREN COUNTY HISTORICAL SOCIETY*, Museum & Library, 105 S Broadway, 45036. SAN 327-7283. Tel: 513-932-1817. FAX: 513-932-8560. E-mail: wchs@wchsmuseum.org. Web Site: wchsmuseum.com. *Exec Dir,* Victoria Van Harlingen; *Educ Dir, Historian,* John J Zimkus
Founded 1945
Library Holdings: Bk Titles 10,000; Per Subs 20
Special Collections: Genealogical & History of Warren County & Southwest Ohio in General; Marcus Mote Coll; Russel Wright Coll; Shaker Coll

GL WARREN COUNTY LAW LIBRARY ASSOCIATION*, 500 Justice Dr, 45036. SAN 313-5640. Tel: 513-695-1381. FAX: 513-695-2947. *Dir,* Lisa M Cook; E-mail: cooklm@co.warren.oh.us
Library Holdings: Bk Vols 5,600
Special Collections: Ohio Law
Wireless access
Open Mon & Tues 1-4:30

LEETONIA

P LEETONIA COMMUNITY PUBLIC LIBRARY, 181 Walnut St, 44431. SAN 313-5659. Tel: 330-427-6635. FAX: 330-427-2378. E-mail: leetonialibrary@gmail.com. Web Site: www.leetonialibrary.org. *Dir,* Lisa Rohrbaugh; Staff 2.5 (MLS 2.5, Non-MLS 0)
Founded 1935. Pop 2,400; Circ 60,969
Jan 2014-Dec 2014 Income State $232,148. Mats Exp $18,500, Books $14,000, Per/Ser (Incl. Access Fees) $2,000, AV Mat $2,500. Sal $130,000
Library Holdings: Bk Vols 40,484; Per Subs 53
Wireless access
Partic in Northeast Ohio Regional Library System
Open Mon, Tues & Thurs 9:30-7, Wed, Fri & Sat 9:30-4
Friends of the Library Group

LIBERTY CENTER

P LIBERTY CENTER PUBLIC LIBRARY*, 124 East St, 43532. (Mail add: PO Box 66, 43532), SAN 313-5675. Tel: 419-533-5721. FAX: 419-533-4849. Web Site: www.libertycenterlibrary.org. *Dir,* Jessica Troyer; E-mail: director@libertycenterlibrary.org; *Dir, Teen Serv,* Jacklyn Farkas; E-mail: jfarkas@libertycenterlibrary.org; *Ch,* Arla Marie Fry; E-mail: afry@libertycenterlibrary.org; Staff 5 (Non-MLS 5)
Founded 1929. Pop 5,400; Circ 33,698
Library Holdings: AV Mats 1,346; Bk Vols 20,236; Per Subs 100
Automation Activity & Vendor Info: (Cataloging) SirsiDynix; (Circulation) SirsiDynix; (ILL) SirsiDynix; (OPAC) SirsiDynix
Database Vendor: EBSCOhost, Gale Cengage Learning, OCLC FirstSearch
Wireless access
Partic in NORWELD
Open Mon, Tues & Thurs 10-8, Wed & Fri 10-5, Sat 9-3
Friends of the Library Group

LIMA

S ALLEN COUNTY HISTORICAL SOCIETY*, Elizabeth M MacDonell Memorial, 620 W Market St, 45801-4604. SAN 313-5683. Tel: 419-222-9426. FAX: 419-222-0649. E-mail: acmuseum@wcoil.com. Web Site: www.allencountymuseum.org. *Dir,* Patricia Smith; *Curator,* Anna B Selfridge; E-mail: aselfridge@wcoil.com; Staff 1 (MLS 1)
Founded 1908
Library Holdings: Bk Titles 10,000; Per Subs 45
Special Collections: History of Ohio, Local History & Genealogy, archives, bks, clippings, micro, mss, photo; Labor, Railroad & Interurban History (John H Keller Railroad & Lima Locomotive Works Coll)
Automation Activity & Vendor Info: (Cataloging) EOS International
Function: Archival coll, Bus archives, For res purposes, ILL available, Newsp ref libr, Photocopying/Printing, Ref & res
Publications: Allen County Historical Society Newsletter; The Allen County Reporter
Open Tues-Sat 1-5
Restriction: Non-circulating, Not a lending libr, Open to pub for ref only, Pub use on premises

L ALLEN COUNTY LAW LIBRARY*, Court of Appeals, Rm 102, 204 N Main St, 45801-4456. SAN 313-5691. Tel: 419-223-1426. E-mail: lawbooks@bright.net. *Librn,* Bonnie Everett; Tel: 419-999-4272; Staff 2 (Non-MLS 2)
Library Holdings: Bk Vols 24,000; Per Subs 18
Function: Res libr
Restriction: Not open to pub, Private libr

G ALLEN OAKWOOD CORRECTIONAL INSTITUTION LIBRARY*, 2338 N West St, 45801. (Mail add: PO Box 4501, 45802), SAN 323-8237. Tel: 419-224-8000. *Librn,* Position Currently Open
Founded 1987
Library Holdings: Bks on Deafness & Sign Lang 4; DVDs 21; High Interest/Low Vocabulary Bk Vols 196; Large Print Bks 163; Bk Titles 14,168; Bk Vols 15,432; Per Subs 73; Videos 848
Special Collections: Afro-American Coll; Law Library; Native American Coll; Re-Entry Coll; Spanish Coll
Automation Activity & Vendor Info: (Acquisitions) Mandarin Library Automation; (Cataloging) Mandarin Library Automation; (Circulation) Mandarin Library Automation; (OPAC) Mandarin Library Automation
Database Vendor: LexisNexis
Special Services for the Blind - Bks on cassette; Bks on CD
Restriction: Non-circulating to the pub, Staff & inmates only

M LIMA MEMORIAL HOSPITAL*, Health Sciences Library, 1001 Bellefontaine Ave, 45804. SAN 313-5705. Tel: 419-228-3335. FAX: 419-226-5061.
Founded 1973
Library Holdings: Bk Titles 1,056; Bk Vols 1,307; Per Subs 60
Subject Interests: Med, Nursing, Pharmacology

P LIMA PUBLIC LIBRARY*, 650 W Market St, 45801. SAN 356-7303. Tel: 419-228-5113. FAX: 419-224-2669. Reference FAX: 419-228-0955. E-mail: lima@oplin.org. Web Site: www.limalibrary.com. *Dir,* Gary Fraser; E-mail: fraser@limalibrary.com; *Head, Adult Serv,* Deborah Keenehan; E-mail: keenehand@limalibrary.com; *Tech Coordr,* Position Currently Open; *Head of Br Serv, Head, Youth Serv,* Debbie Buettner; E-mail: buettnerd@limalibrary.com; Staff 48 (MLS 15, Non-MLS 33)
Founded 1884. Pop 89,689; Circ 847,557
Jan 2009-Dec 2009 Income (Main Library and Branch(s)) $3,121,883, State $2,979,723, Locally Generated Income $107,388, Other $34,772. Mats Exp $197,742, Books $110,925, Per/Ser (Incl. Access Fees) $15,194, AV Mat $49,453, Electronic Ref Mat (Incl. Access Fees) $22,170. Sal $1,111,774 (Prof $790,622)
Library Holdings: AV Mats 56,385; CDs 15,000; DVDs 17,463; e-books 8,334; Large Print Bks 12,474; Bk Vols 344,288; Per Subs 634; Talking Bks 6,774; Videos 896
Special Collections: Art-Architecture Coll; Jewish Culture; Judaic Materials (Dorfmann Coll), State Document Depository; US Document Depository
Subject Interests: Bibliographies
Automation Activity & Vendor Info: (Acquisitions) TLC (The Library Corporation); (Cataloging) TLC (The Library Corporation); (Circulation) TLC (The Library Corporation)
Database Vendor: EBSCOhost, Gale Cengage Learning, OCLC FirstSearch, TLC (The Library Corporation)
Wireless access
Function: e-mail & chat, e-mail serv, E-Reserves, Electronic databases & coll, Handicapped accessible, Home delivery & serv to Sr ctr & nursing homes, Homebound delivery serv, ILL available, Jail serv, Magnifiers for reading, Mail & tel request accepted, Music CDs, Newsp ref libr, Online cat, Online ref, Online searches, Outreach serv, Outside serv via phone, mail, e-mail & web, OverDrive digital audio bks, Photocopying/Printing, Preschool outreach, Prog for adults, Prog for children & young adult, Pub access computers, Ref & res, Ref serv available, Ref serv in person, Res performed for a fee, Senior computer classes, Spoken cassettes & DVDs, Story hour, Summer reading prog, Tax forms, Teen prog, Telephone ref, VHS videos, Video lending libr, Web-catalog, Wheelchair accessible
Partic in OCLC Online Computer Library Center, Inc; OHIONET
Special Services for the Blind - Talking bks
Open Mon, Tues & Thurs 9-8, Wed, Fri & Sat 9-5
Friends of the Library Group

Branches: 5

CAIRO BRANCH, 108 W Main St, Cairo, 45820. (Mail add: PO Box 216, Cairo, 45820-0216), SAN 356-7338. Tel: 419-641-7744. FAX: 419-641-6274. *Libr Assoc,* Kim Sciranka; Staff 2 (Non-MLS 2)
Library Holdings: Bk Vols 11,078
Open Mon & Tues 12-8, Thurs 10-6, Fri & Sat 9-1

ELIDA BRANCH, 200 W Main St, Elida, 45807, SAN 356-7362. Tel: 419-339-6097. FAX: 419-339-6554. *Libr Assoc,* Becky Henderson; E-mail: hendersonb@limalibrary.com; Staff 0.5 (Non-MLS 0.5)
Library Holdings: Bk Vols 13,235
Open Mon & Thurs 1:30-4:30 & 5:30-8, Tues 10-2

LAFAYETTE BRANCH, 225 E Sugar St, Lafayette, 45854, SAN 356-7427. Tel: 419-649-6482. FAX: 419-649-9488. *Libr Assoc,* Marcille Coates; Staff 0.5 (Non-MLS 0.5)
Library Holdings: Bk Vols 11,612
Open Mon & Thurs 12:30-8:30, Wed 5:30-8:30

MEDIAMOBILE, 650 W Market St, 45801. *Head, Tech Serv,* Sue Petty; Tel: 419-228-5113, Ext 126, Fax: 419-224-2669, E-mail: pettys@limalibrary.com; Staff 3 (MLS 1, Non-MLS 2)
Library Holdings: Bk Titles 5,000

SPENCERVILLE BRANCH, 2489 Wisher Dr, Spencerville, 45887, SAN 356-7451. Tel: 419-647-4307. FAX: 419-647-6393. *Libr Assoc,* Susanne Higgins; *Libr Assoc,* Vija Lee; E-mail: vlee@limalibrary.com; Staff 2 (MLS 1, Non-MLS 1)
Library Holdings: Bk Vols 19,884
Open Mon & Tues 12-8, Thurs 10-6, Fri & Sat 9-1
Friends of the Library Group

Bookmobiles: 1. Head, Tech Servs, Sue Petty

S OAKWOOD CORRECTIONAL FACILITY LIBRARY*, 3200 N West St, 45801-2048. SAN 313-5713. Tel: 419-225-8052, Ext 2263. FAX: 419-225-8000. *Librn,* Denise Carter; Staff 1 (MLS 1)
Library Holdings: Audiobooks 55; AV Mats 715; CDs 12; DVDs 47; Large Print Bks 50; Bk Vols 4,000; Per Subs 12; Videos 700
Subject Interests: Music, Video
Special Services for the Blind - Bks on cassette
Restriction: Not open to pub

M ST RITA'S MEDICAL CENTER*, Norman Browning Medical Library, 730 W Market St, 45801-4667. SAN 313-573X. Tel: 419-996-5842. FAX: 419-996-5166. *Coordr,* Kathy Herold
Founded 1948
Library Holdings: Bk Titles 450; Bk Vols 1,041; Per Subs 64
Subject Interests: Med
Wireless access
Partic in Medical Library Association (MLA); Ohio Health Sciences Library Association; Regional Med Libr - Region 3
Open Mon-Fri 8-4

LISBON

L COLUMBIANA COUNTY LAW LIBRARY*, 32 N Park Ave, 44432. SAN 327-7267. Tel: 330-420-3662. FAX: 330-424-7902. E-mail: lcolumbianalaw@neo.rr.com. Web Site: www.columbianacountylawlibrary.com. *Librn,* Ron Vest; E-mail: rvestccll@neo.rr.co
Library Holdings: Bk Vols 15,000
Database Vendor: Westlaw
Restriction: Not open to pub

P LEPPER PUBLIC LIBRARY*, 303 E Lincoln Way, 44432-1400. SAN 313-5748. Tel: 330-424-3117. FAX: 330-424-7343. Web Site: www.lepperlibrary.org. *Dir,* Nancy J Simpson; E-mail: simpsona@oplin.org; Staff 3 (MLS 3)
Founded 1897. Pop 58,000; Circ 179,448
Library Holdings: Bk Titles 45,102; Bk Vols 66,699; Per Subs 184
Subject Interests: Local hist
Automation Activity & Vendor Info: (Cataloging) Innovative Interfaces, Inc; (Circulation) Innovative Interfaces, Inc; (OPAC) Innovative Interfaces, Inc
Partic in Northeast Ohio Regional Library System; Ohio Public Library Information Network
Open Mon & Thurs 9-8, Tues & Wed 9-6, Fri & Sat 9-5
Bookmobiles: 1

LITHOPOLIS

P THE WAGNALLS MEMORIAL LIBRARY*, 150 E Columbus St, 43136. (Mail add: PO Box 217, 43136-0217), SAN 313-5756. Tel: 614-837-4765. FAX: 614-837-0781. Web Site: www.wagnallslibrary.org. *Dir,* Tami Morehart; E-mail: tmore@wagnallslibrary.org; Staff 8 (MLS 4, Non-MLS 4)
Founded 1925. Pop 6,500; Circ 140,000
Library Holdings: Bk Vols 90,000; Per Subs 200
Special Collections: Letters (O Henry to Mabel Wagnalls Jones Coll); Paintings (John Ward Dunsmore Coll); Poetry Hand Written & Framed (Edwin Markham Coll)
Automation Activity & Vendor Info: (Acquisitions) Horizon; (Cataloging) Horizon; (Circulation) Horizon; (Course Reserve) Horizon; (ILL) OCLC; (Media Booking) Horizon; (OPAC) Horizon; (Serials) Horizon
Database Vendor: SirsiDynix
Wireless access
Partic in Cent Libr Consortium
Open Mon-Thurs 10:30-7:30, Sat 10-2
Friends of the Library Group

LOGAN

P LOGAN-HOCKING COUNTY DISTRICT LIBRARY*, 230 E Main St, 43138. SAN 313-5764. Tel: 740-385-2348. FAX: 740-385-9093. Web Site: www.hocking.lib.oh.us. *Dir, Libr Serv,* Andrew D Herold; E-mail: heroldan@oplin.org; *Cat,* Nancy Johnson; *Cat,* Debra Wolfinger; Staff 12 (MLS 1, Non-MLS 11)
Founded 1948. Pop 29,000; Circ 287,575
Library Holdings: Bk Titles 115,590; Per Subs 265
Special Collections: Ohio History & Literature
Automation Activity & Vendor Info: (Acquisitions) Follett Software; (Cataloging) Follett Software; (Circulation) Follett Software; (OPAC) Follett Software; (Serials) Follett Software
Partic in Ohio Public Library Information Network
Open Mon-Thurs 9-8, Fri & Sat 9-5, Sun 1-5

Branches: 1

LAURELVILLE BRANCH, 16240 Maple St, Laurelville, 43135. (Mail add: PO Box 396, Laurelville, 43135-0396). Tel: 740-332-4700. FAX: 740-332-1379. *Librn,* Andrew Harold
Library Holdings: Bk Titles 2,000; Per Subs 70
Open Mon & Tues 9-7, Wed-Fri 9-5, Sat 9-3, Sun 1-5

LONDON

P LONDON PUBLIC LIBRARY*, 20 E First St, 43140. SAN 313-5772. Tel: 740-852-9543. FAX: 740-852-3691. Web Site: www.london.lib.oh.us. *Dir,* Mike Hensel; E-mail: henselmi@oplin.org; *Libr Serv Mgr,* Bryan Howard; E-mail: bhoward@mylondonlibrary.org; *Circ Supvr,* Karla Arnold; E-mail: karnold@mylondonlibrary.org; *Adult Prog Coordr,* Jack Phoenix; E-mail: jphoenix@mylondonlibrary.org; *Coordr, Outreach Serv,* Ruth Gorman; E-mail: rgorman@mylondonlibrary.org; *Youth Serv Coordr,* Mary Anne Wood; E-mail: mwood@mylondonlibrary.org; *Fiscal Officer,* Rebecca Stickel; E-mail: rstickel@mylondonlibrary.org; *AV Spec, Circ Spec,* Helen Keigley; E-mail: hkeigley@mylondonlibrary.org; Staff 14 (MLS 2, Non-MLS 12)
Founded 1905. Pop 11,500; Circ 110,000
Library Holdings: Bks on Deafness & Sign Lang 15; High Interest/Low Vocabulary Bk Vols 25; Bk Titles 36,158; Bk Vols 38,000; Per Subs 106
Automation Activity & Vendor Info: (Cataloging) Innovative Interfaces, Inc; (Circulation) Innovative Interfaces, Inc
Database Vendor: EBSCOhost, TLC (The Library Corporation), Wilson - Wilson Web
Wireless access
Partic in Miami Valley Librs
Open Mon-Thurs 9-8, Fri 10-6, Sat 10-5
Friends of the Library Group

GL MADISON COUNTY LAW LIBRARY*, One N Main, Rm 205, 43140-1068. SAN 313-5780. Tel: 740-852-9515. FAX: 740-852-7144. Web Site: www.co.madison.oh.us. *Librn,* Yvette Wilson; E-mail: ywilson@co.madison.oh.us
Founded 1903
Library Holdings: Bk Titles 20,000
Subject Interests: Fed, Ohio law, Statutes, Texts, Treatises
Database Vendor: LexisNexis, Westlaw
Partic in Westlaw
Open Mon-Fri 8-4

S STATE OF OHIO DEPARTMENT OF CORRECTIONS*, London Correctional Institute Library, 1580 State Rte 56 SW, 43140. (Mail add: PO Box 69, 43140-0069), SAN 313-5799. Tel: 740-852-2454. FAX: 740-852-1591. *Librn,* Gilbert Arthur Hurwood; E-mail: ghurwood@aol.com; Staff 9 (MLS 1, Non-MLS 8)
Founded 1970
Library Holdings: High Interest/Low Vocabulary Bk Vols 900; Bk Titles 16,000; Bk Vols 17,000; Per Subs 45; Spec Interest Per Sub 20
Subject Interests: Westerns
Automation Activity & Vendor Info: (Acquisitions) EOS International; (Cataloging) EOS International; (Circulation) EOS International

LORAIN

P LORAIN PUBLIC LIBRARY SYSTEM*, 351 Sixth St, 44052. SAN 356-7486. Tel: 440-244-1192. Interlibrary Loan Service Tel: 440-277-0672. Toll Free Tel: 800-322-7323. FAX: 440-244-1733. Interlibrary Loan Service FAX: 440-277-0676. Administration FAX: 440-244-4888. TDD: 440-246-3323. E-mail: contact-main@lpls.info. Web Site: www.lorain.lib.oh.us. *Dir,* Joanne Eldridge; Tel: 440-244-1192, Ext 227, E-mail: jeldridge@lpls.info; *Asst Dir,* Toni Whitney; Tel: 440-244-1192, Ext 225, E-mail: twhitney@lpls.info; Staff 25 (MLS 14, Non-MLS 11)
Founded 1901. Pop 135,275; Circ 2,076,434
Jan 2011-Dec 2011 Income (Main Library and Branch(s)) $8,842,248, State $3,674,544, Federal $818,723, Locally Generated Income $4,184,176, Other $164,805. Mats Exp $1,340,409, Books $669,435, Other Print Mats $194,903, AV Mat $393,571, Electronic Ref Mat (Incl. Access Fees) $82,500. Sal $3,865,416
Library Holdings: AV Mats 185,890; Bk Titles 483,366; Per Subs 1,216
Special Collections: Hageman & Toni Morrison Coll
Subject Interests: Ethnic studies, Genealogy, Hist, Spanish (Lang)
Automation Activity & Vendor Info: (Cataloging) SirsiDynix; (Circulation) SirsiDynix; (OPAC) SirsiDynix
Database Vendor: Baker & Taylor, BWI, EBSCOhost, Gale Cengage Learning, H W Wilson, LearningExpress, Medline, Newsbank, OCLC FirstSearch, OCLC WorldShare Interlibrary Loan, OHIONET, Overdrive, Inc, Oxford Online, ReferenceUSA, SirsiDynix, Wilson - Wilson Web, World Book Online
Wireless access
Function: Accelerated reader prog, Adult literacy prog, Audio & video playback equip for onsite use, Audiobks via web, Bilingual assistance for Spanish patrons, Bks on CD, CD-ROM, Children's prog, Computer training, Computers for patron use, Copy machines, Distance learning, Electronic databases & coll, Handicapped accessible, Holiday prog, Homebound delivery serv, Homework prog, ILL available, Instruction & testing, Music CDs, Online cat, Online ref, Online searches, Outreach serv, OverDrive digital audio bks, Printer for laptops & handheld devices, Prog for adults, Prog for children & young adult, Pub access computers, Ref serv available, Spanish lang bks, Summer & winter reading prog, Summer reading prog, Tax forms, Teen prog, Telephone ref, VHS videos, Video lending libr, Wheelchair accessible, Winter reading prog
Partic in CLEVNET; Northeast Ohio Regional Library System; OHIONET
Open Mon-Thurs 9-8:30, Fri & Sat 9-6, Sun (Winter) 1-4
Friends of the Library Group
Branches: 5
AVON BRANCH, 37485 Harvest Dr, Avon, 44011-2812, SAN 356-7516. Tel: 440-934-4743. FAX: 440-934-4165. E-mail: contact-avon@lpls.info. *Br Librn, Supvr,* Donna Kelly; E-mail: dkelly@lpls.info; *Libr Assoc II,* Nancy Tomek; E-mail: ntomek@lpls.info; Staff 5 (MLS 1, Non-MLS 4)
Founded 1956. Pop 21,193; Circ 233,971
Library Holdings: AV Mats 14,987; Bk Titles 42,388; Per Subs 155
Open Mon, Tues & Thurs 10-8:30, Wed 12-8:30, Fri 10-6, Sat 10-5
Friends of the Library Group
COLUMBIA BRANCH, 13824 W River Rd N, Columbia Station, 44028, SAN 356-7540. Tel: 440-236-8751. FAX: 440-236-8956. E-mail: contact-columbia@lpls.info. *Librn Supvr,* Sandra Mitchell; E-mail: smitchell@lpls.info; *Libr Assoc II,* Karlyn Chilenski; E-mail: kchilenski@lpls.info; Staff 4 (MLS 1, Non-MLS 3)
Founded 1955. Pop 7,538; Circ 96,035
Library Holdings: AV Mats 6,594; Bk Titles 24,723; Per Subs 112
Open Mon, Wed & Thurs 12-8, Tues 10-8, Fri 12-6, Sat 10-2
Friends of the Library Group
DOMONKAS BRANCH, 4125 E Lake Rd, Sheffield Lake, 44054, SAN 356-7605. Tel: 440-949-7410. FAX: 440-949-7741. E-mail: contact-domonkas@lpls.info. *Librn Supvr,* Pamela Coghlan; E-mail: pcoghlan@lpls.info; *Libr Assoc II,* Lana Gionfriddo; E-mail: lgionfriddo@lpls.info; Staff 5 (MLS 1, Non-MLS 4)
Founded 1964. Pop 13,123; Circ 156,050
Library Holdings: AV Mats 13,459; Bk Titles 40,340; Per Subs 86
Open Mon, Tues & Thurs 10-8:30, Wed 12-8:30, Fri 2-6, Sat 10-5
Friends of the Library Group
NORTH RIDGEVILLE BRANCH, 35700 Bainbridge Rd, North Ridgeville, 44039. Tel: 440-327-8326. FAX: 440-327-4443. E-mail: contact-northridgeville@lpls.info. *Librn Supvr,* Karen Sigsworth; E-mail: ksigsworth@lpls.info; *Librn,* Susan Spivey; E-mail: sspivey@lpls.info; Staff 9 (MLS 3, Non-MLS 6)
Founded 1958. Pop 29,470; Circ 588,058
Library Holdings: AV Mats 30,563; Bk Titles 82,974; Per Subs 272
Open Mon, Tues & Thurs 10-8:30, Wed 12-8:30, Fri & Sat 10-6, Sun (Winter) 1-5
Friends of the Library Group
SOUTH LORAIN, 2121 Homewood Dr, 44055, SAN 356-763X. Tel: 440-277-5672. FAX: 440-277-5727. E-mail: contact-south@lpls.info. *Librn Supvr,* Norma Preston; E-mail: npreston@lpls.info; *Libr Assoc II,* Veronica Parker; E-mail: vparker@lpls.info; Staff 3 (MLS 1, Non-MLS 2)
Founded 1907. Pop 21,608; Circ 154,581
Library Holdings: AV Mats 20,376; Bk Titles 39,196; Per Subs 128
Automation Activity & Vendor Info: (Cataloging) SirsiDynix; (Circulation) SirsiDynix
Open Mon, Tues & Thurs 11-8, Wed 12-8, Fri 2-6, Sat 11-5
Friends of the Library Group
Bookmobiles: 1. Librn Supvr, Frances Johnson

M MERCY REGIONAL MEDICAL CENTER, Mercy Medical Library, (Formerly Community Health Partners), 3700 Kolbe Rd, 44053. SAN 324-5500. Tel: 440-960-3327. FAX: 440-960-3298. E-mail: ReferenceOnline@mercy.com. *Dir,* Madeline Ventline; Staff 0.5 (MLS 0.5)
Founded 1979
Library Holdings: Bk Titles 3,000; Per Subs 85
Special Collections: Spirituality & Wellness
Subject Interests: Obstetrics, Psychiat, Substance abuse
Automation Activity & Vendor Info: (ILL) LibraryWorld, Inc
Database Vendor: EBSCOhost, Majors, Natural Standard, PubMed, STAT!Ref (Teton Data Systems), Swets Information Services, UpToDate
Function: ILL available
Publications: Library Newsletter
Partic in Medical Library Association (MLA); Midwest Collaborative for Library Services (MCLS); Ohio Libr Coun
Restriction: Circ limited

LOUDONVILLE

P LOUDONVILLE PUBLIC LIBRARY*, 122 E Main St, 44842-1267. SAN 313-5829. Tel: 419-994-5531. FAX: 419-994-4321. Web Site: www.loudonvillelibrary.org. *Dir,* Michael Thornton; E-mail: thorntmi@loudonvillelibrary.org; *Ch,* Deb Knoll; E-mail: knollde@loudonvillelibrary.org; *Ch,* Kristy Spreng; E-mail: sprengkr@loudonvillelibrary.org; *Adult Serv, Ref,* Joy Zemrock; E-mail: zemrocjo@loudonvillelibrary.org; *Fiscal Officer,* Susan Burwell; E-mail: burwelsu@loudonvillelibrary.org; *Pub Relations, Teen Serv,* Mary Mould; E-mail: mouldma@loudonvillelibrary.org; Staff 6 (MLS 2, Non-MLS 4)
Founded 1905. Pop 10,000; Circ 200,374
Library Holdings: Audiobooks 936; CDs 1,746; DVDs 1,196; Large Print Bks 2,007; Bk Vols 49,158; Per Subs 130; Videos 236
Special Collections: Genealogy & Local History Coll; Parent Teacher Coll
Automation Activity & Vendor Info: (Cataloging) OCLC; (Circulation) SirsiDynix
Wireless access
Function: Accelerated reader prog, Adult bk club, After school storytime, Archival coll, Audiobks via web, AV serv, Bk club(s), Children's prog, Computer training, Computers for patron use, Copy machines, Digital talking bks, e-mail & chat, e-mail serv, E-Reserves, Electronic databases & coll, Family literacy, Free DVD rentals, Handicapped accessible, Holiday prog, Home delivery & serv to Sr ctr & nursing homes, Homebound delivery serv, ILL available, Magnifiers for reading, Mail & tel request accepted, Music CDs, Online cat, Online ref, Online searches, Outreach serv, Outside serv via phone, mail, e-mail & web, OverDrive digital audio bks, Photocopying/Printing, Preschool outreach, Prog for adults, Prog for children & young adult, Pub access computers, Ref & res, Ref serv available, Ref serv in person, Scanner, Senior computer classes, Senior outreach, Spoken cassettes & CDs, Spoken cassettes & DVDs, Story hour, Summer reading prog, Tax forms, Teen prog, Telephone ref, VHS videos, Video lending libr, Web-catalog, Wheelchair accessible
Partic in SEO (Serving Every Ohioan) Library Center
Open Mon, Tues & Thurs 10-8, Wed & Fri 10-6, Sat 10-4
Friends of the Library Group

LOUISVILLE

P LOUISVILLE PUBLIC LIBRARY*, 700 Lincoln Ave, 44641-1474. SAN 313-5837. Tel: 330-875-1696. FAX: 330-875-3530. E-mail: info@louisvillelibrary.org. Web Site: www.louisvillelibrary.org. *Dir,* Jason Buydos; E-mail: jbuydos@louisvillelibrary.org; *Head, Adult Serv,* Rachel Sweany; E-mail: rsweany@louisvillelibrary.org; *Head, Ch,* Emily Callan; E-mail: ecallan@louisvillelibrary.org; *AV,* Andrea Bossart; *Circ,* Darla Evans; *Tech Serv,* Jodi Heppe; Staff 4 (MLS 4)
Founded 1935. Pop 13,000
Library Holdings: Bk Vols 120,000; Per Subs 225
Subject Interests: Constitution, Local hist
Automation Activity & Vendor Info: (Acquisitions) Innovative Interfaces, Inc
Database Vendor: SirsiDynix
Wireless access
Partic in Mideastern Ohio Libr Orgn
Open Mon-Thurs 9-9, Fri & Sat 9-5, Sat (June-Aug) 9-1
Friends of the Library Group

MADISON

P MADISON PUBLIC LIBRARY*, 6111 Middle Ridge Rd, 44057-2818. SAN 313-587X. Tel: 440-428-2189. FAX: 440-428-7402. E-mail: info@madison-library.info. Web Site: www.madison-library.info. *Dir/Fiscal*

Officer, Nancy Currie; E-mail: nancy.currie@madison-library.info; Staff 18 (MLS 3, Non-MLS 15)
Founded 1915. Pop 18,500; Circ 565,000
Library Holdings: AV Mats 14,145; Large Print Bks 5,000; Bk Vols 105,764; Per Subs 310
Subject Interests: Genealogy, Local hist
Automation Activity & Vendor Info: (Acquisitions) SirsiDynix; (Cataloging) SirsiDynix; (Circulation) SirsiDynix; (OPAC) BiblioCommons
Database Vendor: EBSCOhost, Gale Cengage Learning, OCLC FirstSearch, Wilson - Wilson Web
Wireless access
Function: Accelerated reader prog, Adult bk club, After school storytime, Art exhibits, Audiobks via web, Bi-weekly Writer's Group, Bk club(s), Bks on CD, Chess club, Children's prog, Computer training, Computers for patron use, Copy machines, Digital talking bks, Distance learning, e-mail serv, E-Reserves, Electronic databases & coll, Exhibits, Family literacy, Free DVD rentals, Handicapped accessible, Home delivery & serv to Sr ctr & nursing homes, ILL available, Mail & tel request accepted, Music CDs, Notary serv, Online cat, Online ref, Orientations, Outreach serv, Outside serv via phone, mail, e-mail & web, OverDrive digital audio bks, Photocopying/Printing, Preschool outreach, Prog for adults, Prog for children & young adult, Pub access computers, Ref serv available, Ref serv in person, Senior computer classes, Senior outreach, Story hour, Summer reading prog, Tax forms, Teen prog, Telephone ref, Web-catalog, Wheelchair accessible
Publications: Dear Friends (Newsletter)
Partic in CLEVNET; Northeast Ohio Regional Library System
Special Services for the Blind - Talking bks
Open Mon-Fri 10-8, Sat 10-5
Friends of the Library Group

MANSFIELD

R FIRST CONGREGATIONAL CHURCH*, Bradford Memorial Library, 640 Millsboro Rd, 44903. SAN 313-5888. Tel: 419-756-3046. FAX: 419-756-5834. *In Charge,* Deana Vail
Library Holdings: Bk Vols 2,500
Open Mon-Fri 9-4:30

R FIRST PRESBYTERIAN CHURCH LIBRARY*, 399 S Trimble Rd, 44906. SAN 313-5896. Tel: 419-756-7066. E-mail: office@mansfield1st.com. *Librn,* Dottie Keaton
Founded 1960
Library Holdings: Bk Titles 3,500
Special Collections: Old Bibles Coll
Open Mon-Thurs 9-4

S KINGWOOD CENTER LIBRARY*, 900 Park Ave W, 44906-2999. SAN 313-590X. Tel: 419-522-0211. FAX: 419-522-0211, Ext 132. E-mail: info@kingwoodcenter.org. Web Site: www.kingwoodcenter.org. *Dir,* Chuck Gleaves
Founded 1953
Library Holdings: AV Mats 50; Bk Titles 8,500; Per Subs 100
Subject Interests: Hort
Friends of the Library Group

S MANSFIELD FINE ARTS GUILD, INC*, Mansfield Art Center Library, 700 Marion Ave, 44903. SAN 313-5926. Tel: 419-756-1700. FAX: 419-756-0860. Web Site: www.mansfieldartcenter.org. *Dir of Educ,* Mary Cooper; E-mail: mary@mansfieldartcenter.org
Library Holdings: Bk Vols 200; Per Subs 150
Open Tues-Sat 11-5, Sun 12-5

P MANSFIELD-RICHLAND COUNTY PUBLIC LIBRARY*, 43 W Third St, 44902-1295. SAN 356-7788. Tel: 419-521-3100. Circulation Tel: 419-521-3140. Reference Tel: 419-521-3110. FAX: 419-525-4750. TDD: 419-521-3113. Web Site: www.mrcpl.org. *Dir,* Joseph C Palmer; Tel: 419-521-3124, Fax: 419-521-3129, E-mail: director@mrcpl.org; *Cat & Proc Mgr,* Marian Benjamin; Tel: 419-521-3134, E-mail: ts@mrcpl.org; *Communications Coordr,* Jean M Ruark; Tel: 419-521-3101, Fax: 419-522-5375, E-mail: communications@mrcpl.org; *IT Coordr,* Peter Moore; Tel: 419-521-3105, Fax: 419-521-3126, E-mail: automation@mrcpl.org; *Coord, Ad Serv, Coordr, AV,* Pamela Lewis; Tel: 419-521-3121; *Coll Develop,* Melinda Garrett; Tel: 419-521-3133, E-mail: collection@mrcpl.org
Founded 1887. Pop 125,000; Circ 1,700,000
Library Holdings: AV Mats 53,000; CDs 36,000; Bk Titles 248,360; Bk Vols 516,231; Talking Bks 12,000; Videos 221,000
Special Collections: Personal Library of Senator John Sherman
Subject Interests: Adult literacy, Found, Genealogy, Grants, Local hist
Automation Activity & Vendor Info: (Acquisitions) SirsiDynix; (Cataloging) SirsiDynix; (Circulation) SirsiDynix; (OPAC) SirsiDynix
Database Vendor: EBSCOhost, Gale Cengage Learning
Function: ILL available
Publications: News From the Mansfield/Richland County Public Library (Newsletter)
Special Services for the Deaf - TDD equip
Friends of the Library Group
Branches: 8
BELLVILLE BRANCH, 97 Bell St, Bellville, 44813, SAN 356-7818. Tel: 419-886-3811. FAX: 419-886-3791. *Br Mgr,* Mary Frankenfield
Founded 1920. Pop 1,568; Circ 127,959
Library Holdings: Bk Vols 14,000
Database Vendor: Dialog, Gale Cengage Learning, ProQuest, Wilson - Wilson Web
Function: ILL available
Open Mon-Thurs 9-8, Fri & Sat 9-5
Friends of the Library Group
BUTLER BRANCH, 21 Elm St, Butler, 44822, SAN 356-7842. Tel: 419-883-2220. FAX: 419-883-2220. *Br Mgr,* Vikki Eckert
Library Holdings: Bk Vols 11,997
Open Mon-Thurs 10-8, Fri 10-5, Sat 9-3
Friends of the Library Group
CRESTVIEW BRANCH, 1575 State Rte 96 E, Ashland, 44805-9262. Tel: 419-895-0010. FAX: 419-895-0010. *Br Mgr,* Ryan Vasko
Library Holdings: Bk Vols 6,825
Open Mon, Tues & Thurs 10-8, Wed & Fri 10-5, Sat 9-3
LEXINGTON BRANCH, 25 Lutz Ave, Lexington, 44904, SAN 356-7877. Tel: 419-884-2500. FAX: 419-884-3695. *Br Mgr,* Katie Gatten
Library Holdings: Bk Vols 39,958
Open Mon-Thurs 9-8, Fri & Sat 9-5
Friends of the Library Group
LUCAS BRANCH, 34 W Main St, Lucas, 44843, SAN 370-9213. Tel: 419-892-2576. FAX: 419-892-2576. *Br Mgr,* Tanaya Silcox; Tel: 419-892-2575; *Ch,* Heather Henderson
Library Holdings: Bk Vols 15,371
Open Mon, Tues & Thurs 11-8, Wed & Fri 11-5, Sat 9-3
Friends of the Library Group
MADISON BRANCH, 1395 Grace St, 44905, SAN 376-1541. Tel: 419-589-7050. FAX: 419-589-7108. *Br Mgr,* Christine Pyles; E-mail: cpyles@mrcp.org
Library Holdings: Bk Vols 27,996
Open Mon-Thurs 9-8, Fri & Sat 9-5
Friends of the Library Group
ONTARIO BRANCH, 2221 Village Mall Dr, 44906, SAN 328-9842. Tel: 419-529-4912. FAX: 419-529-3693. *Br Mgr,* Matt Bachelder
Library Holdings: Bk Vols 35,134
Open Mon-Thurs 9-8, Fri & Sat 9-5
Friends of the Library Group
PLYMOUTH BRANCH, 29 W Broadway, Plymouth, 44865, SAN 356-7907. Tel: 419-687-5655. FAX: 419-687-5655. *Br Mgr,* Danica Perry
Library Holdings: Bk Vols 26,505
Open Mon-Thurs 10-8, Fri 10-5, Sat 9-3
Friends of the Library Group

S RICHLAND CORRECTIONAL INSTITUTION LIBRARY*, 1001 Olivesburg Rd, 44905-1228. (Mail add: PO Box 8107, 44901-8107), SAN 378-3685. Tel: 419-526-2100, Ext 2215. FAX: 419-521-2814. *Librn,* Rebecca Williams; E-mail: rebecca.williams@odrc.state.oh.us; *Libr Assoc,* Dawn Bartram; E-mail: dawn.bartram@odrc.state.oh.us; Staff 2 (MLS 1, Non-MLS 1)
Founded 1998
Jul 2007-Jun 2008 Income $16,000. Mats Exp $14,400, Books $1,000, Per/Ser (Incl. Access Fees) $5,500, Other Print Mats $550, AV Equip $150, AV Mat $200, Presv $7,000. Sal $85,000 (Prof $51,000)
Library Holdings: AV Mats 200; Bks on Deafness & Sign Lang 5; CDs 150; DVDs 25; High Interest/Low Vocabulary Bk Vols 75; Large Print Bks 100; Music Scores 1; Bk Titles 12,000; Bk Vols 13,250; Per Subs 70; Videos 50
Subject Interests: Law
Automation Activity & Vendor Info: (Cataloging) Follett Software; (Circulation) Follett Software; (OPAC) Follett Software
Function: Audio & video playback equip for onsite use, ILL available, Music CDs, VHS videos, Wheelchair accessible
Open Mon-Sun 8-10:30, 11:45-3:30 & 6-8:30
Restriction: Borrowing privileges limited to fac & registered students, Not open to pub, Residents only
Friends of the Library Group

GL RICHLAND COUNTY LAW LIBRARY RESOURCES BOARD*, Richland County Law Library, 50 Park Ave E, 44902. SAN 313-5969. Tel: 419-774-5595. *Law Librn,* Traycee Conner
Library Holdings: Bk Vols 19,000; Per Subs 15

S STATE OF OHIO DEPARTMENT OF CORRECTIONS*, Mansfield Correctional Institution Library, State Rd 545 N, 1150 N Main St, 44903. (Mail add: PO Box 788, 44901-0788), SAN 313-5942. Tel: 419-526-2000,

Ext 3050. FAX: 419-526-1763. *Librn,* John Babajide; E-mail: john.babajide@odrc.state.oh.us; Staff 1 (Non-MLS 1)
Library Holdings: Bk Vols 8,500; Per Subs 160
Subject Interests: Criminal law
Automation Activity & Vendor Info: (Acquisitions) EOS International; (Cataloging) EOS International; (Circulation) EOS International
Partic in State Libr of Ohio
Open Mon-Sun 8-10:45, 1-3:40 & 6-8:30

MARIETTA

C MARIETTA COLLEGE*, Legacy Library, 220 Fifth St, 45750. (Mail add: 215 Fifth St, 45750), SAN 313-5977. Tel: 740-376-4757. Interlibrary Loan Service Tel: 740-376-4544. Reference Tel: 740-376-4543. Administration Tel: 740-376-4758. FAX: 740-376-4843. E-mail: library@marietta.edu. Web Site: library.marietta.edu. *Dir,* Dr Douglas Anderson; E-mail: doug.anderson@marietta.edu; *Head, Tech Serv & Syst,* Angela Burdiss; Tel: 740-376-4537, E-mail: burdissa@marietta.edu; *Ref & Access Serv Librn,* J Peter Thayer; Tel: 740-376-4361, E-mail: thayerp@marietta.edu; *Ref & Instruction Librn,* Joseph Straw; Tel: 740-376-4541, E-mail: joe.straw@marietta.edu. Subject Specialists: *Fine arts, Performing arts,* Dr Douglas Anderson; *Sci,* Angela Burdiss; *Soc sci,* J Peter Thayer; *Educ, Humanities,* Joseph Straw; Staff 11 (MLS 4, Non-MLS 7)
Founded 1835. Enrl 1,512; Fac 108; Highest Degree: Master
Library Holdings: AV Mats 5,141; e-books 20,374; e-journals 14,003; Bk Vols 246,493; Per Subs 547
Special Collections: 16th-19th Century Rare Book Coll; Americana (Stimson Coll); Local History (Fischer Coll & Hoag Coll), photos; Northwest Territory & Early Ohio (Ohio Company of Associates Coll & General Rufus Putnam Papers Coll), docs, ms; Notable Personnages (Slack Coll), autographs & docs; Ohio History & Scientific Coll (Hildreth Coll), bks & ms. State Document Depository; US Document Depository
Automation Activity & Vendor Info: (Acquisitions) Innovative Interfaces, Inc; (Cataloging) Innovative Interfaces, Inc; (Circulation) Innovative Interfaces, Inc; (OPAC) Innovative Interfaces, Inc; (Serials) Innovative Interfaces, Inc
Database Vendor: EBSCOhost, JSTOR
Wireless access
Partic in Ohio Library & Information Network; OHIONET

M MARIETTA MEMORIAL HOSPITAL*, Medical Library, 401 Matthew St, 45750-1699. SAN 373-8329. Tel: 740-374-1400. FAX: 740-374-4959. *Librn,* Angela Hammat; Staff 1 (MLS 1)
Library Holdings: Bk Vols 1,800; Per Subs 175
Subject Interests: Hospital admin, Med, Nursing
Partic in National Network of Libraries of Medicine South Central Region
Restriction: Staff use only

S OHIO HISTORICAL SOCIETY*, Campus Martius Museum Library, 601 Second St, 45750-2122. SAN 313-5985. Tel: 740-373-3750. FAX: 740-373-3680. E-mail: info@campusmartiusmuseum.org. Web Site: ohsweb.ohiohistory.org/places/se04/index.shtml. *Dir,* Le Ann Hendershot; E-mail: lhendershot@campusmatiuscampus.org
Founded 1885
Library Holdings: Bk Titles 500
Subject Interests: Area genealogy prior to 1830, Early Northwest Territory, Ohio, River mat, Wash County
Function: For res purposes
Open Mon-Fri (Nov-Feb) 9:30-5; Wed-Sat (March-Oct) 9:30-5, Sun 12-5

GL WASHINGTON COUNTY LAW LIBRARY*, 205 Putnam St, 45750-3017. SAN 370-3223. Tel: 740-373-6623, Ext 214. FAX: 740-373-2085. E-mail: lawlibrary@washingtongov.org. Web Site: www.co.washington.oh.us/cl-lawlibrary.htm. *Librn,* Juanita Henniger
Library Holdings: Bk Vols 15,050
Special Collections: Ohio Law Cases 1800's Through Current
Open Mon & Wed 8-12 & 1-4, Fri 8-Noon
Restriction: Open to pub for ref only

P WASHINGTON COUNTY PUBLIC LIBRARY*, 615 Fifth St, 45750-1973. SAN 356-7966. Tel: 740-373-1057. Circulation Tel: 740-373-1057, Ext 201. Reference Tel: 740-373-1057, Ext 204, 740-373-1057, Ext 208. Administration Tel: 740-373-1057, Ext 223. Reference FAX: 740-373-2860. Administration FAX: 740-376-2171. Web Site: www.wcplib.info. *Dir,* Justin Mayo; E-mail: j.mayo@wcplib.info; *Circ Mgr,* Melanie Singer; E-mail: msinger@wcplib.info; *Info Serv Mgr,* Andrea Adkins; E-mail: a.adkins@wcplib.info; *Youth Serv Mgr,* Julie Stacy; E-mail: j.stacy@wcplib.info; Staff 68 (MLS 2, Non-MLS 66)
Founded 1829. Pop 62,500; Circ 705,000
Library Holdings: Bk Vols 217,500; Per Subs 245
Special Collections: Local History & Genealogy Coll
Automation Activity & Vendor Info: (Cataloging) SirsiDynix; (Circulation) SirsiDynix; (OPAC) Horizon
Database Vendor: EBSCOhost, OCLC WorldShare Interlibrary Loan, ProQuest, SirsiDynix
Partic in Ohio Public Library Information Network; SEO (Serving Every Ohioan) Library Center; Solo; Southeast Regional Library System
Open Mon-Thurs 9-8:30, Fri & Sat 9-5
Friends of the Library Group
Branches: 5
BARLOW BRANCH, 8370 State Rte 339, Barlow, 45712. (Mail add: PO Box 175, Barlow, 45712-0175), SAN 378-1216. Tel: 740-678-0103. FAX: 740-678-0046. *Br Mgr,* Anna Henry; E-mail: a.henry@wcplib.info; Staff 9 (Non-MLS 9)
Founded 1998. Circ 75,253
Open Mon-Thurs 9-8, Fri 9-6, Sat 10-4
Friends of the Library Group
BELPRE BRANCH, 2012 Washington Blvd, Belpre, 45714, SAN 356-7990. Tel: 740-423-8381. FAX: 740-423-8305. *Br Mgr,* Tam Wamer; E-mail: t.wamer@wcplib.info
Circ 111,478
Open Mon-Wed 9-8, Thurs & Fri 9-6, Sat 9-4
Friends of the Library Group
BEVERLY LIBRARY, MacIntosh St, Beverly, 45715. (Mail add: PO Box 728, Beverly, 45715-0728), SAN 356-8024. Tel: 740-984-4060. FAX: 740-984-2083. *Br Mgr,* Susan Chipps; E-mail: s.chipps@wcplib.info
Open Mon-Wed 10-8, Thurs & Fri 10-5, Sat 10-3
Friends of the Library Group
LOCAL HISTORY & GENEALOGY, 418 Washington St, 45750. Tel: 740-376-2172. FAX: 740-376-2175. E-mail: genealogy@wcplib.lib.oh.us.
Library Holdings: Bk Vols 4,000
Automation Activity & Vendor Info: (Cataloging) Horizon; (Circulation) Horizon
Open Mon, Tues & Thurs 10-7, Fri 10-5, Sat 10-4
NEW MATAMORAS BRANCH, 100 Merchant St, New Matamoras, 45767. (Mail add: PO Box 279, New Matamoras, 45767-0279), SAN 356-8059. Tel: 740-865-3386. FAX: 740-865-2054. *Br Mgr,* Kelly Brady; E-mail: k.brady@wcplib.info
Founded 1936. Circ 29,471
Open Mon-Wed 9-7, Fri 9-6, Sat 9-4
Friends of the Library Group
Bookmobiles: 1

J WASHINGTON STATE COMMUNITY COLLEGE*, Carson K Miller Library, 710 Colegate Dr, 45750. SAN 322-6948. Tel: 740-568-1914. FAX: 740-373-7496. E-mail: refdesk@wscc.edu. Web Site: wscclibrary.wscc.edu. *Libr Spec,* Lindsay McVey; Tel: 740-374-8716, Ext 3101, E-mail: lmcvey@wscc.edu; Staff 7 (MLS 1, Non-MLS 6)
Founded 1990. Enrl 2,209; Fac 174; Highest Degree: Associate
Jul 2007-Jun 2008 Income $247,895. Mats Exp $30,116, Books $11,916, Per/Ser (Incl. Access Fees) $8,000, AV Mat $1,200, Electronic Ref Mat (Incl. Access Fees) $9,000. Sal $212,119
Library Holdings: AV Mats 700; Bk Titles 18,659; Bk Vols 20,245
Subject Interests: Allied health, Computer tech, Nursing
Automation Activity & Vendor Info: (Cataloging) Innovative Interfaces, Inc; (Circulation) Innovative Interfaces, Inc; (Course Reserve) Innovative Interfaces, Inc; (ILL) Innovative Interfaces, Inc; (OPAC) Innovative Interfaces, Inc; (Serials) Innovative Interfaces, Inc
Wireless access
Partic in Ohio Library & Information Network; OHIONET

MARION

S MARION CORRECTIONAL INSTITUTION LIBRARY*, 940 Marion-Williamsport Rd, 43301. (Mail add: PO Box 57, 43301-0057), SAN 313-6000. Tel: 740-382-5781. FAX: 740-382-0595.
Founded 1957
Library Holdings: Bk Titles 15,000; Per Subs 100
Special Collections: Law Library Coll
Automation Activity & Vendor Info: (Cataloging) Follett Software; (Circulation) Follett Software; (OPAC) Follett Software
Function: ILL available, Ref serv available
Partic in State Libr of Ohio
Restriction: Internal circ only

GL MARION COUNTY OHIO LAW LIBRARY*, 258 W Center St, 43302. SAN 313-6019. Tel: 740-223-4170. E-mail: lawlib@ohio.net. *Librn,* Heather Ebert
Library Holdings: Bk Vols 17,000
Wireless access
Open Mon-Fri 8:30-11 & 12-4:30

M MARION GENERAL HOSPITAL*, Medical Library, 1000 McKinnly Park Dr, 43302. SAN 325-4976. Tel: 740-383-8668. FAX: 740-382-2978. *Librn,* Pam Snyder; E-mail: snyderp@ohiohealth.com
Library Holdings: Bk Titles 350; Per Subs 167
Subject Interests: Med, Nursing
Partic in Central Ohio Hospital Library Consortium

P MARION PUBLIC LIBRARY, 445 E Church St, 43302-4290. SAN 356-8083. Tel: 740-387-0992. Web Site: www.marionlibrary.org. *Exec Dir, Fiscal Officer,* Gary Branson; E-mail: director@marionlibrary.org; *Head, Exten Serv,* David Hepp; *Head, Patron Serv,* Gary Butler; *Head, Patron Serv,* Whittney Mahle; *Head, Pub Relations,* Leslie Schifer; *Dept Head, Tech Serv,* Amy Deuble; *Youth Serv Dept Head,* Barbara Moore; Staff 26.21 (MLS 6, Non-MLS 20.21)
Founded 1886. Pop 65,768; Circ 524,819
Jan 2013-Dec 2013 Income (Main Library and Branch(s)) $1,975,318, State $1,886,315, Federal $12,656, Locally Generated Income $76,347. Mats Exp $22,486, Books $123,488, Per/Ser (Incl. Access Fees) $11,106, Other Print Mats $4,213, AV Mat $58,996, Electronic Ref Mat (Incl. Access Fees) $14,682. Sal $1,017,018 (Prof $606,710)
Library Holdings: Audiobooks 5,000; CDs 4,293; DVDs 18,014; Bk Titles 187,061; Bk Vols 191,208; Per Subs 256
Special Collections: Marion Local History. State Document Depository; US Document Depository
Automation Activity & Vendor Info: (Acquisitions) Innovative Interfaces, Inc; (Cataloging) Innovative Interfaces, Inc; (Circulation) Innovative Interfaces, Inc; (OPAC) Innovative Interfaces, Inc; (Serials) Innovative Interfaces, Inc
Database Vendor: Baker & Taylor, BWI, Comprise Technologies Inc, Ingram Library Services, OHIONET, Overdrive, Inc, ProQuest
Wireless access
Function: Prog for adults, Prog for children & young adult, Spoken cassettes & DVDs, Story hour, Summer & winter reading prog, Tax forms, Teen prog, Wheelchair accessible
Partic in OHIONET
Open Mon-Thurs 10-8, Fri & Sat 10-5:30
Friends of the Library Group
Branches: 3
CALEDONIA BRANCH, 112 E Marion St, Caledonia, 43314. (Mail add: PO Box 347, Caledonia, 43314-0347), SAN 356-8113. Tel: 419-845-3666. *Head, Exten Serv,* David Hepp
Library Holdings: Bk Vols 6,359
Open Mon & Thurs 3-6
Friends of the Library Group
HENKLE-HOLLIDAY MEMORIAL, 86 S High, La Rue, 43332. (Mail add: PO Box 342, La Rue, 43332-0342), SAN 356-8148. Tel: 740-499-3066. *Head, Exten Serv,* David Hepp
Library Holdings: Bk Vols 7,195
Open Mon & Thurs 3-6
Friends of the Library Group
PROSPECT BRANCH, 116 N Main, Prospect, 43342. (Mail add: Box 30, Prospect, 43342-0030), SAN 356-8172. Tel: 740-494-2684. *Head, Exten Serv,* David Hepp
Library Holdings: Bk Vols 5,890
Open Mon & Thurs 3-6

MARTINS FERRY

P BELMONT COUNTY DISTRICT LIBRARY*, Martins Ferry Public Library, 20 James Wright Pl, 43935. SAN 356-8202. Tel: 740-633-0314. FAX: 740-633-6242. Web Site: www.mfpl.org. *Dir,* Yvonne O Myers; E-mail: myersyv@oplin.org; *Head, Ref,* Stacy Anderson; E-mail: anserss t@oplin.org; *Br Coordr,* William Cleary; E-mail: clearybi@oplin.org; *Ch Serv, Teen Serv,* Casey Stratton; E-mail: strattca@oplin.org; Staff 22.5 (MLS 2.5, Non-MLS 20)
Founded 1927. Pop 37,000; Circ 422,000
Library Holdings: AV Mats 7,700; High Interest/Low Vocabulary Bk Vols 22; Bk Titles 200,000; Bk Vols 211,377; Per Subs 220; Videos 13,000
Special Collections: James Wright Poetry Coll
Automation Activity & Vendor Info: (Acquisitions) SIRSI WorkFlows; (Cataloging) SIRSI WorkFlows; (Circulation) SIRSI WorkFlows; (OPAC) SIRSI WorkFlows
Database Vendor: OHIONET, SirsiDynix
Wireless access
Partic in SEO (Serving Every Ohioan) Library Center
Open Mon-Thurs 10-7, Fri 10-6, Sat 11-4
Friends of the Library Group
Branches: 5
BETHESDA BRANCH, 112 N Main St, Bethesda, 43719, SAN 356-8237. Tel: 740-484-4532. FAX: 740-484-4732. *Br Mgr,* Karen Davis; E-mail: davisk2@oplin.org; Staff 1 (Non-MLS 1)
Library Holdings: Bk Vols 5,149
Open Mon & Wed 12-7, Fri 12-4, Sat 10-Noon
Friends of the Library Group
BRIDGEPORT BRANCH, 661 Main St, Bridgeport, 43912, SAN 356-8261. Tel: 740-635-2563. FAX: 740-635-6974. *Dir,* Yvonne Myers; E-mail: myersyv@oplin.org; Staff 2 (MLS 1, Non-MLS 1)
Library Holdings: Bk Vols 10,000
Open Mon & Tues 11-6, Thurs & Fri 11-4
POWHATAN POINT BRANCH, 339 N State Rte 7, Powhatan Point, 43942, SAN 356-8350. Tel: 740-795-4624. FAX: 740-795-4624. *Br Mgr,* Jane Stratton; E-mail: jstratton@oplin.org; Staff 1 (Non-MLS 1)
Library Holdings: Bk Vols 3,000
Open Mon & Wed 12-7, Fri 12-4, Sat 11-1
VICTORIA READ FLUSHING BRANCH, 300 High St, Flushing, 43977. (Mail add: PO Box 214, Flushing, 43977-0214), SAN 356-8296. Tel: 740-968-3891. FAX: 740-968-0648. *Br Mgr,* Ferda Shari; E-mail: ferdash@oplin.org; Staff 2 (Non-MLS 2)
Library Holdings: Bk Vols 10,000
Open Mon & Wed 12-7, Fri 12-4, Sat 11-2
Friends of the Library Group
SHADYSIDE BRANCH, 4300 Central Ave, Shadyside, 43947, SAN 356-8385. Tel: 740-676-0506. FAX: 740-676-0123. *Br Mgr,* Lisa Millhouse; E-mail: millholi@oplin.org; Staff 3 (Non-MLS 3)
Library Holdings: Bk Vols 21,838
Open Mon-Wed 11-7, Fri 9-5, Sat 11-3
Friends of the Library Group

MARYSVILLE

P MARYSVILLE PUBLIC LIBRARY, 231 S Plum St, 43040-1596. SAN 356-8415. Tel: 937-642-1876. FAX: 937-642-3457. Web Site: www.marysvillelib.org. *Dir,* Randy Matlow; E-mail: rmatlow@marysvillelib.org; *Head, Youth Serv,* Kate McCartney; E-mail: kmccartney@marysvillelib.org; *Adult Serv,* Patty O'Connor; E-mail: poconnor@marysvillelib.org; Staff 5 (MLS 5)
Founded 1910. Pop 30,912; Circ 600,000
Library Holdings: Audiobooks 10,333; e-books 90,503; e-journals 120; Bk Titles 103,112; Per Subs 237; Videos 20,958
Subject Interests: Genealogy
Automation Activity & Vendor Info: (Acquisitions) Baker & Taylor; (Cataloging) SirsiDynix; (Circulation) SirsiDynix; (OPAC) PALS; (Serials) SirsiDynix
Database Vendor: EBSCOhost, Gale Cengage Learning, H W Wilson, LearningExpress, ProQuest
Open Mon-Thurs 9-8, Fri 9-6, Sat 9-5, Sun 1-5
Friends of the Library Group
Branches: 1
RAYMOND BRANCH, 21698 Main St, Raymond, 43067, SAN 356-844X. Tel: 937-246-4795. FAX: 937-246-2347. *Br Mgr,* Suzi Blue; E-mail: sblue@marysvillelib.org
Library Holdings: Bk Vols 26,612; Per Subs 84
Open Tues-Thurs 11-7, Fri 11-5, Sat 10-2
Friends of the Library Group

S OHIO REFORMATORY FOR WOMEN*, 1479 Collins Ave, 43040-1581. SAN 313-6035. Tel: 937-642-1065, Ext 2064. FAX: 937-645-3835. *Librn,* Frederick Gaieck; E-mail: frederick.gaieck@odrc.state.oh.us; Staff 2 (MLS 1, Non-MLS 1)
Founded 1959
Library Holdings: Large Print Bks 150; Bk Vols 7,000; Per Subs 50
Automation Activity & Vendor Info: (Cataloging) Follett Software; (Circulation) Follett Software

MASON

P MASON PUBLIC LIBRARY*, 200 Reading Rd, 45040-1694. SAN 313-6051. Tel: 513-398-2711. FAX: 513-398-9342. E-mail: masonpl@oplin.org. Web Site: www.masonpl.lib.oh.us. *Dir,* Sarah B Brown
Founded 1978. Pop 56,000; Circ 280,000
Library Holdings: Bk Titles 131,000; Per Subs 260
Special Collections: Mason History Coll
Publications: News & Views; Pulse Journal
Open Mon-Thurs 10-8, Fri & Sat 9-5, Sun (Oct-May) 1-5
Friends of the Library Group

MASSILLON

M AFFINITY MEDICAL CENTER*, Medical Library, 875 Eighth St NE, 44646. SAN 329-9147. Tel: 330-832-8761. FAX: 330-834-4786. *In Charge,* Jessica Bartolone; E-mail: jessica.bartolone@affinitymedicalcenter.com; Staff 2 (MLS 1, Non-MLS 1)
Library Holdings: Bk Titles 300; Bk Vols 1,800; Per Subs 165
Subject Interests: Osteopathy
Restriction: Staff use only

P MASSILLON PUBLIC LIBRARY*, 208 Lincoln Way E, 44646-8416. SAN 356-8474. Tel: 330-832-9831. Interlibrary Loan Service Tel: 330-832-9831, Ext 311. Reference Tel: 330-832-9831, Ext 312. Administration Tel: 330-832-9831, Ext 314. FAX: 330-830-2182. E-mail: mpl.ref@gmail.com. Web Site: www.massillonlibrary.org. *Dir,* Sherie L Brown; E-mail: brownsh@massillonlibrary.org; *Circ Serv Mgr, Tech Mgr,* James Nagy; Tel: 330-832-9831, Ext 332, E-mail: nagyja@massillonlibrary.org; *Coll, Acq & Proc Mgr,* Karen Sykeny; Tel:

330-832-9831, Ext 318, E-mail: sykenyka@massillonlibrary.org; *Mgr, Ch Serv,* Laura Klein; Tel: 330-832-9831, Ext 319, E-mail: kleinla@massillonlibrary.org; *Mgr, Outreach Serv,* Anne Juhasz; Tel: 330-832-9831, Ext 329, E-mail: juhaszan@massillonlibrary.org; *Ref Serv Mgr,* Jessica Watkins; Tel: 330-832-9831, Ext 307, E-mail: watkinje@massillonlibrary.org; *Fiscal Officer,* Amie Lynn; *YA Spec,* Emily Hisey; Staff 54 (MLS 3, Non-MLS 51)
Founded 1897. Pop 30,447; Circ 1,001,434
Special Collections: Early Ohio & Quaker History (Rotch-Wales Coll), mss; Lillian Gish Coll, letters, bks, films, videos, clippings
Subject Interests: Cooking, Gardening
Automation Activity & Vendor Info: (Acquisitions) Innovative Interfaces, Inc - Millenium; (Cataloging) Innovative Interfaces, Inc - Millenium; (Circulation) Innovative Interfaces, Inc - Millenium; (OPAC) Innovative Interfaces, Inc - Millenium; (Serials) Innovative Interfaces, Inc - Millenium
Database Vendor: SirsiDynix
Wireless access
Function: AV serv, Bk club(s), Copy machines, Electronic databases & coll, Fax serv, Genealogy discussion group, Handicapped accessible, Homebound delivery serv, ILL available, Prog for adults, Prog for children & young adult, Ref serv available, Senior computer classes, Spoken cassettes & CDs, Spoken cassettes & DVDs, Summer reading prog, Tax forms, Video lending libr, Wheelchair accessible
Publications: Calendar (Monthly)
Partic in Northeast Ohio Regional Library System; Ohio Public Library Information Network; OHIONET
Open Mon & Tues 10-8, Wed & Thurs 10-6, Fri & Sat 10-5
Friends of the Library Group
Branches: 2
BARRY ASKREN MEMORIAL BRANCH, 1200 Market St NE, Navarre, 44662. SAN 356-8539. Tel: 330-879-2113. FAX: 330-879-5574. *Mgr,* Angel Vaugh; E-mail: vaughnan@massillonlibrary.org
Open Mon-Fri 9-5, Wed 9-8, Sat 9-2
PAM S BELLONI BRANCH, 12000 Navarre Rd SW, Brewster, 44662-9486. SAN 356-8504. Tel: 330-767-9939. FAX: 330-767-0192. *Mgr,* Patty McGrath; E-mail: mcgratpa@massillonlibrary.org
Library Holdings: Bk Vols 12,645
Open Mon & Wed-Fri 8:30-4, Tues 8:30-7
Bookmobiles: 1

MAUMEE

M SAINT LUKE'S HOSPITAL*, Dr R A Hendricks Memorial Library, 5901 Monclova Rd, 43537-1855. Tel: 419-893-7700. FAX: 419-897-8381. *Supvr,* Sandy Sheets; Tel: 419-897-8421
Library Holdings: Bk Vols 500
Open Mon-Fri 6am-Midnight

R SAINT PAUL'S EPISCOPAL CHURCH LIBRARY*, 310 Elizabeth St, 43537. SAN 313-6078. Tel: 419-893-3381. E-mail: office@stpaulsmaumee.org. Web Site: www.stpaulsmaumee.org. *Librn,* Phyllis Gallo; Staff 2 (MLS 2)
Founded 1958
Jan 2005-Dec 2005 Income $2,200, Locally Generated Income $1,200, Parent Institution $1,000. Mats Exp $2,100, Books $1,400, AV Mat $700
Library Holdings: AV Mats 130; Bk Titles 1,790; Bk Vols 1,800
Subject Interests: Anglicana, Church, Relig
Open Mon-Fri 9-4

J STAUTZENBERGER COLLEGE LIBRARY*, 1796 Indian Wood Circle, 43537. Tel: 419-866-0261. Web Site: www.sctoday.edu. *Librn, Res Serv Spec,* Lori Van Liere; E-mail: lori.vanliere@sctoday.edu
Founded 1926. Enrl 750; Highest Degree: Associate
Library Holdings: CDs 2; Bk Titles 558; Per Subs 24; Spec Interest Per Sub 22; Videos 15
Subject Interests: Bus tech, Health & wellness, Info tech, Legal tech, Med tech, Real estate, Veterinary tech
Database Vendor: LexisNexis
Wireless access
Restriction: Access at librarian's discretion, Circ limited, In-house use for visitors, Not open to pub, Open to students, fac & staff

MAYFIELD HEIGHTS

M HILLCREST HOSPITAL*, Medical Library, 6780 Mayfield Rd, 44124. Tel: 440-312-3250. FAX: 440-312-4799. *Med Librn,* Mary Mills; E-mail: mmills@ccf.org; Staff 1 (MLS 1)
Founded 1974
Library Holdings: Bk Titles 1,500; Per Subs 100
Automation Activity & Vendor Info: (Cataloging) CyberTools for Libraries; (Circulation) CyberTools for Libraries; (OPAC) CyberTools for Libraries; (Serials) CyberTools for Libraries
Database Vendor: EBSCO Information Services, Elsevier, Micromedex, OVID Technologies, PubMed, UpToDate
Partic in MLANO
Open Mon-Fri 7:30-4

MCARTHUR

P HERBERT WESCOAT MEMORIAL LIBRARY, 120 N Market St, 45651-1218. SAN 313-5845. Tel: 740-596-5691. FAX: 740-596-2477. Web Site: www.vintoncountypublic.lib.oh.us. *Dir,* Clint Walker; E-mail: walkerer@oplin.org; *Asst Dir, Youth Serv Coordr,* Diana Johnston; E-mail: johnstdi@oplin.org
Founded 1934
Library Holdings: Bk Vols 50,000; Per Subs 171
Subject Interests: Vinton County hist
Wireless access
Open Mon-Fri 9:30-6, Sat 8:30-12:30
Friends of the Library Group
Bookmobiles: 1

MCCOMB

P MCCOMB PUBLIC LIBRARY*, 113 S Todd St, 45858. (Mail add: PO Box 637, 45858-0637), SAN 313-5853. Tel: 419-293-2425. FAX: 419-293-2748. E-mail: mccomb@oplin.org. Web Site: mccomb.oplin.org. *Dir,* Jane Schaffner; E-mail: schaffja@oplin.org; *Asst Dir, Head, Circ,* Laurie Bales; E-mail: balesla@oplin.org; *Ch,* Annette Schroeder; E-mail: aschroeder@oplin.org
Founded 1935. Circ 80,000
Library Holdings: Bk Vols 45,769; Per Subs 95
Special Collections: Art Coll, prints; Civil War (Andrews Raiders), displays
Subject Interests: Local hist
Automation Activity & Vendor Info: (Cataloging) Innovative Interfaces, Inc; (Circulation) Innovative Interfaces, Inc; (OPAC) Innovative Interfaces, Inc
Partic in NORWELD
Open Mon-Wed 9:30-8, Thurs-Sat 9:30-5
Friends of the Library Group

MCCONNELSVILLE

L MORGAN COUNTY BAR ASSOCIATION LIBRARY*, Court House, 19 E Main St, 43756. SAN 327-7224. Tel: 740-962-2262. FAX: 740-962-4522.
Library Holdings: Bk Vols 1,000

P KATE LOVE SIMPSON MORGAN COUNTY LIBRARY*, 358 E Main St, 43756-1130. SAN 313-5861. Tel: 740-962-2533. FAX: 740-962-3316. E-mail: katelove@oplin.org. Web Site: www.morgan.lib.oh.us. *Dir,* Tara Sidwell; E-mail: calendta@oplin.org; Staff 14 (MLS 1, Non-MLS 13)
Founded 1920. Pop 14,897; Circ 132,254
Library Holdings: AV Mats 5,359; Bks on Deafness & Sign Lang 13; Large Print Bks 2,273; Bk Vols 60,890; Per Subs 77
Subject Interests: Genealogy, Local hist
Automation Activity & Vendor Info: (Cataloging) SirsiDynix; (Circulation) SirsiDynix; (ILL) SirsiDynix; (OPAC) SirsiDynix
Wireless access
Function: Handicapped accessible, Home delivery & serv to Sr ctr & nursing homes, Homebound delivery serv, ILL available, Prog for children & young adult, Summer reading prog, Telephone ref, Wheelchair accessible
Partic in SEO (Serving Every Ohioan) Library Center
Open Mon-Fri 9-7, Sat 9-3
Friends of the Library Group
Branches: 1
CHESTERHILL BRANCH, 7520 Marion St, Chesterhill, 43728. Tel: 740-554-7104. FAX: 740-554-7253. *Br Mgr,* Belinda Dalton; E-mail: daltonbe@oplin.org; Staff 3 (Non-MLS 3)
Founded 1936
Library Holdings: Bk Vols 11,000
Function: Handicapped accessible, ILL available, Prog for children & young adult, Summer reading prog, Telephone ref, Wheelchair accessible
Open Mon-Wed 1-7, Fri & Sat 10-4
Bookmobiles: 1

MECHANICSBURG

P MECHANICSBURG PUBLIC LIBRARY*, 60 S Main St, 43044. SAN 313-6108. Tel: 937-834-2004. FAX: 937-834-3396. E-mail: mechanic@oplin.org. Web Site: opac.mechanicsburg.lib.oh.us/front.html. *Dir, Libr Serv,* Tammie Beers
Circ 72,628
Library Holdings: AV Mats 3,500; Bks on Deafness & Sign Lang 40; High Interest/Low Vocabulary Bk Vols 150; Large Print Bks 2,000; Bk Titles 47,000; Per Subs 131
Subject Interests: Bicycling, Family hist, Local hist

Automation Activity & Vendor Info: (Cataloging) TLC (The Library Corporation); (Circulation) TLC (The Library Corporation); (OPAC) TLC (The Library Corporation)
Publications: Between The Covers (Newsletter)
Partic in Miami Valley Librs; Ohio Public Library Information Network
Special Services for the Deaf - Closed caption videos
Special Services for the Blind - Spec prog
Open Mon-Thurs 10-8, Fri & Sat 10-5
Friends of the Library Group

MEDINA

P MEDINA COUNTY DISTRICT LIBRARY*, 210 S Broadway, 44256. SAN 356-8598. Tel: 330-725-0588. Administration Tel: 330-722-6235. FAX: 330-725-2053. Administration FAX: 330-722-4035. TDD: 330-722-6120. Web Site: www.medina.lib.oh.us. *Dir,* Carole Kowell; E-mail: kowell@mcdl.info; *Asst Dir,* Theresa Laffey; E-mail: laffey@mcdl.info; *Coll Res Mgr,* Sylvia Williams; E-mail: williams@mcdl.info; *Tech Serv,* Sue Demis; Staff 170 (MLS 20, Non-MLS 150)
Founded 1905. Pop 130,500; Circ 2,219,488
Library Holdings: Bk Titles 142,547; Bk Vols 575,853; Per Subs 1,289
Subject Interests: Genealogy, Local hist
Automation Activity & Vendor Info: (Circulation) Ex Libris Group
Database Vendor: EBSCOhost, Gale Cengage Learning, ProQuest, SirsiDynix
Function: Archival coll
Publications: Library Live (Newsletter)
Partic in CLEVE-NET
Open Mon-Thurs 9-8:30, Fri 9-6, Sat 9-5, Sun (Sept-May) 1-5
Friends of the Library Group
Branches: 5
BRUNSWICK COMMUNITY, 3649 Center Rd, Brunswick, 44212-0430, SAN 356-8628. Tel: 330-273-4150. FAX: 330-225-0310. *Mgr,* Susan Ungham
Open Mon-Thurs 9-8:30, Fri 9-6, Sat 9-5, Sun (Sept-May) 1-5
Friends of the Library Group
BUCKEYE LIBRARY, 6625 Wolff Rd, 44256-6211. Tel: 330-725-4415. FAX: 330-722-4548. *Mgr,* Holly Camino
Open Mon-Thurs 10-8, Fri & Sat 10-4
Friends of the Library Group
HIGHLAND LIBRARY, 4160 Ridge Rd, 44256-8618. Tel: 330-278-4271. FAX: 330-239-1378. *Mgr,* Diane Dermody
Open Mon-Thurs 10-8, Fri & Sat 10-4
Friends of the Library Group
LODI COMMUNITY, 635 Wooster St, Lodi, 44254-1311, SAN 356-8687. Tel: 330-948-1885. FAX: 330-948-2410. *Mgr,* Betsy Gilder
Library Holdings: Bk Vols 25,534
Open Mon-Thurs 10-8, Fri & Sat 10-4
Friends of the Library Group
SEVILLE COMMUNITY, N Center St, Seville, 44273. (Mail add: PO Box 206, Seville, 44273-0206), SAN 356-8717. Tel: 330-769-2852. FAX: 330-769-1774. *Librn,* Lynn Wiandt
Library Holdings: Bk Vols 22,121
Open Mon-Thurs 10-8, Fri & Sat 10-4
Friends of the Library Group
Bookmobiles: 1

L MEDINA COUNTY LAW LIBRARY ASSOCIATION*, 93 Public Sq, 44256. SAN 320-2232. Tel: 330-725-9744. FAX: 330-723-9608. *Dir,* MaryAnn Lapina; Staff 2 (Non-MLS 2)
Founded 1899
Library Holdings: Bk Vols 20,050
Restriction: Not open to pub

MENTOR

P MENTOR PUBLIC LIBRARY*, 8215 Mentor Ave, 44060. SAN 356-8741. Tel: 440-255-8811. FAX: 440-255-0520. Web Site: www.mentorpl.org. *Exec Dir,* Lynn Hawkins; Tel: 440-255-8811, Ext 232, E-mail: lynn.hawkins@mentorpl.org; *Dep Dir, Human Res Mgr,* Gail Borovic; E-mail: gail.borovic@mentorpl.org; *Adult Info Serv Mgr,* Amanda Densmore; *Mgr, Ch Serv,* Kim Sidorick; *Circ Mgr,* Denise Wright; E-mail: denise.wright@mentorpl.org; *Commun Outreach Coordr,* Jason Lea; *IT Mgr,* Andy Gunsch; *Fiscal Officer,* Colleen Snyder; Staff 55 (MLS 10, Non-MLS 45)
Founded 1819. Pop 65,461; Circ 837,685
Jan 2009-Dec 2009 Income (Main Library and Branch(s)) $4,427,218, State $2,017,050, Locally Generated Income $2,136,818, Other $273,350. Mats Exp $1,089,233, Books $642,199, Per/Ser (Incl. Access Fees) $24,614, AV Mat $299,045, Electronic Ref Mat (Incl. Access Fees) $122,875, Presv $500. Sal $1,784,733
Library Holdings: AV Mats 24,178; CDs 17,044; DVDs 14,843; e-books 65; Electronic Media & Resources 685; Bk Vols 247,256; Per Subs 346
Automation Activity & Vendor Info: (Acquisitions) Innovative Interfaces, Inc; (Cataloging) Innovative Interfaces, Inc; (Circulation) Innovative Interfaces, Inc; (OPAC) Innovative Interfaces, Inc
Database Vendor: Booksite, EBSCO Auto Repair Reference, EBSCOhost, Ex Libris Group, Facts on File, infoUSA, ProQuest, ReferenceUSA, Standard & Poor's, Wiley InterScience, World Book Online
Wireless access
Function: Accelerated reader prog, Adult bk club, After school storytime, Art exhibits, Audiobks via web, AV serv, Bk club(s), Bk reviews (Group), Bks on cassette, Bks on CD, CD-ROM, Children's prog, Computer training, Computers for patron use, Copy machines, Digital talking bks, Electronic databases & coll, Fax serv, Free DVD rentals, Handicapped accessible, Holiday prog, Home delivery & serv to Sr ctr & nursing homes, Homebound delivery serv, ILL available, Instruction & testing, Jail serv, Jazz prog, Magnifiers for reading, Mail & tel request accepted, Monthly prog for perceptually impaired adults, Music CDs, Notary serv, Online cat, Online ref, Online searches, Outreach serv, Outside serv via phone, mail, e-mail & web, OverDrive digital audio bks, Photocopying/Printing, Preschool outreach, Prof lending libr, Prog for adults, Prog for children & young adult, Pub access computers, Ref & res, Ref serv available, Referrals accepted, Scanner, Senior computer classes, Senior outreach, Serves mentally handicapped consumers, Spoken cassettes & CDs, Spoken cassettes & DVDs, Story hour, Summer reading prog, Tax forms, Teen prog, Telephone ref, VHS videos, Web-catalog, Wheelchair accessible, Writing prog
Publications: Cover to Cover (Monthly newsletter)
Partic in Northeast Ohio Regional Library System; Ohio Libr Coun; Ohio Public Library Information Network; OHIONET
Special Services for the Deaf - Bks on deafness & sign lang; Closed caption videos; Staff with knowledge of sign lang
Special Services for the Blind - Assistive/Adapted tech devices, equip & products; Audio mat; Closed circuit TV magnifier; Large print & cassettes; Large print bks; Large print bks & talking machines; Magnifiers; Recorded bks; Ref serv; Talking bk & rec for the blind cat; Talking bk serv referral; Talking bks
Open Mon-Thurs 9-9, Fri & Sat 9-5, Sun (Oct-April) 1-5
Friends of the Library Group
Branches: 2
HEADLANDS, 4669 Corduroy Rd, 44060, SAN 356-8776. Tel: 440-257-2000. *Br Mgr,* Pam Rose
Founded 1964
Open Mon & Wed 1-9, Tues & Thurs-Sat 9-5
MENTOR-ON-THE-LAKE, 5642 Andrews Rd, 44060, SAN 356-8806. Tel: 440-257-2512. FAX: 440-257-6886. *Br Mgr,* Darlene Workman; E-mail: darlene.workman@mentorpl.org
Founded 1998
Open Mon & Wed 1-9, Tues, Thurs & Fri 9-5

METAMORA

P EVERGREEN COMMUNITY LIBRARY*, 253 Maple St, 43540. (Mail add: PO Box E, 43540), SAN 313-6175. Tel: 419-644-2771. Toll Free Tel: 800-308-8603. FAX: 419-644-5778. Web Site: www.evergreencommunitylibrary.org. *Dir,* Jane Dominique; E-mail: dominija@oplin.org; *Ch,* Martie Yunker; *YA Librn,* Debbie Hendricks
Founded 1927. Pop 7,000; Circ 72,943
Library Holdings: Bk Vols 37,000; Per Subs 130
Automation Activity & Vendor Info: (Cataloging) Innovative Interfaces, Inc; (Circulation) Innovative Interfaces, Inc; (OPAC) Innovative Interfaces, Inc
Partic in Northwestern Libr District
Open Mon, Wed & Thurs 10-8, Tues & Fri 10-5, Sat 10-2

MIDDLEBURG HEIGHTS

R MIDDLEBURG HEIGHTS COMMUNITY CHURCH LIBRARY*, United Church of Christ, 7165 Big Creek Pkwy, 44130. SAN 313-6205. Tel: 440-842-7743. FAX: 440-842-7745. Web Site: www.mhccucc.org. *Librn,* Pat Kerslake
Library Holdings: Bk Vols 1,068
Subject Interests: Family, Relig

MIDDLETOWN

M MIDDLETOWN REGIONAL HOSPITAL*, Ada Leonard Memorial Library, 105 McKnight Dr, 45044-8787. SAN 313-6248. Tel: 513-424-2111. *Dir,* Judy Rudokas; Tel: 513-420-5164
Founded 1957
Library Holdings: Bk Titles 50; Per Subs 50
Special Collections: Old Medical Text Coll
Subject Interests: Hist of nursing
Partic in Regional Med Libr - Region 3
Restriction: Staff use only

P MIDPOINTE LIBRARY SYSTEM, (Formerly Middletown Public Library), 125 S Broad St, 45044. SAN 356-889X. Tel: 513-424-1251. Administration Tel: 513-424-0659. FAX: 513-424-6585. Web Site: www.midpointelibrary.org. *Dir,* Anita Carroll; E-mail: acarroll@midpointelibrary.org; *Dir, Human Res,* Katherine A Stengel; E-mail: kstengel@midpointelibrary.org; *Mgr,* Scott Parham; E-mail: sparham@midpointelibrary.org; *IT Mgr,* Ross Brown; E-mail: rbrown@midpointelibrary.org; *Pub Relations Mgr,* Cari Hillman; E-mail: chillman@midpointelibrary.org; *Tech Serv Mgr,* Becky McQuade; E-mail: bmcquade@midpointelibrary.org; Staff 83 (MLS 16.5, Non-MLS 66.5)
Founded 1911. Pop 180,783; Circ 2,125,964
Library Holdings: Audiobooks 48,514; AV Mats 33,377; e-books 142,248; Bk Vols 299,905; Per Subs 820
Special Collections: George C Crout Local History Coll
Subject Interests: Genealogy, Ohioana
Database Vendor: Innovative Interfaces, Inc
Wireless access
Partic in Ohio Library & Information Network
Special Services for the Blind - Talking bks
Open Mon-Thurs 9-9, Fri 9-7, Sat 9-5, Sun 1-5
Friends of the Library Group
Branches: 2
TRENTON BRANCH, 21 E State St, Trenton, 45067, SAN 356-892X. Tel: 513-988-9050. FAX: 513-988-5059. *Br Mgr,* R Diane Current; Tel: 513-988-9930, E-mail: dcurrent@midpointelibrary.org
Founded 1974
Library Holdings: AV Mats 5,120; Bk Vols 15,578; Per Subs 107
Open Mon-Thurs 11-8, Fri & Sat 9-5
Friends of the Library Group
WEST CHESTER BRANCH, 9363 Centre Pointe Dr, West Chester, 45069, SAN 356-8954. Tel: 513-777-3131. FAX: 513-777-8452. *Br Mgr,* Steven Mayhugh; Tel: 513-777-3717, E-mail: smayhugh@middletownlibrary.org
Library Holdings: AV Mats 31,381; Bk Vols 101,481; Per Subs 404
Open Mon-Thurs 9-9, Fri 9-7, Sat 9-5, Sun 1-5
Friends of the Library Group

MILAN

P MILAN-BERLIN TOWNSHIP PUBLIC LIBRARY*, 19 E Church St, 44846. (Mail add: PO Box 1550, 44846-1550), SAN 356-8989. Tel: 419-499-4117. Administration Tel: 419-499-4696. FAX: 419-499-4697. Web Site: www.milan-berlin.lib.oh.us. *Dir,* William Rutger; E-mail: william.rutger@milan-berlin.lib.oh.us; Staff 1 (MLS 1)
Founded 1877. Pop 10,000; Circ 225,042
Library Holdings: AV Mats 12,666; Bk Vols 95,590; Per Subs 199
Special Collections: Barbour Coll; Birth & Death Records; Census Index; Family Genealogies; Immigration Records; Local History (Edison Coll); Local newspaper; Passenger Lists. Oral History
Subject Interests: Genealogy, Local hist
Automation Activity & Vendor Info: (Cataloging) SirsiDynix; (Circulation) SirsiDynix; (ILL) SirsiDynix; (OPAC) SirsiDynix
Partic in Northeast Ohio Regional Library System
Open Mon-Thurs (Winter) 9:30-7:30, Fri 9:30-5, Sat 9:30-1:30; Mon, Wed & Fri (Summer) 9:30-5, Tues & Thurs 9:30-7:30, Sat 9:30-1:30
Branches: 1
BERLIN TOWNSHIP PUBLIC, Four E Main St, Berlin Heights, 44814-9602. (Mail add: PO Box 139, Berlin Heights, 44814-0139), SAN 356-9012. Tel: 419-588-2250. FAX: 419-588-0025. *Br Mgr,* Joanne Chaffee; *Coordr, Youth Serv,* Jo Ann Weaver; E-mail: jo-ann.weaver@milan-berlin.lib.oh.us
Open Mon-Thurs (Winter) 9:30-7:30, Fri 9:30-5, Sat 9:30-1:30; Mon & Wed (Summer) 9:30-7:30, Tues, Thurs & Fri 9:30-5, Sat 9:30-1:30

MILLERSBURG

P HOLMES COUNTY DISTRICT PUBLIC LIBRARY*, 3102 Glen Dr, 44654. SAN 356-9047. Tel: 330-674-5972. Circulation Tel: 330-674-5972, Ext 200. Reference Tel: 330-674-5972, Ext 203. FAX: 330-674-1938. Web Site: www.holmeslibrary.org. *Dir,* William Martino; Tel: 330-674-5972, Ext 201, E-mail: wmartino@holmeslib.org; *Head, Ref,* Susan Corl; E-mail: scorl@holmeslib.org; *Ch Serv,* Laura Lee Wilson; Tel: 330-674-5972, Ext 210, E-mail: lwilson@holmeslib.org; Staff 35 (MLS 5, Non-MLS 30)
Founded 1928. Pop 40,000; Circ 459,837
Library Holdings: Bk Titles 74,500; Bk Vols 145,000; Per Subs 128
Special Collections: Amish & Mennonite Genealogies Coll
Automation Activity & Vendor Info: (Cataloging) SirsiDynix; (Circulation) SirsiDynix; (ILL) SirsiDynix; (OPAC) SirsiDynix
Database Vendor: EBSCOhost, Gale Cengage Learning, OCLC FirstSearch, TLC (The Library Corporation)
Publications: History of Holmes County
Open Mon, Tues & Thurs 9-8, Wed & Fri 9-5, Sat 10-2
Friends of the Library Group
Branches: 2
KILLBUCK BRANCH, 160 W Front St, Killbuck, 44637. (Mail add: PO Box 99, Killbuck, 44637-0099), SAN 356-9136. Tel: 330-276-0882. FAX: 330-276-0882. *Librn,* Sharon Hoxworth
Circ 8,000
Open Mon & Wed 10-5, Tues & Thurs 1-7, Sat 10-2
WALNUT CREEK BRANCH, 4877 Olde Pump St, Walnut Creek, 44687. (Mail add: 3102 Glen Dr, 44654), SAN 356-9195. Tel: 330-893-3464. FAX: 330-893-8464. *Br Mgr,* Kimberli Hiller
Circ 18,000
Open Mon & Wed 10-4, Tues & Thurs 2-8, Sat 10-4
Bookmobiles: 2

L HOLMES COUNTY LAW LIBRARY, Courthouse, Ste 204, One E Jackson St, 44654. SAN 327-3911. Tel: 330-763-2956. FAX: 330-763-2957. E-mail: lawlibrary@co.holmes.oh.us. *Librn,* Pamela Maxfield-Ontko
Partic in Ohio Law Library Consortium
Open Mon-Fri 8:30-4:30

MINERVA

P MINERVA PUBLIC LIBRARY*, 677 Lynnwood Dr, 44657-1200. SAN 313-6256. Tel: 330-868-4101. FAX: 330-868-4267. Web Site: www.minerva.lib.oh.us. *Exec Dir,* Tom Dillie; *Youth Serv Mgr,* Kathy Heller; Staff 13.3 (MLS 2, Non-MLS 11.3)
Founded 1913. Pop 12,289; Circ 320,105
Jan 2012-Dec 2012 Income $674,705, State $646,180, Locally Generated Income $28,525. Mats Exp $102,000, Books $53,600, Per/Ser (Incl. Access Fees) $6,999, Micro $1,048, AV Mat $26,400. Sal $342,000 (Prof $94,700)
Library Holdings: Audiobooks 4,724; CDs 2,656; DVDs 6,561; e-books 31,922; Large Print Bks 2,036; Microforms 69; Bk Vols 90,262; Per Subs 217; Videos 862
Special Collections: Gypsies Coll
Subject Interests: Circus, Clowns, Local genealogy, Local hist
Automation Activity & Vendor Info: (Cataloging) SIRSI WorkFlows; (Circulation) SIRSI WorkFlows; (OPAC) Horizon
Wireless access
Function: Adult bk club, Audiobks via web, Bk club(s), Bks on cassette, Bks on CD, Children's prog, Computer training, Computers for patron use, Copy machines, Digital talking bks, Electronic databases & coll, Exhibits, Fax serv, Free DVD rentals, Handicapped accessible, ILL available, Magnifiers for reading, Mail & tel request accepted, Microfiche/film & reading machines, Music CDs, Online cat, OverDrive digital audio bks, Photocopying/Printing, Preschool outreach, Prog for adults, Prog for children & young adult, Pub access computers, Ref serv in person, Scanner, Spoken cassettes & CDs, Story hour, Summer reading prog, Tax forms, Teen prog, Telephone ref, VHS videos, Web-catalog, Wheelchair accessible
Partic in SEO (Serving Every Ohioan) Library Center
Open Mon-Thurs 10-8, Fri & Sat 10-5

MONROEVILLE

P MONROEVILLE PUBLIC LIBRARY*, 34 Monroe St, 44847. (Mail add: PO Box 276, 44847-0276), SAN 313-6264. Tel: 419-465-2035. FAX: 419-465-2812. Web Site: monroevillepl.org. *Dir,* Heidi Sutter-Voelzke; E-mail: director@monroevillepl.org
Pop 2,000; Circ 46,000
Library Holdings: Bk Vols 21,000; Per Subs 32
Automation Activity & Vendor Info: (Cataloging) SirsiDynix; (Circulation) SirsiDynix; (OPAC) SirsiDynix
Partic in NORWELD
Open Mon & Fri 10-5, Tues-Thurs 10-7, Sat 10-1
Friends of the Library Group

MONTPELIER

P MONTPELIER PUBLIC LIBRARY*, 216 E Main St, 43543-1199. SAN 356-925X. Tel: 419-485-3287. FAX: 419-485-5671. Web Site: montpelierpubliclibrary.oplin.org. *Dir,* Gloria Osburn; E-mail: osburngl@oplin.org; Staff 8 (Non-MLS 8)
Founded 1927. Pop 38,000; Circ 67,066
Library Holdings: Bk Vols 60,150; Per Subs 70
Automation Activity & Vendor Info: (Cataloging) SirsiDynix; (Circulation) SirsiDynix
Partic in NORWELD
Open Mon, Wed & Thurs 10-8, Tues & Fri 10-5, Sat 10-3

S SOCIETY FOR THE STUDY OF MALE PSYCHOLOGY & PHYSIOLOGY LIBRARY*, 321 Iuka, 43543. SAN 326-3061. Tel: 419-485-3602. *Librn,* Dr Jerry Bergman; Staff 1 (MLS 1)
Founded 1974
Jul 2006-Jun 2007. Mats Exp $4,600
Library Holdings: Bk Titles 12,400; Per Subs 43

Special Collections: Male Psychology & Physiology Coll
Wireless access
Function: Res libr
Restriction: Staff & prof res

MORROW

P SALEM TOWNSHIP PUBLIC LIBRARY*, 535 W Pike St, 45152. SAN 313-6272. Tel: 513-899-2588. FAX: 513-899-9420. E-mail: salemtwppl@salem-township.lib.oh.us. Web Site: www.salem-township.lib.oh.us. *Dir,* Jerri A Short; E-mail: shortje@salem-township.lib.oh.us
Founded 1884. Pop 30,822; Circ 211,559
Library Holdings: DVDs 1,146; Bk Titles 74,525; Bk Vols 85,106; Per Subs 226; Talking Bks 14,601; Videos 5,825
Automation Activity & Vendor Info: (Circulation) Innovative Interfaces, Inc; (OPAC) Innovative Interfaces, Inc
Database Vendor: EBSCOhost
Wireless access
Function: ILL available
Partic in Miami Valley Librs; Southwestern Ohio Rural Librs
Open Mon & Tues 10-8, Wed & Thurs 10-6, Fri 10-5, Sat (Winter) 10-2

MOUNT GILEAD

P MOUNT GILEAD PUBLIC LIBRARY*, 41 E High St, 43338-1429. SAN 313-6280. Tel: 419-947-5866. FAX: 419-947-9252. E-mail: mgpl@oplin.org. Web Site: www.mt-gilead.lib.oh.us. *Dir,* Mike Kirk
Founded 1908
Library Holdings: Bk Vols 27,098; Per Subs 104
Automation Activity & Vendor Info: (Cataloging) Follett Software; (Circulation) Follett Software; (OPAC) Follett Software
Wireless access
Open Mon-Thurs 10-8:30, Fri 10-6, Sat 10-3
Friends of the Library Group

MOUNT ORAB

P BROWN COUNTY PUBLIC LIBRARY*, 613 S High St, 45154. (Mail add: PO Box 527, 45154-0527). Tel: 937-444-0181. FAX: 937-444-6502. E-mail: bookly@oplin.org. Web Site: www.browncountypubliclibrary.org. *Exec Dir,* Lynn A Harden; *Asst Dir,* Sandy Smith; E-mail: smithsak@oplin.org; Staff 7.5 (MLS 0.75, Non-MLS 6.75)
Founded 1920. Pop 32,500; Circ 224,726
Library Holdings: Bk Vols 103,050; Per Subs 380
Special Collections: State Document Depository
Automation Activity & Vendor Info: (Cataloging) SirsiDynix; (Circulation) SirsiDynix; (ILL) SirsiDynix; (OPAC) SirsiDynix
Database Vendor: SirsiDynix
Wireless access
Partic in SEO (Serving Every Ohioan) Library Center
Friends of the Library Group
Branches: 4
FAYETTEVILLE-PERRY BRANCH, 406 N East St, Fayetteville, 45118. Tel: 513-875-2665. FAX: 513-875-2738. *Mgr,* Sandra Smith; E-mail: smithsak@oplin.org
Founded 1999
Friends of the Library Group
MT ORAB BRANCH, 613 S High St, 45154. Tel. 937-444-1414. FAX: 937-444-6502. E-mail: bcplmto@oplin.org. *Mgr,* Heather Patten; E-mail: pattenhe@oplin.org
Open Mon, Tues & Thurs 9-8, Fri & Sat 9-4
Friends of the Library Group
SARDINIA BRANCH, 13309 Purdy Rd, Sardinia, 45171. Tel: 937-446-1565. FAX: 937-445-1506. E-mail: bcplsard@oplin.org. *Mgr,* Ginny Bridges; E-mail: bridgegi@oplin.org
Open Mon & Tues 11-6, Wed & Thurs 11-7, Fri & Sat 11-4
Friends of the Library Group
MARY P SHELTON BRANCH, 200 W Grant Ave, Georgetown, 45121. Tel: 937-378-3197. FAX: 937-378-4296. *Mgr,* Tonya Hensley
Open Mon & Tues 10-8, Wed & Thurs 10-7, Fri & Sat 10-4
Friends of the Library Group

MOUNT STERLING

P MOUNT STERLING PUBLIC LIBRARY*, 60 W Columbus St, 43143. SAN 313-6302. Tel: 740-869-2430. FAX: 740-869-3617. E-mail: misi8868@aol.com. Web Site: www.mtsterlingpubliclibrary.org. *Dir,* Christopher Siscoe; *Asst Dir,* Sharon Morgan; *Fiscal Officer,* Vickie Sheets; Staff 12 (Non-MLS 12)
Founded 1913. Pop 10,995; Circ 40,568
Library Holdings: Bks on Deafness & Sign Lang 30; Bk Vols 35,000; Per Subs 40
Automation Activity & Vendor Info: (Acquisitions) SirsiDynix; (Cataloging) SirsiDynix; (Circulation) SirsiDynix; (Course Reserve) SirsiDynix; (OPAC) SirsiDynix
Database Vendor: SirsiDynix
Wireless access
Partic in Ohio Public Library Information Network
Open Mon & Fri 10-5, Tues & Thurs 10-8, Sat 9-1
Friends of the Library Group

MOUNT VERNON

M KNOX COMMUNITY HOSPITAL*, Medical Library, 1330 Coshocton Rd, 43050. SAN 327-5612. Tel: 740-393-9000. FAX: 740-399-3113. *Lead Doc Imaging/Application Spec,* Todd Williams; Tel: 740-393-9616, E-mail: todd.williams@knoxcommhosp.org
Library Holdings: Bk Vols 1,215; Per Subs 15

C MOUNT VERNON NAZARENE UNIVERSITY*, Thorne Library & Learning Resource Center, 800 Martinsburg Rd, 43050-9500. SAN 313-6310. Tel: 740-397-9000, Ext 4240. FAX: 740-397-8847. Web Site: library.mvnu.edu. *Dir,* David Tipton; E-mail: dtipton@mvnu.edu; Staff 8 (MLS 3, Non-MLS 5)
Founded 1968. Enrl 2,455; Fac 155; Highest Degree: Master
Library Holdings: AV Mats 6,449; e-books 35,961; e-journals 7,361; Bk Vols 116,263; Per Subs 250; Videos 1,322
Special Collections: Church of the Nazarene, Doctrine, History & Missions
Automation Activity & Vendor Info: (Acquisitions) Innovative Interfaces, Inc; (Cataloging) Innovative Interfaces, Inc; (Circulation) Innovative Interfaces, Inc; (ILL) OCLC; (Media Booking) Innovative Interfaces, Inc; (OPAC) Innovative Interfaces, Inc; (Serials) Innovative Interfaces, Inc
Database Vendor: EBSCOhost, LexisNexis, OCLC FirstSearch, OVID Technologies
Wireless access
Partic in LOEX; Ohio Library & Information Network; OHIONET

P PUBLIC LIBRARY OF MOUNT VERNON & KNOX COUNTY*, 201 N Mulberry St, 43050-2413. SAN 356-9314. Tel: 740-392-2665. Reference Tel: 740-392-2665, Ext 230. FAX: 740-397-3866. E-mail: library@knox.net. Web Site: www.knox.net. *Dir,* John K Chidester; E-mail: jchidest@knox.net; *Asst Dir,* Mary H McGavick; *Circ,* Violet S Yarman; *Tech Serv,* Sharon Radermacher; *YA Serv,* Hoeffgen Beth; Staff 16 (MLS 3, Non-MLS 13)
Founded 1888. Pop 51,890; Circ 532,985
Library Holdings: Bk Vols 166,395; Per Subs 651
Automation Activity & Vendor Info: (Acquisitions) Innovative Interfaces, Inc; (Cataloging) Innovative Interfaces, Inc; (Circulation) Innovative Interfaces, Inc; (Course Reserve) Innovative Interfaces, Inc; (ILL) Innovative Interfaces, Inc; (Media Booking) Innovative Interfaces, Inc; (OPAC) Innovative Interfaces, Inc; (Serials) Innovative Interfaces, Inc
Wireless access
Open Mon-Fri 9-9, Sat 9-5, Sun 1-5
Friends of the Library Group
Branches: 3
DANVILLE PUBLIC, 512 S Market St, Danville, 43014-9609, SAN 356-9349. Tel: 740-599-2665. FAX: 740-599-2665. *Mgr,* Elizabeth Durbin; Staff 1 (Non-MLS 1)
Library Holdings: Bk Vols 21,000
Open Mon & Tues 1-8, Wed-Fri 10-5, Sat 1-5
Friends of the Library Group
FREDERICKTOWN COMMUNITY, One Burgett Dr, Fredericktown, 43019, SAN 356-9373. Tel: 740-694-2665. FAX: 740-694-3106. *Br Mgr,* Janelle Cothren; Staff 1 (Non-MLS 1)
Library Holdings: Bk Vols 42,500
Open Mon-Thurs 10-8, Fri & Sat 10-5
Friends of the Library Group
GAMBIER PUBLIC, 115 Meadow Lane, Gambier, 43022. (Mail add: PO Box 1984, Gambier, 43022), SAN 370-0194. Tel: 740-427-2665. FAX: 740-427-2665. *Librn,* Elizabeth Durbin; Staff 1 (Non-MLS 1)
Library Holdings: Bk Vols 15,480
Open Mon & Thurs-Sat 10-12:30 & 1:30-5, Tues & Wed 11-8
Friends of the Library Group
Bookmobiles: 1

MOUNT VICTORY

P RIDGEMONT PUBLIC LIBRARY*, 124 E Taylor St, 43340-8811. (Mail add: PO Box 318, 43340-0318), SAN 356-9403. Tel: 937-354-4445. FAX: 937-354-4445. Web Site: www.ridgemont.lib.oh.us. *Dir,* Cindy Zachman; *Librn,* Nancy J Terrill; *Ch Serv,* Beccy Ramsey
Circ 22,396
Library Holdings: Bk Vols 17,000; Per Subs 19
Wireless access
Branches: 1
RIDGEWAY BRANCH, 109 Main St, Ridgeway, 43345. (Mail add: PO Box 2, Ridgeway, 43345-0002), SAN 356-9438. Tel: 937-363-3066. FAX: 937-363-3066. *Librn,* Molly Gallo

NAPOLEON

L HENRY COUNTY LAW LIBRARY*, 609 N Perry St, 43545. SAN 327-6570. Tel: 419-599-1936. FAX: 419-592-4451. *In Charge,* John Donovan
Library Holdings: Bk Titles 5,000

P NAPOLEON PUBLIC LIBRARY*, 310 W Clinton St, 43545-1472. SAN 356-9462. Tel: 419-592-2531. FAX: 419-599-1472. E-mail: NapoleonReference@oplin.org. Web Site: www.napoleon.lib.oh.us. *Dir,* Betsy K Eggers; E-mail: eggersbe@oplin.org; *Fiscal Officer,* Laurie Norden; E-mail: norden@oplin.org; *ILL/Outreach Librn,* Barb George; *Adult Serv,* Su Jones; *Ch Serv,* Mary Hogan; Staff 14.85 (MLS 2, Non-MLS 12.85)
Founded 1906. Pop 28,000; Circ 135,875
Jan 2005-Dec 2005 Income (Main Library and Branch(s)) $809,416, State $549,433, Locally Generated Income $13,519, Other $246,464. Mats Exp $130,461, Books $104,577, Per/Ser (Incl. Access Fees) $13,528, AV Mat $12,356. Sal $504,047 (Prof $95,042)
Library Holdings: AV Mats 10,690; Bk Vols 145,140; Per Subs 252; Videos 1,153
Special Collections: County Papers from 1852, microfilm
Automation Activity & Vendor Info: (Cataloging) Innovative Interfaces, Inc; (Circulation) Innovative Interfaces, Inc; (ILL) Innovative Interfaces, Inc; (OPAC) Innovative Interfaces, Inc
Wireless access
Partic in NORWELD
Open Mon 9:30-8:30, Tues-Fri 9:30-5:30, Sat 9:30-1
Branches: 2
FLORIDA PUBLIC, 671 County Rd 17D, 43545-9215, SAN 356-9470. Tel: 419-762-5876. FAX: 419-762-5645. *Br Head,* Paula Steele
Function: Accelerated reader prog, Audiobks via web, Children's prog, Computers for patron use, Copy machines, e-mail & chat, Electronic databases & coll, Exhibits, Fax serv, ILL available, OverDrive digital audio bks, Photocopying/Printing, Preschool reading prog, Pub access computers, Story hour, Tax forms
Open Mon-Wed 1-5:30, Thurs 2-6:30
MCCLURE COMMUNITY, 110 Cross St, McClure, 43534-0035, SAN 356-9497. Tel: 419-748-8922. FAX: 419-748-8917. *Br Head,* Barbara Dawson
Function: Accelerated reader prog, Computers for patron use, Copy machines, Fax serv, ILL available, Preschool reading prog, Tax forms
Open Mon, Tues & Wed 1-5:30, Thurs 2-6:30

NELSONVILLE

P ATHENS COUNTY PUBLIC LIBRARIES*, Nelsonville Public Library, 95 W Washington, 45764-1177. SAN 356-9527. Tel: 740-753-2118. FAX: 740-753-3543. E-mail: nelpl@athenscounty.lib.oh.us. Web Site: www.myacpl.org. *Dir,* Lauren Miller; E-mail: lmiller@myacpl.org; *Br Mgr,* Laura O'Neil; *Ch,* Mary Van Doren; Staff 11 (MLS 8, Non-MLS 3)
Founded 1936. Pop 61,000; Circ 563,000
Library Holdings: Bk Vols 60,000; Per Subs 189
Open Mon-Thurs 9-7, Fri 9-6, Sat 11-5
Branches: 6
ATHENS PUBLIC LIBRARY, 30 Home St, Athens, 45701, SAN 356-9551. Tel: 740-592-4272. FAX: 740-594-4204. *Br Mgr,* Marilyn Zwayer
Library Holdings: Bk Vols 133,000
Open Tues-Thurs 9-8, Fri & Sat 9-5
Friends of the Library Group
CHAUNCEY PUBLIC, 29 Converse St, Chauncey, 45719. (Mail add: PO Box 3777, Chauncey, 45719), SAN 356-9586. Tel: 740-797-2512. FAX: 740-797-2512. *Br Mgr,* Lee Branner
Library Holdings: Bk Vols 7,000
Open Mon-Fri 11-6
COOLVILLE PUBLIC, 26401 Main St, Coolville, 45723-9059. (Mail add: PO Box 109, Coolville, 45723-0109), SAN 376-8503. Tel: 740-667-3354. FAX: 740-667-3354. *Br Mgr,* Roxanne Rupe; E-mail: rrupe@myacpl.org
Library Holdings: Bk Vols 11,000
Open Mon-Fri 11-6, Sat 11-5
GLOUSTER PUBLIC, 20 Toledo St, Glouster, 45732, SAN 356-9616. Tel: 740-767-3670. FAX: 740-767-3670. *Br Mgr,* Karen M Guffey; E-mail: kguffey@myacpl.org; *Ch,* Deb Couch
Library Holdings: Bk Vols 21,000
Open Mon-Thurs 9-7, Fri 9-5, Sat 9-3
THE PLAINS PUBLIC, 14 S Plains Rd, The Plains, 45780, SAN 375-6009. Tel: 740-797-4579. FAX: 740-797-4579. *Br Mgr,* Ken Robinson; *Ch,* Betty Ranck
Library Holdings: Bk Vols 35,000
Open Mon-Thurs 9-7, Fri & Sat 9-5
WELLS PUBLIC LIBRARY, 5200 Washington Rd, Albany, 45710, SAN 376-8511. Tel: 740-698-3059. FAX: 740-698-3059. *Br Mgr,* Lana Galloway; *Ch,* Taryn Lentes
Library Holdings: Bk Vols 14,000
Open Mon-Thurs 9-7, Fri & Sat 9-3
Bookmobiles: 1

J HOCKING COLLEGE LIBRARY*, 3301 Hocking Pkwy, 45764. SAN 313-6337. Tel: 740-753-6336. Reference Tel: 740-753-6334. FAX: 740-753-6341. E-mail: library@hocking.edu. Web Site: www.hocking.edu/library. *Dir,* Jeff Graffius; Tel: 740-753-6338, E-mail: graffius_j@hocking.edu; *Libr Asst,* Karen Graves; E-mail: graves_k@hocking.edu; Staff 4 (MLS 3, Non-MLS 1)
Founded 1968. Enrl 5,330; Fac 200; Highest Degree: Associate
Library Holdings: AV Mats 5,000; Bk Titles 17,500; Bk Vols 18,000; Per Subs 236
Subject Interests: Culinary arts, Forestry, Natural res, Nursing, Police sci
Automation Activity & Vendor Info: (Cataloging) Innovative Interfaces, Inc; (Circulation) Innovative Interfaces, Inc; (ILL) Innovative Interfaces, Inc; (OPAC) Innovative Interfaces, Inc; (Serials) Innovative Interfaces, Inc
Database Vendor: LexisNexis, ProQuest
Function: ILL available, Online cat, Online ref, Online searches, Photocopying/Printing, Ref & res, Ref serv available, Res libr, Scanner, VHS videos, Wheelchair accessible
Partic in Ohio Library & Information Network
Open Mon-Thurs 7:30am-8pm, Fri 7:30-5

S HOCKING CORRECTIONAL FACILITY LIBRARY*, 16759 Snake Hollow Rd, 45764-9658. (Mail add: PO Box 59, 45764-0059), SAN 322-8134. Tel: 740-753-1917, Ext 213. FAX: 740-753-4277. *Librn,* Daniel Okoro; E-mail: daniel.okoro@odrc.state.oh.us; Staff 1 (MLS 1)
Founded 1983
Library Holdings: Large Print Bks 1,500; Bk Titles 16,000; Per Subs 84; Spec Interest Per Sub 36; Talking Bks 250
Special Collections: Ohio Criminal Law
Special Services for the Deaf - High interest/low vocabulary bks
Special Services for the Blind - Bks on cassette; Large print bks

NEW CARLISLE

P NEW CARLISLE PUBLIC LIBRARY*, 111 E Lake Ave, 45344-1418. SAN 313-6345. Tel: 937-845-3601. FAX: 937-845-0908. Web Site: www.new-carlisle.lib.oh.us. *Dir,* Theodore R Allison; E-mail: allisoth@oplin.org; *Circ Mgr,* Beverly Sparks; *Ch,* Maggie Bollar; Staff 15.98 (MLS 2, Non-MLS 13.98)
Founded 1933. Pop 20,000; Circ 194,108
Library Holdings: Bk Titles 63,522; Per Subs 185
Automation Activity & Vendor Info: (Acquisitions) Horizon; (Cataloging) Horizon; (Circulation) Horizon; (ILL) Horizon; (Media Booking) Horizon; (OPAC) Horizon; (Serials) Horizon
Database Vendor: EBSCOhost, SirsiDynix
Wireless access
Partic in SEO (Serving Every Ohioan) Library Center
Open Tues 10-8, Wed, Fri & Sat 10-6, Thurs 12-8
Friends of the Library Group

NEW CONCORD

CR MUSKINGUM UNIVERSITY LIBRARY, 163 Stormont St, 43762-1199. SAN 313-6353. Tel: 740-826-8152. FAX: 740-826-8404. E-mail: library@muskingum.edu. Web Site: www.muskingum.edu/home/library. *Libr Dir,* Dr Sheila Ellenberger; Tel: 740-826-8260, E-mail: sheilaj@muskingum.edu; *Ref & Instruction Librn,* Nicole Arnold; *Ref & Instruction Librn,* Kristin Cole; *Ref & Instruction Librn,* Linda Hatfield; *Ref & Web Res Librn,* Holly E White; *Circ Supvr,* Kate Hoefler; Tel: 740-826-8156, E-mail: katew@muskingum.edu; Staff 6 (MLS 5, Non-MLS 1)
Founded 1837. Enrl 2,300; Fac 105; Highest Degree: Master
Jul 2014-Jun 2015. Mats Exp $183,900, Books $43,600, Per/Ser (Incl. Access Fees) $15,000, Micro $10,000, AV Mat $10,000, Electronic Ref Mat (Incl. Access Fees) $105,000, Presv $300
Library Holdings: CDs 893; DVDs 531; e-books 25,000; e-journals 12,000; Bk Titles 137,000; Bk Vols 140,000; Per Subs 350; Videos 2,004
Special Collections: Archives Coll. State Document Depository; US Document Depository
Automation Activity & Vendor Info: (Acquisitions) Innovative Interfaces, Inc; (Cataloging) Innovative Interfaces, Inc; (Circulation) Innovative Interfaces, Inc; (Course Reserve) Innovative Interfaces, Inc; (ILL) OCLC FirstSearch; (OPAC) Innovative Interfaces, Inc; (Serials) Innovative Interfaces, Inc
Database Vendor: ABC-CLIO, ACM (Association for Computing Machinery), American Chemical Society, American Physical Society, American Psychological Association (APA), Annual Reviews, Baker & Taylor, Blackwell, Checkpoint Systems, Inc, Cinahl, ebrary, EBSCO Discovery Service, EBSCOhost, Elsevier, Emerald, Ex Libris Group, Facts

on File, H W Wilson, IEEE (Institute of Electrical & Electronics Engineers), Infor Library & Information Solutions, Innovative Interfaces, Inc, ISI Web of Knowledge, LearningExpress, LexisNexis, Marquis Who's Who, Mergent Online, Modern Language Association, Newsbank, OCLC FirstSearch, OCLC WorldShare Interlibrary Loan, OHIONET, OVID Technologies, Safari Books Online, Sage, Springer-Verlag, Swets Information Services, Wilson - Wilson Web, YBP Library Services
Wireless access
Function: 24/7 Online cat, Computers for patron use, Distance learning, Doc delivery serv, e-mail & chat, E-Reserves, Electronic databases & coll, eReaders, Fax serv, Free DVD rentals, ILL available, Instruction & testing, Laminating, Magazines, Microfiche/film & reading machines, Movies, Music CDs, Newsp ref libr, Online cat, Online info literacy tutorials on the web & in blackboard, Online ref, Online searches, Orientations, Outside serv via phone, mail, e-mail & web, Photocopying/Printing, Prof lending libr, Prog for adults, Ref & res, Ref serv available, Ref serv in person, Scanner, Study rm, Wheelchair accessible, Workshops
Partic in Ohio Library & Information Network; Ohio Private Academic Libraries (OPAL)
Restriction: Open to pub for ref & circ; with some limitations

NEW LEXINGTON

P PERRY COUNTY DISTRICT LIBRARY*, 117 S Jackson St, 43764-1382. SAN 356-9640. Tel: 740-342-4194. FAX: 740-342-4204. Web Site: www.pcdl.org. *Dir,* Melissa Marolt; Staff 3 (MLS 3)
Founded 1935. Pop 35,040; Circ 392,461
Library Holdings: Bk Titles 58,300; Bk Vols 137,262; Per Subs 198
Subject Interests: Genealogy, Local hist
Automation Activity & Vendor Info: (Acquisitions) Anacortes Software Inc; (Cataloging) SirsiDynix; (Circulation) SirsiDynix
Wireless access
Open Mon-Thurs 10-8, Fri 10-5, Sat 10-3
Branches: 5
CORNING BRANCH, 113 11th Hill St, Corning, 43730. (Mail add: PO Box 395, Corning, 43730-0395), SAN 356-9675. Tel: 740-347-4763. FAX: 740-347-9219. E-mail: corning@pcdl.org. *Br Mgr,* Peggy Pingle
Open Mon & Wed 10-6, Fri 10-5, Sat 10-1
CROOKSVILLE BRANCH, 111 E Main St, Crooksville, 43731, SAN 356-9705. Tel: 740-982-4821. FAX: 740-982-3133. E-mail: crooksville@pcdl.org. *Br Mgr,* Sonya Saxton
Open Mon & Wed 10-7, Fri 10-5, Sat 10-1
JUNCTION CITY BRANCH, 108 W Main St, Junction City, 43748. (Mail add: PO Box 157, Junction City, 43748), SAN 356-973X. Tel: 740-987-7646. FAX: 740-987-2238. E-mail: junctioncity@pcdl.org. *Br Mgr,* Paula Cotterman
Open Mon & Wed 10-7, Fri 10-5, Sat 10-1
Friends of the Library Group
SOMERSET BRANCH, 103 Public Sq, Somerset, 43783. (Mail add: PO Box 277, Somerset, 43783-0277), SAN 356-9799. Tel: 740-743-1161. FAX: 740-743-9139. E-mail: somerset@pcdl.org. *Br Mgr,* Deborah Boley
Open Mon-Wed 10-7, Fri 10-5, Sat 10-2
Friends of the Library Group
THORNVILLE BRANCH, 99 E Columbus St, Thornville, 43076. (Mail add: PO Box 292, Thornville, 43782-0013), SAN 356-9829. Tel: 740-246-5133. FAX: 740-246-3994. E-mail: thornville@pcdl.org. *Br Mgr,* Sharon Chaffin
Open Mon-Wed 10-7, Fri 10-5, Sat 10-2

NEW LONDON

P NEW LONDON PUBLIC LIBRARY*, 67 S Main St, 44851-1137. SAN 313-6361. Tel: 419-929-3981. FAX: 419-929-0007. E-mail: nwlondon@oplin.org. Web Site: www.newlondonohio.com/library.htm. *Dir,* Anne Lowery; Staff 8 (MLS 1, Non-MLS 7)
Founded 1916. Pop 6,100; Circ 65,000
Library Holdings: AV Mats 1,500; Bk Vols 35,721; Per Subs 98
Subject Interests: Genealogy, Local hist
Automation Activity & Vendor Info: (Acquisitions) Innovative Interfaces, Inc; (Cataloging) Horizon; (Circulation) SirsiDynix; (OPAC) Innovative Interfaces, Inc
Database Vendor: EBSCOhost, Electric Library, OCLC WebJunction
Wireless access
Partic in Ohio Public Library Information Network
Open Mon 9-5, Tues & Thurs 9-8, Wed 12-8, Fri 12-5, Sat 9-3
Friends of the Library Group

NEW MADISON

P NEW MADISON PUBLIC LIBRARY*, 142 S Main St, 45346. (Mail add: PO Box 32, 45346-0032), SAN 313-637X. Tel: 937-996-1741. FAX: 937-996-1473. E-mail: info@newmadisonpubliclibrary.org. Web Site: www.newmadisonpubliclibrary.org. *Dir,* Brenda Miller; Staff 6 (Non-MLS 6)
Founded 1934. Pop 6,000; Circ 100,000
Library Holdings: Bk Vols 47,000; Per Subs 200
Subject Interests: Local hist
Automation Activity & Vendor Info: (Cataloging) SirsiDynix; (Circulation) SirsiDynix; (OPAC) SirsiDynix
Partic in Miami Valley Librs
Open Mon-Wed 9-8, Thurs & Fri 9-5, Sat 9-3
Friends of the Library Group

NEW PHILADELPHIA

C KENT STATE UNIVERSITY*, Tuscarawas Campus Library, 330 University Dr NE, 44663-9452. SAN 313-6388. Tel: 330-308-7471. FAX: 330-308-7553. Web Site: www.tusc.kent.edu/library, www.tusc.kent.edu/student-life/library/index.cfm. *Dir,* Cherie Bronkar; Tel: 330-308-7456, E-mail: cbronkar@kent.edu
Founded 1968. Enrl 817
Library Holdings: Bk Titles 45,000; Bk Vols 58,000; Per Subs 250
Special Collections: Moravian Coll; Ohio Authors Coll; Olmstead Local History Coll
Subject Interests: Local hist, Nursing
Open Mon-Thurs 8am-9pm, Fri 8-5, Sat 9am-1pm

L TUSCARAWAS COUNTY LAW LIBRARY ASSOCIATION*, 101 E High Ave, 44663-2599. SAN 313-640X. Tel: 330-365-3224. FAX: 330-343-5509. *Librn,* Kathy Moreland; E-mail: morelandkathy9@gmail.com
Founded 1865
Jan 2005-Dec 2005 Income $176,012, City $39,962, County $136,050. Mats Exp $154,372, Electronic Ref Mat (Incl. Access Fees) $20,000. Sal $32,000
Library Holdings: Bk Titles 30,000; Per Subs 10; Videos 10
Partic in Westlaw
Open Mon-Fri 8-4:30

P TUSCARAWAS COUNTY PUBLIC LIBRARY*, 121 Fair Ave NW, 44663-2600. SAN 356-9853. Tel: 330-364-4474. FAX: 330-364-8217. E-mail: tuscwref@oplin.org. Web Site: www.tusclibrary.org. *Dir,* Michelle Ramsell; E-mail: ramselmi@oplin.org; *Asst Dir, Mgr, Ad Serv,* Debra Ann Tristano; E-mail: tristade@oplin.org; *Mgr, Ch Serv,* Missy Littell; *Mgr, Extn & Tech Serv,* Andrea Legg; *Mgr, Info Tech,* Richard Wiltrout; E-mail: wiltrari@oplin.org; Staff 5 (MLS 4, Non-MLS 1)
Founded 1905. Pop 54,415; Circ 682,729
Jan 2006-Dec 2006 Income (Main Library and Branch(s)) $1,910,148, State $1,620,840, County $205,737, Locally Generated Income $83,571. Mats Exp $227,418, Books $153,092, Per/Ser (Incl. Access Fees) $15,493, Micro $1,971, AV Mat $56,862. Sal $1,078,391 (Prof $418,215)
Library Holdings: AV Mats 23,717; CDs 7,695; DVDs 4,698; Bk Vols 117,043; Per Subs 372; Videos 5,454
Automation Activity & Vendor Info: (Acquisitions) Horizon; (Cataloging) Horizon; (Circulation) Horizon; (Course Reserve) Horizon; (ILL) Horizon; (Media Booking) Horizon; (OPAC) Horizon
Database Vendor: ALLDATA Online, EBSCOhost, OCLC FirstSearch
Wireless access
Function: Telephone ref
Partic in SEO (Serving Every Ohioan) Library Center
Special Services for the Deaf - Staff with knowledge of sign lang; TDD equip
Open Mon-Thurs 9-8:30, Fri 10-6, Sat 9-5
Friends of the Library Group
Branches: 4
BOLIVAR BRANCH, 455 W Water St SW, Bolivar, 44612-9224. (Mail add: PO Box 588, Bolivar, 44612-0588), SAN 356-9888. Tel: 330-874-2720. *Br Mgr,* Jessica Gard; E-mail: gardje@oplin.org
Library Holdings: CDs 821; DVDs 462; Bk Titles 17,744; Per Subs 45; Talking Bks 305; Videos 682
Open Mon & Fri 10-5m Tues 10-8, Thurs 1-8, Sat 10-2
Friends of the Library Group
EMMA HUBER MEMORIAL LIBRARY, 356 Fifth St SW, Strasburg, 44680, SAN 356-9918. Tel: 330-878-5711. FAX: 330-878-5711. *Br Mgr,* Brenda West; E-mail: westbr@oplin.org
Library Holdings: CDs 655; DVDs 430; Bk Vols 8,920; Per Subs 25; Talking Bks 278; Videos 379
Open Tues 10-5, Wed 10-8, Thurs 1-8, Fri 1-6
Friends of the Library Group
SUGARCREEK BRANCH, 120 S Broadway, Sugarcreek, 44681. (Mail add: PO Box 309, Sugarcreek, 44681-0309), SAN 356-9942. Tel: 330-852-2813. FAX: 330-852-2813. *Br Mgr,* Christine Pierpoint; E-mail: cpierpoint@oplin.org
Library Holdings: CDs 597; DVDs 476; Bk Vols 12,719; Per Subs 49; Talking Bks 164; Videos 954
Open Mon & Wed 10-5, Tues 10-8, Fri 1-8, Sat 10-2
TUSCARAWAS BRANCH, 209 S Main St, Tuscarawas, 44682. (Mail add: PO Box 337, Tuscarawas, 44682-0337), SAN 356-9977. Tel: 740-922-2748. FAX: 740-922-2748. *Br Mgr,* Renee Poland; E-mail: polandre@oplin.org

Library Holdings: CDs 595; DVDs 449; Bk Vols 7,867; Per Subs 27; Talking Bks 23; Videos 413
Bookmobiles: 1

NEW STRAITSVILLE

P NEW STRAITSVILLE PUBLIC LIBRARY*, 102 E Main St, 43766. (Mail add: PO Box 8, 43766-0008), SAN 313-6418. Tel: 740-394-2717. FAX: 740-394-2817. Web Site: www.new-straitsville.lib.oh.us. *Head Librn,* Linda Kemper; E-mail: kemperli@oplin.org; *Asst Librn,* Patty Spencer
Founded 1916. Circ 29,019
Library Holdings: Bk Vols 18,000; Per Subs 35
Automation Activity & Vendor Info: (Cataloging) ComPanion Corp; (Circulation) ComPanion Corp; (OPAC) ComPanion Corp
Open Mon-Fri 2-7, Sat 10-3

NEWARK

S THE DAWES ARBORETUM LIBRARY*, 7770 Jacksontown Rd SE, 43056-9380. SAN 325-2760. Tel: 740-323-2355. Toll Free Tel: 800-443-2937. FAX: 740-323-4058. E-mail: information@dawesarb.org. Web Site: www.dawesarb.org. *Exec Dir,* Luke Messinger
Founded 1970
Library Holdings: Bk Titles 1,400; Per Subs 60
Subject Interests: Gardening, Hort, Juv, Nat hist
Wireless access
Open Mon-Sat 8-5, Sun 1-5
Restriction: Non-circulating

S HEISEY COLLECTORS OF AMERICA, INC*, Louise Ream Library, 169 W Church St, 43055-0027. SAN 324-1555. Tel: 740-345-2932. FAX: 740-345-9638. E-mail: curator@heiseymuseum.org. Web Site: www.heiseymuseum.org. *Curator, Dir,* Jack Burriss; E-mail: curator@heiseymuseum.org; Staff 8 (MLS 1, Non-MLS 7)
Founded 1974
Library Holdings: Bk Titles 600; Per Subs 50
Special Collections: Heisey Company Correspondence & Information
Subject Interests: A H Heisey & Co, Am glass
Publications: Heisey News (Monthly)
Open Tues-Sat 10-4, Sun 1-4
Restriction: Non-circulating

L LICKING COUNTY LAW LIBRARY ASSOCIATION*, 65 E Main St, 43055. SAN 371-439X. Tel: 740-349-6561. FAX: 740-349-6561. *Librn,* James W Pyle; *Adminr,* Sandy Bowers; E-mail: sandybowers@lcounty.com
Library Holdings: Bk Vols 10,000; Per Subs 91

P LICKING COUNTY LIBRARY*, 101 W Main St, 43055-5054. SAN 357-0002. Tel: 740-349-5500. FAX: 740-349-5535. Web Site: www.lickingcountylibrary.info. *Dir,* Babette Wofter; Tel: 740-349-5503, E-mail: bwofter@lickingcountylibrary.info; *Head of Br Serv,* Deb Holman; *Head, Emerging Technologies & Digital Content,* Anne Kennedy; *Head of Outreach Serv,* Brock Hutchison; *Head, Adult Serv,* Mary Harmon; Tel: 740-344-2177; *Head, Ch,* Sadie E Smith; Tel: 740-349-5551, Fax: 740-349-5575, E-mail: sesmith@lickingcountylibrary.info; *Head, Circ,* Doug Stout; *Head, Popular Libr,* Carla Roberts; Tel: 740-349-5550, E-mail: croberts@lickingcountylibrary.info; *Head, Ref (Info Serv),* Jeff Eling; Tel: 740-349-5521, E-mail: jeling@lickingcountylibrary.info; *Head, Teen Serv,* Amy Gantt; Tel: 740-349-5552, E-mail: agantt@lickingcountylibrary.info; *Tech Serv Supvr,* Shirley Smith; *Fiscal Officer,* Sandra Lodge; Tel: 740-349-5505, E-mail: slodge@lickingcountylibrary.info; Staff 26 (MLS 21, Non-MLS 5)
Founded 1908. Pop 109,617; Circ 1,055,130
Jan 2008-Dec 2008 Income (Main Library and Branch(s)) $4,238,830, State $3,137,200. Mats Exp $525,145, Books $398,540, Per/Ser (Incl. Access Fees) $1,734, AV Mat $89,371, Electronic Ref Mat (Incl. Access Fees) $35,500. Sal $2,371,860 (Prof $1,055,000)
Library Holdings: Audiobooks 3,583; AV Mats 34,753; CDs 14,016; DVDs 11,921; Large Print Bks 12,356; Bk Titles 273,994; Bk Vols 428,100; Per Subs 361; Videos 3,641
Special Collections: State Document Depository
Subject Interests: Local hist
Automation Activity & Vendor Info: (Acquisitions) SirsiDynix; (Cataloging) OCLC; (Circulation) SirsiDynix; (OPAC) Horizon
Wireless access
Function: Adult bk club, After school storytime, Audio & video playback equip for onsite use, AV serv, Bk club(s), Bks on cassette, Bks on CD, Children's prog, Computers for patron use, Copy machines, Free DVD rentals, Handicapped accessible, Holiday prog, Home delivery & serv to Sr ctr & nursing homes, Homebound delivery serv, ILL available, Jail serv, Music CDs, Notary serv, Online cat, Online ref, Online searches, Outreach serv, Photocopying/Printing, Prog for adults, Prog for children & young adult, Pub access computers, Ref & res, Ref serv available, Senior outreach, Serves mentally handicapped consumers, Story hour, Summer reading prog, Tax forms, Teen prog, VHS videos, Web-catalog, Workshops
Special Services for the Blind - Large print bks
Open Mon-Thurs 9-8, Fri 9-5:30, Sat 9-5, Sun 1-5
Branches: 5
MARY E BABCOCK BRANCH, 320 N Main St, Johnstown, 43031, SAN 357-0061. Tel: 740-967-2982. FAX: 740-967-0729. *Br Mgr,* Julie McElhaney; E-mail: jmcelhaney@lickingcountylibrary.info; Staff 1 (MLS 1)
Circ 56,334
Library Holdings: Audiobooks 136; AV Mats 1,345; CDs 408; DVDs 794; Bk Titles 29,653; Per Subs 76
Function: Bk club(s), Children's prog, Computers for patron use, Copy machines, Free DVD rentals, Music CDs, Photocopying/Printing, Prog for adults, Prog for children & young adult, Story hour, Summer reading prog, Tax forms, Teen prog, VHS videos
Open Mon-Thurs 10-7, Fri & Sat 10-3
Friends of the Library Group
BUCKEYE LAKE BRANCH, King's Plaza, 4455 Walnut Rd, Rte 79, Buckeye Lake, 43008. Tel: 740-928-0472. FAX: 740-928-0486. *Br Supvr,* Ada Myers; E-mail: amyers@lickingcountylibrary.info; Staff 1 (Non-MLS 1)
Circ 21,206
Library Holdings: Audiobooks 136; AV Mats 1,345; CDs 408; DVDs 794; Per Subs 37
Function: Adult bk club, After school storytime, Bk club(s), Bks on CD, Computers for patron use, Copy machines, Holiday prog, Music CDs, Photocopying/Printing, Prog for adults, Prog for children & young adult, Pub access computers, Story hour, Summer reading prog, Tax forms, Teen prog, Wheelchair accessible
Open Mon-Thurs 10-7, Fri 10-5, Sat 10-3
Friends of the Library Group
HEBRON BRANCH, 934 W Main St, Hebron, 43025, SAN 357-0037. Tel: 740-928-3923. FAX: 740-928-9437. *Br Supvr,* Paula LaFrenierre, E-mail: plafrenierre@lickingcountylibrary.info; Staff 1 (Non-MLS 1)
Circ 41,778
Library Holdings: Audiobooks 136; AV Mats 1,345; CDs 408; DVDs 794; Per Subs 48
Function: Adult bk club, After school storytime, Bk club(s), Bks on cassette, Bks on CD, Children's prog, Computers for patron use, Copy machines, Free DVD rentals, Handicapped accessible, Holiday prog, Music CDs, Photocopying/Printing, Prog for adults, Prog for children & young adult, Pub access computers, Story hour, Summer reading prog, Tax forms, Teen prog
Open Mon-Thurs 10-7, Fri 10-5, Sat 10-3
HERVEY MEMORIAL, 15 N Main, Utica, 43080. (Mail add: PO Box 512, Utica, 43080-0512), SAN 357-0126. Tel: 740-892-2400. FAX: 740-892-2400. *Br Supvr,* Jennifer Mitchell; E-mail: jmitchell@lickingcountylibrary.info; Staff 1 (Non-MLS 1)
Circ 42,663
Library Holdings: Audiobooks 136; AV Mats 1,345; CDs 408; DVDs 794; Per Subs 71
Function: Photocopying/Printing, Prog for adults, Prog for children & young adult, Story hour, Summer reading prog, Tax forms, Teen prog
Open Mon-Thurs 10-7, Fri & Sat 10-3
EMERSON R MILLER BRANCH, 990 W Main St, 43055, SAN 357-0096. Tel: 740-344-2155. FAX: 740-344-4271. *Head of Br Serv,* Deb Holman; E-mail: dholman@lickingcountylibrary.info; Staff 2 (MLS 2)
Circ 114,539
Library Holdings: Audiobooks 136; AV Mats 1,345; CDs 408; DVDs 794; Large Print Bks 150; Per Subs 90
Function: Adult bk club, After school storytime, Bk club(s), Bks on cassette, Bks on CD, Children's prog, Computers for patron use, Copy machines, Free DVD rentals, Handicapped accessible, Holiday prog, Music CDs, Online searches, Photocopying/Printing, Prog for adults, Prog for children & young adult, Pub access computers, Ref serv available, Serves mentally handicapped consumers, Story hour, Summer reading prog, Tax forms, Teen prog, Telephone ref
Open Mon-Thurs 10-8, Fri 10-5, Sat 10-3
Bookmobiles: 1. Supvr, Sharon Bowman. Bk titles 4,700

M LICKING MEMORIAL HOSPITAL*, Ralph E Pickett Medical Library, 1320 W Main St, 43055-3699. SAN 327-3520. Tel: 740-348-4130. FAX: 740-348-4012. *Librn,* Lindsay Freytag; *Asst Librn,* Kathy Bradley
Library Holdings: Bk Vols 250; Per Subs 12

NEWCOMERSTOWN

P NEWCOMERSTOWN PUBLIC LIBRARY*, 123 E Main St, 43832-1093. SAN 313-6450. Tel: 740-498-8228. FAX: 740-498-8221. Web Site: www.newcomerstownlibrary.org. *Dir,* Greg Romer; *Asst Dir,* Michelle Cox; *Youth Serv Librn,* Jennifer Coventry; Staff 3 (MLS 1, Non-MLS 2)
Founded 1935. Pop 6,819; Circ 62,000
Library Holdings: Bk Vols 35,000; Per Subs 79
Wireless access
Partic in SEO (Serving Every Ohioan) Library Center

Open Mon-Thurs 10-8, Fri 10-6, Sat 9-5
Friends of the Library Group

NEWTON FALLS

P NEWTON FALLS PUBLIC LIBRARY*, 204 S Canal St, 44444-1694. SAN 313-6469. Tel: 330-872-1282. FAX: 330-872-9153. Web Site: www.newtonfalls.org. *Dir,* Kerry Reed; E-mail: kerrymccrone@newtonfalls.org; Staff 7 (MLS 5, Non-MLS 2)
Founded 1930. Pop 9,611; Circ 223,898
Subject Interests: Local hist
Automation Activity & Vendor Info: (Cataloging) TLC (The Library Corporation); (Circulation) TLC (The Library Corporation); (OPAC) TLC (The Library Corporation); (Serials) TLC (The Library Corporation)
Database Vendor: TLC (The Library Corporation)
Wireless access
Function: Prog for children & young adult, Ref serv available, Senior computer classes, Spoken cassettes & CDs, Spoken cassettes & DVDs, Summer reading prog, Tax forms, Telephone ref, VHS videos, Video lending libr, Wheelchair accessible, Workshops
Partic in Northeast Ohio Regional Library System
Open Mon-Thurs 9-8, Fri & Sat 9-5, Sun Noon-5
Friends of the Library Group

NILES

P MCKINLEY MEMORIAL LIBRARY*, 40 N Main St, 44446-5082. SAN 313-6477. Tel: 330-652-1704. FAX: 330-652-5788. E-mail: mckinley@mcklib.org. Web Site: www.mckinley.lib.oh.us. *Dir,* Patrick E Finan; Tel: 330-652-1704, Ext 204; Staff 20 (MLS 6, Non-MLS 14)
Founded 1908. Pop 21,000; Circ 277,000
Library Holdings: AV Mats 8,000; CDs 1,200; DVDs 3,300; Large Print Bks 2,400; Bk Vols 72,000; Per Subs 120; Talking Bks 2,200; Videos 700
Special Collections: President William McKinley Coll, bk, micro & mus artifacts
Automation Activity & Vendor Info: (Acquisitions) TLC (The Library Corporation); (Cataloging) TLC (The Library Corporation); (Circulation) TLC (The Library Corporation); (OPAC) TLC (The Library Corporation)
Database Vendor: EBSCOhost, Electric Library, Gale Cengage Learning, Grolier Online, Newsbank, ProQuest, ReferenceUSA, Wilson - Wilson Web
Wireless access
Partic in Northeast Ohio Regional Library System
Friends of the Library Group

NORTH BALTIMORE

P NORTH BALTIMORE PUBLIC LIBRARY*, 230 N Main St, 45872-1125. SAN 313-6493. Tel: 419-257-3621. FAX: 419-257-3859. Web Site: www.nbpubliclibrary.org. *Dir,* Connie Phillips; E-mail: connie@nblibrary.org; *Asst Dir,* Lori Kaufman; *Ch Serv,* Cheryl Heilman; Staff 13 (MLS 1, Non-MLS 12)
Founded 1918. Pop 4,175; Circ 153,366
Library Holdings: AV Mats 3,899; Bk Vols 49,583; Per Subs 146
Special Collections: Film,Television & Theater
Automation Activity & Vendor Info: (Cataloging) SirsiDynix; (Circulation) SirsiDynix; (ILL) SirsiDynix
Wireless access
Function: Adult bk club, After school storytime, CD-ROM, Copy machines, Fax serv, Handicapped accessible, ILL available, Music CDs, Photocopying/Printing, Prog for adults, Prog for children & young adult, Ref serv available, Summer reading prog, Tax forms, Telephone ref, VHS videos, Wheelchair accessible
Partic in NORWELD
Open Mon-Thurs 9-8, Fri 9-5, Sat 9-1

NORTH CANTON

C KENT STATE UNIVERSITY, Stark Campus Library, 6000 Frank Ave NW, 44720-7548. SAN 313-2331. Tel: 330-244-3330, 330-499-9600. FAX: 330-494-6212. E-mail: starklibrary@listserv.kent.edu. Web Site: stark.kent.edu/academics/library. *Dir,* Rob Kairis; Tel: 330-244-3326, E-mail: rkairis@kent.edu; *Online Learning Librn,* Melissa Bauer; Tel: 330-244-3320, E-mail: mbauer10@kent.edu; *Reserves Mgr/Circ,* Position Currently Open; *Acq,* Jeanne Hawley; Tel: 330-244-3321, E-mail: jhawley@kent.edu; *Cat,* Mary Birtalan; Tel: 330-244-3323, E-mail: mbirtalan@kent.edu; *Ref,* Maureen Kilcullen; Tel: 330-244-3322, E-mail: mkilcullen@kent.edu; *Ser,* Roger Davis; Tel: 330-244-3328, E-mail: rdavis@kent.edu; Staff 4 (MLS 3, Non-MLS 1)
Founded 1967. Enrl 5,000; Fac 150; Highest Degree: Master
Jul 2013-Jun 2014 Income $250,000. Mats Exp $99,282, Books $30,817, Per/Ser (Incl. Access Fees) $42,742, AV Mat $6,690, Electronic Ref Mat (Incl. Access Fees) $17,006, Presv $2,027. Sal $470,018 (Prof $303,939)
Library Holdings: Audiobooks 41; AV Mats 4,368; CDs 296; DVDs 1,100; Bk Titles 47,620; Bk Vols 85,819; Per Subs 163; Videos 3,754
Automation Activity & Vendor Info: (Cataloging) Innovative Interfaces, Inc - Millenium; (Circulation) Innovative Interfaces, Inc - Millenium; (Course Reserve) Innovative Interfaces, Inc - Millenium; (ILL) Innovative Interfaces, Inc - Millenium; (Media Booking) Innovative Interfaces, Inc - Millenium; (OPAC) Innovative Interfaces, Inc - Millenium; (Serials) Innovative Interfaces, Inc - Millenium
Database Vendor: ABC-CLIO, ARTstor, Booklist Online, College Source, CQ Press, ebrary, EBSCO Discovery Service, EBSCOhost, Elsevier, Gale Cengage Learning, H W Wilson, IEEE (Institute of Electrical & Electronics Engineers), Innovative Interfaces, Inc, ISI Web of Knowledge, JSTOR, LearningExpress, LexisNexis, Modern Language Association, OCLC, OCLC FirstSearch, OCLC WorldShare Interlibrary Loan, OHIONET, Oxford Online, ProQuest, ReferenceUSA, RefWorks, Safari Books Online, Sage, SerialsSolutions, Springer-Verlag, Standard & Poor's, Westlaw, Wilson - Wilson Web, YBP Library Services
Wireless access
Function: Res libr
Partic in OCLC Online Computer Library Center, Inc; Ohio Library & Information Network
Open Mon-Thurs 7:30am-10pm, Fri 8-5, Sat 9-3, Sun 1-5

P NORTH CANTON PUBLIC LIBRARY, 185 N Main St, 44720-2595. SAN 357-0150. Tel: 330-499-4712. FAX: 330-499-3452. Web Site: www.ncantonlibrary.org. *Dir,* Sandra Lang; Tel: 330-499-4712, Ext 315, E-mail: director@northcantonlibrary.org; *Head, Children's Dept,* Jamie Macris; *Syst Adminr,* Carrie Hayes; Staff 61 (MLS 6, Non-MLS 55)
Founded 1926. Pop 29,575; Circ 966,255
Library Holdings: Audiobooks 7,278; CDs 8,350; DVDs 21,609; e-books 183,874; Electronic Media & Resources 1,170; Bk Vols 111,631
Subject Interests: Art
Automation Activity & Vendor Info: (Acquisitions) Innovative Interfaces, Inc; (Cataloging) Innovative Interfaces, Inc; (Circulation) Innovative Interfaces, Inc; (OPAC) Innovative Interfaces, Inc
Database Vendor: EBSCOhost, Gale Cengage Learning
Wireless access
Function: Handicapped accessible, ILL available, Photocopying/Printing, Prog for adults, Prog for children & young adult, Summer reading prog, Wheelchair accessible
Publications: On The Shelf (Newsletter)
Open Mon-Thurs 10-8, Fri 10-6, Sat 9-5
Friends of the Library Group

S TIMKEN CO, Research Library, 4500 Mt Pleasant Rd NW, WHQ-05, 44720. SAN 313-2382. Tel: 234-262-2049. FAX: 234-262-2282. *Managing Librn,* Patricia Cromi; E-mail: patricia.cromi@timken.com; Staff 1 (MLS 1)
Founded 1966
Library Holdings: Bk Titles 9,000; Per Subs 50
Subject Interests: Eng res, Ferrous metallurgical res
Partic in OHIONET

SR UNITED CHURCH OF CHRIST*, Zion United Church of Christ Memorial Library, 415 S Main St, 44720. SAN 328-1426. Tel: 330-499-8191. FAX: 330-499-8194. E-mail: zionucc@gmail.com. *Librn,* Edlyn Theiss; Staff 1 (MLS 1)
Founded 1964
Library Holdings: AV Mats 31; Bk Titles 3,907
Special Collections: Adult & Children's Books; Religious & Selected Secular Books
Function: Adult literacy prog, Bk reviews (Group), Prog for children & young adult, Ref serv available
Partic in Church & Synagogue Libr Asn
Restriction: Staff & mem only

C WALSH UNIVERSITY*, Brother Edmond Drouin Library, 2020 E Maple St, 44720-3336. SAN 313-2390. Tel: 330-490-7185. Interlibrary Loan Service Tel: 330-490-7204. Reference Tel: 330-244-4942. Automation Services Tel: 330-490-7183. Toll Free Tel: 888-627-1826. FAX: 330-490-7270. E-mail: library@walsh.edu. Web Site: library.walsh.edu. *Dean, Institutional Effectiveness & Libr Serv,* Daniel Suvak; E-mail: dsuvak@walsh.edu; *Asst Librn, Archives & Spec Coll,* Katie Hutchison; Tel: 330-244-4968, E-mail: khutchison@walsh.edu; *Asst Librn, Electronic Content,* Ryan McLaughlin; Tel: 330-244-4658, E-mail: rmclaughlin@walsh.edu; *Asst Librn, Pub Serv,* Shirley Lewis; Tel: 330-490-7187, E-mail: slewis@walsh.edu; *Asst Librn, Tech Serv,* Heidi Beke-Harrigan; Tel: 330-490-7186, E-mail: hbekeharrigan@walsh.edu. Subject Specialists: *Educ, Hist,* Katie Hutchison; *Psychol, Sci,* Ryan McLaughlin; *Nursing, Phys therapy,* Shirley Lewis; *Arts, Lang, Lit,* Heidi Beke-Harrigan; Staff 7.6 (MLS 4.4, Non-MLS 3.2)
Founded 1960. Enrl 2,781; Fac 130; Highest Degree: Doctorate
Jul 2011-Jun 2012 Income $806,253. Mats Exp $806,253, Books $55,000, Per/Ser (Incl. Access Fees) $155,967, AV Mat $12,000, Electronic Ref Mat (Incl. Access Fees) $2,000, Presv $7,000. Sal $369,205 (Prof $219,750)
Library Holdings: AV Mats 17,000; CDs 700; DVDs 3,000; e-books 113,265; e-journals 60,000; Bk Titles 248,368; Bk Vols 277,307; Per Subs 200

Automation Activity & Vendor Info: (Acquisitions) Innovative Interfaces, Inc - Millenium; (Cataloging) Innovative Interfaces, Inc - Millenium; (Circulation) Innovative Interfaces, Inc - Millenium; (Course Reserve) Innovative Interfaces, Inc - Millenium; (ILL) OCLC Online; (OPAC) Innovative Interfaces, Inc - Millenium; (Serials) Innovative Interfaces, Inc - Millenium
Database Vendor: ABC-CLIO, ACM (Association for Computing Machinery), Alexander Street Press, American Chemical Society, American Mathematical Society, American Psychological Association (APA), Annual Reviews, ARTstor, Checkpoint Systems, Inc, CQ Press, Dialog, ebrary, EBSCO Discovery Service, EBSCOhost, Elsevier, Emerald, Ex Libris Group, Factiva.com, Gale Cengage Learning, IBISWorld, Ingram Library Services, Innovative Interfaces, Inc, ISI Web of Knowledge, JSTOR, LearningExpress, LexisNexis, Medline, Mergent Online, Modern Language Association, OCLC, OCLC WorldShare Interlibrary Loan, OHIONET, OVID Technologies, Oxford Online, Project MUSE, ProQuest, PubMed, Safari Books Online, Sage, Scopus, SerialsSolutions, Springer-Verlag, ValueLine, YBP Library Services
Wireless access
Function: Bks on CD, Computers for patron use, Copy machines, e-mail & chat, Electronic databases & coll, Fax serv, ILL available, Music CDs, Online cat, Online searches, Photocopying/Printing, Ref serv available, Scanner, Spoken cassettes & CDs
Publications: New Items List (Acquisition list)
Partic in OCLC Online Computer Library Center, Inc; Ohio Library & Information Network; Ohio Private Academic Libraries (OPAL); OHIONET
Open Mon-Thurs (Winter) 8am-11pm, Fri 8-5, Sat 12-5, Sun 1-10; Mon-Thurs (Summer) 8:15-7, Fri 8-4, Sat 12-5
Restriction: Fee for pub use

NORTH ELYRIA

J LORAIN COUNTY COMMUNITY COLLEGE*, Barbara & Mike Bass Library/Community Resource Center, 1005 Abbe Rd N, 44035-1691. SAN 313-5004. Tel: 440-366-7289. Circulation Tel: 440-366-4026. Interlibrary Loan Service Tel: 440-366-7336. Reference Tel: 440-366-4106. Toll Free Tel: 800-995-5222, Ext 7289. FAX: 440-366-4127. Web Site: www.lorainccc.edu/library. *Interim Dean,* Susan Paul; E-mail: spaul@lorainccc.edu; *Automation Librn, Tech Serv,* Mary Jill Brophy; Tel: 440-366-7285, E-mail: jbrophy@lorainccc.edu; *Instrul Serv/Ref Librn,* Christine Sheetz; Tel: 440-366-7288, E-mail: csheetz@lorainccc.edu; *Ref Librn,* Rita Blanford; *Ref Librn,* Vicki Ceci; *Ref Librn,* Helen DeBalzo Green; *Circ Supvr,* Terry Mazur. Subject Specialists: *Sci,* Christine Sheetz; Staff 31 (MLS 7, Non-MLS 24)
Founded 1964. Enrl 10,000; Fac 263; Highest Degree: Associate
Library Holdings: CDs 300; Bk Titles 93,000; Bk Vols 111,000; Per Subs 610
Automation Activity & Vendor Info: (Acquisitions) Innovative Interfaces, Inc; (Cataloging) Innovative Interfaces, Inc; (Circulation) Innovative Interfaces, Inc; (ILL) Innovative Interfaces, Inc; (OPAC) Innovative Interfaces, Inc
Database Vendor: EBSCOhost, Innovative Interfaces, Inc, LexisNexis, OCLC FirstSearch
Partic in Ohio Library & Information Network; OHIONET
Special Services for the Deaf - Assistive tech
Special Services for the Blind - Accessible computers
Open Mon-Thurs 7:30am-10pm, Fri 7:30-4:30, Sat 10-4, Sun 12-5

NORWALK

R FIRST PRESBYTERIAN CHURCH LIBRARY*, 21 Firelands Blvd, 44857. SAN 313-6531. Tel: 419-668-1923. FAX: 419-663-5115. *Librn,* Linda Busco
Founded 1948
Library Holdings: Bk Titles 3,900; Per Subs 10
Special Collections: Archival Coll, Weekly Bulletin & Monthly Newsletter (1950-1992 complete, 1921-1949 incomplete)
Subject Interests: Biog, Children's educ, Family life, Fiction, Health, Personal problems, Relig related
Publications: Bulletins (Weekly); Newsletter (Monthly)
Open Mon-Fri 9-5, Sun 8-Noon

GL HURON COUNTY LAW LIBRARY ASSOCIATION*, Court House, 3rd Flr, Two E Main St, 44857. SAN 313-654X. Tel: 419-668-5127. FAX: 419-663-5026. E-mail: lawlibrary@hclawlibrary.com. *Librn,* Erin Gail Bartle
Library Holdings: Bk Vols 13,000
Open Mon-Fri 8:30-4:30

P NORWALK PUBLIC LIBRARY*, 46 W Main St, 44857. SAN 313-6558. Tel: 419-668-6063. FAX: 419-663-2190. E-mail: norwalk@oplin.org. Web Site: www.norwalk.lib.oh.us. *Dir,* Sarah Contreras; Staff 2 (MLS 2)
Founded 1861. Pop 54,000; Circ 181,277
Library Holdings: Bk Titles 85,000; Per Subs 210
Special Collections: Huron County History & Genealogy; Local Newspapers, micro
Wireless access
Partic in NORWELD
Open Mon & Wed 9:30-8:30, Tues & Thurs 10:30-6, Fri & Sat 9:30-5
Friends of the Library Group

OAK HARBOR

P OAK HARBOR PUBLIC LIBRARY*, 147 W Main St, 43449-1344. SAN 313-6566. Tel: 419-898-7001. FAX: 419-898-0747. E-mail: oakharpl@oplin.org. Web Site: library.norweld.lib.oh.us/oak-harbor. *Dir,* Lina Hall; E-mail: hallli@oplin.org; Staff 5.59 (MLS 1.63, Non-MLS 3.96)
Founded 1908. Pop 10,300; Circ 108,196
Jan 2006-Dec 2006 Income $359,994, State $313,295, Locally Generated Income $46,699. Mats Exp $64,851, Books $37,976, Per/Ser (Incl. Access Fees) $7,266, AV Mat $10,792, Electronic Ref Mat (Incl. Access Fees) $8,817. Sal $143,070 (Prof $71,853)
Library Holdings: AV Mats 6,180; e-books 35; Large Print Bks 758; Bk Vols 40,008; Per Subs 132
Automation Activity & Vendor Info: (Cataloging) SirsiDynix; (Circulation) SirsiDynix; (ILL) SirsiDynix; (OPAC) SirsiDynix
Database Vendor: OCLC FirstSearch
Wireless access
Partic in NORWELD; Ohio Public Library Information Network; SEO (Serving Every Ohioan) Library Center
Open Mon-Thurs 10-8, Fri 10-5, Sat 10-3
Friends of the Library Group

OAK HILL

P OAK HILL PUBLIC LIBRARY*, 226 S Front St, 45656. Tel: 740-682-6457. FAX: 740-682-3522. Web Site: www.oakhill.lib.oh.us, www.youseemore.com/oakhill. *Dir,* Peggy Johnson; E-mail: johnsope@oplin.org; *Ch Serv,* Lori Williams; *Circ,* Ruth Paulins; *Circ,* Pam Rhodes
Founded 1956
Library Holdings: Bk Vols 35,000
Open Mon & Wed 10-8, Tues, Thurs & Fri 10-6, Sat 10-5

OBERLIN

C OBERLIN COLLEGE LIBRARY, 148 W College St, 44074. SAN 357-0215. Tel: 440-775-8285. FAX: 440-775-6586. E-mail: reference.desk@oberlin.edu. Web Site: www.oberlin.edu/library. *Dir,* Ray English; E-mail: ray.english@oberlin.edu; *Assoc Dir,* Alan Boyd, *Instrul Serv Librn, Ref Serv,* Cynthia Comer; *Circ, ILL,* Allison Gallaher; *Coll Develop,* Jessica Grim; *Electroni & Continuing Res,* Tom Hinders; Staff 2.6 (MLS 1.6, Non-MLS 1)
Founded 1833. Enrl 2,774; Fac 294; Highest Degree: Master
Jul 2012-Jun 2013 Income (Main and Other College/University Libraries) $5,720,831. Mats Exp $2,586,316, Books $986,697, Per/Ser (Incl. Access Fees) $1,516,464, Micro $16,221, Presv $66,934. Sal $3,074,741 (Prof $1,354,497)
Library Holdings: AV Mats 111,150; Music Scores 131,050; Bk Vols 1,475,223; Per Subs 173,326
Special Collections: Aldous Huxley (Robert H Jackson Coll); American Communist Party Pamphlets; American Dime Novels, Anti-Slavery Coll; Archive of the Seal Press, 1976-2001; Book Arts Coll; Civil War Popular Song Lyrics; Early Printed Books; Edwin Arlington Robinson Coll; History of the Book; Illuminated Manuscripts; Jack Schaefer Coll; Japanese Artist Books (Mary Ainsworth Coll); Oberliniana Coll; Orrin W June War of 1812 Coll; Sheet Music Coll; Spanish Drama Coll; The 19th Century Spanish Romantic Novel; Thorton Wilder Coll; Upton Sinclair Coll; Violin Society of America (H K Goodkind Coll), violin construction. US Document Depository
Automation Activity & Vendor Info: (Acquisitions) Innovative Interfaces, Inc; (Cataloging) Innovative Interfaces, Inc; (Circulation) Innovative Interfaces, Inc; (Course Reserve) Blackboard Inc; (ILL) OCLC; (OPAC) Innovative Interfaces, Inc; (Serials) Innovative Interfaces, Inc
Wireless access
Function: AV serv, Computers for patron use, Copy machines, Doc delivery serv, E-Reserves, Electronic databases & coll, Govt ref serv, Handicapped accessible, ILL available, Online cat, Online info literacy tutorials on the web & in blackboard, Online ref, Online searches, Photocopying/Printing, Pub access computers, Ref & res, Scanner, Tax forms, VCDs, VHS videos, Wheelchair accessible
Publications: Library Perspectives (External newsletter)
Partic in Oberlin Group; Ohio Library & Information Network; OHIONET; The Five Colleges of Ohio
Special Services for the Deaf - Assistive tech
Special Services for the Blind - Closed circuit TV; Dragon Naturally Speaking software; Large screen computer & software; ZoomText magnification & reading software
Open Mon-Thurs 8am-2am, Fri 8am-10pm, Sat 10-10, Sun 10am-2am

Restriction: Open to pub for ref & circ; with some limitations, Open to students, fac, staff & alumni
Friends of the Library Group
Departmental Libraries:
SCIENCE, Science Center N174, 119 Woodland St, 44074-1083, SAN 357-0304. Tel: 440-775-8310. Administration Tel: 440-775-5146. E-mail: science.library@oberlin.edu. Web Site: www.oberlin.edu/library/science. *Sci Librn,* Alison Scott Ricker; E-mail: alison.ricker@oberlin.edu; Staff 2 (MLS 1, Non-MLS 1)
Founded 1965
Library Holdings: Bk Vols 93,454
Function: ILL available
MARY M VIAL MUSIC LIBRARY, Oberlin Conservatory of Music, 77 W College St, 44074-1588, SAN 357-0274. Tel: 440-775-8280. Circulation Tel: 440-775-8288. Reference Tel: 440-775-5129. FAX: 440-775-8203. *Librn,* Deborah Campana; E-mail: Deborah.Campana@oberlin.edu; *Pub Serv Librn,* Kathleen Abromeit; E-mail: kathleen.abromeit@oberlin.edu; *Tech Serv Librn,* David Knapp; E-mail: david.knapp@oberlin.edu; *Coordr, Circ,* Greg Solow; Staff 11 (MLS 4, Non-MLS 7)
Founded 1865
Library Holdings: AV Mats 86,752; Bk Vols 217,802
Open Mon-Thurs 8-5:30 & 7-11, Fri 8-5:30 & 7-9, Sat 12-5:30, Sun 1-5:30 & 7-11
CLARENCE WARD ART LIBRARY, Allen Art Bldg, 83 N Main St, 44074-1193, SAN 357-024X. Tel: 440-775-8635. FAX: 440-775-5145. Web Site: www.oberlin.edu/library/libncollect/art/Default.html. *Librn,* Barbara Prior; E-mail: barbara.prior@oberlin.edu; Staff 2 (MLS 1, Non-MLS 1)
Library Holdings: Bk Vols 106,827

P OBERLIN PUBLIC LIBRARY*, 65 S Main St, 44074-1626. SAN 313-6604. Tel: 440-775-4790. FAX: 440-774-2880. Web Site: www.oberlinpl.lib.oh.us. *Dir,* Darren McDonough; *Ch Serv,* Helen Stutzenberger; *Ref,* Eva Greenberg; Staff 3 (MLS 3)
Founded 1947. Pop 11,000; Circ 281,860
Library Holdings: AV Mats 24,415; Bk Titles 130,000; Bk Vols 151,000; Per Subs 235
Subject Interests: Children's lit, Folklore, Ohio
Automation Activity & Vendor Info: (Acquisitions) TLC (The Library Corporation); (Cataloging) TLC (The Library Corporation); (Circulation) TLC (The Library Corporation); (OPAC) TLC (The Library Corporation)
Open Mon-Thurs 10-8:30, Fri & Sat 10-6, Sun (Sept-May) 1-5
Friends of the Library Group

ORIENT

S PICKAWAY CORRECTIONAL INSTITUTION LIBRARY*, 11781 State Rte 762, 43146. (Mail add: PO Box 209, 43146-0209), SAN 371-6031. Tel: 614-877-4362. FAX: 614-877-0735. *Librn,* Igwe Nnacho; Staff 1 (MLS 1)
Library Holdings: High Interest/Low Vocabulary Bk Vols 100; Large Print Bks 50; Bk Titles 25,000; Per Subs 86; Talking Bks 30
Automation Activity & Vendor Info: (Cataloging) EOS International; (Circulation) EOS International; (OPAC) EOS International

ORRVILLE

P ORRVILLE PUBLIC LIBRARY*, 230 N Main St, 44667. SAN 313-6620. Tel: 330-683-1065. FAX: 330-683-1984. TDD: 330-683-6171. E-mail: askus@orrville.lib.oh.us. Web Site: www.orrville.lib.oh.us. *Dir,* Daphne Silchuk-Ashcraft; Staff 4 (MLS 4)
Founded 1925. Pop 11,314; Circ 513,136
Jan 2008-Dec 2008 Income $915,848, State $662,620, County $139,056, Locally Generated Income $16,610, Other $97,562. Mats Exp $1,008,697, Books $97,562, Per/Ser (Incl. Access Fees) $6,995, Micro $1,214, AV Mat $38,356. Sal $367,774 (Prof $158,612)
Library Holdings: Audiobooks 20,570; AV Mats 42,678; Bks on Deafness & Sign Lang 47; CDs 6,875; DVDs 4,671; e-books 17,896; Large Print Bks 518; Bk Vols 60,030; Per Subs 165; Talking Bks 20,570; Videos 6,314
Subject Interests: Railroads
Automation Activity & Vendor Info: (Acquisitions) SirsiDynix; (Cataloging) SirsiDynix; (Circulation) SirsiDynix
Database Vendor: ALLDATA Online, EBSCOhost, Medline, Newsbank, OCLC FirstSearch, OCLC WorldShare Interlibrary Loan, ProQuest, ReferenceUSA, Westlaw, Wilson - Wilson Web, World Book Online
Wireless access
Function: Adult literacy prog, After school storytime, Art exhibits, Audiobks via web, Bks on cassette, Bks on CD, Children's prog, Computer training, Computers for patron use, Copy machines, Digital talking bks, Doc delivery serv, e-mail & chat, e-mail serv, E-Reserves, Electronic databases & coll, Exhibits, Fax serv, Free DVD rentals, Handicapped accessible, Holiday prog, Home delivery & serv to Sr ctr & nursing homes, Homebound delivery serv, ILL available, Large print keyboards, Magnifiers for reading, Mail & tel request accepted, Music CDs, Online cat, Online ref, Online searches, Orientations, Outreach serv, Outside serv via phone, mail, e-mail & web, OverDrive digital audio bks, Photocopying/Printing, Preschool outreach, Prog for adults, Prog for children & young adult, Pub access computers, Ref & res, Ref serv available, Ref serv in person, Scanner, Senior computer classes, Senior outreach, Serves mentally handicapped consumers, Spoken cassettes & CDs, Spoken cassettes & DVDs, Story hour, Summer reading prog, Tax forms, Teen prog, Telephone ref, VHS videos, Video lending libr, Visual arts prog, Wheelchair accessible, Workshops
Partic in CLEVNET; Northeast Ohio Regional Library System
Special Services for the Deaf - TDD equip; TTY equip
Special Services for the Blind - Accessible computers; Aids for in-house use; Assistive/Adapted tech devices, equip & products; Audio mat; BiFolkal kits; Bks on cassette; Bks on CD; Cassettes; Digital talking bk; Handicapped awareness prog; Home delivery serv; Internet workstation with adaptive software; Large print bks; Large screen computer & software; Low vision equip; Magnifiers; PC for handicapped; Playaways (bks on MP3); Recorded bks; Scanner for conversion & translation of mats; Sound rec; Soundproof reading booth; Talking bk serv referral; Videos on blindness & phys handicaps
Open Mon, Tues & Thurs 9-8, Wed & Fri 9-6, Sat 10-3
Friends of the Library Group

J UNIVERSITY OF AKRON LIBRARIES*, Wayne College Library, 1901 Smucker Rd, 44667-9758. SAN 313-6639. Tel: 330-684-8789. Interlibrary Loan Service Tel: 330-684-8950. Administration Tel: 330-684-8951. FAX: 330-683-1381. E-mail: waynelibrary@uakron.edu. Web Site: wayne.uakron.edu/library. *Libr Dir,* Maureen Lerch; E-mail: mlerch@uakron.edu; *Coordr, Libr Serv,* Lisa Nagy; E-mail: lnagy@uakron.edu; Staff 5 (MLS 1, Non-MLS 4)
Founded 1972. Enrl 2,400
Library Holdings: AV Mats 1,700; Bk Vols 18,781; Per Subs 109
Automation Activity & Vendor Info: (Acquisitions) Innovative Interfaces, Inc
Wireless access
Partic in Ohio Library & Information Network

ORWELL

P GRAND VALLEY PUBLIC LIBRARY, One N School St, 44076. (Mail add: PO Box 188, 44076-0188), SAN 313-6647. Tel: 440-437-6545, 440-536-9159. FAX: 440-437-1017. E-mail: grandvalleypubliclibrary@gmail.com. Web Site: www.grandvalley.lib.oh.us. *Dir,* Andrew Davis-Knapp; Tel: 440-536-8951, E-mail: davisan@grandvalley.lib.oh.us; *Asst Dir/ILL/Homebound,* Daniel Tanner; Tel: 440-536-9157, E-mail: tannerda@grandvalley.lib.oh.us; *Fiscal Officer,* Jeannette Gage; Tel: 440-536-9156, E-mail: gageje@grandvalley.lib.oh.us; Staff 4.89 (Non-MLS 4.89)
Founded 1903. Pop 10,229; Circ 68,180
Jan 2011-Dec 2011 Income $180,698. Mats Exp $18,547, Books $8,349, Per/Ser (Incl. Access Fees) $520, AV Equip $497, AV Mat $1,915, Electronic Ref Mat (Incl. Access Fees) $2,622. Sal $96,107
Library Holdings: AV Mats 5,241; DVDs 2,118; e-books 2; Electronic Media & Resources 307; Bk Vols 41,485; Per Subs 64; Videos 3,123
Automation Activity & Vendor Info: (Cataloging) SirsiDynix; (Circulation) SirsiDynix; (OPAC) SirsiDynix
Database Vendor: 3M Library Systems, Baker & Taylor, Booksite, BWI, EBSCO Information Services, EBSCOhost, Ingram Library Services
Wireless access
Function: Accelerated reader prog, Accessibility serv available based on individual needs, Adult bk club, After school storytime, AV serv, Bks on cassette, Bks on CD, CD-ROM, Children's prog, Computer training, Computers for patron use, Copy machines, e-mail & chat, e-mail serv, Electronic databases & coll, Fax serv, Free DVD rentals, Games & aids for the handicapped, Genealogy discussion group, Handicapped accessible, Holiday prog, Home delivery & serv to Sr ctr & nursing homes, Homebound delivery serv, ILL available, Instruction & testing, Large print keyboards, Mail & tel request accepted, Microfiche/film & reading machines, Music CDs, Newsp ref libr, Online cat, Outside serv via phone, mail, e-mail & web, Photocopying/Printing, Preschool outreach, Preschool reading prog, Prof lending libr, Prog for adults, Prog for children & young adult, Pub access computers, Ref & res, Ref serv available, Ref serv in person, Scanner, Senior computer classes, Senior outreach, Story hour, Summer & winter reading prog, Summer reading prog, Teen prog, VHS videos, Video lending libr, Web-catalog, Wheelchair accessible
Partic in Northern Ohio Libr Asn; SEO (Serving Every Ohioan) Library Center
Open Mon-Thurs 9-7, Fri 9-5, Sat 9-1
Friends of the Library Group

OTTAWA

P PUTNAM COUNTY DISTRICT LIBRARY*, The Educational Service Ctr, 124 Putnam Pkwy, 45875-1471. (Mail add: PO Box 230, 45875), SAN 357-0339. Tel: 419-523-3747. FAX: 419-523-6477. Web Site:

www.mypcdl.org. *Dir,* Kelly Ward; E-mail: wardke@oplin.org; *Local Hist Librn,* Ruth Wilhelm; E-mail: wilhelru@oplin.org; *Mgr of Computing,* Alisha Tirey; E-mail: tireyal@oplin.org; *Circ Supvr,* Judy Schroeder; E-mail: schroeju@oplin.org; *Supvr, Extn Serv,* Bev Ricker; E-mail: rickerbe@oplin.org; *Tech Serv Supvr,* Laura Schmitz; E-mail: schmitla@oplin.org; *Br Coordr,* Shirley Beining; E-mail: beininsh@oplin.org; *Ch Serv,* Caryn Tanner; E-mail: richarca@oplin.org; *Ref,* Matthew Ross; *Youth Serv,* Valerie Laukhuf; E-mail: laukhuva@oplin.org
Founded 1924. Circ 282,505
Library Holdings: Bk Vols 163,583; Per Subs 329
Partic in NORWELD
Open Mon-Thurs 9-8, Fri 9-5, Sat 9-Noon
Friends of the Library Group
Branches: 7
COLUMBUS GROVE BRANCH, 317 N Main St, Columbus Grove, 45830, SAN 357-0363. Tel: 419-659-2355. *Br Mgr,* Kelly Ward
Founded 1936
Open Mon 2-8, Tues & Thurs 9-6, Sat 9-3
Friends of the Library Group
CONTINENTAL BRANCH, 301 S Sixth St, Continental, 45831, SAN 357-0371. Tel: 419-596-3727. *Br Mgr,* Theresa Jones
Open Mon & Wed 10-7, Tues 9-5, Thurs & Fri 10-5, Sat 9-12
FORT JENNINGS BRANCH, 655 N Water St, Fort Jennings, 45844-0218, SAN 328-7807. Tel: 419-286-2351. *Br Coordr,* Ruth Fermiller
Founded 1986
Open Tues 9-6, Thurs 2-8, Sat 9-3
Friends of the Library Group
KALIDA BRANCH, 110 S Broad St, Kalida, 45853-0183. (Mail add: PO Box 183, Kalida, 45853-0183), SAN 357-038X. Tel: 419-532-2129. *Br Mgr,* Ruth Hermiller; E-mail: hermilru@oplin.org
Founded 1973
Open Mon 9-6:30, Wed 9-5, Sat 9-Noon
Friends of the Library Group
LEIPSIC MEMORIAL, 305 W Main St, Leipsic, 45856, SAN 357-0398. Tel: 419-943-2604. *Br Coordr,* Laura Schroeder
Founded 1979
Library Holdings: Bk Vols 8,400; Per Subs 30
Open Tues 2-8, Wed & Thurs 9-6, Sat 9-5
Friends of the Library Group
OTTOVILLE-MONTEREY BRANCH, 349 Wayne St, Ottoville, 45876. (Mail add: PO Box 517, Ottoville, 45876-0517), SAN 357-0428. Tel: 419-453-2111. *Br Coordr,* Ruth Fermiller
Founded 1962. Circ 28,000
Library Holdings: Bk Titles 10,000; Per Subs 22
Open Mon 2-8. Wed 9-6, Sat 9-3
Friends of the Library Group
PANDORA-RILEY BRANCH, 118 E Main St, Pandora, 45877-0478. (Mail add: PO Box 478, Pandora, 45877), SAN 328-8544. Tel: 419-384-3232. *Br Mgr,* Laura Schroeder
Founded 1939
Open Mon 2-8, Tues & Wed 9-6, Sat 9-3
Friends of the Library Group
Bookmobiles: 1

OXFORD

C MIAMI UNIVERSITY LIBRARIES, 225 King Library, 45056. (Mail add: 151 S Campus Ave, 45056), SAN 357-0452. Tel: 513-529-2800. Circulation Tel: 513-529-2433. Interlibrary Loan Service Tel: 513-529-6147. Reference Tel: 513-529-4141, FAX: 513-529-3110. Interlibrary Loan Service FAX: 513-529-1682. Web Site: www.lib.miamioh.edu. *Dean & Univ Librn,* Jerome Conley; E-mail: conleyj@miamioh.edu; *Assoc Dean,* Aaron Shrimplin; Tel: 513-529-6823, E-mail: shrimpak@miamioh.edu; *Asst Dean, Assessment & Access Serv,* Belinda Barr; Tel: 513-529-7096, E-mail: barrb@miamioh.edu; *Asst Dean, Instruction & Emerging Tech,* Lisa Santucci; Tel: 513-529-1747, E-mail: santucle@miamioh.edu; *Asst Dean, Tech Serv, Head, Spec Coll & Archives,* Elizabeth Brice; Tel: 513-529-4140, E-mail: bricee@miamioh.edu; *Dir, Libr Tech Serv,* Stan Brown; Tel: 513-529-2351, E-mail: brownsj1@miamioh.edu; *Head, Access Serv,* Rob Withers; Tel: 513-529-6148, E-mail: witherre@miamioh.edu; *Head, Digital Initiatives & Ctr for Digital Scholarship,* John Millard; Tel: 513-529-6789, E-mail: millarj@miamioh.edu; *Educ Librn, Instrul Mat Coordr,* Kathleen Lucey; Tel: 513-529-3340, E-mail: luceyka@miamioh.edu; *Govt Info & Law Librn,* Jeffrey Hartsell-Gundy; Tel: 513-529-4139, E-mail: gundyj@miamioh.edu; Staff 48 (MLS 39, Non-MLS 9)
Founded 1809. Enrl 17,035; Fac 843; Highest Degree: Doctorate
Library Holdings: e-books 625,641; e-journals 31,531; Bk Titles 2,607,746; Bk Vols 2,779,539; Per Subs 1,135
Special Collections: 19th Century Gift Books; 19th Century Trade Cards; Clyde N, Bowden Postcard Coll; Cradle of Coaches (Sports); Early 20th Century Postcards; Early Printed Books; Freedom Summer; Imperial & Revolutionary Russia; James T Farrell; John H James Family Papers; King Coll of Early Juvenile Books & Periodicals; Kuchler Vegetation Maps; Louise Bogan Library; McGuffey Readers & other 19th Century Schoolbooks; Miami University Archives; Native American Women Playwrights Archive; Native Americans/Myaamia (Miami); Northwest Territory and Ohio Regional History; Railroads/Transportation; Rodolfo Usigli Archive; Samual Fulton Covington Coll and Family Papers; Shakespeare First Four Folios; US Civil War/Jefferson Davis & Confederacy; W H McGuffey Family Papers; Western College Memorial Archives; William Dean Howells; World Vegetation Maps. State Document Depository; UN Document Depository; US Document Depository
Automation Activity & Vendor Info: (Acquisitions) Innovative Interfaces, Inc; (Cataloging) Innovative Interfaces, Inc; (Circulation) Innovative Interfaces, Inc; (Course Reserve) Innovative Interfaces, Inc; (ILL) OCLC ILLiad; (OPAC) Innovative Interfaces, Inc; (Serials) Innovative Interfaces, Inc
Database Vendor: Alexander Street Press, EBSCOhost, Factiva.com, ISI Web of Knowledge, JSTOR, OCLC WorldShare Interlibrary Loan, Project MUSE
Wireless access
Partic in Center for Research Libraries; Coalition for Networked Information (CNI); Ohio Library & Information Network; OHIONET
Departmental Libraries:
AMOS MUSIC LIBRARY, Center for the Performing Arts, 45056. (Mail add: 151 S Campus Ave, 45056), SAN 357-0517. Tel: 513-529-2299. FAX: 513-529-1378. *Music Librn,* Barry Zaslow; E-mail: zaslowbj@miamioh.edu; Staff 1 (MLS 1)
Subject Interests: Music, Music educ, Musical theatre, Musicology
BUSINESS, ENGINEERING, SCIENCE, & TECHNOLOGY LIBRARY, Laws Hall, 45056. (Mail add: 551 E High St, 45056), SAN 357-0541. Tel: 513-529-6886. FAX: 513-529-1736. *Interim Head Librn,* Kevin Messner; Tel: 513-529-7204, E-mail: krmessner@miamioh.edu; Staff 5 (MLS 5)
Founded 1978
Special Collections: Kuchler Vegetation Maps
Subject Interests: Bus, Computer sci, Eng, Life sci, Phys sci, Psychol
GARDNER-HARVEY LIBRARY, 4200 N University Blvd, Middletown, 45042-3497, SAN 313-6221. Tel: 513-727-3222. E-mail: midref@lib.muohio.edu. Web Site: www.mid.miamioh.edu/library. *Dir,* John Burke; Tel: 513-727-3293, E-mail: burkejj@miamioh.edu; *Asst Dir,* Beth Tumbleson; Tel: 513-727-3232, E-mail: tumbleb@miamioh.edu; *Pub Serv Librn,* Jessie Long; Tel: 513-727-3225, E-mail: longjh@miamioh.edu; *Acq/Tech Serv Mgr,* Jennifer Hicks; Tel: 513-727-3221, E-mail: hicksjl2@miamioh.edu; *Circ & Reserves Supvr,* Chris Mull; Tel: 513-727-3291, E-mail: mullcr@miamioh.edu; Staff 5 (MLS 3, Non-MLS 2)
Founded 1966. Enrl 2,600; Fac 100; Highest Degree: Bachelor
Jul 2013-Jun 2014 Income $520,993. Mats Exp $128,000, Books $65,000, Per/Ser (Incl. Access Fees) $7,000, Other Print Mats $10,000, Electronic Ref Mat (Incl. Access Fees) $46,000
Library Holdings: AV Mats 4,500; e-books 49,115; Bk Vols 24,000; Per Subs 50
Special Collections: Instructional Materials (IMC Coll), bks & AV
Database Vendor: EBSCO Discovery Service, EBSCOhost, Gale Cengage Learning, LexisNexis, OHIONET, Safari Books Online, YBP Library Services
Function: Accessibility serv available based on individual needs, Adult bk club, Computers for patron use, Copy machines, Electronic databases & coll, Equip loans & repairs, Free DVD rentals, ILL available, Mango lang, Online cat, Online info literacy tutorials on the web & in blackboard, Online ref, Ref serv available, Scanner
Partic in Ohio Library & Information Network; OHIONET
Special Services for the Blind - Assistive/Adapted tech devices, equip & products
Open Mon-Thurs 8am-9pm, Fri 8-5
RENTSCHLER LIBRARY, 1601 University Blvd, Hamilton, 45011, SAN 313-5322. Tel: 513-785-3235. FAX: 513-785-3231. Web Site: www.ham.muohio.edu/library/. *Dir,* Krista McDonald; E-mail: mcdonak@muohio.edu; *Asst Dir,* Mark L Shores; E-mail: shoresml@muohio.edu; *Ref Serv,* Paula Whitaker; E-mail: whitakpj@muohio.edu; *Dir, Tech Serv,* Ya Lan Wu; Staff 6 (MLS 4, Non-MLS 2)
Founded 1968. Fac 38; Highest Degree: Bachelor
Library Holdings: Bk Vols 71,275; Per Subs 356
Automation Activity & Vendor Info: (OPAC) Innovative Interfaces, Inc
Partic in OCLC Online Computer Library Center, Inc; Ohio Library & Information Network; OHIONET
SOUTHWEST OHIO REGIONAL DEPOSITORY, Middletown Campus, Middletown, 45042. (Mail add: 4200 N University Blvd, Middletown, 45042-3458). Tel: 513-727-3474. FAX: 513-727-3478. *Mgr,* Pam Lipscomb; E-mail: lipscope@MiamiOH.edu; Staff 1 (Non-MLS 1)
Library Holdings: Bk Vols 2,450,207
UNIVERSITY ARCHIVES & WESTERN COLLEGE MEMORIAL ARCHIVES, University Archives, Withrow Hall, Western College Memorial Archives, Peabody Hall, 45056. (Mail add: 151 S Campus Ave, 45056). Tel: 513-529-6720. *Interim Univ Archivist,* Jacqueline Johnson; E-mail: johnsoj@miamioh.edu; Staff 1 (MLS 1)

WERTZ ART & ARCHITECTURE LIBRARY, Alumni Hall, 45056. (Mail add: 151 S Campus Ave, 45056), SAN 357-0487. Tel: 513-529-6638. FAX: 513-529-4159. *Archit/Art Librn,* Stacy Brinkman; Tel: 513-529-6650, E-mail: brinkmsn@muohio.edu; Staff 1 (MLS 1)
Subject Interests: Archit, Art, Art educ, Interior design
Friends of the Library Group

P SMITH LIBRARY OF REGIONAL HISTORY, 15 S College Ave, 45056. SAN 329-8027. Tel: 513-523-3035. FAX: 513-523-6661. E-mail: sml@lanepl.org. Web Site: www.lanepl.org/smith. *Mgr,* Valerie E Elliott; E-mail: v.elliott@lanepl.org; Staff 2 (MLS 1, Non-MLS 1)
Founded 1981
Library Holdings: CDs 30; DVDs 18; Microforms 428; Bk Titles 3,598; Bk Vols 3,662; Per Subs 36; Videos 40
Special Collections: Archives of Businesses, Churches, Schools, Cemeteries; Birth, Death & Marriage Records, Wills, Deeds; Clyde Bowden Digital Postcard Coll; Manuscripts (Diaries, Letters); Newspapers; Photographs. Municipal Document Depository; Oral History
Subject Interests: Butler County Ohio, Hist of Oxford Ohio, SW Ohio
Wireless access
Publications: Burial Grounds of Oxford (Local historical information); Ohio 1817-1987; Oxford & Miami University During World War II (Local historical information); To Dwell with Fond Reflection: Families Who Lived in the McGuffey House (Local historical information); Walking Tours of Oxford's Historic Districts (Local historical information)
Open Mon & Wed-Fri 10-12 & 1-5, Tues 10-12 & 1-8, Sat 10-1
Restriction: Non-circulating coll
Friends of the Library Group

PAINESVILLE

S LAKE COUNTY HISTORICAL SOCIETY*, P K Smith Research Library, 415 Riverside Dr, 44077. SAN 313-6124. Tel: 440-639-2945. FAX: 440-255-8980. E-mail: research@lakehistory.org. Web Site: www.lakehistory.org. *Libr Asst,* Janet Decaro
Founded 1938
Library Holdings: Bk Vols 3,500
Subject Interests: Antiques, Garfield family, Genealogy, Local hist
Publications: Here is Lake County, Ohio (1964); Lake County Historical Society (Quarterly)
Open Tues-Fri 9-4

C LAKE ERIE COLLEGE*, James F Lincoln Library, 391 W Washington St, 44077-3309. SAN 313-6663. Tel: 440-375-7400. Reference Tel: 440-375-7403. Administration Tel: 440-375-7405. Web Site: www.lec.edu/library. *Dir,* Christopher Bennett; E-mail: cbennett@lec.edu; *Ref & Media Ctr Librn,* Christine Strlich; E-mail: cstrlich@lec.edu; *Cat,* Lori Greuber; Tel: 440-375-7402; Staff 3 (MLS 2, Non-MLS 1)
Founded 1859. Enrl 1,130; Fac 114; Highest Degree: Master
Library Holdings: AV Mats 1,363; Bk Titles 51,000; Bk Vols 63,200; Per Subs 9,000
Special Collections: College Archives; Thomas Harvey Coll
Subject Interests: Equestrian studies
Automation Activity & Vendor Info: (Cataloging) TLC (The Library Corporation); (Circulation) TLC (The Library Corporation); (Course Reserve) TLC (The Library Corporation); (ILL) OCLC ILLiad; (OPAC) TLC (The Library Corporation)
Database Vendor: 3M Library Systems, American Psychological Association (APA), Facts on File, Gale Cengage Learning, Mergent Online, Newsbank, OCLC, OHIONET, TLC (The Library Corporation)
Wireless access
Function: Archival coll, Computers for patron use, Copy machines, Electronic databases & coll, ILL available, Pub access computers, Ref serv available, Telephone ref
Partic in OHIONET
Restriction: Circ limited

P MORLEY LIBRARY, 184 Phelps St, 44077-3926. SAN 357-0665. Tel: 440-352-3383. FAX: 440-352-2653. E-mail: reference@morleylibrary.org. Web Site: www.morleylibrary.org. *Dir,* Mary-Frances Burns; E-mail: mfb@morleylibrary.org; *Teen Librn,* Jennifer Webster; E-mail: jwebster@morleylibrary.org; *Database Coordr,* Louise Kloss; E-mail: lkloss@morleylibrary.org; *Ref Serv, Ad,* Carl Engel; E-mail: ctengel@morleylibrary.org; *Children's Serv Team Leader,* Deborah Shelton; Tel: 440-352-3383, Ext 207, E-mail: dshelton@morleylibrarylibrary.org; *Circ Serv Team Leader,* Talma Wilkinson; E-mail: twilkinson@morleylibrary.org; *Ref Serv Team Leader,* Charley Voelker; E-mail: cvoelker@morleylibrary.org; *Tech Serv Team Leader,* Laura Bunnell; Tel: 440-352-3383, Ext 302, Fax: 440-352-9097, E-mail: lbunnell@morleylibrary.org. Subject Specialists: *Local hist,* Carl Engel; Staff 39.13 (MLS 10, Non-MLS 29.13)
Founded 1878. Pop 52,404; Circ 552,076
Jan 2013-Dec 2013 Income $2,493,538, State $1,290,641, Locally Generated Income $1,116,380, Other $86,517. Mats Exp $394,125, Books $218,329, Per/Ser (Incl. Access Fees) $31,425, Other Print Mats $347, AV Mat $81,330, Electronic Ref Mat (Incl. Access Fees) $62,694. Sal $1,214,642
Library Holdings: Audiobooks 12,457; AV Mats 955; DVDs 19,126; e-books 3,037; Bk Titles 154,550; Per Subs 330
Special Collections: Foundation Center Resource Center; Obituary Files, 1822 to Present
Subject Interests: Genealogy, Local hist
Automation Activity & Vendor Info: (Acquisitions) TLC (The Library Corporation); (Cataloging) TLC (The Library Corporation); (Circulation) TLC (The Library Corporation); (OPAC) TLC (The Library Corporation)
Database Vendor: EBSCOhost, Gale Cengage Learning
Wireless access
Function: Ref serv available
Partic in Northeast Ohio Regional Library System
Open Mon-Thurs 9-9, Fri 9-6, Sat 9-5, Sun (Oct-April) 1-5
Friends of the Library Group

PARMA

P CUYAHOGA COUNTY PUBLIC LIBRARY, 2111 Snow Rd, 44134-2728. SAN 356-1305. Tel: 216-398-1800. Toll Free Tel: 800-749-5560. FAX: 216-398-1748. Web Site: www.cuyahogalibrary.org. *Exec Dir,* Sari Feldman; *Dep Dir,* Tracy Strobel; *Dir, Literacy & Learning,* Pam Jankowski; *Dir, Tech Serv,* Daniel Barden; *Human Res Dir,* Daniel Hauenstein; *IT Dir,* James Haprian; *Mkt Dir,* Hallie Rich; *Operations Dir,* Scott Morgan; Staff 592.6 (MLS 121.3, Non-MLS 471.3)
Founded 1922. Pop 616,527; Circ 19,743,393
Jan 2013-Dec 2013 Income (Main Library and Branch(s)) $65,699,357. Mats Exp $9,496,838. Sal $29,556,018
Library Holdings: Audiobooks 116,261; Braille Volumes 155; CDs 247,178; DVDs 576,883; e-books 174,527; Large Print Bks 69,511; Microforms 609; Bk Vols 1,762,534; Per Subs 5,185
Special Collections: State Document Depository
Automation Activity & Vendor Info: (Acquisitions) Innovative Interfaces, Inc; (Cataloging) Innovative Interfaces, Inc; (Circulation) Innovative Interfaces, Inc; (OPAC) Innovative Interfaces, Inc; (Serials) Innovative Interfaces, Inc
Wireless access
Partic in OCLC Online Computer Library Center, Inc; OHIONET
Special Services for the Deaf - TTY equip
Open Mon-Thurs 9-9, Fri & Sat 9-5:30, Sun 1-5
Friends of the Library Group
Branches: 27
BAY VILLAGE BRANCH, 502 Cahoon Rd, Bay Village, 44140-2179, SAN 356-133X. Tel: 440-871-6392. FAX: 440-871-5320. *Br Mgr,* Jessica Breslin
Open Mon-Thurs 9-9, Fri & Sat 9-5:30, Sun 1-5
Friends of the Library Group
BEACHWOOD BRANCH, 25501 Shaker Blvd, Beachwood, 44122-2306, SAN 356-1356. Tel: 216-831-6868. FAX: 216-831-0412. *Br Mgr,* William Kelly
Special Collections: Holocaust Coll
Open Mon-Thurs 9-9, Fri & Sat 9-5, Sun 1-5
Friends of the Library Group
BEREA BRANCH, Seven Berea Commons, Berea, 44017-2524, SAN 356-1399. Tel: 440-234-5475. FAX: 440-234-2932. *Br Mgr,* Pamela DeFino
Open Mon-Thurs 9-9, Fri & Sat 9-5:30, Sun 1-5
Friends of the Library Group
BRECKSVILLE BRANCH, 9089 Brecksville Rd, Brecksville, 44141-2313, SAN 356-1429. Tel: 440-526-1102. FAX: 440-526-8793. *Br Mgr,* Melanie Rapp-Weiss
Open Mon-Thurs 9-9, Fri & Sat 9-5:30, Sun 1-5
Friends of the Library Group
BROOK PARK BRANCH, 6155 Engle Rd, Brook Park, 44142-2105, SAN 356-1453. Tel: 216-267-5250. FAX: 216-267-3776. *Br Mgr,* Kevin Payne
Open Mon-Thurs 9-9, Fri & Sat 9-5:30, Sun 1-5
Friends of the Library Group
BROOKLYN BRANCH, 4480 Ridge Rd, Brooklyn, 44144-3353, SAN 356-1488. Tel: 216-398-4600. FAX: 216-398-1545. *Br Mgr,* Lucinda Bereznay
Open Mon-Thurs 9-9, Fri & Sat 9-5:30, Sun 1-5
Friends of the Library Group
CHAGRIN FALLS BRANCH, 100 E Orange St, Chagrin Falls, 44022-2735, SAN 356-1518. Tel: 440-247-3556. FAX: 440-247-0179. *Br Mgr,* Katherine Malmquist
Open Mon-Thurs 9-9, Fri & Sat 9-5:30, Sun 1-5
Friends of the Library Group
FAIRVIEW PARK BRANCH, 21255 Lorain Rd, Fairview Park, 44126-2120, SAN 356-1542. Tel: 440-333-4700. FAX: 440-333-0697. *Br Mgr,* Elaine Wilkinson
Special Collections: State Document Depository
Special Services for the Deaf - TTY equip

Open Mon-Thurs 9-9, Fri & Sat 9-5:30, Sun 1-5
Friends of the Library Group
GARFIELD HEIGHTS BRANCH, 5409 Turney Rd, Garfield Heights, 44125-3203, SAN 356-1577. Tel: 216-475-8178. FAX: 216-475-1015. *Br Mgr,* Lane Edwards
Open Mon-Thurs 9-9, Fri & Sat 9-5:30, Sun 1-5
Friends of the Library Group
GATES MILLS BRANCH, 1491 Chagrin River Rd, Gates Mills, 44040-9703, SAN 356-1607. Tel: 440-423-4808. FAX: 440-423-1363. *Br Mgr,* Katherine Malmquist
Open Mon-Thurs 9-9, Fri & Sat 9-5:30, Sun 1-5
INDEPENDENCE BRANCH, 6361 Selig Dr, Independence, 44131-4926, SAN 356-1631. Tel: 216-447-0160. FAX: 216-447-1371. *Br Mgr,* Melanie Rapp-Weiss
Open Mon-Thurs 9-9, Fri & Sat 9-5:30, Sun 1-5
Friends of the Library Group
MAPLE HEIGHTS BRANCH, 5225 Library Lane, Maple Heights, 44137-1242, SAN 356-1690. Tel: 216-475-5000. FAX: 216-587-7284. *Br Mgr,* Andrew Harant
Open Mon-Thurs 9-9, Fri & Sat 9-5:30, Sun 1-5
Friends of the Library Group
MAYFIELD BRANCH, 500 SOM Ctr Rd, Mayfield Village, 44143-2103, SAN 356-1720. Tel: 440-473-0350. FAX: 440-473-0774. *Br Mgr,* William Rubin
Open Mon-Thurs 9-9, Fri & Sat 9-5:30, Sun 1-5
Friends of the Library Group
MIDDLEBURG HEIGHTS BRANCH, 15600 E Bagley Rd, Middleburg Heights, 44130-4830, SAN 356-1755. Tel: 440-234-3600. FAX: 440-234-0849. *Br Mgr,* Vicki Adams-Cook
Open Mon-Thurs 9-9, Fri & Sat 9-5:30, Sun 1-5
Friends of the Library Group
NORTH OLMSTED BRANCH, 27403 Lorain Rd, North Olmsted, 44070-4037, SAN 356-178X. Tel: 440-777-6211. FAX: 440-777-4312. *Br Mgr,* Valerie Kocin
Open Mon-Thurs 9-9, Fri & Sat 9-5:30, Sun 1-5
Friends of the Library Group
NORTH ROYALTON BRANCH, 5071 Wallings Rd, North Royalton, 44133-5120, SAN 356-181X. Tel: 440-237-3800. FAX: 440-237-6149. *Br Mgr,* Jeanne Cilenti
Open Mon-Thurs 9-9, Fri & Sat 9-5:30, Sun 1-5
Friends of the Library Group
OLMSTED FALLS BRANCH, 8100 Mapleway Dr, Olmsted Falls, 44138, SAN 356-1844. Tel: 440-235-1150. FAX: 440-235-0954. *Br Mgr,* Valerie Kocin
Open Mon-Thurs 9-9, Fri & Sat 9-5, Sun 1-5
Friends of the Library Group
ORANGE BRANCH, 31300 Chagrin Blvd, Pepper Pike, 44124-5916, SAN 356-1879. Tel: 216-831-4282. FAX: 216-831-0714. *Br Mgr,* Julie Liedtke
Open Mon-Thurs 9-9, Fri & Sat 9-5:30, Sun 1-5
Friends of the Library Group
PARMA BRANCH, 6996 Powers Blvd, 44129-6602, SAN 356-1933. Tel: 440-885-5362. FAX: 440-884-2263. *Br Mgr,* Kathleen Sullivan
Open Mon-Thurs 9-9, Fri & Sat 9-5, Sun 1-5
Friends of the Library Group
PARMA HEIGHTS BRANCH, 6206 Pearl Rd, Parma Heights, 44130-3045, SAN 356-1909. Tel: 440-884-2313. FAX: 440-884-2713. *Br Mgr,* Kevin Payne
Open Mon-Thurs 9-9, Fri & Sat 9-5:30, Sun 1-5
Friends of the Library Group
PARMA-SNOW BRANCH, 2121 Snow Rd, 44134-2728, SAN 356-1968. Tel: 216-661-4240. FAX: 216-661-1019. *Br Mgr,* Stacey Boycik
Open Mon-Thurs 9-9, Fri & Sat 9-5:30, Sun 1-5
Friends of the Library Group
RICHMOND HEIGHTS BRANCH, 5235 Wilson Mills Rd, Richmond Heights, 44143-3016, SAN 329-6075. Tel: 440-449-2666. FAX: 440-473-3264. *Br Mgr,* William Rubin
Open Mon-Thurs 9-9, Fri & Sat 9-5:30, Sun 1-5
SOLON BRANCH, 34125 Portz Pkwy, Solon, 44139-6803, SAN 356-1992. Tel: 440-248-8777. FAX: 440-248-5369. *Br Mgr,* Catherine Schultis
Open Mon-Thurs 9-9, Fri & Sat 9-5:30, Sun 1-5
Friends of the Library Group
SOUTH EUCLID-LYNDHURST BRANCH, 4645 Mayfield Rd, South Euclid, 44121-4018, SAN 356-2026. Tel: 216-382-4880. FAX: 216-382-4584. *Br Mgr,* Steven Haynie
Open Mon-Thurs 9-9, Fri & Sat 9-5:30, Sun 1-5
Friends of the Library Group
SOUTHEAST BRANCH, 70 Columbus Rd, Bedford, 44146-2836, SAN 356-1364. Tel: 440-439-4997. FAX: 440-439-5846. *Br Mgr,* Jeanne Sapir
Open Mon-Thurs 9-9, Fri & Sat 9-5:30, Sun 1-5
Friends of the Library Group
STRONGSVILLE BRANCH, 18700 Westwood Dr, Strongsville, 44136-3431, SAN 356-2050. Tel: 440-238-5530. FAX: 440-572-8685. *Br Mgr,* Donna Meyers
Open Mon-Thurs 9-9, Fri & Sat 9-5:30, Sun 1-5
Friends of the Library Group
WARRENSVILLE HEIGHTS BRANCH, 4415 Northfield Rd, Warrensville Heights, 44128-4603, SAN 356-2085. Tel: 216-464-5280. FAX: 216-464-6475. *Br Mgr,* Jesse Sanders
Open Mon-Thurs 9-9, Fri & Sat 9-5:30, Sun 1-5
Friends of the Library Group

PATASKALA

P PATASKALA PUBLIC LIBRARY*, 101 S Vine St, 43062. SAN 313-6698. Tel: 740-927-9986. FAX: 740-964-6204. *Dir/Fiscal Officer,* Jeffrey A Rothweiler; *Asst Dir,* Mary E Kruse; *Ch Serv,* Cathy Lantz; *Circ,* Scott Kammeyer; Staff 3 (MLS 2, Non-MLS 1)
Founded 1937. Pop 12,000; Circ 254,000
Jan 2010-Dec 2010 Income $790,698, State $467,305, Locally Generated Income $289,933, Other $33,460. Mats Exp $115,148, Books $66,657, Per/Ser (Incl. Access Fees) $2,432, AV Mat $46,059
Library Holdings: AV Mats 9,000; Bk Vols 66,000; Per Subs 53
Special Collections: Accords Coll
Open Mon-Thurs (Winter) 10-9, Fri 10-6, Sat 10-5; Mon-Thurs (Summer)) 10-8, Fri & Sat 10-5
Friends of the Library Group

PAULDING

P PAULDING COUNTY CARNEGIE LIBRARY*, 205 S Main St, 45879-1492. SAN 313-6701. Tel: 419-399-2032. FAX: 419-399-2114. Web Site: www.pauldingcountylibrary.org. *Dir,* Susan Pieper; *Asst Dir, Head, Adult Serv,* Vicky Hull; E-mail: vhull@pauldingcountylibrary.org; *Head, Tech Serv,* Teresa Reel; *Head, Youth Serv,* Sara Molitor; Staff 12 (MLS 1, Non-MLS 11)
Founded 1916. Pop 19,432; Circ 205,527
Jan 2009-Dec 2009 Income (Main Library and Branch(s)) $689,823, State $608,578, Other $81,245. Mats Exp $45,314, Books $32,156, Per/Ser (Incl. Access Fees) $5,207, Other Print Mats $294, AV Mat $7,657. Sal $437,135
Library Holdings: DVDs 6,631; Bk Vols 70,915; Per Subs 110
Special Collections: Civil War Interest; High School Yearbooks (County High Schools); Local History & Genealogy; Paulding County Newspapers (1859-present), micro; Paulding County Obituary Card File; Rare Books; World War II Interest
Subject Interests: County genealogy, Local hist
Automation Activity & Vendor Info: (Acquisitions) Innovative Interfaces, Inc; (Circulation) Innovative Interfaces, Inc; (OPAC) Innovative Interfaces, Inc
Database Vendor: Gale Cengage Learning
Wireless access
Function: Bk club(s), Bks on CD, CD-ROM, Children's prog, Computer training, Computers for patron use, Copy machines, Digital talking bks, e-mail & chat, Electronic databases & coll, Exhibits, Family literacy, Fax serv, Free DVD rentals, Genealogy discussion group, Govt ref serv, Handicapped accessible, Health sci info serv, Holiday prog, Homework prog, ILL available, Instruction & testing, Learning ctr, Mail & tel request accepted, Music CDs, Online cat, Online info literacy tutorials on the web & in blackboard, Online searches, Orientations, Photocopying/Printing, Preschool outreach, Prog for adults, Prog for children & young adult, Pub access computers, Ref & res, Ref serv available, Ref serv in person, Scanner, Senior computer classes, Serves mentally handicapped consumers, Story hour, Summer reading prog, Tax forms, Teen prog, Telephone ref, Web-catalog, Wheelchair accessible
Publications: Rural Library Service (Newsletter)
Partic in Ohio Public Library Information Network
Special Services for the Blind - Audio mat; Bks on cassette; Bks on CD; Large print bks; Playaways (bks on MP3); Talking bk & rec for the blind cat
Open Mon-Thurs 9-8, Fri 9-6, Sat 9-1
Friends of the Library Group
Branches: 3
ANTWERP BRANCH, 205 N Madison St, Antwerp, 45813-8411. (Mail add: PO Box 1027, Antwerp, 45813-1027). Tel: 419-258-2855. FAX: 419-258-2855. *Br Mgr,* Laura Woodcox; E-mail: lwoodcox@pauldingcountylibrary.org
Founded 1991
Open Mon & Tues 12-7:30, Wed-Fri 10-5, Sat 9-1
Friends of the Library Group
COOPER COMMUNITY, 206 N First St, Oakwood, 45873. (Mail add: PO Box 348, Oakwood, 45873-0348). Tel: 419-594-3337. FAX: 419-594-3337. *Br Mgr,* Sue Thomas; E-mail: sthomas@pauldingcountylibrary.org
Founded 2000
Open Mon & Tues 12-7:30, Wed-Fri 10-5, Sat 9-1
Friends of the Library Group

PAYNE BRANCH, 101 N Main St, Payne, 45880. (Mail add: PO Box 210, Payne, 45880-0210). Tel: 419-263-3333. FAX: 419-263-3333. *Br Mgr,* Suzi Yenser
Founded 1996
Open Mon & Tues 12-7:30, Wed-Fri 10-5, Sat 9-1
Friends of the Library Group

PEEBLES

P ADAMS COUNTY PUBLIC LIBRARY*, Peebles Public Library, 157 High St, 45660. SAN 356-7753. Tel: 937-587-2085. FAX: 937-587-5043. Web Site: www.adamsco.lib.oh.us. *Exec Dir,* Nicholas Slone; E-mail: sloneni@oplin.org; *Libr Asst,* Beverly Kiser
Open Mon & Wed 10-7, Tues, Thurs, Fri & Sat 10-5
Friends of the Library Group
Branches: 3
MANCHESTER PUBLIC LIBRARY, 401 Pike St, Manchester, 45144, SAN 356-7729. Tel: 937-549-3359. FAX: 937-549-4219. *Libr Asst,* Peggy McCartney
Open Mon & Wed 10-7, Tues, Thurs, Fri & Sat 10-5
Friends of the Library Group
NORTH ADAMS PUBLIC LIBRARY, 2469 Moores Rd, Seaman, 45679. Tel: 937-386-2556. FAX: 937-386-2974. *Libr Asst,* Kris Lanham
Open Mon, Wed, Fri & Sat 10-5, Tues & Thurs 10-7
Friends of the Library Group
WEST UNION PUBLIC LIBRARY, 212 E Sparks Ave, West Union, 45693, SAN 376-9631. Tel: 937-544-2591. FAX: 937-544-2092. *Libr Asst,* Tara Dryden; E-mail: drydenta@oplin.org
Open Mon, Wed, Fri & Sat 10-5, Tues & Wed 10-7
Friends of the Library Group

PEMBERVILLE

P PEMBERVILLE PUBLIC LIBRARY*, 375 E Front St, 43450. (Mail add: PO Box 809, 43450-0809), SAN 357-072X. Tel: 419-287-4012. FAX: 419-287-4620. Web Site: www.pembervillelibrary.org. *Dir,* Jane Kohlenberg; *Ch Serv,* Laurel Rakas; Staff 5 (MLS 2, Non-MLS 3)
Founded 1937. Pop 9,000; Circ 98,000
Library Holdings: High Interest/Low Vocabulary Bk Vols 50; Bk Titles 55,000; Per Subs 145
Subject Interests: Local hist
Automation Activity & Vendor Info: (Cataloging) SirsiDynix; (Circulation) SirsiDynix; (Course Reserve) SirsiDynix; (ILL) SirsiDynix; (OPAC) SirsiDynix; (Serials) SirsiDynix
Function: Doc delivery serv, ILL available, Photocopying/Printing, Ref serv available, Telephone ref
Partic in Northwestern Libr District
Open Mon-Thurs 9-8, Fri 9-2, Sat 10-3
Friends of the Library Group
Branches: 2
LUCKEY BRANCH, PO Box 190, Luckey, 43443, SAN 377-8274. Tel: 419-833-6040. FAX: 419-833-6040. *Dir,* Jane Kohlemberg
Open Mon-Thurs 3:30-7:30, Fri 2-5, Sat 10-Noon
Friends of the Library Group
STONY RIDGE BRANCH, 5805 Fremont Pike, Stony Ridge, 43463, SAN 357-0754. Tel: 419-837-5948. FAX: 419-714-7061. *Br Coordr,* Laura King; E-mail: liblady1@yahoo.com
Library Holdings: Bk Vols 23,000
Open Mon & Tues 12-8, Wed 9-5, Thurs 12-5, Sat 10-12
Friends of the Library Group

PENINSULA

S PENINSULA LIBRARY & HISTORICAL SOCIETY*, 6105 Riverview Rd, 44264. (Mail add: PO Box 236, 44264-0236), SAN 313-671X. Tel: 330-657-2291. FAX: 330-657-2311. E-mail: info@peninsulalibrary.org. Web Site: www.peninsulalibrary.org. *Dir,* Randolph S Bergdorf; *Adult Serv,* Anne M Matusz; *Purchasing,* Corinna A T Short; Staff 13 (MLS 3, Non-MLS 10)
Founded 1943. Pop 553,371
Library Holdings: Bk Vols 38,500; Per Subs 130
Special Collections: Local History Coll
Automation Activity & Vendor Info: (Cataloging) SirsiDynix; (Circulation) SirsiDynix; (OPAC) SirsiDynix
Function: Archival coll, Handicapped accessible, ILL available, Online searches, Photocopying/Printing, Prog for adults, Prog for children & young adult, Ref serv available, Summer reading prog, Telephone ref, Wheelchair accessible
Publications: Bi-monthly Newsletter
Open Mon-Thurs 9-8, Fri & Sat 9-5, Sun (Sept-May) 12-5
Friends of the Library Group
Branches:
CUYAHOGA VALLEY HISTORICAL MUSEUM, 1775 Main St, Second Flr, 44264. (Mail add: PO Box 236, 44264-0236). Tel: 330-657-2892. E-mail: info@peninsulalibrary.org. *Dir,* Randy Bergdorf
Library Holdings: Bk Titles 38,500; Per Subs 124
Automation Activity & Vendor Info: (Acquisitions) SirsiDynix
Open Wed & Fri-Sun 12-4
Friends of the Library Group

PEPPER PIKE

R PARK SYNAGOGUE*, Zehman Library, 27575 Shaker Blvd, 44124. SAN 370-7083. Tel: 216-371-2244, Ext 223, 216-831-5363, Ext 223. FAX: 216-321-0639. *Librn,* Suzanne Arnold
Subject Interests: Judaica, Juv
Friends of the Library Group

R TEMPLE ON THE HEIGHTS*, Jack Jacobson Memorial Library, 27501 Fairmount Blvd, 44124. SAN 313-3931. Tel: 216-831-6555. FAX: 216-831-4599. *Librn,* Dr Ralph R Simon; Staff 2 (MLS 1, Non-MLS 1)
Founded 1928
Library Holdings: Bk Vols 9,000

C URSULINE COLLEGE, Ralph M Besse Library, 2550 Lander Rd, 44124-4398. SAN 313-3885. Tel: 440-449-4202. Interlibrary Loan Service Tel: 440-646-8186. Reference Tel: 440-646-8183. FAX: 440-449-3180. Web Site: www.ursuline.edu/library. *Dir,* Betsey Belkin; E-mail: bbelkin@ursuline.edu; *Head, Bibliog Serv,* Amanda Flower; E-mail: aflower@ursuline.edu; *Head, Electronic & Media Serv,* Suzanna Schroeder; Tel: 440-646-8178, E-mail: sschroeder@ursuline.edu; *Head, Patron Serv & Instruction,* Kathy Fisher; E-mail: kfisher@ursuline.edu; *Archivist, Ref & Instruction Librn,* Mara Dabrishus; E-mail: mdabrishus@ursuline.edu; *Ref & Instruction Librn,* Anita Slack; E-mail: anita.slack@ursuline.edu; *Tech Serv Librn,* Celia Halkovich; E-mail: chalkovich@ursuline.edu; *Acq,* Helen Tramte; E-mail: htramte@ursuline.edu; Staff 13.5 (MLS 7, Non-MLS 6.5)
Founded 1871. Enrl 1,496; Fac 70; Highest Degree: Doctorate
Jul 2012-Jun 2013 Income $733,996. Mats Exp $231,441, Books $38,500, Per/Ser (Incl. Access Fees) $53,500, AV Mat $19,500, Electronic Ref Mat (Incl. Access Fees) $24,000, Presv $1,000. Sal $502,555
Library Holdings: AV Mats 9,220; e-books 88,321; e-journals 46,288; Microforms 4,675; Bk Titles 93,260; Bk Vols 108,546; Per Subs 76
Special Collections: Besse Rivers Coll; Global Studies; Picture Archives Coll
Subject Interests: Art therapy, Educ, Nursing
Automation Activity & Vendor Info: (Acquisitions) Innovative Interfaces, Inc; (Cataloging) Innovative Interfaces, Inc; (Circulation) Innovative Interfaces, Inc; (OPAC) Innovative Interfaces, Inc; (Serials) Innovative Interfaces, Inc
Wireless access
Partic in OCLC Online Computer Library Center, Inc; Ohio Library & Information Network; OHIONET
Open Mon-Thurs 8am-11pm, Fri 8-7, Sat 10-7, Sun 1-11
Friends of the Library Group

PERRY

P PERRY PUBLIC LIBRARY*, 3753 Main St, 44081-9501. SAN 313-6728. Tel: 440-259-3300. FAX: 440-259-3977. E-mail: askus@perry.lib.oh.us. Web Site: www.perrypubliclibrary.org. *Dir,* Virginia Sharp March; E-mail: vmarch@perry.lib.oh.us; *Dept Head, Ref,* Sharon Detering; E-mail: sdetering@perry.lib.oh.us; *Dept Head, Tech Serv,* Kari Betchik; E-mail: kbetchik@perry.lib.oh.us; *Circ Supvr,* Linda Moats; E-mail: lmoats@perry.lib.oh.us; *Ch Serv,* Kara Cervelli; *Ch Serv,* Siobhan McCann; *ILL,* Ginger Hofstetter; E-mail: ghofstetter@perry.lib.oh.us; Staff 5.93 (MLS 4.38, Non-MLS 1.55)
Founded 1929. Pop 9,001; Circ 247,678
Jan 2012-Dec 2012 Income $880,914, State $304,005, Locally Generated Income $530,429, Parent Institution $45,480. Mats Exp $113,583. Sal $635,977
Library Holdings: Audiobooks 8,129; e-books 79,089; Bk Titles 49,123; Per Subs 194; Videos 8,301
Automation Activity & Vendor Info: (Cataloging) SIRSI WorkFlows; (Circulation) SIRSI WorkFlows; (ILL) SIRSI WorkFlows; (OPAC) SirsiDynix
Database Vendor: SirsiDynix
Wireless access
Function: Adult bk club, Audiobks via web, Bk club(s), Bks on CD, CD-ROM, Chess club, Children's prog, Computer training, Computers for patron use, Copy machines, Electronic databases & coll, Fax serv, Free DVD rentals, Handicapped accessible, Homebound delivery serv, ILL available, Magnifiers for reading, Music CDs, OverDrive digital audio bks, Photocopying/Printing, Prog for adults, Prog for children & young adult, Pub access computers, Story hour, Summer reading prog, Tax forms, Teen prog, Web-catalog, Wheelchair accessible
Partic in CLEVNET; Northeastern Ohio Libr Asn
Open Mon-Thurs 9-9, Fri 9-6, Sat 11-4
Friends of the Library Group

PERRYSBURG

J OWENS COMMUNITY COLLEGE LIBRARY*, 30335 Oregon Rd, 43551. (Mail add: PO Box 10000, Toledo, 43699-1947), SAN 313-6736. Tel: 567-661-7221. Circulation Tel: 567-661-7015. Reference Tel: 567-661-7017. Toll Free Tel: 800-466-9367, Ext 7221. FAX: 567-661-7021. E-mail: libhelp@owens.edu. Web Site: www.owens.edu/library. *Dean of Libr Serv,* Thomas R Sink; E-mail: thomas_sink@owens.edu; *Ser Librn,* Matthew Farthing; Tel: 567-661-7023; *Libr Mgr,* Patricia Breno; Tel: 567-661-7020, E-mail: patricia_breno@owens.edu; *Circ Supvr,* Jennifer Blum; Tel: 567-661-7016; *Acq,* Michael Aked; Tel: 567-661-7031; *Cat,* Laurel King; Tel: 567 661 7030; *Ref,* Jane Berger; Tel: 567-661-7223; Staff 14 (MLS 6, Non-MLS 8)
Founded 1966. Enrl 22,000; Fac 1,400; Highest Degree: Associate
Library Holdings: Bk Titles 38,600; Bk Vols 49,800; Per Subs 400
Automation Activity & Vendor Info: (Acquisitions) Innovative Interfaces, Inc; (Cataloging) Innovative Interfaces, Inc; (Circulation) Innovative Interfaces, Inc; (Course Reserve) Docutek; (ILL) Innovative Interfaces, Inc; (Media Booking) Innovative Interfaces, Inc; (OPAC) Innovative Interfaces, Inc; (Serials) Innovative Interfaces, Inc
Database Vendor: EBSCOhost, Innovative Interfaces, Inc, LexisNexis, OCLC WorldShare Interlibrary Loan, ProQuest, Safari Books Online
Wireless access
Partic in OCLC Online Computer Library Center, Inc; Ohio Library & Information Network; OHIONET
Special Services for the Blind - Assistive/Adapted tech devices, equip & products
Open Mon-Thurs (Fall & Spring) 8am-9pm, Fri 8-6, Sat 8-4, Sun 1-8; Mon & Thurs (Summer) 8am-9pm, Tues & Wed 8-6, Fri 8-5, Sat 9-1
Restriction: Open to pub for ref & circ, with some limitations, Open to students, fac & staff, Photo ID required for access

P WAY PUBLIC LIBRARY*, 101 E Indiana Ave, 43551. SAN 313-6744. Tel: 419-874-3135. FAX: 419-874-6129. E-mail: wayref@oplin.org. Web Site: www.way.lib.oh.us. *Dir,* Janel Haas; Tel: 419-874-3135, Ext 102, E-mail: haasja@oplin.org; *Head, Tech Serv,* Linda Rutz; Tel: 419-874-3135, Ext 114, E-mail: rutzli@oplin.org; *Hist Coll Librn,* Richard Baranowski; Tel: 419-874-3135, Ext 110, E-mail: baranori@oplin.org; *Ref Librn,* Wendie Kiskaddon; Tel: 419-874-3135, Ext 107, E-mail: kiskadwe@oplin.org; *Circ Supvr,* Lynn Fleure; Tel: 419-874-3135, Ext 111, E-mail: fleurely@oplin.org; *Coordr, Youth Serv,* Adria Pugh, Tel: 419-874-3135, Ext 109, E-mail: pughad@oplin.org; *Graphic & Visual Design Spec,* Rose Mills; Tel: 419-874-3135, Ext 108, E-mail: millsro@oplin.org; *Syst Admnr,* Travis McAfee; Tel: 419-874-3135, Ext 103, E-mail: mcafeetr@oplin.org; *Youth Serv,* Martha Johns; Tel: 419-874-3135, Ext 127, E-mail: johnsma@oplin.org; Staff 12 (MLS 6, Non-MLS 6)
Founded 1881. Pop 25,000
Library Holdings: Bk Vols 101,156; Per Subs 222
Special Collections: Perrysburg Local History Coll
Automation Activity & Vendor Info: (OPAC) Horizon
Wireless access
Open Mon-Thurs 9-8:30, Fri & Sat 9-5:30, Sun 1-5
Friends of the Library Group

PICKERINGTON

P PICKERINGTON PUBLIC LIBRARY*, 201 Opportunity Way, 43147-1296. SAN 313-6752. Tel: 614-837-4104. Circulation Tel: 614-837-4104, Ext 232. Reference Tel: 614-837-4104, Ext 233. Automation Services Tel: 614-833-1004. FAX: 614-837-8425. Web Site: www.pickerington.lib.oh.us. *Dir,* Suellen Goldsberry; E-mail: sgoldsberry@pickeringtonlibrary.org; *Asst Dir,* Kenton Daniels; E-mail: kdaniels@pickeringtonlibrary.org; *Adult Serv Mgr,* Amanda Fensch; *Youth Serv,* Cathy Burden; Staff 6 (MLS 3, Non-MLS 3)
Founded 1915. Pop 34,000; Circ 366,727
Library Holdings: AV Mats 21,271; Bk Vols 103,143; Per Subs 296
Automation Activity & Vendor Info: (Acquisitions) SirsiDynix; (Cataloging) SirsiDynix; (Circulation) SirsiDynix; (OPAC) SirsiDynix; (Serials) SirsiDynix
Publications: Monthly Newsletter
Partic in Cent Libr Consortium
Open Mon-Thurs (Sept-May) 9-8, Fri 9-6, Sat 9-5, Sun 1-5
Friends of the Library Group

PIQUA

J EDISON COMMUNITY COLLEGE LIBRARY, 1973 Edison Dr, 45356. SAN 313-6779. Tel: 937-778-7950. FAX: 937-778-7958. E-mail: library@edisonohio.edu. Web Site: www.edisonohio.edu/library. *Libr Dir,* Nancy Madden; Tel: 937-778-7955, E-mail: nmadden@edisonohio.edu; *VPres, Info Tech,* David Gansz; Tel: 937-778-7951, E-mail: dgansz@edisonohio.edu; *Cat, Instruction & Ref Librn,* Amanda Hyden; Tel: 937-778-7954, E-mail: ahazenfield@edisonohio.edu; *Libr Asst,* Elsa Barber; Tel: 937-778-7953, E-mail: ebarber@edisonohio.edu; Staff 4 (MLS 3, Non-MLS 1)
Founded 1973. Enrl 3,000; Highest Degree: Associate
Library Holdings: AV Mats 2,019; Bk Vols 23,324; Per Subs 38; Videos 1,108
Subject Interests: Early childhood educ, Nursing
Automation Activity & Vendor Info: (Cataloging) Innovative Interfaces, Inc; (Circulation) Innovative Interfaces, Inc; (Course Reserve) Innovative Interfaces, Inc; (Media Booking) Innovative Interfaces, Inc; (OPAC) Innovative Interfaces, Inc; (Serials) Innovative Interfaces, Inc
Database Vendor: EBSCOhost, Facts on File, Foundation Center, Gale Cengage Learning, LexisNexis, OCLC ArticleFirst, OCLC WorldShare Interlibrary Loan, ProQuest, Safari Books Online
Wireless access
Partic in Ohio Library & Information Network; Southwestern Ohio Council for Higher Education
Open Mon-Thurs 8-8, Fri 8-4, Sat 10-2

P PIQUA PUBLIC LIBRARY*, 116 W High St, 45356. SAN 313-6787. Tel: 937-773-6753. FAX: 937-773-5981. Web Site: www.piqua.lib.oh.us. *Dir,* James C Oda; E-mail: odaja@oplin.org; *Coordr, Circ,* Jill Casto; *Ref Serv Coordr,* Kristen Ruzicka; *Ch Serv,* Nancy Spillane; *Tech Serv,* Tess Graves; Staff 3 (MLS 3)
Founded 1890. Pop 25,000; Circ 260,926
Library Holdings: Bk Vols 136,000; Per Subs 165
Special Collections: Oral History
Subject Interests: Local hist
Automation Activity & Vendor Info: (Cataloging) Brodart; (Circulation) Brodart; (OPAC) Brodart
Partic in Miami Valley Librs
Open Mon-Thurs 9-8:30, Fri & Sat 9-5:30
Friends of the Library Group

PLAIN CITY

P PLAIN CITY PUBLIC LIBRARY*, 305 W Main St, 43064-1148. SAN 313-6795. Tel: 614-873-4912. Circulation Tel: 614-873-4912, Ext 21. Reference Tel: 614-873-4912, Ext 28. FAX: 614-873-8364. E-mail: pcpl@plaincitylib.org. Web Site: www.plaincitylib.org. *Dir,* Chris Long; Tel: 614-873-4912, Ext 23, E-mail: clong@plaincitylib.org; *Circ Mgr,* Barbara Berry; E-mail: bberry@plaincitylib.org; *Cat,* Irena Wallace; Tel: 614-873-4912, Ext 27, E-mail: iwallace@plaincitylib.org; *Pub Serv,* Jane Isaacs; E-mail: jisaacs@plaincitylib.org; *Youth Serv,* Amanda Warner; Tel: 614-873-4912, Ext 30; Staff 19 (MLS 3, Non-MLS 16)
Founded 1944. Circ 142,672
Library Holdings: Bk Titles 54,896; Per Subs 114
Subject Interests: Genealogy, Local hist
Database Vendor: SirsiDynix
Partic in Cent Libr Consortium
Open Mon-Thurs 10-9, Fri & Sat 10-6
Friends of the Library Group

POMEROY

P MEIGS COUNTY DISTRICT PUBLIC LIBRARY*, 216 W Main, 45769-1032. SAN 357-0789. Tel: 740-992-5813. FAX: 740-992-6140. E-mail: meigscty@oplin.org. Web Site: www.meigs.lib.oh.us. *Dir,* Kristi Eblin, E-mail: eblinkr@oplin.org; *Asst Dir,* Olita Heighton; *Coordr, Ch Serv,* Emily Sanders; Staff 4 (Non-MLS 4)
Founded 1881. Pop 23,641; Circ 140,062
Library Holdings: Bk Vols 110,000; Per Subs 300
Automation Activity & Vendor Info: (Cataloging) TLC (The Library Corporation); (Circulation) TLC (The Library Corporation); (OPAC) TLC (The Library Corporation)
Special Services for the Deaf - High interest/low vocabulary bks
Open Mon-Fri 9-9, Sat 9-5, Sun 1-5
Branches: 3
EASTERN, 38850 State Rte 7, Reedsville, 45572. SAN 378-1232. Tel: 740-985-3747. FAX: 740-985-3746. *Dir,* Kristi Eblin
Open Mon-Fri 8-8, Sat 10-6
Friends of the Library Group
MIDDLEPORT BRANCH, 178 S Third St, Middleport, 45760. SAN 357-0819. Tel: 740-992-5713. FAX: 740-992-4207. *Dir,* Kristi Eblin
Open Mon 12-8, Tues-Sat 10-6
Friends of the Library Group
RACINE BRANCH, 210 Tyree Blvd, Racine, 45771. (Mail add: PO Box 370, Racine, 45771-0370), SAN 377-8290. Tel: 740-949-8200. FAX: 740-949-8300. *Asst Dir,* Olita Heighton
Open Mon-Sat 10-6
Friends of the Library Group

PORT CLINTON

P IDA RUPP PUBLIC LIBRARY*, Port Clinton Public Library, 310 Madison St, 43452. SAN 313-6817. Tel: 419-732-3212. Administration Tel: 419-732-3221. FAX: 419-734-9867. E-mail: askida@oplin.org. Web Site:

www.idarupp.org. *Dir,* Deborah Loiacono; *Asst Dir,* Lauren Lemmon; E-mail: lemmonla@oplin.org; *Youth Serv Supvr,* Jennifer Buch; E-mail: buchje@oplin.org; Staff 23 (MLS 4, Non-MLS 19)
Founded 1908. Pop 20,000; Circ 293,827
Library Holdings: Audiobooks 4,000; CDs 4,000; DVDs 4,108; e-books 8,930; Bk Titles 80,817
Special Collections: Bataan Memorial Coll; Coleccion de les Peliculas Mexicanas; Genealogy & Local History Coll; Ohioana & Rare Book Coll; Patricia A Snider Great Lakes Coll
Automation Activity & Vendor Info: (Cataloging) SirsiDynix; (Circulation) SirsiDynix; (OPAC) SirsiDynix
Wireless access
Partic in Ohio Public Library Information Network
Open Mon-Thurs 9:30-8:30, Fri & Sat 9:30-5:30, Sun 1-4
Friends of the Library Group
Branches: 1
ERIE ISLANDS, 281 Concord Ave, Put-In-Bay, 43456. (Mail add: PO Box 147, Put-In-Bay, 43456-0147), SAN 328-0101. Tel: 419-285-4004. FAX: 419-285-4004. *Br Mgr,* Linda Rence; E-mail: renceli@oplin.org; Staff 4 (Non-MLS 4)
Library Holdings: Bk Titles 7,000
Open Mon 10-1, Tues & Thurs 5-8, Wed 10-4, Fri 1-4
Friends of the Library Group

PORTSMOUTH

P PORTSMOUTH PUBLIC LIBRARY*, 1220 Gallia St, 45662-4185. SAN 357-0843. Tel: 740-354-5688. FAX: 740-353-1249. TDD: 740-354-6039. Web Site: www.portsmouth.lib.oh.us. *Dir,* Paige Williams; Staff 70 (MLS 3, Non-MLS 67)
Founded 1831. Pop 80,327; Circ 219,300
Library Holdings: Bk Titles 102,787; Bk Vols 213,680; Per Subs 390
Special Collections: Northwest Territories Coll
Subject Interests: Local hist
Automation Activity & Vendor Info: (Acquisitions) TLC (The Library Corporation); (Cataloging) TLC (The Library Corporation); (Circulation) TLC (The Library Corporation); (ILL) TLC (The Library Corporation); (OPAC) TLC (The Library Corporation); (Serials) TLC (The Library Corporation)
Database Vendor: EBSCOhost, ProQuest
Function: ILL available
Open Mon-Thurs 9-8, Fri & Sat 9-5
Branches: 5
NORTHWEST, 13056 State Rte 73, Rm 12, McDermott, 45652. Tel: 740-372-8314. FAX: 740-372-4315. *Br Mgr,* Jason Stump; Staff 4 (Non-MLS 4)
Founded 2000. Circ 14,875
Open Mon & Wed 1-8, Tues, Thurs & Fri 9-1
VERNAL G RIFFE BRANCH, 3850 Rhodes Ave, New Boston, 45662, SAN 357-0878. Tel: 740-456-4412. FAX: 740-456-4047. *Br Mgr,* Jessica Kamer; Staff 4 (Non-MLS 4)
Founded 1941. Circ 66,112
Open Mon-Wed 9-8, Thurs & Fri 9-6, Sat 9-5:30
W GORDON RYAN BRANCH, 103 Lucasville-Minford Rd, Lucasville, 45648-0744, SAN 370-9027. Tel: 740-259-6119. FAX: 740-259-3168. *Br Mgr,* Gwen Suter; Staff 4 (Non-MLS 4)
Founded 1990. Circ 69,134
Open Mon-Wed 9-8, Thurs & Fri 9-6, Sat 9-5:30
SOUTH WEBSTER BRANCH, 496 Webster St, South Webster, 45682, SAN 326-8462. Tel: 740-778-2122. FAX: 740-778-3436. *Br Mgr,* Lacy Stevenson; Staff 4 (Non-MLS 4)
Founded 1984. Circ 52,434
Open Mon & Tues 9-8, Wed-Fri 9-6, Sat 9-5:30
WHEELERSBURG BRANCH, 10745 Old Gallia Pike, Wheelersburg, 45694, SAN 357-0894. Tel: 740-574-6116. FAX: 740-574-8280. *Br Mgr,* Randi Morrison; Staff 4 (Non-MLS 4)
Founded 1965. Circ 64,426
Open Mon & Tues 9-8, Wed-Fri 9-6, Sat 9-5:30
Bookmobiles: 1

L SCIOTO COUNTY LAW LIBRARY*, Scioto County Court House, 3rd Flr, 602 Seventh St, 45662. SAN 313-6825. Tel: 740-355-8259. FAX: 740-353-9480. E-mail: sclawlibrary@midohio.twcbc.com. *Librn,* Beverly Grimshaw
Library Holdings: Bk Vols 25,100
Database Vendor: LexisNexis
Wireless access
Restriction: External users must contact libr

C SHAWNEE STATE UNIVERSITY*, Clark Memorial Library, 940 Second St, 45662-4344. SAN 357-0967. Tel: 740-351-3323. Circulation Tel: 740-351-3519. Interlibrary Loan Service Tel: 740-351-3353. Reference Tel: 740-351-3321. Administration Tel: 740-351-3267. FAX: 740-351-3432. Web Site: www.shawnee.edu/off/cml/index.html. *Dir,* Rebekah Kilzer; E-mail: rkilzer@shawnee.edu; *Ref Librn,* Mary Cummings; Tel: 740-351-3461, E-mail: mcummings@shawnee.edu; *Syst Librn,* Janet Stewart; Tel: 740-351-3197, E-mail: jstewart@shawnee.edu; *Tech Serv Librn,* Suzanne Johnson Varney; Tel: 740-351-3410, E-mail: svarney@shawnee.edu. Subject Specialists: *Arts, Sci, Teacher educ,* Mary Cummings; Staff 14 (MLS 6, Non-MLS 8)
Founded 1967. Enrl 4,561; Fac 327; Highest Degree: Master
Jul 2010-Jun 2011 Income $1,377,023. Mats Exp $222,794, Books $49,866, Per/Ser (Incl. Access Fees) $33,108, Micro $8,700, AV Mat $11,825, Electronic Ref Mat (Incl. Access Fees) $119,295
Library Holdings: Audiobooks 324; AV Mats 23,036; Bks on Deafness & Sign Lang 96; CDs 1,544; DVDs 802; e-books 56,938; e-journals 64,465; Electronic Media & Resources 309,662; Large Print Bks 39; Microforms 264,999; Music Scores 402; Bk Titles 186,367; Per Subs 218; Videos 4,428
Special Collections: Albert Parry Coll; Bob Wilson Coll; Jessie Stuart Coll; Louis A Brennan Coll; Southern Ohio Valley Writers; Vernal G Riffe Memorabilia. US Document Depository
Automation Activity & Vendor Info: (Acquisitions) Innovative Interfaces, Inc - Millenium; (Cataloging) Innovative Interfaces, Inc - Millenium; (Circulation) Innovative Interfaces, Inc - Millenium; (Course Reserve) Innovative Interfaces, Inc - Millenium; (ILL) OCLC Online; (OPAC) Innovative Interfaces, Inc - Millenium; (Serials) Innovative Interfaces, Inc - Millenium
Database Vendor: 3M Library Systems, ABC-CLIO, Agricola, American Chemical Society, American Mathematical Society, ARTstor, Bowker, College Source, CQ Press, CredoReference, ebrary, EBSCOhost, Elsevier, Ex Libris Group, Facts on File, Gale Cengage Learning, H W Wilson, Ingenta, Innovative Interfaces, Inc, ISI Web of Knowledge, LearningExpress, LexisNexis, McGraw-Hill, Medline, Newsbank, OCLC WorldShare Interlibrary Loan, OHIONET, OVID Technologies, Oxford Online, ProQuest, PubMed, Safari Books Online, Sage, Scopus, SerialsSolutions, Swets Information Services, Thomson - Web of Science, TumbleBookLibrary, ValueLine, Westlaw, Wiley, Wilson - Wilson Web, World Book Online, YBP Library Services
Wireless access
Partic in Ohio Library & Information Network; OHIONET
Special Services for the Deaf - ADA equip; Closed caption videos; Sign lang interpreter upon request for prog
Special Services for the Blind - Daisy reader; Low vision equip; Magnifiers; Rec; Sound rec; Text reader
Open Mon-Thurs (Fall & Spring) 8am-11pm, Fri 8-5, Sat 10-6, Sun Noon-Midnight; Mon-Thurs (Summer) 8am-11pm, Fri 8-5, Sun 1-6

RAVENNA

S PORTAGE COUNTY HISTORICAL SOCIETY MUSEUM & LIBRARY*, 6549 N Chestnut St, 44266. SAN 326-4106. Tel: 330-296-3523. E-mail: pchsohio@neo.rr.com. Web Site: www.history.portage.oh.us. *Pres,* Wayne Enders; *Librn,* Barb Petroski; Staff 9 (Non-MLS 9)
Founded 1951
Library Holdings: Bk Vols 1,000
Special Collections: Frederick J Loudin Coll
Subject Interests: Genealogy, Hist, Local hist
Function: Archival coll, Photocopying/Printing, Res libr
Publications: Newsletter (Quarterly)
Open Thurs & Sun 2-4
Restriction: Not a lending libr, Open to pub with supv only

L PORTAGE COUNTY LAW LIBRARY*, 241 S Chestnut St, 44266. SAN 372-2023. Tel: 330-297-3661. *Librn,* Mary Alice Law
Library Holdings: Bk Vols 17,000; Per Subs 20

P REED MEMORIAL LIBRARY*, 167 E Main St, 44266-3197. SAN 313-6833. Tel: 330-296-2827. FAX: 330-296-3780. Web Site: www.reed.lib.oh.us. *Dir,* Cass Owens; E-mail: owenscass@oplin.org; *Head, Ch,* Angela Young; *Head, Circ,* Karen Ross; *Head, Ref,* Darlene McKenzie; *Head, Tech Serv,* Cindy Wenger; Staff 7 (MLS 7)
Founded 1915. Pop 21,030; Circ 171,172
Library Holdings: AV Mats 10,064; CDs 2,289; DVDs 997; Bk Titles 91,000; Bk Vols 94,241; Per Subs 206; Videos 3,621
Special Collections: Local Paper Film from early 1800-present; Ravenna & Mantua Ohio Glass Coll
Subject Interests: Local hist
Automation Activity & Vendor Info: (Acquisitions) Innovative Interfaces, Inc; (Cataloging) Innovative Interfaces, Inc; (Circulation) Innovative Interfaces, Inc; (OPAC) Innovative Interfaces, Inc; (Serials) Innovative Interfaces, Inc
Database Vendor: Baker & Taylor, EBSCOhost, Gale Cengage Learning, Newsbank, ProQuest
Wireless access
Function: Adult bk club, Chess club, Computer training, Copy machines, Electronic databases & coll, Handicapped accessible, Homebound delivery serv, ILL available, Magnifiers for reading, Mail & tel request accepted, Photocopying/Printing, Prog for adults, Prog for children & young adult,

Ref serv available, Spoken cassettes & CDs, Summer reading prog, Tax forms, Telephone ref, VHS videos, Wheelchair accessible
Publications: Reed the News (Newsletter)
Partic in Portage Library Consortium
Special Services for the Blind - Reader equip; Talking bks & player equip; Videos on blindness & phys handicaps
Open Mon-Fri 9-9, Sat 9-5, Sun 1-5
Friends of the Library Group

RICHWOOD

P RICHWOOD NORTH UNION PUBLIC LIBRARY*, Four E Ottawa St, 43344-1296. SAN 313-6841. Tel: 740-943-3054. FAX: 740-943 9211. Web Site: www.richwoodlibrary.org. *Dir,* Sarah Moore; E-mail: sarahmoore@richwoodlibrary.org; *Ch,* Lisa Holonitch; E-mail: lisaholonitch@richwoodlibrary.org
Founded 1882. Pop 2,200; Circ 44,000
Library Holdings: Bk Titles 72,000; Bk Vols 73,500; Per Subs 149
Special Collections: Oral History
Open Mon-Thurs 11-7, Fri 11-6, Sat 10-2

RIO GRANDE

C UNIVERSITY OF RIO GRANDE*, Jeanette Albiez Davis Library, 218 N College Ave, 45674. SAN 313-685X. Tel: 740-245-7005. Interlibrary Loan Service Tel: 740-245-7398. Reference Tel: 740-245-7344, 740-245-7382. Toll Free Tel: 800-282-7201. FAX: 740-245-7096. E-mail: refdesk@rio.edu. Web Site: library.rio.edu. *Dir,* J David Mauer; E-mail: dmauer@rio.edu; *Cat & Tech Serv Librn,* Gregory Jones; Tel: 740-245-7459, E-mail: gjones@rio.edu; *Outreach Serv Librn,* Amy Wilson; E-mail: awilson@rio.edu; *Ref Librn,* Timothy M Snow; E-mail: tsnow@rio.edu; *Access Serv & Coll Maintenance Assoc,* Deborah T Thompson; E-mail: thompson@rio.edu; Staff 5 (MLS 4, Non-MLS 1)
Founded 1876. Enrl 1,986; Fac 90; Highest Degree: Master
Library Holdings: AV Mats 2,412; Microforms 446,409; Bk Vols 94,197; Per Subs 230
Special Collections: US Document Depository
Automation Activity & Vendor Info: (Acquisitions) Innovative Interfaces, Inc
Function: Computers for patron use, Copy machines, Distance learning, Electronic databases & coll, Exhibits, Govt ref serv, Handicapped accessible, ILL available, Online info literacy tutorials on the web & in blackboard, Photocopying/Printing, Pub access computers, Ref serv in person, Telephone ref, Web-catalog, Wheelchair accessible
Publications: Ex Libris Et Al (Newsletter); Instructional Material (Reference guide); LibGuides (Online only); Pathfinders (Reference guide); Student Newspaper Column (Newsletter)
Partic in Ohio Library & Information Network; OHIONET
Open Mon-Thurs 8am-10pm, Fri 8-5, Sat 1-5, Sun 5-9
Restriction: Circ limited, In-house use for visitors, Open to pub for ref & circ; with some limitations, Open to students, fac & staff, Pub use on premises
Friends of the Library Group

RIPLEY

P UNION TOWNSHIP PUBLIC LIBRARY*, 27 Main St, 45167-1231. SAN 313-6868. Tel: 937-392-4871. FAX: 937-392-1631. E-mail: info@ripleylibrary.com. Web Site: www.ripleylibrary.com. *Dir,* Alison J Gibson; E-mail: gibsonal@oplin.lib.oh.us; *Ch Serv,* Patricia Fithen; *Circ,* Carol Cooper
Founded 1915. Pop 34,966; Circ 155,000
Library Holdings: Bk Vols 45,000; Per Subs 195
Special Collections: Local History, Ripley, Ohio
Automation Activity & Vendor Info: (Acquisitions) SirsiDynix; (Cataloging) SirsiDynix; (Circulation) SirsiDynix; (Serials) SirsiDynix
Database Vendor: Overdrive, Inc
Wireless access
Function: Bks on cassette, Bks on CD, Children's prog, Computer training, Computers for patron use, Copy machines, Electronic databases & coll, Fax serv, Free DVD rentals, Handicapped accessible, Holiday prog, Home delivery & serv to Sr ctr & nursing homes, ILL available, Music CDs, Newsp ref libr, Online cat, Online ref, Online searches, Photocopying/Printing, Prog for children & young adult, Pub access computers, Ref & res, Spoken cassettes & CDs, Story hour, Summer reading prog, Tax forms, VHS videos, Web-catalog, Wheelchair accessible
Partic in SEO (Serving Every Ohioan) Library Center
Open Mon-Thurs 10-8, Fri 10-6, Sat 10-4
Friends of the Library Group
Branches: 2
ABERDEEN BRANCH LIBRARY, 1730 US Rte 52, Aberdeen, 45101-9302. Tel: 937-795-2534. FAX: 937-795-2681. *Dir,* Alison Gibson; Tel: 937-392-4871
Automation Activity & Vendor Info: (Cataloging) SirsiDynix; (Circulation) SirsiDynix; (ILL) SirsiDynix; (Serials) SirsiDynix
Open Mon, Wed & Fri 12-6, Tues & Thurs 12-8, Sat 10-2
Friends of the Library Group
RUSSELLVILLE BRANCH LIBRARY, 280 W Main St, Russellville, 45168-8730. Tel: 937-377-2700. FAX: 937-377-1302. *Dir,* Gibson Alison; Tel: 937-392-4871
Library Holdings: Bk Vols 6,500; Per Subs 39
Automation Activity & Vendor Info: (Cataloging) SirsiDynix; (Circulation) SirsiDynix; (ILL) SirsiDynix; (Serials) SirsiDynix
Open Mon & Wed 12-8, Tues & Thurs 10-6, Fri 12-4, Sat 10-2
Friends of the Library Group

ROCK CREEK

P ROCK CREEK PUBLIC LIBRARY*, 2988 High St, 44084-9703. SAN 313-6876. Tel: 440-563-3340. FAX: 440-563-9566. *Dir,* Janice Despenes; Staff 5 (Non-MLS 5)
Founded 1937. Pop 3,500; Circ 98,000
Library Holdings: Bks on Deafness & Sign Lang 52; Bk Titles 28,000; Per Subs 102
Special Collections: Ruth E Smik Art Coll
Automation Activity & Vendor Info: (Cataloging) SirsiDynix
Database Vendor: Dialog, OCLC FirstSearch
Wireless access
Function: Telephone ref
Partic in Coun of Ashtabula County Librs; Northeast Ohio Regional Library System
Open Mon-Thurs (Sept-May) 9-8, Fri 9-6, Sat 10-2; Mon-Thurs (June-Aug) 9-7, Fri 9-5, Sat 10-2
Friends of the Library Group

ROCKFORD

P ROCKFORD CARNEGIE LIBRARY*, 162 S Main St, 45882-9260. (Mail add: PO Box 330, 45882-0330), SAN 313-6884. Tel: 419-363-2630. FAX: 419-363-3723. Web Site: www.rcpubliclibrary.org. *Dir,* Rozann Maurer; E-mail: rmaurer@rcpubliclibrary.org; Staff 1 (MLS 1)
Founded 1902. Pop 2,000; Circ 58,000
Jan 2010-Dec 2010 Income $175,369, State $171,663, Other $3,706. Mats Exp $16,098, Books $8,983, Per/Ser (Incl. Access Fees) $2,348, AV Mat $4,767. Sal $77,176 (Prof $34,000)
Library Holdings: DVDs 1,664; Large Print Bks 500; Bk Titles 17,087; Bk Vols 20,000; Per Subs 55
Automation Activity & Vendor Info: (Cataloging) SirsiDynix; (Circulation) SirsiDynix; (OPAC) SirsiDynix
Database Vendor: EBSCOhost, SirsiDynix
Wireless access
Partic in NORWELD; SEO (Serving Every Ohioan) Library Center
Open Mon-Thurs 10-8, Fri 10-5:30, Sat 10-2
Friends of the Library Group

ROCKY RIVER

P ROCKY RIVER PUBLIC LIBRARY*, 1600 Hampton Rd, 44116-2699. SAN 313-6892. Tel: 440-333-7610. FAX: 440-333-4184. Web Site: www.rrpl.org. *Dir,* Nick Cronin; Tel; 440-895-3711, E-mail: n.cronin@rrpl.org; *Dep Dir,* Jamie L Mason; E-mail: jmason@rrpl.org; *Dir, Info Tech,* Liz Rowe-Rawlinson; *Mgr, Tech Serv,* Ann Jackson; *Adult Serv,* Steve Haas; *Ch Serv,* Lucy Carney; *Circ,* Louise Russell; *Tech Serv,* Ann Jackson; Staff 15 (MLS 15)
Founded 1928. Pop 22,344; Circ 812,287
Jan 2007-Dec 2007 Income $4,836,311, State $815,919, County $3,236,932, Other $71,396. Mats Exp $654,882, Books $307,207, Per/Ser (Incl. Access Fees) $136,500, AV Mat $130,000, Electronic Ref Mat (Incl. Access Fees) $81,175. Sal $2,416,386 (Prof $816,795)
Library Holdings: Bk Vols 112,743; Per Subs 830
Special Collections: Cowan Pottery Museum
Subject Interests: Rocky River city hist
Automation Activity & Vendor Info: (Circulation) SIRSI-DRA
Database Vendor: SirsiDynix
Wireless access
Function: Art exhibits, Children's prog, Computer training, Electronic databases & coll, Homebound delivery serv, ILL available, OverDrive digital audio bks, Prog for adults
Publications: Between the Covers (Bi-monthly); Cowan Pottery (Journal); Inside View (Newsletter)
Partic in Northeast Ohio Regional Library System
Open Mon-Thurs 9-9, Fri & Sat 9-6, Sun (Sept-May) 1-5
Friends of the Library Group

ROOTSTOWN

CM NORTHEASTERN OHIO UNIVERSITIES COLLEGE OF MEDICINE*, Oliver Ocasek Medical Library, 4209 State Rd 44, 44272. (Mail add: PO Box 95, 44272-0095), SAN 313-6914. Tel: 330-325-6600. Reference Tel: 330-325-6604. FAX: 330-325-0522. Web Site: www.neoucom.edu/audience/library. *Dir,* Beth Layton; Tel: 330-325-6611;

Ref Librn, Heather McEwen; *Circ, Coordr, Access Serv, ILL,* Denise Cardon; *Cat Spec,* Carolyn McSherry; *Acq, Ser & Syst,* Elaine Forsch; Staff 11 (MLS 5, Non-MLS 6)
Founded 1974. Enrl 421; Fac 72; Highest Degree: Master
Library Holdings: Bk Vols 122,569; Per Subs 2,693
Subject Interests: Life sci, Med
Database Vendor: Innovative Interfaces, Inc, LexisNexis, OVID Technologies
Publications: Medical Periodicals in Northeastern Ohio
Partic in Northeast Ohio Regional Library System; Ohio Library & Information Network

ROSSFORD

P ROSSFORD PUBLIC LIBRARY*, 720 Dixie Hwy, 43460-1289. SAN 313-6922. Tel: 419-666-0924. FAX: 419-666-1989. E-mail: rossford@oplin.org. Web Site: www.rossfordlibrary.org. *Dir,* Jeannine Wilbarger; E-mail: wilbarje@oplin.org; *Cataloger, Ch,* Jacky Farkas; *Local Hist Librn, Ref Librn,* Anne Bushel; E-mail: annebushel@rossfordlibrary.org; *YA Librn,* Matt Harbauer; *Ch Serv Spec, Pub Relations Coordr,* Kristine Goldsmith; *Circ Supvr,* Sue Kalinowsk; *Info Tech,* Adam Murphy; E-mail: murphyad@oplin.org; Staff 4 (MLS 4)
Founded 1936. Pop 13,445; Circ 245,667
Library Holdings: e-books 52; Bk Vols 65,332; Per Subs 174
Subject Interests: Local hist
Automation Activity & Vendor Info: (Circulation) SirsiDynix; (OPAC) SirsiDynix
Database Vendor: SirsiDynix
Wireless access
Partic in NORWELD; SE Ohio Regional Librs
Open Mon-Thurs 9-8, Fri & Sat 9-5, Sun (Sept-May) 12-5
Friends of the Library Group

SABINA

P SABINA PUBLIC LIBRARY*, 11 E Elm St, 45169-1330. SAN 313-6930. Tel: 937-584-2751. FAX: 937-584-2751. Web Site: www.sabinalibrary.com. *Dir,* Peggy Dunn; *Asst Dir,* Carolyn G Jarrell
Founded 1937. Circ 32,809
Library Holdings: Bk Vols 32,288; Per Subs 90
Partic in Southwestern Ohio Rural Librs
Open Mon-Thurs 9-8, Fri 9-6, Sat 9-12
Branches: 1
NEW VIENNA LIBRARY, 97 Main St, New Vienna, 45159. Tel: 937-987-4200. *Br Mgr,* Pat Herring-Curtis
Open Mon, Tues & Thurs 12-6, Fri 11-5

SAINT CLAIRSVILLE

J BELMONT COLLEGE*, Learning Resource Center, 120 Fox-Shannon Pl, 43950-9735. SAN 313-6957. Tel: 740-695-9500, Ext 1019. Interlibrary Loan Service Tel: 740-695-9500, Ext 1185. Reference Tel: 740-695-9500, Ext 1186. Toll Free Tel: 800-423-1188 (OH only). FAX: 740-695-2247. E-mail: refdesk@belmontcollege.edu. Web Site: www.belmontcollege.edu. *Dir, Libr & Learning Commons,* Joyce Baker; E-mail: jbaker@belmontcollege.edu; *Coordr, Learning Commons,* Lisa Baker
Founded 1971. Highest Degree: Associate
Library Holdings: AV Mats 2,114; Bk Titles 11,112, Bk Vols 12,600; Per Subs 341
Subject Interests: Allied health, Info tech, Nursing
Automation Activity & Vendor Info: (Acquisitions) Innovative Interfaces, Inc; (Cataloging) Innovative Interfaces, Inc; (Circulation) Innovative Interfaces, Inc; (Course Reserve) Innovative Interfaces, Inc; (ILL) OCLC Connexion; (OPAC) Innovative Interfaces, Inc; (Serials) Innovative Interfaces, Inc
Database Vendor: OCLC FirstSearch, OCLC WorldShare Interlibrary Loan
Wireless access
Function: Archival coll, Audio & video playback equip for onsite use, AV serv, Computer training, Copy machines, Distance learning, Doc delivery serv, Electronic databases & coll, For res purposes, Handicapped accessible, Homework prog, ILL available, Learning ctr, Libr develop, Magnifiers for reading, Mail & tel request accepted, Online searches, Orientations, Photocopying/Printing, Satellite serv, Tax forms, Telephone ref, VHS videos, Wheelchair accessible, Workshops
Partic in OCLC Online Computer Library Center, Inc; Ohio Library & Information Network; OHIONET
Open Mon-Thurs 8-6:30, Fri 8am-1pm

L BELMONT COUNTY LAW LIBRARY*, Court House, 101 W Main St, 43950. SAN 313-6949. Tel: 740-695-2121, Ext 248. FAX: 740-695-4968. *Librn,* Kate Subasic
Library Holdings: Bk Vols 25,000
Database Vendor: LexisNexis, Westlaw
Open Mon-Fri 8:30-4:30

C OHIO UNIVERSITY*, Eastern Campus, Shannon Hall, 1st Flr, 45425 National Rd, 43950-9724. SAN 313-6965. Tel: 740-695-1720, 740-699-2519. Interlibrary Loan Service Tel: 740-699-2332. Reference Tel: 740-699-2344. Administration Tel: 740-699-2490. Toll Free Tel: 800-648-3331, Ext 2519. FAX: 740-695-7075. Web Site: www.eastern.ohiou.edu/directory/library/library.htm. *Head Librn,* Donna Capezzuto; E-mail: capezzut@ohio.edu; *Circ, Sr Libr Assoc,* Brad Cecil; E-mail: cecil@ohio.edu; Staff 3 (MLS 2, Non-MLS 1)
Founded 1957. Enrl 900; Highest Degree: Bachelor
Library Holdings: AV Mats 68,000; CDs 65; DVDs 64; Bk Titles 48,135; Bk Vols 72,869; Per Subs 774; Videos 500
Special Collections: Contemporary American Poetry
Subject Interests: Educ, Nursing
Automation Activity & Vendor Info: (Cataloging) Innovative Interfaces, Inc; (Circulation) Innovative Interfaces, Inc; (Course Reserve) Innovative Interfaces, Inc; (ILL) Innovative Interfaces, Inc; (OPAC) Innovative Interfaces, Inc; (Serials) Innovative Interfaces, Inc
Database Vendor: EBSCOhost, Factiva.com, Innovative Interfaces, Inc, JSTOR, OCLC FirstSearch, OCLC WorldShare Interlibrary Loan, ProQuest, Swets Information Services
Wireless access
Function: Computers for patron use, E-Reserves, Electronic databases & coll, ILL available, Instruction & testing, Online cat, Online ref, Online searches, Orientations, Photocopying/Printing, Pub access computers, Ref serv in person, Spoken cassettes & CDs, Spoken cassettes & DVDs, VHS videos, Wheelchair accessible
Partic in OCLC Online Computer Library Center, Inc; Ohio Library & Information Network; OHIONET
Special Services for the Blind - Assistive/Adapted tech devices, equip & products
Open Mon-Thurs 8-6:30, Fri 8-5
Restriction: Open to fac, students & qualified researchers, Open to pub for ref & circ; with some limitations

P SAINT CLAIRSVILLE PUBLIC LIBRARY*, 108 W Main St, 43950-1225. SAN 313-6973. Tel: 740-695-2062. FAX: 740-695-6420. Web Site: stclibrary.org. *Libr Dir,* Richelle Klug; Staff 1 (Non-MLS 1)
Founded 1941. Pop 6,114; Circ 153,144
Library Holdings: Bk Vols 56,523; Per Subs 161
Subject Interests: Genealogy, Local hist
Automation Activity & Vendor Info: (Acquisitions) SirsiDynix; (Cataloging) SirsiDynix; (Circulation) SirsiDynix; (ILL) SirsiDynix; (OPAC) SirsiDynix
Wireless access
Partic in SE Ohio Regional Librs
Open Mon-Wed 10-8, Thurs & Fri 10-6, Sat 10-2
Friends of the Library Group

SAINT MARTIN

J CHATFIELD COLLEGE LIBRARY*, 20918 State Rte 251, 45118. SAN 313-6981. Tel: 513-875-3344. FAX: 513-875-3912. Web Site: www.chatfield.edu. *Dir, Libr Serv,* Dolores Berish; E-mail: dolores.berish@chatfield.edu
Founded 1860. Enrl 350
Library Holdings: Bk Titles 24,000; Per Subs 25
Subject Interests: Appalachian studies, Children's lit, Fiber arts, Local hist
Automation Activity & Vendor Info: (Cataloging) SirsiDynix; (Circulation) SirsiDynix; (OPAC) SirsiDynix
Wireless access
Partic in SW Ohio Regional Libr Syst

SAINT MARYS

P ST MARYS COMMUNITY PUBLIC LIBRARY*, 140 S Chestnut St, 45885-2307. SAN 313-699X. Tel: 419-394-7471. FAX: 419-394-7291. Web Site: www.stmarys.lib.oh.us. *Dir,* Susan Heckler Pittman; E-mail: pittmasu@oplin.org; *Chief Financial Officer,* Stephanie Hoffer; E-mail: shoffer@oplin.org; *Coord, Ad Serv,* Beth Keuneke; E-mail: keunekbe@oplin.org; Staff 3 (MLS 2, Non-MLS 1)
Founded 1921. Pop 12,000; Circ 125,792
Library Holdings: CDs 1,213; DVDs 1,425; Bk Vols 65,293; Per Subs 135; Talking Bks 1,432; Videos 1,213
Special Collections: Jim Tully Coll
Subject Interests: Local hist
Automation Activity & Vendor Info: (Cataloging) SirsiDynix; (Circulation) SirsiDynix; (OPAC) SirsiDynix
Wireless access
Partic in NORWELD; SE Ohio Regional Librs
Open Mon-Thurs 10-7, Fri 10-5, Sat 10-2
Friends of the Library Group

SAINT PARIS

P SAINT PARIS PUBLIC LIBRARY*, 127 E Main St, 43072. (Mail add: PO Box 740, 43072-0740), SAN 313-7007. Tel: 937-663-4349. FAX: 937-663-0297. E-mail: stparis@oplin.org. Web Site: stparispubliclibrary.org. *Dir,* Nicole Rush; E-mail: rushni@oplin.org; *Circ Supvr,* Jo Ozimek; Staff 11 (Non-MLS 11)
Founded 1936. Pop 10,000; Circ 106,000
Library Holdings: Bks on Deafness & Sign Lang 31; Bk Titles 32,000; Bk Vols 37,000; Per Subs 105
Special Collections: AB Graham Coll
Subject Interests: Genealogy
Friends of the Library Group

SALEM

CR ALLEGHENY WESLEYAN COLLEGE LIBRARY*, 2161 Woodsdale Rd, 44460. SAN 313-7015. Tel: 330-337-6403. FAX: 330-337-6255. *Assoc Prof, Librn,* Alice Weingard; Staff 2 (MLS 1, Non-MLS 1)
Founded 1973. Enrl 57; Fac 8; Highest Degree: Bachelor
Library Holdings: Bk Vols 17,886; Per Subs 118
Automation Activity & Vendor Info: (Cataloging) Follett Software; (Circulation) Follett Software; (Course Reserve) Follett Software; (OPAC) Follett Software
Open Mon-Fri 8-5 & 6:30-10, Sat 10-5

C KENT STATE UNIVERSITY, Salem Campus Library, 2491 State Rte 45-S, 44460-9412. SAN 313-704X. Tel: 330-337-4213. Interlibrary Loan Service Tel: 330-337-4211. FAX: 330-337-4144. *Dir,* Lilith R Kunkel; Tel: 330-337-4215, E-mail: lkunkel@kent.edu; *Libr Assoc,* Maegan Richards; Tel: 330-337-4211, E-mail: mrichar4@kkent.edu; Staff 1 (MLS 1)
Founded 1962. Fac 140
Library Holdings: AV Mats 886; Bk Vols 22,475; Per Subs 98
Automation Activity & Vendor Info: (Cataloging) Innovative Interfaces, Inc; (Circulation) Innovative Interfaces, Inc; (ILL) Innovative Interfaces, Inc; (Media Booking) Innovative Interfaces, Inc; (OPAC) Innovative Interfaces, Inc
Wireless access
Special Services for the Deaf - Video relay serv
Open Mon-Thurs 9-8:30, Fri 9-5

P SALEM PUBLIC LIBRARY*, 821 E State St, 44460-2298. SAN 313-7058. Tel: 330-332-0042. FAX: 330-332-4488. E-mail: library@salem.lib.oh.us. Web Site: www.salem.lib.oh.us. *Dir,* Bradley K Stephens; Tel: 330-332-2458; *Head, Adult Serv, Syst Coordr,* Jane M Massa; E-mail: massaja@oplin.org; *Head, Ch,* Cheryl Kelly; E-mail: kellych@oplin.org; *AV, YA Serv,* June E Drotleff; E-mail: drotleju@oplin.org; *Cataloger, Ref Serv,* Robin J Ludington; E-mail: ludingro@oplin.org; *Mkt, Outreach Coordr,* Teresa Rhodes; E-mail: rhodeste@oplin.org; *Ref Serv,* Jo Ellen Johnston; *Ref Serv, Ad,* Ann D Grimes; E-mail: grimesan@oplin.org; Staff 18 (MLS 5, Non-MLS 13)
Founded 1895. Pop 17,049; Circ 342,864
Library Holdings: AV Mats 13,080; CDs 2,422; DVDs 1,197; Bk Vols 74,678; Per Subs 225; Talking Bks 3,056; Videos 6,405
Special Collections: Columbiana County & Salem History; Quaker History & Biography
Subject Interests: Anti-slavery
Automation Activity & Vendor Info: (Cataloging) Innovative Interfaces, Inc; (Circulation) Innovative Interfaces, Inc; (OPAC) Innovative Interfaces, Inc
Database Vendor: EBSCOhost, Gale Cengage Learning, ProQuest
Wireless access
Open Mon-Thurs 9-9, Fri & Sat 9-6, Sun (Oct-April) 1-5

SANDUSKY

R SAINT STEPHEN UNITED CHURCH OF CHRIST, Centennial Library, 905 E Perkins Ave, 44870. SAN 328-1353. Tel: 419-626-1612. FAX: 419-626-1617. Web Site: www.ststephenucc.org. *Librn,* Edith Balduff; *Librn,* Karen Cassidy; Staff 1 (MLS 1)
Founded 1982
Library Holdings: Bk Titles 4,000
Open Mon-Fri 8:30-4, Sun 8-Noon

GL SANDUSKY BAY LAW LIBRARY ASSOCIATION, INC*, 247 Columbus Ave, 44870. SAN 313-7066. Tel: 419-626-4823. FAX: 419-626-4826. *Librn,* Kelly Del Vecchio
Library Holdings: Bk Vols 14,450; Per Subs 20
Open Mon-Fri 8-4

P SANDUSKY LIBRARY, 114 W Adams St, 44870. SAN 357-1025. Tel: 419-625-3834. FAX: 419-625-4574. E-mail: comments@sanduskylib.org. Web Site: www.sandusky.lib.oh.us. *Exec Dir,* Molly Carver; *Asst Dir,* Terri Estel; *Ref,* Dennis McMullen; Staff 47 (MLS 7, Non-MLS 40)
Founded 1895. Pop 52,000
Library Holdings: Bk Vols 207,692; Per Subs 320
Special Collections: Johnson's Island; Local History Archives
Automation Activity & Vendor Info: (Cataloging) SirsiDynix; (Circulation) SirsiDynix; (OPAC) SirsiDynix
Publications: A View of Sandusky; From the Widow's Walk, Vol I & II
Partic in CLEVE-NET; Ohio Public Library Information Network
Open Mon-Wed 10-8, Thurs & Fri 10-5, Sat 10-5 (10-1 June-Sept)
Branches: 1
KELLEYS ISLAND BRANCH, 528 Division St, Kelleys Island, 43438. Tel: 419-746-9575. *Br Mgr,* Elaine Lickfelt
Library Holdings: Bk Titles 6,000
Open Mon 5-7, Thurs 2:30-4:30, Sat 11-1

SARDIS

P DALLY MEMORIAL LIBRARY*, 37252 Mound St, 43946. (Mail add: PO Box 37, 43946-0037). Tel: 740-483-1288. FAX: 740-483-2311. E-mail: dallylibrary@sbcglobal.net. *Dir,* Tamara R Ellis; Staff 1 (Non-MLS 1)
Founded 2003
Library Holdings: AV Mats 300; Bk Vols 6,000; Per Subs 50
Special Collections: Local History Coll
Automation Activity & Vendor Info: (Cataloging) SirsiDynix; (Circulation) SirsiDynix; (OPAC) SirsiDynix
Wireless access
Function: Computer training, Copy machines, Fax serv, ILL available, Photocopying/Printing, Prog for children & young adult, Ref & res, Summer reading prog, Tax forms, Telephone ref, VHS videos, Wheelchair accessible
Partic in SE Ohio Automation Consortium
Open Tues-Fri 10-6, Sat 10-2
Friends of the Library Group

SHAKER HEIGHTS

P SHAKER HEIGHTS PUBLIC LIBRARY, 16500 Van Aken Blvd, 44120-5318. SAN 357-1084. Tel: 216-991-2030. FAX: 216-991-5951. Web Site: www.shakerlibrary.org, www.shpl.lib.oh.us. *Dir,* Luren E Dickinson; E-mail: ldickinson@shakerlibrary.org; *Dep Dir,* Amy Switzer; E-mail: deputy.director@shakerlibrary.org; *Head, Adult Serv,* Cindy Maxey; E-mail: cindy.maxey@shakerlibrary.org; *Teen Librn,* Audrey Jacobs; E-mail: audrey.jacobs@shakerlibrary.org; *Youth Serv Mgr,* Maureen Brodar; E-mail: maureen.brodar@shakerlibrary.org; *Tech Serv,* Loraine Lamont; E-mail: loraine.lamont@shakerlibrary.org; Staff 71.3 (MLS 20, Non-MLS 51.3)
Founded 1937. Pop 33,963; Circ 1,330,555
Jan 2013-Dec 2013 Income (Main Library and Branch(s)) $4,952,325, State $1,803,821, Locally Generated Income $2,697,122, Other $451,382. Mats Exp $549,160, Books $247,095, Per/Ser (Incl. Access Fees) $38,110, AV Mat $207,851, Electronic Ref Mat (Incl. Access Fees) $55,727, Presv $377. Sal $2,746,713 (Prof $1,496,524)
Library Holdings: AV Mats 37,424; e-books 11,647; Electronic Media & Resources 8,131; Bk Vols 145,156; Per Subs 693
Special Collections: Black Studies; Shaker Heights History, Coll & Archives
Automation Activity & Vendor Info: (Acquisitions) SirsiDynix; (Circulation) SirsiDynix
Wireless access
Publications: Shaker Magazine (Bi-monthly)
Partic in CLEVNET; Northeast Ohio Regional Library System
Special Services for the Blind - Computer with voice synthesizer for visually impaired persons
Open Mon-Thurs 9-9, Fri & Sat 9-5:30, Sun 1-5
Friends of the Library Group
Branches: 1
BERTRAM WOODS BRANCH, 20600 Fayette Rd, 44122-2979, SAN 357-1114. Tel: 216-991-2421. FAX: 216-991-3124. *Br Mgr,* Lynne Miller; E-mail: lynne.miller@shakerlibrary.org
Founded 1960
Library Holdings: AV Mats 24,891; Bk Vols 69,253
Open Mon & Wed 1-9, Tues & Thurs-Sat 9-5:30
Friends of the Library Group

SHAUCK

P PERRY COOK MEMORIAL PUBLIC LIBRARY*, 7406 County Rd 242, 43349. (Mail add: PO Box 214, 43349-0214). Tel: 419-362-7181. FAX: 419-362-1518. E-mail: librarian@perrycooklibrary.org. *Dir,* Sharon Baker
Library Holdings: Bk Titles 25,000; Per Subs 75
Open Mon-Thurs (Sept-May) 10-8, Fri 10-4, Sat 10-2; Mon-Thurs (Jun-Aug) 10-8, Fri 10-4

SHELBY

P MARVIN MEMORIAL LIBRARY*, 29 W Whitney Ave, 44875-1252. SAN 313-7112. Tel: 419-347-5576. FAX: 419-347-7285. Web Site: www.shelbymm.lib.oh.us. *Dir,* Kathy Webb; E-mail: kwebb@oplin.org;

Pub Serv Librn, Shelley Bylica; E-mail: bylicash@oplin.org; *Ch Serv,* Jami Williams; E-mail: jwilliams@oplin.org; Staff 3 (MLS 2, Non-MLS 1)
Founded 1897. Pop 15,000; Circ 127,080
Jul 2005-Jun 2006 Income $618,506, State $540,152, Locally Generated Income $78,354. Mats Exp $102,902, Books $87,575, AV Mat $15,327. Sal $252,232
Library Holdings: AV Mats 4,963; Bk Vols 59,153; Per Subs 142
Automation Activity & Vendor Info: (Acquisitions) TLC (The Library Corporation); (Cataloging) TLC (The Library Corporation); (Circulation) TLC (The Library Corporation); (OPAC) TLC (The Library Corporation)
Open Mon-Thurs 9-8, Fri 9-5, Sat 9-2
Friends of the Library Group

SIDNEY

S AMOS PRESS, INC LIBRARY*, 911 Vandemark Rd, 45365. (Mail add: PO Box 4129, 45365-4129), SAN 323-6048. Tel: 937-498-2111, Ext 276. Toll Free FAX: 800-340-9501. *Librn,* Krista Hesselbein; E-mail: khesselbein@amospress.com; Staff 1 (Non-MLS 1)
Founded 1960
Library Holdings: CDs 180; DVDs 86; Bk Titles 25,000; Per Subs 502; Spec Interest Per Sub 925; Videos 37
Subject Interests: Classic & antique cars, Craft, Numismatics, Philately
Automation Activity & Vendor Info: (Cataloging) Follett Software; (Circulation) Follett Software

P SHELBY COUNTY LIBRARIES*, 230 E North St, 45365-2785. SAN 357-1149. Tel: 937-492-8354. Interlibrary Loan Service Tel: 937-492-6851. FAX: 937-492-9229. Web Site: www.shelbyco.lib.oh.us. *Dir,* Suzanne Cline; E-mail: clinesu@oplin.org; *AV,* Michael Vollmar-Grone; E-mail: vollmami@oplin.org; *Circ, Pub Serv, Ref Serv,* Mark Kister; E-mail: kisterma@oplin.org; *ILL,* Rose Ann Kerns; *Pub Relations,* Peggy Naseman; *Youth Serv,* Bonnie Banks; E-mail: banksbo@oplin.org; Staff 29 (MLS 5, Non-MLS 24)
Founded 1869. Pop 48,183; Circ 494,279
Jan 2009-Dec 2009 Income (Main Library and Branch(s)) $1,699,314. Mats Exp $282,952. Sal $880,127
Library Holdings: AV Mats 19,535; CDs 3,699; DVDs 7,574; Large Print Bks 4,927; Bk Titles 161,380; Bk Vols 168,816; Per Subs 234; Talking Bks 3,573; Videos 13,433
Automation Activity & Vendor Info: (Cataloging) TLC (The Library Corporation); (Circulation) TLC (The Library Corporation); (ILL) OCLC Online; (OPAC) TLC (The Library Corporation)
Database Vendor: Baker & Taylor, Gale Cengage Learning, OCLC WorldShare Interlibrary Loan, OHIONET
Wireless access
Partic in Miami Valley Librs; NORWELD; OCLC Online Computer Library Center, Inc; Ohio Libr Coun; OHIONET
Open Mon, Tues & Thurs 11-8, Wed & Fri 9-6, Sat 11-4
Restriction: 24-hr pass syst for students only
Branches: 5
ANNA COMMUNITY, 304 N Second St, Anna, 45302. (Mail add: PO Box 380, Anna, 45302), SAN 357-1173. Tel: 937-394-2761. FAX: 937-394-2761. *Br Coordr,* Sheila Strunk
Library Holdings: AV Mats 1,518; DVDs 982; Large Print Bks 667; Bk Titles 16,253; Per Subs 13; Talking Bks 350; Videos 312
Special Collections: Lois Lenski Coll
Open Mon & Wed 2-8, Fri 10-6, Sat 10-2
Friends of the Library Group
JACKSON CENTER MEMORIAL, 205 S Linden St, Jackson Center, 45334. (Mail add: PO Box 581, Jackson Center, 45334), SAN 357-1262. Tel: 937-596-5300. FAX: 937-596-5300. *Interim Br Coordr,* Sherri Herring
Library Holdings: AV Mats 550; DVDs 458; Large Print Bks 114; Bk Titles 14,546; Per Subs 19; Talking Bks 65
Open Mon & Wed 2-8, Fri 10-6, Sat 10-2
Friends of the Library Group
RUSSIA BRANCH, 200 Raider St, Russia, 45363. (Mail add: PO Box 445, Russia, 45363-0445), SAN 372-5219. Tel: 937-526-4300. FAX: 937-526-4300. *Br Coordr,* Sheila Barhorst; E-mail: barhorsh@oplin.org
Library Holdings: AV Mats 555; DVDs 525; Large Print Bks 12; Bk Titles 11,133; Per Subs 20; Talking Bks 47
Open Mon & Wed 2-8, Fri 10-6, Sat 10-2
Friends of the Library Group
PHILIP SHEETS FAMILY BOTKINS BRANCH, 109 E Lynn St, Botkins, 45306. (Mail add: PO Box 524, Botkins, 45306), SAN 357-1203. Tel: 937-693-6671. FAX: 937-693-6671. *Br Coordr,* Jane Vehorn
Library Holdings: AV Mats 604; Large Print Bks 103; Bk Titles 16,134; Per Subs 19; Talking Bks 108
Open Mon & Wed 2-8, Fri 10-6, Sat 10-2
Friends of the Library Group
A J WISE FORT LORAMIE BRANCH, 300 E Park St, Fort Loramie, 45845. (Mail add: PO Box 342, Fort Loramie, 45845), SAN 357-1238. Tel: 937-295-3155. FAX: 937-295-3155. *Br Coordr,* Kathy Schafer
Library Holdings: AV Mats 631; DVDs 451; Large Print Bks 138; Bk Titles 14,647; Per Subs 21; Talking Bks 91
Open Mon & Wed 2-8, Fri 10-6, Sat 10-2
Friends of the Library Group

SOLON

S ERICO, INC*, Information Resources Center, 34600 Solon Rd, 44139. SAN 375-1201. Tel: 440-248-0100. FAX: 440-248-0723. *In Charge,* S Sankar
Library Holdings: Bk Titles 6,000; Per Subs 105

SOUTH EUCLID

C NOTRE DAME COLLEGE, Clara Fritzsche Library, 4545 College Rd, 44121. SAN 313-3699. Tel: 216-373-5267. FAX: 216-381-3227. Web Site: www.notredamecollege.edu/library. *Dir,* Karen Zoller; E-mail: kzoller@ndc.edu; *Ser Librn,* James Nickras; E-mail: jnickras@ndc.edu; *Tech Serv/Circ Librn,* Joe Glass; Tel: 216-373-5360, E-mail: jglass@ndc.edu; *Tech Serv,* Kathy Dagenbach; Tel: 216-373-5269, E-mail: kdagenbach@ndc.edu; Staff 2 (MLS 2)
Founded 1922. Enrl 2,136; Fac 332; Highest Degree: Master
Jul 2013-Jun 2014. Mats Exp $100,827, Books $8,112, Per/Ser (Incl. Access Fees) $31,821, AV Mat $192, Electronic Ref Mat (Incl. Access Fees) $60,702. Sal $139,708 (Prof $99,034)
Library Holdings: AV Mats 1,315; Bk Titles 60,308; Bk Vols 88,241; Per Subs 198
Special Collections: Eastern Church Resource Center; Le Cercle des Conferences Francaises French Coll; Tolerance Resource Center (Holocaust, Diversity & Antibias Resources)
Subject Interests: Educ, Lit, Nursing, Theol
Automation Activity & Vendor Info: (Cataloging) Innovative Interfaces, Inc; (Circulation) Innovative Interfaces, Inc; (OPAC) Innovative Interfaces, Inc
Wireless access
Partic in Ohio Library & Information Network; OHIONET
Open Mon-Thurs 8am-10pm, Fri 8-6, Sat 11-3, Sun 1-10

SPRINGFIELD

S CLARK COUNTY HISTORICAL SOCIETY*, Fisher Family Archives & Library, 117 S Fountain Ave, 45502-1207. SAN 320-2240. Tel: 937-324-0657. Reference Tel: 937-324-0657, Ext 234. FAX: 937-324-1992. *Curator,* Kasey Eichensehr; *Curatorial Asst,* Natalie Fritz; E-mail: nataliemfritz@aol.com; Staff 1 (Non-MLS 1)
Founded 1897
Library Holdings: Bk Titles 2,000; Bk Vols 3,000
Special Collections: Periodicals (Crowell-Collier Publishing Company Coll), mags
Subject Interests: County genealogy, County Probate court rec, Early Clark County hist, Manufacturing & commercial rec, Newsps
Wireless access
Open Wed-Sat 10-5
Restriction: Non-circulating

P CLARK COUNTY PUBLIC LIBRARY*, 201 S Fountain Ave, 45506. (Mail add: PO Box 1080, 45501-1080), SAN 357-1297. Tel: 937-323-9751. Circulation Tel: 937-328-6901. Reference Tel: 937-328-6903. FAX: 937-328-6908. Web Site: www.ccpl.lib.oh.us. *Dir,* Sally Rizer; E-mail: srizer@ccpl.lib.oh.us; Staff 12 (MLS 12)
Founded 1872. Pop 140,000; Circ 1,014,667
Library Holdings: AV Mats 36,135; Bks on Deafness & Sign Lang 75; e-books 250; High Interest/Low Vocabulary Bk Vols 200; Bk Vols 436,634; Per Subs 429
Special Collections: Children's Literature (Lois Lenski Coll), bks, mss. State Document Depository; US Document Depository
Automation Activity & Vendor Info: (Acquisitions) Innovative Interfaces, Inc; (Cataloging) Innovative Interfaces, Inc; (Circulation) Innovative Interfaces, Inc; (OPAC) Innovative Interfaces, Inc; (Serials) Innovative Interfaces, Inc
Database Vendor: Baker & Taylor, Newsbank, OCLC FirstSearch, ProQuest, ReferenceUSA, Wilson - Wilson Web
Wireless access
Function: Learning ctr
Partic in Miami Valley Librs
Special Services for the Deaf - High interest/low vocabulary bks; Spec interest per
Special Services for the Blind - Talking bks
Open Mon-Fri 9-9, Sat 9-6, Sun 1-5
Friends of the Library Group

Branches: 5
ENON BRANCH, 209 E Main St, Enon, 45323, SAN 357-1351. Tel: 937-864-2502. *Br Mgr,* Terri Bowman; E-mail: tbowman@ccpl.lib.oh.us
Circ 37,368
Library Holdings: AV Mats 2,180; Bk Vols 18,000; Per Subs 40
Open Mon-Thurs 10-8, Fri & Sat 10-6
HOUSTON, Five W Jamestown St, South Charleston, 45368, SAN 357-1327. Tel: 937-462-8047. *Br Mgr,* Tammy Harshbarger; E-mail: tharshba@ccpl.lib.oh.us
Circ 39,806
Library Holdings: AV Mats 2,997; Bk Vols 30,000; Per Subs 46
Open Mon-Thurs 10-8, Fri & Sat 10-6
Friends of the Library Group
PARK BRANCH, 1119 Bechtle Ave, 45504, SAN 357-1386. Tel: 937-322-2498. *Br Mgr,* Barb Anderson; E-mail: banderson@ccpl.lib.oh.us
Circ 106,290
Library Holdings: AV Mats 7,159; Bk Vols 26,000; Per Subs 53
Open Mon-Fri 10-9, Sat 9-6
SOUTHERN VILLAGE, 1123 Sunset Ave, 45505, SAN 357-1416. Tel: 937-322-2226. *Br Mgr,* Kristin LeMaster; E-mail: klemaster@ccpl.lib.oh.us
Circ 47,819
Library Holdings: AV Mats 4,037; Bk Vols 31,000; Per Subs 38
Open Mon-Fri 10-9, Sat 9-6
WARDER LITERACY CENTER, 137 E High St, 45502, SAN 370-1018. Tel: 937-323-8617. Web Site: www.clarkcountyliteracy.org. *Exec Dir,* David Smiddy
Open Mon-Thurs 11-7:30
Bookmobiles: 2

J CLARK STATE COMMUNITY COLLEGE LIBRARY*, 570 E Leffel Lane, 45505. (Mail add: PO Box 570, 45501-0570), SAN 313-7163. Tel: 937-328-6022. FAX: 937-328-6133. E-mail: library@clarkstate.edu. Web Site: lib2.clarkstate.edu. *Dir of Libr Serv,* Beth Deger; Tel: 937-328-6023, E-mail: degerb@clarkstate.edu; *Ref/Bibliog Instruction Librn,* Judy Johnson; Tel: 937-328-7968, E-mail: johnsonj@clarkstate.edu; *Ref/Bibliog Instruction Librn,* Amy Korpieski; E-mail: korpieskia@clarkstate.edu; *Ref/Bibliog Instruction Librn,* Lisa Pankratz; E-mail: pankratzl@clarkstate.edu; *Tech Serv & Syst Librn,* Sylvia Halladay; Tel: 937-328-6021, Fax: 937-328-6033, E-mail: halladays@clarkstate.edu; *Circ Spec,* Jason Wearly; E-mail: wearlyj@clarkstate.edu; *Ref Asst,* Angela Henry; E-mail: henrya@clarkstate.edu; Staff 6 (MLS 4, Non-MLS 2)
Founded 1966. Enrl 5,000; Fac 65; Highest Degree: Associate
Library Holdings: Audiobooks 500; CDs 2,500; DVDs 1,000; e-books 50,000; e-journals 12,000; Electronic Media & Resources 3,000; Bk Vols 25,000; Videos 3,000
Automation Activity & Vendor Info: (Cataloging) Innovative Interfaces, Inc; (Circulation) Innovative Interfaces, Inc - Millenium; (Course Reserve) Innovative Interfaces, Inc; (OPAC) Innovative Interfaces, Inc - Millenium; (Serials) Innovative Interfaces, Inc - Millenium
Database Vendor: ABC-CLIO, ACM (Association for Computing Machinery), American Chemical Society, American Psychological Association (APA), Blackwell, Cinahl, CQ Press, EBSCO Information Services, EBSCOhost, Elsevier, Facts on File, Gale Cengage Learning, H W Wilson, infoUSA, Innovative Interfaces, Inc, Innovative Interfaces, Inc, LearningExpress, LexisNexis, Medline, Mergent Online, Modern Language Association, OCLC FirstSearch, OCLC WorldShare Interlibrary Loan, OHIONET, OVID Technologies, Oxford Communications, Safari Books Online, Springer-Verlag, Wiley, Wilson - Wilson Web
Wireless access
Function: Archival coll, Bks on CD, Computers for patron use, Copy machines, Distance learning, e-mail serv, Electronic databases & coll, Handicapped accessible, ILL available, Online cat, Online searches, Orientations, Photocopying/Printing, Printer for laptops & handheld devices, Prog for adults, Ref serv available, Scanner, VHS videos, Video lending libr, Wheelchair accessible, Workshops
Partic in Ohio Library & Information Network; Southwestern Ohio Council for Higher Education
Open Mon-Thurs 8am-9pm, Fri 8-5, Sat 10-3

M COMMUNITY HOSPITAL*, Health Sciences Library, 2615 E High St, 45505. SAN 313-7171. Tel: 937-328-9468. FAX: 937-525-2314. *Librn,* Julie Ann McDaniel; Staff 1 (MLS 1)
Library Holdings: Bk Vols 1,000; Per Subs 90
Subject Interests: Nursing
Automation Activity & Vendor Info: (Cataloging) LibraryWorld, Inc; (OPAC) LibraryWorld, Inc
Database Vendor: EBSCOhost
Partic in Ohio-Kentucky Coop Libraries
Open Mon-Fri 8-5

S SPRINGFIELD MUSEUM OF ART LIBRARY*, 107 Cliff Park Rd, 45504-2501. (Mail add: PO Box 34, 45501-0034), SAN 313-7201. Tel: 937-325-4673. FAX: 937-325-4674. Web Site: www.springfieldart.musem. *Exec Dir,* Ann Fortescue; E-mail: afortescue@springfieldart.net
Founded 1946
Library Holdings: Bk Titles 2,500; Per Subs 1
Special Collections: Photography (Alex Bahnsen Coll)
Open Tues-Sat 9-5, Sun 12:30-4:30
Restriction: Non-circulating

C WITTENBERG UNIVERSITY*, Thomas Library, 807 Woodlawn Ave, 45504. (Mail add: PO Box 7207, 45501-7207), SAN 357-1440. Tel: 937-327-7018, Circulation Tel: 937-327-7512. Interlibrary Loan Service Tel: 937-327-7532. Reference Tel: 937-327-7511. FAX: 937-327-6139. E-mail: refdesk@wittenberg.edu. Web Site: www6.wittenberg.edu/lib. *Dir,* Douglas K Lehman; Tel: 937-327-7016, E-mail: dlehman@wittenberg.edu; *Dir, AV,* Lyn McCurdy; Tel: 937-327-7325, E-mail: lmccurdy@wittenberg.edu; *Head, Circ,* Joan Pallant; E-mail: jpallant@wittenberg.edu; *Head, Tech Serv,* Suzanne Smailes; Tel: 937-327-7020, E-mail: ssmailes@wittenberg.edu; *Ref Librn,* Kristen Gibson; Tel: 937-327-7533, E-mail: kgibson@wittenberg.edu; *Ref Librn,* Ken Irwin; Tel: 937-327-7594, E-mail: kirwin@wittenberg.edu; *Ref Librn,* Alisa Mizikar; Tel: 937-327-7515, E-mail: amizikar@wittenberg.edu; Staff 15 (MLS 5, Non-MLS 10)
Founded 1845. Enrl 1,792; Fac 142; Highest Degree: Master
Jul 2011-Jun 2012 Income $1,601,710. Mats Exp $1,601,710, Books $177,424, Per/Ser (Incl. Access Fees) $175,482, AV Mat $7,300, Electronic Ref Mat (Incl. Access Fees) $284,893, Presv $5,510. Sal $810,958 (Prof $408,958)
Library Holdings: AV Mats 26,380; CDs 3,692; DVDs 1,382; e-books 68,552; e-journals 9,334; Microforms 82,850; Bk Titles 400,446; Bk Vols 503,058; Per Subs 14,555; Videos 2,024
Special Collections: Dos Passos Entomological Library; Hymn Book Coll; Japan (Matsumoto Coll); Martin Luther Reformation
Subject Interests: E Asian studies, Music
Automation Activity & Vendor Info: (Acquisitions) Innovative Interfaces, Inc; (Cataloging) Innovative Interfaces, Inc; (Circulation) Innovative Interfaces, Inc; (Course Reserve) Docutek; (Media Booking) Innovative Interfaces, Inc; (OPAC) Innovative Interfaces, Inc; (Serials) Innovative Interfaces, Inc
Database Vendor: ABC-CLIO, ACM (Association for Computing Machinery), American Chemical Society, Dialog, EBSCOhost, Elsevier, Emerald, Gale Cengage Learning, H W Wilson, JSTOR, LearningExpress, LexisNexis, OCLC FirstSearch, OCLC WorldShare Interlibrary Loan, Oxford Online, ProQuest, RefWorks, ScienceDirect, Springer-Verlag, YBP Library Services
Wireless access
Partic in OCLC Online Computer Library Center, Inc; Ohio Library & Information Network; OHIONET; Southwestern Ohio Council for Higher Education
Open Mon-Thurs (Fall & Winter) 8am-Midnight, Fri 8am-9pm, Sat 10-9, Sun Noon-Midnight; Mon-Fri (Summer) 8-4:30

STEUBENVILLE

J EASTERN GATEWAY COMMUNITY COLLEGE LIBRARY*, Jefferson County Campus Library, 4000 Sunset Blvd, 43952-3598. SAN 313-7252. Tel: 740-264-5591, Ext 153. FAX: 740-264-1338. E-mail: libhelp@egcc.edu. Web Site: library.egcc.edu. *Dir, Libr Serv,* Lois Rekowski; Tel: 740-264-5591, Ext 154, E-mail: lrekowski@egcc.edu; Staff 3 (MLS 1, Non-MLS 2)
Founded 1969. Enrl 1,100; Fac 36; Highest Degree: Associate
Library Holdings: Bk Titles 12,925; Bk Vols 14,090; Per Subs 80
Automation Activity & Vendor Info: (Cataloging) Innovative Interfaces, Inc; (Circulation) Innovative Interfaces, Inc; (Course Reserve) Innovative Interfaces, Inc; (ILL) Innovative Interfaces, Inc; (Media Booking) Innovative Interfaces, Inc; (OPAC) Innovative Interfaces, Inc; (Serials) Innovative Interfaces, Inc
Database Vendor: EBSCOhost
Partic in Ohio Library & Information Network
Open Mon-Thurs 8am-9pm, Fri 8-4

C FRANCISCAN UNIVERSITY OF STEUBENVILLE*, John Paul II Library, 1235 University Blvd, 43952-1763. SAN 313-7236. Tel: 740-283-6208. FAX: 740-284-7239. Web Site: www.franciscan.edu. *Dir,* William Jakub; E-mail: wjakub@franciscan.edu; *Ref,* Kathleen Donohue; E-mail: kdonohue@franciscan.edu; *Tech Serv,* Jack Wu; Staff 11 (MLS 4, Non-MLS 7)
Founded 1946. Enrl 2,000; Highest Degree: Master
Library Holdings: Bk Vols 201,000; Per Subs 728
Subject Interests: Catholic orthodoxy, Counseling, Educ, Franciscans, Liberal arts, Mulloy, Phenomenology, Psychol, Theol
Automation Activity & Vendor Info: (Cataloging) OCLC; (Circulation) Innovative Interfaces, Inc; (OPAC) Innovative Interfaces, Inc; (Serials) Innovative Interfaces, Inc

Database Vendor: EBSCOhost
Partic in OCLC Online Computer Library Center, Inc; Ohio Library & Information Network; Ohio Private Academic Libraries (OPAL); OHIONET
Open Mon-Thurs 8:30am-11:45pm, Fri 8:30am-9pm, Sat 9-9, Sun 1-11:45

GL JEFFERSON COUNTY LAW LIBRARY ASSOCIATION*, 301 Market St, 43952. SAN 313-7244. Tel: 740-283-8553. FAX: 740-283-8629. E-mail: law_library@jeffcch.com. *Librn,* Ardis J Stein
Library Holdings: Bk Vols 20,000; Per Subs 30
Database Vendor: Westlaw
Open Mon-Fri 8:30-12 & 1-4:30

P PUBLIC LIBRARY OF STEUBENVILLE & JEFFERSON COUNTY*, 407 S Fourth St, 43952-2942. SAN 357-153X. Tel: 740-282-9782. FAX: 740-282-2919. Administration FAX: 740-282-0615. E-mail: steubnvl@oplin.org. Web Site: www.steubenville.lib.oh.us. *Dir,* Alan Craig Hall; E-mail: alanh@oplin.org; *Asst Dir,* Mike Gray; E-mail: graymi@oplin.org; *Archivist,* Sandy Day; Tel: 740-264-6166, E-mail: daysa@oplin.org; *Pub Serv,* Jennifer Cesta; E-mail: faccinje@oplin.org; Staff 66 (MLS 4, Non-MLS 62)
Founded 1899. Pop 69,709; Circ 771,160
Jan 2012-Dec 2012 Income (Main Library and Branch(s)) $3,395,691, State $2,202,791, County $1,041,882, Locally Generated Income $151,018. Mats Exp $398,226, Books $188,382, Per/Ser (Incl. Access Fees) $10,875, Other Print Mats $36,265, AV Mat $60,916, Electronic Ref Mat (Incl. Access Fees) $101,788. Sal $2,093,277
Library Holdings: Audiobooks 10,188; AV Mats 21,723; CDs 7,648; DVDs 18,437; e-books 33,699; Large Print Bks 8,930; Microforms 991; Bk Titles 138,629; Bk Vols 170,453; Per Subs 85
Special Collections: Electronic Local History (Digital Shoebox); Steubenville & Jefferson County. State Document Depository; US Document Depository
Subject Interests: Local genealogy, Local hist
Automation Activity & Vendor Info: (Cataloging) SirsiDynix; (Circulation) SirsiDynix; (OPAC) SirsiDynix
Database Vendor: SirsiDynix
Wireless access
Publications: PLSJ Library News (Newsletter)
Open Mon-Thurs 9-8, Fri & Sat 9-5
Branches: 6
ADENA BRANCH, 167 Hanna Ave, Adena, 43901-7953. (Mail add: 407 S Fourth St, 43952-2942), SAN 357-1548. Tel: 740-546-3782. FAX: 740-546-3382. *Librn,* Betsy Ford
Open Mon, Tues & Thurs 11-7, Fri & Sat 11-5
BRILLIANT BRANCH, 103 Steuben St, Brilliant, 43913, SAN 357-1564. Tel: 740-598-4028. FAX: 740-598-4456. *Librn,* Karen Merritt
Open Mon-Fri 11-7
DILLONVALE-MT PLEASANT BRANCH, 192 Cole St, Dillonvale, 43917, SAN 357-1599. Tel: 740-769-2090. FAX: 740-769-2771. *Librn,* Sandy Scott
Open Mon, Tues & Thurs 11-7, Fri & Sat 11-5
SCHIAPPA BRANCH, 4141 Mall Dr, 43952, SAN 328-7920. Tel: 740-264-6166. FAX: 740-264-7397. *Librn,* Betsy Ford
Subject Interests: Genealogy, Local hist, Ohio
Open Mon-Fri 9-9, Sat 9-5, Sun 1-5
TILTONSVILLE BRANCH, 702 Walden Ave, Tiltonsville, 43963, SAN 357-1688. Tel: 740-859-5163. FAX: 740-859-0603. *Librn,* Merritt Karen
Open Mon, Tues & Thurs 11-7, Fri & Sat 11-5
TORONTO BRANCH, 607 Daniels St, Toronto, 43964, SAN 357-1718. Tel: 740-537-1262. FAX: 740-537-5447. *Librn,* Bridget Dougherty
Open Mon-Thurs 10-8, Fri & Sat 10-5
Bookmobiles: 1

M TRINITY HEALTH SYSTEMS*, Health Sciences Library, 380 Summit Ave, 43952. SAN 320-9008. Tel: 740-283-7400. FAX: 740-283-7461. *Librn,* Eva Loy; E-mail: eloy@trinityhealth.com; Staff 1 (MLS 1)
Library Holdings: Bk Vols 2,015; Per Subs 75
Special Collections: Rare Book Coll
Subject Interests: Allied health, Med, Nursing
Publications: Library Line (Newsletter)

STOW

P STOW-MUNROE FALLS PUBLIC LIBRARY*, 3512 Darrow Rd, 44224. SAN 313-7279. Tel: 330-688-3295. Administration FAX: 330-688-0448. Web Site: www.smfpl.org. *Dir,* Douglas H Dotterer; *Head, Ch,* Lydia Gamble; *Head, Circ,* Alisha Greenawalt-Johnson; *Head, Ref Serv,* Amy Garrett; *Head, Syst Admin,* Jorge DeCardenas; *Pub Relations & Mkt Mgr,* Ann Malthaner; *Fiscal Officer,* Linda Sutherland; E-mail: sutherli@oplin.org; Staff 40.12 (MLS 13.85, Non-MLS 26.27)
Founded 1924. Pop 37,890; Circ 794,364
Jan 2011-Dec 2011 Income $2,988,495. Mats Exp $366,149, Books $189,237, Per/Ser (Incl. Access Fees) $7,530, AV Mat $110,127, Electronic Ref Mat (Incl. Access Fees) $59,255. Sal $1,257,651 (Prof $489,256)
Library Holdings: Audiobooks 19,095; CDs 11,526; DVDs 18,297; e-books 31,922; Electronic Media & Resources 170; Bk Titles 99,210; Per Subs 168
Subject Interests: Local hist archives
Automation Activity & Vendor Info: (Acquisitions) LibLime; (Cataloging) OCLC; (Circulation) LibLime; (ILL) OCLC WorldShare Interlibrary Loan
Database Vendor: BWI, EBSCOhost, Facts on File, Gale Cengage Learning, Grolier Online, infoUSA, LearningExpress, LibLime, Newsbank, OCLC FirstSearch, OHIONET, Overdrive, Inc, ProQuest, ReferenceUSA, TumbleBookLibrary
Wireless access
Partic in Northeast Ohio Regional Library System; OCLC Online Computer Library Center, Inc
Open Mon-Thurs 9-9, Fri 9-6, Sat 9-5, Sun 1-5
Friends of the Library Group

STRONGSVILLE

S AKZONOBEL*, Strongsville Research Center, Technical Info Services, 16651 Sprague Rd, 44136. SAN 313-7287. Tel: 440-297-5100, 440-297-5538. *Librn,* Pat Starrett; E-mail: patricia.starrett@akzonobel.com; Staff 1 (MLS 1)
Founded 1968
Library Holdings: Bk Vols 2,000; Per Subs 50
Subject Interests: Coating, Paint, Polymer sci, Resin tech
Automation Activity & Vendor Info: (Cataloging) Inmagic, Inc.; (ILL) OCLC; (OPAC) Inmagic, Inc.
Function: Res libr
Partic in OCLC Online Computer Library Center, Inc; OHIONET
Restriction: Not open to pub

S GARDENVIEW HORTICULTURAL PARK LIBRARY*, 16711 Pearl Rd, 44136-6048. SAN 321-0146. Tel: 440-238-6653. E-mail: gardenviewhp@gmail.com. Web Site: sites.google.com/site/gvhpark. *Dir,* Henry A Ross
Founded 1949
Library Holdings: Bk Titles 5,000
Subject Interests: Animals, Birds, Gardening, Self sufficiency, Travel
Function: Ref serv available
Open Sat & Sun (April-Oct) 12-6

SUNBURY

P COMMUNITY LIBRARY*, 44 Burrer Dr, 43074. SAN 313-7295. Tel: 740-965-3901. FAX: 740-965-1258. E-mail: community-library@oplin.org. Web Site: community.lib.oh.us. *Dir,* Chauncey Montgomery; E-mail: montgoc1@oplin.org; Staff 2 (MLS 2)
Founded 1944
Library Holdings: AV Mats 10,000; Bk Titles 90,000; Per Subs 250
Subject Interests: Genealogy, Local hist
Automation Activity & Vendor Info: (Acquisitions) TLC (The Library Corporation); (Cataloging) TLC (The Library Corporation); (Circulation) TLC (The Library Corporation); (ILL) Fretwell-Downing; (OPAC) TLC (The Library Corporation)
Database Vendor: EBSCOhost, ProQuest, Wilson - Wilson Web
Wireless access
Function: Adult bk club, Archival coll, Audio & video playback equip for onsite use, AV serv, Bk club(s), Bks on CD, Chess club, Children's prog, Computer training, Computers for patron use, Copy machines, E-Reserves, Electronic databases & coll, Equip loans & repairs, Family literacy, Fax serv, Free DVD rentals, Govt ref serv, Handicapped accessible, Health sci info serv, Holiday prog, Home delivery & serv to Sr ctr & nursing homes, Homebound delivery serv, ILL available, Instruction & testing, Magnifiers for reading, Mail & tel request accepted, Music CDs, Notary serv, Online cat, Online ref, Online searches, Outside serv via phone, mail, e-mail & web, Photocopying/Printing, Preschool outreach, Prog for adults, Prog for children & young adult, Ref serv available, Scanner, Senior computer classes, Senior outreach, Spoken cassettes & CDs, Summer reading prog, Tax forms, Teen prog, Telephone ref, VHS videos, Web-catalog, Wheelchair accessible, Workshops
Partic in CALICO; Ohio Public Library Information Network
Open Mon-Thurs 9-8, Fri & Sat 9-5
Restriction: Authorized patrons
Friends of the Library Group

SWANTON

P SWANTON LOCAL SCHOOL DISTRICT PUBLIC LIBRARY*, 305 Chestnut St, 43558. SAN 313-7309. Tel: 419-826-2760. FAX: 419-826-1020. E-mail: swantonpl@gmail.com. Web Site: www.swanton.lib.oh.us. *Dir,* Janelle Thomas; *Head, Youth Serv,* Leanna Chappell; Staff 10 (MLS 2, Non-MLS 8)
Founded 1936. Pop 14,700
Library Holdings: Bk Titles 37,750; Per Subs 150

Wireless access
Function: ILL available
Partic in NORWELD
Open Mon-Thurs 10-8:30, Fri & Sat 10-5:30, Sun (Oct-April) 1-5
Friends of the Library Group

SYCAMORE

P MOHAWK COMMUNITY LIBRARY*, 200 S Sycamore Ave, 44882. (Mail add: PO Box 9, 44882-0009), SAN 313-7317. Tel: 419-927-2407. FAX: 419-927-2958. Web Site: www.mohawk.lib.oh.us. *Dir,* Susan Runion; E-mail: susan.runion@mohawkcl.org
Pop 6,603; Circ 109,936
Library Holdings: Bk Vols 20,000; Per Subs 69
Partic in NORWELD
Open Mon-Fri 10-7, Sat 10-1

SYLVANIA

R FIRST UNITED METHODIST CHURCH LIBRARY*, 7000 Erie St, 43560-1920. SAN 328-5855. Tel: 419-882-2205. FAX: 419-882-2205. *Admin Serv,* Jamie Partin
Library Holdings: Bk Vols 1,500; Per Subs 10
Open Mon-Fri 9-4, Sun 8-12

CR LOURDES UNIVERSITY*, Duns Scotus Library, 6832 Convent Blvd, 43560. SAN 313-7325. Tel: 419-824-3761. FAX: 419-824-3511. E-mail: lourdeslibrary@lourdes.edu. Web Site: www.lourdes.edu. *Dir,* Sister Sandra Rutkowski; Tel: 419-824-3762, E-mail: srutkowski@lourdes.edu; Staff 4 (MLS 3, Non-MLS 1)
Founded 1916. Enrl 2,200; Fac 160; Highest Degree: Master
Library Holdings: AV Mats 1,571; Bk Vols 70,000; Per Subs 448
Special Collections: Franciscan Order
Subject Interests: Art, Rare bks
Automation Activity & Vendor Info: (Cataloging) Innovative Interfaces, Inc; (Circulation) Innovative Interfaces, Inc; (OPAC) Innovative Interfaces, Inc; (Serials) Innovative Interfaces, Inc
Partic in Ohio Library & Information Network; Ohio Private Academic Libraries (OPAL)
Open Mon-Thurs 8:30am-9pm, Fri 8:30-2, Sat 9-4
Restriction: Authorized patrons

R TEMPLE - CONGREGATION SHOMER EMUNIM LIBRARY*, 6453 Sylvania Ave, 43560-3999. SAN 313-7341. Tel: 419-885-3341. FAX: 419-882-2778. *Librn,* Alice Applebaum; Staff 2 (MLS 1, Non-MLS 1)
Founded 1875
Library Holdings: Bk Titles 5,000; Per Subs 10
Special Collections: Art (Gertner Memorial Book Shelf)
Subject Interests: Judaica, Related mat
Automation Activity & Vendor Info: (Cataloging) JayWil Software Development, Inc
Function: Res libr
Open Mon, Tues, Thurs & Fri 9-4:30, Wed 4-6, Sun 9:30-12

TALLMADGE

S TALLMADGE HISTORICAL SOCIETY LIBRARY*, PO Box 25, 44278-0025. SAN 327-4551. Tel: 330-630-9760. *Pres,* Fred Wybenga
Library Holdings: Bk Titles 300
Special Collections: Four handwritten Civil War Diaries of Charles H Sackett (1861, 1862, 1864 & 1869); The Bronson Papers Coll (10 large handwritten volumes of local history & family geneaology of Tallmadge from approx 1820 to his death in 1886)
Friends of the Library Group

TIFFIN

C HEIDELBERG UNIVERSITY, Beeghly Library, 10 Greenfield St, 44883-2420. SAN 313-735X. Tel: 419-448-2104. Interlibrary Loan Service Tel: 419-448-2108. Reference Tel: 419-448-2246. Administration Tel: 419-448-2106. FAX: 419-448-2578. E-mail: library@heidelberg.edu. Web Site: www.heidelberg.edu/library. *Dir, Libr Serv,* Nainsi J Houston; E-mail: nhouston@heidelberg.edu; *Asst Dir, Ref Librn,* Laurie Repp; E-mail: lrepp@heidelberg.edu. Subject Specialists: *Irish lit, Women's & gender studies,* Nainsi J Houston; *Bus,* Laurie Repp; Staff 3 (MLS 2.5, Non-MLS 0.5)
Founded 1850. Enrl 1,300; Fac 92; Highest Degree: Master
Jul 2010-Jun 2011. Mats Exp $149,000, Books $4,505, Per/Ser (Incl. Access Fees) $94,733, Electronic Ref Mat (Incl. Access Fees) $45,033. Sal $248,700 (Prof $113,000)
Library Holdings: Bk Titles 120,963; Bk Vols 150,471; Per Subs 392
Special Collections: Correspondence (Besse Coll). US Document Depository
Automation Activity & Vendor Info: (Acquisitions) Innovative Interfaces, Inc; (Cataloging) OCLC Connexion; (Circulation) Innovative Interfaces, Inc; (Course Reserve) Innovative Interfaces, Inc; (ILL) OCLC FirstSearch; (OPAC) Innovative Interfaces, Inc; (Serials) Innovative Interfaces, Inc
Database Vendor: ACM (Association for Computing Machinery), Agricola, American Psychological Association (APA), BioOne, Cinahl, EBSCOhost, Gale Cengage Learning, ISI Web of Knowledge, JSTOR, LearningExpress, LexisNexis, Marcive, Inc, Mergent Online, Modern Language Association, Newsbank-Readex, OCLC, OCLC ArticleFirst, OCLC WorldShare Interlibrary Loan, OHIONET, Oxford Online, Project MUSE, ProQuest, PubMed, Safari Books Online, Sage, Springer-Verlag
Wireless access
Partic in OCLC Online Computer Library Center, Inc; Ohio Library & Information Network; Ohio Private Academic Libraries (OPAL); OHIONET
Open Mon-Thurs 7:45am-11pm, Fri 7:45-5, Sat 1-4, Sun 1-11
Restriction: Open to pub for ref & circ; with some limitations, Open to students, fac, staff & alumni
Friends of the Library Group

M MERCY HOSPITAL OF TIFFIN*, Schriner Memorial Library, 45 St Lawrence Dr, 44883. Tel: 419-455-7000. Toll Free Tel: 800-447-1804 (Ohio only). *Librn,* Kris Fisher
Library Holdings: Bk Vols 500
Wireless access
Restriction: Staff use only

L SENECA COUNTY LAW LIBRARY*, Seneca County Courthouse Annex, 117 E Market St, Ste 4303, 44883. SAN 372-2015. Tel: 567-230-0204. *Law Librn,* Lisa Russell; E-mail: senctylawlibrary@gmail.com
Library Holdings: Bk Vols 17,000; Per Subs 20
Wireless access

P TIFFIN-SENECA PUBLIC LIBRARY*, 77 Jefferson St, 44883. SAN 313-7368. Tel: 419-447-3751. FAX: 419-447-3045. E-mail: tiffin@oplin.org. Web Site: www.tiffinsen.lib.oh.us. *Dir,* Position Currently Open; *Fiscal Officer, Interim Dir,* Mary Powell; *Head, Circ,* Cathy Brandt; E-mail: brandtca@oplin.org; *Head, Computer Serv,* Christopher Brose; *Head, Exten Serv, Senior Citizen Outreach,* Janet Kimmet; *Head, Jr Libr,* Connie Cole; *Head, Media Libr,* Julie Haferd; E-mail: haferdju@opin.org; *Head, Tech Serv,* Jo Anne Schiefer; *Commun Relations Coordr,* Debby Roszman; Staff 14 (MLS 7, Non-MLS 7)
Founded 1880. Pop 31,283; Circ 416,034
Jan 2007-Dec 2007 Income $1,344,243, State $1,166,683. Mats Exp $1,384,977. Sal $739,092
Library Holdings: AV Mats 15,186; Bks on Deafness & Sign Lang 36; High Interest/Low Vocabulary Bk Vols 728; Bk Titles 101,177; Per Subs 313
Special Collections: Sign Language Coll
Subject Interests: Glass, Local hist, Seneca County genealogy
Database Vendor: Civica
Wireless access
Publications: Dimensions (Newsletter)
Partic in NORWELD
Special Services for the Deaf - Captioned film dep
Special Services for the Blind - Talking bks
Open Mon, Tues & Thurs 10-8, Wed & Fri 10-6, Sat 10-3
Friends of the Library Group

C TIFFIN UNIVERSITY, Pfeiffer Library, 139 Miami St, 44883-2162. SAN 313-7376. Tel: 419-448-3435. Reference Tel: 419-448-3436. Automation Services Tel: 419-448-3326. FAX: 419-443-5013. *Dir,* Frances A Fleet; E-mail: ffleet@tiffin.edu; *Ref Serv,* Catherine Carlson; E-mail: carlsonc@tiffin.edu; Staff 2 (MLS 2)
Founded 1956. Enrl 1,650; Highest Degree: Master
May 2012-Apr 2013 Income (Main Library Only) $351,510. Mats Exp $205,790, Books $45,619, Per/Ser (Incl. Access Fees) $61,283, Electronic Ref Mat (Incl. Access Fees) $98,888. Sal $145,720 (Prof $102,252)
Library Holdings: Electronic Media & Resources 70,166; Bk Titles 111,714; Per Subs 125; Videos 145
Subject Interests: Criminal justice, Forensic psychol
Automation Activity & Vendor Info: (Acquisitions) Innovative Interfaces, Inc; (Cataloging) Innovative Interfaces, Inc; (Circulation) Innovative Interfaces, Inc; (Course Reserve) Innovative Interfaces, Inc; (OPAC) Innovative Interfaces, Inc; (Serials) Innovative Interfaces, Inc
Database Vendor: EBSCO Discovery Service, EBSCOhost
Wireless access
Partic in Ohio Library & Information Network; Ohio Private Academic Libraries (OPAL)

TIPP CITY

P TIPP CITY PUBLIC LIBRARY, 11 E Main St, 45371. SAN 313-7384. Tel: 937-667-3826. FAX: 937-667-7968. Web Site: www.tippcitylibrary.org. *Dir,* Anthony Orsini; E-mail: orsinian@oplin.org; *Ad,* Beth Freeman; *Youth Serv Librn,* Heidi Thiele; *IT Mgr,* Garry Burnside; Staff 3 (MLS 3)
Founded 1923. Pop 17,000; Circ 215,000

Library Holdings: Audiobooks 2,000; CDs 1,800; DVDs 3,500; Bk Vols 71,000; Per Subs 92
Automation Activity & Vendor Info: (Circulation) SirsiDynix; (OPAC) SirsiDynix
Wireless access
Partic in Miami Valley Librs; SEO (Serving Every Ohioan) Library Center
Open Mon-Thurs 10-8:30, Fri 10-6, Sat 10-5
Friends of the Library Group

TOLEDO

J DAVIS COLLEGE*, Resource Center, 4747 Monroe St, 43623. SAN 313-7414. Tel: 419-473-2700. FAX: 419-473-2472. *Librn,* Peggy Seniuk; E-mail: pseniuk@daviscollege.edu; Staff 1.75 (MLS 0.75, Non-MLS 1)
Enrl 450; Fac 35; Highest Degree: Associate
Library Holdings: DVDs 55; Electronic Media & Resources 1; Bk Titles 3,125; Bk Vols 3,200; Per Subs 102; Videos 33
Wireless access
Partic in Library & Information Resources Network (LIRN)
Open Mon-Thurs 8am-10pm, Fri 8-5
Restriction: Open to students, fac & staff

R EPWORTH UNITED METHODIST CHURCH LIBRARY*, 3077 Valleyview Dr, 43615-2237. SAN 313-7430. Tel: 419-531-4236. FAX: 419-531-7487. Web Site: www.epworth.com. Staff 5 (MLS 1, Non-MLS 4)
Founded 1960
Library Holdings: Bk Titles 2,550
Automation Activity & Vendor Info: (Cataloging) Book Systems
Open Mon-Fri 9-5, Sun 8-12

L LUCAS COUNTY LAW LIBRARY*, Lucas County Family Court Center, 905 Jackson St, 43604-5512. SAN 313-7570. Tel: 419-213-4747. FAX: 419-213-4287. Web Site: www.toledolawlibrary.org. *Dir,* Galen Avery; E-mail: gvavery@ameritech.net; *Asst Dir,* Patricia Horner; *Asst Dir,* Beverly Wagener; Staff 4 (MLS 1, Non-MLS 3)
Founded 1870
Library Holdings: Bk Vols 76,000; Per Subs 300
Automation Activity & Vendor Info: (Acquisitions) Mandarin Library Automation; (Cataloging) Mandarin Library Automation; (Circulation) Mandarin Library Automation; (OPAC) Mandarin Library Automation
Database Vendor: LexisNexis
Wireless access
Open Mon-Fri 8:30-4:30

L MARSHALL & MELHORN*, Law Library, Four SeaGate, 8th Flr, 43604. SAN 313-7473. Tel: 419-249-7100. FAX: 419-249-7151. *Librn,* Barbara Avery
Founded 1895
Library Holdings: Bk Vols 14,230; Per Subs 26
Subject Interests: Civil, Corporate practice, Intellectual property, Labor law, Litigation, Probate, State, Tax

CR MERCY COLLEGE OF OHIO LIBRARY*, 2221 Madison Ave, 43604. SAN 320-4146. Tel: 419-251-1700. FAX: 419-251-1730. E-mail: library@mercycollege.edu. *Libr Mgr,* Deborah Johnson; Tel: 419-251-1821, E-mail: deborah.johnson@mercycollege.edu. Subject Specialists: *Healthcare,* Deborah Johnson; Staff 4 (MLS 2, Non-MLS 2)
Founded 1996. Enrl 1,204; Fac 63; Highest Degree: Bachelor
Subject Interests: Allied health, Biol, Nursing, Radiology, Relig
Database Vendor: Cinahl, CredoReference, EBSCOhost
Wireless access
Function: Computers for patron use, Copy machines
Partic in Ohio Private Academic Libraries (OPAL); OHIONET
Restriction: Not open to pub

M NORTHCOAST BEHAVIORAL HEALTHCARE LIBRARY*, Toledo Campus Library, 930 S Detroit Ave, 43614-2701. SAN 313-7589. Tel: 419-381-1881, Ext 4780. FAX: 419-389-1967. TDD: 419-381-0815. *In Charge,* Linda Wesson; Staff 1 (Non-MLS 1)
Founded 1937
Library Holdings: Bk Titles 100; Bk Vols 5,000
Subject Interests: Biographies, Educ, Fiction, Psychiat, Psychol, Self help

R SAINT MICHAEL'S IN THE HILLS EPISCOPAL CHURCH*, Parish Library, 4718 Brittany Rd, 43615-2314. SAN 328-137X. Tel: 419-531-1616. FAX: 419-531-9332. E-mail: info@saintmichaelsepiscopal.org. Web Site: www.saintmichaelsepiscopal.org.
Library Holdings: Bk Titles 2,000; Per Subs 13
Special Collections: Summa Theologicae (St Thomas Aquinas), 60 vol
Subject Interests: Relig educ
Special Services for the Deaf - Spec interest per
Open Mon-Fri 9-5

S STATE OF OHIO DEPARTMENT OF CORRECTIONS*, Toledo Correctional Institution Library, 2001 E Central Ave, 43608. Tel: 419-726-7977, Ext 7233. FAX: 419-726-7158. *Librn,* Rose Kuei-Hsiang Shaddy; E-mail: rose.shaddy@odrc.state.oh.us
Library Holdings: Bk Vols 15,500; Per Subs 63
Automation Activity & Vendor Info: (Cataloging) EOS International; (Circulation) EOS International; (OPAC) EOS International

S TOLEDO BLADE-LIBRARY*, 541 N Superior St, 43660. (Mail add: PO Box 921, 43697-0921), SAN 313-7546. Tel: 419-724-6185. Toll Free Tel: 800-245-3317. Web Site: www.toledoblade.com. *Librn,* Jordie W Henry; E-mail: jhenry@theblade.com
Founded 1835
Special Collections: Electronic Library; Newspaper Clippings
Restriction: Not open to pub

M TOLEDO HOSPITAL*, Medical Library, 2142 N Cove Blvd, 43606. SAN 313-7562. Tel: 419-291-3641. Reference Tel: 419-291-4404. FAX: 419-479-6953. *Librn,* Judy Sendelbach
Library Holdings: Bk Titles 3,600; Per Subs 460
Subject Interests: Med, Nursing
Automation Activity & Vendor Info: (ILL) OCLC
Partic in Docline

P TOLEDO-LUCAS COUNTY PUBLIC LIBRARY, 325 N Michigan St, 43604-6614. SAN 357-2013. Tel: 419-259-5200. Circulation Tel: 419-259-5202. Administration Tel: 419-259-5256. Automation Services Tel: 419-259-5373. FAX: 419-255-1334. Administration FAX: 419-255-1332. Automation Services FAX: 419-259-5335. Web Site: www.toledolibrary.org. *Dir,* Clyde Scoles; E-mail: clyde.scoles@toledolibrary.org; *Dep Dir,* Jason Kucsma; *AV Mgr,* Tracy Montri; Tel: 419-259-5285, E-mail: tracy.montri@toledolibrary.org; *Br Serv Mgr,* Susan Skitowski; Tel: 419-259-5221, Fax: 419-259-5119, E-mail: susan.skitowski@toledolibrary.org; *Bus Tech Mgr,* David Topoleski; Tel: 419-259-5209, Fax: 419-259-5243, E-mail: david.topoleski@toledolibrary.org; *Genealogy Mgr, Local Hist Mgr,* Jill Clever; Tel: 419-259-5233, E-mail: jill.clever@toledolibrary.org; *Humanities Mgr,* Ben Malczewski; Tel: 419-259-5218, Fax: 419-259-5243, E-mail: ben.malczewski@toledolibrary.org; *Youth Serv Coordr,* Nancy Eames; *Automation Serv, Tech Serv,* Marilyn Zielinski; Tel: 419-259-5388, Fax: 419-259-5119, E-mail: marilyn.zielinski@toledolibrary.org; Staff 376 (MLS 92, Non-MLS 284)
Founded 1838. Pop 441,815; Circ 5,379,516
Jan 2013-Dec 2013 Income (Main Library and Branch(s)) $35,359,870, State $14,170,986, Locally Generated Income $19,658,117, Other $1,530,767. Mats Exp $4,682,414, Books $1,894,791, Per/Ser (Incl. Access Fees) $181,814, Other Print Mats $22,242, AV Mat $1,130,592, Electronic Ref Mat (Incl. Access Fees) $1,452,975. Sal $15,336,367
Library Holdings: AV Mats 355,842; CDs 118,284; e-books 41,665; Electronic Media & Resources 23,620; Bk Vols 1,876,176; Per Subs 3,413; Videos 172,417
Special Collections: State Document Depository; UN Document Depository; US Document Depository
Subject Interests: Careers, Commun info, Genealogy, Glass technology, Govt proc, Grantsmanship
Automation Activity & Vendor Info: (Acquisitions) Innovative Interfaces, Inc; (Cataloging) Innovative Interfaces, Inc; (Circulation) Innovative Interfaces, Inc; (ILL) OCLC; (OPAC) Innovative Interfaces, Inc; (Serials) Innovative Interfaces, Inc
Wireless access
Open Mon-Thurs 9-8:30, Fri & Sat 9-5:30, Sun (Sept-May) 1:30-5:30
Friends of the Library Group
Branches: 18
BIRMINGHAM, 203 Paine Ave, 43605, SAN 357-2048. Tel: 419-259-5210. FAX: 419-691-8242. *Br Mgr,* Julie McCann; E-mail: julie.mccann@toledolibrary.org
Founded 1920
Library Holdings: Bk Vols 31,951
Open Mon & Tues 9-8:30, Wed-Fri 9-5:30
Friends of the Library Group
HEATHERDOWNS, 3265 Glanzman Rd, 43614, SAN 357-2072. Tel: 419-259-5270. FAX: 419-382-3231. *Br Mgr,* Debbie DiGennaro; E-mail: deborah.digennaro@toledolibrary.org
Founded 1968
Library Holdings: Bk Vols 147,040
Open Mon-Thurs 9-8:30, Fri & Sat 9-5:30, Sun (Sept-May) 1-5
Friends of the Library Group
HOLLAND BRANCH, 1032 S McCord Rd, Holland, 43528, SAN 326-8268. Tel: 419-259-5240. FAX: 419-865-6706. *Br Mgr,* Linda Kerul; E-mail: linda.kerul@toledolibrary.org
Founded 1984
Library Holdings: Bk Vols 126,381
Open Mon-Thurs 9-8:30, Fri & Sat 9-5:30
Friends of the Library Group

KENT, 3101 Collingwood Blvd, 43610, SAN 357-2102. Tel: 419-259-5340. FAX: 419-243-6536. *Br Mgr,* Faith Hairston; E-mail: faith.hairston@toledolibrary.org
Founded 1915
Library Holdings: Bk Vols 67,627
Open Mon & Tues 9-8:30, Wed-Sat 9-5:30
Friends of the Library Group

LAGRANGE, 3422 Lagrange St, 43608, SAN 357-2137. Tel: 419-259-5280. FAX: 419-242-3052. *Br Mgr,* Andrea Hudak; E-mail: andrea.hudak@toledolibrary.org
Founded 1934
Library Holdings: Bk Vols 39,419
Open Mon & Tues 12-9, Wed-Sat 9-5:30
Friends of the Library Group

LOCKE, 703 Miami St, 43605, SAN 357-2161. Tel: 419-259-5310. FAX: 419-691-3237. *Br Mgr,* Mary Kinkus; E-mail: mary.kinkus@toledolibrary.org
Founded 1917
Library Holdings: Bk Vols 58,763
Open Mon & Tues 9-8:30, Wed-Sat 9-5:30
Friends of the Library Group

MAUMEE BRANCH, 501 River Rd, Maumee, 43537, SAN 357-2196. Tel: 419-259-5360. FAX: 419-259-5203. *Br Mgr,* Julie Bursten; E-mail: julie.bursten@toledolibrary.org; Staff 5 (MLS 5)
Founded 1918. Pop 15,000
Library Holdings: DVDs 2,000; Large Print Bks 500; Bk Vols 118,453; Per Subs 200; Talking Bks 500; Videos 3,000
Automation Activity & Vendor Info: (Acquisitions) Innovative Interfaces, Inc; (Cataloging) Innovative Interfaces, Inc; (Circulation) Innovative Interfaces, Inc; (OPAC) Innovative Interfaces, Inc; (Serials) Innovative Interfaces, Inc
Open Mon-Wed 9-8:30, Thurs-Sat 9-5:30
Friends of the Library Group

MOTT, 1085 Dorr St, 43607, SAN 357-2226. Tel: 419-259-5230. FAX: 419-255-4237. *Br Mgr,* Judith Jones; E-mail: judy.jones@toledolibrary.org
Founded 1918
Library Holdings: Bk Vols 63,676
Open Mon & Tues 9-8:30, Wed-Sat 9-5:30
Friends of the Library Group

OREGON BRANCH, 3340 Dustin Rd, Oregon, 43616, SAN 357-2250. Tel: 419-259-5250. FAX: 419-691-3341. *Br Mgr,* Lisa Green; E-mail: lisa.green@toledolibrary.org
Founded 1965
Library Holdings: Bk Vols 109,915
Open Mon-Thurs 9-8:30, Fri & Sat 9-5:30, Sun (Sept-May) 1-5:30
Friends of the Library Group

POINT PLACE, 2727 117th St, 43611, SAN 357-2285. Tel: 419-259-5390. FAX: 419-729-5363. *Br Mgr,* Jessica Luce; E-mail: jessica.luce@toledolibrary.org
Founded 1926
Library Holdings: Bk Vols 83,872
Open Mon-Wed 9-8:30, Thurs-Sat 9-5:30
Friends of the Library Group

REYNOLDS CORNERS, 4833 Dorr St, 43615, SAN 357-2315. Tel: 419-259-5320. *Br Mgr,* Patricia Crosby; E-mail: patricia.crossby@toledolibrary.org
Founded 1958
Library Holdings: Bk Vols 110,184
Open Mon-Wed 9-8:30, Thurs-Sat 9-5:30
Friends of the Library Group

SANGER, 3030 W Central Ave, 43606, SAN 357-234X. Tel: 419-259-5370. FAX: 419-536-9573. *Br Mgr,* Erin Connolly; E-mail: erin.connolly@toledolibrary.org
Founded 1953
Library Holdings: Bk Vols 130,607
Open Mon-Thurs 9-9, Fri & Sat 9-5:30, Sun 1-5:30
Friends of the Library Group

SOUTH, 1736 Broadway, 43609, SAN 357-2374. Tel: 419-259-5395. FAX: 419-243-4217. *Br Mgr,* Jane Thoma
Founded 1918
Library Holdings: Bk Vols 39,985
Open Mon & Tues 12-9, Wed-Sat 9-5:30
Friends of the Library Group

SYLVANIA BRANCH, 6749 Monroe St, Sylvania, 43560, SAN 357-2439. Tel: 419-882-2089. FAX: 419-882-8993. *Br Mgr,* Susan Schafer; E-mail: susan.schafer@toledolibrary.org
Founded 1927
Library Holdings: Bk Vols 146,627
Open Mon-Thurs 9-8:30, Fri & Sat 9-5:30, Sun (May-Sept) 1-5:30
Friends of the Library Group

TOLEDO HEIGHTS, 423 Shasta Dr, 43609, SAN 357-2463. Tel: 419-259-5220. FAX: 419-385-9297. *Br Mgr,* Jeanne McHugh; E-mail: jeanne.mchugh@toledolibrary.org
Founded 1935
Library Holdings: Bk Vols 52,182
Open Mon & Tues 9-8:30, Wed-Sat 9-5:30
Friends of the Library Group

WASHINGTON, 5560 Harvest Lane, 43623, SAN 357-2498. Tel: 419-259-5330. FAX: 419-472-4991. *Br Mgr,* Hannah Lammie; E-mail: hannah.lammie@toledolibrary.org
Founded 1928
Library Holdings: Bk Vols 124,789
Open Mon-Wed 9-8:30, Thurs-Sat 9-5:30
Friends of the Library Group

WATERVILLE BRANCH, 800 Michigan Ave, Waterville, 43566, SAN 357-2528. Tel: 419-878-3055. FAX: 419-878-4688. *Br Mgr,* Karen Wiggins; E-mail: karen.wiggins@toledolibrary.org; Staff 7 (MLS 3.5, Non-MLS 3.5)
Founded 1964
Library Holdings: Bk Vols 76,000
Open Mon-Wed 9-8;30, Thurs-Sat 9-5:30
Friends of the Library Group

WEST TOLEDO, 1320 Sylvania Ave, 43612, SAN 357-2552. Tel: 419-259-5290. FAX: 419-476-0892. *Br Mgr,* Julie Bursten; E-mail: julie.bursten@toledolibrary.org; Staff 16 (MLS 4, Non-MLS 12)
Founded 1930
Library Holdings: Bk Vols 114,402
Open Mon-Thurs 9-8:30, Fri & Sat 9-5:30
Friends of the Library Group

Bookmobiles: 2

S TOLEDO MUSEUM OF ART REFERENCE LIBRARY, 2445 Monroe St, 43620. (Mail add: PO Box 1013, 43697-1013), SAN 313-7597. Tel: 419-255-8000. Circulation Tel: 419-254-5770. Administration Tel: 419-254-5771, Ext 7386. FAX: 419-254-5776. E-mail: library@toledomuseum.org. Web Site: www.toledomuseum.org/learn/reference-library. *Head Librn,* Alison L Huftalen; E-mail: ahuftalen@toledomuseum.org; Staff 3 (MLS 2, Non-MLS 1)
Founded 1901
Library Holdings: Bk Vols 90,000; Per Subs 316
Subject Interests: Hist of art, Music, Studio art
Automation Activity & Vendor Info: (Acquisitions) Spydus; (Cataloging) Spydus; (Circulation) Spydus; (OPAC) Spydus; (Serials) Spydus
Database Vendor: Civica, JSTOR, OCLC
Wireless access
Function: 24/7 Online cat, Archival coll, Computers for patron use, Copy machines, e-mail serv, Free DVD rentals, Magazines, Pub access computers, Ref serv available, Ref serv in person, Scanner
Open Mon-Thurs (Winter) 10-8, Fri & Sat 12-4; Mon-Thurs (Summer) 10-5, Fri & Sat 12-4
Restriction: Circ limited
Friends of the Library Group

S TOLEDO ZOOLOGICAL SOCIETY*, Zoo Library, 2700 Broadway, 43609. (Mail add: PO Box 140130, 43614-0130), SAN 328-0039. Tel: 419-385-5721, Ext 2043. FAX: 419-389-8670. Web Site: www.toledozoo.org. *Librn,* Deborah Aked; E-mail: deborah.aked@toledozoo.org
Founded 1937
Library Holdings: Bk Titles 2,000; Per Subs 112
Subject Interests: Conserv, Ecology, Zoology
Wireless access
Restriction: Open to others by appt, Staff use only

C UNIVERSITY OF TOLEDO*, William S Carlson Library, 2801 W Bancroft St, Mail Stop 509, 43606-3390. SAN 357-2587. Tel: 419-530-4488. Circulation Tel: 419-530-2323. Reference Tel: 419-530-2324. FAX: 419-530-2726. Web Site: www.library.utoledo.edu. *Interim Dir, Libr Serv,* Marcia King-Blandford; Tel: 419-530-2817, E-mail: marcia.king-blandford@utoledo.edu; *Dir, Tech Serv,* Laura Kinner; Tel: 419-530-8532, E-mail: laura.kinner@utoledo.edu; *Coordr, Cat,* Sheryl Stevens; Tel: 419-530-7981, E-mail: sheryl.stevens@utoledo.edu; *Coordr, Coll Develop,* Alice Crosetto; Tel: 419-530-2760, E-mail: alice.crosetto@utoledo.edu; *Libr Syst Coordr,* Christine Rigda; Tel: 419-530-2333, E-mail: christine.rigda@utoledo.edu; *Coordr, Ser & Electronic Res,* Lucy Duhon; Tel: 419-530-2838, E-mail: lucy.duhon@utoledo.edu; *Govt Doc,* Suhasini Kumar; Tel: 419-530-4485, E-mail: suhasini.kumar@utoledo.edu; Staff 18 (MLS 16, Non-MLS 2)
Founded 1917. Enrl 20,173; Fac 591; Highest Degree: Doctorate
Library Holdings: Bk Vols 1,600,000; Per Subs 8,154
Special Collections: Afro-American Literature Since the Harlem Renaissance; American Women's Social History, 1840-1920; Broadside Press Coll; Department of Energy; Etheridge Knight Coll; Eudora Welty; Ezra Pound; Foy D Kohler Coll; Gift Books & Annuals; Glass Manufacturing; Henry David Thoreau Coll; Imagist Poets; Jean Gould Coll; Leigh Hunt; Richard Gosser Coll; Scott & Helen Nearing; Southern Authors; Stock Market; T S Eliot; University of Toledo Archives Coll;

William Dean Howells; William Faulkner & others. US Document Depository
Subject Interests: Educ, Eng, Humanities, Intl relations, Pharm, Psychol, Sci
Database Vendor: Innovative Interfaces, Inc, LexisNexis, OCLC FirstSearch, OVID Technologies, OVID Technologies, ProQuest, Wilson - Wilson Web
Publications: Collections (Newsletter)
Partic in Ohio Library & Information Network; OHIONET
Open Mon-Thurs 8am-Midnight, Fri 8-7, Sat & Sun (Summer) 12-7
Friends of the Library Group

Departmental Libraries:

CL LAVALLEY LAW LIBRARY, Mail Stop 508, 2801 W Bancroft St, 43606-3390, SAN 357-2617. Tel: 419-530-2733. FAX: 419-530-5121. Web Site: www.utoledo.edu/law/library/index.html. *Asst Dean, Assoc Prof,* Rick Goheen; *Sr Electronic/Media Serv Librn,* Ryan Overdorf; *Sr Legal Ref Librn,* Marianne Mussett; *Sr Legal Res Librn,* Robert Jacoby; *Acq,* Claudia Dansby; Staff 5 (MLS 5)
Enrl 317; Fac 28; Highest Degree: Doctorate
Special Collections: US Document Depository
Database Vendor: EBSCOhost, Gale Cengage Learning, HeinOnline, Innovative Interfaces, Inc, OCLC, SerialsSolutions

CM UNIVERSITY OF TOLEDO*, Mulford Health Science Library, Mulford Library Building, 4th Flr, 3025 Library Circle, 43614-8000. (Mail add: Health Science Campus, Mail Stop 1061, 3025 Library Circle, 43610-8000), SAN 357-1807. Tel: 419-383-4225. Interlibrary Loan Service Tel: 419-530-2576. Reference Tel: 419-383-4218. FAX: 419-383-6146. E-mail: mulfordreference@utoledo.edu. Web Site: www.utoledo.edu/library/mulford. *Dir,* Jolene Miller; *Clinical Med Librn,* Bridget Faricy-Beredo; *Health Sci Librn,* Gerald Natal; *Nursing Librn,* Jodi Jameson; Staff 4.2 (MLS 4.2)
Founded 1964. Highest Degree: Doctorate
Library Holdings: Bk Titles 38,272; Bk Vols 154,385; Per Subs 2,376
Subject Interests: Allied health, Med, Nursing
Automation Activity & Vendor Info: (Acquisitions) Innovative Interfaces, Inc; (Cataloging) Innovative Interfaces, Inc; (Circulation) Innovative Interfaces, Inc; (Course Reserve) Innovative Interfaces, Inc; (OPAC) Innovative Interfaces, Inc; (Serials) Innovative Interfaces, Inc
Database Vendor: ABC-CLIO, ACM (Association for Computing Machinery), American Mathematical Society, American Physical Society, Annual Reviews, EBSCOhost, H W Wilson, Innovative Interfaces, Inc, ISI Web of Knowledge, JSTOR, LearningExpress, McGraw-Hill, MD Consult, Micromedex, Nature Publishing Group, Newsbank, OCLC FirstSearch, OCLC WorldShare Interlibrary Loan, OHIONET, OVID Technologies, Oxford Online, Project MUSE, ProQuest, PubMed, Safari Books Online, SerialsSolutions, STAT!Ref (Teton Data Systems), Thomson - Web of Science, UpToDate, Wiley InterScience, Wilson - Wilson Web, YBP Library Services
Wireless access
Function: Health sci info serv
Partic in Ohio Library & Information Network; OHIONET
Open Mon-Thurs 7:30am-Midnight, Fri 7:30am-9pm, Sat 9-9, Sun 9am-Midnight

TROY

S HOBART INSTITUTE OF WELDING TECHNOLOGY*, John H Blankenbuehler Memorial Library, 400 Trade Sq E, 45373-2400. SAN 313-7600. Tel: 937-332-5603. Toll Free Tel: 800-332-9448, Ext 5603. FAX: 937-332-5220. E-mail: hiwt@welding.org. Web Site: www.welding.org. *Mgr, Libr Serv,* Martha A Baker; E-mail: marty.baker@welding.org. Subject Specialists: *Metallurgy, Welding,* Martha A Baker; Staff 1 (Non-MLS 1)
Founded 1964
Library Holdings: Bk Vols 5,000; Per Subs 100
Subject Interests: Chem, Metallurgy, Quality assurance, Radiography, Thermal spraying, Welding
Automation Activity & Vendor Info: (Cataloging) EOS International
Database Vendor: Dialog
Wireless access
Publications: The World of Welding (Newsletter)
Partic in Dialog Corp

L MIAMI COUNTY LAW LIBRARY*, 201 W Main St, 45373. SAN 313-7619. Tel: 937-440-5994. *Librn,* Carolyn Bolin
Library Holdings: Bk Vols 11,000; Per Subs 10
Restriction: Not open to pub

P TROY-MIAMI COUNTY PUBLIC LIBRARY*, 419 W Main St, 45373. SAN 357-2706. Tel: 937-339-0502. FAX: 937-335-4880. E-mail: info@tmcpl.org. Web Site: www.troypubliclibrary.org. *Dir,* Rachelle Miller; *Supvr, Outreach Serv,* Sarah Simon; *Adult Serv,* Deborah Matthews; *Archivist,* Patrick Kennedy; *Children's & Teen Serv,* Nancy Hargrove; *Pub Serv & IT,* Erin Mattan; Staff 16 (MLS 4, Non-MLS 12)
Founded 1896. Pop 43,068; Circ 625,743
Library Holdings: AV Mats 15,707; DVDs 16,008; e-books 10,421; Bk Vols 161,610; Per Subs 146
Special Collections: Local history
Automation Activity & Vendor Info: (Acquisitions) Innovative Interfaces, Inc; (Cataloging) Innovative Interfaces, Inc; (Circulation) Innovative Interfaces, Inc; (OPAC) Innovative Interfaces, Inc; (Serials) Innovative Interfaces, Inc
Database Vendor: ABC-CLIO, ALLDATA Online, EBSCOhost, OHIONET, Overdrive, Inc, ReferenceUSA, TumbleBookLibrary
Wireless access
Partic in Dayton-Miami Valley Consortium
Special Services for the Deaf - Assisted listening device; Bks on deafness & sign lang; High interest/low vocabulary bks
Special Services for the Blind - Low vision equip
Open Mon-Thurs 9-8, Fri 9-6, Sat 9-5, Sun 1-5
Friends of the Library Group

Branches: 1

OAKES-BEITMAN MEMORIAL, 12 N Main St, Pleasant Hill, 45359-0811, SAN 357-2730. Tel: 937-676-2731. FAX: 937-676-2731. *Br Mgr,* Deborah Matthews; Staff 4 (MLS 1, Non-MLS 3)
Library Holdings: Bk Vols 17,000; Per Subs 50
Open Mon & Wed 12-8, Tues & Thurs 10-8, Fri 12-5, Sat 10-3
Friends of the Library Group

Bookmobiles: 1

M UPPER VALLEY MEDICAL CENTER*, Health Sciences Library, 3130 N Dixie Hwy, 45373. Tel: 937-440-4594. FAX: 937-440-4591. *Librn,* Mary J Sutton; E-mail: msutton@premierhealth.com
Library Holdings: Bk Vols 500
Database Vendor: Cinahl
Wireless access
Open Mon-Fri 8-2

TWINSBURG

P TWINSBURG PUBLIC LIBRARY*, 10050 Ravenna Rd, 44087-1796. SAN 313-7627. Tel: 330-425-4268. FAX: 330-425-3622. Web Site: www.twinsburglibrary.org. *Dir,* Laura Leonard; Tel: 330-425-4268, Ext 21, E-mail: leonardla@twinsburglibrary.org; *Youth Serv Mgr,* Katie Lipinski; E-mail: klipinsi@twinsburglibrary.org; *Circ,* Peggy Myers; Tel: 330-425-4268, Ext 141, E-mail: pmyers@twinsburg.lib.oh.us; Staff 12 (MLS 12)
Founded 1910. Circ 581,719
Jan 2006-Dec 2006 Income $2,356,577, State $1,343,418, Locally Generated Income $1,013,159. Mats Exp $457,509, Books $212,825, Per/Ser (Incl. Access Fees) $19,862, Other Print Mats $3,941, AV Mat $100,010, Electronic Ref Mat (Incl. Access Fees) $120,871. Sal $1,271,321 (Prof $412,109)
Library Holdings: AV Mats 34,087; e-books 16,319; Electronic Media & Resources 920; Bk Vols 129,046; Per Subs 419
Subject Interests: Twinsburg hist
Automation Activity & Vendor Info: (Cataloging) SirsiDynix; (Circulation) SirsiDynix; (OPAC) SirsiDynix; (Serials) SirsiDynix
Database Vendor: EBSCOhost, Gale Cengage Learning, OCLC FirstSearch, ProQuest, SirsiDynix, Wilson - Wilson Web
Function: Adult bk club, Adult literacy prog, Audio & video playback equip for onsite use, Audiobks via web, AV serv, Bk club(s), Bk reviews (Group), Bks on cassette, Bks on CD, CD-ROM, Children's prog, Computer training, Computers for patron use, Copy machines, Digital talking bks, E-Reserves, Electronic databases & coll, Fax serv, Free DVD rentals, Home delivery & serv to Sr ctr & nursing homes, Homebound delivery serv, Homework prog, ILL available, Magnifiers for reading, Mail & tel request accepted, Music CDs, Notary serv, Online cat, Online ref, Online searches, Outside serv via phone, mail, e-mail & web, OverDrive digital audio bks, Preschool outreach, Prog for adults, Prog for children & young adult, Pub access computers, Ref & res, Senior computer classes, Web-catalog
Publications: A Librarian Told Me So Blog (Online only); Bestsellers (Online only); Booking for a Look (Online only); Calendar of Events (Bi-monthly); Taste of Twinsburg Blog (Online only); The ABC Book Reviews Blog & Podcast (Online only); TPL Online Newsletter (Online only); Twinsburg Library News Blog (Online only)
Partic in CLEVNET; Northeast Ohio Regional Library System; Ohio Public Library Information Network
Special Services for the Deaf - Am sign lang & deaf culture; Closed caption videos; TTY equip
Special Services for the Blind - Audio mat; Bks on cassette; Bks on CD; Descriptive video serv (DVS); Large print bks; Low vision equip; ZoomText magnification & reading software
Open Mon-Thurs 9:30-8:30, Fri & Sat 9:30-5:30, Sun (Fall & Spring) 1-5
Friends of the Library Group

UHRICHSVILLE

P CLAYMONT PUBLIC LIBRARY*, 215 E Third St, 44683. SAN 357-2765. Tel: 740-922-3626. FAX: 740-922-3500. Web Site: www.claymontlibrary.org. *Dir,* Donna Moody; E-mail: moodyda@oplin.org; *Children's Coordr,* Rene Koile; Staff 2 (MLS 1, Non-MLS 1)
Founded 1934. Pop 12,000; Circ 199,000
Library Holdings: Bk Vols 40,000; Per Subs 104
Special Collections: Clay History Coll; Railroad Coll
Automation Activity & Vendor Info: (Cataloging) SirsiDynix; (Circulation) SirsiDynix; (ILL) SirsiDynix; (OPAC) SirsiDynix
Database Vendor: SirsiDynix
Partic in SE Ohio Regional Librs
Open Mon-Thurs 9-8, Fri 9-6, Sat 9-4
Friends of the Library Group
Branches: 1
DENNISON BRANCH, 15 N Fourth St, Dennison, 44621, SAN 357-279X. Tel: 740-922-5851. FAX: 740-922-6391. *Br Mgr,* Lois Brown; E-mail: brownlo@oplin.org; Staff 2 (MLS 1, Non-MLS 1)
Library Holdings: Bk Vols 23,938; Per Subs 45
Open Mon-Fri 9-6, Sat 9-4
Friends of the Library Group

UNIVERSITY HEIGHTS

C JOHN CARROLL UNIVERSITY*, Grasselli Library & Breen Learning Center, 20700 N Park Blvd, 44118. SAN 313-7635. Tel: 216-397-4233. Interlibrary Loan Service Tel: 216-397-4232. Reference Tel: 216-397-4234. Administration Tel: 216-397-4231. FAX: 216-397-4256. Interlibrary Loan Service FAX: 216-397-4222. Web Site: library.jcu.edu. *Dir,* Michelle Millet; Fax: 216-397-3053, E-mail: library@jcu.edu; *Tech Serv,* Ruth Connell; Tel: 216-397-1635, E-mail: connell@jcu.edu; Staff 14 (MLS 10, Non-MLS 4)
Founded 1886. Enrl 3,696; Fac 477; Highest Degree: Master
Jun 2007-May 2008. Mats Exp $1,104,658, Books $218,500, Per/Ser (Incl. Access Fees) $210,085, Other Print Mats $3,923, Micro $26,691, AV Mat $23,917, Electronic Ref Mat (Incl. Access Fees) $602,135, Presv $19,407
Library Holdings: AV Mats 8,597; e-books 19,416; e-journals 7,485; Microforms 693,759; Bk Vols 761,832; Per Subs 887
Special Collections: Far East (Daniel A Hill Far Eastern Coll); G K Chesterton (John R Bayer Chesterton Coll), bks, micro. State Document Depository; US Document Depository
Subject Interests: Educ, Relig, Theol
Automation Activity & Vendor Info: (Acquisitions) Innovative Interfaces, Inc; (Cataloging) Innovative Interfaces, Inc; (Circulation) Innovative Interfaces, Inc; (Course Reserve) Docutek; (ILL) OCLC ILLiad; (OPAC) Innovative Interfaces, Inc; (Serials) Innovative Interfaces, Inc
Wireless access
Function: Magnifiers for reading, Online cat, Online ref, Orientations, Photocopying/Printing, Pub access computers, Ref & res, Ref serv in person, Scanner, Telephone ref, Workshops
Publications: Library Notes (Newsletter)
Partic in Ohio Library & Information Network; OHIONET
Open Mon-Thurs 7:30am-Midnight, Fri 7:30am-9pm, Sat 10-6, Sun 11am Midnight
Friends of the Library Group

UPPER SANDUSKY

P UPPER SANDUSKY COMMUNITY LIBRARY*, 301 N Sandusky Ave, 43351-1139. SAN 313-7643. Tel: 419-294-1345. FAX: 419-294-4499. Web Site: www.upper-sandusky.lib.oh.us. *Dir,* Kathleen Whitt; *Coordr, Youth Serv,* Jill Stansbery; E-mail: jillst@oplin.org; *Dep Fiscal Officer, Tech Coordr,* Paris Robertson; E-mail: robertpa@oplin.org; *Adult Outreach/Prog Coordr,* Aimee Boes; E-mail: boesai@oplin.org; Staff 4.5 (MLS 1, Non-MLS 3.5)
Founded 1912. Pop 11,542; Circ 154,405
Jan 2011-Dec 2011 Income $588,526, State $251,139, Locally Generated Income $306,436, Other $30,951. Mats Exp $79,549, Books $49,706, Per/Ser (Incl. Access Fees) $4,281, AV Mat $25,362, Electronic Ref Mat (Incl. Access Fees) $200. Sal $214,307 (Prof $121,270)
Library Holdings: Audiobooks 1,790; CDs 64; DVDs 2,935; e-books 63; Large Print Bks 2,972; Bk Vols 43,112; Per Subs 127
Special Collections: State Document Depository
Subject Interests: Genealogy, Local hist
Automation Activity & Vendor Info: (Cataloging) SIRSI WorkFlows; (Circulation) SIRSI WorkFlows; (OPAC) SirsiDynix; (Serials) SIRSI WorkFlows
Database Vendor: SirsiDynix
Wireless access
Function: Audiobks via web, AV serv, Bk club(s), Bks on CD, Children's prog, Computer training, Computers for patron use, Copy machines, Electronic databases & coll, Fax serv, Free DVD rentals, Handicapped accessible, Home delivery & serv to Sr ctr & nursing homes, Homebound delivery serv, ILL available, Mail & tel request accepted, Microfiche/film & reading machines, Online cat, Online searches, OverDrive digital audio bks, Preschool outreach, Preschool reading prog, Printer for laptops & handheld devices, Prog for adults, Prog for children & young adult, Pub access computers, Ref serv available, Scanner, Spoken cassettes & CDs, Story hour, Summer reading prog, Tax forms, Teen prog, Telephone ref, Web-catalog
Partic in NORWELD
Open Mon-Thurs 9-8:30, Fri 9-6, Sat 9-1
Friends of the Library Group

URBANA

P CHAMPAIGN COUNTY LIBRARY*, 1060 Scioto St, 43078. SAN 313-7651. Tel: 937-653-3811. FAX: 937-653-5679. E-mail: champref@oplin.org. Web Site: www.champaign.lib.oh.us. *Dir,* Ty Henderson; E-mail: thenderson@oplin.org; Staff 6 (MLS 1, Non-MLS 5)
Founded 1890. Pop 33,649; Circ 273,947
Library Holdings: CDs 4,743; DVDs 6,070; Electronic Media & Resources 598; Bk Vols 98,334; Per Subs 249
Automation Activity & Vendor Info: (Acquisitions) TLC (The Library Corporation); (Cataloging) TLC (The Library Corporation); (Circulation) TLC (The Library Corporation); (OPAC) TLC (The Library Corporation); (Serials) TLC (The Library Corporation)
Wireless access
Partic in Miami Valley Librs
Special Services for the Blind - Talking bks
Open Mon-Thurs 9-8, Fri & Sat 9-5
Friends of the Library Group
Bookmobiles: 1

C URBANA UNIVERSITY*, Swedenborg Memorial Library, 579 College Way, 43078-2091. SAN 313-766X. Tel: 937-484-1335. Administration Tel: 937-484-1337. FAX: 937-653-8551. E-mail: library@urbana.edu. Web Site: www.urbana.edu. *Dir, Libr Serv,* Julie McDaniel; E-mail: jmcdaniel@urbana.edu; *Coordr, Cat,* Jamie Lattimer; Tel: 937-484-1336, E-mail: jlattimer@urbana.edu; *Coordr, Pub Serv,* Jennifer Midgley; Tel: 937-484-1435, E-mail: jmidgley@urbana.edu; Staff 5 (MLS 1, Non-MLS 4)
Founded 1850. Enrl 1,400; Fac 51; Highest Degree: Master
Library Holdings: AV Mats 2,340; Bk Titles 53,861; Bk Vols 77,132; Per Subs 118
Special Collections: Children's Literature (19th Century); Emanuel Swedenborg; Johnny Appleseed
Subject Interests: Bus, Educ
Automation Activity & Vendor Info: (Acquisitions) Innovative Interfaces, Inc; (Cataloging) Innovative Interfaces, Inc; (Circulation) Innovative Interfaces, Inc; (Course Reserve) Innovative Interfaces, Inc; (ILL) OCLC; (OPAC) Innovative Interfaces, Inc; (Serials) Innovative Interfaces, Inc
Wireless access
Function: Res libr
Partic in OCLC Online Computer Library Center, Inc; Ohio Library & Information Network; Ohio Private Academic Libraries (OPAL); OHIONET; Southwestern Ohio Council for Higher Education
Open Mon-Thurs 8am-10pm, Fri 8-4:30, Sat 12-4, Sun 7pm-10pm

VAN WERT

P BRUMBACK LIBRARY, 215 W Main St, 45891-1695. SAN 313-7678. Tel: 419-238-2168. FAX: 419-238-3180. E-mail: brumback@brumbacklib.com. Web Site: www.brumbacklib.com. *Dir,* John J Carr; E-mail: carrjo@oplin.org; Staff 15 (MLS 2, Non-MLS 13)
Founded 1901. Pop 29,800; Circ 789,350
Jan 2013-Dec 2013 Income (Main Library and Branch(s)) $1,070,905. Mats Exp $147,596. Sal $509,507
Library Holdings: Audiobooks 7,438; Bks on Deafness & Sign Lang 127; Braille Volumes 45; CDs 3,544; DVDs 7,815; e-books 142,248; High Interest/Low Vocabulary Bk Vols 392; Large Print Bks 7,000; Microforms 814; Bk Titles 218,971; Bk Vols 235,143; Per Subs 229; Talking Bks 7,438; Videos 3,268
Special Collections: Local History Coll Rare Books; Van Wert Newspapers, 1855 to present on microfilm
Subject Interests: Bks on CD, Children's bks, Genealogy, Local hist, Popular works
Automation Activity & Vendor Info: (Acquisitions) SirsiDynix; (Cataloging) SirsiDynix; (Circulation) SirsiDynix; (OPAC) SirsiDynix; (Serials) SirsiDynix
Wireless access
Function: Accessibility serv available based on individual needs
Publications: Chapter & Verse Book Review; Chapter Notes (Newsletter)
Partic in NORWELD; Ohio Public Library Information Network
Special Services for the Blind - Accessible computers; BiFolkal kits; Bks available with recordings; Bks on cassette; Bks on CD
Open Mon-Thurs 9-7:30, Fri & Sat 9:30-5

Branches: 5

CONVOY BRANCH, 116 E Tully St, Convoy, 45832. (Mail add: PO Box 607, Convoy, 45832-0607), SAN 377-8886. Tel: 419-749-4000. *Librn,* Cindy Money; Staff 1 (Non-MLS 1)
Library Holdings: Bk Vols 38,427; Per Subs 57
Open Mon-Wed 9-11:30 & 12:30-5:30, Thurs 11-4:30 & 5:30-8, Sat 9am-11:30pm

MIDDLE POINT BRANCH, 102 Railroad St, Middle Point, 45863. (Mail add: PO Box 295, Middle Point, 45863-0295), SAN 377-8908. Tel: 419-968-2553. E-mail: mpbranch@bright.net. *Librn,* Julia Johns; Staff 1 (Non-MLS 1)
Library Holdings: Bk Vols 27,363; Per Subs 41
Open Mon & Wed 12-5:30, Tues 3-8, Thurs 11-4:30, Sat 2-5

OHIO CITY BRANCH, 101 W Carmean St, Ohio City, 45874, SAN 377-8924. Tel: 419-965-2918. *Br Mgr,* Barbara Everidge; Staff 1 (Non-MLS 1)
Library Holdings: Bk Vols 29,819; Per Subs 33
Open Mon & Wed 9-12:30 & 1:30-5:30, Tues 3-8, Thurs 5:30-8, Sat 9-12:30

WILLSHIRE BRANCH, 323 State St, Willshire, 45898, SAN 377-8940. Tel: 419-495-4138. *Librn,* Rose Mowery; Staff 1 (Non-MLS 1)
Library Holdings: Bk Vols 29,311; Per Subs 30
Open Mon 5-8, Tues 11-4, Wed 1-5:30, Thurs 3-8, Sat 9-11:30

WREN BRANCH, 101 Washington St, Wren, 45899, SAN 377-8967. Tel: 419-495-4174. *Br Mgr,* Rose Mowery; Staff 1 (Non-MLS 1)
Library Holdings: Bk Vols 25,500; Per Subs 31
Open Mon 11-4, Tues 5-8, Wed 9-12, Thurs 1:30-5:30, Sat 12:30-5

GL VAN WERT COUNTY LAW LIBRARY ASSOCIATION*, Court House, 3rd Flr, 121 Main St, 45891. SAN 313-7686. Tel: 419-238-6935. FAX: 419-238-2874. *Librn,* Dennis Kimmet
Library Holdings: Bk Vols 17,900
Publications: First Reporter Series in Ultra Fiche; Second Federal Reporter & Supplement
Open Mon-Fri 8-4

VERMILION

S GREAT LAKES HISTORICAL SOCIETY*, Clarence S Metcalf Research Library, Inland Seas Maritime Museum, 480 Main St, 44089. (Mail add: PO Box 435, 44089-0435), SAN 313-7694. Tel: 440-967-3467. Toll Free Tel: 800-893-1485. FAX: 440-967-1519. E-mail: glhs1@inlandseas.org. Web Site: www.inlandseas.org. *Exec Dir,* Christopher Gillcrist
Founded 1944
Library Holdings: Bk Titles 2,400
Special Collections: American Bureau of Shipping 1915-1958; Great Lakes Journal (Inland Seas Coll); Great Lakes Ships Photograph Coll; Lloyd's Inland Register 1873-1907; Lloyd's Register 1926-1970; Marine Review 1883-1931; Maritime Directories (Beeson's Annual 1891-1920 & Green's 1911-1960); Merchant Vessels of the US 1872-1950
Subject Interests: Commercial fishing, Great Lakes hist, Maritime, Original ship's logs, Rec, Yachting
Publications: Chadburn (Newsletter); Inland Seas (Quarterly)
Restriction: Mem only, Open to others by appt

P RITTER PUBLIC LIBRARY*, 5680 Liberty Ave, 44089-1198. SAN 313-7708. Tel: 440-967-3798. FAX: 440-967-5482. E-mail: info@ritter.lib.oh.us. Web Site: www.ritter.lib.oh.us. *Dir,* Janet L Ford; Tel: 440-967-3798, Ext 16, Fax: 440-967-7103, E-mail: janet.ford@ritter.lib.oh.us; *Ref Librn,* Amy L Trotter; Tel: 440-967-3798, Ext 15, E-mail: amy.trotter@ritter.lib.oh.us; *Youth Serv Librn,* Margaret A Townsend; Tel: 440-967-3798, Ext 18, E-mail: marge.townsend@ritter.lib.oh.us; Staff 3 (MLS 3)
Founded 1912. Pop 14,844; Circ 309,608
Jan 2009-Dec 2009 Income $1,343,493, State $616,220, County $530,876, Other $196,397. Mats Exp $171,468, Books $106,194, Per/Ser (Incl. Access Fees) $10,483, Other Print Mats $1,011, AV Mat $44,488, Electronic Ref Mat (Incl. Access Fees) $9,292. Sal $604,853 (Prof $151,803)
Library Holdings: CDs 5,455; DVDs 6,456; e-books 22,807; Microforms 74; Bk Vols 56,146; Per Subs 2,097
Database Vendor: SirsiDynix
Wireless access
Function: Adult bk club, Archival coll, Audio & video playback equip for onsite use, Bk club(s), Bks on cassette, Bks on CD, Children's prog, Computer training, Computers for patron use, Copy machines, Digital talking bks, E-Reserves, Electronic databases & coll, Equip loans & repairs, Fax serv, Free DVD rentals, Handicapped accessible, Home delivery & serv to Sr ctr & nursing homes, Homebound delivery serv, ILL available, Mail & tel request accepted, Music CDs, Newsp ref libr, Notary serv, Online cat, Online ref, Online searches, Outreach serv, Outside serv via phone, mail, e-mail & web, OverDrive digital audio bks, Photocopying/Printing, Preschool outreach, Prog for adults, Prog for children & young adult, Pub access computers, Ref & res, Ref serv available, Senior computer classes, Spoken cassettes & CDs, Story hour, Summer reading prog, Tax forms, Teen prog, Telephone ref, VHS videos, Web-catalog, Wheelchair accessible
Partic in Ohio Libr Coun
Open Mon-Thurs 9:30-8:30, Fri & Sat 9:30-5:30
Restriction: Circ limited, Circ to mem only
Friends of the Library Group

VERSAILLES

P WORCH MEMORIAL PUBLIC LIBRARY*, 790 S Center St, 45380. (Mail add: PO Box 336, 45380-0336), SAN 313-7724. Tel: 937-526-3416. FAX: 937-526-3990. Web Site: www.worch.lib.oh.us. *Dir,* Meme Marlow
Founded 1937. Pop 6,000; Circ 115,000
Library Holdings: Bk Titles 40,000; Per Subs 190
Subject Interests: Area genealogy, Family, Local genealogy
Open Mon-Thurs 9-8, Fri 9-5, Sat 9-2
Friends of the Library Group

WADSWORTH

P ELLA M EVERHARD PUBLIC LIBRARY*, Wadsworth Public Library, 132 Broad St, 44281-1897. SAN 378-4495. Tel: 330-334-5761. Reference Tel: 330-335-1294. Administration Tel: 330-335-1299. Automation Services Tel: 330-335-2600. FAX: 330-334-6605. E-mail: director@wadsworthlibrary.com. Web Site: www.wadsworthlibrary.com. *Dir,* Daniel Slife; *Bus Mgr,* Debi Woodruff; E-mail: debi.woodruff@wadsworthlibrary.com; *Circ Mgr,* Margaret Orchard; *Mgr, Ch Serv, Mgr, Outreach Serv,* Nicole Moore; Tel: 330-335-1296; *Tech Serv Mgr,* Barb Black; E-mail: barb.black@wadsworthlibrary.com; *Tech Mgr,* Trevor Watkins; *Coll Develop Librn,* Abby Hindulak; E-mail: abby.hindulak@wadsworthlibrary.com; *Adult & Teen Serv,* Stacia Gotto; *Mkt, Pub Relations,* Janet Griffing; Tel: 330-335-2604, E-mail: janet.griffing@wadsworthlibrary.com; *YA Serv,* Sean Rapacki; E-mail: sean.rapacki@wadsworthlibrary.com; Staff 11 (MLS 11)
Founded 1922. Pop 27,000; Circ 910,000
Library Holdings: AV Mats 23,628; Bk Vols 156,851; Per Subs 339
Subject Interests: Artwork, Lab kits, Local hist
Automation Activity & Vendor Info: (Acquisitions) Innovative Interfaces, Inc; (Cataloging) Innovative Interfaces, Inc; (Circulation) Innovative Interfaces, Inc; (ILL) Innovative Interfaces, Inc; (OPAC) Innovative Interfaces, Inc; (Serials) Innovative Interfaces, Inc
Database Vendor: ALLDATA Online, Gale Cengage Learning, ProQuest
Wireless access
Function: Home delivery & serv to Sr ctr & nursing homes, Homebound delivery serv, ILL available, Large print keyboards, Magnifiers for reading, Prog for adults, Prog for children & young adult, Summer reading prog, Wheelchair accessible
Publications: Ellagram (Newsletter)
Special Services for the Deaf - ADA equip; Assistive tech; Closed caption videos
Special Services for the Blind - Audio mat; Bks on cassette; Bks on CD; Cassette playback machines; Cassettes; Computer with voice synthesizer for visually impaired persons; Home delivery serv; Large print & cassettes; Large print bks; Large screen computer & software; Magnifiers; Scanner for conversion & translation of mats; Talking bks; Videos on blindness & phys handicaps
Open Mon-Thurs 9-9, Fri & Sat 9-6, Sun (Fall-Spring) 1-5
Friends of the Library Group
Bookmobiles: 2

WAPAKONETA

GL AUGLAIZE COUNTY LAW LIBRARY*, County Courthouse, 201 Willipie St, Ste 405, 45895. SAN 313-7767. Tel: 419-739-6749. E-mail: lawlibrary@auglaizecounty.org. Web Site: www2.auglaizecounty.org/departments/law-library. *Librn,* Lucy Merges
Founded 1898
Library Holdings: Bk Vols 10,000
Database Vendor: LexisNexis, Westlaw
Wireless access
Restriction: Staff & mem only

P AUGLAIZE COUNTY PUBLIC DISTRICT LIBRARY*, 203 S Perry St, 45895-1999. SAN 357-2919. Tel: 419-738-2921. FAX: 419-738-5168. E-mail: acpdl@oplin.org. Web Site: auglaize.oplin.org. *Dir,* Beth Steiner; E-mail: steinebe@oplin.org; *Youth Serv Coordr,* Karie Maurer-Enneking; Staff 15 (MLS 2, Non-MLS 13)
Founded 1925. Pop 33,458; Circ 304,932
Jan 2008-Dec 2008 Income (Main Library and Branch(s)) $1,316,442, State $1,221,976, Locally Generated Income $94,466. Mats Exp $189,653, Books $139,369, Per/Ser (Incl. Access Fees) $11,889, AV Mat $24,753. Sal $581,321 (Prof $166,088)
Library Holdings: Audiobooks 1,982; CDs 963; DVDs 4,909; e-books 7,402; Large Print Bks 3,571; Bk Vols 155,311; Per Subs 311; Videos 693
Subject Interests: Dudley Nichols, Genealogy, Neil Armstrong, Ohio hist

Automation Activity & Vendor Info: (Acquisitions) Innovative Interfaces, Inc; (Cataloging) Innovative Interfaces, Inc; (Circulation) Innovative Interfaces, Inc; (OPAC) Innovative Interfaces, Inc; (Serials) Innovative Interfaces, Inc
Wireless access
Function: Adult bk club, Computers for patron use, Prog for children & young adult, Summer reading prog
Open Mon & Thurs Noon-8, Tues & Wed 10-6, Fri & Sat 10-2
Branches: 5
CRIDERSVILLE PUBLIC LIBRARY, 116 W Main St, Cridersville, 45895, SAN 357-2927. Tel: 419-645-5447. FAX: 419-645-6019. *Br Supvr,* Patricia Stinchfield; E-mail: stinchpa@oplin.org; Staff 2 (Non-MLS 2)
Open Mon 11-6:30, Wed 3-6:30, Sat 10-Noon
NEW BREMEN PUBLIC LIBRARY, 45 W Washington St, New Bremen, 45869, SAN 357-2935. Tel: 419-629-2158. FAX: 419-629-1351. *Br Supvr,* Michelle Parker; E-mail: parkermi@oplin.org; Staff 2 (Non-MLS 2)
Open Mon & Tues 12-7, Thurs 10-2, Sat 10-12
Friends of the Library Group
NEW KNOXVILLE COMMUNITY LIBRARY, 304 S Main St, New Knoxville, 45871. (Mail add: PO Box 370, New Knoxville, 45871-0370), SAN 357-2943. Tel: 419-753-2724. FAX: 419-753-2594. *Br Supvr,* Erin Dodds; E-mail: doddser@oplin.org; Staff 1 (Non-MLS 1)
Open Mon 12-7, Thurs 3-7, Sat 10-12
FRANCIS J STALLO MEMORIAL LIBRARY, 196 E Fourth St, Minster, 45865, SAN 357-2978. Tel: 419-628-2925. FAX: 419-628-4556. *Mgr,* Becky Prenger; E-mail: prengebe@oplin.org; Staff 4 (Non-MLS 4)
Open Mon & Tues 10-7, Wed 3-7, Fri & Sat 10-12
Friends of the Library Group
EDWARD R & MINNIE D WHITE MEMORIAL LIBRARY, 108 E Wapakoneta St, Waynesfield, 45896, SAN 357-3001. Tel: 419-568-5851. FAX: 419-568-2368. *Mgr,* Pamela Kennon; E-mail: kennonpa@oplin.org; Staff 2 (Non-MLS 2)
Partic in NORWELD
Open Mon & Thurs 12-6, Tues 10-4, Sat 10-12
Friends of the Library Group
Bookmobiles: 1. Outreach Servs, Linda Huber

WARREN

C KENT STATE UNIVERSITY*, Trumbull Campus, 4314 Mahoning Ave NW, 44483-1998. Tel: 330-675-8865, 330-847-0571. FAX: 330-675-8825. Web Site: www.trumbull.kent.edu/library/. *Dir,* Rose Guerrieri; Tel: 330-675-8866, E-mail: rguerrie@kent.edu; *Ref Librn,* Harry Packard; E-mail: hpackard@kent.edu; Staff 5 (MLS 2, Non-MLS 3)
Founded 1970. Enrl 2,000; Fac 60; Highest Degree: Bachelor
Library Holdings: Bk Titles 55,000; Bk Vols 75,000; Per Subs 235; Videos 450
Special Collections: Holocaust Coll; Ohio Reference Coll; Science Fiction Coll
Open Mon-Thurs (Winter) 8-8, Fri 9-1, Sat 8-12; Mon-Thurs (Summer) 8-5:30, Fri 9-1

S TRIBUNE CHRONICLE LIBRARY*, 240 Franklin St SE, 44482-5711. (Mail add: PO Box 1431, 44482-1431), SAN 371-8468. Tel: 330-841-1734. FAX: 330 841 1717. Web Site: www.tribune-chronicle.com. *Librn,* Dana Sulonen
Founded 1982
Library Holdings: Bk Titles 391; Bk Vols 533
Special Collections: Tribune 1891-present, microfilm

L TRUMBULL COUNTY LAW LIBRARY*, 120 High St NW, 44481. SAN 372-199X. Tel: 330-675-2525. FAX: 330-675-2527. Web Site: lawlibrary.co.trumbull.oh.us. *Dir,* George Baker; E-mail: gbaker9916@aol.com; *Asst Dir,* Karin L McKinney; Staff 3 (MLS 1, Non-MLS 2)
Library Holdings: Bk Vols 32,000; Per Subs 56
Wireless access
Open Mon-Fri 8:30-4:30

P WARREN-TRUMBULL COUNTY PUBLIC LIBRARY*, 444 Mahoning Ave NW, 44483. SAN 313-7813. Tel: 330-399-8807. Interlibrary Loan Service Tel: 330-399-8807, Ext 110. Reference Tel: 330-399-8807, Ext 400. Administration Tel: 330-399-8807, Ext 124. FAX: 330-395-3988. TDD: 330-393-0784. Web Site: www.wtcpl.org. *Dir,* James Wilkins; E-mail: wilkinsj@wtcpl.org; *Asst Dir,* Jan Vaughn; *Br Coordr,* Pam Daubenspeck; *Cat, Tech Serv,* Ron Hazen; *Circ,* Rob Liste; *ILL,* Jailynn Cronin; *Pub Relations,* Cheryl Bush; *Ref,* Micky Burnsworth; *Youth Serv,* Lori Faust; Staff 34 (MLS 18, Non-MLS 16)
Founded 1890. Pop 160,721; Circ 1,193,268
Jan 2008-Dec 2008 Income (Main Library and Branch(s)) $7,049,023, State $4,267,275, County $2,134,389, Locally Generated Income $647,359. Mats Exp $848,000, Books $546,698, Per/Ser (Incl. Access Fees) $36,000, Micro $12,480, AV Mat $198,822, Electronic Ref Mat (Incl. Access Fees) $54,000. Sal $3,019,016
Library Holdings: CDs 36,779; Bk Vols 415,972; Per Subs 602; Videos 20,117
Subject Interests: Local hist, Ohio
Automation Activity & Vendor Info: (Acquisitions) Innovative Interfaces, Inc; (Cataloging) Innovative Interfaces, Inc; (Circulation) Innovative Interfaces, Inc; (ILL) Innovative Interfaces, Inc; (OPAC) Innovative Interfaces, Inc; (Serials) Innovative Interfaces, Inc
Wireless access
Function: Magnifiers for reading, Mail & tel request accepted, Mail loans to mem, Masonic res mat, Monthly prog for perceptually impaired adults, Music CDs, Online ref, Online searches, Prog for adults, Prog for children & young adult, Pub access computers, Ref serv available, Ref serv in person, Story hour, Summer reading prog, Tax forms, Teen prog, VHS videos, Web-catalog, Wheelchair accessible
Publications: By the Book (Newsletter)
Partic in Northeast Ohio Regional Library System; OHIONET
Special Services for the Blind - Talking bks
Open Mon & Thurs 10-8, Tues & Wed 10-6, Fri 9-6, Sat 9-5
Friends of the Library Group
Branches: 5
BROOKFIELD BRANCH, 7032 Grove St, Brookfield, 44403, SAN 324-251X. Tel: 330-448-8134. *Br Mgr,* Nancy Gaut
Founded 1982. Circ 80,986
Library Holdings: Bk Vols 23,055
Open Mon-Thurs 9-8, Fri 9-5:30, Sat 9-5
Friends of the Library Group
CORTLAND BRANCH, 212 N High St, Cortland, 44410, SAN 324-2528. Tel: 330-638-6335. *Br Mgr,* Karen Murphy
Founded 1977. Circ 101,558
Library Holdings: Bk Vols 25,946
Open Tues & Fri 10-6, Wed & Thurs 12-8, Sat 9-5
Friends of the Library Group
HOWLAND BRANCH, 9095 E Market St, 44484, SAN 370-9000. Tel: 330-856-2011. *Br Mgr,* Diane Thomas
Founded 1990. Circ 173,990
Library Holdings: Bk Vols 35,390
Open Tues & Weds 12-8, Thurs & Fri 10-6, Sat 9-5
Friends of the Library Group
LIBERTY, 415 Churchill-Hubbard Rd, Youngstown, 44505, SAN 377-9971. Tel: 330-759-2589.
Founded 1998. Circ 110,137
Library Holdings: Bk Vols 15,159
Open Tues & Thurs 12-8, Wed & Fri 10-6, Sat 9-5
Friends of the Library Group
LORDSTOWN BRANCH, 1471 Salt Springs Rd SW, 44481, SAN 325-3384. Tel: 330-824-2094. *Br Mgr,* Vera Riffle
Founded 1985. Circ 29,322
Library Holdings: Bk Vols 15,159
Open Mon 12-4 & 4:30-8, Tues-Fri 10-1 & 1:30-6
Friends of the Library Group
Bookmobiles: 1

WARRENSVILLE HEIGHTS

M SOUTH POINTE HOSPITAL LIBRARY*, 4110 Warrensville Center Rd, 44122. SAN 325-1918. Tel: 216-491-7454. FAX: 216-491-7560. *Med Librn,* Mary Pat Harnegie; Staff 1.5 (MLS 0.5, Non-MLS 1)
Founded 1978
Library Holdings: Bk Vols 5,000; Per Subs 200
Subject Interests: Osteopathic med
Automation Activity & Vendor Info: (Circulation) Follett Software
Database Vendor: OVID Technologies
Partic in Greater Midwest Regional Medical Libr Network; Med Libr Asn of NE Ohio; Northeast Ohio Regional Library System

WASHINGTON COURT HOUSE

P CARNEGIE PUBLIC LIBRARY*, 127 S North St, 43160. SAN 313-7848. Tel: 740-335-2540. FAX: 740-335-8409. Web Site: www.cplwcho.org. *Dir,* Poppy Girton; E-mail: girtonpo@oplin.org; *Head, Adult Serv,* Sarah Nichols; *Head, Ch,* Ann Quinn; *Coordr, Tech Support,* Maria Wilburn; Staff 3 (MLS 3)
Founded 1891. Pop 28,500; Circ 214,400
Jan 2006-Dec 2006 Income $1,148,442. Mats Exp $117,571. Sal $679,727 (Prof $194,087)
Library Holdings: Bk Vols 69,461; Per Subs 98
Special Collections: Genealogy & Local History Coll
Automation Activity & Vendor Info: (Acquisitions) SirsiDynix; (Circulation) SirsiDynix; (ILL) SirsiDynix; (OPAC) SirsiDynix
Database Vendor: SirsiDynix
Wireless access
Mem of Carroll & Madison Library System

Partic in SEO (Serving Every Ohioan) Library Center
Open Mon-Fri 10-6, Sat 10-2
Branches: 1
JEFFERSONVILLE BRANCH, Eight S Main St, Jeffersonville, 43128-1063. Tel: 740-426-9292. FAX: 740-426-9284. *Br Mgr,* Susan Davis
Founded 1985. Pop 1,400; Circ 27,000
Library Holdings: Bk Titles 5,000; Per Subs 12
Open Mon-Thurs 10-6

GL FAYETTE COUNTY LAW LIBRARY*, 110 E Court House, 43160-1355. SAN 313-783X. Tel: 740-335-3608. FAX: 740-335-3608. *Librn,* Cindy Seaton
Library Holdings: Bk Vols 14,000
Special Collections: Ohio Laws
Subject Interests: Bankruptcy, Fed reports, Tax
Database Vendor: Westlaw
Open Mon & Wed 8-4

WAUSEON

L FULTON COUNTY ASSOCIATION*, Law Library, Court House, 210 S Fulton, 43567. SAN 327-7208. Tel: 419-337-9260. FAX: 419-337-9293. *Librn,* Sue Behnfeldt
Database Vendor: LexisNexis
Open Mon-Fri 8:30-4:30
Restriction: Open to pub upon request

P WAUSEON PUBLIC LIBRARY*, 117 E Elm St, 43567. SAN 313-7856. Tel: 419-335-6626. FAX: 419-335-0642. Web Site: www.wauseonlibrary.org. *Dir,* Amy Murphy; E-mail: amy.murphy@oplin.org; *Asst Dir,* Maricela DeLeon; Staff 2 (Non-MLS 2)
Founded 1875. Pop 10,638
Library Holdings: AV Mats 3,387; Bk Titles 46,403; Per Subs 141
Special Collections: Local History Coll; Spanish Coll
Subject Interests: Spanish
Automation Activity & Vendor Info: (Cataloging) SirsiDynix; (Circulation) SirsiDynix
Wireless access
Publications: Annual Report
Partic in NW Ohio Libr District; Ohio Public Library Information Network; SEO (Serving Every Ohioan) Library Center
Special Services for the Blind - Large print bks; Talking bks
Open Mon, Tues & Thurs 10-8, Wed & Fri 10-5, Sat 10-2

WAVERLY

P GARNET A WILSON PUBLIC LIBRARY OF PIKE COUNTY*, 207 N Market St, 45690-1176. SAN 313-7864. Tel: 740-947-4921. FAX: 740-947-2918. Web Site: www.pike.lib.oh.us. *Dir,* Thomas S Adkins; E-mail: dirgaw@oplin.org; *Automation Syst Coordr,* Daniel R Moore; E-mail: gawasc@oplin.org; *Pub Serv,* Jennifer Wright; E-mail: gawpcord@oplin.org; *Tech Serv,* Jennifer K Roberts; E-mail: gawtcord@oplin.org; Staff 30 (MLS 1, Non-MLS 29)
Founded 1939. Pop 27,988; Circ 222,623
Library Holdings: Bk Vols 89,005; Per Subs 248
Special Collections: Pike County Local History/Genealogy Room
Automation Activity & Vendor Info: (Cataloging) TLC (The Library Corporation); (Circulation) TLC (The Library Corporation); (OPAC) TLC (The Library Corporation)
Database Vendor: EBSCOhost, Gale Cengage Learning, OVID Technologies, Wilson - Wilson Web
Special Services for the Blind - Talking bks
Open Mon-Thurs 9-8, Fri 9-6, Sat 9-5
Branches: 2
EASTERN BRANCH, 310 E Third St, Beaver, 45613. Tel: 740-226-4408. FAX: 740-226-4408. *Dir,* Thomas S Adkins; Staff 4 (MLS 1, Non-MLS 3)
Founded 2000
Open Mon 10-6, Tues 10-8, Wed-Fri 12-6, Sat 11-4
PIKETON BRANCH, 200 E Second St, Piketon, 45661-8047. (Mail add: PO Box 762, Piketon, 45661-0762), SAN 376-7914. Tel: 740-289-3064. FAX: 740-289-3064. ; Staff 4 (MLS 1, Non-MLS 3)
Founded 1997
Open Mon, Tues & Fri 12-6, Wed 10-6, Thurs 10-8, Sat 11-4

WAYNE

P WAYNE PUBLIC LIBRARY*, 137 E Main St, 43466. SAN 357-3036. Tel: 419-288-2708. FAX: 419-288-3766. Web Site: waynepl.org. *Dir,* Teresa Barnhart; E-mail: barnhate@oplin.org
Founded 1945. Pop 8,800; Circ 93,885
Library Holdings: Bk Vols 37,297; Per Subs 135
Wireless access
Partic in NORWELD
Open Mon-Thurs 10-7, Fri & Sat 10-2
Friends of the Library Group

WAYNESVILLE

P MARY L COOK PUBLIC LIBRARY*, 381 Old Stage Rd, 45068. SAN 313-7872. Tel: 513-897-4826. FAX: 513-897-9215. Web Site: mlcook.lib.oh.us. *Dir,* Linda Swartzel; E-mail: swartzli@oplin.org; *Spec Coll & Archives Librn,* Karen Campbell
Founded 1917. Pop 14,000; Circ 180,892
Library Holdings: AV Mats 6,669; Bk Vols 70,000
Special Collections: Early Quaker Theology; Ohio & Local History
Subject Interests: Genealogy
Function: Adult literacy prog, Archival coll, AV serv, For res purposes, Handicapped accessible, Home delivery & serv to Sr ctr & nursing homes, Homebound delivery serv, ILL available, Large print keyboards, Magnifiers for reading, Photocopying/Printing, Prog for children & young adult, Ref serv available, Summer reading prog, Wheelchair accessible
Publications: Newsletter (Quarterly)
Partic in Miami Valley Librs
Open Mon-Thurs 9-9, Fri 9-5, Sat 9-2, Sun (Winter) 1-4
Friends of the Library Group

WELLINGTON

P HERRICK MEMORIAL LIBRARY*, 101 Willard Memorial Sq, 44090-1342. SAN 313-7880. Tel: 440-647-2120. FAX: 440-647-2103. E-mail: ebooks@oplin.org. Web Site: www.wellington.lib.oh.us. *Dir,* Janet L Hollingsworth; E-mail: hollinja@oplin.org; *Adult Serv,* Lynne Welch; E-mail: welchly@oplin.org; *Ch Serv,* Kathleen Yeager; E-mail: yeagerka@oplin.org; Staff 11 (MLS 2, Non-MLS 9)
Founded 1873. Pop 9,000; Circ 95,000
Library Holdings: Bk Vols 57,042; Per Subs 168
Special Collections: Wellington Historic Photo Coll. Oral History
Subject Interests: Local hist
Automation Activity & Vendor Info: (Cataloging) TLC (The Library Corporation); (Circulation) TLC (The Library Corporation); (OPAC) TLC (The Library Corporation)
Database Vendor: EBSCO Auto Repair Reference, EBSCO Information Services, EBSCOhost
Wireless access
Function: Archival coll
Open Mon-Thurs 9-8:30, Fri & Sat 9-5, Sun (Oct-April) 1-5
Friends of the Library Group

WELLSTON

P SYLVESTER MEMORIAL WELLSTON PUBLIC LIBRARY*, 135 E Second St, 45692. SAN 313-7899. Tel: 740-384-6660. FAX: 740-384-5001. Web Site: www1.youseemore.com/sylvester. *Dir,* Karen A Davis; *Head Cataloger,* Debbie Lewis; *Head, Circ,* Connie Dickerson; *Ch,* Vickie Stephenson; Staff 11 (MLS 1, Non-MLS 10)
Pop 10,000
Library Holdings: Bk Titles 35,000; Bk Vols 40,000
Open Mon & Wed 9-8, Tues, Thurs & Fri 9-6, Sat 9-4

WELLSVILLE

P WELLSVILLE CARNEGIE PUBLIC LIBRARY*, 115 Ninth St, 43968-1431. SAN 313-7902. Tel: 330-532-1526. FAX: 330-532-3127. Web Site: www.wellsville.lib.oh.us. *Dir,* Tracee Murphy; E-mail: murphytr@oplin.org; *Youth Serv Mgr,* Rachel Freed; E-mail: freedra@oplin.org; Staff 6 (MLS 1, Non-MLS 5)
Founded 1908. Pop 14,299; Circ 55,162
Library Holdings: AV Mats 820; Bk Vols 33,000; Per Subs 70
Special Collections: Early History of Columbiana County
Automation Activity & Vendor Info: (Cataloging) Innovative Interfaces, Inc; (Circulation) Innovative Interfaces, Inc; (OPAC) Innovative Interfaces, Inc
Wireless access
Function: Adult bk club, Bks on cassette, Bks on CD, Children's prog, Computers for patron use, Copy machines, Fax serv, Handicapped accessible, ILL available, Notary serv, Photocopying/Printing, Prog for children & young adult, Summer reading prog
Partic in Northeast Ohio Regional Library System
Special Services for the Blind - Bks on cassette; Bks on CD; Talking bks & player equip
Open Mon & Thurs 10-8, Tues, Wed, Fri & Sat 10-6
Friends of the Library Group

WEST JEFFERSON

P HURT-BATTELLE MEMORIAL LIBRARY OF WEST JEFFERSON*, 270 Lily Chapel Rd, 43162-1202. SAN 313-7910. Tel: 614-879-8448. FAX: 614-879-8668. Web Site: www.hbmlibrary.org. *Dir,* Cathy Allen
Founded 1913. Pop 7,500; Circ 81,888

Library Holdings: Bk Vols 44,000; Per Subs 25
Subject Interests: Cookbks, Craft, Med
Automation Activity & Vendor Info: (Cataloging) Follett Software; (Circulation) Follett Software
Wireless access
Function: Bks on CD, Children's prog, Computers for patron use, Copy machines, Electronic databases & coll, Handicapped accessible, Homebound delivery serv, Large print keyboards, Magnifiers for reading, Photocopying/Printing, Prog for adults, Prog for children & young adult, Pub access computers, Scanner, Story hour
Open Mon-Fri 10-8, Sat 10-2
Friends of the Library Group

WEST MILTON

P MILTON-UNION PUBLIC LIBRARY, 560 S Main St, 45383. SAN 313-7929. Tel: 937-698-5515. FAX: 937-698-3774. Web Site: www.mupubliclibrary.org. *Dir,* Carol Netzley Coate; E-mail: coateca@oplin.org; *Adult Serv,* Kimberly Brubaker; *Ch Serv,* Wendy Heisey; E-mail: heiseywe@oplin.org; *IT Spec,* Dori Mort; E-mail: mortdo@oplin.org; *Website Mgr/Teen Serv,* Dawn Merritt; Staff 8 (Non-MLS 8)
Founded 1937. Pop 10,000
Subject Interests: Local hist
Automation Activity & Vendor Info: (Cataloging) SIRSI WorkFlows; (Circulation) SIRSI WorkFlows; (OPAC) Horizon
Database Vendor: EBSCOhost, Electric Library, Gale Cengage Learning, OCLC WebJunction, ProQuest, SirsiDynix
Wireless access
Function: 24/7 Online cat, Activity rm, Adult bk club, Audiobks via web, Bk club(s), Bks on CD, Children's prog, Computer training, Computers for patron use, Copy machines, Electronic databases & coll, eReaders, Free DVD rentals, Handicapped accessible, Holiday prog, Home delivery & serv to Sr ctr & nursing homes, Homebound delivery serv, ILL available, Magazines, Microfiche/film & reading machines, Movies, Music CDs, Online cat, OverDrive digital audio bks, Photocopying/Printing, Preschool outreach, Prog for adults, Prog for children & young adult, Pub access computers, Ref serv available, Scanner, Story hour, Summer reading prog, Tax forms, Teen prog, VHS videos, Wheelchair accessible
Partic in Ohio Public Library Information Network; SEO (Serving Every Ohioan) Library Center
Special Services for the Blind - Audio mat; Bks on CD; Home delivery serv; Large print bks; Playaways (bks on MP3)
Open Mon-Thurs 10-8, Fri & Sat 9-5
Friends of the Library Group

WESTERVILLE

C HONDROS COLLEGE RESOURCE CENTER, Online Learning Library, 4140 Executive Pkwy, 43081-3855. SAN 374-7832. Tel: 614-508-7200. Toll Free Tel: 855-906-8773. FAX: 614-508-7279. E-mail: library@hondros.edu. Web Site: www.nursing.hondros.edu. *Librn,* Beth Smith; Tel: 614-508-6258, Fax: 513-755-9751; Staff 1 (MLS 1)
Enrl 1,200; Highest Degree: Bachelor
Subject Interests: Gen educ, Nursing
Wireless access
Open Mon-Fri 8-5
Restriction: Authorized patrons

S NATIONAL GROUND WATER ASSOCIATION*, Ground Water Information Center, 601 Dempsey Rd, 43081-8978. SAN 327-392X. Tel: 614-898-7791. Toll Free Tel: 800-551-7379. Administration FAX: 614-898-7786. Web Site: www.ngwa.org/gwonline/gwol.cfm. *Dir,* Thad Plumley; E-mail: tplumley@ngwa.org; Staff 2 (MLS 1, Non-MLS 1)
Library Holdings: Bk Vols 24,000; Per Subs 100
Subject Interests: Groundwater protection
Restriction: Mem only, Non-circulating, Not a lending libr

C OTTERBEIN UNIVERSITY, Courtright Memorial Library, 138 W Main St, 43081. (Mail add: One South Grove St, 43081), SAN 313-7937. Tel: 614-823-1215. Interlibrary Loan Service Tel: 614-823-3072. Reference Tel: 614-823-1984. FAX: 614-823-1921. E-mail: library@otterbein.edu. Web Site: library.otterbein.edu, www.otterbein.edu/resources/library/library.htm. *Dir,* Lois F Szudy; Tel: 614-823-1414, E-mail: LSzudy@otterbein.edu; *Cat/Metadata Librn,* Amy Parsons; Tel: 614-823-1026, E-mail: aparsons@otterbein.edu; *Cat/Metadata Librn,* Elizabeth Salt; Tel: 614-823-1939, E-mail: esalt@otterbein.edu; *Electronic Access Librn,* Allen Reichert; Tel: 614-823-1164, E-mail: preichert@otterbein.edu; *Info Literacy Librn,* Rares Piloiu; Tel: 614-823-1314, E-mail: rpiloiu@otterbein.edu; *Syst Librn,* Jane Wu; Tel: 614-823-1027, E-mail: jwu@otterbein.edu; *Coll Develop/Acq Coordr,* Elizabeth Zeitz; Tel: 614-823-1938, E-mail: ezeitz@otterbein.edu; *Ref Serv Coordr,* Jessica Crossfield McIntosh; Tel: 614-823-1366, E-mail: JCrossfieldMcIntosh@otterbein.edu; *Res Sharing Spec,* Rebecca Raeske-Grinch; E-mail: rraeske-grinch@otterbein.edu; *Archivist,* Stephen Grinch; Tel: 614-823-1761, E-mail: sgrinch@otterbein.edu; *Circ,* Rebecca Gale; Tel: 614-823-1799, E-mail: rmmoore@otterbein.edu; *Circ,* William Stoddard; Tel: 614-823-1985, E-mail: wstoddard@otterbein.edu; *Per,* LaVerne Austin; Tel: 614-823-1264, E-mail: laustin@otterbein.edu; Staff 14 (MLS 7, Non-MLS 7)
Founded 1847. Highest Degree: Doctorate
Special Collections: Americana (J Burr & Jessie M Hughes Memorial); Classics (Marshall B & Mary M Fanning Fund); Ethnics & Political Science (Lewis E Myers Memorial); Humanities (NEH Fund); Science (Elvin & Ruth Warrick Fund)
Automation Activity & Vendor Info: (Acquisitions) Innovative Interfaces, Inc; (Cataloging) Innovative Interfaces, Inc; (Circulation) Innovative Interfaces, Inc; (Course Reserve) Innovative Interfaces, Inc; (ILL) Innovative Interfaces, Inc; (OPAC) Innovative Interfaces, Inc; (Serials) Innovative Interfaces, Inc
Database Vendor: ABC-CLIO, Alexander Street Press, American Chemical Society, American Psychological Association (APA), Cinahl, CredoReference, EBSCO Discovery Service, EBSCOhost, Innovative Interfaces, Inc, ISI Web of Knowledge, JSTOR, LexisNexis, Medline, Mergent Online, OCLC FirstSearch, OHIONET, Oxford Online, Project MUSE, ProQuest, PubMed, RefWorks, Safari Books Online, Scopus, SerialsSolutions, Swets Information Services, Thomson - Web of Science, YBP Library Services
Wireless access
Partic in OCLC Online Computer Library Center, Inc; Ohio Library & Information Network; Ohio Private Academic Libraries (OPAL); OHIONET
Open Mon-Thurs 7:45am-2am, Fri 7:45-6, Sat 12-6, Sun Noon-2am
Friends of the Library Group

P WESTERVILLE PUBLIC LIBRARY*, 126 S State St, 43081-2095. SAN 313-7945. Tel: 614-882-7277. Circulation Tel: 614-882-7277, Ext 5. FAX: 614-882-4160. Web Site: www.westervillelibrary.org. *Exec Dir,* Don W Barlow; Tel: 614-882-7277, Ext 2140, Fax: 614-882-5369, E-mail: barlowd@westervillelibrary.org; *Dep Dir,* Karen Albury; Tel: 614-882-7277, Ext 2168, Fax: 614-882-5369, E-mail: kalbury@westervillelibrary.org; *Assoc Dir, Support Serv,* Jessi Crim-Weithman; Tel: 614-882-7277, Ext 134, E-mail: jweithman@westervillelibrary.org; *Coll Develop Mgr,* Belinda Mortensen; Tel: 614-882-7277, Ext 2131; *Mgr, Ad Serv,* Nieca Nowels; Tel: 614-882-7277, Ext 2138, Fax: 614-882-4190, E-mail: nnowels@westervillelibrary.org; *Mgr, Outreach Serv,* Julie Kerns; Tel: 614-882-7277, Ext 2144, E-mail: jkerns@westervillelibrary.org; *Mgr, Youth Serv,* Linda Uhler; Tel: 614-882-7277, Ext 2130, E-mail: luhler@westervillelibrary.org
Founded 1930. Pop 85,093; Circ 1,622,721
Jan 2010-Dec 2010 Income (Main Library Only) $4,962,015, State $2,475,991, Locally Generated Income $1,895,114, Other $590,910. Mats Exp $383,685, Books $247,238, Per/Ser (Incl. Access Fees) $20,308, Manu Arch $5,890, Other Print Mats $405, Micro $4,235, AV Equip $89, AV Mat $40,058, Electronic Ref Mat (Incl. Access Fees) $6,986, Presv $13,476. Sal $2,374,000 (Prof $879,843)
Library Holdings: Bk Vols 283,108; Per Subs 526
Special Collections: Temperance Coll
Subject Interests: Local hist
Automation Activity & Vendor Info: (Acquisitions) Innovative Interfaces, Inc - Millenium; (Cataloging) Innovative Interfaces, Inc; (Circulation) Innovative Interfaces, Inc - Millenium; (ILL) Innovative Interfaces, Inc - Millenium; (Media Booking) Innovative Interfaces, Inc - Millenium; (OPAC) Innovative Interfaces, Inc - Millenium; (Serials) Innovative Interfaces, Inc - Millenium
Database Vendor: 3M Library Systems, ALLDATA Online, BWI, ebrary, EBSCO - WebFeat, EBSCO Auto Repair Reference, EBSCO Information Services, Facts on File, Ingram Library Services, Innovative Interfaces, Inc, Innovative Interfaces, Inc, Inspire, OCLC, OCLC ArticleFirst, OCLC WebJunction, OCLC WorldShare Interlibrary Loan, OHIONET, Overdrive, Inc, ProQuest, ReferenceUSA, ValueLine
Wireless access
Publications: Between the Pages (Newsletter)
Partic in OCLC Online Computer Library Center, Inc; Ohio Library & Information Network; Ohio Public Library Information Network; OHIONET
Special Services for the Deaf - Bks on deafness & sign lang; Captioned film dep; Spec interest per; Videos & decoder
Open Mon-Thurs 9-9, Fri & Sat 9-6, Sun 1-5
Friends of the Library Group
Branches: 1
ANTI SALOON LEAGUE MUSEUM & LOCAL HISTORY RESOURCE CENTER, 126 S State St, 43081, SAN 371-3466. Tel: 614-882-7277, Ext 160. FAX: 614-882-5369. *Librn,* Beth Weinhardt; E-mail: bweinhar@westervillelibrary.org
Open Mon-Fri 9-6
Friends of the Library Group

WESTLAKE

M SAINT JOHN WEST SHORE HOSPITAL*, Jack Brill Medical Library, 29000 Center Ridge Rd, 44145. SAN 313-2064. Tel: 440-827-5569. FAX: 440-827-5573. *Med Librn,* Adora Glorioso; Staff 1 (MLS 1)
Library Holdings: Bk Titles 1,100; Per Subs 50
Special Collections: Osteopathic
Partic in Docline

P WESTLAKE PORTER PUBLIC LIBRARY*, 27333 Center Ridge Rd, 44145-3925. SAN 313-7953. Tel: 440-871-2600. Interlibrary Loan Service Tel: 440-250-5470. Reference Tel: 440-250-5460. FAX: 440-871-6969. Interlibrary Loan Service FAX: 440-250-5470. Web Site: www.westlakelibrary.org. *Dir,* Andrew Mangels; *Asst Dir, Pub Serv,* Mary Worthington; *Asst Dir, Support Serv,* Anita Woods; *Mgr, Popular Mats,* Susan E Cozzens; *Mgr, Ref Serv,* Deborah Ludwig; *Mgr, Tech Serv & Automation,* Tim Donaldson; *Mgr, Youth Serv,* Carolyn Fain
Founded 1884. Pop 33,000; Circ 1,323,226
Jan 2005-Dec 2005 Income $4,675,242, State $1,398,093, Locally Generated Income $3,121,776, Other $15,537. Mats Exp $703,202, Books $358,476, Per/Ser (Incl. Access Fees) $29,250, Other Print Mats $450, Micro $13,936, AV Mat $230,723, Electronic Ref Mat (Incl. Access Fees) $70,363, Presv $4. Sal $2,318,866 (Prof $891,541)
Library Holdings: AV Mats 66,618; CDs 18,443; DVDs 14,494; Large Print Bks 7,325; Bk Vols 176,842; Per Subs 520; Talking Bks 10,522; Videos 18,448
Special Collections: Oral History
Subject Interests: Bus, Genealogy, Local hist
Automation Activity & Vendor Info: (Cataloging) OCLC; (Circulation) SirsiDynix; (ILL) OCLC
Wireless access
Partic in Northeast Ohio Regional Library System; OCLC Online Computer Library Center, Inc; OHIONET
Open Mon-Thurs (Winter) 9-9, Fri & Sat 9-5, Sun 1-5; Mon-Thurs (Summer) 9-9, Fri & Sat 9-5
Friends of the Library Group

WESTON

P WESTON PUBLIC LIBRARY*, 13153 Main St, 43569. (Mail add: PO Box 345, 43569), SAN 313-7961. Tel: 419-669-3415. FAX: 419-669-3216. Web Site: library.norweld.lib.oh.us/weston. *Dir,* Shelen A Stevens; E-mail: dewittsh@oplin.org
Founded 1942. Pop 24,000; Circ 88,989
Library Holdings: Bk Vols 72,000; Per Subs 180
Subject Interests: Local hist
Automation Activity & Vendor Info: (Circulation) SirsiDynix
Publications: Weston Advocate (Monthly)
Partic in NORWELD
Open Mon-Wed 10-8, Thurs & Fri 10-5, Sat 10-3
Friends of the Library Group
Branches: 1
GRAND RAPIDS BRANCH, 17620 Bridge St, Grand Rapids, 43522. (Mail add: PO Box 245, Grand Rapids, 43522), SAN 320-0981. Tel: 419-832-5231. FAX: 419-832-8104. *Mgr,* Darla Froman; E-mail: fromanda@oplin.org
Founded 1978
Open Mon-Wed 10-8, Thurs & Fri 10-5, Sat 10-3
Friends of the Library Group

WICKLIFFE

S LUBRIZOL LIBRARY & RESEARCH CENTER*, 29400 Lakeland Blvd, Mail Drop 152L, 44092. SAN 313-7988. Tel: 440-347-2207. FAX: 440-347-4713. E-mail: library@lubrizol.com. *Mgr,* Rhonda Kidner; Tel: 440-347-2971, E-mail: rek@lubrizol.com; Staff 3 (MLS 2, Non-MLS 1)
Founded 1946
Library Holdings: Bk Titles 6,000; Per Subs 100
Subject Interests: Analytical chem, Chem eng, Organic chem, Petroleum chem, Polymer chem
Automation Activity & Vendor Info: (Acquisitions) Ex Libris Group; (Cataloging) Ex Libris Group; (Circulation) Ex Libris Group; (OPAC) Ex Libris Group; (Serials) Ex Libris Group
Function: Archival coll, Bus archives, Doc delivery serv, For res purposes, Res libr
Restriction: Circ limited, Circulates for staff only, Co libr, Non-circulating coll, Not a lending libr, Not open to pub, Open to staff only

R SAINT MARY SEMINARY*, Bruening-Marotta Library, 28700 Euclid Ave, 44092-2585. SAN 313-380X. Tel: 440-943-7665. FAX: 440-585-3528. Web Site: www.stmarysem.edu/library/. *Librn,* Dr Alan K Rome; E-mail: akrome@dioceseofcleveland.org; Staff 1 (MLS 1)
Founded 1848. Enrl 90; Fac 15
Library Holdings: Bk Vols 69,232; Per Subs 326
Special Collections: Theology (Horstmann Coll)
Subject Interests: Canon law, Church hist, Ecumenism, Liturgy, Pastoral care, Scripture, Spirituality, Theol
Partic in Northeast Ohio Regional Library System
Open Mon-Fri 8-4:30

CR TELSHE YESHIVA COLLEGE*, Rabbi A N Schwartz Library, 28400 Euclid Ave, 44092. SAN 370-4203. Tel: 440-943-5300. FAX: 440-943-5303.
Library Holdings: AV Mats 2,000; Bk Titles 20,000; Per Subs 10

P WICKLIFFE PUBLIC LIBRARY*, 1713 Lincoln Rd, 44092. SAN 313-8003. Tel: 440-944-6010. FAX: 440-944-7264. E-mail: cdesk@wickliffe.lib.oh.us, ref.desk@wickliffe.lib.oh.us. Web Site: www.wickliffe.lib.oh.us. *Dir,* Cheryl Kuonen; *YA Librn,* Monica Waschura; E-mail: mwaschura@wickliffe.lib.oh.us; Staff 11 (MLS 6, Non-MLS 5)
Founded 1934. Pop 13,484; Circ 509,762
Library Holdings: Audiobooks 7,013; CDs 7,013; DVDs 10,958; e-books 11,647; e-journals 4; Electronic Media & Resources 293; High Interest/Low Vocabulary Bk Vols 667; Large Print Bks 3,460; Bk Titles 89,055; Bk Vols 104,159; Per Subs 318; Talking Bks 12,691
Subject Interests: Auto repair, Local hist
Automation Activity & Vendor Info: (Cataloging) SirsiDynix; (Circulation) SirsiDynix; (ILL) SirsiDynix; (OPAC) SirsiDynix
Database Vendor: EBSCOhost, Electric Library
Wireless access
Publications: Your Wickliffe Connection (Quarterly newsletter)
Partic in CLEVNET; Northeast Ohio Regional Library System
Special Services for the Deaf - Bks on deafness & sign lang; TTY equip
Special Services for the Blind - Aids for in-house use; Audio mat; Bks on cassette; Bks on CD; Large print bks; Magnifiers; Reader equip
Open Mon-Thurs 9-9, Fri 9-6, Sat 9-5, Sun (Nov-May) 1-5
Friends of the Library Group

WILBERFORCE

C CENTRAL STATE UNIVERSITY*, Hallie Q Brown Memorial Library, 1400 Brush Row Rd, 45384. (Mail add: PO Box 1006, 45384-1006), SAN 313-8011. Tel: 937-376-6106. Reference Tel: 937-376-6454. FAX: 937-376-6132. Web Site: hallie.ces.edu. *Dir,* Johnny W Jackson; Tel: 937-376-6372, E-mail: jjackson@centralstate.edu; *Archivist,* Sheila Darrow; Tel: 937-376-6521, E-mail: sdarrow@centralstate.edu; *Media Spec,* A Carolyn Sanders; Tel: 937-376-6213, E-mail: csanders@centralstate.edu; *Per, Ref,* Lugene Bailey; Tel: 937-376-6394, E-mail: lbailey@centralstate.edu; *Syst Adminr,* Carolin Sterling; Tel: 937-376-6396, E-mail: csterling@centralstate.edu; Staff 12 (MLS 6, Non-MLS 6)
Founded 1948. Enrl 2,022; Fac 131; Highest Degree: Master
Jul 2007-Jun 2008. Mats Exp $213,831, Books $18,000, Per/Ser (Incl. Access Fees) $99,569, Other Print Mats $10,270, Micro $28,484, Electronic Ref Mat (Incl. Access Fees) $55,508, Presv $2,000. Sal $680,054 (Prof $510,743)
Library Holdings: e-books 21,145; e-journals 5,948; Electronic Media & Resources 1,417; Bk Vols 196,827; Per Subs 386
Special Collections: Afro-American Coll
Automation Activity & Vendor Info: (Acquisitions) Innovative Interfaces, Inc; (Cataloging) Innovative Interfaces, Inc; (Circulation) Innovative Interfaces, Inc; (Course Reserve) Innovative Interfaces, Inc; (ILL) Innovative Interfaces, Inc; (OPAC) Innovative Interfaces, Inc; (Serials) Innovative Interfaces, Inc
Database Vendor: ABC-CLIO, American Physical Society, CredoReference, H W Wilson, Innovative Interfaces, Inc, LexisNexis, Marquis Who's Who, OCLC WorldShare Interlibrary Loan, Oxford Online, Swets Information Services, YBP Library Services
Wireless access
Publications: Index to Periodical Articles by & about Blacks; Primary Sources in African American History
Partic in Dayton-Miami Valley Consortium; OCLC Online Computer Library Center, Inc
Open Mon-Thurs 7:45am-10pm, Fri 7:45-5, Sat 1-5, Sun 1-10
Friends of the Library Group

R PAYNE THEOLOGICAL SEMINARY*, Reverdy C Ransom Memorial Library, 1230 Wilberforce-Clifton Rd, 45384. (Mail add: PO Box 474, 45384-0474), SAN 313-802X. Tel: 937-376-2946, Ext 203, 937-376-2947, Ext 203. Toll Free Tel: 888-816-8933. FAX: 937-376-2888. Web Site: www.payne.edu. *Dir, Libr & Info Serv,* Position Currently Open; Staff 1 (MLS 1)
Founded 1956. Enrl 95; Fac 9; Highest Degree: Master
Library Holdings: Bk Vols 25,000; Per Subs 67
Special Collections: African American Coll
Subject Interests: Biblical studies, Church hist, Doctrinal theol, Ethics, Ethnic studies, Judaica, Philos
Partic in Ohio Private Academic Libraries (OPAL)
Open Mon-Fri 9am-9:30pm, Sat 9-5

C WILBERFORCE UNIVERSITY*, Rembert E Stokes Library & Information Commons, 1055 N Bickett Rd, 45384-5801. (Mail add: PO Box 1003, 45384-1003), SAN 313-8038. Tel: 937-708-5630. Reference Tel: 937-708-5277. FAX: 937-708-5771. E-mail: library@wilberforce.edu. Web Site: www.wilberforce.edu. *Dir, Libr & Info Commons,* Dr Willette Stinson; Tel: 937-708-5629, E-mail: wstinson@wilberforce.edu; *Assoc Librn,* Jacqueline Y Brown; E-mail: jbrown@wilberforce.edu; Staff 2 (MLS 2)
Founded 1856. Enrl 755; Fac 51; Highest Degree: Bachelor
Library Holdings: DVDs 50; e-books 12,000; e-journals 200; Bk Vols 62,000; Per Subs 500; Videos 200
Special Collections: Afro-American History (Arnett-Coppin & Payne), scrapbks, newsp clippings, handbills & some correspondence; History of African Methodist Episcopal Church. State Document Depository
Automation Activity & Vendor Info: (Cataloging) Innovative Interfaces, Inc; (Circulation) Innovative Interfaces, Inc; (Course Reserve) Innovative Interfaces, Inc; (OPAC) Innovative Interfaces, Inc
Wireless access
Partic in OCLC Online Computer Library Center, Inc; Ohio Library & Information Network; Ohio Private Academic Libraries (OPAL)
Open Mon-Thurs 8am-10pm, Fri 8-6, Sat 1-5

WILLARD

P HURON COUNTY COMMUNITY LIBRARY, Willard Memorial Library, Six W Emerald St, 44890-1498. SAN 357-3095. Tel: 419-933-8564. Administration Tel: 419-933-2544. FAX: 419-933-4783. TDD: 800-750-0750. Web Site: www.huroncolib.org. *Dir,* Laura Lee Wilson; E-mail: director@huroncolib.org; *Mgr, Tech Serv,* Margaret White; E-mail: whiteme@huroncolib.org; *Mgr, Youth Serv,* Charlotte Cunningham; E-mail: cunninch@huroncolib.org; *Fiscal Officer,* Adam D Searl; E-mail: fiscalofficer@huroncolib.org; Staff 14 (MLS 1, Non-MLS 13)
Founded 1921. Pop 23,558; Circ 210,014
Jan 2012-Dec 2012 Income (Main Library and Branch(s)) $1,623,931. Mats Exp $82,162. Sal $548,233
Library Holdings: AV Mats 8,911; Electronic Media & Resources 127,623; Bk Vols 76,859; Per Subs 129
Special Collections: Grant Coll; Local History Coll (Huron County); Ohio History Coll; Railroad Books
Automation Activity & Vendor Info: (Cataloging) SirsiDynix; (Circulation) SirsiDynix; (ILL) SirsiDynix; (Media Booking) SirsiDynix; (OPAC) SirsiDynix; (Serials) SirsiDynix
Database Vendor: EBSCO Auto Repair Reference
Wireless access
Function: Accelerated reader prog, Adult bk club, After school storytime, Audio & video playback equip for onsite use, Audiobks via web, Bks on CD, Children's prog, Computer training, Computers for patron use, Copy machines, Digital talking bks, e-mail & chat, e-mail serv, E-Reserves, Electronic databases & coll, Fax serv, Free DVD rentals, Govt ref serv, Handicapped accessible, Holiday prog, Home delivery & serv to Sr ctr & nursing homes, ILL available, Mail & tel request accepted, Microfiche/film & reading machines, Music CDs, Online cat, Online searches, OverDrive digital audio bks, Photocopying/Printing, Preschool outreach, Preschool reading prog, Prog for adults, Prog for children & young adult, Pub access computers, Ref serv available, Scanner, Spanish lang bks, Story hour, Summer reading prog, Tax forms, Teen prog, Wheelchair accessible
Partic in NORWELD
Special Services for the Blind - Accessible computers; Bks on cassette; Bks on CD; Copier with enlargement capabilities; Internet workstation with adaptive software; Large print bks; Large screen computer & software; Magnifiers; Recorded bks; Screen enlargement software for people with visual disabilities; Talking bk serv referral
Open Mon-Thurs 10-8, Fri & Sat 10-5
Friends of the Library Group
Branches: 3
GREENWICH PUBLIC LIBRARY, Four New St, Greenwich, 44837, SAN 357-3125. Tel: 419-752-7331. FAX: 419-752-6801. TDD: 800-750-0750. *Br Mgr,* Stephanie Buchanan; Staff 6 (Non-MLS 6)
Function: Adult bk club, Audiobks via web, Bks on cassette, Bks on CD, Children's prog, Computers for patron use, Copy machines, Electronic databases & coll, Fax serv, Holiday prog, Homebound delivery serv, ILL available, Music CDs, Notary serv, Online cat, Online ref, OverDrive digital audio bks, Prog for children & young adult, Pub access computers, Ref & res, Story hour, Summer reading prog, Tax forms, Teen prog, Telephone ref, VHS videos, Wheelchair accessible
Open Mon-Wed 10-7, Thurs & Fri 10-5, Sat 10-2
Friends of the Library Group
NORTH FAIRFIELD PUBLIC LIBRARY, Five E Main St, North Fairfield, 44855. (Mail add: PO Box 175, North Fairfield, 44855), SAN 357-315X. Tel: 419-744-2285. FAX: 419-744-2115. *Br Mgr,* Gail Cummings; Staff 4 (Non-MLS 4)
Function: Adult bk club, Bks on cassette, Bks on CD, Children's prog, Computers for patron use, Copy machines, Digital talking bks, Fax serv, ILL available, Online cat, Online ref, OverDrive digital audio bks, Photocopying/Printing, Prog for children & young adult, Pub access computers, Ref & res, Story hour, Summer reading prog, Tax forms, Teen prog, Telephone ref, VHS videos, Web-catalog
Open Mon-Wed, 10-7,Thurs & Fri 10-5, Sat 10-2
WAKEMAN COMMUNITY LIBRARY, 33 Pleasant St, Wakeman, 44889-9424, SAN 357-3184. Tel: 440-839-2976. FAX: 440-839-2560. E-mail: wclib@oplin.org. Web Site: willardlibrary.oplin.org/wakemanlibrary/index.htm. *Br Mgr,* Gail Cummings; E-mail: cumminga@oplin.org; Staff 6 (Non-MLS 6)
Founded 1951
Function: After school storytime, Audiobks via web, Bks on cassette, Bks on CD, Children's prog, Computer training, Computers for patron use, Copy machines, Digital talking bks, Electronic databases & coll, Fax serv, Holiday prog, ILL available, Music CDs, Notary serv, Online cat, Online ref, Outreach serv, Photocopying/Printing, Preschool outreach, Prog for adults, Prog for children & young adult, Pub access computers, Ref & res, Story hour, Summer reading prog, Tax forms, Teen prog, Telephone ref, VHS videos, Web-catalog
Open Mon, Thurs & Fri 10-5, Tues 10-8, Wed 10-12
Friends of the Library Group

WILLOWICK

P WILLOUGHBY-EASTLAKE PUBLIC LIBRARY*, 263 E 305th St, 44095. SAN 357-3214. Tel: 440-943-2203. Interlibrary Loan Service Tel: 440-944-5722, Ext 115. FAX: 440-943-2383. Web Site: www.wepl.lib.oh.us. *Interim Dir,* Eric Linderman; E-mail: eric.linderman@welibrary.info; *Dir,* Position Currently Open; *Asst Dir,* Eric Linderman; E-mail: eric.linderman@welibrary.info; *Fiscal Officer,* Vicki Simmons; E-mail: vicki.simmons@welibrary.info; Staff 38 (MLS 14, Non-MLS 24)
Founded 1827. Pop 67,023; Circ 789,490
Library Holdings: Bk Vols 215,048; Per Subs 477
Special Collections: Willoughby Historical Society & News/Herald, micro
Automation Activity & Vendor Info: (Acquisitions) SirsiDynix; (Cataloging) SirsiDynix; (Circulation) SirsiDynix; (OPAC) SirsiDynix; (Serials) SirsiDynix
Wireless access
Partic in Cleveland Integrated Automated Libr Regional Network; Northeast Ohio Regional Library System
Open Mon-Thurs 9-9, Fri & Sat 9-5, Sun (Oct-April) 1-5
Friends of the Library Group
Branches: 4
EASTLAKE BRANCH, 36706 Lake Shore Blvd, Eastlake, 44095, SAN 357-3249. Tel: 440-942-7880. FAX: 440-942-4095. *Br Mgr,* Amy Senning; E-mail: amy.senning@welibrary.info
Founded 1956. Circ 243,125
Library Holdings: High Interest/Low Vocabulary Bk Vols 36
Database Vendor: SirsiDynix
Open Mon-Thurs 9-9, Fri & Sat 9-5, Sun (Oct-April) 1-5
Friends of the Library Group
WILLOUGHBY BRANCH, 30 Public Sq, Willoughby, 44094, SAN 357-3273. Tel: 440-942-3200. FAX: 440-942-4312. *Br Mgr,* Deborah Mullen; E-mail: deborah.mullen@welibrary.info
Founded 1909. Circ 277,109
Library Holdings: High Interest/Low Vocabulary Bk Vols 90
Special Collections: Microfilm Coll; News-Herald Coll; Willoughby Historical Society Coll
Database Vendor: SirsiDynix
Open Mon-Thurs 9-9, Fri & Sat 9-5, Sun (Oct-April) 1-5
Friends of the Library Group
WILLOUGHBY HILLS BRANCH, 35400 Chardon Rd, Willoughby Hills, 44094. Tel: 440-942-3362. FAX: 440-942-3780. *Br Mgr,* Holly Ferkol
Founded 1985
Open Mon-Thurs 11-8, Sat 11-5
Friends of the Library Group
WILLOWICK BRANCH, 263 E 305th St, 44095, SAN 357-3303. Tel: 440-943-4151. FAX: 440-944-6901. *Br Mgr,* Mollie Burns; E-mail: mollie.burns@welibrary.info
Founded 1924. Circ 269,265
Library Holdings: High Interest/Low Vocabulary Bk Vols 56
Database Vendor: SirsiDynix
Open Mon-Thurs 9-9, Fri & Sat 9-5, Sun (Oct-April) 1-5
Friends of the Library Group

WILMINGTON

GL CLINTON COUNTY LAW LIBRARY*, 46 S South St, 45177. SAN 313-8062. Tel: 937-382-2428. FAX: 937-382-7632. E-mail: lclintoncounty@cinci.rr.com. Web Site: co.clinton.oh.us/courts/law-library. *Librn,* Mary Taylor
Founded 1905
Library Holdings: Bk Vols 25,000
Open Tues-Thurs 8-12 & 1-4

C WILMINGTON COLLEGE, Sheppard Arthur Watson Library, Pyle Ctr 1227, 1870 Quaker Way, 45177-2473. SAN 313-8070. Tel: 937-481-2345. Toll Free Tel: 800-341-9318. FAX: 937-383-8571. E-mail: library@wilmington.edu. Web Site: www2.wilmington.edu. *Dir,* Jean Mulhern, PhD; Tel; 937-481-2346, E-mail: jean_mulhern@wilmington.edu; *Head, Ref (Info Serv),* Patti Kinsinger; Tel: 937-481-2441, E-mail: patti_kinsinger@wilmington.edu; *Cataloger, Librn,* Lee Bowman; Tel: 937-481-2394; *Circ Mgr, Mgr, ILL,* Joni Streber; E-mail: joni_streber@wilmington.edu; *Mgr, Tech Serv,* Kathy Hatfield; Tel: 937-481-2398, E-mail: kathernh@wilmington.edu; *Media Ctr Mgr,* Mary Beth Corcoran; Tel: 937-481-2350, E-mail: mediacenter@wilmington.edu. Subject Specialists: *Quaker res,* Patti Kinsinger; *Archives,* Lee Bowman; Staff 6 (MLS 3, Non-MLS 3)
Founded 1870. Enrl 1,350; Fac 76; Highest Degree: Bachelor
Library Holdings: e-books 250,000; e-journals 12,000; Electronic Media & Resources 140; Bk Titles 80,000; Bk Vols 110,000; Per Subs 100; Videos 2,500
Special Collections: College Archives; Peace Resources Center-Hiroshima & Nagasaki Memorial Coll; Quakers-Quakerism Coll, bks, ms, per. US Document Depository
Automation Activity & Vendor Info: (Acquisitions) Innovative Interfaces, Inc; (Cataloging) Innovative Interfaces, Inc; (Circulation) Innovative Interfaces, Inc; (Course Reserve) Innovative Interfaces, Inc; (ILL) OCLC; (OPAC) Innovative Interfaces, Inc; (Serials) Innovative Interfaces, Inc
Database Vendor: 3M Library Systems, ABC-CLIO, Agricola, Baker & Taylor, Brodart, Cinahl, CQ Press, EBSCO Discovery Service, EBSCOhost, Elsevier, Facts on File, H W Wilson, Innovative Interfaces, Inc, ISI Web of Knowledge, LearningExpress, LexisNexis, Medline, Mergent Online, OCLC FirstSearch, OHIONET, Project MUSE, PubMed, Safari Books Online, Sage, Springshare, LLC, Thomson - Web of Science, Wilson - Wilson Web
Wireless access
Function: 24/7 Online cat, Accessibility serv available based on individual needs, Archival coll, Audio & video playback equip for onsite use, AV serv, Computers for patron use, Copy machines, Doc delivery serv, e-mail serv, Electronic databases & coll, Fax serv, Free DVD rentals, Govt ref serv, Handicapped accessible, ILL available, Instruction & testing, Laminating, Magazines, Mail & tel request accepted, Microfiche/film & reading machines, Movies, Music CDs, Newsp ref libr, Online cat, Online info literacy tutorials on the web & in blackboard, Online searches, Orientations, Photocopying/Printing, Printer for laptops & handheld devices, Ref serv available, Ref serv in person, Scanner, Tax forms, Telephone ref, VHS videos, Video lending libr, Web-catalog, Wheelchair accessible
Partic in OCLC Online Computer Library Center, Inc; Ohio Private Academic Libraries (OPAL); OHIONET; Southwestern Ohio Council for Higher Education
Special Services for the Blind - Scanner for conversion & translation of mats
Open Mon-Thurs (Winter) 8am-11pm, Fri 8-5, Sat 1-5, Sun 6pm-11pm; Mon-Fri (Summer) 8-5
Restriction: Access at librarian's discretion, Authorized patrons, Authorized personnel only, Authorized scholars by appt, Borrowing requests are handled by ILL, Circ to mem only, External users must contact libr, In-house use for visitors, Non-circulating of rare bks, Off-site coll in storage - retrieval as requested, Pub use on premises, Registered patrons only, Researchers by appt only

P WILMINGTON PUBLIC LIBRARY OF CLINTON COUNTY*, 268 N South St, 45177-1696. SAN 313-8089. Tel: 937-382-2417. FAX: 937-382-1692. Web Site: www.wilmington.lib.oh.us. *Dir,* Nancy Ehas; E-mail: ehasna@oplin.org; Staff 4 (MLS 2, Non-MLS 2)
Founded 1899. Pop 42,000; Circ 170,061
Library Holdings: Audiobooks 1,476; AV Mats 8,669; Bks on Deafness & Sign Lang 37; CDs 1,341; DVDs 3,994; Large Print Bks 1,422; Bk Vols 46,886; Per Subs 40; Videos 1,858
Special Collections: Ohio Coll; Wilmington News-Journal
Subject Interests: Genealogy, Ohio
Automation Activity & Vendor Info: (Cataloging) Follett Software; (Circulation) Follett Software; (OPAC) Follett Software
Wireless access
Open Mon & Tues 10-8, Wed & Thurs 10-6, Sat 10-5
Friends of the Library Group

WOODSFIELD

P MONROE COUNTY DISTRICT LIBRARY*, 96 Home Ave, 43793. SAN 313-8100. Tel: 740-472-1954. FAX: 740-472-1110. E-mail: mcdl@oplin.org. Web Site: www.monroecounty.lib.oh.us. *Dir,* Kathy South; E-mail: southka@oplin.org
Founded 1939. Pop 15,180; Circ 145,000
Library Holdings: AV Mats 2,514; DVDs 500; Bk Vols 62,918; Per Subs 140; Talking Bks 1,100; Videos 2,014
Automation Activity & Vendor Info: (Acquisitions) SirsiDynix; (Cataloging) SirsiDynix; (Circulation) SirsiDynix; (OPAC) SirsiDynix; (Serials) EBSCO Online
Partic in SEO (Serving Every Ohioan) Library Center
Open Mon-Thurs 10-8, Fri & Sat 10-5
Bookmobiles: 1

WOOSTER

C THE COLLEGE OF WOOSTER LIBRARIES*, 1140 Beall Ave, 44691-2364. SAN 313-8119. Tel: 330-263-2442. Circulation Tel: 330-263-2137. Interlibrary Loan Service Tel: 330-263-2136. Reference Tel: 330-263-2096. Administration Tel: 330-263-2152. FAX: 330-263-2253. Web Site: www.wooster.edu/library/. *Dir,* Mark A Christel; Tel: 330-263-2483, E-mail: mchristel@wooster.edu; *Head, Circ, Media Serv,* Patti McVay-Gorrell; Tel: 330-263-2285, E-mail: pmcvay@wooster.edu; *Mgr, Ser,* Day Logan; Tel: 330-263-2130, E-mail: dlogan@wooster.edu; *Coll Mgr,* Jacob Koehler; Tel: 330-263-2487; *Presv Mgr,* Sue Dunlap; Tel: 330-263-2107, E-mail: sdunlap@wooster.edu; *Access & Res Serv Librn,* Mark Gooch; Tel: 330-263-2522, E-mail: mgooch@wooster.edu; *Res & Info Serv Librn,* Elys Kettling Law; Tel: 330-263-2443, E-mail: ekettling@wooster.edu; *Sci Librn,* Zachary Sharrow; *Spec Coll Librn,* Denise Monbarren; Tel: 330-263-2527, E-mail: dmonbarren@wooster.edu; *Admin Coordr,* Sharon Bodle; *Access Serv,* Julia Gustafson; Tel: 330-263-2315, E-mail: jgustafson@wooster.edu; *Acq Assoc,* Erin Christine; Tel: 330-263-2467; Staff 20 (MLS 8, Non-MLS 12)
Founded 1866. Enrl 1,826; Fac 140; Highest Degree: Bachelor
Library Holdings: AV Mats 23,761; Bk Titles 525,192; Bk Vols 622,273; Per Subs 1,195
Special Collections: 17th Century British Studies (Wallace Notestein Coll); American Politics (Paul O Peters Coll); Drama & Theatre (Gregg D Wolfe Memorial Library of the Theatre). US Document Depository
Automation Activity & Vendor Info: (Acquisitions) Innovative Interfaces, Inc; (Cataloging) Innovative Interfaces, Inc; (Circulation) Innovative Interfaces, Inc; (Course Reserve) Innovative Interfaces, Inc; (ILL) Innovative Interfaces, Inc; (Media Booking) Innovative Interfaces, Inc; (OPAC) Innovative Interfaces, Inc; (Serials) Innovative Interfaces, Inc
Database Vendor: Innovative Interfaces, Inc, OCLC FirstSearch, OVID Technologies, ProQuest, SerialsSolutions, YBP Library Services
Wireless access
Function: Res libr
Partic in OCLC Online Computer Library Center, Inc; Ohio Library & Information Network; OHIONET; The Five Colleges of Ohio
Special Services for the Blind - Assistive/Adapted tech devices, equip & products
Open Mon-Thurs (Winter) 8am-2am, Fri 8am-10pm, Sat 10-10, Sun Noon-1am; Mon-Fri (Summer) 8-5
Restriction: Open to pub for ref & circ; with some limitations
Friends of the Library Group

S OHIO AGRICULTURAL RESEARCH & DEVELOPMENT CENTER LIBRARY, 1680 Madison Ave, 44691-4096. SAN 313-8135. Tel: 330-263-3773. Interlibrary Loan Service Tel: 330-263-3690. FAX: 330-263-3689. E-mail: library_oardc@osu.edu. Web Site: www.oardc.ohio-state.edu/library. *Head Librn,* Constance Britton; E-mail: britton.4@osu.edu; Staff 2 (MLS 1, Non-MLS 1)
Founded 1892
Library Holdings: Bk Vols 69,742; Per Subs 250
Subject Interests: Sci related to agr
Automation Activity & Vendor Info: (Acquisitions) Innovative Interfaces, Inc; (Cataloging) OCLC; (Circulation) Innovative Interfaces, Inc; (ILL) OCLC ILLiad; (OPAC) Innovative Interfaces, Inc; (Serials) Innovative Interfaces, Inc
Database Vendor: Dialog
Wireless access
Partic in Council of Independent Colleges (CIC); OCLC Online Computer Library Center, Inc; Ohio Library & Information Network; OHIONET
Open Mon-Fri 8-5

GL WAYNE COUNTY LAW LIBRARY*, Wayne County Courthouse, 107 W Liberty St, 44691-4850. SAN 313-816X. Tel: 330-287-7721. E-mail: lawlib@sssnet.com. Web Site: www.waynelawlibrary.org. *Librn,* William B Weiss
Founded 1903
Library Holdings: Bk Vols 9,000
Open Mon-Fri 9-1

P WAYNE COUNTY PUBLIC LIBRARY*, 220 W Liberty St, 44691-3593. (Mail add: PO Box 1349, 44691-7086), SAN 357-3338. Tel: 330-262-0916. Circulation Tel: 330-804-4659. Reference Tel: 330-804-4666. FAX: 330-262-1352. Interlibrary Loan Service FAX: 330-804-4745. Reference FAX: 330-804-4747. Administration FAX: 330-262-2905. E-mail: getit@wcpl.info. Web Site: wcpl.info. *Dir,* Jennifer Shatzer; Tel: 330-262-0986, E-mail: jshatzer@wcpl.info; *Mgr, Ad Serv,* Becky Vaeth;

Tel: 330-804-4667, E-mail: rvaeth@wcpl.info; *Mgr, Ch Serv,* Barb Landers; Tel: 330-804-4664, E-mail: blanders@wcpl.info; *Circ Mgr,* Leslie Davenport; Tel: 330-804-4660, E-mail: ldavenport@wcpl.info; *IT & Fac Mgr,* David Tenney; Tel: 330-804-4684, E-mail: dtenney@wcpl.info; *Mgr, Tech Serv,* Stacey Baker; Tel: 330-804-4679, E-mail: sbaker@wcpl.info; *Br Coordr,* Rita Lowe; Tel: 330-804-4686, E-mail: rlowe@wcpl.info; *Fiscal Officer,* Katherine Long; Tel: 330-804-4680, E-mail: klong@wcpl.info; *Human Res,* Desiree Cutright; Tel: 330-804-4683, E-mail: dcutright@wcpl.info; Staff 76 (MLS 13.5, Non-MLS 62.5)
Founded 1897. Pop 103,658; Circ 2,033,725
Jan 2013-Dec 2013 Income (Main Library and Branch(s)) $4,986,817, State $2,731,428, County $1,759,980, Locally Generated Income $260,493, Other $234,916. Mats Exp $823,944, Books $499,349, Per/Ser (Incl. Access Fees) $86,163, Other Print Mats $4,665, AV Mat $169,136, Electronic Ref Mat (Incl. Access Fees) $42,280. Sal $2,203,125
Library Holdings: AV Mats 33,263; CDs 28,024; DVDs 30,680; e-books 115,779; Electronic Media & Resources 101; Bk Vols 319,091; Per Subs 822
Subject Interests: Genealogy, Local hist
Automation Activity & Vendor Info: (Acquisitions) SirsiDynix; (Cataloging) SirsiDynix; (Circulation) SirsiDynix; (ILL) SirsiDynix; (OPAC) SirsiDynix; (Serials) SirsiDynix
Database Vendor: Agricola, ALLDATA Online, BWI, EBSCOhost, Gale Cengage Learning, Newsbank, OCLC FirstSearch, OCLC WorldShare Interlibrary Loan, Overdrive, Inc, ProQuest, ReferenceUSA, ValueLine, Wilson - Wilson Web
Wireless access
Function: Art exhibits, Audiobks via web, Bk club(s), Bks on cassette, Bks on CD, CD-ROM, Children's prog, Computer training, Computers for patron use, Copy machines, Digital talking bks, Distance learning, e-mail serv, Electronic databases & coll, Exhibits, Free DVD rentals, Handicapped accessible, Holiday prog, Home delivery & serv to Sr ctr & nursing homes, Homebound delivery serv, ILL available, Magnifiers for reading, Mail & tel request accepted, Music CDs, Online cat, Online ref, Online searches, Outside serv via phone, mail, e-mail & web, OverDrive digital audio bks, Photocopying/Printing, Preschool outreach, Prog for adults, Prog for children & young adult, Pub access computers, Ref & res, Ref serv available, Ref serv in person, Senior computer classes, Senior outreach, Spoken cassettes & CDs, Spoken cassettes & DVDs, Story hour, Summer reading prog, Tax forms, Teen prog, VHS videos, Video lending libr, Web-catalog, Wheelchair accessible, Workshops
Publications: The Reader's Way (Newsletter)
Partic in CLEVNET; Northeast Ohio Regional Library System; Ohio Public Library Information Network
Special Services for the Deaf - Assistive tech; Bks on deafness & sign lang; Closed caption videos; Described encaptioned media prog; High interest/low vocabulary bks
Special Services for the Blind - Assistive/Adapted tech devices, equip & products; Audio mat; Bks available with recordings; Bks on cassette; Bks on CD; Cassette playback machines; Cassettes; Computer access aids; Descriptive video serv (DVS); Digital talking bk; Extensive large print coll; Home delivery serv; Internet workstation with adaptive software; Large print & cassettes; Large print bks; Large print bks & talking machines; Large screen computer & software; Low vision equip; Magnifiers; Recorded bks; Screen reader software; Sound rec; Talking bk serv referral; Talking bks & player equip; ZoomText magnification & reading software
Open Mon & Tues 9-8, Wed & Thurs 9-6, Fri & Sat 9-2
Friends of the Library Group
Branches: 6
CRESTON BRANCH, 116 S Main St, Creston, 44217. (Mail add: PO Box 396, Creston, 44217-0396), SAN 357-3397. Tel: 330-435-4204. FAX: 330-435-6279. *Br Mgr,* Amy Anderson; E-mail: aanderson@wcpl.info
Subject Interests: Local hist
Open Mon & Thurs 2-8, Wed, Fri & Sat 10-5
Friends of the Library Group
DALTON BRANCH, 127 S Church St, Dalton, 44618. (Mail add: PO Box 597, Dalton, 44618-0597), SAN 323-8342. Tel: 330-828-8486. FAX: 330-828-0255. *Br Mgr,* Teresa Jager; E-mail: tjager@wcpl.info
Founded 1989
Partic in CLEVNET
Open Mon, Tues & Thurs 10-8, Wed & Fri 10-5, Sat 10-2
Friends of the Library Group
DOYLESTOWN BRANCH, 169 N Portage St, Doylestown, 44230, SAN 357-3427. Tel: 330-658-4677. FAX: 330-658-4671. *Br Mgr,* Pat Pond; E-mail: ppond@wcpl.info
Open Mon & Thurs 2-8, Wed, Fri & Sat 10-5
Friends of the Library Group
RITTMAN BRANCH, 49 W Ohio Ave, Rittman, 44270, SAN 357-3451. Tel: 330-925-2761. FAX: 330-925-6217. *Br Mgr,* Martha Scaggs; E-mail: mscaggs@wcpl.info
Open Mon & Thurs 2-8, Wed, Fri & Sat 10-5
Friends of the Library Group
SHREVE BRANCH, 189 W McConkey St, Shreve, 44676-9301. (Mail add: PO Box 612, Shreve, 44676-0612), SAN 357-3362. Tel: 330-567-2219. FAX: 330-567-2791. *Br Mgr,* Nancy Fortune; E-mail: nfortune@wcpl.info
Subject Interests: Local hist
Open Mon & Thurs 2-8, Wed, Fri & Sat 10-5
Friends of the Library Group
WEST SALEM BRANCH, 99 E Buckeye St, West Salem, 44287. Tel: 419-853-4762. *Br Supvr,* Debbie Starcher; Fax: 419-853-4572, E-mail: dstarcher@wcpl.info
Open Tues 10-8, Wed 1-5, Thurs 12-8, Sat 10-2
Friends of the Library Group
Bookmobiles: 2. Mgr, Patti Stevic

WORTHINGTON

S WORTHINGTON HISTORICAL SOCIETY LIBRARY*, 50 W New England Ave, 43085-3536. SAN 327-5639. Tel: 614-885-1247. E-mail: info@worthingtonhistory.org. Web Site: www.worthingtonhistory.org. *Pres,* Jutta Catharine Pegues; E-mail: jcpegues@worthingtonhistory.org; *Coll Curator,* Sue Whitaker; E-mail: curator@worthingtonhistory.org; *Historian,* Virginia McCormick; E-mail: historian@worthingtonhistory.org
Founded 1955
Library Holdings: Bk Vols 5,500
Special Collections: Manuscript Colls
Subject Interests: Archives, Interior design, Local hist
Restriction: Open by appt only

P WORTHINGTON LIBRARIES, Old Worthington Library, 820 High St, 43085. SAN 313-8186. Tel: 614-807-2620. FAX: 614-807-2642. Web Site: www.worthingtonlibraries.org. *Dir,* Chuck Gibson; Tel: 614-807-2601, E-mail: cgibson@worthingtonlibraries.org; *Dep Dir,* Monica Baughman; Tel: 614-807-2602, E-mail: mbaughman@worthingtonlibraries.org; *Dir, Commun Engagement,* Lisa Fuller; Tel: 614-807-2604, E-mail: lfuller@worthingtonlibraries.org; *Bus Mgr/Fiscal Officer,* Margaret Doone; Tel: 614-807-2609, E-mail: mdoone@worthingtonlibraries.org; *Libr Mgr,* Debbie Zimmerman; Tel: 614-807-2622, Fax: 614-807-2659, E-mail: dzimmerman@worthingtonlibraries.org; *Tech Serv Mgr,* Anne Reilly; Tel: 614-807-2631, E-mail: areilly@worthingtonlibraries.org; Staff 99 (MLS 28, Non-MLS 71)
Founded 1925. Pop 73,586; Circ 3,556,803
Library Holdings: Bk Vols 410,843
Special Collections: Worthington History Coll. US Document Depository
Subject Interests: Local authors
Database Vendor: OCLC FirstSearch
Wireless access
Publications: A Page Turner (Newsletter)
Partic in Central Library Consortium (CLC)
Friends of the Library Group
Branches: 2
NORTHWEST LIBRARY, 2280 Hard Rd, Columbus, 43235. Tel: 614-807-2650. FAX: 614-807-2659. *Libr Mgr,* Jeff Regensburger; Tel: 614-807-2652, E-mail: jregensburger@worthingtonlibraries.org
WORTHINGTON PARK LIBRARY, 1389 Worthington Centre Dr, 43085. *Libr Mgr,* Amy Brown; Tel: 614-807-2642, Fax: 614-807-2676, E-mail: abrown@worthingtonlibraries.org

WRIGHT-PATTERSON AFB

AM FRANZELLO AEROMEDICAL LIBRARY*, School of Aerospace Medicine, USAFSAM/EDL, 2510 Fifth St, Bldg 840 Rm 423, 45433. SAN 330-1893, *Chief Librn,* Greg Bidwell; Staff 2 (MLS 2)
Founded 1963
Library Holdings: CDs 70; Bk Titles 5,000; Per Subs 150
Subject Interests: Acoustics, Aviation med, Med, Optics, Psychol, Statistics
Automation Activity & Vendor Info: (Acquisitions) SirsiDynix; (Cataloging) SirsiDynix; (Circulation) SirsiDynix; (ILL) OCLC; (OPAC) SirsiDynix; (Serials) SirsiDynix
Partic in Docline; Fedlink
Open Mon-Fri 7-4

UNITED STATES AIR FORCE

A THE D'AZZO RESEARCH LIBRARY*, AFIT/ENWL, 2950 Hobson Way, Bldg 642, 45433-7765, SAN 357-3664. Tel: 937-255-6565, Ext 4207. Circulation Tel: 937-255-3005. Interlibrary Loan Service Tel: 937-255-6565, Ext 4227. FAX: 937-656-7746. Web Site: www.afit.edu/library. *Dir,* Laurene E Zaporozhetz; Tel: 937-255-6565, Ext 4216, E-mail: laurene.zaporozhetz@afit.edu; Staff 15 (MLS 9, Non-MLS 6)
Founded 1946
Oct 2012-Sept 2013 Income $2,455,545. Mats Exp $1,248,246, Books $25,333, Per/Ser (Incl. Access Fees) $1,219,043, Micro $452, AV Mat $204

Library Holdings: CDs 149; DVDs 1,462; e-journals 213; Microforms 1,225,783; Bk Vols 138,808; Per Subs 574
Special Collections: Air Force Institute of Technology Theses & Dissertations
Subject Interests: Astronautics, Computers, Eng, Math, Mil logistics
Partic in OCLC Online Computer Library Center, Inc; Southwestern Ohio Council for Higher Education
Open Mon-Thurs 8-6, Fri 8-5

A NATIONAL AIR & SPACE INTELLIGENCE CENTER RESEARCH CENTER*, 4180 Watson Way, 45433-5648, SAN 357-363X. Tel: 937-257-3531. FAX: 937-257-0122. *Chief, Acq & Res Flight,* Thomas Rohmiller; E-mail: thomas.rohmiller@wpafb.af.mil; *Ref,* Joseph Burke; E-mail: joseph.burke@wpafb.af.mil; Staff 15 (MLS 9, Non-MLS 6)
Automation Activity & Vendor Info: (Cataloging) EOS International; (Circulation) EOS International; (ILL) OCLC; (OPAC) EOS International

A WRIGHT-PATTERSON AIR FORCE BASE LIBRARY FL2300*, 88 MSG/SVMG, Bldg 1226, 5435 Hemlock St, 45433-5420, SAN 357-3575. Tel: 937-257-4340, 937-257-4815. FAX: 937-656-1776. Web Site: www.88thservices.com/library.htm. *Chief Librn,* Nathaniel Laubner; *Sr Libr Tech,* Deborah Thomas; *Ref Librn,* Amanda Lindsay; Staff 8 (MLS 2, Non-MLS 6)
Founded 1942
Library Holdings: AV Mats 4,600; Bk Titles 36,000; Per Subs 500
Special Collections: Air War Coll; Chief of Staff of the Air Force Reading List; Total Quality Management Coll
Subject Interests: Mil hist
Automation Activity & Vendor Info: (Acquisitions) SirsiDynix; (Cataloging) SirsiDynix; (Circulation) SirsiDynix; (OPAC) SirsiDynix
Database Vendor: Gale Cengage Learning, OCLC FirstSearch, SirsiDynix
Function: AV serv, ILL available, Photocopying/Printing, Prog for children & young adult, Summer reading prog
Open Tues-Thurs 10-9, Fri 10-6, Sat 10-5, Sun 11-6
Restriction: Access for corporate affiliates

A AIR FORCE RESEARCH LABORATORY, WRIGHT RESEARCH SITE TECHNICAL LIBRARY*, Det 1 AFRL/WSC, Bldg 642, Rm 1300, 2950 Hobson Way, 45433-7765, SAN 357-3605. Tel: 937-255-5511. Interlibrary Loan Service Tel: 937-255-5511, Ext 4262. Reference Tel: 937-255-5511, Ext 4238. FAX: 937-656-7746. E-mail: afrl.wsc.library@wpafb.af.mil. Web Site: www.afrl.af.mil/wrslibrary. *Dir,* Annette Sheppard; Tel: 937-255-5511, Ext 4205; *Ref,* Carol Reed; Tel: 937-255-5511, Ext 4271; Staff 11 (MLS 5, Non-MLS 6)
Founded 1919
Library Holdings: Bk Vols 84,000; Per Subs 170
Special Collections: Lahm-Chandler Coll of Aeronautica
Subject Interests: Aeronautical res, Aerospace med, Avionics, Co-applications to aeronaut, Computer sci, Eng, Flight dynamics, Mat, Propulsion
Database Vendor: Dialog, LexisNexis, OCLC FirstSearch, SirsiDynix
Function: ILL available

G UNITED STATES DEPARTMENT OF DEFENSE*, Defense Institute of Security Assistance Management Library, 2475 K St, Rm 315, Bldg 52, 45433-8258. SAN 357-3516. Tel: 937-255-5567. FAX: 937-255-8258. Web Site: disam.osd.mil. *Dir,* Patricia A White; Tel: 937-255-9211, E-mail: patricia.white@disam.dsca.mil; *Acq, ILL,* Brenda Meadows; Tel: 937-255-3030, E-mail: brenda.meadows@disam.dsca.mil; Staff 2 (MLS 1, Non-MLS 1)
Founded 1977
Library Holdings: DVDs 50; Bk Vols 14,000; Per Subs 221; Videos 750
Special Collections: Human Rights; Regional Studies; Security Assistance
Subject Interests: Polit sci
Database Vendor: TLC (The Library Corporation)
Function: Govt ref serv, ILL available, Ref serv available, Telephone ref
Partic in OCLC Online Computer Library Center, Inc
Open Mon-Fri 7-7

XENIA

GL GREENE COUNTY LAW LIBRARY*, Court House, 3rd Flr, 45 N Detroit St, 45385. SAN 313-8194. Tel: 937-562-5115. FAX: 937-562-5116. *Librn,* Nancy Hedges; E-mail: nhedges@co.greene.oh.us
Library Holdings: Bk Vols 12,000; Per Subs 25
Database Vendor: Westlaw
Open Mon-Fri 8-4
Restriction: Open to pub for ref only

P GREENE COUNTY PUBLIC LIBRARY*, 76 E Market St, 45385-3100. (Mail add: PO Box 520, 45385-0520), SAN 357-3729. Tel: 937-352-4000. FAX: 937-372-4673. Web Site: www.greenelibrary.info. *Dir,* Karl Colon; Tel: 937-352-4000, Ext 1201, E-mail: kcolon@gcpl.lib.oh.us; *Dep Dir,* Elizabeth Rumple; *AV,* Steve Raiteri; Tel: 937-352-4000, Ext 1233; *Outreach Serv Librn, Youth Serv,* Kay Webster; Tel: 937-352-4000, Ext 1231; Staff 10 (MLS 6, Non-MLS 4)
Founded 1878. Pop 157,000; Circ 2,279,973
Jan 2006-Dec 2006 Income (Main Library and Branch(s)) $9,770,980, State $5,374,459, County $3,680,822, Locally Generated Income $175,000, Other $250,000. Mats Exp $1,536,252, Books $1,063,246, Per/Ser (Incl. Access Fees) $65,000, AV Mat $328,006, Electronic Ref Mat (Incl. Access Fees) $80,000. Sal $3,555,198
Library Holdings: AV Mats 83,771; Large Print Bks 7,696; Bk Titles 220,100; Bk Vols 547,729; Per Subs 635
Subject Interests: Local hist
Automation Activity & Vendor Info: (Acquisitions) Innovative Interfaces, Inc - Millenium; (Cataloging) Innovative Interfaces, Inc - Millenium; (Circulation) Innovative Interfaces, Inc - Millenium; (ILL) Innovative Interfaces, Inc - Millenium; (OPAC) Innovative Interfaces, Inc; (Serials) Innovative Interfaces, Inc - Millenium
Database Vendor: EBSCOhost, Gale Cengage Learning, Innovative Interfaces, Inc, OCLC FirstSearch
Wireless access
Partic in Miami Valley Librs; OCLC Online Computer Library Center, Inc; Ohio Public Library Information Network; OHIONET
Special Services for the Blind - Bks available with recordings; Bks on cassette; Bks on CD; Computer with voice synthesizer for visually impaired persons; Descriptive video serv (DVS); Home delivery serv; Talking bks
Open Mon-Thurs 9-9, Fri & Sat 9-6, Sun (Sept-May) 1-5
Friends of the Library Group
Branches: 7
BEAVERCREEK COMMUNITY LIBRARY, 3618 Dayton-Xenia Rd, Beavercreek, 45432-2884, SAN 357-3753. Tel: 937-352-4001. FAX: 937-426-0481. *Br Mgr,* Jennifer Ventling; E-mail: jventling@gcpl.lib.oh.us
Library Holdings: AV Mats 18,982; Bk Vols 136,367
Open Mon-Thurs 10-9, Fri & Sat 10-6, Sun (Sept-May) 1-5
Friends of the Library Group
CEDARVILLE COMMUNITY LIBRARY, 20 S Miller St, Cedarville, 45314-8556. (Mail add: PO Box 26, Cedarville, 45314-0026), SAN 357-3818. Tel: 937-352-4006. FAX: 937-766-2847. *Br Mgr,* Diane Hudson
Library Holdings: AV Mats 7,910; Bk Vols 27,817
Open Mon, Tues & Thurs 12:30-8:30, Wed, Fri & Sat 10-6
Friends of the Library Group
FAIRBORN COMMUNITY LIBRARY, One E Main St, Fairborn, 45324-4798, SAN 357-3842. Tel: 937-878-9383. FAX: 937-878-0374. *Br Mgr,* Robin Weinstein
Library Holdings: AV Mats 13,610; Bk Vols 103,277
Open Mon-Thurs 10-9, Fri & Sat 10-6, Sun (Sept-May) 1-5
Friends of the Library Group
JAMESTOWN COMMUNITY LIBRARY, 86B Seaman Dr, Jamestown, 45335, SAN 357-3877. Tel: 937-352-4005. FAX: 937-675-6605. *Br Mgr,* Paul Gregor
Library Holdings: AV Mats 7,662; Bk Vols 32,055
Open Mon, Tues & Thurs 12:30-8:30, Wed, Fri & Sat 10-6
WINTERS-BELLBROOK COMMUNITY LIBRARY, 57 W Franklin St, Bellbrook, 45305-1904, SAN 357-3788. Tel: 937-352-4004. FAX: 937-848-3074. *Br Mgr,* JoEllen Fannin; Staff 3.5 (MLS 2, Non-MLS 1.5)
Founded 1906
Library Holdings: AV Mats 6,276; Bk Vols 33,887
Open Mon, Tues & Thurs 12-8, Wed 10-8, Fri 10-6, Sat 10-5
Friends of the Library Group
XENIA COMMUNITY LIBRARY, 76 E Market St, 45385-0520. Tel: 937-352-4000. FAX: 937-376-5523. *Head Librn,* Travis Bautz; E-mail: tbautz@gcpl.lib.oh.us
Library Holdings: AV Mats 19,820; Bk Vols 138,659
Open Mon, Tues & Thurs 12-8, Wed 10-8, Fri 10-6, Sat 10-5, Sun (Sept-May) 1-5
Friends of the Library Group
YELLOW SPRINGS COMMUNITY LIBRARY, 415 Xenia Ave, Yellow Springs, 45387-1837, SAN 357-3931. Tel: 937-352-4003. FAX: 937-767-2044. *Br Mgr,* Connie Collett
Library Holdings: AV Mats 9,511; Bk Vols 48,122
Open Mon-Thurs 10-9, Fri & Sat 10-6, Sun (Sept-May) 1-5
Friends of the Library Group
Bookmobiles: 1. Coordr, Kay Webster. Bk titles 6,792

YELLOW SPRINGS

C ANTIOCH COLLEGE*, Olive Kettering Memorial Library, One Morgan Pl, 45387-1694. SAN 313-8216. Tel: 937-769-1238. Interlibrary Loan Service Tel: 937-769-1236. Reference Tel: 937-769-1240. FAX: 937-769-1239. Web Site: www.antiochcollege.org/kettering_library.html. *Dir, Libr & Info Serv,* Jim M Kapoun; *Tech Serv Librn,* Ritch Kerns; E-mail: rkerns@antiochcollege.org; *Archivist,* Scott Sanders; Tel: 973-286-5534, E-mail: ssanders@antiochcollege.org; Staff 5 (MLS 2, Non-MLS 3)
Founded 1852. Enrl 110; Fac 13; Highest Degree: Bachelor
Jul 2011-Jun 2012 Income $551,893. Mats Exp $108,215, Books $34,693, Per/Ser (Incl. Access Fees) $30,130, Micro $213, AV Equip $9,848, AV

Mat $4,086, Electronic Ref Mat (Incl. Access Fees) $22,429, Presv $6,816. Sal $293,424 (Prof $158,826)
Library Holdings: AV Mats 6,651; Bks on Deafness & Sign Lang 20; e-books 17,536; Bk Titles 194,203; Bk Vols 295,169; Per Subs 403
Special Collections: Antioch hist; Arthur Morgan Coll, doc, files; Horace Mann (Robert Straker Coll), bks, doc. Oral History
Automation Activity & Vendor Info: (Acquisitions) Innovative Interfaces, Inc; (Cataloging) Innovative Interfaces, Inc; (Circulation) Innovative Interfaces, Inc; (Course Reserve) Innovative Interfaces, Inc; (ILL) Innovative Interfaces, Inc; (Media Booking) Innovative Interfaces, Inc; (OPAC) Innovative Interfaces, Inc; (Serials) Innovative Interfaces, Inc
Database Vendor: OHIONET
Wireless access
Partic in OCLC Online Computer Library Center, Inc; Ohio Library & Information Network; Ohio Private Academic Libraries (OPAL); OHIONET; Southwestern Ohio Council for Higher Education
Open Mon-Wed 8:30-8, Thurs 8:30am-9pm, Fri 8:30-5, Sun 1-5

YOUNGSTOWN

S BUTLER INSTITUTE OF AMERICAN ART, Hopper Research Library, 524 Wick Ave, 44502. SAN 313-8259. Tel: 330-743-1711. FAX: 330-743-9567. E-mail: library@butlerart.com. Web Site: www.butlerart.com. *Librn,* Jean Shreffler; Staff 2 (Non-MLS 2)
Founded 1986
Library Holdings: Bk Titles 5,900; Bk Vols 6,000
Special Collections: American Colonial to Contemporary Art, oils, watercolors, drawings, original prints; Sculpture & Ceramics
Subject Interests: Am art, Artists
Restriction: Mem only, Non-circulating to the pub, Open by appt only

M FORUM HEALTH-WESTERN RESERVE HEALTHCARE*, Northside Medical Center Library, 500 Gypsy Lane, 44501. Tel: 330-884-3476. FAX: 330-884-3494. *Librn,* Dan Dunlany
Library Holdings: e-journals 200; Bk Vols 1,600
Automation Activity & Vendor Info: (Circulation) Innovative Interfaces, Inc; (OPAC) Innovative Interfaces, Inc; (Serials) Innovative Interfaces, Inc
Database Vendor: Cinahl, Medline
Wireless access
Open Mon-Fri 8-4:30

L MAHONING LAW LIBRARY ASSOCIATION*, Courthouse 4th Flr, 120 Market St, 44503-1752. SAN 313-8267. Tel: 330-740-2295. Circulation Tel: 330-740-2295, Ext 7780. Reference Tel: 330-740-2295, Ext 7782. FAX: 330-744-1406. E-mail: mlladir@mahoninglawlibrary.org. Web Site: www.mahoninglawlibrary.org. *Librn,* Anna E Paczelt; Staff 5 (MLS 1, Non-MLS 4)
Founded 1906
Library Holdings: Bk Vols 25,000; Per Subs 140
Special Collections: Ohio Legal Journals. State Document Depository
Subject Interests: Mahoning County legal mat, Ohio, Pa law, Selected city ordinances
Automation Activity & Vendor Info: (Cataloging) Sydney; (Circulation) Sydney; (Media Booking) Sydney; (Serials) Sydney
Open Mon-Fri 8-4:30

P PUBLIC LIBRARY OF YOUNGSTOWN & MAHONING COUNTY*, 305 Wick Ave, 44503. SAN 357-3966. Tel: 330-744-8636. FAX: 330-744-3355. Administration FAX: 330-744-2258. TDD: 330-744-7211. Web Site: www.libraryvisit.org. *Exec Dir,* Heidi M Daniel; E-mail: hdaniel@libraryvisit.org; *Communications & Pub Relations Dir,* Janet S Loew; E-mail: jloew@libraryvisit.org; *Develop Dir,* Deborah Liptak; E-mail: dliptak@libraryvisit.org; *Human Res Dir,* Ruth Bradshaw; E-mail: rbradshaw@libraryvisit.org; *Dir, Tech Serv,* Gary Simon; E-mail: gsimon@libraryvisit.org; *Syst Adminr,* Tom Casey; E-mail: tcasey@libraryvisit.org; *Mgr, Main Libr & Staff Develop,* Diane Vicarel; E-mail: dvicarel@libraryvisit.org; *Mgr, Programming & Youth Serv,* Josephine Nolfi; E-mail: jnolfi@libraryvisit.org; *Mgr, Pub Serv,* Deborah McCullough; E-mail: dmc@libraryvisit.org; *Fiscal Officer,* Susan Merriman; E-mail: sue@libraryvisit.org; *Dep Fiscal Officer,* Tina McBane; E-mail: tmcbane@libraryvisit.org; *Br Mgr,* Kathy Austrino; E-mail: kaustrino@libraryvisit.org; *Br Mgr,* Betsy Ford; *Br Mgr,* Linda Kucalaba; *Br Mgr,* Karen Merritt; *Br Mgr,* Barbara Smith; E-mail: bsmith@libraryvisit.org; *Br Mgr,* Pamela Witte; E-mail: pwitte@libraryvisit.org; Staff 52.8 (MLS 52.2, Non-MLS 0.6)
Founded 1880. Pop 237,270; Circ 1,720,006
Jan 2010-Dec 2010 Income (Main Library and Branch(s)) $11,540,255, State $7,905,562, Federal $48,023, County $3,090,563, Locally Generated Income $496,107. Mats Exp $1,553,981, Books $817,706, Per/Ser (Incl. Access Fees) $100,000, Micro $37,500, AV Mat $313,775, Electronic Ref Mat (Incl. Access Fees) $285,000. Sal $5,838,750 (Prof $2,269,678)
Library Holdings: Audiobooks 21,121; CDs 13,342; DVDs 48,169; e-books 10,413; Large Print Bks 19,652; Bk Vols 262,070; Per Subs 314; Talking Bks 25,209; Videos 4,873
Special Collections: US Document Depository
Subject Interests: Genealogy
Automation Activity & Vendor Info: (Acquisitions) Innovative Interfaces, Inc; (Cataloging) Innovative Interfaces, Inc; (Circulation) Innovative Interfaces, Inc; (OPAC) Innovative Interfaces, Inc
Database Vendor: Bowker, EBSCOhost, Evanced Solutions, Inc, Facts on File, Foundation Center, Gale Cengage Learning, Greenwood Publishing Group, LearningExpress, OCLC FirstSearch, Oxford Communications, ProQuest, ReferenceUSA, Standard & Poor's
Wireless access
Publications: It's Happening This Month
Partic in OCLC Online Computer Library Center, Inc; OHIONET
Open Mon-Thurs 9-9, Fri & Sat 9-5:30
Friends of the Library Group
Branches: 14
AUSTINTOWN, 600 S Raccoon Rd, 44515, SAN 357-3990. *Br Mgr,* Ollie McCurdy
Library Holdings: Bk Vols 63,506
Open Mon-Thurs 9-9, Fri & Sat 9-5:30, Sun (Sept-May) 1-5
Friends of the Library Group
BOARDMAN, 7680 Glenwood Ave, 44512, SAN 357-4024. *Br Mgr,* Anne Martini
Library Holdings: Bk Vols 79,455
Open Mon-Thurs 9-9, Fri & Sat 9-5:30, Sun (Sept-May) 1-5
Friends of the Library Group
BROWNLEE WOODS, 4010 Sheridan Rd, 44514, SAN 357-4059.
Library Holdings: Bk Vols 27,571
Open Mon-Wed, Fri & Sat 10-6
Friends of the Library Group
CAMPBELL BRANCH, 374 Sanderson Ave, Campbell, 44405, SAN 357-4083.
Library Holdings: Bk Vols 19,664
Open Mon & Wed-Sat 10-6
Friends of the Library Group
CANFIELD BRANCH, 43 W Main St, Canfield, 44406, SAN 357-4113.
Library Holdings: Bk Vols 35,188
Open Mon & Tues 9-9, Wed-Sat 9-5:30
Friends of the Library Group
EAST, 430 Early Rd, 44505, SAN 357-4148.
Library Holdings: Bk Vols 13,214
Open Mon-Wed 10-8, Thurs & Sat 10-6
Friends of the Library Group
GREENFORD BRANCH, 7441 W South Range Rd, Greenford, 44422, SAN 369-7835.
Library Holdings: Bk Vols 7,462
Open Tues-Thurs 10-6
Friends of the Library Group
NEWPORT, 3730 Market St, 44507, SAN 357-4415.
Library Holdings: Bk Vols 30,445
Open Mon-Wed 10-8, Thurs-Sat 10-6
Friends of the Library Group
POLAND BRANCH, 311 S Main St, Poland, 44514, SAN 357-4326.
Library Holdings: Bk Vols 70,370
Open Mon-Thurs 9-9, Fri & Sat 9-5:30, Sun (Sept-May) 1-5
Friends of the Library Group
SEBRING BRANCH, 195 W Ohio Ave, Sebring, 44672, SAN 357-4385, Toll Free Tel: 877-715-1233 (Sebring only).
Library Holdings: Bk Vols 25,886
Open Mon-Thurs & Sat 9-5:30
Friends of the Library Group
SPRINGFIELD BRANCH, 10418 Main St, New Middletown, 44442, SAN 369-7851.
Library Holdings: Bk Vols 12,872
Open Mon-Thurs & Sat 10-6
Friends of the Library Group
STRUTHERS, 95 Poland Ave, 44471, SAN 357-444X.
Library Holdings: Bk Vols 31,651
Open Tues-Sat 10-6
Friends of the Library Group
TRI-LAKES BRANCH, 13820 Mahoning Ave, North Jackson, 44451.
Open Mon, Wed, Thurs & Sat 10-6, Tues 10-8
WEST, 2815 Mahoning Ave, 44509, SAN 357-4350.
Library Holdings: Bk Vols 40,300
Open Mon-Thurs & Sat 10-6
Friends of the Library Group

M SAINT ELIZABETH HEALTH CENTER, Medical Library, 1044 Belmont Ave, 44501-1790. SAN 357-4504. Tel: 330-480-3039. FAX: 330-480-3044. *Dir, Med Libr,* Dr Kimbroe Carter; E-mail: kjcarter@mercy.com; *Librn,* Lori Gawdyda; Tel: 330-480-3589, Fax: 330-480-7977, E-mail: lori_gawdyda@mercy.com; Staff 2 (MLS 1, Non-MLS 1)
Founded 1911
Library Holdings: Bk Titles 3,307; Per Subs 66
Subject Interests: Med, Surgery
Open Mon-Fri 7:30-4

C YOUNGSTOWN STATE UNIVERSITY*, William F Maag Jr Library, One University Plaza, 44555-0001. SAN 313-8291. Tel: 330-941-3675. Circulation Tel: 330-941-3678. Interlibrary Loan Service Tel: 330-941-1721. Reference Tel: 330-941-3686. FAX: 330-941-3734. E-mail: library@cc.ysu.edu. Web Site: www.maag.ysu.edu. *Exec Dir,* Position Currently Open; *Head, Access Serv, Interim Co-Dir, Mgr, Libr Operations,* Ana Torres; Tel: 330-941-1717; *Assoc Dir, Info Serv, Interim Co-Dir,* Jeffrey Trimble; Tel: 330-941-2483, E-mail: jtrimble@cc.ysu.edu; *Assoc Ref Librn,* George F Heller, Jr; E-mail: gfheller@ysu.edu; *Acq Librn,* John Popadak; Tel: 330-941-3679, E-mail: jepopadak@ysu.edu; *Bus & Econ Librn,* Christine Adams; Tel: 330-941-3680, E-mail: cmadams02@ysu.edu; *Cat Librn/Interim Head Coll Serv,* Kevin Whitfield; Tel: 330-941-2922, E-mail: kjwhitfield@ysu.edu; *Curric Res Ctr Librn,* Alyssa Annico; *Health Sci Librn,* Maria Barefoot; Tel: 330-941-3681, E-mail: mrbarefoot@ysu.edu; *Multimedia Ctr Librn,* Scott Pfitzinger; *Sci/Eng Librn,* Cynthia Harrison; E-mail: clharrison@ysu.edu; *Info Literacy & Assessment Mgr,* Rebecca K Roberts; Tel: 330-941-1720, E-mail: rkroberts@ysu.edu; *Micro, Ser,* Robert D Ault; Tel: 330-941-1719, E-mail: rdault@ysu.edu; Staff 38 (MLS 17, Non-MLS 21)
Founded 1931. Enrl 15,194; Highest Degree: Doctorate
Library Holdings: Bk Titles 656,990; Bk Vols 792,673; Per Subs 1,344
Special Collections: Early Americana. Oral History; US Document Depository
Subject Interests: Bus, Educ, Mgt, Sci tech
Automation Activity & Vendor Info: (Acquisitions) Innovative Interfaces, Inc; (Cataloging) Innovative Interfaces, Inc; (Circulation) Innovative Interfaces, Inc; (Course Reserve) Innovative Interfaces, Inc; (ILL) Innovative Interfaces, Inc; (OPAC) Innovative Interfaces, Inc; (Serials) Innovative Interfaces, Inc
Database Vendor: EBSCOhost, Innovative Interfaces, Inc, JSTOR, LexisNexis, Newsbank, OCLC FirstSearch, OCLC WorldShare Interlibrary Loan, OVID Technologies, ProQuest, ReferenceUSA, Wilson - Wilson Web
Wireless access
Function: ILL available, Res libr
Partic in NE Ohio Major Acad & Res Librs; Northeast Ohio Regional Library System; OCLC Online Computer Library Center, Inc; Ohio Library & Information Network; OHIONET
Open Mon-Thurs (Fall & Spring) 7:30am-10pm, Fri 7:30-5, Sat 9-5, Sun 1-9; Mon-Thurs (Summer) 7:30am-9pm, Fri 7:30-5, Sat 9-5
Friends of the Library Group

ZANESFIELD

S DR EARL S SLOAN LIBRARY*, 2817 Sandusky St, 43360. (Mail add: PO Box 116, 43360-0116), SAN 374-5759. Tel: 937-592-8343. FAX: 937-592-6474. *Interim Dir, Librn,* Polly Bargar; E-mail: bargarpo@oplin.org; Staff 3 (MLS 1, Non-MLS 2)
Founded 1914
Jan 2005-Dec 2005 Income $85,451. Mats Exp $8,995, Books $6,464, Per/Ser (Incl. Access Fees) $546, AV Mat $748, Electronic Ref Mat (Incl. Access Fees) $1,237. Sal $28,133
Library Holdings: AV Mats 297; Large Print Bks 90; Bk Titles 5,386; Bk Vols 5,390; Per Subs 38
Special Collections: Local Newpaper Originals, 1874-1876; Original Cases, County Historical Society; T & OC Train Depot Photos, Logan County
Publications: Newsletter
Partic in NORWELD; Ohio Libr Coun; Ohio Public Library Information Network
Open Mon, Tues & Thurs 1-7, Wed & Fri 1-5, Sat 10-1

ZANESVILLE

S MUSKINGUM COUNTY GENEALOGICAL SOCIETY LIBRARY*, Muskingum County Chapter OGS Library, c/o John McIntire Public Library, 220 N Fifth St, Second Flr, 43701-3508. (Mail add: PO Box 2427, 43702-2427), SAN 313-8321. Tel: 740-453-0391, Ext 139. FAX: 740-455-6357. Web Site: mccgogs.org. *Libr Dir,* Sandie Plymire
Founded 1975
Library Holdings: Bk Vols 5,000; Per Subs 12
Special Collections: Early Muskingum County Newspapers, micro; Family Histories; Genealogical Society Newsletters; History (Professor Kline Coll), rpts; Marriage & Cemetary Records; Muskingum County & Surrounding Counties Genealogical Materials; Muskingum County History & Genealogy; Norris Schneider Coll, mss; Passenger & Immigration Lists Indexes, Naturalizations, Local Probate Court Records on microfilm, Maps, Atlases, Ancestor Chart File; United States Wars
Publications: books on county marriages, cemeteries, county courthouse dockets; The Muskingum (Monthly Newsletter)
Open Mon & Fri 9-5, Wed 9-8, Sat 9-1

GL MUSKINGUM COUNTY LAW LIBRARY*, 22 N Fifth St, 43701. SAN 313-833X. Tel: 740-455-7154. FAX: 740-588-4362.
Library Holdings: Bk Vols 6,000

P MUSKINGUM COUNTY LIBRARY SYSTEM*, 220 N Fifth St, 43701-3587. SAN 357-4563. Tel: 740-453-0391. FAX: 740-455-6937. Web Site: www.muskingumlibrary.org. *Dir,* Sandi Plymire; Tel: 740-453-0391, Ext 129; *Customer Serv Mgr,* Blair Tom; Tel: 740-453-0391, Ext 131, E-mail: blair@muskingumlibrary.org; *Mgr, Human Res,* Lynn Mercer; Tel: 740-453-0391, Ext 133, E-mail: lynnm@muskingumlibrary.org; *Tech Mgr,* Christy Clark; Tel: 740-453-0391, Ext 122, E-mail: christy@muskingumlibrary.org; *Head, Adult Serv,* Linda Hatfield; Tel: 740-453-0391, Ext 132, E-mail: linda@muskingumlibrary.org; *Ch Serv,* Cheryl West; Tel: 740-453-0391, Ext 115, E-mail: cherylw@muskingumlibrary.org; *Fiscal Officer,* Stacey Russell; Tel: 740-453-0391, Ext 130, E-mail: stacey@muskingumlibrary.org; Staff 8 (MLS 8)
Founded 1903. Pop 85,579; Circ 833,805
Jan 2008-Dec 2008 Income (Main Library and Branch(s)) $3,455,918, State $3,284,102, Locally Generated Income $171,816
Library Holdings: Audiobooks 8,498; AV Mats 2,530; CDs 9,287; DVDs 19,478; Bk Vols 259,915; Per Subs 185; Videos 1,338
Special Collections: Business & Industry; History (Ohio Coll); Zanesville & Muskingum County History
Automation Activity & Vendor Info: (Acquisitions) TLC (The Library Corporation); (Cataloging) TLC (The Library Corporation); (Circulation) TLC (The Library Corporation)
Wireless access
Publications: Newsletter
Partic in OHIONET
Friends of the Library Group
Branches: 5
DRESDEN BRANCH, 816 Main St, Dresden, 43821, SAN 357-4598. Tel: 740-754-1003. *Br Mgr,* Tracy Tom
Circ 70,082
Friends of the Library Group
DUNCAN FALLS-PHILO BRANCH, 222 Main St, Duncan Falls, 43734. (Mail add: PO Box 472, Duncan Falls, 43734), SAN 373-8515. Tel: 740-674-7100. *Br Mgr,* Kathy Kirkbride
Circ 49,273
Friends of the Library Group
NEW CONCORD BRANCH, 77 W Main St, New Concord, 43762, SAN 357-4652. Tel: 740-826-4184. *Br Mgr,* Carmaline Sturtz
Circ 72,358
Friends of the Library Group
ROSEVILLE BRANCH, 41 N Main, Roseville, 43777, SAN 357-4687. Tel: 740-697-0237. *Br Mgr,* Juanita Kinney
Circ 39,266
SOUTH BRANCH, 2530 Maysville Pike, South Zanesville, 43701, SAN 357-4717. Tel: 740-454-1511. *Br Mgr,* Leandra Leffel
Circ 73,603
Friends of the Library Group

C OHIO UNIVERSITY-ZANESVILLE/ZANE STATE COLLEGE*, Zanesville Campus Library, 1425 Newark Rd, 43701. SAN 313-8348. Tel: 740-588-1404. Interlibrary Loan Service Tel: 740-588-1406. Information Services Tel: 740-588-1410. FAX: 740-453-0706. Web Site: www.zanesville.ohiou.edu/zcl. *Dir,* Tony R Hopkins; Tel: 740-588-1409, E-mail: hopkint1@ohio.edu; *Cat Mgr, ILL,* Amy Underwood; E-mail: underwoa@ohio.edu; *Circ Mgr, Educ Res Assoc,* Tracey Humphrey; Tel: 740-588-1405, E-mail: humphret@ohio.edu; *Bibliog Instr, Ref,* Janelle Hubble; Tel: 740-588-1408, E-mail: hubble@ohio.edu; Staff 4 (MLS 2, Non-MLS 2)
Enrl 2,700; Fac 245; Highest Degree: Bachelor
Library Holdings: Bk Titles 62,000; Per Subs 18,000
Special Collections: Muskingum County History (Zanesville Heritage Coll); Zanesville Pottery (Axline Coll)
Subject Interests: Appalachia, Local hist, Pottery
Automation Activity & Vendor Info: (Cataloging) Innovative Interfaces, Inc; (Circulation) Innovative Interfaces, Inc; (Course Reserve) Innovative Interfaces, Inc; (ILL) Inmagic, Inc.; (OPAC) Innovative Interfaces, Inc; (Serials) Innovative Interfaces, Inc
Function: Art exhibits, Doc delivery serv, Handicapped accessible, ILL available, Magnifiers for reading, Online searches, Orientations, Ref serv available, Summer reading prog, Telephone ref, VHS videos, Wheelchair accessible
Partic in OCLC Online Computer Library Center, Inc; Ohio Library & Information Network
Special Services for the Deaf - TTY equip
Open Mon-Thurs 8-8, Fri 8-3, Sat (Fall & Spring) 9-1
Restriction: Authorized patrons
Friends of the Library Group

S ZANESVILLE MUSEUM OF ART LIBRARY*, 620 Military Rd, 43701. SAN 313-8356. Tel: 740-452-0741. FAX: 740-452-0797. *Dir,* Laine Snyder; E-mail: laine@zanesvilleart.org
Founded 1936

Jul 2011-Jun 2012 Income $1,300, Locally Generated Income $300, Parent Institution $1,000. Mats Exp $825, Books $500, Per/Ser (Incl. Access Fees) $225, AV Mat $100
Library Holdings: AV Mats 45; DVDs 20; Bk Titles 2,100
Subject Interests: Art hist, Fine arts
Wireless access
Function: Online searches
Open Wed, Fri & Sat 10-5, Thurs 10-7:30
Restriction: Open to pub for ref only

OKLAHOMA

Date of Statistics: FY 2014
Population, 2010 U.S. Census: 3,751,351
Population, 2011 (est): 3,878,051
Population Served by Public Libraries: 3,160,556
Total Volumes in Public Libraries: 7,101,292
Volumes Per Capita: 1.83
Total Public Library Circulation: 28,400,975
Circulation Per Capita Served: 7.32
Total Public Library Operating Expenditures: $113,580,229
Expenditures Per Capita: $29.29
Expenditures Per Capita Served: $35.94
Grants-in-Aid to Libraries: $2,133,500
Federal (LSTA): $223,934 (direct grants)
Total LSTA: $2,119,065
State Aid: $1,909,566
Number of County or Systems Libraries: 6 multi-county; 2 city-county; 6 county
Counties Served: 29 served by library systems; 6 served by county libraries; 42 counties served by 110 city libraries
Number of Bookmobiles in State: 4

ADA

P ADA PUBLIC LIBRARY*, Hugh Warren Memorial Library, 124 S Rennie, 74820. SAN 313-8364. Tel: 580-436-8121. Interlibrary Loan Service Tel: 580-436-8123. FAX: 580-436-0534. Web Site: www.ada.lib.ok.us. *Dir,* Jennifer Greenstreet; E-mail: jgreenstreet@ada.lib.ok.us; *Ch Serv,* Debbie Whelchel; Tel: 580-436-8122, E-mail: dlwhelchel@ada.lib.ok.us; *Circ,* Betty Blansett; *ILL,* Gary Colbert; *Tech Serv,* Lisa Smith
Founded 1939. Pop 15,820; Circ 140,000
Library Holdings: Bk Titles 55,000; Bk Vols 60,000; Per Subs 200
Automation Activity & Vendor Info: (Acquisitions) Book Systems; (Cataloging) Book Systems; (Circulation) Book Systems
Open Mon-Fri 8-7, Sat 9-1
Friends of the Library Group

C EAST CENTRAL UNIVERSITY*, Linscheid Library, 1100 E 14th St, 74820-6999. SAN 357-4741. Tel: 580-310-5375. Interlibrary Loan Service Tel: 580-310-5374. Reference Tel: 580-310-5371. Information Services Tel: 580-310-5376. FAX: 580-436-3242. Web Site: www.ecok.edu. *Dir,* Dr Adrianna Lancaster, E-mail: alancaster@ecok.edu; *Acq/Per Librn, Asst Libr Dir,* Dana Belcher; Tel: 580-310-5564, E-mail: dbelcher@ecok.edu; *AV, Automation Librn,* Patrick Baumann; Tel: 580-310-5373, E-mail: pbaumann@ecok.edu; *Cat, Govt Doc,* Dr Farooq Ali; Tel: 580-310-5298, E-mail: fali@ecok.edu; *Pub Serv,* Michele McCullar; Tel: 580-310-5370, E-mail: smccullr@ecok.edu; *Ref & Instrul Serv, Instr Coordr,* Angie Brunk; Tel: 580-310-5308, E-mail: abrunk@ecok.edu; Staff 6 (MLS 6)
Founded 1909. Enrl 4,100; Fac 186; Highest Degree: Master
Library Holdings: AV Mats 7,865; e-journals 11,569; Bk Titles 127,376; Bk Vols 176,491; Per Subs 702
Automation Activity & Vendor Info: (Acquisitions) Innovative Interfaces, Inc; (Cataloging) Innovative Interfaces, Inc; (Circulation) Innovative Interfaces, Inc; (Course Reserve) Innovative Interfaces, Inc; (ILL) Innovative Interfaces, Inc; (OPAC) Innovative Interfaces, Inc; (Serials) Innovative Interfaces, Inc
Database Vendor: EBSCOhost, Innovative Interfaces, Inc
Wireless access
Partic in Okla Telecommunications Interlibr Syst
Open Mon-Thurs 8am-10pm, Fri 8-5, Sat 9-1, Sun 2-8

ALLEN

P ALLEN PUBLIC LIBRARY*, 207 S Commerce, 74825. (Mail add: PO Box 343, 74825-0343), SAN 377-2020. Tel: 580-857-2933. FAX: 580-857-2933. E-mail: director@allen.lib.ok.us. *Librn,* Paula Nelson
Library Holdings: Bk Titles 7,000; Per Subs 12
Automation Activity & Vendor Info: (Circulation) Follett Software
Open Mon-Fri 12-6

ALTUS

P ALTUS PUBLIC LIBRARY*, 421 N Hudson, 73521. SAN 313-8380. Tel: 580-477-2890. FAX: 580-477-3626. E-mail: spls@spls.lib.ok.us. Web Site: www.spls.lib.ok.us. *Librn,* Donna Smith; *Automation Syst Coordr,* Janet Howard
Founded 1936. Pop 23,000
Library Holdings: Bk Vols 60,000; Per Subs 75
Automation Activity & Vendor Info: (Cataloging) SirsiDynix; (Circulation) SirsiDynix
Mem of Southern Prairie Library System
Open Mon, Fri & Sat 10-6, Tues-Thurs 10-9
Friends of the Library Group

S OKLAHOMA HISTORICAL SOCIETY-MUSEUM OF THE WESTERN PRAIRIE*, Bernice Ford-Price Memorial Reference Library, 1100 Memorial Dr, 73521. SAN 327-9227. Tel: 580-482-1044. FAX: 580-482-0128. E-mail: muswestpr@okhistory.org. Web Site: www.okhistory.org. *Admin Dir,* Bart McClenny; Staff 1 (Non-MLS 1)
Founded 1973
Library Holdings: Bk Titles 1,899
Special Collections: Southwest Oklahoma Coll. Oral History
Subject Interests: Archival, Local hist, Local oral hist
Function: For res purposes
Restriction: Non-circulating to the pub, Open by appt only

P SOUTHERN PRAIRIE LIBRARY SYSTEM, 421 N Hudson, 73521. (Mail add: PO Box 1141, 73522), SAN 313-8399. Tel: 580-477-2890. Toll Free Tel: 888-302-9053. FAX: 580-477-3626. E-mail: spls@spls.lib.ok.us. Web Site: www.spls.lib.ok.us. *Dir,* Katherine Hale; E-mail: khale@spls.lib.ok.us; *Librn,* Donna Smith; E-mail: dsmith@spls.lib.ok.us; Staff 8 (MLS 2, Non-MLS 6)
Founded 1973. Pop 28,439; Circ 67,901
Library Holdings: AV Mats 1,051; Bk Titles 50,003; Bk Vols 52,003; Per Subs 76
Special Collections: English as a Second Language Coll; Literacy Coll
Subject Interests: African-Am heritage, Alternate sources of energy, Genealogy, Hispanic-Am heritage
Automation Activity & Vendor Info: (Acquisitions) SirsiDynix; (Cataloging) SirsiDynix; (Circulation) SirsiDynix; (ILL) OCLC; (OPAC) SIRSI WorkFlows
Database Vendor: Booklist Online, EBSCO Auto Repair Reference, EBSCOhost, Ingram Library Services, OCLC FirstSearch, OCLC WebJunction, SirsiDynix, WebMD, World Book Online
Wireless access
Member Libraries: Altus Public Library; Hollis Public Library
Partic in OCLC Online Computer Library Center, Inc; OLTN
Special Services for the Blind - Accessible computers; Aids for in-house use; Bks on CD; Copier with enlargement capabilities; Extensive large print coll; Large print bks; Lending of low vision aids; Magnifiers; Screen enlargement software for people with visual disabilities

Open Mon, Fri & Sat 10-6, Tues-Thurs 10-9
Friends of the Library Group

J WESTERN OKLAHOMA STATE COLLEGE*, Learning Resources Center, 2801 N Main St, 73521. SAN 313-8402. Tel: 580-477-7770. FAX: 580-477-7777. Web Site: wosc.edu/library. *Tech Asst,* Joanne Huff; Tel: 580-477-7948, E-mail: joanne.huff@wosc.edu; *Tech Asst,* San Trevino; Tel: 580-477-7951, E-mail: san.trevino@wosc.edu; Staff 2 (Non-MLS 2)
Founded 1926. Enrl 1,853; Fac 150; Highest Degree: Associate
Library Holdings: AV Mats 2,208; Bks on Deafness & Sign Lang 15; Bk Vols 36,756; Per Subs 53
Automation Activity & Vendor Info: (Cataloging) Auto-Graphics, Inc; (Circulation) Auto-Graphics, Inc; (Course Reserve) Auto-Graphics, Inc; (ILL) OCLC Connexion; (OPAC) Auto-Graphics, Inc
Database Vendor: EBSCOhost, Newsbank, OCLC FirstSearch
Wireless access
Open Mon-Thurs 7:30am-9pm, Fri 7:30-5

ALTUS AIR FORCE BASE

A UNITED STATES AIR FORCE*, Altus Air Force Base Library FL4419, 97 FSS/FSDL, 109 E Ave, Bldg 65, 73523-5134. Tel: 580-481-6302. FAX: 580-482-0469. *Libr Dir,* Cheryl Smith-Cook; Tel: 580-481-7693, E-mail: cheryl.smith-cook@altus.af.mil
Founded 1953
Library Holdings: Bk Vols 25,000; Per Subs 53
Subject Interests: Aeronaut, Polit sci
Automation Activity & Vendor Info: (Cataloging) OCLC Connexion; (Circulation) SIRSI Unicorn; (ILL) OCLC WorldShare Interlibrary Loan
Database Vendor: EBSCO Auto Repair Reference, EBSCOhost, Newsbank, OCLC FirstSearch, OCLC WorldShare Interlibrary Loan, ProQuest
Partic in Fedlink; OCLC Online Computer Library Center, Inc
Open Mon-Wed 9-9, Thurs & Sun 1-5, Fri & Sat 9-5

ALVA

P ALVA PUBLIC LIBRARY*, 504 Seventh St, 73717. Tel: 580-327-1833. FAX: 580-327-5329. *Dir,* Sandra Ott-Hamilton; *Asst Dir,* Mandi Schoenhals; Staff 2 (MLS 2)
Pop 5,000; Circ 63,447
Library Holdings: AV Mats 1,548; Bk Vols 49,546; Per Subs 121; Talking Bks 679
Special Collections: Daughters of the American Revolution (DAR) Coll
Subject Interests: Genealogy, Okla
Automation Activity & Vendor Info: (Cataloging) OCLC; (Circulation) Biblionix; (ILL) OCLC; (Serials) DEMCO
Wireless access
Open Mon 10-9, Tues-Sat 10-5:30
Friends of the Library Group

C NORTHWESTERN OKLAHOMA STATE UNIVERSITY*, J W Martin Library, 709 Oklahoma Blvd, 73717. SAN 357-4830. Tel: 580-327-8574. FAX: 580-327-8501. Web Site: www.nwosu.edu/library/index.html. *Dir, Libr Serv,* Susan Jeffries; Tel: 580-327-8570, E-mail: skjeffries@nwosu.edu; *Head Librn,* Marilyn Moore; Tel: 580-213-3111, Fax: 580-213-3140, E-mail: msmoore@nwosu.edu; *Head, Ref,* Cindy Gottsch; Tel: 580-327-8572, E-mail: clgottsch@nwosu.edu; *Govt Doc,* Verna Graybill; Tel: 580-327-8576, E-mail: vpgraybill@nwosu.edu; Staff 11 (MLS 4, Non-MLS 7)
Founded 1897. Enrl 2,000; Fac 75; Highest Degree: Master
Library Holdings: Bk Vols 159,000; Per Subs 1,405
Special Collections: Indian Artifacts; William J Mellor Coll, bks, paintings, sculpture, stereoptican slides, cylinder records & player. US Document Depository
Subject Interests: Agr, Behav sci, Educ, Libr sci, Soc sci
Wireless access
Function: Govt ref serv, ILL available
Restriction: Restricted pub use

ANADARKO

P ANADARKO COMMUNITY LIBRARY*, 215 W Broadway, 73005. SAN 313-8429. Tel: 405-247-7351. Toll Free Tel: 888-607-1747. FAX: 405-247-2024. E-mail: library@cityofanadarko.org. Web Site: www.anadarkopl.okpls.org. *Actg Dir,* Keisha Gordon; *Libr Asst,* Tammy Quoetone
Founded 1901. Pop 8,200; Circ 45,638
Library Holdings: Bk Vols 33,000; Per Subs 80
Special Collections: Oklahoma History
Subject Interests: Art, Native Am, Native Am hist, Okla
Automation Activity & Vendor Info: (Circulation) Follett Software
Database Vendor: EBSCOhost
Wireless access
Open Mon-Thurs 9-6, Fri 9-5, Sat 9-Noon
Friends of the Library Group

ANTLERS

P ANTLERS PUBLIC LIBRARY*, 104 SE Second St, 74523-4000. SAN 313-8437. Tel: 580-298-5649. FAX: 580-298-3567. E-mail: antlerslibrary@antlers.lib.ok.us. Web Site: www.antlerslibrary.okpls.org. *Dir,* Patti Lehman; *Asst Librn,* Sherry Gatheright; Staff 2 (Non-MLS 2)
Founded 1959. Pop 2,989; Circ 12,262
Library Holdings: Bk Vols 14,000
Automation Activity & Vendor Info: (Cataloging) Follett Software; (Circulation) Follett Software; (OPAC) Follett Software
Database Vendor: EBSCOhost
Wireless access
Function: Audio & video playback equip for onsite use, Handicapped accessible, ILL available, Magnifiers for reading, Photocopying/Printing, Preschool outreach, Prog for children & young adult, Spoken cassettes & CDs, Summer reading prog, VHS videos, Wheelchair accessible
Open Tues & Thurs 10-6, Wed 9-5, Fri 10-5, Sat 9-Noon

ARDMORE

P ARDMORE PUBLIC LIBRARY*, 320 E St NW, 73401. SAN 313-8445. Tel: 580-223-8290. Circulation Tel: 580-223-9524. FAX: 580-221-3240. Web Site: www.ardmorelibrary.org. *Dir,* Daniel Gibbs; *Asst Dir,* Lynnette Haggerty; *Tech Serv Librn,* Lorena L Smith; *Youth Serv Librn,* Angela Armstrong; *Circ Supvr,* Terri Wisely; *Tech Serv,* Shirley Strawn; Staff 6 (MLS 2, Non-MLS 4)
Founded 1906. Pop 24,283; Circ 502,271
Jul 2010-Jun 2011 Income $974,337, State $30,641, City $928,362, Other $15,334. Mats Exp $127,919, Books $69,129, Per/Ser (Incl. Access Fees) $5,707, Micro $370, AV Mat $38,209, Electronic Ref Mat (Incl. Access Fees) $14,504. Sal $745,682
Library Holdings: Audiobooks 4,947; DVDs 4,970; Electronic Media & Resources 9; Bk Vols 75,913; Per Subs 153
Special Collections: Eliza Cruce Hall Doll Museum Coll, bks, dolls, slides; McGalliard Local History Coll, clippings, photog, publs
Automation Activity & Vendor Info: (Acquisitions) Innovative Interfaces, Inc; (Cataloging) Innovative Interfaces, Inc; (Circulation) Innovative Interfaces, Inc; (ILL) OCLC; (OPAC) SirsiDynix; (Serials) Innovative Interfaces, Inc
Database Vendor: Bowker, EBSCOhost, Gale Cengage Learning, ProQuest
Wireless access
Function: Adult bk club, Adult literacy prog, Archival coll, Audio & video playback equip for onsite use, Bks on CD, Children's prog, Copy machines, Electronic databases & coll, Fax serv, Free DVD rentals, Genealogy discussion group, Handicapped accessible, ILL available, Music CDs, Notary serv, Online cat, OverDrive digital audio bks, Photocopying/Printing, Ref serv in person, Scanner, Serves mentally handicapped consumers, Summer reading prog, Tax forms, Teen prog, Web-catalog
Partic in Okla Telecommunications Interlibr Syst
Open Mon-Thurs 10-8, Fri 10-6, Sat & Sun 1-5
Friends of the Library Group

P CHICKASAW REGIONAL LIBRARY SYSTEM*, 601 Railway Express, 73401. SAN 357-4954. Tel: 580-223-3164. Toll Free Tel: 888-520-8103 (OK only). FAX: 580-223-3280. E-mail: ardmore@crlsok.org. Reference E-mail: reference@crlsok.org. Web Site: www.crlsok.org. *Exec Dir,* Lynn McIntosh; *Head, Circ,* Elizabeth Negrete; *Bus Mgr,* Treasa Ford; *Br Coordr,* Alyson Vernon; *Mkt Coordr,* Gail Currier; *Ch Serv,* Shawn Brown; *ILL,* Louise Rankin; *Ref,* Pam Bean; *Tech Serv,* David Moran; Staff 12 (MLS 3, Non-MLS 9)
Founded 1960. Pop 95,607; Circ 399,292
Jul 2011-Jun 2012 Income (Main Library and Branch(s)) $1,450,990, State $67,985, County $1,270,605, Other $112,400. Mats Exp $87,503, Books $52,239, Per/Ser (Incl. Access Fees) $9,833, Micro $295, AV Mat $11,138, Electronic Ref Mat (Incl. Access Fees) $13,998. Sal $927,403
Library Holdings: AV Mats 173,443; CDs 5,989; Electronic Media & Resources 35; Bk Titles 97,370; Per Subs 215; Videos 6,690
Subject Interests: Art, Civilized tribes, Okla hist, Texoma
Automation Activity & Vendor Info: (Cataloging) TLC (The Library Corporation); (Circulation) TLC (The Library Corporation)
Wireless access
Open Mon-Thurs 8:30-7:30, Fri 8:30-5, Sat 10-2
Friends of the Library Group
Branches: 7
ATOKA COUNTY LIBRARY, 215 East A St, Atoka, 74525, SAN 357-4989. Tel: 580-889-3555, 580-889-8954. Toll Free Tel: 888-520-8094 (OK only). FAX: 580-889-8860. E-mail: atoka@crlsok.org. *Br Mgr,* Alice Withrow
Open Mon-Thurs 11:30-5:30, Fri 11:30-2:30, Sat 10-1
Friends of the Library Group

DAVIS PUBLIC LIBRARY, 209 E Benton Ave, Davis, 73030, SAN 357-5047. Tel: 580-369-2468, 580-369-3682. Toll Free Tel: 888-520-8095 (OK only). FAX: 580-369-3290. E-mail: davis@crlsok.org. *Br Mgr,* Position Currently Open
Open Mon-Thurs 11:30-5:30, Fri 11:30-2:30, Sat 10-1
Friends of the Library Group

HEALDTON COMMUNITY LIBRARY, 554 S Fourth St, Healdton, 73438, SAN 357-5071. Tel: 580-229-0590. Toll Free Tel: 888-520-8096 (OK only). FAX: 580-229-0654. E-mail: healdton@crlsok.org. *Br Mgr,* Vali Hayes
Open Mon-Thurs 11:30-5:30, Fri 11:30-2:30, Sat 10-1
Friends of the Library Group

JOHNSTON COUNTY, 116 W Main St, Tishomingo, 73460, SAN 357-5160. Tel: 580-371-3006, 580-371-3760. Toll Free Tel: 888-520-8097 (OK only). FAX: 580-371-0042. E-mail: tishomingo@crlsok.org. *Br Mgr,* Michael Henthorn
Open Mon-Thurs 11:30-5:30, Fri 11:30-2:30, Sat 10-1
Friends of the Library Group

LOVE COUNTY, 500 S Hwy 77, Marietta, 73448, SAN 357-5101. Tel: 580-276-3783, 580-276-4574. Toll Free Tel: 888-520-8098 (OK only). FAX: 580-276-1483. E-mail: marietta@crlsok.org. *Br Mgr,* Niki Powell
Open Mon-Thurs 11:30-5:30, Fri 11:30-2:30, Sat 10-1
Friends of the Library Group

MARY E PARKER MEMORIAL LIBRARY, 500 W Broadway, Sulphur, 73086, SAN 357-5136. Tel: 580-622-2889, 580-622-5807. Toll Free Tel: 888-520-8101 (OK only). FAX: 580-622-6395. E-mail: sulphur@crlsok.org. *Br Mgr,* Shannon Bever
Open Mon-Thurs 11:30-5:30, Fri 11:30-2:30, Sat 10-1

WILSON PUBLIC LIBRARY, 1087 US Hwy 70A, Wilson, 73463, SAN 357-5195. Tel: 580-668-2486, 580-668-3056. Toll Free Tel: 888-520-8102 (OK only). FAX. 580-668-9280. E-mail: wilson@crlsok.org. *Br Mgr,* Betty Manley
Open Mon-Thurs 11:30-5:30, Fri 11:30-2:30, Sat 10-1
Friends of the Library Group

Bookmobiles: 1

S SAMUEL ROBERTS NOBLE FOUNDATION, INC*, Noble Foundation Library, 2510 Sam Noble Pkwy, 73401. SAN 313-8453. Tel: 580-224-6260. Interlibrary Loan Service Tel: 580-224-6263. Reference Tel: 580-224-6261. FAX: 580-224-6265. Web Site: www.noble.org. *Dir of Libr,* Position Currently Open
Founded 1951
Library Holdings: e-journals 12,000; Bk Vols 34,100; Per Subs 430
Special Collections: Plant Specimen Identity Coll & Archives. Oral History
Subject Interests: Agr, Chem, Forage, Plant biol
Automation Activity & Vendor Info: (Acquisitions) Ex Libris Group; (Cataloging) Ex Libris Group; (Circulation) Ex Libris Group; (Course Reserve) Ex Libris Group; (ILL) Ex Libris Group; (Media Booking) Ex Libris Group; (OPAC) Ex Libris Group; (Serials) Ex Libris Group
Database Vendor: Dialog, EBSCOhost, OCLC FirstSearch, OVID Technologies
Wireless access
Function: Archival coll, Electronic databases & coll
Publications: Library Guide
Restriction: Co libr

C UNIVERSITY CENTER OF SOUTHERN OKLAHOMA LIBRARY*, Mary Jane Hamilton Library, 611 Veterans Blvd, 73401. SAN 375-426X. Tel: 580-223-1441. *Libr Dir,* Michele Frasier-Robinson; E-mail: mfrasier.robinson@ucso.osrhe.edu; *Asst Libr Dir,* Terri McDowell; E-mail: tmcdowell@ucso.osrhe.edu
Founded 1983. Enrl 1,300; Highest Degree: Master
Library Holdings: e-books 16,000; Bk Titles 14,000; Bk Vols 18,000; Per Subs 130
Automation Activity & Vendor Info: (Cataloging) SirsiDynix; (Circulation) SirsiDynix; (Course Reserve) SirsiDynix; (ILL) OCLC; (OPAC) SirsiDynix; (Serials) SirsiDynix
Database Vendor: Dialog, EBSCOhost, OCLC FirstSearch, OVID Technologies, ProQuest
Wireless access
Function: AV serv, ILL available, Res libr
Open Mon-Thurs 8am-9pm, Fri 9-12 & 1-4

ARKOMA

P ARKOMA PUBLIC LIBRARY*, 1101 Main St, 74901. (Mail add: PO Box 446, 74901-0446), SAN 376-5946. Tel: 918-875-3971. FAX: 918-875-3013. *Dir,* Carol Burgess
Library Holdings: Bk Vols 15,000; Per Subs 18
Automation Activity & Vendor Info: (Circulation) SirsiDynix
Mem of Southeastern Public Library System of Oklahoma
Open Tues 10-7, Wed & Thurs 10-6, Fri 12-5, Sat 9-3
Friends of the Library Group

ATOKA

S HOWARD MCLEOD CORRECTIONAL CENTER LIBRARY*, 1970 E Whippoorwill, 74525-9152. Tel: 580-889-6651. FAX: 580-889-2264. *Supvr,* Position Currently Open
Library Holdings: Bk Vols 7,000; Per Subs 38
Open Wed-Fri 9-8, Sat 8-6

BARNSDALL

P BARNSDALL PUBLIC LIBRARY-ETHEL BRIGGS MEMORIAL LIBRARY*, 410 S Fifth St, 74002. (Mail add: PO Box 706, 74002-0706), SAN 313-8461. Tel: 918-847-2118. FAX: 918-847-2118. *Librn,* Cecilia Hibdon
Founded 1931. Pop 1,400; Circ 8,065
Library Holdings: Bk Titles 12,204
Subject Interests: Hist, Music
Wireless access
Open Mon-Fri 2-6

BARTLESVILLE

P BARTLESVILLE PUBLIC LIBRARY*, 600 S Johnstone, 74003. SAN 313-847X. Tel: 918-338-4161. Circulation Tel: 918-338-4171. Interlibrary Loan Service Tel: 918-338-4168. Reference Tel: 918-338-4169. Automation Services Tel: 918-338-4165. FAX: 918-337-5338. TDD: 918-337-5359. Web Site: www.bartlesville.lib.ok.us. *Dir,* Joan Singleton; Tel: 918-338-4163, Fax: 918-336-7495, E-mail: jsinglet@bartlesville.lib.ok.us; *Asst Dir,* Beth DeGeer; Tel: 918-338-4164, E-mail: bdegeer@bartlesville.lib.ok.us; *Ref Librn,* Katherine Hanson; E-mail: hanson@bartlesville.lib.ok.us; *Tech Serv Librn,* Elsie Green; E-mail: egreen@bartlesville.lib.ok.us; *Youth Serv Librn,* Laura Pryce; Tel: 918-338-4170, E-mail: ljpryce@bartlesville.lib.ok.us; *Circ Supvr,* Sheryl Clark; Tel: 918-338-4162, E-mail: sclark1@bartlesville.lib.ok.us; *Ref Serv Supvr,* Nadine Hawke; Tel: 918-338-4166, E-mail: nhawke@bartlesville.lib.ok.us; Staff 18.6 (MLS 6, Non-MLS 12.6)
Founded 1913. Pop 50,706; Circ 502,399
Jul 2009-Jun 2010 Income $1,127,344, State $23,339, City $1,091,155, Federal $2,850, Other $10,000. Mats Exp $145,241, Books $79,333, Per/Ser (Incl. Access Fees) $6,051, Micro $1,925, AV Mat $21,432, Electronic Ref Mat (Incl. Access Fees) $36,500. Sal $857,121
Library Holdings: AV Mats 5,122; DVDs 10,092; Bk Titles 101,905; Bk Vols 115,315; Per Subs 125
Special Collections: Genealogy Coll; Local Historical Museum; Local History Coll; Oklahoma History Coll. State Document Depository
Subject Interests: Am Indian, Okla tribes
Automation Activity & Vendor Info: (Acquisitions) Horizon; (Cataloging) Horizon; (Circulation) Horizon; (Course Reserve) Horizon; (ILL) Auto-Graphics, Inc
Database Vendor: Amigos Library Services, EBSCOhost, Ingram Library Services, ProQuest, SirsiDynix, ValueLine
Wireless access
Function: Adult bk club, Archival coll, Audio & video playback equip for onsite use, Audiobks via web, BA reader (adult literacy), Bk club(s), Bk reviews (Group), Bks on CD, Children's prog, Citizenship assistance, Computer training, Computers for patron use, Copy machines, Digital talking bks, e-mail & chat, Electronic databases & coll, Exhibits, Family literacy, Fax serv, Free DVD rentals, Genealogy discussion group, Handicapped accessible, Homebound delivery serv, ILL available, Instruction & testing, Literacy & newcomer serv, Magnifiers for reading, Music CDs, Newsp ref libr, Online cat, Online info literacy tutorials on the web & in blackboard, Online ref, Online searches, Outreach serv, Outside serv via phone, mail, e-mail & web, Photocopying/Printing, Preschool outreach, Prog for adults, Prog for children & young adult, Pub access computers, Ref & res, Ref serv in person, Senior computer classes, Story hour, Summer reading prog, Tax forms, Teen prog, Telephone ref, Wheelchair accessible
Publications: The Bartlesville Bookmark (Newsletter)
Special Services for the Deaf - TDD equip
Open Mon-Thurs 9-9, Fri & Sat 9-5:30, Sun (Sept-May) 1:30-5:30
Restriction: Borrowing requests are handled by ILL
Friends of the Library Group

C OKLAHOMA WESLEYAN UNIVERSITY LIBRARY*, Janice & Charles Drake Library, 2201 Silver Lake Rd, 74006-6299. SAN 313-8488. Tel: 918-335-6298. Interlibrary Loan Service Tel: 918-335-6286. Toll Free Tel: 888-279-4536. FAX: 918-335-6220. E-mail: elib@okwu.edu. Web Site: library.okwueagle.com. *Dir, Libr Serv,* Gavin Woltjer; *Off-Campus Librn,* Stephanie Leupp; E-mail: sleupp@okwu.edu; *Pub Serv Librn,* Cheryl Salerno; E-mail: csalerno@okwu.edu; Staff 3 (MLS 2, Non-MLS 1)
Founded 1958. Enrl 969; Fac 55; Highest Degree: Master
Library Holdings: e-books 14,800; Bk Titles 77,378; Bk Vols 93,580; Per Subs 182
Special Collections: Holiness Coll; Josh McDowell Legacy Coll

Automation Activity & Vendor Info: (Cataloging) Auto-Graphics, Inc; (Circulation) Auto-Graphics, Inc; (ILL) Auto-Graphics, Inc; (OPAC) Auto-Graphics, Inc
Database Vendor: CredoReference, EBSCOhost, Gale Cengage Learning, Mergent Online, Newsbank, OCLC FirstSearch, OVID Technologies, Sage
Wireless access
Function: Outside serv via phone, mail, e-mail & web
Partic in Association of Christian Librarians
Open Mon-Thurs 7:30am-Midnight, Fri 7:30am-10pm, Sat 10-10, Sun 2pm-Midnight
Restriction: Access at librarian's discretion

S PHILLIPS 66 RESEARCH LIBRARY*, 180 PLB PRC, 74003-6670. SAN 357-5314. Administration Tel: 918-977-5875. FAX: 918-977-7569. *Dir,* Annabeth Robin; Tel: 981-977-6550, E-mail: Annabeth.Robin@p66.com; *Head Librn,* Laura Allen-Ward; E-mail: Laura.Allen-Ward@p66.com; *Asst Librn,* Debra McConaghy; Tel: 918-977-4701, E-mail: debra.j.mcconaghy@p66.com; Staff 5 (MLS 3, Non-MLS 2)
Founded 1947
Library Holdings: e-books 2,000; e-journals 200; Bk Vols 60,000; Per Subs 100; Videos 100
Subject Interests: Chem, Physics, Plastics, Polymer sci
Automation Activity & Vendor Info: (Cataloging) EOS International; (Circulation) EOS International; (OPAC) EOS International; (Serials) EOS International
Database Vendor: American Chemical Society, Amigos Library Services, CRC Press/Taylor & Francis Group, ebrary, EBSCO Discovery Service, EBSCO Information Services, EBSCOhost, Elsevier, EOS International, IHS, McGraw-Hill, OCLC WorldShare Interlibrary Loan, ScienceDirect, Scopus, Springer-Verlag, Wiley, Wiley InterScience
Wireless access
Function: Doc delivery serv, Electronic databases & coll, For res purposes, Online cat, Online searches, Orientations, Ref & res, Ref serv available, Res libr, Web-catalog
Partic in Amigos Library Services, Inc; OCLC Online Computer Library Center, Inc
Restriction: Access for corporate affiliates, Authorized patrons, Authorized personnel only, By permission only, Co libr, Employees & their associates, Employees only, Not open to pub

S WOOLAROC MUSEUM LIBRARY*, 1925 Woolaroc Ranch Rd, 74003. (Mail add: PO Box 1647, 74005), SAN 370-4149. Tel: 918-336-0307. FAX: 918-336-0084. Web Site: www.woolaroc.org. *Curator,* Linda Stone; Tel: 918-336-0307, Ext 32
Founded 1929
Subject Interests: Anthrop, Ethnology, Firearms, Native Am, Oil, Ranching, Western art, Zoology
Restriction: Lending to staff only, Open to others by appt

BEAVER

P BEAVER COUNTY PIONEER LIBRARY*, 201 Douglas St, 73932. (Mail add: PO Box 579, 73932-0579), SAN 313-850X. Tel: 580-625-3076. FAX: 580-625-3076. Web Site: www.beaverpl.okpls.org. *Librn,* Denise Janko
Circ 8,675
Library Holdings: Bk Vols 16,550; Per Subs 10
Automation Activity & Vendor Info: (Circulation) Follett Software
Wireless access
Open Mon 9:30-7, Tues-Fri 9:30-5:30, Sat 9-12:30
Friends of the Library Group

BETHANY

C SOUTHERN NAZARENE UNIVERSITY*, R T Williams Learning Resources Center, 4115 N College, 73008. SAN 313-8518. Tel: 405-491-6350. Circulation Tel: 405-491-6351. FAX: 405-491-6355. Web Site: www.snu.edu. *Dir,* Jan Reinbold; E-mail: janrein@snu.edu; *Bibliog Instr, Ref,* Joshua Achipa; E-mail: jachipa@snu.edu; *Coordr, Tech Serv,* Joy Pauley; E-mail: jpauley@snu.edu; *Per,* Angela Cape; *Ref,* Ellen Apple; *Ref,* Sybill Connolly; *Ref,* Janice Cramer; *Ref,* Nancy Jurney; Staff 3 (MLS 3)
Founded 1920. Enrl 1,900; Fac 75; Highest Degree: Master
Library Holdings: Bk Titles 80,000; Bk Vols 103,000; Per Subs 200
Special Collections: Hymnological Coll; Ross Hayslip Bible Coll; Signatures (John E Moore Letter Coll)
Subject Interests: Educ, Nursing, Relig, Sciences
Automation Activity & Vendor Info: (Circulation) Follett Software; (OPAC) Follett Software
Database Vendor: EBSCOhost, OCLC FirstSearch
Wireless access
Partic in OCLC Online Computer Library Center, Inc
Open Mon-Thurs 8-11, Fri 8-5, Sat 11-5

CR SOUTHWESTERN CHRISTIAN UNIVERSITY LIBRARY*, SCU Library & Information Center, C H Springer Bldg, 7210 NW 39th Expressway, 73008. (Mail add: PO Box 340, 73008-0340), SAN 313-9654. Tel: 405-789-7661, Ext 3451. FAX: 405-495-0078. E-mail: scu.library@swcu.edu. Web Site: www.swcu.edu/library. *Dir,* Marilyn A Hudson; E-mail: marilyn.hudson@swcu.edu; Staff 1 (MLS 1)
Founded 1946. Enrl 673; Highest Degree: Master
Library Holdings: AV Mats 145; CDs 120; DVDs 25; Bk Titles 28,000; Bk Vols 30,000; Per Subs 50
Special Collections: Noel Brooks Coll, papers & library of a British born author, leader & pastor; Pentecostal Resource Coll, books related to the history of the Charismatic & Pentecostal movements
Automation Activity & Vendor Info: (Cataloging) Follett Software; (Circulation) Follett Software; (OPAC) Follett Software
Database Vendor: EBSCOhost, OCLC FirstSearch, ProQuest
Wireless access
Open Mon-Thurs (Fall & Winter) 8:30am-10pm, Fri 8:30-4, Sat 12-5; Mon & Wed-Fri (Summer) 8:30-4:30, Tues 10-6
Friends of the Library Group

BINGER

P BINGER PUBLIC LIBRARY*, 217 W Main, 73009. (Mail add: 18100 County Rd 1170, 73009-5113), *Dir,* Judy Hill
Founded 1976. Pop 660
Library Holdings: AV Mats 210; DVDs 21; Bk Vols 6,700; Per Subs 10; Talking Bks 107; Videos 12
Function: Photocopying/Printing
Open Mon & Thurs 11-4

BLACKWELL

P BLACKWELL PUBLIC LIBRARY*, 123 W Padon, 74631-2805. SAN 313-8534. Tel: 580-363-1809. FAX: 580-363-7214. E-mail: blklib@4grc.com. *Dir, Pub Libr Serv,* Linda Mayden; Staff 1 (Non-MLS 1)
Founded 1903. Pop 7,500; Circ 117,807
Library Holdings: Bk Titles 34,000; Bk Vols 36,250; Per Subs 79
Subject Interests: Genealogy
Wireless access
Open Mon & Tues 10-8, Wed & Fri 10-6, Sat 10-2
Friends of the Library Group

BOISE CITY

P SOUTAR MEMORIAL LIBRARY*, Seven S Ellis Ave, 73933. (Mail add: PO Box 1088, 73933-1088), SAN 313-8542. Tel: 580-544-2715. FAX: 580-544-2705. E-mail: soutarlib@yahoo.com. Web Site: www.soutarlibrary.okpls.org. *Librn,* Alma Fay Twyman
Founded 1958. Pop 2,475; Circ 11,376
Library Holdings: Bk Vols 15,000
Automation Activity & Vendor Info: (Cataloging) Biblionix/Apollo; (Circulation) Biblionix/Apollo
Wireless access
Open Tues & Thurs 11:30-6, Wed 9-12 & 1-6, Fri 12-6, Sat 9-12
Friends of the Library Group

BOLEY

S JOHN H LILLEY CORRECTIONAL CENTER*, Leisure Library, PO Box 1908, 74829-1908. SAN 371-7070. Tel: 918-667-4246. FAX: 918-667-4245. *In Charge,* Cherri Williams
Library Holdings: Bk Titles 8,000; Bk Vols 8,050; Per Subs 10
Open Mon-Fri 8-4

BRISTOW

P BRISTOW PUBLIC LIBRARY*, Montfort & Allie B Jones Memorial Library, 111 W Seventh Ave, 74010-2401. SAN 313-8550. Tel: 918-367-6562. FAX: 918-367-1156. Web Site: www.bristow.lib.ok.us. *Dir,* Donna Lawrence; E-mail: dlawrence@bristow.lib.ok.us
Pop 4,062; Circ 68,000
Library Holdings: Bk Titles 30,000; Per Subs 65
Special Collections: Henson Room - Olympic memorabila/olympic medals/wrestling bks, art, etc
Subject Interests: Okla
Automation Activity & Vendor Info: (Circulation) Follett Software
Open Mon & Wed 9-6, Tues & Thurs 9-7, Fri 9-3, Sat 9-1

BROKEN BOW

P BROKEN BOW PUBLIC LIBRARY*, 404 Broadway, 74728. SAN 313-8569. Tel: 580-584-2815. FAX: 580-584-9449. *Head Librn,* Judy Williams; E-mail: judyw@oklibrary.net; *Asst Librn,* Angie Fields; *Asst Librn,* Jo Ann Smith; *Asst Librn, Cat,* Mindy Timmons; *Asst Librn, Ch Serv,* Kathleen Stofregen; *Asst Librn, ILL & Distance Libr Serv Spec,* Becky Williams

Founded 1920. Pop 20,000; Circ 110,000
Library Holdings: Bk Titles 33,000; Per Subs 75
Automation Activity & Vendor Info: (Acquisitions) SirsiDynix; (Cataloging) SirsiDynix; (Circulation) SirsiDynix
Database Vendor: EBSCOhost, Electric Library, InfoWorks Technology, OCLC WebJunction, WebMD
Wireless access
Function: Adult bk club, Art exhibits, Audio & video playback equip for onsite use, Bi-weekly Writer's Group, CD-ROM, Copy machines, Electronic databases & coll, Fax serv, Games & aids for the handicapped, Handicapped accessible, Home delivery & serv to Sr ctr & nursing homes, Homebound delivery serv, ILL available, Libr develop, Music CDs, Newsp ref libr, Online info literacy tutorials on the web & in blackboard, Online ref, Online searches, Photocopying/Printing, Preschool outreach, Prog for children & young adult, Ref & res, Spoken cassettes & CDs, Spoken cassettes & DVDs, Summer reading prog, Tax forms, Telephone ref, VHS videos, Workshops
Open Mon-Thurs 9-7, Fri 9-5, Sat 9-3
Friends of the Library Group

BUFFALO

P BUFFALO PUBLIC LIBRARY*, 11 E Turner, 73834. (Mail add: PO Box 265, 73834-0265). Tel: 580-735-2995. FAX: 580-735-6157. Web Site: www.buffalo.lib.ok.us. *Dir,* Kathy Summars
Pop 1,160; Circ 2,210
Library Holdings: AV Mats 554; Bk Vols 8,039; Talking Bks 147
Automation Activity & Vendor Info: (Cataloging) Follett Software; (Circulation) Follett Software; (OPAC) Follett Software
Wireless access
Open Mon, Thurs & Fri 2:30-6, Tues 2-5, Wed 9-12 & 2-5

CARMEN

P CARMEN PUBLIC LIBRARY*, 421 W Main St, 73726. (Mail add: PO Box 98, 73726-0098). Tel: 580-987-2301. FAX: 580-987-2303. *Dir,* Carmen Cain
Pop 389; Circ 1,265
Library Holdings: AV Mats 108; Bk Vols 6,000; Talking Bks 12
Automation Activity & Vendor Info: (Cataloging) Follett Software; (Circulation) Follett Software
Open Mon, Tues & Thurs 2-6, Wed 9-12 & 2-6
Friends of the Library Group

CARNEGIE

P CARNEGIE PUBLIC LIBRARY*, Carnegie Memorial Bldg, 22 S Broadway, 73015. SAN 313-8577. Tel: 580-654-1980. *Librn,* Barbara Cotten
Founded 1953. Pop 1,598; Circ 6,922
Library Holdings: Bk Vols 12,845
Subject Interests: Genealogy, Hist, Relig studies
Partic in Okla Telecommunications Interlibr Syst
Open Mon & Wed 1-6, Fri 11-4

CATOOSA

P CATOOSA PUBLIC LIBRARY*, 105 E Oak, 74015. (Mail add: PO Box 489, 74015-0489). Tel: 918-266-1684. FAX: 918-266-1685. *Libr Dir,* Janie Ducotey; E-mail: jducotey@catoosapubliclibrary.com
Pop 5,449; Circ 16,002
Library Holdings: AV Mats 537; Large Print Bks 100; Bk Vols 14,000; Per Subs 50; Talking Bks 542
Subject Interests: Spanish
Automation Activity & Vendor Info: (Cataloging) Follett Software; (Circulation) Follett Software; (ILL) OCLC ILLiad; (OPAC) Follett Software
Database Vendor: EBSCOhost
Open Mon 1-5, Tues-Thurs 9-7, Fri 9-3, Sat 10-2
Friends of the Library Group

CHANDLER

P CHANDLER PUBLIC LIBRARY*, 1021 Manvel Ave, 74834. SAN 329-7101. Tel: 405-258-3204. FAX: 405-258-3205. Web Site: chandlerlibrary.okpls.org. *Chief Librn,* Carmen Harkins; E-mail: charkins@chandlerok.com; *Asst Librn,* Sandra Helm; Staff 2 (MLS 1, Non-MLS 1)
Founded 1987. Pop 32,199; Circ 10,704
Jul 2005-Jun 2006 Income $73,905. Mats Exp $4,950. Sal $44,747
Library Holdings: Audiobooks 133; CDs 170; DVDs 165; Large Print Bks 245; Bk Titles 13,000; Videos 137
Automation Activity & Vendor Info: (Circulation) Book Systems
Database Vendor: Baker & Taylor, LearningExpress, OCLC WorldShare Interlibrary Loan, TLC (The Library Corporation)
Wireless access
Open Mon-Fri 9-6, Sat 9-12
Friends of the Library Group

CHECOTAH

P JIM LUCAS CHECOTAH PUBLIC LIBRARY, 626 W Gentry, 74426-2218. SAN 313-8593. Tel: 918-473-6715. FAX: 918-473-6603. E-mail: checotahpl@eodls.org. Web Site: www.eodls.lib.ok.us/checotah.html. *Br Mgr,* Kathy Smith; E-mail: kfsmith@eodls.org
Founded 1971
Library Holdings: Bk Vols 30,000; Per Subs 40
Subject Interests: Genealogy, Literacy, Local hist
Automation Activity & Vendor Info: (Circulation) SirsiDynix
Wireless access
Mem of Eastern Oklahoma District Library System
Open Mon 9-7, Tues-Fri 9-6, Sat 9-1
Friends of the Library Group

CHELSEA

P CHELSEA PUBLIC LIBRARY*, 618 Pine St, 74016-0064. SAN 313-8607. Tel: 918-789-3364. FAX: 918-789-4219. *Dir,* Terry Price
Pop 2,500
Library Holdings: Bk Vols 5,400; Per Subs 10
Automation Activity & Vendor Info: (Circulation) Follett Software
Open Tues 9-7, Wed-Fri 9-5, Sat 9-12

CHEROKEE

P CHEROKEE-CITY-COUNTY PUBLIC LIBRARY*, 123 S Grand Ave, 73728. SAN 313-8615. Tel: 580-596-2366. FAX: 580-596-2968. E-mail: cherlb_2000@yahoo.com. *Librn,* Mary Alice McLeod; Staff 1 (Non-MLS 1)
Founded 1907. Pop 6,000
Library Holdings: Bk Vols 15,000
Subject Interests: Agr, Genealogy, Relig studies
Automation Activity & Vendor Info: (Cataloging) Follett Software; (Circulation) Follett Software; (ILL) Follett Software
Wireless access
Open Mon-Thurs 10-6, Fri 10-5, Sat 9-12
Friends of the Library Group

CHICKASHA

P CHICKASHA PUBLIC LIBRARY*, 527 W Iowa Ave, 73018. SAN 313-8623. Tel: 405-222-6075. FAX: 405-222-6072. E-mail: chicklib@chickasha.lib.ok.us. *Dir,* Catharine Cook; Tel: 405-222-6077, E-mail: cathcook@chickasha.lib.ok.us; *Ch Serv,* Lillie Huckaby; E-mail: lhuckaby@chickasha.lib.ok.us; *ILL,* Sandra Robertson; E-mail: sandrar@chickasha.lib.ok.us; Staff 6.5 (MLS 2, Non-MLS 4.5)
Pop 15,800
Library Holdings: AV Mats 2,758; Bk Titles 50,882; Bk Vols 52,170; Per Subs 93
Automation Activity & Vendor Info: (Acquisitions) Follett Software; (Cataloging) Follett Software; (Circulation) Follett Software
Wireless access
Open Mon & Thurs 9:30-8, Tues, Wed & Fri 9:30-6, Sat 10-2
Friends of the Library Group

C UNIVERSITY OF SCIENCE & ARTS OF OKLAHOMA, Nash Library, 1901 S 17th St, 73018. (Mail add: 1727 W Alabama Ave, 73018), SAN 313-8631. Tel: 405-574-1343. FAX: 405-574-1220. E-mail: nashlibrary@usao.edu. Web Site: library.usao.edu. *Dir,* Kelly Brown; Tel: 405-574-1262, E-mail: kbrown@usao.edu; *Electronic Res Librn,* Elizabeth York; Tel: 405-574-1340, E-mail: eyork@usao.edu; *Libr Asst I,* Rhonda Mayo; Tel: 405-574-1263, E-mail: rmayo@usao.edu; *Libr Asst II,* Nicole McMonagle; Tel: 405-574-1341, E-mail: nmcmonagle@usao.edu; Staff 4 (MLS 3, Non-MLS 1)
Founded 1908. Enrl 920; Fac 59; Highest Degree: Bachelor
Jul 2012-Jun 2013 Income $165,000. Mats Exp $130,000, Books $10,000, Per/Ser (Incl. Access Fees) $4,000, Manu Arch $2,000, AV Mat $2,000, Electronic Ref Mat (Incl. Access Fees) $110,000, Presv $2,000. Sal $161,740 (Prof $142,780)
Library Holdings: Bks on Deafness & Sign Lang 300; e-books 50; Bk Titles 65,000; Bk Vols 70,000; Per Subs 30
Special Collections: Oklahoma & Southwestern US History (Anna Lewis Coll); Oklahoma College for Women Archives; Te Ata Coll
Database Vendor: ABC-CLIO, ARTstor, BioOne, Bowker, CQ Press, CredoReference, EBSCOhost, Gale Cengage Learning, JSTOR, Newsbank-Readex, OCLC WorldShare Interlibrary Loan, Oxford Online, Project MUSE, ProQuest
Wireless access
Partic in Amigos Library Services, Inc; OCLC Online Computer Library Center, Inc

Special Services for the Deaf - Bks on deafness & sign lang; Coll on deaf educ; Spec interest per
Friends of the Library Group

CLAREMORE

S J M DAVIS ARMS & HISTORICAL MUSEUM*, Research Library, 330 N JM Davis Blvd, 74017. (Mail add: PO Box 966, 74018), SAN 327-6309. Tel: 918-341-5707. FAX: 918-341-5771. Web Site: www.thegunmuseum.com. *Dir,* Wayne McCombs
Founded 1970
Library Holdings: Bk Titles 3,500
Subject Interests: Firearms
Function: Ref serv available
Open Mon-Sat 1-5

C ROGERS STATE UNIVERSITY LIBRARY*, Stratton Taylor Library, 1701 W Will Rogers Blvd, 74017-3252. SAN 313-864X. Tel: 918-343-7716. Interlibrary Loan Service Tel: 918-343-7720. Administration Tel: 918-343-7715. FAX: 918-343-7897. E-mail: library@rsu.edu. Web Site: www.rsu.edu/library. *Dir,* Alan Lawless; E-mail: alawless@rsu.edu; *Acq, Assoc Dir,* Laura Bottoms; Tel: 918-343-7719, E-mail: lbottoms@rsu.edu; *Access Serv & Distance Learning,* Sarah Clark; E-mail: sclark@rsu.edu; *Govt Doc, Info Serv,* Carolyn Gutierrez; Tel: 918-343-7786, E-mail: cgutierrez@rsu.edu; *Pub Serv,* Janice Ferris; Fax: 918-343-7720, E-mail: jferris@rsu.edu; Staff 5 (MLS 5)
Founded 1909. Enrl 4,632; Highest Degree: Bachelor
Jul 2011-Jun 2012 Income $866,816. Mats Exp $300,000. Sal $308,310 (Prof $229,810)
Library Holdings: CDs 1,263; DVDs 1,263; e-books 43,368; e-journals 40,000; Electronic Media & Resources 70; Bk Vols 76,000
Automation Activity & Vendor Info: (Acquisitions) SirsiDynix; (Cataloging) SirsiDynix; (Circulation) SirsiDynix; (OPAC) SirsiDynix; (Serials) SirsiDynix
Wireless access
Function: Archival coll, Audio & video playback equip for onsite use, AV serv, Bks on CD, Computers for patron use, Copy machines, Digital talking bks, Doc delivery serv, e-mail & chat, e-mail serv, Electronic databases & coll, Equip loans & repairs, Fax serv, Free DVD rentals, Govt ref serv, Handicapped accessible, ILL available, Music CDs, Online cat, Online ref, Orientations, Pub access computers, Ref & res, Ref serv in person, Spoken cassettes & CDs, Spoken cassettes & DVDs, Telephone ref, VHS videos, Wheelchair accessible
Open Mon-Thurs 7:30am-10pm, Fri 7:30-6, Sat 12-8:30, Sun 1:30-10

P WILL ROGERS LIBRARY*, 1515 N Florence Ave, 74017. SAN 313-8658. Tel: 918-341-1564. FAX: 918-342-0362. *Dir,* Sherry Beach; E-mail: sbeach@claremorecity.com; *Asst Dir,* Donna McClellan; Staff 6 (MLS 1, Non-MLS 5)
Founded 1936
Library Holdings: Bk Titles 55,000; Per Subs 42
Special Collections: McClellan Coll; Oklahoma & Indian History Coll
Subject Interests: Okla newsp from before statehood to present day
Automation Activity & Vendor Info: (Acquisitions) TLC (The Library Corporation); (Cataloging) TLC (The Library Corporation); (Circulation) TLC (The Library Corporation)
Database Vendor: EBSCOhost, Gale Cengage Learning, McGraw Hill, Overdrive, Inc, ProQuest
Wireless access
Open Mon & Tues 9:30-8, Wed & Thurs 9:30-6, Fri & Sat 9:30-5
Friends of the Library Group

S WILL ROGERS MEMORIAL MUSEUM LIBRARY*, 1720 W Will Rogers Blvd, 74017. (Mail add: PO Box 157, 74018-0157), SAN 320-2259. Tel: 918-341-0719. Circulation Tel: 918-343-8118. Toll Free Tel: 800-324-9455. FAX: 918-343-8119. Web Site: www.willrogers.com. *Assoc Dir/Librn,* Steven K Gragert; Tel: 918-343-8118, E-mail: skgragert@willrogers.com; Staff 3 (MLS 3)
Founded 1938
Library Holdings: CDs 123; DVDs 26; Bk Vols 2,750; Videos 76
Special Collections: Oral History
Subject Interests: Aviation, Cherokee Indians, Civil War, Film, Genealogy, Local hist, Politics, State hist, Vaudeville, Will Rogers
Publications: Will Rogers, genealogy (bibliographies)
Restriction: Open by appt only

CLEVELAND

P JAY C BYERS MEMORIAL LIBRARY*, 215 E Wichita Ave, 74020. Tel: 918-358-2676. FAX: 918-358-5606. Web Site: jcbyerslibrary.okpls.org. *Libr Dir,* Michelle Miller; E-mail: mmiller@jcbyers.lib.ok.us; *Libr Asst,* Debby Luthy; E-mail: dluthy@jcbyers.lib.ok.us; *Libr Asst,* Dawn Miears; E-mail: dmiears@jcbyers.lib.ok.us
Founded 1936. Pop 3,282; Circ 38,609
Library Holdings: AV Mats 30; Bk Vols 13,000; Per Subs 20; Talking Bks 60
Automation Activity & Vendor Info: (Cataloging) Follett Software; (Circulation) Follett Software
Wireless access
Function: Bk club(s), Handicapped accessible, Home delivery & serv to Sr ctr & nursing homes, Homebound delivery serv, ILL available, Prog for children & young adult, Summer reading prog, VHS videos, Wheelchair accessible
Open Mon-Fri 9:30-6, Sat 9:30-4
Friends of the Library Group

CLINTON

P WESTERN PLAINS LIBRARY SYSTEM*, 501 S 28th St, 73601-3996. SAN 313-8666. Tel: 580-323-0974. FAX: 580-323-1190. Web Site: www.wplibs.com. *Dir,* Jane Janzen; E-mail: jane.janzen@wplibs.com; *Asst Dir,* Dave Timothy Miller; Staff 23 (MLS 3, Non-MLS 20)
Founded 1966. Pop 45,000; Circ 201,000
Special Collections: State Document Depository
Automation Activity & Vendor Info: (Acquisitions) TLC (The Library Corporation); (Cataloging) TLC (The Library Corporation); (Circulation) TLC (The Library Corporation); (ILL) OCLC; (OPAC) TLC (The Library Corporation)
Database Vendor: Amigos Library Services, EBSCO Auto Repair Reference, EBSCOhost, OCLC FirstSearch, OCLC WorldShare Interlibrary Loan, Overdrive, Inc
Wireless access
Function: ILL available, Online searches, Prog for children & young adult, Summer reading prog
Member Libraries: Western Plains Library System
Partic in Amigos Library Services, Inc; OLTN
Special Services for the Blind - Talking bks
Restriction: Non-circulating coll
Friends of the Library Group
Branches: 7

CLINTON PUBLIC LIBRARY, 721 Frisco, 73601-3320, SAN 376-5938. Tel: 580-323-2165. Toll Free Tel: 888-363-9680. FAX: 580-323-7884. E-mail: clinton.public@wplibs.com. *Librn,* Kathy Atchley; Staff 3 (Non-MLS 3)
Founded 1968. Pop 8,833; Circ 44,160
Library Holdings: Bks on Deafness & Sign Lang 50; Bk Vols 75,000; Per Subs 50
Special Collections: State Document Depository
Function: AV serv
Open Mon & Wed 9-6, Tues & Thurs 9-8, Fri 9-5, Sat 9-1
Restriction: Access for corporate affiliates
Friends of the Library Group

CORDELL PUBLIC LIBRARY, 208 S College, Cordell, 73632-5210, SAN 376-5954. Tel: 580-832-3530. FAX: 580-832-3530. E-mail: cordell.public@wplibs.com. *Librn,* Rhonda Schmidt
Library Holdings: Bk Titles 50,000; Per Subs 12
Automation Activity & Vendor Info: (Circulation) TLC (The Library Corporation)
Open Mon, Wed & Thurs 11-6, Tues 9-1, Fri 11-7
Friends of the Library Group

HAZEL CROSS LIBRARY, 111 W Broadway, Thomas, 73669. (Mail add: PO Box 410, Thomas, 73669-0410), SAN 376-6004. Tel: 580-661-3532. FAX: 580-661-3532. *Librn,* Tonya Baldwin
Library Holdings: Bk Titles 5,000; Bk Vols 5,100; Per Subs 10
Automation Activity & Vendor Info: (Circulation) TLC (The Library Corporation)
Open Tues & Thurs 11-6, Wed 8:30-2:30, Fri 11-5, Sat 9-1

SEILING PUBLIC LIBRARY, PO Box 116, Seiling, 73663-0116, SAN 376-5997. Tel: 580-922-4259. FAX: 580-922-4259. *Librn,* Dawn Washington
Library Holdings: Bk Titles 13,000; Bk Vols 13,400; Per Subs 14
Automation Activity & Vendor Info: (Circulation) TLC (The Library Corporation)
Open Tues & Wed 11-6, Thurs 12-6, Fri 11-5, Sat 9-1

SENTINEL PUBLIC LIBRARY, 210 E Main, Sentinel, 73664. (Mail add: PO Box 178, Sentinel, 73664-0178), SAN 376-5989. Tel: 580-393-2244. Toll Free Tel: 888-639-0629. E-mail: sentinel.public@wplibs.com. *Librn,* Janet McEwen; Staff 1 (Non-MLS 1)
Library Holdings: Bk Titles 3,000
Open Tues & Wed 12:30-5:30, Thurs 9-12, Fri 12:30-5

MINNIE R SLIEF MEMORIAL LIBRARY, 201 S Cearlock St, Cheyenne, 73628. (Mail add: PO Box 370, Cheyenne, 73628-0370), SAN 376-5962. Tel: 580-497-3777. Toll Free Tel: 877-730-4206. E-mail: minnier.slief@wplibs.com. *Librn I,* Charlotte Nance; E-mail: charlotte.nance@wplibs.com; Staff 1 (Non-MLS 1)
Founded 1968
Library Holdings: DVDs 67; Bk Vols 9,000; Per Subs 15; Videos 365
Database Vendor: TLC (The Library Corporation)
Mem of Western Plains Library System

Open Mon-Thurs 10:30-5:30, Fri 10:30-5, Sat 9-1
Bookmobiles: 1
WEATHERFORD PUBLIC LIBRARY, 219 E Frankin, Weatherford, 73096-5134, SAN 325-1330. Tel: 580-772-3591. FAX: 580-772-3591. *Librn,* Jamie Hudson; *Asst Librn,* Cynthia Gauger
Founded 1969. Pop 12,000; Circ 42,000
Library Holdings: Bk Vols 63,000; Per Subs 40
Automation Activity & Vendor Info: (Circulation) TLC (The Library Corporation)
Open Mon 1-5, Tues-Fri 8:30-7, Sat 9-1
Friends of the Library Group
Bookmobiles: 1

COALGATE

P COALGATE PUBLIC LIBRARY*, 115 W Ohio St, 74538. (Mail add: PO Box 49, 74538-0049), SAN 376-6446. Tel: 580-927-3103. FAX: 580-927-3846. Web Site: www.coalgate.lib.ok.us. *Librn,* Margie Jump
Library Holdings: Bk Titles 25,000; Per Subs 17
Automation Activity & Vendor Info: (Circulation) SirsiDynix
Mem of Southeastern Public Library System of Oklahoma
Open Mon-Fri 10-6, Sat 10-3

COWETA

P COWETA PUBLIC LIBRARY, 120 E Sycamore, 74429. (Mail add: PO Box 850, 74429-0850). Tel: 918-486-6532. FAX: 918-486-3497. *Dir,* Paula Emmons; Staff 4.5 (MLS 1, Non-MLS 3.5)
Pop 9,569; Circ 60,778
Library Holdings: Audiobooks 385; DVDs 580; Large Print Bks 978; Bk Titles 23,294; Bk Vols 25,270; Per Subs 41; Videos 815
Automation Activity & Vendor Info: (Acquisitions) Book Systems; (Cataloging) Book Systems; (Circulation) Book Systems; (ILL) OCLC WorldShare Interlibrary Loan; (OPAC) Book Systems
Wireless access
Open Mon, Tues & Thurs 10-8, Wed 10-6, Fri 10-5, Sat 10-2
Friends of the Library Group

COYLE

SR ST FRANCIS LIBRARY*, 11414 W Hwy 33, 73027. (Mail add: PO Box 400, 73027-0400), SAN 326-7016. Tel: 405-466-3774. FAX: 405-466-3722. *Dir,* Chris Contreras
Founded 1982
Library Holdings: Bk Titles 19,000; Bk Vols 23,000
Special Collections: C G Jung Writings Coll, bks, journals; Francis of Assisi (St Francis Coll)
Subject Interests: Relig
Publications: Newsletter for St Francis of the Woods (Quarterly)
Open Mon-Fri 9-5

CRESCENT

P CRESCENT COMMUNITY LIBRARY*, 205 N Grand, 73028. (Mail add: PO Box 759, 73028-0759). Tel: 405-969-3779. FAX: 405-969-3779. E-mail: cclib@pldi.net. *Dir,* Shawn Rudd
Pop 1,281; Circ 4,708
Library Holdings: AV Mats 30; Bk Vols 8,000; Per Subs 19; Talking Bks 100
Subject Interests: Mil hist
Automation Activity & Vendor Info: (Cataloging) Follett Software; (Circulation) Follett Software; (OPAC) Follett Software
Open Mon-Fri 9-6
Friends of the Library Group

CUSHING

P CUSHING PUBLIC LIBRARY*, 215 N Steele, 74023-3319. (Mail add: PO Box 551, 74023-0551), SAN 313-8674. Tel: 918-225-4188. FAX: 918-225-6201. *Dir,* Ruth Ann Johnson; E-mail: ruthannjohnson2002@yahoo.com; *Asst Librn,* Roselee Maynard
Founded 1939. Pop 7,500; Circ 56,760
Library Holdings: Bk Vols 65,000; Per Subs 82
Special Collections: Genealogy (Cushing Family), bks, flm, micro; Law (Payne County Law Books); Local History
Subject Interests: Law
Automation Activity & Vendor Info: (Circulation) Innovative Interfaces, Inc
Open Mon-Thurs 9-8, Fri & Sat 9-6

DEWEY

P HERBERT F TYLER MEMORIAL LIBRARY*, 821 N Shawnee, 74029. SAN 313-8682. Tel: 918-534-2106. E-mail: tylerli2001@yahoo.com. *Dir,* Sandy Hadley
Founded 1941. Pop 4,000; Circ 16,012
Library Holdings: AV Mats 800; Large Print Bks 1,000; Bk Vols 15,000; Per Subs 32
Automation Activity & Vendor Info: (Cataloging) Follett Software; (Circulation) Follett Software
Open Mon-Fri 8:30-5:30, Sat 9-Noon
Friends of the Library Group

DRUMRIGHT

P DRUMRIGHT PUBLIC LIBRARY*, 104 E Broadway, 74030. SAN 313-8690. Tel: 918-352-2228. FAX: 918-352-9261. *Librn,* Brenda L Grisham; E-mail: blgrisham@drumright.lib.ok.us
Circ 4,152
Library Holdings: Bk Vols 30,000; Per Subs 15
Automation Activity & Vendor Info: (Cataloging) Follett Software; (Circulation) Follett Software
Open Mon 11-8, Tues, Wed, Fri & Sat 11-4, Thurs 2-8

DUNCAN

P DUNCAN PUBLIC LIBRARY*, 2211 N Hwy 81, 73533. SAN 313-8704. Tel: 580-255-0636. FAX: 580-255-6136. Web Site: www.youseemore.com/duncan. *Dir,* Jan Cole; E-mail: jcole@duncan.lib.ok.us; *Cat,* Brenda Strong; E-mail: bstrong@duncan.lib.ok.us; *Ch Serv,* Darbie LaFontain; E-mail: dlafontain@duncan.lib.ok.us; *ILL,* Lynn Thacker; E-mail: lynnt@duncan.lib.ok.us; *Per,* Amy Ryker; E-mail: aryker@duncan.lib.ok.us; *Tech Serv,* Maria Diaz; E-mail: mdiaz@duncan.lib.ok.us; Staff 11 (MLS 1, Non-MLS 10)
Founded 1921. Pop 22,500; Circ 112,000
Library Holdings: Bk Titles 60,000; Per Subs 140
Subject Interests: Genealogy
Automation Activity & Vendor Info: (Circulation) TLC (The Library Corporation)
Database Vendor: EBSCOhost, OCLC FirstSearch, ProQuest
Wireless access
Partic in Okla Telecommunications Interlibr Syst
Open Mon, Tues & Thurs 9:30-8, Wed & Fri 9:30-6, Sat 9-3
Friends of the Library Group

S HALLIBURTON ENERGY SERVICES*, Research Center Library, 2600 S Second St, 73536-0400, (Mail add: PO Box 1431, 73536-1431), SAN 313-8712. Tel: 580-251-3516. FAX: 580-251-2094. *Librn,* Michele Moren; Staff 1 (MLS 1)
Library Holdings: Bk Titles 13,100; Per Subs 150
Special Collections: Lab Notebooks, micro
Subject Interests: Chem eng, Oil well serv, Petroleum
Function: Res libr
Partic in Sci & Tech Info Network
Restriction: Staff use only

DURANT

P DONALD W REYNOLDS COMMUNITY CENTER & LIBRARY*, 1515 W Main St, 74701. SAN 313-8739. Tel: 580-924-3486, 580-931-0231. Toll Free FAX: 800-521-6529. Web Site: www.donaldwreynolds.okpls.org. *Libr Dir,* Dr Dottie Davis; E-mail: dodavis@durant.org; *Prog Dir,* Robbee Tonubbee; *Asst Librn,* Reba Titsworth; E-mail: rtitsworth@durant.org; *Circ Serv,* Gina Brown; *Circ Serv,* Robert Damron; *Circ Serv,* Taylor Williams; *Tech Serv,* Carla Dalton
Founded 1926. Pop 12,000; Circ 20,000
Library Holdings: Bk Titles 55,000; Bk Vols 66,514; Per Subs 25
Automation Activity & Vendor Info: (Acquisitions) TLC (The Library Corporation); (Cataloging) TLC (The Library Corporation); (Circulation) TLC (The Library Corporation); (ILL) OCLC; (OPAC) TLC (The Library Corporation)
Database Vendor: 3M Library Systems, EBSCOhost, Gale Cengage Learning, Newsbank, OCLC FirstSearch, Overdrive, Inc, Tech Logic
Wireless access
Function: ILL available
Open Mon-Thurs 9-8, Fri & Sat 9-5
Friends of the Library Group

C SOUTHEASTERN OKLAHOMA STATE UNIVERSITY*, Henry G Bennett Memorial Library, 1405 N Fourth Ave, PMB 4105, 74701-0609. Tel: 580-745-2702. Circulation Tel: 580-745-2168. Interlibrary Loan Service Tel: 580-745-2931. Reference Tel: 580-745-2935. Administration Tel: 580-745-3172. FAX: 580-745-7463. TDD: 580-745-3030. Web Site: www.se.edu/lib. *Dir,* Sharon Morrison; E-mail: smorrison@se.edu; *Cat Librn, Circ Librn, Coll Develop Librn,* Susan Webb; Tel: 580-745-2934, E-mail: swebb@se.edu; *Digital Serv Librn, Info Literacy Librn,* Kathryn Plunkett; E-mail: kplunkett@se.edu; *Electronic Res & ILL Librn, Ser Librn,* Sandra Thomas; Tel: 580-745-2933, E-mail: sthomas@se.edu; *Govt Doc Librn,* Brandon Burnette; Tel: 580-745-2795, E-mail: bburnette@se.edu; *Tech/Pub Serv Librn,* Dennis Miles; Tel: 580-745-2396, E-mail: dmiles@se.edu; *Circ Supvr,* Brandi Pate; E-mail: bpate@se.edu;

ILL Spec, Johnathon Sample; Tel: 580-745-2931, E-mail: jsample@se.edu; Staff 11 (MLS 6, Non-MLS 5)
Founded 1913. Enrl 4,075; Highest Degree: Master
Jul 2005-Jun 2006 Income $723,850. Mats Exp $268,433, Books $70,482, Per/Ser (Incl. Access Fees) $101,253, Micro $13,818, AV Mat $4,695, Electronic Ref Mat (Incl. Access Fees) $72,185, Presv $6,000. Sal $348,000 (Prof $284,312)
Library Holdings: CDs 5,082; e-books 8,000; Microforms 513,852; Bk Titles 109,100; Bk Vols 191,240; Per Subs 981; Videos 2,566
Special Collections: Curriculum Materials; Juvenile Literature Coll; Native American Coll. State Document Depository; US Document Depository
Subject Interests: Educ, Hist, Lit
Automation Activity & Vendor Info: (Acquisitions) SirsiDynix; (Cataloging) SirsiDynix; (Circulation) SirsiDynix; (Course Reserve) SirsiDynix; (ILL) SirsiDynix; (OPAC) SirsiDynix; (Serials) SirsiDynix
Database Vendor: Dialog, EBSCOhost, Gale Cengage Learning, Loislaw, Newsbank, OCLC FirstSearch, OCLC WorldShare Interlibrary Loan, ProQuest, PubMed, SirsiDynix, Westlaw
Wireless access
Partic in OCLC Online Computer Library Center, Inc
Open Mon-Thurs (Spring & Fall) 7:30am-10pm, Fri 7:30-5:30, Sat 1-5, Sun 3-10; Mon-Thurs (Summer) 8-8, Sun 3-8

EDMOND

CR OKLAHOMA CHRISTIAN UNIVERSITY, Tom & Ada Beam Library, 2501 E Memorial Rd, 73013. (Mail add: PO Box 11000, Oklahoma City, 73136-1100), SAN 313-945X. Tel: 405-425-5312. Circulation Tel: 405-425-5316. Interlibrary Loan Service Tel: 405-425-5324. Reference Tel: 405-425-5322. Administration Tel: 405-425-5320. FAX: 405-425-5313. E-mail: askalibrarian@oc.edu. Web Site: library.oc.edu. *Dir,* Tamie Lyn Willis; E-mail: tamie.willis@oc.edu; *Archivist, Head, Tech Serv,* Jennifer Compton; Tel: 405-425-5314, E-mail: jennifer.compton@oc.edu; *Electronic Res Librn, Ref Librn,* Dara Tinius; Tel: 405-425-5315, E-mail: dara.tinius@oc.edu; *Instrul Librn, Theological Librn,* Chris Rosser; Tel: 405-425-5323, E-mail: chris.rosser@oc.edu; *Acq Mgr,* April Ford; Tel: 405-425-5319, E-mail: april.ford@oc.edu; *Circ Mgr,* Kathy Fuller; E-mail: kathy.fuller@oc.edu; *ILL Mgr,* Connie Maple; E-mail: connie.maple@oc.edu; *Tech Serv Asst,* Michelle Sheldon; Tel: 405-425-5311, E-mail: michelle.sheldon@oc.edu. Subject Specialists: *Theol,* Chris Rosser; Staff 7.5 (MLS 4.5, Non-MLS 3)
Founded 1950. Enrl 2,200; Fac 100; Highest Degree: Master
Special Collections: Rare Books Coll; Restoration History Coll (A coll of materials from the Stone-Campbell Movement & by Church of Christ authors)
Automation Activity & Vendor Info: (Acquisitions) SirsiDynix; (Cataloging) SirsiDynix; (Circulation) SirsiDynix; (Course Reserve) SirsiDynix; (ILL) OCLC; (OPAC) SirsiDynix; (Serials) SirsiDynix
Database Vendor: Alexander Street Press, American Chemical Society, Amigos Library Services, BioOne, CQ Press, CredoReference, EBSCO Discovery Service, EBSCO Information Services, EBSCOhost, Gale Cengage Learning, JSTOR, Knovel, LearningExpress, LexisNexis, Mergent Online, OCLC, OCLC WorldShare Interlibrary Loan, Oxford Online, ProQuest, Sage, ScienceDirect, SirsiDynix, ValueLine, Wiley
Wireless access
Function: Archival coll, Audio & video playback equip for onsite use, Computers for patron use, Copy machines, Doc delivery serv, e-mail serv, E-Reserves, Electronic databases & coll, Free DVD rentals, ILL available, Magnifiers for reading, Online cat, Online info literacy tutorials on the web & in blackboard, Online ref, Online searches, Orientations, Photocopying/Printing, Pub access computers, Ref & res, Ref serv available, Ref serv in person, Res libr, Scanner, Telephone ref, VHS videos, Web-catalog, Wheelchair accessible
Partic in Amigos Library Services, Inc; Asn of Christian Librs; Christian Col Libr; Oklahoma Council of Academic Libr Directors (OCALD)
Special Services for the Blind - Assistive/Adapted tech devices, equip & products
Open Mon, Tues & Thurs 7:30am-11pm, Wed 7:30-6 & 9-11, Fri 7:30-6, Sat Noon-7, Sun 1:30-5 & 8-11

C UNIVERSITY OF CENTRAL OKLAHOMA*, Max Chambers Library, 100 N University Dr, 73034. (Mail add: PO Box 192, 73034-0192), SAN 313-8747. Tel: 405-974-2884. Circulation Tel: 405-974-3361. Interlibrary Loan Service Tel: 405-974-2876. Reference Tel: 405-974-2878. Automation Services Tel: 405-974-2865. FAX: 405-974-3806, 405-974-3874. E-mail: library@uco.edu. Web Site: library.uco.edu. *Exec Dir,* Dr Bonnie McNeely; Tel: 405-974-2883, E-mail: bmcneely@uco.edu; *Dir, Pub Serv,* Carolyn Mahin; Tel: 405-974-2595, E-mail: cmahin@uco.edu; *Dir, Archives & Spec Coll,* Nicole Williard; Tel: 405-974-2885, E-mail: nwillard@uco.edu; *Dir, Libr Syst & Tech Serv,* Habib Tabatabai; E-mail: htabatabai@uco.edu; *E-Learning Librn,* Deborah Thompson; Tel: 405-974-2880, E-mail: dthompson@uco.edu; *Mgr, Libr Develop,* Carrie Bond; Tel: 405-974-2877, E-mail: cbond@uco.edu; *Coordr, Cat, Metadata Coordr,* Shay Beezley; Tel: 405-974-2872, E-mail: sbeezley@uco.edu; *Coordr, Ref & Instrul Serv,* Ona Britton; Tel: 405-974-2979, E-mail: obritton@uco.edu. Subject Specialists: *Bus,* Carolyn Mahin; *Lit,* Ona Britton; Staff 20 (MLS 18, Non-MLS 2)
Founded 1890. Enrl 12,020; Fac 572; Highest Degree: Master
Library Holdings: Bk Titles 612,720; Bk Vols 960,412; Per Subs 2,147
Special Collections: Alice Ayler Orphan Train Coll, V-tapes; Bill Burchardt Coll; Dale McConathy Coll; Don Betz Coll; John George Coll; Oklahoma Townsite Coll; World War II (Sidney Bray Coll). Oral History; State Document Depository; US Document Depository
Automation Activity & Vendor Info: (Acquisitions) Ex Libris Group; (Cataloging) Ex Libris Group; (Circulation) Ex Libris Group; (Course Reserve) Ex Libris Group; (ILL) OCLC ILLiad; (OPAC) Ex Libris Group; (Serials) Ex Libris Group
Database Vendor: 3M Library Systems, ACM (Association for Computing Machinery), Agricola, Alexander Street Press, American Chemical Society, American Mathematical Society, American Physical Society, American Psychological Association (APA), Amigos Library Services, ARTstor, BioOne, Booklist Online, Bowker, Brodart, Cambridge Scientific Abstracts, Cinahl, College Source, CQ Press, CRC Press/Taylor & Francis Group, Dun & Bradstreet, EBSCOhost, Elsevier, Emerald, Ex Libris Group, Facts on File, Gale Cengage Learning, Haworth Pres Inc, IEEE (Institute of Electrical & Electronics Engineers), IOP, JSTOR, LexisNexis, Medline, Mergent Online, Modern Language Association, Natural Standard, OCLC, OCLC WorldShare Interlibrary Loan, Project MUSE, ProQuest, PubMed, ReferenceUSA, RefWorks, Sage, ScienceDirect, Standard & Poor's, ValueLine, Westlaw, WT Cox, YBP Library Services
Wireless access
Function: Art exhibits, Audio & video playback equip for onsite use, Bks on CD, CD-ROM, Computers for patron use, Copy machines, Distance learning, Doc delivery serv, e-mail & chat, e-mail serv, E-Reserves, Electronic databases & coll, Exhibits, Fax serv, Govt ref serv, Handicapped accessible, Microfiche/film & reading machines, Music CDs, Newsp ref libr, Online cat, Online info literacy tutorials on the web & in blackboard, Online ref, Online searches, Photocopying/Printing, Printer for laptops & handheld devices, Pub access computers, Ref & res, Ref serv available, Ref serv in person, Scanner, Spoken cassettes & CDs, Spoken cassettes & DVDs, Telephone ref, VCDs, VHS videos, Web-catalog, Wheelchair accessible
Partic in Amigos Library Services, Inc; Onenet
Open Mon-Thurs 7:30am-2am, Fri 7:30-6, Sat 10-6, Sun Noon-2am
Restriction: In-house use for visitors
Friends of the Library Group

EL RENO

S BUREAU OF PRISONS*, Federal Correctional Institution Library, PO Box 1000, 73036. SAN 313-8755. Tel: 405-262-4875. FAX: 405-262-6266. *Librn,* Brandon Bowers
Founded 1960
Library Holdings: Bk Vols 5,000; Per Subs 17
Open Mon-Thurs 12-3 & 5-8, Fri 12-3, Sat & Sun 7:30-10 & 11:30-3

S CANADIAN COUNTY HISTORICAL MUSEUM LIBRARY*, 300 S Grand Ave, 73036. SAN 327-571X. Tel: 405-262-5121. *Curator,* Pat Reuter
Library Holdings: Bk Vols 300
Special Collections: Indian Artifacts, Rock Island Railroad Effects, domestic, church & farming implements
Subject Interests: Local hist
Open Wed-Sat 10-5, Sun 1-5

P EL RENO CARNEGIE LIBRARY*, 215 E Wade, 73036-2753. SAN 313-8763. Tel: 405-262-2409. FAX: 405-422-2136. E-mail: library@elrenolibrary.org. Web Site: www.elrenolibrary.org. *Librn,* Kate Shaklee; *Ch Serv,* Penny Beals
Pop 15,000
Library Holdings: Bk Vols 31,700; Per Subs 149
Special Collections: Edna May Armold Archives
Automation Activity & Vendor Info: (Circulation) Biblionix
Wireless access
Open Mon-Thurs 9-7, Fri 9-5, Sat 9-1
Friends of the Library Group

J REDLANDS COMMUNITY COLLEGE*, A R Harrison Learning Resources Center, 1300 S Country Club Rd, 73036. SAN 313-8771. Tel: 405-422-1254. FAX: 405-422-1200. E-mail: library@redlandscc.edu. Web Site: library.redlandscc.edu. *Dir,* Christine Dettlaff; Tel: 405-422-1255, E-mail: dettlaffc@redlandscc.edu; Staff 4 (MLS 1, Non-MLS 3)
Founded 1965. Fac 44; Highest Degree: Associate
Library Holdings: Audiobooks 150; AV Mats 1,200; CDs 20; DVDs 500; e-books 40,000; Bk Titles 12,390; Bk Vols 20,184; Per Subs 100; Videos 390
Automation Activity & Vendor Info: (Cataloging) OCLC WorldShare Interlibrary Loan; (Circulation) TLC (The Library Corporation); (ILL) OCLC WorldShare Interlibrary Loan; (OPAC) TLC (The Library Corporation)

Wireless access
Function: Distance learning, For res purposes, Handicapped accessible, ILL available, Photocopying/Printing, Ref serv available, Telephone ref
Partic in Amigos Library Services, Inc; Oklahoma Council of Academic Libr Directors (OCALD)
Open Mon-Thurs 8-8, Fri 8-5, Sat 10-2

ELGIN

P ELGIN COMMUNITY LIBRARY*, 8183 State Hwy 17, 73538. (Mail add: PO Box 310, 73538-0310). Tel: 580-492-6650. FAX: 580-492-5787. E-mail: cityofelgin@onlineok.com. *Dir,* April Pinion
Pop 1,020
Library Holdings: AV Mats 325; Bk Vols 10,000; Per Subs 16; Talking Bks 166
Open Tues & Thurs 4:30-7

ELK CITY

P ELK CITY CARNEGIE LIBRARY*, 221 W Broadway, 73644. SAN 313-878X. Tel: 580-225-0136. FAX: 580-225-1051. E-mail: library@elkcity.com. *Adult Serv,* Pat Sprowls; *Ch Serv,* Donna McNaught
Founded 1912. Pop 10,000; Circ 76,000
Library Holdings: Bk Vols 47,000; Per Subs 35
Special Collections: Southwest Literature. Oral History
Automation Activity & Vendor Info: (Circulation) Follett Software
Open Mon, Wed & Fri 10-6, Tues & Thurs 10-9, Sat 10-2
Friends of the Library Group

ENID

C NORTHWESTERN OKLAHOMA STATE UNIVERSITY LIBRARIES*, Enid Library, 2929 E Randolph, 73701. Tel: 580-213-3141. FAX: 580-213-3140. E-mail: nwlibraries@nwosu.edu. Web Site: www.nwosu.edu/library. *Dir,* Susan Jeffries; Tel: 580-327-8570, E-mail: skjeffries@nwosu.edu; *Asst Dir & Syst Librn,* Marilyn Moore; Tel: 580-213-3111, E-mail: msmoore@nwosu.edu; Staff 1 (MLS 1)
Founded 1996. Enrl 400; Highest Degree: Master
Library Holdings: Bk Titles 10,000; Bk Vols 10,443; Per Subs 8; Videos 258
Automation Activity & Vendor Info: (Cataloging) Ex Libris Group; (Circulation) Ex Libris Group; (Course Reserve) Ex Libris Group; (ILL) OCLC; (OPAC) Ex Libris Group; (Serials) Ex Libris Group
Database Vendor: American Chemical Society, EBSCOhost, Gale Cengage Learning, JSTOR, Loislaw, OCLC FirstSearch
Wireless access
Function: Computers for patron use, Copy machines, Electronic databases & coll, ILL available, Online cat, Online searches
Open Mon-Thurs 8am-9pm, Fri 8-5
Restriction: Open to students, fac & staff

P PUBLIC LIBRARY OF ENID & GARFIELD COUNTY*, 120 W Maine, 73701-5606. Tel: 580-234-6313. FAX: 580-249-9280. E-mail: publiclibrary@enid.org. Web Site: www.enid.org/library. *Dir,* Michelle R Mears; *Ch Serv,* Kathy Logan; *Pub Serv,* Jade Powell; *Tech Serv,* Mary Shaklee; Staff 19 (MLS 2, Non MLS 17)
Founded 1899. Pop 58,928; Circ 146,404
Library Holdings: Audiobooks 1,762; Bk Titles 74,230; Bk Vols 80,845; Per Subs 160; Videos 1,608
Special Collections: Oklahoma Books & Authors (Marquis James Coll). US Document Depository
Automation Activity & Vendor Info: (Acquisitions) Follett Software; (Cataloging) Follett Software; (Circulation) Follett Software; (OPAC) Follett Software
Database Vendor: EBSCOhost, OCLC FirstSearch, ProQuest
Wireless access
Function: Adult literacy prog, Bks on CD, Copy machines, Electronic databases & coll, Free DVD rentals, Govt ref serv, ILL available, Online cat, Photocopying/Printing, Pub access computers, Ref serv available, Summer reading prog, Tax forms, Wheelchair accessible
Open Mon-Thurs 9-8, Fri & Sat 10-6
Friends of the Library Group

M SAINT MARY'S REGIONAL MEDICAL CENTER*, Medical Library, 305 S Fifth, 73701. (Mail add: PO Box 232, 73701), SAN 320-4154. Tel: 580-249-3092. *Mgr,* Karen Worsham; E-mail: karen.worsham@uhsinc.com
Founded 1964
Library Holdings: AV Mats 400; Bk Titles 2,000; Per Subs 150
Automation Activity & Vendor Info: (Serials) EBSCO Online
Database Vendor: Cinahl, DynaMed, McGraw-Hill, STAT!Ref (Teton Data Systems)
Wireless access
Partic in Basic Health Sciences Library Network; Greater Oklahoma Area Health Sciences Library Consortium; National Network of Libraries of Medicine
Open Mon-Fri 8:30-4:30
Restriction: Non-circulating

ERICK

P ERICK COMMUNITY LIBRARY*, 200 S Sheb Wooley, 73645. (Mail add: PO Box 385, 73645-0385). Tel: 580-526-3425. *Dir,* Jackie Morrow
Pop 1,100
Library Holdings: AV Mats 350; Bk Vols 11,000; Per Subs 17; Talking Bks 179
Open Mon, Wed, Fri & Sat 1-6

EUFAULA

P EUFAULA MEMORIAL LIBRARY, 301 S First St, 74432-3201. SAN 313-8801. Tel: 918-689-2291. FAX: 918-689-4124. E-mail: eufaulapl@eodls.org. Web Site: www.eodls.lib.ok.us/eufaula.html. *Br Mgr,* Peggy Black
Founded 1971
Library Holdings: Bk Titles 28,937; Per Subs 30
Subject Interests: Video
Automation Activity & Vendor Info: (Circulation) SirsiDynix
Mem of Eastern Oklahoma District Library System
Open Mon, Wed & Fri 8:30-5:30, Tues & Thurs 8:30-8, Sat 8:30-12:30
Friends of the Library Group

FAIRFAX

P FAIRFAX PUBLIC LIBRARY*, 158 E Elm, 74637. SAN 313-881X. Tel: 918-642-5535. FAX: 918-642-3350. E-mail: fxpublib@yahoo.com. Web Site: www.fairfax.lib.ok.us. *Librn,* Carol Irons
Founded 1922. Pop 1,555; Circ 4,307
Library Holdings: Bk Vols 17,974; Per Subs 28
Special Collections: Area History
Partic in Okla Telecommunications Interlibr Syst
Open Tues & Thurs 12:30-6, Sat 11-3
Friends of the Library Group

FAIRVIEW

P FAIRVIEW CITY LIBRARY*, 115 S Sixth Ave, 73737-2141. (Mail add: PO Box 419, 73737-0419), SAN 313-8828. Tel: 580-227-2190. FAX: 580 227 2187. E-mail: fairviewlibrary@yahoo.com. Web Site: www.fairview.org. *Dir,* Ernestine Titus; Staff 4 (Non-MLS 4)
Pop 3,730; Circ 15,907
Library Holdings: Bk Titles 20,400; Bk Vols 25,000; Per Subs 38
Special Collections: Oklahoma Heritage Coll
Subject Interests: Genealogy
Automation Activity & Vendor Info: (Circulation) Follett Software
Open Mon-Fri 9-5:30, Tues 9-7, Sat 9-Noon
Friends of the Library Group

FORT GIBSON

P Q B BOYDSTUN LIBRARY, 201 E South Ave, 74434. (Mail add: PO Box 700, 74434-0700), SAN 313-8836. Tel: 918-478-3587. FAX: 918-478-4599. E-mail: fortgibsonpl@eodls.org. Web Site: www.eodls.lib.ok.us/ft gibson.html. *Br Mgr,* Rhonda Lee
Founded 1978
Library Holdings: Large Print Bks 1,500; Bk Vols 22,000; Per Subs 25; Talking Bks 1,000
Subject Interests: Mysteries, Popular, Romances, Western
Automation Activity & Vendor Info: (Cataloging) SirsiDynix; (Circulation) SirsiDynix
Mem of Eastern Oklahoma District Library System
Open Mon & Wed-Fri 9-6, Tues 9-8, Sat 9-2

FORT SILL

UNITED STATES ARMY

A NYE LIBRARY*, 1640 Randolph Rd, 73503-9022, SAN 357-5462. Tel: 580-442-2048, 580-442-3806. FAX: 580-442-7346. Administration FAX: 580-442-7347. E-mail: nye.lib@us.army.mil. Web Site: www.sillmwr.com/recreation-leisure/nye-library. *Librn,* Joan Auwen; E-mail: joan.e.auwen.naf@mail.mil; Staff 10 (MLS 1, Non-MLS 9)
Founded 1953
Library Holdings: Audiobooks 2,004; AV Mats 604; CDs 1,057; DVDs 7,003; Large Print Bks 483; Bk Titles 73,028; Bk Vols 79,378; Per Subs 77
Special Collections: Books for College Libraries, microfiche; College Catalogs, microfiche; Webster University Deposit Coll
Subject Interests: Adult educ, Consumer educ, Family life, Home, Mil sci
Automation Activity & Vendor Info: (Cataloging) Innovative Interfaces, Inc - Millenium; (Circulation) Innovative Interfaces, Inc - Millenium
Database Vendor: Evanced Solutions, Inc, Innovative Interfaces, Inc

Function: Adult bk club, Audio & video playback equip for onsite use, Audiobks via web, Bks on CD, Children's prog, Computer training, Computers for patron use, Copy machines, Digital talking bks, Electronic databases & coll, Exhibits, Fax serv, Free DVD rentals, Handicapped accessible, Holiday prog, Microfiche/film & reading machines, Music CDs, Online cat, Online ref, Online searches, Orientations, OverDrive digital audio bks, Photocopying/Printing, Prog for adults, Prog for children & young adult, Pub access computers, Spanish lang bks, Story hour, Summer reading prog, Teen prog, Web-catalog, Workshops
Partic in OCLC Online Computer Library Center, Inc
Publications: The Tattler (Monthly newsletter)
Special Services for the Deaf - Bks on deafness & sign lang; Closed caption videos
Special Services for the Blind - Bks on CD; Copier with enlargement capabilities; Free checkout of audio mat; Large print bks; Playaways (bks on MP3); Recorded bks
Open Mon-Thurs 10-8, Fri-Sun 10-5
Restriction: Authorized patrons, Mil, family mem, retirees, Civil Serv personnel NAF only

A MORRIS J SWETT TECHNICAL LIBRARY*, Snow Hall 16, Bldg 730, 73503-5100, SAN 357-5438. Tel: 580-442-4525. FAX: 580-442-7300. *Librn,* Jo Ann Knight; E-mail: jo.ann.knight@us.army.mil; *Tech Serv,* Cora Daebler; *Tech Serv,* Daniel Heintzman; Staff 3 (MLS 1, Non-MLS 2)
Founded 1911
Library Holdings: Bk Vols 79,000; Per Subs 65
Special Collections: In-House Indexes; Janes Series; Military Periodical Analytical Index File, VF; Rare Books Coll; Special Bibliographies; Subject Headings to the Library Coll; U Military Science Classification System; Unit Histories-Field Artillery, bk, microfilm, fiche
Subject Interests: Ammunition, Ballistics, Field artillery, Mil hist, Mil sci, Missiles, Ordnance, Weapon systs, Weapons
Partic in OCLC Online Computer Library Center, Inc
Open Mon-Fri 7-5

FREDERICK

P FREDERICK PUBLIC LIBRARY, 200 E Grand, 73542. SAN 313-8844. Tel: 580-335-3601. FAX: 580-335-3601. E-mail: library@frederickok.org. Web Site: www.odl.state.ok.us. *Dir,* Dena Northcutt; E-mail: library@frederickok.org; *Asst Librn,* Kerry Benson; *Asst Librn,* Mark Hazel; Staff 3 (MLS 1, Non-MLS 2)
Founded 1915. Circ 16,384
Library Holdings: Bk Vols 15,000; Per Subs 36
Automation Activity & Vendor Info: (Cataloging) Biblionix/Apollo; (Circulation) Biblionix/Apollo; (ILL) OCLC ILLiad
Wireless access
Open Mon-Thurs 10-6, Fri 10:30-4:30, Sat 9-12
Friends of the Library Group

GEARY

P GEARY PUBLIC LIBRARY*, 106 W Main, 73040. (Mail add: PO Box 216, 73040-0216), SAN 313-8852. Tel: 405-884-2372. FAX: 405-884-2372. E-mail: grylib@pldi.net. Web Site: www.geary.okpls.org. *Dir,* Kay Perkins; Staff 1 (Non-MLS 1)
Founded 1933. Pop 1,200; Circ 14,000
Library Holdings: Bk Titles 10,000; Per Subs 10
Wireless access
Function: Workshops
Open Tues 10-12 & 1-6, Wed & Fri 9-12 & 1-5:30

GOODWELL

C OKLAHOMA PANHANDLE STATE UNIVERSITY*, Marvin E McKee Library, 409 W Sewell, 73939. (Mail add: PO Box 370, 73939-0370), SAN 313-8860. Tel: 580-349-1540. Toll Free Tel: 800-664-6778. FAX: 580-349-1541. E-mail: mckeelib@opsu.edu. Web Site: www.opsu.edu/McKeeLibrary. *Acq Mgr, Dir,* C Evlyn Schmidt; Tel: 580-349-1542, E-mail: ceschmidt@opsu.edu; *Access Serv Librn,* Rhonda Donaldson; Tel: 580-349-1547, E-mail: rdonaldson@opsu.edu; *Archives & Spec Coll Librn, Cat Librn, Tech Serv Librn,* Janet Kravig; Tel: 580-349-1546, E-mail: jkravig@opsu.edu; *Digital Initiatives Librn, Syst & Web Develop Librn, Youth Serv Librn,* Elaina B Stewart; Tel: 580-349-1544, E-mail: estewart@opsu.edu; *Acq Asst,* Dawn Lloyd; Tel: 580-349-1548, E-mail: dlloyd@opsu.edu; Staff 6 (MLS 4, Non-MLS 2)
Founded 1909. Enrl 1,367; Fac 65; Highest Degree: Bachelor
Library Holdings: AV Mats 5,155; Bks on Deafness & Sign Lang 20; e-books 34,616; High Interest/Low Vocabulary Bk Vols 100; Large Print Bks 25; Bk Titles 80,746; Bk Vols 86,000; Per Subs 212; Talking Bks 255
Special Collections: Elementary Education (McKee Library Youth Coll); Howsley Poetry & Shakespeare Coll; K-12 Education (McKee Library Textbook Review Center); McKee Library Archive Coll, bks, ephemera, per; State Public Schools (McKee Library Curriculum Coll). State Document Depository
Automation Activity & Vendor Info: (Acquisitions) Ex Libris Group; (Cataloging) Ex Libris Group; (Circulation) Ex Libris Group; (Course Reserve) Ex Libris Group; (ILL) Clio; (OPAC) Ex Libris Group; (Serials) Ex Libris Group
Database Vendor: 3M Library Systems, Agricola, Alexander Street Press, Amigos Library Services, Baker & Taylor, BioOne, Children's Literature Comprehensive Database Company (CLCD), Cinahl, EBSCOhost, Elsevier, Ex Libris Group, Facts on File, H W Wilson, Medline, OCLC FirstSearch, OCLC WorldShare Interlibrary Loan, Oxford Online, PubMed, Wilson - Wilson Web
Wireless access
Function: Audio & video playback equip for onsite use, CD-ROM, Computers for patron use, Copy machines, Doc delivery serv, e-mail serv, E-Reserves, Electronic databases & coll, Handicapped accessible, ILL available, Music CDs, Online info literacy tutorials on the web & in blackboard, Online searches, Outside serv via phone, mail, e-mail & web, Photocopying/Printing, Ref & res, Ref serv available, Res libr, Spoken cassettes & CDs, Spoken cassettes & DVDs, VHS videos, Video lending libr, Wheelchair accessible
Partic in Amigos Library Services, Inc; Oklahoma Library Technology Network (OLTN)
Special Services for the Blind - ZoomText magnification & reading software
Open Mon-Thurs 8am-10pm, Fri 8-4:30, Sun 5-10
Restriction: Borrowing privileges limited to fac & registered students

GRANDFIELD

P GRANDFIELD PUBLIC LIBRARY*, 101 W Second St, 73546-9449. (Mail add: PO Box 725, 73546-0725), SAN 313-8879. Tel: 580-479-5598. FAX: 580-479-5534. E-mail: grandpl@hotmail.com. *In Charge,* Teresa Speir
Founded 1944. Pop 1,450
Library Holdings: Bk Titles 9,006; Bk Vols 10,092; Per Subs 10
Open Tues & Wed 2-6, Thurs-Sat 9-1
Friends of the Library Group

GRANITE

S OKLAHOMA STATE REFORMATORY LIBRARY*, 1700 E First St, 73547. (Mail add: PO Box 514, 73547-0514), SAN 313-8887. Tel: 580-480-3700. FAX: 580-480-3989. *Librn,* John Slater; E-mail: john.slater@doc.state.ok.us; Staff 1 (MLS 1)
Pop 1,000
Library Holdings: Bk Vols 12,000; Per Subs 50

GROVE

P GROVE PUBLIC LIBRARY*, 1140 Neo Loop, 74344-8602. SAN 313-8895. Tel: 918-786-2945. FAX: 918-786-5233. Web Site: www.eodls.lib.ok.us/grove.html. *Mgr,* Brenda Newnam; E-mail: bnewnam@eodls.lib.ok.us
Founded 1963. Pop 20,000
Library Holdings: Bk Vols 31,000; Per Subs 38
Subject Interests: Genealogy
Automation Activity & Vendor Info: (Circulation) SirsiDynix
Mem of Eastern Oklahoma District Library System
Open Mon, Wed & Fri 8:30-5, Tues & Thurs 8:30-9, Sat 8-12

GUTHRIE

P GUTHRIE PUBLIC LIBRARY*, 201 N Division, 73044-3201. SAN 313-8909. Tel: 405-282-0050. FAX: 405-282-2804. E-mail: library@cityofguthrie.com. Web Site: www.guthrielibrary.com. *Asst Dir,* Candy Ford; E-mail: cford@cityofguthrie.com; Staff 4 (MLS 1, Non-MLS 3)
Founded 1903. Pop 36,301; Circ 78,000
Library Holdings: AV Mats 1,214; Bks on Deafness & Sign Lang 30; Large Print Bks 1,000; Bk Titles 22,302; Bk Vols 22,718; Per Subs 80; Talking Bks 601
Automation Activity & Vendor Info: (Cataloging) Auto-Graphics, Inc; (Circulation) Auto-Graphics, Inc; (ILL) Auto-Graphics, Inc; (OPAC) Auto-Graphics, Inc
Wireless access
Function: Accelerated reader prog, Adult literacy prog, Bks on cassette, Bks on CD, Children's prog, Computer training, Computers for patron use, Copy machines, E-Reserves, Fax serv, Handicapped accessible, Holiday prog, ILL available, Magnifiers for reading, Mail & tel request accepted, Music CDs, Online cat, Photocopying/Printing, Prog for adults, Prog for children & young adult, Ref serv available, Summer reading prog, Telephone ref, VHS videos, Wheelchair accessible, Workshops
Open Mon, Wed & Fri 9-6, Tues & Thurs 9-8, Sat 9-1
Friends of the Library Group

GUYMON

P GUYMON PUBLIC LIBRARY & ARTS CENTER, 1718 N Oklahoma St, 73942. SAN 313-8917. Tel: 580-338-7330. FAX: 580-338-2659. E-mail: guymonpublib@guymon.lib.ok.us. *Dir,* Rachel Sides; E-mail: rsides@guymon.lib.ok.us; Staff 6 (Non-MLS 6)
Pop 12,000; Circ 39,557
Library Holdings: Bk Vols 30,000; Per Subs 45
Automation Activity & Vendor Info: (Acquisitions) Baker & Taylor; (Cataloging) Biblionix/Apollo; (Circulation) Biblionix/Apollo; (ILL) OCLC WorldShare Interlibrary Loan
Database Vendor: EBSCOhost, ProQuest
Wireless access
Function: 24/7 Electronic res, 24/7 Online cat, Adult literacy prog, After school storytime, Archival coll, Art exhibits, Audiobks via web, Bilingual assistance for Spanish patrons, Bks on CD, Children's prog, Citizenship assistance, Computers for patron use, Copy machines, e-mail & chat, Electronic databases & coll, eReaders, Exhibits, Fax serv, Free DVD rentals, Genealogy discussion group, Handicapped accessible, Home delivery & serv to Sr ctr & nursing homes, ILL available, Magazines, Mango lang, Movies, Online cat, OverDrive digital audio bks, Photocopying/Printing, Preschool reading prog, Prog for adults, Prog for children & young adult, Pub access computers, Scanner, Spanish lang bks, Spoken cassettes & CDs, Story hour, Summer reading prog, Telephone ref, Web-catalog, Wheelchair accessible
Open Mon-Thurs 9:30-7, Fri 9:30-5, Sat 9:30-2
Friends of the Library Group

HARTSHORNE

P HARTSHORNE PUBLIC LIBRARY*, 720 Penn Ave, 74547. SAN 376-592X. Tel: 918-297-2113. FAX: 918-297-7004. E-mail: hartshorne@oklibrary.net. Web Site: www.hartshorne.lib.ok.us. *Librn,* Catherine Tucker
Library Holdings: Bk Vols 5,000; Per Subs 20
Automation Activity & Vendor Info: (Circulation) SirsiDynix
Mem of Southeastern Public Library System of Oklahoma
Open Tues & Thurs 10-7, Wed & Fri 10-6, Sat 10-3

HASKELL

P RIEGER MEMORIAL LIBRARY, 116 N Broadway, 74436. (Mail add: PO Box 429, 74436-0429), SAN 313-8925. Tel: 918-482-3614. FAX: 918-482-3266. E-mail: riegerml@eodls.org. Web Site: www.eodls.lib.ok.us/haskell.html. *Br Mgr,* Holly Hughes
Founded 1971
Library Holdings: Bk Vols 13,000; Per Subs 48
Automation Activity & Vendor Info: (Cataloging) SirsiDynix; (Circulation) SirsiDynix
Mem of Eastern Oklahoma District Library System
Open Mon & Wed 12-5:30, Tues 9-6:30, Thurs 9-5:30, Fri 12-4, Sat 9-Noon

HEAVENER

P HEAVENER PUBLIC LIBRARY*, 203 E Ave C, 74937. (Mail add: PO Box 246, 74937-0246), SAN 313-8933. Tel: 918-653-2870. FAX: 918 653 4805. E-mail: heavener@oklibrary.net. Web Site: www.heavener.lib.ok.us. *Librn,* Milena Robinson; *Asst Librn,* Rachael Morton
Pop 2,566; Circ 27,917
Library Holdings: Bk Vols 23,000; Per Subs 25
Automation Activity & Vendor Info: (Circulation) SirsiDynix
Mem of Southeastern Public Library System of Oklahoma
Open Tues & Wed 9-6, Thurs & Fri 10-6, Sat 9-2
Friends of the Library Group

HELENA

S CRABTREE CORRECTIONAL CENTER*, Law Library, Rte 1, Box 8, 73741-9606. Tel: 580-852-3221. *In Charge,* Linda Epps
Library Holdings: Bk Vols 500
Open Mon-Fri 8-4

HENNESSEY

P HENNESSEY PUBLIC LIBRARY*, 525 S Main, 73742. SAN 313-8941. Tel: 405-853-2073. FAX: 405-853-2073. Web Site: www.hennessey.lib.ok.us. *Dir,* Mary L Haney; *Asst Librn,* Karen Vogt; Staff 1 (Non-MLS 1)
Founded 1939. Pop 1,800; Circ 12,191
Library Holdings: Bks on Deafness & Sign Lang 10; Bk Vols 24,000; Per Subs 23
Special Collections: AFI 100 Best Films; Hennessey Clipper from 1890; Hennessey Heritage Coll; National Geographic, complete, leather bound; Ortman Film Memorial
Automation Activity & Vendor Info: (Circulation) Biblionix
Database Vendor: Gale Cengage Learning, OCLC FirstSearch
Wireless access
Function: ILL available
Open Mon-Thurs 9-6, Sat 10-1
Friends of the Library Group

HENRYETTA

P HENRYETTA PUBLIC LIBRARY*, 518 W Main, 74437. SAN 313-895X. Tel: 918-652-7377. FAX: 918-652-2796. E-mail: hplib@henryettalibrary.org. Web Site: www.henryettalibrary.org. *Libr Dir,* Ruby Wesson; E-mail: hplib@henryettalibrary.org; *Asst Librn,* Joann Hott
Founded 1910. Pop 6,096; Circ 36,150
Library Holdings: Audiobooks 108; CDs 150; DVDs 60; Large Print Bks 350; Bk Titles 20,000; Bk Vols 25,000; Per Subs 74; Videos 85
Automation Activity & Vendor Info: (Acquisitions) Winnebago Software Co
Wireless access
Function: CD-ROM, Children's prog, Computers for patron use, Copy machines, Fax serv, Free DVD rentals, Handicapped accessible, Home delivery & serv to Sr ctr & nursing homes, Homebound delivery serv, ILL available, Magnifiers for reading, Music CDs, Photocopying/Printing, Pub access computers, Story hour, Summer reading prog, Tax forms, Wheelchair accessible
Partic in Okla Libr Technology Network
Friends of the Library Group

HINTON

P HINTON PUBLIC LIBRARY*, 115 E Main, 73047. (Mail add: PO Box 34, 73047-0034). Tel: 405-542-6167. FAX: 405-542-6167. E-mail: library1@hintonet.net. *Dir,* Wanda Davis
Pop 2,175; Circ 13,639
Library Holdings: AV Mats 700; Large Print Bks 200; Bk Vols 8,700; Talking Bks 120
Automation Activity & Vendor Info: (Cataloging) Follett Software; (Circulation) Follett Software; (OPAC) Follett Software
Open Mon 10-7, Tues-Fri 9-4, Sat 9-Noon

HOBART

P HOBART PUBLIC LIBRARY*, 200 S Main St, 73651. SAN 313-8968. Tel: 580-726-2535. FAX: 580-726-3600. E-mail: hobartpl@hobart.lib.ok.us. *Dir,* Linda Branam; Staff 3 (Non-MLS 3)
Founded 1912. Circ 39,609
Library Holdings: Bk Vols 24,000; Per Subs 32
Special Collections: Kate F Phelps Genealogical Coll
Wireless access
Open Mon & Tues 9-7, Wed-Fri 9-6
Friends of the Library Group

HODGEN

S JIM E HAMILTON CORRECTIONAL CENTER*, Leisure Library, 53468 Mineral Springs Rd, 74939-3064. SAN 371-7704. Tel: 918-653-7831, Ext 372. FAX: 918-653-3814.
Founded 1970
Jul 2008-Jun 2009 Income $4,500, State $1,500, Federal $3,000. Mats Exp $4,500, Books $3,000, Per/Ser (Incl. Access Fees) $1,500. Sal $36,000
Library Holdings: High Interest/Low Vocabulary Bk Vols 50; Bk Titles 7,480; Per Subs 61; Talking Bks 34
Automation Activity & Vendor Info: (ILL) OCLC ILLiad
Database Vendor: EBSCOhost, OCLC WorldShare Interlibrary Loan
Open Mon-Fri 11-7

HOLDENVILLE

P GRACE M PICKENS PUBLIC LIBRARY*, 209 E Ninth St, 74848. SAN 313-8976. Tel: 405-379-3245. FAX: 405-379-5725. Web Site: www.holdenvillepl.okpls.org. *Dir,* Kim McNaughton; E-mail: readsrus@yahoo.com
Founded 1902. Pop 5,181; Circ 26,912
Library Holdings: Bk Vols 24,000
Automation Activity & Vendor Info: (Acquisitions) Follett Software; (Cataloging) Follett Software; (Circulation) Follett Software
Special Services for the Blind - Bks on cassette
Open Mon-Thurs 9-6, Fri 9-5, Sat 10-1
Friends of the Library Group

HOLLIS

P HOLLIS PUBLIC LIBRARY*, 201 W Broadway & Second St, 73550. (Mail add: PO Box 73, 73550-0073), SAN 313-8984. Tel: 580-688-2744. FAX: 580-688-9736. Web Site: www.spls.lib.ok.us. *Dir,* Dana Cook
Founded 1973. Pop 3,500; Circ 9,991

Library Holdings: Bk Vols 15,000; Per Subs 15
Automation Activity & Vendor Info: (Circulation) SirsiDynix
Open Tues 12-7, Wed & Thurs 10-5, Fri 9-2, Sat 9-1

HOMINY

S DICK CONNER CORRECTIONAL CENTER LEISURE LIBRARY*, PO Box 220, 74035. SAN 324-0126. Tel: 918-594-1300, Ext 4416. FAX: 918-594-1324. *Librn,* Scott Cloud
Founded 1979
Library Holdings: Bk Titles 8,000; Per Subs 35
Partic in Okla Telecommunications Interlibr Syst
Open Mon-Fri 8:30-3

P HOMINY PUBLIC LIBRARY*, 121 W Main, 74035. SAN 313-8992. Tel: 918-885-4486. FAX: 918-885-2837. Web Site: www.hominy.lib.ok.us. *Dir,* Jimmie Rattliff; E-mail: director@hominy.lib.ok.us; Staff 3 (MLS 1, Non-MLS 2)
Founded 1925. Pop 2,274; Circ 12,500
Library Holdings: Bk Vols 10,000
Automation Activity & Vendor Info: (Cataloging) Brodart; (Circulation) Brodart
Database Vendor: Innovative Interfaces, Inc, OVID Technologies
Open Mon, Wed & Fri 9-5, Tues & Thurs 9-6, Sat 10-1

HOOKER

P OLIVE WARNER MEMORIAL LIBRARY*, 111 S Broadway, 73945. (Mail add: PO Box 576, 73945), SAN 313-900X. Tel: 580-652-2835. Toll Free Tel: 800-651-0975. FAX: 580-652-2831. E-mail: owl73945@yahoo.com. *Dir,* Carolyn Blackwelder
Founded 1916. Pop 1,778; Circ 5,992
Library Holdings: AV Mats 210; Bk Vols 16,758; Per Subs 12
Special Collections: Hooker Advance Microfilm, 1907-present
Automation Activity & Vendor Info: (Circulation) Follett Software
Wireless access
Publications: Hooker History, Vol I-III
Open Mon 7pm-9pm, Tues & Thurs 9:30-11:30 & 1:30-5:30, Sat 2-5
Friends of the Library Group

HUGO

P CHOCTAW COUNTY PUBLIC LIBRARY*, 703 E Jackson St, 74743. SAN 313-9018. Tel: 580-326-5591. FAX: 580-326-7388. Web Site: www.oklibrary.net/hugo. *Head Librn,* Lila Swink; E-mail: swink@oklibrary.net; *Asst Librn,* Lisa Heady; *Ad,* Karen C Hart; E-mail: hart@oklibrary.net; *Ch,* Toni Love. Subject Specialists: *Genealogy,* Lila Swink
Pop 17,403
Library Holdings: Audiobooks 350; Bks on Deafness & Sign Lang 5; DVDs 400; Large Print Bks 400; Bk Vols 27,770; Per Subs 20; Spec Interest Per Sub 2; Videos 200
Special Collections: Circus Coll, bks, mags, posters
Automation Activity & Vendor Info: (Circulation) SirsiDynix; (ILL) SirsiDynix; (OPAC) SirsiDynix
Function: Adult bk club, Adult literacy prog, Archival coll, Art exhibits
Mem of Southeastern Public Library System of Oklahoma
Partic in OCLC Online Computer Library Center, Inc
Open Mon, Tues & Thurs 9-7, Wed & Fri 9-6, Sat 9-2
Friends of the Library Group

HULBERT

P HULBERT COMMUNITY LIBRARY, 201 N Broadway, 74441. (Mail add: PO Box 148, 74441-0148). Tel: 918-772-3383. Toll Free Tel: 888-291-8149. FAX: 918-772-3310. E-mail: hulbertpl@eodls.org. Web Site: www.hulbert.lib.ok.us. *Br Mgr,* Cherokee Lowe; E-mail: clowe@eodls.org
Circ 951
Library Holdings: Bk Vols 14,314; Per Subs 10
Automation Activity & Vendor Info: (Cataloging) SirsiDynix; (Circulation) SirsiDynix; (OPAC) SirsiDynix
Wireless access
Mem of Eastern Oklahoma District Library System
Open Mon & Wed 12:30-5:30, Tues 9-5:30, Thurs 9-6:30, Fri 12:30-5, Sat 9-Noon
Friends of the Library Group

IDABEL

P IDABEL PUBLIC LIBRARY*, 103 E Main St, 74745. (Mail add: PO Box 778, 74745-0778), SAN 313-9026. Tel: 580-286-1074, 580-286-6406. FAX: 580-286-3708. E-mail: idabel@oklibrary.net. Web Site: www.idabel.lib.ok.us. *Librn,* Linda Potts; E-mail: potts@oklibrary.net; *Asst Librn,* Julie Woods
Pop 5,946
Library Holdings: Bk Vols 40,000; Per Subs 40
Automation Activity & Vendor Info: (Acquisitions) SirsiDynix; (Cataloging) SirsiDynix; (Circulation) SirsiDynix; (Course Reserve) SirsiDynix; (ILL) SirsiDynix; (Media Booking) SirsiDynix
Mem of Southeastern Public Library System of Oklahoma
Open Mon-Thurs 9-7, Fri 9-5, Sat 9-3
Friends of the Library Group

INOLA

P INOLA PUBLIC LIBRARY*, 15 North Broadway, 74036. (Mail add: PO Box 1237, 74036-1237). Tel: 918-543-8862. Administration Tel: 918-543-3177. FAX: 918-543-3999. E-mail: inolalibrary@inola.lib.ok.us. Web Site: www.inolapubliclibrary.org. *Dir, Libr & Archives, Dir, Libr & Info Serv, Librn,* Claudia E Plett; E-mail: cplett@inola.lib.ok.us; *Asst Librn, Circ,* Gail Oquin Whitworth; Staff 2 (Non-MLS 2)
Founded 1967. Pop 80,757
Special Collections: Indian Cultural Coll
Subject Interests: Indians
Automation Activity & Vendor Info: (Acquisitions) Book Systems; (Cataloging) Book Systems; (Circulation) Book Systems; (ILL) OCLC ILLiad; (OPAC) Book Systems
Database Vendor: EBSCO Information Services, OCLC FirstSearch, OCLC WorldShare Interlibrary Loan
Wireless access
Function: Copy machines, Fax serv, Home delivery & serv to Sr ctr & nursing homes, ILL available, Spoken cassettes & CDs, Summer reading prog, Tax forms, VHS videos, Wheelchair accessible
Open Mon, Wed, Fri 10-4:30, Tues & Thurs 12-7
Restriction: In-house use for visitors, Lending libr only via mail, Lending limited to county residents, Open to pub for ref & circ; with some limitations

JAY

P DELAWARE COUNTY LIBRARY*, 429 S Ninth St, 74346. (Mail add: PO Box 387, 74346-0387), SAN 313-9034. Tel: 918-253-8521. Toll Free Tel: 877-445-6367 (OK only). FAX: 918-253-8726. Web Site: www.eodls.lib.ok.us/jay.html. *Br Mgr,* Karen Alexander; *Circ, Ch,* Carmen Dixon; Staff 3 (Non-MLS 3)
Founded 1970. Pop 3,492; Circ 37,379
Library Holdings: AV Mats 3,015; Bks on Deafness & Sign Lang 49; DVDs 358; Large Print Bks 619; Bk Vols 24,734; Per Subs 25; Videos 1,047
Automation Activity & Vendor Info: (Circulation) SirsiDynix
Wireless access
Function: Copy machines, e-mail serv, Electronic databases & coll, Fax serv, Handicapped accessible
Mem of Eastern Oklahoma District Library System
Open Mon, Wed & Fri 9-6, Tues & Thurs 9-8, Sat 9-1
Restriction: Authorized patrons, Circ to mem only, In-house use for visitors, Lending limited to county residents, Mem only, Non-resident fee
Friends of the Library Group

KANSAS

P KANSAS PUBLIC LIBRARY, Hwy 412 & Oak St, 74347. (Mail add: PO Box 397, 74347-0397). Tel: 918-868-5257. FAX: 918-868-2350. E-mail: kansaspl@eodls.org. Web Site: www.eodls.lib.ok.us/kansas.html. *Br Mgr,* Cherokee Lowe
Library Holdings: Bk Vols 6,000; Per Subs 20
Automation Activity & Vendor Info: (Cataloging) SirsiDynix; (Circulation) SirsiDynix; (OPAC) SirsiDynix
Wireless access
Mem of Eastern Oklahoma District Library System
Open Mon, Wed & Thurs 12-6, Tues 12-7, Fri & Sat 9-1
Friends of the Library Group

KAW CITY

P KAW CITY PUBLIC LIBRARY*, 900 Morgan Sq E, 74641. (Mail add: PO Box 30, 74641-0030), SAN 321-9917. Tel: 580-269-1317. FAX: 580-269-2957. E-mail: kawcitylibrary@yahoo.com. *Librn,* Stacey Richard. Subject Specialists: *Hist,* Stacey Richard; Staff 1 (Non-MLS 1)
Founded 1902. Pop 371; Circ 954
Library Holdings: AV Mats 56; Large Print Bks 80; Bk Vols 3,300
Subject Interests: Indian, Local hist
Wireless access
Function: Bk club(s), Bks on cassette, Bks on CD, CD-ROM, Children's prog, Computer training, Computers for patron use, Copy machines, e-mail serv, Family literacy, Games & aids for the handicapped, Handicapped accessible, ILL available, Music CDs, Notary serv, Online cat, Photocopying/Printing, Prog for children & young adult, Pub access computers, Scanner, Spoken cassettes & CDs, Summer reading prog, Teen prog, VHS videos, Video lending libr, Wheelchair accessible, Workshops
Special Services for the Blind - Audio mat; Bks & mags in Braille, on rec, tape & cassette; Bks available with recordings; Bks on cassette; Bks on

CD; Cassette playback machines; Cassettes; Free checkout of audio mat; Large print bks; Volunteer serv
Open Mon, Tues, Thurs & Fri 8-4:30, Wed 8-7

KELLYVILLE

P KELLYVILLE PUBLIC LIBRARY, 230 E Buffalo, 74039. (Mail add: PO Box 1260, 74039-1260). Tel: 918-247-3740. FAX: 918-247-3740. E-mail: kellyvillelibrary@gmail.com. Web Site: kellyville.biblionix.com. *Dir, Librn,* Jacqueline Case
Pop 906; Circ 10,833
Library Holdings: AV Mats 200; Bk Vols 13,000; Talking Bks 51
Special Collections: Early Literacy Coll
Automation Activity & Vendor Info: (Cataloging) Biblionix/Apollo; (Circulation) Biblionix/Apollo; (OPAC) Biblionix/Apollo
Wireless access
Open Mon 3-8, Tues & Wed 12-6, Thurs 12-7, Fri 8-4
Friends of the Library Group

KINGFISHER

P KINGFISHER MEMORIAL LIBRARY*, 505 W Will Rogers St, 73750. SAN 313-9042. Tel: 405-375-3384. Toll Free Tel: 888-995-9795. FAX: 405-375-3306. Web Site: www.kingfisher.lib.ok.us. *Dir,* Mike Tautkus; *Cat,* Rena S Tollison; *Circ,* Sharon Little; Staff 5 (Non-MLS 5)
Founded 1905. Pop 8,351; Circ 51,960
Library Holdings: Bk Vols 42,000; Per Subs 75
Special Collections: Civil War Coll; Kingfisher Coll; Okla Coll
Automation Activity & Vendor Info: (Cataloging) Follett Software; (Circulation) Follett Software
Database Vendor: EBSCOhost, OCLC FirstSearch, OVID Technologies
Open Mon-Thurs 9-7, Fri 9-5, Sat 9-1
Friends of the Library Group

KONAWA

P KENNEDY LIBRARY OF KONAWA*, 700 W South, 74849. Tel: 580-925-3662. FAX: 580-925-3882. Web Site: www.konawa.k12.ok.us. *Dir,* Karla Davis
Pop 1,479; Circ 18,318
Library Holdings: AV Mats 598; Bk Vols 15,000; Per Subs 25; Talking Bks 30
Subject Interests: Genealogy
Automation Activity & Vendor Info: (Cataloging) ComPanion Corp; (Circulation) ComPanion Corp; (OPAC) ComPanion Corp
Open Mon, Wed-Fri 8-3:30, Tues 8-7
Friends of the Library Group

LANGLEY

P LANGLEY PUBLIC LIBRARY*, 325 W Osage, 74350. (Mail add: PO Box 655, 74350-0655). Tel: 918-782-4461. FAX: 918-782-1056. E-mail: langleypl@gmail.com. *Dir,* Jeanie Norman
Pop 671; Circ 12,910
Library Holdings: AV Mats 250; Bk Vols 9,950; Talking Bks 500
Automation Activity & Vendor Info: (Cataloging) Follett Software; (Circulation) Follett Software
Open Mon 9-12 & 1-8, Tues & Thurs 9-12 & 1-6, Wed & Fri 9-12 & 1-5
Friends of the Library Group

LANGSTON

C LANGSTON UNIVERSITY*, G Lamar Harrison Library, PO Box 1600, 73050-1600. SAN 313-9050. Tel: 405-466-3298. FAX: 405-466-3459. Web Site: www.langston.edu/libraries.aspx. *Dir, Libr Serv,* Bettye Black; Tel: 405-466-3294, E-mail: brblack@langston.edu; *Head of Instruction,* Kate Corbett; Tel: 405-466-2968, E-mail: kcorbett@langston.edu; *Head, Pub Serv,* Joyce Peterson; Tel: 405-466-3604, E-mail: jepeterson@langston.edu; *Res & Instruction Librn,* Sheila Bryant; Tel: 405-466-3457, E-mail: ssbryant@langston.edu; *Res & Instruction Librn,* Shirley Tatum; Tel: 405-466-3463, E-mail: sbtatum@langston.edu; *Spec Res Librn,* Jameka Lewis; Tel: 405-466-3603, E-mail: jblewis@langston.edu
Founded 1949. Enrl 2,172; Fac 69; Highest Degree: Master
Library Holdings: Bk Vols 60,000; Per Subs 972
Special Collections: Black Studies (M B Tolson Black Heritage Center), multi-media. US Document Depository
Subject Interests: Allied health, Muticultural, Urban
Wireless access
Publications: The G Lamar Harrison Library Handbook
Open Mon-Thurs 9am-10pm, Fri & Sat 9-5, Sun 2-10

LAWTON

P LAWTON PUBLIC LIBRARY*, 110 SW Fourth St, 73501-4034. SAN 357-5497. Tel: 580-581-3450. FAX: 580-248-0243. Web Site: www.cityof.lawton.ok.us/library. *Dir,* David Snider; E-mail: dsnider@cityof.lawton.ok.us; *Genealogist,* Paul Follett; *Pub Serv,* Jim Maroon; *Tech Serv,* Denise Flusche
Founded 1904. Pop 108,144; Circ 259,215
Library Holdings: Bk Vols 120,513; Per Subs 327
Special Collections: Oklahoma (Voices of Oklahoma); Southwest Oklahoma Genealogical Research Coll. State Document Depository; US Document Depository
Automation Activity & Vendor Info: (Cataloging) SirsiDynix; (Circulation) SirsiDynix
Wireless access
Partic in Okla Telecommunications Interlibr Syst
Open Mon-Thurs 10-9, Fri & Sat 10-6
Friends of the Library Group
Branches: 1
BRANCH LIBRARY, 1304 NW Kingswood, 73505-4076, SAN 357-5527. Tel: 580-581-3457. *Patron Serv,* Bonnie Ahlquist; *Patron Serv,* Roberta Parham
Library Holdings: Bk Vols 4,200
Open Mon-Fri 1-5, Sat 10-3
Friends of the Library Group
Bookmobiles: 1

S MUSEUM OF THE GREAT PLAINS*, Research Center, 601 NW Ferris Ave, 73507. SAN 313-9077. Tel: 580-581-3460. FAX: 580-581-3458. E-mail: mgp@museumgreatplains.org. Web Site: www.museumgreatplains.org. *Curator,* Deborah Baroff
Founded 1960
Library Holdings: Bk Titles 30,000
Special Collections: Business of Early Lawton (Harry Buckingham Coll), archives; Extensive Hist of Transportation Coll with wagon & carriage manufacturers' catalogs & trade magazines (1869-1926); Manuscript Coll; Plains Indians Photograph Coll; Politics & Law of Early Lawton (Charles Black Coll & L M Gensman Coll), archives; Settlement of Southwestern Oklahoma, agr & hardware cat; Show Business 1900-1940 (Mildred Chrisman Coll), archives; State Politics in 1960s (Fred Harris Coll), archives; Wedel Coll
Subject Interests: Agr, Anthrop, Archaeology, Ecology, Hist of trans-Mississippi West, Settlement on southern plains
Publications: Great Plains Journal; MGP Record (Newsletter)
Restriction: Non-circulating to the pub, Open by appt only

LINDSAY

P LINDSAY COMMUNITY LIBRARY*, 112 W Choctaw, 73052. Tel: 405-756-3449. FAX: 405-756-2268. E-mail: citylibrary@ci.lindsay.ok.us. *Dir,* Jan Blaylock
Pop 2,889; Circ 15,289
Library Holdings: Bk Vols 15,600; Talking Bks 400
Automation Activity & Vendor Info: (Cataloging) Follett Software; (Circulation) Follett Software; (OPAC) Follett Software
Open Mon-Wed & Fri 9-4, Thurs 11-7, Sat 9-Noon

LOCUST GROVE

P LOCUST GROVE PUBLIC LIBRARY*, 715 Harold Andrews Blvd, 74352. (Mail add: PO Box 697, 74352-0697). Tel: 918-479-6585. FAX: 918-479-6582. Web Site: www.lg.lib.ok.us. *Dir,* Annissa Parris
Pop 1,405; Circ 8,283
Library Holdings: AV Mats 265; Bk Vols 9,685
Special Collections: Louis L'Amour Coll
Automation Activity & Vendor Info: (Cataloging) Winnebago Software Co; (Circulation) Winnebago Software Co; (OPAC) Winnebago Software Co
Open Tues Noon-7, Wed-Fri 10-5, Sat 9-Noon

MADILL

P MADILL CITY COUNTY LIBRARY*, 500 W Overton St, 73446. SAN 313-9107. Tel: 580-795-2749. FAX: 580-795-2749. E-mail: madlib@texomaonline.com. Web Site: www.madilllibrary.org. *Dir,* Susan Patton; *Librn,* Shirley Harkins
Founded 1915. Pop 14,000
Library Holdings: Bk Vols 15,000
Automation Activity & Vendor Info: (Acquisitions) Book Systems; (Circulation) Book Systems; (ILL) OCLC WorldShare Interlibrary Loan; (OPAC) EBSCO Online
Database Vendor: EBSCOhost, OCLC FirstSearch, OCLC WorldShare Interlibrary Loan
Wireless access
Open Mon, Tues, Thurs & Fri 9:30-6:30, Wed 9:30-7, Sat 8-Noon
Friends of the Library Group

MANGUM

P MARGARET CARDER PUBLIC LIBRARY*, 201 W Lincoln, 73554. SAN 313-9115. Tel: 580-782-3185. FAX: 580-782-5308. Web Site: www.mangum.okpls.org. *Librn,* Martha Young
Pop 5,849; Circ 10,000
Library Holdings: Bk Titles 12,332; Per Subs 15
Automation Activity & Vendor Info: (Circulation) Follett Software
Open Mon, Wed & Fri 10-5, Tues & Thurs 10-6, Sat 9-Noon
Friends of the Library Group

MANNFORD

P MANNFORD PUBLIC LIBRARY*, 101 Green Valley Park Rd, 74044. (Mail add: PO Box 193, 74044-0193). Tel: 918-865-2665. FAX: 918-865-3429. E-mail: mpl@cimtel.net. *Dir,* Colleen Branson; E-mail: cbranson@mannford.lib.ok.us
Pop 2,800; Circ 23,128
Library Holdings: AV Mats 1,000; CDs 110; DVDs 172; Electronic Media & Resources 1,288; Large Print Bks 339; Bk Vols 19,570; Per Subs 37; Talking Bks 189; Videos 1,288
Special Collections: Mannford History Coll, v-tapes
Automation Activity & Vendor Info: (Cataloging) Book Systems; (Circulation) Book Systems; (ILL) OCLC FirstSearch; (OPAC) Book Systems
Wireless access
Open Mon & Tues 10-6, Wed-Fri 10-5, Sat 9-12
Friends of the Library Group

MARLOW

P GARLAND SMITH PUBLIC LIBRARY*, 407 W Seminole, 73055. SAN 313-9123. Tel: 580-658-5354. FAX: 580-658-9110. *Librn,* Lois Bannister; *Asst Librn,* Pam Wilson; *Ch,* Melinda George; E-mail: cl@gs.lib.ok.us; Staff 2 (Non-MLS 2)
Founded 1938. Pop 5,000; Circ 26,400
Library Holdings: Bk Vols 15,600; Per Subs 25
Automation Activity & Vendor Info: (Circulation) Biblionix
Wireless access
Open Mon, Wed & Fri 12-5, Tues & Thurs 12-8, Sat 8-12
Friends of the Library Group

MAYSVILLE

P ELLIOTT LASATER MAYSVILLE PUBLIC LIBRARY, 506 Williams St, 73057. (Mail add: PO Box 599, 73057-0599), SAN 313-9719. Tel: 405-867-4748. FAX: 405-867-4749. E-mail: maysvillepl@gmail.com. *Librn,* Janet Dinwiddie
Founded 1963. Pop 1,500
Library Holdings: Bk Titles 31,000; Bk Vols 31,500
Automation Activity & Vendor Info: (Circulation) Follett Software
Wireless access
Open Mon-Thurs 8-5:30, Fri 8-Noon

MCALESTER

S JACKIE BRANNON CORRECTIONAL CENTER LIBRARY*, PO Box 1999, 74502. Tel: 918-421-3349. *Librn,* Position Currently Open
Library Holdings: Bk Vols 7,200; Per Subs 33
Automation Activity & Vendor Info: (Cataloging) Follett Software; (Circulation) Follett Software; (OPAC) Follett Software
Open Mon-Fri 8-8

P MCALESTER PUBLIC LIBRARY*, 401 N Second St, 74501. SAN 313-9093. Tel: 918-426-0930. Toll Free Tel: 800-562-9520. FAX: 918-423-5731. *Head Librn,* Christine Sauro; *Asst Librn,* Kathy McGuilberry
Pop 40,524; Circ 122,805
Library Holdings: Bk Vols 70,000; Per Subs 115
Special Collections: Local Newspaper Coll, dating back to 1890's. State Document Depository
Automation Activity & Vendor Info: (Circulation) SirsiDynix
Database Vendor: EBSCOhost, H W Wilson, LearningExpress, Newsbank, OCLC WorldShare Interlibrary Loan, World Book Online
Wireless access
Publications: Book List
Mem of Southeastern Public Library System of Oklahoma
Open Mon-Thurs 9-8, Fri 9-6, Sat 9-5
Friends of the Library Group

P SOUTHEASTERN PUBLIC LIBRARY SYSTEM OF OKLAHOMA, 401 N Second St, 74501. SAN 313-9085. Tel: 918-426-0456. FAX: 918-426-0543. Web Site: www.oklibrary.net. *Exec Dir,* Wayne Hanway; E-mail: whanway@oklibrary.net; *ILL,* Cara Dorrell; E-mail: cara@oklibrary.net; *Tech Serv,* June Doyle; E-mail: doyle@oklibrary.net; Staff 70 (MLS 4, Non-MLS 66)
Founded 1967. Pop 172,281; Circ 799,537
Jul 2013-Jun 2014 Income $4,526,545, State $120,362, County $4,169,437, Locally Generated Income $85,260. Mats Exp $629,811. Sal $2,778,443
Library Holdings: CDs 27,196; DVDs 34,584; e-books 3,027; Microforms 1,968; Bk Vols 425,613; Per Subs 684
Special Collections: All County Newspapers on Microfilm. State Document Depository
Automation Activity & Vendor Info: (Acquisitions) SirsiDynix; (Cataloging) SirsiDynix; (Circulation) SirsiDynix; (OPAC) SirsiDynix; (Serials) SirsiDynix
Wireless access
Member Libraries: Arkoma Public Library; Broken Bow Public Library; Choctaw County Public Library; Coalgate Public Library; Hartshorne Public Library; Heavener Public Library; Idabel Public Library; Latimer County Public Library; Mattie Terry Public Library; McAlester Public Library; Patrick Lynch Public Library; Spiro Public Library; Stigler Public Library; Talihina Public Library; Wister Public Library
Friends of the Library Group

A UNITED STATES ARMY*, John L Byrd Jr Technical Library for Explosives Safety, Bldg 35, One C Tree Rd, 74501. SAN 375-0671. Tel: 918-420-8787. FAX: 918-420-8473. Web Site: www.dac.army.mil. *Librn,* Christine L Holiday; Tel: 918-420-8772, E-mail: christine.holiday@us.army.mil; *Cat,* Blossom Hampton; Tel: 918-420-8707, E-mail: blossom.hampton@us.army.mil; Staff 3 (MLS 2, Non-MLS 1)
Founded 1984
Library Holdings: Bk Titles 4,500; Bk Vols 27,117; Per Subs 16
Special Collections: Accident Reports; Archives Search Reports; Site Plans & Maps; World War II Ordinance Minutes
Automation Activity & Vendor Info: (OPAC) SirsiDynix
Database Vendor: OVID Technologies

MEDFORD

P MEDFORD PUBLIC LIBRARY*, 123 S Main St, 73759. SAN 313-9131. Tel: 580-395-2342. FAX: 580-395-2342. E-mail: medfordpubliclibrary@gmail.com. *Dir,* Rose Towger; Staff 3 (Non-MLS 3)
Founded 1933. Pop 5,000; Circ 11,883
Library Holdings: Bk Titles 6,000; Bk Vols 12,000; Per Subs 10
Special Collections: Oklahoma Geneaology & History Coll
Automation Activity & Vendor Info: (Circulation) Follett Software
Wireless access
Function: Bks on cassette, Bks on CD, Children's prog, Computers for patron use, Copy machines, Large print keyboards, Online cat, Online ref, Online searches, Orientations, Photocopying/Printing, Pub access computers, Ref & res, Story hour, Summer reading prog
Open Mon-Fri 10:30-5:30
Restriction: Non-circulating of rare bks

MIAMI

R FIRST BAPTIST CHURCH*, Library-Media Center, First & A St SW, 74355. (Mail add: PO Box 1030, 74355-1030), SAN 313-914X. Tel: 918-542-1691. FAX: 918-542-1753. *Dir,* Ruth Ann Farris; Staff 8 (MLS 2, Non-MLS 6)
Jan 2007-Dec 2007 Income $3,000
Library Holdings: AV Mats 380; Bk Titles 5,400
Subject Interests: Christian life, Growth, Missions
Open Sun 9am-10:30am, Wed 4-6
Restriction: Mem only

P MIAMI PUBLIC LIBRARY*, 200 N Main, 74354. SAN 313-9158. Tel: 918-541-2292. FAX: 918-542-9363. Web Site: www.miami.lib.ok.us. *Dir,* Marcia Johnson; E-mail: mjohnson@miami.lib.ok.us; *Adult Serv,* Gay Fairchild; E-mail: gfairchild@miami.lib.ok.us; *Ch Serv,* Connie Bradley; E-mail: cbradley@miami.lib.ok.us; Staff 9 (MLS 1, Non-MLS 8)
Founded 1920. Pop 13,565; Circ 142,990
Library Holdings: AV Mats 4,026; Bk Titles 48,776; Bk Vols 51,447; Per Subs 118
Special Collections: Miami NewsRecord: 1901 to present, microfilm; Tar Creek Superfund Site Documents
Subject Interests: Genealogy, Indian hist, Okla
Automation Activity & Vendor Info: (Cataloging) Follett Software; (Circulation) Follett Software; (OPAC) Follett Software
Open Mon, Wed & Thurs 9-8, Tues, Fri & Sat 9-5, Sun 1-5
Friends of the Library Group

J NORTHEASTERN OKLAHOMA A&M COLLEGE*, Learning Resources Center, 200 I NE, 74354. SAN 313-9166. Tel: 918-540-6381. FAX: 918-542-7065. Web Site: www.neoam.cc.ok.us/~library. *Dir,* S C Brown; E-mail: scbrown@neo.edu; *Learning Res Coordr,* Rachel Lloyd; E-mail: rlloyd@neo.edu; Staff 10 (MLS 3, Non-MLS 7)
Founded 1925. Enrl 2,286; Fac 123
Library Holdings: Bk Titles 90,000; Per Subs 476

Partic in Okla Telecommunications Interlibr Syst
Open Mon-Thurs 8-8, Fri 8-4, Sun 2-6

MIDWEST CITY

J ROSE STATE COLLEGE*, Learning Resources Center, 6420 SE 15th St, 73110. SAN 313-9174. Tel: 405-733-7370. Interlibrary Loan Service Tel: 405-733-7338. Reference Tel: 405-733-7543. FAX: 405-736-0260. E-mail: refdesk@rose.edu. Web Site: www.rose.edu/lrc. *Dean,* Chris Meyer; E-mail: cmeyer@rose.edu; *Head Librn,* Melissa Huffman; Tel: 405-733-7538, E-mail: mhuffman@rose.edu; *Ref/Spec Projects Librn,* C Brad Robison; Tel: 405-733-7402, E-mail: crobison@rose.edu; *AV Coordr,* Barb Pfrehm; Tel: 405-733-7914, E-mail: bpfrehm@rose.edu; *Access Serv & Syst,* Mary Kirk; Tel: 405-736-0268, E-mail: mkirk@rose.edu; *Tech Serv,* Carolyn Hust; Tel: 405-736-0204, E-mail: chust@rose.edu; Staff 10 (MLS 6, Non-MLS 4)
Founded 1970. Enrl 5,200; Highest Degree: Associate
Library Holdings: Bk Vols 109,000; Per Subs 425
Special Collections: History of College (Rose State College Colls)
Subject Interests: Hist, Law, Lit
Automation Activity & Vendor Info: (Acquisitions) Ex Libris Group; (Cataloging) Ex Libris Group; (Circulation) Ex Libris Group; (Course Reserve) Ex Libris Group; (ILL) OCLC; (OPAC) Ex Libris Group; (Serials) EBSCO Online
Database Vendor: 3M Library Systems, Baker & Taylor, Career Guidance Foundation, Checkpoint Systems, Inc, Cinahl, College Source, CountryWatch, CQ Press, DynaMed, EBSCO Information Services, EBSCOhost, Ex Libris Group, Facts on File, Gale Cengage Learning, Hoovers, LearningExpress, Marquis Who's Who, Medline, Mergent Online, Newsbank, OCLC WorldShare Interlibrary Loan, ProQuest, PubMed, Westlaw
Wireless access
Function: AV serv, ILL available, Photocopying/Printing, Ref serv available, Telephone ref
Partic in OCLC Online Computer Library Center, Inc
Special Services for the Deaf - Assistive tech; Sorenson video relay syst; TDD equip
Special Services for the Blind - Assistive/Adapted tech devices, equip & products; Magnifiers; Videos on blindness & phys handicaps; ZoomText magnification & reading software
Open Mon-Thurs 7:30am-10pm, Fri 7:30-5, Sat 10-4, Sun 1-8
Restriction: Open to pub for ref & circ; with some limitations
Friends of the Library Group

MOORE

C HILLSDALE FREE WILL BAPTIST COLLEGE LIBRARY*, 3701 S I-35, 73160. (Mail add: PO Box 7208, 73153-1208), SAN 313-9182. Tel: 405-912-9025. Administration Tel: 405-912-9024. FAX: 405-912-9050. Web Site: www.library.hc.edu. *Dir, Libr Serv,* Nancy Draper, III; E-mail: ndraper@hc.edu; *Asst Libr Dir,* Patti Ashby; Staff 2 (MLS 2)
Founded 1968. Enrl 260; Fac 40; Highest Degree: Master
Library Holdings: Bk Titles 22,000; Bk Vols 26,000; Per Subs 232
Special Collections: Free Will Baptist Historical Coll
Automation Activity & Vendor Info: (Cataloging) TLC (The Library Corporation); (Circulation) TLC (The Library Corporation); (OPAC) TLC (The Library Corporation)
Database Vendor: EBSCOhost, OCLC FirstSearch
Wireless access
Restriction: Non-circulating to the pub

MOUNDS

P JULIA CROWDER MCCLELLAN MEMORIAL LIBRARY*, 15 W 14th St, 74047. (Mail add: PO Box 310, 74047-0310). Tel: 918-827-3949. FAX: 918-827-6010. E-mail: moundslibrary@moundsok.com. Web Site: library.moundsok.com. *Dir,* Kristin Haddock; Staff 1 (MLS 1)
Pop 5,000; Circ 14,000
Library Holdings: Audiobooks 300; AV Mats 500; DVDs 200; Large Print Bks 30; Bk Titles 14,000; Talking Bks 200
Special Collections: Local Yearbooks & History Coll, 1971-2002
Automation Activity & Vendor Info: (Acquisitions) Biblionix; (Cataloging) Biblionix; (Circulation) Biblionix; (Course Reserve) Biblionix
Wireless access
Function: After school storytime, Bks on cassette, Bks on CD, Children's prog, Computer training, Computers for patron use, Copy machines, Electronic databases & coll, Fax serv, Handicapped accessible, Notary serv
Open Mon-Fri 9:30-6
Friends of the Library Group

MOUNTAIN VIEW

P ADDIE DAVIS MEMORIAL LIBRARY*, 301 N Fourth St, 73062. (Mail add: PO Box 567, 73062-0567), SAN 372-6614. Tel: 580-347-2397. FAX: 580-347-2397. *Librn,* Kathy Hancock
Founded 1983. Pop 848; Circ 3,089
Library Holdings: Bk Titles 7,500; Bk Vols 8,468; Per Subs 15
Automation Activity & Vendor Info: (Acquisitions) Winnebago Software Co; (Cataloging) Winnebago Software Co; (Circulation) Winnebago Software Co; (Course Reserve) Winnebago Software Co; (ILL) Winnebago Software Co; (Media Booking) Winnebago Software Co; (OPAC) Winnebago Software Co; (Serials) Winnebago Software Co
Open Mon, Wed & Fri 1-6

MULDROW

P MULDROW PUBLIC LIBRARY*, 711 W Shanntel Smith Blvd, 74948. (Mail add: PO Box 449, 74948-0449), SAN 313-9190. Tel: 918-427-6703. FAX: 918-427-7315. Web Site: www.eodls.lib.ok.us/muldrow.html. *Dir,* Bethia Owens
Founded 1979
Library Holdings: Bk Vols 11,000; Per Subs 15
Subject Interests: Local hist
Automation Activity & Vendor Info: (Cataloging) SirsiDynix; (Circulation) SirsiDynix
Publications: Willison Library Bulletin
Mem of Eastern Oklahoma District Library System
Open Tues 10-8, Wed & Fri 10-5, Thurs 10-6, Sat 9-1
Friends of the Library Group

MUSKOGEE

J BACONE COLLEGE LIBRARY*, 2299 Old Bacone Rd, 74403. SAN 313-9204. Tel: 918-781-7263. FAX: 918-687-5913, 918-781-7376. Web Site: www.bacone.edu. *Dir,* Frances Donelson; Staff 1 (MLS 1)
Founded 1880. Enrl 900; Fac 40
Library Holdings: Bk Vols 42,000
Subject Interests: Behav sci, Local hist, Native Am studies, Nursing, Soc sci
Wireless access
Open Mon-Thurs 8-7, Fri 8-5

P EASTERN OKLAHOMA DISTRICT LIBRARY SYSTEM*, 814 W Okmulgee, 74401-6839. SAN 313-9212. Tel: 918-683-2846. FAX: 918-683-0436. Web Site: www.eodls.lib.ok.us. *Exec Dir,* Mary J Moroney; Tel: 918-683-2846, Ext 239, E-mail: mmoroney@eodls.lib.ok.us; Staff 75 (MLS 10, Non-MLS 65)
Founded 1973. Pop 244,790; Circ 1,085,256
Jul 2010-Jun 2011 Income $8,620,309, State $140,668, City $10,181, Federal $2,417, County $4,228,431, Locally Generated Income $4,238,612. Mats Exp $742,251, Books $459,219, Per/Ser (Incl. Access Fees) $40,075, Other Print Mats $9,000, Micro $685, AV Mat $137,902, Electronic Ref Mat (Incl. Access Fees) $95,370. Sal $1,943,681
Library Holdings: AV Mats 59,441; Electronic Media & Resources 26; Bk Titles 240,273; Bk Vols 504,189; Per Subs 775
Special Collections: Local History (Essa Gladney Coll), Tahlequah Branch; Native Americans & Early Oklahoma History (Grant Foreman Coll), Muskogee Branch
Subject Interests: Early hist Indian Territory, Genealogy
Automation Activity & Vendor Info: (Acquisitions) Horizon; (Cataloging) Horizon; (Circulation) Horizon; (ILL) OCLC; (OPAC) Horizon
Database Vendor: EBSCOhost, Gale Cengage Learning, LearningExpress, Newsbank, OCLC FirstSearch, OCLC WorldShare Interlibrary Loan, ProQuest, ReferenceUSA, SerialsSolutions, SirsiDynix, World Book Online
Wireless access
Function: Adult bk club, Adult literacy prog, Archival coll, Audiobks via web, BA reader (adult literacy), Bk club(s), Bks on cassette, Bks on CD, CD-ROM, Children's prog, Citizenship assistance, Computer training, Computers for patron use, Copy machines, e-mail & chat, Electronic databases & coll, Exhibits, Family literacy, Fax serv, Free DVD rentals, Genealogy discussion group, Holiday prog, ILL available, Literacy & newcomer serv, Mail & tel request accepted, Microfiche/film & reading machines, Notary serv, Online cat, Online ref, Online searches, Outreach serv, Photocopying/Printing, Preschool outreach, Preschool reading prog, Prog for adults, Prog for children & young adult, Pub access computers, Ref serv available, Ref serv in person, Scanner, Senior computer classes, Story hour, Summer & winter reading prog, Summer reading prog, Tax forms, Teen prog, Telephone ref, VHS videos, Video lending libr, Web-catalog, Wheelchair accessible
Member Libraries: Delaware County Library; Eufaula Memorial Library; Grove Public Library; Hulbert Community Library; Jim Lucas Checotah Public Library; John F Henderson Public Library; Kansas Public Library; Muldrow Public Library; Muskogee Public Library; Q B Boydstun Library; Rieger Memorial Library; Stanley Tubbs Memorial Library; Stilwell Public Library; Tahlequah Public Library; Warner Public Library
Restriction: 24-hr pass syst for students only
Friends of the Library Group

S JACK C MONTGOMERY VA MEDICAL CENTER*, Health Sciences Library, 1011 Honor Heights Dr, 74401. SAN 313-9263. Tel: 918-680-3753. FAX: 918-680-3752. *Mgr,* Sandra Todd; E-mail: sandra.todd@va.gov; *Nursing Educator,* Hyacinth Rogers; Staff 1 (MLS 1)
Founded 1946
Library Holdings: Bk Vols 6,847
Special Collections: Persian Gulf War Coll; Vietnam Veterans Coll
Subject Interests: Allied health fields, Med, Nursing
Publications: Journal Holdings
Open Mon-Fri 7-3:30

L MUSKOGEE LAW LIBRARY ASSOCIATION*, Muskogee County Court House, 74401. SAN 313-9239. Tel: 918-682-7873. *Law Librn,* Chris James
Library Holdings: Bk Vols 10,000

P MUSKOGEE PUBLIC LIBRARY*, 801 W Okmulgee, 74401. SAN 313-9247. Tel: 918-682-6657. FAX: 918-682-9466. E-mail: muskpublib@eok.lib.ok.us. Web Site: www.eok.lib.ok.us. *Head Librn,* Jan Bryant; E-mail: ljanbryant@eok.lib.ok.us; *Circ,* Debbie Goodwin; Staff 4 (MLS 2, Non-MLS 2)
Founded 1909. Pop 199,225
Library Holdings: Bk Vols 247,015; Per Subs 625
Special Collections: Local Hist (Grant Foreman Room)
Automation Activity & Vendor Info: (Acquisitions) SirsiDynix; (Cataloging) SirsiDynix; (Circulation) SirsiDynix; (Course Reserve) SirsiDynix; (ILL) SirsiDynix; (Media Booking) SirsiDynix; (OPAC) SirsiDynix; (Serials) SirsiDynix
Mem of Eastern Oklahoma District Library System
Open Mon, Tues & Thurs 9-9, Wed & Fri 9-6, Sat 9-5:30
Friends of the Library Group

MUSTANG

P MUSTANG PUBLIC LIBRARY, 1201 N Mustang Rd, 73064. (Mail add: 1501 N Mustang Dr, 73064). Tel: 405-376-2226. FAX: 405-376-9925. Web Site: www.mustanglibrary.org. *Dir,* Desiree Webber; E-mail: dwebber@cityofmustang.org; *Youth Serv Librn,* Lizzy Brown; E-mail: ebrown@cityofmustang.org; *Circ Mgr,* Elsie Purcell; E-mail: epurcell@cityofmustang.org; Staff 3 (MLS 1, Non-MLS 2)
Pop 45,000; Circ 213,580
Jul 2013-Jun 2014 Income $415,762, State $16,524, City $399,238. Mats Exp $55,120, Books $32,550, Per/Ser (Incl. Access Fees) $2,600, AV Mat $9,745, Electronic Ref Mat (Incl. Access Fees) $10,225. Sal $253,031
Library Holdings: Audiobooks 2,230; DVDs 4,344; e-books 23,062; e-journals 234; Electronic Media & Resources 40; Large Print Bks 1,000; Bk Titles 48,999; Bk Vols 57,700; Per Subs 301
Automation Activity & Vendor Info: (Acquisitions) TLC (The Library Corporation); (Cataloging) TLC (The Library Corporation); (Circulation) TLC (The Library Corporation); (ILL) OCLC; (OPAC) TLC (The Library Corporation)
Database Vendor: ALLDATA Online, EBSCOhost
Wireless access
Function: 24/7 Electronic res, 24/7 Online cat, Audiobks via web, Bks on CD, CD-ROM, Children's prog, Computers for patron use, Copy machines, Fax serv, Free DVD rentals, Handicapped accessible, Holiday prog, Life-long learning prog for all ages, Mango lang, Movies, Music CDs, Online cat, OverDrive digital audio bks, Photocopying/Printing, Preschool outreach, Preschool reading prog, Prog for adults, Prog for children & young adult, Pub access computers, Ref serv available, Ref serv in person, Story hour, Study rm, Summer reading prog, Tax forms, Teen prog, Web-catalog, Wheelchair accessible
Open Mon, Wed & Thurs 9-8, Tues 9-9, Fri & Sat 9-5:30
Friends of the Library Group

NEWKIRK

P NEWKIRK PUBLIC LIBRARY*, 116 N Maple St, 74647-4011. SAN 313-9271. Tel: 580-362-3934. FAX: 580-362-1028. Web Site: www.newkirkpl.okpls.org. *Librn,* Carol Kaspar; E-mail: ckaspar@hotmail.com; Staff 1 (Non-MLS 1)
Founded 1910. Pop 2,600; Circ 21,169
Library Holdings: Bk Titles 20,000; Per Subs 33
Automation Activity & Vendor Info: (Cataloging) Follett Software; (Circulation) Follett Software
Function: ILL available, Prog for children & young adult
Special Services for the Deaf - Adult & family literacy prog
Open Mon-Thurs 11-6, Fri 11-5, Sat 9-Noon
Restriction: Circ to mil employees only
Friends of the Library Group

NORMAN

M GRIFFIN MEMORIAL HOSPITAL*, Professional Medical Research Library, Bldg 54W, Rm 221, 900 E Main St, 73071. SAN 313-928X. Tel: 405-321-4880, Ext 2061. FAX: 405-573-6684. *Med Librn,* Emily McEween; Staff 1 (Non-MLS 1)
Library Holdings: Bk Vols 2,000; Per Subs 50
Special Collections: Old Psychiatry Book Archive
Subject Interests: Psychiat
Database Vendor: DynaMed, EBSCOhost, Medline, Micromedex, OCLC FirstSearch, OVID Technologies, PubMed
Function: Archival coll, For res purposes, ILL available, Ref serv available, Res libr, Telephone ref
Publications: Nothing but Psychiatry (Research books & journal)
Partic in Greater Oklahoma Area Health Sciences Library Consortium
Restriction: Med staff only
Friends of the Library Group

S NATIONAL WEATHER CENTER LIBRARY*, 120 David L Boren Blvd, Ste 4300, 73072-7303. SAN 313-9298. Tel: 405-325-1171. FAX: 405-325-1130. Web Site: www.nwc.ou.edu/library.php. *Librn,* Heather Murphy; E-mail: hmurphy@ou.edu. Subject Specialists: *Atmospheric sci,* Heather Murphy; Staff 1 (MLS 1)
Founded 1973
Jul 2009-Jun 2010 Income $137,400. Mats Exp $41,350, Books $6,000, Per/Ser (Incl. Access Fees) $34,100, Other Print Mats $1,250. Sal $67,500 (Prof $52,000)
Library Holdings: DVDs 40; Bk Vols 4,200; Per Subs 35; Videos 25
Subject Interests: Atmospheric physics, Computer prog, Meteorology, Severe storms dynamics, Storm hazards to aircraft, Tornado studies
Wireless access
Function: Computers for patron use, Copy machines, e-mail serv, Electronic databases & coll, Fax serv, Govt ref serv, ILL available, Online cat, Orientations, Ref & res, Res libr, Scanner, Workshops
Restriction: Authorized patrons

M NORMAN REGIONAL HOSPITAL*, Health Sciences Library, 901 N Porter, 73070. (Mail add: PO Box 1308, 73070-1308), SAN 313-9301. Tel: 405-307-1425. FAX: 405-307-1428. *Head Librn,* Amy Picard; E-mail: apicard@nrh-ok.com; Staff 2 (MLS 2)
Founded 1973
Library Holdings: Bk Titles 3,000; Per Subs 150
Subject Interests: Allied health care prof, Med, Nursing
Database Vendor: EBSCOhost, OVID Technologies
Partic in Greater Oklahoma Area Health Sciences Library Consortium
Restriction: Staff use only

G OKLAHOMA DEPARTMENT OF WILDLIFE CONSERVATION*, Fishery Research Laboratory Library, 500 E Constellation, 73072. SAN 325-0857. Tel: 405-325-7288. *Librn,* Sherylann Densow; Staff 1 (Non-MLS 1)
Founded 1949
Library Holdings: Bk Vols 300
Subject Interests: Freshwater fishery biol
Publications: Bulletin of the Oklahoma Fishery Research Laboratory
Restriction: Not open to pub

P PIONEER LIBRARY SYSTEM*, 300 Norman Ctr Ct, 73072. SAN 357-5616. Tel: 405-801-4500. FAX: 405-801-4516. Web Site: www.pioneer.lib.ok.us. *Dir,* Anne Masters; Tel: 405-801-4502, E-mail: amasters@pls.lib.ok.us; *Assoc Dir, Tech,* Andy Peters; Tel: 405-801-4560, E-mail: andy@pls.lib.ok.us; *Asst Dir, Planning & Operations,* Theresa Dickson; Tel: 405-701-2643, E-mail: theresa@pls.lib.ok.us; *Asst Dir, Libr Serv,* Lisa Wells; Tel: 405-801-4503, E-mail: lisa@pls.lib.ok.us; *Bus Mgr,* Doug Buck; Tel: 405-801-4505, E-mail: dbuck@pls.lib.ok.us; Staff 68 (MLS 48, Non-MLS 20)
Founded 1957. Pop 363,796; Circ 2,878,855
Jul 2012-Jun 2013 Income $14,087,627. Mats Exp $1,980,843. Sal $7,074,368
Library Holdings: Bk Titles 207,978; Bk Vols 768,408
Special Collections: Oklahoma Coll
Automation Activity & Vendor Info: (Acquisitions) Brodart; (Cataloging) SirsiDynix; (Circulation) SirsiDynix; (ILL) OCLC
Wireless access
Publications: My Library (Newsletter); Pioneer Library System Annual Report
Member Libraries: Dansville Public Library; Perry Public Library; Sodus Community Library; Williamson Free Public Library
Open Mon-Thurs 9-9, Fri & Sat 9-5, Sun 1-5
Friends of the Library Group
Branches: 10
BLANCHARD PUBLIC, 200 NE Tenth St, Blanchard, 73010. (Mail add: PO Box 614, Blanchard, 73010), SAN 357-5640. Tel: 405-485-2275. FAX: 405-485-9452. *Mgr,* Becky Pauls; E-mail: bpauls@pls.lib.ok.us
Pop 7,600; Circ 115,877
Library Holdings: Bk Titles 22,208; Bk Vols 24,240
Open Mon-Thurs 10-7, Fri 10-6, Sat 10-1, Sun 1-5
Friends of the Library Group

MCLOUD PUBLIC, 133 N Main, McLoud, 74851, SAN 370-9019. Tel: 405-964-2960. FAX: 405-964-5389. *Mgr,* Wanda Haynes; E-mail: whaynes@pls.lib.ok.us
Pop 4,050; Circ 50,875
Library Holdings: Bk Titles 13,828; Bk Vols 14,954
Open Mon-Thurs 10-7, Fri 10-6, Sat 10-1, Sun 1-5
Friends of the Library Group

MOORE PUBLIC, 225 S Howard, Moore, 73160, SAN 357-5675. Tel: 405-793-5100. FAX: 405-793-8755. *Br Mgr,* Ashley Miller; E-mail: amiller@pls.lib.ok.us
Pop 56,315; Circ 764,111
Library Holdings: Bk Titles 134,371; Bk Vols 184,859
Open Mon-Fri 9-9, Sat 9-5, Sun 1-6
Friends of the Library Group

NEWCASTLE PUBLIC, 705 NW Tenth, Newcastle, 73065. (Mail add: PO Box 780, Newcastle, 73065-0780), SAN 357-5691. Tel: 405-387-5076. FAX: 405-387-5204. *Mgr,* Kathie Thomas; E-mail: kathie@pls.lib.ok.us
Pop 7,847; Circ 83,685
Library Holdings: Bk Titles 26,248; Bk Vols 28,315
Open Mon-Thurs 9-7, Fri 9-6, Sat 9-5, Sun 1-5
Friends of the Library Group

NOBLE PUBLIC, 204 N Fifth St, Noble, 73068. (Mail add: PO Box 2120, Noble, 73068), SAN 328-7238. Tel: 405-872-5713. FAX: 405-872-8329. *Br Mgr,* Cathy Adams; E-mail: cadams@pls.lib.ok.us
Pop 6,624; Circ 92,414
Library Holdings: Bk Titles 27,961; Bk Vols 32,167
Open Mon-Thurs 9-7, Fri 9-6, Sat 9-5, Sun 1-5
Friends of the Library Group

NORMAN PUBLIC, 225 N Webster, 73069, SAN 357-5705. Tel: 405-701-2600. FAX: 405-701-2608. *Br Mgr,* Leslie Tabor; E-mail: leslie@pls.lib.ok.us
Pop 113,273; Circ 1,062,842
Library Holdings: Bk Titles 167,244; Bk Vols 251,700
Open Mon-Thurs 9-9, Fri 9-8, Sat 9-5, Sun 1-6
Friends of the Library Group

PURCELL PUBLIC, 919 N Ninth, Purcell, 73080, SAN 357-573X. Tel: 405-527-5546. FAX: 405-527-7140. *County Coordr,* Peggy Cook; E-mail: peggy@pls.lib.ok.us
Pop 6,006; Circ 96,854
Library Holdings: Bk Titles 37,818; Bk Vols 42,419
Open Mon-Thurs 9-7, Fri 9-6, Sat 9-5, Sun 1-5
Friends of the Library Group

SHAWNEE PUBLIC, 101 N Philadelphia, Shawnee, 74801, SAN 357-5764. Tel: 405-275-6353. FAX: 405-273-0590. *County Coordr,* Karen Bays; E-mail: kbays@pls.lib.ok.us
Pop 30,212; Circ 287,035
Library Holdings: Bk Titles 73,607; Bk Vols 86,644
Open Mon-Thurs 9-9, Fri 9-6, Sat 9-5, Sun 1-5
Friends of the Library Group

SOUTHWEST OKLAHOMA CITY PUBLIC LIBRARY, 2201 SW 134th St, Oklahoma City, 73170. Tel: 405-979-2200. FAX: 405-692-6394. *Br Mgr,* Aiden Street; E-mail: astreet@pls.lib.ok.us
Circ 121,643
Library Holdings: Bk Titles 57,523; Bk Vols 62,329
Open Mon-Thurs 9-9, Fri 9-8, Sat 9-5, Sun 1-6

TECUMSEH PUBLIC, 114 N Broadway, Tecumseh, 74873, SAN 357-5799. Tel: 405-598-5955. FAX: 405-598-5416. *Br Mgr,* Elizabeth Lyle; E-mail: bethlyle@pls.lib.ok.us
Pop 6,537; Circ 64,543
Library Holdings: Bk Titles 20,258; Bk Vols 21,823
Open Mon-Thurs 10-7, Fri 10-6, Sat 10-1, Sun 1-5
Friends of the Library Group

C UNIVERSITY OF OKLAHOMA*, Bizzell Memorial Library (Main), 401 W Brooks St, 73019. SAN 357-5829. Tel: 405-325-4142. FAX: 405-325-7550. Web Site: libraries.ou.edu. *Dean, Univ Libr,* Rick Luce; E-mail: rluce@ou.edu; *Assoc Dean of Libr,* Rhonda Cannon; E-mail: rhondacannon@ou.edu; *Dir, Coll Develop & Scholarly Communication,* Karen Rupp-Serrano; E-mail: krs@ou.edu; *Dir, Libr Tech Serv,* John Hennessey; *Head, Access & Delivery Serv,* Janet Brennan Croft; *Head, Acq,* Starla Doescher; Tel: 405-325-2141; *Head, Metadata & Cat,* Katherine Wong; Tel: 405-325-4081; *Head, Outreach Serv,* Karen Antell; *Govt Doc Librn,* Jeffrey Wilhite; Staff 43 (MLS 29, Non-MLS 14)
Founded 1895. Enrl 26,219; Highest Degree: Doctorate
Library Holdings: Bk Vols 5,000,000; Per Subs 75,000
Special Collections: State Document Depository; UN Document Depository; US Document Depository
Automation Activity & Vendor Info: (Circulation) SirsiDynix
Wireless access
Publications: Library Newsletter
Partic in Okla Libr Technology Network
Open Mon-Thurs 7:30am-2am, Fri & Sat 7:30am-10pm, Sun Noon-2am
Friends of the Library Group

Departmental Libraries:

ARCHITECTURE, Architecture Library, LLG8, 830 Van Vleet Oval, 73019, SAN 357-5853. Tel: 405-325-5521. FAX: 405-325-6637. *Librn,* Matt Stock
Library Holdings: Bk Vols 32,169
Open Mon & Wed 8-8, Tues, Thurs & Fri 8-5, Sun 4-8

BASS BUSINESS HISTORY COLLECTION, Bass Collection, 507 NW, 401 W Brooks St, 73019, SAN 357-5845. Tel: 405-325-3941. *Curator,* Daniel Wren; E-mail: dwren@ou.edu
Library Holdings: Bk Vols 23,444
Subject Interests: Biographies, Econ hist, Entrepreneurship, Labor hist, Numismatics, Transportation
Open Mon-Fri 9-4

CHEMISTRY-MATHEMATICS, Physical Sciences Center, Chemistry & Mathematics, Rm 207, 73019, SAN 357-5918. Tel: 405-325-5628. FAX: 405-325-7650. *Librn,* Lina Ortega
Library Holdings: Bk Vols 82,612
Open Mon-Thurs 8-6, Fri 8-5, Sun 1-4

ENGINEERING, Engineering Library, 222FH, 865 Asp Ave, 73019, SAN 357-5977. Tel: 405-325-2941. FAX: 405-325-0345. *Eng Librn,* James Bierman
Library Holdings: Bk Vols 79,076
Open Mon-Thurs 8am-9pm, Fri 8-5, Sat & Sun 1-5

FINE ARTS, Fine Arts Library, 20, 500 W Boyd St, 73019, SAN 357-5888. Tel: 405-325-4243. FAX: 405-325-4243. *Librn,* Matt Stock
Library Holdings: Bk Vols 116,070
Special Collections: Bixler Files (clippings on theater, film & dance)
Subject Interests: Art, Arts mgt, Dance, Music
Open Mon-Thurs 8am-9pm, Fri 8-5, Sat 11-5, Sun 2-9

GEOLOGY, Youngblood Energy Library, R220, 100 E Boyd, 73019, SAN 357-6000. Tel: 405-325-6451. FAX: 405-325-6451. *Geology Librn,* Jody Foote
Library Holdings: Bk Vols 106,059
Open Mon-Thurs 8am-9pm, Fri 8-5, Sat 11-2, Sun 2-7

HISTORY OF SCIENCE COLLECTIONS, Rm 521 NW, 73019, SAN 357-5837. Tel: 405-325-2741. *Curator,* Marilyn Ogilvie; *Librn,* Kerry Magruder
Library Holdings: Bk Vols 92,000
Special Collections: Early Science, per; Histories of Sciences; Histories of Scientific Institutions; History of Science Journals; Science Biographies, Encyclopedias & Dictionaries; Textbooks & Popular Science Works
Subject Interests: Biological sci
Open Mon-Thurs 9-7, Fri 9-5, Sat 10-2

PHYSICS & ASTRONOMY, Physics & Astronomy, 219NH, 440 W Brooks, 73019, SAN 357-6078. Tel: 405-325-2887. FAX: 405-325-3640. *Tech Serv,* Kathryn Caldwell
Library Holdings: Bk Vols 37,534
Open Mon-Thurs 8-6, Fri 8-5

CL DONALD E PRAY LAW LIBRARY, 300 Timberdell Rd, 73019, SAN 357-606X. Tel: 405-325-4311. FAX: 405-325-6282. Web Site: www.law.ou.edu/library. *Dir,* Darin K Fox; *Assoc Dir,* Joel Wegemer; *Tech Serv Librn,* Marilyn Nicely; E-mail: mnicely@ou.edu. Subject Specialists: *Legal res,* Darin K Fox; Staff 14 (MLS 7, Non-MLS 7)
Founded 1909. Enrl 520; Fac 35; Highest Degree: Doctorate
Library Holdings: Bk Vols 207,475; Per Subs 4,371
Special Collections: Native Peoples Law. US Document Depository
Partic in Greater Western Library Alliance; OCLC Online Computer Library Center, Inc
Publications: DataBase Spotlights; Law Library Guide (Reference guide); Law Library Newsletter (Annual); New Books & DataBase List

WESTERN HISTORY COLLECTION, Western History Collection, 452 MH, 630 Parrington Oval, 73019, SAN 357-5861. Tel: 405-325-3641. FAX: 405-325-6069. *Curator,* John Lovett
Library Holdings: Bk Vols 70,838
Special Collections: Abraham Lincoln & the Civil War (Henry B Bass Coll); Congressional Papers (48 Congressmen); History of Kansas & Surrounding States, North American Indians, Cattle Trade, Mining (Alan W Farley Coll); Indian Music Tapes; Indian Nation Papers; Indian-Pioneer Papers; North American Indians & Indian Art (Fred P Schonwald Coll); Oral History of Oklahoma Indian Tribes (Doris Duke Coll); Political Speeches (Helen Gahagan Douglas Coll); Western Americana (Edward Everett Dale Coll). Oral History
Open Mon-Fri 8am-10pm, Sat 9-1

NOWATA

P NOWATA CITY-COUNTY LIBRARY*, 224 S Pine, 74048. (Mail add: PO Box 738, 74048-0738), SAN 324-0002. Tel: 918-273-3363. FAX: 918-273-1818. *Librn,* Marilyn Biggerstaff; Staff 2 (MLS 2)
Founded 1966. Pop 9,992; Circ 16,484
Library Holdings: Bk Titles 23,080; Per Subs 40
Automation Activity & Vendor Info: (Cataloging) Follett Software; (Circulation) Follett Software
Open Mon-Fri 10:30-7:30, Sat 9-2

OKEENE

P OKEENE PUBLIC LIBRARY*, 215 N Main, 73763. (Mail add: PO Box 706, 73763-0706), SAN 313-9328. Tel: 580-822-3306. FAX: 580-822-3309. E-mail: reading@okeene.lib.ok.us. Web Site: www.okeene.okpls.org. *Dir,* Lee Ann Barnes; *Res,* Deborah Nayor/Farhar; Staff 2 (MLS 1, Non-MLS 1)
Founded 1934. Pop 1,500; Circ 2,000
Library Holdings: Bk Vols 6,000
Automation Activity & Vendor Info: (Cataloging) Book Systems; (Circulation) Book Systems; (OPAC) Book Systems
Wireless access
Open Mon-Thurs 2-5:30, Fri 2-5

OKEMAH

P OKEMAH PUBLIC LIBRARY*, 301 S Second, 74859. Tel: 918-623-1915. FAX: 918-623-0489. Web Site: www.okemah.okpls.org. *Dir,* Teresa M Labbe; E-mail: tlabbeopl@yahoo.com
Library Holdings: Bk Vols 27,000
Automation Activity & Vendor Info: (Cataloging) Biblionix; (Circulation) Biblionix
Wireless access
Open Mon-Thurs 10:30-6, Fri 10:30-5:30, Sat 11-2
Friends of the Library Group

OKLAHOMA CITY

M DEACONESS HOSPITAL*, Library Resource Center, 5501 N Portland, 73112-2097. SAN 313-9360. Tel: 405-604-4523. *Mgr,* Ursula Ellis; Staff 2 (MLS 1, Non-MLS 1)
Founded 1972
Library Holdings: AV Mats 200; Bk Titles 600; Per Subs 30
Subject Interests: Auxiliary health serv, Hospital admin, Med, Nursing
Automation Activity & Vendor Info: (Cataloging) Follett Software
Partic in Docline; National Network of Libraries of Medicine
Open Mon-Fri 7-5
Restriction: Hospital staff & commun

GM DEPARTMENT OF VETERANS AFFAIRS*, Medical Center Library, 921 NE 13th St 142D, 73104. SAN 313-9662. Tel: 405-270-0501, Ext 3688. FAX: 405-270-5145. E-mail: vhaoklib@med.va.gov. *In Charge,* Sara Blackwell
Founded 1946
Library Holdings: Bk Vols 1,975; Per Subs 280
Special Collections: Patient Health Education
Publications: Library Notes
Partic in Veterans Affairs Libr Network (VALNET)
Open Mon-Fri 8-4:30

R EMANUEL SYNAGOGUE*, William Davis Memorial Library, 900 NW 47th St, 73118. SAN 313-9387. Tel: 405-528-2113. FAX: 405-528-2121. Web Site: www.emanuelokc.org.
Library Holdings: Bk Vols 3,000; Per Subs 6
Subject Interests: Hebrew, Judaica
Partic in Metronet
Restriction: Not open to pub

FEDERAL AVIATION ADMINISTRATION

S CIVIL AEROSPACE MEDICAL INSTITUTE LIBRARY*, 6500 S MacArthur, AAM-400a, 73169, SAN 357-6213. Tel: 405-954-4398. FAX: 405-954-4379. Web Site: www.faa.gov. *Librn,* Katherine Wade; E-mail: kathy.wade@faa.gov; Staff 2 (MLS 2)
Library Holdings: Bk Vols 6,000; Per Subs 200
Subject Interests: Aerospace med, Aviation psychol, Human factors
Automation Activity & Vendor Info: (Cataloging) EOS International; (ILL) OCLC; (OPAC) EOS International; (Serials) EOS International
Database Vendor: OCLC FirstSearch, OVID Technologies
Partic in Docline; OCLC Online Computer Library Center, Inc
Open Mon-Fri 7:30-5

S MIKE MONRONEY AERONAUTICAL CENTER LIBRARY*, Academy Bldg 14, Rm 114, 6500 S MacArthur Blvd, 73169. (Mail add: AMA-23A, PO Box 25082, 73125-0082), SAN 357-6183. Tel: 405-954-2665. FAX: 405-954-4742. Web Site: www.academy.faa.gov/library. *Librn,* Elaine Regier; Staff 1 (MLS 1)
Founded 1962
Library Holdings: Bk Titles 23,000; Bk Vols 30,000; Per Subs 40; Spec Interest Per Sub 25; Videos 93
Special Collections: FAA Orders; FAA Research Reports
Subject Interests: Aviation, Educ, Electronics, Mgt
Automation Activity & Vendor Info: (Cataloging) OCLC; (ILL) OCLC; (OPAC) CyberTools for Libraries
Database Vendor: EBSCOhost, OCLC FirstSearch, OCLC WorldShare Interlibrary Loan
Function: ILL available, Ref serv available
Partic in OCLC Online Computer Library Center, Inc
Restriction: By permission only

M INTEGRIS BAPTIST MEDICAL CENTER*, Wann Langston Memorial Library, 3300 Northwest Expressway, 73112. SAN 313-9352. Tel: 405-949-3766. FAX: 405-949-3883. *Asst Librn,* Dan Chandler; Staff 3 (MLS 2, Non-MLS 1)
Founded 1968
Library Holdings: Bk Titles 3,100; Bk Vols 3,700; Per Subs 400
Subject Interests: Geriatrics, Hospital admin, Med, Nursing, Transplantation
Database Vendor: OVID Technologies
Partic in National Network of Libraries of Medicine South Central Region

M INTEGRIS SOUTHWEST MEDICAL CENTER*, Scott Hendren Medical Library, 4401 S Western, 73109-3607. SAN 371-5507. Tel: 405-636-7437. FAX: 405-636-7660. *Librn,* Sonya Palmer
Founded 1966
Library Holdings: Bk Titles 2,100; Per Subs 100
Subject Interests: Clinical med
Open Mon-Fri 8-4:30

L MACFEE & TAFT*, Law Library, Two Leadership Sq, 10th Flr, 211 N Robinson, 73102. SAN 326-5900. Tel: 405-235-9621. FAX: 405-235-0439. *Librn,* Patsy Trotter; E-mail: patsy.trotter@mcafeetaft.com; Staff 1 (MLS 1)
Founded 1952
Library Holdings: Bk Vols 14,000; Per Subs 50
Subject Interests: Aviation, Banking, Bankruptcy, Corporate securities, Employee benefits, Environment, Intellectual property, Litigation, Real estate, Tax
Partic in Westlaw
Restriction: Staff use only

M MERCY HOSPITAL OKLAHOMA CITY, Medical Library, 4200 W Memorial Rd, Ste 701, 73120. SAN 329-8922. Tel: 405-752-3390. FAX: 405-752-3670. *Head Librn,* May Harshbarger; E-mail: may.harshbarger@mercy.net
Wireless access
Open Mon-Fri 8-4:30

P METROPOLITAN LIBRARY SYSTEM IN OKLAHOMA COUNTY, 300 Park Ave, 73102. SAN 357-6302. Tel: 405-606-3725. Circulation Tel: 405-606-3860. Interlibrary Loan Service Tel: 405-606-3829. Reference Tel: 405-606-3868. FAX: 405-606-3722. E-mail: director@metrolibrary.org. Web Site: www.metrolibrary.org. *Exec Dir,* Tim Rogers; *Dep Exec Dir, Finance & Support,* Lloyd Lovely; *Dep Exec Dir, Libr Operations,* Kay Bauman; *Dep Exec Dir, Mat & Outreach,* Karen Marriott; *Dep Exec Dir, Tech,* Anne Fischer; Staff 130.55 (MLS 92.84, Non-MLS 37.71)
Founded 1965. Pop 755,245; Circ 6,665,682
Jul 2013-Jun 2014 Income (Main Library and Branch(s)) $33,333,219, State $307,578, County $31,376,535, Other $1,649,106. Mats Exp $5,290,010, Books $2,467,920, Per/Ser (Incl. Access Fees) $182,909, Other Print Mats $1,913, AV Mat $1,284,956, Electronic Ref Mat (Incl. Access Fees) $1,352,312. Sal $16,367,733
Library Holdings: AV Mats 198,634; e-books 44,179; Bk Titles 225,547; Bk Vols 1,042,073; Per Subs 2,916
Special Collections: Black History Coll; Holocaust Resource Coll; Oklahoma Coll. US Document Depository
Wireless access
Publications: Info Magazine (Monthly)
Partic in OCLC Online Computer Library Center, Inc; Oklahoma Library Technology Network (OLTN)
Friends of the Library Group
Branches: 20
ALMONTE LIBRARY, 2914 SW 59th St, 73119-6402. Tel: 405-606-3575. Circulation Tel: 405-606-3577. Reference Tel: 405-606-3576. FAX: 405-606-3579. E-mail: almonte@metrolibrary.org. ; Staff 5 (MLS 3, Non-MLS 2)
Pop 33,702; Circ 172,585
Library Holdings: AV Mats 7,738; Bk Titles 33,788; Bk Vols 35,946; Per Subs 136
Open Mon-Thurs 9-9, Fri 9-6, Sat 9-5, Sun 1-6
BELLE ISLE LIBRARY, 5501 N Villa, 73112-7164, SAN 357-6361. Tel: 405-843-9601. Circulation Tel: 405-606-3208. Reference Tel: 405-606-3211. FAX: 405-843-4560. E-mail: belleisle@metrolibrary.org. *Mgr, Libr Operations,* David Newyear; Staff 8.36 (MLS 7.86, Non-MLS 0.5)
Pop 67,488; Circ 480,506
Library Holdings: AV Mats 15,204; Bk Titles 81,985; Bk Vols 87,220; Per Subs 153
Open Mon-Thurs 9-9, Fri 9-6, Sat 9-5, Sun 1-6
BETHANY LIBRARY, 3510 N Mueller Ave, Bethany, 73008-3971, SAN 357-6396. Tel: 405-789-8363. Circulation Tel: 405-606-3235. Reference Tel: 405-606-3230. FAX: 405-606-3239. E-mail:

bethany@metrolibrary.org. *Mgr, Libr Operations,* Katrina Prince; Staff 5 (MLS 5)
Pop 49,753; Circ 384,442
Library Holdings: AV Mats 10,451; Bk Titles 51,143; Bk Vols 54,409; Per Subs 100
Open Mon-Thurs 9-9, Fri 9-6, Sat 9-5, Sun 1-6

CAPITOL HILL LIBRARY, 334 SW 26th St, 73109-6711, SAN 357-6426. Tel: 405-634-6308. Circulation Tel: 405-606-3249. Reference Tel: 405-606-3247. FAX: 405-606-3244. E-mail: capitolhill@metrolibrary.org. *Mgr, Libr Operations,* Jana Hausburg; Staff 4.5 (MLS 3, Non-MLS 1.5)
Pop 33,702; Circ 135,206
Library Holdings: AV Mats 6,443; Bk Titles 30,288; Bk Vols 32,222; Per Subs 162
Open Mon-Thurs 9-9, Fri 9-6, Sat 9-5, Sun 1-6

CHOCTAW LIBRARY, 2525 Muzzy, Choctaw, 73020-8717, SAN 357-6663. Tel: 405-390-8418. Circulation Tel: 405-606-3260. Reference Tel: 405-606-3256. FAX: 405-606-3269. E-mail: choctaw@metrolibrary.org. *Mgr, Libr Operations,* Todd Podzemny; Staff 4 (MLS 2, Non-MLS 2)
Pop 17,670; Circ 200,624
Library Holdings: AV Mats 11,699; Bk Titles 35,003; Bk Vols 37,239; Per Subs 108
Open Mon-Thurs 9-9, Fri 9-6, Sat 9-5, Sun 1-6

DEL CITY LIBRARY, 4509 SE 15th St, Del City, 73115-3098, SAN 357-6450. Tel: 405-672-1377. Circulation Tel: 405-606-3282. Reference Tel: 405-606-3281. FAX: 405-606-3292. E-mail: delcity@metrolibrary.org. *Mgr, Libr Operations,* Devin McGhee; Staff 4.63 (MLS 1.5, Non-MLS 3.13)
Pop 36,781; Circ 199,582
Library Holdings: AV Mats 9,627; Bk Titles 42,015; Bk Vols 44,697; Per Subs 90
Open Mon-Thurs 9-9, Fri 9-6, Sat 9-5, Sun 1-6

EDMOND LIBRARY, Ten South Blvd, Edmond, 73034-3798, SAN 357-6515. Tel: 405-341-9282. Circulation Tel: 405-606-3413. Reference Tel: 405-606-3403. FAX: 405-606-3411. E-mail: edmond@metrolibrary.org. *Mgr, Libr Operations,* Melody Kellogg; Staff 11.5 (MLS 6.5, Non-MLS 5)
Pop 110,357; Circ 1,212,574
Library Holdings: AV Mats 24,390; Bk Titles 111,158; Bk Vols 118,255; Per Subs 214
Open Mon-Thurs 9-9, Fri 9-6, Sat 9-5, Sun 1-6

RALPH ELLISON LIBRARY, 2000 NE 23rd St, 73111-3402, SAN 357-6485. Tel: 405-424-1437. Circulation Tel: 405-606-3461. Reference Tel: 405-606-3459. FAX: 405-606-3460. E-mail: ralphellison@metrolibrary.org. ; Staff 5 (MLS 3.5, Non-MLS 1.5)
Pop 35,068; Circ 133,779
Library Holdings: AV Mats 7,796; Bk Titles 37,663; Bk Vols 40,068; Per Subs 123
Open Mon-Thurs 9-9, Fri 9-6, Sat 9-5, Sun 1-6
Friends of the Library Group

HARRAH EXTENSION LIBRARY, 1930 N Church Ave, Harrah, 73045. (Mail add: PO Box 893, Harrah, 73045-0893), SAN 327-9960. Tel: 405-454-2001. FAX: 405-454-0322. E-mail: harrah@metrolibrary.org. *Extn Spec,* Jo Nita White; Staff 2 (Non-MLS 2)
Pop 7,080; Circ 60,524
Library Holdings: AV Mats 2,289; Bk Titles 10,912; Bk Vols 10,968, Per Subs 50
Open Mon-Thurs 9:30-12:30 & 1-6, Fri & Sat 9-12:30 & 1-5

JONES EXTENSION LIBRARY, 111 E Main, Jones, 73049-0425, SAN 374-7387. Tel: 405-399-5471. FAX: 405-399-3679. E-mail: jones@metrolibrary.org. *Extn Spec,* Josh Lewis; Staff 0.6 (Non-MLS 0.6)
Pop 837; Circ 18,184
Library Holdings: AV Mats 1,049; Bk Titles 3,626
Open Tues & Thurs 9:30-12:30 & 1-5:30, Sat 9-12:30 & 1-5

LUTHER EXTENSION LIBRARY, 310 NE Third St, Luther, 73054-9999, SAN 374-7395. Tel: 405-277-9967. FAX: 405-277-9238. E-mail: luther@metrolibrary.org. *Extn Spec,* Grant Yokley; Staff 1.5 (Non-MLS 1.5)
Pop 3,052; Circ 54,835
Library Holdings: AV Mats 2,028; Bk Titles 6,524; Per Subs 10
Open Mon-Thurs 9:30-12:30 & 1-6, Fri & Sat 9-12:30 & 1-5

MIDWEST CITY LIBRARY, 8143 E Reno, Midwest City, 73110-3999, SAN 357-654X. Tel: 405-732-4828. Circulation Tel: 405-606-3431. Reference Tel: 405-606-3433. FAX: 405-606-3451. E-mail: midwestcity@metrolibrary.org. *Mgr, Libr Operations,* Chris Kennedy; Staff 8 (MLS 4.5, Non-MLS 3.5)
Pop 81,008; Circ 492,771
Library Holdings: AV Mats 16,726; Bk Titles 71,875; Bk Vols 76,462; Per Subs 184
Open Mon-Thurs 9-9, Fri 9-6, Sat 9-5, Sun 1-6

NICOMA PARK EXTENSION LIBRARY, 2240 Overholser, Nicoma Park, 73066. (Mail add: PO Box 756, Nicoma Park, 73066-0756), SAN 357-6698. Tel: 405-769-9452. FAX: 405-769-4020. E-mail: nicomapark@metrolibrary.org. *Extn Spec,* Victoria Saxton; Staff 0.93 (Non-MLS 0.93)
Pop 1,532; Circ 30,030
Library Holdings: AV Mats 1,196; Bk Titles 4,083; Per Subs 26
Open Tues-Thurs 9:30-12:30 & 1-5:30, Fri & Sat 9-12:30 & 1-5

RONALD J NORICK DOWNTOWN LIBRARY, 300 Park Ave, 73102-3600, SAN 357-6337. Tel: 405-231-8650. Circulation Tel: 405-606-3860. Reference Tel: 405-606-3868. FAX: 405-606-3895. E-mail: downtown@metrolibrary.org. *Mgr, Libr Operations,* Julie Ballou; Staff 16.28 (MLS 13.28, Non-MLS 3)
Pop 60,231; Circ 202,872
Library Holdings: AV Mats 16,304; Bk Titles 132,861; Bk Vols 138,397; Per Subs 887
Special Collections: Genealogy Coll; Holocaust Resource Coll (Preserving the memory & teaching the lessons of the Holocaust); Oklahoma Coll (Materials by Oklahomans or about Oklahoma). US Document Depository
Open Mon-Thurs 9-9, Fri 9-6, Sat 9-5, Sun 1-6

NORTHWEST LIBRARY, 5600 NW 122nd St, 73142-4204. Tel: 405-606-3580. Circulation Tel: 405-606-3569. Reference Tel: 405-606-3568. FAX: 405-606-3570. E-mail: northwest@metrolibrary.org. *Mgr, Libr Operations,* Rachel Kopchick; Staff 9.5 (MLS 8, Non-MLS 1.5)
Pop 110,357; Circ 797,521
Library Holdings: AV Mats 23,859; Bk Titles 127,926; Bk Vols 136,093; Per Subs 282
Open Mon-Thurs 9-9, Fri 9-6, Sat 9-5, Sun 1-6

OUTREACH-BOOK CENTERS & BOOKS BY MAIL, 300 NE 50th St, 73105-1838. Tel: 405-606-3835. FAX: 405-606-3815. E-mail: outreach@metrolibrary.org.
Circ 224,576
Library Holdings: AV Mats 4,517; Bk Vols 44,825

SOUTHERN OAKS LIBRARY, 6900 S Walker, 73139-7203, SAN 357-6574. Tel: 405-631-4468. Circulation Tel: 405-606-3479. Reference Tel: 405-606-3478. FAX: 405-606-3484. E-mail: southernoaks@metrolibrary.org. *Mgr, Libr Operations,* Randy Wayland; Staff 9 (MLS 6.5, Non-MLS 2.5)
Pop 80,398; Circ 395,907
Library Holdings: AV Mats 17,609; Bk Titles 88,355; Bk Vols 93,996; Per Subs 140
Open Mon-Thurs 9-9, Fri 9-6, Sat 9-5, Sun 1-6

THE VILLAGE LIBRARY, 10307 N Pennsylvania Ave, The Village, 73120-4110, SAN 357-6604. Tel: 405-755-0710. Circulation Tel: 405-606-3504. Reference Tel: 405-606-3498. FAX: 405-606-3502. E-mail: village@metrolibrary.org. ; Staff 6.5 (MLS 5, Non-MLS 1.5)
Pop 59,048; Circ 396,712
Library Holdings: AV Mats 13,212; Bk Titles 58,730; Bk Vols 62,480; Per Subs 151
Open Mon-Thurs 9-9, Fri 9-6, Sat 9-5, Sun 1-6
Friends of the Library Group

WARR ACRES LIBRARY, 5901 NW 63rd St, Warr Acres, 73132-7502, SAN 357-6639. Tel: 405-721-2616. Circulation Tel: 405-606-3522. Reference Tel: 405-606-3519. FAX: 405-606-3534. E-mail: warracres@metrolibrary.org. *Mgr, Libr Operations,* Barbara Beasley; Staff 6 (MLS 4, Non-MLS 2)
Pop 57,038; Circ 342,375
Library Holdings: AV Mats 9,619; Bk Titles 50,822; Bk Vols 54,069; Per Subs 73
Open Mon-Thurs 9-9, Fri 9-6, Sat 9-5, Sun 1-6

WRIGHT EXTENSION LIBRARY, 2101 Exchange Ave, 73108-2625, SAN 357-6728. Tel: 405-235-5035. FAX: 405-235-8938. E-mail: wright@metrolibrary.org. *Extn Spec,* Marie Nichols; Staff 0.93 (Non-MLS 0.93)
Pop 1,876; Circ 11,384
Library Holdings: AV Mats 1,138; Bk Titles 5,588; Per Subs 24
Open Tues-Thurs 9:30-12:30 & 1-5:30, Fri & Sat 9-12:30 & 1-5

CR MID-AMERICA CHRISTIAN UNIVERSITY*, Charles Ewing Brown Library, 3500 SW 119th St, 73170-9797. SAN 316-4438. Tel: 405-691-3800. Circulation Tel: 405-691-3800, Ext 174. Interlibrary Loan Service Tel: 405-691-3800, Ext 168. FAX: 405-692-3165. Web Site: www.macu.edu/library/. *Dir,* Michael Foote; *Cat,* Elissa Patadal; Staff 5 (MLS 2, Non-MLS 3)
Founded 1953. Enrl 650; Fac 20; Highest Degree: Bachelor
Library Holdings: Bk Titles 48,000; Per Subs 250; Spec Interest Per Sub 20
Special Collections: Archives of Church of God (Charles Ewing Brown Coll); Wesleyan Holiness Theology (Kenneth E Jones Coll)
Subject Interests: Behav sci, Biblical studies, Bus (non-profit), Christian, Church ministries, English, Sacred music, Teacher educ
Database Vendor: Gale Cengage Learning, OCLC FirstSearch, OVID Technologies
Partic in Metropolitan Libraries Network Of Central Oklahoma Inc; Onenet
Open Mon-Thurs 7:30am-11pm, Fri 7:30-4, Sat 11-4, Sun 8am-11pm

S NATIONAL COWBOY & WESTERN HERITAGE MUSEUM*, Donald C & Elizabeth M Dickinson Research Center, 1700 NE 63rd St, 73111. SAN 327-5655. Tel: 405-478-2250, Ext 289. FAX: 405-478-6421. Web Site: www.nationalcowboymuseum.org/research. *Dir & Librn,* Gerrianne Schaad; Tel: 405-478-2250, Ext 273, E-mail: gschaad@nationalcowboymuseum.org; *Libr Tech,* Karen Spilman; Tel: 405-478-2250, Ext 290, E-mail: kspilman@nationalcowboymuseum.org; Staff 4 (MLS 3, Non-MLS 1)
Founded 1997
Library Holdings: AV Mats 3,480; CDs 357; DVDs 254; Electronic Media & Resources 1,139; Bk Titles 35,000; Per Subs 64; Videos 3,500
Special Collections: Arthur & Shifra Silberman Native American Painting Reference Library Research Files; Blucher Custom Boot Company Coll of Fitting; Contemporary Western Artists' Personal Papers, including Bettina Steinke & Tom Lovell; James E & Laura G Fraser Studio Coll; Joe De Yong Personal Papers; On-Line Image Archive; Photographic Archives (primarily Rodeo); Robert E Cunningham Coll, glass negatives; Saddlery Catalogs (Ron Bledsoe Coll); Western Americana (Glenn D Shirley Coll), Dime novels, movie posters, res files. Oral History
Subject Interests: Conserv, Cowboys, Fine arts, Firearms, Hunting, Ranching, Rodeos, The West, Western art, Western hist
Automation Activity & Vendor Info: (Cataloging) Auto-Graphics, Inc; (Circulation) Auto-Graphics, Inc; (OPAC) Auto-Graphics, Inc
Wireless access
Open Mon-Fri 9-5

S THE NINETY-NINES, INC*, Museum of Women Pilots Library, 4300 Amelia Earhart Rd, 73159-0040. SAN 371-2303. Tel: 405-685-7969. FAX: 405-685-7985. E-mail: president@ninety-nines.org. Web Site: www.ninety-nines.org. *Adminr,* Laura Ohrenberg
Founded 1975
Library Holdings: Bk Vols 850
Special Collections: Amelia Earhart, Louis Thaden, Matilde Moisant, Grace Harris, Hazel Jones, Lucile Wright, Jerri Cobb, Edna Gardner Whyte & Jackie Cochran Colls; Jessie Woods Photo Coll
Restriction: Private libr

J OKLAHOMA CITY COMMUNITY COLLEGE*, Keith Leftwich Memorial Library, 7777 S May Ave, 73159. SAN 313-9646. Tel: 405-682-7564. Reference Tel: 405-682-1611, Ext 7251. FAX: 405-682-7585. Web Site: library.occc.edu. *Dir,* Barbara King; E-mail: bking@occc.edu; *Cataloger/Ref Librn,* MaryGrace Berkowitz; Tel: 405-682-1611, Ext 7229, E-mail: mberkowitz@occc.edu; *Electronic Serv/Ref Librn,* Amanda Lemon; Tel: 405-682-1611, Ext 7146, E-mail: alemon@occc.edu; *ILL/Ref Librn,* Rachel Butler; Tel: 405-682-1611, Ext 7643, E-mail: rbutler@occc.edu; *Ref & Circ Librn,* Linda Boatright; Tel: 405-682-1611, Ext 7468, E-mail: lboatright@occc.edu; *Syst Librn,* Dana Tuley-Williams; Tel: 405-682-1611, Ext 7390, E-mail: dtuley@occc.edu; *Pub Serv,* Jay Ramanjulu; Tel: 405-682-1611, Ext 7202, E-mail: jramanjulu@occc.edu; Staff 7 (MLS 7)
Founded 1972. Enrl 14,300; Fac 140; Highest Degree: Associate
Jul 2008-Jun 2009. Mats Exp $470,000, Books $300,000, Per/Ser (Incl. Access Fees) $70,000, AV Mat $100,000. Sal $434,000 (Prof $272,000)
Library Holdings: e-books 10,000; Bk Vols 120,000; Per Subs 700
Subject Interests: Humanities, Nursing, Soc sci
Automation Activity & Vendor Info: (Acquisitions) SirsiDynix; (Cataloging) SirsiDynix; (Circulation) SirsiDynix; (Course Reserve) SirsiDynix; (ILL) OCLC; (OPAC) SirsiDynix; (Serials) SirsiDynix
Database Vendor: Amigos Library Services, College Source, CountryWatch, CQ Press, EBSCOhost, Gale Cengage Learning, LearningExpress, Newsbank, OCLC FirstSearch, OCLC WorldShare Interlibrary Loan, Oxford Online, ProQuest, PubMed
Wireless access

S OKLAHOMA CITY MUSEUM OF ART*, Library-Resource Center, 415 Couch Dr, 73102. SAN 373-109X. Tel: 405-236-3100. FAX: 405-236-3122. Web Site: www.okcmoa.com. *Curator of Coll,* Alison Amick; *Educ Curator,* Chandra Boyd
Library Holdings: Bk Vols 6,000
Open Tues-Fri 1-5
Restriction: Non-circulating

C OKLAHOMA CITY UNIVERSITY, Dulaney-Browne Library, 2501 N Blackwelder, 73106. SAN 357-6752. Tel: 405-208-5068. Interlibrary Loan Service Tel: 405-208-5874. Reference Tel: 405-208-5065. Administration Tel: 405-208-5072. Automation Services Tel: 405-208-5846. FAX: 405-208-5291. Web Site: www.okcu.edu/library. *Dir,* Victoria Swinney, PhD; E-mail: vswinney@okcu.edu; *Access Serv Librn,* Kristen Burkholder, PhD; E-mail: kburkholder@okcu.edu; *Electronic Res Librn,* Kristal Boulden; E-mail: kboulden@okcu.edu; *Monographs Librn,* Robert Dorman, PhD; E-mail: rdorman@okcu.edu; *Music Librn,* Bonnie Elizabeth Fleming, PhD; E-mail: befleming@okcu.edu; *Archivist, Spec Coll Librn,* Christina Wolf; E-mail: cwolf@okcu.edu; *Theol & Ref LIbrn,* Lee Webb; E-mail: lwebb@okcu.edu; *ILL Spec,* Carissa Maben; E-mail: ckmaben@okcu.edu.
Subject Specialists: *Music,* Bonnie Elizabeth Fleming, PhD; Staff 7 (MLS 7)
Founded 1904. Enrl 3,000; Fac 186; Highest Degree: Doctorate
Jul 2013-Jun 2014 Income $907,890. Mats Exp $195,438, Books $107,513, Per/Ser (Incl. Access Fees) $12,574, Electronic Ref Mat (Incl. Access Fees) $74,851, Presv $500. Sal $677,764 (Prof $320,207)
Library Holdings: CDs 5,586; e-books 89,485; e-journals 19,350; Music Scores 12,486; Bk Vols 209,885; Per Subs 50; Videos 8,181
Special Collections: Methodist History Coll; Oklahoma History (George H Shirk History Center Coll). US Document Depository
Automation Activity & Vendor Info: (Acquisitions) Ex Libris Group; (Cataloging) Ex Libris Group; (Circulation) Ex Libris Group; (Course Reserve) Ex Libris Group; (OPAC) Ex Libris Group; (Serials) Ex Libris Group
Database Vendor: ebrary, EBSCO Information Services, EBSCOhost, JSTOR, OCLC FirstSearch, OCLC WorldShare Interlibrary Loan, Project MUSE, ProQuest
Wireless access
Function: Archival coll, Computers for patron use, Copy machines, Distance learning, Doc delivery serv, e-mail & chat, E-Reserves, Electronic databases & coll, Fax serv, Govt ref serv, Handicapped accessible, ILL available, Music CDs, Online cat, Online info literacy tutorials on the web & in blackboard, Online ref, Online searches, Orientations, Photocopying/Printing, Prof lending libr, Ref serv available, Ref serv in person, Scanner, Tax forms, Telephone ref, VHS videos, Video lending libr, Web-catalog
Partic in OCLC Online Computer Library Center, Inc; Oklahoma Council of Academic Libr Directors (OCALD)
Open Mon-Thurs 7:30am-Midnight, Fri 7:30-7, Sat 10-7, Sun Noon-Midnight
Restriction: Open to pub for ref & circ; with some limitations
Friends of the Library Group

Departmental Libraries:

CL SCHOOL OF LAW LIBRARY, 2501 N Blackwelder, 73106, SAN 357-6787. Tel: 405-208-5271. FAX: 405-208-5172. Web Site: www.law.okcu.edu. *Dir,* Lee Peoples; Tel: 405-208-6030, E-mail: lpeoples@okcu.edu; *Assoc Law Libr Dir,* Jennifer Prilliman; *Asst Dir, Tech Serv,* Nancy A Cowden; *Head, Access Serv,* Jenny Watson; *Head, Ref,* Tim Gatton; *ILL Librn,* Natalie Vaughn; *Syst Librn,* Kathryn Broad; Staff 7 (MLS 7)
Founded 1922. Enrl 620
Library Holdings: Bk Titles 96,875; Bk Vols 317,000
Partic in LexisNexis; Mid-America Law Library Consortium; OCLC Online Computer Library Center, Inc; Westlaw
Open Mon-Fri 7:30am-11pm, Sat 9am-11pm, Sun 1-11

S OKLAHOMA CITY ZOO*, Zoological Library, 2101 NE 50th, 73111. SAN 321-1894. Tel: 405-425-0277. FAX: 405-425-0243. *Librn,* Amy Stephens; E-mail: astephens@okczoo.com
Founded 1970
Library Holdings: Bk Titles 5,000; Per Subs 40
Automation Activity & Vendor Info: (Circulation) Follett Software
Wireless access
Open Mon-Sat 8-5

S OKLAHOMA CORPORATION COMMISSION*, Law Library, Jim Thorpe Bldg, 2101 N Lincoln Blvd, Ste 400, 73105-4904. (Mail add: PO Box 52000, 73152-2000), SAN 313-9476. Tel: 405-521-4257. FAX: 405-521-4150. Web Site: www.occeweb.com. *In Charge,* Brenda Loggins
Library Holdings: Bk Vols 4,000
Restriction: Staff use only

GL OKLAHOMA COUNTY LAW LIBRARY*, 321 Park Ave, Rm 247, 73102-3695. SAN 313-9484. Tel: 405-713-1353. FAX: 405-713-1852. Web Site: www.oklahomacounty.org. *Dir,* Venita L Hoover; E-mail: venhoo@oklahomacounty.org; Staff 1 (MLS 1)
Library Holdings: Bk Vols 33,000; Per Subs 25
Wireless access
Open Mon-Fri 8:30-5

G OKLAHOMA DEPARTMENT OF HUMAN SERVICES*, Records Management Section, 4800 N Stiles Ave, 73105. SAN 313-9506. Tel: 405-524-9863, Ext 28. FAX: 405-521-0789. *Rec Mgt Adminr,* Mary Gail Foster; E-mail: mary.foster@okdhs.org; Staff 1 (MLS 1)
Founded 1966
Special Collections: DHS Archives; History of Oklahoma Department of Human Services
Function: Referrals accepted
Publications: Departmental Publications, Reports & Flyers
Restriction: Staff use only

P OKLAHOMA DEPARTMENT OF LIBRARIES*, 200 NE 18th St, 73105. SAN 313-9514. Tel: 405-521-2502. Reference Tel: 405-522-3505. Toll Free Tel: 800-522-8116. FAX: 405-525-7804. Web Site: www.odl.state.ok.us. *Dir,* Susan McVey; E-mail: smcvey@oltn.odl.state.ok.us; *Dep Dir,* Vicki

Sullivan; E-mail: vsullivan@oltn.odl.state.ok.us; *Head, Libr Develop,* Vicki Mohr; E-mail: vmohr@oltn.odl.state.ok.us; *US Govt Doc Librn,* Steve Beleu; E-mail: sbeleu@oltn.odl.state.ok.us; *Mgr, ILL,* Melecia Caruthers; *Mgr, Libr Serv,* Christine Chen; *LSTA Coordr,* Judy Tirey; E-mail: jtirey@oltn.odl.state.ok.us; *Archivist,* Jan Davis; *Cat, Pub Serv, Ref/Tech Serv,* Kitty Pittman; E-mail: kpittman@oltn.odl.state.ok.us; *Pub Info Officer,* Bill Young; E-mail: byoung@oltn.odl.state.ok.us. Subject Specialists: *Fed docs,* Steve Beleu; *Law, Legis ref,* Christine Chen; Staff 45 (MLS 28, Non-MLS 17)
Founded 1890. Pop 3,450,654
Library Holdings: e-books 575; Bk Vols 270,000; Per Subs 1,604
Special Collections: Oklahoma Coll; State Government Archives. State Document Depository; US Document Depository
Subject Interests: Law
Automation Activity & Vendor Info: (Acquisitions) Ex Libris Group; (Cataloging) Ex Libris Group; (Circulation) Ex Libris Group; (ILL) Ex Libris Group; (OPAC) Ex Libris Group; (Serials) Ex Libris Group
Database Vendor: Dialog, EBSCOhost, Gale Cengage Learning, LexisNexis, OCLC WorldShare Interlibrary Loan, ProQuest, Westlaw
Function: Archival coll, Govt ref serv, ILL available, Libr develop, Online searches, Photocopying/Printing, Ref serv available, Workshops
Publications: Oklahoma Agencies, Boards & Commissions (Annual); Oklahoma Almanac (Reference guide)
Open Mon-Fri 8-5
Restriction: Authorized patrons, Circ limited, Non-circulating to the pub, Open to pub for ref only, Pub use on premises

S OKLAHOMA HISTORICAL SOCIETY*, Research Division, 2401 N Laird Ave, 73105-4997. SAN 357-6825. Tel: 405-522-5225. Administration Tel: 405 522 5209. Automation Services Tel: 405-521-2492. FAX: 405-522-0644. E-mail: mrarchives@okhistory.org. Web Site: www.okhistory.org. *Dir,* William D Welge; Tel: 405-522-5206, E-mail: mrarchives@okhistory.org; *Asst Dir,* Chad A Williams; Tel: 405-522-5205, E-mail: chadw@okhistory.org; *Dir, Pub Serv, Ref Serv,* Laura Martin; Tel: 402-522-5221, E-mail: lmartin@okhistory.org; *Dir, Tech Serv,* Patricia Jones; Tel: 405-522-4025, E-mail: pjones@okhistory.org; *Pub Serv,* Phyllis Adams. Subject Specialists: *Hist of Okla, Indians,* William D Welge; Staff 7 (MLS 3, Non-MLS 4)
Founded 1893
Jul 2006-Jun 2007 Income $2,000,000. Mats Exp $55,200, Books $6,000, Per/Ser (Incl. Access Fees) $1,200, Manu Arch $12,000, Micro $3,000, AV Equip $20,000, AV Mat $1,000, Electronic Ref Mat (Incl. Access Fees) $12,000. Sal $1,500,000 (Prof $37,500)
Library Holdings: CDs 1,000; Microforms 33,000; Bk Titles 8,500; Bk Vols 86,000; Per Subs 80
Special Collections: Alice Robertson Papers; Barde Coll; David L Payne Papers; Emmett Starr's Manuscripts; Frederic B Severs Papers; Grant Foreman Papers; Indian-Pioneer History; Oklahoma Photograph Coll; Robert L Williams Papers; Whipple Coll, bks, mss, photogs. Oral History
Subject Interests: 65 Indian tribes of Okla, Hist of Okla
Automation Activity & Vendor Info: (Cataloging) OCLC; (OPAC) Cuadra Associates, Inc
Function: Archival coll, Homebound delivery serv, Ref serv available, Res libr
Publications: Chronicles of Oklahoma (Quarterly)
Open Mon-Sat 9-4:45
Restriction: Not a lending libr, Open to dept staff only, Open to pub for ref only
Friends of the Library Group

P OKLAHOMA LIBRARY FOR THE BLIND & PHYSICALLY HANDICAPPED*, 300 NE 18th St, 73105. SAN 313-9549. Tel: 405-521-3514. Toll Free Tel: 800-523-0288. FAX: 405-521-4582. TDD: 405-521-4672. E-mail: olbph@okdrs.gov. Web Site: www.library.state.ok.us. *Libr Dir,* Kevin Treese; E-mail: ktreese@okdrs.gov; *Librn,* Julia Alderson; E-mail: jalderson@okdrs.gov; *Librn,* Erin Byrne; E-mail: ebyrne@okdrs.gov; *Librn,* Andrew Shockley; E-mail: ashockley@okdrs.gov; *Librn,* Sammie Willis; E-mail: swillis@okdrs.gov
Founded 1933
Special Collections: Oklahoma History & Oklahoma Authors
Automation Activity & Vendor Info: (Cataloging) Keystone Systems, Inc (KLAS); (Circulation) Keystone Systems, Inc (KLAS); (OPAC) Keystone Systems, Inc (KLAS); (Serials) Keystone Systems, Inc (KLAS)
Database Vendor: Keystone Systems, Inc (KLAS)
Wireless access
Function: Mail loans to mem
Publications: Bright Future (Quarterly)
Special Services for the Deaf - TDD equip
Special Services for the Blind - Bks on cassette; Bks on flash-memory cartridges; Cassette playback machines; Cassettes; Digital talking bk; Digital talking bk machines; Newsletter (in large print, Braille or on cassette); Newsline for the Blind; Newsp reading serv; Production of talking bks; Radio reading serv; Recorded bks; Talking bks; Talking bks & player equip
Open Mon-Fri 8-5
Restriction: Registered patrons only
Friends of the Library Group

J OKLAHOMA STATE UNIVERSITY-OKLAHOMA CITY LIBRARY*, 900 N Portland, 73107-6195. SAN 313-9581. Tel: 405-945-3251. FAX: 405-945-3289. Web Site: www.osuokc.edu/library/. *Dir,* David Robinson; Tel: 405-945-3241, E-mail: dlrtlr@osuokc.edu; *Asst Dir,* Woods Wheeler; Tel: 405-945-9104, E-mail: wheelmw@osuokc.edu; Staff 8 (MLS 3, Non-MLS 5)
Founded 1961. Enrl 4,000; Fac 58; Highest Degree: Associate
Library Holdings: Bks on Deafness & Sign Lang 400; Bk Titles 15,000; Bk Vols 15,373; Per Subs 330
Subject Interests: Fire, Hort, Nursing, Police
Automation Activity & Vendor Info: (Cataloging) Ex Libris Group; (Circulation) Ex Libris Group; (Course Reserve) Ex Libris Group; (OPAC) Ex Libris Group; (Serials) Ex Libris Group
Database Vendor: EBSCOhost, Gale Cengage Learning, OCLC FirstSearch, ProQuest
Wireless access
Publications: Periodical List
Partic in OCLC Online Computer Library Center, Inc
Open Mon-Thurs 8am-9pm, Fri 8-5, Sat 9-5, Sun 1-5
Friends of the Library Group

S OKLAHOMA WATER RESOURCES BOARD LIBRARY*, 3800 N Classen Blvd, 73118. SAN 313-959X. Tel: 405-530-8800. FAX: 405-530-8900. Web Site: www.owrb.ok.gov. *IT Serv Mgr,* Brian Vance; E-mail: brvance@owrb.ok.gov
Library Holdings: Bk Vols 5,500; Per Subs 25
Subject Interests: Dam safety, Flood plain mgt, Geol, Groundwater, Surface water, Water res, Water resources planning
Restriction: Non circulating, Open to pub for ref only, Staff use only

L PHILLIPS, MCFALL, MCCAFFREY, MCVAY & MURRAH PC*, Law Library, Corporate Tower, 13th Flr, 101 N Robinson, 73102. SAN 372-2120. Tel: 405-235-4100. FAX: 405-235-4133. *Librn,* Kathy Schmidt
Library Holdings: Bk Vols 3,500; Per Subs 20
Restriction: Staff use only

M SAINT ANTHONY HOSPITAL*, O'Donoghue Medical Library, 1000 N Lee St, 73102-1080. (Mail add: PO Box 205, 73101-0205), SAN 313-9611. Tel: 405-272-6284. FAX: 405-272-7075. *Librn,* Monica Bread
Founded 1950
Library Holdings: Bk Vols 2,500; Per Subs 178
Subject Interests: Cardiology, Dentistry, Neurology, Nursing, Orthopedics, Psychiat
Partic in S Cent Regional Med Libr Program
Open Mon-Fri 7:30-4

SR SAINT LUKE'S UNITED METHODIST CHURCH LIBRARY*, 222 NW 15th St, 73103-3598. SAN 313-9638. Tel: 405-232-1371. FAX: 405-239-7095.
Founded 1962
Library Holdings: Bk Titles 4,100; Bk Vols 6,000
Subject Interests: Relig
Open Mon-Thurs 8:30-5

S TRONOX LLC*, Technical Center Library, 3301 NW 150th St, 73134. (Mail add: PO Box 268859, 73126-8859), SAN 357-6272. Tel: 405-775-5012, Ext 5755. FAX: 405-775-5027. *Libr Serv Supvr,* Sandy Harris
Founded 1964
Library Holdings: Bk Vols 13,000; Per Subs 50
Special Collections: Patent-Chemicals Coll, flm, microcard & paper; Rare Earth Coll, articles & rpt
Subject Interests: Chem, Chem tech
Wireless access
Restriction: Staff use only

G US COURTS LIBRARY*, 2305 US Courthouse, 200 NW Fourth St, 73102. SAN 374-6038. Tel: 405-609-5460. FAX: 405-609-5461. *Tech Serv,* Sheila Camp; Tel: 405-609-5463, E-mail: sheila_camp@ca10.uscourts.gov; Staff 2 (MLS 1, Non-MLS 1)
Founded 1990
Library Holdings: Bk Titles 2,000; Bk Vols 42,000; Per Subs 450
Special Collections: Oral History
Subject Interests: Law
Restriction: Open to pub for ref only

CM UNIVERSITY OF OKLAHOMA HEALTH SCIENCES CENTER*, Robert M Bird Health Sciences Library, 1000 Stanton L Young Blvd, 73117-1213. (Mail add: PO Box 26901, 73126-0901), SAN 357-6876. Tel:

405-271-2285. Circulation Tel: 405-271-2285, Ext 48701. Interlibrary Loan Service Tel: 405-271-2285, Ext 48753. Reference Tel: 405-271-2285, Ext 48752. Administration Tel: 405-271-2285, Ext 48755. FAX: 405-271-3297. Web Site: library.ouhsc.edu. *Dir,* Clinton M Thompson; E-mail: marty-thompson@ouhsc.edu; *Assoc Dir,* Joy Summers-Ables; Fax: 405-271-6186, E-mail: joy-summers-ables@ouhsc.edu; *Bibliographer,* Shari Clifton; E-mail: shari-clifton@ouhsc.edu; *Cat,* Jack Wagner; Tel: 405-271-2285, Ext 48758, E-mail: jack-wagner@ouhsc.edu; *Circ,* Walee Chotikavanic; Tel: 405-271-2285, Ext 48751, E-mail: walee-chotikavanic@ouhsc.edu; *Ser,* Margaret Garner; Tel: 405-271-2285, Ext 48756; Staff 35 (MLS 8, Non-MLS 27)
Founded 1928. Enrl 3,400; Fac 876; Highest Degree: Doctorate
Jul 2009-Jun 2010 Income $3,565,747. Mats Exp $3,565,747, Books $88,211, Per/Ser (Incl. Access Fees) $1,588,968, AV Mat $23,951, Electronic Ref Mat (Incl. Access Fees) $1,654,370. Sal $1,328,795
Library Holdings: AV Mats 6,205; Bk Titles 103,551; Bk Vols 125,406; Per Subs 4,980
Special Collections: American Indian Health Coll; Medical History Coll; Rare Books
Subject Interests: Allied health, Biomed sci, Dentistry, Med, Nursing, Pub health
Automation Activity & Vendor Info: (Acquisitions) SirsiDynix; (Cataloging) SirsiDynix; (Circulation) SirsiDynix; (OPAC) SirsiDynix; (Serials) SirsiDynix
Database Vendor: Bowker, DynaMed, EBSCO Information Services, EBSCOhost, Gale Cengage Learning, ISI Web of Knowledge, Lexi-Comp, MD Consult, Medline, OCLC FirstSearch, OCLC WorldShare Interlibrary Loan, OVID Technologies, PubMed, RefWorks, SirsiDynix, UpToDate
Wireless access
Function: ILL available
Partic in National Network of Libraries of Medicine South Central Region; OCLC Online Computer Library Center, Inc; Oklahoma Health Sciences Library Association; South Central Academic Medical Libraries Consortium
Friends of the Library Group

S WESTERNERS INTERNATIONAL LIBRARY*, 1700 NE 63rd St, 73111. SAN 328-1310. Tel: 405-478-8408. Toll Free Tel: 800-541-4650. E-mail: wihomeranch@aol.com. Web Site: www.westerners-international.org. *Curator,* Donald Reeves
Library Holdings: Bk Vols 500; Per Subs 10

OKMULGEE

J OKLAHOMA STATE UNIVERSITY*, Institute of Technology Library, 1801 E Fourth, 74447-0088. SAN 313-9697. Tel: 918-293-5080. Reference Tel: 918-293-5078. FAX: 918-293-4628. Web Site: www.osuit.edu/academics/library. *Dir,* Jenny Duncan; Tel: 918-293-5488, E-mail: jenny.duncan@okstate.edu; Staff 3 (MLS 2, Non-MLS 1)
Founded 1946. Enrl 2,039; Fac 118; Highest Degree: Bachelor
Library Holdings: Bk Vols 8,572; Per Subs 350
Subject Interests: Vocational tech
Database Vendor: Agricola, EBSCOhost, Gale Cengage Learning, Newsbank, OCLC FirstSearch, OCLC WorldShare Interlibrary Loan, OVID Technologies, ProQuest
Wireless access
Open Mon-Thurs 7am-8pm, Fri 7-4:30, Sun 2-6

P OKMULGEE PUBLIC LIBRARY*, 218 S Okmulgee Ave, 74447. SAN 313-9700. Tel: 918-756-1448. FAX: 918-758-1148. E-mail: library@okmcity.net. Web Site: www.okmulgeelibrary.org. *Dir,* Kristin Cunningham; *Ch Serv,* Jeana Robinson; Staff 7 (MLS 1, Non-MLS 6)
Founded 1907. Pop 17,906; Circ 139,306
Library Holdings: Audiobooks 1,973; Bk Vols 57,821; Per Subs 150; Videos 2,697
Subject Interests: Creek Indians
Automation Activity & Vendor Info: (Cataloging) Book Systems; (Circulation) Book Systems; (OPAC) Book Systems
Wireless access
Publications: Index to Okmulge Daily Times Obituaries 1950-
Open Mon & Thurs 9-8, Tue & Wed 9-6, Fri 9-5, Sat 8-12
Friends of the Library Group

PAULS VALLEY

P NORA SPARKS WARREN LIBRARY*, 210 N Willow St, 73075. Tel: 405-238-5188. FAX: 405-238-5188. E-mail: nswpub@yahoo.com. Web Site: www.paulsvalley.com. *Dir,* Julia Embree; *Asst Dir,* Tina Hume; *Librn,* Susan Skipper; Staff 120 (Non-MLS 120)
Founded 1951. Pop 6,256
Library Holdings: AV Mats 902; Bk Vols 36,000; Per Subs 66; Talking Bks 200
Subject Interests: Genealogy
Open Mon, Tues, Thurs & Fri 9-5:30, Wed 9-7:30, Sat 8:30-Noon

PAWHUSKA

P PAWHUSKA PUBLIC LIBRARY*, 1801 Lynn Ave, 74056. SAN 313-9735. Tel: 918-287-3989. FAX: 918-287-3989. *Dir,* Lu King; Staff 1 (Non-MLS 1)
Founded 1924. Pop 3,590; Circ 58,887
Library Holdings: Bk Titles 40,000; Per Subs 75
Special Collections: Audio Cassettes & Videos; Genealogy Coll; Newspapers, microfilm; Osage Indian Coll; United States Census, microfilm
Automation Activity & Vendor Info: (Circulation) Follett Software
Publications: Library Brochure
Open Mon-Fri 10-6, Sat 10-4

PAWNEE

P PAWNEE PUBLIC LIBRARY*, 653 Illinois St, 74058. SAN 313-9743. Tel: 918-762-2138. FAX: 918-762-2101. Web Site: www.pawneepubliclibrary.net. *Librn,* Kathy McKinnis
Founded 1936. Pop 2,443; Circ 5,671
Library Holdings: Bk Titles 7,200; Per Subs 12
Automation Activity & Vendor Info: (Circulation) Follett Software
Special Services for the Blind - Talking bks
Open Mon-Fri 10-6, Sat 10-2
Friends of the Library Group

PERKINS

P THOMAS-WILHITE MEMORIAL LIBRARY*, 101 E Thomas, 74059. (Mail add: PO Box 519, 74059-0519), SAN 313-9751. Tel: 405-547-5185. FAX: 405-547-1040. E-mail: perkinslibrary@cityofperkins.net. Web Site: cityofperkins.net/library. *Dir,* Alison Bloyd; E-mail: abloyd@cityofperkins.net; *Circ/Cat Librn,* Jennifer Decker; *Acq,* Carlletta Brown; *Ch Serv,* Lisa Sasser; Staff 2 (MLS 2)
Founded 1954. Pop 4,000; Circ 24,000
Library Holdings: Bk Titles 12,852; Bk Vols 13,281
Special Collections: Frontier Coll; Oklahoma Coll; Will Rogers Coll, bks
Subject Interests: Christian fiction, Frontier, Hispanic, Okla, Pioneer life
Automation Activity & Vendor Info: (Acquisitions) Follett Software; (Cataloging) Follett Software; (Circulation) Follett Software; (OPAC) Follett Software; (Serials) EBSCO Online
Wireless access
Open Mon-Fri 10-6, Sat 9-Noon
Friends of the Library Group

PERRY

P PERRY CARNEGIE LIBRARY*, 302 N Seventh St, 73077. SAN 313-976X. Tel: 580-336-4721. FAX: 580-336-5497. E-mail: staff@perry.lib.ok.us. *Dir,* Jeffrey Courouleau; E-mail: director@perry.lib.ok.us; *Ch Serv,* Barbara Ladson; *Ch Serv,* Trudie Patak; E-mail: tpatak@perry.lib.ok.us; Staff 1 (MLS 1)
Founded 1909. Pop 11,000; Circ 38,800
Library Holdings: Bk Titles 26,503; Bk Vols 29,000; Per Subs 69; Talking Bks 546; Videos 1,604
Automation Activity & Vendor Info: (Cataloging) Follett Software; (Circulation) Follett Software
Open Mon-Fri 9-6, Sat 9-Noon
Friends of the Library Group

PONCA CITY

P PONCA CITY LIBRARY*, 515 E Grand, 74601. SAN 313-9786. Tel: 580-767-0345. Circulation Tel: 580-767-0350. Reference Tel: 580-767-0354. Administration Tel: 580-767-0349. FAX: 580-767-0377. E-mail: library@poncacityok.gov. Web Site: www.poncacityok.gov/index.aspx?nid=155. *Dir,* Holly La Bossiere
Founded 1904. Pop 26,000; Circ 289,855
Library Holdings: Bk Vols 75,000; Per Subs 264
Special Collections: Oriental & 20th Century Western Paintings (Matzene Art Coll)
Subject Interests: Genealogy
Automation Activity & Vendor Info: (Acquisitions) SirsiDynix; (Cataloging) SirsiDynix; (Circulation) SirsiDynix; (ILL) OCLC; (OPAC) SirsiDynix
Partic in OCLC Online Computer Library Center, Inc; OLTN
Open Mon-Thurs 9-9, Fri 9-6, Sat 9-5:30, Sun (Sept-May) 2-5
Friends of the Library Group

POND CREEK

P POND CREEK CITY LIBRARY*, 105 S Second, 73766-9787. (Mail add: PO Box 6, 73766-0006), SAN 323-4711. Tel: 580-532-6319. FAX: 580-532-4913.
Founded 1934. Pop 1,050

Library Holdings: Bk Titles 8,875; Bk Vols 10,000; Per Subs 14; Talking Bks 146; Videos 285
Special Services for the Deaf - Bks on deafness & sign lang; High interest/low vocabulary bks
Open Tues, Thurs & Fri 10-5, Wed 12-7

POTEAU

J CARL ALBERT STATE COLLEGE*, Joe E White Library, 1507 S McKenna, 74953. SAN 313-9808. Tel: 918-647-1310. Interlibrary Loan Service Tel: 918-647-1311. FAX: 918-647-1314. Web Site: www.lib.carlalbert.edu. *Dir,* Terri Carroll; E-mail: tcarroll@carlalbert.edu; *Asst Dir,* T Sutton; E-mail; tsutton@carlalbert.edu
Founded 1934. Enrl 2,300; Fac 75
Library Holdings: e-books 10,000; Bk Vols 25,000; Per Subs 100
Automation Activity & Vendor Info: (Cataloging) SirsiDynix; (Circulation) SirsiDynix; (Course Reserve) SirsiDynix; (OPAC) SirsiDynix
Database Vendor: EBSCOhost, Newsbank, OCLC FirstSearch, ProQuest
Wireless access
Partic in OCLC Online Computer Library Center, Inc
Open Mon-Thurs 8am-8:30pm, Fri 8-4

P PATRICK LYNCH PUBLIC LIBRARY, 206 S McKenna Ave, 74953. SAN 313-9794. Tel: 918-647-4444. FAX: 918-647-8910. E-mail: plpl@oklibrary.net. Web Site: www.oklibrary.net/poteau/home.htm. *Dir,* Nancy B Hamlin; E-mail: hamlin@oklibrary.net; *Ch Serv,* Carole Gill; *Circ,* Nancie Anne Gordon; *Circ,* Donna Musgrove; *Circ,* Debra Kirkendoll; *ILL,* Mona Goodrich
Founded 1929. Pop 19,000; Circ 120,244
Library Holdings: Audiobooks 593; e-books 3,000; Bk Vols 54,000; Per Subs 60
Subject Interests: Genealogy, Literacy
Automation Activity & Vendor Info: (Circulation) SirsiDynix
Mem of Southeastern Public Library System of Oklahoma
Open Mon-Fri 9-7, Sat 9-5
Friends of the Library Group

PRAGUE

P HAYNIE PUBLIC LIBRARY, 1619 W Main St, 74864. SAN 313-9824. Tel: 405-567-4013. *Libr Dir,* Pamela Bea Batson; E-mail: pam.batson@haynielibrary.com
Circ 16,675
Library Holdings: Bk Vols 16,000
Wireless access
Open Tues-Fri 8:30-5:30, Sat 8-Noon
Friends of the Library Group

PRYOR

P PRYOR PUBLIC LIBRARY*, 505 E Graham, 74361. SAN 313-9832. Tel: 918-825-0777. FAX: 918-825-0856. Web Site: www.pryorok.org. *Dir,* Susan Newberry; *Ad,* Lianne Wray; *Ref/Cat Librn,* Marie Reist; *Tech Librn,* Heather Hutto; *Youth Serv Librn,* Jacinda Ramsey
Founded 1939. Pop 32,000; Circ 103,063
Library Holdings: Bk Titles 30,000; Per Subs 100
Special Collections: Autographs of United States Presidents (Harrison Coll), letters; Civil War Coll; Genealogy Coll
Subject Interests: Hist
Automation Activity & Vendor Info: (Cataloging) Follett Software; (Circulation) Follett Software
Open Mon-Thurs 1-9, Tues, Wed & Fri 9-5, Sat 9-Noon
Friends of the Library Group

RUSH SPRINGS

P GLOVER SPENCER MEMORIAL LIBRARY*, 100 S Sixth St, Corner SE Sixth & Blakely Ave, 73082. (Mail add: PO Box 576, 73082-0576), SAN 313-9840. Tel: 580-476-2108. FAX: 580-476-2129. E-mail: director@glover.lib.ok.us. Web Site: www.glover.lib.ok.us. *Librn,* Almata Lindsey
Pop 1,500; Circ 7,440
Library Holdings: AV Mats 1,000; Bk Vols 11,000
Automation Activity & Vendor Info: (Circulation) Follett Software
Open Mon & Wed-Fri Noon-5, Tues Noon-7, Sat 9-Noon
Friends of the Library Group

SALLISAW

P STANLEY TUBBS MEMORIAL LIBRARY*, 101 E Cherokee St, 74955-4621. SAN 313-9859. Tel: 918-775-4481. Toll Free Tel: 888-291-8154 (in 918 area code only). FAX: 918-775-4129. Web Site: www.eodls.lib.ok.us/sallisaw.html. *Br Mgr,* Bethia Owens; Staff 5 (Non-MLS 5)
Founded 1967. Pop 8,000
Library Holdings: Bk Vols 34,000
Automation Activity & Vendor Info: (Acquisitions) SirsiDynix; (Cataloging) SirsiDynix; (Circulation) SirsiDynix
Wireless access
Mem of Eastern Oklahoma District Library System
Open Mon & Thurs 9-8, Tues & Wed 9-6, Fri 9-5, Sat 9-1

SAPULPA

P BARTLETT-CARNEGIE SAPULPA PUBLIC LIBRARY*, 27 W Dewey, 74066. SAN 313-9875. Tel: 918-224-5624. FAX: 918-224-3546. *Dir,* Martha Stalker; *Genealogy Librn,* Barbara Carter; *Genealogy Librn,* Cathy Mattix; *Circ,* Karen Skaggs; Staff 8 (MLS 3, Non-MLS 5)
Founded 1917. Pop 20,000
Library Holdings: Bk Vols 37,000; Per Subs 86
Special Collections: Euchee/Yuchi Indian Tribe Coll; Indians of North America Coll; Oklahoma Coll; Sylvia Welch Genealogical Library Coll, bks, micro
Automation Activity & Vendor Info: (Cataloging) Innovative Interfaces, Inc; (Circulation) Innovative Interfaces, Inc; (OPAC) Innovative Interfaces, Inc
Wireless access
Partic in OLTN
Open Mon, Wed & Thurs 9-6, Tues 9-8, Fri 9-5, Sat 10-2
Friends of the Library Group

SAYRE

P SAYRE PUBLIC LIBRARY*, 113 E Poplar, 73662. SAN 329-8043. Tel: 580-928-2641. Toll Free Tel: 888-363-9678. FAX: 580-928-1189. E-mail: sayrepl1@sayre.lib.ok.us. Web Site: www.sayre.lib.ok.us. *Dir,* Donna Karden
Founded 1921. Pop 2,881; Circ 7,500
Library Holdings: Bk Titles 7,500; Bk Vols 9,000
Special Collections: Genealogical Research, 1900-; Local Newspapers for Sayre Journal & Sayre Record, 1901-; Sayre Record, microfilm
Automation Activity & Vendor Info: (Cataloging) Follett Software; (Circulation) Follett Software; (OPAC) Follett Software
Database Vendor: Gale Cengage Learning, OCLC FirstSearch
Function: ILL available
Open Tues, Wed & Fri 9-4, Thurs 12-7, Sat 9-12
Friends of the Library Group

SEMINOLE

P SEMINOLE PUBLIC LIBRARY*, 424 N Main, 74868. SAN 313-9905. Tel: 405-382-4221. FAX: 405-382-0050. *Dir,* Linda Rhodes; E-mail: libdirector51@yahoo.com
Founded 1929. Pop 17,071; Circ 45,516
Library Holdings: Bk Vols 30,000; Per Subs 65
Special Collections: Large Print Coll
Subject Interests: Native Am - Seminole Tribe
Automation Activity & Vendor Info: (Cataloging) Follett Software; (Circulation) Follett Software
Database Vendor: OCLC FirstSearch
Function: ILL available, Photocopying/Printing, Ref serv available
Partic in Okla Telecommunications Interlibr Syst
Open Mon-Thurs 8:30-6, Fri 8:30-5, Sat 8:30-12:30
Friends of the Library Group

J SEMINOLE STATE COLLEGE*, David L Boren Library, Junction Hwy 9 & David L Boren Blvd, 74818. (Mail add: PO Box 351, 74818-0351), SAN 313-9891. Tel: 405-382-9950, Ext 243. FAX: 405-382-9511. Web Site: www.ssc.cc.ok.us. *Head Librn,* Marguerite Hearod; E-mail: m.hearod@sscok.edu
Founded 1970. Enrl 1,439; Fac 41
Library Holdings: Bk Titles 31,000; Per Subs 301
Special Collections: Library of American Civilization (American History Coll), ultrafiche
Wireless access
Open Mon & Tues 8am-8:30pm, Wed & Thurs 8-7, Fri 8-5

SHATTUCK

P SHATTUCK PUBLIC LIBRARY*, 101 S Main St, 73858. (Mail add: PO Box 129, 73858-0129), SAN 320-5037. Tel: 580-938-5104. FAX: 580-938-5104. E-mail: shattpl@pldi.net. *Librn,* Judy Abbott
Circ 4,837
Library Holdings: Bk Vols 9,118; Per Subs 15
Special Collections: History (Northwest Oklahoman Coll), newsps
Subject Interests: Ellis County hist, Gardening, Laws
Automation Activity & Vendor Info: (Circulation) Follett Software
Partic in Okla Telecommunications Interlibr Syst
Open Mon & Thurs 10-6, Tues & Wed 12-5
Friends of the Library Group

SHAWNEE

CR OKLAHOMA BAPTIST UNIVERSITY*, Mabee Learning Center, 500 W University, OBU Box 61310, 74804-2504. SAN 313-9913. Tel: 405-878-2249. Circulation Tel: 405-878-2251. Interlibrary Loan Service Tel: 405-878-2269. Reference Tel: 405-878-2259. FAX: 405-878-2256. Web Site: www.okbu.edu/library/. *Dean, Libr Serv,* Richard O Cheek; E-mail: richard.cheek@okbu.edu; *Head, Cat, Head, Tech Serv,* Diane Shank; Tel: 405-878-2257, Fax: 405-878-2270, E-mail: diane.shank@okbu.edu; *Access Serv, Curric Center Librn,* Janet Bailey; E-mail: janet.bailey@okbu.edu; *Circ Mgr,* Mary Price; Tel: 405-878-2264, E-mail: mary.price@okbu.edu; *Acq of Monographs,* Nora Inman; Tel: 405-878-2268, E-mail: nora.inman@okbu.edu; *Acq of New Ser/Per,* Vernell Ward; Tel: 405-878-2255, E-mail: vernell.ward@okbu.edu; *Archivist,* Tom Terry; Tel: 405-878-2254, E-mail: tom.terry@okbu.edu; *Govt Doc, Ser,* Denise Jett; Tel: 405-878-2284, E-mail: denise.jett@okbu.edu; *Media Serv,* Cindy Hicks; Tel: 405-878-2253, E-mail: cindy.hicks@okbu.edu. Subject Specialists: *Theol,* Richard O Cheek; Staff 10 (MLS 5, Non-MLS 5)
Founded 1911. Enrl 1,468; Fac 105; Highest Degree: Master
Library Holdings: Bk Vols 225,000; Per Subs 450
Special Collections: Baptist History Center; Brister Pastoral Ministries. US Document Depository
Subject Interests: Archives, Relig
Automation Activity & Vendor Info: (Acquisitions) SirsiDynix; (Cataloging) SirsiDynix; (Circulation) SirsiDynix; (ILL) OCLC Online; (OPAC) SirsiDynix; (Serials) EBSCO Online
Database Vendor: Dialog, EBSCOhost, Gale Cengage Learning, JSTOR, OCLC FirstSearch
Wireless access
Function: Archival coll, AV serv, Govt ref serv, Handicapped accessible, ILL available, Outside serv via phone, mail, e-mail & web, Photocopying/Printing, Ref serv available, Res libr, Telephone ref, Wheelchair accessible
Partic in Dialog Corp; OCLC Online Computer Library Center, Inc
Restriction: Open to students, fac & staff

CR SAINT GREGORY'S UNIVERSITY*, James J Kelly Library, 1900 W MacArthur St, 74804. SAN 313-9921. Tel: 405-878-5111, 405-878-5295. FAX: 405-878-5198. *Dir,* Anita Semtner; E-mail: amsemtner@stgregorys.edu; *Archivist, Cat Librn,* Brother Benet Exton; Tel: 405-878-5109, E-mail: bsexton@stgregorys.edu; *Tech Serv Librn,* Susan Hall; Tel: 405-878-5409, E-mail: sehall@stgregorys.edu; Staff 3 (MLS 3)
Founded 1915. Enrl 802; Fac 36; Highest Degree: Master
Library Holdings: Audiobooks 688; AV Mats 1,438; CDs 73; e-books 3,939; Microforms 3,006; Bk Vols 87,550; Per Subs 106; Videos 426
Special Collections: Treasure Room
Subject Interests: Art, European hist, Native Am, Philos
Automation Activity & Vendor Info: (Acquisitions) Ex Libris Group; (Cataloging) Ex Libris Group; (Circulation) Ex Libris Group; (Course Reserve) Ex Libris Group; (OPAC) Ex Libris Group; (Serials) Ex Libris Group
Database Vendor: Amigos Library Services, EBSCOhost, Ex Libris Group, Gale Cengage Learning, OCLC FirstSearch, ProQuest
Wireless access
Function: Bks on cassette, Computers for patron use, Electronic databases & coll, Handicapped accessible, ILL available, Music CDs, Photocopying/Printing, Spoken cassettes & CDs, VHS videos, Wheelchair accessible
Partic in Oklahoma Council of Academic Libr Directors (OCALD)
Open Mon-Thurs 8am-10pm, Fri 8-4, Sun 4-10
Restriction: In-house use for visitors, Open to students, fac & staff

SPIRO

P SPIRO PUBLIC LIBRARY*, 208 S Main, 74959. SAN 313-993X. Tel: 918-962-3461. FAX: 918-962-5320. *Exec Dir,* Wayne Hanaway; *Librn,* Glenda Stokes; E-mail: stokes@oklibrary.net; *Asst Librn,* Brittany Bell
Pop 2,057; Circ 6,485
Library Holdings: Bk Vols 15,000; Per Subs 15
Automation Activity & Vendor Info: (Cataloging) SirsiDynix; (Circulation) SirsiDynix
Mem of Southeastern Public Library System of Oklahoma
Open Tues-Fri 9-6, Sat 9-2
Friends of the Library Group

STIGLER

P STIGLER PUBLIC LIBRARY*, 402 NE Sixth St, 74462. SAN 313-9948. Tel: 918-967-4801. FAX: 918-967-4470. *Librn,* Lola L Hill
Pop 2,347
Library Holdings: Bk Titles 22,000; Per Subs 32
Automation Activity & Vendor Info: (Circulation) SirsiDynix
Database Vendor: EBSCO Auto Repair Reference, EBSCOhost, LearningExpress, Newsbank, World Book Online
Wireless access
Mem of Southeastern Public Library System of Oklahoma
Open Mon-Thurs 9-7, Fri 9-5, Sat 9-2

STILLWATER

S NATIONAL WRESTLING HALL OF FAME LIBRARY & MUSEUM*, 405 W Hall of Fame Ave, 74075. SAN 313-9972. Tel: 405-377-5243. FAX: 405-377-5244. E-mail: info@wrestlinghalloffame.org. Web Site: www.wrestlinghalloffame.org. *Exec Dir,* LeeRoy Smith; Staff 3 (MLS 3)
Founded 1976
Library Holdings: Bk Titles 112; Bk Vols 170
Subject Interests: Wrestling
Open Mon-Fri 9-4:30

G OKLAHOMA DEPARTMENT OF CAREER & TECHNOLOGY EDUCATION*, Information Commons, 1500 W Seventh Ave, 74074-4364. SAN 313-9956. Tel: 405-377-2000, Ext 161. FAX: 405-743-5142, 405-743-6809. Web Site: www.okcareertech.org/informationcommons/. *Mgr,* Denise Christy; E-mail: dchri@okcareertech.org
Founded 1970
Library Holdings: Bk Titles 14,000; Bk Vols 20,000
Subject Interests: Vocational educ
Wireless access
Open Mon 8-4:30

C OKLAHOMA STATE UNIVERSITY LIBRARIES*, Athletic Ave, 216, 74078-1071. SAN 357-6965. Interlibrary Loan Service Tel: 405-744-9727. Administration Tel: 405-744-6321. FAX: 405-744-5183. Administration FAX: 405-744-7579. E-mail: lib-dls@okstate.edu. Web Site: www.library.okstate.edu. *Dean of Libr,* Sheila Grant Johnson; E-mail: sheila.johnson@okstate.edu; *Assoc Dean, Libr Operations,* Robin Leech; Tel: 405-744-9780, E-mail: robin.leech@okstate.edu; *Assoc Dean, Spec Coll,* Mary Larson; Tel: 405-744-6588, E-mail: mary.larson@okstate.edu; *Dir, Libr Syst,* Rod K McAbee; Tel: 405-744-5955, E-mail: rod.mcabee@okstate.edu; *Dir of Libr Grad & Res Serv,* Victor Baeza; Tel: 405-744-1241, E-mail: victor.baeza@okstate.edu; *Head, Access Serv,* Dr Johnny Johnson; E-mail: johnny.johnson@okstate.edu; *Head, Cat,* Co-Ming Chan; E-mail: co_ming.chan@okstate.edu; *Head, Humanities & Soc Sci,* Steve Locy; E-mail: steven.locy@okstate.edu; *Archit Librn,* Susan Bobo; Tel: 405-744-6034, E-mail: susan.bobo@okstate.edu; *Veterinary Med Librn,* Liz Amos; Tel: 405-744-6655, E-mail: liz.amos@okstate.edu; *Admin Serv,* Karen A Neurohr; Tel: 405-744-2376, E-mail: karen.neurohr@okstate.edu; Staff 106 (MLS 41, Non-MLS 65)
Founded 1894. Enrl 20,956; Fac 893; Highest Degree: Doctorate
Special Collections: Architecture, bks & per; Curriculum Guides & Text Books (Curriculum Materials Library); Oklahoma Governors & Politicians (Papers of Gov Henry S Johnston & Gov Henry Bellmon, Senate Papers of Henry Bellmon); OSU History & Publications, bks, ms; Papers of Angie Debo; Soil Conservation, Water Resources & Agriculture (Oklahoma), bks, ms; US Patent & Trademark Depository Library; Veterinary Medicine, bks & per; Women's Archives, per & ms. Oral History; State Document Depository; US Document Depository
Subject Interests: Agr, Biochem, Botany, Chem, Econ, Educ, Eng, Geol, Hist of the Am West, Math, Physics
Automation Activity & Vendor Info: (Acquisitions) Ex Libris Group; (Cataloging) Ex Libris Group; (Circulation) Ex Libris Group; (Course Reserve) Ex Libris Group; (ILL) OCLC ILLiad; (OPAC) Ex Libris Group; (Serials) Ex Libris Group
Database Vendor: ABC-CLIO, ACM (Association for Computing Machinery), Agricola, Alexander Street Press, American Chemical Society, American Mathematical Society, American Psychological Association (APA), Amigos Library Services, Annual Reviews, ARTstor, ASCE Research Library, Baker & Taylor, BioOne, Blackwell, Bowker, Cambridge Scientific Abstracts, Children's Literature Comprehensive Database Company (CLCD), Community of Science (COS), CQ Press, EBSCOhost, Elsevier, Emerald, Ex Libris Group, Factiva.com, Gale Cengage Learning, IEEE (Institute of Electrical & Electronics Engineers), IOP, ISI Web of Knowledge, JSTOR, Knovel, LexisNexis, Majors, Mergent Online, Modern Language Association, Nature Publishing Group, Newsbank, OCLC FirstSearch, OCLC WebJunction, OCLC WorldShare Interlibrary Loan, OVID Technologies, Oxford Online, ProQuest, PubMed, ScienceDirect, SerialsSolutions, Springer-Verlag, Standard & Poor's, Swets Information Services, Wiley, YBP Library Services
Wireless access
Publications: Perspectives (External newsletter)
Partic in Association of Research Libraries (ARL); Greater Western Library Alliance; Okla Libr Technology Network; Okla Res & Commun Librs Consortium
Friends of the Library Group

Departmental Libraries:

ARCHITECTURE, School of Architecture Bldg, Rm 160, 74078, SAN 357-699X. Tel: 405-744-6047. *Librn,* Susan Bobo; Staff 1 (MLS 1)

CM WILLIAM E BROCK MEMORIAL LIBRARY AT OSU CENTER FOR VETERINARY HEALTH SCIENCES, 102 McElroy Hall, 74078-2013, SAN 357-7023. Tel: 405-744-6655. FAX: 405-744-5609. *Librn,* Liz Amos; Staff 2 (MLS 1, Non-MLS 1)

DIGITAL LIBRARY SERVICES, Edmon Low Library, Rm 215A, 74078-1071. Tel: 405-744-9161. *Head, Digital Initiatives,* Nicole Sump-Crethar; Staff 4 (MLS 3, Non-MLS 1)

DOCUMENTS DEPARTMENT, Edmon Low Library, 5th Flr, 74078-1071, SAN 374-4205. Tel: 405-744-6546. *Head Librn,* John B Phillips; Staff 10 (MLS 4, Non-MLS 6)
Special Collections: UN Document Depository; US Document Depository
Subject Interests: Patent, Trademarks
Open Mon-Fri 8-5

HUMANITIES & SOCIAL SCIENCES DIVISION, Edmon Low Library, 3rd Flr, 74078-1071, SAN 327-9014. *Head Librn,* Steve Locy; Staff 7 (MLS 6, Non-MLS 1)

SCIENCE & ENGINEERING DIVISION, Edmon Low Library, 3rd Flr, 74078-1071, SAN 327-8999. *Actg Head,* Victor Baeza; Staff 5 (MLS 5)

SPECIAL COLLECTIONS & UNIVERSITY ARCHIVES, Library 204, 74078-1071. Tel: 405-744-6311. E-mail: libscua@okstate.edu. Web Site: info.library.okstate.edu/scua/home. *Head, Spec Coll & Archives,* Position Currently Open; Staff 5 (MLS 2, Non-MLS 3)
Special Collections: Oral History
Function: Archival coll, Photocopying/Printing
Restriction: Registered patrons only

MARY L WILLIAMS CURRICULUM MATERIALS LIBRARY, 001 Willard Hall, 74078-1071, SAN 373-8841. Tel: 405-744-6310. FAX: 405-744-1726. Web Site: www.library.okstate.edu/cml/index.htm. *Librn,* Karen T Morris; Tel: 405-744-9769, E-mail: karen.t.morris@okstate.edu. Subject Specialists: *Children's lit, Young adult lit,* Karen T Morris; Staff 2 (MLS 1, Non-MLS 1)
Special Collections: Della Thomas Alice in Wonderland Coll, bks, artifacts; Historical Children's Literature
Open Mon-Fri 8-5

P STILLWATER PUBLIC LIBRARY, 1107 S Duck St, 74074. SAN 313-9964. Tel: 405-372-3633. Interlibrary Loan Service Tel: 405-372-3633, Ext 8119. Reference Tel: 405-372-3633, Ext 8106. Administration Tel: 405-372-3633, Ext 8100. FAX: 405-624-0552. Web Site: library.stillwater.org. *Dir,* Lynda Reynolds; Tel: 405-372-3633, Ext 8101, E-mail: lreynolds@stillwater.org; *Ch,* Elizabeth Murray; Tel: 405-372-3633, Ext 8116, E-mail: emurray@stillwater.org; *Circ Mgr,* Andrea Kane; Tel: 405-372-3633, Ext 8114, E-mail: akane@stillwater.org; *Adult Serv,* Stacy DeLano; Tel: 405-372-3633, Ext 8124, E-mail: sdelano@stillwater.org; *ILL,* Jeanna Shore; E-mail: libraryloan@stillwater.org; *Tech Serv,* Jay Criswell; Tel: 405-372-3633, Ext 8121, E-mail: cataloger@stillwater.org; Staff 10 (MLS 3, Non-MLS 7)
Founded 1923. Pop 77,350; Circ 353,806
Jul 2013-Jun 2014 Income (Main Library Only) $1,511,284, State $27,168, City $124,526, Federal $189,081, Other $48,509. Mats Exp $285,847, Books $83,533, Per/Ser (Incl. Access Fees) $4,547, Micro $245, AV Mat $15,538, Electronic Ref Mat (Incl. Access Fees) $181,984. Sal $777,607 (Prof $409,724)
Library Holdings: AV Mats 18,054; e-books 23,091; Electronic Media & Resources 931; Bk Titles 88,943; Bk Vols 98,826; Per Subs 115
Special Collections: Genealogy Coll; Local Govt Coll; Stillwater Coll. Municipal Document Depository
Automation Activity & Vendor Info: (Cataloging) SirsiDynix; (Circulation) SirsiDynix; (ILL) SirsiDynix; (OPAC) SirsiDynix
Database Vendor: Baker & Taylor, EBSCO Auto Repair Reference, EBSCOhost, Foundation Center, Gale Cengage Learning, Ingram Library Services, OCLC FirstSearch, OCLC WorldShare Interlibrary Loan, Overdrive, Inc, ProQuest, SirsiDynix
Wireless access
Function: Adult bk club, Audio & video playback equip for onsite use, Bilingual assistance for Spanish patrons, Bk club(s), Bks on CD, CD-ROM, Children's prog, Computer training, Computers for patron use, Copy machines, e-mail & chat, e-mail serv, Electronic databases & coll, Exhibits, Fax serv, Free DVD rentals, Genealogy discussion group, Govt ref serv, Handicapped accessible, Home delivery & serv to Sr ctr & nursing homes, Homebound delivery serv, ILL available, Life-long learning prog for all ages, Magazines, Magnifiers for reading, Mail & tel request accepted, Microfiche/film & reading machines, Monthly prog for perceptually impaired adults, Movies, Music CDs, Notary serv, Online cat, Online ref, Online searches, Outreach serv, OverDrive digital audio bks, Photocopying/Printing, Preschool outreach, Preschool reading prog, Printer for laptops & handheld devices, Prog for adults, Prog for children & young adult, Provide serv for the mentally ill, Pub access computers, Ref serv available, Ref serv in person, Scanner, Senior computer classes, Senior outreach, Serves mentally handicapped consumers, Spanish lang bks, Spoken cassettes & CDs, Spoken cassettes & DVDs, Story hour, Study rm, Summer & winter reading prog, Summer reading prog, Tax forms, Teen prog, Telephone ref, VHS videos, Video lending libr, Web-catalog, Wheelchair accessible, Winter reading prog, Workshops
Special Services for the Deaf - Assisted listening device; Bks on deafness & sign lang; Closed caption videos; High interest/low vocabulary bks; Sign lang interpreter upon request for prog
Special Services for the Blind - Accessible computers; Assistive/Adapted tech devices, equip & products; Audio mat; Bks on cassette; Bks on CD; Braille bks; Children's Braille; Copier with enlargement capabilities; Extensive large print coll; Home delivery serv; Internet workstation with adaptive software; Large print bks; Low vision equip; Magnifiers; Micro-computer access & training; Reading & writing aids; Screen enlargement software for people with visual disabilities; Screen reader software; Talking bks; ZoomText magnification & reading software
Open Mon-Thurs 9-9, Fri & Sat 9-6, Sun 1-5
Friends of the Library Group

STILWELL

P STILWELL PUBLIC LIBRARY, Five N Sixth St, 74960. SAN 313-9980. Tel: 918-696-7512. FAX: 918-696-4007. E-mail: stilwellpl@eodls.org. Web Site: www.eodls.lib.ok.us/stilwell.html. *Br Mgr,* Arlene Burton
Founded 1972
Library Holdings: Bk Vols 16,000; Per Subs 10
Automation Activity & Vendor Info: (Circulation) Horizon; (ILL) Horizon
Wireless access
Mem of Eastern Oklahoma District Library System
Open Mon-Fri 9-5:30, Sat 9-1
Friends of the Library Group

STRATFORD

P CHANDLER-WATTS MEMORIAL LIBRARY*, 340 N Oak, 74872. (Mail add: PO Box 696, 74872-0696). Tel: 580-759-2684. FAX: 580-759-3121. *Dir,* Leesa Heckor
Pop 1,474; Circ 19,843
Library Holdings: AV Mats 400; CDs 38; DVDs 200; Bk Vols 19,200; Per Subs 10; Talking Bks 100
Automation Activity & Vendor Info: (Cataloging) Follett Software; (Circulation) Follett Software
Open Mon & Thurs 8-6, Tues, Wed & Fri 8-4
Friends of the Library Group

STROUD

P SAC & FOX NATIONAL PUBLIC LIBRARY, 920883 S Hwy 99, 74079-5178. SAN 374-6690. Tel: 918 968 3526. FAX: 918-968-4837. Web Site: sacandfox.biblionix.com. *Libr Dir,* Kathy J Platt; E-mail: kathy.platt@sacandfoxnation-nsn.gov; *Hist Researcher,* Catherine Joy Walker; E-mail: Cathrine.Walker@sacandfoxnation-nsn.gov; Staff 3 (Non-MLS 3)
Founded 1987. Pop 34,000
Library Holdings: Audiobooks 44; Bks on Deafness & Sign Lang 8; CDs 64; DVDs 1,279; Large Print Bks 64; Bk Titles 6,007; Per Subs 15; Talking Bks 13
Special Collections: Jim Thorpe Coll, lang tapes, restricted bks, treaties; Sac & Fox Archives, newsp, oral hist, photos. Oral History
Automation Activity & Vendor Info: (Cataloging) Biblionix; (Circulation) Biblionix
Database Vendor: Amigos Library Services, Biblionix/Apollo, Bowker, Brodart, EBSCOhost
Wireless access
Open Mon-Fri 8-6, Sat 9-1

P STROUD PUBLIC LIBRARY*, 301 W Seventh St, 74079. (Mail add: PO Box 599, 74079-0599), SAN 313-9999. Tel: 918-968-2567. FAX: 918-968-4700. E-mail: stroudlib@yahoo.com. Web Site: www.cityofstroud.com/dept/library/shtml. *Librn,* Marsha Morgan
Founded 1936. Pop 3,000; Circ 15,000
Library Holdings: Bk Vols 12,000
Special Collections: Oral History
Automation Activity & Vendor Info: (Circulation) Follett Software
Open Mon & Tues 9-1 & 2-6, Wed-Fri 9-1 & 2-5, Sat 9-12
Friends of the Library Group

SULPHUR

S NATIONAL PARK SERVICE*, Travertine Nature Center Library, Chickasaw Nat Recreation Area, 1054 NE Perimeter Rd, 73086. SAN 314-0008. Tel: 580-622-3165. FAX: 580-622-6931. Web Site: www.nps.gov/chic. *Chief of Interpretation,* Ron Parker
Founded 1969
Library Holdings: Bk Vols 1,800; Per Subs 30
Subject Interests: Biol, Botany, Ecology, Geol, Native Am
Open Mon-Sun 9-4:30
Restriction: Ref only

S OKLAHOMA SCHOOL FOR THE DEAF LIBRARY*, 1100 E Oklahoma St, 73086. SAN 314-0016. Tel: 580-622-4900. FAX: 580-622-4959. Web Site: www.osd.k12.ok.us. *Librn,* Sue Galloway; E-mail: sgalloway@osd.k12.ok.us; Staff 1 (MLS 1)
Founded 1898
Library Holdings: Bks on Deafness & Sign Lang 466; Bk Titles 9,407; Bk Vols 9,459; Per Subs 53; Videos 180
Automation Activity & Vendor Info: (Cataloging) Follett Software; (Circulation) Follett Software; (OPAC) Follett Software
Function: Handicapped accessible, Wheelchair accessible
Special Services for the Deaf - Bks on deafness & sign lang; Deaf publ; Sorenson video relay syst; Staff with knowledge of sign lang; TTY equip

TAFT

OKLAHOMA DEPARTMENT OF CORRECTIONS
S JESS DUNN LEISURE LIBRARY*, 601 S 124th St W, 74463. (Mail add: PO Box 316, 74463-0316), SAN 324-4334. Tel: 918-682-7841, Ext 6544. FAX: 918-687-3431. *Head Librn,* Judy Foy; Staff 1 (MLS 1)
Library Holdings: Bk Vols 10,000; Per Subs 10
Function: For res purposes, Orientations
Restriction: Staff & inmates only
S DR EDDIE WARRIOR LEISURE LIBRARY*, 400 N Oak St, 74463. (Mail add: PO Box 315, 74463-0315), SAN 371-5329. Tel: 918-683-8365. FAX: 918-683-1586. *Librn,* Stephany Kash; Staff 1 (MLS 1)
Founded 1989
Library Holdings: Bk Vols 7,600
Special Services for the Deaf - High interest/low vocabulary bks; Spec interest per

TAHLEQUAH

C NORTHEASTERN STATE UNIVERSITY*, John Vaughan Library-Learning Resource Center, 711 N Grand Ave, 74464-2333. SAN 314-2333. Tel: 918-456-5511, Ext 3200. Circulation Tel: 918-456-5511, Ext 3235. Reference Tel: 918-456-5511, Ext 3240. FAX: 918-458-2197. E-mail: library@nsuok.edu. Web Site: library.nsuok.edu. *Exec Dir,* Paula Settoon; E-mail: settoon@nsuok.edu; *Dir, Tech Serv,* Linda West; E-mail: west@nsuok.edu; *Spec Coll Librn,* Delores Sumner; E-mail: sumner@nsuok.edu; *Archivist,* Victoria Sheffler; E-mail: sheffler@nsuok.edu; Staff 32 (MLS 13, Non-MLS 19)
Founded 1909. Enrl 8,833; Fac 340; Highest Degree: Doctorate
Jul 2007-Jul 2008. Mats Exp $708,408, Books $87,623, Per/Ser (Incl. Access Fees) $620,785
Library Holdings: e-books 75,241; e-journals 13,941; Bk Titles 324,379; Bk Vols 415,275; Per Subs 5,685
Special Collections: Native American History Coll. State Document Depository; US Document Depository
Automation Activity & Vendor Info: (Acquisitions) Innovative Interfaces, Inc; (Cataloging) Innovative Interfaces, Inc; (Circulation) Innovative Interfaces, Inc; (Course Reserve) Innovative Interfaces, Inc; (ILL) OCLC ILLiad; (OPAC) Innovative Interfaces, Inc; (Serials) Innovative Interfaces, Inc
Database Vendor: EBSCOhost, OCLC FirstSearch, ProQuest, Westlaw, Wilson - Wilson Web
Wireless access
Partic in Amigos Library Services, Inc; Dialog Corp; Grateful Med; OCLC Online Computer Library Center, Inc; Okla Libr Technology Network; WebDocs
Special Services for the Deaf - ADA equip
Special Services for the Blind - Assistive/Adapted tech devices, equip & products
Open Mon-Thurs 7:30am-2am, Fri 7:30-5, Sat 1-5, Sun 2-2
Departmental Libraries:
BROKEN ARROW CAMPUS LIBRARY, 3100 E New Orleans St, Broken Arrow, 74014. Tel: 918-449-6459. Administration Tel: 918-449-6452. FAX: 918-449-6454. Web Site: library.nsuok.edu/nsuba/index.html. *Dir,* Dr Pamela Louderback; Tel: 918-449-6453, E-mail: louderba@nsuok.edu; *Instruction Librn,* Tom Rink; Tel: 918-449-6457, E-mail: rink@nsuok.edu; *Instruction Librn,* Karl Siewert; Tel: 918-449-6449, E-mail: siewert@nsuok.edu; Staff 6 (MLS 4, Non-MLS 2)
Founded 2001. Enrl 3,300; Fac 60; Highest Degree: Master
Jul 2007-Jun 2008. Mats Exp $42,000, Books $15,000, Per/Ser (Incl. Access Fees) $27,000
Library Holdings: e-books 35,000; e-journals 11,000; Bk Titles 11,000; Bk Vols 17,000; Per Subs 138
Database Vendor: Amigos Library Services, ebrary, Gale Cengage Learning, H W Wilson, JSTOR, Mergent Online, Newsbank, OCLC WorldShare Interlibrary Loan, OVID Technologies, ProQuest, PubMed, Standard & Poor's, ValueLine
Partic in Dialog Corp; Grateful Med; OCLC Online Computer Library Center, Inc; Oklahoma Council of Academic Libr Directors (OCALD); OLTN
Special Services for the Deaf - Assisted listening device
Special Services for the Blind - Assistive/Adapted tech devices, equip & products
Open Mon-Thurs 8:30am-9pm, Fri & Sat 8:30-5
MUSKOGEE CAMPUS LIBRARY, 2400 W Shawnee St, Muskogee, 74401. (Mail add: PO Box 549, Muskogee, 74402). Tel: 918-456-5511, Ext 5021. FAX: 918-458-2101. *Dir,* Behnam Etemad; E-mail: etemad@nsuok.edu; *Libr Tech,* Sandra Fuller
Library Holdings: AV Mats 200; e-books 75,241; e-journals 13,941; Bk Titles 2,500; Per Subs 60
Open Mon-Thurs 8-8, Fri 8-5

P TAHLEQUAH PUBLIC LIBRARY*, 120 S College Ave, 74464. SAN 376-6438. Tel: 918-456-2581. Toll Free Tel: 888-291-8129. FAX: 918-458-0590. Web Site: www.tahlequah.lib.ok.us. *Librn,* Robin Mooney
Library Holdings: Bk Vols 50,000; Per Subs 20
Automation Activity & Vendor Info: (Cataloging) Horizon; (Circulation) Horizon
Wireless access
Mem of Eastern Oklahoma District Library System
Open Mon-Thurs 9-8, Fri 9-6, Sat 9-1
Friends of the Library Group

TALIHINA

P TALIHINA PUBLIC LIBRARY*, 900 Second St, 74571. SAN 314-0059. Tel: 918-567-2002. Toll Free Tel: 800-650-6630. FAX: 918-567-2921. *Head Librn,* Lee Toliver; E-mail: toliver@oklibrary.net
Founded 1969
Library Holdings: Bk Vols 22,000; Per Subs 20
Special Collections: Oklahoma Coll
Automation Activity & Vendor Info: (Circulation) SirsiDynix
Database Vendor: EBSCOhost, OCLC FirstSearch
Wireless access
Function: Children's prog, Copy machines, Fax serv, Free DVD rentals, Genealogy discussion group, ILL available, Music CDs, Online searches, Prog for adults, Prog for children & young adult, Scanner, Teen prog, VHS videos
Mem of Southeastern Public Library System of Oklahoma
Open Tues & Thurs 1-5, Sat 9-Noon

TECUMSEH

S CENTRAL OKLAHOMA JUVENILE CENTER LIBRARY*, 700 S Ninth, 74893. Tel: 405-598-4146. FAX: 405-598-4158. *Librn,* Diane Houston
Library Holdings: Bk Vols 9,000; Per Subs 30
Open Mon-Fri 8-3:30

TEXHOMA

P TEXHOMA PUBLIC LIBRARY*, PO Box 647, 73949-0647. SAN 314-0067. Tel: 580-423-7150. *Librn,* Carol Coble
Founded 1926. Pop 1,200; Circ 4,708
Library Holdings: Bk Vols 16,000
Open Tues-9-12 & 1-5

TINKER AFB

A UNITED STATES AIR FORCE*, Tinker Air Force Base Library FL2030, 72nd FSS/FSDL, Bldg 5702, 6120 Arnold St, 73145-8101. SAN 357-7058. Tel: 405-734-2626. FAX: 405-734-9511. Web Site: www.tinker.af.mil. *Librn,* Samuel Richards
Founded 1943
Library Holdings: Bk Vols 10,500; Per Subs 115
Special Collections: Total Quality Management
Subject Interests: Aeronautical eng, Recreational
Wireless access
Partic in OCLC Online Computer Library Center, Inc
Open Mon-Thurs 8-7, Fri 8-5, Sat 9-5, Sun 11-5

TISHOMINGO

J MURRAY STATE COLLEGE LIBRARY*, Learning Resource Center, One Murray Campus St LS 101, 73460. SAN 314-0075. Tel: 580-371-2371. FAX: 580-371-9844. Web Site: www.msc.cc.ok.us/lrc. *Dir,* Mary Rixen; E-mail: mrixen@mscok.edu; Staff 3 (MLS 1, Non-MLS 2)
Founded 1930. Enrl 1,958; Fac 43; Highest Degree: Associate
Library Holdings: Bk Titles 22,879; Bk Vols 25,495; Per Subs 177
Automation Activity & Vendor Info: (Cataloging) TLC (The Library Corporation); (Circulation) TLC (The Library Corporation); (Course Reserve) TLC (The Library Corporation); (OPAC) TLC (The Library Corporation)
Database Vendor: EBSCOhost, OCLC FirstSearch
Publications: Library Handbook; Student Worker's Handbook
Partic in OCLC Online Computer Library Center, Inc

TONKAWA

J NORTHERN OKLAHOMA COLLEGE*, Vineyard Library, 1220 E Grand Ave, 74653-4022. (Mail add: PO Box 310, 74653-0310), SAN 314-0083. Tel: 580-628-6250. FAX: 580-628-6209. Web Site: www.noc.edu. *Dir, Libr Serv,* Benjamin Hainline; Tel: 580-628-6253, E-mail: ben.hainline@noc.edu; Staff 6 (MLS 2, Non-MLS 4)
Founded 1901. Enrl 1,600; Fac 65; Highest Degree: Associate
Library Holdings: Bk Titles 41,000; Per Subs 227
Special Collections: Oklahoma Coll. Oral History
Subject Interests: Native Am hist
Automation Activity & Vendor Info: (Acquisitions) Ex Libris Group; (Cataloging) Ex Libris Group; (Circulation) Ex Libris Group; (OPAC) Ex Libris Group
Database Vendor: EBSCOhost, Gale Cengage Learning, ProQuest
Function: Res libr
Open Mon-Thurs 7:30am-9pm, Fri 7:30-5

P TONKAWA PUBLIC LIBRARY*, 216 N Seventh, 74653. SAN 314-0091. Tel: 580-628-3366. FAX: 580-628-3688. *Librn,* Elda Moore; E-mail: e_moore_us@yahoo.com
Founded 1922. Pop 3,127; Circ 33,412
Library Holdings: Bk Titles 18,000; Per Subs 36
Special Collections: Oklahoma Coll
Automation Activity & Vendor Info: (Circulation) Biblionix
Wireless access
Open Mon, Tues, Thurs & Fri 10-6, Wed 12-7, Sat 10-1
Friends of the Library Group

TRYON

P TRYON PUBLIC LIBRARY*, 25 S Main St, 74875. (Mail add: PO Box 65, 74875-0065). Tel: 918-374-2227. FAX: 918-374-2228. E-mail: tlibrary@brightok.net. *Dir,* Wanda Sullivan
Library Holdings: Bk Vols 3,800; Per Subs 10
Open Tues & Thurs 10-2, Wed 9-2 & 5-7

TULSA

S AMERICAN ASSOCIATION OF PETROLEUM GEOLOGISTS FOUNDATION, Energy Resources Library, 1444 S Boulder, 74101-3604. (Mail add: PO Box 979, 74101-0979), SAN 321-1185. Tel: 918-560-2620. FAX: 918-560-2642. E-mail: library@aapg.org. Web Site: foundation.aapg.org/library. *Coll Develop, Geoscience Librn,* Karen Gail Piqune. Subject Specialists: *Geol,* Karen Gail Piqune; Staff 1 (MLS 1)
Founded 1976
Library Holdings: Bk Titles 4,000; Per Subs 85
Special Collections: AAPG Published Material
Subject Interests: Geol with emphasis on petroleum exploration
Automation Activity & Vendor Info: (Cataloging) LibraryWorld, Inc; (ILL) Auto-Graphics, Inc
Database Vendor: OCLC FirstSearch, ProQuest
Function: Res libr
Partic in Amigos Library Services, Inc
Open Mon Thurs 12:30-5, Fri 12:30-4

R FIRST UNITED METHODIST CHURCH LIBRARY*, 1115 S Boulder, 74119-2492. SAN 314-0121. Tel: 918-587-9481, Ext 152. FAX: 918-584-5228. Web Site: www.fumctulsa.org. *Librn,* Joan Spears; E-mail: joanspears@fumctulsa.org; Staff 12 (Non-MLS 12)
Founded 1940
Library Holdings: Bk Titles 15,263; Per Subs 20
Special Collections: Children's Library; Famous Christian Art Reproductions; John Charles Wesley Coll; Methodist Rare Book Coll
Subject Interests: Christian life, Educ
Open Mon-Thurs 10-3, Sun 9-12:30
Friends of the Library Group

L GABLE & GOTWALS, INC*, Law Library, 1100 Oneok Plaza, 100 W Fifth St, 74103-4217. SAN 372-2236. Tel: 918-595-4800. FAX: 918-595-4990. Web Site: gablelaw.com. *Adminr,* Shelley J Bradley; Tel: 918-595-4938, E-mail: sbradley@gablelaw.com; Staff 4 (MLS 2, Non-MLS 2)
Founded 1944
Library Holdings: Bk Vols 10,000; Per Subs 100

S THOMAS GILCREASE INSTITUTE OF AMERICAN HISTORY & ART LIBRARY*, 1400 Gilcrease Museum Rd, 74127-2100. SAN 314-0148. Tel: 918-596-2700. FAX: 918-596-2770. *Sr Curator,* Robert B Pickering; E-mail: bob-pickering@utulsa.edu; *Asst Librn,* Renee Harvey; E-mail: renee-harvey@utulsa.edu; Staff 2 (MLS 1, Non-MLS 1)
Founded 1942
Library Holdings: Bk Titles 40,000; Per Subs 15
Special Collections: Manuscripts
Subject Interests: Native Am hist, Western hist

M HILLCREST MEDICAL CENTER LIBRARY*, 1120 S Utica Ave, 74104-4090. SAN 357-7201. Tel: 918-579-8357. Reference Tel: 918-579-8356. FAX: 918-579-8388. *Librn,* Peggy Miller Cook; E-mail: pcook@hillcrest.com; *Doc Delivery, ILL,* Sandra K Webb; Tel: 918-579-8356, E-mail: swebb@hillcrest.com. Subject Specialists: *Med, Nursing,* Peggy Miller Cook; Staff 2 (MLS 1, Non-MLS 1)
Founded 1976
Library Holdings: CDs 100; e-books 139; e-journals 7,170; Bk Titles 2,063; Bk Vols 2,270; Per Subs 137; Videos 133
Special Collections: Hillcrest Patient/Family Health Information Center
Subject Interests: Allied health, Med, Nursing
Automation Activity & Vendor Info: (Cataloging) CyberTools for Libraries; (Circulation) CyberTools for Libraries; (OPAC) CyberTools for Libraries; (Serials) CyberTools for Libraries
Database Vendor: DynaMed, EBSCOhost, Elsevier, OCLC FirstSearch, OCLC WorldShare Interlibrary Loan, OVID Technologies, PubMed, STAT!Ref (Teton Data Systems), UpToDate
Function: Doc delivery serv, Health sci info serv, ILL available, Online searches, Orientations, Photocopying/Printing, Ref serv available
Publications: List of Recent Acquisitions (Acquisition list)
Partic in Health Libraries of Eastern Oklahoma; Medical Library Association (MLA); National Network of Libraries of Medicine; Oklahoma Health Sciences Library Association; SCC/MLA
Open Mon-Fri 8-4:30
Restriction: In-house use for visitors

CM OKLAHOMA STATE UNIVERSITY - CENTER FOR HEALTH SCIENCES*, Medical Library, 1111 W 17th St, 74107-1898. SAN 314-0156. Tel: 918-561-8449. Interlibrary Loan Service Tel: 918-561-8448. Reference Tel: 918-561-1119. Administration Tel: 918-561-8451. FAX: 918-561-8412. Web Site: www.healthsciences.okstate.edu/medlibrary/index.html. *Dir,* Beth Anne Freeman; E-mail: beth.freeman@okstate.edu; *Assoc Dir,* Dohn H Martin; E-mail: dohn.martin@okstate.edu; *Access Serv Librn, Media Serv Librn,* Jamey Lamb; Tel: 918-561-1114, E-mail: jamey.lamb@okstate.edu; *Ref Librn,* Linda London; Tel: 918-561-8466, E-mail: linda.london@okstate.edu; *Ref & Instruction,* Melissa Kash-Holley; Tel: 918-561-8457, E-mail: david.money@okstate.edu. Subject Specialists: *Med ref,* Dohn H Martin; *Med ref,* Linda London; *Med ref,* Melissa Kash-Holley; Staff 3 (MLS 3)
Founded 1974. Enrl 380; Highest Degree: Doctorate
Library Holdings: AV Mats 4,142; e-books 170; e-journals 11,498; Bk Titles 28,077; Bk Vols 57,979; Per Subs 356; Videos 687
Special Collections: Anatomical Models & Realia; Case Histories for Massachusetts General Hospital; College Archives; National Library of Medicine Literature Searches; Osteopathic Literature
Subject Interests: Med
Automation Activity & Vendor Info: (Acquisitions) Ex Libris Group; (Cataloging) Ex Libris Group; (Circulation) Ex Libris Group; (Course Reserve) Ex Libris Group; (OPAC) Ex Libris Group; (Serials) Ex Libris Group
Database Vendor: Blackwell, EBSCOhost, Elsevier MDL, Factiva.com, ISI Web of Knowledge, Newsbank, OCLC WorldShare Interlibrary Loan, OVID Technologies, ProQuest, PubMed, ScienceDirect, STAT!Ref (Teton Data Systems), UpToDate, Wiley
Wireless access
Partic in National Network of Libraries of Medicine; SCAMeL
Open Mon-Thurs 7am-Midnight, Fri 7am-9pm, Sat 9-9, Sun 9am-Midnight
Restriction: Open to pub for ref only

C OKLAHOMA STATE UNIVERSITY - TULSA LIBRARY*, 700 N Greenwood Ave, 74106-0702. SAN 326-8993. Tel: 918-594-8130. Interlibrary Loan Service Tel: 918-594-8138. Reference Tel: 918-594-8137. Administration Tel: 918-594-8132. Automation Services Tel: 918-594-8140. FAX: 918-594-8145. E-mail: tulsa.libraryreference@okstate.edu. Web Site: osu-tulsa.okstate.edu/library/index.asp. *Dir,* Beth Anne Freeman; E-mail: beth.freeman@okstate.edu; *Assoc Dir, Head, Tech Serv,* Jerrie Hall; E-mail: jerrie.hall@okstate.edu; *Access Serv Librn, Coll Serv Librn,* Lynn Wallace; Tel: 918-594-8451, E-mail: lynn.wallace@okstate.edu; *Assessment Librn, Ref Librn,* Mary Hujsak; Tel: 918-594-8453, E-mail: mary.hujsak@okstate.edu; *Curric Mat Librn, Ref Librn,* Robert David Bell; Tel: 918-594-8136, E-mail: rd.bell@okstate.edu; *Instruction Librn, Ref Librn,* Thomas Thorisch; Tel: 918-594-8146, E-mail: thomas.thorisch@okstate.edu; *Coordr, Pub Serv,* Dona Davidson; Tel: 918-594-8139, E-mail: dona.davidson@okstate.edu. Subject Specialists: *Eng, Sci,* Robert David Bell; Staff 7 (MLS 7)
Founded 1999. Enrl 2,700; Fac 63; Highest Degree: Doctorate
Jul 2009-Jun 2010 Income $1,379,180. Mats Exp $425,338. Sal $600,160 (Prof $388,610)
Library Holdings: Audiobooks 24; AV Mats 2,897; Bks on Deafness & Sign Lang 260; CDs 1,272; DVDs 615; e-books 83,000; Electronic Media & Resources 150; Bk Vols 145,597; Per Subs 67,241; Videos 2,236

Special Collections: Center for Poets & Writers Manuscript Coll; Cyrus Stevens Avery Papers; Eric Coll (from 1980); Michael Wallis Manuscript Coll; Michael Wallis Route 66 Archive; Tulsa Race Riot of 1921
Subject Interests: Computer sci, Educ, Eng, Psychol
Automation Activity & Vendor Info: (Acquisitions) Ex Libris Group; (Cataloging) Ex Libris Group; (Circulation) Ex Libris Group; (Course Reserve) Ex Libris Group; (ILL) OCLC ILLiad; (OPAC) Ex Libris Group; (Serials) Ex Libris Group
Database Vendor: 3M Library Systems, ACM (Association for Computing Machinery), Alexander Street Press, American Chemical Society, American Mathematical Society, American Psychological Association (APA), Amigos Library Services, ARTstor, Baker & Taylor, BioOne, Blackwell, Brodart, Cambridge Scientific Abstracts, Children's Literature Comprehensive Database Company (CLCD), CountryWatch, CQ Press, CredoReference, Dun & Bradstreet, ebrary, EBSCOhost, Elsevier, Elsevier MDL, Emerald, Factiva.com, Gale Cengage Learning, IEEE (Institute of Electrical & Electronics Engineers), infoUSA, ISI Web of Knowledge, JSTOR, Knovel, LexisNexis, Medline, Mergent Online, Nature Publishing Group, OCLC WorldShare Interlibrary Loan, Oxford Online, ProQuest, PubMed, ReferenceUSA, RefWorks, Sage, ScienceDirect, SerialsSolutions, Springer-Verlag, Standard & Poor's, Wiley InterScience, YBP Library Services
Wireless access
Partic in Greater Western Library Alliance; OCLC Online Computer Library Center, Inc; Oklahoma Council of Academic Libr Directors (OCALD)
Special Services for the Deaf - Accessible learning ctr; Bks on deafness & sign lang
Special Services for the Blind - ZoomText magnification & reading software
Open Mon-Thurs 8am-10pm, Fri 8-5, Sat 9-5, Sun 1-9
Restriction: Open to pub for ref & circ; with some limitations

C ORAL ROBERTS UNIVERSITY LIBRARY*, John D Messick Learning Resources Center, 7777 S Lewis Ave, 74171. SAN 314-0199. Tel: 918-495-6723. Circulation Tel: 918-495-6391. Interlibrary Loan Service Tel: 918-495-7377. Reference Tel: 918-495-6887. FAX: 918-495-6893. Interlibrary Loan Service FAX: 918-495-7428. E-mail: libref@oru.edu. Web Site: www.oru.edu/university/library. *Dean, Univ Libr, Theological Librn,* Dr William W Jernigan; E-mail: wjernigan@oru.edu; *Asst Dir, Pub Serv,* Jane Malcolm; Tel: 918-495-7495, E-mail: jmalcolm@oru.edu; *Asst Dir, Tech Serv,* Judy Stubbs; Tel: 918-495-6889, Fax: 918-495-6727, E-mail: justubbs@oru.edu; *Head Ref Librn, ILL,* Annette Villines; Tel: 918-495-7378, E-mail: avillines@oru.edu; *Head, Cat & Computer Serv,* Dana Higeons; Tel: 918-495-6885, E-mail: dhigeons@oru.edu; *Acq, Electronic Res Librn,* Mary Ann Walker; Tel: 918-495-6896, E-mail: mwalker@oru.edu; *Circ Supvr,* Jilda Elk; Tel: 918-495-6392, E-mail: jelk@oru.edu; *Archivist,* Roger Rydin; Tel: 918-495-6750, Fax: 918-495-6751, E-mail: rrydin@oru.edu; *Bibliog Instruction/Ref,* Myra Bloom; Tel: 918-495-7174, E-mail: mbloom@oru.edu; *Cat,* Jennifer Horton; Tel: 918-495-6881, E-mail: jehorton@oru.edu; *Cat Spec,* Janelle Sullivan; Tel: 918-495-6882, E-mail: jsullivan@oru.edu; *Circ/Reserves,* Cheryle Holeman; Tel: 918-495-6028, E-mail: choleman@oru.edu; *Coll Develop & Acq,* Judith Rigsby; Tel: 918-495-6895, Fax: 918-495-6895, E-mail: jrigsby@oru.edu; *Libr Info/Fac Facilitator,* Sally Jo Shelton; Tel: 918-495-6902, E-mail: sshelton@oru.edu; *Ref,* Peggy Pixley; Tel: 918-495-6732, E-mail: ppixley@oru.edu. Subject Specialists: *Theol,* Dr William W Jernigan; *Bus,* Jane Malcolm; *Theol,* Sally Jo Shelton; Staff 16 (MLS 8, Non-MLS 8)
Founded 1963. Enrl 3,067; Fac 281; Highest Degree: Doctorate
May 2011-Apr 2012 Income (Main Library Only) $1,218,362. Mats Exp $386,061, Books $91,615, Per/Ser (Incl. Access Fees) $46,109, Other Print Mats $1,866, Micro $2,452, Electronic Ref Mat (Incl. Access Fees) $242,306, Presv $1,713. Sal $768,996 (Prof $454,192)
Library Holdings: Audiobooks 733; AV Mats 15,627; CDs 137; DVDs 1,509; e-books 105,000; e-journals 25,348; Microforms 40,431; Music Scores 5,430; Bk Titles 229,893; Bk Vols 322,059; Per Subs 28,400; Videos 863
Special Collections: Elmar Camillo Dos Santos Coll; Holy Spirit Research Center; Jewish Theological Coll; Oral Roberts Ministry Archives; William Sanford LaSor Coll
Subject Interests: Biblical studies, Missions, Pentecostalism, Theol
Automation Activity & Vendor Info: (Acquisitions) Innovative Interfaces, Inc; (Cataloging) Innovative Interfaces, Inc; (Circulation) Innovative Interfaces, Inc; (Course Reserve) Innovative Interfaces, Inc; (OPAC) Innovative Interfaces, Inc; (Serials) Innovative Interfaces, Inc
Database Vendor: Amigos Library Services, Baker & Taylor, Bowker, Cambridge Scientific Abstracts, CountryWatch, CQ Press, CredoReference, Dun & Bradstreet, DynaMed, ebrary, EBSCOhost, Elsevier, Gale Cengage Learning, Innovative Interfaces, Inc, Marcive, Inc, McGraw-Hill, Mergent Online, Micromedex, MITINET, Inc, OCLC ArticleFirst, OCLC FirstSearch, OCLC WorldShare Interlibrary Loan, OVID Technologies, Oxford Online, ProQuest, Sage, ScienceDirect, SerialsSolutions, Standard & Poor's, Thomson - Web of Science, ValueLine
Wireless access
Function: Archival coll, Audio & video playback equip for onsite use, Audiobks via web, Bks on CD, Computers for patron use, Copy machines, Distance learning, E-Reserves, Electronic databases & coll, ILL available, Microfiche/film & reading machines, Online cat, Online searches, Orientations, Outside serv via phone, mail, e-mail & web, Photocopying/Printing, Ref serv available, Ref serv in person, Scanner, Spoken cassettes & CDs, Spoken cassettes & DVDs, Workshops
Partic in OCLC Online Computer Library Center, Inc; Oklahoma Health Sciences Library Association
Open Mon-Thurs 7:30am-11:30pm, Fri 7:30-7:30, Sat 12-11:30, Sun 3-11:30
Restriction: Access at librarian's discretion, Badge access after hrs, ID required to use computers (Ltd hrs), In-house use for visitors, Open to fac, students & qualified researchers, Open to researchers by request, Open to students, fac, staff & alumni, Res pass required for non-affiliated visitors
Departmental Libraries:
HOLY SPIRIT RESEARCH CENTER, 7777 S Lewis Ave, 74171. Tel: 918-495-6391. Reference Tel: 918-495-6887. FAX: 918-495-6662. E-mail: hsrc@oru.edu. Web Site: library.oru.edu. *Dir, Holy Spirit Res Ctr,* Dr Mark E Roberts; Tel: 918-495-6868, E-mail: mroberts@oru.edu; *Archivist,* Roger Rydin; Tel: 918-495-6750. Subject Specialists: *Biblical studies,* Dr Mark E Roberts; Staff 1 (Non-MLS 1)
Fac 1
Library Holdings: AV Mats 8,265; CDs 66; DVDs 115; Microforms 37; Music Scores 51; Bk Vols 15,829; Per Subs 60; Videos 822
Special Collections: Howard M Ervin Coll
Subject Interests: Charismatic, Divine healing, Pentecostal, Pneumatology
Open Mon-Fri 12:30-4:20

S PALOMINO HORSE BREEDERS OF AMERICA LIBRARY*, 15253 E Skelly Dr, 74116-2637. SAN 326-4130. Tel: 918-438-1234. FAX: 918-438-1232. Web Site: www.palominohba.com. *Librn,* Terri Green
Founded 1941
Library Holdings: Bk Vols 500; Per Subs 175
Open Mon-Fri 8:30-4:30

S PHILBROOK MUSEUM OF ART*, H A & Mary K Chapman Library, 2727 S Rockford Rd, 74114-4104. (Mail add: PO Box 52510, 74152-0510), SAN 314-0210. Tel: 918-748-5306. FAX: 918-748-5303. E-mail: library@philbrook.org. Web Site: www.philbrook.org. *Librn,* Thomas Elton Young; E-mail: tyoung@philbrook.org; Staff 1 (MLS 1)
Founded 1940
Library Holdings: Bk Vols 24,000; Per Subs 105
Special Collections: American Indian (Roberta C Lawson Library); Native American Artists Coll, VF; Oklahoma Artists Coll, VF
Subject Interests: Fine arts, Visual arts
Automation Activity & Vendor Info: (Cataloging) Follett Software; (Circulation) Follett Software; (OPAC) Follett Software
Database Vendor: Gale Cengage Learning, OCLC FirstSearch, Wilson - Wilson Web
Function: Archival coll, ILL available, Ref serv available, Telephone ref
Partic in OCLC Online Computer Library Center, Inc
Open Mon-Fri 10-12 & 1-5
Restriction: Circulates for staff only

CR PHILLIPS THEOLOGICAL SEMINARY LIBRARY*, 901 N Mingo Rd, 74116. SAN 357-5403. Tel: 918-270-6437. Administration Tel: 918-270-6459. FAX: 918-270-6490. E-mail: ptslibrary@ptstulsa.edu. Web Site: www.ptstulsa.edu. *Libr Dir,* Sandy Shapoval; E-mail: sandy.shapoval@ptstulsa.edu; *Electronic Res & Instruction Librn,* Clair Powers; Tel: 918-270-6431, E-mail: clair.powers@ptstulsa.edu; *Reserves Librn,* Mary Coniglio; Tel: 918-270-6427, E-mail: mary.coniglio@ptstulsa.edu; Staff 5 (MLS 3.5, Non-MLS 1.5)
Founded 1950. Enrl 119; Fac 15; Highest Degree: Doctorate
Subject Interests: Relig, Theol
Automation Activity & Vendor Info: (Acquisitions) Ex Libris Group; (Cataloging) Ex Libris Group; (Circulation) Ex Libris Group; (Course Reserve) Ex Libris Group; (ILL) OCLC FirstSearch; (OPAC) Ex Libris Group; (Serials) EBSCO Online
Database Vendor: Amigos Library Services, Baker & Taylor, CredoReference, EBSCO Information Services, EBSCOhost, Ex Libris Group, JSTOR, OCLC, OCLC FirstSearch, OCLC WorldShare Interlibrary Loan, Oxford Online
Wireless access
Partic in OCLC Online Computer Library Center, Inc

M SAINT FRANCIS HEALTH SYSTEM*, Health Sciences Library, 6161 S Yale Ave, 74136. SAN 314-0253. Tel: 918-494-1210. FAX: 918-494-1893. *Librn,* Beth Treaster; E-mail: bhtreaster@saintfrancis.com; Staff 3 (MLS 2, Non-MLS 1)
Founded 1962
Library Holdings: e-books 90; e-journals 8,000; Bk Titles 1,000; Per Subs 100

Subject Interests: Hospitals, Med, Nursing, Pharm
Automation Activity & Vendor Info: (Circulation) Follett Software; (OPAC) Follett Software
Database Vendor: EBSCOhost, Gale Cengage Learning, Lexi-Comp, OCLC FirstSearch, OCLC WorldShare Interlibrary Loan, OVID Technologies, PubMed, ScienceDirect
Open Mon-Fri 8-5
Restriction: In-house use for visitors

M SAINT JOHN MEDICAL CENTER*, Health Sciences Library, 1923 S Utica, 74104. SAN 314-0261. Tel: 918-744-2970. FAX: 918-744-3209. E-mail: library@sjmc.org. *Librn,* James M Donovan
Founded 1946
Library Holdings: Bk Vols 12,000; Per Subs 135
Subject Interests: Behav sci, Catholic bio ethics, Educ, Med, Nursing, Soc sci
Open Mon-Fri 8-4:30

C SPARTAN COLLEGE OF AERONAUTICS & TECHNOLOGY LIBRARY*, 8820 E Pine St, 74115. Tel: 918-836-6886. FAX: 918-831-5245. Web Site: www.spartan.edu. *Dir,* Melody Watts; E-mail: mwatts@mail.spartan.edu
Library Holdings: Bk Vols 13,000
Automation Activity & Vendor Info: (Acquisitions) Follett Software; (Cataloging) Follett Software; (Circulation) Follett Software; (OPAC) Follett Software
Wireless access
Open Mon-Thurs 7am-9pm, Fri 7-7, Sat 9-5

P TULSA CITY-COUNTY LIBRARY*, 400 Civic Ctr, 74103. SAN 357-735X. Tel: 918-596-7977. Interlibrary Loan Service Tel: 918-596-7963. FAX: 918-596-7964. TDD: 918-596-7978. Web Site: www.tulsalibrary.org. *Chief Exec Officer,* Gary Shaffer; E-mail: gshaffe@tulsalibrary.org; *Chief Operating Officer,* Laurie Sundborg; E-mail: lsundbo@tulsalibrary.org; *Dep Dir, Cent Libr,* Suanne Wymer; E-mail: swymer@tulsalibrary.org; *Dep Dir, Support Serv,* Charlotte Frazier; E-mail: cfrazie@tulsalibrary.org; Staff 289 (MLS 67, Non-MLS 222)
Founded 1961. Pop 613,816; Circ 6,027,407
Jul 2012-Jun 2013 Income $28,343,478. Mats Exp $3,792,641, Books $1,979,894, Per/Ser (Incl. Access Fees) $626,174, AV Mat $462,475, Electronic Ref Mat (Incl. Access Fees) $295,808. Sal $17,037,031
Library Holdings: Bk Titles 1,691,103
Special Collections: A J Levorsen Geology Coll, bks, maps; Land Office Survey Map Coll; Shakespeare Coll. State Document Depository; US Document Depository
Subject Interests: African-Am hist, Indust
Automation Activity & Vendor Info: (Acquisitions) Innovative Interfaces, Inc; (Cataloging) Innovative Interfaces, Inc; (Circulation) Innovative Interfaces, Inc; (ILL) Innovative Interfaces, Inc; (OPAC) Innovative Interfaces, Inc
Wireless access
Publications: Annual Report; Open Book (Quarterly)
Partic in Okla Libr Technology Network; SDC Search Serv
Special Services for the Deaf - High interest/low vocabulary bks; TDD equip
Special Services for the Blind - Home delivery serv
Open Mon-Thurs 9-9, Fri & Sat 9-5, Sun 1-5
Friends of the Library Group
Branches: 26
BIXBY BRANCH, 20 E Breckinridge, Bixby, 74008, SAN 357-7449. Tel: 918-549-7514. FAX: 918-549-7517. *Br Mgr,* Carolyn Trammell; Staff 2 (MLS 1, Non-MLS 1)
Library Holdings: Bk Vols 35,485
Open Mon 10-8, Tues-Thurs 12-8, Fri 12-6, Sat 10-5
BROKEN ARROW BRANCH, 300 W Broadway, Broken Arrow, 74012, SAN 357-7473. Tel: 918-549-7500. FAX: 918-549-7504. *Br Mgr,* Rebecca Howard
Library Holdings: Bk Vols 61,372
Open Mon-Thurs 10-8, Fri 10-6, Sat 10-5
BROOKSIDE, 1207 E 45th Pl, 74105, SAN 357-7503. Tel: 918-549-7507. FAX: 918-549-7510. *Br Mgr,* Ellen Cummings; Staff 5 (MLS 2, Non-MLS 3)
Library Holdings: Bk Vols 45,493
Open Mon-Thurs 10-8, Fri 10-6, Sat 10-5
CENTRAL LIBRARY, 400 Civic Ctr, 74103, SAN 357-7414. Tel: 918-549-7323. *Dep Dir,* Suanne Wymer
Library Holdings: Bk Vols 539,000
Open Mon-Thurs 9-9, Fri & Sat 9-5, Sun (Sept-May) 1-5
COLLINSVILLE BRANCH, 1223 Main, Collinsville, 74021, SAN 357-7538. Tel: 918-549-7528. FAX: 918-549-7531. *Br Mgr,* Rhonda Weldon; Staff 2 (MLS 1, Non-MLS 1)
Library Holdings: Bk Vols 30,957
Open Mon-Thurs 12-8, Fri 12-5, Sat 10-5
GENEALOGY CENTER, 8316 E 93rd St, 74133. Tel: 918-549-7691. E-mail: genaskus@tulsalibrary.org. *Librn,* Kathy Huber
Library Holdings: CDs 300; Bk Vols 9,295
Special Collections: All Census Records for Oklahoma; Passenger & Immigration Lists Index; Roster of Confederate Soldiers; Roster of the Union Soldiers; The DAR Lineage Book; The Final Rolls of the Five Civilized Tribes; The New England Historical & Genealogical Register; The War of the Rebellion; Tulsa City Funeral Home Records; Tulsa County Cemetery Records
Subject Interests: Genealogy
Open Mon-Thurs 9-9, Fri 9-6, Sat 9-5, Sun 1-5
GLENPOOL BRANCH, 730 E 141st St, Glenpool, 74033. (Mail add: PO Box 580, 74101), SAN 326-7954. Tel: 918-549-7535. FAX: 918-549-7538. *Br Mgr,* Ron Cook
Library Holdings: Bk Vols 32,117
Open Mon-Thurs 12-8, Fri 12-5, Sat 10-5
NATHAN HALE LIBRARY, 6038 E 23rd St, 74114, SAN 357-7627. Tel: 918-549-7617. FAX: 918-549-7620. *Br Mgr,* Ann Gaebe; Staff 4 (MLS 1, Non-MLS 3)
Library Holdings: Bk Vols 39,000
Open Mon 10-8, Tues-Thurs 10-6, Fri & Sat 10-5
HARDESTY REGIONAL LIBRARY, 8316 E 93rd St, 74133, SAN 357-7937. Tel: 918-549-7550. FAX: 918-549-7559. *Br Mgr,* Emily Archibald
Library Holdings: Bk Vols 163,504
Open Mon-Thurs 9-9, Fri 9-6, Sat 9-5, Sun 1-5
PEGGY V HELMERICH LIBRARY, 5131 E 91st St, 74137, SAN 371-4942. Tel: 918-549-7631. FAX: 918-549-7634. *Br Mgr,* Marilyn Neal; Staff 7 (MLS 1, Non-MLS 6)
Library Holdings: Bk Vols 66,512
Open Mon-Thurs 10-8, Fri & Sat 10-5
JENKS BRANCH, 523 West B St, Jenks, 74037, SAN 357-7651. Tel: 918-549-7570. FAX: 918-549-7573. *Br Mgr,* Cheryl Newman; Staff 2 (MLS 1, Non-MLS 1)
Library Holdings: Bk Vols 35,812
Open Mon & Tues 12-8, Wed & Thurs 10-6, Fri 12-5, Sat 10-5
HERMAN & KATE KAISER LIBRARY, 5202 S Hudson Ave, Ste B, 74135. Tel: 918-549-7542. FAX: 918-549-7545. *Br Mgr,* Buddy Ingalls; Staff 4 (MLS 3, Non-MLS 1)
Founded 2008
Library Holdings: Bk Vols 58,689
Function: Free DVD rentals, Handicapped accessible, ILL available, Music CDs, Online cat, Preschool outreach, Preschool reading prog, Prog for children & young adult, Pub access computers, Spanish lang bks, Story hour, Summer & winter reading prog, Tax forms, Teen prog, Telephone ref
Open Mon-Thurs 10-8, Fri 10-6, Sat 10-5
KENDALL-WHITTIER BRANCH, 21 S Lewis St, 74104, SAN 357-7562. Tel: 918-549-7584. FAX: 918-549-7587. *Br Mgr,* David Nofire
Library Holdings: Bk Vols 34,624
Open Mon-Thurs 10-8, Fri & Sat 10-5
JUDY Z KISHNER LIBRARY, 10150 N Cincinnati Ave E, 74073, SAN 357-7953. Tel: 918-549-7577. FAX: 918-549-7580. *Br Mgr,* Suzi Smith; Staff 2 (MLS 1, Non-MLS 1)
Library Holdings: Bk Vols 18,680
Open Mon, Tues & Thurs 12-7, Wed & Sat 10-5, Fri 12-5
MARTIN REGIONAL LIBRARY, 2601 S Garnett Rd, 74129, SAN 357-7686. Tel: 918-549-7590. *Br Mgr,* Amy Stephens; Staff 12 (MLS 4, Non-MLS 8)
Library Holdings: Bk Vols 110,016
Open Mon-Thurs 9-9, Fri 9-6, Sat 9-5, Sun 1-5
MAXWELL PARK, 1313 N Canton, 74115, SAN 328-7947. Tel: 918-549-7610. FAX: 918-549-7613. *Br Mgr,* Rosella Lindh; Staff 4 (MLS 1, Non-MLS 3)
Library Holdings: Bk Vols 35,788
Open Mon-Fri 10-6, Sat 10-5
OUTREACH SERVICES, 2901 S Harvard, Ste A, 74114. Tel: 918-549-7480. *Mgr,* Tracy Warren; Staff 7 (MLS 1, Non-MLS 6)
Founded 1970
Library Holdings: Bk Vols 23,751
Special Collections: Blindness & Other Handicaps Reference Material
Open Mon-Fri 9-5
OWASSO BRANCH, 103 W Broadway, Owasso, 74055, SAN 357-7775. Tel: 918-549-7624. FAX: 918-549-7627. *Br Mgr,* Barbara Barnes; Staff 4 (MLS 1, Non-MLS 3)
Library Holdings: Bk Vols 52,432
Open Mon-Thurs 10-8, Fri 10-6, Sat 10-5
CHARLES PAGE BRANCH, 551 E Fourth St, Sand Springs, 74063, SAN 357-7805. Tel: 918-549-7521. FAX: 918-549-7524. *Br Mgr,* Mark Carlson; Staff 2 (MLS 1, Non-MLS 1)
Library Holdings: Bk Vols 29,352
Open Mon-Thurs 10-8, Fri & Sat 10-5

PRATT, 3219 S 113th West Ave, Sand Springs, 74063, SAN 357-783X. Tel: 918-549-7638. FAX: 918-549-7641. *Br Mgr,* Chris Lair; Staff 3 (MLS 1, Non-MLS 2)
Library Holdings: Bk Vols 46,619
Open Mon-Thurs 10-8, Fri & Sat 10-5

RUDISILL REGIONAL LIBRARY, 1520 N Hartford, 74106, SAN 357-7740. Tel: 918-549-7645. *Br Mgr,* Keith Jemison; Staff 6 (MLS 1, Non-MLS 5)
Library Holdings: Bk Vols 71,156
Open Mon-Thurs 9-9, Fri & Sat 9-5, Sun 1-5

SCHUSTERMAN-BENSON LIBRARY, 3333 E 32nd Pl, 74135, SAN 357-7597. Tel: 918-549-7670. FAX: 918-549-7672. *Br Mgr,* Brad Thomas; Staff 7 (MLS 2, Non-MLS 5)
Founded 1955
Library Holdings: Bk Vols 47,561
Open Mon-Thurs 10-8, Fri & Sat 10-5

SKIATOOK BRANCH, 316 E Rogers Blvd, Skiatook, 74070, SAN 357-7929. Tel: 918-549-7676. FAX: 918-549-7679. *Br Mgr,* Michelle Beckes
Library Holdings: Bk Vols 28,963
Open Mon 12-8, Tues-Thurs 10-6, Fri & Sat 11-5

SOUTH BROKEN ARROW, 3600 S Chestnut, Broken Arrow, 74011, SAN 374-7093. Tel: 918-549-7662. FAX: 918-549-7665. *Br Mgr,* Emily Tichenor; Staff 5 (MLS 2, Non-MLS 3)
Library Holdings: Bk Vols 36,692
Open Mon-Thurs 10-8, Fri & Sat 10-5

SUBURBAN ACRES, 4606 N Garrison Ave, 74126, SAN 357-7988. Tel: 918-549-7655. FAX: 918-549-7658. E-mail: sa@tulsalibrary.org. *Br Mgr,* Sherrie Wallace
Library Holdings: Bk Vols 23,556
Open Mon-Thurs 10-6, Fri & Sat 11-5

ZARROW REGIONAL LIBRARY, 2224 W 51st, 74107, SAN 357-8003. Tel: 918-549-7683. *Br Mgr,* Barry Hensley; Staff 5 (MLS 1, Non-MLS 4)
Library Holdings: Bk Vols 58,172
Open Mon-Thurs 9-9, Fri & Sat 9-5, Sun 1-5

Bookmobiles: 1

TULSA COMMUNITY COLLEGE LIBRARIES, (Formerly Tulsa Community College Learning Resources Center)

J METRO CAMPUS*, 909 S Boston Ave, 74119-2011, SAN 357-8046. Tel: 918-595-7172. Reference Tel: 918-595-7296. FAX: 918-595-7179. E-mail: mlibrarian@tulsacc.edu. Web Site: lrc.tulsacc.edu. *Dean,* Paula Settoon; Tel: 918-595-7461, E-mail: paula.settoon@tulsacc.edu; *Sr Cat Librn,* Cary Isley; Tel: 918-595-7177, E-mail: cisley@tulsacc.edu; *Ref Librn,* Adam Brennan; Tel: 918-595-7330, E-mail: abrennan@tulsacc.edu; *Syst Librn,* Robert Holzmann; Tel: 918-595-7173, E-mail: bholzmann@tulsacc.edu; *Supvr,* Casey Ashe; Tel: 918-595-7285, E-mail: cashe@tulsacc.edu; *Acq,* Mary Kent; Tel: 918-595-7175, E-mail: mkent@tulsacc.edu
Founded 1970. Highest Degree: Associate
Library Holdings: DVDs 301; Bk Vols 38,775; Per Subs 242; Videos 1,501
Subject Interests: Allied health, Computer sci, Foreign lang, Nursing, Paralegal
Function: Electronic databases & coll, Photocopying/Printing
Open Mon-Thurs 7:30am-9:30pm, Fri 7:30-5, Sat 9-1

J NORTHEAST CAMPUS, 3727 E Apache St, 74115-3151, SAN 357-8070. Tel: 918-595-7501. Interlibrary Loan Service Tel: 918-595-7493. Reference Tel: 918-595-7555. Administration Tel: 918-595-7568. Web Site: library.tulsacc.edu. *Dir,* Emily Tichenor; E-mail: emily.tichenor@tulsacc.edu; *Ref & Instruction Librn,* Gisele A McDaniel; Tel: 918-595-7502, E-mail: gisele.mcdaniel@tulsacc.edu; Staff 7 (MLS 4, Non-MLS 3)
Founded 1978. Enrl 4,088; Fac 61; Highest Degree: Associate
Library Holdings: Audiobooks 100; Bks on Deafness & Sign Lang 200; DVDs 291; Bk Titles 29,122; Per Subs 152; Videos 1,301
Subject Interests: Eng, Hort, Human serv, Humanities, Technologies
Function: Electronic databases & coll, Photocopying/Printing
Open Mon-Thurs 7:30am-9pm, Fri 7:30-6, Sat 8:30am-12:30pm

J SOUTHEAST CAMPUS*, 10300 E 81st St, 74133-4513, SAN 357-8089. Tel: 918-595-7703. Administration Tel: 918-595-7701. FAX: 918-595-7706. *Libr Mgr,* Stephanie Ingold; Tel: 918-595-7730, E-mail: stephanie.ingold@tulsacc.edu; *Ref & Instruction Librn,* Suzanne Haynes; Tel: 918-595-7704, E-mail: shaynes@tulsacc.edu; *Ref & Instruction Librn,* Amy Norman; Tel: 918-595-7702, E-mail: anorman@tulsacc.edu; Staff 5 (MLS 3, Non-MLS 2)
Founded 1984. Enrl 6,385; Fac 82; Highest Degree: Associate
Library Holdings: DVDs 402; Bk Titles 29,355; Per Subs 150; Videos 2,142
Subject Interests: Math, Performing arts
Automation Activity & Vendor Info: (Circulation) Ex Libris Group
Function: Electronic databases & coll, Photocopying/Printing
Partic in Tulsa Area Libr Coop
Open Mon-Fri 7:30am-9:30pm, Sat 8:30-12:30

J WEST CAMPUS LIBRARY*, 7505 W 41st St, 74107-8633, SAN 376-9542. Tel: 918-595-8010. Administration Tel: 918-595-8011. FAX: 918-595-8016. Web Site: www.tulsacc.edu/. *Libr Mgr,* Amanda Kuhns; E-mail: amanda.kuhns@tulsacc.edu; *Ref & Instruction Librn,* Megan Donald; Staff 4 (MLS 2, Non-MLS 2)
Founded 1995. Enrl 2,700; Fac 35; Highest Degree: Associate
Library Holdings: CDs 41; Bk Titles 9,034; Per Subs 61; Videos 1,000
Subject Interests: Bus, Early childhood develop, Hospitality, Veterinary tech
Function: Electronic databases & coll, Photocopying/Printing
Open Mon-Thurs 7:30am-9:30pm, Fri 7:30-5, Sat 8:30-12:30

GL TULSA COUNTY LAW LIBRARY*, 500 S Denver Ave, 74103. SAN 314-027X. Tel: 918-596-5404. FAX: 918-596-4509. E-mail: lawlibrary@tulsacounty.org. Web Site: www.tulsalawlib.com. *Dir,* Joyce M Pacenza; *Mgr,* Kathleen Marrs; Staff 2 (MLS 1, Non-MLS 1)
Founded 1949
Library Holdings: Bk Titles 900; Bk Vols 30,000
Open Mon-Fri 8:30-5

S TULSA WORLD*, Library Department, 315 S Boulder Ave, 74103-3401. (Mail add: PO Box 1770, 74102-1770), SAN 314-0288. Tel: 918-582-0921. FAX: 918-581-8425. Web Site: www.tulsaworld.com. *Librn,* Debbie Jackson; *Librn,* Hilary Pittman
Founded 1941
Library Holdings: Bk Vols 1,000
Special Collections: The Tulsa Tribune; Tulsa World
Partic in LexisNexis

GL UNITED STATES COURT OF APPEALS, Tenth Circuit Library, 333 W Fourth St, 74103. SAN 372-2163. Tel: 918-699-4744. FAX: 918-699-4743. *Librn,* Leslie B McGuire; E-mail: leslie_mcguire@ca10.uscourts.gov; Staff 1 (MLS 1)
Library Holdings: Bk Titles 150; Bk Vols 5,000; Per Subs 10
Wireless access
Restriction: Not open to pub

C UNIVERSITY OF OKLAHOMA*, Tulsa Library, Schusterman Ctr, 4502 E 41st St, 74135. SAN 321-9771. Tel: 918-660-3220. Interlibrary Loan Service Tel: 918-660-3219. FAX: 918-660-3215. Web Site: tulsa.ou.edu/library. *Dir,* Stewart Brower; Tel: 918-660-3222, E-mail: stewart-brower@ouhsc.edu; *Ref & Instruction Librn,* Toni Hoberecht; E-mail: toni-hoberecht@ouhsc.edu; *Tech Serv Librn,* Junie C Janzen; Tel: 918-660-3224, E-mail: junie-janzen@ouhsc.edu; *Coordr of Educ & Outreach,* Lynn Yeager; Tel: 918-660-3216, E-mail: lynn-yeager@ouhsc.edu; Staff 13 (MLS 3, Non-MLS 10)
Founded 1976. Enrl 1,800; Highest Degree: Doctorate
Library Holdings: AV Mats 600; Bk Vols 55,000; Per Subs 675
Subject Interests: Allied health, Med, Nursing, Pharmacology, Pub health, Soc work
Automation Activity & Vendor Info: (Cataloging) SirsiDynix; (Circulation) SirsiDynix; (Course Reserve) Docutek; (ILL) OCLC ILLiad; (OPAC) SirsiDynix; (Serials) SirsiDynix
Database Vendor: Blackwell, Community of Science (COS), EBSCOhost, Gale Cengage Learning, OCLC FirstSearch, OVID Technologies, PubMed, STAT!Ref (Teton Data Systems)
Wireless access
Function: Audio & video playback equip for onsite use, CD-ROM, Computer training, Copy machines, Distance learning, e-mail serv, E-Reserves, Electronic databases & coll, Health sci info serv, ILL available, Instruction & testing, Online cat, Online info literacy tutorials on the web & in blackboard, Online ref, Online searches, Ref & res, Ref serv available, Telephone ref, Web-catalog, Workshops
Partic in SCAMeL
Restriction: Circ limited, Limited access for the pub, Open to students, fac & staff

C UNIVERSITY OF TULSA LIBRARIES*, McFarlin Library, 2933 E Sixth St, 74104-3123. SAN 357-8135. Tel: 918-631-2873. Reference Tel: 918-631-2880. FAX: 918-631-3791. TDD: 918-631-2873. Web Site: www.lib.utulsa.edu. *Dir,* Francine Fisk; Tel: 918-631-2495, Fax: 918-631-2150, E-mail: francine-fisk@utulsa.edu; *Acq,* Steve Nobles; Tel: 918-631-2869, E-mail: sjn@utulsa.edu; *Cat,* James Hoffman; Tel: 918-631-3486, E-mail: james-hoffman@utulsa.edu; *Ref,* Ann Blakely; Tel: 918-631-3061, E-mail: ann-blakely@utulsa.edu; Staff 37 (MLS 14, Non-MLS 23)
Founded 1894. Enrl 4,171; Highest Degree: Doctorate
Library Holdings: Bk Titles 537,580; Bk Vols 793,884; Per Subs 2,258
Special Collections: American Indian Law & History (Robertson-Shleppey-Milam Coll); Modernist Literature including libraries of Edmond Wilson & Cyril Connelly; Papers of Jean Rhys, Anna Kavan, Stevie Smith, Rebecca West, Richard Ellmann, Richard Murphy, V S Naipaul, publisher Andre Deutsch, & others; Strong holdings of James

Joyce, Robert Graves, D H Lawrence & others. State Document Depository; US Document Depository
Subject Interests: Am, British, Earth sci, Irish lit, Liberal arts, Modern hist, Modernist, Petroleum
Automation Activity & Vendor Info: (Acquisitions) Innovative Interfaces, Inc; (Cataloging) Innovative Interfaces, Inc; (Circulation) Innovative Interfaces, Inc; (Course Reserve) Innovative Interfaces, Inc; (ILL) Innovative Interfaces, Inc; (OPAC) Innovative Interfaces, Inc; (Serials) Innovative Interfaces, Inc
Database Vendor: Innovative Interfaces, Inc
Wireless access
Partic in OCLC Online Computer Library Center, Inc; OCLC Research Library Partnership; OCLC-LVIS
Open Mon-Thurs 7:30am-Midnight, Fri 7:30-6, Sat 12-8, Sun 1-Midnight
Departmental Libraries:

CL MABEE LEGAL INFORMATION CENTER, 3120 E Fourth Pl, 74104-3189, SAN 357-8194. Tel: 918-631-2404. Reference Tel: 918-631-2460. FAX: 918-631-3556. Web Site: www.utulsa.edu/law/library. *Dir,* Richard E Ducey; E-mail: richard-ducey@utulsa.edu; *Assoc Dir,* Lou Lindsey; E-mail: louise-lindsey@utulsa.edu; *Head, Tech Serv,* Mira Greene; E-mail: mira-greene@utulsa.edu; *Intl Law Librn,* David Gay; E-mail: william-gay@utulsa.edu; *Coll Develop Mgr,* Courtney Selby; E-mail: courtney-selby@utulsa.edu; *Access Serv,* Carol Arnold; E-mail: carol-arnold@utulsa.edu; *Ref & Info Serv, Team Leader,* Melanie Nelson; E-mail: melanie-nelson@utulsa.edu; *Ref & Info Serv, Web Coordr,* Daniel Bell; *Ref Serv,* Hadley Faye; E-mail: m-hadley@utulsa.edu. Subject Specialists: *Native Am,* Hadley Faye; Staff 17 (MLS 9, Non-MLS 8)
Founded 1923. Enrl 624; Fac 56; Highest Degree: Doctorate
Library Holdings: Bk Titles 181,591; Bk Vols 375,359; Per Subs 3,253
Special Collections: Bernard Schwartz Archives; College of Law History Archives. US Document Depository
Subject Interests: Energy, Environ, Native Am
Partic in Mid-America Law Library Consortium; OCLC Online Computer Library Center, Inc
Publications: Library Guide
Open Mon-Thurs 7:30am-1am, Fri 7:30am-9pm, Sat 9-9, Sun 9am-11pm
Restriction: Mem only

VALLIANT

P MATTIE TERRY PUBLIC LIBRARY*, 311 N Johnson, 74764. (Mail add: PO Box 630, 74764-0630). Tel: 580-933-4883. FAX: 580-933-5532. *Head Librn,* Jessica Brents
Founded 1998
Library Holdings: Bk Vols 14,409; Per Subs 10
Special Collections: Arts & Crafts Coll; Oklahoma Coll
Automation Activity & Vendor Info: (Cataloging) SirsiDynix; (Circulation) SirsiDynix; (OPAC) SirsiDynix
Database Vendor: EBSCOhost, Electric Library, LearningExpress, Newsbank, OCLC FirstSearch, OCLC WebJunction, OCLC WorldShare Interlibrary Loan, SirsiDynix, World Book Online
Wireless access
Mem of Southeastern Public Library System of Oklahoma
Open Tues & Thurs 10-6, Wed & Fri 10-5, Sat 10-3

VANCE AFB

A UNITED STATES AIR FORCE*, Vance Air Force Base Library, 71 FTW/CSC-CSSL, 446 McAffrey Ave, Bldg 314, Ste 24, 73705-5710. SAN 357-8259. Tel: 580-213-7368. FAX: 580-237-8106. Web Site: www.youseemore.com/vanceafb. *Librn,* Mary Arthur; E-mail: mary.arthur.ctr@vance.af.mil
Founded 1941
Library Holdings: Bk Vols 20,000; Per Subs 50
Subject Interests: Aviation, Flying
Wireless access
Open Mon-Thurs 10-9, Fri & Sat 10-6, Sun 12-6

VINITA

P VINITA PUBLIC LIBRARY*, 215 W Illinois Ave, 74301. Tel: 918-256-2115. FAX: 918-256-2309. Web Site: www.vinitapl.okpls.org. *Dir,* Susan Walters
Founded 1923. Pop 6,472
Library Holdings: AV Mats 400; Bk Vols 29,500; Per Subs 12; Talking Bks 500
Special Collections: Cherokee Nation Genealogy & History Coll; Will Rogers Coll
Automation Activity & Vendor Info: (Cataloging) Follett Software; (Circulation) Follett Software
Open Mon, Wed & Fri 11-6, Tues 11-7, Sat 12-3

WAGONER

P WAGONER CITY PUBLIC LIBRARY*, 302 N Main St, 74467-3834. SAN 314-0318. Tel: 918-485-2126. FAX: 918-485-0179. E-mail: wagonercitypubliclibrary@ymail.com. Web Site: wagonercitypubliclibrary.webs.com. *Dir,* Barnett Janie; *Children's Coordr,* Heather Cameron; *Circ,* Leila Frisby; *Circ,* Lori Hall
Founded 1912. Pop 7,700; Circ 45,012
Library Holdings: Large Print Bks 592; Bk Vols 20,000; Per Subs 21
Automation Activity & Vendor Info: (Cataloging) Follett Software; (Circulation) Follett Software; (ILL) Follett Software; (OPAC) Follett Software
Open Mon-Thurs 9-6, Fri 9-5, Sat 10-2
Friends of the Library Group

WALTERS

P WALTERS PUBLIC LIBRARY*, 202 N Broadway St, 73572-1226. (Mail add: PO Box 485, 73572-0485), SAN 314-0326. Tel: 580-875-2006. FAX: 580-875-2023. E-mail: walterspl@yahoo.com. *Librn,* Gina Suson; Staff 2 (Non-MLS 2)
Founded 1922. Pop 6,198; Circ 30,400
Library Holdings: Audiobooks 157; AV Mats 278; CDs 35; DVDs 40; Large Print Bks 300; Bk Titles 30,000; Per Subs 25; Videos 275
Special Collections: Oklahoma Section
Subject Interests: Genealogy
Automation Activity & Vendor Info: (Cataloging) Book Systems; (Circulation) Book Systems; (Course Reserve) Book Systems; (ILL) Book Systems
Database Vendor: Gale Cengage Learning, Innovative Interfaces, Inc
Wireless access
Open Mon-Fri 11-5:30, Sat 10-1

WARNER

J CONNORS STATE COLLEGE, Carl O Westbrook Library Learning Center, 1000 College Rd, 74469-9700. SAN 314-0334. Tel: 918-463-6210. Administration Tel: 918-463-6236. FAX: 918-463-6314. Web Site: connorsstate.edu. *Librn,* Jolene Armstrong; Tel: 918-463-6249, E-mail: jolene.armstrong@connorsstate.edu; *Librn,* Karen Harmon; Staff 2 (MLS 2)
Founded 1909. Enrl 2,200; Highest Degree: Associate
Jul 2013-Jun 2014 Income (Main and Other College/University Libraries) $393,391. Mats Exp $100,000. Sal $265,715
Library Holdings: DVDs 240; Bk Vols 24,000; Per Subs 25
Automation Activity & Vendor Info: (Acquisitions) Ex Libris Group; (Cataloging) OCLC Online; (Circulation) Ex Libris Group; (Course Reserve) Ex Libris Group; (ILL) OCLC Online; (OPAC) Ex Libris Group
Database Vendor: Baker & Taylor, Brodart, Cinahl, CQ Press, CredoReference, DynaMed, EBSCO Information Services, EBSCOhost, Ex Libris Group, Gale Cengage Learning, Medline, Newsbank, OCLC, OCLC FirstSearch, OCLC WorldShare Interlibrary Loan, ProQuest, WebMD
Wireless access
Function: Computers for patron use, Copy machines, Distance learning, e-mail & chat, e-mail serv, E-Reserves, Electronic databases & coll, Exhibits, Free DVD rentals, Handicapped accessible, ILL available, Instruction & testing, Magnifiers for reading, Microfiche/film & reading machines, Online cat, Online info literacy tutorials on the web & in blackboard, Online searches, Orientations, Photocopying/Printing, Printer for laptops & handheld devices, Pub access computers, VHS videos, Video lending libr, Web-catalog, Wheelchair accessible, Workshops
Open Mon-Thurs (Fall & Spring) 8am-9pm, Fri 8-4
Restriction: Borrowing privileges limited to fac & registered students, In-house use for visitors, Open to students, fac & staff, Open to students, fac, staff & alumni, Photo ID required for access
Departmental Libraries:

MUSKOGEE CAMPUS LIBRARY, 201 Court St, Muskogee, 74401. Tel: 918-684-5408. FAX: 918-684-0404. *Librn,* Izoro Dathane Kerley; E-mail: idkerle@connorsstate.edu
Automation Activity & Vendor Info: (Cataloging) Ex Libris Group; (OPAC) Ex Libris Group
Open Mon-Thurs (Fall & Spring) 8am-9pm, Fri 8-3:30

P WARNER PUBLIC LIBRARY*, 207 Eighth St, 74469. (Mail add: PO Box 120, 74469-0120), SAN 376-5970. Tel: 918-463-2363. Toll Free Tel: 888-234-0606. FAX: 918-463-2711. Web Site: www.eodls.lib.ok.us/warner.html. *Br Mgr, Librn,* Peggy Matthews
Founded 1981
Library Holdings: DVDs 1,700; Bk Vols 18,000; Videos 700
Automation Activity & Vendor Info: (Circulation) SirsiDynix
Mem of Eastern Oklahoma District Library System
Open Tues 9-6:30, Wed-Fri 9-5:30, Sat 9-Noon
Friends of the Library Group

WATONGA

P WATONGA PUBLIC LIBRARY*, 301 N Prouty, 73772. SAN 314-0342. Tel: 580-623-7748. FAX: 580-623-7747. E-mail: bookwoman@watonga.lib.ok.us. Web Site: www.watonga.lib.ok.us. *Dir,* Terri Crawford; *Asst Dir,* Sharon Barnes; Staff 4 (MLS 2, Non-MLS 2)
Founded 1906. Pop 5,000; Circ 38,313
Library Holdings: Bk Titles 28,000; Bk Vols 32,000; Per Subs 34
Special Collections: Local History (Blaine County Coll), bks & interviews tapes
Subject Interests: Local genealogy, Local hist
Automation Activity & Vendor Info: (Circulation) Follett Software
Publications: Books in Print; Publishers Weekly; Subject Guide to Books in Print
Partic in Ohio Public Library Information Network; Okla Telecommunications Interlibr Syst
Open Mon-Fri 10-5:30, Sat 10-1
Friends of the Library Group

WAURIKA

P WAURIKA LIBRARY*, 98 Meridian St, 73573. SAN 314-0350. Tel: 580-228-3274. FAX: 580-228-3274. E-mail: waurikalibrary@yahoo.com. *Dir,* Billie Porter
Circ 17,938
Library Holdings: Bk Vols 10,048
Open Mon, Wed, Thurs & Fri 10-5, Tues 10-7

WAYNOKA

P WAYNOKA PUBLIC LIBRARY*, 1659 Cecil St, 73860. SAN 314-0369. Tel: 580-824-6181. FAX: 580-824-0282. *Librn,* Jo Ann Bellmon
Pop 1,370; Circ 5,404
Library Holdings: Bk Vols 5,000
Automation Activity & Vendor Info: (Circulation) Follett Software
Open Mon-Fri 1:30-5:30

WEATHERFORD

C SOUTHWESTERN OKLAHOMA STATE UNIVERSITY*, Al Harris Library, 100 Campus Dr, 73096-3002. SAN 357-8283. Tel: 580-774-7023. Circulation Tel: 580-774-3130. Interlibrary Loan Service Tel: 580-774-7026. Reference Tel: 580-774-7082. Administration Tel: 580-774-7081. Automation Services Tel: 580-774-7074. Information Services Tel: 580-774-3031. FAX: 580-774-3112. Web Site: www.swosu.edu/library/. *Interim Dir,* Jason Dupree; *Instrul Serv Librn,* Frederic Murray; Tel: 580-774-7113, E-mail: frederic.murray@swosu.edu; *Per & Govt Doc Librn,* Jane Long; Tel: 580-774-3731, E-mail: jane.long@swosu.edu; *Pub Serv Librn,* Jason Dupree; E-mail: jason.dupree@swosu.edu; *Ref & Digitization Librn,* Phillip Fitzsimmons; Tel: 580-774-3030, E-mail: phillip.fitzsimmons@swosu.edu; *Syst & Web Mgt Librn,* Jonathan Woltz; E-mail: jonathan.woltz@swosu.edu; *Tech Serv Librn,* Linda Pye; Tel: 580-774-7021, E-mail: linda.pye@swosu.edu; *Circ Coordr,* Position Currently Open; *Coordr, ILL & Doc Delivery Serv,* Mary Roberson; E-mail: mary.roberson@swosu.edu; *Purchasing Coordr,* Janet Grabeal; E-mail: janet.grabeal@swosu.edu; *Acq Tech,* Dale Evans; Tel: 580-774-3737, E-mail: dale.evans@swosu.edu; *Digitization & Virtual Ref Tech,* Jason Henderson; Tel: 580-774-7024, E-mail: jason.henderson@swosu.edu; *Govt Doc Tech,* Doug Reichmann; Tel: 580-774-7069, E-mail: doug.reichmann@swosu.edu; *Media Serv, Syst Tech,* Brandon Schwartz; Tel: 580-774-7061, E-mail: brandon.schwartz@swosu.edu; *Per & Binding Tech,* Barbara Roddam; Tel: 580-774-7022, E-mail: barbara.roddam@swosu.edu; *Tech Serv Technician,* Janet Black; Tel: 580-774-3089, E-mail: janet.black@swosu.edu; Staff 16 (MLS 7, Non-MLS 9)
Founded 1902. Enrl 4,362; Fac 256; Highest Degree: Doctorate
Library Holdings: Audiobooks 1,000; AV Mats 8,000; e-books 150,000; e-journals 39,100; Bk Vols 300,000; Per Subs 300; Videos 500
Special Collections: SWOSU Digital Repository; SWOSU University Publications (Southwestern Room). State Document Depository; US Document Depository
Subject Interests: Educ, Humanities, Sciences
Automation Activity & Vendor Info: (Acquisitions) Ex Libris Group; (Cataloging) Ex Libris Group; (Circulation) Ex Libris Group; (Course Reserve) Ex Libris Group; (ILL) OCLC; (OPAC) Ex Libris Group; (Serials) Ex Libris Group
Database Vendor: ABC-CLIO, Alexander Street Press, American Chemical Society, American Mathematical Society, American Psychological Association (APA), Amigos Library Services, Annual Reviews, Cinahl, CQ Press, CredoReference, Discovery Education, Dun & Bradstreet, ebrary, EBSCO Information Services, EBSCOhost, Ex Libris Group, Gale Cengage Learning, Hoovers, Ingram Library Services, ISI Web of Knowledge, JSTOR, LearningExpress, Lexi-Comp, LexisNexis, Marcive, Inc, Medline, OCLC ArticleFirst, OCLC FirstSearch, OCLC WorldShare Interlibrary Loan, OVID Technologies, Oxford Online, Project MUSE, ProQuest, PubMed, RefWorks, Springshare, LLC, Swets Information Services, Thomson - Web of Science, ValueLine
Wireless access
Function: Audiobks via web, Computers for patron use, Doc delivery serv, e-mail & chat, E-Reserves, Electronic databases & coll, Fax serv, Free DVD rentals, Govt ref serv, Handicapped accessible, ILL available, Instruction & testing, Learning ctr, Mail & tel request accepted, Microfiche/film & reading machines, Online cat, Online ref, Online searches, Photocopying/Printing, Printer for laptops & handheld devices, Pub access computers, Ref serv available, Ref serv in person, Spoken cassettes & CDs, Telephone ref, Web-catalog, Wheelchair accessible, Writing prog
Partic in Amigos Library Services, Inc; OCLC Online Computer Library Center, Inc
Special Services for the Deaf - ADA equip
Open Mon-Thurs 7:30am-11pm, Fri 7:30-5, Sat 12-5, Sun 3-11
Restriction: In-house use for visitors, Open to students, fac, staff & alumni, Pub use on premises

Departmental Libraries:

O H MCMAHAN LIBRARY, 409 E Mississippi, Sayre, 73662. Tel: 580-928-5533, Ext 2157, 580-928-5533, Ext 2185. FAX: 580-928-5533, Ext 2135. Web Site: www.swosu.edu/library/sayre/index.asp. *Interim Dir,* Jason Dupree; E-mail: jason.dupree@swosu.edu; *Librn,* April Miller; E-mail: april.miller@swosu.edu; *Libr Tech,* Dianna Mosburg; E-mail: dianna.mosburg@swosu.edu; Staff 2 (MLS 1, Non-MLS 1)
Founded 1971. Enrl 558; Fac 18; Highest Degree: Associate
Library Holdings: Bk Titles 6,500; Per Subs 54
Special Collections: Medical Reserve
Automation Activity & Vendor Info: (Acquisitions) Ex Libris Group; (Circulation) Ex Libris Group; (OPAC) Ex Libris Group
Database Vendor: EBSCO Information Services, EBSCOhost, Medline, OCLC ArticleFirst, OCLC FirstSearch, OCLC WorldShare Interlibrary Loan

WESTVILLE

P JOHN F HENDERSON PUBLIC LIBRARY, 116 N Williams, 74965. (Mail add: PO Box 580, 74965-0580), SAN 314-0377. Tel: 918-723-5002. FAX: 918-723-3400. E-mail: westvillepl@eodls.org. Web Site: www.eodls.lib.ok.us/westville.html. *Librn,* Sue Ann Ghormley
Founded 1969. Pop 1,049
Library Holdings: Bk Vols 17,693; Per Subs 20
Automation Activity & Vendor Info: (Circulation) SirsiDynix
Wireless access
Mem of Eastern Oklahoma District Library System
Open Mon-Fri 8:30-5:30, Sat 9-Noon

WETUMKA

P WETUMKA PUBLIC LIBRARY*, 202 N Main, 74883. SAN 324-0347. Tel: 405-452-3785. FAX: 405-452-5825. *Librn,* Joan Hill; E-mail: joanhill29@gmail.com
Pop 1,451
Library Holdings: Bk Titles 10,000; Bk Vols 17,547; Videos 483
Wireless access
Open Mon & Tues 2-6, Wed-Fri 1-5

WEWOKA

S SEMINOLE NATION MUSEUM LIBRARY*, 524 S Wewoka Ave, 74884. (Mail add: PO Box 1532, 74884-1532), SAN 375-6718. Tel: 405-257-5580. FAX: 405-257-5580. Web Site: theseminolenationmuseum.org. *Pres,* Dr Steve Walker; *Dir,* Richard Ellwanger; E-mail: director@theseminolemuseum.org
Founded 1974
Library Holdings: Bk Titles 2,000
Subject Interests: African-Am hist, Cultural hist
Open Mon-Sat 10-5
Restriction: In-house use for visitors

P WEWOKA PUBLIC LIBRARY*, 118 W Fifth St, 74884. SAN 314-0385. Tel: 405-257-3225. E-mail: librarian@cityofwewoka.com. Web Site: www.cityofwewoka.com/library.html. *Librn,* Carolyn Trimble; *Asst Librn,* Dorothy McNally
Founded 1928
Library Holdings: Bk Vols 15,000
Wireless access
Open Mon-Fri 9:30-5:30, Sat 9-Noon

WILBURTON

C EASTERN OKLAHOMA STATE COLLEGE*, Library Media Center, Bill H Hill Library Bldg, 2nd & 3rd Flrs, 1301 W Main St, 74578. SAN 314-0393. Tel: 918-465-1875. FAX: 918-465-0112. Web Site: www.eosc.edu/library. *Dir, Libr & Media Serv,* Maria Martinez; Tel: 918-465-1711, E-mail: mmartinez@eosc.edu; *Libr Asst,* Kim Pendergraft;

Tel: 918-465-1783, E-mail: kdpendergraft@eosc.edu; Staff 5 (MLS 2, Non-MLS 3)
Founded 1909. Enrl 1,800; Fac 48
Library Holdings: Bks on Deafness & Sign Lang 12; Bk Titles 38,000; Bk Vols 41,000; Per Subs 200
Special Collections: Native American Coll. Oral History
Database Vendor: EBSCOhost, Gale Cengage Learning
Function: Photocopying/Printing
Open Mon-Thurs (Fall & Spring) 7:30am-9pm, Fri 7:30-4:30, Sun 5-9; Mon-Thurs (Summer) 7:30-4:30

P LATIMER COUNTY PUBLIC LIBRARY*, 301 W Ada Ave, 74578. (Mail add: PO Box 126, 74578-0126), SAN 314-0407. Tel: 918-465-3751. FAX: 918-465-4287. *Librn,* Latoyah Pendergraft; E-mail: pendergraft@oklibrary.net; *Asst Librn,* Dana Malone
Pop 3,000
Library Holdings: Bk Vols 15,000; Per Subs 25
Automation Activity & Vendor Info: (Cataloging) SirsiDynix; (Circulation) SirsiDynix; (Serials) EBSCO Online
Wireless access
Mem of Southeastern Public Library System of Oklahoma
Open Mon 9-6, Tues-Thurs 10-6, Fri 10-5, Sat 10-3

WISTER

P WISTER PUBLIC LIBRARY*, 211 Plum St, 74966. SAN 314-0415. Tel: 918-655-7654. FAX: 918-655-3267. E-mail: wister@oklibrary.net. Web Site: www.wister.lib.ok.us. *Head Librn,* Leslie Langley; E-mail: langley@oklibrary.net; *Ch Serv,* Sheila Pickering Reid; Staff 2 (Non-MLS 2)
Pop 1,200; Circ 13,000
Library Holdings: Bk Titles 10,500; Per Subs 15
Automation Activity & Vendor Info: (Circulation) SirsiDynix
Function: ILL available
Mem of Southeastern Public Library System of Oklahoma
Open Tues-Thurs 10-6, Fri 10-5, Sat 9-2

WOODWARD

P WOODWARD PUBLIC LIBRARY, 1500 Main St, 73801. SAN 314-0423. Tel: 580-254-8544. FAX: 580-254-8546. Web Site: woodwardlibrary.okpls.org. *Dir,* Connie Terry; E-mail: cterry@woodward.lib.ok.us; *Adult Serv,* Paula Odell; Staff 6 (Non-MLS 6)
Founded 1899. Pop 12,340; Circ 75,448
Library Holdings: Audiobooks 1,803; DVDs 2,745; e-books 23,437; e-journals 243; Bk Titles 29,182; Per Subs 57
Special Collections: Genealogy; Oklahoma History Coll, bks, pamphlets
Subject Interests: Genealogy, Literacy
Automation Activity & Vendor Info: (Cataloging) Auto-Graphics, Inc; (Circulation) Auto-Graphics, Inc; (OPAC) Auto-Graphics, Inc
Database Vendor: Auto-Graphics, Inc, Baker & Taylor, EBSCO Auto Repair Reference, EBSCOhost, Gale Cengage Learning, Newsbank, Overdrive, Inc, TumbleBookLibrary
Wireless access
Special Services for the Blind - Bks on cassette
Open Mon-Thurs 9-7, Fri 9-5, Sat 9-4
Friends of the Library Group

WYNNEWOOD

P WYNNEWOOD PUBLIC LIBRARY*, 108 N Dean A McGee Ave, 73098. Tel: 405-665-2512. FAX: 405-665-4619. E-mail: wynnelib@wynnewood.lib.ok.us. *Dir,* Debbie Daugherty; Staff 1 (Non-MLS 1)
Pop 2,400
Library Holdings: AV Mats 400; Bk Vols 15,000; Talking Bks 300
Special Collections: Local & Native American Genealogy Coll; Roster of Union & Confederate Soldiers
Automation Activity & Vendor Info: (Acquisitions) Follett Software; (Cataloging) Follett Software; (Circulation) Follett Software; (OPAC) Follett Software
Database Vendor: EBSCO Information Services
Wireless access
Open Mon, Wed & Fri 9-12 & 1-5, Tues & Thurs 9-12 & 1-6, Sat 9-Noon
Friends of the Library Group

YALE

P YALE PUBLIC LIBRARY*, 213 N Main, 74085. SAN 314-0431. Tel: 918-387-2135. FAX: 918-387-2616. *Dir,* Janice Clark; E-mail: jclark@yale.lib.ok.us; *Asst Librn,* Linda Butcher; Staff 2 (Non-MLS 2)
Founded 1919. Pop 1,392; Circ 24,429
Jul 2010-Jun 2011 Income $78,682, State $2,765, City $75,917. Mats Exp $78,682, Books $3,915, Per/Ser (Incl. Access Fees) $187, Other Print Mats $631, AV Mat $330. Sal $42,392
Library Holdings: Audiobooks 267; AV Mats 1,575; CDs 38; DVDs 675; Large Print Bks 220; Bk Vols 22,715; Per Subs 24
Automation Activity & Vendor Info: (Acquisitions) Follett Software; (Cataloging) Follett Software; (ILL) CLSI; (OPAC) Follett Software
Database Vendor: Brodart
Wireless access
Function: ILL available
Partic in OLTN
Open Mon 10-7, Tues-Fri 10-5:30
Friends of the Library Group

YUKON

P MABEL C FRY PUBLIC LIBRARY*, 1200 Lakeshore Dr, 73099. SAN 314-044X. Tel: 405-354-8232. FAX: 405-350-5930. *Librn,* Sara Schieman; E-mail: sschieman@cityofyofyukonok.gov; *Asst Librn,* Carla Hickey
Founded 1905. Circ 48,300
Library Holdings: Bk Vols 33,000; Per Subs 80
Automation Activity & Vendor Info: (Cataloging) Follett Software; (Circulation) Follett Software
Open Mon-Thurs 9:30-9, Fri 9:30-5, Sat 9:30-2
Friends of the Library Group

OREGON

Date of Statistics: FY 2013-2014
Population, 2010 U.S. Census: 3,831,074
Population, July 1, 2013: 3,919,020
Population Served by Public Libraries: 3,755,011
Unserved: 164,009
Total Volumes in Public Libraries: 11,740,033. Note: this number does not contain duplicates of downloadable materials purchased by statewide consortium
Volumes Per Capita: 3.13
Total Public Library Circulation: 57,168,132
Circulation Per Capita: 15.22
Total Public Library Expenditures: $192,512,176
Expenditures Per Capita: $51.27
Grants-in-Aid to Public Libraries: $683,406
LSTA Federal Funds Received by State Library: $2,288,648
Grants to Public Libraries from Federal Sources (LSTA): $386,904 (does not include federal funds that subsidize statewide database licensing support. Subsidies included with state library share.)
State Library's Share from Federal Sources (LSTA): $119,976
Number of County Libraries: 16
Counties Served: 36
Number of Bookmobiles in State: 7

ADAMS

P ADAMS PUBLIC LIBRARY*, 190 Main St, 97810. (Mail add: PO Box 20, 97810-0020), SAN 328-9079. Tel: 541-566-3038. FAX: 541-566-2077. E-mail: adamspl@wtechlink.us. Web Site: www.adams.plinkit.org. *Libr Dir,* Jennifer Davison
Pop 401
Library Holdings: Large Print Bks 200; Bk Vols 5,000; Per Subs 12
Automation Activity & Vendor Info: (Acquisitions) Evergreen
Wireless access
Mem of Umatilla County Special Library District
Open Tues-Thurs 1-6
Friends of the Library Group

AGNESS

P AGNESS COMMUNITY LIBRARY*, 3905 Cougar Lane, 97406. (Mail add: PO Box 33, 97406-0033), SAN 314-0458. Tel: 541-247-6323. FAX: 541-247-6323. E-mail: agnesslibrary@hughes.net. Web Site: www.agnesslibrary.plinkit.org. *Dir,* Jhanna Stutzman-Fry; Staff 4 (Non-MLS 4)
Founded 1943. Pop 220; Circ 5,921
Library Holdings: Bk Vols 12,000; Per Subs 30
Subject Interests: Local Native Am
Automation Activity & Vendor Info: (Cataloging) TLC (The Library Corporation)
Open Mon & Thurs 10-5

ALBANY

P ALBANY PUBLIC LIBRARY*, 2450 14th Ave SE, 97322. SAN 357-8348. Tel: 541-917-7580. Circulation Tel: 541-917-7581, 541-917-7588. Interlibrary Loan Service Tel: 541-917-7582. FAX: 541-917-7586. Web Site: library.cityofalbany.net. *Dir,* Ed Gallagher; Tel: 541-917-7589, E-mail: ed.gallagher@cityofalbany.net; *Supv Librn,* Marcia Timm; Tel: 541-917-7592, E-mail: marcia.timm@cityofalbany.net; *Ch Serv,* Scott Keeney; Tel: 541-917-7591, E-mail: scott.keeney@cityofalbany.net; *Ref Serv,* John Burton; Tel: 541-917-7580, Ext 4702, E-mail: john.burton@cityofalbany.net; *Ref Serv,* Diane Moody; Tel: 541-917-7580, Ext 4701, E-mail: diane.moody@cityofalbany.net; *Tech Serv,* Laurel Langenwalter; Tel: 541-917-7580, Ext 4700, E-mail: laurel.langenwalter@cityofalbany.net; *YA Serv,* Doris Hicks; Tel: 541-917-7580, Ext 4704, E-mail: doris.hicks@cityofalbany.net; Staff 11 (MLS 7, Non-MLS 4)
Founded 1907. Pop 45,560; Circ 576,723
Jul 2005-Jun 2006 Income (Main Library and Branch(s)) $762,416. Mats Exp $207,724
Library Holdings: AV Mats 10,792; Bk Vols 132,633; Per Subs 270
Special Collections: Oregon History Coll
Automation Activity & Vendor Info: (Acquisitions) SirsiDynix; (Cataloging) SirsiDynix; (Circulation) SirsiDynix; (OPAC) SirsiDynix
Database Vendor: 3M Library Systems, BWI, EBSCOhost, Gale Cengage Learning, OCLC FirstSearch, OCLC WorldShare Interlibrary Loan, ReferenceUSA, SirsiDynix
Wireless access
Partic in OCLC Online Computer Library Center, Inc
Open Mon-Wed 10-8, Thurs & Fri 10-6, Sat 10-5
Friends of the Library Group
Branches: 1
DOWNTOWN CARNEGIE, 302 Ferry St SW, 97321-2216, SAN 357-8372. Tel: 541-917-7585. Circulation Tel: 541-917-7588. Administration Tel: 541-917-7584. *Br Mgr,* Jason Darling; E-mail: jason.darling@cityofalbany.net; Staff 2 (MLS 1, Non-MLS 1)
Founded 1913
Library Holdings: Bk Vols 24,000
Subject Interests: Historic home renovation
Open Mon-Fri 10-6
Friends of the Library Group

J LINN-BENTON COMMUNITY COLLEGE LIBRARY*, 6500 SW Pacific Blvd, 97321-3799. SAN 314-0466. Tel: 541-917-4638. FAX: 541-917-4659. E-mail: libref@linnbenton.edu. Web Site: lib.linnbenton.edu, www.linnbenton.edu/library. *Asst Dean,* Kristen Jones; *Chair,* Jorry Rolfe; Tel: 541-917-4649; *Circ,* Cheryl Seaders; E-mail: seaderc@linnbenton.edu; Staff 2 (MLS 2)
Founded 1969. Enrl 6,042; Fac 160
Library Holdings: AV Mats 6,997; e-books 2,318; Electronic Media & Resources 250; Bk Titles 42,480; Bk Vols 48,000; Per Subs 169
Subject Interests: Linn-Benton County hist, Nursing, Vocational tech mat
Automation Activity & Vendor Info: (Cataloging) SirsiDynix; (Circulation) SirsiDynix; (ILL) OCLC; (OPAC) SirsiDynix
Partic in OCLC Online Computer Library Center, Inc; Valley Link
Open Mon-Thurs 8-8, Fri 8-4:30

M SAMARITAN ALBANY GENERAL HOSPITAL*, Stanley K Davis Library, 1046 Sixth Ave SW, 97321. SAN 325-7835. Tel: 541-812-4446. FAX: 541-812-4482. *Librn,* Douglas Hambley; Staff 1 (MLS 1)
Library Holdings: Bk Vols 400; Per Subs 40
Automation Activity & Vendor Info: (Cataloging) LibraryWorld, Inc; (OPAC) LibraryWorld, Inc
Database Vendor: EBSCOhost, MD Consult, OVID Technologies
Wireless access

G UNITED STATES DEPARTMENT OF ENERGY*, NETL-Albany Library, 1450 Queen Ave SW, 97321-2152. SAN 314-0490. Tel: 541-967-5864. FAX: 541-967-5936. *Libr Tech,* Nellie McKay; E-mail: nellie.mckay@NETL.DOE.GOV; Staff 1 (Non-MLS 1)
Founded 1943
Library Holdings: e-journals 3,000; Bk Titles 20,000; Bk Vols 30,000; Per Subs 25
Subject Interests: Chem, Energy, Mat sci, Metallurgy, Mineralogy, Physics

Automation Activity & Vendor Info: (Cataloging) EOS International; (Circulation) EOS International; (ILL) OCLC; (OPAC) EOS International; (Serials) EOS International
Database Vendor: American Chemical Society, Dialog, Elsevier, EOS International, ISI Web of Knowledge, OCLC FirstSearch, OCLC WorldShare Interlibrary Loan, ScienceDirect, Springer-Verlag
Function: ILL available, Online cat, Res libr
Partic in OCLC Online Computer Library Center, Inc
Restriction: Open to pub for ref only, Open to pub with supv only, Photo ID required for access

AMITY

P AMITY PUBLIC LIBRARY*, 307 Trade St, 97101. (Mail add: PO Box 470, 97101-0470), SAN 376-3315. Tel: 503-835-8181. *Librn,* Eileen Lewis
Library Holdings: Bk Vols 15,000
Automation Activity & Vendor Info: (Acquisitions) Innovative Interfaces, Inc; (Cataloging) Innovative Interfaces, Inc; (OPAC) Innovative Interfaces, Inc
Partic in Chemeketa Cooperative Regional Library Service
Open Mon, Tues, Thurs & Fri 1-5, Wed 5-9, Sat 10-1
Friends of the Library Group

ARLINGTON

P ARLINGTON PUBLIC LIBRARY*, City Hall, 500 W First St, 97812. (Mail add: PO Box 339, 97812-0339), SAN 357-8704. Tel: 541-454-2444. FAX: 541-454-2568. *Librn,* Mary Mitchell
Pop 818; Circ 2,900
Library Holdings: Bk Vols 8,000
Automation Activity & Vendor Info: (Cataloging) Evergreen; (Circulation) Evergreen; (OPAC) Evergreen
Open Mon & Wed 2-6, Tues, Thurs & Fri 10-2
Friends of the Library Group

ASHLAND

C SOUTHERN OREGON UNIVERSITY*, Lenn & Dixie Hannon Library, 1250 Siskiyou Blvd, 97520-5076. SAN 314-0504. Tel: 541-552-6441. Circulation Tel: 541-552-6860. Interlibrary Loan Service Tel: 541-552-6823. Reference Tel: 541-552-6442. FAX: 541-552-6429. Web Site: hanlib.sou.edu. *Dean, Univ Libr,* Paul Adalian; Tel: 541-552-6833, E-mail: adalianp@sou.edu; *Head, Ref,* Connie Anderson; Tel: 541-552-6820, E-mail: anderson@sou.edu; *Access Serv Coordr,* Judy Dye; Tel: 541-552-6825, E-mail: dyej@sou.edu; *Coordr, Cat,* Kate Cleland-Sipfle; Tel: 541-552-6839, E-mail: clelandk@sou.edu; *E-Res Coll Develop Coordr,* Teresa Montgomery; Tel: 541-552-6837, E-mail: montgomery@sou.edu; *E-Res Syst & Web Coordr,* Emily Miller-Francisco; Tel: 541-552-6819, E-mail: millere@sou.edu; *Per Coordr,* Kathy Hoxmeier; Tel: 541-552-6844, E-mail: hoxmeier@sou.edu; *Syst Coordr,* Jim Rible; Tel: 541-552-6821, E-mail: rible@sou.edu; *Bibliog Instr,* Dale Vidmar; Tel: 541-552-6842, E-mail: vidmar@sou.edu; *Coll Develop,* Mary Jane Cedar-Face; Tel: 541-552-6836, E-mail: cedarface@sou.edu; *Govt Doc,* Deborah Hollens; Tel: 541-552-6850, E-mail: hollens@sou.edu; *ILL,* Anna Beauchamp; E-mail: beauchamp@sou.edu. Subject Specialists: *Hist,* Paul Adalian; *Bus, Econ,* Connie Anderson; *Foreign lang, Geog,* Kate Cleland-Sipfle; *Performing arts, Visual arts,* Teresa Montgomery; *Crime, Philos, Psychol,* Emily Miller-Francisco; *Sciences,* Jim Rible; *Communication, Educ,* Dale Vidmar; *Anthrop, Sociol,* Mary Jane Cedar-Face; *English, Polit sci,* Deborah Hollens; Staff 21 (MLS 9, Non-MLS 12)
Founded 1926. Enrl 5,772; Fac 278; Highest Degree: Master
Library Holdings: Bk Titles 241,000; Bk Vols 310,000; Per Subs 2,028
Special Collections: Oregon State Documents; Shakespeare-Renaissance (Bailey). State Document Depository; US Document Depository
Subject Interests: Ecology, Educ, Local hist, Shakespeare studies
Automation Activity & Vendor Info: (Acquisitions) Innovative Interfaces, Inc; (Cataloging) Innovative Interfaces, Inc; (Circulation) Innovative Interfaces, Inc; (Course Reserve) Innovative Interfaces, Inc; (OPAC) Innovative Interfaces, Inc; (Serials) Innovative Interfaces, Inc
Database Vendor: Cambridge Scientific Abstracts, Dialog, EBSCOhost, Gale Cengage Learning, JSTOR, LexisNexis, OCLC FirstSearch, OCLC WorldShare Interlibrary Loan, ProQuest, Springer-Verlag, Wiley, Wilson - Wilson Web
Partic in OCLC Online Computer Library Center, Inc; Orbis Cascade Alliance
Open Mon-Thurs 7:45am-11pm, Fri 7:45-5, Sat 12-5, Sun 1-11
Friends of the Library Group

ASTORIA

P ASTORIA PUBLIC LIBRARY*, 450 Tenth St, 97103. SAN 314-0512. Tel: 503-325-7323. Web Site: astorialibrary.org. *Dir,* Jane Tucker; E-mail: jtucker@astoria.or.us; Staff 5 (MLS 2, Non-MLS 3)
Founded 1892. Pop 10,000
Library Holdings: Bk Vols 53,000; Per Subs 30
Automation Activity & Vendor Info: (Cataloging) TLC (The Library Corporation); (Circulation) TLC (The Library Corporation); (OPAC) TLC (The Library Corporation)
Function: ILL available
Open Tues-Thurs 10-7, Fri & Sat 10-5
Friends of the Library Group

J CLATSOP COMMUNITY COLLEGE-LEARNING RESOURCE CENTER, Dora Badollet Library, 1680 Lexington, 97103. SAN 314-0520. Tel: 503-338-2462. FAX: 503-338-2387. E-mail: libcirc@clatsop.edu. Web Site: lrc.clatsopcc.edu. *Dir,* Candice Watkins; Tel: 503-388-2466, E-mail: cwatkins@clatsopcc.edu; Staff 5 (MLS 2, Non-MLS 3)
Founded 1962. Enrl 1,352; Fac 40; Highest Degree: Associate
Library Holdings: High Interest/Low Vocabulary Bk Vols 225; Bk Vols 35,000; Per Subs 670
Subject Interests: Marine tech, Regional hist
Automation Activity & Vendor Info: (Acquisitions) Ex Libris Group; (Cataloging) Ex Libris Group; (Circulation) Ex Libris Group; (Course Reserve) Ex Libris Group; (OPAC) Ex Libris Group; (Serials) Ex Libris Group
Database Vendor: ebrary
Wireless access
Function: Ref serv available
Partic in OCLC Online Computer Library Center, Inc
Open Mon-Thurs (Fall & Spring) 8-6, Fri 8-5, Sun 12-5; Mon-Thurs (Summer) 8-8
Restriction: Restricted access

S COLUMBIA RIVER MARITIME MUSEUM*, Ted M Natt Research Library, 1792 Marine Dr, 97103. SAN 314-0539. Tel: 503-325-2323. FAX: 503-325-2331. Web Site: www.crmm.org. *Librn,* Arline LaMear; *Curator,* Jeffrey Smith
Founded 1962
Library Holdings: Bk Titles 8,000; Per Subs 194
Special Collections: Maritime Photo Archive; Vessel Plans Coll
Subject Interests: Folklore, Maritime hist
Publications: Quarterdeck (Newsletter)
Restriction: Non-circulating to the pub, Open by appt only

ATHENA

P ATHENA PUBLIC LIBRARY*, 418 E Main St, 97813. (Mail add: PO Box 450, 97813-0450), SAN 358-0474. Tel: 541-566-2470. FAX: 541-566-2470. E-mail: athenalibrary@cityofathena.com. Web Site: www.uci.net/~athenalibrary. *Dir,* Carrie Bremer; Staff 1 (Non-MLS 1)
Founded 1914. Pop 1,799
Jul 2009-Jun 2010 Income $47,950, City $10,950, Other $37,000. Mats Exp $7,800, Books $6,000, Per/Ser (Incl. Access Fees) $300, AV Equip $1,500. Sal $27,000
Library Holdings: Audiobooks 300; CDs 450; DVDs 10; Electronic Media & Resources 13; Bk Titles 10,000; Per Subs 20; Videos 350
Automation Activity & Vendor Info: (Acquisitions) Follett Software; (Cataloging) Follett Software; (Circulation) Follett Software; (ILL) Innovative Interfaces, Inc - Millenium; (Media Booking) Innovative Interfaces, Inc - Millenium
Database Vendor: Gale Cengage Learning
Wireless access
Mem of Umatilla County Special Library District
Open Mon 1-7, Tues 7:30-1:30, Wed 12-5, Thurs 7:30-10:30 & 1-5
Friends of the Library Group

BAKER CITY

P BAKER COUNTY PUBLIC LIBRARY*, 2400 Resort St, 97814-2798. SAN 357-8437. Tel: 541-523-6419. FAX: 541-523-9088. E-mail: ask@bakerlib.org. Web Site: www.bakerlib.org. *Libr Dir,* Perry N Stokes; E-mail: director@bakerlib.org; *IT Serv Mgr,* Jim White; E-mail: tech@bakerlib.org; *ILL,* Carmen Wickam; E-mail: ill@bakerlib.org; Staff 13.4 (MLS 1, Non-MLS 12.4)
Founded 1906. Pop 16,750; Circ 153,607
Jul 2007-Jun 2008 Income (Main Library and Branch(s)) $780,851, State $8,229, County $749,972, Locally Generated Income $13,500, Other $9,150. Mats Exp $83,000, Books $61,900, Per/Ser (Incl. Access Fees) $5,500, AV Mat $5,000, Electronic Ref Mat (Incl. Access Fees) $10,600. Sal $378,925 (Prof $229,855)
Library Holdings: DVDs 2,317; e-books 2,557; Large Print Bks 3,285; Music Scores 73; Bk Vols 117,363; Per Subs 349; Talking Bks 3,401; Videos 4,261
Special Collections: Baker County Coll; Oregon History Coll
Automation Activity & Vendor Info: (Cataloging) Innovative Interfaces, Inc; (Circulation) Innovative Interfaces, Inc; (OPAC) Innovative Interfaces, Inc
Database Vendor: EBSCO Auto Repair Reference, EBSCOhost, infoUSA, LearningExpress, Newsbank, Overdrive, Inc
Wireless access

Function: Audio & video playback equip for onsite use, Audiobks via web, Bks on cassette, Bks on CD, CD-ROM, Children's prog, Computer training, Computers for patron use, Copy machines, Fax serv, Handicapped accessible, ILL available, Jail serv, Magnifiers for reading, Music CDs, Newsp ref libr, Online cat, Online ref, Online searches, Outside serv via phone, mail, e-mail & web, OverDrive digital audio bks, Photocopying/Printing, Prog for adults, Prog for children & young adult, Scanner, Spoken cassettes & CDs, Summer reading prog, Tax forms, VHS videos, Web-catalog, Wheelchair accessible
Partic in Libraries of Eastern Oregon (LEO); Sage Library System of Eastern Oregon
Special Services for the Deaf - Bks on deafness & sign lang; Closed caption videos
Special Services for the Blind - Bks on cassette; Bks on CD; Magnifiers
Open Mon-Thurs 9-8, Fri 9-5, Sat 10-4, Sun 12-4
Restriction: Lending limited to county residents, Non-circulating of rare bks
Friends of the Library Group
Branches: 4
HAINES BRANCH, 818 Cole St, Haines, 97833, SAN 357-8461. Tel: 541-856-3309. *Br Mgr,* Donna Kilgore; Staff 2 (Non-MLS 2)
Founded 1961. Pop 590
HALFWAY BRANCH, 260 Gover Lane, Halfway, 97834. (Mail add: PO Box 922, Halfway, 97834-0922), SAN 357-8496. Tel: 541-742-5279. E-mail: halfway@bakerlib.org. *Br Mgr,* Linda Bergeron; Staff 0.475 (Non-MLS 0.475)
Pop 550
Open Wed 2-5, Thurs 4-7, Fri 9-12 & 1-4, Sat 9-12
Friends of the Library Group
HUNTINGTON BRANCH, 55 E Jefferson, Huntington, 97907. (Mail add: PO Box 130, Huntington, 97907), SAN 357-8526. Tel: 541-869-2440. FAX: 541-869-2440. E-mail: huntington@bakerlib.org. *Libr Asst,* Julynn Phalen
Open Mon & Tues 2-5, Wed 4-7, Fri 10-5, Sat 10-1
RICHLAND BRANCH, 42008 Moody Rd, Richland, 97870, SAN 357-8550. Tel: 541-893-6088. E-mail: richland@bakerlib.org. *Br Mgr,* B J Pierce
Open Mon & Wed 1-5, Tues 8-12, Sat 9-12
Bookmobiles: 1. Bk vols 2,300

BANDON

P BANDON PUBLIC LIBRARY*, 1204 11th St SW, 97411. (Mail add: PO Box 128, 97411-0128), SAN 314-0563. Tel: 541-347-3221. FAX: 541-347-9363. Web Site: www.bandon.cclsd.org. *Dir,* Rosalyn McGarva; *Asst Dir,* Susan Kling; *Ch,* Julie Tipton; Staff 6 (MLS 1, Non-MLS 5)
Pop 3,000; Circ 159,651
Library Holdings: Bk Vols 63,046; Per Subs 93
Automation Activity & Vendor Info: (Cataloging) Innovative Interfaces, Inc; (Circulation) Innovative Interfaces, Inc; (ILL) Innovative Interfaces, Inc; (OPAC) Innovative Interfaces, Inc
Wireless access
Publications: Friends (Newsletter)
Mem of Coos County Library Service District
Open Tues, Wed & Thurs 10:30-8:30, Fri & Sat 10:30-5
Friends of the Library Group

BANKS

P BANKS PUBLIC LIBRARY*, 111 Market St, 97106-9019. SAN 314-0571. Tel: 503-324-1382. FAX: 503-324-9132. Web Site: www.wccls.org/libraries/banks. *Libr Dir,* Denise Holmes
Founded 1976
Library Holdings: Bk Vols 20,893; Per Subs 64; Talking Bks 1,394; Videos 1,075
Automation Activity & Vendor Info: (Cataloging) Innovative Interfaces, Inc; (Circulation) Innovative Interfaces, Inc; (OPAC) Innovative Interfaces, Inc
Wireless access
Partic in Washington County Cooperative Library Services
Open Mon, Fri & Sat 11-5, Tues-Thurs 11-7
Friends of the Library Group

BEAVERTON

P BEAVERTON CITY LIBRARY*, 12375 SW Fifth St, 97005-2883. SAN 314-058X. Tel: 503-644-2197. Reference Tel: 503-526-2577. FAX: 503-526-2636. Administration FAX: 503-574-3436. TDD: 503-574-4606. E-mail: librarymail@beavertonoregon.gov. Web Site: www.beavertonlibrary.org. *Dir,* Abigail Elder; Tel: 503-526-3705, E-mail: aelder@beavertonoregon.gov; *Adult Serv Mgr,* Linda Fallon; Tel: 503-526-2676, E-mail: lfallon@beavertonoregon.gov; *Br Mgr,* John Finn; Tel: 503-526-2381, Fax: 503-350-3645, E-mail: jfinn@beavertonoregon.gov; *Circ Mgr,* Melissa Little; E-mail: mlittle@beavertonoregon.gov; *Tech Serv Mgr,* Michele Caldwell; Tel: 503-526-2209, E-mail: mcaldwell@beavertonoregon.gov; *Youth Serv Mgr,* Victoria Campbell; Tel: 503-526-2599, E-mail: vcampbell@beavertonoregon.gov; *Vols Serv Coordr,* Jennifer Johnson; Tel: 503-526-3703, E-mail: jjohnson@beavertonoregon.gov; Staff 85 (MLS 17, Non-MLS 68)
Founded 1938. Pop 136,000; Circ 2,700,000
Jul 2009-Jun 2010 Income $6,329,873, State $15,317, City $1,815,781, County $4,284,088, Locally Generated Income $214,687. Mats Exp $465,086, Books $299,099, Per/Ser (Incl. Access Fees) $88,055, Micro $12,544, AV Mat $60,585, Electronic Ref Mat (Incl. Access Fees) $4,803. Sal $2,707,479
Special Collections: Local History Coll; World Languages Coll
Automation Activity & Vendor Info: (Acquisitions) Innovative Interfaces, Inc; (Cataloging) Innovative Interfaces, Inc; (Circulation) Innovative Interfaces, Inc; (ILL) OCLC; (OPAC) Innovative Interfaces, Inc; (Serials) Innovative Interfaces, Inc
Database Vendor: Gale Cengage Learning
Wireless access
Function: Audiobks via web, Bks on CD, Children's prog, Computer training, Computers for patron use, Copy machines, Digital talking bks, E-Reserves, Electronic databases & coll, Family literacy, Fax serv, Free DVD rentals, Handicapped accessible, Health sci info serv, Homework prog, ILL available, Magnifiers for reading, Mail & tel request accepted, Music CDs, Online cat, Prog for adults, Prog for children & young adult, Pub access computers, Ref & res, Ref serv in person, Spoken cassettes & CDs, Story hour, Summer reading prog, Tax forms, Teen prog, Telephone ref, Video lending libr, Web-catalog, Wheelchair accessible
Partic in Washington County Cooperative Library Services
Special Services for the Deaf - Assisted listening device; Bks on deafness & sign lang; Closed caption videos; TDD equip
Special Services for the Blind - Assistive/Adapted tech devices, equip & products; Bks on cassette; Bks on CD; Computer with voice synthesizer for visually impaired persons; Large print bks; Magnifiers; Scanner for conversion & translation of mats; Screen enlargement software for people with visual disabilities
Open Mon-Thurs 10-9, Fri & Sat 10-5, Sun 1-5
Friends of the Library Group

CM OREGON NATIONAL PRIMATE RESEARCH CENTER*, McDonald Library, 505 NW 185th Ave, 97006. SAN 314-061X. Tel: 503-690-5311. FAX: 503-690-5243. Web Site: www.ohsu.edu/library/primate.shtml. *Br Mgr,* Denise Urbanski; E-mail: urbanskd@ohsu.edu. Subject Specialists: *Primatology,* Denise Urbanski; Staff 1 (Non-MLS 1)
Founded 1961
Jul 2006-Jun 2007. Mats Exp $100,158, Books $2,158, Per/Ser (Incl. Access Fees) $98,000
Library Holdings: Bk Titles 3,900; Bk Vols 14,765; Per Subs 81
Special Collections: Primatology Coll
Subject Interests: Biomed lit, Primates
Automation Activity & Vendor Info: (Circulation) Innovative Interfaces, Inc; (ILL) OCLC ILLiad; (OPAC) Innovative Interfaces, Inc; (Serials) Innovative Interfaces, Inc
Function: For res purposes
Partic in Washington County Libr Network

BEND

J CENTRAL OREGON COMMUNITY COLLEGE BARBER LIBRARY*, 2600 NW College Way, 97701-5998. SAN 314-0636. Tel: 541-383-7560. Interlibrary Loan Service Tel: 541-383-7561. Reference Tel: 541-383-7567. FAX: 541-383-7406. Web Site: campuslibrary.cocc.edu. *Col Librn,* David Bilyeu; Tel: 541-383-7563, E-mail: dbilyeu@cocc.edu; *Acq, Assoc Col Librn, Coll,* Catherine Finney; Tel: 541-383-7559; *Assoc Col Librn, Info & Access Serv Librn,* Tina Hovekamp; Tel: 541-383-7295, E-mail: thovekamp@cocc.edu; Staff 4.5 (MLS 4.5)
Founded 1950. Enrl 5,742; Fac 155; Highest Degree: Associate
Jul 2009-Jun 2010 Income $861,140. Mats Exp $137,984, Books $38,615, Per/Ser (Incl. Access Fees) $44,079, AV Mat $10,000, Electronic Ref Mat (Incl. Access Fees) $45,290. Sal $449,702 (Prof $269,897)
Library Holdings: AV Mats 1,962; Bks on Deafness & Sign Lang 93; e-books 7,262; Bk Titles 65,285; Per Subs 236
Special Collections: Harold Wynne (Papers related to Rajnesshpuram); Records of the Oregon Superintendency of Indian Affairs 1848-1873; USDA Farm Service Agency (National Forest Service Aerial Photograph Coll). US Document Depository
Subject Interests: Native Am
Automation Activity & Vendor Info: (Acquisitions) Innovative Interfaces, Inc; (Cataloging) Innovative Interfaces, Inc; (Circulation) Innovative Interfaces, Inc; (Course Reserve) Innovative Interfaces, Inc; (ILL) OCLC; (Media Booking) Innovative Interfaces, Inc; (OPAC) Innovative Interfaces, Inc; (Serials) Innovative Interfaces, Inc
Database Vendor: BioOne, College Source, CQ Press, CredoReference, EBSCOhost, JSTOR, LexisNexis, Modern Language Association, Newsbank, OCLC FirstSearch, OCLC WorldShare Interlibrary Loan, Oxford Online, ProQuest, SerialsSolutions
Wireless access

Function: Outside serv via phone, mail, e-mail & web
Partic in Orbis Cascade Alliance
Open Mon-Thurs 8am-10pm, Fri 8-5, Sat 10-5, Sun 12-6
Restriction: Authorized patrons

P DESCHUTES PUBLIC LIBRARY DISTRICT, 507 NW Wall St, 97701-2698. SAN 357-8585. Tel: 541-312-1021. FAX: 541-389-2982. Web Site: www.deschuteslibrary.org. *Dir,* Todd Dunkelberg; E-mail: toddd@deschuteslibrary.org; *Asst Dir, Operational Serv,* Lynne Mildenstein; Tel: 541-617-7061, Fax: 541-617-7061, E-mail: lynnem@deschuteslibrary.org; *Asst Dir, Pub Serv,* Kevin Barclay; Tel: 541-312-1046, E-mail: kevinb@deschuteslibrary.org; *Youth Serv Mgr,* Heather McNeil; Tel: 541-617-7099, Fax: 541-617-7097, E-mail: heatherm@deschuteslibrary.org; *Network Tech,* Mark Hovey; Tel: 541-312-1040, E-mail: markh@deschuteslibrary.org; Staff 78 (MLS 22, Non-MLS 56)
Founded 1920. Pop 140,000; Circ 1,808,402
Library Holdings: Bk Titles 199,699; Bk Vols 396,020; Per Subs 849
Automation Activity & Vendor Info: (Acquisitions) Innovative Interfaces, Inc; (Cataloging) Innovative Interfaces, Inc; (Circulation) Innovative Interfaces, Inc; (OPAC) Innovative Interfaces, Inc; (Serials) Innovative Interfaces, Inc
Wireless access
Partic in OCLC Online Computer Library Center, Inc
Special Services for the Blind - Computer with voice synthesizer for visually impaired persons
Open Mon-Fri 8-12 & 1-4
Friends of the Library Group
Branches: 5
BEND BRANCH, 601 NW Wall St, 97701, SAN 376-9402. Tel: 541-617-7040. Reference Tel: 541-617-7080. FAX: 541-617-7044. Reference FAX: 541-617-7083. *Mgr,* Jo Caisse; Tel: 541-617-7087, E-mail: joc@deschuteslibrary.org
Pop 70,328; Circ 1,009,376
Library Holdings: Bk Titles 172,526; Bk Vols 216,007; Per Subs 274
Open Mon-Wed 10-8, Thurs & Fri 10-6, Sat & Sun 12-5
Friends of the Library Group
LA PINE BRANCH, 16425 First St, La Pine, 97739. (Mail add: PO Box 40, La Pine, 97739-0040), SAN 325-3236. Tel: 541-312-1090. FAX: 541-536-0752. *Commun Librn,* Josie Hanneman; E-mail: lapineinfo@dpls.lib.or.us; *Supvr,* Cathy Zgraggen
Founded 2000. Pop 8,602; Circ 121,124
Library Holdings: Bk Titles 35,229; Bk Vols 36,892; Per Subs 75
Open Mon-Fri 10-6, Sat 10-5, Sun 1-5
Friends of the Library Group
REDMOND BRANCH, 827 SW Deschutes Ave, Redmond, 97756, SAN 357-8615. Tel: 541-312-1050. FAX: 541-548-6358. *Br Mgr,* Linda Olson; Tel: 541-312-1051, E-mail: lindao@dpls.us
Founded 1917. Pop 21,109; Circ 441,698
Library Holdings: Bk Titles 80,676; Bk Vols 86,313; Per Subs 133
Open Mon & Wed-Fri 10-6, Tues 10-8, Sat 10-5
Friends of the Library Group
SISTERS BRANCH, 110 N Cedar St, Sisters, 97759. (Mail add: PO Box 1209, Sisters, 97759), SAN 357-864X. Tel: 541-312-1070. FAX: 541-549-9620. *Commun Librn,* Colleen Galvin; E-mail: sistersinfo@dpls.lib.or.us; *Supvr,* Zoe Schumacher
Founded 1939. Pop 1,430; Circ 101,952
Library Holdings: Bk Titles 25,229; Bk Vols 26,517; Per Subs 72
Open Mon & Thurs 10-6, Wed 10-8, Fri & Sat 11-5, Sun 1-5
Friends of the Library Group
SUNRIVER AREA BRANCH, 56855 Venture Lane, Sunriver, 97707, SAN 377-6700. Tel: 541-312-1080. FAX: 541-593-9286. *Commun Librn,* Sheila Grier; Tel: 541-312-1081, E-mail: sunriverinfo@dpls.lib.or.us; *Supvr,* Heidi Powers
Founded 1998. Pop 1,700; Circ 96,677
Library Holdings: Bk Titles 29,081; Bk Vols 30,291; Per Subs 86
Open Mon & Thurs 10-6, Tues & Wed 10-8, Fri & Sat 10-5
Friends of the Library Group

C OREGON STATE UNIVERSITY*, Cascades Campus Library Services, 2600 NW College Way, 97701-5998. FAX: 541-383-7507. Web Site: osulibrary.oregonstate.edu/cascades. *Libr Dir,* Tina Hovekamp; Tel: 541-383-7295, E-mail: thovekamp@cocc.edu; *Ref & Instruction Librn,* Beverly Adler; Tel: 541-383-7795, E-mail: badler@cocc.edu; *Librn,* Sara Thompson; E-mail: sara.thompson@osucascade.edu
Automation Activity & Vendor Info: (Acquisitions) Innovative Interfaces, Inc; (Cataloging) Innovative Interfaces, Inc; (Circulation) Innovative Interfaces, Inc; (OPAC) Innovative Interfaces, Inc; (Serials) Innovative Interfaces, Inc
Database Vendor: EBSCOhost
Wireless access
Partic in Orbis Cascade Alliance
Open Mon-Thurs (Spring) 8am-10pm, Fri 8-5, Sat 10-5, Sun 12-6

S SCIENTISTS CENTER FOR ANIMAL WELFARE LIBRARY*, 2660 NE Hwy 20, Ste 610-115, 97701. SAN 372-7262. Tel: 301-345-3500. FAX: 541-383-4655. E-mail: info@scaw.com. Web Site: www.scaw.com. *Managing Dir,* Linda Tockey
Founded 1978
Library Holdings: Bk Vols 1,000
Publications: SCAW (Newsletter)
Restriction: Mem only

BLUE RIVER

P FRANCES O'BRIEN MEMORIAL LIBRARY*, 51790 McKenzie St, 97413. (Mail add: PO Box 291, 97413-0291). Tel: 541-822-3249. *Pres,* Ellen Sather
Founded 1929
Library Holdings: Bk Vols 40,000
Open Mon-Sat 10-4:30

BOARDMAN

P OREGON TRAIL LIBRARY DISTRICT*, Boardman Library, 200 South Main St, 97818. Tel: 541-481-3365. FAX: 541-481-2668. Web Site: www.oregontrail.plinkit.org. *Dir,* Marsha Richmond; Tel: 541-481-3365
Automation Activity & Vendor Info: (Cataloging) Innovative Interfaces, Inc - Millenium; (Circulation) Innovative Interfaces, Inc - Millenium; (ILL) Innovative Interfaces, Inc - Millenium; (OPAC) Innovative Interfaces, Inc - Millenium
Database Vendor: EBSCO Information Services, Gale Cengage Learning, ProQuest
Partic in Sage Library System of Eastern Oregon
Open Mon & Wed 11-8, Thurs Noon-5, Fri 10-5, Sat 10-2
Friends of the Library Group
Branches: 2
HEPPNER BRANCH, 444 North Main St, Heppner, 97836. (Mail add: PO Box 325, Heppner, 97836). Tel: 541-676-9964. Administration Tel: 541-481-3365. FAX: 541-676-5900.
Partic in Sage Library System of Eastern Oregon
Open Tues & Wed 11-8, Thurs Noon-5, Fri 10-5, Sat 11-3
Friends of the Library Group
IRRIGON BRANCH, Irrigon, 97844. Tel: 541-481-2665.
Open Tues & Thurs 10:30-4
Friends of the Library Group

BROOKINGS

P CHETCO COMMUNITY PUBLIC LIBRARY*, 405 Alder St, 97415. SAN 314-0644. Tel: 541-469-7738. FAX: 541-469-6746. Web Site: www.chetcolibrary.org. *Dir,* Susana Fernandez; E-mail: susanaf@nwtec.com
Founded 1947. Pop 12,909; Circ 164,770
Library Holdings: Large Print Bks 3,230; Bk Titles 48,961; Bk Vols 51,126; Per Subs 118; Talking Bks 2,644; Videos 1,612
Subject Interests: NW hist
Automation Activity & Vendor Info: (Cataloging) SirsiDynix; (Circulation) SirsiDynix; (OPAC) SirsiDynix
Wireless access
Partic in Ore Libr Asn; Southern Oregon Library Federation
Open Mon & Fri 10-6, Tues & Thurs 10-7, Wed 10-8, Sat 10-5
Friends of the Library Group

BROWNSVILLE

P BROWNSVILLE COMMUNITY LIBRARY, 146 Spaulding, 97327. (Mail add: PO Box 68, 97327-0068), SAN 314-0652. Tel: 541-466-5454. E-mail: library@ci.brownsville.or.us. *Dir,* Sherri Lemhouse; Staff 12 (Non-MLS 12)
Founded 1911. Pop 1,500; Circ 19,000
Library Holdings: Large Print Bks 350; Bk Vols 18,500; Per Subs 15; Talking Bks 300
Special Collections: Linn County Cemetaries; Oregon Trail Coll
Subject Interests: Genealogy, NW hist
Automation Activity & Vendor Info: (Cataloging) Follett Software; (Circulation) Follett Software
Wireless access
Open Tues, Wed & Fri 10-5, Thurs 1-7, Sat 10-2
Friends of the Library Group

BURNS

P HARNEY COUNTY LIBRARY*, 80 West D St, 97720-1299. SAN 314-0679. Tel: 541-573-6670. FAX: 541-573-1571. Web Site: www.harneycountylibrary.org. *Dir,* Cheryl Hancock; E-mail: cheryl@harneycountylibrary.org; Staff 2.5 (MLS 1, Non-MLS 1.5)
Founded 1903. Pop 7,000; Circ 38,482
Library Holdings: AV Mats 4,800; Bk Vols 25,000; Per Subs 70
Special Collections: Western History Room. Oral History

Automation Activity & Vendor Info: (Cataloging) Evergreen; (Circulation) Evergreen; (OPAC) Evergreen
Database Vendor: Gale Cengage Learning, LearningExpress, Library Ideas, LLC, Overdrive, Inc
Wireless access
Function: Bks on cassette, Bks on CD, Children's prog, Computers for patron use, Copy machines, Electronic databases & coll, Fax serv, Free DVD rentals, Handicapped accessible, ILL available, Mail & tel request accepted, Music CDs, Online cat, OverDrive digital audio bks, Photocopying/Printing, Prog for adults, Prog for children & young adult, Story hour, Summer reading prog
Partic in Sage Library System of Eastern Oregon
Open Mon & Tues 10:30-7, Wed 12-7, Thurs & Fri 10:30-6, Sat 12-4

CANBY

P CANBY PUBLIC LIBRARY, 292 N Holly St, 97013-3732. SAN 314-0687. Tel: 503-266-3394. Administration Tel: 503-266-4021, Ext 230. FAX: 503-266-1709. E-mail: canbyinfo@lincc.org. Web Site: canbylibrary.org. *Dir,* Melissa Kelly; E-mail: kellym@ci.canby.or.us; *Ch,* Peggy Wickwire; E-mail: pwickwire@lincc.org; *Pub Relations,* Hanna Hofer; E-mail: hoferh@ci.canby.or.us
Pop 22,000; Circ 300,000
Library Holdings: Bk Vols 60,000; Per Subs 70
Special Collections: Emma Wakefield Coll (materials on herbs)
Subject Interests: Children's bks, Christianity, Computer, Herbs, Ore
Automation Activity & Vendor Info: (Cataloging) SirsiDynix; (Circulation) SirsiDynix; (OPAC) SirsiDynix
Wireless access
Open Mon, Wed & Fri 10-6, Tues & Thurs 1-8, Sat 1-6, Sun 12-5
Friends of the Library Group

CANNON BEACH

P CANNON BEACH LIBRARY, 131 N Hemlock, 97110. (Mail add: PO Box 486, 97110-0486). Tel: 503-436-1391. E-mail: info@cannonbeachlibrary.org. Web Site: cannonbeachlibrary.org/home.php. *Mgr,* Buddie Anderson
Founded 1927
Library Holdings: Bk Vols 13,000
Special Collections: Haystack Rock Coll; Northwest Coll
Wireless access
Open Mon, Tues & Fri 12-5, Wed & Thurs 12-6, Sat 10-5
Friends of the Library Group

CHARLESTON

C UNIVERSITY OF OREGON*, Loyd & Dorothy Rippey Library, Institute of Marine Biology, 63466 Boat Basin Dr, 97420-1221. (Mail add: PO Box 5389, 97420-0605). Tel: 541-888-2581, Ext 219. E-mail: oimbref@uoregon.edu. Web Site: library.uoregon.edu. *Librn,* Barbara Butler; E-mail: butler@uoregon.edu
Library Holdings: Bk Vols 6,000; Per Subs 60
Wireless access
Open Mon-Thurs 8-4

CLACKAMAS

M KAISER PERMANENTE NORTHWEST REGIONAL*, Health Sciences Library, Kaiser Sunnyside Medical Ctr, 10180 SE Sunnyside Road, 97015. Tel: 503-571-4293. Interlibrary Loan Service Tel: 503-571-4165. FAX: 503-571-4291. *Mgr,* Ann H Haines; E-mail: ann.h.haines@kp.org; Staff 3 (MLS 1, Non-MLS 2)
Founded 1975
Library Holdings: Bk Titles 1,000; Per Subs 225
Special Collections: Consumer Health Coll
Subject Interests: Med, Nursing
Automation Activity & Vendor Info: (OPAC) Innovative Interfaces, Inc
Database Vendor: American Psychological Association (APA), Cinahl, DynaMed, EBSCOhost, Natural Standard, OVID Technologies, ProQuest
Wireless access
Partic in Oregon Health Sciences Libraries Association
Open Mon-Thurs 7-4:30, Fri 7:30-4

CLATSKANIE

P CLATSKANIE LIBRARY DISTRICT*, 11 Lillich St, 97016. (Mail add: PO Box 577, 97016-0577), SAN 314-0695. Tel: 503-728-3732. E-mail: clpublic@clatskanie.com. Web Site: www.clatskanie.com. *Dir,* Elizabeth A Kruse; Staff 1 (Non-MLS 1)
Pop 3,190; Circ 23,801
Jul 2005-Jun 2006 Income $134,366. Mats Exp $31,504, Books $7,718. Sal $64,062
Library Holdings: Bk Vols 23,801; Per Subs 38
Subject Interests: Columbia County hist
Automation Activity & Vendor Info: (Cataloging) SirsiDynix; (Circulation) SirsiDynix; (ILL) OCLC
Wireless access
Open Mon-Wed 10-7, Thurs-Sat 10-5:30
Friends of the Library Group

CONDON

P GILLIAM COUNTY LIBRARY*, 310 S Main, 97823. (Mail add: PO Box 34, 97823-0034), SAN 357-8674. Tel: 541-384-6052. FAX: 541-384-6052. *Dir,* Mary Geser
Circ 5,905
Library Holdings: Bk Vols 10,000; Per Subs 15
Automation Activity & Vendor Info: (Cataloging) Follett Software; (Circulation) Follett Software; (OPAC) Follett Software
Open Mon-Fri 12-4

COOS BAY

P COOS BAY PUBLIC LIBRARY*, 525 Anderson St, 97420-1678. SAN 314-0717. Tel: 541-269-1101. FAX: 541-269-7567. Web Site: bay.cooslibraries.org, www.cooslibraries.org. *Dir,* Sami Pierson; E-mail: spierson@cclsd.org; *Asst Dir,* Ellen Thompson; E-mail: ethompson@cclsd.org; *Acq,* Ann Couture; *Ch Serv,* Patricia Flitcroft; Staff 6 (MLS 3, Non-MLS 3)
Founded 1910. Pop 24,164; Circ 343,485
Jul 2008-Jun 2009 Income $1,068,194, State $4,218, Locally Generated Income $866,082, Other $197,894. Mats Exp $134,332, Books $91,580, Per/Ser (Incl. Access Fees) $12,942, Micro $210, AV Mat $26,400, Electronic Ref Mat (Incl. Access Fees) $3,200. Sal $516,072
Library Holdings: AV Mats 15,463; Bk Vols 117,749; Per Subs 254
Special Collections: Oregon History (Helene Stack Bower Oregon Coll). Oral History
Automation Activity & Vendor Info: (Cataloging) Innovative Interfaces, Inc; (Circulation) Innovative Interfaces, Inc; (OPAC) Innovative Interfaces, Inc; (Serials) Innovative Interfaces, Inc
Database Vendor: 3M Library Systems, EBSCOhost, Ingram Library Services, Innovative Interfaces, Inc, ProQuest
Wireless access
Mem of Coos County Library Service District
Partic in Southern Oregon Library Federation
Open Mon-Thurs 10-7, Fri & Sat 12-6
Friends of the Library Group

P COOS COUNTY LIBRARY SERVICE DISTRICT*, Tioga Hall, 1988 Newmark Ave, 97420. SAN 322-4279. Tel: 541-888-1529. FAX: 541-888-1529. Web Site: www.cooslibraries.org. *Dir,* Mary Jane Fisher; Tel: 541-888-7393, E-mail: mjfisher@socc.edu; *Outreach Serv Librn,* Irene Luoto; Tel: 541-888-7273, E-mail: iluoto@socc.edu; *Network Adminr,* Sean Park; Tel: 541-888-7459, E-mail: spark@cclsd.org
Founded 1980
Member Libraries: Bandon Public Library; Coos Bay Public Library; Coquille Public Library; Dora Public Library; Hazel M Lewis Library; Lakeside Public Library; Myrtle Point Library; North Bend Public Library

J SOUTHWESTERN OREGON COMMUNITY COLLEGE LIBRARY*, 1988 Newmark Ave, 97420-2956. SAN 314-0725. Tel: 541-888-7431. Circulation Tel: 541-888-7270. Interlibrary Loan Service Tel: 541-888-7262. Reference Tel: 541-888-7448. FAX: 541-888-7605. Web Site: www.socc.edu/library. *Dir,* Sharon Smith; E-mail: ssmith@socc.edu; *Libr Tech,* Mike Cole; Tel: 541-888-7429, E-mail: mcole@socc.edu; Staff 2 (MLS 2)
Founded 1962. Highest Degree: Associate
Library Holdings: Bks on Deafness & Sign Lang 40; Bk Titles 35,220; Bk Vols 39,626; Per Subs 219
Automation Activity & Vendor Info: (Cataloging) Innovative Interfaces, Inc; (Circulation) Innovative Interfaces, Inc; (Course Reserve) Innovative Interfaces, Inc; (ILL) OCLC; (OPAC) Innovative Interfaces, Inc
Database Vendor: CredoReference, EBSCOhost, Facts on File, Gale Cengage Learning
Wireless access
Partic in Coastline; OCLC Online Computer Library Center, Inc; Southern Oregon Library Federation
Open Mon-Thurs 9-6, Fri 9-4, Sun 1-5

COQUILLE

P COQUILLE PUBLIC LIBRARY*, 105 N Birch St, 97423-1299. SAN 314-0733. Tel: 541-396-2166. FAX: 541-396-2174. Web Site: www.cityofcoquille.org. *Dir,* Anne Conner; *Cat,* Mary Graham; *Ch Serv,* Sherri Erwin; Staff 2 (MLS 1, Non-MLS 1)
Pop 6,500; Circ 88,201
Jul 2009-Jun 2010 Income $293,250. Mats Exp $45,750. Sal $234,000
Library Holdings: Bk Titles 35,082; Per Subs 96

Automation Activity & Vendor Info: (Cataloging) Innovative Interfaces, Inc; (Circulation) Innovative Interfaces, Inc; (OPAC) Innovative Interfaces, Inc
Wireless access
Mem of Coos County Library Service District
Open Mon-Thurs 10-6, Fri 10-5, Sat 12-5
Friends of the Library Group

CORNELIUS

P CORNELIUS PUBLIC LIBRARY*, 1355 N Barlow St, 97113-8912. SAN 314-075X. Tel: 503-992-5307. FAX: 503-357-7775. E-mail: library@ci.cornelius.or.us. Web Site: www.ci.cornelius.or.us. *Dir,* Stephanie Lind; Staff 4 (MLS 1, Non-MLS 3)
Founded 1913. Pop 10,000; Circ 40,000
Library Holdings: Bk Vols 21,230; Per Subs 49
Special Collections: Educational CD-ROMs
Subject Interests: Spanish
Automation Activity & Vendor Info: (Cataloging) Innovative Interfaces, Inc; (Circulation) Innovative Interfaces, Inc; (OPAC) Innovative Interfaces, Inc
Partic in Washington County Cooperative Library Services
Open Mon-Thurs 12-8, Fri & Sat 10-5
Friends of the Library Group

CORVALLIS

L BENTON COUNTY LAW LIBRARY, 559 NW Monroe Ave, 97330. (Mail add: Sunset Bldg, 4077 SW Research Way, 97333), SAN 373-6652. Tel: 541-766-6673. FAX: 541-766-6893. *Librn,* Martha A Jenkins; E-mail: martha.a.jenkins@co.benton.or.us; Staff 1 (MLS 1)
Jul 2014-Jun 2015 Income $55,000. Mats Exp $26,000
Library Holdings: Bk Titles 255; Bk Vols 5,797
Function: Res libr
Restriction: Pub use on premises

S CH2M HILL*, Engineering Information Center Library, 2300 NW Walnut Blvd, 97330-3596. (Mail add: PO Box 428, 97339-0428), SAN 321-5172. Tel: 541-752-4271, Ext 3652. FAX: 541-752-0276. *Librn,* Shirley Drake; E-mail: sdrake@ch2m.com; *Librn,* Suzanne Robb; Tel: 208-345-5310, Ext 26222
Founded 1946
Library Holdings: Bk Vols 12,110; Per Subs 250
Restriction: Staff use only

P CORVALLIS-BENTON COUNTY PUBLIC LIBRARY*, 645 NW Monroe Ave, 97330. SAN 357-8739. Tel: 541-766-6926. Reference Tel: 541-766-6793. Administration Tel: 541-766-6928. Reference FAX: 541-766-6726. Administration FAX: 541-766-6915. TDD: 541-766-6988. Web Site: www.library.ci.corvalis.or.us/corvalis/default.asp. *Dir,* Carolyn Rawles-Heiser; Tel: 541-766-6910; *Head, Access Serv,* Felicia Uhden; Tel: 541-766-6997; *Head, Adult Serv,* Mary Finnegan; Tel: 541-766-6993; *Youth Serv Mgr,* Curtis Kiefer; Tel: 541-766-6962; Staff 46 (MLS 19, Non-MLS 27)
Founded 1899. Pop 84,000; Circ 1,594,973
Library Holdings: Bk Titles 221,092; Bk Vols 370,055; Per Subs 1,072
Automation Activity & Vendor Info: (Cataloging) TLC (The Library Corporation); (Circulation) TLC (The Library Corporation); (OPAC) TLC (The Library Corporation)
Database Vendor: EBSCOhost, Gale Cengage Learning, LexisNexis, OCLC FirstSearch, SirsiDynix, Wilson - Wilson Web
Wireless access
Function: Adult bk club
Open Mon-Fri 10-9, Sat 10-6, Sun 12-6
Friends of the Library Group
Branches: 3
ALSEA COMMUNITY LIBRARY, 19192 Alsea Hwy, Alsea, 97324, SAN 357-8798. Tel: 541-487-5061. FAX: 541-487-5061. *Librn,* Mary Rounds
Open Mon, Wed & Sat 10-4:30, Tues & Thurs 2-8
Friends of the Library Group
MONROE COMMUNITY LIBRARY, 668 Commercial St, Monroe, 97456, SAN 314-1284. Tel: 541-847-5174. FAX: 541-847-5174. *Br Mgr,* Lori Pelkey; E-mail: lori.pelkey@ci.corvallis.or.us
Open Mon 1:30-4:30, Tues & Thurs 10-4:30, Wed 3-8, Sat 10-3
Friends of the Library Group
PHILOMATH COMMUNITY LIBRARY, 1050 Applegate St, Philomath, 97370. (Mail add: PO Box 400, Philomath, 97370-0569), SAN 325-3953. Tel: 541-929-3016. FAX: 541-929-5934. *Asst Dir,* Teresa Landers; Tel: 541-766-6995, E-mail: teresa.landers@ci.corvallis.or.us
Open Mon & Thurs-Sat 10-5, Tues & Wed 10-8
Friends of the Library Group
Bookmobiles: 1. Librn, Linda Kahlbaum

M GOOD SAMARITAN REGIONAL MEDICAL CENTER*, Murray Memorial Library, 3600 NW Samaritan Dr, 97330. SAN 371-8557. Tel: 541-768-6200. Administration Tel: 541-768-4899. FAX: 541-768-5087. E-mail: info@samlib.com, samlib5@gmail.com. Web Site: www.samlib.com. *Mgr, Libr Serv,* Kenneth H Willer; E-mail: kwiller@samhealth.org; *Librn,* Stefani Sackinger; E-mail: ssackinger@samhealth.org; Staff 2 (MLS 1, Non-MLS 1)
Founded 1976
Library Holdings: e-books 90; e-journals 270; Bk Titles 1,100; Per Subs 110
Subject Interests: Med
Automation Activity & Vendor Info: (OPAC) LibraryWorld, Inc
Wireless access
Function: Health sci info serv
Partic in Docline; Oregon Health Sciences Libraries Association
Open Mon-Fri 8:30-5
Restriction: Open to pub for ref & circ; with some limitations

C OREGON STATE UNIVERSITY LIBRARIES*, The Valley Library, 121 The Valley Library, 97331-4501. SAN 314-0792. Tel: 541-737-3331. Circulation Tel: 541-737-2538. Interlibrary Loan Service Tel: 541-737-4488. Reference Tel: 541-737-7295. Administration Tel: 541-737-4633. FAX: 541-737-3453. Circulation FAX: 541-737-1328. Reference FAX: 541-737-8224. TDD: 541-737-4594. E-mail: library.web@oregonstate.edu. Web Site: osulibrary.oregonstate.edu. *Univ Librn/OSU Press Dir,* Faye Chadwell; E-mail: faye.chadwell@oregonstate.edu; *Assoc Univ Librn, Learning & Engagement,* Cheryl Middleton; Tel: 541-737-4667, E-mail: cheryl.middleton@oregonstate.edu; *Assoc Univ Librn, Res & Scholarly Communication,* Shan Sutton; Tel: 541-908-1655, E-mail: shan.sutton@oregonstate.edu; *Head, Emerging Tech & Serv,* Evviva Weinraub; Tel: 541-737-2458, E-mail: evviva.weinraub@oregonstate.edu; *Head, Guin & Cascades Campus Libr,* Janet Webster; Tel: 541-867-0108, Fax: 541-867-0105, E-mail: janet.webster@oregonstate.edu; *Head, Tech Serv,* Michael Boock; Tel: 541-737-9155, Fax: 541-737-8267, E-mail: michael.boock@oregonstate.edu; *Head, Univ Archives,* Larry Landis; Tel: 541-737-0540, Fax: 541-737-0541, E-mail: larry.landis@oregonstate.edu; Staff 44 (MLS 32, Non-MLS 12)
Founded 1887. Enrl 23,507; Fac 44; Highest Degree: Doctorate
Jul 2009-Jun 2010. Mats Exp $10,164,539. Sal $4,116,389 (Prof $2,407,679)
Library Holdings: AV Mats 43,000; e-journals 33,080; Microforms 2,220,487; Bk Vols 1,620,937; Per Subs 38,748
Special Collections: Ava Helen & Linus Pauling Coll; Northwest Coll. US Document Depository
Subject Interests: Agr, Environ studies, Forestry, Natural sci, Oceanography
Automation Activity & Vendor Info: (Acquisitions) Innovative Interfaces, Inc; (Cataloging) Innovative Interfaces, Inc; (Circulation) Innovative Interfaces, Inc; (Course Reserve) Innovative Interfaces, Inc; (ILL) OCLC; (OPAC) Innovative Interfaces, Inc; (Serials) Innovative Interfaces, Inc
Database Vendor: ABC-CLIO, ACM (Association for Computing Machinery), Agricola, American Chemical Society, American Mathematical Society, Annual Reviews, ASCE Research Library, BCR: Christian Periodical Index, BioOne, Blackwell, Cambridge Scientific Abstracts, Children's Literature Comprehensive Database Company (CLCD), Cinahl, CIOS (Communication Institute for Online Scholarship), CISTI Source, College Source, Dialog, EBSCOhost, Elsevier, H W Wilson, Haworth Pres Inc, IEEE (Institute of Electrical & Electronics Engineers), IHS, Innovative Interfaces, Inc, IOP, ISI Web of Knowledge, JSTOR, LexisNexis, Marcive, Inc, Medline, Micromedex, Modern Language Association, Nature Publishing Group, Newsbank, OCLC ArticleFirst, OCLC FirstSearch, OCLC WorldShare Interlibrary Loan, OCLC-RLG, OVID Technologies, Project MUSE, ProQuest, PubMed, ReferenceUSA, ScienceDirect, SerialsSolutions, Springer-Verlag, Standard & Poor's, STN International, Swets Information Services, Thomson - Web of Science, ValueLine, Wiley, Wilson - Wilson Web
Wireless access
Function: Archival coll, Doc delivery serv, ILL available, Libr develop, Online searches, Photocopying/Printing, Ref serv available, Res libr
Publications: Library Messenger (Newsletter)
Partic in Greater Western Library Alliance; Orbis Cascade Alliance
Open Mon-Sun 10-10
Restriction: Open to pub for ref & circ; with some limitations
Friends of the Library Group
Departmental Libraries:
UNIVERSITY ARCHIVES & SPECIAL COLLECTIONS, 121 Valley Library, 97331-4501. Tel: 541-737-2165. FAX: 541-737-3453. E-mail: archives@oregonstate.edu. Web Site: osulibrary.oregonstate.edu/archives. *Head, Archives & Spec Coll,* Larry A Landis; Tel: 541-737-0540, E-mail: larry.landis@oregonstate.edu; *Hist of Sci Librn/Curator,* Anne Bahde; *Multicultural Librn,* Natalia Fernandez; Tel: 541-737-2195, E-mail: natalia.fernandez@oregonstate.edu; *Sr Archivist,* Elizabeth A Nielsen; Tel: 541-737-0543, E-mail: elizabeth.nielsen@oregonstate.edu; *Archivist,* Tiah K Edmunson-Morton; Tel: 541-737-7387, E-mail:

tiah.edmunson-morton@oregonstate.edu; *Archivist,* Karl R McCreary; Tel: 541-737-0539, E-mail: karl.mccreary@oregonstate.edu; *Info Tech,* Ryan Wick; Tel: 541-737-2075, E-mail: ryan.wick@oregonstate.edu; *Libr Tech,* Trevor Sandgathe; E-mail: trevor.sandgathe@oregonstate.edu; *Res Asst,* Chris Petersen; Tel: 541-737-2810
Open Mon-Fri 9-5

G US ENVIRONMENTAL PROTECTION AGENCY, ORD/NHEERL/Western Ecology Division Library, 200 SW 35th St, 97333. SAN 314-0768. Tel: 541-754-4731. FAX: 541-754-4799. *Librn,* Mary C O'Brien; E-mail: obrien.mary@epamail.epa.gov; Staff 1 (MLS 1)
Founded 1966
Library Holdings: Bk Titles 7,000; Bk Vols 8,000; Per Subs 30
Subject Interests: Environ monitoring & assessment, Global climate change, Habitat res, Modeling wildlife populations, Monitoring freshwater ecosystems, Pesticide res
Automation Activity & Vendor Info: (Cataloging) OCLC; (ILL) OCLC
Database Vendor: BioOne, JSTOR
Function: For res purposes, ILL available, Mail & tel request accepted
Partic in EPA National Libr Network
Restriction: Borrowing requests are handled by ILL, Circulates for staff only, Staff use, pub by appt, Visitors must make appt to use bks in the libr

COTTAGE GROVE

P COTTAGE GROVE PUBLIC LIBRARY*, 700 E Gibbs Ave, 97424. SAN 314-0806. Tel: 541-942-3828. FAX: 541-942-1267. Web Site: library.cottagegrove.org. *Dir,* Pete Barrell; Staff 4 (MLS 1, Non-MLS 3)
Founded 2000. Pop 9,010; Circ 86,997
Library Holdings: Bk Titles 42,098; Per Subs 51; Talking Bks 1,483; Videos 2,030
Special Collections: Oregon Coll
Automation Activity & Vendor Info: (Cataloging) SirsiDynix; (Circulation) SirsiDynix; (OPAC) SirsiDynix
Wireless access
Open Mon & Tues 10-8, Wed-Sat 10-6
Friends of the Library Group

COVE

S COVE LIBRARY*, 606 Main, 97824. (Mail add: 1005 Haefer Lane, 97824-8723). Tel: 541-568-4758, 541-568-5001. *Learning Res Ctr Adminr,* Yvonne Oliver
Founded 1903
Jul 2008-Jun 2009 Income $3,000, County $2,000, Locally Generated Income $300. Mats Exp $600, Books $200, Electronic Ref Mat (Incl. Access Fees) $400
Library Holdings: Audiobooks 80; Bks-By-Mail 3; Bks on Deafness & Sign Lang 3; CDs 40; DVDs 60; High Interest/Low Vocabulary Bk Vols 43; Large Print Bks 32; Bk Titles 3,700; Talking Bks 76; Videos 161
Special Collections: Oregon History Coll. Municipal Document Depository; Oral History; State Document Depository; US Document Depository
Automation Activity & Vendor Info: (Acquisitions) A-G Canada Ltd
Partic in Sage Library System of Eastern Oregon
Special Services for the Deaf - Bks on deafness & sign lang
Special Services for the Blind - Assistive/Adapted tech devices, equip & products; Talking bks
Open Tues & Thurs 10-6

CRESWELL

P LANE LIBRARY DISTRICT*, Creswell Library, 64 W Oregon Ave, 97426. (Mail add: PO Box 366, 97426-0366). Tel: 541-895-3053. FAX: 541-895-3507. *Dir,* Su Liudahl; Staff 3 (MLS 2, Non-MLS 1)
Founded 2004. Pop 8,000; Circ 60,223
Library Holdings: Bk Vols 31,000; Per Subs 54
Automation Activity & Vendor Info: (Acquisitions) SIRSI WorkFlows; (Cataloging) SirsiDynix; (Circulation) SIRSI WorkFlows; (ILL) SIRSI WorkFlows; (OPAC) SIRSI WorkFlows
Database Vendor: EBSCO Auto Repair Reference, EBSCOhost, ProQuest
Wireless access
Function: Adult bk club, Art exhibits, Audiobks via web, Bilingual assistance for Spanish patrons, Bks on cassette, Bks on CD, Children's prog, Computers for patron use, Copy machines, Electronic databases & coll, Free DVD rentals, Genealogy discussion group, Handicapped accessible, Holiday prog, Home delivery & serv to Sr ctr & nursing homes, Homebound delivery serv, ILL available, Mail & tel request accepted, Music CDs, Online cat, OverDrive digital audio bks, Photocopying/Printing, Preschool outreach, Prog for adults, Prog for children & young adult, Pub access computers, Ref serv available, Story hour, Summer reading prog, Tax forms, Teen prog, VHS videos, Video lending libr, Web-catalog, Wheelchair accessible
Special Services for the Blind - Audio mat; Bks on cassette; Bks on CD; Large print bks; Large type calculator

Open Mon & Fri 12-6, Tues-Thurs 10-7, Sat 10-4
Restriction: Borrowing requests are handled by ILL
Friends of the Library Group

DALLAS

P DALLAS PUBLIC LIBRARY*, 950 Main St, 97338-2802. SAN 314-0822. Tel: 503-623-2633. FAX: 503-623-7357. Web Site: www.ci.dallas.or.us/index.aspx?nid=102. *Lead Librn,* Rosalyn E McGarva; E-mail: rosalyn.mcgarva@dallasor.gov; Staff 7 (MLS 1, Non-MLS 6)
Founded 1905. Pop 18,500; Circ 189,500
Library Holdings: Bk Titles 68,000; Per Subs 135
Subject Interests: Ore hist
Automation Activity & Vendor Info: (Cataloging) Innovative Interfaces, Inc - Millenium; (Circulation) Innovative Interfaces, Inc - Millenium; (OPAC) Innovative Interfaces, Inc - Millenium
Database Vendor: Gale Cengage Learning
Wireless access
Partic in Chemeketa Cooperative Regional Library Service
Open Mon, Thurs & Fri 11-5, Tues & Wed 11-3
Friends of the Library Group

DAYTON

P MARY GILKEY CITY LIBRARY*, 416 Ferry St, 97114-9774. (Mail add: PO Box 339, 97114-0339), SAN 329-7586. Tel: 503-864-2221. FAX: 503-864-2956. *Librn,* Debra Lien; E-mail: debralien@ci.dayton.or.us
Founded 1923. Pop 2,495
Library Holdings: Bk Vols 11,000; Per Subs 10
Automation Activity & Vendor Info: (Cataloging) Innovative Interfaces, Inc; (Circulation) Innovative Interfaces, Inc; (OPAC) Innovative Interfaces, Inc
Partic in Chemeketa Cooperative Regional Library Service
Open Mon 9-7, Tues-Fri 9-5
Friends of the Library Group

DEXTER

S CASCADE FOOTHILLS LIBRARY*, 39095 Dexter Rd, 97431. (Mail add: PO Box 12, 97431-0012). Tel: 541-937-2625. E-mail: cfllib@epud.net. *Dir,* Candy Lanfear
Mar 2005-Feb 2006 Income $7,500
Library Holdings: Audiobooks 200; CDs 50; DVDs 100; Large Print Bks 200; Bk Vols 8,000; Videos 60
Wireless access
Function: CD-ROM, Handicapped accessible, Home delivery & serv to Sr ctr & nursing homes, Homebound delivery serv, Homework prog, Prog for adults, Prog for children & young adult, Spoken cassettes & CDs, Spoken cassettes & DVDs, Summer reading prog, VHS videos, Video lending libr, Workshops
Open Mon 2-6, Wed 1-6, Thurs & Fri 10-4, Sat 10-2
Restriction: Private libr
Friends of the Library Group

DUFUR

P DUFUR SCHOOL-COMMUNITY LIBRARY*, 802 NE Fifth St, 97021-3034. Tel: 541-467-2588. FAX: 541-467-2589. Web Site: www.dufur.k12.or.us. *Librn,* Louise Walkowiak; E-mail: lwalk@dufur.k12.or.us
Pop 1,887
Library Holdings: Bk Vols 21,000
Open Mon & Wed (Winter) 8-4, Tues & Thurs 8-4 & 6-8, Fri 8-3:30; Tues & Thurs (Summer) 10-12, 1-3 & 6-8

ECHO

P ECHO PUBLIC LIBRARY*, 20 S Bonanza, 97826. (Mail add: PO Box 9, 97826-0009), SAN 358-0539. Tel: 541-376-8411. FAX: 541-376-8218. E-mail: ecpl@centurytel.net. Web Site: www.echo-oregon.com. *Dir,* Diane Berry; *Asst Librn,* Karen Beacham
Library Holdings: Bk Vols 12,000; Per Subs 20
Mem of Umatilla County Special Library District
Open Mon, Tues, Thurs & Fri 9-5, Wed 9-5 & 5:30-8:30

ELGIN

P ELGIN PUBLIC LIBRARY*, 1699 Division St, 97827. (Mail add: PO Box 67, 97827-0067), SAN 314-0830. Tel: 541-437-2860. FAX: 541-437-2860. *Dir,* Theresa Chandler; Staff 1 (Non-MLS 1)
Founded 1911. Pop 2,600
Library Holdings: Bk Vols 15,447
Special Collections: Northwest
Function: Computers for patron use, Handicapped accessible, Homebound delivery serv, ILL available, Magnifiers for reading, Mail & tel request

accepted, Music CDs, Prog for children & young adult, Spoken cassettes & CDs, Summer reading prog, Tax forms, VHS videos, Wheelchair accessible
Open Mon, Tues & Fri 1-6, Wed 2-8, Thurs 10-6

ENTERPRISE

P ENTERPRISE PUBLIC LIBRARY*, 101 NE First St, 97828-1173. SAN 314-0849. Tel: 541-426-3906. E-mail: enterpl@eoni.com. *Librn,* Denine Rautenstrauch
Founded 1911. Pop 3,199; Circ 20,000
Library Holdings: Bk Vols 15,000; Per Subs 57
Automation Activity & Vendor Info: (Cataloging) Follett Software; (Circulation) Follett Software
Open Mon & Fri 12-6, Tues-Thurs 10-6, Sat 10-2

P WALLOWA COUNTY LIBRARY, 207 NW Logan, 97828-0186. SAN 314-0857. Tel: 541-426-3969. FAX: 541-426-3969. Interlibrary Loan Service E-mail: wclib@eoni.com. Web Site: www.co.wallowa.or.us/library. *Dir,* Susan Polumsky; Staff 1 (Non-MLS 1)
Founded 1964. Pop 3,140; Circ 6,633
Library Holdings: Bks on Deafness & Sign Lang 22; Bk Vols 21,000
Subject Interests: Local hist, Nez Perce Indians, Ore hist, Pac NW hist
Restriction: Pub access by telephone only
Branches: 2
IMNAHA STATION, Imnaha Hwy, Imnaha, 97842. Tel: 541-577-2308. *Librn,* Mellica McIntire
Library Holdings: Bk Vols 2,000
Open Tues & Thurs 12-4
TROY LIBRARY STATION, 66247 Redmond Grade, 97828. Tel: 541-828-7788. FAX: 541-828-7748. *Librn,* Jane Curry
Library Holdings: AV Mats 1,500; Bk Vols 1,800
Open Mon-Thurs (Winter) 3:30-4:30, Sun 11-3; Mon-Wed (Summer) 3:30-4:30, Thurs 8-4, Sun 11-3
Bookmobiles: 2

ESTACADA

P ESTACADA PUBLIC LIBRARY*, 825 NW Wade St, 97023. SAN 314-0865. Tel: 503-630-8273. FAX: 503-630-8282. Web Site: www.estacada.lib.or.us. *Dir,* Anna Stavinoha; E-mail: esref@lincc.org; *Librn,* Michele Kinnamon; E-mail: michelek@lincc.org; *Youth Serv Librn,* Jennifer Fleenor; *Circ Mgr,* Sarah Hibbert; *Per,* Laurie Ellicott; Staff 6.5 (MLS 1.5, Non-MLS 5)
Founded 1904. Pop 18,000; Circ 301,754
Jul 2007-Jun 2008 Income $350,000, City $6,000, County $315,000, Locally Generated Income $11,500. Mats Exp $60,000. Sal $200,000 (Prof $85,000)
Library Holdings: AV Mats 16,384; CDs 5,838; DVDs 3,285; Large Print Bks 734; Bk Vols 59,242; Per Subs 223; Talking Bks 2,538; Videos 3,552
Special Collections: Estacada History
Automation Activity & Vendor Info: (Acquisitions) SirsiDynix; (Cataloging) SirsiDynix; (Circulation) SirsiDynix; (ILL) OCLC; (OPAC) SirsiDynix
Database Vendor: EBSCOhost, Newsbank
Wireless access
Function: Audiobks via web, Bks on cassette, Bks on CD, Children's prog, Computers for patron use, Copy machines, Electronic databases & coll, Free DVD rentals, ILL available, Magnifiers for reading, Mail & tel request accepted, Mus passes, Music CDs, Online cat, Online ref, Online searches, Outside serv via phone, mail, e-mail & web, OverDrive digital audio bks, Photocopying/Printing, Prog for children & young adult, Ref & res, Ref serv available, Summer reading prog, Tax forms, Teen prog, Telephone ref, VHS videos
Partic in Library Information Network of Clackamas County
Open Mon-Thurs 9-8, Fri-Sun 10-5

EUGENE

P EUGENE PUBLIC LIBRARY*, 100 W Tenth Ave, 97401. SAN 314-0881. Tel: 541-682-5450. FAX: 541-682-5898. Web Site: www.eugene-or.gov/library. *Libr Serv Dir,* Connie J Bennett; *Adult Serv Mgr,* Nancy Horner; *Br Serv Mgr,* Angie Bray; *Circ Mgr,* Maresa Kirk; *Customer Experience Mgr,* LaVena Nohrenberg; *Tech Serv Mgr,* Kristynn Johnson; *Virtual Br & Tech Innovation Mgr,* Margaret Hazel; Staff 99.2 (MLS 18.4, Non-MLS 80.8)
Founded 1904. Pop 156,295; Circ 3,000,000
Jul 2011-Jun 2012 Income (Main Library and Branch(s)) $12,056,330, State $17,226, City $10,267,874, Federal $60,585, Other $1,710,645. Mats Exp $837,328, Books $458,109, Per/Ser (Incl. Access Fees) $37,593, AV Mat $195,449, Electronic Ref Mat (Incl. Access Fees) $146,777. Sal $7,387,935
Library Holdings: AV Mats 89,066; e-books 30,444; Electronic Media & Resources 20,552; Bk Titles 401,616; Per Subs 398
Special Collections: State Document Depository
Automation Activity & Vendor Info: (Acquisitions) Innovative Interfaces, Inc; (Cataloging) Innovative Interfaces, Inc; (Circulation) Innovative Interfaces, Inc; (OPAC) Innovative Interfaces, Inc
Database Vendor: ABC-CLIO, Alexander Street Press, ALLDATA Online, Booklist Online, CQ Press, EBSCOhost, Facts on File, Foundation Center, Gale Cengage Learning, infoUSA, LearningExpress, Newsbank, P4 Performance Management, Inc, ReferenceUSA, Safari Books Online, TumbleBookLibrary
Wireless access
Special Services for the Deaf - ADA equip; Assisted listening device; Assistive tech; Coll on deaf educ; Sign lang interpreter upon request for prog; Staff with knowledge of sign lang; Video relay serv
Special Services for the Blind - Accessible computers; Assistive/Adapted tech devices, equip & products; Bks on CD; Braille equip; Braille paper; Digital talking bk; Extensive large print coll; Home delivery serv; Internet workstation with adaptive software; Large screen computer & software; Large type calculator; Low vision equip; Magnifiers; Multimedia ref serv (large print, Braille using CD-ROM tech); Networked computers with assistive software; PC for handicapped; Rental typewriters & computers; Screen enlargement software for people with visual disabilities; Screen reader software; Text reader; ZoomText magnification & reading software
Open Mon-Thurs 10-8, Fri-Sun 10-6
Friends of the Library Group
Branches: 2
BETHEL BRANCH, 1990 Echo Hollow Rd, 97402-7004. Tel: 541-682-5450. FAX: 541-682-5898. *Br Mgr,* Angela Bray; Staff 6.4 (MLS 0.5, Non-MLS 5.9)
Founded 2000
Special Services for the Deaf - ADA equip; Assistive tech; Bks on deafness & sign lang; Sign lang interpreter upon request for prog
Special Services for the Blind - ABE/GED & braille classes for the visually impaired & print handicapped; Assistive/Adapted tech devices, equip & products; Bks on CD; Digital talking bk; Internet workstation with adaptive software; Large print bks; Screen enlargement software for people with visual disabilities; ZoomText magnification & reading software
Open Tues-Thurs 2-6, Fri & Sat 11-6
SHELDON BRANCH, 1566 Coburg Rd, 97401-4802. Tel: 541-682-5450. FAX: 541-682-5898. *Br Mgr,* Angela Bray; Staff 6.3 (MLS 0.5, Non-MLS 5.8)
Founded 2000
Special Services for the Deaf - ADA equip; Assistive tech; Bks on deafness & sign lang; Sign lang interpreter upon request for prog
Special Services for the Blind - Assistive/Adapted tech devices, equip & products; Bks on CD; Digital talking bk; Internet workstation with adaptive software; Large print bks; Screen enlargement software for people with visual disabilities; ZoomText magnification & reading software
Open Tues-Thurs 2-6, Fri & Sat 11-6

C GUTENBERG COLLEGE, McKenzie Study Center, 1883 University St, 97403. Tel: 541-683-5141. FAX: 541-683-6997. E-mail: office@gutenberg.edu. Web Site: gutenberg.edu. *Supvr,* Ron Julian
Library Holdings: Bk Vols 2,600
Open Mon-Fri 8:30-Midnight

J LANE COMMUNITY COLLEGE LIBRARY*, 4000 E 30th Ave, 97405-0640. SAN 314-0903. Tel: 541-463-5220. Circulation Tel: 541-463-5273. Interlibrary Loan Service Tel: 541-463-3168. Reference Tel: 541-463-5355. Administration Tel: 541-463-5770. FAX: 541-463-4150. E-mail: library@lanecc.edu. Web Site: www.lanecc.edu/library. *Interim Dir,* Marika Pineda; E-mail: pinedam@lanecc.edu; *Ref Serv,* David Doctor; Tel: 541-463-5278, E-mail: doctord@lanecc.edu; *Ref Serv,* Jen Ferro; Tel: 541-463-5825, E-mail: ferroj@lanecc.edu; *Ref Serv,* Jen Klaudinyi; Tel: 541-463-5357, E-mail: klaudinyij@lanecc.edu; *Ref Serv,* Don Macnaughtan; Tel: 541-463-5359, E-mail: macnaughtand@lanecc.edu; Staff 5 (MLS 5)
Founded 1964. Enrl 29,743; Fac 585; Highest Degree: Associate
Library Holdings: AV Mats 6,831; Bks on Deafness & Sign Lang 48; e-books 1,311; e-journals 10; High Interest/Low Vocabulary Bk Vols 77; Bk Titles 58,771; Bk Vols 66,846; Per Subs 5,250
Special Collections: English as a Second Language
Automation Activity & Vendor Info: (Acquisitions) Innovative Interfaces, Inc; (Cataloging) Innovative Interfaces, Inc; (Circulation) Innovative Interfaces, Inc; (Course Reserve) Innovative Interfaces, Inc; (OPAC) Innovative Interfaces, Inc; (Serials) Innovative Interfaces, Inc
Database Vendor: ARTstor, EBSCOhost, Gale Cengage Learning, ProQuest, SerialsSolutions, STN International
Wireless access
Function: Handicapped accessible, ILL available, Photocopying/Printing, Ref serv available
Publications: Eugene Register-Guard Index, 1970 to 1980 (Index to newspapers)
Partic in OCLC Online Computer Library Center, Inc; Orbis Cascade Alliance

Special Services for the Deaf - Bks on deafness & sign lang; Closed caption videos
Special Services for the Blind - Closed circuit TV; Computer with voice synthesizer for visually impaired persons
Open Mon-Thurs 7:30-7, Fri 7:30-5:30
Restriction: In-house use for visitors

GL LANE COUNTY LAW LIBRARY*, Lane County Public Service Bldg, 125 E Eighth Ave, 97401. SAN 314-0911. Tel: 541-682-4337. FAX: 541-682-4315. E-mail: LCLAWLIB@co.lane.or.us. Web Site: www.lanecounty.org/Departments/CAO/LawLibrary/pages/default.aspx. *Law Librn,* Neil Miller; E-mail: neil.miller@co.lane.or.us; Staff 2 (MLS 1, Non MLS 1)
Founded 1948
Library Holdings: Bk Vols 19,200; Per Subs 10
Special Collections: Oregon Law
Automation Activity & Vendor Info: (Cataloging) LibraryWorld, Inc
Database Vendor: LexisNexis, Westlaw
Publications: Lane County Law Library Newsletter (Quarterly)
Open Mon-Fri 8-5

CR NEW HOPE CHRISTIAN COLLEGE, Flint Memorial Library, 2155 Bailey Hill Rd, 97405. SAN 314-0873. Tel: 541-485-1780, Ext 3309. FAX: 541-343-5801. E-mail: library@newhope.edu. Web Site: www.newhope.edu/library. *Libr Dir,* Jan Kelley; E-mail: jankelley@newhope.edu; Staff 1 (MLS 1)
Founded 1925. Enrl 200; Fac 18; Highest Degree: Bachelor
Jul 2014-Jun 2015. Mats Exp $33,300, Books $13,000, Per/Ser (Incl. Access Fees) $20,000, Presv $300. Sal $35,000
Library Holdings: AV Mats 1,500; e-books 1,179; Bk Titles 32,500; Bk Vols 35,000; Per Subs 50
Special Collections: Flint Coll
Automation Activity & Vendor Info: (Cataloging) EOS International; (Circulation) EOS International; (Course Reserve) EOS International; (ILL) OCLC WorldShare Interlibrary Loan; (OPAC) EOS International
Database Vendor: EBSCOhost, Gale Cengage Learning, LearningExpress
Wireless access
Open Mon-Thurs 8:30am-10pm, Fri 8:30-5, Sat 2-8, Sun 6pm-10pm

CR NORTHWEST CHRISTIAN UNIVERSITY*, Edward P Kellenberger Library, 1188 Kincade, 97401. (Mail add: 828 E 11th Ave, 97401), SAN 314-0938. Tel: 541-684-7235. Circulation Tel: 541-684-7233. Interlibrary Loan Service Tel: 541-684-7234. Reference Tel: 541-684-7278. Toll Free Tel: 877-463-6622. FAX: 541-684-7307. E-mail: libraryoffice@nwcu.edu. Web Site: www.nwcu.edu/library. *Dir,* Steve Silver; Tel: 541-684-7237, E-mail: ssilver@nwcu.edu; *Ref & Instruction Librn,* Scott Gallagher-Starr; E-mail: sgallagherstarr@nwcu.edu; *Supvr, Pub Serv,* Karen Head; E-mail: khead@nwcu.edu; *Tech Serv Supvr,* Debbie DuTell; Tel: 541-684-7246, E-mail: ddutell@nwcu.edu; Staff 4 (MLS 2, Non-MLS 2)
Founded 1895. Enrl 623; Fac 53; Highest Degree: Master
Library Holdings: AV Mats 11,147; Bk Vols 64,899; Per Subs 109
Special Collections: Christian Church History (Disciples of Christ, Disciplianа); Museum Coll of African, Asian & Northwest Pioneer Artifacts Archives; Museum Coll of English Bible (Bushnell Coll), rare bks & Bibles; William E. Paul English Bible Coll
Subject Interests: Biblical studies, Bus & mgt, Counseling, Teacher educ
Automation Activity & Vendor Info: (Acquisitions) Ex Libris Group; (Cataloging) Ex Libris Group; (Circulation) Ex Libris Group; (Course Reserve) Ex Libris Group; (ILL) OCLC; (OPAC) Ex Libris Group; (Serials) Ex Libris Group
Database Vendor: Annual Reviews, EBSCOhost, Gale Cengage Learning, LexisNexis, OCLC FirstSearch, OCLC WebJunction, OCLC WorldShare Interlibrary Loan, Oxford Online, WT Cox
Wireless access
Partic in Council for Christian Colleges & Universities; Northwest Association of Private Colleges & Universities (NAPCU); OCLC Online Computer Library Center, Inc; Online Private Academic Library Link (OPALL)
Open Mon-Thurs 8am-10pm, Fri 8-5, Sun 3-8
Friends of the Library Group

S OREGON RESEARCH INSTITUTE LIBRARY*, 1776 Millrace Dr, 97403-1983. SAN 325-8122. Tel: 541-484-2123. FAX: 541-484-1108. Web Site: www.ori.org. *Libr Mgr,* Amy Greenwold; E-mail: amy@ori.org; *Electronic Res Librn,* Elaine Shuman; E-mail: elaines@ori.org; Staff 2 (MLS 2)
Library Holdings: Bk Vols 5,000; Per Subs 85
Subject Interests: Adolescence, Behav sci, Chronic disease, Eating disorders, Psychol, Substance abuse, Tobacco cessation
Automation Activity & Vendor Info: (Cataloging) Inmagic, Inc.; (Circulation) Inmagic, Inc.; (OPAC) Inmagic, Inc.; (Serials) Inmagic, Inc.
Database Vendor: EBSCOhost, OCLC FirstSearch
Wireless access
Partic in Docline; OCLC Online Computer Library Center, Inc
Restriction: Open to staff only

C UNIVERSITY OF OREGON LIBRARIES*, Knight Library, 1501 Kincaid St, 97403-1299. (Mail add: 1299 University of Oregon, 97403-1299), SAN 357-8976. Tel: 541-346-3056. Circulation Tel: 541-346-3065. Interlibrary Loan Service Tel: 541-346-3055. Reference Tel: 541-346-1818. FAX: 541-346-3485. Web Site: www.libweb.uoregon.edu. *Dean of Libr,* Position Currently Open; *Assoc Univ Librn/Media & Instrul Serv,* Andrew R Bonamici; *Assoc Univ Librn, Res Serv,* Mark R Watson; *Dir, Res Mgt & Assessment,* Nancy Slight-Gibney; *Head, Access Serv,* Laura L Willey; *Head, Coll Serv,* Ann Miller; *Head, Doc Ctr,* Thomas A Stave; *Head, Ref & Res Serv,* Paul Frantz; *Head, Spec Coll & Archives,* James Fox; Staff 74 (MLS 52, Non-MLS 22)
Founded 1883. Enrl 21,507; Fac 1,209; Highest Degree: Doctorate
Jul 2009-Jun 2010 Income (Main and Other College/University Libraries) $21,624,941, Federal $217,171, Locally Generated Income $902,508, Parent Institution $19,232,009, Other $1,273,253. Mats Exp $6,224,006. Sal $8,050,987 (Prof $4,200,741)
Library Holdings: e-books 291,531; e-journals 70,866; Microforms 4,198,103; Bk Titles 1,932,872; Bk Vols 3,138,936; Per Subs 46,879
Special Collections: American History (The American West), ms; American Missions & Missionaries, ms; Children's Literature, Book & Magazine Illustrations, bks, ms; East Asian Literature & Art; Esperanto; Politics (20th Century American Politics, particularly Conservatism), ms; Zeppelins. Can & Prov; State Document Depository; UN Document Depository; US Document Depository
Subject Interests: Archit, Art, Law, Math, Music, Sci
Automation Activity & Vendor Info: (Acquisitions) Innovative Interfaces, Inc; (Cataloging) Innovative Interfaces, Inc; (Circulation) Innovative Interfaces, Inc; (Course Reserve) Innovative Interfaces, Inc; (ILL) OCLC ILLiad; (Media Booking) Innovative Interfaces, Inc; (OPAC) OCLC WorldShare Interlibrary Loan; (Serials) Innovative Interfaces, Inc
Wireless access
Partic in Association of Research Libraries (ARL); Center for Research Libraries; Coun of Libr Info Resources; Greater Western Library Alliance; OCLC Online Computer Library Center, Inc; Pacific Rim Digital Library Alliance (PRDLA)
Open Mon-Thurs 8am-Midnight, Fri 8-7, Sat 11-7, Sun 11am-Midnight

Departmental Libraries:

ARCHITECTURE & ALLIED ARTS, 200 Lawrence Hall, 97403, SAN 357-900X. Tel: 541-346-3637. FAX: 541-346-2205. *Head Librn,* Edward Teague; E-mail: ehteague@uoregon.edu; Staff 3 (MLS 3)
Founded 1915
Library Holdings: Bk Vols 52,000
Open Mon-Thurs 8am-11pm, Fri 8-7, Sat 11-7, Sun 11-11

CL JOHN E JAQUA LAW LIBRARY, William W Knight Law Ctr, 2nd Flr, 1515 Agate St, 97403-1221. (Mail add: 1221 University of Oregon, 270 Knight Law Ctr, 97403-1221), SAN 357-9093. Tel: 541-346-3088. FAX: 541-346-1669. Web Site: lawlibrary.uoregon.edu. *Dir,* Mary Ann Hyatt; Tel: 541-346-3097, E-mail: mahyatt@uoregon.edu; *Libr Mgr,* Dannie Helm; Tel: 541-346-8271, E-mail: dhelm@uoregon.edu; *Coll Librn,* Ilona Tsutsui; Tel: 541-346-1657, E-mail: itsutsui@uoregon.edu; *Ref Librn,* Jaye Barlous; Tel: 541-346-1901, E-mail: barlous@uoregon.edu; *Ref Librn,* Stephanie Midkiff; Tel: 541-346-1661, E-mail: smidkiff@uoregon.edu; *Ref Librn,* Angus Nesbit; Tel: 541-346-1673, E-mail: anesbit@law.uoregon.edu; *Tech Serv Librn,* Joni Herbst; Tel: 541-346-1655, E-mail: herbst@uoregon.edu; *Evening Coordr,* Ben Farrell; Tel: 541-346-1658, E-mail: bfarrell@uoregon.edu; *Ser Spec,* Elena Chertok; Tel: 541-346-1659, E-mail: echertok@uoregon.edu; *Acq Tech,* Lisa Levitt; Tel: 541-346-3802, E-mail: llevitt@uoregon.edu; *Metadata Serv Tech,* Diane Haas; Tel: 541-346-1656, E-mail: dkhaas@uoregon.edu; Staff 12 (MLS 6, Non-MLS 6)
Founded 1893
Library Holdings: e-books 32,533; e-journals 1,950; Bk Vols 206,065; Per Subs 2,264
Partic in Orbis Cascade Alliance
Open Mon-Thurs (Winter) 7:30am-Midnight, Fri 7:30am-9pm, Sat 9-9, Sun 9am-Midnight; Mon-Thurs (Summer) 8am-9pm, Fri 8-5, Sat & Sun Noon-9

MATHEMATICS, 210 Fenton Hall, University of Oregon, 97403, SAN 357-9131. Tel: 541-346-3023. FAX: 541-346-3012. Web Site: www.libweb.uoregon.edu/scilib/mathlib. *Head of Libr,* Victoria Mitchell; Tel: 541-346-3076, E-mail: vmitch@uoregon.edu; *Coll Develop, Ref & Instrul Serv Librn,* Ann Zeidman-Karpinski; Tel: 541-346-2663, E-mail: annie@uoregon.edu; *Access Serv,* Donald Swain; Tel: 541-346-2656, E-mail: dswain@uoregon.edu
Founded 1980. Highest Degree: Doctorate
Library Holdings: Bk Vols 26,000; Per Subs 350

SCIENCE, Onyx Bridge, Lower Level, University of Oregon, 97403, SAN 357-9158. Tel: 541-346-3075. Information Services Tel: 541-346-2661. FAX: 541-346-3012. Web Site: www.libweb.uoregon.edu/scilib. *Head of Libr,* Margaret Bean; Tel: 541-346-1876, E-mail: mbean@uoregon.edu; *Librn,* Ann Zeidman-Karpinski; Tel: 541-346-2663, E-mail: annie@uoregon.edu; *Data Serv Librn,* Brian Westra; Tel: 541-346-2654,

E-mail: bwestra@uoregon.edu; *Ref Librn,* Dean Walton; Tel: 541-346-2871, E-mail: dpwalton@uoregon.edu; *Br Mgr,* Lara Nesselroad; Tel: 541-346-2664, E-mail: lnessel@uoregon.edu. Subject Specialists: *Physics,* Margaret Bean; *Computer sci, Environ studies, Math,* Ann Zeidman-Karpinski; *Chem,* Brian Westra; *Biol, Molecular biol, Neuroscience,* Dean Walton; Staff 8 (MLS 4, Non-MLS 4)
Founded 1968. Highest Degree: Doctorate
Library Holdings: Bk Vols 175,000; Per Subs 2,500
Open Mon-Thurs (Fall-Spring) 8am-11pm, Fri 8-6, Sat Noon-6, Sun 11-11; Mon-Thurs (Summer) 8am-9pm, Fri 8-7, Sat Noon-7, Sun Noon-9

FAIRVIEW

S NACCO MATERIALS HANDLING GROUP, INC*, CBDC Technical Support Resource Center, 4000 NE Blue Lake Rd, 97025. SAN 314-1594. Tel: 503-721-6234. FAX: 503-721-1364. Web Site: www.nmhg.com. *Librn,* Melissa Hardenbergh
Founded 1961
Library Holdings: Bk Titles 16,000; Bk Vols 20,000; Per Subs 60
Subject Interests: Construction safety, Domestic societies, Eng design for mat handling equip, Foreign societies, Indust safety
Restriction: Not open to pub

FALLS CITY

P WAGNER COMMUNITY LIBRARY*, 111 N Main St, 97344-9776. SAN 320-5045. Tel: 503-787-3521, Ext 319. FAX: 503-787-1507. E-mail: wagner-library@ccrls.org. Web Site: www.wagner.plinkit.org. *Dir,* Holly Kraus; Staff 1 (MLS 1)
Pop 1,200
Library Holdings: AV Mats 3,118; Large Print Bks 40; Bk Titles 8,500; Bk Vols 394,000
Automation Activity & Vendor Info: (Cataloging) Innovative Interfaces, Inc; (Circulation) Innovative Interfaces, Inc; (OPAC) Innovative Interfaces, Inc
Function: Summer reading prog
Partic in Chemeketa Cooperative Regional Library Service
Open Mon (Winter) 1-6, Tues-Thurs 1-5, Sat 10-1; Tues (Summer) 1-6, Wed-Fri 1-5, Sat 10-1

FLORENCE

P SIUSLAW PUBLIC LIBRARY DISTRICT*, 1460 Ninth St, 97439-0022. SAN 314-0954. Tel: 541-997-3132. Circulation Tel: 541-997-3132, Ext 201, 541-997-3132, Ext 203. Reference Tel: 541-997-3132, Ext 205. Administration Tel: 541-997-3132, Ext 211. Automation Services Tel: 541-997-3132, Ext 208. FAX: 541-997-6473. Web Site: www.siuslawlibrary.org. *Dir,* Stephen C Skidmore; E-mail: skidmore@siuslaw.lib.or.us; *Asst Libr Dir, Ch Serv,* Gayle Waiss; E-mail: gwaiss@siuslaw.lib.or.us; *Tech Coordr,* Linda Weight; E-mail: lweight@siuslaw.lib.or.us; *Circ,* Mary Colgan-Bennetts; E-mail: bennetts@siuslaw.lib.or.us; *Ref Serv, Ad,* Kevin Mittge; E-mail: mittge@siuslaw.lib.or.us; Staff 5 (MLS 3, Non-MLS 2)
Founded 1985. Pop 17,146; Circ 202,526
Jul 2011-Jun 2012 Income (Main Library and Branch(s)) $879,888, State $1,988, Federal $7,534, Locally Generated Income $802,082, Other $68,284. Mats Exp $106,373, Books $58,970, Per/Ser (Incl. Access Fees) $18,660, AV Mat $22,374, Electronic Ref Mat (Incl. Access Fees) $6,369. Sal $377,180 (Prof $180,996)
Library Holdings: AV Mats 12,595; e-books 30,174; High Interest/Low Vocabulary Bk Vols 600; Bk Vols 84,721; Per Subs 334
Special Collections: Newspapers published in Florence, 1891 to date, micro; Oregon Past & Present Coll; Reference Library of Frank Herbert. Oral History
Automation Activity & Vendor Info: (Cataloging) OCLC; (Circulation) SIRSI WorkFlows; (ILL) SIRSI WorkFlows; (OPAC) SIRSI-iBistro
Database Vendor: EBSCO Auto Repair Reference, Gale Cengage Learning, ProQuest
Wireless access
Function: Art exhibits, Audiobks via web, AV serv, Bk club(s), Bks on cassette, Bks on CD, Computer training, Computers for patron use, Copy machines, Digital talking bks, e-mail & chat, e-mail serv, Electronic databases & coll, Exhibits, Free DVD rentals, Genealogy discussion group, Handicapped accessible, Home delivery & serv to Sr ctr & nursing homes, Homebound delivery serv, ILL available, Large print keyboards, Magnifiers for reading, Mail & tel request accepted, Music CDs, Online ref, Online searches, Outreach serv, OverDrive digital audio bks, Photocopying/Printing, Preschool outreach, Prog for adults, Prog for children & young adult, Pub access computers, Ref & res, Ref serv available, Ref serv in person, Spoken cassettes & CDs, Spoken cassettes & DVDs, Story hour, Summer reading prog, Tax forms, Telephone ref, VHS videos, Wheelchair accessible
Publications: The Bookmark (Newsletter)
Open Mon & Thurs-Sat 10-6, Tues & Wed 10-8, Sun 1-5
Friends of the Library Group

Branches: 1
MAPLETON BRANCH, 88148 Riverview Ave, Mapleton, 97453. (Mail add: 1460 Ninth St, 97439). Tel: 541-268-4033. *Br Mgr,* Kevin K Mittge; Tel: 541-997-3132, Fax: 541-997-6473, E-mail: mittge@siuslaw.lib.or.us; Staff 1 (Non-MLS 1)
Library Holdings: Bk Titles 3,000; Per Subs 12
Automation Activity & Vendor Info: (Acquisitions) SirsiDynix
Open Tues-Sat 12-5

FOREST GROVE

P FOREST GROVE CITY LIBRARY*, 2114 Pacific Ave, 97116-9019. SAN 314-0962. Tel: 503-992-3247. Reference Tel: 503-992-3337. FAX: 503-992-3333. Web Site: www.fglibrary.plinkit.org. *Dir,* Colleen Winters; Tel: 503-992-3246, E-mail: winters@wccls.org; *Ch Serv,* Ann Dondero; E-mail: anndo@wccls.org; *Ch Serv,* Linda Stiles Taylor; E-mail: lindast@wccls.org; Staff 12 (MLS 4, Non-MLS 8)
Founded 1909. Pop 22,500; Circ 292,198
Jul 2005-Jun 2006 Income $735,517, State $2,997, City $296,489, County $424,814. Mats Exp $48,140, Books $28,310, Per/Ser (Incl. Access Fees) $9,300, AV Mat $10,530. Sal $615,955
Library Holdings: AV Mats 13,520; Bk Vols 87,788; Per Subs 212
Special Collections: Large Print Coll; Spanish Language Coll
Automation Activity & Vendor Info: (Acquisitions) Innovative Interfaces, Inc; (Cataloging) Innovative Interfaces, Inc; (Circulation) Innovative Interfaces, Inc; (OPAC) Innovative Interfaces, Inc
Partic in Washington County Cooperative Library Services
Open Mon-Wed 10-8, Thurs-Sat 10-5
Friends of the Library Group

C PACIFIC UNIVERSITY LIBRARY*, 2043 College Way, 97116. SAN 357-9182. Tel: 503-352-1400. Interlibrary Loan Service Tel: 503-352-1413. Reference Tel: 503-352-1418. Administration Tel: 503-352-1402. FAX: 503-352-1416. E-mail: reference@pacificu.edu. Web Site: www.pacificu.edu/library. *Dir, Univ Librn,* Marita Kunkel; Tel: 503-352-1401, E-mail: marita.kunkel@pacificu.edu; *Dir, Educ Tech & Curricular Innovation,* Al Weiss; Tel: 503-352-1417, E-mail: alweiss@pacificu.edu; *Archives/Spec Coll & Instrul Serv Librn,* Eva Guggemos; Tel: 503-352-1415, E-mail: guggemos@pacificu.edu; *Digital Res/Metadata Librn,* Erica Findley; Tel: 503-352-1411, E-mail: erica.findley@pacificu.edu; *Health Sci Librn,* Nancy Henderson; Tel: 503-352-7208, Fax: 503-352-7230, E-mail: henderson@pacificu.edu; *Instrul Serv & Res Librn,* Lynda R Irons; Tel: 503-352-1409, E-mail: larremol@pacificu.edu; *Libr Syst & Applications Librn,* Megan Banasek; Tel: 503-352-1407, E-mail: megan.banasek@pacificu.edu; *Scholarly Communications & Res Serv Librn,* Isaac Gilman; Tel: 503-352-7209, E-mail: gilmani@pacificu.edu; *Project Mgr - Wash County Hist Online,* Lindsay Zaborowski; E-mail: lindsay.prescott@pacificu.edu. Subject Specialists: *Archives, Soc sci,* Eva Guggemos; *Educ,* Erica Findley; *Health sci,* Nancy Henderson; *Humanities, Natural sci,* Lynda R Irons; *Health sci,* Isaac Gilman; Staff 20 (MLS 8, Non-MLS 12)
Founded 1849. Enrl 3,378; Fac 256; Highest Degree: Doctorate
Jul 2011-Jun 2012. Mats Exp $2,398,299. Sal $1,236,641
Library Holdings: AV Mats 13,787; e-books 73,652; Bk Vols 195,610; Per Subs 15,871
Special Collections: Oregon Hist. US Document Depository
Subject Interests: Arts & Sci, Health sci
Automation Activity & Vendor Info: (Acquisitions) Innovative Interfaces, Inc; (Cataloging) Innovative Interfaces, Inc; (Circulation) Innovative Interfaces, Inc; (OPAC) Innovative Interfaces, Inc; (Serials) Innovative Interfaces, Inc
Wireless access
Partic in OCLC Online Computer Library Center, Inc; Orbis Cascade Alliance
Open Mon-Thurs 7:30am-Midnight, Fri 7:30am-10pm, Sat 10-10, Sun 10am-Midnight

FOSSIL

P FOSSIL PUBLIC LIBRARY*, 401 Main St, 97830. (Mail add: PO Box 487, 97830-0487). Tel: 541-763-2046. FAX: 541-763-2124. E-mail: fplib@centurytel.net. *In Charge,* Teresa Hunt
Library Holdings: AV Mats 228; Bk Titles 4,500
Open Tues-Thurs 1-4

GASTON

P GASTON COMMUNITY LIBRARY*, 116 Front St, 97119. (Mail add: PO Box 129, 97119-0129). Tel: 503-985-3464. FAX: 503-985-1014. E-mail: gastonlibrarian@comcast.net. Web Site: gastonlibrarian.home.comcast.net. *Dir,* Diana Watkins; E-mail: teach@pacificu.edu; *Head Librn,* Nancy Watt; Tel: 503-639-8458, E-mail: wattn11@verizon.net; *IT Tech,* Debby Townsend; Tel: 503-662-4104, E-mail: dstown@coho.net
Library Holdings: Audiobooks 81; AV Mats 20; CDs 80; DVDs 256; Large Print Bks 518; Bk Vols 16,743; Per Subs 5; Spec Interest Per Sub 1; Talking Bks 55; Videos 524

Automation Activity & Vendor Info: (Acquisitions) JayWil Software Development, Inc; (Cataloging) JayWil Software Development, Inc; (Circulation) JayWil Software Development, Inc
Database Vendor: JayWil Software Development, Inc
Wireless access
Open Tues & Thurs 2-5 & 6-8:30, Sat 11-5

GERVAIS

CR SALEM BIBLE COLLEGE LIBRARY*, 12234 River Rd NE, 97026. (Mail add: PO Box 9248, Salem, 97305-0248). Tel: 503-304-0092. FAX: 503-304-0899. *Dean,* Debbie Lamm Bray
Library Holdings: Bk Vols 9,000
Open Mon & Tues 8:30am-9:30pm, Wed-Fri 8:30-5

GLADSTONE

P GLADSTONE PUBLIC LIBRARY, 135 E Dartmouth St, 97027-2435. SAN 314-0970. Tel: 503-656-2411. FAX: 503-655-2438. E-mail: glref@lincc.lib.or.us. *Dir,* Irene Green
Pop 17,859; Circ 178,150
Library Holdings: Bk Titles 46,000; Bk Vols 55,000; Per Subs 120
Automation Activity & Vendor Info: (Cataloging) SirsiDynix; (Circulation) SirsiDynix; (OPAC) SirsiDynix
Wireless access
Partic in Library Information Network of Clackamas County
Open Mon-Thurs 10-8, Fri & Sat 11-5:30, Sun 1-5
Friends of the Library Group

GOLD BEACH

P CURRY PUBLIC LIBRARY, 94341 Third St, 97444. SAN 314-0989. Tel: 541-247-7246. FAX: 541-247-4411. E-mail: currylibrary@cplib.net. Web Site: www.currypubliclibrary.org. *Dir,* Jeremy Skinner; E-mail: jeremy@cplib.net; *Cataloger,* Jordan Popoff; E-mail: jordan@cplib.net; *Ch Serv,* Alta Denton; E-mail: alta@cplib.net
Founded 1955. Pop 4,949; Circ 53,868
Library Holdings: Bk Vols 30,000; Per Subs 100
Automation Activity & Vendor Info: (Cataloging) TLC (The Library Corporation); (Circulation) TLC (The Library Corporation); (OPAC) TLC (The Library Corporation)
Wireless access
Open Mon-Thurs 10-7, Fri & Sat 10-5, Sun 12-4
Friends of the Library Group

GRANTS PASS

P JOSEPHINE COMMUNITY LIBRARIES, INC, 200 NW C St, 97526-2094. (Mail add: PO Box 1684, 97528), SAN 357-9247. Tel: 541-476-0571. FAX: 541-479-0685. E-mail: info@josephinelibrary.org. Web Site: www.josephinelibrary.org. *Exec Dir,* Kate Lasky; Staff 5 (MLS 0.5, Non-MLS 4.5)
Founded 1913. Pop 81,026; Circ 295,476
Jul 2009-Jun 2010 Income (Main Library and Branch(s)) $341,069, State $13,455, City $5,000, Locally Generated Income $322,614. Mats Exp $40,500, Books $29,000, Per/Ser (Incl. Access Fees) $6,000, Electronic Ref Mat (Incl. Access Fees) $5,500. Sal $142,594
Library Holdings: Audiobooks 8,000; AV Mats 5,160; CDs 1,000; DVDs 4,400; e-books 25,000; Electronic Media & Resources 24; Large Print Bks 2,200; Bk Vols 145,800; Per Subs 157; Videos 4,200
Subject Interests: Genealogy, Ore hist
Automation Activity & Vendor Info: (Cataloging) Innovative Interfaces, Inc; (Circulation) Innovative Interfaces, Inc; (OPAC) Innovative Interfaces, Inc
Database Vendor: Gale Cengage Learning, LearningExpress, Overdrive, Inc, ProQuest, World Book Online
Wireless access
Function: Bks on CD, Children's prog, Computers for patron use, Copy machines, E-Reserves, Electronic databases & coll, Free DVD rentals, Handicapped accessible, ILL available, Life-long learning prog for all ages, Magazines, Music CDs, Online cat, OverDrive digital audio bks, Photocopying/Printing, Prog for children & young adult, Pub access computers, Ref serv in person, Spoken cassettes & DVDs, Story hour, Summer reading prog, Teen prog, VHS videos, Writing prog
Publications: News of the Grants Pass, Illinois Valley, Williams & Wolf Creek libraries (Newsletter)
Partic in Southern Oregon Library Federation
Open Tues & Thurs 2-7, Wed & Fri 11-4, Sat Noon-4
Restriction: ID required to use computers (Ltd hrs)
Friends of the Library Group
Branches: 3
ILLINOIS VALLEY, 209 W Palmer St, Cave Junction, 97523-0190, SAN 357-9271. Tel: 541-592-4778. *Br Mgr,* Roberta Lee
Library Holdings: Bk Vols 25,000
Friends of the Library Group
WILLIAMS BRANCH, 20695 Williams Hwy, Williams, 97544, SAN 357-9301. Tel: 541-846-7020. *Br Mgr,* Debbie Gonnella; E-mail: dgonnella@josephinelibrary.org
Library Holdings: Bk Vols 7,000
Friends of the Library Group
WOLF CREEK BRANCH, 102 Ruth Ave, Wolf Creek, 97497, SAN 357-9336. Tel: 541-866-2606.
Library Holdings: Bk Vols 7,000
Friends of the Library Group

S JOSEPHINE COUNTY HISTORICAL SOCIETY, Research Library, 512 SW Fifth St, 97526. SAN 326-1891. Tel: 541-479-7827. E-mail: josephine@historicalsociety.us. Web Site: www.jocohistorical.org/research-library. *Exec Dir,* Rose Scott; Staff 1 (MLS 1)
Founded 1960
Library Holdings: Bk Vols 945
Special Collections: Josephine County (Amos Voorhies Coll), photog
Subject Interests: Local hist
Function: Res libr
Publications: The Oldtimer (Newsletter)
Open Tues-Fri 10-4
Restriction: Not a lending libr

L JOSEPHINE COUNTY LAW LIBRARY*, Justice Bldg, 2nd Flr, 500 NW Sixth St, 97526. SAN 325-8343. Tel: 541-474-5488. FAX: 541-474-5223. *Law Librn,* Beecher Ellison; E-mail: bellison@co.josephine.or.us
Library Holdings: Bk Vols 15,000
Open Mon-Fri 9-12 & 1-3

J ROGUE COMMUNITY COLLEGE*, Redwood Campus Library, Wiseman Ctr, 3345 Redwood Hwy, 97527. SAN 314-0997. Tel: 541-956-7152. FAX: 541-471-3588. Web Site: learn.roguecc.edu/library. *Dir, Libr Serv,* Lynda Kettler; Tel: 541-956-7500, Ext 7147, E-mail: lkettler@roguecc.edu; *Ref Librn,* Fran Cardoza; Tel: 541-956-7153, E-mail: fcardoza@roguecc.edu; *Ref Librn,* Robert Felthousen; Tel: 541-956-7149, E-mail: rfelthousen@roguecc.edu; *Ref Librn,* Mary Pierce; Tel: 541-956-7151, E-mail: mpierce@roguecc.edu; *Circ Serv Coordr,* Marian Stoner; Tel: 541-956-7150, E-mail: mstoner@roguecc.edu; Staff 4 (MLS 4)
Founded 1971. Enrl 1,400; Fac 100
Library Holdings: Bk Titles 33,600; Per Subs 350
Special Collections: Oregon Outdoors
Subject Interests: Allied health, Nursing, Small bus
Automation Activity & Vendor Info: (Cataloging) Innovative Interfaces, Inc; (Circulation) Innovative Interfaces, Inc; (OPAC) Innovative Interfaces, Inc
Partic in OCLC Online Computer Library Center, Inc; Southern Oregon Library Federation
Open Mon-Thurs (Winter) 7:30am-8pm, Fri 7:30-5, Sat 9-12; Mon, Tues & Thurs (Summer) 8-5, Wed 8-7
Friends of the Library Group
Departmental Libraries:
RIVERSIDE CAMPUS LIBRARY, 205 S Central, Medford, 97501. Tel: 541-245-7512. FAX: 541-774-1046. *Head Librn,* Tom Miller; E-mail: tmiller@roguecc.edu
Library Holdings: Bk Vols 55,000
Database Vendor: CQ Press, EBSCOhost, Gale Cengage Learning, LexisNexis
Open Mon-Thurs 8-8, Fri 8-5, Sat 12-4
TABLE ROCK CAMPUS LIBRARY, 7800 Pacific Ave, White City, 97503. Tel: 541-245-7820. FAX: 541-245-7975. *Circ,* Bonnie Conard
Library Holdings: Bk Vols 900; Per Subs 13
Automation Activity & Vendor Info: (Course Reserve) Innovative Interfaces, Inc
Open Mon & Thurs 9-4, Tues & Wed 9-5

GRESHAM

J MOUNT HOOD COMMUNITY COLLEGE LIBRARY*, 26000 SE Stark St, 97030. SAN 314-1004. Tel: 503-491-7161. Reference Tel: 503-491-7516. FAX: 503-491-7389. E-mail: reference@mhcc.edu. Web Site: www.mhcc.edu/library. *Coll Develop Librn, Fac Librn,* Stephanie Debner; Tel: 503-491-7150, E-mail: stephanie.debner@mhcc.edu; *Fac Librn, Instruction Coordr,* Jennifer Snoek-Brown; Tel: 503-491-7693, E-mail: jennifer.snoek-brown@mhcc.edu; *Tech Serv Coordr,* Heather White; Tel: 503-491-7106, E-mail: heather.white@mhcc.edu; *Libr Tech Spec,* Matt Anderson; Tel: 503-491-7617, E-mail: matthew.anderson@mhcc.edu; Staff 6 (MLS 4, Non-MLS 2)
Founded 1965. Highest Degree: Associate
Library Holdings: AV Mats 3,760; e-books 1,824; Bk Titles 49,580; Per Subs 437
Automation Activity & Vendor Info: (Acquisitions) Innovative Interfaces, Inc; (Cataloging) Innovative Interfaces, Inc; (Circulation) Innovative Interfaces, Inc; (Course Reserve) Innovative Interfaces, Inc; (Media

Booking) Innovative Interfaces, Inc; (OPAC) Innovative Interfaces, Inc; (Serials) Innovative Interfaces, Inc
Wireless access
Partic in Orbis Cascade Alliance
Open Mon-Thurs (Winter) 8-7, Fri 8-5, Sat & Sun 12-5; Mon-Thurs (Summer) 7:30-7, Fri 8-5

HAMMOND

P WARRENTON COMMUNITY LIBRARY*, 861 Pacific Dr, 97121. (Mail add: PO Box 250, Warrenton, 97146-0250). Tel: 503-861-3919. Administration Tel: 503-861-2233. FAX: 503-861-2351. *Mgr,* Gillian Maggert
Founded 1991. Pop 4,230
Library Holdings: Bk Titles 13,000; Per Subs 10
Open Mon-Fri 1-5, Sat 10-Noon
Friends of the Library Group

HARRISBURG

P HARRISBURG PUBLIC LIBRARY*, 354 Smith St, 97446. (Mail add: PO Box 724, 97446-0724). Tel: 541-995-6949. FAX: 541-995-9244. Web Site: www.ci.harrisburg.or.us. *Librn,* Cheryl Spangler; E-mail: cspangler@ci.harrisburg.or.us
Library Holdings: Bk Titles 6,500
Automation Activity & Vendor Info: (Acquisitions) Follett Software; (Cataloging) Follett Software; (OPAC) Follett Software
Open Mon 3-8:30, Tues-Thurs 12-6, Fri 10-4:30
Friends of the Library Group

HELIX

P HELIX PUBLIC LIBRARY*, 119 Columbia St, 97835. (Mail add: PO Box 324, 97835-0324), SAN 358-0504. Tel: 541-457-6130. FAX: 541-457-6130. E-mail: helixlibrary@helixtel.com. *Dir,* Tina Williams; Staff 1 (Non-MLS 1)
Founded 1906. Pop 277
Library Holdings: Bk Vols 5,216; Per Subs 15
Special Collections: Oral History
Subject Interests: Local hist
Automation Activity & Vendor Info: (Cataloging) Follett Software; (Circulation) Follett Software; (OPAC) Follett Software
Mem of Umatilla County Special Library District
Open Mon 3:30-6, Tues 9-4, Wed 9:30-Noon, Thurs 2-7, Fri 9-Noon
Friends of the Library Group

HERMISTON

P HERMISTON PUBLIC LIBRARY*, 235 E Gladys Ave, 97838-1827. SAN 358-0563. Tel: 541-567-2882. FAX: 541-667-5055. E-mail: library@hermiston.or.us. Web Site: www.hermistonlibrary.us. *Dir,* Marie Baldo; E-mail: mbaldo@hermiston.or.us; *Internet Serv, Ref Librn,* Heidi Florenzen; E-mail: hFlorenzen@hermiston.or.us; *Outreach Serv Librn, Pub Serv,* Kelly Martinez; E-mail: kmartinez@hermiston.or.us; *Tech Serv,* Leeann Baldwin; E-mail: lbaldwin@hermiston.or.us; Staff 8 (MLS 2, Non-MLS 6)
Founded 1916. Pop 19,500
Library Holdings: AV Mats 1,102; Bks on Deafness & Sign Lang 10; e-books 3,431; High Interest/Low Vocabulary Bk Vols 25; Large Print Bks 2,000; Bk Vols 47,586; Per Subs 75; Talking Bks 930; Videos 1,200
Special Collections: National Geographic 1899-present
Automation Activity & Vendor Info: (Cataloging) Innovative Interfaces, Inc; (Circulation) Innovative Interfaces, Inc; (OPAC) Innovative Interfaces, Inc
Database Vendor: EBSCOhost, Newsbank
Function: Archival coll, AV serv, Distance learning, For res purposes, Handicapped accessible, Homebound delivery serv, ILL available, Libr develop, Newsp ref libr, Online searches, Photocopying/Printing, Prog for adults, Prog for children & young adult, Ref serv available, Serves mentally handicapped consumers, Summer reading prog, Telephone ref, Wheelchair accessible, Workshops
Partic in Umatilla County Spec Libr District
Special Services for the Deaf - High interest/low vocabulary bks
Special Services for the Blind - Audio mat; Bks available with recordings; Bks on cassette; Bks on CD; Cassettes; Copier with enlargement capabilities; Extensive large print coll; Large print bks; Spec prog; Talking bks
Open Mon-Thurs 11-7, Fri & Sat 10-5
Friends of the Library Group

HILLSBORO

P HILLSBORO PUBLIC LIBRARY*, Hillsboro Main Library, 2850 NE Brookwood Pkwy, 97124-5327. SAN 314-1837. Tel: 503-615-6500. FAX: 503-615-6601. TDD: 503-648-9181. E-mail: libraryfeedback@ci.hillsboro.or.us. Web Site: www.hillsboro-oregon.gov/library. *Dir,* Michael R Smith; *Asst Dir,* Linda Lybecker; *Circ Mgr,* Linda Osuna; *Coll Develop Mgr, Tech Serv Coordr,* Karen Muller; *Reader Serv Mgr,* Carol Reich
Founded 1914. Pop 133,000; Circ 2,829,680
Jul 2012-Jun 2013 Income (Main Library and Branch(s)) $7,435,002, State $13,268, City $2,855,712, County $4,255,421, Locally Generated Income $310,601. Mats Exp $721,303, Books $435,218, Per/Ser (Incl. Access Fees) $32,472, AV Mat $252,113, Electronic Ref Mat (Incl. Access Fees) $1,500. Sal $3,532,267
Library Holdings: AV Mats 55,960; CDs 19,069; DVDs 38,014; Bk Vols 250,850; Per Subs 488
Automation Activity & Vendor Info: (Acquisitions) Innovative Interfaces, Inc; (Cataloging) Innovative Interfaces, Inc; (Circulation) Innovative Interfaces, Inc; (ILL) Innovative Interfaces, Inc; (OPAC) Innovative Interfaces, Inc
Database Vendor: Gale Cengage Learning, OCLC FirstSearch, OCLC WorldShare Interlibrary Loan, ReferenceUSA, SerialsSolutions, TumbleBookLibrary
Wireless access
Partic in Washington County Cooperative Library Services
Special Services for the Deaf - TDD equip
Special Services for the Blind - Accessible computers; Assistive/Adapted tech devices, equip & products
Open Mon-Fri 10-9, Sat 10-6, Sun Noon-6
Friends of the Library Group
Branches: 1
SHUTE PARK BRANCH LIBRARY, 775 SE Tenth Ave, 97123, SAN 314-1020. Tel: 503-615-6500. FAX: 503-615-6501. *Br Mgr,* Hillary Ostlund
Special Collections: Spanish Language Coll
Open Mon-Wed 10-8, Thurs-Sat 10-6
Friends of the Library Group

TUALITY HEALTHCARE
M HEALTH SCIENCES LIBRARY*, 335 SE Eighth Ave, 97123, SAN 326-3401. Tel: 503-681-1121. FAX: 503-681-1729. E-mail: tuality.library@tuality.org. *Librn,* Judith Hayes; E-mail: judith.hayes@tuality.org; *Libr Tech,* Meredith I Solomon; E-mail: meredith.solomon@tuality.org; Staff 1 (Non-MLS 1)
Library Holdings: Bk Titles 750; Bk Vols 800; Per Subs 140
Subject Interests: Clinical med, Hospital admin, Nursing
Database Vendor: EBSCOhost, OVID Technologies
Partic in Docline; National Network of Libraries of Medicine; Oregon Health Sciences Libraries Association
Open Mon-Fri 9-5
Restriction: Open to others by appt, Staff use only

M TUALITY HEALTH INFORMATION RESOURCE CENTER*, 334 SE Eighth Ave, 97123-4201, SAN 371-3563. Tel: 503-681-1702. FAX: 503-681-1932. E-mail: tuality.library@tuality.org. Web Site: www.wccls.org. *Libr Serv Mgr,* Judith Hayes. Subject Specialists: *Consumer health, Med,* Judith Hayes; Staff 1.25 (MLS 1, Non-MLS 0.25)
Founded 1988
Oct 2012-Sept 2013 Income (Main Library and Branch(s)) $70,000. Mats Exp $70,000
Library Holdings: Audiobooks 2; AV Mats 800; Bks on Deafness & Sign Lang 10; CDs 5; DVDs 250; e-books 1,700; e-journals 2,400; Electronic Media & Resources 10; Large Print Bks 5; Bk Titles 900; Per Subs 5
Special Collections: Model/Poster Coll
Subject Interests: Consumer health
Automation Activity & Vendor Info: (Cataloging) Innovative Interfaces, Inc; (Circulation) Innovative Interfaces, Inc; (OPAC) Innovative Interfaces, Inc
Database Vendor: Cinahl, EBSCOhost, Medline, Micromedex, OCLC WorldShare Interlibrary Loan, PubMed
Function: Computers for patron use, Doc delivery serv, Electronic databases & coll, Free DVD rentals, Health sci info serv, ILL available, Mail & tel request accepted, Online searches, Pub access computers, Ref serv available, Spanish lang bks, Telephone ref
Partic in Docline; National Network of Libraries of Medicine; Washington County Cooperative Library Services
Open Mon, Tues & Thurs 11-3, Wed & Fri 1-5
Restriction: Open to pub for ref & circ; with some limitations

GL WASHINGTON COUNTY LAW LIBRARY, 111 NE Lincoln St, 97124. SAN 314-1039. Tel: 503-846-8880. FAX: 503-846-3515. E-mail: lawlibrary@co.washington.or.us. Web Site: www.co.washington.or.us/lawlibrary. *Law Librn,* Laura Orr; Staff 2 (MLS 2)
Founded 1926
Library Holdings: Bk Vols 17,000
Subject Interests: Legal res, Ore
Automation Activity & Vendor Info: (Cataloging) LibraryWorld, Inc
Database Vendor: Fastcase, HeinOnline, LexisNexis, Westlaw

Wireless access
Open Mon-Fri 8-5

INDEPENDENCE

P INDEPENDENCE PUBLIC LIBRARY*, 175 Monmouth St, 97351-2423. SAN 314-1047. Tel: 503-838-1811. FAX: 503-838-4486. Web Site: www.ccrls.org/independence. *Dir,* Robin Puccetti; E-mail: robinp@ccrls.org; Staff 2 (MLS 1, Non-MLS 1)
Founded 1912. Pop 7,200; Circ 77,500
Jul 2006-Jun 2007 Income $254,849, State $1,014, City $208,587, Locally Generated Income $14,707, Other $30,541. Mats Exp $21,459, Books $15,505, Per/Ser (Incl. Access Fees) $1,492, AV Mat $3,854, Electronic Ref Mat (Incl. Access Fees) $608. Sal $185,753 (Prof $88,648)
Library Holdings: AV Mats 5,958; Bk Vols 32,408; Per Subs 57
Special Collections: Local History Coll; Oregon History Coll; Spanish Language Coll
Automation Activity & Vendor Info: (Acquisitions) Innovative Interfaces, Inc; (Cataloging) Innovative Interfaces, Inc; (Circulation) Innovative Interfaces, Inc; (OPAC) Innovative Interfaces, Inc
Database Vendor: EBSCOhost
Wireless access
Function: Audiobks via web, AV serv, Bilingual assistance for Spanish patrons, Bks on cassette, Bks on CD, CD-ROM, Children's prog, Computers for patron use, Copy machines, Handicapped accessible, Homebound delivery serv, ILL available, Music CDs, Online cat, Photocopying/Printing, Prog for adults, Prog for children & young adult, Spoken cassettes & CDs, Spoken cassettes & DVDs, Summer reading prog, Tax forms, Teen prog, Telephone ref, VHS videos, Video lending libr, Web-catalog, Wheelchair accessible
Partic in Chemeketa Cooperative Regional Library Service
Open Mon & Thurs 10-7, Tues, Wed & Fri 1-7, Sat 10-5
Friends of the Library Group

JEFFERSON

P JEFFERSON PUBLIC LIBRARY*, 128 N Main St, 97352. (Mail add: PO Box 1068, 97352-1068), SAN 376-3323. Tel: 541-327-3826. FAX: 541-327-3120. *Dir,* Valerie Hauser; Staff 2 (MLS 1, Non-MLS 1)
Founded 1938. Pop 2,500; Circ 12,854
Library Holdings: Bk Vols 18,000; Per Subs 31
Subject Interests: State hist
Automation Activity & Vendor Info: (Cataloging) Innovative Interfaces, Inc; (Circulation) Innovative Interfaces, Inc; (OPAC) Innovative Interfaces, Inc
Database Vendor: EBSCOhost
Partic in Chemeketa Cooperative Regional Library Service
Open Tues-Thurs 10-6, Sat 10-4
Friends of the Library Group

JOHN DAY

P GRANT COUNTY LIBRARY*, 507 S Canyon Blvd, 97845-1050. SAN 314-1055. Tel: 541-575-1992. E-mail: grant047@centurytel.net. *Chief Librn,* Melody Jackson; *Asst Librn,* Vicki Waters
Pop 8,250; Circ 60,567
Library Holdings: AV Mats 618; Bk Titles 33,948; Bk Vols 60,000; Per Subs 24; Videos 277
Open Mon, Wed, Fri & Sat 1-5, Tues 10-12 & 1-7, Thurs 1-5 & 7-9

JOSEPH

P JOSEPH CITY LIBRARY, 201 N Main, 97846. (Mail add: PO Box 15, 97846-0015), SAN 314-1063. Tel: 541-432-0141. FAX: 541-432-3832. E-mail: joseph97846@hotmail.com. *Librn,* Genene Kingsford
Founded 1912. Pop 1,890; Circ 11,069
Library Holdings: AV Mats 800; Bk Vols 12,000; Per Subs 30
Special Collections: Wallowa County History
Automation Activity & Vendor Info: (Cataloging) Evergreen; (Circulation) Evergreen; (OPAC) Evergreen
Wireless access
Open Tues-Sat 12-4
Friends of the Library Group

JUNCTION CITY

P JUNCTION CITY PUBLIC LIBRARY*, 726 Greenwood St, 97448-1628. (Mail add: PO Box 280, 97448-0280), SAN 314-1071. Tel: 541-998-8942. Web Site: www.ci.junction-city.or.us/library. *Libr Dir,* Lynn Frost; E-mail: lfrost@ci.junction-city.or.us; *Asst Librn,* Freda Darling
Founded 1924. Pop 5,000; Circ 35,712
Library Holdings: High Interest/Low Vocabulary Bk Vols 50; Large Print Bks 200; Bk Vols 25,000; Per Subs 30
Special Collections: Scandinavian Coll
Automation Activity & Vendor Info: (Cataloging) SirsiDynix; (Circulation) SirsiDynix; (OPAC) SirsiDynix
Publications: JCPL: A Plan for Service
Open Mon & Tues 12-7, Wed & Thurs 12-6, Sat 10-3
Friends of the Library Group

KLAMATH FALLS

J KLAMATH COMMUNITY COLLEGE, Learning Resource Center, 7390 S Sixth St, 97603. Tel: 541-880-2206. E-mail: kcclrc@klamathcc.edu. Web Site: www.klamathcc.edu, www.klamathcc.edu/lrc/default.aspx. *Dir,* Mark Peterson; Staff 2 (MLS 1, Non-MLS 1)
Founded 1996. Enrl 723; Fac 49; Highest Degree: Associate
Library Holdings: Audiobooks 90; Bks on Deafness & Sign Lang 6; CDs 108; DVDs 267; Bk Titles 5,125; Bk Vols 5,602; Per Subs 83; Videos 1,182
Automation Activity & Vendor Info: (Acquisitions) Evergreen; (Cataloging) Evergreen; (Circulation) Evergreen
Database Vendor: EBSCO Information Services, EBSCOhost
Wireless access
Function: Audio & video playback equip for onsite use, Computer training, Computers for patron use, Copy machines, Electronic databases & coll, Equip loans & repairs, Exhibits, Free DVD rentals, Handicapped accessible, ILL available, Instruction & testing, Learning ctr, Literacy & newcomer serv, Online info literacy tutorials on the web & in blackboard, Online searches, Orientations, Photocopying/Printing, Pub access computers, Ref & res, Res libr, Senior computer classes, VHS videos, Web-catalog
Open Mon-Thurs 8-6, Fri 8-4:30
Restriction: Use of others with permission of librn

P KLAMATH COUNTY LIBRARY SERVICES DISTRICT*, 126 S Third St, 97601-6394. SAN 357 9484. Tel: 541-882-8894. Reference Tel: 541-882-8897. Toll Free Tel: 800-230-3871. FAX: 541-882-6166. TDD: 541-885-7183. Web Site: www.klamathlibrary.plinkit.org. *Dir,* Andy Swanson; Tel: 541-882-8896, E-mail: aswanson@klamathlibrary.org; *Supv Librn,* Christy Davis; E-mail: cdavis@klamathlibrary.org; *Supv Librn,* Nathalie Johnston; E-mail: njohnston@klamathlibrary.org; *Youth Serv Librn,* Drucilla Curtis; E-mail: dcurtis@klamathlibrary.org; Staff 7 (MLS 3, Non-MLS 4)
Founded 1913. Pop 70,085; Circ 472,976
Jul 2010-Jun 2011 Income (Main Library and Branch(s)) $2,404,869, State $14,290, County $41,596, Locally Generated Income $2,309,764, Other $39,219. Mats Exp $313,800, Books $190,314, Per/Ser (Incl. Access Fees) $13,680, Micro $6,915, AV Mat $81,433, Electronic Ref Mat (Incl. Access Fees) $21,458. Sal $979,335 (Prof $345,695)
Library Holdings: AV Mats 12,808; CDs 11,026; DVDs 11,402; e-books 12,295; Microforms 1,785; Bk Titles 137,961; Bk Vols 185,930; Per Subs 286; Videos 4,510
Subject Interests: Genealogy, Ore
Automation Activity & Vendor Info: (Acquisitions) Innovative Interfaces, Inc; (Cataloging) Innovative Interfaces, Inc; (Circulation) Innovative Interfaces, Inc; (ILL) OCLC ILLiad; (OPAC) Innovative Interfaces, Inc; (Serials) EBSCO Online
Database Vendor: BCR: Christian Periodical Index, Bowker, EBSCO Auto Repair Reference, EBSCO Information Services, Gale Cengage Learning, H W Wilson, LearningExpress, Overdrive, Inc, ProQuest
Wireless access
Function: Bk club(s), Computers for patron use, Homebound delivery serv, ILL available, Jail serv, OverDrive digital audio bks
Special Services for the Deaf - Bks on deafness & sign lang; Closed caption videos; TDD equip
Special Services for the Blind - Bks available with recordings; Bks on cassette; Bks on CD; Talking bks & player equip
Open Mon, Fri & Sat 10-5, Tues & Thurs 10-8, Wed 1-8, Sun 1-5
Friends of the Library Group
Branches: 11
BLY BRANCH, Gearhart School, 61100 Metler St, Bly, 97622. (Mail add: PO Box 366, Bly, 97622-0366), SAN 377-7677. Tel: 541-353-2299. FAX: 541-353-2299. E-mail: blystaff@klamathlibrary.org. *In Charge,* Roseann Sciurba; Staff 1 (Non-MLS 1)
Circ 8,263
Library Holdings: CDs 137; DVDs 458; Large Print Bks 180; Bk Titles 3,105; Per Subs 7; Videos 232
Open Tues-Thurs 10-4
BONANZA BRANCH, 31703 Hwy 70, Bonanza, 97623. (Mail add: PO Box 218, Bonanza, 97623-0218), SAN 357-9549. Tel: 541-545-6944. FAX: 541-545-6944. E-mail: bonanzastaff@klamathlibrary.org. *Librn,* Helen Hankins; Staff 2 (MLS 0.5, Non-MLS 1.5)
Library Holdings: CDs 176; DVDs 363; Large Print Bks 341; Bk Titles 7,109; Per Subs 8; Videos 132
Open Tues & Thurs 10-6, Wed 9-1, Sat 11-3, Sun 12-4
CHEMULT BRANCH, 120 Damon St, Chemult, 97731. (Mail add: PO Box 155, Chemult, 97731-0155), SAN 377-7693. Tel: 541-365-2412. FAX: 541-365-2412. E-mail: chemultstaff@klamathlibrary.org. *In Charge,* Christine Shuey; Staff 1 (Non-MLS 1)
Circ 1,884

Library Holdings: CDs 176; DVDs 363; Large Print Bks 139; Bk Titles 3,240; Per Subs 6; Videos 156
Open Thurs & Fri 10:30-5, Sat 2-5
CHILOQUIN BRANCH, 140 First Ave, Chiloquin, 97624. (Mail add: PO Box 666, Chiloquin, 97624-0666), SAN 357-9573. Tel: 541-783-3315. FAX: 541-783-3315. E-mail: chiloquinstaff@klamathlibrary.org. *In Charge,* Liliana Mendonca; Staff 1 (Non-MLS 1)
Circ 17,381
Library Holdings: CDs 247; DVDs 587; Large Print Bks 368; Bk Titles 9,690; Per Subs 8; Videos 517
Open Mon & Sat 10-2, Tues 10-4, Wed & Thurs 10-6
Friends of the Library Group

L LOYD DELAP LAW LIBRARY, 126 S Third St, 97601-6388, SAN 357-9662. Tel: 541-883-5128. FAX: 541-885-3624. *Law Libr Asst,* Teresal Penner; E-mail: tpenner@klamathlibrary.org; Staff 1 (Non-MLS 1)
Founded 1929
Jul 2010-Jun 2011 Income $100,547, State $93,723, County $365, Other $6,459. Mats Exp $24,532, Books $10,038, Electronic Ref Mat (Incl. Access Fees) $14,494. Sal $41,596
Library Holdings: Bk Vols 2,500
Database Vendor: LexisNexis
Open Mon & Fri 10-12 & 12:30-5, Tues & Thurs 10-12 & 12:30-6, Wed 1-6
GILCHRIST BRANCH, 138306 Michigan Ave, Gilchrist, 97737. (Mail add: PO Box 633, Gilchrist, 97737-0633), SAN 378-1461. Tel: 541-433-2186. FAX: 541-433-2186. E-mail: gilchriststaff@klamathlibrary.org. *In Charge,* Coleen Thomas-Burbank; Staff 1 (Non-MLS 1)
Circ 1,422
Library Holdings: CDs 142; DVDs 9; Large Print Bks 135; Bk Titles 5,027; Per Subs 6; Videos 169
Open Tues & Sat 10-12:30 & 1-5, Wed 10-2
KENO BRANCH, Keno Plaza, Unit 8, 15555 Hwy 66, Keno, 97627. (Mail add: PO Box 283, Keno, 97627-0283). Tel: 541-273-0750. FAX: 541-273-0750. E-mail: kenostaff@klamathlibrary.org. *In Charge,* Linda Ward
Circ 6,553
Library Holdings: AV Mats 244; CDs 168; DVDs 281; Large Print Bks 179; Bk Titles 4,312; Per Subs 6; Videos 106
Open Tues & Wed 12:30-4:30, Thurs 10-12 & 12:30-4:30, Sat 10-2
MALIN BRANCH, 2307 Front St, Malin, 97632. (Mail add: PO Box 525, Malin, 97632-0525), SAN 357-9697. Tel: 541-723-5210. FAX: 541-723-5930. E-mail: malinstaff@klamathlibrary.org. *In Charge,* Christa Moore; Staff 1 (Non-MLS 1)
Circ 5,731
Library Holdings: CDs 130; DVDs 220; Large Print Bks 252; Bk Titles 5,188; Per Subs 7; Videos 103
Open Tues & Thurs 9-12 & 1-5:30, Wed 1-5:30, Sat 9-12
Friends of the Library Group
MERRILL BRANCH, 365 W Front, Merrill, 97633. (Mail add: PO Box 1001, Merrill, 97633-1001), SAN 377-7715. Tel: 541-798-5393. FAX: 541-798-5393. E-mail: merrillstaff@klamathlibrary.org. *In Charge,* Christa Moore; Staff 1 (Non-MLS 1)
Circ 6,547
Library Holdings: CDs 138; DVDs 230; Large Print Bks 182; Bk Titles 4,135; Per Subs 6; Videos 111
Open Mon, Wed & Fri 9-12 & 1-5:30, Sat 1-5:30
Friends of the Library Group
SOUTH SUBURBS, 3706 S Sixth St, 97603. Tel: 541-273-3679. E-mail: ssubstaff@klamathlibrary.org. *In Charge,* Hankins Helen; Staff 1 (Non-MLS 1)
Circ 24,862
Library Holdings: CDs 380; DVDs 425; Large Print Bks 299; Bk Titles 7,018; Per Subs 7; Videos 425
Open Mon, Tues & Thurs 12-5, Wed, Fri & Sat 9-1 & 2-5
SPRAGUE RIVER BRANCH, Sprague River Hwy, Sprague River, 97639-8602. (Mail add: PO Box 29, Sprague River, 97639-0029), SAN 377-7731. Tel: 541-533-2769. E-mail: spragueriverstaff@klamathlibrary.org. *In Charge,* Joyce Hardman; Staff 1 (Non-MLS 1)
Circ 14,654
Library Holdings: CDs 134; DVDs 367; Large Print Bks 145; Bk Titles 4,433; Per Subs 6; Videos 214
Open Tues-Thurs 11-4, Sat 12-3
Friends of the Library Group

S KLAMATH COUNTY MUSEUM & BALDWIN HOTEL MUSEUM*, Research Library, 1451 Main St, 97601. SAN 314-108X. Tel: 541-883-4208. FAX: 541-883-5170. Web Site: www.co.klamath.or.us, www.ohwy.com/or/k/klamatcm.htm. *Mgr,* Todd Kepple; E-mail: tkepple@co.klamath.or.us; *Curator,* Lynn Jeche
Founded 1960
Library Holdings: Bk Titles 10,000
Special Collections: Early Photographs (Floyd), negatives-prints; Photo Glass Plates (Baldwin), negatives-prints; Photographs, Modoc Indian War & Logging & Lumbering (Ogle), negatives-prints, bks, doc & micro
Subject Interests: Hist, Natural sci, Pre-hist, Wildlife of area
Function: Res libr
Publications: Research Papers
Restriction: Open by appt only

C OREGON INSTITUTE OF TECHNOLOGY LIBRARY, 3201 Campus Dr, 97601-8801. SAN 314-1098. Tel: 541-885-1772. Circulation Tel: 541-885-1771. Reference Tel: 541-885-1773. FAX: 541-885-1777. E-mail: libtech@oit.edu. Web Site: www.oit.edu/libraries. *Dir,* Kelly Peterson-Fairchild; Tel: 541-885-1783, E-mail: kelly.petersonfairchild@oit.edu; *Info Syst Librn,* Karen Kunz; Tel: 541-885-1769, E-mail: karen.kunz@oit.edu; *Instruction Librn,* Aja Bettencourt-McCarthy; *Instrul Serv Librn,* Alla Powers; Tel: 541-885-1774, E-mail: alla.powers@oit.edu; *Tech Serv Librn,* Iris Goodwin; Tel: 541-885-1965, E-mail: iris.godwin@oit.edu; *Wilsonville Librn,* Dawn Lowe-Wincentsen; Tel: 503-821-1258, E-mail: dawn.lowewincentsen@oit.edu; *Mgr, Access Serv,* Jan A Abeita; *Acq/Cat Tech, Govt Doc,* Deniece Davis; *Cat Tech, Govt Doc, ILL,* Chris Haupt; Tel: 541-885-1099, E-mail: christine.haupt@oit.edu; *Operating Syst/Network Analyst,* Joe Hurlbut; *Ser Tech,* Hsiu-Ling Lin. Subject Specialists: *Manufacturing, Mechanical eng,* Kelly Peterson-Fairchild; *Computer eng, Math,* Karen Kunz; *Humanities, Soc sci,* Alla Powers; *Health sci,* Iris Goodwin; *Distance educ,* Dawn Lowe-Wincentsen; Staff 12 (MLS 6, Non-MLS 6)
Founded 1950. Enrl 3,927; Fac 218; Highest Degree: Master
Library Holdings: Bk Titles 91,528; Bk Vols 155,560; Per Subs 2,110
Special Collections: Shaw Historical Library Coll; Western History (Klamath Basin Coll). State Document Depository; US Document Depository
Subject Interests: Computer sci, Eng tech, Hist of sci & tech, Med
Automation Activity & Vendor Info: (Acquisitions) Ex Libris Group; (Cataloging) Ex Libris Group; (Circulation) Ex Libris Group; (Course Reserve) Ex Libris Group; (ILL) Clio; (OPAC) Ex Libris Group; (Serials) Ex Libris Group
Database Vendor: CIOS (Communication Institute for Online Scholarship), CRC Press/Taylor & Francis Group, CredoReference, ebrary, EBSCOhost, Ex Libris Group, Faulkner Information Services, Foundation Center, Gale Cengage Learning, H W Wilson, LearningExpress, LexisNexis, Marcive, Inc, OCLC ArticleFirst, OCLC FirstSearch, OCLC WorldShare Interlibrary Loan, PubMed, Safari Books Online, Sage, ScienceDirect, Springer-Verlag, Standard & Poor's, Wiley InterScience, Wilson - Wilson Web, YBP Library Services
Wireless access
Function: Audio & video playback equip for onsite use, Computers for patron use, Copy machines, E-Reserves, Electronic databases & coll, Online cat, Pub access computers, Ref serv available, Scanner, Telephone ref
Publications: Journal of the Shaw Historical Library (Local historical information)
Partic in OCLC Online Computer Library Center, Inc; Orbis Cascade Alliance
Restriction: Borrowing privileges limited to fac & registered students, Non-circulating coll, Non-circulating of rare bks, Open to pub for ref & circ; with some limitations

LA GRANDE

C EASTERN OREGON UNIVERSITY*, Pierce Library, One University Blvd, 97850. SAN 314-1101. Tel: 541-962-3540. Circulation Tel: 541-962-3864. Interlibrary Loan Service Tel: 541-962-3735. Reference Tel: 541-962-3605. Automation Services Tel: 541-962-3579. FAX: 541-962-3335. Web Site: pierce.eou.edu. *Dir,* Karen Clay; Tel: 541-962-3792, E-mail: kclay@eou.edu; *Outreach Serv Librn,* Shirley J Roberts; E-mail: sroberts@eou.edu; *Pub Serv,* Ken Watson; Tel: 541-962-3546, E-mail: kwatson@eou.edu; *Ref,* Theresa Gillis; E-mail: tgillis@eou.edu. Subject Specialists: *Bus,* Shirley J Roberts; *Sciences,* Ken Watson; Staff 13 (MLS 4, Non-MLS 9)
Founded 1929. Enrl 2,334; Fac 125; Highest Degree: Master
Library Holdings: Bk Titles 115,809; Bk Vols 156,402; Per Subs 854
Special Collections: Native American Literature; Oregon, bks & doc. US Document Depository
Subject Interests: Genealogy, Local hist
Automation Activity & Vendor Info: (Acquisitions) Innovative Interfaces, Inc; (Cataloging) Innovative Interfaces, Inc; (Circulation) Innovative Interfaces, Inc; (OPAC) Innovative Interfaces, Inc; (Serials) Innovative Interfaces, Inc
Database Vendor: EBSCOhost, OCLC FirstSearch, OVID Technologies, ProQuest
Publications: Newsletter
Partic in Orbis Cascade Alliance
Open Mon-Thurs 7:30am-11pm, Fri 7:30-6, Sat 11-7, Sun 2-11
Friends of the Library Group

P LA GRANDE PUBLIC LIBRARY*, F Maxine & Thomas W Cook Memorial Library, 2006 Fourth St, 97850-2496. SAN 314-111X. Tel: 541-962-1339. FAX: 541-962-1338. Web Site: www.cityoflagrande.org/library. *Dir,* Terri Lynn Washburn; Tel: 541-962-1335, E-mail: libdirector@cityoflagrande.org
Founded 1912. Pop 25,000; Circ 162,506
Jul 2011-Jun 2012 Income $504,469. Mats Exp $53,180, Books $37,000, Per/Ser (Incl. Access Fees) $4,180, AV Mat $12,000. Sal $351,447 (Prof $65,000)
Library Holdings: Audiobooks 3,554; AV Mats 3,469; e-books 12,295; Electronic Media & Resources 25; Large Print Bks 2,000; Bk Vols 57,145; Per Subs 112
Special Collections: Oregon History Coll
Automation Activity & Vendor Info: (Cataloging) Evergreen; (Circulation) Evergreen; (OPAC) Evergreen
Database Vendor: EBSCOhost, Gale Cengage Learning, Ingram Library Services, LearningExpress, Loislaw, OCLC, Overdrive, Inc, World Book Online
Wireless access
Partic in Sage Library System of Eastern Oregon
Open Mon 11-8, Tues-Fri 11-6, Sat 9-4

LAKE OSWEGO

P LAKE OSWEGO PUBLIC LIBRARY*, 706 Fourth St, 97034-2399. SAN 314-1128. Tel: 503-636-7628. Reference Tel: 503-675-2540. Administration Tel: 503-697-6583. FAX: 503-635-4171. Reference FAX: 503-675-2536. Web Site: www.lakeoswegolibrary.org. *Dir,* Bill Baars; E-mail: bbaars@ci.oswego.or.us; *Mgr,* Jacqueline Rose; Tel: 503-675-2539, E-mail: jrose@ci.oswego.or.us; *Head, Ref, Mgr, Tech Serv,* Jane Carr; *Circ Supvr,* Donna Ainslie; Tel: 503-675-3996, E-mail: dainslie@ci.oswego.or.us; Staff 23 (MLS 9, Non-MLS 14)
Founded 1930. Pop 42,904; Circ 1,285,371
Library Holdings: AV Mats 39,348; Bk Vols 153,395; Per Subs 282
Special Collections: Northwest Coll, bks & files. Oral History
Subject Interests: Art, Compact discs, Genealogy, Graphic novels, Pacific Northwest
Automation Activity & Vendor Info: (Acquisitions) SirsiDynix; (Cataloging) SirsiDynix; (Circulation) SirsiDynix; (ILL) OCLC
Database Vendor: EBSCOhost, Gale Cengage Learning, OCLC FirstSearch, ProQuest, SirsiDynix
Wireless access
Partic in Library Information Network of Clackamas County; OCLC Online Computer Library Center, Inc
Open Mon-Thurs 10-9, Fri & Sat 10-6, Sun 1-6
Friends of the Library Group

LAKESIDE

P LAKESIDE PUBLIC LIBRARY*, 915 N Lake Rd, 97449. (Mail add: PO Box R, 97449-0811), SAN 329-7608. Tel: 541-759-4432. FAX: 541-759-4752. Web Site: lakeside.cclsd.org. *Librn,* Nadine O Goodrich; E-mail: ngoodrich@cclsd.org; Staff 0.53 (Non-MLS 0.53)
Founded 1987. Pop 2,044; Circ 22,758
Library Holdings: Bk Titles 26,724; Per Subs 32
Automation Activity & Vendor Info: (Acquisitions) Innovative Interfaces, Inc; (Cataloging) Innovative Interfaces, Inc; (OPAC) Innovative Interfaces, Inc
Wireless access
Mem of Coos County Library Service District
Open Mon-Fri 10:30-5, Sat 12-4
Friends of the Library Group

LAKEVIEW

P LAKE COUNTY LIBRARY DISTRICT*, 513 Center St, 97630-1582. SAN 357-9786. Tel: 541-947-6019. FAX: 541-947-6034. E-mail: library@co.lake.or.us. Web Site: www.lakecountylibrary.org. *Dir,* Amy Hutchinson; Staff 4.3 (MLS 1, Non-MLS 3.3)
Founded 1948. Pop 7,500; Circ 55,039
Jul 2006-Jun 2007 Income (Main Library and Branch(s)) $231,689, State $13,591, County $9,675, Locally Generated Income $14,432, Other $193,991. Mats Exp $28,765, Books $20,176, Per/Ser (Incl. Access Fees) $3,884, Other Print Mats $165, AV Mat $4,218, Electronic Ref Mat (Incl. Access Fees) $322. Sal $104,926
Library Holdings: AV Mats 5,011; e-journals 1; Electronic Media & Resources 26; Bk Titles 47,655; Per Subs 63
Special Collections: Oregon Coll. State Document Depository
Subject Interests: Agr, Americana
Automation Activity & Vendor Info: (Cataloging) Innovative Interfaces, Inc; (Circulation) Innovative Interfaces, Inc; (Course Reserve) Innovative Interfaces, Inc; (OPAC) Innovative Interfaces, Inc
Database Vendor: EBSCOhost
Wireless access
Function: Computers for patron use, Copy machines, Electronic databases & coll, ILL available, Magnifiers for reading, Music CDs, Online ref, Photocopying/Printing, Prog for adults, Prog for children & young adult, Ref & res, Summer reading prog, Tax forms, Telephone ref, VHS videos
Partic in Libraries of Eastern Oregon (LEO)
Special Services for the Deaf - Bks on deafness & sign lang
Special Services for the Blind - Audio mat; Bks on cassette; Bks on CD; Copier with enlargement capabilities; Home delivery serv; Large print bks; Magnifiers
Open Mon & Wed-Fri 8:30-6, Tues 8:30am-9pm, Sat 12-4
Restriction: Lending limited to county residents
Branches: 3
CHRISTMAS VALLEY BRANCH, Christmas Tree Lane, Christmas Valley, 97641. (Mail add: PO Box 87, Christmas Valley, 97641), SAN 357-9794. Tel: 541-576-2336. FAX: 541-576-2336. E-mail: cvlibrary@internetextension.com. *Librn,* Barbara Remy
Open Tues & Thurs 10-6, Sat 10-2
Friends of the Library Group
PAISELY BRANCH, 513 Mill St, Paisley, 97636. (Mail add: PO Box 99, Paisley, 97636), SAN 357-9816. Tel: 541-943-3911. FAX: 541-943-3911. *Librn,* Jan Murphy
Library Holdings: Bk Titles 6,500
Open Tues & Wed 10-6
Friends of the Library Group
SILVER LAKE BRANCH, Hwy 31, Silver Lake, 97638. (Mail add: PO Box 87, Silver Lake, 97638), SAN 357-9840. Tel: 541-576-2146. FAX: 541-576-2146. *Librn,* Rosa Villigrana
Library Holdings: Bk Titles 3,046
Open Mon 10-6

LANGLOIS

P LANGLOIS PUBLIC LIBRARY*, 48234 Hwy 101, 97450. (Mail add: PO Box 277, 97450-0277), SAN 314-1144. Tel: 541-348-2066. FAX: 541-348-2066. E-mail: langlibrary@harborside.com. Web Site: www.langlois.plinkit.org. *Dir,* Scott Alan Smith; E-mail: scott.alan.smith@langloislibrary.net; Staff 2 (MLS 1, Non-MLS 1)
Founded 1955. Pop 1,000; Circ 12,562
Library Holdings: Bk Vols 13,500; Per Subs 45
Special Collections: Oregon Coll
Automation Activity & Vendor Info: (Cataloging) TLC (The Library Corporation); (Circulation) TLC (The Library Corporation); (OPAC) TLC (The Library Corporation)
Database Vendor: Overdrive, Inc
Wireless access
Function: Adult bk club, Art exhibits, Audiobks via web, Bks on cassette, Bks on CD, Children's prog, Computers for patron use, Copy machines, Electronic databases & coll, Exhibits, Fax serv, Free DVD rentals, ILL available, Instruction & testing, Mail & tel request accepted, Music CDs, Newsp ref libr, Online cat, OverDrive digital audio bks, Photocopying/Printing, Prog for adults, Pub access computers, Ref serv available, Ref serv in person, Scanner, Story hour, Summer reading prog
Open Mon-Sat 11-6
Friends of the Library Group

LEBANON

P LEBANON PUBLIC LIBRARY*, 55 Academy St, 97355-3320. SAN 314-1152. Tel: 541-258-4926. FAX: 541-258-4958. *Libr Serv Mgr,* Carol Dinges; Tel: 541-258-4232, E-mail: cdinges@ci.lebanon.or.us; Staff 11 (Non-MLS 11)
Founded 1910. Pop 15,000; Circ 194,000
Jul 2012-Jun 2013 Income $601,396, State $2,051, City $517,657, Federal $7,891, Locally Generated Income $73,797. Mats Exp $56,903, Books $32,411, Per/Ser (Incl. Access Fees) $6,955, Micro $150, AV Mat $9,176, Electronic Ref Mat (Incl. Access Fees) $8,211. Sal $341,141
Library Holdings: Audiobooks 2,848; Bks-By-Mail 293; Braille Volumes 2; Electronic Media & Resources 22; High Interest/Low Vocabulary Bk Vols 400; Large Print Bks 1,000; Microforms 223; Bk Vols 44,867; Per Subs 74; Videos 3,457
Special Collections: Genealogy (End of the Trail Research Coll)
Automation Activity & Vendor Info: (Acquisitions) Evergreen; (Cataloging) Evergreen; (Circulation) Evergreen; (ILL) OCLC FirstSearch; (OPAC) Evergreen
Database Vendor: Booklist Online, EBSCO Auto Repair Reference, Gale Cengage Learning, Ingram Library Services, OCLC FirstSearch, OCLC WorldShare Interlibrary Loan, Overdrive, Inc, ProQuest
Wireless access
Function: Audiobks via web, Bks on cassette, Bks on CD, Children's prog, Computer training, Computers for patron use, Copy machines, Digital talking bks, e-mail & chat, E-Reserves, Electronic databases & coll, Fax serv, Free DVD rentals, Handicapped accessible, ILL available, Music CDs, Online cat, OverDrive digital audio bks, Photocopying/Printing, Preschool outreach, Prog for adults, Prog for children & young adult, Pub access computers, Ref & res, Ref serv in person, Res performed for a fee, Spoken cassettes & CDs, Story hour, Summer reading prog, Tax forms, Teen prog, Telephone ref, VHS videos, Web-catalog, Wheelchair accessible

Open Mon & Thurs 10-7, Fri & Sat 10-5
Restriction: Circ to mem only, Non-resident fee
Friends of the Library Group

LINCOLN CITY

P DRIFTWOOD PUBLIC LIBRARY, 801 SW Hwy 101, Ste 201, 97367-2720. SAN 314-1160. Tel: 541-996-2277. FAX: 541-996-1262. E-mail: librarian@driftwoodlib.org. Web Site: www.driftwoodlib.org. *Libr Dir,* Kirsten Brodbeck-Kenney; E-mail: kbrodbeck-kenney@lincolncity.org; *Ref Librn,* Morgan Sohl; E-mail: msohl@lincolncity.org; *Circ Supvr,* Ken Hobson; E-mail: kenh@lincolncity.org; *Outreach Coordr,* Mackie Welch; E-mail: mwelch@driftwoodlib.org; *Children's Prog,* Teena Nelson; E-mail: tnelson@driftwoodlib.org; Staff 8 (MLS 3, Non-MLS 5)
Founded 1965. Pop 12,465; Circ 115,147
Library Holdings: AV Mats 14,225; High Interest/Low Vocabulary Bk Vols 127; Large Print Bks 4,514; Bk Titles 86,000; Per Subs 110; Spec Interest Per Sub 50; Talking Bks 2,677
Subject Interests: Pacific Northwest
Automation Activity & Vendor Info: (Cataloging) OCLC; (Circulation) Innovative Interfaces, Inc; (OPAC) Innovative Interfaces, Inc
Wireless access
Publications: Driftwood Gazette
Special Services for the Blind - Closed circuit TV
Open Mon-Wed 10-8, Thurs-Sat 10-6, Sun 1-5
Friends of the Library Group

LYONS

P LYONS PUBLIC LIBRARY, 279 Eighth St, 97358-2122. (Mail add: 448 Cedar St, 97358-2124), SAN 376-3293. Tel: 503-859-2366. E-mail: lyonspl@ccrls.org. Web Site: www.lyons.plinkit.org. *Librn,* Brenda Harris; *Asst Librn,* Molly Freeman
Pop 2,296; Circ 17,369
Library Holdings: AV Mats 554; Bks on Deafness & Sign Lang 25; CDs 100; High Interest/Low Vocabulary Bk Vols 100; Large Print Bks 250; Bk Vols 23,232; Per Subs 35; Talking Bks 290; Videos 530
Subject Interests: Vietnam
Automation Activity & Vendor Info: (Cataloging) Innovative Interfaces, Inc; (Circulation) Innovative Interfaces, Inc
Wireless access
Function: ILL available, Photocopying/Printing, Ref serv available
Partic in Chemeketa Cooperative Regional Library Service
Special Services for the Deaf - Staff with knowledge of sign lang
Open Tues-Thurs 1-6:30, Fri 1-5, Sat 10-3:30
Restriction: Mem only
Friends of the Library Group

MADRAS

P JEFFERSON COUNTY LIBRARY DISTRICT, 241 SE Seventh St, 97741. SAN 314-1209. Tel: 541-475-3351. FAX: 541-475-7434. E-mail: library@jcld.org. Web Site: www.jcld.org. *Dir,* DeRese Hall; E-mail: DeRese@jcld.org; *Adult Acq Spec,* Susie Green; E-mail: Susie@jcld.org; *Cat/ILL Spec,* Jackie May; E-mail: Jackie@jcld.org; *Spanish Serv Spec,* Yirah Marrero; E-mail: Yirah@jcld.org; *Youth Serv Spec,* Lorene Forman; E-mail: Lorene@jcld.org. Subject Specialists: *Spanish,* Yirah Marrero
Founded 1915
Special Collections: Oregon Coll
Automation Activity & Vendor Info: (Cataloging) Innovative Interfaces, Inc; (Circulation) Innovative Interfaces, Inc; (OPAC) Innovative Interfaces, Inc
Wireless access
Function: 24/7 Online cat, Children's prog, Computers for patron use, Copy machines, ILL available, Magazines, Movies, Music CDs, Online cat, Photocopying/Printing, Pub access computers, Spanish lang bks, Spoken cassettes & CDs, Summer reading prog, Tax forms, VHS videos
Open Mon-Thurs 10-8, Sat 10-4
Friends of the Library Group

MANZANITA

S INFORMATION MASTERS LIBRARY*, 37980 Reed Rd, 97130. (Mail add: PO Box 525, 97130), SAN 372-2171. Tel: 503-368-6990. FAX: 503-368-7118. *Librn,* Signe E Larson; E-mail: slarson@teleport.com
Library Holdings: Bk Vols 11,300; Per Subs 50
Subject Interests: Bus, Bus law
Wireless access
Open Mon-Sat 9-5

MARYLHURST

C MARYLHURST UNIVERSITY*, Shoen Library, 17600 Pacific Hwy (Hwy 43), 97036-7036. (Mail add: PO Box 261, 97036-0261), SAN 314-1217. Tel: 503-699-6261. Toll Free Tel: 800-634-9982, Ext 6261. FAX: 503-636-1957. E-mail: library@marylhurst.edu. Web Site: www.marylhurst.edu/shoenlibrary/. *Univ Librn,* Nancy Hoover; Tel: 503-699-6261, Ext 3372; *Dir, Tech Serv,* Judy Voges; Tel: 503-699-6261, Ext 3374; *Circ Mgr,* C Quill West; Tel: 503-699-6261, Ext 4435, E-mail: cwest@marylhurst.edu; *Supvr, Ser,* Sarah-Lynda Johnson; *Acq, Cat,* Patti Russell; Tel: 503-699-6261, Ext 3373, E-mail: prussell@marylhurst.edu; *Electronic Res,* Canon Crawford; Tel: 503-699-6261, Ext 3379, E-mail: ccrawford@marylhurst.edu; *ILL,* Position Currently Open; *Media Spec,* Ross Ludeman; Tel: 503-699-6261, Ext 4443, E-mail: rludeman@marylhurst.edu; *Pub Serv,* Kirk Howard; Tel: 503-699-6261, Ext 3375, E-mail: khoward@marylhurst.edu. Subject Specialists: *Eng lit,* Nancy Hoover; Staff 9 (MLS 4, Non-MLS 5)
Founded 1893. Enrl 1,200; Highest Degree: Doctorate
Jul 2005-Jun 2006 Income $46,970. Mats Exp $242,460, Books $130,726, Per/Ser (Incl. Access Fees) $51,522, AV Equip $6,000, AV Mat $14,403, Electronic Ref Mat (Incl. Access Fees) $39,809. Sal $241,687
Library Holdings: AV Mats 3,064; CDs 1,292; DVDs 378; e-books 7,255; e-journals 419; Music Scores 3,993; Bk Titles 76,826; Bk Vols 81,772; Per Subs 304; Talking Bks 132; Videos 1,256
Special Collections: Sacred Music
Subject Interests: Art, Art therapy, Music, Pacific Northwest, Relig
Automation Activity & Vendor Info: (Acquisitions) Innovative Interfaces, Inc; (Cataloging) Innovative Interfaces, Inc; (Circulation) Innovative Interfaces, Inc; (Course Reserve) Innovative Interfaces, Inc; (OPAC) Innovative Interfaces, Inc; (Serials) Innovative Interfaces, Inc
Database Vendor: EBSCOhost, LexisNexis, OCLC FirstSearch
Wireless access
Partic in Northwest Association of Private Colleges & Universities (NAPCU); Orbis Cascade Alliance
Open Mon-Thurs 8:30am-10pm, Fri-Sat 8:30-7, Sun 11-7
Restriction: Open to students, fac & staff, Pub use on premises, Residents only
Friends of the Library Group

MAUPIN

P SOUTHERN WASCO COUNTY LIBRARY, Maupin Library, 410 Deschutes Ave, 97037. (Mail add: PO Box 328, 97037-0328). Tel: 541-395-2208. FAX: 541-395-2208. E-mail: southernwascolibrary@gmail.com. Web Site: www.geocities.com/maupinlibrary. *Libr Dir,* Valerie D Stephenson; Staff 1 (Non-MLS 1)
Pop 750
Library Holdings: AV Mats 1,425; Large Print Bks 200; Bk Titles 6,950; Per Subs 12
Special Collections: Ivan Donaldson Botanical Coll; Local Newspapers, circa 1914-1930
Subject Interests: Genealogy, Local hist
Open Tues-Thurs 1-6, Fri 11-4

MCMINNVILLE

C LINFIELD COLLEGE*, Jereld R Nicholson Library, 900 SE Baker St, 97128. SAN 314-1187. Tel: 503-883-2261. Reference Tel: 503-883-2518. FAX: 503-883-2566. E-mail: library-circulation@linfield.edu. Interlibrary Loan Service E-mail: ill@linfield.edu. Web Site: www.linfield.edu/linfield-libraries.html. *Libr Dir,* Susan Barnes Whyte; Tel: 503-883-2517, E-mail: swhyte@linfield.edu; *Dir, Res Sharing,* Rich Schmidt; Tel: 508-883-2534, E-mail: rschmidt@linfield.edu; *Coll Mgt Librn,* Kathleen Spring; Tel: 503-883-2263, E-mail: kspring@linfield.edu; *Ref & Instruction Librn,* Jean Caspers; Tel: 503-883-2262, E-mail: jcaspers@linfield.edu; *Ref/Distance Learning Librn,* Carol McCulley; Tel: 503-883-2595, E-mail: cmccull@linfield.edu; *Syst Librn,* Barbara Valentine; Tel: 503-883-2573, E-mail: bvalen@linfield.edu; Staff 12 (MLS 8, Non-MLS 4)
Founded 1849. Enrl 2,186; Fac 143; Highest Degree: Bachelor
Jul 2006-Jun 2007. Mats Exp $646,264, Books $160,180, Per/Ser (Incl. Access Fees) $366,322, Electronic Ref Mat (Incl. Access Fees) $112,443, Presv $7,319. Sal $687,868 (Prof $596,107)
Library Holdings: Bk Vols 182,713; Per Subs 1,268
Special Collections: Baptist Pioneer History Coll. US Document Depository
Subject Interests: Canadiana, Environ studies, Gender studies, Pac NW hist
Automation Activity & Vendor Info: (Acquisitions) Innovative Interfaces, Inc; (Cataloging) Innovative Interfaces, Inc; (Circulation) Innovative Interfaces, Inc; (Serials) Innovative Interfaces, Inc
Database Vendor: EBSCOhost, Gale Cengage Learning, Innovative Interfaces, Inc, LexisNexis, OCLC FirstSearch, OVID Technologies, ProQuest
Wireless access
Publications: Nicholson News (Newsletter)
Partic in OCLC Online Computer Library Center, Inc; Orbis Cascade Alliance

Open Mon-Thurs 7:30am-1am, Fri 7:30-6, Sat 10-6, Sun Noon-1am; Mon-Fri (Summer) 8-5
Friends of the Library Group
Departmental Libraries:
PORTLAND CAMPUS, 2255 NW Northrup, Portland, 97210. (Mail add: 1015 NW 22nd Ave, Portland, 97210), SAN 370-4793. Tel: 503-413-7335. Interlibrary Loan Service Tel: 503-413-7448. Administration Tel: 503-413-7820. FAX: 503-413-8016. *Dir,* Patrice O'Donovan; E-mail: odonovan@linfield.edu; *Head, Access Serv,* Matthew Gage; Tel: 503-413-7696, E-mail: mgage@linfield.edu; *Libr Tech Spec,* April Younglove; E-mail: ayoungl@linfield.edu
Library Holdings: Bk Vols 13,468; Per Subs 155
Subject Interests: Nursing
Database Vendor: Cinahl
Open Mon-Thurs 8am-9pm, Fri 8-5, Sat 11-5, Sun 3-9

P MCMINNVILLE PUBLIC LIBRARY*, 225 NW Adams St, 97128-5425. SAN 314-1195. Tel: 503-435-5562. Circulation Tel: 503-435-5561. Interlibrary Loan Service Tel: 503-435-5553. Reference Tel: 503-435-5568. Administration Tel: 503-435-5550. E-mail: libref@ci.mcminnville.or.us. Web Site: www.maclibrary.org. *Libr Dir,* Jenny Berg; E-mail: jenny.berg@ci.mcminnville.or.us; *Librn III/Ref,* Alice Darnton; E-mail: alice.darnton@ci.mcminnville.or.us; *Libr Serv Mgr,* Wendy Whitesitt; E-mail: wendy.whitesitt@ci.mcminnville.or.us; *Ch Serv,* Kimbre Chapman; Tel: 503-435-5569, E-mail: kimbre.chapman@ci.mcminnville.or.us; *Circ,* Sheila McAlexander; Staff 8.5 (MLS 4.5, Non-MLS 4)
Founded 1912. Pop 50,029; Circ 352,211
Jul 2012-Jun 2013 Income (Main Library and Branch(s)) $1,483,799. Mats Exp $92,742, Books $65,034, Per/Ser (Incl. Access Fees) $4,831, AV Mat $12,377, Electronic Ref Mat (Incl. Access Fees) $10,500. Sal $703,905
Library Holdings: Audiobooks 4,609; DVDs 5,467; e-books 25,761; Bk Titles 78,750; Per Subs 113
Automation Activity & Vendor Info: (Acquisitions) Innovative Interfaces, Inc; (Cataloging) Innovative Interfaces, Inc; (Circulation) Innovative Interfaces, Inc; (OPAC) Innovative Interfaces, Inc; (Serials) Innovative Interfaces, Inc
Database Vendor: EBSCOhost
Wireless access
Function: Adult bk club, Audiobks via web, Bilingual assistance for Spanish patrons, Bk club(s), Bks on CD, Children's prog, Computer training, Computers for patron use, Copy machines, Digital talking bks, e-mail & chat, e-mail serv, Electronic databases & coll, Free DVD rentals, Home delivery & serv to Sr ctr & nursing homes, Homebound delivery serv, ILL available, Magnifiers for reading, Mail & tel request accepted, Music CDs, Online cat, Online ref, Online searches, Outreach serv, Outside serv via phone, mail, e-mail & web, OverDrive digital audio bks, Photocopying/Printing, Preschool outreach, Preschool reading prog, Prog for children & young adult, Pub access computers, Ref serv available, Ref serv in person, Scanner, Senior computer classes, Spanish lang bks, Spoken cassettes & CDs, Spoken cassettes & DVDs, Story hour, Summer reading prog, Tax forms, Teen prog, Telephone ref, Video lending libr, Wheelchair accessible
Publications: Friends of the Library News
Partic in Chemeketa Cooperative Regional Library Service
Open Tues-Thurs 10-8, Fri-Sun 10-5
Friends of the Library Group
Bookmobiles: 1

MEDFORD

L JACKSON COUNTY LAW LIBRARY*, Justice Bldg, Basement, 100 S Oakdale Ave, 97501. SAN 325-8149. Tel: 541-774-6437. FAX: 541-774-6767. Web Site: www.co.jackson.or.us. *Librn,* Pam Pfeil; E-mail: pfeilpd@jacksoncounty.org
Library Holdings: Bk Vols 15,000; Per Subs 10
Open Mon-Fri 8-12 & 1-5

P JACKSON COUNTY LIBRARY SERVICES*, 205 S Central Ave, 97501-2730. SAN 357-9875. Tel: 541-774-8679. Circulation Tel: 541-774-8682. Interlibrary Loan Service Tel: 541-774-6421. FAX: 541-774-6748. Reference FAX: 541-734-3997. E-mail: infolib@jcls.org. Web Site: www.jcls.org. *Dir,* Kim Wolfe; Tel: 541-774-6980, E-mail: kwolfe@jcls.org; *Br Serv Mgr,* Wende Glimpse; Tel: 541-774-6443, E-mail: wglimpse@jcls.org; *Cent Libr Mgr,* Kimberly Laura; E-mail: lkimberly@jcls.org; *Ch Serv, Coll Mgr,* Marian Barker; Tel: 541-774-6423, E-mail: mbarker@jcls.org; *Tech Serv,* Stroud Crystal; Tel: 541-774-6573, E-mail: cstroud@jcls.org; Staff 18 (MLS 10, Non-MLS 8)
Founded 1908. Pop 192,992; Circ 35,000,000
Jul 2007-Jun 2008 Income (Main Library and Branch(s)) $3,000,000, State $29,624, Federal $10, Locally Generated Income $10. Mats Exp $690,000, Books $453,213, Per/Ser (Incl. Access Fees) $58,000, AV Mat $50,000, Electronic Ref Mat (Incl. Access Fees) $39,338
Library Holdings: Bk Vols 567,118; Per Subs 1,560
Special Collections: Oregon Coll; Werner Sheet Music Coll. State Document Depository
Automation Activity & Vendor Info: (Cataloging) Innovative Interfaces, Inc; (Circulation) Innovative Interfaces, Inc
Database Vendor: EBSCOhost
Wireless access
Partic in Southern Oregon Library Federation
Open Mon 12-7, Tues 12-6, Wed 10-5, Sat 12-4
Friends of the Library Group
Branches: 14
APPLEGATE BRANCH, 18484 N Applegate Rd, Applegate, 97530. (Mail add: PO Box 3308, Applegate, 97530-3308), SAN 358-0261. Tel: 541-846-7346. FAX: 541-846-7346. *Br Mgr,* Lisa Martin; E-mail: lmartin@jcls.org
Open Tues & Fri 2-6, Sat 10-2
Friends of the Library Group
ASHLAND BRANCH, 410 Siskiyou Blvd, Ashland, 97520-2136, SAN 357-9905. Tel: 541-774-6980. Reference FAX: 541-774-6892. E-mail: ashlib@jcls.org. *Br Mgr,* Amy Blossom
Special Collections: Shakespeare
Open Mon 10-8, Tues & Wed 10-6, Thurs & Sat Noon-5, Sun Noon-4
Friends of the Library Group
BUTTE FALLS BRANCH, 626 Fir Ave, Butte Falls, 97522. (Mail add: PO Box 138, Butte Falls, 97522-0138), SAN 357-993X. Tel: 541-865-3511. FAX: 541-865-3511. *Br Mgr,* Lee Ann Pierce; E-mail: lpierce@jcls.org; Staff 1 (Non-MLS 1)
Open Tues 10-2, Thurs 1-5
Friends of the Library Group
CENTRAL POINT BRANCH, 116 S Third St, Central Point, 97502, SAN 357-9964. Tel: 541-664-3228. *Br Mgr,* Position Currently Open
Open Mon 11-6, Wed 1-6, Thurs 1-7, Fri 11-5
Friends of the Library Group
EAGLE POINT BRANCH, 239 W Main St, Eagle Point, 97524. (Mail add: PO Box 459, Eagle Point, 97524-0459), SAN 357-9999. Tel: 541-826-3313. FAX: 541-826-3313. *Br Mgr,* Charlene Prinsen
Open Wed, Fri & Sat 10-4, Thurs Noon-6
Friends of the Library Group
GOLD HILL BRANCH, 202 Dardanelles St, Gold Hill, 97525-0136. (Mail add: PO Box 258, Gold Hill, 97525-0258), SAN 358-0024. Tel: 541-855-1994. FAX: 541-855-1994. *Br Mgr,* Cindy Oldfield; E-mail: coldfield@jcls.org; Staff 2 (Non-MLS 2)
Open Mon 11-6, Wed 2-7, Fri 1-5
Friends of the Library Group
JACKSONVILLE BRANCH, 340 West C St, Jacksonville, 97530. (Mail add: PO Box 490, Jacksonville, 97530-0490), SAN 358-0059. Tel: 541-899-1665. FAX: 541-899-1665. *Br Mgr,* Laurel Prchal; E-mail: lprchal@jcls.org; Staff 2 (Non-MLS 2)
Open Mon Noon-5, Wed 10-5, Thurs 2-6, Sat 10-2
Friends of the Library Group
PHOENIX BRANCH, 510 W First St, Phoenix, 97535. (Mail add: PO Box 277, Phoenix, 97535-0277), SAN 358-0083. Tel: 541-535-7090. FAX: 541-535-7090. *Br Mgr,* Jody Flemming; Staff 2 (Non-MLS 2)
Open Mon 1-7, Tues & Thurs 11-4
Friends of the Library Group
PROSPECT BRANCH, 150 Mill Creek Dr, Prospect, 97536. (Mail add: PO Box 39, Prospect, 97536-0039), SAN 358-0113. Tel: 541-560-3668. FAX: 541-560-3668. *Br Mgr,* Lee Ann Pierce; E-mail: lpierce@jcls.org; Staff 1 (Non-MLS 1)
Open Wed 10-2, Fri 1-5
Friends of the Library Group
ROGUE RIVER BRANCH, 412 E Main St, Rogue River, 97537. (Mail add: PO Box 1075, Rogue River, 97537-1075), SAN 358-0148. Tel: 541-864-8850. FAX: 541-864-8871. *Br Mgr,* Seline Pierson
Open Mon & Fri 10-4, Tues & Thurs 1-7, Sat Noon-4
Friends of the Library Group
RUCH BRANCH, 7919 Hwy 238, Ruch, 97530-9728, SAN 329-6628. Tel: 541-899-7438. *Br Mgr,* Thalia Truedell; E-mail: ttruedell@jcls.org
Open Tues 11-5, Thurs 1-7, Sat 12-4
Friends of the Library Group
SHADY COVE BRANCH, 22477 Hwy 62, Shady Cove, 97539-9718. (Mail add: PO Box 502, Shady Cove, 97539-0502), SAN 358-0172. Tel: 541-878-2270. FAX: 541-878-2270. *Br Mgr,* Sue Anne Torres; E-mail: atorres@jcls.org
Open Tues 12-6, Wed 1-7, Fri 10-2
Friends of the Library Group
TALENT BRANCH, 101 Home St, Talent, 97540. (Mail add: PO Box 597, Talent, 97540-0597), SAN 358-0202. Tel: 541-535-4163. FAX: 541-535-4163. *Br Mgr,* Patrick Mathewes
Open Tues 10-6, Wed & Thurs 12-7, Fri & Sat 10-5
Friends of the Library Group
WHITE CITY BRANCH, 3143 Ave C, White City, 97503-1443, SAN 358-0237. Tel: 541-864-8880. FAX: 541-864-8889. *Br Mgr,* Jo Ann Crosby; E-mail: jcrosby@jcls.org
Open Mon 11-6, Tues 10-2, Thurs 12-5, Sat 10-4
Friends of the Library Group

MILL CITY

P MILL CITY LIBRARY*, 260 SW Second Ave, 97360. (Mail add: PO Box 1194, 97360-1194). Tel: 503-897-4143. *In Charge,* Susann Heller
Library Holdings: AV Mats 300; Bk Vols 10,000; Per Subs 35; Talking Bks 25
Open Mon-Thurs 10-12 & 1:30-3:30, Fri & Sat 10-12
Friends of the Library Group

MILTON-FREEWATER

P MILTON-FREEWATER PUBLIC LIBRARY, Eight SW Eighth Ave, 97862-1501. SAN 358-0598. Tel: 541-938-8247. Interlibrary Loan Service Tel: 541-938-8239. Administration Tel: 541-938-8246. FAX: 541-938-8254. Web Site: www.mfcity.com/library. *Dir,* Erin Wells; E-mail: erin.wells@milton-freewater-or.gov; *Ch Serv, YA Serv,* Lili Schmidt; Tel: 541-938-8248, E-mail: lili.schmidt@milton-freewater-or.gov; *Circ, ILL,* Donna Sheridan; E-mail: donna.sheridan@milton-freewater-or.gov; *Local Hist/Genealogy,* Sandy Nelson; Tel: 541-938-8251, E-mail: genealogy@milton-freewater-or.gov; Staff 1 (MLS 1)
Founded 1913. Pop 12,000; Circ 50,583
Jul 2013-Jun 2014 Income $333,819, State $1,088, City $128,140, Locally Generated Income $15,401, Other $189,190. Mats Exp $25,000. Sal $178,654
Library Holdings: AV Mats 2,624; Electronic Media & Resources 26; Bk Vols 43,000; Per Subs 54; Videos 1,078
Subject Interests: Genealogy, Local hist
Automation Activity & Vendor Info: (Cataloging) Evergreen; (Circulation) Evergreen; (ILL) Evergreen; (OPAC) Evergreen
Database Vendor: EBSCO Auto Repair Reference, EBSCOhost
Wireless access
Function: Archival coll, Audiobks via web, Bks on cassette, Bks on CD, Children's prog, Computers for patron use, Copy machines, E-Reserves, Electronic databases & coll, Exhibits, Fax serv, Free DVD rentals, Handicapped accessible, ILL available, Magnifiers for reading, Mail & tel request accepted, Microfiche/film & reading machines, Music CDs, Newsp ref libr, Online cat, Online searches, OverDrive digital audio bks, Photocopying/Printing, Preschool outreach, Preschool reading prog, Prog for adults, Prog for children & young adult, Pub access computers, Spanish lang bks, Spoken cassettes & CDs, Spoken cassettes & DVDs, Story hour, Summer reading prog, Tax forms, VHS videos, Video lending libr, Web-catalog, Wheelchair accessible
Mem of Umatilla County Special Library District
Partic in Libraries of Eastern Oregon (LEO); Sage Library System of Eastern Oregon
Special Services for the Deaf - Bks on deafness & sign lang
Special Services for the Blind - Audio mat; Bks on cassette; Bks on CD; Home delivery serv; Large print bks; Talking bks
Open Mon-Wed 12-8, Thurs & Fri 10-6, Sat 10-2
Restriction: Non-resident fee, Open to pub for ref & circ; with some limitations
Friends of the Library Group

MILWAUKIE

P LEDDING LIBRARY OF MILWAUKIE*, 10660 SE 21st Ave, 97222. SAN 314-1241. Tel: 503-786-7580. Reference Tel: 503-786-7546. Administration Tel: 503-786-7584. FAX: 503-659-9497. Web Site: www.ci.milwaukie.or.us/library. *Dir,* Josef Sandfort; *Ch Serv,* Jana Hoffman; Tel: 503-786-7585; *Circ,* Nancy Wittig; Tel: 503-786-7582; *Ref Serv,* Robert Lanxon; Staff 5 (MLS 4, Non-MLS 1)
Founded 1934. Pop 30,000; Circ 671,554
Jul 2009-Jun 2010 Income $2,453,871. Mats Exp $130,000. Sal $854,804 (Prof $828,747)
Library Holdings: Bk Vols 88,749; Per Subs 210; Videos 12,010
Subject Interests: Local hist, Northwest
Automation Activity & Vendor Info: (Acquisitions) SirsiDynix; (Cataloging) SirsiDynix; (Circulation) SirsiDynix; (OPAC) SirsiDynix
Database Vendor: Gale Cengage Learning
Wireless access
Function: Handicapped accessible, Homebound delivery serv, ILL available, Photocopying/Printing, Prog for children & young adult, Ref serv available, Summer reading prog, Telephone ref
Partic in Library Information Network of Clackamas County
Open Mon-Thurs 10-9, Fri & Sat 10-6, Sun 12-6
Friends of the Library Group

MOLALLA

P MOLALLA PUBLIC LIBRARY*, 201 E Fifth St, 97038. (Mail add: PO Box 1289, 97038-1289), SAN 314-125X. Tel: 503-829-2593. FAX: 503-759-3486. E-mail: moref@lincc.lib.or.us. *Dir,* Glenda Triebwasser
Pop 19,950; Circ 115,000
Library Holdings: Bk Vols 35,365; Per Subs 212
Special Collections: Animal Husbandry Coll
Automation Activity & Vendor Info: (Cataloging) SirsiDynix; (Circulation) SirsiDynix; (OPAC) SirsiDynix
Partic in Library Information Network of Clackamas County
Open Mon-Thurs 10-8, Fri & Sat 10-5
Friends of the Library Group

MONMOUTH

P MONMOUTH PUBLIC LIBRARY, 168 S Ecols St, 97361. (Mail add: PO Box 10, 97361-0010), SAN 314-1268. Tel: 503-838-1932. FAX: 503-838-3899. Web Site: www.ci.monmouth.or.us/library. *Libr Dir,* Krist Obrist; E-mail: kobrist@ci.monmouth.or.us; *IT/Ref Librn,* Howard Feltmann; E-mail: hfeltmann@ci.monmouth.or.us; *Youth Serv Librn,* Carrie Kasperick; E-mail: ckasperick@ci.monmouth.or.us; *Circ Supvr,* Terry Alvarez; E-mail: talvarez@ci.monmouth.or.us; Staff 9 (MLS 3, Non-MLS 6)
Founded 1934. Pop 17,125; Circ 155,000
Jul 2005-Jun 2006 Income $545,377. Mats Exp $43,693. Sal $223,363
Library Holdings: High Interest/Low Vocabulary Bk Vols 100; Bk Vols 66,652; Per Subs 174
Automation Activity & Vendor Info: (Acquisitions) Innovative Interfaces, Inc; (Cataloging) Innovative Interfaces, Inc; (OPAC) Innovative Interfaces, Inc
Wireless access
Partic in Chemeketa Cooperative Regional Library Service
Open Tues-Thurs 10-8, Fri 10-6, Sat 10-5
Friends of the Library Group

WESTERN OREGON UNIVERSITY

C WAYNE & LYNN HAMERSLY LIBRARY*, 345 N Monmouth Ave, 97361-1396, SAN 314-1276. Tel: 503-838-8418. Circulation Tel: 503-838-8902. Reference Tel: 503-838-8899. Administration Tel: 503-838-8240. FAX: 503-838-8399. Interlibrary Loan Service FAX: 503-838-8645. E-mail: refdesk@wou.edu. Web Site: www.wou.edu/library. *Dean of Libr,* Dr Allen McKiel; Tel: 503-838-8886, E-mail: mckiela@wou.edu; *Adjunct Instruction,* Tracy Scharn; Tel: 503-838-8892, E-mail: scharnt@wou.edu; *Archives & Exhibits,* Erin Passehl; Tel: 503-838-8893, E-mail: passehl@wou.edu; *Coll Develop, Tech Serv,* Camila Gabaldon Winningham; Tel: 503-838-8653, E-mail: gabaldonc@wou.edu; *Instruction & Outreach,* Robert Monge; Tel: 803-838-8887, E-mail: monger@wou.edu; *Libr Instruction,* Shirley Lincicum; Tel: 503-838-8890, E-mail: lincics@wou.edu; *Pub Serv,* Janeanne Rockwell-Kincannon; Tel: 503-838-9493, E-mail: kincanj@wou.edu. Subject Specialists: *Computer sci, Health,* Camila Gabaldon Winningham; *English,* Robert Monge; *Creative arts, Hist,* Shirley Lincicum; *Gender studies, Humanities,* Janeanne Rockwell-Kincannon; Staff 17.25 (MLS 6, Non-MLS 11.25)
Founded 1856. Enrl 5,500; Highest Degree: Master
Jul 2007-Jun 2008 Income $1,889,995. Mats Exp $689,196, Books $138,681, Per/Ser (Incl. Access Fees) $344,609, AV Mat $11,171, Electronic Ref Mat (Incl. Access Fees) $189,714, Presv $5,021. Sal $922,266 (Prof $493,085)
Library Holdings: AV Mats 9,984; e-books 3,149; e-journals 2,600; Bk Titles 187,340; Bk Vols 236,684; Per Subs 798
Special Collections: Archival Materials & Special Coll Relating to University History & Former Governor Robert W Straub; State Adopted Textbooks. State Document Depository; US Document Depository
Automation Activity & Vendor Info: (Acquisitions) Innovative Interfaces, Inc; (Cataloging) Innovative Interfaces, Inc; (Circulation) Innovative Interfaces, Inc; (ILL) Innovative Interfaces, Inc; (OPAC) Innovative Interfaces, Inc; (Serials) Innovative Interfaces, Inc
Partic in OCLC Online Computer Library Center, Inc; Orbis Cascade Alliance
Publications: Hamersly Library Guide (Library handbook)
Special Services for the Deaf - TTY equip

C JENSEN ARCTIC MUSEUM-WESTERN RESEARCH LIBRARY*, 590 W Church St, 97361, SAN 329-1952. Tel: 503-838-8468. FAX: 503-838-8289. E-mail: arctic@wou.edu. Web Site: www.wou.edu/president/advancement/jensen/index.php. *Curator,* Roben Jack Larrison
Founded 1985
Library Holdings: Bk Titles 1,400
Subject Interests: Arctic, Native Am
Publications: Paglan (Newsletter)
Open Wed-Sat 10-4

MOSIER

P MOSIER VALLEY LIBRARY*, 1003 Third Ave, 97040. (Mail add: PO Box 525, 97040-0525). Tel: 541-478-3495. *Pres,* Glenna McCargar
Pop 2,000
Library Holdings: Bk Vols 3,500
Wireless access
Open Mon, Thurs & Fri 1-3, Wed 10-12 & 1-3, Sat 10-12
Friends of the Library Group

MOUNT ANGEL

P MOUNT ANGEL PUBLIC LIBRARY*, 290 E Charles St, 97362. (Mail add: PO Box 870, 97362-0870), SAN 314-1306. Tel: 503-845-6401. FAX: 503-845-6261. *Dir,* Collette Decock; *Librn,* Marilyn Clouser; *Ch,* Samantha McDermott
Founded 1946. Pop 3,700; Circ 34,711
Library Holdings: AV Mats 2,081; Bk Vols 30,413; Per Subs 58
Function: After school storytime
Partic in Chemeketa Cooperative Regional Library Service
Open Tues 12-6:30, Wed 11-5, Thurs & Fri 12-5, Sat 1-5
Friends of the Library Group

MYRTLE POINT

P DORA PUBLIC LIBRARY*, 56125 Goldbrick Rd, 97458. SAN 376-7256. Tel: 541-572-6009. Interlibrary Loan Service Tel: 541-888-7260. Web Site: www.doralibrary.plinkit.org. *Dir,* Betty H Vaughn; Staff 2 (Non-MLS 2)
Pop 350
Library Holdings: Bk Vols 11,326; Per Subs 35; Talking Bks 470; Videos 1,344
Automation Activity & Vendor Info: (Cataloging) Innovative Interfaces, Inc; (Circulation) Innovative Interfaces, Inc; (OPAC) Innovative Interfaces, Inc
Database Vendor: EBSCOhost
Function: ILL available
Mem of Coos County Library Service District
Open Mon, Wed & Fri 1-6, Tues & Thurs 6pm-8pm, Sat 10-2

P MYRTLE POINT LIBRARY*, Flora M Laird Memorial Library, 435 Fifth St, 97458-1113. SAN 314-1314. Tel: 541-572-2591. FAX: 541-572-5168. *Libr Dir,* Barbara Caffey; E-mail: bcaffey@cclsd.org
Founded 1925. Pop 4,308; Circ 53,827
Jul 2006-Jun 2007 Income $159,501. Mats Exp $54,655. Sal $132,325
Library Holdings: Bk Vols 35,306; Per Subs 77
Automation Activity & Vendor Info: (Cataloging) Innovative Interfaces, Inc; (Circulation) Innovative Interfaces, Inc; (OPAC) Innovative Interfaces, Inc
Wireless access
Mem of Coos County Library Service District
Open Mon-Wed 10-8, Thurs-Sat 12-5

NEWBERG

C GEORGE FOX UNIVERSITY*, Murdock Learning Resource Center, 416 N Meridian St, 97132. SAN 314-1322. Tel: 503-554-2410. Interlibrary Loan Service Tel: 503-554-2423. Reference Tel: 503-554-2419. FAX: 503-554-3599. Web Site: library.georgefox.edu. *Dean of Libr,* Merrill Johnson; *Pub Serv Librn,* Jane Scott; *Ref Librn,* Rodney Birch; *Ref Librn,* Rob Bohall; *Tech Serv & Syst Librn,* Alexander Rolfe; *ILL Coordr,* Laurie Lieggi
Founded 1891. Enrl 3,485; Highest Degree: Doctorate
Jul 2011-Jun 2012. Mats Exp $968,662, Books $137,575, Per/Ser (Incl. Access Fees) $390,961, AV Mat $12,224, Electronic Ref Mat (Incl. Access Fees) $425,815, Presv $2,087. Sal $596,001 (Prof $277,189)
Library Holdings: AV Mats 5,649; CDs 524; DVDs 2,003; e-books 148,608; e-journals 56,042; Bk Titles 293,000; Bk Vols 357,000; Videos 1,515
Special Collections: Herbert Hoover Coll, bks, pamphlets, per, photog; Peace Coll, bks, per; Society of Friends (Quaker Coll), bks, pamphlets, per, photog
Automation Activity & Vendor Info: (Acquisitions) Innovative Interfaces, Inc; (Cataloging) Innovative Interfaces, Inc; (Circulation) Innovative Interfaces, Inc; (Course Reserve) Innovative Interfaces, Inc; (OPAC) Innovative Interfaces, Inc; (Serials) Innovative Interfaces, Inc
Wireless access
Partic in OCLC Online Computer Library Center, Inc; Orbis Cascade Alliance

Departmental Libraries:

PORTLAND CENTER LIBRARY, Hampton Plaza, 12753 SW 68th Ave, Portland, 97223, SAN 314-1934. Tel: 503-554-6130. Interlibrary Loan Service Tel: 503-554-6132. Reference Tel: 503-554-6136. FAX: 503-554-6134. *Librn,* Charlie Kamilos; Tel: 503-554-6131, E-mail: ckamilos@georgefox.edu; *E-Learning & Ref Librn,* Robin Ashford
Highest Degree: Doctorate
Jul 2011-Jun 2012 Income $321,192. Mats Exp $79,502, Books $14,741, Per/Ser (Incl. Access Fees) $34,110, AV Mat $7,851, Electronic Ref Mat (Incl. Access Fees) $22,750, Presv $50
Library Holdings: AV Mats 2,533; CDs 11; DVDs 300; e-journals 28,950; Bk Titles 49,687; Bk Vols 57,612; Per Subs 293; Videos 303
Subject Interests: Counseling, Theol

P NEWBERG PUBLIC LIBRARY, 503 E Hancock St, 97132-2899. SAN 314-1330. Tel: 503-538-7323. FAX: 503-538-9720. E-mail: nplibrary@newbergoregon.gov. Web Site: www.newbergoregon.gov/library. *Dir,* Leah Griffith; Tel: 503-537-1256, E-mail: leah.griffith@newbergoregon.gov; *Asst Dir,* Korie Buerkle; E-mail: korie.buerkle@newbergoregon.gov; *Vols Serv Coordr,* Rea Andrew; E-mail: rea.andrew@newbergoregon.gov; *Cat, YA Serv,* K'lyn Hann; E-mail: klyn.hann@newbergoregon.gov; *Ch Serv,* Mary Lynn Thomas; E-mail: mary.thomas@newbergoregon.gov; Staff 13 (MLS 2, Non-MLS 11)
Founded 1912. Pop 22,000; Circ 288,555
Jul 2009-Jun 2010 Income $1,143,135, State $3,500, City $683,646, County $61,000, Locally Generated Income $50,000, Other $344,989. Mats Exp $78,700, Books $60,400, Per/Ser (Incl. Access Fees) $6,800, AV Mat $9,000, Electronic Ref Mat (Incl. Access Fees) $2,500. Sal $744,843 (Prof $172,496)
Library Holdings: AV Mats 3,500; Bks on Deafness & Sign Lang 10; High Interest/Low Vocabulary Bk Vols 100; Large Print Bks 828; Bk Titles 64,000; Bk Vols 70,000; Per Subs 268; Talking Bks 2,500
Special Collections: Municipal Document Depository
Automation Activity & Vendor Info: (Acquisitions) Innovative Interfaces, Inc; (Cataloging) Innovative Interfaces, Inc; (Circulation) Innovative Interfaces, Inc; (OPAC) Innovative Interfaces, Inc
Database Vendor: Gale Cengage Learning, Overdrive, Inc
Wireless access
Function: Audio & video playback equip for onsite use, Handicapped accessible, Home delivery & serv to Sr ctr & nursing homes, ILL available, Online searches, Photocopying/Printing, Prog for adults, Prog for children & young adult, Ref serv available, Spoken cassettes & CDs, Summer reading prog, Telephone ref, VHS videos, Wheelchair accessible
Partic in Chemeketa Cooperative Regional Library Service
Open Tues & Thurs 10-8, Wed 10-5, Fri 12-5, Sat 10-3
Friends of the Library Group

NEWPORT

P LINCOLN COUNTY LIBRARY DISTRICT*, 1247 NW Grove St, Ste 2, 97365. (Mail add: PO Box 2027, 97365-0144). Tel: 541-265-3066. FAX: 541-265-3066. E-mail: lcld@lincolncolibrarydist.org. Web Site: lcldinfo.wikispaces.com. *Dir,* Diedre Conkling; E-mail: diedre@lincolncolibrarydist.org; *Cat,* Jane Cothron; E-mail: jcothron@lincolncolibrarydist.org; Staff 2 (MLS 2)
Founded 1988. Pop 23,590
Jul 2012-Jun 2013 Income $1,471,165, State $3,354, County $1,251,123, Other $216,688. Mats Exp $21,739, Books $7,134, Per/Ser (Incl. Access Fees) $941, AV Mat $1,585, Electronic Ref Mat (Incl. Access Fees) $12,079. Sal $202,313 (Prof $130,361)
Library Holdings: AV Mats 2,679; CDs 901; DVDs 1,778; e-books 113,995; Bk Vols 17,900; Per Subs 33
Special Collections: Native American Coll
Automation Activity & Vendor Info: (Acquisitions) ByWater Solutions; (Cataloging) OCLC CatExpress; (Circulation) ByWater Solutions; (Course Reserve) ByWater Solutions; (ILL) OCLC FirstSearch; (OPAC) ByWater Solutions; (Serials) ByWater Solutions
Database Vendor: Gale Cengage Learning, LearningExpress, OCLC FirstSearch, OCLC WorldShare Interlibrary Loan
Wireless access
Function: Doc delivery serv, ILL available, Libr develop, Prof lending libr
Partic in Chinook Library Network
Open Mon-Fri 8:30-6:30
Restriction: Prof mat only
Friends of the Library Group

P NEWPORT PUBLIC LIBRARY, 35 NW Nye St, 97365-3714. SAN 314-1349. Tel: 541-265-2153. FAX: 541-574-9496. TDD: 800-735-2900. E-mail: reference@newportlibrary.org. Web Site: www.newportlibrary.org. *Libr Dir,* Ted J Smith; *Asst Dir,* Kay Eldon; *Ref Librn, Supv Librn,* Sheryl Eldridge; *Supv Librn, Youth Serv Librn,* Rebecca Cohen; *Outreach Serv Librn,* Alice MacGougan; *Cataloger,* Stacy Johns; Staff 12 (MLS 5, Non-MLS 7)
Founded 1945. Pop 17,500; Circ 287,214
Library Holdings: Bk Vols 71,688
Automation Activity & Vendor Info: (Cataloging) SirsiDynix; (Circulation) SirsiDynix; (ILL) OCLC; (OPAC) Innovative Interfaces, Inc; (Serials) SirsiDynix
Database Vendor: Gale Cengage Learning, Innovative Interfaces, Inc, OCLC, OCLC WorldShare Interlibrary Loan, ReferenceUSA
Wireless access
Function: After school storytime, Audiobks via web, AV serv, Bilingual assistance for Spanish patrons, Bk club(s), Bks on CD, Children's prog, Computer training, Computers for patron use, Copy machines, Digital talking bks, e-mail & chat, e-mail serv, Electronic databases & coll, Free DVD rentals, Handicapped accessible, Holiday prog, Home delivery & serv to Sr ctr & nursing homes, Homebound delivery serv, ILL available, Magnifiers for reading, Mail & tel request accepted, Music CDs, Online cat, Online ref, Online searches, OverDrive digital audio bks, Photocopying/Printing, Preschool outreach, Prog for adults, Prog for children & young adult, Pub access computers, Ref serv available, Ref serv

in person, Summer reading prog, Tax forms, Teen prog, Telephone ref, VHS videos, Video lending libr, Web-catalog, Wheelchair accessible
Special Services for the Deaf - Bks on deafness & sign lang
Special Services for the Blind - Assistive/Adapted tech devices, equip & products; VisualTek equip
Open Mon-Wed 10-9, Thurs-Sat 10-6, Sun 12-5
Friends of the Library Group

J OREGON COAST COMMUNITY COLLEGE LIBRARY*, 332 SW Coast Hwy, 97365-4928. SAN 374-5945. Tel: 541-574-7126. FAX: 541-265-3820. E-mail: library@occc.cc.or.us. Web Site: www.occc.cc.or.us/library/. *Dir, Libr & Media,* Kathleen Searles; E-mail: ksearles@occc.cc.or.us; Staff 2 (MLS 2)
Founded 1993. Enrl 474; Fac 35; Highest Degree: Associate
Library Holdings: e-books 1,800; Bk Vols 8,132; Per Subs 50; Videos 1,500
Automation Activity & Vendor Info: (Cataloging) SirsiDynix; (Circulation) SirsiDynix; (OPAC) SirsiDynix
Database Vendor: EBSCOhost, Gale Cengage Learning, LexisNexis, OCLC FirstSearch, ProQuest, SirsiDynix, SirsiDynix
Partic in Chinook Library Network
Open Mon-Thurs 9-6, Fri 9-4:30

S OREGON COAST HISTORY CENTER LIBRARY*, 545 SW Ninth St, 97365. SAN 370-548X. Tel: 541-265-7509. FAX: 541-265-3992. E-mail: coasthistory@newportnet.com. Web Site: www.oregoncoasthistory.org. *Archivist,* Jodi Weeber; Staff 1 (Non-MLS 1)
Founded 1961
Library Holdings: Bk Titles 600
Special Collections: Lincoln County History, bks, docs, photos; Siletz Tribal History, docs, maps, photos, artifacts
Function: Res libr
Open Tues-Sat 11-4

C OREGON STATE UNIVERSITY*, Marilyn Potts Guin Library, 2030 Marine Science Dr, 97365. SAN 321-5342. Tel: 541-867-0249. FAX: 541-867-0105. E-mail: hmsc.library@oregonstate.edu. Web Site: osulibrary.oregonstate.edu/guin. *Head of Libr,* Janet G Webster; Tel: 541-867-0108, E-mail: janet.webster@oregonstate.edu; Staff 3 (MLS 1, Non-MLS 2)
Founded 1967
Library Holdings: Bk Titles 20,000; Bk Vols 35,000; Per Subs 310
Subject Interests: Aquaculture, Marine fisheries, Marine mammals, Marine sci
Automation Activity & Vendor Info: (Acquisitions) Innovative Interfaces, Inc; (Cataloging) Innovative Interfaces, Inc; (Circulation) Innovative Interfaces, Inc; (Course Reserve) Innovative Interfaces, Inc; (ILL) Innovative Interfaces, Inc; (Media Booking) Innovative Interfaces, Inc; (OPAC) Innovative Interfaces, Inc; (Serials) Innovative Interfaces, Inc
Database Vendor: Cambridge Scientific Abstracts, EBSCOhost, LexisNexis, OCLC FirstSearch, OVID Technologies, ProQuest, Thomson - Web of Science, Wilson - Wilson Web
Wireless access
Function: Res libr
Partic in OCLC Online Computer Library Center, Inc
Open Mon-Fri 8-5
Friends of the Library Group

NORTH BEND

G BUREAU OF LAND MANAGEMENT*, Coos Bay District Office Library, 1300 Airport Lane, 97459-2000. SAN 314-0709. Tel: 541-756-0100. FAX: 541-751-4303. E-mail: BLM_OR_CB_Mail@blm.gov. Web Site: www.or.blm.gov/coosbay. *Supvr,* Linda Petterson
Library Holdings: Bk Vols 2,500
Restriction: Not open to pub

P NORTH BEND PUBLIC LIBRARY*, 1800 Sherman Ave, 97459. SAN 314-1357. Tel: 541-756-0400. FAX: 541-756-1073. Web Site: northbendlibrary.org. *Dir,* Gary Sharp; *Asst Dir,* Buzzy Nielsen; Staff 4 (MLS 4)
Founded 1914. Pop 18,000; Circ 242,168
Library Holdings: Bk Titles 95,000; Bk Vols 112,000; Per Subs 214
Special Collections: City; Oregoniana (Oregon Coll), bks, clippings, pamphlets. Oral History
Automation Activity & Vendor Info: (Acquisitions) Innovative Interfaces, Inc; (Circulation) Innovative Interfaces, Inc; (OPAC) Innovative Interfaces, Inc
Wireless access
Mem of Coos County Library Service District
Partic in OCLC Online Computer Library Center, Inc; Southern Oregon Library Federation
Open Mon-Wed 11-8, Thurs & Fri 11-6, Sat 12-5, Sun (Fall-Spring) 12-5
Friends of the Library Group

NORTH POWDER

P NORTH POWDER LIBRARY*, 290 E St, 97867. (Mail add: PO Box 309, 97867-0309). Tel: 541-898-2175. FAX: 541-898-2175. *Librn,* Nancy Friedkline
Library Holdings: Bk Titles 900
Wireless access
Open Mon 2-7, Sat 2-6

NYSSA

P NYSSA PUBLIC LIBRARY*, 319 Main St, 97913-3845. Tel: 541-372-2978. FAX: 541-372-3278. E-mail: nyssalibrary@yahoo.com. *Librn,* Faith Adams; *Asst Librn, Circ,* Cathy Hutton; *Cat,* Jenny Simpson
Pop 6,227
Library Holdings: Bk Vols 24,000; Per Subs 30
Automation Activity & Vendor Info: (Acquisitions) Innovative Interfaces, Inc; (Cataloging) Innovative Interfaces, Inc; (Circulation) Innovative Interfaces, Inc; (Course Reserve) Innovative Interfaces, Inc; (ILL) Innovative Interfaces, Inc; (OPAC) Innovative Interfaces, Inc; (Serials) Innovative Interfaces, Inc
Open Tues & Thurs 12-7, Wed 10-5, Sat 12-4

OAK GROVE

P CLACKAMAS COUNTY LIBRARY*, Oak Lodge, 16201 SE McLoughlin Blvd, 97267-4653. SAN 314-139X. Tel: 503-655-8543. Web Site: www.co.clackamas.us/lib/. *Dir,* Doris Grolbert; Tel: 503-650-3112, E-mail: dorisgro@co.clackamas.or.us; Staff 1.88 (MLS 0.94, Non-MLS 0.94)
Founded 1938. Pop 84,411; Circ 937,898
Jul 2006-Jun 2007 Income (Main Library and Branch(s)) $1,503,044, State $29,537, County $1,390,069, Locally Generated Income $83,438. Mats Exp $78,165, Books $44,011, Per/Ser (Incl. Access Fees) $11,046, AV Mat $23,108. Sal $929,010
Library Holdings: AV Mats 27,354; e-books 2,557; Bk Vols 141,879; Per Subs 276
Automation Activity & Vendor Info: (Acquisitions) SirsiDynix; (Cataloging) SirsiDynix; (Circulation) SirsiDynix; (OPAC) SirsiDynix
Database Vendor: OCLC FirstSearch
Partic in Library Information Network of Clackamas County
Open Tues-Thurs 12:30-8, Fri & Sat 10:30-6
Friends of the Library Group
Branches: 2
CLACKAMAS CORNER, 11750 SE 82nd Ave, Ste D, Portland, 97086, SAN 328-7106. Tel: 503-722-6222. Reference Tel: 503-722-6227. *Dir,* Doris Grolbert; Tel: 503-650-3112, E-mail: dorisgro@co.clackamas.or.us; *Ref Serv,* Doug Jones
Open Tues-Thurs 12:30-8, Fri & Sat 10:30-6
Friends of the Library Group
HOODLAND, 68256 E Hwy 26, Welches, 97067. Tel: 503-622-3460. *Dir,* Doris Grolbert; Tel: 503-650-3112, E-mail: dorisgro@co.clackamas.or.us
Open Tues-Thurs 12-8, Fri & Sat 12-5
Friends of the Library Group

OAKRIDGE

P OAKRIDGE PUBLIC LIBRARY, 48326 E First St, 97463. (Mail add: PO Box 1410, 97463-1410), SAN 314-1365. Tel: 541-782-2258. FAX: 541-782-1081. E-mail: oakridgelibrary@ci.oakridge.or.us. Web Site: www.ci.oakridge.or.us. *Coordr,* Sheri Cameron; Staff 1 (Non-MLS 1)
Founded 1950. Pop 3,200; Circ 11,000
Library Holdings: Bk Vols 18,000; Per Subs 30
Automation Activity & Vendor Info: (Cataloging) SirsiDynix; (Circulation) SirsiDynix
Wireless access
Open Mon, Wed & Fri 1-5, Tues & Thurs 9-12 & 1-5, Sat 10-2

ONTARIO

P MALHEUR COUNTY LIBRARY*, 388 SW Second Ave, 97914. SAN 358-0350. Tel: 541-889-6371. FAX: 541-889-4279. E-mail: malheurlibrary@yahoo.com. Web Site: www.malheur.or.us/library.html. *Dir,* Patricia Bradshaw; *ILL,* Betty Lee; Staff 10 (MLS 1, Non-MLS 9)
Founded 1909. Pop 32,065; Circ 190,085
Library Holdings: Bk Titles 100,847; Per Subs 88
Special Collections: Oregon & Idaho Coll. State Document Depository
Subject Interests: Literacy
Automation Activity & Vendor Info: (Cataloging) Innovative Interfaces, Inc; (Circulation) Innovative Interfaces, Inc; (ILL) Innovative Interfaces, Inc; (OPAC) Innovative Interfaces, Inc
Database Vendor: EBSCOhost, Innovative Interfaces, Inc, OCLC FirstSearch
Function: Prof lending libr, Ref serv available
Open Tues & Wed 11-6, Thurs 11-8, Fri 11-5, Sat 11-4
Friends of the Library Group
Bookmobiles: 1

J TREASURE VALLEY COMMUNITY COLLEGE LIBRARY*, 650 College Blvd, 97914-3423. Tel: 541-881-5929. FAX: 541-881-2724. E-mail: librarian@tvcc.cc. Web Site: www.tvcc.cc/library/index.cfm. *Dept Chair,* Dennis Gill; Tel: 541-881-5915; *Libr Mgr,* Christina Macklin; Tel: 541-881-5928, E-mail: cmacklin@tvcc.cc; *Libr Tech,* Virginia Crow; Tel: 541-881-5927. Subject Specialists: *Cataloging, Info literacy,* Christina Macklin; Staff 4 (Non-MLS 4)
Founded 1963. Enrl 3,200; Highest Degree: Associate
Jul 2011-Jun 2012. Mats Exp $35,000. Sal $225,000
Library Holdings: Audiobooks 250; CDs 100; DVDs 900; e-books 5,000; e-journals 8; Bk Titles 38,000; Bk Vols 42,000; Per Subs 80; Spec Interest Per Sub 40
Special Collections: Japanese American Oral History Project, videos. Oral History
Automation Activity & Vendor Info: (Acquisitions) Evergreen; (Cataloging) Evergreen; (Circulation) Evergreen; (ILL) OCLC FirstSearch; (OPAC) Evergreen; (Serials) Evergreen
Database Vendor: EBSCOhost, Facts on File, Gale Cengage Learning, H W Wilson, LearningExpress, Newsbank, ProQuest
Wireless access
Function: Archival coll, Audio & video playback equip for onsite use, Bks on CD, Computers for patron use, Digital talking bks, Distance learning, e-mail serv, Electronic databases & coll, Free DVD rentals, Handicapped accessible, ILL available, Instruction & testing, Music CDs, Online cat, Online ref, Online searches, Orientations, Pub access computers, Ref & res, Ref serv available, Ref serv in person, Spoken cassettes & CDs
Partic in Sage Library System of Eastern Oregon
Special Services for the Deaf - ADA equip
Open Mon-Thurs 7am-9pm, Fri 8-5, Sun 1-9

OREGON CITY

J CLACKAMAS COMMUNITY COLLEGE, Marshall N Dana Memorial Library, 19600 Molalla Ave, 97045. SAN 314-1381. Tel: 503-594-6323. Reference Tel: 503-594-6042. E-mail: reference@clackamas.edu. Web Site: www.clackamas.edu. *Librn,* Terry Mackey; Tel: 503-594-3315, E-mail: terrym@clackamas.edu; *Librn,* Sarah Nolan; Tel: 503-594-3316, E-mail: sarahn@clackamas.edu; *Libr Serv Coordr,* Ali Ihrke; Tel: 503-594-3312, E-mail: alison.ihrke@clackamas.edu; *Libr Serv Coordr,* Rose Taylor; Tel: 503-594-3491, E-mail: roset@clackamas.edu; Staff 4 (MLS 2, Non-MLS 2)
Founded 1967. Enrl 4,987; Fac 150; Highest Degree: Associate
Library Holdings: Bk Vols 52,600; Per Subs 300
Special Collections: Oregon Coll
Automation Activity & Vendor Info: (Acquisitions) Innovative Interfaces, Inc; (Cataloging) Innovative Interfaces, Inc; (Circulation) Innovative Interfaces, Inc; (Course Reserve) Innovative Interfaces, Inc; (ILL) Innovative Interfaces, Inc; (OPAC) Innovative Interfaces, Inc; (Serials) Innovative Interfaces, Inc
Database Vendor: 3M Library Systems, Baker & Taylor, EBSCOhost, Gale Cengage Learning, Innovative Interfaces, Inc, LexisNexis, OCLC FirstSearch, OCLC WorldShare Interlibrary Loan, ProQuest
Wireless access
Function: Res libr
Open Mon-Thurs 7:30am-8pm, Fri 7:30-5, Sat 11-3

P OREGON CITY PUBLIC LIBRARY*, 362 Warner Milne Rd, 97045. SAN 314-1403. Tel: 503-657-8269. FAX: 503-657-3702. Web Site: www.orcity.org/library. *Libr Dir,* Maureen Cole; E-mail: mcole@orcity.org; *Mgr, Libr Serv,* Lynda Ackerson; E-mail: lackerson@orcity.org; *Tech Serv,* Betty Joe Armstrong; E-mail: barmstrong@orcity.org
Founded 1904. Pop 53,000; Circ 518,000
Jul 2007-Jun 2008 Income $803,958, State $9,800, City $175,366, County $618,792. Mats Exp $79,843, Books $49,200, Per/Ser (Incl. Access Fees) $4,465, AV Mat $26,178. Sal $358,324
Library Holdings: AV Mats 13,227; Bk Vols 99,558; Per Subs 208
Special Collections: Oregon History (The Oregon Coll), bk, micro
Subject Interests: Genealogy, Local hist, Ore
Automation Activity & Vendor Info: (Acquisitions) SirsiDynix; (Cataloging) SirsiDynix; (Circulation) SirsiDynix; (OPAC) SirsiDynix
Function: Bks on cassette, Bks on CD, CD-ROM, Children's prog, Computers for patron use, Copy machines, Handicapped accessible, Homebound delivery serv, ILL available, Magnifiers for reading, Mus passes, Music CDs, Online cat, OverDrive digital audio bks, Photocopying/Printing, Prog for children & young adult, Pub access computers, Ref serv in person, Story hour, Summer reading prog, Tax forms, Teen prog, VHS videos, Wheelchair accessible
Partic in Library Information Network of Clackamas County
Open Mon-Wed 10-7, Thurs-Sat 10-6, Sun Noon-5
Friends of the Library Group

M WILLAMETTE FALLS HOSPITAL*, Health Sciences Library, 1500 Division St, 97045. SAN 375-0647. Tel: 503-650-6757. FAX: 503-650-6836. *Librn,* Heather Martin; E-mail: heather.martin@providence.org
Library Holdings: Bk Vols 800; Per Subs 450
Subject Interests: Consumer health
Open Mon-Thurs 8-1

PENDLETON

J BLUE MOUNTAIN COMMUNITY COLLEGE LIBRARY*, 2411 NW Carden Ave, 97801. (Mail add: PO Box 100, 97801), SAN 314-1411. Tel: 541-278-5915. Interlibrary Loan Service Tel: 541-278-5912. Administration Tel: 541-278-5916. Automation Services Tel: 541-276-1470. FAX: 541-276-6119. Web Site: www.bluecc.edu/library. *Dir,* Position Currently Open; *Cat, Electronic Res,* Heather Estrada; Tel: 541-278-5913, E-mail: heather.estrada@bluecc.edu; Staff 4 (MLS 2, Non-MLS 2)
Founded 1963. Enrl 2,108; Fac 79
Library Holdings: AV Mats 3,518; Bk Titles 34,821; Bk Vols 36,972; Per Subs 367
Special Collections: State Document Depository; US Document Depository
Automation Activity & Vendor Info: (Cataloging) OCLC; (Circulation) Innovative Interfaces, Inc; (Course Reserve) Innovative Interfaces, Inc; (ILL) OCLC; (OPAC) Innovative Interfaces, Inc
Database Vendor: EBSCOhost, Gale Cengage Learning, OVID Technologies
Function: AV serv, Res libr
Partic in Sage Library System of Eastern Oregon
Open Mon-Thurs 7:30am-9pm, Fri 7:30-4, Sun (Spring) 1-5

P PENDLETON PUBLIC LIBRARY*, 502 SW Dorion Ave, 97801-1698. SAN 358-0601. Tel: 541-966-0210. FAX: 541-966-0382. Web Site: www.pendleton.plinkit.org. *Dir,* Kat Davis; Staff 7 (MLS 2, Non-MLS 5)
Founded 1987. Pop 23,500; Circ 122,000
Library Holdings: AV Mats 7,685; CDs 317; DVDs 241; Electronic Media & Resources 22; High Interest/Low Vocabulary Bk Vols 221; Large Print Bks 1,954; Bk Titles 60,000; Per Subs 140; Talking Bks 5,175; Videos 2,269
Special Collections: Northeast Oregon; Pacific Northwest; Rodeo & Western Literature
Automation Activity & Vendor Info: (Cataloging) Evergreen; (Circulation) Evergreen; (OPAC) Evergreen
Wireless access
Mem of Umatilla County Special Library District
Open Mon-Thurs 10-8, Fri & Sat 10-5
Friends of the Library Group

PILOT ROCK

P PILOT ROCK PUBLIC LIBRARY*, 144 N Alder Pl, 97868. (Mail add: PO Box 520, 97868-0520), SAN 358-0628. Tel: 541-443-3285. FAX: 541-443-2253. E-mail: pilotrockpl@centurytel.net. *Librn,* Susan Hilliard
Library Holdings: Bk Titles 6,000; Per Subs 30
Partic in Umatilla County Spec Libr District
Open Mon-Fri 11-6

PORT ORFORD

P PORT ORFORD PUBLIC LIBRARY DISTRICT*, 1421 Oregon St, 97465. (Mail add: PO Box 130, 97465-0130), SAN 314-1446. Tel: 541-332-5622. E-mail: polibrary2012@gmail.com. Web Site: www.polibrary.org. *Dir,* Tobe Porter
Pop 3,232; Circ 25,539
Library Holdings: Bk Titles 22,986; Bk Vols 23,331; Per Subs 50
Automation Activity & Vendor Info: (Acquisitions) TLC (The Library Corporation); (Cataloging) TLC (The Library Corporation); (OPAC) TLC (The Library Corporation)
Open Mon-Fri 10-5, Sat & Sun 1-5
Friends of the Library Group

PORTLAND

C ART INSTITUTE OF PORTLAND LIBRARY*, 1122 NW Davis St, 97209-2911. SAN 314-1454. Tel: 503-228-6528. Toll Free Tel: 800-547-0937, 888-228-6528. FAX: 503-228-2895. E-mail: aipdlibrary@aii.edu. Web Site: www.aii.edu. *Dir,* Jennifer Cox; Staff 1 (MLS 1)
Founded 1966. Enrl 1,500; Highest Degree: Bachelor
Library Holdings: Bk Vols 27,000; Per Subs 125
Subject Interests: Advertising, Apparel design, Art, Culinary arts, Digital film, Digital video, Fashion hist, Graphic design, Indust design, Interior design, Liberal arts, Media arts & animation
Automation Activity & Vendor Info: (Acquisitions) Baker & Taylor; (Cataloging) Marcive, Inc
Database Vendor: Baker & Taylor, Brodart, Discovery Education, EBSCOhost, Electric Library, H W Wilson, Marcive, Inc, OCLC WorldShare Interlibrary Loan, Oxford Online, Wilson - Wilson Web, YBP Library Services
Wireless access

Open Mon-Thurs 7:30am-8:30pm, Fri 7:30-5, Sat 11-4
Restriction: Borrowing requests are handled by ILL

L ATER & WYNNE, LLP*, Law Library, KOIN Ctr, Ste 1800, 222 SW Columbia, 97201. SAN 372-2201. Tel: 503-226-1191. FAX: 503-226-0079. Web Site: www.aterwynne.com. *Librn,* Doreen Smith; E-mail: dss@aterwynne.com
Library Holdings: Bk Vols 20,000; Per Subs 50
Open Mon-Fri 8:30-5

G BONNEVILLE POWER ADMINISTRATION LIBRARY - 1*, 905 NE 11th Ave, 97232. (Mail add: PO Box 3621, 97208-3621), SAN 314-1853. Tel: 503-230-4171. Reference Tel: 503-230-4178. FAX: 503-230-5911. E-mail: library@bpa.gov. *Librn,* Tina L Kay; *Mgr,* Kaye Silver; Staff 2 (MLS 2)
Founded 1937
Library Holdings: Bk Titles 35,000; Bk Vols 50,000; Per Subs 200
Special Collections: BPA Coll. US Document Depository
Subject Interests: Computer sci, Electrical eng, Fish, Utilities industry, Wildlife
Automation Activity & Vendor Info: (Cataloging) SirsiDynix; (Circulation) SirsiDynix; (ILL) OCLC; (OPAC) SirsiDynix; (Serials) EBSCO Online
Database Vendor: Factiva.com, OCLC FirstSearch, ProQuest, SirsiDynix
Function: Telephone ref
Publications: Book lists; Brochure; Pathfinders
Open Mon-Fri 7:30-4:30

L BULLIVANT, HOUSER & BAILEY*, Law Library, 300 Pioneer Tower, 888 SW Fifth Ave, 97204-2089. SAN 372-221X. Tel: 503-228-6351. FAX: 503-295-0915. Web Site: www.bullivant.com. *Librn,* Laurie Daley
Founded 1938
Library Holdings: Bk Vols 10,000; Per Subs 80
Open Mon-Fri 7:30-5

P CEDAR MILL COMMUNITY LIBRARY*, 12505 NW Cornell Rd, Ste 13, 97229. SAN 314-1470. Tel: 503-644-0043. Interlibrary Loan Service Tel: 503-644-0043, Ext 133. Reference Tel: 503-644-0043, Ext 114. Administration Tel: 503-644-0043, Ext 110. FAX: 503-644-3964. E-mail: askuscml@wccls.org. Web Site: library.cedarmill.org. *Dir,* Peter Leonard; E-mail: peterl@wccls.org; *Adult Serv,* Lynne Erlandson; *Circ,* Shannon Caster; *Tech Serv,* Rita Rivera; *Youth Serv,* Nancy Spaulding; Staff 18 (MLS 17, Non-MLS 1)
Founded 1974. Pop 73,110; Circ 2,636,200
Jul 2013-Jun 2014 Income (Main Library and Branch(s)) $4,085,391, County $3,395,391, Locally Generated Income $690,000. Mats Exp $377,000, Books $224,000, Per/Ser (Incl. Access Fees) $20,000, AV Equip $500, AV Mat $112,000, Electronic Ref Mat (Incl. Access Fees) $21,000. Sal $2,925,375
Library Holdings: AV Mats 41,939; Bk Vols 205,764; Per Subs 420
Special Collections: Oregon & Pacific Northwest, bks, per; Parent-Teacher Res Coll
Automation Activity & Vendor Info: (Acquisitions) Innovative Interfaces, Inc; (Cataloging) Innovative Interfaces, Inc; (Circulation) Innovative Interfaces, Inc; (OPAC) Innovative Interfaces, Inc
Wireless access
Function: Adult bk club, Archival coll, Audiobks via web, AV serv, Bilingual assistance for Spanish patrons, Bk club(s), Bks on CD, Children's prog, Computer training, Computers for patron use, Copy machines, Digital talking bks, e-mail & chat, Electronic databases & coll, Free DVD rentals, Handicapped accessible, ILL available, Magnifiers for reading, Mail & tel request accepted, Mus passes, Music CDs, Online cat, Outreach serv, OverDrive digital audio bks, Preschool outreach, Preschool reading prog, Prog for adults, Prog for children & young adult, Pub access computers, Ref serv available, Ref serv in person, Senior computer classes, Senior outreach, Summer reading prog, Teen prog, Telephone ref, Web-catalog, Wheelchair accessible, Workshops
Publications: Library News (Newsletter)
Partic in Washington County Cooperative Library Services
Open Mon-Fri 10-8, Sat 10-5, Sun 12-5
Friends of the Library Group
Branches: 1
BETHANY BRANCH, 15325 NW Central Dr, Ste J-8, 97229. Tel: 503-617-7323. Web Site: library.cedarmill.org/bethany-branch. *Br Mgr,* Marianne Coalson; Staff 9.15 (MLS 1.38, Non-MLS 7.77)
Founded 2007
Library Holdings: Audiobooks 1,806; CDs 2,732; DVDs 5,632; Electronic Media & Resources 483; Large Print Bks 244; Bk Vols 44,423; Per Subs 49
Open Mon-Fri 10-8, Sat 10-5, Sun 12-5
Friends of the Library Group

C CONCORDIA UNIVERSITY LIBRARY*, 2811 NE Holman St, 97211-6067. SAN 314-1497. Tel: 503-280-8507. Reference Tel: 503-493-6462. FAX: 503-280-8697. E-mail: library@cu-portland.edu. Web Site: www.cu-portland.edu/library. *Univ Librn,* Brent Mai; Tel: 503-493-6460, E-mail: bmai@cu-portland.edu; *Head, Ref,* Judy Anderson; Tel: 503-493-6453, E-mail: juanderson@cu-portland.edu; *Cat Librn,* Nolan Bremer; Tel: 503-493-6210, E-mail: nbremer@cu-portland.edu; *Ref & Instruction Librn,* Krista Reichard; Tel: 503-493-6246, E-mail: kreichard@cu-portland.edu; *Access Serv, Acq Mgr,* Patrick Cox; Tel: 503-493-6461, E-mail: pcox@cu-portland.edu; Staff 5 (MLS 4, Non-MLS 1)
Founded 1905. Enrl 1,522; Fac 137; Highest Degree: Master
Library Holdings: CDs 311; DVDs 768; e-books 72,985; e-journals 25,589; Bk Vols 88,236; Per Subs 250
Special Collections: Children's Literature Coll; Religious History (Luther & Reformation Research Coll); Volga German Studies
Subject Interests: Behav sci, Nursing, Soc sci, Theol
Automation Activity & Vendor Info: (Acquisitions) Innovative Interfaces, Inc - Millenium; (Cataloging) Innovative Interfaces, Inc - Millenium; (Circulation) Innovative Interfaces, Inc - Millenium; (Course Reserve) Innovative Interfaces, Inc - Millenium; (ILL) OCLC; (OPAC) Innovative Interfaces, Inc - Millenium; (Serials) Innovative Interfaces, Inc - Millenium
Database Vendor: Alexander Street Press, American Chemical Society, American Psychological Association (APA), ARTstor, Children's Literature Comprehensive Database Company (CLCD), College Source, CredoReference, ebrary, EBSCOhost, Facts on File, JSTOR, LexisNexis, Modern Language Association, Newsbank, OCLC FirstSearch, OCLC WorldShare Interlibrary Loan, OVID Technologies, Oxford Online, ProQuest, Sage, SBRnet (Sports Business Research Network), ScienceDirect, SerialsSolutions, Wilson - Wilson Web
Wireless access
Partic in Lyrasis; OCLC Online Computer Library Center, Inc
Open Mon-Thurs 7am-11pm, Fri 7-6, Sat 9-6, Sun 2-11
Friends of the Library Group

S EDUCATION NORTHWEST*, Professional Library, 101 SW Main St, Ste 500, 97204. SAN 314-1667. Tel: 503-275-9554. FAX: 503-275-0458. *Librn,* Linda Fitch; E-mail: linda.fitch@educationnorthwest.org; Staff 2 (MLS 1, Non-MLS 1)
Founded 1965
Library Holdings: Bk Titles 10,000; Per Subs 200
Special Collections: ERIC Coll
Subject Interests: Educ, Educ K-12 curriculum, Educ res, Pre-sch children

P GARDEN HOME COMMUNITY LIBRARY*, 7475 SW Oleson Rd, 97223-7474. Tel: 503-245-9932. Web Site: www.gardenhome.plinkit.org. *Dir,* Cooky Abrams
Library Holdings: Bk Titles 18,000; Per Subs 35
Automation Activity & Vendor Info: (Cataloging) Innovative Interfaces, Inc; (Circulation) Innovative Interfaces, Inc; (OPAC) Innovative Interfaces, Inc
Wireless access
Partic in Washington County Cooperative Library Services
Open Mon-Thurs 9-8, Fri 9-5, Sat 9-3

S GENEALOGICAL FORUM OF OREGON, INC LIBRARY*, 2505 SE 11th Ave, Suite B-18, 97202. SAN 321-5377. Tel: 503-963-1932. E-mail: library@gfo.org. Web Site: www.gfo.ind.opalsinfo.net/bin/home, www.gfo.org.
Founded 1946
Library Holdings: Audiobooks 298; CDs 1,020; Microforms 6,934; Bk Titles 22,078; Spec Interest Per Sub 55
Subject Interests: Genealogy, Hist
Database Vendor: FileMaker
Wireless access
Function: Archival coll, Computers for patron use, Copy machines, Electronic databases & coll, Genealogy discussion group, Masonic res mat, Microfiche/film & reading machines, Online cat, Orientations, Photocopying/Printing, Printer for laptops & handheld devices, Prog for adults, Ref & res, Ref serv available, Ref serv in person, Res libr, Res performed for a fee, Spoken cassettes & CDs, Workshops, Writing prog
Publications: The Bulletin of the Genealogical Forum of Oregon, Inc. (Quarterly); The Forum Insider (Newsletter)
Open Mon, Tues & Thurs 9:30-5, Wed 9:30-8, Fri & Sat 9:30-3, Sun 12-5
Restriction: Circ to mem only, Fee for pub use, Mem only

S INTERCULTURAL COMMUNICATION INSTITUTE*, Research Library, 8835 SW Canyon Lane, Ste 238, 97225. SAN 323-5866. Tel: 503-297-4622. FAX: 503-297-4695. E-mail: ici@intercultural.org. Web Site: www.intercultural.org. *Dir,* Sandra L Garrison-Whitmore
Founded 1987. Enrl 300; Fac 73; Highest Degree: Master
Library Holdings: AV Mats 1,069; Bks on Deafness & Sign Lang 49; CDs 36; DVDs 64; Bk Titles 10,528; Per Subs 15; Spec Interest Per Sub 3; Videos 778
Special Collections: Anthropologist Edward T Hall Coll; Dean Barnlund Bequeathment Photographic Coll; IJIR Complete Coll; Indonesia (Monroe

Sweetland Coll); Intercultural Press Beginnings (David Hoope's Coll); Japan (John Condon Coll); Native American Education (Floy C Pepper Coll); Roots of Intercultural Communication (LaRay Barna Coll)
Subject Interests: Intercultural communication
Wireless access
Function: Res libr
Restriction: Open evenings by appt
Friends of the Library Group

J ITT TECHNICAL INSTITUTE*, Learning Resource Center, 9500 NE Cascades Pkwy, 97220. Tel: 503-255-6500. Toll Free Tel: 800-234-5488. FAX: 503-335-1715. Web Site: www.itt-tech.edu. *Learning Res Ctr Asst,* Hailey McAllister
Library Holdings: AV Mats 200; Bk Vols 500; Per Subs 60
Wireless access
Open Mon-Fri 9-9, Sat 9-2

M KAISER PERMANENTE*, Center for Health Research, 3800 N Interstate Ave, 97227-1098. SAN 374-5899. Tel: 503-335-6744. E-mail: library@kpchr.org. Web Site: www.kpchr.org. *Dir,* Daphne Plaut; Staff 1 (MLS 1)
Library Holdings: Bk Titles 9,000; Per Subs 150
Restriction: Open by appt only

L LANE POWELL PC*, Law Library, 601 SW Second Ave, No 2100, 97204. SAN 371-6023. Tel: 503-778-2100. FAX: 503-778-2200. Web Site: www.lanepowell.com. *Mgr,* Linda Tobiska; E-mail: tobiskal@lanepowell.com; *Librn,* Alys Tryon; E-mail: tryona@lanepowell.com; Staff 2 (MLS 2)
Founded 1889
Library Holdings: Bk Vols 10,000; Per Subs 100
Automation Activity & Vendor Info: (Cataloging) Inmagic, Inc.; (Serials) Inmagic, Inc.
Wireless access
Partic in OCLC Online Computer Library Center, Inc
Restriction: Private libr

M LEGACY EMANUEL HOSPITAL & HEALTH CENTER LIBRARY*, 2801 N Gantenbein Ave, 97227. SAN 314-1519. Tel: 503-413-2558. FAX: 503-413-2544. *Libr Mgr,* Carol Galganski; E-mail: cgalgans@lhs.org; *Tech Spec Librn,* Bonnie Mastel; *Ref Serv,* Cindy Muller
Founded 1949
Library Holdings: Bk Titles 2,200; Bk Vols 2,700; Per Subs 200
Subject Interests: Emergency med, Pediatrics, Surgery, Trauma med
Function: Res libr
Partic in National Network of Libraries of Medicine
Open Mon-Fri 8-4:30

M LEGACY GOOD SAMARITAN HOSPITAL & MEDICAL CENTER*, Health Sciences Library, 1015 NW 22nd Ave, 97210. SAN 314-1586. Tel: 503-413-7335. FAX: 503-413-8016. *Mgr, Ref Serv,* Carol Galganski; *Tech Serv,* Kelly Ferkovich; Staff 3 (MLS 2, Non-MLS 1)
Library Holdings: Bk Vols 10,000; Per Subs 531
Subject Interests: Med, Nursing
Restriction: Staff use only

LEWIS & CLARK COLLEGE
CL PAUL L BOLEY LAW LIBRARY*, Lewis & Clark Law School, 10015 SW Terwilliger Blvd, 97219, SAN 358-0830. Tel: 503-768-6776. Reference Tel: 503-768-6688. FAX: 503-768-6760. E-mail: lawlib@lclark.edu. Web Site: lawlib.lclark.edu. *Dir,* Peter S Nycum; *Assoc Dir,* Tami Gierloff; *Head, Ref,* Seneca Gray; *Head, Tech Serv,* Kathy Faust; *Electronic Res,* Rob Truman; *Reader Serv,* Lynn Williams; Staff 9 (MLS 7, Non-MLS 2)
Founded 1884. Enrl 720; Fac 40; Highest Degree: Doctorate
Library Holdings: Bk Vols 213,961; Per Subs 4,840
Special Collections: Crime Victim Coll; Milton S Pearl Environmental Law Library; Patent Law Coll; Samuel S Johnson Public Land Law Review Commission Coll. State Document Depository; US Document Depository
Subject Interests: Am law, Antitrust, Environ studies, Intellectual property, Taxation
Automation Activity & Vendor Info: (Acquisitions) Innovative Interfaces, Inc; (Cataloging) Innovative Interfaces, Inc; (Circulation) Innovative Interfaces, Inc; (Course Reserve) Innovative Interfaces, Inc; (ILL) OCLC WorldShare Interlibrary Loan; (Media Booking) Innovative Interfaces, Inc; (OPAC) Innovative Interfaces, Inc; (Serials) Innovative Interfaces, Inc
Database Vendor: EBSCOhost, H W Wilson, Innovative Interfaces, Inc, JSTOR, LexisNexis, Loislaw, Newsbank, OCLC FirstSearch, OCLC WorldShare Interlibrary Loan, ProQuest, SerialsSolutions, Westlaw, Wilson - Wilson Web
Function: ILL available, Ref serv available
Partic in OCLC Online Computer Library Center, Inc
Publications: Handbook (Annual); Subject Bibliographies
Open Mon-Thurs 7am-Midnight, Fri 7am-10pm, Sat & Sun 9am-Midnight

C AUBREY R WATZEK LIBRARY*, 0615 SW Palatine Hill Rd, 97219-7899, SAN 358-0806. Tel: 503-768-7274. Circulation Tel: 503-768-7270. Interlibrary Loan Service Tel: 503-768-7280. Reference Tel: 503-768-7285. Administration Tel: 503-768-7275. FAX: 503-768-7282. Web Site: library.lclark.edu. *Interim Dir,* Mark Dahl; Tel: 503-768-7339, E-mail: dahl@lclark.edu; *Assoc Dir,* Elaine Heras; Tel: 503-768-7277, E-mail: heras@lclark.edu; *Acq & Coll Develop Librn,* Jim Bunnelle; E-mail: bunnelle@lclark.edu; *Cat Librn,* Laura Ayling Tucker; E-mail: ayling@lclark.edu; *Fac Outreach Librn,* Dan Kelley; E-mail: dkelley@lclark.edu; *Ref Librn,* Betty Ann Smith; E-mail: smithb@lclark.edu; *Mgr, Access Serv,* Rick Peterson; E-mail: rjp@lclark.edu; Staff 13 (MLS 11, Non-MLS 2)
Founded 1867. Enrl 2,466; Fac 163; Highest Degree: Master
Library Holdings: Bk Vols 290,000
Special Collections: Lewis & Clark Expedition Coll. US Document Depository
Subject Interests: Gender studies, Pac NW hist
Automation Activity & Vendor Info: (Acquisitions) Innovative Interfaces, Inc; (Cataloging) Innovative Interfaces, Inc; (Circulation) Innovative Interfaces, Inc; (OPAC) Innovative Interfaces, Inc; (Serials) Innovative Interfaces, Inc
Partic in OCLC Online Computer Library Center, Inc; Orbis Cascade Alliance
Friends of the Library Group

S MAZAMAS LIBRARY & ARCHIVES*, 527 SE 43rd Ave, 97215. SAN 325-8165. Tel: 503-227-2345, Ext 2. FAX: 503-227-0862. E-mail: library@mazamas.org. Web Site: www.mazamas.org. *Librn,* Robert William Lockerby; *Archives Dir,* Barbara Marquam; *Photo Archivist,* Jeff Thomas. Subject Specialists: *Ore climbing hist,* Jeff Thomas; Staff 1 (MLS 1)
Founded 1915
Library Holdings: Bk Vols 8,000; Per Subs 36
Subject Interests: Mountaineering
Function: Photocopying/Printing
Restriction: Mem only
Friends of the Library Group

L MILLER NASH LLP LIBRARY*, 111 SW Fifth Ave, 3400 US Bancorp Tower, 97204-3699. SAN 314-1624. Tel: 503-224-5858. Toll Free Tel: 877-220-5858. FAX: 503-224-0155. Web Site: www.millernash.com. *Dir, Libr Serv,* Elise Brickner-Schulz; Tel: 503-205-2427, E-mail: elise.brickner-schulz@millernash.com; *Ref Librn,* Douglas Hull; E-mail: hull@millernash.com; Staff 5 (MLS 3, Non-MLS 2)
Founded 1873
Library Holdings: Bk Titles 8,000; Bk Vols 20,000; Per Subs 400
Subject Interests: Law

P MULTNOMAH COUNTY LIBRARY*, 205 NE Russell St, 97212-3708. SAN 358-0865. Tel: 503-988-5402. Interlibrary Loan Service Tel: 503-988-5245. Reference Tel: 503-988-5234. TDD: 503-988-5246. Web Site: www.multcolib.org. *Dir,* Vailey Oehlke; Tel: 503-988-5403, E-mail: vaileyo@multcolib.org; *Dep Dir,* Becky Cobb; E-mail: beckyc@multcolib.org; *Dir, Mkt & Communications,* Jeremy Graybill; Tel: 503-988-5498, E-mail: jeremyg@multcolib.org; *Dir, Neighborhood Libr,* Rita Jimenez; *Youth Serv Dir,* Katie O'Dell; Staff 437 (MLS 94, Non-MLS 343)
Founded 1864. Pop 685,950; Circ 2,639,698
Library Holdings: Bk Vols 1,696,686
Special Collections: John Wilson Room; McCormack Coll, bks, rec; Oregon Coll; Roses (Thomas Newton Cook Rose Library & Jesse A Currey Memorial Rose Coll). State Document Depository; US Document Depository
Automation Activity & Vendor Info: (Circulation) Innovative Interfaces, Inc
Wireless access
Partic in OCLC Online Computer Library Center, Inc
Open Mon-Fri 8-5
Friends of the Library Group
Branches: 19
ALBINA, 3605 NE 15th Ave, 97212-2358, SAN 358-089X. Tel: 503-988-5362. FAX: 503-988-5482. *In Charge,* Lisa White
Founded 1906
Open Mon & Tues 12-8, Wed-Sat 10-6, Sun 12-5
Friends of the Library Group
BELMONT, 1038 SE Cesar E Chavez Blvd, 97214-4318, SAN 358-092X. Tel: 503-988-5382. FAX: 503-988-5481. *In Charge,* Matthew Yake
Founded 1924
Open Mon, Fri & Sat 10-6, Tues 10-8, Wed & Thurs 12-8, Sun 10-5
Friends of the Library Group
CAPITOL HILL, 10723 SW Capitol Hwy, 97219-6816, SAN 358-0954. Tel: 503-988-5385. FAX: 503-988-5479. *In Charge,* Patti Vincent
Founded 1972

Open Mon & Tues 12-8, Wed-Sat 10-6, Sun 12-5
Friends of the Library Group
CENTRAL, 801 SW Tenth Ave, 97205-2520. Tel: 503-988-5123. FAX: 503-988-5226. *In Charge,* Dave Ratliff; Tel: 503-988-5231
Founded 1913
Open Mon 10-8, Tues & Wed Noon-8, Thurs-Sat 10-6, Sun 10-5
Friends of the Library Group
FAIRVIEW-COLUMBIA BRANCH, 1520 NE Village St, Fairview, 97024. Tel: 503-988-5655. FAX: 503-988-6111. *In Charge,* David Lee
Founded 2001
Open Mon & Tues Noon-8, Wed-Sat 10-6, Sun Noon-5
Friends of the Library Group
GREGORY HEIGHTS, 7921 NE Sandy Blvd, 97213-7150, SAN 358-0989. Tel: 503-988-5386. FAX: 503-988-5278. *In Charge,* May Dea
Open Mon & Tues Noon-8, Wed-Sat 10-6, Sun Noon-5
Friends of the Library Group
GRESHAM BRANCH, 385 NW Miller Ave, Gresham, 97030-7204, SAN 358-1012. Tel: 503-988-5387. FAX: 503-988-5198. *In Charge,* Martha Flotten
Open Mon, Fri & Sat 10-6, Tues 10-8, Wed & Thurs Noon-8, Sun 10-5
Friends of the Library Group
HILLSDALE, 1525 SW Sunset Blvd, 97239, SAN 358-1349. Tel: 503-988-5388. FAX: 503-988-5197. *In Charge,* Peg Solonika
Open Mon, Fri & Sat 10-6, Tues 10-8, Wed & Thurs Noon-8, Sun 10-5
Friends of the Library Group
HOLGATE, 7905 SE Holgate Blvd, 97206-3367, SAN 358-1047. Tel: 503-988-5389. FAX: 503-988-5194. *In Charge,* Victoria Oglesbee
Open Mon & Tues Noon-8, Wed-Sat 10-6, Sun Noon-5
Friends of the Library Group
HOLLYWOOD, 4040 NE Tillamook St, 97212, SAN 358-1071. Tel: 503-988-5391. FAX: 503-988-5192. *In Charge,* Bryan Fearn
Founded 1917
Open Mon, Fri & Sat 10-6, Tues 10-8, Wed & Thurs Noon-8, Sun 10-5
Friends of the Library Group
KENTON, 8226 N Denver Ave, 97217. Tel: 503-988-5370. FAX: 503-988-5163. *In Charge,* David Miles
Founded 2010
Open Mon & Tues Noon-8, Wed-Sat 10-6, Sun Noon-5
Friends of the Library Group
MIDLAND, 805 SE 122nd Ave, 97233-1107, SAN 358-1160. Tel: 503-988-5392. FAX: 503-988-5189. *In Charge,* Carol Parten
Open Mon, Fri & Sat 10-6, Tues 10-8, Wed & Thurs Noon-8, Sun 10-5
Friends of the Library Group
NORTH PORTLAND, 512 N Killingsworth St, 97217-2330, SAN 358-1225. Tel: 503-988-5394. FAX: 503-988-5187. *In Charge,* Patricia Welch
Founded 1909
Special Collections: Black Resource Coll
Open Mon & Tues Noon-8, Wed-Sat 10-6, Sun Noon-5
Friends of the Library Group
NORTHWEST, 2300 NW Thurman St, 97210. Tel: 503-988-5560. FAX: 503-988-3486. *In Charge,* Kim Anderson
Founded 2001
Open Mon & Tues Noon-8, Wed-Sat 10-6, Sun Noon-5
Friends of the Library Group
ROCKWOOD, 17917 SE Stark St, 97233-4825, SAN 358-125X. Tel: 503-988-5396. FAX: 503-988-5178. *In Charge,* Kylie Park
Founded 1963
Open Mon & Tues Noon-8, Wed-Sat 10-6, Sun Noon-5
Friends of the Library Group
ST JOHNS, 7510 N Charleston Ave, 97203-3709, SAN 358-1284. Tel: 503-988-5397. FAX: 503-988-5176. *In Charge,* Nancy Arvesen
Founded 1913
Open Mon & Tues Noon-8, Wed-Sat 10-6, Sun Noon-5
Friends of the Library Group
SELLWOOD-MORELAND, 7860 SE 13th Ave, 97202-6300, SAN 358-1314. Tel: 503-988-5398. FAX: 503-988-5175. *In Charge,* Jenna Scott
Founded 1905
Open Mon & Tues Noon-8, Wed-Sat 10-6, Sun Noon-5
Friends of the Library Group
TROUTDALE, 2451 SW Cherry Park Rd, Troutdale, 97060. Tel: 503-988-5355. FAX: 503-988-5145. *In Charge,* Sarah Oliver
Founded 2010
Open Mon & Tues Noon-8, Wed-Sat 10-6, Sun Noon-5
Friends of the Library Group
WOODSTOCK, 6008 SE 49th Ave, 97206-6117, SAN 358-1373. Tel: 503-988-5399. FAX: 503-988-5173. *In Charge,* Carol Uhte
Open Mon & Tues Noon-8, Wed-Sat 10-6, Sun Noon-5
Friends of the Library Group

L MULTNOMAH LAW LIBRARY*, County Courthouse, 4th Flr, 1021 SW Fourth Ave, 97204. SAN 314-1632. Tel: 503-988-3394. FAX: 503-988-3395. E-mail: multlawlib@yahoo.com. Web Site: multlawlib.org. *Law Librn,* Jacquelyn Jurkins
Founded 1890
Library Holdings: Bk Vols 216,500
Database Vendor: HeinOnline
Wireless access
Partic in LexisNexis; Westlaw

CR MULTNOMAH UNIVERSITY, John & Mary Mitchell Library, 8435 NE Glisan St, 97220-5898. SAN 314-1640. Tel: 503-251-5322. Circulation Tel: 503-251-5321. Reference Tel: 503-251-5317. FAX: 503-254-1268. E-mail: library@multnomah.edu. Web Site: www.multnomah.edu/resources/library. *Dir,* Dr Philip M Johnson; Tel: 503-251-5323, E-mail: pjohnson@multnomah.edu; *Head, Pub Serv,* Pam Middleton; E-mail: pamm@multnomah.edu; *Ref Librn,* Suzanne Smith; E-mail: ssmith@multnomah.edu; *Tech Serv,* Susan Spirz; Tel: 503-251-5316, E-mail: sspirz@multnomah.edu; Staff 4 (MLS 2, Non-MLS 2)
Founded 1936. Enrl 828; Fac 40; Highest Degree: Doctorate
Library Holdings: e-books 11,325; Bk Titles 64,000; Bk Vols 77,489; Per Subs 402
Special Collections: Bible Coll
Subject Interests: Biblical studies, Christian educ, Church hist, Practical theol, Theol
Automation Activity & Vendor Info: (Acquisitions) Ex Libris Group; (Cataloging) Ex Libris Group; (Circulation) Ex Libris Group; (Course Reserve) Ex Libris Group; (ILL) OCLC; (Media Booking) Ex Libris Group; (OPAC) Ex Libris Group; (Serials) Ex Libris Group
Database Vendor: EBSCOhost
Wireless access
Partic in OCLC Online Computer Library Center, Inc; Online Private Academic Library Link (OPALL)
Open Mon-Thurs 7:30am-11pm, Fri 7:30-7, Sat 10-5:30, Sun 3-11

S MUSEUM OF CONTEMPORARY CRAFT LIBRARY*, 724 NW Davis St, 97209. SAN 323-519X. Tel: 503-223-2654. FAX: 503-223-0190. E-mail: info@museumofcontemporarycraft.org. Web Site: www.contemporarycrafts.org. *Actg Dir,* Nicole Nathan; E-mail: nnathan@museumofcontemporarycraft.org; *Dir,* Position Currently Open
Founded 1937
Library Holdings: Bk Vols 750; Per Subs 1,000
Subject Interests: Craft, Craft hist
Open Tues-Sun 11-6, Thurs 11-8
Restriction: Restricted access

CM NATIONAL COLLEGE OF NATUROPATHIC MEDICINE LIBRARY*, 049 SW Porter, 97201. SAN 314-1659. Tel: 503-552-1542. FAX: 503-219-9709. E-mail: circulation@ncnm.edu. Web Site: www.ncnm.edu. *Head Librn,* Rick Severson; *Librn,* Friedhelm Kirchfeld
Founded 1956. Enrl 450; Fac 45; Highest Degree: Doctorate
Library Holdings: AV Mats 1,600; Bk Titles 12,000; Per Subs 160
Special Collections: Homeopathic Coll, journals; Naturopathic Coll, journals, rare bks
Subject Interests: Acupuncture, Botanical med, Homeopathy, Naturopathic med, Nutrition, Phys therapy
Automation Activity & Vendor Info: (Cataloging) Innovative Interfaces, Inc; (Circulation) Innovative Interfaces, Inc; (OPAC) Innovative Interfaces, Inc; (Serials) Innovative Interfaces, Inc
Open Mon-Thurs 7am-9pm, Fri 7-6, Sat 9-5

C OREGON COLLEGE OF ART & CRAFT LIBRARY, 8245 SW Barnes Rd, 97225. SAN 314-1683. Tel: 503-297-5544. FAX: 503-297-9651. E-mail: library@ocac.edu. Web Site: sites.google.com/a/ocac.edu/library/home, www.ocac.edu/campus-life/library. *Dir,* Elsa Loftis; Tel: 503-297-5544, Ext 119, E-mail: eloftis@ocac.edu; Staff 1 (MLS 1)
Highest Degree: Master
Library Holdings: Bk Vols 12,000; Per Subs 90
Subject Interests: Craft hist, Design
Partic in Washington County Cooperative Library Services
Open Mon-Fri 9-5

CM OREGON COLLEGE OF ORIENTAL MEDICINE LIBRARY*, 75 NW Couch St, 97209. SAN 375-4952. Tel: 503-253-3443, Ext 132. Web Site: library.ocom.edu. *Col Librn,* Candise Branum; E-mail: cbranum@ocom.edu; *Pub Serv Librn,* Nyssa Walsh; E-mail: nwalsh@ocom.edu; *Syst Librn,* Veronica Vichit-Vadakan; E-mail: vvv@ocom.edu; Staff 3 (MLS 3)
Founded 1991. Enrl 230; Fac 15; Highest Degree: Master
Library Holdings: AV Mats 720; Bk Titles 2,000; Bk Vols 2,500; Per Subs 40
Subject Interests: Acupuncture
Automation Activity & Vendor Info: (Cataloging) Inmagic, Inc.; (OPAC) Inmagic, Inc.
Partic in Docline
Open Mon-Thurs 8-7, Fri 8-5, Sat 11-4

G OREGON DEPARTMENT OF GEOLOGY & MINERAL INDUSTRIES LIBRARY*, Ste 965, No 28, 800 NE Oregon St, 97232-2162. SAN 314-1691. Tel: 971-673-1555. FAX: 971-673-1562. Web Site: www.oregongeology.com. *Librn,* Margaret D Jenks; Tel: 971-673-1546, E-mail: margi.jenks@dogami.state.or.us; Staff 1 (Non-MLS 1)
Founded 1937
Library Holdings: Bk Titles 10,000; Bk Vols 30,000
Special Collections: Archival Mining Report; Theses & Dissertations on Geology of Oregon; Unpublished Data & Reports on Geology of Oregon includes site-specific seismic studies
Subject Interests: Geol of Ore
Function: For res purposes, Govt ref serv, ILL available, Photocopying/Printing, Ref serv available, Res libr, Telephone ref
Open Mon-Fri 7:30-4:30
Restriction: Circulates for staff only, In-house use for visitors, Non-circulating to the pub, Not a lending libr, Pub use on premises

CM OREGON HEALTH & SCIENCE UNIVERSITY LIBRARY*, 3181 SW Sam Jackson Park Rd, 97239-3098. (Mail add: PO Box 573, 97207-0573), SAN 358-1551. Tel: 503-494-3460. FAX: 503-494-3227. E-mail: library@ohsu.edu. Web Site: www.ohsu.edu/library. *Libr Dir, Univ Librn,* Chris Shaffer; Tel: 503-494-6057, E-mail: shafferc@ohsu.edu; *Head, Access Serv, Spec Projects Librn,* Judith Norton; Tel: 503-494-3481, E-mail: norton@ohsu.edu; *Head, Admin Serv, Head, Syst,* Janet Crum; Tel: 503-494-0691, E-mail: crumj@ohsu.edu; *Head, Coll Develop, Head, Scholarly Communications,* Emily McElroy; Tel: 503-494-6659, E-mail: mcelroye@ohsu.edu; *Head, Archives, Head, Historical Coll,* Sara Piasecki; Tel: 503-418-2287, E-mail: piasecki@ohsu.edu; *Head, Instruction & Outreach, Head, Res Serv,* Dolores Judkins; Tel: 503-494-3478, E-mail: judkinsd@ohsu.edu; *Acq Librn, Electronic Res Librn,* Kristina DeShazo; Tel: 503-494-1637, E-mail: deshazok@ohsu.edu; *Metadata Librn, Ser Librn,* Friday Valentine; Tel: 503-494-0883, E-mail: valentif@ohsu.edu; *Ref Librn,* Emily Ford; *Ref Librn,* Andrew Hamilton; *Ref Librn,* Todd Hannon; *Ref Librn,* Loree Hyde; *Cataloger, Syst Librn,* Carla Pealer; Tel: 503-494-5114, E-mail: pealerc@ohsu.edu; *Syst Librn, Web Develop Librn,* Laura Zeigen; *Circ Mgr,* Mary Hultine; *Mgr, Ser,* Kathleen Stewart; *Web Serv Mgr,* Shannon Carr; Tel: 503 494-3484, E-mail: carrsh@ohsu.edu; *Circ Coordr,* Michael Mackin; *Ref/Outreach Coordr,* Steve Teich; Tel: 503-494-3444, E-mail: teich@ohsu.edu; *Archivist,* Karen Peterson; *Cat, ILL Spec,* Kris Roley; Staff 34 (MLS 13.5, Non-MLS 20.5)
Founded 1919. Enrl 2,586; Fac 2,142; Highest Degree: Doctorate
Jul 2006-Jun 2007. Mats Exp $2,037,913, Books $204,433, Per/Ser (Incl. Access Fees) $1,678,428, AV Mat $2,769, Electronic Ref Mat (Incl. Access Fees) $129,795, Presv $22,488
Library Holdings: Bk Titles 66,929; Bk Vols 221,001; Per Subs 2,429
Special Collections: Historical Photograph Coll; History of Dentistry Coll; History of Medicine Coll; Manuscripts & Archives; Medical Museum, artifacts; OHSU Oral History Project; Oregon Memorial Library for Bereaved Parents; Pacific Northwest & OHSU Publications (PNW Archives)
Automation Activity & Vendor Info: (Acquisitions) Innovative Interfaces, Inc; (Cataloging) Innovative Interfaces, Inc; (Circulation) Innovative Interfaces, Inc; (Course Reserve) Innovative Interfaces, Inc; (ILL) OCLC ILLiad; (Media Booking) Innovative Interfaces, Inc; (OPAC) Innovative Interfaces, Inc; (Serials) Innovative Interfaces, Inc
Database Vendor: EBSCOhost, Nature Publishing Group, OCLC FirstSearch, OCLC WorldShare Interlibrary Loan, OVID Technologies, ScienceDirect, STAT!Ref (Teton Data Systems), Wiley
Wireless access
Function: Prof lending libr
Partic in National Network of Libraries of Medicine Pacific Northwest Region; OCLC Online Computer Library Center, Inc; Orbis Cascade Alliance

S OREGON HISTORICAL SOCIETY RESEARCH LIBRARY*, 1200 SW Park Ave, 97205. SAN 314-1675. Tel: 503-306-5243. Reference Tel: 503-306-5240. FAX: 503-219-2040. E-mail: libreference@ohs.org. Web Site: www.ohs.org. *Dir,* MaryAnn Campbell; Staff 14 (MLS 7, Non-MLS 7)
Founded 1898
Library Holdings: Bk Vols 33,000; Per Subs 420
Subject Interests: Hist Pacific NW
Function: Res libr
Partic in OCLC Online Computer Library Center, Inc

S OREGON ZOO ANIMAL MANAGEMENT LIBRARY*, 4001 SW Canyon Rd, 97221. SAN 325-8262. Tel: 503-220-5763. FAX: 503-226-0074. Web Site: www.oregonzoo.org. *Conserv Librn, Res,* Karen Lewis; E-mail: karen.lewis@oregonzoo.org
Library Holdings: Bk Titles 1,152
Subject Interests: Biol, Conserv, Natural hist
Automation Activity & Vendor Info: (Cataloging) Follett Software
Restriction: Open by appt only

C PACIFIC NORTHWEST COLLEGE OF ART*, Charles Voorhies Fine Art Library, 1241 NW Johnson St, 97209. Tel: 503-821-8966. E-mail: librarycirc@pnca.edu. Web Site: library.pnca.edu. *Dir, Libr Serv,* Dan McClure; Tel: 503-821-8970, E-mail: dmcclure@pnca.edu; Staff 5 (MLS 3, Non-MLS 2)
Founded 2001
Library Holdings: DVDs 1,500; Electronic Media & Resources 99,000; Bk Vols 29,000; Per Subs 100; Videos 800
Special Collections: Oral History
Automation Activity & Vendor Info: (Acquisitions) ComPanion Corp; (Cataloging) ComPanion Corp; (Circulation) ComPanion Corp; (Course Reserve) ComPanion Corp; (ILL) OCLC FirstSearch; (OPAC) ComPanion Corp; (Serials) ComPanion Corp
Database Vendor: ARTstor, EBSCOhost, Gale Cengage Learning, OCLC FirstSearch, OCLC WorldShare Interlibrary Loan, Oxford Online, ProQuest, Wilson - Wilson Web
Wireless access
Function: Archival coll, Art exhibits, Audio & video playback equip for onsite use, CD-ROM, ILL available, Learning ctr, Online searches, Orientations, Photocopying/Printing, VHS videos
Open Mon-Thurs 7:30am-Midnight, Fri 8-8, Sat & Sun 12-8
Restriction: Circ limited, Open to students, fac & staff, Pub use on premises

L PERKINS COIE*, Law Library, 1120 NW Couch St, 10th Flr, 97209-4128. SAN 372-2260. Tel: 503-727-2051. FAX: 503-727-2222. Web Site: www.perkinscoie.com. *Electronic Res Mgr,* Catherine Horan; E-mail: choran@perkinscoie.com; *Dir,* Position Currently Open
Library Holdings: Bk Vols 10,000; Per Subs 50
Restriction: Not open to pub

S PORTLAND ART MUSEUM*, Anne & James F Crumpacker Family Library, 1219 SW Park Ave, 97205-2486. SAN 314-1756. Tel: 503-276-4215. E-mail: library@pam.org. Web Site: www.pam.org. *Dir,* Debra Royer; Tel: 503-276-4526; Staff 3 (Non-MLS 3)
Founded 1892
Library Holdings: Bk Titles 33,000; Per Subs 60
Special Collections: Arts of the Pacific Northwest Coast Indians; Auction Catalogs; Contemporary Art; English Silver; Japanese Prints; Northwest Artists File
Subject Interests: Art hist
Open Mon-Thurs 10-5, Sun Noon-5

J PORTLAND COMMUNITY COLLEGE LIBRARY*, Administration, 12000 SW 49th AV, 97219. (Mail add: PO Box 19000, 97280), SAN 358-1403. Circulation Tel: 971-722-4935. Reference Tel: 503-614-7239, 503-978-5269. Administration Tel: 971-722-4497. Automation Services Tel: 971-722-4678. Information Services Tel: 971-722-4500. FAX: 971-722-8397. Administration FAX: 971-722-8398. TDD: 503-978-5269. Web Site: www.pcc.edu/library/. *Dir,* Donna L Reed; Tel: 971-722-4497, E-mail: donna.reed@pcc.edu; *Fac Librn-Cascade Campus,* Stephanie Debner; Tel: 971-722-5697, E-mail: stephanie.debner@pcc.edu; *Fac Librn-Cascade Campus,* Anthony (Tony) Greiner; Tel: 971-722-5333, E-mail: anthony.greiner@pcc.edu; *Fac Librn-Cascade Campus,* Torie Scott; Tel: 971-722-5433, E-mail: vscott@pcc.edu; *Fac Librn-Rock Creek Campus,* Pam Kessinger; Tel: 971-722-7051, E-mail: pkessing@pcc.edu; *Fac Librn-Rock Creek Campus,* Roberta Richards; Tel: 971-722-7374; *Fac Librn-Rock Creek Campus,* Robin Shapiro; Tel: 971-722-7126, E-mail: robin.shapiro@pcc.edu; *Fac Librn-Sylvania Campus,* Allie Flanary; Tel: 971-722-4686, E-mail: allinee.flanary@pcc.edu; *Fac Librn-Sylvania Campus,* Bob Kingston; Tel: 971-722-4962, E-mail: bob.kingston@pcc.edu; *Fac Librn-Sylvania Campus,* Jane Rognlie; Tel: 971-722-4590, E-mail: jrognlie@pcc.edu; *Ref Librn-Sylvania Campus,* Al Cordle; Tel: 971-722-4592, E-mail: acordle@pcc.edu; *Tech Mgr,* Maria Wagner; Tel: 503-977-4631, E-mail: maria.wagner@pcc.edu; *Acq Spec,* Jay Brewster; Tel: 971-722-4633, E-mail: jbrewster@pcc.edu; *Circ,* Katherine M Stevens; Tel: 503-977-4678, E-mail: kstevens@pcc.edu; *Digital Serv,* David Lippert; E-mail: dlippert@pcc.edu; *Digital Serv,* Donna Meeds; Tel: 971-722-4460, E-mail: dmeeds@pcc.edu; *ILL,* Leslie Gretchen; Tel: 971-722-7190, E-mail: intlib@pcc.edu. Subject Specialists: *Virtual ref,* Stephanie Debner; *Assessment,* Torie Scott; *Assessment,* Pam Kessinger; *Developmental educ,* Roberta Richards; *Develop,* Robin Shapiro; *Developmental educ,* Jane Rognlie; *Cataloging,* Maria Wagner; *Purchasing,* Jay Brewster; Staff 15 (MLS 11, Non-MLS 4)
Founded 1964
Jul 2005-Jun 2006 Income $2,446,096. Mats Exp $606,077. Sal $1,252,971
Library Holdings: AV Mats 8,397; Bks on Deafness & Sign Lang 212; e-books 374; High Interest/Low Vocabulary Bk Vols 552; Bk Titles 172,324; Bk Vols 260,942; Per Subs 1,394; Talking Bks 1,679
Automation Activity & Vendor Info: (Acquisitions) Innovative Interfaces, Inc; (Cataloging) Innovative Interfaces, Inc; (Circulation) Innovative Interfaces, Inc; (Course Reserve) Innovative Interfaces, Inc; (ILL) Innovative Interfaces, Inc; (Media Booking) Innovative Interfaces, Inc; (OPAC) Innovative Interfaces, Inc; (Serials) Innovative Interfaces, Inc

Database Vendor: EBSCOhost, Gale Cengage Learning, OCLC FirstSearch, ProQuest, Wilson - Wilson Web
Partic in Orbis Cascade Alliance
Open Mon-Fri 7:30-5
Friends of the Library Group

C PORTLAND STATE UNIVERSITY LIBRARY, 1875 SW Park Ave, 97201-3220. (Mail add: PO Box 1151, 97207-1151), SAN 314-1772. Tel: 503-725-5874. Interlibrary Loan Service Tel: 503-725-3879. Administration Tel: 503-725-4616. FAX: 503-725-4524. Web Site: library.pdx.edu. *Dean, Univ Libr,* Marilyn Moody; E-mail: marilynmoody@pdx.edu; *Asst Univ Librn, Res Serv & Tech,* Barbara Glackin; Tel: 503-725-4575, E-mail: barbaraglackin@pdx.edu; *Asst Univ Librn, Admin Serv, Planning & Digital Initiatives,* Tom Bielavitz; Tel: 503-725-4576, E-mail: bielavit@pdx.edu; *Head, Acq & Presv,* Mary Ellen Kenreich; Tel: 503-725-5780, E-mail: kenreichm@pdx.edu; *Head, Monographic Cat,* Tom Larsen; Tel: 503-725-8179, E-mail: larsent@pdx.edu; *Head, Spec Coll, Univ Archivist,* Cristine Paschild; Tel: 503-725-9883, E-mail: paschild@pdx.edu; *Interim Asst Univ Librn, Pub Serv,* Claudia Weston; Tel: 503-725-4542, E-mail: westonc@pdx.edu
Founded 1946. Enrl 28,000; Highest Degree: Doctorate
Special Collections: US Document Depository
Wireless access
Partic in Orbis Cascade Alliance

GM PORTLAND VA MEDICAL CENTER LIBRARY*, 3710 SW US Veterans Hospital Rd, P6LIB, 97239-2964. (Mail add: PO Box 1034, 97207-1034), SAN 314-1888. Tel: 503-220-8262, Ext 55955. Interlibrary Loan Service Tel: 503-220-8262, Ext 55039. FAX: 503-721-7816. E-mail: portland.library@med.va.gov. *Chief, Libr Serv,* Rose Campbell; E-mail: rose.campbell@va.gov; *Consumer Health Librn,* Kaye Martin; E-mail: kaye.martin@va.gov; Staff 2 (MLS 2)
Library Holdings: AV Mats 1,190; Bk Titles 9,096; Per Subs 191
Subject Interests: Geriatrics, Liver transplant, Med, Nursing, Patient health info, Post-traumatic stress, Psychol
Database Vendor: EBSCOhost, Elsevier, RefWorks, STAT!Ref (Teton Data Systems), UpToDate
Partic in National Network of Libraries of Medicine Pacific Northwest Region; OCLC Online Computer Library Center, Inc; Oregon Health Sciences Libraries Association; Veterans Affairs Libr Network (VALNET)
Restriction: Hospital staff & commun

M PROVIDENCE SAINT VINCENT HOSPITAL & MEDICAL CENTER*, Health Sciences Library, 9205 SW Barnes Rd, 97225. SAN 314-1810. Tel: 503-216-2257. FAX: 503-216-6085. *Dir,* Ann M Von Segen
Library Holdings: Bk Titles 4,000; Bk Vols 5,000; Per Subs 570
Subject Interests: Cancer, Cardiology, Hospital admin, Internal med, Nursing
Wireless access
Partic in Ore Health Info Network
Restriction: Not open to pub

C REED COLLEGE, Eric V Hauser Memorial Library, 3203 SE Woodstock Blvd, 97202-8199. SAN 314-1802. Tel: 503-777-7702. Interlibrary Loan Service Tel: 503-777-7750. Reference Tel: 503-777-7554. Administration Tel: 503-777-7780. FAX: 503-777-7786. Web Site: www.library.reed.edu. *Col Librn,* Dena Hutto; Tel: 503-777-7572, E-mail: dhutto@reed.edu; *Head, Access Serv,* James Holmes; *Head, Coll Serv,* Xan Arch; *Head, Res Serv,* Annie Downey; *Data Serv Librn,* Ryan Clement; *Digital Assets Librn,* Angie Beiriger; *Performing Arts Librn,* Erin Conor; *Spec Coll & Archives Librn,* Gay Walker; *Cat & Metadata,* Abigail Bibee; *Circ,* Mark McDaniel; *Sci,* Linda Maddux; *Syst,* Rosalie Carlson; *Visual Res,* Booke Sansosti; *Web Serv,* Joe Marquez; Staff 25.25 (MLS 11, Non-MLS 14.25)
Founded 1911. Enrl 1,433; Fac 132; Highest Degree: Master
Jul 2012-Jun 2013 Income $5,383,770. Mats Exp $2,999,859, Books $604,980, Per/Ser (Incl. Access Fees) $2,027,901, AV Equip $32,779, AV Mat $58,113, Electronic Ref Mat (Incl. Access Fees) $200,022, Presv $16,617. Sal $1,270,466 (Prof $751,460)
Library Holdings: AV Mats 33,673; Bk Titles 1,221,867
Special Collections: US Document Depository
Automation Activity & Vendor Info: (Acquisitions) Innovative Interfaces, Inc; (Cataloging) Innovative Interfaces, Inc; (Circulation) Innovative Interfaces, Inc; (ILL) OCLC ILLiad; (OPAC) Innovative Interfaces, Inc; (Serials) Innovative Interfaces, Inc
Wireless access
Partic in Northwest Association of Private Colleges & Universities (NAPCU); OCLC Online Computer Library Center, Inc; Orbis Cascade Alliance

L SCHWABE, WILLIAMSON & WYATT LIBRARY, Pacwest Ctr, 1211 SW Fifth Ave, Ste 1500, 97204-3795. SAN 373-6067. Tel: 503-796-2071. Reference Tel: 503-796-2854. FAX: 503-796-2900. Web Site: www.schwabe.com. *Mgr,* LaJean Humphries; Staff 3 (MLS 3)
Founded 1892
Library Holdings: e-books 103; Bk Titles 2,500; Bk Vols 10,000; Per Subs 200
Subject Interests: Law
Automation Activity & Vendor Info: (Cataloging) EOS International; (OPAC) EOS International
Restriction: Not open to pub

L STOEL RIVES LLP*, Law Library, 900 SW Fifth Ave, Ste 2600, 97204. SAN 314-1500. Tel: 503-294-9576. FAX: 503-220-2480. Web Site: www.stoel.com. *Librn,* Tony Haas; *Ref Serv,* Shannon Marich; Staff 10 (MLS 3, Non-MLS 7)
Founded 1906
Library Holdings: Bk Vols 30,000
Automation Activity & Vendor Info: (Cataloging) Inmagic, Inc.
Partic in Dialog Corp; Westlaw
Restriction: Staff use only

L TONKON TORP LLP*, Law Library, 888 SW Fifth Ave, Ste 1600, 97204-2099. SAN 372-2244. Tel: 503-221-1440. FAX: 503-972-3789. Web Site: www.tonkon.com. *Librn,* Richard LaSasso; Tel: 503-802-2089, E-mail: rich@tonkon.com
Founded 1974
Library Holdings: Bk Vols 10,000; Per Subs 50
Automation Activity & Vendor Info: (Cataloging) Inmagic, Inc.
Open Mon-Fri 8-6
Restriction: Staff use only

A UNITED STATES ARMY CORPS OF ENGINEERS*, Portland District Technical Library, CENWP-SP-RL, 333 SW First Ave, 97204. (Mail add: PO Box 2946, 97208-2946), SAN 358-1527. Tel: 503-808-5140. FAX: 503-808-5142. E-mail: cenwp.library@usace.army.mil. Web Site: www.nwp.usace.army.mil/References.aspx. *Librn,* Mary Ellen Y Haug; E-mail: maryellen.y.haug@usace.army.mil; *Cataloger,* Shiela K Osheroff; E-mail: shiela.k.osheroff@usace.army.mil; *Libr Tech,* Barbara A Boyd; E-mail: barbara.a.boyd@usace.army.mil; Staff 2.5 (MLS 1.5, Non-MLS 1)
Founded 1938
Library Holdings: Bk Titles 15,125; Bk Vols 24,153; Per Subs 40
Special Collections: Portland District Reports
Subject Interests: Civil eng, Cultural res, Dredging, Environ eng, Water resources planning
Automation Activity & Vendor Info: (Cataloging) EOS International; (Circulation) EOS International; (ILL) OCLC FirstSearch; (OPAC) EOS International; (Serials) EOS International
Database Vendor: ASCE Research Library, BioOne, HeinOnline, IHS, ISI Web of Knowledge, JSTOR, Knovel, OCLC, OCLC WorldShare Interlibrary Loan, ProQuest, Safari Books Online, ScienceDirect, Springer-Verlag, Thomson - Web of Science, Wiley
Open Mon-Fri 8-4

GL US COURT OF APPEALS LIBRARY*, Pioneer Courthouse, 700 SW Sixth Ave, Ste 109, 97204. Tel: 503-833-5310. FAX: 503-833-5315. *Librn,* Scott M McCurdy; E-mail: scott_mccurdy@lb9.uscourts.gov; *Asst Librn,* Elaine Thomas; Staff 3 (MLS 2, Non-MLS 1)
Restriction: Circ to mem only

GL UNITED STATES COURTS LIBRARIES*, 7A40 Mark O Hatfield, US Courthouse, 1000 SW Third Ave, 97204. SAN 321-3862. Tel: 503-326-8140. FAX: 503-326-8144. *Librn,* Scott McCurdy; *Asst Librn,* Elaine Thomas; Staff 3 (MLS 3)
Library Holdings: Bk Titles 850; Bk Vols 18,000; Per Subs 50
Automation Activity & Vendor Info: (Cataloging) SirsiDynix; (OPAC) SirsiDynix
Restriction: In-house use for visitors, Lending to staff only, Non-circulating to the pub, Open to others by appt, Restricted pub use, Secured area only open to authorized personnel

C UNIVERSITY OF PORTLAND*, Clark Library, 5000 N Willamette Blvd, 97203-5743. SAN 314-1861. Tel: 503-943-7111. Interlibrary Loan Service Tel: 503-943-7526. Reference Tel: 503-943-7788. Toll Free Tel: 800-841-8261. FAX: 503-943-7491. E-mail: library@up.edu. Web Site: library.up.edu. *Dir,* Drew Harrington; E-mail: harringd@up.edu; *Head, Pub Serv,* Caroline Mann; E-mail: mann@up.edu; *Head, Coll Serv,* Susan E Hinken; E-mail: hinken@up.edu; *Coll Tech Librn,* Bonnie Parks; E-mail: parks@up.edu; *Ref & Instruction Librn,* Stephanie Michel; E-mail: michel@up.edu; *Ref & Instruction Librn,* Heidi Senior; E-mail: senior@up.edu; *Ref & Instruction Librn,* Diane Sotak; E-mail: sotak@up.edu; Staff 7 (MLS 7)
Founded 1901. Enrl 3,357; Fac 277; Highest Degree: Doctorate
Library Holdings: Bk Titles 190,000; Bk Vols 360,000; Per Subs 1,600
Subject Interests: Catholic theol, Philos
Database Vendor: Innovative Interfaces, Inc
Wireless access

Partic in Northwest Association of Private Colleges & Universities (NAPCU); OCLC Online Computer Library Center, Inc; Orbis Cascade Alliance
Open Mon-Thurs 7:30am-Midnight, Fri 7:30am-9pm, Sat 10-9, Sun 10am-Midnight

CM UNIVERSITY OF WESTERN STATES*, W A Budden Library, 2900 NE 132nd Ave, 97230-3099. SAN 314-1942. Tel: 503-251-5752. Interlibrary Loan Service Tel: 503-206-3202. Administration Tel: 503-251-5757. FAX: 503-251-5759. E-mail: librarian@uws.edu. Web Site: www.uws.edu. *Univ Librn,* Janet Tapper; E-mail: jtapper@uws.edu; *Electronic Res Librn,* Katie Lockwood; E-mail: klockwood@uws.edu; *Media Spec,* Tom Olsen; Tel: 503 251 5755, E mail: tolsen@uws.edu; *Cat, ILL, Libr Asst,* Tania Wisotzke; E-mail: twisotzke@uws.edu; *Access Serv Asst,* Robin Milford; E-mail: rmilford@uws.edu; Staff 5 (MLS 2, Non-MLS 3)
Founded 1904. Enrl 425; Fac 50; Highest Degree: Doctorate
Library Holdings: AV Mats 3,000; Bk Titles 9,000; Bk Vols 13,500; Per Subs 300
Subject Interests: Anatomy, Chiropractic, Exercise & sports sci, Manual therapy, Nutrition
Automation Activity & Vendor Info: (Cataloging) Innovative Interfaces, Inc; (Circulation) Innovative Interfaces, Inc; (ILL) Clio; (OPAC) Innovative Interfaces, Inc; (Serials) EBSCO Online
Database Vendor: Cinahl, DynaMed, EBSCOhost, Gale Cengage Learning, Innovative Interfaces, Inc, Natural Standard, OCLC ArticleFirst, OCLC FirstSearch, OCLC WorldShare Interlibrary Loan, OVID Technologies, PubMed, RefWorks, ScienceDirect
Wireless access
Function: Archival coll, Doc delivery serv, ILL available
Partic in Chiropractic Libr Consortium; Medical Library Association (MLA); OCLC Online Computer Library Center, Inc
Restriction: Open to fac, students & qualified researchers, Open to pub for ref only

CR WARNER PACIFIC COLLEGE*, Otto F Linn Library, 2219 SE 68th Ave, 97215-4099. SAN 314-190X. Tel: 503-517-1102. Reference Tel: 503-517-1033. FAX: 503-517-1351. Web Site: www.warnerpacific.edu/library. *Dir, Libr Serv,* Sue Kopp; Tel: 503-517-1032, E-mail: skopp@warnerpacific.edu; *Electronic Res, Instruction Librn,* Doug McClay; Tel: 503-517-1118, E-mail: dmcclay@warnerpacific.edu; *Circ Supvr,* Jeff Barnhardt; Tel: 503-517-1037, E-mail: jbarnhardt@warnerpacific.edu; *Acq, Ser,* Mari Bettineski; Tel: 503-517-1023, E-mail: mbettineski@warnerpacific.edu; Staff 4 (MLS 2, Non-MLS 2)
Founded 1937. Enrl 970; Highest Degree: Master
Library Holdings: Bk Titles 47,621; Bk Vols 59,251; Per Subs 315
Special Collections: Church of God Archives
Automation Activity & Vendor Info: (Acquisitions) Innovative Interfaces, Inc; (Cataloging) Innovative Interfaces, Inc; (Circulation) Innovative Interfaces, Inc; (Course Reserve) Innovative Interfaces, Inc; (ILL) OCLC FirstSearch; (Serials) Innovative Interfaces, Inc
Database Vendor: OCLC WorldShare Interlibrary Loan
Wireless access
Function: ILL available
Partic in Northwest Association of Private Colleges & Universities (NAPCU); Orbis Cascade Alliance
Restriction: Open to fac, students & qualified researchers

S WASHINGTON COUNTY HISTORICAL SOCIETY & MUSEUM LIBRARY*, 17677 NW Springville Rd, 97229. SAN 329-2460. Tel: 503-645-5353. FAX: 503-645-5650. E-mail: info@washingtoncountymuseum.org, librarian@washingtoncountymuseum.org. Web Site: www.washingtoncountymuseum.org. *Res Librn,* Winn Herrschaft; Staff 4 (Non-MLS 4)
Founded 1956
Library Holdings: Bk Vols 650
Special Collections: Photograph Coll. Municipal Document Depository; Oral History
Subject Interests: Hist, Presv
Publications: This Far-Off Sunset Land
Restriction: Non-circulating to the pub, Not a lending libr, Open by appt only

P WEST SLOPE COMMUNITY LIBRARY*, 3678 SW 78th Ave, 97225-9019. SAN 324-248X. Tel: 503-292-6416. Administration Tel: 503-297-1428. FAX: 503-292-6932. Web Site: www.wccls.org/libraries/westslope. *Libr Mgr,* Veronica Eden; Staff 7.2 (MLS 2, Non-MLS 5.2)
Founded 1950. Pop 11,000; Circ 280,000
Jul 2010-Jun 2011 Income $679,500, State $2,000, County $675,000, Locally Generated Income $2,500. Mats Exp $80,000, Books $65,000, Per/Ser (Incl. Access Fees) $4,000, AV Mat $11,000
Library Holdings: CDs 5,282; DVDs 8,311; e-books 12,396; Electronic Media & Resources 130; Bk Vols 44,700; Per Subs 134
Automation Activity & Vendor Info: (Circulation) Innovative Interfaces, Inc
Wireless access
Partic in Washington County Cooperative Library Services
Open Mon-Thurs 9:30-8, Fri & Sat 9:30-4
Friends of the Library Group

R WESTERN SEMINARY, Cline-Tunnell Library, 5511 SE Hawthorne Blvd, 97215-3367. SAN 314-1926. Tel: 503-517-1840. Interlibrary Loan Service Tel: 503-517-1842. Toll Free Tel: 877-517-1800. FAX: 503-517-1801. Web Site: www.westernseminary.edu/library/pdx/index.htm. *Head of Libr,* Dr Robert A Krupp; Tel: 503-517-1838, E-mail: rakrupp@westernseminary.edu; *Acq, Circ,* Vivian J Woo; Tel: 503-517-1843, E-mail: vjwoo@westernseminary.edu; *ILL,* Sherry Atkins; E-mail: satkins@westernseminary.edu; *Tech Serv,* Karen J Arvin; Tel: 503-517-1841, E-mail: kjarvin@westernseminary.edu; Staff 1.5 (MLS 1.5)
Founded 1927. Enrl 471; Fac 98; Highest Degree: Doctorate
Jul 2012-Jun 2013 Income $4,607. Mats Exp $29,544, Books $4,381, Per/Ser (Incl. Access Fees) $11,124, Electronic Ref Mat (Incl. Access Fees) $14,039. Sal $106,042 (Prof $69,782)
Library Holdings: AV Mats 226; Bks on Deafness & Sign Lang 40; CDs 441; DVDs 73; e-books 136,498; Microforms 31,874; Bk Titles 80,340; Bk Vols 86,651; Per Subs 183; Videos 229
Special Collections: Baptist History Coll
Automation Activity & Vendor Info: (Acquisitions) Ex Libris Group; (Cataloging) Ex Libris Group; (Circulation) Ex Libris Group; (ILL) Ex Libris Group; (OPAC) Ex Libris Group
Database Vendor: EBSCOhost, Gale Cengage Learning
Wireless access
Function: ILL available
Publications: Library Handbook; Library Online Resources
Partic in OCLC Online Computer Library Center, Inc; Online Private Academic Library Link (OPALL); WIN Library Network
Special Services for the Deaf - Bks on deafness & sign lang
Open Mon 8-6, Tues-Thurs 8-5, Fri 8-4, Sat 10-2

S WORLD FORESTRY CENTER*, World Forest Institute Library, 4033 SW Canyon Rd, 97221. SAN 375-0639. Tel: 503-228-1367. FAX: 503-228-4608. Web Site: www.worldforestry.org. *Dir,* Sara Wu; E-mail: swu@worldforestry.org
Founded 1989
Library Holdings: Bk Vols 1,000
Function: Res libr
Restriction: Open by appt only

POWERS

P HAZEL M LEWIS LIBRARY*, 511 Third Ave, 97466. (Mail add: PO Box 559, 97466-0559), SAN 314-1969. Tel: 541-439-5311. FAX: 541-439-5311. E-mail: hazelmlewis@yahoo.com. *Dir,* Joanie Bedwell; *Ch Serv,* Phyllis Pearce; Staff 2 (Non-MLS 2)
Founded 1935. Pop 680; Circ 26,101
Library Holdings: Bk Vols 25,385; Per Subs 44
Subject Interests: Hist
Automation Activity & Vendor Info: (Cataloging) Innovative Interfaces, Inc; (Circulation) Innovative Interfaces, Inc; (OPAC) Innovative Interfaces, Inc
Database Vendor: EBSCOhost, Innovative Interfaces, Inc, OCLC FirstSearch
Wireless access
Function: ILL available
Mem of Coos County Library Service District
Open Mon & Wed 10-6, Tues & Thurs 10-12 & 4-8, Fri & Sat 10-4

PRINEVILLE

P CROOK COUNTY LIBRARY*, 175 NW Meadow Lakes Dr, 97754-1997. SAN 920-7287. Tel: 541-447-7978. FAX: 541-447-1308. E-mail: library@crooklib.org. Web Site: www.crooklib.org. *Dir,* Camille Wood; Tel: 541-447-7978, Ext 301, E-mail: cwood@crooklib.org; *Ad, Youth Serv Librn,* Barratt Miller; Tel: 541-447-7978, Ext 303, E-mail: bmiller@crooklib.org; *Circ Serv Mgr,* Cindy York; Tel: 541-447-7978, Ext 304, E-mail: cyork@crooklib.org; Staff 11 (MLS 2, Non-MLS 9)
Founded 1931. Pop 22,566; Circ 150,032
Jul 2012-Jun 2013 Income $561,555, State $6,406, County $555,149. Mats Exp $71,300
Library Holdings: AV Mats 19,746; DVDs 6,785; e-books 12,295; Bk Titles 47,664; Per Subs 141
Automation Activity & Vendor Info: (Acquisitions) Innovative Interfaces, Inc; (Cataloging) Innovative Interfaces, Inc; (Circulation) Innovative Interfaces, Inc; (ILL) OCLC; (OPAC) Innovative Interfaces, Inc; (Serials) Innovative Interfaces, Inc

Database Vendor: Baker & Taylor, EBSCO Auto Repair Reference, Gale Cengage Learning, Ingram Library Services, LearningExpress, OCLC FirstSearch, OCLC WorldShare Interlibrary Loan, Overdrive, Inc
Wireless access
Function: Audiobks via web, Bks on CD, Children's prog, Computers for patron use, Copy machines, e-mail & chat, Electronic databases & coll, Family literacy, Fax serv, Free DVD rentals, Handicapped accessible, ILL available, Magnifiers for reading, Mail & tel request accepted, Music CDs, Online cat, Outreach serv, OverDrive digital audio bks, Photocopying/Printing, Preschool reading prog, Printer for laptops & handheld devices, Prog for adults, Prog for children & young adult, Pub access computers, Ref serv available, Spanish lang bks, Story hour, Summer reading prog, Tax forms, Teen prog, Telephone ref, Wheelchair accessible
Member Libraries: Jefferson County District Library
Open Mon-Wed 9-8, Thurs & Fri 9-6, Sat 10-4
Restriction: Authorized patrons
Friends of the Library Group
Bookmobiles: 1. Mary Ryan, Bk vols 900

RAINIER

P RAINIER CITY LIBRARY*, 106 B St W, 97048. (Mail add: PO Box 100, 97048-0100), SAN 314-1993. Tel: 503-556-7301. FAX: 503-556-3200. E-mail: rainier_library@yahoo.com. *Librn,* Patricia Stanley
Pop 1,800; Circ 9,000
Library Holdings: Bk Vols 12,000; Per Subs 30
Special Collections: Rainier History Coll
Open Mon-Fri 9:30-12 & 1-5

ROSEBURG

L DOUGLAS COUNTY LAW LIBRARY*, Justice Bldg, Rm 305, 97470. SAN 372-2252. Tel: 541-440-4341. E-mail: dclawlib@co.douglas.or.us. Web Site: www.co.douglas.or.us/LawLib/. *Librn,* Diana L Hadley; Staff 0.5 (MLS 0.5)
Jul 2012-Jun 2013 Income $93,000. Mats Exp $60,000, Books $40,000, Electronic Ref Mat (Incl. Access Fees) $20,000. Sal $33,000
Library Holdings: Electronic Media & Resources 25; Bk Vols 10,000; Per Subs 10
Subject Interests: Legal mat
Wireless access
Function: Copy machines, For res purposes, Govt ref serv, Ref & res, Ref serv in person, Res libr
Open Mon, Tues & Thurs 9-12 & 1-4, Wed 8:30-12
Restriction: Non-circulating, Open to pub for ref only, Pub access for legal res only

P DOUGLAS COUNTY LIBRARY SYSTEM, 1409 NE Diamond Lake Blvd, 97470. SAN 358-1616. Tel: 541-440-4305. Interlibrary Loan Service Tel: 541-440-4304. Administration Tel: 541-440-4311. FAX: 541-957-7798. TDD: 541-957-4783. Web Site: dclibrary.us. *Dir,* Harold A Hayes; *Pub Serv,* Darla Schofield; Tel: 541-957-4635, E-mail: djschofi@co.douglas.or.us; *Tech Serv,* Jeremiah S Elliott; Tel: 541-440-6005, E-mail: jelliott@co.douglas.or.us; Staff 9 (MLS 4, Non-MLS 5)
Founded 1955. Pop 107,000; Circ 512,988
Library Holdings: Audiobooks 8,846; AV Mats 15,655; e-books 30,806; Bk Vols 223,125; Per Subs 381; Talking Bks 21,575
Subject Interests: Commun needs
Automation Activity & Vendor Info: (Acquisitions) SirsiDynix; (Cataloging) SirsiDynix; (Circulation) SirsiDynix; (ILL) SirsiDynix; (OPAC) SirsiDynix
Wireless access
Partic in Southern Oregon Library Federation
Special Services for the Deaf - TDD equip
Open Tues 12-7, Wed 11-6, Thurs 11-5, Sat 10-2
Friends of the Library Group
Branches: 10
CANYONVILLE BRANCH, 250 N Main St, Canyonville, 97417. (Mail add: PO Box 216, Canyonville, 97417-0216), SAN 358-1640. Tel: 541-839-4727. FAX: 541-839-4727. *Br Librn,* Carol Hilderbrand; E-mail: cahilder@co.douglas.or.us
Library Holdings: Bk Vols 14,276
Open Mon 12-5, Wed 10-4, Thurs 2-7
Friends of the Library Group
GLENDALE BRANCH, Third & Willis, Glendale, 97442. (Mail add: PO Box 680, Glendale, 97442-0680), SAN 358-1705. Tel: 541-832-2360. FAX: 541-832-2360. *Librn,* Linda Kitchens; E-mail: lskitche@co.douglas.or.us
Library Holdings: Bk Vols 11,195
Open Tues 1-6, Wed & Fri 11-4:30
Friends of the Library Group
PAUL B & DOROTHY F HULT LIBRARY, 440 SE Grape, Winston, 97496. (Mail add: PO Box 640, Winston, 97496-0640), SAN 358-1918. Tel: 541-679-5501. *Librn,* Pete Tano; E-mail: pktano@co.douglas.or.us
Library Holdings: Bk Vols 18,477
Open Mon, Tues & Thurs 12-6, Fri 11-5
C GILES HUNT MEMORIAL, 210 E Central St, Sutherlin, 97479. (Mail add: PO Box 429, Sutherlin, 97479-0429), SAN 358-1764. Tel: 541-459-9161. FAX: 541-459-9161. Web Site: www.co.douglas.or.us/library/sutherlin.htm. *Librn,* Juanita Steiner; E-mail: jmsteiner@co.douglas.or.us
Library Holdings: Bk Vols 20,068
Open Tues 12-6, Wed 10-6, Fri & Sat 11-4
Friends of the Library Group
MYRTLE CREEK BRANCH, 231 Division, Myrtle Creek, 97457. (Mail add: PO Box 5006, Myrtle Creek, 97457-0041), SAN 358-1799. Tel: 541-863-5945. FAX: 541-863-5945. *Librn,* Joy Sanada; E-mail: jesanada@co.douglas.or.us
Library Holdings: Bk Vols 19,874
Open Mon & Thurs 12-6, Tues & Wed 11-5
OAKLAND BRANCH, 637 NE Locust St, Oakland, 97462. (Mail add: PO Box 87, Oakland, 97462-0087), SAN 358-1829. Tel: 541-459-9784. FAX: 541-459-9784. *Librn,* Glenn Hansen; E-mail: glhansen@co.douglas.or.us
Library Holdings: Bk Vols 9,862
Open Mon 1-5, Wed 1-6, Fri 10-5
REEDSPORT BRANCH, 395 Winchester St, Reedsport, 97467, SAN 358-1853. Tel: 541-271-3500. FAX: 541-271-1027. *Librn,* Sue Cousineau; E-mail: smcusin@co.douglas.or.us
Library Holdings: Bk Vols 17,906
Open Tues 12-7, Wed 10-4, Thurs 12-6, Fri 11-4
Friends of the Library Group
RIDDLE BRANCH, 637 First Ave, Riddle, 97469. (Mail add: PO Box 33, Riddle, 97469-0033), SAN 358-1888. Tel: 541-874-2070. FAX: 541-874-2070. *Librn,* Patti Rieman; E-mail: parieman@co.douglas.or.us
Library Holdings: Bk Vols 14,185
Open Tues 12-6, Wed, 12-5, Fri 11-4
Friends of the Library Group
MILDRED WHIPPLE LIBRARY, 205 West A Ave, Drain, 97435. (Mail add: PO Box 128, Drain, 97435-0128), SAN 358-1675. Tel: 541-836-2648. FAX: 541-836-2304. *Librn,* Elizabeth Land; E-mail: ebland@co.douglas.or.us
Library Holdings: Bk Vols 18,703
Open Mon 2-7, Tue 10-5, Fri 12-4
Friends of the Library Group
YONCALLA BRANCH, 194 Birch, Yoncalla, 97499. (Mail add: PO Box 157, Yoncalla, 97499-0157), SAN 358-1942. Tel: 541-849-2128. FAX: 541-849-2128. *Librn,* Jill Cunningham; E-mail: jccunnin@co.douglas.or.us
Library Holdings: Bk Vols 12,417
Open Wed 10-5, Thurs 2-7, Sat 10-2
Friends of the Library Group

S DOUGLAS COUNTY MUSEUM*, Lavola Bakken Research Library, 123 Museum Dr, 97470. SAN 314-2019. Tel: 541-957-7007. FAX: 541-957-7017. E-mail: museum@co.douglas.or.us. Web Site: www.douglasmuseum.com. *Res,* Karen Bratton; E-mail: kabratto@co.douglas.or.us
Founded 1969
Library Holdings: Bk Vols 2,800
Special Collections: Herbarium Coll of Douglas County; History of Douglas County Coll, ledgers, scrapbooks, county records, unpublished articles, letters, diaries, mss, census & cemetery records, genealogies. Oral History
Subject Interests: Agr, Dougla develop, Douglas county hist, Logging mills, Marine hist, Mining, Natural hist, Railroads, Saw mills, Umpqua Indians
Open Mon-Fri 11-4:30

J UMPQUA COMMUNITY COLLEGE LIBRARY*, 1140 Umpqua College Rd, 97470. (Mail add: PO Box 967, 97470), SAN 314-2035. Tel: 541-440-4640. Interlibrary Loan Service Tel: 541-677-3245. Reference Tel: 541-677-3244. Toll Free Tel: 800-820-5161. FAX: 541-440-4637. TDD: 541-440-4626. Web Site: www.umpqua.edu/library/libhome.htm. *Dir, Libr Serv,* David Hutchison; Tel: 541-440-4638, E-mail: david.hutchison@umpqua.edu; *Libr Spec,* Kristen Moser; Tel: 541-440-7682, E-mail: kristen.moser@umpqua.edu; *Circ,* Susan Leek; E-mail: susan.leek@umpqua.edu; *Ref,* Katherine Cunnion; Tel: 541-440-7681, E-mail: katherine.cunnion@umpqua.edu; Staff 8 (MLS 2, Non-MLS 6)
Founded 1964. Enrl 3,000; Fac 69; Highest Degree: Associate
Library Holdings: Bk Vols 50,000; Per Subs 188
Special Collections: Fire Science; Grant
Automation Activity & Vendor Info: (Cataloging) SirsiDynix; (Circulation) SirsiDynix; (Course Reserve) SirsiDynix; (ILL) SirsiDynix; (OPAC) SirsiDynix

Database Vendor: EBSCOhost, Gale Cengage Learning, LexisNexis, ProQuest, SirsiDynix
Wireless access
Function: ILL available
Publications: Oregon Regional Union List of Serials
Partic in OCLC Online Computer Library Center, Inc; Orbis Cascade Alliance
Open Mon-Thurs 7:30am-9pm

SAINT BENEDICT

C MOUNT ANGEL ABBEY LIBRARY*, One Abbey Dr, 97373. SAN 314-2051. Tel: 503-845-3303, 503-845-3317. Reference Tel: 503-845-3102. FAX: 503-845-3500. Web Site: www.mtangel.edu/library. *Adminr,* Victoria Ertelt; E-mail: victoriae@mtangel.edu; *Acq,* Laurie Jiricek; E-mail: lauriej@mtangel.edu; *Cat,* Bruce Flath; E-mail: bflath@mtangel.edu; *ILL,* Sandi Ritchey; E-mail: sandir@mtangel.edu; *Tech Serv,* Bede Partridge; E-mail: bedep@mtangel.edu; Staff 4 (MLS 2, Non-MLS 2)
Founded 1882. Enrl 230; Fac 40; Highest Degree: Master
Library Holdings: Bk Vols 230,000; Per Subs 380
Special Collections: Civil War; McKuen Philosophy Coll; Patristic & Latin Christian Studies
Subject Interests: Humanities, Philos, Theol
Automation Activity & Vendor Info: (Acquisitions) Ex Libris Group; (Cataloging) Ex Libris Group; (Circulation) Ex Libris Group; (Course Reserve) Ex Libris Group; (OPAC) Ex Libris Group; (Serials) Ex Libris Group
Database Vendor: EBSCOhost
Partic in OCLC Online Computer Library Center, Inc; Online Private Academic Library Link (OPALL)
Open Mon-Thurs 8:30-5 & 6:30-9:30, Fri 8:30-5, Sat 10-4, Sun 1-4 & 6:30-9:30
Friends of the Library Group

SAINT HELENS

P SAINT HELENS PUBLIC LIBRARY*, 375 S 18th St, Ste A, 97051-2022. SAN 314-206X. Tel: 503-397-4544. FAX: 503-366-3020. E-mail: shpl@ci.st-helens.or.us. Web Site: sthelens.plinkit.org. *Interim Dir,* Diane Barbee; Tel: 503-397-4544, Ext 1, E-mail: DianeB@ci.st-helens.or.us; Staff 5.5 (MLS 3, Non-MLS 2.5)
Founded 1914. Pop 12,075; Circ 125,000
Jul 2006-Jun 2007 Income $539,513. Mats Exp $51,740, Books $30,000, Per/Ser (Incl. Access Fees) $5,240, AV Mat $15,500, Electronic Ref Mat (Incl. Access Fees) $1,000. Sal $330,984 (Prof $143,112)
Library Holdings: AV Mats 4,400; CDs 837; DVDs 455; Large Print Bks 907; Bk Titles 35,514; Bk Vols 38,609; Per Subs 100; Talking Bks 1,900; Videos 2,500
Special Collections: Municipal Document Depository
Automation Activity & Vendor Info: (Cataloging) TLC (The Library Corporation); (Circulation) TLC (The Library Corporation); (ILL) OCLC; (OPAC) TLC (The Library Corporation)
Database Vendor: EBSCOhost, TLC (The Library Corporation)
Function: Art exhibits, CD-ROM, Copy machines, Digital talking bks, Electronic databases & coll, ILL available, Magnifiers for reading, Music CDs, Orientations, Preschool outreach, Prog for adults, Prog for children & young adult, Summer reading prog, VHS videos
Open Mon-Thurs 10-7, Fri 10-5, Sat 10-2
Friends of the Library Group

SALEM

J CHEMEKETA COMMUNITY COLLEGE LIBRARY, Bldg 9, 2nd Flr, 4000 Lancaster Dr NE, 97305-1500. (Mail add: PO Box 14007, 97309-7070), SAN 314-2094. Tel: 503-399-5043. Reference Tel: 503-399-5231. FAX: 503-399-5214. E-mail: reference@chemeketa.edu. Web Site: library.chemeketa.edu. *Dir,* Natalie Beach; Tel: 503-399-5105, E-mail: nbeach@chemeketa.edu; Staff 16.13 (MLS 5.75, Non-MLS 10.38)
Founded 1962. Enrl 11,109; Fac 5; Highest Degree: Associate
Library Holdings: e-books 111,000; Bk Vols 65,000
Automation Activity & Vendor Info: (Acquisitions) Ex Libris Group; (Cataloging) Ex Libris Group; (Circulation) Ex Libris Group; (Course Reserve) Ex Libris Group; (ILL) OCLC WorldShare Interlibrary Loan; (OPAC) Ex Libris Group; (Serials) Ex Libris Group
Database Vendor: Alexander Street Press, ARTstor, CQ Press, ebrary, EBSCOhost, Ex Libris Group, Facts on File, Gale Cengage Learning, H W Wilson, JSTOR, LexisNexis, OCLC, OVID Technologies, Oxford Online, PubMed, ReferenceUSA, Safari Books Online, Sage, ScienceDirect, YBP Library Services
Wireless access
Function: Audio & video playback equip for onsite use, Doc delivery serv, E-Reserves, Electronic databases & coll, Fax serv, Handicapped accessible, ILL available, Magnifiers for reading, Online cat, Online ref, Photocopying/Printing, Pub access computers
Partic in Chemeketa Cooperative Regional Library Service; OCLC Online Computer Library Center, Inc; Orbis Cascade Alliance; Valley Link

CR CORBAN UNIVERSITY LIBRARY*, 5000 Deer Park Dr SE, 97317-9392. SAN 314-2221. Tel: 503-375-7016. FAX: 503-375-7196. E-mail: library@corban.edu. Web Site: www.corban.edu/library. *Dir,* Floyd M Votaw; E-mail: fvotaw@corban.edu; *Acq,* Holly Flores; *Circ,* Gary Taylor; *ILL, Ref Serv,* Garrett Trott; E-mail: gtrott@corban.edu; *Tech Serv,* Connie Edgar; Staff 2 (MLS 2)
Founded 1935. Enrl 1,100; Fac 55; Highest Degree: Doctorate
Jul 2008-Jun 2009. Mats Exp $89,449, Books $37,973, Per/Ser (Incl. Access Fees) $17,483, AV Mat $1,192, Electronic Ref Mat (Incl. Access Fees) $31,079, Presv $1,722. Sal $204,554 (Prof $107,635)
Library Holdings: AV Mats 5,237; e-books 8,326; Microforms 7,508; Bk Vols 105,469; Per Subs 528
Special Collections: Prewitt-Allen Archaeology Museum
Subject Interests: Bible, Missions, Theol
Automation Activity & Vendor Info: (Acquisitions) Ex Libris Group; (Cataloging) Ex Libris Group; (Circulation) Ex Libris Group; (Course Reserve) Ex Libris Group; (OPAC) Ex Libris Group; (Serials) Ex Libris Group
Database Vendor: CQ Press, EBSCOhost, Facts on File, H W Wilson, Oxford Online, ProQuest, ReferenceUSA, Westlaw
Wireless access
Partic in Christian Library Consortium; Northwest Association of Private Colleges & Universities (NAPCU); Online Private Academic Library Link (OPALL)
Open Mon-Thurs 7:45am-11pm, Fri 7:45-6, Sat 11:30-6, Sun 3-11

R FIRST BAPTIST CHURCH*, Curry Memorial Library, 395 Marion St NE, 97301. SAN 314-2116. Tel: 503-364-2285. FAX: 503-391-9272. E-mail: fbc@fbcsalem.org. Web Site: www.fbcsalem.org. *Librn,* Willene Peterson
Library Holdings: Bk Vols 6,000
Subject Interests: Biblical studies, Christian fiction, Christian living
Open Wed 5:30-8:30, Sun 8:30-12 & 5-7:30

L MARION COUNTY LAW LIBRARY*, 555 Court St, 97309. (Mail add: PO Box 14500, 97309), SAN 372-2155. Tel: 503-588-5090. FAX: 503-373-4386. E-mail: lawlibrary@co.marion.or.us. Web Site: legal.co.marion.or.us/lawlibrary. *Librn,* Martha Renick
Library Holdings: Bk Vols 10,000; Per Subs 50
Partic in Midwest Collaborative for Library Services (MCLS)
Open Mon-Fri 8:30-5

G OREGON DEPARTMENT OF TRANSPORTATION LIBRARY*, 355 Capitol St NE, Rm 22, 97301-3871. SAN 358-1977. Tel: 503-986-3280. FAX: 503-986-4025. Web Site: www.oregon.gov/odot/cs/bss/library.shtml. *Librn,* Laura Wilt; E-mail: laura.e.wilt@odot.state.or.us; Staff 1 (MLS 1)
Founded 1937
Library Holdings: Bk Titles 12,000; Bk Vols 18,000; Per Subs 50
Special Collections: Safety costumes; Transportation Safety, v-tapes
Subject Interests: Aeronaut, Eng, Environ, Motor vehicles, Planning, Soils, Transit, Transportation
Automation Activity & Vendor Info: (Cataloging) EOS International; (OPAC) EOS International
Database Vendor: OCLC FirstSearch
Open Mon-Fri 8-4:30

G OREGON LEGISLATIVE LIBRARY*, 900 Court St NE, Rm 446, 97301. SAN 374-5635. Tel: 503-986-1668. FAX: 503-986-1005. Web Site: www.leg.state.or.us/comm/commsrvs/home.htm. *Legis Ref Coordr,* Patricia Nielsen; Staff 1 (Non-MLS 1)
Library Holdings: Bk Titles 6,000; Per Subs 20; Videos 40
Special Collections: Oral History
Wireless access
Function: Ref & res
Open Mon-Fri 8-5

S OREGON SCHOOL FOR THE DEAF LIBRARY*, 999 Locust St NE, 97301-0954. SAN 314-2140. Tel: 503-378-3825, 503-378-6779. FAX: 503-378-3378. Web Site: www.osd.k12.or.us. *Librn,* Peggy Breen; E-mail: peggy.breen@osd.k12.or.us
Founded 1870
Library Holdings: Bk Vols 14,500; Per Subs 30
Wireless access
Restriction: Not open to pub

S OREGON STATE CORRECTIONAL INSTITUTION LIBRARY*, 3405 Deer Park Dr SE, 97310-3985. SAN 314-2159. Tel: 503-373-7523. FAX: 503-378-8919. *Librn,* Greg Hunter; Staff 1 (MLS 1)
Founded 1959
Library Holdings: Bk Vols 40,289
Restriction: Not open to pub, Staff & inmates only

P OREGON STATE LIBRARY*, 250 Winter St NE, 97301-3950. SAN 358-206X. Tel: 503-378-4243. Interlibrary Loan Service Tel: 503-378-4498. FAX: 503-585-8059. Web Site: oregon.gov/osl. *State Librn,* MaryKay Dahlgreen; E-mail: marykay.dahlgreen@state.or.us; *Bus Mgr,* Shawn Range; Tel: 503-378-3870, E-mail: shawn.range@state.or.us; *Prog Mgr, Talking Bk & Libr Develop,* Susan Westin; Tel: 503-378-5435, E-mail: susan.b.westin@state.or.us; *Prog Mgr, Govt Res Serv,* Margie Harrison; Tel: 503-378-5030, E-mail: margie.harrison@state.or.us; Staff 39.26 (MLS 14, Non-MLS 25.26)
Founded 1905. Pop 2,742,750; Circ 121,079
Library Holdings: AV Mats 2,566; Large Print Bks 315; Bk Titles 63,260; Bk Vols 63,276; Per Subs 301; Talking Bks 127,353
Special Collections: Family History (Genealogy Coll), bks, micro; Grants & Funding, Patent, US Census; Oregon History (Oregoniana); State & Federal Government, bks, doc. State Document Depository; US Document Depository
Subject Interests: Agr, Forestry, Govt
Automation Activity & Vendor Info: (Circulation) Innovative Interfaces, Inc; (OPAC) Innovative Interfaces, Inc
Wireless access
Publications: Letter to Libraries Online
Partic in OCLC Online Computer Library Center, Inc
Special Services for the Blind - Braille bks; Talking bks
Open Mon-Fri 8-5

P OREGON STATE LIBRARY TALKING BOOK & BRAILLE SERVICES*, 250 Winter St NE, 97301-3950. SAN 314-2124. Tel: 503-378-5389. Toll Free Tel: 800-452-0292. FAX: 503-585-8059. E-mail: tbabs.info@state.or.us. Web Site: www.oregon.gov/osl/tbabs, www.tbabs.org. *Pub Serv Librn,* Elke Bruton; Tel: 503-378-5455, E-mail: elke.bruton@state.or.us; *Prog Mgr,* Susan Westin; Tel: 503-378-5435, E-mail: susan.b.westin@state.or.us
Founded 1932
Library Holdings: Bk Titles 60,000; Bk Vols 158,126
Subject Interests: Ore
Automation Activity & Vendor Info: (Circulation) Keystone Systems, Inc (KLAS); (OPAC) Keystone Systems, Inc (KLAS)
Publications: Talking Book & Braille News (Quarterly)
Special Services for the Deaf - TDD equip
Special Services for the Blind - Descriptive video serv (DVS)
Open Mon-Fri 8-5

S OREGON STATE PENITENTIARY LIBRARY*, OSP Maximum, 2605 State St, 97310. SAN 358-2124. Tel: 503-378-2081. *Librn,* M Davidson
Founded 1953
Library Holdings: Bk Vols 10,000
Special Collections: Indian History Coll
Subject Interests: Agr, Archit, Art, Hort, Philos
Special Services for the Deaf - High interest/low vocabulary bks; Spec interest per
Restriction: Not open to pub, Staff & inmates only
Branches:
COFFEE CREEK CORRECTIONAL FACILITY, 24499 SW Grahams Ferry Rd, Wilsonville, 97070. Tel: 503-570-6783. FAX: 503-570-6786. *Librn,* Angela Wheeler
Library Holdings: Bk Vols 8,500
Restriction: Staff & inmates only
OSP MINIMUM, 2809 State St, 97310, SAN 358-2272. Tel: 503-378-2081. *Librn,* M Davidson
Library Holdings: Bk Titles 8,000
Special Collections: Legal Materials
Restriction: Staff & inmates only

M SALEM HOSPITAL COMMUNITY EDUCATION CENTER*, Staff Library & Resource Center, 890 Oak St SE, 97301. (Mail add: PO Box 14001, 97309-5014), SAN 321-5474. Tel: 503-814-1598. Toll Free Tel: 866-977-2432 (Ore only). FAX: 503-814-1599. Web Site: www.salemhospital.org/chec. *Librn,* Paul Howard; Staff 3 (MLS 1, Non-MLS 2)
Founded 1972
Library Holdings: Bk Titles 2,500; Per Subs 600
Subject Interests: Med
Automation Activity & Vendor Info: (Acquisitions) Inmagic, Inc.; (Cataloging) Inmagic, Inc.; (Circulation) Inmagic, Inc.; (Serials) Inmagic, Inc.
Wireless access
Partic in OCLC Online Computer Library Center, Inc
Open Mon-Thurs 9-7, Fri 9-6

P SALEM PUBLIC LIBRARY*, 585 Liberty St SE, 97301. (Mail add: PO Box 14810, 97309), SAN 358-2396. Tel: 503-588-6052. Circulation Tel: 503-588-6060. Interlibrary Loan Service Tel: 503-588-6078. Administration Tel: 503-588-6071. Automation Services Tel: 503-589-7740. FAX: 503-588-6055. Administration FAX: 503-589-2011. TDD: 503-588-6021. E-mail: library@cityofsalem.net. Web Site: www.salemlibrary.org. *Libr Adminr,* BJ Toewe; Tel: 503-588-6084, E-mail: bjtoewe@cityofsalem.net; *Adult Serv Mgr,* Christopher Rumbaugh; Tel: 503-588-6449, E-mail: crumbaugh@cityofsalem.net; *Tech Serv Mgr,* Paul Lightcap; Tel: 503-588-6020, E-mail: plightcap@cityofsalem.net; *Youth Serv Mgr,* Karen Fisher; Tel: 503-588-6039, E-mail: kfisher@cityofsalem.net; *Circ Supvr,* Karen Kinzie; Tel: 503-588-6090, E-mail: kkinzie@cityofsalem.net; *Mgt Analyst,* Cyndi Easterly; Tel: 503-588-6064, E-mail: ceasterly@cityofsalem.net; Staff 78 (MLS 13, Non-MLS 65)
Founded 1904. Pop 140,000; Circ 1,338,355
Library Holdings: AV Mats 22,233; Bk Titles 228,312; Bk Vols 485,152; Per Subs 839
Special Collections: Oregon History Coll; Original Art; Salem Historic Photos Coll
Subject Interests: Local hist
Automation Activity & Vendor Info: (Cataloging) Innovative Interfaces, Inc; (Circulation) Innovative Interfaces, Inc; (ILL) OCLC; (OPAC) Innovative Interfaces, Inc
Database Vendor: Dialog, EBSCOhost, OCLC FirstSearch
Wireless access
Function: ILL available, Photocopying/Printing, Ref serv available
Publications: Online Newsletter; Salem Public Library (Newsletter)
Partic in Chemeketa Cooperative Regional Library Service
Open Tues-Thurs 10-9, Fri & Sat 10-6, Sun (Sept-May) 1-5
Friends of the Library Group
Branches: 1
WEST SALEM, 395 Glen Creek Rd NW, 97304, SAN 358-2426. Tel: 503-588-6301. FAX: 503-588-6397. Administration FAX: 503-589-2011. *Libr Mgr,* Karen Fischer; Tel: 503-588-6039, E-mail: kfischer@cityofsalem.net
Circ 132,144
Library Holdings: Bk Vols 35,000; Per Subs 45
Automation Activity & Vendor Info: (Acquisitions) Innovative Interfaces, Inc; (Serials) Innovative Interfaces, Inc
Open Mon, Tues, Thurs & Fri 2-6
Friends of the Library Group

S SANTIAM CORRECTIONAL INSTITUTION LIBRARY*, 4005 Aumsville Hwy, 97317. Tel: 503-378-3678, Ext 522. FAX: 503-378-8520. *Librn,* Shawn Jenne
Library Holdings: Bk Vols 2,000

GL STATE OF OREGON LAW LIBRARY*, Supreme Court Bldg, 1163 State St, 97301-2563. SAN 314-2205. Tel: 503-986-5640. FAX: 503-986-5623. E-mail: state.law.library@ojd.state.or.us. Web Site: www.oregon.gov/SOLL/index.shtml. *Electronic Serv Librn, Law Librn,* Cathryn Bowie; Tel: 503-986-5921, E-mail: cathryn.e.bowie@ojd.state.or.us; *Cat Librn, Doc Librn,* Gary Morgan; Tel: 503-986-5737, E-mail: gary.w.morgan@ojd.state.or.us; *Ref Librn,* Peter Howard; E-mail: peter.a.howard@ojd.state.or.us; Staff 4 (MLS 3, Non-MLS 1)
Founded 1848
Library Holdings: Bk Titles 12,000; Bk Vols 100,000; Per Subs 200
Automation Activity & Vendor Info: (Acquisitions) Innovative Interfaces, Inc; (Circulation) Innovative Interfaces, Inc; (OPAC) Innovative Interfaces, Inc; (Serials) Innovative Interfaces, Inc
Database Vendor: OCLC FirstSearch
Function: Res libr
Open Mon-Fri 8-5

C WILLAMETTE UNIVERSITY*, Mark O Hatfield Library, 900 State St, 97301. SAN 358-2450. Tel: 503-370-6312. Interlibrary Loan Service Tel: 503-370-6018. Reference Tel: 503-370-6560. Automation Services Tel: 503-370-6610. FAX: 503-370-6141. E-mail: library@willamette.edu. Web Site: library.willamette.edu. *Univ Librn,* Deborah B Dancik; Tel: 503-370-6561, E-mail: ddancik@willamette.edu; *Assoc Univ Librn, Pub Serv & Coll,* Joni R Roberts; Tel: 503-370-6741, E-mail: jroberts@willamette.edu; *Assoc Univ Librn, Tech Serv,* Carol A Drost; Tel: 503-370-6715, E-mail: cdrost@willamette.edu; *Assoc Univ Librn, Syst,* Michael Spalti; Tel: 503-370-6356, E-mail: mspalti@willamette.edu; *Head, Ref,* Ford Schmidt; Tel: 503-375-5407, E-mail: fschmidt@willamette.edu; *Bus Librn,* Gary Klein; Tel: 503-370-6743, E-mail: gklein@willamette.edu; *Digital Assets Librn,* Sara Amato; Tel: 503-370-6719; *Humanities Librn,* Doreen Simonsen; Tel: 503-375-5343, E-mail: dsimonse@willamette.edu; *Syst Librn,* Bill Kelm; Tel: 503-375-5332, E-mail: bkelm@willamette.edu; *Access Serv Mgr,* Melissa Treichel; Tel: 503-370-4217, E-mail: mtreiche@willamette.edu; *Monographs & Acq Mgr,* Elizabeth Butterfield; Tel: 503-370-6616, E-mail: ebutterf@willamette.edu; *Mgr, Per,* Erica Miller; Tel: 503-370-6739, E-mail: emiller@willamette.edu; *Circ & Stacks Supvr,* Shanel Parette; *Doc Delivery, Libr Serv Coordr,* Rich Schmidt; E-mail: rschmidt@willamette.edu; *Univ Archivist,* Mary McRobinson; Tel: 503-370-6764, E-mail: mcrobin@willamette.edu; *Archivist,* Rose Marie Walter; Tel: 503-370-6845, E-mail: rwalter@willamette.edu; *Sci,* John Repplinger; Tel: 503-370-6525, E-mail: jrepplin@willamette.edu; *Tech Serv,* Alice French; Tel: 503-370-6476, E-mail: afrench@willamette.edu.

Subject Specialists: *Anthrop, Northwest, Sociol,* Joni R Roberts; *Children's lit, Fiction, Women's studies,* Carol A Drost; *Film studies, Hist, Politics,* Ford Schmidt; *Econ, Psychol, Pub policy,* Gary Klein; *Fine arts, Humanities,* Doreen Simonsen; *Biol, Chem,* John Repplinger; Staff 18 (MLS 12, Non-MLS 6)
Founded 1842. Fac 279; Highest Degree: Master
Jun 2012-May 2013 Income $1,907,511. Mats Exp $759,272. Sal $830,086 (Prof $692,728)
Library Holdings: AV Mats 11,596; e-books 4,785; Music Scores 6,636; Bk Titles 220,527; Bk Vols 244,734; Per Subs 2,485
Special Collections: Mark O Hatfield Archives; University Archives. US Document Depository
Subject Interests: Pacific Northwest
Automation Activity & Vendor Info: (Acquisitions) Innovative Interfaces, Inc; (Cataloging) Innovative Interfaces, Inc; (Circulation) Innovative Interfaces, Inc; (OPAC) Innovative Interfaces, Inc; (Serials) Innovative Interfaces, Inc
Database Vendor: EBSCOhost, LexisNexis, OCLC FirstSearch, OVID Technologies, ScienceDirect, SerialsSolutions
Wireless access
Partic in New England Law Library Consortium, Inc; OCLC Online Computer Library Center, Inc; Orbis Cascade Alliance
Open Mon-Thurs (Winter) 7:45am-2am, Fri 7:45am-9pm, Sat 10-9, Sun 10am-2am; Mon-Fri (Summer) 8-4:30
Friends of the Library Group

Departmental Libraries:

CL J W LONG LAW LIBRARY, 245 Winter St SE, 97301, SAN 358-2485. Tel: 503-370-6386. FAX: 503-375-5426. Web Site: www.willamette.edu/law/longlib. *Dir,* Ann Kitchel; Tel: 503-375-5345, E-mail: akitchel@willamette.edu; *Head, Ref & Res Serv,* Timothy Kelly; Tel: 503-375-5326, E-mail: tkelly@willamette.edu; *Head, Tech Serv,* Elysabeth Hall; Tel: 503-375-5318, E-mail: ehall@willamette.edu. Subject Specialists: *Legal res,* Ann Kitchel; Staff 9.65 (MLS 3, Non-MLS 6.65)
Founded 1883. Enrl 400; Fac 30; Highest Degree: Doctorate
Library Holdings: Bk Titles 39,880; Bk Vols 300,000; Per Subs 1,200
Special Collections: US Document Depository
Automation Activity & Vendor Info: (Acquisitions) Ex Libris Group; (Cataloging) Ex Libris Group; (Circulation) Ex Libris Group; (Course Reserve) Ex Libris Group; (ILL) OCLC ILLiad; (OPAC) Ex Libris Group
Database Vendor: Cassidy Cataloguing Services, Inc, EBSCO Information Services, Fastcase, Gale Cengage Learning, HeinOnline, LexisNexis, OCLC WorldShare Interlibrary Loan, Oxford Online, Paratext, ProQuest, Westlaw
Function: Outside serv via phone, mail, e-mail & web, Ref serv available
Partic in OCLC Online Computer Library Center, Inc
Open Mon-Fri 7:30-7 (9-5 Summer)
Restriction: 24-hr pass syst for students only, Open to students, fac, staff & alumni, Pub access for legal res only

SANDY

P SANDY PUBLIC LIBRARY, 38980 Proctor Blvd, 97055-8040. (Mail add: PO Box 578, 97055-0578), SAN 314-223X. Tel: 503-668-5537. FAX: 503-668-3153. E-mail: saref@lincc.lib.or.us. Web Site: www.cityofsandy.com/library. *Libr Dir,* Sarah McIntyre; Tel: 503-489-2168, E-mail: smcintyre@ci.sandy.or.us; *Ch,* Monica Smith; E-mail: msmith@ci.sandy.or.us; *Ref Librn,* Maureen Skinner; E-mail: mskinner@ci.sandy.or.us. Subject Specialists: *Early literacy,* Monica Smith; Staff 11.73 (MLS 3, Non-MLS 8.73)
Founded 1934. Pop 30,123; Circ 439,362
Jul 2012-Jun 2013 Income $1,027,188, State $3,851, Locally Generated Income $988,607, Other $34,730. Mats Exp $95,677, Books $63,089, Per/Ser (Incl. Access Fees) $5,491, AV Mat $18,642, Electronic Ref Mat (Incl. Access Fees) $8,455. Sal $768,924
Library Holdings: CDs 4,252; DVDs 7,297; e-books 25,910; Bk Vols 63,850; Per Subs 166; Talking Bks 1,362
Automation Activity & Vendor Info: (Cataloging) SirsiDynix; (Circulation) SirsiDynix; (OPAC) SirsiDynix
Database Vendor: EBSCOhost, Gale Cengage Learning, ProQuest, SirsiDynix
Wireless access
Function: 24/7 Electronic res, 24/7 Online cat, Adult bk club, Art exhibits, Bk club(s), Bks on CD, Children's prog, Computer training, Computers for patron use, Copy machines, Digital talking bks, Electronic databases & coll, Free DVD rentals, Handicapped accessible, ILL available, Magazines, Mus passes, Music CDs, Online cat, Online ref, OverDrive digital audio bks, Photocopying/Printing, Prog for adults, Prog for children & young adult, Pub access computers, Ref serv available, Ref serv in person, Spanish lang bks, Story hour, Summer reading prog, Tax forms, Teen prog, Telephone ref, Wheelchair accessible
Partic in Library Information Network of Clackamas County
Open Mon-Fri 10-7, Sat 10-5, Sun 1-5
Friends of the Library Group

SCAPPOOSE

P SCAPPOOSE PUBLIC LIBRARY*, 52469 SE Second St, 97056. (Mail add: PO Box 400, 97056-0400), SAN 314-2248. Tel: 503-543-7123. FAX: 503-543-7161. Web Site: scappooselibrary.org. *Libr Dir,* Dan White; E-mail: dwhite@scappooselibrary.org; *Cataloger,* David Sale; E-mail: dsale@scappooselibrary.org; *Youth Serv,* Ruth Silen; E-mail: rsilen@scappooselibrary.org; *Libr Tech,* Donna Worley; E-mail: dworley@scappooselibrary.org; Staff 3.5 (MLS 1.7, Non-MLS 1.8)
Founded 1929. Pop 11,688
Library Holdings: AV Mats 4,212; Bks on Deafness & Sign Lang 10; CDs 91; DVDs 201; e-journals 1; Electronic Media & Resources 9; Large Print Bks 828; Bk Vols 34,273; Per Subs 106; Videos 2,238
Subject Interests: Northwest
Automation Activity & Vendor Info: (Cataloging) SirsiDynix; (Circulation) SirsiDynix; (OPAC) SirsiDynix
Database Vendor: Gale Cengage Learning, SirsiDynix
Wireless access
Open Mon & Fri 10-6, Tues-Thurs 10-8, Sat 10-4
Friends of the Library Group

SCIO

P SCIO PUBLIC LIBRARY*, Town Hall, 38957 NW First Ave, 97374. (Mail add: PO Box 37, 97374-0037), SAN 329-3262. Tel: 503-394-3342. FAX: 503-394-2340. E-mail: slibrary@smt-net.com. *Librn,* LaVonne Murray
Founded 1940. Pop 2,000
Library Holdings: Bks on Deafness & Sign Lang 10; Bk Vols 12,852
Database Vendor: OCLC FirstSearch
Open Mon & Wed-Fri 9-12 & 1-5, Tues 3-8, Sat 1-4
Friends of the Library Group

SEASIDE

P SEASIDE PUBLIC LIBRARY, 1131 Broadway, 97138. SAN 314-2256. Tel: 503-738-6742. FAX: 503-738-6742. Web Site: www.seasidelibrary.org. *Dir,* Esther Moberg
Founded 1935
Library Holdings: Bk Vols 32,000; Per Subs 68
Wireless access
Open Tues-Thurs 9-8, Fri & Sat 9-5, Sun 1-5
Friends of the Library Group

SHERIDAN

P SHERIDAN PUBLIC LIBRARY*, 142 NW Yamhill, 97378-1843. (Mail add: PO Box 248, 97378-0248), SAN 314-2264. Tel: 503-843-3420. FAX: 503-843-2561. E-mail: sheridan@ccrls.org. *Dir,* Toni Rose
Pop 2,260; Circ 12,852
Library Holdings: AV Mats 3,000; Bk Vols 25,000; Per Subs 35; Talking Bks 500
Automation Activity & Vendor Info: (Cataloging) Innovative Interfaces, Inc; (Circulation) Innovative Interfaces, Inc
Partic in Chemeketa Cooperative Regional Library Service
Open Tues-Fri 10-6, Sat 12-5
Friends of the Library Group

SHERWOOD

P SHERWOOD PUBLIC LIBRARY, 22560 SW Pine St, 97140-9019. SAN 314-2272. Tel: 503-625-6688. Administration Tel: 503-625-4272. FAX: 503-625-4254. E-mail: askusspl@wccls.org. Web Site: www.sherwoodoregon.gov/library. *Libr Mgr,* Adrienne Doman Calkins; E-mail: adriennec@wccls.org; Staff 5.6 (MLS 5.6)
Founded 1935. Pop 18,575; Circ 367,240
Library Holdings: AV Mats 9,968; e-books 30,806; Electronic Media & Resources 22,860; Bk Vols 36,545; Per Subs 181
Automation Activity & Vendor Info: (Acquisitions) Innovative Interfaces, Inc; (Cataloging) Innovative Interfaces, Inc; (Circulation) Innovative Interfaces, Inc; (OPAC) Innovative Interfaces, Inc
Wireless access
Function: 24/7 Electronic res, 24/7 Online cat, Audiobks via web, AV serv, Bks on CD, Chess club, Children's prog, Computer training, Computers for patron use, Copy machines, Digital talking bks, e-mail serv, Electronic databases & coll, Free DVD rentals, ILL available, Life-long learning prog for all ages, Magazines, Mango lang, Music CDs, Online cat, Online ref, Online searches, Orientations, Outreach serv, OverDrive digital audio bks, Photocopying/Printing, Prof lending libr, Prog for adults, Prog for children & young adult, Provide serv for the mentally ill, Pub access computers, Ref serv available, Ref serv in person, Referrals accepted, Spanish lang bks, Story hour, Summer reading prog, Tax forms, Teen prog,

Telephone ref, Video lending libr, Wheelchair accessible, Workshops, Writing prog
Partic in Washington County Cooperative Library Services
Open Mon-Thurs 10-8, Fri & Sat 10-6, Sun 1-5
Restriction: Authorized scholars by appt
Friends of the Library Group

SILETZ

P SILETZ PUBLIC LIBRARY*, 255 S Gaither St, 97380. (Mail add: PO Box 130, 97380-0130), SAN 376-7248. Tel: 541-444-2855. FAX: 541-444-2855. E-mail: siletz@lincolncolibrarydist.org. *Head Librn,* Carol Rasmussen-Schramm
Founded 1954. Pop 3,000
Library Holdings: Bk Titles 15,000; Per Subs 15
Automation Activity & Vendor Info: (Acquisitions) SirsiDynix; (Cataloging) SirsiDynix; (Circulation) SirsiDynix; (Course Reserve) SirsiDynix; (ILL) SirsiDynix; (Media Booking) SirsiDynix; (OPAC) SirsiDynix; (Serials) SirsiDynix
Database Vendor: SirsiDynix
Wireless access
Partic in Chinook Library Network
Open Wed, Fri & Sat 10-6, Thurs 10-8
Friends of the Library Group

SILVERTON

P SILVER FALLS LIBRARY DISTRICT*, 410 S Water St, 97381-2137. SAN 314-2280. Tel: 503-873-5173. Reference Tel: 503-873-8796. FAX: 503-873-6227. E-mail: silvfals@ccrls.org. Web Site: www.silverfalls.plinkit.org. *Dir,* Marlys Swalboski; *Youth Serv Librn,* Kristy Kemper Hodge; E-mail: kkhodge@ccrls.org; *Adult Serv,* Spring Quick; E-mail: squick@ccrls.org; *Circ,* Marilyn Shadburne; E-mail: marilyn.shadburne@ccrls.org; Staff 12 (MLS 3, Non-MLS 9)
Founded 1911. Pop 29,913; Circ 196,605
Library Holdings: Bk Vols 69,229; Per Subs 148; Talking Bks 2,897; Videos 4,762
Automation Activity & Vendor Info: (Cataloging) Innovative Interfaces, Inc; (Circulation) Innovative Interfaces, Inc; (OPAC) Innovative Interfaces, Inc
Wireless access
Function: Adult bk club, Art exhibits, Audiobks via web, Bi-weekly Writer's Group, Bks on cassette, Bks on CD, Children's prog, Computers for patron use, Copy machines, e-mail & chat, Electronic databases & coll, Free DVD rentals, Genealogy discussion group, Homebound delivery serv, ILL available, Music CDs, Online cat, Online searches, OverDrive digital audio bks, Photocopying/Printing, Prog for adults, Prog for children & young adult, Pub access computers, Ref serv available, Summer reading prog, Tax forms, VHS videos, Web-catalog, Wheelchair accessible
Partic in Chemeketa Cooperative Regional Library Service
Open Tues-Thurs 10-9, Fri 10-6, Sat 10-5
Friends of the Library Group

SPRINGFIELD

M SACRED HEART MEDICAL CENTER AT RIVERBEND*, Library Services, 3333 RiverBend Dr, 97477. (Mail add: PO Box 10905, Eugene, 97440-2905), SAN 314-0946. Tel: 541-222-2280. E-mail: libraryshmc@peacehealth.org. *Dir,* Kim Tyler; *Ref Serv,* Beverly Schriver; *Ref Serv,* Bonnie Starks; Staff 5 (MLS 3, Non-MLS 2)
Founded 1971
Library Holdings: Bk Vols 8,000; Per Subs 450
Special Collections: Archives (School of Nursing, 1942-70), print, tapes & transcription; Nurse Dolls in Uniform
Subject Interests: Computers in health care, Med, Mgt develop, Nursing
Automation Activity & Vendor Info: (Acquisitions) EOS International; (Cataloging) EOS International; (Circulation) EOS International; (OPAC) EOS International
Database Vendor: EBSCOhost, OCLC FirstSearch, OCLC WorldShare Interlibrary Loan, OVID Technologies, PubMed
Wireless access
Function: Doc delivery serv, ILL available, Photocopying/Printing, Ref serv available
Open Mon-Fri 7:30-5

P SPRINGFIELD PUBLIC LIBRARY*, 225 Fifth St, 97477-4697. SAN 314-2299. Tel: 541-726-3766. FAX: 541-726-3747. E-mail: library@ci.springfield.or.us. Web Site: wheremindsgrow.org. *Dir,* Robert Everett; *Cat Librn,* Rita Eberle; *Ref Librn,* Carrie Schindele-Cupples; *Mgr, Support Serv,* Debbie Steinman; *Mrg/Youth & Adult Serv,* Barbara Thompson; *Tech Spec,* Brad Sargeant; Staff 7 (MLS 5, Non-MLS 2)
Founded 1908. Pop 55,000; Circ 345,000
Library Holdings: AV Mats 9,249; Electronic Media & Resources 26; Bk Vols 142,300; Per Subs 122
Special Collections: Mystery & Detective Fiction Coll (1920 to present)
Automation Activity & Vendor Info: (Acquisitions) SirsiDynix; (Cataloging) SirsiDynix; (Circulation) SirsiDynix; (OPAC) SirsiDynix; (Serials) SirsiDynix
Wireless access
Partic in OCLC Online Computer Library Center, Inc
Open Mon & Tues 10-8, Wed & Thurs 10-6, Fri & Sat Noon-5
Friends of the Library Group

STANFIELD

P STANFIELD PUBLIC LIBRARY*, 180 W Coe Ave, 97875. (Mail add: PO Box 489, 97875-0489), SAN 358-0652. Tel: 541-449-1254. FAX: 541-449-3264. E-mail: stanfieldpubliclibrary001@hotmail.com. *Librn,* Barbara Duncan; Staff 2 (Non-MLS 2)
Founded 1914. Pop 2,900; Circ 6,900
Jul 2007-Jun 2008 Income $48,000, City $5,000, Parent Institution $43,000. Mats Exp $14,000. Sal $16,000
Library Holdings: AV Mats 520; Large Print Bks 40; Bk Titles 7,445; Talking Bks 120
Special Collections: NE Oregon History Coll
Subject Interests: Diabetes, Local hist
Wireless access
Mem of Umatilla County Special Library District
Partic in Sage Library System of Eastern Oregon
Open Mon-Thurs 2-6, Sat 10-2

STAYTON

P STAYTON PUBLIC LIBRARY*, 515 N First Ave, 97383-1703. SAN 314-2302. Tel: 503-769-3313. FAX: 503-769-3218. E-mail: staytonpl@ccrls.org. Web Site: www.stayton.plinkit.org. *Dir,* Position Currently Open; *Ch Serv,* Cassandra Portner; Staff 1 (MLS 1)
Founded 1938. Pop 11,000; Circ 237,000
Jul 2012-Jun 2013 Income $427,568, City $260,200, County $80,250, Locally Generated Income $27,500, Other $25,000. Mats Exp $44,200, Books $31,500, Per/Ser (Incl. Access Fees) $3,200, AV Equip $3,000, AV Mat $6,500. Sal $247,534 (Prof $62,412)
Library Holdings: Audiobooks 4,356; DVDs 4,478; Bk Vols 49,230; Per Subs 69; Videos 4,478
Automation Activity & Vendor Info: (Acquisitions) Innovative Interfaces, Inc; (Cataloging) Innovative Interfaces, Inc; (Circulation) Innovative Interfaces, Inc; (ILL) Innovative Interfaces, Inc; (OPAC) Innovative Interfaces, Inc
Database Vendor: Gale Cengage Learning
Wireless access
Function: Audiobks via web, Bk club(s), Bks on cassette, Bks on CD, Children's prog, Computer training, Computers for patron use, Copy machines, Digital talking bks, e-mail & chat, e-mail serv, E-Reserves, Electronic databases & coll, Exhibits, Family literacy, Fax serv, Free DVD rentals, Handicapped accessible, ILL available, Mail & tel request accepted, Microfiche/film & reading machines, Music CDs, Notary serv, Online cat, Online info literacy tutorials on the web & in blackboard, Online ref, Online searches, Outreach serv, Outside serv via phone, mail, e-mail & web, OverDrive digital audio bks, Photocopying/Printing, Preschool outreach, Preschool reading prog, Prog for adults, Prog for children & young adult, Pub access computers, Ref & res, Ref serv available, Ref serv in person, Spoken cassettes & CDs, Spoken cassettes & DVDs, Story hour, Summer reading prog, Tax forms, Teen prog, Telephone ref, Video lending libr
Partic in Chemeketa Cooperative Regional Library Service
Open Mon & Tues 10-5:30, Wed 12-8:30, Thurs 10-8:30, Fri 12-5:30, Sat 10-4
Friends of the Library Group

SWEET HOME

P SWEET HOME PUBLIC LIBRARY*, 1101 13th Ave, 97386-2197. SAN 314-2310. Tel: 541-367-5007. FAX: 541-367-3754. Web Site: www.sweet-home.or.us. *Dir,* Rose Peda; E-mail: rpeda@ci.sweet-home.or.us; Staff 3 (Non-MLS 3)
Founded 1942. Pop 8,500; Circ 48,461
Jul 2006-Jun 2007 Income $199,498. Mats Exp $50,825. Sal $101,234
Library Holdings: Bk Vols 41,000; Per Subs 72
Subject Interests: Cooking, Northwest
Open Mon, Tues & Thurs 10-6, Fri & Sat 10-3
Friends of the Library Group

THE DALLES

J COLUMBIA GORGE COMMUNITY COLLEGE LIBRARY*, 400 E Scenic Dr, 97058. SAN 375-3395. Tel: 541-506-6081. Administration Tel: 541-506-6080. FAX: 541-506-6082. E-mail: cgcclibrary@cgcc.cc.or.us. Web Site: www.cgcc.cc.or.us/library.
Founded 1995. Enrl 1,010; Highest Degree: Associate
Jul 2010-Jun 2011 Income $371,400

Library Holdings: Bks on Deafness & Sign Lang 62; CDs 550; DVDs 284; e-books 47,000; Bk Titles 19,500; Per Subs 98; Videos 800
Automation Activity & Vendor Info: (Cataloging) Evergreen; (Circulation) Evergreen; (Course Reserve) Evergreen; (ILL) OCLC; (OPAC) Evergreen
Database Vendor: ABC-CLIO, CQ Press, ebrary, EBSCOhost, Elsevier, Gale Cengage Learning, McGraw-Hill, OCLC FirstSearch, OCLC WorldShare Interlibrary Loan, Oxford Online, PubMed
Wireless access
Function: Audio & video playback equip for onsite use, Bks on CD, Computers for patron use, Copy machines, Distance learning, e-mail serv, Electronic databases & coll, Equip loans & repairs, Handicapped accessible, ILL available, Literacy & newcomer serv, Music CDs, Online cat, Pub access computers, Ref serv available, Scanner, VHS videos
Partic in Sage Library System of Eastern Oregon
Open Mon-Thurs 8-6, Fri 8-1, Sat 8-Noon

P THE DALLES-WASCO COUNTY LIBRARY*, 722 Court St, 97058-2270. SAN 357-8852. Tel: 541-296-2815. FAX: 541-296-4179. E-mail: cityinfo@ci.the-dalles.or.us. Web Site: www.ci.the-dalles.or.us. *Dir, Libr Serv,* Sheila Dooley; E-mail: sheila_dooley@ci.the-dalles.or.us; Staff 6 (MLS 1, Non-MLS 5)
Founded 1909. Pop 21,285; Circ 109,966
Jul 2006-Jun 2007 Income $391,762. Mats Exp $22,943. Sal $274,095
Library Holdings: AV Mats 2,116; Bk Vols 65,441; Per Subs 114; Talking Bks 2,326
Subject Interests: Ore hist
Automation Activity & Vendor Info: (Acquisitions) SirsiDynix; (Cataloging) SirsiDynix; (Circulation) SirsiDynix; (OPAC) SirsiDynix
Partic in Gorge LINK Library Consortium
Open Tues & Wed 11-8:30, Thurs & Fri 10-6, Sat 10-3
Friends of the Library Group

M MID-COLUMBIA MEDICAL CENTER*, Planetree Health Resource Center, 200 E Fourth St, 97058. SAN 377-628X. Tel: 541-296-8444. FAX: 541-296-6054. Web Site: www.mcmc.net. *Coordr,* Linda Stahl; *Libr Asst,* Molly Hamlin; Staff 3 (MLS 1, Non-MLS 2)
Founded 1992
Library Holdings: AV Mats 500; Bk Vols 4,000; Per Subs 50
Subject Interests: Consumer health info, Med info
Automation Activity & Vendor Info: (Circulation) Evergreen; (OPAC) Evergreen
Database Vendor: Gale Cengage Learning
Wireless access
Function: Doc delivery serv, Handicapped accessible, Health sci info serv, ILL available, Online searches, Photocopying/Printing, Ref serv available
Partic in Docline; Sage Library System of Eastern Oregon
Open Tues-Fri 10-5

TIGARD

P TIGARD PUBLIC LIBRARY*, 13500 SW Hall Blvd, 97223-8111. SAN 314-2329. Tel: 503-684-6537. Reference Tel: 503-718-2517. FAX: 503-598-7515, 503-718-2797. TDD: 503-644-2197. Web Site: www.tigard-or.gov/library/default.asp. *Dir of Libr Serv,* Margaret Barnes; Tel: 503-684-6537, Ext 2501, E-mail: margaret@tigard-or.gov; *Circ Mgr,* Craig Carter, Tel: 503-684-6537, Ext 2509, E-mail: craigc@tigard-or.gov, *Reader Serv Mgr,* Molly Carlisle; Tel: 503-684-6537, Ext 2519, E-mail: molly@tigard-or.gov; *Tech Serv Mgr,* Teresa Ferguson; Tel: 503-684-6537, Ext 2505, E-mail: teresaf@tigard-or.gov; *Supvr, Ad Serv,* Sarah Jesudason; Tel: 503-684-6537, Ext 2649, E-mail: sarah@tigard-or.gov; *Supvr, Circ,* David Abbey; Tel: 503-684-6537, Ext 2510, E-mail: davida@tigard-or.gov; *Supvr, Circ,* Sandra Hughes; Tel: 503-684-6537, Ext 2515, E-mail: sandra@tigard-or.gov; *Supvr, Youth Serv,* Amber Bell; Tel: 503-684-6537, Ext 2812, E-mail: amber@tigard-or.gov; *Coordr, Acq,* Amy Emery; Tel: 503-684-6537, Ext 2513, E-mail: amye@tigard-or.gov; *Communications Coordr,* Paula Walker; Tel: 503-684-6537, Ext 2508, E-mail: paula@tigard-or.gov; *Vols Serv Coordr,* Trish Stormont; Tel: 503-684-6537, Ext 2516, E-mail: trish@tigard-or.gov; Staff 38.8 (MLS 15.2, Non-MLS 23.6)
Founded 1963. Pop 67,278; Circ 1,481,715
Jul 2009-Jun 2010 Income $3,800,100, State $8,349, City $977,106, County $2,812,137, Other $2,508. Mats Exp $2,433,307, Books $387,691, Other Print Mats $14,862, Micro $3,880, AV Mat $154,871, Presv $1,872,003. Sal $2,218,944
Library Holdings: Audiobooks 865; AV Mats 3,317; CDs 1,182; DVDs 5,570; Large Print Bks 362; Bk Titles 30,857; Per Subs 256
Automation Activity & Vendor Info: (Acquisitions) Innovative Interfaces, Inc; (Cataloging) Innovative Interfaces, Inc; (Circulation) Innovative Interfaces, Inc; (ILL) Innovative Interfaces, Inc; (OPAC) Innovative Interfaces, Inc
Wireless access
Partic in Washington County Cooperative Library Services
Special Services for the Deaf - Assistive tech; Bks on deafness & sign lang; Closed caption videos; TDD equip
Special Services for the Blind - Bks on cassette; Bks on CD; Computer with voice synthesizer for visually impaired persons; Descriptive video serv (DVS); Home delivery serv; Internet workstation with adaptive software; Large print bks; PC for handicapped; Volunteer serv
Open Mon-Wed & Fri 10-9, Sat 10-6, Sun Noon-6
Friends of the Library Group

TILLAMOOK

J TILLAMOOK BAY COMMUNITY COLLEGE LIBRARY*, 2510 First St, Rm 7, 97141. Tel: 503-842-8222, Ext 1126. FAX: 503-842-2214. Web Site: tillamookbay.cc/library.html. *Dir,* Rebecca Thurman; E-mail: thurman@tillamookbay.cc
Library Holdings: AV Mats 200; Bk Vols 1,500; Per Subs 12
Automation Activity & Vendor Info: (Cataloging) SirsiDynix; (Circulation) SirsiDynix; (OPAC) SirsiDynix
Database Vendor: EBSCOhost, Gale Cengage Learning
Partic in Chinook Library Network
Open Mon-Thurs 8:30-7:30, Fri 8:30-4:30

P TILLAMOOK COUNTY LIBRARY*, 1716 Third St, 97141. SAN 358-2515. Tel: 503-842-4792. FAX: 503-815-8194. Web Site: www.tillamook.plinkit.org. *Dir,* Sara Charlton; E-mail: charlton@co.tillamook.us.org; *Co-Mgr,* Sarah Beeler; *Co-Mgr,* Bill Landeau; *Ch,* Melanie Hetrick; Staff 27 (MLS 7, Non-MLS 20)
Founded 1907. Pop 25,000; Circ 352,290
Jul 2012-Jun 2013 Income (Main Library and Branch(s)) $4,670,000. Mats Exp $836,500, Books $90,000, AV Mat $21,000. Sal $1,113,500
Library Holdings: Bk Vols 179,150; Per Subs 424
Special Collections: Local History (Oregon). State Document Depository
Automation Activity & Vendor Info: (Cataloging) Innovative Interfaces, Inc - Millenium; (Circulation) Innovative Interfaces, Inc - Millenium; (OPAC) Innovative Interfaces, Inc - Millenium
Database Vendor: EBSCO Auto Repair Reference, EBSCO Information Services, LearningExpress, OCLC WorldShare Interlibrary Loan, ProQuest
Wireless access
Partic in OCLC Online Computer Library Center, Inc
Open Mon-Thurs 9-9, Fri & Sat 9-5:30
Friends of the Library Group
Branches: 5
BAY CITY, 1716 Third St, 97141, SAN 358-254X. Tel: 503-377-0231. FAX: 503-815-1911. *In Charge,* Debbie Riley; Staff 1 (Non-MLS 1)
Open Tues-Fri 12-5, Sat 10-3
Friends of the Library Group
GARIBALDI BRANCH, City Hall, Garibaldi, 97118, SAN 358-2574. Tel: 503-322-2100. FAX: 503-322-2100. *In Charge,* Norma Johansen
Open Mon-Fri 12-5, Sat 10-3
Friends of the Library Group
MANZANITA BRANCH, 571 Laneda, Manzanita, 97130. (Mail add: PO Box 147, Manzanita, 97130-0147), SAN 358-2604. Tel: 503-368-6665. FAX: 503-368-6665. *In Charge,* Charlotte Forster
Open Mon, Wed & Fri 12-5, Tues & Thurs 12-8, Sat 10-3
Friends of the Library Group
ROCKAWAY BEACH BRANCH, 120 N Coral, Rockaway Beach, 97136. (Mail add: PO Box 185, Rockaway Beach, 97136). Tel: 503-355-2665. FAX: 503-355-2665. *In Charge,* Linda Werner
Open Mon-Fri 12-5, Sat 10-3
Friends of the Library Group
SOUTH COUNTY, 6200 Camp St, Pacific City, 97135. (Mail add: PO Box 66, Pacific City, 97135-0066), SAN 358-2639. Tel: 503-965-6163. FAX: 503-965-6163. *In Charge,* Carolyn Evenson
Open Mon, Thurs & Fri 12-5, Tues & Wed 12-8, Sat 10-3
Friends of the Library Group
Bookmobiles: 1

S TILLAMOOK COUNTY PIONEER MUSEUM*, Research Library, 2106 Second St, 97141. SAN 375-510X. Tel: 503-842-4553. FAX: 503-842-4553. Web Site: www.tcpm.org. *Dir of Mus,* Gary Albright; E-mail: director@tcpm.org; *Res,* Ruby Fry-Matson; E-mail: ruby@tcpm.org
Library Holdings: Bk Titles 4,000
Special Collections: Oral History
Function: ILL available, Telephone ref
Restriction: Non-circulating to the pub, Not a lending libr, Open by appt only, Open to pub with supv only

TILLER

P TILLER COMMUNITY LIBRARY*, 27812 Tiller Trail Hwy, 97484. (Mail add: PO Box 185, 97484-0185), *Librn,* Chris Rusch; Tel: 541-825-3837, E-mail: crusch@hughes.net
Library Holdings: Bk Vols 2,500
Open Wed, Fri & Sat 4-7
Friends of the Library Group

TOLEDO

P TOLEDO PUBLIC LIBRARY*, 173 NW Seventh St, 97391. SAN 314-2337. Tel: 541-336-3132. FAX: 541-336-3428. Web Site: www.cityoftoledo.org/library.htm. *Dir,* Deborah Trusty; E-mail: librarydirector@cityoftoledo.org; *Asst Dir,* Lisa A Miller; *Cat, Tech Serv,* Andrea Haller; Staff 3.4 (Non-MLS 3.4)
Founded 1916. Pop 5,965; Circ 70,884
Library Holdings: Bk Vols 35,000; Per Subs 70
Special Collections: Yaquina Genealogical Society Coll
Subject Interests: Genealogy
Automation Activity & Vendor Info: (Cataloging) OCLC; (Circulation) ByWater Solutions; (ILL) OCLC; (OPAC) ByWater Solutions
Database Vendor: Baker & Taylor, ebrary, EBSCO Information Services, Gale Cengage Learning, OCLC, TLC (The Library Corporation)
Wireless access
Partic in Chinook Library Network
Open Mon & Tues 12-8, Wed-Fri 10-6, Sat 10-4, Sun 1-5

TUALATIN

P TUALATIN PUBLIC LIBRARY*, 18878 SW Martinazzi, 97062. SAN 314-2345. Tel: 503-691-3074. Information Services Tel: 503-691-3071. FAX: 503-692-3512. E-mail: librarymail@ci.tualatin.or.us. Web Site: www.tualatin.or.us/departments/community/services/library. *Mgr,* Position Currently Open; Staff 15 (MLS 6, Non-MLS 9)
Founded 1977. Pop 25,000; Circ 580,000
Jul 2007-Jun 2008 Income $1,513,000, City $240,000, County $1,200,000, Locally Generated Income $56,000, Other $17,000. Mats Exp $240,000
Library Holdings: Bk Vols 90,000; Per Subs 180
Automation Activity & Vendor Info: (Cataloging) Innovative Interfaces, Inc; (Circulation) Innovative Interfaces, Inc; (OPAC) Innovative Interfaces, Inc
Database Vendor: ALLDATA Online, EBSCO Auto Repair Reference, Gale Cengage Learning, OCLC FirstSearch, ValueLine
Wireless access
Partic in Washington County Cooperative Library Services
Open Mon-Thurs 10-9, Fri & Sat 10-6, Sun 1-6
Friends of the Library Group

UKIAH

P UKIAH PUBLIC LIBRARY*, 201 Hill St, 97880. (Mail add: PO Box 218, 97880-0218), SAN 376-3285. Tel: 541-427-3435. FAX: 541-427-3730. *Librn,* Sherri Contreras
Library Holdings: Audiobooks 250; CDs 150; DVDs 425; High Interest/Low Vocabulary Bk Vols 25; Large Print Bks 85; Bk Titles 11,125; Videos 350
Wireless access
Partic in Umatilla County Spec Libr District
Open Mon, Tues & Thurs 9-2, Wed 1-6
Friends of the Library Group

UMATILLA

S TWO RIVERS CORRECTIONAL INSTITUTE LIBRARY*, 82911 Beach Access Rd, 97882. Tel: 541-922-2177. *Librn,* Sharon Justus
Library Holdings: Bk Vols 12,000

P UMATILLA PUBLIC LIBRARY*, 700 Sixth St, 97882-9507. (Mail add: PO Box 820, 97882-0820), SAN 358-0687. Tel: 541-922-5704. FAX: 541-922-5708. Web Site: umatilla.plinkit.org. *Libr Dir,* Kellie Lamoreaux; *Asst Librn,* Pam Johnson
Library Holdings: Bk Vols 21,604; Per Subs 12
Automation Activity & Vendor Info: (Cataloging) Innovative Interfaces, Inc; (Circulation) Innovative Interfaces, Inc; (OPAC) Innovative Interfaces, Inc
Wireless access
Open Mon 10-7, Tues-Thurs 10-6, Fri 9-5, Sat 10-2
Friends of the Library Group

UNION

P UNION CARNEGIE PUBLIC LIBRARY*, 182 N Main St, 97883. (Mail add: PO Box 928, 97883-0928), SAN 314-2353. Tel: 541-562-5811. FAX: 541-562-5811. E-mail: uclib@eoni.com. *Dir,* Louise Shelden
Founded 1913. Pop 972; Circ 168,364
Library Holdings: Bk Vols 10,000
Subject Interests: Alternate energy res
Function: ILL available
Open Mon, Tues & Thurs 1-6, Wed 6-7:30, Fri 9:30-2:30

VALE

P EMMA HUMPHREY LIBRARY*, 150 A St E, 97918-1345. Tel: 541-473-3902. *Librn,* Margaret Tolman
Library Holdings: Bk Titles 15,000; Per Subs 20
Automation Activity & Vendor Info: (Cataloging) Evergreen; (Circulation) Evergreen; (OPAC) Evergreen
Wireless access
Open Mon & Tues 12-5, Wed & Fri 1-5, Thurs 7pm-9pm

VENETA

P FERN RIDGE LIBRARY DISTRICT*, 88026 Territorial Rd, 97487. (Mail add: PO Box 397, 97487-0397), SAN 314-2361. Tel: 541-935-7512. FAX: 541-935-8013. E-mail: staff@fernridgelibrary.org. Web Site: www.fernridgelibrary.org. *Dir,* Rozella Van Meter; Staff 5 (Non-MLS 5)
Founded 1966. Pop 10,750; Circ 76,210
Library Holdings: Bk Titles 34,794; Per Subs 68
Automation Activity & Vendor Info: (Cataloging) SirsiDynix; (Circulation) SirsiDynix; (OPAC) SirsiDynix
Database Vendor: EBSCOhost
Publications: Friends of the Library (Newsletter)
Open Tues & Thurs 10-8, Wed & Fri 9:30-6, Sat 9-5
Friends of the Library Group

VERNONIA

P VERNONIA PUBLIC LIBRARY*, 701 Weed Ave, 97064-1102. SAN 314-237X. Tel: 503-429-1818. FAX: 503-429-0729. E-mail: library@vernonia-or.gov. *Dir,* Nancy Burch
Founded 1925. Pop 1,750; Circ 9,633
Library Holdings: Bk Vols 20,000; Per Subs 30
Automation Activity & Vendor Info: (Cataloging) Follett Software; (Circulation) Follett Software
Open Mon, Wed & Fri 10-5, Tues & Thurs 2-7, Sat 10-2
Friends of the Library Group

WALDPORT

P WALDPORT PUBLIC LIBRARY*, 460 Hemlock St, 97394. (Mail add: PO Box 1357, 97394-1357), SAN 314-2388. Tel: 541-563-5880. FAX: 541-563-6237. E-mail: waldportlibrary@waldport.org. Web Site: www.waldport.org/Departments/library.php, www.waldportlibrary.plinkit.org. *Libr Dir,* Jill E Tierce; E-mail: jtierce@waldport.org; Staff 2 (Non-MLS 2)
Founded 1919. Pop 4,900; Circ 68,238
Library Holdings: AV Mats 1,936; Electronic Media & Resources 27; Bk Titles 21,000; Per Subs 41
Automation Activity & Vendor Info: (Cataloging) SirsiDynix; (Circulation) SirsiDynix; (OPAC) SirsiDynix
Database Vendor: EBSCOhost
Wireless access
Open Mon & Thurs 10-7, Tues, Wed & Fri 10-5, Sat 10-4
Friends of the Library Group

WALLOWA

P WALLOWA PUBLIC LIBRARY*, 201 N Main, 97885. (Mail add: PO Box 486, 97885-0486). Tel: 541-886-4265. E-mail: wallowapubliclibrary@gmail.com. Web Site: wallowapubliclibrary.org. *Dir,* Debbie Lind
Library Holdings: Bk Titles 8,000
Open Mon, Tues, Thurs & Fri 1-5, Wed 10-2

WASCO

P WASCO CITY/COMMUNITY LIBRARY*, 1017 Clarke St, 97065. (Mail add: PO Box 202, 97065-0202). Tel: 541-442-8505. FAX: 541-442-5001. *Dir,* Danee Rankin
Library Holdings: Bk Vols 7,000
Special Collections: Biographies; Children's Coll; Non-Fiction & Fiction; Oregon History & Authors; US Presidents Coll
Wireless access
Open Mon & Wed 9-12:15 & 1-5:30, Tues & Thurs 9-12:15 & 1-7:30, Fri 9-2
Friends of the Library Group

WEST LINN

P WEST LINN PUBLIC LIBRARY*, 1595 Burns St, 97068-3231. SAN 314-240X. Tel: 503-656-7853. Reference Tel: 503-656-7853, Ext 3026. Information Services Tel: 503-656-7853, Ext 6. FAX: 503-656-2746. E-mail: wlref@lincc.org. Web Site: westlinnoregon.gov/library. *Dir,* Holly Mercer; Tel: 503-656-7853, Ext 3021, E-mail: hmercer@westlinnoregon.gov; *Teen Serv Librn,* Elaine Spence; Tel: 503-656-7853, Ext 3030, E-mail: espence@westlinnoregon.gov; *Circ Mgr,*

Sarah McIntyre; Tel: 503-656-7853, Ext 3019, E-mail: smcintyre@westlinnoregon.gov
Founded 1939
Library Holdings: AV Mats 19,486; Bk Vols 82,481; Per Subs 285
Automation Activity & Vendor Info: (Cataloging) SirsiDynix; (Circulation) SirsiDynix; (OPAC) SirsiDynix
Wireless access
Publications: Newsletter
Partic in Library Information Network of Clackamas County
Open Mon-Wed 10-8, Thurs & Fri 10-6, Sat & Sun 12-5
Friends of the Library Group

WESTFIR

P WESTFIR CITY LIBRARY*, 47441 Westoak Rd, 97492. (Mail add: PO Box 296, 97492-0296). Tel: 541-782-3733. FAX: 541-782-3983.
Library Holdings: Bk Titles 9,500
Open Mon, Wed & Fri 9-2

WESTON

P WESTON PUBLIC LIBRARY*, 108 E Main St, 97886. SAN 358-0717. Tel: 541-566-2378. FAX: 541-566-2378. E-mail: wcolibrary@qwestoffice.net. Web Site: westonpubliclibrary.com. *Librn,* Kathleen Schmidtgall
Library Holdings: Bk Titles 9,000; Per Subs 50
Open Mon, Wed & Fri 8-12 & 1-5, Tues & Thurs 1:30-7

WHITE CITY

GM DEPARTMENT OF VETERANS AFFAIRS*, Hospital Library, VA Domiciliary, 142-D, 8495 Crater Lake Hwy, 97503. SAN 314-2418. Tel: 541-826-2111, Ext 3297. FAX: 541-830-3503. *Chief Librn,* Sarah L Fitzpatrick; E-mail: sarah.fitzpatrick@med.va.gov; Staff 3 (MLS 1, Non-MLS 2)
Library Holdings: AV Mats 600; Bk Titles 14,000; Per Subs 159; Talking Bks 25
Special Collections: World War II Coll

WILLAMINA

P WILLAMINA PUBLIC LIBRARY*, 385 NE C St, 97396. (Mail add: PO Box 273, 97396-0273), SAN 376-3307. Tel: 503-876-6182. FAX: 503-876-1121. E-mail: willapl@ccrls.org. Web Site: www.ccrls.org/willamina. *Dir,* Melissa Hansen; *Ch Serv,* Denise Williams
Pop 2,000; Circ 15,100
Library Holdings: AV Mats 2,000; Large Print Bks 300; Bk Titles 28,744; Bk Vols 29,618; Per Subs 64; Talking Bks 510
Automation Activity & Vendor Info: (Acquisitions) Innovative Interfaces, Inc; (Cataloging) Innovative Interfaces, Inc; (Circulation) Innovative Interfaces, Inc
Partic in Chemeketa Cooperative Regional Library Service
Open Mon-Fri 10-7
Friends of the Library Group

WILSONVILLE

C PIONEER PACIFIC COLLEGE LIBRARY*, 27375 SW Parkway Ave, 97070. Tel: 503-682-1862. Web Site: www.pioneerpacific.edu. *Head Librn,* Jill Sled; Staff 3 (MLS 1, Non-MLS 2)
Enrl 1,200
Library Holdings: e-books 21,000; Bk Titles 3,000
Database Vendor: ebrary, EBSCOhost, Westlaw
Wireless access
Open Mon-Thurs 7:30am-10:30pm

P WILSONVILLE PUBLIC LIBRARY*, 8200 SW Wilsonville Rd, 97070. SAN 329-9287. Tel: 503-682-2744. FAX: 503-682-8685. E-mail: reference@wilsonvillelibrary.org. Web Site: www.wilsonvillelibrary.org. *Dir,* Patrick Duke; Tel: 503-570-1590, E-mail: duke@wilsonvillelibrary.org; *Mgr, Libr Operations,* Kimberly Robben; Tel: 503-570-1597, E-mail: robben@wilsonvillelibrary.org; *Ad,* Greg Martin; Tel: 503-570-1591, E-mail: martin@wilsonvillelibrary.org; *Youth Serv Librn,* Stephen Engelfried; Tel: 503-570-1592, E-mail: engelfried@wilsonvillelibrary.org; Staff 15 (MLS 5, Non-MLS 10)
Founded 1982. Pop 25,000; Circ 498,000
Library Holdings: AV Mats 20,516; Large Print Bks 3,318; Bk Vols 82,995; Per Subs 181
Special Collections: Japanese Language Children's Books; Local History & Oregon Genealogy (Heritage Coll)
Subject Interests: Genealogy, Japan, Pacific Northwest
Automation Activity & Vendor Info: (Acquisitions) SirsiDynix; (Cataloging) SirsiDynix; (Circulation) SirsiDynix; (OPAC) SirsiDynix; (Serials) SirsiDynix
Wireless access
Function: Adult bk club, Audio & video playback equip for onsite use, Audiobks via web, Bk club(s), Bks on cassette, Bks on CD, CD-ROM, Children's prog, Computer training, Computers for patron use, Copy machines, Digital talking bks, Electronic databases & coll, Fax serv, Home delivery & serv to Sr ctr & nursing homes, Homebound delivery serv, ILL available, Instruction & testing, Music CDs, Notary serv, Online cat, Online ref, Online searches, OverDrive digital audio bks, Photocopying/Printing, Prog for adults, Prog for children & young adult, Pub access computers, Ref serv available, Senior computer classes, Story hour, Summer reading prog, Tax forms, Teen prog, Telephone ref, VHS videos, Video lending libr, Web-catalog, Wheelchair accessible, Workshops, Writing prog
Open Mon-Wed 10-8, Thurs-Sat 1-6
Friends of the Library Group

WOODBURN

P WOODBURN PUBLIC LIBRARY*, 280 Garfield St, 97071-4698. SAN 314-2442. Tel: 503-982-5252. Circulation Tel: 503-982-5262. FAX: 503-982-5258. E-mail: woodburn@ccrls.org. Web Site: www.woodburnlibrary.org. *Mgr,* John Hunter; Tel: 503-982-5259, E-mail: john.hunter@ci.woodburn.or.us; *ILL, Ref Serv,* Elvira Sanchez-Kisser; Tel: 503-982-5254, E-mail: elvira.sanchez-kisser@ci.woodburn.or.us; *Youth Serv,* Gladis Martinez; Tel: 503-982-5260, E-mail: gladis.martinez@ci.woodburn.or.us; Staff 9.75 (MLS 3.75, Non-MLS 6)
Founded 1914. Pop 25,000; Circ 158,719
Library Holdings: Bk Vols 55,000; Per Subs 50
Special Collections: Language (Russian & Spanish Coll)
Automation Activity & Vendor Info: (Acquisitions) Innovative Interfaces, Inc; (Cataloging) Innovative Interfaces, Inc; (Circulation) Innovative Interfaces, Inc; (ILL) Innovative Interfaces, Inc; (OPAC) Innovative Interfaces, Inc; (Serials) EBSCO Online
Wireless access
Partic in Chemeketa Cooperative Regional Library Service
Open Mon-Wed 10-7, Thurs & Fri 10-5, Sat 1-5
Friends of the Library Group

YACHATS

P YACHATS PUBLIC LIBRARY*, 560 W Seventh, 97498. (Mail add: PO Box 817, 97498-0817), SAN 314-2450. Tel: 541-547-3741. FAX: 541-547-3741. E-mail: yachatspl@actionnet.net. *Librn,* Annette Howarth
Pop 695; Circ 4,580
Library Holdings: Bk Vols 15,000; Per Subs 14
Automation Activity & Vendor Info: (Cataloging) Library Concepts
Open Mon-Fri 12-4, Sat 10-4
Friends of the Library Group

PENNSYLVANIA

Date of Statistics: FY 2012
Population, 2010 U.S. Census: 12,702,379
Population Served by Public Libraries: 12,411,468
Unserved: 290,911
Total Volumes in Public Libraries: 31,372,907
Volumes Per Capita: 2.653
Total Public Circulation: 69,080,603
Circulation Per Capita: 5.57 (population served)
Total Public Library Income: $329,786,912
Source of Income:
Public Funds: $211,630,557
State Funds: $56,970,206
Federal: $2,201,734
Private Funds (including gifts): $58,984,415

Total Operating Expenditures: $324,441,985
Total Capital Expenditures: $15,908,167
Operating Expenditures Per Capita: $26 (population served)
Grants-in-Aid to Public Libraries:
Federal (Library Services & Technology Act 2012-2013): $5,544,252
State Aid (2012-2013): $53,507,000
Apportionment: To be eligible for state aid, the local financial effort of a library or library system must be at least $5 per capita unless the library serves an economically distressed municipality
Number of County or Multi-County (Regional) Libraries: 54
Counties Served: 67
Number of Bookmobiles in State: 30

ABINGTON

M ABINGTON MEMORIAL HOSPITAL*, Wilmer Memorial Medical Library, 1200 York Rd, 19001. SAN 314-2469. Tel: 215-481-2096. Web Site: www.amh.org. *Dir,* Marion Chayes; Staff 4 (MLS 3, Non-MLS 1)
Founded 1914
Library Holdings: Bk Titles 5,196; Bk Vols 5,300; Per Subs 450
Subject Interests: Dentistry, Med, Nursing, Surgery
Partic in NY Regional Med Libr
Open Mon-Fri 9-4:30

R ABINGTON PRESBYTERIAN CHURCH LIBRARY*, 1082 Old York Rd, 19001-4593. SAN 314-2477. Tel: 215-887-4530. FAX: 215-887-5988. Web Site: www.apcusa.org. *Librn,* Eleanor Barwis
Founded 1956
Library Holdings: Bk Vols 6,046
Subject Interests: Environ studies, Local Presbyterian church hist, Mostly non-fiction
Open Mon-Fri 8:30-4:30

P ABINGTON TOWNSHIP PUBLIC LIBRARY*, Abington Free Library, 1030 Old York Rd, 19001-4594. SAN 358-2663. Tel: 215-885-5180. Circulation Tel: 215-885-5180, Ext 10. Reference Tel: 215-885-5180, Ext 13. FAX: 215-885-9242. TDD: 215-572-1483. Web Site: abingtonfreelibrary.org. *Exec Dir,* Nancy Hammeke Marshall; Tel: 215-885-5180, Ext 14; *Cat,* Michael Rechel; *Ch Serv,* Carolyn DuBois; *Ref,* Mimi Satterthwaite; Staff 46.35 (MLS 10.56, Non-MLS 35.79)
Founded 1966. Pop 57,853; Circ 502,424
Jan 2011-Dec 2011 Income (Main Library and Branch(s)) $2,349,484, State $182,392, City $2,044,213, Locally Generated Income $21,074, Other $101,805. Mats Exp $278,153, Books $117,005, Per/Ser (Incl. Access Fees) $48,631, AV Mat $20,195, Electronic Ref Mat (Incl. Access Fees) $15,657. Sal $1,504,462 (Prof $41,000)
Library Holdings: Audiobooks 7,522; DVDs 4,768; Electronic Media & Resources 31; Bk Vols 153,893; Per Subs 266
Automation Activity & Vendor Info: (Acquisitions) Innovative Interfaces, Inc; (Cataloging) Innovative Interfaces, Inc; (Circulation) Innovative Interfaces, Inc; (ILL) Innovative Interfaces, Inc; (OPAC) Innovative Interfaces, Inc; (Serials) Innovative Interfaces, Inc
Database Vendor: ProQuest
Wireless access
Partic in Montgomery County Library & Information Network Consortium
Open Mon-Thurs 9:30-9, Fri & Sat 9:30-5, Sun 1-5
Friends of the Library Group
Branches: 1
ROSLYN BRANCH, 2412 Avondale Ave, Roslyn, 19001-4203, SAN 358-2698. Tel: 215-886-9818. FAX: 215-886-9818. *Librn,* Celia Frankford; E-mail: cfrankford@mclinc.org
Library Holdings: Bk Vols 23,620; Per Subs 43
Open Mon 11-9, Tues, Thurs & Fri 11-6, Sat 11-2
Friends of the Library Group

R OLD YORK ROAD TEMPLE BETH AM LIBRARY*, 971 Old York Rd, 19001. SAN 314-2493. Tel: 215-886-8000. FAX: 215-886-8320. Web Site: www.oyrtbetham.org. *Librn,* Marlena Rossman
Founded 1964
Library Holdings: AV Mats 187; Bk Titles 5,000; Talking Bks 49
Subject Interests: Judaica, Relig studies
Wireless access
Open Tues 4-9, Sun 9:30-Noon
Restriction: Non-circulating

C PENNSYLVANIA STATE UNIVERSITY*, Abington College Library, 1600 Woodland Rd, 19001. SAN 314-2507. Tel: 215-881-7424. Interlibrary Loan Service Tel: 215-881-7428. Reference Tel: 215-881-7462. FAX: 215-881-7423. Web Site: www.libraries.psu.edu/abington. *Head Librn,* Samuel R Stormont; Tel: 215-881-7425; *Assoc Librn,* Binh P Le; Tel: 215-881-7426, E-mail: bpl1@psu.edu; *Assoc Librn,* Mathew Wayman; Tel: 215-881-7497, E-mail: mjw13@psu.edu; *Ref Librn,* Paula Smith; E-mail: pms20@psu.edu; *Supvr, Access Serv,* Rebecca Herwatic; Tel: 215-881-7431, E-mail: rlh181@psu.edu; Staff 6 (MLS 2, Non-MLS 4)
Founded 1950. Enrl 2,493; Fac 90; Highest Degree: Master
Library Holdings: Bk Titles 63,483; Bk Vols 68,950; Per Subs 163; Talking Bks 139, Videos 751
Wireless access
Function: Audio & video playback equip for onsite use, Copy machines
Partic in OCLC Online Computer Library Center, Inc; RLIN (Research Libraries Information Network)
Open Mon-Thurs 7:30am-8pm, Fri (Summer) 7:30-5

ADAMSTOWN

P ADAMSTOWN AREA LIBRARY*, 3000 N Reading Rd, Rte 272, 19501. (Mail add: PO Box 356, 19501-0356). Tel: 717-484-4200. FAX: 717-484-0738. Web Site: www.adamstown.lib.pa.us. *Dir,* Kathy Thren; Staff 7 (MLS 1, Non-MLS 6)
Founded 1945. Pop 28,317; Circ 52,816
Library Holdings: AV Mats 940; Bks on Deafness & Sign Lang 21; Large Print Bks 90; Bk Titles 19,859; Bk Vols 21,110; Per Subs 33; Talking Bks 320; Videos 280
Special Collections: Antiques & Collectibles
Automation Activity & Vendor Info: (Cataloging) Innovative Interfaces, Inc; (Circulation) Innovative Interfaces, Inc; (OPAC) Innovative Interfaces, Inc
Database Vendor: EBSCOhost, Gale Cengage Learning, ProQuest
Function: ILL available
Mem of Library System of Lancaster County
Open Mon-Thurs 9:30-8, Fri 9:30-5, Sat 9:30-4:30
Friends of the Library Group

ALBION

P ALBION AREA PUBLIC LIBRARY*, 111 E Pearl St, 16401-1202. SAN 314-2523. Tel: 814-756-5400. FAX: 814-756-5400. Web Site: www.albionarealibrary.org. *Dir,* Janice Petrus; *Asst Librn,* Jeri Harrington
Pop 1,607; Circ 25,783
Library Holdings: Bk Vols 15,000; Per Subs 24
Automation Activity & Vendor Info: (Cataloging) Infor Library & Information Solutions; (Circulation) Infor Library & Information Solutions
Open Mon & Wed 9-7, Sat 9-3
Friends of the Library Group

S STATE CORRECTIONAL INSTITUTION*, Albion Library, 10745 Rte 18, 16475-0001. Tel: 814-756-5778. FAX: 814-756-9735. *Librn,* Gene Zarnick
Library Holdings: Bk Vols 25,000; Per Subs 75
Automation Activity & Vendor Info: (Cataloging) Follett Software; (Circulation) Follett Software; (OPAC) Follett Software
Partic in HSLC/Access PA/POWER Library
Open Mon, Tues, Thurs & Sun 9-11, 1-4 & 6-8, Wed, Fri & Sat 9-11 & 1-4

ALEXANDRIA

P MEMORIAL PUBLIC LIBRARY OF THE BOROUGH OF ALEXANDRIA, 313 Main St, Ste 1, 16611. SAN 314-254X. Tel: 814-669-4313. *Librn,* Martha Brenneman; Staff 3 (MLS 1, Non-MLS 2)
Founded 1899. Pop 3,465; Circ 12,445
Library Holdings: Audiobooks 586; CDs 173; DVDs 310; Large Print Bks 108; Bk Titles 20,401; Bk Vols 22,611; Per Subs 29; Talking Bks 90; Videos 179
Special Collections: Oral History
Wireless access
Open Mon & Thurs 10:30-5 & 6:30-8, Tues & Fri 9-5
Friends of the Library Group

ALIQUIPPA

P BEAVER COUNTY LIBRARY SYSTEM*, 109 Pleasant Dr, Ste 101, 15001. SAN 314-2558. Tel: 724-378-6227. Web Site: www.beaverlibraries.org. *Dir,* Jodi Oliver; E-mail: joliver@beavercountypa.gov; *Tech Coordr,* Mark Stevenson; *Ch Serv,* Rose Celio
Pop 211,420; Circ 526,453
Library Holdings: Bk Vols 309,325; Per Subs 50
Special Collections: Record Album Coll
Automation Activity & Vendor Info: (Cataloging) Innovative Interfaces, Inc; (Circulation) Innovative Interfaces, Inc; (OPAC) Innovative Interfaces, Inc
Publications: Newsletter (Quarterly); Resources for Program Planning
Member Libraries: B F Jones Memorial Library; Baden Memorial Library; Beaver Area Memorial Library; Carnegie Free Library; Chippewa Library Information Center; Laughlin Memorial Library; Monaca Public Library; New Brighton Public Library; Rochester Public Library
Partic in OCLC Online Computer Library Center, Inc; Pittsburgh Regional Libr Consortium
Open Mon-Fri 8:30-4:30

P B F JONES MEMORIAL LIBRARY, 663 Franklin Ave, 15001-3736. SAN 314-2566. Tel: 724-375-2900. FAX: 724-375-3274. Web Site: www.beaverlibraries.org/aliquippa.asp. *Libr Dir,* Linda Helms; E-mail: lhelms@beaverlibraries.org; Staff 3 (MLS 2, Non-MLS 1)
Founded 1921. Pop 30,000; Circ 90,000
Library Holdings: Bk Vols 66,000; Per Subs 130
Special Collections: LPDR for Nuclear Reg Com for Beaver Valley I & II Power Stations; PA Airhelp Resource Center
Automation Activity & Vendor Info: (Acquisitions) Innovative Interfaces, Inc; (Cataloging) Innovative Interfaces, Inc; (Circulation) Innovative Interfaces, Inc; (Course Reserve) Innovative Interfaces, Inc; (ILL) Innovative Interfaces, Inc; (OPAC) Innovative Interfaces, Inc; (Serials) Innovative Interfaces, Inc
Database Vendor: OCLC FirstSearch
Wireless access
Function: 24/7 Electronic res, 24/7 Online cat, Accessibility serv available based on individual needs, Adult bk club, Archival coll, Bk club(s), Bks on CD, Chess club, Children's prog, Computer training, Computers for patron use, Copy machines, Digital talking bks, E-Reserves, Electronic databases & coll, Fax serv, Free DVD rentals, ILL available, Laminating, Libr develop, Magazines, Magnifiers for reading, Microfiche/film & reading machines, Movies, Newsp ref libr, Online cat, Outreach serv, OverDrive digital audio bks, Photocopying/Printing, Preschool outreach, Prof lending libr, Prog for adults, Prog for children & young adult, Pub access computers, Ref & res, Ref serv in person, Referrals accepted, Scanner, Senior computer classes, Summer reading prog, Tax forms, Teen prog, Telephone ref, Wheelchair accessible
Mem of Beaver County Library System
Partic in Interlibrary Delivery Service of Pennsylvania; OCLC Online Computer Library Center, Inc; Pittsburg Regional Libr Ctr
Open Mon-Wed 9-7:30, Thurs-Sat 9-5
Friends of the Library Group

ALLENTOWN

P ALLENTOWN PUBLIC LIBRARY*, 1210 Hamilton St, 18102. SAN 358-2728. Tel: 610-820-2400. FAX: 610-820-0640. Web Site: www.allentownpl.org. *Dir,* Renee Haines; *Acq,* Bejamin Bertalan; *Adult Serv, ILL,* Diana Defanti; *Adult Serv,* Nanci Jeanne Fenselau; *Cat,* Peg Gordon; *Ch Serv,* Joan Kneiss; Staff 12 (MLS 12)
Founded 1912. Pop 133,271; Circ 858,994
Library Holdings: Bk Vols 270,946; Per Subs 351
Special Collections: State Document Depository
Subject Interests: Local hist
Automation Activity & Vendor Info: (Acquisitions) SirsiDynix; (Cataloging) SirsiDynix; (Circulation) SirsiDynix; (Course Reserve) SirsiDynix; (ILL) SirsiDynix; (Media Booking) SirsiDynix; (OPAC) SirsiDynix; (Serials) SirsiDynix
Wireless access
Partic in OCLC Online Computer Library Center, Inc
Open Mon-Thurs 9-9, Fri 9-6, Sat 9-5
Friends of the Library Group

C CEDAR CREST COLLEGE*, Cressman Library, 100 College Dr, 18104-6196. SAN 314-2620. Tel: 610-606-4666, Ext 3387. Interlibrary Loan Service Tel: 610-606-3543. Information Services Tel: 610-606-3536. FAX: 610-740-3769. Web Site: library.cedarcrest.edu. *Dir,* MaryBeth Freeh; E-mail: mafreeh@cedarcrest.edu; *Electronic Res, Info & Instrul Serv Librn,* Sheri Schneider; *Tech Serv Librn,* Scott Parkinson; *Lending Serv Coordr,* Kyle Suzanne Crimi; *Media Serv,* Judy Titus; *Ref,* James Gilbert; Staff 5 (MLS 3, Non-MLS 2)
Founded 1867. Enrl 1,320; Fac 90; Highest Degree: Master
Library Holdings: AV Mats 20,069; e-books 7,686; e-journals 27,978; Microforms 14,979; Bk Vols 140,653; Per Subs 28,278; Videos 4,175
Special Collections: American Poetry, bks, journals; Social Work, bks, journals; Women in the United States, bks, journals
Subject Interests: Women studies
Automation Activity & Vendor Info: (Acquisitions) SirsiDynix; (Cataloging) SirsiDynix; (Circulation) SirsiDynix; (Course Reserve) SirsiDynix; (OPAC) SirsiDynix; (Serials) SirsiDynix
Database Vendor: American Chemical Society, American Psychological Association (APA), BioOne, Blackwell, Checkpoint Systems, Inc, CRC Press/Taylor & Francis Group, H W Wilson, Hoovers, Ingenta, LexisNexis, Modern Language Association, Nature Publishing Group, OCLC ArticleFirst, OCLC FirstSearch, OCLC WorldShare Interlibrary Loan, OVID Technologies, Oxford Online, Project MUSE, Sage, ScienceDirect, SirsiDynix, Springer-Verlag, Wiley, Wilson - Wilson Web
Wireless access
Function: Archival coll, Art exhibits, Audio & video playback equip for onsite use
Publications: Library Services Information Leaflets
Partic in Dialog Corp; Lehigh Valley Association of Independent Colleges; Lyrasis; OCLC Online Computer Library Center, Inc; Pennsylvania Academic Library Consortium, Inc (PALCI)
Open Mon-Thurs (Winter) 8am-11pm, Fri 8-5, Sat 9am-10pm, Sun Noon-11; Mon & Tues (Summer) 9am-11pm, Wed & Thurs 9-7, Fri 9-5, Sat & Sun Noon-5

M GOOD SHEPHERD MEDICAL LIBRARY*, 850 S Fifth St, 18103. SAN 374-8626. Tel: 610-776-3294. FAX: 610-776-8336. Web Site: www.goodshepherdrehab.org.
Library Holdings: Bk Titles 536; Bk Vols 600; Per Subs 51
Subject Interests: Med, Pub health
Partic in Basic Health Sciences Library Network
Open Mon-Fri 8-Noon
Restriction: Employees & their associates

S LEHIGH COUNTY HISTORICAL SOCIETY*, Scott Andrew Trexler II Memorial Library, Lehigh Valley Heritage Museum, 432 W Walnut St, 18102-5428. SAN 314-2655. Tel: 610-435-1074. FAX: 610-435-9812. Web Site: www.lchs.museum. *Exec Dir,* Joseph Garrera; Tel: 610-435-1074, Ext 19, E-mail: j_garrera@lchs.museum; *Curator, Dir, Libr & Archives,* Jill Youngken; Tel: 610-435-1074, Ext 20, E-mail: j_youngken@lchs.museum; *Ref Librn,* Carol Herrity; Tel: 610-435-1074, Ext 12, E-mail: c_herrity@lchs.museum; Staff 2 (MLS 1, Non-MLS 1)
Founded 1906
Library Holdings: Bk Titles 10,000; Per Subs 20
Special Collections: Allentown Imprints; City Directories; Early German Newspapers; Local Church Records; Manuscript Coll; Photograph Coll
Subject Interests: Lehigh County
Open Mon-Fri 10-4, Sat 10-1 & 1:30-4

GL LEHIGH COUNTY LAW LIBRARY*, County Court House, 455 W Hamilton St, 18101-1614. SAN 314-2663. Tel: 610-782-3385. FAX: 610-820-3311. Web Site: www.lccpa.org. *Dir,* Lorelei A Broskey; E-mail: loreleibroskey@lehighcounty.org; Staff 4 (MLS 1, Non-MLS 3)
Founded 1869
Library Holdings: Bk Titles 2,500; Bk Vols 21,074; Per Subs 35
Special Collections: Ordinances Coll; Pennsylvania Law, Local Municipal & Legislative History
Open Mon-Fri 8-4:30

M LEHIGH VALLEY HOSPITAL*, Medical Library, Cedar Crest & I-78, 18105. (Mail add: PO Box 689, 18105-1556), SAN 371-5426. Tel: 610-402-8410. FAX. 610-402-8409. *Dir,* Barbara J Iobst, E-mail. barbara.iobst@lvh.com
Founded 1974
Library Holdings: Bk Vols 2,800; Per Subs 350
Automation Activity & Vendor Info: (Cataloging) CyberTools for Libraries; (Circulation) CyberTools for Libraries
Function: Photocopying/Printing
Partic in Cooperating Hospital Libraries of the Lehigh Valley Area
Open Mon-Fri 8:30-5:30
Restriction: Open to pub for ref only
Branches:
HEALTH LIBRARY & LEARNING CENTER, 17th & Chew, 18105. (Mail add: PO Box 7017, 18105-7017), SAN 314-2582. Tel: 610-402-2263. FAX: 610-402-2548. *Dir,* Barbara J Iobst; Tel: 610-402-8410, Fax: 610-402-8409, E-mail: barbara.iobst@lvh.com; *Dir, Br Serv,* Denise Parker
Founded 1940
Library Holdings: Bk Titles 1,000; Per Subs 85
Restriction: Not open to pub
MUHLENBERG MEDICAL LIBRARY, 2545 Schoenersville Rd, Bethlehem, 18017, SAN 327-0904. Tel: 484-884-2237. FAX: 484-861-0711. *Dir,* Barbara J Iobst; Tel: 610-402-8410, Fax: 610-402-8409, E-mail: barbara.iobst@lvh.com
Library Holdings: Bk Vols 750; Per Subs 70

S THE MORNING CALL*, Newspaper Archives, 101 N Sixth St, 18101. (Mail add: PO Box 1260, 18105-1260), SAN 314-2612. Tel: 610-820-6500. FAX: 610-820-6693. *Librn,* Dianne Knauss; *Asst Librn,* Jessica Johnson; Staff 2 (MLS 1, Non-MLS 1)
Founded 1932
Library Holdings: Bk Vols 1,500
Special Collections: Newspaper Microfilm, 1870-present, micro, photog
Restriction: Employees only

C MUHLENBERG COLLEGE*, Trexler Library, 2400 Chew St, 18104-5586. SAN 314-2671. Tel: 484-664-3500. Interlibrary Loan Service Tel: 484-664-3510. Reference Tel: 484-664-3600. Administration Tel: 484-664-3551. FAX: 484-664-3511. E-mail: refdesk@muhlenberg.edu. Web Site: www.muhlenberg.edu/library. *Dir,* Tina Hertel; Tel: 484-664-3550, E-mail: thertel@muhlenberg.edu; *Head, Coll Res Mgt,* Penny Lochner; Tel: 484-664-3561; *Head, Libr Syst & Info Transfer Serv,* Tim Clarke; Tel: 484-664-3520; *Head, Pub Outreach & Info Literacy Serv,* Jennifer Jarson; Tel: 484-664-3552; *Cat/Metadata Librn,* Catherine Hodge-Bodart; Tel: 484 664 3575; *Outreach & Scholarly Communication Librn,* Kelly Cannon; Tel: 484-664-3602, E-mail: kelly.cannon@gw.muhlenberg.edu; *Ref Serv Librn,* Rachel Hamelers; *Spec Coll & Archives Librn,* Diane Koch; Tel: 484-664-3694, E-mail: dkoch@muhlenberg.edu; *Acq & Budget Mgr,* Karen A Gruber; Tel: 484-664-3570, E-mail: gruber@muhlenberg.edu; *Mgr, ILL,* Kristin Brodt; E-mail: kbrodt@muhlenberg.edu. Subject Specialists: *Soc sci,* Jennifer Jarson; *Bus, Humanities,* Kelly Cannon; Staff 14 (MLS 8, Non-MLS 6)
Founded 1867. Enrl 2,500; Fac 260; Highest Degree: Bachelor
Library Holdings: AV Mats 6,599; Bks on Deafness & Sign Lang 70; CDs 2,189; e-journals 13,622; Bk Titles 173,484; Bk Vols 226,746; Per Subs 14,760; Talking Bks 406; Videos 3,996
Special Collections: Abram Samuels Sheet Music Coll; Muhlenberg Family mss; Pennsylvania German Coll; Rare Book Coll; Ray R Brennan Map Coll. Oral History; US Document Depository
Subject Interests: European hist, German lit
Automation Activity & Vendor Info: (Acquisitions) Innovative Interfaces, Inc; (Cataloging) Innovative Interfaces, Inc; (Circulation) Innovative Interfaces, Inc; (Course Reserve) Innovative Interfaces, Inc; (ILL) Innovative Interfaces, Inc; (Media Booking) Innovative Interfaces, Inc; (OPAC) Innovative Interfaces, Inc; (Serials) Innovative Interfaces, Inc
Database Vendor: Dialog, EBSCOhost, JSTOR, LexisNexis, Newsbank, OCLC FirstSearch, OCLC WorldShare Interlibrary Loan, OVID Technologies, SerialsSolutions, Wilson - Wilson Web
Wireless access
Function: Art exhibits, Audio & video playback equip for onsite use, Bk club(s), Bks on CD, Computer training, Copy machines, E-Reserves, Electronic databases & coll, Govt ref serv, Handicapped accessible, ILL available, Instruction & testing, Music CDs, Online cat, Online info literacy tutorials on the web & in blackboard, Online ref, Online searches, Outreach serv, Photocopying/Printing, Prog for adults, Pub access computers, Ref serv available, Tax forms, VHS videos, Wheelchair accessible
Partic in Lyrasis
Special Services for the Deaf - Bks on deafness & sign lang; Closed caption videos
Special Services for the Blind - Assistive/Adapted tech devices, equip & products; Computer with voice synthesizer for visually impaired persons; Reader equip; ZoomText magnification & reading software
Open Mon-Fri (Winter) 9-5; Mon-Thurs (Spring) 8am-1am, Fri 8am-10pm, Sat 11-7, Sun 11am-1am; Mon-Thurs (Summer) 9am-10pm, Fri 9-5, Sat & Sun 12-5
Restriction: Authorized patrons

P PARKLAND COMMUNITY LIBRARY*, 4422 Walbert Ave, 18104-1619. SAN 314-5646. Tel: 610-398-1361. Administration Tel: 610-398-1333. FAX: 610-398-3538. E-mail: info@parklandlibrary.org. Web Site: parklandlibrary.org. *Dir,* Debbie Jack; E-mail: jackd@parklandlibrary.org; *Head, Ref, Tech Coordr,* Noah Roth; E-mail: rothn@parklandlibrary.org; *Adult Serv,* Maryellen Kanarr; E-mail: kanarrm@parklandlibrary.org; *Youth Serv,* Hannah Killian; E-mail: killianh@parklandlibrary.org; Staff 23 (MLS 7, Non-MLS 16)
Founded 1973. Pop 54,000; Circ 250,730
Library Holdings: Audiobooks 2,619; AV Mats 8,336; Bks on Deafness & Sign Lang 57; CDs 1,413; DVDs 4,259; e-books 1,502; Electronic Media & Resources 20; Large Print Bks 1,559; Bk Titles 75,000; Per Subs 118
Special Collections: Local History Coll; Penna-German Society Publications
Automation Activity & Vendor Info: (Acquisitions) TLC (The Library Corporation); (Cataloging) TLC (The Library Corporation); (Circulation) TLC (The Library Corporation); (ILL) TLC (The Library Corporation); (OPAC) TLC (The Library Corporation)
Database Vendor: Baker & Taylor, EBSCOhost, Gale Cengage Learning, Overdrive, Inc, ProQuest, ReferenceUSA, TLC (The Library Corporation), TumbleBookLibrary, Wilson - Wilson Web, WT Cox
Wireless access
Function: Adult bk club, Computer training, Computers for patron use, Copy machines, Electronic databases & coll, Free DVD rentals, Home delivery & serv to Sr ctr & nursing homes, Homebound delivery serv, ILL available, Magnifiers for reading, Music CDs, Online cat, Online ref, Online searches, OverDrive digital audio bks, Photocopying/Printing, Prof lending libr, Prog for adults, Prog for children & young adult, Pub access computers, Ref serv available, Spoken cassettes & CDs, Summer reading prog, Telephone ref, VHS videos, Web-catalog, Wheelchair accessible, Workshops
Publications: Friends of the Library Information Paper (FLIP); Newsletter
Special Services for the Blind - Audio mat; Bks on cassette; Bks on CD; Large print bks; Talking bks
Open Mon-Thurs 10-9, Fri & Sat 10-5
Friends of the Library Group

M SACRED HEART HOSPITAL*, Medical Library, 421 Chew St, 18102. SAN 314 268X. Tel: 610 776 4500. FAX: 610-606-4422. Web Site: www.shh.org. *Librn,* Position Currently Open
Founded 1949
Library Holdings: Bk Vols 6,668; Per Subs 128
Subject Interests: Dental, Diagnostic radiology, Family practice, Ophthalmology, Otolaryngology
Partic in National Network of Libraries of Medicine
Open Mon-Fri 8-4:30

M ST LUKE'S HOSPITAL-ALLENTOWN CAMPUS*, Learning Resource Center, 1736 Hamilton St, 18104. SAN 322-8266. Tel: 610-770-8355. FAX: 610-770-8736. *Dir,* Maria Collette; Tel: 610-954-4650, Fax: 610-954-4651, E-mail: colletm@slhn.org; *Librn,* Vanessa Reis-Bradley; Staff 3 (MLS 2, Non-MLS 1)
Library Holdings: Bk Vols 2,000; Per Subs 75
Database Vendor: EBSCOhost, OVID Technologies
Function: Archival coll, ILL available, Photocopying/Printing
Partic in Basic Health Sciences Library Network; Cooperating Hospital Libraries of the Lehigh Valley Area
Open Mon-Fri 9-1
Restriction: Open to others by appt, Open to pub for ref only

ALLISON PARK

P HAMPTON COMMUNITY LIBRARY*, 3101 McCully Rd, 15101. Tel: 412-684-1098. FAX: 412-684-1097. E-mail: hampton@einetwork.net. Web Site: www.hamptoncommunitylibrary.org. *Dir,* Position Currently Open
Founded 1990. Pop 17,526
Library Holdings: Bk Vols 40,000; Per Subs 50
Subject Interests: Early children's bks
Automation Activity & Vendor Info: (Acquisitions) Innovative Interfaces, Inc; (Cataloging) Innovative Interfaces, Inc; (Circulation) Innovative

Interfaces, Inc; (ILL) Innovative Interfaces, Inc; (OPAC) Innovative Interfaces, Inc
Mem of Allegheny County Library Association
Open Tues-Thurs 9:30-8, Fri 9:30-5, Sat 9-4
Friends of the Library Group

ALTOONA

P ALTOONA AREA PUBLIC LIBRARY*, 1600 Fifth Ave, 16602-3693. SAN 358-2817. Tel: 814-946-0417. Circulation Tel: 814-946-0417, Ext 125. Interlibrary Loan Service Tel: 814-946-0417, Ext 126. Reference Tel: 814-946-0417, Ext 131. Administration Tel: 814-946-0417, Ext 120. FAX: 814-946-3230. Web Site: www.altoonalibrary.org. *Exec Dir,* Jennifer Knisely; Tel: 814-946-0417, Ext 122; *Ch Serv,* Adrienne Brown; Staff 25.6 (MLS 6, Non-MLS 19.6)
Founded 1927. Pop 62,348; Circ 225,543
Jul 2005-Jun 2006 Income $1,197,672, State $493,328, City $2,400, Federal $48,065, County $60,370, Locally Generated Income $165,185, Parent Institution $361,947, Other $66,377. Mats Exp $134,214, Books $97,550, Per/Ser (Incl. Access Fees) $11,396, Micro $3,832, AV Mat $10,664, Electronic Ref Mat (Incl. Access Fees) $5,458, Presv $5,314. Sal $620,869 (Prof $216,572)
Library Holdings: AV Mats 21,772; CDs 1,805; Bk Vols 135,314; Per Subs 220; Talking Bks 4,978; Videos 2,002
Special Collections: Local History (Pennsylvania Room); Railroad Photographs. State Document Depository; US Document Depository
Subject Interests: Adult literacy, Railroad hist
Automation Activity & Vendor Info: (Cataloging) SirsiDynix; (Circulation) SirsiDynix; (OPAC) SirsiDynix
Database Vendor: EBSCOhost, OCLC FirstSearch, OCLC WebJunction, OCLC WorldShare Interlibrary Loan
Wireless access
Function: Homebound delivery serv, Large print keyboards, Magnifiers for reading, Outside serv via phone, mail, e-mail & web, Photocopying/Printing, Prof lending libr, Prog for children & young adult, Ref serv available, Serves mentally handicapped consumers, Summer reading prog, Telephone ref, Wheelchair accessible
Mem of Blair County Library System
Partic in Interlibrary Delivery Service of Pennsylvania; OCLC Online Computer Library Center, Inc
Special Services for the Deaf - TTY equip
Open Mon 8:30-8, Tues, Wed & Fri 8:30-5, Thurs 8:30-7, Sat 9-4
Friends of the Library Group

M ALTOONA HOSPITAL*, Glover Memorial Library, 620 Howard Ave, 16601-4899. SAN 314-2728. Tel: 814-946-2318. FAX: 814-889-3176. Web Site: www.altoonaregional.org/healthlibrary_glover.htm. *Dir,* Katherine Terlinsky; E-mail: kterlinsky@altoonaregional.org; Staff 2 (MLS 1, Non-MLS 1)
Founded 1940
Library Holdings: Bk Titles 4,020; Bk Vols 4,238; Per Subs 300
Special Collections: Altoona Hospital (Historical Coll), bks, doc, artifacts, photogs
Subject Interests: Allied health, Cancer, Med, Nursing
Function: ILL available, Ref serv available
Partic in National Network of Libraries of Medicine
Open Mon-Fri 7:30-3:30
Restriction: Circulates for staff only, Non-circulating to the pub, Open to pub for ref only, Pub use on premises
Friends of the Library Group

P BLAIR COUNTY LIBRARY SYSTEM*, 1600 Fifth Ave, 16601. SAN 314-2744. Tel: 814-946-0417, Ext 132. FAX: 814-946-3230. E-mail: bcl@altoonalibrary.org. Web Site: www.blaircountylibraries.org. *Syst Adminr,* Timothy Salony; Staff 1 (MLS 1)
Pop 129,026
Automation Activity & Vendor Info: (Circulation) Follett Software; (OPAC) Follett Software
Member Libraries: Altoona Area Public Library; Bellwood-Antis Public Library; Claysburg Area Public Library; Holidaysburg Area Public Library; Martinsburg Community Library; Roaring Spring Community Library; Tyrone-Snyder Public Library
Open Mon-Fri 8:30-5

GM DEPARTMENT OF VETERANS AFFAIRS*, Medical Center Library, 2907 Pleasant Valley Blvd, 16602-4305. SAN 314-2760. Tel: 814-943-8164, Ext 7156. FAX: 814-940-7895. *Prog Spec,* Eileen Anslinger; Staff 1 (Non-MLS 1)
Founded 1950
Library Holdings: AV Mats 414; Bk Titles 2,524; Per Subs 129
Special Collections: Medical Journal Coll, microfilm
Subject Interests: Med, Patient educ
Partic in Veterans Affairs Libr Network (VALNET)
Restriction: Staff use only

C PENNSYLVANIA STATE ALTOONA*, Robert E Eiche Library, 3000 Ivyside Park, 16601-3760. SAN 314-2752. Tel: 814-949-5255. Circulation Tel: 814-949-5256. Interlibrary Loan Service Tel: 814-949-5519. Reference Tel: 814-949-5253. FAX: 814-949-5246, 814-949-5520. Web Site: www.aa.psu.edu. *Head Librn,* Timothy Wherry; E-mail: tlw6@psu.edu; *Asst Librn,* Amy Deuink; Tel: 814-949-5252, E-mail: ald120@psu.edu; *Coordr, Instruction,* Position Currently Open; *Info Tech,* Bonnie Imler; Tel: 814-949-5499, E-mail: bbil@psu.edu; *Ref,* Mila Su; E-mail: mcs1@psu.edu; Staff 6 (MLS 3, Non-MLS 3)
Founded 1939. Enrl 3,485; Fac 105
Library Holdings: Bk Vols 90,000
Special Collections: Drama & The Dance (Cutler Coll); Drama on Records (Buzzard Coll); Lincoln Coll (Klevan Coll)
Partic in OCLC Online Computer Library Center, Inc; RLIN (Research Libraries Information Network)
Open Mon-Thurs (Winter) 8am-11pm, Fri 8-5, Sat 12-5, Sun 3-11; Mon-Fri (Summer) 8-5

J SOUTH HILLS SCHOOL OF BUSINESS & TECHNOLOGY LIBRARY*, 508 58th St, 16602. SAN 314-2736. Tel: 814-944-6134. Toll Free Tel: 888-282-7427. FAX: 814-944-4684. Web Site: www.southhills.edu. *Dir,* Marianne Beyer
Library Holdings: Bk Vols 1,000; Per Subs 14

AMBLER

S LTK ENGINEERING SERVICES LIBRARY*, 100 W Butler Ave, 19002. Tel: 215-641-8833. Administration Tel: 215-542-0700. FAX: 215-542-7676. *Librn,* Sabina D Tannenbaum; E-mail: stannenbaum@ltk.com
Founded 1974
Library Holdings: Bk Titles 5,500; Per Subs 100
Subject Interests: Urban transportation
Automation Activity & Vendor Info: (Cataloging) EOS International; (Circulation) EOS International; (OPAC) EOS International
Database Vendor: EOS International, IEEE (Institute of Electrical & Electronics Engineers)

TEMPLE UNIVERSITY LIBRARIES
See Philadelphia

AMBRIDGE

P LAUGHLIN MEMORIAL LIBRARY*, 99 Eleventh St, 15003-2305. SAN 314-2795. Tel: 724-266-3857. FAX: 724-266-5670. *Dir,* Emilee Waldo; E-mail: ewaldo@beaverlibraries.org; Staff 2 (MLS 1, Non-MLS 1)
Founded 1929. Pop 13,298; Circ 49,755
Jan 2012-Dec 2013 Income $190,000. Mats Exp $20,000. Sal $110,000 (Prof $35,000)
Library Holdings: AV Mats 930; CDs 50; DVDs 200; Large Print Bks 200; Bk Titles 24,000; Per Subs 50; Talking Bks 200; Videos 100
Special Collections: Local History (Pennsylvania), bks, maps, slides; Music Coll, cassettes, rec, tapes
Subject Interests: Econ, Hist, Music
Automation Activity & Vendor Info: (Course Reserve) Innovative Interfaces, Inc; (Serials) Innovative Interfaces, Inc
Database Vendor: Overdrive, Inc
Wireless access
Function: Adult literacy prog, Archival coll, BA reader (adult literacy), Games & aids for the handicapped, Handicapped accessible, ILL available, Magnifiers for reading, Online searches, Outside serv via phone, mail, e-mail & web, Photocopying/Printing, Prof lending libr, Prog for adults, Prog for children & young adult, Ref serv available, Spoken cassettes & CDs, Summer reading prog, VHS videos, Wheelchair accessible
Mem of Beaver County Library System
Special Services for the Deaf - TTY equip
Open Mon-Thurs 10-7, Fri 10-4, Sat 9-4

S PENNSYLVANIA HISTORICAL & MUSEUM COMMISSION*, Old Economy Village Historical Site Museum, 270 16th St, 15003-2298. SAN 314-2809. Tel: 724-266-4500. FAX: 724-266-3010. Web Site: www.oldeconomyvillage.org. *Curator,* Sarah Buffington; Staff 2 (Non-MLS 2)
Founded 1805
Library Holdings: Bk Titles 6,180; Bk Vols 6,591; Per Subs 27
Special Collections: Harmony Society (1805-1905), music, papers
Subject Interests: 19th Century indust, German lit, Music
Open Tues-Sat 10-5, Sun 12-5

R TRINITY EPISCOPAL SCHOOL FOR MINISTRY LIBRARY*, 311 11th St, 15003. SAN 371-6937. Tel: 724-266-3838. Circulation Tel: 724-266-3838, Ext 267. Interlibrary Loan Service Tel: 724-266-3838, Ext 223. FAX: 724-266-4617. E-mail: library@tsm.edu. Web Site: www.tsm.edu/academics/library.html. *Libr Dir,* Susanah Hanson; E-mail: shanson@tsm.edu; *Asst Librn,* Carrie Wardzinski; Tel: 724-266-3838, Ext

265, E-mail: cwarzinski@tsm.edu; *Libr Tech,* Justin Hostutler; E-mail: jhostutler@tsm.edu; Staff 2 (MLS 2)
Founded 1975. Enrl 105; Fac 22; Highest Degree: Doctorate
Library Holdings: Bk Vols 85,000; Per Subs 390
Subject Interests: Biblical studies, Theol
Automation Activity & Vendor Info: (Cataloging) TLC (The Library Corporation); (Circulation) TLC (The Library Corporation); (OPAC) TLC (The Library Corporation); (Serials) TLC (The Library Corporation)
Database Vendor: EBSCOhost
Wireless access
Partic in Pittsburgh Regional Libr Consortium
Open Mon-Thurs 9-9, Fri 9-5

ANDALUSIA

R THE KING LIBRARY, 1065 Bristol Pike, 19020. SAN 314-2817. Tel: 215-639-4387. *Librn,* Nicholas W Medvedeff; Tel: 215-637-6516, Fax: 209-370-9697, E-mail: medvedeff@aol.com; Staff 1 (Non-MLS 1)
Founded 1882
Nov 2005-Oct 2006 Income $3,800. Mats Exp $1,260
Library Holdings: Bk Titles 12,568; Bk Vols 13,111; Per Subs 16
Special Collections: Key Coll
Subject Interests: Classical lit, Hist, Relig
Restriction: Access at librarian's discretion, Private libr

ANNVILLE

P ANNVILLE FREE LIBRARY*, 216 E Main St, 17003-1599. SAN 314-2825. Tel: 717-867-1802. FAX: 717-867-5754. Web Site: www.lclibs.org/annville/index.php. *Dir,* Dee L Neff; E-mail: dln@lclibs.org; Staff 5 (MLS 1, Non-MLS 4)
Founded 1941. Pop 12,891; Circ 78,019
Library Holdings: Large Print Bks 136; Bk Titles 36,998; Bk Vols 38,110; Per Subs 105; Talking Bks 651; Videos 1,233
Subject Interests: Archit, Art
Automation Activity & Vendor Info: (Cataloging) Innovative Interfaces, Inc; (Circulation) Innovative Interfaces, Inc; (OPAC) Innovative Interfaces, Inc
Function: ILL available
Mem of Lebanon County Library System
Open Mon-Thurs 10-8, Fri & Sat 10-5
Friends of the Library Group

C LEBANON VALLEY COLLEGE*, Vernon & Doris Bishop Library, 101 N College Ave, 17003-1400. SAN 314-2833. Tel: 717-867-6977. Interlibrary Loan Service Tel: 717-867-6974, 717-867-6976. Reference Tel: 717-867-6972, 717-867-6987. Administration Tel: 717-867-6985. Automation Services Tel: 717-867-6973. FAX: 717-867-6979. Web Site: www.lvc.edu/library. *Dir,* Position Currently Open; *Access Serv Librn,* Maureen Bentz; E-mail: bentz@lvc.edu; *Instruction & Ref Librn,* Donna Lynn Miller; E-mail: miller@lvc.edu; *Syst/Electronic Serv Librn,* Lori Nyce, E-mail: nyce@lvc.edu; *Tech Serv,* Julia L Harvey; Tel: 717-867-6971, E-mail: harvey@lvc.edu; Staff 9 (MLS 5, Non-MLS 4)
Founded 1867. Enrl 1,731; Fac 100; Highest Degree: Doctorate
Jul 2012-Jun 2013 Income $1,318,974. Mats Exp $746,739, Books $153,912, Per/Ser (Incl. Access Fees) $329,631, Micro $1,326, AV Mat $9,508, Electronic Ref Mat (Incl. Access Fees) $250,055, Presv $2,307. Sal $440,773 (Prof $312,737)
Library Holdings: AV Mats 18,996; CDs 8,427; DVDs 8,368; e-books 139,523; e-journals 48,822; Microforms 7,509; Music Scores 8,104; Bk Titles 154,749; Bk Vols 171,158; Per Subs 4,777; Videos 1,295
Special Collections: Early Iron Industry (C B Montgomery Coll); Pennsylvania German (Hiram Herr Shenk Coll)
Subject Interests: Behav sci, Music, Soc sci
Automation Activity & Vendor Info: (Acquisitions) SirsiDynix; (Cataloging) SirsiDynix; (Circulation) SirsiDynix; (Course Reserve) Blackboard Inc; (ILL) OCLC ILLiad; (OPAC) SirsiDynix; (Serials) SirsiDynix
Database Vendor: Agricola, Alexander Street Press, American Chemical Society, American Mathematical Society, ARTstor, Bowker, Cinahl, CredoReference, ebrary, EBSCOhost, Elsevier, Gale Cengage Learning, H W Wilson, JSTOR, LexisNexis, McGraw-Hill, MD Consult, Medline, Mergent Online, Modern Language Association, Newsbank, OCLC, OCLC ArticleFirst, OCLC FirstSearch, OCLC WorldShare Interlibrary Loan, Oxford Online, Paratext, ProQuest, PubMed, RefWorks, Sage, ScienceDirect, SerialsSolutions, SirsiDynix, Springshare, LLC, Standard & Poor's, YBP Library Services
Wireless access
Partic in Lyrasis; OCLC Online Computer Library Center, Inc
Open Mon-Thurs 7:30am-Midnight, Fri 7:30am-9pm, Sat 10-7, Sun Noon-Midnight

APOLLO

P APOLLO MEMORIAL LIBRARY*, 219 N Pennsylvania Ave, 15613. SAN 314-2841. Tel: 724-478-4214. FAX: 724-478-1693. E-mail: apollolibrary@hotmail.com. Web Site: home.alltel.net/apollolibrary, www.armstronglibraries.org. *Chief Librn,* Tina Zins
Founded 1908. Pop 3,699; Circ 28,000
Library Holdings: Bk Vols 30,000; Per Subs 108
Subject Interests: Genealogy, Local hist
Wireless access
Publications: Newsletter (Quarterly)
Open Tues-Thurs 11-7, Fri & Sat 9-4

ARDMORE

P ARDMORE FREE LIBRARY*, 108 Ardmore Ave, 19003-1399. SAN 314-2868. Tel: 610-642-5187. FAX: 610-649-2618. E-mail: ardmorelibrary@lmls.org. Web Site: www.lmls.org. *Head Librn,* Jane Quin; *Ch Serv,* Dawnita Brown; Staff 2.8 (MLS 1, Non-MLS 1.8)
Founded 1899. Pop 58,000; Circ 109,066
Library Holdings: AV Mats 5,794; Bk Titles 36,000; Per Subs 62
Subject Interests: African-Am studies
Automation Activity & Vendor Info: (Acquisitions) Innovative Interfaces, Inc; (Cataloging) Innovative Interfaces, Inc; (Circulation) Innovative Interfaces, Inc; (OPAC) Innovative Interfaces, Inc
Wireless access
Function: Adult bk club, Adult literacy prog, Bks on cassette, Bks on CD, Children's prog, Computers for patron use, Copy machines, E-Reserves, Electronic databases & coll, Free DVD rentals, Handicapped accessible, Holiday prog, ILL available, Music CDs, Photocopying/Printing, Prog for adults, Prog for children & young adult, Ref serv in person, Story hour, Summer reading prog, Tax forms
Mem of Lower Merion Library System
Open Mon, Tues & Thurs 10-8, Wed 1-8, Fri & Sat 10-5

R FIRST PRESBYTERIAN CHURCH*, William Faulds Memorial Library, Five W Montgomery Ave, 19003-1599. SAN 314-2876. Tel: 610-642-6650. FAX: 610-645-0517. E-mail: admin@ardmorepres.org. Web Site: www.ardmorepres.org. *Adminr,* Raelyn Harman; *Librn,* Connie Hoelscher; Staff 1 (MLS 1)
Founded 1962
Library Holdings: Bk Titles 3,000
Subject Interests: Behav sci, Relig studies, Soc sci

P LOWER MERION LIBRARY SYSTEM*, 75 E Lancaster Ave, 19003-2388. SAN 314-3589. Tel: 610-645-6110. FAX: 610-649-8835. E-mail: lmls@lmls.org. Web Site: www.lmls.org. *Dir,* Christine Steckel; *Ref,* Marcia Bass; Staff 14 (MLS 14)
Founded 1935. Pop 58,003; Circ 1,330,166
Library Holdings: Bk Titles 215,694; Bk Vols 424,931; Per Subs 350
Subject Interests: Archit, Art, Hort, Local hist, Music
Member Libraries: Ardmore Free Library; Bala Cynwyd Library; Belmont Hills Public Library; Gladwyne Free Library; Ludington Public Library; Penn Wynne Library

ASHLAND

P ASHLAND PUBLIC LIBRARY*, 1229 Center St, 17921-1207. SAN 314-2884. Tel: 570-875-3175. FAX: 570-875-2699. Web Site: www.ashlandpubliclibrary.org. *Librn,* Irene Hardnock
Pop 20,212; Circ 18,006
Library Holdings: Bk Vols 14,900; Per Subs 50
Automation Activity & Vendor Info: (Cataloging) Follett Software; (Circulation) Follett Software; (OPAC) Follett Software
Open Mon, Tues & Thurs 10-6, Fri 9-4, Sat 8-12

ASTON

P ASTON PUBLIC LIBRARY*, 3270 Concord Rd, 19014. SAN 320-8494. Tel: 610-494-5877. FAX: 610-494-1314. Web Site: www.astonlibrary.org. *Dir,* Stephen Sarazin; Staff 7 (MLS 1, Non-MLS 6)
Pop 16,203; Circ 79,168
Library Holdings: Bk Vols 35,000; Per Subs 60
Automation Activity & Vendor Info: (Cataloging) Innovative Interfaces, Inc; (Circulation) Innovative Interfaces, Inc; (OPAC) Innovative Interfaces, Inc
Function: Adult bk club, Bk club(s), Computers for patron use, Copy machines, Fax serv, Music CDs, Online cat, Prog for children & young adult, Spoken cassettes & CDs, Story hour, Summer reading prog, Tax forms, Web-catalog
Mem of Delaware County Library System
Open Mon-Thurs 10-8, Fri & Sat 10-5
Friends of the Library Group

C NEUMANN COLLEGE LIBRARY*, One Neumann Dr, 19014-1298. SAN 325-2841. Tel: 610-558-5545. Interlibrary Loan Service Tel: 610-361-5216. Reference Tel: 610-361-5313. FAX: 610-459-1370. E-mail: library@neumann.edu. Web Site: www.neumann.edu/academics/library.asp. *Interim Dir, Ref Librn,* Tiffany McGregor; Tel: 610-361-2487, E-mail: mcgregot@neumann.edu; *Acq Librn,* Richard Ridgway; Tel: 610-361-5316, E-mail: ridgwayr@neumann.edu; *Ref Librn,* Maureen Williams; Tel: 610-558-5541, E-mail: williamm@neumann.edu; *Archives,* Sister Marie Therese Carr; Tel: 610-361-5206, E-mail: carrm@neumann.edu; *Circ,* Andy Miller; *ILL, Reserves,* Barbara Selletti; E-mail: sellettb@neumann.edu; *Tech Serv,* Jessica Gibney; Tel: 610-361-5416; Staff 9 (MLS 4, Non-MLS 5)
Founded 1965. Enrl 2,800; Fac 200; Highest Degree: Doctorate
Library Holdings: AV Mats 3,000; CDs 300; e-books 2,000; Bk Titles 78,000; Bk Vols 90,000; Per Subs 400; Videos 3,000
Special Collections: Betty Neuman Archives; Curriculum; Franciscan Coll
Subject Interests: Nursing, Pastoral counseling
Automation Activity & Vendor Info: (Acquisitions) EOS International; (Cataloging) SirsiDynix; (Circulation) SirsiDynix; (Course Reserve) Docutek; (ILL) OCLC Online; (OPAC) SirsiDynix; (Serials) SirsiDynix
Database Vendor: EBSCOhost, JSTOR, LexisNexis, OCLC FirstSearch, OCLC WorldShare Interlibrary Loan, ProQuest, PubMed, SirsiDynix, Wilson - Wilson Web
Wireless access
Partic in Lyrasis; OCLC Online Computer Library Center, Inc; Southeastern Pa Consortium for Higher Educ; Tri-State College Library Cooperative
Open Mon-Thurs (Winter) 8am-11pm, Fri 8-5, Sat 10-5, Sun 1-6; Mon-Thurs (Summer) 8am-10pm, Fri 8-5, Sat 10-3, Sun 12-4

ATGLEN

P ATGLEN PUBLIC LIBRARY*, 413 Valley Ave, 19310-1402. SAN 314-2906. Tel: 610-593-6848. FAX: 610-593-6848. Web Site: www.ccls.org. *Dir,* Carey Bresler; E-mail: cbresler@ccls.org; Staff 2 (Non-MLS 2)
Pop 1,217; Circ 20,186
Library Holdings: Audiobooks 530; AV Mats 1,014; Bk Vols 11,333; Per Subs 33
Database Vendor: EBSCOhost
Wireless access
Function: Adult bk club, Bk club(s), Children's prog, Computers for patron use, Copy machines, Fax serv, Free DVD rentals, Photocopying/Printing, Prog for adults, Prog for children & young adult, Pub access computers, Story hour, Summer reading prog, Writing prog
Mem of Chester County Library System
Open Mon & Wed-Fri 1-6, Sat 9-1

ATHENS

P SPALDING MEMORIAL LIBRARY*, 724 S Main St, 18810-1010. SAN 314-2914. Tel: 570-888-7117. Administration Tel: 570-882-1247. FAX: 570-882-9202. E-mail: spalding@stny.rr.com. Web Site: www.spaldinglibrary.org. *Dir,* Janet S Gigee; E-mail: gigee@stny.rr.com; *Asst Dir, Ch,* Diane Sidey; Staff 5 (Non-MLS 5)
Founded 1897. Pop 8,795; Circ 34,334
Library Holdings: Bk Vols 30,081; Per Subs 45
Subject Interests: County hist for genealogy, State hist for genealogy
Automation Activity & Vendor Info: (Cataloging) Follett Software; (Circulation) Follett Software
Wireless access
Mem of Bradford County Library System
Open Mon-Thurs 12-8, Fri 9-3, Sat 9-4
Friends of the Library Group

AVALON

P AVALON PUBLIC LIBRARY, 317 S Home Ave, 15202. SAN 314-2922. Tel: 412-761-2288. FAX: 412-761-7745. E-mail: avalon@einetwork.net. Web Site: www.avalonlibrary.org. *Dir,* Rania S Sullivan; E-mail: sullivanr@einetwork.net; Staff 4 (MLS 1, Non-MLS 3)
Founded 1940. Pop 4,705; Circ 49,343
Automation Activity & Vendor Info: (Cataloging) Innovative Interfaces, Inc - Millenium; (Circulation) Innovative Interfaces, Inc - Millenium
Wireless access
Function: Adult bk club, After school storytime, Bi-weekly Writer's Group, Bks on CD, Children's prog, Computers for patron use, Copy machines, E-Reserves, Electronic databases & coll, Fax serv, Free DVD rentals, Handicapped accessible, ILL available, Magazines, Magnifiers for reading, Mango lang, Movies, Music CDs, Online cat, OverDrive digital audio bks, Photocopying/Printing, Prog for adults, Prog for children & young adult, Pub access computers, Senior computer classes, Story hour, Summer reading prog, Tax forms, Teen prog, Wheelchair accessible
Mem of Allegheny County Library Association
Partic in eiNetwork
Special Services for the Blind - Bks on cassette; Bks on CD; Large print bks
Open Mon & Wed 10-6, Tues & Thurs 12-8, Fri 10-5, Sat 9-4
Friends of the Library Group

AVELLA

P AVELLA AREA PUBLIC LIBRARY*, 11 School Ct, 15312-2356. (Mail add: PO Box 547, 15312-0547), SAN 376-5725. Tel: 724-587-5688. FAX: 724-587-3432. Web Site: www.avellapubliclibrary.org. *Dir,* Lynn Maidment Clarchick; Staff 3 (MLS 1, Non-MLS 2)
Library Holdings: AV Mats 1,169; Large Print Bks 78; Bk Titles 10,111; Bk Vols 10,841; Per Subs 16; Talking Bks 233; Videos 708
Open Mon & Thurs 1-7, Tues & Wed 9-7, Sat 9-4

AVONMORE

P AVONMORE PUBLIC LIBRARY*, 619 Allegheny Ave, 15618. SAN 314-2930. Tel: 724-697-4828. FAX: 724-697-1322. *Librn,* Peggy Shearer; *Ch Serv,* Mitsy Veneziani; Staff 2 (Non-MLS 2)
Pop 3,271; Circ 9,110
Library Holdings: Bk Titles 6,184; Bk Vols 6,415; Per Subs 19; Videos 248
Mem of Westmoreland County Federated Library System
Open Mon & Thurs 5-7, Tues 11-2, Wed 10-7

BADEN

P BADEN MEMORIAL LIBRARY*, 385 State St, 15005-1946. SAN 314-2949. Tel: 724-869-3960. FAX: 724-869-8816. Staff 3 (MLS 1, Non-MLS 2)
Founded 1941. Pop 5,331; Circ 29,116
Library Holdings: Bk Titles 26,840; Bk Vols 27,390; Per Subs 48; Talking Bks 315; Videos 387
Automation Activity & Vendor Info: (Acquisitions) Innovative Interfaces, Inc; (Cataloging) Innovative Interfaces, Inc; (Circulation) Innovative Interfaces, Inc; (Course Reserve) Innovative Interfaces, Inc; (ILL) Innovative Interfaces, Inc; (OPAC) Innovative Interfaces, Inc; (Serials) Innovative Interfaces, Inc
Mem of Beaver County Library System
Open Mon, Wed & Thurs 1-8, Tues 12-8, Sat 10-5

BALA CYNWYD

P BALA CYNWYD LIBRARY*, 131 Old Lancaster Rd, 19004-3037. SAN 314-2957. Tel: 610-664-1196. FAX: 610-664-5534. E-mail: balacynwydlibrary@lmls.org. Web Site: lmls.org. *Librn,* Jean Knapp; *Circ,* Carol Cobaugh; *Ch Serv,* Jane France; *ILL,* Karen Frederick; *Ref Serv,* Maria Lerman
Founded 1915. Pop 14,538; Circ 408,387
Library Holdings: Bk Vols 122,449; Per Subs 188
Special Collections: Children's Historical Book Coll; Music Coll, bks, cassettes, scores, compact discs
Subject Interests: Judaica, Music
Automation Activity & Vendor Info: (Acquisitions) Innovative Interfaces, Inc; (Cataloging) Innovative Interfaces, Inc; (Circulation) Innovative Interfaces, Inc; (Course Reserve) Innovative Interfaces, Inc; (OPAC) Innovative Interfaces, Inc
Mem of Lower Merion Library System
Open Mon-Thurs 10-9, Fri & Sat 10-5, Sun 12-5

P BELMONT HILLS PUBLIC LIBRARY*, 120 Mary Watersford Rd, 19004. SAN 314-2965. Tel: 610-664-8427. FAX: 610-664-8427. *Head Librn,* Patricia Rayfield; Tel: 610-664-1063, E-mail: prayfield@lmls.org; Staff 3 (MLS 1, Non-MLS 2)
Founded 1935. Pop 9,812; Circ 63,510
Jan 2007-Dec 2007 Income $154,890, State $14,390, County $9,000, Locally Generated Income $16,000, Other $115,500. Mats Exp $26,800, Books $25,600, Per/Ser (Incl. Access Fees) $1,200. Sal $122,300 (Prof $64,000)
Library Holdings: AV Mats 1,040; Large Print Bks 114; Bk Titles 24,610; Bk Vols 26,080; Per Subs 73; Videos 359
Mem of Lower Merion Library System
Open Mon & Tues 10-8, Wed & Thurs 12-8, Sat 10-5

BANGOR

P BANGOR PUBLIC LIBRARY*, 39 S Main St, 18013-2690. SAN 314-2981. Tel: 610-588-4136. FAX: 610-588-1931. E-mail: bngrpl@epix.net. Web Site: www.bangorlibrary.org. *Dir,* Barbara Brandt; Staff 1 (Non-MLS 1)
Founded 1922. Pop 18,745; Circ 32,091
Jul 2011-Jun 2012 Income $135,000, State $26,000, City $8,000, Locally Generated Income $101,000
Library Holdings: Bk Vols 32,000; Per Subs 44
Special Collections: Local Newspaper, flm

Subject Interests: Local hist
Automation Activity & Vendor Info: (Acquisitions) Follett Software; (Cataloging) Follett Software; (Circulation) Follett Software; (OPAC) Follett Software
Wireless access
Publications: Footnotes (Quarterly)
Special Services for the Blind - Bks & mags in Braille, on rec, tape & cassette
Open Mon & Wed 1-8, Tues & Thurs 10-8, Fri 1-5, Sat 10-4
Friends of the Library Group

BEAVER

S MICHAEL BAKER CORPORATION LIBRARY*, 4301 Dutch Ridge Rd, 15009. SAN 314-3007. Tel: 724-495-4021. Toll Free Tel: 800-553-1153. FAX: 724-495-4001. E-mail: library@mbakercorp.com. *Librn,* Regina Hart; Staff 1 (MLS 1)
Founded 1972
Library Holdings: Audiobooks 200; e-books 79; Electronic Media & Resources 281; Bk Titles 11,425; Per Subs 295; Videos 106
Subject Interests: Archit, Aviation eng, Civil eng, Construction mgt, Environ eng, Geospatial info tech, Pipeline eng, Railroad planning, Transportation planning
Function: Bus archives, Doc delivery serv, Handicapped accessible, Online searches, Ref serv available
Restriction: Employee & client use only, Open to pub upon request

P BEAVER AREA MEMORIAL LIBRARY*, 100 College Ave, 15009-2794. SAN 314-3015. Tel: 724-775-1132. FAX: 724-775-6982. *Dir,* Diane Wakefield; E-mail: dwakefield@beaverlibraries.org; *Asst Librn,* Mary Jane Ulmer; *Ch Serv,* Erin Funkhouser; Staff 3 (MLS 2, Non-MLS 1)
Founded 1948. Pop 18,833; Circ 177,647
Jan 2009-Dec 2009 Income $366,247, State $118,228, Provincial $31,500, City $42,350, County $17,300, Locally Generated Income $99,979, Other $56,890. Mats Exp $64,087, Books $50,556, Per/Ser (Incl. Access Fees) $3,414, AV Mat $10,117. Sal $208,027
Library Holdings: AV Mats 13,670; Bk Vols 52,286; Per Subs 67
Automation Activity & Vendor Info: (Cataloging) Innovative Interfaces, Inc; (Circulation) Innovative Interfaces, Inc; (OPAC) Innovative Interfaces, Inc
Wireless access
Mem of Beaver County Library System
Open Mon-Thurs 9:30-8, Fri & Sat 9:30-5
Friends of the Library Group

GL BEAVER COUNTY LAW LIBRARY*, Court House, 810 Third St, 15009. SAN 314-3023. Tel: 724-770-4659. FAX: 724-728-4133. Web Site: www.beavercountycourts.org/lawlibrary. *Dir,* Bette Sue Dengel; E-mail: bdengel@beavercountypa.gov; Staff 2 (MLS 1, Non-MLS 1)
Founded 1972
Jan 2006-Dec 2006 Income $140,800, County $138,800, Locally Generated Income $2,000. Mats Exp $82,000, Books $71,500, Per/Ser (Incl. Access Fees) $500, Electronic Ref Mat (Incl. Access Fees) $10,000. Sal $40,000 (Prof $38,500)
Library Holdings: Bk Titles 900; Bk Vols 25,000; Per Subs 20
Special Collections: Local court opinions & ordinances
Subject Interests: Pa legal practice
Function: ILL available
Open Mon-Fri 8:30-12 & 1-4:30
Restriction: Circ limited

M HERITAGE VALLEY HEALTH SYSTEM*, Health Sciences Library, 1000 Dutch Ridge Rd, 15009. SAN 326-3827. Tel: 724-773-1941. FAX: 724-728-7429. Web Site: www.heritagevalley.org. Staff 2 (MLS 1, Non-MLS 1)
Library Holdings: Bk Vols 3,600; Per Subs 195
Subject Interests: Internal med, Nursing, Oncology
Partic in Basic Health Sciences Library Network
Open Mon-Thurs 8-4, Fri 7-3

BEAVER FALLS

P CARNEGIE FREE LIBRARY*, 1301 Seventh Ave, 15010-4219. SAN 314-304X. Tel: 724-846-4340. FAX: 724-846-0370. Web Site: www.beaverlibraries.org/carnegiefree.htm. *Dir,* Jean Ann Barsotti; E-mail: jabarsotti@beaverlibraries.org; Staff 1 (MLS 1)
Founded 1902. Pop 19,127; Circ 45,000
Library Holdings: Bk Vols 50,000; Per Subs 204
Special Collections: Beaver Falls Historical Museum; Resource & Research Center for Local History
Subject Interests: Genealogy, Pa
Automation Activity & Vendor Info: (Circulation) Innovative Interfaces, Inc; (OPAC) Innovative Interfaces, Inc
Database Vendor: EBSCOhost, Innovative Interfaces, Inc
Wireless access
Mem of Beaver County Library System
Open Mon-Wed 10-7, Thurs & Sat 10-5:30

P CHIPPEWA LIBRARY INFORMATION CENTER*, 2811 Darlington Rd, 15010. Tel: 724-847-1450. FAX: 724-847-1449. Web Site: beaverlibraries.org. *Dir,* Heather Metheny; E-mail: hmetheny@beaverlibraries.org
Library Holdings: Bk Vols 3,000
Automation Activity & Vendor Info: (Circulation) Innovative Interfaces, Inc
Mem of Beaver County Library System
Open Mon & Wed 10-4, Tues 10-8, Thurs 1-8, Sat 10-2, Sun 1-5

C GENEVA COLLEGE*, McCartney Library, 3200 College Ave, 15010-3599. SAN 358-2930. Tel: 724-847-6563. Interlibrary Loan Service Tel: 724-847-6764. Reference Tel: 724-847-6740. Administration Tel: 724-847-6690. Automation Services Tel: 724-847-6637. FAX: 724-847-6687. Web Site: www.geneva.edu. *Dir,* John Doncevic; E-mail: jgdoncev@geneva.edu; *Asst Mgr,* Caren Turnbull; E-mail: cturnbul@geneva.edu; *Acq/Ser Librn,* Kimberly Kaufman; *Syst Librn,* John Delivuk; E-mail: jdelivuk@geneva.edu; *Ref & Instrul Serv, Instr Coordr,* Miriam Stauffer Fairfield; E-mail: mfairfie@geneva.edu; *Archivist,* Kae Hirschy Kirkwood; Tel: 724-847-6694, E-mail: kkirkwoo@geneva.edu; *Cat,* Kathryn Floyd; Tel: 724-847-6688, E-mail: kefloyd@geneva.edu; *Circ,* Sharon Glover; E-mail: sglover@geneva.edu; *Ser,* Robert Triance; Tel: 724-847-6693, E-mail: rtriance@geneva.edu; Staff 16 (MLS 6, Non-MLS 10)
Founded 1931. Enrl 2,100; Fac 131; Highest Degree: Master
Library Holdings: AV Mats 13,767; CDs 1,806; e-journals 25; Electronic Media & Resources 223,044; Bk Titles 173,029; Per Subs 857; Videos 2,380
Special Collections: Early American Imprints, microcard, microfiche; Geneva Author Shelf, bks published by Geneva College alumni, faculty, administration & students; Library of American Civilization, microfiche; Personal Library & Papers of Dr Clarence Macartney (Macartney Coll); Reformed Presbyterian Church (Covenanter Coll); Shaw Shoemaker Coll, microfiche
Automation Activity & Vendor Info: (Acquisitions) Ex Libris Group; (Cataloging) Ex Libris Group; (Circulation) Ex Libris Group; (Course Reserve) Ex Libris Group; (ILL) OCLC; (Media Booking) Ex Libris Group; (OPAC) Ex Libris Group; (Serials) Ex Libris Group
Database Vendor: Cambridge Scientific Abstracts, EBSCOhost, Gale Cengage Learning, LexisNexis, ProQuest
Function: Archival coll, Audio & video playback equip for onsite use, AV serv, Distance learning, ILL available, Online searches, Photocopying/Printing, Ref serv available, Satellite serv, Telephone ref
Publications: Miscellaneous Guides; Miscellaneous Pathfinders
Partic in Keystone Library Network; Lyrasis; OCLC Online Computer Library Center, Inc; Pennsylvania Academic Library Consortium, Inc (PALCI)
Open Mon-Thurs 8am-Midnight, Fri 8-8, Sat 10-5:30
Restriction: Access for corporate affiliates, Authorized scholars by appt, Open to fac, students & qualified researchers, Open to pub with supv only, Open to students, Open to students, fac & staff, Photo ID required for access, Restricted borrowing privileges

BEDFORD

P BEDFORD COUNTY LIBRARY*, 240 S Wood St, 15522. SAN 314-3066. Tel: 814-623-5010. FAX: 814-623-2676. Web Site: bedfordcountylibrary.com. *Dir,* Matt Godissart; E-mail: godissartm@bedfordcountylibrary.com; *Asst Dir/Ch,* Rebecca Claar; E-mail: claarb@bedfordcountylibrary.com; *Cataloger, Computer Tech,* Teresa McGinnes; E-mail: mcginnest@bedfordcountylibrary.com. Subject Specialists: *Children's lit,* Rebecca Claar; Staff 8 (MLS 1, Non-MLS 7)
Founded 1944. Pop 29,419; Circ 67,360
Jan 2009-Dec 2009 Income $280,770, State $140,831, County $82,875, Locally Generated Income $40,100, Other $16,964. Mats Exp $280,770, Books $36,500, Per/Ser (Incl. Access Fees) $4,100, AV Mat $5,000. Sal $204,855 (Prof $46,000)
Library Holdings: Audiobooks 916; DVDs 1,000; Bk Vols 39,000; Per Subs 26
Automation Activity & Vendor Info: (Acquisitions) Baker & Taylor; (Cataloging) Follett Software; (Circulation) Follett Software; (OPAC) Follett Software
Database Vendor: EBSCOhost
Wireless access
Mem of Bedford County Library System
Open Mon-Fri 9-7, Sat 9-2
Bookmobiles: 1. In Charge, Lorna Pokryfke. Bk vols 3,000

S PIONEER HISTORICAL SOCIETY OF BEDFORD COUNTY INC, Bedford County Historical Society & Pioneer Library, 6441 Lincoln Hwy, 15522. SAN 374-4930. Tel: 814-623-2011. FAX: 814-623-2011. E-mail:

bedfordhistory@embarqmail.com. Web Site: www.bedfordpahistory.com. *Exec Dir,* Gillian K Leach; Staff 2 (Non-MLS 2)
Subject Interests: Bedford County, County records, Genealogy, Local hist
Wireless access
Publications: The Pioneer Magazine (Quarterly)
Open Tues-Fri (Jan-March) 9-4; Mon-Fri (April-Dec) 9-4

BELLE VERNON

P BELLE VERNON PUBLIC LIBRARY*, 505 Speer St, 15012-1540. SAN 314-3074. Tel: 724-929-6642. FAX: 724-929-4197. E-mail: bvlibrary@comcast.net. Web Site: www.bellevernonlibrary.org. *Dir,* Bonnie Egros
Founded 1937. Circ 9,514
Library Holdings: Bk Vols 20,500; Per Subs 20
Automation Activity & Vendor Info: (Cataloging) Follett Software; (Circulation) Follett Software; (OPAC) Follett Software
Mem of Westmoreland County Federated Library System
Open Mon & Wed 11-5, Tues & Thurs 11-7, Sat 9-4 (9-1 Summer)

P ROSTRAVER PUBLIC LIBRARY*, 700 Plaza Dr, 15012. SAN 370-7466. Tel: 724-379-5511. FAX: 724-379-6090. E-mail: r.library@comcast.net. *Dir,* Ruth Ann Zupan; *Asst Dir,* Fran Rendulic; *Ch Serv,* Kelly Yoskosky
Founded 1958. Pop 12,000; Circ 4,828
Library Holdings: Bk Titles 20,000; Per Subs 25
Subject Interests: Local hist
Wireless access
Mem of Westmoreland County Federated Library System
Open Mon-Thurs 10-7, Fri 10-1, Sat 9-4
Friends of the Library Group

BELLEFONTE

S AMERICAN PHILATELIC RESEARCH LIBRARY, 100 Match Factory Pl, 16823. SAN 315-243X. Tel: 814-933-3803. FAX: 814-933-6128. E-mail: aprl@stamps.org. Web Site: www.stamplibrary.org. *Libr Dir,* Tara Murray; Staff 4 (MLS 3, Non-MLS 1)
Founded 1968
Library Holdings: Bk Titles 22,000; Per Subs 375
Special Collections: American First Day Cover Society Archives; Daniel Hines Air Mail Coll; Piper File; Richard B Graham Papers; Thomas J Alexander Papers; United States Stamp Files; W Wallace Cleland Papers
Subject Interests: Philately, Postal hist
Automation Activity & Vendor Info: (Cataloging) Inmagic, Inc.
Wireless access
Publications: Philatelic Literature Review (Quarterly)
Open Mon-Fri 8-4:30

GL CENTRE COUNTY LAW LIBRARY*, Court House, 3rd Flr, 16823. SAN 314-3082. Tel: 814-355-6754. FAX: 814-355-6707. *Dir,* Barbara Gallo; Tel: 814-355-6727, E-mail: bggallo@co.centre.pa.us
Library Holdings: Bk Vols 20,000; Per Subs 15
Database Vendor: LexisNexis
Open Mon-Fri 8:30-5

P CENTRE COUNTY LIBRARY & HISTORICAL MUSEUM*, 200 N Allegheny St, 16823-1601. SAN 358-3058. Tel: 814-355-1516. FAX: 814-355-2700. Interlibrary Loan Service FAX: 814-355-0334. Web Site: www.centrecountylibrary.org. *Exec Dir,* Lisa Erickson; E-mail: lerickson@centrecountylibrary.org; *Syst & Emerging Tech Librn,* Stefanie Gorzelsky; E-mail: sgorzelsky@centrecountylibrary.org; *Youth Serv Librn,* Katie Nicholson; E-mail: knicholson@centrecountylibrary.org; *Dir, Pub Serv,* Tracy Carey; E-mail: tcarey@centrecountylibrary.org; Staff 16 (MLS 5, Non-MLS 11)
Founded 1938. Pop 58,709; Circ 337,675
Library Holdings: Bk Titles 159,962; Bk Vols 199,553; Per Subs 256
Special Collections: County Documents; Genealogy (Spangler Coll). Oral History
Subject Interests: Hist
Automation Activity & Vendor Info: (Acquisitions) SirsiDynix; (Cataloging) SirsiDynix; (Circulation) SirsiDynix; (OPAC) SirsiDynix
Database Vendor: EBSCOhost
Partic in Interlibrary Delivery Service of Pennsylvania; OCLC Online Computer Library Center, Inc
Special Services for the Deaf - Accessible learning ctr
Open Mon-Thurs 9-8, Fri 9-6, Sat 9-5, Sun 1-5
Friends of the Library Group
Branches: 3
CENTRE HALL AREA BRANCH, 109 W Beryl St, Centre Hall, 16828. (Mail add: PO Box 492, Centre Hall, 16828-0492). Tel: 814-364-2580. FAX: 814-364-2598. *Br Mgr,* J A Babay; Staff 2 (Non-MLS 2)
Library Holdings: Bk Titles 13,684; Bk Vols 15,011; Per Subs 37
Open Mon, Wed & Fri 10-5, Tues & Thurs 4-5 & 6-8, Sat 9-1
EAST PENNS VALLEY BRANCH, Millheim Borough Bldg, 225 E Main St, Millheim, 16854. (Mail add: PO Box 70, Aaronsburg, 16820-0070), SAN 358-3082. Tel: 814-349-5328. FAX: 814-349-5288.
Library Holdings: Bk Titles 19,112; Bk Vols 21,290; Per Subs 39
Open Mon & Fri 10-5, Tues & Thurs 1-8, Sat 11-2
Friends of the Library Group
HOLT MEMORIAL, Nine W Pine St, Philipsburg, 16866, SAN 358-3112. Tel: 814-342-1987. FAX: 814-342-0530. *Librn,* Theresa Hutton; Staff 2 (MLS 1, Non-MLS 1)
Library Holdings: Bk Titles 21,290; Bk Vols 22,417; Per Subs 39
Open Mon & Thurs 1-8, Tues & Wed 9-5, Fri 1-5, Sat 9-2
Bookmobiles: 1. Dir, Lisa Erickson. Bk vols 3,000

S STATE CORRECTIONAL INSTITUTION*, Rockview Library, Box A, 16823-0820. Tel: 814-355-4874. *Librn,* Alan Riggall
Library Holdings: Bk Vols 14,000; Per Subs 50

BELLEVUE

P ANDREW BAYNE MEMORIAL LIBRARY*, 34 N Balph Ave, 15202-3297. SAN 314-3104. Tel: 412-766-7447. FAX: 412-766-3620. Web Site: www.baynelibrary.org. *Dir,* Denise Plaskon; E-mail: plaskond@einetwork.net; Staff 7 (MLS 1, Non-MLS 6)
Founded 1927. Pop 9,848; Circ 29,610
Library Holdings: AV Mats 2,400; Bk Vols 24,000; Per Subs 32; Talking Bks 2,300; Videos 1,600
Subject Interests: Bellevue genealogy, Bellevue hist
Wireless access
Mem of Allegheny County Library Association
Partic in Pittsburgh Regional Libr Consortium
Open Mon & Wed 10-8, Tues & Thurs 10-6, Fri 10-5, Sat 10-2, Sun 1-5
Friends of the Library Group

BELLWOOD

P BELLWOOD-ANTIS PUBLIC LIBRARY, 526 Main St, 16617-1910. SAN 314-3112. Tel: 814-742-8234. FAX: 814-742-8235. *Librn,* Hazel A Bilka; E-mail: hab@blwd.k12.pa.us; *Webmaster,* Mike Lingenfelter; E-mail: mwl@tuckahoe.blwd.k12.pa.us
Founded 1965. Circ 50,675
Library Holdings: Bk Vols 36,783; Per Subs 75
Automation Activity & Vendor Info: (Cataloging) Follett Software; (Circulation) Follett Software; (OPAC) Follett Software
Wireless access
Mem of Blair County Library System
Open Mon-Thurs 1-8, Sat 9-4

BENTLEYVILLE

P BENTLEYVILLE PUBLIC LIBRARY*, 931 Main St, 15314-1119. SAN 314-3120. Tel: 724-239-5122. FAX: 724-239-5196. E-mail: bentpub@bentcom.net. Web Site: www.bentcom.net/~bentpub.
Founded 1941. Pop 9,843; Circ 38,000
Library Holdings: Bk Titles 22,000; Per Subs 18
Automation Activity & Vendor Info: (Circulation) Follett Software
Database Vendor: EBSCOhost
Function: ILL available
Open Mon-Thurs 12-7:30, Fri 10-4, Sat 10-5

BERNVILLE

P BERNVILLE AREA COMMUNITY LIBRARY*, 6721 Bernville Rd, 19506. (Mail add: PO Box 580, 19506-0580). Tel: 610-488-1302. FAX: 270-479-1302. E-mail: bernvilleacl@berks.lib.pa.us. Web Site: www.berks.lib.pa.us/bernvilleacl. *Co-Dir,* Ruth E Darling; E-mail: ruadarling@berks.lib.pa.us
Founded 1994. Pop 4,652
Library Holdings: Bk Vols 13,000; Per Subs 20
Automation Activity & Vendor Info: (Cataloging) SirsiDynix; (Circulation) SirsiDynix
Wireless access
Function: Audio & video playback equip for onsite use, CD-ROM, Digital talking bks, Handicapped accessible, Homebound delivery serv, ILL available, Online searches, Orientations, Photocopying/Printing, Prog for adults, Prog for children & young adult, Ref serv available, Serves mentally handicapped consumers, Spoken cassettes & CDs, Summer reading prog, Telephone ref, VHS videos, Wheelchair accessible
Mem of Berks County Public Libraries
Special Services for the Deaf - Bks on deafness & sign lang; Closed caption videos; High interest/low vocabulary bks
Special Services for the Blind - Assistive/Adapted tech devices, equip & products; Audio mat; Bks on cassette; Bks on CD; Computer with voice synthesizer for visually impaired persons; Home delivery serv; Talking bks
Open Mon-Thurs 11-7, Sat 10-2, Sun 2-5

BERWICK

P MCBRIDE MEMORIAL LIBRARY*, 500 Market St, 18603. SAN 314-3139. Tel: 570-752-2241. FAX: 570-752-8893. Web Site: www.mcbridelibrary.org. *Dir, Libr Serv,* Position Currently Open; *Dir of Circ,* Alice Zaikoski; Staff 10 (MLS 1, Non-MLS 9)
Founded 1916. Pop 17,325; Circ 58,302
Library Holdings: CDs 190; DVDs 700; Bk Titles 40,000; Per Subs 60; Talking Bks 468; Videos 200
Special Collections: Landmark Audio Book Leasing; McNaughton Book Leasing, large print
Subject Interests: Pa hist
Wireless access
Function: ILL available
Open Mon & Tues 10-8, Wed 10-6, Thurs & Fri 12-6, Sat 10-2
Friends of the Library Group

BERWYN

P EASTTOWN LIBRARY & INFORMATION CENTER*, 720 First Ave, 19312-1769. SAN 314-3147. Tel: 610-644-0138. FAX: 610-251-9739. Web Site: www.easttownlibrary.org. *Dir,* Alan Silverman; E-mail: asilverman@ccls.org; *Head, Circ,* Susan Harris; E-mail: sharris@ccls.org; *Head, Ref,* Audrey Young; E-mail: ayoung@ccls.org; *Head, Tech Serv,* Susanne Martin; E-mail: smartin@ccls.org; *Head, Youth Serv,* Rebecca Sheridan; E-mail: bsheridan@ccls.org; Staff 14.5 (MLS 3.6, Non-MLS 10.9)
Founded 1905. Pop 10,477; Circ 299,615
Jan 2011-Dec 2011 Income $889,265, State $56,918, City $583,000, County $61,347, Locally Generated Income $188,000. Mats Exp $107,041, Books $75,677, Per/Ser (Incl. Access Fees) $6,209, AV Mat $21,555, Electronic Ref Mat (Incl. Access Fees) $3,600. Sal $626,469
Library Holdings: Audiobooks 1,960; CDs 2,237; DVDs 4,147; Large Print Bks 1,428; Bk Vols 56,909; Per Subs 110
Special Collections: Local History Coll
Automation Activity & Vendor Info: (Acquisitions) Innovative Interfaces, Inc; (Cataloging) Innovative Interfaces, Inc; (Circulation) Innovative Interfaces, Inc; (ILL) Innovative Interfaces, Inc; (OPAC) Innovative Interfaces, Inc; (Serials) Innovative Interfaces, Inc
Wireless access
Function: Adult bk club, Art exhibits, Bks on CD, Children's prog, Computer training, Computers for patron use, Copy machines, Electronic databases & coll, Exhibits, Handicapped accessible, Homebound delivery serv, ILL available, Music CDs, Notary serv, Online cat, Photocopying/Printing, Preschool outreach, Ref serv in person, Scanner, Story hour, Summer reading prog, Tax forms, Telephone ref
Publications: Easttown Library Newsletter (Online only)
Mem of Chester County Library System
Special Services for the Blind - Bks on CD; Internet workstation with adaptive software; Large print bks; Magnifiers
Open Mon-Thurs 9:30-9, Fri 9:30-6, Sat 10-5, Sun 1:30-5
Friends of the Library Group

BESSEMER

P FRANK D CAMPBELL MEMORIAL LIBRARY*, 17 S Main St, 16112-2535. SAN 314-3155. Tel: 724-667-7939. FAX: 724 667 0898. Web Site: fdclibrary.org. *Librn,* Lorena Williams; E-mail: lwilliams@fdclibrary.org; Staff 1 (Non-MLS 1)
Founded 1920. Pop 8,655
Library Holdings: AV Mats 660; Bks on Deafness & Sign Lang 4; Braille Volumes 2; CDs 160; DVDs 196; Large Print Bks 330; Bk Titles 14,700; Bk Vols 14,800; Per Subs 25; Videos 415
Database Vendor: SirsiDynix
Mem of Lawrence County Federated Library System
Open Mon & Wed 9:30-7, Tues 4-8, Thurs 11:30-7, Fri 9:30-5, Sat 9:30-4:30

BETHANY

P BETHANY PUBLIC LIBRARY*, Eight Court St, 18431-9516. SAN 314-6227. Tel: 570-253-4349. *Librn,* Tamara Murray; Staff 3 (Non-MLS 3)
Founded 1936. Pop 1,180; Circ 4,000
Library Holdings: DVDs 100; Large Print Bks 75; Bk Titles 6,200; Per Subs 25
Automation Activity & Vendor Info: (Cataloging) TLC (The Library Corporation); (Circulation) TLC (The Library Corporation)
Database Vendor: TLC (The Library Corporation)
Function: Archival coll, Audio & video playback equip for onsite use, BA reader (adult literacy), ILL available, Online searches, Photocopying/Printing, Prog for adults, Prog for children & young adult, Summer reading prog, Telephone ref, Workshops
Open Tues-Thurs 9-5, Wed 9-6, Fri 9-12, Sat 9-4
Friends of the Library Group

BETHEL

P BETHEL-TULPEHOCKEN PUBLIC LIBRARY*, 8601 Lancaster Ave, 19507. SAN 314-3163. Tel: 717-933-4060. FAX: 717-933-9655. E-mail: bethelpl@berks.lib.pa.us. Web Site: www.berks.lib.pa.us/bethelpl. *Dir,* Chris Ritter; *Asst Librn,* Eldyne Bordner; *Asst Librn,* Daphne Meyer; *Asst Librn,* Louise Schwartz
Founded 1963. Pop 7,456
Library Holdings: Bk Titles 15,000; Per Subs 60
Subject Interests: Behav sci, Educ, Environ studies, Local hist, Soc sci
Automation Activity & Vendor Info: (Cataloging) SirsiDynix; (Circulation) SirsiDynix; (OPAC) SirsiDynix
Mem of Berks County Public Libraries
Open Mon-Thurs 10-8, Fri 10-5, Sat 9-4

BETHEL PARK

P BETHEL PARK PUBLIC LIBRARY*, 5100 W Library Ave, 15102. SAN 314-3171. Tel: 412-835-2207. Reference Tel: 412-835-2207, Ext 246. FAX: 412-835-9360. E-mail: bethelpark@einetwork.net. Web Site: www.bethelparklibrary.org. *Dir,* Christine McIntosh; E-mail: mcintoshc@einetwork.net; *Ref Serv, Ad,* Robert Kalchthaler; E-mail: kalchthalerr@einetwork.net; *Tech Serv,* James Huttenhower; E-mail: huttenhowerj@einetwork.net; Staff 41 (MLS 11, Non-MLS 30)
Founded 1955. Pop 33,724; Circ 346,000
Library Holdings: Bk Titles 97,300; Bk Vols 101,425; Per Subs 123
Special Collections: Municipal Document Depository; US Document Depository
Subject Interests: Adult, Aging, Bus serv, Career, Employment, Investment serv, Literacy, Local hist, Parenting res, Pre-sch daycare, Teacher res ctr
Automation Activity & Vendor Info: (Acquisitions) Innovative Interfaces, Inc; (Cataloging) Innovative Interfaces, Inc; (Circulation) Innovative Interfaces, Inc; (Course Reserve) Innovative Interfaces, Inc; (ILL) Innovative Interfaces, Inc; (OPAC) Innovative Interfaces, Inc; (Serials) Innovative Interfaces, Inc
Wireless access
Function: Adult literacy prog, AV serv, Bus archives, Govt ref serv, Handicapped accessible, Home delivery & serv to Sr ctr & nursing homes, Homebound delivery serv, ILL available, Libr develop, Online searches, Photocopying/Printing, Prog for adults, Prog for children & young adult, Ref serv available, Summer reading prog, Telephone ref, Wheelchair accessible
Mem of Allegheny County Library Association
Special Services for the Blind - Reader equip
Open Mon-Thurs 9-9, Fri & Sat 9-5, Sun 1-5

R CHRIST UNITED METHODIST CHURCH LIBRARY*, 44 Highland Rd, 15102. SAN 314-318X. Tel: 412-835-6621. FAX: 412-835-9130. E-mail: mail@christumc.net. Web Site: christumc.net. Staff 1 (Non-MLS 1)
Founded 1960
Library Holdings: Bk Titles 3,741; Bk Vols 3,910; Per Subs 14
Open Mon-Fri 10-3

BETHLEHEM

P BETHLEHEM AREA PUBLIC LIBRARY, 11 W Church St, 18018. SAN 358-3147. Tel: 610-867-3761. Circulation Tel: 610-867-3761, Ext 203. Interlibrary Loan Service Tel: 610-867-3761, Ext 233. Reference Tel: 610-867-3761, Ext 224. FAX: 610-867-2767. E-mail: info@bapl.org. Web Site: www.bapl.org. *Exec Dir,* Josh Berk; E-mail: jberk@bapl.org; *Asst Dir,* Erin Poore; *Head, Acq, Syst & Tech,* Dan Solove; Tel: 610-867-3761, Ext 216, E-mail: dsolove@bapl.org; *Head, Info Serv,* M Rayah Levy; Tel: 610-867-3761, Ext 212, E-mail: mlevy@bapl.org; *Head, Youth Serv,* Edana Hoy; Tel: 610-867-3761, Ext 218, E-mail: ehoy@bapl.org; *ILL,* Valerie Mann; E-mail: vmann@bapl.org; Staff 33 (MLS 8, Non-MLS 25)
Founded 1901. Pop 118,458; Circ 792,435
Subject Interests: Local hist, Spanish
Automation Activity & Vendor Info: (Cataloging) Innovative Interfaces, Inc - Millenium; (Circulation) Innovative Interfaces, Inc - Millenium; (OPAC) Innovative Interfaces, Inc - Millenium; (Serials) Innovative Interfaces, Inc - Millenium
Wireless access
Partic in Lyrasis
Open Mon-Wed 9-9, Thurs & Fri 9-6, Sat 9-5
Friends of the Library Group
Branches: 1
SOUTH SIDE, 400 Webster St, 18015, SAN 358-3171. Tel: 610-867-7852. FAX: 610-867-9821. *Br Mgr,* Brenda Grow; E-mail: bgrow@bapl.org; *Adult Serv,* Position Currently Open; *Youth Serv,* Position Currently Open; Staff 4 (MLS 1, Non-MLS 3)
Subject Interests: Literacy, Spanish
Open Tues-Thurs 11-8, Wed & Sat 11-5
Friends of the Library Group
Bookmobiles: 1. Librn, Michael Henninger

S HISTORIC BETHLEHEM PARTNERSHIP LIBRARY*, 427 N New St, 18018-5802. (Mail add: 459 Old York Rd, 18018-5830), SAN 327-0947. Tel: 610-882-0450. Administration FAX: 610-882-0460. E-mail: info@historicbethlehem.org. Web Site: www.historicbethlehem.org. *Archivist, Librn,* Bonnie Stacy
Library Holdings: Bk Vols 3,000
Subject Interests: Decorative art, Local hist
Restriction: Non-circulating, Open by appt only

C LEHIGH UNIVERSITY*, Library & Technology Services, Fairchild-Martindale Library, Eight A E Packer Ave, 18015-3170. SAN 358-3295. Circulation Tel: 610-758-3030. Interlibrary Loan Service Tel: 610-758-3055. Reference Tel: 610-758-4357. Administration Tel: 610-758-3025. FAX: 610-758-6524. Web Site: www.lehigh.edu/library. *Vice Provost for Libr & Tech Serv,* Bruce M Taggart; E-mail: bmt2@lehigh.edu; *Admin Dir,* James Young; Tel: 610-758-4645, Fax: 610-758-3004; *Acq,* Helen Mack; Tel: 610-758-3035, E-mail: hpm0@lehigh.edu; *Cat,* Doreen Herold; Tel: 610-758-2639, E-mail: dok205@lehigh.edu; Staff 26 (MLS 18, Non-MLS 8)
Founded 1865. Enrl 5,600; Fac 410; Highest Degree: Doctorate
Library Holdings: Bk Titles 770,440; Bk Vols 1,145,980; Per Subs 12,000
Special Collections: Bayer Galleria of Rare Books; Lehigh Coll. State Document Depository; US Document Depository
Automation Activity & Vendor Info: (Acquisitions) SirsiDynix; (Cataloging) OCLC; (Circulation) SirsiDynix; (ILL) OCLC; (Media Booking) SirsiDynix; (OPAC) SirsiDynix
Publications: LTS Connection (Newsletter); Special Collections Flyer
Partic in Interlibrary Delivery Service of Pennsylvania; Lehigh Valley Association of Independent Colleges; OCLC Online Computer Library Center, Inc; Pa Academic Librs Connection Coun
Special Services for the Blind - Reader equip
Open Mon-Thurs 7:30am-2am, Fri 7:30am-10pm, Sat 10-10, Sun 10am-2am
Friends of the Library Group

Departmental Libraries:

LINDERMAN LIBRARY, 30 Library Dr, 18015, SAN 358-3325. Tel: 610-758-4506 (Special Collections). Reference Tel: 610-758-3050. FAX: 610-758-6091. E-mail: inspc@lehigh.edu. *Mgr Fac,* Kathleen Dugan; Tel: 610-758-4925, E-mail: kpk4@lehigh.edu
Founded 1878. Enrl 6,800; Highest Degree: Doctorate
Special Collections: History of Technology Coll. US Document Depository
Subject Interests: Eng, Hist, Humanities, Sci, Tech
Automation Activity & Vendor Info: (Acquisitions) SIRSI WorkFlows; (Cataloging) SIRSI WorkFlows; (Circulation) SIRSI WorkFlows; (Serials) SIRSI Unicorn
Database Vendor: Project MUSE
Function: Archival coll
Friends of the Library Group

R MORAVIAN ARCHIVES*, 41 W Locust St, 18018-2757. SAN 314-321X. Tel: 610-866-3255. FAX: 610-866-9210. E-mail: info@moravianchurcharchives.org. Web Site: www.moravianchurcharchives.org. *Archivist,* Dr Paul M Peucker; Staff 4 (MLS 3, Non-MLS 1)
Founded 1751
Library Holdings: Bk Vols 20,000; Per Subs 12
Special Collections: Bethlehem Gemeinbibliothek, Library of the Early Moravian Community of Bethlehem; History of Unitas Fratrum (Malin Library)
Subject Interests: Moravian Church hist
Wireless access
Open Mon-Fri 8:30-4:30
Restriction: In-house use for visitors, Not a lending libr
Friends of the Library Group

C MORAVIAN COLLEGE & MORAVIAN THEOLOGICAL SEMINARY*, Reeves Library, 1200 Main St, 18018-6650. SAN 314-3228. Tel: 610-861-1541. Circulation Tel: 610-861-1544. Interlibrary Loan Service Tel: 610-861-1545. Reference Tel: 610-861-1543. Administration Tel: 610-861-1540. FAX: 610-861-1577. Web Site: www.moravian.edu/public/reeves/index.htm. *Dir,* Rita Berk; E-mail: berkr@moravian.edu; *Archivist,* Jan Ballard; Tel: 610-861-1594, E-mail: mejsb01@moravian.edu; *Electronic Res,* Wendy Juniper; Tel: 610-861-1546, E-mail: wajuniper@moravian.edu; *Info Literacy,* Dorothy Glew; Tel: 610-861-1579, E-mail: medfg01@moravian.edu; *Pub Serv, Ref,* Bonnie Falla; Tel: 610-861-1676, E-mail: fallab@moravian.edu; *Ref Serv,* Beth Fuchs; Tel: 610-625-7965, E-mail: fuchsb@moravian.edu; *Tech Serv,* Linda LaPointe; Tel: 610-861-1547, E-mail: lapointe@moravian.edu; Staff 12 (MLS 6, Non-MLS 6)
Founded 1742. Enrl 1,789; Fac 108; Highest Degree: Master
Jul 2006-Jun 2007 Income $1,137,016. Mats Exp $492,770, Books $160,416, Per/Ser (Incl. Access Fees) $253,180, AV Mat $17,900, Electronic Ref Mat (Incl. Access Fees) $61,274. Sal $509,601 (Prof $286,199)
Library Holdings: CDs 1,975; DVDs 536; e-books 25,787; e-journals 14,378; Music Scores 13,350; Bk Titles 253,000; Bk Vols 263,020; Per Subs 1,037; Videos 2,467
Special Collections: History & Development of the Moravian Church (Groenfeldt Moravian Coll); Rare Books Coll
Subject Interests: Liberal arts, Relig, Theol
Automation Activity & Vendor Info: (Acquisitions) SirsiDynix; (Cataloging) SirsiDynix; (Circulation) SirsiDynix; (Course Reserve) SirsiDynix; (ILL) OCLC Connexion; (OPAC) SirsiDynix; (Serials) SirsiDynix
Database Vendor: ABC-CLIO, Cambridge Scientific Abstracts, EBSCOhost, Elsevier MDL, IOP, ISI Web of Knowledge, JSTOR, LexisNexis, OCLC FirstSearch, OCLC WorldShare Interlibrary Loan, ScienceDirect, SerialsSolutions, SirsiDynix, ValueLine, Westlaw, Wiley
Wireless access
Function: Archival coll, Handicapped accessible, ILL available, Online searches, Photocopying/Printing, Ref serv available, VHS videos, Wheelchair accessible
Partic in Lehigh Valley Association of Independent Colleges; OCLC Online Computer Library Center, Inc; Pennsylvania Academic Library Consortium, Inc (PALCI); Southeastern Pennsylvania Theological Library Association
Open Mon-Thurs 8am-Midnight, Fri 8am-10pm, Sat 10-10, Sun Noon-Midnight
Restriction: Restricted borrowing privileges
Friends of the Library Group

J NORTHAMPTON COMMUNITY COLLEGE, Paul & Harriett Mack Library, College Ctr, 3835 Green Pond Rd, 18020-7599. (Mail add: Northampton Community College, 3835 Green Pond Rd, 18020), SAN 314-3236. Tel: 610-861-3360. Reference Tel: 610-861-5359. Administration Tel: 610-861-5358. FAX: 610-861-5373. Web Site: www.northampton.edu/library.htm. *Dir, Libr Serv,* Sandra Sander; E-mail: ssander@northampton.edu; *Acq Librn,* Evonne Loomis; E-mail: eloomis@northampton.edu; *Cat Librn,* Anne Bittner; E-mail: abittner@northampton.edu; *Info Serv Librn,* Courtney Eger; E-mail: ceger@northampton.edu; *Info Serv Librn,* Audrey Harvey; E-mail: aharvey@northampton.edu; *Info Serv Librn,* Lauri Miller; E-mail: lmiller@northampton.edu; *Info Serv Librn,* Elehna Shores; E-mail: eshores@northampton.edu; Staff 6.5 (MLS 6, Non-MLS 0.5)
Founded 1967. Enrl 13,000; Fac 1,200; Highest Degree: Associate
Library Holdings: Audiobooks 275; CDs 261; DVDs 2,572; e-books 18,599; Electronic Media & Resources 56; Bk Titles 58,050; Bk Vols 67,497; Per Subs 201
Special Collections: College Archives; Dornish Coll of Children's Materials; Foundations & Grants
Automation Activity & Vendor Info: (Acquisitions) SIRSI WorkFlows; (Cataloging) SIRSI WorkFlows; (Circulation) SIRSI WorkFlows; (ILL) OCLC; (OPAC) SIRSI WorkFlows; (Serials) SIRSI WorkFlows
Database Vendor: ABC-CLIO, Alexander Street Press, Baker & Taylor, Cinahl, CQ Press, CRC Press/Taylor & Francis Group, CredoReference, EBSCOhost, Facts on File, Foundation Center, Gale Cengage Learning, Hoovers, JSTOR, Knovel, McGraw-Hill, Mergent Online, ProQuest, SirsiDynix, Springshare, LLC, Westlaw
Wireless access
Partic in Lyrasis
Open Mon-Thurs 7:30am-10pm, Fri 7:30-5, Sat 8:30-4:30, Sun 1-8

Departmental Libraries:

MONROE CAMPUS LIBRARY, Keystone Hall, 2411 Rte 715, Tannersville, 18372. Tel: 570-369-1810. *Mgr,* Emily Mroff
Open Mon-Thurs 8am-9pm, Fri 8-5, Sat 9-4:30

M ST LUKE'S HOSPITAL & HEALTH NETWORK*, W L Estes Jr Memorial Library, 801 Ostrum St, 18015. SAN 358-335X. Tel: 610-954-4650. Interlibrary Loan Service Tel: 610-954-4652. FAX: 610-954-4651. E-mail: estes.library@slhn.org. Web Site: www.mystlukesonline.org/locations/library-services/index.aspx. *Dir, Libr Serv,* Maria D Collette; E-mail: colletm@slhn.org; *Asst Dir,* Diane Frantz; Tel: 610-954-3407, E-mail: frantzd@slhn.org; *Librn,* Vanessa Reis-Bradley; Tel: 610-770-8355, Fax: 610-770-8736, E-mail: reisbrv@slhn.org; Staff 5 (MLS 3, Non-MLS 2)
Founded 1947
Jul 2007-Jun 2008 Income $603,980. Mats Exp $378,380, Books $20,940, Per/Ser (Incl. Access Fees) $186,294, Micro $18,900, AV Mat $4,500, Electronic Ref Mat (Incl. Access Fees) $60,706, Presv $3,560. Sal $225,600 (Prof $153,200)
Library Holdings: Audiobooks 10; CDs 100; DVDs 200; e-books 25; e-journals 75; Bk Titles 8,300; Bk Vols 9,500; Per Subs 300; Videos 250
Special Collections: Nursing (Historical Coll)
Subject Interests: Allied health, Med, Nursing, Surgery
Automation Activity & Vendor Info: (Cataloging) LibraryWorld, Inc; (Circulation) LibraryWorld, Inc; (OPAC) LibraryWorld, Inc
Database Vendor: Checkpoint Systems, Inc, Cinahl, EBSCO Information Services, EBSCOhost, Medlib, Medline, Micromedex, Natural Standard,

OCLC FirstSearch, OVID Technologies, PubMed, STAT!Ref (Teton Data Systems), UpToDate
Wireless access
Partic in Cooperating Hospital Libraries of the Lehigh Valley Area; Greater NE Regional Med Libr Program; National Network of Libraries of Medicine
Open Mon-Thurs 8-8, Fri 8-5:30

S URBAN RESEARCH & DEVELOPMENT CORP LIBRARY*, 28 W Broad St, 18018. SAN 314-3244. Tel: 610-865-0701. FAX: 610-868-7613. E-mail: urdc@urdc.com. *Pres,* Martin C Gilchrist; *Librn,* Charlie Schmehl
Founded 1968
Library Holdings: Bk Titles 3,500; Per Subs 25
Subject Interests: Archit, Art, Econ, Eng, Geog, Graphic design, Landscape archit, Regional planning, Soc sci, Urban planning
Restriction: Non-circulating to the pub

BIGLERVILLE

P HARBAUGH-THOMAS LIBRARY*, 50 W York St, 17307. (Mail add: PO Box 277, 17307-0277). Tel: 717-677-6257. FAX: 717-677-6357. Web Site: www.adamslibrary.org/ht. *Librn,* Jessica Laganosky; E-mail: jessical@adamslibrary.org
Library Holdings: Bk Vols 20,000
Automation Activity & Vendor Info: (Circulation) TLC (The Library Corporation)
Mem of Adams County Library System
Open Mon 12-6, Tues & Thurs 12-8, Wed & Fri 10-6, Sat 9-5

BIRDSBORO

P BOONE AREA LIBRARY, 129 N Mill St, 19508-2340. SAN 314-3252. Tel: 610-582-5666. FAX: 610-582-6826. E-mail: boone@berks.lib.pa.us. Web Site: booneareallibrary.com. *Dir,* Wayne R Lahr; *Asst Librn,* Shelley E Grapes; *Asst Librn,* Lisa Strouse; *Children's/Teen Coordr,* Lisa Kraljevich; Staff 1 (MLS 1)
Founded 1963. Pop 21,249
Library Holdings: Bk Vols 26,341; Per Subs 65
Automation Activity & Vendor Info: (Cataloging) SirsiDynix; (Circulation) SirsiDynix; (OPAC) SirsiDynix
Database Vendor: SirsiDynix
Wireless access
Function: 24/7 Online cat, Activity rm, Adult bk club, Audiobks via web, Bk club(s), Bks on CD, Children's prog, Computer training, Computers for patron use, Copy machines, e-mail & chat, e-mail serv, E-Reserves, Electronic databases & coll, Fax serv, Free DVD rentals, Handicapped accessible, ILL available, Instruction & testing, Magazines, Mail & tel request accepted, Movies, Mus passes, Music CDs, Online cat, Online ref, Online searches, Outside serv via phone, mail, e-mail & web, OverDrive digital audio bks, Photocopying/Printing, Preschool outreach, Preschool reading prog, Prog for adults, Prog for children & young adult, Pub access computers, Ref serv available, Ref serv in person, Scanner, Summer reading prog, Tax forms, Telephone ref
Mem of Berks County Public Libraries
Open Mon 10-8, Tues & Thurs 1-8, Wed, Fri & Sat 9-4

BLACK LICK

P BURRELL TOWNSHIP LIBRARY*, 190 Park Dr, 15716. (Mail add: PO Box 424, 15716), SAN 324-3702. Tel: 724-248-7122. FAX: 724-248-1803. E-mail: burrelltownshiplibrary@gmail.com. Web Site: www.burrelltownshiplibrary.org. *Dir,* Kate Abner
Founded 1977. Pop 3,669
Library Holdings: Bk Titles 15,000; Per Subs 29
Wireless access
Open Tues 10-6, Wed 11-5, Thurs 1-7, Fri 1-5, Sat 9-3
Friends of the Library Group

BLAIN

P COMMUNITY LIBRARY OF WESTERN PERRY COUNTY*, Main St, 17006. (Mail add: PO Box 56, 17006-0056). Tel: 717-536-3761. FAX: 717-536-3761. *Dir,* Lois Parker; Staff 3 (MLS 1, Non-MLS 2)
Pop 3,148; Circ 14,916
Library Holdings: Bk Titles 8,846; Bk Vols 9,190; Per Subs 15; Talking Bks 98; Videos 167
Wireless access
Open Tues, Thurs & Fri 2-7, Wed & Sat 8-2

BLAIRSVILLE

P BLAIRSVILLE PUBLIC LIBRARY*, 113 N Walnut St, 15717-1348. SAN 314-3260. Tel: 724-459-6077. FAX: 724-459-6097. Web Site: www.bssd.k12.pa.us/bplib. *Librn,* Joni Melnick
Pop 3,595; Circ 75,000
Library Holdings: Bk Vols 26,000; Per Subs 52
Automation Activity & Vendor Info: (Cataloging) Follett Software; (Circulation) Follett Software; (OPAC) Follett Software
Open Mon & Wed 1:30-8:30, Tues & Fri 1:30-5, Wed & Sat 10-5

BLOOMSBURG

P BLOOMSBURG PUBLIC LIBRARY*, 225 Market St, 17815-1726. SAN 314-3287. Tel: 570-784-0883. FAX: 570-784-8541. E-mail: bloompl@epix.net. Web Site: www.bloomsburgpl.org. *Dir,* Hal Pratt; *Asst Librn,* Kathleen Taylor; *Ch Serv,* Karen Roszel; Staff 9 (MLS 1, Non-MLS 8)
Founded 1889. Pop 19,017; Circ 132,500
Library Holdings: Bk Titles 33,000; Per Subs 90
Special Collections: Genealogy Coll
Open Mon-Thurs 9-8, Fri 9-5, Sat 9-1
Friends of the Library Group

C BLOOMSBURG UNIVERSITY OF PENNSYLVANIA*, Harvey A Andruss Library, 400 E Second St, 17815-1301. SAN 314-3295. Tel: 570-389-4224. Circulation Tel: 570-389-4205. Interlibrary Loan Service Tel: 570-389-4218. Reference Tel: 570-389-4204. FAX: 570-389-3066. Interlibrary Loan Service FAX: 570-389-3895. Web Site: www.library.bloomu.edu. *Interim Dir, Libr Serv,* Dr Magolis David; Tel: 570-389-4921; *Res Librn,* Darla Bressler; *Res Librn,* Michael J Coffta; *Archivist & Spec Coll Librn, Historian, Res Librn,* Robert A Dunkelberger; *Database Coordr, Res Librn,* Linda Neyer; *Res Librn,* Kathryn Yelinek; *Coordr, Cat,* Marilou Z Hinchcliff. Subject Specialists: *Educ,* Darla Bressler; *Bus,* Michael J Coffta; *Health sci, Sci,* Linda Neyer; *Govt doc,* Kathryn Yelinek; Staff 19 (MLS 7, Non-MLS 12)
Founded 1839. Enrl 10,091; Fac 520; Highest Degree: Doctorate
Jul 2009-Jun 2010. Mats Exp $2,965,795, Books $201,205, Per/Ser (Incl. Access Fees) $1,079,906, Presv $19,962. Sal $1,195,933 (Prof $693,865)
Library Holdings: AV Mats 13,565; e-books 12,201; Microforms 2,136,526; Bk Titles 611,044; Per Subs 52,438
Special Collections: Art Exhibit Catalogs; Bloomsburg University Archives; Covered Bridges Newbery & Caldecott Awards (Elinor R Keefer Coll). State Document Depository; US Document Depository
Subject Interests: Children's lit
Automation Activity & Vendor Info: (Acquisitions) Ex Libris Group; (Cataloging) Ex Libris Group; (Circulation) Ex Libris Group; (Course Reserve) Ex Libris Group; (ILL) OCLC ILLiad; (Media Booking) Ex Libris Group; (OPAC) Ex Libris Group; (Serials) Ex Libris Group
Database Vendor: ABC-CLIO, ACM (Association for Computing Machinery), Agricola, American Psychological Association (APA), EBSCO - WebFeat, EBSCOhost, JSTOR, LexisNexis, OCLC FirstSearch, OVID Technologies, ProQuest, RefWorks, Sage, Thomson - Web of Science, WebMD, Westlaw, Wiley, Wiley InterScience, Wilson - Wilson Web, YBP Library Services
Wireless access
Partic in Interlibrary Delivery Service of Pennsylvania; Lyrasis; OCLC Online Computer Library Center, Inc; Pennsylvania Academic Library Consortium, Inc (PALCI)
Open Mon-Thurs 7:30am-Midnight, Fri 7:30-4:30, Sat 9-5, Sun Noon-Midnight
Friends of the Library Group

S COLUMBIA COUNTY HISTORICAL & GENEALOGICAL SOCIETY LIBRARY*, 225 Market St, 17815-0360. (Mail add: PO Box 360, 17815-0360), SAN 314-3309. Tel: 570-784-1600. E-mail: research@colcohist-gensoc.org. Web Site: www.colcohist-gensoc.org. *Exec Dir,* Bonnie Lou Farver
Founded 1914
Library Holdings: Bk Titles 2,000
Subject Interests: Columbia County, Genealogy, Local hist, Mat culture
Function: Handicapped accessible
Publications: Historical Leaflets; Monographs; The Columbian
Open Tues & Fri 9-3, Thurs 9-7:30, Sat 9-11:30
Restriction: Non-circulating to the pub

P COLUMBIA COUNTY TRAVELING LIBRARY*, 702 Sawmill Rd, Ste 101, 17815. SAN 320-8125. Tel: 570-387-8782. E-mail: cctl@epix.net. Web Site: www.cctlibrary.org. *Libr Dir,* Dr Lydia Kegler; Staff 2 (MLS 1, Non-MLS 1)
Founded 1941. Pop 30,000; Circ 22,000
Jan 2012-Dec 2012 Income $98,094, State $21,531, County $64,863, Locally Generated Income $11,700. Mats Exp $12,000, Books $11,000, Per/Ser (Incl. Access Fees) $100, AV Mat $900. Sal $56,000 (Prof $27,456)
Library Holdings: Audiobooks 400; DVDs 150; Large Print Bks 2,600; Bk Vols 22,000; Per Subs 7
Automation Activity & Vendor Info: (Cataloging) Book Systems; (Circulation) Book Systems; (OPAC) Book Systems
Special Services for the Blind - Assistive/Adapted tech devices, equip & products
Open Mon-Fri 8-3

Friends of the Library Group
Bookmobiles: 1

BLOSSBURG

P BLOSSBURG MEMORIAL LIBRARY, 307 Main St, 16912. SAN 314-3317. Tel: 570-638-2197. FAX: 570-638-2197. E-mail: blosslib@epix.net. *Dir,* Elisabeth Miranda; Staff 2 (Non-MLS 2)
Founded 1946. Pop 3,899; Circ 11,977
Library Holdings: Audiobooks 379; AV Mats 855; CDs 54; DVDs 577; Large Print Bks 445; Bk Vols 13,149; Per Subs 43; Videos 278
Automation Activity & Vendor Info: (Cataloging) AmLib Library Management System; (Circulation) AmLib Library Management System; (OPAC) AmLib Library Management System
Wireless access
Function: Adult bk club, CD-ROM, Children's prog, Computer training, Computers for patron use, Copy machines, e-mail & chat, Electronic databases & coll, Fax serv, Free DVD rentals, Holiday prog, ILL available, Online cat, Online ref, Preschool outreach, Prog for adults, Prog for children & young adult, Pub access computers, Ref serv available, Senior outreach, Story hour, Summer reading prog, VHS videos
Mem of Potter-Tioga Library System
Open Mon-Thurs 12-7, Fri 12-5, Sat 9-3
Friends of the Library Group

BLUE BELL

J MONTGOMERY COUNTY COMMUNITY COLLEGE*, The Brendlinger Library, 340 DeKalb Pike, 19422-0796. SAN 314-3333. Tel: 215-641-6300, 215-641-6596. FAX: 215-619-7182. E-mail: libraries@mc3.edu. Web Site: www.mc3.edu/. *Dir, Libr Serv,* Diane Lovelace; *Asst Dir, Access Serv,* Deborah Dulepski
Founded 1966. Enrl 11,000
Special Collections: College Archives. US Document Depository
Automation Activity & Vendor Info: (Acquisitions) SIRSI Unicorn; (Cataloging) OCLC Connexion; (Circulation) SIRSI WorkFlows; (Course Reserve) SIRSI WorkFlows; (ILL) OCLC ILLiad; (Media Booking) SIRSI WorkFlows; (OPAC) SIRSI-iLink; (Serials) SIRSI WorkFlows
Database Vendor: ABC-CLIO, CQ Press, EBSCOhost, JSTOR, LexisNexis, Newsbank, OCLC FirstSearch, ProQuest, RefWorks, Wilson - Wilson Web
Wireless access
Function: Archival coll, Art exhibits, Audio & video playback equip for onsite use
Partic in OCLC Online Computer Library Center, Inc; Tri-State College Library Cooperative

R REFORMED EPISCOPAL SEMINARY*, Fred C Kuehner Memorial Library, 826 Second Ave, 19422. SAN 314-9919. Tel: 610-292-9852. FAX: 610-292-9853. Web Site: library.lts.org/septla/pts.htm. *Librn,* Jonathan S Riches; E-mail: jonathan.riches@reseminary.edu
Founded 1887
Library Holdings: Bk Vols 21,000
Subject Interests: British church hist, Liturgy, Puritans, Reformed Episcopal church
Partic in Southeastern Pennsylvania Theological Library Association
Open Mon-Thurs 8am-9pm

S UNISYS CORP*, Corporate Library, One Unisys Way, Ste E3-112, 19424. SAN 328-7211. Tel: 215-986-2324. *Mgr,* Susan H Hahn; Staff 2 (MLS 2)
Founded 1952
Library Holdings: Bk Vols 7,000; Per Subs 200
Special Collections: Market Research; Photo Archives
Subject Interests: Electronics, Mkt

P WISSAHICKON VALLEY PUBLIC LIBRARY*, 650 Skippack Pike, 19422. SAN 358-2906. Tel: 215-643-1320. Circulation Tel: 215-643-1320, Ext 10. Reference Tel: 215-643-1320, Ext 19. FAX: 215-643-6611. E-mail: library@wvpl.org. Web Site: www.wvpl.org. *Dir,* David J Roberts; Tel: 215-643-1320, Ext 11, E-mail: droberts@wvpl.org; *Asst Librn, Ch Serv,* Kathleen Berry; Tel: 215-643-1320, Ext 14, E-mail: kberry@wvpl.org; *Asst Librn,* Gertrude Buri; Tel: 215-643-1320, Ext 12, E-mail: tburi@wvpl.org; *Circ,* Marva Jones; Staff 40 (MLS 6, Non-MLS 34)
Founded 1934. Pop 35,410; Circ 398,000
Jul 2005-Jun 2006 Income (Main Library and Branch(s)) $1,214,000, State $173,000, City $900,000, Locally Generated Income $141,000. Mats Exp $205,700, Books $145,450, Per/Ser (Incl. Access Fees) $11,385, AV Mat $48,865. Sal $607,655
Library Holdings: AV Mats 12,857; CDs 1,870; DVDs 2,363; Large Print Bks 2,102; Bk Vols 117,797; Per Subs 220; Talking Bks 4,383; Videos 4,216
Automation Activity & Vendor Info: (Cataloging) TLC (The Library Corporation); (Circulation) SirsiDynix; (OPAC) SirsiDynix
Database Vendor: EBSCOhost
Function: ILL available
Open Mon-Thurs 10-9, Fri & Sat 10-5, Sun 1-4
Friends of the Library Group
Branches: 1
AMBLER BRANCH, 209 Race St, Ambler, 19002, SAN 358-2876. Tel: 215-646-1072. FAX: 215-654-0161. E-mail: reference@wvpl.org. *Librn,* Lois McMullen; Staff 5 (MLS 5)
Founded 1923. Pop 35,410; Circ 110,000
Library Holdings: Bk Titles 37,500; Per Subs 74
Subject Interests: Art, Educ, Natural sci
Publications: Annual Report
Open Mon-Thurs 10-9, Fri & Sat 10-5
Friends of the Library Group

BLUE RIDGE SUMMIT

P ALEXANDER HAMILTON MEMORIAL FREE LIBRARY*, Blue Ridge Summit Free Library, 13676 Monterey Lane, 17214. (Mail add: PO Box 34, 17214-0034), SAN 314-335X. Tel: 717-794-2240. FAX: 717-794-5929. E-mail: brsummit@yahoo.com. Web Site: www.brsfl.org. *Librn,* Nancy L Bert; *Asst Librn,* Norma Hudson; Staff 2 (Non-MLS 2)
Founded 1922. Pop 9,000
Library Holdings: Bk Vols 26,333; Per Subs 20
Automation Activity & Vendor Info: (Cataloging) Follett Software; (Circulation) Follett Software
Open Mon-Thurs 3-8, Sat 10-4

BOYERTOWN

P BOYERTOWN COMMUNITY LIBRARY*, 29 E Philadelphia Ave, 19512-1124. SAN 376-5741. Tel: 610-369-0496. FAX: 610-369-0542. E-mail: boyertowncl@berks.lib.pa.us. Web Site: www.berks.lib.pa.us/boyertowncl. *Libr Dir,* Lindsey Riegner; *Head, Circ,* Sue Elphick; *Children's Prog Coordr,* Lopez Susan; *Asst Circ Mgr,* Debra Focht; Staff 9 (MLS 1, Non-MLS 8)
Founded 1989. Pop 32,060; Circ 215,220
Jan 2012-Dec 2012 Income $329,364. Mats Exp $229,531. Sal $124,535 (Prof $28,210)
Library Holdings: Audiobooks 2,284; CDs 781; DVDs 3,271; e-books 4,734; e-books 4,734; Electronic Media & Resources 20; Electronic Media & Resources 20; Bk Vols 33,688; Per Subs 78
Automation Activity & Vendor Info: (Circulation) Horizon; (OPAC) Horizon
Wireless access
Function: Adult bk club, After school storytime, Audiobks via web, Bk club(s), Bks on CD, Children's prog, Computers for patron use, Copy machines, Electronic databases & coll, Fax serv, Free DVD rentals, Handicapped accessible, ILL available, Mus passes, Music CDs, Online cat, Online searches, OverDrive digital audio bks, Passport agency, Photocopying/Printing, Prog for adults, Prog for children & young adult, Pub access computers, Spoken cassettes & CDs, Spoken cassettes & DVDs, Story hour, Summer reading prog, Tax forms, Teen prog, Telephone ref, VHS videos, Web-catalog, Wheelchair accessible, Writing prog
Mem of Berks County Public Libraries
Open Mon-Wed 10-8, Thurs-Sat 10-5
Friends of the Library Group

S CABOT PERFORMANCE MATERIALS LIBRARY*, County Line Rd, 19512. SAN 314-3368. Tel: 610-369-8414. FAX: 610-367-2068. *Librn,* Joyce Bollard; Staff 1 (Non-MLS 1)
Library Holdings: Bk Titles 1,142; Bk Vols 1,236; Per Subs 25
Subject Interests: Alloys, Chem, Metals
Partic in Dialog Corp
Restriction: Staff use only

BRADDOCK

P BRADDOCK CARNEGIE LIBRARY*, 419 Library St, 15104-1609. Tel: 412-351-5356. FAX: 412-351-6810. Web Site: www.braddocklibrary.org. *Exec Dir,* Vicki Vargo; Staff 2 (MLS 2)
Pop 18,307; Circ 46,810
Library Holdings: Bk Titles 31,261; Bk Vols 32,690; Per Subs 58; Talking Bks 538; Videos 1,170
Automation Activity & Vendor Info: (Cataloging) Innovative Interfaces, Inc; (Circulation) Innovative Interfaces, Inc; (OPAC) Innovative Interfaces, Inc
Database Vendor: Innovative Interfaces, Inc
Mem of Allegheny County Library Association
Open Mon-Thurs 2-7, Sat 10-4

BRADFORD

P BRADFORD AREA PUBLIC LIBRARY*, 67 W Washington St, 16701-1234. SAN 314-3392. Tel: 814-362-6527. FAX: 814-362-4168. E-mail: bapublib@atlanticbb.net. Web Site: www.bradfordlibrary.org. *ILL,* Cathy Doyle; Staff 6 (Non-MLS 6)
Founded 1901. Pop 21,772; Circ 54,159

Library Holdings: AV Mats 3,043; CDs 1,285; Large Print Bks 3,915; Bk Titles 55,258; Per Subs 54; Talking Bks 1,216; Videos 1,041
Special Collections: Local Authors Coll; Local Newspaper (1878-present), micro
Automation Activity & Vendor Info: (Cataloging) Follett Software; (Circulation) Follett Software; (ILL) Follett Software; (OPAC) Follett Software
Wireless access
Open Mon & Wed 10-7, Tues & Thurs-Sat 10-5
Friends of the Library Group

M BRADFORD REGIONAL MEDICAL CENTER*, Huff Memorial Library, 116 Interstate Pkwy, 16701. SAN 324-640X. Tel: 814-362-8572. FAX: 814-362-8632. Web Site: www.brmc.com. *In Charge,* Anita J Herbert; Staff 1 (Non-MLS 1)
Library Holdings: Bk Titles 1,126; Bk Vols 1,291; Per Subs 47
Restriction: Staff use only

C UNIVERSITY OF PITTSBURGH AT BRADFORD*, T Edward & Tullah Hanley Library, 300 Campus Dr, 16701. SAN 314-3406. Tel: 814-362-7610. Reference Tel: 814-362-7615. FAX: 814-362-7688. Web Site: www.library.pitt.edu/bradford. *Dir,* Marietta A Frank; Tel: 814-362-7614, E-mail: marietta@pitt.edu; *Ref & Instruction Librn,* Kimberly Bailey; E-mail: hanold@pitt.edu; *Acq, Archivist,* Dianna Beaver; E-mail: dbeaver@pitt.edu; *Cat, ILL,* Jean Luciano; E-mail: jluciano@pitt.edu; *Cat, Ser,* Sherri Lothridge; E-mail: sherril@pitt.edu; *Circ,* Dina Whitehouse; E-mail: did13@pitt.edu; Staff 6 (MLS 2, Non-MLS 4)
Founded 1963. Enrl 1,500; Fac 141; Highest Degree: Bachelor
Library Holdings: Audiobooks 1,190; AV Mats 4,323; CDs 620; DVDs 1,300; Microforms 14,125; Bk Vols 93,522; Per Subs 134; Videos 1,066
Special Collections: Fesenmyer Scrap Books; Forres Stewart Photos; Lowenthal Coll; Pennsylvania Civilian Conservation Corps Material
Subject Interests: Am studies (lit & hist), Behav sci, Bus admin, Criminal law & justice, Environ studies, Liberal arts, Soc sci, Sports
Automation Activity & Vendor Info: (Acquisitions) Ex Libris Group; (Cataloging) Ex Libris Group; (Circulation) Ex Libris Group; (ILL) Ex Libris Group; (OPAC) Ex Libris Group; (Serials) Ex Libris Group
Wireless access
Function: Ref serv available
Publications: Hanley Happenings (Newsletter)
Partic in OCLC Online Computer Library Center, Inc; Pennsylvania Academic Library Consortium, Inc (PALCI)
Open Mon-Thurs 8am-11:30pm, Fri 8-5, Sat 1-5, Sun 1-11:30
Restriction: Open to pub for ref & circ; with some limitations, Restricted access
Friends of the Library Group

BRIDGEVILLE

P BRIDGEVILLE PUBLIC LIBRARY*, 505 McMillen St, 15017. SAN 314-3414. Tel: 412-221-3737. FAX: 412-220-8124. Web Site: www.bridgevillelibrary.org. *Pres,* Nino Petrocelli, Sr; *Dir,* Donna Taylor; E-mail: taylord@cincwork.net; Staff 2 (MLS 1.5, Non-MLS 0.5)
Founded 1962. Pop 5,341; Circ 65,177
Library Holdings: Bk Titles 18,878
Automation Activity & Vendor Info: (Cataloging) Innovative Interfaces, Inc; (Circulation) Innovative Interfaces, Inc
Database Vendor: SirsiDynix
Wireless access
Mem of Allegheny County Library Association
Partic in Electronic Info Network (eiNetwork)
Open Mon-Thurs 9-8, Fri-Sat 9-5, Sun (Sept-May) 1-5
Friends of the Library Group

BRISTOL

P MARGARET R GRUNDY MEMORIAL LIBRARY*, 680 Radcliffe St, 19007-5199. SAN 314-3422. Tel: 215-788-7891. FAX: 215-788-4976. Web Site: www.buckslib.org/libraries/bristol. *Dir,* Position Currently Open; *Adult Serv,* Denise Kolber; *Ch Serv,* Shirley Hickey; Staff 17 (MLS 5, Non-MLS 12)
Founded 1966. Pop 22,161; Circ 161,590
Library Holdings: AV Mats 1,082; Large Print Bks 192; Bk Titles 71,911; Bk Vols 74,681; Per Subs 121; Talking Bks 91; Videos 310
Special Collections: Bucks County Census 1790-1910, microfilm; Bucks County Courier Times 1911-Present, microfilm
Subject Interests: Local hist
Automation Activity & Vendor Info: (Acquisitions) SirsiDynix; (Circulation) SirsiDynix; (OPAC) SirsiDynix
Open Mon-Thurs 11-9, Fri & Sat 11-4

J PENNCO TECH LIBRARY*, 3815 Otter St, 19007. SAN 314-3430. Tel: 215-824-3200. Toll Free Tel: 800-575-9399. FAX: 215-785-1945. E-mail: placement@penncotech.edu. Web Site: www.penncotech.edu. *Librn,* Deborah Rexon; Staff 1 (MLS 1)
Founded 1973. Enrl 400; Fac 45; Highest Degree: Associate
Library Holdings: Bk Titles 2,450; Bk Vols 3,000; Per Subs 33
Special Collections: Automotive Technology; Medical Secretary; Pharmacy Technician
Open Mon, Wed & Thurs 8-4 & 6:30-8:30, Tues & Fri 8-4
Restriction: Open to students, fac & staff

BROCKWAY

P MENGLE MEMORIAL LIBRARY*, 324 Main St, 15824-0324. SAN 314-3457. Tel: 814-265-8245. FAX: 814-265-1125. E-mail: mengle@usachoice.net. Web Site: menglelibrary.org/. *Asst Dir,* Leslie Barr; *Librn,* Darlene Marshall. Subject Specialists: *Prog, Tech,* Leslie Barr; Staff 2 (MLS 2)
Founded 1965. Pop 7,900; Circ 39,000
Jan 2007-Dec 2007 Income $130,530, State $42,618, City $5,300, County $5,833, Locally Generated Income $26,479, Other $50,300. Mats Exp $13,000, Books $10,000, Per/Ser (Incl. Access Fees) $3,000. Sal $87,000 (Prof $28,500)
Library Holdings: Bk Titles 35,000; Per Subs 85
Automation Activity & Vendor Info: (Acquisitions) AmLib Library Management System
Wireless access
Function: Adult bk club, Bks on cassette, Bks on CD, Chess club, Children's prog, Computer training, Computers for patron use, E-Reserves, Family literacy, Fax serv, Free DVD rentals, ILL available, Music CDs, Outreach serv, OverDrive digital audio bks, Photocopying/Printing, Preschool reading prog, Prog for adults, Prog for children & young adult, Pub access computers, Story hour, Summer reading prog, Tax forms, Teen prog, VHS videos
Mem of Jefferson County Library System
Friends of the Library Group

BRODHEADSVILLE

P WESTERN POCONO COMMUNITY LIBRARY, 131 Pilgrim Way, 18322. (Mail add: PO Box 318, 18322-0318), SAN 320-2313. Tel: 570-992-7934. FAX: 570-992-7915. Web Site: www.wpcl.lib.pa.us. *Dir/Chief Exec Officer,* Carol H Kern; Staff 10.6 (MLS 1, Non-MLS 9.6)
Founded 1974. Pop 29,053
Library Holdings: Audiobooks 6,712; Audiobooks 6,712; Audiobooks 6,712; Bks on Deafness & Sign Lang 10; Bks on Deafness & Sign Lang 10; Bks on Deafness & Sign Lang 10; CDs 2,878; CDs 2,878; CDs 2,878; DVDs 2,707; DVDs 2,707, DVDs 2,707; e-books 1,142; e-books 1,142; e-books 1,142; Electronic Media & Resources 32; Large Print Bks 3,109; Large Print Bks 3,109; Large Print Bks 3,109; Bk Titles 72,394; Bk Titles 72,394; Bk Titles 72,394; Bk Vols 65,732; Bk Vols 65,732; Bk Vols 65,732; Talking Bks 6,712; Talking Bks 6,712; Talking Bks 6,712; Videos 2,707; Videos 2,707; Videos 2,707
Special Collections: Monroe County History
Automation Activity & Vendor Info: (Cataloging) Innovative Interfaces, Inc - Millenium; (Circulation) Innovative Interfaces, Inc - Millenium; (ILL) Innovative Interfaces, Inc; (OPAC) Innovative Interfaces, Inc - Millenium
Database Vendor: ABC-CLIO, Access Pennsylvania, EBSCOhost
Wireless access
Function: Adult bk club, Adult literacy prog, Bks on cassette, Bks on CD, CD-ROM, Children's prog, Citizenship assistance, Computer training, Computers for patron use, Copy machines, Electronic databases & coll, Exhibits, Free DVD rentals, Handicapped accessible, Home delivery & serv to Sr ctr & nursing homes, ILL available, Literacy & newcomer serv, Magnifiers for reading, Online cat, Online ref, Outreach serv, Photocopying/Printing, Preschool outreach, Prog for adults, Prog for children & young adult, Pub access computers, Ref & res, Ref serv available, Ref serv in person, Senior computer classes, Senior outreach, Serves mentally handicapped consumers, Spoken cassettes & CDs, Spoken cassettes & DVDs, Story hour, Summer reading prog, Tax forms, Teen prog, Telephone ref, VHS videos, Web-catalog, Wheelchair accessible, Workshops
Open Mon, Wed & Thurs 9-8, Tues & Fri 9-5, Sat 9-4
Restriction: Non-resident fee
Friends of the Library Group

BROOKVILLE

P REBECCA M ARTHURS MEMORIAL LIBRARY*, 223 Valley St, 15825-0223. SAN 314-3465. Tel: 814-849-5512. FAX: 814-849-6211. E-mail: rmarthurlib@comcast.net. Web Site: www.rmalib.com. *Librn,* Rosalee Pituch; Staff 2 (MLS 1, Non-MLS 1)
Founded 1958. Pop 11,758; Circ 65,938
Library Holdings: Bk Vols 34,717; Per Subs 70; Talking Bks 1,517; Videos 2,619
Subject Interests: Local hist

Automation Activity & Vendor Info: (Cataloging) Brodart; (Circulation) Brodart; (OPAC) Brodart
Function: Adult bk club, After school storytime, Bks on cassette, Bks on CD, Children's prog, Computers for patron use, Copy machines, Fax serv, Handicapped accessible, Holiday prog, Home delivery & serv to Sr ctr & nursing homes, Homebound delivery serv, ILL available, Photocopying/Printing, Prog for adults, Prog for children & young adult, Ref serv available, Summer reading prog, Tax forms, Telephone ref, VHS videos, Wheelchair accessible
Mem of Oil Creek District Library Center
Open Tues, Thurs & Fri 11:30-8, Wed 9:30-8, Sat 10-3, Sun 1-5
Friends of the Library Group

BROOMALL

R BETH EL NER TAMID LIBRARY*, 715 Paxon Hollow Rd, 19008-9998. SAN 314-3473. Tel: 610-356-8700, 610-544-1111. FAX: 610-544-7364. *Librn,* Dr Joyce Freedman; E-mail: billyjoyf@aol.com; Staff 1 (MLS 1)
Founded 1959
Library Holdings: Bk Titles 2,791; Bk Vols 2,990; Per Subs 12
Subject Interests: Jewish hist, Judaica
Open Mon-Thurs 10-3

SR CHURCH OF JESUS CHRIST OF LATTER-DAY SAINTS-PHILADELPHIA*, Stake Family History Center, 721 Paxon Hollow Rd, 19008. SAN 375-2402. Tel: 610-356-8507. Web Site: www.familysearch.org. *Dir,* Wayne Burton; Staff 1 (Non-MLS 1)
Library Holdings: Bk Vols 500
Special Collections: Philadelphia Coll. Oral History; US Document Depository
Subject Interests: Genealogy
Open Tues-Thurs 9:30-1:30 & 7-9, Sat 9:30-2:30

P MARPLE PUBLIC LIBRARY*, 2599 Sproul Rd, 19008-2399. SAN 314-3481. Tel: 610-356-1510. FAX: 610-356-3589. E-mail: marple@delcolibraries.org. Web Site: www.marplelibrary.org. *Dir,* Deborah Parsons; *Head, Adult Serv,* Bridgette Crockett; *Head, Tech Serv,* Antoinette Stabinski; *Ch Serv,* Andrea Mandel; Staff 5 (MLS 5)
Founded 1951. Pop 23,642
Library Holdings: Bk Titles 90,000; Bk Vols 92,000; Per Subs 90
Automation Activity & Vendor Info: (Circulation) Innovative Interfaces, Inc
Wireless access
Mem of Delaware County Library System
Open Mon-Thurs 10-9, Fri 10-6, Sat 10-5, Sun 1-5
Friends of the Library Group

R TEMPLE SHOLOM OF BROOMALL LIBRARY*, 55 N Church Lane, 19008. SAN 314-349X. Tel: 610-356-5165. FAX: 610-356-6713. Web Site: www.templeshalom.org. *Librn,* Barbara Clarke
Library Holdings: Bk Vols 2,500; Per Subs 50
Special Collections: Judaica Coll
Publications: Jerusalem Post; Jewish Exponent; Reform Judaism Inside

BROWNSVILLE

P BROWNSVILLE FREE PUBLIC LIBRARY, 100 Seneca St, 15417-1974. SAN 314-3511. Tel: 724-785-7272. FAX: 724-785-6087. E-mail: brpublib@gmail.com. Web Site: www.bfpl.org. *Dir,* Kristina L Haluska; Staff 3 (MLS 1, Non-MLS 2)
Founded 1927. Pop 14,769
Library Holdings: Bk Vols 23,031; Per Subs 43; Talking Bks 109; Videos 62
Automation Activity & Vendor Info: (Cataloging) Follett Software; (OPAC) Follett Software
Wireless access
Mem of Fayette County Library System
Open Mon-Sat 9:30-5

BRYN ATHYN

C BRYN ATHYN COLLEGE*, Swedenborg Library, 2925 College Dr, 19009. (Mail add: PO Box 740, 19009-0740), SAN 314-352X. Tel: 267-502-2547. Circulation Tel: 267-502-2524. Interlibrary Loan Service Tel: 267-502-2536. FAX: 267-502-2637. E-mail: library@brynathyn.edu. Web Site: www.brynathyn.edu/academics/swedenborg-library. *Dir,* Carroll C Odhner; E-mail: carroll.odhner@brynathyn.edu; *Tech Serv Librn,* Carol Traveny; E-mail: carol.traveny@brynathyn.edu; Staff 5.25 (MLS 2.75, Non-MLS 2.5)
Founded 1877. Enrl 237; Fac 33; Highest Degree: Master
Library Holdings: e-journals 7,422; Microforms 1,617; Bk Titles 79,447; Bk Vols 95,729; Per Subs 152
Special Collections: Religion (Swedenborgiana); Scientific Books (Published in 16th, 17th & 18th Centuries)
Subject Interests: Behav sci, Educ, Hist, Natural sci, Relig studies, Soc sci
Automation Activity & Vendor Info: (Cataloging) SirsiDynix; (Circulation) SirsiDynix; (OPAC) SirsiDynix; (Serials) SirsiDynix
Database Vendor: American Psychological Association (APA), CredoReference, Facts on File, Gale Cengage Learning, JSTOR, Wilson - Wilson Web
Wireless access
Publications: Bi-Lines (Newsletter)
Partic in Health Sci Libr Info Consortium; Lyrasis; OCLC Online Computer Library Center, Inc; Tri-State College Library Cooperative
Open Mon-Thurs 7:30-6 & 7:30-10:30, Fri 7:30-5, Sun 7:30pm-10:30pm
Friends of the Library Group

BRYN MAWR

C AMERICAN COLLEGE*, Vane B Lucas Memorial Library, 270 S Bryn Mawr Ave, 19010-2196. SAN 314-3538. Tel: 610-526-1307. FAX: 610-526-1310. E-mail: library@theamericancollege.edu. Web Site: library.theamericancollege.edu. *Dir,* John H Whitham; Staff 2 (MLS 1, Non-MLS 1)
Founded 1927. Enrl 30,000; Fac 21; Highest Degree: Master
Special Collections: Insurance (Solomon S Huebner Coll), bks, papers & flm; Insurance History Coll. Oral History
Subject Interests: Ins (finance), Taxation
Automation Activity & Vendor Info: (Acquisitions) EOS International; (Cataloging) OCLC WorldShare Interlibrary Loan; (Circulation) EOS International; (ILL) OCLC; (OPAC) EOS International; (Serials) EOS International
Database Vendor: Checkpoint Systems, Inc, EBSCO Discovery Service, EBSCOhost, ProQuest, Westlaw
Wireless access
Publications: Library Bulletin
Partic in Tri-State College Library Cooperative; Westchester Academic Library Directors Organization (WALDO)
Open Mon-Fri 8:30-4:30

C BRYN MAWR COLLEGE*, Mariam Coffin Canaday Library, 101 N Merion Ave, 19010-2899. SAN 314-3546. Circulation Tel: 610-526-5276. Interlibrary Loan Service Tel: 610-526-5278. Reference Tel: 610-526-5279. Administration Tel: 610-526-5271. FAX: 610-526-7480. E-mail: library@brynmawr.edu. Web Site: www.brynmawr.edu/library. *Chief Info Officer, Dir of Libr,* Position Currently Open; *Assoc Chief Info Officer,* Florence D Goff; Tel: 610-526-5275, E-mail: fgoff@brynmawr.edu; *Dir, Libr Coll, Head, Spec Coll,* Eric Pumroy; Tel: 610-526-5272, E-mail: epumroy@brynmawr.edu; *Dir, Planning & Communication,* Melissa Kramer; Tel: 610-527-5287, E-mail: mkramer@brynmawr.edu; *Head, Res Support & Educ Tech,* David Consiglio; Tel: 610-526-6534, E-mail: dconsiglio@brynmawr.edu; *Coordr, Info Access & Delivery,* Berry Chamness; Tel: 610-526-5295, E-mail: bchamness@brynmawr.edu; Staff 25 (MLS 18, Non-MLS 7)
Founded 1885. Enrl 1,478; Fac 126; Highest Degree: Doctorate
Library Holdings: Electronic Media & Resources 5,240; Bk Titles 891,443; Per Subs 1,712
Special Collections: Books about Books; College Archives; English & Dutch History Coll; Fine & Graphic Arts Coll; History of & Writing by Women; History of Religion Coll; History of Science Coll; Natural History Coll; Press Books; Theater & Performing Arts Coll; Travel & Exploration Coll; Twentieth Century Lithography Coll; Urban History Coll (New York, London, Paris)
Automation Activity & Vendor Info: (Acquisitions) Innovative Interfaces, Inc; (Cataloging) Innovative Interfaces, Inc; (Circulation) Innovative Interfaces, Inc; (OPAC) Innovative Interfaces, Inc; (Serials) Innovative Interfaces, Inc
Database Vendor: Cambridge Scientific Abstracts, Elsevier MDL, Gale Cengage Learning, JSTOR, LexisNexis, OCLC FirstSearch, OCLC WorldShare Interlibrary Loan, OVID Technologies, ProQuest, ScienceDirect
Publications: Bryn Mawr Library Card Catalog (Annual); Mirabile Dictu (Periodical)
Partic in Pennsylvania Academic Library Consortium, Inc (PALCI); Philadelphia Area Consortium of Special Collections Libraries; Tri-College University Libraries Consortium
Open Mon-Thurs 8am-Midnight, Fri 8am-10pm, Sat 10-10, Sun 10am-Midnight
Friends of the Library Group
Departmental Libraries:
RHYS CARPENTER LIBRARY FOR ART, ARCHAEOLOGY & CITIES, 101 N Merion Ave, 19104-2899. Circulation Tel: 610-526-7912. FAX: 610-526-7975. *Head of Libr,* Camilla MacKay; Tel: 610-526-7910, E-mail: cmackay@brynmawr.edu
Open Mon-Thurs 8am-Midnight, Fri 8-8, Sat 10-7, Sun 12-Midnight

LOIS & REGINALD COLLIER SCIENCE LIBRARY, 101 N Merion Ave, 19104-2899. Tel: 610-526-5118. Circulation Tel: 610-526-7463. FAX: 610-526-7464. *Head of Libr,* Terri Freedman; E-mail: tfreedma@brynmawr.edu
Open Mon-Thurs 8am-Midnight, Fri 8am-10pm, Sat 10-10, Sun 10-Midnight
Friends of the Library Group

M BRYN MAWR HOSPITAL LIBRARY, Joseph N Pew Jr Medical Library, 130 S Bryn Mawr Ave, 19010. SAN 314-3554. Tel: 484-337-3160. FAX: 610-525-5931. E-mail: bmhlibrary@mlhs.org. *Med Librn,* Joan Wolff; E-mail: wolffj@mlhs.org; Staff 1 (MLS 1)
Founded 1893
Special Collections: Medical Antique Instrument Coll
Automation Activity & Vendor Info: (Cataloging) Innovative Interfaces, Inc; (Serials) Innovative Interfaces, Inc
Database Vendor: EBSCOhost, ProQuest
Wireless access
Partic in Basic Health Sciences Library Network; Delaware Valley Information Consortium
Open Mon-Fri 9-5
Restriction: Authorized personnel only, Circulates for staff only, In-house use for visitors

R BRYN MAWR PRESBYTERIAN CHURCH, Converse Library, 625 Montgomery Ave, 19010-3599. SAN 314-3562. Tel: 610-525-2821. Web Site: www.bmpc.org. *Librn,* Kathleen R MacMurray; E-mail: carolschmidt@bmpc.org; Staff 7 (MLS 1, Non-MLS 6)
Founded 1878
Library Holdings: Audiobooks 15; AV Mats 100; CDs 10; DVDs 50; Large Print Bks 25; Bk Vols 2,000; Per Subs 13; Videos 100
Subject Interests: Presbyterian Church, Soc issues, Spirituality, Theol
Automation Activity & Vendor Info: (Acquisitions) ResourceMATE; (Cataloging) Marcive, Inc
Database Vendor: JayWil Software Development, Inc, Marcive, Inc
Wireless access
Publications: Conversations (Annual report)
Open Mon-Sat 9-5, Sun 8-1

J HARCUM COLLEGE LIBRARY*, 750 Montgomery Ave, 19010-3476. SAN 314-3570. Tel: 610-526-6085. Interlibrary Loan Service Tel: 610-526-6066. Reference Tel: 610-526-6062. Administration Tel: 610-526-6084. FAX: 610-526-6086. Web Site: www.harcum.edu/library. *Dir of Libr Serv,* Ann Ranieri; E-mail: aranieri@harcum.edu; *Instruction Librn, Ref Librn,* Katie McGowan; E-mail: cmcgowan@harcum.edu; *Bibliographer, Ref Librn,* Clara Salloom; E-mail: csalloom@harcum.edu; *Acq, ILL,* Margaret Langberg; E-mail: mlangberg@harcum.edu; *AV,* Grant Polley; E-mail: gpolley@harcum.edu; *Cataloger,* Roxanne Sutton; Tel: 610-526-6022, E-mail: rsutton@harcum.edu; *Circ, Reserves,* Miriam Burstein; E-mail: mburstein@harcum.edu; *Circ,* Carol Martin; E-mail: cmartin@harcum.edu; *Educ Technologist,* Dennis Lecker; Tel: 610-526-6665, E-mail: dlecker@harcum.edu; Staff 7 (MLS 4.5, Non-MLS 2.5)
Founded 1915. Enrl 1,500; Fac 120; Highest Degree: Associate
Library Holdings: AV Mats 1,340; Electronic Media & Resources 178; Bk Titles 35,714; Bk Vols 40,440; Per Subs 233
Subject Interests: Dental, Liberal studies, Nursing, Occupational therapy, Phys therapy, Radiology, Veterinary tech
Automation Activity & Vendor Info: (Acquisitions) SirsiDynix; (Cataloging) SirsiDynix; (Circulation) SirsiDynix; (Course Reserve) SirsiDynix; (ILL) OCLC; (OPAC) SirsiDynix; (Serials) SirsiDynix
Database Vendor: CredoReference, EBSCOhost, Gale Cengage Learning, Lexi-Comp, ProQuest
Wireless access
Partic in HSLC/Access PA/POWER Library; Lyrasis; OCLC Online Computer Library Center, Inc; OCLC-LVIS; Tri-State College Library Cooperative
Restriction: Open to pub for ref only

P LUDINGTON PUBLIC LIBRARY*, Five S Bryn Mawr Ave, 19010-3471. SAN 314-3597. Tel: 610-525-1776. FAX: 610-525-1783. Web Site: www.lmls.org. *Head Librn,* Margery Hall; E-mail: mhall@lmls.org; *Head, Circ,* Jennifer Wark; E-mail: jwark@lmls.org; *Head, Ref,* Marcia Bass; E-mail: mbass@lmls.org; *Coordr, Youth Serv,* Darlene Davis; E-mail: ddavis@lmls.org; Staff 6 (MLS 6)
Founded 1916. Pop 13,000; Circ 641,574
Library Holdings: Bk Vols 150,000; Per Subs 300
Subject Interests: Archit, Art, Hort
Automation Activity & Vendor Info: (Acquisitions) Innovative Interfaces, Inc; (Cataloging) Innovative Interfaces, Inc; (Circulation) Innovative Interfaces, Inc; (OPAC) Innovative Interfaces, Inc
Wireless access
Function: Audiobks via web, Bks on CD, Children's prog, Computer training, Computers for patron use, Copy machines, Handicapped accessible, Homebound delivery serv, ILL available, Music CDs, Online cat, Online ref, OverDrive digital audio bks, Photocopying/Printing, Prog for adults, Prog for children & young adult, Pub access computers, Ref serv available, Story hour, Summer reading prog, Tax forms, Telephone ref
Publications: Main Line; Union List of Periodicals & Newspapers
Mem of Lower Merion Library System
Open Mon-Thurs 9-9, Fri 9-6, Sat 9-5, Sun 12-5
Friends of the Library Group

BURGETTSTOWN

P BURGETTSTOWN COMMUNITY LIBRARY*, Two Kerr St, 15021-1127. SAN 314-3600. Tel: 724-947-9780. FAX: 724-947-5116. E-mail: burglib@cobweb.net. Web Site: www.burglibrary.org. *Libr Dir,* Patty Parrish; Staff 1.5 (Non-MLS 1.5)
Founded 1946. Pop 10,500
Library Holdings: Audiobooks 100; DVDs 20; Large Print Bks 200; Bk Vols 18,900; Per Subs 10; Videos 200
Automation Activity & Vendor Info: (Cataloging) Follett Software; (Circulation) Follett Software
Database Vendor: EBSCOhost, Gale Cengage Learning
Wireless access
Function: Adult bk club, Bks on CD, Computers for patron use, Copy machines, Fax serv, Handicapped accessible, ILL available, Story hour, VHS videos
Mem of Washington County Library System
Open Mon-Thurs 12-8, Fri & Sat 10-5
Friends of the Library Group

BUTLER

P BUTLER AREA PUBLIC LIBRARY*, 218 N McKean St, 16001-4971. SAN 314-3643. Tel: 724-287-1715. FAX: 724-285-5090. TDD: 724-287-1781. Web Site: www.butlerlibrary.info. *Exec Dir,* Lori Hinderliter; Tel: 724-287-1715, Ext 106; *Head, Ref,* Apryl Gilliss; Tel: 724-287-1715, Ext 113, E-mail: agilliss@bcfls.org; *Youth Serv Librn,* Peter Bess; Tel: 724-287-1715, Ext 109; Staff 9 (MLS 4, Non-MLS 5)
Founded 1894. Pop 31,005; Circ 348,068
Library Holdings: Bk Vols 100,748; Per Subs 140
Special Collections: Genealogy
Automation Activity & Vendor Info: (Acquisitions) TLC (The Library Corporation); (Cataloging) TLC (The Library Corporation); (Circulation) TLC (The Library Corporation); (OPAC) TLC (The Library Corporation)
Wireless access
Publications: Annual Report; Newsletter
Mem of Butler County Federated Library System
Partic in Lyrasis, OCLC Online Computer Library Center, Inc
Special Services for the Deaf - Assistive tech; Bks on deafness & sign lang; TDD equip; TTY equip
Special Services for the Blind - Bks on CD; Home delivery serv; Large print bks; Playaways (bks on MP3); Volunteer serv
Open Mon-Thurs 8-8, Fri 8-5, Sat 8-4
Friends of the Library Group

J BUTLER COUNTY COMMUNITY COLLEGE*, John A Beck Jr Library, College Dr, Oak Hills, 16002. (Mail add: PO Box 1203, 16003-1203), SAN 314-3619. Tel: 724-284-8511. FAX: 724-285-6047. Web Site: www.bc3.edu/index.asp. *Dean of Libr Serv,* Stephen Joseph; *Media Librn, Ref Librn,* Jean Schumway; *Tech Serv Librn,* Martin Miller; Staff 3 (MLS 3)
Founded 1966. Enrl 2,500; Fac 165
Library Holdings: Bk Titles 41,218; Bk Vols 45,122; Per Subs 255
Subject Interests: Allied health, Lit, Soc issues
Automation Activity & Vendor Info: (Acquisitions) Ex Libris Group; (Cataloging) Ex Libris Group; (Circulation) Ex Libris Group; (Course Reserve) Ex Libris Group; (OPAC) Ex Libris Group; (Serials) Ex Libris Group
Database Vendor: CQ Press, EBSCOhost, Facts on File, Hoovers, ReferenceUSA
Publications: Acquisitions List; Bibliographies; Library Instruction on Video; Newsletter; Periodicals List; Student Handbook
Partic in OCLC Online Computer Library Center, Inc
Open Mon-Thurs 8am-9pm, Fri 8-4

P BUTLER COUNTY FEDERATED LIBRARY SYSTEM*, 218 N McKean St, 16001. Tel: 724-283-1880. FAX: 724-841-0433. Web Site: www.bcfls.org. *Adminr,* Lori Hinderliter; E-mail: lhinderliter@bcfls.org; Staff 8 (MLS 1, Non-MLS 7)
Founded 1987
Library Holdings: Bk Vols 28,269; Per Subs 30
Automation Activity & Vendor Info: (Cataloging) TLC (The Library Corporation); (Circulation) TLC (The Library Corporation); (OPAC) TLC (The Library Corporation)
Wireless access

Member Libraries: Butler Area Public Library; Cranberry Public Library; Evans City Public Library; Mars Area Public Library; North Trails Public Library; Prospect Community Library; Slippery Rock Community Library; South Butler Community Library; Zelienople Area Public Library
Special Services for the Deaf - TTY equip
Friends of the Library Group
Bookmobiles: 1

GL BUTLER COUNTY LAW LIBRARY*, Courthouse, 124 W Diamond St, 16001. SAN 314-3627. Interlibrary Loan Service Tel: 724-284-5206. FAX: 724-284-5210. *Librn,* Susan Megarry; E-mail: smegarry@co.butler.pa.us
Library Holdings: Bk Titles 20,000; Per Subs 60
Subject Interests: Law, Pa
Database Vendor: Westlaw
Open Mon-Fri 8:30-4:30
Restriction: Open to pub for ref only

GM DEPARTMENT OF VETERANS AFFAIRS*, Medical Center Library, 325 New Castle Rd, 16001. SAN 314-366X. Tel: 724-285-2250. FAX: 724-477-5073. E-mail: library529@va.gov. *Libr Mgr,* Christine Meyer; Tel: 724-285-2246; *Libr Tech,* Mary Ann Wagner; Tel: 724-477-5024; Staff 2 (Non-MLS 2)
Founded 1946
Library Holdings: Bk Titles 1,327; Per Subs 131
Subject Interests: Geriatrics, Med, Nursing, Psychol, Soc work
Partic in Veterans Affairs Library Network (VALNET)
Restriction: Pub use on premises, Staff use only

CALIFORNIA

P CALIFORNIA AREA PUBLIC LIBRARY*, 100 Wood St, 15419. SAN 314-3678. Tel: 724-938-2907. FAX: 724-938-9119. E-mail: calpublib@zoominternet.net. Web Site: calpublib.org. *Libr Dir,* David L Porterfield; Staff 2 (MLS 1, Non-MLS 1)
Founded 1934. Pop 9,650
Library Holdings: Audiobooks 65; AV Mats 415; Bks on Deafness & Sign Lang 7; Braille Volumes 2; DVDs 182; Large Print Bks 200; Bk Titles 14,500; Bk Vols 20,000; Per Subs 15; Spec Interest Per Sub 1; Videos 415
Special Collections: Local Hist Coll; Railroads Coll
Automation Activity & Vendor Info: (Cataloging) Follett Software; (Circulation) Follett Software; (OPAC) Follett Software
Wireless access
Function: ILL available
Publications: California Journal (Newsletter)
Mem of Washington County Library System
Friends of the Library Group

C CALIFORNIA UNIVERSITY OF PENNSYLVANIA*, Louis L Manderino Library, 250 University Ave, 15419-1394. SAN 314-3686. Tel: 724-938-4091. Interlibrary Loan Service Tel: 724-938-4049. Reference Tel: 724-938-4094. Administration Tel: 724-938-4096. Automation Services Tel: 724-938-5772. FAX: 724-938-5901. Administration FAX: 724-938-4088. E-mail: reference@calu.edu. Web Site: www.library.calu.edu. *Dean, Libr Serv,* Douglas A Hoover; E-mail: hoover@calu.edu; *Chairperson, Electronic Res Librn, Webmaster,* Loring Prest; Tel: 724-938-5769, E-mail: prest@calu.edu; *Govt Doc/Distance Learning Librn,* William Denny; Tel: 724-938-4451, E-mail: denny_w@calu.edu; *Info Literacy/Instrul Tech Librn,* Ryan Sittler; Tel: 724-938-4923, E-mail: sittler@calu.edu; *Res & Electronic Coll Librn,* William Meloy; Tel: 724-938-4067, E-mail: meloy@calu.edu; *Res & Instruction Librn,* Monica Ruane Rogers; E-mail: ruane@calu.edu; *Tech Serv Librn,* Julia F McGinnis; Tel: 724-938-5472, Fax: 724-938-4490, E-mail: mcginnis@calu.edu; *Supvr, Acq,* Cora Russell; Tel: 724-938-5702, E-mail: russell@calu.edu; *Coordr, Circ,* Barbara L Sabo; Tel: 724-938-4092, E-mail: sabo@calu.edu; *ILL,* Diane Greenlief; Tel: 724-938-5539, E-mail: Greenlief@calu.edu; *Pub Serv, Syst Adminr,* Carol Otto; E-mail: otto@calu.edu; Staff 21 (MLS 8, Non-MLS 13)
Founded 1852. Enrl 8,243; Fac 253; Highest Degree: Master
Library Holdings: Bk Vols 389,566; Per Subs 9,314
Special Collections: State Document Depository; US Document Depository
Automation Activity & Vendor Info: (Acquisitions) Ex Libris Group; (Cataloging) Ex Libris Group; (Circulation) Ex Libris Group; (Course Reserve) Docutek; (ILL) Ex Libris Group; (OPAC) Ex Libris Group; (Serials) Ex Libris Group
Database Vendor: EBSCOhost, LexisNexis, OCLC FirstSearch, OVID Technologies, ProQuest, SirsiDynix, Wilson - Wilson Web
Wireless access
Partic in Interlibrary Delivery Service of Pennsylvania; Keystone Library Network; Lyrasis; Pennsylvania Academic Library Consortium, Inc (PALCI); State System of Higher Education Library Cooperative
Open Mon-Thurs 7:30am-11pm, Fri 7:30-5, Sat & Sun 12-8

CAMBRIDGE SPRINGS

P CAMBRIDGE SPRINGS PUBLIC LIBRARY*, 158 McClellan St, 16403-1018. SAN 314-3716. Tel: 814-398-2123. FAX: 814-398-2123. E-mail: cspl@ccfls.org. Web Site: ccfls.org/cambridge. *Dir,* Connie Bullock
Founded 1928. Pop 6,805; Circ 25,388
Library Holdings: AV Mats 608; Bks on Deafness & Sign Lang 25; Large Print Bks 155; Bk Titles 20,000; Bk Vols 21,669; Per Subs 80; Talking Bks 290
Automation Activity & Vendor Info: (Cataloging) Follett Software; (Circulation) Follett Software; (OPAC) Follett Software
Mem of Crawford County Federated Library System
Open Mon 12-8, Tues & Thurs 10-8, Wed & Fri 12-5, Sat 9-4

CAMP HILL

P CLEVE J FREDRICKSEN LIBRARY*, 100 N 19th St, 17011-3900. SAN 314-3732. Tel: 717-761-3900. FAX: 717-761-5493. E-mail: fredricksen@ccpa.net. Web Site: www.fredricksenlibrary.org. *Dir,* Bonnie Goble; *Asst Dir,* Jackie Barton; *Head, Ch,* Mary Alice Spiegel; *Head, Circ,* Cheryl Condon; Staff 6 (MLS 6)
Founded 1957. Pop 74,064; Circ 404,089
Library Holdings: Bk Vols 99,796
Automation Activity & Vendor Info: (Acquisitions) SirsiDynix; (Cataloging) SirsiDynix; (Circulation) SirsiDynix; (OPAC) SirsiDynix
Wireless access
Mem of Cumberland County Library System
Friends of the Library Group
Branches: 1
EAST PENNSBORO, 98 S Enola Dr, Enola, 17025, SAN 376-5695. Tel: 717-732-4274. FAX: 717-732-6478. E-mail: eastpennsboro@ccpa.net. Web Site: www.eastpennsborobranch.org. *Libr Dir,* Bonnie Goble
Pop 26,305; Circ 54,933
Library Holdings: Bk Vols 13,601
Open Mon, Tues & Thurs 10-8, Wed 10-5, Fri 12-5
Friends of the Library Group

M HOLY SPIRIT HOSPITAL*, Medical Library, 503 N 21st St, 17011. SAN 325-0164. Tel: 717-763-2664. FAX: 717-763-2136. E-mail: info@hsh.org. Web Site: www.hsh.org. *Librn,* Edie Asbury; E-mail: easbury@hsh.org; Staff 1 (MLS 1)
Library Holdings: Bk Titles 2,651; Bk Vols 2,780; Per Subs 145
Subject Interests: Consumer health, Med, Mental health
Function: Copy machines, Doc delivery serv, ILL available, Online cat, Online searches, Orientations
Publications: Medical Library Newsletter
Partic in Basic Health Sciences Library Network; Central Pennsylvania Health Sciences Library Association; OCLC Online Computer Library Center, Inc
Open Mon-Fri 7-6
Restriction: Badge access after hrs, Hospital staff & commun

S STATE CORRECTIONAL INSTITUTION*, Camp Hill Library, PO Box 8837, 17011-8837. Tel: 717-737-4531. FAX: 717-737-2202. *Librn,* Lizhu Zhong; E-mail: lzhong@state.pa.us
Library Holdings: AV Mats 200; Bk Vols 12,000; Per Subs 40
Automation Activity & Vendor Info: (Cataloging) Follett Software; (Circulation) Follett Software; (OPAC) Follett Software
Open Mon-Fri 8am-8:30pm, Sat & Sun 8-4:30

CANONSBURG

P FRANK SARRIS PUBLIC LIBRARY*, 36 N Jefferson Ave, 15317. SAN 314-3740. Tel: 724-745-1308. FAX: 724-745-4958. Web Site: www.franksarrislibrary.org. *Libr Dir,* Peggy Tseng; E-mail: ptseng@franksarrislibrary.org; *Asst Dir,* Jackie Zataweski; E-mail: jzataweski@franksarrislibrary.org; Staff 11 (MLS 1, Non-MLS 10)
Founded 1879
Library Holdings: Bk Titles 70,000; Per Subs 64
Special Collections: Canonsburg Notes, micro; Federal Census; History of Western Pennsylvania (Johnson Memorial Coll)
Automation Activity & Vendor Info: (Cataloging) AmLib Library Management System; (Circulation) AmLib Library Management System; (OPAC) AmLib Library Management System
Wireless access
Function: Accelerated reader prog, Adult bk club, Archival coll, Bk club(s), Bks on CD, Children's prog, Computers for patron use, Copy machines, E-Reserves, Electronic databases & coll, Fax serv, Free DVD rentals, Handicapped accessible, ILL available, Online cat, Photocopying/Printing, Preschool outreach, Prog for children & young adult, Pub access computers, Ref serv in person, Story hour, Summer & winter reading prog, Tax forms, Teen prog, Telephone ref, VHS videos, Web-catalog, Wheelchair accessible
Mem of Washington County Library System
Partic in Washington County Cooperative Library Services

Special Services for the Blind - ZoomText magnification & reading software
Open Mon-Thurs 11-8, Fri & Sat 10-5
Friends of the Library Group
Bookmobiles: 1

CANTON

P GREEN FREE LIBRARY*, 38 N Center St, 17724-1304. SAN 314-3767. Tel: 570-673-5744. FAX: 570-673-5005. E-mail: greenfre@frontiernet.net. Web Site: www.cantonlibrary.org. *Dir,* Cathy Golder
Pop 6,449; Circ 16,460
Library Holdings: Bk Vols 24,000; Per Subs 25
Automation Activity & Vendor Info: (Cataloging) Follett Software; (Circulation) Follett Software
Wireless access
Mem of Bradford County Library System
Open Mon, Tues & Thurs 11-7, Fri 9-12& 2-5, Sat 9-2, Sun 6:30pm-8:30-pm
Friends of the Library Group

CARBONDALE

P CARBONDALE PUBLIC LIBRARY*, Five N Main St, 18407-2303. SAN 314-3775. Tel: 570-282-4281. FAX: 570-282-7031. Web Site: www.lclshome.org. *Dir,* Marie Ann Zaccone; E-mail: mzaccone@albright.org; *ILL,* Joan Cosgrove; E-mail: jcosgrove@albright.org; *Youth Serv,* Sandy Longo; E-mail: slongo@albright.org
Founded 1874. Pop 12,808; Circ 26,169
Library Holdings: Bk Vols 22,936; Per Subs 65
Automation Activity & Vendor Info: (Acquisitions) SirsiDynix; (Cataloging) SirsiDynix; (Circulation) SirsiDynix; (ILL) SirsiDynix; (OPAC) SirsiDynix
Wireless access
Function: Adult bk club, Chess club, Handicapped accessible, ILL available, Magnifiers for reading, Music CDs, Newsp ref libr, Online searches, Outside serv via phone, mail, e-mail & web, Photocopying/Printing, Prog for adults, Prog for children & young adult, Ref & res, Ref serv available, Spoken cassettes & CDs, Spoken cassettes & DVDs, Summer reading prog, Telephone ref, VHS videos, Video lending libr, Wheelchair accessible
Mem of Lackawanna County Library System
Open Mon-Thurs 10-8, Fri & Sat 10-5
Friends of the Library Group

CARLISLE

P BOSLER FREE LIBRARY*, 158 W High St, 17013-2988. SAN 314-3791. Tel: 717-243-4642. FAX: 717-243-8281. *Dir,* Linda K Rice; E-mail: lrice@ccpa.net; *Asst Dir,* Tienya B Smith; E-mail: tsmith@ccpa.net; *Ch Serv,* Melissa A Killinger; E-mail: mkillinger@ccpa.net; *ILL, Ref,* Connie Weaver; E-mail: cweaver@ccpa.net; *Ref Serv,* Jean Bahner; E-mail: jbahner@ccpa.net; *Ref Serv,* Kathy Byers; E-mail: khyers@ccpa.net; *Ref Serv,* Michael Monahan; E-mail: mmonahan@ccpa.net; Staff 7 (MLS 3, Non-MLS 4)
Founded 1900. Pop 48,312; Circ 351,905
Library Holdings: AV Mats 5,680; CDs 220; Large Print Bks 341; Bk Titles 96,490; Bk Vols 98,190; Per Subs 172; Talking Bks 130; Videos 782
Subject Interests: Local hist
Automation Activity & Vendor Info: (Circulation) SirsiDynix
Mem of Cumberland County Library System
Open Mon-Fri 10-9, Sat 10-5, Sun 1-5
Friends of the Library Group

S CUMBERLAND COUNTY HISTORICAL SOCIETY*, Hamilton Library, 21 N Pitt, 17013-2945. (Mail add: PO Box 626, 17013-0626), SAN 314-3805. Tel: 717-249-7610. FAX: 717-258-9332. E-mail: info@historicalsociety.com. Web Site: www.historicalsociety.com. *Dir,* Linda Franklin Witmer; *Librn,* Cara Holtry Curtis; Staff 5 (MLS 2, Non-MLS 3)
Founded 1874
Library Holdings: Per Subs 20
Special Collections: A A Line, J N; Carlisle; Cartography (John V Miller, M D Coll), maps; Choate & Carlisle Indian School, photog; Cumberland County; Cumberland County Firms Business Records, bd; Genealogy, VF; Index to Cumberland County Church & Cemetery Records; John S Steckbeck Coll (Carlisle Indian School Coll. Author of Fabulous Redmen); Judge James Hamilton (papers, bks & mss); Newspapers, 1749-present & Carlisle Indian School Publications, 1880-1917, bd & micro; Official Cumberland County, records, bks & mss; Papers of Robert Whitehill, Sylvester B Sadler, Jeremiah Zeamer & others, mss
Subject Interests: Architect, Genealogy, Local hist, Property
Function: Archival coll, For res purposes
Publications: Annual Journal; Monographs
Restriction: Closed stack, Fee for pub use, Not a lending libr

L CUMBERLAND COUNTY LAW LIBRARY*, One Courthouse Sq, 17013-3387. SAN 327-098X. Tel: 717-240-6200. FAX: 717-240-6462. Web Site: www.ccpa.net. *Librn,* Michelle Sibert; Staff 1 (Non-MLS 1)
Library Holdings: Electronic Media & Resources 54; Bk Titles 150
Database Vendor: Westlaw
Wireless access
Open Mon-Fri 8-4:30

P CUMBERLAND COUNTY LIBRARY SYSTEM*, 19 S West St, 17013-2839. SAN 314-3813. Tel: 717-240-6175. E-mail: ccls@cumberlandcountylibraries.org. Web Site: cumberlandcountylibraries.org. *Exec Dir,* Jonelle Prether Darr; E-mail: jdarr@cumberlandcountylibraries.org; *Outreach Serv Librn,* Carol Linderman-Justice; Tel: 717-240-7771, E-mail: clindermanjustice@cumberlandcountylibraries.org; *Automation Syst Coordr,* Barbara Leach; Tel: 717-240-7735, E-mail: bleach@cumberlandcountylibraries.org; *Tech Serv Coordr,* Sharon Scott; Tel: 717-240-7872, E-mail: sscott@cumberlandcountylibraries.org; Staff 5 (MLS 5)
Founded 1961. Pop 244,731
Jan 2007-Dec 2007 Income $2,104,765, State $477,765, Federal $15,385, County $1,370,294, Locally Generated Income $119,500, Other $121,821. Mats Exp $148,681, Books $24,535, Per/Ser (Incl. Access Fees) $967, Other Print Mats $48,175, AV Mat $9,000, Electronic Ref Mat (Incl. Access Fees) $66,004. Sal $700,709
Library Holdings: Bk Titles 7,992; Per Subs 26
Automation Activity & Vendor Info: (Acquisitions) Horizon; (Cataloging) Horizon; (Circulation) Horizon; (OPAC) Horizon; (Serials) Horizon
Database Vendor: Baker & Taylor, EBSCOhost, OCLC, OCLC WebJunction, SirsiDynix
Wireless access
Member Libraries: Amelia S Givin Free Library; Bosler Free Library; Cleve J Fredricksen Library; John Graham Public Library; Joseph T Simpson Public Library; New Cumberland Public Library; Shippensburg Public Library
Partic in Capital Area Library District
Open Mon-Fri 8-4:30

C DICKINSON COLLEGE*, Waidner-Spahr Library, 333 W High St, 17013-2896. (Mail add: College & High St, 17013), SAN 314-3821. Tel: 717-245-1397. FAX: 717-245-1439. E-mail: library@dickinson.edu. Web Site: lis.dickinson.edu/library/. *Dir,* Eleanor Mitchell; Tel: 717-245-1142, E-mail: mitchelle@dickinson.edu; *Assoc Dir, Libr Res & Admin,* Theresa Arndt; *Assoc Dir, Info Literacy & Res Serv,* Christine Bombaro; *Asst Dir, Access Serv,* Maureen Dermott; *Spec Coll Librn,* Malinda Triller; *Tech Serv Librn,* Kirk Doran; *Col Archivist,* James Gerencser; Staff 27 (MLS 8, Non-MLS 19)
Founded 1784. Enrl 2,300; Fac 227; Highest Degree: Bachelor
Library Holdings: Bk Titles 388,000; Bk Vols 479,000; Per Subs 12,500
Special Collections: Carl Sandburg Coll, bks, letters, mss; Eli Slifer Coll, letters; Isaac Norris Coll; Jacobs Asian Coll, James Buchanan Coll, letters, mss, John Drinkwater Coll, bks, letters, mss; John F Kennedy Coll, artifacts, bks, per; Joseph Priestly Coll, bks, mss; Marianne Moore Coll, bks, letters; Martin Native American Coll; Moncure Conway Coll, letters. US Document Depository
Subject Interests: E European hist, Russian hist, Russian lit
Automation Activity & Vendor Info: (Acquisitions) SirsiDynix; (Cataloging) SirsiDynix; (Circulation) SirsiDynix; (Course Reserve) SirsiDynix; (ILL) OCLC; (OPAC) SirsiDynix; (Serials) SirsiDynix
Wireless access
Publications: John & Mary's Journal; Manuscript Collections of Dickinson College; Spahr Library Notes
Partic in Central Pennsylvania Consortium; Lyrasis; Oberlin Group; Pennsylvania Academic Library Consortium, Inc (PALCI); Westchester Academic Library Directors Organization (WALDO)
Open Mon-Thurs 8am-2am, Fri 8am-10pm, Sat 10-10, Sun 10am-2am
Friends of the Library Group

CL PENNSYLVANIA STATE UNIVERSITY - DICKINSON SCHOOL OF LAW*, The H Laddie Montague, Jr Law Library, 1170 Harrisburg Pike, 17013-1617. SAN 314-383X. Tel: 717-240-5267. FAX: 717-240-5127. Web Site: www.dsl.psu.edu/library. *Assoc Dean, Libr & Info Serv, Dir, Law Libr,* Steven Hinckley; Tel: 814-867-0390, E-mail: sdh14@psu.edu; *Assoc Dir, Law Librn,* Gail Partin; Tel: 717-240-5294, E-mail: gap6@psu.edu; *Asst Dir, Law Librn,* Kevin Gray; E-mail: kpg3@psu.edu; *Assoc Law Librn, Bibliog/Ser Control,* Debra Jones; Tel: 717-240-5222, E-mail: daj6@psu.edu; *Assoc Law Librn, Govt Doc/Acq,* Cecily A H Giardina; Tel: 717-240-5226, E-mail: chg3@psu.edu; *Archivist, Assoc Law Librn, Ref,* Mark W Podvia; Tel: 717-240-5015, E-mail: mwp3@psu.edu; *Assoc Law Librn, Ref,* Judy L Swarthout; Tel: 717-240-5229, E-mail: jsx2@psu.edu;

Asst Law Librn, Access Serv, David McCaslin; Tel: 814-865-8863, E-mail: djm200@psu.edu; *Asst Law Librn, Cat,* Richard O Paone; Tel: 717-240-5011, E-mail: rop2@psu.edu; *Asst Law Librn, Ref,* Lauren Gluckman; Tel: 814-865-8875, E-mail: lig2@psu.edu; *Asst Law Librn, Ref,* Kimberli Morris; Tel: 814-863-0885, E-mail: kam59@psu.edu; *Asst Law Librn, Ref, Circ/ILL,* Laura J Ax-Fultz; Tel: 717-241-3541, E-mail: lja10@psu.edu; *Circ Supvr,* Mary Foster; Tel: 717-240-5009, E-mail: mrf6@psu.edu; *Tech Serv Coordr,* Susan Zullinger; Tel: 717-240-5225, E-mail: suz2@psu.edu; Staff 14 (MLS 6, Non-MLS 8)
Founded 1834. Enrl 620; Fac 35; Highest Degree: Doctorate
Library Holdings: Bk Titles 103,610; Bk Vols 451,196; Per Subs 1,482
Special Collections: US Document Depository
Subject Interests: European commun law, Intl human rights
Database Vendor: Innovative Interfaces, Inc
Function: ILL available, Prof lending libr, Ref & res, VHS videos
Partic in Interlibrary Delivery Service of Pennsylvania; Mid-Atlantic Law Library Cooperative; OCLC Online Computer Library Center, Inc
Open Mon-Thurs 8am-9pm, Fri 8-5

A UNITED STATES ARMY HERITAGE & EDUCATION CENTER*, US Army Military History Institute, 950 Soldiers Dr, 17013-5021. SAN 321-3684. Tel: 717-245-3972. Interlibrary Loan Service Tel: 717-245-3130. Reference Tel: 717-245-3949. FAX: 717-245-3067. E-mail: usarmy.carlisle.awc.mbx.ahec-ves@mail.mil. Web Site: www.carlisle.army.mil/ahec. *Dir,* Dr Conrad C Crane; Tel: 717-245-4483, E-mail: conrad.crane@us.army.mil; *Mus Dir,* Jack Leighow; *Coll Mgt Mgr,* Greg Statler. Subject Specialists: *Mil hist,* Dr Conrad C Crane; Staff 29 (MLS 5, Non-MLS 24)
Founded 1967
Library Holdings: Bk Vols 283,865; Per Subs 185
Special Collections: Army Doctrinal Publications; Army Heritage Museum Artifacts; Army Unit Histories; Personal Manuscript Coll, paper & photog; Rare Books. Oral History
Subject Interests: Land warfare, US Army hist
Wireless access
Function: Exhibits, Handicapped accessible, Photocopying/Printing, Pub access computers
Partic in Associated College Libraries of Central Pennsylvania; Fedlink; Military Education Research Library Network (MERLN)
Open Tues-Sat 9-5, Sun 11-5
Restriction: Circ limited, Closed stack, Open to pub for ref & circ; with some limitations, Restricted borrowing privileges
Friends of the Library Group

A US ARMY WAR COLLEGE LIBRARY*, 122 Forbes Ave, 17013-5220. SAN 314-3848. Tel: 717-245-4300. Circulation Tel: 717-245-4288. Interlibrary Loan Service Tel: 717-245-4298. Reference Tel: 717-245-3660. FAX: 717-245-3323. Web Site: www.carlisle.army.mil/library/. *Dir,* Bohdan Kohutiak; E-mail: bohdan.kohutiak@us.army.mil; *Dept Head, User Serv,* Ginny Shope; Tel: 717-245-4280, E-mail: virginia.shope@us.army.mil; *Syst Coordr,* William Rotella; Tel: 717-245-4704, E-mail: william.rotella@us.army.mil; Staff 20 (MLS 9, Non-MLS 11)
Highest Degree: Master
Library Holdings: AV Mats 4,800; e-books 3,799; e-journals 447; Microforms 117,413; Bk Titles 107,616; Bk Vols 170,078; Per Subs 471
Subject Interests: Area studies, Econ, Foreign policy, Intl law, Intl relations, Leadership, Mgt, Mil sci, Mil strategy, Strategy
Automation Activity & Vendor Info: (Cataloging) SirsiDynix; (Circulation) SirsiDynix; (Course Reserve) SirsiDynix; (ILL) SirsiDynix; (OPAC) SirsiDynix
Wireless access
Function: Govt ref serv, ILL available, Res libr
Partic in Fedlink
Open Mon-Fri 8-4:30
Restriction: In-house use for visitors

CARMICHAELS

P FLENNIKEN PUBLIC LIBRARY*, 102 E George St, 15320-1202. SAN 314-3856. Tel: 724-966-5263. FAX: 724-966-9511. Web Site: www.flenniken.org. *Dir,* Linda R Orsted; *Asst Dir,* Jessica Miller; *Ch Serv,* Tina Gresko; Staff 4 (MLS 2, Non-MLS 2)
Founded 1946. Pop 12,356; Circ 40,000
Library Holdings: AV Mats 1,500; Bk Vols 34,000; Per Subs 89; Talking Bks 1,000
Subject Interests: Coal, Fiction, Local hist, Women
Automation Activity & Vendor Info: (Cataloging) Innovative Interfaces, Inc - Millenium; (Circulation) Innovative Interfaces, Inc - Millenium; (ILL) Innovative Interfaces, Inc - Millenium; (OPAC) Innovative Interfaces, Inc - Millenium; (Serials) Innovative Interfaces, Inc - Millenium
Database Vendor: H W Wilson, Innovative Interfaces, Inc, Newsbank, ProQuest
Wireless access
Function: Adult bk club, Bks on cassette, Bks on CD, CD-ROM, Children's prog, Computer training, Computers for patron use, Copy machines, Electronic databases & coll, Fax serv, Free DVD rentals, Homework prog, ILL available, Music CDs, Online cat, Outreach serv, Photocopying/Printing, Preschool outreach, Prog for adults, Prog for children & young adult, Pub access computers, Ref serv available, Ref serv in person, Spoken cassettes & CDs, Spoken cassettes & DVDs, Story hour, Summer reading prog, Tax forms, Teen prog, Telephone ref, VHS videos
Mem of Greene County Library System
Open Mon-Thurs 10-7, Fri & Sat 10-5
Friends of the Library Group

CARNEGIE

P ANDREW CARNEGIE FREE LIBRARY & MUSIC HALL*, 300 Beechwood Ave, 15106-2699. SAN 314-3864. Tel: 412-276-3456. FAX: 412-276-9472. Web Site: www.carnegiecarnegie.com. *Exec Dir,* Maggie Forbes; *Libr Dir,* Diane Klinefelter; Tel: 412-276-3456, Ext 5, E-mail: klinefelter@eiworknet.net; *Children & Youth Serv Librn,* Erin Tipping
Founded 1899. Pop 10,864; Circ 30,855
Library Holdings: Bk Vols 32,600; Per Subs 72
Special Collections: Civil War Memorabilia Coll; Local Newspapers, back to Jan 7, 1872
Mem of Allegheny County Library Association
Open Tues-Thurs 10-8, Fri 10-5, Sat 9-5
Friends of the Library Group

CARROLLTOWN

P CARROLLTOWN PUBLIC LIBRARY*, 140 E Carroll St, 15722. (Mail add: PO Box 316, 15722-9998), SAN 314-3880. Tel: 814-344-6300. FAX: 814-344-6355. *Librn,* Deborah Gresco
Pop 5,318; Circ 10,068
Library Holdings: Bk Vols 8,100; Per Subs 15
Automation Activity & Vendor Info: (Cataloging) Follett Software; (Circulation) Follett Software
Mem of Cambria County Library System & District Center
Open Mon 11:30-7, Tues 11-5, Wed 10-5, Thurs 10-4:30, Fri 10-4, Sat 9-4

CASTLE SHANNON

P COMMUNITY LIBRARY OF CASTLE SHANNON*, 3677 Myrtle Ave, 15234-2198. SAN 314-3899. Tel: 412-563-4552. FAX: 412-563-8228. Web Site: castleshannonlibrary.org. *Dir,* Heather Myrah; Staff 13 (MLS 4, Non-MLS 9)
Founded 1953. Pop 8,556; Circ 76,674
Library Holdings: AV Mats 5,792; CDs 68; Large Print Bks 342; Bk Vols 42,733; Per Subs 221; Talking Bks 2,311; Videos 3,481
Automation Activity & Vendor Info: (Cataloging) Innovative Interfaces, Inc; (Circulation) Innovative Interfaces, Inc; (OPAC) Innovative Interfaces, Inc
Database Vendor: EBSCOhost, Gale Cengage Learning
Mem of Allegheny County Library Association
Open Mon & Wed 1-9, Tues & Thurs 10-9, Fri & Sun 1-5, Sat 10-5
Friends of the Library Group

CATASAUQUA

P PUBLIC LIBRARY OF CATASAUQUA*, 302 Bridge St, 18032-2510. (Mail add: PO Box 127, 18032-0127), SAN 314-3902. Tel: 610-264-4151. FAX: 610-264-4593. Web Site: www.catasauquapl.org. *Dir,* Martha L Birtcher; Staff 4 (MLS 1, Non-MLS 3)
Founded 1923. Pop 11,315; Circ 33,285
Library Holdings: AV Mats 840; Bk Vols 18,304; Per Subs 49; Videos 410
Subject Interests: Local hist
Open Mon-Thurs 2-7:30, Fri 2-5, Sat 9-4 (9-1 Summer)
Friends of the Library Group

CENTER VALLEY

C DESALES UNIVERSITY*, Trexler Library, 2755 Station Ave, 18034. SAN 314-3910. Tel: 610-282-1100, Ext 1266. Interlibrary Loan Service Tel: 610-282-1100, Ext 1257. FAX: 610-282-2342. Web Site: www.desales.edu/library. *Dir,* Debbie Malone; Tel: 610-282-1100, Ext 1253, E-mail: debbie.malone@desales.edu; *Dir, Tech Serv,* Phyllis Vogel; E-mail: phyllis.vogel@desales.edu; *Syst Librn,* Kimberley Sando; E-mail: kim.sando@desales.edu; *Circ Mgr,* Gloria Biser; E-mail: gloria.biser@desales.edu; *Pub Serv,* Lynne Kvinnesland; E-mail: lynne.kvinnesland@desales.edu; *Pub Serv,* Michele Mrazik; E-mail: michele.mrazik@desales.edu; *Pub Serv,* Loretta Ulincy; E-mail: loretta.ulincy@desales.edu; Staff 6 (MLS 5, Non-MLS 1)
Founded 1965. Enrl 2,500; Fac 102; Highest Degree: Doctorate
Library Holdings: DVDs 1,377; e-books 130,000; e-journals 8,000; Music Scores 587; Bk Titles 115,676; Bk Vols 147,270; Per Subs 272; Videos 11,530

Special Collections: American Theatre (John Y Kohl Coll), bks & pamphlets; St Francis De Sales Coll; St Thomas More Coll; Theatre Criticism (Walter Kerr Coll)
Subject Interests: Nursing, Philos, Roman Catholic relig
Automation Activity & Vendor Info: (Acquisitions) Innovative Interfaces, Inc; (Cataloging) Innovative Interfaces, Inc; (Circulation) Innovative Interfaces, Inc; (Media Booking) Innovative Interfaces, Inc; (OPAC) Innovative Interfaces, Inc; (Serials) Innovative Interfaces, Inc
Wireless access
Publications: Newsletter
Partic in Lehigh Valley Association of Independent Colleges; Lyrasis; OCLC Online Computer Library Center, Inc
Open Mon-Thurs 8:30am-Midnight, Fri 8:30am-9pm, Sat 9-5, Sun Noon Midnight
Restriction: Access for corporate affiliates

P SOUTHERN LEHIGH PUBLIC LIBRARY*, 3200 Preston Lane, 18034. (Mail add: PO Box 279, 18034-0279), SAN 314-4283. Tel: 610-282-8825. FAX: 610-282-8828. E-mail: staff@solehipl.org. Web Site: www.solehipl.org. *Dir, Librn,* Lynnette Saeger; *Asst Dir,* Gail Shearer; Staff 3.5 (MLS 1.5, Non-MLS 2)
Founded 1963. Pop 18,138; Circ 94,476
Library Holdings: Bk Vols 46,482; Per Subs 166
Automation Activity & Vendor Info: (Cataloging) TLC (The Library Corporation); (Circulation) TLC (The Library Corporation); (OPAC) TLC (The Library Corporation); (Serials) TLC (The Library Corporation)
Wireless access
Open Mon-Thurs 10-9, Fri & Sat 10-5
Friends of the Library Group

CHADDS FORD

S BRANDYWINE CONSERVANCY, INC*, Brandywine River Museum Library, US Rte 1, Box 141, 19317. SAN 314-3929. Tel: 610-388-2700. FAX: 610-388-1197. E-mail: library@brandywine.org. *Librn,* Ruth Bassett; *Librn,* Gail Stanislow
Founded 1971
Library Holdings: Bk Titles 3,622; Bk Vols 5,171; Per Subs 22
Special Collections: American Illustration; N C Wyeth Coll, prints, posters, proofs, calendars; Stanley Arthurs (Blanche Swayne Coll), scrapbks
Subject Interests: Am art, Andrew Wyeth, Howard Pyle, James Wyeth, Local artists, N C Wyeth
Database Vendor: OCLC FirstSearch
Restriction: Open by appt only, Open to pub for ref only

CHAMBERSBURG

P COYLE FREE LIBRARY*, 102 N Main St, 17201-1676. SAN 314-3945. Tel: 717-263-1054. Interlibrary Loan Service Tel: 717-263-1054, Ext 203. Reference Tel: 717-263-1054, Ext 205. FAX: 717-709-0288. Web Site: fclspa.org/coyle-free-library. *Dir,* Denice Bigham; E-mail: dbigham@fclspa.org
Founded 1924. Pop 26,811; Circ 169,290
Library Holdings: AV Mats 4,161; Large Print Bks 2,701; Bk Titles 70,000; Per Subs 175; Talking Bks 2,099
Special Collections: State Document Depository
Subject Interests: Genealogy, Local hist, Spanish
Automation Activity & Vendor Info: (Acquisitions) Brodart; (Cataloging) Brodart; (Circulation) Brodart; (ILL) Brodart; (OPAC) Brodart; (Serials) Brodart
Wireless access
Mem of Franklin County Library System
Special Services for the Blind - Talking bks
Open Mon-Fri 9-8:30, Sat 9-5
Friends of the Library Group

GL FRANKLIN COUNTY LAW LIBRARY ASSOCIATION*, Franklin County Law Library, 100 Lincoln Way E, Ste E, 17201-2291. SAN 314-3953. Tel: 717-263-4809. FAX: 717-264-1992. E-mail: lawlibrary@franklinbar.org.
Database Vendor: Westlaw

P FRANKLIN COUNTY LIBRARY SYSTEM*, 101 Ragged Edge Rd S, 17202. SAN 314-3937. Tel: 717-709-0282. FAX: 717-263-2248. Web Site: www.fclspa.org. *Dir,* Bernice Crouse; *Cat,* Kay Heller; *Ref,* Moriah Miller; Staff 13 (MLS 8, Non-MLS 5)
Founded 1998. Pop 121,825; Circ 492,052
Library Holdings: AV Mats 13,952; CDs 302; Bk Titles 133,842; Bk Vols 267,684; Per Subs 360; Videos 791
Special Collections: Family Place; Spanish Coll
Subject Interests: Genealogy, Local hist
Automation Activity & Vendor Info: (Cataloging) OCLC; (Circulation) AmLib Library Management System; (ILL) OCLC; (OPAC) AmLib Library Management System
Wireless access
Member Libraries: Alexander Hamilton Memorial Free Library; Coyle Free Library; Fort Loudon Community Library; Grove Family Library; Lilian S Besore Memorial Library; Saint Thomas Library
Partic in HSLC/Access PA/POWER Library; OCLC Online Computer Library Center, Inc
Special Services for the Blind - Assistive/Adapted tech devices, equip & products; Descriptive video serv (DVS)
Bookmobiles: 1. Librn, Amanda Flagle. Bk titles 6,582

P GROVE FAMILY LIBRARY*, 101 Ragged Edge Rd S, 17202. SAN 314-3961. Tel: 717-264-9663. FAX: 717-264-6055. *Dir,* Joan Peiffer; E-mail: jpeiffer@fclspa.org; Staff 3 (MLS 1, Non-MLS 2)
Founded 1948. Pop 25,384; Circ 72,501
Jan 2005-Dec 2005. Mats Exp $22,893
Library Holdings: Bk Vols 51,113
Special Collections: Family Place
Subject Interests: Local hist, Needlework
Automation Activity & Vendor Info: (Circulation) AmLib Library Management System; (OPAC) AmLib Library Management System
Mem of Franklin County Library System
Partic in HSLC/Access PA/POWER Library
Open Mon & Tues 9-8, Wed & Fri 9-5, Thurs 12-8, Sat 9-3
Friends of the Library Group
Bookmobiles: 2

S KITTOCHTINNY HISTORICAL SOCIETY LIBRARY*, 175 E King St, 17201. SAN 374-9231. Tel: 717-264-1667. *Head Librn,* Lillian Colletta; Staff 1 (Non-MLS 1)
Library Holdings: Bk Titles 26,810; Bk Vols 28,000; Per Subs 21
Subject Interests: Genealogy, Local hist
Open Thurs-Sat 9:30-4

C WILSON COLLEGE*, John Stewart Memorial Library, 1015 Philadelphia Ave, 17201-1285. SAN 314-397X. Tel: 717-264-4141. Circulation Tel: 717-262-2008. Interlibrary Loan Service Tel: 717-264-4141, Ext 3380. Reference Tel: 717-264-4141, Ext 3294. Administration Tel: 717-264-4141, Ext 5114. Information Services Tel: 717-264-4141, Ext 3295. Web Site: www.wilson.edu. *Dir,* Kathleen Murphy; E-mail: kmurphy@wilson.edu; *Cat Librn,* Kelly Spiese; E-mail: kspiese@wilson.edu; *Pub Serv Librn,* Andrew Frank; E-mail: andrew.frank@wilson.edu; *ILL, Libr Tech,* Jonathan Clark; E-mail: joclark@wilson.edu; Staff 3 (MLS 3)
Founded 1869. Enrl 776; Fac 77; Highest Degree: Master
Library Holdings: Bk Vols 175,372; Per Subs 312
Subject Interests: Art, Local hist, Veterinary med, Women's studies
Automation Activity & Vendor Info: (Acquisitions) LibLime; (Cataloging) LibLime; (Circulation) LibLime; (Course Reserve) LibLime; (ILL) OCLC; (OPAC) LibLime; (Serials) LibLime
Database Vendor: Agricola, Alexander Street Press, American Psychological Association (APA), Annual Reviews, ARTstor, Atlas Systems, BioOne, Checkpoint Systems, Inc, CQ Press, CredoReference, ebrary, EBSCOhost, Gale Cengage Learning, JSTOR, LexisNexis, LibLime, Medline, Modern Language Association, OCLC, OCLC ArticleFirst, OCLC CAMIO, OCLC FirstSearch, OCLC WorldShare Interlibrary Loan, ProQuest, ScienceDirect, SerialsSolutions, YBP Library Services
Wireless access
Partic in Lyrasis; OCLC Online Computer Library Center, Inc
Open Mon-Thurs 8am-11pm, Fri 8-4, Sat 9-5, Sun 1-11

CHARLEROI

P JOHN K TENER LIBRARY*, 638 Fallowfield Ave, 15022-1996. SAN 314-3988. Tel: 724-483-8282. FAX: 724-483-3478. E-mail: charlibrary@comcast.net. Web Site: www.charleroilibrary.org. *Dir,* Toni Gajan
Founded 1941. Pop 13,175; Circ 16,000
Library Holdings: DVDs 525; Bk Vols 23,746; Per Subs 35; Talking Bks 1,100; Videos 750
Function: Home delivery & serv to Sr ctr & nursing homes, Homebound delivery serv, ILL available, Prog for adults, Prog for children & young adult, Summer reading prog, VHS videos
Open Mon-Thurs 10-8, Fri & Sat 10-5
Friends of the Library Group

CHESTER

P J LEWIS CROZER LIBRARY*, 620 Engle St, 19013-2199. SAN 314-4011. Tel: 610-494-3454. Interlibrary Loan Service Tel: 610-494-3459. FAX: 610-494-8954. E-mail: crdirector@delcolibraries.org. *Exec Dir,* LaTanya C Burno; *Asst Dir,* Barbara Lidle; E-mail: crill@delcolibraries.org; Staff 2 (MLS 2)
Founded 1894. Pop 36,854
Library Holdings: AV Mats 1,500; Large Print Bks 175; Bk Titles 18,100; Bk Vols 52,000; Per Subs 90; Talking Bks 250

Subject Interests: African-Am hist, Chester City hist, Del County hist
Automation Activity & Vendor Info: (Cataloging) Innovative Interfaces, Inc; (Circulation) Innovative Interfaces, Inc; (ILL) Innovative Interfaces, Inc
Mem of Delaware County Library System
Open Mon-Thurs 9-6, Fri 9-5, Sat 9-4 (9-1 Summer)

S DELAWARE COUNTY HISTORICAL SOCIETY*, Museum & Research Library, 408 Avenue of the States, 19013. SAN 314-402X. Tel: 610-872-0502. Administration Tel: 610-359-0832. FAX: 610-872-0503. Administration FAX: 610-359-0839. Web Site: www.delawarecountyhistoricalsociety-pa.org. *Librn,* Margaret F Johnson; E-mail: mfdjohnson@gmail.com; Staff 1 (Non-MLS 1)
Founded 1895
Library Holdings: Bk Titles 7,280; Bk Vols 8,100; Per Subs 19
Special Collections: Atlases & Maps; Borough Township Files, articles, booklets, news clippings, photos; Chester & Upland Borough Birth Records; Chester County Tax Records, 1715-1800, microfilm; Chester F Baker Notebooks; Church Records; Genealogy Coll, bks, ms; Local Historical Places & People (Dr Anna Broomall Notebook Coll), info, news clippings, photos; New Jersey Archives; Newspaper Coll, microfilm; Pennsylvania Archives; Pennsylvania Cemetery Records, Obituaries & Funeral Records; Pennsylvania Census Information; Pennsylvania Colonial Records; Pennsylvania Magazine of History & Biography, 1877 to date; Photograph Coll. Oral History
Subject Interests: Genealogy, Hist of Delaware county, Maps
Wireless access
Function: Res libr
Publications: The Bulletin (Newsletter)
Open Tues 1-8, Wed 9-4, Sat 9-2

C WIDENER UNIVERSITY*, Wolfgram Memorial Library, One University Pl, 19013-5792. SAN 358-3503. Tel: 610-499-4067. Interlibrary Loan Service Tel: 610-499-4070. FAX: 610-499-4588. Web Site: www.widener.edu/libraries. *Dir,* Robert Danford; Tel: 610-499-4087, E-mail: redanford@widener.edu; *Head, Pub Serv,* Susan Tsiouris; *Head, Ref & Instruction,* Samuel Stormont; Tel: 610 499-4080, E-mail: srstormont@widener.edu; *Ref Librn,* Jill Borin; *Ref Librn,* Molly Wolf; *Syst Adminr, Tech Serv,* Deborah Holl; Tel: 610-499-4299; *Archivist, Ref,* Janet Alexander; Tel: 610-449-4591; *Cat,* Rosalyn Goldstein; Tel: 610-499-4079. Subject Specialists: *Psychol,* Susan Tsiouris; *Hist, Soc work,* Jill Borin; *Educ, Human sexuality,* Molly Wolf; Staff 12 (MLS 12)
Founded 1821. Enrl 5,042; Fac 273; Highest Degree: Doctorate
Library Holdings: Bk Titles 157,631; Bk Vols 403,889; Per Subs 2,256
Special Collections: Lindsay Law; Wolfgram Coll (English & American Literature)
Subject Interests: Bus mgt, Clinical psychol, Educ, Eng, Hotel mgt, Humanities, Nursing, Phys therapy, Soc work
Database Vendor: Innovative Interfaces, Inc
Publications: AV Catalog; Faculty Handbook; User Guides; WolfGRAM (Newsletter)
Partic in Lyrasis; OCLC Online Computer Library Center, Inc; Pennsylvania Academic Library Consortium, Inc (PALCI)
Open Mon-Thurs (Winter) 8am-11:30pm, Fri 8am-9pm, Sat 9-5, Sun Noon-11:30; Mon-Thurs (Summer) 7:30am-10pm, Fri 7:30-5, Sat 10-3, Sun 1-6

CHESTER SPRINGS

P CHESTER SPRINGS LIBRARY*, 1685A Art School Rd, 19425-1402. SAN 320-8508. Tel: 610-827-9212. FAX: 610-827-1148. Web Site: www.ccls.org. *Dir,* Nancy Mclaughlin; E-mail: nmclaughlin@ccls.org; Staff 5 (MLS 1, Non-MLS 4)
Founded 1978. Pop 13,626; Circ 1,463
Library Holdings: AV Mats 1,524; Large Print Bks 281; Bk Vols 19,338; Per Subs 38; Talking Bks 397
Subject Interests: Local hist
Automation Activity & Vendor Info: (Acquisitions) Innovative Interfaces, Inc; (Cataloging) Innovative Interfaces, Inc; (Circulation) Innovative Interfaces, Inc; (OPAC) Innovative Interfaces, Inc; (Serials) Innovative Interfaces, Inc
Wireless access
Function: ILL available, Photocopying/Printing, Prog for children & young adult, Ref serv available, Summer reading prog
Mem of Chester County Library System
Open Mon & Wed 10-6, Tues & Thurs 12-6, Fri 10-5, Sat 10-4, Sun 12-4
Friends of the Library Group

CHEYNEY

C CHEYNEY UNIVERSITY*, Leslie Pinckney Hill Library, 1837 University Circle, 19319. (Mail add: PO Box 200, 19319-0200), SAN 314-4062. Tel: 610-399-2203. FAX: 610-399-2491. Web Site: www.cheyney.edu. *Dean,* Lut R Nero; E-mail: lnero@cheyney.edu; *Archives,* Bingham F Keith; E-mail: kbingham@cheyney.edu; *Circ,* Jim Plank; *Govt Doc, Pub Serv,* Abdul Aden; E-mail: aaden@cheyney.edu; *Info Serv,* B J Mullaney; E-mail: bmullane@cheyney.edu; *Tech Serv,* Lily Qi; E-mail: lqi@cheyney.edu; Staff 10 (MLS 6, Non-MLS 4)
Founded 1853. Enrl 1,692; Fac 107; Highest Degree: Master
Library Holdings: Bk Titles 198,641; Bk Vols 228,421; Per Subs 1,126; Videos 1,279
Special Collections: Afro-American studies; Ethnic Coll; University Archives. State Document Depository; US Document Depository
Automation Activity & Vendor Info: (Cataloging) Ex Libris Group; (Circulation) Ex Libris Group; (ILL) OCLC; (OPAC) Ex Libris Group
Database Vendor: EBSCOhost
Publications: Annual Report; Newsletter; Student & Faculty Handbooks
Partic in OCLC Online Computer Library Center, Inc; State System of Higher Education Library Cooperative; Tri-State College Library Cooperative
Open Mon-Thurs 8:30am-10pm, Fri 8:30-5, Sat 11-4, Sun 4-10

CHRISTIANA

P MOORES MEMORIAL LIBRARY*, Nine W Slokom Ave, 17509-1202. SAN 314-4070. Tel: 610-593-6683. FAX: 610-593-7044. E-mail: chrlib@christianalibrary.org. Web Site: www.christianalibrary.org. *Dir,* Claudia Roun; Staff 3 (Non-MLS 3)
Founded 1881. Pop 6,000; Circ 60,000
Library Holdings: AV Mats 400; Bks on Deafness & Sign Lang 25; DVDs 800; High Interest/Low Vocabulary Bk Vols 50; Large Print Bks 200; Bk Titles 13,000; Per Subs 32; Talking Bks 50; Videos 150
Special Collections: Christiana Riot of 1851 - Prelude to Civil War. State Document Depository
Subject Interests: Local hist
Wireless access
Function: Homework prog, ILL available, Learning ctr, Mus passes, Music CDs, Online cat, Online ref, Online searches, OverDrive digital audio bks, Photocopying/Printing, Prog for adults, Prog for children & young adult, Spoken cassettes & CDs, Story hour, Summer reading prog, Tax forms
Mem of Library System of Lancaster County
Open Tues-Thurs 1-7, Fri 1-6, Sat 10-4
Friends of the Library Group

CLAIRTON

P CLAIRTON PUBLIC LIBRARY*, 616 Miller Ave, 15025-1497. SAN 358-3538. Tel: 412-233-7966. FAX: 412-233-2536. Web Site: www.clairtonlibrary.org. *Dir,* Emma J Anderson; Staff 1 (MLS 1)
Founded 1920. Pop 9,656; Circ 35,000
Library Holdings: Bk Vols 35,600; Per Subs 66
Automation Activity & Vendor Info: (Cataloging) Innovative Interfaces, Inc; (Circulation) Innovative Interfaces, Inc; (OPAC) Innovative Interfaces, Inc
Wireless access
Mem of Allegheny County Library Association
Open Mon 9-8, Tues-Thurs 9-5, Fri 10-5, Sat 9-4
Friends of the Library Group

CLARION

S CLARION COUNTY HISTORICAL SOCIETY*, Ralph J & Virginia A Fulton Library, 17 S Fifth Ave, 16214-1501. SAN 326-2871. Tel: 814-226-4450. FAX: 814-226-7106. E-mail: clarionhistory@comcast.net. Web Site: www.orgsites.com/pa/clarioncountyhistoricalsociety. *Exec Dir,* Mary Lea Lucas; *Librn,* Mary Jane Miller. Subject Specialists: *Genealogy, Local hist,* Mary Lea Lucas; Staff 1 (Non-MLS 1)
Founded 1955
Library Holdings: Bk Titles 2,500; Per Subs 20
Special Collections: Birth & Delayed Birth Certificates; Bound Local Newspaper Books 1894-1970; Civil War Regimentals; Clarion County Documents & Photographs; County Cemetery Records; Death Certificates; Family Histories; Genealogy, bks & mss; Native American Coll; Obituaries; Western Pennsylvania & County History. Oral History
Subject Interests: County hist, Genealogy
Wireless access
Function: Archival coll, Copy machines, Genealogy discussion group, Handicapped accessible, Wheelchair accessible, Workshops
Publications: Iron County Chronicle (Newsletter)
Partic in OCLC via Clarion District Libr Asn
Open Mon-Fri 10-4
Restriction: Not a lending libr, Open evenings by appt

P CLARION FREE LIBRARY*, 644 Main St, 16214. SAN 314-4119. Tel: 814-226-7172. FAX: 814-226-6750. E-mail: director@clarionfreelibrary.org. Web Site: www.clarionfreelibrary.org. *Exec Dir,* Daniel R Parker; E-mail: dparker@clarionfreelibrary.org; *Ch Serv,* Jean Smith; E-mail: jsmith@clarionfreelibrary.org; *ILL,* Mary O'Hara; E-mail: mohara@clarionfreelibrary.org; Staff 6 (MLS 1, Non-MLS 5)
Founded 1914. Pop 21,254; Circ 121,215

Library Holdings: AV Mats 2,160; Bks on Deafness & Sign Lang 25; High Interest/Low Vocabulary Bk Vols 400; Large Print Bks 1,486; Bk Titles 45,453; Bk Vols 47,753; Per Subs 76; Talking Bks 930
Special Collections: Census 1790 to 1920, microfiche; Clarion News & Leader-Vindicator, 1868-present, newsp on micro
Subject Interests: Local hist
Automation Activity & Vendor Info: (Cataloging) TLC (The Library Corporation); (Circulation) TLC (The Library Corporation); (OPAC) TLC (The Library Corporation)
Database Vendor: EBSCOhost, ProQuest
Function: AV serv, Handicapped accessible, ILL available, Newsp ref libr, Photocopying/Printing, Prof lending libr, Prog for children & young adult, Summer reading prog, Telephone ref, Wheelchair accessible
Mem of Oil Creek District Library Center
Open Mon-Thurs 9-8, Fri 9-5, Sat 8:30-3:30

C CLARION UNIVERSITY OF PENNSYLVANIA, Rena M Carlson Library, 840 Wood St, 16214. SAN 358-3597. Tel: 814-393-2343. Circulation Tel: 814-393-2301. Interlibrary Loan Service Tel: 814-393-2481. Reference Tel: 814-393-1841. FAX: 814-393-2344. Reference FAX: 814-393-1862. E-mail: libsupport@clarion.edu. Web Site: www.clarion.edu/library. *Dean,* Dr Terry S Latour; Tel: 814-393-1931, E-mail: tlatour@clarion.edu; *Cataloger, Librn, Tech Serv Coordr,* Shirley M Johnson; Tel: 814-393-2746, E-mail: sjohnson@clarion.edu; *Archivist, Ref Librn,* Corene Glotfelty; Tel: 814-393-1805, E-mail: cglotfelty@clarion.edu; *Coll Develop Coordr, Ref Librn,* Basil D Martin; Tel: 814-393-2303, E-mail: bmartin@clarion.edu; *Ref Librn/Info Literacy Coordr,* Mary Buchanan; Tel: 814-393-1811, E-mail: mbuchanan@clarion.edu; *Virtual Learning & Outreach Librn,* Linda Cheresnowski; Tel: 814-393-2329, E-mail: lcheresnowsk@clarion.edu; *AV Coordr, Syst Mgr,* William Trimble; Tel: 814-393-2017, E-mail: wtrimble@clarion.edu; *Per Coordr,* Sandy Chen; Tel: 814-393-2748, E-mail: schen@clarion.edu; *ILL, Libr Tech,* Ginger McGiffin; E-mail: gmcgiffin@clarion.edu; *Circ, Libr Tech, Reserves,* Melissa Pierce; Tel: 814-393-2304, E-mail: mpierce@clarion.edu; *Database Mgt/Bibliog Access & Control Librn,* Pat Johner; Tel: 814-393-2749, E-mail: pjohner@clarion.edu; Staff 21 (MLS 9, Non-MLS 12)
Founded 1867. Enrl 6,080; Highest Degree: Master
Library Holdings: AV Mats 7,303; e-books 146,296; e-journals 40,951; Microforms 1,504,927; Bk Titles 439,647; Bk Vols 593,203; Per Subs 30,836
Special Collections: Harvey Center for Study of Oil Heritage. State Document Depository
Subject Interests: British Commonwealth
Automation Activity & Vendor Info: (Acquisitions) Ex Libris Group; (Cataloging) Ex Libris Group; (Circulation) Ex Libris Group; (ILL) OCLC ILLiad; (OPAC) Ex Libris Group; (Serials) Ex Libris Group
Database Vendor: ABC-CLIO, Access Pennsylvania, American Chemical Society, American Psychological Association (APA), Bowker, Cambridge Scientific Abstracts, Cinahl, College Source, CQ Press, CRC Press/Taylor & Francis Group, CredoReference, Dialog, Dun & Bradstreet, ebrary, EBSCO Discovery Service, EBSCOhost, Elsevier, Emerald, Gale Cengage Learning, Infotrieve, infoUSA, JSTOR, LexisNexis, Mergent Online, OCLC CAMIO, OCLC FirstSearch, OCLC WorldShare Interlibrary Loan, OVID Technologies, Oxford Online, ProQuest, ScienceDirect, STN International, Westlaw, Wilson - Wilson Web, YBP Library Services
Wireless access
Function: Archival coll, ILL available, Photocopying/Printing
Publications: The United Kingdom of Great Britain & Ireland: An Annotated Bibliography of Documentary Sources in Carlson Library
Partic in Interlibrary Delivery Service of Pennsylvania; Keystone Library Network; Lyrasis; Northwest Interlibrary Cooperative of Pennsylvania; Pennsylvania Academic Library Consortium, Inc (PALCI)
Special Services for the Blind - Computer with voice synthesizer for visually impaired persons; Magnifiers
Open Mon-Thurs 7:45am-Midnight, Fri 7:45-5, Sat 9-5, Sun 1-Midnight
Friends of the Library Group

CLARKS SUMMIT

P ABINGTON COMMUNITY LIBRARY*, 1200 W Grove St, 18411-9501. SAN 314-4127. Tel: 570-587-3440. Web Site: www.lclshome.org/abington. *Dir,* Leah Rudolph; Staff 4 (MLS 3, Non-MLS 1)
Founded 1961. Pop 22,523; Circ 260,019
Library Holdings: Bk Vols 70,000; Per Subs 100
Special Collections: Classical Sheet Music Coll. Oral History
Automation Activity & Vendor Info: (Cataloging) SirsiDynix; (Circulation) SirsiDynix; (ILL) OCLC; (OPAC) SirsiDynix
Mem of Lackawanna County Library System
Open Mon-Fri 9-9, Sat 9-5, Sun 2-5
Friends of the Library Group

CR BAPTIST BIBLE COLLEGE & SEMINARY*, Murphy Memorial Library, 538 Venard Rd, 18411-1250. SAN 358-3627. Tel: 570-585-9281. Circulation Tel: 570-585-9284. Interlibrary Loan Service Tel: 570-585-9282. FAX: 570-585-9244. Web Site: www.bbc.edu. *Libr Dir,* Joshua Michael; E-mail: jmichael@bbc.edu; Staff 3 (MLS 3)
Founded 1932. Enrl 942; Highest Degree: Doctorate
Library Holdings: AV Mats 14,000; e-journals 10,777; Bk Vols 103,819; Per Subs 356
Subject Interests: Biblical studies, Christian educ, Church hist, Church ministries, Church music, Counseling, Theol
Automation Activity & Vendor Info: (Cataloging) TLC (The Library Corporation); (Circulation) TLC (The Library Corporation); (OPAC) TLC (The Library Corporation)
Database Vendor: BCR: Christian Periodical Index, EBSCOhost, JSTOR, Newsbank, OCLC FirstSearch, OCLC WorldShare Interlibrary Loan, ProQuest, SerialsSolutions, TLC (The Library Corporation)
Wireless access
Open Mon-Thurs 8am-10pm, Fri 8-5, Sat 11-5, Sun 2-5 & 8-10

CLAYSBURG

P CLAYSBURG AREA PUBLIC LIBRARY*, 957 Bedford St, 16625. (Mail add: PO Box 189, 16625-0189), SAN 314-4135. Tel: 814-239-8647. FAX: 814-239-2782. *Libr Dir,* Jane Knisely; *Asst Librn,* Pam Musselman; *Libr Tech,* Margie Ebersole; Staff 3 (Non-MLS 3)
Founded 1965. Pop 6,650; Circ 22,000
Library Holdings: Bks on Deafness & Sign Lang 12; Braille Volumes 1; CDs 111; DVDs 253; Large Print Bks 280; Bk Titles 25,207; Bk Vols 25,257; Per Subs 55; Talking Bks 448; Videos 149
Wireless access
Mem of Blair County Library System
Open Mon & Thurs 10-7, Tues & Wed 10-5
Friends of the Library Group

CLEARFIELD

L CLEARFIELD COUNTY LAW LIBRARY*, Courthouse, 2nd Flr, Ste 228, 230 E Market St, 16830. SAN 327-1102. Tel: 814-765-2641. FAX: 814-765-7649. *Librn,* Carol Mease; Staff 1 (Non-MLS 1)
Library Holdings: Bk Titles 11,421; Bk Vols 13,559; Per Subs 71
Subject Interests: Pa law
Database Vendor: Westlaw
Open Mon-Fri 8:30-4
Friends of the Library Group

P JOSEPH & ELIZABETH SHAW PUBLIC LIBRARY, One S Front St, 16830. SAN 314-4143. Tel: 814-765-3271. FAX: 814-765-6316. Web Site: www.clearfield.org/shaw. *Dir,* Paula J Collins; E-mail: pcollins@clearfield.org; *Youth Serv,* Erin Wills; E-mail: shawyouthservices@clearfield.org; *Tech Asst,* Deborah Shope; Staff 8 (MLS 1, Non-MLS 7)
Founded 1940. Pop 16,930; Circ 78,000
Library Holdings: Bk Titles 55,000; Per Subs 80
Special Collections: Art (Thomas Murray Chase Coll); Pennsylvania & Clearfield County PA History Coll
Subject Interests: Genealogy, Local hist
Automation Activity & Vendor Info: (Cataloging) TLC (The Library Corporation); (Circulation) TLC (The Library Corporation); (Serials) TLC (The Library Corporation)
Database Vendor: EBSCOhost, Overdrive, Inc, TLC (The Library Corporation), TumbleBookLibrary
Wireless access
Function: ILL available
Partic in Cent Pa District
Open Mon, Wed & Sat 10-5, Tues & Thurs 10-9, Fri 12-5
Friends of the Library Group

COALPORT

P GLENDALE AREA PUBLIC LIBRARY INC, Community Bldg, 961 Forest St, 16627. Tel: 814-672-4378. E-mail: gapli814@gmail.com. Web Site: glendaleareapubliclibrary.org. *Dir,* Nancy Washell; Fax: 814-672-5973; Staff 1 (Non-MLS 1)
Founded 1979
Library Holdings: Bk Titles 10,640; Bk Vols 11,031; Per Subs 12
Subject Interests: Local hist
Wireless access
Open Mon-Wed 10-4, Thurs 12-8, Sun 1-4
Friends of the Library Group

COATESVILLE

M BRANDYWINE HOSPITAL & TRAUMA CENTER*, Health Sciences Library, 201 Reeceville Rd, 19320. SAN 322-7340. Tel: 610-383-8147. FAX: 610-383-8243. *Dir,* Margo P Dinniman; Staff 1 (MLS 1)
Library Holdings: Bk Titles 3,000; Per Subs 250
Special Collections: Nursing Education & Research Coll

Automation Activity & Vendor Info: (Acquisitions) Winnebago Software Co; (Cataloging) Winnebago Software Co; (Circulation) Winnebago Software Co
Database Vendor: EBSCOhost, ProQuest
Partic in Docline
Restriction: Open by appt only

P COATESVILLE AREA PUBLIC LIBRARY*, 501 E Lincoln Hwy, 19320-3413. SAN 314-4151. Tel: 610-384-4115. FAX: 610-384-7551. Web Site: www.coatesvilleareallibrary.org. *Interim Dir,* Kim Belknap; Tel: 610-384-9647; *Youth Serv Spec,* Sherry Christman; E-mail: schristman@ccls.org; Staff 5 (MLS 2, Non-MLS 3)
Founded 1936. Pop 53,400
Jan 2005-Dec 2005 Income $310,000. Mats Exp $5,500. Sal $179,000 (Prof $48,000)
Library Holdings: Bks on Deafness & Sign Lang 15; DVDs 200; Bk Vols 65,000; Per Subs 85; Talking Bks 760; Videos 1,600
Special Collections: Oral History
Subject Interests: Local hist, Multicultural
Automation Activity & Vendor Info: (Cataloging) Innovative Interfaces, Inc; (Circulation) Innovative Interfaces, Inc; (ILL) Innovative Interfaces, Inc; (OPAC) Innovative Interfaces, Inc
Database Vendor: Innovative Interfaces, Inc
Wireless access
Publications: Annual Report
Mem of Chester County Library System
Open Mon & Thurs 10-8, Tues & Wed 10-6, Fri 10-5, Sat 9-4 (July-Aug 10-2)

GM DEPARTMENT OF VETERANS AFFAIRS*, Medical Center Library, 1400 Black Horse Hill Rd, 19320-2040. SAN 314-4178. Tel: 610-383-0288, 610-384-7711. FAX: 610-383-0245. Web Site: www.coatesville.va.gov. *Chief Librn,* Andrew Henry; E-mail: andrew.henry@med.va.gov; Staff 1 (MLS 1)
Founded 1931
Library Holdings: Bk Titles 13,680; Bk Vols 14,390; Per Subs 392
Subject Interests: Neurology, Patient health educ, Psychiat
Database Vendor: OVID Technologies
Partic in BRS; Consortium for Health Information & Library Services; Docline; National Network of Libraries of Medicine; Veterans Affairs Libr Network (VALNET)
Restriction: Staff use only

COCHRANTON

P COCHRANTON AREA PUBLIC LIBRARY*, 107 W Pine St, 16314-0296. SAN 314-4186. Tel: 814-425-3996. FAX: 814-425-3996. E-mail: cochpl@hotmail.com. Web Site: www.ccfls.org/cochranton. *Librn,* Deanna Gray; *Asst Librn,* Jennifer Winger
Founded 1969. Pop 5,390; Circ 12,411
Library Holdings: Bk Vols 19,000; Per Subs 30
Automation Activity & Vendor Info: (Cataloging) Follett Software; (Circulation) Follett Software
Mem of Crawford County Federated Library System
Open Mon & Wed 5-9, Tues & Thurs 9-5, Fri 10-2, Sat 9-4 (9-1 Summer)

COLLEGEVILLE

C URSINUS COLLEGE LIBRARY*, Myrin Library, 601 E Main St, 19426. (Mail add: PO Box 1000, 19426-1000), SAN 314-4194. Tel: 610-409-3607. FAX: 610-489-0634. Web Site: www.ursinus.edu. *Libr Dir,* Charles A Jamison; Tel: 610-409-3243, E-mail: cjamison@ursinus.edu; *Info Literacy Librn,* Diane Skorina; Tel: 610-409-3022, E-mail: dskorina@ursinus.edu; *IT Librn,* David H Mill; Tel: 610-409-3301, E-mail: dmill@ursinus.edu; *Tech Serv Librn,* Kerry Gibson; Tel: 610-409-3460, E-mail: kgibson@ursinus.edu; *Circ Supvr,* Maureen Damiano; E-mail: mdamiano@ursinus.edu; Staff 11 (MLS 4, Non-MLS 7)
Founded 1870. Enrl 1,570; Fac 100; Highest Degree: Bachelor
Library Holdings: Bk Vols 420,000; Per Subs 1,200
Special Collections: Linda Grace Hoyer Updike Literary Papers; Pennsylvania German Studies Archives; The Pennsylvania Folklife Society Coll; Ursinusiana Coll. State Document Depository; US Document Depository
Subject Interests: Behav sci, Hist, Natural sci, Pa German, Recreation studies, Soc sci, Women's studies
Automation Activity & Vendor Info: (Circulation) SirsiDynix
Database Vendor: SirsiDynix
Wireless access
Publications: Myrin Library News
Partic in Interlibrary Delivery Service of Pennsylvania; Tri-State College Library Cooperative
Open Mon-Thurs (Fall & Spring) 8am-2am, Fri 8am-9pm, Sat 9-9, Sun 10am-2am; Mon-Thurs (Summer) 8-7, Fri 8-4:30
Friends of the Library Group

COLLINGDALE

P COLLINGDALE PUBLIC LIBRARY*, 823 MacDade Blvd, 19023-1422. SAN 314-4208. Tel: 610-583-2214. FAX: 610-583-0172. E-mail: collingdale@delcolibraries.org. Web Site: www.delco.lib.pa.us. *Dir,* Gerry Finley
Founded 1937. Pop 9,100; Circ 16,463
Library Holdings: Bk Vols 14,300; Per Subs 15
Mem of Delaware County Library System
Open Mon-Fri 1-7, Sat 10-5

COLUMBIA

P COLUMBIA PUBLIC LIBRARY*, 24 S Sixth St, 17512-1599. SAN 314-4224. Tel: 717-684-2255. FAX: 717-684-5920. Web Site: www.columbia.lib.pa.us. *Adminr,* Lisa Greybill; E-mail: lgreybill@columbia.lib.pa.us; Staff 1 (Non-MLS 1)
Pop 10,311; Circ 36,910
Library Holdings: Bk Titles 26,817; Bk Vols 27,410; Per Subs 58; Talking Bks 416; Videos 722
Special Collections: Lloyd Mifflin Works
Subject Interests: Civil War, Local art, Local hist
Automation Activity & Vendor Info: (Serials) EBSCO Online
Wireless access
Publications: Newsletter (Monthly)
Mem of Library System of Lancaster County
Open Mon-Thurs 10-8, Fri 10-6, Sat 9-4

S NATIONAL WATCH & CLOCK MUSEUM*, Library & Research Center, 514 Poplar St, 17512-2124. SAN 321-0251. Tel: 717-684-8261. FAX: 717-684-0142. Web Site: www.nawcc.org. *Libr Dir,* Sara Butler Dockery; Tel: 717-684-8261, Ext 224, E-mail: sdockery@nawcc.org; *Archivist, Librn,* Nancy Dyer; Tel: 717-684-8261, Ext 214, E-mail: ndyer@nawcc.org
Founded 1965
Library Holdings: Bk Vols 30,000; Per Subs 50
Special Collections: Hamilton Watch Co Records & Publications; Seth Thomas Ledgers & Publications
Open Mon-Thurs 8-5, Fri 8-4, Sat 12-4
Restriction: Open to pub for ref only

CONNEAUT LAKE

P MARGARET SHONTZ MEMORIAL LIBRARY*, Conneaut Lake Public Library, 145 Second St, 16316-5117. SAN 320-5053. Tel: 814-382-6666. FAX: 814-382-6666. E-mail: shontzpl@ccfls.org. *Librn,* Betty Ecklund
Founded 1971. Pop 4,300
Library Holdings: Bk Titles 14,000; Per Subs 26
Automation Activity & Vendor Info: (Circulation) Follett Software
Mem of Crawford County Federated Library System
Open Mon 10-4, Tues & Thurs 1-5, Wed 6-8

CONNEAUTVILLE

P STONE MEMORIAL LIBRARY*, 1101 Main St, 16406. (Mail add: PO Box 281, 16406-0281), SAN 314-4240. Tel: 814-587-2142. FAX: 814-587-2142. Web Site: ccfls.org/stone/. *Librn,* Doreen Nelson; *Asst Librn, Ch Serv,* Telce McCann
Founded 1903. Pop 2,086; Circ 19,681
Library Holdings: Bk Titles 20,000; Per Subs 41
Mem of Crawford County Federated Library System
Open Mon 2-8, Tues & Thurs 10-6, Fri 1-7, Sat 8-3

CONNELLSVILLE

P CARNEGIE FREE LIBRARY*, 299 S Pittsburgh St, 15425-3580. SAN 314-4259. Tel: 724-628-1380. FAX: 724-628-5636. E-mail: carnegie@zoominternet.net. Web Site: www.carnegiefreelib.org. *Dir,* Casey Sirochman; E-mail: casey.ccfl@gmail.com; Staff 5 (MLS 2, Non-MLS 3)
Founded 1903. Pop 34,835; Circ 45,000
Library Holdings: Audiobooks 380; DVDs 150; Bk Titles 42,265; Per Subs 108; Videos 159
Special Collections: Local & Fayette County History (Pennsylvania Coll)
Automation Activity & Vendor Info: (Cataloging) Follett Software; (Circulation) Follett Software; (OPAC) Follett Software
Wireless access
Publications: Newsletter
Open Mon & Wed (Winter) 10-8, Tues & Thurs 10-6, Fri & Sat 10-5; Mon (Summer) 10-8, Tues-Thurs 10-6, Fri & Sat 10-5
Friends of the Library Group

CONSHOHOCKEN

S PQ CORP*, Information Services Center, 280 Cedar Grove Rd, 19428-2240. SAN 314-6731. Tel: 610-651-4629. FAX: 610-832-2931. *Mgr,* Dolores A Whitehurst; E-mail: dori.whitehurst@pqcorp.com; Staff 1 (MLS 1)

Founded 1925
Library Holdings: Bk Titles 3,000; Per Subs 90
Subject Interests: Bus, Ceramics, Chem, Potassium silicates, Sodium
Database Vendor: Dialog, Factiva.com, STN International
Function: For res purposes, ILL available, Online searches, Res libr
Publications: Bulletin
Partic in OCLC Online Computer Library Center, Inc; Piers; Questal Orbit
Restriction: Private libr

COOPERSTOWN

P COOPERSTOWN PUBLIC LIBRARY*, 182 N Main St, 16317. (Mail add: PO Box 264, 16317-0264), SAN 371-5442. Tel: 814-374-4605. FAX: 814-374-4606. Web Site: www.cooperstownlibrary.org. *Dir,* Jane Beach; E-mail: jane@cooperstownlibrary.org; Staff 1 (Non-MLS 1)
Founded 1987. Pop 4,153
Library Holdings: Bks on Deafness & Sign Lang 22; CDs 164; DVDs 118; Large Print Bks 573; Bk Titles 11,811; Per Subs 30; Talking Bks 759; Videos 613
Automation Activity & Vendor Info: (Cataloging) Follett Software; (Circulation) Follett Software; (OPAC) Follett Software
Wireless access
Mem of Oil Creek District Library Center
Open Mon & Thurs 1-8, Tues & Fri 9-5

COPLAY

P COPLAY PUBLIC LIBRARY*, 49 S Fifth, 18037-1398. SAN 314-4291. Tel: 610-262-7351. FAX: 610-262-4937. E-mail: coplaypubliclibrary@gmail.com. Web Site: www.coplaypubliclibrary.wordpress.com. *Dir,* Julie Hughes, Staff 7 (Non-MLS 7)
Founded 1962. Pop 3,411; Circ 15,000
Library Holdings: Large Print Bks 78; Bk Titles 15,000; Per Subs 30; Talking Bks 490; Videos 1,424
Open Mon & Wed (Winter) 1:30-7:30, Tues 11-7:30, Thurs 1:30-8:30, Fri 1:30-7, Sat 10-5; Mon, Wed & Thurs (Summer) 1:30-7:30, Tues 10-7:30, Fri 1:30-7, Sat 10-2

CORAOPOLIS

P CORAOPOLIS MEMORIAL LIBRARY*, 601 School St, 15108-1196. SAN 314-4305. Tel: 412-264-3502. FAX: 412-269-8982. Web Site: coraopolislibrary.org. *Librn,* Susan McClellan; E-mail: mcclellans@einetwork.net; Staff 6 (MLS 1, Non-MLS 5)
Founded 1937. Pop 6,131; Circ 19,300
Library Holdings: AV Mats 3,000; Bks on Deafness & Sign Lang 25; Large Print Bks 300; Bk Vols 28,800; Per Subs 44
Special Collections: Story Coll
Subject Interests: Genealogy, Pa
Automation Activity & Vendor Info: (Cataloging) Innovative Interfaces, Inc; (Circulation) Innovative Interfaces, Inc
Wireless access
Mem of Allegheny County Library Association
Partic in Electronic Info Network (eiNetwork)
Open Mon-Thurs 10-8, Fri & Sat 10-5

CORRY

P CORRY PUBLIC LIBRARY*, 117 W Washington St, 16407. SAN 314-4321. Tel: 814-664-4404, 814-664-7611. FAX: 814-663-0742. Web Site: www.corrylibrary.org. *Libr Dir,* Marcia Stiller; *Ch Serv,* Tracy Blair; Staff 7.72 (MLS 1, Non-MLS 6.72)
Founded 1900. Pop 12,270; Circ 97,415
Library Holdings: Audiobooks 1,890; AV Mats 2,035; Bk Vols 69,911; Per Subs 108; Spec Interest Per Sub 98
Special Collections: Local Newspaper (Corry Journal, 1902-present), micro
Subject Interests: Genealogy, Pa hist
Automation Activity & Vendor Info: (Acquisitions) SIRSI WorkFlows; (Cataloging) SIRSI WorkFlows; (Circulation) SIRSI WorkFlows; (ILL) SIRSI WorkFlows; (OPAC) SIRSI-iBistro; (Serials) SIRSI WorkFlows
Database Vendor: EBSCOhost, SirsiDynix
Wireless access
Function: Adult bk club, Art exhibits, Bk club(s), Bks on cassette, Bks on CD, CD-ROM, Children's prog, Computers for patron use, Copy machines, e-mail & chat, e-mail serv, Electronic databases & coll, Fax serv, Free DVD rentals, Genealogy discussion group, Handicapped accessible, ILL available, Instruction & testing, Mail & tel request accepted, Music CDs, Online cat, Online searches, Outreach serv, OverDrive digital audio bks, Photocopying/Printing, Preschool outreach, Prog for adults, Prog for children & young adult, Pub access computers, Ref serv available, Ref serv in person, Res performed for a fee, Story hour, Summer reading prog, Tax forms, Telephone ref, VHS videos, Web-catalog, Wheelchair accessible
Partic in Share NW Consortium
Open Mon, Tues & Thurs 10-8, Wed 1-8, Fri 10-6, Sat 10-2, Sun 1-4
Friends of the Library Group

COUDERSPORT

P COUDERSPORT PUBLIC LIBRARY*, 502 Park Ave, 16915-1672. SAN 314-433X. Tel: 814-274-9382. FAX: 814-274-9137. E-mail: coudy502@hotmail.com. *Librn,* Barb Wagner
Founded 1850. Pop 5,405; Circ 36,711
Library Holdings: Bk Titles 20,000; Bk Vols 23,000; Per Subs 76
Mem of Potter-Tioga Library System
Open Mon-Thurs 10-8, Fri 10-6, Sat 10-5

P POTTER-TIOGA LIBRARY SYSTEM*, 502 Park Ave, 16915-1672. SAN 314-7290. Tel: 814-274-7422. FAX: 814-274-7422. E-mail: pottertioga@yahoo.com, pottertioga@zitomedia.net. Web Site: www.pottertiogalibrary.org. *County Librn,* Jody Cole; *Asst County Librn,* Barb Hogan
Founded 1975. Pop 60,343; Circ 224,862
Library Holdings: Bk Vols 209,608; Per Subs 373
Member Libraries: Blossburg Memorial Library; Coudersport Public Library; Elkland Area Community Library; Galeton Public Library; Genesee Area Library; Green Free Library; Knoxville Public Library; Mansfield Free Public Library; Oswayo Valley Memorial Library; Ulysses Library Association; Westfield Public Library
Open Mon-Fri 9-5

CRANBERRY TOWNSHIP

P CRANBERRY PUBLIC LIBRARY*, Municipal Center, 2525 Rochester Rd, Ste 300, 16066-6423. SAN 314-7339. Tel: 724-776-9100. FAX: 724-776-2490. E-mail: cranberry@bcfls.org. Web Site: www.cranberrytownship.org. *Dir,* Leslie Pallotta; Tel: 724-776-9100, Ext 1125; *Ad,* Patricia DiFiore; Tel: 724-776-9100, Ext 1126; *Tech Serv Librn,* Rebecca Bess; Tel: 724-776-9100, Ext 1147; *Teen Serv Librn,* Rachael Troianos; *Youth Serv Librn,* Annemarie Lamperski; Staff 4 (MLS 2, Non-MLS 2)
Founded 1974. Pop 28,098; Circ 294,366
Jan 2013-Dec 2013 Income $592,825. Mats Exp $545,752. Sal $309,567
Library Holdings: Bk Vols 89,335; Per Subs 86
Automation Activity & Vendor Info: (Cataloging) TLC (The Library Corporation); (Circulation) TLC (The Library Corporation); (OPAC) TLC (The Library Corporation)
Database Vendor: EBSCOhost, Gale Cengage Learning
Wireless access
Function: AV serv, Handicapped accessible, ILL available, Magnifiers for reading, Photocopying/Printing, Prog for children & young adult, Ref serv available, Summer reading prog, Telephone ref, Wheelchair accessible
Mem of Butler County Federated Library System
Partic in Midwest Libr Consortium
Special Services for the Deaf - Closed caption videos; High interest/low vocabulary bks
Special Services for the Blind - Computer with voice synthesizer for visually impaired persons
Open Mon-Thurs 10-8, Fri 10-5, Sat 10-4, Sun 1-4
Restriction: In-house use for visitors
Friends of the Library Group

CRESCO

P BARRETT PARADISE FRIENDLY LIBRARY*, 6500 Rte 191, Corner Rte 191/390 & Sand Spring Dr, 18326. SAN 314-7894. Tel: 570-595-7171. FAX: 570-595-7879. E-mail: brfpubli@ptd.net. Web Site: www.barrettlibrary.org. *Libr Dir,* Cindy DeLuca; Staff 1 (Non-MLS 1)
Founded 1909. Pop 6,551; Circ 100,000
Library Holdings: Bk Titles 21,000; Per Subs 250
Automation Activity & Vendor Info: (Cataloging) Innovative Interfaces, Inc - Millenium; (Circulation) Innovative Interfaces, Inc - Millenium; (OPAC) Innovative Interfaces, Inc - Millenium
Wireless access
Function: Adult bk club, Audiobks via web, Bk club(s), Bks on cassette, Bks on CD, Children's prog, Computer training, Computers for patron use, Copy machines, e-mail serv, Electronic databases & coll, Family literacy, Free DVD rentals, Genealogy discussion group, Handicapped accessible, ILL available, Online searches, Preschool outreach, Prog for adults, Prog for children & young adult, Pub access computers, Ref serv available, Ref serv in person, Senior computer classes, Spoken cassettes & CDs, Spoken cassettes & DVDs, Story hour, Summer reading prog, Tax forms, Teen prog, Wheelchair accessible
Open Mon-Thurs 10-8, Fri & Sat 10-5
Friends of the Library Group

CRESSON

P CRESSON PUBLIC LIBRARY*, 231 Laurel Ave, 16630-1118. SAN 314-4356. Tel: 814-886-2619. FAX: 814-886-9564. Web Site: www.cclsys.org/cresson. *Libr Dir,* Ashley N Flynn
Founded 1927. Pop 4,923; Circ 18,904
Library Holdings: Bk Vols 11,041; Per Subs 13
Automation Activity & Vendor Info: (Cataloging) Evergreen; (Circulation) Evergreen; (OPAC) Evergreen
Wireless access
Mem of Cambria County Library System & District Center
Open Mon-Thurs 1-7, Fri 1-5, Sat 8-3

C MOUNT ALOYSIUS COLLEGE LIBRARY*, 7373 Admiral Peary Hwy, 16630-1999. SAN 314-4364. Tel: 814-886-6445. FAX: 814-886-5767. Web Site: www.mtaloy.edu. *Libr Dir,* Position Currently Open; *Coll Mgt Librn,* Robert Stere; E-mail: rstere@mtaloy.edu; *Info Literacy Librn,* Shamim Rajpar; *Cat,* Joan Mix; Staff 7 (MLS 3, Non-MLS 4)
Founded 1939. Enrl 1,600; Fac 55; Highest Degree: Master
Library Holdings: Bk Vols 80,000; Per Subs 275
Special Collections: Ecumenical Studies Coll
Subject Interests: Law
Automation Activity & Vendor Info: (Cataloging) SirsiDynix; (Circulation) SirsiDynix; (OPAC) SirsiDynix
Database Vendor: LexisNexis, ProQuest, Wilson - Wilson Web
Wireless access
Partic in OCLC Online Computer Library Center, Inc; Pennsylvania Academic Library Consortium, Inc (PALCI)
Open Mon-Thurs 8am-11pm, Fri 8-4, Sat 12-5, Sun 12-8

CURWENSVILLE

P CLEARFIELD COUNTY PUBLIC LIBRARY*, 601 Beech St, 16833. SAN 358-3716. Tel: 814-236-0589. FAX: 814-236-3620. E-mail: staff@clearfieldcountylibrary.org. Web Site: www.youseemore.com/clearfieldcounty/directory.asp. *Dir,* Daniel Bogey
Founded 1940. Pop 46,046; Circ 141,741
Library Holdings: Bk Titles 84,328; Per Subs 129
Special Collections: Oral History of Curwensville
Automation Activity & Vendor Info: (Cataloging) TLC (The Library Corporation); (OPAC) TLC (The Library Corporation)
Partic in Cent Pa District
Open Mon-Fri 9-5
Branches: 1
CURWENSVILLE BRANCH, 601 Beech St, 16833. Tel: 814-236-0355. FAX: 814-236-3620. *Libr Mgr,* Shirley Bennett; Staff 2 (MLS 1, Non-MLS 1)
Library Holdings: Audiobooks 610; DVDs 160; Large Print Bks 2,086; Bk Titles 26,833; Bk Vols 27,915; Per Subs 59; Videos 22
Open Mon & Wed 12:30-8, Tues, Thurs & Fri 10-5, Sat 9-3
Friends of the Library Group
Bookmobiles: 1. Coordr, Mark Kercenneck. Bk vols 39,337

DALLAS

P BACK MOUNTAIN MEMORIAL LIBRARY*, 96 Huntsville Rd, 18612. SAN 314-4372. Tel: 570-675-1182. FAX: 570-674-5863. Web Site: backmountainlibrary.org. *Dir,* Martha Butler; *Ch Serv,* Janet Bauman; Staff 1 (MLS 1)
Founded 1945. Pop 34,824; Circ 106,468
Jan 2005-Dec 2005 Income $411,400, State $81,000, County $86,000, Locally Generated Income $244,400. Mats Exp $81,847, Books $68,000, Per/Ser (Incl. Access Fees) $5,847, AV Equip $5,000, Electronic Ref Mat (Incl. Access Fees) $3,000. Sal $182,644 (Prof $45,000)
Library Holdings: CDs 202; DVDs 103; Large Print Bks 1,008; Bk Vols 76,000; Per Subs 145; Talking Bks 982; Videos 800
Automation Activity & Vendor Info: (Cataloging) Innovative Interfaces, Inc; (Circulation) Innovative Interfaces, Inc; (ILL) Innovative Interfaces, Inc; (OPAC) Innovative Interfaces, Inc
Wireless access
Mem of Luzerne County Library System
Open Mon-Thurs 9:30-8:30, Fri & Sat 9:30-5:30
Friends of the Library Group

C MISERICORDIA UNIVERSITY, Mary Kintz Bevevino Library, 301 Lake St, 18612-1098. SAN 314-4380. Tel: 570-674-6231. Administration Tel: 570-674-6225. FAX: 570-674-6342. E-mail: reference@misericordia.edu. Web Site: www.misericordia.edu/library. *Dir of Libr Serv,* Jennifer Luksa; E-mail: jsluzele@misericordia.edu; *Head, Ref & Outreach,* Lisa Galico; Tel: 570-674-6353, E-mail: lgalico@misericordia.edu; *Access Serv Mgr,* Colleen Newhart; Tel: 570-674-3036, E-mail: cnewhart@misericordia.edu; *Archivist,* Jessica Garner; Tel: 570-674-6420, E-mail: jreeder@misericordia.edu; Staff 15 (MLS 7, Non-MLS 8)
Founded 1924
Special Collections: Childrens's Literature; Comics & Graphic Novels; Sister Mary Carmel McGarigle Archives
Automation Activity & Vendor Info: (Acquisitions) SirsiDynix; (Cataloging) SirsiDynix; (Circulation) SirsiDynix; (Course Reserve) SirsiDynix; (ILL) OCLC ILLiad; (OPAC) SirsiDynix; (Serials) SirsiDynix
Database Vendor: EBSCOhost, JSTOR, LexisNexis, Newsbank, OCLC, Project MUSE, RefWorks, SBRnet (Sports Business Research Network), ScienceDirect, SerialsSolutions, SirsiDynix, YBP Library Services
Wireless access
Publications: Book Marks: the Library Newsletter
Partic in Lyrasis; Pennsylvania Academic Library Consortium, Inc (PALCI)
Open Mon-Thurs 8am-11pm, Fri 8-5, Sat 10-7, Sun 11-11
Friends of the Library Group

DALTON

P DALTON COMMUNITY LIBRARY*, 113 E Main St, 18414. (Mail add: PO Box 86, 18414-0086), SAN 314-4399. Tel: 570-563-2014. FAX: 570-563-2512. Web Site: www.lclshome.org/dalton. *Dir,* Shu Qiu; E-mail: sqiu@albright.org; Staff 1 (MLS 1)
Founded 1948
Library Holdings: Bk Vols 20,000; Per Subs 40
Special Collections: Local History
Subject Interests: Lackawana County hist
Automation Activity & Vendor Info: (Acquisitions) SirsiDynix; (Cataloging) SirsiDynix; (Circulation) SirsiDynix; (Course Reserve) SirsiDynix; (ILL) SirsiDynix; (Media Booking) SirsiDynix; (OPAC) SirsiDynix; (Serials) SirsiDynix
Database Vendor: SirsiDynix
Wireless access
Mem of Lackawanna County Library System
Open Mon-Thurs 10-8, Fri & Sat 10-5
Friends of the Library Group
Bookmobiles: 1

DANVILLE

P THOMAS BEAVER FREE LIBRARY*, 205 Ferry St, 17821-1939. (Mail add: PO Box 177, 17821-0177), SAN 314-4410. Tel: 570-275-4180. FAX: 570-275-8480. Web Site: www.tbflibrary.org. *Dir,* Bonnie White; *Head, Cat,* Joette Shalongo; *Ch Serv, Pub Serv, YA Serv,* Beth Lynn; *ILL, Per,* Jane Bradford; *Pub Serv,* Cynthia Dark. Subject Specialists: *Geog,* Joette Shalongo; Staff 7 (MLS 1, Non-MLS 6)
Founded 1886. Pop 21,286
Library Holdings: Bks on Deafness & Sign Lang 15; Bk Vols 33,027; Per Subs 108
Automation Activity & Vendor Info: (Cataloging) EOS International; (Circulation) EOS International; (OPAC) EOS International
Database Vendor: EBSCOhost
Open Mon 1-8, Tues 10:30-5, Wed 11-5, Thurs 10:30-8, Fri 12-5, Sat 11-3
Friends of the Library Group

M GEISINGER HEALTH SYSTEM*, Health Sciences Library, 100 N Academy Ave, 17822-2101. SAN 358-383X. Tel: 570-271-6463. FAX: 570-271-5738. *Dir,* Jack Latshaw; Tel: 570-271-8197, E-mail: jlatshaw@geisinger.edu; *Asst Dir,* Susan Robishaw; Tel: 570-271-8198, E-mail: srobishaw@geisinger.edu; *Librn,* Claire Huntington; Tel: 570-271-6288, E-mail: chuntington@geisinger.edu; Staff 8 (MLS 4, Non-MLS 4)
Founded 1927
Library Holdings: AV Mats 925; e-books 78; e-journals 511; Electronic Media & Resources 35; Bk Titles 5,004; Per Subs 511
Special Collections: Geisinger Archives
Subject Interests: Allied health, Hist of med, Med, Med specialities
Automation Activity & Vendor Info: (Cataloging) OCLC; (ILL) OCLC; (OPAC) Softlink America; (Serials) Infotrieve
Publications: Audiovisual Listing; Guide to Use & Services - Health Sciences Library; Library Bulletin; Periodical Holdings List
Partic in Dialog Corp; Lyrasis; National Network of Libraries of Medicine; OCLC
Restriction: In-house use for visitors
Friends of the Library Group

DARBY

P DARBY FREE LIBRARY*, 1001 Main St, 19023-0169. (Mail add: PO Box 164, 19023-0164), SAN 314-4429. Tel: 610-586-7310. FAX: 610-586-2781. E-mail: darby@delcolibraries.org. Web Site: darbylibrary.org. *Dir,* Susan Borders; *Circ Mgr,* Albert Renzulli; Staff 6 (Non-MLS 6)
Founded 1743. Pop 10,299; Circ 11,127
Library Holdings: Bk Vols 16,260; Per Subs 38
Subject Interests: Darby hist
Database Vendor: EBSCOhost, Gale Cengage Learning, OCLC FirstSearch
Wireless access

Mem of Delaware County Library System
Open Mon, Wed, Fri & Sat 10-5, Tues & Thurs 10-7

M MERCY FITZGERALD HOSPITAL*, Health Sciences Library, 1500 Lansdowne Ave, MS No 0127, 19023-1295. SAN 314-4437. Tel: 610-237-4150. FAX: 610-237-4830. *Mgr, Libr Serv,* Ellen Aberamowitz; Staff 1 (MLS 1)
Founded 1933
Jan 2008-Dec 2008. Mats Exp $80,730, Books $3,000, Per/Ser (Incl. Access Fees) $61,000
Library Holdings: CDs 55; DVDs 156; e-journals 26; Bk Titles 806; Bk Vols 912; Per Subs 127; Videos 262
Subject Interests: Med, Nursing, Surgery
Database Vendor: EBSCOhost, OCLC FirstSearch
Partic in Basic Health Sciences Library Network; Consortium of Health Info; HSLC/Access PA/POWER Library
Open Mon-Fri 7:30-5

DAWSON

P BROWNFIELD COMMUNITY LIBRARY*, 291 Banning Rd, 15428. Tel: 724-529-7680. FAX: 724-529-7680. *Dir,* Nancy Ober
Library Holdings: Bk Vols 14,000; Per Subs 13
Mem of Fayette County Library System
Open Mon & Wed 12-2, Tues & Thurs 12-2 & 6-8

DELMONT

P DELMONT PUBLIC LIBRARY*, 77 Greensburg St, 15626. SAN 314-4445. Tel: 724-468-5329. FAX: 724-468-5329. E-mail: delmlib@comcast.net. Web Site: www.delmontlibrary.org. *Dir,* Denni Grassel; Staff 2 (Non-MLS 2)
Founded 1931. Pop 3,401; Circ 39,000
Library Holdings: Bk Titles 16,400; Per Subs 24
Special Collections: Desert Storm War Coll; War on Drugs
Automation Activity & Vendor Info: (Acquisitions) Follett Software; (Cataloging) Follett Software; (Circulation) Follett Software; (Course Reserve) Follett Software; (OPAC) Follett Software
Wireless access
Function: Adult bk club, After school storytime, Art exhibits, Bk club(s), Bks on cassette, Bks on CD, CD-ROM, Children's prog, Computer training, Computers for patron use, Copy machines, Digital talking bks, e-mail serv, E-Reserves, Electronic databases & coll, Exhibits, Free DVD rentals, Handicapped accessible, ILL available, Magnifiers for reading, Mail & tel request accepted, Music CDs, Online cat, Online searches, Outreach serv, Photocopying/Printing, Prog for adults, Prog for children & young adult, Provide serv for the mentally ill, Pub access computers, Senior computer classes, Serves mentally handicapped consumers, Spoken cassettes & CDs, Spoken cassettes & DVDs, Story hour, Summer reading prog, Tax forms, Teen prog, VHS videos, Video lending libr, Web-catalog, Wheelchair accessible, Workshops, Writing prog
Open Mon-Thurs 10-7, Sat 9-4
Friends of the Library Group

DILLSBURG

P DILLSBURG AREA PUBLIC LIBRARY*, 17 S Baltimore St, 17019. SAN 314-4453. Tel: 717-432-5613. FAX: 717-432-7641. E-mail: dllib@yorklibraries.org. Web Site: www.yorklibraries.org/dillsburg. *Dir,* Kate Purcel; E-mail: kpurcel@yorklibraries.org; Staff 7 (MLS 2, Non-MLS 5)
Founded 1953. Pop 21,073; Circ 69,479
Library Holdings: Large Print Bks 200; Bk Vols 35,800; Per Subs 16
Automation Activity & Vendor Info: (Circulation) Innovative Interfaces, Inc - Millenium
Wireless access
Mem of York County Library System
Open Mon-Thurs 10-8, Fri 10-3, Sat 10-5 (10-3 Summer)

DINGMANS FERRY

P DELAWARE TOWNSHIP LIBRARY ASSOCIATION*, PO Box 303, 18328-0303. Tel: 570-828-2226. *In Charge,* Patti Barone; Tel: 570-828-2626; Staff 1 (Non-MLS 1)
Library Holdings: Bk Titles 3,280; Bk Vols 3,410; Per Subs 16
Open Mon & Wed 1-4, Sat 11-1

DONORA

P DONORA PUBLIC LIBRARY*, 510 Meldon Ave, 15033-1333. SAN 314-4461. Tel: 724-379-7940. FAX: 724-379-8809. E-mail: donlibr@comcast.net. Web Site: www.donorapublibrary.org. *Dir, Operations,* Beth Vaccaro; Staff 2 (MLS 1, Non-MLS 1)
Founded 1930. Pop 11,739; Circ 16,783
Library Holdings: Bks on Deafness & Sign Lang 12; Bk Titles 27,000; Bk Vols 29,000; Per Subs 83
Automation Activity & Vendor Info: (Cataloging) Follett Software; (Circulation) Follett Software; (OPAC) Follett Software
Mem of Washington County Library System
Open Mon 11-6, Tues-Thurs 11-7, Fri 11-4, Sat 9-4
Friends of the Library Group

DOUGLASSVILLE

S STV INC LIBRARY, 205 W Welsh Dr, 19518. SAN 315-1352. Tel: 610-385-8200, 610-385-8280. FAX: 610-385-8501. *Librn,* C Leh; E-mail: carol.leh@stvinc.com; Staff 1 (MLS 1)
Subject Interests: Archit, Eng
Publications: Notable Websites (Online only); What's New in the Library (Online only)
Restriction: Co libr, Employees only, Open to pub by appt only

DOWNINGTOWN

P DOWNINGTOWN LIBRARY CO*, 330 E Lancaster Ave, 19335-2946. SAN 314-447X. Tel: 610-269-2741. FAX: 610-269-3639. Web Site: www.ccls.org/libs/dowingtown.htm. *Dir,* Karen Miller; Staff 2 (MLS 1, Non-MLS 1)
Founded 1876. Pop 27,613; Circ 55,618
Library Holdings: Bk Titles 23,817; Bk Vols 25,490; Per Subs 61; Talking Bks 374; Videos 610
Special Collections: Oral History
Subject Interests: Local hist
Automation Activity & Vendor Info: (Cataloging) Innovative Interfaces, Inc; (Circulation) Innovative Interfaces, Inc; (OPAC) Innovative Interfaces, Inc
Mem of Chester County Library System
Open Mon-Thurs 9:30-8, Fri 9:30-5, Sat 9-4
Friends of the Library Group

DOYLESTOWN

P BUCKS COUNTY FREE LIBRARY*, Headquarters, 150 S Pine St, 18901-4932. SAN 358-3899. Tel: 215-348-0332. Circulation Tel: 215-348-9081, Ext 1223. Interlibrary Loan Service Tel: 215-348-1866. Reference Tel: 215-348-9081, Ext 1211. FAX: 215-348-4760. Interlibrary Loan Service FAX: 215-348-9458. E-mail: hello@buckslib.org. Web Site: www.buckslib.org. *Exec Dir,* Martina Kominiarek; Tel: 215-348-0332, Ext 1101; *Dir, Coll Mgt,* Janet Marnatti; Tel: 215-348-0332, Ext 1141, E-mail: marnattij@buckslib.org; *Pub Serv Dir,* Susan Ziegler; Tel: 215-348-0332, Ext 1102, E-mail: ziegler@buckslib.org; *Syst Serv Dir,* Javier Lanchang; Tel: 215-348-0332, Ext 1103, E-mail: lanchangj@buckslib.org; *District Consult Librn,* Jan O'Rourke; Tel: 215-348-0332, Ext 1131, E-mail: orourkej@buckslib.org; *Tech Serv Mgr,* Christina M Snyder; Tel. 215-348-9083, Ext 1171, E-mail: snyderc@buckslib.org; *Youth Serv Consult,* Dianne Malvoso; Tel: 215-348-0332, Ext 1135, E-mail: malvosod@buckslib.org; Staff 37 (MLS 37)
Founded 1956. Pop 464,092; Circ 2,249,396
Library Holdings: AV Mats 85,933; Bk Titles 769,357; Bk Vols 925,144; Per Subs 1,013
Special Collections: The Woods Handicapped & Gifted Coll. State Document Depository; US Document Depository
Subject Interests: Foreign fiction
Automation Activity & Vendor Info: (Acquisitions) SirsiDynix; (Cataloging) SirsiDynix; (Circulation) SirsiDynix; (ILL) OCLC FirstSearch; (OPAC) SirsiDynix
Database Vendor: Baker & Taylor, EBSCOhost, Factiva.com, Gale Cengage Learning, Hoovers, LearningExpress, OCLC FirstSearch, Overdrive, Inc, ProQuest, Standard & Poor's
Wireless access
Publications: Directory of Libraries in Bucks County; One Calendar - Programs & Events
Member Libraries: Free Library of New Hope & Solebury; Free Library of Northampton Township; Riegelsville Public Library; Township Library of Lower Southampton; Village Library of Wrightstown; Warminster Township Free Library
Special Services for the Blind - Assistive/Adapted tech devices, equip & products
Friends of the Library Group
Branches: 7
BENSALEM BRANCH, 3700 Hulmeville Rd, Bensalem, 19020-4449, SAN 358-3929. Tel: 215-638-2030. FAX: 215-638-2192. *Br Mgr,* Lisa Kern; E-mail: kernl@buckslib.org; *Youth Serv Librn,* Teresa Heebner; E-mail: heebnert@buckslib.org; Staff 4 (MLS 2, Non-MLS 2)
Pop 58,434; Circ 278,655
Library Holdings: AV Mats 11,677; Bk Vols 110,212; Per Subs 89
Function: Passport agency
Friends of the Library Group
LEVITTOWN BRANCH, 7311 New Falls Rd, Levittown, 19055-1006, SAN 358-3988. Tel: 215-949-2324. *Br Mgr,* Pat Hartman; Staff 2 (MLS 2)
Pop 102,340; Circ 493,930

Library Holdings: AV Mats 19,771; Bk Vols 168,569; Per Subs 130
Open Mon-Thurs 10-9, Fri 10-6, Sat 9-5
Friends of the Library Group

LIBRARY CENTER AT DOYLESTOWN, 150 S Pine St, 18901-4932, SAN 358-3953. Tel: 215-348-9081. FAX: 215-348-9489. *Youth Serv Mgr,* Roberta Yakovich; Tel: 215-348-0332, Ext 1240; Staff 6 (MLS 6)
Pop 100,977; Circ 1,018,713
Library Holdings: AV Mats 27,816; Bk Vols 191,922; Per Subs 130
Special Collections: US Document Depository
Function: Homebound delivery serv
Friends of the Library Group

JAMES A MICHENER BRANCH, 401 W Mill St, Quakertown, 18951-1248, SAN 358-4011. Tel: 215-536-3306. FAX: 215-536-8397. *Br Mgr,* Diane Malvaso; E-mail: malvosod@buckslib.org; *Ch Serv Librn,* Edna Hoy; Staff 4 (MLS 3, Non-MLS 1)
Pop 42,082; Circ 289,101
Library Holdings: AV Mats 8,449; Bk Vols 95,123; Per Subs 105
Open Mon-Wed 10-9, Thurs-Sat 10-5
Friends of the Library Group

PENNWOOD, 301 S Pine St, Langhorne, 19047-2887, SAN 358-4046. Tel: 215-757-2510. FAX: 215-757-9579. *Br Librn,* Jan Dickler; E-mail: dicklerj@buckslib.org; Staff 3 (MLS 2, Non-MLS 1)
Pop 70,880; Circ 204,627
Library Holdings: AV Mats 20,228; Bk Vols 72,596; Per Subs 84
Special Collections: Handicapped & Gifted Individual (The Wood Coll)
Special Services for the Deaf - TTY equip

SAMUEL PIERCE BRANCH, 491 Arthur Ave, Perkasie, 18944-1033, SAN 358-4070. Tel: 215-257-9718. FAX: 215-257-0759. *Br Librn,* Elizabeth Anderson; E-mail: andersonb@buckslib.org; *Youth Serv Librn,* Jennifer Cogan; Staff 3 (MLS 2, Non-MLS 1)
Pop 47,020; Circ 269,870
Library Holdings: AV Mats 10,977; Bk Vols 70,324; Per Subs 90
Friends of the Library Group

YARDLEY-MAKEFIELD BRANCH, 1080 Edgewood Rd, Yardley, 19067-1648, SAN 358-4100. Tel: 215-493-9020. *Libr Mgr,* Anne Reiser; *Youth Serv Librn,* Jessica Gruber; Staff 3 (MLS 1, Non-MLS 2)
Pop 42,359; Circ 415,662
Library Holdings: Bk Vols 77,182
Friends of the Library Group

S BUCKS COUNTY HISTORICAL SOCIETY, Mercer Museum Library, 84 S Pine St, 18901-4999. SAN 314-4496. Tel: 215-345-0210, Ext 141. FAX: 215-230-0823. E-mail: mmlib@mercermuseum.org. Web Site: www.mercermuseum.org. *Coll Mgr,* Sara Good; E-mail: sgood@mercermuseum.org; Staff 2 (Non-MLS 2)
Founded 1880
Library Holdings: Bk Vols 18,000
Special Collections: Bucks County History & Genealogy Coll; Early American Technology Coll; Henry C Mercer Coll
Subject Interests: Antiques
Automation Activity & Vendor Info: (Cataloging) Cuadra Associates, Inc; (OPAC) Cuadra Associates, Inc
Function: Archival coll, Copy machines, Doc delivery serv, e-mail serv, Online cat, Prog for adults, Wheelchair accessible
Open Tues-Thurs 1-5, Fri & Sat 10-5
Restriction: Not a lending libr, Ref only, Restricted pub use

GL BUCKS COUNTY LAW LIBRARY*, Court House, 55 E Court St, First Flr, 18901. SAN 314-450X. Tel: 215-343-6023, 215-348-6000. FAX: 215-348-6827. Web Site: www.buckscounty.org. *Chief Info Officer,* Donald W Jacobs; Staff 3 (MLS 2, Non-MLS 1)
Library Holdings: Bk Titles 33,690; Bk Vols 35,190; Per Subs 100
Special Collections: Case Law; Court Rules; Dictionaries; Digests; Federal Statutes; Form Books; Law Encyclopedias; Law-Related Periodicals; National Reporter & System; State Statutes (PA,NJ,NY,DE,FL,MD); Treaties
Subject Interests: Pa law
Automation Activity & Vendor Info: (Cataloging) SirsiDynix; (Circulation) SirsiDynix; (OPAC) SirsiDynix
Database Vendor: LexisNexis, Westlaw
Open Mon-Fri 8:30-5

C DELAWARE VALLEY COLLEGE OF SCIENCE & AGRICULTURE*, Joseph Krauskopf Memorial Library, 700 E Butler Ave, 18901-2699. SAN 314-4534. Tel: 215-489-2254. Circulation Tel: 215-489-2953. Interlibrary Loan Service Tel: 215-489-4968. FAX: 215-230-2967. Web Site: www.delval.edu. *Dir,* Peter Kupersmith; E-mail: peter.kupersmith@delval.edu; *Instrul Serv Librn,* Janet Klaessig; Tel: 215-489-4957, E-mail: janet.klaessig@delval.edu; *Cataloger,* Marian Schad; Tel: 215-489-2385; *Grad & Distance Educ,* Sarah Penniman; E-mail: sarah.penniman@delval.edu; Staff 6 (MLS 5, Non-MLS 1)
Founded 1896. Enrl 1,950; Fac 90; Highest Degree: Master
Library Holdings: e-books 1,200; Bk Vols 48,900; Per Subs 250
Special Collections: Joseph Krauskopf Coll
Subject Interests: Animal sci, Plant sci
Automation Activity & Vendor Info: (Acquisitions) SirsiDynix; (Cataloging) SirsiDynix; (Circulation) SirsiDynix; (Course Reserve) SirsiDynix; (OPAC) SirsiDynix; (Serials) SirsiDynix
Partic in Lyrasis; OCLC Online Computer Library Center, Inc; Tri-State College Library Cooperative
Open Mon-Thurs (Winter) 8am-11pm, Fri 8-5:30, Sat 9:30-5:30, Sun 1-11; Mon-Thurs (Summer) 8:30-6:30, Fri 8:30-12, Sat 10-4

DRESHER

R TEMPLE SINAI*, The Martin Josephs Library, 1401 N Limekiln Pike, 19025. SAN 315-0119. Tel: 215-643-6510, Ext 110. FAX: 215-643-9441. Web Site: www.tsinai.com. *Libr Dir,* Shelia Gendelman; *Exec Dir,* Steve Friedrich; E-mail: sfriedrich@tsinai.com; *Educ Dir,* Faith B Rubin; E-mail: frubin@tsinai.com
Library Holdings: Bk Vols 7,500
Subject Interests: Judaica
Open Tues & Wed 12-6, Sun 9:30-12:30
Friends of the Library Group

DU BOIS

P DU BOIS PUBLIC LIBRARY*, 31 S Brady St, 15801. SAN 314-4577. Tel: 814-371-5930. FAX: 814-371-2282. E-mail: director@duboispubliclibrary.org. Web Site: www.duboispubliclibrary.org. *Dir,* Rebecca J McTavish; Staff 5 (MLS 1, Non-MLS 4)
Founded 1920. Pop 19,600; Circ 96,000
Jan 2013-Dec 2013 Income $237,580, State $60,380, City $134,000, Locally Generated Income $43,200. Mats Exp $27,600, Books $22,250, Per/Ser (Incl. Access Fees) $1,600, AV Mat $3,250, Electronic Ref Mat (Incl. Access Fees) $500. Sal $176,550
Library Holdings: Audiobooks 800; AV Mats 2,800; CDs 550; DVDs 1,150; Large Print Bks 2,466; Bk Vols 43,250; Per Subs 25; Videos 150
Special Collections: Pennsylvania Room (History & Geneaology). Oral History
Automation Activity & Vendor Info: (Cataloging) AmLib Library Management System; (Circulation) AmLib Library Management System; (OPAC) AmLib Library Management System
Database Vendor: EBSCO Auto Repair Reference, EBSCO Information Services, EBSCOhost, LearningExpress, Overdrive, Inc
Wireless access
Function: Audiobks via web, Bks on CD, Children's prog, Computers for patron use, Electronic databases & coll, Family literacy, Fax serv, Holiday prog, Home delivery & serv to Sr ctr & nursing homes, Homebound delivery serv, ILL available, Magnifiers for reading, Microfiche/film & reading machines, Mus passes, Music CDs, Online cat, OverDrive digital audio bks, Photocopying/Printing, Preschool outreach, Preschool reading prog, Prog for adults, Prog for children & young adult, Pub access computers, Ref serv in person, Story hour, Summer reading prog, Tax forms, Teen prog, Web-catalog
Partic in Central Pennsylvania Consortium
Open Mon, Tues & Thurs 9-8, Wed & Fri 9-5, Sat 9-4
Restriction: 24-hr pass syst for students only
Friends of the Library Group

C PENNSYLVANIA STATE UNIVERSITY*, DuBois Campus Library, College Pl, Hiller Bldg, Rm 113, 301 E DuBois Ave, 15801. SAN 314-4585. Tel: 814-375-4756. FAX: 814-375-4784. Web Site: www.libraries.psu.edu/psul/dubois.html. *Head Librn,* Karen Fuller; *Ref Librn,* Carrie Bishop; Staff 4 (MLS 2, Non-MLS 2)
Founded 1935. Enrl 920; Fac 50
Library Holdings: Bk Vols 43,000; Per Subs 125
Special Collections: Wildlife Technology (Paul A Handwerk & David D Wanless Coll)
Automation Activity & Vendor Info: (Acquisitions) SirsiDynix; (Cataloging) SirsiDynix; (Circulation) SirsiDynix; (Course Reserve) SirsiDynix; (ILL) OCLC; (OPAC) SirsiDynix; (Serials) SirsiDynix
Database Vendor: Factiva.com, LexisNexis, ProQuest
Partic in OCLC Online Computer Library Center, Inc; RLIN (Research Libraries Information Network)
Open Mon-Thurs 8-8, Fri 8-4:30

DUNBAR

P DUNBAR COMMUNITY LIBRARY*, 60 Connellsville St, 15431. Tel: 724-277-4775. FAX: 724-277-4775. E-mail: dunbarcommunityfreelibrary@yahoo.com, dunlib@cvzoom.net. *Coordr,* Sandy Rosensteel; Tel: 724-322-6109, E-mail: sandyrosensteel@zoominternet.net
Library Holdings: Audiobooks 20; DVDs 15; Large Print Bks 30; Bk Vols 12,000; Per Subs 5; Videos 50
Wireless access
Function: Accelerated reader prog, After school storytime, Bks on cassette, Bks on CD, Children's prog, Computer training, Computers for patron use, Copy machines, e-mail & chat, Fax serv, Handicapped

accessible, Homework prog, ILL available, Photocopying/Printing, Pub access computers, Story hour, Summer reading prog, Tax forms, Teen prog, VHS videos, Wheelchair accessible
Mem of Fayette County Library System
Open Mon 9-12 & 5-8, Tues & Wed 12-3 & 5-8, Fri 12-3, Sat 11-2

DUNMORE

C PENNSYLVANIA STATE UNIVERSITY*, Worthington Scranton Commonwealth College Library, 120 Ridge View Dr, 18512-1699. SAN 314-4593. Tel: 570-963-2630. Circulation Tel: 570-963-2636. Automation Services Tel: 570-963-2632. Information Services Tel: 570-963-2633. FAX: 570-963-2635. Web Site: www.libraries.psu.edu/psul/scranton. *Head of Libr,* Billie Walker; E-mail: bcw11@psu.edu; *Ref Librn,* Tierney Lyons
Founded 1923. Highest Degree: Bachelor
Library Holdings: Bk Vols 66,000; Per Subs 100
Wireless access
Partic in OCLC Online Computer Library Center, Inc; RLIN (Research Libraries Information Network)
Open Mon-Thurs 8am-10pm, Fri 8-4:30

DUSHORE

P SULLIVAN COUNTY LIBRARY*, 206 Center St, 18614. (Mail add: PO Box 309, 18614-0309), SAN 314-4615. Tel: 570-928-9352. Web Site: sullivancountylibrary.org. *Dir,* Carol Roinick
Founded 1947. Pop 6,556; Circ 35,500
Library Holdings: Bk Vols 16,847; Per Subs 60
Subject Interests: Local hist
Wireless access
Open Tues & Wed 10-6, Thurs 12-7, Fri 10-5, Sat 9-4

EAGLEVILLE

M EAGLEVILLE HOSPITAL*, Henry S Louchheim Medical Library, 100 Eagleville Rd, 19403. (Mail add: PO Box 45, 19408-0045), SAN 314-4623. Tel: 610-539-6000. Web Site: www.eaglevillehospital.org.
Founded 1971
Library Holdings: Bk Titles 3,780; Bk Vols 4,062; Per Subs 131
Special Collections: Black History & Culture; Change; Homosexuality; Management & Organizational; Therapeutic Community Life
Subject Interests: Alcoholism, Drug addiction, Psychol, Soc work
Partic in Consortium of Health Info; Delaware Valley Information Consortium
Restriction: Non-circulating to the pub, Staff & patient use

P LOWER PROVIDENCE COMMUNITY LIBRARY, 50 Parklane Dr, 19403-1171. SAN 375-3115. Tel: 610-666-6640. FAX: 610-666-5109. Web Site: www.lowerprovidencelibrary.org. *Dir,* Lynn Burkholder; E-mail: LBurkholder@mclinc.org; *Head, Children's & Teen Serv,* Sandrah Moles; E-mail: SMoles@mclinc.org; *Head, Circ,* Kathleen Sharkey; E-mail: KSharkey@mclinc.org; *Head, Support Serv,* Jill Kozol; E-mail: JKozol@mclinc.org; *Cat & Coll Mgt Librn,* Emily Rabson; E-mail: ERabson@mclinc.org; *Ref & Ad Serv Librn,* Barbara Loewengart; E-mail: BLoewengart@mclinc.org; Staff 4 (MLS 3, Non-MLS 1)
Founded 1985. Pop 25,400; Circ 250,000
Automation Activity & Vendor Info: (Cataloging) Innovative Interfaces, Inc; (Circulation) Innovative Interfaces, Inc; (OPAC) Innovative Interfaces, Inc
Database Vendor: Access Pennsylvania, Booklist Online, Gale Cengage Learning, LearningExpress, Library Ideas, LLC, ReferenceUSA, TumbleBookLibrary, World Book Online
Wireless access
Partic in Montgomery County Library & Information Network Consortium
Special Services for the Deaf - Bks on deafness & sign lang
Open Mon-Thurs (Winter) 10-8:30, Fri & Sat 10-5, Sun 1-5; Mon-Thurs (Summer) 10-8:30, Fri 10-5, Sat 10-2
Friends of the Library Group

EAST BERLIN

P EAST BERLIN COMMUNITY LIBRARY*, 105 Locust St, 17316. (Mail add: PO Box 1014, 17316-1014), SAN 321-6640. Tel: 717-259-9000. FAX: 717-259-7651. E-mail: eblib@adamslibrary.org. Web Site: www.adamslibrary.org/eb, www.eastberlinlibrary.org. *Dir,* Brandt Ensor; Staff 0.75 (Non-MLS 0.75)
Founded 1975. Pop 8,515; Circ 94,295
Library Holdings: Audiobooks 932; AV Mats 2,588; Bk Vols 25,376; Per Subs 26
Automation Activity & Vendor Info: (Cataloging) TLC (The Library Corporation); (Circulation) TLC (The Library Corporation); (OPAC) TLC (The Library Corporation)
Wireless access
Mem of Adams County Library System
Open Mon & Wed 10-6, Tues & Thurs 12-8, Fri & Sat 9-4

EAST STROUDSBURG

C EAST STROUDSBURG UNIVERSITY*, Kemp Library, 200 Prospect Ave, 18301-2999. SAN 314-4666. Tel: 570-422-3465. Circulation Tel: 570-422-3126. Interlibrary Loan Service Tel: 570-422-3914. Reference Tel: 570-422-3594. FAX: 570-422-3151. Web Site: www4.esu.edu/library/index.cfm. *Dean of Libr & Univ Coll,* Dr Edward Owusu-Ansah; Tel: 570-422-3467, E-mail: owusu-ansah@esu.edu; *Electronic Res Librn,* Leslie A Berger; Tel: 570-422-3597, E-mail: lberger@esu.edu; *Govt Doc Librn,* Ramona Hylton; Tel: 570-422-3150, E-mail: rhylton@esu.edu; *Acq Asst,* Leslie Fawcett; Tel: 570-422-3186, E-mail: lfawcett@esu.edu; Staff 22 (MLS 10, Non-MLS 12)
Founded 1893. Enrl 6,272; Fac 283; Highest Degree: Master
Library Holdings: AV Mats 12,367; Bk Vols 459,839; Per Subs 1,100
Special Collections: State Document Depository; US Document Depository
Automation Activity & Vendor Info: (Cataloging) Ex Libris Group; (Circulation) Ex Libris Group; (Course Reserve) Docutek; (OPAC) Ex Libris Group; (Serials) Ex Libris Group
Database Vendor: EBSCOhost, Gale Cengage Learning, JSTOR, LexisNexis, OCLC WorldShare Interlibrary Loan, OVID Technologies, TLC (The Library Corporation)
Wireless access
Partic in Keystone Library Network; Lyrasis; Northeastern Pennsylvania Library Network; Pennsylvania Academic Library Consortium, Inc (PALCI)
Special Services for the Deaf - Assistive tech
Special Services for the Blind - Assistive/Adapted tech devices, equip & products
Open Mon-Thurs (Fall-Spring) 7:30am-Midnight, Fri 7:30-6, Sat 10-6, Sun 10am-Midnight; Mon-Fri (Summer) 10am-Midnight

M POCONO MEDICAL CENTER*, Marshall R Metzgar Medical Library, 206 E Brown St, 18301. SAN 327-1048. Tel: 570-476-3515. *Librn,* Position Currently Open
Founded 1976
Library Holdings: e-books 11; e-journals 7; Electronic Media & Resources 4; Bk Titles 500; Per Subs 100
Database Vendor: EBSCOhost, OVID Technologies
Wireless access
Partic in Basic Health Sciences Library Network; CinaHL
Open Mon-Fri 7-3:30

EASTON

P EASTON AREA PUBLIC LIBRARY & DISTRICT CENTER, 515 Church St, 18042-3587. SAN 314-4682. Tel: 610-258-2917. FAX: 610-253-2231. E-mail: director@eastonpl.org. Web Site: www.eastonpl.org. *Dir,* Jennifer Stocker; Tel: 610-258-2917, Ext 310, E-mail: jenns@eastonpl.org; *Adult Serv, Head, Ref,* Gail Coakley; *Coordr, Computer Serv,* Georgia Weber; *Cat, Tech Serv Coordr,* Annette Bon Lore; *Youth Serv Coordr,* Audrey Kantner; *Acq, Extn Serv,* Susan Gardner; Staff 6 (MLS 6)
Founded 1811. Pop 59,000; Circ 400,000
Library Holdings: Bk Vols 187,668; Per Subs 416
Special Collections: Genealogy & Local History, Pennsylvania, Eastern Ohio & Western New Jersey (Henry F Marx Local History Room)
Subject Interests: Hist, Literary criticism
Automation Activity & Vendor Info: (Acquisitions) Innovative Interfaces, Inc - Millenium; (Cataloging) Innovative Interfaces, Inc - Millenium; (Circulation) Innovative Interfaces, Inc - Millenium; (OPAC) Innovative Interfaces, Inc - Millenium
Database Vendor: Gale Cengage Learning, OCLC FirstSearch
Wireless access
Publications: Exlibris (Newsletter)
Partic in OCLC Online Computer Library Center, Inc
Open Mon-Thurs 9-9, Fri 9-6, Sat 9-5
Friends of the Library Group
Branches: 2
PALMER MEMORIAL LIBRARY, One Weller Pl, 18045, SAN 320-054X. Tel: 610-258-7492. *Br Mgr,* Stephanie Supinski
Library Holdings: Bk Vols 15,380; Per Subs 38
Open Mon, Fri & Sat 9-5, Tues-Thurs 11-7
Friends of the Library Group
SOUTHSIDE, 401 W Berwick St, 18042, SAN 321-9461. Tel: 610-258-3121. *Br Mgr,* Debbie Osmun; E-mail: debbieo@eastonpl.org
Library Holdings: Bk Vols 8,033; Per Subs 17
Open Mon & Fri 10-3, Tues & Wed 12-6, Thurs 10-4

M EASTON HOSPITAL*, Frank J D'Agostino MD Medical Library, 250 S 21st St, 18042-3892. SAN 326-3207. Tel: 610-250-4131. FAX: 610-250-4905. E-mail: library_easton@chs.net. Web Site: www.eastonmedicallibrary.com.
Library Holdings: e-journals 1,800; Bk Titles 2,780; Bk Vols 3,091; Per Subs 180
Subject Interests: Med, Nursing, Pediatrics, Surgery

Automation Activity & Vendor Info: (Cataloging) LibraryWorld, Inc; (Circulation) LibraryWorld, Inc
Database Vendor: EBSCOhost, MD Consult, Medline, PubMed, STAT!Ref (Teton Data Systems), UpToDate
Restriction: Staff use only

C LAFAYETTE COLLEGE*, David Bishop Skillman Library, 710 Sullivan Rd, 18042-1797. SAN 358-4194. Tel: 610-330-5151. Interlibrary Loan Service Tel: 610-330-5157. Reference Tel: 610-330-5155. FAX: 610-252-0370. Web Site: www.library.lafayette.edu. *Dir,* Neil J McElroy; Tel: 610-330-5150, E-mail: mcelroyn@lafayette.edu; *Head, Info Serv,* Terese Heidenwolf; Tel: 610-330-5153, E-mail: heidenwt@lafayette.edu; *Spec Coll Librn,* Diane W Shaw; Tel: 610-330-5401, E-mail: shawd@lafayette.edu; *Syst Librn,* Robert Duncan; Tel: 610-330-5156, E-mail: duncanr@lafayette.edu; *Access Serv,* Katherine Furlong; Tel: 610-330-5669, E-mail: furlongk@lafayette.edu; *Acq, Ser,* Michael Hanson; Tel: 610-330-5636, E-mail: hansonm@lafayette.edu; *Cat,* Helen Dungan; Tel: 610-330-5160, E-mail: dunganh@lafayette.edu; *Ref,* Amy Abruzzi; Tel: 610-330-5631, E-mail: abruzzia@lafayette.edu; *Ref,* Rebecca Metzger; Tel: 610-330-5154, E-mail: metzgerr@lafayette.edu; Staff 20 (MLS 12, Non-MLS 8)
Founded 1826. Enrl 2,250; Fac 184; Highest Degree: Bachelor
Library Holdings: Bk Titles 494,000; Bk Vols 510,000; Per Subs 8,767; Videos 3,000
Special Collections: American Friends of Lafayette; Conahay Tinsman & Fox Angling Coll; Howard Chandler Christy Coll; Jay Parini Coll; Marquis de LaFayette Coll; Robt & Helen Meyner Coll; Stephen Crane Coll; Wm E Simon Coll
Automation Activity & Vendor Info: (Acquisitions) Innovative Interfaces, Inc; (Cataloging) Innovative Interfaces, Inc; (Circulation) Innovative Interfaces, Inc; (Course Reserve) Innovative Interfaces, Inc; (ILL) Innovative Interfaces, Inc; (Media Booking) Innovative Interfaces, Inc; (OPAC) Innovative Interfaces, Inc; (Serials) Innovative Interfaces, Inc
Publications: Bytes & Books
Partic in Interlibrary Delivery Service of Pennsylvania; Lehigh Valley Association of Independent Colleges; Pennsylvania Academic Library Consortium, Inc (PALCI)
Open Mon-Thurs 8:30am-1am, Fri 8:30am-10pm, Sat 10-10, Sun 10am-1am
Friends of the Library Group
Departmental Libraries:

CL KIRBY LIBRARY OF GOVERNMENT & LAW, Kirby Hall of Civil Rights, 716 Sullivan Rd, 18042-1780, SAN 358-4224. Tel: 610-330-5398. FAX: 610-330-5397. *Br Librn, Cataloger/Ref Librn, Coll Develop,* Mercedes Benitez-Sharpless; E-mail: sharplem@lafayette.edu. Subject Specialists: *Constitutional law, Intl law, Polit sci,* Mercedes Benitez-Sharpless; Staff 8 (MLS 1, Non-MLS 7)
Founded 1930
Library Holdings: Bk Titles 29,690; Bk Vols 31,410; Per Subs 126
Subject Interests: Civil rights, Intl relations, Polit sci
Open Mon-Fri 8:45-5

P MARY MEUSER MEMORIAL LIBRARY*, 1803 Northampton St, 18042-3183. SAN 314-4690. Tel: 610-258-3040. Web Site: www.meuserlib.org. *Dir,* Daniel L Redington; *Adult Serv,* Wende Fazio; *Ch Serv,* Natasha Stanton; Staff 3 (Non-MLS 3)
Founded 1962. Pop 15,000; Circ 5,500
Library Holdings: Bk Vols 49,000; Per Subs 80
Subject Interests: Art, Poetry
Automation Activity & Vendor Info: (Acquisitions) Brodart; (Cataloging) Evolve; (Circulation) Evolve; (OPAC) Evolve
Wireless access
Open Tues-Thurs 9:45-8, Fri 9:45-5, Sat 9-4
Friends of the Library Group

S NORTHAMPTON COUNTY HISTORICAL & GENEALOGICAL SOCIETY*, Jane S Moyer Library, 342 Northampton St, 18042. SAN 314-4712. Tel: 610-253-1222. FAX: 610-253-4701. Web Site: www.northamptonctymuseum.org. *Librn,* Jane S Moyer
Founded 1906
Library Holdings: Bk Titles 9,000; Bk Vols 11,000
Special Collections: Deed Coll; Family Photo Coll; Genealogical File Coll; Manuscript Coll; Merchants' Ledgers; Picture Coll; Postal Card Coll. Oral History
Subject Interests: County hist of Pa, Genealogy, Hist rec, Northampton County
Wireless access
Function: Res libr
Publications: Tales from the Grapevine (Newsletter)
Restriction: Open by appt only, Open to pub for ref only

GL NORTHAMPTON COUNTY LAW LIBRARY*, 669 Washington St, 18042-7468. SAN 314-4704. Tel: 610-559-6751. FAX: 610-559-6750. E-mail: ncll@nccpa.org. Web Site: www.nccpa.org. *Librn,* Anita L DeBona
Founded 1860
Library Holdings: Bk Titles 23,399
Special Collections: Typical Coll for Pa County Law Libr
Open Mon-Fri 8:30-4:30

EBENSBURG

GL CAMBRIA COUNTY FREE LAW LIBRARY*, Court House, S Center St, 15931. SAN 314-4739. Tel: 814-472-1501. Toll Free Tel: 800-540-2525, Ext 1501. FAX: 814-472-4799. *Librn,* Sandy Papcunik; Staff 2 (MLS 1, Non-MLS 1)
Founded 1920
Library Holdings: Bk Titles 38,919; Bk Vols 40,410; Per Subs 58; Videos 182
Subject Interests: Pa law
Open Mon-Fri 9-4

S CAMBRIA COUNTY HISTORICAL SOCIETY LIBRARY*, 615 N Center St, 15931. (Mail add: PO Box 278, 15931-0278), SAN 314-4747. Tel: 814-472-6674. Web Site: www.cambriacountyhistorical.com. *Curator,* Kathy Jones
Founded 1925
Library Holdings: Bk Titles 2,400; Bk Vols 3,100
Subject Interests: Genealogy of families within Cambria County, Hist of Cambria county, Indust, Pa soc & relig life of citizens
Publications: Heritage (Newsletter)
Open Tues-Fri 10-4, Sat 9-1

P EBENSBURG CAMBRIA PUBLIC LIBRARY*, 225 W Highland Ave, 15931-1507. SAN 314-4755. Tel: 814-472-7957. FAX: 814-472-2037. E-mail: ebenpl@yahoo.com. Web Site: www.cclib.lib.pa.us/ebensburg. *Librn,* Mary Makin
Founded 1923. Pop 4,818; Circ 20,751
Library Holdings: AV Mats 1,420; Large Print Bks 204; Bk Titles 25,584; Bk Vols 25,998; Per Subs 24
Special Collections: Local History Coll
Automation Activity & Vendor Info: (Cataloging) Innovative Interfaces, Inc; (Circulation) Innovative Interfaces, Inc; (OPAC) Innovative Interfaces, Inc
Wireless access
Mem of Cambria County Library System & District Center
Open Mon, Tues, Thurs & Fri 1-8, Sun 12-7

EDGEWOOD

P C C MELLOR MEMORIAL LIBRARY*, Edgewood Library, One Pennwood Ave, 15218-1627. SAN 315-0844. Tel: 412-731-0909. FAX: 412-731-8969. Web Site: ccmellorlibrary.org. *Dir,* Sally Bogie; *Tech Mgr,* Sue Philippi; *Ch Serv,* Andrea McNeill; Staff 7 (MLS 2, Non-MLS 5)
Founded 1918. Pop 22,623; Circ 108,143
Library Holdings: Large Print Bks 210; Bk Titles 42,819; Bk Vols 44,141; Per Subs 88; Talking Bks 1,291; Videos 1,014
Automation Activity & Vendor Info: (Cataloging) Innovative Interfaces, Inc; (Circulation) Innovative Interfaces, Inc; (OPAC) Innovative Interfaces, Inc
Mem of Allegheny County Library Association
Open Mon-Thurs 10-8, Fri 10-5, Sat 10-3, Sun 12-3

EDINBORO

C EDINBORO UNIVERSITY OF PENNSYLVANIA*, Baron-Forness Library, 200 Tartan Ave, 16444. SAN 358-4259. Tel: 814-732-2779. Circulation Tel: 814-732-2273. Interlibrary Loan Service Tel: 814-732-2946. Reference Tel: 814-732-2253. FAX: 814-732-2883. E-mail: library@edinboro.edu. Web Site: www.edinboro.edu/cwis/library/menu.html. *Assoc VPres,* Dr Donald Dilmore; E-mail: ddilmore@edinboro.edu; *Archivist & Spec Coll Librn,* David Obringer; E-mail: obringer@edinboro.edu; *Curric Mat Librn,* Dr Andrea Wyman; E-mail: awyman@edinboro.edu; *Instrul Serv Librn, Online Serv,* Dr Monty McAdoo; E-mail: mmcadoo@edinboro.edu; *Soc Media Librn,* Jessica Lasher; Tel: 814-732-1704, E-mail: jlasher@edinboro.edu; *Syst Librn,* Anthony McMullen; E-mail: amcmullen@edinboro.edu; *Acq,* Loralyn Whitney; E-mail: whitney@edinboro.edu; *Cat, Tech Serv,* Barry Gray; E-mail: bgray@edinboro.edu; *Circ,* Judy Wilson; E-mail: wilsonj@edinboro.edu; *ILL,* Judy Rauenswinter; E-mail: rauenswinter@edinboro.edu; *Ref,* Jack Widner; E-mail: widner@edinboro.edu; *Ser,* Christine Troutman; E-mail: ctroutman@edinboro.edu; Staff 22 (MLS 10, Non-MLS 12)
Founded 1857. Enrl 7,080; Fac 380; Highest Degree: Master
Jul 2009-Jun 2010. Mats Exp $939,534, Books $153,527, Per/Ser (Incl. Access Fees) $294,225, AV Mat $34,049, Electronic Ref Mat (Incl. Access Fees) $429,295, Presv $14,901. Sal $1,322,579
Library Holdings: AV Mats 10,111; CDs 1,550; DVDs 1,126; e-books 20,720; e-journals 35,738; Microforms 688,352; Bk Titles 309,638; Bk Vols 482,442; Per Subs 844; Videos 2,965

Special Collections: Art Coll; Southeast Asia Coll. State Document Depository
Subject Interests: Educ
Automation Activity & Vendor Info: (Acquisitions) Ex Libris Group; (Cataloging) Ex Libris Group; (Circulation) Ex Libris Group; (Course Reserve) Docutek; (ILL) OCLC; (OPAC) Ex Libris Group; (Serials) Ex Libris Group
Database Vendor: Cambridge Scientific Abstracts, Dialog, EBSCOhost, Gale Cengage Learning, JSTOR, LexisNexis, OCLC FirstSearch, OVID Technologies, SerialsSolutions
Wireless access
Publications: Faculty Guide; Student Guide
Partic in Keystone Library Network; Northwest Interlibrary Cooperative of Pennsylvania; Pennsylvania Academic Library Consortium, Inc (PALCI)
Special Services for the Blind - Large screen computer & software; Reader equip
Open Mon-Thurs 8am-Midnight, Fri 8-6, Sat 9-5, Sun 1:30-10
Friends of the Library Group

ELDRED

S ENSANIAN PHYSICOCHEMICAL INSTITUTE*, Institute Library, Barden Brook Rd, 16731. (Mail add: PO Box 98, 16731-0098), SAN 358-4313. Tel: 814-225-3296. *Chief Librn,* Elisabeth Anahid Ensanian; Staff 3 (MLS 1, Non-MLS 2)
Founded 1963
Library Holdings: Bk Titles 3,510; Bk Vols 3,790; Per Subs 136
Special Collections: Cosmology (Structure of the Universe), bks, rpt; Geotropism (Gravitation Biology), rpt; Gravitation (Information Center for Gravitation Chemistry), bks, rpt; Non-Destructive Testing of Materials, bks, rpt; Physiochemical Robotic Sensors; Quantum Physics; Robotics & Robot Sensors (Tactile); Stored Energy in Metals (Electrotopography Information Center), rpt
Subject Interests: Artificial intelligence, Automation, Bioeng, Biol diagnostic med, Conceptual foundations of quantum physics, Econ, Energy conversion, Evaluations of metals, Fingerprinting of odors, Manufacturing in zero gravity, Mat sci, Math, Metallurgy, Non-destructive testing, Non-linear thermodynamics, Pattern recognition, Plant physiology, Quantum computers, Robots, Solid state, Theoretical physics, Total automated manufacturing in the metalworking industries, Water structure
Restriction: Staff use only

ELIZABETHTOWN

C ELIZABETHTOWN COLLEGE, The High Library, One Alpha Dr, 17022-2227. SAN 314-4771. Tel: 717-361-1451. Circulation Tel: 717-361-1222. Interlibrary Loan Service Tel: 717-361-1455. Reference Tel: 717-361-1461. FAX: 717-361-1167. Web Site: www.etown.edu/library. *Col Librn, Dir,* Sarah Penniman; Tel: 717-361-1428, E-mail: pennimans@etown.edu; *Head, Libr Database,* Susan Krall; Tel: 717-361-1457, E-mail: kralls@etown.edu; *Head, Coll Mgt,* Sylvia T Morra; Tel: 717-361-1452, E-mail: morrast@etown.edu; *Head, Reader Serv,* Elizabeth Young Miller; Tel: 717-361-1456, E-mail: younge@etown.edu; *Access Serv Librn,* Louise M Hyder-Darlington; Tel: 717-361-1454, E-mail: hyderl@etown.edu; *Ref Librn,* Peter J DePuydt; Tel: 717-361-1453, E-mail: depuydtp@etown.edu; *Archivist,* Rachel Grove Rohrbaugh; Tel: 717-361-1506, E-mail: grover@etown.edu; Staff 9 (MLS 6, Non-MLS 3)
Founded 1899. Enrl 1,856; Fac 132; Highest Degree: Master
Jul 2013-Jun 2014. Mats Exp $532,659, Books $103,893, Per/Ser (Incl. Access Fees) $263,447, Electronic Ref Mat (Incl. Access Fees) $161,412, Presv $3,907. Sal $364,569 (Prof $269,924)
Library Holdings: CDs 1,373; DVDs 1,612; e-books 5,305; e-journals 82,076; Electronic Media & Resources 72; Music Scores 3,275; Bk Titles 197,390; Bk Vols 263,974; Per Subs 512; Videos 2,044
Special Collections: Brethren Heritage Coll
Automation Activity & Vendor Info: (Acquisitions) SirsiDynix; (Cataloging) SirsiDynix; (Circulation) SirsiDynix; (Course Reserve) SirsiDynix; (ILL) OCLC ILLiad; (OPAC) SirsiDynix; (Serials) SirsiDynix
Database Vendor: American Chemical Society, American Mathematical Society, ARTstor, Cambridge Scientific Abstracts, Career Guidance Foundation, CQ Press, EBSCOhost, Gale Cengage Learning, JSTOR, LexisNexis, OCLC WorldShare Interlibrary Loan, ProQuest, PubMed, SirsiDynix, STN International
Wireless access
Partic in HSLC/Access PA/POWER Library; Inter-University Consortium for Political & Social Research (ICPSR); Lyrasis; OCLC Online Computer Library Center, Inc; Pennsylvania Academic Library Consortium, Inc (PALCI)
Open Mon-Thurs 7:45am-1am, Fri 7:45am-10pm, Sat 10-9, Sun Noon-1am
Restriction: Authorized patrons
Friends of the Library Group

P ELIZABETHTOWN PUBLIC LIBRARY*, Ten S Market St, 17022-2307. SAN 314-478X. Tel: 717-367-7467. FAX: 717-367-5019. E-mail: information@etownpubliclibrary.org. Web Site: www.etownpubliclibrary.org. *Exec Dir,* Deborah Drury; Staff 14 (MLS 3, Non-MLS 11)
Founded 1925. Pop 37,950; Circ 280,000
Library Holdings: AV Mats 1,000; Bks on Deafness & Sign Lang 75; Large Print Bks 750; Bk Titles 42,000; Bk Vols 45,000; Per Subs 80; Talking Bks 150
Special Collections: Braille & Vision Impaired; Business; Community Development; Deaf & Hard of Hearing; Parenting
Automation Activity & Vendor Info: (Cataloging) Innovative Interfaces, Inc; (Circulation) Innovative Interfaces, Inc; (OPAC) Inlex
Database Vendor: Baker & Taylor, Dialog, EBSCOhost, Gale Cengage Learning, LexisNexis, ProQuest, Wilson - Wilson Web
Function: Audio & video playback equip for onsite use, AV serv, Bus archives, CD-ROM, Distance learning, Games & aids for the handicapped, Handicapped accessible, ILL available, Large print keyboards, Libr develop, Magnifiers for reading, Music CDs, Online searches, Photocopying/Printing, Prof lending libr, Prog for adults, Prog for children & young adult, Ref serv available, Spoken cassettes & CDs, Summer reading prog, Telephone ref, VHS videos, Wheelchair accessible, Workshops
Mem of Library System of Lancaster County
Special Services for the Deaf - Bks on deafness & sign lang; Deaf publ; Staff with knowledge of sign lang
Special Services for the Blind - Bks & mags in Braille, on rec, tape & cassette; Bks available with recordings; Bks on cassette; Bks on CD; Braille bks; Cassettes; Large print bks; Magnifiers; PC for handicapped
Open Mon-Thurs 7am-8pm, Sat 9-4
Friends of the Library Group

ELKINS PARK

R BETH SHOLOM CONGREGATION*, Joseph & Elizabeth Schwartz Library, 8231 Old York Rd, 19027. SAN 314-4798. Tel: 215-887-1342. FAX: 215-887-6605. Web Site: www.bethsholomcongregation.org. *In Charge,* Deana Baker; Staff 1 (Non-MLS 1)
Founded 1959
Library Holdings: Bk Titles 7,549; Bk Vols 7,610; Per Subs 16
Special Collections: Jewish Music (Gedaliah Rabinowitz Library); Judaica
Subject Interests: Jewish art
Open Mon-Fri 10-2

CM PENNSYLVANIA COLLEGE OF OPTOMETRY AT SALUS UNIVERSITY*, Gerard Cottet Library, 8360 Old York Rd, 19027. SAN 314-9625. Tel: 215-780-1260. FAX: 215-780-1263. E-mail: gcottet@salus.edu. *Dir,* Keith Lammers; E-mail: keith@salus.edu; *Asst Librn,* Luminita Vulcu; Tel: 215-780-1262, E-mail: luminita@salus.edu; *ILL,* Marian Weber; Tel: 215-780-1261, E-mail: marian@salus.edu; Staff 4 (MLS 2, Non-MLS 2)
Founded 1919. Enrl 585; Fac 31
Library Holdings: Bk Titles 24,610; Bk Vols 25,818; Per Subs 316
Special Collections: Antique Eyewear & Ophthalmic Instruments; Old Visual Science Books
Subject Interests: Audiology, Blindness, Clinical med, Low vision, Ocular anatomy, Ocular pharmacology, Ophthalmology, Optometry, Rehabilitation optics, Vision res, Visually impaired
Automation Activity & Vendor Info: (Cataloging) Mandarin Library Automation; (Circulation) Mandarin Library Automation; (OPAC) Mandarin Library Automation
Wireless access
Publications: Infovision (Newsletter); Ocular Bibliographies
Partic in Basic Health Sciences Library Network; Delaware Valley Information Consortium; Docline; Health Sci Libr Info Consortium; National Network of Libraries of Medicine; Regional Med Libr Network
Open Mon-Fri 8am-11:45pm, Sat & Sun 10am-11:45pm

R REFORM CONGREGATION KENESETH ISRAEL*, Meyers Library, 8339 Old York Rd, 19027. SAN 314-4836. Tel: 215-887-8700. FAX: 215-887-1070. Web Site: www.kenesethisrael.org. *Librn,* Norma Meshkov; E-mail: mnorma1@aol.com; Staff 3 (MLS 1, Non-MLS 2)
Library Holdings: Bk Titles 10,000; Bk Vols 14,000; Per Subs 30
Subject Interests: Judaica
Open Tues 4-6, Wed 10-3:30, Sun 9:15-12:15

ELKLAND

P ELKLAND AREA COMMUNITY LIBRARY*, 110 Parkway Ave, 16920-1311. SAN 314-4844. Tel: 814-258-7576. FAX: 814-258-7414. E-mail: eacl@epix.net. Web Site: www.elklandlibrary.com. *Librn,* Rosemary Hackett
Pop 3,927; Circ 12,599
Library Holdings: Bk Vols 14,000; Per Subs 60
Special Collections: Elkland Journal Coll, bd copies & microfilm
Automation Activity & Vendor Info: (Cataloging) Brodart; (Circulation) Brodart

Mem of Potter-Tioga Library System
Open Mon, Tues & Thurs 4-8, Wed & Fri 8-4, Sat 8-3

ELLWOOD CITY

P ELLWOOD CITY AREA PUBLIC LIBRARY, 415 Lawrence Ave, 16117-1944. SAN 314-4852. Tel: 724-758-6458. FAX: 724-758-0115. E-mail: Ellwood_Library@lawrencecountylibrary.org. Web Site: www.ellwoodlibrary.org. *Dir,* Veronica Pacella; Staff 5 (Non-MLS 5)
Founded 1914. Pop 18,146
Library Holdings: Bk Vols 48,138; Per Subs 75
Database Vendor: SirsiDynix
Mem of Lawrence County Federated Library System
Open Mon-Thurs 10-8, Fri 10-4, Sat 9-4
Friends of the Library Group

ELVERSON

S US DEPARTMENT OF INTERIOR, NATIONAL PARK SERVICE*, Hopewell Furnace National Historic Site Resource Center, Two Mark Bird Lane, 19520. Tel: 610-582-8773, Ext 240. FAX: 610-582-2768. TDD: 610-582-2093. E-mail: hofu_superintendent@nps.gov. Web Site: www.nps.gov/hofu/index.html. *In Charge,* Rebecca Ross; E-mail: rebecca_ross@nps.gov; Staff 1 (Non-MLS 1)
Founded 1938
Library Holdings: Bk Vols 1,200; Videos 20
Special Collections: Hopewell Furnace Charcoal Iron Industry Coll, microfiche & microfilm; Hopewell Furnace Reports; Old & Rare Books on the History of Iron Making. Oral History
Subject Interests: Hist
Special Services for the Deaf - TDD equip
Restriction: Not open to pub, Open by appt only, Open to researchers by request

ELYSBURG

P RALPHO TOWNSHIP PUBLIC LIBRARY*, 32B Market St, 17824. (Mail add: PO Box 315, 17824-0315), SAN 314-4860. Tel: 570-672-9449. Web Site: www.schiu.k12.pa.us/ralpl. *Dir,* Patricia Bidding; Staff 1 (MLS 1)
Founded 1974. Pop 3,131; Circ 14,058
Library Holdings: Bk Titles 15,706; Bk Vols 18,872; Per Subs 42
Open Mon, Tues & Thurs 2-8:30, Wed 10-8:30, Fri 2-6:30, Sat 9-3
Friends of the Library Group

EMMAUS

P EMMAUS PUBLIC LIBRARY*, 11 E Main St, 18049. SAN 314-4879. Tel: 610-965-9284. FAX: 610-965-6446. E-mail: emmauspl@cliu.org. Web Site: www.emmauspl.org. *Dir,* Frances A Larash; *ILL,* Maralie Rowell; *Ref,* Dorothy Russell; Staff 10 (MLS 4, Non-MLS 6)
Founded 1966. Pop 21,000; Circ 160,000
Library Holdings: Bk Vols 90,000; Per Subs 60
Special Collections: Local History (Shelter House Coll); Roeder Coll, art & ref bks
Automation Activity & Vendor Info: (Acquisitions) Civica; (Cataloging) Civica; (Circulation) Civica; (Course Reserve) Civica; (ILL) Civica; (Media Booking) Civica; (OPAC) Civica; (Serials) Civica
Function: AV serv, ILL available, Prog for children & young adult, Ref serv available, Summer reading prog, Wheelchair accessible
Open Mon-Thurs 10-9, Sat 10-5
Restriction: Open to pub for ref & circ; with some limitations
Friends of the Library Group

S RODALE INC, Library & Information Services, 400 S Tenth St, 18098. SAN 324-7805. Tel: 610-967-8729, 610-967-8880. Interlibrary Loan Service Tel: 610-967-8189. FAX: 610-967-8100. *Chief Librn,* Lynn Donches; E-mail: lynn.donches@rodale.com; *Per Librn,* Carla Lindenmuth; Tel: 610-967-8153; *Ref Librn,* Gina Kelchner; Tel: 610-967-7569; *ILL,* Jennifer Keiser; Staff 6 (MLS 2, Non-MLS 4)
Founded 1976
Library Holdings: e-journals 15; Bk Titles 40,000; Bk Vols 42,000; Per Subs 700
Subject Interests: Agr, Fitness, Gardening, Health, Nutrition, Sports
Automation Activity & Vendor Info: (Acquisitions) Sydney; (Cataloging) Sydney; (Circulation) Sydney; (OPAC) Sydney; (Serials) Sydney
Database Vendor: EBSCOhost, Factiva.com, LexisNexis, ProQuest
Publications: Abstract Bulletins; Periodical List
Restriction: Open by appt only

EMPORIUM

GL CAMERON COUNTY LAW LIBRARY*, Court House, 20 E Fifth St, 15834. SAN 328-0047. Tel: 814-486-2315. FAX: 814-486-0464. Web Site: www.cameroncountypa.com. *Librn,* Brenda Munz
Founded 1890
Library Holdings: Bk Titles 18,910; Bk Vols 20,000; Per Subs 57
Open Mon-Fri 8:30-4

P CAMERON COUNTY PUBLIC LIBRARY*, Barbara Moscato Brown Memorial Library, 27 W Fourth St, 15834. (Mail add: PO Box 430, 15834-0430), SAN 358-4526. Tel: 814-486-8011. FAX: 814-486-3725. E-mail: brocampl@zitomedia.net. Web Site: www.barbaramoscatobrownlibrary.org, www.cameroncountypubliclibrary.org, www.emporiumlibrary.org. *Dir,* Anna Marie English; *ILL,* Richard A Sarick; Staff 4 (MLS 1, Non-MLS 3)
Founded 1940. Pop 5,974
Library Holdings: Large Print Bks 450; Bk Vols 30,300; Per Subs 74
Subject Interests: Pa hist
Automation Activity & Vendor Info: (Cataloging) Follett Software; (Circulation) Follett Software; (OPAC) Follett Software
Database Vendor: Dialog, EBSCOhost
Open Mon, Tues, Thurs & Fri 11-8, Wed 9-1, Sat 9-4
Friends of the Library Group

EPHRATA

P EPHRATA PUBLIC LIBRARY*, 550 S Reading Rd, 17522. SAN 314-4887. Tel: 717-738-9291. FAX: 717-721-3003. Web Site: www.ephratapubliclibrary.org. *Exec Dir,* Joseph Zappacosta; *Pub Relations,* Penny Talbert; Staff 2 (MLS 2)
Founded 1962. Pop 30,460; Circ 351,000
Library Holdings: Bk Vols 72,000; Per Subs 35
Automation Activity & Vendor Info: (Cataloging) Innovative Interfaces, Inc; (Circulation) Innovative Interfaces, Inc; (OPAC) Innovative Interfaces, Inc
Mem of Library System of Lancaster County
Open Mon-Thurs 9-8, Fri 9-6, Sat 9-1, Sun (Sept-May) 2-5
Friends of the Library Group

S THE HISTORICAL SOCIETY OF THE COCALICO VALLEY LIBRARY*, 237 W Main St, 17522. (Mail add: PO Box 193, 17522), SAN 326-5331. Tel: 717-733-1616. *Librn,* Cynthia Marquet; Staff 1 (MLS 1)
Founded 1957
Library Holdings: Bk Titles 1,750; Bk Vols 2,075
Special Collections: Ephrata Cloister Imprints (Walter Moyer Coll); Historical Photographs
Subject Interests: Local genealogy, Local hist
Publications: Annual Journal
Open Mon, Wed & Thurs 9:30-6, Sat 8:30-5
Restriction: Non-circulating to the pub

ERDENHEIM

J ANTONELLI INSTITUTE*, Art & Photography Library, 300 Montgomery Ave, 19038. SAN 372-6967. Tel: 215-836-2222. FAX: 215-836-2794. E-mail: admissions@antonelli.edu. Web Site: www.antonelli.edu. *Pres,* Dr Thomas Treacy
Founded 1938. Enrl 150; Fac 22
Library Holdings: Bk Titles 1,145; Per Subs 62
Open Mon-Fri 8am-10pm

ERIE

SR ANSHE HESED TEMPLE LIBRARY*, 930 Liberty St, 16502. SAN 328-6363. Tel: 814-454-2426. FAX: 814-454-2427. *Librn,* Janine Dreyfus
Library Holdings: Bk Vols 4,000
Special Collections: Congregational Archives

GM DEPARTMENT OF VETERANS AFFAIRS MEDICAL CENTER*, Medical Library, 135 E 38th St, 16504-1559. SAN 314-5050. Tel: 814-868-8661. FAX: 814-860-2469. *Librn,* Mary E Nourse; E-mail: mary.nourse@med.va.gov; Staff 2 (MLS 1, Non-MLS 1)
Founded 1951
Library Holdings: Bk Vols 35,000; Per Subs 125
Subject Interests: Nursing, Primary health care
Partic in Docline; Erie Area Health Information Library Cooperative; National Network of Libraries of Medicine; NICOP
Open Mon-Fri 8-4:30

S ERIE COUNTY HISTORICAL SOCIETY*, Library & Archives, Erie County History Ctr, 419 State St, 16501. SAN 324-7619. Tel: 814-454-1813, Ext 26. Reference Tel: 814-454-1813, Ext 28. FAX: 814-454-6890. Web Site: www.eriecountyhistory.org. *Dir, Libr & Archives,* Annita Andrick; E-mail: aandrick@eriecountyhistory.org; Staff 1.75 (MLS 1, Non-MLS 0.75)
Founded 1903
Library Holdings: Bk Vols 5,800; Per Subs 20
Special Collections: Oral History
Subject Interests: Civil War, Local hist, Pa hist
Function: Workshops

Publications: Ethnic Erie Archives Series (Local historical information); Journal of Erie Studies (Bi-annually)
Partic in Northwest Interlibrary Cooperative of Pennsylvania; OCLC Online Computer Library Center, Inc
Open Tues-Sat 11-4
Restriction: Staff & prof res

GL ERIE COUNTY LAW LIBRARY, Court House, Rm 01, 140 W Sixth St, 16501. SAN 314-4933. Tel: 814-451-6319. FAX: 814-451-6320. *Dir,* Max C Peaster; E-mail: mpeaster@eriecountygov.org; Staff 1 (MLS 1)
Founded 1876
Library Holdings: Bk Vols 10,000; Per Subs 10
Subject Interests: Law
Database Vendor: LexisNexis, Westlaw
Partic in NICOP
Open Mon-Fri 8-4:30

P ERIE COUNTY PUBLIC LIBRARY*, Raymond M Blasco MD Memorial Library, 160 E Front St, 16507. SAN 358-4585. Tel: 814-451-6900. Circulation Tel: 814-451-6929. Interlibrary Loan Service Tel: 814-451-6922. Reference Tel: 814-451-6927. Administration Tel: 814-451-6952. Automation Services Tel: 814-451-6923, 814-451-6925. FAX: 814-451-6907. Administration FAX: 814-451-6969. TDD: 814-451-6931. E-mail: reference@erielibrary.org. Web Site: www.erielibrary.org. *Exec Dir,* Margaret Z Stewart; E-mail: mstewart@eriecountygov.org; *Mgr, Ad Serv,* Ann Marie Schlindwein; E-mail: aschlindwein@eriecountygov.org; *Mgr, Ch Serv,* Susan Miceli; Tel: 814-451-6928, E-mail: smiceli@eriecountygov.org; *Mgr, Circ Serv,* Evelyn Wesman; Tel: 814-451-6908, E-mail: ewesman@eriecountygov.org; *Outreach Serv Mgr,* Marcy Hall; Tel: 814-451-6959, E-mail: mhall@eriecountygov.org; *Mgr, Tech Serv,* Anitra Gates; Tel: 814-451-6919, E-mail: agates@eriecountygov.org; *Br Coordr,* Mary Rennie; Tel: 814-451-6910, E-mail: mrennie@erielibrary.org; *Main Libr Coordr,* Joan Duke; Tel: 814-451-6911, E-mail: jduke@erielibrary.org; *Tech Coordr,* Ann Randall-Dill; E-mail: ardill@erielibrary.org; Staff 21.5 (MLS 16, Non-MLS 5.5)
Founded 1895. Pop 245,275; Circ 1,560,203
Jan 2009-Dec 2009 Income (Main Library and Branch(s)) $5,926,600, State $1,882,993, Federal $75,489, County $3,696,344, Locally Generated Income $271,774. Mats Exp $610,209, Books $373,481, Per/Ser (Incl. Access Fees) $22,689, Micro $882, AV Mat $96,700, Electronic Ref Mat (Incl. Access Fees) $111,457, Presv $5,000. Sal $4,188,147 (Prof $32,370)
Library Holdings: Audiobooks 29,448; AV Mats 27,881; DVDs 18,452; e-books 325; Bk Vols 433,943; Per Subs 269; Videos 21,723
Special Collections: Genealogy (Western Pennsylvania). State Document Depository; US Document Depository
Automation Activity & Vendor Info: (Acquisitions) SIRSI WorkFlows; (Cataloging) SIRSI WorkFlows; (Circulation) SIRSI WorkFlows; (OPAC) SIRSI-iBistro
Database Vendor: 3M Library Systems, Auto-Graphics, Inc, Baker & Taylor, Booksite, Facts on File, Foundation Center, Gale Cengage Learning, infoUSA, LearningExpress, OCLC WorldShare Interlibrary Loan, Overdrive, Inc, ProQuest, ReferenceUSA, SirsiDynix, Wilson - Wilson Web
Wireless access
Partic in Lyrasis
Open Mon-Thurs 9-8:30, Fri & Sat 9-5, Sun 1-5
Friends of the Library Group

Branches: 4

EDINBORO BRANCH, 413 W Plum St, Edinboro, 16412-2508, SAN 358-4615. Tel: 814-451-7081. *Br Coordr,* Mary Rennie; Tel: 814-451-6910, E-mail: mrennie@erielibrary.org

IROQUOIS AVENUE, 4212 Iroquois Ave, 16511-2198, SAN 358-4674. Tel: 814-451-7082. FAX: 814-451-7092. *Br Coordr,* Mary Rennie; Tel: 814-451-6910, Fax: 814-451-6969, E-mail: mrennie@erielibrary.org
Open Mon-Thurs 10-8, Fri & Sat 10-5

LINCOLN COMMUNITY CENTER, 1255 Manchester Rd, 16505-2614, SAN 358-4763. Tel: 814-451-7085. FAX: 814-451-7095. *Br Coordr,* Mary Rennie; Tel: 814-451-6910, Fax: 814-451-6969, E-mail: mrennie@erielibrary.org

MILLCREEK, 2088 Interchange Rd, Ste 280, 16565-0601, SAN 358-4739. Tel: 814-451-7084. FAX: 814-451-7094. *Br Coordr,* Mary Rennie; Tel: 814-451-6910, Fax: 814-451-6969, E-mail: mrennie@erielibrary.org

Bookmobiles: 1

R FIRST PRESBYTERIAN CHURCH OF THE COVENANT, Brittain Library, 250 W Seventh St, 16501. SAN 314-4909. Tel: 814-456-4243. FAX: 814-454-3350. *Librn,* Jean Ann Tauber; Staff 0.25 (MLS 0.25)
Founded 1954
Library Holdings: Large Print Bks 100; Bk Vols 7,000; Per Subs 12; Videos 50
Function: Handicapped accessible, Summer reading prog, Video lending libr, Wheelchair accessible
Restriction: Restricted access, Restricted borrowing privileges

C GANNON UNIVERSITY*, Nash Library, 109 University Sq, 16541. SAN 314-4968. Tel: 814-871-7557. Interlibrary Loan Service Tel: 814-871-5529. FAX: 814-871-5666. Web Site: library.gannon.edu. *Dir,* Ken Brundage; *Archivist, Asst Dir,* Robert Dobiesz; *Outreach Librn,* Emmett Lombard; *Syst Librn,* Betsy Garloch; *Circ Supvr,* Robert Sparks; *Coll Develop,* Lawrence Maxted; *ILL,* Mary Beth Earll; *Ref & Instruction,* Deborah West; *Tech Serv,* Lori Grossholz; Staff 18 (MLS 9, Non-MLS 9)
Founded 1925. Enrl 3,408; Fac 201; Highest Degree: Doctorate
Jul 2011-Jun 2012. Mats Exp $506,971, Books $96,978, Per/Ser (Incl. Access Fees) $124,569, AV Mat $11,034, Electronic Ref Mat (Incl. Access Fees) $188,707, Presv $5,280. Sal $726,013
Library Holdings: AV Mats 2,853; e-journals 46,118; Bk Vols 265,863; Per Subs 152
Automation Activity & Vendor Info: (Acquisitions) SIRSI WorkFlows; (Cataloging) SIRSI WorkFlows; (Circulation) SIRSI WorkFlows; (ILL) OCLC ILLiad; (OPAC) SirsiDynix; (Serials) SIRSI WorkFlows
Database Vendor: ACM (Association for Computing Machinery), Alexander Street Press, American Chemical Society, American Psychological Association (APA), CredoReference, ebrary, EBSCOhost, HeinOnline, IEEE (Institute of Electrical & Electronics Engineers), JSTOR, OCLC FirstSearch, OCLC WorldShare Interlibrary Loan, OVID Technologies, ProQuest, Sage, ScienceDirect, Westlaw
Wireless access
Partic in Lyrasis; Pennsylvania Academic Library Consortium, Inc (PALCI)
Open Mon-Thurs 7:30am-Midnight, Fri 8-7, Sat 11-7, Sun 12:30-Midnight

CM LAKE ERIE COLLEGE OF OSTEOPATHIC MEDICINE*, Learning Resource Center, 1858 W Grandview Blvd, 16509-1025. Tel: 814-866-8451. Administration Tel: 814-866-8151. FAX: 814-868-6911. E-mail: library@lecom.edu. Web Site: www.lecom.edu. *Dir,* Daniel Welch; E-mail: dwelch@lecom.edu; Staff 5 (MLS 3, Non MLS 2)
Founded 1993. Highest Degree: Doctorate
Library Holdings: e-journals 800; Bk Vols 8,500; Per Subs 200
Subject Interests: Osteopathic med
Automation Activity & Vendor Info: (Cataloging) EOS International; (Circulation) EOS International; (OPAC) EOS International; (Serials) EOS International
Database Vendor: EBSCO Information Services, OVID Technologies
Wireless access
Partic in Lyrasis
Open Mon-Fri 7am-11pm, Sat & Sun 8am-11pm
Restriction: Open to students, fac & staff

C MERCYHURST UNIVERSITY, Hammermill Library - Main Campus, 501 E 38th St, 16546. SAN 314-5018. Tel: 814-824-2234. Interlibrary Loan Service Tel: 814-824-2236. Administration Tel: 814-824-2232. FAX: 814-824-2219. Web Site: library.mercyhurst.edu. *Dir, Univ Libr & Distance Learning,* Darci Jones; Tel: 814-824-2237, E-mail: djones@mercyhurst.edu; *Cat Librn,* Therese Lancaster; Tel: 814-824-2231, E-mail: tlancaster@mercyhurst.edu; *Archivist, Ref Librn,* Earleen Glaser; Tel: 814-824-2190, E-mail: eglaser@mercyhurst.edu; *Ser Librn,* Penny Wise; Tel: 814-824-3309, E-mail: pwise@mercyhurst.edu; *Syst & Teaching Librn,* Rebecca Crago; Tel: 814-824-3305, E-mail: rcrago@mercyhurst.edu; *ILL Coordr,* Ashley Lambert; E-mail: alambert@mercyhurst.edu; *Acq,* Lynn Falk; E-mail: lfalk@mercyhurst.edu; Staff 8 (MLS 4, Non-MLS 4)
Founded 1926. Highest Degree: Master
Special Collections: Ethnic History Concentrating on Northwest Pennsylvania, bks
Automation Activity & Vendor Info: (Acquisitions) ByWater Solutions; (Cataloging) ByWater Solutions; (Circulation) ByWater Solutions; (Course Reserve) ByWater Solutions; (ILL) ByWater Solutions; (OPAC) ByWater Solutions; (Serials) ByWater Solutions
Database Vendor: 3M Library Systems, ByWater Solutions, CredoReference, ebrary, EBSCO Discovery Service, EBSCOhost, Gale Cengage Learning, JSTOR, LexisNexis, OCLC, OCLC WorldShare Interlibrary Loan, ProQuest, RefWorks
Wireless access
Partic in Interlibrary Delivery Service of Pennsylvania; Lyrasis; Northwest Interlibrary Cooperative of Pennsylvania; OCLC Online Computer Library Center, Inc; Pennsylvania Academic Library Consortium, Inc (PALCI)
Open Mon-Thurs 8am-2am, Fri 8am-10pm, Sat 9-9, Sun Noon-2am

Departmental Libraries:

RIDGE LIBRARY - NORTH EAST CAMPUS, 16 W Division St, North East, 16428, SAN 378-4460. Tel: 814-725-6116. Circulation Tel: 814-725-6324. FAX: 814-725-6112. Web Site: northeast.mercyhurst.edu/text/library_web_page/index.htm. *Dir,* Caitlyn Russman; Staff 4 (MLS 2, Non-MLS 2)
Enrl 700; Highest Degree: Associate
Library Holdings: Bk Vols 6,933; Per Subs 58
Open Mon-Thurs 7:45am-9pm, Fri 7:45-4, Sat 10-2

C PENN STATE ERIE*, John M Lilley Library, 4951 College Dr, 16563-4115. SAN 314-5026. Tel: 814-898-6106. FAX: 814-898-6350. Web Site: www.pserie.psu.edu/library/bdindex.htm. *Dir,* Richard L Hart; *Acq, Ser,* Melissa Osborn; *Archives, Ref Serv,* Jane Ingold; *Bibliog Instr,*

Patience Simmonds; *Circ,* Lisa Moyer; *ILL,* Patti Mrozowski; Staff 7 (MLS 4, Non-MLS 3)
Founded 1948. Enrl 4,500; Fac 200; Highest Degree: Master
Library Holdings: Bk Vols 133,000; Per Subs 575; Videos 2,500
Special Collections: Behrend Family Coll; Hammermill Paper Company Coll
Wireless access

M SAINT VINCENT HEALTH CENTER*, Health Sciences Library, 232 W 25th St, 16544. SAN 314-5042. Tel: 814-452-5736. FAX: 814-452-7131. *Coordr,* Tina Burling; E-mail: tburling@svhs.org; Staff 1 (Non-MLS 1)
Founded 1940
Library Holdings: Bk Titles 3,596; Per Subs 378
Special Collections: History of Medicine
Subject Interests: Dentistry, Hospital admin, Med, Nursing
Database Vendor: OVID Technologies
Function: Archival coll, Doc delivery serv, Health sci info serv, ILL available
Partic in Basic Health Sciences Library Network; Central Pennsylvania Health Sciences Library Association; Mid-Atlantic Regional Med Libr Prog
Restriction: Staff use only

M UPMC HAMOT*, Library Services, 201 State St, 16550. SAN 314-4984. Tel: 814-877-3628. FAX: 814-877-6188. Web Site: upmchamot.org. *Mgr,* Linda Jeffery; E-mail: jefferyll@upmc.edu; Staff 1 (Non-MLS 1)
Founded 1964
Library Holdings: e-books 35; e-journals 124; Bk Titles 1,500; Bk Vols 2,186; Per Subs 100
Subject Interests: Emergency med, Gen surgery, Hospital admin, Internal med, Neurology, Orthopedics, Trauma med
Automation Activity & Vendor Info: (Cataloging) Follett Software; (Circulation) OVID Technologies; (ILL) OCLC FirstSearch
Database Vendor: EBSCOhost, OVID Technologies
Wireless access
Publications: Columns In-house
Partic in Erie Area Health Information Library Cooperative; NICOP
Open Mon-Fri 7:30-4

ESSINGTON

P TINICUM MEMORIAL PUBLIC LIBRARY*, 620 Seneca St, 19029-1199. SAN 314-5085. Tel: 610-521-9344. FAX: 610-521-3463. E-mail: tinicum@delcolibraries.org. *Dir,* Agnes Davis; *Asst Librn,* Esther Berry
Pop 4,906; Circ 31,379
Library Holdings: Bk Vols 18,203; Per Subs 30
Mem of Delaware County Library System
Open Mon & Wed 10-4:30 & 6-8, Tues 2-6, Thurs 5:30-8, Fri 10-4, Sat 9-4

EVANS CITY

P EVANS CITY PUBLIC LIBRARY, 204 S Jackson St, 16033-1138. SAN 314-5093. Tel: 724-538-8695. FAX: 724-538-5630. E-mail: evanscity@bcfls.org. Web Site: www.bcfls.org/evanscity.htm. *Ch Serv Librn, Libr Dir,* Michelina Stickney
Founded 1932. Pop 4,836; Circ 10,000
Library Holdings: Bk Titles 17,000; Per Subs 30
Automation Activity & Vendor Info: (Cataloging) TLC (The Library Corporation); (Circulation) TLC (The Library Corporation); (OPAC) TLC (The Library Corporation)
Mem of Butler County Federated Library System
Open Mon-Thurs 10-6, Sat 9-4 (9-1 Summer)

EVERETT

P EVERETT FREE LIBRARY*, 137 E Main St, 15537-1259. SAN 314-5115. Tel: 814-652-5922. FAX: 814-652-5425. Web Site: www.everettlibrary.org. *Dir,* Judy Hillegas; *Ref,* Susan Myers; Staff 4 (MLS 2, Non-MLS 2)
Founded 1923. Pop 12,903; Circ 47,396
Library Holdings: Bks on Deafness & Sign Lang 27; Bk Titles 41,000; Per Subs 61
Special Collections: Bedford County History; Everett Bicentennial Records Coll; Genealogy; Pennsylvania History
Subject Interests: Local census data
Automation Activity & Vendor Info: (Circulation) Follett Software; (OPAC) Follett Software
Function: ILL available
Publications: Directory of Pennsylvania Libraries
Mem of Bedford County Library System
Open Mon & Thurs 11-6, Tues 1-8, Wed 10-5, Fri 9-7, Sat 9-4

EXTON

P CHESTER COUNTY LIBRARY SYSTEM*, 450 Exton Square Pkwy, 19341-2496. SAN 315-3312. Tel: 610-280-2600. FAX: 610-280-2688. Interlibrary Loan Service FAX: 610-280-2693. Web Site: www.ccls.org. *Exec Dir, Syst,* Joseph L Sherwood; Tel: 610-280-2611, E-mail: jsherwood@ccls.org; *Libr Dir,* Marguerite Dube; E-mail: mdube@ccls.org; *Acq, Coll Develop,* Jenna Persick; *Circ,* Barbara Bailey; *ILL,* Carol Welch; *Multimedia,* Stephanie Sharon; *Ref,* Susan Frederick; *Youth Serv,* Jeanne Clancy; Staff 75 (MLS 19, Non-MLS 56)
Founded 1928. Pop 412,170
Library Holdings: Bk Vols 282,907; Per Subs 1,117
Special Collections: Adult Reading Large Type Coll; AGR (Adult Graded Reading); Chester County Coll; Chester's Reading Large Type Coll; Children's Reading Large Type Coll; Computer Software Coll; Literacy Coll; Local Newspaper Coll; State & Local Government Rare Books Coll; Work Place Job & Career Information Coll
Automation Activity & Vendor Info: (Acquisitions) Innovative Interfaces, Inc; (Cataloging) Innovative Interfaces, Inc; (Circulation) Innovative Interfaces, Inc; (ILL) Innovative Interfaces, Inc; (OPAC) Innovative Interfaces, Inc; (Serials) Innovative Interfaces, Inc
Wireless access
Publications: Chester County Library Business News; Chester County Library System (Newsletter)
Member Libraries: Atglen Public Library; Avon Grove Library; Bayard Taylor Memorial Library; Chester Springs Library; Coatesville Area Public Library; Downingtown Library Co; Easttown Library & Information Center; Honey Brook Community Library; Oxford Public Library; Parkesburg Free Library; Phoenixville Public Library; Spring City Free Public Library; Tredyffrin Public Library; West Chester Public Library
Partic in Interlibrary Delivery Service of Pennsylvania; OCLC Online Computer Library Center, Inc
Friends of the Library Group
Bookmobiles: 1

FACTORYVILLE

P FACTORYVILLE PUBLIC LIBRARY*, 163 College Ave, 18419. (Mail add: PO Box 238, 18419-0238), SAN 314-5131. Tel: 570-945-3788. *Dir,* Georgianna Fields
Pop 1,500; Circ 4,715
Library Holdings: Bk Vols 6,300
Open Mon 7pm-9pm, Tues 2-5, Wed 11-4, Thurs 10:30-12:30 & 1-6, Sat 10-Noon

FAIRFIELD

P FAIRFIELD AREA LIBRARY, 31 Wortz Dr, 17320. Tel: 717-642-6009. FAX: 717-642-6430. E-mail: fairfield@adamslibrary.org. Web Site: www.adamslibrary.org. *Mgr,* Sherrie DeMartino
Mem of Adams County Library System
Open Mon & Thurs 2-8, Tues, Wed & Fri 11-5, Sat 10-4

FALLSINGTON

P FALLSINGTON LIBRARY*, 139 Yardley Ave, 19054-1119. SAN 314-514X. Tel: 215-295-4449. Web Site: www.buckslib.org/libraries/fallsington. *Dir,* Karen Suscovich; Staff 2 (Non-MLS 2)
Founded 1800. Pop 35,891; Circ 43,512
Library Holdings: AV Mats 590; Large Print Bks 72; Bk Titles 23,910; Bk Vols 25,611; Per Subs 49; Talking Bks 72; Videos 161
Special Collections: Bucks County; History Coll; Pennsylvania State History Coll; Society of Friends Coll
Automation Activity & Vendor Info: (Cataloging) SirsiDynix; (Circulation) SirsiDynix; (OPAC) SirsiDynix
Open Mon-Thurs 1-4:30 & 6-9, Fri 1-4:30, Sat 10-3

FARMINGTON

S NATIONAL PARK SERVICE, DEPARTMENT OF INTERIOR, Fort Necessity National Battlefield Research Library, One Washington Pkwy, 15437. SAN 323-8644. Tel: 724-329-5512. FAX: 724-329-8682. Web Site: www.nps.gov/fone. *Curator,* Brian Reedy; Tel: 724-329-5811, E-mail: brian_reedy@nps.gov
Founded 1979
Library Holdings: Bk Vols 3,000
Special Collections: French & Indian War/National Road
Restriction: Open by appt only

FARRELL

P STEY-NEVANT PUBLIC LIBRARY*, 1000 Roemer Blvd, 16121-1899. Tel: 724-983-2714. FAX: 724-983-2710. E-mail: info@steynevantlibrary.com. Web Site: www.steynevantlibrary.com. *Librn,* Margaret Orchard; Staff 4 (Non-MLS 4)

Founded 1931. Pop 6,841
Library Holdings: Bk Vols 34,218; Per Subs 90
Special Collections: Black Studies Coll
Automation Activity & Vendor Info: (Cataloging) Follett Software; (Circulation) Follett Software; (OPAC) Follett Software
Open Mon & Thurs 11-7, Tues & Wed 10-6, Fri & Sat 7-2

M UPMC HORIZON*, Shenango Valley Campus Medical Library, 2200 Memorial Dr, 16121. SAN 326-6443. Tel: 724-589-6322, 724-983-7558. FAX: 724-589-6587. *Librn,* Carrie Gault
Library Holdings: e-books 2,500; e-journals 2,000; Bk Titles 250
Wireless access
Open Mon-Fri 7-5
Restriction: Borrowing privileges limited to fac & registered students, Hospital employees & physicians only, Not open to pub
Branches:
GREENVILLE CAMPUS MEDICAL LIBRARY, 110 N Main St, Greenville, 16125. Tel: 724-589-6672. FAX: 724-589-6631. *Librn,* Tammy Buckley
Library Holdings: e-books 2,500; e-journals 2,000; Bk Vols 300
Open Mon-Fri 7-3
Restriction: Non-circulating

FEASTERVILLE

P TOWNSHIP LIBRARY OF LOWER SOUTHAMPTON*, 1983 Bridgetown Pike, 19053-4493. SAN 314-5166. Tel: 215-355-1183. FAX: 215-364-5735. Web Site: www.buckslib.org. *Librn,* Sally Pollock; E-mail: pollocks@buckslib.org; *Ch Serv,* Bonnie Reeves; Staff 2 (MLS 2)
Founded 1956. Pop 18,909
Library Holdings: Audiobooks 3,999; AV Mats 7,310; e-books 1,295; Bk Vols 75,175; Per Subs 86
Automation Activity & Vendor Info: (Circulation) SirsiDynix; (OPAC) SirsiDynix
Wireless access
Mem of Bucks County Free Library
Open Mon & Wed 10-9, Tues & Thurs 12-9, Fri 12-6, Sat 9-4
Friends of the Library Group

FLEETWOOD

P FLEETWOOD AREA PUBLIC LIBRARY*, 110 W Arch St, Ste 209, 19522-1301. SAN 376-5857. Tel: 610-944-0146. FAX: 610-944-9064. E-mail: fleetwoodapl@berks.lib.pa.us. Web Site: www.berks.lib.pa.us/fleetwoodapl. *Dir,* Lois A Bailey; Staff 5 (Non MLS 5)
Founded 1990. Pop 14,071
Library Holdings: Bk Titles 15,000; Per Subs 12
Automation Activity & Vendor Info: (Cataloging) SirsiDynix; (Circulation) SirsiDynix; (OPAC) SirsiDynix
Database Vendor: Dialog
Mem of Berks County Public Libraries
Open Mon, Wed & Thurs 9-8, Tues 2:30-8, Fri 9-1, Sat 9-4

FOGELSVILLE

C PENNSYLVANIA STATE LEHIGH VALLEY LIBRARY*, 8380 Mohr Lane, 18051-9999. SAN 314-5174. Tel: 610-285-5027. FAX: 610-285-5158. Web Site: www.lv.psu.edu/library. *Dir,* Dennis J Phillips; E-mail: djp3@psu.edu; *Supvr,* Stephanie Derstine; Tel: 610-285-5031, E-mail: sad14@psu.edu; *Ref Serv,* Judy Sandt; Tel: 610-285-5028, E-mail: jsandt@psu.edu; Staff 4 (MLS 2, Non-MLS 2)
Founded 1912. Enrl 624; Fac 20
Library Holdings: Bk Vols 40,000; Per Subs 172
Automation Activity & Vendor Info: (Circulation) SirsiDynix; (OPAC) SirsiDynix
Partic in OCLC Online Computer Library Center, Inc; RLIN (Research Libraries Information Network)
Open Mon-Thurs (Winter) 8am-9pm, Fri 8-5, Sat 10-3; Mon-Thurs (Summer) 8-8, Fri 8-5

FOLCROFT

P BOROUGH OF FOLCROFT PUBLIC LIBRARY*, Delmar Dr & Ashland Ave, 19032-2002. SAN 314-5182. Tel: 610-586-1690. FAX: 610-586-2179. *Head Librn,* Sue Ann Smith; Staff 2 (MLS 1, Non-MLS 1)
Pop 8,231; Circ 14,910
Library Holdings: Bk Titles 14,390; Bk Vols 15,871; Per Subs 32; Talking Bks 91; Videos 203
Mem of Delaware County Library System
Open Mon-Wed & Fri 12-5, Thurs 9-5, Sat 9-4

FOLSOM

P RIDLEY TOWNSHIP PUBLIC LIBRARY*, 100 E MacDade Blvd, 19033-2592. SAN 314-5190. Tel: 610-583-0593. Circulation Tel: 610-583-0593, Ext 202. Interlibrary Loan Service Tel: 610-583-0593, Ext 214. Reference Tel: 610-583-0593, Ext 205. Administration Tel: 610-583-0593, Ext 207. Automation Services Tel: 610-583-0593, Ext 204. FAX: 610-583-9505. E-mail: info@ridleylibrary.org. Web Site: www.ridleylibrary.org. *Dir,* Catherine Bittle; *Ch Serv,* Lauren Longbottom; *ILL,* Karen Sacco; *Pub Serv,* Kathleen Ferguson; *Ref Serv,* Mary Tobin; Staff 25 (MLS 5, Non-MLS 20)
Founded 1957. Pop 30,791; Circ 200,000
Jan 2011-Dec 2011 Income $691,880. Mats Exp $137,275, Books $95,000, Per/Ser (Incl. Access Fees) $11,000, Micro $9,000, AV Mat $16,500, Presv $5,775. Sal $414,000
Library Holdings: AV Mats 5,459; Bk Vols 73,559; Per Subs 199
Automation Activity & Vendor Info: (Acquisitions) Innovative Interfaces, Inc; (Cataloging) Innovative Interfaces, Inc; (Circulation) Innovative Interfaces, Inc; (Course Reserve) Innovative Interfaces, Inc; (ILL) Innovative Interfaces, Inc; (Media Booking) Innovative Interfaces, Inc; (OPAC) Innovative Interfaces, Inc; (Serials) Innovative Interfaces, Inc
Database Vendor: Innovative Interfaces, Inc
Wireless access
Function: After school storytime, Audiobks via web, AV serv, Bilingual assistance for Spanish patrons, Bks on CD, Bus archives, Children's prog, Computer training, Computers for patron use, Copy machines, e-mail & chat, e-mail serv, Electronic databases & coll, Handicapped accessible, Holiday prog, ILL available, Jazz prog, Music CDs, Online cat, Online ref, Online searches, OverDrive digital audio bks, Photocopying/Printing, Preschool outreach, Prog for adults, Prog for children & young adult, Pub access computers, Ref serv available, Ref serv in person, Spoken cassettes & CDs, Story hour, Summer reading prog, Tax forms, Teen prog, Telephone ref, VHS videos, Video lending libr, Wheelchair accessible
Publications: Annual report
Mem of Delaware County Library System
Open Mon-Wed 9-8, Thurs & Fri 9-5, Sat 12-4, Sun 1-4:30
Friends of the Library Group

FORD CITY

P FORD CITY PUBLIC LIBRARY*, 1136 Fourth Ave, 16226-1202. SAN 314-5204. Tel: 724-763-3591. FAX: 724-763-2705. Web Site: www.armstronglibraries.org/ford-city. *Dir,* Anita Bowser; Staff 2.5 (Non-MLS 2.5)
Founded 1945. Pop 3,410; Circ 23,131
Library Holdings: Bk Titles 33,029; Per Subs 58
Special Collections: 75th Anniversary Book of Ford City (Ford City History Coll); Ancestry (Claypool Family in America, Jack Family & Schall/Shaull Family Coll), pamphlets; Apollo People Coll; Armstrong County of Pennsylvania (J H Beers Coll, 1914); Bethel Evangelical Lutheran Church Cemetery Listing 1979; Bethel Township 1878-1978 Centennial; Decendants of Jacob Nunamaker & Katherine (Zell) Nunamaker Coll; Dulany-Furlong & Kindred Families Coll; Easley-Rooker Family History Coll, 2nd draft; Elderton Plumcreek Area-Through the Years; Ford City Centennial 1887-1987; History of Armstrong County (R W Smith Coll, 1883); History of Manorville, pamphlets; History of Slate Lick Presbyterian Church Coll, pamphlets; Lives & Letters From Kiester House; Michael A Sheely Family Coll; The Anderson Family History Coll; The Family of Samuel Wysalin America Coll; Thomas Graham Benner Family Coll
Automation Activity & Vendor Info: (Cataloging) Follett Software; (Circulation) Follett Software; (OPAC) Follett Software
Wireless access
Open Mon-Wed (Winter) 12-7, Thurs & Fri 10-5, Sat 9-4; Mon, Tues, Thurs & Fri (Summer) 9-4, Wed 12-7, Sat 9-1

FORT LOUDON

P FORT LOUDON COMMUNITY LIBRARY*, 210 Mullen St, 17224. (Mail add: PO Box 39, 17224-0039). Tel: 717-369-4704. FAX: 717-369-4757. E-mail: ftloudon@fclspa.org. Web Site: www.fclspa.org. *Br Mgr,* Gail D Sacho
Library Holdings: Bk Vols 2,500
Automation Activity & Vendor Info: (Cataloging) Brodart; (Circulation) Brodart; (OPAC) Brodart
Wireless access
Mem of Franklin County Library System
Open Mon-Thurs 3:30-7:30, Sat 9-12

FORT WASHINGTON

C DEVRY UNIVERSITY*, Pennsylvania Library, 1140 Virginia Dr, 19034. Tel: 215-591-5700, Ext 5786. Circulation Tel: 215-591-5783. FAX: 215-591-5754. E-mail: ftw-library@devry.edu. Web Site: www.philly.devry.edu/academics_library.html. *Dir, Libr Serv,* Pam Johnson; E-mail: pjohnson4@devry.edu; Staff 1 (MLS 1)

Founded 2002. Highest Degree: Master
Library Holdings: Audiobooks 67; CDs 859; DVDs 462; e-books 117,500; Bk Vols 12,826; Per Subs 42; Videos 76
Automation Activity & Vendor Info: (Cataloging) Ex Libris Group; (Circulation) Ex Libris Group; (ILL) OCLC FirstSearch; (OPAC) Ex Libris Group
Database Vendor: ABC-CLIO, Agricola, Cinahl, ebrary, EBSCOhost, Faulkner Information Services, IBISWorld, IEEE (Institute of Electrical & Electronics Engineers), LexisNexis, Plunkett Research, Ltd, Safari Books Online
Function: Computers for patron use, Electronic databases & coll, ILL available, Literacy & newcomer serv, Online cat, Online ref, Photocopying/Printing, Writing prog
Open Mon-Thurs 8am-9pm, Fri 8-5, Sat 9-2
Restriction: Circ privileges for students & alumni only, Circulates for staff only, Open to students, fac & staff

P UPPER DUBLIN PUBLIC LIBRARY*, 805 Loch Alsh Ave, 19034. SAN 358-4135. Tel: 215-628-8744. E-mail: upperdublinlibrary@mclinc.org. Web Site: www.upperdublinlibrary.org. *Dir,* Cherilyn Fiory; *Asst Dir,* Lauren Smyth; *Circ Mgr,* Judy Fraser; *Ch Serv,* Barbara McNutt; *Mkt & Communications Spec,* India Frazier; *Ref Serv,* Kay Klocko; *Tech Serv,* Kathy Brannon; *Teen Serv,* Molly Kane; Staff 13.51 (MLS 5.43, Non-MLS 8.08)
Founded 1932. Pop 25,878; Circ 249,090
Library Holdings: AV Mats 10,903; Bk Vols 106,772; Per Subs 125
Automation Activity & Vendor Info: (Acquisitions) Innovative Interfaces, Inc; (Cataloging) Innovative Interfaces, Inc; (Circulation) Innovative Interfaces, Inc; (OPAC) Innovative Interfaces, Inc
Wireless access
Function: Adult bk club, Audiobks via web, AV serv, Bk club(s), Bks on cassette, Bks on CD, Children's prog, Computer training, Computers for patron use, Copy machines, Digital talking bks, e-mail & chat, e-mail serv, Free DVD rentals, Handicapped accessible, Holiday prog, ILL available, Instruction & testing, Mail & tel request accepted, Music CDs, Online cat, Outreach serv, Outside serv via phone, mail, e-mail & web, OverDrive digital audio bks, Photocopying/Printing, Preschool outreach, Prog for adults, Prog for children & young adult, Pub access computers, Ref serv available, Senior computer classes, Spoken cassettes & CDs, Spoken cassettes & DVDs, Story hour, Summer reading prog, Tax forms, Teen prog, Telephone ref, VHS videos, Web-catalog, Wheelchair accessible, Workshops
Partic in Montgomery County Library & Information Network Consortium
Open Mon-Thurs 9:30-9, Fri & Sat 9:30-5, Sun 12-5
Friends of the Library Group

FOXBURG

P FOXBURG FREE LIBRARY*, 31 Main St, 16036. (Mail add: PO Box 304, 16036-0304), SAN 314-5255. Tel: 724-659-3431. FAX: 724-659-3214. E-mail: foxburgdir@embarqmail.com. Web Site: www.youseemore.com/foxburg. *Dir,* Brenda Beikert; *Asst Dir,* Caroll Timblin; Staff 1.5 (MLS 0.5, Non-MLS 1)
Founded 1910. Pop 5,516; Circ 11,346
Library Holdings: Bk Vols 16,479; Per Subs 11
Automation Activity & Vendor Info: (Cataloging) Follett Software
Mem of Oil Creek District Library Center
Open Mon, Tues 12-7, Fri & Sat 10-5
Friends of the Library Group

FRACKVILLE

P FRACKVILLE FREE PUBLIC LIBRARY*, 56 N Lehigh Ave, 17931-1424. SAN 314-5263. Tel: 570-874-3382. FAX: 570-874-3382. Web Site: www.frackvillelibrary.com. *Dir,* Joan Farrell; E-mail: joanfarrell@frackvillelibrary.com; *Asst Librn,* Marge Rench; Staff 2 (MLS 1, Non-MLS 1)
Founded 1939. Pop 9,348; Circ 10,293
Library Holdings: Bk Titles 19,124; Per Subs 41; Talking Bks 128; Videos 145
Subject Interests: Local hist
Automation Activity & Vendor Info: (Acquisitions) Follett Software; (Cataloging) SirsiDynix; (Circulation) Follett Software
Function: Adult bk club, After school storytime, Bk club(s), Chess club, ILL available, Magnifiers for reading, Photocopying/Printing, Prog for children & young adult, Ref serv available, Senior computer classes, Spoken cassettes & CDs, Summer reading prog, Telephone ref, VHS videos, Wheelchair accessible, Workshops
Partic in OCLC Online Computer Library Center, Inc
Open Mon-Thurs 12-7, Fri 12-5, Sat 9-1

S STATE CORRECTIONAL INSTITUTION*, Frackville Library, 1111 Altamont Blvd, 17931. Tel: 570-874-4516. *Librn,* Jean Bahner
Founded 1987
Library Holdings: Bk Vols 12,000; Per Subs 40
Automation Activity & Vendor Info: (Circulation) Follett Software
Open Mon, Tues & Sat 8-10:30 & 1-3:30, Wed-Fri 8-10:30, 1-3:30 & 6-8

FRANKLIN

P FRANKLIN PUBLIC LIBRARY, 421 12th St, 16323-0421. SAN 314-5271. Tel: 814-432-5062. FAX: 814-432-8998. E-mail: franklinpl@franklinlibrary.org. Web Site: www.franklinlibrary.org. *Librn,* Deborah Oaks; *Ch Serv,* Abby Rosen; *ILL,* Stephen Snyder; Staff 8 (MLS 1, Non-MLS 7)
Founded 1894. Pop 21,577; Circ 80,034
Library Holdings: AV Mats 2,734; CDs 327; DVDs 97; Large Print Bks 1,355; Bk Titles 43,278; Per Subs 105; Talking Bks 1,229; Videos 1,315
Special Collections: Pennsylvania & Venango County History Coll
Automation Activity & Vendor Info: (Acquisitions) Follett Software; (Cataloging) Follett Software; (Circulation) Follett Software; (OPAC) Follett Software
Wireless access
Function: Activity rm, Adult bk club, Adult literacy prog, Bk club(s), Bks on CD, Children's prog, Computers for patron use, e-mail & chat, Electronic databases & coll, Fax serv, Free DVD rentals, Handicapped accessible, Home delivery & serv to Sr ctr & nursing homes, ILL available, Magazines, Mail & tel request accepted, Microfiche/film & reading machines, Movies, Music CDs, Online cat, Outreach serv, OverDrive digital audio bks, Photocopying/Printing, Preschool outreach, Prog for adults, Pub access computers, Senior outreach, Story hour, Summer reading prog, Tax forms, Teen prog, VHS videos
Open Mon-Fri 10-8, Sat 10-5
Restriction: Non-resident fee
Friends of the Library Group

GL VENANGO COUNTY LAW LIBRARY*, Venango County Court House, 1168 Liberty St, 16323. (Mail add: PO Box 831, 16323-0831), SAN 324-1173. Tel: 814-432-9612. FAX: 814-432-3149. E-mail: sbaker@co.venango.pa.us. Web Site: www.co.venango.pa.us. *Law Librn,* Sandra L Baker; E-mail: sbaker@co.venango.pa.us
Library Holdings: Bk Titles 10,000
Subject Interests: Law cases from 25 reporter systs
Open Mon-Fri 8:30-4:30

FREDERICKSBURG

P MATTHEWS PUBLIC LIBRARY*, 102 W Main St, 17026. Tel: 717-865-5523. FAX: 717-865-5523. Web Site: www.lclibs.org/matthews. *Dir,* Sheila Redcay; E-mail: redcay@lclibs.org; Staff 6 (MLS 1, Non-MLS 5)
Founded 1982
Library Holdings: Bks on Deafness & Sign Lang 10; Bk Vols 30,000; Per Subs 25
Automation Activity & Vendor Info: (Cataloging) Innovative Interfaces, Inc; (Circulation) Innovative Interfaces, Inc; (OPAC) Innovative Interfaces, Inc
Mem of Lebanon County Library System
Open Mon-Thurs 9-8, Fri 9-5, Sat 9-4
Friends of the Library Group

FREDERICKTOWN

P FREDERICKTOWN AREA PUBLIC LIBRARY*, 38 Water St, 15333. (Mail add: PO Box 625, 15333-0625), SAN 376-575X. Tel: 724-377-0017. FAX: 724-377-2924. E-mail: fredpl@atlanticbbn.net. Web Site: www.fredpl.org/. *Dir,* Dawn M Bell
Library Holdings: Bk Titles 10,551; Per Subs 20
Function: Audiobks via web, For res purposes, ILL available, Photocopying/Printing, Prog for children & young adult, Summer reading prog
Open Mon, Wed & Thurs 9-7, Tues 9-5, Sat 9-4
Friends of the Library Group

FREEPORT

P FREEPORT AREA LIBRARY*, 428 Market St, 16229-1122. SAN 314-5301. Tel: 724-295-3616. FAX: 724-295-3616. E-mail: fala@salsgiver.com. Web Site: freeportlibrary.org. *Librn,* Nancy R Hagins; *Asst Librn,* Sara Jones
Founded 1936. Pop 9,856; Circ 19,234
Library Holdings: AV Mats 641; Bks on Deafness & Sign Lang 15; DVDs 106; High Interest/Low Vocabulary Bk Vols 375; Large Print Bks 1,595; Microforms 27; Bk Titles 33,431; Bk Vols 36,991; Per Subs 21; Talking Bks 519; Videos 667
Wireless access
Open Mon & Tues 10-6, Wed 10-7, Thurs & Fri 12-5, Sat 10-3

GALETON

P GALETON PUBLIC LIBRARY*, Five Park Ln, 16922. SAN 314-531X. Tel: 814-435-2321. FAX: 814-435-2321. *Librn,* Darlene Jackson; *Librn,* Kay Sutton
Founded 1907. Pop 2,131; Circ 6,025
Library Holdings: Bk Vols 10,000; Per Subs 21
Subject Interests: Local hist
Mem of Potter-Tioga Library System
Open Mon & Wed 1-5, Tues 11-5, Thurs 11-8, Fri 1-8, Sat 10-5

GALLITZIN

P GALLITZIN PUBLIC LIBRARY*, DeGol Plaza, Ste 30, 411 Convent St, 16641-1244. SAN 314-5328. Tel: 814-886-4041. FAX: 814-886-2125. E-mail: gallitzin@cclsys.org, gallitzinpublib@yahoo.com. Web Site: www.cclsys.org/gallitzin. *Dir,* Inge Zerbee; *Librn,* Connie Boldizar
Founded 1957. Pop 2,003; Circ 28,000
Library Holdings: Audiobooks 100; Bk Titles 14,633; Per Subs 40
Automation Activity & Vendor Info: (Cataloging) Evergreen; (Circulation) Evergreen; (OPAC) Evergreen
Mem of Cambria County Library System & District Center
Open Tues 1-7, Wed & Fri 9-5, Thurs 9-7, Sat 9-4 (9-1 Summer)

GENESEE

P GENESEE AREA LIBRARY*, 301 Main St, 16923-8805. (Mail add: PO Box 135, 16923-0135), SAN 376-7272. Tel: 814-228-3328. FAX: 814-228-3328. E-mail: gal@zitomedia.net. Web Site: www.geneseelibrary.com. *Dir,* Kate Miller
Founded 1985
Library Holdings: Bk Vols 7,000; Per Subs 16
Wireless access
Mem of Potter-Tioga Library System
Open Tues, Wed & Fri 11-6, Sat 9-4

GETTYSBURG

S ADAMS COUNTY HISTORICAL SOCIETY LIBRARY*, Lutheran Theological Seminary Campus, 368 Springs Ave, 17325. (Mail add: PO Box 4325, 17325-4325), SAN 314-5336. Tel: 717-334-4723. FAX: 717-334-0722. E-mail: info@achs-pa.org. *Exec Dir,* Benjamin K Neely
Founded 1940
Library Holdings: Bk Titles 2,000; Per Subs 10
Special Collections: The Battle of Gettysburg Research Center
Subject Interests: Adams County hist
Publications: Adams County History; Newsletter (Annual)

L ADAMS COUNTY LAW LIBRARY*, Court House, 111-117 Baltimore St, 17325. SAN 327-1080. Tel: 717-337-9812. FAX: 717-334-1625. *Librn,* Cecelia Brown
Library Holdings: Bk Vols 50,000; Per Subs 10
Open Mon-Fri 8-4:30
Restriction: Non-circulating

P ADAMS COUNTY LIBRARY SYSTEM*, Central Library, 140 Baltimore St, 17325-2311. SAN 358-4887. Tel: 717-334-5716. FAX: 717-334-7992. E-mail: adams@adamslibrary.org. Web Site: www.adamslibrary.org. *Dir,* Robin Lesher; Tel: 717-334-0163, E-mail: robinl@adamslibrary.org; *Asst Dir,* Laura Goss; *Adult Serv, Outreach/Commun Relations Librn,* Sara Edminston; Staff 35 (MLS 5, Non-MLS 30)
Founded 1945. Pop 101,407; Circ 737,770
Jan 2012-Dec 2012 Income $2,097,071, State $581,674, County $1,083,128, Locally Generated Income $423,269. Mats Exp $320,097, Books $162,402, Per/Ser (Incl. Access Fees) $10,636, AV Mat $101,489, Electronic Ref Mat (Incl. Access Fees) $45,570. Sal $1,236,229
Library Holdings: Bk Vols 141,155; Per Subs 354
Special Collections: Art; Eisenhower Room Coll (Civil War & Local Hist)
Automation Activity & Vendor Info: (Cataloging) TLC (The Library Corporation); (Circulation) TLC (The Library Corporation); (OPAC) TLC (The Library Corporation)
Wireless access
Function: Art exhibits, Handicapped accessible, Homebound delivery serv, ILL available, Magnifiers for reading, Music CDs, Prog for adults, Prog for children & young adult, Ref serv available, Summer reading prog, Telephone ref, VHS videos
Member Libraries: East Berlin Community Library; Fairfield Area Library; Harbaugh-Thomas Library; Littlestown Library; New Oxford Area Library
Open Mon-Thurs 9-8:30, Fri & Sat 9-5, Sun 1-5
Friends of the Library Group
Bookmobiles: 1

C GETTYSBURG COLLEGE*, Musselman Library, 300 N Washington St, 17325. SAN 314-5344. Tel: 717-337-6604. Circulation Tel: 717-337-7024. Interlibrary Loan Service Tel: 717-337-6893. Reference Tel: 717-337-6600. FAX: 717-337-7001. Web Site: www.gettysburg.edu/library/index.dot. *Dir, Libr Serv,* Robin Wagner; Tel: 717-337-6768, E-mail: rowagner@gettysburg.edu; *Asst Dir, User Serv (ILL),* Natalie Hinton; Tel: 717-337-7032, E-mail: nhinton@gettysburg.edu; *Head, Music & Media Serv,* Timothy Sestrick; Tel: 717-337-7045, E-mail: tsestric@gettysburg.edu; *Head, Ref,* Janelle Wertzberger; Tel: 717-337-7010, E-mail: jwertzbe@gettysburg.edu; *Archivist, Head, Spec Coll,* Karen Drickamer; Tel: 717-337-7015, E-mail: kdrickam@gettysburg.edu; *Head, Tech Serv,* Kathy D'Angelo; Tel: 717-337-7007, E-mail: kdangelo@gettysburg.edu; *Head, User Serv,* Ronalee Ciocco; Tel: 717-337-6994, E-mail: rciocco@gettysburg.edu; *Asst Archivist,* Christine Ameduri; Tel: 717-337-7006, E-mail: cameduri@gettysburg.edu; *Circ,* Susan Pinkey; Tel: 717-337-7005, E-mail: spinkey@gettysburg.edu; *Media Spec,* Nancy Bernardi; Tel: 717-337-7022, E-mail: nbernard@gettysburg.edu; *Syst Adminr,* Alice Huff; Tel: 717-337-7020, E-mail: ahuff@gettysburg.edu; Staff 28 (MLS 12, Non-MLS 16)
Founded 1832. Enrl 2,529; Fac 200; Highest Degree: Bachelor
Library Holdings: Bk Vols 349,466; Per Subs 2,600
Special Collections: Civil War Maps Coll; College History. Oral History
Subject Interests: Asian art, Rare bks, World War II
Automation Activity & Vendor Info: (Acquisitions) Innovative Interfaces, Inc; (Cataloging) Innovative Interfaces, Inc; (Circulation) Innovative Interfaces, Inc; (Course Reserve) Innovative Interfaces, Inc; (ILL) OCLC ILLiad; (OPAC) Innovative Interfaces, Inc; (Serials) Innovative Interfaces, Inc
Database Vendor: TLC (The Library Corporation)
Wireless access
Publications: Friends of Musselman Library (Newsletter)
Partic in Associated College Libraries of Central Pennsylvania; Central Pennsylvania Consortium; Lyrasis; Pennsylvania Academic Library Consortium, Inc (PALCI)
Friends of the Library Group

S GETTYSBURG NATIONAL MILITARY PARK LIBRARY*, 1195 Baltimore Pike, Ste 100, 17325. SAN 314-5352. Tel: 717-334-1124, Ext 1231. FAX: 717-334-1997. E-mail: gett_library@nps.gov. Web Site: www.nps.gov/gett. *Supvr,* D Scott Hartwig; E-mail: scott_hartwig@nps.gov; *Historian,* John S Heiser; E-mail: john_heiser@nps.gov. Subject Specialists: *Battle of Gettysburg, Civil War, Mil hist,* D Scott Hartwig; *Am Civil War,* John S Heiser; Staff 1 (Non-MLS 1)
Founded 1895
Library Holdings: AV Mats 24; CDs 48; DVDs 12; Bk Titles 5,155; Bk Vols 7,700; Per Subs 10; Spec Interest Per Sub 2; Videos 143
Special Collections: Al Gambone Coll (Civil War, Personalities); Gregory Coco Coll (Civil War Personal Accounts), Harry Pfanz Research Coll (Civil War- Gettysburg); Personnel, Battle of Gettysburg, photos
Subject Interests: Battle of Gettysburg, Campaign, Cycloramas, Eisenhower at Gettysburg, Gettysburg National Cemetery, Lincoln's Gettysburg Address
Function: Res libr
Restriction: Circulates for staff only, In-house use for visitors, Open to pub by appt only, Open to researchers by request

J HACC CENTRAL PENNSYLVANIA'S COMMUNITY COLLEGE*, Gettysburg Campus Library, 731 Old Harrisburg Rd, 17325. Tel: 717-337-1644. Interlibrary Loan Service Tel: 717-780-2623. FAX: 717-337-2329. E-mail: gettlibr@hacc.edu. Web Site: lib2.hacc.edu/campus/GBG/gbg.html. *Dir,* Beth A Evitts; Tel: 717-337-3855, Ext 3027, E-mail: baevitts@hacc.edu; *Adjunct Fac Librn,* Kathleen Heidecker; E-mail: kbheidec@hacc.edu; *Adjunct Fac Librn,* Sandra Negro; E-mail: senegro@hacc.edu; *Adjunct Fac Librn,* P Edward Sprenkle; E-mail: psprenkl@hacc.edu; *Libr Spec,* Mike Wallace; E-mail: mfwallac@hacc.edu; *Libr Tech,* Sally Feeser; E-mail: safeeser@hacc.edu; *Libr Tech,* Keri McLucas; E-mail: ksmcluca@hacc.edu; Staff 4.25 (MLS 2.25, Non-MLS 2)
Founded 1999. Enrl 2,375; Fac 116; Highest Degree: Associate
Library Holdings: AV Mats 436; e-books 1,773; Bk Titles 8,424; Bk Vols 8,821; Per Subs 76
Automation Activity & Vendor Info: (Acquisitions) SirsiDynix; (Cataloging) SirsiDynix; (Circulation) SirsiDynix; (Course Reserve) Docutek; (ILL) SirsiDynix; (Media Booking) SirsiDynix; (OPAC) SirsiDynix; (Serials) SirsiDynix
Database Vendor: ARTstor, EBSCOhost, Gale Cengage Learning, LexisNexis, Newsbank, ProQuest, Safari Books Online, Wilson - Wilson Web
Wireless access
Open Mon-Thurs (Fall & Spring) 7:30-9, Fri 7:30-5, Sat 8-1
Restriction: In-house use for visitors, Non-circulating to the pub

R LUTHERAN THEOLOGICAL SEMINARY*, A R Wentz Library, 66 Seminary Ridge, 17325. SAN 314-5360. Tel: 717-338-3014. Toll Free Tel: 800-658-8437. FAX: 717-337-1611. E-mail: library@ltsg.edu. Web Site:

www.ltsg.edu/Resources/Wentz-Library. *Archivist, Libr Dir,* Dr B Bohleke; E-mail: bbohleke@ltsg.edu; *Tech Serv Librn,* Susann Posey; Tel: 717-338-3032, E-mail: sposey@ltsg.edu; *Acq,* Roberta Brent; Tel: 717-334-6286, Ext 2102, E-mail: rbrent@ltsg.edu. Subject Specialists: *Ancient Egypt, Ancient Near East,* Dr B Bohleke; Staff 3 (MLS 2, Non-MLS 1)
Founded 1826. Enrl 277; Fac 17; Highest Degree: Master
Jul 2008-Jun 2009. Mats Exp $55,000, Books $25,000, Per/Ser (Incl. Access Fees) $28,000, AV Mat $2,000. Sal $99,000
Library Holdings: Bk Vols 178,000; Per Subs 450
Special Collections: Lutheran Church History in America
Subject Interests: Biblical studies, Church hist, Church-related subjects, Lutheran church, Pastoral studies, Philos, Preaching, Stewardship, Theol, Worship
Automation Activity & Vendor Info: (Acquisitions) Ex Libris Group; (Cataloging) Ex Libris Group; (Circulation) Ex Libris Group; (Course Reserve) Ex Libris Group; (ILL) OCLC; (OPAC) Ex Libris Group; (Serials) Ex Libris Group
Database Vendor: OCLC FirstSearch, OCLC WorldShare Interlibrary Loan
Wireless access
Function: Outside serv via phone, mail, e-mail & web, VHS videos
Partic in Southeastern Pennsylvania Theological Library Association; Washington Theological Consortium
Open Mon-Thurs (Winter) 8am-9pm, Fri 8-5, Sat 9-12 & 1-4:30; Mon-Fri (Summer) 8:30-4:30

GIBSONIA

P NORTHERN TIER REGIONAL LIBRARY, 4015 Dickey Rd, 15044-9713. SAN 314-5379. Tel: 724-449-2665. FAX: 724-443-6755. E-mail: northerntier@einetwork.net. Web Site: www.northerntierlibrary.org. *Dir,* Diane C Illis; Staff 5 (MLS 3, Non-MLS 2)
Founded 1954. Pop 22,597; Circ 246,496
Library Holdings: AV Mats 8,000; Bk Vols 64,655; Per Subs 65
Automation Activity & Vendor Info: (Cataloging) Innovative Interfaces, Inc; (Circulation) Innovative Interfaces, Inc; (OPAC) Innovative Interfaces, Inc
Database Vendor: EBSCOhost, Gale Cengage Learning, ProQuest, SirsiDynix
Wireless access
Function: Adult bk club, Audiobks via web, Bks on CD, Children's prog, Computer training, Computers for patron use, Copy machines, Digital talking bks, Electronic databases & coll, Handicapped accessible, ILL available, Music CDs, Online cat, Photocopying/Printing, Prog for adults, Prog for children & young adult, Ref serv available, Summer reading prog, Tax forms, Telephone ref
Publications: The Library Link (Monthly)
Mem of Allegheny County Library Association
Partic in Electronic Info Network (eiNetwork)
Open Mon-Thurs 10-8, Fri 10-4, Sat 9-4
Friends of the Library Group
Branches: 1
PINE CENTER, 700 Warrendale Rd, 15044. Tel: 724-625-5655.
Library Holdings: Large Print Bks 27; Bk Titles 4,190; Bk Vols 4,360; Per Subs 55
Function: Audiobks via web, Bks on CD, Computers for patron use, ILL available, Online searches, OverDrive digital audio bks, Pub access computers, Telephone ref
Open Mon-Thurs 2:30-5:30

GIRARD

P RICE AVENUE COMMUNITY PUBLIC LIBRARY*, 705 Rice Ave, 16417-1122. SAN 314-5387. Tel: 814-774-4982. E-mail: racpl@riceavenuelibrary.org. Web Site: www.riceavenuelibrary.org. *Dir,* Stacey M Serrano; Staff 3 (MLS 1, Non-MLS 2)
Founded 1999. Pop 6,500; Circ 31,000
Library Holdings: Bk Vols 16,000; Per Subs 35
Open Mon 3-8, Tues 1-8, Wed 10-12 & 1-8, Thurs 1-4, Fri 11-4, Sat 9-3
Friends of the Library Group

GLADWYNE

R BETH DAVID REFORM CONGREGATION, Jewel K Markowitz Library, 1130 Vaughans Lane, 19035-0287. SAN 314-8661. Tel: 610-896-7485. FAX: 610-642-5406. Web Site: www.bdavid.org.
Founded 1947
Library Holdings: Bk Vols 4,500
Special Collections: Judaica for Children
Subject Interests: Judaica

P GLADWYNE FREE LIBRARY*, 362 Righters Mill Rd, 19035-1587. SAN 314-5395. Tel: 610-642-3957. FAX: 610-642-3985. Web Site: www.lmls.org. *Librn,* Carolyn G Conti; *Ch Serv,* Alicemarie Collins; Staff 9 (MLS 1, Non-MLS 8)
Founded 1931. Pop 5,720; Circ 101,942
Jan 2007-Dec 2007 Income $498,757, State $20,180, Locally Generated Income $47,858. Mats Exp $81,615, Books $46,913, Per/Ser (Incl. Access Fees) $8,703, AV Mat $25,999. Sal $254,477
Library Holdings: Bk Vols 44,569; Per Subs 105
Special Collections: Cookbooks; Pennsylvania History Coll
Wireless access
Mem of Lower Merion Library System
Open Mon, Tues & Thurs 10-9, Wed, Fri & Sat 10-5
Friends of the Library Group

GLASSPORT

P SAMUEL A WEISS COMMUNITY LIBRARY*, 440 Monongahela Ave, 15045-1474. SAN 314-5425. Tel: 412-672-7400. *Librn,* Ann Dzurko
Founded 1943. Pop 7,000
Library Holdings: Large Print Bks 100; Bk Vols 12,000
Open Tues 6:30pm-8pm

GLEN MILLS

P RACHEL KOHL COMMUNITY LIBRARY*, 687 Smithbridge Rd, 19342-1225. SAN 376-3129. Tel: 610-358-3445. FAX: 610-558-0693. E-mail: kohllibrary@delcolibraries.org. Web Site: www.kohllibrary.org. *Dir,* Gena Kerrigan
Library Holdings: Bk Titles 27,000; Bk Vols 29,200; Per Subs 58
Automation Activity & Vendor Info: (Cataloging) Innovative Interfaces, Inc; (Circulation) Innovative Interfaces, Inc
Wireless access
Mem of Delaware County Library System
Partic in Am Pub Libr Asn; Pennsylvania Library Association
Open Mon-Thurs 10-8, Fri & Sat 10-5, Sun 1-5
Friends of the Library Group

GLEN ROCK

P ARTHUR HUFNAGEL PUBLIC LIBRARY OF GLEN ROCK*, 32 Main St, 17327. SAN 314-5433. Tel: 717-235-1127. FAX: 717-235-0330. E-mail: grlib@yorklibraries.org. Web Site: www.yorklibraries.org/glenrock. *Dir,* Gina Mumaw; Staff 2 (Non-MLS 2)
Founded 1936. Pop 5,455
Library Holdings: Bk Vols 17,500; Per Subs 70
Special Collections: Pamphlet Coll
Subject Interests: Local hist
Mem of York County Library System
Open Mon & Tues 11-4 & 6-8, Wed & Thurs 10-4 & 6-8, Sat 9-4
Friends of the Library Group

GLENOLDEN

P GLENOLDEN LIBRARY*, 211 S Llanwellyn Ave, 19036-2118. SAN 314-545X. Tel: 610-583-1010. FAX: 610-583-7610. E-mail: glenolden@delcolibraries.org. Web Site: charlotte.delco.lib.pa.us. *Dir,* Andrea Boothby; E-mail: gldirector@delcolibraries.org; *Ch Serv,* Peggy Bauer
Founded 1894. Pop 7,633; Circ 17,116
Library Holdings: Bk Titles 16,500; Per Subs 50
Automation Activity & Vendor Info: (Cataloging) Innovative Interfaces, Inc; (Circulation) Innovative Interfaces, Inc
Mem of Delaware County Library System
Open Mon & Wed 10-5 & 6-8:30, Tues & Thurs 1-5 & 6-8:30, Fri 10-5, Sat 9-4

GLENSHAW

P GLENSHAW PUBLIC LIBRARY*, 1504 Butler Plank Rd, 15116-2397. SAN 314-5468. Tel: 412-487-2121. *Dir,* Violet F Rowe
Founded 1895. Circ 7,334
Library Holdings: Bk Titles 12,704; Talking Bks 111
Open Mon 7pm-8pm, Wed 2-4, Fri 1-4, Sat 10-Noon

P SHALER NORTH HILLS LIBRARY*, 1822 Mount Royal Blvd, 15116. SAN 314-5476. Tel: 412-486-0211. FAX: 412-486-8286. E-mail: shaler@einetwork.net. Web Site: www.shalerlibrary.org. *Dir,* Sharon McRae; *Ch,* Karen Hathaway; *Ch,* Joy Herrington; *Teen Serv Librn,* Kara Falck; *Acq,* Betty Kakavis; *Adult Serv,* Marie Jackson; *Ch Serv,* Ingrid Kalchthaler; *Ref Serv,* Carolyn Cunningham; *Tech Serv,* Lesle Dunn; Staff 4 (MLS 4)
Founded 1942. Pop 29,757; Circ 339,021
Library Holdings: AV Mats 10,460; Bk Titles 98,268; Per Subs 216
Special Collections: Puppets
Automation Activity & Vendor Info: (Cataloging) Innovative Interfaces, Inc; (Circulation) Innovative Interfaces, Inc; (OPAC) Innovative Interfaces, Inc; (Serials) Innovative Interfaces, Inc
Database Vendor: Baker & Taylor, Gale Cengage Learning, H W Wilson, Newsbank, ReferenceUSA

Wireless access
Mem of Allegheny County Library Association
Partic in Electronic Info Network (eiNetwork)
Special Services for the Blind - Assistive/Adapted tech devices, equip & products
Open Mon-Thurs 10-8, Fri 10-6, Sat 10-5, Sun (Sept-May) 1-5
Friends of the Library Group

GLENSIDE

C ARCADIA UNIVERSITY*, Bette E Landman Library, 450 S Easton Rd, 19038-3295. SAN 314-5484. Tel: 215-572-2975. Reference Tel: 215-572-2138. FAX: 215-572-0240. Reference E-mail: reference@arcadia.edu. Web Site: www.arcadia.edu/library. *Assoc Dean, Libr Serv, Instrul Tech,* Jeanne Buckley; Tel: 215-572-4019, E-mail: buckleyj@arcadia.edu; *Ref Librn,* Larissa Gordon; Tel: 215-572-2136, E-mail: gordonl@arcadia.edu; *Ref Librn,* Calvin Wang; Tel: 215-572-4097, E-mail: wangc@arcadia.edu; *Access Serv Librn,* Michelle Reale; Tel: 215-572-2139, E-mail: realem@arcadia.edu; *Digital Res Librn,* Eric Jeitner; Tel: 215-572-2842, E-mail: jeitnere@arcadia.edu; *Coll Develop Mgr,* Karen Kohn; Tel: 215-572-8528, E-mail: kohnk@arcadia.edu; Staff 10 (MLS 4, Non-MLS 6)
Founded 1963. Enrl 3,200; Fac 289; Highest Degree: Doctorate
Library Holdings: AV Mats 3,396; e-books 300; e-journals 7,000; Bk Titles 99,415; Bk Vols 144,232; Per Subs 832
Automation Activity & Vendor Info: (Acquisitions) SirsiDynix; (Cataloging) SirsiDynix; (Circulation) SirsiDynix; (Course Reserve) SirsiDynix; (OPAC) SirsiDynix; (Serials) SirsiDynix
Database Vendor: Cambridge Scientific Abstracts, Dialog, JSTOR, LexisNexis, Newsbank, OCLC FirstSearch, OCLC WorldShare Interlibrary Loan, OVID Technologies, ProQuest, SerialsSolutions
Wireless access
Partic in Delaware Valley Information Consortium; Interlibrary Delivery Service of Pennsylvania; Lyrasis; OCLC Online Computer Library Center, Inc; Southeastern Pa Consortium for Higher Educ; Tri State Col Libr Coop
Open Mon-Thurs (Fall-Spring) 8:30-8, Fri 8:30-5; Mon-Thurs (Summer) 8am-10pm, Fri 8-5, Sat 12-5
Friends of the Library Group

P CHELTENHAM TOWNSHIP LIBRARY SYSTEM*, 215 S Keswick Ave, 19038-4420. SAN 314-5506. Tel: 215-885-0457. FAX: 215-885-1239. Web Site: www.cheltenhamlibraries.org. *Admin Dir,* Carrie L Turner; E-mail: cturner@mclinc.org; *Acq, Head, Tech Serv, Purchasing,* Dorothy L Sutton; E-mail: dsutton@mclinc.org; *Cat,* Jeanine Pringle; E-mail: jpringle@mclinc.org; Staff 43 (MLS 8, Non-MLS 35)
Founded 1966. Pop 36,875; Circ 296,162
Library Holdings: AV Mats 10,249; Bk Vols 124,191; Per Subs 466
Subject Interests: African-Am hist, Art, Bus ref, Educ software, Handicrafts, Local hist, Multicultural mat
Automation Activity & Vendor Info: (Cataloging) Innovative Interfaces, Inc; (Circulation) Innovative Interfaces, Inc; (OPAC) Innovative Interfaces, Inc
Partic in Montgomery County Library & Information Network Consortium
Open Mon-Fri 9-5
Branches: 4
EAST CHELTENHAM FREE LIBRARY, Rowland Community Center, 400 Myrtle Ave, Cheltenham, 19012-2038, SAN 314-3996. Tel: 215-379-2077. FAX: 215-379-1275. *Head Librn,* Angela Lane; Staff 8 (MLS 1, Non-MLS 7)
Founded 1957. Pop 7,906; Circ 34,077
Library Holdings: AV Mats 2,056; Bk Vols 29,008; Per Subs 75
Subject Interests: Handicrafts, Multicultural mat
Open Mon 10-9, Tues 10-6, Wed 1-9, Thurs & Fri 1-6, Sat 10-4
Friends of the Library Group
ELKINS PARK FREE LIBRARY, 563 E Church Rd, Elkins Park, 19027-2499, SAN 314-481X. Tel: 215-635-5000. FAX: 215-635-5844. E-mail: elkinspark@mclinc.org. *Head Librn,* Beth Cackowski; E-mail: bcackowski@mclinc.org; *Head, Circ,* Susan Kettner; E-mail: skettner@mclinc.org; *Adult Serv, Ref,* Kerry Birnbaum; E-mail: kbirnbaum@mclinc.org; *Ch Serv,* Elizabeth McGoran; E-mail: emcgoran@mclinc.org; Staff 14 (MLS 3, Non-MLS 11)
Founded 1958. Pop 20,995; Circ 186,565
Library Holdings: AV Mats 9,570; Bk Vols 58,522; Per Subs 110
Subject Interests: Popular mat
Automation Activity & Vendor Info: (Acquisitions) Baker & Taylor
Open Mon & Wed 10-9, Tues, Thurs & Fri 10-6, Sat 10-4, Sun 1-4
Friends of the Library Group
GLENSIDE FREE LIBRARY, 215 S Keswick Ave, 19038-4420, SAN 314-5514. Tel: 215-885-0455. FAX: 215-885-1019. E-mail: glenside@mclinc.org. *Head Librn,* Stephanie Campbell; E-mail: scampbell@mclinc.org; *Head, Circ,* Christina Sirianni; E-mail: csirianni@mclinc.org; *ILL, Ref Librn,* Christina Riehman-Murphy; E-mail: criehman-murphy@mclinc.org; *Youth Serv Librn,* Allison Frick; E-mail: africk@mclinc.org; Staff 14 (MLS 4, Non-MLS 10)
Founded 1928. Pop 13,210; Circ 101,849
Library Holdings: AV Mats 15,000; Bk Vols 33,000; Per Subs 110
Automation Activity & Vendor Info: (Cataloging) Innovative Interfaces, Inc; (Circulation) Innovative Interfaces, Inc; (OPAC) Innovative Interfaces, Inc
Database Vendor: Evanced Solutions, Inc, LearningExpress, Overdrive, Inc, ReferenceUSA, World Book Online
Open Mon, Wed & Fri 10-6, Tues & Thurs 10-9, Sat 10-4, Sun 1-4
Friends of the Library Group
LAMOTT FREE LIBRARY, 7420 Sycamore Ave, LaMott, 19027-1005, SAN 320-1732. Tel: 215-635-4419. FAX: 215-635-4419. E-mail: lamott@mclinc.org. *Br Mgr,* Carolyn Turner-Harris; Staff 3 (Non-MLS 3)
Founded 1966. Pop 1,590; Circ 8,255
Library Holdings: AV Mats 601; Bk Vols 4,954; Per Subs 51
Subject Interests: African-Am hist
Automation Activity & Vendor Info: (Cataloging) Innovative Interfaces, Inc; (Circulation) Innovative Interfaces, Inc; (OPAC) Innovative Interfaces, Inc
Open Mon & Wed 3-8:30, Tues 2-6, Thurs 10-6, Fri 3-6, Sat 12-4
Friends of the Library Group

S CHILD CUSTODY EVALUATION SERVICES, INC*, Child Custody Library, PO Box 202, 19038-0202. SAN 326-6184. Tel: 215-576-0177. *Dir,* Dr Ken Lewis; E-mail: drkenlewis@snip.net
Founded 1980
Library Holdings: Bk Titles 800; Per Subs 40
Restriction: Open by appt only, Open to researchers by request

CR WESTMINSTER THEOLOGICAL SEMINARY, Montgomery Library, 2960 W Church Rd, 19038. (Mail add: PO Box 27009, 19118-7009), SAN 315-0267. Tel: 215-572-3821. Reference Tel: 215-935-3880. FAX: 215-887-3412. E-mail: library@wts.edu. Web Site: www.wts.edu/library. *Dir,* Sandy Finlayson; Tel: 215-572-3823, E-mail: sfinlayson@wts.edu; *Asst Librn,* Marsha Blake; E-mail: mblake@wts.edu; *Archives & Rare Bk Librn,* Karla Grafton; Tel: 215-572-3856, E-mail: kgrafton@wts.edu; *Tech Serv & Syst Librn,* Donna Campbell; Tel: 215-935-3872, E-mail: acquisitions@wts.edu; *Circ Mgr,* Donna Roof; Tel: 215-572-3822, E-mail: droof@wts.edu; Staff 5 (MLS 4, Non-MLS 1)
Founded 1929. Enrl 450; Fac 13; Highest Degree: Doctorate
Library Holdings: Bk Vols 133,063; Per Subs 695
Special Collections: Bible Texts & Versions; Early Reformed Theology
Subject Interests: Biblical studies, Reformation, Systematic theol
Automation Activity & Vendor Info: (Acquisitions) Innovative Interfaces, Inc; (Cataloging) Innovative Interfaces, Inc; (Circulation) Innovative Interfaces, Inc; (Course Reserve) Innovative Interfaces, Inc; (ILL) OCLC; (OPAC) Innovative Interfaces, Inc
Database Vendor: EBSCOhost, Elsevier
Wireless access
Partic in OCLC Online Computer Library Center, Inc; Southeastern Pennsylvania Theological Library Association
Open Mon-Thurs (Winter) 8am-10pm, Fri 8-6, Sat 12-4; Mon-Fri (Summer) 9-5
Restriction: Open to fac, students & qualified researchers

GREENCASTLE

P LILIAN S BESORE MEMORIAL LIBRARY*, 305 E Baltimore St, 17225-1004. SAN 314-5530. Tel: 717-597-7920. FAX: 717-597-5320. Web Site: www.fclspa.org/besore/besore.htm. *Librn,* Barbara Schuit; Staff 1 (MLS 1)
Founded 1963. Pop 16,226; Circ 49,931
Jan 2005-Dec 2005. Mats Exp $44,674
Library Holdings: Bk Vols 38,528; Per Subs 57
Special Collections: Local History
Automation Activity & Vendor Info: (Circulation) AmLib Library Management System; (OPAC) AmLib Library Management System
Wireless access
Mem of Franklin County Library System
Partic in HSLC/Access PA/POWER Library
Open Mon, Tues & Thurs 9-8, Wed & Fri 9-5, Sat 9-1
Friends of the Library Group

GREENSBURG

M EXCELA HEALTH*, Westmoreland Hospital Library, 532 W Pittsburgh St, 15601-2282. SAN 358-500X. Tel: 724-832-4088. FAX: 724-832-4661. *Librn,* Janet C Petrak
Founded 1952
Library Holdings: Bk Titles 3,000; Per Subs 60
Special Collections: Hospital archives
Open Mon-Fri 8-4:30
Restriction: Restricted pub use, Staff use only

P GREENSBURG HEMPFIELD AREA LIBRARY*, 237 S Pennsylvania Ave, 15601-3086. SAN 314-5557. Tel: 724-837-5620. Reference Tel: 724-837-8441. FAX: 724-836-0160. Web Site: www.ghal.org. *Dir,* Cesare J Muccari; *Ch Serv,* Mary Jane Mason; Staff 6 (MLS 3, Non-MLS 3)
Founded 1936. Pop 79,181; Circ 150,000
Library Holdings: AV Mats 3,716; Large Print Bks 190; Bk Titles 67,431; Bk Vols 82,911; Per Subs 149; Talking Bks 1,511; Videos 580
Special Collections: Pennsylvania Room (Pa History & Geneology)
Subject Interests: Genealogy
Automation Activity & Vendor Info: (Cataloging) TLC (The Library Corporation); (Circulation) TLC (The Library Corporation); (OPAC) TLC (The Library Corporation)
Database Vendor: EBSCOhost
Mem of Westmoreland County Federated Library System
Open Mon-Thurs (Winter) 10-7:50, Fri & Sat 10-4:50; Mon & Thurs (Summer) 10-7:50, Tues, Wed, Fri & Sat 10-4:50

CR SETON HILL UNIVERSITY, Reeves Memorial Library, One Seton Hill Dr, 15601. SAN 314-5565. Tel: 724-838-4291. Interlibrary Loan Service Tel: 724-830-1584. Administration Tel: 724-838-4270. Automation Services Tel: 724-830-4616. FAX: 724-838-4203. E-mail: reeves@setonhill.edu. Web Site: setonhill.edu/academics/reeves_library. *Dir,* Dr David H Stanley; E-mail: stanley@setonhill.edu; *Cat & Acq,* Adam Pellman; Tel: 724-838-2438, E-mail: pellman@setonhill.edu; *Pub Serv Librn,* Kelly Clever; E-mail: clever@setonhill.edu; *Syst Librn,* Dana Krydick; E-mail: krydick@setonhill.edu; *Per,* Judith Koveleskie; Tel: 724-838-7828, E-mail: kovelesk@setonhill.edu; Staff 7 (MLS 5, Non-MLS 2)
Founded 1918. Enrl 2,000; Fac 100; Highest Degree: Master
Jul 2013-Jun 2014. Mats Exp $159,523, Books $18,000, Per/Ser (Incl. Access Fees) $16,523, Electronic Ref Mat (Incl. Access Fees) $125,000
Library Holdings: AV Mats 6,665; CDs 970; DVDs 1,406; e-books 88,320; Bk Vols 70,000; Per Subs 192; Videos 2,490
Subject Interests: Entrepreneurship, Fine arts
Automation Activity & Vendor Info: (Acquisitions) Innovative Interfaces, Inc; (Cataloging) Innovative Interfaces, Inc; (Circulation) Innovative Interfaces, Inc; (Course Reserve) Innovative Interfaces, Inc; (OPAC) Innovative Interfaces, Inc; (Serials) Innovative Interfaces, Inc
Database Vendor: American Chemical Society, ARTstor, EBSCOhost, Elsevier, Gale Cengage Learning, Hoovers, JSTOR, OCLC WorldShare Interlibrary Loan, Sage
Wireless access
Partic in Lyrasis; Share Westmoreland Consortium; Westmoreland Acad Librs Consortium
Open Mon-Thurs 8am-11:50pm, Fri 8-4:50, Sat 9-4:50, Sun 1-11:50

C UNIVERSITY OF PITTSBURGH AT GREENSBURG*, Millstein Library, 150 Finoli Dr, 15601-5804. SAN 314-5573. Tel: 724-836-9687. FAX: 724-836-7043. Web Site: www.library.pitt.edu/greensburg. *Dir,* Position Currently Open; *Pub Serv/Instruction Librn,* Anna Mary Williford; E-mail: annamary@pitt.edu; *Ref & Pub Serv Librn,* Amanda Folk; E-mail: alfolk@pitt.edu; Staff 7 (MLS 3, Non-MLS 4)
Founded 1963. Enrl 1,753; Fac 94; Highest Degree: Bachelor
Jul 2011-Jun 2012. Mats Exp $75,451, Books $47,892, Per/Ser (Incl. Access Fees) $5,257, Other Print Mats $5,989, Micro $4,020, AV Mat $9,939, Electronic Ref Mat (Incl. Access Fees) $265, Presv $552. Sal $368,617
Library Holdings: Audiobooks 162; CDs 660; DVDs 1,674; Microforms 9,744; Music Scores 143; Bk Vols 74,623; Per Subs 72; Videos 2,025
Special Collections: UPG Archives. Oral History
Subject Interests: Hist, Info sci, Lit
Automation Activity & Vendor Info: (Acquisitions) Ex Libris Group; (Cataloging) Ex Libris Group; (Circulation) Ex Libris Group; (Course Reserve) Ex Libris Group; (ILL) Ex Libris Group; (OPAC) Ex Libris Group; (Serials) Ex Libris Group
Database Vendor: YBP Library Services
Wireless access
Partic in Lyrasis; OCLC Online Computer Library Center, Inc; Pennsylvania Academic Library Consortium, Inc (PALCI); Westmoreland Acad Librs Consortium
Special Services for the Blind - Assistive/Adapted tech devices, equip & products; Computer with voice synthesizer for visually impaired persons; Reader equip
Open Mon-Thurs 8:30am-11pm, Fri 8:30-5, Sat 10-6, Sun 2-10
Friends of the Library Group

P WESTMORELAND COUNTY FEDERATED LIBRARY SYSTEM*, 226 Donohoe Rd, 15601. Tel: 724-420-5638. *Dir,* Nancy Gresko; E-mail: nancy.gresko@wlnonline.org; Staff 3 (MLS 2, Non-MLS 1)
Founded 1995. Pop 367,000
Library Holdings: Bk Vols 760,000; Per Subs 2,000
Member Libraries: Avonmore Public Library; Belle Vernon Public Library; Greensburg Hempfield Area Library; Hyde Park Public Library; Jeannette Public Library Association; Ligonier Valley Library Association, Inc; Mount Pleasant Free Public Library; Murrysville Community Library; New Florence Community Library; Norwin Public Library Association Inc; Penn Area Library; Peoples Library; Rostraver Public Library; Scottdale Public Library; Sewickley Township Public Library; Smithton Public Library; Trafford Community Public Library; Vandergrift Public Library Association; West Newton Public Library; Youngwood Area Public Library
Open Mon-Fri 9-4:30

S WESTMORELAND COUNTY HISTORICAL SOCIETY, Calvin E Pollins Memorial Library, 362 Sand Hill Rd, Ste 1, 15601. SAN 326-3940. Tel: 724-532-1935. FAX: 724-532-1938. E-mail: library@westmorelandhistory.org. Web Site: www.westmorelandhistory.org. *Coordr,* Anita Zanke
Library Holdings: Bk Vols 4,200
Special Collections: Archival Coll; Genealogy Coll
Subject Interests: Genealogy, Local hist
Wireless access
Publications: Westmoreland Chronicle (Newsletter); Westmoreland History Magazine
Open Tues, Thurs & Fri 9-5, Wed 9-8
Restriction: Not a lending libr

L WESTMORELAND COUNTY LAW LIBRARY*, Two N Main St, Ste 202, 15601. SAN 314-5549. Tel: 724-830-3266. FAX: 724-830-3042. Web Site: www.co.westmoreland.pa.us. *Librn,* Betty Ward; E-mail: eward@co.westmoreland.pa.us
Library Holdings: Bk Vols 24,000; Per Subs 35
Subject Interests: Legal mat
Partic in Share Westmoreland Consortium
Open Mon, Tues, Thurs & Fri 8:30-4, Wed 8:30-7:30

GREENVILLE

P GREENVILLE AREA PUBLIC LIBRARY, 330 Main St, 16125-2615. SAN 314-5603. Tel: 724-588-5490. FAX: 724-588-5481. E-mail: director@greenvillelibrary.net. *Dir,* Jeanne Ball; *Cat,* Amanda Graul; Staff 3.5 (Non-MLS 3.5)
Founded 1921. Pop 12,582; Circ 67,710
Library Holdings: AV Mats 2,279; Large Print Bks 750; Bk Vols 37,784; Per Subs 80
Automation Activity & Vendor Info: (Cataloging) Follett Software; (Circulation) Follett Software
Wireless access
Function: Copy machines, ILL available, Magnifiers for reading, Mail & tel request accepted, Music CDs, Newsp ref libr, Photocopying/Printing, Prog for children & young adult, Ref & res, Spoken cassettes & CDs, Summer reading prog, Tax forms, Telephone ref, Video lending libr
Open Tues-Thurs 9:30-8, Fri & Sat 9:30-4:30
Restriction: Authorized patrons
Friends of the Library Group

C THIEL COLLEGE*, Langenheim Memorial Library, 75 College Ave, 16125-2183. SAN 314-5611. Tel: 724-589-2124, 724-589-2205. Interlibrary Loan Service Tel: 724-589-2121. Reference Tel: 724-589-2119. FAX: 724-589-2122. Web Site: www.thiel.edu. *Dir,* Allen S Morrill; E-mail: amorrill@thiel.edu; *Circ Supvr,* Maryann Cardillo; Tel: 724-589-2118, E-mail: mcardillo@thiel.edu; *Acq, Ser,* Lida Mason; Tel: 724-589-2128, E-mail: lmason@thiel.edu; *Circ,* Richard Walcott; E-mail: rwalcott@thiel.edu; *Instruction & Outreach,* Jeanne Ball; E-mail: jball@thiel.edu; *ILL, Tech Serv,* Dorothy Brenoel; E-mail: dbrenoel@thiel.edu; *Govt Doc, Tech Support,* Deborah Ross; Tel: 724-589-2127, E-mail: dross@thiel.edu; Staff 7 (MLS 5, Non-MLS 2)
Founded 1866. Enrl 1,200; Fac 65; Highest Degree: Bachelor
Library Holdings: CDs 477; DVDs 38; e-books 4,177; e-journals 124; Electronic Media & Resources 31; Bk Titles 148,556; Bk Vols 186,643; Per Subs 460
Special Collections: State Document Depository; US Document Depository
Automation Activity & Vendor Info: (Acquisitions) MultiLIS; (Cataloging) OCLC Connexion; (Circulation) MultiLIS; (Course Reserve) MultiLIS; (ILL) OCLC; (OPAC) MultiLIS; (Serials) MultiLIS
Database Vendor: EBSCOhost, Gale Cengage Learning, LexisNexis, OCLC WorldShare Interlibrary Loan
Wireless access
Function: Govt ref serv, ILL available, Ref serv available
Partic in Lyrasis; OCLC Online Computer Library Center, Inc
Open Mon-Thurs 8am-10pm, Fri 8-5, Sat 12-4, Sun 2-10
Restriction: Limited access for the pub

GROVE CITY

S GEORGE JUNIOR REPUBLIC LIBRARY*, 200 George Junior Rd, 16127. (Mail add: PO Box 1058, 16127-5058), *Librn,* Mary McKinley
Library Holdings: Bk Vols 20,000; Per Subs 20

Automation Activity & Vendor Info: (Cataloging) Follett Software; (Circulation) Follett Software; (OPAC) Follett Software
Open Mon-Fri 8-3:30

C GROVE CITY COLLEGE, Henry Buhl Library, 300 Campus Dr, 16127-2198. SAN 314-562X. Tel: 724-458-2047. FAX: 724-458-2181. *Coll Develop, Dir,* Barbra Munnell; Tel: 724-458-3824, E-mail: bmmunnell@gcc.edu; *Asst Dir, Bibliog Instr, Ref Librn,* Kim Marks; Tel: 724-450-1532, E-mail: ksmarks@gcc.edu; *Outreach Librn, Ref,* Megan Babal; Tel: 724-264-1007, E-mail: mebabal@gcc.edu; *Acq,* Jill Forsythe; *Bibliog Instr, Ref,* Amy C Cavanaugh; Tel: 724-458-2148, E-mail: accavanaugh@gcc.edu; *Ref,* Carol Singleton; Tel: 724-450-4038; *Ser,* Joyce M Kebert; Tel: 724-458-3821, E-mail: jmkebert@gcc.edu; *Tech Serv,* Janet Elder; Tel: 724-458-3823, E-mail: jleleder@gcc.edu; *Tech Serv,* Conni L Shaw; Tel: 724-458-3842, E-mail: clshaw@gcc.edu; Staff 9 (MLS 6, Non-MLS 3)
Founded 1900. Enrl 2,480; Fac 120; Highest Degree: Bachelor
Library Holdings: Audiobooks 390; e-books 140,000; Microforms 4,000; Bk Vols 138,000; Videos 4,000
Special Collections: Ludwig von Mises Papers, letters, ms & pamphlets
Subject Interests: Am, Behav sci, British, English, European hist, Soc sci
Automation Activity & Vendor Info: (Cataloging) TLC (The Library Corporation); (Circulation) TLC (The Library Corporation); (OPAC) TLC (The Library Corporation)
Database Vendor: 3M Library Systems, ABC-CLIO, American Chemical Society, American Psychological Association (APA), Annual Reviews, ARTstor, Bowker, Cambridge Scientific Abstracts, CQ Press, CRC Press/Taylor & Francis Group, EBSCOhost, Hoovers, ISI Web of Knowledge, JSTOR, LexisNexis, Medline, Modern Language Association, Nature Publishing Group, OCLC FirstSearch, Oxford Online, Plunkett Research, Ltd, Project MUSE, ProQuest, PubMed, ScienceDirect, TLC (The Library Corporation), Wilson - Wilson Web
Wireless access
Partic in Lyrasis

P GROVE CITY COMMUNITY LIBRARY*, 125 W Main St, 16127-1569. SAN 314-5638. Tel: 724-458-7320. FAX: 724-458-7332. E-mail: gccl@grovecitypalibrary.org. Web Site: www.grovecitypalibrary.org. *Dir,* Apryl Flynn Gilliss; E-mail: director@grovecitypalibrary.org; *Cataloger/Ref Librn,* Wendy Riggi; *Children's & Teen Serv Coordr,* Heather Baker; *Circ, ILL,* Janis Stiner
Founded 1958. Pop 14,309; Circ 32,353
Library Holdings: Bk Vols 31,858; Per Subs 60
Automation Activity & Vendor Info: (Cataloging) Follett Software; (Circulation) Follett Software; (OPAC) Follett Software
Database Vendor: Baker & Taylor, EBSCOhost, Gale Cengage Learning, Oxford Online
Wireless access
Open Mon & Fri 10-8, Tues-Thurs 10-5, Sat 8-3
Friends of the Library Group

GWYNEDD VALLEY

C GWYNEDD MERCY UNIVERSITY*, Lourdes Library, 1325 Sumneytown Pike, 19437. (Mail add: PO Box 901, 19437-0901), SAN 314-5654. Tel: 215-646-7300, Ext 474. FAX: 215-641-5596. E-mail: library@gmc.edu. Web Site: www.gmc.edu/library. *Dir,* Daniel Schabert; E-mail: schabert.d@gmc.edu; *Asst Dir & Syst Librn,* Nancy McGarvey; E-mail: mcgarvey.n@gmc.edu; *Coordr, Circ,* Peggy Lopuzanski; E-mail: lopuzanski.m@gmc.edu; *Acq, ILL,* Pat Smith; *AV, Circ,* Eileen Wood; *Cat, Ref Serv,* Dee Simms; E-mail: simms.d@gmc.edu; *Instrul Serv/Ref Librn,* Heather Burychka; E-mail: burychka.h@gmc.edu; Staff 9 (MLS 4, Non-MLS 5)
Founded 1948. Enrl 1,952; Fac 85; Highest Degree: Doctorate
Library Holdings: AV Mats 10,552; e-books 950; e-journals 13,506; Microforms 17,868; Bk Titles 91,133; Bk Vols 93,910; Per Subs 173
Special Collections: Institute for New Orleans History & Culture
Subject Interests: Ireland
Automation Activity & Vendor Info: (Cataloging) SirsiDynix; (Circulation) SirsiDynix; (Course Reserve) SirsiDynix; (ILL) OCLC; (OPAC) SirsiDynix; (Serials) SirsiDynix
Database Vendor: EBSCOhost, OVID Technologies, Wilson - Wilson Web
Partic in OCLC Online Computer Library Center, Inc; Southeastern Pa Consortium for Higher Educ; Tri-State College Library Cooperative
Open Mon-Thurs 8:30am-10pm, Fri 8:30-4:30, Sat 10-5, Sun 11-6

HAMBURG

P HAMBURG PUBLIC LIBRARY*, 35 N Third St, 19526-1502. SAN 314-5670. Tel: 610-562-2843. FAX: 610-562-8136. E-mail: hamburgpl@berks.lib.pa.us. Web Site: www.berk.lib.pa.us/hamburgpl/index.htm. *Dir,* Daniel LaRue; *Librn,* Mary Laurie; *Ch Serv,* Donna Sweigert; Staff 3 (MLS 1, Non-MLS 2)
Founded 1903. Pop 13,190; Circ 39,197
Library Holdings: Audiobooks 800; AV Mats 1,000; CDs 450; Large Print Bks 1,000; Bk Vols 17,000; Per Subs 80; Talking Bks 600
Special Collections: Hamburg Items 1902-Present, microfilm
Wireless access
Open Mon 10-8, Tues & Thurs 12-8, Wed & Fri 10-5, Sat 9-4

HAMLIN

P SALEM PUBLIC LIBRARY*, 562 Easton Tpk, 18427-9720. (Mail add: Box 98, 18427-0098), SAN 314-5689. Tel: 570-689-0903. FAX: 570-689-4432. E-mail: salemlake@waynelibraries.org. *Dir,* Amy Alpaugh; Staff 2 (Non-MLS 2)
Founded 1969. Pop 8,732
Library Holdings: Bk Vols 7,000
Special Collections: Civil War Coll; Lincoln Coll; Railroad Coll; Zane Grey Coll
Partic in Midwest Collaborative for Library Services (MCLS)
Open Tues 10-6, Wed & Thurs 10-8, Fri 10-4, Sat 10-2
Friends of the Library Group

HANOVER

P GUTHRIE MEMORIAL LIBRARY*, Two Library Pl, 17331-2283. SAN 314-5697. Tel: 717-632-5183. FAX: 717-632-7565. E-mail: gulibrary@yorklibraries.org. Web Site: www.yorklibraries.org. *Dir,* Fletcher Hiigel; *Dir of Develop,* Lisa Kane; *Assoc Dir, Teens,* Melody Dewberry; *Ad,* Connie McInturff; *Ch Serv Librn,* Kelly Horner; *ILL,* Linda Gladfelter; Staff 15 (MLS 2, Non-MLS 13)
Founded 1911. Pop 40,711; Circ 406,026
Library Holdings: Bk Vols 99,685; Per Subs 157
Special Collections: Pennsylvania Room
Subject Interests: Genealogy, Local hist, Pa
Automation Activity & Vendor Info: (Circulation) Innovative Interfaces, Inc
Database Vendor: Baker & Taylor, EBSCOhost, Gale Cengage Learning, Wilson - Wilson Web
Wireless access
Publications: Weekly Newspaper Column
Mem of York County Library System
Special Services for the Deaf - TDD equip
Open Mon-Thurs 10-8, Fri & Sat 10-5
Friends of the Library Group

HARLEYSVILLE

S MENNONITE HISTORIANS OF EASTERN PENNSYLVANIA*, Mennonite Historical Library & Archives, 565 Yoder Rd, 19438. SAN 326-3444. Tel: 215-256-3020. FAX: 215-256-3023. E-mail: info@mhep.org. Web Site: www.mhep.org. *Coll Mgr,* Joel D Alderfer; E-mail: alderferjoel@mhep.org; Staff 1 (Non-MLS 1)
Founded 1967
Library Holdings: Bk Titles 6,910; Bk Vols 8,384; Per Subs 125
Special Collections: Franconia Mennonite Mission Board Coll, 1917-1971; J C Clemens Coll; Jacob B Mensch Coll; Jacob Fretz Coll; John E Lapp Coll; Local History (Robert C Bucher Coll); Mennonite Church History (Towamencin Mennonite Coll); Salford Mennonite Church Coll, 1718-2000
Subject Interests: Archives, Genealogy, Local biog, Mennonite hist, Montgomery counties, Pa German studies, Peace studies, Theol
Function: Res libr
Publications: MHEP (Newsletter)
Restriction: Non-circulating to the pub

HARRISBURG

L COMMONWEALTH COURT LIBRARY*, 603 Irvis Office Bldg, Commonwealth & Walnut Aves, 17120. SAN 314-5719. Tel: 717-255-1615. FAX: 717-255-1784. Web Site: www.aopc.org/index/cwealth/indexcwealth.asp. *Librn,* Pam Shoop
Founded 1970
Library Holdings: Bk Titles 500; Bk Vols 20,000
Database Vendor: LexisNexis, Westlaw
Restriction: Not open to pub

GL DAUPHIN COUNTY LAW LIBRARY*, Dauphin County Courthouse, Front & Market Sts, 4th Flr, 17101. SAN 314-5735. Tel: 717-780-6605. FAX: 717-780-6481. Web Site: www.dauphinc.org. *Law Librn,* Tracey McCall; E-mail: tmccall@dauphinc.org; *Asst Law Librn,* M Ellen V Gladfelter; E-mail: mgladfelter@dauphinc.org; *Asst Law Librn,* Laura Motter; E-mail: lmotter@dauphinc.org; Staff 1 (Non-MLS 1)
Founded 1865
Jan 2010-Dec 2010 Income $6,500. Mats Exp $345,000. Sal $124,000 (Prof $60,000)
Library Holdings: Bk Vols 36,500; Per Subs 9
Open Mon-Fri 8-4:30
Restriction: Circ limited

P DAUPHIN COUNTY LIBRARY SYSTEM, 101 Walnut St, 17101. SAN 358-5034. Tel: 717-234-4961. FAX: 717-234-7479. E-mail: discover@dcls.org. Web Site: www.dcls.org. *Exec Dir,* Richard Bowra; Tel: 717-234-4961, Ext 102; *Dir, Commun Relations,* Karen Cullings; Tel: 717-234-4961, Ext 104; *Pub Serv Dir,* Lisa Appelt; Tel: 717-234-4961, Ext 105; Staff 35 (MLS 21, Non-MLS 14)
Founded 1889. Pop 221,283; Circ 1,114,970
Library Holdings: AV Mats 60,503; CDs 26,228; Large Print Bks 6,504; Per Subs 532; Talking Bks 14,992; Videos 17,715
Special Collections: Grants Info; Job/Career Ctr
Subject Interests: Local hist, Pa
Automation Activity & Vendor Info: (Acquisitions) SirsiDynix; (Cataloging) SirsiDynix; (Circulation) SirsiDynix; (ILL) OCLC; (OPAC) SirsiDynix
Database Vendor: EBSCOhost, Gale Cengage Learning, LearningExpress, Medline, Newsbank, ReferenceUSA, TumbleBookLibrary
Wireless access
Publications: Connect Newsletter (Quarterly); Information Place (Quarterly); Passport (Bi-monthly)
Open Mon-Fri 10-5
Friends of the Library Group
Branches: 8
WILLIAM H & MARION C ALEXANDER FAMILY LIBRARY, 200 W Second St, Hummelstown, 17036, SAN 314-6278. Tel: 717-566-0949. FAX: 717-566-7178. E-mail: WebMailAFL@dcls.org. *Libr Mgr,* John Miller; Staff 2 (MLS 2)
Circ 102,340
Library Holdings: AV Mats 6,603; CDs 2,713; Large Print Bks 827; Per Subs 74; Talking Bks 1,467; Videos 2,138
Open Tues-Thurs 10-8, Fri 10-6, Sat 10-3
Friends of the Library Group
EAST SHORE AREA LIBRARY, 4501 Ethel St, 17109, SAN 358-5093. Tel: 717-652-9380. FAX: 717-545-3584. Interlibrary Loan Service FAX: 717-652-5012. E-mail: WebMailESA@dcls.org. *Adminr,* Marjorie McKensie; Tel: 717-652-9380, Ext 122; Staff 11 (MLS 8, Non-MLS 3)
Circ 608,774
Library Holdings: AV Mats 18,346; CDs 7,921; Large Print Bks 2,525; Per Subs 158; Talking Bks 5,325; Videos 4,637
Open Mon-Thurs 10-9, Fri-Sun 10-5
Friends of the Library Group
ELIZABETHVILLE AREA LIBRARY, 80 N Market St, Elizabethville, 17023, SAN 358-5123. Tel: 717-362-9825. Circulation Tel: 717-362-9825, Ext 307. FAX: 717-362-8119. E-mail: WebMailEV@dcls.org. *Libr Mgr,* Holly Etzweiller; Staff 2 (MLS 1, Non-MLS 1)
Circ 104,253
Library Holdings: AV Mats 7,307; CDs 2,958; Large Print Bks 463; Per Subs 58; Talking Bks 1,465; Videos 2,722
Open Tues-Thurs 10-8, Fri 10-5, Sat 10-2
Friends of the Library Group
JOHNSON MEMORIAL, 799 E Center St, Millersburg, 17061, SAN 314-7622. Tel: 717-692-2658. FAX: 717-692-5003. E-mail: WebMailJOH@dcls.org. *Libr Mgr,* Holly Etzweiler; Staff 1 (Non-MLS 1)
Founded 1931. Circ 44,138
Library Holdings: AV Mats 3,892; CDs 1,907; Large Print Bks 337; Per Subs 40; Talking Bks 1,072; Videos 863
Open Mon-Fri 3:30-8, Sat 10-3
KLINE LIBRARY, 530 S 29th St, 17104, SAN 358-5212. Tel: 717-234-3934. FAX: 717-234-7713. E-mail: WebMailKL@dcls.org. *Libr Mgr,* John Miller; Staff 2 (MLS 1, Non-MLS 1)
Circ 83,264
Library Holdings: AV Mats 8,377; CDs 3,274; Large Print Bks 764; Per Subs 52; Talking Bks 1,762; Videos 3,046
Open Tues-Thurs 10-8, Fri 10-6, Sat 10-5
Friends of the Library Group
MCCORMICK RIVERFRONT LIBRARY, 101 Walnut St, 17101, SAN 358-5069. Tel: 717-234-4976. FAX: 717-234-7479. E-mail: WebMailMRL@dcls.org. *Libr Mgr,* Dawn Weiman; Staff 2 (MLS 1, Non-MLS 1)
Circ 60,084
Library Holdings: AV Mats 6,469; CDs 3,347; Large Print Bks 554; Per Subs 48; Talking Bks 1,130; Videos 1,896
Open Mon-Thurs 10-6, Fri 10-5
Friends of the Library Group
NORTHERN DAUPHIN LIBRARY, 683 Main St, Lykens, 17048, SAN 358-5247. Tel: 717-453-9315. FAX: 717-453-9524. E-mail: WebMailND@dcls.org. *Libr Mgr,* Holly Etzwiler; Staff 2 (MLS 1, Non-MLS 1)
Circ 57,221
Library Holdings: AV Mats 4,101; CDs 1,756; Large Print Bks 535; Per Subs 44; Talking Bks 1,074; Videos 1,163
Open Mon, Wed & Fri 10-5, Tues & Thurs 1-8
Friends of the Library Group
MADELINE L OLEWINE MEMORIAL LIBRARY, 2410 N Third St, 17110, SAN 358-5158. Tel: 717-232-7286. FAX: 717-232-9707. E-mail: WebMailMOM@dcls.org. *Libr Mgr,* Dawn Weiman; Staff 1 (Non-MLS 1)
Circ 54,896
Library Holdings: AV Mats 5,408; CDs 2,352; Large Print Bks 499; Per Subs 43; Talking Bks 1,697; Videos 1,250
Open Mon-Thurs 10-6, Fri 10-5

J HARRISBURG AREA COMMUNITY COLLEGE*, McCormick Library, One HACC Dr, 17110-2999. SAN 314-5778. Tel: 717-780-2460. Reference Tel: 717-780-2624. FAX: 717-780-2462. E-mail: library@hacc.edu. Web Site: lib2.hacc.edu/campus/hbg/hbg.html. *Dir,* laura Wukovitz; *Coll Develop Librn,* Beverly Segina; Tel: 717-780-2466, E-mail: basegina@hacc.edu; *Ref & Instruction Librn,* Kathleen Conley; Tel: 717-780-1186, E-mail: ksconley@hacc.edu; *Ref & Instruction Librn,* Katie Margolis; *Ref & Instruction Librn,* Judi Ungar; *Circ Mgr,* Edyta Lonon; *Libr Spec,* Lucy Kucynski; *Libr Tech,* Borany Kanal-Scott; Staff 11.5 (MLS 7, Non-MLS 4.5)
Founded 1964. Enrl 7,659; Fac 205; Highest Degree: Associate
Jul 2011-Jun 2012 Income $1,135,000. Mats Exp $199,000, Books $112,000, Per/Ser (Incl. Access Fees) $73,000, AV Mat $14,000. Sal $715,188 (Prof $507,569)
Library Holdings: AV Mats 5,361; e-books 47; Bk Vols 86,656; Per Subs 375
Special Collections: Cooper Law Library
Automation Activity & Vendor Info: (Circulation) SirsiDynix; (Course Reserve) SirsiDynix; (Media Booking) SirsiDynix; (OPAC) SirsiDynix; (Serials) SirsiDynix
Wireless access

M HARRISBURG HOSPITAL LIBRARY AT PINNACLEHEALTH SYSTEM*, Main Bldg, 2nd Flr, 111 S Front St, 17101-2099. SAN 314-5786. Tel: 717-782-5533. FAX: 717-782-5512. E-mail: libraries@pinnaclehealth.org. Web Site: www2.pinnaclehealth.org. *Mgr, Libr Serv,* Laurie J Schwing; Tel: 717-782-5534, E-mail: lschwing@pinnaclehealth.org; *Doc Delivery, Librn,* Elizabeth Morgan; Tel: 717-782-5511, E-mail: emorgan@pinnaclehealth.org; *Librn, Tech Serv,* Helen Houpt; Tel: 717-657-7247, Fax: 717-657-7248, E-mail: hhoupt@pinnaclehealth.org. Subject Specialists: *Mgt, Mobile res,* Laurie J Schwing; *Nursing res,* Elizabeth Morgan; *Health literacy,* Helen Houpt; Staff 1.2 (MLS 1.2)
Founded 1936
Library Holdings: Audiobooks 1; CDs 9; DVDs 80; e-books 157; e-journals 2,085; Bk Titles 963; Per Subs 128
Special Collections: Archives of PinnacleHealth System; History of Medicine Coll
Subject Interests: Allied health, Clinical med, Consumer health, Hospital admin, Nursing
Automation Activity & Vendor Info: (Cataloging) EOS International; (Circulation) EOS International; (OPAC) EOS International; (Serials) EOS International
Database Vendor: EBSCOhost, Elsevier, EOS International, MD Consult, Medianet, Micromedex, OCLC, OVID Technologies, PubMed, ScienceDirect, STAT!Ref (Teton Data Systems), UpToDate
Wireless access
Partic in Central Pennsylvania Health Sciences Library Association; National Network of Libraries of Medicine; OCLC Online Computer Library Center, Inc
Restriction: Badge access after hrs, Hospital employees & physicians only

C HARRISBURG UNIVERSITY OF SCIENCE & TECHNOLOGY*, Learning Commons, 326 Market St, 17101. Tel: 717-901-5188. E-mail: library@harrisburgu.edu. Web Site: library.harrisburgu.edu. *Univ Librn,* David Runyon; E-mail: drunyon@harrisburg.edu; Staff 1 (MLS 1)
Highest Degree: Master
Special Collections: Board Games (Coll of board games showcasing a wide variety of mechanics and game types); Electronic Games (Coll of video games for PS3, xBox360, and Wii)
Subject Interests: Sci, Tech
Function: CD-ROM, Copy machines, Electronic databases & coll, Online cat, Photocopying/Printing, Ref serv available
Partic in Associated College Libraries of Central Pennsylvania; Keystone Library Network; Lyrasis; Pennsylvania Academic Library Consortium, Inc (PALCI)
Restriction: Access at librarian's discretion, Borrowing privileges limited to fac & registered students, External users must contact libr, Open to students, fac & staff, Secured area only open to authorized personnel, Use of others with permission of librn

S HISTORICAL SOCIETY OF DAUPHIN COUNTY LIBRARY*, 219 S Front St, 17104. SAN 326-4270. Tel: 717-233-3462. FAX: 717-233-6059. E-mail: library@dauphincountyhistory.org. Web Site: dauphincountyhistoricalsociety.org. *Librn,* Evelyn L James; Staff 1 (Non-MLS 1)

Library Holdings: Bk Titles 5,151; Bk Vols 5,260; Per Subs 16
Subject Interests: Genealogy, Local hist
Function: Res libr
Open Mon-Thurs 12:45-4:15

L MCNESS, WALLACE & NURICK LLC*, Information Center, 100 Pine St, 17108. (Mail add: PO Box 1166, 17108-1166), SAN 326-9361. Tel: 717-232-8000. FAX: 717-237-5300. Web Site: www.mwn.com. *Dir, Info Serv,* Margaret J Ross; Tel: 717-237-5205, E-mail: mross@mwn.com; Staff 3 (MLS 2, Non-MLS 1)
Library Holdings: Bk Vols 15,000; Per Subs 200
Automation Activity & Vendor Info: (Acquisitions) SIMA, Inc; (Cataloging) SIMA, Inc; (Circulation) SIMA, Inc; (OPAC) SIMA, Inc; (Serials) SIMA, Inc
Database Vendor: Dialog, LexisNexis, OCLC FirstSearch, Westlaw
Open Mon-Fri 8-5:30

G PENNSYLVANIA DEPARTMENT OF TRANSPORTATION*, Library & Research Center, Commonwealth Keystone Bldg, 6th Flr, 400 North St, 17120-0041. (Mail add: PO Box 3054, 17105-3054). Tel: 717-787-5796. FAX: 717-783-9152. E-mail: penndot_library@state.pa.us. Web Site: www.dot.state.pa.us.
Founded 1979
Library Holdings: Bk Titles 21,719; Bk Vols 23,452; Per Subs 250
Special Collections: Transportation Research Board Series
Subject Interests: Bus, Eng, Transportation
Automation Activity & Vendor Info: (Circulation) EOS International; (Serials) EOS International
Database Vendor: Dialog
Restriction: Open by appt only, Open to pub for ref only

G PENNSYLVANIA JOINT STATE GOVERNMENT COMMISSION LIBRARY*, 108 Finance Bldg, Rm G-16, 17120. SAN 314-5921. Tel: 717-787-6803. FAX: 717-787-7020. *Librn,* Yelena Khanzhina; Tel: 717-787-6851, E-mail: ykhanzhina@legis.state.pa.us; Staff 1 (Non-MLS 1)
Library Holdings: Bk Titles 3,500; Per Subs 75
Subject Interests: Educ, Finance, Govt, Legis ref mat from other states, Pa statutes
Automation Activity & Vendor Info: (OPAC) Ex Libris Group; (Serials) Ex Libris Group
Database Vendor: OCLC FirstSearch
Wireless access
Restriction: Non-circulating to the pub

GL PENNSYLVANIA LEGISLATIVE REFERENCE BUREAU LIBRARY*, Main Capitol, Rm 641, 17120-0033. SAN 314-5956. Tel: 717-787-4816. FAX: 717-783-2396. *Librn,* Susan K Zavacky; Staff 1 (Non-MLS 1)
Founded 1909
Library Holdings: Bk Vols 12,000; Per Subs 25
Subject Interests: Law, Pa legislature
Automation Activity & Vendor Info: (Acquisitions) LibraryWorld, Inc; (Cataloging) LibraryWorld, Inc
Function: For res purposes
Open Mon-Fri 8:45-4:45
Restriction: Not a lending libr

GL PENNSYLVANIA OFFICE OF ATTORNEY GENERAL*, Law Library, 1525 Strawberry Sq, 17120. SAN 314-5891. Tel: 717-787-3176. FAX: 717-772-4526. *Admin Officer,* Bob Robitaille; Staff 3 (MLS 1, Non-MLS 2)
Founded 1873
Library Holdings: Bk Vols 26,500
Database Vendor: LexisNexis, Westlaw
Partic in Mead Data Cent
Restriction: Staff use only

G PENNSYLVANIA PUBLIC UTILITY COMMISSION LIBRARY*, Commonwealth Keystone Bldg, 400 North St, 17120-0079. (Mail add: PO Box 3265, 17105-3265), SAN 324-6078. Tel: 717-783-1740. FAX: 717-783-3458. *Librn,* Sherri Del Biondo; Staff 2 (MLS 1, Non-MLS 1)
Founded 1977
Library Holdings: Bk Titles 10,241; Bk Vols 11,690; Per Subs 39
Subject Interests: Econ, Energy, Eng, Law, Pub utilities
Restriction: Not open to pub

M PINNACLEHEALTH LIBRARY SERVICES*, Community General Osteopathic Hospital Library, 4300 Londonderry Rd, 17103. (Mail add: PO Box 3000, 17105-3000), SAN 314-5727. Tel: 717-657-7247. FAX: 717-657-7248. E-mail: libraries@pinnaclehealth.org. Web Site: www2.pinnaclehealth.org. *Librn,* Helen L Houpt; E-mail: hhoupt@pinnaclehealth.org; Staff 0.8 (MLS 0.8)
Founded 1977
Library Holdings: e-books 157; e-journals 2,085; Bk Vols 721; Per Subs 8; Videos 10
Subject Interests: Allied health, Hospital admin, Med, Nursing
Automation Activity & Vendor Info: (Acquisitions) EOS International; (Cataloging) EOS International; (Circulation) EOS International; (OPAC) EOS International; (Serials) EOS International
Database Vendor: EBSCOhost, EOS International, McGraw-Hill, MD Consult, OCLC, OVID Technologies, PubMed, ScienceDirect, STAT!Ref (Teton Data Systems), UpToDate
Wireless access
Function: Copy machines, Doc delivery serv, Electronic databases & coll, Online searches, Photocopying/Printing
Partic in Central Pennsylvania Health Sciences Library Association; National Network of Libraries of Medicine
Restriction: Badge access after hrs, Hospital employees & physicians only

G SENATE LIBRARY OF PENNSYLVANIA*, Main Capitol Bldg, Rm 157, 17120-0030. SAN 314-5999. Tel: 717-787-6120. FAX: 717-772-2366. E-mail: senlib@os.pasen.gov. Web Site: www.pasen.gov/senate_library.html. *Librn,* Evelyn F Andrews; E-mail: eandrews@os.pasen.gov
Library Holdings: Bk Vols 10,000; Per Subs 15
Special Collections: Histories of Legislation for Senate & House of Representatives of Pennsylvania; Legislative Journals for Senate and House of Representatives of Pennsylvania; Transcripts of Hearings for Senate & House of Representatives of Pennsylvania
Open Mon-Fri 8-5

P STATE LIBRARY OF PENNSYLVANIA, Forum Bldg, 607 South Dr, 17120-0600. SAN 314-6022. Tel: 717-787-2646. Circulation Tel: 717-787-3169. Interlibrary Loan Service Tel: 717-787-4782. Reference Tel: 717-783-5950, 717-787-3273. Administration Tel: 717-783-5968. FAX: 717-772-3265. TDD: 717-783-8445. E-mail: ra-reflib@pa.gov. Web Site: www.portal.state.pa.us/portal/server.pt/community/bureau_of_state_library/8811. *State Librn,* Stacey Aldrich; Tel: 717-783-2466, E-mail: saldrich@pa.gov; *Dir, Libr Serv,* Alice Lubrecht; E-mail: alubrecht@pa.gov; *Head, Pub Serv, Regional Dep Librn,* Kathleen Hale; Tel: 717-787-2327, E-mail: kahale@pa.gov; *Digital Librn,* William T Fee; Tel: 717-783-7014, E-mail: wfee@pa.gov; *Rare Bk Librn,* Dr Iren Snavely; Tel: 717-783-5982, E-mail: irsnavely@pa.gov; *State Doc Cataloger,* Mary Spila; Tel: 717-783-3884, E-mail: mspila@pa.gov; *Cat, Coll,* Thomas Duszak; Tel: 717-772-5616, E-mail: tduszak@pa.gov. Subject Specialists: *Fed docs, State doc,* Kathleen Hale; *Digitization,* William T Fee; *Pa hist, Rare bks,* Dr Iren Snavely; *Cataloging,* Thomas Duszak; Staff 33 (MLS 21, Non-MLS 12)
Founded 1745
Jul 2013-Jun 2014 Income $9,344,249. Mats Exp $716,129. Sal $2,939,199
Library Holdings: Audiobooks 5; AV Mats 365; CDs 6,647; DVDs 1,714; e-books 30,351; e-journals 48,532; Electronic Media & Resources 78,807; Microforms 726,444; Bk Titles 1,258,216; Bk Vols 1,709,599; Per Subs 455; Videos 347
Special Collections: Central Pennsylvania Genealogy Coll; Jansen Manuscript Letters Coll; Jansen-Shirk Bookplate Coll; Pennsylvania Colonial Assembly Coll; Pennsylvania Comics; Pennsylvania Imprints, 1689-1865; Pennsylvania Newspapers-Historic & Current. State Document Depository; US Document Depository
Subject Interests: Hist, Law, Pa
Automation Activity & Vendor Info: (Acquisitions) Ex Libris Group; (Cataloging) Ex Libris Group; (Circulation) Ex Libris Group; (ILL) OCLC Online; (OPAC) Ex Libris Group; (Serials) Ex Libris Group
Database Vendor: Access Pennsylvania, Cinahl, EBSCOhost, Emerald, Ex Libris Group, Gale Cengage Learning, HeinOnline, JSTOR, LexisNexis, Marcive, Inc, Medline, Newsbank-Readex, OCLC, OCLC FirstSearch, OCLC WebJunction, OCLC WorldShare Interlibrary Loan, Oxford Online, ProQuest, PubMed, ReferenceUSA, Westlaw
Wireless access
Function: 24/7 Electronic res, 24/7 Online cat, Computers for patron use, Copy machines, e-mail serv, Electronic databases & coll, Exhibits, Govt ref serv, Handicapped accessible, ILL available, Libr develop, Magnifiers for reading, Mail & tel request accepted, Microfiche/film & reading machines, Newsp ref libr, Online cat, Online ref, Orientations, Photocopying/Printing, Pub access computers, Ref serv available, Scanner, Web-catalog, Wheelchair accessible
Publications: Checklist of Official Pennsylvania Publications; Directory-Pennsylvania Libraries; First 100 Years of Pennsylvania Imprints; Revised Classification Scheme for Pennsylvania State Publications
Partic in Interlibrary Delivery Service of Pennsylvania; Keystone Library Network; Lyrasis; Pennsylvania Academic Library Consortium, Inc (PALCI); Philadelphia Area Consortium of Special Collections Libraries
Special Services for the Deaf - ADA equip
Special Services for the Blind - Accessible computers; Large screen computer & software; Magnifiers; Screen reader software
Open Tues-Thurs 9:30-5
Restriction: Circ limited, Non-circulating of rare bks

J THOMPSON INSTITUTE*, Kaplan Career Institute Resource Room, 5650 Derry St, 17111. SAN 314-6049. Tel: 717-564-4112, 717-901-5867. Toll Free Tel: 800-272-4632. FAX: 717-558-1344. Web Site: www.kaplan.edu. *Exec Dir,* Sherry Rosenberg; *Librn,* Jo Hendren; E-mail: jhendren@kaplan.edu
Library Holdings: Bk Vols 1,900; Per Subs 30
Subject Interests: Electronics, Med, Secretarial
Wireless access
Open Mon-Fri 8am-10pm

HARRISON CITY

P PENN AREA LIBRARY*, 2001 Municipal Court, 15636. (Mail add: PO Box 499, 15636-0499), SAN 359-5897. Tel: 724-744-4414. FAX: 724-744-0226. E-mail: library@pennlib.org. Web Site: www.pennlib.org. *Dir,* Dorene Miller; E-mail: dmiller@pennlib.org; *Ref Librn,* Dawn Corall; E-mail: dcorrall@pennlib.org; *Coordr, Ch Serv,* Pat Cappeta; E-mail: pcappeta@pennlib.org; Staff 4 (MLS 1, Non-MLS 3)
Founded 1970. Pop 16,178; Circ 52,610
Library Holdings: Large Print Bks 300; Bk Titles 33,002; Bk Vols 35,375; Per Subs 101; Talking Bks 560; Videos 1,500
Subject Interests: Civil War, Local hist
Automation Activity & Vendor Info: (Acquisitions) Follett Software; (Cataloging) Follett Software; (Circulation) Follett Software; (Course Reserve) Follett Software; (ILL) Follett Software; (Media Booking) Follett Software; (OPAC) Follett Software; (Serials) Follett Software
Mem of Westmoreland County Federated Library System
Open Mon-Thurs 10-8, Fri & Sat 10-5
Friends of the Library Group

HASTINGS

P HASTINGS PUBLIC LIBRARY*, 312 Beaver St, 16646. (Mail add: PO Box 515, 16646-0515), SAN 314-6065. Tel: 814-247-8231. FAX: 814-247-8871. E-mail: hastings@cclsys.org. Web Site: www.cclib.lib.pa.us/hastings. *Dir, Libr & Info Serv,* Bernadette Dillon
Pop 2,846; Circ 13,510
Jan 2006-Dec 2006 Income $41,131, State $11,221, City $550, County $12,551, Locally Generated Income $16,809. Mats Exp $8,768, Books $5,568, Per/Ser (Incl. Access Fees) $1,200, AV Mat $500, Electronic Ref Mat (Incl. Access Fees) $395. Sal $15,983
Library Holdings: AV Mats 400; Large Print Bks 500; Bk Titles 14,115; Per Subs 45; Talking Bks 150
Automation Activity & Vendor Info: (Cataloging) Follett Software; (Circulation) Follett Software
Wireless access
Function: Handicapped accessible, Home delivery & serv to Sr ctr & nursing homes, Homebound delivery serv, ILL available, Online searches, Photocopying/Printing, Prog for children & young adult, Summer reading prog, Wheelchair accessible
Mem of Cambria County Library System & District Center
Open Mon & Wed 12-6, Tues & Thurs 2-8, Fri 1-5, Sat 9-4

HATBORO

R HATBORO BAPTIST CHURCH LIBRARY*, 32 N York Rd, 19040. SAN 314-6073. Tel: 215-675-8400. FAX: 215-675-4697. Web Site: www.hatborobaptistchurch.org. *Librn,* Carolyn Zimmerman; Staff 1 (Non-MLS 1)
Founded 1950
Library Holdings: Bk Titles 4,682; Bk Vols 4,720; Per Subs 11
Subject Interests: Christian living, Devotionals, Missions, Relig, Sermons
Open Mon-Fri 9-5

P UNION LIBRARY COMPANY OF HATBOROUGH*, 243 S York Rd, 19040-3429. SAN 323-5475. Tel: 215-672-1420. FAX: 215-672-1546. E-mail: hat.lib@verizon.net. Web Site: www.hatborogov.org/library. *Librn,* Harriet Ehrsam; Staff 4 (MLS 1, Non-MLS 3)
Founded 1775. Pop 7,380; Circ 39,000
Library Holdings: Bk Titles 22,000; Per Subs 41
Special Collections: American Civil War Coll; American Revolution; Colonial Subscription Library, circa 1770; Pennsylvania History Coll
Automation Activity & Vendor Info: (Acquisitions) Follett Software; (Cataloging) Follett Software; (Circulation) Follett Software; (OPAC) Follett Software
Database Vendor: EBSCOhost, ProQuest
Wireless access
Open Mon 1-5, Tues 10-6, Wed & Thurs 10-8, Fri 10-4, Sat 10-5
Friends of the Library Group

HATFIELD

R BIBLICAL THEOLOGICAL SEMINARY LIBRARY, 200 N Main St, 19440-2499. SAN 314-609X. Tel: 215-368-5000, Ext 123. FAX: 215-368-6906. E-mail: library@biblical.edu. Web Site: library.biblical.edu, www.biblical.edu/library. *Interim Adminr,* Susan Disston; E-mail: librarydirector@biblical.edu; *Coordr, Ser,* Lydia Putnam; *Tech Serv Coordr,* Dave Evans; Staff 3 (Non-MLS 3)
Founded 1971. Enrl 300; Fac 12; Highest Degree: Doctorate
Library Holdings: e-journals 65; Electronic Media & Resources 5,969; Bk Titles 35,000; Bk Vols 38,000; Per Subs 250; Videos 118
Special Collections: Biblical Seminary Theses (New York Coll)
Subject Interests: Theol
Automation Activity & Vendor Info: (Acquisitions) Ex Libris Group; (Cataloging) Ex Libris Group; (Circulation) Ex Libris Group; (Course Reserve) Ex Libris Group; (ILL) OCLC WorldShare Interlibrary Loan; (OPAC) Ex Libris Group; (Serials) Ex Libris Group
Database Vendor: American Psychological Association (APA), EBSCO Information Services, EBSCOhost, OCLC FirstSearch, OCLC WorldShare Interlibrary Loan
Wireless access
Function: 24/7 Electronic res, 24/7 Online cat, Computers for patron use, Copy machines, Distance learning, e-mail serv, Electronic databases & coll, Free DVD rentals, ILL available, Microfiche/film & reading machines, Online cat, Online info literacy tutorials on the web & in blackboard, Referrals accepted
Partic in Southeastern Pennsylvania Theological Library Association; Tri-State College Library Cooperative
Open Mon & Tues 9-8, Wed-Fri 9-5, Sat 9-2
Restriction: Open to pub for ref & circ; with some limitations, Open to students, fac & staff

HAVERFORD

C HAVERFORD COLLEGE, James P Magill Library, 370 Lancaster Ave, 19041-1392. SAN 358-5514. Tel: 610-896-1175. Interlibrary Loan Service Tel: 610-896-1171. Reference Tel: 610-896-1356. FAX: 610-896-1102. E-mail: library@haverford.edu. Web Site: library.haverford.edu. *Librn of the Col,* Terry Snyder; Tel: 610-896-1272, E-mail: tsnyder@haverford.edu; *Assoc Librn, Coordr, Coll Mgt & Metadata Serv,* Norm Medeiros; Tel: 610-896-1173, E-mail: nmedeiro@haverford.edu; *Head, Acq & Ser,* Mike Persick; Tel: 610-896-2971, E-mail: mpersick@haverford.edu; *Curator of Rare Bks & Ms, Head, Spec Coll,* Sarah Horowitz; Tel: 610-896-2948, E-mail: shorowitz@haverford.edu; *Cat Librn,* Richard Aldred; Tel: 610-896-1273, E-mail: raldred@haverford.edu; *Digital Scholarship Librn,* Mike Zarafonetis; Tel: 610-896-4965, E-mail: mzarafon@haverford.edu; *Electronic Res Librn,* Johanna Riordan; Tel: 610-896-1168, E-mail: jriordan@haverford.edu; *Lead Res & Instruction Librn,* Margaret Schaus; Tel: 610-896-1166, E-mail: mschaus@haverford.edu; *Music Librn, Web Coordr,* Adam Crandell; Tel: 610-896-1169, E-mail: acrandell@haverford.edu; *Ref Librn,* James Gulick; Tel: 610-896-1170, E-mail: jgulick@haverford.edu; *Res & Instruction Librn,* Caroline (Charlie) McNabb; E-mail: cmcnabb@haverford.edu; *Res & Instruction Librn,* Jeremiah Mercurio; Tel: 610-896-2976, E-mail: jmercuri@haverford.edu; *Sci Librn,* Dora Wong; Tel: 610-896-1416, E-mail: dwong@haverford.edu; *Visual Res Librn,* Julie Coy; Tel: 610-896-1128, E-mail: jcoy@haverford.edu; *Circ Serv Supvr & Bldg Projects Mgr,* Dawn Heckert; Tel: 610-896-1163, E-mail: dheckert@haverford.edu; *Col Archivist, Rec Mgr,* Krista Oldham; Tel: 610-896-1284, E-mail: koldham@haverford.edu; *Coordr, Digital Scholarship & Serv,* Laurie Allen; Tel: 610-896-4226, E-mail: lallen@haverford.edu; *ILL Spec,* Rob Haley; E-mail: rhaley@haverford.edu; *Conservator,* Bruce Bumbarger; Tel: 610-896-1165, E-mail: bbumbarg@haverford.edu; *Curator of Quaker Coll,* Ann Upton; Tel: 610-896-1158, E-mail: aupton@haverford.edu; Staff 19 (MLS 17, Non-MLS 2)
Founded 1833. Enrl 1,205; Fac 118; Highest Degree: Bachelor
Jul 2013-Jun 2014. Mats Exp $1,583,000, Books $353,000, Per/Ser (Incl. Access Fees) $1,230,000
Special Collections: Christopher Morley Coll; Cricket Coll; Elizabethan Studies (Philips Coll); Maxfield Parrish Coll; Mysticism (Jones Coll); Near Eastern Manuscripts (Harris Coll); Photography Coll; Quakerism: Friends Tracts of 17th Century (Jenks Coll), archives, doc, journals, maps, meeting minutes, ms, papers, pictures, rec; Roberts Manuscripts Coll; Rufus Jones Writings (Tobias Coll)
Automation Activity & Vendor Info: (Acquisitions) Innovative Interfaces, Inc; (Cataloging) Innovative Interfaces, Inc; (Circulation) Innovative Interfaces, Inc; (Course Reserve) Innovative Interfaces, Inc; (ILL) Innovative Interfaces, Inc; (OPAC) Innovative Interfaces, Inc; (Serials) Innovative Interfaces, Inc
Wireless access
Publications: Connections (Newsletter); Feminae: Medieval Women & Gender Index
Partic in Five Colleges, Inc; Lyrasis; OCLC Online Computer Library Center, Inc; Pennsylvania Academic Library Consortium, Inc (PALCI); Philadelphia Area Consortium of Special Collections Libraries; Tri-College University Libraries Consortium
Departmental Libraries:
ASTRONOMY, Observatory, 370 W Lancaster Ave, 19041. Tel: 610-896-1291. FAX: 610-896-1102. *Sci,* Dora Wong; Tel: 610-896-1416, E-mail: dwong@haverford.edu; Staff 1 (MLS 1)
Subject Interests: Astronomy

MUSIC, Union Bldg, 370 W Lancaster Ave, 19041. Tel: 610-896-1005. FAX: 610-896-1102. *Librn,* Adam Crandell; Tel: 610-896-1169, E-mail: acrandel@haverford.edu; Staff 1 (MLS 1)
WHITE SCIENCE, 370 W Lancaster Ave, Haversford, 19041. Tel: 610-896-1291. FAX: 610-896-1102. *Sci,* Dora Wong; Tel: 610-896-1416, E-mail: dwong@haverford.edu; Staff 1 (MLS 1)
Open Mon-Thurs 9am-1am, Fri 9-9, Sat 11-9, Sun 11am-1am

HAVERTOWN

P HAVERFORD TOWNSHIP FREE LIBRARY*, 1601 Darby Rd, 19083-3798. SAN 314-6111. Tel: 610-446-3082. Interlibrary Loan Service Tel: 610-446-3082, Ext 206. Reference Tel: 610-446-3082, Ext 202. FAX: 610-853-3090. E-mail: haverford@delcolibraries.org, reference@haverfordlibrary.org. Web Site: www.haverfordlibrary.org. *Dir,* Adeline Ciannella; Tel: 610-446-3082, Ext 213, E-mail: htfl@comcast.net; *Head, Circ,* Donna Jones; Tel: 610-446-3082, Ext 201; *Head, Ref,* Sue Vision; E-mail: hareference@delco.lib.pa.us; *Head, Tech Serv,* Christine Faris; Tel: 610-446-3082, Ext 210, E-mail: havgirltech@comcast.net; *Ch Serv,* Patricia Evans; Tel: 610-446-3082, Ext 205, E-mail: hacsd@delco.lib.pa.us; *ILL,* Joanne Cahill; E-mail: illha@delco.lib.pa.us; *Webmaster, YA Serv,* Deborah Purdy; Tel: 610-446-3082, Ext 207, E-mail: havteen@comcast.net; Staff 34 (MLS 7, Non-MLS 27)
Founded 1934. Pop 48,498; Circ 259,881
Library Holdings: AV Mats 9,588; Bk Titles 124,870; Per Subs 177
Function: Handicapped accessible, Homebound delivery serv, ILL available, Photocopying/Printing, Prog for children & young adult, Ref serv available, Summer reading prog, Telephone ref, Wheelchair accessible
Mem of Delaware County Library System
Open Mon-Thurs 9:30-9, Fri 9-6, Sat 9:30-5, Sun 1-5
Friends of the Library Group

HAWLEY

P HAWLEY LIBRARY*, 103 Main Ave, 18428-1325. SAN 314-6138. Tel: 570-226-4620. FAX: 570-226-8233. E-mail: hawlib@ptd.net. Web Site: www.plowc.org. *Dir,* Maura Rottmund
Founded 1961. Circ 28,000
Library Holdings: Bk Vols 34,000; Per Subs 75
Special Collections: Large Print Books Coll; Memorial Art Coll (von Hake)
Open Mon 1-5, Tues & Thurs 10-7, Wed, Fri & Sat 10-5

HAZLETON

P HAZLETON AREA PUBLIC LIBRARY*, 55 N Church St, 18201-5893. SAN 358-5603. Tel: 570-454-2961. FAX: 570-454-0630. Web Site: www.hazletonlibrary.org. *Dir,* Jim Reinmiller; *Br Coordr,* Alexis Neapolitan, Jr; *Ch Serv,* Michele Kushmeder; *ILL, Ref,* Jane Dougherty; *Tech Serv,* Melissa O'Connell-Cook; Staff 18 (MLS 2, Non MLS 16)
Founded 1907. Pop 73,057; Circ 221,591
Library Holdings: CDs 109; Large Print Bks 352; Bk Titles 151,116; Bk Vols 137,819; Per Subs 471; Talking Bks 1,496; Videos 2,296
Special Collections: Hazleton-Mining History (Local History Coll), photog, maps, bks; Pennsylvania History
Automation Activity & Vendor Info: (Cataloging) Innovative Interfaces, Inc; (Circulation) Innovative Interfaces, Inc
Mem of Luzerne County Library System
Open Mon-Thurs (Winter) 8:30am-9pm, Fri & Sat 8:30-5; Mon-Thurs (Summer) 8:30-8, Fri 8:30-5, Sat 8:30-4
Branches: 4
FREELAND BRANCH, 515 Front St, Freeland, 18224, SAN 358-5662. Tel: 570-636-2125. *Librn,* Colleen Tatar; Staff 3 (MLS 1, Non-MLS 2)
Library Holdings: AV Mats 1,142; Large Print Bks 66; Bk Titles 42,811; Bk Vols 44,112; Per Subs 63; Talking Bks 88; Videos 381
Open Mon & Wed (Winter) 1-5 & 6-9, Tues, Thurs & Sat 10-12 & 1-5, Fri 1-5; Mon & Wed (Summer) 1-5 & 6-8, Tues & Thurs 9-12 & 1-5, Fri 12-4
MCADOO, SOUTHSIDE BRANCH, 15 Kelayres Rd, McAdoo, 18237, SAN 358-5697. Tel: 570-929-1120. *Librn,* Sue Piacenti; Staff 2 (MLS 1, Non-MLS 1)
Library Holdings: AV Mats 508; Bk Titles 16,830; Bk Vols 18,510; Per Subs 51; Talking Bks 53; Videos 171
Open Mon-Wed (Winter) 3-8; Mon-Thurs (Summer) 10-3
NUREMBERG BRANCH, Mahanoy St, Nuremberg, 18241. (Mail add: PO Box 36, Nuremberg, 18241-0036), SAN 358-5727. Tel: 570-384-4101. *Librn,* Alice Lisefski; Staff 2 (MLS 1, Non-MLS 1)
Library Holdings: AV Mats 752; Bk Titles 18,751; Bk Vols 19,991; Per Subs 61; Talking Bks 81; Videos 192
Open Mon & Tues (Winter) 10-12 & 1-5, Wed 4-8, Fri 1-5; Mon & Tues (Summer) 10-12 & 1-5, Wed 4-8, Fri 12-4
VALLEY, 211 Main St, Conyngham, 18219, SAN 358-5638. Tel: 570-788-1339. *Librn,* Pat Walser; Staff 3 (MLS 1, Non-MLS 2)
Library Holdings: AV Mats 825; Bk Titles 18,911; Bk Vols 19,902; Per Subs 51; Talking Bks 102; Videos 191
Open Mon & Wed (Winter) 1-5 & 6-9, Tues, Thurs & Sat 10-12 & 1-5, Fri 1-5; Mon & Wed (Summer) 1-5 & 6-8, Tues & Thurs 9-12 & 1-5, Fri 12-4

M LEHIGH VALLEY HOSPITAL-HAZLETON*, Medical Library, 700 E Broad St, 18201. SAN 328-0136. Tel: 570-501-4800. FAX: 570-501-4840. Web Site: hazleton.lvhn.org/library/medical-library.html. *Librn,* Sharon Hrabina
Library Holdings: AV Mats 500; Bk Titles 1,545; Per Subs 266
Subject Interests: Allied health, Consumer health, Med, Nursing
Automation Activity & Vendor Info: (Cataloging) Professional Software
Database Vendor: Cinahl, EBSCOhost, MD Consult, OVID Technologies, PubMed, STAT!Ref (Teton Data Systems)
Partic in Basic Health Sciences Library Network; Docline; Health Information Library Network of Northeastern Pennsylvania (HILNNEP); Northeastern Pennsylvania Library Network
Open Mon-Fri 8-4

C PENNSYLVANIA STATE UNIVERSITY LIBRARIES*, Hazleton Library, 76 University Dr, 18202-8025. SAN 314-6146. Tel: 570-450-3170. FAX: 570-450-3128. E-mail: UL-HAZLETON@lists.psu.edu. Web Site: libraries.psu.edu/psul/hazleton.html. *Head Librn,* Lynn A Valerie; Tel: 570-450-3172, E-mail: vag3@psu.edu; *Ref & Instruction Librn,* Shannon G Richie; Tel: 570-450-3562, E-mail: sgr1@psu.edu; *Libr Supvr,* Ron Harman; Tel: 570-450-3171, E-mail: rrh13@psu.edu; *Info Res & Serv Support Spec,* Lisa Hartz; Tel: 570-450-3127, E-mail: Lah41@psu.edu; *Info Res & Serv Support Spec,* Michael Kattner; Tel: 570-450-3115, E-mail: mpk7@psu.edu; Staff 6 (MLS 2, Non-MLS 4)
Founded 1934. Enrl 1,316; Fac 69
Library Holdings: Bk Vols 80,500; Per Subs 230
Partic in OCLC Online Computer Library Center, Inc; RLIN (Research Libraries Information Network)

HEGINS

P TRI-VALLEY FREE PUBLIC LIBRARY*, 633 E Main St, 17938-9303. SAN 320-8427. Tel: 570-682-8922. FAX: 570-682-8922. E-mail: trvpl@epix.net. Web Site: www.schiu.k12.pa.us/tripl. *Librn,* Lorraine Oldham
Founded 1978. Pop 3,600
Library Holdings: Bks on Deafness & Sign Lang 12; Bk Titles 19,385; Bk Vols 21,000; Per Subs 20
Special Collections: Puppets
Open Mon, Wed & Fri 9-12 & 1-5, Tues & Thurs 1-5 & 6-8, Sat 8-3 (9-1 Jun-Aug)
Friends of the Library Group

HELLERTOWN

P HELLERTOWN AREA LIBRARY*, 409 Constitution Ave, 18055-1928. Tel: 610-838-8381. FAX: 610-838-8466. E-mail: readabook@hellertownlibrary.org. Web Site: www.hellertownlibrary.org. *Dir,* Robin Rotherham
Library Holdings: Bk Vols 30,000; Per Subs 38
Automation Activity & Vendor Info: (Cataloging) Follett Software; (Circulation) Follett Software; (OPAC) Follett Software
Open Mon & Wed 12-8, Tues & Thurs 10-6, Fri 9-5, Sat 9-4 (9-1 Summer)
Friends of the Library Group

HERMINIE

P SEWICKLEY TOWNSHIP PUBLIC LIBRARY*, 201 Highland Ave, 15637-1311. SAN 314-6162. Tel: 724-446-9940. FAX: 724-446-9114. E-mail: sewtwp@nb.net. *Librn,* Manda L Luchs; Staff 1 (MLS 1)
Founded 1952. Pop 6,250; Circ 17,785
Library Holdings: DVDs 250; Large Print Bks 320; Bk Vols 17,000; Per Subs 30; Talking Bks 350; Videos 400
Function: Photocopying/Printing, Prog for adults, Prog for children & young adult, Senior computer classes, Spoken cassettes & CDs, Spoken cassettes & DVDs, Summer reading prog, Tax forms, VHS videos, Video lending libr
Mem of Westmoreland County Federated Library System
Open Mon & Wed 10-7, Thurs 4-7, Fri 10-5, Sat 9-4
Friends of the Library Group

HERMITAGE

S MERCER COUNTY REGIONAL PLANNING COMMISSION LIBRARY*, 2491 Highland Rd, 16148. SAN 329-8825. Tel: 724-981-2412. FAX: 724-981-7677. E-mail: mail@mcrpc.com. Web Site: www.mcrpc.com. *Librn,* Dennis G Puko
Library Holdings: Bk Vols 350

HERSHEY

S ANTIQUE AUTOMOBILE CLUB OF AMERICA*, Library & Research Center, 501 W Governor Rd, 17033-2219. (Mail add: PO Box 417, 17033-0417), SAN 325-0377. Tel: 717-534-2082. FAX: 717-534-9101. Web Site: www.aaca.org. *Head Librn,* Chris M Ritter; Staff 4 (MLS 1, Non-MLS 3)
Founded 1977
Library Holdings: Bk Vols 4,000; Per Subs 220
Special Collections: Marmon Coll
Subject Interests: Automotive
Open Mon-Fri 8:30-3:45

M LOIS HIGH BERSTLER COMMUNITY HEALTH LIBRARY*, 35 Hope Dr, HS-07, 17033. Tel: 717-531-4032. FAX: 717-531-5942. E-mail: chil@hmc.psu.edu. Web Site: www.pennstatehershey.org/web/commhealth/home. *Librn,* Patrice Hall; Staff 1 (MLS 1)
Founded 1998
Library Holdings: AV Mats 100; Electronic Media & Resources 4; Bk Vols 1,000; Per Subs 15
Automation Activity & Vendor Info: (Cataloging) Innovative Interfaces, Inc; (Circulation) Innovative Interfaces, Inc; (OPAC) Innovative Interfaces, Inc
Partic in Community Libraries Information Consortium
Open Mon & Wed 9-6, Tues & Thurs 9-7, Fri 9-4

P HERSHEY PUBLIC LIBRARY*, 701 Cocoa Ave, 17033. SAN 314-6170. Tel: 717-533-6555. FAX: 717-534-1666. E-mail: library@derrytownship.org. Web Site: www.hersheylibrary.org. *Dir,* Barbara S Ellis; Tel: 717-533-6555, Ext 3715, E-mail: barbellis@derrytownship.org; *Head, Ref,* Donna Small; E-mail: donnasmall@derrytownship.org; *Coll Develop, Head, Tech Serv,* Barbara Nwoke; E-mail: barbaranwoke@derrytownship.org; *Coordr, Circ,* Chris Gawron; E-mail: chrisgawron@derrytownship.org; *Tech Coordr,* Jeff Cothren; *Children's & Youth Serv,* Rita Hunt Smith; E-mail: ritahuntsmith@derrytownship.org; *ILL,* Denise Phillips; E-mail: denisephillips@derrytownship.org; *Prog & PR Spec,* Julie Brnik; E-mail: jebrnik@derrytownship.org; Staff 23 (MLS 7, Non-MLS 16)
Founded 1913. Pop 21,273; Circ 406,000
Jan 2010-Dec 2010 Income $1,164,682, State $74,716, City $986,102, Locally Generated Income $103,864. Mats Exp $151,454, Books $83,687, Per/Ser (Incl. Access Fees) $15,993, AV Mat $16,468, Electronic Ref Mat (Incl. Access Fees) $23,282, Presv $850. Sal $625,446 (Prof $302,808)
Library Holdings: Bk Vols 77,930; Per Subs 176
Special Collections: Chocolate, Pennsylvania Coll
Automation Activity & Vendor Info: (Circulation) Innovative Interfaces, Inc; (OPAC) Innovative Interfaces, Inc
Database Vendor: Gale Cengage Learning
Wireless access
Partic in Community Libraries Information Consortium; Lyrasis; OCLC Online Computer Library Center, Inc
Open Mon-Thurs 9:30-9, Fri 9:30-6, Sat 9:30-5, Sun 1-5
Friends of the Library Group

CM PENNSYLVANIA STATE UNIVERSITY, COLLEGE OF MEDICINE*, George T Harrell Health Sciences Library, Penn State Hershey, 500 University Dr, 17033. (Mail add: PO Box 850, 17033-0850), SAN 314-6189. Tel: 717-531-8626. Interlibrary Loan Service Tel: 717-531-8633. Reference Tel: 717-531-8634. Administration Tel: 717-531-8631. Information Services Tel: 717-531-8011. FAX: 717-531-8635. Web Site: www.med.psu.edu/library. *Dir,* Cynthia Robinson; Tel: 717-531-8628, Fax: 717-531-8636, E-mail: crobinson1@psu.edu; *Assoc Dir & Coordr of Educ & Instruction,* Nancy Adams; Tel: 717-531-8989, E-mail: nadams@hmc.psu.edu; *Biomedical Info & Emerging Technologies,* Robyn Reed; Tel: 717-531-6137, E-mail: rreed4@hmc.psu.edu; *Coll Access & Support Serv,* Lauren Kime; Tel: 717-531-8640, E-mail: lkime@hmc.psu.edu; *Coll Develop & Digital Res Mgt,* David Brennan; Tel: 717-531-0003, Ext 285323, E-mail: dbrennan@hmc.psu.edu; *ILL, Ref Serv,* Esther Dell; E-mail: eyd1@psu.edu; *Ref & Instruction,* Elaine Dean; Tel: 717-531-8581, E-mail: edean@hmc.psu.edu. Subject Specialists: *Computer tech,* Robyn Reed; *Educ,* David Brennan; Staff 7 (MLS 7)
Founded 1965. Enrl 660; Fac 643; Highest Degree: Doctorate
Jul 2011-Jun 2012. Mats Exp $1,555,527, Books $7,482. Sal $767,561 (Prof $483,240)
Library Holdings: e-journals 12,170; Bk Titles 17,201; Per Subs 12,177
Subject Interests: Bioeng, Biomed sci, Humanities, Med, Med educ, Nursing
Automation Activity & Vendor Info: (Acquisitions) SIRSI WorkFlows; (Cataloging) SIRSI WorkFlows; (Circulation) SIRSI WorkFlows; (OPAC) SirsiDynix
Database Vendor: Agricola, Cambridge Scientific Abstracts, Cinahl, CQ Press, DynaMed, EBSCOhost, Elsevier MDL, Gale Cengage Learning, JSTOR, Lexi-Comp, Medline, Micromedex, OCLC WorldShare Interlibrary Loan, OVID Technologies, Oxford Online, ProQuest, PubMed, Safari Books Online, ScienceDirect, SirsiDynix, UpToDate
Wireless access
Partic in Association of Academic Health Sciences Libraries; Docline; Greater NE Regional Med Libr Program; National Network of Libraries of Medicine; OCLC Online Computer Library Center, Inc
Special Services for the Deaf - Assistive tech
Open Mon-Thurs 8am-Midnight, Fri & Sat 8am-10pm, Sun 10am-Midnight
Restriction: Open to students, fac & staff

HOLLIDAYSBURG

GL BLAIR COUNTY LAW LIBRARY, Blair County Courthouse, Ste 227, 423 Allegheny St, 16648. SAN 314-6197. Tel: 814-693-3090. FAX: 814-693-3289. E-mail: lawlibrary@blairco.org. *Librn,* Lucille H Wolf; Staff 1 (Non-MLS 1)
Founded 1900
Library Holdings: Bk Vols 8,000; Per Subs 20
Special Collections: Law Reviews/Law Journals Coll (From various counties in Pennsylvania, dating back to 1800s), bks
Database Vendor: Westlaw
Open Mon-Fri 8:30-4:30

P HOLIDAYSBURG AREA PUBLIC LIBRARY, One Furnace Rd, 16648-1051. SAN 314-6200. Tel: 814-695-5961. FAX: 814-695-6824. Web Site: www.hollidaysburglibrary.org. *Dir,* Janet Marie Eldred; E-mail: hapldirector@atlanticbb.net; *Libr Serv Mgr,* Crystal Sue Crissman; E-mail: hapldirectorcc@atlanticbbn.net; *Ch Serv,* Melanie Ramsey; Staff 2 (MLS 1, Non-MLS 1)
Founded 1943. Pop 24,291; Circ 72,000
Library Holdings: AV Mats 1,762; DVDs 50; Bk Titles 41,632; Bk Vols 42,000; Per Subs 82; Talking Bks 1,162
Subject Interests: Pa
Automation Activity & Vendor Info: (Cataloging) Follett Software; (Circulation) Follett Software; (OPAC) Follett Software
Mem of Blair County Library System
Open Mon-Thurs 10-8, Fri & Sat 10-5
Friends of the Library Group

HONESDALE

P WAYNE COUNTY PUBLIC LIBRARY*, 1406 N Main St, 18431-2006. SAN 314-6235. Tel: 570-253-1220. FAX: 570-253-1240. Web Site: waynelibraries.org. *Dir,* Molly Rodgers; Staff 2 (MLS 2)
Pop 24,500; Circ 104,000
Library Holdings: AV Mats 3,000; Bks on Deafness & Sign Lang 12; Large Print Bks 3,000; Bk Titles 28,000; Per Subs 95
Automation Activity & Vendor Info: (Cataloging) TLC (The Library Corporation); (Circulation) TLC (The Library Corporation); (OPAC) TLC (The Library Corporation)
Friends of the Library Group

HONEY BROOK

P HONEY BROOK COMMUNITY LIBRARY*, 687 Compass Rd, 19344. (Mail add: PO Box 1082, 19344-1082), SAN 314-6243. Tel: 610-273-3303. FAX: 610-273-9382. Web Site: www.ccls.org/libs/hbrook.htm. *Dir,* Paula McGinness; E-mail: pmcginness@ccls.org; Staff 1 (MLS 1)
Founded 1963. Pop 8,000; Circ 63,974
Library Holdings: AV Mats 3,036; Bks on Deafness & Sign Lang 18; CDs 99; DVDs 34; Large Print Bks 415; Bk Titles 24,085; Per Subs 39; Talking Bks 702; Videos 2,201
Special Collections: Home Schooling Coll
Subject Interests: Local hist
Automation Activity & Vendor Info: (Cataloging) Innovative Interfaces, Inc; (Circulation) Innovative Interfaces, Inc; (ILL) Innovative Interfaces, Inc; (OPAC) Innovative Interfaces, Inc
Mem of Chester County Library System
Open Mon & Wed 10-6, Tues & Thurs 10-8, Fri & Sat 10-5

HORSHAM

P HORSHAM TOWNSHIP LIBRARY, 435 Babylon Rd, 19044-1224. SAN 378-4525. Tel: 215-443-2609. FAX: 215-443-2697. Web Site: www.horshamlibrary.org. *Libr Dir,* Laurie Tynan; Tel: 215-443-2609, Ext 205, E-mail: ltynan@mclinc.org; *Asst Dir/Ref Librn,* Erin Halovanic; Tel: 215-443-2609, Ext 208, E-mail: ehalovanic@mclinc.org; *Ch,* Ellyn Benner; Tel: 215-443-2609, Ext 206, E-mail: ebenner@mclinc.org; *Circ Supvr,*

Stephanie McKenna; Tel: 215-443-2609, Ext 207, E-mail: smckenna@mclinc.org; *Cataloger,* Frances Penner; Tel: 215-443-2609, Ext 211, E-mail: fpenner@mclinc.org; Staff 5 (MLS 4, Non-MLS 1)
Founded 2004. Pop 26,147; Circ 336,377
Jan 2013-Dec 2013 Income $1,122,931, State $72,939, City $999,921, Locally Generated Income $50,071. Mats Exp $129,376, Books $74,306, Per/Ser (Incl. Access Fees) $10,584, AV Mat $14,384, Electronic Ref Mat (Incl. Access Fees) $29,102, Presv $1,000. Sal $381,536 (Prof $216,077)
Library Holdings: Audiobooks 3,515; CDs 2,023; DVDs 5,891; e-books 663; e-journals 110; Bk Vols 98,834; Per Subs 133
Special Collections: Environmental Remediation (Willow Grove Naval Air Station Administrative Records), print & PDF doc
Automation Activity & Vendor Info: (Acquisitions) Innovative Interfaces, Inc; (Cataloging) Innovative Interfaces, Inc; (Circulation) Innovative Interfaces, Inc; (OPAC) Innovative Interfaces, Inc; (Serials) Innovative Interfaces, Inc
Database Vendor: Booklist Online, EBSCOhost, Gale Cengage Learning, Overdrive, Inc, ReferenceUSA, TumbleBookLibrary, World Book Online
Wireless access
Function: 24/7 Online cat, Adult bk club, Art exhibits, Audiobks via web, Bk club(s), Bks on CD, Children's prog, Computers for patron use, Copy machines, Electronic databases & coll, Free DVD rentals, Handicapped accessible, ILL available, Magnifiers for reading, Mango lang, Mus passes, Music CDs, OverDrive digital audio bks, Photocopying/Printing, Prog for adults, Prog for children & young adult, Pub access computers, Story hour, Summer reading prog, Tax forms, Teen prog, Wheelchair accessible
Partic in Montgomery County Library & Information Network Consortium
Open Mon 12:30-9, Tues-Thurs 10-9, Fri 10-6, Sat 10-5
Friends of the Library Group

HOUSTON

P CHARTIERS-HOUSTON COMMUNITY LIBRARY*, 730 W Grant St, 15342. SAN 314-6251. Tel: 724-745-4300. FAX: 724-745-4233. E-mail: chlibrary@comcast.net. Web Site: www.chartiershoustonlibrary.org. *Libr Dir,* Daniel J Burniston; Staff 4 (MLS 1, Non-MLS 3)
Founded 1960. Pop 9,500; Circ 24,822
Library Holdings: Bk Vols 37,717; Per Subs 30
Automation Activity & Vendor Info: (Acquisitions) Follett Software; (Cataloging) Follett Software; (Circulation) Follett Software
Wireless access
Function: Bks on cassette, Bks on CD, Children's prog, Computers for patron use, Copy machines, Electronic databases & coll, Fax serv, Free DVD rentals, Genealogy discussion group, Holiday prog, ILL available, Online ref, Online searches, Photocopying/Printing, Preschool outreach, Prog for adults, Prog for children & young adult, Spoken cassettes & CDs, Spoken cassettes & DVDs, Summer reading prog, Tax forms, VHS videos, Video lending libr, Wheelchair accessible
Publications: On & Off the Shelf
Open Mon-Fri 10-8, Sat 9-4
Friends of the Library Group

HOUTZDALE

S STATE CORRECTIONAL INSTITUTION*, Houtzdale Library, State Rte 2007, 16698. (Mail add: PO Box 1000, 16698-1000). Tel: 814-378-1000, Ext 1556. FAX: 814-378-1030. *Librn,* Roane Lytle
Library Holdings: Per Subs 75
Automation Activity & Vendor Info: (Cataloging) Follett Software; (Circulation) Follett Software
Open Mon-Fri 8:30-11, 1-3:30 & 5:45-8, Sat & Sun 8:30-11 & 1-3:30

HUGHESVILLE

P HUGHESVILLE AREA PUBLIC LIBRARY*, 146 S Fifth St, 17737. SAN 314-626X. Tel: 570-584-3762. FAX: 570-584-2689. E-mail: hapl@jvbrown.edu. Web Site: www.hughesvillelibrary.org. *Librn,* Lena Carichner; *Asst Librn,* Phyllis Stevens; Staff 4 (MLS 1, Non-MLS 3)
Founded 1941. Pop 5,000; Circ 28,000
Library Holdings: Bk Vols 22,000; Per Subs 32
Automation Activity & Vendor Info: (Circulation) SirsiDynix
Database Vendor: EBSCOhost
Wireless access
Mem of Lycoming County Libr Syst
Open Mon, Tues & Thurs 10-8, Fri & Sat 10-5
Friends of the Library Group

HUNLOCK CREEK

S STATE CORRECTIONAL INSTITUTION*, Retreat Library, 660 State Rte 11, 18621. Tel: 570-735-8754, Ext 373. FAX: 570-740-2406. *Librn,* Karen Stroup
Library Holdings: Bk Vols 9,000; Per Subs 25
Automation Activity & Vendor Info: (Cataloging) Follett Software; (Circulation) Follett Software
Open Mon-Sun 9-8:15

HUNTINGDON

P HUNTINGDON COUNTY LIBRARY*, 330 Penn St, 16652-1487. SAN 358-5816. Tel: 814-643-0200. FAX: 814-643-0132. E-mail: library@huntingdon.net. Web Site: www.huntingdon.net/library. *Dir,* Nancy Holland; *Acq,* Linda Swinnerton; Staff 1 (MLS 1)
Founded 1935. Pop 45,600
Library Holdings: DVDs 150; Large Print Bks 2,000; Bk Titles 56,000; Bk Vols 74,437; Per Subs 95; Videos 1,000
Special Collections: State & Local History (Pennsylvania Room)
Automation Activity & Vendor Info: (Cataloging) Follett Software; (Circulation) Follett Software; (OPAC) Follett Software
Open Mon & Thurs 10-8, Tues & Wed 10-6, Fri 10-5, Sat 9-4
Friends of the Library Group
Bookmobiles: 1

C JUNIATA COLLEGE*, Beeghly Library, 1815 Moore St, 16652-2120. SAN 314-6286. Tel: 814-641-3450. FAX: 814-641-3435. Web Site: www.juniata.edu/services/library. *Dir,* John Mumford; Tel: 814-641-3452, E-mail: mumford@juniata.edu; *Asst Dir, Head, Libr Syst & Tech,* Julie Woodling; Tel: 814-641-3454, E-mail: woodling@juniata.edu; *Head, Ref Serv,* Andrew Dudash; Tel: 814-641-3479, E-mail: dudash@juniata.edu; *Circ Supvr, ILL Coordr,* Lynn Jones; Tel: 814-641-3449, E-mail: ljones@juniata.edu; *Coordr, Acq,* Beth Yocum; Tel: 814-641-3455, E-mail: yocum@juniata.edu; *Coordr, Cat,* Patricia Lightner; Tel: 814-641-3458, E-mail: lightner@juniata.edu; *Col Archivist,* Janice Hartman; Tel: 814-641-5315, E-mail: hartmaj@juniata.edu; Staff 8.5 (MLS 4, Non-MLS 4.5)
Founded 1876. Enrl 1,450; Fac 90; Highest Degree: Bachelor
Library Holdings: Bk Titles 140,000; Bk Vols 200,000; Per Subs 1,000
Special Collections: Church of the Brethren (College Archives), bks, ms; Early Pennsylvania German Imprints (Abraham Harley Cassel Coll), bks & pamphlets; Pennsylvania Folklore (Henry W Shoemaker Coll); Snow Hill Coll
Automation Activity & Vendor Info: (Acquisitions) SirsiDynix; (Cataloging) SirsiDynix; (Circulation) SirsiDynix; (Course Reserve) SirsiDynix; (ILL) SirsiDynix; (Media Booking) SirsiDynix; (OPAC) SirsiDynix; (Serials) SirsiDynix
Database Vendor: SirsiDynix
Wireless access
Partic in Associated College Libraries of Central Pennsylvania; Dialog Corp; Lyrasis; OCLC Online Computer Library Center, Inc; Pennsylvania Academic Library Consortium, Inc (PALCI)
Friends of the Library Group

S STATE CORRECTIONAL INSTITUTION*, Smithfield Library, 1120 Pike St, 16652. (Mail add: PO Box 999, 16652-0999). Tel: 814-643-6520. FAX: 814-506-1022. *Librn,* Renee Lubert
Library Holdings: Bk Vols 19,000; Per Subs 58

S SWIGART MUSEUM LIBRARY*, Museum Park, Rte 22 E, 16652. (Mail add: PO Box 214, 16652-0214), SAN 327-6201. Tel: 814-643-0885. FAX: 814-643-2857. E-mail: tours@swigartmuseum.com. *Pres,* Patricia B Swigart
Library Holdings: Bk Titles 1,000
Restriction: Open by appt only

HUNTINGDON VALLEY

P HUNTINGDON VALLEY LIBRARY*, 625 Red Lion Rd, 19006-6297. SAN 314-6294. Tel: 215-947-5138. FAX: 215-938-5894. Web Site: www.hvlibrary.org. *Dir,* Sharon Moreland-Sender; *Youth Serv,* Alice Turman; Staff 8 (MLS 2, Non-MLS 6)
Founded 1953. Pop 13,000
Jan 2007-Dec 2007 Income $750,000
Library Holdings: Bk Vols 90,000; Per Subs 115
Automation Activity & Vendor Info: (Cataloging) Innovative Interfaces, Inc; (Circulation) Innovative Interfaces, Inc; (ILL) Innovative Interfaces, Inc; (OPAC) Innovative Interfaces, Inc
Database Vendor: EBSCOhost, Gale Cengage Learning, Newsbank, ReferenceUSA
Wireless access
Function: Adult literacy prog, Audio & video playback equip for onsite use, AV serv, Handicapped accessible, Health sci info serv, Homebound delivery serv, ILL available, Online searches, Photocopying/Printing, Prog for adults, Prog for children & young adult, Ref serv available, Summer reading prog, Telephone ref, Wheelchair accessible, Workshops
Publications: Huntingdon Valley Library (Newsletter)
Partic in Montgomery County Library & Information Network Consortium
Special Services for the Deaf - Bks on deafness & sign lang
Special Services for the Blind - Audio mat; Bks on cassette; Bks on CD; Large print bks; Reader equip; Ref serv; Talking bks; Videos on blindness & phys handicaps

Open Mon-Thurs 10-9, Fri & Sat 10-5
Friends of the Library Group

HYDE PARK

P HYDE PARK PUBLIC LIBRARY*, 700 Main St, 15641. (Mail add: PO Box 162, 15641-0162). Tel: 724-845-1944. *Pres,* Holly Tusing; E-mail: tholl@comcast.net; Staff 1 (Non-MLS 1)
Founded 1976. Pop 540; Circ 2,120
Library Holdings: Bk Titles 3,178; Bk Vols 3,391; Per Subs 23
Mem of Westmoreland County Federated Library System
Open Mon 5:30-7:30

HYNDMAN

P HYNDMAN LONDONDERRY PUBLIC LIBRARY*, 161 Clarence St, 15545. (Mail add: PO Box 733, 15545-0733), SAN 376-5733. Tel: 814-842-3782. FAX: 814-842-3737. E-mail: info@hyndmanlibrary.org. Web Site: www.hyndmanlibrary.org. *Dir,* Mary Ellis; E-mail: marye@hyndmanlibrary.org; *Asst Librn,* Polly Groves; Staff 2 (Non-MLS 2)
Founded 1991. Pop 2,902; Circ 4,278
Library Holdings: Bk Titles 13,084; Bk Vols 13,575; Per Subs 10; Talking Bks 235; Videos 1,227
Automation Activity & Vendor Info: (Cataloging) Follett Software
Wireless access
Function: CD-ROM, Copy machines, E-Reserves, Fax serv, Handicapped accessible, ILL available, Photocopying/Printing, Spoken cassettes & CDs, Spoken cassettes & DVDs, Summer reading prog, Tax forms, VHS videos, Wheelchair accessible
Mem of Bedford County Library System
Partic in Pennsylvania Library Association
Open Mon-Thurs 1-7, Fri 1-5

IMMACULATA

C IMMACULATA UNIVERSITY*, Gabriele Library, 1145 King Rd, 19345-0705. SAN 314-6308. Tel: 610-647-4400, Ext 3839. Reference Tel: 610-647-4400, Ext 3829. FAX: 610-640-5828. Web Site: library.immaculata.edu. *Dir,* Jeff Rollison; Tel: 610-647-4400, Ext 3841, E-mail: jrollison@immaculata.edu; *Archivist,* Sister Marita David Kirsch; Tel: 610-647-4400, Ext 3828, E-mail: mkirsch@immaculata.edu; *ILL,* Sister Alice Schaebler; Tel: 610-647-4400, Ext 3838, E-mail: aschaebler@immaculata.edu; *Ref,* Carol Howe; Tel: 610-647-4400, Ext 3832, E-mail: chowe@immaculata.edu; *Ref,* Janice Wilson; Tel: 610-647-4400, Ext 3831, E-mail: jwilson@immaculata.edu; *Ser,* Marguerite Buck; Tel: 610-647-4400, Ext 3833, E-mail: mbuck@immaculata.edu; Staff 17 (MLS 5, Non-MLS 12)
Founded 1920. Enrl 1,599; Fac 88; Highest Degree: Doctorate
Library Holdings: Bk Titles 138,416; Bk Vols 141,910; Per Subs 755; Videos 504
Special Collections: Dietetics; Spanish American & Chicano Literature Coll
Automation Activity & Vendor Info: (Acquisitions) SirsiDynix; (Cataloging) SirsiDynix; (Circulation) SirsiDynix; (Course Reserve) SirsiDynix; (OPAC) SirsiDynix; (Serials) Sydney
Database Vendor: EBSCOhost, LexisNexis, OCLC FirstSearch, OVID Technologies
Function: Res libr
Publications: The Gabriele Herald (Newsletter)
Partic in Consortium for Health Information & Library Services; OCLC Online Computer Library Center, Inc; Southeastern Pa Consortium for Higher Educ; Tri-State College Library Cooperative
Open Mon-Thurs 8:30am-11pm, Fri 8:30-5, Sat 10-5, Sun Noon-11
Restriction: In-house use for visitors

SR SISTERS, SERVANTS OF THE IMMACULATE HEART OF MARY ARCHIVES*, Villa Maria House of Studies, 1140 King Rd, 19345. (Mail add: PO Box 200, 19345-0200), SAN 375-6408. Tel: 610-647-2160. Reference Tel: 610-647-2160, Ext 522. FAX: 610-889-4874. *Archivist,* Sister M St Michel Mullany; E-mail: sstmmullany@yahoo.com; *Asst Archivist,* Sister Francis Bernard Butt
Library Holdings: Bk Titles 1,000
Wireless access

INDIANA

S HISTORICAL & GENEALOGICAL SOCIETY OF INDIANA COUNTY*, 621 Wayne Ave, 15701-3042. (Mail add: Silas M Clark House, 200 S 6th St, 15701), SAN 326-9302. Tel: 724-463-9600. FAX: 724-463-9899. E-mail: ichistoricalsociety@gmail.com. Web Site: www.rootsweb.com/~paicgs. *Exec Dir,* Coleen Chambers
Founded 1939
Library Holdings: Bk Titles 5,000; Bk Vols 8,000; Spec Interest Per Sub 200
Special Collections: Cecil Smith Coll, bks mss; Frances Strong Helman Coll, bks, mss
Subject Interests: Antiques, Genealogy, Local hist, Pa hist, State hist
Automation Activity & Vendor Info: (Acquisitions) EOS International; (Cataloging) EOS International; (OPAC) EOS International; (Serials) EOS International
Publications: Newsletter (Monthly)
Restriction: In-house use for visitors, Non-circulating coll

GL INDIANA COUNTY LAW LIBRARY*, County Court House, 825 Philadelphia St, 15701. SAN 314-6316. Tel: 724-465-3956. FAX: 724-465-3152. *Admin Librn,* Robin Orr; Staff 1 (Non-MLS 1)
Library Holdings: Bk Titles 15,612; Bk Vols 17,080; Per Subs 135
Open Mon-Fri 8:30-12 & 1-4
Restriction: Non-circulating to the pub

P INDIANA FREE LIBRARY, INC*, 845 Philadelphia St, 15701-3908. SAN 320-8516. Tel: 724-465-8841. FAX: 724-465-9902. Web Site: www.indianafreelibrary.org. *Dir,* Kate Geiger; E-mail: publib.kate@gmail.com; *Circ Librn,* John Swanson; *Ch Serv,* Joanne Mast; *Youth Serv,* Lauri Steffy
Founded 1934. Pop 32,118; Circ 139,684
Library Holdings: Bk Vols 88,000; Per Subs 123
Wireless access
Special Services for the Blind - Computer with voice synthesizer for visually impaired persons
Open Mon & Wed 10-9, Tues & Thurs 10-6, Fri & Sat 10-5
Friends of the Library Group

M INDIANA REGIONAL MEDICAL CENTER*, Learning Resources Center, 835 Hospital Rd, 15701. (Mail add: PO Box 788, 15701-0788), SAN 314-6332. Tel: 724-357-7055. FAX: 724-357-7094. Web Site: www.indianarmc.org. *Librn,* James Kinneer; Staff 1 (Non-MLS 1)
Library Holdings: e-journals 12; Bk Vols 360; Per Subs 40
Partic in Laurel Highlands Health Science Library Consortium
Restriction: Non-circulating to the pub

C INDIANA UNIVERSITY OF PENNSYLVANIA*, Stapleton Library, 431 S 11th St, Rm 203, 15705-1096. SAN 358-5905. Tel: 724-357-2330. Circulation Tel: 724-357-2340. Reference Tel: 724-357-3006. FAX: 724-357-4891. Web Site: www.iup.edu/library. *Dean, Univ Libr,* Luis Gonzalez; E-mail: lgonzal@iup.edu; *Asst Dean of Libr, Assessment & Develop,* Kate E Jenkins; E-mail: kjenkins@iup.edu; *Asst Dean of Libr, Syst & Tech,* D Edward Zimmerman; E-mail: edzimmer@iup.edu; *Acq/Ser Librn,* Jin Ping; E-mail: jinpang@iup.edu; *Coll Develop/E-Res Librn,* Joann C Janosko; E-mail: janosko@iup.edu; *Govt Info/Ref Librn,* Theresa R McDivitt; E-mail: mcdivitt@iup.edu; *Pub Serv Librn,* Blaine E Knupp; Tel: 724-357-2338, E-mail: beknupp@iup.edu; *Bibliographer, Ref Librn,* Carol E Connell; E-mail: cconnell@iup.edu; *Ref Librn,* Sandra L Janicki; E-mail: cspslj@iup.edu; *Spec Coll Librn, Univ Archivist,* Harrison Wick; Tel: 724-357-3039, E-mail: hwick@iup.edu; Staff 36 (MLS 15, Non-MLS 21)
Founded 1875. Enrl 13,020; Fac 763; Highest Degree: Doctorate
Library Holdings: AV Mats 50,000; Bk Titles 582,453; Bk Vols 800,000; Per Subs 16,000
Special Collections: Charles Darwin Coll; Herman Melville Coll; James Abbott McNeill Whistler Coll; John Greenleaf Whittier Coll; Nathaniel Hawthorne Coll; Norman Mailer Coll; Regional Coal & Steel Labor & Industrial Archives. State Document Depository; US Document Depository
Subject Interests: Educ, Liberal arts
Automation Activity & Vendor Info: (Acquisitions) Ex Libris Group; (Cataloging) Ex Libris Group; (Circulation) Ex Libris Group; (Course Reserve) Docutek; (ILL) OCLC; (Media Booking) Ex Libris Group; (OPAC) Ex Libris Group; (Serials) Ex Libris Group
Database Vendor: EBSCOhost, LexisNexis, OCLC FirstSearch, OVID Technologies
Wireless access
Publications: Monumentae: A Union List of Music Monuments in Pennsylvania Chapter, Music Library Assn
Partic in Keystone Library Network; Pennsylvania Academic Library Consortium, Inc (PALCI)
Open Mon-Thurs 7:45am-12:45am, Fri 7:45-7, Sat 11-5
Friends of the Library Group

Departmental Libraries:

NORTHPOINTE REGIONAL CAMPUS LIBRARY, Academic Bldg, 167 Northpointe Blvd, Freeport, 16229, SAN 314-6634. Tel: 724-294-3300. FAX: 724-294-3307. *Libr Supvr,* William Daugherty; E-mail: william.daugherty@iup.edu; *Librn,* Portia Diaz; E-mail: portia@iup.edu; Staff 4 (MLS 1, Non-MLS 3)
Founded 1962. Enrl 180; Fac 23; Highest Degree: Master
Library Holdings: e-books 16,020; e-journals 14,858; Bk Vols 5,000; Per Subs 10; Videos 231

HAROLD S ORENDORFF LIBRARY, 101 Cogswell Hall, 422 S 11th St, 15705-1071, SAN 358-5921. Tel: 724-357-2892. Circulation Tel: 724-357-3058. FAX: 724-357-4891. Web Site: www.lib.iup.edu/depts/musiclib/music.html. *Librn,* Dr Carl Rahkonen;

Tel: 724-357-5644, E-mail: rahkonen@iup.edu; *Tech Serv,* Terice McFerron; Staff 2 (MLS 1, Non-MLS 1)
Founded 1969
Library Holdings: Bk Titles 43,610; Bk Vols 45,811; Per Subs 56; Videos 391
Automation Activity & Vendor Info: (Cataloging) Ex Libris Group; (Circulation) Ex Libris Group
Partic in Pennsylvania Academic Library Consortium, Inc (PALCI)
Open Mon, Wed & Thurs 8-8, Tues 8am-10pm, Sun 8-4:30

PUNXSUTAWNEY CAMPUS LIBRARY, 1012 Winslow St, Punxsutawney, 15767, SAN 315-1425. Tel: 814-938-4870. FAX: 814-938-5900. *Tech Serv,* Carol Asamoah; E-mail: carasam@iup.edu
Founded 1962. Enrl 250
Library Holdings: Bk Titles 18,000; Bk Vols 19,842; Per Subs 82; Videos 742
Automation Activity & Vendor Info: (Acquisitions) Ex Libris Group; (Cataloging) Ex Libris Group; (Circulation) Ex Libris Group; (OPAC) Ex Libris Group; (Serials) Ex Libris Group
Partic in Center for Research Libraries; OCLC Online Computer Library Center, Inc
Open Mon-Thurs 8am-10:30pm, Fri 8-4, Sat 10-5, Sun 6pm-10:30pm

S STATE CORRECTIONAL INSTITUTION*, Pine Grove Library, 189 Fryock Rd, 15701. Tel: 724-465-9630. FAX: 724-464-5135. *Dir, Libr Serv,* Katherine Manners; E-mail: kmanners@pa.gov; Staff 2 (MLS 1, Non-MLS 1)
Library Holdings: Bk Vols 6,300; Per Subs 100
Automation Activity & Vendor Info: (Cataloging) Follett Software; (Circulation) Follett Software
Open Mon & Sun 12:15-7:45, Tues-Thurs 8:15-7:45, Fri 8:15-8:15

INTERCOURSE

P PEQUEA VALLEY PUBLIC LIBRARY*, 31 Center St, 17534. (Mail add: PO Box 617, 17534-0617). Tel: 717-768-3160. FAX: 717-768-3888. Web Site: www.pvpl.org/pequeavalley/site/default.asp. *Dir,* Margaret Perella; E-mail: director@pvpl.org
Founded 1975. Pop 19,588
Library Holdings: AV Mats 1,172; Bk Vols 16,793; Per Subs 92; Videos 505
Automation Activity & Vendor Info: (Cataloging) Innovative Interfaces, Inc; (Circulation) Innovative Interfaces, Inc; (OPAC) Innovative Interfaces, Inc
Wireless access
Mem of Library System of Lancaster County
Open Mon-Thurs 11-8, Fri 11-5, Sat 8-3 (8-12 Summer)

IRWIN

P NORWIN PUBLIC LIBRARY ASSOCIATION INC*, 100 Caruthers Ln, 15642. SAN 358-5964. Tel: 724-863-4700. Circulation Tel: 724-863-4700, Ext 103. Interlibrary Loan Service Tel: 724-863-4700, Ext 104. FAX: 724-863-6195. Web Site: norwinlibrary.nb.net, www.norwinpubliclibrary.org. *Dir,* Falk Diana; *Asst Dir,* Bill Mausteller; *Ch Serv,* Barbara Flynn; *Mat,* Brian Kissler; *ILL,* Krista Brown; Staff 4 (MLS 3, Non-MLS 1)
Founded 1937. Pop 40,363; Circ 117,291
Library Holdings: Bk Vols 61,000; Per Subs 55
Special Collections: Standard-Observer (local newspaper)
Database Vendor: LearningExpress
Publications: Online Serials Database Full Text
Mem of Westmoreland County Federated Library System
Open Mon-Thurs 10-8, Fri & Sat 10-5
Friends of the Library Group

JEANNETTE

P JEANNETTE PUBLIC LIBRARY ASSOCIATION*, 500 Magee Ave, 15644-3416. SAN 314-6359. Tel: 724-523-5702. FAX: 724-523-2357. E-mail: jeannettepl@hotmail.com. Web Site: www.jeannettepubliclibrary.com, www.jeannettepubliclibrary.org. *Dir,* Hope Sehring; *Asst Librn,* Ann Porreca; Staff 10 (MLS 1, Non-MLS 9)
Founded 1932. Pop 15,413; Circ 36,478
Jan 2008-Dec 2008 Income $178,708, State $64,520, City $15,000, County $3,935, Locally Generated Income $60,000, Parent Institution $33,253, Other $2,000. Mats Exp $31,232, Books $20,053, Per/Ser (Incl. Access Fees) $4,654, AV Equip $1,686, AV Mat $4,654, Electronic Ref Mat (Incl. Access Fees) $185. Sal $96,786 (Prof $29,550)
Library Holdings: Audiobooks 739; AV Mats 5,936; Bks on Deafness & Sign Lang 13; CDs 1,117; DVDs 1,391; Electronic Media & Resources 3; High Interest/Low Vocabulary Bk Vols 25; Large Print Bks 407; Bk Titles 37,533; Bk Vols 37,735; Per Subs 110; Spec Interest Per Sub 50; Talking Bks 25; Videos 2,620
Special Collections: Jeannette Coll, artifacts, historic doc
Subject Interests: Glass industry, Local hist
Automation Activity & Vendor Info: (Acquisitions) Innovative Interfaces, Inc; (Cataloging) Innovative Interfaces, Inc; (Circulation) Innovative Interfaces, Inc; (Course Reserve) Innovative Interfaces, Inc; (ILL) Innovative Interfaces, Inc; (OPAC) Innovative Interfaces, Inc
Wireless access
Function: Adult literacy prog, Archival coll, Art exhibits, Bk club(s), Bks on CD, Children's prog, Computer training, Computers for patron use, Copy machines, e-mail serv, ILL available, Music CDs, Online cat, Online ref, Online searches, Photocopying/Printing, Preschool outreach, Prog for children & young adult, Ref & res, Senior computer classes, Summer reading prog, Tax forms, Telephone ref, VHS videos
Mem of Westmoreland County Federated Library System
Partic in HSLC/Access PA/POWER Library; Share Westmoreland Consortium; WIN Library Network
Special Services for the Deaf - Bks on deafness & sign lang
Special Services for the Blind - Bks on CD
Open Mon-Fri 12-7, Sat 10-5
Friends of the Library Group

JEFFERSON HILLS

P JEFFERSON HILLS LIBRARY*, 925 Old Clairton Rd, 15025-3158. SAN 314-4097. Tel: 412-655-7741. FAX: 412-655-4003. Web Site: www.jeffersonhillslibrary.org. *Dir, Tech Coordr,* Jan Reschenthaler; E-mail: reschenthalerj@einetwork.net; Staff 11 (MLS 1, Non-MLS 10)
Founded 1959. Pop 9,666
Library Holdings: Bk Vols 36,000; Per Subs 50
Automation Activity & Vendor Info: (Circulation) Innovative Interfaces, Inc
Wireless access
Mem of Allegheny County Library Association
Open Mon-Thurs 10-8:30, Sat 10-3, Sun 1-4
Friends of the Library Group

JENKINTOWN

S GRA INC LIBRARY*, 115 West Ave, Ste 201, 19046. SAN 314-6383. Tel: 215-884-7500. FAX: 215-884-1385. Web Site: www.gra-inc.com. *Ref Librn,* Gail Kostinko; Staff 1 (MLS 1)
Founded 1975
Library Holdings: Bk Titles 8,500; Per Subs 115
Special Collections: US Airline Annual Reports
Subject Interests: Aviation, Econ analysis, Regulatory analysis, Transportation
Automation Activity & Vendor Info: (Cataloging) Inmagic, Inc.
Restriction: Pub ref by request, Staff use only

R GRACE PRESBYTERIAN CHURCH*, Cecil Harding Jones Library, 444 Old York Rd, 19046. SAN 314-6391. Tel: 215-887-6117. FAX: 215-887-5724. Web Site: www.gracejenkintown.org. *Librn,* Mary Parker; Staff 1 (Non-MLS 1)
Founded 1952
Library Holdings: Bk Titles 3,560; Bk Vols 4,100; Per Subs 19
Special Collections: Bibles; Religious Art
Subject Interests: Children's bks, Christian educ, Current soc problems, Ecology, Meditation & pvt relig, Travel
Open Mon-Fri 8:30-4

P JENKINTOWN LIBRARY, 460 Old York Rd, 19046-2829. SAN 314-6405. Tel: 215-884-0593. FAX: 215-884-2243. *Dir,* Rosalind Lubeck; *Acq,* Edith Prout; *ILL,* Bonnie Miller; Staff 8 (MLS 1, Non-MLS 7)
Founded 1803. Pop 4,422; Circ 65,000
Automation Activity & Vendor Info: (Acquisitions) Innovative Interfaces, Inc; (Cataloging) Innovative Interfaces, Inc; (Circulation) Innovative Interfaces, Inc; (ILL) Innovative Interfaces, Inc; (OPAC) Innovative Interfaces, Inc; (Serials) Innovative Interfaces, Inc
Wireless access
Function: Bk club(s), Bks on cassette, Bks on CD, Children's prog, Computer training, Computers for patron use, Copy machines, Fax serv, Free DVD rentals, Handicapped accessible, Holiday prog, ILL available, Mus passes, Music CDs, Online cat, OverDrive digital audio bks, Passport agency, Photocopying/Printing, Preschool outreach, Preschool reading prog, Prog for adults, Prog for children & young adult, Pub access computers, Ref & res, Story hour, Summer & winter reading prog, Tax forms, Teen prog, Wheelchair accessible
Partic in Montgomery County Library & Information Network Consortium
Open Mon-Thurs 10-9, Fri & Sat 10-5

J MANOR COLLEGE*, Basileiad Library, 700 Fox Chase Rd, 19046-3399. SAN 314-6413. Tel: 215-885-2360. Circulation Tel: 215-885-2360, Ext 238. Reference Tel: 215-885-2360, Ext 240. FAX: 215-576-6564. E-mail: basileiad@manor.edu. Web Site: library.manor.edu. *Dir,* Beth Lander; E-mail: blander@manor.edu; Staff 4 (MLS 2, Non-MLS 2)
Founded 1947. Enrl 700; Highest Degree: Associate

Jul 2006-Jun 2007 Income $119,372. Mats Exp $32,000, Books $10,000, Per/Ser (Incl. Access Fees) $8,500, AV Equip $1,000, Electronic Ref Mat (Incl. Access Fees) $12,500. Sal $76,972
Library Holdings: AV Mats 800; e-books 1,500; High Interest/Low Vocabulary Bk Vols 200; Bk Vols 40,000; Per Subs 85
Special Collections: Civil War Coll; Ukrainian Coll
Automation Activity & Vendor Info: (Cataloging) OCLC Online; (Circulation) Follett Software; (OPAC) Follett Software; (Serials) EBSCO Online
Database Vendor: EBSCOhost
Wireless access
Open Mon-Thurs 8am-9:30pm, Fri 8-5, Sat 10-2

JERSEY SHORE

P JERSEY SHORE PUBLIC LIBRARY*, 110 Oliver St, 17740. SAN 314-6421. Tel: 570-398-9891. FAX: 570-398-9897. E-mail: jspl@jvbrown.edu. Web Site: www.jerseyshorepubliclibrary.org. *Dir,* Charlene Brungard; Staff 6 (MLS 1, Non-MLS 5)
Founded 1950. Pop 6,115
Library Holdings: Bk Vols 13,634; Per Subs 30
Wireless access
Mem of Lycoming County Libr Syst
Open Mon & Fri 9-5, Tues-Thurs 9-8, Sat 9-4
Friends of the Library Group

JIM THORPE

GL CARBON COUNTY LAW LIBRARY*, Carbon County Courthouse, Four Broadway, 2nd Flr, 18229. (Mail add: PO Box 207, 18229-0207), SAN 314-643X. Tel: 570-325-3111. FAX: 570-325-9449. Web Site: www.carboncourts.com.
Open Mon-Fri 8:30-4:30

P DIMMICK MEMORIAL LIBRARY*, 54 Broadway, 18229-2022. SAN 314-6448. Tel: 570-325-2131. FAX: 570-325-9339. E-mail: thorpepl@ptd.net. Web Site: www.dimmicklibrary.org. *Dir,* Susan Sterling; Staff 4 (MLS 1, Non-MLS 3)
Founded 1889. Pop 14,000; Circ 23,182
Jan 2006-Dec 2006 Income $260,056. Mats Exp $23,741. Sal $79,167
Library Holdings: Bks on Deafness & Sign Lang 15; Large Print Bks 22; Bk Titles 20,000; Bk Vols 22,000; Per Subs 60; Talking Bks 436
Special Collections: Census Coll, 1780-, microfilm; Firemen Materials; Local Genealogies; Local History Books; Local Newspapers, microfilm
Subject Interests: Census, Genealogy, Local hist, Mining, Railroads
Automation Activity & Vendor Info: (Cataloging) TLC (The Library Corporation); (Circulation) TLC (The Library Corporation); (OPAC) TLC (The Library Corporation)
Database Vendor: EBSCOhost, TLC (The Library Corporation)
Wireless access
Function: ILL available, Mail & tel request accepted, Photocopying/Printing, Prog for children & young adult, Ref serv available, Summer reading prog, Telephone ref
Open Mon-Wed & Fri (Winter) 9-5, Thurs 11-7, Sat 9-4; Mon-Wed & Fri (Summer) 9-5, Thurs 11-7, Sat 9-1
Friends of the Library Group

JOHNSONBURG

P JOHNSONBURG PUBLIC LIBRARY*, 520 Market St, 15845-0240. SAN 314-6456. Tel: 814-965-4110. FAX: 814-965-3320. E-mail: jburglib@windstream.net. Web Site: www.johnsonburglibrary.org. *Dir,* Melinda Lewis; Staff 1 (Non-MLS 1)
Founded 1939. Pop 3,003; Circ 22,000
Library Holdings: AV Mats 600; Bks on Deafness & Sign Lang 10; Large Print Bks 130; Bk Vols 18,000; Per Subs 51; Talking Bks 250
Subject Interests: Genealogy, Local hist, Pa hist
Automation Activity & Vendor Info: (Cataloging) Follett Software; (Circulation) Follett Software; (OPAC) Follett Software
Open Mon & Fri 11-5, Tues, Wed & Thurs 11-7, Sat 9-4

JOHNSTOWN

P CAMBRIA COUNTY LIBRARY SYSTEM & DISTRICT CENTER*, 248 Main St, 15901. SAN 358-6022. Tel: 814-536-5131. Reference Tel: 814-536-5131, Ext 210. FAX: 814-536-6905. Interlibrary Loan Service FAX: 814-535-4140. E-mail: campub@cclsys.org. Reference E-mail: reference@cclsys.org. Web Site: www.cclsys.org. *Dir,* Lyn Meek; E-mail: meekl@cclsys.org; *Head, Ch,* Becky Pollino; E-mail: pollinor@cclsys.org; *Head, Circ,* Dolores Berg; E-mail: bergd@cclsys.org; *Head, Ref,* Christine Goch; E-mail: gochcl@cclsys.org; *Network Adminr,* Joel Koss; E-mail: koss@cclsys.org; Staff 7 (MLS 7)
Founded 1870. Pop 111,715; Circ 161,745
Library Holdings: AV Mats 4,332; Bk Vols 146,304; Per Subs 176; Talking Bks 2,633
Special Collections: State Document Depository; US Document Depository
Automation Activity & Vendor Info: (Cataloging) Innovative Interfaces, Inc; (Circulation) Innovative Interfaces, Inc; (OPAC) Innovative Interfaces, Inc
Wireless access
Member Libraries: Carrolltown Public Library; Cresson Public Library; Ebensburg Cambria Public Library; Gallitzin Public Library; Hastings Public Library; Highland Community Library; Lilly-Washington Public Library; Mary S Biesecker Public Library; Nanty Glo Public Library; Northern Cambria Public Library; Patton Public Library; Portage Public Library; South Fork Public Library
Partic in OCLC Online Computer Library Center, Inc
Open Mon & Tues 8-8, Wed & Thurs 8-6, Fri & Sat 9-4
Friends of the Library Group

C CAMBRIA-ROWE BUSINESS COLLEGE*, Resource Center, 221 Central Ave, 15902. Tel: 814-536-5168. FAX: 814-536-5160. Web Site: www.crbc.edu. *Dir of Educ,* Jonathan Wolf; Staff 2 (Non-MLS 2)
Library Holdings: Bk Titles 341; Bk Vols 500; Per Subs 50
Open Mon-Thurs 8-4

M CONEMAUGH MEMORIAL MEDICAL CENTER*, Health Sciences Library, 1086 Franklin St, 15905-4398. SAN 314-6472. Tel: 814-534-5960, 814-534-9111. Circulation Tel: 814-534-9411. Interlibrary Loan Service Tel: 814-534-9636. Reference Tel: 814-534-9413. FAX: 814-534-3244. Web Site: www.conemaugh.org. *ILL, Librn,* Kris Kalina; E-mail: kkalina@conemaugh.org; *Libr Asst,* Stephanie Porter; E-mail: sporter@conemaugh.org; Staff 2 (MLS 1, Non-MLS 1)
Automation Activity & Vendor Info: (Cataloging) Marcive, Inc; (Circulation) Follett Software; (OPAC) Follett Software
Database Vendor: EBSCOhost, McGraw-Hill, MD Consult, OVID Technologies, TDNet, UpToDate
Wireless access
Partic in Central Pennsylvania Health Sciences Library Association; Medical Library Association (MLA)
Open Mon-Fri 6:30-4

R FIRST LUTHERAN CHURCH*, Walden M Holl Parish Library, 415 Vine St, 15901. SAN 314-6480. Tel: 814-536-7521. FAX: 814-536-0855. *Librn,* Carol S Massingill; Staff 2 (MLS 1, Non-MLS 1)
Founded 1954
Library Holdings: Bk Vols 5,032; Per Subs 2
Open Mon-Fri 9-3, Sun 9-12

P HIGHLAND COMMUNITY LIBRARY, 330 Schoolhouse Rd, 15904-2924. SAN 314-6499. Tel: 814-266-5610. FAX: 814-262-0130. E-mail: highland@cclsys.org. Web Site: www.cclsys.org/highland.
Founded 1962. Pop 15,153; Circ 67,862
Library Holdings: Bk Titles 30,000; Per Subs 75
Automation Activity & Vendor Info: (Cataloging) Evergreen
Mem of Cambria County Library System & District Center
Friends of the Library Group

J PENNSYLVANIA HIGHLANDS COMMUNITY COLLEGE LIBRARY*, 101 Community College Way, 15904. SAN 375-4413. Tel: 814-262-6458. FAX: 814-269-9744. E-mail: library@pennhighlands.edu. Web Site: www.pennhighlands.edu. *Assoc Dean,* Dr Barbara A Zaborowski; Tel: 814-262-6425, E-mail: bzabor@pennhighlands.edu; *Info Literacy & eLearning Librn,* Alexander Kirby; Tel: 814-262-6484, E-mail: akirby@pennhighlands.edu. Subject Specialists: *Hist,* Alexander Kirby; Staff 2 (MLS 2)
Founded 1994. Enrl 1,565; Fac 22; Highest Degree: Associate
Jul 2009-Jun 2010. Mats Exp $144,600, Books $60,760, Per/Ser (Incl. Access Fees) $8,000, Electronic Ref Mat (Incl. Access Fees) $75,840. Sal $137,015 (Prof $101,580)
Library Holdings: Bk Titles 10,952; Bk Vols 12,289; Per Subs 104
Special Collections: Greater Johnstown Genealogy Coll
Automation Activity & Vendor Info: (Acquisitions) Follett Software; (Cataloging) Follett Software; (Circulation) Follett Software; (ILL) OCLC FirstSearch; (OPAC) Follett Software
Database Vendor: EBSCOhost, Gale Cengage Learning, LexisNexis, ProQuest, Wilson - Wilson Web
Partic in HSLC/Access PA/POWER Library; Pennsylvania Community College Library Consortium (PCCLC)
Open Mon-Thurs 8am-9pm, Fri 8-4, Sat 10-4

C UNIVERSITY OF PITTSBURGH, JOHNSTOWN CAMPUS*, Owen Library, 450 Schoolhouse Rd, 15904. SAN 314-6537. Tel: 814-269-7300. Interlibrary Loan Service Tel: 814-269-7292. Reference Tel: 814-269-7295. Administration Tel: 814-269-7289. FAX: 814-269-7286. Administration FAX: 814-269-7283. Web Site: www.library.pitt.edu/johnstown. *Dir,* Deborah Rinderknecht; Tel: 814-269-7288, E-mail: drinderk@pitt.edu; *Access Serv Librn,* David Kupas; Tel: 814-269-1983, E-mail:

dmk24@pitt.edu; *Coll Mgt Librn,* Patricia Balko; Tel: 814-269-7290, E-mail: balko@pitt.edu; *Ref Librn,* James Langan; E-mail: jlangan@pitt.edu; *Coordr, Libr Instruction,* Paul Bond; Tel: 814-269-7287, E-mail: paulbond@pitt.edu; Staff 9 (MLS 5, Non-MLS 4)
Founded 1927. Enrl 3,134; Fac 136; Highest Degree: Bachelor
Library Holdings: AV Mats 656; Bk Vols 151,322; Per Subs 360
Automation Activity & Vendor Info: (Acquisitions) Ex Libris Group; (Cataloging) Ex Libris Group; (Circulation) Ex Libris Group; (Course Reserve) Ex Libris Group; (ILL) Ex Libris Group; (Media Booking) Ex Libris Group; (OPAC) Ex Libris Group; (Serials) Ex Libris Group
Wireless access
Partic in OCLC Online Computer Library Center, Inc; Pennsylvania Academic Library Consortium, Inc (PALCI); Pittcat
Open Mon-Thurs (Sept-May) 8am-10:30pm, Fri 8-5, Sat 10-6, Sun 2-10:30; Mon-Thurs (June-Aug) 8-6, Fri 8-5

KANE

P FRIENDS MEMORIAL PUBLIC LIBRARY*, 230 Chase St, 16735. SAN 358-612X. Tel: 814-837-7010. FAX: 814-837-7010. E-mail: friendslibrarykanepa@gmail.com. Web Site: www.friendslibrary.org/. *Dir,* Cindy Parker
Library Holdings: Bk Vols 14,000; Per Subs 40
Automation Activity & Vendor Info: (Circulation) Follett Software
Open Tues 10-2 & 5-7, Wed 10-5, Thurs 12-7, Sat 9-3

KENNETT SQUARE

S LONGWOOD GARDENS LIBRARY*, 409 Conservatory Rd, 19348-1805. (Mail add: PO Box 501, 19348-0501), SAN 314-6545. Tel: 610-388-1000, Ext 510. FAX: 610-388-2078. E-mail: library@longwoodgardens.org. *Librn,* Venice Bayrd. Subject Specialists: *Hort,* Venice Bayrd; Staff 3 (MLS 1, Non-MLS 2)
Founded 1960
Library Holdings: Bk Vols 25,000; Per Subs 350; Videos 300
Special Collections: Rare Books
Subject Interests: Botany, Hort, Landscape archit
Automation Activity & Vendor Info: (Acquisitions) EOS International; (Cataloging) EOS International; (Circulation) EOS International; (Course Reserve) EOS International; (ILL) OCLC FirstSearch; (OPAC) EOS International; (Serials) EOS International
Database Vendor: EOS International, OCLC FirstSearch
Function: ILL available, Photocopying/Printing
Partic in Council on Botanical & Horticultural Libraries, Inc (CBHL); Lyrasis
Open Mon-Fri 8-5
Restriction: Circulates for staff only, Co libr, In-house use for visitors, Lending libr only via mail, Open to pub for ref only

P BAYARD TAYLOR MEMORIAL LIBRARY*, 216 E State St, 19348-3112. (Mail add: PO Box 730, 19348-0730), SAN 314-6553. Tel: 610-444-2702. Interlibrary Loan Service Tel: 610-444-2988. FAX: 610-444-1752. Web Site: www.bayardtaylor.org. *Dir,* Donna L Murray; E-mail: dmurray@ccls.org; *ILL,* Ana M Feliciano; *Tech Serv,* Michael R Cooney; Staff 8 (MLS 2, Non-MLS 6)
Founded 1895. Pop 24,611; Circ 138,130
Library Holdings: AV Mats 4,394; CDs 278; Large Print Bks 235; Bk Titles 46,955; Bk Vols 51,444; Per Subs 161; Talking Bks 992; Videos 490
Special Collections: Antiques (Harlan R Cole Coll); Literature (Bayard Taylor Coll); Local History (Chester County)
Subject Interests: Antiques, Archit, Art, Environ studies, Hist, Hort
Automation Activity & Vendor Info: (Cataloging) Innovative Interfaces, Inc; (Circulation) Innovative Interfaces, Inc
Wireless access
Publications: Views a-Foot
Mem of Chester County Library System
Open Mon-Thurs 9-8, Fri 9-5, Sat 9-4

KING OF PRUSSIA

G UNITED STATES NATIONAL PARK SERVICE, Horace Wilcox Memorial Library at Valley Forge National Historical Park, 151 Library Lane, 19406. (Mail add: Valley Forge National Historical Park, 1400 N Outer Line Dr, 19406-1000), SAN 375-2011. Tel: 610-296-2593. Administration Tel: 610-783-1034. Administration FAX: 610-783-1060. Web Site: www.nps.gov/vafo. *Archivist,* Dona M McDermott; E-mail: dona_mcdermott@nps.gov. Subject Specialists: *Am Revolution,* Dona M McDermott; Staff 1 (Non-MLS 1)
Library Holdings: Bk Vols 8,700; Per Subs 25
Subject Interests: Am Revolution
Function: For res purposes
Restriction: Open by appt only, Ref only to non-staff

P UPPER MERION TOWNSHIP LIBRARY*, 175 W Valley Forge Rd, 19406-2399. SAN 314-6596. Tel: 610-265-1196. Circulation Tel: 610-265-4805. FAX: 610-265-3398. E-mail: uppermerionlibrary@mclinc.org. Web Site: www.umtownship.org/library/index.html. *Dir,* Karl Helicher; Tel: 610-205-8548, E-mail: khelicher@mclinc.org; Staff 18 (MLS 6, Non-MLS 12)
Founded 1963. Pop 27,000; Circ 189,000
Library Holdings: Bk Vols 100,000; Per Subs 180
Special Collections: Oral History
Automation Activity & Vendor Info: (Circulation) Innovative Interfaces, Inc; (OPAC) Innovative Interfaces, Inc
Publications: Township Lines (Newsletter)
Partic in Montgomery County Library & Information Network Consortium
Open Mon-Thurs 9-9, Sat 10-5
Friends of the Library Group

KINGSTON

L HOURIGAN, KLUGER & QUINN*, Law Library, 600 Third Ave, 18704-5815. SAN 372-1833. Tel: 570-287-3000. Toll Free Tel: 800-760-1529. FAX: 570-287-8005. E-mail: hkq@hkqpc.com. Web Site: www.hkqpc.com. *Librn,* Michael J Reilly
Library Holdings: Bk Vols 9,000; Per Subs 50
Restriction: Staff use only

P HOYT LIBRARY*, 284 Wyoming Ave, 18704-3597. SAN 314-660X. Tel: 570-287-2013. FAX: 570-283-2081. E-mail: hoytlib@ptd.net. Web Site: www.hoytlibrary.org. *Exec Dir,* Melissa A Szafran; E-mail: mszafran@osterhout.lib.pa.us; *Circ Coordr,* Jessica Fountain; *Youth Serv Coordr,* Maryann Hovan; *Cat,* Carrie Murray; *Info Serv,* Diane Rebar; Staff 1 (MLS 1)
Founded 1928. Pop 33,309; Circ 121,661
Library Holdings: Audiobooks 3,659; DVDs 1,691; Bk Vols 62,451; Per Subs 144
Special Collections: Early Americana (William Brewster Coll), bks, maps; Holocaust (Reuben Levy Coll); Jewish History (Levison Coll)
Database Vendor: EBSCOhost
Wireless access
Mem of Luzerne County Library System
Open Mon & Thurs 1-8, Tues, Wed & Fri 9-5, Sat 9-4
Friends of the Library Group

R WYOMING SEMINARY*, Kirby Library, 201 N Sprague Ave, 18704-3593. SAN 314-6626. Tel: 570-270-2169. FAX: 570-270-2178. Web Site: www.youseemore.com/wyomingseminary/kirby. *Dir of Libr,* Courtney Lewis; E-mail: clewis@wyomingseminary.org; *Upper Sch Librn,* Ivy Miller; Tel: 570-270-2168, E-mail: imiller@wyomingseminary.org
Library Holdings: Bk Vols 20,000; Per Subs 125
Automation Activity & Vendor Info: (Acquisitions) TLC (The Library Corporation); (Cataloging) TLC (The Library Corporation); (Circulation) TLC (The Library Corporation); (Course Reserve) TLC (The Library Corporation); (ILL) TLC (The Library Corporation); (OPAC) TLC (The Library Corporation)
Database Vendor: Discovery Education, Facts on File, Gale Cengage Learning, Greenwood Publishing Group, ProQuest, TLC (The Library Corporation)
Wireless access
Function: ILL available
Restriction: Not open to pub
Friends of the Library Group

KITTANNING

P KITTANNING PUBLIC LIBRARY*, 280 N Jefferson, 16201. SAN 314-6642. Tel: 724-543-1383. FAX: 724-543-1621. E-mail: kittanninglibrary@hotmail.com. Web Site: www.armstronglibraries.org/kittanning.php. *Dir,* Amanda Gearhart; Staff 1 (MLS 1)
Founded 1923. Pop 5,432; Circ 63,750
Library Holdings: AV Mats 175; High Interest/Low Vocabulary Bk Vols 30; Large Print Bks 1,000; Bk Titles 30,000; Per Subs 75; Talking Bks 600
Special Collections: County Histories Coll (including Allegheny, Armstrong, Butler, Clarion, Clearfield, Indiana, Jefferson, Washington & Westmoreland); Family Histories Coll (including Adams, Anderson, Barrackman, Bowser, Booth, Boyer, Claypool, Corbett, Hawk, Lookabaugh, McCullough, Marshall, Minteer, Oblinger, Ralston, Schall, Shellhamer & Wolfe); Kittanning & Armstrong County Notebooks Coll; Newspaper Coll (Armstrong Democrat 1828-1841 & Kittanning Gazette 1825-1833)
Partic in Midwest Libr Consortium
Special Services for the Blind - BiFolkal kits
Open Mon-Wed 12-7, Thurs & Fri 10-5, Sat 9-4
Friends of the Library Group

KNOX

P KNOX PUBLIC LIBRARY*, 620 S Main St, 16232. (Mail add: PO Box 510, 16232-0510), SAN 314-6650. Tel: 814-797-1054. FAX: 814-797-1054. E-mail: knoxpl@windstream.net. *Dir,* Roxanne J Miller; *Ch,* Erin Lloyd; Staff 3 (MLS 1, Non-MLS 2)
Founded 1935. Pop 7,589; Circ 23,500
Library Holdings: AV Mats 2,697; CDs 190; DVDs 60; Large Print Bks 340; Bk Titles 20,947; Per Subs 46; Videos 560
Automation Activity & Vendor Info: (Cataloging) Follett Software; (Circulation) Follett Software; (OPAC) Follett Software
Function: Bks on CD, Children's prog, Computers for patron use, Copy machines, Fax serv, Handicapped accessible, ILL available, Music CDs, Online cat, Prog for children & young adult, Pub access computers, Ref serv available, Story hour, Summer reading prog, Tax forms, VHS videos
Mem of Oil Creek District Library Center
Partic in HSLC/Access PA/POWER Library
Special Services for the Deaf - Closed caption videos
Special Services for the Blind - BiFolkal kits; Bks on cassette; Bks on CD; Large print bks; Magnifiers
Open Mon, Tues & Thurs 9:30-8, Fri & Sat 9:30-2

KNOXVILLE

P KNOXVILLE PUBLIC LIBRARY, 112 E Main St, 16928. (Mail add: PO Box 277, 16928-0277), SAN 314-6669. Tel: 814-326-4448. E-mail: kpblibrary@gmail.com. Web Site: www.knoxvillepubliclibrary.com. *Librn,* Ellen Williams; *Asst Librn,* Debby Berdanier
Founded 1921. Pop 1,668; Circ 7,649
Jan 2007-Dec 2007 Income $29,599. Mats Exp $5,921. Sal $13,876
Library Holdings: AV Mats 790; Bk Vols 11,570; Per Subs 36
Subject Interests: Genealogy, State hist
Wireless access
Mem of Potter-Tioga Library System
Open Mon 9-8:30, Wed 9-6:30, Fri 9-6, Sat 11-4

KUTZTOWN

P KUTZTOWN COMMUNITY LIBRARY*, 70 Bieber Alley, 19530-1113. SAN 314-6677. Tel: 610-683-5820. FAX: 610-683-8155. E-mail: kutztownpl@berks.lib.pa.us. Web Site: www.berks.lib.pa.us/louisagonsercl. *Dir,* Janet Yost; *Youth Serv Librn,* Lisa Nuss; E-mail: skuchild@berks.lib.pa.us; Staff 1 (MLS 1)
Founded 1949. Pop 16,000; Circ 28,000
Library Holdings: Bk Vols 27,000; Per Subs 20
Subject Interests: City hist, County hist, Quilting, Quilts
Wireless access
Function: Summer reading prog, Tax forms, VHS videos, Wheelchair accessible
Mem of Berks County Public Libraries
Restriction: Authorized patrons
Friends of the Library Group

C KUTZTOWN UNIVERSITY*, Rohrbach Library, 15200 Kutztown Rd, Bldg 5, 19530-0735. SAN 314-6685. Tel: 610-683-4484. Circulation Tel: 610-683-4480. Interlibrary Loan Service Tel: 610-683-4158. Reference Tel: 610-683-4165. FAX: 610-683-4747. Web Site: www.kutztown.edu/library/home.html. *Dean, Libr Serv,* Position Currently Open; *Ref Librn,* Sylvia Pham; E-mail: spham@kutztown.edu; *Info Literacy, Ref Librn,* Krista Prock; E-mail: prock@kutztown.edu; *Syst Coordr,* Bruce Gottschall; E-mail: gottscha@kutztown.edu; *Access Serv, Distance Educ, Univ Archivist,* Susan Czerny; E-mail: czerny@kutztown.edu; *Cat,* Michael Weber; E-mail: weber@kutztown.edu; *Curric Mats Ctr,* Karen Wanamaker; *Electronic Res, ILL, Per,* Bob Flatley; E-mail: flatley@kutztown.edu; *Info Commons/Voices & Choices Ctr,* R Bruce Jensen; E-mail: rjenson@kutztown.edu; *Info Literacy, Ref,* Ruth Perkins; E-mail: perkins@kutztown.edu; *Tech Serv,* Stephanie Steely; E-mail: steely@kutztown.edu; Staff 25 (MLS 11, Non-MLS 14)
Founded 1866. Enrl 10,200; Fac 401; Highest Degree: Master
Library Holdings: Bks on Deafness & Sign Lang 112; CDs 181; e-journals 80,000; Large Print Bks 388; Bk Vols 517,000; Per Subs 795
Special Collections: Library Science Coll, bks & per; Pennsylvania Coll, bks, per & micro
Subject Interests: Art, Educ, Hist
Automation Activity & Vendor Info: (Acquisitions) Ex Libris Group; (Cataloging) Ex Libris Group; (Circulation) Ex Libris Group; (Course Reserve) Docutek; (ILL) OCLC ILLiad; (OPAC) Ex Libris Group; (Serials) Ex Libris Group
Database Vendor: ABC-CLIO, ACM (Association for Computing Machinery), American Chemical Society, Annual Reviews, ARTstor, ASCE Research Library, Baker & Taylor, BioOne, Blackwell, Bloomberg, Booklist Online, Bowker, Brodart, Children's Literature Comprehensive Database Company (CLCD), CountryWatch, CQ Press, Dialog, Dun & Bradstreet, Ebooks Corporation, ebrary, EBSCO - WebFeat, EBSCOhost, Elsevier, Emerald, Ex Libris Group, Facts on File, JSTOR, LexisNexis, Marquis Who's Who, McGraw-Hill, Medline, Mergent Online, Newsbank, OCLC, OCLC ArticleFirst, OCLC FirstSearch, Project MUSE, ProQuest, ReferenceUSA, RefWorks, Safari Books Online, Sage, ScienceDirect, SerialsSolutions, Springshare, LLC, Thomson - Web of Science, ValueLine, WebMD, Wilson - Wilson Web
Wireless access
Publications: Rohrbach Library Newsletter
Partic in Associated College Libraries of Central Pennsylvania; Interlibrary Delivery Service of Pennsylvania; Pennsylvania Academic Library Consortium, Inc (PALCI); State System of Higher Education Library Cooperative
Special Services for the Deaf - TTY equip
Special Services for the Blind - Reader equip
Open Mon-Thurs 7:45-Midnight, Fri 7:45-5, Sat 9-5, Sun 2-Midnight

S PENNSYLVANIA GERMAN HERITAGE LIBRARY*, 22 Luckenbill Rd, 19530. SAN 326-1050. Tel: 484-646-4165. E-mail: pagermanlibrary@kutztown.edu. Web Site: www.kutztown.edu/community/pgchc/lib.htm, www.kutztown.edu/hcl. *Exec Dir,* Dr Robert Reynolds; Fax: 610-683-4638, E-mail: reynolds@kutztown.edu; *Librn,* Lucy Kern
Founded 1998
Library Holdings: Bk Titles 7,500
Special Collections: Pennsylvania German Society Publications; Yoder Coll
Subject Interests: Folklore, Genealogy, Local hist
Function: Res libr
Open Mon-Fri 10-12 & 1-4

LA PLUME

C KEYSTONE COLLEGE*, Miller Library, One College Green, 18440-0200. SAN 314-6707. Tel: 570-945-8332. Circulation Tel: 570-945-8335. Interlibrary Loan Service Tel: 570-945-3333. FAX: 570-945-8969. E-mail: millerlibrary@keystone.edu. Web Site: www.keystone.edu. *Dir,* Mari Flynn; E-mail: mari.flynn@keystone.edu; *Access & Ser Librn,* Paula Yunko; *Ref & Tech Librn,* Bill Zeranski; *ILL,* Carole Green; *Res & Instrul Serv Librn,* Ann Patrick; Staff 11 (MLS 1, Non-MLS 10)
Founded 1934. Enrl 1,660; Fac 250; Highest Degree: Bachelor
Library Holdings: Bk Vols 42,400; Per Subs 283
Special Collections: Local History (Christy Mathewson Coll)
Automation Activity & Vendor Info: (Acquisitions) TLC (The Library Corporation); (Cataloging) OCLC Online; (Circulation) TLC (The Library Corporation); (OPAC) TLC (The Library Corporation)
Publications: Library Guides
Partic in Northeastern Pennsylvania Library Network; OCLC Online Computer Library Center, Inc
Open Mon-Thurs 7:30am-10pm, Fri 7:30-5, Sat 12-5

LACEYVILLE

P LACEYVILLE PUBLIC LIBRARY*, W Main St, 18623. (Mail add: PO Box 68, 18623-0068), SAN 314-6715. Tel: 570-869-1958. *Librn,* Mary Tyler
Circ 5,751
Library Holdings: Bk Vols 8,000; Per Subs 10
Open Mon 3-6, Tues 1-5, Thurs 10-5, Fri 4-7, Sat 9-12
Friends of the Library Group

LAFAYETTE HILL

P WILLIAM JEANES MEMORIAL LIBRARY*, 4051 Joshua Rd, 19444-1400. SAN 314-6723. Tel: 610-828-0441. FAX: 610-828-4049. Web Site: wjl.mclinc.org. *Dir,* Sheila Mikkelson; E-mail: smikkelson@mclinc.org; *Asst Ch,* Linda Poland; E-mail: lpoland@mclinc.org; *Circ Mgr,* Crommarty Cecelia; E-mail: ccrommarty@mclinc.org; *Teen Prog Coordr,* Kate DiGiacomo; E-mail: kdigiacomo@mclinc.org; *Cataloger, Vols Serv Coordr,* Lucille Leap; E-mail: lleap@mclinc.org; *Adult Serv, Ref,* Robyn Train; E-mail: rtrain@mclinc.org; *Cataloger,* Meredith Brunel; E-mail: mbrunel@mclinc.org; *Ch Serv,* Beth Hargis; E-mail: bhargis@mclinc.org; Staff 15 (MLS 3, Non-MLS 12)
Founded 1933. Pop 16,700; Circ 145,000
Library Holdings: Bk Titles 51,000; Per Subs 210
Subject Interests: Quaker hist
Automation Activity & Vendor Info: (Cataloging) Innovative Interfaces, Inc; (Circulation) Innovative Interfaces, Inc; (OPAC) Innovative Interfaces, Inc
Database Vendor: EBSCOhost
Wireless access
Function: Bks on CD, Children's prog, E-Reserves, Electronic databases & coll, Free DVD rentals, Handicapped accessible, ILL available, Mail & tel request accepted, Mus passes, Music CDs, Online cat, Online ref, Online searches, OverDrive digital audio bks, Photocopying/Printing, Preschool outreach, Prog for adults, Prog for children & young adult, Pub access

computers, Ref serv in person, Spoken cassettes & CDs, Story hour, Summer reading prog, Tax forms, Teen prog, Video lending libr, Web-catalog, Wheelchair accessible
Partic in Montgomery County Library & Information Network Consortium
Open Mon 12-9, Tues-Thurs 10-9, Fri & Sat 10-5, Sun 1-5
Friends of the Library Group

LAKEWOOD

P NORTHERN WAYNE COMMUNITY LIBRARY*, 11 Library Rd, 18439. Tel: 570-798-2444. FAX: 570-798-2444. E-mail: nwcl@nep.net. Web Site: www.waynelibraries.org/northernwayne.
Library Holdings: Bks on Deafness & Sign Lang 12; Bk Vols 14,000; Per Subs 35
Automation Activity & Vendor Info: (Cataloging) TLC (The Library Corporation); (Circulation) TLC (The Library Corporation); (OPAC) TLC (The Library Corporation)
Open Tues & Thurs 8:30-6, Wed 6pm-9pm, Fri 9-6, Sat 9-4

LANCASTER

R THE EVANGELICAL & REFORMED HISTORICAL SOCIETY, 555 W James St, 17603. SAN 314-6758. Tel: 717-290-8734. E-mail: erhs@lancasterseminary.edu. Web Site: www.erhs.info. *Archivist,* Phillip B Anglin; E-mail: panglin@lancasterseminary.edu; *Archives Asst,* Jennifer Groff; Staff 1.25 (MLS 1.25)
Founded 1863
Library Holdings: Bk Titles 7,000
Special Collections: Colonial Coll; Congregations (German Reformed) in Pennsylvania & Surrounding States, church recs; History (William J Hinke Manuscript Coll); Mercersburg Theology Coll; Missionary History (German Reformed Church Manuscript Coll), ms, off doc; Missions (A R Bartholomew Coll); US Church Records of the Reformed Church, the Evangelical & Reformed Church
Function: 24/7 Online cat, Archival coll, Exhibits
Publications: Evangelical & Reformed Historical Society (Newsletter)
Restriction: Non-circulating coll

SR FIRST BAPTIST CHURCH LIBRARY*, 612 N Duke St, 17602. SAN 326-3509. Tel: 717-392-8818. FAX: 717-392-2182. *Librn,* Sally Perry; Staff 1 (Non-MLS 1)
Library Holdings: Bk Titles 1,276; Bk Vols 1,509; Per Subs 29
Special Collections: Church Archives, membership lists & minutes
Subject Interests: Relig
Open Mon-Fri 9-2

C FRANKLIN & MARSHALL COLLEGE*, Shadek-Fackenthal Library, 450 College Ave, 17603-3318. (Mail add: PO Box 3003, 17603-3003), SAN 358-626X. Tel: 717-291-4223. Interlibrary Loan Service Tel: 717-291-4224. Reference Tel: 717-291-4217. FAX: 717-291-4160. Web Site: library.fandm.edu. *Dir,* Pamela Snelson; Tel: 717-291-3896, E-mail: pamela.snelson@fandm.edu; *Coordr,* Linda M Danner; Tel: 717-291-4216, E-mail: linda.danner@fandm.edu; *Syst Coordr,* Denise Chmielewski; Tel: 717-358-7192, E-mail: denise.chmielewsk@fandm.edu; *Acq,* Martin Gordon; Tel: 717-291-3842, E-mail: marty.gordon@fandm.edu; *Cat,* Renate Sachse; Tel: 717-399-4435, E-mail: renate.sachse@fandm.edu; *Coll Develop,* Thomas A Karel; Tel: 717-291-3845, E-mail: tom.karel@fandm.edu; *Electronic Serv,* Andrew Gulati; Tel: 717-291-4261, E-mail: andy.gulati@fandm.edu; *Info Literacy,* Lisa Stillwell; Tel: 717-291-3844, E-mail: lisa.stillwell@fandm.edu; *Ref Serv,* Scott Vine; Tel: 717-291-3840, E-mail: scott.vine@fandm.edu; *Spec Coll & Archives Librn,* Christopher Raab; Tel: 717-291-4225, E-mail: christopher.raab@fandm.edu; *Visual Res,* Louise A Kulp; Tel: 717-291-4242, E-mail: louise.kulp@fandm.edu. Subject Specialists: *Art,* Louise A Kulp; Staff 26 (MLS 10, Non-MLS 16)
Founded 1787. Enrl 2,005; Fac 199; Highest Degree: Bachelor
Library Holdings: AV Mats 5,651; CDs 2,671; Bk Titles 491,089; Bk Vols 501,611; Per Subs 2,025; Videos 4,033
Special Collections: German Language Books in America (German American Imprint Coll); Lincoln (W W Griest Coll), photog; Theatre Arts (Anne Figgat Coll); Theatre Memorabilia (Alexander Corbett Coll), photog. US Document Depository
Automation Activity & Vendor Info: (Acquisitions) SirsiDynix; (Cataloging) SirsiDynix; (Circulation) SirsiDynix; (ILL) SirsiDynix; (OPAC) SirsiDynix; (Serials) SirsiDynix
Database Vendor: Dialog, EBSCOhost, OCLC FirstSearch, OVID Technologies, ProQuest, Wilson - Wilson Web
Function: Archival coll
Partic in Associated College Libraries of Central Pennsylvania; Interlibrary Delivery Service of Pennsylvania; OCLC Online Computer Library Center, Inc; Pennsylvania Academic Library Consortium, Inc (PALCI)
Open Mon-Thurs 8am-Midnight, Fri 8am-10pm, Sat 11-10, Sun 11am-2am
Friends of the Library Group

Departmental Libraries:
MARTIN LIBRARY OF THE SCIENCES, PO Box 3003, 17604-3003, SAN 370-7075. Tel: 717-291-3843. FAX: 717-291-4088. *Dir,* Pamela Snelson; Tel: 717-291-3896, E-mail: psnelson@fandm.edu; *Sci Librn,* Dale Riordan; E-mail: driordan@fandm.edu; Staff 3 (MLS 1, Non-MLS 2)
Founded 1991
Library Holdings: Bk Titles 33,652; Bk Vols 35,091; Per Subs 109; Videos 52
Subject Interests: Astronomy, Biol, Chem, Computer sci, Geol, Physics, Psychol
Open Mon-Thurs 8-2, Fri 8am-Midnight, Sat 9am-Midnight, Sun 11-2
Friends of the Library Group

J HARRISBURG AREA COMMUNITY COLLEGE*, D&E Library Lancaster Campus, 1641 Old Philadelphia Pike, 17602. Tel: 717-358-2986. Interlibrary Loan Service Tel: 717-780-2623. FAX: 717-358-2952. E-mail: lanclibrary@hacc.edu. Web Site: lib2.hacc.edu. *Dir,* Joseph V McIlhenney; Tel: 717-358-2222, E-mail: jvmcilhe@hacc.edu; *Fac Librn,* Lisa J Weigard; Tel: 717-358-2226, E-mail: ejweigar@hacc.edu; *Adjunct Fac Librn,* Andrea J Chemero; E-mail: achemero@hacc.edu; *Adjunct Fac Librn,* Allyson F Dawson-Valentine; E-mail: afdawson@hacc.edu; *Adjunct Fac Librn,* Kathleen Dragann; E-mail: kmdragan@hacc.edu; *Adjunct Fac Librn,* Sayre Turney; E-mail: sgturney@hacc.edu; *Libr Spec,* Janice Hackman; E-mail: jmhackma@hacc.edu; *Libr Spec,* Bernadette Lynch; E-mail: blynch@hacc.edu; *Libr Tech,* Melissa Farr; E-mail: mfarr@hacc.edu; Staff 8 (MLS 5.5, Non-MLS 2.5)
Founded 1989. Enrl 21,000; Fac 273; Highest Degree: Associate
Library Holdings: AV Mats 898; Bks on Deafness & Sign Lang 43; Large Print Bks 14; Bk Titles 16,754; Bk Vols 28,199; Per Subs 115
Automation Activity & Vendor Info: (Acquisitions) SirsiDynix; (Cataloging) SirsiDynix; (Circulation) SirsiDynix; (Course Reserve) Docutek; (ILL) SirsiDynix; (Media Booking) SirsiDynix; (OPAC) SirsiDynix; (Serials) SirsiDynix
Database Vendor: EBSCOhost, Gale Cengage Learning, LexisNexis, ProQuest, Wilson - Wilson Web
Wireless access
Partic in Interlibrary Delivery Service of Pennsylvania
Open Mon-Thurs (Winter) 7:30am-9:30pm, Fri 7:30-4, Sat 8-2, Sun 12:30-6; Mon-Thurs (Summer) 7:30am-9:30pm
Restriction: Non-circulating to the pub

CR LANCASTER BIBLE COLLEGE*, Charles & Gloria Jones Library, Teague Learning Commons, 901 Eden Rd, 17601-5036. SAN 314-6766. Tel: 717-560-8250. Circulation E-mail: circdesk@lbc.edu. Web Site: www.lbc.edu/community/library/index. *Tech Dir,* Gerald Lincoln; Tel: 717-569-7071, Ext 5362, E-mail: glincoln@lbc.edu; *Assoc Libr Dir,* Deb Hunt; Tel: 717-569-7071, Ext 5349, E-mail: dhunt@lbc.edu; *Head, Tech Serv,* Jocelyn Abel; Tel: 717-569-7071, Ext 5361, E-mail: jabel@lbc.edu; *Ref Librn,* Randall Dick; Tel: 717-569-7071, Ext 5412, E-mail: rdick@lbc.edu; *Acq Asst,* Lisa Swarr; Tel: 717-569-7071, Ext 5385, E-mail: lswarr@lbc.edu; *Circ Asst,* Bethany Fethkenher; Tel: 717-569-7071, Ext 5311, E-mail: bfethkenher@lbc.edu; Staff 6 (MLS 4, Non-MLS 2)
Founded 1933. Enrl 1,525; Fac 58; Highest Degree: Doctorate
Library Holdings: e-books 190,000; e-journals 50,000; Bk Vols 203,000; Per Subs 388
Special Collections: LBC Coll; Lloyd M Perry Coll (Pastoral Theology)
Subject Interests: Bible, Christian educ, Missions, Music, Theol
Automation Activity & Vendor Info: (Acquisitions) Ex Libris Group; (Cataloging) Ex Libris Group; (Circulation) Ex Libris Group; (OPAC) Ex Libris Group; (Serials) Ex Libris Group
Database Vendor: Alexander Street Press, BCR: Christian Periodical Index, CountryWatch, CredoReference, ebrary, EBSCO Discovery Service, EBSCOhost, Facts on File, Gale Cengage Learning, H W Wilson, LexisNexis, Medline, OCLC FirstSearch, OCLC WorldShare Interlibrary Loan, ProQuest, Sage, Wilson - Wilson Web
Wireless access
Partic in Lyrasis; OCLC Online Computer Library Center, Inc; Southeastern Pennsylvania Theological Library Association
Open Mon-Thurs 7am-12am, Fri 7am-10pm, Sat 8-8, Sun 2-12
Restriction: Fee for pub use

S LANCASTER COUNTY HISTORICAL SOCIETY*, James Buchanan Foundation for the Preservation of Wheatland Library, 230 N President Ave, 17603-3125. Tel: 717-392-4633. Web Site: www.lancasterhistory.org. *Dir of Libr Serv,* Marjorie R Bardeen; Tel: 717-392-4633, Ext 119; *Libr Asst,* Linda Stienstra; Tel: 717-392-4633, Ext 111
Library Holdings: Bk Vols 175

GL LANCASTER COUNTY LAW LIBRARY*, 50 N Duke St, 17602. (Mail add: PO Box 83480, 17608-3480), SAN 314-6790. Tel: 717-299-8090. FAX: 717-295-2509. Web Site: www.co.lancaster.pa.us/lawlibrary. *Librn,* Eleanor Gerlott; E-mail: gerlott@co.lancaster.pa.us; Staff 1 (MLS 1)
Founded 1867
Library Holdings: Bk Vols 27,000; Per Subs 25

Open Mon-Fri 8:30-5
Restriction: Non-circulating to the pub

S LANCASTER COUNTY PRISON LIBRARY*, 625 E King St, 17602-3199. Tel: 717-299-7814. Web Site: www.co.lancaster.pa.us. *Coordr,* Dan Brazill; Staff 1 (Non-MLS 1)
Library Holdings: Bk Titles 2,159; Bk Vols 2,308; Per Subs 16
Branches:
LAW, 625 E King St, 17602-3199. Tel: 717-299-7814. *Coordr,* Tom Romanowski; Staff 1 (Non-MLS 1)
Library Holdings: Bk Titles 362; Bk Vols 910; Per Subs 10
Open Mon-Fri 9-5

S LANCASTER COUNTY'S HISTORICAL SOCIETY LIBRARY*, 230 N President Ave, 17603-3125. SAN 314-6782. Tel: 717-392-4633. E-mail: reference@lancasterhistory.org. Web Site: www.lancasterhistory.org. *Dir of Libr Serv,* Marjorie R Bardeen; E-mail: marjorie.bardeen@lancasterhistory.org; Staff 4 (MLS 1, Non-MLS 3)
Founded 1886
Library Holdings: Microforms 3,000; Bk Titles 15,000; Per Subs 35
Special Collections: 18th & 19th Century Law Library (Judge Jasper Yeates Coll); Lancaster County Archives-Legal Records, 1729-1929, ms; Lancaster History Coll, ms
Subject Interests: Genealogy, Lancaster County, Pa hist
Automation Activity & Vendor Info: (Cataloging) Ex Libris Group; (OPAC) Ex Libris Group; (Serials) Ex Libris Group
Database Vendor: OCLC, ProQuest
Wireless access
Function: Archival coll, ILL available, Online cat, Photocopying/Printing, Prog for adults, Ref serv available, Web-catalog, Wheelchair accessible
Publications: Journal of Lancaster County's Historical Society (Quarterly); The Historian (Newsletter)
Open Mon, Wed & Fri 9:30-5, Tues & Thurs 9:30-8
Restriction: In-house use for visitors, Non-circulating

S LANCASTER MENNONITE HISTORICAL SOCIETY LIBRARY, 2215 Millstream Rd, 17602-1499. SAN 314-6812. Tel: 717-393-9745. FAX: 717-393-8751. E-mail: library@lmhs.org.
Founded 1958
Library Holdings: Bk Titles 32,953; Per Subs 256
Subject Interests: Amish, Hist, Lancaster County, Mennonites
Automation Activity & Vendor Info: (Cataloging) Follett Software; (Circulation) Follett Software; (OPAC) Follett Software
Database Vendor: ProQuest
Wireless access
Open Tues-Sat 8:30-4:30

P LANCASTER PUBLIC LIBRARY, 125 N Duke St, 17602-2883. SAN 358-6324. Tel: 717-394-2651. FAX: 717-394-3083. E-mail: admin@lancaster.lib.pa.us. Web Site: www.lancaster.lib.pa.us. *Exec Dir,* Herbert B Landau; E-mail: hlandau@lancaster.lib.pa.us; *Dep Dir,* Joyce Sands; Tel: 717-396-9313, Ext 110, Fax: 717-606-4599, E-mail: jsands@lancaster.lib.pa.us; *Dir, Finance & Fac,* Cindy Farley; Tel: 717-394-2651, Ext 130, E-mail: cfarley@lancaster.lib.pa.us; *Circ Mgr,* Katharine M Leader; Tel: 717-394-2651, Ext 102, Fax: 717-394-2651, E-mail: kleader@lancaster.lib.pa.us; *Commun Relations Mgr,* Heather Sharpe; Tel: 717-394-2651, Ext 119, E-mail: hsharpe@lancaster.lib.pa.us; *Mgr, Vols Serv,* Anna Thomas; Tel: 717-394-2651, Ext 273, E-mail: athomas@lancaster.lib.pa.us; *Supvr, Coll Develop,* Karin Rezendes; E-mail: krezendes@lancaster.lib.pa.us
Founded 1759. Pop 221,485; Circ 864,259
Library Holdings: AV Mats 29,190; Bk Vols 249,313; Per Subs 176
Special Collections: Oral History; State Document Depository
Subject Interests: Health, Local hist, Popular lit, Wellness
Wireless access
Mem of Library System of Lancaster County
Partic in OCLC Online Computer Library Center, Inc
Special Services for the Blind - ABE/GED & braille classes for the visually impaired & print handicapped
Open Mon-Thurs 10-8, Fri & Sat 10-5
Friends of the Library Group
Branches: 2
LANCASTER PUBLIC LIBRARY EAST - LEOLA BRANCH, 46 Hillcrest Ave, Leola, 17540, SAN 358-6413. Tel: 717-656-7920. *Br Mgr,* Corinne Brumbach; E-mail: cbrumbach@lancaster.lib.pa.us
Founded 1976. Circ 72,054
Library Holdings: Bk Vols 23,635; Per Subs 11
Friends of the Library Group
LANCASTER PUBLIC LIBRARY WEST - MOUNTVILLE BRANCH, 120 College Ave, Mountville, 17554, SAN 358-6472. Tel: 717-285-3231. *Br Mgr,* Lissa Holland; E-mail: lholland@lancaster.lib.pa.us
Founded 1963. Circ 157,210
Library Holdings: Bk Vols 31,498; Per Subs 9
Friends of the Library Group

R LANCASTER THEOLOGICAL SEMINARY, Schaff Library, 555 W James St, 17603-9967. SAN 314-6839. Tel: 717-290-8707. Interlibrary Loan Service Tel: 717-290-8742. FAX: 717-393-4254. E-mail: library@lancasterseminary.edu. Web Site: www.lancasterseminary.edu/library. *Librn,* Myka Kennedy Stephens; Tel: 717-290-8704, E-mail: mkstephens@lancasterseminary.edu; Staff 2 (MLS 1, Non-MLS 1)
Founded 1825. Enrl 114; Fac 9; Highest Degree: Doctorate
Library Holdings: AV Mats 8,148; Bk Vols 138,000; Per Subs 283
Special Collections: Church History & Liturgics (Albright Coll)
Subject Interests: Biblical studies, Educ, Hist, Theol
Automation Activity & Vendor Info: (Acquisitions) TLC (The Library Corporation); (Cataloging) TLC (The Library Corporation); (Circulation) TLC (The Library Corporation); (OPAC) TLC (The Library Corporation); (Serials) TLC (The Library Corporation)
Database Vendor: EBSCOhost, H W Wilson, OCLC, OCLC ArticleFirst, OCLC CAMIO, OCLC FirstSearch, OCLC WorldShare Interlibrary Loan, Project MUSE
Wireless access
Partic in Lyrasis; OCLC Online Computer Library Center, Inc; Southeastern Pennsylvania Theological Library Association
Open Mon-Thurs 7:30am-10:30pm, Fri 7:30-4:30, Sat 12-4, Sun 2-5
Friends of the Library Group

S LANDIS VALLEY MUSEUM*, Reference Library, 2451 Kissel Hill Rd, 17601. SAN 314-6847. Tel: 717-569-0401. FAX: 717-560-2147. Web Site: www.landisvalleymuseum.org. *Dir,* Stephen S Miller
Founded 1925
Library Holdings: Bk Vols 12,000
Subject Interests: Arts, Folklife, Folklore, Hist, Pa agr hist, Pa rural life & culture, Trade catalogs
Open Mon-Fri 9-5

P LIBRARY SYSTEM OF LANCASTER COUNTY*, 1866 Colonial Village Lane, Ste 107, 17601. Tel: 717-207-0500. FAX: 717-207-0504. E-mail: administration@lancasterlibraries.org. Web Site: www.lancasterlibraries.org. *Adminr,* Bill Hudson; E-mail: bhudson@lancasterlibraries.org; *Commun Relations Mgr,* Mary Ann Heltshe-Steinhauer; E-mail: mheltshe@lancasterlibraries.org; *Econ Develop Mgr & Consult,* Rhonda Kleiman; E-mail: rkleiman@lancasterlibraries.org; *Financial Mgr,* James D Showalter; E-mail: jshowalter@lancasterlibraries.org; *Mgr, Info Serv,* Dan Coleman; E-mail: dcoleman@lancasterlibraries.org; *Internal Operations Mgr,* Donna J Westerhoff; E-mail: dwesterhoff@lancasterlibraries.org; *Spec Serv Mgr,* Ed Miller; E-mail: emiller@lancasterlibraries.org; *Youth Serv Mgr,* Renee Christiansen; E-mail: rchristiansen@lancasterlibraries.org; *Training & Develop Coordr,* Stephanie Zimmerman; E-mail: szimmerman@lancasterlibraries.org
Founded 1987
Jan 2011-Dec 2011 Income $3,691,158, State $1,552,355, Federal $45,840, County $2,075,000, Locally Generated Income $17,963
Library Holdings: Bk Titles 404,672
Wireless access
Member Libraries: Adamstown Area Library; Columbia Public Library; Eastern Lancaster County Library; Elizabethtown Public Library; Ephrata Public Library; Lancaster Public Library; Lititz Public Library; Manheim Community Library; Manheim Township Public Library; Milanof-Schock Library; Moores Memorial Library; Pequea Valley Public Library; Quarryville Library; Strasburg-Heisler Library
Bookmobiles: 1

P MANHEIM TOWNSHIP PUBLIC LIBRARY*, 595 Granite Run Dr, 17601. Tel: 717-560-6441. FAX: 717-560-0570. E-mail: info@mtpl.info. Web Site: www.mtpl.info. *Exec Dir,* Katrina Anderson; Tel: 717-509-4604, Ext 303, E-mail: kanderson@mtpl.info; *Cir & Fac Mgr,* Marcia Beckwith; E-mail: mbeckwith@mtpl.info; *Coll Develop & Tech Serv Mgr,* Greta Kernicky; E-mail: gkernicky@mtpl.info; *Operations Mgr,* Janet Bailey; E-mail: jbailey@mtpl.info; *Youth Serv Mgr,* Mary Anne Stanley; E-mail: mstanley@mtpl.info
Founded 2007. Pop 38,133; Circ 318,617
Library Holdings: CDs 100; DVDs 2,400; Bk Vols 28,900; Per Subs 59; Talking Bks 1,600
Automation Activity & Vendor Info: (Acquisitions) Innovative Interfaces, Inc; (Cataloging) Innovative Interfaces, Inc; (Circulation) Innovative Interfaces, Inc; (OPAC) Innovative Interfaces, Inc; (Serials) Innovative Interfaces, Inc
Wireless access
Function: Adult bk club, Art exhibits, Audio & video playback equip for onsite use, Audiobks via web, Bi-weekly Writer's Group, Bk club(s), Bks on CD, Chess club, Children's prog, Computer training, Computers for patron use, Copy machines, Digital talking bks, Doc delivery serv, For res purposes, Free DVD rentals, Handicapped accessible, Holiday prog, ILL available, Instruction & testing, Magnifiers for reading, Mail & tel request accepted, Mus passes, Music CDs, Online cat, Online info literacy tutorials

on the web & in blackboard, Online ref, Online searches, OverDrive digital audio bks, Photocopying/Printing, Preschool reading prog, Printer for laptops & handheld devices, Prog for adults, Prog for children & young adult, Pub access computers, Ref & res, Ref serv available, Scanner, Senior computer classes, Senior outreach, Spanish lang bks, Story hour, Summer reading prog, Tax forms, Teen prog, Telephone ref, Web-catalog, Wheelchair accessible, Workshops, Writing prog
Mem of Library System of Lancaster County
Open Mon-Wed 10-8, Thurs & Fri 10-5, Sat 9-4
Friends of the Library Group

M PENNSYLVANIA COLLEGE OF HEALTH SCIENCES*, Health Sciences Library, Lancaster General Hospital, 555 N Duke St, 17604. SAN 314-6804. Tel: 717-544-5698. FAX: 717-544-4923. E-mail: library@lghealth.org, library@PAcollege.edu. Web Site: www.pacollege.edu.library. *Dir,* Cynthia McClellan; Tel: 717-544-5697, E-mail: cm057@lghealth.org; *Asst Librn,* Marie Fitzsimmons; E-mail: mf023@lghealth.org; Staff 1 (MLS 1)
Founded 1967
Library Holdings: Bk Titles 8,000; Per Subs 340
Automation Activity & Vendor Info: (Cataloging) EOS International; (Circulation) EOS International; (OPAC) EOS International; (Serials) EOS International
Database Vendor: EBSCOhost, OVID Technologies
Wireless access
Partic in Basic Health Sciences Library Network; Central Pennsylvania Health Sciences Library Association; Docline; Medical Library Association (MLA)
Open Mon-Thurs 8am-9pm, Fri 8-5, Sat 12-5; Mon-Fri (Summer) 8-5

§S SHUTS ENVIRONMENTAL LIBRARY, Three Nature's Way, 17602. Tel: 717-295-2055. FAX: 717-295-3688. E-mail: parks@co.lancaster.pa.us. Web Site: www.lancastercountyparks.org.
Founded 1991
Library Holdings: Bk Titles 4,500
Subject Interests: Environ, Gardening, Health, Native Am
Open Mon-Fri 8:30-5, Sat 9-3

S STEINMAN ENTERPRISES*, Lancaster Newspapers, Inc Library, Eight W King St, 17603-3824. (Mail add: PO Box 1328, 17608-1328), SAN 314-6820. Tel: 717-291-8773. E-mail: library@lnpnews.com. *Mgr,* Kim Gomoll; E-mail: kgomoll@lnpnews.com; Staff 7 (MLS 1, Non-MLS 6)
Founded 1952
Library Holdings: Bk Titles 1,000
Special Collections: Archived articles of local interest published by Lancaster Newspapers, 1950-, unindexed earlier publications, 1800-1950, micro; Biography Clippings on World, National, State & Local People; Remington Rand Lektrievers Subject & Biography Coll, VF
Subject Interests: Amish, Local art, Local politics
Database Vendor: ProQuest

J THADDEUS STEVENS COLLEGE OF TECHNOLOGY*, Kenneth W Schuler Learning Resources Center, 750 E King St, 17602-3198. SAN 370-7539. Tel: 717-299-7753. Interlibrary Loan Service Tel: 717-391-3502. Administration Tel. 717-299-7734. FAX: 717-396-7186. Web Site: www.stevenscollege.edu. *Dir,* Diane Ambruso; E-mail: ambruso@stevenscollege.edu; *Librn,* Tim Creamer; Tel: 717-391-3503, E-mail: creamer@stevenscollege.edu; *Librn,* Suzanne Waddell; Tel: 717-396-7176, E-mail: waddell@stevenscollege.edu; *Libr Tech,* Brenda Smith; Tel: 717-391-3502, E-mail: smith@stevenscollege.edu; Staff 3 (MLS 3)
Founded 1976. Enrl 680; Fac 55; Highest Degree: Associate
Library Holdings: e-books 1,188; Bk Titles 27,000; Per Subs 305
Automation Activity & Vendor Info: (Acquisitions) Ex Libris Group; (Cataloging) Ex Libris Group; (Circulation) Ex Libris Group; (Course Reserve) Ex Libris Group; (OPAC) Ex Libris Group; (Serials) Ex Libris Group
Partic in HSLC/Access PA/POWER Library; Keystone Library Network; OCLC Online Computer Library Center, Inc
Open Mon-Thurs 7am-10pm, Fri 7-5, Sun 2-10

LANGHORNE

CR CAIRN UNIVERSITY, Masland Library, 200 Manor Ave, 19047. SAN 314-9684. Tel: 215-702-4370. Interlibrary Loan Service Tel: 215-702-4520. Reference Tel: 215-702-4225. Administration Tel: 215-702-4376. FAX: 215-702-4374. E-mail: library@cairn.edu. Web Site: library.cairn.edu. *Dir,* Timothy K Hui; E-mail: thui@cairn.edu; *Asst Dir, Automation Syst Coordr, Head, Tech Serv,* Stephanie S Kaceli; E-mail: stephaniekaceli@cairn.edu; Staff 5.25 (MLS 5.25)
Founded 1913. Highest Degree: Master
Library Holdings: AV Mats 12,688; e-books 129,089; e-journals 30,186; Bk Titles 105,341; Bk Vols 138,408; Per Subs 661
Subject Interests: Archives, Biblical studies, Educ, Music, Theol studies
Automation Activity & Vendor Info: (Acquisitions) Innovative Interfaces, Inc; (Cataloging) Innovative Interfaces, Inc; (Circulation) Innovative Interfaces, Inc; (Course Reserve) Innovative Interfaces, Inc; (ILL) OCLC ILLiad; (OPAC) Innovative Interfaces, Inc; (Serials) Innovative Interfaces, Inc
Wireless access
Function: 24/7 Electronic res, 24/7 Online cat, Archival coll, Art exhibits, Distance learning, e-mail & chat, e-mail serv, E-Reserves, Electronic databases & coll, Fax serv, ILL available, Online cat, Online info literacy tutorials on the web & in blackboard, Online ref, Outside serv via phone, mail, e-mail & web, Printer for laptops & handheld devices, Ref & res, Ref serv available, Ref serv in person, Scanner, Study rm
Partic in Lyrasis; OCLC Online Computer Library Center, Inc; Southeastern Pennsylvania Theological Library Association; Tri-State College Library Cooperative
Restriction: Open to fac, students & qualified researchers, Open to pub for ref only, Open to students, fac & staff

LANSDALE

P LANSDALE PUBLIC LIBRARY*, 301 Vine St, 19446-3690. SAN 314-6898. Tel: 215-855-3228. FAX: 215-855-6440. E-mail: inforequests@lansdalelibrary.org. Web Site: www.lansdalelibrary.org. *Dir,* Anne M Frank; *Adult Serv,* Tom Meyor; E-mail: adultservices@lansdalelibrary.org; Staff 4 (MLS 3, Non-MLS 1)
Founded 1928. Pop 16,362; Circ 77,289
Library Holdings: AV Mats 2,532; Bk Titles 42,054; Bk Vols 46,131; Per Subs 168
Subject Interests: Local hist
Automation Activity & Vendor Info: (Cataloging) TLC (The Library Corporation); (Circulation) TLC (The Library Corporation); (OPAC) TLC (The Library Corporation); (Serials) EBSCO Online
Database Vendor: EBSCOhost
Open Mon-Fri 10-9, Sat 10-3

LANSDOWNE

R FIRST PRESBYTERIAN CHURCH*, DRA Carson Memorial Library, 140 N Lansdowne Ave, 19050. (Mail add: PO Box 277, 19050-0277), SAN 314-6901. Tel: 610-622-0800. FAX: 610-622-0881. Web Site: www.lansdownepresbyterian.org. *In Charge,* Rona Shirdan; Staff 1 (Non-MLS 1)
Founded 1945
Library Holdings: Bk Titles 3,260; Bk Vols 3,591; Per Subs 12
Special Collections: Lansdowne & Lansdowne Presbyterian Church, clippings, brochures, mss, photos & pictures
Open Mon-Fri 9-3, Sun 10-1

P LANSDOWNE PUBLIC LIBRARY*, 55 S Lansdowne Ave, 19050-2804. SAN 314-691X. Tel: 610-623-0239. FAX: 610-623-6825. E-mail: lansdowne@delcolibraries.org. Web Site: www.delco.lib.pa.us. *Dir,* Amy Gillespie; Staff 10 (MLS 2, Non-MLS 8)
Founded 1898. Pop 11,712; Circ 147,005
Library Holdings: Bk Vols 54,000; Per Subs 87
Mem of Delaware County Library System
Open Mon-Thurs 9-9, Fri 9-6, Sat 10-4 (10-2 July & Aug)
Friends of the Library Group

LAPORTE

GL SULLIVAN COUNTY LAW LIBRARY*, Court House, Main & Muncy St, 18626. (Mail add: PO Box 157, 18626-0157), SAN 375-247X. Tel: 570-946-4053. FAX: 570-946-4609. Web Site: www.sullivancounty-pa.us. *Law Librn,* Terri K Baran
Library Holdings: Bk Vols 500
Open Mon-Fri 8:30-4

LATROBE

P ADAMS MEMORIAL LIBRARY*, 1112 Ligonier St, 15650. SAN 314-6928. Tel: 724-539-1972. FAX: 724-537-0338. E-mail: library@adamslib.org. Web Site: www.adamslib.org. *Dir,* Tracy Trotter; *Br Mgr,* Aurea Lucas; *Br Mgr,* Kathryn Orndorff-Tauber; *Ch Serv,* Tarrah Dean; *Ch Serv,* Karen Herc; *Tech Coordr,* Joseph Joyner; Staff 25 (MLS 5, Non-MLS 20)
Founded 1927. Pop 51,000; Circ 260,000
Library Holdings: Bk Vols 110,000; Per Subs 50
Automation Activity & Vendor Info: (Cataloging) Follett Software; (Circulation) Follett Software; (OPAC) Follett Software
Database Vendor: EBSCOhost
Partic in Monessen District Libr Ctr
Special Services for the Blind - Assistive/Adapted tech devices, equip & products
Open Mon-Thurs 10-8, Sat 10-5
Friends of the Library Group

Branches: 2
CALDWELL MEMORIAL LIBRARY, 982 N Chestnut St Extension, Derry, 15627. Tel: 724-694-5765. FAX: 724-694-8546. *Br Mgr,* Aurea Lucas
Library Holdings: Bk Vols 9,731
Open Mon-Thurs 3-8, Sat 10-3
UNITY, 156 Beatty County Rd, 15650. Tel: 724-532-1840. FAX: 724-532-1841. *Br Mgr,* Kathryn Orndorff-Tauber
Library Holdings: Bk Vols 9,323; Per Subs 10
Open Mon & Wed 2-7, Fri 10-3, Sun 1-6
Bookmobiles: 1. In Charge, Jennifer Nemcheck. Bk vols 7,000

M EXCELA HEALTH LATROBE HOSPITAL*, Health Sciences Library, One Mellon Way, 15650-1096. SAN 314-6944. Tel: 724-537-1275. FAX: 724-537-1890. *Mgr,* Marilyn Daniels; E-mail: mdaniels@excelahealth.org; Staff 1 (MLS 1)
Founded 1963
Library Holdings: Bk Titles 2,830; Bk Vols 3,052; Per Subs 162
Subject Interests: Allied health, Med, Nursing
Partic in Basic Health Sciences Library Network; National Network of Libraries of Medicine; Share Westmoreland Consortium
Open Mon-Fri 9:30-6

CR SAINT VINCENT COLLEGE & SEMINARY LIBRARY*, 300 Fraser Purchase Rd, 15650-2690. SAN 314-6952. Tel: 724-805-2966. Interlibrary Loan Service Tel: 724-805-2484. Reference Tel: 724-805-2370. Administration Tel: 724-805-2307. FAX: 724-805-2905. E-mail: library@stvincent.edu. Web Site: www.stvincent.edu. *Dir,* Brother David Kelly; E-mail: david.kelly@stvincent.edu; *Acq, Asst Dir,* Denise A Hegemann; E-mail: denise.hegemann@email.stvincent.edu; *Cataloger, Head, Tech Serv,* Elizabeth DiGiustino; E-mail: elizabeth.digustino@stvincent.edu; *Circ & ILL, Pub Serv Librn,* Bridget Hornyak; E-mail: bridget.hornyak@email.stivincent.edu; *Ser Librn,* Fr Matthias Martinez; E-mail: mathias.martinez@email.stvincent.edu; *Spec Coll Librn,* Fr Chrysostom V Schlimm; E-mail: chrysostom.schlimm@email.stvincent.edu; Staff 10 (MLS 5, Non-MLS 5)
Founded 1846. Enrl 1,800; Highest Degree: Master
Library Holdings: Bk Titles 382,266; Per Subs 387
Special Collections: Medievalia; Patrology
Subject Interests: Benedictina, Ecclesiastical hist, Hist, Incunabula, Pa, Relig studies, Theol
Automation Activity & Vendor Info: (Circulation) Innovative Interfaces, Inc; (OPAC) Innovative Interfaces, Inc
Database Vendor: EBSCOhost, JSTOR, LexisNexis, Project MUSE
Wireless access
Function: Audio & video playback equip for onsite use, Bks on cassette, Bks on CD, CD-ROM, Computers for patron use, Copy machines, Electronic databases & coll, ILL available, Microfiche/film & reading machines, Music CDs, Online cat, Ref & res, Ref serv in person, Scanner, Spoken cassettes & CDs, Spoken cassettes & DVDs, VCDs, VHS videos, Web-catalog
Partic in Lyrasis; OCLC Online Computer Library Center, Inc
Special Services for the Blind - Reader equip
Open Mon-Thurs 8:15am-11:45pm, Fri 8:15-4:45, Sat 10-4:45, Sun 12-11:45

LAURELDALE

P MUHLENBERG COMMUNITY LIBRARY*, 3612 Kutztown Rd, 19605-1842. SAN 314-6960. Tel: 610-929-0589. FAX: 610-929-8165. E-mail: muhlenbergcl@berks.lib.pa.us. Web Site: www.berks.lib.pa.us/muhlenbergcl/. *Dir,* Position Currently Open
Founded 1960. Pop 23,753; Circ 150,000
Library Holdings: Bk Vols 28,000; Per Subs 76
Special Collections: Autism Society of Berks; Berks County, PA History Coll
Automation Activity & Vendor Info: (Acquisitions) Horizon; (Cataloging) Horizon; (Circulation) Horizon; (Course Reserve) Horizon; (ILL) Horizon; (Media Booking) Horizon; (OPAC) Horizon; (Serials) Horizon
Wireless access
Mem of Berks County Public Libraries
Open Mon-Thurs (Winter) 10-8, Fri 10-5, Sat 9-4; Tues-Thurs (Summer) 10-8, Fri 10-5, Sat 9-2

LAURELTON

P WEST END LIBRARY*, 1724 State Rte 235, 17835. (Mail add: PO Box 111, 17835-0111). Tel: 570-922-4773. FAX: 570-922-1162. E-mail: wellib@westendlibrary.org. Web Site: www.westendlibrary.org. *Dir,* Susan L Epley; *Asst Librn,* Judy A Bowersox; *Ch Serv,* Denise A Hosterman; Staff 3 (Non-MLS 3)
Founded 1980. Pop 1,735
Library Holdings: Bk Vols 9,194; Per Subs 26
Automation Activity & Vendor Info: (Cataloging) TLC (The Library Corporation); (Circulation) TLC (The Library Corporation); (OPAC) TLC (The Library Corporation)
Mem of Union County Library System
Open Mon & Thurs 1-8, Tues & Fri 9:30-4:30, Sat 9-4

LEBANON

J HARRISBURG AREA COMMUNITY COLLEGE*, Pushnik Family Library Lebanon Campus, 735 Cumberland St, 17042. Tel: 717-270-6328. Interlibrary Loan Service Tel: 717-780-2623. Administration Tel: 717-270-6320. Web Site: lib2.hacc.edu. *Libr Dir,* Deborah G Lovett; E-mail: dglovett@hacc.edu; *Electronic Serv Librn,* Judith Nagata; Tel: 717-780-2535, E-mail: jmnagata@hacc.edu; *Automation Syst Coordr,* Michael L Bowden; Tel: 717-780-1936, E-mail: mlbowden@hacc.edu; *Acq,* Kim McGovern; Tel: 717-780-2465, E-mail: kbmcgove@hacc.edu; *Cat,* Position Currently Open; *ILL,* Diane Wiedemann; E-mail: dlweiden@hacc.edu; Staff 3 (MLS 2, Non-MLS 1)
Founded 1990. Enrl 1,317; Fac 100; Highest Degree: Associate
Library Holdings: AV Mats 364; Bks on Deafness & Sign Lang 17; e-books 2,598; e-journals 2,490; Electronic Media & Resources 82; Bk Titles 15,676; Per Subs 54; Videos 375
Subject Interests: Career, Pa German culture
Automation Activity & Vendor Info: (Acquisitions) SirsiDynix; (Cataloging) SirsiDynix; (Circulation) SirsiDynix; (Course Reserve) Docutek; (ILL) SirsiDynix; (Media Booking) SirsiDynix; (OPAC) SirsiDynix; (Serials) SirsiDynix
Database Vendor: ARTstor, CredoReference, EBSCOhost, Elsevier, Gale Cengage Learning, LexisNexis, Newsbank, ProQuest, SirsiDynix, Wilson - Wilson Web
Wireless access
Special Services for the Blind - Assistive/Adapted tech devices, equip & products; Large screen computer & software; Low vision equip; Reader equip; Screen enlargement software for people with visual disabilities; Screen reader software; ZoomText magnification & reading software
Open Mon-Thurs 7:30am-9pm, Fri 7:30-4
Restriction: In-house use for visitors, Non-circulating to the pub

M KROHN MEMORIAL LIBRARY, Good Samaritan Hospital Medical Library, Fourth & Walnut St, 17042. (Mail add: PO Box 1281, 17042-1281), SAN 371-8719. Tel: 717-270-7826. FAX: 717-270-3882. E-mail: librarian@gshleb.org. *Med Librn,* Georgeanna E Ledgerwood; E-mail: gledgerwood@gshleb.org; Staff 1 (MLS 1)
Library Holdings: Bk Titles 1,028; Per Subs 130
Subject Interests: Clinical med, Hospital admin, Nursing
Automation Activity & Vendor Info: (Acquisitions) Professional Software; (Cataloging) Professional Software
Database Vendor: EBSCOhost, Elsevier
Wireless access
Function: Computers for patron use, Copy machines, Doc delivery serv, Fax serv, For res purposes, Handicapped accessible, Health sci info serv, ILL available, Online cat, Online searches, Orientations, Photocopying/Printing, Prof lending libr, Ref serv available, Res libr
Partic in Basic Health Sciences Library Network; Central Pennsylvania Health Sciences Library Association
Open Mon-Fri 8-4:30
Restriction: Circ limited, Circulates for staff only, Hospital employees & physicians only, In-house use for visitors, Med & health res only, Open to pub for ref only, Prof mat only, Pub use on premises

P LEBANON COMMUNITY LIBRARY, DISTRICT CENTER, 125 N Seventh St, 17046-5000. SAN 320-4189. Tel: 717-273-7624. FAX: 717-273-2719. Web Site: www.lclibs.org/lebanon. *Libr Dir,* Michelle Hawk; E-mail: hawk@lclibs.org; Staff 19 (MLS 2, Non-MLS 17)
Founded 1925. Pop 60,000; Circ 300,000
Library Holdings: AV Mats 6,000; Bks on Deafness & Sign Lang 10; CDs 200; High Interest/Low Vocabulary Bk Vols 300; Large Print Bks 2,000; Bk Titles 98,471; Bk Vols 101,628; Per Subs 120; Talking Bks 2,721; Videos 4,621
Special Collections: Spanish Coll
Subject Interests: Local hist
Automation Activity & Vendor Info: (Cataloging) Innovative Interfaces, Inc; (Circulation) Innovative Interfaces, Inc; (ILL) Innovative Interfaces, Inc; (OPAC) Innovative Interfaces, Inc
Wireless access
Publications: Books 'n More
Mem of Lebanon County Library System
Open Mon-Wed 8-8, Thurs 8-7, Fri & Sat 8-5
Friends of the Library Group

S LEBANON COUNTY HISTORICAL SOCIETY LIBRARY*, 924 Cumberland St, 17042-5186. SAN 314-6979. Tel: 717-272-1473. FAX: 717-272-7474. E-mail: office@lchsociety.org. Web Site: www.lchsociety.org. *Librn,* Brian Kissler

Founded 1898
Library Holdings: Bk Titles 2,000; Bk Vols 2,200; Per Subs 12
Special Collections: Coleman-Cornwall Papers, 1757-1940
Subject Interests: Genealogy, German immigrants in Pa, Lebanon County hist, Lebanon County newspapers, Pa hist
Wireless access
Open Mon & Fri 1-8, Thurs 9-4:30, Sat 9-3, Sun 1-4:30

GL LEBANON COUNTY LAW LIBRARY*, 400 S Eighth St, Rm 305, 17042. SAN 377-1202. Tel: 717-274-2801, Ext 2280. FAX: 717-273-7490. *Librn,* Luz Rosario; E-mail: lrosario@lebcnty.org; Staff 1 (Non-MLS 1)
Library Holdings: Bk Titles 7,284; Bk Vols 16,191; Per Subs 84
Database Vendor: Westlaw
Open Mon-Fri 8:30-4:30

P LEBANON COUNTY LIBRARY SYSTEM*, 125 N Seventh St, 17046. SAN 358-6561. Tel: 717-273-7624. FAX: 717-273-2719. Web Site: lclibs.org. *Adminr,* Anne Hall; Tel: 717-273-7624, Ext 212, E-mail: ahall@lclibs.org; Staff 1 (MLS 1)
Founded 1969
Jan 2005-Dec 2005 Income $184,000, State $34,000, County $150,000. Sal $27,000
Automation Activity & Vendor Info: (Acquisitions) Innovative Interfaces, Inc; (Cataloging) Innovative Interfaces, Inc; (Circulation) Innovative Interfaces, Inc; (ILL) Innovative Interfaces, Inc; (OPAC) Innovative Interfaces, Inc; (Serials) Innovative Interfaces, Inc
Wireless access
Member Libraries: Annville Free Library; Lebanon Community Library, District Center; Matthews Public Library; Myerstown Community Library; Palmyra Public Library; Richland Community Library
Restriction: Not a lending libr

G LEBANON VA MEDICAL CENTER LIBRARY*, 1700 S Lincoln Ave, 17042-7597. SAN 314-6987. Tel: 717-272-6621, Ext 4746. Toll Free Tel: 800-409-8771. FAX: 717-228-6069. E-mail: lib.lebvamc@va.gov. *Librn,* Kristine Scannell; Staff 1 (MLS 1)
Library Holdings: Bk Titles 3,500; Per Subs 700
Automation Activity & Vendor Info: (Cataloging) EOS International; (Circulation) EOS International
Database Vendor: EBSCOhost, EOS International, MD Consult, Nature Publishing Group, OVID Technologies, ProQuest, PubMed, RefWorks, UpToDate, Wiley InterScience
Function: ILL available
Partic in Dept of Vet Affairs Libr Network
Restriction: Open to pub upon request

LEECHBURG

P LEECHBURG PUBLIC LIBRARY*, 215 First St, 15656-1375. SAN 314-6995. Tel: 724-845-1911. *Librn,* Joseph Kantor
Founded 1926. Pop 2,581; Circ 3,192
Library Holdings: Bk Titles 12,183; Bk Vols 12,910; Per Subs 100; Talking Bks 50
Automation Activity & Vendor Info: (Cataloging) ComPanion Corp; (Circulation) ComPanion Corp
Open Mon-Thurs 3-8

LEESPORT

P BERKS COUNTY PUBLIC LIBRARIES*, 1040 Berk Rd, 19533. (Mail add: PO Box 689, 19533-0689). Tel: 610-378-5260. FAX: 610-378-1525. Web Site: www.berks.lib.pa.us. *Adminr,* Denise Sticha; *Asst Admin,* Jennifer Smilko; E-mail: jennifer@berks.lib.pa.us; Staff 16 (MLS 5, Non-MLS 11)
Founded 1986. Pop 362,483
Library Holdings: Bk Vols 301,654; Per Subs 1,166
Automation Activity & Vendor Info: (Cataloging) SirsiDynix; (Circulation) SirsiDynix; (OPAC) SirsiDynix
Wireless access
Member Libraries: Bernville Area Community Library; Bethel-Tulpehocken Public Library; Boone Area Library; Boyertown Community Library; Brandywine Community Library; Exeter Community Library; Fleetwood Area Public Library; Kutztown Community Library; Mifflin Community Library; Muhlenberg Community Library; Robesonia Community Library; Schuylkill Valley Community Library; Sinking Spring Public Library; Spring Township Library; Village Library of Morgantown; Wernersville Public Library; West Lawn-Wyomissing Hills Library; Womelsdorf Community Library
Open Mon-Fri 8-4
Friends of the Library Group
Bookmobiles: 2

P SCHUYLKILL VALLEY COMMUNITY LIBRARY*, 1310 Washington Rd, 19533-9708. SAN 370-6842. Tel: 610-926-1555. FAX: 610-926-3710. E-mail: svcl@berks.lib.pa.us. Web Site: www.berks.lib.pa.us/svcl/. *Dir,* Susan L Shipe; Staff 1 (MLS 1)
Founded 1989. Pop 13,738; Circ 51,013
Library Holdings: Bk Vols 16,156; Per Subs 38
Database Vendor: EBSCOhost
Wireless access
Function: Adult bk club, Audiobks via web, Bks on cassette, Bks on CD, Chess club, Children's prog, Computer training, Computers for patron use, Copy machines, Electronic databases & coll, Free DVD rentals, Holiday prog, ILL available, Mus passes, Music CDs, Online cat, Online searches, OverDrive digital audio bks, Prog for adults, Prog for children & young adult, Pub access computers, Scanner, Spoken cassettes & CDs, Spoken cassettes & DVDs, Story hour, Summer reading prog, Tax forms, VHS videos, Wheelchair accessible
Mem of Berks County Public Libraries
Open Mon 3-8, Tues-Thurs 9-8, Fri 9-2, Sat 9-4
Friends of the Library Group

LEHIGHTON

P LEHIGHTON AREA MEMORIAL LIBRARY*, 124 North St, 18235-1589. SAN 314-7002. Tel: 610-377-2750. FAX: 610-377-5803. E-mail: liblehtn@ptd.net. Web Site: www.library.cpals.com. *Dir,* Becky Wanamaker; Staff 1 (MLS 1)
Founded 1948. Pop 17,131; Circ 3,500
Jan 2008-Dec 2008 Income $92,195. Mats Exp $14,000, Books $12,500, Per/Ser (Incl. Access Fees) $1,500
Library Holdings: AV Mats 1,050; DVDs 200; Large Print Bks 500; Bk Titles 17,800; Bk Vols 18,300; Per Subs 30; Talking Bks 700; Videos 150
Automation Activity & Vendor Info: (Cataloging) TLC (The Library Corporation); (Circulation) TLC (The Library Corporation)
Open Mon, Wed & Fri 10-4:50, Tues & Thurs 1:30-7:50, Sat 9-2:50

LEHMAN

C PENNSYLVANIA STATE UNIVERSITY, WILKES-BARRE COMMONWEALTH COLLEGE*, Nesbitt Library, PO Box PSU, 18627-0217. SAN 315-3460. Tel: 570-675-9212. Circulation Tel: 570-675-9214. Reference Tel: 570-675-9261. Administration Tel: 570-675-9295. FAX: 570-675-7436. Web Site: www.wb.psu.edu/. *Head Librn,* Bruce D Reid; Staff 5 (MLS 2, Non-MLS 3)
Founded 1916. Enrl 825; Fac 88; Highest Degree: Bachelor
Library Holdings: Bk Vols 34,212; Per Subs 425
Subject Interests: Eng
Partic in OCLC Online Computer Library Center, Inc; Pennsylvania Academic Library Consortium, Inc (PALCI); RLIN (Research Libraries Information Network)
Open Mon-Thurs 8-8, Fri 8-4:30, Sun Noon-5

LEVITTOWN

S BUCKS COUNTY COURIER TIMES LIBRARY*, 8400 Rte 13, 19057-5198. SAN 371-2036. Tel: 215-949-4000. FAX: 215-949-4177. Web Site: www.buckscountycouriertimes.com. *Librn,* Carol Calvello; Staff 1 (Non-MLS 1)
Library Holdings: Bk Titles 830; Bk Vols 952; Per Subs 16
Special Collections: Newspaper Coll
Open Mon-Fri 8-4

LEWISBURG

C BUCKNELL UNIVERSITY*, Ellen Clarke Bertrand Library, Library & Information Technology, 221 Ellen Clarke Bertrand Library, 17837. SAN 314-7010. Tel: 570-577-1557. Circulation Tel: 570-577-1882. Interlibrary Loan Service Tel: 570-577-3249. FAX: 570-577-3313. Web Site: www.bucknell.edu/libraryit. *VPres, Libr & Info Tech,* Param Bedi; E-mail: param.bedi@bucknell.edu; *Dir, Libr Serv & Instrul Tech,* Carrie Rampp; E-mail: cer013@bucknell.edu; *Asst Dir, Res Serv,* Kathleen McQuiston; Tel: 570-577-3309, E-mail: mcquisto@bucknell.edu; *Asst Dir, Libr Coll Develop & Access Serv,* Jennifer Clarke; Tel: 570-577-3252, E-mail: jclarke@bucknell.edu; *Curator, Spec Coll & Univ Archives,* Isabella O'Neill; Tel: 570-577-3230, E-mail: ioneill@bucknell.edu; Staff 30 (MLS 10, Non-MLS 20)
Founded 1846. Enrl 3,470; Fac 325; Highest Degree: Master
Special Collections: Fine Presses; Irish Literature. State Document Depository; US Document Depository
Subject Interests: Eng, Liberal arts
Automation Activity & Vendor Info: (Acquisitions) SirsiDynix; (Cataloging) OCLC WorldShare Interlibrary Loan; (Circulation) OCLC WorldShare Interlibrary Loan; (Course Reserve) OCLC WorldShare Interlibrary Loan; (ILL) OCLC ILLiad; (Media Booking) OCLC WorldShare Interlibrary Loan; (OPAC) OCLC WorldShare Interlibrary Loan
Wireless access

Partic in Associated College Libraries of Central Pennsylvania; Coalition for Networked Information (CNI); OCLC Online Computer Library Center, Inc; Pennsylvania Academic Library Consortium, Inc (PALCI); Susquehanna Library Cooperative
Open Mon-Thurs 7am-2am, Fri 7am-10pm, Sat 9am-10pm, Sun 9am-2am
Friends of the Library Group
Departmental Libraries:
ACQUISITIONS, Library & Information Technology, 17837. Tel: 570-577-3252. *Asst Dir, Libr Coll Develop & Access Serv,* Jennifer Clarke; E-mail: jclarke@bucknell.edu
Friends of the Library Group
CATALOGING, 117 Bertrand Library, 17837. Tel: 570-577-3252. *Asst Dir, Libr Coll Develop & Access Serv,* Jennifer Clarke
Automation Activity & Vendor Info: (Acquisitions) OCLC; (Cataloging) OCLC; (Circulation) OCLC; (ILL) OCLC ILLiad; (OPAC) OCLC WorldShare Interlibrary Loan
Open Mon-Thurs 7am-2am, Fri 7am-10pm, Sat 9am-10pm, Sun 9am-2am
Friends of the Library Group
CIRCULATION, Library & Information Technology, 130 Bertrand Library, 17837. Tel: 570-577-1882, 570-577-3287. *Access Serv Mgr,* Mary Jean Moser; E-mail: woland@bucknell.edu
Friends of the Library Group
INTERLIBRARY LOAN, Library & Information Technology, 17837. Tel: 570-577-3249. *Mgr, ILL & E-Res,* Dan Heuer; E-mail: rheuer@bucknell.edu
RESEARCH SERVICES, Library & Information Technology, 17837. Tel: 570-577-1462, 570-577-3228. *Mgr, Ref & Info Serv,* Martha Holland; Tel: 570-577-1673, E-mail: holland@bucknell.edu
Special Collections: US Document Depository
Friends of the Library Group
SERIALS, Library & Information Technology, 17837. Tel: 570-577-1663. *Libr Asst,* Kathryn Dalius; E-mail: kdalius@bucknell.edu
Friends of the Library Group

P PUBLIC LIBRARY FOR UNION COUNTY*, 255 Reitz Blvd, 17837-9211. SAN 314-7029. Tel: 570-523-1172. FAX: 570-524-7771. Web Site: www.publibuc.org. *Dir,* Roberta Greene; E-mail: rgreene@publibuc.org; *Head, Adult Serv,* Melanie Weber; E-mail: mweber@publibuc.org; *Head, Ch,* Mary Harrison; E-mail: mharrison@publibuc.org; Staff 12 (MLS 2, Non-MLS 10)
Founded 1910. Pop 37,000; Circ 220,600
Library Holdings: Bk Vols 108,000; Per Subs 103
Subject Interests: Local hist, Pa hist
Automation Activity & Vendor Info: (Cataloging) TLC (The Library Corporation); (Circulation) TLC (The Library Corporation); (OPAC) TLC (The Library Corporation)
Database Vendor: TLC (The Library Corporation)
Wireless access
Function: Home delivery & serv to Sr ctr & nursing homes, Homebound delivery serv, ILL available, Magnifiers for reading, Photocopying/Printing, Prog for adults, Prog for children & young adult, Ref serv available, Summer reading prog, Telephone ref, Wheelchair accessible
Publications: Newsletter (Quarterly)
Mem of Union County Library System
Open Mon, Tues & Thurs 9:30-8:30, Wed, Fri & Sat 9:30-5

S UNION COUNTY HISTORICAL SOCIETY LIBRARY*, Union County Courthouse, S Second & St Louis Sts, 17837. SAN 327-618X. Tel: 570-524-8666. FAX: 570-524-8743. Web Site: www.unioncountyhistoricalsociety.org. *Pres,* Jeannette Lasansky; E-mail: lasansky@bucknell.edu
Founded 1963
Library Holdings: Bk Titles 500
Special Collections: Business & Craftsmen Ledgers (slides & videos). Oral History
Subject Interests: Genealogy
Publications: Union County Heritage
Open Mon-Fri 8:30-12 & 1-4:30

P UNION COUNTY LIBRARY SYSTEM*, 255 Reitz Blvd, 17837-9211. Tel: 570-523-1172. FAX: 570-524-7771. Web Site: unioncountylibrarysystem.com. *Adminr,* Roberta Greene; E-mail: rgreene@publibuc.org; Staff 4 (MLS 2, Non-MLS 2)
Founded 1998. Pop 43,000
Library Holdings: Bk Vols 147,000; Per Subs 219
Automation Activity & Vendor Info: (Cataloging) TLC (The Library Corporation); (Circulation) TLC (The Library Corporation); (OPAC) TLC (The Library Corporation)
Wireless access
Function: Handicapped accessible, Home delivery & serv to Sr ctr & nursing homes, Homebound delivery serv, ILL available, Magnifiers for reading, Photocopying/Printing, Prog for adults, Prog for children & young adult, Ref serv available, Summer reading prog, Telephone ref, Wheelchair accessible
Member Libraries: Jane I & Annetta M Herr Memorial Library; Public Library for Union County; West End Library

LEWISTOWN

M LEWISTOWN HOSPITAL*, Jane Karn Medical Library, 400 Highland Ave, 17044-9983. SAN 314-7037. Tel: 717-242-7242, 717-248-5411. FAX: 717-242-7245. *Med Libr Tech,* Stephanie Marie Bilger; E-mail: sbilger@lewistownhospital.org; Staff 1 (Non-MLS 1)
Founded 1974
Library Holdings: Bk Titles 1,656; Bk Vols 1,980; Per Subs 55
Subject Interests: Health, Med, Nursing
Partic in Greater NE Regional Med Libr Program
Restriction: Staff use only

S MIFFLIN COUNTY HISTORICAL SOCIETY LIBRARY & MUSEUM, One W Market St, 17044-1746. SAN 326-9205. Tel: 717-242-1022. FAX: 717-242-3488. E-mail: info@mifflincountyhistoricalsociety.org. *Librn,* Jean A Laughlin
Founded 1921
Subject Interests: Genealogy, Local hist
Publications: Notes from Monument Square (Newsletter)
Open Tues & Wed 10-4
Restriction: Open to pub for ref only

P MIFFLIN COUNTY LIBRARY*, 123 N Wayne St, 17044-1794. SAN 358-6626. Tel: 717-242-2391. FAX: 717-242-2825. Web Site: www.mifflincountylibrary.org. *Dir,* Molly Kinney; E-mail: mollykinney@mifcolib.org; *Youth Serv Librn,* Susan Miriello; Staff 13.02 (MLS 2, Non-MLS 11.02)
Founded 1842. Pop 46,486; Circ 172,812
Jan 2014-Dec 2014 Income (Main Library and Branch(s)) $387,000, State $211,000, County $166,000, Locally Generated Income $10,000. Mats Exp $106,928, Books $93,200, Per/Ser (Incl. Access Fees) $3,500, AV Mat $8,228, Electronic Ref Mat (Incl. Access Fees) $2,000. Sal $290,000
Library Holdings: AV Mats 3,870; High Interest/Low Vocabulary Bk Vols 1,815; Bk Titles 65,703; Bk Vols 91,184; Per Subs 159
Automation Activity & Vendor Info: (Cataloging) TLC (The Library Corporation); (Circulation) TLC (The Library Corporation); (OPAC) TLC (The Library Corporation)
Wireless access
Partic in Cent Pa District
Open Mon, Thurs, Fri & Sat 9-4, Tues & Wed 9-8, Sun 1:30-5
Friends of the Library Group
Branches: 2
KISHACOQUILLAS BRANCH, 194 N Penn St, Belleville, 17004. (Mail add: PO Box 996, Belleville, 17004-0996). Tel: 717-935-2880. FAX: 717-935-2880. E-mail: kish@mifflincountylibrary.org. ; Staff 0.75 (Non-MLS 0.75)
Founded 1961. Pop 3,913; Circ 20,793
Library Holdings: High Interest/Low Vocabulary Bk Vols 317; Bk Titles 11,564; Bk Vols 11,697; Per Subs 16
Open Mon & Tues 12-4:30 & 5:30-8, Wed & Thurs 9-12:30 & 1:30-5, Sat 9-1
ROTHROCK BRANCH, Ten N Queen St, McVeytown, 17051. (Mail add: PO Box 331, McVeytown, 17051-0331), SAN 358-674X. Tel: 717-899-6851. FAX: 717-899-6851. E-mail: rothrock@mifflincountylibrary.org. *Br Mgr,* Sandra Hummel; Staff 0.75 (Non-MLS 0.75)
Founded 1988. Pop 3,724; Circ 11,137
Library Holdings: High Interest/Low Vocabulary Bk Vols 353; Bk Titles 7,766; Bk Vols 8,069; Per Subs 14
Open Mon & Thurs 12-5 & 6-8, Tues & Wed 9-12 & 1-5, Sat 9-1

LIGONIER

P LIGONIER VALLEY LIBRARY ASSOCIATION, INC, 120 W Main St, 15658-1243. SAN 314-7061. Tel: 724-238-6451. FAX: 724-238-6989. E-mail: lvlibrary@wpa.net. Web Site: www.ligonierlibrary.org. *Dir,* M Janet Hudson; E-mail: lvldirector@wpa.net; *Circ Supvr,* Mary Boyd; *Archivist,* Shirley G Iscrupe; E-mail: lvlparoom@yahoo.com; *Ch Serv,* Linda Norris; E-mail: lvlkids@ligonierlibrary.org. Subject Specialists: *City hist, Genealogy, State hist,* Shirley G Iscrupe; Staff 12 (MLS 2, Non-MLS 10)
Founded 1945. Pop 16,644; Circ 130,213
Jan 2014-Dec 2014 Income $526,807, State $65,525, City $1,500, County $6,000, Parent Institution $453,782
Special Collections: Large Print Coll; Ligonier Echo, micro; Newbery-Caldecott Coll; Pennsylvania History (Pennsylvania Room), bks & micro; Writer's Coll
Subject Interests: County hist, Genealogy

Automation Activity & Vendor Info: (Cataloging) Innovative Interfaces, Inc; (Circulation) Innovative Interfaces, Inc; (ILL) OCLC; (OPAC) Innovative Interfaces, Inc
Database Vendor: Baker & Taylor, ProQuest
Wireless access
Function: 24/7 Online cat, Bk club(s), Bks on CD, Children's prog, Computers for patron use, Copy machines, Digital talking bks, Electronic databases & coll, Exhibits, Free DVD rentals, Genealogy discussion group, Handicapped accessible, Holiday prog, ILL available, Life-long learning prog for all ages, Magazines, Microfiche/film & reading machines, Music CDs, Online cat, Online searches, OverDrive digital audio bks, Preschool reading prog, Prog for adults, Prog for children & young adult, Pub access computers, Scanner, Story hour, Study rm, Summer reading prog
Publications: Happenings (Newsletter)
Mem of Westmoreland County Federated Library System
Partic in Share Westmoreland Consortium
Open Mon-Thurs 10-8:30, Fri & Sat 10-5

LILLY

P LILLY-WASHINGTON PUBLIC LIBRARY*, 520 Church St, Ste 1, 15938-1118. SAN 314-707X. Tel: 814-886-7543. FAX: 814-886-3925. E-mail: lillywash@cclsys.org. Web Site: www.cclsys.org/lillywash. *Dir,* Brenda Marsh
Founded 1963. Pop 1,162; Circ 14,529
Jan 2012-Dec 2012 Income $30,154, State $8,233, County $13,111, Locally Generated Income $8,810. Mats Exp $4,706, Books $3,806, Per/Ser (Incl. Access Fees) $400, AV Mat $500. Sal $16,443
Library Holdings: Bk Vols 6,987; Per Subs 21
Automation Activity & Vendor Info: (Circulation) Brodart
Database Vendor: Gale Cengage Learning
Wireless access
Mem of Cambria County Library System & District Center
Open Mon-Wed & Fri (Winter) 10-5, Sat 8:30-3:30; Mon-Wed (Summer) 9-5, Thurs 9-1, Sat 8:30-12:30

LIMA

P MIDDLETOWN FREE LIBRARY*, 21 N Pennell Rd, 19037. (Mail add: PO Box 275, 19037-0275), SAN 314-7088. Tel: 610-566-7828. FAX: 610-892-0880. E-mail: middletown@delcolibraries.org. *Dir,* Mary Glendening; E-mail: midirector@delcolibraries.org; *Ad,* Laura Kuchmay; E-mail: miref@delcolibraries.org; *Youth Serv Librn,* Jason Fialkovich; E-mail: micsd@delcolibraries.org; Staff 3 (MLS 1, Non-MLS 2)
Founded 1956. Pop 15,807; Circ 143,983
Library Holdings: AV Mats 2,564; DVDs 2,076; Bk Vols 58,257; Per Subs 166
Wireless access
Function: Adult bk club, Audiobks via web, Bks on CD, Children's prog, Computers for patron use, Copy machines, Family literacy, Genealogy discussion group, ILL available, Music CDs, Online cat, OverDrive digital audio bks, Preschool outreach, Preschool reading prog, Prog for adults, Prog for children & young adult, Pub access computers, Story hour, Summer reading prog, Tax forms, Teen prog
Mem of Delaware County Library System
Open Mon-Thurs 10-8, Fri 10-5, Sat 11-4, Sun 1-4
Restriction: 24-hr pass syst for students only
Friends of the Library Group

LINCOLN UNIVERSITY

C LINCOLN UNIVERSITY*, Langston Hughes Memorial Library, 1570 Old Baltimore Pike, 19352. (Mail add: PO Box 147, 19352-0147), SAN 314-7096. Tel: 610-932-8300, Ext 3367. Circulation Tel: 610-932-8300, Ext 3366. Interlibrary Loan Service Tel: 610-932-8300, Ext 3356. Reference Tel: 610-932-8300, Ext 3371. Administration Tel: 610-932-8300, Ext 3261. FAX: 610-932-1206. Web Site: www.lincoln.edu/library. *Assoc Prof, Dir,* Tracey J Hunter Hayes; Tel: 484-365-7370, E-mail: thunterhayes@lincoln.edu; *Access Serv Librn, Asst Prof,* Joseph McIlhenney; Tel: 484-365-7366, E-mail: jmcilhenney@lincoln.edu; *Acq Librn, Asst Prof,* Elizabeth Pitt; Tel: 484-365-7357, E-mail: epitt@lincoln.edu; *Asst Prof, Cat Librn,* Albert Bryson; Tel: 484-365-7358, E-mail: bryson@lincoln.edu; *Prof, Ref Librn,* Mahinder Chopra; Tel: 484-365-7371, E-mail: chopra@lincoln.edu; *Assoc Prof, Ser Librn,* Neal Carlson; Tel: 484-365-7262, E-mail: carlson@lincoln.edu; *Asst Prof, Spec Coll Librn,* Susan Pevar; Tel: 484-365-7266, E-mail: spevar@lincoln.edu; *ILL & Distance Libr Serv Spec,* Bonnie Horn; Tel: 484-365-7356, E-mail: bhorn@lincoln.edu; Staff 7 (MLS 6, Non-MLS 1)
Founded 1898. Fac 7; Highest Degree: Master
Special Collections: African Studies, bks, per; Afro-American Studies, micro, vf; Langston Hughes (Personal Library); Larry Neal Spec Coll; Therman O'Daniel Spec Coll
Subject Interests: Liberal arts, Presbyterianism lit, Protestant theol, Sci
Publications: Accessions List; Catalog of the Special Negro & African Collection, 2 vols & supplement
Partic in Interlibrary Delivery Service of Pennsylvania; Lyrasis; OCLC Online Computer Library Center, Inc; Tri State Col Libr Coop

LINESVILLE

P LINESVILLE COMMUNITY PUBLIC LIBRARY*, 111 Penn St, 16424. (Mail add: PO Box 97, 16424-0097), SAN 376-5709. Tel: 814-683-4354. FAX: 814-683-4354. Web Site: www.ccfls.org/linesville. *Librn,* Telce Varee; Staff 2 (MLS 1, Non-MLS 1)
Pop 5,661; Circ 10,080
Library Holdings: Bk Titles 18,700; Bk Vols 18,900; Per Subs 61; Talking Bks 434; Videos 172
Wireless access
Mem of Crawford County Federated Library System
Open Mon 9-5, Tues & Thurs 4-8, Wed 9-1 & 4-8, Fri 9-1, Sat 8-12
Friends of the Library Group

LIONVILLE

M PENNSYLVANIA STATE DEPARTMENT OF HEALTH*, Herbert Fox Memorial Library, 110 Pickering Way, 19353. (Mail add: PO Box 500, Exton, 19341-0500), SAN 327-8689. Tel: 610-280-3464. FAX: 610-450-1932. *Librn,* Dr M Jeffrey Shoemaker; *Asst Librn,* Andrea O'Leary; E-mail: aoleary@health.state.pa.us; Staff 2 (MLS 2)
Library Holdings: Bk Titles 2,120; Bk Vols 2,460; Per Subs 58
Subject Interests: Pub health
Restriction: Staff use only

LITITZ

P LITITZ PUBLIC LIBRARY*, 651 Kissel Hill Rd, 17543. SAN 314-7118. Tel: 717-626-2255. FAX: 717-627-4191. Web Site: www.lititzlibrary.org. *Dir,* Susan Miller Tennant; E-mail: stennant@lititzlibrary.org; *Asst Dir, Ch Serv,* Karen Payonk; E-mail: kpayonk@lititzlibrary.org; *Coordr, Spec Serv,* Linda Skelly; E-mail: lskelly@lititzlibrary.org; Staff 19 (MLS 4, Non-MLS 15)
Founded 1936. Pop 28,337; Circ 279,096
Library Holdings: Bk Vols 54,916; Per Subs 50
Mem of Library System of Lancaster County
Open Mon-Thurs 9-8, Fri 9-6, Sat 9-4
Friends of the Library Group

LITTLESTOWN

P LITTLESTOWN LIBRARY*, 232 N Queen St, 17340. Tel: 717-359-0446. FAX: 717-359-1359. Web Site: www.adamslibrary.org/about-2/branch-libraries. *Librn,* Valli Hoski; E-mail: vallih@adamslibrary.org; *Asst Br Mgr,* Kat Clements
Library Holdings: Bk Titles 8,391; Bk Vols 9,211; Per Subs 25
Automation Activity & Vendor Info: (Cataloging) TLC (The Library Corporation); (Circulation) TLC (The Library Corporation); (OPAC) TLC (The Library Corporation)
Wireless access
Mem of Adams County Library System
Open Tues & Thurs 2-8, Wed & Fri 12-6, Sat 10-4
Friends of the Library Group

LOCK HAVEN

C LOCK HAVEN UNIVERSITY OF PENNSYLVANIA*, George B Stevenson Library, 401 N Fairview Ave, 17745-2390. SAN 314-7134. Tel: 570-484-2309. Interlibrary Loan Service Tel: 570-484-2545. Reference Tel: 570-484-2468. Administration Tel: 570-484-2310. Automation Services Tel: 570-484-2466. FAX: 570-484-2506. Web Site: www.lhup.edu/library/home.htm. *Dir, Libr & Info Serv,* Joby Topper; E-mail: jtopper@lhup.edu; Staff 17 (MLS 9, Non-MLS 8)
Founded 1870. Enrl 4,900; Fac 250; Highest Degree: Master
Library Holdings: Bk Titles 244,123; Bk Vols 353,198; Per Subs 848
Special Collections: Eden Phillpotts Coll
Automation Activity & Vendor Info: (Acquisitions) Ex Libris Group; (Cataloging) Ex Libris Group; (Circulation) Ex Libris Group; (Course Reserve) Ex Libris Group; (ILL) Ex Libris Group; (Media Booking) Ex Libris Group; (OPAC) Ex Libris Group; (Serials) Ex Libris Group
Partic in Interlibrary Delivery Service of Pennsylvania; OCLC Online Computer Library Center, Inc; Pennsylvania Academic Library Consortium, Inc (PALCI); State System of Higher Education Library Cooperative; Susquehanna Library Cooperative
Open Mon-Fri 7:30am-11pm, Sat 9-5, Sun 2-11

P ANNIE HALENBAKE ROSS LIBRARY*, 232 W Main St, 17745-1241. SAN 358-6774. Tel: 570-748-3321. FAX: 570-748-1050. E-mail: ross1@rosslibrary.org. Web Site: www.rosslibrary.org. *Exec Dir,* Diane Whitaker; *County Librn,* Joseph Bitner; *Coordr, Youth Serv,* Nancy Antram;

Adult Serv, Louis Bernard; *Cat,* Tracey Dow; *ILL,* Marilyn Morrison; Staff 11 (MLS 2, Non-MLS 9)
Founded 1910. Pop 37,914; Circ 126,546
Jan 2012-Dec 2012 Income (Main Library Only) $423,058, State $142,866, City $22,500, Federal $4,000, County $80,000, Locally Generated Income $173,692. Mats Exp $76,127, Books $44,579, Per/Ser (Incl. Access Fees) $4,972, Micro $3,818, AV Mat $4,843, Electronic Ref Mat (Incl. Access Fees) $6,639, Presv $11,276. Sal $257,618 (Prof $50,882)
Library Holdings: AV Mats 3,474; CDs 150; DVDs 3,472; Large Print Bks 5,000; Bk Titles 85,763; Bk Vols 121,962; Per Subs 120
Special Collections: Local Genealogical Materials; Pennsylvaniana (Pennsylvania Room), bks, census reports, local photo coll, micro
Automation Activity & Vendor Info: (Cataloging) EOS International; (Circulation) EOS International; (OPAC) EOS International
Database Vendor: Brodart, Overdrive, Inc, TumbleBookLibrary
Wireless access
Function: Art exhibits, Bk club(s), CD-ROM, Computer training, Copy machines, Family literacy, Handicapped accessible, Home delivery & serv to Sr ctr & nursing homes, ILL available, Magnifiers for reading, Newsp ref libr, Online searches, Photocopying/Printing, Preschool outreach, Prog for adults, Prog for children & young adult, Ref serv available, Senior computer classes, Summer reading prog, Telephone ref, VHS videos, Video lending libr, Wheelchair accessible, Workshops
Publications: A Final Peek at the Past; Another Peek at the Past; Clinton County: A Journey Through Time; Flemington Mosaic; Indians of Clinton County; Journal of Travels, Adventures & Remarks of Jerry Church; Maynard's Historical Clinton County; Mountain Folks: Fragments of Central Pennsylvania Folklore; No Rain in Heaven; Old Town: A History of Early Lock Haven; Peek at the Past; Third Peek at the Past
Special Services for the Deaf - Accessible learning ctr; High interest/low vocabulary bks
Special Services for the Blind - BiFolkal kits; Bks on cassette; Bks on CD; Internet workstation with adaptive software; Large print bks; Magnifiers
Open Mon, Tues & Thurs 10-8, Wed, Fri & Sat 10-6
Friends of the Library Group
Branches: 2
FRIENDSHIP COMMUNITY LIBRARY, Main St, Beech Creek, 16822. (Mail add: PO Box 478, Beech Creek, 16822-0478). Tel: 570-962-2048. *Asst Br Mgr,* Susan M Gibson; Staff 1 (Non-MLS 1)
Founded 1981. Pop 1,727
Jan 2012-Dec 2012 Income $10,162, Locally Generated Income $500, Parent Institution $4,462, Other $5,200. Mats Exp $682, Books $500, Per/Ser (Incl. Access Fees) $182. Sal $4,462
Library Holdings: Large Print Bks 150; Bk Vols 8,000; Videos 50
Function: AV serv, Handicapped accessible, ILL available, Online searches, Summer reading prog
Open Mon, Tues & Thurs 3-7
RENOVO AREA LIBRARY, 317 Seventh St, Renovo, 17764, SAN 358-6804. Tel: 570-923-0390. *Br Mgr,* Barbara Rauch; Staff 1 (Non-MLS 1)
Founded 1968. Pop 5,000; Circ 7,729
Jan 2007-Dec 2007 Income $72,119, State $24,176, County $9,252, Locally Generated Income $32,380, Parent Institution $6,311. Mats Exp $6,177, Books $5,320, Per/Ser (Incl. Access Fees) $707, Presv $150. Sal $21,669
Library Holdings: AV Mats 63; Large Print Bks 150; Bk Vols 11,405; Per Subs 10
Function: Children's prog, Computers for patron use, Copy machines, Exhibits, Handicapped accessible, Holiday prog, ILL available, OverDrive digital audio bks, Preschool reading prog, Prog for children & young adult, Pub access computers, Ref serv available, Summer reading prog, Wheelchair accessible
Open Tues 12:30-5:30 & 6-8, Wed-Fri 9-1 & 1:30-5

LORETTO

CR SAINT FRANCIS UNIVERSITY, Library & Learning Commons, 106 Franciscan Way, 15940. (Mail add: PO Box 600, 15940-0600), SAN 358-6839. Tel: 814-472-3011. Circulation Tel: 814-472-3160. Interlibrary Loan Service Tel: 814-472-3155. Reference Tel: 814-472-3161. Automation Services Tel: 814-472-3163. Information Services Tel: 814-472-3162. FAX: 814-472-3154. Interlibrary Loan Service FAX: 814-472-3093. E-mail: cirli@francis.edu. *Dean of Libr Serv,* Sandra A Balough; Tel: 814-472-3153, E-mail: sbalough@francis.edu; *Assoc Dean,* Janie Rager; E-mail: jrager@francis.edu; *Info Serv Librn,* Brad Coffield; Tel: 814-472-3315, E-mail: bcoffield@francis.edu; *Info Serv Librn,* Renee Hoffman; Tel: 814-472-3152, E-mail: rhoffman@francis.edu; *Archivist, Tech Serv Librn,* Rebecca Kopanic; Tel: 814-472-3156, E-mail: rkopanic@francis.edu
Founded 1847. Enrl 1,700; Fac 120; Highest Degree: Doctorate
Jul 2013-Jun 2014. Mats Exp $390,514, Books $25,449, Per/Ser (Incl. Access Fees) $29,386, Electronic Ref Mat (Incl. Access Fees) $263,649, Presv $2,005. Sal $572,560 (Prof $443,545)
Library Holdings: CDs 144; DVDs 516; e-books 39,053; e-journals 44,444; Electronic Media & Resources 70; Bk Titles 67,132; Bk Vols 20,829; Per Subs 50; Videos 3,080
Automation Activity & Vendor Info: (Acquisitions) OCLC; (Cataloging) OCLC Connexion; (Circulation) OCLC; (Course Reserve) OCLC; (ILL) OCLC ILLiad; (Media Booking) OCLC; (OPAC) OCLC; (Serials) OCLC
Database Vendor: ABC-CLIO, Alexander Street Press, American Chemical Society, American Physical Society, American Psychological Association (APA), ARTstor, Atlas Systems, BioOne, Bowker, Cambridge Scientific Abstracts, Checkpoint Systems, Inc, Cinahl, CQ Press, CredoReference, ebrary, EBSCOhost, Elsevier, Facts on File, Gale Cengage Learning, Haworth Pres Inc, Hoovers, JSTOR, MD Consult, Medline, Nature Publishing Group, OCLC, OCLC ArticleFirst, OCLC FirstSearch, OCLC WebJunction, OCLC WorldShare Interlibrary Loan, OCLC Worldshare Management Services, OVID Technologies, Project MUSE, ProQuest, PubMed, Sage, ScienceDirect, SerialsSolutions, Standard & Poor's, Thomson - Web of Science, ValueLine
Wireless access
Partic in Lyrasis; Pennsylvania Academic Library Consortium, Inc (PALCI)
Open Mon-Thurs 7am-11pm, Fri 7-6, Sat 12-5, Sun 1-11

MACUNGIE

P LOWER MACUNGIE LIBRARY*, 3450 Brookside Rd, 18062. Tel: 610-966-6864. FAX: 610-965-0384. Web Site: www.lowermaclib.org. *Dir,* Kathee Rhode
Library Holdings: AV Mats 4,290; Bk Vols 35,398; Per Subs 105
Automation Activity & Vendor Info: (Cataloging) Horizon; (Circulation) Horizon; (Course Reserve) Horizon; (ILL) Horizon; (OPAC) Horizon
Open Mon 10-9, Tues, Wed & Thurs 10-8, Fri & Sat 9-5

MAHANOY CITY

P MAHANOY CITY PUBLIC LIBRARY*, 17-19 W Mahanoy Ave, 17948-2615. SAN 314-7231. Tel: 570-773-1610. Web Site: www.mahanoycitypubliclibrary.org. *Dir,* Linda Ernst; *Asst Dir,* Carol Keims
Pop 10,749; Circ 14,162
Library Holdings: Bk Vols 30,000; Per Subs 28
Open Mon-Fri 10-7, Sat 10-2

MALVERN

P MALVERN PUBLIC LIBRARY*, One E First Ave, 19355-2743. SAN 314-724X. Tel: 610-644-7259. FAX: 610-644-5204. Web Site: www.ccls.org. *Dir,* Rosalie Dietz; E-mail: rdietz@ccls.org; Staff 3 (MLS 1, Non-MLS 2)
Founded 1873. Pop 34,222; Circ 51,861
Library Holdings: Bk Titles 37,259; Bk Vols 39,116; Per Subs 94; Talking Bks 2,175; Videos 1,682
Automation Activity & Vendor Info: (Cataloging) Innovative Interfaces, Inc; (Circulation) Innovative Interfaces, Inc; (OPAC) Innovative Interfaces, Inc
Wireless access
Open Mon-Wed 9-9, Thurs 9-8, Fri 9-5, Sat 9-4
Friends of the Library Group

C PENNSYLVANIA STATE UNIVERSITY*, Great Valley Library (University Libraries), 30 E Swedesford Rd, 19355. SAN 315-1492. Tel: 610-648-3215. FAX: 610-725-5223. Web Site: www.libraries.psu.edu/greatvalley. *Head Librn,* Dr Dolores Fidishun; Tel: 610-648-3227, E-mail: dxf19@psu.edu; *Head, Circ,* Carol Riley; Tel: 610-648-3205, E-mail: cmr18@psu.edu; *Ref Librn,* Alexia Hudson; Tel: 610-648-3364, E-mail: aih3@psu.edu; *Ref Librn,* James Sauer; Tel: 610-648-3354, E-mail: jls51@psu.edu; *Coordr, Acq, Coordr, Ser,* Carol Folk; Tel: 610-648-3228, E-mail: cfj11@psu.edu; *Instrul Design/Web Serv,* Julie Meyer; Tel: 610-648-3358, E-mail: jmm49@psu.edu; Staff 14 (MLS 3, Non-MLS 11)
Founded 1963. Enrl 1,700; Fac 80; Highest Degree: Master
Library Holdings: Bk Vols 40,000; Per Subs 380
Special Collections: Curriculum; Eric Documents; Psychological Tests; Thesis
Subject Interests: Computer sci, Educ, Eng, Math, Mgt
Automation Activity & Vendor Info: (Cataloging) SirsiDynix; (Circulation) SirsiDynix; (OPAC) SirsiDynix; (Serials) SirsiDynix
Wireless access
Partic in OCLC Online Computer Library Center, Inc; RLIN (Research Libraries Information Network); Tri State Col Libr Coop
Open Mon-Thurs 9:30-9:30, Fri 9:30-6, Sat 8-4:30

MANHEIM

P MANHEIM COMMUNITY LIBRARY*, 15 E High St, 17545-1505. Tel: 717-665-6700. FAX: 717-665-2470. *Dir,* Barbara A Brosey; Staff 3 (MLS 1, Non-MLS 2)
Pop 17,091; Circ 32,815

Library Holdings: Bk Titles 19,642; Bk Vols 21,718; Per Subs 29; Talking Bks 674; Videos 705
Automation Activity & Vendor Info: (Cataloging) Innovative Interfaces, Inc; (Circulation) Innovative Interfaces, Inc; (OPAC) Innovative Interfaces, Inc
Mem of Library System of Lancaster County
Open Mon-Thurs 10-8, Fri 10-6, Sat 9-4
Friends of the Library Group

MANOR

P MANOR PUBLIC LIBRARY*, 44 Main St, 15665. Tel: 724-864-6850. FAX: 724-864-6850. E-mail: manorpublic.library@comcast.net. Web Site: www.manorpubliclibrary.org. *Dir,* Shannon Metcalf, *Libr Asst,* Vicki Monaco
Founded 1944
Library Holdings: Bk Vols 18,000; Per Subs 14
Automation Activity & Vendor Info: (Cataloging) Follett Software; (Circulation) Follett Software; (OPAC) Follett Software
Open Mon & Wed 12-7, Tues & Thurs 10-5, Sat 10-2

MANSFIELD

P MANSFIELD FREE PUBLIC LIBRARY*, 71 N Main St, 16933. SAN 314-7274. Tel: 570-662-3850. FAX: 570-662-7423. E-mail: mfpl@epix.net. Web Site: www.ncldistrict.org/mansfield. *Dir,* Mary Sirgey
Founded 1901. Pop 5,929; Circ 20,694
Library Holdings: Audiobooks 250; Bks on Deafness & Sign Lang 5; Braille Volumes 1; DVDs 700; Large Print Bks 300; Bk Vols 17,000; Per Subs 40
Special Collections: Books on tape; Large Print Coll; Pennsylvania & Tioga County
Automation Activity & Vendor Info: (Circulation) EOS International
Wireless access
Mem of Potter-Tioga Library System
Open Mon, Tues & Thurs 1-8, Wed 10-8, Sat 9-4
Friends of the Library Group

C MANSFIELD UNIVERSITY, North Hall Library, Five Swan St, 16933. SAN 314-7282. Tel: 570-662-4670. Interlibrary Loan Service Tel: 570-662-4683. Administration Tel: 570-662-4689. Information Services Tel: 570-662-4671. FAX: 570-662-4993. Web Site: www.mnsfld.edu/depts/. *Dir,* Scott R DiMarco; E-mail: sdimarco@mansfield.edu; *Coordr, Tech Serv,* Jamey Harris; E-mail: jharris@mansfield.edu; *Ref,* Frances S Garrison; Tel: 570-662-4688, E-mail: fgarriso@mansfield.edu; *Ref,* Sheila M Kasperek; Tel: 570-662-4675, E-mail: skaspere@mansfield.edu; *Ref,* Matt Syrett; Tel: 570-662-4679, E-mail: msyrett@mansfield.edu; Staff 16 (MLS 5, Non-MLS 11)
Founded 1857. Enrl 2,970; Fac 180; Highest Degree: Master
Jul 2013-Jun 2014 Income $1,351,263. Mats Exp $475,798. Sal $875,465
Library Holdings: Bk Vols 240,352; Per Subs 26,050
Special Collections: Annual Report. Oral History; US Document Depository
Subject Interests: Criminal justice, Educ, Music
Automation Activity & Vendor Info: (Acquisitions) Ex Libris Group; (Cataloging) Ex Libris Group; (Circulation) Ex Libris Group; (ILL) Ex Libris Group; (OPAC) Ex Libris Group; (Serials) Ex Libris Group
Database Vendor: Cambridge Scientific Abstracts, Dialog, EBSCOhost, Gale Cengage Learning, LexisNexis, OCLC FirstSearch, OVID Technologies, ProQuest, SerialsSolutions, Wilson - Wilson Web
Partic in Keystone Library Network; Lyrasis; Pennsylvania Academic Library Consortium, Inc (PALCI); State System of Higher Education Library Cooperative; Susquehanna Library Cooperative
Special Services for the Deaf - ADA equip

MAPLE GLEN

SR SUPPLEE MEMORIAL PRESBYTERIAN CHURCH LIBRARY*, 855 Welsh Rd, 19002. SAN 328-3410. Tel: 215-646-4123. FAX: 215-646-8895. Web Site: www.suppleepc.org. *Librn,* Johanna Sorkness
Library Holdings: AV Mats 43; Bk Vols 2,133
Special Collections: Antique Bible Coll
Open Mon-Fri 1-3, Sun 8-12

MARCUS HOOK

P MARY M CAMPBELL PUBLIC LIBRARY*, Tenth & Green Sts, 19061-4592. SAN 314-7304. Tel: 610-485-6519. E-mail: marcushook@delcolibraries.org. *Librn,* Irene H Wallin; Staff 4 (MLS 1, Non-MLS 3)
Founded 1923. Pop 2,314; Circ 11,826
Library Holdings: Bk Vols 23,000; Per Subs 60
Mem of Delaware County Library System
Open Mon, Wed & Fri 10-5:30, Tues & Thurs 2:30-8, Sat 10-5 (9-1 Summer)
Friends of the Library Group

MARIANNA

P MARIANNA COMMUNITY PUBLIC LIBRARY*, 247 Jefferson Ave, 15345. (Mail add: PO Box 457, 15345-0457), SAN 314-7320. Tel: 724-267-3888. FAX: 724-267-3888. E-mail: mclib@roadlynx.net. Web Site: www.mariannalibrary.org. *Dir,* Susan Casper
Founded 1968. Pop 2,486; Circ 8,331
Library Holdings: Bk Vols 8,054; Per Subs 43
Open Mon-Fri 11-5, Sat 8:30-3:30 (8:30-12:30 Summer)
Friends of the Library Group

MARIENVILLE

P FOREST COUNTY LIBRARY*, Marienville Area Public Library, 106 Pine St, 16239. (Mail add: Box 306, 16239-0306), SAN 358-6898. Tel: 814-927-8552. FAX: 814-927-8552. Web Site: www.csonline.net/marienvillelibrary. *Librn,* Sue Watson; *Asst Librn,* Kathy Henschel
Founded 1969. Pop 2,426; Circ 17,000
Library Holdings: DVDs 744; Bk Vols 11,000; Per Subs 30
Automation Activity & Vendor Info: (Cataloging) Follett Software; (Circulation) Follett Software
Database Vendor: Baker & Taylor, EBSCOhost, Gale Cengage Learning
Wireless access
Open Mon-Wed 10:30-5:30, Thurs 10:30-8, Sat 9-4
Friends of the Library Group

MARS

P MARS AREA PUBLIC LIBRARY*, 107 Grand Ave, 16046. (Mail add: PO Box 415, 16046-0415), SAN 314-7347. Tel: 724-625-9048. FAX: 724-625-2871. Web Site: www.bcfls.org/mars-area-public-library. *Dir,* J Ford; E-mail: jford@bcfls.org; Staff 1 (Non-MLS 1)
Founded 1947. Pop 6,000; Circ 48,000
Jan 2005-Dec 2005 Income $113,000. Mats Exp $13,500. Sal $70,000 (Prof $32,000)
Library Holdings: Bk Titles 32,000; Per Subs 52
Automation Activity & Vendor Info: (Cataloging) TLC (The Library Corporation); (Circulation) TLC (The Library Corporation)
Database Vendor: EBSCOhost, Gale Cengage Learning
Wireless access
Mem of Butler County Federated Library System
Special Services for the Blind - Audio mat; Large print bks
Open Mon & Wed 10-8, Tues 10-5, Thurs 10-7, Fri 10-3, Sat 9-4 (Summer) 9-1
Friends of the Library Group

MARTINSBURG

P MARTINSBURG COMMUNITY LIBRARY*, 201 S Walnut St, 16662-1129. SAN 314-7355. Tel: 814-793-3335. FAX: 814-793-9755. E-mail: mclibrary@atlanticbbn.net. Web Site: www.martinsburgcommunitylibrary.org. *Dir,* Jackie Rhule; Staff 2 (Non-MLS 2)
Founded 1918. Pop 5,181; Circ 50,000
Library Holdings: AV Mats 1,214; Large Print Bks 211; Bk Titles 29,919; Bk Vols 31,684; Per Subs 25; Talking Bks 108; Videos 714
Special Collections: Genealogy (George H Liebegott Coll); Genealogy (John Memorial Coll)
Subject Interests: County hist, Family hist, Town hist
Automation Activity & Vendor Info: (Cataloging) Follett Software; (Circulation) Follett Software; (OPAC) Follett Software
Database Vendor: EBSCOhost
Wireless access
Function: Archival coll
Mem of Blair County Library System
Open Mon, Tues, Thurs & Fri 10-4, Sat 10-2
Friends of the Library Group

MARYSVILLE

P MARYSVILLE-RYE LIBRARY*, 198 Overcrest Rd, 17053-1157. SAN 314-7363. Tel: 717-957-2851. FAX: 717-957-3054. Web Site: www.freewebs.com/marysvillerye/. *Dir,* Wendy Holler; Staff 2 (MLS 1, Non-MLS 1)
Founded 1966. Pop 6,122; Circ 14,198
Library Holdings: AV Mats 590; Bk Titles 14,272; Bk Vols 16,891; Per Subs 46; Talking Bks 211; Videos 197
Automation Activity & Vendor Info: (Cataloging) TLC (The Library Corporation); (Circulation) TLC (The Library Corporation)
Open Mon-Wed 1-8, Thurs 12-8, Sat 9-4
Friends of the Library Group

MASONTOWN

P GERMAN-MASONTOWN PUBLIC LIBRARY*, Nine S Washington St, 15461-2025. SAN 314-7371. Tel: 724-583-7030. FAX: 724-583-0979. E-mail: germaslibrary01@yahoo.com. Web Site: www.germaslibrary.org. *Dir,* Amy Ryan; *Admin Supvr,* Shirley Renaldi
Founded 1965. Pop 11,500; Circ 30,779
Library Holdings: Bk Vols 24,328; Per Subs 42
Subject Interests: Local hist
Automation Activity & Vendor Info: (Cataloging) LibraryWorld, Inc; (Circulation) LibraryWorld, Inc; (OPAC) LibraryWorld, Inc; (Serials) LibraryWorld, Inc
Wireless access
Mem of Fayette County Library System
Open Mon 3-7, Tues & Thurs 10-5, Wed 10-6, Sat 9-3
Friends of the Library Group

MCCONNELLSBURG

P FULTON COUNTY LIBRARY*, 227 N First St, 17233-1003, SAN 321-5105. Tel: 717-485-5327. FAX: 717-485-5646. Web Site: www.fclspa.org/fulton/home.htm. *Dir,* Jamie Brambley; E-mail: jbrambley@fclspa.org; Staff 6 (MLS 1, Non-MLS 5)
Founded 1975. Pop 14,283; Circ 29,812
Library Holdings: Large Print Bks 110; Bk Titles 37,411; Bk Vols 38,910; Per Subs 96; Talking Bks 309; Videos 584
Special Collections: Handicapped; Special Needs
Subject Interests: Civil War
Automation Activity & Vendor Info: (Cataloging) Brodart; (Circulation) Brodart; (OPAC) Brodart
Open Mon, Wed & Fri 9-6, Tues & Thurs 9-8, Sat 9-4
Friends of the Library Group
Branches: 1
HUSTONTOWN BRANCH, 313 Pitt St, Ste B, Hustontown, 17229. (Mail add: PO Box 426, Hustontown, 17229-0426), SAN 329-3653. Tel: 717-987-3606. FAX: 717-987-3606. *Br Mgr,* Trudy Fix; E-mail: tfix@fclspa.org; Staff 2 (MLS 1, Non-MLS 1)
Library Holdings: Bk Titles 23,019; Bk Vols 25,642; Per Subs 51; Talking Bks 90; Videos 209
Open Mon-Wed & Fri 10-5, Thurs 12-5
Friends of the Library Group

MCDONALD

P HERITAGE PUBLIC LIBRARY*, 52 Fourth St, 15057-1166. SAN 314-7142. Tel: 724-926-8400. FAX: 724-926-4686. E-mail: heritagelibrary@comcast.net. Web Site: www.heritagepublib.org. *Interim Dir,* Rebecca Skirpan; Staff 4 (Non-MLS 4)
Founded 1907. Pop 8,000; Circ 27,000
Library Holdings: Bks on Deafness & Sign Lang 20; Large Print Bks 630; Bk Titles 23,000; Per Subs 35; Talking Bks 340
Automation Activity & Vendor Info: (Acquisitions) Follett Software; (Cataloging) Follett Software
Database Vendor: EBSCOhost
Wireless access
Function: Accelerated reader prog, Adult bk club, Bks on CD, Computers for patron use, Copy machines, Fax serv, Free DVD rentals, Handicapped accessible, ILL available, Microfiche/film & reading machines, Scanner, Story hour, Tax forms, VHS videos, Wheelchair accessible
Mem of Washington County Library System
Open Tues-Thurs 10-8, Sat 10-4
Friends of the Library Group

MCEWENSVILLE

P MONTGOMERY HOUSE LIBRARY*, Warrior Run Area Public, 20 Church St, 17749. (Mail add: PO Box 5, 17749-0005), SAN 314-7150. Tel: 570-538-1381. FAX: 570-538-1381. E-mail: director@montgomeryhouselibrary.org. Web Site: www.montgomeryhouselibrary.org. *Dir,* J A Babay; *Mgr, Libr Serv,* Cindy Batdorf; E-mail: cindy.batdorf@montgomeryhouselibrary.org; *Pub Serv,* Harriet Moyer; E-mail: harriet.moyer@montgomeryhouselibrary.org; Staff 1 (MLS 1)
Founded 1967. Pop 9,463; Circ 43,179
Special Collections: Pennsylvania Coll
Subject Interests: Local hist
Automation Activity & Vendor Info: (Acquisitions) LibLime
Database Vendor: Access Pennsylvania
Wireless access
Open Mon & Thurs 1-8, Tues & Wed 11-7, Fri 10-6, Sat 9-4
Friends of the Library Group

MCKEES ROCKS

P FOR STO-ROX LIBRARY*, 500 Chartiers Ave, 15136. SAN 314-7177. Tel: 412-771-1222. FAX: 412-771-2340. Web Site: www.storoxlibrary.org. *Dir,* Brad Wulfkuhle; *Youth Serv Coordr,* Sue Ann Orange; E-mail: oranges@einetwork.net; Staff 2 (Non-MLS 2)
Founded 1995. Pop 13,328; Circ 24,848
Library Holdings: Large Print Bks 93; Bk Titles 11,559; Bk Vols 14,162; Per Subs 43; Videos 310
Automation Activity & Vendor Info: (Cataloging) Innovative Interfaces, Inc; (Circulation) Innovative Interfaces, Inc; (OPAC) Innovative Interfaces, Inc; (Serials) Innovative Interfaces, Inc
Mem of Allegheny County Library Association
Open Mon-Thurs 12-7, Sat 12-4
Friends of the Library Group

M OHIO VALLEY GENERAL HOSPITAL LIBRARY*, 25 Heckel Rd, 15136. SAN 314-7169. Tel: 412-777-6159. FAX: 412-777-6866. *Mgr, Continued Educ,* Lynn Scanga
Founded 1905
Library Holdings: Bk Vols 1,900; Per Subs 90
Subject Interests: Consumer health info, Gen med, Nursing
Open Mon-Fri 9-5

MCKEESPORT

P CARNEGIE LIBRARY OF MCKEESPORT*, 1507 Library Ave, 15132-4796. SAN 314-7185. Tel: 412-672-0625. FAX: 412-672-7860. Web Site: www.einetwork.net/ein/mckeespt. *Interim Dir,* Kelley Moten; E-mail: motenk@einetwork.net; *Dir,* Position Currently Open; *Cat,* Nancy Henderson; *Ch Serv,* Chris Kritikos; Staff 3 (MLS 1, Non-MLS 2)
Founded 1902. Pop 63,291; Circ 101,681
Library Holdings: AV Mats 10,811; Large Print Bks 384; Bk Titles 112,658; Bk Vols 114,390; Per Subs 211; Talking Bks 3,742; Videos 4,682
Special Collections: Local History (Western Pennsylvania), bks, pamphlets, pictures; Pennsylvania Archives
Subject Interests: Educ, Hist, Lit
Automation Activity & Vendor Info: (Cataloging) Innovative Interfaces, Inc; (Circulation) Innovative Interfaces, Inc; (OPAC) Innovative Interfaces, Inc; (Serials) Innovative Interfaces, Inc
Mem of Allegheny County Library Association
Open Mon-Wed (Winter) 8-8, Thurs & Fri 8-6, Sat 8-3, Sun 11-3; Mon-Wed (Summer) 8-8, Thurs & Fri 8-6, Sat 8-1
Friends of the Library Group
Branches: 2
ELIZABETH FORWARD BRANCH, Central Elementary School, 401 Rock Run Rd, Elizabeth, 15037. Tel: 412-896-2371. *Br Mgr,* Jill Dahl; Staff 2 (MLS 1, Non-MLS 1)
Library Holdings: Bk Titles 12,816; Bk Vols 14,919; Per Subs 21
Open Tues-Thurs (Winter) 1-7, Fri & Sat 10-2; Tues & Wed (Summer) 1-7, Thurs-Sat 10-2
Friends of the Library Group
WHITE OAK BRANCH, McAllister Lodge, 169 Victoria Dr, White Oak, 15131. Tel: 412-678-2002. *Br Mgr,* Frances Trimble; *Br Coordr,* Mary Jane DeParma; Staff 2 (MLS 1, Non-MLS 1)
Library Holdings: Bk Titles 5,290; Bk Vols 5,460; Per Subs 15
Open Mon & Tues (Winter) 1-5, Wed & Thurs 3-7, Sat 10-2; Mon, Tues & Sat (Summer) 10-2, Wed & Thurs 3-7
Friends of the Library Group

M MCKEESPORT HOSPITAL*, Health Service Library, 1500 Fifth Ave, 15132. SAN 314-7193. Tel: 412-664-2363. FAX: 412-664-2581. *Librn,* Karen Zundel; E-mail: zundelkm@msx.upmc.edu; Staff 1 (Non-MLS 1)
Founded 1975
Library Holdings: Bk Titles 3,811; Bk Vols 4,091; Per Subs 80
Subject Interests: Hospital admin, Med, Nursing
Open Mon, Wed & Fri 9-3, Tues & Thurs 7-7

C PENNSYLVANIA STATE UNIVERSITY, GREATER ALLEGHENY, J Clarence Kelly Library, 4000 University Dr, 15132-7698. SAN 314-7207. Tel: 412-675-9110. Reference Tel: 412-675-9119. FAX: 412-675-9113. Web Site: www.libraries.psu.edu/psul/greaterallegheny.html. *Head Librn,* Kay Ellen Harvey; Tel: 412-580-7814, E-mail: keh4@psu.edu; Staff 6 (MLS 2, Non-MLS 4)
Founded 1948. Enrl 878; Fac 59; Highest Degree: Bachelor
Library Holdings: Bk Vols 43,000; Per Subs 70
Automation Activity & Vendor Info: (OPAC) SirsiDynix
Database Vendor: ACM (Association for Computing Machinery), Agricola, American Mathematical Society, Annual Reviews, ARTstor, ASCE Research Library, BioOne, Cinahl, College Source, CQ Press, EBSCOhost, Elsevier, Factiva.com, GalleryWatch, HeinOnline, Hoovers, IBISWorld, IEEE (Institute of Electrical & Electronics Engineers), Ingenta, JSTOR, Knovel, LexisNexis, MD Consult, Medianet, Mergent Online, Newsbank, OCLC FirstSearch, OVID Technologies, Oxford Online, Project MUSE, ProQuest, PubMed, RefWorks, Safari Books Online, SirsiDynix,

ValueLine, Westlaw, Wiley InterScience, Wilson - Wilson Web, YBP Library Services
Wireless access
Partic in OCLC Online Computer Library Center, Inc; RLIN (Research Libraries Information Network)
Open Mon-Thurs 8-8, Fri 8-5, Sat 12-5, Sun 3-8

MCMURRAY

P PETERS TOWNSHIP PUBLIC LIBRARY*, 616 E McMurray Rd, 15317-3495. SAN 314-7215. Tel: 724-941-9430. FAX: 724-941-9438. Web Site: www.ptlibrary.org. *Admin Dir,* Pier M Lee; E-mail: plee@ptlibrary.org; *Adult Serv, Ref,* Margaret Deitzer; E-mail: mdeitzer@ptlibrary.org; *Ch Serv,* Joanne Robinson; E-mail: jrobinson@ptlibrary.org; Staff 22 (MLS 6, Non-MLS 16)
Founded 1957. Pop 17,566; Circ 397,672
Jan 2006-Dec 2006 Income $831,000. Mats Exp $220,000. Sal $559,000
Library Holdings: Bk Vols 120,604; Per Subs 200
Special Collections: Oral History; State Document Depository
Automation Activity & Vendor Info: (Cataloging) SirsiDynix; (Circulation) SirsiDynix; (OPAC) SirsiDynix
Database Vendor: EBSCOhost, Facts on File, Gale Cengage Learning, Grolier Online, Newsbank, ProQuest
Wireless access
Mem of Washington County Library System
Open Mon-Thurs 9-9, Fri 9-5, Sat 9-4, Sun 1-5
Friends of the Library Group

MEADVILLE

C ALLEGHENY COLLEGE LIBRARY, Lawrence Lee Pelletier Library, 555 N Main St, 16335. (Mail add: 520 N Main St, 16335), SAN 314-738X. Tel: 814-332-3768. Interlibrary Loan Service Tel: 814-332-3790. Reference Tel: 814-332-3769. Administration Tel: 814-332-3363. Automation Services Tel: 814-332-2740. FAX: 814-337-5673. Web Site: library.allegheny.edu. *Dir,* Linda Gail Bills; Tel: 814-332-3362, E-mail: lbills@allegheny.edu; *Head, Res & Instrul Serv,* Michael Hurley; Tel: 814-332-2890, E-mail: mhurley@allegheny.edu; *Head, Res & Metadata Mgt,* Brian Kern; Tel: 814-332-3792, E-mail: bkern@allegheny.edu; *Quantitative Data Librn/Technologist,* Position Currently Open; *Res & Instruction Librn,* Cynthia Burton; Tel: 814-332-2982, E-mail: cburton@allegheny.edu; *Res & Instruction Librn, Spec Coll Librn,* Jane Westenfeld; Tel: 814-332-3789, E-mail: jwestenf@allegheny.edu; *Syst Librn,* Alan E Bartlett; E-mail: abartlett@allegheny.edu; *Coordr, Circ & Communications,* Aimee Reash; E-mail: areash@allegheny.edu; *Col Archivist,* Ruth Andel; Tel: 814-332-2398, E-mail: randel@allegheny.edu; *Acq Spec,* Nancy L Brenot; E-mail: nbrenot@allegheny.edu; *Circ Spec,* William Burlingame; Tel: 814-332-3359, E-mail: wburlingame@allegheny.edu; *ILL Spec,* Linda Ernst; E-mail: lernst@allegheny.edu; *Ser/Gifts/Acq Spec,* Sherree Byers; Tel: 814-332-2968, E-mail: sbyers@allegheny.edu; *Instructional Technologist,* Helen McCullough; Tel: 814-332-3364, E-mail: hmccull@allegheny.edu; Staff 9 (MLS 7, Non-MLS 2)
Founded 1815. Enrl 2,100; Fac 135; Highest Degree: Bachelor
Jul 2007-Jun 2008. Mats Exp $594,700, Books $165,000, Per/Ser (Incl. Access Fees) $264,000, Micro $5,000, AV Equip $2,000, AV Mat $10,700, Electronic Ref Mat (Incl. Access Fees) $148,000
Library Holdings: AV Mats 8,600; CDs 905; DVDs 936; e-books 150; e-journals 21,750; Electronic Media & Resources 100; Microforms 493,740; Bk Titles 306,660; Bk Vols 796,800; Per Subs 800; Videos 8,612
Special Collections: Atlantic & Great Western Railroad Letters, papers, photog; Ida M Tarbell, letters, ms, bks; Lincoln, bks, pamphlets; Original Library, 1819-23 (Gifts of James Winthrop, Isaiah Thomas & William Bentley). State Document Depository; US Document Depository
Automation Activity & Vendor Info: (Acquisitions) Innovative Interfaces, Inc; (Cataloging) Innovative Interfaces, Inc; (Circulation) Innovative Interfaces, Inc; (ILL) OCLC ILLiad; (Media Booking) Innovative Interfaces, Inc; (OPAC) Innovative Interfaces, Inc; (Serials) Innovative Interfaces, Inc
Database Vendor: ACM (Association for Computing Machinery), Agricola, Alexander Street Press, American Chemical Society, American Mathematical Society, American Physical Society, American Psychological Association (APA), Annual Reviews, ARTstor, Atlas Systems, BioOne, Blackwell, CRC Press/Taylor & Francis Group, CredoReference, ebrary, EBSCOhost, Elsevier, Facts on File, Gale Cengage Learning, H W Wilson, Innovative Interfaces, Inc, IOP, ISI Web of Knowledge, JSTOR, LexisNexis, Luna Imaging/Insight, Mergent Online, Modern Language Association, Nature Publishing Group, OCLC ArticleFirst, OCLC FirstSearch, OCLC WorldShare Interlibrary Loan, Oxford Online, Paratext, Project MUSE, ProQuest, PubMed, RefWorks, Safari Books Online, Sage, ScienceDirect, SerialsSolutions, Springer-Verlag, Thomson - Web of Science, Wiley InterScience, Wilson - Wilson Web
Wireless access
Partic in Coun of Libr Info Resources; Lyrasis; National Institute for Technology & Liberal Education (NITLE); Northwest Interlibrary Cooperative of Pennsylvania; OCLC Online Computer Library Center, Inc; Pennsylvania Academic Library Consortium, Inc (PALCI)
Open Mon-Thurs 7:30am-1am, Fri 7:30am-9pm, Sat 9-9, Sun 11:30am-1am

P CRAWFORD COUNTY FEDERATED LIBRARY SYSTEM*, 848 N Main St, 16335-2689. SAN 314-7398. Tel: 814-336-1773. FAX: 814-333-8173. Web Site: www.ccfls.org. *Syst Adminr,* John Brice; Staff 15 (MLS 4, Non-MLS 11)
Founded 1978. Pop 86,090; Circ 361,028
Library Holdings: AV Mats 11,364; Large Print Bks 701; Bk Titles 103,667; Bk Vols 104,323; Per Subs 261; Talking Bks 3,648; Videos 2,072
Special Collections: Rotating Books on Cassette Coll
Member Libraries: Benson Memorial Library; Cambridge Springs Public Library; Cochranton Area Public Library; Linesville Community Public Library; Margaret Shontz Memorial Library; Meadville Public Library; Saegertown Area Library; Springboro Public Library; Stone Memorial Library
Open Mon-Thurs 9-9, Fri 9-6, Sat 9-5

S CRAWFORD COUNTY HISTORICAL SOCIETY*, Research Center for Crawford County History, 411 Chestnut St, 16335. (Mail add: PO Box 411, 16335-0411), SAN 314-7401. Tel: 814-724-6080. FAX: 814-724-6080. E-mail: cchsresearch@zoominternet.net. Web Site: www.crawfordhistorical.org. *Res Librn,* Anne W Stewart; Staff 2 (MLS 1, Non-MLS 1)
Founded 1879
Library Holdings: Bk Vols 2,600; Spec Interest Per Sub 15
Special Collections: Bulen Music Coll; Civil War Coll; Huidekoper, Reynolds & Dick Families; Photograph Coll; Railroad Coll (Erie, Bessemer); Talon Coll. Municipal Document Depository; Oral History
Subject Interests: Crawford County hist
Wireless access
Function: Res libr
Publications: Colorful Crawford County; Crawford County History (Newsletter); European Capital, British Iron & an American Dream: The Story of the Atlantic & Great Western Railroad; Images of America: Meadville; Images of Meadville: Meadville's Architectural Heritage; In French Creek Valley, 1938; Naturalization Abstracts, Crawford County, PA 1800-1906; Place Names of Crawford County, PA; Stories from French Creek Valley; The Diary of William Reynolds; The First 100 Years: Settlement & Growth in Crawford Count, PA; Treads of Tradition: Northwest Pennsylvania Quilts
Open Mon-Wed & Fri 1-5, Thurs 1-8, Sat 9-3
Restriction: Non-circulating

M MEADVILLE MEDICAL CENTER*, Winslow Medical Library, 751 Liberty St, 16335. SAN 314-7428. Tel: 814-333-5740. FAX: 814-333-5714. *Librn,* Barbara Ewing; Staff 1 (Non-MLS 1)
Library Holdings: Bk Vols 732; Per Subs 156
Subject Interests: Med, Med tech, Nursing
Function: ILL available, Res libr
Partic in Erie Area Health Information Library Cooperative; National Network of Libraries of Medicine; Northwest Interlibrary Cooperative of Pennsylvania
Open Mon-Fri 9:30-6
Restriction: Non-circulating to the pub, Pub access by telephone only

P MEADVILLE PUBLIC LIBRARY*, 848 N Main St, 16335-2689. SAN 314-7436. Tel: 814-336-1773. FAX: 814-333-8173. Web Site: www.meadvillelibrary.org. *Exec Dir,* John J Brice, III; E-mail: jbrice@ccfls.org; *Asst Dir, Ch Serv,* Mary Lee Minnis; *Adult Serv, Circ,* Patricia Bailey; *ILL,* Linda Eidell; *Online Serv, Ref,* Roseann Dies; Staff 20 (MLS 5, Non-MLS 15)
Founded 1812. Pop 38,911; Circ 248,896
Library Holdings: AV Mats 10,601; Large Print Bks 586; Bk Titles 88,901; Bk Vols 90,142; Per Subs 249; Talking Bks 3,591; Videos 2,079
Special Collections: Crawford County Historical Coll, bks & mss. Oral History
Subject Interests: Hist
Wireless access
Publications: Snippets from the Shelves (Newsletter)
Mem of Crawford County Federated Library System
Partic in Lyrasis; Northwest Interlibrary Cooperative of Pennsylvania
Open Mon-Thurs 9-9, Fri 9-6, Sat 9-5 (9-2 Summer)
Friends of the Library Group

MECHANICSBURG

CR MESSIAH COLLEGE, Murray Library & Learning Commons, One College Ave, Ste 3002, 17055. SAN 358-4941. Tel: 717-691-6006. Circulation Tel: 717-691-6006, Ext 3860. Interlibrary Loan Service Tel: 717-691-6006, Ext 7242. Reference Tel: 717-691-6006, Ext 3910. FAX: 717-691-2356. Web Site: www.messiah.edu/murraylibrary. *Dir,* Jonathan D

Lauer; Tel: 717-691-6006, Ext 3820, E-mail: jlauer@messiah.edu; *Spec Projects Adminr, Curator of Bk Arts,* Cherie Fieser; Tel: 717-691-6006, Ext 7181, E-mail: cfieser@messiah.edu; *Circ Supvr,* Deb K Roof; Tel: 717-691-6006, Ext 7293, E-mail: droof@messiah.edu; *ILL Supvr,* Barb Syvertson; E-mail: bsyverts@messiah.edu; *Coll Develop Coordr,* Beth Transue; Tel: 717-691-6006, Ext 3810, E-mail: btransue@messiah.edu; *Electronic Res Coordr,* Michael Rice; Tel: 717-691-6006, Ext 7069, E-mail: mrice@messiah.edu; *Libr Instruction Coordr,* Beth L Mark; Tel: 717-691-6006, Ext 3590, E-mail: bmark@messiah.edu; *Pub Serv Coordr,* Lawrie Merz; Tel: 717-691-6006, Ext 3880, E-mail: lmerz@messiah.edu; *Tech Serv Coordr,* Liz Y Kielley; Tel: 717-691-6006, Ext 3850, E-mail: ekielley@messiah.edu; *Acq Tech,* Amanda Flagle; Tel: 717-691-6006, Ext 7073, E-mail: aflagle@messiah.edu; *Ser Tech,* Sharon Berger; Tel: 717-691-6006, Ext 7017, E-mail: sberger@messiah.edu; *Archivist,* Glen Pierce; Tel: 717-691-6006, Ext 6048, E-mail: gpierce@messiah.edu; Staff 16 (MLS 6, Non-MLS 10)
Founded 1909. Enrl 2,746; Fac 175; Highest Degree: Master
Special Collections: Artists' Books; Brethren in Christ Archives, bks, ms, micro; Canadian Literature; Ruth E Engle Memorial Coll of Children's Book Illustration; Science & Religion (W Jim Neidhardt Coll)
Subject Interests: Music, Nursing, Relig
Automation Activity & Vendor Info: (Acquisitions) Ex Libris Group; (Cataloging) Ex Libris Group; (Circulation) Ex Libris Group; (Course Reserve) Ex Libris Group; (ILL) OCLC Online; (OPAC) Ex Libris Group; (Serials) EBSCO Online
Database Vendor: EBSCOhost, Gale Cengage Learning, JSTOR, OCLC FirstSearch, OVID Technologies, ProQuest, Wilson - Wilson Web
Wireless access
Partic in Interlibrary Delivery Service of Pennsylvania; Lyrasis; OCLC Online Computer Library Center, Inc
Open Mon-Thurs (Winter) 7:30am-Midnight, Fri 7:30-6, Sat 10-8, Sun 2-Midnight; Mon & Wed (Summer) 8-8, Tues, Thurs & Fri 8-5
Friends of the Library Group

Departmental Libraries:

BRETHREN IN CHRIST HISTORICAL LIBRARY & ARCHIVES, One College Ave, Grantham, 17027-9795. (Mail add: PO Box 3002, Grantham, 17027-9999), SAN 374-9835. Tel: 717-691-6048. FAX: 717-691-6042. E-mail: archives@messiah.edu. Web Site: www.messiah.edu/archives. *Dir,* Glen A Pierce; Staff 1 (Non-MLS 1)
Founded 1952
Library Holdings: Bk Titles 600; Per Subs 20
Special Collections: Anabaptist, Pietist & Wesleyan Studies; Archives of Brethren in Christ Church; Archives of Messiah College; Manuscripts Coll. Oral History
Function: Archival coll
Open Mon-Thurs 9-12 & 1-3

P JOSEPH T SIMPSON PUBLIC LIBRARY*, 16 N Walnut St, 17055-3362. SAN 314-7444. Tel: 717-766-0171. FAX: 717-766-0152. E-mail: mechanicsburg@ccpa.net. Web Site: www.ccpa.net/simpson. *Dir,* Sue Erdman; Staff 17 (MLS 5, Non-MLS 12)
Founded 1961. Pop 42,023; Circ 428,000
Jan 2005-Dec 2005 Income $637,974, State $200,851, County $270,723. Mats Exp $91,300, Books $67,000, Per/Ser (Incl. Access Fees) $9,300, AV Mat $15,000. Sal $366,600
Library Holdings: Bk Vols 82,000; Per Subs 135
Special Collections: Irving College, Mechanicsburg, Pennsylvania (women's college that closed in 1929)
Automation Activity & Vendor Info: (Acquisitions) SirsiDynix; (Cataloging) SirsiDynix; (Circulation) SirsiDynix; (OPAC) SirsiDynix
Database Vendor: EBSCOhost, Gale Cengage Learning
Mem of Cumberland County Library System
Open Mon-Thurs 10-9, Fri & Sat 10-5, Sat (July-Aug) 10-2, Sun (Sept-June) 1-5
Friends of the Library Group

MEDIA

S COLONIAL PENNSYLVANIA PLANTATION*, Sol Feinstone Library, Ridley Creek State Park, 19063. SAN 314-4763. Tel: 610-566-1725. Web Site: www.colonialplantation.org. *In Charge,* Joy Woppert; E-mail: info@colonialplantation.org
Founded 1973
Library Holdings: Bk Vols 1,500
Special Collections: Southeastern Pennsylvania History-Folklore, VF
Subject Interests: Hist, Soc life & customs of the Am Colonial
Restriction: Open by appt only

J DELAWARE COUNTY COMMUNITY COLLEGE LIBRARY*, 901 S Media Line Rd, 19063-1094. SAN 314-7452. Tel: 610-359-5149. Reference Tel: 610-359-5146. Administration Tel: 610-359-5150. FAX: 610-359-5272. E-mail: library@dccc.edu. Web Site: library.dccc.edu. *Dir,* Dr Karen Rege; Staff 7.5 (MLS 7.5)
Founded 1967. Enrl 9,589; Highest Degree: Associate
Library Holdings: Audiobooks 188; CDs 554; DVDs 653; e-books 1,374; Bk Vols 23,726; Per Subs 104
Subject Interests: Law, Nursing
Automation Activity & Vendor Info: (Acquisitions) Innovative Interfaces, Inc; (Cataloging) Innovative Interfaces, Inc; (Circulation) Innovative Interfaces, Inc; (Course Reserve) Innovative Interfaces, Inc; (ILL) OCLC; (OPAC) Innovative Interfaces, Inc; (Serials) Innovative Interfaces, Inc
Database Vendor: American Psychological Association (APA), ARTstor, CQ Press, CredoReference, Dialog, EBSCO Discovery Service, EBSCOhost, Gale Cengage Learning, H W Wilson, Infotrieve, JSTOR, OCLC WorldShare Interlibrary Loan, ProQuest, PubMed, Safari Books Online, Springshare, LLC, Westlaw
Wireless access
Partic in OCLC Online Computer Library Center, Inc; Tri State Col Libr Coop
Special Services for the Deaf - Assistive tech
Special Services for the Blind - Accessible computers; Assistive/Adapted tech devices, equip & products; Bks on CD; Closed circuit TV magnifier; Digital talking bk machines; Internet workstation with adaptive software; Low vision equip; Scanner for conversion & translation of mats; Screen enlargement software for people with visual disabilities; Screen reader software
Open Mon-Thurs 8am-10pm, Fri 8-5, Sat 9-4
Restriction: Circ privileges for students & alumni only, ID required to use computers (Ltd hrs), In-house use for visitors, Lending libr only via mail, Pub use on premises

P DELAWARE COUNTY LIBRARY SYSTEM, Bldg 19, 340 N Middletown Rd, 19063-5597. SAN 320-2267. Tel: 610-891-8622. FAX: 610-891-8641. E-mail: support@delcolibraries.org. Web Site: www.delcolibraries.org. *Dir,* David L Belanger; *Asst Dir,* Janis T Stubbs; *IT Dir,* Rene Kelly; *Law Librn,* Perretta Susan; *Digital Libr & Ref Coordr,* Position Currently Open; *Tech Serv,* Kristin Suda; *Youth Serv,* Margie Stern. Subject Specialists: *Law,* Perretta Susan; Staff 23 (MLS 6, Non-MLS 17)
Founded 1981. Pop 550,000; Circ 2,606,607
Library Holdings: AV Mats 12,000; Bk Titles 16,000; Per Subs 76
Subject Interests: Libr sci
Automation Activity & Vendor Info: (Acquisitions) Innovative Interfaces, Inc; (Cataloging) Innovative Interfaces, Inc; (Circulation) Innovative Interfaces, Inc; (ILL) Innovative Interfaces, Inc; (Media Booking) Innovative Interfaces, Inc; (OPAC) Innovative Interfaces, Inc; (Serials) Innovative Interfaces, Inc
Database Vendor: EBSCOhost, Gale Cengage Learning
Wireless access
Member Libraries: Aston Public Library; Borough of Folcroft Public Library; Collingdale Public Library; Darby Free Library; Glenolden Library; Haverford Township Free Library; Helen Kate Furness Free Library; J Lewis Crozer Library; Lansdowne Public Library; Marple Public Library; Mary M Campbell Public Library; Middletown Free Library; Newtown Public Library; Norwood Public Library; Prospect Park Free Library; Rachel Kohl Community Library; Radnor Memorial Library; Ridley Park Public Library; Ridley Township Public Library; Sharon Hill Public Library; Swarthmore Public Library; Tinicum Memorial Public Library; Upper Darby Township & Sellers Memorial Free Public Library; Yeadon Public Library
Open Mon-Fri 8:30-4:30
Friends of the Library Group

S FRANK C FARNHAM COMPANY INC LIBRARY*, 210 W Front St, Ste 5, 19063-3101. SAN 325-9676. Tel: 610-892-8008. FAX: 610-892-8050. *Pres,* Frank C Farnham; E-mail: fcfarnham@f-c-farnham.com; Staff 1 (Non-MLS 1)
Library Holdings: Bk Titles 4,500; Bk Vols 6,000; Per Subs 18
Restriction: Staff use only

GL JUDGE FRANCIS J CATANIA LAW LIBRARY*, Court House, 201 W Front St, 19063. SAN 314-7460. Tel: 610-891-4462. FAX: 610-891-4480. Web Site: www.delcolibraries.org/lawlibrary. *Dir,* Susan R Perretta; Staff 2 (MLS 1, Non-MLS 1)
Founded 1902
Library Holdings: Bk Vols 30,000; Per Subs 30
Function: Ref serv available, Res libr
Open Mon-Fri 8-4:30

P MEDIA-UPPER PROVIDENCE FREE LIBRARY*, One E Front St, 19063. SAN 314-7487. Tel: 610-566-1918. FAX: 610-566-9056. Web Site: www.medialibrary.org. *Dir,* Brandi Whitesell; *Ref Librn,* John Kennedy; *Youth Serv Librn,* Brittany Eastman; Staff 8 (MLS 4, Non-MLS 4)
Founded 1901. Pop 15,678
Library Holdings: Bk Titles 52,000; Per Subs 85
Automation Activity & Vendor Info: (Cataloging) Innovative Interfaces, Inc; (Circulation) Innovative Interfaces, Inc
Open Mon 10-8, Tues-Thurs 10-9, Fri 10-6, Sat 10-4, Sun 1-4
Friends of the Library Group

J PENNSYLVANIA INSTITUTE OF TECHNOLOGY LIBRARY*, 800 Manchester Ave, 19063-4098. SAN 328-5839. Tel: 610-892-1524. Toll Free Tel: 800-422-0025. FAX: 610-892-1523. E-mail: library@pit.edu. Web Site: my.pit.edu/content/studentservices/library.aspx. *Dir of Libr Serv,* Lynea Anderman; E-mail: landerman@pit.edu; *Ref & Info Literacy Librn,* Jessica Richter; E-mail: jrichter@pit.edu; Staff 1.5 (MLS 1.5)
Founded 1962. Enrl 756; Highest Degree: Associate
Jul 2010-Jun 2011 Income $223,269, Parent Institution $173,903, Other $49,366. Mats Exp $61,338, Books $16,964, Per/Ser (Incl. Access Fees) $24,461, AV Mat $8,269, Electronic Ref Mat (Incl. Access Fees) $11,644. Sal $85,755
Library Holdings: Audiobooks 12; AV Mats 20; CDs 12; DVDs 823; e-books 52,000; Electronic Media & Resources 6; Bk Titles 15,000; Bk Vols 18,500; Per Subs 30; Videos 325
Special Collections: Architecture & Archaelogy (Hinderliter Coll); Early 20th Century or Earlier Publications (Founder's Coll); Honeywell Technology Coll; Professional Development Coll
Subject Interests: Allied health, Archit, Bus admin, Computer sci, Eng, Tech
Automation Activity & Vendor Info: (Acquisitions) TLC (The Library Corporation); (Cataloging) TLC (The Library Corporation); (Circulation) TLC (The Library Corporation); (ILL) OCLC; (OPAC) TLC (The Library Corporation)
Database Vendor: ebrary, Facts on File, Gale Cengage Learning, JSTOR, McGraw-Hill, OCLC, Springshare, LLC, TLC (The Library Corporation)
Wireless access
Function: Archival coll, Audio & video playback equip for onsite use, CD-ROM, Computers for patron use, Copy machines, Electronic databases & coll, Exhibits, Free DVD rentals, ILL available, Libr develop, Online cat, Online searches, Orientations, Outside serv via phone, mail, e-mail & web, Photocopying/Printing, Pub access computers, Ref serv available, Ref serv in person, Res libr, Telephone ref, VHS videos, Video lending libr, Web-catalog, Workshops
Publications: Off the Shelf (Periodical)
Partic in HSLC/Access PA/POWER Library; Lyrasis; OCLC Online Computer Library Center, Inc
Open Mon, Tues & Thurs 8:30-7, Wed & Fri 8:30-5
Restriction: Non-circulating coll, Open to pub for ref & circ; with some limitations, Open to students, fac, staff & alumni

C PENNSYLVANIA STATE UNIVERSITY LIBRARIES*, John D Vairo Library, Brandywine Campus, 25 Yearsley Mill Rd, 19063-5596. SAN 314-7495. Tel: 610-892-1386. FAX: 610-892-1359. Web Site: www.brandywine.psu.edu. *Head Librn,* Susan Ware; E-mail: saw4@psu.edu; Staff 4 (MLS 2, Non-MLS 2)
Founded 1967. Enrl 1,734; Fac 75
Library Holdings: Bk Vols 75,000; Per Subs 100
Partic in OCLC Online Computer Library Center, Inc; RLIN (Research Libraries Information Network)
Open Mon-Thurs 8am-9:30pm, Fri 8-5

MEHOOPANY

P MEHOOPANY AREA LIBRARY*, Schoolhouse Hill Rd, 18629. (Mail add: PO Box 202, 18629-0202). Tel: 570-833-2818. FAX: 570-833-2818. *Dir,* Norma J Trowbridge
Founded 1982. Circ 1,052
Library Holdings: AV Mats 68; Large Print Bks 180; Bk Vols 10,395; Talking Bks 216
Special Collections: Accelerated Readers Coll
Function: Summer reading prog
Open Wed 10-7, Thurs & Fri 10:30-5

MELROSE PARK

C GRATZ COLLEGE, The Tuttleman Library, 7605 Old York Rd, 19027. SAN 359-0550. Tel: 215-635-7300, Ext 159. FAX: 215-635-7320. Web Site: www.gratzcollege.edu. *Dir of Libr Serv,* Nancy H Nitzberg; E-mail: NNitzberg@gratz.edu; Staff 1 (MLS 1)
Founded 1895. Highest Degree: Doctorate
Library Holdings: Bk Titles 93,781; Bk Vols 96,210; Per Subs 181; Videos 792
Special Collections: Anti-Semitica Coll; Archives Coll; Hebraica & Judaica; Holocaust Oral History Archive; Materials for Training Teachers of Hebrew Language & Culture. Oral History
Subject Interests: Bible, Hebrew lang, Hist, Holocaust, Israel studies, Jewish educ, Lit, Music, Rabbinics, Rare bks
Automation Activity & Vendor Info: (Cataloging) TLC (The Library Corporation); (Circulation) TLC (The Library Corporation)
Function: ILL available
Partic in Tri State Col Libr Coop
Open Mon-Thurs 9-5:30, Fri 9-3

Departmental Libraries:
ABNER & MARY SCHREIBER JEWISH MUSIC LIBRARY, 7605 Old York Rd, 19027. Tel: 215-635-7300. FAX: 215-635-7320. *Dir,* Eliezer M Wise; *Music,* Randi Cohen; E-mail: rcohen@gratz.edu; Staff 2 (Non-MLS 2)
Founded 1950
Library Holdings: Bk Titles 28,410; Bk Vols 29,112; Per Subs 68
Special Collections: Choral Jewish Music of the 16th-20th Centuries (Eric Mandell Coll); Folk, Liturgical, Secular, Popular, Manuscripts & Published Music; Music For Small Ensembles, Virtuoso Instruments & Symphonic Scores by Jewish Composers or on Jewish; Preserved From Nazi Holocaust-Liturgical & Secular, Vocal, Instrumental & Choral (Arno Nadel Estate); Themes (Joseph Kutler Instrumental Library of Jewish Music)
Partic in OCLC Online Computer Library Center, Inc
Open Mon-Wed 9-9, Thurs 9-7, Fri 9-1, Sun 9-3

MERCER

P MERCER AREA LIBRARY*, 143 N Pitt St, 16137-1283. SAN 314-7517. Tel: 724-662-4233. FAX: 724-662-8893. E-mail: mercerarealib@htol.net. *Dir,* Connie Jewell
Founded 1916. Pop 11,100; Circ 59,022
Library Holdings: Bk Vols 20,087; Per Subs 51
Special Collections: Video Colls
Automation Activity & Vendor Info: (Acquisitions) Follett Software; (Cataloging) Follett Software; (Circulation) Follett Software; (Course Reserve) Follett Software; (ILL) Follett Software; (Media Booking) Follett Software; (OPAC) Follett Software; (Serials) Follett Software
Partic in Tri County Libr Consortium
Open Mon & Fri 9:30-5, Tues-Thurs 9:30-8, Sat 8-3 (8-12 Summer)
Friends of the Library Group

GL MERCER COUNTY LAW LIBRARY*, 305 Mercer County Courthouse, 16137-0123. SAN 327-0653. Tel: 724-662-3800, Ext 2302. Toll Free Tel: 800-711-9124. FAX: 724-662-0620. Web Site: www.mcc.co.mercer.pa.us/library. *Dir,* Jean Heckathorn; Staff 1 (Non-MLS 1)
Founded 1913
Library Holdings: Bk Vols 17,500; Per Subs 30
Function: Res libr
Open Mon-Fri 8:30-4:30
Restriction: Not a lending libr

S STATE REGIONAL CORRECTIONAL FACILITY LIBRARY*, 801 Butler Pike, 16137. SAN 371-6155. Tel: 724-662-1837, Ext 1126. FAX: 724-662-1940. *Librn,* Colleen Mojock; Staff 1 (MLS 1)
Library Holdings: Audiobooks 291; Large Print Bks 82; Bk Titles 13,669; Per Subs 80; Videos 791
Special Collections: Black History; Spanish Coll
Automation Activity & Vendor Info: (Cataloging) Follett Software; (Circulation) Follett Software; (OPAC) Follett Software
Special Services for the Deaf - Bks on deafness & sign lang; High interest/low vocabulary bks
Open Sun-Fri 8-4

MERCERSBURG

P FENDRICK LIBRARY*, 20 N Main St, 17236-1612. Tel: 717-328-9233. Web Site: www.fendricklibrary.com. *Dir,* Cheryl Custer
Library Holdings: Audiobooks 250; DVDs 20; Large Print Bks 64; Bk Vols 50,000; Per Subs 18; Videos 100
Wireless access
Open Mon 2:30-8, Wed & Fri 10-8, Sat 10-2

MERION STATION

R TEMPLE ADATH ISRAEL*, Ruben Library, 250 N Highland Ave, 19066. SAN 314-755X. Tel: 610-934-1919. FAX: 610-664-0959. E-mail: info@adathisrael.org. Web Site: www.adathisrael.org. *Exec Dir,* Lori Dafilou; Tel: 610-934-1903, E-mail: Ldafilou@adathisrael.org
Founded 1955
Library Holdings: Bk Titles 6,000; Per Subs 10
Subject Interests: Judaica
Restriction: Mem only, Use of others with permission of librn

MESHOPPEN

P FRANCES E KENNARD PUBLIC LIBRARY*, Auburn & Canal Sts, 18630. SAN 314-7568. Tel: 570-833-5060. FAX: 570-833-4238. *Pres,* Herbert Smith; *Librn,* Marcia Bertram; Staff 1 (Non-MLS 1)
Founded 1900. Pop 981; Circ 6,500
Library Holdings: Bk Titles 4,681; Bk Vols 4,926; Per Subs 16; Videos 90
Open Mon, Tues & Thurs 4-8, Wed 3-8

MEYERSDALE

P MEYERSDALE PUBLIC LIBRARY*, 210 Center St, 15552-1323. (Mail add: PO Box 98, 15552-0098), SAN 314-7576. Tel: 814-634-0512. FAX: 814-634-0512. Web Site: www.meyersdalelibrary.com. *Dir,* Vida Vaughn; Staff 2 (MLS 1, Non-MLS 1)
Founded 1939. Pop 19,000; Circ 35,355
Library Holdings: Bks on Deafness & Sign Lang 20; Bk Vols 33,822; Per Subs 40
Subject Interests: Local hist
Automation Activity & Vendor Info: (Acquisitions) Innovative Interfaces, Inc; (Cataloging) Innovative Interfaces, Inc; (Circulation) Innovative Interfaces, Inc; (Course Reserve) Innovative Interfaces, Inc; (ILL) Innovative Interfaces, Inc; (OPAC) Innovative Interfaces, Inc; (Serials) Innovative Interfaces, Inc
Function: Accelerated reader prog, Adult bk club, Adult literacy prog, Archival coll, Audio & video playback equip for onsite use, Audiobks via web, Bks on cassette, Bks on CD, Children's prog, Citizenship assistance, Computer training, Computers for patron use, Copy machines, Digital talking bks, e-mail serv, E-Reserves, Electronic databases & coll, Family literacy, Fax serv, Games & aids for the handicapped, Genealogy discussion group, Handicapped accessible, Home delivery & serv to Sr ctr & nursing homes, ILL available, Instruction & testing, Large print keyboards, Learning ctr, Magnifiers for reading, Mail & tel request accepted, Outreach serv, OverDrive digital audio bks, Photocopying/Printing, Preschool outreach, Prog for adults, Prog for children & young adult, Pub access computers, Ref serv available, Scanner, Senior outreach, Story hour, Summer reading prog, Tax forms, Telephone ref, Wheelchair accessible
Mem of Somerset County Federated Library System
Open Mon-Fri 10-7, Sat 10-5
Friends of the Library Group

MIDDLEBURG

S SNYDER COUNTY HISTORICAL SOCIETY, INC LIBRARY*, 30 E Market St, 17842-1017. (Mail add: PO Box 276, 17842-0276), SAN 328-8188. Tel: 570-837-6191. FAX: 570-837-4282. *Librn,* Helen Keiser
Founded 1898
Library Holdings: Bk Titles 3,200
Publications: Snyder Co Historical Society Bulletin
Open Thurs & Fri (Winter) 10-3:30; Thurs, Fri & Sun (Summer) 1:30-5

MIDDLETOWN

S AMERGEN ENERGY*, Three Mile Island Technical Library, Three Mile Island Nuclear Generating Sta, PO Box 480, 17057. SAN 320-992X. Tel: 717-948-8105. FAX: 717-948-8824. *Librn,* Joan H Slavin; Staff 1 (MLS 1)
Library Holdings: Bk Titles 2,679; Bk Vols 2,910; Per Subs 225
Subject Interests: Nuclear power, Radiation
Open Mon-Fri 7-3:30

P MIDDLETOWN PUBLIC LIBRARY, 20 N Catherine St, 17057-1401. SAN 314-7584. Tel: 717-944-6412. FAX: 717-930-0510. E-mail: info@middletownpubliclib.org. Web Site: www.middletownpubliclib.org. *Dir,* John Grayshaw; *Librn,* Barbara Scull; Staff 4.5 (MLS 1, Non-MLS 3.5)
Founded 1926. Pop 9,242; Circ 55,108
Special Collections: Interviews from Early 1970s, indexed; Middletown Journal, 1886-present, newsp; Press & Journal Coll. Oral History
Automation Activity & Vendor Info: (Acquisitions) Innovative Interfaces, Inc; (Cataloging) Innovative Interfaces, Inc; (Circulation) Innovative Interfaces, Inc; (OPAC) Innovative Interfaces, Inc
Database Vendor: Comprise Technologies Inc, Evanced Solutions, Inc, OCLC WorldShare Interlibrary Loan, Overdrive, Inc, ProQuest, ReferenceUSA
Wireless access
Function: Adult bk club, Audiobks via web, Bks on cassette, Bks on CD, Children's prog, Computers for patron use, Copy machines, Electronic databases & coll, Fax serv, Free DVD rentals, Handicapped accessible, Holiday prog, ILL available, Outreach serv, OverDrive digital audio bks, Photocopying/Printing, Preschool outreach, Prog for adults, Prog for children & young adult, Pub access computers, Story hour, Summer & winter reading prog, Summer reading prog, Tax forms, Teen prog, VHS videos
Partic in Community Libraries Information Consortium
Special Services for the Blind - Audio mat; Bks on cassette; Bks on CD; Large print bks; Playaways (bks on MP3); Recorded bks
Open Mon, Tues & Thurs 9:30-8, Wed 9:30-4, Sat 9-4 (9-2 Summer)
Friends of the Library Group

G PENNSYLVANIA DEPARTMENT OF CONSERVATION & NATURAL RESOURCES*, Bureau of Topographic & Geologic Survey Library, 3240 Schoolhouse Rd, 17057-3534. SAN 358-5336. Tel: 717-702-2017. FAX: 717-702-2065. Web Site: www.dcnr.state.pa.us/topogeo/library/index.htm. *Librn,* Jody Smale; Tel: 717-702-2020, E-mail: jsmale@pa.gov; Staff 3 (MLS 1, Non-MLS 2)
Founded 1850
Library Holdings: Bk Titles 11,300; Bk Vols 12,951; Per Subs 65
Special Collections: Aerial Photography, contact prints; Maps (United States Geologic Survey Seven & One Half Minute Maps)
Subject Interests: Earth sci, Geog, Geol
Automation Activity & Vendor Info: (Acquisitions) Ex Libris Group; (Cataloging) Ex Libris Group; (OPAC) Ex Libris Group
Database Vendor: Access Pennsylvania, EBSCOhost
Function: Ref serv available
Publications: In House Newsletter
Open Mon-Fri 9-12 & 1-4

C PENNSYLVANIA STATE UNIVERSITY-HARRISBURG LIBRARY, 351 Olmsted Dr, 17057-4850. SAN 314-7592. Tel: 717-948-6070. Interlibrary Loan Service Tel: 717-948-6071. Reference Tel: 717-948-6073. Administration Tel: 717-948-6079. Interlibrary Loan Service FAX: 717-948-6381. E-mail: gln1@psu.edu. Web Site: www.libraries.psu.edu/psul/harrisburg.html. *Dir,* Dr Gregory A Crawford; E-mail: gac2@psu.edu; *Behav Sci & Educ Ref Librn, Coordr, Instruction & Outreach,* Bernadette A Lear; Tel: 717-948-6360, E-mail: bal19@psu.edu; *Bus & Pub Admin Ref Librn, Ref & Pub Serv Coordr,* Glenn McGuigan; Tel: 717-948-6078, E-mail: gxm22@psu.edu; *Cat Librn,* Eileen Zagon; E-mail: ekz1@psu.edu; *Col Archivist, Coordr, Archives & Spec Coll, Humanities Librn,* Heidi Abbey; Tel: 717-948-6056, E-mail: hna2@psu.edu; *Coord, Coll Develop, Sci, Eng & Tech Ref Librn,* Eric Delozier; Tel: 717-948-6373, E-mail: epd103@psu.edu; *Circ Mgr,* Fay Youngmark; E-mail: fay1@psu.edu; *Electronic Serv,* Alan Mays; E-mail: axm22@psu.edu; *Per,* Henry Koretzky; Tel: 717-948-6563, E-mail: hrk2@psu.edu. Subject Specialists: *Archaeology, Classical Mediterranean, Humanities,* Dr Gregory A Crawford; *Educ, Libr instruction, Soc sci,* Bernadette A Lear; *Bus, Criminal justice, Pub admin,* Glenn McGuigan; *Holocaust studies, Jewish studies,* Eileen Zagon; *Am studies, Communications, Humanities,* Heidi Abbey; *Computer sci, Eng, Health sci,* Eric Delozier; Staff 15 (MLS 6, Non-MLS 9)
Founded 1966. Enrl 4,500; Fac 250; Highest Degree: Doctorate
Special Collections: Holocaust & Genocide Studies Coll; PA Culture Studies; Women's History Coll
Subject Interests: Am studies, Behav sci, Computer sci, Criminal justice, Educ, Eng, Humanities, Pub affairs
Automation Activity & Vendor Info: (Acquisitions) SirsiDynix; (Cataloging) SirsiDynix; (Circulation) SirsiDynix; (Course Reserve) SirsiDynix; (ILL) OCLC; (OPAC) SirsiDynix; (Serials) SirsiDynix
Wireless access
Function: Archival coll, Audio & video playback equip for onsite use, e-mail & chat, E-Reserves, Electronic databases & coll, Equip loans & repairs, Exhibits, Handicapped accessible, Microfiche/film & reading machines, Music CDs, Online cat, Photocopying/Printing, Ref serv available, Scanner, Wheelchair accessible
Special Services for the Deaf - Assistive tech
Special Services for the Blind - Assistive/Adapted tech devices, equip & products
Open Mon-Thurs 7:30am-11pm, Fri 7:30am-9pm, Sat 10-6, Sun 2-11

MIDLAND

P CARNEGIE FREE LIBRARY*, 61 Ninth St, 15059-1503. SAN 314-7606. Tel: 724-643-8980. FAX: 724-643-8985. Web Site: www.beaverlibraries.org. *Dir,* Linda Slopek; E-mail: lslopek@beaverlibraries.org
Founded 1916. Pop 4,684; Circ 22,111
Jan 2011-Dec 2011 Income $83,297, State $22,768, County $4,944, Locally Generated Income $55,585. Mats Exp $8,951, Books $4,157, Per/Ser (Incl. Access Fees) $3,324, AV Mat $1,470. Sal $48,414 (Prof $19,000)
Library Holdings: Audiobooks 841; Large Print Bks 23; Bk Vols 16,576; Per Subs 44; Videos 2,332
Automation Activity & Vendor Info: (Acquisitions) Innovative Interfaces, Inc - Millenium; (Cataloging) Innovative Interfaces, Inc; (Circulation) Innovative Interfaces, Inc; (ILL) Innovative Interfaces, Inc; (OPAC) Innovative Interfaces, Inc
Database Vendor: LearningExpress
Wireless access
Mem of Beaver County Library System
Open Mon-Thurs 12-7, Sat 9-4

MIFFLINBURG

P JANE I & ANNETTA M HERR MEMORIAL LIBRARY*, 500 Market St, 17844. SAN 314-7614. Tel: 570-966-0831. FAX: 570-966-0106. E-mail: herr@herrlibrary.org. Web Site: www.herrlibrary.org. *Dir,* Kelly Walter
Founded 1945. Pop 7,600
Library Holdings: Bk Vols 18,000; Per Subs 35

Automation Activity & Vendor Info: (Circulation) TLC (The Library Corporation)
Wireless access
Mem of Union County Library System
Open Mon & Fri 7pm-9pm, Tues-Thurs 11-5 & 7-9, Sat 10-2

MIFFLINTOWN

P JUNIATA COUNTY LIBRARY*, 498 Jefferson St, 17059-1424. SAN 358-7010. Tel: 717-436-6378. FAX: 717-436-9324. E-mail: juniatalibrary@juniatalibrary.org. Web Site: www.juniatalibrary.org. *Dir,* Brady Clemens; E-mail: bclemens@juniatalibrary.org; Staff 1 (MLS 1)
Founded 1966. Pop 25,000; Circ 90,000
Library Holdings: Bk Titles 51,000; Per Subs 70
Subject Interests: Local hist
Automation Activity & Vendor Info: (Cataloging) Evergreen; (Circulation) Evergreen; (OPAC) Evergreen
Wireless access
Open Mon, Tues, Thurs & Fri 10-8, Wed & Sat 9-4
Friends of the Library Group

MILFORD

P PIKE COUNTY PUBLIC LIBRARY*, 201 Broad St, 18337-1398. SAN 358-707X. Tel: 570-296-8211. FAX: 570-296-8987. E-mail: admin@pcpl.org. Web Site: www.pcpl.org. *Libr Dir,* Ellen Schaffner; *Tech Serv Mgr,* Joan VanFelton
Founded 1902. Pop 46,302; Circ 114,030
Library Holdings: Bk Vols 66,547
Automation Activity & Vendor Info: (Cataloging) TLC (The Library Corporation)
Publications: Print & Email Newsletters
Partic in Evergreen Indiana Consortium; Midwest Collaborative for Library Services (MCLS)
Open Mon-Thurs 10-8, Fri & Sat 10-5
Friends of the Library Group
Branches: 2
DINGMAN TOWNSHIP, 100 Bond Ct, 18337-7793. Tel: 570-686-7045. FAX: 570-686-1798. E-mail: dingman@pcpl.org. *Br Mgr,* Pamela DeMeis
Open Mon, Tues & Fri 10-6, Wed & Thurs 2-8, Sun 10-2
LACKAWAXEN TOWNSHIP, 223 Rte 590, Greeley, 18425-9718, SAN 371-3776. Tel: 570-685-3100. FAX: 570-685-9450. *In Charge,* Helen Badoud
Open Tues, Wed & Fri 2-7, Sun 10-3

MILLERSVILLE

C MILLERSVILLE UNIVERSITY*, Helen A Ganser Library, Nine N George St, 17551. (Mail add: PO Box 1002, 17551-0302), SAN 314-7630. Tel: 717-872-3608. Circulation Tel: 717-872-3612. Interlibrary Loan Service Tel: 717-872-3853. Reference Tel: 717-872-3611. FAX: 717-872-3854. Interlibrary Loan Service FAX: 717-872-3854. Web Site: library.millersville.edu. *Interim Dir,* Dr Marjorie Warmkessel; Tel: 717-872-3618, E-mail: marjorie.warmkessel@millersville.edu; *Ref Librn,* Leo Shelly; Tel: 717-872-3610, E-mail: leo.shelly@millersville.edu; *Cat,* Teresa Weisser; Tel: 717-872-3604, E-mail: teresa.weisser@millersville.edu; Staff 13 (MLS 13)
Founded 1855. Enrl 7,919; Fac 334; Highest Degree: Master
Jul 2005-Jun 2006. Mats Exp $901,882, Books $270,673, Per/Ser (Incl. Access Fees) $554,696, Micro $42,359, AV Mat $17,680, Presv $16,474
Library Holdings: AV Mats 13,770; e-books 3,556; Bk Vols 565,281; Per Subs 10,105
Special Collections: Archives of American Industrial Arts Association; The Carl Van Vechten Memorial Coll of Afro American Arts & Letters, bks, photog; Wickersham Coll of 19th Century Textbooks. State Document Depository; US Document Depository
Subject Interests: Educ, Ethnic studies, Holocaust, Local hist
Automation Activity & Vendor Info: (Acquisitions) Ex Libris Group; (Cataloging) Ex Libris Group; (Circulation) Ex Libris Group; (Course Reserve) Docutek; (ILL) Ex Libris Group; (OPAC) Ex Libris Group; (Serials) Ex Libris Group
Partic in Associated College Libraries of Central Pennsylvania; Keystone Library Network; OCLC Online Computer Library Center, Inc; Pa Syst of Higher Educ Libr Coun; Pennsylvania Academic Library Consortium, Inc (PALCI)
Open Mon-Thurs 8am-Midnight, Fri 8am-9pm, Sat 9-9, Sun 1-Midnight
Friends of the Library Group

MILTON

P MILTON PUBLIC LIBRARY*, 23 S Front St, 17847. SAN 314-7649. Tel: 570-742-7111. FAX: 570-742-7137. Web Site: www.milton.lib.de.us/. *Dir,* Mary Catherine Hopkins; E-mail: milton-director@lib.de.us; *Circ,* Kathy Eisley
Founded 1923. Pop 12,000
Special Collections: Milton Daily Standard Newspaper, 1816 to present, micro
Subject Interests: Hist of Milton, Northumberland County
Automation Activity & Vendor Info: (Cataloging) Follett Software; (Circulation) Follett Software; (OPAC) Follett Software
Wireless access
Open Mon-Fri 10-8, Sat 10-4
Friends of the Library Group

MINERSVILLE

P MINERSVILLE PUBLIC LIBRARY ASSOCIATION INC*, Minersville Public Library, 220 S Fourth St, 17954. SAN 314-7657. Tel: 570-544-5196. FAX: 570-544-5196. E-mail: mpl@minersvillelibrary.org. Web Site: www.minersvillelibrary.org. *Libr Dir,* Mary Grigalonis
Founded 1934. Pop 4,552; Circ 11,777
Jan 2007-Dec 2007 Income $99,989, State $22,223, City $11,350, County $1,244, Locally Generated Income $39,911, Other $25,261. Mats Exp $9,278, Books $6,490, Per/Ser (Incl. Access Fees) $343, Other Print Mats $434, AV Mat $459, Electronic Ref Mat (Incl. Access Fees) $1,552. Sal $24,827
Library Holdings: AV Mats 532; DVDs 10; Large Print Bks 525; Bk Vols 16,208; Per Subs 29; Talking Bks 513; Videos 613
Automation Activity & Vendor Info: (Acquisitions) AmLib Library Management System; (Cataloging) AmLib Library Management System; (Circulation) AmLib Library Management System; (ILL) Fretwell-Downing; (OPAC) AmLib Library Management System
Database Vendor: EBSCOhost
Wireless access
Function: Bks on cassette, Bks on CD, Children's prog, Computers for patron use, Copy machines, Fax serv, Free DVD rentals, Holiday prog, ILL available, Large print keyboards, Magnifiers for reading, Mail & tel request accepted, Online searches, Photocopying/Printing, Prog for children & young adult, Ref serv available, Summer reading prog, Tax forms, Telephone ref, VHS videos
Special Services for the Blind - Bks on cassette; Bks on CD; Computer access aids; Copier with enlargement capabilities; Extensive large print coll; Large print & cassettes; Large print bks; Magnifiers
Open Mon, Wed & Thurs 12-7, Tues & Sat 10-5, Fri 12-5
Friends of the Library Group

MONACA

J COMMUNITY COLLEGE OF BEAVER COUNTY LIBRARY*, One Campus Dr, 15061-2588. SAN 314-7665. Tel: 724-775-8561. Circulation Tel: 724-775-8561, Ext 116. FAX: 724-728-8024. Web Site: www.ccbc.edu/lib. *Libr Mgr,* Cheryl Herrington; Tel: 724-775-8561, Ext 316, E-mail: cheryl.herrington@ccbc.edu; *Ref Librn,* Leila Mandel; Tel: 724-775-8561, Ext 113; *Circ,* Angie Pope; *Circ,* Pat Smith; Staff 1 (MLS 1)
Founded 1967. Enrl 2,545; Fac 41; Highest Degree: Associate
Jul 2005-Jun 2006. Mats Exp $90,000, Books $40,000, Per/Ser (Incl. Access Fees) $20,000, Electronic Ref Mat (Incl. Access Fees) $30,000. Sal $120,000 (Prof $35,000)
Library Holdings: Bk Titles 46,324; Bk Vols 52,281; Per Subs 89
Subject Interests: Aviation, Law enforcement, Nursing
Automation Activity & Vendor Info: (Cataloging) Innovative Interfaces, Inc; (Circulation) Innovative Interfaces, Inc; (Course Reserve) Innovative Interfaces, Inc; (ILL) Innovative Interfaces, Inc; (OPAC) Innovative Interfaces, Inc
Database Vendor: EBSCOhost, Gale Cengage Learning, LexisNexis, ProQuest, Wilson - Wilson Web
Function: ILL available, Magnifiers for reading, Orientations, Ref serv available
Open Mon-Thurs 7:30am-8pm, Fri 7:30-4

P MONACA PUBLIC LIBRARY*, 609 Pensylvania Ave, 15061. SAN 314-7673. Tel: 724-775-9608. FAX: 724-775-1637. E-mail: monacapl@hotmail.com. Web Site: www.monacapa.net. *Librn,* Patricia Smith
Founded 1973. Pop 7,661; Circ 20,014
Library Holdings: Bk Vols 14,500; Per Subs 26
Automation Activity & Vendor Info: (Cataloging) Innovative Interfaces, Inc; (Circulation) Innovative Interfaces, Inc
Mem of Beaver County Library System
Open Mon, Tues & Thurs 2-8, Wed 10-8, Sat 9-4

C PENNSYLVANIA STATE UNIVERSITY*, Beaver Campus Library, 100 University Dr, 15061. SAN 314-7681. Tel: 724-773-3790. FAX: 724-773-3793. Web Site: www.libraries.psu.edu/beaver. *Head Librn,* Martin Goldberg; Tel: 724-773-3791, E-mail: mxg35@psu.edu; *Ref Librn,* Courtney L Young; Tel: 724-773-3796, E-mail: cly11@psu.edu; Staff 2 (MLS 2)
Founded 1965. Enrl 900; Fac 63; Highest Degree: Master

Library Holdings: Bk Titles 52,435; Bk Vols 54,614; Per Subs 142; Talking Bks 108; Videos 761
Special Collections: Afro-American Autobiographies
Subject Interests: Steel indust
Partic in OCLC Online Computer Library Center, Inc; RLIN (Research Libraries Information Network)
Open Mon-Thurs 8am-9pm, Fri (Summer) 8-4:30

MONESSEN

P MONESSEN PUBLIC LIBRARY*, 326 Donner Ave, 15062-1182. SAN 314-7703. Tel: 724-684-4750. FAX: 724-684-0206. E-mail: Monessen.Public.Library@gmail.com. Web Site: www.monessenlibrary.org. *Dir,* Dave Zilka; E-mail: dzilka@hotmail.com; *Ch,* Jill Godlewski; *Ref Librn,* Allen Feryok; *Ref Librn,* Mary Matovich; *Cat,* Daniel Zyglowicz; Staff 7 (MLS 7)
Founded 1936. Pop 259,824
Library Holdings: High Interest/Low Vocabulary Bk Vols 1,500; Bk Vols 108,900; Per Subs 345
Special Collections: State Document Depository; US Document Depository
Partic in OCLC Online Computer Library Center, Inc; Westmoreland Library Network (WLN)
Open Mon-Wed 10-7, Thurs 10-5, Fri & Sat 10-2
Friends of the Library Group

MONONGAHELA

P MONONGAHELA AREA LIBRARY*, 813 W Main St, 15063-2815. SAN 314-7711. Tel: 724-258-5409. FAX: 724-258-5440. E-mail: monongahelalib@gmail.com. Web Site: www.monarealibrary.org. *Dir,* E J Filander; Staff 1 (Non-MLS 1)
Founded 1905. Pop 17,000; Circ 27,000
Library Holdings: Audiobooks 205; Bks on Deafness & Sign Lang 5; CDs 52; DVDs 168; Large Print Bks 652; Bk Titles 30,764; Per Subs 28
Special Collections: Genealogical Coll; Monongahela Daily Newspapers, 1851-1982 (micro)
Subject Interests: Local hist
Automation Activity & Vendor Info: (Acquisitions) Innovative Interfaces, Inc; (Cataloging) Innovative Interfaces, Inc; (Circulation) Innovative Interfaces, Inc; (Course Reserve) Innovative Interfaces, Inc; (OPAC) Innovative Interfaces, Inc; (Serials) Innovative Interfaces, Inc
Database Vendor: EBSCOhost
Wireless access
Function: Children's prog
Mem of Washington County Library System
Open Mon-Thurs 11-7, Fri 11-5, Sat 10-5
Friends of the Library Group

MONROETON

P MONROETON PUBLIC LIBRARY*, 149 Dalpiaz Dr, 18832. (Mail add: PO Box 145, 18832-0145), SAN 314-772X. Tel: 570-265-2871. FAX: 570-265-7995. E-mail: monroetonlibrary@comcast.net. Web Site: www.monroetonlibrary.org. *Librn,* Karen S Troup; Staff 3 (Non-MLS 3)
Founded 1939. Pop 633; Circ 3,000
Library Holdings: Bk Vols 5,900; Per Subs 15
Automation Activity & Vendor Info: (Cataloging) Follett Software; (Circulation) Follett Software
Mem of Bradford County Library System
Open Mon & Wed 1-6, Tues & Thurs 9-2, Sat 10-2
Friends of the Library Group

MONROEVILLE

J COMMUNITY COLLEGE OF ALLEGHENY COUNTY*, Boyce Campus Library, 595 Beatty Rd, 15146. SAN 358-7134. Tel: 724-325-6798. FAX: 724-325-6696. E-mail: library@ccac.edu. Web Site: ccac.edu/library. *Dir,* Position Currently Open; *Dept Head, Librn,* Mary Ellen Benson; Tel: 724-325-6713, E-mail: mbenson@ccac.edu; *Dept Head, Librn,* Raymond Martin; Tel: 724-325-6796, E-mail: rmartin@ccac.edu; Staff 8 (MLS 5, Non-MLS 3)
Founded 1966. Enrl 5,400; Fac 80
Library Holdings: Bk Titles 68,512; Bk Vols 71,910; Per Subs 182; Videos 559
Special Collections: Paralegal Coll
Subject Interests: Allied health, Food serv, Hospitality, Nursing, Paralegal
Automation Activity & Vendor Info: (Cataloging) SirsiDynix; (Circulation) SirsiDynix; (OPAC) SirsiDynix; (Serials) SirsiDynix
Database Vendor: EBSCOhost, OCLC FirstSearch
Publications: Acquisitions Lists; Bibliographies; Library Handbook; Library Newspaper
Partic in OCLC Online Computer Library Center, Inc; Pittsburgh Regional Libr Consortium
Open Mon-Thurs 8-8, Fri 8-4, Sat 9-1

M FORBES REGIONAL HOSPITAL*, Health Sciences Library, 2570 Haymaker Rd, 15146. (Mail add: 320 E North Ave, Pittsburgh, 15212), SAN 314-7746. E-mail: forbeslibrary@wpahs.org. Web Site: www.wpahs.org/health-sciences-library/forbes-regional-hospital-health-services. Staff 1 (MLS 1)
Founded 1978
Library Holdings: e-books 20; e-journals 900; Electronic Media & Resources 8; Bk Titles 500; Per Subs 80
Special Collections: Forbes History Coll
Subject Interests: Family practice, Gynecology, Obstetrics, Oncology, Pediatrics, Psychiat
Automation Activity & Vendor Info: (OPAC) LibraryWorld, Inc
Database Vendor: EBSCOhost, Micromedex, OVID Technologies, PubMed, STAT!Ref (Teton Data Systems), UpToDate
Partic in Basic Health Sciences Library Network; Pittsburgh Basic Health Sciences Libr Consortium (PBHSL)
Open Mon-Fri 8-3:30

P MONROEVILLE PUBLIC LIBRARY, 4000 Gateway Campus Blvd, 15146-3381. SAN 314-7770. Tel: 412-372-0500. Circulation Tel: 412-372-0500, Ext 15. Reference Tel: 412-372-0500, Ext 4. Administration Tel: 412-372-0500, Ext 11. Automation Services Tel: 412-372-0500, Ext 23. FAX: 412-372-1168. Web Site: www.monroevillelibrary.org. *Dir,* Nicole Henline; *Automation Syst Librn,* Janet L Balas; *Teen Librn,* Pam Bodziock; *Adult Serv,* Mark Hudson; Tel: 412-372-0500, Ext 13; *Ch Serv,* Lou Anne Sokolowski; Tel: 412-372-0500, Ext 21; *Ref Serv,* Marlene Dean; *Tech Serv,* Sally Michalski; Staff 19 (MLS 9, Non-MLS 10)
Founded 1964. Pop 33,162; Circ 221,476
Jan 2010-Dec 2010 Income $1,398,830, State $119,897, City $933,404, County $266,614, Other $53,826. Mats Exp $174,608, Books $107,069, Per/Ser (Incl. Access Fees) $7,957, Micro $5,632, AV Mat $50,948. Sal $872,810
Library Holdings: CDs 6,382; DVDs 5,227; Bk Vols 119,514; Per Subs 219
Special Collections: Local Newspaper 1976-Present, microfilm; New Reader Coll; Newbery & Caldecott Coll; NY Times 1940-Present, microfilm
Subject Interests: Careers, Local hist
Automation Activity & Vendor Info: (Acquisitions) Innovative Interfaces, Inc; (Cataloging) Innovative Interfaces, Inc; (Circulation) Innovative Interfaces, Inc; (OPAC) Innovative Interfaces, Inc
Database Vendor: Innovative Interfaces, Inc
Wireless access
Publications: Program Calendar (Monthly bulletin)
Mem of Allegheny County Library Association
Special Services for the Blind - Accessible computers; Bks & mags in Braille, on rec, tape & cassette; Bks on CD; Large print bks; Ref serv
Open Mon-Thurs 9-9, Fri & Sat 9-5, Sun (Sept-May) 2-5
Friends of the Library Group

MONT ALTO

C PENNSYLVANIA STATE UNIVERSITY, Mont Alto Campus Library, One Campus Dr, 17237-9703. SAN 314-7797. Tel: 717-749-6040. Circulation Tel: 717-749-6182. Interlibrary Loan Service Tel: 717-749-6042. Reference Tel: 717-749-6041. FAX: 717-749-6059. Web Site: www.libraries.psu.edu/psul/montalto.html. *Head Librn,* Alica Lisa White; Tel: 717-749-6044, E-mail: acw3@psu.edu; *Ref Librn,* Tom Reinsfelder; E-mail: tlr15@psu.edu; *Info Res & Serv Support Spec,* Jonathan Hindman; E-mail: jwh5116@psu.edu; *Info Res & Serv Support Spec,* Andrea Pritt; E-mail: alp5088@psu.edu; *ILL,* Position Currently Open; Staff 4 (MLS 2, Non-MLS 2)
Founded 1963. Enrl 1,261; Fac 53
Library Holdings: Bk Vols 36,000; Per Subs 180
Wireless access
Partic in OCLC Online Computer Library Center, Inc; RLIN (Research Libraries Information Network)
Open Mon-Fri 8am-10pm, Sat & Sun 4pm-10pm

MONTGOMERY

P MONTGOMERY AREA PUBLIC LIBRARY*, One S Main St, 17752-1150. SAN 314-7800. Tel: 570-547-6212. FAX: 570-547-0648. E-mail: mapl@jvbrown.edu. *Librn,* Susan Thomas; Staff 2 (Non-MLS 2)
Founded 1911. Pop 4,785; Circ 14,995
Library Holdings: Bk Vols 16,000; Per Subs 42
Automation Activity & Vendor Info: (Cataloging) SirsiDynix; (Circulation) SirsiDynix
Open Mon-Wed & Fri 12-8, Thurs 9-2, Sat 10-3

MONTOURSVILLE

P DR W B KONKLE MEMORIAL LIBRARY*, 384 Broad St, 17754-2206. SAN 314-7819. Tel: 570-368-1840. FAX: 570-368-7416. E-mail: konkle@jvbrown.edu. Web Site: www.jvbrown.edu. *Librn,* Jean Reeder
Founded 1943. Pop 7,694

Library Holdings: Bk Titles 23,000; Per Subs 45
Special Collections: Pennsylvania Coll, bks & pamphlets
Automation Activity & Vendor Info: (Cataloging) SirsiDynix; (Circulation) SirsiDynix; (OPAC) SirsiDynix
Mem of Lycoming County Libr Syst
Open Mon-Fri 10-7:30, Sat 9-4
Friends of the Library Group

MONTROSE

P SUSQUEHANNA COUNTY HISTORICAL SOCIETY & FREE LIBRARY ASSOCIATION*, Two Monument Sq, 18801-1115. SAN 358-7169. Tel: 570-278-1881. FAX: 570-278-9336. E-mail: dirsusqcolib@stny.rr.com. Web Site: www.susqcolibrary.org. *Dir,* Susan Stone; *Asst Librn,* Amy LaRue; *Ch Serv,* Frances Allen; *Pub Serv,* Hilary Caws-Elwitt; *Tech Serv,* Yasuko Ely; Staff 14 (MLS 2, Non-MLS 12)
Founded 1907. Pop 42,238; Circ 218,822
Library Holdings: Bk Vols 49,495; Per Subs 159
Special Collections: Genealogy (Census Records), micro; Genealogy (New England Historical & Genealogical Register); Local newspapers, micro
Function: Home delivery & serv to Sr ctr & nursing homes, Homebound delivery serv, ILL available, Prog for children & young adult, Summer reading prog
Publications: Centennial History of Susquehanna County, Pennsylvania; County Atlas; History of Susquehanna County, Pennsylvania
Open Mon-Fri 9-9, Sat 9-4
Friends of the Library Group
Branches: 3
FOREST CITY BRANCH, 531 Main St, Forest City, 18421-1421, SAN 358-7193. Tel: 570-785-5590. FAX: 570-785-4822. E-mail: fclib@nep.net. *Librn,* Diana Junior
Library Holdings: Bk Vols 14,802; Per Subs 57
Open Mon, Wed & Thurs, 10-1 & 2-5, Tues & Fri 10-1 & 2-7, Sat 10-1
HALLSTEAD-GREAT BEND BRANCH LIBRARY, 135 Franklin Ave, Hallstead, 18822, SAN 314-5662. Tel: 570-879-2227. FAX: 570-879-0982. E-mail: hallib@epix.net. *Dir,* Angie Hall
Founded 1917. Pop 6,000; Circ 24,631
Library Holdings: Bk Vols 9,089; Per Subs 36
Database Vendor: EBSCOhost
Function: ILL available
Open Mon, Wed & Thurs 9-1 & 2-5, Tues 9-1 & 2-6, Fri 9-1
Friends of the Library Group
SUSQUEHANNA BRANCH, 83 Erie Blvd, Ste C, Susquehanna, 18847, SAN 358-7223. Tel: 570-853-4106. FAX: 570-853-3265. E-mail: sqbrlib@epix.net. *Librn,* Laura Nichols
Circ 33,004
Library Holdings: Bk Vols 13,313; Per Subs 55
Open Mon-Wed 9-1 & 2-5, Thurs 9-1 & 2-6, Fri 9-1
Friends of the Library Group

GL SUSQUEHANNA COUNTY LAW LIBRARY*, Court House, 18801. (Mail add: PO Box 218, 18801-0218), SAN 372-9044. Tel: 570-278-4600. *Dir,* Mary Foster
Library Holdings: Bk Vols 12,500
Database Vendor: Westlaw
Open Mon-Fri 9-4:30

MOON TOWNSHIP

P MOON TOWNSHIP PUBLIC LIBRARY*, 1700 Beaver Grade Rd, Ste 100, 15108-2984. SAN 378-4231. Tel: 412-269-0334. FAX: 412-269-0136. E-mail: moontwp@einetwork.net. Web Site: www.moonlibrary.org. *Dir,* Maria Joseph; Staff 4 (MLS 4)
Pop 22,361; Circ 123,633
Jan 2010-Dec 2010 Income $445,000. Mats Exp $88,000. Sal $246,000
Library Holdings: Audiobooks 1,000; CDs 800; DVDs 3,000; Bk Vols 50,000; Per Subs 105
Automation Activity & Vendor Info: (Cataloging) Innovative Interfaces, Inc; (Circulation) Innovative Interfaces, Inc; (OPAC) Innovative Interfaces, Inc
Database Vendor: EBSCOhost, Gale Cengage Learning
Wireless access
Function: Adult bk club, Bks on CD, Chess club, Children's prog, Computer training, Computers for patron use, Copy machines, e-mail & chat, e-mail serv, Electronic databases & coll, Free DVD rentals, Handicapped accessible, Holiday prog, ILL available, Magnifiers for reading, Music CDs, Online cat, Online searches, Photocopying/Printing, Preschool outreach, Prog for adults, Prog for children & young adult, Pub access computers, Ref & res, Ref serv in person, Senior computer classes, Spoken cassettes & CDs, Spoken cassettes & DVDs, Story hour, Summer reading prog, Tax forms, Teen prog, Telephone ref, Wheelchair accessible
Mem of Allegheny County Library Association
Special Services for the Blind - Bks on CD; Large print bks; Magnifiers
Open Mon-Thurs 10-8, Fri & Sat 10-5, Sun (Sept-June) 1-5
Friends of the Library Group

C ROBERT MORRIS UNIVERSITY LIBRARY*, 6001 University Blvd, 15108-1189. SAN 358-3686. Tel: 412-397-6871. Circulation Tel: 412-397-6882. FAX: 412-397-4288. E-mail: library@rmu.edu. Web Site: www.rmu.edu/library. *Dean of Libr,* Frances Caplan; Tel: 412-397-6868, E-mail: caplan@rmu.edu; *Acq,* Donald Luisi; Tel: 412-397-6865, E-mail: luisi@rmu.edu; *Cat,* Abiodum Ibraheem; Tel: 412-397-6875, E-mail: ibraheem@rmu.edu; *ILL,* Bruce Johnston; Tel: 412-397-6877, E-mail: johnston@rmu.edu; *Pub Serv,* Christopher Devine; Tel: 412-397-6872, E-mail: devinec@rmu.edu; Staff 17 (MLS 9, Non-MLS 8)
Founded 1962. Enrl 4,156; Fac 189; Highest Degree: Doctorate
Jun 2011-May 2012 Income $1,684,770. Mats Exp $642,354, Books $170,323, Per/Ser (Incl. Access Fees) $119,808, Micro $28,249, AV Mat $21,530, Electronic Ref Mat (Incl. Access Fees) $302,444. Sal $821,210 (Prof $603,790)
Library Holdings: e-books 1,932; Bk Titles 93,847; Bk Vols 111,496; Per Subs 432
Database Vendor: Cambridge Scientific Abstracts, CQ Press, EBSCOhost, Elsevier, Emerald, Ex Libris Group, ISI Web of Knowledge, JSTOR, LexisNexis, OCLC FirstSearch, OCLC WorldShare Interlibrary Loan, Project MUSE, ProQuest, ReferenceUSA, RefWorks, Sage, SerialsSolutions, Thomson - Web of Science, Westlaw, Wiley, Wilson - Wilson Web
Wireless access
Function: ILL available
Partic in Lyrasis; OCLC Online Computer Library Center, Inc; Pennsylvania Academic Library Consortium, Inc (PALCI)

MORGAN

P SOUTH FAYETTE TOWNSHIP LIBRARY*, 515 Millers Run Rd, 15064. Tel: 412-257-8660. FAX: 412-257-8682. E-mail: southfayette@einetwork.net. Web Site: southfayettelibrary.org. *Dir,* Position Currently Open; *Ch Serv,* Jody Wilson; E-mail: wilsonj@einetwork.net; Staff 4 (MLS 2, Non-MLS 2)
Founded 1994
Mem of Allegheny County Library Association
Open Mon-Thurs 10-8, Fri & Sat 10-5
Friends of the Library Group

MORGANTOWN

P VILLAGE LIBRARY OF MORGANTOWN*, 207 N Walnut St, 19543. (Mail add: PO Box 797, 19543-0797), SAN 314-7827. Tel: 610-286-1022. FAX: 610-286-1024. E-mail: village.library@villagelibrary.org. Web Site: www.villagelibrary.org. *Dir,* Susan Shipe; *Ch,* Pam Mohl; E-mail: pam.mohl@villagelibrary.org; Staff 1 (MLS 1)
Founded 1965. Pop 9,216; Circ 78,886
Library Holdings: Bk Titles 22,000; Per Subs 47
Special Collections: Small Business Coll
Wireless access
Function: After school storytime, Bks on cassette, Bks on CD, Children's prog, Computer training, Computers for patron use, Copy machines, Fax serv, Free DVD rentals, Handicapped accessible, Holiday prog, ILL available, Magnifiers for reading, Music CDs, Online cat, Orientations, OverDrive digital audio bks, Photocopying/Printing, Prog for adults, Prog for children & young adult, Pub access computers, Senior outreach, Story hour, Summer reading prog, Tax forms, VHS videos, Wheelchair accessible, Workshops
Mem of Berks County Public Libraries
Special Services for the Deaf - Closed caption videos
Special Services for the Blind - Audio mat; Bks on cassette; Bks on CD; Large print bks; Magnifiers; Reader equip; Talking bks
Open Mon 9-7, Tues & Thurs 9-5, Wed 9-6, Fri 9-1, Sat 9-4
Friends of the Library Group

MORRISVILLE

P MORRISVILLE FREE LIBRARY ASSOCIATION*, 300 N Pennsylvania Ave, 19067-6621. SAN 314-7835. Tel: 215-295-4850. FAX: 215-295-4851. *Librn,* Diane Hughes; Staff 5 (MLS 1, Non-MLS 4)
Founded 1904. Pop 10,023; Circ 36,911
Library Holdings: AV Mats 1,181; Large Print Bks 171; Bk Titles 26,791; Bk Vols 28,411; Per Subs 73; Talking Bks 265; Videos 391
Automation Activity & Vendor Info: (Cataloging) SirsiDynix; (Circulation) SirsiDynix
Open Mon-Thurs 11-8, Sat 10-5
Friends of the Library Group

MOSCOW

P NORTH POCONO PUBLIC LIBRARY*, 113 Van Brunt St, 18444-9254. SAN 376-5717. Tel: 570-842-4700. FAX: 570-842-1304. Web Site: www.lclshome.org/npocono. *Dir,* Susan Jeffery; E-mail: susanjeffery@albright.org; Staff 8 (MLS 1, Non-MLS 7)
Founded 1985. Pop 18,925

Library Holdings: Bk Titles 35,000; Per Subs 55
Automation Activity & Vendor Info: (Cataloging) SirsiDynix; (Circulation) SirsiDynix; (ILL) SirsiDynix; (OPAC) SirsiDynix
Database Vendor: EBSCOhost
Wireless access
Mem of Lackawanna County Library System
Open Mon-Thurs 9-7, Fri & Sat 9-4

MOUNT CARMEL

P MOUNT CARMEL AREA PUBLIC LIBRARY*, 30 S Oak St, 17851-2185. SAN 314-7843. Tel: 570-339-0703. E-mail: mountcarmelpubliclibrary@verizon.net. Web Site: www.geocities.com/mcpublib. *Librn,* Vivian McCracken
Founded 1961. Pop 12,832; Circ 50,000
Library Holdings: Bk Vols 54,000; Per Subs 90
Special Collections: Proceedings Northunderland County, Hist Soc, Local Hist Coll
Subject Interests: Handicrafts, World War II
Wireless access
Open Mon & Tues 8-6, Wed 8-1, Thurs 9-6, Fri 9-4, Sat 9-1

MOUNT HOLLY SPRINGS

P AMELIA S GIVIN FREE LIBRARY*, 114 N Baltimore Ave, 17065-1201. SAN 314-7851. Tel: 717-486-3688. FAX: 717-486-7170. E-mail: amelia@ccpa.net. Web Site: ccpa.net. *Dir,* Cynthia Stratton Thomson; Staff 5 (MLS 1, Non-MLS 4)
Founded 1889. Pop 9,421; Circ 61,112
Library Holdings: Bk Titles 27,991; Bk Vols 29,411; Per Subs 116; Talking Bks 943; Videos 1,287
Mem of Cumberland County Library System
Open Mon-Thurs 10-9, Fri 10-6, Sat 9-4

MOUNT JEWETT

P MOUNT JEWETT MEMORIAL LIBRARY, Seven E Main St, 16740. (Mail add: PO Box Y, 16740), SAN 314-786X. Tel: 814-778-5588. FAX: 814-778-5588. E-mail: librarian@mtjewettlibrary.org. *Dir,* Debbie Deane
Founded 1938. Pop 1,992; Circ 3,966
Library Holdings: Audiobooks 200; e-books 4,000; Bk Vols 16,842; Per Subs 12
Open Mon-Thurs 10-12, 2-5 & 7-9, Fri 10-12 & 2-5, Sat 10-2

MOUNT JOY

P MILANOF-SCHOCK LIBRARY*, 1184 Anderson Ferry Rd, 17552. SAN 314-7878. Tel: 717-653-1510. FAX: 717-653-6590. Web Site: www.mslibrary.org. *Exec Dir,* Debra Rosser-Hogben; E-mail: drosser-hogben@mountjoy.lib.pa.us; *Asst Dir,* Nancy L Behney; E-mail: nbehney@lancaster.lib.pa.us; *Circ Coordr,* Susan Craine; *Commun Relations Coordr,* Kirsen Rhoads; *Coordr, Ch & Youth Serv,* Jan Betty; Staff 5.7 (MLS 1, Non-MLS 4.7)
Founded 1964. Pop 25,442; Circ 211,148
Jan 2011-Dec 2011 Income $343,766, State $76,756, City $94,447, County $8,271, Locally Generated Income $152,617, Other $15,916. Mats Exp $40,895, Books $27,327, Per/Ser (Incl. Access Fees) $2,053, AV Mat $8,207. Sal $202,321 (Prof $48,000)
Library Holdings: Audiobooks 3,290; DVDs 4,954; e-books 6; Large Print Bks 600; Bk Vols 35,881; Per Subs 72
Wireless access
Function: Adult bk club, Adult literacy prog, Bk club(s), Bks on cassette, Bks on CD, Chess club, Children's prog, Computer training, Computers for patron use, Copy machines, e-mail serv, E-Reserves, Electronic databases & coll, Free DVD rentals, Handicapped accessible, ILL available, Magnifiers for reading, Mus passes, Music CDs, Notary serv, Online cat, Online ref, Orientations, OverDrive digital audio bks, Passport agency, Photocopying/Printing, Preschool outreach, Prog for adults, Prog for children & young adult, Pub access computers, Ref serv available, Senior computer classes, Summer reading prog, Tax forms, Teen prog, Telephone ref, VHS videos, Web-catalog, Wheelchair accessible
Mem of Library System of Lancaster County
Open Mon-Thurs 10-8, Sat 9-1
Restriction: Authorized patrons, In-house use for visitors, Lending limited to county residents, Non-resident fee, Pub ref by request, Pub use on premises
Friends of the Library Group

MOUNT PLEASANT

M FRICK HOSPITAL*, Joseph F Bucci Health Sciences Library, 508 S Church St, 15666. SAN 329-0689. Tel: 724-547-1352. FAX: 724-547-1693. *Librn,* Marilyn Daniels; Staff 2 (MLS 1, Non-MLS 1)
Founded 1980
Library Holdings: AV Mats 40; Bk Titles 871; Per Subs 90
Database Vendor: EBSCOhost
Publications: The Next Chapter (Newsletter)
Partic in National Network of Libraries of Medicine Middle Atlantic Region
Open Mon, Wed & Thurs 9:30-3, Tues & Fri 8-Noon

P MOUNT PLEASANT FREE PUBLIC LIBRARY*, 120 S Church St, 15666-1879. SAN 314-7886. Tel: 724-547-3850. FAX: 724-547-0324. E-mail: librarian@mountpleasantpalibrary.org. Web Site: www.mountpleasantpalibrary.org. *Dir, Libr Serv,* Jamie K Falo; *Librn,* Carole A Klocek; Staff 5 (Non-MLS 5)
Founded 1936. Pop 15,000; Circ 24,000
Library Holdings: AV Mats 200; Large Print Bks 20; Bk Titles 22,972; Per Subs 63; Talking Bks 200
Special Collections: Math Coll; Teen Coll; Whiskey Rebellion
Automation Activity & Vendor Info: (Cataloging) Follett Software; (Circulation) Follett Software
Mem of Westmoreland County Federated Library System
Partic in Share Westmoreland Consortium
Open Mon-Thurs 11-8, Fri 11-5, Sat 9:30-4:30

MOUNTAIN TOP

P MARIAN SUTHERLAND KIRBY LIBRARY*, 35 Kirby Ave, 18707-1214. SAN 376-5687. Tel: 570-474-9313. FAX: 570-474-2587. E-mail: info@kirbylib.org. Web Site: www.kirbylib.org. *Dir,* Dr Marcia McGann; Staff 5 (MLS 1, Non-MLS 4)
Library Holdings: Bk Titles 32,000; Per Subs 80
Wireless access
Mem of Luzerne County Library System
Partic in Pennsylvania Library Association
Open Mon, Thurs & Fri 9-5, Tues & Wed 9-9, Sat 9-4 (9-1 Summer)
Friends of the Library Group

MUNCY

S MUNCY HISTORICAL SOCIETY & MUSEUM OF HISTORY*, Historical Library, 40 N Main St, 17756-1004. (Mail add: PO Box 11, 17756-0011), SAN 372-9060. Tel: 570-546-5917. E-mail: muncyhistorical@aol.com. Web Site: www.muncyhistoricalsociety.org. *Curator,* Linda Poulton
Library Holdings: Bk Vols 400
Open Mon-Fri 9-3
Friends of the Library Group

P MUNCY PUBLIC LIBRARY*, 108 S Main St, 17756-0119. SAN 314-7916. Tel: 570-546-5014. FAX: 570-546-5014. Web Site: www.muncylibrary.com. *Librn,* Laurie Cressman
Pop 7,207; Circ 41,624
Library Holdings: AV Mats 1,025; DVDs 500; Large Print Bks 200; Bk Vols 25,200; Per Subs 40; Talking Bks 325; Videos 200
Special Collections: Luminary-Local Newspaper on Microfilm; Pennsylvania History, micro
Wireless access
Mem of Lycoming County Libr Syst
Open Mon, Tues & Thurs 1-9, Wed & Sat 9-4, Fri 11-6
Friends of the Library Group

MUNHALL

P CARNEGIE LIBRARY OF HOMESTEAD*, 510 E Tenth Ave, 15120-1910. Tel: 412-462-3444. FAX: 412-462-4669. *Dir,* Tyrone Ward; Staff 2 (MLS 1, Non-MLS 1)
Pop 19,368; Circ 22,350
Library Holdings: Large Print Bks 188; Bk Titles 48,919; Bk Vols 50,191; Per Subs 132; Talking Bks 903; Videos 657
Mem of Allegheny County Library Association
Open Mon-Fri 9-8, Sat 9-5

MURRYSVILLE

P MURRYSVILLE COMMUNITY LIBRARY*, 4130 Sardis Rd, 15668-1120. SAN 314-7924. Tel: 724-327-1102. FAX: 724-327-7142. E-mail: murrysville@wlnonline.org. Web Site: www.murrysvillelibrary.org. *Dir,* Jamie Falo; Tel: 724-327-1102, Ext 153; *Cat,* Susan Lyons; *Ch Serv,* Carol Siefken; Staff 9 (MLS 2, Non-MLS 7)
Founded 1922. Pop 25,940; Circ 149,800
Library Holdings: AV Mats 4,280; Large Print Bks 1,080; Bk Vols 55,500; Per Subs 125
Subject Interests: Local newsp
Automation Activity & Vendor Info: (Acquisitions) Innovative Interfaces, Inc; (Cataloging) Innovative Interfaces, Inc; (Circulation) Innovative Interfaces, Inc; (ILL) Innovative Interfaces, Inc; (OPAC) Innovative Interfaces, Inc; (Serials) Innovative Interfaces, Inc
Database Vendor: Baker & Taylor, Brodart, ProQuest, ReferenceUSA
Wireless access
Mem of Westmoreland County Federated Library System

Partic in Westmoreland Library Network (WLN)
Open Mon-Wed 9-8:30, Thurs-Sat 9-5, Sun (Sept-May) 1-5

MYERSTOWN

R EVANGELICAL SCHOOL OF THEOLOGY*, Rostad Library, 121 S College St, 17067. SAN 314-7932. Tel: 717-866-5775. FAX: 717-866-4667. Web Site: www.evangelical.edu. *Librn,* Dr Terry M Heisey; E-mail: theisey@evangelical.edu; *Circ,* Julie Miller; E-mail: jmiller@evangelical.edu; Staff 1 (MLS 1)
Founded 1954. Enrl 200; Fac 9; Highest Degree: Master
Library Holdings: Bk Titles 73,490; Bk Vols 76,810; Per Subs 550
Special Collections: Evangelical Association; Evangelical Congregational Church Archives; Pietism
Subject Interests: Biblical studies
Automation Activity & Vendor Info: (Cataloging) TLC (The Library Corporation); (Circulation) TLC (The Library Corporation); (OPAC) TLC (The Library Corporation)
Database Vendor: EBSCOhost
Function: Archival coll, ILL available, Online searches, Photocopying/Printing, Ref serv available
Partic in Southeastern Pennsylvania Theological Library Association
Open Mon, Tues & Thurs (Winter) 8am-10pm, Wed & Fri 8-5, Sat 9-3; Mon-Fri (Summer) 8-5

P MYERSTOWN COMMUNITY LIBRARY*, 199 N College St, 17067. (Mail add: PO Box 246, 17067-0246), SAN 314-7940. Tel: 717-866-2800. FAX: 717-866-5898. Web Site: www.lclibs.org. *Dir,* Linda Manwiller; E-mail: llm@lclibs.org; Staff 2 (MLS 1, Non-MLS 1)
Founded 1936. Pop 13,341; Circ 72,692
Jan 2010-Dec 2010 Income $176,331. Mats Exp $13,308. Sal $73,248
Library Holdings: AV Mats 1,918; Bk Vols 43,367; Per Subs 46
Subject Interests: Local counties, Local genealogies, Pa archives, Pa German Folklore Society, Pa hist
Automation Activity & Vendor Info: (Acquisitions) Baker & Taylor; (Cataloging) Innovative Interfaces, Inc; (Circulation) Innovative Interfaces, Inc; (OPAC) Innovative Interfaces, Inc
Wireless access
Mem of Lebanon County Library System
Open Mon, Wed & Thurs 12-8, Tues 12-6, Fri 10-5, Sat 9-4 (9-1 Summer)

NANTICOKE

J LUZERNE COUNTY COMMUNITY COLLEGE LIBRARY, 1333 S Prospect St, 18634-3899. SAN 314-7959. Tel: 570-740-0415. Interlibrary Loan Service Tel: 570-740-0424. Reference Tel: 570-740-0661. Toll Free Tel: 800-377-5222, Ext 7415. FAX: 570-735-6130. Web Site: depts.luzerne.edu/library. *Dir,* Mia Wang Bassham; Tel: 800-377-5222, Ext 7420, E-mail: mbassham@luzerne.edu; *Electronic Res Librn,* Position Currently Open; *Ref Librn,* Position Currently Open; Staff 3 (MLS 3)
Founded 1966. Enrl 4,887; Fac 138; Highest Degree: Associate
Jul 2013-Jun 2014 Income $654,729. Mats Exp $169,404, Books $60,155, Per/Ser (Incl. Access Fees) $21,000, Micro $11,950, AV Mat $14,599, Electronic Ref Mat (Incl. Access Fees) $60,000, Presv $1,700. Sal $453,969 (Prof $186,932)
Library Holdings: Audiobooks 65; AV Mats 14,669; Bks-By-Mail 100; DVDs 336; e-books 129,568; Music Scores 407; Bk Titles 56,414; Bk Vols 60,527; Per Subs 102; Videos 1,470
Special Collections: Criminal Justice Coll; Fire Science Technology Coll
Subject Interests: Dental assisting, Hotel, Hygiene, Nursing, Restaurant mgt
Automation Activity & Vendor Info: (Acquisitions) SirsiDynix; (Cataloging) SirsiDynix; (Circulation) SirsiDynix; (Course Reserve) SirsiDynix; (ILL) OCLC; (OPAC) SirsiDynix; (Serials) SirsiDynix
Database Vendor: Access Pennsylvania, Bowker, CQ Press, CredoReference, EBSCOhost, Gale Cengage Learning, JSTOR, Lexi-Comp, LexisNexis, OCLC, OCLC FirstSearch, OCLC WorldShare Interlibrary Loan, Oxford Online, ProQuest, SirsiDynix
Wireless access
Partic in Lyrasis; OCLC Online Computer Library Center, Inc
Open Mon-Thurs 8-6:30, Fri 8-5
Restriction: Borrowing requests are handled by ILL

P MILL MEMORIAL LIBRARY*, 495 E Main St, 18634-1897. SAN 314-7967. Tel: 570-735-3030. FAX: 570-735-0340. Web Site: www.gnasd.com/millmemorial.htm. *Dir,* Cliff Farides; Staff 5 (MLS 1, Non-MLS 4)
Founded 1945. Pop 22,803; Circ 43,910
Library Holdings: Large Print Bks 380; Bk Titles 53,410; Bk Vols 56,980; Per Subs 142; Talking Bks 92; Videos 725
Automation Activity & Vendor Info: (Cataloging) Innovative Interfaces, Inc; (Circulation) Innovative Interfaces, Inc; (ILL) Innovative Interfaces, Inc; (OPAC) Innovative Interfaces, Inc
Mem of Luzerne County Library System
Open Tues-Thurs 10-8, Fri & Sat 10-5
Friends of the Library Group

NANTY GLO

P NANTY GLO PUBLIC LIBRARY*, 942 Roberts St, 15943-0296. SAN 314-7975. Tel: 814-749-0111. FAX: 814-749-0111. E-mail: nantyglo@cclsys.org. Web Site: cclsys.org/nantyglo. *Librn,* Sharon Gallaher; *Asst Librn,* Janet Llewllyn
Founded 1962. Pop 10,000; Circ 25,000
Library Holdings: Bk Vols 28,000; Per Subs 40
Special Collections: Library of America
Subject Interests: Accelerated readers
Automation Activity & Vendor Info: (Cataloging) Follett Software; (Circulation) Follett Software
Wireless access
Mem of Cambria County Library System & District Center
Special Services for the Blind - Audio mat
Open Mon, Tues & Thurs 1-7, Wed 10-4, Fri 1-5, Sat 9-4

NARBERTH

P NARBERTH COMMUNITY LIBRARY*, 80 Windsor Ave, 19072-2296. SAN 314-7991. Tel: 610-664-2878. FAX: 610-667-3245. E-mail: narcirc1@mclinc.org. Web Site: nar.mclinc.org. *Dir,* Janine Waters; E-mail: jwatersg@mclinc.org; Staff 5.5 (MLS 1.5, Non-MLS 4)
Founded 1921. Pop 4,300; Circ 45,617
Library Holdings: AV Mats 1,420; Large Print Bks 600; Bk Vols 48,760; Per Subs 45
Special Collections: Pennsylvania & Philadelphia Area History (Pennsylvania Coll)
Automation Activity & Vendor Info: (Acquisitions) Innovative Interfaces, Inc; (Cataloging) Innovative Interfaces, Inc; (Circulation) Innovative Interfaces, Inc; (ILL) Innovative Interfaces, Inc; (OPAC) Innovative Interfaces, Inc
Database Vendor: Overdrive, Inc, World Book Online
Wireless access
Function: Audiobks via web, Bks on cassette, Bks on CD, Children's prog, Computers for patron use, Copy machines, Electronic databases & coll, Free DVD rentals, ILL available, Mail & tel request accepted, Mus passes, Online cat, OverDrive digital audio bks, Photocopying/Printing, Preschool outreach, Prog for adults, Prog for children & young adult, Pub access computers, Ref serv in person, Story hour, Summer reading prog, Tax forms, Teen prog
Partic in Montgomery County Library & Information Network Consortium
Open Mon-Thurs (Sept-June) 10-8, Fri & Sat 10-5; Sat (July & Aug) 10-2

NATRONA HEIGHTS

M ALLEGHENY VALLEY HOSPITAL*, Medical Library, 1301 Carlisle St, 15065. Tel: 724-226-7092. FAX: 724-226-7303. *Librn,* Craig Arvid Jones; E-mail: cjones2@wpahs.org
Library Holdings: Bk Vols 700; Per Subs 50
Subject Interests: Med
Database Vendor: OVID Technologies, PubMed
Function: ILL available
Open Mon-Fri 8:30-12:30

P COMMUNITY LIBRARY OF ALLEGHENY VALLEY*, 1522 Broadview Blvd, 15065. SAN 378-1674. Tel: 724-226-3491. FAX: 724-226-3821. Web Site: alleghenyvalleylibrary.org. *Dir,* Kathy Firestone; Staff 15 (MLS 2, Non-MLS 13)
Founded 1923. Pop 23,284; Circ 153,372
Jan 2011-Dec 2011 Income (Main Library and Branch(s)) $377,925, State $74,153, Locally Generated Income $117,765, Other $126,958. Mats Exp $35,201, Books $24,175, Per/Ser (Incl. Access Fees) $3,842, Micro $1,208, AV Mat $4,769, Electronic Ref Mat (Incl. Access Fees) $1,207. Sal $228,248
Library Holdings: Audiobooks 2,308; AV Mats 7,152; CDs 521; DVDs 1,150; e-books 24,568; Bk Vols 68,802; Per Subs 83
Automation Activity & Vendor Info: (Acquisitions) Innovative Interfaces, Inc; (Cataloging) Innovative Interfaces, Inc; (Circulation) Innovative Interfaces, Inc; (Course Reserve) Innovative Interfaces, Inc; (ILL) Innovative Interfaces, Inc; (OPAC) Innovative Interfaces, Inc; (Serials) Innovative Interfaces, Inc
Wireless access
Mem of Allegheny County Library Association
Open Mon-Thurs 11:30-8:30, Fri 10-2, Sat 9-4
Friends of the Library Group
Branches: 1
TARENTUM BRANCH, 400 Lock St, Tarentum, 15084, SAN 315-2650. Tel: 724-226-0770. FAX: 724-226-3526. *Dir,* Kathy Firestone; E-mail: firestonek@einetwork.net; Staff 3 (Non-MLS 3)
Founded 1923
Library Holdings: Bk Titles 16,702; Per Subs 27

Open Mon 11-8, Tues & Wed 9-6, Fri 9-4, Sat 10-2
Friends of the Library Group

NAZARETH

P MEMORIAL LIBRARY OF NAZARETH & VICINITY*, 295 E Center St, 18064-2298. SAN 314-8009. Tel: 610-759-4932. FAX: 610-759-9513. E-mail: nazlib1@nazarethlibrary.org. Web Site: www.nazarethlibrary.org. *Dir,* Position Currently Open; *Asst Dir, Ch Serv,* Catherine Stewart; E-mail: nazlib1@nazarethlibrary.org; Staff 10 (MLS 1, Non-MLS 9)
Founded 1949. Pop 22,690; Circ 139,000
Jan 2009-Dec 2009 Income $473,314, State $100,404, Locally Generated Income $325,410, Other $47,500. Mats Exp $78,428. Sal $280,201 (Prof $56,000)
Library Holdings: Audiobooks 1,559; e-books 2,087; Large Print Bks 350; Bk Titles 53,300; Bk Vols 58,764; Per Subs 103; Videos 1,818
Subject Interests: Genealogy, Hist
Automation Activity & Vendor Info: (Cataloging) TLC (The Library Corporation); (Circulation) TLC (The Library Corporation); (Course Reserve) TLC (The Library Corporation); (ILL) TLC (The Library Corporation); (Media Booking) TLC (The Library Corporation); (OPAC) TLC (The Library Corporation); (Serials) TLC (The Library Corporation)
Database Vendor: EBSCO Auto Repair Reference, EBSCO Information Services, EBSCOhost, Grolier Online, H W Wilson, ProQuest, PubMed, ReferenceUSA, TLC (The Library Corporation), World Book Online
Wireless access
Open Mon, Fri & Sat 10-5, Tues-Thurs 10-8
Friends of the Library Group

S THE MORAVIAN HISTORICAL SOCIETY*, Museum & Library, 214 E Center St, 18064. SAN 374-552X. Tel: 610-759-5070. FAX: 610-759-2461. E-mail: info@moravianhistoricalsociety.org. Web Site: www.moravianhistoricalsociety.org. *Exec Dir,* Wendy S Weida; E-mail: director@moravianhistoricalsociety.org
Founded 1857
Library Holdings: Bk Titles 5,000; Per Subs 10
Function: Res libr
Open Mon-Fri 1-4
Restriction: Not a lending libr

NEW ALBANY

P NEW ALBANY COMMUNITY LIBRARY*, 98 Front St, 18833. (Mail add: Rte 2, Box 162, 18833-0054), SAN 314-8017. Tel: 570-363-2418. *In Charge,* Debbie McComb
Founded 1963
Library Holdings: Bk Vols 5,000
Mem of Bradford County Library System
Open Tues 9am-11am, Thurs 6pm-7pm, Sat 2-4
Friends of the Library Group

NEW ALEXANDRIA

P NEW ALEXANDRIA PUBLIC LIBRARY*, Keystone Plaza, Rte 22, 15670-9703. (Mail add: PO Box 405, 15670-0405), SAN 314-8025. Tel: 724-668-7747. Web Site: www.newalexandriapa.com/library. *Librn,* Jacqueline Snyder; E-mail: jackiesnyder65@hotmail.com; Staff 1 (Non-MLS 1)
Founded 1921. Pop 742; Circ 1,081
Library Holdings: Bk Titles 8,462; Bk Vols 10,000; Per Subs 18
Open Mon & Wed 2-7, Tues 12-5, Thurs 1-7, Sat 10-12

NEW BETHLEHEM

P REDBANK VALLEY PUBLIC LIBRARY*, 720 Broad St, 16242-1107. SAN 314-8033. Tel: 814-275-2870. FAX: 814-275-2875. E-mail: newbiepl@comcast.net. Web Site: www.youseemore.com/newbethlehem. *Dir,* Joyce Erin; E-mail: newbethdirector@gmail.com; Staff 4 (MLS 1, Non-MLS 3)
Founded 1955. Pop 8,081; Circ 29,796
Jan 2006-Dec 2006 Income $82,418, State $37,000, County $3,709, Locally Generated Income $40,000, Other $1,709. Mats Exp $10,680, Books $9,000, Per/Ser (Incl. Access Fees) $700, Electronic Ref Mat (Incl. Access Fees) $180, Presv $800. Sal $51,000 (Prof $25,400)
Library Holdings: AV Mats 800; Bks on Deafness & Sign Lang 35; CDs 230; DVDs 504; Large Print Bks 366; Bk Titles 23,898; Bk Vols 23,921; Per Subs 40; Talking Bks 344
Special Collections: Local Newspaper, microfilm
Automation Activity & Vendor Info: (Cataloging) TLC (The Library Corporation); (Circulation) TLC (The Library Corporation); (OPAC) TLC (The Library Corporation)
Database Vendor: EBSCOhost
Wireless access
Function: Adult bk club, After school storytime, Bks on CD, Children's prog, Computer training, Computers for patron use, Copy machines, Fax serv, Free DVD rentals, Handicapped accessible, Holiday prog, ILL available, Music CDs, Passport agency, Photocopying/Printing, Preschool outreach, Prog for adults, Prog for children & young adult, Story hour, Summer reading prog, Tax forms, Wheelchair accessible
Mem of Oil Creek District Library Center
Special Services for the Deaf - Bks on deafness & sign lang; Closed caption videos; Spec interest per
Special Services for the Blind - Audio mat; Bks on cassette; Bks on CD; Copier with enlargement capabilities; Extensive large print coll; Home delivery serv; Large print bks
Open Mon, Wed & Fri 10-5, Tues & Thurs 11-7, Sat 10-1

NEW BLOOMFIELD

P BLOOMFIELD PUBLIC LIBRARY*, 19 E McClure St, Borough Bldg, 17068. (Mail add: PO Box 558, 17068-0558). Tel: 717-582-7426. FAX: 717-582-0051. E-mail: circdesk@bloomfieldpl.org. Web Site: www.bloomfieldpl.org. *Dir,* Linda Wilson
Library Holdings: Bks on Deafness & Sign Lang 13; Bk Vols 15,000; Per Subs 30
Automation Activity & Vendor Info: (Cataloging) Follett Software; (Circulation) Follett Software
Database Vendor: Gale Cengage Learning
Open Mon & Fri 1-5, Tues & Thurs 2-7, Wed 9-7, Sat 9-4

L PERRY COUNTY LAW LIBRARY, Perry County Courthouse, Center Sq, Two E Main St, 17068. (Mail add: PO Box 668, 17068-0668), SAN 372-9079. Tel: 717-582-5143. FAX: 717-582-5144. *Court Adminr,* Christina L Zook; E-mail: czook@perryco.org
Library Holdings: Bk Vols 100; Per Subs 100
Database Vendor: LexisNexis
Open Mon-Fri 8-4

S PERRY HISTORIANS LIBRARY*, Harry W Lenig Library, 763 Dix Hill Rd, 17068. (Mail add: PO Box 73, Newport, 17074-0073), SAN 371-8336. Tel: 717-582-4896. E-mail: staff@theperryhistorians.org. Web Site: www.theperryhistorians.org. *Librn,* Donna Heller Zinn
Founded 1976
Library Holdings: Bk Titles 5,000; Per Subs 25
Special Collections: Court House Records; Land Surveys; Stoneware; Taufscheins
Subject Interests: Genealogy, Local hist
Publications: The Airy View (Newsletter); The Perry Review (Annual)
Open Wed 9-9

NEW BRIGHTON

P NEW BRIGHTON PUBLIC LIBRARY*, 1021 Third Ave, 15066-3011. SAN 314-8041. Tel: 724-846-7991. FAX: 724-846-7995. E-mail: newbrightonpubliclibrary@yahoo.com. Web Site: www.beaverlibraries.org/newbrighton.asp. *Dir,* Kate Weidner; E-mail: kweidner@beaverlibraries.org; Staff 1 (Non-MLS 1)
Pop 8,341; Circ 29,432
Library Holdings: Bk Titles 29,231; Bk Vols 30,908; Per Subs 34; Talking Bks 515; Videos 331
Mem of Beaver County Library System
Open Tues-Thurs 11-7, Fri 11-5, Sat 9-4

NEW CASTLE

S ERIE BUSINESS CENTER SOUTH*, Blackmer Library, 170 Cascade Galleria, 16101. SAN 372-9087. Tel: 814-456-7504. Web Site: www.eriebc.edu/newcastle. *Dir,* Hanni Nazario; E-mail: hanni.nazario@eriebc.edu; Staff 1 (Non-MLS 1)
Library Holdings: Bk Titles 1,890; Bk Vols 2,080; Per Subs 121
Subject Interests: Acctg
Open Mon-Fri 8-5

SR FIRST CHRISTIAN CHURCH LIBRARY*, 23 W Washington St, 16101. SAN 320-2275. Tel: 724-652-6657. *In Charge,* Trudy Chandler; Staff 1 (Non-MLS 1)
Founded 1959
Library Holdings: Bk Titles 4,390; Bk Vols 4,670; Per Subs 26
Special Collections: Historical
Subject Interests: Relig
Open Mon-Fri 9-3

SR HIGHLAND PRESBYTERIAN CHURCH*, Elizabeth Milholland Library, 708 Highland Ave, 16101. SAN 329-8450. Tel: 724-654-7391. *Librn,* Anne M Graham; Staff 1 (Non-MLS 1)
Library Holdings: Bk Titles 2,581; Bk Vols 2,790; Per Subs 11
Special Collections: Ministry of Encouragement
Subject Interests: Relig
Open Mon-Fri 9-2

M JAMESON HEALTH SYSTEM LIBRARY*, Jameson Memorial Hospital School of Nursing Library, 1211 Wilmington Ave, 16105-2595. SAN 358-7258. Tel: 724-656-4050. FAX: 724-656-4267. *Librn*, Lori A Graham; E-mail: lgraham@jamesonhealth.org; Staff 2 (MLS 1, Non-MLS 1)
Founded 1898
Library Holdings: Bk Titles 3,198; Bk Vols 4,561; Per Subs 120
Subject Interests: Med, Nursing
Partic in National Network of Libraries of Medicine Middle Atlantic Region
Open Mon-Fri 8-4:30

P LAWRENCE COUNTY FEDERATED LIBRARY SYSTEM*, 207 E North St, 16101-3691. Tel: 724-658-6659. FAX: 724-658-7209. Web Site: lawrencecountylibrary.org. *Dir*, Sandra Collins; E-mail: scollins@ncdlc.org; Staff 45 (MLS 6, Non-MLS 39)
Founded 1998. Pop 97,000; Circ 250,000
Library Holdings: Bk Titles 110,000; Bk Vols 171,000; Per Subs 125
Special Collections: US Document Depository
Subject Interests: Genealogy
Automation Activity & Vendor Info: (Cataloging) Evergreen; (Circulation) Evergreen; (OPAC) Evergreen
Wireless access
Function: Prof lending libr, Ref serv available
Member Libraries: Ellwood City Area Public Library; Frank D Campbell Memorial Library; New Castle Public Library
Restriction: Non-circulating
Friends of the Library Group
Bookmobiles: 1

L LAWRENCE COUNTY LAW LIBRARY*, 430 Court St, 16101. SAN 328-0551. Tel: 724-656-2136. FAX: 724-658-4489. *Librn*, Jo Helen Thomas; Staff 1 (MLS 1)
Jan 2006-Dec 2006 Income $122,454. Mats Exp $81,235, Books $52,000, Per/Ser (Incl. Access Fees) $75, Electronic Ref Mat (Incl. Access Fees) $29,160. Sal $26,439
Library Holdings: CDs 15; Bk Vols 25,000; Per Subs 15
Special Collections: State Document Depository
Database Vendor: LexisNexis, Westlaw
Function: Res libr
Open Mon-Fri 8-4
Restriction: Not a lending libr

P NEW CASTLE PUBLIC LIBRARY*, 207 E North St, 16101-3691. SAN 314-8068. Tel: 724-658-6659. FAX: 724-658-7209. Reference FAX: 724 658 9012. Web Site: www.ncdlc.org. *Dir*, Sandra Collins; E mail: scollins@ncdlc.org; *District Librn*, Amy Geisinger; E-mail: ageisinger@ncdlc.org; *Head, Ch*, Kathleen Lebby, E-mail: klebby@ncdlc.org; *Head, Per, Ref Serv, Ad*, Mike Orwell; E-mail: morwell@ncdlc.org; *Govt Doc, Head, Ref*, Jennifer Joseph; E-mail: reference@ncdlc.org; *Circ Supvr*, Susan Morgan; E-mail: smorgan@ncdlc.org; *IT & Security Mgr*, Ron Davis; E-mail: rdavis@ncdlc.org; *Cat, Tech Serv*, Julie Mulcahy; E-mail: jmulcahy@ncdlc.org; Staff 8 (MLS 7, Non-MLS 1)
Founded 1908. Pop 68,588; Circ 181,000
Library Holdings: Bk Vols 11,300; Per Subs 138
Special Collections: Architecture (Jane Jackson Coll), bks, microflm; Brotherhood (Joshua A Kaplan Coll); Gardening, Landscape (Wylie McCaslin Coll); Judaism (Council Corner Coll); Local History Coll; Pharmacy (Lawrence C Pharmaceutical Coll); Polish Culture (Polish Falcons Coll); Women's World (Federation Coll). State Document Depository; US Document Depository
Subject Interests: Hist
Automation Activity & Vendor Info: (Cataloging) Evergreen; (Circulation) Evergreen
Database Vendor: OCLC FirstSearch
Wireless access
Mem of Lawrence County Federated Library System
Partic in Tri County Libr Consortium
Open Mon & Thurs 8:30-8:30, Tues, Wed, Fri & Sat 8:30-5
Friends of the Library Group
Bookmobiles: 1

R NORTHMINSTER PRESBYTERIAN CHURCH*, Alice M Sterling Memorial Library, 2434 Wilmington Rd, 16105. SAN 314-8076. Tel: 724-658-9051. FAX: 724-658-9613. *Librn*, Susan Dexter
Founded 1957
Library Holdings: Bk Vols 4,000
Subject Interests: Christian educ, Relig
Open Mon-Fri 8:30-4, Sun 10:45-12:45

NEW CUMBERLAND

P NEW CUMBERLAND PUBLIC LIBRARY*, One Benjamin Plaza, 17070-1597. SAN 314-8084. Tel: 717-774-7820. FAX: 717-774-7824. E-mail: newcumberland@ccpa.net. Web Site: www.ccpa.net. *Dir*, Judith Dillen; *Cat*, Denise Shellehamer; *Ch Serv*, Eilleen Franz; *ILL*, Leatrice Calderelli; Staff 4 (MLS 1, Non-MLS 3)
Founded 1941. Pop 7,665; Circ 192,707
Library Holdings: Bk Titles 57,418; Bk Vols 59,861; Per Subs 131; Talking Bks 491; Videos 3,408
Subject Interests: Local hist
Automation Activity & Vendor Info: (OPAC) SirsiDynix
Mem of Cumberland County Library System
Open Mon-Thurs 10-9, Fri & Sat 10-5
Friends of the Library Group

NEW FLORENCE

P NEW FLORENCE COMMUNITY LIBRARY, 122 Ligonier St, 15944. SAN 314-8092. Tel: 724-235-2249. FAX: 724-235-2249. E-mail: nflibrary@comcast.net. Web Site: www.newflorencelibrary.org. *Librn*, Margaret Betz; Staff 1 (Non-MLS 1)
Pop 2,667; Circ 24,383
Library Holdings: Audiobooks 453; DVDs 744; Large Print Bks 1,424; Bk Titles 22,591; Bk Vols 23,486; Per Subs 10; Videos 95
Automation Activity & Vendor Info: (OPAC) Innovative Interfaces, Inc
Database Vendor: Gale Cengage Learning
Wireless access
Function: Bks on cassette, Bks on CD, Children's prog, Computers for patron use, Copy machines, Electronic databases & coll, Fax serv, Free DVD rentals, Handicapped accessible, ILL available, Online cat, Online ref, Photocopying/Printing, Prog for adults, Prog for children & young adult, Summer & winter reading prog, Tax forms, VHS videos
Mem of Westmoreland County Federated Library System
Open Mon & Wed 11-6, Tues 11-8, Thurs & Fri 11-4, Sat 10-5

NEW HOLLAND

P EASTERN LANCASTER COUNTY LIBRARY*, 11 Chestnut Dr, 17557-9437. SAN 314-8114. Tel: 717-354-0525. FAX: 717-354-7787. Web Site: www.elancolibrary.org. *Dir*, Donna Brice; E-mail: dbrice@elancolibrary.org; *Youth Serv Librn*, Heather Smith; E-mail: hsmith@elancolibrary.org; Staff 3 (MLS 1, Non-MLS 2)
Pop 22,579; Circ 51,211
Library Holdings: Bk Titles 29,430; Bk Vols 32,611; Per Subs 71; Talking Bks 685; Videos 903
Automation Activity & Vendor Info: (Cataloging) Innovative Interfaces, Inc; (Circulation) Innovative Interfaces, Inc; (ILL) Innovative Interfaces, Inc; (OPAC) Innovative Interfaces, Inc; (Serials) Innovative Interfaces, Inc
Database Vendor: Baker & Taylor, Booklist Online, BWI, Ingram Library Services, OCLC FirstSearch, OCLC WebJunction, OCLC WorldShare Interlibrary Loan, Overdrive, Inc, ProQuest, ReferenceUSA, WebMD
Wireless access
Mem of Library System of Lancaster County
Open Mon-Thurs 10-8, Fri & Sat 10-1
Friends of the Library Group

NEW HOPE

P FREE LIBRARY OF NEW HOPE & SOLEBURY, 93 W Ferry St, 18938-1332. SAN 314-8122. Tel: 215-862-2330. E-mail: nhspubliclibrary@gmail.com. Web Site: www.nhslibrary.org. *Dir*, Connie Hillman; Staff 1 (MLS 1)
Founded 1894. Pop 9,995; Circ 45,479
Special Collections: New Hope Reference Coll; Performing & Fine Arts Coll
Subject Interests: Archit, Art
Wireless access
Function: Adult bk club, Audiobks via web, Bk club(s), Bks on cassette, Bks on CD, Computers for patron use, Copy machines, Homebound delivery serv, ILL available, Music CDs, Online cat, OverDrive digital audio bks, Preschool outreach, Prog for adults, Prog for children & young adult, Pub access computers, Story hour, Summer reading prog, Tax forms, VHS videos
Mem of Bucks County Free Library
Open Mon-Wed 10-7, Thurs-Sat 10-5

S THE FREEDONIA GAZETTE*, Marx Brothers Library & Archives, 335 Fieldstone Dr, 18938-1012. SAN 326-1808. Tel: 215-862-9734. *Dir, Ref*, Paul G Wesolowski
Founded 1982
Library Holdings: Bk Titles 140
Special Collections: Effect of Marx Brothers on popular culture (Gloria Teasdale Coll), toys, games, T-shirts, greeting cards, cups & statues
Publications: The Freedonia Gazette - The magazine devoted to the Marx Brothers

NEW KENSINGTON

S ALCOA TECHNICAL CENTER LIBRARY*, 100 Technical Dr, 15069. SAN 314-2531. Tel: 724-337-5300. FAX: 724-337-2394. Web Site: www.alcoa.com. *Librn,* Earl Mounts; E-mail: earl.mounts@alcoa.com; Staff 6 (MLS 3, Non-MLS 3)
Founded 1919
Library Holdings: Bk Titles 21,615; Bk Vols 23,249; Per Subs 116
Special Collections: Alcoa Laboratories History; Alcoa Publications; Technical Translations
Subject Interests: Aluminum, Auto tech, Light metals, Mat sci, Packaging, Surface sci
Automation Activity & Vendor Info: (Cataloging) Cuadra Associates, Inc
Database Vendor: Dialog
Publications: Intranet
Partic in OCLC Online Computer Library Center, Inc
Open Mon-Fri 9-5
Restriction: Employees & their associates, Use of others with permission of librn

P PEOPLES LIBRARY*, New Kensington, 880 Barnes St, 15068. SAN 358-7371. Tel: 724-339-1021. Circulation Tel: 724-339-1021, Ext 10. Interlibrary Loan Service Tel: 724-339-1021, Ext 13. FAX: 724-339-2027. E-mail: peoplesnk@peopleslibrary.net. Web Site: www.peopleslibrary.org, www.peopleslink.org. *Dir,* David Hrivnak; Tel: 724-339-1021, Ext 12, E-mail: hrivnakd@peopleslibrary.net; *Head, Circ,* Denise Blose; E-mail: dblose@peopleslibrary.net; *Ch Serv,* Mary Wesolek; Tel: 724-339-1021, Ext 15, E-mail: mwesolek@peopleslibrary.net; *Network Adminr,* John Michael Polczynski; Tel: 724-339-1021, Ext 17, E-mail: johnpolczynski@peopleslibrary.net; Staff 15 (MLS 1, Non-MLS 14)
Founded 1928. Pop 46,312; Circ 92,207
Library Holdings: High Interest/Low Vocabulary Bk Vols 134; Bk Titles 35,851; Bk Vols 37,815; Per Subs 36
Subject Interests: Careers, Cookbks, Local hist, Westerns
Automation Activity & Vendor Info: (Acquisitions) Innovative Interfaces, Inc; (Cataloging) Innovative Interfaces, Inc; (Circulation) Innovative Interfaces, Inc; (OPAC) Innovative Interfaces, Inc
Database Vendor: EBSCOhost
Publications: Library Newsletter
Mem of Westmoreland County Federated Library System
Partic in Monessen District Libr Ctr; Share Westmoreland Consortium; Westmoreland Library Network (WLN)
Open Mon-Thurs 9-6, Fri & Sat 9-5
Friends of the Library Group
Branches: 1
LOWER BURRELL, 3052 Wachter Ave, Lower Burrell, 15068-3543, SAN 358-7401. Tel: 724-339-1565. Circulation Tel: 724-339-1565, Ext 10. Interlibrary Loan Service Tel: 724-339-1565, Ext 11. FAX: 724-339-5132. E-mail: peopleslb@peopleslibrary.net. *Br Mgr,* Carole Bauer; Fax: 724-339-2027, E-mail: cbauer@peopleslibrary.net
Library Holdings: Bk Titles 25,251; Bk Vols 26,363
Open Mon & Wed 11-8, Tues & Thurs 10-8, Fri 10-5, Sat 9-3
Friends of the Library Group

NEW MILFORD

P PRATT MEMORIAL LIBRARY*, 752 Main St, 18834. (Mail add: PO Box 407, 18834), SAN 314-8157. Tel: 570-465-3098. E-mail: prattml@nep.net. Web Site: prattmemoriallibrary.org. *Librn,* Betty Mitchell
Founded 1903. Pop 2,400; Circ 7,400
Library Holdings: Bk Vols 9,000; Per Subs 23; Talking Bks 125
Wireless access
Open Mon & Sat 2-5, Wed 2-7, Fri 6:30-8:30

NEW OXFORD

P NEW OXFORD AREA LIBRARY*, 122 N Peter St, 17350-1229. SAN 324-5764. Tel: 717-624-2182. FAX: 717-624-1358. Web Site: www.adamslibrary.org. *Br Mgr,* Wilma Krepps; E-mail: wilmak@adamslibrary.org; Staff 3 (MLS 1, Non-MLS 2)
Founded 1983. Pop 3,162; Circ 14,189
Library Holdings: AV Mats 984; Bk Vols 15,000; Per Subs 29; Talking Bks 103; Videos 171
Automation Activity & Vendor Info: (Acquisitions) TLC (The Library Corporation); (Cataloging) TLC (The Library Corporation); (Circulation) TLC (The Library Corporation); (Course Reserve) TLC (The Library Corporation); (ILL) TLC (The Library Corporation); (Media Booking) TLC (The Library Corporation); (OPAC) TLC (The Library Corporation); (Serials) TLC (The Library Corporation)
Mem of Adams County Library System
Open Mon & Thurs 2-8, Tues, Wed & Fri 11-5, Sat 10-4
Friends of the Library Group

NEW WILMINGTON

C WESTMINSTER COLLEGE*, McGill Library, S Market St, 16172-0001. SAN 358-7436. Tel: 724-946-7330. FAX: 724-946-6220. Web Site: www.westminster.edu/library. *Dir,* Molly P Spinney; E-mail: mspinney@westminster.edu; *Cat, Syst Coordr,* Erin T Smith; E-mail: smithet@westminster.edu; *Per,* David K Brautigarm; E-mail: dbrautig@westminster.edu; *Ref,* Dorita F Bolger; E-mail: dbolger@westminster.edu; Staff 4 (MLS 4)
Founded 1852. Enrl 1,350; Fac 100; Highest Degree: Master
Library Holdings: Bk Titles 228,421; Bk Vols 247,000; Per Subs 864
Special Collections: Autographed Books; Bibles in Foreign Languages; James Fenimore Cooper, early eds; K C Constantine, papers
Automation Activity & Vendor Info: (Cataloging) SirsiDynix; (Circulation) SirsiDynix; (OPAC) SirsiDynix
Database Vendor: SirsiDynix
Publications: Friends of the Library Newsletter
Partic in Dialog Corp; OCLC Online Computer Library Center, Inc; Utah Academic Library Consortium
Open Mon-Thurs 8am-Midnight, Fri 8am-9pm, Sat 9-8, Sun 1-11
Friends of the Library Group

NEWFOUNDLAND

S CINEMA ARTS, INC*, Motion Picture Archives, 207 Lincoln Green Lane, 18445. (Mail add: PO Box 452, 18445-0452), SAN 323-7206. Tel: 570-676-4145. FAX: 570-676-9194. E-mail: jeainc@gmail.com. *VPres,* Beverley Allen; *Acq,* Janice E Allen; *Tech Serv,* Mike Kolvek; Staff 6 (MLS 3, Non-MLS 3)
Founded 1987
Library Holdings: CDs 390; Bk Titles 10,141; Bk Vols 14,961; Per Subs 52; Videos 1,082
Special Collections: Kinograms & Telenews, reels; Posters; Silent Film Coll; Still Photographs
Subject Interests: Educ, Transportation, Travel, World War I, World War II
Restriction: Open by appt only

P NEWFOUNDLAND AREA PUBLIC LIBRARY*, Main St, 18445. (Mail add: PO Box 214, 18445-0214), SAN 314-8165. Tel: 570-676-4518. FAX: 570-676-4518. *Dir,* Carol Shaheen; Staff 3 (MLS 1, Non-MLS 2)
Pop 4,210; Circ 9,812
Library Holdings: AV Mats 982; Large Print Bks 84; Bk Titles 18,129; Bk Vols 19,981; Per Subs 39; Talking Bks 154; Videos 269
Automation Activity & Vendor Info: (Cataloging) TLC (The Library Corporation); (Circulation) TLC (The Library Corporation)
Open Wed 10-4, Thurs 10-8, Fri 9-4, Sat 10-2
Friends of the Library Group

NEWPORT

P NEWPORT PUBLIC LIBRARY, 316 N Fourth St, 17074-1203. SAN 314-8173. Tel: 717-567-6860. FAX: 717-567-3373. E-mail: nppublib@pa.net. Web Site: pecoinfo.org. *Dir,* Jeanne Heicher; *Asst Dir,* Mary Jane Zentichko; *Ch Serv,* Cheryl Johnson; Staff 3 (Non-MLS 3)
Founded 1914. Pop 9,169
Wireless access
Function: Art exhibits, Copy machines, Fax serv, ILL available, Mail & tel request accepted, Music CDs, Online searches, Prog for children & young adult, Spoken cassettes & CDs, Summer reading prog, Tax forms, Telephone ref, VHS videos, Wheelchair accessible
Open Mon, Wed & Fri 1-8, Tues, Thurs & Sat 10-6
Friends of the Library Group

NEWTOWN

J BUCKS COUNTY COMMUNITY COLLEGE LIBRARY*, 275 Swamp Rd, 18940-0999. SAN 314-8181. Tel: 215-968-8009. Interlibrary Loan Service Tel: 215-968-8555. Reference Tel: 215-968-8013. FAX: 215-968-8142. Web Site: www.bucks.edu/library. *Dir, Libr Serv,* Linda McCann; Tel: 215-968-8003, E-mail: mccannl@bucks.edu; *Dean, Learning Res,* Maureen McCreadie; Tel: 215-968-8004, E-mail: mccreadi@bucks.edu; *Coll Mgt Librn,* Marzenna Ostrowski; Tel: 215-504-8619, E-mail: ostrowsk@bucks.edu; *Digital Res Librn,* Brian Johnstone; Tel: 215-504-8554, E-mail: johnston@bucks.edu; *Emerging Tech Librn,* Matthew Seibert; Tel: 215-968-8304, E-mail: seibert@bucks.edu; *Info Literacy Librn,* Margaret Montet; Tel: 215-968-8373, E-mail: montetm@bucks.edu; *New Media Librn,* Paul Proces; Tel: 215-497-8711, E-mail: procesp@bucks.edu; *Online Learning Librn,* William Hemmig; Tel: 215-504-8611, E-mail: hemmigw@bucks.edu; Staff 17 (MLS 10, Non-MLS 7)
Founded 1965. Enrl 9,274; Fac 201
Special Collections: US Document Depository
Automation Activity & Vendor Info: (Acquisitions) SirsiDynix; (Cataloging) SirsiDynix; (Circulation) SirsiDynix; (ILL) OCLC; (OPAC) SirsiDynix; (Serials) SirsiDynix

Wireless access
Partic in OCLC Online Computer Library Center, Inc
Open Mon-Thurs 8am-9pm, Fri 8-3:30, Sat 8-3:30, Sun 1-5:30
Friends of the Library Group

S NEWTOWN HISTORIC ASSOCIATION, INC*, Research Center & Barnsley Room of Newtown History, Court St & Centre Ave, 18940. (Mail add: PO Box 303, 18940-0303), SAN 326-4289. Tel: 215-968-4004. Web Site: www.newtownhistoric.org. *Curator,* Harriet Beckert; Staff 11 (MLS 5, Non-MLS 6)
Founded 1982
Library Holdings: CDs 20; DVDs 20; Bk Vols 1,500; Per Subs 30
Special Collections: Hicks Family (Edward Hicks Coll); New Century Club Records, 1890-present; Newtown (Barnsley Coll), clippings, original doc; Newtown Genealogy Coll; Newtown Records of Local Insurance Company 1831-1989; People & Places in Early Newtown, pictures & postcards; Reliance Company Records. Municipal Document Depository
Function: Bus archives, Copy machines, e-mail serv, Electronic databases & coll, Mail & tel request accepted, Newsp ref libr, Photocopying/Printing, Ref & res, Res libr
Publications: Half Moon (Newsletter)
Open Tues 9-3, Thurs 7pm-9pm
Restriction: Non-circulating to the pub, Not a lending libr, Open to fac, students & qualified researchers, Open to pub for ref only
Friends of the Library Group

P NEWTOWN LIBRARY CO*, 114 Centre Ave, 18940. SAN 314-8203. Tel: 215-968-7659. E-mail: librarian@newtownlibrary.com. Web Site: www.newtownlibrary.com. *Librn,* Karolyn Fisher; *Pub Relations,* Louis Saurman; *Strategic Planning,* Glen Beasley
Founded 1760
Library Holdings: Bk Vols 21,135; Per Subs 30; Talking Bks 119
Special Collections: Civil War; Old Books for Children (19th Century); Pa & Local Area Coll; Revolutionary War Coll
Subject Interests: 19th Century, Pa hist
Publications: Newtown Borough Council; Newtown Library Under Two Kings; Newtown's First Library Building
Open Mon-Fri 10-5 & 6:30-8:30, Thurs & Fri 10-5, Sat 9:30-2:30
Friends of the Library Group

NEWTOWN SQUARE

P NEWTOWN PUBLIC LIBRARY*, 201 Bishop Hollow Rd, 19073 4176. SAN 314-8211. Tel: 610-353-1022. FAX: 610-353-2611. E-mail: newtown@delcolibraries.org. Web Site. www.newtownlibrary.org. *Dir,* Susan Knorr; Staff 1 (MLS 1)
Founded 1974. Pop 11,940; Circ 56,000
Library Holdings: Bk Vols 55,000; Per Subs 90
Special Collections: Nedurian Law Coll
Database Vendor: EBSCOhost, Gale Cengage Learning, Innovative Interfaces, Inc
Wireless access
Mem of Delaware County Library System
Open Mon-Thurs 10-8, Fri 10-5, Sat 10-3, Sun (Sept-June) 1-4
Friends of the Library Group

NEWVILLE

P JOHN GRAHAM PUBLIC LIBRARY*, Nine Parsonage St, 17241-1399. SAN 314-822X. Tel: 717-776-5900. FAX: 717-776-4408. Web Site: www.ccpa.net. *Librn,* SallyAnn M Smith; E-mail: sasmith@ccpa.net; Staff 7 (MLS 1, Non-MLS 6)
Founded 1960. Pop 11,115; Circ 62,811
Library Holdings: AV Mats 1,591; Bk Titles 26,811; Bk Vols 27,919; Per Subs 98; Talking Bks 418; Videos 601
Subject Interests: Genealogy, Pa, Relig
Automation Activity & Vendor Info: (Cataloging) Horizon; (Circulation) Horizon; (OPAC) Horizon
Database Vendor: EBSCOhost, SirsiDynix
Mem of Cumberland County Library System
Open Mon, Tues, Thurs & Fri 10-8, Wed & Sat 10-5
Friends of the Library Group

NORRISTOWN

GL LAW LIBRARY OF MONTGOMERY COUNTY*, Court House, Swede & Airy Streets, 19404. (Mail add: PO Box 311, 19404-0311), SAN 314-8254. Tel: 610-278-3806. FAX: 610-278-5998. Web Site: llmc.montcopa.org. *Law Librn,* Denise C Mines; *Ref Librn,* Jeanne M Ottinger; Staff 4 (MLS 3, Non-MLS 1)
Founded 1869
Library Holdings: Bk Vols 70,400; Per Subs 100
Automation Activity & Vendor Info: (Cataloging) Softlink America; (Circulation) Softlink America; (OPAC) Softlink America; (Serials) Softlink America
Open Mon-Fri 8:30-4:15

P MONTGOMERY COUNTY-NORRISTOWN PUBLIC LIBRARY*, 1001 Powell St, 19401-3817. SAN 358-7495. Tel: 610-278-5100. Web Site: mnl.mclinc.org. *Exec Dir,* Kathleen M Arnold-Yergel; Tel: 610-278-5100, Ext 140; *Head, Circ,* Asha Verma; Tel: 610-278-5100, Ext 112; *Head, Ref,* Loretta Righter; Tel: 610 278 5100, Ext 201; *Head, Tech Serv,* Beth Slating; Tel: 610-278-5100, Ext 118; *Head, Youth Serv,* Traycee Yawger; Tel: 610-278-5100, Ext 205; *Supvr, ILL,* Valerie Johnson; Tel: 610-278-5100, Ext 120; *Automation Serv,* Leslie Rush; Tel: 610-278-5100, Ext 125; *Bkmobile/Outreach Serv,* Russell Rush; Tel: 610-278-5100, Ext 123; Staff 85 (MLS 19, Non-MLS 66)
Founded 1794. Pop 315,547; Circ 637,861
Library Holdings: AV Mats 21,168; High Interest/Low Vocabulary Bk Vols 675; Large Print Bks 10,079; Bk Vols 479,242; Per Subs 831
Special Collections: Carolyn Wicker Field Coll (autographed children's books & correspondence from children's authors & illustrations); Old Fiction (before 1969-closed bookstacks); Pennsylvania (Steinbright Local History). State Document Depository; US Document Depository
Subject Interests: Pa hist
Automation Activity & Vendor Info: (Cataloging) Innovative Interfaces, Inc; (Circulation) Innovative Interfaces, Inc; (OPAC) Innovative Interfaces, Inc
Wireless access
Partic in Interlibrary Delivery Service of Pennsylvania; Montgomery County Library & Information Network Consortium; OCLC Online Computer Library Center, Inc; OCLC, Inc through Palinet; Pa Area Libr Network
Special Services for the Deaf - Bks on deafness & sign lang; High interest/low vocabulary bks; Spec interest per
Open Mon-Thurs 9-8, Fri 9-6, Sat 9-5 (10-2 Summer)
Friends of the Library Group
Branches: 4
CONSHOHOCKEN FREE LIBRARY, 301 Fayette St, Conshohocken, 19428, SAN 358-7525. Tel: 610-825-1656. FAX: 610-825-1685. *Br Mgr,* Rachel Fecho; Staff 2 (MLS 1, Non-MLS 1)
Library Holdings: Large Print Bks 250; Bk Titles 23,610; Bk Vols 25,911; Per Subs 62; Talking Bks 90; Videos 300
Open Mon & Wed 12-9, Tues & Thurs 10-5, Fri 1-5, Sat 9-12, Sun 1-5
Friends of the Library Group
PERKIOMEN VALLEY, 290 Second St, Schwenksville, 19473, SAN 376-8074. Tel: 610-287-8360. FAX: 610-287-8360. Web Site: www.pvlibrary.net. *Br Mgr,* Aileen Johnson; Staff 1 (Non-MLS 1)
Founded 1930. Pop 33,000; Circ 55,000
Library Holdings: Large Print Bks 182; Bk Titles 21,614; Bk Vols 23,911; Per Subs 25; Videos 800
Function: Adult bk club, After school storytime, Audiobks via web, Bk club(s), Bks on cassette, Bks on CD, Children's prog, Computers for patron use, Copy machines, Digital talking bks, e-mail serv, E Reserves, Electronic databases & coll, Free DVD rentals, Govt ref serv, Handicapped accessible, Holiday prog, Home delivery & serv to Sr ctr & nursing homes, Homebound delivery serv, ILL available, Jail serv, Magnifiers for reading, Mail & tel request accepted, Mail loans to mem, Newsp ref libr, Online cat, Online ref, Online searches, Outreach serv, OverDrive digital audio bks, Photocopying/Printing, Prog for adults, Prog for children & young adult, Pub access computers, Ref & res, Ref serv available, Spoken cassettes & CDs, Spoken cassettes & DVDs, Story hour, Summer reading prog, Tax forms, Teen prog, Telephone ref, Web-catalog, Wheelchair accessible
Open Mon-Thurs 12-8, Fri 12-6, Sat 10-2
Friends of the Library Group
ROYERSFORD PUBLIC, 200 S Fourth Ave, Royersford, 19468, SAN 375-4758. Tel: 610-948-7277. FAX: 610-948-7277. *Br Mgr,* Eileen McNamara; E-mail: emcnamara@mclinc.org; Staff 1 (MLS 1)
Pop 31,211; Circ 62,859
Library Holdings: Bk Titles 19,610; Bk Vols 20,541; Per Subs 27; Talking Bks 59; Videos 119
Open Mon-Thurs 10-8, Fri & Sat 10-2
Friends of the Library Group
UPPER PERKIOMEN VALLEY, 350 Main St, Red Hill, 18076, SAN 358-755X. Tel: 215-679-2020. E-mail: upvlibrary@comcast.net. Web Site: www.upvlibrary.org. *Br Mgr,* Jeanne Cove; *Head, Youth Serv,* Wendy Kramer; Staff 3 (Non-MLS 3)
Founded 1970. Pop 19,327
Library Holdings: DVDs 1,100; Bk Titles 28,000; Bk Vols 29,111; Per Subs 31
Open Mon-Thurs 10-8, Fri 10-5, Sat 10-2
Friends of the Library Group
Bookmobiles: 4. Head, Bkmobile Serv, Russell Rush

S MONTGOMERY COUNTY PLANNING COMMISSION LIBRARY*, One Montgomery Plaza, 425 Swede St, 19401. SAN 314-8262. Tel: 610-278-3722. FAX: 610-278-3941. Web Site: planning.montcopa.org/planning/site/default.asp. *Adminr,* William T Morgan; Tel: 610-278-3732, E-mail: bmorgan@montcopa.org; Staff 1 (Non-MLS 1)
Founded 1950
Library Holdings: Bk Titles 4,000; Per Subs 40
Special Collections: 1980 Census of Population & Housing (Computer; 1990 Census; Printouts); Subdivision Files: Maps & Correspondence, micro & flm
Subject Interests: Environ studies, Housing, Land use, Landscape archit, Recreation, Transportation planning
Open Mon-Fri 8:30-4:15

M MONTGOMERY HOSPITAL*, Medical Library, 1301 Powell St, 19404. SAN 324-4946. Tel: 610-270-2232. *Librn,* Margaret Almon; Staff 1 (MLS 1)
Founded 1978
Library Holdings: e-journals 1,100; Bk Titles 275
Subject Interests: Family practice
Partic in Basic Health Sciences Library Network; Delaware Valley Information Consortium
Restriction: Not open to pub

M NORRISTOWN STATE HOSPITAL*, Noyes Memorial Library, Kaleidoscope, Bldg 53 CR, 1001 Sterigere St, 19401. SAN 358-7584. Tel: 610-313-1180, 610-313-5369. FAX: 610-313-5370. *Dir,* Elizabeth Sorg; Staff 1 (MLS 1)
Founded 1975
Jul 2007-Jun 2008 Income $65,271, Locally Generated Income $50, Parent Institution $65,221. Mats Exp $2,319, Books $1,030, Per/Ser (Incl. Access Fees) $160, AV Mat $344. Sal $62,952 (Prof $62,952)
Library Holdings: AV Mats 1,241; Bk Titles 9,710; Per Subs 5
Special Collections: 19th Century Psychiatric Journals & Annual Reports NSH-Archives; Patient Coll; Staff Coll
Subject Interests: Alcoholism, Drug abuse, Hort therapy, Music, Nutrition-diet therapy, Pastoral psych-counseling, Pharmacology-psychopharmacology, Psychiat neurology, Psychiat nursing, Psychotherapy-psychoanalysis, Recreational
Automation Activity & Vendor Info: (Cataloging) Ex Libris Group; (Circulation) Ex Libris Group; (OPAC) Ex Libris Group
Function: Audio & video playback equip for onsite use, AV serv, Bks on cassette, Bks on CD, CD-ROM, Computers for patron use, Copy machines, e-mail serv, Electronic databases & coll, Free DVD rentals, Health sci info serv, ILL available, Magnifiers for reading, Mail & tel request accepted, Mail loans to mem, Online cat, Prof lending libr, Prog for adults, Provide serv for the mentally ill, Ref serv available, VHS videos, Video lending libr, Wheelchair accessible
Partic in DEVIC; National Network of Libraries of Medicine South Central Region
Special Services for the Deaf - Assisted listening device
Open Mon-Fri 8:15-4:15
Restriction: Access at librarian's discretion, Authorized patrons, Authorized scholars by appt

NORTH EAST

S LAKE SHORE RAILWAY HISTORICAL SOCIETY MUSEUM & LIBRARY*, 31 Wall St (at Robinson St), 16428-1223. (Mail add: PO Box 571, 16428-0571), SAN 326-6206. Tel: 814-725-1911. FAX: 814-725-1911. E-mail: lsrhs@velocity.net. Web Site: www.velocity.net/~lsrhs. *Librn,* Ray Grabowski
Library Holdings: Bk Titles 1,600; Per Subs 40
Special Collections: Locomotive Builder's Photogs (General Electric Co), film negs; Locomotive Builder's Photogs (Heisler Locomotive Works), glass plate, film negs. Oral History
Restriction: Open by appt only

P MCCORD MEMORIAL LIBRARY*, 32 W Main St, 16428. SAN 314-8319. Tel: 814-725-4057. E-mail: mccord@ccfls.org. Web Site: www.mccordlibrary.org. *Dir,* Mary Kieffer; *Ch Serv,* Rae Lindsey; Staff 1 (MLS 1)
Founded 1899. Pop 11,214; Circ 79,000
Library Holdings: Bks on Deafness & Sign Lang 37; Bk Titles 32,000; Bk Vols 35,087; Per Subs 93; Spec Interest Per Sub 20
Subject Interests: Agr, Arts & crafts, Genealogy, Local hist, Quilting
Automation Activity & Vendor Info: (Cataloging) Infor Library & Information Solutions; (Circulation) Infor Library & Information Solutions; (OPAC) Infor Library & Information Solutions
Function: Adult literacy prog
Partic in Share NW Consortium
Friends of the Library Group

NORTH VERSAILLES

P NORTH VERSAILLES PUBLIC LIBRARY*, 1401 Greensburg Ave, 15137. SAN 314-8270. Tel: 412-823-2222. FAX: 412-823-2012. Web Site: www.northversailleslibrary.org. *Dir,* Michael A Kowalcheck; *Asst Dir, Prog Coordr,* Karen Schmidt-Ramsey; Staff 2 (MLS 1, Non-MLS 1)
Founded 1974. Pop 12,419; Circ 24,239
Library Holdings: Bk Titles 23,419; Bk Vols 24,312; Per Subs 59
Automation Activity & Vendor Info: (Cataloging) Innovative Interfaces, Inc; (Circulation) Innovative Interfaces, Inc
Mem of Allegheny County Library Association
Open Mon & Wed 10-6, Tues & Thurs 10-8, Fri 10-5, Sat 9-4
Friends of the Library Group

NORTH WALES

S MADLYN & LEONARD ABRAMSON CENTER FOR JEWISH LIFE*, Library of the Polisher Research Institute, 1425 Horsham Rd, 19454-1320. SAN 322-7758. Tel: 215-371-1333. FAX: 215-371-3015. E-mail: librarian@abramsoncenter.org. Web Site: www.abramsoncenter.org/pri. *Res Librn,* Rachel R Resnick; E-mail: rresnick@abramsoncenter.org. Subject Specialists: *Geriatrics, Gerontology,* Rachel R Resnick; Staff 1 (MLS 1)
Founded 1959
Jul 2007-Jun 2008. Mats Exp $26,400, Books $3,000, Per/Ser (Incl. Access Fees) $23,400
Library Holdings: AV Mats 53; Bk Titles 7,622; Per Subs 58; Spec Interest Per Sub 58
Special Collections: Gerontology & Geriatrics Research Coll, bks, CDs, videos; M Powell Lawton Coll, bks, videos
Subject Interests: Death, Dying, Geriatrics, Gerontology, Long term care admin, Psychol, Sociol
Automation Activity & Vendor Info: (Acquisitions) EOS International; (Cataloging) EOS International; (Circulation) EOS International; (OPAC) EOS International; (Serials) EOS International
Database Vendor: EBSCOhost
Function: For res purposes, ILL available, Res libr
Partic in Basic Health Sciences Library Network; Delaware Valley Information Consortium; National Network of Libraries of Medicine
Open Mon-Fri 8:30-4
Restriction: Authorized scholars by appt, Circulates for staff only, In-house use for visitors, Open to pub by appt only, Prof mat only, Pub use on premises

P NORTH WALES AREA LIBRARY*, 233 S Swartley St, 19454. SAN 314-8297. Tel: 215-699-5410. FAX: 215-699-5901. Web Site: www.northwalesborough.org/general/library.aspx, www.northwaleslibrary.org. *Dir,* Jayne Blackledge; E-mail: jayne@northwaleslibrary.org
Founded 1923. Pop 3,342; Circ 41,000
Library Holdings: Audiobooks 842; DVDs 599; Large Print Bks 609; Bk Vols 35,489; Per Subs 20; Talking Bks 200
Subject Interests: Bks on CD
Automation Activity & Vendor Info: (Acquisitions) Innovative Interfaces, Inc - Millenium
Database Vendor: Baker & Taylor
Wireless access
Function: Bk club(s), Children's prog, Computers for patron use, Copy machines, E-Reserves, Handicapped accessible, ILL available, Photocopying/Printing, Prog for adults, Prog for children & young adult, Pub access computers, Story hour, Summer reading prog, Teen prog, Web-catalog, Workshops, Writing prog
Open Mon & Thurs 1-9, Tues & Wed 10-9, Fri 1-5, Sat 10-4
Friends of the Library Group

NORTH WARREN

M WARREN STATE HOSPITAL*, Library Services Department, 33 Main Dr, 16365. SAN 359-6524. Tel: 814-726-4223. FAX: 814-726-4562. *Librn,* Karen Ervin; E-mail: kervin@state.pa.us; Staff 1 (MLS 1)
Library Holdings: Bk Titles 12,000; Bk Vols 10,000; Per Subs 80
Special Collections: Self-help/patient recovery Coll
Subject Interests: Alcohol abuse, Death/dying, Drug abuse, Gerontology, Med, Neurology, Nursing, Occupational therapy, Psychiat, Psychiat nursing, Psychol, Psychotherapy, Sociol
Automation Activity & Vendor Info: (Cataloging) Ex Libris Group; (Circulation) Ex Libris Group; (OPAC) Ex Libris Group
Function: ILL available
Publications: Periodicals Union List
Partic in OCLC Online Computer Library Center, Inc
Open Mon-Fri 8-4
Restriction: Open to pub by appt only, Open to students, fac & staff

NORTHAMPTON

P NORTHAMPTON AREA PUBLIC LIBRARY*, 1615 Laubach Ave, 18067-1597. SAN 358-7673. Tel: 610-262-7537. FAX: 610-262-4356. Web Site: www.northamptonapl.org. *Actg Dir,* Karen Hein; E-mail: khein@northamptonapl.org; *Ch,* Cheryl DiGiacoma; E-mail: cdigiacoma@northamptonapl.org; Staff 2 (MLS 2)
Founded 1965. Pop 38,251; Circ 133,918
Jul 2008-Jun 2009 Income $480,256, State $147,452, City $247,490, Other $85,314. Mats Exp $68,576, Books $37,525, Per/Ser (Incl. Access Fees) $2,757, AV Mat $21,454, Electronic Ref Mat (Incl. Access Fees) $1,675, Presv $5,165. Sal $273,902 (Prof $45,000)
Library Holdings: CDs 3,611; DVDs 5,247; Large Print Bks 1,171; Bk Titles 53,004; Bk Vols 53,761; Per Subs 95; Talking Bks 1,233
Subject Interests: Local hist
Automation Activity & Vendor Info: (Acquisitions) TLC (The Library Corporation); (Cataloging) TLC (The Library Corporation); (Circulation) TLC (The Library Corporation)
Database Vendor: EBSCOhost, TLC (The Library Corporation)
Wireless access
Open Mon-Thurs 9-8, Sat 9-4
Friends of the Library Group

NORTHERN CAMBRIA

P NORTHERN CAMBRIA PUBLIC LIBRARY*, 1030 Philadelphia Ave, 15714-1399. Tel: 814-948-8222. FAX: 814-948-2813. E-mail: ncambria@cclsys.org. Web Site: www.cclsys.org/ncambria. *Libr Dir,* Vanessa Funyak; *Asst Dir,* Michaelene McCombie
Library Holdings: Bks on Deafness & Sign Lang 12; Bk Titles 15,858; Bk Vols 16,891; Per Subs 38
Automation Activity & Vendor Info: (Cataloging) Follett Software; (Circulation) Follett Software; (OPAC) Follett Software
Mem of Cambria County Library System & District Center
Open Mon-Wed 12-7, Thurs & Sat 9-4

NORTHUMBERLAND

P PRIESTLEY FORSYTH MEMORIAL LIBRARY, 100 King St, 17857-1670. SAN 314-8327. Tel: 570-473-8201. FAX: 570-473-8807. E-mail: pfml@ptd.net. Web Site: www.priestleyforsyth.org. *Dir,* Jeff Johnstonbaugh; Staff 5 (MLS 1, Non-MLS 4)
Founded 1926. Pop 7,400; Circ 52,000
Library Holdings: Bk Vols 27,000; Per Subs 100
Special Collections: Joseph Priestley Coll
Subject Interests: Local hist
Automation Activity & Vendor Info: (Circulation) ComPanion Corp; (OPAC) ComPanion Corp
Friends of the Library Group

NORWOOD

P NORWOOD PUBLIC LIBRARY*, 513 Welcome Ave, 19074-1425. SAN 314-8335. Tel: 610-534-0693. FAX: 610-532-8785. Web Site: www.nplibrary.com. *Dir,* Jane Lloyd
Founded 1938. Pop 6,162; Circ 25,698
Library Holdings: Bk Vols 21,800; Per Subs 40
Automation Activity & Vendor Info: (Cataloging) Innovative Interfaces, Inc; (Circulation) Innovative Interfaces, Inc
Database Vendor: Innovative Interfaces, Inc
Wireless access
Open Mon, Tues & Thurs 11-8:30, Wed 9-8:30, Sat 9-4

OAKDALE

J PITTSBURGH TECHNICAL INSTITUTE*, Library Resource Center, 1111 McKee Rd, 15071. SAN 315-0976. Tel: 412-809-5223. FAX: 412-809-5219. E-mail: library@pti.edu. Web Site: www.pti.edu. *Dir,* Ruth Walter; Staff 3 (MLS 1, Non-MLS 2)
Founded 1946. Enrl 2,100; Fac 91; Highest Degree: Associate
Library Holdings: Bk Titles 5,500; Bk Vols 7,500; Per Subs 170
Automation Activity & Vendor Info: (Acquisitions) Innovative Interfaces, Inc - Millenium; (Cataloging) Innovative Interfaces, Inc - Millenium; (Circulation) Innovative Interfaces, Inc; (Course Reserve) Innovative Interfaces, Inc - Millenium; (Media Booking) Innovative Interfaces, Inc - Millenium; (OPAC) Innovative Interfaces, Inc - Millenium; (Serials) Innovative Interfaces, Inc - Millenium
Database Vendor: 3M Library Systems, Cinahl, EBSCOhost, Facts on File, Hoovers, Medline
Wireless access
Partic in HSLC/Access PA/POWER Library
Open Mon-Thurs 7am-7:30pm, Fri 7-5

P WESTERN ALLEGHENY COMMUNITY LIBRARY*, 181 Bateman Rd, 15071-3906. SAN 370-730X. Tel: 724-695-8150. FAX: 724-695-2860. Web Site: westernalleghenylibrary.org. *Libr Dir,* Marianne A Sforza; E-mail: sforzam@einetwork.net; *Head, Youth Serv,* Amanda Kirby; E-mail: kirbya@einetwork.net; *Dir, Mkt & Develop, Teen Librn,* Carrie Nurnberger; *Asst Youth Serv, Circ Librn,* Caitlyn Bovard; *Tech Serv Librn,* Heather Blake; Staff 10 (MLS 3, Non-MLS 7)
Founded 1990. Pop 18,950; Circ 68,027
Library Holdings: AV Mats 1,994; CDs 225; DVDs 297; Large Print Bks 259; Bk Titles 31,467; Bk Vols 34,261; Per Subs 82; Talking Bks 852; Videos 620
Automation Activity & Vendor Info: (Cataloging) Innovative Interfaces, Inc; (Circulation) Innovative Interfaces, Inc; (OPAC) Innovative Interfaces, Inc; (Serials) Innovative Interfaces, Inc
Database Vendor: EBSCOhost, Gale Cengage Learning, Innovative Interfaces, Inc, ProQuest
Wireless access
Function: Handicapped accessible, Prog for children & young adult, Ref serv available, Summer reading prog
Mem of Allegheny County Library Association
Partic in Electronic Info Network (eiNetwork)
Open Mon-Thurs 10-8, Fri 10-4, Sat 9-4, Sun (Sept-June) 1-5
Friends of the Library Group

OAKMONT

P OAKMONT CARNEGIE LIBRARY*, 700 Allegheny River Blvd, 15139. SAN 314-8343. Tel: 412-828-9532. FAX: 412-828-5979. E-mail: oakmont@einetwork.net. Web Site: www.oakmontlibrary.org. *Dir,* Beth Ann Mellor; E-mail: mellorb1@einetwork.net; *Archivist/Ref Librn,* Stephanie Zimble; E-mail: zimbles@einetwork.net; *Youth Serv Librn,* Karen Crowell; E-mail: crowellk@einetwork.net; Staff 7 (MLS 2, Non-MLS 5)
Founded 1901. Pop 6,911; Circ 75,150
Library Holdings: CDs 228; DVDs 195; Large Print Bks 100; Bk Vols 38,000; Per Subs 55
Special Collections: Local Geneaology Coll; Local Newspaper (Advance Leader 1917-1945), micro; Local Photography Archive, digitized photog. Oral History
Automation Activity & Vendor Info: (Cataloging) Innovative Interfaces, Inc; (Circulation) Innovative Interfaces, Inc; (OPAC) Innovative Interfaces, Inc; (Serials) Baker & Taylor
Database Vendor: EBSCOhost, Gale Cengage Learning, Ingram Library Services, Innovative Interfaces, Inc, Innovative Interfaces, Inc, OCLC, ProQuest, ReferenceUSA
Wireless access
Function: Adult literacy prog
Mem of Allegheny County Library Association
Partic in Electronic Info Network (eiNetwork)
Open Mon-Thurs 10-8, Fri & Sat 10-4, Sun 1-4
Friends of the Library Group

OIL CITY

P OIL CITY LIBRARY*, Two Central Ave, 16301-2795. SAN 314-8378. Tel: 814-678-3072. FAX: 814-676-8028. Web Site: www.oilcitylibrary.org. *Dir,* Bruce George; E-mail: director@oilcitylibrary.org; *Cataloger,* Sharon A Duarte; Tel: 814-678-3071, E-mail: sduarte@oilcitylibrary.org; *ILL,* Deborah Rider; *Ch Serv,* Sandee Lalley; Staff 3 (MLS 3)
Founded 1904. Pop 15,206; Circ 153,159
Jan 2010-Dec 2010 Income $636,500, State $204,000, City $327,500, Locally Generated Income $105,000. Mats Exp $111,600, Books $81,000, Per/Ser (Incl. Access Fees) $7,500, AV Mat $5,100, Electronic Ref Mat (Incl. Access Fees) $18,000. Sal $270,000
Library Holdings: AV Mats 152; DVDs 800; Large Print Bks 3,000; Bk Vols 103,000; Per Subs 250; Talking Bks 2,000; Videos 3,500
Special Collections: Genealogy (Selden Coll). State Document Depository
Subject Interests: Hist of oil
Automation Activity & Vendor Info: (Cataloging) SirsiDynix; (Circulation) SirsiDynix; (OPAC) SirsiDynix
Database Vendor: SirsiDynix
Mem of Oil Creek District Library Center
Open Mon-Wed 8:30am-9pm, Thurs 8:30-6, Fri & Sat 8:30-5
Friends of the Library Group

C VENANGO COLLEGE OF CLARION UNIVERSITY OF PENNSYLVANIA*, Charles L Suhr Library, 1801 W First St, 16301. SAN 314-836X. Tel: 814-676-6591. Toll Free Tel: 877-836-2646. FAX: 814-677-3987. Web Site: www.clarion.edu/395. *Librn/Unit Coordr,* Nancy Clemente; Tel: 814-676-6591, Ext 1245, E-mail: nclemente@clarion.edu; *ILL, Libr Tech,* Brenda Sturtz; Tel: 814-676-6591, Ext 1244, E-mail: sturtz@clarion.edu; *Libr Tech,* Sylvia Wiegel; Tel: 814-676-6591, Ext 1246, E-mail: swiegel@clarion.edu; Staff 3 (MLS 1, Non-MLS 2)
Founded 1961. Enrl 809; Fac 63; Highest Degree: Master
Library Holdings: Bk Titles 45,691; Bk Vols 48,715; Per Subs 182
Special Collections: Barbara Morgan Harvey Center for the Study of Oil Heritage
Subject Interests: Nursing, Paralegal

Automation Activity & Vendor Info: (Acquisitions) Ex Libris Group; (Cataloging) Ex Libris Group; (Circulation) Ex Libris Group; (Course Reserve) Ex Libris Group; (ILL) OCLC; (Media Booking) Ex Libris Group; (OPAC) Ex Libris Group; (Serials) Ex Libris Group
Database Vendor: EBSCOhost, Gale Cengage Learning, LexisNexis, OVID Technologies, ProQuest, Wilson - Wilson Web
Wireless access
Partic in Erie Area Health Information Library Cooperative
Open Mon-Thurs 8-8, Fri 8-4

ORANGEVILLE

P ORANGEVILLE PUBLIC LIBRARY*, 301 Mill St, 17859-0177. (Mail add: PO Box 268, 17859-0268). Tel: 570-683-5354. E-mail: orangevillelibrary@pa.metrocast.net. Web Site: www.orangevillelibrary.org. *Librn,* Pamela Simpson; *Asst Librn,* Melinda Spaid; Staff 2 (Non-MLS 2)
Founded 1927
Library Holdings: Audiobooks 422; DVDs 443; e-books 130; Large Print Bks 140; Bk Titles 10,510; Videos 767
Special Collections: Local Hist (Orangeville, Columbia County, Pennsylvania); Military Fiction; Military Hist
Automation Activity & Vendor Info: (Cataloging) ComPanion Corp; (Circulation) ComPanion Corp; (OPAC) ComPanion Corp
Wireless access
Function: Bks on cassette, Bks on CD, Children's prog, Computers for patron use, Copy machines, Free DVD rentals, Handicapped accessible, Photocopying/Printing, Prog for adults, Prog for children & young adult, Pub access computers, Story hour, Summer reading prog, VHS videos, Video lending libr
Open Mon-Thurs 2-7, Sat 9-Noon
Friends of the Library Group

ORWIGSBURG

S ACOPIAN CENTER FOR CONSERVATION LEARNING*, Hawk Mountain Sanctuary Library, 410 Summer Valley Rd, 17961. SAN 375-3638. Tel: 570-943-3411, Ext 101. FAX: 570-943-2284. Web Site: www.hawkmountain.org. *Dir,* Keith Bildstein; E-mail: bildstein@hawkmtn.org; Staff 2 (MLS 1, Non-MLS 1)
Founded 1934
Library Holdings: Bk Titles 5,350; Bk Vols 6,110; Per Subs 61; Videos 72
Special Collections: Oral History
Function: Res libr
Restriction: Mem only, Not a lending libr, Open by appt only, Open to students

P ORWIGSBURG AREA FREE PUBLIC LIBRARY*, 214 E Independent St, 17961-2304. SAN 320-5061. Tel: 570-366-1638. FAX: 570-366-5414. E-mail: orwigsburglibrary@comcast.net. *Actg Libr Dir,* Claudia Gross; Staff 2 (Non-MLS 2)
Founded 1978. Pop 12,000; Circ 21,000
Library Holdings: Bk Vols 20,000; Per Subs 41
Automation Activity & Vendor Info: (Cataloging) Follett Software; (Circulation) Follett Software; (OPAC) Follett Software
Open Mon-Thurs 10-7, Fri 10-5, Sat 9-4

OXFORD

P OXFORD PUBLIC LIBRARY*, 48 S Second St, 19363-1377. SAN 314-8394. Tel: 610-932-9625. FAX: 610-932-9251. E-mail: oxfordlibrary@ccls.org. Web Site: www.ccls.org, www.oxfordpubliclibrary.org. *Dir,* Carey Bresler; E-mail: cbresler@ccls.org; *Ch Serv Librn,* Nancy Kodish; *Circ,* Linda M Teel; Staff 3 (MLS 1, Non-MLS 2)
Founded 1784. Pop 21,000; Circ 130,000
Library Holdings: AV Mats 2,147; CDs 200; DVDs 950; Large Print Bks 88; Bk Titles 39,410; Bk Vols 40,678; Per Subs 97; Talking Bks 1,027; Videos 388
Special Collections: Local History (Holcombe Coll)
Automation Activity & Vendor Info: (Cataloging) Innovative Interfaces, Inc; (Circulation) Innovative Interfaces, Inc
Wireless access
Function: Adult bk club, Adult literacy prog, After school storytime, Art exhibits, Chess club, Digital talking bks, E-Reserves, Electronic databases & coll, Family literacy, Handicapped accessible, Home delivery & serv to Sr ctr & nursing homes, Homebound delivery serv, Homework prog, ILL available, Magnifiers for reading, Mail & tel request accepted, Music CDs, Online ref, Online searches, Orientations, Photocopying/Printing, Prog for adults, Prog for children & young adult, Ref & res, Spoken cassettes & CDs, Spoken cassettes & DVDs, Summer reading prog, Telephone ref, VHS videos, Wheelchair accessible, Workshops
Open Mon-Thurs 9:30-8, Fri 9:30-5, Sat 9-5 (9:30-3 Summer)
Friends of the Library Group

PALMERTON

P PALMERTON AREA LIBRARY ASSOCIATION*, 402 Delaware Ave, 18071-1995. SAN 314-8416. Tel: 610-826-3424. FAX: 610-826-6248. E-mail: plapalm@ptd.net. Web Site: www.palmertonarealibrary.com. *Dir,* Diane M Danielson; Staff 1 (Non-MLS 1)
Founded 1928. Pop 12,300; Circ 37,000
Jan 2006-Dec 2006 Income $167,400, State $43,000, City $7,400, County $1,500, Locally Generated Income $59,000, Other $56,500. Mats Exp $26,500, Books $20,000, Per/Ser (Incl. Access Fees) $2,000, Other Print Mats $500, AV Mat $4,000. Sal $82,000 (Prof $25,000)
Library Holdings: CDs 369; DVDs 225; Music Scores 35; Bk Vols 40,000; Per Subs 55; Talking Bks 1,525; Videos 2,789
Subject Interests: Local hist, Pa hist
Database Vendor: TLC (The Library Corporation)
Wireless access
Function: Adult bk club, Audiobks via web, Bks on cassette, Bks on CD, Children's prog, Computers for patron use, Copy machines, Free DVD rentals, Handicapped accessible, ILL available, Mail & tel request accepted, Music CDs, Online cat, Online searches, Photocopying/Printing, Pub access computers, Senior computer classes, Story hour, Summer reading prog, Tax forms, Teen prog, VHS videos, Video lending libr, Web-catalog, Wheelchair accessible
Open Mon & Tues 10-8, Wed, Thurs & Fri 10-5, Sat 9-4
Friends of the Library Group

PALMYRA

P PALMYRA PUBLIC LIBRARY*, Borough Bldg, 325 S Railroad St, 17078-2492. SAN 314-8424. Tel: 717-838-1347. FAX: 717-838-1236. Web Site: www.lclibs.org/palmyra. *Exec Dir,* Karla J Marsteller; E-mail: kmarsteller@lclibs.org; *Circ Coordr, Tech Serv Coordr,* Elise Jackson; E-mail: ejackson@lclibs.org; *Ch Serv,* Amy Shaffer-Duong; E-mail: missamy@lclibs.org; *ILL,* Lorna Melhorn; E-mail: lkmelhorn@lclibs.org; Staff 14 (MLS 1, Non-MLS 13)
Founded 1954. Pop 19,325; Circ 120,000
Library Holdings: Large Print Bks 98; Bk Titles 51,610; Bk Vols 53,901; Per Subs 121; Talking Bks 190; Videos 316
Automation Activity & Vendor Info: (Cataloging) Innovative Interfaces, Inc; (Circulation) Innovative Interfaces, Inc
Wireless access
Mem of Lebanon County Library System
Open Mon-Wed 10-8, Thurs & Fri 10-5, Sat 9-4 (9-1 July & Aug)
Friends of the Library Group

PAOLI

M JEFFERSON HEALTH SYSTEM, PAOLI MEMORIAL HOSPITAL*, Robert M White Memorial Library, 255 W Lancaster Ave, 19301. SAN 314-8467. Tel: 610-648-1570. FAX: 610-648-1551. Web Site: www.jeffersonhealth.org. *Librn,* Ellen Sandford
Founded 1970
Library Holdings: Bk Titles 800; Per Subs 50
Subject Interests: Allied health, Med, Nursing
Publications: News Leaf (Monthly)
Partic in Basic Health Sciences Library Network; Consortium for Health Information & Library Services; Delaware Valley Information Consortium; National Network of Libraries of Medicine

PARKESBURG

P PARKESBURG FREE LIBRARY*, 105 West St, 19365-1499. SAN 314-8475. Tel: 610-857-5165. FAX: 610-857-1193. Web Site: www.ccls.org. *Dir,* Thomas Peter Knecht; E-mail: tknecht@ccls.org; *Ch,* Sandra McLaughlin; E-mail: smclaughlin@ccls.org; Staff 2 (MLS 1, Non-MLS 1)
Founded 1916. Pop 4,711; Circ 76,394
Library Holdings: DVDs 1,000; Large Print Bks 188; Bk Titles 27,191; Bk Vols 28,420; Per Subs 59; Talking Bks 755; Videos 1,454
Special Collections: Local Historical Files
Automation Activity & Vendor Info: (Circulation) Innovative Interfaces, Inc
Wireless access
Mem of Chester County Library System
Open Mon-Thurs 12-8, Fri 12-6, Sat 9-4 (9-1 Summer)

PATTON

P PATTON PUBLIC LIBRARY*, 444 Magee Ave, 16668-1210. SAN 314-8483. Tel: 814-674-8231. FAX: 814-674-6188. E-mail: patton@cclsys.org. Web Site: www.cclsys.org/patton. *Librn,* Monica Burkhart; *Asst Librn,* Mary Joriner; *Asst Librn,* Patricia Yencho
Founded 1962. Pop 2,023; Circ 28,920
Jan 2010-Dec 2010 Income $55,000. Mats Exp $8,500. Sal $24,000
Library Holdings: Audiobooks 275; DVDs 500; e-books 400; Large Print Bks 643; Microforms 45; Bk Titles 15,235; Per Subs 24; Videos 525

Automation Activity & Vendor Info: (Cataloging) Innovative Interfaces, Inc - Millenium; (Circulation) Innovative Interfaces, Inc - Millenium; (OPAC) Innovative Interfaces, Inc - Millenium
Wireless access
Mem of Cambria County Library System & District Center
Open Mon-Thurs (Winter) 10-7, Fri & Sat 10-5; Mon-Thurs (Summer) 10-7, Fri 10-5, Sat 10-2
Friends of the Library Group

PECKVILLE

P VALLEY COMMUNITY LIBRARY*, 739 River St, 18452. SAN 328-0578. Tel: 570-489-1765. Web Site. www.lackawannacountylibrarysystem.org/interboro. *Dir,* Mary Barna; E-mail: mbarna@albright.org; *Head, Ch, Head, Youth Serv,* Karen Slachta; Staff 8 (MLS 1, Non-MLS 7)
Founded 1985. Pop 33,000; Circ 124,687
Jan 2006-Dec 2006 Income $470,833, County $410,883, Locally Generated Income $59,950. Mats Exp $43,830, Books $33,000, Per/Ser (Incl. Access Fees) $2,800, AV Mat $8,030. Sal $228,857
Library Holdings: AV Mats 4,790; Bk Vols 32,158; Per Subs 52; Talking Bks 1,840
Special Collections: Joseph McDonald Pearl Harbor Transcripts; Medal of Honor Recipent Gino Merli Memorabilia
Subject Interests: Lackawana County hist, Local hist
Automation Activity & Vendor Info: (Circulation) SirsiDynix
Mem of Lackawanna County Library System
Open Mon-Thurs 10-8, Fri & Sat 10-5
Friends of the Library Group

PENN VALLEY

SR HAR ZION TEMPLE*, Ida & Matthew Rudofker Library, 1500 Hagys Ford Rd, 19072. SAN 327-8662. Tel: 610-667-5000. FAX: 610-667-2032. E-mail: hzt@harziontemple.org. Web Site: www.harziontemple.org. *Librn,* Bill Moody; *Asst Librn,* Anne Stein
Library Holdings: Bk Vols 9,000; Per Subs 23
Open Mon-Thurs 3:30-6, Sun 9-1

PENNSBURG

P SCHWENKFELDER LIBRARY & HERITAGE CENTER*, 105 Seminary St, 18073. SAN 314-8491. Tel: 215-679-3103. FAX: 215-679-8175. E-mail. info@schwenkfelder.com. Web Site: www.schwenkfelder.com. *Exec Dir,* David W Luz; Tel: 215 679 3103, Ext 11; *Assoc Dir,* Allen L Viehmeyer; Tel: 215-679-3103, Ext 17, E-mail: allen@schwenkfelder.com; *Archivist,* Hunt Schenkel; Tel: 215-679-3103, Ext 13, E-mail: hunt@schwenkfelder.com; *Curator,* Candace Perry; Tel: 215-679-3103, Ext 12, E-mail: candace@schwenkfelder.com; Staff 3 (Non-MLS 3)
Founded 1884. Pop 20,000
Library Holdings: Bk Titles 25,000
Special Collections: Montgomery County History, bks, ms; Reformation Coll; Schwenkfelder History & Theology, bks, ms; Silesian History Coll
Subject Interests: Hist
Function: Archival coll, Res libr
Open Tues, Wed & Fri 9-4, Thurs 9-8, Sat 10-3, Sun 1-4
Restriction: Non-circulating
Friends of the Library Group

PERKASIE

SR TRINITY EVANGELICAL LUTHERAN CHURCH*, Library & Media Center, 19 S Fifth St, 18944. SAN 328-4530. Tel: 215-257-6801. FAX: 215-258-5685. E-mail: trinityperkasie@verizon.net. Web Site: www.trinityperkasie.org.
Library Holdings: Bk Titles 7,200
Special Collections: Children (gen & relig)
Publications: AV Catalog (periodically); Monthly Reviews-New Material in Church Newsletter Trinity Chimes
Friends of the Library Group

PERKIOMENVILLE

S AMERICAN ASSOCIATION OF BIRTH CENTERS LIBRARY*, 3123 Gottschall Rd, 18074-9604. SAN 326-7385. Tel: 215-234-8068. Toll Free Tel: 866-542-4784. FAX: 215-234-8829. E-mail: aabc@birthcenters.org. Web Site: www.birthcenters.org. *Exec Dir,* Kate Bauer; Staff 2 (MLS 2)
Library Holdings: Bk Titles 1,000; Per Subs 25
Special Collections: Birth Centers; CBCN News Coll; NACC News Coll, doc bd & newsletters
Publications: AABC News; Maternity Care in Ferment; Policies & Procedures Manual; Public Information Flyer; Quality Assurance Manual; Workshop Manual

PERRYOPOLIS

P MARY FULLER FRAZIER SCHOOL COMMUNITY LIBRARY*, 142 Constitution St, 15473-1390. SAN 314-8513. Tel: 724-736-8480. FAX: 724-736-8481. *Librn,* Valerie Madorma; Staff 2 (MLS 2)
Founded 1960. Pop 2,573; Circ 18,000
Library Holdings: Bk Titles 26,114; Bk Vols 28,911; Per Subs 44
Subject Interests: Fayette County hist
Mem of Fayette County Library System
Open Mon-Thurs (Winter) 3-9, Sat 9-1; Mon & Wed (Summer) 6pm-9pm, Sat 9-1

PHILADELPHIA

S ACADEMY OF NATURAL SCIENCES OF PHILADELPHIA*, Ewell Sale Stewart Library, 1900 Benjamin Franklin Pkwy, 19103-1195. SAN 314-8521. Tel: 215-299-1040. FAX: 215-299-1144. E-mail: library@ansp.org. Web Site: www.ansp.org/library. *Libr Dir,* Clare Flemming; Tel: 215-299-1175, E-mail: flemming@ansp.org; Staff 4 (MLS 3, Non-MLS 1)
Founded 1812
Special Collections: Entomology (Library of the American Entomological Society); Manuscripts (Academy History & Archives); Photograph Coll; Portrait & Drawing Coll; Pre-Linnaean Coll
Subject Interests: Botany, Entomology, Environ res, Evolution, Exploration, Hist of sci, Limnology, Malacology, Ornithology, Systematic biol, Zoology
Automation Activity & Vendor Info: (Acquisitions) Innovative Interfaces, Inc; (Cataloging) Innovative Interfaces, Inc; (OPAC) Innovative Interfaces, Inc; (Serials) Innovative Interfaces, Inc
Function: Archival coll, Copy machines, Electronic databases & coll, Exhibits, ILL available, Photocopying/Printing, Res libr, Res performed for a fee
Publications: Guide to Microfilm Publication of Academy Minutes & Correspondence; Guide to the Manuscripts Collections of ANSP; Library Catalog; Serial Titles; Wolf Room Rare Book Collection Checklist
Partic in Lyrasis; OCLC Online Computer Library Center, Inc; Philadelphia Area Consortium of Special Collections Libraries
Restriction: Open by appt only, Restricted borrowing privileges
Friends of the Library Group

S AIDS LIBRARY*, 1233 Locust St, 2nd Flr, 19107. (Mail add: 1233 Locust St, 5th Flr, 19107), SAN 370-7601. Tel: 215-985-4851. FAX: 215-985-4492. TDD: 215-985-0458. Web Site: www.aidslibrary.org. *Head, Coll Serv,* Allie Fraser; *Access Serv & Syst, Publ Librn, Web Serv,* Val Sowell; *Archives & Spec Coll Librn, Client Serv Librn, Computer Instrul Serv Librn,* Marc Miller; *Ref Serv,* Adam Feldman; Staff 5 (MLS 2, Non-MLS 3)
Founded 1987
Library Holdings: Bk Titles 2,710; Bk Vols 5,423; Per Subs 131
Function: Audio & video playback equip for onsite use, Computer training, Computers for patron use, Copy machines, e-mail serv, For res purposes, Handicapped accessible, Health sci info serv, Homebound delivery serv, Online searches, Outside serv via phone, mail, e-mail & web, Photocopying/Printing, Prog for adults, Ref serv available, Res libr, Telephone ref, VHS videos, Wheelchair accessible, Workshops
Special Services for the Deaf - TDD equip
Open Mon-Fri 10-12 & 1-5

L AMERICAN LAW INSTITUTE LIBRARY*, 4025 Chestnut St, 19104. SAN 314-8556. Tel: 215-243-1654. Toll Free Tel: 800-253-6397. FAX: 215-243-1636. *Librn,* Harry Kyriakodis; Staff 1 (MLS 1)
Founded 1965
Library Holdings: Bk Vols 5,500; Per Subs 30
Special Collections: ALI Publications, microfiche; ALI-ABA Materials & Periodicals
Subject Interests: Law

S AMERICAN MEDICAL FOUNDATION FOR PEER REVIEW & EDUCATION LIBRARY*, The Barclay on Rittenhouse Sq, 237 S 18th St, Ste 11-D, 19103-6164. SAN 329-4323. Tel: 215-545-6363. FAX: 215-545-2163. E-mail: medfoundation@aol.com. Web Site: www.medicalfoundation.org. *Dir,* Dr Evelyn Baram-Clothier
Library Holdings: Bk Vols 400
Restriction: Open by appt only

S AMERICAN PHILOSOPHICAL SOCIETY LIBRARY, 105 S Fifth St, 19106-3386. SAN 314-8564. Tel: 215-440-3400. FAX: 215-440-3423. E-mail: books@amphilsoc.org, manuscripts@amphilsoc.org. Web Site: www.amphilsoc.org. *Librn,* Dr Martin L Levitt; Tel: 215-440-3403, E-mail: mlevitt@amphilsoc.org; *Head, Ms Proc & Libr Registrar,* Valerie-Anne Lutz; Tel: 215-440-3444, E-mail: vlutz@amphilsoc.org; *Head, Conserv,* Anne Downey; Tel: 215-440-3412, E-mail: adowney@amphilsoc.org; *Assoc Librn, Curator of Ms,* Charles B Greifenstein; Tel: 215-440-3404, E-mail: cgreifenstein@amphilsoc.org; *Assoc Librn, Tech Serv & Security,* Stephanie

Glass; Tel: 215-440-3409, E-mail: sglass@amphilsoc.org; *Asst Librn, Curator, Printed Mat,* Roy Goodman; Tel: 215-440-3408, E-mail: rgoodman@amphilsoc.org; *Cat Librn,* Marian Christ; Tel: 215-440-3407, E-mail: mchrist@amphilsoc.org; *Ref Archivist & Libr Prog Coordr,* Earle Spamer; Tel: 215-440-3443, E-mail: espamer@amphilsoc.org; *Conservator,* Denise Carbone; Tel: 215-440-3413; *Proc Archivist,* Michael Miller; Tel: 215-440-3420, E-mail: mmiller@amphilsoc.org; *Spec Projects,* Ann Reinhardt; Staff 22 (MLS 13, Non-MLS 9)
Founded 1743
Library Holdings: Bk Titles 275,000; Per Subs 420
Special Collections: American Indian Linguistics (Franz Boas et al Coll); Benjamin Franklin & his Circle; Medical Research (Simon Flexner et al Coll); Stephen Girard Papers, film; Thomas Jefferson
Subject Interests: Am hist to 1840, Biochem, Darwin, Electricity, European background, Evolution, Genetics, Hist of sci in Am, Lewis & Clark expedition, Modern physics, Paleontology, Polar exploration, Quantum physics, Thomas Paine
Publications: Annual Report of the Committee on Library; Mendel Newsletter
Open Mon-Fri 9-4:45
Friends of the Library Group

S AMERICAN SWEDISH HISTORICAL MUSEUM LIBRARY*, 1900 Pattison Ave, 19145. SAN 314-8580. Tel: 215-389-1776. FAX: 215-389-7701. E-mail: info@americanswedish.org. Web Site: www.americanswedish.org. *Exec Dir,* Tracey Rae Beck; E-mail: tbeck@americanswedish.org
Founded 1926
Library Holdings: Bk Titles 5,000; Per Subs 30
Special Collections: Fredrika Bremer Coll; Jenny Lind Coll; John Ericsson Coll
Subject Interests: Genealogy, Original correspondence, Scandinavian hist, Swedish hist, Swedish-Am hist
Function: Res libr
Publications: Newsletter
Open Tues-Fri 10-4, Sat & Sun 12-4
Restriction: Non-circulating

ARIA HEALTH
M HEALTH SCIENCES LIBRARIES*, Red Lion & Knights Rds, 19114-1436, SAN 324-6302. Tel: 215-612-4135, 215-831-2182. FAX: 215-612-4946. *Dir, Libr Serv,* Gary Jay Christopher; Tel: 215-949-5160, Fax: 215-949-7821, E-mail: gchristopher@ariahealth.org; Staff 3 (Non-MLS 3)
Founded 1950
Library Holdings: Bk Titles 5,121; Bk Vols 5,560; Per Subs 412
Subject Interests: Allied health, Consumer health, Nursing
Database Vendor: EBSCOhost, OVID Technologies
Function: Prof lending libr
Partic in DEVIC
Restriction: Open to pub upon request, Staff use only
M SCHOOL OF NURSING LIBRARY*, Three Neshaminy Interflex, Trevose, 19053, SAN 324-7481. Tel: 215-710-3510, Ext 23523. FAX: 215-710-3543. *Librn,* Sophia Kim; E-mail: skim@ariahealth.org; Staff 1 (MLS 1)
Library Holdings: Bk Vols 2,500; Per Subs 89
Subject Interests: Nursing
Automation Activity & Vendor Info: (Serials) EBSCO Online
Database Vendor: OVID Technologies
Function: Doc delivery serv, ILL available
Partic in Basic Health Sciences Library Network; DEVIC; National Network of Libraries of Medicine
Open Mon-Fri 8-4
Restriction: Access at librarian's discretion, Access for corporate affiliates, Authorized scholars by appt, By permission only, Internal circ only, Open by appt only, Open to fac, students & qualified researchers, Open to pub for ref only, Open to pub upon request, Open to pub with supv only, Open to students, fac & staff, Prof mat only, Pub ref by request

C ART INSTITUTE OF PHILADELPHIA LIBRARY, 1622 Chestnut St, 19103. SAN 322-8347. Tel: 215-567-7080. Circulation Tel: 215-405-6471. E-mail: aiphlibrary2@aii.edu. Web Site: aii.campusguides.com/aiph. *Librn,* Marie Burkitt; Tel: 215-405-6794, E-mail: mburkitt@aii.edu; Staff 1 (MLS 1)
Founded 1974. Enrl 300; Fac 200; Highest Degree: Bachelor
Library Holdings: AV Mats 5,000; Bk Vols 16,000; Per Subs 101
Subject Interests: Animation, Applied arts, Fashion design, Graphic design, Interactive media design, Video production
Automation Activity & Vendor Info: (Cataloging) Ex Libris Group; (Circulation) Ex Libris Group; (OPAC) Ex Libris Group
Database Vendor: Wilson - Wilson Web
Wireless access
Partic in Tri-State College Library Cooperative

S ATHENAEUM OF PHILADELPHIA, East Washington Sq, 219 S Sixth St, 19106-3794. SAN 314-8610. Tel: 215-925-2688. FAX: 215-925-3755. E-mail: athena@philaathenaeum.org. Web Site: www.philaathenaeum.org, www.philadelphiabuildings.org. *Dir,* Sandra L Tatman, PhD; E-mail: sltatman@philaathenaeum.org; *Asst Dir,* Eileen Magee; E-mail: magee@philaathenaeum.org; *Circ Librn,* Jill Lemin Lee; E-mail: jilly@philaathenaeum.org; *Archivist,* Michael Seneca; E-mail: mseneca@philaathenaeum.org; *Cat,* Lois Reibach; E-mail: lreibach@athenaonline.org; *Curator of Archit,* Bruce Laverty; E-mail: laverty@philaathenaeum.org. Subject Specialists: *Archit hist,* Sandra L Tatman, PhD; *Bk illustr & design,* Jill Lemin Lee; *Archives, Digital presv,* Michael Seneca; *Archit, City hist,* Bruce Laverty; Staff 5.5 (MLS 2.5, Non-MLS 3)
Founded 1814
Library Holdings: Bk Vols 98,000
Special Collections: Architectural Drawings; Architecture & Design, 1814-1940; Historic Photographs; History of Books, 16th to 20th centuries (Turner Coll)
Subject Interests: Archit, Bk illustr & design, Local hist, Manuscripts
Automation Activity & Vendor Info: (Cataloging) Auto-Graphics, Inc; (OPAC) Auto-Graphics, Inc
Database Vendor: EBSCOhost
Wireless access
Function: Archival coll, Art exhibits, Bks on cassette, Bks on CD, Electronic databases & coll, Mail loans to mem, Online cat, Online searches, Prog for adults, Prog for children & young adult, Ref & res, Res libr
Publications: Athenaeum Newsletter (Online only)
Partic in Lyrasis; OCLC Online Computer Library Center, Inc; Philadelphia Area Consortium of Special Collections Libraries
Open Mon-Fri 9-5
Restriction: Circ to mem only, In-house use for visitors, Non-circulating of rare bks, Researchers by appt only
Friends of the Library Group

L BALLARD, SPAHR LLP LIBRARY*, 1735 Market St, 51st Flr, 19103-7599. SAN 314-8645. Tel: 215-864-8150. FAX: 215-864-8999. *Dir,* David Proctor; E-mail: proctor@ballardspahr.com; *Admin Mgr,* Eugenie Tyburski; E-mail: tyburski@ballardspahr.com; Staff 6 (MLS 4, Non-MLS 2)
Library Holdings: Bk Vols 25,000; Per Subs 400
Subject Interests: Law
Wireless access

L THE BEASLEY FIRM, LLC*, Law Library, 1125 Walnut St, 19107-4997. SAN 372-9095. Tel: 215-592-1000. FAX: 215-592-8360. Web Site: www.beasleyfirm.com. *Res,* Joel Tuckman

C BEREAN INSTITUTE LIBRARY*, 1901 W Girard Ave, 19130. SAN 326-436X. Tel: 215-763-4833, Ext 117. FAX: 215-236-6011. Web Site: www.bereaninstitute.edu. *Dir, Libr Res Ctr,* Dr Loraine Poole-Naranjo; Staff 1 (MLS 1)
Founded 1899. Enrl 300; Fac 16
Library Holdings: Bk Titles 4,362; Bk Vols 5,291; Per Subs 32
Automation Activity & Vendor Info: (Circulation) Follett Software; (OPAC) Follett Software
Function: ILL available
Publications: List of Acquisitions
Open Mon-Thurs 8:30-6:30, Fri 8:30-2
Restriction: Borrowing privileges limited to fac & registered students
Friends of the Library Group

L BLANK ROME LLP*, Law Library, One Logan Sq, 18th & Cherry Sts, 19103-6998. SAN 372-2309. Tel: 215-569-5500. Interlibrary Loan Service Tel: 215-569-5500 Ext 4290. FAX: 215-569-5546. E-mail: librarygroup@blankrome.com. Web Site: www.blankrome.com. *Dir,* Mary Sheridan Newman; Tel: 215-569-5490, Fax: 215-832-5490, E-mail: newman-ms@blankrome.com; *Bus Res Librn,* Cheryl P Halvorsen; Tel: 215-988-6978, E-mail: halvorsen@blankrome.com; *Electronic Serv,* Joseph Keslar; Staff 6 (MLS 3, Non-MLS 3)
Library Holdings: Bk Titles 3,400; Bk Vols 20,000; Per Subs 400
Automation Activity & Vendor Info: (Cataloging) Inmagic, Inc.; (OPAC) Inmagic, Inc.; (Serials) Inmagic, Inc.
Database Vendor: LexisNexis, OCLC FirstSearch, Westlaw
Partic in LibraryLinkNJ, The New Jersey Library Cooperative; Lyrasis
Open Mon-Fri 9-5
Restriction: By permission only

L BUCHANAN INGERSOLL & ROONEY PC*, Philadelphia Branch, Two Liberty Pl, 50 S 16th St, Ste 3200, 19102-2555. Tel: 215-665-5311. FAX: 215-665-8760. Web Site: www.bipc.com. *Librn,* Jeffrey Kreiling; Staff 2 (MLS 1, Non-MLS 1)

Library Holdings: Bk Titles 17,810; Bk Vols 18,410; Per Subs 312
Open Mon-Fri 8:30-4:30

C CENTER FOR ADVANCED JUDAIC STUDIES LIBRARY*, 420 Walnut St, 19106-3703. SAN 314-8939. Tel: 215-238-1290. FAX: 215-238-1540. Web Site: www.library.upenn.edu/cjs. *Curator,* Dr Arthur Kiron; E-mail: kiron@pobox.upenn.edu; *Circ, ILL,* Judith Leifer; E-mail: leifer@mail.cjs.upenn.edu; Staff 4 (MLS 1, Non-MLS 3)
Founded 1907
Library Holdings: Bk Titles 162,410; Bk Vols 180,000; Per Subs 92
Special Collections: American-Jewish History, archives; Arabica (Prof Skoss Coll); Bible (Prof Max Margolis Coll); Geniza Fragments; Hebrew Manuscripts; History of Jewish & Oriental Studies; History of Philadelphia; Oriental Manuscripts & Papyri; Poland & Hungary Coll; Rare Printed Judaica; USSR Coll
Subject Interests: Biblical studies, Judaica, Near Eastern studies
Automation Activity & Vendor Info: (Acquisitions) Innovative Interfaces, Inc; (Cataloging) Innovative Interfaces, Inc; (Circulation) Innovative Interfaces, Inc; (Course Reserve) Innovative Interfaces, Inc; (ILL) Innovative Interfaces, Inc; (Media Booking) Innovative Interfaces, Inc; (OPAC) Innovative Interfaces, Inc; (Serials) Innovative Interfaces, Inc
Publications: The Jewish Quarterly Review
Partic in Dialog Corp; OCLC Online Computer Library Center, Inc; Philadelphia Area Consortium of Special Collections Libraries; RLIN (Research Libraries Information Network)
Open Mon-Fri 9-4:30

CR CHESTNUT HILL COLLEGE*, Logue Library, 9601 Germantown Ave, 19118-2695. SAN 314-8769. Tel: 215-248-7050. FAX: 215-248-7056. Web Site: www.chc.edu/library. *Dean of Libr,* Mary Jo Larkin; Tel: 215-248-7055, E-mail: mjlarkin@chc.edu; *Cat,* Gail Cathey; Tel: 215-248-7053; *Circ,* Marian Ehnow; Tel: 215-248-7052; *ILL,* Carol Consorto; Tel: 215-242-9982; *Per,* Diane Arnold; Tel: 215-248-7054; Staff 8 (MLS 5, Non-MLS 3)
Founded 1924. Highest Degree: Doctorate
Library Holdings: Bk Titles 141,260; Bk Vols 144,910; Per Subs 543
Special Collections: Catholic Church Music (Montani Coll); Irish History & Literature Coll
Subject Interests: Educ, Liberal arts, Relig studies
Automation Activity & Vendor Info: (Acquisitions) SirsiDynix; (Cataloging) SirsiDynix; (Circulation) SirsiDynix; (ILL) SirsiDynix; (OPAC) SirsiDynix; (Serials) SirsiDynix
Database Vendor: EBSCOhost, LexisNexis, OCLC FirstSearch, ProQuest, Wilson - Wilson Web
Partic in SEPCHE; Tri-State College Library Cooperative
Open Mon-Thurs 8am-Midnight, Fri 8am-9pm, Sat 9-5, Sun Noon-Midnight

M CHESTNUT HILL HOSPITAL*, Medical Library, 8835 Germantown Ave, 19118. SAN 314-8777. Tel: 215-248-8206. FAX: 215-248-8240. *Librn,* Jacquelyn B Knuckle; Staff 2 (Non-MLS 2)
Founded 1930
Library Holdings: Bk Titles 1,180; Bk Vols 1,500; Per Subs 150
Special Collections: Rare Medical Books, Medical Humanities, Hospital Archives
Subject Interests: Consumer health, Med, Nursing, Pediatrics, Surgery
Automation Activity & Vendor Info: (Cataloging) CyberTools for Libraries
Database Vendor: EBSCOhost
Publications: Library Bulletin
Partic in Basic Health Sciences Library Network; Delaware Valley Information Consortium
Open Mon-Fri 8:30-5

S CHINATOWN BUILDING & EDUCATION FOUNDATION*, Chinese Cultural & Community Center, 125 N Tenth St, 19107. SAN 370-9574. Tel: 215-923-6767. FAX: 610-623-6775. *In Charge,* T T Chang; Staff 1 (Non-MLS 1)
Library Holdings: Bk Titles 2,162; Bk Vols 2,491; Per Subs 14
Special Collections: Chinese Language Coll
Subject Interests: Far East
Open Mon-Fri 9-4:30

S COLLEGE OF PHYSICIANS OF PHILADELPHIA*, Historical Library, 19 S 22nd St, 19103-3097. SAN 358-7762. Tel: 215-563-3737. FAX: 215-561-6477. E-mail: library@collegeofphysicians.org. Web Site: www.collegeofphysicians.org. *Col Librn,* Annie Brogran; Tel: 215-399-2304, E-mail: abrogan@collegeofphysicians.org; *The S Gordon Castigliano Dir of Libr Digital Initiatives,* Michelle DiMeo, PhD; Tel: 215-399-2306, E-mail: mdimeo@collegeofphysician.org; *Sr Libr Asst & Cataloguer,* Sofie Sereda; Tel: 215-399-2305, E-mail: ssereda@collegeofphysicians.org. Subject Specialists: *Hist of med,* Annie Brogran; *Hist of med, Hist of sci,* Michelle DiMeo, PhD; Staff 4 (MLS 1, Non-MLS 3)
Founded 1788
Library Holdings: Bk Titles 170,000; Bk Vols 350,000; Per Subs 12
Special Collections: Archives of the College of Physicians; Early Printed Books in Medicine, incunables; Gerontology (Joseph T Freeman Coll); Helfand-Radbill Medical Bookplate Coll; Medical Autograph Coll; Medical Portraits Coll; Otto & Gisela Fleischmann Psychoanalytic Coll; Sadoff Library of Forensic Psychiatry & Legal Medicine; Samuel Gross Library of Surgery; Samuel Lewis Curio Coll; Samuel X Radbill Pediatric Historical Library; William Harvey Coll
Subject Interests: Hist of med
Automation Activity & Vendor Info: (Cataloging) Ex Libris Group; (Circulation) Ex Libris Group; (ILL) OCLC; (OPAC) Ex Libris Group
Database Vendor: OCLC, OCLC FirstSearch
Wireless access
Function: For res purposes
Partic in OCLC Online Computer Library Center, Inc; Philadelphia Area Consortium of Special Collections Libraries
Restriction: Circ limited, Closed stack, In-house use for visitors, Open by appt only
Friends of the Library Group

J COMMUNITY COLLEGE OF PHILADELPHIA LIBRARY*, 1700 Spring Garden St, 19130. SAN 314-9730. Tel: 215-751-8000. Circulation Tel: 215-751-8383. Reference Tel: 215-751-8394. FAX: 215-751-8762. Web Site: path.ccp.edu/vpacaff/library. *Dept Chair,* Jessica Rossi; E-mail: jward@ccp.edu; *Regional Librn,* Jaroslaw Fedorijczuk; E-mail: jfedorijczuk@ccp.edu; *Regional Librn,* Carol Jewett; E-mail: cjewett@ccp.edu; *Access Serv,* Jacquelyn Bryant; E-mail: jbryant@ccp.edu; *Electronic Res,* Jalyn Warren; *Ref,* Nicole Duncan-Kinard; Tel: 215-751-8407, E-mail: nkinard@ccp.edu; *Ser,* Nicole Karam; Tel: 215-751-8388, E-mail: nkaram@ccp.edu; Staff 21 (MLS 10, Non-MLS 11)
Founded 1964. Enrl 22,691; Highest Degree: Associate
Library Holdings: Bk Vols 100,000; Per Subs 300
Automation Activity & Vendor Info: (Acquisitions) Innovative Interfaces, Inc; (Cataloging) Innovative Interfaces, Inc; (Circulation) Innovative Interfaces, Inc; (ILL) OCLC; (OPAC) Innovative Interfaces, Inc; (Serials) Innovative Interfaces, Inc
Database Vendor: EBSCOhost, Gale Cengage Learning, JSTOR, LexisNexis
Wireless access
Partic in Lyrasis; Tri-State College Library Cooperative
Restriction: Open to students, fac & staff, Photo ID required for access

R CONGREGATION RODEPH SHALOM*, Philadelphia & Elkins Park Suburban Center Library, 615 N Broad St, 19123. SAN 358-8009. Tel: 215-627-6747 (Philadelphia Center), 215-635-2500 (Elkins Park Center). FAX: 215-627-1313. E-mail: info@rodephshalom.org. Web Site: www.rodephshalom.org. *Librn,* Lois Hirsch
Founded 1802
Library Holdings: Bk Vols 10,300; Per Subs 22
Special Collections: (Roberta Lee Magaziner Memorial), bks, music; Children's Books; Family Life (Sadie Goldberg Memorial); Jewish Music
Subject Interests: Hist, Judaica-Jewish biog, Relig
Restriction: Open to pub for ref only

S COUNCIL FOR RELATIONSHIPS LIBRARY*, 4025 Chestnut St, 1st Flr, 19104. SAN 327-0610. Tel: 215-382-6680. FAX: 215-386-1743. Web Site: councilforrelationships.org. *Dir,* Shirley Jacoby; Staff 1 (Non-MLS 1)
Library Holdings: Bk Titles 2,890; Bk Vols 3,140; Per Subs 58
Open Mon-Thurs 9-9, Fri 9-5

L COZEN O'CONNOR, Law Library, 1900 Market St, 3rd Flr, 19103. SAN 372-1965. Tel: 215-665-2000. Interlibrary Loan Service Tel: 215-665-4748. Reference Tel: 215-665-2083. FAX: 215-665-2013. Web Site: www.cozen.com. *Dir of Libr Serv,* Loretta F Orndorff; E-mail: lorndorff@cozen.com; Staff 9 (MLS 6, Non-MLS 3)
Library Holdings: Bk Titles 7,003
Automation Activity & Vendor Info: (Cataloging) Inmagic, Inc.; (Circulation) Inmagic, Inc.; (OPAC) Inmagic, Inc.; (Serials) Inmagic, Inc.
Database Vendor: LexisNexis, Westlaw
Wireless access
Partic in Greater Philadelphia Law Library Association
Open Mon-Fri 9-5
Restriction: External users must contact libr

S CURTIS INSTITUTE OF MUSIC, John de Lancie Library, 1720 Locust St, 19103. (Mail add: 1726 Locust St, 19103), SAN 314-8831. Tel: 215-893-5265. Circulation Tel: 215-717-3156. Interlibrary Loan Service Tel: 215-717-3147. Reference Tel: 215-717-3122. Administration Tel: 215-717-3121. FAX: 215-717-3170. E-mail: library@curtis.edu. Web Site: library.curtis.edu. *Libr Dir,* Michelle Oswell; E-mail: michelle.oswell@curtis.edu; *Asst Librn,* Emily Butler; Tel: 215-717-3123, E-mail: emily.butler@curtis.edu; *Media Librn,* Molly O'Brien; E-mail: molly.obrien@curtis.edu; *Circ Mgr,* Darryl Hartshorne; E-mail:

darryl.hartshorne@curtis.edu; *Archivist,* Helen van Rossum; Tel: 215-717-3148; *Archives Asst,* Barbara Benedett; Tel: 215-717-3139, E-mail: barbara.benedett@curtis.edu; Staff 5.5 (MLS 3.5, Non-MLS 2)
Founded 1926. Enrl 163; Fac 107; Highest Degree: Master
Jun 2009-May 2010 Income $389,576. Mats Exp $106,357, Books $7,108, Per/Ser (Incl. Access Fees) $5,059, Manu Arch $18,351, Other Print Mats $47,812, AV Mat $4,671, Electronic Ref Mat (Incl. Access Fees) $3,322, Presv $20,034. Sal $234,376 (Prof $180,195)
Library Holdings: AV Mats 12,041; CDs 18,236; DVDs 1,231; Electronic Media & Resources 3,322; Music Scores 54,523; Bk Titles 7,184; Bk Vols 9,797; Per Subs 70; Videos 1,184
Special Collections: Music Scores
Subject Interests: Music
Automation Activity & Vendor Info: (Cataloging) Innovative Interfaces, Inc; (Circulation) Innovative Interfaces, Inc; (Course Reserve) Innovative Interfaces, Inc; (ILL) OCLC Online; (OPAC) Innovative Interfaces, Inc
Database Vendor: OCLC FirstSearch, Oxford Online
Wireless access
Function: Archival coll, Audio & video playback equip for onsite use, Computers for patron use, Copy machines, Electronic databases & coll, ILL available, Music CDs, Online cat, Ref serv in person
Partic in Lyrasis
Open Mon-Fri 9-6:30, Sun 1-6
Restriction: Open to researchers by request, Open to students, fac & staff

S EDWARD M DAVID RESEARCH LIBRARY*, Woodmere Art Museum, 9201 Germantown Ave, 19118. SAN 325-2191. Tel: 215-247-0948. FAX: 215-247-2387. Web Site: www.woodmereartmuseum.org. *Dir of Mus,* William R Valerio; Staff 2 (MLS 1, Non-MLS 1)
Founded 1981
Library Holdings: Bk Titles 2,310; Bk Vols 2,570; Per Subs 16
Special Collections: American 19th Century (Charles Knox Smith Coll), paintings; Philadelphia 20th Century (Woodmere Coll), paintings
Subject Interests: Philadelphia artists
Automation Activity & Vendor Info: (Cataloging) TLC (The Library Corporation); (Circulation) TLC (The Library Corporation)
Restriction: Circ limited, Not open to pub

L DECHERT LIBRARY*, Cira Ctr, 2929 Arch St, 19104. SAN 314-8858. Tel: 215-994-4000. FAX: 215-994-2222. Web Site: www.dechert.com. *Librn,* Karen Anello; *Librn,* Elaine Walker; Staff 3 (MLS 3)
Subject Interests: Law
Automation Activity & Vendor Info: (Acquisitions) EOS International; (Cataloging) EOS International; (Circulation) EOS International; (OPAC) EOS International; (Serials) EOS International
Database Vendor: Bloomberg, Dialog, EOS International, Factset, Fastcase, GalleryWatch, HeinOnline, LexisNexis, OCLC FirstSearch, OneSource, Swets Information Services, Westlaw
Restriction: Staff use only

DREXEL UNIVERSITY LIBRARIES

C HAGERTY LIBRARY*, 33rd & Market Sts, 19104-2875. (Mail add: 3141 Chestnut St, 19104-2875), SAN 314-8912. Tel: 215-895-2750. Circulation Tel: 215-895-2767. Interlibrary Loan Service Tel: 215-895-2769. Reference Tel: 215-895-2755. Toll Free Tel: 888-278-8825. FAX: 215-895-2070. Web Site: www.library.drexel.edu. *Dean, Univ Libr,* Danuta Nitecki; E-mail: dan44@drexel.edu; *Dir, Libr Acad Partnerships,* Elizabeth Ten Have; Tel: 215-895-2751, E-mail: elizabeth.tenhave@drexel.edu; *Dir, Libr Admin Serv,* Lenore Hardy; Tel: 215-895-2758, E-mail: hardy@drexel.edu; *Dir, Libr Serv & Quality Improvement,* John W Wiggins; Tel: 215-895-2773, E-mail: jww@drexel.edu; *Head, Access Serv,* Deirdre Childs; Tel: 215-895-6785, E-mail: dparker@drexel.edu; *Head, Libr Syst,* Peter Ivanick; Tel: 215-895-2090, E-mail: pdi23@drexel.edu; *Electronic Res Librn,* Noelle Egan; Tel: 215-895-2752, E-mail: nme26@drexel.edu; *Emerging Tech Librn,* Rebekah Kilzer; Tel: 215-895-6783, E-mail: rdk26@drexel.edu; *Ref Librn,* Jay Bhatt; Tel: 215-895-1873, E-mail: bhattjj@drexel.edu; *Ref Librn,* Peggy Dominy; Tel: 215-895-2754, Fax: 215-895-6950, E-mail: dominymf@drexel.edu; *Ref Librn,* Ann Keith Kennedy; Tel: 215-895-2772, E-mail: ann.keith.kennedy@drexel.edu; *Ref Librn,* Larry Milliken; Tel: 215-895-2765, E-mail: larry.milliken@drexel.edu; *Ref Librn,* Emily Missner; Tel: 215-895-6164, E-mail: edm25@drexel.edu; *Ref Librn,* Tim Siftar; Tel: 215-895-2762, E-mail: siftar@drexel.edu; *Evening Ref Librn,* Nancy Bellafante; *Evening Ref Librn,* Steven Bogel; *Evening/Weekend Ref Librn,* Amy Kwasnicki; *Evening/Weekend Ref Librn,* Nancy Thorne; *Evening/Weekend Ref Librn,* Katelyn Wolfrom; *Evening/Weekend Supvr,* Joshua Fore; *Evening/Weekend Supvr,* Jimenez Oreste; *Univ Archivist,* Robert Sieczkiewicz; Tel: 215-895-1757, E-mail: robs@drexel.edu; *Webmaster,* Katherine Lynch; Tel: 215-895-1344, E-mail: klynch@drexel.edu. Subject Specialists: *Eng,* Jay Bhatt; *Math, Sciences,* Peggy Dominy; *Media arts & design,* Ann Keith Kennedy; *Humanities, Soc sci,* Larry Milliken; *Bus,* Emily Missner; *Educ, Info sci, Tech,* Tim Siftar; Staff 34 (MLS 12, Non-MLS 22)
Founded 1891. Highest Degree: Doctorate
Library Holdings: AV Mats 2,700; e-books 127,535; e-journals 27,000; Bk Titles 266,821; Bk Vols 323,638; Per Subs 190
Special Collections: A J Drexel & Family; Charles Lukens Huston, Jr Ethics Coll; Drexel Archives; History of the Book
Subject Interests: Art, Design, Libr sci, Sci
Automation Activity & Vendor Info: (Acquisitions) Innovative Interfaces, Inc; (Cataloging) Innovative Interfaces, Inc; (Circulation) Innovative Interfaces, Inc; (Course Reserve) Innovative Interfaces, Inc; (ILL) OCLC ILLiad; (Media Booking) Innovative Interfaces, Inc; (OPAC) Innovative Interfaces, Inc; (Serials) SerialsSolutions
Database Vendor: American Psychological Association (APA), Blackwell, Community of Science (COS), DynaMed, ebrary, EBSCO Information Services, EBSCOhost, Elsevier, Ex Libris Group, IEEE (Institute of Electrical & Electronics Engineers), Ingenta, Innovative Interfaces, Inc, ISI Web of Knowledge, JSTOR, LexisNexis, MD Consult, Medline, Natural Standard, Nature Publishing Group, OCLC FirstSearch, OCLC WorldShare Interlibrary Loan, OVID Technologies, ProQuest, PubMed, RefWorks, ScienceDirect, SerialsSolutions, Springer-Verlag, Thomson - Web of Science, Wiley, Wiley InterScience, YBP Library Services
Partic in HSLC/Access PA/POWER Library; Lyrasis; Pennsylvania Academic Library Consortium, Inc (PALCI)
Open Mon-Fri 8am-Midnight, Sat & Sun 10-10

CM HAHNEMANN LIBRARY*, 245 N 15th St MS 449, 19102-1192, SAN 314-9234. Circulation Tel: 215-762-7631. Interlibrary Loan Service Tel: 215-762-7630. Reference Tel: 215-762-7184. FAX: 215-762-8180. Web Site: www.library.drexel.edu/healthsciences. *Dir, Health Sci Libr, Dir, Libr Admin Serv,* Lenore Hardy; Tel: 215-762-7022; *Assoc Dir, Health Sci Libr,* Linda M Katz; Tel: 215-762-7632, E-mail: linda.katz@drexel.edu; *Access Serv Librn, Evening Supvr,* Katherine Fisher; Tel: 215-762-1069; *Educ Librn,* Gary Childs; *Evening Supvr, Outreach Librn,* Kathleen Turner; *Ref Librn,* Steven Bogel; *Computer Ctr Mgr,* Albert Gerhold; *Evening Supvr,* Paul Hunter; *Evening Supvr,* Elizabeth Warner; *Fac Coordr, Human Res,* Antonello Dinallo; Tel: 215-762-7186; *ILL Coordr,* Lynda Sadusky; Staff 17 (MLS 7, Non-MLS 10)
Founded 1868. Highest Degree: Doctorate
Library Holdings: AV Mats 1,434; e-books 3,002; e-journals 7,982; Bk Titles 34,734; Bk Vols 36,266; Per Subs 72
Subject Interests: Creative arts therapies, Health sci, Med, Nursing, Pub health
Automation Activity & Vendor Info: (Acquisitions) Innovative Interfaces, Inc; (Cataloging) Innovative Interfaces, Inc; (Circulation) Innovative Interfaces, Inc; (Course Reserve) Innovative Interfaces, Inc; (ILL) OCLC ILLiad; (OPAC) Innovative Interfaces, Inc; (Serials) SerialsSolutions
Database Vendor: American Psychological Association (APA), Blackwell, DynaMed, ebrary, EBSCO Information Services, EBSCOhost, Elsevier, Ex Libris Group, IEEE (Institute of Electrical & Electronics Engineers), Ingenta, Innovative Interfaces, Inc, ISI Web of Knowledge, JSTOR, LexisNexis, MD Consult, Medline, Natural Standard, Nature Publishing Group, OCLC WorldShare Interlibrary Loan, OVID Technologies, ProQuest, PubMed, RefWorks, Sage, ScienceDirect, SerialsSolutions, Springer-Verlag, Thomson - Web of Science, UpToDate, Wiley, Wiley InterScience
Partic in Lyrasis; OCLC Online Computer Library Center, Inc
Special Services for the Blind - Assistive/Adapted tech devices, equip & products
Open Mon-Thurs 7:45am-11pm, Fri 7:45-8, Sat & Sun 10-10

CM QUEEN LANE LIBRARY*, 2900 Queen Lane, 19129, SAN 372-8447. Tel: 215-991-8740. FAX: 215-843-0840. Web Site: www.library.drexel.edu/healthsciences. *Circ Librn, Ref Librn,* Adrienne Jenness; E-mail: adrienne.jenness@drexel.edu; *Coordr,* Martha Kirby; E-mail: martha.kirby@drexel.edu; *Circ & ILL,* David Wagner; Staff 5 (MLS 2, Non-MLS 3)
Highest Degree: Doctorate
Library Holdings: AV Mats 628; e-books 127,535; e-journals 27,000; Bk Titles 7,780; Bk Vols 9,911; Per Subs 4
Subject Interests: Anatomy, Biochem, Immunology, Med educ, Microbiology, Neurobiol, Pharmacology, Physiology
Automation Activity & Vendor Info: (Cataloging) Innovative Interfaces, Inc - Millenium; (Circulation) Innovative Interfaces, Inc - Millenium; (ILL) OCLC ILLiad; (OPAC) Innovative Interfaces, Inc - Millenium; (Serials) SerialsSolutions
Database Vendor: American Psychological Association (APA), Annual Reviews, Blackwell, Cinahl, Community of Science (COS), DynaMed, ebrary, EBSCO Information Services, EBSCOhost, Elsevier, Ex Libris Group, IEEE (Institute of Electrical & Electronics Engineers), Ingenta, Innovative Interfaces, Inc, ISI Web of Knowledge, JSTOR, LexisNexis, MD Consult, Medline, Natural Standard, Nature Publishing Group, OCLC WorldShare Interlibrary Loan, OVID Technologies, ProQuest, PubMed, RefWorks, Sage, ScienceDirect, SerialsSolutions, Springer-Verlag, Thomson - Web of Science, Wiley, Wiley InterScience
Partic in Lyrasis; OCLC Online Computer Library Center, Inc

Publications: Queen Lane Library Guide (Library handbook)
Open Mon-Fri 8-5

L DRINKER BIDDLE & REATH LLP*, Law Library, One Logan Sq, Ste 2000, 19103-6996. SAN 314-8920. Tel: 215-988-2700. Reference Tel: 215-988-2952. FAX: 215-988-2757. *Dir,* Jennifer Schroth-Tusche; E-mail: jennifer.schroth@dbr.com; *Res,* Janet A Moore; Staff 4 (MLS 3, Non-MLS 1)
Founded 1970
Library Holdings: Bk Titles 4,000; Bk Vols 20,000; Per Subs 350
Special Collections: Historic Patent Model Coll; Rare PA Law Books
Automation Activity & Vendor Info: (Cataloging) SydneyPlus; (Serials) Sydney
Database Vendor: OCLC FirstSearch, OCLC WorldShare Interlibrary Loan
Partic in Lyrasis
Restriction: Open by appt only

L DUANE MORRIS LLP LIBRARY*, 30 S 17th St, 19103-4196. SAN 314-8955. Tel: 215-979-1720. Interlibrary Loan Service Tel: 215-979-1724. FAX: 215-979-1020. Web Site: www.duanemorris.com. *Dir, Libr & Res Serv,* Christine Scherzinger; *Asst Libr Dir,* Jennifer Brank; Staff 13 (MLS 9, Non-MLS 4)
Founded 1904
Library Holdings: Bk Vols 9,000
Subject Interests: Law
Automation Activity & Vendor Info: (Acquisitions) SydneyPlus; (Cataloging) SydneyPlus; (OPAC) SydneyPlus; (Serials) SydneyPlus
Database Vendor: OCLC FirstSearch
Partic in OCLC Online Computer Library Center, Inc
Restriction: Not open to pub

M ALBERT EINSTEIN HEALTHCARE NETWORK*, Luria Medical Library, 5501 Old York Rd, 19141. SAN 358-8068. Tel: 215-456-6345. Reference Tel: 215-456-6346. Administration Tel: 215-456-5882. FAX: 215-456-8267. E-mail: library@einstein.edu. Web Site: www.einstein.edu. *Dir, Libr Serv,* Lillian Brazin; E-mail: brazinl@einstein.edu; *Coordr,* Florence Rosenthal; E-mail: rosenthf@einstein.edu; *Automation Syst Coordr, ILL,* David Kitchen; E-mail: kitchend@einstein.edu; Staff 3 (MLS 1, Non-MLS 2)
Founded 1952
Library Holdings: AV Mats 150; Bk Titles 1,500; Bk Vols 2,000; Per Subs 270
Subject Interests: Med, Med admin, Nursing
Database Vendor: OVID Technologies
Function: Res libr
Partic in DEVIC; National Network of Libraries of Medicine
Restriction: Open to others by appt, Staff use only

S FEDERAL RESERVE BANK OF PHILADELPHIA*, Library & Research Center, 100 N Sixth St, 4th Flr, 19106. (Mail add: Ten Independence Mall, 19106), SAN 314-9021. Tel: 215-574-6540. FAX: 215-574-3847. E-mail: phil.library.mailbox@phil.frb.org. *Mgr,* Christine Le; E-mail: christine.le@phil.frb.org; *Supvr, Info & Digital Serv,* Wendy Parker; E-mail: wendy.b.parker@phil.frb.org; *Cat, e-Publ,* Position Currently Open; *Info Spec,* Cristine M McCollum; Tel: 215-574-6626, E-mail: cristine.m.mccollum@phil.frb.org; *Tech Serv Spec,* Beth Paul; E-mail: beth.paul@phil.frb.org. Subject Specialists: *Cataloging,* Beth Paul; Staff 4 (MLS 4)
Founded 1922
Library Holdings: Bk Titles 15,000; Bk Vols 30,000; Per Subs 400
Special Collections: Federal Reserve System Publications
Subject Interests: Banking, Econ
Automation Activity & Vendor Info: (Cataloging) SirsiDynix; (Circulation) SirsiDynix; (ILL) OCLC; (OPAC) SirsiDynix; (Serials) SirsiDynix
Database Vendor: Dun & Bradstreet, EBSCOhost, Elsevier, Factiva.com, Hoovers, ISI Web of Knowledge, JSTOR, LexisNexis, OCLC, Oxford Online, ScienceDirect, SerialsSolutions, Springer-Verlag, Wiley InterScience
Partic in OCLC Online Computer Library Center, Inc
Restriction: Open by appt only, Open to pub for ref only

GL FIRST JUDICIAL DISTRICT OF PENNSYLVANIA*, Alex Bonavitacola Law Library, City Hall, Rm 600, Broad & Market Sts, 19107. SAN 321-0596. Tel: 215-686-3799. FAX: 215-686-3737. Web Site: www.courts.phila.gov/departments/lawlibrary.asp. *Law Librn,* Stephanie Shepard; E-mail: Stephanie.Shepard@courts.phil.gov
Founded 1970
Library Holdings: Bk Vols 40,000; Per Subs 132
Subject Interests: US law (Penna)
Partic in OCLC Online Computer Library Center, Inc
Open Mon-Fri 9-5
Restriction: Open to pub for ref only

S FOREIGN POLICY RESEARCH INSTITUTE LIBRARY*, 1528 Walnut St, Ste 610, 19102. SAN 314-9072. Tel: 215-732-3774, Ext 102. FAX: 215-732-4401. E-mail: fpri@fpri.org. Web Site: www.fpri.org. *VPres,* Alan Luxenberg
Founded 1962
Library Holdings: Per Subs 150
Special Collections: Foreign Broadcast Information Service Reports
Subject Interests: Area studies, Intl econ, Intl relations, Mil, Polit sci
Open Mon-Fri 9-5

L FOX ROTHSCHILD LLP*, Law Library, 2000 Market St, 19103-3291. SAN 325-965X. Tel: 215-299-2732. FAX: 215-299-2150. E-mail: library@foxrothschild.com. *Dir,* Catherine M Monte
Library Holdings: Bk Vols 20,000

S FRANKLIN INSTITUTE LIBRARY*, 222 N 20th St, 19103-1194. SAN 314-9080. Tel: 215-448-1239. FAX: 215-448-1364. Web Site: www.fi.edu. *Librn,* Irene D Coffey; Staff 2 (MLS 1, Non-MLS 1)
Founded 1824
Library Holdings: AV Mats 4,000; Bk Titles 19,500; Per Subs 150
Special Collections: Underwater Man Coll; Ware Sugar Coll
Subject Interests: Math, Phys sci, Sci educ
Partic in OCLC Online Computer Library Center, Inc

P FREE LIBRARY OF PHILADELPHIA*, 1901 Vine St, 19103-1116. SAN 358-8181. Tel: 215-686-5322. Interlibrary Loan Service Tel: 215-686-5360. FAX: 215-563-3628. TDD: 215-963-0202. Web Site: www.freelibrary.org. *Pres & Dir,* Siobhan Reardon; Tel: 215-686-5300, Fax: 215-686-5368, E-mail: reardons@freelibrary.org; *Assoc Dir,* Joseph McPeak; Tel: 215-686-5325, E-mail: mcpeakj@freelibrary.org; *Chief of Staff,* Indira Scott; E-mail: Scottl@freelibrary.org; Staff 841 (MLS 263, Non-MLS 578)
Founded 1891. Pop 1,517,550; Circ 7,419,466
Jul 2013-Jun 2014. Mats Exp $8,242,782, Books $1,620,938, Per/Ser (Incl. Access Fees) $483,011, Manu Arch $156,260, Other Print Mats $846,770, Micro $149,596, AV Mat $1,635,591, Electronic Ref Mat (Incl. Access Fees) $821,833, Presv $23,303
Library Holdings: Audiobooks 47,669; AV Mats 971,389; Bks on Deafness & Sign Lang 1,200; Braille Volumes 64,292; CDs 100,687; DVDs 190,888; e-books 18,871; Electronic Media & Resources 145; Large Print Bks 56,434; Microforms 119,202; Music Scores 36,401; Bk Titles 28,260; Bk Vols 3,477,434; Per Subs 2,383; Talking Bks 791,700; Videos 110,863
Special Collections: US Document Depository
Automation Activity & Vendor Info: (Cataloging) SirsiDynix; (Circulation) SirsiDynix
Wireless access
Partic in OCLC Online Computer Library Center, Inc
Special Services for the Deaf - Bks on deafness & sign lang; Captioned film dep; High interest/low vocabulary bks; Spec interest per; TDD equip
Open Mon-Thurs 9-9, Fri 9-6, Sat 9-5, Sun 1-5
Friends of the Library Group

Branches: 72

ACCESS SERVICES, 1901 Vine St, 19103-1116. Tel: 215-686-5412. FAX: 215 686 5353. *Dir,* Laura Moore; Staff 3 (MLS 1, Non MLS 2)
Library Holdings: Bk Titles 10,840; Bk Vols 12,911
Open Mon-Fri 9-5
Friends of the Library Group

ANDORRA BRANCH, 705 E Cathedral Rd, 19128-2106, SAN 358-8998. Tel: 215-482-4350, 215-685-2552. FAX: 215-478-7635. *Br Mgr,* Ann Blasberg; Staff 6 (MLS 2, Non-MLS 4)
Founded 1975
Library Holdings: CDs 2,480; DVDs 5,142; Bk Vols 50,741
Open Mon, Wed, Fri & Sat 10-5, Tues & Thurs 12-8
Friends of the Library Group

ART, 1901 Vine St, 19103-1116. Tel: 215-686-5403. *Head Librn,* Karen Lightner; Staff 5 (MLS 4, Non-MLS 1)
Library Holdings: Bk Titles 11,619; Bk Vols 15,085; Per Subs 152
Special Collections: (American Institute of Architects, Philadelphia Chapter Coll); Fine Prints & Print Making; Illustrations (Joseph Pennell Coll); John Frederick Lewis Coll; Old Philadelphia Survey: Restorations & Measured Drawings; Stained Glass (Lawrence Saint Coll & Henry Lee Willet Coll)
Subject Interests: Archit, Costume, Decorative art, Fine arts, Graphic arts
Open Mon-Thurs 9-9, Fri 9-6, Sat 9-5, Sun 1-5
Friends of the Library Group

AUTOMOBILE REFERENCE COLLECTION, 1901 Vine St, 19103-1116. Tel: 215-686-5404. *Curator,* Kim Bravo; Staff 1 (MLS 1)
Library Holdings: Bk Titles 25,611; Bk Vols 30,910; Per Subs 84
Special Collections: Books & Photographs Tracing the Automobile from 1896 to date; Instruction, Parts & Shop Manuals; Sales Catalogs
Subject Interests: Automobiles

Open Mon-Fri 9-5
Friends of the Library Group
LUCIEN E BLACKWELL WEST PHILADELPHIA REGIONAL, 125 S 52nd St, 19139-3408, SAN 358-8963. Tel: 215-685-7424. FAX: 215-685-7438. *Regional Librn,* Roben Manker; Staff 22 (MLS 7, Non-MLS 15)
Library Holdings: CDs 4,071; DVDs 6,993; Bk Vols 77,820
Open Tues & Wed 12-8, Thurs-Sat 10-5
Friends of the Library Group
BUSHROD BRANCH, 6304 Castor Ave, 19149-2731, SAN 358-9021. Tel: 215-685-1471, 215-685-1472. FAX: 215-685-1079. *Br Mgr,* Catherine Krystopowicz; Staff 8 (MLS 2, Non-MLS 6)
Library Holdings: CDs 2,480; DVDs 5,146; Bk Vols 32,064
Open Mon, Wed & Fri 10-5, Tues & Thurs 12-8
Friends of the Library Group
BUSINESS, SCIENCE & INDUSTRY, 1901 Vine St, 19103-1116. Tel: 215-686-5394. *Head Librn,* Paul Savedow; Staff 7.5 (MLS 6, Non-MLS 1.5)
Library Holdings: Bk Titles 31,412; Bk Vols 34,119; Per Subs 306
Special Collections: Trade Periodical Literature
Subject Interests: Bus, Computers, Consumer info, Philatelic lit
Open Mon-Thurs 9-9, Fri 9-6, Sat 9-5, Sun 1-5
Friends of the Library Group
BUSTLETON AVENUE BRANCH, 10199 Bustleton Ave, 19116-3718, SAN 358-9056. Tel: 215-685-0472. FAX: 215-698-8892. *Br Mgr,* Kristin Sawka; Staff 9 (MLS 3, Non-MLS 6)
Library Holdings: CDs 2,349; DVDs 4,520; Bk Vols 40,128
Open Mon, Wed, Fri & Sat 10-5, Tues & Thurs 1-9
Friends of the Library Group
CENTRAL CHILDREN'S DEPARTMENT, 1901 Vine St, 19103-1116. Tel: 215-686-5369. *Head Librn,* Irene Wright; Staff 9.5 (MLS 4, Non-MLS 5.5)
Library Holdings: AV Mats 9,411; Bk Titles 50,119; Bk Vols 52,311; Per Subs 46; Videos 911
Special Collections: Bibliographies; Bibliographies for the Adult Researcher; Children's Books in 60 Different Languages; Folklore Coll; Foreign Language Coll; Historical Bibliography: Books about Children's Literature; Historical Coll of Children's Literature from 1837 to present; Kathrine McAlarney Coll of Illustrated Children's Books; Original Children's Book Illustrations & Manuscripts
Open Mon-Thurs 9-7, Fri 9-6, Sat 9-5, Sun 1-5
Friends of the Library Group
CHESTNUT HILL BRANCH, 8711 Germantown Ave, 19118-2716, SAN 358-9080. Tel: 215-685-9290. FAX: 215-685-9291. *Br Mgr,* Margaret Brunton; Staff 8 (MLS 3, Non-MLS 5)
Library Holdings: CDs 2,934; DVDs 3,760; Bk Vols 44,813
Open Mon & Wed 1-9, Tues, Thurs & Sat 10-5
Friends of the Library Group
DAVID COHEN OGONTZ BRANCH, 6017 Ogontz Ave, 19141-1311, SAN 376-8554. Tel: 215-685-3566, 215-685-3567. FAX: 215-685-3568. *Br Mgr,* Veronica Britto; Staff 4 (MLS 1, Non-MLS 3)
Library Holdings: CDs 1,664; DVDs 3,635; Bk Vols 25,389
Open Mon & Wed 12-8, Tues, Thurs & Sat 10-5
Friends of the Library Group
JOSEPH E COLEMAN NORTHWEST REGIONAL, 68 W Chelten Ave, 19144-2795, SAN 358-8939. Tel: 215-685-2150. FAX: 215-848-7790. *Regional Librn,* Patricia McLaughlin; Staff 28 (MLS 10, Non-MLS 18)
Library Holdings: AV Mats 1,861; Large Print Bks 209; Bk Titles 38,790; Bk Vols 42,610; Per Subs 79; Videos 410
Open Tues & Wed 12-8, Thurs-Sat 10-5, Sun 1-5
Friends of the Library Group
RAMONITA G DE RODRIGUEZ BRANCH, 600 W Girard Ave, 19123-1311, SAN 358-9897. Tel: 215-686-1767, 215-686-1768. FAX: 215-686-1769. *Br Mgr,* Lisa Chianese-Lopez; Staff 7 (MLS 2, Non-MLS 5)
Library Holdings: CDs 2,145; DVDs 4,662; Bk Vols 32,149
Open Mon & Wed 12-8, Tues, Thurs & Fri 10-5
Friends of the Library Group
THOMAS F DONATUCCI SR BRANCH, 1935 Shunk St, 19145-4234, SAN 358-9803. Tel: 215-685-1653, 215-685-1755. FAX: 215-685-1652. *Br Mgr,* David Mariscotti; Staff 4 (MLS 2, Non-MLS 2)
Library Holdings: CDs 1,858; DVDs 4,364; Bk Vols 32,901
Open Mon, Wed, Fri & Sat 10-5, Tues & Thurs 12-8, Sun 1-5
Friends of the Library Group
KATHARINE DREXEL BRANCH, 11099 Knights Rd, 19154-3516, SAN 358-9447. Tel: 215-685-9383. FAX: 215-685-9384. *Br Mgr,* Richard Krawczyk; Staff 6 (MLS 2, Non-MLS 4)
Library Holdings: CDs 2,657; DVDs 3,675; Bk Vols 38,173
Open Mon & Wed 12-8, Tues, Thurs & Fri 10-5
Friends of the Library Group
CHARLES L DURHAM BRANCH, 3320 Haverford Ave, 19104-2021, SAN 358-9641. Tel: 215-685-7436, 215-685-7677. FAX: 215-685-7439. *Br Mgr,* Joel Nichols; Staff 4 (MLS 1, Non-MLS 3)
Library Holdings: CDs 1,860; DVDs 3,011; Bk Vols 26,021
Open Mon & Wed 11-7, Tues, Thurs & Fri 10-5
Friends of the Library Group
EASTWICK BRANCH, 2851 Island Ave, 19153-2314, SAN 359-0224. Tel: 215-685-4170, 215-685-4171. FAX: 215-937-0412. *Br Mgr,* Jeff Wheeler; Staff 5 (MLS 1, Non-MLS 4)
Library Holdings: CDs 2,162; DVDs 3,563; Bk Vols 38,001
Open Mon & Wed 12-8, Tues & Thurs-Sat 10-5
Friends of the Library Group
EDUCATION, PHILOSOPHY & RELIGION, 1901 Vine St, 19103-1116. Tel: 215-686-5392. *Head Librn,* Position Currently Open; Staff 7 (MLS 6, Non-MLS 1)
Library Holdings: Bk Titles 26,511; Bk Vols 27,291; Per Subs 68
Special Collections: Bibles; Judaica-Hebraica; Moses Marx Coll; The Workplace - Job & Career Information Center
Subject Interests: Educ, Libr, Librarianship, Philos, Psychol, Relig studies
Open Mon-Thurs 9-9, Fri 9-6, Sat 9-5, Sun 1-5
Friends of the Library Group
FALLS OF SCHUYLKILL BRANCH, 3501 Midvale Ave, 19129-1633, SAN 358-920X. Tel: 215-685-2093. FAX: 215-685-2092. *Br Mgr,* Valerie Samuel; Staff 6 (MLS 2, Non-MLS 4)
Library Holdings: CDs 4,005; DVDs 4,967; Bk Vols 42,401
Open Mon & Wed 12-8, Tues, Thurs & Sat 10-5
Friends of the Library Group
FISHTOWN COMMUNITY BRANCH, 1217 E Montgomery Ave, 19125-3445, SAN 358-917X. Tel: 215-685-9990, 215-685-9991. FAX: 215-685-9989. *Br Mgr,* Allison Freyermuth; Staff 6 (MLS 2, Non-MLS 4)
Library Holdings: CDs 1,381; DVDs 2,881; Bk Vols 15,794
Open Mon, Wed & Fri 10-5, Tues & Thurs 12-8
Friends of the Library Group
EDWIN A FLEISHER COLLECTION OF ORCHESTRAL MUSIC, 1901 Vine St, 19103-1116. Tel: 215-686-5313. *Asst Curator,* Stu Serio; Staff 5 (MLS 1, Non-MLS 4)
Library Holdings: Bk Titles 16,840; Bk Vols 20,092; Per Subs 76
Special Collections: Archives of American Composers; Conductor's scores & complete instrumental parts for approximately 15,000 orchestral works & approximately 1500 reference scores available for loan on application; Reference files on over 1500 composers; Repository for discs & cassettes of works from the coll; Repository for tapes of American-International Music Fund's Recording Guarantee Project
Open Mon-Fri 9-5
Friends of the Library Group
FOX CHASE BRANCH, 501 Rhawn St, 19111-2504, SAN 358-9234. Tel: 215-685-0547. FAX: 215-685-0546. *Br Mgr,* Paul Daka; Staff 8 (MLS 2, Non-MLS 6)
Library Holdings: CDs 2,327; DVDs 4,008; Bk Vols 35,290
Open Mon & Wed 1-9, Tues, Thurs & Fri 10-5
Friends of the Library Group
FRANKFORD BRANCH, 4634 Frankford Ave, 19124-5804, SAN 358-9269. Tel: 215-685-1473, 215-685-1474. FAX: 215-289-6914. *Br Mgr,* Betsy Baxter; Staff 5 (MLS 2, Non-MLS 3)
Library Holdings: CDs 1,867; DVDs 5,321; Bk Vols 40,316
Open Mon & Wed 11-7, Tues, Thurs & Fri 10-5
Friends of the Library Group
FUMO FAMILY BRANCH, 2437 S Broad St, 19148-3508, SAN 358-9951. Tel: 215-685-1758. FAX: 215-685-1757. *Br Mgr,* Renee Pokorny; Staff 5 (MLS 2, Non-MLS 3)
Library Holdings: CDs 1,532; DVDs 3,136; Bk Vols 26,368
Open Mon & Wed 10-8, Tues & Thurs-Sat 10-5
Friends of the Library Group
GENERAL INFORMATION, 1901 Vine St, 19103-1116. Tel: 215-686-5322. *Head Librn,* Lori Morse; Staff 9 (MLS 1, Non-MLS 8)
Library Holdings: Bk Titles 1,192; Bk Vols 1,794; Per Subs 14
Special Collections: Telephone Directories
Open Mon-Thurs 9-9, Fri 9-6, Sat 9-5, Sun 1-5
Friends of the Library Group
GOVERNMENT PUBLICATIONS, 1901 Vine St, 19103-1116. Tel: 215-686-5330. *Head Librn,* David Utz; Staff 8.5 (MLS 6.5, Non-MLS 2)
Library Holdings: Bk Titles 19,801; Bk Vols 21,212; Per Subs 42
Special Collections: US Patent Coll; US Patents. State Document Depository; UN Document Depository; US Document Depository
Open Mon-Thurs 9-9, Fri 9-6, Sat 9-5, Sun 1-5
Friends of the Library Group
GREATER OLNEY BRANCH, 5501 N Fifth St, 19120-2805, SAN 358-9323. Tel: 215-685-2845, 215-685-2846. FAX: 215-548-2605. *Br Mgr,* Bob Sisson; Staff 7 (MLS 2, Non-MLS 5)
Library Holdings: CDs 1,727; DVDs 4,093; Bk Vols 33,673
Open Mon & Wed 12-8, Tues, Thurs & Sat 10-5
Friends of the Library Group
HADDINGTON BRANCH, 446 N 65th St, 19151-4003, SAN 358-9382. Tel: 215-685-1970. FAX: 215-685-1971. *Br Mgr,* Frank Bonifante; Staff 4 (MLS 2, Non-MLS 2)
Library Holdings: CDs 1,086; DVDs 2,806; Bk Vols 24,659

Open Mon, Wed & Fri 10-5, Tues & Thurs 11-7
Friends of the Library Group
HAVERFORD AVENUE BRANCH, 5543 Haverford Ave, 19139-1432, SAN 358-9390. Tel: 215-685-1964, 215-685-1965. FAX: 215-685-1966. *Br Mgr,* Christina Pie; Staff 4 (MLS 1, Non-MLS 3)
Library Holdings: CDs 2,532; DVDs 3,742; Bk Vols 35,533
Open Mon & Wed 12-8, Tues, Thurs & Fri 10-5
Friends of the Library Group
HOLMESBURG BRANCH, 7810 Frankford Ave, 19136-3013, SAN 358-9412. Tel: 215-685-8756. FAX: 215-685-8759. *Br Mgr,* Carol Barta Weidner; Staff 6 (MLS 2, Non-MLS 4)
Library Holdings: CDs 1,972; DVDs 3,619; Bk Vols 33,015
Open Mon & Wed 12-8, Tues & Thurs-Sat 10-5
Friends of the Library Group
INDEPENDENCE BRANCH, 18 S Seventh St, 19106-2314. Tel: 215-685-1633. FAX: 215-685-1844. *Br Mgr,* Marianne Banbor; Staff 9 (MLS 3, Non-MLS 6)
Library Holdings: CDs 3,657; DVDs 6,407; Bk Vols 45,628
Open Mon & Wed 12-8, Tues, Thurs & Fri 10-5
Friends of the Library Group
INTERLIBRARY LOAN, 1901 Vine St, 19103-1116. Tel: 215-686-5360. FAX: 215-563-3628. *Head Librn,* Sandra Miller; Staff 5.5 (MLS 2, Non-MLS 3.5)
Library Holdings: Bk Vols 304,100
Open Mon-Wed 9-6, Thurs & Fri 9-5
Friends of the Library Group
KENSINGTON BRANCH, 104 W Dauphin St, 19133-3701, SAN 358-9471. Tel: 215-685-9996. FAX: 215-685-9997. *Br Mgr,* Marcela Franco; Staff 5 (MLS 2, Non-MLS 3)
Library Holdings: CDs 1,657; DVDs 3,610; Bk Vols 22,725
Open Mon & Wed 10-6, Tues, Thurs & Sat 10-5
Friends of the Library Group
KINGSESSING BRANCH, 1201 S 51st, 19143-4353, SAN 358-9501. Tel: 215-685-2690. FAX: 215-685-2691. *Br Mgr,* Conita Pierson; Staff 4 (MLS 2, Non-MLS 2)
Library Holdings: CDs 1,514; DVDs 3,909; Bk Vols 27,414
Open Mon, Wed & Sat 10-5, Tues & Thurs 11-7
Friends of the Library Group
LAWNCREST BRANCH, 6098 Rising Sun Ave, 19111-6009, SAN 358-9536. Tel: 215-685-0549. FAX: 215-685-0548. *Br Mgr,* Debra Mikus; Staff 6 (MLS 2, Non-MLS 4)
Library Holdings: CDs 2,029; DVDs 3,988; Bk Vols 31,246
Open Mon, Wed & Sat 10-5, Tues & Thurs 12-8
Friends of the Library Group
P LIBRARY FOR THE BLIND & PHYSICALLY HANDICAPPED, 919 Walnut St, 19107-5289, SAN 314-9102. Tel: 215-683-3214. Toll Free Tel: 800-222-1754. FAX: 215-683-3211. E-mail: flphlind@freelibrary.org *Head Librn,* Keri Wilkins; *Tech Serv,* Patricia Shotzbarger; Staff 5 (MLS 5)
Founded 1897. Pop 12,745; Circ 1,125,725
Jul 2008-Jun 2009 Income State $1,770,105
Library Holdings: AV Mats 500; Bk Titles 95,000
Special Collections: Blindness & Handicaps
Publications: 919 News Insider for Children & Teens (Bi-annually); 919 News, Reader Newsletter (Quarterly)
Special Services for the Blind - ABE/GED & braille classes for the visually impaired & print handicapped; Braille equip; Braille servs; Closed circuit TV; Info on spec aids & appliances; Magnifiers; Mags & bk reproduction/duplication; Reader equip; Volunteer serv
Open Mon-Fri 9-5
Friends of the Library Group
LITERATURE, 1901 Vine St, 19103-1116. Tel: 215-686-5402. *Head Librn,* Position Currently Open; Staff 6 (MLS 5, Non-MLS 1)
Library Holdings: Bk Titles 42,818; Bk Vols 48,908; Per Subs 142
Special Collections: Granger Coll; Ottemiller Coll
Subject Interests: Belles lettres, Folklore, Journalism, Lang arts, Lit
Open Mon-Thurs 9-9, Fri 9-6, Sat 9-5, Sun 1-5
Friends of the Library Group
LOGAN BRANCH, 1333 Wagner Ave, 19141-2916, SAN 358-9595. Tel: 215-685-9156, 215-686-9157. FAX: 215-456-2285. *Br Mgr,* Belita Thornton; Staff 5 (MLS 2, Non-MLS 3)
Library Holdings: CDs 1,310; DVDs 3,409; Bk Vols 34,174
Open Mon, Wed & Fri 10-5, Tues & Thurs 12-8
Friends of the Library Group
LOVETT MEMORIAL BRANCH, 6945 Germantown Ave, 19119-2189, SAN 358-9625. Tel: 215-685-2095. FAX: 215-685-2094. *Br Mgr,* Lynn Ruthrauff; Staff 6 (MLS 2, Non-MLS 4)
Library Holdings: CDs 3,415; DVDs 4,519; Bk Vols 43,082
Open Mon & Wed 1-9, Tues & Thurs-Sat 10-5
Friends of the Library Group
MAP COLLECTION, 1901 Vine St, 19103-1116. Tel: 215-686-5397. *Curator,* Richard C Boardman; Staff 1 (MLS 1)
Library Holdings: Bk Titles 9,841; Bk Vols 11,293
Special Collections: 19th & 20th Century Philadelphia Fire Insurance Atlases, suburban atlases; 19th Century Pennsylvania County Atlases; Decorative Maps & Maps of Imaginary Lands; Historical Philadelphia Map Coll; William G Kelzo Coll of Jansson-Visscher Maps of America
Subject Interests: Cartobibliography, Geog, Hist of cartography, Map librarianship
Open Mon-Fri 9-5
Friends of the Library Group
LILLIAN MARRERO BRANCH, 601 W Lehigh Ave, 19133-2228, SAN 358-9560. Tel: 215-685-9794. FAX: 215-685-9689. *Br Mgr,* Rebekah Ray; Staff 5 (MLS 2, Non-MLS 3)
Library Holdings: CDs 1,607; DVDs 3,471; Bk Vols 31,823
Open Mon & Wed 11-7, Tues & Thurs-Sat 10-5
Friends of the Library Group
MCPHERSON SQUARE BRANCH, 601 E Indiana Ave, 19134-3042, SAN 358-965X. Tel: 215-685-9994, 215-685-9995. FAX: 215-685-9984. *Br Mgr,* Judi Moore; Staff 5 (MLS 2, Non-MLS 3)
Library Holdings: CDs 1,553; DVDs 3,911; Bk Vols 31,325
Open Mon & Wed 10-6, Tues, Thurs & Fri 10-5
Friends of the Library Group
CECIL B MOORE BRANCH, 2320 W Cecil B Moore Ave, 19121-2927, SAN 358-9145. Tel: 215-685-2766. FAX: 215-685-3893. *Br Mgr,* Stephanie Bujak; Staff 9 (MLS 2, Non-MLS 7)
Library Holdings: CDs 1,352; DVDs 3,598; Bk Vols 30,825
Open Mon & Wed 10-6, Tues, Thurs & Fri 10-5
Friends of the Library Group
MUSIC, 1901 Vine St, 19103-1116. Tel: 215-686-5316. *Head Librn,* Steve Landstreet; Staff 8 (MLS 5, Non-MLS 3)
Library Holdings: Bk Titles 10,691; Bk Vols 12,510
Special Collections: Coll of Musical Fund Society; Drinker Library of Choral Music; Harvey Husten & Huber Jazz Libraries, rec; Historical Record Coll; Sheet Music (incl Americana)
Subject Interests: Bibliog, Biog, Chamber, Collected works, Criticism, Dance, Essays, Instrumental music, Manuscripts
Open Mon-Thurs 9-9, Fri 9-6, Sat 9-5, Sun 1-5
Friends of the Library Group
NEWSPAPER & MICROFILM CENTER, 1901 Vine St, 19103-1116. Tel: 215-686-5431. FAX: 215-567-0398. *Head Librn,* Position Currently Open; Staff 9 (MLS 5, Non-MLS 4)
Library Holdings: Bk Titles 12,680; Bk Vols 14,310; Per Subs 221
Subject Interests: Current events
Open Mon-Fri 9-6, Sat 9-5, Sun 1-5
Friends of the Library Group
NICETOWN-TIOGA BRANCH, 3720 N Broad St, 19140-3608, SAN 358-9684. Tel: 215-685-9789, 215-685-9790. FAX: 215-685-9788. *Br Mgr,* Marsha Stender; Staff 5 (MLS 2, Non-MLS 3)
Library Holdings: CDs 766; DVDs 3,225; Bk Vols 22,078
Open Mon, Wed & Sat 10-5, Tues & Thurs 10-6
Friends of the Library Group
BLANCHE A NIXON LIBRARY - COBBS CREEK BRANCH, 5800 Cobbs Creek Pkwy, 19143-3036, SAN 358-9110. Tel: 215-685-1973. FAX: 215-685-1974. *Br Mgr,* Darren Cottman; Staff 6 (MLS 2, Non-MLS 4)
Library Holdings: CDs 1,221; DVDs 3,176; Bk Vols 22,078
Open Mon & Wed 12-8, Tues & Thurs-Sat 10-5
Friends of the Library Group
NORTHEAST REGIONAL, 2228 Cottman Ave, 19149-1297, SAN 358-8904. Tel: 215-685-0300. FAX: 215-742-3225. *Regional Librn,* Jennifer Chang; Staff 40 (MLS 15, Non-MLS 25)
Library Holdings: CDs 6,343; DVDs 7,178; Bk Vols 124,416
Open Tues & Wed 1-9, Thurs-Sat 10-5, Sun 1-5
Friends of the Library Group
OAK LANE BRANCH, 6614 N 12th St, 19126-3299, SAN 358-9714. Tel: 215-685-2848. FAX: 215-685-2847. *Br Mgr,* Debra Ahrens; Staff 6 (MLS 2, Non-MLS 4)
Library Holdings: CDs 2,019; DVDs 3,640; Bk Vols 31,007
Open Mon & Wed 12-8, Tues, Thurs & Fri 10-5
Friends of the Library Group
OVERBROOK PARK, 7422 Haverford Ave, 19151-2995, SAN 358-9749. Tel: 215-685-0182. FAX: 215-685-0183. *Actg Br Mgr,* Marvin DeBose; Staff 6 (MLS 2, Non-MLS 4)
Library Holdings: CDs 1,713; DVDs 3,761; Bk Vols 45,874
Open Mon, Wed & Sat 10-5, Tues & Thurs 11-7
Friends of the Library Group
PASCHALVILLE BRANCH, 6942 Woodland Ave, 19142-1823, SAN 358-9773. Tel: 215-685-2662, 215-685-2663. FAX: 215-685-2656. *Br Mgr,* Emily Anne Livingston; Staff 4 (MLS 2, Non-MLS 2)
Library Holdings: CDs 1,588; DVDs 3,748; Bk Vols 28,617
Open Mon, Wed & Fri 10-5, Tues & Thurs 11-7
Friends of the Library Group
PHILADELPHIA CITY INSTITUTE, 1905 Locust St, 19103-5730, SAN 358-9838. Tel: 215-685-6621, 215-685-6623. FAX: 215-685-6622. *Br Mgr,* Joseph Paradin; Staff 9 (MLS 3, Non-MLS 6)
Library Holdings: CDs 4,068; DVDs 6,707; Bk Vols 41,863
Open Mon & Wed 12-8, Tues, Thurs & Sat 10-5
Friends of the Library Group

PHILBRICK POPULAR LIBRARY, 1901 Vine St, 19103-1116. Tel: 215-686-5320. *Head Librn,* Dena Heilik; Staff 24 (MLS 6, Non-MLS 18)
Library Holdings: Bk Titles 11,211; Bk Vols 13,497
Open Mon-Thurs 9-9, Fri 9-6, Sat 9-5, Sun 1-5
Friends of the Library Group

PRINT & PICTURE, 1901 Vine St, 19103-1116. Tel: 215-686-5405. *Curator,* Aurora Deshauteurs; Staff 2 (MLS 1, Non-MLS 1)
Library Holdings: Bk Titles 20,681; Bk Vols 23,942; Per Subs 51
Special Collections: Centennial Exhibition of 1876 Photographs; Circulating Coll of Pictures on all Subjects; Contemporary Graphic Arts Coll; Greeting Cards; Napoleonica (Carson Coll); Philadelphia Coll; Portrait Prints (Lewis Coll)
Open Mon-Fri 9-5
Friends of the Library Group

QUEEN MEMORIAL BRANCH, 1201 S 23rd St, 19146-4316, SAN 374-7328. Tel: 215-685-1869, 215-685-1899. FAX: 215-685-1654. *Br Mgr,* Mark Wolfe; Staff 4 (MLS 1, Non-MLS 3)
Library Holdings: CDs 1,491; DVDs 3,261; Bk Vols 23,155
Open Mon & Wed 10-6, Tues, Thurs & Fri 10-5
Friends of the Library Group

RARE BOOK, 1901 Vine St, 19103-1116. Tel: 215-686-5416. *Head Librn,* Janine Pollock; Staff 5 (MLS 4, Non-MLS 1)
Library Holdings: Bk Titles 41,192; Bk Vols 43,411
Special Collections: A B Frost (C Barton Brewster Coll); A E Newton (Swift Newton Coll) American Pamphlets (Charles J Biddle Coll); Agnes Repplier (Anne Von Moschzisker Coll); American Historical Autographs incl Jay Treaty Papers (Elkins Coll); American Sunday School Union Publications; Americana (William M Elkins Coll); Angling Prints (Evan Randolph Coll); Arthur Rackham (Grace Clark Haskell Coll); Beatrix Potter (Collamore, Cridland, Elkins & Stevens Coll); Bookplates (J Somers Smith Coll); Bret Harte (Edward F R Wood Coll); British Engravers (Lewis Coll); Calligraphy (9th-20th Centuries Coll); Children's Books Printed in America, 1682-1850 (ASW Rosenbach, Emerson Greenaway, Mrs William H Allen, Frederick R Gardner Coll); Christopher Morley Coll; Common Law (Hampton L Carson Coll); Cuneiform Tablets (John Frederick Lewis Coll); Dickens First Editions, Letters & Memoriabilia (Elkins Coll); Dickens Letters (Benoliel Coll); Early Bibles; Edgar Allan Poe (Richard Gimbel Coll); English & Irish Pamphlets; European Manuscripts (Lewis & Widener Coll); Four Folios of Shakespeare (Joseph E Widener Coll); Gift Books; Goldsmith First Editions & Papers (Elkins Coll); Horace (Moncure Biddle Coll); Horn Books (Elisabeth Ball Coll); Howard Pyle & His School (Thornton Oakley Coll); Incunabula (Copinger-Widener Coll); James Branch Cabell (D Jaques Benoliel Coll); John Gilpin (Brewster Coll); Kate Greenaway Coll; Letters of the Presidents (Strouse Coll); Margaret Leaf Coll; Munro Leaf Coll; Oriental Manuscripts & Miniatures (Lewis Coll); Palmer Cox; Pennsylvania German Imprints, Manuscripts & Fraktur (Henry S Borneman & Others Coll); Philadelphia Views (Randolph Coll); Press Books; Robert Lawson (Frederick R Gardner Coll); Title Pages & Printer's Marks (John Ashhurst Coll); Wing, Short Title Catalogue Books
Open Mon-Sat 9-5
Friends of the Library Group

REGIONAL FOUNDATION CENTER, 1901 Vine St, 19103-1116. Tel: 215-686-5423. *Head Librn,* Janet Puchino; Staff 2 (MLS 2)
Library Holdings: Bk Titles 5,683; Bk Vols 7,981; Per Subs 26
Subject Interests: Fundraising, Info on area foundations, Nat foundations, Nonprofit organization mgt, Philanthropy
Open Mon, Tues, Thurs & Fri 9-5, Wed 9-7, Sat 10-5
Friends of the Library Group

RICHMOND BRANCH, 2987 Almond St, 19134-4955, SAN 358-9927. Tel: 215-685-9992, 215-685-9993. FAX: 215-291-5312. *Br Mgr,* Gerald Franklin; Staff 5 (MLS 2, Non-MLS 3)
Library Holdings: CDs 1,999; DVDs 4,436; Bk Vols 37,688
Open Mon, Wed & Sat 10-5, Tues & Thurs 12-8
Friends of the Library Group

ROXBOROUGH BRANCH, 6245 Ridge Ave, 19128-2630, SAN 358-9986. Tel: 215-685-2550. FAX: 215-685-2551. *Br Mgr,* Bruce Siebers; Staff 4 (MLS 2, Non-MLS 2)
Library Holdings: CDs 1,999; DVDs 4,436; Bk Vols 37,866
Open Mon & Wed 12-8, Tues, Thurs & Fri 10-5
Friends of the Library Group

CHARLES SANTORE BRANCH, 932 S Seventh St, 19147-2932, SAN 359-0046. Tel: 215-686-1766. FAX: 215-686-1765. *Br Mgr,* Jeanne Hamann; Staff 6 (MLS 2, Non-MLS 4)
Library Holdings: CDs 2,036; DVDs 5,233; Bk Vols 33,837
Open Mon & Wed 12-8, Tues & Thurs-Sat 10-5
Friends of the Library Group

SOCIAL SCIENCE & HISTORY, 1901 Vine St, 19103-1116. Tel: 215-686-5396. *Head Librn,* David Ninemire; Staff 6 (MLS 4, Non-MLS 2)
Library Holdings: Bk Titles 48,691; Bk Vols 51,408; Per Subs 122
Special Collections: American Imprint Series, micro; American Indian (Wilberforce Eames Coll); Chess (Charles Willing Coll); Confederate Imprints (Simon Gratz Coll); Rowing (Lewis H Kenney Coll)
Subject Interests: Anthrop, Archaeology, Behav sci, Bibliog, Biog, Hist, Intl relations, Polit sci, Soc sci, Sports, Travel
Open Mon-Thurs 9-9, Fri 9-6, Sat 9-5, Sun 1-5
Friends of the Library Group

SOUTH PHILADELPHIA BRANCH, 1700 S Broad St, 19145-2392, SAN 359-0011. Tel: 215-685-1866, 215-685-1867. FAX: 215-685-1868.
Library Holdings: CDs 2,036; DVDs 6,266; Bk Vols 40,498
Closed due to demolition & construction of new building.12/31/2013-11/01/2015
Open Mon & Wed 12-8, Tues, Thurs & Sat 10-5
Friends of the Library Group

TACONY BRANCH, 6742 Torresdale Ave, 19135-2416, SAN 359-0070. Tel: 215-685-8755, 215-685-8758. FAX: 215-685-8718. *Br Mgr,* Suzin Weber; Staff 6 (MLS 2, Non-MLS 4)
Library Holdings: CDs 2,099; DVDs 5,002; Bk Vols 36,696
Open Mon & Wed 12-8, Tues, Thurs & Fri 10-5
Friends of the Library Group

TORRESDALE BRANCH, 3079 Holme Ave, 19136-1101, SAN 359-0100. Tel: 215-685-0494. FAX: 215-685-0495. *Br Mgr,* Ann Hornbach; Staff 6 (MLS 2, Non-MLS 4)
Library Holdings: CDs 2,328; DVDs 3,542; Bk Vols 31,097
Open Mon & Wed 12-8, Tues, Thurs & Sat 10-5
Friends of the Library Group

WADSWORTH AVENUE BRANCH, 1500 Wadsworth Ave, 19150-1699, SAN 359-0135. Tel: 215-685-9293, 215-685-9294. FAX: 215-685-9293. *Br Mgr,* Juanita Vega-DeJoseph; Staff 5 (MLS 2, Non-MLS 3)
Library Holdings: CDs 1,327; DVDs 2,941; Bk Vols 31,085
Open Mon & Wed 12-8, Tues, Thurs & Fri 10-5
Friends of the Library Group

WALNUT STREET WEST BRANCH, 201 S 40th St, 19104-3542, SAN 359-016X. Tel: 215-685-7671, 215-685-7672, 215-685-7678. FAX: 215-685-7679. *Br Mgr,* Tiffany Nardella; Staff 8 (MLS 3, Non-MLS 5)
Library Holdings: CDs 3,982; DVDs 6,088; Bk Vols 57,648
Open Mon & Wed 12-8, Tues, Thurs & Sat 10-5
Friends of the Library Group

WELSH ROAD BRANCH, 9233 Roosevelt Blvd, 19114-2205, SAN 359-0194. Tel: 215-685-0497, 215-685-0498. FAX: 215-685-0496. *Br Mgr,* Brook Freeman; Staff 7 (MLS 2, Non-MLS 5)
Library Holdings: CDs 2,469; DVDs 5,067; Bk Vols 46,415
Open Mon & Wed 12-8, Tues, Thurs & Sat 10-5
Friends of the Library Group

WEST OAK LANE BRANCH, 2000 Washington Lane, 19138-1344, SAN 325-4097. Tel: 215-685-2843. FAX: 215-685-2844. *Br Mgr,* Irene Klemas; Staff 6 (MLS 2, Non-MLS 4)
Library Holdings: CDs 2,866; DVDs 3,607; Bk Vols 35,463
Open Mon, Wed, Fri & Sat 10-5, Tues & Thurs 12-8
Friends of the Library Group

WHITMAN BRANCH, 200 Snyder Ave, 19148-2620, SAN 359-0259. Tel: 215-685-1754. FAX: 215-685-1753. *Br Mgr,* Allen Merry; Staff 5 (MLS 2, Non-MLS 3)
Library Holdings: CDs 2,171; DVDs 4,206; Bk Vols 35,963
Open Mon & Wed 12-8, Tues, Thurs & Sat 10-5
Friends of the Library Group

WIDENER BRANCH, 2808 W Lehigh Ave, 19132-3296, SAN 359-0283. Tel: 215-685-9798, 215-685-9799. FAX: 215-685-9716. *Br Mgr,* Prather Egan; Staff 5 (MLS 2, Non-MLS 3)
Library Holdings: CDs 1,907; DVDs 4,068; Bk Vols 28,810
Open Mon & Wed 10-6, Tues & Thurs-Sat 10-5
Friends of the Library Group

WYNNEFIELD BRANCH, 5325 Overbrook Ave, 19131-1498, SAN 359-0313. Tel: 215-685-0298, 215-685-0299. FAX: 215-685-0294. *Br Mgr,* Alex Bender; Staff 6 (MLS 2, Non-MLS 4)
Library Holdings: CDs 1,947; DVDs 3,692; Bk Vols 37,859
Open Mon & Wed 12-8, Tues, Thurs & Sat 10-5
Friends of the Library Group

WYOMING BRANCH, 231 E Wyoming Ave, 19120-4439, SAN 359-0348. Tel: 215-685-9158. FAX: 215-685-9159. *Br Mgr,* Rebecca Shaknovich; Staff 4 (MLS 1, Non-MLS 3)
Library Holdings: CDs 1,723; DVDs 4,821; Bk Vols 35,220
Open Mon & Wed 12-8, Tues, Thurs & Fri 10-5
Friends of the Library Group

P FRIENDS FREE LIBRARY OF GERMANTOWN*, 5418 Germantown Ave, 19144. SAN 314-9129. Tel: 215-951-2355. FAX: 215-951-2697. Web Site: www.germantownfriends.org. *Dir,* Katherine St Clair; Staff 3 (MLS 1, Non-MLS 2)
Founded 1845. Circ 27,841
Library Holdings: Bk Titles 61,414; Bk Vols 63,981; Per Subs 198; Videos 411
Special Collections: Irvin C Poley Theatre Coll 1900-1975
Subject Interests: African-Am studies, Natural sci, Quaker hist
Open Mon-Thurs (Winter) 8-4, Fri 8-3; Tues & Thurs (Summer) 10-4, Wed 12-6

S GERMAN SOCIETY OF PENNSYLVANIA*, Joseph Horner Memorial Library, 611 Spring Garden St, 19123. SAN 314-917X. Tel: 215-627-2332. FAX: 215-627-5297. E-mail: librarian@germansociety.org. Web Site: www.germansociety.org. *VPres, Culture & Heritage,* Dr Maria Sturm; *Spec Coll Librn,* Chrissy Bellizzi; *Cataloger,* Bettina Hess; Staff 2 (MLS 1, Non-MLS 1)
Founded 1817
Library Holdings: Bk Vols 60,000; Per Subs 4; Spec Interest Per Sub 4
Special Collections: Carl-Schurz-Association Holdings; German American Archives (Printed & Manuscript Coll 18th to 20th Century); German-American Newspapers (19th & Early 20th Century)
Subject Interests: Hist, Lit, Politics
Database Vendor: OCLC WorldShare Interlibrary Loan, TLC (The Library Corporation)
Wireless access
Publications: German Society of Pennsylvania-German Historical Institute Reference Guide 20 (Research guide)
Open Tues & Thurs 10-4

S GERMANTOWN HISTORICAL SOCIETY*, Library & Archives, 5501 Germantown Ave, 19144-2291. SAN 314-9188. Tel: 215-844-1683. FAX: 215-844-2831. E-mail: library@germantownhistory.org. Web Site: www.germantownhistory.org. *Archivist, Librn,* Sandra L Chaff; Staff 1 (MLS 1)
Founded 1900
Library Holdings: Bk Vols 4,100
Special Collections: African-American Genealogy Archives; German Emigrants Coll; Germantown Hospital Records, 1860s to 1990s; Germantown Industries & Architecture Coll; Horticulture (Edwin C Jellett & Thomas Meehan Coll), bks, graphic works, personal papers; Local History Coll; PG & N Railroad Coll, 1800s to 1900s; Photograph Coll, 1849 to present; Pre-Photographic Images, etchings, paintings, posters; War of the Revolution & Civil War Colls. Oral History
Subject Interests: African-Am hist, Chestnut Hill, Philadelphia, Genealogy, Germantown, Philadelphia, Mount Airy, Philadelphia, Philadelphia hist, 17th-20th Centuries
Wireless access
Function: Archival coll, Audio & video playback equip for onsite use, Copy machines, e-mail serv, Exhibits, Ref & res, Ref serv available, Ref serv in person, Res libr, Scanner, Spoken cassettes & CDs
Publications: Germantown Crier (Bi-annually)
Open Tues 9-1, Thurs & Sun 1-5
Restriction: Fee for pub use, In-house use for visitors, Limited access for the pub, Non-circulating, Not a lending libr, Open to pub for ref only, Pub use on premises, Restricted pub use
Friends of the Library Group

GLAXOSMITHKLINE PHARMACEUTICALS

S MARKETING LIBRARY*, One Franklin Plaza, 19101. (Mail add: PO Box 7929 FP 1260, 19101-7929), SAN 359-1271. Tel: 215-751-5576. FAX: 215-751-5509. *Bibliog Instr, Librn, Online Serv,* Doris Shalley; Staff 1 (Non-MLS 1)
Founded 1946
Library Holdings: Bk Titles 2,268; Bk Vols 2,391; Per Subs 216
Publications: Acquisitions Bulletin; Mark Alert (Quarterly)
Open Mon-Fri 8:30-4:30

S RESEARCH & DEVELOPMENT LIBRARY*, UW2322, 709 Swedeland Rd, King of Prussia, 19406-2799. (Mail add: PO Box 1539, King of Prussia, 19406-0939), SAN 359-1247. Tel: 610-270-6400. FAX: 610-270-4127. *Librn,* Robert Guerrero; Staff 12 (MLS 12)
Founded 1947
Library Holdings: Bk Titles 15,856; Bk Vols 17,510; Per Subs 800
Subject Interests: Biochem, Chem, Med, Microbiology, Pharm, Pharmacology
Publications: List of Recent Acquisitions
Restriction: Not open to pub

S GRAND ARMY OF THE REPUBLIC MUSEUM & LIBRARY*, 4278 Griscom St, 19124-3954. SAN 372-9176. Tel: 215-289-6484. E-mail: garmuslib@verizon.net. Web Site: www.garmuslib.org. *Pres,* Elmer Atkinson
Founded 1926
Library Holdings: Bk Vols 3,000
Special Collections: Original copies of Philadelphia Inquirer newspapers published 1861-1865
Subject Interests: Civil War
Function: Res libr
Open Tues 12-4, Wed 10-2
Restriction: Not a lending libr
Friends of the Library Group

S WILLET HAUSER ARCHITECTURAL GLASS LIBRARY*, 811 E Cayuga St, 19124. SAN 315-0275. Tel: 215-247-5721. Toll Free Tel: 877-709-4106. FAX: 215-533-2309. *Ref Serv,* Amy Pulliam. Subject Specialists: *Iconography of Philadelphia to 1930, Stained glass,* Amy Pulliam; Staff 1 (Non-MLS 1)
Library Holdings: Bk Titles 1,000; Per Subs 10
Special Collections: Out-of-Print Research Books on Costumes, Animals & Art; Willet Studio Archives
Subject Interests: Bible commentaries, Christian symbolism, Church archit, Lives of saints, Stained glass
Function: Ref serv available
Restriction: Not open to pub

S HAY GROUP*, Corporate Library, Wanamaker Bldg, 100 Penn Square E, 19107-3388. SAN 314-9242. Tel: 215-861-2434. FAX: 215-861-2102. *Librn,* Claire DiPardo; E-mail: claire_dipardo@haygroup.com
Library Holdings: Bk Vols 300; Per Subs 60
Subject Interests: Human res
Restriction: Not open to pub

S HISTORICAL SOCIETY OF PENNSYLVANIA, Library Division, 1300 Locust St, 19107-5699. SAN 314-9250. Tel: 215-732-6200. Interlibrary Loan Service Tel: 215-732-6200, Ext 219. Reference Tel: 215-732-6200, Ext 209. Administration Tel: 215-732-6200, Ext 237. FAX: 215-732-2680. E-mail: library@hsp.org, readyref@hsp.org. Web Site: www.hsp.org. *Sr Dir, Libr & Coll,* Lee Arnold; E-mail: larnold@hsp.org; *Dir, Presv & Conserv,* Tara O'Brien; Tel: 215-732-6200, Ext 245, E-mail: tobrien@hsp.org; *Dir, Archives & Coll Mgt,* Matthew Lyons; Tel: 215-732-6200, Ext 301, E-mail: mlyons@hsp.org; *Dir, Digital Coll,* Cathleen Lu; Tel: 215-732-6200, Ext 249, E-mail: clu@hsp.org; *Dir, Res Serv,* David Haugaard; E-mail: dhaugaard@hsp.org; *Asst Dir, Res Serv,* Sarah Heim; Tel: 215-732-6200, Ext 261, E-mail: sheim@hsp.org; *Head, Ref Serv, Historian,* Dr Daniel N Rolph; Tel: 215-732-6200, Ext 203, E-mail: drolph@hsp.org; *Cataloger,* Willhem Echevarria; Tel: 215-732-6200, Ext 206, E-mail: wechevarria@hsp.org. Subject Specialists: *Archives, Genealogy,* Lee Arnold; *Bk arts, Conserv, Presv,* Tara O'Brien; *Archives, Manuscripts,* Matthew Lyons; *Copyright, Digital asset mgt,* Cathleen Lu; *Biog, Genealogy, Pa hist,* David Haugaard; *Hist of med, Women's hist,* Sarah Heim; *Civil War, Folklore, Genealogy,* Dr Daniel N Rolph; *Cataloging, Music hist, Music performance,* Willhem Echevarria; Staff 17 (MLS 7, Non-MLS 10)
Founded 1824
Library Holdings: AV Mats 1,235; Microforms 28,000; Bk Vols 560,000; Per Subs 2,000; Videos 164
Special Collections: Atlantis National Daily Greek Newspapers; Delaware Valley, architectural drawings & maps, photos, prints; Economic, Social & Political History of Middle Colonies & States, 1650s-present (including Papers of William Penn & the Penn Family, John Dickinson, James Buchanan, George Mifflin Dallas, Jay Cooke, James Logan, Salmon P Chase & Joel R Poinsett); Ethnic & Immigrant Experience in the US since 1877 (Balch Institute Coll), audio rec, bks, newsp, organizational rec, pamphlets, personal papers, photos; Fiorani Radio Production Records; Indian Rights Association Archives; Leonard Covello Papers; Nelson Diaz Papers; Pennsylvania Abolition Society Archives; Scots Thistle Society Coll; Shigezo & Sonoko Iwata Papers; Simon Gratz & Ferdinand J Dreer Autograph Colls
Subject Interests: Genealogical, Hist, Mats dealing with the Delaware Valley region, Original thirteen colonies
Automation Activity & Vendor Info: (Acquisitions) Ex Libris Group; (Cataloging) Ex Libris Group; (OPAC) Ex Libris Group; (Serials) Ex Libris Group
Database Vendor: Ex Libris Group
Wireless access
Function: Res libr
Publications: Guide to the Balch Collections (Collection catalog); Guide to the Manuscript Collection of the Historical Society of Pennsylvania (Collection catalog); HSP Sidelights (Newsletter); Pennsylvania Legacies (Periodical); Pennsylvania Magazine of History & Biography (Quarterly); Serving History in a Changing World by Sally Griffith
Partic in Philadelphia Area Consortium for the History of Science (PACHS); Philadelphia Area Consortium of Special Collections Libraries
Open Tues & Thurs 12:30-5:30, Wed 12:30-8:30, Fri 10-5:30
Restriction: Non-circulating

CR HOLY FAMILY UNIVERSITY LIBRARY*, 9801 Frankford Ave, 19114. SAN 314-9269. Tel: 267-341-3315, 267-341-3316. Interlibrary Loan Service Tel: 267-341-3584. Administration Tel: 267-341-3314. Automation Services Tel: 267-341-3312. FAX: 215-632-8067. E-mail: reference@holyfamily.edu. Web Site: www.holyfamily.edu/library. *Dir of Libr Serv,* Denise Avellino; *Ref Serv Librn,* Robert Ellermeyer; *Syst Librn,* Richard James; *Tech Serv Librn,* Shannon Brown; *ILL Coordr,* Debby Kramer; *Learning Res Ctr Coordr,* Katherine Ruppel; Tel: 267-341-4010, Fax: 215-504-2050; *Acq/Ser Asst,* Florence Tilsner; *Circ/Ser Asst,* Lee Carr; *Learning Res Ctr Asst,* Cris Runowski; Staff 5 (MLS 5)
Founded 1954. Enrl 2,178; Fac 350; Highest Degree: Doctorate
Library Holdings: DVDs 2,930; e-books 17,776; Bk Vols 96,900
Subject Interests: Arts, Bus, Catholicism, Counseling psychol, Criminal justice, Educ, Nursing, Relig, Sciences

Automation Activity & Vendor Info: (Acquisitions) SirsiDynix; (Cataloging) SirsiDynix; (Circulation) SirsiDynix; (Course Reserve) SirsiDynix; (ILL) OCLC Online; (OPAC) SirsiDynix; (Serials) SirsiDynix
Database Vendor: Alexander Street Press, American Psychological Association (APA), Annual Reviews, Children's Literature Comprehensive Database Company (CLCD), CredoReference, EBSCO Information Services, EBSCOhost, Facts on File, Faulkner Information Services, Hoovers, JSTOR, OCLC FirstSearch, OCLC WorldShare Interlibrary Loan, Sage, SirsiDynix
Wireless access
Function: Archival coll, Audio & video playback equip for onsite use, Computers for patron use, Electronic databases & coll, Handicapped accessible, ILL available, Online cat, Online info literacy tutorials on the web & in blackboard, Online ref, Orientations, Photocopying/Printing, Ref serv available, Scanner, Telephone ref, Workshops
Publications: Library & Search Guides (Research guide)
Partic in Lyrasis; OCLC Online Computer Library Center, Inc; Southeastern Pa Consortium for Higher Educ; Tri State Col Libr Coop
Open Mon-Thurs 7:30am-11pm, Fri 7:30-5, Sat 11-5, Sun 11-11
Restriction: ID required to use computers (Ltd hrs), In-house use for visitors

S INDEPENDENCE SEAPORT MUSEUM LIBRARY, 211 S Columbus Blvd, 19106. SAN 314-9781. Tel: 215-413-8640. E-mail: library@phillyseaport.org. Web Site: www.phillyseaport.org. *Dir, Libr & Archives,* Sarah Newhouse; E-mail: snewhouse@phillyseaport.org; Staff 1 (MLS 1)
Founded 1974
Library Holdings: Bk Titles 14,000; Bk Vols 15,000; Per Subs 35
Special Collections: Manuscript Coll; Map & Chart Coll; Philadelphia Area Shipbuilding (NY Shipbuilding Corp, Cramp Shipbuilding Co), vessel registers; Photograph Coll; Rare Book Coll
Subject Interests: Maritime heritage of the Delaware, Naval sci, Port of Philadelphia, S Jersey maritime hist
Function: Archival coll, Exhibits, Ref & res, Ref serv available, Res libr
Publications: John Lenthall, Naval Architect: A Guide to Plans & Drawings of American Naval & Merchant Vessels 1790-1874; Massachusetts Steam Navigation Company, Salem, Massachusetts Records (1816-1818) & the Newhall Family Business Papers (1809-1852): A Descriptive Guide; Shipbuilding at Cramp & Sons: A History & Guide to Collections of the William Cramp & Sons Ship & Engine Building Company (1830-1927) & the Cramp Shipbuilding Company (1941-46) of Philadelphia
Partic in OCLC Online Computer Library Center, Inc
Restriction: Non-circulating, Open by appt only

L JENKINS LAW LIBRARY, 833 Chestnut St, Ste 1220, 19107-4429. SAN 314-9366. Tel: 215-574-7900. Circulation Tel: 215-574-1500. Interlibrary Loan Service Tel: 215-574-7933. Reference Tel: 215-574-1505. Automation Services Tel: 215-574-7907. FAX: 215-574-7920. Circulation FAX: 215-574-7921. Reference FAX: 215-925-2105. Automation Services FAX: 215-574-7910. E-mail: research@jenkinslaw.org. Web Site: www.jenkinslaw.org. *Exec Dir,* Regina L Smith; Tel: 215-574-7904, E-mail: rsmith@jenkinslaw.org; *Asst Dir, Bus Serv,* Ida Weingram; Tel: 215-574-7935, E-mail: iweingram@jenkinslaw.org; *Asst Dir, Knowledge Serv,* Nancy Garner; Tel: 215-574-7944, E-mail: ngarner@jenkinslaw.org; *Asst Dir, Tech,* Andrew Sather; Tel: 215-574-7903, E-mail: asather@jenkinslaw.org; *Cat Librn,* Sheila Walker; Tel: 215-574-7957, E-mail: swalker@jenkinslaw.org; *Ref Librn,* Michelle Buhalo; Tel: 215-574-7911, E-mail: mbuhalo@jenkinslaw.org; *Ref Librn,* Geoff Matis; Tel: 215-574-7930, E-mail: gmatis@jenkinslaw.org; *Ref Librn,* Carey Sias; Tel: 215-574-7948, E-mail: csias@jenkinslaw.org; *Ref Librn,* Michael Sweeney; Tel: 215-574-7946, E-mail: msweeney@jenkinslaw.org; *Educ Serv Mgr,* Dan Giancaterino; Tel: 215-574-7945, E-mail: dgiancaterino@jenkinslaw.org; *Libr Syst Mgr,* Katrina Piechnik; Tel: 215-574-7907, E-mail: kpiechnik@jenkinslaw.org; *Res Serv Mgr,* Jenny Hohenstein; Tel: 215-574-7941, E-mail: jhohenstein@jenkinslaw.org; *ILL Coordr,* Matthew Thomas; E-mail: mthomas@jenkinslaw.org; Staff 28 (MLS 13, Non-MLS 15)
Founded 1802
Jan 2013-Dec 2013 Income $4,883,066, Locally Generated Income $1,235,042, Other $3,648,024. Mats Exp $1,532,502, Books $50,286, Per/Ser (Incl. Access Fees) $988,682, Other Print Mats $1,132, Micro $7,431, AV Mat $189, Electronic Ref Mat (Incl. Access Fees) $478,777, Presv $6,005. Sal $1,756,023 (Prof $1,056,125)
Special Collections: Roman & Canon Law (John Marshall Gest Coll). State Document Depository
Automation Activity & Vendor Info: (Acquisitions) Innovative Interfaces, Inc; (Cataloging) Innovative Interfaces, Inc; (Circulation) Innovative Interfaces, Inc; (ILL) OCLC; (OPAC) Innovative Interfaces, Inc; (Serials) SerialsSolutions
Database Vendor: 3M Library Systems, Bloomberg, Dialog, Dun & Bradstreet, Fastcase, Gale Cengage Learning, HeinOnline, Innovative Interfaces, Inc, LexisNexis, Medline, Newsbank, OCLC, OCLC FirstSearch, OCLC WorldShare Interlibrary Loan, ProQuest, SerialsSolutions, Standard & Poor's, Westlaw
Wireless access
Function: Audio & video playback equip for onsite use, Copy machines, Distance learning, Doc delivery serv, e-mail serv, Electronic databases & coll, ILL available, Online cat, Online searches, Orientations, Photocopying/Printing, Ref & res, Ref serv available, Spoken cassettes & CDs, Spoken cassettes & DVDs, Tax forms, Telephone ref, Web-catalog, Wheelchair accessible, Workshops
Publications: Jenkins Flash (Current awareness service)
Partic in Mid-Atlantic Law Library Cooperative; OCLC Online Computer Library Center, Inc
Special Services for the Blind - Screen enlargement software for people with visual disabilities
Open Mon, Tues, Thurs & Fri 8:30-6, Wed 8:30-7
Restriction: Fee for pub use, Limited access for the pub, Mem only, Non-circulating to the pub, Restricted pub use, Sub libr

L KLEHR, HARRISON, HARVEY, BRANZBURG & ELLERS*, Law Library, 260 S Broad St, 19102-5003. SAN 376-1584. Tel: 215-568-6060. FAX: 215-568-6603. Web Site: www.klehr.com. *Librn,* Margaret S Fallon; Tel: 215-569-3091, E-mail: mfallon@klehr.com; Staff 3 (MLS 1, Non-MLS 2)
Library Holdings: Bk Titles 12,198; Bk Vols 15,160; Per Subs 32
Database Vendor: LexisNexis

C LA SALLE UNIVERSITY*, Connelly Library, 1900 W Olney Ave, 19141-1199. SAN 314-9382. Tel: 215-951-1287. Circulation Tel: 215-751-1293. Interlibrary Loan Service Tel: 215-951-1862. FAX: 215-951-1595. Web Site: www.lasalle.edu/library. *Dir,* John S Baky; Tel: 215-951-1286, E-mail: baky@lasalle.edu; *Access Serv, Circ Serv,* Christopher Kibler; *Bibliog Instr,* Bernetta Doane; Tel: 215-951-1962, E-mail: doane@lasalle.edu; Staff 14 (MLS 10, Non-MLS 4)
Founded 1863. Enrl 4,000; Fac 150; Highest Degree: Doctorate
Library Holdings: Bk Titles 362,819; Bk Vols 365,411; Per Subs 4,789; Videos 1,088
Special Collections: Charles Willson Peale Coll; Germantowniana Coll; Graham Green; Japanese Tea Ceremony; Katherine Ann Porter Coll; Lasalliana; Vietnam War; Walker Percy Coll
Subject Interests: Holocaust, Vietnam War
Database Vendor: Dialog, EBSCOhost, Innovative Interfaces, Inc, JSTOR, LexisNexis, OCLC FirstSearch, OVID Technologies, ProQuest, SirsiDynix
Function: Res libr
Publications: Connelly Chronicle; Newsletter (Quarterly)
Partic in Pennsylvania Academic Library Consortium, Inc (PALCI)
Open Mon-Thurs 8am-Midnight, Fri 8-8, Sat 10-6, Sun Noon-Midnight

S LIBRARY COMPANY OF PHILADELPHIA, 1314 Locust St, 19107-5698. SAN 314-9404. Tel: 215-546-3181. FAX: 215-546-5167. Web Site: www.librarycompany.org. *Dir,* Dr Richard S Newman; E-mail: rsnewman@librarycompany.org; *Librn,* James N Green; E-mail: jgreen@librarycompany.org; *Chief of Ref,* Cornelia S King; E-mail: cking@librarycompany.org; *Curator, Photog & Prints,* Sarah Weatherwax; E-mail: printroom@librarycompany.org; Staff 17 (MLS 5, Non-MLS 12)
Founded 1731
Library Holdings: Bk Titles 500,000
Special Collections: American Imprints to 1880; American Judaica to 1850; American Technology & Business to 1860; Early American Imprints (Zinman Coll); Early American Natural History, Agriculture, Education & Philanthropy (Afro-American Coll); English & American Literature Coll; German Americana to 1830; Libraries of William Byrd, Benjamin Franklin, James Logan, Benjamin Rush & other Early American Book Collectors; Philadelphiana bks, prints; Popular Medicine to 1880; Prints & Photographs of Philadelphia to 1930
Subject Interests: 18th Century med, 18th Century sci, 19th Century women's hist, African-Am, Am archit, Am political hist, Background of Am civilization to 1880, Bookbinding, Early 19th Century med, Early 19th Century sci, Econ hist, Hist, Iconography of Philadelphia to 1930, Women's hist
Automation Activity & Vendor Info: (Cataloging) OCLC Connexion; (OPAC) Ex Libris Group
Database Vendor: Backstage Library Works, Ex Libris Group, Newsbank, OCLC-RLG
Wireless access
Publications: Annual Report; Exhibition Catalogues; Newsletter
Partic in Independent Res Libr Asn; Philadelphia Area Consortium for the History of Science (PACHS); Philadelphia Area Consortium of Special Collections Libraries
Open Mon-Fri 9-4:45
Friends of the Library Group

R LUTHERAN THEOLOGICAL SEMINARY, Krauth Memorial Library, 7301 Germantown Ave, 19119-1794. SAN 314-9412. Tel: 215-248-6329. Interlibrary Loan Service Tel: 215-248-6334. FAX: 215-248-6327. E-mail: request@ltsp.edu. Web Site: www.ltsp.edu/krauth/index.html. *Coll Develop,*

Dir, Karl Krueger; Tel: 215-248-6330, E-mail: kkrueger@ltsp.edu; *Acq, ILL Librn,* Ronald Townsend; E-mail: rtownsend@ltsp.edu; *Archivist,* John Peterson; Tel: 215-248-6383, E-mail: mtairyarchives@ltsp.edu; *Pub Serv Asst,* Sharon Baker; Staff 4 (MLS 2, Non-MLS 2)
Founded 1864. Enrl 450; Fac 18; Highest Degree: Doctorate
Library Holdings: Bk Titles 200,000; Per Subs 470
Special Collections: Lutheran Archives, Region 7
Subject Interests: Archit, Evangelical Lutheran Church in Am, Liturgy, Lutheran hist, Relig, Relig art, Urban studies, Women
Automation Activity & Vendor Info: (Cataloging) Ex Libris Group; (Circulation) Ex Libris Group; (OPAC) Ex Libris Group
Wireless access
Partic in Lyrasis; OCLC Online Computer Library Center, Inc; Philadelphia Area Consortium of Special Collections Libraries; Southeastern Pennsylvania Theological Library Association
Open Mon-Thurs (Fall & Spring) 8:30am-9pm, Fri 8:30-4:30, Sat 9-3; Mon-Fri (Summer) 8:30-4:30

M MAGEE REHABILITATION HOSPITAL*, Patient Learning Resource Center Library, 1513 Race St, 19102. SAN 326-1611. Tel: 215-587-3423. FAX: 215-568-3533. *Libr Serv Mgr,* Vera Bradley; E-mail: vbradley@mageerehab.org
Library Holdings: Bk Titles 500; Bk Vols 550; Per Subs 80
Open Mon, Wed & Thurs 9:30-8, Tues & Fri 9:30-5, Sat 12-3, Sun 12-5

S THE MASONIC LIBRARY & MUSEUM OF PENNSYLVANIA, Masonic Temple, One N Broad St, 19107-2520. SAN 314-9099. Tel: 215-988-1933. FAX: 215-988-1953. Web Site: www.pagrandlodge.org. *Librn,* Dr Glenys A Waldman; Tel: 215-988-1908, E-mail: gawaldman@pagrandlodge.org; *Asst Librn,* Catherine L Giaimo; E-mail: clgiaimo@pagrandlodge.org; *Curator,* Dennis P Buttleman; Tel: 215-988-1485, E-mail: dpbuttleman@pagrandlodge.org; Staff 3 (MLS 2, Non-MLS 1)
Founded 1817
Library Holdings: Bk Vols 75,000; Spec Interest Per Sub 90
Special Collections: General Works on Freemasonry; Masonic Biography & General History; Masonic Manuscript Coll
Subject Interests: Freemasonry, Hist, Philos, Relig
Automation Activity & Vendor Info: (Cataloging) SydneyPlus
Function: Archival coll, Ref serv available
Publications: Grand Lodge Proceedings (Annual); The Pennsylvania Freemason (Quarterly)
Restriction: Circ to mem only, Fee for pub use, In-house use for visitors

M MERCY PHILADELPHIA HOSPITAL*, Medical Library, 501 S 54th St, 2 Main, Rm 234, 19143. SAN 320-4596. Tel: 215-748-9415. FAX: 215-748-9341. *Mgr, Libr Serv,* Ann Marie Zglinicki; E-mail: azglinicki@mercyhealth.org; Staff 1 (MLS 1)
Founded 1918
Library Holdings: Bk Vols 1,035; Per Subs 85
Subject Interests: Med
Partic in Basic Health Sciences Library Network; Consortium for Health Information & Library Services; Health Science Library Information Consortium
Open Mon-Fri 8:30-5

S MONELL CHEMICAL SENSES CENTER*, Morley R Kare Library, 3500 Market St, 19104-3308. SAN 322-9181. Tel: 215-898-6666. FAX: 215-898-2084. Web Site: www.monell.org. *Librn,* Joseph Brand; *Asst Librn,* Douglas Bayley; Staff 2 (Non-MLS 2)
Library Holdings: Bk Titles 830; Bk Vols 951; Per Subs 16
Subject Interests: Chem senses, Nutrition
Restriction: Open by appt only

L MONTGOMERY, MCCRACKEN, WALKER & RHOADS LLP LIBRARY*, 123 S Broad St, 19109. SAN 314-948X. Tel: 215-772-7611. FAX: 215-772-7620. Web Site: www.mmwr.com. *Dir,* Kathleen Coon; E-mail: kcoon@mmwr.com; Staff 3 (MLS 2, Non-MLS 1)
Library Holdings: Bk Titles 8,961; Bk Vols 15,000; Per Subs 162
Subject Interests: Law
Open Mon-Fri 8:30-4:30

C MOORE COLLEGE OF ART & DESIGN*, Connelly Library, 20th St & The Parkway, 19103-1179. SAN 314-9498. Tel: 215-965-4054. FAX: 215-965-8544. Web Site: library.moore.edu. *Cat, Dir,* Sharon Watson-Mauro; Tel: 215-965-8582, E-mail: swmauro@moore.edu; *Curator,* Helen F McGinnis; Tel: 215-965-4058, E-mail: hmcginnis@moore.edu; *Archivist,* Annabelle Curran; Tel: 215-965-4057, E-mail: acurran@moore.edu; *AV, Media Spec,* Charles Duquesne; Tel: 215-965-4060, E-mail: cduquesne@moore.edu; *Circ Supvr,* Alison Macrina; E-mail: amacrina@moore.edu; Staff 6 (MLS 3, Non-MLS 3)
Founded 1848. Enrl 400; Highest Degree: Bachelor
Library Holdings: Bk Vols 40,000; Per Subs 110
Special Collections: Bookworks Coll, artists' books; Joseph Moore Jr Coll; Philadelphia School of Design for Women Archives
Subject Interests: Art hist, Prof, Studio arts, Women's studies in visual arts
Automation Activity & Vendor Info: (Cataloging) Innovative Interfaces, Inc; (Circulation) Innovative Interfaces, Inc; (ILL) Innovative Interfaces, Inc; (OPAC) Innovative Interfaces, Inc; (Serials) Innovative Interfaces, Inc
Partic in OCLC Online Computer Library Center, Inc; Tri State Col Libr Coop
Open Mon-Thurs 8am-10pm, Fri 8-5, Sat 8:30-5

L MORGAN, LEWIS & BOCKIUS LLP*, Law Library, 1701 Market St, 13th Flr, 19103-2921. SAN 314-9501. Tel: 215-963-5000. FAX: 215-963-5001. Toll Free FAX: 877-432-9652. Web Site: www.morganlewis.com. *Dir, Libr Serv, Head Librn,* Connie Smith; E-mail: cbsmith@morganlewis.com; Staff 8 (MLS 5, Non-MLS 3)
Founded 1873
Library Holdings: Bk Titles 47,890; Bk Vols 49,610; Per Subs 212
Subject Interests: Legal mat, Pa law
Automation Activity & Vendor Info: (Acquisitions) Innovative Interfaces, Inc; (Cataloging) Innovative Interfaces, Inc; (Circulation) Innovative Interfaces, Inc; (OPAC) Innovative Interfaces, Inc; (Serials) Innovative Interfaces, Inc
Database Vendor: LexisNexis, Westlaw
Restriction: Open to pub upon request, Staff use only

NATIONAL ARCHIVES & RECORDS ADMINISTRATION

G MID ATLANTIC REGION (CENTER CITY PHILADELPHIA), 14700 Townsend Rd, 19154. Tel: 215-305-9347. FAX: 215-305-2052. E-mail: philadelphia.archives@nara.gov. Web Site: www.archives.gov/philadelphia. *Archives Dir,* Leslie Simon; E-mail: leslie.simon@nara.gov; *Admin Officer,* Brenda Bernard; Tel: 215-305-2007, E-mail: brenda.bernard@nara.gov
Special Collections: Archival Records of Federal Agencies & Courts in Delaware, Maryland, Pennsylvania, Virginia & West Virginia; Indian Affairs Records, microfilm; Passenger Arrival & Naturalization Records, microfilm; Population Censuses for All States, 1790-1930, microfilm; Pre-Federal & Early Federal History, microfilm; Pre-World War I Military Service Records, microfilm; US Diplomacy Records, microfilm; World War II Fourth Enumeration Draft Cards
Function: Photocopying/Printing
Open Mon-Fri 8-5
Restriction: Ref only to non-staff

G MID ATLANTIC REGION (NORTHEAST PHILADELPHIA), 14700 Townsend Rd, 19154-1096. SAN 314-9528. Tel: 215-305-9347. FAX: 215-305-2052. Web Site: www.archives.gov/midatlantic. *Dir,* Leslie Simon; Staff 8 (MLS 3, Non-MLS 5)
Founded 1968
Library Holdings: Bk Titles 350
Special Collections: Genealogy (United States Census Schedules, 1790-1920), micro; United States District Courts Records (Delaware, Maryland, Pennsylvania, Virginia, West Virginia)
Publications: Research Sources in the Archives Branch
Open Mon-Fri 8-4:30

S NATIONAL PARK SERVICE INDEPENDENCE NATIONAL HISTORICAL PARK*, Library & Archives, Merchants Exchange Bldg, 3rd Flr, 143 S Third St, 19106. SAN 314-9536. Tel: 215-597-8047. FAX: 215-597-3969. Web Site: www.nps.gov/inde/library-and-archives.htm. *Archivist, Libr Mgr,* Christina Higgins; Tel: 215-597-2069; *Libr Tech,* Andrea Ashby; E-mail: andrea_ashby@nps.gov; Staff 2 (MLS 1, Non-MLS 1)
Founded 1951
Library Holdings: Bk Titles 11,292; Bk Vols 12,631; Per Subs 10
Special Collections: Edwin Owen Lewis Papers, 1927-1974; History & Restoration of Independence Hall (Horace Wells Sellers Coll, 1730-1930); Isidor Ostroff Papers, 1941-1968; National Museum Board of Managers Records, 1873-1918 (collected by William H Staake, Ellen Waln Harrison & Mary B Chew); Philadelphia Bureau of City Property, Independence Hall Records, 1896-1950; The Independence Hall Association Records, 1906-1962; The Morris Family Papers associated with the Deshler-Morris House in Germantown. Oral History
Subject Interests: 18th Century Philadelphia, Am decorative arts of the 18th century, Constitution politics, Hist
Function: Archival coll, Ref serv available
Restriction: Circulates for staff only, In-house use for visitors, Open by appt only

S NATIONAL RAILWAY HISTORICAL SOCIETY LIBRARY*, 100 N 20th St, 4th Flr, 19103. SAN 327-0572. Tel: 215-557-6606. FAX: 215-557-6740. E-mail: info@nrhs.com. Web Site: www.nrhs.com. *Exec Dir,* Kristen Olszewski
Library Holdings: Bk Vols 10,000
Subject Interests: Railway hist of N Am
Function: Res libr

S NEW YEAR SHOOTERS & MUMMERS MUSEUM LIBRARY*, 1100 S Second St, 19147. SAN 328-297X. Tel: 215-336-3050. FAX: 215-389-5630. E-mail: mummersmus@aol.com. Web Site: www.mummers.com. *Dir,* Palma Lucas; *Curator,* Jack Cohen
Library Holdings: Per Subs 200
Restriction: Open by appt only
Friends of the Library Group

S DONALD F & MILDRED TOPP OTHMER LIBRARY OF CHEMICAL HISTORY, 315 Chestnut St, 19106. SAN 326-6885. Tel: 215-873-8205. Circulation Tel: 215-873-8250. Reference Tel: 215-873-8269. Automation Services Tel: 215-873-8257. FAX: 215-629-5205. Reference FAX: 215-629-5269. Automation Services FAX: 215-629-5257. E-mail: reference@chemheritage.org. Web Site: chemheritage.org/library/library.html, othmerlib.chemheritage.org. *Dir, Libr Serv,* Elsa B Atson; E-mail: eatson@chemheritage.org; *Arnold Thackray Dir,* Ronald Brashear; E-mail: rbrashear@chemheritage.org; *Librn I,* Victoria Valusek; E-mail: vvalusek@chemheritage.org; *Tech Serv Librn,* Andrea Tomlinson; E-mail: andreat@chemheritage.org; *Ref Librn/Fel Coordr,* Ashley Augustniak; E-mail: aaugustyniak@chemheritage.org; *Chief Curator, Archives & Ms,* Patrick Shea; E-mail: PShea@chemheritage.org; *Curator, Rare Bks,* James Voelkel; E-mail: jvoelkel@chemheritage.org; *Digital Coll Curator,* Michelle DiMeo; E-mail: meimeo@chemheritage.org; *Image Coll,* Hillary S Kativa; E-mail: HKativa@chemheritage.org; *Sr Archivist,* Andrew Mangravite; E-mail: AndrewM@chemheritage.org
Founded 1988
Library Holdings: e-books 3,307; e-journals 1,954; Microforms 336; Bk Titles 61,338; Bk Vols 115,702; Per Subs 100; Videos 400
Special Collections: Roy G Neville Historical Chemical Library. Oral History
Subject Interests: Hist of chem
Automation Activity & Vendor Info: (Cataloging) Innovative Interfaces, Inc; (Circulation) Innovative Interfaces, Inc; (ILL) Innovative Interfaces, Inc; (OPAC) Innovative Interfaces, Inc; (Serials) Innovative Interfaces, Inc
Database Vendor: 3M Library Systems, Dialog, Innovative Interfaces, Inc, JSTOR, Marquis Who's Who, OCLC FirstSearch, OCLC WorldShare Interlibrary Loan, OCLC-RLG, Project MUSE
Wireless access
Function: Res libr
Publications: Boltonia (Newsletter); Chemical Heritage
Partic in OCLC Online Computer Library Center, Inc; Philadelphia Area Consortium of Special Collections Libraries; RLIN (Research Libraries Information Network)
Open Mon-Fri 10-4
Restriction: Non-circulating to the pub

C PEIRCE COLLEGE LIBRARY*, 1420 Pine St, 19102-4699. SAN 314-9846. Tel: 215-670-9269. FAX: 215-670-9338. E-mail: library@peirce.edu. Web Site: library.peirce.edu. *Chief Librn,* Debra S Schrammel; Tel: 215-670-9269, Ext 9270; *Access Serv, Ref Serv,* John Powell; *Ref,* Gary Shecter; *Ref & Instruction Librn,* Bart Everts; Staff 6 (MLS 4, Non-MLS 2)
Founded 1963
Library Holdings: Bk Titles 42,610; Bk Vols 44,190; Per Subs 161
Special Collections: Law Coll
Automation Activity & Vendor Info: (Cataloging) Softlink America; (Circulation) Softlink America; (Course Reserve) Softlink America; (OPAC) Softlink America
Database Vendor: CredoReference, ebrary, EBSCOhost, Hoovers, LexisNexis, ProQuest, Westlaw
Wireless access
Open Mon-Thurs 8am-8:30pm, Fri 8-7, Sat 10-4

M PENN PRESBYTERIAN MEDICAL CENTER*, Health Sciences Library, 39th & Market St, 19104. SAN 314-9862. Tel: 215-662-9575. FAX: 215-243-3200. *Librn,* Rebecca Landau; E-mail: rebecca.landau@uphs.upenn.edu
Founded 1972
Library Holdings: Bk Vols 100
Subject Interests: Allied health, Med, Nursing
Wireless access
Restriction: Not open to pub

S PENNSYLVANIA ACADEMY OF FINE ARTS LIBRARY*, 128 N Broad St, 19102. SAN 314-9617. Tel: 215-972-7600, Ext 2030. FAX: 215-569-0153. E-mail: library@pafa.org. *Head Librn,* Brian Duffy; E-mail: bduffy@pafa.edu; *Asst Librn,* Rick Henderson; Staff 2 (MLS 1, Non-MLS 1)
Library Holdings: Bk Titles 14,500; Per Subs 89
Subject Interests: Visual arts
Wireless access

S PENNSYLVANIA HORTICULTURAL SOCIETY*, McLean Library, 100 N 20th St, 19103-1495. SAN 314-9641. Tel: 215-988-8772. Reference Tel: 215-988-8782. FAX: 215-988-8783. E-mail: mcleanlibrary@pennhort.org. Web Site: www.pennsylvaniahorticulturalsociety.org. *Mgr,* Janet Evans; E-mail: jevans@pennhort.org
Founded 1827
Library Holdings: Bk Titles 14,000; Per Subs 200
Special Collections: 15th-20th Century Horticultural Material; Pennsylvania Horticulture, Herbals, Medical Botany, rare bks
Subject Interests: Botany, Early Am horticulture, Landscape design, Specifically Pennsylvania
Partic in Lyrasis; OCLC Online Computer Library Center, Inc; Philadelphia Area Consortium of Special Collections Libraries
Open Mon-Fri 9-5

PENNSYLVANIA HOSPITAL

M HISTORIC LIBRARY*, Three Pine Ctr, 800 Spruce St, 19107-6192, SAN 359-0763. Tel: 215-829-5434. FAX: 215-829-7155. Web Site: www.uphs.upenn.edu/paharc/collections/library.html. *Archivist,* Stacey C Peeples; E-mail: peepless@pahosp.com; Staff 1 (Non-MLS 1)
Founded 1762
Library Holdings: Bk Titles 13,681; Bk Vols 15,459; Per Subs 16
Special Collections: Benjamin Smith Barton; Lloyd Zachary; The Meigs Family; Thomas Story Kirkbride; William Byrd of Westover
Subject Interests: Anatomy, Botany, Med texts from 1700 to 1930, Natural hist, Obstetrics, Psychiat, Surgery
Function: Archival coll
Open Mon-Fri 9-4:30
Restriction: Non-circulating
Friends of the Library Group

M MEDICAL LIBRARY*, Three Pine Ctr, 800 Spruce St, 19107-6192, SAN 359-0798. Tel: 215-829-3370. FAX: 215-829-7155. E-mail: libraryservices@pahosp.com. Web Site: www.uphs.upenn.edu/pahedu/library. *Dir,* Position Currently Open; *Librn,* Lydia Witman; *Archivist, Curator,* Stacey Peeples; E-mail: stacey.peeples@uphs.upenn.edu; *Libr Asst,* Tom Hanley; Staff 3 (MLS 2, Non-MLS 1)
Founded 1940
Library Holdings: Bk Titles 19,782; Bk Vols 22,640; Per Subs 200
Subject Interests: Allied health, Hist of med, Hist of Pa hosp, Hist of psychiat, Med, Nursing, Psychiat, Psychoanalysis
Open Mon-Fri 9-4

S PENNSYLVANIA SCHOOL FOR THE DEAF LIBRARY*, 100 W School House Lane, 19144. SAN 327-0599. Tel: 215-951-4743. FAX: 215-951-4708. E-mail: library@psd.org. *Librn,* Janice VanGorden; E-mail: jvangorden@psd.org
Founded 1820
Library Holdings: Bks on Deafness & Sign Lang 4,000; DVDs 600; Bk Vols 24,000; Per Subs 13; Spec Interest Per Sub 5
Wireless access
Special Services for the Deaf - Adult & family literacy prog; Assistive tech; Bks on deafness & sign lang; Closed caption videos; Coll on deaf educ; Deaf publ; Staff with knowledge of sign lang; TDD equip; Video & TTY relay via computer
Open Mon-Fri 8-4

L PEPPER HAMILTON LLP*, Law Library, 3000 Two Logan Sq, 18th & Arch Sts, 19103-2799. SAN 314-965X. Tel: 215-981-4100, 215-981-4636. Circulation Tel: 215-981-4107. Interlibrary Loan Service Tel: 215-981-4105. Reference Tel: 215-981-4104. Automation Services Tel: 215-981-4101. FAX: 215-981-4750. E-mail: library@pepperlaw.com. *Dir, Libr & Res Serv,* Robyn L Beyer; E-mail: beyerr@pepperlaw.com; Staff 9 (MLS 5, Non-MLS 4)
Library Holdings: Bk Vols 35,000; Per Subs 500
Subject Interests: Law, Med
Automation Activity & Vendor Info: (Acquisitions) Softlink America; (Cataloging) Softlink America; (Circulation) Softlink America; (OPAC) Softlink America; (Serials) Softlink America
Database Vendor: Dialog, LexisNexis, OCLC FirstSearch, Westlaw
Function: For res purposes, ILL available
Partic in Dialog Corp; Westlaw
Restriction: Access at librarian's discretion, Private libr

CM PHILADELPHIA COLLEGE OF OSTEOPATHIC MEDICINE*, O J Snyder Memorial Library, 4170 City Ave, 19131-1694. SAN 314-9692. Tel: 215-871-6470. FAX: 215-871-6489. E-mail: library@pcom.edu. Web Site: library.pcom.edu. *Exec Dir,* Etheldra Templeton; *Assoc Dir,* Stephanie Ferretti; Tel: 215-871-6475, E-mail: stephaniefe@pcom.edu; *Electronic Res Librn,* Christine Davidian; *Cat,* Mitzi Killeen; *Circ,* Julia Lewis; *ILL,* Randall Blackwell; Staff 10 (MLS 4, Non-MLS 6)
Founded 1899. Enrl 2,736; Highest Degree: Doctorate
Library Holdings: Bk Titles 18,501; Bk Vols 38,824; Per Subs 525
Special Collections: Archival History of Medicine; First Editions in Osteopathy; Osteopathic Periodicals
Subject Interests: Med, Osteopathic med, Psychol

Database Vendor: EBSCOhost, OVID Technologies, ProQuest
Publications: Archival Coll; Audio-Visual Coll; Bibliographies; Library Handbook; Library Newsletter; Osteopathic Coll; Osteopathic Colleges & Hospital Libraries Survey Book; Periodicals & Pamphlets; Union List of Osteopathic Literature
Partic in Pennsylvania Academic Library Consortium, Inc (PALCI); Tri-State College Library Cooperative
Restriction: 24-hr pass syst for students only, Authorized personnel only

S PHILADELPHIA CORPORATION FOR AGING LIBRARY*, 642 N Broad St, 19130-3049. SAN 327-0696. Tel: 215-765-9000, Ext 5062. FAX: 215-765-9066. Web Site: www.pcacares.org/pca_learn_pca_library_online.aspx. *Librn,* Scott Spencer, E-mail: sspencer@pcaphl.org. Subject Specialists: *Aging,* Scott Spencer; Staff 2 (MLS 1, Non-MLS 1)
Founded 1978
Library Holdings: Bk Titles 3,839; Per Subs 100
Automation Activity & Vendor Info: (Acquisitions) Inmagic, Inc.; (Cataloging) Inmagic, Inc.; (Circulation) Inmagic, Inc.; (ILL) Inmagic, Inc.; (OPAC) Inmagic, Inc.; (Serials) Inmagic, Inc.
Partic in National Network of Libraries of Medicine
Restriction: Open by appt only

S PHILADELPHIA HISTORICAL COMMISSION LIBRARY*, City Hall, Rm 576, 19107. Tel: 215-686-7660. FAX: 215-686-7674. Web Site: www.phila.gov/historical. *Presv Officer,* John Farnham
Library Holdings: Bk Titles 2,500; Bk Vols 3,000; Per Subs 10
Open Mon-Fri 8:30-5

S PHILADELPHIA MUSEUM OF ART LIBRARY*, Ruth & Raymond G Perelman Bldg, 2525 Pennsylvania Ave, 19130. (Mail add: PO Box 7646, 19101-7646), SAN 314-979X. Tel: 215-684-7650. FAX: 215-236-0534. E-mail: library@philamuseum.org. Web Site: www.philamuseum.org/library. *Arcadia Dir, Libr & Archives,* Position Currently Open; *Coll Develop Librn,* Mary Wassermann; Tel: 215-684-7654, E-mail: mwassermann@philamuseum.org; *Reader Serv Librn,* Evan Towle; Tel: 215-684-7645, E-mail: etowle@philamuseum.org; *Asst Reader Serv Librn,* Richard Sieber; Tel: 215-684-7646, E-mail: rsieber@philamuseum.org; *Tech Serv Librn,* Linda Martin-Schaff; Tel: 215-684-7655, E-mail: lschaff@philamuseum.org; *Martha Hamilton Morris Archivist,* Susan K Anderson; Tel: 215-684-7659, E-mail: skanderson@philamuseum.org; *Project Archivist,* Bertha Adams; Tel: 215-684-7643, E-mail: badams@philamuseum.org; Staff 10 (MLS 7, Non-MLS 3)
Founded 1876
Library Holdings: Bk Vols 210,000; Per Subs 450
Special Collections: Arms & Armor (Kienbusch Coll); Ars Medica; Art Auction Catalogues, 1741-present; European Painting (John G Johnson Coll)
Subject Interests: Am art, Arms, Ceramics, Conserv, Costumes, Decorative art, Drawings, Dutch hist, E Asian art, European painting, Indian arts, Photog, Prints, Sculpture, Textiles
Automation Activity & Vendor Info: (Acquisitions) Ex Libris Group; (Cataloging) Ex Libris Group; (Circulation) Ex Libris Group; (ILL) OCLC; (OPAC) Ex Libris Group; (Serials) Ex Libris Group
Database Vendor: ARTstor, EBSCOhost, Ex Libris Group, H W Wilson, Ingenta, JSTOR, OCLC FirstSearch, OCLC WorldShare Interlibrary Loan, OCLC-RLG, ProQuest, Wilson - Wilson Web
Wireless access
Partic in Lyrasis; OCLC Online Computer Library Center, Inc; Philadelphia Area Consortium of Special Collections Libraries
Open Tues-Fri 10-4
Restriction: Non-circulating

S PHILADELPHIA ORCHESTRA LIBRARY*, 300 S Broad St, 19102-4297. SAN 321-060X. Tel: 215-670-2343. FAX: 215-985-0746. *Head Librn,* Robert Grossman; E-mail: rgrossman@philorch.org; *Librn,* Nancy M Bradburd; Tel: 215-670-2342, E-mail: nbradburd@philorch.org; Staff 3 (MLS 1, Non-MLS 2)
Founded 1900
Library Holdings: Bk Titles 5,000; Bk Vols 10,000
Subject Interests: Orchestra performance, Sheet music
Function: Archival coll
Publications: Marcato (Newsletter)
Restriction: Mem only

C PHILADELPHIA UNIVERSITY*, Paul J Gutman Library, 4201 Henry Ave, 19144-5497. SAN 314-9722. Tel: 215-951-2840. Reference Tel: 215-951-2848. FAX: 215-951-2574. Web Site: www.philau.edu/library. *Dir,* Karen M Albert; Tel: 215-951-2847, E-mail: albertk@philau.edu; *Coll Develop Coordr, Spec Coll Librn,* Stanley Gorski; Tel: 215-951-2581, E-mail: gorskis@philau.edu; *Syst Librn,* Michael Cabus; Tel: 215-951-5365, E-mail: cabusm@philau.edu; *Circ Supvr,* Dee Linke; Tel: 215-951-2841, E-mail: linked@philau.edu; *Supvr, Ser,* Melvyn Brown; Tel: 215-951-2572, E-mail: brownm@philau.edu; *Coordr, Info Literacy,* Jordana Shane; Tel: 215-951-2629, E-mail: shanej@philau.edu; *Coordr, Libr Syst & Mat Proc,* Barbara Lowry; Tel: 215-951-2842, E-mail: lowryb@philau.edu; *Ref & ILL Serv Coordr,* Brynne Norton; Tel: 215-951-2580, E-mail: nortonb@philau.edu. Subject Specialists: *Health sci,* Karen M Albert; Staff 6 (MLS 5, Non-MLS 1)
Founded 1884. Enrl 2,100; Fac 105; Highest Degree: Master
Library Holdings: Bk Vols 110,000; Per Subs 950
Special Collections: Textile History Coll
Subject Interests: Apparel, Archit, Design, Fashion, Hist of textile, Indust, Textiles, Textiles manufacture
Automation Activity & Vendor Info: (Acquisitions) SirsiDynix; (Cataloging) SirsiDynix; (Circulation) SirsiDynix
Database Vendor: SirsiDynix
Wireless access
Partic in OCLC Online Computer Library Center, Inc; Pennsylvania Academic Library Consortium, Inc (PALCI); Tri-State College Library Cooperative
Open Mon-Thurs (Fall & Spring) 8am-Midnight, Fri 8-7:30, Sat 10-5, Sun Noon-Midnight; Mon–Thurs (Summer) 8am–9pm, Fri 8:30–4:30, Sat 10-5
Restriction: Authorized scholars by appt, Open to students, fac & staff

GM PHILADELPHIA VA MEDICAL CENTER*, Library Service (142D), 3900 Woodland Ave, 19104. SAN 359-2472. Tel: 215-823-5860. FAX: 215-823-5108. E-mail: vhaphilibrarystaff@va.gov. *Chief,* Priscilla L Stephenson; *Med Librn,* Mark Marchino; Staff 3 (MLS 2, Non-MLS 1)
Library Holdings: Bk Titles 4,360; Bk Vols 4,750; Per Subs 225
Subject Interests: Behav health, Clinical med, Healthcare mgt, Nursing
Automation Activity & Vendor Info: (Cataloging) CyberTools for Libraries; (Circulation) CyberTools for Libraries; (OPAC) CyberTools for Libraries; (Serials) CyberTools for Libraries
Database Vendor: Cinahl, ebrary, EBSCOhost, Lexi-Comp, McGraw-Hill, MD Consult, Medline, Natural Standard, OCLC, ProQuest, PubMed, STAT!Ref (Teton Data Systems), Swets Information Services, UpToDate
Function: Doc delivery serv, Health sci info serv, ILL available, Ref & res
Publications: New Books (Quarterly); Special Interest Bibliographies
Partic in Veterans Affairs Libr Network (VALNET)
Restriction: Lending to staff only, Staff & patient use

SR PHILADELPHIA YEARLY MEETING OF THE RELIGIOUS SOCIETY OF FRIENDS*, Henry J Cadbury Library, 1515 Cherry St, 19102. SAN 315-0046. Tel: 215-241-7220. FAX: 215-567-2096. E-mail: library@pym.org. Web Site: www.pym.org/library. *Head Librn,* Rita Varley; Tel: 215-241-7219
Founded 1961
Library Holdings: Bk Titles 18,000
Special Collections: Non Violent Alternatives; Peace Education Resources; Quakerism & Quaker History; Religion & Psychology (Dora Wilson Coll), bks & papers
Subject Interests: African-Am, Civil rights, Criminal justice, Environ studies, Family life, Peace, Quaker hist, Quakers, Relig educ, Spiritual life, Women's studies
Automation Activity & Vendor Info: (Cataloging) Follett Software; (Circulation) Follett Software; (OPAC) Follett Software
Wireless access
Restriction: Mem only

S PHILADELPHIA ZOO LIBRARY*, 3400 W Girard Ave, 19104. SAN 314-9838. Tel: 215-243-5216. FAX: 215-243-0219. E-mail: library@phillyzoo.org. Web Site: www.phillyzoo.org. *Libr Serv Mgr,* Stephanie Julianna Eller; E-mail: eller.stephanie@phillyzoo.org; Staff 1 (Non-MLS 1)
Founded 1874
Library Holdings: Bk Vols 3,000; Per Subs 70
Special Collections: Videos, Conference Proceedings & Pathology Reports
Subject Interests: Animal behavior, Biol, Birds, Botany, Conserv, Ecology, Herpetology, Hort, Ichthyology, Mammals, Natural hist, Nutrition, Pathology, Veterinary med, Zool mgt, Zoology

L POST & SCHELL, PC*, Law Library, Four Penn Center, 1600 JFK Blvd, 15th Flr, 19103-2808. SAN 372-1825. Tel: 215-587-1100. FAX: 215-587-1444. Web Site: www.postschell.com. *Librn,* Kathryn Brewer; E-mail: kbrewer@postschell.com; Staff 1 (MLS 1)
Founded 1968
Library Holdings: Bk Vols 2,000
Automation Activity & Vendor Info: (Cataloging) SIMA, Inc
Database Vendor: Dun & Bradstreet, LexisNexis, MD Consult, OCLC FirstSearch
Partic in American Association of Law Libraries (AALL); Greater Philadelphia Law Library Association

R PRESBYTERIAN HISTORICAL SOCIETY, 425 Lombard St, 19147-1516. SAN 315-0178. Tel: 215-627-1852. FAX: 215-627-0115. E-mail: refdesk@history.pcusa.org. Web Site: www.history.pcusa.org. *Dir, Prog & Serv,* Nancy J Taylor; Staff 13 (MLS 11, Non-MLS 2)

Founded 1852
Library Holdings: Bk Titles 200,000; Per Subs 150
Special Collections: Alaska (Sheldon Jackson Coll); American Indian Missionary Correspondence; American Sunday School Union; Archives of Presbyterian Church (USA) & Predecessor Denominations; Board of Foreign Missions; National & Foreign Missions; National Council of Churches Archives; Religious News Service
Subject Interests: Am Presbyterian hist
Wireless access
Function: 24/7 Online cat, Archival coll, Exhibits, Microfiche/film & reading machines, Ref & res
Publications: Journal of Presbyterian History (Journal); PHS Matters (Monthly newsletter); Presbyterian Heritage (Newsletter)
Partic in OCLC Online Computer Library Center, Inc
Open Mon-Fri 8:30-4:30
Restriction: Non-circulating
Friends of the Library Group

S PSYCHOANALYTIC CENTER OF PHILADELPHIA LIBRARY*, Rockland-East Fairmount Park, 3810 Mount Pleasant Dr, 19121-1002. SAN 314-2973. Tel: 215-235-2345. FAX: 215-235-2388. E-mail: pcop@philanalysis.org. Web Site: philanalysis.org. *Librn,* Zoe Friedberg
Library Holdings: Bk Titles 1,260; Per Subs 12; Videos 13
Subject Interests: Psychoanalysis
Function: ILL available, Ref serv available
Open Mon-Fri 9-5

L RAWLE & HENDERSON*, Law Library, The Widener Bldg, One S Penn Sq, 17th Fl, 19107. SAN 314-9897. Tel: 215-575-4480. FAX: 215-563-2583. *Librn,* Christine Harvan
Founded 1783
Library Holdings: Bk Vols 14,500
Subject Interests: Admiralty law, General law
Partic in Dialog Corp; Westlaw

L REED SMITH LLP*, Law Library, 2500 One Liberty Pl, 1650 Market St, 19103. SAN 372-1701. Tel: 215-851-1413. FAX: 215-851-1420. Web Site: www.reedsmith.com. *Mgr,* Scott Demaris
Library Holdings: Bk Vols 8,500; Per Subs 100
Open Mon-Fri 8-5

S RMA INFORMATION CENTER*, 1801 Market St, Ste 300, 19103. SAN 329-2800. Tel: 215-446-4111. FAX: 215-446-4101. Web Site: www.rmahq.org. *Mgr,* Heng You; Tel: 215-446-4113, E-mail: hyou@rmahq.org; Staff 2 (MLS 1, Non-MLS 1)
Library Holdings: Bk Titles 2,000; Per Subs 150
Automation Activity & Vendor Info: (Acquisitions) Inmagic, Inc.; (Cataloging) Inmagic, Inc.; (Circulation) Inmagic, Inc.; (Serials) Inmagic, Inc.
Database Vendor: Factiva.com
Function: Res libr
Publications: The RMA Journal (Monthly)
Restriction: Staff use only

S ROSENBACH MUSEUM & LIBRARY*, 2010 DeLancey Pl, 19103. SAN 314-9935. Tel: 215-732-1600. FAX: 215-545-7529. E-mail: info@rosenbach.org. Web Site: www.rosenbach.org. *Dir,* Derick Dreher; Tel: 215-732-1600, Ext 121, E-mail: ddreher@rosenbach.org; *Librn,* Elizabeth E Fuller; Tel: 215-732-1600, Ext 115, E-mail: eefuller@rosenbach.org; *Curator,* Judith M Guston; Tel: 215-732-1600, Ext 112, E-mail: jmguston@rosenbach.org; Staff 20 (MLS 1, Non-MLS 19)
Founded 1954
Library Holdings: Bk Vols 30,000
Special Collections: Marianne Moore Coll, bks, drawings, furnishings, mss, photos; Maurice Sendak Coll, bks, drawings, mss; Rosenbach Company Archives, bks, mss; Rush-Williams-Biddle Family Papers, mss
Subject Interests: 20th Century Am lit, Americana, Bk illustr, British lit, Hist of bks, Latin Americana, Printing
Function: Outside serv via phone, mail, e-mail & web, Res libr
Publications: Collection Guides; Exhibition Catalogs; Fine Press & Facsimile Editions of Rare Books & Mss
Partic in OCLC Research Library Partnership
Restriction: Not a lending libr, Open by appt only
Friends of the Library Group

M ROXBOROUGH MEMORIAL HOSPITAL*, School of Nursing & Medical Libraries, 5800 Ridge Ave, 19128. SAN 325-2868. Tel: 215-487-4345. FAX: 215-487-4350. *Librn,* Christine Johnson; Staff 1 (MLS 1)
Founded 1945
Library Holdings: CDs 316; Bk Titles 2,000; Per Subs 151; Videos 102
Subject Interests: Allied health, Med, Nursing
Automation Activity & Vendor Info: (Cataloging) New Generation Technologies Inc. (LiBRARYSOFT); (OPAC) New Generation Technologies Inc. (LiBRARYSOFT)
Wireless access
Partic in Basic Health Sciences Library Network; Delaware Valley Information Consortium; Docline
Restriction: Circ limited

S RYERSS MUSEUM & LIBRARY*, Burholme Park, 7370 Central Ave, 19111-3055. SAN 314-9943. Tel: 215-685-0544, 215-685-0599. E-mail: ryerssmuseum@gmail.com. Web Site: ryerssmuseum.org. *Librn,* Beth Atkinson
Founded 1910
Library Holdings: Bk Vols 20,000; Per Subs 10
Special Collections: Local History Coll; Victoriana Coll
Open Fri-Sun 10-4
Friends of the Library Group

M SAINT CHRISTOPHER'S HOSPITAL FOR CHILDREN*, Margery H Nelson Medical Library, 160 E Erie Ave, 19134. SAN 329-2940. Tel: 215-427-5374. FAX: 215-427-6872. *Librn,* Position Currently Open
Library Holdings: Bk Titles 4,400; Per Subs 60
Open Mon-Fri 8:30-5

M SAINT JOSEPH'S HOSPITAL*, Medical Library, 16th St & Girard Ave, 19130-1615. SAN 314-9978. Tel: 215-787-9000, 215-787-9156. *Librn,* Sister Mary Carmelita
Library Holdings: Bk Vols 200; Per Subs 30
Open Mon-Fri 6-5

SAINT JOSEPH'S UNIVERSITY

C CAMPBELL LIBRARY*, Mandeville Hall, 5600 City Ave, 19131. Tel: 610-660-1195. Circulation Tel: 610-660-1197. Reference Tel: 610-660-1196. FAX: 610-660-1604. *Dir,* Sonia Bennett; E-mail: sbennett@sju.edu; Staff 2 (MLS 1, Non-MLS 1)
Founded 1965
Library Holdings: Electronic Media & Resources 1,698; Bk Titles 2,369; Per Subs 200
Special Collections: USDA Yearbooks
Subject Interests: Food mkt
Automation Activity & Vendor Info: (Acquisitions) Innovative Interfaces, Inc; (Cataloging) Innovative Interfaces, Inc; (Circulation) Innovative Interfaces, Inc; (OPAC) Innovative Interfaces, Inc
Database Vendor: EBSCOhost, LexisNexis, OCLC FirstSearch, ProQuest
Partic in Lyrasis
Publications: Subject Bibliographies
Open Mon-Thurs 8:30am-11pm, Fri 8:30-5, Sat 10-6, Sun 1-11

C FRANCIS A DREXEL LIBRARY*, 5600 City Ave, 19131-1395, SAN 359-0976. Tel: 610-660-1905. Circulation Tel: 610-660-1900. Interlibrary Loan Service Tel: 610-660-1907. Reference Tel: 610-660-1904. Automation Services Tel: 610-660-1914. FAX: 610-660-1916. Web Site: www.sju.edu/libraries/drexel. *Dir, Libr Serv,* Anne Krakow; *Assoc Dir, Res Mgt,* Marjorie Rathbone; Tel: 610-660-1912, E-mail: rathbone@sju.edu; *Assoc Dir, Syst & Tech,* Marvin Weaver; E-mail: mweaver@sju.edu; *Bus Librn,* Cynthia Slater; Tel: 610-660-1139, E-mail: cslater@sju.edu; *Web Serv & Ref Librn,* Linda Kubala; Tel: 610-660-1531, E-mail: lkubala@sju.edu; *Archives & Ref,* Christopher Dixon; E-mail: cdixon@sju.edu; *Cat & Syst Adminr,* Susan Cheney; Tel: 610-660-1976, E-mail: scheney@sju.edu; *Circ Supvr,* Dolores McCaughan; Tel: 610-660-1926, E-mail: dmccaugh@sju.edu; *Instruction & Outreach,* Sara Franks; Tel: 610-660-1913, E-mail: sfranks@sju.edu; *ILL,* Mary Martinson; E-mail: martinson@sju.edu; *Per & Shared Res,* Kris Mudrick; Tel: 610-660-3215, E-mail: kmudrick@sju.edu; *Ref Serv,* Naomi Cohen; Tel: 610-660-1057, E-mail: ncohen@sju.edu; Staff 11 (MLS 11)
Founded 1851. Enrl 7,000; Fac 392; Highest Degree: Doctorate
Library Holdings: e-journals 7,480; Bk Titles 206,362; Bk Vols 355,556; Per Subs 1,418
Special Collections: SJU Publications Coll
Subject Interests: Hist, Philos, Theol
Automation Activity & Vendor Info: (Acquisitions) Innovative Interfaces, Inc; (Cataloging) Innovative Interfaces, Inc; (Circulation) Innovative Interfaces, Inc; (ILL) Innovative Interfaces, Inc; (OPAC) Innovative Interfaces, Inc; (Serials) Innovative Interfaces, Inc
Database Vendor: EBSCOhost, JSTOR, LexisNexis, OCLC FirstSearch, OCLC WorldShare Interlibrary Loan, OVID Technologies, ProQuest, ScienceDirect
Partic in OCLC Online Computer Library Center, Inc; Pa Tri-State Col Libr Coop; Pennsylvania Academic Library Consortium, Inc (PALCI)
Publications: Library Lines (Newsletter)
Open Mon-Thurs 8:30am-Midnight, Fri 8:30am-9pm, Sat 10-6, Sun Noon-Midnight

SR SAINT MARK'S CHURCH*, Isaiah V Williamson Library, 1625 Locust St, 19103. SAN 314-9986. Tel: 215-735-1416. FAX: 215-735-0572. Web Site: www.saintmarksphiladelphia.org.
Library Holdings: Bk Vols 1,800; Per Subs 17

Subject Interests: Anglo-Catholicism, Episcopal church, Spirituality
Open Mon-Fri 9-4

L SAUL EWING LLP*, Law Library, Centre Sq W, 1500 Market St, 38th Flr, 19102. SAN 325-9757. Tel: 215-972-7873. FAX: 215-972-1945. Web Site: www.saul.com. *Libr Dir,* Stacey Digan; *Assoc Libr Dir,* Richard Weston; *Ref Librn,* Jerilynn Donaldson; Staff 4 (MLS 2, Non-MLS 2)
Library Holdings: Bk Vols 24,500; Per Subs 100
Open Mon-Fri 8-5

L SCHNADER, HARRISON, SEGAL & LEWIS LIBRARY*, 1600 Market St, Ste 3600, 19103. SAN 315-0011. Tel: 215-751-2111. FAX: 215-751-2205. Web Site: www.schnader.com. *Dir,* Bobbi Cross; Tel: 215-751-2399, E-mail: bcross@schnader.com; *Res,* Kathy Cater; E-mail: kcater@schnader.com; *Res,* Annemarie Lorenzen; E-mail: alorenzen@schnader.com; Staff 7 (MLS 3, Non-MLS 4)
Library Holdings: Bk Vols 35,000; Per Subs 1,000
Subject Interests: Law
Automation Activity & Vendor Info: (Cataloging) EOS International; (Circulation) EOS International; (OPAC) EOS International; (Serials) EOS International
Database Vendor: Dialog, Dun & Bradstreet, EBSCOhost, Fastcase, LexisNexis, Westlaw
Partic in OCLC Online Computer Library Center, Inc; RLIN (Research Libraries Information Network)
Restriction: Open to employees & special libr

S SETTLEMENT MUSIC SCHOOL*, Mary Louise Curtis Library, 416 Queen St, 19147-3094. (Mail add: PO Box 63966, 19147-3966), SAN 359-1158. Tel: 215-320-2604. FAX: 215-551-0483. Web Site: www.smsmusic.org. *Dir,* Eric Anderson; Tel: 215-320-2602, E-mail: eanderson@smsmusic.org; *Librn,* Jean Peoples; Staff 1 (Non-MLS 1)
Founded 1969. Enrl 3,100
Library Holdings: Bk Titles 800
Special Collections: Chamber Music (Mischa Schneider & J Gershon Cohen Coll), scores & parts; Flute Music (William Kincaid Coll), scores & parts

Branches:

GERMANTOWN LIBRARY, 6128 Germantown Ave, 19144, SAN 359-1182. Tel: 215-320-2610. FAX: 215-438-7133. *Br Dir,* Eric Anderson; E-mail: eanderson@smsmusic.org; Staff 1 (Non-MLS 1)
Founded 1959
Library Holdings: Bk Vols 300

KARDON-NORTHEAST - SOL SCHOENBACH LIBRARY, 3745 Clarendon Ave, 19114, SAN 359-1212. Tel: 215-320-2620. FAX: 215-637-8716. *Dir,* William Peters; Tel: 215-320-2622, E-mail: wpeters@smsmusic.org
Founded 1976
Library Holdings: Bk Titles 1,500

WILLOW GROVE BRANCH LIBRARY, 318 Davisville Rd, Willow Grove, 19090, SAN 328-8501. Tel: 215-320-2630. *Br Dir,* Patricia Manley; E-mail: pmanley@smsmusic.org; Staff 1 (Non-MLS 1)
Library Holdings: Bk Titles 500

M TALBOT RESEARCH LIBRARY*, Fox Chase Cancer Center, 333 Cottman Ave, 3rd Flr, 19111-2497. SAN 314-9323. Tel: 215-728-2711. FAX: 215-728-3655. E-mail: lib_reference@fccc.edu. Web Site: www.fccc.edu/library/index.html. *Dir,* Beth A Lewis; E-mail: beth.lewis@fccc.edu; *Librn,* Alex Pfundt; Staff 7 (MLS 3, Non-MLS 4)
Founded 1926
Library Holdings: Bk Vols 5,000; Per Subs 450
Subject Interests: Biochem, Cancer, Cell biol, Clinical res, Crystallography, Genetics
Automation Activity & Vendor Info: (Acquisitions) SirsiDynix; (Cataloging) SirsiDynix; (Circulation) SirsiDynix; (OPAC) SirsiDynix; (Serials) SirsiDynix
Database Vendor: Dialog, OVID Technologies
Partic in Health Science Library Information Consortium; Lyrasis; National Network of Libraries of Medicine Middle Atlantic Region
Restriction: Open to pub for ref only

JM TEMPLE UNIVERSITY HEALTH SYSTEM*, Northeastern Hospital School of Nursing Library, 2301 E Allegheny Ave, 19134. SAN 314-9579. Tel: 215-926-3168. FAX: 215-926-3159. Web Site: www.nehson.templehealth.org. *Dir of Libr/Media Serv,* Victoria Newton; E-mail: Victoria.Newton@tuhs.temple.edu. Subject Specialists: *Med, Nursing,* Victoria Newton; Staff 2.5 (MLS 1, Non-MLS 1.5)
Founded 1925. Enrl 85; Fac 12; Highest Degree: Associate
Jul 2007-Jun 2008 Income $111,000. Mats Exp $50,000, Books $2,000, AV Equip $500, AV Mat $2,000, Electronic Ref Mat (Incl. Access Fees) $23,000, Presv $400. Sal $61,000 (Prof $50,500)
Library Holdings: AV Mats 550; CDs 10; DVDs 10; Electronic Media & Resources 75; Bk Titles 2,550; Per Subs 80; Videos 240
Subject Interests: Nursing
Database Vendor: EBSCOhost, OVID Technologies
Function: Computer training, Computers for patron use, Electronic databases & coll, Health sci info serv, ILL available, Online searches
Partic in Basic Health Sciences Library Network; Delaware Valley Information Consortium; HSLC/Access PA/POWER Library
Open Mon-Thurs 8-7, Fri 8-12:30, Sun 1-5
Restriction: Borrowing privileges limited to fac & registered students, Employee & client use only, Hospital staff & commun, In-house use for visitors, Med staff & students, Mem organizations only, Non-circulating to the pub, Open to pub for ref only, Open to pub upon request, Open to students, fac & staff, Restricted pub use

M TEMPLE UNIVERSITY HOSPITAL, EPISCOPAL CAMPUS*, Medical Library, Front St & Lehigh Ave, 19125. SAN 314-8998. Tel: 215-707-0286. FAX: 215-707-0291. *Med Librn,* Marita J Krivda. Subject Specialists: *Med bibliog,* Marita J Krivda; Staff 1 (MLS 1)
Founded 1962
Jul 2005-Jun 2006 Income $85,000. Mats Exp $85,000, Books $5,000, Per/Ser (Incl. Access Fees) $20,000, Other Print Mats $5,000, Electronic Ref Mat (Incl. Access Fees) $10,000, Presv $5,000. Sal $45,000
Library Holdings: Bk Titles 2,700; Bk Vols 9,500; Per Subs 110
Special Collections: Hospital Archives Coll
Subject Interests: Internal med, Nursing, Psychiat
Database Vendor: EBSCOhost, OVID Technologies, PubMed, ScienceDirect
Partic in BSHL; Delaware Valley Information Consortium; Docline; National Network of Libraries of Medicine South Central Region
Open Mon-Fri 9-5

C TEMPLE UNIVERSITY LIBRARIES*, Samuel Paley Library, 1210 W Berks St, 19122-6088. SAN 359-1301. Tel: 215-204-8231. Circulation Tel: 215-204-0744. Reference Tel: 215-204-8212. FAX: 215-204-5201. Web Site: library.temple.edu. *Dean, Univ Libr,* Larry Alford; *Assoc Univ Librn,* Steven Bell; *Sr Assoc Univ Librn,* Jonathan LeBreton; Tel: 215-204-3184, E-mail: lebreton@temple.edu; *Head, Access Serv,* Penelope Myers; Tel: 215-204-0749, Fax: 215-204-0769, E-mail: pmyers@temple.edu; *Head, Coll Develop,* Frank Immler; Tel: 215-204-9244, E-mail: fimmler@temple.edu; *Head, Libr Syst & Tech,* Byron C Mayes; Tel: 215-204-5797, E-mail: bcmayes@temple.edu; *Spec Coll Librn,* Thomas Whitehead; Tel: 215-204-4371, E-mail: whitetm@temple.edu; *Archivist,* Margaret Jerrido; Tel: 215-204-6639, E-mail: mj@temple.edu; *Ref,* Jennifer Baldwin; Tel: 215-204-4585, E-mail: jbaldwin@temple.edu
Founded 1892. Enrl 28,126; Fac 1,045; Highest Degree: Doctorate
Library Holdings: Bk Vols 2,971,988; Per Subs 23,567
Special Collections: Mid 19th Century Philadelphia Urban Planning, Housing Social Welfare, Education & Labor records (Urban Archives); Philadelphia News Photographs from the Philadelphia Inquirer & Bulletin from Individuals & Organizations; Richard Ellis Library, War Posters (Rare Book & Manuscript Coll); Russell H Conwell & Temple University archives, publications, sermons, lectures, faculty & alumni publications, oral history (Cornwellana-Templana Coll); Science Fiction & Fantasy; Small Press & Alternative Press Publications, 1960's-date (Contemporary Culture Coll); Symbolist Literature, 20th Century English Literature, Richard Aldington, Walter de la Mare, 17th Century English History & Religion, Bibles, Herbals & Horticulture, Business & Accounting History, Printing, Publishing & Graphic Arts. Oral History; State Document Depository; US Document Depository
Automation Activity & Vendor Info: (Acquisitions) Innovative Interfaces, Inc
Database Vendor: Innovative Interfaces, Inc
Publications: Descriptive Guide to the University Archives; Manuscript Register Series; Monitor; Temple University Libraries Newsletter; Urban Archives Notes
Partic in Association of Research Libraries (ARL); Coalition for Networked Information (CNI); Northeast Research Libraries Consortium (NERL); OCLC Online Computer Library Center, Inc; Pennsylvania Academic Library Consortium, Inc (PALCI)

Departmental Libraries:

AMBLER, 580 Meetinghouse Rd, Ambler, 19002, SAN 314-2779. Tel: 267-468-8640. Circulation Tel: 215-283-1393. FAX: 267-468-8641. *Head of Libr,* Sandra Thompson; Tel: 267-468-8642, E-mail: sandi@temple.edu; Staff 8 (MLS 3, Non-MLS 5)
Highest Degree: Doctorate
Library Holdings: Bk Vols 90,000; Per Subs 446

BLOCKSON AFRO-AMERICAN COLLECTION, Sullivan Hall, 1st Flr, 1330 W Berks St, 19122, SAN 376-2262. Tel: 215-204-6632. FAX: 215-204-5197. *Librn,* Aslaku Berhanu; E-mail: aberhanu@temple.edu
Special Collections: Prints & Photographs; Slave Narrative Coll; Underground Railroad Coll. Oral History

CM GINSBURG HEALTH SCIENCES LIBRARY, 3500 N Broad St, 19140, SAN 359-1425. Tel: 215-707-2665. FAX: 215-707-4135. *Interim Dir,* Barbara Kuchan; Tel: 215-707-2402, E-mail: bkuchan@temple.edu
Founded 1901. Enrl 2,282; Highest Degree: Doctorate
Library Holdings: Bk Vols 131,315; Per Subs 1,410
Subject Interests: Allied health, Dentistry, Med, Nursing, Pharm

Partic in Interlibrary Delivery Service of Pennsylvania; OCLC Research Library Partnership
Friends of the Library Group

CL LAW LIBRARY, Charles Klein Law Bldg, 1719 N Broad St, 19124, SAN 359-145X. Tel: 215-204-7891. FAX: 215-204-1785. Web Site: www2.law.temple.edu. *Dir,* John Necci; Tel: 215-204-4538, E-mail: john.necci@temple.edu; Staff 10 (MLS 10)
Library Holdings: Bk Vols 550,000; Per Subs 850
Special Collections: Historic Trials (Temple University Trials Coll)
Automation Activity & Vendor Info: (Cataloging) Innovative Interfaces, Inc; (Circulation) Innovative Interfaces, Inc; (Course Reserve) Innovative Interfaces, Inc; (ILL) Innovative Interfaces, Inc; (OPAC) Innovative Interfaces, Inc; (Serials) Innovative Interfaces, Inc
Database Vendor: LexisNexis, Westlaw
Partic in HSLC/Access PA/POWER Library
Open Mon-Thurs 8am-11pm, Fri 8am-9pm, Sat 9-5, Sun 1-8

SCIENCE, ENGINEERING & ARCHITECTURE LIBRARY, Engineering Bldg, Rm 201, 1947 N 12th St, 19122, SAN 359-1395. Tel: 215-204-7828. FAX: 215-204-7720. *Head of Libr,* Gretchen Sneff; Tel: 215-204-4724, E-mail: gsneff@temple.edu; Staff 1 (MLS 1)
Subject Interests: Archit, Civil, Electrical, Environ, Mechanical eng

CM TEMPLE UNIVERSITY SCHOOL OF PODIATRIC MEDICINE*, Charles E Krausz Library, Eighth St at Race, 19107. SAN 359-0674. Tel: 215-625-5275. FAX: 215-629-1622. Web Site: podiatry.temple.edu. *Head Librn,* Carol Vincent; Staff 2 (MLS 1, Non-MLS 1)
Founded 1962. Enrl 445; Fac 114; Highest Degree: Master
Library Holdings: Bk Titles 10,500; Per Subs 150
Special Collections: Anthony Sabatella Coll; Center for the History of Foot Care; Stewart E Reed Coll, bks, prints, per, monographs
Subject Interests: Med, Orthopedics, Podiatry
Automation Activity & Vendor Info: (Acquisitions) Innovative Interfaces, Inc; (Cataloging) Innovative Interfaces, Inc; (Circulation) Innovative Interfaces, Inc; (Course Reserve) Innovative Interfaces, Inc; (ILL) Innovative Interfaces, Inc; (Media Booking) Innovative Interfaces, Inc; (OPAC) Innovative Interfaces, Inc; (Serials) Innovative Interfaces, Inc
Database Vendor: OVID Technologies
Wireless access
Partic in Health Science Library Information Consortium
Open Mon-Thurs 8am-11:30pm, Fri 8-4:45, Sat 9-5, Sun Noon-10:30

CM THOMAS JEFFERSON UNIVERSITY*, Scott Memorial Library, 1020 Walnut St, 19107. SAN 359-1603. Tel: 215-503-6994. Circulation Tel: 215-503-6995. Interlibrary Loan Service Tel: 215-503-6773. Reference Tel: 215-503-8150. FAX: 215-923-3203. Web Site: jeffline.jefferson.edu. *Univ Librn,* Edward W Tawyea; E-mail: edward.tawyea@jefferson.edu; *Dep Univ Librn,* Rod MacNeil; Tel: 215-503-2827, E-mail: rod.macneil@jefferson.edu; *Dir, Coll Develop,* Diana Ryan; Tel: 215-503-2829, E-mail: diana.ryan@jefferson.edu; *Head, Info Serv,* Margy Grasberger; Tel: 215-503-7815, E-mail: margy.grasberger@jefferson.edu; *Mgr, Access Serv,* Rebecca Pernell; Tel: 215-503-2828, E-mail: rebecca.pernell@jefferson.edu; *Archivist,* F Michael Angelo; Tel: 215-503-8097, E-mail: michael.angelo@jefferson.edu; *Ser,* Brad Long; *Syst Librn,* Gary Spahn; Tel: 215-503-3123, E-mail: gary.spahn@jefferson.edu; *Web Coordr,* Ann Koopman; Tel: 215-503-0441, E-mail: ann.koopman@jefferson.edu; Staff 14 (MLS 14)
Founded 1896. Enrl 2,028; Fac 611; Highest Degree: Doctorate
Library Holdings: Bk Titles 81,718; Bk Vols 203,790; Per Subs 1,872
Special Collections: Obstetrics & Gynecology (Bland)
Subject Interests: Med
Database Vendor: SirsiDynix
Publications: JEFFLINE Forum (Newsletter)
Partic in Lyrasis; National Network of Libraries of Medicine Middle Atlantic Region; OCLC Online Computer Library Center, Inc
Open Mon-Fri 8am-2am, Sat 11am-2am, Sun 10am-2am

S THOMSON REUTERS INC SCIENTIFIC*, Custom Information Services, 1500 Spring Garden St, 4th Flr, 19130. SAN 314-9331. Tel: 215-386-0100, 215-823-1890. FAX: 215-243-2235. Web Site: www.thomsonreuters.com.
Founded 1961
Subject Interests: Biblometrics, Hist of sci, Scientometrics
Partic in BRS; Dialog Corp; SDC
Open Mon-Fri 9-5
Restriction: Staff use only

S UNION LEAGUE OF PHILADELPHIA LIBRARY*, 140 S Broad St, 19102. SAN 315-0151. Tel: 215-587-5594. FAX: 215-587-5598. E-mail: library@unionleague.org. Web Site: www.unionleague.org. *Dir,* Jim Mundy; E-mail: mundj@unionleague.org; *Librn,* Beth DeGeorge; E-mail: degeorgeb@unionleague.org; Staff 1 (MLS 1)
Founded 1862
Library Holdings: AV Mats 1,500; CDs 200; DVDs 500; Bk Titles 25,000; Bk Vols 26,000; Per Subs 61; Videos 2,000
Special Collections: American Civil War; Lincolniana; Philadelphia & Pennsylvania History Coll
Automation Activity & Vendor Info: (Cataloging) EOS International; (Circulation) EOS International; (OPAC) EOS International
Database Vendor: EBSCOhost
Wireless access
Partic in Philadelphia Area Consortium of Special Collections Libraries
Restriction: Researchers by appt only
Friends of the Library Group

A UNITED STATES ARMY*, Army Corps of Engineers Philadelphia District Library, Wanamaker Bldg, 100 Penn Square E, 19107-3390. SAN 359-1662. Tel: 215-656-6821. FAX: 215-656-6828. *Info Spec,* Linda Carnevale Skale; E-mail: linda.c.skale@usace.army.mil; Staff 1 (MLS 1)
Founded 1969
Library Holdings: Bk Vols 9,500; Per Subs 60
Special Collections: Congressional Documents: Rivers & Harbors, from 1933; Transactions of the ASCE, from 1941
Subject Interests: Eng, Sciences
Publications: Accessions List (Monthly); Bibliography Series
Open Mon-Fri 9-5

GL UNITED STATES COURT OF APPEALS*, William H Hastie Library, Burn Courthouse, 1st Flr, 601 Market St, Room 1609, 19106. SAN 315-0186. Tel: 267-299-4300. FAX: 267-299-4328. *Circuit Librn,* Judith F Ambler; *Head, Res Serv,* Michelle Ayers; E-mail: michelle_ayers@ca3.uscourts.gov; *Head, Tech Serv,* Susan E McGahey; E-mail: susan_mcgahey@ca3.uscourts.gov; Staff 12 (MLS 6, Non-MLS 6)
Library Holdings: Bk Vols 100,000; Per Subs 150
Subject Interests: Judicial admin
Automation Activity & Vendor Info: (Acquisitions) SirsiDynix; (Cataloging) SirsiDynix; (Circulation) SirsiDynix; (Serials) SirsiDynix
Database Vendor: SirsiDynix, TLC (The Library Corporation)
Open Mon-Fri 8:30-4:30

S US DEPARTMENT OF LABOR*, Region III Library, Curtis Bldg, Ste 740 W, 170 S Independence Mall W, 19106-3309. SAN 370-2766. Tel: 215-861-4900. FAX: 215-861-4904. *Librn,* Barbara Bray; Tel: 215-861-4912, E-mail: bray.barbara@dol.gov; Staff 1 (MLS 1)
Library Holdings: Bk Vols 2,000
Subject Interests: Occupational health, Occupational safety
Partic in Fedlink

G UNITED STATES ENVIRONMENTAL PROTECTION*, Region 3 Library, 1650 Arch St, 3PM52, 19103. SAN 314-898X. Tel: 215-814-5254. FAX: 215-814-5253. E-mail: library-reg3@epa.gov. Web Site: www.epa.gov/reg3rcei/. *Admin Librn,* Nick Lazzaro; Tel: 215-814-5256, E-mail: lazzaro.nick@epa.gov; *Ref,* Anne Gold; Tel: 215-814-5362, E-mail: gold.anne@epa.gov; *Info Spec,* Angelina Brown; Tel: 215-814-5537, E-mail: brown.angelina@epa.gov; Staff 3 (MLS 3)
Founded 1972
Library Holdings: Bk Titles 9,500; Bk Vols 14,000; Per Subs 200
Subject Interests: Biodiversity, Ecology, Environ law, Hazardous waste, Pollution control, Toxicology, Wetland ecology
Database Vendor: Dialog, LexisNexis, OCLC FirstSearch
Function: Computers for patron use, ILL available, Ref serv available
Restriction: Borrowing requests are handled by ILL

A UNITED STATES NAVY*, Naval Surface Warfare Center - Carderock Division, 1000 Kittyhawk Ave, Bldg 77L, 19112. SAN 359-1816. Tel: 215-897-7078. FAX: 215-897-8380. *Tech Info Spec,* Belinda Sagan; E-mail: belinda.sagan@navy.mil
Founded 1909
Library Holdings: Bk Vols 10,000; Per Subs 40
Special Collections: Navy Technical Manuals
Subject Interests: Chem, Electrical, Marine eng, Mechanical, Metallurgy
Partic in Dialog Corp
Restriction: Not open to pub

C UNIVERSITY OF PENNSYLVANIA LIBRARIES*, Van Pelt Library, 3420 Walnut St, 19104-6206. SAN 359-1840. Tel: 215-898-7556. Circulation Tel: 215-898-7566. Interlibrary Loan Service Tel: 215-898-7559. Information Services Tel: 215-898-7555. FAX: 215-898-0559. E-mail: library@pobox.upenn.edu. Web Site: www.library.upenn.edu. *Vice Provost & Dir,* Carton Rogers; E-mail: rogers@pobox.upenn.edu; *Dir, Coll Develop & Scholarly Communication,* Position Currently Open; *Dir, Logistics & Access Serv,* Position Currently Open; *Dir, Info Tech & Digital Develop,* Michael Winkler; Staff 294 (MLS 118, Non-MLS 176)
Founded 1750. Enrl 20,643; Fac 2,475; Highest Degree: Doctorate
Library Holdings: e-books 508,696; e-journals 79,220; Bk Vols 6,065,122; Videos 19,787
Special Collections: 16th Century Imprints Coll; 18th Century English Fiction (Singer-Mendenhall Coll); American Drama Coll (Clothier, Speiser, Edwin Forrest Library & Manuscripts); Aristotle Texts & Commentaries;

Benjamin Franklin Imprints (Curtis Coll); Bibles (Ross & Block Coll); Church History, Spanish Inquisition, Canon Law & Witchcraft (Henry Charles Lea Library); Cryptography (Mendelsohn Coll); Early Americana (Dechert Coll); Elzevier Imprints (Krumbhaar Coll); English Economic History (Colwell Coll, Carey Coll); Eugene Ormandy Archive; Franz Werfel (Alma Mahler Werfel Coll); French Plays of the 18th & 19th Century Coll; French Revolution Pamphlets (McClure Coll); History of Alchemy & Chemistry (Edgar Fahs Smith Library); Indic Manuscripts Coll; Italian Renaissance Literature (Macaulay Coll); James Fenimore Cooper Coll; James T Farrell Coll; Jonathan Swift (Teerink Coll); Leibniz (Schrecker Coll); Lewis Mumford Coll; Marian Anderson Coll; Mark Twain Coll; Neo-Latin Literature (Neufforge Coll); Robert Montgomery Bird Coll; Shakespeariana, Tudor & Stuart Drama (Horace Howard Furness Library); Spanish Golden Age Literature (Rennert & Crawford Coll); Spanish-American Texts, 17th-19th Centuries (Keil Coll); Theodore Dreiser Coll; Van Wyck Brooks Coll; Waldo Frank Coll; Walt Whitman Coll; Washington Irving Coll. UN Document Depository; US Document Depository
Wireless access
Publications: Penn Library Facts; Penn Library News; Penn Library Resource Guide
Partic in Association of Research Libraries (ARL); HSLC/Access PA/POWER Library; OCLC Online Computer Library Center, Inc; OCLC Research Library Partnership
Friends of the Library Group

Departmental Libraries:

ANNENBERG SCHOOL OF COMMUNICATION, 3620 Walnut St, 19104-6220, SAN 359-1905. Tel: 215-898-7027. FAX: 215-898-5388. *Head of Libr,* Sharon Black; Tel: 215-898-6106, E-mail: sblack@asc.upenn.edu
Founded 1962
Library Holdings: Bk Vols 9,566; Per Subs 305; Videos 500
Special Collections: Faculty Publications; Film (16mm) catalogs; Financial Reports of the Communication Companies & Public TV Stations of the US; Sol Worth Archive; Television Script Archive
Subject Interests: Attitude & opinion res, Communications, Hist & tech of communication, Interpersonal communications, Res in mass media, Theory
Publications: Reference Sources in Communications; Selected Acquisitions

CL BIDDLE LAW LIBRARY, 3501 Sansom St, 19104, SAN 359-193X. Tel: 215-898-7488. Circulation Tel: 215-898-7478, 215-898-9012. Interlibrary Loan Service Tel: 215-898-9013. Reference Tel: 215-898-7853. FAX: 215-898-6619. E-mail: bll@law.upenn.edu. Web Site: www.law.upenn.edu/library. *Assoc Dean & Dir,* Paul M George; E-mail: pmgeorge@law.upenn.edu; *Assoc Dir, Pub Serv,* Edwin J Greenlee; Tel: 215-898-4169, E-mail: egreenle@law.upenn.edu; *Assoc Dir, Tech Serv,* Jeffrey Grillo; Tel: 215-898-7690, E-mail: jgrillo@law.upenn.edu; *Head, Access Serv,* Joseph F Parsio; Tel: 215-746-1755, E-mail: jparsio@law.upenn.edu; *Head, Ref Serv,* Timothy C Von Dulm; Tel: 215-898-0844, E-mail: tvondulm@law.upenn.edu
Library Holdings: Bk Vols 601,030
Special Collections: 16th Century English Year Books; Anglo-American & Foreign Law, bks, monographs, digests; Early American & English Law Books; Early American Legal, ms; Records & Briefs of Pennsylvania Supreme & Superior Courts, United States Court of Appeals for Third Circuit & United States Supreme Court, micro. US Document Depository
Subject Interests: Admin regulations, Anglo-Am, Canon law, Decisions, Foreign, Intl law, Judicial rpts, Roman law

CM BIOMEDICAL LIBRARY, Johnson Pavilion, 3610 Hamilton Walk, 19104-6060, SAN 359-2111. Tel: 215-898-5817. Interlibrary Loan Service Tel: 215-898-4113. Administration Tel: 215-898-4290. Information Services Tel: 215-898-5818. FAX: 215-573-4143. E-mail: libref@mail.med.upenn.edu. Web Site: www.library.upenn.edu/biomed. *Dir,* Barbara Cavanaugh; E-mail: bbc@pobox.upenn.edu
Subject Interests: Biol, Clinical med, Nursing
Partic in RML
Open Mon-Thurs 8am-Midnight, Fri 8am-10pm, Sat 10-6, Sun 10am-Midnight

CHEMISTRY, 3301 Spruce St, 5th Flr, 19104-6323, SAN 359-1964. Tel: 215-898-2177. FAX: 215-898-0741. E-mail: chemlib@pobox.upenn.edu. *Librn,* Judith Currano; E-mail: currano@pobox.upenn.edu
Library Holdings: Bk Vols 39,017
Subject Interests: Biochem, Inorganic, Organic
Open Mon-Fri 9-5

FISHER FINE ARTS LIBRARY, Furness Bldg, 220 S 34th St, 19104-6308, SAN 359-2022. Tel: 215-898-8325. FAX: 215-573-2066. *Fine Arts Librn,* William Keller; E-mail: wkeller@pobox.upenn.edu
Library Holdings: Bk Vols 250,000
Special Collections: Rare Architectural Books, 16th to 20th Century; Urban Maps & Views
Subject Interests: Archit, City, Hist of art, Hist presv, Landscape archit, Regional planning, Urban design

CM LEON LEVY DENTAL MEDICINE LIBRARY, 240 S 40th St, 19104-6030, SAN 359-1999. Tel: 215-898-8969. FAX: 215-898-7985. *Head of Libr,* Pat Heller; Tel: 215-898-8978, E-mail: heller@pobox.upenn.edu
Library Holdings: Bk Vols 59,447
Special Collections: Dental Catalogs; Dental Patents; Foreign Dental Dissertations; Thomas W Evans Historical Documents
Subject Interests: Dentistry, Hist of dent, Oral biol
Partic in Mid-Atlantic Law Library Cooperative; RML
Publications: Acquisitions List of Books & Periodicals

LIPPINCOTT-WHARTON SCHOOL, 3420 Walnut St, 19104-3436, SAN 359-2057. Tel: 215-898-5924. FAX: 215-898-2261. E-mail: lippinco@wharton.upenn.edu. *Dir,* Michael Halperin; Tel: 215-898-9434, E-mail: halperin@wharton.upenn.edu
Library Holdings: Bk Vols 188,976
Special Collections: Corporation Annual Reports; Financial; Investment Sources; Lipman Criminology Coll; New York Stock Exchange & American Stock Exchange, microfiche
Subject Interests: Finance, Labor, Mgt incl acctg, Mkt, Real property, Taxation, Transportation

MATH-PHYSICS-ASTRONOMY LIBRARY, David Rittenhouse Lab, 209 S 33rd St, 19104-6317, SAN 359-2081. Tel: 215-898-8173. FAX: 215-573-2009. E-mail: mpalib@pobox.upenn.edu. *Head of Libr,* Lauren Gala; E-mail: milaur@pobox.upenn.edu
Library Holdings: Bk Vols 52,707
Subject Interests: Astronomy, Math, Physics

MORRIS ARBORETUM LIBRARY, 100 Northwestern Ave, 19118-2697, SAN 359-2359. Tel: 215-247-5777, Ext 115. FAX: 215-248-4439. *Librn,* Matthew Sibert
Founded 1933
Library Holdings: Bk Vols 6,700; Per Subs 44
Special Collections: 19th Century Historical Botanical Books
Subject Interests: Botany, Conserv, Ecology, Garden design, Hist, Hort, Plant pathology, Urban forestry

MUSEUM, 3260 South St, 19104-6324, SAN 359-2170. Tel: 215-898-4021. FAX: 215-573-2008. E-mail: muselib@pobox.upenn.edu. *Head of Libr,* John Weeks; E-mail: weeksj@pobox.upenn.edu
Library Holdings: Bk Vols 139,864
Special Collections: Aboriginal American Linguistics & Ethnology (Daniel Garrison Brinton Coll); Egyptology
Subject Interests: Anthrop, Archaeology, Ethnology

RARE BOOK & MANUSCRIPT LIBRARY, 3420 Walnut St, 19104. Tel: 215-898-7088. E-mail: rbml@pobox.upenn.edu. Web Site: www.library.upenn.edu/rbm. *Dir,* David McKnight; Tel: 215-746-5829, E-mail: dmcknigh@pobox.upenn.edu; *Curator of Printed Bks,* Lynne Farrington; Tel: 215-746-5828, E-mail: lynne@pobox.upenn.edu
Library Holdings: Bk Vols 250,000
Automation Activity & Vendor Info: (Cataloging) Ex Libris Group; (OPAC) Ex Libris Group
Function: Res libr
Restriction: Non-circulating

CM VETERINARY LIBRARY, 380 S University Ave, 19104-4539, SAN 359-226X. Tel: 215-898-8895. FAX: 215-573-2007. E-mail: vetlib@pobox.upenn.edu. Web Site: www.library.upenn.edu/vet. *Head of Libr,* Margaret Lindem; Tel: 215-898-8874, E-mail: mlindem@pobox.upenn.edu
Library Holdings: Bk Vols 33,777
Special Collections: Fairman Rogers Coll on Equitation & Horsemanship

C UNIVERSITY OF THE ARTS UNIVERSITY LIBRARIES*, Albert M Greenfield Library, Anderson Hall, 1st Flr, 333 S Broad St, 19102. (Mail add: 320 S Broad St, 19102-4994), SAN 359-0828. Tel: 215-717-6280. Interlibrary Loan Service Tel: 215-717-6283. Reference Tel: 215-717-6282. FAX: 215-717-6287. Web Site: library.uarts.edu. *Assoc Provost, Dir, Univ Libr,* Carol H Graney; Tel: 215-717-6281, E-mail: cgraney@uarts.edu; *Access Serv Librn,* Kimberly Lesley; Tel: 215-717-6284, E-mail: klesley@uarts.edu; *Digital Initiatives & Syst Librn,* Joshua Roberts; Tel: 215-717-6244, E-mail: joroberts@uarts.edu; *Music Librn,* Dr Mark Germer; Tel: 215-717-6293, E-mail: mgermer@uarts.edu; *Pub Serv Librn,* Sara J MacDonald; E-mail: smacdonald@uarts.edu; *Ref Librn,* Mary Louise Castaldi; E-mail: mcastaldim@uarts.edu; *Tech Serv Librn,* Kathryn Coyle; Tel: 215-717-6285, E-mail: kcoyle@uarts.edu; *Visual Res Librn,* Laura Grutzeck; Tel: 215-717-6294, E-mail: lgrutzeck@uarts.edu; Staff 8 (MLS 8)
Founded 1876. Enrl 2,126; Fac 505; Highest Degree: Master
Library Holdings: CDs 10,476; DVDs 2,804; e-books 90,272; Electronic Media & Resources 43; Microforms 461; Music Scores 19,056; Bk Titles 88,121; Bk Vols 111,872; Per Subs 314; Videos 1,112
Special Collections: Book Arts; Published Works by or about University of the Arts Faculty; Textiles Coll
Subject Interests: Design, Media, Performing arts, Visual arts
Automation Activity & Vendor Info: (Acquisitions) Innovative Interfaces, Inc; (Cataloging) Innovative Interfaces, Inc; (Circulation) Innovative

Interfaces, Inc; (Course Reserve) Innovative Interfaces, Inc; (OPAC) Innovative Interfaces, Inc; (Serials) Innovative Interfaces, Inc
Database Vendor: ABC-CLIO, Alexander Street Press, ARTstor, Bowker, Dialog, ebrary, EBSCOhost, Gale Cengage Learning, Greenwood Publishing Group, H W Wilson, Innovative Interfaces, Inc, JSTOR, LexisNexis, Marcive, Inc, Material ConneXion, OCLC, OCLC FirstSearch, OCLC WorldShare Interlibrary Loan, Oxford Online, ProQuest, Wilson - Wilson Web, YBP Library Services
Wireless access
Function: ILL available
Partic in Association of Independent Colleges of Art & Design (AICAD); Lyrasis
Restriction: Researchers by appt only
Departmental Libraries:
MUSIC LIBRARY, Merriam Theater, 3rd Flr, 250 S Broad St, 19102. (Mail add: 320 S Broad St, 19102-4994), SAN 328-7122. Tel: 215-717-6292. FAX: 215-717-6287. *Librn,* Dr Mark Germer; Tel: 215-717-6293, E-mail: mgermer@uarts.edu; Staff 1 (MLS 1)
Open Mon-Thurs (Winter) 8:15am-8pm, Fri 8:15-6, Sat Noon-5, Sun 4-9; Mon-Thurs (Summer) 9-5, Fri 9-4
VISUAL RESOURCES & SPECIAL COLLECTIONS, Anderson Hall, Mezzanine, 333 S Broad St, 19102. (Mail add: 320 S Broad St, 19102-4994), SAN 359-0852. Tel: 215-717-6290. FAX: 215-717-6287. *Spec Coll Librn, Visual Res,* Laura Grutzeck; Tel: 215-717-6294, E-mail: lgrutzeck@uarts.edu; Staff 1 (MLS 1)
Founded 1958
Open Mon 9-5, Tues-Thurs 9-7, Fri 9-6

C UNIVERSITY OF THE SCIENCES IN PHILADELPHIA*, Joseph W England Library, 4200 Woodland Ave, 19104-4491. SAN 314-9714. Tel: 215-596-8960. Interlibrary Loan Service Tel: 215-596-8969. Reference Tel: 215-596-8967. FAX: 215-596-8760. Web Site: www.usip.edu/library. *Dir,* Charles J Myers; Tel: 215-596-8790, E-mail: c.myers@usip.edu; *Coordr, Access Serv,* Cynthia McClellan; Tel: 215-596-8961, E-mail: c.mcclell@usip.edu; *Coordr, Electronic Res,* Jeanette McVeigh; Tel: 215-895-1197, E-mail: j.mcveig@usip.edu; *Coordr, Instruction,* Leslie Bowman; Tel: 215-596-8964, E-mail: l.bowman@usip.edu; *Coordr, Ref (Info Serv),* Sylvia Tarzanin; Tel: 215-596-8731, E-mail: s.tarzan@usip.edu; *Coordr, Tech Serv,* Gina Kaiser; Tel: 215-596-8963, E-mail: g.kaiser@usip.edu; *Media Serv,* Jacqueline Smith; Tel: 215-596-8994, E-mail: j.smith@usip.edu; *Tech Spec,* Eva Agbada; Tel: 215-596-8962, E-mail: e.agbada@usip.edu; Staff 20 (MLS 8, Non-MLS 12)
Founded 1822. Enrl 2,600; Fac 150; Highest Degree: Doctorate
Jul 2005-Jun 2006 Income $1,876,928. Mats Exp $618,300, Books $45,000, Per/Ser (Incl. Access Fees) $522,000, AV Equip $40,100, AV Mat $4,000, Presv $7,200. Sal $828,422 (Prof $489,755)
Library Holdings: AV Mats 1,236; CDs 169; DVDs 51; e-books 40; e-journals 11,100; Bk Vols 84,403; Per Subs 318; Videos 785
Special Collections: College Archives Coll; Rare Books Coll
Subject Interests: Biol, Chem, Pharm, Pharmacognosy, Pharmacology, Phys therapy, Related health sci, Toxicology
Automation Activity & Vendor Info: (Acquisitions) Ex Libris Group; (Cataloging) Ex Libris Group; (Circulation) Ex Libris Group; (Course Reserve) Docutek; (ILL) OCLC ILLiad; (OPAC) Ex Libris Group; (Serials) Ex Libris Group
Database Vendor: 3M Library Systems, Dialog, EBSCOhost, Gale Cengage Learning, Haworth Pres Inc, Lexi-Comp, LexisNexis, Newsbank, OCLC FirstSearch, OCLC WorldShare Interlibrary Loan, OVID Technologies, ProQuest, PubMed, ScienceDirect, STAT!Ref (Teton Data Systems), STN International, Swets Information Services, TDNet, Wiley
Wireless access
Partic in HSLC/Access PA/POWER Library; National Network of Libraries of Medicine; OCLC Online Computer Library Center, Inc; Pennsylvania Academic Library Consortium, Inc (PALCI); Tri-State College Library Cooperative
Open Mon-Fri 9-5
Restriction: Limited access for the pub

S WAGNER FREE INSTITUTE OF SCIENCE LIBRARY*, 1700 W Montgomery Ave, 19121. SAN 315-0240. Tel: 215-763-6529, Ext 12. FAX: 215-763-1299. E-mail: library@wagnerfreeinstitute.org. Web Site: www.wagnerfreeinstitute.org. *Librn,* Lynn Dorwaldt; Staff 2 (MLS 1, Non-MLS 1)
Founded 1855
Library Holdings: Bk Titles 13,000; Bk Vols 45,000; Per Subs 10
Special Collections: 19th Century US & State Geological Surveys; History of Science Coll; Natural Science Coll; Science Education Coll; William Wagner Coll
Subject Interests: Anthrop, Astronomy, Botany, Chem, Geol, Natural sci, Paleontology, Phys sci
Automation Activity & Vendor Info: (Cataloging) Ex Libris Group; (ILL) OCLC; (OPAC) Ex Libris Group
Function: Res libr
Partic in OCLC Online Computer Library Center, Inc; Philadelphia Area Consortium of Special Collections Libraries
Restriction: Non-circulating, Open by appt only

L WHITE & WILLIAMS, LLP*, Law Library, 1800 One Liberty Pl, 19103-7395. SAN 329-0484. Tel: 215-864-7000. FAX: 215-864-7123. Web Site: www.whiteandwilliams.com. *Libr Serv Supvr,* Evelyn Quillen; Staff 2 (MLS 1, Non-MLS 1)
Library Holdings: Bk Vols 15,092
Open Mon-Fri 7-6

S JOHN J WILCOX JR LGBT LIBRARY OF PHILADELPHIA*, William Way Community Ctr, 1315 Spruce St, 19107. SAN 377-2500. Tel: 215-732-2220. FAX: 215-732-0770. Web Site: www.waygay.org.
Founded 1976
Library Holdings: Bk Titles 6,500; Bk Vols 11,000; Per Subs 10; Spec Interest Per Sub 10
Special Collections: Personal & Organizational Coll related to GLBT people in the Greater Delaware Valley (dating from the early 1960s onward), papers & AV mats; Rare Book Coll (from the late 19th century)
Function: Res libr

M WILLS EYE HOSPITAL*, Charles D Kelman Library, 840 Walnut St, 19107. SAN 315-0283. Tel: 215-928-3288. FAX: 215-928-7247. Web Site: www.willseye.org/physicians/library. *Librn,* Gloria Birkett-Parker; Staff 1 (MLS 1)
Founded 1944
Library Holdings: AV Mats 3,165; Electronic Media & Resources 15; Bk Vols 10,000; Videos 150
Special Collections: History of Ophthalmology
Subject Interests: Ophthalmology
Automation Activity & Vendor Info: (Cataloging) SydneyPlus; (Circulation) SydneyPlus; (OPAC) SydneyPlus; (Serials) SydneyPlus
Function: Audio & video playback equip for onsite use, CD-ROM, Doc delivery serv, Handicapped accessible, Health sci info serv, ILL available, Online searches, Orientations, Photocopying/Printing, Res libr, Spoken cassettes & CDs, Telephone ref, VHS videos, Wheelchair accessible
Partic in Association of Vision Science Librarians (AVSL); National Network of Libraries of Medicine
Special Services for the Blind - Spec cats
Open Mon-Fri 8:30-6
Restriction: Circulates for staff only, Fee for pub use, Open to pub for ref only, Pub use on premises

S WISTAR INSTITUTE LIBRARY*, 3601 Spruce St, Rm 215, 19104-4268. SAN 320-5851. Tel: 215-898-3826. Interlibrary Loan Service Tel: 215-898-3816. FAX: 215-898-3856. Web Site: www.wistar.org. *Archivist, Dir, Libr Serv,* Nina P Long; E-mail: nlong@wistar.org; Staff 2 (MLS 2)
Founded 1892
Library Holdings: Bk Vols 2,900; Per Subs 85
Special Collections: Archives, ephemera, ms; Historical Book Coll; Isaac J Wistar Civil War Coll; Wistar Institute & Family Papers
Subject Interests: Biochem, Cell biol, Genetics, Immunology, Oncology, Virology
Automation Activity & Vendor Info: (OPAC) CASPR; (Serials) CASPR
Database Vendor: Dialog, Medline, Swets Information Services
Wireless access
Restriction: Open to pub by appt only

PHOENIXVILLE

R FIRST PRESBYTERIAN CHURCH LIBRARY*, 145 Main St, 19460. SAN 315-0313. Tel: 610-933-8816. FAX: 610-933-8060. *Librn,* Lynn Schmitt
Library Holdings: Bk Vols 2,500
Publications: Christianity Today-Virtue-Concern

P PHOENIXVILLE PUBLIC LIBRARY*, 183 Second Ave, 19460-3420. SAN 315-0321. Tel: 610-933-3013. FAX: 610-933-4338. Web Site: www.phoenixvillelibrary.org. *Dir of Develop, Interim Exec Dir,* Susan Mostek; *Exec Dir,* Position Currently Open; *Dir, Adult Serv, Head, Ref,* Mark Pinto; Tel: 610-933-3013, Ext 32, E-mail: mpinto@ccls.org; *Dir of Develop,* Dorian Wells; Tel: 610-933-3013, Ext 31, E-mail: dwells@ccls.org; *Dir, Children & YA,* Rebecca Krause; Tel: 610-933-3013, Ext 27; *Circ Mgr, ILL,* Kay Price; Tel: 610-933-3013, Ext 22, E-mail: kprice@ccls.org
Founded 1896. Pop 26,500; Circ 138,000
Library Holdings: Bk Vols 70,000; Per Subs 120
Special Collections: Local History
Automation Activity & Vendor Info: (Cataloging) Innovative Interfaces, Inc; (Circulation) Innovative Interfaces, Inc; (OPAC) Innovative Interfaces, Inc
Mem of Chester County Library System
Open Mon-Thurs 9:30-9, Fri & Sat 9:30-5, Sun (Oct-May) 1-5
Friends of the Library Group

CR VALLEY FORGE CHRISTIAN COLLEGE*, Storms Research Center, 1401 Charlestown Rd, 19460. SAN 315-033X. Tel: 610-917-2001. FAX: 610-917-2008. E-mail: research@vfcc.edu. Web Site: www.vfcc.edu. *Libr Dir,* Deborah G Hirneisen; Tel: 610-917-2003, E-mail: dghirneisen@vfcc.edu; *Pub Serv,* Julia Patton; Tel: 610-917-2004, E-mail: jgpatton@vfcc.edu; Staff 2 (MLS 2)
Founded 1939. Enrl 760; Fac 35; Highest Degree: Master
Library Holdings: AV Mats 2,939; e-books 110,000; e-journals 28,000; Bk Vols 71,000; Per Subs 47
Special Collections: Valley Forge General Hospital
Subject Interests: Bible, Relig
Automation Activity & Vendor Info: (Acquisitions) SIRSI WorkFlows; (Cataloging) SIRSI WorkFlows; (Circulation) SIRSI WorkFlows; (Course Reserve) SIRSI WorkFlows; (ILL) OCLC Online; (Media Booking) SIRSI WorkFlows; (OPAC) SIRSI-iBistro; (Serials) SIRSI WorkFlows
Database Vendor: Alexander Street Press, CredoReference, EBSCOhost, Gale Cengage Learning, Hoovers, JSTOR, LexisNexis, OCLC FirstSearch, OCLC WorldShare Interlibrary Loan, Oxford Online, SirsiDynix
Wireless access
Partic in Christian Libr Network; Lyrasis; Southeastern Pennsylvania Theological Library Association; Tri-State College Library Cooperative
Special Services for the Deaf - Am sign lang & deaf culture; Bks on deafness & sign lang; Closed caption videos; Sign lang interpreter upon request for prog
Special Services for the Blind - Large print bks; ZoomText magnification & reading software
Open Mon-Thurs 7:30am-11pm, Fri 7:30-5, Sat 1-5, Sun 8pm-11pm

PIPERSVILLE

P PIPERSVILLE FREE LIBRARY*, 7114 Durham Rd, 18947-9998. (Mail add: PO Box 122, 18947-0122). Tel: 215-766-7880. *Librn,* Marylou Wenner
Library Holdings: Bk Vols 12,000
Open Mon & Fri 3-5, Tues & Wed 3-5 & 7-9, Thurs 10-12, 3-5 & 7-9

PITTSBURGH

S AIR & WASTE MANAGEMENT ASSOCIATION LIBRARY*, One Gateway Ctr, 3rd Flr, 420 Fort Duquesne Blvd, 15222. SAN 329-8957. Tel: 412-232-3444. Toll Free Tel: 800-270-3444. FAX: 412-232-3450. E-mail: info@awma.org. Web Site: www.awma.org. *Coordr,* Nancy Bernheisel; E-mail: nbernheisel@awma.org
Founded 1951
Library Holdings: Bk Vols 800; Per Subs 15

GM ALLEGHENY COUNTY HEALTH DEPARTMENT LIBRARY*, 301 39th St, 15201. SAN 315-0348. Tel: 412-578-8028. FAX: 412-578-8144. *Dir,* Dr Bruce Dixon; Staff 1 (Non-MLS 1)
Founded 1973
Library Holdings: Bk Titles 656; Bk Vols 1,090; Per Subs 28
Subject Interests: Air pollution, Environ studies, Pub health med
Restriction: Staff use only

GL ALLEGHENY COUNTY LAW LIBRARY*, 921 City-County Bldg, 414 Grant St, 15219-2543. SAN 315-0356. Tel: 412-350-5353. Circulation Tel: 412-350-5354. FAX: 412-350-5889. Web Site: www.duq.edu/academics/schools/law/law-library/allegheny-county-law-library. *Dir,* Frank Y Liu; Tel: 412-396-5018, E-mail: liu@duq.edu; *Asst Dir, Lawyer Serv,* Dr Joel Fishman; Tel: 412-350-5727, E-mail: fishman@duq.edu; *Ref/Circ Supvr,* Paul Recht; E-mail: recht@duq.edu; Staff 4 (MLS 2, Non-MLS 2)
Founded 1867
Library Holdings: Bk Titles 91,462; Bk Vols 110,000; Per Subs 109
Special Collections: Alaskan Boundary Dispute 1893; Manuscripts of D T Watson; United States Supreme Court Records & Briefs, 1912 to present. US Document Depository
Automation Activity & Vendor Info: (Acquisitions) Innovative Interfaces, Inc; (Cataloging) Innovative Interfaces, Inc; (Circulation) Innovative Interfaces, Inc; (OPAC) Innovative Interfaces, Inc
Database Vendor: LexisNexis, Westlaw
Wireless access
Publications: Allegheny County Law Library Law; History & Genealogy Series
Open Mon-Thurs 8:30-7, Fri 8:30-5, Sat 12-5

M ALLEGHENY GENERAL HOSPITAL*, Health Sciences Library, 320 E North Ave, 15212-4772. SAN 315-0364. Tel: 412-359-3040. FAX: 412-359-4420. E-mail: aghlibrary@wpahs.org. Web Site: www.ahn.org. Staff 10 (MLS 6, Non-MLS 4)
Founded 1935
Library Holdings: Bk Titles 11,219; Bk Vols 12,684; Per Subs 750
Subject Interests: Anesthesiology, Cancer res, Cardiology, Gynecology, Heart surgery, Internal med, Neurology, Obstetrics, Oncology, Oral surgery, Orthopedics, Pathology, Pediatrics, Rehabilitation, Renal med, Respiratory diseases, Thoracic
Automation Activity & Vendor Info: (Cataloging) EOS International; (Circulation) EOS International
Database Vendor: OVID Technologies
Publications: What's New
Partic in Basic Health Sciences Library Network; Dialog Corp; Greater NE Regional Med Libr Program; Inc; National Network of Libraries of Medicine
Open Mon-Fri 8-5:30

C ART INSTITUTE OF PITTSBURGH LIBRARY*, 420 Boulevard of the Allies, 15219-1328. Tel: 412-291-6357. FAX: 412-263-3715, 412-291-6300. *Dir, Libr Serv,* Amanda DeKnight; E-mail: adeknight@aii.edu; Staff 4 (MLS 2, Non-MLS 2)
Enrl 2,499; Highest Degree: Bachelor
Library Holdings: AV Mats 4,000; Bk Vols 15,000; Per Subs 150
Subject Interests: Advertising, Animation, Culinary, Digital media, Game art design, Graphic design, Interior design, Photog, Video, Web design
Automation Activity & Vendor Info: (Circulation) Follett Software; (Course Reserve) Follett Software; (OPAC) Follett Software; (Serials) Follett Software
Database Vendor: EBSCOhost, ProQuest
Wireless access
Function: For res purposes, Handicapped accessible, Photocopying/Printing
Open Mon-Thurs 7:30am-9:30pm, Fri 7:30-5, Sat 10-4
Restriction: Non-circulating to the pub, Not open to pub, Open to students, fac & staff, Photo ID required for access

P BALDWIN BOROUGH PUBLIC LIBRARY*, Wallace Bldg, 41 Macek Dr, 15227-3638. SAN 324-3982. Tel: 412-885-2255. FAX: 412-885-5255. Web Site: www.baldwinborolibrary.org. *Dir,* Joyce Chiappetta; E-mail: chiappettaj@einetwork.net; *Adult Serv,* Nancy Musser; E-mail: mussern@einetwork.net; *Youth Serv,* Position Currently Open; Staff 9 (MLS 2, Non-MLS 7)
Founded 1965. Pop 22,088; Circ 63,410
Library Holdings: Bk Titles 33,846; Bk Vols 34,759; Per Subs 142; Talking Bks 1,568; Videos 2,479
Automation Activity & Vendor Info: (Cataloging) Innovative Interfaces, Inc
Database Vendor: EBSCOhost, Gale Cengage Learning
Mem of Allegheny County Library Association
Open Mon, Wed & Thurs 10-9, Tues 4-9, Fri & Sat 10-5
Friends of the Library Group

P BRENTWOOD LIBRARY*, 3501 Brownsville Rd, 15227-3115. SAN 315-0437. Tel: 412-882-5694. E-mail: brentwood@einetwork.net. Web Site: www.brentwoodlibrarychanginglives.org. *Dir,* Dennis Luther; *Ch Serv,* Dolores Colarosa; Staff 7 (MLS 1, Non-MLS 6)
Founded 1951. Pop 10,466; Circ 134,000
Automation Activity & Vendor Info: (Acquisitions) Innovative Interfaces, Inc; (Cataloging) Innovative Interfaces, Inc; (Circulation) Innovative Interfaces, Inc; (OPAC) Innovative Interfaces, Inc
Wireless access
Mem of Allegheny County Library Association
Open Mon-Thurs 10-8:30, Fri 1-5, Sat 10-3, Sun 12-4
Friends of the Library Group

R BYZANTINE CATHOLIC SEMINARY OF SAINTS CYRIL & METHODIUS LIBRARY, 3605 Perrysville Ave, 15214-2297. SAN 315-0445. Tel: 412-321-8383. FAX: 412-321-9936. Web Site: www.bcs.edu. *Dir,* Sandra A Collins; E-mail: scollins@bcs.edu. Subject Specialists: *Byzantine studies, Relig studies, Theol,* Sandra A Collins; Staff 1.5 (MLS 1.5)
Founded 1950. Enrl 20; Fac 12; Highest Degree: Master
Library Holdings: AV Mats 150; CDs 25; DVDs 25; Bk Titles 35,000; Per Subs 70; Videos 25
Special Collections: Church Slavonic Language (Byzantine Catholic Liturgical Books Coll); History of the Byzantine Catholic Church in Carpatho-Ruthenia & in the United States; Ruthenian Cultural Coll; Ruthenian Historical Coll
Subject Interests: Byzantine studies, Eastern Christian theology, Ruthenian studies
Wireless access
Partic in HSLC/Access PA/POWER Library
Open Mon-Fri 9-9
Restriction: 24-hr pass syst for students only, Access at librarian's discretion, Authorized scholars by appt, Circ limited, Non-circulating of rare bks

CR CARLOW UNIVERSITY*, Grace Library, 3333 Fifth Ave, 15213. SAN 315-0453. Tel: 412-578-6139. FAX: 412-578-6242. *Univ Librn,* Elaine J Misko; E-mail: ejmisko@carlow.edu; *Cat Librn,* Karyn L Kwiatkowski; Tel: 412-578-6143, E-mail: klkwiatkowski@carlow.edu; *Syst Librn,* Carrie E Nelson; Tel: 412-578-6137, E-mail: cenelson@carlow.edu; *Coordr, Pub Serv,* Andrea K Leyko; E-mail: akleyko@carlow.edu; *Coordr, Tech Serv,*

Karen M Goldbach; Tel: 412-578-6145, E-mail: kmgoldbach@carlow.edu; *Pub Serv,* Emily M Szitas; Tel: 412-578-2049, E-mail: emszitas@carlow.edu; Staff 7 (MLS 6, Non-MLS 1)
Founded 1929. Enrl 2,310; Fac 280; Highest Degree: Doctorate
Jul 2011-Jun 2012 Income $717,777, Locally Generated Income $1,570, Parent Institution $716,207. Mats Exp $292,153, Books $65,495, Per/Ser (Incl. Access Fees) $77,975, AV Mat $4,055, Electronic Ref Mat (Incl. Access Fees) $93,776, Presv $3,703. Sal $392,721 (Prof $339,035)
Library Holdings: AV Mats 5,625; Bks-By-Mail 2; Bks on Deafness & Sign Lang 173; DVDs 266; e-books 922; e-journals 137; Bk Titles 89,586; Bk Vols 109,371; Per Subs 356; Videos 1,322
Special Collections: African American Studies; Career Resources; Peace Studies
Subject Interests: Early childhood educ, English lit, Irish lit, Theol, Women's studies
Automation Activity & Vendor Info: (Acquisitions) SirsiDynix; (Cataloging) SirsiDynix; (Circulation) SirsiDynix; (Course Reserve) SirsiDynix; (OPAC) SirsiDynix
Database Vendor: Alexander Street Press, Bowker, CQ Press, EBSCOhost, Facts on File, Gale Cengage Learning, OCLC FirstSearch, ProQuest, RefWorks
Wireless access
Publications: Grace Library Student Handbook
Partic in Lyrasis; OCLC Online Computer Library Center, Inc; Pennsylvania Academic Library Consortium, Inc (PALCI); Pittsburgh Council on Higher Education (PCHE)
Open Mon-Thurs 8am-Midnight, Fri 8am-9pm, Sat 8-4:30, Sun 12:30-4:30

P CARNEGIE LIBRARY OF PITTSBURGH*, 4400 Forbes Ave, 15213-4007. SAN 359-2561. Tel: 412-622-3114. Interlibrary Loan Service Tel: 412-920-4535. Reference Tel: 412-622-3175. FAX: 412-622-6278. Reference FAX: 412-687-8982. TDD: 412-622-3167. E-mail: info@carnegielibrary.org. Web Site: www.carnegielibrary.org. *Pres & Dir,* Mary Frances Cooper; Tel: 412-622-8874, E-mail: director@carnegielibrary.org; *Dep Dir,* Susan Banks; Tel: 412-622-1911, E-mail: bankssu@carnegielibrary.org; *Dir, Digital Strategy & Tech Integration,* Toby Greenwalt; Staff 104.4 (MLS 104.4)
Founded 1895. Pop 458,597; Circ 3,540,244
Jan 2012-Dec 2012 Income (Main Library and Branch(s)) $28,128,409, State $3,357,529, City $40,000, Federal $214,734, Locally Generated Income $18,681,200, Other $5,834,946. Mats Exp $3,842,127. Sal $15,497,075
Library Holdings: Bk Vols 1,895,092; Per Subs 3,405
Special Collections: 19th Century American & German Music Journals (Merz Music Library); Architecture & Design (Bernd Coll); Atomic Energy Commission Reports, micro; Cartoons (Cy Hungerford Coll), originals on pasteboard; English Translation of DIN Standards, trade cats; Local History (Isaac Craig Coll, Pittsburgh Newspapers, 1786-date, Pittsburgh Photographic Library); Narratives (Imbrie Memorial Coll); US Government Research Reports (PB Reports incl OTS Translations), micro; US Patents, 1872-date & British Patents, 1617-date, bks, micro; World War I Personal Coll. State Document Depository; US Document Depository
Subject Interests: Archit, Art, Children's lit, Genealogy, Humanities, Indust, Local hist, Music, Natural sci, Soc sci
Automation Activity & Vendor Info: (Acquisitions) Innovative Interfaces, Inc; (Cataloging) Innovative Interfaces, Inc; (Circulation) Innovative Interfaces, Inc; (ILL) Innovative Interfaces, Inc; (OPAC) Innovative Interfaces, Inc; (Serials) Innovative Interfaces, Inc
Database Vendor: Innovative Interfaces, Inc
Wireless access
Publications: A Purchase Guide for Branch & Public Libraries; Science & Technology Desk Reference; The Bridges of Pittsburgh & Allegheny County
Mem of Allegheny County Library Association
Partic in Electronic Info Network (eiNetwork); Oakland Library Consortium (OLC)
Special Services for the Deaf - TDD equip
Open Mon-Thurs 10-8, Fri & Sat 10-5:30, Sun 12-5
Friends of the Library Group
Branches: 17
BEECHVIEW, 1910 Broadway Ave, 15216-3130, SAN 359-2685. Tel: 412-563-2900. FAX: 412-563-7530. E-mail: beechview@carnegielibrary.org. Web Site: www.carnegielibrary.org/locations/beechview. *Mgr,* Audrey Iacone; E-mail: iaconea@carnegielibrary.org
Circ 56,153
Library Holdings: Bk Vols 32,983; Per Subs 64
Open Mon, Tues & Thurs 10-8, Wed, Fri & Sat 10-5
Friends of the Library Group
BROOKLINE, 708 Brookline Blvd, 15226, SAN 359-2715. Tel: 412-561-1003. E-mail: brookline@carnegielibrary.org. Web Site: www.carnegielibrary.org/locations/brookline. *Mgr,* Jessica Clark; E-mail: clark2@carnegielibrary.org
Circ 131,039
Library Holdings: Bk Vols 37,837; Per Subs 50
Open Mon-Thurs 10-8, Fri & Sat 10-5
Friends of the Library Group
CARRICK, 1811 Brownsville Rd, 15210-3907, SAN 359-274X. Tel: 412-882-3897. FAX: 412-882-0131. E-mail: carrick@carnegielibrary.org. Web Site: www.carnegielibrary.org/locations/carrick. *Mgr,* Julie Kuchta; E-mail: kuchtaj@carnegielibrary.org
Circ 67,647
Library Holdings: Bk Vols 25,733; Per Subs 64
Open Mon, Fri & Sat 10-5, Tues-Thurs 10-8
Friends of the Library Group
DOWNTOWN & BUSINESS, 612 Smithfield St, 15222-2506, SAN 359-2626. Tel: 412-281-7141. FAX: 412-471-1724. E-mail: downtown@carnegielibrary.org. Web Site: www.carnegielibrary.org/locations/downtown. *Dept Head,* Karen Rossi; E-mail: rossik@carnegielibrary.org
Circ 270,852
Library Holdings: Bk Vols 60,815; Per Subs 145
Special Collections: Industrial & Trade Directories; Pittsburgh Company Index
Subject Interests: Computer sci, Finance, Mkt, Performing arts
Publications: Bibliographies; Pathfinders; What's New
Special Services for the Blind - Computer with voice synthesizer for visually impaired persons
Open Mon-Thurs 8:30-6, Fri 8:30-5, Sat 10-5
Friends of the Library Group
EAST LIBERTY, 130 S Whitfield St, 15206-3806, SAN 359-2804. Tel: 412-363-8232. FAX: 412-363-8272. E-mail: eastliberty@carnegielibrary.org. Web Site: www.carnegielibrary.org/locations/eastliberty. *Dept Head,* Chris Gmiter; E-mail: gmiter@carnegielibrary.org
Circ 189,177
Library Holdings: Bk Vols 77,268; Per Subs 97
Open Mon-Thurs 10-8, Fri & Sat 10-5
Friends of the Library Group
HAZELWOOD, 4901 Second Ave, 15207-1674, SAN 359-2839. Tel: 412-421-2517. FAX: 412-422-9845. E-mail: hazelwood@carnegielibrary.org. Web Site: www.carnegielibrary.org/locations/hazelwood. *Mgr,* Mary Ann McHarg; E-mail: mchargm@carnegielibrary.org
Circ 49,949
Library Holdings: Bk Vols 17,285; Per Subs 40
Open Mon, Fri & Sat 10-5, Tues-Thurs 10-8
Friends of the Library Group
HILL DISTRICT, 2177 Centre Ave, 15219-6316, SAN 359-3134. Tel: 412-281-3753. FAX: 412-281-6272. E-mail: hilldistrict@carnegielibrary.org. Web Site: www.carnegielibrary.org/locations/hilldistrict. *Mgr,* Joyce Broadus; E-mail: broadusj@carnegielibrary.org; Staff 5 (MLS 3, Non-MLS 2)
Circ 22,746
Library Holdings: Bk Vols 22,935; Per Subs 34
Open Mon-Wed 10-8, Thurs-Sat 10-5
Friends of the Library Group
HOMEWOOD, 7101 Hamilton Ave, 15208-1052, SAN 359-2863. Tel: 412-731-3080. E-mail: homewood@carnegielibrary.org. Web Site: www.carnegielibrary.org/locations/homewood. *Mgr,* Denise Graham; E-mail: grahamd@carnegielibrary.org
Circ 86,648
Library Holdings: Bk Vols 39,056; Per Subs 65
Subject Interests: African-Am culture
Open Mon & Wed 10-7, Tues, Thurs & Sat 10-5
Friends of the Library Group
KNOXVILLE, 400 Brownsville Rd, 15210-2251, SAN 359-2898. Tel: 412-381-6543. FAX: 412-381-9833. E-mail: knoxville@carnegielibrary.org. Web Site: www.carnegielibrary.org/locations/knoxville. *Mgr,* Jennifer Pickle; E-mail: picklej@carnegielibrary.org
Circ 50,682
Library Holdings: Bk Vols 24,515; Per Subs 56
Open Mon-Wed 10-8, Thurs-Sat 10-5
Friends of the Library Group
LAWRENCEVILLE, 279 Fisk St, 15201-2847, SAN 359-2928. Tel: 412-682-3668. FAX: 412-682-5943. E-mail: lawrenceville@carnegielibrary.org. Web Site: www.carnegielibrary.org/locations/lawrenceville. *Mgr,* LeeAnn Anna
Library Holdings: Bk Vols 24,110; Per Subs 38
Open Mon-Wed 10-8, Thurs-Sat 10-5
Friends of the Library Group

P LIBRARY FOR THE BLIND & PHYSICALLY HANDICAPPED, Leonard C Staisey Bldg, 4724 Baum Blvd, 15213-1321, SAN 315-0461. Tel: 412-687-2440. Toll Free Tel: 800-242-0586. FAX: 412-687-2442. E-mail: lbph@carnegielibrary.org. Web Site: www.carnegielibrary.org/lbph. *Dir,* Kathleen Kappel; E-mail: kappelk@carnegielibrary.org
Special Collections: Materials on Disabilities
Publications: Three Rivers News (Newsletter); Three Rivers News Junior (Newsletter)

Special Services for the Blind - Assistive/Adapted tech devices, equip & products; Bks on cassette; Cassette playback machines; Closed circuit TV; Computer with voice synthesizer for visually impaired persons; Copier with enlargement capabilities; Descriptive video serv (DVS); Digital talking bk; Digital talking bk machines; Large print bks; Large screen computer & software; Newsletter (in large print, Braille or on cassette); Newsline for the Blind; Ref serv; Tel Pioneers equip repair group; Volunteer serv; Web-Braille
Open Mon-Fri 9-5
Friends of the Library Group

MOUNT WASHINGTON, 315 Grandview Ave, 15211-1549, SAN 359-2952. Tel: 412-381-3380. FAX: 412-381-9876. E-mail: mtwashington@carnegielibrary.org. Web Site: www.carnegielibrary.org/locations/mtwashington. *Dept Head,* Marian Streiff; E-mail: streiffm@carnegielibrary.org
Circ 77,303
Library Holdings: Bk Vols 25,634; Per Subs 68
Open Mon, Fri & Sat 10-5, Tues-Thurs 10-8
Friends of the Library Group

SHERADEN, 720 Sherwood Ave, 15204-1724, SAN 359-2987. Tel: 412-331-1135. E-mail: sheraden@carnegielibrary.org. Web Site: www.carnegielibrary.org/locations/sheraden. *Mgr,* Ian Eberhardt; Staff 6 (MLS 2, Non-MLS 4)
Circ 42,993
Library Holdings: Bk Vols 22,442; Per Subs 25
Open Mon-Wed 10-8, Thurs-Sat 10-5
Friends of the Library Group

SOUTH SIDE, 2205 E Carson St, 15203, SAN 359-3010. Tel: 412-431-0505. FAX: 412-431-7968. E-mail: southside@carnegielibrary.org. Web Site: www.carnegielibrary.org/locations/southside. *Mgr,* Suzy Waldo; E-mail: waldos@carnegielibrary.org
Circ 74,382
Library Holdings: Bk Vols 27,331; Per Subs 68
Open Mon-Wed 10-8, Thurs-Sat 10-5
Friends of the Library Group

SQUIRREL HILL, 5801 Forbes Ave, 15217-1601, SAN 359-3045. Tel: 412-422-9650. FAX: 412-422-5811. E-mail: squirrelhill@carnegielibrary.org. Web Site: www.carnegielibrary.org/locations/squirrelhill. *Dept Head,* Jody Bell
Circ 511,546
Library Holdings: Bk Vols 106,728; Per Subs 147
Special Collections: Jewish History & Culture (Olender Foundation)
Open Mon-Thurs 10-8, Fri & Sat 10-5, Sun 1-5
Friends of the Library Group

WEST END, 47 Wabash St, 15220-5422, SAN 359-307X. Tel: 412-921-1717. FAX: 412-921-3494. E-mail: westend@carnegielibrary.org. Web Site: www.carnegielibrary.org/locations/westend. *Mgr,* Mark Lee; E-mail: leem@carnegielibrary.org
Circ 32,983
Library Holdings: Bk Vols 22,307; Per Subs 35
Open Mon, Fri & Sat 10-5, Tues-Thurs 10-8
Friends of the Library Group

WOODS RUN, 1201 Woods Run Ave, 15212-2335, SAN 359-310X. Tel: 412-761-3730. FAX: 412-761-3445. E-mail: woodsrun@carnegielibrary.org. Web Site: www.carnegielibrary.org/locations/woodsrun. *Br Mgr,* Ellen Paul
Circ 100,305
Library Holdings: Bk Vols 32,239; Per Subs 53
Open Mon, Fri & Sat 10-5, Tues-Thurs 10-8
Friends of the Library Group

C CARNEGIE MELLON UNIVERSITY*, University Libraries, Hunt Library, 4909 Frew St, 15213-3833. SAN 359-3193. Tel: 412-268-2446. Reference Tel: 412-268-2442. FAX: 412-268-2793. E-mail: ul-huntref@andrew.cmu.edu. Web Site: www.library.cmu.edu. *Dean, Univ Libr,* Keith G Webster; E-mail: kwebster@andrew.cmu.edu; *Assoc Dean,* Erika Linke; Tel: 412-268-7800, E-mail: elo8@andrew.cmu.edu; *Head of Acq Serv,* Denise Novak; *Head, Access Serv,* Joan Stein; *Head, Archives,* Gabrielle V Michalek; *Head, Cat,* Terry Hurlbert; *Head, Libr Info Tech,* Melanie Myers; *Head, Library Info Tech, Res & Develop,* Chris Kellen; *Interim Head, Ref, Soc Sci Librn,* Afeworki Paulos; E-mail: apaulos2@andrew.cmu.edu; *Head, Spec Coll,* Martin Aurand; *Bus & Econ Librn,* Roye Werner; *Music Librn,* Kristin Heath; *Ref Librn,* Sue Collins; Tel: 412-268-5019; *Ref Librn,* Ethan Pullman; *Ser Librn,* Alice Bright; *Spec Coll Librn,* Mary Kay Johnsen; Tel: 412-268-6622; *Computer Serv Mgr,* Richard Schall; *Syst Mgr,* Ken Rose; *Syst Mgr,* Rashid Siddiqui; *Circ Supvr,* Ona Taylor; *Ref Serv Supvr,* Precious Jones; *Admin Coordr,* Andrea Cohen; *Cat Spec,* Jan Hardy; *Libr Syst Spec,* Jon Singletary; *Cataloger,* Linda Dujmic; *Univ Archivist,* Patrick Trembeth; Tel: 412-268-7402, E-mail: ptrembet@andrew.cmu.edu; Staff 94 (MLS 26, Non-MLS 68)
Founded 1920. Enrl 8,687; Fac 525; Highest Degree: Doctorate
Library Holdings: Bk Vols 1,021,423; Per Subs 2,945
Special Collections: Architecture Archives; Bookbindings (including Edwards of Halifax); Early Scientific Works; Important Early Printers (Aldus, Plantin & Estienne Coll); Private Presses (Kimscott & Doves Coll); Senator John Heinz III Archives
Automation Activity & Vendor Info: (Acquisitions) SirsiDynix; (Cataloging) SirsiDynix; (Circulation) SirsiDynix; (Course Reserve) SirsiDynix; (ILL) OCLC; (OPAC) SirsiDynix; (Serials) SirsiDynix
Database Vendor: EBSCOhost, Gale Cengage Learning, JSTOR, LexisNexis, OCLC FirstSearch, ProQuest, SirsiDynix, Wilson - Wilson Web
Wireless access
Function: ILL available, Photocopying/Printing
Partic in Center for Research Libraries; Digital Libr Fedn; Interlibrary Delivery Service of Pennsylvania; Lyrasis; Oakland Library Consortium (OLC); OCLC Online Computer Library Center, Inc; Pennsylvania Academic Library Consortium, Inc (PALCI)

Departmental Libraries:

HUNT INSTITUTE FOR BOTANICAL DOCUMENTATION, Hunt Library Bldg, 5th Flr, 4909 Frew St, 15213-3833, SAN 315-0739. Tel: 412-268-7301. Reference Tel: 412-268-2436. FAX: 412-268-5677. E-mail: huntinst@andrew.cmu.edu. Web Site: huntbot.andrew.cmu.edu. *Librn,* Charlotte A Tancin; E-mail: ctancin@cmu.edu; *Asst Librn,* Jeannette McDevitt; E-mail: jmcdevit@andrew.cmu.edu; Staff 2 (MLS 2)
Founded 1961
Library Holdings: Bk Titles 29,950; Per Subs 200
Special Collections: 18th Century Taxonomy (Michel Adanson Coll), bks, ms; Linnaeana (Strandell Coll), bks, clippings
Subject Interests: Biog of people in plant sci, Botanical bibliography, Botanical illustration, Hist of bot, Hist of sci
Function: Archival coll, Art exhibits, For res purposes, Mail & tel request accepted, Online cat, Ref & res, Ref serv available, Ref serv in person, Res libr
Restriction: Closed stack, Non-circulating, Not a lending libr, Restricted loan policy

MELLON INSTITUTE LIBRARY, 4400 Fifth Ave, 4th Flr, 15213-2617, SAN 359-3258. Tel: 412-268-3171. FAX: 412-268-6945. E-mail: sciref@andrew.cmu.edu. Web Site: guides.library.cmu.edu/melloninstitute. *Head, Sci Libr,* Matthew Marsteller; *Chem & Biol Librn,* Diane Covington; *Computer Sci Librn,* Jillian Miller. Subject Specialists: *Biol, Chem,* Diane Covington
Founded 1911
Subject Interests: Biological sci, Chem
Open Mon-Fri 8:30-5

SOFTWARE ENGINEERING INSTITUTE LIBRARY, 4500 Fifth Ave, 15213-2612. Tel: 412-268-7733. FAX: 412-268-1340. E-mail: library@sei.cmu.edu. *Mgr, Libr Serv,* Sheila Rosenthal; E-mail: slr@sei.cmu.edu; *Ref Librn,* Rachel Callison; E-mail: callison@sei.cmu.edu; *ILL, Libr Assoc,* Terry Ireland; E-mail: tas@sei.cmu.edu; *Libr Spec,* Michelle C Fried; E-mail: mfried@sei.cmu.edu; Staff 4 (MLS 2, Non-MLS 2)
Founded 1986. Fac 2
Library Holdings: Bk Vols 12,600; Per Subs 245
Subject Interests: Computer sci, Software eng, Syst eng
Function: Res libr
Open Mon-Fri 8:30-5
Restriction: Access at librarian's discretion

SORRELLS ENGINEERING & SCIENCE LIBRARY, 4400 Wean Hall, 15213, SAN 359-3223. Tel: 412-268-2426. *Head, Sci Libr,* Matthew Marsteller; *Principal Librn,* G Lynn Berard; *Computer Sci Librn,* Jillian Miller; *Eng Librn,* Donna Beck. Subject Specialists: *Math sci, Physics,* Matthew Marsteller; *Civil eng, Environ eng, Mechanical eng,* G Lynn Berard; *Chem eng, Mat sci,* Donna Beck
Founded 1971
Special Collections: Energy & Environment; Robotics & Computer Science
Subject Interests: Computer sci, Energy, Eng, Environ, Math, Physics, Robotics

S CARNEGIE MUSEUM OF NATURAL HISTORY LIBRARY, 4400 Forbes Ave, 15213-4080. SAN 315-047X. Tel: 412-622-3284. FAX: 412-622-8837. E-mail: cmnhweb@carnegiemnh.org. Web Site: www.carnegiemnh.org/science/default.aspx?=8923. *Libr Mgr,* Xianghua Sun; E-mail: sunx@carnegiemnh.org; Staff 4 (MLS 2, Non-MLS 2)
Founded 1896
Library Holdings: Bk Titles 26,200; Bk Vols 132,000; Per Subs 1,500
Subject Interests: Amphibians, Anthrop, Archaeology, Birds, Botany, Invertebrate paleontology, Invertebrate zool, Mammals, Reptiles, Vertebrate paleontology
Automation Activity & Vendor Info: (Cataloging) Innovative Interfaces, Inc; (OPAC) Innovative Interfaces, Inc; (Serials) Innovative Interfaces, Inc
Database Vendor: BioOne
Function: For res purposes
Open Mon-Fri 9-5

C CHATHAM COLLEGE*, Jennie King Mellon Library, Woodland Rd, 15232. SAN 315-0496. Tel: 412-365-1245. Reference Tel: 412-365-1670. FAX: 412-365-1465. Web Site: www.chatham.edu/academics/library.cfm. *Dir,* Jill Ausel; Tel: 412-365-1244, E-mail: jausel@chatham.edu; *Head, Tech Serv,* Dan Nolting; Tel: 412-365-1243, E-mail: dnolting@chatham.edu; *Access Serv,* Jamie Peretich; Tel: 412-365-1619; *Ref,* Dana Mastroinni; Tel: 412-365-1602, E-mail: dmoore@chatham.edu; *Ref,* Irma Smith; Tel: 412-365-1247; Staff 7 (MLS 4, Non-MLS 3)
Founded 1869. Enrl 1,000; Fac 50; Highest Degree: Master
Library Holdings: Bk Titles 94,000; Bk Vols 97,000; Per Subs 365
Special Collections: African-American (Wray Coll); Mayan Art & Civilization (Snowdon Coll)
Subject Interests: Women studies
Automation Activity & Vendor Info: (Acquisitions) Innovative Interfaces, Inc; (Cataloging) Innovative Interfaces, Inc; (Circulation) Innovative Interfaces, Inc; (Course Reserve) Innovative Interfaces, Inc; (ILL) Innovative Interfaces, Inc; (Media Booking) Innovative Interfaces, Inc; (OPAC) Innovative Interfaces, Inc; (Serials) Innovative Interfaces, Inc
Database Vendor: Dialog, EBSCOhost, LexisNexis, OCLC FirstSearch, ProQuest
Partic in OCLC Online Computer Library Center, Inc; OHIONET
Open Mon-Thurs 7:45am-Midnight, Fri 7:45-5, Sat 8-7, Sun Noon-Midnight

S CHILDREN'S INSTITUTE LIBRARY*, 1405 Shady Ave, 15217-1350. SAN 315-1115. Tel: 412-420-2247. FAX: 412-420-2510. Web Site: www.amazingkids.org. *Med Librn,* Karen Liljequist; E-mail: kli@the-institute.org; Staff 1 (MLS 1)
Founded 1972
Library Holdings: Bk Vols 2,100; Per Subs 70
Subject Interests: Asthma, Burn injury, Cerebral palsy, Children's lit, Head injury, Learning disabilities, Pediatrics, Prader-Willi, Rehabilitation, Spina bifida, Unusual syndromes (staff libr)
Automation Activity & Vendor Info: (Acquisitions) Innovative Interfaces, Inc; (Cataloging) Innovative Interfaces, Inc; (Circulation) Innovative Interfaces, Inc
Database Vendor: EBSCOhost, PubMed
Open Mon-Fri 8:30-5

L COHEN & GRIGSBY PC*, Law Library, 625 Liberty Ave, 15222-3152. SAN 374-6224. Tel: 412-297-4870. FAX: 412-209-0672. Web Site: www.cohenlaw.com. *Librn,* Tony Chan; Staff 1 (MLS 1)
Library Holdings: Bk Titles 839; Bk Vols 961; Per Subs 160
Subject Interests: Employment, Immigration
Automation Activity & Vendor Info: (Acquisitions) Inmagic, Inc.; (Cataloging) Inmagic, Inc.
Wireless access
Restriction: Open by appt only

COMMUNITY COLLEGE OF ALLEGHENY COUNTY

J ALLEGHENY CAMPUS LIBRARY*, 808 Ridge Ave, 15212-6003, SAN 315-0526. Tel: 412-237-2585. FAX: 412-237-6563. E-mail: library@ccac.edu. Web Site: www.ccac.edu/library. *Dir,* Anne Tanski; *Librn,* Dennis Hennessey; *Librn,* Ruth Byers; *Librn, Web Coordr,* Elora Cunningham; *Librn,* David Mooney; *Archivist,* Pat Moran; Staff 4 (MLS 4)
Founded 1966. Enrl 5,400; Fac 177
Library Holdings: Bk Titles 75,682; Per Subs 294
Automation Activity & Vendor Info: (Cataloging) SirsiDynix; (Circulation) SirsiDynix; (Course Reserve) SirsiDynix; (OPAC) SirsiDynix; (Serials) SirsiDynix
Database Vendor: EBSCOhost, Gale Cengage Learning, OCLC FirstSearch, ProQuest
Partic in Knight-Ridder Info, Inc; Lyrasis; OCLC Online Computer Library Center, Inc
Open Mon-Thurs 8-8, Fri 8-4, Sat 9-3

J NORTH CAMPUS LIBRARY & LEARNING SERVICES*, 8701 Perry Hwy, 15237-5372. Tel: 412-369-3681. FAX: 412-369-3626. Web Site: www.ccac.edu/library. *Operations Mgr,* Anne Tanski; E-mail: atanski@ccac.edu; *Dept Head, Librn,* Barbara Thompson; Tel: 412-369-3671, E-mail: bthompson@ccac.edu; Staff 6 (MLS 3, Non-MLS 3)
Highest Degree: Associate
Library Holdings: Bk Titles 20,599; Bk Vols 24,073; Per Subs 167
Automation Activity & Vendor Info: (Cataloging) SirsiDynix; (Circulation) SirsiDynix; (OPAC) SirsiDynix
Database Vendor: EBSCOhost, OCLC FirstSearch
Open Mon-Thurs 8-9, Fri 8-4, Sat 8-2:30

S CONSAD RESEARCH CORP LIBRARY*, 121 N Highland Ave, 15206. SAN 371-0211. Tel: 412-363-5500. FAX: 412-363-5509. Web Site: www.consad.com. *Pres,* W A Steger; E-mail: wasteger@consad.com; Staff 1 (Non-MLS 1)
Library Holdings: Bk Titles 1,891; Bk Vols 1,940; Per Subs 160
Wireless access
Open Mon-Fri 9-5

P COOPER-SIEGEL COMMUNITY LIBRARY*, 403 Fox Chapel Rd, 15238. Tel: 412-828-9520. FAX: 412-828-4960. Web Site: www.coopersiegelcommunitylibrary.org. *Exec Dir,* Stephanie Flom; E-mail: sflom@boydcommunitycenter.org; *Libr Dir,* Kathy Amrhein; E-mail: amrheink@einetwork.net; *Libr Mgr,* Jill McConnell; Staff 17 (MLS 8, Non-MLS 9)
Library Holdings: Bk Vols 81,438; Per Subs 237
Special Collections: Lauri Ann West Children's Coll, bks, cds
Automation Activity & Vendor Info: (Acquisitions) Innovative Interfaces, Inc; (Cataloging) Innovative Interfaces, Inc; (Circulation) Innovative Interfaces, Inc; (OPAC) Innovative Interfaces, Inc; (Serials) Innovative Interfaces, Inc
Mem of Allegheny County Library Association
Open Mon, Wed & Thurs 10-8, Tues & Fri 10-5, Sat 10-4 (Summer 9-4), Sun (Sept-June) 1-5
Branches: 1
SHARPSBURG BRANCH, 1212 Main St, 15215. Tel: 412-781-0783. *Br Mgr,* Kathy Amrhein; E-mail: amrheink@einetwork.net
Library Holdings: Bk Vols 12,990
Open Mon 10-6, Tues 10-2, Thurs 2-8, Sat 10-4

P CRAFTON PUBLIC LIBRARY, 140 Bradford Ave, 15205. SAN 378-424X. Tel: 412-922-6877. FAX: 412-922-7637. Web Site: www.craftonpubliclibrary.com. *Dir,* Kathryn Robinson; *Ch Serv,* Carolyn Rosenquest; Staff 2 (MLS 2)
Founded 1937. Pop 5,971
Library Holdings: Bk Vols 30,000; Per Subs 75
Automation Activity & Vendor Info: (Cataloging) Innovative Interfaces, Inc; (Circulation) Innovative Interfaces, Inc; (OPAC) Innovative Interfaces, Inc
Wireless access
Mem of Allegheny County Library Association
Partic in Electronic Info Network (eiNetwork)
Open Mon & Fri 9-5, Tues-Thurs 12-8, Sat 9-4
Friends of the Library Group

R CRAFTON UNITED PRESBYTERIAN CHURCH LIBRARY*, 80 Bradford Ave, 15205. SAN 315-0550. Tel: 412-921-2293. FAX: 412-921-0348. *Adminr,* Jennifer A Elo
Library Holdings: Bk Vols 600
Open Mon-Fri 9-2:30

SR DIOCESE OF PITTSBURGH*, Learning Media Center, 2900 Noblestown Rd, 15205. SAN 315-0577. Tel: 412-928-5817. FAX: 412-928-5833. E-mail: lmc@diopitt.org. Web Site: www.diopitt.org. *Dir,* Jeff Hirst
Library Holdings: Bk Vols 3,500; Per Subs 81
Open Mon-Fri 9-4

P DORMONT PUBLIC LIBRARY*, 2950 W Liberty Ave, 15216-2594. SAN 315-0585. Tel: 412-531-8754. FAX: 412-531-1601. Web Site: www.dormontlibrary.org. *Dir,* Cindy D'Agostino; E-mail: DAgostinoc@einetwork.net; Staff 1 (Non-MLS 1)
Founded 1936. Pop 8,600; Circ 43,096
Jan 2007-Dec 2007 Income $388,342, State $46,867, City $76,150, County $64,524, Locally Generated Income $200,801. Mats Exp $32,350, Books $26,658, Per/Ser (Incl. Access Fees) $1,571, AV Mat $2,873, Presv $1,248. Sal $108,101 (Prof $36,000)
Library Holdings: AV Mats 2,574; e-books 15,073; Electronic Media & Resources 2,376; Bk Vols 26,361; Per Subs 64
Subject Interests: Accelerated readers, Classics, Small bus
Automation Activity & Vendor Info: (Acquisitions) Innovative Interfaces, Inc; (Cataloging) Innovative Interfaces, Inc; (Circulation) Innovative Interfaces, Inc; (Course Reserve) Innovative Interfaces, Inc; (ILL) Innovative Interfaces, Inc; (Media Booking) Innovative Interfaces, Inc; (OPAC) Innovative Interfaces, Inc; (Serials) Innovative Interfaces, Inc
Wireless access
Mem of Allegheny County Library Association
Open Mon-Thurs 9-9, Fri & Sat 9-5

CR DUQUESNE UNIVERSITY*, Gumberg Library, 600 Forbes Ave, 15282. SAN 359-3282. Tel: 412-396-6130. Circulation Tel: 412-396-6131. Interlibrary Loan Service Tel: 412-396-5341. Reference Tel: 412-396-6133. Administration Tel: 412-396-6136. Interlibrary Loan Service FAX: 412-396-1800. Web Site: www.duq.edu/library. *Univ Librn,* Dr Laverna Saunders; E-mail: lsaunders@duq.edu; *Dir, Info Serv,* Maureen Diana Sasso; Tel: 412-396-5680, E-mail: sasso@duq.edu; *Head, Coll Mgt,* Tracie Ballock; Tel: 412-396-4560, Fax: 412-396-5639, E-mail: ballockt@duq.edu; *Health Sci Librn, Libr Assessment Coordr,* David Nolfi; Tel: 412-396-4931, E-mail: nolfi@duq.edu; Staff 24 (MLS 18, Non-MLS 6)
Founded 1878. Enrl 9,312; Fac 983; Highest Degree: Doctorate

Jul 2011-Jun 2012 Income (Main Library Only) $5,493,939. Mats Exp $2,123,979. Sal $1,961,666 (Prof $1,256,922)
Library Holdings: Audiobooks 126; AV Mats 89,421; CDs 10,993; DVDs 4,265; e-books 74,771; e-journals 101,487; Microforms 252,149; Music Scores 16,322; Bk Titles 415,900; Bk Vols 532,777; Per Subs 369; Videos 1,125
Special Collections: Cardinal John Wright Coll; Judge Michael Musmanno Coll; Maureen Sullivan Curriculum Center; Rabbi Herman Hailperin Coll; Simon Silverman Phenomenology Coll
Subject Interests: Catholic studies, Ethics, Philos, Theol
Automation Activity & Vendor Info: (Acquisitions) SirsiDynix; (Cataloging) SirsiDynix; (Circulation) SirsiDynix; (ILL) OCLC ILLiad; (OPAC) SirsiDynix; (Serials) Ex Libris Group
Database Vendor: ACM (Association for Computing Machinery), Agricola, American Chemical Society, American Mathematical Society, American Physical Society, American Psychological Association (APA), Annual Reviews, ARTstor, Blackwell, Bowker, Cambridge Scientific Abstracts, CIOS (Communication Institute for Online Scholarship), CQ Press, CRC Press/Taylor & Francis Group, CredoReference, EBSCOhost, Elsevier, Emerald, Ex Libris Group, Facts on File, Gale Cengage Learning, Haworth Pres Inc, ISI Web of Knowledge, JSTOR, Lexi-Comp, LexisNexis, MD Consult, Mergent Online, Micromedex, Nature Publishing Group, OCLC FirstSearch, OCLC WorldShare Interlibrary Loan, OVID Technologies, Oxford Online, Project MUSE, ProQuest, PubMed, RefWorks, Sage, ScienceDirect, Scopus, SirsiDynix, Springer-Verlag, ValueLine, Wiley InterScience, Wilson - Wilson Web, YBP Library Services
Wireless access
Publications: BiblioBrief (Online only)
Partic in Basic Health Sciences Library Network; Lyrasis; National Network of Libraries of Medicine; Pennsylvania Academic Library Consortium, Inc (PALCI)
Special Services for the Blind - Bks on cassette; Bks on CD; Copier with enlargement capabilities; Duplicating spec requests; Recorded bks; Ref serv; Sound rec; Videos on blindness & phys handicaps
Open Mon-Thurs 7am-1am, Fri 7-9, Sat 10-9, Sun 11am-1am

Departmental Libraries:

CL CENTER FOR LEGAL INFORMATION, 900 Locust St, 15282. (Mail add: Center for Legal Information, 600 Forbes Ave, 15282). Tel: 412-396-5017. Reference Tel: 412-396-1697. FAX: 412-396-6294. E-mail: lawlibrary@duq.edu. Web Site: www.duq.edu/academics/schools/law/law-library. *Dir,* Frank Y Liu; Tel: 412-396-5018, E-mail: liu@duq.edu; *Assoc Dir,* Dittakavi Rao; Tel: 412-396-5014, E-mail: rao@duq.edu; *Asst Dir, Pub Serv,* Tsegaye Beru; Tel: 412-396-4423, E-mail: beru@duq.edu; *Asst Dir, Tech Serv,* Patricia Horvath; Tel: 412-396-5016, E-mail: horvath@duq.edu; *Ref Librn/Circ Syst,* Charles Sprowls; Tel: 412-396-5533, E-mail: sprowlsc@duq.edu; *Mgr, Database Syst/Cat,* Amy Lovell; Tel: 412-396-6292, E-mail: lovell@duq.edu; Staff 11 (MLS 6, Non-MLS 5)
Founded 1911
Library Holdings: Bk Titles 182,390; Bk Vols 265,903; Per Subs 5,126
Special Collections: UN Document Depository; US Document Depository
Automation Activity & Vendor Info: (Acquisitions) Innovative Interfaces, Inc; (Cataloging) Innovative Interfaces, Inc; (Circulation) Innovative Interfaces, Inc; (Course Reserve) Innovative Interfaces, Inc; (ILL) Innovative Interfaces, Inc; (Media Booking) Innovative Interfaces, Inc; (OPAC) Innovative Interfaces, Inc; (Serials) Innovative Interfaces, Inc
Publications: DuqLawWire (Newsletter)
Open Mon-Thurs 7:30 am-Midnight, Fri 7:30am-10pm, Sat 9-9, Sun Noon-Midnight

R EAST LIBERTY PRESBYTERIAN CHURCH LIBRARY*, 116 S Highland Ave, 15206. SAN 315-0615. Tel: 412-441-3800. FAX: 412-441-4422. Web Site: www.cathedralofhope.org.
Library Holdings: Bk Titles 2,160; Bk Vols 2,340; Per Subs 7

P GREEN TREE PUBLIC LIBRARY*, Ten W Manilla Ave, 1st Flr, 15220-3310. SAN 315-0666. Tel: 412-921-9292. FAX: 412-921-4004. TDD: 412-921-9004. E-mail: greentree@einetwork.net. Web Site: www.einetwork.net/ein/greentree. *Dir,* Suzy Ruskin; *Asst Dir,* Stephanie Ross; E-mail: rosss@einetwork.net; Staff 8 (MLS 2, Non-MLS 6)
Pop 4,938; Circ 55,000
Library Holdings: AV Mats 2,342; Large Print Bks 710; Bk Titles 35,691; Bk Vols 36,780; Per Subs 92
Automation Activity & Vendor Info: (Acquisitions) Innovative Interfaces, Inc; (Cataloging) Innovative Interfaces, Inc; (Circulation) Innovative Interfaces, Inc; (Course Reserve) Innovative Interfaces, Inc; (ILL) Innovative Interfaces, Inc; (Media Booking) Innovative Interfaces, Inc; (OPAC) Innovative Interfaces, Inc; (Serials) Innovative Interfaces, Inc
Publications: Chapter Notes (Newsletter)
Mem of Allegheny County Library Association
Special Services for the Deaf - TDD equip
Special Services for the Blind - Talking bks
Open Mon-Thurs 10-9, Fri & Sat 10-5
Friends of the Library Group

M HEALTHSOUTH HARMARVILLE REHABILITATION HOSPITAL*, Resource Room, Guys Run Rd, 15238. (Mail add: PO Box 11460, 15238-0460), SAN 325-9536. Tel: 412-828-1300, Ext 7511. FAX: 412-826-6722. *Mgr,* Bonnie Lewetag; Staff 1 (Non-MLS 1)
Library Holdings: Bk Titles 1,129; Bk Vols 1,252; Per Subs 18
Publications: Acquisitions & Holdings Lists; Bibliographies; Current Awareness
Partic in BRS; Docline; Pittsburgh-East Hospital Libr Coop
Open Mon-Fri 7:30-4

S HISTORICAL SOCIETY OF WESTERN PENNSYLVANIA*, Library & Archives, 1212 Smallman St, 15222. SAN 315-0712. Tel: 412-454-6364. FAX: 412-454-6028. E-mail: library@hswp.org. Web Site: www.heinzhistorycenter.org. *Dir,* Dr Alexis Macklin; E-mail: asmacklin@heinzhistorycenter.org; *Chief Librn,* Art Louderback; Tel: 412-454-6360, E-mail: calouderback@heinzhistorycenter.org; *Acq,* Robert Stakeley; *Archivist,* David Grinnell; *Image Librn,* Lauren Zabelski; Tel: 412-454-6402; *Ref Serv,* Jolene Wertz; Tel: 412-454-6365, E-mail: jlwertz@hswp.org; Staff 6 (MLS 3, Non-MLS 3)
Founded 1879
Library Holdings: Bk Titles 18,000; Bk Vols 35,000; Per Subs 300
Special Collections: African-American Archives; Business Coll; Italian Archives; Jewish Archives; Polish Archives; Slovak Archives; Women's Coll
Subject Interests: Genealogy, Hist of Western Pa
Function: Archival coll, Res libr
Open Thurs-Sat 10-5
Restriction: Non-circulating

S JEFFERSON REGIONAL MEDICAL CENTER*, Behan Health Science Library, Coal Valley Rd, 15236. (Mail add: PO Box 18119, 15236-0119), SAN 371-1625. Tel: 412-469-5786. FAX: 412-469-5468. *Librn,* Ann Ferrari
Library Holdings: Bk Vols 300; Per Subs 200
Open Mon-Fri 8-4:30

L JONES DAY*, Law Library, 500 Grant St, 31st Flr, 15219. SAN 372-1884. Tel: 412-394-7226. FAX: 412-394-7959. *Libr Serv Mgr,* Nancy S Seymour
Library Holdings: Bk Vols 15,000

L K&L GATES LIBRARY*, The K&L Gates Ctr, 210 Sixth Ave, 15222. SAN 315-0798. Tel: 412-355-6311. FAX: 412-355-6501. Web Site: www.klgates.com. *Dir of Libr Serv,* Gwen Vargas; Tel: 412-355-6718, E-mail: gwen.vargas@klgates.com
Founded 1956
Subject Interests: Corp, Securities, Tax

S KTA-TATOR INC LIBRARY*, 115 Technology Dr, 15275-1085. SAN 372-9184. Tel: 412-788-1300. FAX: 412-788-1306. *Mgr,* Greg Shahen; Staff 1 (Non-MLS 1)
Library Holdings: Bk Titles 286; Bk Vols 320; Per Subs 13
Restriction: Staff use only

C LA ROCHE COLLEGE*, John J Wright Library, 9000 Babcock Blvd, 15237. SAN 315-081X. Tel: 412-536-1063. Circulation Tel: 412-536-1064. Interlibrary Loan Service Tel: 412 536-1057. Reference Tel: 412 536-1061. Administration Tel: 412 536-1059. FAX: 412-536-1062. Web Site: www.intranet.laroche.edu/library. *Dir,* LaVerne P Collins; E-mail: laverne.collins@laroche.edu; *Asst Dir,* Darlene Veghts; Tel: 412-536-1055, E-mail: veghtsd1@laroche.edu; *Ref Serv Coordr,* Jacqueline Bolte; E-mail: boltej1@laroche.edu; Staff 3 (MLS 3)
Founded 1963. Enrl 1,469; Fac 60; Highest Degree: Master
Library Holdings: Bk Titles 70,000; Per Subs 578
Special Collections: US Document Depository
Automation Activity & Vendor Info: (Acquisitions) Innovative Interfaces, Inc; (Cataloging) Innovative Interfaces, Inc; (Circulation) Innovative Interfaces, Inc; (Course Reserve) Innovative Interfaces, Inc; (ILL) Innovative Interfaces, Inc; (Media Booking) Innovative Interfaces, Inc; (OPAC) Innovative Interfaces, Inc; (Serials) Innovative Interfaces, Inc
Partic in Lyrasis; OCLC Online Computer Library Center, Inc
Open Mon-Thurs 8:30am-Midnight, Fri & Sat 8:30-4:30, Sun 1-Midnight

P MT LEBANON PUBLIC LIBRARY, 16 Castle Shannon Blvd, 15228-2252. SAN 315-0917. Tel: 412-531-1912. FAX: 412-531-1161. TDD: 412-531-5268. E-mail: mtlebanon@einetwork.net. Web Site: www.mtlebanonlibrary.org. *Dir,* Cynthia K Richey; E-mail: richeyc@einetwork.net; *Assoc Dir, Fac & Info Tech,* Jeremy White; E-mail: whitej@einetwork.net; *Assoc Dir, Pub Serv,* Position Currently Open; *Sr*

Librn, Ch Serv, Holly Visnesky; E-mail: visneskyh@einetwork.net; Staff 8 (MLS 8)
Founded 1932. Pop 33,137; Circ 554,384
Jan 2013-Jan 2014 Income $2,107,273, State $171,141, City $1,363,791, County $318,794, Locally Generated Income $253,547. Mats Exp $569,976, Books $226,188, Per/Ser (Incl. Access Fees) $14,244, AV Mat $96,948, Electronic Ref Mat (Incl. Access Fees) $62,762, Presv $169,834. Sal $975,395 (Prof $445,089)
Library Holdings: AV Mats 19,864; e-books 82,416; Electronic Media & Resources 20,842; Bk Vols 131,272; Per Subs 269
Special Collections: Local History Coll; Pennsylvania Coll; Special Needs/Disabilities
Subject Interests: Study guides
Automation Activity & Vendor Info: (Cataloging) Innovative Interfaces, Inc; (Circulation) Innovative Interfaces, Inc; (ILL) Innovative Interfaces, Inc; (OPAC) Innovative Interfaces, Inc; (Serials) Innovative Interfaces, Inc
Database Vendor: Alexander Street Press, Booksite, Career Guidance Foundation, Dun & Bradstreet, EBSCOhost, Evanced Solutions, Inc, Facts on File, Foundation Center, Gale Cengage Learning, Grolier Online, LearningExpress, LexisNexis, Medline, Newsbank, OCLC WebJunction, Overdrive, Inc, Oxford Online, ProQuest, ReferenceUSA, Standard & Poor's, TumbleBookLibrary, ValueLine, Westlaw, World Book Online
Wireless access
Function: 24/7 Electronic res, 24/7 Online cat, Accessibility serv available based on individual needs, Activity rm, Adult bk club, Adult literacy prog, After school storytime, Art exhibits, Audiobks via web, AV serv, Bk club(s), Bks on CD, Chess club, Children's prog, Computer training, Computers for patron use, Copy machines, e-mail & chat, E-Reserves, Electronic databases & coll, eReaders, Exhibits, Family literacy, Genealogy discussion group, Handicapped accessible, Holiday prog, Home delivery & serv to Sr ctr & nursing homes, Homebound delivery serv, ILL available, Large print keyboards, Life-long learning prog for all ages, Literacy & newcomer serv, Magazines, Magnifiers for reading, Mango lang, Microfiche/film & reading machines, Movies, Music CDs, Online cat, Online ref, Outreach serv, OverDrive digital audio bks, Photocopying/Printing, Preschool outreach, Preschool reading prog, Prog for adults, Prog for children & young adult, Pub access computers, Scanner, Senior computer classes, Senior outreach, Serves mentally handicapped consumers, Spanish lang bks, Story hour, Study rm, Summer reading prog, Tax forms, Teen prog, Telephone ref, Wheelchair accessible
Publications: More Friends Library Newsletter
Mem of Allegheny County Library Association
Partic in Electronic Info Network (eiNetwork)
Special Services for the Deaf - Bks on deafness & sign lang; Coll on deaf educ; High interest/low vocabulary bks; TTY equip
Special Services for the Blind - Closed circuit TV magnifier; Computer with voice synthesizer for visually impaired persons; Home delivery serv; Large screen computer & software; Magnifiers; Reader equip; Ref serv
Open Mon-Thurs 9-9, Fri & Sat 9-5, Sun 1-5
Friends of the Library Group

S NATIONAL CENTER FOR JUVENILE JUSTICE*, Technical Assistance Resource Center, 3700 S Water St, Ste 200, 15203. SAN 372-9214. Tel: 412-227-6950. FAX: 412-227-6955. Web Site: www.ncjj.org. *Dir,* Melissa Sickmund; Tel: 412-246-0824, E-mail: msickmund@ncjfcj.org; Staff 1 (MLS 1)
Founded 1973
Library Holdings: Bk Titles 16,000; Per Subs 50
Subject Interests: Juv delinquency
Function: Res libr
Open Mon-Fri 8-5

S NATIONAL INSTITUTE FOR OCCUPATIONAL SAFETY & HEALTH*, Pittsburgh Library, Cochrans Mill Rd, 15236. (Mail add: PO Box 18070, 15236-8070), SAN 370-2758. Tel: 412-386-4431. FAX: 412-386-4592. E-mail: kis2@cdc.gov. *Dir,* Kathleen Stabryla; *Librn,* Carolyn Biglow; Staff 2 (MLS 2)
Library Holdings: Bk Vols 165,000; Per Subs 100
Automation Activity & Vendor Info: (OPAC) Livelink for Libraries
Partic in National Network of Libraries of Medicine South Central Region

S NEVILLE CHEMICAL CO*, Research & Development Library, 2800 Neville Rd, 15225-1496. SAN 371-6899. Tel: 412-331-4200. FAX: 412-771-0226. Web Site: www.nevchem.com. *Dir, Res & Develop,* Gary Scheeser; E-mail: gscheeser@nevchem.com; Staff 1 (MLS 1)
Library Holdings: Bk Titles 1,800; Bk Vols 2,100; Per Subs 200
Subject Interests: Chem
Function: Res libr

P NORTHLAND PUBLIC LIBRARY, 300 Cumberland Rd, 15237-5455. SAN 315-0941. Tel: 412-366-8100. Toll Free Tel: 888-292-2798. FAX: 412-366-2064. E-mail: northland@einetwork.net. Web Site: www.northlandlibrary.org. *Exec Dir,* Amy M Steele; Tel: 412-366-8100, Ext 101, E-mail: steelea@einetwork.net; *Dir, Mkt & Communications,* Santina Balestreire; Tel: 412-366-8100, Ext 103, E-mail: balestreires@einetwork.net; *Dir, Support Serv,* Robert Kolessar; Tel: 412-366-8100, Ext 106, E-mail: kolessarr@einetwork.net; *Found Dir,* Position Currently Open; *Ad/Coll Develop/e-Res,* Karen Shah; Tel: 412-3366-8100, Ext 113, E-mail: shahk@einetwork.net; *Mgr, Ad Serv,* Jane Jubb; Tel: 412-366-8100, Ext 110, E-mail: jubbj@einetwork.net; *Mgr, Children's & YA,* Susan Claus; Tel: 412-366-8100, Ext 120, E-mail: clauss@einetwork.net; *Circ Mgr,* Kim Ann Smith; Tel: 412-366-8100, Ext 115, E-mail: smithk@einetwork.net; *Supvr, Computer Serv,* Tricia Fisher; Tel: 412-366-8100, Ext 144, E-mail: fishert@einetwork.net; *Supvr, Tech Serv,* Debra Martin; Tel: 412-366-8100, Ext 166, E-mail: martind@einetwork.net; *ILL,* Karen Wingrove; Tel: 412-366-8100, Ext 119, E-mail: wingrovek@einetwork.net. Subject Specialists: *Computer sci,* Tricia Fisher; Staff 58.17 (MLS 13.46, Non-MLS 44.71)
Founded 1968. Pop 81,658; Circ 986,986
Jan 2013-Dec 2013 Income $2,520,156, State $291,566, City $1,453,799, County $487,384, Locally Generated Income $212,542, Other $74,865. Mats Exp $293,630, Books $180,654, Per/Ser (Incl. Access Fees) $8,000, AV Mat $41,650, Electronic Ref Mat (Incl. Access Fees) $3,400. Sal $1,475,064
Library Holdings: Audiobooks 7,071; AV Mats 340; Bks on Deafness & Sign Lang 48; Braille Volumes 3; CDs 5,675; DVDs 12,445; e-books 29,726; e-journals 300; Electronic Media & Resources 236; Large Print Bks 2,909; Microforms 2; Music Scores 132; Bk Titles 134,858; Bk Vols 168,573; Per Subs 211; Videos 963
Special Collections: Northland Historical Image Coll (over 1300 digitized images of local historical images)
Subject Interests: Genealogy, Local hist
Automation Activity & Vendor Info: (Cataloging) Innovative Interfaces, Inc; (Circulation) Innovative Interfaces, Inc; (OPAC) Innovative Interfaces, Inc
Database Vendor: Access Pennsylvania, CQ Press, EBSCO Auto Repair Reference, EBSCOhost, Gale Cengage Learning, Ingram Library Services, ProQuest, TumbleBookLibrary, ValueLine
Wireless access
Function: Adult bk club, Audiobks via web, Bks on cassette, Bks on CD, CD-ROM, Children's prog, Computer training, Computers for patron use, Copy machines, Digital talking bks, E-Reserves, Electronic databases & coll, Free DVD rentals, Genealogy discussion group, Handicapped accessible, Holiday prog, Homebound delivery serv, ILL available, Magnifiers for reading, Microfiche/film & reading machines, Music CDs, Online cat, Online ref, Online searches, Outreach serv, OverDrive digital audio bks, Photocopying/Printing, Preschool outreach, Prog for adults, Prog for children & young adult, Pub access computers, Ref serv available, Ref serv in person, Satellite serv, Scanner, Senior computer classes, Spanish lang bks, Story hour, Summer & winter reading prog, Summer reading prog, Tax forms, Teen prog, Telephone ref, VHS videos, Web-catalog, Wheelchair accessible, Winter reading prog, Writing prog
Publications: Northland News (Newsletter)
Mem of Allegheny County Library Association
Partic in Electronic Info Network (eiNetwork)
Special Services for the Deaf - Assistive tech; Bks on deafness & sign lang; Closed caption videos
Special Services for the Blind - Aids for in-house use; Assistive/Adapted tech devices, equip & products; Bks on cassette; Bks on CD; Braille bks; Closed circuit TV; Computer with voice synthesizer for visually impaired persons; Digital talking bk; Internet workstation with adaptive software; Large print bks; Low vision equip; Playaways (bks on MP3); Talking bks
Open Mon-Thurs 9-9, Fri 9-6, Sat 9-5, Sun (Winter) 1-5

P PENN HILLS LIBRARY*, 1037 Stotler Rd, 15235-2099. SAN 315-0968. Tel: 412-795-3507. FAX: 412-798-2186. E-mail: phlibrary@einetwork.net. Web Site: www.pennhillslibrary.org. *Dir,* Tyrone Ward; E-mail: wardt@einetwork.net; *Librn,* Mary Ann Zeak; E-mail: zeakm@einetwork.net; Staff 31 (MLS 3, Non-MLS 28)
Founded 1966. Pop 46,807; Circ 278,969
Library Holdings: Bk Titles 112,121; Per Subs 225
Special Collections: Penn Hills Historical Committee Coll
Automation Activity & Vendor Info: (Acquisitions) SirsiDynix; (Cataloging) SirsiDynix; (Circulation) SirsiDynix; (Course Reserve) SirsiDynix; (ILL) SirsiDynix; (Media Booking) SirsiDynix; (OPAC) SirsiDynix; (Serials) SirsiDynix
Wireless access
Publications: The Book Shelf (Newsletter)
Mem of Allegheny County Library Association
Partic in Electronic Info Network (eiNetwork)
Open Mon-Thurs 9-9, Fri & Sat 9-5, Sun (Sept-May) 1-5
Friends of the Library Group
Branches: 1
LINCOLN PARK SATELLITE, 7300 Ridgeview Ave, 15235. Tel: 412-362-7729. FAX: 412-362-7729. *Br Mgr,* Elizabeth Randolph; Staff 1 (Non-MLS 1)
Pop 749; Circ 1,256
Library Holdings: Bk Titles 8,190; Bk Vols 9,100; Per Subs 22

Open Mon-Thurs 2-7, Fri 2-5
Friends of the Library Group

S PITTSBURGH HISTORY & LANDMARKS FOUNDATION*, James D Van Trump Library, 100 W Station Square Dr, Ste 450, 15219. SAN 315-100X. Tel: 412-471-5808. FAX: 412-471-1633. Web Site: www.phlf.org. *Hist Coll Dir,* Albert M Tannler; E-mail: al@phlf.org; *Asst Librn,* Frank Stroker; E-mail: frank@phlf.org
Founded 1964
Library Holdings: Bk Vols 5,000; Per Subs 10
Subject Interests: Archit hist, Pittsburgh hist
Function: Res libr
Restriction: Open by appt only

S PITTSBURGH INSTITUTE OF MORTUARY SCIENCE, William J Musmanno Memorial Library, 5808 Baum Blvd, 15206. SAN 315-1018. Tel: 412-362-8500. FAX: 412-362-1684. E-mail: pims5808@aol.com. Web Site: www.pims.edu. *Librn,* Melanie Cline; E-mail: librarian@pims.edu; Staff 1 (MLS 1)
Founded 1939. Enrl 130; Fac 20; Highest Degree: Associate
Library Holdings: Audiobooks 1; AV Mats 79; CDs 6; DVDs 58; Bk Vols 2,309; Per Subs 30; Videos 162
Subject Interests: Death care industry
Automation Activity & Vendor Info: (Cataloging) Follett Software; (Circulation) Follett Software
Wireless access
Open Mon-Fri 9-4

S PITTSBURGH POST GAZETTE*, Library, 34 Boulevard of the Allies, 15222. SAN 327-0726. Tel: 412-263-1184. Reference Tel: 412-263-1619. FAX: 412-471-1987. E-mail: library@post-gazette.com. Web Site: www.post-gazette.com. *Head Librn,* Angelika Kane; Tel: 412-263-1397, E-mail: angelikakane@post-gazette.com; *Info Spec,* Stephen Karlinchak; Tel: 412-263-2585, E-mail: skarlinchak@post-gazette.com; Staff 4 (MLS 1, Non-MLS 3)
Founded 1930
Library Holdings: Electronic Media & Resources 10; Microforms 2,000; Bk Titles 300; Spec Interest Per Sub 5
Special Collections: Photo Files & Digital Photo Archives (both PG & former Pittsburgh Press); Picture Files - Pittsburgh Clipping Files Dating Back to 1930s (both PG & former Pittsburgh Press)
Database Vendor: Dialog, Factiva.com, LexisNexis, Newsbank, ProQuest
Function: For res purposes, Newsp ref libr, Online searches, Photocopying/Printing, Telephone ref
Special Services for the Blind - Radio reading serv
Restriction: Access at librarian's discretion, Access for corporate affiliates, By permission only, Co libr, Employees & their associates, Non-circulating, Not a lending libr, Not open to pub, Private libr, Pub access by telephone only

R PITTSBURGH THEOLOGICAL SEMINARY*, Clifford E Barbour Library, 616 N Highland Ave, 15206-2596. SAN 315-1042. Tel: 412-924-1354. FAX: 412-362-2329. Web Site: www.barbourlibrary.org, www.pts.edu. *Dir,* Sharon Taylor; Tel: 412-924-1350, E-mail: staylor@pts.edu; *Head, Pub Serv,* Position Currently Open; *Head, Tech Serv, Lead Cataloger,* Position Currently Open; *Electronic Res Librn,* Anthony Rogers; Tel: 412-924-1352, E-mail: arogers@pts.edu; *Archivist, Rec Mgt Librn,* Elizabeth M Scott; Tel: 412-924-1353, E-mail: emscott@pts.edu; *Evening/Weekend Supvr, ILL,* Alexis Stapp; Tel: 412-924-1356, E-mail: astapp@pts.edu; *Acq,* Mariam Sogoian; Tel: 412-924-1361, E-mail: msogoian@pts.edu; *Cat,* Sandra Howard; Tel: 412-924-1359, E-mail: showard@pts.edu; *Ser,* Diane Faust; Tel: 412-924-1360, E-mail: dfaust@pts.edu; Staff 6 (MLS 6)
Founded 1794. Fac 21; Highest Degree: Doctorate
Jun 2010-May 2011. Mats Exp $237,762. Sal $499,705
Library Holdings: Microforms 88,311; Bk Vols 296,142; Per Subs 860
Special Collections: Hymnology (Warrington Coll); Reformation Theology (John M Mason Coll)
Subject Interests: Bible, Church hist, Practical theol, Theol
Automation Activity & Vendor Info: (Acquisitions) Innovative Interfaces, Inc; (Cataloging) Innovative Interfaces, Inc; (Circulation) Innovative Interfaces, Inc; (Course Reserve) Innovative Interfaces, Inc; (OPAC) Innovative Interfaces, Inc; (Serials) Innovative Interfaces, Inc
Database Vendor: EBSCOhost, Innovative Interfaces, Inc, OCLC WorldShare Interlibrary Loan
Wireless access
Partic in Lyrasis; OCLC Online Computer Library Center, Inc
Open Mon-Thurs (Sept-May) 8:30am-10pm, Fri 8:30-5, Sat 9-4:30, Sun 5-10; Mon-Fri (June-Aug) 9-4:30

S PITTSBURGH TOY LENDING LIBRARY*, c/o First United Methodist Church, 5401 Centre Ave, Rear, 15232. SAN 372-5502. Tel: 412-682-4430. E-mail: pghtll@yahoo.com. Web Site: trfn.clpgh.org/toylibrary. *Pres,* Susy Moran
Founded 1974
Library Holdings: Bk Titles 100
Special Collections: Parenting; Toys (imaginative & cognitive)
Publications: Networks (Newsletter); Networks (Bi-monthly)
Special Services for the Deaf - Bks on deafness & sign lang
Restriction: Mem only

S PITTSBURGH ZOO & PPG AQUARIUM LIBRARY*, One Wild Pl, 15206. SAN 370-7113. Tel: 412-665-3640. Toll Free Tel: 800-474-4966. FAX: 412-665-3661. Web Site: www.pittsburghzoo.com.
Founded 1983
Library Holdings: Bk Titles 14,000; Per Subs 15
Special Collections: Ciguatera (Inia geoffrensis) Poisoning, research papers; Gambierdiscus toxicus; Platanistidae Dolphins, research papers
Restriction: Staff use only

S PLANNED PARENTHOOD OF WESTERN PENNSYLVANIA, INC*, Mary Richards Culbertson Resource Center, 933 Liberty Ave, 15222-3701. Tel: 412-434-8969. Toll Free Tel: 800-230-7526. FAX: 412-434-8974. Web Site: www.ppwp.org. *In Charge,* Brenda Lee Green. Subject Specialists: *Educ,* Brenda Lee Green
Founded 1979
Library Holdings: AV Mats 200; Bk Titles 1,200; Per Subs 13
Subject Interests: Admin, Educ curricula, Family planning, Family studies, Human sexuality, Marriage, Med ref, Pop, Prof educ, Relig perspectives, Sexuality, Women
Partic in Laurel Highlands Health Science Library Consortium
Restriction: Open by appt only

C POINT PARK UNIVERSITY LIBRARY*, 414 Wood St, 15222. (Mail add: 201 Wood St, 15222). Tel: 412-392-3171. FAX: 412-392-3168. E-mail: library@pointpark.edu. Web Site: www.pointpark.edu. *Dir,* Elizabeth Evans; Tel: 412-392-3161, E-mail: eevans@pointpark.edu; *Assoc Dir,* Brenton Wilson; Tel: 412-392-3163, E-mail: bwilson@pointpark.edu; *Circ & Stacks Coordr,* Melanie Kirchartz; Tel: 412-392-3165, E-mail: mkirchartz@pointpark.edu; *Tech Serv Coordr,* Margie Stampahar; Tel: 412-392-3167, E-mail: mstampahar@pointpark.edu; *Ref & Instrul Serv, Instr Coordr,* Anna Mihalega; Tel: 412-392-3166, E-mail: amihalega@pointpark.edu; *Ref Librn,* Joan Hamby; Tel: 412-392-3162, E-mail: jhamby@pointpark.edu; Staff 8 (MLS 5, Non-MLS 3)
Enrl 3,523; Highest Degree: Master
Library Holdings: AV Mats 1,439; e-books 30,000; e-journals 17,000; Bk Vols 95,000; Per Subs 270
Special Collections: Plays & Musicals Cores (Performing Arts Coll)
Automation Activity & Vendor Info: (Acquisitions) Innovative Interfaces, Inc; (Cataloging) Innovative Interfaces, Inc; (Circulation) Innovative Interfaces, Inc; (Course Reserve) Innovative Interfaces, Inc; (ILL) Innovative Interfaces, Inc; (OPAC) Innovative Interfaces, Inc; (Serials) Innovative Interfaces, Inc
Database Vendor: EBSCOhost, JSTOR, LexisNexis, ProQuest, PubMed, ScienceDirect, SerialsSolutions
Wireless access
Partic in Lyrasis; Pennsylvania Academic Library Consortium, Inc (PALCI); Pittsburgh Council on Higher Education (PCHE)
Special Services for the Blind - Closed circuit TV; ZoomText magnification & reading software
Open Mon-Thurs 8am-Midnight, Fri 8-5, Sat 8-7, Sun 11-9

M HOWARD ANDERSON POWER MEMORIAL LIBRARY*, Magee-Womens Hospital of UPMC, 300 Halket St, Ste 1205, 15213. SAN 359-4548. Tel: 412-641-4288. FAX: 412-641-4854. E-mail: librarystaff@mail.magee.edu. *Mgr, Libr Serv,* Carrie Everstine; E-mail: ceverstine@magee.edu; Staff 1.2 (MLS 1, Non-MLS 0.2)
Founded 1965
Library Holdings: e-journals 9; Bk Titles 1,681; Bk Vols 1,799; Per Subs 57
Subject Interests: Med
Database Vendor: PubMed
Wireless access
Function: Computers for patron use, Copy machines, Doc delivery serv, ILL available, Online searches
Partic in Basic Health Sciences Library Network; National Network of Libraries of Medicine
Open Mon-Fri 8-4:30
Restriction: Med & nursing staff, patients & families

PPG INDUSTRIES, INC
S CHEMICALS TECHNICAL INFORMATION CENTER*, 440 College Park Dr, Monroeville, 15146. SAN 370-7784. Tel: 724-325-5221. FAX: 724-325-5289. Web Site: www.ppg.com. *Mgr,* Denise Callihan; E-mail: callihan@ppg.com; *Info Spec,* Audrey Anderson; Staff 3 (MLS 1, Non-MLS 2)
Library Holdings: Bk Vols 14,000; Per Subs 120
Subject Interests: Organic chem

Automation Activity & Vendor Info: (Cataloging) SydneyPlus; (Circulation) SydneyPlus; (OPAC) SydneyPlus
Database Vendor: Factiva.com, STN International
Partic in Lyrasis
Publications: Technical Reports Abstract Bulletin
Restriction: Open by appt only

S GLASS TECHNOLOGY CENTER*, Guys Run Rd, Harmar Township, 15238. (Mail add: PO Box 11472, 15238-0472), SAN 359-3673. Tel: 412-820-8568. FAX: 412-820-8696. E-mail: harmarlib@ppg.com. Web Site: www.ppg.com. *Mgr, Libr Serv,* Denise Callihan; *Info Spec,* Audrey Anderson; Tel: 412-820-8517; *Info Spec,* Amy Watson; *Tech Serv,* Beverly Weston; Tel: 412-820-4936; Staff 4 (MLS 2, Non-MLS 2)
Founded 1975
Library Holdings: Bk Titles 25,000; Per Subs 160
Special Collections: Internal Documents Coll
Subject Interests: Ceramics, Chem, Fiber glass, Glass, Mat sci, Physics
Automation Activity & Vendor Info: (ILL) OCLC; (OPAC) Sydney; (Serials) EBSCO Online
Database Vendor: Dialog
Partic in Lyrasis
Publications: Journal List

S TECHNICAL INFORMATION CENTER*, 4325 Rosanna Dr, Allison Park, 15101, SAN 359-3762. Tel: 412-492-5443. FAX: 412-492-5509. Web Site: www.ppg.com. *Dir, Libr Serv,* Denise Callihan; Tel: 724-325-5221, E-mail: callihan@ppg.com; *Assoc Librn,* Cherese Benson; E-mail: bensonc@ppg.com; *Info Spec,* Mary Lee Richner; Tel: 412-492-5268, E-mail: richner@ppg.com; Staff 3 (MLS 2, Non-MLS 1)
Library Holdings: Bk Vols 10,000; Per Subs 200
Subject Interests: Coatings, Paints, Polymers, Resins
Restriction: Co libr, In-house use for visitors, Open by appt only

S PSP METRICS LIBRARY, The Frick Bldg, 437 Grant St, Ste 1900, 15219-6110. SAN 372-6290. Tel: 412-261-1333. FAX: 412-261-5014. Web Site: www.pspmetrics.com. *Librn/Communications Spec,* Lauren J Williams; E-mail: lwilliams@pspmetrics.com; Staff 1 (MLS 1)
Founded 1946
Library Holdings: Bk Titles 500; Per Subs 15
Special Collections: Industrial-Organizational Psychology; Management Development; Work Motivation

L REED SMITH LLP*, Law Library, 225 Fifth Ave, 15222. SAN 315-1093. Tel: 412-288-3377. Interlibrary Loan Service Tel: 412-288-5931. FAX: 412-288-3063. Web Site: www.reedsmith.com. *Dir,* Ronda W Fisch; E-mail: rfisch@reedsmith.com; Staff 7 (MLS 3, Non-MLS 4)
Founded 1970
Library Holdings: Bk Titles 10,000; Bk Vols 35,000; Per Subs 2,000
Subject Interests: Pa law
Automation Activity & Vendor Info: (Acquisitions) SirsiDynix; (Cataloging) SirsiDynix; (Circulation) SirsiDynix; (OPAC) SirsiDynix; (Serials) SirsiDynix
Database Vendor: Dialog, HeinOnline, LexisNexis, OCLC FirstSearch, OneSource, ReferenceUSA, SerialsSolutions, SirsiDynix, Westlaw
Partic in OCLC Online Computer Library Center, Inc
Open Mon-Fri 8-6

R REFORMED PRESBYTERIAN THEOLOGICAL SEMINARY LIBRARY*, 7418 Penn Ave, 15208-2594. SAN 315-1107. Tel: 412-731-6000, 412-731-8690. FAX: 412-731-4834. Web Site: www.rpts.edu. *Dir,* Thomas Reid; E-mail: treid@rpts.edu; Staff 1.5 (MLS 1, Non-MLS 0.5)
Founded 1810. Enrl 120; Fac 15; Highest Degree: Doctorate
Jan 2013-Dec 2013 Income $114,000, Parent Institution $110,000, Other $4,000. Mats Exp $35,600, Books $20,000, Per/Ser (Incl. Access Fees) $8,000, Other Print Mats $300, AV Mat $200, Electronic Ref Mat (Incl. Access Fees) $4,300, Presv $2,800. Sal $54,800 (Prof $47,500)
Library Holdings: AV Mats 1,400; Braille Volumes 10; CDs 40; DVDs 40; Electronic Media & Resources 20; Microforms 1,500; Bk Vols 79,000; Per Subs 210; Videos 250
Special Collections: 16th-18th Century Rare Theological Works; Reformed Presbyterian Coll
Subject Interests: Bible, Church-state, Theol, Worship
Automation Activity & Vendor Info: (Cataloging) TLC (The Library Corporation); (Circulation) TLC (The Library Corporation); (Course Reserve) TLC (The Library Corporation); (ILL) TLC (The Library Corporation); (OPAC) TLC (The Library Corporation)
Database Vendor: TLC (The Library Corporation)
Wireless access
Function: Computers for patron use, Electronic databases & coll, ILL available, Mail & tel request accepted, Online cat, Photocopying/Printing, Ref serv available, Spoken cassettes & CDs, Spoken cassettes & DVDs, VHS videos
Publications: Library Handbook
Partic in OCLC Online Computer Library Center, Inc

SR SAINT PAUL'S EPISCOPAL CHURCH LIBRARY*, 1066 Washington Rd, 15228-2024. SAN 329-9724. Tel: 412-531-7153. FAX: 412-531-9820. Web Site: www.stpaulspgh.org. *Librn,* Celeste Nalwasky
Library Holdings: Bk Titles 4,000
Open Mon-Fri 8:30-4:30, Sat & Sun 7-3

A US ARMY CORPS OF ENGINEERS LIBRARY, PITTSBURGH DISTRICT*, 1000 Liberty Ave, 15222-4186. Tel: 412-395-7422. FAX: 412-644-2811. *Librn,* Deborah Barker; Staff 1 (MLS 1)
Library Holdings: Bk Vols 7,000
Automation Activity & Vendor Info: (Cataloging) LibraryWorld, Inc; (OPAC) LibraryWorld, Inc; (Serials) LibraryWorld, Inc
Database Vendor: Dialog, OCLC FirstSearch, ProQuest
Open Mon-Fri 6:30-3

C UNIVERSITY OF PITTSBURGH*, Hillman Library, 3960 Forbes Ave, 15260. SAN 359-3916. Tel: 412-648-7710. FAX; 412-648-7887. Web Site: www.library.pitt.edu. *Univ Librn,* Rush Miller; E-mail: rgmiller@pitt.edu; *Assoc Univ Librn,* Fern Brody; E-mail: feb@pitt.edu; Staff 260 (MLS 108, Non-MLS 152)
Founded 1873. Enrl 43,347; Fac 1,846
Special Collections: 18th & 20th Century historical records & ms including photog, glass plates & negatives of organizations, societies, institutions, businesses, city & county governmental agencies in Southwestern Penn (Archives of Industrial Society); 19th & 20th Century American & English Theatre (Ford & Harriet Curtis Coll); 20th Century Children's Literature (Clifton Fadiman Coll); Archive of Popular Culture; Canadian; Flora & Norman Winkler Coll; Foundation Center Coll; Frank P Ramsey Papers; Hervey Allen Coll, ms, bks; Historical Children's Literature, dating to 18th century, incl Mr Rogers Neighborhood (Elizabeth Nesbitt Room), tv archives, videotapes, puppets, ms; Human Relations Area Files; Izaak Walton's Compleat Angler (Bernard S Horne Coll); John A Nietz Textboook Coll (Early America School Books); Mary Roberts Rinehart Coll, ms, bks; Music & Memorabilia of Stephen Collins Foster (Foster Memorial Library); Pavlowa-Heinrich Ballet Coll; Pennsylvania Industry, Institutions, Ethnic Organizations (Archives of Industrial Society), legis papers, hist rec; Ramon Gomez de la Serna Coll, bks, ms; Rudolf Carnap & Hans Reichenbach Coll, bks, ms; Walter & Martha Leuba Coll; Western Pennsylvania, Early History & Travel (Darlington Memorial Library); William Steinberg Coll. State Document Depository; UN Document Depository; US Document Depository
Subject Interests: Bolivia, Cuba, E Asian, E European, Latin Am, Russia
Automation Activity & Vendor Info: (Cataloging) Ex Libris Group
Wireless access
Publications: Bibliographies; Guide to Libraries
Partic in Association of Research Libraries (ARL); Center for Research Libraries; Lyrasis; Northeast Research Libraries Consortium (NERL); Pennsylvania Academic Library Consortium, Inc (PALCI)

Departmental Libraries:

AFRICAN-AMERICAN COLLECTION, Hillman Library, 1st Flr, 15260, SAN 359-3932. Tel: 412-648-7714. FAX: 412-648-7733. Web Site: www.library.pitt.edu/african-american-collection. *Head Librn,* Arif Jamal; Tel: 412-648-7759, E-mail: ajamal@pitt.edu

CL BARCO LAW LIBRARY, Law Bldg, 3900 Forbes Ave, 4th Flr, 15260, SAN 359-4513. Tel: 412-648-1325, 412-648-1330. Interlibrary Loan Service Tel: 412-648-1356. FAX: 412-648-1352. Web Site: www.law.pitt.edu/library. *Actg Dir,* Mark Silverman; Tel: 412-648-1376; *Acq, Ser Librn,* Patricia Roncevich; Tel: 412-648-1321, E-mail: roncevich@pitt.edu; *Syst & Cat Librn,* Sallie Smith; Tel: 412-648-1326, E-mail: sas67@pitt.edu
Founded 1915
Library Holdings: Bk Vols 185,466; Per Subs 4,674
Database Vendor: LexisNexis, Westlaw
Partic in OCLC Online Computer Library Center, Inc; Westlaw
Publications: Research Guides; User's Guide
Open Mon-Thurs 7:30am-10pm, Fri 7:30-5, Sat 10-6, Sun 12-8

BEVIER ENGINEERING LIBRARY, G33 Benedum Hall, 15261, SAN 359-4122. Tel: 412-624-9620. FAX: 412-624-8103. E-mail: uls-engineeringlibrary@mail.pitt.edu. Web Site: www.library.pitt.edu/engineering. *Head Librn,* Judith Ann Brink; Tel: 412-624-0859, E-mail: jbrink@pitt.edu

BUHL SOCIAL WORK COLLECTION, Hillman Library, 1st Flr, 3960 Forbes Ave, 15260, SAN 359-3975. Web Site: www.library.pitt.edu/buhl-social-work-collection. *Librn,* Arif Jamal; Tel: 412-648-7759, E-mail: ajamal@pitt.edu
Open Mon-Thurs 8am-10pm, Fri 8-6, Sat 10-6, Sun 12-9

BUSINESS, 118 Mervis Hall, 15260, SAN 359-436X. Tel: 412-648-1669. FAX: 412-648-1809. Web Site: www.library.pitt.edu/business. *Head Librn,* Eve Wider; Tel: 412-648-3356, E-mail: ewider@pitt.edu; Staff 3 (MLS 2, Non-MLS 1)
Library Holdings: Bk Vols 15,000; Per Subs 600
Partic in Northeast Research Libraries Consortium (NERL)

CHEMISTRY, 130 Chevron Science Ctr, 15261, SAN 359-4009. Tel: 412-624-8294. FAX: 412-624-1809. Web Site: www.library.pitt.edu/chemistry. *Head Librn,* Margarete Bower; Tel: 412-624-3714, E-mail: bower@pitt.edu

CM FALK LIBRARY OF THE HEALTH SCIENCES, 200 Scaife Hall, 3550 Terrace St, 15261, SAN 359-4335. Circulation Tel: 412-648-8866. Interlibrary Loan Service Tel: 412-648-2037. Reference Tel: 412-648-8824. FAX: 412-648-9020. E-mail: medlibq@pitt.edu. Web Site: www.hsls.pitt.edu. *Dir,* Barbara A Epstein; E-mail: bepstein@pitt.edu; Staff 24 (MLS 24)

Library Holdings: Bk Vols 447,014; Per Subs 3,182

Special Collections: History of Medicine

Subject Interests: Dentistry, Health, Health & rehabilitation sci, Med, Nursing, Pharm, Pub health

Publications: HSLS Update (Newsletter)

Open Mon-Thurs 7am-Midnight, Fri 7am-10pm, Sat 9:30am-10pm, Sun 11am-Midnight

THEODORE M FINNEY MUSIC LIBRARY, Music Bldg B28, 15260, SAN 359-4246. Tel: 412-624-4130. FAX: 412-624-4180. Web Site: www.library.pitt.edu/music. *Head of Libr,* James P Cassaro; Tel: 412-624-4131, E-mail: cassaro@pitt.edu; Staff 3 (MLS 2, Non-MLS 1)

Founded 1966. Fac 37; Highest Degree: Doctorate

Library Holdings: CDs 30,000; DVDs 900; Microforms 10,000; Music Scores 50,000; Bk Vols 65,000; Per Subs 250; Videos 1,500

Special Collections: Eric Moe Coll, first drafts, ms; Mirskey Coll; Polish Singers Alliance of America Coll

Automation Activity & Vendor Info: (Acquisitions) Ex Libris Group; (Circulation) Ex Libris Group; (Course Reserve) Ex Libris Group; (ILL) OCLC ILLiad; (OPAC) Ex Libris Group

Function: Audio & video playback equip for onsite use, CD-ROM, Computers for patron use, Copy machines, Doc delivery serv, E-Reserves, Electronic databases & coll, Handicapped accessible, ILL available, Music CDs, Online cat, Online info literacy tutorials on the web & in blackboard, Online ref, OverDrive digital audio bks, Photocopying/Printing, Ref serv in person, Res libr, Telephone ref, VCDs, VHS videos, Web-catalog, Wheelchair accessible

Restriction: Borrowing privileges limited to fac & registered students, Borrowing requests are handled by ILL, Non-circulating of rare bks, Off-site coll in storage - retrieval as requested, Restricted borrowing privileges

FRICK FINE ARTS LIBRARY, Frick Fine Arts Bldg, 1st Flr, 15260, SAN 359-4157. Tel: 412-648-2410. FAX: 412-648-7568. E-mail: uls-fineartslibrary@mail.pitt.edu. Web Site: www.library.pitt.edu/fine-arts. *Head of Libr,* Position Currently Open; Staff 4 (MLS 2, Non-MLS 2)

Library Holdings: Bk Vols 85,000; Per Subs 350

Subject Interests: Archit hist, Art hist

HILLMAN LIBRARY, 271 Hillman Library, 15260, SAN 359 419X. Circulation Tel: 412-648-7800. Reference Tel: 412-648-3330. FAX: 412-648-7887. Web Site: www.library.pitt.edu/hillman. *Dir,* Rush Miller; E-mail: rgmiller@pitt.edu

Library Holdings: Bk Vols 1,500,000

LANGLEY LIBRARY, 217 Langley Hall, 15260, SAN 359-4181. Tel: 412-624-4490. FAX: 412-624-1809. Web Site: www.library.pitt.edu/langley. *Head of Libr,* Margarete Bower; Tel: 412-624-3714, E-mail: bower@pitt.edu; *Libr Spec,* Laura Dougherty; E-mail: lmac@pitt.edu; *Libr Spec,* Laurel Povazan Scholnick; E-mail: laurelp@pitt.edu

Open Mon-Thurs 8:30-6, Fri 8:30-5

M UNIVERSITY OF PITTSBURGH MEDICAL CENTER SHADYSIDE*, Hopwood Library, 5230 Centre Ave, 15232. SAN 315-1166. Tel: 412-623-2620. *Coordr, Libr Serv,* Heidi Patterson; Staff 1 (MLS 1)

Founded 2001

Library Holdings: Bk Vols 8,000; Per Subs 225

Subject Interests: Clinical med, Consumer health info, Nursing

Automation Activity & Vendor Info: (Acquisitions) Ex Libris Group; (Cataloging) Ex Libris Group; (Circulation) Ex Libris Group; (OPAC) Ex Libris Group

Database Vendor: Dialog, EBSCOhost, OVID Technologies

Wireless access

Open Mon-Fri 8-5

M UPMC MERCY HOSPITAL OF PITTSBURGH*, Brady Library of the Health Sciences, 1400 Locust St, 15219. SAN 359-3614. Tel: 412-232-7520. FAX: 412-232-8422. Web Site: www.upmc.com/locations/hospitals/mercy/Pages/default.aspx. *Archivist, Doc Delivery,* Kathleen Washy; *Circ, Coll Develop,* Susan Walko; *Pub Serv, Ser,* Robert Neumeyer; Staff 3 (MLS 3)

Founded 1922

Library Holdings: Bk Vols 4,000; Per Subs 450

Subject Interests: Gen surgery, Med

Automation Activity & Vendor Info: (Acquisitions) EOS International; (Cataloging) EOS International; (Circulation) EOS International; (OPAC) EOS International; (Serials) EOS International

Database Vendor: Dialog

Function: Archival coll, Doc delivery serv, ILL available, Ref serv available

Partic in Pittsburgh Basic Health Sciences Libr Consortium (PBHSL); Pittsburgh-East Hospital Libr Coop

Restriction: Co libr

M UPMC PASSAVANT*, Medical Library, 9100 Babcock Blvd, 15237-5842. SAN 315-0933. Tel: 412-367-6320. FAX: 412-367-6889. *Med Librn,* Linda D'Antonio; E-mail: dantoniolm@upmc.edu

Founded 1971

Library Holdings: Per Subs 200

Special Collections: Consumer Health Pamphlets

Subject Interests: Med, Nursing

Database Vendor: OVID Technologies

Partic in Basic Health Sciences Library Network; National Network of Libraries of Medicine; Pittsburgh-East Hospital Libr Coop

Open Mon-Fri 8-4:30

M UPMC ST MARGARET*, Health Sciences Library, 815 Freeport Rd, 15215. SAN 359-3827. Tel: 412-784-4121, 412-784-4238. FAX: 412-784-4989. *Dir,* Amy Haugh; E-mail: haughaj@upmc.edu; Staff 2 (MLS 1, Non-MLS 1)

Founded 1951

Library Holdings: Bk Vols 2,500; Per Subs 200

Special Collections: Historical Coll (Harry M Margolis MD)

Subject Interests: Family med, Gerontology, Nursing educ, Occupational therapy, Orthopedics, Rheumatoid arthritis

Partic in Basic Health Sciences Library Network

Open Mon-Fri 8-4:30

G VA PITTSBURGH HEALTHCARE SYSTEM*, Medical Library Highland Drive Div, 7180 Highland Dr, 15206. SAN 359-4602. Tel: 412-365-5515. FAX: 412-365-5510. *Librn,* Jane Rish

Founded 1954

Partic in National Network of Libraries of Medicine

Open Mon-Fri 8-4:30

Branches:

MEDICAL LIBRARY HEINZ DIVISION, 1010 Delafield Rd, 15215. (Mail add: Aspinwall Library 142D-A, Delafield Road, 15240). Tel: 412-784-3747. FAX: 412-784-3508. *Librn,* James R Johnson; E-mail: james.johnson6@va.gov; Staff 1 (MLS 1)

Open Mon-Fri 8-4:30

MEDICAL LIBRARY UNIVERSITY DRIVE DIVISION, University Dr, 15240. Tel: 412-688-6000, Ext 814718. FAX: 412-688-6586. *Librn,* Jane Rish; E-mail: jane.rish@va.gov; Staff 1 (MLS 1)

Open Mon-Fri 8-4:30

M WESTERN PENNSYLVANIA HOSPITAL*, Richard M Johnston Health Sciences Library, 4800 Friendship Ave, 15224. SAN 359-4696. Tel: 412-578-4708. FAX: 412-578-7317. E-mail: medlib@wpahs.org. Web Site: www.wpahs.org/education/library/wph/index.html. *Librn,* Heidi O Patterson; Tel: 412-578-5556, E-mail: hpatters@wpahs.org

Library Holdings: e-journals 300; Bk Vols 5,000; Per Subs 150

Subject Interests: Nursing

Database Vendor: OVID Technologies

Partic in CinaHL; Pittsburgh-East Hospital Libr Coop

Open Mon-Thurs 8am-10am, Fri 8-6, Sat & Sun 12-10

P WHITEHALL PUBLIC LIBRARY*, 100 Borough Park Dr, 15236-2098. SAN 315-1239. Tel: 412-882-6622. FAX: 412-882-9556. E-mail: whitehall@einetwork.net. Web Site: www.whitehallpubliclibrary.org. *Dir,* Paula Kelly

Founded 1963

Library Holdings: Bk Vols 62,000; Per Subs 100

Special Collections: Bks on tapes; Business Coll; College Career Information; Large Print Coll; Parenting Coll; Toddler Board & Cloth Books Coll

Subject Interests: Mysteries, Popular fiction, Popular paperbacks, Travel info

Mem of Allegheny County Library Association

Open Mon-Thurs 9-9, Fri 1-5, Sat 9-5, Sun 12-4

Friends of the Library Group

P WILKINSBURG PUBLIC LIBRARY*, 605 Ross Ave, 15221-2195. SAN 315-1247. Tel: 412-244-2940. FAX: 412-243-6943. Web Site: www.einetwork.net/ein/wlksbrg/. *Dir,* Joel D Minnigh; Tel: 412-244-2941, E-mail: minnighj@einetwork.net; *Librn, Outreach Serv Librn,* Tom Shaw; Tel: 412-244-4378, E-mail: shawt@einetwork.net; *Assoc Librn,* Linda Jennings; Tel: 412-244-2942, E-mail: jenningsl@einetwork.net; *Ch Serv,* Lisa Barnes; Tel: 412-244-2944; Staff 3 (MLS 3)

Founded 1899. Pop 19,196; Circ 95,632

Library Holdings: AV Mats 6,500; Bks on Deafness & Sign Lang 17; High Interest/Low Vocabulary Bk Vols 150; Large Print Bks 5,000; Bk Titles 73,297; Per Subs 140

Special Collections: Wilkinsburg History Coll, large print coll
Subject Interests: Biographies, Local hist, Mysteries
Automation Activity & Vendor Info: (Cataloging) Innovative Interfaces, Inc; (Circulation) Innovative Interfaces, Inc; (OPAC) Innovative Interfaces, Inc
Mem of Allegheny County Library Association
Open Mon & Wed 10-8, Tues & Thurs 10-6, Fri & Sat 10-5
Friends of the Library Group
Branches: 1
EASTRIDGE, 1900 Graham Blvd, 15235. Tel: 412-342-0056. *Dir,* Joel D Minnigh; *Assoc Librn,* Linda Jennings
Founded 2003
Library Holdings: AV Mats 2,000; Bk Vols 8,000; Per Subs 25
Open Tues & Thurs 10-8, Wed, Fri & Sat 10-5, Sun 1-5
Friends of the Library Group

PITTSTON

S NORTHEASTERN PENNSYLVANIA ALLIANCE*, Northeastern Pennsylvania Nonprofit & Community Assistance Center, 1151 Oak St, 18640-3795. SAN 329-0824. Tel: 570-655-5581. FAX: 570-654-5137. E-mail: ncac@nepa-alliance.org. Web Site: www.nepa-alliance.org/ncac.htm. *Mgr,* Kurt R Bauman; Tel: 570-655-5581, Ext 237; Staff 2 (MLS 2)
Founded 1980
Library Holdings: Bk Titles 305; Bk Vols 500; Per Subs 35; Spec Interest Per Sub 10; Videos 20
Special Collections: Pennsylvania State Data Center Foundation Library
Wireless access
Publications: Annual Report; Newsletters; Weekly Funding Updates by Email
Open Mon-Fri 7:30-5
Restriction: Non-circulating

P PITTSTON MEMORIAL LIBRARY, 47 Broad St, 18640. SAN 315-1255. Tel: 570-654-9565. FAX: 570-654-6078. E-mail: pittstonlibrary@luzernelibraries.org. Web Site: www.pittstonmemoriallibrary.org. *Dir,* Anne Hogya; E-mail: ahogya@luzernelibraries.org
Founded 1971. Pop 8,104; Circ 54,435
Library Holdings: AV Mats 3,000; Bk Vols 40,000; Per Subs 75
Automation Activity & Vendor Info: (Cataloging) SirsiDynix; (Circulation) SirsiDynix
Wireless access
Function: Adult bk club, Audiobks via web, Bk club(s), Bks on cassette, Bks on CD, Children's prog, Computers for patron use, Copy machines, Electronic databases & coll, Exhibits, Fax serv, Free DVD rentals, Handicapped accessible, Holiday prog, ILL available, Photocopying/Printing, Preschool outreach, Prog for adults, Prog for children & young adult, Pub access computers, Ref & res, Story hour, Summer reading prog, Tax forms, Teen prog, Telephone ref, Wheelchair accessible
Mem of Luzerne County Library System
Open Mon & Thurs 11-7, Tues, Wed & Fri 9-5, Sat 9-4
Friends of the Library Group

PLEASANT HILLS

P PLEASANT HILLS PUBLIC LIBRARY*, 302 Old Clairton Rd, 15236-4399. SAN 315-1263. Tel: 412-655-2424. FAX: 412-655-2292. E-mail: pleasanthills@einetwork.net. Web Site: www.pleasanthillslibrary.org. *Dir,* Sharon Julian-Milas
Founded 1945. Pop 8,268; Circ 119,585
Jan 2011-Dec 2011 Income $303,000
Library Holdings: Bk Titles 57,800; Per Subs 105
Subject Interests: Lit
Automation Activity & Vendor Info: (Cataloging) Innovative Interfaces, Inc; (Circulation) Innovative Interfaces, Inc
Wireless access
Mem of Allegheny County Library Association
Open Mon-Thurs 10-8:30, Fri 10-4, Sat 9-4
Friends of the Library Group

PLEASANT MOUNT

P PLEASANT MOUNT PUBLIC LIBRARY*, 375 Great Bend Tpk, 18453-9801. (Mail add: PO Box 33, 18453-9801), SAN 320-8389. Tel: 570-448-2573. FAX: 570-448-9713. E-mail: pmpl@nep.net. Web Site: www.plowc.org. *Librn,* William Bower
Founded 1975. Pop 1,500
Library Holdings: CDs 171; DVDs 61; Large Print Bks 123; Bk Titles 5,351; Per Subs 15; Talking Bks 111; Videos 555
Open Tues-Fri Noon-7, Sat 9-4
Friends of the Library Group

PLUM BOROUGH

P PLUM BOROUGH COMMUNITY LIBRARY*, 445 Center-New Texas Rd, 15239. Tel: 412-798-7323. FAX: 412-798-9245. Web Site: www.einetwork.net/ein/plumboro. *Dir,* Marilyn Klingensmith; E-mail: klingensmithm@einetwork.net
Pop 26,940
Library Holdings: AV Mats 3,457; Bk Vols 28,000; Per Subs 75; Videos 3,040
Automation Activity & Vendor Info: (Cataloging) Innovative Interfaces, Inc; (Circulation) Innovative Interfaces, Inc; (OPAC) Innovative Interfaces, Inc
Mem of Allegheny County Library Association
Open Mon-Thurs 10-8, Fri & Sat 10-5

PLYMOUTH

P PLYMOUTH PUBLIC LIBRARY*, 107 W Main St, 18651-2919. SAN 315-128X. Tel: 570-779-4775. FAX: 570-779-5616. Web Site: www.luzerneco.lib.pa.us/plymouth.htm. *Dir,* Suzanne Youngblood; E-mail: syoungblood@osterhout.lib.pa.us; Staff 1 (MLS 1)
Founded 1938. Pop 11,201; Circ 18,473
Jan 2005-Dec 2005 Income $149,827, State $42,000, Provincial $24,739, City $5,800, County $39,000, Locally Generated Income $29,805, Other $8,483. Mats Exp $19,500, Books $19,500, Micro $180, Presv $25. Sal $94,927 (Prof $28,000)
Library Holdings: AV Mats 905; High Interest/Low Vocabulary Bk Vols 52; Large Print Bks 450; Bk Titles 42,721; Per Subs 72; Talking Bks 350
Subject Interests: Children's bks, Cookbks, Local hist
Automation Activity & Vendor Info: (Cataloging) Innovative Interfaces, Inc; (Circulation) Innovative Interfaces, Inc; (OPAC) Innovative Interfaces, Inc
Mem of Luzerne County Library System
Partic in Midwest Collaborative for Library Services (MCLS)
Open Mon-Thurs 9:30-7, Sat 10-5
Friends of the Library Group

PLYMOUTH MEETING

S ECRI INSTITUTE LIBRARY*, 5200 Butler Pike, 19462. SAN 315-1301. Tel: 610-825-6000, Ext 5309. FAX: 610-834-7366. *Chief Librn,* Evelyn Kuserk; E-mail: ekuserk@ecri.org; Staff 3 (MLS 3)
Founded 1966
Library Holdings: AV Mats 600; e-journals 400; Bk Titles 11,000; Per Subs 2,000
Special Collections: Medical & Health Care Related Devices (Health Devices Evaluation Services)
Subject Interests: Med tech
Automation Activity & Vendor Info: (Acquisitions) Inmagic, Inc.; (Cataloging) Inmagic, Inc.; (Circulation) Inmagic, Inc.; (OPAC) Inmagic, Inc.; (Serials) Inmagic, Inc.
Database Vendor: Dialog, EBSCOhost, LexisNexis, Medline, OVID Technologies, PubMed, ScienceDirect, Scopus
Wireless access
Partic in Delaware Valley Information Consortium; National Network of Libraries of Medicine
Restriction: Employees only, Limited access based on advanced application

POCONO PINES

P CLYMER LIBRARY*, 115 Firehouse Rd, 18350-9705. SAN 324-3974. Tel: 570-646-0826. FAX: 570-646-6181. E-mail: clymer@clymerlibrary.org. Web Site: www.clymerlibrary.org. *Dir,* Laura Laspee; E-mail: llaspee@clymerlibrary.org; Staff 1 (Non-MLS 1)
Founded 1902. Pop 15,343
Library Holdings: Bk Titles 50,007; Per Subs 50
Automation Activity & Vendor Info: (Circulation) Innovative Interfaces, Inc
Database Vendor: EBSCOhost
Wireless access
Function: ILL available, Photocopying/Printing, Telephone ref
Open Mon, Wed, Fri & Sat 10-5, Tues & Thurs 10-8

POINT MARION

P POINT MARION PUBLIC LIBRARY*, 399 Ontario St, 15474. SAN 370-7458. Tel: 724-725-9553. FAX: 724-725-9553. E-mail: pmlibrary@verizon.net. Web Site: www.pointmarionlibrary.com. *In Charge,* Joyce Dills
Founded 1928. Pop 2,067; Circ 7,675
Library Holdings: Bk Titles 6,550
Mem of Fayette County Library System
Open Mon-Thurs 6pm-9pm, Tues 2-4, Sat 12-2

PORT ALLEGANY

P SAMUEL W SMITH MEMORIAL PUBLIC LIBRARY*, 201 E Maple St, 16743. SAN 315-131X. Tel: 814-642-9210. FAX: 814-642-7555. E-mail: swsmith@swsmithlibrary.org. Web Site: www.swsmithlibrary.org. *Dir,* Janna C Shaffer; Staff 3.14 (MLS 1, Non-MLS 2.14)
Founded 1930. Pop 9,208; Circ 35,662
Jan 2005-Dec 2005 Income $122,700, State $37,832, City $22,722, Locally Generated Income $54,071. Mats Exp $16,631, Books $13,674, Per/Ser (Incl. Access Fees) $1,775, AV Mat $1,182. Sal $43,753 (Prof $23,000)
Library Holdings: CDs 64; DVDs 95; Large Print Bks 2,886; Bk Titles 26,670; Bk Vols 27,438; Per Subs 40; Talking Bks 558; Videos 867
Subject Interests: Glass
Automation Activity & Vendor Info: (Circulation) Follett Software; (OPAC) Follett Software
Wireless access
Open Mon, Tues & Thurs 11-7, Wed, Fri & Sat 9-4
Friends of the Library Group
Bookmobiles: 1. Librn, Gertrude Whipkey. Bk titles 2,000

PORT CARBON

P PORT CARBON PUBLIC LIBRARY*, 111 Pike St, 17965-1814. SAN 315-1328. Tel: 570-622-6115. FAX: 570-622-6115. E-mail: ptclib@wtvaccess.com. *Board Pres,* Janet Eich; *Libr Dir,* Jason Abati; Staff 3 (Non-MLS 3)
Pop 2,105
Library Holdings: DVDs 1,000; Bk Titles 13,000; Per Subs 10; Videos 100
Open Mon, Wed & Thurs 1-7, Tues & Fri 1-6, Sat 9-4

PORTAGE

P PORTAGE PUBLIC LIBRARY*, 704 Main St, 15946-1715. SAN 315-1336. Tel: 814-736-4340. FAX: 814-736-4413. E-mail: portage@cclsys.org. Web Site: www.cclsys.org/portage/. *Librn,* Rebecca Pollino
Founded 1927. Pop 6,879; Circ 31,259
Library Holdings: Large Print Bks 566; Bk Titles 15,147; Bk Vols 15,587; Per Subs 22; Talking Bks 460
Wireless access
Mem of Cambria County Library System & District Center; South Central Library System
Open Mon 9-12 & 4-8, Tues, Wed & Thurs 12-7, Sat 9-4

POTTSTOWN

M POTTSTOWN MEMORIAL MEDICAL CENTER*, Medical Library, 1600 E High St, 19464. SAN 372-9230. Tel: 610-327-7468. FAX: 610-705-6903. *Librn,* Cindy Yeager; E-mail: cindy_yeager@chs.net
Library Holdings: Bk Titles 400; Per Subs 50
Subject Interests: Med, Nursing, Surgery
Partic in Basic Health Sciences Library Network; DEVIC
Restriction: Med staff only, Open to others by appt

P POTTSTOWN REGIONAL PUBLIC LIBRARY, 500 E High St, 19464-5656. SAN 315-1344. Tel: 610-970-6551. FAX: 610-970-6553. E-mail: pottstownlibrary@mclinc.org. Web Site: ppl.mclinc.org. *Exec Dir,* Susan E Davis; E-mail: sdavis@mclinc.org; Staff 3 (MLS 3)
Founded 1921. Pop 43,625; Circ 130,642
Library Holdings: Bk Vols 82,957; Per Subs 178
Special Collections: Limerick Nuclear Power Plant
Subject Interests: Pa hist
Automation Activity & Vendor Info: (Cataloging) Innovative Interfaces, Inc; (Circulation) Innovative Interfaces, Inc; (OPAC) Innovative Interfaces, Inc; (Serials) Innovative Interfaces, Inc
Database Vendor: Booklist Online, EBSCO Auto Repair Reference, EBSCOhost, Foundation Center, Gale Cengage Learning, H W Wilson, Newsbank, ProQuest, ReferenceUSA, TumbleBookLibrary
Wireless access
Function: Adult bk club, After school storytime, Audiobks via web, Bks on CD, Computer training, Computers for patron use, Copy machines, E-Reserves, Electronic databases & coll, Fax serv, Handicapped accessible, Holiday prog, Homework prog, ILL available, Microfiche/film & reading machines, Music CDs, Newsp ref libr, Online cat, Online searches, Outreach serv, Outside serv via phone, mail, e-mail & web, Passport agency, Photocopying/Printing, Preschool outreach, Preschool reading prog, Prog for adults, Prog for children & young adult, Pub access computers, Ref serv available, Scanner, Senior computer classes, Story hour, Summer reading prog, Tax forms, Teen prog, Telephone ref, Web-catalog, Wheelchair accessible
Partic in Montgomery County Library & Information Network Consortium
Open Mon-Wed 10-8, Thurs & Fri 10-6, Sat 9-4
Friends of the Library Group

POTTSVILLE

M JOSEPH F MCCLOSKEY SCHOOL OF NURSING AT SCHUYLKILL HEALTH*, Medical Library, 420 S Jackson St, 17901. SAN 326-5439. Tel: 570-621-5000, 570-621-5033. Web Site: www.schuylkillhealthschoolofnursing.com. *Librn,* Christina Steffy; E-mail: csteffy@schuylkillhealth.com
Library Holdings: Bk Vols 1,850; Per Subs 15
Subject Interests: Med
Wireless access
Publications: Newsletter (Quarterly)
Restriction: Med staff only

P POTTSVILLE FREE PUBLIC LIBRARY*, 215 W Market St, 17901-4304. SAN 315-1379. Tel: 570-622-8105, 570-622-8880. FAX: 570-622-2157. E-mail: potpublib@pottsvillelibrary.org. Web Site: www.pottsvillelibrary.org. *Dir,* Nancy Smink; *Adult Serv,* Denise Miller; E-mail: potcirc@iu29.org; *ILL,* Gina Bensinger; E-mail: potill@iu29.org; *Ref,* Becki White; E-mail: potref@iu29.org; Staff 6 (MLS 6)
Founded 1911. Pop 94,130; Circ 114,350
Jan 2010-Dec 2010 Income $745,020, State $461,378, City $51,000, County $37,642, Locally Generated Income $120,000, Other $75,000. Mats Exp $64,920, Books $39,120, Per/Ser (Incl. Access Fees) $13,127, AV Mat $12,663. Sal $400,162 (Prof $263,494)
Library Holdings: AV Mats 15,266; CDs 1,307; DVDs 576; Large Print Bks 4,246; Bk Titles 99,315; Bk Vols 109,980; Per Subs 200; Talking Bks 4,074; Videos 3,128
Special Collections: Anthracite Coll; Lincoln Coll; Molly Maguires Coll. State Document Depository; US Document Depository
Automation Activity & Vendor Info: (Acquisitions) Baker & Taylor; (Cataloging) OCLC Connexion; (Circulation) AmLib Library Management System; (ILL) OCLC ILLiad; (OPAC) AmLib Library Management System
Function: Adult bk club, Art exhibits, Bk club(s), Bks on cassette, Bks on CD, CD-ROM, Children's prog, Computers for patron use, Copy machines, Doc delivery serv, e-mail serv, Electronic databases & coll, Free DVD rentals, Handicapped accessible, ILL available, Magnifiers for reading, Photocopying/Printing, Prog for adults, Prog for children & young adult, Ref & res, Summer reading prog, Tax forms, VHS videos
Open Mon, Tues & Thurs 8:30-8:30, Wed, Fri & Sat 8:30-5
Friends of the Library Group

GL SCHUYLKILL COUNTY LAW LIBRARY*, Schuylkill County Court House, 401 N Second St, 17901. SAN 315-1395. Tel: 570-628-1235. FAX: 570-628-1017. *Librn,* D Susan Kost; *Asst Librn,* Dorothy Lazovi
Founded 1888
Library Holdings: Bk Vols 30,000; Per Subs 20
Database Vendor: Westlaw
Open Mon-Fri 8:30-4:30

M SCHUYLKILL MEDICAL CENTER EAST*, Health Science Library, 700 E Norwegian St, 17901-2798. SAN 372-6215. Tel: 570-621-4466. FAX: 570-621-4891. Staff 0.5 (MLS 0.5)
Jul 2011-Jun 2012. Mats Exp $19,100, Books $3,700, Per/Ser (Incl. Access Fees) $15,000, Other Print Mats $400. Sal $33,000
Library Holdings: CDs 24; Bk Titles 755; Bk Vols 810; Per Subs 20; Videos 50
Subject Interests: Med, Nursing, Pub health
Automation Activity & Vendor Info: (Cataloging) Follett Software; (OPAC) Follett Software
Function: Health sci info serv
Partic in Central Pennsylvania Health Sciences Library Association; National Network of Libraries of Medicine
Open Mon-Fri 9-5
Restriction: Hospital staff & commun

PROSPECT

P PROSPECT COMMUNITY LIBRARY, 357 Main St, 16052. SAN 315-1417. Tel: 724-865-9718. FAX: 724-865-9261. Web Site: www.bcfls.org/prospect. *Dir,* Lou Pocchiari; E-mail: lou.pocchiari@prospectlibrary.org; Staff 2 (MLS 1, Non-MLS 1)
Founded 1922. Pop 7,000; Circ 14,000
Library Holdings: Bk Vols 14,000; Per Subs 20
Subject Interests: Gardening, Genealogy, Local hist
Automation Activity & Vendor Info: (Cataloging) TLC (The Library Corporation); (Circulation) TLC (The Library Corporation); (OPAC) TLC (The Library Corporation)
Wireless access
Mem of Butler County Federated Library System
Open Mon 1-8, Tues & Wed 10-5, Thurs 1-7, Fri 10-2, Sat 8-3
Restriction: Lending limited to county residents
Friends of the Library Group

PROSPECT PARK

P PROSPECT PARK FREE LIBRARY*, 720 Maryland Ave, 19076. Tel: 610-532-4643. FAX: 610-532-5648. E-mail: prospectpark@delcolibraries.org. Web Site: www.delcolibraries.org, www.prospectparklibrary.org. *Dir,* Mariann Jennings
Pop 6,594
Library Holdings: AV Mats 305; Bk Vols 20,000; Per Subs 25
Automation Activity & Vendor Info: (Cataloging) Innovative Interfaces, Inc; (Circulation) Innovative Interfaces, Inc; (OPAC) Innovative Interfaces, Inc
Wireless access
Mem of Delaware County Library System
Open Mon & Thurs 12-8, Tues & Fri 11-5, Sat 8:30-3:30 (8:30-12:30 Summer)

PUNXSUTAWNEY

P PUNXSUTAWNEY MEMORIAL LIBRARY*, 301 E Mahoning St, 15767-2198. SAN 315-145X. Tel: 814-938-5020. FAX: 814-938-3180. E-mail: info@punxsutawneylibrary.org. Web Site: www.punxsutawneylibrary.org. *Libr Dir,* Coral Ellshoff
Founded 1916. Pop 16,225; Circ 50,000
Library Holdings: Bk Vols 36,000; Per Subs 50
Automation Activity & Vendor Info: (Cataloging) AmLib Library Management System; (Circulation) AmLib Library Management System; (OPAC) AmLib Library Management System
Database Vendor: EBSCO Information Services, EBSCOhost
Wireless access
Mem of Oil Creek District Library Center
Partic in Jefferson County Library System
Open Mon-Fri 9-6, Sat 9-4
Friends of the Library Group

QUARRYVILLE

P QUARRYVILLE LIBRARY*, 357 Buck Rd, 17566. Tel: 717-786-1336. FAX: 717-786-9220. Web Site: www.quarryvillelibrary.org. *Dir,* Frances Vita; *Asst Dir,* Dolly Spence
Library Holdings: Audiobooks 1,797; AV Mats 2,115; Bks on Deafness & Sign Lang 10; Bk Vols 42,298; Per Subs 55
Automation Activity & Vendor Info: (Cataloging) Innovative Interfaces, Inc; (Circulation) Innovative Interfaces, Inc; (OPAC) Innovative Interfaces, Inc
Mem of Library System of Lancaster County
Open Tues-Thurs 10-8, Fri 10-5, Sat 10-2
Friends of the Library Group
Bookmobiles: 1. Spec Servs Coordr, Ed Miller

RADNOR

C CABRINI COLLEGE LIBRARY*, 610 King of Prussia Rd, 19087-3698. SAN 315-1476. Tel: 610-902-8538. FAX: 610-902-8539. E-mail: library@cabrini.edu. Web Site: www.cabrini.edu/library. *Dir,* Dr Roberta C Jacquet; Tel: 610-902-8260, E-mail: jacquet@cabrini.edu; *Asst Libr Dir,* Anne Schwelm; Tel: 610-902-8536, E-mail: aschwelm@cabrini.edu; *Electronic Res Librn,* Sara Drew; Tel: 610-902-8249, E-mail: sara@cabrini.edu; *Syst & Emerging Tech Librn,* Lawral Wornek; Tel: 610-902-8568, E-mail: lawral@cabrini.edu; Staff 7 (MLS 4, Non-MLS 3)
Founded 1957. Enrl 2,256; Fac 71; Highest Degree: Master
Jul 2007-Jun 2008. Mats Exp $289,500, Books $86,500, Per/Ser (Incl. Access Fees) $70,000, Electronic Ref Mat (Incl. Access Fees) $125,000, Presv $8,000. Sal $320,500 (Prof $200,000)
Library Holdings: DVDs 1,000; e-books 600; Bk Titles 76,500; Bk Vols 85,000; Per Subs 340
Special Collections: Cabriniana Coll; Franklin Delano Roosevelt Coll
Subject Interests: Educ, Immigration
Automation Activity & Vendor Info: (Acquisitions) SirsiDynix; (Cataloging) SirsiDynix; (Circulation) SirsiDynix; (OPAC) SirsiDynix; (Serials) SirsiDynix
Database Vendor: EBSCOhost, JSTOR, LexisNexis, OCLC FirstSearch, ProQuest
Wireless access
Function: e-mail serv, E-Reserves
Partic in Southeastern Pa Consortium for Higher Educ; Tri State Col Libr Coop
Restriction: Open to students, fac & staff

S WELLINGTON MANAGEMENT CO, LLP*, Four Radnor Corporate Ctr, Ste 500, 19087-8613. SAN 329-3300. Tel: 610-631-3500. FAX: 610-631-3505. *In Charge,* Dena Monastero; E-mail: dlmonastero@wellington.com
Library Holdings: Per Subs 100
Subject Interests: Coop finance, Indust
Restriction: Staff use only

READING

C ALBRIGHT COLLEGE*, F Wilbur Gingrich Library, 13th & Exeter Sts, 19604. (Mail add: PO Box 15234, 19612-5234), SAN 315-1514. Tel: 610-921-7517. Interlibrary Loan Service Tel: 610-921-7209. Reference Tel: 610-921-7211. FAX: 610-921-7509. E-mail: libraryref@alb.edu. Web Site: www.albright.edu/library/. *Dir,* Rosemary L Deegan; Tel: 610-921-7202, E-mail: rdeegan@alb.edu; *AV,* George E Missonis; Tel: 610-921-7203, E-mail: gmissonis@alb.edu; *ILL,* Christine L Kantner; E-mail: ckantner@alb.edu; *Cat,* Arlene Breiner; Tel: 610-921-7204, E-mail: abreiner@alb.edu; *Tech Serv,* Fianna D Holt; Tel: 610-921-7201, E-mail: fholt@alb.edu; *Ref,* Sandra L Stump; Tel: 610-921-7205, E-mail: sstump@alb.edu; *Circ,* Barbara Anderson; Tel: 610-921-7200, E-mail: banderson@alb.edu; Staff 14 (MLS 6, Non-MLS 8)
Founded 1856. Enrl 1,753
Library Holdings: Bks on Deafness & Sign Lang 60; Bk Vols 218,300; Per Subs 700
Special Collections: Albrightiana; Dick Coll of the Limited Editions Club; Norse-American Coll; Reading & Berks County (J Bennett Nolan Coll)
Subject Interests: Behav sci, Holocaust, Natural sci, Soc sci
Automation Activity & Vendor Info: (Acquisitions) BiblioMondo; (Cataloging) BiblioMondo; (Circulation) BiblioMondo; (OPAC) BiblioMondo; (Serials) BiblioMondo
Database Vendor: Dialog, Gale Cengage Learning, LexisNexis, OCLC FirstSearch, OVID Technologies, ProQuest, Wilson - Wilson Web
Function: ILL available
Publications: eLibris; Library Link (Newsletter); Pathfinders; Serials List; User's Guide
Partic in Associated College Libraries of Central Pennsylvania; Berks County Library Association; Dialog Corp; Hoover; Interlibrary Delivery Service of Pennsylvania; OCLC Online Computer Library Center, Inc; OCLC-LVIS
Open Mon-Thurs 8am-Midnight, Fri 8-7, Sat 9-5, Sun 1-Midnight
Friends of the Library Group

C ALVERNIA UNIVERSITY*, Dr Frank A Franco Library Learning Center, 400 St Bernardine St, 19607-1737. SAN 315-1522. Tel: 610-796-8223. Interlibrary Loan Service Tel: 610-796-8224. FAX: 610-796-8347. Web Site: www.alvernia.edu/library. *Libr Dir,* Sharon Neal; Tel: 610-796-1465, E-mail: sharon.neal@alvernia.edu; *Access Serv Librn,* Curtis Datko; Tel: 610-568-1534, E-mail: curtis.datko@alvernia.edu; *Distance Educ Librn,* Marietta Dooley; Tel: 215-635-4734, E-mail: marietta.dooley@alvernia.edu; *Evening/Weekend Librn,* Heidi Ziemer; Tel: 610-796-8355, E-mail: heidi.ziemer@alvernia.edu; *Instrul & Ref Librn,* Leon Weber; Tel: 610-796-8352, E-mail: leon.weber@alvernia.edu; *Tech Serv Librn,* Rebecca Rishar; Tel: 610-796-8395, E-mail: rebecca.rishar@alvernia.edu; Staff 12 (MLS 6, Non-MLS 6)
Founded 1958. Enrl 2,201; Highest Degree: Doctorate
Jul 2010-Jun 2011 Income $403,400. Mats Exp $265,876, Books $52,160, Per/Ser (Incl. Access Fees) $71,814, Manu Arch $300, Other Print Mats $9,500, AV Mat $9,346, Electronic Ref Mat (Incl. Access Fees) $117,056, Presv $3,000. Sal $353,523 (Prof $205,851)
Library Holdings: Audiobooks 95; AV Mats 2,277; CDs 969; DVDs 698; e-books 22,000; e-journals 91,041; Bk Titles 71,170; Bk Vols 71,244; Per Subs 150; Videos 2,277
Special Collections: Italian-American Cultural Center; Polish Coll
Subject Interests: Bus, Criminal justice, Educ, Nursing, Occupational therapy
Automation Activity & Vendor Info: (Acquisitions) Innovative Interfaces, Inc; (Cataloging) Innovative Interfaces, Inc; (Circulation) Innovative Interfaces, Inc; (Course Reserve) Innovative Interfaces, Inc; (ILL) Innovative Interfaces, Inc; (OPAC) Innovative Interfaces, Inc; (Serials) Innovative Interfaces, Inc
Database Vendor: 3M Library Systems, CQ Press, ebrary, EBSCOhost, Gale Cengage Learning, Innovative Interfaces, Inc, JSTOR, LexisNexis, OCLC FirstSearch, OCLC WorldShare Interlibrary Loan, ProQuest, PubMed, Westlaw
Wireless access
Partic in Lyrasis; OCLC Online Computer Library Center, Inc
Open Mon-Thurs 7:30am-Midnight, Fri 7:30-4:30, Sat 9-5, Sun Noon-Midnight

GL BERKS COUNTY LAW LIBRARY, Courthouse, 10th Flr, 633 Court St, 19601-4302. SAN 315-1549. Tel: 610-478-3370. Circulation Tel: 610-478-3370, Ext 3177. Administration Tel: 610-478-6208, Ext 3684. Information Services Tel: 610-478-3370, Ext 3171. FAX: 610-478-6375. E-mail: lawlibrary@countyofberks.com. Web Site: www.co.berks.pa.us/lawlibrary. *Adminr,* Tracy Barlet; Tel: 610-478-6208; *Law Libr Asst,* Catrina L Mackes; E-mail: cmackes@countyofberks.com; *Law Libr Asst,* Melanie Marinaccio; E-mail: mmarinaccio@countyofberks.com. Subject Specialists: *Labor law,* Melanie Marinaccio; Staff 2 (Non-MLS 2)
Founded 1859
Library Holdings: Bk Titles 4,750; Bk Vols 34,000; Per Subs 1,300

Automation Activity & Vendor Info: (OPAC) Innovative Interfaces, Inc - Millenium
Database Vendor: HeinOnline, LexisNexis, Westlaw
Function: Doc delivery serv, Fax serv
Open Mon-Fri 8:30-4:30
Restriction: Open to pub for ref only, Restricted borrowing privileges

S CARPENTER TECHNOLOGY CORP, Research & Development Library, 1600 Centre Ave, 19601. (Mail add: PO Box 14662, 19612-4662), SAN 315-1557. Tel: 610-208-2807. E-mail: randdlibrary@cartech.com. *Librn,* Mindy L Peters; Staff 1 (MLS 1)
Founded 1950
Subject Interests: Mat sci, Metallurgy
Wireless access
Function: Ref & res
Partic in Berks County Library Association
Restriction: Employees only, Open to others by appt, Open to researchers by request

P EXETER COMMUNITY LIBRARY*, 4569 Prestwick Dr, 19606. Tel: 610-406-9431. FAX: 610-406-9415. E-mail: exetercl@berks.lib.pa.us. Web Site: www.berks.lib.pa.us/exetercl. *Asst Dir,* Mallory McConnell; *Ch Serv,* Laura C Kauffman; Staff 3 (Non-MLS 3)
Founded 1999. Pop 25,000; Circ 221,158
Library Holdings: CDs 2,489; DVDs 3,625; Bk Vols 18,000; Per Subs 58
Automation Activity & Vendor Info: (Cataloging) SirsiDynix; (Circulation) SirsiDynix; (OPAC) SirsiDynix
Database Vendor: Baker & Taylor
Wireless access
Function: Adult bk club, Bk club(s), Copy machines, e-mail serv, Electronic databases & coll, Fax serv, Handicapped accessible, ILL available, Mail & tel request accepted, Music CDs, Prog for adults, Prog for children & young adult, Spoken cassettes & CDs, Summer reading prog, Tax forms, VHS videos, Wheelchair accessible
Mem of Berks County Public Libraries
Open Mon-Thurs 10-8, Fri & Sat 10-5
Friends of the Library Group

S HISTORICAL SOCIETY OF BERKS COUNTY*, Museum & Library, 940 Centre Ave, 19601. SAN 315-1581. Tel: 610-375-4375. FAX: 610-375-4376. Web Site: www.berksweb.com/histsoc. *Archivist, Dir,* Kimberly Richards
Founded 1869
Library Holdings: CDs 200; Bk Titles 16,000
Special Collections: Berks County Family Histories; German & English Newspapers of Reading & Berks County 1797-1907, newsp bd; Iron History of Berks County; Original Manuscripts
Publications: The Historical Review of Berks County
Open Tues-Sat 9-4

R KESHER ZION SYNAGOGUE SISTERHOOD LIBRARY*, 1245 Perkiomen Ave, 19602-1318. SAN 315-1603. Tel: 610-374-1763. FAX: 610-375-1352. *Adult Serv,* Karol Page; *Ch Serv, YA Serv,* Rachel Yaffee; Staff 2 (Non-MLS 2)
Library Holdings: Bk Titles 2,780; Bk Vols 3,010
Subject Interests: Hebraica, Judaica

C PENNSYLVANIA STATE UNIVERSITY*, Thun Library, Berks Campus, Tulpehocken Rd, 19610. (Mail add: PO Box 7009, 19610-7009), SAN 315-1611. Tel: 610-396-6240. FAX: 610-396-6249. Web Site: www.libraries.psu.edu/berks/. *Head Librn,* Deena J Morganti; Tel: 610-396-6246, E-mail: djm12@psu.edu; *Ref Librn,* Nancy H Dewald; Tel: 610-396-6243, E-mail: nxd7@psu.edu; *Ref Librn,* Billie E Walker; Tel: 610-396-6242, E-mail: bew11@psu.edu; Staff 4 (MLS 4)
Founded 1958. Enrl 2,400; Fac 100
Library Holdings: Bk Vols 50,000; Per Subs 130
Partic in OCLC Online Computer Library Center, Inc; RLIN (Research Libraries Information Network)
Open Mon-Thurs (Winter) 7:30am-Midnight, Fri 7:30-5, Sat Noon-5, Sun 2-10; Mon-Thurs (Summer) 8am-10pm, Fri 8-5

J READING AREA COMMUNITY COLLEGE, The Yocum Library, Ten S Second St, 19602. (Mail add: PO Box 1706, 19603-1706), SAN 315-1638. Tel: 610-607-6237. Interlibrary Loan Service Tel: 610-372-4721, Ext 5051. Reference Tel: 610-372-4721, Ext 5057. Administration Tel: 610-372-4721, Ext 5061. Toll Free Tel: 800-626-1665, Ext 6237. FAX: 610-607-6254. E-mail: library@racc.edu. Web Site: www.racc.edu/library/. *Asst Dean, Libr Serv,* Mary Ellen G Heckman; E-mail: mheckman@racc.edu; *Instrul Serv Librn, Ref Serv,* Kim R Stahler; *Tech Serv,* Brenna Corbit; Tel: 610-372-4721, Ext 5033, E-mail: bcorbit@racc.edu; Staff 9 (MLS 3, Non-MLS 6)
Founded 1971. Enrl 2,951; Fac 60; Highest Degree: Associate
Library Holdings: Bk Vols 32,000; Per Subs 225
Special Collections: Comic Books; Music Score Coll; Schuylkill Navigation Co Maps
Subject Interests: Film, Nursing
Function: ILL available, Magnifiers for reading, Wheelchair accessible
Special Services for the Blind - Aids for in-house use
Open Mon-Thurs 8am-10pm, Fri 8-5, Sat 9:30-1:30, Sun 1:30-4:30
Restriction: Open to pub for ref & circ; with some limitations

P READING PUBLIC LIBRARY*, 100 S Fifth St, 19602. SAN 359-4963. Tel: 610-655-6350. Reference Tel: 610-655-6355. Administration Tel: 610-655-6365. Interlibrary Loan Service FAX: 610-655-6354. Reference FAX: 610-655-6609. Administration FAX: 610-478-9035. E-mail: reference@reading.lib.pa.us. Web Site: www.reading.lib.pa.us. *Dir,* Frank Kasprowicz; *Asst Dir,* Joseph Zappacosta; *Ch Serv,* Lynn Miller; *ILL, Ref Serv,* Pamela Hehr; *Tech Serv,* Virginia Lash
Founded 1763. Pop 382,000; Circ 529,603
Library Holdings: Bk Titles 297,582; Bk Vols 311,785; Per Subs 305
Special Collections: John Updike Coll; Local Imprints, Berks Authors Coll; Pennsylvania German Coll. State Document Depository; US Document Depository
Automation Activity & Vendor Info: (Cataloging) SirsiDynix; (Circulation) SirsiDynix; (OPAC) SirsiDynix
Database Vendor: EBSCOhost, Gale Cengage Learning
Wireless access
Partic in OCLC Online Computer Library Center, Inc
Open Mon-Wed 8:15am-9pm, Thurs & Fri 8:15-5:30, Sat 8:45-5
Friends of the Library Group
Branches: 3
NORTHEAST, 1348 N 11th St, 19604-1509, SAN 359-4998. Tel: 610-655-6361. FAX: 610-655-6668. E-mail: rplne@reading.lib.pa.us. *Librn,* Bronwen Gillette
Library Holdings: Bk Vols 28,336
Open Mon & Wed 1-9, Tues, Thurs & Sat 9-5
Friends of the Library Group
NORTHWEST, 901 Schuylkill Ave, 19601, SAN 359-5021. Tel: 610-655-6360. FAX: 610-655-6667. *Br Mgr,* Emily McNulty
Founded 1939
Library Holdings: Bk Vols 14,966
Open Mon & Wed 1-5 & 6-9, Tues, Thurs & Sat 9-12 & 1-5
SOUTHEAST, 1426 Perkiomen Ave, 19602-2136, SAN 359-5056. Tel: 610-655-6362. FAX: 610-655-6669. E-mail: rplse@reading.lib.pa.us. *Br Mgr,* Sue Belz
Library Holdings: Bk Vols 23,291
Open Mon & Wed 1-9, Tues, Thurs & Sat 9-5
Friends of the Library Group
Bookmobiles: 1

S READING PUBLIC MUSEUM LIBRARY*, 500 Museum Rd, 19611-1425. SAN 315-1654. Tel: 610-371-5850. FAX: 610-371-5632. Web Site: www.readingpublicmuseum.org. *In Charge,* Ashley Hamilton
Founded 1904
Library Holdings: Bk Titles 8,000
Subject Interests: Anthrop, Archit, Art, Astronomy, Natural sci
Restriction: Open by appt only, Open to pub for ref only

RED LION

P KALTREIDER-BENFER LIBRARY*, 147 S Charles St, 17356. SAN 315-1689. Tel: 717-244-2032. FAX: 717-246-2394. E-mail: kalib@yorklibraries.org. Web Site: www.kaltreider-benfer.org. *Dir,* Don Dellinger; E-mail: ddellinger@yorklibraries.org; Staff 6 (MLS 1, Non-MLS 5)
Founded 1963. Pop 59,157; Circ 215,000
Library Holdings: Bk Titles 51,000; Per Subs 45
Publications: Red Lion Community Directory
Mem of York County Library System
Open Mon-Thurs 10-8, Fri 10-5, Sat 9-4 (10-2 July & Aug)
Friends of the Library Group

REPUBLIC

P REPUBLIC COMMUNITY LIBRARY*, 13 DeGregory Circle, 15475. (Mail add: PO Box 165, 15475-0165). Tel: 724-246-0404. FAX: 724-246-0404. *Dir,* Margaret Wyatt
Library Holdings: Bk Vols 10,500
Automation Activity & Vendor Info: (Cataloging) Brodart; (Circulation) Brodart
Open Tues-Fri (Winter) 2-5; Tues-Fri (Summer) 1-4

REYNOLDSVILLE

P REYNOLDSVILLE PUBLIC LIBRARY*, 460 Main St, 15851-1251. SAN 315-1700. Tel: 814-653-9471. FAX: 814-653-9471. Web Site: home.adelphia.net/~reylib. *Dir,* Sharon Bobal
Founded 1929. Pop 6,870; Circ 35,212
Library Holdings: Bk Vols 12,500; Per Subs 50

Mem of Oil Creek District Library Center
Open Mon-Fri 1-8, Sat 10-5

RICHBORO

P FREE LIBRARY OF NORTHAMPTON TOWNSHIP*, 25 Upper Holland Rd, 18954-1514. SAN 315-1719. Tel: 215-357-3050. Web Site: www.buckslib.org/northampton. *Dir,* Elizabeth Baugh; *Ch,* Barbara Lewis; *Ref,* Amy Wardle; Staff 4 (MLS 4)
Founded 1970. Pop 40,692; Circ 277,870
Jan 2009-Dec 2009 Income $841,000, City $778,800, Locally Generated Income $62,200. Mats Exp $121,000, Books $89,000, Per/Ser (Incl. Access Fees) $5,000, AV Mat $27,000. Sal $535,000
Library Holdings: AV Mats 11,406; Bk Vols 101,673; Per Subs 128
Automation Activity & Vendor Info: (Circulation) SirsiDynix; (OPAC) SirsiDynix
Wireless access
Mem of Bucks County Free Library
Open Mon-Thurs 12-9, Fri 10-5, Sat 10-5
Friends of the Library Group

RICHLAND

P RICHLAND COMMUNITY LIBRARY*, 111 E Main St, 17087. SAN 315-1727. Tel: 717-866-4939. FAX: 717-866-2661. Web Site: www.lclibs.org/richland. *Dir,* Amy Davis; E-mail: adavis@lclibs.org
Founded 1886. Pop 3,958; Circ 34,467
Library Holdings: Bk Titles 15,000; Per Subs 20
Mem of Lebanon County Library System
Open Mon-Wed 12:30-8, Thurs 10:30-5, Fri 12:30-5, Sat 9-4

RIDGWAY

P RIDGWAY PUBLIC LIBRARY*, 329 Center St, 15853. SAN 315-1735. Tel: 814-773-7573. FAX: 814-776-1093. Web Site: www.ridgwaylibrary.org. *Dir,* Lann Yurchick; E-mail: Library_director@ridgwaylibrary.org; *Ch Serv, ILL,* Sophia Duffield; Staff 1 (Non-MLS 1)
Founded 1899. Pop 9,280; Circ 35,286
Library Holdings: Bk Titles 16,000; Per Subs 70
Automation Activity & Vendor Info: (Acquisitions) Follett Software; (Cataloging) Follett Software; (Circulation) Follett Software; (ILL) Follett Software; (OPAC) Follett Software
Wireless access
Function: Adult bk club, Copy machines, Fax serv, ILL available, Large print keyboards, Magnifiers for reading, Prog for children & young adult, Spoken cassettes & CDs, Summer reading prog, Tax forms, VHS videos
Open Mon & Fri 11-5, Tues-Thurs 11-8, Sat 9-4
Bookmobiles: 1

RIDLEY PARK

P RIDLEY PARK PUBLIC LIBRARY*, 107 E Ward St, 19078-3097. SAN 315-1743. Tel: 610-583-7207. FAX: 610-583-2160. E-mail: ridleypark@delcolibraries.org. *Dir,* Catherine Bittle; *Ch Serv,* Mary Ellen Keeney
Founded 1888. Pop 7,183; Circ 27,525
Library Holdings: Bk Vols 20,000; Per Subs 35
Mem of Delaware County Library System
Open Mon Noon-8:30, Tues & Thurs Noon-5, & 6:30-8:30, Wed 10-8:30, Sat 10-5
Friends of the Library Group

M TAYLOR HOSPITAL*, Medical Library, 175 E Chester Pike, 19078. SAN 372-6134. Tel: 610-595-6000, 610-595-6027. Web Site: virtuallibrary.crozer.org. *Dir,* Judy Ziegler
Founded 1977
Library Holdings: Bk Titles 400; Per Subs 90
Automation Activity & Vendor Info: (OPAC) Inmagic, Inc.
Database Vendor: EBSCOhost, OVID Technologies
Open Mon-Fri 7:30-5

RIEGELSVILLE

P RIEGELSVILLE PUBLIC LIBRARY*, 615 Easton Rd, 18077. (Mail add: PO Box 65, 18077-0065), SAN 320-8397. Tel: 610-749-2357. E-mail: librarian@riegelsvillelibrary.info. Web Site: www.riegelsvillelibrary.info. *Dir,* Zeau Modig; *Children's Serv Coordr,* Julia Sefton; *Tech Serv,* Terri Randolph; Staff 3 (MLS 1, Non-MLS 2)
Founded 1886. Pop 2,176; Circ 16,500
Library Holdings: Bk Vols 16,500; Per Subs 31
Special Collections: Riegelsville Historic Room Coll
Wireless access
Function: Adult bk club, Archival coll, Audiobks via web, Bks on cassette, Bks on CD, Children's prog, Computers for patron use, Copy machines, Digital talking bks, Free DVD rentals, Handicapped accessible, Holiday prog, ILL available, Music CDs, Online cat, Photocopying/Printing, Preschool outreach, Prog for adults, Prog for children & young adult, Pub access computers, Scanner, Story hour, Summer reading prog, VHS videos
Mem of Bucks County Free Library
Open Tues & Thurs 9-7, Sat 9-3
Friends of the Library Group

RIMERSBURG

P ECCLES-LESHER MEMORIAL LIBRARY*, 673 Main St, 16248-4817. (Mail add: PO Box 359, 16248-0359), SAN 315-1751. Tel: 814-473-3800. FAX: 814-473-8200. Web Site: www.eccles-lesher.org. *Dir,* Rachel Campbell; E-mail: director@eccles-lesher.org; *Ch Serv,* Nancy Shanafelt; E-mail: programs@eccles-lesher.org; *ILL,* Sherri Campbell; *Ref,* Sharon Custer; E-mail: reference@eccles-lesher.org; Staff 1 (MLS 1)
Founded 1968. Pop 6,003; Circ 29,398
Jan 2006-Dec 2006 Income $115,539, State $32,500, County $3,039, Locally Generated Income $5,000, Other $75,000. Mats Exp $14,400, Books $11,000, Per/Ser (Incl. Access Fees) $1,900, Micro $100, AV Mat $1,400. Sal $77,500 (Prof $27,000)
Library Holdings: AV Mats 2,910; Bks on Deafness & Sign Lang 10; DVDs 269; Large Print Bks 375; Bk Titles 25,500; Bk Vols 23,200; Per Subs 52; Talking Bks 641; Videos 2,000
Special Collections: Genealogy Histories of Local Families; Local Newspapers, microfilm
Subject Interests: Fishing, Hunting, Relig studies
Automation Activity & Vendor Info: (Circulation) Follett Software; (OPAC) Follett Software
Wireless access
Publications: Biweekly Newspaper Article
Mem of Oil Creek District Library Center
Open Mon, Tues & Thurs 9-6, Fri & Sat 9-4
Friends of the Library Group

RINGTOWN

P RINGTOWN AREA LIBRARY*, 132 W Main St, 17967-9538. (Mail add: PO Box 120, 17967), SAN 320-8400. Tel: 570-889-5503. Toll Free FAX: 570-889-5503. E-mail: ringtownlibrary@epix.net. Web Site: iu29.schiu.k12.pa.us/rinpl/. *Librn,* Tanya Savitsky
Founded 1976. Pop 1,535; Circ 3,750
Library Holdings: Bk Vols 11,000; Per Subs 23
Open Mon & Fri 11-5, Tues 1-5, Weds 1-7, Thurs 10-4, Sat 8-3 (8-12 July-Aug)
Friends of the Library Group

ROARING SPRING

P ROARING SPRING COMMUNITY LIBRARY*, 320 E Main St, 16673-1009. SAN 315-176X. Tel: 814-224-2994. FAX: 814-224-4472. Web Site: www.roaringspringlibrary.org. *Dir,* Michelle McIntyre
Founded 1959. Pop 6,287; Circ 16,332
Library Holdings: Bk Titles 23,679; Per Subs 88
Automation Activity & Vendor Info: (Cataloging) Follett Software; (Circulation) Follett Software; (OPAC) Follett Software
Function: ILL available
Mem of Blair County Library System
Open Mon & Wed 3-7, Tues, Thurs & Fri 9-4, Sat 9-2
Friends of the Library Group

ROBESONIA

P ROBESONIA COMMUNITY LIBRARY*, 75-A S Brooke St, 19551-1500. SAN 315-1778. Tel: 610-693-3264. FAX: 610-693-6864. E-mail: robesoniacl@berks.lib.pa.us. Web Site: www.berks.lib.pa.us/sro. *Dir,* Stephanie D Williams; Staff 1 (MLS 1)
Founded 1969. Pop 4,995; Circ 59,308
Library Holdings: Bk Titles 21,756; Per Subs 70
Automation Activity & Vendor Info: (Cataloging) Horizon; (Circulation) Horizon; (OPAC) Horizon
Wireless access
Function: ILL available, Photocopying/Printing, Prog for adults, Prog for children & young adult, Summer reading prog
Mem of Berks County Public Libraries
Open Mon-Thurs 9:30-8, Fri & Sat 9-1
Friends of the Library Group

ROCHESTER

P ROCHESTER PUBLIC LIBRARY*, 252 Adams St, 15074-2137. SAN 315-1786. Tel: 724-774-7783. FAX: 724-774-9158. Web Site: www.beaverlibraries.org/rochester.asp. *Dir,* Terri Gallagher; E-mail: tgallagher@beaverlibraries.org
Founded 1922. Pop 4,739; Circ 9,084
Library Holdings: Bk Titles 28,000; Per Subs 25

Mem of Beaver County Library System
Open Mon & Wed 12-7, Tues & Thurs 9-4, Sat 9-4 (10-2 Summer)

ROSEMONT

C ROSEMONT COLLEGE LIBRARY, Gertrude Kistler Memorial Library, 1400 Montgomery Ave, 19010-1631. SAN 315-1794. Tel: 610-527-0200, Ext 2271. Reference Tel: 610-527-0200, Ext 2273. Administration Tel: 610-527-0200, Ext 2973. Information Services Tel: 610-527-0200, Ext 2976. Web Site: www.rosemont.edu/library/index.aspx. *Exec Dir, Libr Serv,* Catherine Fennell; E-mail: fennell@rosemont.edu; *Asst Dir, Libr Serv,* Joseph Tresnan; Tel: 610-527-0200, Ext 2206, E-mail: jtresnan@rosemont.edu; *Head, Access Serv & ILL,* Kathleen Deeming; E-mail: kdeeming@rosemont.edu; *Ref & Instrul Tech Librn,* Brendan Johnson; Tel: 610-527-0200, Ext 2287, E-mail: brendan.johnson@rosemont.edu; Staff 9 (MLS 4, Non-MLS 5)
Founded 1921. Enrl 900; Fac 150; Highest Degree: Master
Library Holdings: AV Mats 3,966; Bks on Deafness & Sign Lang 47; CDs 59; DVDs 2,115; e-books 5,539; e-journals 16,295; Microforms 22,509; Bk Titles 123,699; Bk Vols 155,634; Per Subs 77; Videos 979
Special Collections: African American Coll; Children's Coll; Publisher's Binding Coll; Rosemont Coll; Women's Poetry Coll
Subject Interests: Gen liberal arts
Automation Activity & Vendor Info: (Cataloging) SirsiDynix; (Circulation) SirsiDynix; (Course Reserve) SirsiDynix; (OPAC) SirsiDynix
Database Vendor: Alexander Street Press, Annual Reviews, CredoReference, JSTOR, LexisNexis, OCLC FirstSearch, OCLC WorldShare Interlibrary Loan, OVID Technologies, Project MUSE, ProQuest, SerialsSolutions, SirsiDynix, Wilson - Wilson Web
Wireless access
Partic in Interlibrary Delivery Service of Pennsylvania; OCLC Online Computer Library Center, Inc; Southeastern Pa Consortium for Higher Educ; Tri-State College Library Cooperative
Special Services for the Deaf - Staff with knowledge of sign lang
Special Services for the Blind - Assistive/Adapted tech devices, equip & products; Computer with voice synthesizer for visually impaired persons; Dragon Naturally Speaking software; Magnifiers; ZoomText magnification & reading software
Friends of the Library Group

SAEGERTOWN

P SAEGERTOWN AREA LIBRARY*, 325 Broad St, 16433. (Mail add: PO Box 871, 16433-0871), SAN 376-642X. Tel: 814-763-5203. FAX: 814-763-4979. E-mail: sal@ccfls.org. Web Site: www.ccfls.org/saegertown. *Dir,* Heather J Wakefield; *Librn,* Judith L Miller
Founded 1984
Library Holdings: Bk Vols 14,200; Per Subs 30
Automation Activity & Vendor Info: (Cataloging) Follett Software; (Circulation) Follett Software; (OPAC) Follett Software
Wireless access
Mem of Crawford County Federated Library System
Partic in Share NW Consortium
Open Mon-Thurs 12-7, Fri 9-1, Sat 9-4
Friends of the Library Group

SAINT DAVIDS

C EASTERN UNIVERSITY, Warner Memorial Library, 1300 Eagle Rd, 19087-3696. SAN 315-1824. Tel: 610-341-5981. Interlibrary Loan Service Tel: 610-341-5958. Reference Tel: 610-341-1777. Interlibrary Loan Service FAX: 610-341-1375. E-mail: reference1777@eastern.edu. Web Site: www.eastern.edu/warner-memorial-library. *Dir,* James L Sauer; Tel: 610-341-5957, E-mail: jsauer@eastern.edu; *Info Serv Librn,* Mark D Puterbaugh; Tel: 610-341-1461, E-mail: mputerba@eastern.edu; *Tech Serv Librn,* Jonathan Beasley; Tel: 610-225-5003, E-mail: jbeasley@eastern.edu; Staff 10 (MLS 7, Non-MLS 3)
Founded 1952. Enrl 3,400; Fac 140; Highest Degree: Doctorate
Jul 2013-Jun 2014. Mats Exp $375,000, Books $75,000, Per/Ser (Incl. Access Fees) $60,000, AV Mat $3,500, Electronic Ref Mat (Incl. Access Fees) $235,000, Presv $1,500
Library Holdings: Audiobooks 500; e-books 171,000; e-journals 80,000; Microforms 870,000; Bk Vols 178,000; Per Subs 225; Videos 5,199
Special Collections: Bruce Rogers Coll; Harry C Goebel Coll on Fine Printing; Marcus Aurelius
Automation Activity & Vendor Info: (Acquisitions) TLC (The Library Corporation); (Cataloging) TLC (The Library Corporation); (Circulation) TLC (The Library Corporation); (Course Reserve) TLC (The Library Corporation); (OPAC) TLC (The Library Corporation); (Serials) TLC (The Library Corporation)
Database Vendor: Access Pennsylvania, Annual Reviews, Cinahl, CredoReference, ebrary, EBSCOhost, H W Wilson, JSTOR, LexisNexis, Newsbank, OCLC FirstSearch, OVID Technologies, ProQuest, RefWorks, Sage, SirsiDynix, TLC (The Library Corporation), Wilson - Wilson Web
Wireless access
Partic in Asn of Christian Librs; OCLC Online Computer Library Center, Inc; Pennsylvania Academic Library Consortium, Inc (PALCI); Tri-State College Library Cooperative
Open Mon-Thurs 8am-11pm, Fri 8-5, Sat 10-3
Friends of the Library Group

SAINT MARYS

P SAINT MARY'S PUBLIC LIBRARY*, 127 Center St, 15857. SAN 315-1859. Tel: 814-834-6141. FAX: 814-834-9814. E-mail: library@stmaryslibrary.org. Web Site: www.stmaryslibrary.org. *Dir, Tech Serv,* Jane Vavala; *Coll Develop,* Velma Gross; *Ch Serv,* Vicki Miller; *ILL,* Diana Smith; *Purchasing,* Justine McCafferty; Staff 7 (MLS 1, Non-MLS 6)
Founded 1921. Pop 15,225
Library Holdings: Bk Titles 38,124; Per Subs 85
Subject Interests: Elk County, St Mary's area hist
Open Mon & Wed 10-8, Tues & Thurs 12-8, Fri 10-5, Sat 9-4 (9-1 July-Aug)
Friends of the Library Group

SAINT THOMAS

P SAINT THOMAS LIBRARY*, 30 School House Lane, 17252-9650. Tel: 717-369-4716. FAX: 717-369-4896. E-mail: stthomaspublib@yahoo.com. Web Site: www.fclspa.org. *Mgr,* Deanna Snider
Founded 1977. Pop 5,775; Circ 12,699
Jan 2005-Dec 2005. Mats Exp $6,504
Library Holdings: Bk Vols 9,416; Per Subs 16
Special Collections: Family Place
Automation Activity & Vendor Info: (Cataloging) AmLib Library Management System; (Circulation) AmLib Library Management System; (OPAC) AmLib Library Management System
Wireless access
Mem of Franklin County Library System
Open Mon, Tues, Thurs & Fri 2-6, Wed 10-6, Sat 9-12

SANDY LAKE

P LAKEVIEW AREA PUBLIC LIBRARY*, 3271 S Main St, 16145. (Mail add: PO Box 622, 16145-0622). Tel: 724-376-4217. *Pres,* Theresa Panneri
Library Holdings: Bk Vols 3,000
Open Tues 10-6, Fri 10-3, Sat 10-1

SAXONBURG

P SOUTH BUTLER COMMUNITY LIBRARY*, 240 W Main St, 16056. (Mail add: PO Box 454, 16056-0454), SAN 320-5096. Tel: 724-352-4810. FAX: 724-352-1815. Web Site: www.southbutlerlibrary.org. *Dir,* Erin Wincek; E-mail: erin.wincek@southbutlerlibrary.org; Staff 2 (MLS 2)
Founded 1978. Pop 7,993; Circ 32,028
Library Holdings: Bk Vols 23,000; Per Subs 48; Videos 877
Special Collections: Butler County History
Subject Interests: Cooking, Craft, Gardening
Mem of Butler County Federated Library System
Open Mon, Wed & Thurs 10-6, Tues 10-8, Fri 10-3, Sat 9-4
Friends of the Library Group

SAXTON

P SAXTON COMMUNITY LIBRARY*, 315 Front St, 16678-8612. (Mail add: PO Box 34, 16678-0034), SAN 315-1891. Tel: 814-635-3533. FAX: 814-635-3001. E-mail: saxtonlibrary@verizon.net. *Libr Dir,* Judy Williams
Founded 1968. Pop 4,182; Circ 11,611
Jan 2011-Dec 2011 Income $71,943, State $13,950, City $1,400, County $10,027, Locally Generated Income $46,566. Mats Exp $9,004, Books $7,097, Per/Ser (Incl. Access Fees) $730, AV Mat $323, Electronic Ref Mat (Incl. Access Fees) $529, Presv $325. Sal $33,917
Library Holdings: Audiobooks 311; Bks on Deafness & Sign Lang 12; Braille Volumes 1; CDs 5; DVDs 55; High Interest/Low Vocabulary Bk Vols 14; Large Print Bks 411; Bk Titles 19,719; Bk Vols 20,380; Per Subs 35; Videos 106
Special Collections: Nuclear Regulatory Commission Local Public Document Room
Automation Activity & Vendor Info: (Cataloging) Follett Software; (Circulation) Follett Software
Database Vendor: EBSCO - WebFeat, EBSCO Auto Repair Reference, EBSCOhost
Wireless access
Mem of Bedford County Library System
Open Mon & Wed 10:30-7:30, Tues & Thurs 2:30-7:30, Sat 9-4

SAYRE

M WILLIAM C BECK HEALTH SCIENCE LIBRARY & RESOURCE CENTER*, One Guthrie Sq, 18840. SAN 315-1905. Tel: 570-882-4700. FAX: 570-882-4703. Web Site: www.guthrie.org. *Tech Spec,* Brad Zehr; E-mail: zehr_brad@ghs.guthrie.org
Founded 1922
Library Holdings: Bk Titles 4,200; Bk Vols 7,673; Per Subs 500
Special Collections: Mayock Coll
Subject Interests: Hist, Med, Med ethics, Nursing
Partic in South Central Regional Library Council; Susquehanna Library Cooperative
Open Mon-Fri 8-5

P SAYRE PUBLIC LIBRARY, INC*, 122 S Elmer Ave, 18840. SAN 315-1913. Tel: 570-888-2256. FAX: 570-888-3355. E-mail: sayrepl@stny.rr.com. Web Site: www.sayrepl.org. *Dir,* Tiffany R Robbins; Staff 2 (Non-MLS 2)
Founded 1936. Pop 5,813; Circ 6,483
Library Holdings: AV Mats 1,525; Large Print Bks 655; Bk Titles 25,663; Per Subs 45; Talking Bks 510
Subject Interests: Local hist
Automation Activity & Vendor Info: (Cataloging) Follett Software; (Circulation) Follett Software
Database Vendor: EBSCOhost
Mem of Bradford County Library System
Open Tues & Thurs 10-7:30, Wed, Fri & Sat 10-5
Friends of the Library Group

SCHNECKSVILLE

J LEHIGH CARBON COMMUNITY COLLEGE LIBRARY*, 4525 Education Park Dr, 18078-9372. SAN 315-1921. Tel: 610-799-1196. Circulation Tel: 610-799-1150. Reference Tel: 610-799-1769. FAX: 610-779-1159. Web Site: www.lccc.edu. *Dean, Libr Serv,* David Stephen Voros; Tel: 610-799-1164, E-mail: dvoros@lccc.edu; *Coordr, Ref,* Rick Paterick; E-mail: rpaterick@lccc.edu; *Acq,* Rose Boettger; E-mail: rboettger@lccc.edu; *AV,* Joann Warmkessel; Tel: 610-799-1124, E-mail: jwarmkessel@lccc.edu; *Cat,* Jane Yagerhofer; Tel: 610-799-1160, E-mail: jyagerhofer@lccc.edu; *Circ,* Barbara Hoffman; E-mail: bhoffman@lccc.edu; *ILL,* Susan Mattern; Tel: 610-799-1163, E-mail: smattern@lccc.edu; *Ref,* Barbara Balas; Tel: 610-799-1770, E-mail: bbalas@lccc.edu; *Ser,* Darlene Coleman; E-mail: dcoleman@lccc.edu; Staff 19 (MLS 7, Non-MLS 12)
Founded 1967. Enrl 6,400; Fac 80; Highest Degree: Associate
Library Holdings: Bk Titles 42,293; Bk Vols 50,834; Per Subs 550
Special Collections: College Archives; New York Times, 1851-present, micro
Subject Interests: Allied health, Criminal justice
Automation Activity & Vendor Info: (Acquisitions) Innovative Interfaces, Inc; (Cataloging) Innovative Interfaces, Inc; (Circulation) Innovative Interfaces, Inc; (Course Reserve) Innovative Interfaces, Inc; (ILL) Innovative Interfaces, Inc; (Media Booking) Innovative Interfaces, Inc; (OPAC) Innovative Interfaces, Inc; (Serials) Innovative Interfaces, Inc
Database Vendor: EBSCOhost, Gale Cengage Learning, LexisNexis, OCLC FirstSearch, ProQuest, Wilson - Wilson Web
Publications: Library Skills Workbook (Research guide)
Partic in ARIEL; Interlibrary Delivery Service of Pennsylvania; Lyrasis
Open Mon-Thurs 7:30am-9:45pm, Fri 7:30-5, Sat (Fall-Spring) 8:30-1:30

SCHUYLKILL HAVEN

C PENNSYLVANIA STATE UNIVERSITY, SCHUYLKILL CAMPUS*, Ciletti Memorial Library, 240 University Dr, 17972-2210. SAN 315-193X. Tel: 570-385-6234. FAX: 570-385-6232. E-mail: mwl2@psu.edu. Web Site: www.hbg.psu.edu/library/ciletti/index.html. *Librn,* Michael W Loder; Staff 6 (MLS 2, Non-MLS 4)
Founded 1934. Enrl 1,124; Fac 45
Library Holdings: CDs 300; DVDs 800; Bk Vols 44,000; Per Subs 170
Special Collections: County Coll (Pennsylvania German & Dutch Materials, Coal Industry); O'Hara Coll (materials by & on John O'Hara); Richter Coll (materials by & on Conrad Richter); Treasure Coll (Jones' family bks & recs)
Automation Activity & Vendor Info: (Acquisitions) SirsiDynix; (Cataloging) SirsiDynix; (Circulation) SirsiDynix; (Course Reserve) SirsiDynix; (OPAC) SirsiDynix
Wireless access
Partic in OCLC Online Computer Library Center, Inc; Pennsylvania Academic Library Consortium, Inc (PALCI); RLIN (Research Libraries Information Network)
Open Mon-Thurs 7:45am-10pm, Fri 7:45-5, Sat 9-2, Sun 1-9

P SCHUYLKILL HAVEN FREE PUBLIC LIBRARY*, 104 Saint John St, 17972-1614. SAN 315-1948. Tel: 570-385-0542. FAX: 570-385-2523. E-mail: sch@iu29.org. Web Site: www.haven.k12.pa.us/havenpl. *Pres,* John Dudley; *Dir,* Lynette Moyer; Staff 2 (MLS 1, Non-MLS 1)
Founded 1934. Pop 8,200; Circ 34,356
Library Holdings: Audiobooks 400; DVDs 2,000; Large Print Bks 706; Bk Titles 30,735; Per Subs 47; Talking Bks 200; Videos 12
Automation Activity & Vendor Info: (Cataloging) Follett Software; (Circulation) Follett Software
Open Mon, Tues & Thurs 11-8, Wed & Fri 9-6, Sat 9-4

SCOTT TOWNSHIP

P SCOTT TOWNSHIP PUBLIC LIBRARY*, 301 Lindsay Rd, 15106-4206. Tel: 412-429-5380. FAX: 412-429-5370. Web Site: www.scottlibrary.org. *Dir,* Gina Leone; *Librn,* Gina Leone; *Librn,* Jill Morse; *Librn,* Becky Shetler; *Circ Mgr,* Nancy K George; *Youth Serv Mgr,* Sherry Small; Staff 5 (MLS 2, Non-MLS 3)
Founded 2001. Pop 46,900; Circ 87,500
Library Holdings: Bk Vols 32,000
Automation Activity & Vendor Info: (Cataloging) Innovative Interfaces, Inc; (Circulation) Innovative Interfaces, Inc; (OPAC) Innovative Interfaces, Inc
Wireless access
Mem of Allegheny County Library Association
Special Services for the Deaf - Adult & family literacy prog; Bks on deafness & sign lang; Closed caption videos
Open Mon & Tues 10-8, Wed & Thurs 12-8, Fri 1-5, Sat 10-5
Friends of the Library Group

SCOTTDALE

P SCOTTDALE PUBLIC LIBRARY*, 235 Pittsburgh St, 15683-1796. SAN 315-1956. Tel: 724-887-6140. FAX: 724-887-6140. E-mail: bookworm@cvzoom.net. Web Site: scottdalelibrary.org. *Librn,* Patricia E Miller; *Asst Librn,* Rhonda Allison
Founded 1910. Pop 5,833; Circ 26,294
Library Holdings: Bk Vols 30,000; Per Subs 61
Automation Activity & Vendor Info: (Cataloging) Follett Software; (Circulation) Follett Software; (OPAC) Follett Software
Mem of Westmoreland County Federated Library System
Open Mon & Tues 10-7, Wed 10-6, Thurs 12-8, Fri 10-2, Sat 9-4
Friends of the Library Group

SCRANTON

J JOHNSON COLLEGE LIBRARY, 3427 N Main Ave, 18508-1995. SAN 315-1999. Tel: 570-702-8953. FAX: 570-348-2181. Web Site: www.johnson.edu. *Dir,* Ronald Krysiewski; E-mail: rkrysiewski@johnson.edu; Staff 2 (MLS 1, Non-MLS 1)
Founded 1969. Enrl 349; Fac 21
Library Holdings: Bk Titles 4,410; Bk Vols 5,217; Per Subs 118
Open Mon-Thurs 8-8, Fri 8-4

L LACKAWANNA BAR ASSOCIATION*, Law Library, Courthouse, Ground Flr, 200 N Washington Ave, 18503. SAN 315-2006. Tel: 570-963-6712. FAX: 570-344-2944. *Librn,* Marita E Paparelli; Staff 1 (Non-MLS 1)
Founded 1879
Library Holdings: Bk Titles 21,619; Bk Vols 25,411; Per Subs 127
Subject Interests: Law
Open Mon-Fri 8:30-5
Restriction: Non-circulating to the pub

J LACKAWANNA COLLEGE*, Seeley Memorial Library, 501 Vine St, 18509. SAN 359-5145. Tel: 570-961-7831. Toll Free Tel: 877-346-3552. FAX: 570-961-7817. Web Site: library.lackawanna.edu. *Dir, Libr Serv,* Mary Beth Roche; Tel: 570-504-1589, E-mail: rochem@lackawanna.edu; *Librn,* Rhett Perdew; E-mail: perdewr@lackawanna.edu; *Media Librn,* Elaine Pencek; Tel: 570-961-7875, E-mail: penceke@lackawanna.edu; Staff 5 (MLS 3, Non-MLS 2)
Founded 1965. Enrl 1,269; Fac 20; Highest Degree: Associate
Library Holdings: Electronic Media & Resources 12; Large Print Bks 14; Bk Titles 15,356; Bk Vols 18,674; Per Subs 46; Spec Interest Per Sub 12; Videos 683
Automation Activity & Vendor Info: (Cataloging) Follett Software; (Circulation) Follett Software; (Course Reserve) Follett Software; (OPAC) Follett Software; (Serials) Follett Software
Database Vendor: Gale Cengage Learning, ProQuest
Open Mon-Thurs (Fall & Spring) 8am-9pm, Fri 8-4, Sun 2-9; Mon-Fri (Summer) 8-4

P LACKAWANNA COUNTY LIBRARY SYSTEM*, 520 Vine St, 18509-3298. SAN 324-8062. Tel: 570-348-3003. Interlibrary Loan Service Tel: 570-348-3018. FAX: 570-348-3028. Web Site: www.lackawannacountylibrarysystem.org. *Adminr,* Mary Garm; Staff 98 (MLS 17, Non-MLS 81)
Founded 1983. Pop 213,385; Circ 1,320,801

Jan 2006-Dec 2006 Income $4,948,366, State $1,244,002, Federal $28,674, County $3,599,140, Locally Generated Income $76,550. Mats Exp $780,697. Sal $2,784,591
Library Holdings: Bk Titles 521,107; Per Subs 690
Automation Activity & Vendor Info: (Acquisitions) SirsiDynix; (Cataloging) SirsiDynix; (Circulation) SirsiDynix; (OPAC) SirsiDynix; (Serials) SirsiDynix
Member Libraries: Abington Community Library; Carbondale Public Library; Dalton Community Library; North Pocono Public Library; Scranton Public Library; Taylor Community Library; Valley Community Library
Open Mon-Fri 9-5
Bookmobiles: 1

S LACKAWANNA HISTORICAL SOCIETY LIBRARY*, 232 Monroe Ave, 18510. SAN 315-2014. Tel: 570-344-3841. FAX: 570-344-3815. E-mail: lackawannahistory@gmail.com. *Exec Dir,* Mary Ann Savakinus-Moran
Founded 1886
Library Holdings: Bk Vols 2,500
Special Collections: Lackawanna County & Pennsylvania History; Scranton History, ms, photog & newsp files bd
Subject Interests: Antiques, Archit, Coal mining, Ethnic hist, Family hist, Local hist, Transportation
Publications: Lackawana Historical Society Journal (Quarterly)

C MARYWOOD UNIVERSITY LIBRARY*, 2300 Adams Ave, 18509-1598. SAN 315-2022. Tel: 570-961-4707. Interlibrary Loan Service Tel: 570-348-6205. Reference Tel: 570-961-4714. FAX: 570-961-4769. E-mail: libraryhelp@marywood.edu. Web Site: www.marywood.edu/library. *Libr Dir,* Position Currently Open; *Coll Develop Librn, Interim Dir,* Jim Frutchey; E-mail: frutchey@maryu.marywood.edu; *Digital Ser & Scholarly Res Librn,* Michelle Sitko; E-mail: sitko@maryu.marywood.edu; *Head, Tech Proc, Syst/Electronic Res Librn,* Zhong Geng; E-mail: geng@maryu.marywood.edu; *Info Literacy Librn,* Annette Fisher; E-mail: fisher@maryu.marywood.edu; *Outreach & Assessment Librn,* Amanda Avery; E-mail: aavery@maryu.marywood.edu; *Res & Instruction Librn,* Hong Miao; E-mail: hongm@maryu.marywood.edu; *Res Librn,* Julie Watson; E-mail: jawatson@maryu.marywood.edu; *User Serv Librn,* Leslie Christianson; E-mail: lchristianson@maryu.marywood.edu; Staff 8 (MLS 8)
Founded 1915. Enrl 2,926; Fac 168; Highest Degree: Doctorate
Subject Interests: Art, Behav sci, Educ, Music, Nutrition, Relig studies, Soc sci, Soc work
Automation Activity & Vendor Info: (Acquisitions) SirsiDynix; (Cataloging) SirsiDynix; (Circulation) SirsiDynix; (Course Reserve) SirsiDynix; (ILL) OCLC; (OPAC) SirsiDynix; (Serials) SirsiDynix
Wireless access
Partic in Lyrasis; OCLC Online Computer Library Center, Inc; Pennsylvania Academic Library Consortium, Inc (PALCI)
Open Mon-Thurs 8am-11pm, Fri 8-7, Sat 8:30-5:30, Sun Noon-11

P SCRANTON PUBLIC LIBRARY*, Albright Memorial Library, Albright Memorial Bldg, 500 Vine St, 18509-3298. SAN 359-5269. Tel: 570-348-3000. FAX: 570-348-3020. Web Site: www.lclshome.org/albright. *Dir,* Jack Finnerty; Tel: 570-348-3013, E-mail: jrf@albright.org; *Ch Serv,* Laureen Maloney; *ILL,* Roxanne Tigue; E-mail: ill@albright.org; *Pub Serv,* Marie Crispino, *Ref,* Richard McGuire, *Tech Coordr,* Scott Thomas
Founded 1893. Pop 213,000
Library Holdings: Bk Vols 180,000; Per Subs 300
Special Collections: State Document Depository; US Document Depository
Subject Interests: Local hist
Automation Activity & Vendor Info: (Acquisitions) SirsiDynix; (Cataloging) SirsiDynix; (Circulation) SirsiDynix; (OPAC) SirsiDynix; (Serials) SirsiDynix
Database Vendor: EBSCOhost, OCLC FirstSearch
Wireless access
Mem of Lackawanna County Library System
Open Mon-Thurs 9-9, Fri 9-5:30, Sat 9-5, Sun 2-5
Friends of the Library Group
Branches: 2
NANCY KAY HOLMES BRANCH, 1032 Green Ridge St at Wyoming Ave, 18509, SAN 359-5293. Tel: 570-207-0764. E-mail: grcirc@albright.org. *Actg Br Mgr,* Diane Demko
Founded 1889
Library Holdings: Bk Vols 8,700; Per Subs 25
Open Mon-Thurs 11-7, Fri 11-5:30
LACKAWANNA COUNTY CHILDREN'S LIBRARY, 520 Vine St, 18509-3298. Tel: 570-348-3000, Ext 3015. FAX: 570-348-3020. Web Site: www.lclshome.org/childrenslibrary/index.php. *Head, Ch,* Laureen Maloney
Library Holdings: Bks on Deafness & Sign Lang 25; Bk Vols 30,000; Per Subs 12
Open Mon-Thurs 9-8, Fri 9-5:30, Sat 9-5, Sun 2-5
Bookmobiles: 1

S SCRANTON TIMES-TRIBUNE*, Reference Library, 149 Penn Ave, 18503. SAN 315-2030. Tel: 570-348-9140. Toll Free Tel: 800-228-4637, Ext 9140. FAX: 570-348-9135. *Mgr,* Brian Fulton
Founded 1920
Library Holdings: Bk Vols 3,200
Subject Interests: Anthracite mining, Coal, Govt, Local hist, Railroads
Restriction: Open by appt only

CR UNIVERSITY OF SCRANTON*, Harry & Jeanette Weinberg Memorial Library, Monroe & Linden, 18510-4634. SAN 315-2049. Tel: 570-941-4000, 570-941-4008. Circulation Tel: 570-941-7524. Interlibrary Loan Service Tel: 570-941-4003. FAX: 570-941-7817. Interlibrary Loan Service FAX: 570-941-4002. Web Site: www.scranton.edu/library. *Dean,* Charles E Kratz; E-mail: charles.kratz@scranton.edu; *Assoc Dean,* Bonnie Strohl; Tel: 570-941-4006, E-mail: bonnie.strohl@scranton.edu; *Asst Dean,* Jean Lenville; Tel: 570-941-4009, E-mail: jena.lenville@scranton.edu; *Dept Chair, Head, Ref Serv,* Betsey Moylan; E-mail: betsey.moylan@scranton.edu; *Digital Serv & Emerging Tech Librn,* Kristen Yarmey; E-mail: kristen.yarmey@scranton.edu; *Coordr, Info Literacy,* Bonnie Oldham; E-mail: bonnie.oldham@scranton.edu; *Libr Syst Coordr,* Mary Kovalcin; Tel: 570-941-6135, E-mail: mary.kovalcin@scranton.edu; *Media Res Coordr,* Sharon Finnerty; Tel: 570-941-6330, E-mail: sharon.finnerty@scranton.edu; *Acq & Continuing Res,* Narda Tafuri; Tel: 570-941-7811, Fax: 570-941-7809, E-mail: narda.tafuri@scranton.edu; *Archives, Spec Coll,* Michael Knies; Tel: 570-941-6341, E-mail: michael.knies@scranton.edu; *Cat & Metadata,* Michelle McHugh; Tel: 570-941-4004, Fax: 570-941-7818, E-mail: michelle.mchugh@scranton.edu; *Circ,* Patricia Savitts; Tel: 570-941-7526, E-mail: patricia.savitts@scranton.edu; *ILL,* Magdalene Restuccia; E-mail: magdalene.restuccia@scranton.edu; *Online Serv,* Kevin Norris; E-mail: kevin.norris@scranton.edu; *Outreach Serv, Pub Serv,* George Aulisio; E-mail: george.aulisio@scranton.edu; *Pub Serv, Virtual Ref,* Donna Witek; E-mail: donna.witek@scranton.edu. Subject Specialists: *Counseling, Psychol,* Bonnie Strohl; *Bus, Educ,* Betsey Moylan; *Sciences,* Kristen Yarmey, *Nursing, Occupational therapy, Phys therapy,* Bonnie Oldham; *Hist, Lang, Polit sci,* Kevin Norris; *Commun, Computer sci, Math,* George Aulisio; *English, Soc, Theol,* Donna Witek; Staff 39 (MLS 14, Non-MLS 25)
Founded 1888. Enrl 5,337; Fac 428; Highest Degree: Doctorate
Jun 2012-May 2013 Income $5,674,218. Mats Exp $1,499,456, Books $208,464, Per/Ser (Incl. Access Fees) $562,903, Manu Arch $11,000, Other Print Mats $39,255, Micro $17,886, AV Mat $35,937, Electronic Ref Mat (Incl. Access Fees) $589,611, Presv $34,400. Sal $1,653,470 (Prof $1,040,194)
Library Holdings: AV Mats 21,871; Bks on Deafness & Sign Lang 302; e-books 75,481; e-journals 45,972; Electronic Media & Resources 165,969; Bk Vols 565,916; Per Subs 48,971
Special Collections: Congressman Joseph McDade Coll; Early Printed Books & Manuscripts (William W Scranton Coll); International Correspondence School; Joseph Polakoff Coll, papers; Passionist Congregation Historical Archives; University Archives Coll; Zaner-Bloser
Automation Activity & Vendor Info: (Acquisitions) Innovative Interfaces, Inc; (Cataloging) Innovative Interfaces, Inc; (Circulation) Innovative Interfaces, Inc; (Course Reserve) Innovative Interfaces, Inc; (ILL) OCLC; (OPAC) Innovative Interfaces, Inc; (Serials) Innovative Interfaces, Inc
Database Vendor: ABC-CLIO, ACM (Association for Computing Machinery), Alexander Street Press, American Chemical Society, American Mathematical Society, American Psychological Association (APA), Annual Reviews, Bowker, Cambridge Scientific Abstracts, Cinahl, CredoReference, Dun & Bradstreet, ebrary, EBSCO Information Services, EBSCOhost, Elsevier, Emerald, Gale Cengage Learning, H W Wilson, Haworth Pres Inc, Hoovers, IEEE (Institute of Electrical & Electronics Engineers), Infotrieve, Innovative Interfaces, Inc, IOP, JSTOR, LexisNexis, Medline, Modern Language Association, Nature Publishing Group, OCLC ArticleFirst, OCLC FirstSearch, OCLC WorldShare Interlibrary Loan, OVID Technologies, Project MUSE, ProQuest, PubMed, RefWorks, Sage, ScienceDirect, SerialsSolutions, Springer-Verlag, Springshare, LLC, Standard & Poor's, STN International, ValueLine, Wiley InterScience, Wilson - Wilson Web, YBP Library Services
Wireless access
Function: Archival coll, Audio & video playback equip for onsite use, Distance learning, Doc delivery serv, e-mail & chat, E-Reserves, Electronic databases & coll, Fax serv, ILL available, Microfiche/film & reading machines, Online ref, Photocopying/Printing, Pub access computers
Publications: A Modern Renaissance Library: 200 Selections from the Collection of Edward R Leahy; Faculty & Student Guides; Newsletters; Reference Bibliographies; Weinberg Memorial Library Information Update (Newsletter); William Morris & the Kelmscott Press Exhibition Catalog
Partic in Interlibrary Delivery Service of Pennsylvania; Lyrasis; Northeastern Pennsylvania Library Network; OCLC Online Computer Library Center, Inc; Pennsylvania Academic Library Consortium, Inc (PALCI); Westchester Academic Library Directors Organization (WALDO)
Open Mon-Thurs 8am-11:30pm, Fri 8am-10pm, Sat 12-8, Sun Noon-11:30

Restriction: Badge access after hrs
Friends of the Library Group

SELINSGROVE

P SNYDER COUNTY LIBRARIES*, Community Bldg, One N High St, 17870-1599. SAN 359-5382. Tel: 570-374-7163. FAX: 570-374-2120. Web Site: www.snydercountylibraries.org. *Exec Dir,* Pam Ross; E-mail: scldir@ptd.net; *Youth Serv Coordr,* Barbara McGary; E-mail: bsmcgary@ptd.net; Staff 11 (MLS 2, Non-MLS 9)
Founded 1976. Pop 37,546; Circ 103,488
Library Holdings: Bk Titles 66,148; Bk Vols 75,000; Per Subs 172
Automation Activity & Vendor Info: (Acquisitions) EOS International; (Cataloging) EOS International; (Circulation) EOS International; (OPAC) EOS International
Database Vendor: SirsiDynix
Open Mon-Thurs 10-8, Fri & Sat 10-5
Friends of the Library Group
Branches: 3
BEAVERTOWN COMMUNITY LIBRARY, 111 W Walnut St, Beavertown, 17813-9730, SAN 359-5412. Tel: 570-658-3437. FAX: 570-658-3437. *Br Mgr,* Sherri Sellers; Staff 2 (Non-MLS 2)
Founded 1977
Library Holdings: Bk Vols 4,384; Per Subs 19
Open Mon & Tues 2-7, Thurs 12-5, Fri 2-5, Sat 10-Noon
Friends of the Library Group
MCCLURE COMMUNITY LIBRARY, PO Box 370, McClure, 17841-0370, SAN 359-5447. Tel: 570-658-7700. FAX: 570-658-7700. E-mail: mcclurelibrary@verizon.net. *Librn,* Joe Hall; Staff 1 (Non-MLS 1)
Founded 1977
Library Holdings: Bk Vols 4,562; Per Subs 28
Open Mon & Thurs 2-7, Tues & Fri 12-5, Sat 10-12
MIDDLEBURG COMMUNITY LIBRARY, 13 N Main St, Middleburg, 17842. (Mail add: PO Box 43, Middleburg, 17842-0043), SAN 359-5471. Tel: 570-837-5931. FAX: 570-837-5931. E-mail: midduser@ptd.net. *Librn,* Shirley Carroll; *Librn,* Chris Snyder; Staff 2 (Non-MLS 2)
Founded 1982
Library Holdings: Bk Titles 6,607; Per Subs 34
Open Mon & Thurs 1-8, Tues 10-8, Fri 1-5, Sat 10-12

C SUSQUEHANNA UNIVERSITY*, Blough-Weis Library, 514 University Ave, 17870-1050. SAN 315-2065. Tel: 570-372-4319. Circulation Tel: 570-372-4022. Interlibrary Loan Service Tel: 570-372-4016. Reference Tel: 570-372-4160. FAX: 570-372-4310. Web Site: www.susqu.edu/library. *Dir,* Kathleen Gunning; Tel: 570-372-4320, E-mail: gunning@susqu.edu; *Assoc Dir,* Rebecca Wilson; Tel: 570-372-4321, E-mail: wilsonb@susqu.edu; *Syst Librn,* Robert Gessner; Tel: 570-372-4322, E-mail: gessnerr@susqu.edu; *ILL,* Sheila Fisher; Tel: 570-372-4326, E-mail: fishers@susqu.edu; *Pub Serv,* Cindy Whitmoyer; Tel: 570-372-4459; *Ref Serv, YA,* Kathleen Dalton; E-mail: dalton@susqu.edu. Subject Specialists: *Info serv,* Kathleen Dalton; Staff 8 (MLS 6, Non-MLS 2)
Founded 1858. Enrl 2,100; Fac 180; Highest Degree: Bachelor
Library Holdings: Bk Titles 202,682; Bk Vols 367,146; Per Subs 50,390
Special Collections: Jane Apple Shakespeare Coll; Music (Wilt Coll); Pennsylvania Coll
Subject Interests: Bus, Environ studies, Music
Automation Activity & Vendor Info: (Acquisitions) SirsiDynix; (Cataloging) SirsiDynix; (Circulation) SirsiDynix; (Course Reserve) SirsiDynix; (ILL) OCLC; (Media Booking) SirsiDynix; (OPAC) SirsiDynix; (Serials) SirsiDynix
Database Vendor: EBSCOhost, Gale Cengage Learning, LexisNexis, OCLC FirstSearch, Wilson - Wilson Web
Wireless access
Function: Res libr
Partic in Associated College Libraries of Central Pennsylvania; Pennsylvania Academic Library Consortium, Inc (PALCI); Susquehanna Library Cooperative
Open Mon-Thurs 8am-1am, Fri 8-8, Sat 10-8, Sun 11am-1am

SELLERSVILLE

M GRAND VIEW HOSPITAL*, Edward F Burrow Memorial Library, 700 Lawn Ave, 18960. SAN 324-5519. Tel: 215-453-4000, 215-453-4632. FAX: 215-453-4133. *Tech Serv,* Annette McGough; Staff 1 (Non-MLS 1)
Library Holdings: Bk Titles 891; Bk Vols 900; Per Subs 70
Subject Interests: Med, Nursing, Surgery
Open Mon-Fri 8:30-4:30

SENECA

M UPMC NORTHWEST*, Medical Library, 100 Fairfield Dr, 16346-2130. SAN 324-6930. Tel: 814-437-7000, Ext 5331. *Librn,* Ann L Lucas
Library Holdings: Bk Titles 850; Bk Vols 900; Per Subs 100
Subject Interests: Med, Nursing
Partic in Erie Area Health Information Library Cooperative; National Network of Libraries of Medicine South Central Region; Northwest Interlibrary Cooperative of Pennsylvania
Open Mon-Fri 8-4:30

SEWICKLEY

P SEWICKLEY PUBLIC LIBRARY, INC*, 500 Thorn St, 15143-1333. SAN 315-2081. Tel: 412-741-6920. FAX: 412-741-6099. E-mail: sewickley@einetwork.net. Web Site: sewickleylibrary.org. *Dir,* Carolyn Toth; *Asst Dir,* Lynne Schneider
Founded 1873. Pop 14,089; Circ 183,443
Library Holdings: Bk Vols 89,400; Per Subs 220
Subject Interests: Western Pa hist
Automation Activity & Vendor Info: (Cataloging) Innovative Interfaces, Inc; (Circulation) Innovative Interfaces, Inc; (OPAC) Innovative Interfaces, Inc
Publications: Newsletter
Mem of Allegheny County Library Association
Partic in Electronic Info Network (eiNetwork)
Open Mon-Thurs 9:30-9, Fri & Sat 9:30-5, Sun 1-5
Friends of the Library Group

SHAMOKIN

P SHAMOKIN & COAL TOWNSHIP PUBLIC LIBRARY, INC*, 210 E Independence St, 17872-6888. SAN 315-209X. Tel: 570-648-3202. FAX: 570-648-4255. E-mail: shamlib@ptd.net. Web Site: www.sctpubliclibrary.lib.pa.us. *Dir,* Mary Ellen Lowe; Staff 6 (MLS 1, Non-MLS 5)
Founded 1941. Pop 20,092; Circ 54,153
Library Holdings: Audiobooks 209; CDs 642; DVDs 771; Large Print Bks 1,292; Bk Titles 53,004; Per Subs 85; Videos 437
Special Collections: History of Pennsylvania, Northcumberland County & Shamokin (Pennsylvania Coll)
Automation Activity & Vendor Info: (Cataloging) Follett Software; (Circulation) Follett Software; (OPAC) Follett Software
Open Mon-Thurs 10-6, Fri 10-5, Sat 9-4

SHARON

C PENNSYLVANIA STATE UNIVERSITY*, Lartz Memorial Library, Shenango Campus, 177 Vine Ave, 16146. SAN 315-2111. Tel: 724-983-2876. FAX: 724-983-2881. Web Site: www.libraries.psu.edu/shenango. *Head Librn,* Matthew Ciszek; Tel: 724-983-2880, E-mail: mpc16@psu.edu; *Ref Librn,* Jonathan Megill; Tel: 724-983-2883, E-mail: jdm38@psulias.psu.edu; Staff 4 (MLS 2, Non-MLS 2)
Founded 1965. Enrl 990; Fac 35; Highest Degree: Master
Library Holdings: Bk Vols 35,000; Per Subs 319
Automation Activity & Vendor Info: (Cataloging) SirsiDynix; (Circulation) SirsiDynix; (OPAC) SirsiDynix
Partic in OCLC Online Computer Library Center, Inc; OCLC Research Library Partnership; RLIN (Research Libraries Information Network)
Open Mon-Thurs (Fall & Spring) 8-8, Fri 8-5, Sun 11-5; Mon-Thurs (Summer) 8-6, Fri 8-5

M SHARON REGIONAL HEALTH SYSTEM*, School of Nursing Library, 740 E State St, 16146. SAN 329-5206. Tel: 724-983-3911, Ext 3873. FAX: 724-983-5621. *Res Mgr,* Dick Davis; E-mail: ddavis@srhs-pa.org
Library Holdings: Bk Titles 300; Per Subs 35
Subject Interests: Healthcare admin, Hist, Med, Nursing
Partic in Docline; Erie Area Health Information Library Cooperative
Open Mon-Fri 7-5

P SHENANGO VALLEY COMMUNITY LIBRARY*, 11 N Sharpsville Ave, 16146. SAN 315-2103. Tel: 724-981-4360. FAX: 724-981-5208. E-mail: svalleylib@yahoo.com. *Dir,* Karen L Spak; *Adult Serv,* Rima Selius; *Ch Serv,* Valerie J Ellenberger; Staff 2 (MLS 2)
Founded 1923. Pop 32,813; Circ 80,000
Library Holdings: Bk Vols 60,000; Per Subs 125
Special Collections: State Document Depository
Subject Interests: Genealogy, Local hist
Publications: The Bookmark (Quarterly); The Bookmark (Newsletter)
Open Mon-Thurs 10-8, Fri & Sat 10-4, Sun 1-5
Friends of the Library Group

SHARON HILL

P SHARON HILL PUBLIC LIBRARY*, 246 Sharon Ave, 19079-2098. SAN 315-2138. Tel: 610-586-3993. FAX: 610-586-8233. E-mail: sharonhill@delcolibraries.org. *Dir,* Sue Borders
Founded 1938. Pop 7,464; Circ 14,426
Library Holdings: AV Mats 112; Bk Vols 16,594; Per Subs 20; Talking Bks 200

Wireless access
Mem of Delaware County Library System
Open Mon, Wed & Thurs 1-7, Tues, Fri & Sat 10-5
Friends of the Library Group

SHEFFIELD

P SHEFFIELD TOWNSHIP LIBRARY*, 20 Leather St, 16347. SAN 315-2146. Tel: 814-968-3439. FAX: 814-968-5761. E-mail: librarian@sheffieldlibrary.org. Web Site: www.sheffieldlibrary.org. *Dir,* Janet L Gustafson
Pop 2,793; Circ 4,127
Library Holdings: Bk Vols 11,000; Per Subs 33
Open Mon 6pm-8pm, Tues 10:30-5, Wed 2-8, Thurs & Fri 1-5, Sat 9-3:30

SHENANDOAH

P SHENANDOAH AREA FREE PUBLIC LIBRARY, 15 W Washington St, 17976-1708. SAN 315-2154. Tel: 570-462-9829. E-mail: safpl@shenhgts.net. Web Site: www.iu29.org/shenandoahpl. *Libr Dir,* Robert Sluzis; Staff 1 (Non-MLS 1)
Founded 1975. Pop 5,624; Circ 15,416
Library Holdings: DVDs 248; Large Print Bks 166; Bk Vols 11,519; Per Subs 23; Videos 453
Automation Activity & Vendor Info: (Acquisitions) Follett Software; (Cataloging) Follett Software; (Circulation) Follett Software
Database Vendor: Baker & Taylor, EBSCOhost, Gale Cengage Learning, OCLC FirstSearch, ProQuest, Wilson - Wilson Web
Wireless access
Special Services for the Deaf - Adult & family literacy prog
Open Mon, Tues, Thurs & Fri 11-5, Wed 11-7, Sat 9-1

SHILLINGTON

P MIFFLIN COMMUNITY LIBRARY, Six Philadelphia Ave, 19607. Tel: 610-777-3911. FAX: 610-777-5516. E-mail: mifflincl@berks.lib.pa.us. Web Site: www.berks.lib.pa.us/mifflincl. *Dir,* Helen Flynn; *Youth Serv Librn,* Kristin Brumbach
Library Holdings: Audiobooks 1,046; CDs 1,088; DVDs 2,633; Large Print Bks 1,134; Bk Vols 27,211; Per Subs 60; Videos 390
Automation Activity & Vendor Info: (Cataloging) SirsiDynix; (Circulation) SirsiDynix; (OPAC) SirsiDynix; (Serials) SirsiDynix
Wireless access
Mem of Berks County Public Libraries
Open Mon, Tues & Thurs 9-8, Wed 9-5, Fri 9-1, Sat 9-4 (9-1 Summer)
Friends of the Library Group

SHINGLEHOUSE

P OSWAYO VALLEY MEMORIAL LIBRARY*, 103 N Pleasant St, 16748. (Mail add: PO Box 188, 16748-0188), SAN 315-2162. Tel: 814-697-6691. FAX: 814-697-6691. E-mail: ovml@yahoo.com. Web Site: www.ovmlibrary.org. *Librn,* Tammyann Ray; *Asst Librn,* Fran Fox
Founded 1915. Pop 3,568; Circ 29,411
Library Holdings: Bk Vols 18,000; Per Subs 35
Wireless access
Mem of Potter-Tioga Library System
Open Mon 10-8, Wed & Fri 9-6, Sat 9-4

SHIPPENSBURG

P SHIPPENSBURG PUBLIC LIBRARY*, 73 W King St, 17257-1299. SAN 315-2170. Tel: 717-532-4508. FAX: 717-532-2454. E-mail: shippensburg@ccpa.net. Web Site: www.ccpa.net. *Librn,* Susan Sanders; Staff 15 (MLS 2, Non-MLS 13)
Founded 1933. Pop 24,796; Circ 122,399
Library Holdings: Bk Vols 60,000; Per Subs 107
Automation Activity & Vendor Info: (Cataloging) SirsiDynix; (Circulation) SirsiDynix
Mem of Cumberland County Library System
Open Mon-Thurs 9-9, Fri 9-5, Sat 10-5
Friends of the Library Group

C SHIPPENSBURG UNIVERSITY*, Ezra Lehman Memorial Library, 1871 Old Main Dr, 17257-2299. SAN 359-5560. Tel: 717-477-1463. Circulation Tel: 717-477-1465. Interlibrary Loan Service Tel: 717-477-1462. Reference Tel: 717-477-1474. FAX: 717-477-1389. E-mail: library@ship.edu. Web Site: library.ship.edu. *Dean, Libr & Acad Tech Support Serv,* Dr Dennis Mathes; E-mail: dhm@ship.edu; *Assoc Dean & Dir of Libr Serv,* Dr Michelle Foreman; Tel: 717-477-1475, E-mail: mtforeman@ship.edu; *Chair,* Kirk Moll; Tel: 717-477-1473, E-mail: kamoll@ship.edu; *Advocacy, Outreach, Events & Exhibits Librn,* Chantana Charoenpanitkul; Tel: 717-477-1634, E-mail: chchar@ship.edu; *Ref Librn,* Signe Kelker; Tel: 717-477-1289, E-mail: sjkelk@ship.edu; *Scholarly Communications, E-Res & Web Librn,* Aaron Dobbs; Tel: 717-477-1018, E-mail: awdobbs@ship.edu; *Spec Coll & Archives Librn,* Karen Daniel; Tel: 717-477-1516, E-mail: kdd@ship.edu; *Coll Mgt, Coordr, Tech Serv,* Barbara Rotz; Tel: 717-477-1027, E-mail: bdrotz@ship.edu; *Access Serv,* Mary Mowery; Tel: 717-477-1461, E-mail: mamowe@ship.edu; *ILL,* Diane Kalathas; E-mail: dmkala@ship.edu; *Libr Tech,* Kathy Coy; Tel: 717-477-1466, E-mail: kjcoy@ship.edu; *Libr Tech,* Joyce Harding; Tel: 717-477-1123, Ext 3289, E-mail: jyhard@ship.edu; *Libr Tech,* Melanie Reed; Tel: 717-477-1325, E-mail: mareed@ship.edu; *Libr Tech,* Karen Thomas; Tel: 717-477-1123, Ext 3597, E-mail: kjthom@ship.edu; Staff 22 (MLS 9, Non-MLS 13)
Founded 1871. Enrl 7,500; Fac 360; Highest Degree: Master
Library Holdings: Bk Vols 449,125; Per Subs 1,243
Special Collections: University Archives. US Document Depository
Subject Interests: Criminal justice, Curric, Educ, Media
Automation Activity & Vendor Info: (Acquisitions) Ex Libris Group; (Cataloging) Ex Libris Group; (Circulation) Ex Libris Group; (Course Reserve) Ex Libris Group; (Media Booking) Ex Libris Group; (OPAC) Ex Libris Group; (Serials) Ex Libris Group
Database Vendor: EBSCOhost, LexisNexis, OCLC FirstSearch, OVID Technologies, ProQuest, Wilson - Wilson Web
Partic in Lyrasis; OCLC Online Computer Library Center, Inc; Pa Syst of Higher Educ Libr Coun

SHREWSBURY

P PAUL SMITH LIBRARY OF SOUTHERN YORK COUNTY*, 80 Constitution Ave, 17361-1710. Tel: 717-235-4313. FAX: 717-235-8553. E-mail: sycstaff@yorklibraries.org. Web Site: www.yorklibraries.org. *Dir,* Demi Fair; E-mail: dfair@yorklibraries.org
Library Holdings: Bk Vols 48,000; Per Subs 54
Automation Activity & Vendor Info: (Acquisitions) Innovative Interfaces, Inc; (Cataloging) Innovative Interfaces, Inc; (Circulation) Innovative Interfaces, Inc; (OPAC) Innovative Interfaces, Inc
Wireless access
Mem of York County Library System
Open Mon-Wed 10-8, Thurs, Fri & Sat 10-5 (10-2 Summer)
Friends of the Library Group

SINKING SPRING

P SINKING SPRING PUBLIC LIBRARY*, 3940 Penn Ave, 19608. SAN 315-2189. Tel: 610-678-4311. FAX: 610-670-4826. Web Site: www.berks.lib.pa.us/sinkingspringpl/. *Dir,* Sondra Westbrook; *Ch Serv,* Patricia Shoff
Founded 1965. Pop 8,467; Circ 27,070
Library Holdings: Bk Titles 10,000; Per Subs 40
Mem of Berks County Public Libraries
Open Mon-Thurs 10-8, Fri 10-3, Sat 8-3
Friends of the Library Group

SLATINGTON

P SLATINGTON LIBRARY*, 650 Main St, 18080. SAN 315-2197. Tel: 610-767-6461. FAX: 610-767-6461. *Librn,* Rosanne Pugh
Founded 1962. Pop 13,395; Circ 20,310
Library Holdings: Bk Vols 24,027

S WILDLIFE INFORMATION CENTER*, Donald S Heintzelman Wildlife Library, 8844 Paint Mill Rd, 18080. (Mail add: PO Box 198, 18080-0198), SAN 375-1864. Tel: 610-760-8889. FAX: 610-760-8889. E-mail: lgnc@ptd.net. Web Site: www.lgnc.org. *Exec Dir,* Dan R Kunkle
Founded 1986
Library Holdings: Bk Titles 5,000; Per Subs 125
Subject Interests: Conserv, Ecology, Ornithology, Wildlife
Restriction: Open by appt only

SLICKVILLE

P SALEM TOWNSHIP PUBLIC LIBRARY-CIVIC CENTER*, 114 Main St, 15684. (Mail add: PO Box 157, 15684-0157), SAN 315-2200. Tel: 724-468-4492.
Founded 1965. Pop 12,000
Library Holdings: Bk Vols 9,000; Per Subs 12
Automation Activity & Vendor Info: (Cataloging) Innovative Interfaces, Inc
Open Tues & Thurs 6pm-9pm, Sat 10:30-2:30

SLIPPERY ROCK

P SLIPPERY ROCK COMMUNITY LIBRARY*, 316 N Main St, 16057. (Mail add: PO Box 25, 16057-0025). Tel: 724-738-9179. E-mail: srcl@bcfls.org. Web Site: www.slipperyrocklibrary.com. *Dir & Librn,* Karen Pierce
Library Holdings: Audiobooks 50; Bk Titles 5,000; Per Subs 10
Automation Activity & Vendor Info: (Cataloging) TLC (The Library Corporation); (Circulation) TLC (The Library Corporation)
Wireless access

Mem of Butler County Federated Library System
Open Mon & Tues 9-2, Thurs 12-7, Sat 10-2
Friends of the Library Group

C SLIPPERY ROCK UNIVERSITY OF PENNSYLVANIA*, Bailey Library, 16057-9989. SAN 315-2219. Tel: 724-738-2058. Circulation Tel: 724-738-2637. Interlibrary Loan Service Tel: 724-738-2580. Information Services Tel: 724-738-2641. FAX: 724-738-2661. Web Site: academics.sru.edu/library/new/index.htm. *Dir,* Philip Tramdack; Tel: 724-738-2630, E-mail: philip.tramdack@sru.edu; *Acq Librn,* Heather Love; *Archivist, Art Librn,* Judith Silva; Tel: 724-738-2658, E-mail: judith.silva@sru.edu; *Coll Mgt Librn, Dept Chair,* Jessica Marshall; Tel: 724-738-2663, E-mail: jessica.marshall@sru.edu; *Educ Librn, Instrul Mat Coordr,* Renee Tkacik; *Govt Doc, Instrul Serv Librn,* Jane Smith; Tel: 724-738-2638, E-mail: jane.smith@sru.edu; *Ref & Access Serv Librn,* Lynn Hoffmann; Tel: 724-738-2666, E-mail: lynn.hoffmann@sru.edu; *Bus Serv, Soc Sci Librn,* Catherine Rudowsky; Tel: 724-738-2657, E-mail: catherine.marshall@sru.edu; *Syst Librn,* Martina Malvasi-Haines; Tel: 724-738-2664, E-mail: martina.malvasi@sru.edu; *Tech Serv Librn,* Aiping Chen-Gaffey; Tel: 724-738-2660, E-mail: aiping.chen-gaffey@sru.edu; *Evening Supvr,* Karen Mason; *Acq,* Mary Purdy; *Archives, Govt Doc,* Kevin McLatchy; *Circ,* Kathy Manning; *ILL,* Rita McClelland; *Ser,* Joe Drobney; *Outreach Coordr, Syst,* Kathy Frampton; *Tech Serv,* Robert Krzanowski. Subject Specialists: *Art, Dance, Theatre,* Judith Silva; *Math, Music, Sciences,* Jessica Marshall; *English, Polit sci,* Jane Smith; *Hist, Philos,* Lynn Hoffmann; *Anthrop, Bus, Sociol,* Catherine Rudowsky; *Modern lang, Psychol,* Aiping Chen-Gaffey; Staff 21 (MLS 9, Non-MLS 12)
Founded 1889. Enrl 7,734; Fac 405; Highest Degree: Doctorate
Library Holdings: Bk Vols 599,974; Per Subs 820
Special Collections: Italy, bks, flm, micro; Japan, bks, flm, micro; Physical Education, Recreation & Sports, bks, flm, micro. Oral History; State Document Depository; US Document Depository
Automation Activity & Vendor Info: (Acquisitions) Ex Libris Group; (Cataloging) Ex Libris Group; (Circulation) Ex Libris Group; (Course Reserve) Docutek; (ILL) OCLC; (Media Booking) Ex Libris Group; (OPAC) Ex Libris Group; (Serials) Ex Libris Group
Database Vendor: Cambridge Scientific Abstracts, EBSCOhost, Gale Cengage Learning, LexisNexis, OCLC FirstSearch, OVID Technologies, SerialsSolutions, Wilson - Wilson Web
Publications: Japanese Collection; Japanese Collection Supplement
Partic in Interlibrary Delivery Service of Pennsylvania; OCLC Online Computer Library Center, Inc; Pennsylvania Academic Library Consortium, Inc (PALCI); State System of Higher Education Library Cooperative
Open Mon-Thurs 8-11, Fri 8-5, Sat 9-5, Sun 1-11
Friends of the Library Group

SMETHPORT

P HAMLIN MEMORIAL LIBRARY*, 123 S Mechanic St, 16749. (Mail add: PO Box 422, 16749-0422), SAN 315-2235. Tel: 814-887-9262. FAX: 814-887-9234. E-mail: library@hamlinlibrary.org. Web Site: www.hamlinlibrary.org. *Dir,* Lorine Rounsville; Staff 1 (Non-MLS 1)
Founded 1967. Pop 5,933; Circ 22,605
Library Holdings: AV Mats 1,143; Large Print Bks 970; Bk Vols 25,429; Per Subs 42; Talking Bks 1,116
Subject Interests: Automotive hist, Civil War
Open Mon & Tues 12-5 & 7-9, Wed 10-5, Thurs 7pm-9pm, Fri 12-5, Sat 9-1
Friends of the Library Group

GL MCKEAN COUNTY LAW LIBRARY*, 500 W Main St, 16749-1149. SAN 315-2227. Tel: 814-887-3325. FAX: 814-887-2712. *Librn,* Joanne Bly; Staff 1 (Non-MLS 1)
Library Holdings: Bk Titles 10,908; Bk Vols 15,180; Per Subs 15
Subject Interests: Pa law
Database Vendor: Westlaw
Open Mon-Fri 8:30-4:30

SMITHFIELD

P FAYETTE COUNTY LIBRARY SYSTEM*, 14 Water St, 15478. (Mail add: PO Box 497, 15478-0497), SAN 371-7216. Tel: 724-569-1777. FAX: 724-569-1772. *Pres,* Marilyn Miller
Founded 1989. Pop 25,964
Jan 2006-Dec 2006 Income $22,400, County $20,000, Other $2,400
Member Libraries: Brownfield Community Library; Brownsville Free Public Library; Dunbar Community Library; German-Masontown Public Library; Mary Fuller Frazier School Community Library; Point Marion Public Library; Smithfield Public Library

P SMITHFIELD PUBLIC LIBRARY*, 14 Water St, 15478. (Mail add: PO Box 497, 15478-0497). Tel: 724-569-1777. *Librn,* Jean Kennedy
Library Holdings: Bk Vols 10,000
Open Tues & Thurs 2-6

SMITHTON

P SMITHTON PUBLIC LIBRARY*, Center & Second St, 15479. (Mail add: PO Box 382, 15479-0382), SAN 315-2243. Tel: 724-872-0701. FAX: 724-872-0701. *Librn,* Beth Vaccaro
Founded 1959. Pop 552; Circ 6,884
Library Holdings: Bk Vols 6,000; Per Subs 15
Mem of Westmoreland County Federated Library System
Special Services for the Blind - Bks on cassette; Bks on CD
Open Mon & Thurs 4:30-8, Sat 10-1

SOMERSET

M BEDFORD-SOMERSET MENTAL HEALTH*, Mental Retardation Center Library, 245 W Race St, 15501. SAN 320-7277. Tel: 814-443-4891. FAX: 814-443-4898. *In Charge,* Randy Hay; E-mail: randyh@besmhmr.dst.pa.us; Staff 2 (Non-MLS 2)
Library Holdings: Bk Titles 325; Bk Vols 400; Per Subs 12
Restriction: Staff use only

P MARY S BIESECKER PUBLIC LIBRARY*, 230 S Rosina Ave, 15501. SAN 315-2251. Tel: 814-445-4011. FAX: 814-443-0725. E-mail: info@maryslibrary.com. Web Site: www.maryslibrary.com. *Dir,* Lee Ann Schrock; Staff 3 (Non-MLS 3)
Founded 1914. Pop 6,762; Circ 46,829
Jan 2005-Dec 2005. Mats Exp $21,000
Library Holdings: Bk Titles 26,723; Bk Vols 33,275
Special Collections: Civil War; Geneaology; Local & Pennsylvania History; Somerset County Newspapers, microfilms
Automation Activity & Vendor Info: (Cataloging) Follett Software; (Circulation) Follett Software
Database Vendor: Access Pennsylvania, Overdrive, Inc
Function: Adult bk club, Handicapped accessible, Homework prog, ILL available, Magnifiers for reading, Music CDs, Newsp ref libr, Online searches, Photocopying/Printing, Prog for adults, Prog for children & young adult, Ref serv available, Spoken cassettes & CDs, Spoken cassettes & DVDs, Summer reading prog, Telephone ref, VHS videos, Video lending libr
Mem of Cambria County Library System & District Center
Partic in Pennsylvania Library Association
Open Mon-Fri 10-6, Sat 9-4

P SOMERSET COUNTY FEDERATED LIBRARY SYSTEM, 6022 Glades Pike, Ste 120, 15501-0043. Tel: 814-445-5907. Administration Tel: 814-445-2556. FAX: 814-443-0650. E-mail: somerset@somersetcountypalibraries.org. Web Site: www.scfls.org. *Adminr,* Cheryl Morgan; E-mail: cmorgan@somersetcountypalibraries.org; *Asst Syst Adminr,* Kathy Plaso; E-mail: kplaso@somersetcountypalibraries.org; Staff 2 (MLS 2)
Library Holdings: Bk Vols 143,757; Per Subs 297
Automation Activity & Vendor Info: (Cataloging) Evergreen; (Circulation) Evergreen; (OPAC) Evergreen
Database Vendor: ProQuest
Wireless access
Function: Audiobks via web, Bks on cassette, Bks on CD, Computer training, Computers for patron use, Copy machines, e-mail serv, Electronic databases & coll, Fax serv, Free DVD rentals, Games & aids for the handicapped, Handicapped accessible, Home delivery & serv to Sr ctr & nursing homes, Homebound delivery serv, ILL available, Mail & tel request accepted, Online ref, Online searches, OverDrive digital audio bks, Photocopying/Printing, Preschool outreach, Provide serv for the mentally ill, Pub access computers, Ref serv in person, Serves mentally handicapped consumers, Story hour, Summer reading prog, Tax forms, Telephone ref, VHS videos, Video lending libr, Wheelchair accessible
Member Libraries: Meyersdale Public Library; Somerset County Library; Windber Public Library
Special Services for the Blind - Bks on CD; Cassettes; Large print & cassettes; Large print bks; Large screen computer & software
Bookmobiles: 1. Bk vols 7,427

GL SOMERSET COUNTY LAW LIBRARY*, Court House, 111 E Union St, Ste 60, 15501. SAN 315-2278. Tel: 814-445-1508, 814-445-1510. FAX: 814-445-1455. *Law Librn,* Sara Andreyo
Library Holdings: Bk Vols 21,785; Per Subs 75
Database Vendor: Westlaw
Open Mon-Fri 8:30-4

P SOMERSET COUNTY LIBRARY, 6022 Glades Pike, Ste 120, 15501-4300. SAN 315-2286. Tel: 814-445-5907. Administration Tel: 814-445-2556. FAX: 814-443-0650. E-mail: somerset@somersetcountypalibraries.org. Web Site: somersetcolibrary.org. *Dir,* Cheryl Morgan; E-mail: cmorgan@somersetcountypalibraries.org; Staff 7 (MLS 2, Non-MLS 5)
Founded 1947. Pop 39,320; Circ 116,435

Library Holdings: Bk Titles 60,339; Bk Vols 100,361; Per Subs 176; Talking Bks 2,309; Videos 3,670
Automation Activity & Vendor Info: (Cataloging) Evergreen; (Circulation) Evergreen; (OPAC) Evergreen
Database Vendor: TumbleBookLibrary
Wireless access
Function: 24/7 Electronic res, 24/7 Online cat, Audiobks via web, Bk club(s), Bks on cassette, Bks on CD, Children's prog, Computers for patron use, Copy machines, e-mail & chat, e-mail serv, Electronic databases & coll, Fax serv, Free DVD rentals, Games & aids for the handicapped, Handicapped accessible, Home delivery & serv to Sr ctr & nursing homes, ILL available, Large print keyboards, Magazines, Magnifiers for reading, Mail & tel request accepted, Newsp ref libr, Online cat, Online ref, Online searches, Outreach serv, OverDrive digital audio bks, Photocopying/Printing, Preschool outreach, Preschool reading prog, Pub access computers, Ref serv in person, Scanner, Senior outreach, Serves mentally handicapped consumers, Story hour, Summer reading prog, Tax forms, Telephone ref, VHS videos, Video lending libr
Mem of Somerset County Federated Library System
Special Services for the Blind - Low vision equip
Open Mon-Thurs 8-8, Fri 8-5, Sat 8-4
Friends of the Library Group
Bookmobiles: 1. In Charge, Christine Bowser

STATE CORRECTIONAL INSTITUTION
S LAUREL HIGHLANDS LIBRARY*, 5706 Glades Pike, 15501. (Mail add: PO Box 631, 15501-0631). Tel: 814-445-6501. FAX: 814-443-0208. *Corrections Librn,* Sandra Pletcher; *Libr Asst II,* Margaret Foreback; Staff 2 (MLS 1, Non-MLS 1)
Library Holdings: Audiobooks 906; Bk Vols 13,900; Per Subs 57; Videos 261
Automation Activity & Vendor Info: (Acquisitions) Follett Software; (Cataloging) Follett Software; (Circulation) Follett Software; (ILL) Follett Software; (OPAC) Follett Software
Open Mon 1-9, Tues-Thurs 7am-9pm, Fri-Sun 7-3

S SOMERSET LIBRARY*, 1590 Walters Mill Rd, 15510-0001. Tel: 814-443-8100. FAX: 814-443-8157. *Librn,* Marcia Roman
Library Holdings: Bk Vols 15,000; Per Subs 70
Automation Activity & Vendor Info: (Cataloging) Follett Software; (Circulation) Follett Software; (OPAC) Follett Software
Open Mon-Fri 8:30-8, Sat & Sun 8:30-3:30

SOUDERTON

P ZION MENNONITE CHURCH & PUBLIC LIBRARY*, 149 Cherry Lane, 18964. SAN 320-7285. Tel: 215-723-3592. FAX: 215-723-0573. Web Site: www.zionmennonite.org. *Librn,* Gwen Hartzell
Founded 1945
Library Holdings: Bk Vols 5,500; Per Subs 15
Subject Interests: Bibles, Mennonite hist
Publications: Christianity Today; Mennonite Weekly Review
Open Mon-Fri 9-4

SOUTH CANAAN

R SAINT TIKHON'S ORTHODOX THEOLOGICAL SEMINARY, Patriarch Saint Tikhon Library, St Tikhon's Rd, 18459. (Mail add: PO Box 130, 18459-0130), SAN 315-2316. Tel: 570-561-1818, Ext 111. Interlibrary Loan Service Tel: 570-937-3209. Administration Tel: 570-567-1818, Ext 105. Web Site: www.stots.edu/library.htm. *Librn,* Sergei Arhipov; Staff 4 (MLS 2, Non-MLS 2)
Founded 1938. Highest Degree: Master
Library Holdings: Bk Vols 36,000; Per Subs 230
Special Collections: Russian & Church Slavic Theological & Literature Coll
Subject Interests: Orthodox Eastern church, Orthodox theol
Automation Activity & Vendor Info: (Serials) Gateway
Partic in Southeastern Pennsylvania Theological Library Association

SOUTH FORK

P SOUTH FORK PUBLIC LIBRARY*, 320 Main St, 15956-9998. SAN 315-2324. Tel: 814-495-4812. FAX: 814-495-7369. *Dir,* Sheila Ferchalk
Pop 1,600; Circ 13,782
Library Holdings: Bk Vols 11,000; Per Subs 12
Mem of Cambria County Library System & District Center
Open Mon-Fri 12-6
Friends of the Library Group

SOUTH PARK

P SOUTH PARK TOWNSHIP LIBRARY*, 2575 Brownsville Rd, 15129-8527. SAN 314-7053. Tel: 412-833-5585. FAX: 412-833-7368. Web Site: www.einpgh.org/ein/southprk. *Dir,* Sharon Jean Bruni; *Asst Libr Dir, Ch Serv,* Mary Caryl Planiczki; *Adult Serv Coordr,* Donna Neiport; *Tech Serv,* Jane McCullough; *Tech Serv,* Blanche McManus; Staff 3 (MLS 3)
Founded 1970. Pop 14,251; Circ 60,000
Library Holdings: Bk Titles 36,000; Bk Vols 50,000; Per Subs 105
Mem of Allegheny County Library Association
Partic in Electronic Info Network (eiNetwork)
Open Mon & Thurs 1-9, Tues & Wed 10-9, Sat 10-5
Friends of the Library Group

SOUTHAMPTON

P SOUTHAMPTON FREE LIBRARY*, 947 Street Rd, 18966. SAN 315-2332. Tel: 215-322-1415. FAX: 215-396-9375. Web Site: www.southamptonpa.com/library. *Dir,* Kim Ingram; *Head, Ch,* Lora Terifay; *Head, Circ,* Debbie Stroup; *Head, Ref (Info Serv),* Jeannie Kim; Staff 6 (MLS 3, Non-MLS 3)
Founded 1921. Pop 15,764; Circ 175,000
Jan 2008-Dec 2008 Income $526,283
Library Holdings: Bk Vols 80,000; Per Subs 85
Automation Activity & Vendor Info: (Acquisitions) SirsiDynix; (Cataloging) SirsiDynix; (Circulation) SirsiDynix; (OPAC) SirsiDynix
Wireless access
Open Mon-Thurs 10-8, Fri & Sat 10-5
Friends of the Library Group

SPRING CITY

P SPRING CITY FREE PUBLIC LIBRARY*, 245 Broad St, 19475-1702. SAN 315-2367. Tel: 610-948-4130. FAX: 610-948-9478. Web Site: www.ccls.org. *Dir,* Anita Regester; E-mail: aregeste@ccls.org; *Asst Dir,* Nancy Robinson
Founded 1910. Pop 8,798; Circ 33,611
Library Holdings: Bk Vols 16,500; Per Subs 54
Automation Activity & Vendor Info: (Cataloging) Innovative Interfaces, Inc; (Circulation) Innovative Interfaces, Inc; (OPAC) Innovative Interfaces, Inc
Database Vendor: EBSCOhost
Wireless access
Function: ILL available, Photocopying/Printing
Mem of Chester County Library System
Open Mon-Wed 10-8, Thurs 12-8, Sat 10-5

SPRING GROVE

P GLATFELTER MEMORIAL LIBRARY*, 101 Glenview Rd, 17362. SAN 315-2383. Tel: 717-225-3220. FAX: 717-225-9808. E-mail: gmlib@yorklibraries.org. Web Site: www.yorklibraries.org/glatfelter. *Dir,* Deborah Van de Castle; E-mail: dvandecastle@yorklibraries.org; Staff 6 (MLS 1, Non-MLS 5)
Founded 1937. Pop 20,309; Circ 78,422
Library Holdings: Bk Vols 35,423; Per Subs 40
Mem of York County Library System
Open Mon 12-8, Tues 9:30-8, Wed 9:30-3, Thurs 1-8, Sat (Sept-June) 9-4

SPRING HOUSE

S ROHM & HAAS CO*, Research Division, Knowledge Center, 727 Norristown Rd, 19477-0439. (Mail add: PO Box 904, 19477-0904). SAN 359-5625. FAX: 215-641-7811. *Mgr,* Andrea Kirk; *Online Serv,* Joanne L Witiak; Staff 19 (MLS 8, Non-MLS 11)
Library Holdings: Bk Titles 3,500; Per Subs 400
Subject Interests: Chem, Coatings, Leather, Paper, Plastics, Polymers, Resins, Toxicology
Partic in OCLC Online Computer Library Center, Inc
Restriction: Staff use only

SPRINGBORO

P SPRINGBORO PUBLIC LIBRARY*, 110 S Main St, 16435-1108. (Mail add: PO Box 51, 16435-0051), SAN 315-2391. Tel: 814-587-3901. FAX: 814-587-3901. Web Site: www.ccfls.org/springboro. *Librn,* Joy Post
Pop 2,800; Circ 10,000
Library Holdings: Bk Vols 10,000; Per Subs 15
Mem of Crawford County Federated Library System
Open Mon, Wed & Sat 10-5, Tues & Thurs 2-9

SPRINGDALE

P SPRINGDALE FREE PUBLIC LIBRARY*, 331 School St, 15144-1343. SAN 315-2405. Tel: 724-274-9729. FAX: 724-274-6125. E-mail: springdale@einetwork.net. Web Site: www.springdalepubliclibrary.org. *Librn,* Janet Tyree; Staff 1 (Non-MLS 1)
Founded 1933. Pop 9,798; Circ 43,740
Library Holdings: Bk Titles 35,000; Per Subs 50
Database Vendor: Innovative Interfaces, Inc
Wireless access
Function: Adult bk club, Adult literacy prog, After school storytime, Art exhibits, Audiobks via web, Bi-weekly Writer's Group, Bk club(s), Bk

reviews (Group), Bks on CD, Computer training, Computers for patron use, Copy machines, Doc delivery serv, e-mail & chat, e-mail serv, E-Reserves, Electronic databases & coll, Exhibits, Family literacy, Fax serv, Free DVD rentals, Genealogy discussion group, Handicapped accessible, Health sci info serv, Holiday prog, Home delivery & serv to Sr ctr & nursing homes, Homebound delivery serv, Homework prog, ILL available, Learning ctr, Magnifiers for reading, Mail & tel request accepted, Mail loans to mem, Online cat, Online searches, Outreach serv, OverDrive digital audio bks, Photocopying/Printing, Preschool outreach, Preschool reading prog, Printer for laptops & handheld devices, Prog for adults, Prog for children & young adult, Pub access computers, Ref serv available, Senior computer classes, Senior outreach, Spoken cassettes & DVDs, Story hour, Summer & winter reading prog, Tax forms, Teen prog, Telephone ref, VHS videos, Wheelchair accessible, Workshops, Writing prog
Mem of Allegheny County Library Association
Open Mon, Wed & Thurs 12-8, Tues & Fri 10-5, Sat 9-4
Friends of the Library Group

SPRINGFIELD

R COVENANT UNITED METHODIST CHURCH LIBRARY*, 212 W Springfield Rd, 19064-2402. SAN 315-2413. Tel: 610-544-1400. FAX: 610-544-2862. Web Site: www.covumc.com. *In Charge,* Robin Bratz; Staff 1 (Non-MLS 1)
Library Holdings: Bk Titles 1,960; Bk Vols 2,205; Per Subs 15
Open Mon-Fri 9-5

M SPRINGFIELD HOSPITAL MEDICAL LIBRARY*, 190 W Sproul Rd, 19064-2097. SAN 329-2908. Tel: 610-328-8700, 610-328-8749. *Librn,* Judith Ziegler
Library Holdings: Bk Vols 1,000; Per Subs 105
Subject Interests: Med, Nursing, Osteopathic med

P SPRINGFIELD TOWNSHIP LIBRARY*, 70 Powell Rd, 19064-2446. SAN 315-2421. Tel: 610-543-2113. FAX: 610-543-1356. E-mail: springfield@delcolibraries.org. Web Site: www.delcolibraries.org, www.springfieldlibrary.org. *Dir,* Audrey Blossic; *Outreach Librn,* Christine Palmer; *Pub Serv Mgr,* Harold Boyer; *Tech Serv,* Christine Rushton; Staff 13.14 (MLS 4, Non-MLS 9.14)
Founded 1937. Pop 23,677; Circ 179,167
Jan 2010-Dec 2010 Income $1,071,632, State $83,287, County $7,505, Locally Generated Income $980,840. Mats Exp $115,890, Books $64,226, Per/Ser (Incl. Access Fees) $24,393, AV Mat $17,514, Electronic Ref Mat (Incl. Access Fees) $1,141, Presv $8,616. Sal $560,443
Library Holdings: AV Mats 5,386; Bk Vols 109,346; Per Subs 131; Videos 6,862
Special Collections: Genealogy Coll; Local History Coll
Automation Activity & Vendor Info: (Cataloging) Innovative Interfaces, Inc; (Circulation) Innovative Interfaces, Inc; (Course Reserve) Innovative Interfaces, Inc; (ILL) Innovative Interfaces, Inc; (Media Booking) Innovative Interfaces, Inc; (OPAC) Innovative Interfaces, Inc; (Serials) Innovative Interfaces, Inc
Database Vendor: EBSCOhost, Facts on File, Gale Cengage Learning, OCLC FirstSearch, ReferenceUSA
Wireless access
Open Mon-Thurs 9-9, Fri 9-6, Sat 9-4, Sun 1-4
Friends of the Library Group

STATE COLLEGE

S INTERNATIONAL INSTITUTE FOR SPORT HISTORY LIBRARY*, PO Box 175, 16804-0175. Tel: 814-321-4018. Web Site: www.iisoh.org. *Pres,* Harvey Lee Abrams; E-mail: habrams@iisoh.org. Subject Specialists: *Hist of sport, Olympic games, Phys educ,* Harvey Lee Abrams; Staff 1 (Non-MLS 1)
Founded 2001
Library Holdings: Bk Vols 10,000
Special Collections: History of Dance Coll; History of Recreation Coll; History of Sport Coll; Olympic Games Coll; Physical Education & Recreation Coll; Sport in Art Coll; Sports Organization & Federation Documents. Oral History
Subject Interests: Dance, Hist of sport, Olympic games, Phys educ, Recreation
Function: Res libr
Publications: Newsletter (Quarterly)
Restriction: Non-circulating
Friends of the Library Group

M MOUNT NITTANY MEDICAL CENTER*, Esker W Cullen Health Sciences Library, 1800 E Park Ave, 16803. SAN 326-419X. Tel: 814-234-6191. FAX: 814-231-7031. *Dir,* Elinor Snow; *Librn,* Gini Horn; Staff 2 (MLS 2)
Library Holdings: e-journals 1; Electronic Media & Resources 3; Bk Vols 1,500; Per Subs 100
Subject Interests: Allied health, Med, Nursing
Wireless access
Publications: List of Journals; Orientation Info Sheet
Partic in Basic Health Sciences Library Network; Central Pennsylvania Health Sciences Library Association; National Network of Libraries of Medicine
Open Mon-Fri 8-5

G PENNSYLVANIA FISH & BOAT COMMISSION*, Benner Spring Fish Research Station Library, 1735 Shiloh Rd, 16801-8495. SAN 314-3090. Tel: 814-355-4837. FAX: 814-355-8264. Web Site: www.fish.state.pa.us/images/fisheries/fcs/benner/fcs.htm. *Mgr,* Sherry Lucas; E-mail: shlucas@state.pa.us; Staff 2 (Non-MLS 2)
Founded 1953
Library Holdings: Bk Titles 510; Bk Vols 680; Per Subs 59
Special Collections: Fisheries & fisheries related texts, journals & reprints
Open Mon-Fri 8-3:30

S PENNSYLVANIA STATE UNIVERSITY*, Applied Research Laboratory Information Services, N Atherton St, 16801. (Mail add: PO Box 30, 16804-0030), SAN 315-2464. Tel: 814-863-9940. FAX: 814-863-5568. E-mail: library@arl.psu.edu. Web Site: www.arl.psu.edu. *Dept Head,* Patricia G Hayes; E-mail: pgh1@psu.edu; *Tech Libr Spec,* Richard W Brown; *Libr Asst,* Wanda Andrews; Staff 3 (Non-MLS 3)
Founded 1945
Library Holdings: Bk Titles 4,580; Bk Vols 4,790; Per Subs 30
Special Collections: Children's Diversity Coll; Eric Walker Coll. Oral History
Subject Interests: Applied math, Computers, Electronics, Eng, Manufacturing eng, Oceanography, Physics
Automation Activity & Vendor Info: (Acquisitions) Inmagic, Inc.; (Cataloging) Inmagic, Inc.; (Circulation) Inmagic, Inc.; (Serials) Inmagic, Inc.
Partic in DTIC
Open Mon-Fri 8-5
Restriction: Authorized personnel only, Circ limited, Internal use only, Not open to pub, Researchers only, Secured area only open to authorized personnel
Friends of the Library Group

P SCHLOW CENTRE REGION LIBRARY*, 211 S Allen St, 16801-4806. SAN 315-2472. Tel: 814-237-6236. Circulation Tel: 814-235-7815. Reference Tel: 814-235-7816. Administration Tel: 814-235-7814. FAX: 814-238-8508. E-mail: refdesk@schlowlibrary.org. Web Site: www.schlowlibrary.org. *Dir,* Elizabeth Allen; *Acq,* Linda Lorich; *Adult Serv,* Patricia Griffith; *Ch Serv,* Anita Ditz; Tel: 814-235-7817; *Tech Serv,* Ann Lindsay; Staff 24 (MLS 5, Non-MLS 19)
Founded 1957. Pop 79,406; Circ 591,851
Library Holdings: AV Mats 13,052; Bk Vols 109,691; Per Subs 202
Special Collections: Oral History
Automation Activity & Vendor Info: (Acquisitions) SirsiDynix; (Cataloging) SirsiDynix; (Circulation) SirsiDynix; (OPAC) SirsiDynix
Wireless access
Function: Art exhibits, Chess club, Free DVD rentals, Handicapped accessible, ILL available, Music CDs, Online ref, Online searches, Prog for adults, Prog for children & young adult, Senior computer classes, Spoken cassettes & DVDs, Summer reading prog, Tax forms, Telephone ref
Partic in Centre County Fed of Pub Librs; Lyrasis; OCLC Online Computer Library Center, Inc
Open Mon-Wed 9-9, Thurs 12-9, Fri 9-6, Sat 9-5, Sun (Sept-May) 1:30-5
Friends of the Library Group

STEWARTSTOWN

P MASON-DIXON PUBLIC LIBRARY*, 250 Bailey Dr, 17363. SAN 315-2499. Tel: 717-993-2404. FAX: 717-993-9210. Web Site: www.yorklibraries.org/mason-dixon. *Dir,* Carol Stampler; E-mail: cstampler@yorklibraries.org; Staff 1 (MLS 1)
Founded 1961. Pop 12,731; Circ 60,885
Library Holdings: CDs 119; Bk Vols 35,000; Per Subs 103; Talking Bks 382; Videos 254
Wireless access
Mem of York County Library System
Open Mon & Wed 10-8, Tues & Thurs 12-8, Fri 10-5, Sat 9-4 (10-2 Summer)
Friends of the Library Group

STRAFFORD

P TREDYFFRIN PUBLIC LIBRARY*, 582 Upper Gulph Rd, 19087-2096. SAN 315-2502. Tel: 610-688-7092. FAX: 610-688-2014. Web Site: www.ccls.org, www.tredyffrinlibraries.org. *Dir,* Michael Packard; Staff 8 (MLS 6, Non-MLS 2)
Founded 1965. Pop 34,067; Circ 464,914
Library Holdings: e-books 38; Bk Titles 86,185; Bk Vols 90,962; Per Subs 412

Subject Interests: Local hist
Automation Activity & Vendor Info: (Circulation) Innovative Interfaces, Inc; (OPAC) Innovative Interfaces, Inc
Mem of Chester County Library System
Partic in OCLC Online Computer Library Center, Inc
Open Mon-Thurs 9:30-9, Fri 9:30-6, Sat 9:30-5, Sun 1-5
Friends of the Library Group
Branches: 1
PAOLI BRANCH, 18 Darby Rd, Paoli, 19301-1416, SAN 321-8708. Tel: 610-296-7996. FAX: 610-296-9708. *Br Mgr,* Beverly Michaels; Staff 11 (MLS 1, Non-MLS 10)
Pop 34,067; Circ 106,279
Library Holdings: Bk Titles 24,692; Bk Vols 25,991; Per Subs 72
Subject Interests: Local hist
Open Mon-Thurs 9:30-8, Fri 9:30-6, Sat 9:30-5, Sun 1-5
Friends of the Library Group

STRASBURG

P STRASBURG-HEISLER LIBRARY*, 143 Precision Ave, 17579. SAN 376-6055. Tel: 717-687-8969. FAX: 717-687-9795. E-mail: staff@strasburglibrary.org. Web Site: www.strasburglibrary.org. *Dir,* Kristin Fernitz; *Youth Serv Coordr,* Linda Kaan
Library Holdings: Bk Titles 16,000; Bk Vols 18,000; Per Subs 25
Mem of Library System of Lancaster County
Open Mon-Thurs 10-8, Fri 10-5, Sat 10-2, Sun 1-4

S TRAIN COLLECTORS ASSOCIATION*, Toy Train Reference Library, 300 Paradise Lane, 17579. (Mail add: PO Box 248, 17579-0248), SAN 326-2553. Tel: 717-687-8623. FAX: 717-687-0742. E-mail: ref-library@traincollectors.org. Web Site: www.traincollectors.org. *Librn,* Jan Athey; Staff 1 (MLS 1)
Founded 1982
Library Holdings: Bk Titles 1,400; Bk Vols 1,405; Per Subs 75
Special Collections: Toy Manufacturers Coll of: Catalogs, Instruction Sheets, Advertising & Dealer Ephemera. Oral History
Publications: National Headquarters News (Newsletter); Train Collectors Quarterly (Periodical)
Open Mon-Fri 8:30-4:30
Restriction: Open to pub for ref only
Friends of the Library Group

STROUDSBURG

P EASTERN MONROE PUBLIC LIBRARY, 1002 N Ninth St, 18360. SAN 315-2529. Tel: 570-421-0800. Circulation Tel: 570-421-0800,Ext 301. Interlibrary Loan Service Tel: 570-421-0800, Ext 310. Reference Tel: 570-421-0800, Ext 316. FAX: 570-421-0212. E-mail: reference@monroepl.org. Web Site: www.monroepl.org. *Dir,* Barbara J Keiser; *Dept Head, Adult Serv,* Mary Stewart Erm; *Head, Tech Serv,* Linnae Cintron; *Admin Serv Mgr,* Korey Rustici; *Ch Serv,* Julie Bonser; *ILL,* Carol Varipapa; Staff 36 (MLS 6, Non-MLS 30)
Founded 1913. Pop 74,003; Circ 493,285
Jan 2014-Dec 2014 Income (Main Library and Branch(s)) $1,831,858, State $400,202, County $1,256,669, Locally Generated Income $100,000. Mats Exp $194,000. Sal $1,027,602
Special Collections: Monroe County History Coll
Subject Interests: Local hist
Automation Activity & Vendor Info: (Acquisitions) Baker & Taylor; (Cataloging) SIRSI WorkFlows; (Circulation) SIRSI WorkFlows; (ILL) OCLC; (OPAC) SIRSI-iBistro
Database Vendor: ABC-CLIO, Alexander Street Press, Baker & Taylor, ebrary, EBSCOhost, Gale Cengage Learning, Greenwood Publishing Group, JSTOR, LearningExpress, Overdrive, Inc, ProQuest, ReferenceUSA, TumbleBookLibrary, World Book Online
Wireless access
Function: ILL available
Special Services for the Deaf - Assistive tech
Special Services for the Blind - Assistive/Adapted tech devices, equip & products
Friends of the Library Group
Branches: 2
POCONO TOWNSHIP BRANCH, Municipal Bldg, Rte 611, Tannersville, 18372. (Mail add: 1002 N Ninth St, 18360-1210), SAN 320-8370. Tel: 570-629-5858. E-mail: ptl@monroepl.org. *Br Librn,* Patti Marra; Staff 1 (Non-MLS 1)
Founded 1987. Circ 24,765
Library Holdings: Audiobooks 281; AV Mats 1,626; CDs 134; DVDs 1,096; High Interest/Low Vocabulary Bk Vols 50; Large Print Bks 393; Bk Vols 13,287; Per Subs 21; Videos 115
Database Vendor: Evanced Solutions, Inc, Project MUSE, SirsiDynix
Open Mon 9-1 & 2-6, Tues & Fri 1-6, Wed 3-7, Thurs 9-2, Sat 10-2
Friends of the Library Group

SMITHFIELDS BRANCH, RGB Plaza, Rte 209, 507 Seven Bridges Rd, East Stroudsburg, 18301. (Mail add: 507 Seven Bridges Rd, Ste 102, East Stroudsburg, 18301), SAN 371-9308. Tel: 570-223-1881. E-mail: smf@monroepl.org. *Br Librn,* C Sue Young; Staff 2 (MLS 1, Non-MLS 1)
Founded 1991. Circ 34,197
Library Holdings: Audiobooks 529; AV Mats 2,272; CDs 196; DVDs 1,131; High Interest/Low Vocabulary Bk Vols 69; Large Print Bks 913; Bk Vols 16,476; Per Subs 35; Videos 416
Automation Activity & Vendor Info: (Cataloging) SirsiDynix; (Circulation) SirsiDynix; (OPAC) SIRSI WorkFlows
Database Vendor: Evanced Solutions, Inc, Project MUSE, SirsiDynix
Open Mon-Thurs 10-7, Fri & Sat 10-4
Friends of the Library Group
Bookmobiles: 1

S MONROE COUNTY HISTORICAL ASSOCIATION*, Elizabeth D Walters Library, 900 Main St, 18360. SAN 325-5344. Tel: 570-421-7703. FAX: 570-421-9199. E-mail: mcha@ptd.net. Web Site: mcha-pa.org. *Exec Dir,* Amy Leiser
Founded 1921
Library Holdings: Bk Titles 5,000; Bk Vols 10,000; Per Subs 17
Special Collections: Monroe County History & Genealogy Coll, bks, docs, mss, photogs. Oral History
Function: Res libr
Publications: Fanlight
Open Tues-Fri 9-4, Sat 10-4

L MONROE COUNTY LAW LIBRARY*, Court House, 18360. SAN 327-0866. Tel: 570-420-3642. *Librn,* Roy Kleinle; Staff 1 (Non-MLS 1)
Library Holdings: Bk Vols 7,000; Per Subs 12
Database Vendor: Westlaw
Open Mon-Fri 8:30-4:30

SUGAR GROVE

P SUGAR GROVE FREE LIBRARY, 22 Harmon St, 16350. (Mail add: PO Box 313, 16350-0313), SAN 315-2537. Tel: 814-489-7872. FAX: 814-489-7872. E-mail: sgfreelibrary@gmail.com. Web Site: www.sgfreelibrary.org. *Dir,* Leslie LaBarte; *Asst Dir,* Julie Greenman; Staff 1 (MLS 1)
Founded 1936. Pop 5,720
Library Holdings: Bk Titles 19,136; Per Subs 50
Special Collections: Artist Coll, bks
Subject Interests: Early oil industry, Gardening, Relig
Automation Activity & Vendor Info: (Cataloging) Innovative Interfaces, Inc; (Circulation) Innovative Interfaces, Inc; (OPAC) Innovative Interfaces, Inc
Database Vendor: Access Pennsylvania, Overdrive, Inc
Wireless access
Function: Adult bk club, Audio & video playback equip for onsite use, Audiobks via web, Bks on CD, Children's prog, Computer training, Computers for patron use, Copy machines, Distance learning, Electronic databases & coll, Equip loans & repairs, eReaders, Fax serv, Free DVD rentals, Holiday prog, ILL available, Instruction & testing, Magazines, Movies, Music CDs, Online cat, Outside serv via phone, mail, e-mail & web, OverDrive digital audio bks, Photocopying/Printing, Prog for children & young adult, Pub access computers, Ref serv available, Ref serv in person, Scanner, Senior computer classes, Story hour, Summer reading prog, Tax forms, Teen prog, Telephone ref, Web-catalog, Wheelchair accessible, Workshops
Partic in Warren County Libr Syst
Open Mon & Wed 11-8, Tues & Thurs 11-4

SUMMERDALE

C CENTRAL PENNSYLVANIA COLLEGE LIBRARY*, Charles T Jones Library, 600 Valley Rd, 17093. (Mail add: PO Box 309, 17093). Tel: 717-728-2227. FAX: 717-728-2300. Web Site: www.centralpenn.edu/library. *Libr Dir,* Diane Porterfield; E-mail: dianeporterfield@centralpenn.edu; *Librn,* Jill Hallam-Miller; Staff 3.5 (MLS 3.5)
Founded 2002. Enrl 1,000; Highest Degree: Bachelor
Automation Activity & Vendor Info: (Acquisitions) Innovative Interfaces, Inc; (Cataloging) Innovative Interfaces, Inc; (Circulation) Innovative Interfaces, Inc; (Course Reserve) Innovative Interfaces, Inc; (OPAC) Innovative Interfaces, Inc; (Serials) Innovative Interfaces, Inc
Database Vendor: EBSCOhost, Gale Cengage Learning, Hoovers, Oxford Online, Westlaw
Wireless access
Restriction: Open to students, fac, staff & alumni

SUMMERVILLE

P SUMMERVILLE PUBLIC LIBRARY*, 114 Second Ave, 15864. (Mail add: PO Box 301, 15864-0301), SAN 315-2545. Tel: 814-856-3169. FAX: 814-856-3169. E-mail: sulibrary@usachoice.net. Web Site: users.usachoice.net/~sulibrary. *Dir,* A Jennifer Coleman
Founded 1932. Pop 1,897; Circ 6,000
Library Holdings: High Interest/Low Vocabulary Bk Vols 80; Bk Titles 12,000; Bk Vols 16,000; Per Subs 46
Special Collections: Oral History
Subject Interests: Cookery, Local hist
Automation Activity & Vendor Info: (Acquisitions) AmLib Library Management System
Database Vendor: Overdrive, Inc, ProQuest
Wireless access
Mem of Oil Creek District Library Center
Open Mon, Tues & Thurs 12:30-8, Wed 12:30-6, Sat 9-1

SUNBURY

P DEGENSTEIN COMMUNITY LIBRARY*, 40 S Fifth St, 17801. SAN 315-2553. Tel: 570-286-2461. FAX: 570-286-4203. E-mail: kaufflib@ptd.net. Web Site: www.degensteinlibrary.org. *Dir,* Gail E Broome
Founded 1937. Pop 16,717; Circ 66,564
Library Holdings: Bk Vols 64,000; Per Subs 98
Special Collections: Pennsylvania History Room. State Document Depository; UN Document Depository; US Document Depository
Subject Interests: Local hist
Automation Activity & Vendor Info: (Circulation) EOS International
Open Mon 1-9, Tues, Wed & Fri 10-6, Thurs 10-9, Sat 9-5
Friends of the Library Group

GL NORTHUMBERLAND COUNTY LAW LIBRARY*, Court House, 201 Market St, 17801-3471. SAN 315-2561. Tel: 570-988-4162. FAX: 570-988-4497.
Founded 1886
Jan 2008-Dec 2008 Income $40,000. Mats Exp $40,500
Special Collections: Municipal Document Depository; State Document Depository
Database Vendor: Westlaw
Function: Res libr
Open Mon-Fri 9-4:30
Restriction: Open to pub for ref only

SWARTHMORE

S FRIENDS HISTORICAL LIBRARY OF SWARTHMORE COLLEGE, 500 College Ave, 19081-1399. SAN 315-2588. Tel: 610-328-8496. Interlibrary Loan Service Tel: 610-328-8498. FAX: 610-690-5728. E-mail: friends@swarthmore.edu. Web Site: www.swarthmore.edu/library/friends. *Curator,* Christopher Densmore; Tel: 610-328-8499, E-mail: cdensmo1@swarthmore.edu; Staff 2 (Non-MLS 2)
Founded 1871
Library Holdings: Bk Vols 44,000; Per Subs 212
Special Collections: Archival Records of Swarthmore College; Archives of Philadelphia Yearly Meeting, New York Yearly Meeting, Baltimore Yearly Meeting & other Quaker Meetings; Papers of Quakers including Lucretia Mott, Elias Hicks, John Woolman & John G Whittier; Records of Quaker Organizations including Friends General Conference; Society of Friends Coll, bks, per, printed mat
Subject Interests: Quaker hist
Publications: Catalog of the Book & Serials Collections of the Friends Historical Library; Guide to the Manuscript Collections of Friends Historical Library of Swarthmore College; Guide to the Records of Philadelphia Yearly Meeting
Partic in OCLC, Inc through Palinet; Philadelphia Area Consortium of Special Collections Libraries
Open Mon-Fri 8:30-4:30, Sat 10-1

C SWARTHMORE COLLEGE*, McCabe Library, 500 College Ave, 19081-1081. SAN 359-5773. Tel: 610-328-8489. Circulation Tel: 610-328-8477. Interlibrary Loan Service Tel: 610-328-7822. Reference Tel: 610-328-8493. FAX: 610-328-7329. E-mail: librarian@swarthmore.edu. Web Site: www.swarthmore.edu/library. *Head, Digital Libr Prog & Tech Planning,* Spencer Lamm; Tel: 610-328-8541, E-mail: slamm1@swarthmore.edu; *Col Librn,* Peggy Seiden; E-mail: pseiden1@swarthmore.edu; *Assoc Col Librn, Tech Serv & Digital Initiatives,* Barb Weir; Tel: 610-328-8443, E-mail: bweir1@swarthmore.edu; *Humanities Librn,* Anne Garrison; Tel: 610-328-8492, E-mail: agarris1@swarthmore.edu; *Outreach & Instruction Librn,* Pam Harris; Tel: 610-690-2056, E-mail: pharris1@swarthmore.edu; *Performing Arts Librn,* Donna Fournier; Tel: 610-328-8231, E-mail: dfourni1@swarthmore.edu; *Sci Librn,* Meg Spencer; Tel: 610-328-7685, E-mail: mspence1@swarthmore.edu; *Soc Sci Librn,* Melanie Maksin; Tel: 610-690-5786, E-mail: mmaksin1@swarthmore.edu; *Access Serv, Circ,* Alison Masterpasqua; Tel: 610-328-8478, E-mail: amaster1@swarthmore.edu; *ILL,* Sandy Vermeychuk; E-mail: sverney1@swarthmore.edu. Subject Specialists: *Dance, Music,* Donna Fournier; Staff 18 (MLS 11.7, Non-MLS 6.3)
Founded 1864. Enrl 1,514; Fac 180; Highest Degree: Bachelor
Jul 2009-Jun 2010. Mats Exp $2,040,007, Books $447,473, Per/Ser (Incl. Access Fees) $1,500,566, AV Mat $67,832, Presv $24,136
Library Holdings: e-journals 15,164; Bk Vols 860,000; Per Subs 1,174; Videos 11,604
Special Collections: British Writings on Travel in America (British Americana Coll); History of Technology (Bathe Coll); Private Press (Charles B Shaw Coll); Recorded Literature (Potter Coll); Romantic Poetry (Wells Wordsworth & Thomson Coll); W H Auden Coll. State Document Depository; US Document Depository
Automation Activity & Vendor Info: (Acquisitions) Innovative Interfaces, Inc; (Cataloging) Innovative Interfaces, Inc; (Circulation) Innovative Interfaces, Inc; (Course Reserve) Innovative Interfaces, Inc; (ILL) Innovative Interfaces, Inc; (Media Booking) Innovative Interfaces, Inc; (OPAC) Innovative Interfaces, Inc; (Serials) Innovative Interfaces, Inc
Wireless access
Partic in Interlibrary Delivery Service of Pennsylvania; Lyrasis; OCLC Online Computer Library Center, Inc; OCLC Research Library Partnership; Pennsylvania Academic Library Consortium, Inc (PALCI); Tri-College Consortium
Open Mon-Thurs 8am-2am, Fri 8am-11pm, Sat 10am-8pm, Sun 10am-2am
Restriction: Open to students, fac & staff
Friends of the Library Group
Departmental Libraries:
CORNELL SCIENCE & ENGINEERING, 500 College Ave, 19081-1399. Tel: 610-328-7685. FAX: 610-690-5776. *Sci,* Meg E Spencer
Library Holdings: Bk Vols 92,575
Open Mon-Thurs 8:15am-1am, Fri 8:15-11, Sat 10-10, Sun 11:30am-1am
DANIEL UNDERHILL MUSIC & DANCE, 500 College Ave, 19081-1399. Tel: 610-328-8232. *Librn,* Donna Fournier; Tel: 610-328-8231
Library Holdings: Bk Vols 40,936
Open Mon-Thurs 9am-1am, Fri 9-6, Sat 10-6, Sun 11:30am-1am

P SWARTHMORE PUBLIC LIBRARY*, Borough Hall, 121 Park Ave, 19081-1536. SAN 315-260X. Tel: 610-543-0436, 610-543-3171. FAX: 610-328-6699. E-mail: Swarthmore@delcolibraries.org. Web Site: www.delcolibraries.org, www.swarthmorepubliclibrary.org. *Dir,* Sharon Ford; E-mail: swdirector@delcolibraries.org; *Asst Librn,* Karen Robinson; *Children's Programmer,* Kristin Grossi; *Circ, Tech Serv & Automation,* Carol Mackin; Staff 1 (MLS 1)
Founded 1929. Pop 6,157; Circ 115,000
Library Holdings: Bk Vols 48,500; Per Subs 96
Automation Activity & Vendor Info: (Circulation) Innovative Interfaces, Inc
Database Vendor: EBSCOhost, Gale Cengage Learning
Wireless access
Function: ILL available
Mem of Delaware County Library System
Open Mon-Thurs 10-9, Fri 10-12 & 2-7, Sat 10-5, Sun 1-5 (10-2 Summer)
Friends of the Library Group

SWISSVALE

P CARNEGIE FREE LIBRARY OF SWISSVALE*, 1800 Monongahela Ave, 15218-2312. SAN 315-2618. Tel: 412-731-2300. FAX: 412-731-6716. Web Site: swissvalelibrary.org. *Dir,* Kate Grannemann; E-mail: grannemannk@einetwork.net; Staff 5 (MLS 2, Non-MLS 3)
Founded 1916. Pop 13,182; Circ 28,419
Library Holdings: Large Print Bks 107; Bk Titles 19,679; Bk Vols 21,410; Per Subs 116; Talking Bks 310; Videos 268
Automation Activity & Vendor Info: (Cataloging) Innovative Interfaces, Inc; (Circulation) Innovative Interfaces, Inc; (ILL) Innovative Interfaces, Inc; (OPAC) Innovative Interfaces, Inc
Database Vendor: EBSCOhost, Gale Cengage Learning, SirsiDynix
Wireless access
Mem of Allegheny County Library Association
Open Mon, Tues & Thurs 10-8, Wed & Fri 10-4, Sat 9-4
Friends of the Library Group

SYKESVILLE

P SYKESVILLE PUBLIC LIBRARY*, 21 E Main St, 15865-0021. SAN 315-2626. Tel: 814-894-5243. FAX: 814-894-5243. *Librn,* Ruth Sackash
Founded 1968. Pop 2,973; Circ 7,025
Library Holdings: Bk Titles 10,625; Bk Vols 9,000; Per Subs 35
Mem of Oil Creek District Library Center

TAMAQUA

P TAMAQUA PUBLIC LIBRARY*, 30 S Railroad St, 18252. SAN 315-2642. Tel: 570-668-4660. FAX: 570-668-3047. E-mail: tamaquapubliclibrary@hotmail.com. Web Site: www.tamaquapl.com, www.tamaquapubliclibrary.com. *Libr Dir,* Gayle R Heath
Founded 1934. Pop 17,144
Library Holdings: Bk Titles 39,000; Per Subs 52

TAYLOR

P TAYLOR COMMUNITY LIBRARY*, 710 Main St, 18517-1774. SAN 315-2677. Tel: 570 562 3180. FAX: 570 562 3140. Web Site: www.lclshome.org/taylor. *Librn,* Jeanie Sluck
Founded 1954. Pop 7,200; Circ 10,249
Library Holdings: Bk Vols 41,000; Per Subs 20
Automation Activity & Vendor Info: (Cataloging) SirsiDynix; (Circulation) SirsiDynix; (OPAC) SirsiDynix
Mem of Lackawanna County Library System
Open Mon-Thurs 9-9, Fri 9-5, Sat 9-4
Bookmobiles: 1

TELFORD

P INDIAN VALLEY PUBLIC LIBRARY*, 100 E Church Ave, 18969. SAN 315-2685. Tel: 215-723-9109. FAX: 215-723-0583. Web Site: www.ivpl.org. *Dir,* Linda Beck; E-mail: lbeck@ivpl.org; *Adult Serv,* Deborah Faulkner; E-mail: dfaulkner@ivpl.org; *Ch Serv,* Sara Parisi; E-mail: sparisi@ivpl.org; *Ref Serv,* Melanie Ford; E-mail: mford@ivpl.org; *Ref Serv,* Bob Rekuc; E-mail: brekuc@ivpl.org; *Tech Serv,* Mary Porter; E-mail: mporter@ivpl.org; Staff 22 (MLS 6, Non-MLS 16)
Founded 1963. Pop 41,000; Circ 520,000
Library Holdings: AV Mats 9,450; Large Print Bks 925; Bk Vols 130,000; Per Subs 130
Special Collections: Charles Price Genealogy Coll; Chinese Culture Coll; Local Newspaper 1881-date; Pennsylvania Archives
Automation Activity & Vendor Info: (Cataloging) SirsiDynix; (Circulation) SirsiDynix
Database Vendor: EBSCOhost, Gale Cengage Learning, OCLC FirstSearch, ProQuest, SirsiDynix
Wireless access
Open Mon-Thurs 9-9, Fri 10-9, Sat 10-5, Sun 1-5
Friends of the Library Group

TIDIOUTE

P TIDIOUTE PUBLIC LIBRARY*, 197 Main St, 16351. (Mail add: PO Box T, 16351-0225), SAN 315-2693. Tel: 814-484-3581. FAX: 814-484-3581. *Librn,* Elizabeth Nicholson
Founded 1921. Pop 939; Circ 10,815
Library Holdings: Bk Vols 12,000; Per Subs 45
Open Mon 1-8, Wed 10-5, Fri 12-6, Sat 9-3
Friends of the Library Group

TIONESTA

P SARAH STEWART BOVARD MEMORIAL LIBRARY*, 156 Elm St, 16353. (Mail add: PO Box 127, 16353-0127), SAN 315-2707. Tel: 814-755-4454. FAX: 814-755-4333. E-mail: ssbml@zoominternet.net. Web Site: www.tionestalibrary.org. *Dir,* Brenda McGraw
Founded 1942. Pop 5,072; Circ 14,000
Library Holdings: Bk Titles 19,000; Per Subs 47
Special Collections: Artifacts (Forest County Logging & Boat Building Tools Coll); Forest County History & Geography, bks, pamphlets, photog, etc
Automation Activity & Vendor Info: (Cataloging) Follett Software; (Circulation) Follett Software; (OPAC) Follett Software
Open Tues, Fri & Sat 10-5, Wed & Thurs 12-7

TITUSVILLE

P BENSON MEMORIAL LIBRARY*, 213 N Franklin St, 16354-1788. SAN 315-2715. Tel: 814-827-2913. FAX: 814-827-9836. *Dir,* Gail K Myer; *Ch Serv,* Tara Bartley; Staff 5 (MLS 4, Non-MLS 1)
Founded 1902. Pop 16,355; Circ 103,690
Library Holdings: Audiobooks 891; CDs 579; DVDs 731; Large Print Bks 649; Bk Titles 54,027; Per Subs 200; Videos 704
Special Collections: Oil City Births & Marriages (1882-1909); Titusville Births & Deaths (1857-1917); Titusville Herald (1865-present), micro; US Census for Crawford Forest, Venango & Warren Counties (1850-1900), micro
Subject Interests: Early petroleum indust, Genealogy, Local hist
Automation Activity & Vendor Info: (Cataloging) LibLime; (Circulation) LibLime; (OPAC) LibLime
Mem of Crawford County Federated Library System
Open Mon-Thurs 10-8, Fri & Sat 10-5
Friends of the Library Group

S PENNSYLVANIA HISTORICAL & MUSEUM COMMISSION*, Drake Well Museum Library, 202 Museum Lane, 16354-8902. SAN 315-2723. Tel: 814-827-2797. FAX: 814-827-4888. Web Site: www.drakewell.org. *Dir,* Melissa Mann
Founded 1934
Library Holdings: Bk Titles 4,000; Per Subs 16
Special Collections: Early Petroleum Industry (Brewer), doc; Early Petroleum Industry (Townsend), doc; Nitroglycerine (Roberts), doc; Personal Papers (Fletcher), doc; Standard Oil Company (Ida M Tarbell), doc. Oral History
Subject Interests: Hist of region, Petroleum indust
Function: Res libr
Restriction: Not a lending libr, Open by appt only
Friends of the Library Group

C UNIVERSITY OF PITTSBURGH AT TITUSVILLE*, Haskell Memorial Library, 504 E Main St, 16354. SAN 315-2731. Tel: 814-827-4439. FAX: 814-827-4449. Web Site: www.library.pitt.edu/titusville. *Head of Libr,* Marc Ross; Tel: 814-827-4452, E-mail: marcross@pitt.edu
Founded 1963
Library Holdings: Bk Vols 47,200; Per Subs 90
Automation Activity & Vendor Info: (Circulation) Ex Libris Group; (OPAC) Ex Libris Group; (Serials) Ex Libris Group
Wireless access
Partic in OCLC Online Computer Library Center, Inc

TOBYHANNA

P POCONO MOUNTAIN PUBLIC LIBRARY*, 5540 Memorial Blvd, 18466. SAN 372-7289. Tel: 570-894-8860. FAX: 570-894-8852. E-mail: pmpl_library@yahoo.com. Web Site: www.poconomountpl.org. *Dir,* Ann Shincovich; *Ad,* Cathy Conway; *Ch,* Susanne Mocerino; *Cat Librn,* Kathryn Ritter-Vicich; *ILL Librn, Purchasing,* Bev Abel; *YA Librn,* Mary Ann Lewis; *Pub Serv,* Jo Collins; *Pub Serv,* Linda Fernandez; *Pub Serv,* Linda Salmon; *Pub Serv,* Kristen Sullivan; *Pub Serv,* Sarah Rieder; *Pub Serv, Tech Serv,* Alex Goodstein; *ESL Coordr,* Judite Maldonando-Colombani; Staff 8 (MLS 1, Non-MLS 7)
Founded 1975. Pop 17,947; Circ 160,962
Library Holdings: Bk Titles 31,458; Bk Vols 38,000; Per Subs 100
Automation Activity & Vendor Info: (Cataloging) Follett Software; (Circulation) Follett Software; (OPAC) Follett Software
Database Vendor: EBSCOhost
Open Mon & Wed 10-8, Tues, Thurs, Fri & Sat 10-5
Friends of the Library Group

A UNITED STATES ARMY*, Tobyhanna Army Depot Post Library, 11 Hap Arnold Blvd, 18466-5099. Tel: 570-615-7584, 570-615-8851. FAX: 570-895-7419. *Librn,* Lee Muzi
Founded 1959
Library Holdings: CDs 400; DVDs 2,000; Bk Vols 7,000; Per Subs 28
Partic in OCLC Online Computer Library Center, Inc
Open Mon-Fri 8am-1pm

TOPTON

P BRANDYWINE COMMUNITY LIBRARY*, 60 Tower Dr, 19562-1301. SAN 323-9411. Tel: 610-682-7115. FAX: 610-682-7385. E-mail: brandywinecl@berks.lib.pa.us. Web Site: www.berks.lib.pa.us/brandywinecl. *Librn,* Cheryl DuBois Knight; *Asst Librn,* Lynne Priester; *Ch,* Charlotte Puff; Staff 4 (MLS 1, Non-MLS 3)
Founded 1989. Pop 12,770; Circ 82,092
Library Holdings: AV Mats 5,323; Large Print Bks 1,086; Bk Titles 21,608; Per Subs 81; Talking Bks 1,821
Automation Activity & Vendor Info: (Acquisitions) Innovative Interfaces, Inc; (Cataloging) Innovative Interfaces, Inc; (Circulation) Innovative Interfaces, Inc; (Course Reserve) Innovative Interfaces, Inc; (ILL) Innovative Interfaces, Inc; (Media Booking) Innovative Interfaces, Inc; (OPAC) Innovative Interfaces, Inc; (Serials) Innovative Interfaces, Inc
Database Vendor: SirsiDynix
Function: Adult bk club
Publications: Just Between Friends (Newsletter)
Mem of Berks County Public Libraries
Special Services for the Blind - Closed circuit TV magnifier
Open Mon-Thurs 10-8, Fri & Sat (Winter) 10-5
Friends of the Library Group

TOWANDA

S OSRAM SYLVANIA LIBRARY*, Hawes St, 18848. SAN 315-274X. Tel: 570-268-5322. FAX: 570-268-5350. *Librn,* Kathy Hammerly; E-mail: kathy.hammerly@sylvania.com; Staff 1 (Non-MLS 1)
Founded 1956
Library Holdings: Bk Titles 11,281; Bk Vols 12,452; Per Subs 351

Subject Interests: Ceramics, Chem, Metallurgy
Restriction: Staff use only

P TOWANDA PUBLIC LIBRARY*, 104 Main St, 18848-1895. SAN 315-2758. Tel: 570-265-2470. FAX: 570-265-7212. E-mail: towandapublib@gmail.com. Web Site: www.towandapubliclibrary.org. *Dir,* June Houghtaling; Staff 5 (MLS 1, Non-MLS 4)
Founded 1880. Pop 10,461; Circ 48,100
Library Holdings: Bk Vols 30,000; Per Subs 76
Special Collections: Local History Coll
Subject Interests: Civil War
Automation Activity & Vendor Info: (Acquisitions) Evergreen
Database Vendor: LearningExpress, Overdrive, Inc, TumbleBookLibrary
Wireless access
Mem of Bradford County Library System; South Central Kansas Library System
Open Mon-Thurs 10-8, Fri & Sat 10-5
Friends of the Library Group

TOWER CITY

P TOWER-PORTER COMMUNITY LIBRARY*, 230 E Grand Ave, 17980-1124. SAN 315-2766. Tel: 717-647-4900. E-mail: toweport@comcast.net. Web Site: www.iu29.org/towpl. *Pres of Board,* Edward Gobrecht; *Libr Dir,* Thomas Houtz
Pop 4,185
Library Holdings: Bk Vols 8,500; Per Subs 10
Wireless access
Open Mon-Thurs 1-8, Sat 9-4

TRAFFORD

P TRAFFORD COMMUNITY PUBLIC LIBRARY*, 416 Brinton Ave, 15085. (Mail add: PO Box 173, 15085-0173), SAN 315-2774. Tel: 412-372-5115. FAX: 412-372-0993. *Librn,* Sharon Peacock
Pop 3,662; Circ 12,715
Library Holdings: Bk Vols 12,000; Per Subs 25
Mem of Westmoreland County Federated Library System
Open Mon-Wed 10-3 & 6:30-8, Thurs 10-4, Sat 9:30-4:30

TREMONT

P TREMONT AREA FREE PUBLIC LIBRARY*, 19 N Pine St, 17981-1410. (Mail add: PO Box 54, 17981-0054), SAN 315-2782. Tel: 570-695-3325. E-mail: tafpl@epix.net. *Librn,* Bonnie Wiscount
Pop 1,796; Circ 3,308
Library Holdings: Bk Vols 7,902; Per Subs 15
Open Mon & Wed 10-4 & 6-8, Tues & Thurs 11-2 & 6-8, Fri 10-4, Sat 8-3

TREVOSE

S GE BETZ*, Technology Library, 4636 Somerton Rd, 19053-6783. SAN 315-2790. Tel: 215-953-2546. E-mail: gebetz.library@ge.com. Web Site: www.gewater.com. *Adminr,* Dianne E Rose; E-mail: dianne.rose@ge.com; Staff 1 (MLS 1)
Founded 1925
Library Holdings: Electronic Media & Resources 50; Bk Titles 4,500; Bk Vols 5,500; Per Subs 200
Subject Interests: Corrosion, Indust wastes, Water pollution, Water treatment
Publications: Acquisitions List
Partic in Dialog Corp; National Network of Libraries of Medicine
Restriction: Access at librarian's discretion

TROY

P BRADFORD COUNTY LIBRARY SYSTEM*, 16093 Rte 6, 16947. SAN 315-2812. Tel: 570-297-2436. FAX: 570-297-4197. E-mail: bclibrary@bradfordco.org. Web Site: bradfordcountylibrary.org. *Dir,* Jeffrey Singer; E-mail: singerj@bradfordco.org; *Youth Librn,* Sarah Vargason; E-mail: stoodys@bradfordco.org; *ILL,* Theresa Fritchman; E-mail: fritchmant@bradfordco.org; Staff 11 (MLS 3, Non-MLS 8)
Founded 1941. Pop 75,000; Circ 144,069
Library Holdings: Bk Vols 194,396
Subject Interests: Local hist
Automation Activity & Vendor Info: (Acquisitions) Brodart; (Cataloging) Follett Software; (Circulation) Follett Software
Wireless access
Member Libraries: Allen F Pierce Free Library; Green Free Library; Mather Memorial Library; Monroeton Public Library; New Albany Community Library; Sayre Public Library, Inc; Spalding Memorial Library; Towanda Public Library; Wyalusing Public Library
Open Mon-Thurs 8-8, Fri 8-6, Sat 10-5
Friends of the Library Group
Bookmobiles: 1. In Charge, Rosemary Wynott

P ALLEN F PIERCE FREE LIBRARY*, 115 Center St, 16947-1125. SAN 315-2820. Tel: 570-297-2745. FAX: 570-297-2745. Web Site: www.piercelibrary.org. *Librn,* Susan Wolfe; E-mail: s16@epix.net; Staff 2 (MLS 1, Non-MLS 1)
Founded 1912. Pop 5,197; Circ 8,312
Library Holdings: Bk Titles 17,219; Bk Vols 18,100; Per Subs 53; Talking Bks 100; Videos 63
Automation Activity & Vendor Info: (Circulation) Follett Software; (Course Reserve) Follett Software; (OPAC) Follett Software
Database Vendor: EBSCOhost, Gale Cengage Learning
Mem of Bradford County Library System
Open Tues & Thurs 1-7, Wed & Fri 9-5, Sat 8-3 (8-12 Summer)

TUNKHANNOCK

P TUNKHANNOCK PUBLIC LIBRARY*, 220 W Tioga St, 18657-6611. SAN 315-2839. Tel: 570-836-1677. FAX: 570-836-2148. E-mail: tunpubli@epix.net. Web Site: www.tunkhannock.com/library. *Librn,* Susan Turrell
Founded 1890. Pop 28,080; Circ 148,914
Jan 2006-Dec 2006 Income $273,619, State $65,337, County $45,000, Locally Generated Income $163,282. Mats Exp $37,227, Books $30,738, Per/Ser (Incl. Access Fees) $2,203, AV Mat $4,286. Sal $121,121 (Prof $46,911)
Library Holdings: AV Mats 4,431; CDs 798; DVDs 96; High Interest/Low Vocabulary Bk Vols 69; Large Print Bks 2,317; Bk Titles 39,794; Bk Vols 45,024; Per Subs 75; Talking Bks 2,115; Videos 2,021
Automation Activity & Vendor Info: (Acquisitions) Brodart; (Cataloging) Brodart; (Circulation) Follett Software; (OPAC) Follett Software
Wireless access
Open Mon-Fri 10-9, Sat 9-3
Friends of the Library Group

TYRONE

P TYRONE-SNYDER PUBLIC LIBRARY*, 1000 Pennsylvania Ave, 16686. SAN 315-2847. Tel: 814-684-1133. FAX: 814-684-1878. E-mail: info@tyronelibrary.org. Web Site: www.tyronelibrary.org. *Dir,* Jessica Ford Cameron; Tel: 814-684-1133, Ext 3; *Asst Dir,* Judie Adams; Tel: 814-684-1133, Ext 4
Founded 1964. Circ 36,020
Library Holdings: Bk Vols 24,050; Per Subs 52
Special Collections: Local history
Automation Activity & Vendor Info: (Cataloging) Follett Software; (Circulation) Follett Software; (OPAC) Follett Software
Function: Homebound delivery serv, Photocopying/Printing
Mem of Blair County Library System
Open Mon & Fri 12-5, Tues & Thurs 12-8, Wed 11-5, Sat 10-5
Friends of the Library Group

ULSTER

P MATHER MEMORIAL LIBRARY, 23866 Rte 220, 18850. (Mail add: PO Box 230, 18850-0230), SAN 315-2855. Tel: 570-358-3595. FAX: 570-358-3595. E-mail: matherpl@epix.net. Web Site: matherlibrary.org. *Dir,* Deneen Roach
Founded 1921. Pop 2,685; Circ 13,787
Library Holdings: Audiobooks 248; DVDs 427; Large Print Bks 398; Bk Vols 13,830; Per Subs 33; Videos 194
Automation Activity & Vendor Info: (Circulation) Biblionix
Wireless access
Function: 24/7 Online cat, Bks on CD, Computers for patron use, Copy machines, ILL available, Magazines, Mango lang, Online cat, OverDrive digital audio bks, Photocopying/Printing, Preschool reading prog, Pub access computers, Story hour, Summer reading prog
Mem of Bradford County Library System
Open Tues 10-7, Wed & Thurs 11-7, Fri 2-6, Sat 9-4

ULYSSES

P ULYSSES LIBRARY ASSOCIATION*, 401 N Main St, 16948. (Mail add: PO Box 316, 16948-0316), SAN 315-2863. Tel: 814-848-7226. FAX: 814-848-7226. E-mail: ulylib@verizon.net. Web Site: www.ulysseslibrary.com. *Librn,* Sheri Graves; *Asst Librn,* Bonnie Merkey
Founded 1916. Pop 1,375; Circ 11,547
Library Holdings: Bk Vols 15,824; Per Subs 15
Automation Activity & Vendor Info: (Acquisitions) Brodart; (Cataloging) Brodart; (Circulation) Brodart
Function: Summer reading prog
Mem of Potter-Tioga Library System
Open Tues, Thurs & Fri 1-7, Wed 9-6, Sat 9-5

UNION CITY

P UNION CITY PUBLIC LIBRARY*, Two Stranahan St, 16438-1322. SAN 315-2871. Tel: 814-438-3209. FAX: 814-438-8031. Interlibrary Loan Service E-mail: unioncitypl@gmail.com. Web Site: www.ucpl.org. *Librn,* Christine Slocum
Founded 1908. Pop 6,491; Circ 7,111
Library Holdings: Bk Titles 24,678; Per Subs 46
Special Collections: Local Newspaper, micro
Automation Activity & Vendor Info: (Circulation) Follett Software; (OPAC) Follett Software
Wireless access
Open Mon & Thurs 9-7.30, Tues & Fri 9-5.30, Sat 9-4 (10 2 Summer)
Friends of the Library Group

UNIONTOWN

GL FAYETTE COUNTY LAW LIBRARY, Court House, 61 E Main St, Ste D, 15401-3514. SAN 315-288X. Tel: 724-430-1228. FAX: 724-430-4886. E-mail: falawlib@atlanticbbn.net. *Law Librn,* Barry Richard Blaine; *Asst Law Librn,* Barbara Pasqua; Staff 2 (MLS 1, Non-MLS 1)
Founded 1927
Library Holdings: Bk Vols 25,000
Open Mon-Fri 8-4:30
Restriction: Non-circulating

C PENNSYLVANIA STATE UNIVERSITY*, Fayette Library, One University Dr, 15401. (Mail add: PO Box 519, 15401-0519), SAN 315-2898. Tel: 724-430-4155. FAX: 724-430-4152. Web Site: www.libraries.psu.edu/fayette/. *Head of Libr,* John Riddle; Tel: 724-430-4156, E-mail: jsr13@psu.edu; *Ref Serv,* Gerry Dorobish; Tel: 724-430-4154, E-mail: gxd6@psu.edu; Staff 2 (MLS 1, Non-MLS 1)
Founded 1965. Enrl 994; Fac 48
Library Holdings: Bk Vols 50,000; Per Subs 125
Partic in OCLC Online Computer Library Center, Inc; RLIN (Research Libraries Information Network)
Open Mon-Thurs 8-8, Fri 8-5, Sat 10-3

M UNIONTOWN HOSPITAL*, Professional Library, 500 W Berkeley St, 15401. SAN 327-084X. Tel: 724-430-5178. FAX: 724-430-3349. *Librn,* Rosemary Panichella; E-mail: panichella@utwn.org; Staff 1 (MLS 1)
Jul 2012-Jun 2013. Mats Exp $23,900, Books $2,000, Per/Ser (Incl. Access Fees) $5,900, Electronic Ref Mat (Incl. Access Fees) $18,000
Library Holdings: e-books 80; Bk Titles 268; Bk Vols 270; Per Subs 22
Partic in Basic Health Sciences Library Network; National Network of Libraries of Medicine Middle Atlantic Region; Pittsburgh Basic Health Sciences Libr Consortium (PBHSL)
Open Tues & Thurs 8:30-4

P UNIONTOWN PUBLIC LIBRARY*, 24 Jefferson St, 15401-3602. SAN 315-2901. Tel: 724-437-1165. FAX: 724-439-5689. Web Site: www.uniontownlib.org. *Libr Dir,* Lynne E Tharan; Staff 8 (MLS 1, Non-MLS 7)
Founded 1928. Pop 10,372; Circ 66,386
Jan 2012-Dec 2012 Income $437,159, State $43,151, City $226,000, Other $168,008. Mats Exp $37,636, Books $35,500, Per/Ser (Incl. Access Fees) $2,136. Sal $184,556
Library Holdings: Bk Vols 98,673; Per Subs 75
Special Collections: Pennsylvania Room. Oral History
Subject Interests: Local hist
Automation Activity & Vendor Info: (Cataloging) Innovative Interfaces, Inc; (Circulation) Innovative Interfaces, Inc; (ILL) Innovative Interfaces, Inc; (OPAC) Innovative Interfaces, Inc
Wireless access
Function: Adult bk club, Archival coll, Art exhibits, Bks on CD, Children's prog, Computers for patron use, Copy machines, e-mail serv, E-Reserves, Free DVD rentals, Handicapped accessible, ILL available, Learning ctr, Magnifiers for reading, Mail & tel request accepted, Microfiche/film & reading machines, Newsp ref libr, Online cat, OverDrive digital audio bks, Prog for adults, Prog for children & young adult, Pub access computers, Ref serv available, Serves mentally handicapped consumers, Story hour, Summer reading prog, Web-catalog, Wheelchair accessible
Special Services for the Blind - Audio mat; Bks on CD; Copier with enlargement capabilities; Large print bks; Low vision equip; Magnifiers; Recorded bks; Sec-Tec enlarger
Open Mon 11-8, Tues-Thurs 10:30-6, Fri 10:30-5, Sat 10-5
Friends of the Library Group

UNIVERSITY PARK

C PENNSYLVANIA STATE UNIVERSITY LIBRARIES*, Pattee Library & Paterno Library, 510 Paterno Library, 16802. SAN 359-601X. Tel: 814-865-0401. FAX: 814-865-3665. E-mail: slb3@psu.edu. Web Site: www.libraries.psu.edu. *Dean of Univ Libr & Scholarly Communications,* Barbara I Dewey; *Assoc Dean, Coll, Info & Access Serv,* Lisa German; *Assoc Dean, Res & Scholarly Communication & Co-Dir of Digital Publ, Copyright Librn,* Michael Furlough; *Assoc Dean, Undergrad & Learning Serv,* Jack Sulzer; *Head of Scholarly Communications Serv,* Linda Friend; *Head of Ser & Acq Serv,* Robert Alan; *Head, Access Serv,* Ann Snowman; *Head, Digital Libr Tech,* Mairead Martin; *Head, Digitization & Presv Dept,* Sue Kellerman; *Head, Libr Serv,* Debora Cheney; Tel: 814-863-1345, E-mail: dlc13@psu.edu; *Asst Head, Access Serv,* Barbara Coopey; *Archivist, Spec Coll Cat Librn,* Ann Copeland; *Mgr, Pub Relations & Mkt,* Catherine S Grigor; Tel: 814-863-4240, Fax: 814-865-2344, E-mail: cqg3@psu.edu; *Electronic Res,* James Jamison; Tel: 814-867-0886, E-mail: jaj115@psu.edu; *Univ Archivist,* Jackie Esposito; Staff 531 (MLS 161, Non-MLS 370)
Founded 1857. Enrl 91,061; Fac 5,625; Highest Degree: Doctorate
Library Holdings: Bk Vols 5,365,489; Per Subs 99,091
Special Collections: Ambit Magazine Archives; American Literature (Hay & Pattee Coll); Amy Bonner Coll; Australiana (Moody & Sutherland Coll), bks & pictures; Barbara Hackman Franklin Papers; Be Glad Then America, opera recs & papers; Bibles (Plumb Coll); Black Literature Coll; Boal Family Papers; Christopher Logue Papers; Conrad Richter Coll, ms; Edward Lucie-Smith Papers; Eric A Walker Papers; Erwin Mueller Papers; Eugene Wettstone Coll; Evan Pugh Coll & Papers; Fay S Lincoln Photography Coll; Fred L Pattee Papers; Fred Waring Archives & Music Library; George M Rhodes Papers; George W Atherton Papers; German-American Literature (Allison-Shelley Coll), bks, ms; Glass Bottle Blowers Association Archives; Henry M Shoemaker Coll; I W Abel Papers; Jacques Brunius Coll; John C Griffiths Papers; John O'Hara Coll; Joseph Priestley Coll; Kenneth Burke Coll; Maurice Goddard Papers; National Committee for Citizens in Education Archives; Noran Kersta Television History Coll; Pennsylvania AFL-CIO Archives; Pennsylvania Art Education Association Archives; Pennsylvania German Imprints (Ammon Stapleton Coll); Pennsylvania Imprints; Peter Porter Coll; Ramon del Valle-Inclan Coll; Richard Henry Stoddard & Elizabeth Drew Barstow Stoddard Coll, ms; Roxburghe Club Coll; Russell E Marker Papers; Science Fiction Coll; Sebastian Martorana Papers; United Wallpaper Craftsmen of North America Archives; Vance Packard Papers; Warren S Smith Papers; William C Darrah Cartes de Visite Coll; William Frear Papers; William G Waring Papers
Subject Interests: Agr, Archit, Art, Behav sci, Commonwealth, Feminism, Hist, Latin Am lit, Natural sci, Soc sci
Wireless access
Function: Archival coll, AV serv, Distance learning, Doc delivery serv, E-Reserves, Electronic databases & coll, Family literacy, Homebound delivery serv, ILL available, Libr develop, Online info literacy tutorials on the web & in blackboard, Photocopying/Printing, Ref serv available
Publications: Guide to the University Libraries; Library Bibliographical Series; The Library (Newsletter)
Partic in Association of Research Libraries (ARL); Committee on Institutional Cooperation; OCLC Online Computer Library Center, Inc; Pennsylvania Academic Library Consortium, Inc (PALCI)
Special Services for the Blind - Assistive/Adapted tech devices, equip & products; Low vision equip; Reader equip; Reading & writing aids; ZoomText magnification & reading software

Departmental Libraries:

ARCHITECTURE & LANDSCAPE ARCHITECTURE, 111 Stuckeman Family Bldg, 16802-1912. SAN 359-6044. Tel: 814-865-3614. FAX: 814-865-5073. E-mail: qum7@psu.edu. Web Site: www.libraries.psu.edu/psul/architecture.html. *Head Librn,* Henry Pisciotta; Tel: 814-865-3665, E-mail: henryp@psu.edu; Staff 4 (MLS 1, Non-MLS 3)

FLETCHER L BYROM EARTH & MINERAL SCIENCES LIBRARY, 105 Deike Bldg, 16802, SAN 359-6079. Tel: 814-865-9517. FAX: 814-865-1379. Web Site: www.libraries.psu.edu/psul/emsl.html. *Head of Libr,* Linda Musser; Tel: 814-863-7073, E-mail: lrm4@psu.edu; *Sci Librn,* Robert L Tolliver; E-mail: rlt17@psu.edu; Staff 4 (MLS 2, Non-MLS 2)
Founded 1931. Highest Degree: Doctorate
Subject Interests: Earth sci, Geog, Mat sci, Meteorology, Mining

EBERLY FAMILY SPECIAL COLLECTIONS LIBRARY, 104 Paterno Library, 16802-1808. Tel: 814-865-1793, 814-865-7931. FAX: 814-863-5318. Web Site: www.libraries.psu.edu/psul/speccolls.html. *Head & Dorothy Foehr Huck Chair,* Timothy D Pyatt; E-mail: tdp11@psu.edu; *Head, Hist Coll & Labor Archives,* James Quigel; Tel: 814-863-3181, E-mail: jpq1@psu.edu; *Curator of Rare Bks & Ms,* Sandra K Stelts; Tel: 814-863-5388, E-mail: sks5@psu.edu; Staff 21 (MLS 4, Non-MLS 17)
Founded 1904. Highest Degree: Doctorate
Subject Interests: Archives, Manuscripts, Rare bks
Open Mon-Thurs 8-6, Fri 8-5, Sun 4-8
Restriction: Non-circulating

EDUCATION & BEHAVIORAL SCIENCES, 501 Paterno Library, 16802-1812, SAN 371-8638. Tel: 814-865-2842. Web Site: www.libraries.psu.edu/psul/ebsl.html. *Dir, Pa Ctr for the Bk, Head Librn,* Steven Herb; Tel: 814-863-2141, E-mail: slh18@psu.edu; *Asst Dir, Pa Ctr for the Bk, Educ & Behav Sci Librn,* Karla M Schmit; Tel:

814-863-5521, E-mail: kms454@psu.edu; *Asst Head, Learning Serv, Educ & Behav Sci Librn,* Ellysa Stern Cahoy; E-mail: esc10@psu.edu; Staff 6 (MLS 3, Non-MLS 3)

ENGINEERING, 325 Hammond Bldg, 16802, SAN 359-6109. Tel: 814-865-3451. FAX: 814-863-5989. Web Site: www.libraries.psu.edu/psul/eng.html. *Eng Librn,* Angela R Davis; Tel: 814-865-7005, E-mail: ard21@psu.edu; *Eng Librn,* Vanessa Eyer; Tel: 814-865-3698, E-mail: vld5011@psu.edu; *Eng Librn,* Bonnie Osif; Tel: 814-865-3697, E-mail: bao2@psu.edu; Staff 7 (MLS 3, Non-MLS 4)

THE DONALD W HAMER MAPS LIBRARY, 001 Pattee Library, B-level, Curtin Rd, 16802-1807. Tel: 814-863-0094. E-mail: maproom@psu.edu. Web Site: www.libraries.psu.edu/psul/maps.html. *Head of Libr,* Helen Sheehy; E-mail: hms2@psu.edu; Staff 3 (MLS 1, Non-MLS 2)

LIBRARY LEARNING SERVICES, 305 Pattee Library, Tower, 16802-1803. Tel: 814-865-9257. FAX: 814-865-3665. Web Site: www.libraries.psu.edu/psul/lls.html. *Head, Learning Serv,* Loanne Snavely; Tel: 814-865-3064, Fax: 814-865-9256, E-mail: lls11@psu.edu; *Info Literacy Librn,* Anne Behler; Tel: 814-863-3832, E-mail: acb10@psu.edu; *Info Literacy Librn,* Glenn N Masuchika; Tel: 814-867-2229, E-mail: gnm1@psu.edu; *Info Literacy Librn, Learning Technologies Coordr, Sally W Kalin Librn, Learning Innovations,* Emily Rimland; Tel: 814-863-7355, E-mail: elf113@psu.edu; *Learning Design Librn,* Amanda S Clossen; Tel: 814-863-7455, E-mail: asc17@psu.edu; *Ref Librn,* Dawn Amsberry; Tel: 814-865-5093, E-mail: dua4@psu.edu; Staff 10 (MLS 6, Non-MLS 4)

LIFE SCIENCES, 401 Paterno Library, 16802-1811. Tel: 814-865-7056. Web Site: www.libraries.psu.edu/psul/lifesciences.html. *Head Librn,* Amy Paster; Tel: 814-865-3708, E-mail: alp4@psu.edu; *Librn,* Kathy Fescemyer; Tel: 814-865-3703, E-mail: kaf12@psu.edu; *Librn,* Nancy Henry; Tel: 814-863-3713, E-mail: nih1@psu.edu; *Librn,* Janet Hughes; Tel: 814-865-3705, E-mail: jah19@psu.edu; *Librn,* Helen Smith; Tel: 814-865-3706, E-mail: hfs1@psu.edu. Subject Specialists: *Entomology, Mycology, Turfgrass,* Amy Paster; *Entomology, Plant sci,* Kathy Fescemyer; *Biological sci,* Janet Hughes; *Agr sci,* Helen Smith; Staff 7 (MLS 5, Non-MLS 2)
Founded 1888. Highest Degree: Doctorate
Special Collections: Kneebone Mushroom Reference Library

GEORGE & SHERRY MIDDLEMAS ARTS & HUMANITIES LIBRARY, Pennsylvania State University, W 202 Pattee Library, 16802-1801. Tel: 814-865-6481. FAX: 814-863-7502. Web Site: www.libraries.psu.edu/psul/artshumanities.html. *Actg Head, Libr,* Eric Novotny; Tel: 814-865-1014, E-mail: ecn1@psu.edu; *Librn,* Jade Atwill; Tel: 814-863-0738, E-mail: yya2@psu.edu; *Librn,* Amanda Maple; Tel: 814-863-1401, E-mail: alm8@psu.edu; *Librn,* Henry Pisciotta; Tel: 814-863-6778, E-mail: hap10@psu.edu; *Humanities Liaison Librn,* Manuel Ostos; Tel: 814-865-3693, E-mail: muo16@psu.edu; *Humanities Librn for Technological Innovations, Sally W Kalin Librn,* C Dawn Childress; Tel: 814-865-0660, E-mail: cdc17@psu.edu; *Paterno Family Librn for Lit,* William Brockman; Tel: 814-865-9718, E-mail: uxb5@psu.edu; *Tombros Librn for Classics & Humanities,* Charles E Jones; Tel: 814-867-4872, E-mail: cej14@psu.edu. Subject Specialists: *Hist, Middle Eastern studies, Philos of sci,* Eric Novotny; *Asian studies,* Jade Atwill; *Dance, Music,* Amanda Maple; *Archit, Arts,* Henry Pisciotta; Staff 10 (MLS 8, Non-MLS 2)
Open Mon-Thurs 7:45am-10pm, Fri 7:45-5, Sat 10-5, Sun 1-10

NEWS & MICROFORMS LIBRARY, 21 Pattee Library, 16802-1804. Tel: 814-863-0377. Web Site: www.libraries.psu.edu/psul/nml.html. *Actg Head, Libr,* Eric Novotny; E-mail: enc1@psu.edu; Staff 4 (MLS 1, Non-MLS 3)

PHYSICAL & MATHEMATICAL SCIENCES, 201 Davey Lab, 16802-6301, SAN 359-6168. Tel: 814-865-7617. FAX: 814-865-2565. Web Site: www.libraries.psu.edu/psul/pams.html. *Librn,* Nancy J Butkovich; Tel: 814-865-3716, E-mail: njb2@psu.edu; *Sci Librn,* John J Meier; Tel: 814-867-1448, E-mail: meier@psu.edu. Subject Specialists: *Math, Statistics,* Nancy J Butkovich; Staff 4 (MLS 2, Non-MLS 2)
Founded 2005
Special Collections: US Patent Depository
Subject Interests: Astronomy, Astrophysics, Chem, Math, Physics, Statistics

WILLIAM & JOAN SCHREYER BUSINESS LIBRARY, 301 Paterno Library, 16802-1810. Tel: 814-865-6369. FAX: 814-863-6370. E-mail: business_ref@psulias.psu.edu. Web Site: www.libraries.psu.edu/psul/business.html. *Actg Head Librn,* Diane W Zabel; Tel: 814-865-1013, E-mail: dxz2@psu.edu; *Foster Communications Librn,* Jeffrey A Knapp; *Librn,* Kevin Harwell; Tel: 814-865-0141, E-mail: krh@psulias.psu.edu; *Bus Liaison Librn,* Lauren Reiter; Tel: 814-865-4414, E-mail: lmr29@psu.edu; *Info, Sci & Tech Bus Liaison Librn,* Penny Huffman; Tel: 814-865-6493, E-mail: jph22@psu.edu; Staff 6 (MLS 4, Non-MLS 2)

SOCIAL SCIENCES, 201 Paterno Library, 16802-1809. Tel: 814-865-4861. FAX: 814-865-1403. Web Site: www.libraries.psu.edu/psul/socialsciences.html. *Head of Libr,* Helen M Sheehy; Tel: 814-863-1347, E-mail: hms2@psu.edu; *Librn,* Sylvia A Owiny; Tel: 814-865-8864, E-mail: san17@psu.edu; *Librn,* Vernon Schlotzhauer; Tel: 814-863-4644, E-mail: vxs120@psu.edu; *Ref Librn,* Paula Contreras; Tel: 814-865-3621, E-mail: pcc10@psu.edu; *Ref Librn,* Cheryl McCallips; Tel: 814-863-1365, E-mail: cam42@psu.edu; *US Govt Doc Librn,* Stephen Woods; Tel: 814-865-0665, E-mail: sjw31@psu.edu. Subject Specialists: *Law, Polit sci,* Helen M Sheehy; *African-Am studies, Ethnic studies,* Sylvia A Owiny; *African studies, Anthrop, Global studies,* Vernon Schlotzhauer; *Criminal justice, Sociol,* Stephen Woods; Staff 8 (MLS 6, Non-MLS 2)
Library Holdings: Per Subs 1,200

UPPER BURRELL

C PENNSYLVANIA STATE UNIVERSITY, NEW KENSINGTON*, Elisabeth S Blissell Library, 3550 Seventh St Rd, Rte 780, 15068-1798. SAN 314-8149. Tel: 724-334-6071. FAX: 724-334-6113. Web Site: www.libraries.psu.edu/newken/. *Head Librn,* Jennifer R Gilley; Tel: 724-334-6076, E-mail: jrg15@psu.edu; *Ref Librn,* Amy Rustic; Tel: 724-334-6072, E-mail: aer123@psu.edu; Staff 2 (Non-MLS 2)
Founded 1958. Enrl 983; Fac 40
Library Holdings: Bk Vols 36,000; Per Subs 100
Partic in OCLC Online Computer Library Center, Inc; RLIN (Research Libraries Information Network)
Open Mon-Thurs (Winter) 8am-9pm, Fri 8-5, Sun 1-5; Mon-Thurs (Summer) 8-7, Fri 8-5

UPPER DARBY

P UPPER DARBY TOWNSHIP & SELLERS MEMORIAL FREE PUBLIC LIBRARY*, 76 S State Rd, 19082. SAN 359-6192. Tel: 610-789-4440. Reference FAX: 610-789-6363. Administration FAX: 610-789-5319. E-mail: upperdarby@delcolibraries.org. Web Site: www.udlibraries.org. *Dir, Libr Serv,* Nancy L Hallowell; *Asst Dir, Tech Serv,* Elaine Irwin; E-mail: techservices@udlibraries.org; *Head, Adult Serv,* Maria Polymenakos; E-mail: circservices@udlibraries.org; *Head, Ch, Head, Youth Serv,* Charlotte Ryan; E-mail: udcsd@delco.lib.pa.us; Staff 22 (MLS 9, Non-MLS 13)
Founded 1930. Pop 81,831; Circ 293,318
Jan 2007-Dec 2007 Income (Main Library and Branch(s)) $1,464,497. Mats Exp $150,516. Sal $1,051,608
Library Holdings: Bk Vols 122,050; Per Subs 251
Subject Interests: Local hist
Automation Activity & Vendor Info: (Circulation) Innovative Interfaces, Inc
Database Vendor: EBSCOhost, Gale Cengage Learning
Wireless access
Function: Homebound delivery serv, ILL available, Prog for adults, Prog for children & young adult, Ref serv available, Summer reading prog
Mem of Delaware County Library System
Open Mon-Fri 9-9, Sat 9-5, Sun (Sept-May) 1:30-5
Friends of the Library Group
Branches: 2

MUNICIPAL, 501 Bywood Ave, 19082, SAN 359-6222. Tel: 610-734-7649. FAX: 610-734-5781. *Br Librn,* Karen Healy
Library Holdings: Bk Titles 23,504; Per Subs 44
Open Mon & Tues 10-9, Wed & Thurs 10-6, Fri 10-5, Sat 10-3
Friends of the Library Group

PRIMOS BRANCH, 409 Ashland Rd, Secane, 19018, SAN 359-6249. Tel: 610-622-8091. FAX: 484-461-9026. E-mail: upperdarbyprimos@delcolibraries.org. *Br Librn,* Caroline Jushchyshyn
Library Holdings: Bk Vols 30,260; Per Subs 53
Open Mon-Thurs 9-9, Fri 9-5, Sat 10-3
Friends of the Library Group

UPPER ST CLAIR

P UPPER ST CLAIR TOWNSHIP LIBRARY*, 1820 McLaughlin Run Rd, 15241-2397. SAN 315-1204. Tel: 412-835-5540. FAX: 412-835-6763. Web Site: www.twpusc.org/library/index.html. *Dir,* Helen Palascak; *Head, Ch,* Debra Conn; *Head, Tech Serv,* Maureen Case; *Circ Coordr,* Vanessa Ryzner; Staff 11 (MLS 11)
Founded 1957. Pop 20,053; Circ 394,641
Jan 2009-Dec 2009 Income $1,030,210, City $761,106, Federal $600, County $218,504, Locally Generated Income $50,000. Mats Exp $227,000, Books $110,000, Per/Ser (Incl. Access Fees) $85,000, AV Mat $32,000. Sal $718,619
Library Holdings: AV Mats 11,724; CDs 2,825; DVDs 3,155; Large Print Bks 945; Bk Titles 94,903; Per Subs 191; Videos 1,401
Automation Activity & Vendor Info: (Acquisitions) Innovative Interfaces, Inc - Millenium; (Cataloging) Innovative Interfaces, Inc - Millenium; (Circulation) Innovative Interfaces, Inc - Millenium; (OPAC) Innovative Interfaces, Inc - Millenium; (Serials) Innovative Interfaces, Inc - Millenium
Database Vendor: SirsiDynix
Wireless access
Function: Adult bk club, After school storytime, Art exhibits, Audiobks via web, Bk club(s), Bk reviews (Group), Chess club, Children's prog, Computers for patron use, Copy machines, Digital talking bks, Fax serv,

Free DVD rentals, Holiday prog, Home delivery & serv to Sr ctr & nursing homes, Music CDs, Online cat, OverDrive digital audio bks, Photocopying/Printing, Preschool outreach, Printer for laptops & handheld devices, Prog for adults, Prog for children & young adult, Pub access computers, Summer & winter reading prog, Tax forms, Teen prog, Web-catalog, Wheelchair accessible
Mem of Allegheny County Library Association
Open Mon-Thurs 9:30-9, Fri & Sat 9:30-5, Sun (Sept-May) 1-5
Friends of the Library Group

R WESTMINSTER PRESBYTERIAN CHURCH LIBRARY*, 2040 Washington Rd, 15241. SAN 315-1220. Tel: 412-835-6630. FAX: 412-835-5690. Web Site: www.westminster-church.org. *Head Librn,* Tom Sanders; E-mail: tsanders1018@hotmail.com; *Coordr,* Mary Kay Mitchell; E-mail: mitchell@westminster-church.org
Library Holdings: Bk Vols 5,000
Friends of the Library Group

VALLEY FORGE

S HOUGHTON INTERNATIONAL*, Technical Center Library, Madison & Van Buren Aves, 19482. (Mail add: PO Box 930, 19482-0930), SAN 314-8246. Tel: 610-666-4121. FAX: 610-666-7354. *Librn,* Nan Burch; E-mail: nburch@houghtonintl.com; Staff 1 (Non-MLS 1)
Founded 1921
Library Holdings: Bk Titles 7,291; Bk Vols 7,542; Per Subs 181
Subject Interests: Analytical tech, Biol, Chem, Hydraulic oils, Metal working proc, Microbiology
Restriction: Staff use only

VANDERGRIFT

P VANDERGRIFT PUBLIC LIBRARY ASSOCIATION*, 128C Washington Ave, 15690-1214. SAN 315-2952. Tel: 724-568-2212. FAX: 724-568-3862. E-mail: vandergriftpubliclibrary@comcast.net. Web Site: vandergriftpubliclibrary.org. *Dir,* Charlene Hoffer
Founded 1901. Pop 5,904; Circ 23,963
Library Holdings: Bk Titles 19,000; Per Subs 40
Mem of Westmoreland County Federated Library System
Open Mon, Tues & Thurs 1-8, Wed 10-8, Fri 10-5, Sat 8-3

VENANGO

P CLARK MEMORIAL LIBRARY*, 21713 Cussewago St, 16440. (Mail add: PO Box 197, 16440-0197), SAN 315-2960. Tel: 814-398-9956. *Librn,* Allie Lasher; Staff 1 (Non-MLS 1)
Pop 310; Circ 1,389
Library Holdings: Bk Titles 5,784; Bk Vols 6,112; Per Subs 14
Partic in Crawford County Federated Libr Bd; Ocean State Libraries
Open Tues & Thurs 6-8, Sat 10-1

VILLANOVA

S DEVEREUX FOUNDATION*, Behavioral Healthcare Library, 444 Devereux Dr, 19085. (Mail add: PO Box 638, 19085-0638), SAN 321-6349. Tel: 610-542-3056. Interlibrary Loan Service Tel: 610-542-3051. FAX: 610-542-3092. *Dir,* Wanda Newton; E-mail: wnewton@devereux.org; *Assoc Librn,* Christina Evans; E-mail: cevans2@devereux.org
Founded 1957
Library Holdings: Bk Titles 2,100; Per Subs 135
Special Collections: Mental Health (ICTR Coll), A-tapes; Psychology (ICTR Psychodiagnostic Test Coll)
Subject Interests: Psychiat, Spec educ
Automation Activity & Vendor Info: (OPAC) Sydney
Partic in DEVIC; Dialog Corp; Docline; National Network of Libraries of Medicine New England Region; OCLC Online Computer Library Center, Inc
Open Mon-Fri 9-5

S ENVIRONMENTAL RESEARCH ASSOCIATES INC LIBRARY*, PO Box 219, 19085-0219. SAN 372-9354. Tel: 610-449-7400. FAX: 610-449-7404. *Librn,* Dr M H Levin
Library Holdings: Bk Titles 2,670; Bk Vols 3,100; Per Subs 35
Restriction: Not open to pub

C VILLANOVA UNIVERSITY*, Falvey Memorial Library, 800 Lancaster Ave, 19085. SAN 359-6346. Tel: 610-519-4270. Circulation Tel: 610-519-4271. Interlibrary Loan Service Tel: 610-519-4274. Reference Tel: 610-519-4273. Administration Tel: 610-519-4291. FAX: 610-519-5018. Web Site: www.library.villanova.edu. *Dean of Libr,* Joseph Lucia; Tel: 610-519-4290, E-mail: joseph.lucia@villanova.edu; Staff 26 (MLS 19, Non-MLS 7)
Founded 1842. Enrl 10,367; Fac 570; Highest Degree: Doctorate
Jun 2005-May 2006 Income (Main Library Only) $4,544,800. Mats Exp $3,094,143, Books $656,500, Per/Ser (Incl. Access Fees) $1,668,500, Manu Arch $34,000, Micro $65,000, AV Equip $8,143, AV Mat $50,000, Electronic Ref Mat (Incl. Access Fees) $550,000, Presv $62,000. Sal $2,680,462 (Prof $1,616,698)
Library Holdings: AV Mats 6,980; e-books 2,425; Bk Titles 586,591; Bk Vols 682,713; Per Subs 12,000; Talking Bks 93
Special Collections: Digital Library; Elbert G Hubbard Coll; Irish American History & Literature (Joseph McGarrity Coll); Mendel Coll; Saint Augustine Coll; Sherman-Thackara Coll. State Document Depository
Automation Activity & Vendor Info: (Acquisitions) Ex Libris Group; (Cataloging) Ex Libris Group; (Circulation) Ex Libris Group
Wireless access
Partic in Lyrasis; OCLC Online Computer Library Center, Inc; Pennsylvania Academic Library Consortium, Inc (PALCI); Philadelphia Area Consortium of Special Collections Libraries
Open Mon-Thurs 8am-Midnight, Fri 8-8, Sat 9-8, Sun 10am-Midnight

Departmental Libraries:

CL LAW LIBRARY, Garey Hall, 299 N Spring Mill Rd, 19085, SAN 359-6370. Tel: 610-519-7020. Interlibrary Loan Service Tel: 610-519-7830. Reference Tel: 610-519-7024. Administration Tel: 610-519-7022. FAX: 610-519-7033. *Assoc Dean of Libr,* Feliu Vicenc; Tel: 610-519-7023, E-mail: feliu@law.villanova.edu; *Assoc Dir, Res & Info Serv,* Amy Spare; Tel: 610-519-7188, E-mail: spare@law.villanova.edu; *Assoc Dir, Coll Mgt,* Steve Elkins; Tel: 610-519-7780, E-mail: elkins@law.villanova.edu; *Cat Librn,* Mary Jo Heacock; Tel: 610-519-7896, E-mail: heacock@law.villanova.edu; *Electronic Res Librn,* Lori Strickler; Tel: 610-519-7235, E-mail: strickler@law.villanova.edu; *Circ Coordr, Ref Librn,* Mary Cornelius; Tel: 610-519-7189, E-mail: mcorneli@law.villanova.edu; *Ref Librn,* Robert Hegadorn; Tel: 610-519-7021, E-mail: hegadorn@law.villanova.edu; *Ref Librn,* Matthew McGovern; Tel: 610-519-3893, E-mail: mcgovern@law.villanova.edu; *Circ,* Regina Kuzul; E-mail: rkuzul@law.villanova.edu; Staff 23 (MLS 10, Non-MLS 13)
Founded 1953. Enrl 750; Fac 35; Highest Degree: Doctorate
Library Holdings: Microforms 1,121,935; Bk Titles 146,361; Bk Vols 337,075; Per Subs 3,703
Special Collections: Church & State Coll. US Document Depository
Subject Interests: Tax law
Automation Activity & Vendor Info: (Acquisitions) Innovative Interfaces, Inc; (Cataloging) Innovative Interfaces, Inc; (Circulation) Innovative Interfaces, Inc; (ILL) OCLC; (OPAC) Innovative Interfaces, Inc; (Serials) Innovative Interfaces, Inc
Database Vendor: Bloomberg, HeinOnline, LexisNexis, Westlaw
Publications: New Aquisitions

WALLINGFORD

P HELEN KATE FURNESS FREE LIBRARY*, 100 N Providence Rd, 19086. SAN 315-3002. Tel: 610-566-9331. FAX: 610-566-9337. E-mail: furnesslibrary@delcolibraries.org. Web Site: www.hkflibrary.org. *Dir,* Jennifer Stock; *Ch,* Lori L Friedgen-Veitch; *Evening Ref Librn,* Maricela Ayala; *Evening Ref Librn,* Meg Hawkins; *Evening Ref Librn,* Martha Trzepacz; *Tech Serv,* Position Currently Open; Staff 5 (MLS 4, Non-MLS 1)
Founded 1902. Pop 15,000; Circ 76,500
Library Holdings: Bk Titles 44,400; Per Subs 90; Talking Bks 392
Wireless access
Mem of Delaware County Library System
Open Mon-Thurs 10-5 & 7-9, Fri 10-5, Sat 10-3, Sun 1-4

R OHEV SHALOM SYNAGOGUE, Ray Doblitz Memorial Library, Two Chester Rd, 19086. SAN 315-3010. Tel: 610-874-1465. FAX: 610-874-1466. E-mail: library@ohev.net. Web Site: www.ohev.net. *Librn,* Amy Graham
Founded 1955
Library Holdings: Bk Titles 5,300; Bk Vols 5,500; Per Subs 14
Subject Interests: Judaica
Automation Activity & Vendor Info: (Cataloging) JayWil Software Development, Inc
Wireless access

R PENDLE HILL LIBRARY*, 338 Plush Mill Rd, 19086. SAN 372-9281. Tel: 610-566-4507. Toll Free Tel: 800-742-3150. FAX: 610-566-3679. E-mail: info@pendlehill.org. Web Site: www.pendlehill.org. *Librn,* Position Currently Open
Library Holdings: Bk Vols 8,000; Per Subs 20
Subject Interests: Quakers, Relig
Wireless access

WARMINSTER

R NESHAMINY-WARWICK PRESBYTERIAN CHURCH LIBRARY*, 1401 Meetinghouse Rd, 18974. SAN 315-3037. Tel: 215-343-6060. *Librn,* Bernard E Deitrick
Founded 1959

Library Holdings: CDs 250; DVDs 100; Bk Titles 8,600; Per Subs 10; Videos 450
Special Collections: History of Presbyterians in Local Area
Subject Interests: Christian educ, Inspirational lit, Relig studies
Publications: Church & Synagogue Libraries
Open Mon-Fri 9-5, Sun 9-12:30

P WARMINSTER TOWNSHIP FREE LIBRARY*, 1076 Emma Lane, 18974. SAN 315-3053. Tel: 215-672-4362. FAX: 215-672-3604. Web Site: www.warminstertownship.org/public-services/library. *Dir,* Peggy Lindner; E-mail: plindner@warminsterpa.org; *Adult Serv,* Lisa Clancy; E-mail: clancyl@bucklib.org; *Children's & Teen Serv,* Katie Hansen; E-mail: swallowk@buckslib.org; Staff 11.97 (MLS 3.37, Non-MLS 8.6)
Founded 1960. Pop 31,875; Circ 221,485
Jan 2006-Dec 2006 Income $687,580, State $147,364, City $452,921, Locally Generated Income $87,295. Mats Exp $102,694, Books $76,365, Per/Ser (Incl. Access Fees) $5,321, Micro $262, AV Equip $2,522, AV Mat $14,099, Presv $4,125. Sal $497,181
Library Holdings: AV Mats 5,720; Bk Vols 100,936; Per Subs 91
Automation Activity & Vendor Info: (Circulation) SIRSI WorkFlows; (OPAC) SIRSI-iBistro
Wireless access
Function: Bk club(s), Bks on cassette, Bks on CD, Children's prog, Computers for patron use, Copy machines, E-Reserves, Electronic databases & coll, ILL available, Music CDs, Online cat, Online searches, OverDrive digital audio bks, Photocopying/Printing, Prog for adults, Prog for children & young adult, Pub access computers, Spoken cassettes & CDs, Spoken cassettes & DVDs, Summer reading prog, Tax forms, Teen prog, VHS videos, Web-catalog
Publications: Newsletter
Mem of Bucks County Free Library
Open Mon-Wed 10-9, Thurs & Sat 10-5, Fri 12-5
Friends of the Library Group

WARREN

S WARREN COUNTY HISTORICAL SOCIETY*, Library & Archives, 210 Fourth Ave, 16365. (Mail add: PO Box 427, 16365-0427), SAN 327-0459. Tel: 814-723-1795. FAX: 814-723-1795. E-mail: warrenhistory@kinzua.net. Web Site: www.warrenhistory.org. *Managing Dir,* Michelle Gray; *Prog Coordr,* Emily Sailor; *Curator,* Jennifer Mazzu; Staff 3 (Non-MLS 3)
Founded 1900
Library Holdings: Bk Vols 2,200
Special Collections: Allegheny River Travel & History; Chief Cornplanter & the Seneca Indians; Historic Images 1900-2000; Horton Genealogy Coll; Lieutenant Governor Stone Coll
Subject Interests: Local hist
Publications: Cavalcade-Warren County's Second Century; Stepping Stones Magazine, 1955-Present
Open Mon-Fri 8:30-4:30, Sat (April-Nov) 9-Noon
Restriction: Not a lending libr

M WARREN GENERAL HOSPITAL*, Health Sciences Library, Two Crescent Park W, 16365. SAN 370-6931. Tel: 814-723-4973, Ext 1825. FAX: 814-723-3785. Automation Services FAX: 814-723-2248. *Dir,* Nancy Bean; E-mail: bnancy@wgh.org; Staff 1 (Non-MLS 1)
Library Holdings: Bk Titles 800; Per Subs 100
Database Vendor: OVID Technologies
Partic in National Network of Libraries of Medicine
Restriction: Staff use only

P WARREN LIBRARY ASSOCIATION*, Warren Public Library, 205 Market St, 16365. SAN 315-3061. Tel: 814-723-4650. FAX: 814-723-4521. E-mail: wla@westpa.net. Web Site: www.warrenlibrary.org. *Dir,* Patricia Sherbondy; E-mail: psherbondy@warrenlibrary.org; *IT & Security Mgr,* Barbara Tracey; E-mail: btracey@warrenlibrary.org; *Adult Serv,* Sharon Gage; E-mail: sgage@warrenlibrary.org; *Cat,* Jenna Derr; E-mail: jderr@warrenlibrary.org; *Ch Serv,* Susan Slater; E-mail: sslater@warrenlibrary.org; *Extn Serv,* Kelli Knapp; E-mail: kknapp@warrenlibrary.org; *ILL,* Barbara C Tubbs; E-mail: btubbs@warrenlibrary.org; *Ref,* Penelope Wolboldt; E-mail: pwolboldt@warrenlibrary.org; Staff 30 (MLS 6, Non-MLS 24)
Founded 1873. Pop 41,815; Circ 349,765
Library Holdings: Bk Vols 167,257; Per Subs 242
Special Collections: Local History; Local Newspapers 1824-current; Petroleum History Coll, bks, maps, pamphlets; Sheet Music, Popular Show Tunes, 1834-1955 (Robertson Music Coll). State Document Depository; US Document Depository
Automation Activity & Vendor Info: (Cataloging) SirsiDynix; (Circulation) SirsiDynix; (OPAC) SirsiDynix
Database Vendor: OCLC WorldShare Interlibrary Loan, ReferenceUSA, SirsiDynix
Wireless access
Publications: The Fulcrum (Newsletter)
Open Mon-Thurs 10-8, Fri & Sat 10-5
Friends of the Library Group

WASHINGTON

P CITIZENS LIBRARY*, 55 S College St, 15301. SAN 315-3088. Tel: 724-222-2400. Circulation Tel: 724-222-2400, Ext 222. Interlibrary Loan Service Tel: 724-222-2400, Ext 225. Reference Tel: 724-222-2400, Ext 223. FAX: 724-222-2606. E-mail: citlib@citlib.org. Web Site: www.washlibs.org/Citizens. *Dir,* Diane L Ambrose; E-mail: ambrose@citlib.org; *Asst Dir, District Consult Librn,* Melinda Tanner; E-mail: mtanner@citlib.org; *Genealogy Librn,* Ella Hatfield; E-mail: ehatfield@citlib.org; *Ch Mgr,* Rebecca Smiley; E-mail: rsmiley@citlib.org; *Circ Serv Mgr,* Kathy Pienkowski; E-mail: kpien@citlib.org; *Coll Develop Mgr,* Carol Levy; E-mail: clevy@citlib.org; *Digital Serv Mgr,* Jackie Wright; E-mail: jwright@citlib.org; *ILL Mgr,* Bret Stiffler; E-mail: bstiffler@citlib.org; *Circ Asst,* Taryn King; E-mail: tking@citlib.org; *Teen Serv,* Katy Pretz; E-mail: kpretz@citlib.org; Staff 7 (MLS 7)
Founded 1870. Pop 54,519; Circ 170,024
Special Collections: Genealogy & Local History (Iams Coll), ms. State Document Depository
Automation Activity & Vendor Info: (Acquisitions) Innovative Interfaces, Inc; (Cataloging) Innovative Interfaces, Inc; (Circulation) Innovative Interfaces, Inc; (OPAC) Innovative Interfaces, Inc
Database Vendor: EBSCOhost, ProQuest
Wireless access
Function: Archival coll, ILL available
Partic in Asn for Libr Info; OCLC Online Computer Library Center, Inc
Special Services for the Deaf - Bks on deafness & sign lang; High interest/low vocabulary bks; Spec interest per; TDD equip
Open Mon-Thurs 10-8, Fri & Sat 10-5:30
Friends of the Library Group

J PENN COMMERCIAL BUSINESS/TECHNICAL SCHOOL*, 242 Oak Spring Rd, 15301-2871. Tel: 724-222-5330. Toll Free Tel: 888-309-7484. FAX: 724-222-4722. Web Site: www.penncommercial.net. *Librn,* Ellen Deutsch; Staff 2 (MLS 1, Non-MLS 1)
Founded 1929
Library Holdings: Bk Titles 2,120; Bk Vols 2,350; Per Subs 29
Open Mon-Fri 8-5

C WASHINGTON & JEFFERSON COLLEGE LIBRARY*, U Grant Miller Library, 60 S Lincoln St, 15301. SAN 315-310X. Tel: 724-223-6070. Reference Tel: 724-223-6072. Administration Tel: 724-223-6071. FAX: 724-223-5272. Web Site: www.washjeff.edu/library. *Dir, Tech Serv, Interim Dir, Libr Serv, Librn,* Rebecca H Keenan; Tel: 724-223-6069, E-mail: rkeenan@washjeff.edu; *Circ Supvr,* Rachael Bolden; E-mail: rbolden@washjeff.edu; *Acq, Tech Serv,* Cheri L Duball; Tel: 724-223-6104, E-mail: cduball@washjeff.edu; *Archives, Coll, Tech Serv,* Anna Mae Moore; Tel: 724-223-6068, E-mail: amoore@washjeff.edu; *Metadata Librn,* Alexis D Rittenberger; Tel: 724-503-1001, Ext 3039, E-mail: arittenberger@washjeff.edu; *Ser, Tech Serv,* Carla V Myers; Tel: 724-223-6547, E-mail: cmyers@washjeff.edu; *Syst,* Jayne Silfee; Tel: 724-223-6071, E-mail: jsilfee@washjeff.edu; Staff 5 (MLS 5)
Founded 1781
Library Holdings: AV Mats 8,484; e-books 13,000; Bk Titles 153,257; Bk Vols 161,130; Per Subs 522
Special Collections: College History; Washington County (Historical); Western Pennsylvania & Upper Ohio Valley, mss
Subject Interests: Behav sci, Hist, Natural sci, Soc sci
Automation Activity & Vendor Info: (Acquisitions) SirsiDynix; (Cataloging) SirsiDynix; (Circulation) SirsiDynix; (Course Reserve) SirsiDynix; (OPAC) SirsiDynix; (Serials) SirsiDynix
Partic in Dialog Corp; Lyrasis; OCLC Online Computer Library Center, Inc; OHIONET
Open Mon-Thurs 8am-2am, Fri 8am-9pm, Sat 9-6, Sun 11am-2am

S WASHINGTON COUNTY HISTORICAL SOCIETY LIBRARY*, 49 E Maiden St, 15301. SAN 327-0637. Tel: 724-225-6740. FAX: 724-225-8495. Interlibrary Loan Service E-mail: info@wchspa.org. Web Site: www.wchspa.org. *Admin Dir,* James Ross
Founded 1900
Library Holdings: Bk Titles 1,847
Special Collections: Military History of Washington County
Open Tues-Fri 11-4

GL WASHINGTON COUNTY LAW LIBRARY*, One S Main St, Ste G004, 15301-6813. SAN 315-3118. Tel: 724-228-6747. Web Site: www.washingtoncourts.us/pages/lawLibrary.aspx. *Law Librn,* Jamie Yancich; E-mail: jamie.yancich@washingtoncourts.us; *Asst Law Librn,* Megan Beekman; Tel: 724-250-4026; Staff 2 (MLS 1, Non-MLS 1)
Founded 1867
Jan 2009-Dec 2009 Income $204,271. Mats Exp $107,500. Sal $71,407
Library Holdings: Bk Titles 1,250; Bk Vols 22,000; Per Subs 20; Spec Interest Per Sub 19

Subject Interests: Legal res, Local hist
Database Vendor: LexisNexis, Westlaw
Open Mon-Fri 9-4:30
Restriction: Non-circulating to the pub

M WASHINGTON HOSPITAL*, Health Sciences Libraries, 155 Wilson Ave, 15301-3398. SAN 315-3126. Tel: 724-223-3144. FAX: 724-223-4096. *Dir,* Heidi L Marshall; E-mail: hmarshall@washingtonhospital.org; Staff 4 (MLS 1, Non-MLS 3)
Founded 1927
Library Holdings: Bk Vols 2,500
Subject Interests: Family practice, Internal med, Med, Nursing
Open Mon-Fri 7:30-4

WASHINGTON CROSSING

S DAVID LIBRARY OF THE AMERICAN REVOLUTION*, 1201 River Rd, 18977. (Mail add: PO Box 748, 18977-0748), SAN 315-3134. Tel: 215-493-6776. FAX: 215-493-9276. Administration FAX: 215-493-5492. Web Site: www.dlar.org. *Chief Operating Officer,* Meg McSweeney; Tel: 215-493-6776, Ext 106, E-mail: mcsweeney@dlar.org; *Librn,* Katherine A Ludwig; Tel: 215-493-6776, Ext 102, E-mail: librarian@dlar.org; *Fac Mgr,* Anthony M Russo; Tel: 215-493-6776, Ext 110, E-mail: tony@dlar.org
Founded 1959
Jan 2006-Dec 2006. Mats Exp $40,800, Books $20,000, Per/Ser (Incl. Access Fees) $800, Micro $10,000, AV Mat $5,000, Presv $5,000
Library Holdings: Bk Titles 8,000; Per Subs 25
Special Collections: 18th Century American Manuscripts (Sol Feinstone Coll); American History - circa 1750-1800 (18th & Early 19th Century), pamphlets, rare bks
Subject Interests: Am hist, Am Revolution
Automation Activity & Vendor Info: (OPAC) EOS International
Function: Res libr
Publications: Guide to Sol Feinstone Collection of the David Library of the American Revolution (Library handbook)
Open Tues-Sat 10-5
Restriction: Non-circulating

WATERFORD

P WATERFORD PUBLIC LIBRARY*, 24 S Park Row, 16441. (Mail add: PO Box 820, 16441-0820), SAN 315-3150. Tel: 814-796-4729. FAX: 814-796-4729. E-mail: wplpa@velocity.net. Web Site: www.waterfordlibrary.org. *Librn,* Bethany Schaaf; Staff 2 (Non-MLS 2)
Founded 1936. Pop 1,517; Circ 21,476
Jul 2011-Jun 2012 Income $39,107, State $3,742, City $12,942, County $6,795, Locally Generated Income $15,628. Mats Exp $7,578
Library Holdings: Audiobooks 312; Bk Vols 18,196; Per Subs 29
Automation Activity & Vendor Info: (Circulation) SirsiDynix; (OPAC) SirsiDynix
Wireless access
Open Mon & Fri 1-5, Tues 10-2, Wed 11-5, Thurs 7pm-9pm, Sat 9-3

WAVERLY

P WAVERLY MEMORIAL LIBRARY*, 1115 N Abington Rd, 18471. (Mail add: PO Box 142, 18471-0142), SAN 315-3169. Tel: 570 586 8191. FAX: 570-586-0185. E-mail: info@waverlycomm.org. Web Site: www.waverlycomm.com. *Exec Dir,* Maria Wilson
Pop 1,800; Circ 4,100
Library Holdings: Bk Vols 3,000
Subject Interests: Children's bks, Fiction
Open Mon-Fri 9-5, Sat 10-12

WAYMART

S STATE CORRECTIONAL INSTITUTION*, Waymart Library, PO Box 256, 18472-0256. Tel: 570-488-5811. FAX: 570-488-2551, 570-488-2609. *Librn,* Maria Suhadolnik
Library Holdings: Bk Vols 5,000; Per Subs 40
Automation Activity & Vendor Info: (Cataloging) Follett Software; (Circulation) Follett Software
Open Mon-Fri 8-8, Sat & Sun 8-4

WAYNE

P RADNOR MEMORIAL LIBRARY*, 114 W Wayne Ave, 19087-4098. SAN 315-3185. Tel: 610-687-1124. Information Services Tel: 610-687-1124, Ext 21. FAX: 610-687-1454. E-mail: radnor@delcolibraries.org. Web Site: www.radnorlibrary.org. *Exec Dir,* Kathy Mulroy; *Head, Ch,* Carrie Sturgill; *Head, Info Serv,* Joanne Iantorno; Staff 12 (MLS 5, Non-MLS 7)
Founded 1892. Pop 46,872; Circ 256,811
Library Holdings: AV Mats 9,362; Bk Vols 109,421; Per Subs 209
Special Collections: Pennsylvania History; Reader Development Coll. Oral History
Subject Interests: Archit, Art, Drama, Foreign lang, Hist, Lit
Automation Activity & Vendor Info: (Acquisitions) Innovative Interfaces, Inc; (Cataloging) Innovative Interfaces, Inc; (Circulation) Innovative Interfaces, Inc; (Course Reserve) Innovative Interfaces, Inc; (ILL) Innovative Interfaces, Inc; (Media Booking) Innovative Interfaces, Inc; (OPAC) Innovative Interfaces, Inc; (Serials) Innovative Interfaces, Inc
Wireless access
Mem of Delaware County Library System
Open Mon-Fri 9-9, Sat 9-5, Sun 1-5
Friends of the Library Group

J VALLEY FORGE MILITARY ACADEMY & COLLEGE*, May H Baker Memorial Library, 1001 Eagle Rd, 19087-3695. SAN 315-3193. Tel: 610-989-1200, 610-989-1364. FAX: 610-975-9642. Web Site: www.vfmac.edu/academics_library.html. *Dir, Libr Serv,* Jean Smith; E-mail: jsmith@vfmac.edu; *Academy Librn,* Christine Ackerson; Tel: 610-989-1438, E-mail: cackerson@vfmac.edu; *Libr Tech,* Susan Morris; Staff 4 (MLS 2, Non-MLS 2)
Founded 1928. Enrl 535; Fac 72; Highest Degree: Associate
Library Holdings: AV Mats 500; Electronic Media & Resources 17; High Interest/Low Vocabulary Bk Vols 200; Bk Titles 50,000; Bk Vols 80,000; Per Subs 60
Special Collections: Military & Naval History Coll
Subject Interests: Classical lit, Govt, Mil sci, World hist
Automation Activity & Vendor Info: (Cataloging) Mandarin Library Automation; (Circulation) Mandarin Library Automation; (OPAC) Mandarin Library Automation
Database Vendor: CQ Press, CredoReference, EBSCO Auto Repair Reference, EBSCO Information Services, EBSCOhost, Electric Library, Facts on File, Gale Cengage Learning, JSTOR, LexisNexis, Newsbank, TLC (The Library Corporation)
Wireless access
Publications: Competency Handbook; Faculty Library Partnership Project; How to Effectively Use the Library Information; Library Policies & Procedures; PathFinders; Strategic Developmental Plan for Library Services, Plans & Operations; Webs of the Week
Partic in Lyrasis; Tri-State College Library Cooperative
Open Mon-Thurs 7:45am-10pm, Fri 7:45-4, Sat 2-5, Sun 3-10
Restriction: Badge access after hrs

R WAYNE PRESBYTERIAN CHURCH LIBRARY*, 125 E Lancaster Ave, 19087. SAN 315-3207. Tel: 610-688-8700. FAX: 610-688-8743. Web Site: www.waynepres.org. *Librn,* Leslie O'Heir
Founded 1957
Library Holdings: Bk Vols 6,000; Per Subs 15

WAYNESBURG

P EVA K BOWLBY PUBLIC LIBRARY*, 311 N West St, 15370-1238. SAN 359-6559. Tel: 724-627-9776. FAX: 724-852-1900. Web Site: www.alltel.net/bowlby. *Admin Dir,* Barbara Ferguson; *Ch Serv,* Kathy McClure; Tel: 724-727-9776, Ext 15; Staff 13 (MLS 1, Non-MLS 12)
Founded 1943. Pop 40,476; Circ 71,573
Library Holdings: Bk Vols 55,000; Per Subs 100
Special Collections: Local History Coll, rare bks; W & W Railroad (Roach Coll), photog
Subject Interests: Agr
Automation Activity & Vendor Info: (Acquisitions) Follett Software; (Cataloging) Follett Software; (Circulation) Follett Software; (Course Reserve) Follett Software; (ILL) Follett Software; (OPAC) Follett Software
Publications: Newsletter (Quarterly)
Mem of Greene County Library System
Partic in OCLC Online Computer Library Center, Inc
Open Mon 12-6, Tues & Thurs 10-8, Wed 10-6, Fri 11-5, Sat 9-3

GL GREENE COUNTY LAW LIBRARY*, Greene County Courthouse, 10 E High St, 15370. SAN 315-3223. Tel: 724-852-5237. FAX: 724-627-4716. *Court Adminr,* Sheila S Rode
Library Holdings: Bk Vols 1,250

P GREENE COUNTY LIBRARY SYSTEM*, 22 W High St, 2nd Flr, Rm 209, 15370. SAN 359-6613. Tel: 724-852-5396. E-mail: gcls@windstream.net. Web Site: www.greenecolib.org. *Syst Adminr,* Therese M Barry; Staff 3 (MLS 1, Non-MLS 2)
Founded 1976. Pop 40,476; Circ 101,969
Special Collections: Local History Coll. Municipal Document Depository; State Document Depository
Automation Activity & Vendor Info: (Cataloging) Follett Software; (Circulation) Follett Software
Wireless access
Member Libraries: Eva K Bowlby Public Library; Flenniken Public Library
Special Services for the Blind - Bks on cassette; Bks on CD; Cassettes; Large print bks; Recorded bks
Open Tues & Thurs 1-6, Wed & Sat 10-3

Friends of the Library Group
Bookmobiles: 1. Mobile Servs, Judith Saska

C WAYNESBURG COLLEGE*, Eberly Library, 93 Locust Ave, 15370-1242. SAN 315-3231. Tel: 724-852-3278. Administration Tel: 724-852-3419. FAX: 724-627-4188. E-mail: library@waynesburg.edu. Web Site: www.waynesburg.edu/depts/eberly. *Interim Dir,* Rea Andrew Redd; Tel: 724-852-3254, E-mail: rredd@waynesburg.edu; *Cat,* Beth Boehm; Tel: 724-852-7640, E-mail: bboehm@waynesburg.edu; *ILL, Syst Librn,* John Walters Thompson; Tel: 724-852-7668, E-mail: jthompso@waynesburg.edu; Staff 7 (MLS 5, Non-MLS 2)
Founded 1849. Enrl 2,159; Fac 141; Highest Degree: Master
Library Holdings: AV Mats 2,070; CDs 709; DVDs 439; Bk Titles 83,893; Bk Vols 86,702; Per Subs 395; Talking Bks 582; Videos 1,747
Special Collections: Western Pennsylvania History (Trans-Appalachian Coll)
Subject Interests: Criminal justice, Educ, Nursing
Automation Activity & Vendor Info: (Cataloging) OCLC; (Circulation) Innovative Interfaces, Inc; (Course Reserve) Innovative Interfaces, Inc; (ILL) OCLC; (OPAC) Innovative Interfaces, Inc; (Serials) EBSCO Online
Database Vendor: EBSCOhost, Innovative Interfaces, Inc
Function: Adult literacy prog, AV serv, Distance learning, ILL available, Photocopying/Printing, Res libr, Satellite serv
Publications: Library Brochure
Partic in OCLC Online Computer Library Center, Inc; OHIONET; Pittsburgh Regional Libr Consortium
Open Mon-Thurs 7:30am-Midnight, Fri 7:30-5, Sat 10-4, Sun 2-Midnight
Restriction: Open to fac, students & qualified researchers
Friends of the Library Group

WEATHERLY

P WEATHERLY AREA COMMUNITY LIBRARY*, 20 Carbon St, Unit 1, 18255. Tel: 570-427-5085. *Pres,* Ruth Isenberg
Founded 1995
Library Holdings: DVDs 10; Large Print Bks 200; Bk Vols 20,000; Per Subs 10; Talking Bks 203; Videos 103
Special Collections: Municipal Document Depository
Special Services for the Blind - Talking bks
Open Mon 10-12 & 2-5, Tues & Sat 2-5, Wed 9-12 & 3:30-5, Thurs 10-12 & 7-8:30, Fri 3:30-5

WELLSBORO

P GREEN FREE LIBRARY*, 134 Main St, 16901-1412. SAN 315-324X. Tel: 570-724-4876. FAX: 570-724-7605. E-mail: greenlib@epix.net. Web Site: www.greenfreelibrary.org. *Dir,* Leslie A Wishard; Staff 6 (MLS 1, Non-MLS 5)
Founded 1911. Pop 11,435; Circ 45,000
Jan 2006-Dec 2006 Income $230,400, State $51,700, County $12,400, Locally Generated Income $166,300. Mats Exp $50,000, Books $32,000, Per/Ser (Incl. Access Fees) $5,800, Micro $3,000, Electronic Ref Mat (Incl. Access Fees) $4,200. Sal $115,000 (Prof $30,000)
Library Holdings: AV Mats 1,100; Large Print Bks 1,300; Bk Titles 37,200; Per Subs 101
Subject Interests: Civil War, Genealogy, Local hist
Automation Activity & Vendor Info: (Cataloging) Innovative Interfaces, Inc; (Circulation) Innovative Interfaces, Inc; (OPAC) Innovative Interfaces, Inc
Database Vendor: EBSCOhost
Wireless access
Function: ILL available
Mem of Potter-Tioga Library System
Open Mon-Fri 10-8, Sat 10-5
Friends of the Library Group

WERNERSVILLE

P WERNERSVILLE PUBLIC LIBRARY*, 100 N Reber St, 19565-1412. SAN 315-3266. Tel: 610-678-8771. FAX: 610-678-3025. E-mail: wernersvillepl@berks.lib.pa.us. Web Site: www.berks.lib.pa.us/wernersvillepl. *Dir,* Janet L Moore
Founded 1906. Pop 11,791; Circ 15,000
Library Holdings: DVDs 1,000; Bk Titles 18,000; Per Subs 70; Talking Bks 900
Subject Interests: Civil War, Local hist
Wireless access
Mem of Berks County Public Libraries
Open Mon-Wed 10-8, Thurs 12-8, Sat 9-4
Friends of the Library Group

WEST CHESTER

G CHESTER COUNTY ARCHIVES & RECORDS SERVICES LIBRARY*, 601 Westtown Rd, Ste 080, 19382-4958. (Mail add: PO Box 2747, 19380-0990), SAN 323-5181. Tel: 610-344-6760. Reference Tel: 610-344-6763. FAX: 610-344-5616. E-mail: ccarchives@chesco.org. Web Site: www.chesco.org/archives. *Dir,* Laurie A Rofini; Staff 3 (MLS 1, Non-MLS 2)
Founded 1982
Special Collections: Municipal Document Depository
Subject Interests: Hist of Chester county
Function: Archival coll
Open Mon-Fri 9-4

S CHESTER COUNTY HISTORICAL SOCIETY LIBRARY*, 225 N High St, 19380. SAN 315-3304. Tel: 610-692-4800. FAX: 610-692-4357. Web Site: www.chestercohistorical.org. *Librn,* Diane P Rofini; *Archivist,* Pamela C Powell; Staff 2 (MLS 2)
Founded 1893
Library Holdings: Bk Titles 16,000; Bk Vols 25,000; Per Subs 50
Special Collections: Chester County Newspapers; Chester County School Records; Photograph Coll; Postal History Coll; William Penn (Albert Cook Myers Coll)
Subject Interests: Decorative art, Genealogy, Hist of Chester county, Local family hist, Local hist
Wireless access
Partic in OCLC Online Computer Library Center, Inc
Open Wed-Sat 10-5
Restriction: Non-circulating

M CHESTER COUNTY HOSPITAL LIBRARY*, Health Care Library, 701 E Marshall St, 19380. SAN 329-7063. Tel: 610-431-5204. FAX: 610-696-8411. *Librn,* Ginny Moll; E-mail: gmoll@cchosp.com; *Librn,* Inger Wallin; E-mail: iwallin@cchosp.com; Staff 2 (MLS 2)
Library Holdings: CDs 100; DVDs 50; e-books 110; e-journals 60; Bk Titles 1,000; Per Subs 30
Special Collections: Diversity Coll; Medical Ethics Coll
Automation Activity & Vendor Info: (Cataloging) EOS International; (Media Booking) EOS International
Database Vendor: EBSCOhost, OVID Technologies, PubMed
Wireless access
Partic in Basic Health Sciences Library Network
Open Mon-Fri 8-4:30

L CHESTER COUNTY LAW LIBRARY*, Bar Association Bldg, 15 W Gay St, 19380-3014. SAN 315-3290. Tel: 610-344-6166. FAX: 610-344-6994. E-mail: lawlibrary@chesco.org. Web Site: dsf.chesco.org. *Librn,* Jeannie Naftzger; *Asst Librn,* Ritza Hazen
Founded 1862
Library Holdings: Bk Titles 31,611; Bk Vols 33,190; Per Subs 40
Subject Interests: Pa law
Partic in Westlaw
Open Mon-Fri 8:30-4:30
Restriction: Open to pub for ref only

S EVALUATION ASSOCIATES INC LIBRARY*, 1350 Telegraph Rd, 19380. SAN 373-1103. Tel: 610-692-7686. FAX: 610-692-7687. *In Charge,* Clark Hanrahan; Staff 1 (Non-MLS 1)
Library Holdings: Bk Titles 3,290; Bk Vols 3,410; Per Subs 60
Restriction: Staff use only

R GROVE UNITED METHODIST CHURCH LIBRARY*, 490 W Boot Rd, 19380. SAN 315-3320. Tel: 610-696-2663. FAX: 610-696-5625. *Librn,* Seybold Linda; Staff 1 (Non-MLS 1)
Founded 1774
Library Holdings: Bk Titles 1,116; Bk Vols 1,208
Subject Interests: Bible, Christianity, Methodism
Open Mon-Fri 10-3

SR SWEDENBORG FOUNDATION LIBRARY, 320 N Church St, 19380. SAN 327-0319. Tel: 610-430-3222. FAX: 610-430-7982. E-mail: info@swedenborg.com. Web Site: www.swedenborg.com. *Operations Mgr,* Morgan Beard; E-mail: mbeard@swedenborg.com
Founded 1874
Library Holdings: Bk Vols 1,500
Wireless access
Open Mon-Fri 10-5

P WEST CHESTER PUBLIC LIBRARY*, 415 N Church St, 19380-2401. SAN 315-3339. Tel: 610-696-1721. FAX: 610-429-1077. E-mail: wcpubliclibrary@gmail.com. Web Site: www.wcpubliclibrary.org. *Dir,* Victoria E Dow; E-mail: vdow@ccls.org; Staff 13 (MLS 2, Non-MLS 11)
Founded 1872. Pop 60,000; Circ 155,000
Library Holdings: Bk Titles 50,000; Per Subs 110
Subject Interests: Local hist
Automation Activity & Vendor Info: (Circulation) Innovative Interfaces, Inc; (OPAC) Innovative Interfaces, Inc

Database Vendor: EBSCOhost, Innovative Interfaces, Inc, LearningExpress, Overdrive, Inc
Wireless access
Function: Adult bk club, Adult literacy prog, Bks on CD, Chess club, Children's prog, Computers for patron use, Copy machines, Handicapped accessible, ILL available, Music CDs, OverDrive digital audio bks, Photocopying/Printing, Preschool reading prog, Prog for adults, Prog for children & young adult, Pub access computers, Ref serv available, Scanner, Spanish lang bks, Story hour, Summer reading prog, Web-catalog, Wheelchair accessible
Publications: The eStory (Online only); WCPL (Online only); WCPL Pa (Online only); WCPLNews (Online only)
Mem of Chester County Library System
Friends of the Library Group

C WEST CHESTER UNIVERSITY*, Francis Harvey Green Library, 25 W Rosedale Ave, 19383. SAN 359-6672. Tel: 610-436-2747. Circulation Tel: 610-436-2946. Interlibrary Loan Service Tel: 610-436-3454. Reference Tel: 610-436-2453. Interlibrary Loan Service FAX: 610-636-2251. Administration FAX: 610-738-0554. E-mail: libcirc@wcupa.edu, refdesk@wcupa.edu. Web Site: www.wcupa.edu/library.fhg. *Dir,* Richard H Swain; E-mail: rswain@wcupa.edu; *Assoc Dir,* Dr Adele Bane; Tel: 610-436-2263, E-mail: abane@wcupa.edu; *Head, Acq, Head, Ser,* Dr Christina McCawley; Tel: 610-436-2167;610-436-2656, Fax: 610-738-0555, E-mail: cmccawley@wcupa.edu; *Head, ILL,* Tracie Meloy; *Instrul Serv Librn,* Patricia Lenkowski; Tel: 610-436-3393, E-mail: plenkowski@wcupa.edu; *Govt Doc, Maps Librn,* Reyes Awilda; Tel: 610-436-3206, E-mail: areyes@wcupa.edu; *Coll Develop, Ref Librn,* Mame Purce; Tel: 610-738-0467, E-mail: mpurce@wcupa.edu; *Rare Bks, Spec Coll Librn,* Tara Wink; Tel: 610-436-3456, E-mail: twink@wcupa.edu; *Circ Supvr,* Dana McDonnell; Tel: 610-436-1098, E-mail: dmcdonnell@wcupa.edu; *Ref Coordr,* Stephen Marvin; Tel: 610-436-1068, E-mail: smarvin@wcupa.edu; *Access Serv, ILL,* Clayton Garthwait; Tel: 610-436-3409, E-mail: cgarthwait@wcupa.edu; *Cat,* Jean Burton; Tel: 610-436-2917, E-mail: jburton@wcupa.edu; *Electronic Res, Web Serv,* Jane Hutton; Tel: 610-436-3453, E-mail: jhutton@wcupa.edu; *Info Literacy,* Rachel McMullin; Tel: 610-738-0510, E-mail: rmcmullan@wcupa.edu; *Music,* Tim Sestrick; Tel: 610-436-2379, E-mail: tsestrick@wcupa.edu; *Sci,* Dr Walter Cressler; Tel: 610-436-1072, E-mail: wcressler@wcupa.edu; *Syst,* Kathie Marvin; Tel: 610-436-1044, E-mail: kmarvin@wcupa.edu. Subject Specialists: *Educ,* Patricia Lenkowski; *Criminal justice, Geog, Polit sci,* Reyes Awilda; *Anthrop, Diversity, Sociol,* Mame Purce; *Hist,* Tara Wink; *Bus, Soc sci,* Stephen Marvin; *Communication,* Clayton Garthwait; *Women's studies,* Jean Burton; *Computer sci, Math,* Jane Hutton; *Humanities,* Rachel McMullin; *Music,* Tim Sestrick; *Health sci, Sci,* Dr Walter Cressler; Staff 16 (MLS 16)
Founded 1871. Enrl 12,822; Fac 768; Highest Degree: Master
Library Holdings: AV Mats 81,070; CDs 13,236; DVDs 3,601; e-books 640,761; e-journals 17,249; Music Scores 34,604; Bk Vols 759,153; Per Subs 2,958; Videos 5,211
Special Collections: Anthony Wayne Letters (Rare Book), bks, letters; History of County (Chester County Coll, incl Darlington Coll of Rare Scientific & Botanical); Holocaust Studies (Frejdowicz Coll); John Sanderson's Biographies of the Signers of the Declaration of Independence, Philips Coll of Autographed Books & Letters; Physical Education (Ehinger Coll); Shakespeare Folios; Stanley Weintraub Coll, ms & related mats. Oral History; State Document Depository; US Document Depository
Subject Interests: Art, Educ, Health, Humanities, Kinesiology, Music, Nursing
Automation Activity & Vendor Info: (Acquisitions) Ex Libris Group; (Cataloging) Ex Libris Group; (Circulation) Ex Libris Group; (Course Reserve) Docutek; (ILL) OCLC ILLiad; (OPAC) Ex Libris Group; (Serials) Ex Libris Group
Database Vendor: Alexander Street Press, Cambridge Scientific Abstracts, EBSCOhost, Gale Cengage Learning, ISI Web of Knowledge, JSTOR, LexisNexis, OCLC WorldShare Interlibrary Loan, OVID Technologies, ProQuest, SerialsSolutions, STN International
Wireless access
Function: Archival coll, Audio & video playback equip for onsite use, Handicapped accessible, ILL available, Photocopying/Printing, Ref serv available, Spoken cassettes & CDs, Telephone ref, VHS videos
Partic in Keystone Library Network; Lyrasis; OCLC Online Computer Library Center, Inc; State System of Higher Education Library Cooperative; Tri-State College Library Cooperative
Special Services for the Deaf - Assistive tech; TTY equip
Special Services for the Blind - Assistive/Adapted tech devices, equip & products
Open Mon-Wed 7:30am-2am, Thurs 7:30am-Midnight, Fri 7:30-5, Sat 10-6, Sun Noon-2am
Friends of the Library Group
Departmental Libraries:
PRESSER MUSIC LIBRARY, School of Music & Performing Arts Center, 19383. Tel: 610-436-2379, 610-436-2430. FAX: 610-436-2873. *Music Librn,* Tim Sestrick; E-mail: tsestrick@wcupa.edu; *Music Libr Supvr,* Hunter King; E-mail: tking@wcupa.edu; *Music Libr Tech,* Lucille Stroud; E-mail: lstroud@wcupa.edu
Library Holdings: AV Mats 43,459; CDs 12,872; DVDs 79; Music Scores 34,604; Bk Titles 10,452
Automation Activity & Vendor Info: (ILL) Ex Libris Group
Open Mon-Thurs (Fall & Spring) 8am-10pm, Fri 8-4:30, Sat 1-5, Sun 5pm-9pm; Mon-Fri (Summer) 8-4
Friends of the Library Group

S WESTON SOLUTIONS INC*, Weston Information Center, 1400 Weston Way, 19380-0903. (Mail add: PO Box 2653, 19380-2653), SAN 315-3347. Tel: 610-701-3080. FAX: 610-701-3158. Web Site: www.westonsolutions.com. *Mgr,* Jack V Morris, II; E-mail: jack.morris@westonsolutions.com; Staff 2 (MLS 1, Non-MLS 1)
Founded 1965
Library Holdings: Bk Titles 3,000; Per Subs 150
Subject Interests: Air pollution, Energy, Environ studies, Health, Land use planning, Nuclear wastes, Solid waste, Toxicology, Water pollution
Database Vendor: Dialog, LexisNexis
Publications: Newsletter
Restriction: Co libr, Employees & their associates, Not open to pub, Private libr

WEST ELIZABETH

S EASTMAN CHEMICAL*, Research Library, State Hwy 837, 15088-0567. SAN 314-4089. Tel: 412-384-2520. FAX: 412-384-9634. *Mgr,* George Kutzik; Staff 1 (Non-MLS 1)
Founded 1940
Library Holdings: Bk Titles 2,160; Bk Vols 2,390; Per Subs 21
Open Mon-Fri 8:30-4:30

WEST GROVE

P AVON GROVE LIBRARY*, 117 Rosehill Ave, 19390-1214. (Mail add: PO Box 100, 19390-0100), SAN 315-3355. Tel: 610-869-2004. FAX: 610-869-2957. Web Site: www.ccls.org. *Dir,* Kim Ringler; E-mail: kringler@ccls.org; *Head, Circ,* Nancy Gardner; Staff 6 (MLS 1, Non-MLS 5)
Pop 21,959; Circ 36,840
Library Holdings: Bk Titles 18,000; Bk Vols 19,500; Per Subs 48; Talking Bks 471; Videos 391
Mem of Chester County Library System
Open Mon 10-6, Tues-Thurs 10-8, Fri 10-4, Sat 9-4
Friends of the Library Group

WEST LAWN

P WEST LAWN-WYOMISSING HILLS LIBRARY*, 101 Woodside Ave, 19609. SAN 315-3363. Tel: 610-678-4888. FAX: 610-678-9210. Web Site: www.berks.lib.pa.us/wlwhl/. *Dir,* Paparella Bonnie; *Librn,* Dennis McAfee; Staff 4 (Non-MLS 4)
Founded 1937. Pop 10,000
Library Holdings: Bk Vols 9,000; Per Subs 25
Mem of Berks County Public Libraries
Friends of the Library Group

WEST MIFFLIN

J COMMUNITY COLLEGE OF ALLEGHENY COUNTY*, South Campus Library, 1750 Clairton Rd, 15122-3097. SAN 315-3371. Tel: 412-469-6295. FAX: 412-469-6370. E-mail: library@ccac.edu. Web Site: www.ccac.edu/library. *Head Librn,* Irene Grimm; E-mail: igrimm@ccac.edu; *Librn,* Sally Caldrone; E-mail: scaldrone@ccac.edu; Staff 11 (MLS 6, Non-MLS 5)
Founded 1967
Library Holdings: Bk Vols 42,126; Per Subs 144
Subject Interests: Allied health, Nursing
Automation Activity & Vendor Info: (Cataloging) SirsiDynix; (Circulation) SirsiDynix; (Course Reserve) SirsiDynix; (ILL) OCLC; (OPAC) SirsiDynix; (Serials) SirsiDynix
Database Vendor: EBSCOhost, Gale Cengage Learning, OCLC FirstSearch, ProQuest
Special Services for the Blind - Assistive/Adapted tech devices, equip & products
Open Mon-Thurs 7:30am-9pm, Fri 7:30-4, Sat 8-4

J PITTSBURGH INSTITUTE OF AERONAUTICS*, Clifford Ball Learning Resource Center, Five Allegheny County Airport, 15122-2674. (Mail add: PO Box 10897, Pittsburgh, 15236). Tel: 412-346-2100, 412-462-9011. Toll Free Tel: 800-444-1440. FAX: 412-466-0513.
Founded 1929. Fac 20; Highest Degree: Associate
Library Holdings: Bk Vols 4,000; Per Subs 20
Open Mon-Fri 7:15-8 & 2:30-3:30

WEST NEWTON

P WEST NEWTON PUBLIC LIBRARY*, 124 N Water St, 15089. SAN 370-7474. Tel: 724-872-8555. FAX: 724-872-8555. *Dir,* Deborah McCallister
Founded 1939. Circ 3,250
Library Holdings: AV Mats 468; Large Print Bks 311; Bk Titles 9,992; Bk Vols 10,091; Per Subs 12; Talking Bks 137; Videos 322
Subject Interests: Civil War
Automation Activity & Vendor Info: (Cataloging) Follett Software; (Circulation) Follett Software
Mem of Westmoreland County Federated Library System
Open Mon, Wed & Fri 10-3, Sat 10-12

WEST PITTSTON

P WEST PITTSTON LIBRARY*, 200 Exeter Ave, 18643-2442. SAN 315-3398. Tel: 570-654-9847. FAX: 570-654-8037. Web Site: www.wplibrary.org. *Dir,* Anne Bramblett Barr
Founded 1873. Pop 5,000
Library Holdings: Bk Vols 26,000; Per Subs 32
Database Vendor: Innovative Interfaces, Inc, OCLC FirstSearch
Wireless access
Mem of Luzerne County Library System
Special Services for the Blind - Reader equip; Talking bks
Open Mon-Thurs 12-8, Fri 12-6, Sat 10-5
Friends of the Library Group

WEST SUNBURY

P NORTH TRAILS PUBLIC LIBRARY, 1553 W Sunbury Rd, 16061-1211. Tel: 724-476-1006. FAX: 724-637-2700. Web Site: www.bcfls.org/northtrails. *Dir, Extn Serv,* Kathy D Kline; E-mail: kkline@bcfls.org; Staff 1 (MLS 1)
Founded 2004. Pop 30,000; Circ 330,000
Jan 2013-Jan 2014 Income $76,000, County $60,000, Locally Generated Income $10,000
Automation Activity & Vendor Info: (Acquisitions) OCLC CatExpress; (Cataloging) TLC (The Library Corporation); (Circulation) TLC (The Library Corporation)
Database Vendor: Access Pennsylvania, EBSCOhost, ReferenceUSA
Wireless access
Function: Adult bk club, Computers for patron use, Copy machines, E-Reserves, ILL available, Music CDs, Online cat, Online searches, OverDrive digital audio bks, Preschool outreach, Prof lending libr, Prog for children & young adult, Spoken cassettes & CDs, Spoken cassettes & DVDs
Mem of Butler County Federated Library System
Open Mon & Tues 11-6, Thurs & Fri 10-5
Friends of the Library Group

WESTFIELD

P WESTFIELD PUBLIC LIBRARY*, 147 Maple St, 16950-1616. SAN 315-3401. Tel: 814-367-5411. FAX: 814-367-5411. E-mail: wplibrary@verizon.net. Web Site: www.westfieldpubliclibrary.com. *Libr Dir,* Rebecca Nagy
Pop 2,441; Circ 26,000
Library Holdings: Bk Vols 12,900; Per Subs 23
Mem of Potter-Tioga Library System
Open Mon, Wed & Fri 1-7, Tues 10-5, Thurs, 9-12, Sat 8-3

WHITE HAVEN

P WHITE HAVEN AREA COMMUNITY LIBRARY, 99 Towanda St, 18661. Tel: 570-443-8776. E-mail: Whacl.Library@yahoo.com. *Chair,* Patricia Heamen
Library Holdings: Bk Vols 6,000; Per Subs 10
Wireless access

WHITEHALL

P WHITEHALL TOWNSHIP PUBLIC LIBRARY*, 3700 Mechanicsville Rd, 18052-3399. SAN 315-341X. Tel: 610-432-4339. FAX: 610-432-9387. E-mail: whitehallpl@cliu.org. Web Site: www.whitehallpl.org. *Dir,* Nancy J Adams; *AV,* Cheryl Hixson; *Ref,* Christine Andrews; *Youth Serv,* Lorraine Santaliz; *Tech Coordr,* James Gilbert; Staff 6 (MLS 2, Non-MLS 4)
Founded 1964. Pop 26,768
Jul 2010-Jun 2011 Income $576,551. Mats Exp $87,917, Books $32,555, Per/Ser (Incl. Access Fees) $10,814, AV Mat $20,443, Electronic Ref Mat (Incl. Access Fees) $16,027, Presv $7,719. Sal $396,590
Library Holdings: Bk Vols 103,933; Per Subs 131
Special Collections: Adult Easy Readers Coll; Braille Bible Coll; Juvenile Braille Picture Books Coll
Subject Interests: Local hist, Songbooks
Automation Activity & Vendor Info: (Cataloging) TLC (The Library Corporation); (Circulation) TLC (The Library Corporation); (OPAC) TLC (The Library Corporation)
Database Vendor: Baker & Taylor, EBSCO Auto Repair Reference, Gale Cengage Learning, Grolier Online, infoUSA, LearningExpress, Newsbank, Overdrive, Inc, ProQuest, ReferenceUSA, Sage, TLC (The Library Corporation), TumbleBookLibrary
Wireless access
Function: Accelerated reader prog, Adult bk club, Art exhibits, Audiobks via web, AV serv, Bks on cassette, Bks on CD, Children's prog, Computer training, Computers for patron use, Copy machines, e-mail & chat, e-mail serv, E-Reserves, Electronic databases & coll, Exhibits, ILL available, Large print keyboards, Microfiche/film & reading machines, Music CDs, Online cat, OverDrive digital audio bks, Preschool outreach, Preschool reading prog, Prog for adults, Prog for children & young adult, Pub access computers, Ref serv available, Referrals accepted, Senior computer classes, Spoken cassettes & CDs, Spoken cassettes & DVDs, Story hour, Summer & winter reading prog, Summer reading prog, Tax forms, Teen prog, Telephone ref, VHS videos, Video lending libr, Web-catalog
Publications: Brochure for New Members; Monthly Bibliography of New Acquisitions
Open Mon-Thurs 9:30-9, Fri 9:30-6, Sat 9:30-5
Friends of the Library Group

WILCOX

P WILCOX PUBLIC LIBRARY*, 105 Clarion St, 15870. (Mail add: PO Box 58, 15870-0058), SAN 315-3428. Tel: 814-929-5639. FAX: 814-929-9934. E-mail: staff@wilcoxlibrary.net. Web Site: www.wilcoxlibrary.net. *Dir,* Barbara DePonceau
Founded 1963. Pop 1,781; Circ 4,600
Library Holdings: Bk Vols 7,720; Per Subs 10
Automation Activity & Vendor Info: (OPAC) Follett Software
Wireless access
Open Mon & Fri 10-4, Tues & Thurs 12-4, Sat 9-3

WILKES-BARRE

GM DEPARTMENT OF VETERANS AFFAIRS*, Medical Center Library, 1111 E End Blvd, 18711. SAN 315-3479. Tel: 570-824-3521. FAX: 570-821-7264. Web Site: www.wilkes-barre.va.gov. *Librn,* Jay Suffren; Staff 1 (Non-MLS 1)
Founded 1950
Library Holdings: Bk Titles 4,500; Bk Vols 5,200; Per Subs 280
Subject Interests: Med
Restriction: Staff & mem only

M GEISINGER WYOMING VALLEY MEDICAL CENTER LIBRARY*, 1000 E Mountain Dr, 18711. SAN 372-7939. Tel: 570-826-7809. FAX: 570-826-7682. Web Site: www.geisinger.edu. *In Charge,* Kay L Johnstone; Staff 2 (MLS 1, Non-MLS 1)
Founded 1981
Library Holdings: Bk Titles 2,160; Bk Vols 2,780; Per Subs 25
Subject Interests: Pub health
Database Vendor: OVID Technologies
Function: Doc delivery serv, ILL available, Photocopying/Printing, Ref serv available, Res libr
Special Services for the Deaf - Bks on deafness & sign lang; TTY equip
Open Mon-Fri 8:30-3:30

C KING'S COLLEGE, D Leonard Corgan Library, 14 W Jackson St, 18701-2010. SAN 315-3436. Tel: 570-208-5840. FAX: 570-208-6022. Web Site: www.kings.edu. *Dir,* Dr Terrence Mech; Tel: 570-208-5943, E-mail: terrencemech@kings.edu; *Asst Tech Prof, Electronic Res & Syst Librn,* Adam Balcziunas; *Asst Tech Prof, Instruction & Ref Librn,* Marianne Sodoski; *Asst Tech Prof, Instruction & Ref Librn,* Rebecca Thompson; *Asst Tech Prof, Instrul & Ref Serv Coordr,* Jordana Shane; *Circ Supvr,* Kenya Flash; Staff 5 (MLS 5)
Founded 1946. Enrl 2,184; Fac 155; Highest Degree: Master
Jul 2013-Jun 2014 Income $1,162,055. Mats Exp $514,421, Books $99,600, Per/Ser (Incl. Access Fees) $104,787, Micro $3,952, AV Mat $295, Electronic Ref Mat (Incl. Access Fees) $252,322, Presv $1,062. Sal $479,479 (Prof $319,458)
Library Holdings: AV Mats 2,179; CDs 464; DVDs 809; Electronic Media & Resources 49; Microforms 579,471; Bk Vols 185,081; Per Subs 181; Videos 2,134
Special Collections: Public & Private Papers of Honorable Daniel J Flood, MC; Public & Private Papers of The Honorable James L Nelligan
Automation Activity & Vendor Info: (Acquisitions) Innovative Interfaces, Inc; (Cataloging) Innovative Interfaces, Inc; (Circulation) Innovative Interfaces, Inc; (OPAC) Innovative Interfaces, Inc
Database Vendor: Dialog, EBSCOhost, LexisNexis, ProQuest
Wireless access

Publications: Daniel J Flood Collection Register; Edward Welles Catalog of Artists
Partic in Lyrasis; Northeastern Pennsylvania Library Network; OCLC Online Computer Library Center, Inc

S LUZERNE COUNTY HISTORICAL SOCIETY*, Bishop Memorial Library, 49 S Franklin St, 18701. SAN 315-3517. Tel: 570-823-6244. FAX: 570-823-9011. Web Site: www.luzernecountyhistory.com. *Exec Dir,* Anthony T Brooks; *Archivist, Librn,* Amanda Fontenova; E-mail: afontenova@luzernehistory.org
Founded 1858
Library Holdings: Bk Vols 7,000; Per Subs 15
Special Collections: Business Records of Coal Companies; Manuscripts of Personal & Family Papers of Prominent Wyoming Valley Individuals
Subject Interests: Anthracite mining, Hist of Wyoming Valley, Local hist, Pa
Function: Archival coll
Open Tues-Fri 12-4, Sat 10-4

P OSTERHOUT FREE LIBRARY*, 71 S Franklin St, 18701-1287. SAN 359-6850. Tel: 570-823-0156. FAX: 570-823-5477. *Exec Dir,* Richard Miller; E-mail: rmiller@osterhout.lib.pa.us; *Head, Automation, Head, Tech Serv,* Gail Frew; E-mail: gfrew@osterhout.lib.pa.us; *Head, Circ,* Elaine Schall; E-mail: eschall@osterhout.lib.pa.us; *Head, Info Serv,* Elaine Stefanko; E-mail: estafanko@osterhout.lib.pa.us; *Head, Youth Serv,* Elaine Rash; E-mail: erash@osterhout.lib.pa.us; *ILL,* Sandra Schimmel; E-mail: sschimmel@osterhout.lib.pa.us
Founded 1889. Pop 154,707; Circ 258,489
Library Holdings: Bk Vols 200,000; Per Subs 300
Subject Interests: Local hist
Wireless access
Publications: Osterhout Free Library Newsletter (Quarterly)
Mem of Luzerne County Library System
Partic in Northeastern Pennsylvania Library Network
Special Services for the Deaf - Bks on deafness & sign lang; High interest/low vocabulary bks
Open Mon-Thurs 8:30-8:30, Fri & Sat 8:30-5
Friends of the Library Group
Branches: 3
NORTH, 28 Oliver St, 18705, SAN 359-6885. Tel: 570-822-4660. FAX: 570-822-4660. *Supvr,* Joanne Austin; E-mail: jaustin@osterhout.lib.pa.us; Staff 2 (Non-MLS 2)
Library Holdings: Bk Titles 15,659; Bk Vols 17,818; Per Subs 23; Talking Bks 88; Videos 219
Open Mon 1-5:30 & 6:30-8:30, Tues & Thurs 12:30-5:30, Wed 1-5:30, Fri 1-5
Friends of the Library Group
PLAINS TOWNSHIP, 126 N Main St, Plains, 18705, SAN 359-6915. Tel: 570-824-1862. FAX: 570-824-1862. *In Charge,* Kathleen Szafran; Staff 1 (Non-MLS 1)
Library Holdings: Large Print Bks 78; Bk Titles 13,691; Bk Vols 15,081; Per Subs 29; Talking Bks 219; Videos 179
Open Wed 1-5:30, Thurs 6:30-8:30, Fri 1-5
SOUTH, Two Airy St, 18702, SAN 359-694X. Tel: 570-823-5544. FAX: 570-823-5544. *In Charge,* Melissa Jones; Staff 1 (Non-MLS 1)
Library Holdings: Large Print Bks 116; Bk Titles 9,690; Bk Vols 10,115; Per Subs 29; Talking Bks 189; Videos 209
Open Mon & Tues 12:30-5:30, Wed 1-5:30, Thurs 1-5:30 & 6:30-8:30, Fri 1-5
Friends of the Library Group

M WILKES-BARRE GENERAL HOSPITAL*, Library Services, 575 N River St, 18764. SAN 315-3495. Tel: 570-552-1175. FAX: 570-552-1183. E-mail: library@commonwealthhealth.net. *Mgr,* Rosemarie Kazda Taylor; Staff 1 (MLS 1)
Founded 1935
Library Holdings: e-books 150; e-journals 18,000; Bk Vols 3,500; Per Subs 58
Special Collections: Health Resource Center, Consumer Health Coll
Subject Interests: Med, Nursing
Automation Activity & Vendor Info: (Acquisitions) Professional Software; (Cataloging) Professional Software; (Circulation) Professional Software; (OPAC) Professional Software; (Serials) Professional Software
Database Vendor: DynaMed, EBSCOhost, Elsevier, McGraw-Hill, MD Consult, Micromedex, OCLC FirstSearch, OVID Technologies, PubMed, ScienceDirect
Publications: Infobits (Newsletter)
Partic in Basic Health Sciences Library Network; Health Information Library Network of Northeastern Pennsylvania (HILNNEP); Middle Atlantic Regional Med Libr Prog
Open Mon-Fri 7-3:30

L WILKES-BARRE LAW & LIBRARY ASSOCIATION, Hon Max Rosenn Memorial Law Library, 200 N River St, Rm 23, 18711-1001. SAN 315-3509. Tel: 570-822-6712. FAX: 570-822-8210. E-mail: law.library@luzernecounty.org. Web Site: www.wblawlibrary.org. *Dir & Law Librn-in-Chief,* Joseph Paul Justice Burke, III; E-mail: JoeatWBLLA@aol.com
Founded 1850
Library Holdings: Bk Vols 40,000; Per Subs 40
Database Vendor: Westlaw
Open Mon-Fri 9-4

C WILKES UNIVERSITY*, Farley Library, 187 S Franklin St, 18766-0998. (Mail add: 84 W South St, 18766), SAN 359-6974. Tel: 570-408-4250. Interlibrary Loan Service Tel: 570-408-4256. Administration Tel: 570-408-4254. FAX: 570-408-7823. E-mail: library@wilkes.edu. Web Site: www.wilkes.edu/library. *Dean,* Robert Shaddi; *Ref,* Brian Sacolic; E-mail: brian.sacolic@wilkes.edu; *Computer Syst Librn,* Giselle Romanace; E-mail: gisele.romanace@wilkes.edu; *Tech Serv Librn,* Helenmary Selecky; Tel: 570-408-4258, E-mail: helenmary.selecky@wilkes.edu; *Circ Asst,* Frederick Krohle; E-mail: frederick.krohle@wilkes.edu; *Coordr,* Lawrence Kopenis; E-mail: lawrence.kopenis@wilkes.edu; *Supvr,* Jean Krohle; E-mail: jean.krohlej@wilkes.edu; Staff 19 (MLS 5, Non-MLS 14)
Founded 1933. Enrl 3,010; Fac 188; Highest Degree: Doctorate
Library Holdings: Bk Titles 172,742; Bk Vols 201,686; Per Subs 522
Special Collections: Admiral Howard Stark Coll; McClintock Room, mss; Northeast Pennsylvania History; Poland, Culture & History (Polish Room)
Publications: Library News Brief
Partic in Northeastern Pennsylvania Library Network; OCLC Online Computer Library Center, Inc
Open Mon-Thurs 8am-11:45pm, Fri 8-5, Sat 11-5, Sun 11am-11:45pm
Restriction: In-house use for visitors, Open to students, fac & staff

WILLIAMSBURG

P WILLIAMSBURG PUBLIC LIBRARY*, 511 W Second St, 16693. SAN 315-3525. Tel: 814-832-3367. FAX: 814-832-3845. Web Site: www.williamspl.net. *Librn,* Lugene Shelley; Staff 1 (MLS 1)
Founded 1950. Pop 5,993; Circ 7,853
Library Holdings: Bk Vols 15,000; Per Subs 60
Subject Interests: Pa hist
Automation Activity & Vendor Info: (Cataloging) Follett Software; (Circulation) Follett Software; (OPAC) Follett Software
Open Mon & Wed 1-8, Tues 1-5, Thurs 1-7, Fri 11-4, Sat 9-4

WILLIAMSPORT

P JAMES V BROWN LIBRARY OF WILLIAMSPORT & LYCOMING COUNTY*, 19 E Fourth St, 17701-6390. SAN 359-7067. Tel: 570-326-0536. Reference Tel: 570-327-2954. FAX: 570-326-1671. E-mail: jvbrown@jvbrown.edu. Web Site: www.jvbrown.edu. *Dir,* Barbara S McGary; E-mail: bmcgary@jvbrown.edu; *Asst Dir/District Consult,* Melissa A Rowse; E-mail: mrowse@jvbrown.edu; *Youth Serv Coordr,* Nina Edgerton; E-mail: nedgerton@jvbrown.edu; *Ref,* Beth Schetroma; *Tech Serv,* Laura Spencer; Staff 36 (MLS 6, Non-MLS 30)
Founded 1905. Pop 84,702; Circ 561,942
Library Holdings: Audiobooks 8,318; DVDs 21,060; e-books 3,469; Bk Titles 120,043; Per Subs 198
Special Collections: Pennsylvania Coll
Subject Interests: Adoption, Parenting coll
Automation Activity & Vendor Info: (Cataloging) Innovative Interfaces, Inc; (Circulation) Innovative Interfaces, Inc; (OPAC) Innovative Interfaces, Inc
Wireless access
Mem of Lycoming County Libr Syst
Special Services for the Blind - Closed circuit TV magnifier; Reader equip
Open Mon-Fri 9-8, Sat & Sun Noon-5
Friends of the Library Group
Branches: 1
L LYCOMING COUNTY LAW LIBRARY, 19 E Fourth St, 17701. Tel: 570-326-0536. FAX: 570-326-1671.
Founded 1927
Library Holdings: Bk Titles 20,500; Per Subs 15
Open Mon-Fri 9-5
Bookmobiles: 2

C LYCOMING COLLEGE*, John G Snowden Memorial Library, 700 College Pl, 17701-5192. SAN 315-355X. Tel: 570-321-4053. Interlibrary Loan Service Tel: 570-321-4091. FAX: 570-321-4090. Web Site: www.lycoming.edu/library. *Assoc Dean, Dir, Libr Serv,* Janet M Hurlbert; Tel: 570-321-4082, E-mail: hurlbjan@lycoming.edu; *Head, Coll Mgt,* Susan K Beidler; Tel: 570-321-4084, E-mail: beidler@lycoming.edu; *Mgr, Ser,* Wilma Reeder; *Instrul Serv Librn & Coordr, Info Literacy & Outreach,* Alison Gregory; Tel: 570-321-4087, E-mail: gregory@lycoming.edu; *Instrul Serv Librn & Coordr of Ref & Assessment,* Mary Broussard; Tel: 570-321-4068, E-mail: brousm@lycoming.edu; *Circ Supvr,* Alysha Russo; Staff 12 (MLS 5, Non-MLS 7)
Founded 1812. Enrl 1,450; Fac 92; Highest Degree: Bachelor

Library Holdings: e-books 2,500; Bk Vols 186,000; Per Subs 1,140
Special Collections: Religion (Central Pennsylvania Conference of the United Methodist Church Archives). US Document Depository
Subject Interests: Psychol, Relig studies, Sociol
Automation Activity & Vendor Info: (Acquisitions) TLC (The Library Corporation); (Cataloging) TLC (The Library Corporation); (Circulation) TLC (The Library Corporation); (OPAC) TLC (The Library Corporation); (Serials) TLC (The Library Corporation)
Partic in Associated College Libraries of Central Pennsylvania; Pennsylvania Academic Library Consortium, Inc (PALCI); Susquehanna Library Cooperative
Open Mon-Thurs (Winter) 7:30am-1am, Fri 7:30am-9pm, Sat 10-9, Sun 1-1; Mon-Fri (Summer) 7:30-4
Friends of the Library Group

C ROGER & PEGGY MADIGAN LIBRARY, 999 Hagan Way, 17701. (Mail add: One College Ave, DIF No 69, 17701), SAN 315-3576. Tel: 570-327-4523. Interlibrary Loan Service Tel: 570-320-2400, Ext 7788. Reference Tel: 570-320-2409. Administration Tel: 570-320-2400, Ext 7104. Toll Free Tel: 800-367-9222. FAX: 570-327-4503. E-mail: library@pct.edu, refdesk@pct.edu. Web Site: www.pct.edu/library. *Dir,* Tracey Amey; E-mail: tamey@pct.edu; *Asst Dir, Libr Serv,* Joann Eichenlaub; E-mail: jeichenl@pct.edu; *Librn, Archives & Digital Coll Initiatives,* Patricia Scott; E-mail: pscott@pct.edu; *Librn, Cat & Metadata Initiatives,* Alan Buck; E-mail: abuck@pct.edu; *Librn, Fac Outreach Initiatives,* Judy McConnell; E-mail: jmcconne@pct.edu; *Librn, Info Literacy Initiatives,* Judith Zebrowski; E-mail: jzebrows@pct.edu; *Access Serv Mgr,* Patricia Bilbay; E-mail: pbilbay@pct.edu; *Access Serv Mgr,* Cynthia Ennis; E-mail: cke1@pct.edu; *Acq & Tech Serv Mgr,* Lynne Koskie; E-mail: lkoskie@pct.edu; *Libr Operations & Pub Serv Mgr,* Jean Bremigen; E-mail: jbremige@pct.edu; *Ref & Res Initiative,* Georgia Laudenslager; E-mail: glaudens@pct.edu. Subject Specialists: *Budgeting, Coll & resource mgt,* Tracey Amey; *Communications, Humanities,* Patricia Scott; *Natural res mgt, Transportation tech,* Alan Buck; *Health sci,* Judy McConnell; *Bus, Hospitality,* Judith Zebrowski; *Civil eng, Indust tech, Plastics,* Georgia Laudenslager; Staff 18 (MLS 6, Non-MLS 12)
Founded 1965. Enrl 6,000; Highest Degree: Bachelor
Library Holdings: AV Mats 8,000; e-books 18,000; e-journals 36,000; Electronic Media & Resources 85; Microforms 800; Bk Titles 102,000; Bk Vols 131,136; Per Subs 800
Special Collections: Sloan Art Coll; Williamsport Technical Institute 1914-1965 black & white photographs & other information. State Document Depository
Subject Interests: Archit, Art, Aviation, Civil eng, Construction, Culinary arts, Health sci, Natural res conservation, Tech
Automation Activity & Vendor Info: (Acquisitions) SirsiDynix; (Cataloging) SirsiDynix; (Circulation) SirsiDynix; (ILL) OCLC ILLiad; (Media Booking) SirsiDynix; (OPAC) OCLC; (Serials) SirsiDynix
Database Vendor: 3M Library Systems, Access Pennsylvania, ACM (Association for Computing Machinery), ALLDATA Online, Atlas Systems, Cinahl, College Source, EBSCOhost, Faulkner Information Services, Gale Cengage Learning, JSTOR, LexisNexis, McGraw-Hill, Mergent Online, OCLC FirstSearch, OCLC WorldShare Interlibrary Loan, OVID Technologies, Oxford Online, ProQuest, Sage, SirsiDynix, UpToDate, ValueLine, Westlaw
Wireless access
Partic in Interlibrary Delivery Service of Pennsylvania; Lyrasis; OCLC Online Computer Library Center, Inc; Pennsylvania Academic Library Consortium, Inc (PALCI); Susquehanna Library Cooperative
Special Services for the Deaf - Assistive tech; Closed caption videos; High interest/low vocabulary bks; Sorenson video relay syst
Special Services for the Blind - Assistive/Adapted tech devices, equip & products
Open Mon-Thurs 7:30am-11pm, Fri 7:30-5, Sat 1-5, Sun 1-11

M SUSQUEHANNA HEALTH MEDICAL LIBRARY*, 777 Rural Ave, 17701-3198. SAN 315-3584. Tel: 570-321-2266. E-mail: medical_library@susquehannahealth.org. Web Site: www.susquehannahealth.org/services/lrc/index.asp. *Dir,* Michael Heyd; E-mail: mheyd@susquehannahealth.org; Staff 4 (MLS 1, MLS 1, Non-MLS 1, Non-MLS 1)
Founded 1951
Library Holdings: Bk Vols 4,300; Per Subs 130
Subject Interests: Allied health, Med, Nursing
Automation Activity & Vendor Info: (Cataloging) AmLib Library Management System; (Circulation) AmLib Library Management System; (OPAC) AmLib Library Management System
Database Vendor: EBSCOhost, EBSCOhost
Function: Audio & video playback equip for onsite use, Audio & video playback equip for onsite use, AV serv, AV serv, Computer training, Computer training, Doc delivery serv, Doc delivery serv, Electronic databases & coll, Electronic databases & coll, Health sci info serv, Health sci info serv
Partic in Susquehanna Library Cooperative
Open Mon-Fri 8-4:30
Restriction: Hospital staff & commun, Open to pub for ref only, Pub use on premises

WILLOW GROVE

M ABINGTON MEMORIAL HOSPITAL*, Dixon School of Nursing Library, 2500 Maryland Rd, 19090-1284. SAN 373-7349. Tel: 215-481-5591. FAX: 215-481-5550. Web Site: amh.org. *Dir, Libr Serv,* Marion Chayes; E-mail: mchayes@amh.org; Staff 2 (MLS 1, Non-MLS 1)
Founded 1914
Library Holdings: Bk Vols 5,000; Per Subs 75; Videos 54
Subject Interests: Nursing
Partic in Basic Health Sciences Library Network; Delaware Valley Information Consortium; National Network of Libraries of Medicine
Open Mon-Thurs 9-9, Fri 9-4:30

P UPPER MORELAND FREE PUBLIC LIBRARY, 109 Park Ave, 19090-3277. SAN 315-3630. Tel: 215-659-0741. Web Site: www.uppermorelandlibrary.org. *Dir,* Margie Repka-Peters; *Asst Dir,* Cathy Gilmore; *Head, Tech Serv,* Katie Fitzpatrick; *Ch,* James Moran; *Pub Serv Librn,* Adam Cole; *Circ Mgr,* Karen Wilton; Staff 5 (MLS 4, Non-MLS 1)
Founded 1959. Pop 24,015; Circ 215,972
Jan 2013-Dec 2013 Income $821,633. Mats Exp $92,590, Books $46,866, Per/Ser (Incl. Access Fees) $10,121, AV Mat $16,949, Electronic Ref Mat (Incl. Access Fees) $18,654. Sal $485,385 (Prof $252,889)
Library Holdings: Audiobooks 3,853; AV Mats 8,654; Bks on Deafness & Sign Lang 58; CDs 1,187; DVDs 4,732; e-books 9,187; e-journals 110; Electronic Media & Resources 14; High Interest/Low Vocabulary Bk Vols 40; Large Print Bks 2,512; Music Scores 39; Bk Titles 62,815; Per Subs 111
Subject Interests: English as a second lang, Local hist
Automation Activity & Vendor Info: (Cataloging) Innovative Interfaces, Inc; (Circulation) Innovative Interfaces, Inc; (OPAC) Innovative Interfaces, Inc; (Serials) Innovative Interfaces, Inc
Wireless access
Function: Adult bk club, Bks on CD, Children's prog, Computer training, Computers for patron use, Copy machines, E-Reserves, Electronic databases & coll, Free DVD rentals, ILL available, Mus passes, Music CDs, Online cat, Photocopying/Printing, Prog for adults, Prog for children & young adult, Spoken cassettes & DVDs, Summer reading prog
Partic in Montgomery County Library & Information Network Consortium
Special Services for the Blind - Large screen computer & software
Open Mon-Thurs 10-9, Fri & Sat 10-5, Sun 1-5
Friends of the Library Group

R WILLOW GROVE BAPTIST CHURCH LIBRARY*, 1872 Kimball Ave, 19090. SAN 318-9392. Tel: 215-659-4505. *Librn,* Debbie Monaghan
Library Holdings: Bk Vols 1,100
Subject Interests: Children's videos, Christian living, Christian novels, Family life, Music, Psychol, Recreation

WINDBER

M WINDBER MEDICAL CENTER*, Medical Library, 600 Somerset Ave, 15963. SAN 315-3657. Tel: 814-467-3000. FAX: 814-266-8230. *Librn,* Heather Brice
Library Holdings: Bk Vols 150; Per Subs 13
Automation Activity & Vendor Info: (Cataloging) Book Systems
Publications: Current Awareness Listings
Partic in Greater NE Regional Med Libr Program; Laurel Highlands Health Science Library Consortium; National Network of Libraries of Medicine
Restriction: Open to staff only

P WINDBER PUBLIC LIBRARY*, 1909 Graham Ave, 15963-2011. SAN 315-3665. Tel: 814-467-4950. FAX: 814-467-0960. E-mail: windlib@somersetcountypalibraries.org. *Dir,* Susan Brandau; E-mail: sbrandau@somersetcountypalibraries.org; Staff 1 (Non-MLS 1)
Founded 1918. Pop 13,969; Circ 15,079
Library Holdings: Bk Vols 26,467
Automation Activity & Vendor Info: (Cataloging) Innovative Interfaces, Inc; (Circulation) Innovative Interfaces, Inc; (OPAC) Innovative Interfaces, Inc
Function: Handicapped accessible, ILL available, Outside serv via phone, mail, e-mail & web, Photocopying/Printing, Prog for adults, Prog for children & young adult, Summer reading prog, VHS videos
Mem of Somerset County Federated Library System
Open Mon, Tues & Thurs 12-8, Wed 1-8, Fri & Sat 10-5

WOMELSDORF

P WOMELSDORF COMMUNITY LIBRARY*, 203 W High St, 19567-1307. Tel: 610-589-1424. FAX: 610-589-5022. E-mail: womelsdorfcl@berks.lib.pa.us. Web Site: www.berks.lib.pa.us/womelsdorfcl. *Dir,* Carol Hugar
Founded 1978. Circ 21,700

Library Holdings: AV Mats 500; Bk Vols 7,770; Per Subs 36
Automation Activity & Vendor Info: (Acquisitions) SirsiDynix; (Cataloging) SirsiDynix; (ILL) SirsiDynix; (OPAC) SirsiDynix
Mem of Berks County Public Libraries
Friends of the Library Group

WORCESTER

S PETER WENTZ FARMSTEAD LIBRARY*, 2100 Schultz Rd, 19490. (Mail add: PO Box 240, 19490), SAN 374-8820. Tel: 610-584-5104. FAX: 610-584-6860. E-mail: peterwentzfarmstead@montcopa.org. Web Site: www.montcopa.org. *Curator,* Morgan T McMillan; Staff 1 (Non-MLS 1)
Founded 1744
Library Holdings: Bk Titles 800
Special Collections: Wentz & Schultz Family Geneology Coll
Subject Interests: Decorative art, Local hist, Pa
Function: Ref serv available
Restriction: Not a lending libr, Open by appt only, Private libr
Friends of the Library Group

WORTHINGTON

P WORTHINGTON WEST FRANKLIN COMMUNITY LIBRARY*, 214 E Main St, 16262. (Mail add: PO Box 85, 16262-0085), SAN 370-7326. Tel: 724-297-3762. FAX: 724-297-3762. E-mail: wwlibrary@comcast.net. Web Site: armstronglibraries.org/worthington. *Dir,* Timi Kost; Staff 1 (MLS 1)
Founded 1985. Pop 2,800
Library Holdings: Audiobooks 96; CDs 33; DVDs 92; Large Print Bks 628; Bk Titles 10,856; Per Subs 12; Videos 459
Automation Activity & Vendor Info: (Cataloging) Follett Software; (Circulation) Follett Software; (OPAC) Follett Software
Function: Bks on cassette, Bks on CD, Children's prog, Computers for patron use, Copy machines, Distance learning, e-mail serv, Electronic databases & coll, Exhibits, Fax serv, Handicapped accessible, ILL available, Mail & tel request accepted, Music CDs, Online cat, Prog for adults, Pub access computers, Scanner, Story hour, Summer reading prog, Tax forms, Telephone ref, VHS videos
Special Services for the Blind - Cassettes; Large print bks; Sound rec
Open Tues & Wed 12-5, Thurs & Fri 10:30-6, Sat 10:30-4:30

WRIGHTSTOWN

P VILLAGE LIBRARY OF WRIGHTSTOWN*, 727 Penns Park Rd, 18940-9605. SAN 315-3681. Tel: 215-598-3322. FAX: 215-598-9659. Web Site: www.buckslib.org/libraries/wrightstown. *Dir,* Lisa Lieberson
Founded 1958. Pop 2,839; Circ 25,281
Library Holdings: Bk Titles 18,000; Per Subs 59
Publications: Newsletter (Bi-annually)
Mem of Bucks County Free Library
Open Mon, Tues & Fri 9-5, Wed & Thurs 9-7, Sat (Sept-June) 10-1, Sun 1-5

WYALUSING

P WYALUSING PUBLIC LIBRARY*, 115 Church St, 18853. (Mail add: PO Box 98, 18853-0098), SAN 315-369X. Tel: 570-746-1711. FAX: 570-746-1674. E-mail: wyalusingpl@gmail.com. Web Site: wyalusinglibrary.org. *Dir,* Cathy Brady; *Circ Libra,* Melody Brace; *Circ Librn,* Amy Girven; *Circ Librn,* Judy Higley
Founded 1902. Pop 1,927; Circ 11,987
Library Holdings: Bk Vols 13,000; Per Subs 28
Subject Interests: Local hist
Mem of Bradford County Library System
Open Mon, Wed, & Fri 10-8, Tues & Thurs 3-6, Sat 9-4

WYNCOTE

CR RECONSTRUCTIONIST RABBINICAL COLLEGE LIBRARY*, Mordecai M Kaplan Library, 1299 Church Rd, 19095. SAN 314-9900. Tel: 215-576-0800, Ext 232. Administration Tel: 215-576-0800, Ext 234. FAX: 215-576-6143. E-mail: kaplanlibrary@rrc.edu. Web Site: www.rrc.edu. *Dir,* Deborah Stern; E-mail: dstern@rrc.edu; *Asst Librn,* Alan Lapayover; E-mail: alapayover@rrc.edu. Subject Specialists: *Jewish relig texts,* Alan Lapayover; Staff 2.25 (MLS 1, Non-MLS 1.25)
Founded 1968. Enrl 50; Fac 12; Highest Degree: Master
Library Holdings: Electronic Media & Resources 10; Bk Vols 47,000; Per Subs 120
Subject Interests: Jewish studies, Rabbinics
Automation Activity & Vendor Info: (Cataloging) SirsiDynix; (Circulation) SirsiDynix; (ILL) OCLC; (OPAC) SirsiDynix; (Serials) SirsiDynix
Database Vendor: EBSCOhost, Gale Cengage Learning, OCLC FirstSearch
Wireless access
Function: Copy machines, Electronic databases & coll, Handicapped accessible, ILL available, Online cat, Ref & res, Res libr
Partic in Asn of Jewish Librs; Lyrasis; Southeastern Pennsylvania Theological Library Association
Open Mon-Thurs 8-6, Fri 9-4

WYNDMOOR

P FREE LIBRARY OF SPRINGFIELD TOWNSHIP*, 1600 Paper Mill Rd, 19038. SAN 372-7726. Tel: 215-836-5300. FAX: 215-836-2404. E-mail: springfieldlibrary@mclinc.org. Web Site: fls.mclinc.org. *Dir,* Marycatherine McGarvey; E-mail: mmcgarvey@mclinc.org; *Asst Dir, Acq,* Joy Utz; E-mail: jutz@mclinc.org; *Head, Ref Serv,* Ann Cartelli; E-mail: acartelli@mclinc.org; *Ch Serv,* Leslie Talon; E-mail: ltalon@mclinc.org; *Circ,* Patricia Ennis; E-mail: ennis@mclinc.org; *ILL,* Marylou Hughes; E-mail: mlhughes@mclinc.org; *Reader Serv, YA Serv,* Marie Keissling; E-mail: mkeissling@mclinc.org; Staff 7 (MLS 2, Non-MLS 5)
Founded 1965. Pop 19,708; Circ 57,161
Library Holdings: Bk Titles 68,410; Bk Vols 70,890; Per Subs 133; Talking Bks 977; Videos 412
Special Collections: Aircraft (Lamason Coll); Art (Malta Fund); Business; Gardening (Swain Coll); Outdoor Sports (Brodsky Fund); Performing Arts (Quillian Coll); Popular Medicine (Ramsey Coll)
Automation Activity & Vendor Info: (Circulation) Innovative Interfaces, Inc
Wireless access
Partic in Montgomery County Library & Information Network Consortium
Special Services for the Blind - Talking bks
Open Mon-Thurs (Winter) 9-9, Fri 9-5, Sat 10-5, Sun 1-4; Mon-Thurs (Summer) 9-9, Fri 9-5, Sat 10-2
Friends of the Library Group

WYNNEWOOD

R ANTHONY CARDINAL BEVILACQUA THEOLOGICAL RESEARCH CENTER*, Ryan Memorial Library, 100 E Wynnewood Rd, 19096. SAN 359-0917. Tel: 610-785-6274. Reference Tel: 610-785-6277. FAX: 610-664-7913. Web Site: www.scs.edu/library. *Dir, Libr Serv,* Cait Kokolus; E-mail: ckokolus@adphila.org; *Pub Serv,* Ene Andrilli; Staff 8 (MLS 3, Non-MLS 5)
Founded 1832. Enrl 350; Fac 35; Highest Degree: Master
Library Holdings: AV Mats 16,021; e-journals 2,000; Electronic Media & Resources 34; Bk Titles 103,118; Bk Vols 127,112; Per Subs 565
Special Collections: Nineteenth Century Devotional Literature; Pre-Vatican II Liturgical Books; Rare Books
Subject Interests: Catholic theol, Patristics, Philos, Scripture studies
Automation Activity & Vendor Info: (Acquisitions) Ex Libris Group; (Cataloging) Ex Libris Group; (Circulation) Ex Libris Group; (Course Reserve) Ex Libris Group; (ILL) Ex Libris Group; (OPAC) Ex Libris Group; (Serials) Ex Libris Group
Database Vendor: EBSCOhost
Partic in Southeastern Pennsylvania Theological Library Association; Tri-State College Library Cooperative
Open Mon-Tues 8:30am-11pm, Wed & Thurs 8:30am-10pm, Fri 8:30-4:30, Sat 9:30-4:30, Sun 1-10

M LANKENAU HOSPITAL*, Medical Library, 100 Lancaster Ave, 19096. SAN 359-0615. Tel: 610-645-2698. FAX: 610-645-3425. *Dir,* Mazen Hassan; *Librn,* Kary Heller; *Librn,* Maria Panoc; Staff 2 (MLS 2)
Founded 1860
Library Holdings: Bk Titles 6,281; Bk Vols 6,419; Per Subs 321
Special Collections: Collected Papers of the Lankenau Research Center
Subject Interests: Gen med, Surgery
Partic in National Network of Libraries of Medicine; Regional Med Libr Network
Open Mon-Fri 8:30-5

R MAIN LINE REFORM TEMPLE*, Beth Elohim Library, 410 Montgomery Ave, 19096. SAN 315-3711. Tel: 610-649-7800. FAX: 610-642-6338. *Librn,* Sally Brown; E-mail: sbrown@mlrt.org; Staff 2 (MLS 1, Non-MLS 1)
Founded 1961
Library Holdings: Bk Titles 10,184; Bk Vols 14,990; Per Subs 23; Talking Bks 25
Special Collections: Young Adult (Steven Berman Memorial Coll)
Subject Interests: Jewish hist, Judaica
Open Mon-Thurs 10-3, Sun 10-1

R PALMER THEOLOGICAL SEMINARY*, Austen K deBlois Library, Six Lancaster Ave, 19096. SAN 314-8963. Tel: 610-645-9318. E-mail: semlibr@eastern.edu. Web Site: www.palmerseminary.edu/library. *Dir,* Melody Mazuk; Tel: 610-645-9319, E-mail: mazuk@eastern.edu; *Tech Serv Librn,* Nancy R Adams; Tel: 610-645-9317, E-mail: nadams@eastern.edu; *Libr Serv Mgr,* Wayne Hopkins; Tel: 610-645-9318, E-mail: whopkins@eastern.edu; *Bibliog Instr,* Mayra Picos-Lee; Tel: 610-645-9332, E-mail: mpicosle@eastern.edu; Staff 6 (MLS 2, Non-MLS 4)
Founded 1925

Library Holdings: AV Mats 1,345; Bk Vols 122,378; Per Subs 394; Videos 504
Special Collections: Barbour Black Studies; MacBride Coll; Soto-Fontanz Hispanic Studies
Automation Activity & Vendor Info: (Cataloging) TLC (The Library Corporation); (Circulation) TLC (The Library Corporation); (OPAC) TLC (The Library Corporation)
Function: ILL available
Partic in Southeastern Pennsylvania Theological Library Association
Open Mon, Tues & Thurs (Fall & Spring) 8:30am-11pm, Wed 8:30am-10pm, Fri 8:30-4:30, Sat 10-5
Friends of the Library Group

P PENN WYNNE LIBRARY, 130 Overbrook Pkwy, 19096-3211. SAN 314-9609. Tel: 610-642-7844. FAX: 610-642-2761. E-mail: pennwynnelibrary@lmls.org. Web Site: www.lmls.org. *Librn,* Judy Soret; Staff 5 (MLS 2, Non-MLS 3)
Founded 1929
Library Holdings: Audiobooks 1,334; CDs 1,290; DVDs 3,138; Large Print Bks 1,030; Bk Vols 44,170; Per Subs 30
Special Collections: Judaica
Automation Activity & Vendor Info: (Acquisitions) Innovative Interfaces, Inc; (Cataloging) Innovative Interfaces, Inc; (Circulation) Innovative Interfaces, Inc; (OPAC) Innovative Interfaces, Inc
Wireless access
Function: ILL available, Prog for adults, Prog for children & young adult, Summer reading prog, Telephone ref, Wheelchair accessible
Mem of Lower Merion Library System
Open Mon-Thurs 10-9, Fri & Sat 10-5

R PHILADELPHIA ARCHDIOCESAN HISTORICAL RESEARCH CENTER*, Archives & Historical Collections, 100 E Wynnewood Rd, 19096-3001. SAN 359-0941. Tel: 610-667-2125. FAX: 610-667-2730. Web Site: www.rc.net/philadelphia/pahrc/index.html. *Dir,* Joseph J Casino
Library Holdings: Bk Vols 8,000
Special Collections: American Catholic Newspapers (19th Century) Religious American Coll; Catechism Coll; Popular Piety Coll
Subject Interests: Immigration
Restriction: Open to pub for ref only

WYOMING

P WYOMING FREE LIBRARY*, 358 Wyoming Ave, 18644-1822. SAN 315-372X. Tel: 570-693-1364. FAX: 570-693-0189. *Librn,* Jonah Alben
Library Holdings: Bk Vols 12,000; Per Subs 15
Mem of Luzerne County Library System
Open Mon 11-6, Tues-Fri 11-5, Sat 9-4

WYOMISSING

P SPRING TOWNSHIP LIBRARY*, 78C Commerce Dr, 19610. Tel: 610-373-9888. FAX: 610-373-0334. E-mail: springtwp@berks.lib.pa.us. Web Site: www.berks.lib.pa.us/springtwp. *Dir,* Celia Colby; *Ch,* Tracee Yawger; Staff 2 (MLS 1, Non-MLS 1)
Founded 2004. Pop 25,000; Circ 82,000
Jan 2007-Dec 2007 Income $186,800, City $90,000, County $73,800, Locally Generated Income $23,000. Mats Exp $28,300, Books $15,400, Per/Ser (Incl. Access Fees) $1,000, AV Mat $6,600, Electronic Ref Mat (Incl. Access Fees) $5,300
Library Holdings: Bk Vols 15,171; Per Subs 34
Automation Activity & Vendor Info: (Cataloging) Horizon; (Circulation) Horizon; (OPAC) Horizon; (Serials) Horizon
Database Vendor: ProQuest
Wireless access
Function: Art exhibits, Bks on cassette, Bks on CD, Children's prog, Computer training, Computers for patron use, Copy machines, Digital talking bks, e-mail serv, Electronic databases & coll, Fax serv, Free DVD rentals, ILL available, Mail & tel request accepted, Mus passes, Music CDs, Online cat, Online searches, Orientations, Outreach serv, Outside serv via phone, mail, e-mail & web, OverDrive digital audio bks, Photocopying/Printing, Preschool outreach, Prog for adults, Prog for children & young adult, Pub access computers, Senior computer classes, Spoken cassettes & CDs, Spoken cassettes & DVDs, Story hour, Summer reading prog, Tax forms, Teen prog, Telephone ref, VHS videos, Wheelchair accessible
Mem of Berks County Public Libraries
Open Mon-Thurs 9-8, Fri 9-2, Sat 9-4
Friends of the Library Group

P WYOMISSING PUBLIC LIBRARY*, Nine Reading Blvd, 19610-2084. SAN 315-3738. Tel: 610-374-2385. FAX: 610-374-8424. Web Site: www.wyopublib.org. *Dir,* Joan S King
Founded 1913. Pop 11,155; Circ 83,470
Library Holdings: Bk Vols 27,295; Per Subs 92
Automation Activity & Vendor Info: (Cataloging) Follett Software; (Circulation) Follett Software; (OPAC) Follett Software

YEADON

P YEADON PUBLIC LIBRARY*, 809 Longacre Blvd, 19050-3398. SAN 315-3762. Tel: 610-623-4090. FAX: 610-394-9374. E-mail: yeadon@delcolibraries.org. Web Site: www.yeadonlibrary.org. *Interim Libr Mgr,* Darlene Walker; *Youth Serv Librn,* LaTina Bedford-Dean; *Circ & ILL Mgr,* Ja'Nelle Schretzenmaire; Staff 4 (Non-MLS 4)
Founded 1937. Pop 11,727
Library Holdings: Bk Vols 38,000; Per Subs 100
Special Collections: African-American Cultural Center; Brodie/Johnson African-American Cultural Center for Children; Fifty-Plus Center; Parenting Center
Wireless access
Mem of Delaware County Library System
Open Mon-Thurs 10-9, Fri 10-6, Sat 10-5
Friends of the Library Group

YORK

R FIRST CHURCH OF THE BRETHREN LIBRARY*, 2710 Kingston Rd, 17402-3799. SAN 315-3797. Tel: 717-755-0307. *Librn,* Helen Lehman; Staff 1 (Non-MLS 1)
Founded 1966
Library Holdings: Bk Titles 7,280; Bk Vols 7,500; Per Subs 26
Special Collections: Church of the Brethren Coll
Subject Interests: Biog, Family studies, Fiction, Inspiration, Recreation, Relig studies
Open Mon-Fri 10-4

J HARRISBURG AREA COMMUNITY COLLEGE*, York Campus Library, 2010 Pennsylvania Ave, 17404. Tel: 717-718-0328, Ext 3520. Interlibrary Loan Service Tel: 717-780-2623. FAX: 717-718-8967. Web Site: lib2.hacc.edu. *Dir,* Laura Wukovitz; Tel: 717-780-2468; *Adjunct Fac Librn,* Amy A Grapes; E-mail: aagrapes@hacc.edu; *Adjunct Fac Librn,* Jennifer L Hummel; E-mail: jlhummel@hacc.edu; *Adjunct Fac Librn,* Amy L Pajewski; E-mail: alpajews@hacc.edu; *Ref & Instruction Librn,* Lisa A Hartman; Tel: 717-718-0328, Ext 3556, E-mail: lahartma@hacc.edu; *Libr Spec,* Kathleen O Frederick; E-mail: kofreder@hacc.edu; *Libr Tech,* Rebecca C Anstine; E-mail: rcanstin@hacc.edu; Staff 4.9 (MLS 3.4, Non-MLS 1.5)
Founded 2005. Enrl 3,157; Fac 140; Highest Degree: Associate
Library Holdings: AV Mats 96; Bks on Deafness & Sign Lang 1; DVDs 39; Large Print Bks 2; Bk Vols 2,984; Per Subs 72; Talking Bks 1; Videos 57
Automation Activity & Vendor Info: (Acquisitions) SirsiDynix; (Cataloging) SirsiDynix; (Circulation) SirsiDynix; (Course Reserve) Docutek; (ILL) SirsiDynix; (Media Booking) SirsiDynix; (OPAC) SirsiDynix; (Serials) SirsiDynix
Database Vendor: EBSCOhost, Gale Cengage Learning, LexisNexis, ProQuest
Wireless access
Open Mon-Thurs (Winter) 7:30am-9pm, Fri 7:30-4, Sat 8:30am-12:30pm; Mon-Thurs (Summer) 7:30am-9pm

P MARTIN MEMORIAL LIBRARY*, 159 E Market St, 17401-1269. SAN 315-3819. Tel: 717-846-5300. FAX: 717-848-2330. Web Site: www.yorklibraries.org. *Exec Dir,* William Schell; E-mail: wschell@yorklibraries.org; *Coll Develop, Head, Tech Serv,* Lora-Lynn Stevens; E-mail: lstevens@yorklibraries.org; *Head, Youth Serv,* Paula Gilbert; E-mail: pgilbert@yorklibraries.org; *Info Serv,* Lora Yourst; E-mail: lyourst@yorklibraries.org; *ILL,* Ruth Schaeberle; Staff 54 (MLS 8, Non-MLS 46)
Founded 1935. Pop 112,500; Circ 585,300
Library Holdings: Bk Vols 150,000; Per Subs 200
Automation Activity & Vendor Info: (Circulation) SirsiDynix
Mem of York County Library System
Open Mon-Thurs 9-9, Fri & Sat 9-5:30
Friends of the Library Group

M MEMORIAL HOSPITAL LIBRARY, 325 S Belmont St, 17403-2609. (Mail add: PO Box 15118, 17405-7118), SAN 315-3827. Tel: 717-849-5305. FAX: 717-815-2482. E-mail: library@mhyork.org. *Librn,* Laurie Yourist; Staff 2 (MLS 1, Non-MLS 1)
Library Holdings: Per Subs 64
Subject Interests: Health admin, Med
Wireless access
Partic in Greater NE Regional Med Libr Serv
Open Mon & Thurs 1:30-5:30, Tues & Fri 8-Noon, Wed 12-4
Restriction: Open to pub for ref & circ; with some limitations

C PENN STATE UNIVERSITY YORK*, Lee R Glatfelter Library, 1031 Edgecomb Ave, 17403-3398. SAN 315-3835. Tel: 717-771-4020. Interlibrary Loan Service Tel: 717-771-4021. Reference Tel: 717-771-4024. FAX: 717-771-4022. Web Site: www.libraries.psu.edu/psul/york.html. *Actg Head Librn,* Barbara Eshbach; Tel: 717-771-4023, E-mail: bee11@psu.edu; *Circ Supvr, ILL,* Dawn Oswald; E-mail: djo10@psu.edu; *Info Res & Serv Support Spec,* Angela Caldwell; Staff 3.5 (MLS 1, Non-MLS 2.5)
Enrl 1,329; Fac 110; Highest Degree: Master
Library Holdings: CDs 500; DVDs 2,000; Bk Vols 65,000; Per Subs 150
Automation Activity & Vendor Info: (Circulation) SIRSI WorkFlows; (Course Reserve) SIRSI WorkFlows; (OPAC) SirsiDynix
Wireless access
Function: Art exhibits, Copy machines, E-Reserves, Electronic databases & coll, Free DVD rentals, Handicapped accessible, Music CDs, Online cat, Online info literacy tutorials on the web & in blackboard, Ref serv in person
Partic in OCLC Online Computer Library Center, Inc; RLIN (Research Libraries Information Network)
Open Mon-Thurs (Winter) 8am-9pm, Fri 8-5, Sat 10-4, Sun 1-6; Mon-Thurs (Summer) 8-8, Fri 8-5, Sat 11-4
Restriction: Open to pub for ref & circ; with some limitations, Open to students, fac & staff

M WELLSPAN YORK HOSPITAL*, Philip A Hoover MD Library, 1001 S George St, 17405-7198. SAN 315-3878. Tel: 717-851-2495. Circulation Tel: 717-851-4256. Interlibrary Loan Service Tel: 717-851-3322. Reference Tel: 717-851-3323. FAX: 717-851-2487. E-mail: libserv@wellspan.org. Web Site: www.wellspan.org/body.cfm?id=246. *Dir, Libr Serv,* Catherine Kelly; Staff 5 (MLS 2, Non-MLS 3)
Founded 1929
Library Holdings: e-journals 2,000; Bk Titles 7,000; Bk Vols 31,300; Per Subs 375
Subject Interests: Clinical med, Hist of med, Nursing
Automation Activity & Vendor Info: (Acquisitions) SirsiDynix; (Cataloging) SirsiDynix; (Circulation) SirsiDynix; (ILL) OCLC; (OPAC) SIRSI-iLink; (Serials) EBSCO Online
Database Vendor: EBSCOhost, OVID Technologies, PubMed, SirsiDynix
Wireless access
Function: Res libr
Partic in Basic Health Sciences Library Network
Open Mon-Fri 7:30-4:30

C YORK COLLEGE OF PENNSYLVANIA*, Schmidt Library, 441 Country Club Rd, 17403-3651. SAN 315-3843. Tel: 717-815-1304. Interlibrary Loan Service Tel: 717-815-1485. Reference Tel: 717-815-1356. Administration Tel: 717-815-1577. FAX: 717-849-1608. E-mail: library@ycp.edu. Web Site: library.ycp.edu. *Dir,* Denise Shorey; Tel: 717-815-1353, E-mail: dshorey@ycp.edu; *Coll Develop,* Beth Jacoby; Tel: 717-815-1950, E-mail: bjacoby@ycp.edu; *Info Serv,* Susan McMillan; Tel: 717-815-1480, E-mail: smcmilla@ycp.edu; *Info Serv,* Zehao Zhou; Tel: 717-815-1518, E-mail: zzhou@ycp.edu; *Instrul Media,* Patricia Poet; Tel: 717-815-1458, E-mail: ppoet@ycp.edu; *Syst,* Vickie Kline; Tel: 717-815-1459, E-mail: vkline@ycp.edu; *Info Literacy,* Joel Burkholder; Tel: 717-815-1726, E-mail: jburkhol@ycp.edu; Staff 7 (MLS 7)
Founded 1787. Enrl 4,745; Fac 543; Highest Degree: Doctorate
Library Holdings: CDs 2,527; DVDs 5,069; e-books 104,757; e-journals 11,122; Electronic Media & Resources 11,708; Music Scores 527; Bk Titles 117,576; Videos 1,708
Special Collections: Lincoln Coll
Subject Interests: Bus admin, Educ, Nursing
Automation Activity & Vendor Info: (Acquisitions) SIRSI Unicorn; (Cataloging) SirsiDynix; (Circulation) SirsiDynix; (Course Reserve) Docutek; (ILL) Relais International; (OPAC) SirsiDynix; (Serials) SerialsSolutions
Database Vendor: Alexander Street Press, EBSCOhost, Gale Cengage Learning, LexisNexis, ProQuest, Sage
Wireless access
Partic in Lyrasis; OCLC Online Computer Library Center, Inc; Pennsylvania Academic Library Consortium, Inc (PALCI)
Open Mon-Thurs 8am-2am, Fri 8-8, Sat 10-6, Sun Noon-2am

S YORK COUNTY HERITAGE TRUST*, Historical Society of York County Library & Archives, 250 E Market St, 17403. SAN 315-3800. Tel: 717-848-1587. FAX: 717-812-1204. E-mail: library@yorkheritage.org. Web Site: www.yorkheritage.org. *Librn,* Lila Fourhman-Shaull; E-mail: lshaull@yorkheritage.org; Staff 2 (Non-MLS 2)
Founded 1895
Library Holdings: Bk Vols 25,000; Per Subs 50
Special Collections: Art (Lewis Miller Folk Drawing Coll), mss; Folk Coll; Genealogy of York & Adams County (York County Genealogical Coll), bks, mss; General Jacob Devers Coll; Governmental Archives (Archives of York City & York County), mss; History (York County Historical Coll), bks, mss; James Shettel Circus & Theater in America Coll, broadsides, mss, photog; Local Newspapers Coll, 1789 to present, micro; York Gazette & Daily, 1815-1970, micro
Subject Interests: Decorative art, Fine arts, Genealogy, Local hist
Open Tues-Sat 9-5
Restriction: Non-circulating to the pub

P YORK COUNTY LIBRARY SYSTEM*, 159 E Market St, 3rd Flr, 17401. SAN 315-386X. Tel: 717-846-5300. Administration Tel: 717-849-6969. FAX: 717-849-6999. Web Site: www.yorklibraries.org. *Pres,* Patricia Calvani; *Automation Syst Coordr,* Barbara Summers; Tel: 717-840-7435
Pop 381,751; Circ 1,553,057
Library Holdings: Bk Vols 453,646; Per Subs 661
Wireless access
Member Libraries: Arthur Hufnagel Public Library of Glen Rock; Dillsburg Area Public Library; Glatfelter Memorial Library; Guthrie Memorial Library; Kaltreider-Benfer Library; Martin Memorial Library; Mason-Dixon Public Library; Paul Smith Library of Southern York County
Branches: 5
COLLINSVILLE COMMUNITY, 2632 Delta Rd, Brogue, 17309. (Mail add: PO Box 8, Brogue, 17309), SAN 324-007X. Tel: 717-927-9014. FAX: 717-927-9664. E-mail: cllib@yorklibraries.org. Web Site: www.yorklibraries.org/collinsville. *Librn,* Victoria Dick; Staff 3 (MLS 1, Non-MLS 2)
Pop 14,025; Circ 38,575
Library Holdings: Bk Vols 13,600; Per Subs 30
Open Mon, Wed & Fri 10-5, Tues & Thurs 1-8, Sat 9-1
Friends of the Library Group
DOVER AREA COMMUNITY, 3700-3 Davidsburg Rd, Dover, 17315, SAN 377-7154. Tel: 717-292-6814. FAX: 717-292-9774. E-mail: dolib@yorklibraries.org. Web Site: www.yorklibraries.org/dover. *Librn,* Debbie Van de Castle; E-mail: dvandecastle@yorklibraries.org; Staff 1 (MLS 1)
Pop 22,349; Circ 88,585
Library Holdings: Bk Titles 17,505; Bk Vols 19,126; Per Subs 24
Open Mon 12-8, Tues & Wed 10-8, Thurs 10-5, Fri & Sat 9-1
Friends of the Library Group
KREUTZ CREEK VALLEY, 66 Walnut Springs Rd, Hellam, 17406, SAN 377-7170. Tel: 717-252-4080. FAX: 717-252-0283. E-mail: kclib@yorklibraries.org. Web Site: www.yorklibraries.org/kc. *Librn,* Susan Nenstiel; E-mail: snenstiel@yorklibraries.org; Staff 1 (MLS 1)
Pop 10,363; Circ 49,245
Library Holdings: Bk Titles 13,008; Bk Vols 13,803
Open Mon, Wed & Fri 10-5, Tues & Thurs 12-8, Sat 10-1
Friends of the Library Group
RED LAND COMMUNITY LIBRARY, 48 Robin Hood Dr, Etters, 17319, SAN 324-0088. Tel: 717-938-5599. E-mail: rnlib@yorklibraries.org. Web Site: www.yorklibraries.org/red-land. *Librn,* Mary Beth Long; E-mail: mblong@yorklibraries.org; Staff 1 (MLS 1)
Pop 44,865; Circ 62,783
Library Holdings: Bk Titles 22,241; Bk Vols 25,595; Per Subs 18
Open Mon & Wed 10-5, Tues 1-8, Thurs 10-8, Fri & Sat 10-2
Friends of the Library Group
VILLAGE, 35-C N Main St, Jacobus, 17407, SAN 324-3184. Tel: 717-428-1034. FAX: 717-428-3869. E-mail: sflib@yorklibraries.org. Web Site: www.yorklibraries.org/village. *Librn,* Becky Shives; E-mail: rshives@yorklibraries.org; Staff 4 (Non-MLS 4)
Pop 7,514, Circ 82,000
Library Holdings: Bk Vols 18,000; Per Subs 26
Open Mon, Wed & Fri 10-5, Tues & Thurs Noon-8, Sat 10-1
Friends of the Library Group

YORK HAVEN

P YORK HAVEN COMMUNITY LIBRARY*, Two N Front St, 17370. SAN 315-3886. Tel: 717-266-4712. *Actg Dir,* Cynthia Owad
Library Holdings: Bk Titles 10,009; Per Subs 17
Open Tues & Wed 5-8

YOUNGSVILLE

P YOUNGSVILLE PUBLIC LIBRARY*, 100 Broad St, 16371-1421. SAN 315-3894. Tel: 814-563-7670. FAX: 814-563-7670. Web Site: www.youngsvillelibrary.org. *Dir, Libr Serv,* Kristy L Wallace
Founded 1931. Pop 5,421; Circ 10,671
Library Holdings: Bk Titles 10,000; Per Subs 30
Open Mon & Tues Noon-7:3, Wed 10-5, Fri 12-4
Friends of the Library Group

YOUNGWOOD

J WESTMORELAND COUNTY COMMUNITY COLLEGE*, Learning Resources Center, 400 Armbrust Rd, 15697-1895. SAN 315-3908. Tel: 724-925-4100. Interlibrary Loan Service Tel: 724-925-4102. Reference Tel: 724-925-4101. Administration Tel: 724-925-4097. Toll Free Tel: 800-262-2103. FAX: 724-925-1150. *Dir,* Kathleen Keefe; E-mail: keefek@my.wccc.edu; *Tech Serv,* Belinda Sedlak; Tel: 724-925-4096, E-mail: sedlakb@wccc-pa.edu; Staff 6 (MLS 4, Non-MLS 2)

Founded 1970. Enrl 6,400; Fac 82; Highest Degree: Associate
Library Holdings: AV Mats 3,000; Electronic Media & Resources 19; Bk Titles 65,000; Bk Vols 70,000; Per Subs 500; Videos 2,830
Special Collections: State Document Depository; US Document Depository
Automation Activity & Vendor Info: (Acquisitions) SirsiDynix; (Cataloging) SirsiDynix; (Circulation) SirsiDynix; (Course Reserve) SirsiDynix; (ILL) SirsiDynix; (OPAC) SirsiDynix; (Serials) SirsiDynix
Database Vendor: EBSCOhost, LexisNexis, ProQuest, SirsiDynix
Partic in OCLC Online Computer Library Center, Inc; Share Westmoreland Consortium
Open Mon, Wed, Thurs & Fri 10-5, Tues 10-8, Sat 10-1

P YOUNGWOOD AREA PUBLIC LIBRARY*, 17 S Sixth St, 15697-1623. SAN 320-8540. Tel: 724-925-9350. FAX: 724-925-9350. E-mail: yaplib@hotmail.com. Web Site: www.youngwoodapl.org. *Librn*, Jean Antoline
Founded 1954. Pop 3,749; Circ 11,272
Library Holdings: Large Print Bks 372; Bk Vols 14,396; Per Subs 24; Talking Bks 552
Automation Activity & Vendor Info: (Cataloging) Innovative Interfaces, Inc; (Circulation) Innovative Interfaces, Inc
Mem of Westmoreland County Federated Library System
Partic in Share Westmoreland Consortium
Open Mon & Thurs 10-7:30, Tues & Fri 10-5

ZELIENOPLE

P ZELIENOPLE AREA PUBLIC LIBRARY*, 227 S High St, 16063-1319. SAN 315-3916. Tel: 724-452-9330. FAX: 724-452-9318. E-mail: zelienople@bcfls.org. Web Site: www.bcfls.org/zelienople. *Dir*, Janice Lawrence; *Adult Serv*, Amy Kellner; *Online Serv & Tech*, Jolene Thompson; Staff 3 (MLS 1, Non-MLS 2)
Founded 1919. Pop 11,500; Circ 95,000
Jan 2011-Dec 2011 Income $196,810, State $35,520, City $50, County $22,795, Locally Generated Income $77,495. Mats Exp $34,585, Books $24,975, Per/Ser (Incl. Access Fees) $2,095, AV Equip $540, AV Mat $5,975, Presv $1,000. Sal $86,825 (Prof $27,000)
Library Holdings: Audiobooks 355; AV Mats 1,500; CDs 300; DVDs 750; e-books 50; Large Print Bks 825; Bk Titles 6,500; Per Subs 75; Talking Bks 250; Videos 75
Special Collections: Preschool AV Coll, puppets, teaching devices, videos
Automation Activity & Vendor Info: (Cataloging) TLC (The Library Corporation); (Circulation) TLC (The Library Corporation); (ILL) TLC (The Library Corporation); (OPAC) TLC (The Library Corporation)
Database Vendor: EBSCO Auto Repair Reference, EBSCOhost, Gale Cengage Learning, Grolier Online, Ingram Library Services, OCLC, TLC (The Library Corporation)
Wireless access
Function: Adult bk club, Audiobks via web, Bk club(s), Bks on CD, Children's prog, Computer training, Computers for patron use, E-Reserves, Electronic databases & coll, Family literacy, Free DVD rentals, Handicapped accessible, Holiday prog, ILL available, Music CDs, Online cat, Online ref, OverDrive digital audio bks, Preschool reading prog, Prog for adults, Prog for children & young adult, Pub access computers, Ref serv available, Senior computer classes, Story hour, Summer reading prog, Tax forms, Teen prog, Telephone ref, Web-catalog, Wheelchair accessible
Mem of Butler County Federated Library System
Special Services for the Deaf - TTY equip
Special Services for the Blind - Bks on cassette; Bks on CD; Large print bks; Playaways (bks on MP3)
Open Mon 10-8, Tues-Thurs 10-6, Sat 9-1
Restriction: Use of others with permission of librn
Friends of the Library Group